WINE ENTHUS[I]
MAGAZIN[E]

Essential

BUYING GUIDE

2008

RUNNING PRESS
PHILADELPHIA · LONDON

9 8 7 6 5 4 3 2 1
Digit on the right indicates the number of this printing

Library of Congress Control Number: 2007920547

ISBN-13: 978-0-7624-3137-3
ISBN-10: 0-7624-3137-7

Cover design by Bill Jones
Interior design by Jan Greenberg and Bill Jones
Edited by Sarah O'Brien, Jennifer Leczkowski, and Diana von Glahn
Typography: Garamond and Helvetica Neue Condensed

This book may be ordered by mail from the publisher.
Please include $2.50 for postage and handling.
But try your bookstore first!

Running Press Book Publishers
2300 Chestnut Street
Philadelphia, Pennsylvania 19103-4371

Visit us on the web!
www.runningpresscooks.com
www.wineenthusiast.com/magazine

PHOTOGRAPHY CREDITS

Cover photo: Courtesy of *Wine Enthusiast Magazine*
p.1: © Susie M. Eising Food Photography/Stockfood America
p.3 top: © Ted Stefanski/Cephas, bottom: © Kevin Judd/Cephas
p.4: © Nigel Blythe/Cephas
p.5: Courtesy of *Wine Enthusiast Magazine*
p.7: © Mick Rock/Cephas
p.8: © Mick Rock/Cephas
pp.10-11 all: Courtesy of *Wine Enthusiast Magazine*
p.12: © Louis de Rohan/Cephas
p.58: © Kevin Judd/Cephas
p.186: © Walter Geiersperger/Cephas

p.210: © Steven Morris/Cephas
p.280: © Mick Rock/Cephas
p.383: © Mick Rock/Cephas
p.418: © Mike Newton/Cephas
p.588: © Kevin Judd/Cephas
p.637: © Mick Rock/Cephas
p.676: © Juan Espi/Cephas
p.720: © Mick Rock/Cephas
p.821: © Ted Stefanski/Cephas
p.823: © Mick Rock/Cephas
p.824: © Clay McLachlan/Cephas

Contents

Foreword

It sounds like a dream come true for many wine enthusiasts: making a living by sipping and evaluating the greatest wines from all over the world. Yes, it's true that members of our tasting panel sample thousands of wines every year. But of course, there is a great deal of work involved in actually tasting wine for review purposes (see How We Taste and Rate on page 8). But even given all the procedures and pressures, there is sublime pleasure to be had in trying new wines, whether the wine is a new grape variety, was produced in an unfamiliar region, or is just a new vintage of an old favorite. Every time we uncork, there is a new experience to be had. It's almost always pleasurable at some level; sometimes, it's simply sublime. And that brings us to this book.

The *Wine Enthusiast Essential Buying Guide 2008* includes more than 40,000 ratings and reviews of wines, the best that our tasting panel has sampled since we established the tasting and review program in 1999. We've arranged the reviews so that the book is as easy to use as possible—divided according to countries and alphabetized by producer name. Three other crucial bits of information are presented as prominently as possible: the quality score (based on the *Wine Enthusiast* 100-point scale), the vintage, and the grape variety, wherever possible. Experienced wine enthusiasts can go straight to the producing countries and producers whose wines they've enjoyed in the past

or have currently cellared to check scores. Novices will find this guide an indispensable tool to peruse before treks to the retail store. The *Wine Enthusiast Essential Buying Guide 2008* makes it easy to find values, track the performance of certain producers' wines over time, and get an idea of the general characteristics of wines from a certain region.

It's all about enjoyment: drinking what you like while continuing to experiment, trying some new wines, and taking advantage of the charm and power of wine. It's mind-boggling, the diversity that variables of grape variety, climate, soil, vineyard technique, and winemaking skill can produce.

We also encourage you to check us out online at www.wineenthusiast.com/magazine for our continually updated wine database, as well as the world's best vintage chart. It is the ideal companion to this book, providing you with everything you need to make wise buying decisions when at the retail store or restaurant.

Cheers,

Adam Strum
Publisher and Editor-in-Chief
Wine Enthusiast Magazine

Wine-Buying Strategies

SMART WINE BUYING TAKES PLANNING

In America, most wine is consumed the night it is bought. Whether it is a bottle of Opus One for a dinner party or a box of Franzia White Zin to improve Tuesday-night leftovers, it's often opened immediately with little thought.

Unfortunately, buying wine that way sacrifices a great deal of the pleasure of wine, and rarely provides the best deal. Pretentious though it may seem, it's worthwhile to develop a strategy for acquiring wine. It's both fun and rewarding.

There are a number of reasons for planning your purchases, but they almost all lead to having a supply on hand, ideally in a wine cellar or refrigerated storage cabinet. The most obvious advantage is that some wines improve with age, and even if you can afford to buy properly aged vintages, they may be very difficult to find. Buying young saves money, but also means that you'll be able to enjoy the wine when it's at its peak.

Of course, most wine doesn't improve with age, but if you're reading this, you most likely appreciate the wine that does. Most better reds certainly improve with a few years, and though many of today's wines are made to reach their peaks within a decade, most are released when they're only two or three years old. Hold them for even three or four years and they will improve tremendously. But if you buy wines at that peak stage, you will have to pay a premium.

Serious collectors, of course, often see wine as an investment that can be sold at an appreciated value in the future. Others see the real value in having far better wines to drink themselves.

Of course, some wines just keep on improving for decades: top Bordeaux, Burgundies, Napa Cabs, Barolos, and many Spanish wines fall in this category. It's not wise to drink them when they're only a few years old; if you do, they probably won't be much better than ordinary wines. Some people even develop a taste for old wines that many would consider past their prime, while others enjoy learning what happens to wines as they age.

You can obviously save a great deal when you cellar wines yourself, but even cursory planning can also save a lot of money. Buying wine on sale can be very rewarding. Almost every retailer offers at least 10 percent off for full cases, sometimes mixed cases, and that's like getting more than a bottle free with each case.

Some wines are even sold as futures. This primarily applies to top labels, but even some relatively modest wineries sell wine this way if it's in short supply. For example, after disastrous fires and earthquakes in wine warehouses, some producers in California offered attractive futures for their wines to maintain cash flow.

When all is said and done, however, perhaps the best reason for planning ahead is to have the right wine on hand when you want it. It's awful nice to be able to go into your cellar and grab a perfectly aged bottle that's the perfect match for dinner, or to take a special treat to a celebration without a trip to the wine store. In many areas, finding a special bottle could require ordering ahead, or a long drive to a state-controlled liquor store that is open during limited hours.

The only downside to having good wines on hand is a mixed one: You're more likely to enjoy it!

WHAT DO YOU LIKE?

Of course, it doesn't make much sense to have a cellar full of wine you don't like. Wine-buying guides provide good reference points for wines you've never tasted, but you'll probably want to buy only one bottle of a wine you haven't tasted instead of many, even if the producer has a good reputation or a well-known reviewer has awarded it a high score. Reputation and wine scores should be starting points, since people's tastes differ widely. Fortunately, there are a lot of ways to help guide your purchases.

One way to improve your odds is to learn which reviewers have tastes that mirror yours. For example, if you love massive Cabernets, which are extremely full bodied and high in alcohol, find which critics rave over them. Also learn which reviewers prefer more restrained wines that might be more suitable for enjoying with food.

All that said, the best way to learn what you like is by tasting wine. Take wine-tasting classes at wine stores or local colleges and adult schools. Attend wine events where you can taste a wide variety of wines. Try wines by the glass when available at restaurants and bars. Wine clubs and tasting parties with friends can be both great fun and very informative. Take recommendations from friends, but be sure to consider whether their tastes are similar to yours. Whatever you do, pay attention and take notes. And don't forget to spit (when you're at a tasting, not at a restaurant!)—otherwise, all the wine will taste great!

You'll almost always find some surprises, particularly with some inexpensive wines. Most important, accept your own tastes. Drinking wine isn't about forcing yourself to learn to like wines that don't suit you. Remember, above all of the terminology and technicality, the most important thing about wine should be the ability to get the most out of every glass, so that you actually enjoy what you're drinking. Drink—and buy—what you like and don't apologize or try to impress others.

MAKING THE PURCHASE

Once you've decided what wine you like, buy more of it. Although wine choices were once very limited, and still are in some states, in most areas, choices have multiplied, and expand daily as restrictive laws fall to lawsuits or change to reflect today's attitudes and to increase tax revenues.

The old-time wine store—and its modern counterpart—remains one of the best places to buy wines. Clerks in these stores tend to be knowledgeable about wine, and if you become a regular, they can learn more about your tastes and steer you toward wines you'll likely enjoy. Many shops now offer classes, wine tastings, and other events, and some will even order special wines and ship or deliver them to your home.

In many states, you can buy wine in supermarkets, giant discounters, club stores, discount wine and liquor outlets, and even convenience stores. And they're not just selling basic wine, either. Costco has emerged as one of the nation's largest retailers of fine wines including some that cost hundreds of dollars a bottle.

With barriers to interstate shipping of wine falling, direct purchases from wineries are making more and more sense. While it hardly pays to buy widely distributed wines direct from the wineries and pay shipping when you can buy the same wine at a neighborhood store many times for less, often the only place to get some wines is from the winery. This includes special bottles from big producers, including limited production bottlings and library wines.

For these wines, the most fun of all is to visit the winery, where you can taste before buying. As wineries spring up all over the country, that may not require a trip to Napa Valley. Many wineries also sell directly over the Internet, by brochure or mail, or by phone, and many independent firms sell wines from many producers as well.

If you're especially fond of certain wineries' wines, it can be fun to sign up for their wine clubs. They typically send a few bottles to members a few times a year, generally at a discount, often including wines not available except to club members or at the winery. Most wine clubs have special events, too, often at the wineries but some in other locations.

Whatever you do, don't forget the wine once it's in your cellar. While some wines improve with age, most don't.

How We Taste and Rate

Although *Wine Enthusiast* was first published in 1988, the magazine didn't regularly publish its own wine reviews until 1999. Beginning that year, the magazine's *Buying Guide* began to include the reviews of its own editors and other qualified tasters. The *Wine Enthusiast Essential Buying Guide 2008* focuses on new releases and selected older wines.

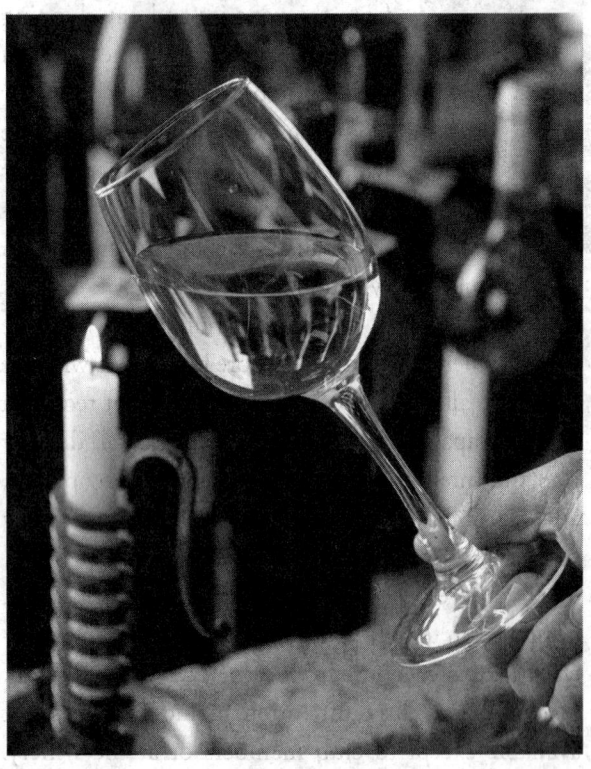

Today, approximately 500 wine reviews are included in each issue of *Wine Enthusiast Magazine*. Each review contains a score on the 100-point scale, the full name of the wine, its suggested national retail price, and a tasting note. If a price cannot be confirmed, $NA (not available) will be printed. Prices are for 750 ml bottles unless otherwise indicated.

This compilation contains all of the wines formally reviewed by the *Wine Enthusiast* tasting panel from its inception through the final issue of 2006.

Regular contributors to our Buying Guide include Tasting Director/Senior Editor Joe Czerwinski, Senior Editor Susan Kostrzewa, and Contributing Editor Michael Schachner in New York; European Editor Roger Voss in Bordeaux; Italian Editor Monica Larner in Rome; West Coast Editor Steve Heimoff in California; and Contributing Editor Paul Gregutt in Seattle. Past contributors whose initials may appear in this guide include former Tasting Directors Mark Mazur and Chuck Simeone, former Senior Editor Daryna Tobey, former Tasting Coordinator Kristen Fogg, Contributing Editor Jeff Morgan, and former contributing tasters Martin Neschis and Larry Walker.

If a wine was evaluated by a single reviewer, that taster's initials appear following the note. When no initials appear, the wine was evaluated by two or more reviewers and the score and tasting note reflect the input of all tasters.

TASTING METHODOLOGY AND GOALS

Tastings are conducted individually or in a group setting and performed blind or in accordance with accepted industry practices (it is not possible to taste the wines blind when visiting producers, for example). When wines are tasted in our offices or for specific tasting features, they are tasted blind, in flights defined by grape variety, place of origin, and vintage.

We assess quality by examining five distinct characteristics: appearance, bouquet, flavor, mouthfeel, and finish. Above all, our tasters are looking for balance and harmony, with additional consideration given for ability to improve with age. Price is not a factor in assigning scores to wines. When possible, wines considered flawed or uncustomary are retasted.

ABOUT THE SCORES

Ratings reflect what our editors felt about a particular wine. Beyond the rating, we encourage you to read the accompanying tasting note to learn about a wine's special characteristics.

Classic 98–100: The pinnacle of quality.

Superb 94–97: A great achievement.

Excellent 90–93: Highly recommended.

Very Good 87–89: Often good value; well recommended.

Good 83–86: Suitable for everyday consumption; often good value.

Acceptable 80–82: Can be employed in casual, less-critical circumstances.

Wines receiving a rating below 80 are not reviewed.

SPECIAL DESIGNATIONS

Best Buys are wines that offer a high level of quality in relation to price. There are no specific guidelines or formulae for determining Best Buys, but they are generally priced below $15.

Editors' Choice wines are those that offer excellent quality at a price above our Best Buy range, or a wine at any price with unique qualities that merit special attention.

Cellar Selections are wines deemed highly collectible and/or requiring time in a temperature-controlled wine cellar to reach their maximum potential. A Cellar Selection designation does not mean that a wine must be stored to be enjoyed, but that cellaring will probably result in a more enjoyable bottle. In general, an optimum time for cellaring will be indicated.

Contributors

Tasting Director and Senior Editor Joe Czerwinski joined *Wine Enthusiast Magazine* in 1999 as an associate editor. In addition to managing the entire tasting and review program, he reviews wines from France, Germany, Australia, and New Zealand.

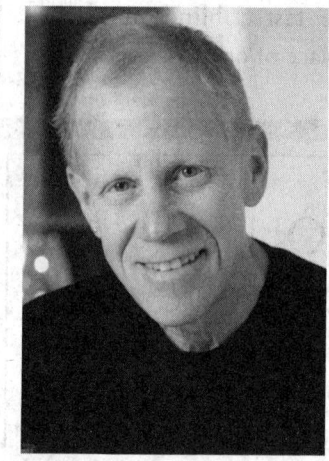

West Coast Editor Steve Heimoff was born in New York City and moved to California to attend grad school. He quickly discovered wine, which became his passion. He has been with *Wine Enthusiast Magazine* for 13 years and reviews virtually all of the California wines. His book, *A Wine Journey along the Russian River*, was published in 2005 by University of California Press. His most recent book was published in Fall 2007.

Susan Kostrzewa is a senior editor and Web editor for *Wine Enthusiast magazine* and *Wine Enthusiast* online. Kostrzewa has written and edited wine, food and travel stories for the past 10 years, and in addition to editing *Wine Enthusiast*'s print magazine and online publication, currently reviews wines from South Africa, Greece, Hungary, Israel, and all the U.S., except California and Washington.

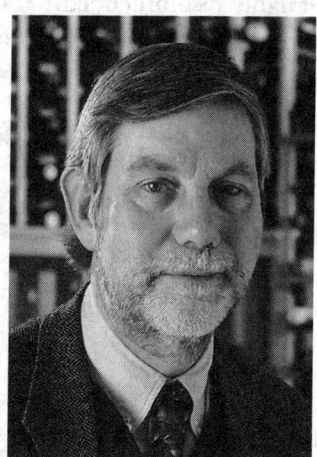

European Editor Roger Voss is a wine and food author and journalist. He has been writing on wine and food for the past 25 years. His books include *France: A Feast of Food and Wine*, *The Wines of the Loire*, *Pocket Guide to the Wines of the Loire, Alsace, and the Rhône;* and *Fortified Wines*. He is based in Bordeaux, France, from where he reviews the wines of Austria, France, and Portugal.

Monica Larner has lived in Italy on and off for the past 15 years and is *Wine Enthusiast Magazine*'s Italian Editor. Based in Rome, she is a member of the Italian Association of Sommeliers and has published three books on her adopted home. When not in Europe,  she can be found with pruning shears in hand on the family-run Larner Vineyard in Santa Barbara Country, California.

In addition to reviewing Pacific Northwest wines for *Wine Enthusiast Magazine*, Seattle-based **Contributing Editor Paul Gregutt** writes on wine for the *Seattle Times*, the *Yakima Herald-Republic*, the *Walla Walla Union-Bulletin*, and *Pacific*  *Northwest* magazine. He has written two editions of Northwest Wines, and his book, *Washington Wines and Wineries*, was published by the University of California Press in 2007.

Michael Schachner is a New York-based journalist specializing in wine, food, and travel. His articles appear regularly in *Wine Enthusiast Magazine*, for which he is a contributing editor and a member of the magazine's tasting panel. In addition, he is a wine consultant and profes-  sional speaker. His areas of wine expertise include Spain, Italy, and South America.

Argentina

Argentina features a vaunted winemaking history that began some five hundred years ago when Spanish missionaries first arrived and planted vines. But it wasn't until about two hundred years ago that Argentina developed a commercial wine industry, largely centered in the province of Mendoza, located about four hundred miles directly west of Buenos Aires.

For all intents and purposes, Argentina's wine industry was until fairly recently geared toward domestic consumption. Nineteenth and early twentieth-century immigrants from Spain and Italy had a huge thirst for wine, and the vineyards that they planted along the western edge of the country, where the climate is dry, the temperatures are warm, and there's plenty of water available from the mighty Andes, produced copious amounts of varietal and blended reds that the Argentine population drank with nary a complaint.

Harvesting grapes in a vineyard of Peñaflor, Mendoza, Argentina

To a large extent, that's still the case. Argentineans remain the primary consumers of their own wines. But as the global wine market began to take shape in the latter half of the twentieth century, Argentina refocused its winemaking and marketing efforts to highlight exports. Today, there are approximately one hundred wineries throughout Argentina that are sending their wines overseas. Mendoza, with its numerous subzones, remains front and center among wine regions, with areas like San Rafael, La Rioja, San Juan, Salta, and Cafayate vying for second chair.

Due to a pervasive hot, dry climate, it's safe to say that red wines outperform white wines in almost all parts of Argentina; although the higher one goes into the Andes, the cooler it gets and the crisper the white wines become. And with such deep Italian and Spanish roots running through the country's people, that makes sense.

Malbec, which was brought to Argentina from France some 150 years ago, has emerged as Argentina's signature grape. It is grown throughout the country, and while it varies in style, one can safely call it fruity, aromatic, and lush. In flatter, warmer vineyards, Malbec can be soft and simple, an easy wine for everyday drinking and blending. But if taken into the foothills of the mountains or grown in old vineyards, it can be a wine of immense character.

Joining Malbec on the red roster is Cabernet Sauvignon, which is flavorful and serious when coming from top wineries like Terrazas de Los Andes, Catena Zapata, Norton, Cobos, or Chakana, to name several. Picked ripe, like in California and aged mostly in French oak barrels, Argentinean Cabernet has what it takes.

Other red grapes one frequently encounters are Bonarda and Sangiovese, both of which were brought over from Italy, as well as Merlot, Syrah, Tempranillo, and even some Pinot Noir.

Among white wines, one of Argentina's best and most distinctive offerings is Torrontès, an import from Galicia in Spain. Floral and occasionally exotic in scent and taste, Torrontès seems to do best in the more northern Salta region, where there's higher humidity and more rain than in Mendoza.

And as stated before, the Andean foothills are proving to be the prime spot for Chardonnay. At elevations of more than 3,000 feet above sea level, warm days and cool nights yield naturally fresh and properly acidic wines. Flavors of pineapple, green banana, and other tropical fruits are common among Argentina's modern-day Chardonnays.

[Ñ]

[ñ] 2003 Malbec (Uco Valley) $30. Freixenet, the big cava producer from Catalonia, Spain, has entered Argentina via this cutely named winery. The wine, however, is pretty much your standard-fare Malbec. The nose and palate are fruity and bold, while the finish offers spice and coffee. Good but not up to the price. **86** —*M.S. (12/1/2006)*

1919

1919 2004 Cabernet Sauvignon (Mendoza) $10. Flat and basic, with charred secondary aromas. Simple red fruit with rubbery tannins make for an average palate. Easy enough but hard to find anything special or exciting to go on about. **83** —*M.S. (8/1/2006)*

1919 2004 Malbec (Mendoza) $10. Black cherry mixes with raisin on the dark, meaty nose. Additional black cherry and plum flavors are thick and a bit prune-based, but if you enjoy ripeness you'll like the style. Bitter chocolate and toast carry the finish. **85 Best Buy** —*M.S. (8/1/2006)*

1919 2004 Syrah (Mendoza) $10. Smells like cherry sucking candy and immature red fruit. Very colorful and bold, with sharp flavors and a jumpy mouthfeel. Limited in what it has to offer. **81** —*M.S. (11/1/2006)*

ACHÁVAL-FERRER

Achával-Ferrer 2002 Finca Altamira Malbec (Mendoza) $85. The nose is all bacon, game, and leather along with graphite and berry fruit. Surprisingly firm and juicy on the palate; the acidity is rather sharp, which manufactures a racy, hard mouthfeel. No complaints with the exotic flavors coming from this old-vines wine. But the feel is astringent and the finish has some heat. Unconventional. **88** —*M.S. (7/1/2005)*

Achával-Ferrer 2000 Finca Altamira Malbec (Mendoza) $85. Very dark and extracted, with brooding aromas of ink and lots and lots of wood. In the mouth, plum and blueberry fruit gets a boost from some chocolaty flavors, but that same fruit also gets covered up by some very heavy oak. The finish is rather grapy and heavy, with a cooling hint of menthol. **86** —*M.S. (5/1/2003)*

Achával-Ferrer 2001 Quimera Red Blend (Mendoza) $55. This blend of Cabernet, Malbec, and Merlot is round and intense, with aromatic notes of iodine, rubber, and smoked meat. At first taste, the palate is like a confection—something similar to cherry lollipops. And the finish is acidic and sharp. With time it settles down, indicating that it could improve with age. But now it's clumsy and aggressive. **85** —*M.S. (5/1/2003)*

ACORDEÓN

Acordeón 2004 Syrah (Mendoza) $10. Starts out smoky and seemingly ripe, but the nose is the best part. The palate, by contrast, is tight, gritty, and the flavors are awkward at best. Really not that consistent and loses focus the more you get into it. **81** —*M.S. (11/1/2006)*

ALAMOS

Alamos 2003 Bonarda (Mendoza) $10. Vegetal on the nose, with flavors of stewed plum and black olive. Salinity on the finish doesn't really help this wine, which struggles across the board. **81** —*M.S. (11/15/2005)*

Alamos 2002 Bonarda (Mendoza) $10. This varietal bottling uses an old Italian grape that's still popular in Argentina. The wine is fresh and snappy, with lots of simple, sweet fruit and mild tannins. A touch of creamy vanillin from short-term oak aging is a welcome addition. **86** —*M.S. (7/1/2004)*

Alamos 2000 Bonarda (Mendoza) $13. Heavy aromas of wood, dark chocolate, and black plums get this uncommon varietal going. Chewy strawberry and chocolate run rough over the palate, and the finish is large and packed with coffee flavor. Fans of fruit balls may dig this, but if balance and complexity are what you're after, keep looking. **84** —*M.S. (11/1/2002)*

Alamos 2002 Cabernet Sauvignon (Mendoza) $10. Leathery and light, and not strong in the area of true Cabernet character. Meaning there isn't much richness or weight, and the berry fruit is bland. Okay, but lacks punch. **84** —*M.S. (7/1/2004)*

Alamos 2001 Cabernet Sauvignon (Mendoza) $10. Some spicy red-fruit aromas along with hints of citrus rind and pine needles signal freshness.

Solid plum and raspberry flavors confirm its medium weight and middle-of-the-road aspirations. On the back end, smooth oak is a good touch. **86** —*M.S. (5/1/2003)*

Alamos 1999 Cabernet Sauvignon (Mendoza) $13. Some dusty, leathery aromas start this wine out, and the bouquet never matures beyond leaf and forest floor. Some sweet grapey flavors chime in on the palate, and that taste is something similar to sugar beets. The light cherry-tinged finish offers a bit of depth, but not much. **84** —*M.S. (11/1/2002)*

Alamos 2004 Chardonnay (Mendoza) $10. Lean smelling, with apple, beeswax, and a spot of iodine on the nose. Flavors of melon, apple, and pepper are forward and real if a bit oak-driven. Weighty throughout. **85 Best Buy** —*M.S. (11/15/2005)*

Alamos 2003 Chardonnay (Mendoza) $10. Despite spending just five months on oak staves, the nose is toasty. There's also good pear and banana notes as well as some vanilla. Tasted shortly after bottling; it should round out by the time you're reading this review. The balance seems to be right on the spot. **87** —*M.S. (7/1/2004)*

Alamos 2002 Chardonnay (Mendoza) $10. Like virtually every wine from the Catena family, oak is at the lead. You can smell clear notes of butterscotch and wood. In the mouth, a creamy sensation takes over, while flavors of vanilla and lemon show the show. The finish is long and oaky, with plenty of vanillin. What some might see as overoaked will be a pleasure to others. **86** —*M.S. (5/1/2003)*

Alamos 2001 Chardonnay (Mendoza) $13. Simple aromas of fruit and wheat are touched up by toasted oak. Lemon, citrus, and pear flavors vie for attention here, but nothing really stands out. It finishes on the spicy side, but with a sweetness that seems to come from residual sugar. **83** —*M.S. (7/1/2002)*

Alamos 2004 Malbec (Mendoza) $10. Clean and smooth, with vanilla and boysenberry defining the nose. Not a complex wine, but one made for everyday drinking; thus the plum and berry fruit is ripe and forward, while the finish is just toasty enough. Flawless even though it lacks sophistication. No high gears but still a good ride. **87 Best Buy** —*M.S. (11/15/2005)*

Alamos 2003 Malbec (Mendoza) $10. Saturated and extracted, with an incredibly deep purple tint paving the way for manly aromas of espresso, campfire, and toasted coconut. The palate, meanwhile, runs a bit sweet, with boysenberry and plum. Soft on the back end, but with enough spine to see it through. For fans of bold reds. **88 Best Buy** —*M.S. (3/1/2005)*

Alamos 2002 Malbec (Mendoza) $11. Plenty of char greets you, which is typical of a Catena wine; oak is always in play. The palate is ultraripe, with cherry and boysenberry fruit receiving a boost from bold acidity. With nuances of earth and pepper, but ultimately a lean body, this wine steers the course while never overreaching its limits. **86** —*M.S. (12/1/2003)*

Alamos 2001 Malbec (Mendoza) $11. At first the nose is somewhat dull and closed, but patience and swirling reveals black fruit, some wood notes, and a bit of rubber. Boysenberry fruit drives the palate. The finish goes heavy on the oak, but there's also some nice layering. **86** —*M.S. (5/1/2003)*

Alamos 2000 Malbec (Mendoza) $13. Wood-driven spicy aromas dominate the bouquet, which offers too little fruit and only a hint of clove. Raspberry and red cherry flavors come before a dry, simple woody finish. Given the light, lean body weight of this wine, the oak comes on a bit strong and drying. **83** —*M.S. (11/1/2002)*

Alamos 2002 Pinot Noir (Mendoza) $10. Comes from the cooler Tupungato area, and shows a rooty, spicy, berry nose along with good color. The palate offers some true Pinot character, a bit of pepper and some leather before turning thin. Finishes light, with a hint of chocolate. **85** —*M.S. (7/1/2004)*

Alamos 2004 Viognier (Mendoza) $10. Floral and light, with encouraging aromas. Doesn't have the glycerol of a Rhône Viognier, but shows nice apple and peach flavors in front of a lightweight but clean finish. Fairly bright and lively, and solid on the surface. **87 Best Buy** —*M.S. (11/15/2005)*

Alamos 2003 Viognier (Mendoza) $10. Hailing from the high-altitude, rugged Tupungato subregion, this Viognier is purely Argentine in style. Yes, it has true honeysuckle aromas and pure honey flavors, but it's also rather lemony and lean, with a thin midpalate and a tight, light finish. **86** —M.S. (7/1/2004)

ALBERTI 154

Alberti 154 2003 Cabernet Sauvignon (Mendoza) $10. Spicy and saucy on the nose, with hints of barnyard and leather. Opens to show crisp plum and berry flavors in front of a spicy, grippy finish. Not tannic per se, but fairly tight. **86 Best Buy** —M.S. (11/15/2005)

Alberti 154 2002 Cabernet Sauvignon (Mendoza) $10. Cherry and earth aromas have a hint of leather, which adds rusticity to the wine. Can't-miss notes of clove and nutmeg seriously bolster flavors of cherry and plum, and by the time the finish rolls around, that clove quality is magnified. Ultimately this is a spicy, leaner Cab, but good acids and tannins keep it upright. **86 Best Buy** —M.S. (7/1/2004)

Alberti 154 2003 Merlot (Mendoza) $10. Inviting enough, with some buttery oak on the palate along with fresh red-fruit flavors. Finishes solid, with a smoky side. Crisp, bordering on lean, with hard tannins and a lot of aggressive tang. **83** —M.S. (11/15/2005)

Alberti 154 2002 Merlot (Mendoza) $10. Short on freshness and focus; the wine starts out a touch musty, and in the mouth, flavors of cotton candy, strawberry, and red licorice seem confectionary. Caramel on the finish and a chewy ending texture are the lasting impressions. **83** —M.S. (7/1/2004)

ALFREDO ROCA

Alfredo Roca 2002 Cabernet Sauvignon (San Rafael) $12. Aromas of jammy fruit mix with smoky bacon, and the whole is inviting. The palate maintains a soft, simple character, while the finish pours on toasty oak notes. Quite meaty and chewy, without much overt acidity. **85** —M.S. (11/15/2005)

Alfredo Roca 2004 Chardonnay (San Rafael) $12. Waxy and oily, with flavors of orange and other citrus fruits. The feel is kind of flat and heavy, with chunky melon on the finish. **82** —M.S. (11/15/2005)

Alfredo Roca 2003 Malbec (San Rafael) $11. An entirely different breed. The nose hints strongly at bacon and spice, but it also weaves in subtle red-fruit notes. Out of the ordinary on the palate, too, where cherry flavors are light but savory. A touch odd and slick, but good because it's not standard. **85** —M.S. (12/1/2006)

Alfredo Roca 2002 Malbec (San Rafael) $12. Starts out exotic, with clove and other spice notes. The palate is somewhat racy, with crisp acids pushing juicy black fruit. On the edges you'll find oaky, spicy notes. Finishes peppery and snappy, with some length. **86** —M.S. (12/31/2005)

Alfredo Roca 2004 Tocai Friulano (San Rafael) $12. Heavy on the nose, with a strong scent of mineral and vitamins. Soft in the mouth, with a round texture but little flavor backing it up. Registers more vapid than anything. **81** —M.S. (12/31/2005)

ALTA VISTA

Alta Vista 2002 Premium Bonarda (Mendoza) $10. One of the better Bonardas out there. It's full, solid, and surprisingly plush. Aromas of leather and earth mix with berry fruit, followed by a spicy plum and berry palate. Finishes with notes of smoked meat and oak. **86 Best Buy** —M.S. (10/1/2004)

Alta Vista 2003 Premium Cabernet Sauvignon (Mendoza) $13. Lively from the beginning, where red-fruit aromas are toughened up by notes of leather, earth, and spice. Fairly robust in the mouth, with plum, berry, and pepper flavors. Substantive throughout, with firm tannins and enough oak to create mocha and vanilla on the finish. **87** —M.S. (11/1/2006)

Alta Vista 2005 Premium Chardonnay (Mendoza) $13. Light citrus, grapefruit, and oak notes are nice openers. Peach, melon, and other fruits grace the palate. Shows crispness in addition to oak, and the finish is lasting and round. Easy to get; pretty solid overall. **85** —M.S. (11/1/2006)

Alta Vista 2002 Premium Chardonnay (Mendoza) $10. The nose is heavy and a bit odd; the mix of pears and white pepper doesn't really work. In the mouth, potent flavors of butterscotch and Bartlett pear bolster things, but overall it still seems out of whack. **84** —M.S. (5/1/2003)

Alta Vista 2001 Premium Chardonnay (Mendoza) $10. At first the nose is distant, bordering on weak. But it comes around and functions as a good entrée to the spicy pear and apple palate. The finish is dry, with plenty of wood spice poking in and out. Elegance may not be its strong suit, but it has power and size. **85** —M.S. (5/1/2003)

Alta Vista 1999 Malbec (Mendoza) $12. Considering how universally solid the '99 vintage was in this country, this wine is a disappointment. It has stemmy, green aromas, only a modicum of cherry and raspberry fruit, and a fiery hot finish. As a whole, it's raw and difficult to recommend. **82** —M.S. (11/1/2002)

Alta Vista 2002 Alto Malbec (Mendoza) $60. Begins with smoky bacon aromas that are followed by ripe black cherry and blackberry. Very plump and earthy, with a flush mouthfeel and lively acidity. Severely oaked, but that wood is of quality, so it yields vanilla and pepper rather than resin or sawdust. A blend of 85% Malbec and 15% Cabernet. **91** —M.S. (7/1/2005)

Alta Vista 1998 Alto Malbec (Mendoza) $60. In 1997 Jean-Michel Arcaute of Château Clinet in Bordeaux began this Argentinean venture, and this blend of 80% Malbec and 20% Cabernet is supposed to be the best wine from the property. Admittedly, 1998 was a wet year, but this wine has green bean aromas, a clumsy, bulky palate of nondescript red fruit, and wall-to-wall tannins on top of sweet, sugary flavors. **84** —M.S. (11/1/2002)

Alta Vista 2000 Grand Reserve Malbec (Mendoza) $20. The first whiff is of peanuts, and with time some ink and smoked meat emerge. The flavors are ample and satisfying, with black fruit, roast meat, and bitter chocolate vying for the front row. The finish is only slightly bitter, with chocolate and coffee sticking out. **87** —M.S. (5/1/2003)

Alta Vista 2002 Grande Reserve Malbec (Mendoza) $20. Almost floral, but with aromas of crushed minerals and tar. Airing reveals some coconut, but swirling unleashes an onslaught of balancing snappy red fruit. Definitely an oaky Malbec, with powerful finishing flavors of coffee, bitter chocolate, and vanilla. **89** —M.S. (7/1/2005)

Alta Vista 2004 Premium Malbec (Mendoza) $13. Jammy and attractive. The nose is wide open and full of dark berry aromas. The palate is also pretty deep, and in addition to the requisite beaming fruit you'll find licorice and molasses. Finishes on the money, and with richness. **88 Best Buy** —M.S. (11/1/2006)

Alta Vista 2002 Premium Malbec (Mendoza) $10. This wine captures all that is good about affordable Malbec. It's endowed with ripe red and black fruits, a bit of violet on the nose, and just the right hint of leather. The palate is nice and sweet, with dry tannins and a dense finish. Sound like a balanced, ready-to-go red wine? It is. **89 Best Buy** —M.S. (10/1/2004)

Alta Vista 2001 Premium Malbec (Mendoza) $10. Though not offputting, there's nothing particularly "premium" about this sweet, woody wine. Cloying mocha aromas and flavors mask indistinct red fruit and create a wine that's much like a milk chocolate bar. A very easy mouthfeel, but nothing complex. **83** —M.S. (1/1/2004)

Alta Vista 2000 Premium Malbec (Mendoza) $10. The nose is lean and thin, while the palate is slick, dark, and smoky. The finish is light and nondescript, and there seems to be a weedy note at the core. This wine is like a chameleon; it changes a lot but never seems to hit much of a stride. **82** —M.S. (5/1/2003)

Alta Vista 2003 Alto Malbec-Cabernet Sauvignon (Mendoza) $60. Full, dense, and powerful is this blend of Malbec and Cabernet, but it's also ultraripe and loaded with new oak. Earth, cola, and blackberry are all attractive aromas, while the berry fruit is commendable. Where this wine slumps, if you can say that, is in the complexity department; it seems almost too simple and easy. **88** —M.S. (8/1/2006)

Alta Vista 2000 Red Blend (Mendoza) $8. Lean in the nose, with aromas of spearmint and grass. The strawberry is on the candied side, while tomato and cherry flavors come up toward the end. The feel in the mouth is good but the flavors aren't up to par. **82** —*M.S. (5/1/2003)*

Alta Vista 2000 Cosecha Tempranillo Blend (Mendoza) $8. The berry aromas are faint, much weaker than the grassy notes alongside. The flavors are of candied red fruit: think red licorice. The finish is heavy and expansive. While not bad, there is no complexity here. **84** —*M.S. (11/1/2002)*

Alta Vista 2002 Malbec-Tempranillo Tempranillo Blend (Mendoza) $8. Light on the nose, with shy strawberry and cherry aromas. Quite skinny on the palate, with inconsistent cherry cola and oak flavors. Very light on the finish, but buttery. Shows questionable barrel notes. **82** —*M.S. (10/1/2004)*

Alta Vista 2005 Premium Torrontès (Salta) $13. Floral and sweet, but not that light or ethereal. At 14.5% this represents the heavy, seriously ripe side of Torrontès. Flavors of pineapple and nectarine are borderline oily, while the finish toes the line of being aggressive. Flavorful but a rumbler. **85** —*M.S. (11/1/2006)*

Alta Vista 2003 Premium Torrontès (Mendoza) $10. Floral and potent, with classic Torrontès aromas and flavors. Look for taste notes of lemongrass, lychee, papaya, and citrus, and then a forward, lemony finish with solid acidity. If you have any interest in Torrontès, this is a good place to start. **86** —*M.S. (7/1/2004)*

Alta Vista 2002 Premium Torrontès (Mendoza) $10. The bouquet rings of peaches; the flavor profile is like fruit cocktail, with some grapefruit added in for edge. The finish is long, and here the acids do their thing. **83** —*M.S. (5/1/2003)*

Alta Vista 2003 Chardonnay-Torrontès White Blend (Mendoza) $8. This 50/50 blend offers aromas of lime, talcum powder, and wet stones. Flavors of apple, melon, and citrus are standard and tangy, without too much strength. Lemony acids keep it lively. **84** —*M.S. (10/1/2004)*

Alta Vista 2000 Cosecha White Blend (Mendoza) $8. Bright yellow in color, with a heavy scoop of honey, cream, and overripe tropical fruit to the nose. The flavors are dull and a little bit vegetal. Not flawed but not inspiring. Even worse, it tastes old. **80** —*M.S. (5/1/2003)*

ALTAS CUMBRES

Altas Cumbres 2002 Cabernet Sauvignon (Mendoza) $9. Aromas of campfire, baked fruit, black licorice and cherry create a pleasant bouquet. The cherry and cassis fruit that flows on the palate is juicy and live-wire. Finishes with coffee, chocolate, and black pepper. Full and forward, with a dark personality. **88 Best Buy** —*M.S. (11/15/2004)*

Altas Cumbres 2002 Cabernet Sauvignon-Malbec (Mendoza) $9. Quite flowery and round, with pure grape, cherry, and berry aromas and flavors. Very fresh and spunky, and well made. Finishes with lots of fruit, integrated oak and hints of coffee and chocolate. **88 Best Buy** —*M.S. (11/15/2004)*

Altas Cumbres 2002 Malbec (Mendoza) $9. Cotton candy and flower-petal aromas are a bit sweet and youthful, but the nose is no turn off. Flavors of berry and molasses convey some thickness, while the finish is equally creamy and thick. Spicy and full of fruit. **87 Best Buy** —*M.S. (11/15/2004)*

Altas Cumbres 2003 Viognier (Mendoza) $9. A bit of celery interferes with the otherwise clean fruit on the bouquet. Flavors of apple, lemon and lime are sweet and satisfactory. Finishes full, with a grabby feel. **84** —*M.S. (11/15/2004)*

ALTOCEDRO

Altocedro 2004 Año Cero Malbec (Mendoza) $12. Violet in color, with chunky, ripe aromas of earth and berries that win you over. Structured and full, but also dry and layered. The fruit comes across ripe, while on the finish everything folds into a nice little square. Not spectacular but very easy to drink and enjoy. **87 Best Buy** —*M.S. (12/1/2006)*

Altocedro 2001 Año Cero Malbec (Mendoza) $12. Earthy and leathery, with some deeper fruit notes below the rustic exterior. The palate shows raisin, carob, and bitter chocolate flavors, while coffee and mocha carry the finish. Strains to keep it together, but has its attributes. **83** —*M.S. (11/15/2005)*

Altocedro 2001 Reserva Malbec (Mendoza) $17. Fresh-cut oak sits front and center, and behind it there's textbook plum and berry fruit. Racy and tannic, but solid and fruity. Almost exactly as expected, although a bit thin as it gets more air. **85** —*M.S. (11/15/2005)*

ALTOS DE MEDRANO

Altos de Medrano 2001 Reserva Viña Hormigas Malbec (Mendoza) $24. Altos is a six-man, predominantly Italian joint venture that makes great Malbec. Their reserva is richly extracted, with legs that want to climb up rather than down. The nose is full of mint, leather and blueberry, while the thick palate stays balanced and tight. The fact that oak is complementary and not dominant is the coup de grace. **92** —*M.S. (12/1/2003)*

ALTOS LAS HORMIGAS

Altos Las Hormigas 2003 Malbec (Mendoza) $12. Starts full and oaky, but not sappy or overly creamy. Settles to offer aromas of campfire, lavender, black peppercorn, and plenty of snappy berry fruit. Fine texture and depth of flavor, with cherry, plum, and vanilla. A complete wine with an intense spice element. **89 Best Buy** —*M.S. (7/1/2005)*

Altos Las Hormigas 2001 Malbec (Mendoza) $9. On the nose, smooth berry aromas turn chocolaty courtesy of the high-toast barrels used. In the mouth, the plump fruit seems up to the oak. There's raspberry and raisin, and some blueberry, too. For the curious, Altos de Medrano is the winery and hormigas, in Spanish, are ants. Fortunately, I've seen no such critters at the winery. **88 Best Buy** —*M.S. (11/15/2003)*

Altos Las Hormigas 2004 Reserva Viña Hormigas Malbec (Mendoza) $23. Potent and piercing right off the bat. The color says a lot, and the nose is confirmation that with this Malbec you're not playing around. The berry level is up there, and the flavors of blackberry, cassis, and plum are deep and satisfying. A nice layer of roasted fruit and oak carry the finish, and overall this wine offers a lot of juice per sip. **91** —*M.S. (12/31/2005)*

Altos Las Hormigas 2002 Reserva Viña Hormigas Malbec (Mendoza) $25. Saturated in color. Smells rugged, like tire rubber and tar mixed with blackberry. Beautiful tasting, with black cherry, licorice, and minerality on a firm, no-flab palate. Fairly big tannins create structure; a touch of crushed pepper and burnt toast darken up the finish. **92 Editors' Choice** —*M.S. (7/1/2005)*

ALTOSUR

Altosur 2002 Estate Bottled Cabernet Sauvignon (Mendoza) $10. Tobacco, sugar beet, and cough drop aromas don't offer much, while blatant wood resin on the palate is wrapped tightly around blowsy blackberry fruit. Tough and tannic. **81** —*M.S. (7/1/2005)*

Altosur 2002 Chardonnay (Mendoza) $10. This wine from Finca Sophenia is tiring and should be drunk immediately. In the meantime, there are cornflake and wheat bread aromas in front of a creamy palate marked by honey and flan. Warm, doughy, and losing form. **83** —*M.S. (7/1/2005)*

Altosur 2002 Merlot (Mendoza) $10. Quite jumbled and big at 14.2% alcohol. This wine is cast in stone, it's so hard and tannic, even for Merlot. But under the bombarding tannic wall there's racy dark berry fruit. Ripped and hard, it badly needs meat to ease the tannins. By itself it's no joy ride. **85 Best Buy** —*M.S. (7/1/2005)*

AMBIENTE

Ambiente 2004 Malbec (Mendoza) $12. Not a lot of ambience to talk about. The nose is almost peanutty in its murkiness, while the flavors of cherry, burnt toast, and green pepper are less than impressive. Not an overly bad wine; it just fails to impress at any juncture. **81** —*M.S. (12/1/2006)*

Ambiente 2003 Tempranillo (Mendoza) $12. Argentinean Tempranillo is a slippery slope, as evidenced by this mossy, olive-ridden red that has its moments as well as its faults. Positives include a nice spice element and good intentions. But beware of the herbal flavors and rock-hard mouthfeel. **84** —*M.S. (12/1/2006)*

AMOR DE LOS ANDES

Amor de los Andes 2002 Malbec (Mendoza) $15. Jammy, sweet aromas conjure notes of a rose garden in bloom, but the palate is more scattered. On offer is basic cherry, raisin and cotton candy. Sweet on the finish, yet good in a simple way. **84** —*M.S. (3/1/2005)*

Amor de los Andes 2002 Syrah (La Rioja) $11. Rustic berry and leather on the nose is backed up by modest cherry and plum flavors. A touch gritty and hot on the finish, with slight tomato and leather notes. **83** —*M.S. (3/1/2005)*

Amor de los Andes 2002 Tempranillo (Mendoza) $15. Fairly overripe, with jammy aromas touched by raspberry and mocha. Somewhat lactic on the palate, with strawberry and other berry notes. Finishes flat although it never offends. **83** —*M.S. (3/1/2005)*

ANASTASIA

Anastasia 2001 Chardonnay (Mendoza) $10. Very nice aromas of pear and pineapple crowd the big, powerful bouquet. The mouth is expressive, with pear, apple, spice, and vanilla flavors; it's a step up from most of the competition. The finish is simultaneously smooth and cooling. Healthy acidity and plenty of extract make for a well-balanced whole. **88 Best Buy** —*M.S. (5/1/2003)*

ANDALHUE

Andalhue 2004 Organico Malbec (Mendoza) $12. Good in color, with modest black-fruit aromas. Sports some tartness along with typical cherry and chocolate flavors. Fine in terms of size, but with an electric streak of acidity running through the center. Finishes chocolaty. **84** —*M.S. (11/15/2005)*

ANDEAN

Andean 2004 Finca La Escondida Reserva Chardonnay (San Juan) $16. A classic modern wine with plenty of vanilla, almond, and baked apple on the rich, nutty bouquet. Flavors of peach, toasted nuts, and bread are stylish and elegant, while a beam of acidity keeps it perfectly balanced. A great little find from Argentina. **90 Editors' Choice** —*M.S. (11/1/2006)*

ANDELUNA

Andeluna 2003 Grand Reserve Pasionado Bordeaux Blend (Mendoza) $50. From the beginning you can tell that this Bordeaux-style blend has the requisite components to make the grade. The bouquet offers baking spices, berry, and vanilla in large doses, while the palate is ample, fresh, and fairly racy. Nothing dull or clumsy here; it's a balanced, structured wine with aging ability. Drink now or hold through 2009. **91** —*M.S. (6/1/2006)*

Andeluna 2003 Limited Release Cabernet Franc (Mendoza) $50. Young and disjointed at first, the nose finally settles on almond paste and berry syrup. This is Andeluna's most pricey wine, and while it delivers deep plum and blackberry followed by a smoky coffee and chocolate-tinged finish, it's grabby and awkward. Good but not a star. **86** —*M.S. (8/1/2006)*

Andeluna 2003 Reserve Cabernet Sauvignon (Mendoza) $23. Ripe and cushy, with deeply defined fruit aromas that carry enough soft touches to make you want to dig in. Delicate but daring on the palate, with chocolate notes darkening the cassis and cherry flavors. Very round and exceedingly mouthfilling. **90** —*M.S. (6/1/2006)*

Andeluna 2003 Winemaker's Selection Cabernet Sauvignon (Mendoza) $13. Ruby in color, with attractive mint, leather, and black-fruit aromas. Like all Andeluna reds, which are made by the talented Silvio Alberto, it is ripe and lush; the black cherry, raspberry, and chocolate flavors satisfy on their way to a toasted, smooth finish. Cushy and right for the times, and a bargain given that we're talking Cabernet Sauvignon. **88 Best Buy** —*M.S. (8/1/2006)*

Andeluna 2003 Reserve Chardonnay (Mendoza) $23. The color is a rich gold hue, while the nose offers a collection of apple, cinnamon, mineral, and toast. This is a full-bodied and well-made wine, with baked-fruit flavors offset by spice and white pepper. Then it finishes creamy and sweet, highlighting toffee, caramel and vanilla. With proper weight and acids, it's balanced. **88** —*M.S. (6/1/2006)*

Andeluna 2004 Winemaker's Selection Chardonnay (Mendoza) $13. Heavy and unfocused, with sweet, candied flavors that are neither here nor there. Finishes with oaky resin and vanilla. **81** —*M.S. (4/1/2006)*

Andeluna 2003 Reserve Malbec (Mendoza) $23. Winemaker Silvio Alberto, working with consultant Michel Rolland, is clearly a proponent of the bigger-is-better school, and he deserves credit for making big wines that are balanced despite being brawny. This high-end Malbec, which is very reasonably priced, blasts with menthol, prune, chocolate, and cassis. It's modern and chewy, but has enough tannin, acid, and grit to keep it in fine form. Drink now through 2008. **92 Editors' Choice** —*M.S. (6/1/2006)*

Andeluna 2003 Winemaker's Selection Malbec (Mendoza) $13. Dark and harmonious, with a heavy coating of toast on the nose. Round, meaty, colorful, and rich, with jammy plum and berry flavors coasting on a cuddly, easy body. A fairly big Malbec with just enough spice and charred character to balance it off. **89 Best Buy** —*M.S. (8/1/2006)*

Andeluna 2003 Reserve Merlot (Mendoza) $23. Big and ripe, with chewy fruit and a lot of plum and blackberry character. At 15.3% it hides its alcohol amid berry, cassis, and black-pepper flavors. Modern in style, with tannin and texture. Very nice and fairly natural despite its heft. **88** —*M.S. (6/1/2006)*

Andeluna 2003 Winemaker's Selection Merlot (Mendoza) $13. Big and fruity, with notes of rubber and graphite on the bouquet. Textured and pretty full-bodied, the berry, cassis, and pepper flavors come across as dedicated and real. Kind of short and basic on the finish, but by then it has made its point. **86** —*M.S. (6/1/2006)*

ANDES GRAPES

Andes Grapes 2002 Maia Cabernet Sauvignon (Mendoza) $8. Murky and slightly chemical, with tart, bland flavors and a hard mouthfeel. Not much else to speak of. **81** —*M.S. (10/1/2004)*

Andes Grapes 2002 Maia Malbec (Mendoza) $8. Light from the beginning, with simple cherry, raisin, and spice aromas. Somewhat hollow in the midpalate, with cherry and raspberry flavors. Finishes light; good enough but lacking body. **84** —*M.S. (10/1/2004)*

Andes Grapes 2002 Maia Merlot (Mendoza) $8. Prune and raisin aromas mix with leather to create a stewy, overripe whole. Despite the hefty aromas, there's not much stuffing to this wine. It goes down trim, with little flesh or excitement. **82** —*M.S. (10/1/2004)*

Andes Grapes 2002 Maia Syrah (Mendoza) $8. Smells of Sherry and caramel, while the fruit is just okay at the core and weak around the edges. Finishes flat. **81** —*M.S. (10/1/2004)*

Andes Grapes 2002 Maia Tempranillo (Mendoza) $8. Dusty red fruit, cola, and a touch of sourness make for only an adequate nose. It's an easygoing red without a whole lot of true Tempranillo character. The raspberry and red cherry flavors are lean, with woody accents. **83** —*M.S. (10/1/2004)*

ANGARO

Angaro 2002 Finca la Celia Cabernet Sauvignon-Tempranillo (Uco Valley) $6. The nose is potent if not obviously pretty; there's way too much barrel char and sulfur. Dull strawberry flavors mix with some cherry on the palate, while the finish is light and a tad weedy. **83** —*M.S. (5/1/2003)*

Angaro 2001 Finca la Celia Cabernet Sauvignon-Tempranillo (Uco Valley) $6. The rustic nose is leathery and a bit sulfuric, but it isn't unappealing. Nor is the bold cherry and cassis palate, which is touched up by some coffee. The finish is loaded with berry fruit. The only fault here is its depth: Everything positive is front and forward and there's nothing underneath. The blend is 55% Cabernet and 45% Tempranillo. **86** —*M.S. (11/1/2002)*

Angaro 2002 Finca la Celia Chardonnay (Uco Valley) $6. The nose is fresh at first, but it has little staying power so it gets funky fast. Grapefruit is the dominant flavor, that and some lime and green apple. The finish features pink grapefruit, but there's a burning feel to it. **83** —*M.S. (5/1/2003)*

Angaro 2002 Finca la Celia Merlot (Uco Valley) $6. At this price it's hard to argue with the spicy, smoky nose and likable black cherry and plum flavors. And it finishes peppery and fairly long. Yes, it's a bit hard and short on depth, but it's only six bucks. **84** —*M.S. (5/1/2003)*

Angaro 2002 Finca la Celia Red Blend (Uco Valley) $6. The nose is sulfuric and gassy, and it takes forever for that to blow off. Flavors of beet, cherry, raspberry, and plum are adequate, but the finish is disjointed, dry, and buttery. **81** —*M.S. (5/1/2003)*

Angaro 2000 Finca la Celia Red Blend (Uco Valley) $6. What some might generously call "terroir" will probably come across as funky and barnyardy to most. It just doesn't smell that great. Flavors of berry syrup, currant, and rhubarb are present on the palate and the finish. This is clearly not the best that Argentina has to offer. It's 75% Malbec and 25% Syrah. **81** —*M.S. (11/1/2002)*

Angaro 2002 Finca la Celia Sauvignon Blanc (Uco Valley) $6. Some apple is evident on the nose prior to flavors of lemon and green beans. The finish is warm, with a good feel to it. But it's quite heavy with green-bean notes, much like the palate. **82** —*M.S. (5/1/2003)*

ANTIS

Antis 2004 Cabernet Sauvignon (Mendoza) $12. Less than ripe on the nose, with hay and green notes. Yet the palate is sweet and sugary. Hence the front end and back end are at odds with each other. **80** —*M.S. (8/1/2006)*

Antis 2003 Malbec (Mendoza) $12. Very solid, with full ripeness and smooth cherry and raspberry aromas. The mouth is defined and dense, with clean berry flavors and just the right touch of oak. Feels round and to scale in the mouth, with a smooth finish that shows a touch of chocolate. Tasty and easy. **88 Best Buy** —*M.S. (4/1/2006)*

Antis 2004 Reserve Malbec (Mendoza) $17. Purple and large, and that makes it easy to peg as young. With so much color and extract the palate can only be big, and it's holding rich, almost syrupy blackberry flavors that are mountainous but unrefined. **86** —*M.S. (8/1/2006)*

Antis 2003 Cuvee Celebration Reserve Red Blend (Mendoza) $24. Here's a good but rugged blend of Merlot, Malbec, and Cabernet that starts out with smoked meat, rubber, and pure red-fruit aromas. The feel may seem a touch hard if sipped alone, but with food it will sing a pretty tune. On the finish it's burly and tannic, but it's healthy as can be and should age nicely for several years. **88** —*M.S. (8/1/2006)*

ANTONIO NERVIANI

Antonio Nerviani 2001 Reserve Cabernet Sauvignon (Mendoza) $16. Brownish in color, and clearly on its way to maturity. The nose is herbal and spicy, but in a good way, rather than conveying green notes. Tobacco, olive, and dried plum and cherry flavors make for a more complex palate than many. Finishes simple and nice, which is why it goes no higher than this. **86** —*M.S. (11/15/2005)*

Antonio Nerviani 2001 Reserve Malbec (Mendoza) $16. Green and funky at first, but it changes rapidly. There's also candy and raisin on the nose. The mouth is sort of lean and herky-jerky, with sugar beet and spice. Finishes heavy and syrupy, with a hint of sour weediness. **81** —*M.S. (11/15/2005)*

Antonio Nerviani 2001 Reserve Meritage (Mendoza) $16. Shows initial aromas of cherry and raspberry along with leather and raisin, but after some airing the bouquet dulls down and becomes murky. Lots of buttery, nonintegrated oak covers the red-fruit flavors and then dominates the finish. Ultimately that oak is the downfall. **85** —*M.S. (7/1/2005)*

ARGENTINE BEEF

Argentine Beef 2003 Cabernet Sauvignon (Cafayate) $10. Fairly vegetal, with olive and bell pepper aromas. Light and green, without much fruit besides strawberry and plum. Acceptable mouthfeel with medium tannins. Less than rosy and ripe. **81** —*M.S. (12/31/2005)*

ATILIO AVENA

Atilio Avena 2002 Roble Malbec (Mendoza) $10. Light berry aromas with a hint of green is the opening act. Next you taste basic plum fruit with a touch of grassiness mixed in. Finishes light and disappears in a flash. Has its moments but also its weaknesses. **84** —*M.S. (4/1/2006)*

ATILIO AVENA

Atilio Avena 2004 Torrontès (Mendoza) $10. Neutral at best, with some chemical aromas on the nose. Underdeveloped apple and lemon flavors ride along the raw palate. Tasted twice. **80** —*M.S. (4/1/2006)*

BALBI

Balbi 1997 Reserve Cabernet Sauvignon (Mendoza) $13. **87 Best Buy** *(8/1/2000)*

Balbi 2002 Malbec (Mendoza) $8. The nose consists of berry jam, wintergreen, and burnt popcorn. Angular and lean, with flavors of pie cherries, tomato, and peppers; in some ways it has similar flavors to a mild salsa. A clean finish with some body is the high point. **83** —*M.S. (12/1/2003)*

Balbi 1999 Malbec (Mendoza) $8. In the mouth and on the finish, expect very tart black fruit, movie popcorn and an underlying metallic edge. Opens with aromas of blackgrapes, oak, plum, and a little earthiness. **82** —*D.T. (5/1/2002)*

Balbi 1998 Malbec (Mendoza) $8. Light in color, almost translucent, with green, sharp aromas. The flavor on the surface is all sour cherries, with just a little richer black fruit hidden well underneath. Although not flawed, it's extremely lean and tart. **80** —*M.S. (11/15/2001)*

Balbi 1998 Red Blend (Mendoza) $7. **85 Best Buy** *(8/1/2000)*

Balbi 2002 Syrah (Mendoza) $8. Lean and short, with aromas of mustard and cured meats. The palate is modest at best, with sour raspberry and pie-cherry flavors. An herbal, sharp finish leaves a pickled lasting note. **81** —*M.S. (2/1/2004)*

Balbi 1999 Syrah (Mendoza) $8. A solid example of the varietal, with deeply earthy, peppery aromas, and it is certainly as clean as any wine on earth. Yet the flavors have been stretched. This leaves the strong tannins alone on the palate. Still, with almost anything you could fit on a backyard barbecue, this would be fine. **85** —*S.H. (11/1/2002)*

Balbi 1998 Syrah (Mendoza) $8. Soft and well balanced, this ink-colored Argentinean Syrah oozes with jammy blackberry, black cherry, and grape jelly flavors from start to finish. The palate also shows some creamy vanilla notes. Any easy, economical, everyday quaff. **86 Best Buy** *(10/1/2001)*

Balbi 1998 Syrah (Mendoza) $10. **83** *(8/1/2000)*

Balbi 1997 White Blend (Mendoza) $7. **83** *(8/1/2000)*

BAUDRON

Baudron 1999 Malbec (Mendoza) $8. Forest aromas, with nutmeg and clove, initiate a very pleasing start. The palate becomes hollow in the middle then drops off, finishing with lean fruit and coarse tannins. **85 Best Buy** —*C.S. (5/1/2002)*

BEC

BEC 2005 Nuevo Malbec (Mendoza) $12. Quite roasted and ripe up front, with a heavy burnt/toasted scent that covers up most of the fruit that might want to get out. Plump and candied on the palate, with a sweetness that seems simple and out of place. Creamy and warm on the finish, with thickness. Questionable in terms of its polish and finesse. **84** —*M.S. (8/1/2006)*

BENMARCO

BenMarco 2004 Cabernet Sauvignon (Mendoza) $20. Berry, pine, and cinnamon aromas make for a good opening, while the palate is lean yet endowed with solid plum and black cherry flavors. Quite pure and streamlined, with full tannins and perky acids. This is not a fat, flat New World Cabernet. **88** —*M.S. (12/1/2006)*

BenMarco 2002 Malbec (Mendoza) $20. This full-bodied wine veers toward jammy, with obvious chocolate-tinged oak. The palate is broad and brash, with floral notes accenting plum and black-cherry fruit. BenMarco, which boasts 12% Bonarda, is from Pedro Marchevsky, Catena's former vineyard manager. It's a tribute to his father, made by his wife, Susana Balbo. **90** —*M.S. (12/1/2003)*

BIG DADDY VINEYARDS

Big Daddy Vineyards 2003 Bodega Polo Gran Reserva Bordeaux Blend (Carodilla) $8. Candied caramel and milk chocolate aromas are the result of an oaking program gone wrong. The wine is so thick and overdone that it tastes like carob. **82** —*M.S. (7/1/2004)*

Big Daddy Vineyards 2002 Bodega Polo Cabernet Sauvignon (La Consulta) $8. Big, meaty aromas yield to flavors of plum and clove. The finish features coffee notes and some vanilla. The weakness here is heavy, cheek-starching tannins that throw it out of balance. **82** —*M.S. (5/1/2003)*

Big Daddy Vineyards 2002 Bodega Polo Cabernet Sauvignon (San Martin) $8. The nose has an artificial quality to it, something akin to cream soda. The palate offers muddled cassis and plum flavors, while it finishes rough, with coffee and burnt toast notes. Tannic and drying. **81** —*M.S. (5/1/2003)*

Big Daddy Vineyards 2003 Chardonnay (Mendoza) $9. Heavy and flat, with dull apple aromas. The palate delivers simple yellow fruit, while the finish is soft and devoid of spunk. There isn't a whole lot more to say about this wine; it's a cipher. **82** —*M.S. (6/1/2006)*

Big Daddy Vineyards 2003 Bodega Polo Chardonnay (San Martin) $8. Strange aromas of campfire and grilled hot dogs barely resemble Chardonnay. In the mouth, coconut, vanilla, and wood resin are odd and overwhelming. Is that the flavor of oak dust on the finish? **80** —*M.S. (2/1/2004)*

Big Daddy Vineyards 2003 Malbec (Mendoza) $9. Basically a simple, creamy red; the strawberry and chocolate flavors are easy to like and not hard to get. Not as purple and lush as many, as it deals road tar, raspberry, and citrus peel on the nose. **84** —*M.S. (8/1/2006)*

Big Daddy Vineyards 2003 Bodega Polo Malbec (Carodilla) $8. Fat and vegetal, with a lactic ring to the nose. Flavors of cough syrup and boysenberry border on cloying, while the finish is burnt and leathery. Too heavy for its own good. **81** —*M.S. (7/1/2004)*

Big Daddy Vineyards 2002 Bodega Polo Malbec (San Martin) $8. This bargain wine features jammy aromas of black fruit and milk chocolate. The juicy palate delivers plenty of sweet blackberry along with coffee and vanilla. The finish is smooth and creamy. **85** —*M.S. (5/1/2003)*

Big Daddy Vineyards 2002 Bodega Polo Malbec (Maipú) $8. Popcorn, maple, and mocha pour off of the heavily toasted nose, while the palate, which has ample black fruit, is overrun with more oak flavor. A buttery, cloying finish with thick carob/chocolate flavors is the lasting impression. Awkward and bulky. **82** —*M.S. (5/1/2003)*

Big Daddy Vineyards 2002 Sanes SA Malbec (Mendoza) $8. Spicy and smooth on the nose, with piquant hints to the plum-styled fruit. The palate boasts cherry and plum accented by ample but balanced oak spice. Some buttery wood notes are evident on the long, layered finish. Seemingly well made and modern, and a nice example of affordable Malbec. **86 Best Buy** —*M.S. (5/1/2003)*

Big Daddy Vineyards 2001 Tawert SA Malbec (Tupungato) $8. Sweet, candied aromas kick it off, and underneath there's some blueberry and cotton candy. The mouth pops with cherry and raspberry flavors and some buttery oak. The finish is also kind of oaky and, all things considered, it's a bit over the top. **84** —*M.S. (5/1/2003)*

Big Daddy Vineyards 2003 Merlot (Mendoza) $9. Mute on the nose, with only rubber cement and anonymous dark fruit showing up. Tastes of ripe plum, carob, and burnt toast, while the finish offers vanilla shadings then a blast of heat. Not a smooth operator. **82** —*M.S. (8/1/2006)*

Big Daddy Vineyards 2003 Bodega Polo Merlot (Carodilla) $8. Sweet to the nose, with caramel and green bean aromas vying with the fruit notes. More green interjects itself into the flavor profile, while some okay caramel pops up on the warm, clinging finish. Good texture and feel, but not quite right in terms of flavor. **83** —*M.S. (7/1/2004)*

Big Daddy Vineyards 2002 Bodega Polo Merlot (Carodilla) $8. Cola and vanilla aromas kick off the nose, which is solid if not overtly fruity. Raspberry and cream flavors dominate the palate prior to a round,

smooth finish that features some charred meat and vanilla. Weighty, with a spicy element throughout. **85** —*M.S. (5/1/2003)*

Big Daddy Vineyards 2002 Bodega Polo Merlot (Uco Valley) $8. Despite having no track record in the U.S., this wine has a lot of positives. The leathery nose has fresh red fruit, bacon, and even some sugar-beet aromas. The flavor profile veers toward black plums, bacon, and mocha, while the fully oaked finish is lengthy, powerful, and full of vanilla and cherry candy. From the Polo stable, this is the best wine. **87 Best Buy** —*M.S. (5/1/2003)*

Big Daddy Vineyards 2001 Tawert SA Merlot (Mendoza) $8. Deep, rich, and gaudy, with a few exotic aromatic notes that create interest. The palate is round and ripe, with clean berry fruit. The finish, while flimsy and somewhat hollow at its center, is chewy and sweet. **85** —*M.S. (5/1/2003)*

Big Daddy Vineyards 2002 Sanes SA Red Blend (Mendoza) $8. Offers simple but clean aromas of raspberry and earth. Some light cherry and raspberry fruit comes before an oaky, broad finish. On the whole, it's lean. **83** —*M.S. (5/1/2003)*

Big Daddy Vineyards 2001 Tawert SA Red Blend (Mendoza) $8. "Roble" means oak, but there isn't much positive oak to this low-impact wine that smells of green herbs and animal hide. Some tart pie cherry fruit seems adequate at first, but it doesn't hold on for long. Thin, tart, and angular. **80** —*M.S. (5/1/2003)*

Big Daddy Vineyards 2003 Syrah (Mendoza) $9. This wine is rock solid and well worth a go. The nose is smoky, rubbery, and full of fruit. In the mouth, vanilla softens and supports pure plum and cherry flavors. Mouthfilling and balanced. If only all value wines were this well made. **88 Best Buy** —*M.S. (8/1/2006)*

Big Daddy Vineyards 2002 Sanes SA Syrah (Mendoza) $8. Cherry and vanilla aromas set the stage for this clean, bold Syrah that delivers tasty raspberry and cherry fruit. The finish is smooth and textured, yet not terribly tannic. It's a complete wine that offers a lot for the price. **86 Best Buy** —*M.S. (5/1/2003)*

Big Daddy Vineyards 2001 Tawert SA Syrah (Mendoza) $8. Cheese is the overriding note on the nose, that and some maple. Black fruit softens the palate, which doesn't seem 100% ripe. And the finish is fairly bland. Clean but dull; decent but unexciting. **83** —*M.S. (5/1/2003)*

Big Daddy Vineyards 2002 Sanes SA Tempranillo (Mendoza) $8. Mocha and maple aromas make more of an olfactory impression than does any particular fruit. Once you taste the wine you'll find tart cherry and some racy acids. The finish is expansive and warm, with plenty of oak spice. There are also solid tannins. **84** —*M.S. (5/1/2003)*

BLASON

Blason 2002 Chardonnay (Mendoza) $10. Forward and fruity, if a bit clumsy and unrefined. The palate is crisp and fresh, with good apple, pear, and herb flavors. And the finish is just as easygoing; it's very clean and simple, with no heavy oak. **85** —*M.S. (5/1/2003)*

BODEGA CATENA ZAPATA

Bodega Catena Zapata 1999 Nicolas Catena Zapata Cabernet Blend (Mendoza) $90. For Bordeaux lovers, this wine from one of Argentina's undisputed leaders establishes a new benchmark. The aromas are herbal, earthy, and subdued, with forest floor, plum, cassis, and a hint of buttery oak. The palate is all about ripe cassis and blackberry, with a welcome note of rustic woodiness. And the finish is perfectly creamy and satisfying. A triumph of a wine in just its second vintage. **92 Cellar Selection** —*M.S. (5/1/2003)*

Bodega Catena Zapata 2001 Cabernet Sauvignon (Mendoza) $60. Grapes from three vineyards were blended to create this lighter-framed Cab that won't be confused for a powerhouse. It's more rosy and fresh than most New World reds, with red berry flavors and rather high acidity. Best with food due to its racier qualities. **87** —*M.S. (7/1/2004)*

Bodega Catena Zapata 2002 Nicolas Catena Zapata Cabernet Sauvignon-Malbec (Mendoza) $95. When this powerhouse icon red was introduced with the '97 vintage it was heavily weighted to Cabernet Sauvignon. But now Malbec accounts for 32% of the blend. The result in this excellent year is a forward wine with laser-beam acidity framing bright blueberry and cassis flavors. It has perfect structure and avoids any of the softness and heaviness that sometimes plague New World super reds. **92 Editors' Choice** —*M.S. (11/1/2006)*

Bodega Catena Zapata 2002 Chardonnay (Mendoza) $30. This barrel fermented, full-bodied wine delivers lots of depth, clean apple, and pear fruit, and big, yummy toast and spice notes. It's a round, well-balanced Chardonnay that screams of the terroir of Mendoza—which means there's size, acidity, and power. **89** —*M.S. (7/1/2004)*

Bodega Catena Zapata 2001 Malbec (Mendoza) $50. Bodega Catena Zapata's high-end Malbec deserves credit for its balance and focus on fruit. It's smooth, with cola and cinnamon notes accenting pulsating sweet and tart berries. The frame is solid, the tannins integrated, and it goes down easy. **90** —*M.S. (12/1/2003)*

Bodega Catena Zapata 2001 Nicolas Catena Zapata Red Blend (Mendoza) $90. This signature wine from Nicolas Catena offers wonderful aromatics, including deep black fruit, coffee, and fancy oak. The palate on this blended wine (it's mostly Cabernet) deals ample black cherry and cassis, and the finish is snappy, not heavy. A bit leaner and lighter in the midpalate than one might expect. Definitely food-friendly more than lush. **90** —*M.S. (11/15/2005)*

BODEGA ELVIRA CALLE

Bodega Elvira Calle 2003 Alberti 154 Malbec (Mendoza) $10. Big and bulky, with aromatic hints of cheddar cheese, tobacco, licorice, and espresso. The palate is sweet and chewy, while the finish delivers a wave of black pepper and mushroom. **84** —*M.S. (11/15/2004)*

BODEGA FAMILIA BARBERIS

Bodega Familia Barberis 2002 Blason Malbec (Mendoza) $10. The light berry nose does not excite, nor does the syrupy palate that runs heavy with plum and pepper. The finish is fat, bulky and unrefined. Only some vital acids save it from a worse fate. **81** —*M.S. (5/1/2003)*

Bodega Familia Barberis 2003 Cava Negra Malbec (Mendoza) $8. Jammy, with bubble gum aromas. Along the way there's some talcum powder and mint scents. Fairly fruity and modestly smooth, with fresh, friendly flavors but also a touch of grassy green at the center. **84 Best Buy** —*M.S. (11/15/2005)*

Bodega Familia Barberis 2003 Finca La Daniela Malbec (Mendoza) $10. Rather creamy and jammy to the nose, with flavors of cherry, plum, and vanilla. Soft and fleshy, and a bit short on zest. Good enough with no overt faults; it's just a bit flat and lazy. **84** —*M.S. (7/1/2005)*

Bodega Familia Barberis 2002 Blason Tempranillo (Mendoza) $10. Some funky thistle-like aromas start things in the wrong direction, and from then on everything seems awkward. The palate is overdone with beet and coffee flavors, while the finish is really weighty, bordering on syrupy. **81** —*M.S. (5/1/2003)*

BODEGA FILIPPO FIGARI

Bodega Filippo Figari 2003 Single Vineyard Reserve Malbec (Mendoza) $26. Light years better than the winery's basic Malbec, this single-vineyard, reserve-level wine shows oak and power on the nose along with bright cherry. The palate deals red fruit and moderate sweetness, while chocolate works the finish. A serious wine that weighs in at 14.5%. Only 500 cases produced. **88** —*M.S. (12/1/2006)*

BODEGA JOSÉ QUATTROCCHI

Bodega José Quattrocchi 2002 Nino Franco Torrontès (Mendoza) $13. The dark hue and thick, sweet aromas announce that, just like the label says, this wine was oaked. What emerges from the glass is a cloying honey and orange-laden confection. It's pretty aggressive stuff with too many odd and out of place flavors, i.e. creamed corn. Acceptable, but just. **80** —*M.S. (5/1/2003)*

BODEGA LA RURAL

Bodega La Rural 2000 Felipe Rutini Chardonnay (Tupungato) $17. Aromas of lemon curd and oak are about all you get from this fading Chard. The flavors are of lemon and lime, and the finish, while clean, is basic at best. Thin, lean, and acidic, but still zestless. Go figure. **82** —*M.S. (5/1/2003)*

BODEGA LOPEZ

Bodega Lopez 2002 Cabernet Xero Cabernet Sauvignon (Mendoza) $9. Sweaty on the nose, with faded oak along with modest plum and berry. The palate is tangy, with raspberry fruit flavors and some resin. Finishes grainy and thin, with dry wood notes. **83** —*M.S. (11/15/2004)*

Bodega Lopez 2002 Malbec Xero Malbec (Mendoza) $9. Light to the eye, with lean strawberry and alfalfa aromas. The fruit is basic, with light pepper and spice nuances to the finish. Some broad-brushed oak adds sweetness and vanilla to the flavor profile. **84** —*M.S. (11/15/2004)*

BODEGA LURTON

Bodega Lurton 2003 Bonarda (Uco Valley) $7. This youngster tastes like cherry skins and red plums. It's quite acidic, which produces a juicy, tangy mouthfeel. Ultimately it's rather sour and lean. **82** —*M.S. (11/15/2004)*

Bodega Lurton 2005 Cabernet Sauvignon (Uco Valley) $9. Turned earth, berry jam, and candied sweetness on the nose portend full-force black-fruit flavors that are grainy, bold, and not terribly refined. Standard fare Cabernet, yet a little on the simple, hard side. **84** —*M.S. (11/1/2006)*

Bodega Lurton 2003 Cabernet Sauvignon (Uco Valley) $9. The nose features a mish-mash of rubber, cinnamon, and red fruit, and then turns toward tomato upon airing. Cherry and raspberry flavors are best called "fresh," while the finish is light and modestly tannic. **84** —*M.S. (11/15/2004)*

Bodega Lurton 2004 Gran Lurton Cabernet Sauvignon (Mendoza) $18. Blackberry, tar, and other dark notes coat the masculine bouquet, while cherry and cassis work the palate. This is a solid, big wine with structure; it's also fairly tannic and hard. Has its merits; pretty full and rugged. **87** —*M.S. (12/1/2006)*

Bodega Lurton 2002 Reserva Cabernet Sauvignon (Uco Valley) $12. Clean and flush throughout, with baked-fruit, chocolate, and earth aromas. Very big on the palate, but soft and chewy. Finishing notes of coffee along with wide tannins create a lasting, long impression. Fine for the price. **89 Best Buy** —*M.S. (11/15/2004)*

Bodega Lurton 2005 Reserva Chardonnay (Mendoza) $13. Intensely yellow in color, with heavy popcorn and toast aromas. Runs decidedly bitter and nutty across the palate, while the feel is oily and dull. Not that pleasurable. **81** —*M.S. (11/1/2006)*

Bodega Lurton 2005 Malbec (Uco Valley) $9. Jumpy and leathery at first, although time in the glass settles it down. The palate offers blackberry as the lead flavor, although there's some lemon peel and citrus in the background. Finishes simple and short. **84** —*M.S. (12/1/2006)*

Bodega Lurton 2003 Malbec (Uco Valley) $9. Moderately perfumed, with a mostly smooth, likable bouquet. It runs fairly sweet, with a good mix of fruit and oak. Finishes in a clean, wavy ride. Notes of chocolate and blueberry accent the flavor profile. **86 Best Buy** —*M.S. (11/15/2004)*

Bodega Lurton 2004 Reserva Malbec (Mendoza) $13. Slightly brambly but otherwise dominated by strong red-fruit aromas and flavors. The palate is fairly rich and full, as it should be, with chocolate and herbal/pepper notes sneaking in. Doesn't have a lot of finish or sweetness. Pretty good mouthfeel and core acidity. **86** —*M.S. (12/1/2006)*

Bodega Lurton 2005 Pinot Gris (Uco Valley) $8. Heavy and tropical in style, with honey and creamy pear aromas. Very sweet and ripe, with punchless Bartlett pear and syrupy peach flavors. Thick and textured; almost unctuous. But it tastes fine and doesn't offend. **83** —*M.S. (2/1/2006)*

Bodega Lurton 2005 Rosé Blend (Mendoza) $8. This rosado is made from Bonarda and Malbec grapes. It's a touch vegetal on the nose, with hints of vanilla to sweeten it up. The palate is tart and dry, with peach, nectarine, and apple flavors. Decent feel and body keep it afloat. **83** —*M.S. (12/1/2006)*

Bodega Lurton 2005 Torrontès (Mendoza) $9. Aromas of melon and baby powder are light but attractive, while the peach and citrus flavors are wet, zesty, and fresh. Finishes with dried-fruit flavors and a sprinkle of minerality. Commendable for its simplicity. **85 Best Buy** —*M.S.* *(12/1/2006)*

Bodega Lurton 2004 Torrontès (Uco Valley) $7. Aromas of lemon and floor wax are a bit stunted, while the creamy palate has a cloying feel to it. Flavorwise, look for litchi and tarragon. **83** —*M.S.* *(11/15/2004)*

Bodega Lurton 2003 Torrontès (Mendoza) $7. What a score! Torrontès, a little-known Spanish white winegrape, turns out to be a superstar in Mendoza. Packed tight with bright, vivid, penetrating fruit, this strikingly flavorful wine begins with lovely scents of citrus, orange peel, and tangerine and takes off from there. It moves into still more complexity, with traces of diesel, talc, and flower petal. Think Viognier, Gewürztraminer, and Riesling, blended and punched up with a full-bodied, lingering finish. **90 Best Buy** —*P.G.* *(11/15/2004)*

Bodega Lurton 2005 Flor de Torrontès Reserva Torrontès (Uco Valley) $13. Smells lifeless, with mild bitterness and banana flavors. Sort of waxy on the finish, despite sharp acidity. Not as good as the winery's basic Torrontès. **80** —*M.S. (12/1/2006)*

BODEGA NANNI

Bodega Nanni 2001 Single Estate Vineyard Cabernet Sauvignon (Cafayate) $11. Distant but not overpowering aromas of green tobacco and canned veggies bring ripeness into question, yet in the mouth, it's more about berry fruit and cassis than outright green character. A large, coffee-tinged finish is vibrant and juicy due to sharp yet controlled acidity. Has its merits as well as faults; certified organic. **84** —*M.S. (2/1/2004)*

Bodega Nanni 2001 Single Estate Vineyard Malbec (Cafayate) $11. This organic wine is interesting if not amazing. First off, it is more acidic than most; but it's also made in a different vein, coming from up north in Cafayete. Look for zippy rhubarb and cranberry nuances as well as a touch of stewed character at the core. Not unlike a German or Austrian red. **84** —*M.S. (12/1/2003)*

Bodega Nanni 2001 Tannat (Cafayate) $11. This certified organic Tannat from northern Argentina is a good but simple wine, one with a deep color, flavors of plum, blackberry, and liquid smoke, and serious tannin. The back end yields little flavor. Depth is not its strong point. **85** —*M.S. (2/1/2004)*

BODEGA NOEMÍA DE PATAGONIA

Bodega Noemía de Patagonia 2005 A Lisa Malbec (Río Negro Valley) $24. A lovely, crisp-styled Malbec (with 10% Merlot) that does the Río Negro region of Patagonia proud. A Lisa is in its inaugural vintage, and the wine boasts toast, mineral, and black fruit both on the nose and in the mouth. Not exactly streamlined but tighter than most Malbecs. Drink now into 2008. **90** —*M.S. (12/15/2006)*

Bodega Noemía de Patagonia 2004 J. Alberto Malbec (Río Negro Valley) $38. Not a hair is out of place on this pure and potent Malbec. The bouquet is crusty and rich, with berry and bitter chocolate aromas. The palate is chock-full of mulberry, black cherry, nutmeg and cocoa powder; the finish is smooth and rewarding. Good through 2008. **91** —*M.S. (12/15/2006)*

Bodega Noemía de Patagonia 2004 Noemía Malbec (Río Negro Valley) $110. Noemía's signature Malbec, now in its third vintage, is one of the country's best. It starts out herbal and smoky, with a lot of dark French oak. The mouth is powerful and pure, with at least three layers of complex flavors and textures. The fruit is both subtle and loud. Simply an excellent wine of world-class character. Best in 2008–09. **92** —*M.S. (12/15/2006)*

Bodega Noemía de Patagonia 2003 Noemía Malbec (Río Negro Valley) $152. It doesn't take a great brain to figure out that this is a rocking, beautifully crafted international red wine. Mint, spice, and chocolate aromas are dipped in lovely new oak, while the palate is all about bold plum backed by coffee and mocha. Stellar now and shows all signs of a wine that will only get better. **93 Editors' Choice** —*M.S. (4/1/2006)*

Bodega Noemía de Patagonia 2002 Noemía Malbec (Río Negro Valley) $140. Exotic and refined, with a stately bouquet of violets, mineral, and cassis. Sensational quality for a wine from rugged Patagonia. It bursts

with black raspberry propelled by firm acids. Then it folds back into a darker space, where fudge and pepper notes make for a warming, spicy finish. Shows off the skill of Danish winemaker Hans Vinding-Diers. **92** —*M.S. (7/1/2005)*

BODEGA NORTON

Bodega Norton 2002 Barbera (Mendoza) $8. As with Norton's Sangiovese, you must scratch all impressions of Italian Barbera if you are going to like this wine. Because what it offers is candied fruit, a juicy mouthfeel and a fresh, simple finish. Yes, it's kind of strange. But it's also kind of good. **85** —*M.S. (7/1/2004)*

Bodega Norton 2002 Cabernet Sauvignon (Mendoza) $8. A bit light, but it shows snap and spice. Has a mild streak of vegetal green, yet the feel is rich enough and the balance good enough to help it hold its own. **84** —*M.S. (7/1/2004)*

Bodega Norton 1999 Cabernet Sauvignon (Mendoza) $8. With strawberry and candied cherry aromas, stewed rhubarb, and butter flavors, and a warm, round finish, this wine is what it is: a sweet and chewy red whose best purpose is an introduction to the potential of Mendoza. **84** —*M.S. (11/1/2002)*

Bodega Norton 1999 Chardonnay (Mendoza) $8. Could the scent of microwaved popcorn be any stronger? Obviously, it's heavily oaked, and that carries onto the palate where you'll find heavy, woody flavors in addition to banana and lemon. This needs a lot more charm and style; in all honesty, it's not delivering much. **80** —*M.S. (7/1/2002)*

Bodega Norton 2002 Reserve Chardonnay (Mendoza) $14. A sweet, friendly wine with mostly pear flavors and some hints of lemon and citrus. Easygoing and refreshing is the style, and for the most part it delivers what it aims to. **86** —*M.S. (7/1/2004)*

Bodega Norton 2002 Malbec (Mendoza) $8. Blackberry and raisins on the nose, and then a round, sweet palate that's nice and slightly smoky. Pretty good Malbec, especially for the price, and rather tasty. **86** —*M.S. (7/1/2004)*

Bodega Norton 1999 Malbec (Mendoza) $8. Lean raspberry aromas carry a tinge of wheat and smoked meat. Cherry, bacon, and buttery wood flavors steer the palate into a finish that's basically more of the same. This is the prototype of easy-drinking Malbecs. It's light and clean if not overwhelming or complex. **85 Best Buy** —*M.S. (11/1/2002)*

Bodega Norton 1998 Malbec (Mendoza) $9. 80 *(5/1/2002)*

Bodega Norton 2003 Reserve Malbec (Mendoza) $21. Ripe and dense, with aromas of balsamic reduction, berry fruit, and bread dough. The palate runs exceptionally sweet and rich, but it's not cloying or syrupy. Totally holes-free, with can't-miss flavors and solid tannins. Drink now or hold through 2007. **89** —*M.S. (11/15/2005)*

Bodega Norton 2002 Reserve Malbec (Mendoza) $16. Norton has hit a home run with this Malbec, one of the best wines we've ever tried from the bodega. Aged in all new French oak, the wine is pure, deep, and sweet, with ample spice and chocolate rounding out the body. A big wine with balance and pizzazz. **90** —*M.S. (7/1/2004)*

Bodega Norton 1999 Reserve Malbec (Mendoza) $14. From this stellar vintage, Norton has crafted a tasty, sturdy, affordable Malbec, one that captures the meaty violet character of the grape but doesn't go overboard with extract or oak. In the mouth, plum and licorice flavors lead into a dry finish that also yields some butter and coffee. Mouthfilling and wholesome. **87 Best Buy** —*M.S. (11/1/2002)*

Bodega Norton 1999 Merlot (Mendoza) $8. The bouquet is kind of flat and mute; what does emerge is mostly bubble gum and far-off bramble. The palate is better, as it offers some cassis, earthy mushroom, and also a little bit of green bell pepper. The warm, moderately tannic finish is solid, but the wine isn't terribly rich or structured. It has a candied personality, which fans of sweeter wines should like. **85 Best Buy** —*M.S. (11/1/2002)*

Bodega Norton 2002 Reserve Merlot (Mendoza) $16. A powerful Merlot, one with a nose of violets, perfume, and muddled fruit. Very big in the mouth, with fairly full and sharp tannins. Has a lot of what people are looking for, but is a touch short in finesse. **87** —*M.S. (7/1/2004)*

Bodega Norton 2002 La Privada Red Blend (Mendoza) $20. Norton's proprietary house blend features a sensuous mix of Cabernet, Merlot, and Malbec, all from the scintillating '02 harvest. This is one of the best wines Norton has made in ages, if not in its history. Tobacco, tar, and chocolate aromas accent the deep, saturated bouquet. And the flavors and feel are pure New World in that ripeness and drinkability take precedence over complexity. **91 Editors' Choice** —*M.S. (7/1/2004)*

Bodega Norton 1999 Privada Red Blend (Mendoza) $21. This bodega's top-of-the-line offering is comprised of 40% Malbec, 30% Cabernet Sauvignon, and 30% Merlot. But something in here isn't quite ripe, because the green aromatics and flavors are strong. So is the tomato-like flavor at the core of the palate. For some reason the wine lacks potency. **83** —*M.S. (11/1/2002)*

Bodega Norton 1998 Privada Red Blend (Mendoza) $14. Strong aromas of black fruit, wet leaves, and violets. Very chunky in the mouth, with heavy tannins. Overall, it's slightly awkward. On the plus side, big blackberry fruit adds life to this blend of Cabernet Sauvignon, Malbec, and Merlot. **83** —*M.S. (11/15/2001)*

Bodega Norton 2002 Sangiovese (Mendoza) $8. Expunge all ideas of conventional Chianti and then you can get after the sweet cherry fruit and the soft, chewy palate that come with this Argentine Sangiovese. Totally New World, with moderate depth and a weak finish. **85** —*M.S. (7/1/2004)*

Bodega Norton 1998 Sangiovese (Mendoza) $9. **81** *(5/1/2002)*

Bodega Norton 2003 Sauvignon Blanc (Mendoza) $8. Grapefruit aromas precede a surprisingly plump, full body and then an avalanche of tropical fruit flavors. Shows enough true SB character to earn a recommendation, but it's a bit chunkier than most in this range. **85** —*M.S. (7/1/2004)*

Bodega Norton 2002 Sauvignon Blanc (Mendoza) $8. The broad aromas of apple and pineapple carry just a hint of green vegetables. The palate is pure Sauvignon Blanc in the New Zealand style, with pear, grapefruit, and some bell pepper. The finish is long and zesty. **85** —*M.S. (5/1/2003)*

Bodega Norton 2000 Sauvignon Blanc (Mendoza) $8. Light whiffs of melon with stronger hints of celery and green pepper. Sweet and tart, tasting of lemon-lime and green apples. An appetizer wine that could work with seafood. Very acidic. **83** —*M.S. (11/15/2001)*

Bodega Norton 2003 Torrontès (Mendoza) $8. Smells like it should, with light, exotic lychee aromas as well as notes of wildflower. In the mouth, it's a bit more meaty and a touch less zesty than ideal, and it finishes soft. But along the way it's tasty and would match well with take-out Chinese food. **85** —*M.S. (7/1/2004)*

BODEGA NQN

Bodega NQN 2004 Malma Malbec (Neuquén) $10. Slightly rugged at first, with strong scents of leather, earth, and subdued dark fruit. The palate is classic Malbec: soft, chewy, and medium in depth. Not terribly complex or long on the finish, but satisfying. **87 Best Buy** —*M.S. (12/15/2006)*

Bodega NQN 2004 Malma Reserva Malbec (Neuquén) $20. Gets going with a lot of barrel and leather, but maybe not as much fruit as one might hope for. Makes its point with a round, creamy mouthfeel that supports jammy plum and blackberry flavors. A very good Malbec that will be better once the vines age. **88** —*M.S. (12/15/2006)*

Bodega NQN 2005 Picada 15 Red Blend (Neuquén) $8. This lighter-bodied blend has a lot in common with a good Côtes-du-Rhône. It's mildly spicy but also quite fruity; the nose exudes red-berry and cinnamon aromas, while the palate is warm and just slightly oaky. A nice bistro wine. **87 Best Buy** —*M.S. (12/15/2006)*

Bodega NQN 2005 Malma Sauvignon Blanc (Neuquén) $10. This new Patagonian winery is doing better with its reds. This SB is honeyed and slightly mealy; the palate starts out soft and chunky, with apple and peach flavors that are less than zesty and slightly oxidized. Still, complexity arises as there's a lasting butterscotch taste that is not unpleasant. **84** —*M.S. (12/15/2006)*

BODEGA PRIVADA

Bodega Privada 2002 Cabernet Sauvignon (Mendoza) $8. Vegetal, with prune and syrup aromas. It is sour and simultaneously sweet. For most folks, it won't cut the mustard. **81** —*M.S. (7/1/2004)*

Bodega Privada 2003 Chardonnay (Mendoza) $8. Sweet at the core, with a bouquet that's rimmed by applesauce and canned-pear aromas. Flavors of lettuce greens, apple, and pear create a light mix, while the finish is simple and largely clean. **84** —*M.S. (7/1/2004)*

Bodega Privada 2002 Malbec (Mendoza) $8. Plump and open, albeit bland. The nose offers basic berry and plum fruit. Flavors of cherry, apple skins, and red licorice create a sweet whole, while the finish is spicy, with an emphasis on black pepper. **84** —*M.S. (7/1/2004)*

Bodega Privada 2002 Merlot (Mendoza) $8. A touch rusty and thin to the eye, but mostly lean and clean on the nose, despite some leafiness. Modest tannins support flavors of dried cherry, raisin, and spice, and while it's not multidimensional by any stretch, it's not hard to drink, either. **84** —*M.S. (7/1/2004)*

Bodega Privada 2003 Sauvignon Blanc (Mendoza) $8. Soda-like up front, as if you were sniffing a glass of Sprite. The palate is thin, with a modicum of pear and apple but far more white pepper and celery. Nothing much on the finish seals this wine's fate. **81** —*M.S. (7/1/2004)*

Bodega Privada 2002 Syrah (Mendoza) $8. Chewy and meaty, with chunky black fruit on the nose and jammy cherry and raspberry notes on the palate. Finishes smooth and solid for the most part, with a pretty good mouthfeel. A good everyday wine. **85 Best Buy** —*M.S. (7/1/2004)*

Bodega Privada 2002 Torrontès (Salta) $8. Heavily perfumed and flowery, but lacking verve and precision. The mouth tosses up meaty apple fruit accented by cinnamon and nutmeg, while the finish is spicy and forward. **83** —*M.S. (7/1/2004)*

BODEGA Y CAVAS DE WEINERT

Bodega Y Cavas De Weinert 2000 Gran Vino Bordeaux Blend (Luján de Cuyo) $26. Sharp, spiky, and raw to start, with sassy fruit and aromas of smoked meat and polished leather. In the mouth, more identifiable flavors of plum, raspberry, and beet take over, and time allows for it to unfold. Finishes sturdy, with perfect tannins and perky acids. Match this with grilled beef and you're on your way. Sophisticated yet antique. How nice to see an individual wine like this. **90 Editors' Choice** —*M.S. (7/1/2005)*

BODEGAS CARO

Bodegas Caro 2002 Cabernet Sauvignon-Malbec (Mendoza) $45. After an earthy, aggressive, almost sweaty start, this joint-venture red from Nicolas Catena and Eric de Rothschild finds its course and manages to improve. The palate is full of acid-driven, amplified cherry and plum flavors, and while there's a hint of buttery oak resting on the finish, that should subside with airing and a good food pairing. **90** —*M.S. (6/1/2006)*

Bodegas Caro 2001 Cabernet Sauvignon-Malbec (Mendoza) $40. This Cabernet/Malbec blend comes from a joint venture between the Lafite-driven Rothschilds and Nicolás Catena. It's oaky and earthy, with bright black fruit that falls squarely into the cherry-cassis-plum category. A hint of graham cracker graces the sweet finish, which turns slightly lemony upon airing. Drink through 2005. **90** —*M.S. (2/1/2004)*

Bodegas Caro 2003 Amancaya Cabernet Sauvignon-Malbec (Mendoza) $15. Our highest praise goes out to Lafite-Rothschild and Nicolas Catena for putting together this excellent, highly affordable red blend. It smells cool, minty, and deeply fruity, with developed blackberry, cassis, and smoked meat flavors. Textbook across the board. Masculine and impressive. **92 Editors' Choice** —*M.S. (3/1/2005)*

Bodegas Caro 2004 Amancaya Malbec-Cabernet Sauvignon (Mendoza) $18. This has to rank as one of the world's best wines for the money. The depth is impeccable and the balance and pop are commendable. All hail Argentina, or at least Barons de Rothschild and Nicolas Catena for coming up with this affordable blend of Malbec and Cabernet that pulses with berry fruit, waves of chocolate, and so much toasty persistence that it almost requires brakes. For under $20 this is faultless stuff. **91 Editors' Choice** —*M.S. (12/31/2005)*

BODEGAS DEL TUPUN

Bodegas del Tupun 2005 Marlena Cabernet Sauvignon (Mendoza) $10. Smells varietally correct, like cassis and black plum, and it delivers what you'd expect: bold New World Cabernet flavors, albeit with a touch of tartness and rusticity. **84** *(11/15/2006)*

Bodegas del Tupun 2006 Marlena Chardonnay-Viognier (Mendoza) $10. This 50-50 blend of Chardonnay and Viognier is a bit oily and heavy in the mouth. It's thickly textured, with broad pear and spice flavors that lack the crisply delineated floral notes Viognier should bring to the table. Solid, rather than exciting. **83** *(11/15/2006)*

Bodegas del Tupun 2005 Marlena Malbec (Mendoza) $10. Starts with bright cherry-berry scents, and never moves much beyond that. It's a simple, fruity wine that's clean, crisp, and easy to drink; a solid choice for a weekday dinner. **84** *(11/15/2006)*

BODEGAS ESCORIHUELA

Bodegas Escorihuela 2003 High Altitude Cabernet Sauvignon-Malbec (Agrelo) $10. Purple in color, with potent berry aromas. The blend is 65% in favor of Malbec, and the wine boasts black raspberry and plum flavors. Finishes hefty and warm, with notes of cola. **86 Best Buy** —*M.S. (11/15/2004)*

Bodegas Escorihuela 2002 High Altitude Cabernet Sauvignon-Malbec (Mendoza) $10. Good as it is on its own, Malbec only gets better when blended with Cabernet, as it is here, in a 2:1 proportion. This wine explodes with spice and tight, tart fruit. Berries, currants, and cherries highlight the full, round mid-palate, leading confidently into a finish folded in cocoa and toast. Clean, elegant and stylish, it carries none of the mushroom or funk flavors that often come with inexpensive Argentine reds. Part of the Escorihuela Group, who also make the One Bunch and Gascón wines. **90 Best Buy** —*P.G. (11/15/2004)*

Bodegas Escorihuela 2002 High Altitude Red Blend (Mendoza) $10. Dark and pretty, with a great attack. The nose is full and black, with all the trimmings. The mouth is lush with cassis, plum, and tobacco. A very nice wine, but somewhat flat and soft on the finish. There's more up front than on the back side. **88 Best Buy** —*M.S. (2/1/2004)*

Bodegas Escorihuela 2002 High Altitude White Blend (Mendoza) $10. This made-for-export line features sleek packaging picturing Argentinean wildlife, and in the bottle what's coming out seems good. This white blend is ripe, with loads of apple and lemon on the nose, and lemon meringue on the palate. It's unwooded, yet naturally spicy. **86** —*M.S. (7/1/2004)*

BODEGAS HISPANO ARGENTINAS

Bodegas Hispano Argentinas 2002 Martins Malbec (Mendoza) $9. At first it's minty and licorice-tinged, but with time some raisin and oak come up. A bit lower in acidity than many, but with big tannins that stretch out across the palate. Chocolate and coffee carry the finish. **86 Best Buy** —*M.S. (12/1/2003)*

BODEGAS Y VINEDOS SANTA SOFIA

Bodegas y Vinedos Santa Sofia 2002 Urban Oak Red Blend (Uco Valley) $9. Smooth and burly, with meaty, berry aromas preceding a friendly, hefty palate that's chock full of black plum, chocolate, and vanilla. With its open-knit finish, this has most of what the average wine lover seeks. This Tempranillo-Malbec blend is solid. **88 Best Buy** —*M.S. (2/1/2004)*

BROQUEL

Broquel 2002 Cabernet Sauvignon (Mendoza) $15. Aromas of berry compote, marinade, wood smoke, and leather are scattered about. The flavors of blackberry and cassis are good and plump, but ultimately kind of simple. In the end, the wine loses structure and fades away without leaving a lasting impression. **86** —*M.S. (10/1/2004)*

Broquel 2000 Cabernet Sauvignon (Mendoza) $15. There is some fine, ripe fruit to this clean, medium-bodied Cabernet. The nose is hefty and fairly rich, with campfire like smoky oak. The round palate delivers plummy fruit and some drying oak flavor. The finish is long, with hints of vanilla and butter. **87** —*M.S. (5/1/2003)*

Broquel 2003 Chardonnay (Argentina) $15. Pretty big, with aromas of buttered toast and nearly overripe fruit. Forceful acidity drives lemon

and apple flavors, and the final act is a run of pineapple. An aggressive, acidic, broad-shouldered Chard. **85** —*M.S. (10/1/2004)*

Broquel 2002 Chardonnay (Mendoza) $15. Trapiche's high-end Chardonnay scores points for its heft, power, and all-important balance. The nose features baked apple, popcorn, and some wood, but it's not over the top. Flavors of apple, pineapple, and butterscotch are smooth and soft, while a bracing shot of acidity keeps everything in line. **88** —*M.S. (7/1/2004)*

Broquel 2001 Chardonnay (Mendoza) $15. Well oaked, with coconut and fruit vying for center stage. The mouthfeel is soft, evidence of low acidity. But the flavor profile is rewarding: there's custard, lemon, and lots of barrel char. When you hear of wines that taste and smell like the inside of a barrel, this one might qualify. Still, it has enough fruit to save it from its oaky self. **86** —*M.S. (5/1/2003)*

Broquel 2002 Malbec (Argentina) $15. This upper middle-class Trapiche brand seems to be here to stay, and the Malbec offers round, chunky aromas of sweet berries and vanilla, followed by a juicy palate loaded with plum and cherry. Some dark campfire notes to the finish let you know this is real wine. **89** —*M.S. (10/1/2004)*

Broquel 2001 Malbec (Mendoza) $15. Solid and sturdy; this is a berry-filled, muscled-up wine with a pounding nose that bodes well for what's to come—a chewy palate with broad, smooth tannins and deep, developed black fruit. Nuances of coffee, chili pepper, and tobacco render it classy and elevate it to a higher echelon. **88** —*M.S. (12/1/2003)*

Broquel 2000 Malbec (Mendoza) $15. Creamy aromas of mocha and coffee carry just a whiff of cheese and dill, possibly remnants of the oak treatment. The palate, meanwhile, delivers a nice punch of berries and wood, and like the nose, the finish is creamy. Overall, the wine is generous and pleasant. **88** —*M.S. (5/1/2003)*

BUDINI

Budini 2004 Cabernet Sauvignon (Mendoza) $11. Black cherry, citrus peel, and a touch of charcoal and grilled meat make for a solid nose. Ripe blackberry and dark plum work the palate, while coffee, licorice, and spice grace the firm, grabby, mildly tannic finish. **85** —*M.S. (12/1/2006)*

Budini 2005 Chardonnay (Mendoza) $11. Apple cider and caramel on the nose, and that aromatic combo doesn't stir much interest. Tastes like mulled cider, while the finish is thick with caramel and toffee. A heavy, oily Chardonnay that could use better balance and flavors. **81** —*M.S. (11/1/2006)*

BYBLOS

Byblos 2004 Bonarda (Mendoza) $8. A kosher Bonarda with hard, spicy aromas but not a whole lot of fruit. Lean and peppery in the mouth, with toasty, bitter finishing flavors. Deep diggers will find some black cherry in the center. **83** —*M.S. (11/15/2005)*

Byblos 2004 Semi-Sweet Bonarda (Mendoza) $8. A sugary kosher brother to the dry Bonarda; this is basically a replacement for sweet Concord-based wines. It offers cotton candy and cherry flavors, and a sticky yet not too heavy mouthfeel. **82** —*M.S. (11/15/2005)*

CABRA MONTES

Cabra Montes 2004 Cabernet Sauvignon (Agrelo) $9. Sweet cherry aromas seem almost like Grenache atop graham crackers, while the palate is lean, green, and topped off by brandied cherry. Adequate as a cheap quaffer but not up to the next level. **82** —*M.S. (8/1/2006)*

Cabra Montes 2004 Chardonnay (Uco Valley) $9. Fresh, tropical, and welcoming. Sweet and lush in the mouth with a full blast of mango and melon flavors. Medium-bodied with good acidity. Finishes correct and everything seems to be united and put together. Above-average value Chardonnay from Argentina. **86 Best Buy** —*M.S. (8/1/2006)*

Cabra Montes 2004 Merlot (Agrelo) $9. Bright and open, and for the most part everything about this easygoing red is pleasant. Tasty plum and raspberry flavors are simple but ripe, while the overall expression is balanced and measured. Finishes with some sweet chocolate and vanilla for good measure. **85 Best Buy** —*M.S. (8/1/2006)*

CABRINI

Cabrini 2000 Cabernet Sauvignon (Mendoza) $11. Eight months in French and American oak has left a strong barrel influence on this wine, which features a heavily charred nose before a palate of cassis, cherry, and rhubarb. The oak is powerful toward the end, manifesting itself in the flavors of molasses and coffee. A sturdy structure and a solid core of fruit are the high points. **88 Best Buy** —*M.S. (11/1/2002)*

Cabrini 2000 Malbec (Mendoza) $11. This is an idiosyncratic Malbec that you will probably love or hate. Yet we found ourselves somewhat undecided. First off, it's sweet in the nose, barely different from Port. The beet, red plum and cassis flavors are forward but awkward, and overall it seems like a confection. Think chocolate-covered frozen bananas from the county fair. **86 Best Buy** —*M.S. (11/1/2002)*

CAOBA

Caoba 2004 Reserve Chardonnay (Mendoza) $13. Honey, cornflakes, and apple juice aromas sit in front of lively but basic apple and melon flavors. Fairly full in weight, with ripe forward flavors. Not a polished gem by any means but decent enough. **83** —*M.S. (11/1/2006)*

Caoba 2005 Malbec (Mendoza) $10. Lightly candied at first, but airing unveils more pure plum and raspberry aromas. Cherry, raspberry, and plum flavors are standard but good, while the mouthfeel is firm and smooth enough. Mainstream all the way but likable. **86 Best Buy** —*M.S. (11/1/2006)*

CARINAE

Carinae 2004 Malbec (Mendoza) $11. Green and raisiny at the same time, which isn't a good combination. The wine seems ultra ripe and lacking in red fruit, acids, and other balancing elements. Harvested too late? Regardless, it isn't working. **81** —*M.S. (11/1/2006)*

Carinae 2004 Reserva Malbec (Mendoza) $15. Best at the beginning, where balsamic notes blend with earth and leather to create a dark, brooding nose. The palate, however, is dull and reduced; it's like a bite of devil's food cake: one bite is enough. Seems like the grapes were picked too late; it's stewy. **82** —*M.S. (11/1/2006)*

CARLOS BASSO

Carlos Basso 2000 Cabernet Sauvignon (San Carlos) $12. The lean, racy aromas are akin to red currants, green tobacco, and grass. The flavor profile is fairly one-dimensional, featuring red plum and little else. The finish has a full tannic grip along with licorice, but the same green from the bouquet rises up in the form of additional underripe flavors. **85** — *M.S. (11/1/2002)*

Carlos Basso 2004 Dos Fincas Cabernet Sauvignon-Malbec (Uco Valley) $10. An excellent wine for the money. All of Basso's current wines are rock solid, including this blend of Cabernet and Malbec, which shows jammy berry aromas backed by plump blackberry and strawberry flavors. Solid and flush throughout, with nary a flaw. **90 Best Buy** —*M.S. (12/1/2006)*

Carlos Basso 2004 Dos Fincas Cabernet Sauvignon-Merlot (Uco Valley) $10. Sensational wine for the money. The Cab and Merlot work together seamlessly, as the nose exudes raspberry and sweet leather. Tastes warm and toasty, with ripe fruit softened by chocolate and pillowy tannins. Argentine red at its affordable best. **91 Best Buy** —*M.S. (12/1/2006)*

Carlos Basso 2004 Malbec (Luján de Cuyo) $13. Smooth, fruity, and a touch earthy on the nose, with pure raspberry, plum, and cassis in proper doses. Quite comfortable across the palate, where juicy acids wrestle with full tannins. Finishes big, with chocolate. **90 Best Buy** —*M.S. (12/1/2006)*

Carlos Basso 2000 Malbec (Mendoza) $12. The nose is a bit stemmy and the mouth is hard, but the fruit is bright and snappy. If the tannins were softer and the feel more charming, this would have much more going for it. Alas, as it is it's rather unforgiving. **83** —*M.S. (11/1/2002)*

CARMELO PATTI

Carmelo Patti 2003 Extra Brut Sparkling Blend (Mendoza) $17. Toasty and dry in a Champagne style, with flavors of lemon rind, dry apple, and plenty of earthy mushroom. In fact, it's that mushroomy quality that takes over, leaving you wanting a bit more freshness. Still, it has its merits. **85** —*M.S. (12/31/2005)*

Carmelo Patti 2002 Extra Brut Sparkling Blend (Mendoza) $19. More of an artisan bubbly from a small producer in Argentina. Gold-amber in color, with mild toast and cornflake aromas. A bit heavy on the tongue, with apple as the main course. Turns almondy and rounder on the finish. Definitely shows some Champagne personality. **87** —*M.S. (12/31/2004)*

CASA BOHER

Casa Boher 2003 Cabernet Sauvignon (Mendoza) $11. A lot of open-cut wood on the nose, which results in aggressive citrus notes along with hard blasts of oak shavings. The mouth is gritty and firm, with jumpy cherry and raspberry flavors. Quite tannic; not a lot of love here. **83** — *M.S. (11/15/2005)*

Casa Boher 2003 Malbec (Mendoza) $11. Smooth and full of berry, marzipan, and Christmas spice aromas. Comes on strong as it opens, revealing blueberry and black cherry flavors. Quite fresh and snappy, but with ample heft. A fine everyday red with guts. **87 Best Buy** —*M.S. (7/1/2005)*

Casa Boher 2003 Merlot (Mendoza) $11. Green on the nose, with hints of beet and tomato. Quite snappy on the tongue, with acid-based cherry and raspberry flavors mixed with some green. Not caustic, but verging on astringent. **83** —*M.S. (11/15/2005)*

Casa Boher 2003 Sauvignon Blanc (Mendoza) $11. Blunt and clumsy, with a slight vegetal streak to the chunky nose. The flavor profile is sweet and candied, while the finish hits with a wave of applesauce and peach flavors. Hangs rather heavily on the palate. **83** —*M.S. (7/1/2005)*

CASA DE TANGO

Casa de Tango 1998 Reserve Syrah (Mendoza) $12. Superdark fruit—grape, prune, and fig—meets chocolate and leather on the nose of this Argentine offering. More of the same show on the palate, where the mouthfeel is creamy, but on the lean side. Flash-finish has coffee-mocha notes. **83** *(10/1/2001)*

CASA MONTES

Casa Montes 2001 Alzamora Grand Reserve Oak Malbec (San Juan) $14. A spicy sort of red, with earth, leather, and forest aromas. Cassis, cherry, and chocolate make for a tasty palate, although there's a bit of outsized tannin, oak, and heat. Sturdy, medium in terms of lushness, and broad. **87** —*M.S. (11/1/2006)*

Casa Montes 2001 Alzamora Grand Reserve Oak Syrah (San Juan) $14. Leafy red fruit, candied licorice, and a touch of toast add up to the bare basics on the nose. Tangy and short in the mouth, with a bit too much acidity resulting in a scratchy mouthfeel. Cherry and red raspberry are the dominant flavors. **83** —*M.S. (11/1/2006)*

CASATERRA

Casaterra 2002 Cabernet Sauvignon (Mendoza) $7. Not on a par with the brand's more impressive Chardonnay; this Cabernet is aggressive and unbalanced. The palate is sweet. **80** —*M.S. (7/1/2004)*

Casaterra 2003 Chardonnay (Mendoza) $8. A perfectly nice South American Chard, one with pineapple, creamy pear, and apple on the nose. More apple and pear comes on strong in the mouth, followed by a sizable, smooth finish. Nothing in this wine is too overdone or thrilling, but the total package is likable. **86 Best Buy** —*M.S. (7/1/2004)*

Casaterra 2002 Malbec (Mendoza) $8. Run-of-the-mill berry and earth on the nose, followed by adequate blackberry and cherry flavors. A leathery mouthfeel created by stiff tannins pushes life into the finish. Doesn't stand up to intense airing and swirling. **84** —*M.S. (10/1/2004)*

Casaterra 2002 Merlot (Mendoza) $7. Berry jam and light leather up front, followed by medium-grade plum and cherry flavors. Vanilla and chocolate notes add thickness to the finish. The balance is not in question; standard acidity and tannins create a good mouthfeel. **84** —*M.S. (2/1/2004)*

CASTLE VIEW

Castle View 2004 Cabernet Sauvignon (Mendoza) $6. Limited red-fruit aromas mix with violets on the nose, while the mouth is tight, linear, and flat, with basic red fruits. Not bad but not complex, with a touch of artificiality on the finish. **83 Best Buy** —*M.S. (11/15/2005)*

Castle View 2004 Chardonnay (Mendoza) $6. A chalky wine with aromas of flowers and powdered sugar. Light in the mouth and striving for focus. Shows some lemon rind and dryness on the finish. **82** —*M.S. (11/15/2005)*

Castle View 2004 Malbec (Mendoza) $6. Soft red fruit on the nose is followed by a creamy, almost lactic strawberry flavor. Seems kind of empty and rough, with candied heat and milk chocolate on the finish. **82** —*M.S. (12/31/2005)*

Castle View 2004 Merlot (Mendoza) $6. More than acceptable aromas of red plum and light berries set the stage for simple but fresh cherry and currant flavors. Medium-bodied and clean, with a snappy finish and an easygoing overall personality. **84 Best Buy** —*M.S. (12/31/2005)*

CATENA

Catena 2002 Cabernet Sauvignon (Mendoza) $20. Snappy and polished, with more around the edges than in the middle. Nonetheless it's got nice black fruit, some tar and rubber, and ample vanilla. Well oaked but not "woody," with raspberry, red currant, and vanilla on the palate. Easy on the finish, if simple. **87** —*M.S. (11/15/2005)*

Catena 1999 Agrelo Cabernet Sauvignon (Mendoza) $20. Made in a woody style, but there's enough sweet blackberry fruit to compensate. Scents of toasty oak and a hint of menthol waft from the glass; oak adds cinnamon and other dried spices to the palate. Juicy, lemony acids keep the flavors lively through the finish. **87** —*J.C. (5/1/2002)*

Catena 2001 Agrelo Vineyard Cabernet Sauvignon (Mendoza) $23. Very woody, with some cola notes to the bouquet. The palate is tart and snappy, with more cranberry and cherry pie than opulent Cabernet fruit. Some buttery oak is detectable on the tannic finish. Has forcefulness but no supple richness. **84** —*M.S. (5/1/2003)*

Catena 2000 Alta Cabernet Sauvignon (Mendoza) $60. Fairly lean and a bit grassy on the nose, with plenty of red fruit but not much of the heft or extract that one expects from a higher-end, modern-style Cabernet. Everything comes in a reserved, quiet way, from the fruit to the background notes of toast and chocolate. **87** —*M.S. (7/1/2004)*

Catena 2004 Chardonnay (Mendoza) $18. Peach, melon, and apple carry the clean but ordinary bouquet, and behind that comes a round palate full of ripe banana, pear, caramel, and vanilla. Fully oaked but not overdone, with toast on the finish. Good Argentine Chardonnay. **86** —*M.S. (6/1/2006)*

Catena 2003 Chardonnay (Mendoza) $18. Very good and fresh; one of the better examples of a balanced Argentine Chardonnay that you'll encounter. Aromas of pear, vanilla, and oak are solid and well blended, while the peach and pear flavors are exact. Some citrus, mineral, and baking spice on the finish create a fine ending. **90 Editors' Choice** —*M.S. (3/1/2005)*

Catena 2001 Agrelo Vineyards Chardonnay (Mendoza) $20. Here's a wine with body and power. The nose is chunky and meaty, with lots of oak and banana. The palate is big, with full flavors of vanilla, custard, lemon, and more banana. Toasted marshmallow and coconut, both indicators of an aggressive, powerful barrel regimen, are front and center on the finish. **87** —*M.S. (5/1/2003)*

Catena 2000 Agrelo Vineyards Chardonnay (Mendoza) $15. Custard, melon, citrus, and toasted-wood aromas. Pineapple and lemon flavors are offset by a lacquer-like note on the tail end and a heavy mouthfeel. So in that sense, it struggles for balance. **85** —*M.S. (7/1/2002)*

Catena 2002 Alta Chardonnay (Mendoza) $30. Made from Catena's Adrianna Vineyard, this bulky reserve-level wine deals mature aromas of corn, wheat, and melon more than anything zingy or zesty. The full-bodied palate is ripe and meaty, with chunky cantaloupe and peach flavors. Warm and oaky on the back end, if maybe a little too heavy. Drink now. **88** —*M.S. (3/1/2005)*

Catena 2002 Alta Chardonnay (Mendoza) $30. Toasty and ripe, with nice cinnamon and vanilla shadings. Lots of apple, pineapple, and spice grace the palate of this single-vineyard wine. Shows modest wood on the finish and plenty of length. Borders on weighty but maintains its elegance. **88** —*M.S. (11/15/2005)*

Catena 2001 Alta Chardonnay (Mendoza) $33. A single-vineyard wine from Tupungato, and barrel fermented as well as fully oaked throughout aging. The result is a spicy, creamy, thick Chard with baked apple fruit, cinnamon, and just enough acidity to carry it all to fruition. Very Catena and very Argentinean in style. **90** —*M.S. (7/1/2004)*

Catena 2000 Alta Chardonnay (Mendoza) $32. The color is brownish-gold. Butter, coconut, and a distant note of apple on the nose. The flavors are thick and buttery, and with little acidity working in its favor the wine seems tired. Very oaky at the end. Tasted twice, with consistent results. **84** —*M.S. (5/1/2003)*

Catena 1999 Alta Adrianna Vineyard Chardonnay (Mendoza) $30. This pricey, mature wine is richly colored, and features an expected blast of toasted oak on the nose as well as some lemon and scrambled eggs. The oak element is heavy, but interesting. It definitely drives the wine and provides plenty of spicy nuances. If it's missing anything, it's defined, clean fruit, and brighter acidity. Drink immediately. **88** —*M.S. (7/1/2002)*

Catena 2003 Malbec (Mendoza) $20. Balsamic vinegar and earth aromas get it started, with baked fruit and chocolate playing second fiddle. Solid, spicy, and in no way flabby; in fact, it's rather firm on the palate. Not quite rich and fruity enough to make the highest echelon, but still a very good Malbec. **88** —*M.S. (11/15/2005)*

Catena 2002 Malbec (Mendoza) $22. Full and toasty, with an overt, burnt, almost charred nose. Mineral, charcoal, and red plum carry the zesty palate to an open, tasty, long finish. Closing notes of espresso, tree bark, and bitter chocolate are obvious and appropriate. **88** —*M.S. (3/1/2005)*

Catena 1999 Alta Malbec (Mendoza) $55. Sweet and soft black cherry aromas are couched in cream and a slight woody heat. On the palate, black berry fruit smolders under earthy, forest-floor flavors. It's a little rough and rustic in the mouth, thanks to a dose of drying tannins. Finishes with more oak and a metallic twinge. **86** —*D.T. (5/1/2002)*

Catena 2000 Alta Angelica Vineyard Malbec (Mendoza) $55. Oak is a dominating factor, but if you can handle that, like the fruit can, you should enjoy this burly Malbec. Aromas of charred wood and sawdust lead into black cherry and blackberry. The finish is pure mocha and vanilla, and at all points it's tannic, layered, and satisfying. **90** —*M.S. (5/1/2003)*

Catena 2001 Bodega Catena Zapata Malbec (Mendoza) $25. Once again, the house style awaits: toast and char on the nose. But it's not masking anything; instead, that smoky edge not only carries but also adds a buttery edge to the strawberry, raspberry, chocolate, and coffee that complete this textbook Malbec. A blend of two vineyards, and proprietary in its flavors. **88** —*M.S. (12/1/2003)*

CATENA ALTA

Catena Alta 2002 Malbec (Mendoza) $45. Impressive and saturated, with ripe aromas. The mouth is focused and, generally speaking, quite rewarding. The blackberry and dark plum flavors are big and aggressive. If there's any one place the wine doesn't wow, it's on the finish, which is short and a bit sharp-edged. Needs food. **89** —*M.S. (4/1/2006)*

CAVA NEGRA

Cava Negra 2002 Malbec (Mendoza) $8. Although this isn't overly stuffed, it manages to handle the spicy wood that was thrown at it during aging. With cinnamon and foresty accents, the fruit comes across light and distant. Still, the wine finishes clean and proper, so it should do well with basic foods. **85 Best Buy** —*M.S. (3/1/2005)*

CAVAS DE CHACRAS

Cavas de Chacras 1999 Reserve Malbec (Mendoza) $13. Not sure why this 1999 would still be on the market as a current release, but at the very least it shows that Malbec ages fairly well. The nose is still largely fresh, while the red fruit flavors fall into the raspberry, plum, and cassis category. Not terribly lush but solid. **85** —*M.S. (8/1/2006)*

Cavas de Chacras 2004 Rosé Reserve Rosé Blend (Mendoza) $10. Slightly harsh aromas of radish and leather are a little raw. Tastes like fresh nectarines and berries, then turns a bit mealy on the finish. **80** —*M.S. (8/1/2006)*

CAVAS DE SANTOS

Cavas de Santos 2002 Cabernet Sauvignon (Mendoza) $11. Light and brushy, with aromas of red cherry, citrus peel, and leather. Decent cherry and chocolate flavors take care of the palate, which is limited but not bad. Scratchy on the finish, with an initial push that does better than the lasting notes. **83** —*M.S. (11/15/2005)*

Cavas de Santos 2002 Gran Malbec (Mendoza) $17. Round and woody, with dry fruit on the nose. Cherry, blackberry and some meatiness make for a recognizable, easy-to-like palate. Finishes a bit soft, with little acidity or kick. Drink now. **85** —*M.S. (11/15/2005)*

CAVAS DEL CONDE

Cavas del Conde 2002 Cabernet Sauvignon (Mendoza) $9. The bouquet is all about stewed, raisiny fruit. Heavy as lead, with sticky raisin and prune flavors. Finishes ponderous, with zero agility. **80** —*M.S. (11/15/2005)*

Cavas del Conde 2002 Malbec (Mendoza) $9. Jammy and woody, but not terribly complex. The fruit falls squarely into the grape and plum category, but there's also some distracting green notes up front and on the herbal finish. Decent, but has issues. Tasted twice with identical impressions. **83** —*M.S. (11/15/2005)*

Cavas del Conde 2004 Primacia Merlot (Mendoza) $7. A lot of raisin and heavy cola aromas weigh down the bouquet in front of reduced, almost condensed baked-fruit flavors. A stewy wine with a saving streak of acidity in the middle tier. **81** —*M.S. (6/1/2006)*

Cavas del Conde 2002 Piedra del Molino Syrah (Mendoza) $7. Tired and lacking, with dusty herbal fruit aromas and hardly any richness or ripeness. Finishes rough while stirring no enthusiasm. Just acceptable. **80** —*M.S. (4/1/2006)*

Cavas del Conde 2004 Primacia Syrah (Mendoza) $7. Flat and raisiny, with a hint of orange peel on the nose. More saturated in the mouth, but bland in terms of primary flavors and jagged in terms of feel. Finishing flavors of prune, licorice, and coffee are thick and less than convincing. **83** —*M.S. (4/1/2006)*

CAVAS DEL VALLE

Cavas del Valle 2000 Malbec (Tupungato) $15. This old-vines red features an intriguing nose of lavender, citrus peel, sandalwood, and cherry. In the mouth, though, it's only medium in body and depth, with sharp acids driving red-berry fruit. Lushness, frequently the premier component of Argentinean Malbec, just isn't here. **85** —*M.S. (11/1/2002)*

CHAKANA

Chakana 2004 Bonarda (Mendoza) $12. This unusual varietal wine doesn't offer much in the way of aromas but it's saturated and full of nice dark-fruit flavors, particularly roast plum and blackberry. Has power, purity, and spice at its core, with chocolate on the finish. Well made, a touch rubbery and offers a good introduction to the Bonarda grape. **87 Best Buy** —*M.S. (11/15/2005)*

Chakana 2004 Cabernet Sauvignon (Mendoza) $12. The spice-to-fruit ratio on the bouquet is solid if not out of the ordinary. Tight cherry, plum, and raspberry flavors carry the palate, while the finish is largely on the money. A deep and chewy, full-bodied Cabernet. **87 Best Buy** —*M.S. (11/15/2005)*

Chakana 2003 Reserve Cabernet Sauvignon (Mendoza) $23. Hard and slightly chemical, with heavy fruit that is almost stewed. Very firm tannins and plenty of oak on the finish result in a grabby, chunky wine that registers as forceful, yet short on charm. **82** —*M.S. (11/15/2005)*

Chakana 2004 Malbec (Mendoza) $12. Serious stuff that requires at least 10 minutes of airing to shed its rusticity and reveal its charms and qualities, among which are smoky plum aromas and flavors that bring spice and chocolate along for the ride. Layered and warm on the finish, with plumpness and hard spice. **88 Best Buy** —*M.S. (11/15/2005)*

Chakana 2003 Malbec (Mendoza) $11. Starts out dense, with aromas of fruit cake, prune, and hard cheese, but time allows it to show its sweet side, where currant, blackberry, and sautéed mushroom carry the palate to a forward, likable finish. Made in a fresh but sizable style; it's not syrupy yet it packs power. **89 Best Buy** —*M.S. (3/1/2005)*

Chakana 2003 Reserve Malbec (Mendoza) $23. Attractive lavender and violet notes accent typical black-fruit aromas, and the result is a mix of syrup and fresh summer plums. The palate is exceedingly ripe as it bursts with blackberry flavors and a heavy underblast of chocolate. Tight on the finish, but only at first. Soon it expands to reveal toasty, burly flavors and tannins. Delicious and sporty. **90** —*M.S. (11/15/2005)*

Chakana 2005 Rosé Malbec (Mendoza) $12. Leafy and herbal, with a bit of a cooked quality on the nose. Quite tangy, with citrus, green melon, and red currant flavors. Lasting due to outsized acidity. **83** —*M.S. (4/1/2006)*

Chakana 2004 Shiraz (Mendoza) $12. It doesn't take a genius to realize that this is a very nicely made, fully healthy Shiraz. The bouquet is just right, with smoky nuances to the full-fledged dark fruit aromas. The palate is racy and juicy, but plush with blackberry and plum. And the balance is right on. Smells good, tastes good, and feels good. **90 Best Buy** —*M.S. (10/1/2005)*

CHEVAL DES ANDES

Cheval des Andes 2002 Cabernet Sauvignon-Malbec (Mendoza) $75. A serious wine for serious wine drinkers. It's 60% Cabernet and the rest Malbec. Deep, deep, and deeper is how to best describe the chewy, fruit-saturated palate, but even better, this wine has guts, balance, and aging capacity. Best to hold this joint-venture red from Chateau Cheval-Blanc and Terrazas de Los Andes for at least three years. **93 Cellar Selection** —*M.S. (7/1/2005)*

CINCO TIERRAS

Cinco Tierras 2003 Malbec (Mendoza) $10. Ripe and smoky, with attractive nuances to the forward bouquet. This is a nice wine with spunky plum flavors balanced by adequate but not overpowering oak. Cola, wood grain, and toast notes help the finish along. Medium in weight and pure; mildly tannic. **85 Best Buy** —*M.S. (12/31/2005)*

Cinco Tierras 2003 Reserve Malbec (Mendoza) $14. Sweet and oaky, with graham cracker and wood grain on the nose. Tastes fairly fruity at first, with initial blackberry and plum flavors. Turns crisp and acidic on the finish, almost to the point of scouring. Not a step up from the regular, less expensive 2003 Malbec. **84** —*M.S. (12/31/2005)*

CLOS DE LOS SIETE

Clos de los Siete 2003 Malbec (Mendoza) $16. Pure and inky. The nose offers graphite, earth, and a huge amount of blackberry. The ripe palate is deep and defined, with a layer or two of complexity. Finishes with oak shadings, a splash of mint, and chocolate. Because the vineyards that yield this wine are still young, expect only better things in the future. Congratulations to Clos leader Michel Rolland and his gang of seven. **91 Editors' Choice** —*M.S. (7/1/2005)*

Clos de los Siete 2002 7 Red Blend (Mendoza) $15. This new Malbec comes courtesy of Michel Rolland, who has shown his skill before with the grape, at Yacochuya in Cafayete. This wine is sweet and lush, with plum and cassis in droves. In the mouth, it's round, textured, and masculine, yet devoid of hard tannins. High in alcohol (14.5%) but not hot. Derived from seven Mendoza vineyards. **90 Best Buy** —*M.S. (10/1/2004)*

Clos de los Siete 2004 Red Wine Red Blend (Mendoza) $17. A bit of marmalade and violets accent the bold, dark nose. Not at all subtle, with syrupy berry flavors offset by a whack of bitter chocolate. Full-bodied, with chewy tannins and plenty of oak on the finish. A ripe, untamed, candied wine that will settle with more bottle age. **89** —*M.S. (6/1/2006)*

COIRON

Coiron 2003 Malbec (Mendoza) $9. A lot of funk on the nose, and it never really goes away. Aromas of burnt coffee, sulfur, and charred meat are less than attractive, while the palate runs weedy. Just too shaky and off to rate better. **81** —*M.S. (12/1/2006)*

COLOMÉ

Colomé 2004 Estate Red Blend (Calchaqui Valley) $25. This new wine from Donald Hess of the Hess Collection is a big, bold mix of black cherry and currants. It's ripe and cushioned by full tannins and a lot of spirit. The blend is 66% Malbec, 20% Cabernet, and 14% Tannat from high-altitude vineyards in Salta. Will go nicely with steak and other meat dishes. A truly excellent, modern-styled Argentine red. **91 Editors' Choice** —*M.S. (12/1/2006)*

Colomé 2003 Reserva Red Blend (Calchaqui Valley) $90. Here's one heck of a black, saturated wine. Cola and tar aromas abound, while the palate is borderline medicinal due to its extreme ripeness. If you like a rich, sun-drenched red with heft and body, this is it. The blend is 80% Malbec and 20% Cabernet Sauvignon, and it hails from vines with up to 150 years of history behind them. Weighs in at a whopping 15.5%. **92** —*M.S. (12/1/2006)*

Colomé 2006 Torrontès (Calchaqui Valley) $13. Normally a wine with this score and price would earn front-line Best Buy status. But because it's brand new and total production is only 600 cases, you're going to have to work to find it. But if you do, expect a melon-driven wine with clean lines, good acidity, and a long finish. It's refined Torrontès; aromatic and complex to the point that you might mistake it for a Rhône Valley Viognier or something similar. **90 Editors' Choice** —*M.S. (12/1/2006)*

COLONIA LAS LIEBRES

Colonia Las Liebres 2005 Bonarda (Mendoza) $9. From the Altos Las Hormigas gang comes this Bonarda that hits with more power than precision, yet in the long run it makes the grade as a fun wine with plenty to offer. The nose is full of dark fruit, coffee, vanilla and marzipan, while the palate and finish are equally fruity and forward. The perfect red for burgers. **87 Best Buy** —*M.S. (11/1/2006)*

CONCHA Y TORO

Concha y Toro 2002 Xplorador Malbec (Mendoza) $7. Lots of black fruit with a touch of earth and an herbal undercurrent. Forward and jammy, with solid black cherry, plum, and pepper. Finishes a bit spicy, with chocolate to sweeten it up. Nothing to take issue with here; quite good value. **86 Best Buy** —*M.S. (11/15/2005)*

Concha y Toro 2001 Xplorador Malbec (Mendoza) $7. Once again, this brand offers a lot of flavor for a song. Dark aromas of pencil lead and rubber mix with ripe fruit. It's balanced, not heavy, yet not wimpy or watery. For everyday Malbec you can't do much better. **86 Best Buy** — *M.S. (10/1/2004)*

Concha y Toro 2000 Xplorador Malbec (Mendoza) $8. For the times where you want a good, clean red wine but still want to keep it under ten bucks, give this a try. Full and forceful plum and licorice aromas start it off, followed by full berry fruit on the palate and then a spicy, dry finish. **85 Best Buy** —*M.S. (11/1/2002)*

CONQUISTA

Conquista 2004 Malbec (Mendoza) $8. Light, with cherry and orange peel on the nose. So it's not surprising that snappy cherry and raspberry flavors follow. Shows a lot of pop and acidity, yet it manages to fold in some pepper and chocolate. **84 Best Buy** —*M.S. (11/15/2005)*

CRISTOBAL 1492

Cristobal 1492 2003 Bonarda (Mendoza) $10. Violet and rich to the eye, with full-force boysenberry aromas. Aggressive and full-bodied, with rubbery tannins and massive flavors of bacon, molasses, and black fruits. Very good Bonarda, a grape that usually fails to impress. And for the price it's well worth a try. **87 Best Buy** —*M.S. (11/15/2005)*

Cristobal 1492 2003 Cabernet Sauvignon (Mendoza) $10. Good color and condensed, with a lot of tar and rubber. In the mouth, there's brightness as well as flavors of cherry and raspberry. Finishes creamy, with a shot of coconut. **85 Best Buy** —*M.S. (11/15/2005)*

Cristobal 1492 2003 Malbec (Mendoza) $10. Bubble gum and spice aromas, with chunky, off-centered fruit. Smells as if it might have gone through carbonic maceration, meaning it's candied and rubbery, with bright, gummy fruit flavors. **80** —*M.S. (12/31/2005)*

Cristobal 1492 2003 Oak Reserve Malbec (Mendoza) $15. Toasty and smoky, with rubber and powerful dark-fruit aromas. Plum and black cherry work the palate, while on the back end black fruit is spiced up by strong hints of pepper. Standard but good; plump and satisfying. **87** — *M.S. (11/15/2005)*

Cristobal 1492 2003 Oak Reserve Shiraz (Mendoza) $19. The oak here has resulted in bacon and wet-dog aromas, and the bouquet stays funky. Bold berry, carob, and pepper on the palate set the stage for a warm, almost lactic finish. Has merits but doesn't sing. **83** —*M.S. (11/15/2005)*

Cristobal 1492 2004 Verdelho (Mendoza) $10. Floral and different, with papaya, peach, and melon. This is not Spanish-style Verdejo, which is much more racy and acidic. This one is soft, smooth, a bit flat and flabby, but nonetheless it grows on you. **84** —*M.S. (11/15/2005)*

CROTTA

Crotta 2001 Tempranillo (Mendoza) $8. The bouquet is exotic at first, with spice and pepper mixing with red fruit. Black cherry and black pepper define the flavor profile, and the finish is spicy yet surprisingly sweet. **84** —*M.S. (5/1/2003)*

CUQ

CUQ 2004 Merlot-Bonarda Red Blend (Mendoza) $15. Tannic and raisiny, with no cushion to speak of. The blend is Merlot and Bonarda, a marriage that could work but barely makes the grade in this case. Comes across loud and rough. **81** —*M.S. (12/31/2005)*

DAVIS FAMILY

Davis Family 2000 Gusto Vita Malbec (Mendoza) $30. With licorice, pepper, coffee, wet rubber, and mocha, this is a highly aromatic table wine, one that's owned and made by the Davis family from California. The mouth features cola, blueberry, and coffee notes, and the mouthfeel is simultaneously stylish yet lush. It's immensely smooth, big and bold. **90** —*M.S. (5/1/2003)*

DIABLO DE UCO

Diablo de Uco 2002 Cabernet Sauvignon (Mendoza) $13. Pretty on the nose, as the violet, cocoa, and subtle fruit tones work well together. The palate is juicy, typically acidic and penetrating. A long finish that's clean but a bit thin closes the show. Displays some spiky qualities, primarily sharp acidity. **86** —*M.S. (11/15/2004)*

Diablo de Uco 2003 Malbec (Mendoza) $13. Solid up front, with earth, root beer, and black-fruit aromas. The feel, however, is quite zippy, with sharp acidity pushing the plum and black cherry flavors toward the realm of tangy. It's no surprise that it finishes kind of rowdy and jumpy. Still, it tastes good and clean. **85** —*M.S. (12/31/2005)*

Diablo de Uco 2002 Malbec (Mendoza) $13. Sports a dark luster, with large, equally black aromas that match the robust color. Mouthfeel is where this wine racks up its points; the palate is plush and rich. Flavorwise, you get plum and berry riding on a wave of sharp acidity. **87** —*M.S. (11/15/2004)*

Diablo de Uco 2002 Merlot (Mendoza) $13. Murky aromas of earth and coal turn bland before veering toward cheesy. Flavors of red raspberry and pie cherry are tart, while the mouthfeel is scouring due to high acidity. Ultra tart and fresh, but ultimately sour and short. **82** —*M.S. (11/15/2004)*

DOMAINE CHANDON

Domaine Chandon NV Fresco Brut Champagne Blend (Mendoza) $11. **85 Best Buy** —*D.T. (11/15/2002)*

DOMAINE JEAN BOUSQUET

Domaine Jean Bousquet 2003 Cabernet Sauvignon (Mendoza) $12. Alive and spicy, with a lot of oak but also some pretty good fruit in support. Tastes of cherry and cassis, with good acid-to-tannin balance. Some herbal, leafy notes on the finish conjure memories of cru bourgeois Bordeaux. Shows some complexity and style for a $12 Cab. **87 Best Buy** —*M.S. (11/15/2005)*

Domaine Jean Bousquet 2004 Chardonnay (Tupungato) $11. Full-bodied and ripe, starting with the butterscotch and toast aromas and continuing on to the sweet-styled palate that offers pear, apple butter and walnut flavors. Thick more than lean, with one of the roundest and creamiest mouthfeels going. **86 Best Buy** —*M.S. (7/1/2005)*

Domaine Jean Bousquet 2005 Organic Chardonnay (Tupungato) $13. Yellowish in color, with a heavy, somewhat creamy nose that deals vanilla and melon. More sweet vanilla is woven into the anonymous fruit flavors, while slight oakiness rears up on the finish. Not bad but oaky and unfocused. **84** —*M.S. (8/1/2006)*

Domaine Jean Bousquet 2004 Malbec (Mendoza) $11. Entirely attractive and smooth. The nose offers appropriate milk chocolate, crushed berry, and jam-like aromas, while the palate is ripe, fruity, and balanced. Good on the palate, with sweet but dark finishing notes. A winner in its price range. **89 Best Buy** —*M.S. (11/15/2005)*

Domaine Jean Bousquet 2005 Organic Malbec (Tupungato) $13. Dark and dense, with extracted black cherry, leather, and earth aromas. Shows a ton of body and darkness but only limited flavors. Chocolate and vanilla appear on the finish, but there's also a blast of green to bring it down. **84** —*M.S. (8/1/2006)*

Domaine Jean Bousquet 2005 Rosé Malbec-Cabernet Sauvignon (Tupungato) $10. Light in color, with fresh yet slightly perfumed aromas. Sweet yet kind of bland, with a candied finish. Very sugary, with a lot of residual sweetness. A lot like White Zin. **84** —*M.S. (4/1/2006)*

Domaine Jean Bousquet 2004 Merlot (Mendoza) $11. This Merlot from Tupungato has clean, proper aromas and a fair amount of zesty cherry and raspberry flavors. Tangy on the finish, if a bit lean. Still, there's enough purity and power to elevate it to the quality level. Young and ready to go; a BBQ wine of the first order. **86 Best Buy** —*M.S. (11/15/2005)*

Domaine Jean Bousquet 2005 Organic Merlot (Tupungato) $13. Kind of reedy and covered with a veneer of wood that holds in the red cherry and raspberry aromas and flavors. Feels lean and wispy on the palate, where a bell pepper note creeps into the picture. Loses body the longer it sits. **84** —*M.S. (8/1/2006)*

DOMINGO HERMANOS

Domingo Hermanos 2001 Palo Domingo Red Blend (Salta) $49. This small-production tribute wine hails from Salta. It's a firm, thick wine with full-force plum, berry, and caramel aromas and flavors. The finish is rich and saturated, and overall it's a good, brooding wine with some class and style. Just 116 cases produced. **87** —*M.S. (7/1/2004)*

DOMINGO MOLINA

Domingo Molina 2000 Malbec (Argentina) $15. The nose offers maple, roasted nuts, and some deep black fruit. The palate is grapy and chunky, and the finish is heavily dosed with coffee and burnt wood. The overall sensation is slightly hot and tannic. For those interested, it's from Yacochuya, in the northern Salta region. **86** —*M.S. (5/1/2003)*

DON MIGUEL GASCÓN

Don Miguel Gascón 2004 Malbec (Mendoza) $13. Bright purple in color, with heavy smoke and rubber aromas that together come across as bacon and bitter chocolate. Cassis, plum, and tobacco rest comfortably on the palate, while the finish is grapy, extracted, and toasty. In recent years this wine has carved out its own style, and this vintage fits the model. **87** — *M.S. (11/15/2005)*

Don Miguel Gascón 2003 Malbec (Mendoza) $12. Round and smoky, as is the house style. There's also the full allotment of asphalt, leather, and black-plum aromas. Full and ripe on the palate, with additional plum and black cherry flavors. Finishes with a tingle, the result of slightly sharp acidity. **87 Best Buy** —*M.S. (10/1/2004)*

Don Miguel Gascón 2002 Malbec (Mendoza) $12. Heavily oaked and offering the full monty in terms of toast and char. But that burnt quality works well here, largely because the fruit is healthy and ripe. Flavors of black plum and nutmeg-tinged berry define the heart of this full-extract red. Yet another wine from the Catena stable. **87** —*M.S. (12/1/2003)*

Don Miguel Gascón 2000 Malbec (Mendoza) $10. Malbec, a Bordeaux grape often used in blending, makes its mark in the Argentina's Mendoza region, where it yields sturdy, flavorful reds characterized by inky color and chewy texture. The black cherry fruit has an appealing coffee-chocolate overlay and dense mouthfeel. Tangy, peppery tannins and an earthy note on the back end show a more rustic side of the personality of this great grilled-meat companion. **88** *(11/15/2001)*

Don Miguel Gascón 2003 President's Blend Malbec (Mendoza) $22. Anyone looking for a whole lot of wine for not too much cash will be pleased with this blend, named for former Argentinean president Juan Perón, husband of Evita. Back to the wine: it's rich, heady, and borderline opulent, with ripe tannins, plumpness and hedonistic fruit. Incorporates 10% Cabernet and 5% Syrah. **91 Editors' Choice** —*M.S. (6/1/2006)*

Don Miguel Gascón 2000 President's Blend Malbec (Mendoza) $20. This is a dark, heavily oaked wine, one that contains 10% Cabernet Sauvignon and 5% Syrah in addition to Malbec. The nose is less about fruit and more about wood, with sawdust aromas front and center. The plum and black currant fruit is masked by the heavy barrel influence, and the mouthfeel is heavy. **86** —*M.S. (11/1/2002)*

Don Miguel Gascón 2003 Syrah (Mendoza) $12. Dark and saturated; it's black as night, a thick, chewy wine. The bouquet is overflowing with fresh-roasted coffee and earth, while the meaty palate is deep, with blackberry and black currant flavors. Plenty of warmth, pepper, and vanilla on the finish. A big, extracted bruiser, very much in this brand's style. **87 Best Buy** —*M.S. (10/1/2004)*

Don Miguel Gascón 2002 Syrah (Mendoza) $12. Inky purple in color, with a dense bouquet of bacon, coffee grinds, and plum. The palate is grapey at first, while a textured but mildly tangy finish comes next. Fairly high-voltage and powerful, but not very elegant. Best for fans of thick, extracted reds. **84** —*M.S. (2/1/2004)*

Don Miguel Gascón 2000 Syrah (Mendoza) $12. Anyone who enjoys a meaty, over-the-top Syrah, one that's full of bacon, leather, and super-charged tannins, should try this. The palate is like blueberry pie, but with smoky bacon on top. The finish is chewy and long. This wine borders on being cloying—it's that rich. Best with fatty ribs or cheeseburgers. **85** —*M.S. (11/1/2002)*

Don Miguel Gascón 2005 Viognier (Mendoza) $13. For some time now this wine has been the measuring stick for Argentine Viognier, and the '05 vintage is one of the best yet. Mineral, melon, and peaches coat the bouquet, while the balanced palate is full of sweet melon flavors. This is a warm, ripe, slightly creamy wine that's meant to be drunk as soon as possible, before it loses steam. **88 Best Buy** —*M.S. (6/1/2006)*

Don Miguel Gascón 2004 Viognier (Mendoza) $12. Lively, with young legs. The bouquet blasts forth with lemon curd and ripe apple aromas, which are followed by a plump yet racy palate full of spicy apple, pear, and mild mineral notes. Not meant for the long haul. **86** —*M.S. (11/15/2004)*

Don Miguel Gascón 2003 Viognier (Mendoza) $12. Fairly light and fruity as a result of only 20% barrel fermentation. Shows lemony, clean aromas and a medium-size body. With just a hint of barrel influence, it's zesty but short. Good for parties. **85** —*M.S. (7/1/2004)*

Don Miguel Gascón 2002 Viognier (Mendoza) $12. A meaty, bold wine, with peach, custard, and crushed vitamin comprising the nose. Tastes sweet and cloying, with sugary citrus flavors. A sticky, heavy finish is saturated with tropical fruit and sweet almond candy. The feeling here is that this is too ponderous. **83** —*M.S. (2/1/2004)*

DON RODOLFO

Don Rodolfo 2003 High Altitude Vineyards Cabernet Sauvignon (Cafayate) $10. Syrupy and strange, with a lactic palate feel and cloying cherry fruit. Finishes bitter as well as candied. **82** —*M.S. (11/15/2004)*

Don Rodolfo 2004 High Altitude Vineyards Malbec (Cafayate) $10. Fairly earthy and stewy, but not too baked to suffer. The palate is expectedly chunky and meaty, with full-weight dark fruits and some rooty depth. Fairly easygoing and likable, but a tad muddled. **84** —*M.S. (12/1/2006)*

Don Rodolfo 2003 High Altitude Vineyards Malbec (Cafayate) $10. Pickle and sauerkraut notes mix with raisins and leather on the nose. It maintains that funky, pickled flavor throughout. Along the way there's red-berry fruit and some heat-bearing spice. Unconventional and strange, but acceptable. **82** —*M.S. (11/15/2004)*

Don Rodolfo 2003 High Altitude Vineyards Shiraz (Cafayate) $10. Begins with leather, earth and stewed plum aromas. The body is big and manly, with smooth tannins and a chunky mouthfeel. Flavors of plum, berry, and rhubarb are lively, accented by a touch of milk chocolate. **87 Best Buy** —*M.S. (11/15/2004)*

Don Rodolfo 2004 High Altitude Vineyards Tannat (Cafayate) $10. Tannat by nature is a hard, brooding grape, and this version from northern Argentina's Salta region is funky, with olive, horse hide, and plenty of dark-fruit aromas and flavors. The palate is leathery but proportioned, with spice and length. Could use a touch more cushion, but hey, that's Tannat. **86 Best Buy** —*M.S. (12/1/2006)*

Don Rodolfo 2002 High Altitude Vineyards Tannat (Cafayate) $10. Candied and sweet on the nose, but sour on the tongue. Simply put, it's astringent, lean, and acidic, all common traits of this hard-to-master grape more frequently found in Uruguay. **81** —*M.S. (3/1/2005)*

Don Rodolfo 2005 High Altitude Vineyards Torrontès (Cafayate) $10. Yellowish rather than pale in color, which indicates some overripeness that's confirmed on the chunky, apple-driven nose. Big on the palate as well, with tropical fruit preceding a lazy finish. Big in flavor but lacks touch. **83** —*M.S. (11/1/2006)*

Don Rodolfo 2003 High Altitude Vineyards Torrontès (Cafayate) $10. Floral as it should be, with lemon and litchi aromas. Citrus controls the palate, aided by notes of green herbs. Long and zesty on the finish. A good Torrontès that's meant to be served well chilled. **85 Best Buy** —*M.S. (11/15/2004)*

DOÑA CRISTINA

Doña Cristina 2001 Red Blend (Mendoza) $14. The plum, raisin, and oak aromas are familiar, while the cherry-based palate is snappy and abrasive. Gritty, without much flesh, yet not off in terms of taste. A blend of 65% Malbec, 35% Tempranillo. **82** —*M.S. (11/15/2005)*

DOÑA PAULA

Doña Paula 2003 Estate Cabernet Sauvignon (Luján de Cuyo) $15. Good value in Cabernet, blending ripe cassis with just enough weedy, tobaccoey complexities. Medium-weight, folding in hints of cedar on the midpalate. Simultaneously mouthwatering and chewy on the finish. Drink now with burgers or hold another 2–3 years and serve with roast beef. **89** *(12/31/2004)*

Doña Paula 2002 Estate Cabernet Sauvignon (Luján de Cuyo) $15. A mix of rusticity and richness defines the liqueur and leather aromas. The fruit is somewhat candied and heavy, with peppery notes darkening things up. Lots of sweet chocolate appears on the finish, which clamps down with firm, spicy tannins. **86** —*M.S. (2/1/2004)*

Doña Paula 2005 Los Cardos Cabernet Sauvignon (Luján de Cuyo) $10. A bit heavy and muddled up front, but that could be construed as being earthy. The flavors run a touch green, but along with that leaning there's zesty red fruit and some tannin. Grabby but not harsh. **83** —*M.S. (11/1/2006)*

Doña Paula 2003 Los Cardos Cabernet Sauvignon (Luján de Cuyo) $10. Round on the nose, with a fair amount of candied, spicy fruit. Ripe and regular, with berry and cherry flavors, firm tannins, and a touch of oak. Robust acidity makes it a zinger across the tongue. **85** —*M.S. (10/1/2004)*

Doña Paula 2002 Los Cardos Cabernet Sauvignon (Luján de Cuyo) $8. The nose deals earth, soy sauce, game, and a distant note of green pepper. There's good extract and color throughout, with some syrupy sweetness to offset the mildest note of green bean. Pepper and other spices on the finish create interest. **85 Best Buy** —*M.S. (2/1/2004)*

Doña Paula 2003 Estate Chardonnay (Luján de Cuyo) $15. Toasty and nutty on the nose, this is a big, woody wine that's barrel-fermented in 80% new French oak. Peach and pear notes support the wood on the palate, and the wine finishes crisp, with a hint of grapefruit. **86** *(12/31/2004)*

Doña Paula 2002 Estate Chardonnay (Luján de Cuyo) $15. Pear and honey aromas belie a palate that's mostly citrus, tangerine, and sweet grapefruit. Finishes persistent, with a juicy, clean, mildly watery mouthfeel. Not bad within its category. **86** —*M.S. (10/1/2004)*

Doña Paula 2005 Los Cardos Chardonnay (Mendoza) $10. The bouquet initially yields iodine and ham aromas, but airing settles it down. Sweet and full of apple flavors in the mouth, while the finish veers dangerously close to cider-like. Struggles to make its mark. **82** —*M.S. (11/1/2006)*

Doña Paula 2004 Los Cardos Chardonnay (Mendoza) $9. From the yellow tint through the ripe tropical fruit, this is Argentinean Chardonnay in its truest form. Los Cardos is the second label from Doña Paula, itself a spinoff of Chile's Santa Rita. The nose offers popcorn along with pear and licorice, and the texture and flavors are solid as a statue. "Cardos," in Spanish, are thistles, but there's nothing prickly about this well-priced Chard. **86 Best Buy** —*M.S. (11/15/2005)*

Doña Paula 2004 Los Cardos Chardonnay (Luján de Cuyo) $9. A soft, fruity, medium-weight Chardonnay, with obvious flavors of peach and vanilla. Finishes with a touch of grapefruit. **85** *(12/31/2004)*

Doña Paula 2003 Los Cardos Chardonnay (Luján de Cuyo) $10. Smooth and round on the nose, with aromas of melon and honey. A bit soft but not flaccid, with a sweet, creamy flavor profile that blends apple and pear. Finishes light and clean, with a hint of vanilla. **86 Best Buy** —*M.S. (10/1/2004)*

Doña Paula 2002 Los Cardos Chardonnay (Luján de Cuyo) $8. With its soft pear and banana aromas, the bouquet is welcoming. Flavors of mango and lychee are sweet, while a note of white pepper adds spice. Licorice and nutmeg provide depth to the lemony finish. Nice and drinkable. **85 Best Buy** —*M.S. (2/1/2004)*

Doña Paula 2002 Séleccion de Bodega Single Vineyard Chardonnay (Luján de Cuyo) $29. The richest and most concentrated on Doña Paula's Chards, this one has enough fruit intensity to support the oak treatment. Melon and citrus aromas lead the way, accented by light toasted-oat scents. Melon and white peach flavors flow easily across the palate, riding a rich, viscous mouthfeel. Smooth finish, nicely integrating fruit and oak. **89** *(12/31/2004)*

Doña Paula 1999 Malbec (Mendoza) $12. Muscular, chunky, and a bit sun-baked. The nose is smothered by sweaty leather and barnyard, while a bit of everything is accounted for on the palate: red berries, jamminess, even red cabbage. In the final analysis, it's got force but it's not focused or harnessed. **83** —*M.S. (12/1/2003)*

Doña Paula 2003 Estate Malbec (Luján de Cuyo) $15. Nicely done, with bright raspberry aromas that leap from the glass. Mixed berries and vanilla on the palate, a fleshy, creamy mouthfeel and a supple finish make this deceptively easy to drink. **87** *(12/31/2004)*

Doña Paula 2003 Los Cardos Malbec (Luján de Cuyo) $10. The bouquet kicks off with a hard, cheesy scent. Then come rubber and asphalt along with dark berry notes. It tastes of raspberry jam, then goes soft before veering toward strawberry on the finish. Lighter in weight, and without much depth. **84** —*M.S. (11/15/2004)*

Doña Paula 1999 Los Cardos Malbec (Mendoza) $8. Big and barrel heavy, with burnt aromas dominating the nose. Underneath is sweet black-cherry fruit, although it's so rich and forward that it risks being considered medicinal. Some heavy wood creates a chocolaty flavor and feel. **84** —*M.S. (12/1/2003)*

Doña Paula 2005 Los Cardos Rosé Malbec (Mendoza) $10. Hard and spiky on the nose, and not a whole lot better in the mouth. The flavors are tart and juicy, while the lean finish is ultratangy and sharp. **80** —*M.S. (12/1/2006)*

Doña Paula 1999 Séleccion de Bodega Single Vineyard Malbec (Luján de Cuyo) $12. Better flavors than aromas. The nose begins gassy and burnt, and it never quite sheds that harsh barrel smell. But in the mouth, it has sweet, chunky fruit and a pleasant softness. Our bet is that if given time to properly open, folks will like it because of its easiness. **84** —*M.S. (12/1/2003)*

Doña Paula 2003 Estate Merlot (Tupungato) $15. Black cherry and coffee aromas tinged with herbs upfront, followed by slightly earthy flavors. Seems soft at first, but the acidity builds on the finish, closing with tart flavors and hints of caramel and graham crackers. **85** *(12/31/2004)*

Doña Paula 2002 Estate Merlot (Tupungato) $15. Crisp and tight, with firm tannins and acids. Also a bit vegetal, but not overly. Flavors of black fruit and licorice are standard fare. A pedestrian, drinkable Merlot with some style. **85** —*M.S. (10/1/2004)*

Doña Paula 2003 Los Cardos Merlot (Tupungato) $10. Boisterous and over-cooked, with heavily roasted aromas and flavors. Not a polished, prime-time wine. **80** —*M.S. (10/1/2004)*

Doña Paula 2002 Los Cardos Merlot (Tupungato) $8. Aromas of leather and root beer are rustic and inviting. Flavors of berries, pepper, and red beets create a sweet palate, while firm tannins push the finish. A touch lactic and creamy, but good overall. **85 Best Buy** —*M.S. (2/1/2004)*

Doña Paula 2002 Estate Red Blend (Luján de Cuyo) $15. This 60-40 blend begins with creamy chocolate and vanilla aromas atop standard-fare red fruit. Flavors of rhubarb, cherry, and pepper exert themselves on the woody, peppery palate. The weakness here is a thin middle; things start out solid and then shorten rapidly. **84** —*M.S. (2/1/2004)*

Doña Paula 2005 Los Cardos Sauvignon Blanc (Mendoza) $10. Pungent grapefruit aromas carry the aggressive yet fragile nose. Sheer and citric in the mouth, with sharp lemon-lime flavors. Zesty almost to the point of scouring. **82** —*M.S. (12/1/2006)*

Doña Paula 2004 Los Cardos Sauvignon Blanc (Tupungato) $9. The must for this wine spends up to two weeks refrigerated on its gross lees prior to fermentation, according to winemaker Gandolini. The result is a grapefruity, slightly grassy wine that's rounder and softer on the mid-palate, filling in with flavors of melon and fig. Tart on the finish. **85 Best Buy** *(12/31/2004)*

Doña Paula 2003 Estate Shiraz-Malbec (Luján de Cuyo) $15. Boasts an extra measure of complexity over the unblended Malbec, adding smoke, spice, and herb notes to the lush, fruity base. Peppery and briary on the finish. **88** *(12/31/2004)*

Doña Paula 2003 Los Cardos Syrah (Luján de Cuyo) $10. Chunky, grapy, and a bit weedy. The palate is one part sticky sweet and one part tart, while the finish is hot and spicy. **82** —*M.S. (10/1/2004)*

Doña Paula 2002 Los Cardos Syrah (Luján de Cuyo) $8. Some funky leather, barnyard, and charred beef gets it going, followed by ripe flavors of berry and sweet chocolate. A finish with sweetness, vanilla, and carob is borderline cloying, but not quite. **85 Best Buy** —*M.S. (2/1/2004)*

DURIGUTTI

Durigutti 2003 Malbec (Mendoza) $12. Purple in color, with oaky aromas manifested in the form of sawdust, cinnamon, and chocolate. Ripe berry and plum notes carry the toasty palate, and the finish comes back with additional chocolate, toast, and vanilla. Rich and solid. **88 Best Buy** —*M.S. (12/31/2005)*

Durigutti 2003 Reserva Malbec (Mendoza) $29. Violet in color, with persistent, potent aromas of mint, marzipan, and black cherry. This is not your run-of-the-mill soft Malbec; on the contrary, it's peppered with piercing acidity, which yields a can't-miss freshness. Flavorwise, we're talking zesty boysenberry and raspberry. **90** —*M.S. (12/1/2006)*

ECOS

Ecos 2002 Malbec (Mendoza) $12. Violet and pretty, with a forceful bouquet that starts out rustic before finding its stride. The palate is flush with fruit, primarily black currant and boysenberry. The finish, however, is not too long and loses clarity quickly. **85** —*M.S. (10/1/2004)*

Ecos 2003 Syrah (Mendoza) $12. A touch saucy and spicy on the nose, but there's also plenty of plum and berry fruit. Laudable texture and color, with just enough butter and vanilla on the finish to give it a creamy, rich aftertaste. A good entry into the ever-growing global Syrah sweepstakes. **87 Best Buy** —*M.S. (10/1/2004)*

EL NIÑO

El Niño 2003 Malbec (Mendoza) $19. Cranberry and sweet beet aromas are gritty but pure, while the palate pushes high-octane black fruit along with chocolate and raisin flavors. Lively in terms of feel, with very nice acidity providing balance. Finishes long and smoky, with pop. **88** —*M.S. (7/1/2005)*

ENRIQUE FOSTER

Enrique Foster 2004 Ique Malbec (Mendoza) $11. Quite basic and innocuous. The nose offers simple berry and plum, but nothing exciting. The palate is earthy, fruity, and solid; but again, nothing out of the ordinary. And it's short on the finish. Good but leaves you wanting more. **84** —*M.S. (12/1/2006)*

Enrique Foster 2003 Ique Malbec (Mendoza) $12. Dark purple in color, with equally dark aromas of black fruit, road tar, and mustard greens. The mouth is balanced and rich, dealing jammy blueberry and black cherry along with a serving of melted fudge. What Malbec from Argentina should be. **88 Best Buy** —*M.S. (11/15/2004)*

Enrique Foster 2002 Limited Edition Malbec (Luján de Cuyo) $36. Starts a little sour, pickled, and funky, but airing lets it find its legs and shine. Plum and snappy berry fruit is a touch tart, but not too much so. With time, it fattens up, displaying charcoal, coffee, and chocolate on the finish. **87** —*M.S. (11/15/2004)*

Enrique Foster 2002 Reserva Malbec (Luján de Cuyo) $23. The earthy nose offers leather and red fruit, but it's far short of overdone. Raspberry and cherry flavors dominate, while the lighter-weight palate is racy but not that plump in the middle. A good wine that improves with airing. **87** —*M.S. (11/15/2004)*

ESCALERA AL SOL

Escalera al Sol 1999 Syrah (Mendoza) $6. The berry–rhubarb fruit here shows a dry, sour note and also a slight mustiness. The mouthfeel is even and the wine has balance—it's not too short or too sharp—there's just not enough material here. Pepper and meat notes show on the short finish. **83** *(10/1/2001)*

ESTANCIA

Estancia 2000 Ancon Malbec (Mendoza) $25. **88** —*C.S. (5/1/2002)*

ETCHART

Etchart 1999 Chardonnay (Cafayate) $NA. A toasty, milky creaminess plays heavily on the bouquet, and in the mouth there's a lot of coconut. Sharp acidity pushes pineapple and green-apple characteristics. Has its virtues, but awkward at all points. **83** —*M.S. (9/1/2001)*

Etchart 1999 Rio de Plata Malbec (Mendoza) $7. Some marshmallow and black cherry aromas peek through a veil of woody scents, but overall the wine is short on fruit. The primary flavors are woody and smoky, like the inside of a charred barrel; the finish hollow. **81** —*J.C. (5/1/2002)*

Etchart 1999 Torrontès (Cafayate) $NA. Overt and akin in some ways to Gewurztraminer. Flowery, lemony, and fairly ebullient. Driving acidity keeps it fresh, and it tails away with a dry, soda-like snap. But drink soon; it's not getting younger. **84** —*M.S. (9/1/2001)*

EZIO

Ezio 2004 Merlot (Famatina Valley) $6. Dry and full of savory plum and spice aromas. With zesty and developed raspberry and cherry flavors along with a mostly fresh and balanced mouthfeel, this is a pretty good bargain Merlot. **85 Best Buy** —*M.S. (6/1/2006)*

Ezio 2004 Pinot Grigio (Famatina Valley) $6. Waxy and somewhat bland, with a touch of melon on the nose. Dilute apple and melon flavors on a full, thick palate. A lot of mouthfeel here and some stickiness. **82** —*M.S. (2/1/2006)*

FABRE MONTMAYOU

Fabre Montmayou 2005 Malbec (Luján de Cuyo) $10. Always one of the best Malbecs for the money. This French-owned estate doesn't cut corners, so you get a serious red wine that's heady, vigorous, and authentic. The color is perfect, the bouquet smoky and penetrating, and the taste of berry fruit, spicy wood, and vanilla convincing. **89 Best Buy** —*M.S. (12/1/2006)*

Fabre Montmayou 2002 Malbec (Mendoza) $10. Big and burly at 14.5% alcohol, with blueberry, blackberry, fudge, and earth on the nose. Very ripe and heady, with sweet fruit flavors and a ton of oak. Nothing wrong whatsoever, but it locks into a place and doesn't budge. As a result, complexity is lacking. **87 Best Buy** —*M.S. (7/1/2005)*

Fabre Montmayou 2002 Gran Reserva Malbec (Mendoza) $15. This you just have to love, especially for the price. Starts with graham cracker, kirsch, and black cherry aromas before transitioning to chocolate, vanilla, and coffee. Shows subtle touches but a lot of Argentinean power and pizzazz. Restrained but ripe; robust yet suave. **90 Best Buy** —*M.S. (7/1/2005)*

ARGENTINA

FALLING STAR

Falling Star 2004 Cabernet Sauvignon (Cuyo) $5. Artificially jammy and sweet, with medicinal cherry aromas and flavors. Fairly hard, with gritty tannins. More of an effort than it should be. **82** —*M.S. (7/1/2005)*

Falling Star 2002 Cabernet Sauvignon (Mendoza) $6. Trapiche is behind this fruity, somewhat sweet Cabernet that should have mass appeal. The bouquet is packed with rubber, smoked meat and plum, while the palate runs sweet, with raspberry and beet flavors. Some milk chocolate on the finish leaves a chewy, sweet impression. **84 Best Buy** —*M.S. (2/1/2004)*

Falling Star 2004 Chardonnay (Cuyo) $5. Smells fine, with flowers and mixed stone fruits. The palate is thin but sweet, with ripe apple and mango flavors. As might be expected from a value Chard, the finish is syrupy and a touch hot, but not offensively so. **83 Best Buy** —*M.S. (3/1/2005)*

Falling Star 2002 Chardonnay (Mendoza) $5. Aromas of gumdrop, lemon juice, and anise create a stylish impression, however, the wine turns more zesty and tangy in the mouth. Flavors of grapefruit, lemon, and apple are open yet ultimately rather simple. **84 Best Buy** —*M.S. (2/1/2004)*

Falling Star 2001 Chardonnay (Mendoza) $5. The bouquet offers mango, wild flower, and other sweet aromas. Flavors of apple and pear control the palate, while a dry and balanced finish closes things out. **85 Best Buy** —*M.S. (5/1/2003)*

Falling Star 2000 Chardonnay (Mendoza) $5. This wine from Trapiche has a banana bouquet and clashing flavors of lemon, papaya, grapefruit, and toast. It's lean and tangy, and almost tastes like bits of Sauvignon Blanc and/or Viognier were thrown in. **80** —*M.S. (11/15/2001)*

Falling Star 2004 Merlot-Malbec (Cuyo) $5. For a five-spot you get syrupy but fairly deep red fruit in the cherry, raspberry, and plum category. The mouthfeel is more than acceptable, while the overriding jammy sweetness could muster mass appeal. **84 Best Buy** —*M.S. (3/1/2005)*

Falling Star 2001 Merlot-Malbec (Mendoza) $6. Very light in color and strange in the nose; the cherry aromas are candied and downright strange. The palate is of little consequence and the finish is lean and tastes of cherry infused tea. **80** —*M.S. (5/1/2003)*

Falling Star 2004 Sauvignon Blanc-Semillon (Cuyo) $5. Fairly round and solid, with citrus, nectarine, and honey aromas. Tastes a bit more like orange juice than a fine white, but the mouthfeel and acid-fruit balance is acceptable. Best with simple Asian foods and salads. **84 Best Buy** —*M.S. (7/1/2005)*

FAMILIA CASSONE

Familia Cassone 2001 Malbec (Luján de Cuyo) $9. If this truly comes from 90-year-old vines, as advertised, then it's fairly light. It begins with simple dried-fruit and wintergreen aromas before picking up speed. Notes of citrus peel, buttery oak, and blueberry dominate. For a light ride, it's moderately smooth. **84** —*M.S. (12/1/2003)*

Familia Cassone 1999 Reserva Malbec (Mendoza) $13. The full-force nose is redolent of lavender, cinnamon, leather, and fresh black plums. Similar chewy plum fruit carries the palate, which is undoubtedly more fruity than it is dark. The vivacious finish has full tannins and plenty of verve. This is the type of wine that just flows down the pipe. **88 Best Buy** —*M.S. (11/1/2002)*

FAMILIA LLAVER ORO

Familia Llaver Oro 2001 Sauvignon Blanc (Mendoza) $16. Gold in color, with a mute nose that doesn't offer much in the way of typical SB character. The palate deals apple and pear, and while that's not usual, neither is the mouthfeel, which is plump and flat. **82** —*M.S. (2/1/2004)*

Familia Llaver Oro 1999 Syrah (Mendoza) $18. The luster on this older wine is beginning to fade. The nose tosses up a hint of syrup, pine needle, and tree bark. The palate is filled with cherry and some medicinal, herbal accents. Not bad but something is missing, namely focus and identifiable Syrah-like flavors of fruit and pepper. **83** —*M.S. (2/1/2004)*

FAMILIA SCHROEDER

Familia Schroeder 2004 Saurus Patagonia Cabernet Sauvignon (Argentina) $9. Good color but the nose and palate don't offer that Cabernet lushness that most of us seek. The red-fruit nose is kind of lean, probably a reflection of Patagonia's cool climate. And the palate is peppery and starchy, with hard tannins. **82** —*M.S. (6/1/2006)*

Familia Schroeder 2005 Saurus Patagonia Select Chardonnay (Argentina) $13. Pickled at first, while oak comes on strong as it airs out. The palate shows a lot of butter and toast, with only mild fruit hanging out in the background. Dry and short in the long run. **83** —*M.S. (6/1/2006)*

Familia Schroeder 2004 Saurus Patagonia Malbec (Argentina) $9. Mildly funky and pickled at first, but that herbal, vegetal quality lifts after airing. Throughout, there's a touch of a saucy, salty note but alongside that there's good red-fruit character that's eager to please. **85 Best Buy** —*M.S. (4/1/2006)*

Familia Schroeder 2004 Saurus Patagonia Select Malbec (Argentina) $13. Among the new crop of Patagonian Malbecs, this wine shows a sly style. It's not that full of bells and whistles but it does offer plenty of ripe red fruit such as cassis, cherry, and strawberry. Blended in are touches of tobacco and leather. Goes down smooth and easy; registers more lush and ripe than anything. **89 Best Buy** —*M.S. (4/1/2006)*

Familia Schroeder 2004 Saurus Patagonia Merlot (Argentina) $9. Ripe, jammy, and forward, with very little besides heavy berry fruit to offer. The palate is overtly oaky, with butter and wood notes. Grapy and a raw in the middle, with some displaced tannins. **83** —*M.S. (6/1/2006)*

Familia Schroeder 2004 Saurus Patagonia Select Merlot (Argentina) $13. The nose offers hints of rubber and smoked meat, but the fruit is difficult to peg. The mouth is ripe enough, with notes of blackberry and chocolate. Mouthcoating, but with soft tannins. **84** —*M.S. (6/1/2006)*

Familia Schroeder 2004 Saurus Patagonia Select Pinot Noir (Argentina) $13. Round, red, ripe, and rubbery. It weighs in at 14% but seems like a mystery wine when tasted blind. Yields little Pinot character but as generic red wine it's acceptable. Tastes mostly of anonymous berry and chocolate. **81** —*M.S. (6/1/2006)*

Familia Schroeder 2005 Saurus Patagonia Select Sauvignon Blanc (Argentina) $13. Round and toasty, with obvious barrel notes of vanilla and baked apple. Exhibits round, low-density toasted fruit on a creamy palate; finishes soft and short, with extra pear and vanilla bean. **85** —*M.S. (4/1/2006)*

FANTELLI

Fantelli 2002 Cabernet Sauvignon (Mendoza) $8. Damp and pruney, with a sour edge to the nose. Candied fruit, a bit sweet and sour, and mildly oaky. **81** —*M.S. (10/1/2004)*

Fantelli 2003 Chardonnay (Mendoza) $8. Gold in color, with apricot and peach aromas. It's heavy and ripe, with baked apple and orange flavors. Soft on the palate, without much force or acidity. Drink now to enjoy the chunky body and caramel-laden finish. **84** —*M.S. (10/1/2004)*

Fantelli 2001 Chardonnay (Mendoza) $9. Lean and snappy, with pear notes on the nose. The palate offers sugary apple and melon fruit, while the finish is a touch bawdy. Banana notes come on strong late in the game. **83** —*M.S. (2/1/2004)*

Fantelli 2000 Chardonnay (Mendoza) $9. The color is a brownish gold, which isn't terribly inviting. The smell of cream soda is about all that emanates from the otherwise dull nose. Sour apple is the prime flavor, while popping acids make for a good mouthfeel. The problem here is the taste more than the body or balance. **82** —*M.S. (7/1/2002)*

Fantelli 2004 Malbec (Mendoza) $9. Speechless at first as the nose offers very little. The mouth offers basic dark fruit with some tannins. Grabby at first, but better as it opens up. Rubbery but fairly ripe. **83** —*M.S. (6/1/2006)*

Fantelli 2002 Malbec (Mendoza) $8. Nice and sensible, with open but restrained berry aromas. A bold enough wine, with raspberry and cherry flavors and a full, chewy finish. With good tannins and ripe fruit, this is basic Malbec in show form. **86 Best Buy** —*M.S. (10/1/2004)*

Fantelli 2001 Malbec (Mendoza) $9. Ruby in color, and light almost to the point of transparency. Flavors of cherry and toast define the palate, while the finish is a bit raw. Otherwise, it's a pleasing enough wine because of simple oak-driven raspberry flavors. **84** —*M.S. (12/1/2003)*

Fantelli 1999 Malbec (Mendoza) $10. **83** *(5/1/2002)*

Fantelli 2002 Merlot (Mendoza) $8. Sweet cherry and cotton candy aromas emanate from the nose, while dark berry fruit and earth notes carry the palate. A touch prickly and acidic for Merlot, but not bad. Finishes with above-average fruit and mild tannins. **86 Best Buy** —*M.S. (10/1/2004)*

Fantelli 1999 Merlot (Mendoza) $10. Aromas of fresh earth and dark berries match what lies on the palate—basic Merlot flavors of black raspberry fruit and earth. Tannins are soft. Not complex, but enjoyable. **83** —*C.S. (5/1/2002)*

Fantelli 1999 Sangiovese (Mendoza) $10. Overall, the Sangiovese did not show well from most of the producers. Fantelli made a simple but interesting and very pleasant wine that shows aromas of cherry and cinnamon with black pepper and sour cherry flavors. A good wine for a picnic with dried meats and cheeses. **84** —*C.S. (5/1/2002)*

Fantelli 2004 Syrah (Mendoza) $9. Raspberry, bramble, and leather are convincing opening aromas, while the ripe black cherry on the palate is spiced up by some light wood notes. Textured on the tongue, with vanilla and cherry notes to the finish. Not all that Syrah-like, but good as red wine goes. **85 Best Buy** —*M.S. (6/1/2006)*

Fantelli 2002 Syrah (Mendoza) $8. Reserved on the nose, with entirely correct leather, plum, and cola aromas. The palate is nice and balanced, with a good feel supporting black cherry and plum flavors. Finishes first with fruit and then a second wave of buttery oak. **86 Best Buy** —*M.S. (10/1/2004)*

Fantelli 2001 Syrah (Mendoza) $9. Basic plum and berry fruit aromas have a note of rubber that gets more aggressive with time. Simple, with open raspberry, plum, and mild vanilla flavors. A light, buttery, chocolaty finish leaves a round, friendly impression. **85** —*M.S. (2/1/2004)*

Fantelli 2005 Torrontès (Mendoza) $9. Floral and spring-like up front, but also smells too much like air freshener or dish soap. Plump pear and cantaloupe flavors are adequate, but the candied finish and heavy sweetness lean toward dull and heavy. Not bad but has faults. **83** —*M.S. (8/1/2006)*

Fantelli 2004 Torrontès (Mendoza) $8. Mildly floral with lemon-lime and anise. But that's initially; after that it really doesn't hold its form. Flavors of melon and honey are sweet but not that convincing, while the feel is textured, bordering on syrupy. **83** —*M.S. (12/31/2005)*

Fantelli 2003 Torrontès (Mendoza) $8. Very light in color, with matching lightweight aromas of hay, licorice gumdrop, and papaya. Not terribly complex, but light and easy, with honeydew and tropical fruit flavors. Critics could equate it to water while admirers will laud its freshness. **85 Best Buy** —*M.S. (10/1/2004)*

FELIPE RUTINI

Felipe Rutini 2004 Chardonnay (Tupungato) $18. Closed and heavy on the nose, with baked-apple flavors and caramel. Weighs in as full-bodied, with toffee and bitter pith notes on the finish. Aims fairly high and delivers up to an extent: there's size and substance but also some over-ripeness, corn, and pith. Not perfect, but not bad. **85** —*M.S. (6/1/2006)*

Felipe Rutini 2002 Chardonnay (Mendoza) $19. Here's a nice mix of tropical fruit set on a full, balanced, racy frame. The nose kicks off with a bit of banana, light oak, and vanilla. In the mouth, bracing acidity meets ripe fruit with nice results. Finishes sly, with hints of wood resin and licorice. **88** —*M.S. (7/1/2004)*

Felipe Rutini 1999 Reserve Chardonnay (Mendoza) $19. Potent, mature aromas give you a lot to ponder. There's lemon, stone, and also an unfortunate vegetal note. The mouth offers tangy edges, due to still-vital acids. All in all, however, it's just not really there the way it should be. **83** —*M.S. (7/1/2002)*

Felipe Rutini 2003 Malbec (La Consulta) $18. Yet again this relatively affordable wine shows the charms and potential of Argentinean Malbec. It has a beautiful color and full, fruity aromas. The palate runs a bit snappy and upright, with cherry-based fruit that will go great with any type of grilled or braised meat. Clean, ripe, and tasty, with the slightest bit of perky acids. **89** —*M.S. (4/1/2006)*

Felipe Rutini 2002 Malbec (Mendoza) $19. Winemaker Mariano Di Paola has a way with La Consulta-area Malbec. His are structured, tight when young, and elegant when they hit three years in bottle. This youngster is full of pop and color. It's true Malbec, with broad shoulders, layered fruit, and a toasty, full finish. A drink-or-hold type, and not expensive for what you're getting. **90** —*M.S. (7/1/2004)*

Felipe Rutini 2001 Malbec (Mendoza) $20. The label stresses that the wine comes from a single vineyard in the La Consulta subregion of Mendoza. That said, what's in the bottle is fine juice, with cinnamon, red licorice, and blueberry aromas and flavors. The fruit is high-end and amplified by zesty acidity. Very much the mode in terms of new-wave Argentine Malbec. **89** —*M.S. (12/1/2003)*

Felipe Rutini 2000 Malbec (Tupungato) $18. A delicious, deeply fruited wine that's packed with meaty aromas, a hint of iodine, and some sweet perfume. The palate is defined not by individual fruit flavors but a wholeness and lushness that you can't ignore. Overall it's perfectly balanced and rewarding to drink; a stellar Malbec at an affordable price. **91 Editors' Choice** —*M.S. (5/1/2003)*

Felipe Rutini 2003 Encuentro Malbec-Merlot (Tupungato) $25. The polar opposite of boring, this lovely blend offers aromas of mint, herbs, flower petals, and sandalwood. The palate, meanwhile, is all about pure, robust blackberry, and plum. It's a chunky, rich wine with a bit of burnt toast on the lusty finish. Thorough and textured. A bona fide winner. **90 Editors' Choice** —*M.S. (6/1/2006)*

Felipe Rutini 2003 Merlot (Tupungato) $18. Sweet and rooty on the nose, with hints of cola and earth. This is a solid red wine, with plum, berry, and some mild astringency to the palate. Finishes a bit tart but still makes it to the quality level. Likely better with food than by itself. **85** —*M.S. (6/1/2006)*

Felipe Rutini 2002 Merlot (Mendoza) $20. This is La Rural's top line, and before we've been a fan of the Malbec. But this wine has serious balance issues; it's acidic and sour at the core, with heavy oak and not enough flesh. Hails from the cooler Tupungato region, something that's evident in the wine's thin structure. **82** —*M.S. (3/1/2005)*

Felipe Rutini 2002 Merlot (Mendoza) $19. With tangy plum, cranberry, and red currant fruit, you can't call this a fat, modern Merlot. It's fairly tight, with some pronounced acidity. But it's also a fresh breeze in a world of so many fruit-and-oak monsters. Best as a food wine, maybe with spaghetti and meatballs or something similar. **87** —*M.S. (7/1/2004)*

Felipe Rutini 2000 Merlot (Tupungato) $18. With briar and oak aromas, the fruit seems a bit subdued. The palate, however, delivers ample sweet cherry and plum flavors and the finish is nicely structured and tight, albeit a bit oaky. A nicely made wine. **86** —*M.S. (5/1/2003)*

Felipe Rutini 1999 Apartado Red Blend (Mendoza) $60. This blend of Malbec, Cabernet, Merlot, and Syrah is smooth and leafy, and one whiff tells you it's well crafted. The palate features some high-toned red fruit, while the finish is soft and smooth with full tannins. **90** —*M.S. (5/1/2003)*

FILLIPO FIGAR

Fillipo Figar 2000 Anastasia Cabernet Sauvignon (Mendoza) $10. The wine kicks off with raisin and lemon pith notes. Next come sweet but off-kilter flavors of prune, boysenberry, and sugar beet. The finish is packed in tight, but the core is a bit sour. This wine is like the proverbial hare: It starts out fast but fades before the finish line. **84** —*M.S. (11/1/2002)*

Fillipo Figar 2001 Anastasia Malbec (Mendoza) $10. This is a youthful wine that's a bit rough right now. It starts out with bacon and tar-like aromas before shifting into a mouthful of cherry fruit. The finish is tight and grainy, while the overall profile is tannic and jumpy. Some time in the bottle should help it all come together. **85 Best Buy** —*M.S. (11/1/2002)*

FILUS

Filus 2003 Reserve Malbec (Mendoza) $16. Sweet and woody from start to finish. In between the powerful oak waves you'll find smoked meat and leather. Ripe in the mouth, with blueberry and blackberry flavors, then tannic and very woody on the finish. In fact, oak takes over as the dominant characteristic about halfway through. **85** —*M.S. (12/31/2005)*

FINCA DE DOMINGO

Finca de Domingo 1999 Malbec (Argentina) $12. The nose is dry, dusty, and a tiny bit green. The flavor profile matches that bouquet, as green notes ride side by side with raspberry fruit. Some sweetness and licorice grace the finish, but don't expect much complexity here. It's a simple wine, albeit a pretty good one. **85** —*M.S. (5/1/2003)*

Finca de Domingo 2003 Torrontès (Argentina) $8. Sharp on the nose, with aromas of lemon-lime. Basic apple and spice flavors control the lean, subdued palate. Finishes heavy and fairly bland. **82** —*M.S. (7/1/2004)*

Finca de Domingo 2001 Torrontès (Cafayate) $7. The pleasant flowery aromas that first arise unfortunately get tangled up with something akin to floor polish. There's lemon, white peach, and green herb flavors on the palate, followed by a finish that's clean and persistent. But the body is rather thin and the consistency is that of commercial fruit juice. **82** —*M.S. (5/1/2003)*

FINCA DEL VALLE

Finca del Valle 2001 Cabernet Sauvignon (Mendoza) $8. Lean and clean, but very thin. Aromas of cherry and raisins lead into a strawberry-raspberry palate that packs little punch. The midpalate is tangy, while the finish fails to register much beyond tart fruit and dry earth. **83** —*M.S. (2/1/2004)*

Finca del Valle 2000 Lazzaro Coleccion Familia Cabernet Sauvignon (Mendoza) $12. The extraction on this wine is just right, and there's a nice black plum, cherry, and coffee character. But the nose is marred by a strong hint of wet dog that reared up on two different samples. Without that strange aroma, this wine might even rate higher. Even with it, the wine shows restraint, balance and style. **88 Best Buy** —*M.S. (11/1/2002)*

Finca del Valle 2001 Chardonnay (Mendoza) $7. Bland and indifferent, with butterscotch and chemical aromas. Some apple and citrus carry the palate into a forward but midland finish. Thick and sweet mango and banana flavors are what's left behind. **81** —*M.S. (2/1/2004)*

Finca del Valle 2001 Malbec (Mendoza) $7. Rusty in color, especially for the normally dark Malbec. Some mint and licorice aromas lead it off, followed by malty oak. Rather lean and dry across the palate, with more acids than flesh. **82** —*M.S. (12/1/2003)*

Finca del Valle 2001 Merlot (Mendoza) $7. Starts off with cola and rooty aromas, but turns stewed rather quickly. A bit syrupy and green in the mouth, with a fairly strong oak veneer. Some drying wood and a touch of cough drop define the finish. **82** —*M.S. (2/1/2004)*

Finca del Valle 2003 Lazzaro Coleccion Familia Merlot (Mendoza) $9. Don't be surprised if the aromas of beets and cranberry fail to lure you in. The palate, meanwhile, features heavy, awkward flavors prior to a fat, buttery finish. Lacks balance. **81** —*M.S. (10/1/2004)*

Finca del Valle 2002 Trinomium Red Blend (Mendoza) $10. Light, with raspberry and citrus-rind aromas. Flavors of cherry, cola, and burnt meat lead into a creamy, oaky finish. Fairly low-acid, with a soft feel. The mix is Malbec (70%) along with Cab and Merlot. **86 Best Buy** —*M.S. (2/1/2004)*

FINCA EL PORTILLO

Finca El Portillo 2004 Cabernet Sauvignon (Mendoza) $9. Starts with a strong blast of smoked meat and coffee, and the palate holds onto the coffee character as it deals plum and berry flavors. Limited in scope, with a touch of toast. **84** —*M.S. (11/15/2005)*

Finca El Portillo 2005 Chardonnay (Uco Valley) $9. Fresh, tropical, and welcoming. Sweet and lush in the mouth with a full blast of mango and melon flavors. Medium-bodied with good acidity. Finishes correct and everything seems to be united and put together. Above-average value Chardonnay from Argentina. **87 Best Buy** —*M.S. (8/1/2006)*

Finca El Portillo 2004 Chardonnay (Mendoza) $9. Chunky and forward, with nectarine and pineapple flavors. Zesty and fairly intense, with a

simple, forward finish. Fruity for sure, with balance and an easy personality. **85 Best Buy** —*M.S. (11/15/2005)*

Finca El Portillo 2004 Malbec (Mendoza) $9. Salentein's large-production second label is anchored by this dandy lighter-weight Malbec, which features a brilliant color, sweet berry aromas, and a snappy palate. And while most big-boy Malbecs from Argentina are syrupy, this wine resides on the other side of the fence. It doesn't require a huge hunk of steak to balance it off; the tannins are mild and the acidity more than manageable. **86 Best Buy** —*M.S. (11/15/2005)*

Finca El Portillo 2004 Merlot (Alto Valle de Uco) $9. Fairly charred and leathery for what's here, meaning the fruit isn't really up to the oak. The palate is tangy and slightly candied, with berry flavors covered by a burnt overlay. The finish is acidic and a touch raw. **83** —*M.S. (12/31/2005)*

Finca El Portillo 2005 Sauvignon Blanc (Uco Valley) $9. Heavy and basic, with melon and pineapple aromas. Full-flavored with a ton of apple and cinnamon character. Made in the round, fruit-forward style. Not a complex, overly serious wine. A solid quaffer. **84** —*M.S. (8/1/2006)*

Finca El Portillo 2004 Sauvignon Blanc (Alto Valle de Uco) $9. Not much in the way of aromas, with tangerine and mango flavors. Finishes short, but fruity enough, with lasting flavors of pineapple and orange. **83** —*M.S. (7/1/2005)*

Finca El Portillo 2005 Syrah (Mendoza) $10. A nice step up from previous vintages; this affordable Syrah sports dark-fruit aromas and muscle, while the flavors veer toward jammy blackberry. Not a tannic, spicy, complex wine; instead it's easy as pie. **87 Best Buy** —*M.S. (12/1/2006)*

FINCA EL RETIRO

Finca El Retiro 2003 Cabernet Sauvignon (Mendoza) $11. Broad up front but pasty, with olive and soy sauce added in. The cherry and berry flavors are zesty but nondistinct, while the finish is lean and hits with cranberry and cherry. Also shows a bit of compost. **82** —*M.S. (8/1/2006)*

Finca El Retiro 2003 Malbec (Mendoza) $11. Open, friendly aromas of black cherry, sugar beet, violets, and talcum powder start this wine on a nice, simple, satisfying path. Tastes of blueberry, cherry, and pretty much all the berry and tree fruits you can think of. Ripe and sweet on the finish. By the book. **86 Best Buy** —*M.S. (8/1/2006)*

Finca El Retiro 2003 Reserva Especial Malbec (Mendoza) $17. Earthy and ripe, with lots of black cherry and raspberry on both the bouquet and palate. Comes on equally juicy and smooth, with good length on the back end and plenty of acidity to push the flavor. Balanced and on the money. **88** —*M.S. (6/1/2006)*

Finca El Retiro 2003 Syrah (Mendoza) $11. Bright in color and jammy on the nose, with aromas of bubble gum and blueberry. Candied in the mouth, with flavors of sugary plum and cherry. More of a junior varsity wine; it shows some talent but needs more practice. **83** —*M.S. (8/1/2006)*

Finca El Retiro 2003 Reserva Especial Tempranillo (Mendoza) $17. Intensely colored and miles better than the label's troubled basic Tempranillo, this is an Argentinean rendition of Spain's workhorse grape that showcases berry and plum flavors, plenty of oak, and ample chocolate and espresso on the finish. More impressive when taken as a whole; best to drink with barbecue and not get too analytical. **85** —*M.S. (6/1/2006)*

FINCA FLICHMAN

Finca Flichman 1999 Syrah (Mendoza) $10. Light berry aromas and flavors make up this simple quaffer that nonetheless offers enough substance to satisfy. Similar to Côtes-du-Rhône; it closes with licorice notes and sweet, creamy oak. Of interest, Flichman made one of Argentina's very first Syrahs back in 1974. **83** —*M.S. (11/15/2001)*

Finca Flichman 1998 Reserva Syrah (Mendoza) $13. Argentina's wines are, it seems, as meaty as its national dishes. This Mendoza Reserva shows roast beef, spice, and smoke on the nose, and a full, rich, even mouthfeel. The palate delivers dark oak, blackberry, and meat flavors with a healthy dose of black pepper. Finishes dark and peppery, with decent length. **86** *(10/1/2001)*

FINCA KOCH

Finca Koch 2003 Cabernet Sauvignon (Tupungato) $15. A wine that's seriously muscled up with tannin and oak. That's what you get with this rugged Argentinean Cabernet that comes with leafy notes of tobacco and mint along with raspy, grippy berry fruit. Maybe another year in bottle will help; now it's not that pleasant. **83** —*M.S. (12/1/2006)*

Finca Koch 2001 Cabernet Sauvignon (Mendoza) $19. Big and burly, but also stylish. The nose throws off roasted plum, rubber, road tar, and tree bark. All together the bouquet stirs interest. The mouth offers bright acidity in support of drying cherry and raspberry fruit, while the finish is firm, with rising tannins. About as good an Argentinean Cab as you'll find these days. **89 Editors' Choice** —*M.S. (7/1/2004)*

Finca Koch 2001 Cabernet Sauvignon (Tupungato) $17. Pretty root beer, prune, and cassis aromas start out fast but fade a bit upon airing. The palate is primarily cassis and blackberry, and while the finish is tannic and full, it lacks that final touch of polish you look for in a great red. Nevertheless, it's a good wine from a label that bears watching. Only 200 cases were made. **88** —*M.S. (5/1/2003)*

Finca Koch 2003 Martin Koch Thirteen Months Cabernet Sauvignon (Tupungato) $14. A better overall ride than the more oaky Koch Cabernet, this bottling, aged 13 months in barrel, is crisp and fruity, with firm tannins that clamp down on the finish. Along the way there's bright raspberry and pie cherry flavors that are fresh albeit stark. **87** — *M.S. (12/1/2006)*

Finca Koch 2004 Martin Koch Six Months Malbec (Luján de Cuyo) $14. An earthy specimen, with leather and crude-oil aromas blended with dark fruit. The palate is extracted and chewy, with berry and cherry flavors that should please. With its body and thickness, it registers as a modern-styled red. **88** —*M.S. (12/1/2006)*

Finca Koch 2004 Torrontès (Cafayate) $9. Light up front, with slight floral and banana aromas. Flavors of lemon and apple are short and clean, while a tangy finish closes it out. Fairly big for Torrontès but not offering much in the way of character. **83** —*M.S. (12/1/2006)*

FINCA LA ANITA

Finca La Anita 1996 Syrah (Mendoza) $50. Though almost fading, with a brick edge in the glass, there is still style in this wine's pruney fruit, tobacco-leather accents, and earthy shadings. Thin but smooth-bodied, the fig and wood elements will appeal to lovers of mature wines, but fans of youthful fruit should take a pass here. Drink now. **85** *(11/1/2001)*

FINCA LA DANIELA

Finca La Daniela 2002 Malbec (Mendoza) $11. Earthy yet fresh, with red fruit aromas that flow directly onto the sweet, oozing palate. Quite simple, but ready to drink. It's got chocolate and fruit syrup on the finish along with integrated tannins and acidity. Textbook fashion. **86 Best Buy** —*M.S. (5/1/2005)*

FINCA LA NINA

Finca La Nina 2003 Cabernet Sauvignon (Mendoza) $9. Jammy raspberry up front, with some earth and zest. The mouth pulses with lively raspberry and cherry, while the finish hits firmly with initial fruit that gives way to chocolate. Harmonious and well priced. **87 Best Buy** —*M.S. (11/15/2005)*

FINCA SIMONASSI

Finca Simonassi 2003 Reserve Malbec (Mendoza) $10. Starts out with bubble gum and sweet candy aromas, which are followed by black cherry flavors. Seems a little hard and grating at first, although airing does open it up. Ultimately it's a basic Malbec with good flavors and adequate mouthfeel. **84** —*M.S. (12/1/2006)*

FINCA SOPHENIA

Finca Sophenia 2003 Synthesis Bordeaux Blend (Tupungato) $40. Gets going with aromas of molasses, black olive, and pencil lead, which accent the rich black fruit that's prominently on display. Intense in the mouth, where dark plum and black cherry dominate. The mouthfeel is ripe and warm, and the finishing notes of licorice, chocolate and coffee are sturdy and refined. **90** —*M.S. (6/1/2006)*

Finca Sophenia 2003 Estate Cabernet Sauvignon (Tupungato) $18. If you like a dark, saturated wine with a ton of ripeness and richness, then this is it. The color is opaque, the bouquet full of rubber, blackberry, and chocolate. It's intense stuff, with black cherry and cassis flavors preceding

a finish dense with bitter notes, licorice, and vanilla. Solid to the core.. **90 Editors' Choice** —*M.S. (11/15/2005)*

Finca Sophenia 2003 Chardonnay (Mendoza) $15. Michel Rolland consults on this Chard from Tupungato, which shows powdered sugar, apple, and pineapple on the nose. A bit confusing to the taste, with olive oil and white pepper supporting distant flavors of papaya and green melon. Round but short on the finish. **84** —*M.S. (3/1/2005)*

Finca Sophenia 2005 Altosur Chardonnay (Tupungato) $11. Light on the nose, with modest peach and apple. Apple, pineapple, and a touch of toast carry the palate, which is clean and acid-based. Arguably a touch sweet, but overall it's a good South American Chardonnay. **86 Best Buy** —*M.S. (6/1/2006)*

Finca Sophenia 2003 Malbec (Mendoza) $17. Purple to the eye, with intense aromas of mint, licorice, and saturated black fruit. The mouth is like blueberry-blackberry compote, while the oak seems heavy given the wine's higher acids and limited depth. Has plenty of positives but sings just one note. **87** —*M.S. (3/1/2005)*

Finca Sophenia 2005 Altosur Malbec (Tupungato) $18. Round, ripe, and showing no cracks, although there is a touch of dill weed on the nose that's not altogether unwelcome. The palate is forward and standard, with ripe plum and berry flavors. Fairly squat and tannic on the finish, with a full mouthfeel. **87** —*M.S. (8/1/2006)*

Finca Sophenia 2002 Altosur Malbec (Mendoza) $10. Hailing from high-altitude Tupungato, this dense but fresh Malbec issues good plum, berry, and earth aromas along with some smokiness and tree bark. It's fairly rich and full across the tongue, showing blackberry, blueberry, and chocolate. Finishes warm and spicy, with good girth and weight. **88 Best Buy** —*M.S. (3/1/2005)*

Finca Sophenia 2005 Altosur Rosé Malbec (Tupungato) $10. Reddish in color, which announces that it's Malbec. The nose is sizable but fresh, with riper, sweeter aromas. A bit more zesty in the mouth than you might expect, with an expansive, almost Beaujolais-like finish. Well balanced; a good pink wine. **86 Best Buy** —*M.S. (6/21/2006)*

Finca Sophenia 2002 Merlot (Mendoza) $17. Somewhat heavy and over-ripe, with plum and earth aromas. The palate carries a heavy, weighty feel, with rather murky flavors. Rubbery tannins create a stick-to-the-cheeks sensation. Seems like the winemaking effort was here but maybe not the grapes. **84** —*M.S. (3/1/2005)*

Finca Sophenia 2003 Estate Merlot (Tupungato) $18. Fairly roasted, with touches of brown sugar and burnt caramel on the bouquet. Solid in the mouth, with cherry and plum flavors along with some hard tannins. Finishes clean, with a touch of beet juice and astringency **85** —*M.S. (11/15/2005)*

Finca Sophenia 2004 Altosur Rose Merlot-Malbec (Tupungato) $10. Bright and fruity, but low in acid and a touch funky, especially as it warms and opens. While chilled it'll show good raspberry and cherry aromas and flavors, but warming reveals cough syrup and some horsehide. Made from Malbec and Merlot. **83** —*M.S. (4/1/2006)*

Finca Sophenia 2004 Altosur Sauvignon Blanc (Mendoza) $10. This snappy, high-altitude version from Finca Sophenia scores points for its attractive nose of citrus and wet stones, and the palate holds form. Flavors of grapefruit, tangerine, and cantaloupe aren't fancy but they are nice and fresh. Cleansing acidity and crispness help it along. **86 Best Buy** —*M.S. (11/15/2005)*

FINCA URQUIZA

Finca Urquiza 2001 Cabernet Sauvignon (Mendoza) $12. Sweet and mature, with earth, plum, and raspberry aromas and flavors. A main-stream red with little texture or complexity, but it goes down well with a medium body and no overt flaws. For everyday consumption. **85** —*M.S. (3/1/2005)*

Finca Urquiza 2001 Malbec (Mendoza) $12. Fruity and floral on the nose, which is by far the wine's high point. The palate, however, is too acidic to handle the weight of the fruit, which isn't much. In the end, the wine's racy and intense, offering more on the nose than in the mouth. **83** —*M.S. (3/1/2005)*

ARGENTINA

FLOURISH

Flourish 2004 Malbec (Mendoza) $11. An organic entry into the crowded Mendocino Malbec category. Fleshy and fruity, with a hint of barnyard and leather on the nose. Fairly bright on the palate, with cherry, plum and vanilla flavors. Shows grip and body on the finish. Not spectacular but solid in a pedestrian way. **85** —*M.S. (11/15/2005)*

FUNDACION DE MENDOZA

Fundacion de Mendoza 1999 Prestigio Cabernet Blend (Mendoza) $15. This oak-aged blend has a very odd mix of aromas: green herbs, baking spices, and strawberry sucking candy (but very little fruit). The palate is lean and dry, while the finish is surprisingly sweet, with a flavor of red licorice. Some coffee and wood spice also is detectable. **83** —*M.S. (11/1/2002)*

FUNKY LLAMA

Funky Llama 2004 Cabernet Sauvignon (Mendoza) $6. Leather, burnt bush, and leafy, green Cabernet aromas get it off the mark in questionable fashion. The palate offers some berry flavor but it's chewy, buttery and off-center. Not a whole lot going for it. **81** —*M.S. (8/1/2006)*

Funky Llama 2003 Cabernet Sauvignon (Mendoza) $6. Rubbery and jammy, with condensed aromas of cough drops and cherry sucking candy. Finishes astringent and cloying. **80** —*M.S. (7/1/2005)*

Funky Llama 2004 Chardonnay (Mendoza) $6. Simple and floral; not concentrated. This lightweight is tasty enough and overall it's balanced. The palate deals citrus, melon, and crispness, and the feel is lively and juicy. Tastes more like Spanish Albariño than Chardonnay. **84 Best Buy** —*M.S. (6/1/2006)*

Funky Llama 2003 Chardonnay (Mendoza) $6. A little oily and heavy, but the buttercup and candle wax aromas seem more real than artificial. The palate is plump, a bit sugary, but the apple and orange notes are clear. Finishes juicy enough and not overly cloying. **84 Best Buy** —*M.S. (3/1/2005)*

Funky Llama 2004 Malbec (Mendoza) $6. Ripe and solid, with big, bold aromas and flavors. It's full of cherry and raspberry, and the feel and balance seem right. Medium in length and strength, with a hint of toast on the finish. **85 Best Buy** —*M.S. (4/1/2006)*

Funky Llama 2003 Malbec (Mendoza) $6. Raw and lacking in concentration, this wine delivers pedestrian fruit with a lactic, buttery consistency. Finishes sweet but sort of gritty, and slightly medicinal. **82** —*M.S. (3/1/2005)*

Funky Llama 2004 Rosé Malbec (Mendoza) $6. Fairly lively and forward, with sturdy plum and berry characteristics. This is a surprisngly solid Malbec rosé; you get a secure and crisp finish, not too much wayward sugar, and pretty good quality overall. Served chilled you might just enjoy a glass, or even a bottle. **85 Best Buy** —*M.S. (4/1/2006)*

Funky Llama 2004 Merlot (Mendoza) $6. Light and candied, with strawberry drink mix as the main aroma. In the mouth, it's rather sticky and sweet, with basic characteristics. Adequate in terms of feel and balance. **82** —*M.S. (6/1/2006)*

Funky Llama 2004 Shiraz (Mendoza) $6. Moderately fruity on the nose, with a hint of leafiness and pickle. Raspberry and strawberry flavors are generally sweet, while the feel is a bit on the sharp side. Simple and straightforward, but with hardly any recognizable Shiraz character. **83** —*M.S. (6/1/2006)*

Funky Llama 2004 Tempranillo (Mendoza) $6. Transparent in color, with bubblegum and candied fruit on the nose. Sweet and rubbery on the palate, with a lean, burnt personality. Not horrible but surely nothing to rave about. **80** —*M.S. (6/1/2006)*

Funky Llama 2003 Tempranillo (Mendoza) $6. Generally gimmicky names draw no applause from these parts, but here we like this wine's raspberry, graham cracker, and orange-peel nose along with its crystallized raspberry and strawberry flavors. It's slightly gritty and sugary, but overall it's still fresh enough to handle the sweetness. **84 Best Buy** —*M.S. (3/1/2005)*

GENTILE COLLINS

Gentile Collins 2001 Chardonnay (Mendoza) $8. Subdued aromas lean toward acacia and pear. The mouthfeel is kind of thick and beefy, and the flavors of ripe apple and honey seem to work with that type of weight. Given the price it has plenty going for it, including a warm and satisfying finish. **86 Best Buy** —*M.S. (5/1/2003)*

Gentile Collins 2001 Malbec (Mendoza) $8. The nose is floral and sweet, if a bit candied. In the mouth, full and fresh blueberries mix nicely with the essences of clove and anise. The finish is smooth and sturdy, and surprisingly long. This is a good wine from a little-known producer, one that gets better with airing. **86** —*M.S. (5/1/2003)*

Gentile Collins 2002 Gran Syrah (Mendoza) $15. More lean and tight than bulky, with licorice, pepper, and leather aromas. Compact in the mouth, with spice and cherry flavors leading into a peppery, drying finish. Balanced and more traditional than many modern, beefy, unidentifiable reds. **87** —*M.S. (11/1/2006)*

Gentile Collins 2002 Tempranillo (Mendoza) $8. The heavy, rough nose is strange; it smells much like coffee grounds. The palate is chewy and big, and rather out of balance. Even the chocolaty notes to the finish aren't quite right; bitterness is what you take from it. **80** —*M.S. (5/1/2003)*

GOUGUENHEIM WINERY

Gouguenheim Winery 2004 Cabernet Sauvignon (Mendoza) $10. Lots of clove and oak on the nose, with some green aromas and coffee bean. Core black cherry with spice shadings carries the palate, while the finish is constricted and mildly tannic. Fairly hard in terms of mouthfeel. **84** —*M.S. (8/1/2006)*

Gouguenheim Winery 2004 Malbec (Mendoza) $10. Starts hard and rubbery before opening to show more wood and toast than clean, approachable fruit. Kind of buttery and woody on the palate, where red fruit sits in reserve. Sort of lean in terms of flavor; limited. **83** —*M.S. (8/1/2006)*

Gouguenheim Winery 2003 Flores de Valle Melosa Azul Malbec (Mendoza) $26. Deep, a touch rugged, and lively, with berry aromas accented by strong whiffs of citrus peel, especially lemon rind. Flavors of black raspberry and cassis are convincing, while the palate is textured, with smooth tannins and integrated acids. Balanced overall; one of this winery's best offerings to date. **87** —*M.S. (11/1/2006)*

Gouguenheim Winery 2003 Otoño Malbec (Mendoza) $10. Sweet and extracted, with medicinal aromas of kirsch meeting chocolate bon-bons. Carob, malted milk, and raspberry liqueur are the dominant flavors, while the finish is spirited, i.e. grabby and aggressive. Best if you like yours saturated and big-boned. **86 Best Buy** —*M.S. (7/1/2005)*

Gouguenheim Winery 2004 Verano Merlot (Mendoza) $10. Probably this winery's best current release; the nose is forward, spicy, fruity, and convincing. Follow that with bright cherry and berry flavors along with a finish that's got medium tannins in support of spice and coffee, and you have a well-priced winner. What affordable red wine was meant to be. **88 Best Buy** —*M.S. (8/1/2006)*

Gouguenheim Winery 2003 Verano Merlot (Mendoza) $10. Spunky and upright, with herbal red fruit on the nose and short, staccato flavors of rhubarb and pie cherry. Finishes tangy and hard, with a slight bitterness. **83** —*M.S. (7/1/2005)*

Gouguenheim Winery 1999 Silvestre Red Blend (Tupungato) $15. Seems like time forgot this Cabernet-Merlot-Malbec trio, and now it's unstable. The nose is pure barnyard, with hints of peanut and saddle. The palate is cooked and tired. Not horrible but still best to skip. **80** —*M.S. (3/1/2005)*

Gouguenheim Winery 2004 Primavera Syrah (Mendoza) $10. Pretty solid aromatically, and nicely colored, but goes sharp, lean, and tart in the mouth. Shows some cherry flavor, but also displaced citrus. Too much austerity and overt acidity. **82** —*M.S. (8/1/2006)*

GRAFFIGNA

Graffigna 1998 Selección Especial Cabernet Sauvignon (Tulum Valley) $10. Herbal and grapey in the nose, with violets and green vegetables. Plummy flavors, with drying tannins. As a whole, it's simple and flat, without much complexity. It also shows signs of overripe fruit and dilution. **81** —*M.S. (11/15/2001)*

Graffigna 1999 Selección Especial Cabernet Sauvignon (Tulum Valley) $10. **82** —*C.S. (5/1/2002)*

Graffigna 2004 Malbec (San Juan) $11. Gets going with some murky, rubbery notes as well as hints of sugar beet and rhubarb. Caramel, milk chocolate, and marshmallow flavors override basic fruit on the tongue, leaving a sticky, quasi-artificial quality. **82** —*M.S. (11/15/2005)*

Graffigna 2001 Don Santiago Malbec (San Juan) $20. Violet in color, with pickled aromas marring black plum. Flavors of red cabbage and plum are tart, and the mouthfeel is that of a citrus-based juice. From the more eastern district of San Juan. **81** —*M.S. (3/1/2005)*

Graffigna 2000 Don Santiago Malbec (San Juan) $11. This is meant to be a special selection from the Tulum Valley, but it's rather thick, tarry, and candied. A sugary palate the consistency of berry syrup is the vehicle for this oaky, black-fruit heavyweight that is sweet beyond what it should be. **82** —*M.S. (12/1/2003)*

Graffigna 2003 G Malbec (Pedernal Valley) $18. Cola, mint, vanilla, and black fruit control the bouquet, with acid-propelled cherry and red plum flavors coming next. Freshness and clarity are attributes although some might say it's too much of a tart, straight-shooter. Alive and snappy for sure. **85** —*M.S. (12/31/2005)*

Graffigna 2001 Selección Especial Estate Bottled Malbec (Tulum Valley) $10. Cheesy aromas kick start it, and the wine never really recovers. It's pungent, sharp, and angular, with some weedy flavors that intermingle with a blanket of oak. Decent in the mouth, as it gets a bit better with airing. **81** —*M.S. (12/1/2003)*

Graffigna 1999 Selección Especial Malbec (Tulum Valley) $10. A deep purple color that holds true to the rim shows the extraction achieved in this wine. The nose was a bit closed with fruit, but exhibits green herbs and a nutty earthiness. The palate brings trail mix flavors with a sweet blackberry finish, for an easy quaffing. **85 Best Buy** —*C.S. (5/1/2002)*

Graffigna 2005 Pinot Grigio (San Juan) $10. Pink and orange in color, a result of more extended skin contact. Slightly meaty and strange in flavor, with papaya and bread dough controlling the palate. Sort of sweet in the center; generally unfocused and weird. **80** —*M.S. (2/1/2006)*

Graffigna 2000 Selección Especial Estate Bottled Red Blend (San Juan) $10. Leathery aromas mix with the smell of beets and field greens. The palate is awkward, while the finish is overly tannic given the size and quality of the fruit. **80** —*M.S. (5/1/2003)*

Graffigna 2004 Shiraz (San Juan) $11. Ordinary plum and berry aromas to start, followed by a more jammy palate that tastes of berry compote. A touch of chocolate and pepper carry the finish. All totaled this is decent wine with middle-of-the-road characteristics. **83** —*M.S. (6/1/2006)*

Graffigna 2003 G Shiraz (Pedernal Valley) $18. Leather and spice on the nose complement basic berry aromas. The palate is fairly acidic and zingy, with red fruit and a touch of oak. Finishes bright and jumpy; little to nothing in the way of nuance. **83** —*M.S. (4/1/2006)*

Graffigna 1999 Syrah (Tulum Valley) $18. **81** *(1/1/2004)*

Graffigna 2001 Don Santiago Syrah (San Juan) $18. Gets going with mocha, coffee, and other oak-based aromas. The flavor profile is developed and fruity, emphasizing plum, blackberry, and raspberry. Plenty of pop and a tight, mouth-filling finish make it lively. **86** —*M.S. (11/15/2004)*

Graffigna 2000 Don Santiago Syrah (Tulum Valley) $18. Strange aromas lead you to a palate of canned fruit and sugar. This is a weird wine with no balance and too much radical sweetness. Definitely not ready for the big leagues. **80** —*M.S. (2/1/2004)*

Graffigna 1999 Selección Especial Syrah (Tulum Valley) $10. Lots of wood, camphor, and decaying vegetables on the nose made this wine hard to like from the get-go. Mouthfeel is lean (some said thin), with tart berry fruit, musty cedar, and white pepper flavors. There isn't much of a finish, but what's there is pretty woody. **82** *(10/1/2001)*

Graffigna 2001 Selección Especial Syrah-Cabernet (Tulum Valley) $10. Sharp at first, with funky, sulfuric aromas. The palate is heavily pickled and out of whack. A medicinal finish with a note of sugar beet won't win many fans. **80** —*M.S. (2/1/2004)*

HACIENDA DEL PLATA

Hacienda del Plata 2002 Reserve Cabernet Sauvignon (Mendoza) $24. Too many things to take issue with here for it to rate any higher. The nose features chocolate-covered raisin and tomato sauce, while the lean palate deals brambly cherry and berry flavors. Lacks persistence and notable bright spots. **82** —*M.S. (8/1/2006)*

Hacienda del Plata 2003 Zagal Cabernet Sauvignon (Mendoza) $15. So woody at first you'd think you had entered a sawmill, but with time it settles down. Red berries, milk chocolate, and wood spice work the palate, followed by lean fruit leftovers and vanilla. **83** —*M.S. (6/1/2006)*

Hacienda del Plata 2002 Zagal Malbec (Mendoza) $15. Green and austere, with burnt grass on the nose and palate. Cranberry fruit is sharp; not a prime-timer. Barely acceptable. **80** —*M.S. (6/1/2006)*

Hacienda del Plata 2005 Sauvignon Blanc (Mendoza) $15. Light yellow in tint, with big tropical aromas centering on melon. Tastes more lemony and dry than the nose might suggest, with a strong, astringent blast of green apple on the finish. **82** —*M.S. (8/1/2006)*

HENRY LAGARDE

Henry Lagarde 1999 Estate Bottled Cabernet Sauvignon (Luján de Cuyo) $10. Aromas of cool earth, coffee, and plenty of oak-driven mocha and toffee comprise the bouquet, while the palate offers supple cherry and berry fruit with oak shadings. The finish is rather light, with a hint of vegetable at the center. **85** —*M.S. (5/1/2003)*

Henry Lagarde 2000 Malbec (Luján de Cuyo) $12. Soft, but with the stuffing to make it appealing. Dark and rich, with modest acids and tannins but plenty of oomph. The nose is all cigar box, barnyard, and black fruit. Very chunky and a bit herbal. Frankly, it's all over the map; probably should be drunk now—with braised short ribs or something similar. **86** —*M.S. (12/1/2003)*

Henry Lagarde 1999 Malbec (Luján de Cuyo) $10. This is a bit lighter than most Mendoza Malbecs, but it has some healthy berry fruit and spice along with aromatic notes of pine and resin. The finish is oaky and airy. Easygoing and very drinkable. **86** —*M.S. (5/1/2003)*

Henry Lagarde 2000 Merlot (Luján de Cuyo) $10. Aromas of mint, earth, and mocha along with berries get it started, followed by flavors of plum, cherry, and blackberry. It's really a mixed bag of fruit with some oak shadings in the form of coffee and toffee. As a whole it's a good, fruity wine with a fairly big, lush character. **87** —*M.S. (5/1/2003)*

Henry Lagarde 2002 Viognier (Luján de Cuyo) $10. Sweet and honeyed in the nose, but rather indistinct. The flavors are lemon and banana, while a hint of bitterness frames the palate. Citrusy and tangy throughout due to aggressive acids. Like liquid sucking candy. **83** —*M.S. (5/1/2003)*

HIGH ALTITUDE

High Altitude 2005 Chardonnay-Viognier (Agrelo) $12. The nose bears a strong resemblance to canned fruit, particularly peaches. The palate offers some zesty nectarine and even more fruit cocktail. Moderately snappy, with some solid core acidity. The blend is 50% Chardonnay and 50% Viognier. **84** —*M.S. (6/1/2006)*

High Altitude 2005 Malbec-Cabernet Sauvignon (Agrelo) $12. Fairly dense on the nose, with aromas of coffee grounds, leather, and beef stew along with berry fruit. The palate is true, with plum and brambly berry flavors. However, the feel is a bit choppy due to sharp acidity. A good blend that will do well with food. **86** —*M.S. (12/1/2006)*

High Altitude 2004 Malbec-Cabernet Sauvignon (Mendoza) $10. Ripe and fruity from start to finish. The bouquet is fresh and clean, with a bit of citrus peel and red raspberry. A lot of easy red fruit carries the palate, primarily strawberry, raspberry, and currant. Chocolaty at the end, but not oaky. A bona fide crowd-pleaser for a very good price. **88 Best Buy** —*M.S. (11/15/2005)*

HUMBERTO BARBERIS

Humberto Barberis 1999 Malbec (Mendoza) $13. The nose is duller than it should be, with some syrupy, creamy qualities. The flavors veer toward black plum, but there's a hint of vegetation there, too. **83** —*M.S. (5/1/2003)*

ARGENTINA

ICHANKA

Ichanka 2005 Syrah (La Rioja) $10. Ripe, bulky and fruity, with simple, granular aromas. The mouthfeel is full and warm, but generally speaking the balance is where it's supposed to be. Smooth and chocolaty across the palate and onto the finish. Shows power and density. **85 Best Buy** —*M.S. (12/1/2006)*

Ichanka 2005 Torrontès (La Rioja) $10. Lightly waxy, with inoffensive but innocuous floral aromas. The palate shows citrus candy and weight, while the finish is more or less the same. Registers as a pulpy, chunky white as opposed to something lithe and snappy. **83** —*M.S. (12/1/2006)*

INCA

Inca 2002 Barbera-Merlot Barbera (Salta) $NA. A bit grapy and cloying, but mostly it's a pure, fruity wine that adds credence to the potential of blending Barbera with Merlot. The ripe palate offers plum and blackberry, while the finish is steady, albeit condensed. Chewy in the mouth, and forward. **84** —*M.S. (7/1/2004)*

Inca 2004 Cabernet Sauvignon-Malbec (Calchaqui Valley) $9. A tiny bit heavy and soupy at first, but the palate brings things into perspective as it delivers sweet berry and spice flavors and only modest acids and tannins. It's a wine for now, with lasting jammy notes that are generally quite pleasant. **86 Best Buy** —*M.S. (12/1/2006)*

Inca 2002 Cabernet Sauvignon-Malbec (Salta) $NA. Sweet at first, then it turns toward beet juice and bell pepper. The flavor profile is defined by cola, licorice and green pepper, while the spicy finish is marinade-like. **81** —*M.S. (7/1/2004)*

Inca 2003 Barbera-Merlot Red Blend (Calchaqui Valley) $9. A good and interesting red from Salta. The blend is 80% Barbera with 20% Merlot, and the final result is positive. Cherry, plum, and earth work the nose, followed by cherry, raspberry, and cassis flavors. A thorough, different type of wine for those looking to explore what's lurking on the fringes of the wine world. **87 Best Buy** —*M.S. (12/1/2006)*

Inca 2002 Tannat (Salta) $NA. Sweet and dark, with a jammy, black-licorice quality. In the mouth, bitter chocolate and pepper seem to mask the weak, low-acid fruit that lies below. Finishes heavy, with strong barrel notes. In many ways, it's borderline Port-like. **83** —*M.S. (7/1/2004)*

Inca 2003 Torrontès (Salta) $NA. From high-altitude vineyards in the northern Salta region comes this well-made, zippy white blend. On the nose, tarragon combines with citrus, peach, and nectarine, while in the mouth, things are solid and even a touch creamy. Finishing flavors of banana, melon, and lychee are typical of Torrontès. **86** —*M.S. (7/1/2004)*

Inca 2005 Torrontès-Chardonnay White Blend (Calchaqui Valley) $9. Opens with a full punch bowl of light, flowery, fruity aromas and backs that up with mixed fruit flavors along with touches of mineral, green herbs, and fresh lettuce. With 20% Chardonnay stiffening 80% Torrontès, this wine shows a little something different. **86 Best Buy** —*M.S. (11/1/2006)*

INFINITUS

Infinitus 2004 Malbec (Río Negro Valley) $13. Shows some young-vine raciness but also the sappy red cherry that is Rio Negro Malbec. Balanced and nicely oaked, with a comfortable finish that carries both chocolate and vanilla. From the maker of Fabre Montmayou. **86** —*M.S. (12/15/2006)*

Infinitus 2005 Gran Reserva Merlot (Río Negro Valley) $25. Smells a little hot and peppery, but the palate is big and expansive, with generous flavors of blackberry and vanilla. Round on the finish, if a bit generic, and not overly identifiable as Merlot. Still, it's an attractive, spicy red wine. **86** —*M.S. (12/15/2006)*

J. & F. LURTON

J. & F. Lurton 2001 Gran Lurton Reserve Cabernet Blend (Uco Valley) $18. Attractive mint, blackberry, leather, and earth scents precede a chewy palate bulked up by thick plum and blackberry flavors. The mouthfeel is round and soft, although some tannin pokes through to spike it up. Finishes with vanilla, coffee, and mocha. **86** —*M.S. (11/15/2004)*

J. & F. Lurton 2002 Gran Lurton Cabernet Sauvignon (Mendoza) $18. Starts out showing red-fruit aromas of currant, plum, and raspberry. The palate stays the course, offering raspberry and strawberry flavors. Shows plenty of ripeness, moderate tannins, and some buttery, vanilla-based oak. Fresh but simple. Drink now. **87** —*M.S. (7/1/2005)*

J. & F. Lurton 2004 Reserva Chardonnay (Mendoza) $12. Gold in color, with good texture. Somewhat short on intensity, however, with ample oak, almond, apple, and pear flavors. Weighty but not terribly expressive. Appropriate acidity, good with salmon and the like. **85** —*M.S. (7/1/2005)*

J. & F. Lurton 2003 Chacayes Malbec (Mendoza) $75. For the second straight year, Chacayes scores major points among serious Argentine wines competing for the world's attention. This blend of 80% Malbec and 20% Cabernet is deep, dark, and seductive. It's all about compact, intense fruit supported by hefty tannins. Very nice and perfectly ripe. Hold a couple of years for best results. **92 Cellar Selection** —*M.S. (12/1/2006)*

J. & F. Lurton 2002 Chacayes Malbec (Mendoza) $75. This is what full-force, high-elevation Malbec is all about. The color is opaque, the nose a potent brew of herbal mint, blackberry, and earth. With layers of warmth and depth on the finish, this wine represents the bigger is better school of thought. **92** —*M.S. (11/15/2004)*

J. & F. Lurton 2003 Piedra Negra Malbec (Uco Valley) $28. An impressive encore to the 2002. This wine hits with a bolt of leather, graphite, and blackberry before moving on to a pure, tasty palate that's loaded with concentrated berry flavors. Very bright and bouncy, and just a level below the Lurton brothers' studly Chacayes. **90** —*M.S. (12/1/2006)*

J. & F. Lurton 2002 Piedra Negra Malbec (Uco Valley) $30. Gorgeous aromas of pipe tobacco, mint, and sweet oak create a full, meaty bouquet when combined with the blasting fruit that's on display. Flavors of blackberry and plum are ripe and refined, while the tannins grab but don't slam at your palate. Textured and chocolaty, with ample freshness. A winner. **90** —*M.S. (11/15/2004)*

J. & F. Lurton 2002 Reserva Malbec (Mendoza) $13. The bouquet springs with red licorice, black cherry, and blueberry, but also a hint of minty green. Not sharp but piquant on the tongue, with hints of cherry candy and grainy oak. Good on the surface but there's not a whole lot underneath. A solid quaff to match with burgers or pizza. **86** —*M.S. (7/1/2005)*

J. & F. Lurton 2004 Bodega Lurton Pinot Gris (Uco Valley) $7. Yellow in color, with buttercup and citrus aromas. Not bad on the palate, where kiwi, melon, and citrus flavors are fairly solid if unexciting. Where the wine completely fails to resemble Pinot Gris is on the scale; here it offers virtually no acidity and thus too much weight. **84 Best Buy** —*M.S. (7/1/2005)*

J. & F. Lurton 2003 Tierra del Fuego Red Blend (Mendoza) $6. Lighter framed than your average Argentinean red, but good in its red-fruit base. The nose shows red berry, vanilla, and adequate depth, while the palate is dry and lean, with cherry the dominant fruit. **85 Best Buy** —*M.S. (11/15/2004)*

J. & F. Lurton 2004 Tierra del Fuego White Blend (Mendoza) $6. This white blend from the Lurton brothers is full-bodied and creamy, with pear, apple, and melon aromas and flavors. Finishes fat and off-dry, with a ripe aftertaste. Fairly sticky and big across the tongue. **85 Best Buy** —*M.S. (11/15/2004)*

J. ALBERTO

J. Alberto 2004 Malbec (Río Negro Valley) $40. The second wine from Bodega Noemía de Patagonia is an unbridled winner in 2004. It's ripe and saturated, with a warm and spicy nose that blends just the right amount of rusticity with blackberry and plum. Quite a heavyweight with some raw oak, chocolate, and mocha. Everything that fans of Argentine Malbec are looking for is on stage here. **90** —*M.S. (4/1/2006)*

JOFFRÉ E HIJAS

Joffré e Hijas 2004 Grand Cabernet Sauvignon (Uco Valley) $21. A weird wine with early sneaker-sole aromas that change to root beer and liqueur later on. The palate is soft, almost devoid of tannin, with sugary black fruit that seems either a touch cooked or a close cousin of recioto. Lacks the edge of a balanced wine. **82** —*M.S. (11/1/2006)*

Joffré e Hijas 2004 Grand Chardonnay (Mendoza) $21. Nice and sweet at first, with aromas of flowers and tropical fruit. Plump on the palate, without much noticeable acidity. The flavors, therefore, run toward banana, pear and ripe apple. Finishes creamy and soft; teetering on flaccid. **85** —*M.S. (4/1/2006)*

Joffré e Hijas 2004 Grand Malbec (Uco Valley) $19. Starts with coffee and burnt toast, and next comes deep blueberry, black plum, and spice flavors. Begins racy on the palate and then mellows into cushy softness. Good in its depth of flavor, with chewy tannins. **87** —*M.S. (12/1/2006)*

Joffré e Hijas 2003 Grand Malbec (Mendoza) $21. A bit of burnt character clouds the grapy nose, but it's not a heavy, overoaked wine. In fact, the palate is a touch tangy, with zesty black cherry and a decent amount of protruding acidity. Rigid but solid, with full fruit flavors. **86** —*M.S. (6/1/2006)*

Joffré e Hijas 2003 Reserve Malbec (Uco Valley) $40. Heavily oaked and minty on the nose, but the problems really arise on the palate, where outsized acidity and not enough richness amount to too much tang and tartness. For a good-vintage Malbec, there's not nearly enough body and flavor here. **82** —*M.S. (4/1/2006)*

Joffré e Hijas 2003 Grand Merlot (Mendoza) $21. Roasted and deep at first, which is encouraging. But it doesn't really stand the test, showing tart plum and berry flavors, out-of-place tannin and shortness on the palate. Finishes too thin and hard. **82** —*M.S. (6/1/2006)*

Joffré e Hijas 2003 Reserva Merlot (Uco Valley) $40. Very oaky, with coconut and raw wood making up the bulk of the bouquet. Wood is the recurring theme throughout, with just a bit of dark fruit making an appearance. Very hard, tannic, and tough. **83** —*M.S. (8/1/2006)*

KAIKEN

Kaiken 2003 Cabernet Sauvignon (Mendoza) $13. Starts out heavily smoked, almost woodsy. Stays oaky throughout, while showing an overt candied, sweet, medicinal core. Not very edgy, with a lot of marshmallow, vanilla, and syrup. Made at twice the production level as the inaugural 2002, and with a new premium wine competing for top fruit; still good but not special like the '02. **86** —*M.S. (7/1/2005)*

Kaiken 2002 Cabernet Sauvignon (Mendoza) $13. Lauded Chilean winemaker Aurelio Montes traveled across the Andes to make this wine, just like the Kaiken bird does when it migrates. It's quite stunning, especially given the price. Look for black plum, licorice, cassis, earth, and coffee aromas and flavors. The bitter chocolate finish is dynamite in terms of tannic structure and length. **90 Editors' Choice** —*M.S. (11/15/2004)*

Kaiken 2003 Ultra Cabernet Sauvignon (Mendoza) $23. Clumsy at first, but admittedly tasted a month prior to release. Time frees up deep, sturdy fruit overlayed with a sheet of creamy oak that yields vanilla, resin, and subtle spice flavors. Chunky and ripe; the berry fruit is 100% mature. Will knit together with more time in bottle. Better in 2006. **90 Editors' Choice** —*M.S. (7/1/2005)*

Kaiken 2003 Malbec (Mendoza) $13. Round and rambunctious, with aromas of leather, herbs, cherry, and cassis. Veers toward grapey in the mouth, but holds the line while offering soft, buttery plum, raspberry, and vanilla flavors. Warm and spicy on the finish, with a heaping portion of chocolate and cream. **89 Best Buy** —*M.S. (7/1/2005)*

Kaiken 2002 Malbec (Mendoza) $13. This new brand from Montes in Chile scored big with its inaugural Cabernet and the Malbec is just as good, if not better. The tint is a purple haze, while the nose is dark, masculine, and full of ultraripe black fruit. Deep and rich throughout—and totally delicious—it's what good South American reds are all about: bursting fruit, body, and value. **91 Best Buy** —*M.S. (3/1/2005)*

Kaiken 2003 Ultra Malbec (Mendoza) $23. The inaugural premium Malbec from Montes S.A.'s fledgling Argentinean venture displays round, attractive aromas of concentrated black fruit and hefty oak. The palate is bold, chewy, and rich, while fine tannins and lively acidity keep any potential holes well plugged. Tastes sweet, dark, fruity, and ripe, with vanilla and coffee on the finish. Tremendously satisfying. **91** —*M.S. (7/1/2005)*

LA PUERTA

La Puerta 2004 Cabernet Sauvignon (La Rioja) $8. Big and dark, with smoked meat and bacon aromas sitting side by side with damp, soupy notes. Has its strong points, such as the dark plum and bacon flavors and the wideness of the finish. Strikes against include extra hard tannins that result in a scouring, lasting feel. **84 Best Buy** —*M.S. (8/1/2006)*

La Puerta 2005 Chardonnay (La Rioja) $8. Overtly floral and jumpy, with potent aromas of perfume. Heavy in the mouth, with odd, bland flavors of applesauce and spice. Soft and sticky. **80** —*M.S. (6/1/2006)*

La Puerta 2005 Malbec (La Rioja) $8. Jammy and oaky, with raisin, graham cracker, and blackberry thrown in for good measure. The palate teeters on syrupy but holds the line to show sweet, ripe berry, and plum flavors. Mild tannins and some coffee on the healthy finish. **86 Best Buy** —*M.S. (4/1/2006)*

La Puerta 2005 Merlot (La Rioja) $8. Granular and reduced on the nose, with bulky fruit flavors and an awkward mouthfeel. Finishes rather heavy and a bit burnt. **80** —*M.S. (6/1/2006)*

La Puerta 2005 Shiraz (La Rioja) $8. Full plum and raspberry aromas are not overpowering, but they are big and set the stage for plum, coffee, and pepper flavor components. Displays a bit of heat and bitterness late on the finish, but for the most part this wine is varietally correct and tastes not unlike a sun-drenched Côtes-du-Rhône. **84 Best Buy** —*M.S. (8/1/2006)*

La Puerta 2005 Torrontès (La Rioja) $8. Honey, flowers, and a bit of mineral on the solid nose. This is full and ripe, with pretty melon, anise, and other Southeast Asian flavors. A bit more full and extracted than most, but it's neither flabby nor heavy. **86 Best Buy** —*M.S. (4/1/2006)*

LA YUNTA

La Yunta 2005 Torrontès (La Rioja) $10. Light-bodied and more in line with traditional, quaffable Torrontès, this one offers a whiff of orange blossom and lemon in front of melon, kiwi, and lime flavors. Good in texture, as it doesn't try to do too much. **85 Best Buy** —*M.S. (11/1/2006)*

La Yunta 2002 Torrontès (Famatina Valley) $9. From the La Rioja region, this colorless white offers virtually nothing in terms of aromas and then barely a smack of candied fruit flavor. It's overly thin, with microscopic amounts of citrus. **80** —*M.S. (7/1/2004)*

La Yunta 2001 Torrontès (Argentina) $9. Some cheesiness jumbles up the pineapple aromas on the nose, but the palate is clean, offering tropical fruit and peaches. The finish is smooth and satisfying, with a slight bitterness. It's much like a blended fruit juice with bite. Hails from the province of La Rioja (but not Spain). **84** —*M.S. (5/1/2003)*

LAS MORAS

Las Moras 2005 Bonarda (San Juan) $9. A touch of mulch and smoked meat make for a confounding, less than pure bouquet. And in the mouth, there's rubbery black cherry followed by an almost salty finish. Doesn't seem complete; something is missing, namely polish and purity of fruit. **82** —*M.S. (11/1/2006)*

Las Moras 2004 Bonarda (San Juan) $8. Broad and clean, with solid berry and cherry aromas along with some citrus zest. The palate offers bright berry flavors, while the finish is full, leathery, and tight. Commendable for its forward fruit and quality mouthfeel. A good introduction to Bonarda. **85 Best Buy** —*M.S. (11/15/2005)*

Las Moras 2004 Reserva Cabernet Sauvignon-Shiraz (San Juan) $13. Smooth and ripe, with woody aromas of toasted coconut and vanilla. The palate is all black cherry and cassis, while the finish is smooth and easy, with a light wave of mocha at the base. Overall it's an integrated wine with balance. **88 Best Buy** —*M.S. (12/1/2006)*

Las Moras 2005 Reserva Chardonnay (San Juan) $13. A fat Chard made in the New World style, meaning it pushes a block of oak across the bouquet and then pours on the textured apple, nut, and butterscotch flavors. Lacks complexity and vitality, but offers ample size and richness. Drink immediately. **84** —*M.S. (11/1/2006)*

Las Moras 2004 Reserva Chardonnay (San Juan) $12. Gold in color, with full, ripe, and generally pleasant aromas. Chewy and round in the mouth, with apple and citrus flavors. Vanilla and pepper notes work the finish, which also offers touches of smoke and toast. **85** —*M.S. (11/15/2005)*

Las Moras 2005 Malbec (San Juan) $9. Robust red wine, with ever-changing aromas of earth, leather, baked fruit, and more. Shows glimpses of complexity amid standard, chunky Malbec flavors of plum and blackberry. **84** —*M.S. (12/1/2006)*

Las Moras 2002 Mora Negra Red Blend (Tulum Valley) $36. Fully oaked, so the nose deals plenty of coffee and maple. Under that there's vibrant red-cherry and cassis flavors amid firm tannins. The finish is solid and spicy, with chocolate folded in. Although it is a bit gritty and hard now, each additional month you hold it the hardness will dissipate. Made of 70% Malbec and 30% Bonarda. **90** —*M.S. (4/1/2006)*

Las Moras 2005 Sauvignon Blanc (San Juan) $9. Modest, unfocused tangerine and passion fruit aromas lead to a plump, flat palate with dried apricot and passion fruit flavors. Seems soft on the finish, as if the acidity is low. **81** —*M.S. (12/1/2006)*

Las Moras 2005 Shiraz (San Juan) $9. Nicely put together, with a solid blend of spice, leather, and smoked meat vying with juicy berry aromas. The palate is tangy and fresh, with flashy cherry flavors. Finishes strong, with coffee and chocolate. A good wine for the money; recommended for everyday Shiraz. **86 Best Buy** —*M.S. (12/1/2006)*

Las Moras 2004 Shiraz (San Juan) $8. Sturdy and solid, with some leather and spice to the nose. Loud and racy on the palate, with some heat and spice on the back side. This is yet another solid, forward wine from Argentina, and for the money you can't really go wrong. **87 Best Buy** —*M.S. (10/1/2005)*

Las Moras 2004 Reserva Tannat (San Juan) $13. You don't see much South American Tannat outside Uruguay, but this one scores points for its dark charcoal and cola nose as well as its deep black cherry and plum flavors. Yes, it's kind of hard and tannic, but it's also got some verve and length to it. With meat, it would be worth the gamble. **86** —*M.S. (12/1/2006)*

Las Moras 2003 Reserva Tannat (San Juan) $10. An Argentinean Tannat that strikes a lot of good chords. The nose is full of blackberry and prune, while the palate seems racy courtesy of core acidity that can't be shaken. Good for those eager to expand their wine horizons. It's both dark and jumpy. **85 Best Buy** —*M.S. (8/1/2006)*

Las Moras 2005 Viognier (San Juan) $8. Chunky and on the verge of overripe, with soft peach and melon aromas. Additional peach and melon flavors define the overweight palate, while the finish is heavy but flavorful. Tasty stuff with merits, but its lifespan is going to be short. **84 Best Buy** —*M.S. (6/1/2006)*

Las Moras 2004 Viognier (San Juan) $8. Simple and doughy, with plump, sugary aromas of canned pears and applesauce. The palate features soft melon and nectarine, while the finish has punch and some lingering fruit notes. Low in acidity. **84 Best Buy** —*M.S. (11/15/2005)*

LAUREL GLEN

Laurel Glen 2003 Terra Rosa Malbec (Mendoza) $14. Pure and linear, without a spot of funk or wayward oak. The nose is beefed up with aromas of tar, smoke, leather, and blackberry, yet the palate is a bit candied. Easygoing enough to rank as a very good everyday wine. And you'll never say "corchado" after opening it; it's sealed with a screw cap. **87** —*M.S. (7/1/2005)*

Laurel Glen 2002 Vale La Pena Malbec (Mendoza) $34. A totally different breed of fox. The nose deals blueberry but also a thin, floral note that teeters on the edge of piercing. Almost crisp and prickly on the palate, with little of the heft and overt oak that so many premier Malbecs show. Racy stuff, but if you match it with food it might actually do better than some of the heavyweights. **87** —*M.S. (7/1/2005)*

Laurel Glen 2001 Vale La Pena Malbec (Mendoza) $30. The name implies that the wine is "worth the effort"; taste it and we think you'll agree. It's from Patrick Campbell of California, and it comes from 80-year-old vines. The concentration and power are up front, as are the oak and tannin. The nose offers dried fruit, cedar, espresso, and mocha, and it tastes of ripe black fruit. Just 300 cases made in conjunction with Achàval-Ferrer. **91** —*M.S. (12/1/2003)*

LOS CIELOS

Los Cielos 2005 Cabernet Sauvignon-Malbec (Mendoza) $9. Chunky and full, but not totally pure. The palate holds form, showing sharp flavors of strawberry and cherry. Some light oak and vanilla works the finish, while some leftover acidity creates a tangy overall impression. **83** —*M.S. (11/1/2006)*

Los Cielos 2005 Trebbiano-Chardonnay White Blend (Mendoza) $9. Fresh and full of zesty apple aromas that lead into a palate of cider, citrus, and spice. Light in the mouth, with proper acidity. Generally fits the bill as a good, easy quaffer. **84** —*M.S. (11/1/2006)*

LUCA

Luca 2000 Chardonnay (Mendoza) $32. This bold, burly wine has a pretty shine to it. Attractive honey, melon, and buttered-toast aromas dance on the nose, and the creamy yet structured palate offers coconut and banana flavors along with proper acids. It's very much like the inaugural '99 wine, maybe a bit better balanced, but less concentrated. Regardless, it's still potent Chardonnay featuring plenty of high-grade oak. **89** —*M.S. (7/1/2002)*

Luca 2000 Malbec (Altos de Mendoza) $37. Raspberry jam aromas greet you as the bouquet exudes power: There's bursting fruit, campfire, earth, and chocolate rolled into one. The palate is healthy but not overdone; oak is present but not overwhelming. Quite healthy and spunky, and can age. Luca is the private label of Laura Catena. **90** —*M.S. (12/1/2003)*

LUIGI BOSCA

Luigi Bosca 2003 Gala 2 Bordeaux Blend (Mendoza) $37. Why this vintage is so much more monotone and raisiny than the lovely '02 is anyone's guess. However, that's the case. The nose starts out with game and bacon but it shifts to raisin and prune with airing. The palate, meanwhile, is also lively at first and then goes raisiny. Very dark but it settles on a single plane and then stays there. Tannic as well. **85** —*M.S. (8/1/2006)*

Luigi Bosca 2002 Gala 2 Bordeaux Blend (Mendoza) $33. Well made and satisfying, from start to finish. This is about as good as it gets when Argentina tries its hand at blending: the mix is Cabernet Sauvignon, Cab Franc, and Merlot. Smooth and meaty on the palate, with pure plum, currant, and cherry flavors. Spice and extract dominate the finish, with hints of chocolate and coffee. It's the whole package. **90 Editors' Choice** —*M.S. (3/1/2005)*

Luigi Bosca 2002 Finca La Linda Cabernet Sauvignon (Mendoza) $10. Somewhat complex, as it begins with heavy bacon and tire rubber aromas that ultimately give way to more floral notes. Fairly thick on the palate, with sweet red fruits, glycerol, and tannins. Finishes a touch flat and sugary, with some Port-like heat. A hard one to peg. **86 Best Buy** —*M.S. (3/1/2005)*

Luigi Bosca 2003 Reserva Cabernet Sauvignon (Mendoza) $18. In general, we've been liking Bosca's wines. But this Cabernet is murky and tomatoey, with too much stagnant character to earn a better score. Not really up to par. **81** —*M.S. (12/1/2006)*

Luigi Bosca 2004 Finca La Linda Chardonnay (Mendoza) $10. Ripe and a bit prickly on the nose, but it's way more sturdy than dirty. Flavors of apple, lemon, and orange peel are fine, while the fresh finish is bittered up a bit by citrus pith. **86 Best Buy** —*M.S. (3/1/2005)*

Luigi Bosca 2005 Reserva Chardonnay (Mendoza) $18. Opens with a nice combination of mineral dust and orange marmalade, while the palate is smooth with the flavors of banana and lemon curd. Suave with a splash of necessary acidity. As always, Luigi Bosca delivers a very good wine. **88** —*M.S. (11/1/2006)*

Luigi Bosca 2004 Reserva Chardonnay (Mendoza) $15. Quite full and plump, with oily aromas along with hints of wood resin and nectarine. More citrus than expected on the tongue, primarily overripe white grapefruit. Somewhat low-acid on the finish, but good overall. **86** —*M.S. (3/1/2005)*

Luigi Bosca 2003 Malbec (Luján de Cuyo) $20. Violet in color, with sweet lilac, plum, and graham cracker aromas. A fruitball of the first order, but one that's ripe and balanced. The palate pours on blackberry and chocolate in spades, while the tannins and acids meet in the middle. **90** —*M.S. (8/1/2006)*

Luigi Bosca 2003 Finca La Linda Malbec (Mendoza) $10. Chunky and spicy on the nose, with mid-level plum and black-cherry flavors. More light than dark, with fleshy fruit that makes an O.K. impression before heading for the exit. Good but unexciting. **84** —*M.S. (7/1/2005)*

Luigi Bosca 2002 Finca La Linda Malbec (Mendoza) $10. Intriguingly herbal, with spice, leather, and oregano aromas as opposed to Malbec's more common jammy blueberry and blackberry characteristics. The palate is moderately juicy, with hints of pepper, baking spices, and earth. Different than the pack, which is admirable. **87 Best Buy** —*M.S. (3/1/2005)*

Luigi Bosca 2003 Reserva Malbec (Mendoza) $18. Meaty and slightly savory, with roasted aromas and spice notes mixed in. The palate is rich and ripe, with blackberry and fudge-based flavors. It's also rather different than the average Malbec: the flavor profile doesn't just feature jammy berry fruit. There's smoked meat, raisin, and other interesting things going on. **89** —*M.S. (12/1/2006)*

Luigi Bosca 2001 Reserva Malbec (Mendoza) $16. Slightly sharp but snappy enough to keep you interested. Flavors of red apple, raspberry, and plum control the palate, while moderately hard tannins on the finish seem to stretch and thin the wine. **84** —*M.S. (3/1/2005)*

Luigi Bosca 2001 Reserva Merlot (Mendoza) $16. Rusty in color, with "country" aromas of sweaty leather, horsehide, and hay. Ponderous on the palate, with sour plum and murky baked fruit. Surely not a disaster but brings with it some heavy overriding characteristics. **82** —*M.S. (3/1/2005)*

Luigi Bosca 1997 Finca Los Nobles Cabernet Bouchet Red Blend (Argentina) $70. There's plenty of life in this eight-year-old blend, and the nose is like a brew of game, herbs, heirloom tomato, and savory spices. The palate is plenty deep, with cherry, blackberry, cumin, oregano, and raisin flavors, while the finish is forward and lively. Put it this way: this is a unique look at Argentinean winemaking circa the 1990s. **89** —*M.S. (7/1/2005)*

Luigi Bosca 1997 Finca Los Nobles Malbec Verdot Red Blend (Mendoza) $58. This is a stylish throwback, like the new Knicks putting on vintage Frazier jerseys. The nose is spicy and slightly herbal, with fresh basil, cinnamon, and leather mixing with dried black fruits. Still vital and kicking on the palate, with juicy plum, blueberry, coffee, and chocolate flavors. Toasty and spicy on the finish; drink or continue to hold. **91** —*M.S. (7/1/2005)*

Luigi Bosca 2002 Gala 1 Red Blend (Mendoza) $33. Big and rubbery, with an extreme oaky nose. The unconventional blend is Malbec, Petit Verdot, and Tannat, and it focuses mostly on red fruits like rhubarb and plum. Slightly tannic and hot, but also inspired and properly made. **86** —*M.S. (3/1/2005)*

Luigi Bosca 2004 Reserva Sauvignon Blanc (Maipú) $15. Dull passion fruit is about the best you get from the bouquet, while the palate is weak and watery, with light tropical fruit flavors. Finishes with banana notes. **81** —*M.S. (7/1/2005)*

Luigi Bosca 2002 Reserva Syrah (Mendoza) $16. Ripe and rich, with jammy black fruit and plenty of oak-driven bacon on the nose. This is your prototype modern Syrah, one with cola, raspberry, plum, and chocolate flavors. The tannins are firm but forgiving, and the spice element is not light years from that of a Rhône wine. Syrah like this could give Malbec some competition. **89 Editors' Choice** —*M.S. (3/1/2005)*

Luigi Bosca 2004 Finca La Linda Tempranillo (Mendoza) $10. Among the small field that is Argentinean Tempranillo, this is a standout. The nose is full, meaty, and ripe, with bacon in the mix. The palate is full-bore and delivers a blend of cherry, cola, and coffee flavors. Big but balanced, and not to be confused with something Spanish. **88 Best Buy** —*M.S. (12/1/2006)*

Luigi Bosca 2003 Finca La Linda Tempranillo (Mendoza) $10. Perfect color combined with one of the more atypical but interesting bouquets you'll find stirs intrigue. Aromas of mint, berry syrup, and most of all clove are intense, while the black licorice and espresso accents on the palate work. Not Spanish in style nor is it reserved. This is a bruising wine with a unique Mendoza identity. **87 Best Buy** —*M.S. (3/1/2005)*

Luigi Bosca 2004 Finca La Linda Viognier (Luján de Cuyo) $10. A strange wine with heavy, overripe aromas of burnt grass and melon. No real fruit to hang your hat on, and nothing much in the way of nuance, feel, or finish. Made by Luigi Bosca. **80** —*M.S. (7/1/2005)*

Luigi Bosca 2005 Gala 3 White Blend (Mendoza) $30. Heavily toasted up front, yielding popcorn, cream soda, and ultimately a touch of pear. The blend is an uncommon trio of Viognier, Chardonnay, and Riesling that results in a meaty palate with hidden acidity and dry citrus flavors. Unusual, with interesting qualities. As a whole, however, it isn't outstanding. **86** —*M.S. (11/1/2006)*

LUIS CORREAS

Luis Correas 1997 Malbec (Mendoza) $9. 82 —*C.S. (5/1/2002)*

MARCUS JAMES

Marcus James 2000 Chardonnay (Mendoza) $11. To get the best results, you'd better chill this one down. That way you'll get more of the refreshing apple and pear element of the wine and less of its fat, chunky body and rough, unpolished edges. **80** —*M.S. (7/1/2002)*

MARTINO

Martino 2002 Malbec (Luján de Cuyo) $19. Herbal and spicy, with lactic notes and ripe blueberry aromas. Quite fruity and sprawling, with big plum and berry flavors. Thick in the mouth and large on the finish, with syrup and just enough acid to keep it balanced. **87** —*M.S. (12/31/2005)*

Martino 2002 Old Vines Malbec (Mendoza) $55. Deep mocha and coffee greet you on the nose, backed by intense fruit and lavender aromas. And in between you catch some perfume and lilac. Rich and creamy in the mouth, with a full allotment of berry fruits, including blueberry and blackberry. Finishes a bit oaky and short, but that's a small complaint. **90** —*M.S. (11/15/2004)*

MAYOL

Mayol 2003 Pircas Vineyard Bonarda (Mendoza) $15. Dense and dark, with a color akin to purple ink. Catchy and well-made, the fruit is ripe and abnormally friendly, while the structure is solid. What makes this an above-average wine in its class is that the acidity is mellow, not shrill as is often the case. **87** —*M.S. (11/15/2004)*

Mayol 2002 Pircas Vineyard Bonarda (Vista Flores) $15. This is about as good as it gets with Bonarda, a thinner, juicier red with lots of acidity and true red-fruit flavors. Plum, cherry, and a touch of oak define the palate, while the finish is dry and expansive. A bit grapy and grabbing, but still a good example of this mostly lost Italian variety. **85** —*M.S. (7/1/2004)*

Mayol 2003 Sebastian Vineyard Cabernet Sauvignon (Tupungato) $15. Basic and juicy, with olive on the nose along with black fruit. Ripe and tannic, with berry and plum flavors and a robust, somewhat tannic mouthfeel. Pushes cherry and blackberry late; good but standard. **84** —*M.S. (12/31/2005)*

Mayol 2003 Montuiri Vineyard Malbec (Luján de Cuyo) $15. Rubbery and firm on the nose, yet soft in the mouth. The flavors are of pure red fruit, mostly raspberry and currants. Mild on the finish, clean and easy, with a touch of buttery oak. Not that deep but decent. **84** —*M.S. (12/31/2005)*

Mayol 2002 Montuiri Vineyard Malbec (Luján de Cuyo) $15. A single-vineyard heavyweight with sweet aromas of oak, caramel, and berry syrup. The palate is stewy and dark, with blackberry and pepper notes. The feel across the tongue is stand-up, with chocolate and coffee notes coming on late. **88** —*M.S. (7/1/2004)*

Mayol 2002 Pircas Vineyard Syrah (Vista Flores) $15. Only a mild vegetal hint to the nose holds this back. Otherwise, it's round and chunky, and quite well balanced. The red fruit on the palate is vivid, and the vanilla-tinged oak seems to grace that fruit. The texture throughout is good, as is the color. **87** —*M.S. (7/1/2004)*

MAYU

Mayu 2003 Malbec (San Juan) $11. Dark and jammy on the nose, with a spot of vinegar and sharp leather. Tangy plum and cherry flavors on the palate, with sharp-edged tannins. The puckery finish shows coffee and mocha shadings. **82** —*M.S. (11/15/2005)*

MEDANOS

Medanos 2004 Cabernet Sauvignon (Mendoza) $13. Flat and vinegary, with mulchy aromas. An organic wine with not a lot going for it. It's chewy, with no overt edge or balance. **80** —*M.S. (11/15/2005)*

MEDRANO

Medrano 2001 Cabernet Sauvignon (Maipú) $9. This American-owned label provides just enough quality and true flavor to merit a look. The nose is syrupy and a touch cooked, but the plum and berry flavors are solid. Some coffee and chocolate notes on the finish make up for the wine's specious balance. **84** —*M.S. (7/1/2004)*

Medrano 2002 Chardonnay (Tupungato) $9. Light and stony, with flimsy apricot and butterscotch aromas. Flavors of peach, pear, and melon lead to a clean, easy finish. Some smokiness and a touch of lees stir interest. **84** —*M.S. (2/1/2004)*

Medrano 2001 Malbec (Luján de Cuyo) $9. Raspberry and cherry pie aromas are at first sharp but turn earthy in time. In the mouth, it has a proper feel and expressive cherry and blackberry flavors. The finish is round, with grip and bitter chocolate notes. It goes down easy, with a dab of toasty oak flavor. **86** —*M.S. (2/1/2004)*

Medrano 2001 Merlot (Luján de Cuyo) $9. Has aromas of barbecue sauce and/or marinade, the mouthfeel is sticky, while the flavors are sweet and artificial. With spiked tannins and low acidity, this one struggles to make the grade. **82** —*M.S. (7/1/2004)*

Medrano 2001 Syrah (Mendoza) $9. Standard black fruit and unwelcome green notes carry the nose, while an odd mix of oak and indistinct berry fruit man the palate. This wine offers body and grabby tannins, but also some pickled flavors and an unfocused structure. **84** —*M.S. (7/1/2004)*

MELIPAL

Melipal 2004 Malbec (Mendoza) $20. Big and earthy, with secondary aromas of pepper, chocolate, and smoke supporting bold black fruit. Cassis and black cherry are the leading flavors, while the zesty yet oak-heavy finish is right on. A very good Malbec from what was an average year. **88** —*M.S. (11/1/2006)*

Melipal 2003 Malbec (Mendoza) $20. Pure and potent, with dark aromas that are softened slightly by hints of coconut and rose petals. The palate may be slightly syrupy, but the raspberry and plum flavors are fine, and the chocolaty aftertaste is hard to discount. Quite ripe and serious; just juicy enough to avoid being heavy. **89** —*M.S. (11/15/2005)*

Melipal 2005 Malbec Rosé Malbec (Mendoza) $14. Fresh on the bouquet, with spring flowers and cherry blossom. Simple melon and peach flavors are less than ideal, while the finish is soft and easy but devoid of much nuance or flavor. Clean enough; not terribly thrilling. **84** —*M.S. (11/1/2006)*

Melipal 2004 Reserve Malbec (Mendoza) $42. Rock steady from opening to close. The nose is earthy and toasty, but it's the dark-fruit notes that score the major points. Zesty and full of ribald black cherry, raspberry, and chocolate flavors. Finishes with another helping of fudge, and in the final analysis it fills the tank to the brim. **90** —*M.S. (11/1/2006)*

Melipal 2003 Reserve Malbec (Mendoza) $40. Driving and powerful. The nose offers balsamic notes along with piercing hints of road tar, crude oil, crushed lavender, and leather. The palate is packed full of tobacco, citrus and bright berry fruit. Not the least bit soft, with a zesty mouthfeel that toes the line between balanced and overt. Will show its best in 2006–07. **91** —*M.S. (11/15/2005)*

MICHEL LAROCHE/JORGE CODERCH

Michel Laroche/Jorge Coderch 2002 Colina Negra Cabernet Sauvignon (San Rafael) $15. Fairly rich, chewy, and structured, this is a sturdy, good-value red from an area 250 miles south of Santiago. Blackberry and cassis flavors are accented by vanilla and tobacco. Has some firm tannins on the finish, but they're ripe, not harsh or green. **88** *(2/1/2004)*

MICHEL TORINO

Michel Torino 2001 Cabernet Sauvignon (Cafayate) $14. Slightly weedy and green, with sour cherry and weak raspberry flavors. Finishes tight and solid, but without much flavor to back things up. **82** —*M.S. (7/1/2004)*

Michel Torino 2003 Don David Cabernet Sauvignon (Cafayate) $15. Spicy and alluring, with molasses, earth, and barbecue on the nose. Bold blackberry, plum, and cough syrup work the palate, while the finish is tannic and firm. Not particularly plush, but lively and tasty. **87** — *M.S. (6/1/2006)*

Michel Torino 2002 Don David Cabernet Sauvignon (Cafayate) $14. Exhibits a nice blend of licorice, vanilla, and berry aromas in front of a wall of cherry, blackberry, and raspberry fruit. Tobacco and chocolate on the finish, completing the package. **87** —*M.S. (10/1/2004)*

Michel Torino 1999 Don David Cabernet Sauvignon (Cafayate) $14. 83 *(5/1/2002)*

Michel Torino 2002 Don David Chardonnay (Cafayate) $14. Mushy and flat on the bouquet, but not oxidized. The palate is also heavy and overdone, with dull apple and oak flavors. Hints of marshmallow and caramel create a sweet finish. **83** —*M.S. (7/1/2004)*

Michel Torino 2006 Ciclos Fumé Blanc (Cafayate) $27. There are fumé blancs that are oak-backed and others that aren't. This one is the former. The nose is full of toast and vanilla, while the fruit is on the ripe, weighty side, with peach, melon, and lemon flavors. Fairly rich in the mouth, with whetting acidity. **86** —*M.S. (12/15/2006)*

Michel Torino 2000 Malbec (Cafayate) $10. 81 —*D.T. (5/1/2002)*

Michel Torino 2001 Colección Michel Torino Malbec (Cafayate) $10. Cafayate is not Mendoza, nor does this wine taste like a Mendoza wine. It's aromatic and racy, with sharp acids and a piercing mouthfeel. Sour cherry and cassis flavors dominate, while a hint of enrichening blueberry sweetens things up. **84** —*M.S. (12/1/2003)*

Michel Torino 2003 Don David Malbec (Cafayate) $15. In recent years Michel Torino has been making better and better Malbec, and this vintage is the best we've tasted. It offers sweet fruit and marzipan on the nose, while the big, chewy palate is lush and packed with berries, vanilla, and chocolate nesting on pillowy tannins. Very chummy and almost lavish. **90 Best Buy** —*M.S. (4/1/2006)*

Michel Torino 2002 Don David Malbec (Cafayate) $14. Compact, potent, and saturated, with plenty of leather and licorice aromas along with leather. Fairly fruity, with blackberry and cherry, a hint of bitter chocolate, and buttery oak. A big red, but tasty and made for grilled meats. **87** —*M.S. (10/1/2004)*

Michel Torino 2001 Don David Malbec (Cafayate) $14. Aromas of tomato, molasses, and plum jam are bulked up by oak and earth, and the end result is a bit scrambled. In the mouth, things don't really get better; the flavors are of raspberry and sour cherry, while the finish is astringent and acidic. **83** —*M.S. (7/1/2004)*

Michel Torino 2001 Don David Malbec (Cafayate) $14. This wine comes from the northern part of the country, thus it's quite different than your typical Mendoza fruitball. Snappy red-berry fruit with piercing acidity is what it's about. Think northern Italian wines for a reference, and try to appreciate its fit shape without giving up on it. **85** —*M.S. (12/1/2003)*

Michel Torino 2004 Don David Reserve Malbec (Cafayate) $15. Inky black in color, with a pretty nose defined by toast, minerality, stout plum and berry fruit. Round and vigorous in the mouth, with vibrant dark-berry flavors. A muscled-up wine from Salta with just enough finesse to balance everything out. Ready to drink. **88** —*M.S. (12/15/2006)*

Michel Torino 2004 Ciclos Malbec-Merlot (Cafayate) $25. Chocolate and mint with the essence of coffee drives the bouquet. In the mouth, this Malbec-Merlot blend is ripe as can be, with cassis, blackberry, and chocolate all making their mark. The finish is secure and mildly tannic, while the overall take is that this is a ribald, rich South American red. **92 Editors' Choice** —*M.S. (12/1/2006)*

Michel Torino 2003 Altimus Red Blend (Cafayate) $50. Pitch dark in color, with a huge, oaky/earthy nose that cuddles deep black-plum fruit. Ultraripe and modern in style, with mounds of plum and blackberry flavors. Toasty and minty on the round finish. This is one rich wine; a massive improvement over the 2000 vintage, the last Altimus we rated. **91** —*M.S. (6/1/2006)*

Michel Torino 2000 Altimus Red Blend (Cafayate) $45. Huge and grapey, with a meaty, plum-packed palate that is over the top. The finish is equally round and large, and it's loaded on the back end with bitter espresso. Try as you might, this one is tough to like. It just doesn't have much harmony despite its top-shelf price. **82** —*M.S. (5/1/2003)*

Michel Torino 2004 Ciclos Sauvignon Blanc (Cafayate) $25. The label says fumé and the nose leaves no doubt that the wine was barrel aged because cinnamon and toast are all over it. Yet the flavor profile is rather tangy, with mango and apple leading the way. Holds form on the finish. Not a common style for Sauvignon Blanc. **85** —*M.S. (8/1/2006)*

ARGENTINA

Michel Torino 2004 Don David Torrontès (Cafayate) $15. The yellow color and can't-miss nose work in tandem to announce that this wine was barrel aged, which isn't necessarily the way we like this grape to be processed. But since that's the way it is, get ready for toast, vanilla, and resin along with apple and lemon notes. At least it's properly acidic and shows good balance and feel. **84** —*M.S. (4/1/2006)*

Michel Torino 2003 Don David Torrontès (Cafayate) $14. Attractive aromas of flowers and lemon-lime kick it off, followed by cinnamon-baked apple, star anise, tarragon and white pepper. The attitude is forward and bold, and the finish dry and long. A good Torrontès that pops on the palate. **86** —*M.S. (10/1/2004)*

Michel Torino 2002 Don David Torrontès (Cafayate) $14. Highly aromatic, with exotic scents of lilac, honey, and lychee fruit. Flavors of melon, green apple, lemon, and more lychee are round and fulfilling, while the finish is forward. Shows modest power and finesse, even on a bulky frame. **85** —*M.S. (7/1/2004)*

Michel Torino 2000 Don David Torrontès (Cafayate) $14. Potent yet clean aromas of pineapple create the nose, which is followed by a tangy palate redolent of oranges and lemons. The finish provides more of that citrus flavor and also some balancing zestiness. For being a couple years old already it is fresh. **84** —*M.S. (5/1/2003)*

Michel Torino 2005 Don David Reserve Torrontès (Cafayate) $15. This wine is always a bit waxy and heavy, as vanilla and baked-corn aromas are prominent. In the mouth, potent acidity propels apple, mango, and peach flavors, while the finish is lively to say the least. At 13.9% it's a heavyweight. **84** —*M.S. (11/1/2006)*

MIL PIEDRAS

Mil Piedras 2003 Cabernet Sauvignon (Mendoza) $12. Quite fresh and juicy, with raw black cherry aromas and flavors of raspberry and plum. Zesty is the mouthfeel, with not a whole lot in the center. Juicy but devoid of any Cabernet heft. **84** —*M.S. (11/15/2005)*

Mil Piedras 2003 Malbec (Mendoza) $12. Raisiny, with a texture that's flat as Kansas. Finishes hard, with dull flavors. **80** —*M.S. (11/15/2005)*

Mil Piedras 2003 Tempranillo (Mendoza) $12. More lightweight than most, with strawberry aromas and accents of cinnamon cookie. Not that complex in the mouth, where plum and cherry flavors are consistent if unexciting. Generally speaking, it's likable and zesty. **84** —*M.S. (11/15/2005)*

MJ GALLIARD

MJ Galliard 2004 Cabernet Sauvignon (Mendoza) $16. Mint and tomato blend with red fruit on the nose. The palate is tight and tannic, with limited cherry and cassis flavors. Finishes dry and blanched, with little to offer. **81** —*M.S. (12/1/2006)*

MJ Galliard 2003 Malbec (Mendoza) $20. At 14.5% alcohol, this wine is too big to have the flaws that it does. The nose is muddy, dark, and heavy, while the palate is short and bitter, with strange rubbery flavors peeking through the heavy tannins. **82** —*M.S. (7/1/2004)*

MJ Galliard 2003 Merlot (Mendoza) $20. Rubber, wood smoke, and black fruit vie for center stage. In the mouth, you'll find the earth, coffee, and berries. Finishes dry, firm, and traditional. A well enough made wine that doesn't reach the summit of the mountain. **85** —*M.S. (7/1/2004)*

MJ Galliard 2003 Sauvignon Blanc (Mendoza) $20. Bland, with oak-driven aromas of butter and roast corn. In the mouth, there's banana, pineapple, and other sweet, ripe fruits, but to say it's traditional Sauvignon Blanc would be a stretch of great magnitude. And the alcohol, which clocks in at 14.2%, seems high. **83** —*M.S. (7/1/2004)*

MONTE CINCO

Monte Cinco 2003 Oak Malbec (Mendoza) $42. A defined, balanced, artistic rendition of Malbec. Cola and hard spices mix with leather and sweet marshmallow on the bouquet, then it dishes berry pie, coffee, and mocha flavors. Plenty of charcoal and chocolate create a sturdy but delectable finish. An excellent Malbec. **91** —*M.S. (11/15/2004)*

MURVILLE

Murville NV Brut Nature Champagne Blend (San Rafael) $14. This Argentinean sparkler is forward but not terribly fruity. The flavors are hard to describe, probably a result of this being a no-dosage wine. Some spice on the finish adds character to otherwise standard apple and pear. **83** —*M.S. (1/1/2004)*

ÑANDÚ

Ñandú 2004 Malbec (Mendoza) $12. Smells of coffee syrup and green beans, with fudge and gamy fruit in support. Rather cloying on the palate, with a bitter, black-pepper finish. Very hard and bordering on too tough to drink. **81** —*M.S. (11/15/2005)*

Ñandú 2003 Malbec (San Rafael) $12. This new wine comes courtesy of Bernard Portet (Clos du Val) and son, and for the most part it's on the money. The aromas are a touch horsey to start, and the red fruit is racy more than beefy. But it has a lot of flavor, full tannins, and good balance. If aired out and served with meat or stew, it won't disappoint. **86** —*M.S. (7/1/2005)*

NATIVO

Nativo 2002 El Felino Malbec (Mendoza) $16. This meaty wine weighs in at a barely manageable 14.7% alcohol. It's a new product from Paul Hobbs and his Argentinean partners, and it's dark, saturated, and carries leather and roasted aromas. When it opens, robust blackberry and pepper pour forth. Spice and glycerin carry the finish toward a booming crescendo. **88** —*M.S. (12/1/2003)*

NAVARRO CORREAS

Navarro Correas 2001 Ultra Bordeaux Blend (Mendoza) $27. Aromatic, with blueberry and dried jerky scents. Good fruit with earthy, chocolaty nuances creates a pretty palate that follows the nose nicely. On the downside, it turns thin toward the end. But it manages to stay juicy; in some ways it tastes like Zinfandel. **87** —*M.S. (2/1/2004)*

Navarro Correas 2002 Colección Privada Cabernet Sauvignon (Mendoza) $11. A touch of rubber mixes with aromas of cassis and blackberry to set the stage for a juicy, fresh palate loaded with cherry and plum flavors. Nothing crazy here, just solid red wine that makes the grade at all check points. **87 Best Buy** —*M.S. (11/15/2005)*

Navarro Correas 2000 Colección Privada Cabernet Sauvignon (Mendoza) $16. Some leafy, rustic notes emerge from the bouquet. Ripe plum dominates the palate, but unfortunately there's a sticky grapeskin quality to the mouthfeel. The tannins are hard, too. The flavor profile is better than the texture. **82** —*M.S. (11/1/2002)*

Navarro Correas 2002 Gran Reserva Cabernet Sauvignon (Mendoza) $19. Moderately powerful, with red plum, tomato, and spicy wood to the nose. The palate registers as nondescript, with standard fruit and oak. Grabby tannins, butter and vanilla dominate the finish. Seems more acidic and hard than ideal. **84** —*M.S. (11/15/2005)*

Navarro Correas 2001 Gran Reserva Altos del Rio Cabernet Sauvignon (Mendoza) $23. Big and attractive, with a nice blend of black cherry, rose petal, cinnamon, and rubber. Quite bright on the palate, with cherry, blackberry, coffee and chocolate. With all these descriptors you can see that it's flavorful. It's also spunky and fairly dark. **89** —*M.S. (2/1/2004)*

Navarro Correas 2001 Colección Privada Chardonnay (Mendoza) $16. Flowery, fresh aromas with a hint of butterscotch get things going, followed by an ordinary Chardonnay palate of apples and pears. The finish is full and textured, but a tad clumsy, too. Good, but somewhat ordinary. **84** —*M.S. (11/1/2002)*

Navarro Correas 2003 Colección Privada Chardonnay (Mendoza) $11. Apple, wax bean, and vanilla carry the nose to a palate of ripe melon and lemon. Shows good weight and balance, with a touch of oily meatiness. **85** —*M.S. (11/15/2005)*

Navarro Correas 2003 Colección Privada Malbec (Mendoza) $10. Jammy and fresh, with hints of raspberry and rhubarb. In the mouth, it's fairly rich, with black plum and chocolate. It successfully plays both sides of the fence: It's medium-weight and not overdone, yet it packs punch and offers layers of creamy fruit. A high-water mark for this winery. **89 Best Buy** —*M.S. (3/1/2005)*

Navarro Correas 2000 Colección Privada Malbec (Mendoza) $16. 85 — *M.S. (11/1/2002)*

Navarro Correas 2001 Gran Reserva Altos del Rio Malbec (Mendoza) $23. Deeply colored, with a potent bouquet of leather, earth, lavender, chocolate, and boysenberry. Tastes and feels fresh, courtesy of pulsing acidity. That same acidity works to amplify the berry-cherry fruit, which is nicely accented by notes of coffee. One of NC's best Malbec efforts we've tried. **89** —*M.S. (12/1/2003)*

Navarro Correas 2003 Colección Privada Merlot (Mendoza) $11. Displays character and moderate richness, as any good Merlot should. The palate offers enough dark, smoky fruit to satisfy red-wine lovers, while there's a pleasant smoothness to the mouthfeel. Finishes with a smack of hickory and smoked meat along with blackberry and zest. **86 Best Buy** —*M.S. (11/15/2005)*

Navarro Correas 2000 Colección Privada Merlot (Mendoza) $16. That there are clear, unmistakable aromatics of smoked meats and violets could lead you into believing that this is Malbec, but it's not. Plum, cassis, and chocolate flavors push it more toward traditional Merlot, as does the airy, round finish. The tannins are full and aggressive, yet the overall balance and depth are solid. **86** —*M.S. (11/1/2002)*

Navarro Correas 2003 Colección Privada Syrah (Mendoza) $11. Adequately spicy, with some meatiness to the nose. In the mouth, there's tangy cherry, modest tannin, and some minor chocolate notes. Starts out tight and rubbery before opening up some; finishes deeper than it begins. **85** —*M.S. (4/1/2006)*

Navarro Correas 2000 Colección Privada Syrah (Mendoza) $16. Although this wine is more flowery in the nose than it is meaty or spicy, the flavors of blueberry, blackberry, nutmeg, and chocolate work well together. And the finish is bright and powerful, with full tannins, but it isn't overwhelming or starching. **87** —*M.S. (11/1/2002)*

NIETO SENETINER

Nieto Senetiner 2002 Limited Edition Bonarda (Luján de Cuyo) $30. Strong and bulky, with leather, oak, and dark-fruit aromas. Starts better than it finishes. Along the way are moderately rich plum and berry fruit. A heavy whack of wood late brings it down a notch. **84** —*M.S. (10/1/2004)*

Nieto Senetiner 2003 Don Nicanor Bordeaux Blend (Mendoza) $12. Jammy and condensed to start with, but ultimately the nose checks in as unexpressive. Intense in the mouth but limited in its depth and scope. There's blackberry early and mocha late, but the feel is hard. Quite tannic and unyielding. It's one-third each Cabernet, Malbec and Merlot. **86** —*M.S. (11/1/2006)*

Nieto Senetiner 2001 Don Nicanor Bordeaux Blend (Luján de Cuyo) $15. A blend of Cabernet, Malbec, and Merlot that sits in the glass like a brick; it's opaque purple in color. The nose offers an oak-driven swirl of coconut and mocha on top of brooding, dark fruit. In the mouth, however, it's a tannic bomb. Needs airing and a steak. **85** —*M.S. (10/1/2004)*

Nieto Senetiner 2000 Cadus Cabernet Sauvignon (Luján de Cuyo) $40. Saucy and woody, with nondescript yet powerful black-fruit aromas. Like the Cadus Malbec, this wine has fierce tannins that form a barrier around the body. Inside is the fruit and good stuff; outside are the tannins and a lot of nonintegrated French oak. **85** —*M.S. (10/1/2004)*

Nieto Senetiner 2001 Reserva Nieto Cabernet Sauvignon-Shiraz (Luján de Cuyo) $10. All wood, from first sniff to final swallow. Licorice and mint aromas flow off the oak, while the palate is lemony and hard as nails. If you must, air it out for as long as possible. **82** —*M.S. (10/1/2004)*

Nieto Senetiner 2005 Reserva Chardonnay (Mendoza) $10. For a lighter-bodied wine, this sure shows a lot of aggressive, resiny oak. The nose has sawmill qualities, while the palate is woody and spicy, with apple in the background. Seemed better in 2004; wasn't nearly as oaky. **83** —*M.S. (12/1/2006)*

Nieto Senetiner 2004 Reserva Chardonnay (Mendoza) $10. If it seems dilute and distant up front, the palate packs more punch. There's melon, pear, and citrus rolled into an amorphous mish-mash, while the finish delivers mostly ripe melon. Runs a touch watery at the core, but with freshening acidity. **86 Best Buy** —*M.S. (7/1/2005)*

Nieto Senetiner 2001 Cadus Malbec (Mendoza) $37. Opaque purple in color, with harsh aromas of cigar ash, green beans, and pencil lead. Flavors of carob and beet are not that friendly, while the mouthfeel is rock hard; the tannins are piercing and the feel is scouring. **81** —*M.S. (11/15/2005)*

Nieto Senetiner 2000 Cadus Malbec (Luján de Cuyo) $40. Not an easy wine to grade. It's very dark and oaky, with hefty mint, coffee, and charcoal aromas. The palate is tight, with dense black fruit and rock-hard tannins that are tight at first and then expand to the point of being aggressive. Already an "older" wine but showing no signs of backing up. **88** —*M.S. (10/1/2004)*

Nieto Senetiner 2000 Cadus Estiba 39 Malbec (Mendoza) $60. Inky as night, with lush, ripe aromas of berries, tree bark, cola, and all sorts of other herb-infused elixirs. The palate is totally seductive, with cherry and blackberry overflowing. Chewy and round on the finish, with lemony oak kicking in. This is a block wine from a single vineyard and it's all the way strong. **92 Editors' Choice** —*M.S. (12/31/2005)*

Nieto Senetiner 2002 Cadus Single Vineyard Malbec (Mendoza) $45. Deep, dark, and rubbery, with masculine plum and blackberry flavors. This wine is like midnight; it's pure and black as can be, with huge berry and plum flavors and all the bitter chocolate you can imagine. Bold and built like a fort; the best Nieto to date. Tight, centered, and delicious. **92 Editors' Choice** —*M.S. (12/31/2005)*

Nieto Senetiner 2004 Reserva Malbec (Mendoza) $10. Bright purple in color, a sure indicator that what's to come will be jammy and rich. The nose is all boysenberry and wood, with a hint of mineral. The palate is ultraripe but a bit clumsy and oversized. Not complex but very nice in a fruit-forward, knife-and-fork manner. **87 Best Buy** —*M.S. (11/1/2006)*

Nieto Senetiner 2003 Reserva Malbec (Mendoza) $10. A huge amount of smoke, rubber, herbs, and black fruit pour out of the nose, and that same intensity is carried onto the palate, where bright, juicy, spicy fruit is raring and ready to go. Espresso and black licorice on the finish convey power, the cornerstone of the wine. Correct and snappy; the formula for good-drinking Malbec. **89 Best Buy** —*M.S. (7/1/2005)*

Nieto Senetiner 2002 Reserva Nieto Malbec (Luján de Cuyo) $10. A bit quiet on the nose, but clean and properly fruity. Black cherry, blackberry, and chocolate flavors make for a sweet, lively mouthful. Finishes both sugary and dark, almost like a dessert. **88 Best Buy** —*M.S. (10/1/2004)*

Nieto Senetiner 2003 Reserva Merlot (Mendoza) $10. Solid but overrun with heavy sawdust-based aromas and flavors. Here's a wine with body and balance but far too much racy oak. The result is not a lot of fruit but a ton of mint, vanilla, and licorice flavors. **84** —*M.S. (11/15/2005)*

Nieto Senetiner 2002 Cadus Syrah (Mendoza) $37. Saturated, with aromas of moist earth, prune, tightly woven oak, and leather. It's not a funky, animal-driven style of Syrah; just the opposite, it's creamy and rich, with waves of chocolate and vanilla crashing alongside chunky black fruit. Seems apparent that the Nieto Senetiner winery found its stride in 2002; all its top wines are excellent. **91 Editors' Choice** —*M.S. (12/31/2005)*

NOVUS

Novus 2005 Cabernet Sauvignon (Mendoza) $10. Straightforward plum and rubber aromas seem slightly baked or burnt, while the palate features hard peppery flavors at the center of a powerful yet mildly scouring red-fruit palate. Not offensive but basic and raw. **83** —*M.S. (11/1/2006)*

Novus 2003 Cabernet Sauvignon (Mendoza) $10. Damp earth and a leafy accent render the nose less than fruity, while the mouth is round and grabby, with basic Cabernet flavors and hard tannins. Short on the finish. **83** —*M.S. (8/1/2006)*

Novus 2004 Chardonnay (Mendoza) $11. Gold in color and on the dry, waxy side. Shows mineral and dried fruits on the nose, with heavy pear and apple bulking up the palate. Finishes short, with some pithy bitterness. But good overall, with a roundness that's appealing. **85** —*M.S. (6/1/2006)*

Novus 2005 Malbec (Mendoza) $10. A very nice wine given the price. The nose features a likable combination of dense berry and leathery spice, while the palate is juicy, ripe, and full of black fruit. Not ultra complicated or complex; it's just pure, ripe Malbec in its most approachable form. **89 Best Buy** —*M.S. (12/1/2006)*

Novus 2003 Malbec (Mendoza) $11. Starts out reserved then comes on strong. Aromas of bright red fruits and leather are more austere than lush, and the palate delivers raspberry, cherry, and plum in balanced fashion. Light oak creates a chocolate sensation on the finish. Structured nicely. **87 Best Buy** —*M.S. (4/1/2006)*

Novus 2005 Syrah (Mendoza) $10. Novus is a label to watch if you're into well-made, full-force wines that are balanced and easy to drink. The current Syrah features berry aromas in front of cassis, berry, and plum flavors. It isn't particularly varietal or foxy, but it is solid, masculine, dark, and chocolaty. **88 Best Buy** —*M.S. (12/1/2006)*

Novus 2003 Syrah (Mendoza) $11. Standard fare, but nice. The nose offers some burnt sugar in addition to black fruit, while the palate is full of plum, cherry, and spice. Chocolate and vanilla are detectable on the medium-length finish, while the feel and balance are proper. **85** —*M.S. (6/1/2006)*

O. FOURNIER

O. Fournier 2001 A Crux Red Blend (Mendoza) $42. The big brother and precursor to B Crux, this wine has 70% Tempranillo, 20% Malbec, and 10% Merlot. It's a big, chewy sweet wine with a lot of character as well as some heavy oak and heat toward the end. Since it's the very first wine from O. Fournier, and because 2001 was an average year, expect even better offerings in 2002 and '03. **89** —*M.S. (7/1/2005)*

O. Fournier 2002 B Crux Red Blend (Mendoza) $21. Intense and saucy, with strong aromatic hints of barbecued meat, marinade, and crushed red pepper. Deeper down there's cherry and baked plum flavors. Smooth but just racy enough, with excellent acid-tannin balance. Finishes with vanilla, pepper, and fresh tomato. It's 60% Tempranillo, 20% Malbec, and 20% Merlot. **89** —*M.S. (7/1/2005)*

PALO ALTO

Palo Alto 2004 Amadores Malbec (Argentina) $21. The nose displays some tree bark and sawmill, but underneath there's savory spice alongside black fruit. The palate is ripe and deep, with berry essence and clove. Dark chocolate carries the finish, which is firmly tannic but not overly hard. **86** —*M.S. (12/1/2006)*

Palo Alto 2005 Amadores Limited Edition Pinot Noir (Mendoza) $16. Dry and toasty on the nose, but tart, racy, and raspy on the palate. The raspberry and cherry flavors are sharp and fall off to dry and lean as the wine progresses. **82** —*M.S. (12/1/2006)*

PASCUAL TOSO

Pascual Toso 2002 Reserve Cabernet Sauvignon (Mendoza) $18. Heavily smoked, with nuances of sweet caramel and marshmallow poking through the oaky cover. In the mouth, a couple of layer's worth of cassis and cherry stir interest, while late in the game you get a steady flow of hard tannins and roasty-toasty afternotes. **87** —*M.S. (7/1/2004)*

Pascual Toso 2005 Maipo Vineyards Chardonnay (Mendoza) $11. Fans of ripe, round Chardonnays should look no further than this. The apple, pear, and melon flavors are nice and sweet, with hints of butter and toast backing them up. Good on the palate, with body and texture. An easy drinker. **87 Best Buy** —*M.S. (12/1/2006)*

Pascual Toso 2004 Maipo Vineyards Malbec (Mendoza) $11. This jumpy, lively Malbec is a hulk that starts with funky aromas of wet dog and bacon before settling to reveal bold blackberry and plum notes. It's saturated and solid in the mouth, where black-fruit flavors dominate. On the finish comes spice and mocha. A full-force wine that needs time in the glass to show its best. **87 Best Buy** —*M.S. (12/1/2006)*

Pascual Toso 2002 Reserve Malbec (Mendoza) $18. Fairly round and inviting, but with a leafiness that brings total ripeness into question. Flavors of blueberry and plums are textbook Malbec, while the lasting, fruity finish is deep and features a hint or two of spice and chocolate. **86** —*M.S. (7/1/2004)*

Pascual Toso 2003 Estate Bottled Merlot (Maipú) $NA. Piercing aromas of bulky fruit and horseradish are tough to handle, and underneath there's little to no redeeming sweetness. Menacing in its tannic profile. **80** —*M.S. (7/1/2005)*

Pascual Toso 2005 Maipo Vineyards Sauvignon Blanc (Mendoza) $11. For Argentine Sauvignon Blanc, Toso's version is nice. There's light green-apple aromas in front of green melon and grapefruit flavors. Finishes fairly full and grabby, with likable flavors. Not to be confused with Sancerre or anything, but solid. **86 Best Buy** —*M.S. (12/1/2006)*

PIATTELLI

Piattelli 2003 Cabernet Sauvignon (Tupungato) $14. Fairly smooth and berry dominated, with almost rubbery fruit flavors that are at once tangy and satisfying. In terms of mouthfeel it's a bit hard and tannic, especially given the depth of fruit. But the flavors and intensity are there. **86** — *M.S. (12/1/2006)*

Piattelli 2001 Cabernet Sauvignon (Mendoza) $15. Despite the cheesy note to the nose, the rest of this wine is rock solid. The bouquet features solid oak cloaking berry fruit, while on the palate you'll find cherry, cassis, and licorice. With its soft, simple finish along with bits of chocolate and vanilla, it's a nice Cabernet. From the Tupungato subregion. **87** —*M.S. (7/1/2004)*

PIRCAS NEGRAS

Pircas Negras 2005 Organic Torrontès (Famatina Valley) $10. Clean, light, and fresh; it's the perfect white wine for a picnic. Lithe, lucid flavors of tangerine and pink grapefruit are sweet and ripe, and worthwhile. The stony, citric tail is good, too. **85 Best Buy** —*M.S. (8/1/2006)*

PLAZA DE MULAS

Plaza de Mulas 2005 Chardonnay (Mendoza) $8. Peach, melon, and other slightly sweet tropical aromas lead into green melon and citrus flavors. Medium-bodied and a bit chewy, with a light, uneven finish that pushes grapefruit and soda cracker. **84 Best Buy** —*M.S. (8/1/2006)*

PRELUDIO

Preludio 2004 Malbec (Mendoza) $18. Granular aromas of berry, earth, and tar precede a vivacious, rather deep palate of lumbering, chewy black-fruit flavors. It feels right, sits right, and tastes right while leaving chocolate and nutmeg on the finish. Fairly classy and definitely well made. Only 400 cases made. **89** —*M.S. (12/1/2006)*

Preludio 2003 Malbec (Mendoza) $16. Rubber and cinnamon aromas along with sweet fruits and bubble gum make for an attractive, easy-to-get nose. Very ripe and saturated in the mouth, with blackberry and plum flavors. Not ultra complex, in fact it's kind of monotone. But what's here is easy to like and tasty. **87** —*M.S. (12/31/2005)*

Preludio 2003 Acorde #1 Reserve Malbec-Cabernet Sauvignon (Mendoza) $36. This blend of Malbec and Cabernet Sauvignon is very woody, so much so that the nose offers mostly cinnamon and green lumber. The palate, however, is ultracreamy, with vanilla and milk chocolate running the show. Seems a bit sticky and oaky. Could use more uncut fruit. **85** — *M.S. (6/1/2006)*

Preludio 2004 Tempranillo (Mendoza) $16. A full-octane wine with notes of olive and berry on the bouquet. It runs bright in the mouth, with zippy cherry and cassis flavors. Later on you detect olive at the core, but that's admirably covered by a blanket of fine oak. Good in its class. **86** — *M.S. (12/1/2006)*

Preludio 2003 Tempranillo (Mendoza) $14. Rustic and bulky, but not without its merits. The bouquet begins with sweet maple syrup aromas that set the stage for cassis and black plum flavors. It's a touch stewy and chocolaty, but the earthy tannins manage to add edge and teeth. **85** — *M.S. (11/15/2005)*

PULMARY

Pulmary 2004 Donaria Bonarda (Mendoza) $20. Rather rubbery and raisiny, with some fruitcake on the nose. Additional raisin and plum on the palate is backed by hard tannins. Like many Bonarda, this wine is tough and brawny. Subtlety is not its hallmark. **83** —*M.S. (12/31/2005)*

Pulmary 2004 Donaria Malbec (Mendoza) $20. A touch lean and green, with hints of rhubarb and burning brush. Raspberry and strawberry flavors are dominant, but there's a hole in the middle of the palate that renders the mouthfeel somewhat hollow. Finishes top-heavy, with a sweet superficiality. **83** —*M.S. (12/31/2005)*

QUARA

Quara 2004 Cabernet Sauvignon (Cafayate) $9. Plum and leather work the nose, while jammy, jumbled red-fruit flavors carry the palate. Coffee and mocha on the finish are offset by spiky acidity. Very unusual Cabernet. **84** —*M.S. (11/15/2005)*

Quara 2004 Malbec (Cafayate) $9. Damp and murky, with aromas of burnt toast and flavors of beets and raspberry. The feel is round and lactic, with unfocused grapy fruit. **82** —*M.S. (11/15/2005)*

Quara 2004 Merlot (Cafayate) $9. Easygoing, with plum and berry flavors. Turns a bit snappy and upright in the mouth, but maintains a fresh, fruit-packed personality. While nothing really stands out, the whole is solid and largely likable. **84** —*M.S. (11/15/2005)*

Quara 2004 Tannat (Cafayate) $9. Solid enough, with standard black-fruit aromas that show raisin but also adequate freshness. Black cherry is the dominant flavor component, backed by a finish that's decently textured and a touch chocolaty. Not great, but not bad for Tannat. **83** —*M.S. (8/1/2006)*

Quara 2004 Torrontès (Cafayate) $9. Floral and fresh, with some blossom and honey aromas. Rather plump and soft, but with enough acidity to keep the feel solid. Flavors of banana, papaya, citrus, and stone fruit are fresh and tasty. Proves that Cafayate is the prime region for Torrontès. **85 Best Buy** —*M.S. (12/31/2005)*

RAZA

Raza 2003 Limited Edition Malbec (Famatina Valley) $40. Dense and full of plum, spice, smoke, and char. The palate is up to the task, offering lively, concentrated berry and black cherry flavors. A complete wine with good balance. It has a purpose and a way of getting there. **89** —*M.S. (11/1/2006)*

Raza 2004 Silver Reserve Malbec (Famatina Valley) $13. Nice and spicy, with exotic aromatics like citrus peel, coriander, and browned butter. Of course, there's solid berry fruit in there as well. Seems a touch pastry-like in the mouth, where sugars and cream come in waves. Chunky in the long run, but fun and big. **86** —*M.S. (11/1/2006)*

Raza 2003 Limited Edition Syrah (Famatina Valley) $40. Heavy and dark, with raisin, animal crackers, and tobacco aromas. Offbeat on the palate, with forceful but awkward blackberry flavors and cloying, hard-hitting tannins. Short flavors; hot and baked. **83** —*M.S. (11/1/2006)*

Raza 2004 Silver Reserve Syrah (Famatina Valley) $13. Standard aromas in the berry and beet range is what you get on the nose. The body hits hard on the palate, where the fruit flavors seem rugged, juicy, and a bit tangy. Settles on the finish, offering clarity in a tight, modest package. **84** —*M.S. (8/1/2006)*

Raza 2004 Silver Reserve Torrontès (Famatina Valley) $13. This is an active, zesty Torrontès, which is the best way to find it. Grapefruit and fresh celery are intertwined on the nose, while fresh apple and citrus fruits work the palate. Totally clean and easy. **86** —*M.S. (8/1/2006)*

RELINCHO

Relincho 2002 Cabernet Sauvignon-Merlot (Mendoza) $7. This 50/50 blend features apple skin, cherry, and other berry aromas and flavors, all wrapped in a coating of hard candy. The finish is like a sucking lozenge and the mouthfeel is rock hard. **82** —*M.S. (3/1/2005)*

RENACER

Renacer 2004 Punto Final Malbec (Perdriel) $11. One of the year's best red wine values has to be this fully ripe and totally structured Malbec made by Alberto Antonini (winemaker for Altos Las Hormigas) and Hector Durigutti. The color almost gives away its power; and if not, the aromas of marinated meat, plum, and blackberry essence will. Saturated, thick and modern, but made right. Perfect with beef. **91 Best Buy** — *M.S. (11/1/2006)*

Renacer 2004 Punto Final Reserva Malbec (Perdriel) $18. Charcoal and ripe berry fruit announce this as a serious, masculine Malbec. The palate answers the bell, delivering tight blackberry and cassis flavors in front of a tannic, sturdy finish. Shows great foundation and potential; best in late 2007 into 2008. **92 Editors' Choice** —*M.S. (12/1/2006)*

RICARDO SANTOS

Ricardo Santos 2005 La Madras Vineyard Malbec (Mendoza) $18. Savory and ripe. The nose starts with earthy fruit combined with leather and mushroom. The palate is deep and full, with notes of brandied cherries, sautéed porcini, and chocolate. Fades a bit on the finish, leaving coffee and bitter chocolate. Very good, with just the slightest herbal character. **89** —*M.S. (12/1/2006)*

Ricardo Santos 2004 La Madras Vineyard Malbec (Mendoza) $17. Bright boysenberry aromas offer a touch of sugar beet and perfume, while the palate is all about jammy berry flavors with dark, lush shadings. Firm on the finish, with no holes to speak of. Undeniably ripe, with a good feel and plenty of richness. **88** —*M.S. (6/1/2006)*

Ricardo Santos 2003 La Madras Vineyard Malbec (Mendoza) $18. Far more lean and raw than expected, with an overriding green tobacco note to the nose. Grassy on the palate, with raspberry and a bit of rhubarb. Finishes sweety and jammy, with some protruding tannins. Not a bad wine but disappointing compared to the previous vintage. **84** —*M.S. (12/31/2005)*

Ricardo Santos 2002 La Madras Vineyard Malbec (Maipú) $17. Smooth and full of cool aromas like cola, damp earth, and berry pie. The mouth comes alive with vivacious plum and blackberry fruit, while the finish features drive and length. Juicy and lush, with a saturated palate and fine balance. A single-vineyard wine with poise and class. **90 Editors' Choice** —*M.S. (7/1/2004)*

RINCON PRIVADO

Rincon Privado 1996 Special Reserve Cabernet Sauvignon (San Rafael) $20. This is quite an old wine, yet it's still alive and kicking. The bouquet is mature, with oak and briar showing strongly. The fruit, however, is fading toward cranberry and underripe plum, while the finish is discordant: It's fat and chewy, unlike the lean palate. **83** —*M.S. (5/1/2003)*

Rincon Privado 1999 Malbec (San Rafael) $11. Floral aromas lead the way, followed by some lavender. The palate, however, doesn't keep with the program; it's peppery and sharp, with only a dab of cherry and cranberry fruit. With its lean structure and racy acidity, this must be served with food. **84** —*M.S. (5/1/2003)*

Rincon Privado 1999 Merlot (San Rafael) $11. Offers some spice and tobacco, but also some green character. The palate is snappy and fresh, with cherry flavors. And despite some aggressive tannins, the finish is fairly positive. **84** —*M.S. (5/1/2003)*

Rincon Privado 1999 Pinot Noir (San Rafael) $11. One sniff tells you this is something different, but what exactly it might be is harder to determine. The nose is spicy, if a bit stemmy, and the palate delivers some raspberry and vanilla. The finish is lean and not too forward, and ultimately it tastes little like the Pinot Noir most of us are used to. **84** —*M.S. (5/1/2003)*

ROMANCE

Romance 2002 Red Blend (Mendoza) $8. A concept wine aimed at capitalizing on Argentina's reputation as a romantic, tango-loving country. The blend of Bonarda, Malbec, and Cabernet is out of the ordinary, with strange, ultrasweet flavors that turn sour upon deeper inspection. **82** —*M.S. (7/1/2004)*

ROSELL BOHER

Rosell Boher NV Brut Champagne Blend (Argentina) $27. A touch gassy, with mild but heavy orange and other citrus flavors. Good in terms of feel and bead, with a welcome overall character. Has its good points, but not quite complete in all categories. **85** —*M.S. (12/31/2004)*

Rosell Boher 1999 Grande Cuvée Champagne Blend (Argentina) $40. A little bit amber as it shows off nice Pinot Noir color. Quite yeasty, toasty, and stylish. A pleasant surprise from Argentina; this bubbly shows style and polish. The palate is bodied, with spicy peach and light berry flavors. Peppery and long, with a plump, laudable mouthfeel. **89 Editors' Choice** —*M.S. (12/31/2004)*

SALENTEIN

Salentein 2003 Cabernet Sauvignon (Uco Valley) $19. A wine of character. The bouquet takes time to unfold, dealing earthy aromas and desert sage. Flavors of black cherry and cassis are firm and forceful, while the tannins are pronounced. A little clumsy and rugged now; should be better in a year or so. **89 Cellar Selection** —*M.S. (12/1/2006)*

Salentein 2002 Cabernet Sauvignon (Mendoza) $18. Nice and full, with aromas of stewed fruit, tobacco, leather, and black pepper. Impeccably sturdy and upright, but never hard nor tannic. Instead it's full of plum, liqueur, and chocolate flavors as well as some smoky espresso. Throughout it shows the right touch of power and pizzazz. **90** —*M.S. (3/1/2005)*

Salentein 2001 Cabernet Sauvignon (Mendoza) $18. A New World Cabernet close in structure to a good Sonoma bottling. Rich and ripe, with black currant, cassis, and herb flavors and rich, distinguished tannins. Oak adds subtlely and does not overwhelm. Easily as good as many California bottlings costing 2 or 3 times as much. **91** —*S.H. (1/1/2002)*

Salentein 2002 El Portillo Cabernet Sauvignon (Mendoza) $9. Piquant, with red bell pepper and faint plum and cherry aromas. Too weedy in the mouth to rate higher. **81** —*M.S. (7/1/2004)*

Salentein 2003 El Portillo Chardonnay (Mendoza) $9. Creamy yet dry on the nose, with a dusty overall bouquet and not too much fruit. The fruit on the palate is sweet but nondescript. Possibly too acidic as well. **84** —*M.S. (7/1/2004)*

Salentein 2004 Malbec (Uco Valley) $19. Lovely up front, with lavender, licorice, and pepper accenting live-wire blackberry aromas. Jammy and extracted in the mouth, with pure berry flavors. This is a mountain of a wine that doesn't pull its punches. Expect weight, tannin, and extract but also a lot of flavor. **90** —*M.S. (12/1/2006)*

Salentein 2003 Malbec (Mendoza) $18. Rich and sweet, with kirsch and blueberry fruit aromas mixed with molasses and marzipan. It keeps that sweet profile on the palate, where baked plum, brandied prune, and fruitcake take over. Finishes fairly spicy and chocolaty, with a saturated, meaty body. **88** —*M.S. (12/31/2005)*

Salentein 2002 Malbec (Mendoza) $18. Better than the '01, but still acidic and tannic. That said, it does offer attractive coffee and coconut aromas, and also interplay between cocoa and plum. The flavor mix is mostly complete, and there's some nice spice to the finish. **86** —*M.S. (7/1/2004)*

Salentein 2001 Malbec (Mendoza) $9. A slight wine with rosy aromas and not much else. Far from overpowering, it's kind of meek, with lean but clean fruit. Given Salentein's wondrous production facility and lofty intentions, this is disappointing. **84** —*M.S. (7/1/2004)*

Salentein 2001 Malbec (Mendoza) $18. This is a strong wine, similar in flavor and structure to a big mountain Cabernet, but with distinctive flavors. It pours very dark and closed. Airing reveals grilled meat, cassis, and plum aromas. Drinks dry and powerful, with big but accessible tannins. **91** —*S.H. (1/1/2002)*

Salentein 2002 El Portillo Malbec (Mendoza) $9. Lots of oak and chunky aromas lead it astray. In the mouth, it's better, with racy red fruit and some pepper. Still, it's not warm and cuddly like a Malbec of this type should be. **84** —*M.S. (7/1/2004)*

Salentein 2001 Finca el Portillo Malbec (Uco Valley) $9. A winery to watch is Salentein, the maker of this densely colored wine that features inky blackberry aromas along with hints of spice and tobacco. Lush but firm, with moderate tannins that make themselves felt. A streak of toasty oak creates coffee and pepper on the back palate. **87 Best Buy** —*M.S. (12/1/2003)*

Salentein 2002 Merlot (Mendoza) $18. Lugubrious, earthy, and stewy, with leather, mint, and barnyard aromas. The palate, once aired out, shows muscled-up plum and burnt coffee, while the finish deals chocolate and starchy tannin. Seems to be aiming higher than it reaches. **83** —*M.S. (11/15/2005)*

Salentein 2001 Merlot (Mendoza) $19. Quite nice, with heavy, masculine aromas of leather and charcoal spicing up the dark berry fruit that's on display. Round in the mouth, with cherry and raspberry flavors preceding a chewy, chocolaty finish. Spreads out nicely from front to back. **88** —*M.S. (7/1/2004)*

Salentein 2002 El Portillo Merlot (Mendoza) $9. Spicy and dull throughout, with peppery aromas and a tannic mouthfeel. Out of proportion and missing something. **82** —*M.S. (7/1/2004)*

Salentein 2003 Pinot Noir (Uco Valley) $19. This funky Argentinean Pinot pours on the rubber, turned earth, and heavy fruit aromas, and then backs them up with a full, meaty, starchy palate that's loaded with dry cherry and red-pepper flavors. A robust, grabby wine with virtues and question marks. **86** —*M.S. (12/1/2006)*

Salentein 2003 Finca el Portillo Sauvignon Blanc (Mendoza) $9. The nose is slightly more vegetal than ideal, but in the mouth there is both good acids and body. Flavors of baked apples and dried mangoes seem sweet, and that's because residual sugar is present. **85** —*M.S. (7/1/2004)*

Salentein 2001 Shiraz (Mendoza) $18. Like a big Aussie Shiraz, young and jammy, opening with a blast of blueberry, blackberry, cassis, white chocolate, and vanilla. Huge in the mouth, collossal, stuffed with fruity-berry flavors, but very dry. The tannins are especially rich and well-textured. Great drinking, and best paired with roasts or even game. **90** —*S.H. (1/1/2002)*

Salentein 2002 Syrah (Mendoza) $18. Jammy and saturated, with ripe plum, berry, and tar aromas. It's fairly sweet and hedonistic in the mouth, but with enough pulsing acidity to keep things in balance. Smoky, racy, and juicy on the back palate; this is one of the better Salentein wines we've tried lately. **88** —*M.S. (3/1/2005)*

Salentein 2003 Syrah (Uco Valley) $19. Salentein, after a few years of finding its way in Tupungato, has hit the mark with this tobacco- and spice-driven Syrah. The bouquet is ripe, with a hint of prune and earth, while the palate is full, juicy, and full of berries, vanilla, and coconut. Modern and woody, but satisfying. **90** —*M.S. (12/1/2006)*

Salentein 2004 Finca El Portillo Syrah (Alto Valle de Uco) $9. Stewy and condensed, with beet, rhubarb, and baked beans on the nose. Jumbled and hard to define in the mouth, with a soft finish that introduces a touch of green bean. **82** —*M.S. (4/1/2006)*

Salentein 2002 El Portillo Tempranillo (Mendoza) $9. Hot and spicy aromas mix with raspberry notes, while the core is tart and leathery. This wine needs some work. **82** —*M.S. (7/1/2004)*

SAN HUBERTO

San Huberto 2005 Bonarda (Aminga Valley) $9. The bouquet on this bold red amounts to one big blast of fruit, nothing more or less. The palate matches the nose, with black plum, blueberry, and cola flavors. Broad in the mouth and fiercely tannic. Spirited but a little untamed. **84** —*M.S. (12/1/2006)*

San Huberto 2002 Bonarda (Aminga Valley) $7. Open and light, with raspberry and foresty aromas. Very lean on the palate. Shows red raspberry and pepper flavors in front of an innocuous, flyweight finish. A thin wine that manages to taste decent. **82** —*M.S. (10/1/2004)*

San Huberto 2002 Cabernet Sauvignon (Aminga Valley) $8. Reduced and tight on the nose, with sharp, foresty cherry and berry flavors. Straightforward and firm. **83** —*M.S. (10/1/2004)*

San Huberto 2003 Crianza Cabernet Sauvignon (Argentina) $10. A little bit of bramble and green on the nose, but by and large this wine is solid. The palate offers sweetness and brown sugar along with zesty fruit, while the tannic structure and persistence are unavoidable. **85 Best Buy** —*M.S. (6/1/2006)*

San Huberto 2005 Chardonnay (Aminga Valley) $10. Sweet as can be, with strong aromas of talcum powder and air freshener. Rather lean in the mouth, with a watery, processed flavor profile. Not awful but not much to write home about. **80** —*M.S. (6/1/2006)*

San Huberto 2002 Chardonnay (Aminga Valley) $8. Light pear, pineapple, and honey aromas don't hold up to much airing or swirling. In the mouth, it's all citrus, largely lemon, and orange. Finishes perky and zesty, but without much focus. Hails from La Rioja. **83** —*M.S. (10/1/2004)*

San Huberto 2005 Malbec (Aminga Valley) $10. A wine that seems to be striving for more than it can deliver. The nose is jammy and big, with maple, toast, and other sweet wood-driven notes. Candied and ripe throughout, with marshmallow and vanilla on the finish. Clumsy in the final analysis. **83** —*M.S. (4/1/2006)*

San Huberto 2002 Malbec (La Rioja) $8. This La Rioja Malbec is warm and leathery, with basic fruit and pickle-barrel aromas. The flavor profile

ARGENTINA

is made up of meaty plum and chocolate, yet the finish is lean and woody. **83** —*M.S. (10/1/2004)*

San Huberto 1997 Malbec (Argentina) $9. This sweet and slightly syrupy blend of cola and raspberries turns tart and lemony on the finish—a combination of flavors and textures that don't quite meld together. **82** —*J.C. (5/1/2002)*

San Huberto 2003 Crianza Malbec (Argentina) $10. Displays a nice ruby tint in front of full, ripe, almost smoky aromas. The palate is a bit fat and sweet, with dark plum and blackberry flavors offset by a slight dab of buttery oak. A simple, one-note kind of red, but a good one nonetheless. **85 Best Buy** —*M.S. (4/1/2006)*

San Huberto 2002 Medalla d'Oro Crianza Malbec (Aminga Valley) $10. Heavy and burnt, with tire-rubber aromas perched aside leather and black olive. Carob and plum flavors with a soy sauce note to the finish. Not a lot going on here. **81** —*M.S. (10/1/2004)*

San Huberto 2005 Torrontès (Aminga Valley) $9. Pale in color, almost silver, with light but fresh floral aromas. A touch simple on the palate, but still round and tasty enough to earn points; you'll find attractive pear and cinnamon flavors. Lightweight yet fluid on the finish. An easygoing but likable rendition of Torrontès. **86 Best Buy** —*M.S. (4/1/2006)*

San Huberto 2002 Torrontès (Aminga Valley) $7. Pungent, with aromas of green herbs, litchi fruit, and green melon. Starts better than it finishes, and along the way you'll find moderate peach and melon flavors riding on a competent palate. **84** —*M.S. (10/1/2004)*

SAN POLO

San Polo 2003 Auka Malbec (San Carlos) $15. Dark as night, with shiny edges to the violet luster. Pretty, floral, and fairly deep on the nose, with caramel and chocolate. This is a forward, power-packed red with extract and intensity of flavor. Aggressive but with a full tank that should allow it to go the distance. **88** —*M.S. (7/1/2005)*

San Polo 2004 Auka Merlot (San Carlos) $15. Simple red-fruit aromas are o.k. but fail to register above that. The palate is tasty enough, with sweet plum and blackberry flavors. Creamy on the finish, yet a bit candied and cloying. Improves with airing. **84** —*M.S. (12/31/2005)*

San Polo 2003 Auka Merlot (San Carlos) $15. Standard jammy fruit sets the stage for moderate black cherry and plum flavors. Seems hard on the palate, with jagged tannins that will drill away if left unwashed. Fairly flavorful, but lacking in charm. **83** —*M.S. (7/1/2005)*

SAN TELMO

San Telmo 2000 Cabernet Sauvignon (Mendoza) $10. **82** —*C.S. (5/1/2002)*

San Telmo 2003 Chardonnay (Mendoza) $7. Smells hot but neutral, with meek flavors of citrus and pineapple. Lots of vibrant acidity creates a scouring mouthfeel, but what is there to say about the bland flavors of soda crackers and citrus pith? **82** —*M.S. (7/1/2005)*

San Telmo 2000 Chardonnay (Mendoza) $10. Very light in color, much like hay. A mute nose follows, barely offering something akin to applesauce. It's sugary on the palate, with a buttery finish. Potent acidity prevents it from being ponderous, yet it's still a heavyweight. **82** —*M.S. (11/15/2001)*

San Telmo 2004 Malbec (Mendoza) $7. Gritty on the nose, with hints of raisin and chocolate. Big in the mouth, but bulky and wobbly, with cooked plum and raisin flavors. Finishes a touch flat, with black cherry notes. **83** —*M.S. (11/15/2005)*

San Telmo 2003 Malbec (Mendoza) $7. Jammy, sweet, and leathery on the nose, with a kick of sourness. The palate is common, with medium red fruit that's strawberry-raspberry in style. Adequate on the palate, and generally satisfying. **84 Best Buy** —*M.S. (3/1/2005)*

San Telmo 2003 Merlot (Mendoza) $7. Starts with sweaty leather and peanut aromas before moving on to linear, sour flavors. Pure acid on the finish does nothing to make it chummier. **80** —*M.S. (7/1/2005)*

San Telmo 2003 Shiraz (Mendoza) $7. A bit rubbery and raw, but with a hearty backbone. The nose deals plum and black cherry along with some smoky wet leather, while the palate is grapey with a touch of blueberry. Finishes clean and simple. **86 Best Buy** —*M.S. (3/1/2005)*

SANTA EUGENIA

Santa Eugenia 1999 Malbec (Mendoza) $7. **82** —*C.S. (5/1/2002)*

SANTA FAUSTINA

Santa Faustina 2002 Alto Lunlunta Vineyard Malbec (Mendoza) $20. Ripe, with leather, balsamic, and prune aromas. Saturated in the mouth, but ultimately it's narrow in scope. On the finish, creamy oak rises up to leave butter and resin flavors. A fairly big wine with ample barrel influence. **85** —*M.S. (11/1/2006)*

Santa Faustina 2002 Medrano Vineyard Syrah (Mendoza) $20. A heavy load, with berry jam, marshmallow, and other unconvincing aromas. Dark as night but clumsy as can be, with thick flavors and a core sweetness that doesn't seem natural. **80** —*M.S. (11/1/2006)*

SANTA JULIA

Santa Julia 2001 Cabernet Sauvignon (Mendoza) $8. The nose is simple, featuring briar patch, earth, and smoke. Strawberry and cherry flavors ride along the solid palate, and the finish is mostly sweet cherry and some vanilla. **84** —*M.S. (5/1/2003)*

Santa Julia 2000 Cabernet Sauvignon (Mendoza) $8. Flavorful, but very brisk, with moderate-to-high acidity. It's a modest wine, with blackberry and coffee aromas and flavors, slight tobacco accents and a short finish. It's good, but not as satisfying an overall package as the other reds at the same level of the range. **84** *(12/15/2001)*

Santa Julia 1996 Oak Reserva Malbec Cabernet Sauvignon (Mendoza) $10. **87 Best Buy** *(5/1/2000)*

Santa Julia 2005 Organica Cabernet Sauvignon (Mendoza) $9. Easy, light, and mildly candied, with pure cherry and berry aromas. Cherry and raspberry flavors are ripe and open, with good balance. Not the deepest, most dense wine on the market but classy and solid. Good for the money. **86 Best Buy** —*M.S. (8/1/2006)*

Santa Julia 2004 Reserva Cabernet Sauvignon (Mendoza) $12. A lot of up-front oak greets you, with sweet fruit and brown sugar in reserve. Cassis, plum, and vanilla work the palate, which has some edge and tannin to it. Fairly well balanced, with some structure. No one will mistake it for sophisticated but what's here works. **85** —*M.S. (11/1/2006)*

Santa Julia 2002 Reserva Cabernet Sauvignon (Mendoza) $10. Rosy and floral on the bouquet, with chalk, black fruit, and raisin. Healthy across the palate, with big, grabby tannins driving home plum, cherry, and chocolate flavors. Plenty of energy and verve on display. **87 Best Buy** —*M.S. (10/1/2004)*

Santa Julia 2000 Reserva Cabernet Sauvignon (Mendoza) $11. Full, with blackberry aromas, tobacco, and a big, dry palate with plenty of dark fruit and wood. There's not a lot of nuance or dimension, but plenty of scale and wood-driven length. As with the reserve Chardonnay, a modest scaling back on the oak regimen would allow the fruit to show more, yielding a more balanced and attractive wine. **86** *(12/15/2001)*

Santa Julia 1999 Reserva Cabernet Sauvignon (Mendoza) $10. At first, the oak element is strong, so much so that you smell sawdust. But after it airs out, black fruit takes over. Although it's not made for the cellar, it should evolve over the next year or so based on its healthy tannins and tight structure. **84** —*M.S. (11/15/2001)*

Santa Julia 2005 Chardonnay (Mendoza) $8. Awkward, with early aromatics akin to sauerkraut. Airing doesn't totally shake that funky character, and the fruit seems on the cooked side. Acceptable mouthfeel. **81** —*M.S. (6/1/2006)*

Santa Julia 2002 Chardonnay (Mendoza) $9. Creamy and sweet up front, with some butterscotch on the nose. Pear and papaya flavors are tropical and sweet, and the melony finish is warm and satisfying. Quite fruity and fun to drink. **85** —*M.S. (2/1/2004)*

Santa Julia 2001 Chardonnay (Mendoza) $7. The better side of the nose takes time to reveal itself. At first it's all apple cider, peanuts, and popcorn, but then fresh apples and spice appear. In the mouth it's a little chewy, with more of that dominant apple character. A serviceable, drinkable wine, but nothing special. **83** —*M.S. (7/1/2002)*

Santa Julia 2000 Chardonnay (Mendoza) $7. The distinct aroma of butterscotch plays heavily on the nose, followed by pear and nectarine flavors.

Good, healthy acidity drives the flavors home. Finishes with equally full flavors and plenty of pop. **84 Best Buy** —*M.S. (11/15/2001)*

Santa Julia 2005 Organica Chardonnay (Mendoza) $9. Starts with apple covered in oak-based caramel and vanilla, but loses its focus as it evolves. The palate is a mishmash of melon, citrus, and papaya, while the overall take is that its less than stellar but not offensive. In this case, the organic qualifier isn't a boost. **83** —*M.S. (6/1/2006)*

Santa Julia 2004 Reserva Chardonnay (Mendoza) $12. With its vanilla and caramel accents on pure pear and apple fruit, this is a good, basic Argentinean Chard. The palate is clean and forward, with solid apple forming the framework. Shows just enough butter and toast to warm it up, but it's not a heavy wine. Smooth and easy. **87 Best Buy** —*M.S. (6/1/2006)*

Santa Julia 2002 Reserva Chardonnay (Mendoza) $10. Smoky and toasty at the edges, with lots of fresh oak resulting in a nose defined by coconut. Apple, melon, and banana flavors precede a finish that's light and oaky, with some pepper. Arguably a bit too woody for this level of Chardonnay. **85** —*M.S. (10/1/2004)*

Santa Julia 2000 Reserva Chardonnay (Mendoza) $9. This straightforward apple and toast-dominated Chardonnay has medium weight and decent length. It's decidedly mainstream, a bit too one-dimensionally so. But it's still tasty in that mode, and oak-lovers will savor the spicy wood that comes up very strongly on the close. Again, good, but here a more reserved use of oak might yield a wine of more nuance and better balance. **85** *(12/15/2001)*

Santa Julia 2003 Malbec (Mendoza) $9. Sweet and candied on the nose, with a blueberry core. In the mouth, you get sweet, grapy fruit prior to a large, meaty finish. A bit awkward and gangly now, and it shouldn't really progress much. **84** —*M.S. (10/1/2004)*

Santa Julia 2001 Malbec (Mendoza) $9. A lightly extracted Malbec with clean, pure flavors. Some floral, lavender aromas accent blueberry notes, while flavors of pepper and baking spice add character to more typical black plum and blueberry. The finish is lengthy, dry, and warming. Balance, freshness, and a soft mouthfeel are all pluses. **87 Best Buy** — *M.S. (5/1/2003)*

Santa Julia 2000 Malbec (Mendoza) $7. Earthy, dark cherry aromas and flavors are up-front in this moderately full, slightly rustic wine. Big on the palate, with just a hint of a bitter note, it closes with a peppery quality not entirely unlike Zinfandel. This solid red will be a great companion to grilled meats. **86** *(12/15/2001)*

Santa Julia 2004 Reserva Malbec (Mendoza) $12. Solid, ripe, and tasty, with hard rubber, dark berry, and toast on the nose. Jammy and big on first take, yet it runs a bit thin once you bore your way to the center. Still, everything is lively and easy to like. Would be just right with a burger fresh off the grill. **87 Best Buy** —*M.S. (11/1/2006)*

Santa Julia 2002 Reserva Malbec (Mendoza) $10. Leather and char define the bouquet of this rather reserved reserva. Hardly a grape avalanche, this Malbec is dry, peppery, and displays hints of cherry and coffee. Fairly rugged and tight, with firm tannins. Good for everyday drinking or as an introduction to Malbec. **86** —*M.S. (12/1/2003)*

Santa Julia 2000 Reserva Malbec (Mendoza) $11. A bouquet of dark, earthy Malbec fruit and tangy oak opens this dense, compact red. The mouth shows similar flavors and a full, chewy feel. Finishes with firm but not harsh tannins, spice, and earth notes. A fine candidate for a few years' cellaring, which should allow it to open it up hopefully adding elegance to its considerable power. **88 Best Buy** *(12/15/2001)*

Santa Julia 1999 Reserva Malbec (Mendoza) $10. Strong oak along with some rubbery notes on the nose. It's positively woody from start to finish, with a taste profile of plummy fruit and black licorice. All in all it's typical of the grape type and region, but maybe a tad too woody. **84** — *M.S. (11/15/2001)*

Santa Julia 2000 Merlot (Mendoza) $8. This tangy and light-to-medium weight wine offers bright red fruit with slightly darker berry, chocolate, and earth shadings. Good acidity keeps it lively on the palate, as does the tannic tang of the moderately long finish. Just what a value Merlot should be. **85 Best Buy** *(12/15/2001)*

Santa Julia 2001 Merlot (Mendoza) $8. The bouquet offers briar, tomato, and spice, but not much fruit. The palate deals a lean hand of rhubarb

and cherry, while the finish is fair to middling, but does deliver length. Firm tannins and healthy acids keep it in balance. **85** —*M.S. (5/1/2003)*

Santa Julia 2005 Pinot Grigio (Mendoza) $8. Hints of melon and citrus on the nose, but the palate is limited in what it offers. Flavors of dried apricot is the best you get from this short, somewhat bitter wine. Not concentrated; stretched thin. **80** —*M.S. (11/1/2006)*

Santa Julia 2000 Malbec-Cab Sauv Red Blend (Mendoza) $7. Like the straight Malbec, this blend has an attractive, slightly rustic quality. Here the Cabernet fruit adds both a darker note and perhaps palate smoothness. Full-flavored and nicely textured, it ends with moderate tannins, cassis flavors, earth, and meaty accents. **86** *(12/15/2001)*

Santa Julia 2001 Red Blend (Mendoza) $9. The nose borders on being neutral, and the palate is leafy and dry, offering just a touch of strawberry flavor. On the finish, spice notes rise up, but they're short-lived and lack power. **83** —*M.S. (5/1/2003)*

Santa Julia NV Extra Brut Sparkling Blend (Mendoza) $13. Sweet from the start, with maple and pear on the bouquet. More soft than sturdy, with a candied palate that offers round, almost sugary citrus flavors. Easy for a glass or two, but without the voltage to go further. **85** —*M.S. (6/1/2006)*

Santa Julia 2005 Torrontès (Mendoza) $8. Not unkind aromas of bath oil and flowers set the stage for slightly pithy citrus and melon flavors. Registers as chunky in the mouth, with additional pith and a slight bitterness to the finish. Pretty good overall. **84 Best Buy** —*M.S. (8/1/2006)*

Santa Julia 2003 Torrontès (Mendoza) $7. Look at it and it's nearly colorless. The nose, however, is out there: there's lychee fruit, flowers, and pine sol in abundance. Lime is the predominant fruit, and there is a zesty acidic beam through the middle. Doesn't seem as complete as past examples. **83** —*M.S. (2/1/2004)*

Santa Julia 2002 Torrontès (Argentina) $8. After Chardonnay, Torrontès is Argentina's other white. This one is light and semisweet, with nice acids, a pretty floral bouquet, and simple but clean melon, kiwi, and lychee flavors. Once the white grape of 16th-century Spanish missionaries, Torrontès has adapted well to Argentina, just about the only place it's grown these days. **85** —*M.S. (11/15/2003)*

Santa Julia 2001 Torrontès (Mendoza) $7. This bright, spicy white made from an uncommon variety, is a notable value that deserves attention. The vibrant lime, tangerine, and lychee aromas and full, well-fruited mouthfeel are a winning combination. Turns drier on the finish, maintaining interest from stem to stern. Lovely on its own, and will pair well with spicy foods, too. **87 Best Buy** *(12/15/2001)*

Santa Julia 2000 Torrontès (Mendoza) $7. This bright, spicy white of an uncommon variety is a notable value deserving attention. The vibrant lime, tangerine, and lychee aromas and full, well-fruited mouthfeel are a winning combination. Turns drier on the finish, maintaining interest from stem to stern. Lovely on its own, and will pair well with spicy foods, too. **87 Best Buy** *(12/15/2001)*

Santa Julia 2000 Torrontès (Mendoza) $7. Litchi and nectarine are prominent in this vivacious white, rarely found outside of Argentina. This version is fun and lively, with plenty of zip. Finishes in crisp, defined, lengthy layers. Definitely worth a try. **86 Best Buy** —*M.S. (11/15/2001)*

Santa Julia 2000 Tardio Torrontès (Mendoza) $10. Very sweet and inviting aromas of litchi and gardenias are major components of the pleasant bouquet on this late-harvest wine. Honey and clove flavors; perfectly fresh and balanced. If you like Moscato d'Asti, (minus the bubbles) try this. **85 Best Buy** —*M.S. (11/15/2001)*

Santa Julia 2004 Tardío Torrontès (Mendoza) $13. Floral as always, with pineapple and lemon aromas. Lemon-lime is the lead player on the palate, with freshness present throughout. Has good feel and balance but limited depth of flavor and almost no complexity. An easy drinker. **86** — *M.S. (8/1/2006)*

Santa Julia 2001 Tardio Late Harvest Torrontès (Mendoza) $12. Fresh and light, with pineapple aromas and some citrus zest. The palate is lithe, pretty, and packed with spicy peach and pear flavors. The finish comes in layers. This is one of Argentina's best Torrontès. **86** —*M.S. (5/1/2003)*

Santa Julia 2005 Viognier (Mendoza) $9. Smells like a tropical fruit salad, with chunky, flat pineapple in the lead. Diluted melon is the main flavor,

ARGENTINA

with some grapefruit coming on late. Short on texture and depth. **82** —*M.S. (11/1/2006)*

Santa Julia 2002 Viognier (Mendoza) $12. Although this wine has little in common with French or Californian Viognier, it's fairly solid yet bland. Toasty, nutty aromas mingle with pear and melon, while in the mouth it tastes of apples and lemon rind. Some pineapple, vanilla, and banana are the lasting flavors. **83** —*M.S. (2/1/2004)*

Santa Julia 2002 Viognier (Mendoza) $8. The bouquet of flowers, honey, and apples is nice, as is the palate, which is round and full of coconut, banana, and other exotic fruits. Some tangerines and limes dance together on the rather big and full finish. **85** —*M.S. (5/1/2003)*

SEPTIMA

Septima 2003 Cabernet Sauvignon (Mendoza) $8. Funky on the nose, with aromas of cream cheese, green bean, and red fruit. Beets and cherries carry the palate to a cloying, immensely sugary palate. Struggles as Cabernet. **81** —*M.S. (3/1/2005)*

Septima 2001 Cabernet Sauvignon (Mendoza) $9. A mix of leather, hard cheese, and grass on the nose lacks the rich cassis and cherry notes Cabernet is known for. The palate is compact and chewy, with carob and herbs mixed into the fruit. A finish of oak and dill turns dull upon inspection. **84** —*M.S. (2/1/2004)*

Septima 2002 Reserva Cabernet Sauvignon-Malbec (Mendoza) $14. This Cab-Malbec mix starts with sweet, syrupy aromas that grow more masculine with airing, with violet and rose petal scents along with some oak-driven caramel. The palate is round and sizable, with chocolate and plum flavors. Finishes meaty and chunky. From a newer winery owned by Codorníu of Spain. **88** —*M.S. (11/15/2004)*

Septima 2003 Malbec (Mendoza) $8. Powerfully oaked, with initial aromas of cedar shavings and asphalt. Airing softens it up, revealing black cherry, smoke, leather, and protruding, firm tannins. **87 Best Buy** —*M.S. (11/15/2004)*

Septima 2002 Malbec (Mendoza) $9. From the prime growing area of Agrelo, this relative newcomer is owned by the Codorníu company from Spain, and it's really a find. The nose is perfectly pure and round, with fine berry aromas and a light boost of oak. Otherwise, it's simply a tasty, luscious easy drinker with cola, cherry, and raspberry in spades. Fine balance and poise make it a steal. **88 Best Buy** —*M.S. (12/1/2003)*

Septima 2001 Red Blend (Mendoza) $8. Very bland aromas and equally bland fruit with some rubbery notes make this underwhelming. While not offensive or bad, it's just mute, offering the consumer little to sink his or her teeth into. **81** —*M.S. (5/1/2003)*

SIMONASSI

Simonassi 2003 Estate Malbec (San Rafael) $10. Aromas of light raspberry and cookie dough are a bit sweet, but taken together they are attractive. The palate delivers snappy berry flavors and plenty of tannic kick. It loses a touch of focus as it opens but at $10 it offers more than enough quality. **87 Best Buy** —*M.S. (12/1/2006)*

Simonassi 2004 Premium Malbec (Mendoza) $12. Gets out of the blocks with grassy, almost murky aromas. The palate is loaded with clipped, pinched fruit that's overly acidic and leaves a harsh impression on the cheeks and tongue. A wine that needs better balance and more. **81** —*M.S. (12/1/2006)*

SOLALTO

SolAlto 2005 Chardonnay (San Juan) $8. Here's an inexpensive wine that delivers tasty pear and melon flavors. The body is solid, maybe a bit hefty, but there's enough acidity to keep it on track. Easygoing stuff with no surprises. **85 Best Buy** —*M.S. (6/1/2006)*

SolAlto 2004 Malbec (San Juan) $8. Jumbled, with sweet, soft fruit that is sugary and quite strange. Not exactly off the mark but a hard wine to like. It's sweet and candied and unfocused. **81** —*M.S. (6/1/2006)*

SolAlto 2004 Pinot Grigio (San Juan) $8. Solid if a bit creamy, with apple, pear, and a hint of spice on the nose. Chunky melon and spice flavors work fairly nicely on the soft, smooth palate. Not the most zesty or lively wine, but what's on offer is pretty good. **84 Best Buy** —*M.S. (2/1/2006)*

SORBUS

Sorbus 2004 Malbec (Mendoza) $8. Clean and in your face, with touches of mint and leather to the cherry-dominate bouquet. Good in the mouth, with a nice feel, moderate but noticeable tannins, and fresh plum, berry and integrated oak flavors. Competent and lengthy on the finish. **86 Best Buy** —*M.S. (12/31/2005)*

SOUTHERN WILLOWS

Southern Willows 2002 Merlot (Mendoza) $9. Sharp and sour, with cherry, sucking candy and scouring acidity. Not poor but rather harsh on the palate. **81** —*M.S. (3/1/2005)*

SUBLIMIS

Sublimis 2004 Limited Edition Cabernet Sauvignon (Mendoza) $12. Foresty and damp on the nose, with just a touch of standard red fruit propping things up. Runs leafy and dry in the mouth, with a hard, almost bitter finish. Too tough and tannic to really enjoy. **81** —*M.S. (12/1/2006)*

SUSANA BALBO

Susana Balbo 2001 Malbec (Mendoza) $27. Over two decades of working in Argentina, Susana Balbo has picked up a thing or two about winemaking. Her eponymous Malbec features masculine high-voltage fruit coddled in French oak. The result is a snappy, deep wine with lemony edges and a strong foundation. With 10% each of Cabernet and Bonarda. **89** —*M.S. (12/1/2003)*

Susana Balbo 2005 Crios Malbec (Mendoza) $15. Subtle and smooth from start to finish. The aromas are sly but sturdy, with mocha and blackberry sticking out. The flavor profile is pure black fruit with underlayers of spice and chocolate. A ripe, really good example of approachable Malbec. **90 Best Buy** —*M.S. (12/1/2006)*

TAMARÍ

Tamarí 2004 Reserva Malbec (Mendoza) $12. Smooth and lifted, with bold berry aromas backed by strong lemony oak. Plum and boysenberry form a solid foundation, and off that you get texture and chocolate. Tight, tannic, and with far more good qualities than bad. **85** —*M.S. (8/1/2006)*

Tamarí 2003 Reserva Malbec (Mendoza) $10. Plump, woody, and ultimately too weedy to score better. And the palate and finish are both tight as nails, with heavy tannins. Nowhere near balanced, as it goes in every direction. **80** —*M.S. (11/15/2005)*

TANGO

Tango 2002 Cabernet Sauvignon (Mendoza) $9. Rubbery on the nose, with bold lactic aromas along with spice and red fruit. The sketchy palate reveals cherry and chocolate, and those flavors come with a kick. Fairly aggressive given the depth of fruit and polish. **84** —*M.S. (11/15/2004)*

Tango 2002 Reserve Cabernet Sauvignon (Mendoza) $12. Full and wholesome on the nose, with blackberry, cherry, and smoke aromas. Tastes good as a full package, with a pure finish. A rock-solid wine, clearly the best in the Tango line. **89 Best Buy** —*M.S. (11/15/2004)*

Tango 2002 Chardonnay (Mendoza) $9. A little old by now, but the smooth, light aromas convey additional life and freshness. The palate mixes citrus and apple, while there's some white-pepper spice on the finish. Fairly full, but low-acid. **84** —*M.S. (3/1/2005)*

Tango 2002 Malbec (Mendoza) $9. Prickly aromas are sour; there's just too much rhubarb and bramble to the nose. Texture is the wine's main attribute; the palate is firm and structured, yet soft enough to enjoy. Problem is the flavor profile is marred by mild weediness and green flavors. Incongruous as a whole. **83** —*M.S. (11/15/2004)*

Tango 2001 Malbec (Mendoza) $10. At first you almost have to laugh at the name. Would the Spanish call one of theirs "Bullfight?" That said, the wine itself isn't bad. It's a bit heavy, forceful, and unrefined. What hinders it is a rubbery mouthfeel and a mild burn to the finish. **83** —*M.S. (12/1/2003)*

Tango 2002 Reserve Malbec (Mendoza) $12. A bit uncommon and scattered on the bouquet, but deep digging reveals mincemeat and blueberry notes. The palate offers simple red-fruit flavors prior to a light, tart finish. Fresh and likable. **85** —*M.S. (11/15/2004)*

Tango 2002 Merlot (Mendoza) $9. Quite funky at first, with initial cotton candy aromas that mix in hints of leather and light red fruit. Things find a more even keel aided by time in the glass, and finally it ends softly. Not much stuffing but not bad. **85 Best Buy** —*M.S. (11/15/2004)*

Tango 2002 Syrah (Mendoza) $9. Aromas of leather, tobacco, and rubber border on artificial but hold the line. The fat palate features plum fruit, while the finish turns oaky, buttery, and tangy. Even if this doesn't hit the bull's eye, it's nice enough. **84** —*M.S. (11/15/2004)*

TANGO SUR

Tango Sur 2004 Cabernet Sauvignon (Mendoza) $9. Nondistinguished red wine is how to best describe this one. It has some rhubarb as well as berry, while the feel is racy and zesty. Arguably scratchy and a bit green. **82** —*M.S. (8/1/2006)*

Tango Sur 2003 Cabernet Sauvignon (Mendoza) $8. Raisiny and fat, not exactly the most welcoming notes. Tastes overripe and sugary, with a finish too much like sherry. **80** —*M.S. (3/1/2005)*

Tango Sur 2004 Chardonnay (Mendoza) $9. Light and easy, with honey aromas. White peach and underripe cantaloupe work the flavor profile, followed by almond notes and some creaminess on the finish. Pleasant enough. **83** —*M.S. (4/1/2006)*

Tango Sur 2003 Chardonnay (Mendoza) $8. Clean, simple, and unadulterated, with a pleasant roundness and pure, ripe fruit. The flavors veer toward green apple, citrus, and pineapple, while the finish is warm and clean. An easy, satisfying wine. **85 Best Buy** —*M.S. (3/1/2005)*

Tango Sur 2004 Malbec (Mendoza) $9. Tasty and juicy, like a value Malbec should be. The nose hints at rubber and bacon, but mostly it sports round plum and berry aromas. The palate offers equal amounts of black cherry and raspberry, and the finish is mildly toasty, with a smack of pepper. Shows guts and substance. **86 Best Buy** —*M.S. (4/1/2006)*

Tango Sur 2003 Malbec (Mendoza) $8. Ripe and heavy on the nose, with hints of stewed plum, berries, and chocolate. More chunky prune and plum follows in the mouth. Entirely drinkable but not refined. **83** —*M.S. (3/1/2005)*

Tango Sur 2004 Rosé Malbec (Mendoza) $9. Rubber and funk on the nose give way to cleaner cherry. Flavors of strawberry and raspberry are a bit dilute but not watery. Light and smooth enough late, with a bit of bubble gum but no flab. **84** —*M.S. (4/1/2006)*

Tango Sur 2004 Merlot (Mendoza) $9. Ripe, tight, and fresh, this is what everyday Merlot should be like. There's some roast meat and leather atop cherry on the nose, and behind that there's black fruit, leather, bacon, and pepper flavors. A totally legitimate table wine for a good price. **87 Best Buy** —*M.S. (6/1/2006)*

Tango Sur 2004 Shiraz (Mendoza) $9. Blueberry jam and some violet-like aromas get it off the mark, with plum and black cherry flavors playing second fiddle. Mildly tart and zesty in terms of feel, with a light finish. Mainstream all the way. **84** —*M.S. (6/1/2006)*

Tango Sur 2003 Shiraz (Mendoza) $8. The earthy plum aromas seem common, as if you've been there before. Flavors of plum, berry, and rhubarb, however, are fresh and zesty. Good on the palate and healthy, with decent tannins and some chocolate to the finish. **85 Best Buy** —*M.S. (3/1/2005)*

Tango Sur 2003 Tempranillo (Mendoza) $8. Clean and medium weight, with simple red-fruit and cherry-cola aromas. Forward plum and berry carry the palate, which spreads out with no frills over the finish. Somewhat smoky and burnt on the aftertaste, but still pretty good mainstream stuff. **85 Best Buy** —*M.S. (3/1/2005)*

TAPIZ

Tapiz 2000 Cabernet Sauvignon (Mendoza) $8. The immediate take on the bouquet is one of sweetness and freshness, but deeper down it's earthy, meaty, and mildly green. Vibrant cassis and chocolate flavors grace the palate, but again a hint of green rises up. With good heft, racy acidity, and solid tannins, this qualifies as a good bargain Cab. **85** —*M.S. (11/1/2002)*

Tapiz 1999 Cabernet Sauvignon (Mendoza) $8. Clean, classic Cabernet aromas do a good job of inviting you in. Cassis, vanilla, and herbs mix nicely. The deep-purple color accurately announces the big blackberry flavor. Underneath is some pleasant oak. It finishes mildly hot, but overall it's smooth. **85 Best Buy** —*M.S. (11/15/2001)*

Tapiz 2001 Chardonnay (Mendoza) $8. The flavors are somewhat candied and sweet, but the finish is bold and full of vanilla. Possibly too sweet for high-end drinkers but potentially a mainstream winner. **85** —*M.S. (5/1/2003)*

Tapiz 2000 Chardonnay (Mendoza) $8. Fully ripened fruit was no problem, to judge by the bright, expressive peach, pear, and guava-breadfruit flavors. Good structure, with crisp acids. But one big problem is super oakiness, in one form or another, that's so heavy handed, the wine tastes salty. Sometimes less is more. **84** —*S.H. (7/1/2002)*

Tapiz 1999 Chardonnay (Mendoza) $8. Heavily toasted oak dominates a nose that also features some tropical fruit, mostly bananas. Oak in the form of burnt toast and butter are the leading flavors. Thick-bodied and heavy in the finish. **83** —*M.S. (11/15/2001)*

Tapiz 2002 Malbec (Mendoza) $8. Deep purple in hue, with saturated dark-fruit aromas along with pinches of cola and creamy oak. Fairly concentrated for a wine of this stature; for less than $10 you get vanilla and chocolate accents atop youthful, bouncy blackberry. The mouthfeel is plump, and there's a toasted coconut flavor on the finish. **87 Best Buy** —*M.S. (2/1/2004)*

Tapiz 2001 Malbec (Mendoza) $8. Fuller than most, with all of the qualities of Argentinean Malbec. The palate is redolent with black cherry and blueberry, and the finish is fairly relaxed, which is somewhat surprising yet welcome given the wine's jammy quality. Pretty much a sure bet for fans of American Zinfandel; there are a lot of similarities between the two. **87 Best Buy** —*M.S. (5/1/2003)*

Tapiz 2000 Malbec (Mendoza) $8. The sturdy but hardly overpowering nose of violets and bacon is pure Malbec. So is the black cherry fruit and notes of coffee that you get on the palate. A fairly clean cherries-and-vanilla finish is solid at first before fading quickly. Very typical for its class, but a tad thin and monotone. **85** —*M.S. (11/1/2002)*

Tapiz 1999 Malbec (Mendoza) $8. Aromas of grape bubble gum set the stage. The palate is warm and expansive. But it's entirely one-dimensional and ultimately quite basic. Most drinkers should find it pleasant if they're not seeking something spectacular. **83** —*M.S. (11/15/2001)*

Tapiz 2001 Merlot (Mendoza) $8. A rustic wine, although it's well made and clean. Very full-bodied, very dry, and tannic. The flavors are vaguely like Merlot. Not a bad price for a decent, everyday red you can serve with roasts, pizza, burgers, and similar fare. **84** —*S.H. (1/1/2002)*

Tapiz 2000 Merlot (Mendoza) $8. Although this wine doesn't scream "Merlot" when you smell or taste it, it is nonetheless a good value red. It has fresh plum aromas with vanilla shadings along with cherry and cassis fruit that carries a buttery underlay. The finish is dry and creamy, with some chocolate flavor peeking through. This wine has stuffing even if it lacks distinct varietal character. **86 Best Buy** —*M.S. (11/1/2002)*

TEKIAH

Tekiah 2003 Syrah (Argentina) $11. Scents of dull plum give way to brighter, more candied fruit and a dose of caramel. Medium in body, finishing on a note of slightly bitter dark chocolate. **84** —*J.C. (4/1/2005)*

TEMPUS ALBA

Tempus Alba 2003 Preludio Syrah (Mendoza) $15. A touch damp and mealy at first, although it clears up when given time. The palate features slightly salty fruit in the plum and blackberry family, while the mouthfeel is sticky, bordering on rich. Stays the course with little to no variation, but what's here is pretty good. **85** —*M.S. (10/1/2005)*

TERRA ROSA

Terra Rosa 2002 Cabernet Sauvignon (Mendoza) $10. Hard on the nose, with cracked pepper and rubber. Once it opens, you get spicy plum, cherry, and meaty tannins. Finishes with overt wood notes and some sweet and sour. Spicy and unconventional, but not bad. **85** —*M.S. (10/1/2004)*

ARGENTINA

TERRAZAS

Terrazas 1999 Alto Cabernet Sauvignon (Mendoza) $9. 83 *(5/1/2002)*

Terrazas 1999 Reserva Cabernet Sauvignon (Mendoza) $17. Toasted almond and vanilla aromas match with continued earth flavors of cedar and a dried dirt. Soil qualities show more prominent than fruit, in a velvety wine with only a little cassis. A well-balanced wine that finishes soft and nonaggressive. **87** —*C.S. (5/1/2002)*

Terrazas 1999 Reserva Malbec (Mendoza) $17. 83 *(5/1/2002)*

TERRAZAS DE LOS ANDES

Terrazas de Los Andes 2004 Cabernet Sauvignon (Mendoza) $12. Dark and chewy, with cassis, blackberry, and a slight hint of green to the nose. A solid red made for early consumption, this Cab has soft tannins, lots of oak-based vanilla, and an easygoing personality. **86** *(5/1/2005)*

Terrazas de Los Andes 2001 Afincado Los Aromos Vineyard Cabernet Sauvignon (Mendoza) $38. Black in color, with the full allotment of earth, leather, and black-fruit aromas. Fairly tight on the palate, with flavors of black cherry, cough syrup, and espresso. Finishes stark but nice; good but just short of the big leagues. **87** —*M.S. (3/1/2005)*

Terrazas de Los Andes 2002 Alto Cabernet Sauvignon (Mendoza) $9. Rubbery, smoky aromas to the cranberry and blueberry fruit. Tastes sweet and ripe, with ample cherry and blackberry notes. A tight finish with coffee notes and big tannins render it substantive. **85** —*M.S. (2/1/2004)*

Terrazas de Los Andes 1999 Gran Cabernet Sauvignon, Vineyard los Aromos Cabernet Sauvignon (Mendoza) $38. Still hard and tannic five years removed from harvest, but also loaded with deep molasses and smoked-meat aromas and flavors. This is a thick, unforgiving wine, but the cherry, cassis, and black plum fruit is masculine and gritty. Best with a juicy steak or a rack of ribs. **88** —*M.S. (7/1/2004)*

Terrazas de Los Andes 2003 Reserva Cabernet Sauvignon (Mendoza) $16. Big and sassy, with smoky aromas of barbecued meat, baked dark fruits, eucalyptus, and leather. In the mouth, it's more sweet than subdued, with cassis, blackberry, and hints of chocolate. Very much in the modern style, with a plush feel and the aftertaste of coffee meeting cola. **90** *(5/1/2005)*

Terrazas de Los Andes 2002 Reserva Cabernet Sauvignon (Mendoza) $16. Starts with a slight hint of lemony oak before revealing herb, leather, and blackberry aromas. Cassis and a toffee-like caramel flavor work the palate, followed by a rich, fruity finish with only modest tannins. Pretty much ready to go now. **88** *(5/1/2005)*

Terrazas de Los Andes 2001 Reserva Cabernet Sauvignon (Mendoza) $15. Somewhat restrained and dark to the nose, but within there's buried sweet fruit, leather, and pepper. The mouthfeel is round, with only modest tannins making themselves felt. Finishes roasty and spicy, with proper balance and overall integration. **87** —*M.S. (7/1/2004)*

Terrazas de Los Andes 2000 Reserva Cabernet Sauvignon (Mendoza) $17. Prune, chocolate, and tree bark can be detected on the nose. The mouth is thick and chewy, with low acidity not providing the balance to offset that richness. The finish is heavy and dark, and oddly some green flavors come through. This wine has good attributes but it's also searching for balance. **85** —*M.S. (5/1/2003)*

Terrazas de Los Andes 2004 Chardonnay (Mendoza) $12. Lemon, cream, and toasty aromas are backed by flavors of melon, pineapple, and banana. A typical but simple New World Chard: meaning it's a blend of sweet fruit, light oak, and modest acidity. **85** *(5/1/2005)*

Terrazas de Los Andes 2002 Alto Chardonnay (Mendoza) $8. A hint of fresh oak creates popcorn aromas on top of fairly ripe fruit, and while the palate doesn't offer overt, classic flavors, the overall package of wood, apple, and melon is satisfying. Definitely a middle-of-the-road wine, but the balance is admirable and the acids are lively. **86 Best Buy** —*M.S. (7/1/2004)*

Terrazas de Los Andes 2000 Alto Chardonnay (Mendoza) $8. Given this Chandon-owned winery's success with Malbec, you might hope for more here. But this fading Chardonnay doesn't have much going for it.

It's flat, with pleasant clove-like aromas and cider-like flavors. It also finishes flat, indicating a short lifespan ahead of it. **83** —*M.S. (7/1/2002)*

Terrazas de Los Andes 2004 Reserva Chardonnay (Mendoza) $16. Fairly lemony and a bit buttery, with ripe tropical fruit sitting in wait. Aromas of butterscotch, baking spices, and honey are largely attractive, as is the melon and citrus on the palate. Possibly too oaky for opponents of heavily barreled wines, but for most folks it'll satisfy. **88** *(5/1/2005)*

Terrazas de Los Andes 2002 Reserva Chardonnay (Mendoza) $15. From Tupungato, this is a very good Chardonnay that offers aromas of pear, vanilla, and toasted bread. It's almost Burgundian in style, with almond and white pepper accenting apple and mild citrus. Would be a good choice with fish or fowl. **89** —*M.S. (7/1/2004)*

Terrazas de Los Andes 2001 Reserva Chardonnay (Mendoza) $17. This offering from a respected winery seems a touch ponderous and flat, as if it's starting to lose its zip already. The nose has vanilla and coconut, but the palate is dominated by sweet flavors that don't taste like anything in particular. The finish is rich and powerful, yet it leaves a vegetal aftertaste. **85** —*M.S. (5/1/2003)*

Terrazas de Los Andes 2005 Malbec (Mendoza) $10. Ripe and a bit heavy, with aromas of leather and charcoal. A dark-styled but basic Malbec with chunky plum and cassis flavors. Round in the mouth, with a chalky, mildly tannic finish. Nothing exceptional but a good, balanced specimen. **86 Best Buy** —*M.S. (11/1/2006)*

Terrazas de Los Andes 2004 Malbec (Mendoza) $12. Aggressive and a tad bit rough, but it's still young. Time should soften it up, and what will then be waiting is a ton of rugged black fruit, some creamy oak, and a whole lot of vanilla and carob. Made for the masses; loaded with power. **86** *(5/1/2005)*

Terrazas de Los Andes 2003 Afincado Las Compuertas Vineyard Malbec (Mendoza) $45. Quite dense and ripe, with prune, earth, and rubber on the nose. The depth of color coincides with the meatiness and grapiness you find on the palate, which is pleasing but modest in depth and complexity. Weighs in as a full, easy, chewy wine. **88** —*M.S. (11/1/2006)*

Terrazas de Los Andes 2001 Afincado Las Compuertas Vineyard Malbec (Mendoza) $38. Boasting plum, bitter chocolate, and some earth, this is a fairly full Malbec, but not one that shows off the best this winery can do. For that, wait for the 2002 and '03 vintages, which are measurably better. Here, however, there's bulky fruit, coffee notes, and some woody spice that are more than acceptable. **86** —*M.S. (3/1/2005)*

Terrazas de Los Andes 2002 Alto Malbec (Mendoza) $8. Sweet at first, with graham-cracker aromas. Upon airing, leather and stable aromas emerge. Still, it's a good wine with plump plum fruit and the full allotment of chocolate and wood on the finish. A touch of late heat, however, riles it up, making it less round than ideal. **85 Best Buy** —*M.S. (12/1/2003)*

Terrazas de Los Andes 1999 Gran Malbec Vineyard las Compuertas Malbec (Mendoza) $38. A saturated, deeply colored heavyweight that could win a competition for the biggest Malbec going. It's opulent, with oak-based coconut aromas to go along with prune, maple, and black cherry. Almost like Port, with blatant wood, dark fruit, and large tannins. Still young and driving and entirely hedonistic. **91** —*M.S. (12/1/2003)*

Terrazas de Los Andes 2004 Reserva Malbec (Mendoza) $16. Rich and borderline syrupy, but restrained enough to keep its focus. The mouth deals brawny red and black fruit encased in meaty tannins. And with some oak-based mocha and coffee on the finish, it is solid as a rock. **88** —*M.S. (11/1/2006)*

Terrazas de Los Andes 2003 Reserva Malbec (Mendoza) $16. Lots of color and intensity. The bouquet blasts with heavy-metal blackberry and blueberry aromas, while the palate is rich and soft yet structured enough to avoid mushiness. That said, this is a ripe, beefy red, exactly the type of jammy, fruity Malbec that has helped solidify Argentina's name. **89** *(5/1/2005)*

Terrazas de Los Andes 2001 Reserva Malbec (Mendoza) $17. Grapey and inky, with intense earth, leather, and berry aromas. Frankly, it may be a touch too oaky for its own good; things seem slightly muddled, and there's a distant flavor of chicken fat. Nonetheless, it's sweet and ripe at the core, with cola and espresso notes. **87** —*M.S. (12/1/2003)*

Terrazas de Los Andes 2000 Reserva Malbec (Mendoza) $17. The nose announces that it's a muscled-up wine, one that resembles Bordeaux. Aromas of leather and prune are front and center, and the palate is broad and deep, with additional prune and some Port notes. Coffee, fudge, and burnt toast all make appearances on the finish. **87** —*M.S. (5/1/2003)*

TERZA

Terza 2005 Volta Rosé Malbec (Mendoza) $10. Light strawberry aromas lead the way, with a touch of almond candy as background. The palate is fruity but nondescript, with tangy acidity and good mouthfeel. This is a perfectly competent rosé, especially for Argentina, which isn't really known for the style. **85** —*M.S. (12/1/2006)*

TIKAL

Tikal 2001 Amorío Malbec (Mendoza) $30. Based on the surreal label and heavy bottle, you almost expect the richest version of Malbec, but it's actually a bit reserved, emphasizing zingy red-berry fruit, modest oak, and a racy mouthfeel. Ernesto Catena, son of Nicolas, is the proprietor, and he's done well in channeling the zest that Malbec can deliver. **89** —*M.S. (12/1/2003)*

TITTARELLI

Tittarelli 2004 Bonarda (Mendoza) $10. Bright but kind of light, with attractive red-fruit aromas. The mouth, however, is a touch stark and zesty, with juicy, jumpy cherry, and plum flavors. Not overly stellar nor does it try to reach very far; good for Bonarda. **85 Best Buy** —*M.S. (11/1/2006)*

Tittarelli 2004 Reserva Bonarda (Mendoza) $13. Ripeness is apparent from the first whiff of blackberry and prune. Yet the palate features tangy flavors that lead straight to a rubbery, almost bouncy finish. Full for sure but not very polished. **82** —*M.S. (12/1/2006)*

Tittarelli 2004 Reserva de Familia Bonarda (Mendoza) $20. Root beer, wintergreen, and black plum aromas announce a certain level of ripeness, and in the mouth it's even riper, with syrupy flavors and very little snap or pop. This a heavy wine that takes soft and creamy to the outer limits. Corpulent and too low in acidity. **81** —*M.S. (11/1/2006)*

Tittarelli 2004 Chardonnay (Mendoza) $10. Floral and zesty on the nose, with just a hint of butterscotch. The mouth, however, is live-wire and tangy, as the fruit is citrusy and shrill but definitely clean. Finishes racy and free. A no-oak style that mostly works. **84** —*M.S. (11/1/2006)*

Tittarelli 2004 Reserva Malbec (Mendoza) $13. Scattershot aromas of wet paint and berries are the opening salvo. Acid-based red fruit carries the palate, while the mouthfeel is electric to the point of overbearing. Tastes alright but doesn't have the cuddly feel or lushness that's the signature of a good Malbec. **83** —*M.S. (12/1/2006)*

Tittarelli 2003 Reserva de Familia Tempranillo (Mendoza) $20. The color and aromas stir intrigue, but the brutally sharp palate that runs on steam-roller acidity does it no favors. Succulent to the point of sour, and giant to the point of overdone, this wine needs to head back to the garage for a tune-up. **80** —*M.S. (12/1/2006)*

TRAPICHE

Trapiche 2004 Broquel Bonarda (Mendoza) $15. It's not often that Bonarda makes a point, but this new one from Trapiche's Broquel label is exemplary. The bouquet pumps out mint, tobacco, black cherry, and toasted oak, while the blackberry-drenched palate is pure pleasure. With a steak, this is a sure bet. And it won't break the bank. **90 Best Buy** —*M.S. (11/1/2006)*

Trapiche 2005 Cabernet Sauvignon (Mendoza) $8. Fairly serious for a value wine, with touches of spice, mint, and dark fruit on the bouquet. The palate features solid red-fruit flavors that may be stretched thin but are good nonetheless. Snappy, upright and just solid enough. **85 Best Buy** —*M.S. (8/1/2006)*

Trapiche 2003 Cabernet Sauvignon (Mendoza) $7. Dense and heavy, with dull black fruit that falls apart with time. Basic raspberry and vanilla flavors lead the way to a thick, creamy finish that shows little life. Flat and lacking complexity, with a strange aftertaste. **82** —*M.S. (7/1/2004)*

Trapiche 1999 Cabernet Sauvignon (Mendoza) $10. 83 *(5/1/2002)*

Trapiche 2004 Broquel Cabernet Sauvignon (Mendoza) $14. Nice color and plenty of fruit on the nose add up to a welcome mat. The palate deals berry fruit galore, especially raspberry, cassis, and black cherry. Juicy but still a little plump on the finish, with overall balance equal to that of a dancer. **89 Best Buy** —*M.S. (6/1/2006)*

Trapiche 2004 Medalla Cabernet Sauvignon (Mendoza) $35. Mildly dusty and herbal on the nose, but not the least bit green or weedy. Flavors of tobacco, cassis, and blackberry carry accents of cedar and vanilla, while the soft tannins make for a full, easy mouthfeel. Aged 18 months in French oak but it's not overly toasty or dark. **89** *(12/1/2006)*

Trapiche 2003 Medalla Cabernet Sauvignon (Mendoza) $25. Sawdust and mint smother the oaky nose, while the palate pushes dark fruit and even more resiny wood. Clearly the intent was to offer a barrique-style wine, but the result, while not bad, doesn't really click. What you get is coffee, vanilla and resin but not a lot of fruit. **84** —*M.S. (12/31/2005)*

Trapiche 2002 Medalla Cabernet Sauvignon (Mendoza) $25. Extremely woody given the depth and quality of the fruit. Simply put: The body and flavors don't match the overpowering vanilla notes and resiny tannins stemming from the oak. In fact, the finish is all butter and little fruit. **83** —*M.S. (11/15/2005)*

Trapiche 2004 Oak Cask Cabernet Sauvignon (Mendoza) $10. Ripe and plummy, with blackberry on the inviting nose. Sizable on the palate, with raspberry and cassis in spades. Wholesome and nice, with no noticeable flaws. Good, affordable Cabernet doesn't come around every day, but this is an exception to the rule. **87 Best Buy** —*M.S. (6/1/2006)*

Trapiche 2003 Oak Cask Cabernet Sauvignon (Mendoza) $10. Lightly but properly oaked, with strong, likable hints of mocha, coffee, and mint. It's a textbook New World, bargain-priced Cab, with plum and cassis flavors that are fresh and easy. Shows good structure, tannin, and ripeness, with yet more finishing oak. A quintessential by-the-glass pour. **86 Best Buy** —*M.S. (12/31/2005)*

Trapiche 2002 Oak Cask Cabernet Sauvignon (Mendoza) $10. Lots of oak in lemony form controls the nose, which paves the way for dark plum and cherry flavors, and then a sturdy, broad finish loaded with milk chocolate and vanilla. Full, mouth-grabbing tannins are supported by ample flesh and extract. **85** —*M.S. (7/1/2004)*

Trapiche 2000 Oak Cask Cabernet Sauvignon (Mendoza) $9. Root beer and cola notes stand out on the nose, which gives way to a mouthful of plum fruit and buttery oak. A smooth, light finish cements the quality status of this easygoing, clean wine. **87 Best Buy** —*M.S. (5/1/2003)*

Trapiche 2005 Chardonnay (Mendoza) $7. Flowery and lively, with apple and mild citrus flavors. More than decent on the tongue, with good balance. More steady and solid than spectacular, with varietal correctness and ample weight. **84 Best Buy** —*M.S. (6/1/2006)*

Trapiche 2004 Chardonnay (Mendoza) $8. A bit of pumpkin and squash on the early nose, with apple coming later. Comes across with orange and honey on the palate, and there's soft melon on the finish. Sort of sweet but it works. **84 Best Buy** —*M.S. (6/1/2006)*

Trapiche 2005 Broquel Chardonnay (Mendoza) $14. Broquel is Trapiche's higher-end label, and generally speaking this Chardonnay is one of the best Argentineans going. Yes, there's a heavy dose of wood, but with time it meshes nicely into the apple, melon, and citrus fruit that's prominently on display. Pure on the finish, with forward acidity. **88** —*M.S. (6/1/2006)*

Trapiche 2004 Broquel Chardonnay (Mendoza) $14. Nice if not enigmatic, with pear, talc, and apricot on the healthy bouquet. Trapiche's higher-end Chardonnay offers baked fruit on the sides of the palate and citrus at the center. It's more round and chewy than tight, but with decent acids. **87** —*M.S. (4/1/2006)*

Trapiche 2005 Oak Cask Chardonnay (Mendoza) $10. Fairly oaky, as the name might indicate. Flavors of lemon, apple, and pineapple are complete, if a bit common, while the feel is round and a touch resiny. Finishes solid, with a modicum of butter. On the heavier side, but acidic enough to maintain its balance. **85 Best Buy** —*M.S. (6/1/2006)*

Trapiche 2004 Oak Cask Chardonnay (Mendoza) $10. Gold in color, with a waxy nose full of apricot and/or orange marmalade. Due to some acidic push in the middle, the wine has good feel. Flavorwise, however, it's a bit lacking: there's overt apricot but not much else. Finishes with butterscotch and vanilla. **84** —*M.S. (4/1/2006)*

Trapiche 2002 Oak Cask Chardonnay (Mendoza) $10. Heavy toast and cream on the nose, with lemon, green apple, and wood resin on the palate. Wood takes the wheel on the finish and just won't let go. **83** —*M.S. (2/1/2004)*

Trapiche 2001 Oak Cask Chardonnay (Mendoza) $9. The apple, pear, and banana aromas seem standard, but develop a varnishy note. Citrus fruits form the palate, and the finish is schizophrenic: at first it's sour and then it runs sweet. Finally, the mouthfeel is sharp due to piercing acids. **84** —*M.S. (5/1/2003)*

Trapiche 2005 Malbec (Mendoza) $8. Ripe like pie, with a strong, deep, fruity bouquet and body. Lots of cherry and raspberry cover the palate, and there's enough gritty acidity to keep it fresh and lip-smacking. Nice Malbec for the money; a perfect pizza or hamburger wine. **86 Best Buy** —*M.S. (4/1/2006)*

Trapiche 2003 Malbec (Mendoza) $7. Open and fruity, with lots of cherry, strawberry, and red-licorice aromas. The palate is smooth and healthy, with raspberry, cherry, and vanilla flavors. Good length and drive ensure that this one will satisfy the average Merlot bargain hunter. **86 Best Buy** —*M.S. (7/1/2004)*

Trapiche 1999 Malbec (Mendoza) $10. Wood and wood-derived flavors take center stage in the aptly named Oak Cask Malbec. On the nose, buttercream and oak aromas envelop black fruit. Flavors in the mouth are quite cedary, with tart mixed berries underneath. More cedar, fleshy red plum and a metallic tinge rounds out the finish. **83** —*D.T. (5/1/2002)*

Trapiche 2004 Broquel Malbec (Mendoza) $15. Dark as night, with a rich, round, deep nose. Overt on the palate, with cherry, blackberry, and plum. Juicy enough, with chewy tannins and firm acidity. Beefy enough to match with any meat and dark enough to substitute for paint. **87** —*M.S. (6/1/2006)*

Trapiche 2004 Oak Cask Malbec (Mendoza) $10. Full and toasty, with medium depth of fruit but a lot of friendliness. Forward in the mouth, with pretty black cherry and plum flavors that are warm and ride smoothly on a bed of solid tannins. Well knit and solid. Offers a lot for the money. A good by-the-glass red. **88 Best Buy** —*M.S. (8/1/2006)*

Trapiche 2003 Oak Cask Malbec (Mendoza) $10. Smooth and ripe, with a sweet, doughy character to the nose. Ripe, lush, and healthy, with cassis and chocolate oozing off the palate. For the money this is rock-solid Malbec, saturated and chewy, with ample tannins. **88 Best Buy** —*M.S. (6/1/2006)*

Trapiche 2002 Oak Cask Malbec (Mendoza) $10. Bright purple in color, with an approachable bouquet that features chunky cherry and earth notes. Probably best at first (it doesn't stand up to too much airing), but with enough tight, grabby tannins to push it until the end. Shrill acidity creates the aura of a fresh, lively mouthfeel but also calls out for food as an accompaniment. **86 Best Buy** —*M.S. (7/1/2004)*

Trapiche 2001 Oak Cask Malbec (Mendoza) $10. Creamy and woody, but loaded with enough succulent fruit to offset any potential overoaking. The texture is rich and meaty, while flavor-wise, a streak of black licorice runs down the middle to accent the blackberry that dominates the palate. As good a basic wine as Trapiche has recently made. **87** —*M.S. (12/1/2003)*

Trapiche 2000 Oak Cask Malbec (Mendoza) $9. Some spice-driven raspberry notes as well as the scent of licorice gum drops define the nose prior to a palate of snappy berry fruit with solid oak in support. The finish is mild but long. Solid Malbec. **86** —*M.S. (5/1/2003)*

Trapiche 2004 Viña Carlos Gei Berra Malbec (Mendoza) $50. A modern-styled Malbec even though it comes from 33-year-old vines grown in a cool subsection of Mendoza. The aromas are warm, smoky, and earthy as they set the stage for bright boysenberry and currant flavors. Balanced and sturdy, with fine natural acidity. Drink now through 2015. **90** *(12/1/2006)*

Trapiche 2003 Viña Felipe Villafañe Malbec (La Consulta) $35. Spicy and woody at first, with tons of black fruit. The nose shows a hint of dill, but for the most part the wine's pure and full of plum, blackberry, vanilla, and good tannins. Firm and loaded, with cola on the finish. Yet

another success in Trapiche's new line of old-vine, single-vineyard Malbecs. **90** —*M.S. (6/1/2006)*

Trapiche 2003 Viña José Blanco Malbec (Mendoza) $34. Very big and brawny is this single-vineyard, new-to-the-market Malbec from grower Jose Blanco. Expect lots of fresh-cut cinnamon on the nose along with leather, earth, and gum. Heavy but balanced, with big tannins wrapped in plenty of coconut and mint. Takes a while to grasp; it's a giant with huge fruit and some clumsiness. Better from 2007–2009. **91 Cellar Selection** —*M.S. (6/1/2006)*

Trapiche 2004 Viña Pedro Gonzalez Malbec (Mendoza) $50. Ripe and smooth, with hints of molasses, toast, and vanilla as well as mulberry and blackberry. The wine runs sweet but masculine, with chocolate as the prime secondary flavor. Finishes long and broad, with supple tannins. Made from 8-year-old vines. Drink now through 2015. **91** *(12/1/2006)*

Trapiche 2003 Viña Pedro Gonzalez Malbec (Mendoza) $35. This is one of three new single-vineyard Malbecs from venerable Trapiche, and it proves that with rich, old-vine fruit winemaker Daniel Pi can make ultramodern vino that will please New World palates the world over. This particular bottling is a potent brew of well-oaked juice that shows wintergreen, menthol, and a ton of blackberry, black cherry, and coffee. It isn't fooling around, that's for sure. **91 Editors' Choice** —*M.S. (4/1/2006)*

Trapiche 2004 Viña Victorio Coletto Malbec (Mendoza) $50. While all of Trapiche's single-vineyard Malbecs are excellent, this is the rock star of the group. From 50-year-old vines, Coletto offers prune, fruitcake,, and cedary aromas in front of a jammy but structured palate. Smooth as silk with hints of Port. A lovely, lush wine that should age well through 2012. **93 Editors' Choice** *(12/1/2006)*

Trapiche 2005 Merlot (Mendoza) $7. Nondescript in terms of fruit flavors, with a strong hint of green pepper. Decent feel and length, with spice. But just too much green character to score better. **81** —*M.S. (6/1/2006)*

Trapiche 2002 Merlot (Mendoza) $7. Cherry, spice, and tree bark make for a good nose, despite a hint of green. The berry fruit on the palate is a bit thin, as is the finish. For some basic plum flavors and a good body, this wine delivers the goods. **84** —*M.S. (5/1/2003)*

Trapiche 2004 Iscay Merlot-Malbec (Mendoza) $55. Iscay means "two" in a native Incan language, and it represents the wine's composition of 50% Malbec and 50% Merlot. The wine is intense and inky, with aromas of mocha, black fruit, asphalt, and rubber. The palate is juicy and lively, with full but not too aggressive tannins. Very nice but not as interesting as the single-vineyard Malbecs. **90** *(12/1/2006)*

Trapiche 2003 Iscay Merlot-Malbec (Mendoza) $48. Aggressive and oaky, with lactic aromas as well as heavy burnt-toast notes. This is Trapiche's flagship blend of Cabernet and Malbec, and every year it seems less than up to its price. The '03 version is tart in the middle, with a ton of tannin and raw wood. Maybe it'll round into form with time in the cellar. But maybe not. **85** —*M.S. (8/1/2006)*

Trapiche 2005 Oak Cask Pinot Noir (Mendoza) $9. Saucy and herbal, with leather and citrus peel on the nose. Heavy and undistinguished on the palate, with atypical plum and blackberry flavors. Hard to identify as Pinot Noir. **80** —*M.S. (6/1/2006)*

Trapiche 2000 Falling Star Red Blend (Mendoza) $5. 80 *(5/1/2002)*

Trapiche 1999 Iscay Red Blend (Mendoza) $50. Flavors of coffee and pine tar interact with aromas of cedar, varnish, and coconut. This wine has huge oak that will need time to integrate. The potential is there, but will there be any fruit when the oak settles? Drink in 3–10 years. **87** —*C.S. (5/1/2002)*

Trapiche 2004 Oak Cask Shiraz (Mendoza) $9. Spins a ton of raw berry and plum aromas along with oak, and the wine is plenty flavorful. Problem is, it's pretty bumpy and aggressive, with jagged tannins and a fiery feel. Good in some ways; rough in others. **83** —*M.S. (8/1/2006)*

Trapiche 2006 Torrontès (Mendoza) $8. Varietally floral, with spice, tropical fruit and citrus on the nose. Clean and wispy on the palate, with touches of lemon extract, banana, and pineapple. A zesty, easy white wine; best as an apéritif. **86 Best Buy** *(12/1/2006)*

TRIVENTO

Trivento 2004 Select Chardonnay (Mendoza) $15. Light in color and rather sweet, with aromas of pineapple, white corn, and candied yams. Plump but not overly oaky, with spiced pear and melon flavors. Leaves somewhat of a canned-fruit impression on the finish. **84** —M.S. (11/15/2005)

Trivento 2003 Golden Reserve Malbec (Mendoza) $20. After a few years of stumbling around in Mendoza, this Concha y Toro project seems to have found its way. This wine, albeit oaky, is full of dark fruit, dill, and toast aromas. The palate is balanced and tight, with firm tannins and plenty of black cherry, plum, and coffee flavors. Toasty and lasting. Shows a lot of power and purity. **91** —M.S. (12/1/2006)

Trivento 2002 Golden Reserve Malbec (Mendoza) $20. Concha y Toro's Argentinean branch makes this heavyweight wine, which goes heavy on the oak, toast, and horseradish. It's opaque in color, with monster tannins backing plum and blackberry fruit. Finishes hot, peppery, and short, but with a lot of texture. **87** —M.S. (3/1/2005)

TRUMPETER

Trumpeter 2003 Cabernet Sauvignon (Mendoza) $9. From the Maipú subsection of Mendoza, this one runs on the heavy side, with plum and berry aromas, a chewy mouthfeel, and lots of sugar on the finish. Lacks finesse but delivers plenty of flavor along the way. **84** —M.S. (3/1/2005)

Trumpeter 2002 Cabernet Sauvignon (Mendoza) $9. More oak than balance, and the fruit seems tart. Grippy tannins and racy acids create a tougher than usual mouthfeel, and overall the flavors just aren't that exciting. Good enough, but better to stick with the Malbec. **84** —M.S. (7/1/2004)

Trumpeter 1999 Maipú Cabernet Sauvignon (Argentina) $12. This Catena brand starts off light and leafy before gathering its legs and emitting a full blast of charcoal oak. The cherry and raspberry flavors flow on the medium-bodied palate, with chewy black fruit and chocolate appearing late on the finish. Although nothing in particular stands out, it's yet another solid Argentinean Cab for the cost-conscious shopper. **85** —M.S. (11/1/2002)

Trumpeter 2004 Chardonnay (Tupungato) $9. Lightweight in its approach, but still sturdy. The bouquet offers melon, tropical notes, and white flowers, while the palate deals mostly cantaloupe and banana. A modestly oaked wine without a ton of stuffing. Good for basic sipping. **85 Best Buy** —M.S. (6/1/2006)

Trumpeter 2002 Chardonnay (Mendoza) $9. Fresh and forward, with full tropical fruit aromas accented by some oak. Flavors of pineapple, mango, and vanilla work because there's some crisp acidity pushing it all while not allowing it to feel heavy. **85** —M.S. (7/1/2004)

Trumpeter 2001 Chardonnay (Argentina) $9. Fresher and tastier than the 2000 version, this is a nice cocktail party Chardonnay that won't fail at the dinner table. Pineapple graces the sweet, refreshing nose, while lemon and green apple carry the racy palate. It's a wine that offers the essence of Chardonnay in a clean, basic package. **85** —M.S. (7/1/2002)

Trumpeter 2000 Tupungato Chardonnay (Argentina) $12. 85 —M.S. (7/1/2002)

Trumpeter 2004 Malbec (Tupungato) $9. A big blast of oak rises up from the glass, a barrier to what fruit might lie below. Once you get to the palate, there's tight but somewhat tart raspberry and a touch of leather. Not nearly as ripe and rich as the oak on the nose calls for; thus the end result is almost sour, which isn't an attribute when it comes to Malbec. **83** —M.S. (6/1/2006)

Trumpeter 2003 Malbec (Mendoza) $9. Heavily extracted, with roasted aromas of charred wood, beef, and coconut. The mouth pushes bold cherry, blackberry, and plum flavors, while the finish is slick yet tangy. This wine shows bulk around the edges but is leaner and more acidic in its center. Solid for everyday action, assuming you like yours big. **87 Best Buy** —M.S. (3/1/2005)

Trumpeter 2002 Malbec (Mendoza) $9. Deep berry fruit, sweet perfume, and beyond average complexity. From an excellent vintage, it offers violets on the nose and a sweet, rich body. A no-brainer among under-$10 reds. **87 Best Buy** —M.S. (7/1/2004)

Trumpeter 2000 Malbec (Argentina) $12. This clean, fresh, racy Malbec from the Catena family of wineries hails from an elevated section of Mendoza. The palate features zippy cherry and red plum fruit, while the finish is dry, properly oaky, and smooth. The acid-driven fruit successfully fights through any overt wood or tannins, providing newcomers a nice introduction to Malbec. **86 Best Buy** —M.S. (11/1/2002)

Trumpeter 2004 Malbec-Syrah (Tupungato) $9. Heady and well choreographed, with roasted sweet aromas to get things going. Some char and weight appear next, setting up solid cherry and blackberry flavors. Juicy, ripe and structured. An unusual blend that works nicely. **86 Best Buy** — M.S. (6/1/2006)

Trumpeter 2003 Malbec-Syrah (Mendoza) $9. From cooler Tupungato, this blend seems marinated on the nose, with rubbery accents to the dark fruit. The bulky palate spills over with raspberry and plum, while the finish is mildly acidic. Nonetheless it's a full-force red with plenty of fuel in the tank. **85 Best Buy** —M.S. (3/1/2005)

Trumpeter 2002 Malbec-Syrah (Mendoza) $9. A new and fairly intense blend from the folks at La Rural that features tight berry fruit with leather and smoke accents. There's cherry, plum, and firm, meaty tannins —that, and plenty of acidity. **86** —M.S. (7/1/2004)

Trumpeter 2004 Merlot (Tupungato) $9. Although it kicks off on the stewy, baked side of the fence, airing reveals good fruit and ample wood; indeed, there's brandied cherry, vanilla, and chocolate to ponder. Long on the finish, albeit a finish that's one-note simple. A little stark in terms of feel. **85 Best Buy** —M.S. (6/1/2006)

Trumpeter 2003 Merlot (Mendoza) $9. The bouquet is downright saucy, with molasses, brown sugar, and leather aromas. Standard plum and berry make for an average palate, while modest coffee and spice carry the finish. Generally good, but fails to make an impression. **84** —M.S. (3/1/2005)

Trumpeter 2002 Merlot (Tupungato) $9. This Tupungato Merlot has a deep color and chewy, chocolaty fruit that has enough berry fruit to make the grade. With mild earthy touches and some spice notes, it's enjoyable, especially given the price. **85** —M.S. (7/1/2004)

Trumpeter 2000 Merlot (Tupungato) $12. From high-altitude vineyards near the Andes comes this earthy, muscle-bound Merlot. It features bright cherry fruit and a hint of green pepper, but only a hint (it is ripe). The finish is mostly oak, but with drying, full tannins and a firm grip, it can handle that woodiness. A touch of barnyard renders it out of the ordinary, which is better than being dull and generic. **86 Best Buy** —M.S. (11/1/2002)

Trumpeter 2002 Syrah (Mendoza) $9. Certainly not the most complex Syrah you'll encounter, but it has meaty, strong, dark fruit, adequate spice, and lots of forceful acids that push the package. **85** —M.S. (7/1/2004)

Trumpeter 2000 Syrah (Luján de Cuyo) $12. Like every other Trumpeter red, the Syrah features bold fruit, ample spice, and good balance. The bouquet is dusty and leathery, the palate extracted and full of plum and cherry fruit. The feel to the wine is lively, more spring-loaded than dense or dull. **85** —M.S. (11/1/2002)

VALENTIN BIANCHI

Valentin Bianchi 2002 Elsa Barbera (San Rafael) $9. Tart and peppery on the nose, with a smoky character. Oddly, some sweetness gets folded into the flavor package, but that creates a gummy sensation. **83** —M.S. (7/1/2004)

Valentin Bianchi 2001 Elsa Barbera (San Rafael) $8. The nose is prickly and spicy, with some leather notes, but the palate doesn't follow suit; it's rather dull, with only modest strawberry fruit. The finish is too heavy, so the final impression is one of roughness. Unfortunately it's nothing like Barbera from Italy **82** —M.S. (5/1/2003)

Valentin Bianchi 2000 Elsa Barbera (San Rafael) $8. 80 (5/1/2002)

Valentin Bianchi 2002 Cabernet Sauvignon (San Rafael) $18. Shows full plum and blackberry aromas, but not necessarily textbook Cabernet aromas. It's pretty soft and chunky across the tongue, leaving a creamy sensation. Has some oak, but it's not a huge factor. Finishes blunt. **87** — M.S. (7/1/2004)

Valentin Bianchi 2002 Cabernet Sauvignon (San Rafael) $18. More than 50,000 cases of this wine are made, and it's ripe, with cherry and plum carrying things from front to back. Decent tannins and the lack of green flavors or aromas make it worth a taste. **84** —*M.S. (7/1/2004)*

Valentin Bianchi 1999 Cabernet Sauvignon (Mendoza) $14. The smoky, minty deep-berry nose is forward and expressive, even if it has a whiff of green to it. Rich black cherry and chocolate flavors are a bit candied, as if county fair cotton candy were added in. The finish is a simple, seamless continuation of the palate's flavors and feel. The body of this wine is full, the tannins somewhat coarse. **87** —*M.S. (11/1/2002)*

Valentin Bianchi 2005 Elsa Cabernet Sauvignon (San Rafael) $9. Red plum pushed by hard smoke aromas create a firm, rubbery bouquet. Sweet and oozing on the palate, with a lot of run-away flavors. Not terribly soft or refined but full of flavor and power. Base-level. **83** —*M.S. (11/1/2006)*

Valentin Bianchi 2004 Elsa Cabernet Sauvignon (San Rafael) $9. Simple but tasty, with berry and cherry aromas framed by a light touch of oak. This is more of a live-wire red, with nice acidity pushing black cherry and mocha flavors. Nice mouthfeel and a good finish make it good for the money. **85 Best Buy** —*M.S. (12/31/2005)*

Valentin Bianchi 2001 Elsa Cabernet Sauvignon (San Rafael) $8. Foresty aromas more than fruit are what you get fromthe clean, fresh bouquet. The palate offers a healthy dose of cherry fruit and black pepper, while the spicy finish rings with clarity. Good value. **85** —*M.S. (5/1/2003)*

Valentin Bianchi 2000 Enzo Bianchi Gran Cru Cabernet Sauvignon (San Rafael) $53. It's 86% Cabernet with some Malbec and Merlot, and the fruit is of the masculine, sturdy stock. The nose offers dusty red fruit, oak, leather, and earth. In the mouth, a core of cherry and cassis is surrounded by spice. It's almost elegant but not quite; it's bigger than that, but neither heavy nor overripe. **89** —*M.S. (7/1/2004)*

Valentin Bianchi 2004 Famiglia Bianchi Cabernet Sauvignon (San Rafael) $18. Full barrique aromas work great with the wine's overriding ripe, rubbery black fruit. Aromas of lemon peel, char, and pulsing berry lead toward lively raspberry, plum and herb flavors. Smooth and well rounded. An elevated wine. **89** —*M.S. (8/1/2006)*

Valentin Bianchi 2003 Famiglia Bianchi Cabernet Sauvignon (Argentina) $18. Aggressive and saucy, a reflection of the wine's 14.7% alcohol level. Below that stewy, marinated nose is sweet, saturated Cabernet fruit that pushes the envelope toward richness. Finishes with meaty notes and a blast of coconut. **84** —*M.S. (11/15/2005)*

Valentin Bianchi 2002 Famiglia Bianchi Cabernet Sauvignon (San Rafael) $18. Shows a touch of heat to the fully ripe flavors of plum and blackberry, but otherwise shines, with the emphasis on fruit rather than oak. Picks up some leafy notes on the finish. **88** *(10/1/2004)*

Valentin Bianchi 2003 Particular Cabernet Sauvignon (Mendoza) $30. As convincing an Argentinean Cabernet as you'll find. The nose offers tight oak, spice, mint, and vanilla along with dark, expressive fruit. The palate is right where you'd want it; the cassis, cherry and earth notes are just right. Finishes with vanilla and a touch of cola. **90** —*M.S. (11/15/2005)*

Valentin Bianchi 1997 Particular Proprietor's Reserve Cabernet Sauvignon (San Rafael) $28. This is Valentin Bianchi's attempt at a high-end reserve wine, and frankly, it falls short of the target. The nose is flat and fading, with simple but sharp red-fruit aromas. The palate is broad, but it lacks purity and definition. **84** —*M.S. (5/1/2003)*

Valentin Bianchi 2003 Chardonnay (San Rafael) $18. Clean and whole, with a good texture and pure aromas of banana, tropical fruits, and gentle oak. Some pear flavor works nicely on the palate, which is balanced and mildly smoky. A pretty solid everyday Chardonnay. **86** —*M.S. (7/1/2004)*

Valentin Bianchi 2000 Chardonnay (San Rafael) $15. This is forward and oaky, almost bulky in the nose, but not overdone. The palate offers some nice orange flavors, along with a dose of ripe tropical fruit. The mouthfeel is right on, with proper acids providing necessary balance. The finish is clean and smooth, although a little sweet. **87** —*M.S. (7/1/2002)*

Valentin Bianchi 2001 Elsa Chardonnay (San Rafael) $11. Clear as day in the glass, with forced oak and spring flowers in the nose. In a word, it's strange. In the mouth, you'll get sweetness and other flavors not generally associated with Chardonnay. It's not necessarily a bad white wine, but it is definitely at odds with typical Chardonnay. **80** —*M.S. (7/1/2002)*

Valentin Bianchi 2004 Famiglia Bianchi Chardonnay (Argentina) $18. Light in color, with simple pear and applesauce aromas touched up by a whiff of wood smoke. Pineapple and banana flavors carry the palate to a sugary, vanilla-laden finish. Along the way jumpy acidity keeps it fresh. **83** —*M.S. (11/15/2005)*

Valentin Bianchi 2003 Famiglia Bianchi Chardonnay (San Rafael) $18. **85** *(10/1/2004)*

Valentin Bianchi 2002 Malbec (San Rafael) $18. Ripe and raisiny, with Port-like aromas and a chewy, rich body. If you appreciate berry fruit with a full texture and chocolaty nuances, then this will do the trick. Mostly simple in the end, but tasty along the way. **88** —*M.S. (7/1/2004)*

Valentin Bianchi 2002 Malbec (San Rafael) $18. Clean and tad bit earthy, but sort of thin and simple. Among grapey reds that are quaffable and not offensive, this can lead the list. **84** —*M.S. (7/1/2004)*

Valentin Bianchi 2001 Malbec (Mendoza) $16. From outside the Mendoza region, this is a tasty wine with cola and root beer aromas that turn tighter and more like coffee if given time. Prune and chocolate flavors lean into a mouthfilling finish that stands up to scrutiny. A slightly out-of-the-ordinary wine, one with herbal hints and style. **88** —*M.S. (12/1/2003)*

Valentin Bianchi 1999 Malbec (Mendoza) $13. One look at the deep purple color followed by a sniff of the robust nose and you know that this Malbec is the real thing. Huge cassis and black cherry flavors stand sentry on the black fruit palate. The finish is equally dark and wonderfully rich, emphasizing yet more cassis as well as espresso. It's pure and clean, chewy and big, but not thick. **89 Best Buy** —*M.S. (11/1/2002)*

Valentin Bianchi 2005 Elsa Malbec (San Rafael) $9. The price on this perennial bargain brand from Valentin Bianchi has crept up in recent years, and thus its value potential has stalled somewhat. But it's still a fruity number that once it opens and settles delivers jammy aromas and solid red-berry flavors. We like that it's neither candied nor weedy. 60,000 cases proves that good wine can be made in quantity. **85 Best Buy** —*M.S. (12/1/2006)*

Valentin Bianchi 2004 Elsa Malbec (Mendoza) $9. Generic berry aromas come with hints of tomato, herbs, and leather, while the palate deals cassis and cherry alongside roasted meat and carob. Heavy in the mouth with a syrupy, almost jammy mouthfeel. **84** —*M.S. (12/31/2005)*

Valentin Bianchi 2003 Elsa Malbec (San Rafael) $9. A bit soft and simple, but fine as an everyday quaffer. Plum and blackberry fruit is front and center, accented by hints of chocolate, leather, and spice. **84** *(10/1/2004)*

Valentin Bianchi 2001 Elsa Malbec (San Rafael) $8. This wine from Valentin Bianchi always carries some interesting aromatics, such as clove and licorice. Flavors of blueberries and black pepper control the clean palate. On the back end, dry woody notes remain after the fruitiness does its fade. **86 Best Buy** —*M.S. (5/1/2003)*

Valentin Bianchi 1999 Elsa Malbec (San Rafael) $7. This bargain-priced wine from Valentin Bianchi offers proper licorice, spiced plum, bacon, and bramble aromas along with meaty black cherry and plum flavors. It finishes only mildly tannic, with no holes. It's an easy yet rich wine, not a big-boned bruiser but one with substance. **86 Best Buy** —*M.S. (11/1/2002)*

Valentin Bianchi 2003 Famiglia Bianchi Malbec (San Rafael) $18. A lot of funk on the nose, with strong but passing aromas of clam shell and cleanser. Better in the mouth, where grapy fruit takes over. Very extracted, with coffee and vanilla on the full-weight finish. **83** —*M.S. (11/15/2005)*

Valentin Bianchi 2002 Famiglia Bianchi Malbec (San Rafael) $18. **87** *(10/1/2004)*

Valentin Bianchi 2003 Particular Malbec (San Rafael) $30. A big, ripe, saturated offering, the type of wine most red-wine enthusiasts want, and also the type of wine that has earned Argentina its reputation for making serious Malbec. The color is purple, the bouquet rubbery and smoky. The palate is dynamite; the black-fruit flavors are superb and the coffee and dark chocolate nuances just right. A stud of a wine that could use about a year in bottle to reach its peak. **91 Editors' Choice** —*M.S. (7/1/2005)*

Valentin Bianchi 2002 Particular Malbec (San Rafael) $30. Excellent color and dark aromas announce this wine as a major league player. The nose represents pure intensity, with tar, oil, and heavy blackberry scents. Plum, licorice, and more blackberry dominate the ripe palate, while the finish spreads out nicely. Very nice Malbec, but with a price. **90** —*M.S. (3/1/2005)*

Valentin Bianchi 2003 Particular Merlot (Mendoza) $30. Potent and layered, as it begins with sharp, spicy aromas before opening to show deeper black fruit. Saturated plum and blackberry flavors are touched up by a certain saucy spiciness, while the resonating mouthfeel is beefy and rich. This is serious Argentinean Merlot, yet it doesn't quite register as great. **88** —*M.S. (11/15/2005)*

Valentin Bianchi 2001 Enzo Bianchi Red Blend (San Rafael) $53. This top-of-the-line Cabernet (there's also 16% Merlot) boasts an impressive texture that's remarkably smooth and supple. Aromas are complex, combining cinnamon and brown sugar with ripe blackberries and cassis; this wine just needs a little more length to reach the next level. **89** *(10/1/2004)*

Valentin Bianchi 2003 Sauvignon Blanc (San Rafael) $18. Light in color, with equally light pear and cream notes to the nose. Californian Bob Pepi consults on this wine, which shows flavors of fresh lettuce, honey, citrus, and stones. Not bad, but a tad sour. **85** —*M.S. (7/1/2004)*

Valentin Bianchi 2002 Sauvignon Blanc (San Rafael) $12. With fresh pineapple and peach, some bread dough and a note of pine, this wine has all the right things going on aromatically. The feel on the palate is also right, due to good acids, while the flavors of pear, pineapple, and apricot more than do the trick. **88** —*M.S. (5/1/2003)*

Valentin Bianchi 2005 Famiglia Bianchi Sauvignon Blanc (San Rafael) $15. Runs toward the sweet side, with fruit syrup and candied apple on the nose. Lemon-lime is the front and center flavor component, while the finish runs sweet and sour, with a sugary aftertaste. **83** —*M.S. (8/1/2006)*

Valentin Bianchi 2004 Famiglia Bianchi Sauvignon Blanc (San Rafael) $15. Nice as a total package, with pear, citrus, and mineral aromas. Tangy and fresh on the palate, with grab and medium-strength citrus and melon flavors. Zesty and long, yet ultimately it settles at fresh and simple. **84** —*M.S. (11/15/2005)*

Valentin Bianchi 2002 Elsa Semillon-Chardonnay (San Rafael) $8. Some mint and licorice to the nose along with talcum powder render it unusual. The palate delivers a heavy load of sweet banana and papaya, but also a strong hint of green. The finish is on the sweet and thick side, and overall things seem a bit flat and unexciting. **83** —*M.S. (5/1/2003)*

Valentin Bianchi 2003 Elsa Syrah (San Rafael) $9. Hints of coffee and black pepper enliven basic blackberry fruit. Quite tart on the palate, finishing with a trace of bitterness. **84** *(10/1/2004)*

Valentin Bianchi 2003 Elsa White Blend (San Rafael) $9. Totally fresh and likable, with apple aromas and flavors as well as an easygoing attitude. Fairly neutral as whites go, but good for salads and Asian foods. **83** —*M.S. (7/1/2004)*

VALERO

Valero 2003 Especial Syrah (Mendoza) $10. Has some bold chocolaty notes that resemble carob or fudge to go along with hints of raisin and stewed strawberries. Medium-bodied, with a finish that stays with you. **83** —*J.C. (4/1/2005)*

VIEJA BODEGA

Vieja Bodega 2003 Reserve Malbec (Mendoza) $9. This is a traditional-styled Malbec, one with leaner cherry and raspberry fruit as opposed to heavy blackberry. It's a bit racy and acidic, but it's stylish as well. Big enough to satisfy but complex enough to intrigue. **86 Best Buy** —*M.S. (6/1/2006)*

Vieja Bodega 2003 Reserve Syrah (Mendoza) $9. Solid from start to finish, with bramble and spice on the nose along with ripe plum and berry compote. Easy, basic, and satisfying on the palate, where full dark-fruit flavors get a boost from subtle, appropriate oak. Medium density and concentration make it a wine to drink now. **87 Best Buy** —*M.S. (8/1/2006)*

VIENTO SUR

Viento Sur 2003 Cabernet Sauvignon (Mendoza) $9. Quite good for the money, with mild coconut and caramel aromas on top of berry fruit. The palate is ripe and sweet, with cinnamon, chocolate, and coffee notes mingling with berries and currants. Shows the slightest hint of grass at the core but overall it's very good. **87 Best Buy** —*M.S. (6/1/2006)*

Viento Sur 2003 Malbec (Mendoza) $9. Solid and fruity, with plump berry aromas, spice, and mint on the nose. The mouth is full and chewy, with good tannins, a correct feel, and proper balance. No issues here; this is a mouthfilling Malbec with some spice and character. And the price is definitely right. **87 Best Buy** —*M.S. (4/1/2006)*

Viento Sur 2003 Syrah (Mendoza) $9. Dark fruit and leather on the nose seem fine, yet the palate is high-toned and starchy, with sharp flavors of cherry, plum, and mushroom doing battle with severe tannins. And it's a touch saucy and salty on the finish. **83** —*M.S. (8/1/2006)*

Viento Sur 2005 Torrontès (Mendoza) $9. Tropical fruit and a whiff of talcum powder on the bulky, ripe nose. Shows ample zest, spice, and pear notes on the palate, followed by a long, full finish. Nice acidity and body ensure commendable balance. **85 Best Buy** —*M.S. (4/1/2006)*

VIMINI

Vimini 2005 Chardonnay (Uco Valley) $13. A gold-colored heavy wine with butterscotch and apricot aromas followed by a tangy palate that features a beam of acidity running through the middle. Remains tangy and narrow through the finish. **82** —*M.S. (12/1/2006)*

VIÑA ANTIGUA

Viña Antigua 2004 Sangiovese-Bonarda Red Blend (Maipú) $7. Simple earth, rubber, and berry aromas come prior to cranberry, plum, and cherry flavors. Finishes quickly, with drying tannins. A tight, limited wine that won't offend or excite. **83** —*M.S. (12/1/2006)*

VINA COBOS

Vina Cobos 1999 Malbec (Mendoza) $65. Could this be Argentina's best wine right now? If you can find a bottle, give it a shot and decide for yourself. The aromas of mint, eucalyptus, cola, and bitter chocolate are intense yet pure. The monstrous palate is overflowing with black cherry, plum, and licorice, but it maintains a racy, balanced edge. The oak is heavy but not overwhelming. It's a wonderful Malbec, a leader in its class made by Paul Hobbs of California. **92 Cellar Selection** —*M.S. (11/1/2002)*

Vina Cobos 1999 Bramare Malbec (Mendoza) $37. The little brother to Cobos; this wine is filled with tobacco, cedar, and milk chocolate aromas and all the plum, berry, coffee, and licorice flavors one might expect from excellent Malbec. The finish is tight but smooth, with a fine underlay of vanilla oak. This wine has perfect balance; it's properly acidic yet rich, with freshness and weight but no syrupy qualities. **90** —*M.S. (11/1/2002)*

Viña Cobos 2002 Cobos Malbec (Mendoza) $60. This ultra extracted, inky Malbec comes from a partnership that includes Paul Hobbs, and while you cannot argue with the wine's density, purity, and power, it probably isn't for everyone. With 14.8% alcohol, a ton of color, and loads of clove-packed oak, it's giant. Perhaps you wish it less aggressive and more approachable. Or maybe you outright love it, like we did. Regardless, it needs three years of bottle age, that or several hours of air if you plan to drink it now. **93 Editors' Choice** —*M.S. (3/1/2005)*

VIÑA MAIPÚ

Viña Maipú 2003 Malbec (Maipú) $8. Starts with aromas of strawberry and raspberry, but to be honest they're a touch green and grassy. On the palate, there's plum and chocolate, and late in the game it's all about milk chocolate. Not complex but decent. **83** —*M.S. (12/1/2006)*

VINITERRA

Viniterra 1999 Lujan de Cuyo Malbec (Mendoza) $15. This straggler from the fine '99 vintage really sings. The first act is a smooth and luscious nose of blueberry jam and spice. The palate then delivers richness and loads of bursting berry fruit. It's made to please and is ready to drink now. **90 Best Buy** —*M.S. (5/1/2003)*

Viniterra 1999 Syrah (Mendoza) $10. Smooth, deep, and very attractive, with sensational ripeness and layer upon layer of quality. The nose is sweet and inviting, while the blackberry fruit is ideal. The layered finish offers coffee and chocolate and the mouthfeel is right on the money. A fine example of Argentinean Syrah, something you don't come across every day. **90 Best Buy** —*M.S. (5/1/2003)*

WEINERT

Weinert 2003 Carrascal Bordeaux Blend (Mendoza) $13. Dry and a bit herbal, with red-fruit aromas and a spot of green. The palate deals good red-berry flavor with accents of black pepper and vanilla. Persistent on the finish, with moderate tannic grab. Streamlined but not what you'd call thin. **87** —*M.S. (6/1/2006)*

Weinert 2002 Weinert Carrascal Bordeaux Blend (Mendoza) $13. Leathery and reserved, with aromas of wet earth, black pepper, jalapeños, and bell pepper. And while that may sound unripe to you, in the mouth the wine deals snappy red fruit and bona fide ripeness. Yes, it's a touch tight in terms of feel, but for a real taste of old-style South American wine, this is it. **87** —*M.S. (7/1/2005)*

Weinert 2000 Cabernet Sauvignon (Mendoza) $22. Typcially rustic, as are most of Weinert's wines. Tree bark, earth, and cola are apparent on the saucy, traditional bouquet, while the palate is a touch raw and herbal, with tomato and oregano accenting medium-weight red fruit. For some this is the right style; for others it won't do the trick. **84** —*M.S. (8/1/2006)*

Weinert 2000 Malbec (Mendoza) $23. Round and full, with plenty of toasty, smoky aromas to go with graphite and ripe fruit. Plenty of solid berry flavors grace the palate, and they vie with woody notes for prime billing. Vanilla, char, and leather make for a solid finish. If there's any weakness, it's that the wine's middle is quiet. **86** —*M.S. (11/15/2005)*

Weinert 2005 Montfleury Gran Rosé Rosé Blend (Mendoza) $12. Salmon colored, with light melon and almond aromas that are hardly distinct but by the same token are nice enough. Sweet and simple in the mouth, with no discernible fruit flavor to latch onto. **83** —*M.S. (8/1/2006)*

Weinert 2003 Cosecha de Otoño Sauvignon Blanc (Mendoza) $72. Heavy, with aromas of cornflakes and peach syrup. Unctuous and chunky as can be, with sweetness dialed up to the max. Finishes like a bull in a China shop, with canned pear, honey, and raw sugar. **80** —*M.S. (8/1/2006)*

Weinert 2005 Carrascal White Blend (Mendoza) $13. Light apple and honey aromas precede apple cider and spice flavors. Basic white wine with some juiciness. Very little depth or style, however. **83** —*M.S. (4/1/2006)*

XUMEK

Xumek 2003 Sol Huarpe Malbec (San Juan) $18. Dark in color and rich on the nose, with marzipan, blackberry, and a touch of leather. This is a powerful, modern-style Malbec with exciting, deep fruit and several layers of depth. Mildly syrupy in the middle, but not the least bit out of whack. Hails from the warm, somewhat northern San Juan zone. **90 Editors' Choice** —*M.S. (12/31/2005)*

Xumek 2003 Sol Huarpe Syrah (Zonda Valley) $14. Very forward and correct, with a bit of piquant snap to the nose. That same perky quality carries over to the palate, where some coffee character darkens blackberry fruit. Racy and solid, and on the money. **88** —*M.S. (10/1/2005)*

YACOCHUYA

Yacochuya 2000 Malbec (Cafayate) $48. Renowned French consultant Michel Rolland and his wife, Dany, make this bruiser in northern Argentina, and it's unique to say the least. It sizzles at 16% alcohol, with subdued ink and smoke aromas, fiery flavors of blackberry, licorice and pepper, and firm, probing tannins. Call it a wine warrior's wine, a collector's special; and try to cellar it for several years before drinking. **93** —*M.S. (12/1/2003)*

ZOLO

Zolo 2004 Cabernet Sauvignon (Mendoza) $14. A Cabernet that resides on the dark side. The nose is baked and earthy, with coffee notes. Dark plum and chocolate flavors run wild on the tannic palate, while the lengthy finish is slightly bitter with the taste of espresso. **85** —*M.S. (6/1/2006)*

Zolo 2003 Cabernet Sauvignon (Mendoza) $14. Fairly attractive on the nose, with licorice, tobacco, and black fruit. Based on that, you're

encouraged; but the palate fails to go beyond the solid and simple. Black-fruit flavors along with coffee and chocolate score points, while the short, buttery finish gives them back. **85** —*M.S. (11/15/2005)*

Zolo 2005 Chardonnay (Mendoza) $11. Round, plump, and creamy up front, with intensely sweet flavors of apple juice, pineapple, candied lemon peel, and oranges. If you like easy tropical flavors it has its merits. Chardonnay connoisseurs, however, may find it too simple and sweet. **84** —*M.S. (11/1/2006)*

Zolo 2004 Chardonnay (Mendoza) $14. Not a whole lot to say about the soft, flat nose. It's o.k., but that's really about it. The palate, meanwhile, turns sweet, nearly to the point of candied. And the finish is downright sugary. Decent weight and feel help it along. **82** —*M.S. (6/1/2006)*

Zolo 2003 Chardonnay (Mendoza) $14. Heavy and flat, with bulky butterscotch and ultraripe peach aromas. Starts better than it finishes; the initial citrus and melon flavors show some pop, but airing turns it mealy. **82** —*M.S. (11/15/2005)*

Zolo 2004 Reserve Chardonnay (Mendoza) $19. A typical New World Chardonnay in that it starts with corny aromas that are matched by heavy toast notes. Act two is an ultra sweet palate that seems more sugary than ideal. Very tropical as well, with sweet mango and pineapple flavors. Too sweet to be convincing as a dry white. **83** —*M.S. (12/1/2006)*

Zolo 2003 Malbec (Mendoza) $14. Fresh and fruity even if it lacks the precision and depth of a higher-end wine. The fruit is forward and fairly big, and the nose comes around to show character and moderate oak. Good in the mouth; more than fits the bill. **86** —*M.S. (12/31/2005)*

Zolo 2003 Merlot (Mendoza) $14. Fresh and alert, with snappy red raspberry and pie cherry flavors. Seems almost citrusy due to perky acids, while outsized tannins make sure there's length to the finish. **84** —*M.S. (11/15/2005)*

Zolo 2005 Sauvignon Blanc (Mendoza) $13. Melon and other light floral aromas set up nectarine, tangerine, and grapefruit flavors. Quite a lot of free-flowing citrus with a juicy, lively mouthfeel. Rugged but ripe. **84** —*M.S. (4/1/2006)*

Zolo 2004 Sauvignon Blanc (Mendoza) $13. Crisp and firm on the nose, but more sweet and cloying on the palate. Flavors of pear and roasted corn are not quite as sharp as ideal, while the finish is barely of medium depth. A bit plump and slick, as it falls off with time. **83** —*M.S. (11/15/2005)*

Zolo 2005 Torrontès (Mendoza) $14. Granular aromas of crushed vitamin, iodine, and citrus aren't terribly impressive, and there's some aggressive flavors on the palate. Registers a bit spiky, with tropical fruit and reduced but bold melon notes. **83** —*M.S. (4/1/2006)*

ZUCCARDI

Zuccardi 2000 Q Cabernet Sauvignon (Mendoza) $20. Ample leather and dark-fruit aromas yield to tobacco and oak on the nose. Flavors of sweet plums and chocolate create a masculine palate, and the finish is deeply charred and toasty. The extraction is big and the tannins full. **87** —*M.S. (2/1/2004)*

Zuccardi 1999 Q Cabernet Sauvignon (Mendoza) $22. 89 *(5/1/2002)*

Zuccardi 2000 Q Chardonnay (Mendoza) $20. Brownish gold and losing speed with each passing moment. The oxidized, buttery nose is overdone and waxy, while the palate yields cider and cinnamon, seemingly the leftovers from the oaking it went through. The mouthfeel is flat, and overall it's much like apricot juice. **81** —*M.S. (2/1/2004)*

Zuccardi 1999 Q Chardonnay (Mendoza) $22. Aged 100% in new French oak, this Chardonnay succeeds admirably in balancing full, ripe fruit, good acidity, and creamy vanillin elements. Apple, orange, pumpkin-spice, and vanilla notes on the nose open to a round, similarly flavored palate. The long finish shows elegant, tangy oak notes and apple and cream echoes. Drink through 2004. **89** *(12/15/2001)*

Zuccardi 2002 Q Malbec (Mendoza) $20. This Malbec is easy, ripe, stylish, and 100% attractive. The plump black fruit is distinguished and solid, while the mouthfeel is tight yet proper, with good tannic structure and pulsing acidity. Drink now through 2008. **90 Editors' Choice** —*M.S. (6/1/2006)*

Zuccardi 2000 Q Malbec (Mendoza) $20. There's plenty to like about this tight yet forgiving wine. Sweet berry aromas mix with copious maple-tinged oak, while hints of raisin and leather poke through. Solid through the middle, with a finish of mocha and espresso. Saturated but not over the top, and it gets better with airing. **88** —*M.S. (12/1/2003)*

Zuccardi 1999 Q Malbec (Mendoza) $22. Everything comes together handsomely in this elegant rendering of Argentina's premier red grape. A full, briary nose with dark-berry, earth, and chocolate aromas opens to a smooth palate, with very good fruit to wood balance. The close is solid and spicy, with tangy tannins and pepper notes. Tasty now, the wine should improve through mid-decade. **90 Editors' Choice** *(12/15/2001)*

Zuccardi 1998 Q Malbec (Mendoza) $22. Solid and fruity, if a little muddled in the bouquet. Bold and full of black fruit on the palate, with a rich, round mouthfeel. Finishes with tannic grip and powerful oaky influences. Spicy and deep throughout. **84** —*M.S. (11/15/2001)*

Zuccardi 2000 Q Merlot (Mendoza) $20. Forward and bright, yet the aromas score more points than the hard, tannic palate. A bouquet of baked cherries, licorice, and earth is encouraging; the wild-style cherry palate, however, leaves something to be desired. The mouthfeel is tough as nails and the tannic structure is hard. **83** —*M.S. (2/1/2004)*

Zuccardi 1999 Q Merlot (Mendoza) $22. Familia Zuccardi has shown well with the "Q" series of varietally labeled wines. The Merlot's rich blackberry fruit held its intensity and remained interesting throughout the mouth, accented with a lush creaminess that was supported by the firm tannins. Made to drink now, but will last for a few years. **90** —*C.S. (5/1/2002)*

Zuccardi 2002 Zeta Red Blend (Argentina) $45. This Malbec-Tempranillo blend is trying to be one of those new-wave super bruisers and it achieves that goal, but only to a point. It's big, round, savory, and lush, but it's shallow in the midsection because it lacks acidity and punch. Beefy but incomplete. **86** —*M.S. (6/1/2006)*

Zuccardi 2003 Q Tempranillo (Mendoza) $20. Year after year I taste this wine, and it always seems oaky and short on fruit. That said, it's a balanced, serious wine from well-tended vines, and it's made by folks who care. If you take the plunge, look for coconut and vanilla from the oak and dry fruit with touches of tomato and herbs. **84** —*M.S. (12/1/2006)*

Zuccardi 2002 Q Tempranillo (Mendoza) $20. Very oaky, with a can't-miss scent of butter, and also some maple. Sweet and syrupy on first take but then it settles down to deliver licorice, cooked brown sugar, and toast. What's best about this wine is its feel. **86** —*M.S. (6/1/2006)*

Zuccardi 2001 Q Tempranillo (Mendoza) $20. Tastes like an Argentine version of Rioja, which it probably should. The nose is spicy, oaky, and a bit pickled. Flavors of wood grain, plum, and leather lead into a dry, spiced-up finish that carries a chili pepper flavor. A bit overoaked. **84** —*M.S. (10/1/2004)*

Zuccardi 2000 Q Tempranillo (Mendoza) $20. The nose is heavily barrel dominated: aromas of barbecue sauce and sawdust overwhelm any piquant red fruit that might be hanging around. Flavors of light cherry, molasses, and red chilies turn lemony as the oak takes over the palate. This wine really pushes the oak, so much so that it falters. **82** —*M.S. (2/1/2004)*

Australia

Although Philip Schaffer was the first to plant a successful vineyard in Australia in 1791, it was not until the mid-nineteenth century that grape growing and viticulture was more widespread throughout South Australia, Victoria, and New South Wales. In the 1880s, however, phylloxera (see Glossary) spread through Victoria and New South Wales. South Australia's very stringent (and still existent) quarantine policy spared its vines from the louse and, to this day, the state is the seat of Australia's wine production.

It's only been during the past twenty or so years that Australia has become known on the world stage as a premium wine-producing nation. It is now home to about 1,800 wineries and is the fourth-largest wine-exporting country

Zinfandel vines of Cape Mentelle, Margaret River, Western Australia.

(behind France, Italy, and Spain), with export sales topping $2.7 billion in 2004. The country's biggest export markets are the United States and the United Kingdom, though Australian wine is exported to over one hundred countries.

Australia is vast; at over 7.6 million square kilometers, it is roughly the size of the continental United States, but is home to only about 15 percent of America's population. In spite of its size, many wine drinkers outside Australia have it in their heads that Oz wines all taste the same. To characterize them all as broad-shouldered, plum- and berry-flavored, well-oaked wines that are high in alcohol is as short-sighted as saying that all Americans—from the Bronx to Alabama—have the same accent. With that in mind, here's a broad overview of some of the country's best-

known winemaking regions, or Geographical Indications (GIs), and the wines for which each region is best known.

The general area around Perth, in the southwestern corner of Western Australia, is home to some of the country's most coveted, premium-quality wines. The Margaret River GI is the most renowned of the GIs in Western Australia. The region's maritime climate yields structured, age-worthy Cabernet Sauvignons, and some of the country's best Chardonnays. Semillon and Sauvignon Blanc blends are successful here, too.

In South Australia, where most of Australia's wine is produced, most GIs are located within a drive of the port city of Adelaide. It is in this state that Shiraz flourishes—just about every winery makes one.

Clare Valley, home to some of Australia's best Riesling (all of which is sealed with a screwcap), is located about eighty-five miles north of Adelaide. It has an altitude of 400 to 500 meters above sea level, and benefits from cool evening breezes and warm summers. Barossa Valley, just southwest of Clare, is hot, dry, and flat, with summertime temperatures that can top 100 degrees Fahrenheit. Most of Australia's flagship Shirazes come from Barossa Valley. The wines are generally big and broad, with luscious, extracted plum and berry fruit. Grenache and Cabernet Sauvignon, too, are very good here. Eden Valley, just south of Barossa, succeeds with both reds and whites, but you'll find that its Rieslings, Chardonnays, and Viogniers are among the country's best.

Directly south of Adelaide are McLaren Vale and, to its east, the Adelaide Hills. Like Barossa Valley, McLaren Vale also specializes in Shiraz and Grenache (and to a lesser degree, Cabernet). The Vale's microclimates are varied—some areas are flat and hot, others cooler, yielding wines from one GI that can taste very different. Most McLaren Vale reds, though, are lush in the mid-palate, often with a silky, chalky feel. The Adelaide Hills, at an altitude of about 400 meters above sea level, specializes in wines that thrive in cooler climates: Sauvignon Blanc, Chardonnay, Pinot Noir, Riesling, and other aromatic whites. Other reds can thrive in the region's warmest sites. Coonawarra, even farther south from Adelaide, is famed for its terra rossa soils, from which yield long-lived Cabernet Sauvignon.

Though there are a number of winegrowing regions in the state of Victoria, the best known is the Yarra Valley, from whence come some very good Chardonnays and Pinot Noirs. Wines from this region are often delicate and understated, rather than powerful, which again proves just how broad the spectrum is on Australia's wine styles. Rutherglen, in northeastern Victoria, is home to the country's (and really, some of the world's) most renowned fortified Muscats. Tasmania, the island just south of Victoria, is home to some of Australia's coolest grape-growing sites. As such, Riesling, Chardonnay, and Pinot Noir thrive here; production of sparkling wines containing the latter two grapes is also a specialty.

Just north of Sydney in New South Wales lies the Hunter Valley, an area with hot temperatures moderated by mild maritime breezes, and rain in the months leading up to harvest. This is Semillon country; the region's famed white wine is known for its long aging potential. Shiraz and Chardonnay are also very good here.

AUSTRALIA

AUSTRALIA

2 UP

2 Up 2004 Shiraz (South Australia) $14. Made by Kevin O'Brien at Kangarilla Road winery, but this is not as enjoyable as that brand's wines. This one offers confected aromas, and tangy, acidic berry flavors. Simple and entry-level. **83** —D.T. (6/1/2006)

3 HILLS HIGH

3 Hills High 2001 Cabernet Sauvignon (South Australia) $20. Right out of the gate, this Cab is very fragrant, like blackberries and cinnamon, and turns nutty, almost Porty, the longer it sits in the glass. The palate, on the other hand, takes a while to come around. Straightaway, the palate is a little dumb, but with time it opens nicely, turning out fine plum flavors framed in oak and nutshells. Wooly tannins come through on the finish. **87** —D.T. (12/31/2005)

3 Hills High 2002 Sangiovese-Shiraz Red Blend (South Australia) $20. Sangiovese really dominates here, adding pretty notes of cherry, leather, cedar, and orange liqueur to Shiraz's plummy core. Round in the mouth, with approachable but textured tannins. A very nice wine. 1,000 cases produced. **89** —D.T. (4/1/2006)

3 Hills High 2005 Watervale Riesling (South Australia) $20. This is a dry, tasty wine, but a very wiry, puckery style of Riesling—meaning, if you don't like your Rieslings tart, you may have some difficulty here. Its a very good wine (full of citrus and cilantro, with a minerally, stony, bony quality) but not a giving one. Will probably show its best with seafood or salads. **87** —D.T. (12/1/2005)

3 Hills High 2004 Sauvignon Blanc (Adelaide Hills) $18. A Sauvignon with a lot of heart, if not a lot of complexity. Offers citrus and tropical fruit edged with minerals; a good, everyday wine. **86** —D.T. (12/1/2005)

3 Hills High 2001 Shiraz (South Australia) $20. Most of this wine's fruit is from McLaren Vale, despite the label's broader appellation. Firm, black fruit and medium weight mark this wine, which also has accents of Sweet Tart. Flavors are pretty nice, though obscured by a papery-oaky veneer. **86** —D.T. (12/31/2005)

9 MILE ROAD

9 Mile Road 2004 Shiraz (South Australia) $15. The brand's name refers to a stretch in Langhorne Creek. Has nice nutmeg aromas and moderate plum and berry flavors, but an odd, artificial sweetener-like note is a detraction. **83** —D.T. (10/1/2006)

ABBEY ROCK

Abbey Rock 2000 Cabernet Sauvignon-Merlot (South Eastern Australia) $10. The full-force bouquet is big, round, and chunky, and the palate, as might be expected, is full force, generating a big blast of plum fruit. It's 60% Cab and 40% Merlot, a nice melange that finishes in tight, stream-lined fashion. While there are no gaping holes in this wine, it is a trifle sugary. **86 Best Buy** —M.S. (12/15/2002)

Abbey Rock 2001 Chardonnay (South Eastern Australia) $10. Opens with a big burst of yellow fruit (particularly peach and nectarine) and some cream and oak; this profile rides the wine out through the finish. It's not a complicated wine, but it's enjoyable and utterly quaffable, which makes it an ideal choice (given its price and its flavor profile) for large, gotta-please-everyone gatherings. **86** —D.T. (6/1/2003)

Abbey Rock 2001 Shiraz (South Eastern Australia) $10. Forward aromas of fresh baked bread, pork, and ripe red fruit are accented by salinity, cinnamon, and white pepper. The fruit reads very sweet at palate entry, with meatiness and firm acidity throughout. **85** —K.F. (3/1/2003)

ABBEY VALE

Abbey Vale 1999 Chardonnay (Margaret River) $14. This is a nice, easygoing Chardonnay. Apple with a touch of oak are the flavors. Crisp acidity and a creamy mouthfeel lead into a long finish. A seafood salad would make good company for this one. **85** —M.N. (6/1/2001)

Abbey Vale 2004 Vat 351 Chardonnay (Margaret River) $9. So light in color, it's almost clear. Talc-powder aromas waft from the nose; on the palate, delicate yellow fruit is accented by floral notes. It's very unusual to find Margaret River wines at this price, so grab it up. **87 Best Buy** — D.T. (5/1/2005)

Abbey Vale 1999 Verdelho (Margaret River) $16. **86** —M.M. (10/1/2000)

Abbey Vale 2000 Verdelho (Margaret River) $14. Banana, cream, and a hint of cilantro characterize this Verdelho's nose. The palate is, at first, bright and lively with hints of cream; a split second later, it is supertart. Finish is bitter, with an odd metallic flavor. **83** —D.T. (9/1/2001)

ADAMS BROTHERS

Adams Brothers 2001 Reserve Selection Shiraz (Clare Valley) $28. An export-only wine, I'm betting that you'll see plenty of this Stateside. A joint effort between Tim Adams and his brother, Simon Adams, once winemaker at Yalumba and now general manager at Cellarmasters. Creamy in the mouth, with tight plum and blackberry fruit on the palate. Black pepper and fresh herb notes surface on the finish. **89** —D.T. (2/1/2004)

ALDINGA BAY

Aldinga Bay 2001 Sangiovese (McLaren Vale) $19. Brown sugar and molasses coat generic red fruit on the palate—you'd never peg this as Sangiovese (but then, who would ever guess Australian Sangiovese?). Starts off with marshmallow on the nose, and finishes with juicy, lips-macking fruit. **85** —D.T. (5/1/2004)

ALICE WHITE

Alice White 2003 Cabernet Sauvignon (South Eastern Australia) $7. There's an unusual but interesting note that accompanies the dusty blackberry aromas—apple, maybe? On the palate, ripe red plum and berry fruit is enveloped by dusty tannins. Fresh, easy to drink, and just the thing for pizza night. **86 Best Buy** —D.T. (11/15/2004)

Alice White 2001 Cabernet Sauvignon (South Eastern Australia) $8. Chalky cement-like aromas start, then turn to cinnamon and blackberries. The flavors are of spicy, zingy raspberries with bright acidity on the palate. A wine that should be drunk young. **84** —C.S. (6/1/2002)

Alice White 2000 Cabernet Sauvignon (South Eastern Australia) $8. The mouthfeel on this wine is pretty nice, though it's a bit high on acid. Hickory, smoke, and an underlying meatiness are present here from beginning to end. Fruit (stewed fruit, to be specific) doesn't show until the back end. **83** —D.T. (9/1/2001)

Alice White 1999 Cabernet Sauvignon (South Eastern Australia) $7. This simple Cabernet opens with berry and tobacco aromas. There's a sweet and sour quality to the fruit, like stewed cherries and rhubarb. It's light and easy on the palate. All in all, a decent straightforward quaff. **84** (6/1/2001)

Alice White 2005 Cabernet Sauvignon-Shiraz (South Eastern Australia) $7. This 65-35 blend feels pretty light on the palate, but it plumps out a bit with some air. It offers pedestrian red plum and cherry fruit and a decent texture, particularly for the price. **83** —D.T. (11/15/2006)

Alice White 2004 Cabernet Sauvignon-Shiraz (South Eastern Australia) $7. Smells like root beer, and tastes like roasted fruit. Dilute, too. **81** —D.T. (10/1/2005)

Alice White 2000 Cabernet Sauvignon-Shiraz (South Eastern Australia) $7. A well made 50-50 blend, this is loaded with black fruit. Perfect balance, a velvety mouthfeel and a long finish are other attributes. Food-wise, prime rib would be just fine. **87 Best Buy** —M.N. (6/1/2001)

Alice White 2005 Chardonnay (South Eastern Australia) $7. Light honey and peach aromas intensify briefly on the palate—think grilled peaches. Has a sawdusty veneer of oak; will do for casual circumstances. **83** — D.T. (6/1/2006)

Alice White 2003 Chardonnay (South Eastern Australia) $7. Very acidic, with a sharply clean, almost green streak of citrus, although there are richer nuances of peaches and tropical fruits. This eminently drinkable wine doesn't have a lot of stuffing, but it's a great value, and very versatile with food. **86** —S.H. (9/1/2004)

Alice White 2002 Chardonnay (South Eastern Australia) $8. Medium-bodied and a little viscous in the mouth, this value Chard is no fruit bomb, as are many others at this price. It's rather interesting—look for white stone fruit and floral notes on the palate, and peach and passion fruit notes on the nose. Finishes with a peppery-herbaceous bite. **86 Best Buy** —D.T. (8/1/2003)

Alice White 2004 Merlot (South Eastern Australia) $7. This wine is quite simple and candied, with raspberry and blackberry flavors. Simple; finishes with a woody, sawdusty note. **82** —*D.T. (10/1/2005)*

Alice White 2003 Merlot (South Eastern Australia) $7. Big, big fruit, a total blast of blackberry jam and subtler layerings of cherries, briary berries, and milk chocolate. It's a lip-smackingly tasty wine, quite dry, with a bright burst of acidity, and a great value from Down Under. **85** —*S.H. (9/1/2004)*

Alice White 2002 Merlot (South Eastern Australia) $8. This Merlot-for-the-masses is nothing fancy, but it has simplicity and bounciness on its side. Smells just as it tastes: fleshy, red, plums, with just the slightest hint of oak on the finish. There are few red wines that this reviewer would ever put on ice, or in the frige for a few minutes, but this Merlot is one of them. **84** —*D.T. (6/1/2003)*

Alice White 2005 Lexia Muscat of Alexandria Muscat (South Eastern Australia) $7. Totally uncomplicated, but certainly an easy-drinking, unusual white. Orange blossom and honey notes waft from the nose, and the palate deals more orange, plus peach, pear, and lemon notes. Low in acid, but this will have many fans. **84 Best Buy** —*D.T. (11/15/2006)*

Alice White 2005 Semillon-Chardonnay (South Eastern Australia) $7. Not all that concentrated on the palate, with just modest pear and melon flavors. Soft—a little flabby, even—in feel. **83** —*D.T. (4/1/2006)*

Alice White 2004 Semillon-Chardonnay (South Eastern Australia) $7. This white's aromas are quite nice and feminine, but the palate disappoints. Vague yellow fruit and chalk flavors are dilute and over before it starts. If the flavors showed the promise that the nose showed, it would have been a much better wine. **82** —*D.T. (3/1/2005)*

Alice White 2005 Shiraz (South Eastern Australia) $7. Nose is both sweet and saline; has simple, sweet fruit on the palate and goes flat toward the finish. **82** —*D.T. (6/1/2006)*

Alice White 2003 Shiraz (South Eastern Australia) $7. A great value in a big, full-bodied red, and one that has the complexities of far more expensive ones. It combines fruity plums and cherries with deeper, darker expressions of earth, cured leather, and bitter chocolate. There's also a spicy streak of white pepper. Very dry, with smooth, rich tannins. **87** —*S.H. (9/1/2004)*

Alice White 2001 Shiraz (South Eastern Australia) $8. Starts mute, but aromas build to butterscotch, cranberry, and raisin scone. This really takes shape on the palate, with summer-ripe raspberry, white pepper and grilled meats. Finishes with a note of sweet green herbs. **86 Best Buy** —*K.F. (3/1/2003)*

Alice White 2000 Shiraz (South Eastern Australia) $8. Plenty of cool mint and eucalyptus aromas show on the nose of the solid, simple quaff. It's light but juicy, with plenty of strawberry-raspberry flavor and a slight drying mineral note. Coffee and spice add interest to the close. **86 Best Buy** *(10/1/2001)*

Alice White 1999 Shiraz (South Eastern Australia) $8. After the fairly hearty sulfur on the nose blows off, the berry and chocolate aromas and flavors here are light and wear a lot of wood for the weight of the fruit. There's decent mouthfeel and some woody tannins on the back end of this simple quaffer. **83** —*M.N. (6/1/2001)*

ALKOOMI

Alkoomi 2001 Cabernet Sauvignon (Frankland River) $25. The black plum fruit is sturdy but soft; still, make no mistake: This wine's focus is its chewy tannins. There's no killer oak or caramel flavors—just fat plum and moist soil, and maybe a little wheat. A very nice wine, and well tempered. **91 Editors' Choice** —*D.T. (5/1/2004)*

Alkoomi 2000 Southlands Red Blend (Western Australia) $11. Aromas of cranberry and green olive don't reveal a dominant varietal in this three-grape blend. Very light and simple, but soft and tartly sour with hints of cherry and blackberry that accompany the green olive tinges. **84** *(9/1/2001)*

Alkoomi 2002 Riesling (Frankland River) $17. Though it is in the unscrewcapped minority, this is a well-built Riesling, and one that somehow seems engineered to please a wide-reaching audience. It offers white peach and other subtle fruit flavors dusted with sweet talc. Make no mistake—its dry, minerally mouthfeel is the key player here. Has a little spritz in the mouth, with white pepper and a burst of peach fruit on the back end. **88** —*D.T. (8/1/2003)*

Alkoomi 2004 Sauvignon Blanc (Frankland River) $20. Crisp and minerally on the nose, but with a backing of passion fruit, fresh-cut grass, and citrus. Quite zesty and acidic, with lean, stylish grapefruit flavors. Long and pure, with mild spritz and a cleansing quality to it. **88** *(7/1/2005)*

Alkoomi 2002 Sauvignon Blanc (Frankland River) $17. An excellent Sauvignon Blanc, with invigorating grass, gooseberry, and lemon-lime flavors, and a mouthfeel that manages to be both zesty and viscous. Opens with permeating, fragrant melon, green apple, and fresh herbal flavors. **91 Editors' Choice** —*D.T. (10/1/2003)*

Alkoomi 2001 Sauvignon Blanc (Frankland River) $17. Grapefruit and mint make for an interesting and attractive couple on the nose, while tart citrus and a bit of grass make up the flavor profile. It hails from Western Australia, and overall it gets the job done. On the down side, however, is a slight vinegar note. **87** *(8/1/2002)*

Alkoomi 2000 Sauvignon Blanc (Frankland River) $15. A bright citrus-herb nose opens this Sauvignon Blanc with distinct style and character. Grapefruit, lime, lemon peel, and green grassy flavors unfold on the round medium-full palate, but the herbaceous element is assertive, and continues to come to the fore with time in the glass. Fans of this style will find this a winner; if that's not you, you probably won't. **85** —*J.F. (9/1/2001)*

Alkoomi 2001 Shiraz (Frankland River) $22. Shows rustic flavors like hay and earth over its red plum fruit. In spite of its earthiness, this feels like a wiry, bright wine, probably thanks to its undercurrent of eucalyptus. On the nose, you'll find grape, plum, chalk, and earth flavors. Another very good wine from this always dependable Oz winery. **88** —*D.T. (5/1/2004)*

Alkoomi 1999 Shiraz (Frankland River) $20. Shows rich, meaty aromas of black peppercorn-crusted steak, soy, and Asian spices that segue smoothly into flavors of black cherries and plums accented by pepper and roasted meat. Finishes long, with persistent pepper notes and some firm tannins. Drink now through 2008. **89** *(10/1/2001)*

Alkoomi 2000 Southlands White Blend (Western Australia) $11. This unusual blend of Semillon, Chenin Blanc, and Sauvignon Blanc is good but isn't for everyone—the bouquet is a garden-fresh blend of gooseberries, green bananas, and leafy lettuce; the palate shows clean, zingy green pea and cilantro flavors. It's lightweight, with a slightly tart, fresh-cut wood and citrus finish. Would go well with shrimp or white fish. **86 Best Buy** —*D.T. (9/1/2001)*

Alkoomi 2001 Southlands Frankland River White Blend (Western Australia) $11. 89 Best Buy —*C.S. (11/15/2002)*

ALL SAINTS

All Saints 1999 Cabernet Sauvignon (Rutherglen) $30. A rich, decadent wine oozing with sweet oak, vanilla, and char scents riding over amazingly ripe berry-cherry fruits. Tastes strongly of sweet black cherries that are framed in supple, complex, firm tannins. The finish lasts for a long time. **92** —*S.H. (1/1/2002)*

All Saints 1998 Shiraz (Rutherglen) $28. Very dark, with cola and spiced-plum aromas. This big boy weighs in at 14.5%, and you can tell the moment it hits your palate. The flavor profile deals apple skins, plum, licorice, and vanilla, while the back end is warm and overtly tannic. It's not your basic Shiraz, yet something seems missing, which proves that sometimes grand intentions aren't met. **86** —*M.S. (3/1/2003)*

All Saints 1999 Carlyle Reserve Shiraz (Rutherglen) $40. Anyone itching for a huge old-vine Shiraz with the thickness of motor oil and powerful Port and barrel influences will love this 15%-alcohol bruiser. Which means fans of leaner, more graceful wines need not apply. The palate is more about weight than particular flavors, while the finish is equally sweet and oaky. Now it's satisfying to drink in a young Port way; in about four more years it should be properly settled. **90 Cellar Selection** —*M.S. (3/1/2003)*

AUSTRALIA

ALLANDALE

Allandale 2001 Cabernet Sauvignon (Mudgee) $23. This wine will appeal most to folks who like their fruit bolstered by lots of creamy, buttery accents. The nose offers plenty of butterscotch and vanilla, and the palate shows stewy mixed plums, more vanilla, and woody tannins. A very good wine, but people who favor these characteristics may find this review conservative. **87** —D.T. (12/31/2004)

Allandale 2003 Chardonnay (Hunter Valley) $15. Accented by new French and American oak, this is a rich Chardonnay. Aromas of nut and grilled meats are echoed on the palate, giving interest to pear and citrus zest notes underneath. Any more wood would be too much, but as it stands it's a harmonious, hedonistic white. **90 Best Buy** —D.T. (4/1/2006)

Allandale 2002 Chardonnay (Hunter Valley) $18. On the nose, smoke and pineapple take on a milky quality. Yellow peach fruit is sturdy, rather than fleshy and juicy, in the mouth, and is dressed in a buttery-creamy cloak. Medium-weight, with a long, tangy finish. **86** (7/2/2004)

Allandale 2000 Chardonnay (Hunter Valley) $13. A soft, oaky style, with lots of barrel-char and burnt-sugar aromas backed by lemon and grapefruit. Toasted marshmallow and sautéed pineapple flavors finish gently. **84** —J.C. (7/1/2002)

Allandale 2002 Semillon (Hunter Valley) $15. Light resin and hay aromas on the nose; coats the insides of the mouth with olive oil, river rock, and lemon flavors. Understated, with a piquant citrusy bite on the finish. **88** —D.T. (4/1/2006)

Allandale 2002 Matthew Shiraz (Hunter Valley) $20. This is a very classy Shiraz with aromas of clay and earth, and crisp plum and cherry fruit at its core. It's not a broad wine, yet it really does leave a powerful impression on the palate. Medium-sized and Old World in style; drink after 2008. **91** —D.T. (4/1/2006)

AMBERLEY

Amberley 1997 Reserve Cabernet Sauvignon (Margaret River) $45. 1997 is the current vintage on this reserve wine, but it already feels tired. Brown-red in color; monotone and lean on the palate. **82** —D.T. (8/1/2005)

Amberley 2001 Cabernet Sauvignon-Merlot (Margaret River) $24. Shows odd aromas of anise, rhubarb, pickle barrel, and wheat flour on the nose, but what you get in the mouth is more enjoyable, and more straightforward. Chewy tannins are set against blackberry, oak, and tea flavors, picking up a little wheat toast on the finish. **87** —D.T. (12/31/2004)

Amberley 2002 Charlotte Street Chardonnay (Western Australia) $11. A pleasant wine, and one in which pineapple is the principal note. The nose also shows citrus and white pepper, and the palate, a slick, soft creamsicle flavor and feel. Straightforward, and a good bet for wine novices. **84** (7/2/2004)

Amberley 2004 Chenin Blanc (Margaret River) $12. This isn't a wine to age or mull over, but I like it very much. It has aromas of white stone fruit and fresh grass, and tastes like yellow peach, mango, and other tropical fruit. It's upbeat, summery and pleasing. **87 Best Buy** —D.T. (5/1/2005)

Amberley 2003 Proprietary Chenin Blanc (Margaret River) $13. Chenin from Australia isn't something we see often in these parts. This version is round and soft in the mouth, with medium body and loads of peach flavors and aromas. The fruit is a little sweet, but it's an easy, enjoyable choice. **86** —D.T. (11/15/2004)

Amberley 2003 Semillon-Sauvignon Blanc (Margaret River) $17. Aromas are crisp—citrus peel, green apple, honey—flavors are of apples and exotic fruits, all the way through the finish. Fresh, supple, and very likeable, though somewhat soft. **87** —D.T. (11/15/2004)

Amberley 2001 Proprietary Semillon-Sauvignon Blanc (Margaret River) $15. 83 —D.T. (5/1/2004)

ANDREW GARRETT ESTATES

Andrew Garrett Estates 2001 Kelly's Promise Cabernet Sauvignon-Merlot (South Eastern Australia) $9. The wine has some nice aromas of dense wheat bread, nuts, and dried fruit; as well as a meaty, stick-to-your-ribs

feel. The red fruit core, though, verges on stewy. Still, it's a good wine, and one that won't break the bank. **84** —D.T. (9/1/2004)

Andrew Garrett Estates 2002 Kelly's Promise Chardonnay (South Eastern Australia) $9. Like white shoes—so fresh and summery that it would almost be a sin to drink after Labor Day, when you're spending time indoors. This is bright, sunny, and just the thing to gulp down on the porch. Tropcial and citrus fruit through and through, with a smokiness accenting the fruit on the nose. **86** (7/1/2004)

ANDREW HARRIS

Andrew Harris 1999 Premium Chardonnay (Mudgee) $13. A zesty, citrus-accented wine that features aromas and flavors of lemons and limes, pie crust, and minty herbs. Finishes clean and refreshing—a racy wine that nevertheless isn't lightweight. **87** —J.C. (7/1/2002)

Andrew Harris 2000 Reserve Chardonnay (Mudgee) $23. There's nothing subtle about this wine, which layers tropical fruit and pecan aromas over flavors of buttered nuts and citrus. Turns lemony on the finish. The intense flavors are all powered by an undercurrent of gravelly nuttiness. **89** —J.C. (7/1/2002)

ANDREW PEACE

Andrew Peace 2004 Masterpeace Cabernet Sauvignon-Merlot (South Eastern Australia) $9. The feel is unusual—like papery tannins—but other aspects of the wine are pretty good for a value sipper. Has aromas of raspberry, talc, and fresh whipping cream. On the palate, the fruit is slightly sweet, but will certainly appeal to a young audience. **84** —D.T. (12/31/2005)

Andrew Peace 2002 Chardonnay (South Eastern Australia) $8. Has smoky, buttery scents, along with some peach and corn. Its body is fairly full, with flavors that turn odd just after palate entry—sour, vegetal, steely. Short and dilute on the finish. A surprising finish, considering Peace's red wines have performed much better. **80** (7/2/2004)

Andrew Peace 2004 Masterpeace Chardonnay (South Eastern Australia) $9. This Chard has a soft feel and creamy aromas and flavors. The core is built of peach fuzz and mango. Simple, easy and quaffable. 5,000 cases produced. **84** —D.T. (10/1/2005)

Andrew Peace 2002 Red Blend (South Eastern Australia) $8. Juicy and fruit-driven, this wine's a simple solution for large gatherings. Bouncy and Beaujolais-weight, there's cherry fruit with some earth and brown sugar in the background. Finishes toasty. A blend of Shiraz, Cabernet Sauvignon, Grenache, and Mataro. **86 Best Buy** —D.T. (5/1/2004)

Andrew Peace 2004 Masterpeace Red Blend (South Eastern Australia) $9. Masterpeace? More like, Masterblend. This hodgepodge blend of Shiraz, Cab, Grenache and Mataro offers plummy, purply aromas and fruity, albeit sweetish, berry-basket flavors. Not complicated, and well priced. **85 Best Buy** —D.T. (8/1/2005)

Andrew Peace 2002 Shiraz (South Eastern Australia) $8. Hippie-types will pick this up for the peace sign-emblazoned label, but there's plenty to like otherwise. It's medium-bodied, with mixed plum fruit and a smooth mouthfeel. It's a little acidic on the finish, where there's also some mocha and nut notes. **85** —D.T. (12/31/2003)

ANGOVE'S

Angove's 2000 Classic Reserve Cabernet Sauvignon (South Australia) $10. On the soft side for a Cab, which isn't at all a bad thing. Plum and oak mark the palate, with more of the same on the finish. Smoky, barbecue-like aromas start things off. **85** —D.T. (6/1/2003)

Angove's 1999 Classic Reserve Cabernet Sauvignon (South Eastern Australia) $10. Lighter and more red-fruited than most Australian Cabs, Port-like qualities show in this wine's tawny hues and cherry, burnt sugar and earth bouquet. A mouth of slightly overripe berry fruit and the creamy, smooth texture are appealing, as is the attractively sweet, slightly hot finish. It's unusual, but that's not a bad thing. **86 Best Buy** (9/1/2001)

Angove's 1997 Classic Reserve Cabernet Sauvignon (South Eastern Australia) $12. 85 (4/1/2000)

Angove's 2002 Long Row Cabernet Sauvignon (South Australia) $10. A sturdy, good choice for a $10 wine. Flavors and aromas are light and red (think plum and watermelon). The soft red-pencil-eraser finish comes to a gentle close. **84** —*D.T. (11/15/2004)*

Angove's 1999 Sarnia Farm Cabernet Sauvignon (Padthaway) $9. Seems a little unbalanced, but there's so much wood here it's hard to discern what the discordance is, exactly. The palate and finish are all about toffee, with tart red cherry fruit underneath—the butterscotch on the nose should have tipped me off. **82** —*D.T. (1/1/2002)*

Angove's 2003 Vineyard Select Cabernet Sauvignon (Coonawarra) $20. This is a pretty solid Cab, crisp and smooth on the palate, with black cherry fruit at the fore. On the nose, it offers more black cherry, plus unusual rice-cracker and marinade aromas. **87** —*D.T. (12/31/2005)*

Angove's 2002 Vineyard Select Cabernet Sauvignon (Coonawarra) $20. A well-made Cab without frills: Plum dominates on the nose, but there's also a hint of herb. Plum and cherry fruit in the mouth has a slightly taut pucker, and brown earthy accents. **87** —*D.T. (12/31/2004)*

Angove's 2003 Bear Crossing Cabernet Sauvignon-Merlot (South Australia) $7. Straightahead and no-frills, but also quite a deal. Taut red cherries and plums are at the heart of this wine, with dry, spicy-earthy accents on both the nose and palate. **84 Best Buy** —*D.T. (2/1/2006)*

Angove's 2002 Bear Crossing Cabernet Sauvignon-Merlot (South Australia) $7. Chewy red plum on the palate is countered with brown earth; you'll find similar earthy-meaty notes and red fruit, plus a whisper of eucalyptus, on the nose. Finishes with a slightly tangy, acidic bite. **84** —*D.T. (6/1/2003)*

Angove's 2000 Bear Crossing Cabernet Sauvignon-Merlot (South Australia) $7. We don't usually think of Cabernet as a pizza-pasta sort of wine, but this one would do that job admirably. It has a lean, Chianti-like feel to it, along with tart cherry, milk chocolate and leather flavors, finishing with a burst of lemony acidity. **86 Best Buy** —*J.C. (6/1/2002)*

Angove's 2003 Bear Crossing Chardonnay (South Australia) $7. Nose doesn't reveal much more than butter, or light coconut, aromas. In the mouth, there's an odd filminess to the texture, and flavors of gold apple that are punctuated by bright herb (and maybe some alcohol) on the finish. **82** —*D.T. (11/15/2004)*

Angove's 2002 Bear Crossing Chardonnay (South Australia) $7. An approachable wine that starts off with floral, peachy aromas and ripe peach and yellow fruit flavors. On the back palate, there's a burst of tropical fruit, plus some oak. Easy to drink, and easily to like. **85** —*D.T. (8/1/2003)*

Angove's 2001 Bear Crossing Chardonnay (South Australia) $7. This boldly flavored wine is loaded with buttered pears, tropical fruits, and citrus. Orange peel, mint, and tea notes add interest to the finish, which is a bit syrupy-sweet and bitter-pithy at the same time—just enough to balance each other out. **85 Best Buy** —*J.C. (7/1/2002)*

Angove's 2002 Classic Reserve Chardonnay (South Australia) $9. Has a round, custardy mouthfeel that says Chardonnay, but flavors that may remind you more of Sauvignon Blanc. Zesty citrus and mineral notes foil modest yellow fruit on the palate, with white pepper notes brightening up the nose and finish. **87 Best Buy** —*D.T. (6/1/2003)*

Angove's 2000 Classic Reserve Chardonnay (South Australia) $9. This starts off great with gobs of melon and other tropical fruits. The palate has refreshing acidity, a medium to full body and an unctuous mouthfeel. The close, however, comes too quickly. **86** —*M.N. (6/1/2001)*

Angove's 2004 Long Row Chardonnay (South Australia) $10. This value Chard offers a moderate amount of wood and cream bolstering pineapple and peach flavors. Offers similar notes on the nose. Just the kind of wine to enjoy well chilled, in warm weather **84** —*D.T. (10/1/2005)*

Angove's 2003 Long Row Chardonnay (South Australia) $10. Creamy, buttery aromas hint at what's to come in the mouth: yellow fruit gussied up with some cream and toast, with a heavyish, clumsy mouthfeel. Good, but pretty straightforward. **84** —*D.T. (12/31/2004)*

Angove's 2003 Sarnia Farm Chardonnay (Padthaway) $14. Medium-bodied in the mouth, but flavors are very lean and crisp (think herb, citrus pith, stone fruit). Finishes with a buttery slickness. **84** —*D.T. (12/31/2004)*

Angove's 2005 Nine Vines Rosé Grenache-Syrah (South Australia) $10. Dark red-garnet in color, with aromas of meat, mineral, and plum. I like this rosé for its full body and dark berry-and-chalk flavor profile. It's 70% Grenache and 30% Shiraz, a grownup (read: dry and full) version of rosé at an affordable price. Its modern, sleek packaging, too, belies its cost. **86 Best Buy** —*D.T. (11/15/2005)*

Angove's 2002 Long Row Merlot (South Australia) $10. Pencil eraser aromas with a slight stemminess. It's a straighforward Merlot, with red plum and cherry notes. Light in body and concentration. **84** —*D.T. (12/31/2004)*

Angove's 2001 Classic Reserve Pinot Noir (South Australia) $10. This Pinot has sturdy red fruit going for it, plus a smooth mouthfeel and medium body. But it also had a strange powdery accent to it that reminded me somewhat of instant iced tea—sure, it gave the wine a more interesting texture, but the flavor I could have done without.. **84** —*D.T. (6/1/2003)*

Angove's 2003 Vineyard Select Riesling (Clare Valley) $19. Olive oil and passion fruit aromas are expressive; the citrus and stone fruit flavors are less so. It's also a little weightier on the palate than is typical of a Riesling, but it's still an enjoyable sip. **86** —*D.T. (3/1/2005)*

Angove's 2001 Classic Reserve Sauvignon Blanc (South Australia) $10. Waxy canned pineapple aromas lead the way into a palate that's entirely lemon, lime, and grapefruit. It's sharp and light, which means that well chilled it will come across as being refreshing. On the negative side of things, there's a strong candied quality to the wine that can't be ignored. **84** *(1/1/2004)*

Angove's 2004 Long Row Sauvignon Blanc (South Australia) $10. Aromas are of white pepper and lemon zest. This is a bright, dry, citrusy Sauvignon—perhaps a little overzealously so. Its flavors are very lemony, and a bit sour to this reviewer's taste. Good, but is not a goes-down-easy sipper. At its best at the raw bar. **83** —*D.T. (11/15/2004)*

Angove's 2004 Vineyard Select Sauvignon Blanc (Adelaide Hills) $19. A spare, austere, lemony sort of Sauvignon. It is almost unforgiving at first, but after a few sips, you get used to the style and begin to appreciate the minerally, chalky feel. A natural with white fish, or any rich sauces that beg to be cut with a laser-edged white. **87** —*D.T. (12/1/2005)*

Angove's 2002 Bear Crossing Semillon-Chardonnay (South Australia) $7. That it's neither sweet nor flabby is what I most appreciate about this value-priced white. Yellow fruit (peach, pear, and banana, mostly) is the key player here, though there are mineral accents here and there. Fun, forward, and very drinkable. **86 Best Buy** —*D.T. (12/31/2003)*

Angove's 2002 Bear Crossing Shiraz (South Australia) $7. Easy-drinking but pleasurable, with woodsy-charred tannins, I'd drink this with barbecue all the time, if only I had a barbecue. Cherry and dark plum fruit is ripe and accessible on the nose and the palate. It's not a complicated, nuanced wine, but that's no reason not to buy a few bottles to have around the house. **86 Best Buy** —*D.T. (11/15/2003)*

Angove's 2000 Classic Reserve Shiraz (South Australia) $10. The aromas are slightly peppery and green, leading one to anticipate some under-ripeness. However, there is no green to the palate, as raspberry rides high. The finish is full and round, if a bit flat. A bit of a candied quality mars the freshness and clarity. **85** —*M.S. (3/1/2003)*

Angove's 1999 Classic Reserve Shiraz (South Australia) $9. The dark cherry currant and cocoa fruit has an overripe, candied quality. It's wrapped in deep caramel-toasted oak, and has a plump, rather sappy feel. Almost Port-like, it's sweet and herbal at once—it's a bit out there, but will have appeal for the adventurous. **83** *(10/1/2001)*

Angove's 2003 Long Row Shiraz (South Australia) $10. Aromas run the gamut between raspberry and cherry, to spice, cedar, and chocolate. The palate delivers crisp berry and cherry fruit at first, but the flavors are fleeting, leaving tannins, but not much flavor, on the tongue. **84** —*D.T. (2/1/2006)*

Angove's 2002 Red Belly Black Shiraz (Limestone Coast) $13. This new Angove's label has cherry, wood and anise aromas. Straightforward berry-plum flavors take on hints of earth and herb. Mouthfeel is soft; finish shows some wood. **84** —*D.T. (11/15/2004)*

AUSTRALIA

Angove's 2002 Sarnia Farm Shiraz (Padthaway) $14. A conservative, buttoned-up wine: It has a rigid core of black fruit, with graham cracker and oak accents. It has a nice fatness in midpalate, and smooths out into a juicy finish. A very good wine, and one that won't break the bank. **88** —*D.T. (12/31/2004)*

Angove's 2003 Vineyard Select Shiraz (McLaren Vale) $20. This is a substantial Shiraz, sure to please everyone at your next dinner party. Black cherry and raspberry aromas take on wheat flour and amaretto accents, with just the black cherry and flour notes galloping through the medium-length finish. **89** —*D.T. (12/31/2005)*

Angove's 2002 Vineyard Select Shiraz (McLaren Vale) $20. Smooth, chewy tannins on the palate with ripe red fruit flavors (plum, cherry, raspberry) are a tasty, winning combination. The sweet accents on the nose (caramel, sweet tart, toffee) may appeal more to others than they did me—still, the quibble is a minor one. **89** —*D.T. (3/1/2005)*

ANNIE'S LANE

Annie's Lane 2002 Cabernet Sauvignon-Merlot (Clare Valley) $13. Though the wine's flavors and aromas are dark—earth, black cherry, black plum—it still presents a cheerful, not black and brooding, face. Cooler-climate cherry fruit on the palate is tart and sweet. Chewy and medium-bodied, and a very nice value. **88 Best Buy** —*D.T. (12/31/2004)*

Annie's Lane 2003 Chardonnay (Clare Valley) $13. Has light, pleasant vanilla, paraffin, and white peach aromas. It's plump in the mouth, with lots of wood and spice, and a side order of stone fruit. Finishes a little thin. A nice wine; it's hard to come by a Clare appellation bottle at this price. **85** *(7/2/2004)*

Annie's Lane 2003 Chardonnay (Clare Valley) $NA. A little alcoholic on the nose, but there's bright tropical fruit and stone fruit flavors on the palate. Good, textbook Chard that finishes with decent length. **86** —*D.T. (1/1/2002)*

Annie's Lane 2002 Chardonnay (Clare Valley) $13. This is a bright, balanced Chard with a clean, chalky mouthfeel and nice Golden Delicious apple, passion fruit, and peach flavors on the palate. Finishes with dry citrus flavors. It screams summer, so enjoy it outside while the weather's fine. **88** —*D.T. (8/1/2003)*

Annie's Lane 2000 Coppertrail Shiraz-Grenache-Mourvedre Red Blend (Clare Valley) $20. Though the plum fruit on the nose smells fresh and red, with a nice dusty overlay, the fruit turns a little sour on the palate—like plums mixed in with a few cranberries. Finishes with herb and oak; this is a wine would benefit from being served with food to show its best. **84** —*D.T. (9/1/2004)*

Annie's Lane 2004 Riesling (Clare Valley) $14. Very dry, as Clare Rieslings should be, this is an ideal pre-dinner sip. Its flavors are palate cleansing and subtle—think citrus peel and mineral/stone, and its acidity is just tangy enough. Olive oil, cracker and citrus aromas start it all off. **87** —*D.T. (8/1/2006)*

Annie's Lane 2003 Riesling (Clare Valley) $14. Nose is a nice mix of lime, gooseberry, and jasmine, and the mouthfeel is a mix of chalky smoothness and a dash of viscosity. Peach, pear and lime peel flavors fade into a medium-length finish. **88 Best Buy** —*D.T. (5/1/2004)*

Annie's Lane 2002 Riesling (Clare Valley) $14. A straightforward but pleasant wine, with a yellow-fruit core that wears a chalky cloak. The nose offers zippy citrus aromas, and the first strains of the yellow fruit-and-mineral duo. **86** —*D.T. (8/1/2003)*

Annie's Lane 2004 Coppertrail Riesling (Clare Valley) $14. Some Rieslings bowl you over with flavor and acid, but this isn't one of them. You know all that talk you hear about the grape's versatility with food? They could have been talking about this wine, and its wet-stone texture, and lemon and pear flavors. **87** —*D.T. (10/1/2005)*

Annie's Lane 2002 Semillon (Clare Valley) $NA. This Semillon has perky yellow fruit and a viscous mouthfeel; has some weight and fullness, particularly considering the variety, and the fact that it's unoaked. Hay, honey, flowers, and fresh-mown grass on the nose is the best part. **88** —*D.T. (2/1/2004)*

Annie's Lane 1999 Copper Trail Shiraz (Clare Valley) $32. A lighter-style Shiraz from Clare. Nose offers fruitcake, bready aromas with candied fruit. The palate is a fruit bonanza—think red plum, black plum, and raspberry. A fleeting herbal, or metallic, edge at the back of the palate, and a finish that fades a little too fast are my only quibbles. **86** —*D.T. (12/31/2003)*

Annie's Lane 2001 Coppertrail Shiraz (Clare Valley) $30. Shows sweet vanilla and candied nut on the nose, followed by cool, black-cherry notes in the mouth. It's a focused wine, not a mouthfilling one, with a lovely soil-mineral texture. Very good; 750 cases produced. **89** —*D.T. (12/1/2005)*

ANNVERS

Annvers 2001 Cabernet Sauvignon (Langhorne Creek) $28. A very good wine, but not an opulent, fleshy wine. It's medium-weight, with plum skin and tea accents on the palate, and a nose that takes a little while to open. There's a fair amount of oak here as well—if that bothers you, look elsewhere. **87** —*D.T. (5/1/2004)*

Annvers 2001 Shiraz (McLaren Vale) $30. Much of the winedrinking public will like this better than I did, but I found the sweet, creamy flavors through and through just a bit over the top—this wine's ripe mixed berry fruit is swimming in toffee, caramel, coffee, and the like. It's still a nice wine, with fruit that just regrettably doesn't get its due. **85** —*D.T. (5/1/2004)*

ANTIPODEAN

Antipodean 1999 Chardonnay (Eden Valley) $NA. Yellow fruit dominates the palate, which also has an unusual powdery mouthfeel. The yellow fruit on the finish is a little dilute. Nose is smoky, almost barbecuey, with a petrol note. **83** —*D.T. (8/1/2003)*

AQUILA

Aquila 2001 Cabernet Sauvignon (Margaret River) $15. Medium-bodied, with black fruit that doesn't overwhelm you, this is a Cab you can enjoy easily with food—and it wouldn't have to be steak, either. The real draw here is the chalky texture. **86** —*D.T. (10/1/2003)*

Aquila 2000 Cabernet Sauvignon (Margaret River) $15. 84 —*D.T. (10/1/2003)*

Aquila 1999 Shiraz (Blackwood Valley) $17. From a new growing region in Western Australia, this wine possesses mounds of menthol-scented oak, which ride heavy over the black cherry fruit. Finishes short, probably the result of young vines, but shows a glimmer of the potential that may exist in some of Australia's newer regions. **83** *(10/1/2001)*

ARAMIS

Aramis 2003 Shiraz (McLaren Vale) $21. Shows a bit of unintegrated oak on the nose—dry toast and vanilla notes stick out—but there's also a fair dose of blackberry fruit to go with it. In the mouth, the taut berry flavors continue to wear a dry, cedary veneer; give this another year to pull the disparate elements together. **87** —*J.C. (12/15/2006)*

ARCHETYPE

Archetype 2004 Old Vine Reserve Shiraz (Barossa Valley) $35. Stylized and excellent Shiraz. Briar and chili powder aromas are subtle; the wine is broad on the palate, with flavors of plum, raspberry, and vanilla bean. Tannins are soft and approachable at first, but feel thick and wooly by the time you reach for a second glass. 1,000 cases produced. **91** —*D.T. (8/1/2006)*

ARMSTRONG

Armstrong 1999 Shiraz (Victoria) $54. A promising sweet cherry, vanillin oak, and spice nose opens to a very black, very smooth palate. The forward fruit and vanilla of the front end is overtaken by loads of dark oak, rendering it a bit more monolithic than expected, but still pleasurable. Finishes tart-sweet, with modest length. **88** *(11/1/2001)*

ARTHUR'S CREEK

Arthur's Creek 1996 Estate Cabernet Sauvignon (Yarra Valley) $40. Herbaceous almost to the point of being vegetal, the weedy tobacco aromas flirt dangerously with green bean scents. The tart cherry and bell pepper flavors turn lemony on the finish, giving an impression of less-than-fully-ripe fruit. **84** —*J.C. (6/1/2002)*

AUSTRALIA

Arthur's Creek 1995 Estate Cabernet Sauvignon (Yarra Valley) $40.
Unusual aromas of jam, figs, and curry lead to a spicy, grapey—though slightly acidic—palate. Finishes short, with too much tannin for the fruit. **84** *(9/1/2001)*

Arthur's Creek 1999 Chardonnay (Yarra Valley) $25. Wow—talk about contrasts. The nose is way over the top, a grotesque parody of a butterscotch sundae. The finish is multilayered and complex, featuring echoes of toast and white peaches. In between is a somewhat neutral-tasting wine. You may love it or you may hate it—it's that kind of wine. **85** —*J.C. (7/1/2002)*

ARUNDA

Arunda 1999 Cabernet Sauvignon-Merlot (South Eastern Australia) $9. A bit rough and ready but overall a nice, fruity wine. It's satisfactorily dry, with a good balance acidity, tannins, and alcohol. There's a tart sharpness but if you can overlook it, it's not too bad. **85** —*S.H. (6/1/2002)*

Arunda 2000 Chardonnay (South Eastern Australia) $9. What's nice about this wine is the acidity: It burns; it sparkles; it makes your mouth water and prepares it for yummy food. It's not all about fruit, oak and lees—a meal in itself. The flavors are of apples and peaches dusted with pepper and cinnamon. **87 Best Buy** —*S.H. (9/1/2002)*

Arunda 2001 Shiraz-Cabernet Sauvignon (South Eastern Australia) $9. If you like your red wines jammy and young, with forceful acids, you'll like this one from Oz. Shiraz stars with peppery notes, but the blend works well and the wine is clean and fresh and dry, at a value price. **86** —*S.H. (1/1/2002)*

AUSTRALIAN DOMAINE WINES

Australian Domaine Wines 1999 Alliance Shiraz (South Eastern Australia) $18. This is a smooth mouthful of blackberry, tobacco, espresso, anise, and toast flavors that turns a little sour and leathery on the finish even as it blends in some hints of cocoa. A solid mainstream effort. **86** *(10/1/2001)*

AUSVETIA

AusVetia 1997 Shiraz (South Australia) $60. Sixty bucks for a night in the wilderness? This Shiraz will take you there, with its wood, eucalyptus, and smoke aromas, and a palate that is more piney, spicy, and sappy than fruity. Those that like smooth wines with outdoorsy flavors would do well to set up camp here. **89** *(11/1/2001)*

BALGOWNIE ESTATE

Balgownie Estate 2000 Cabernet Sauvignon (Bendigo) $25. From Victoria, this inky Cab offers mineral and pure, densely packed cassis and blackberry fruit. It's spicy, racy, and full-throttle, but by no means overextracted or mushy; just the opposite, in fact. On the finish, bright layered fruit is the opening act followed by oak. **91** —*M.S. (12/15/2002)*

Balgownie Estate 2002 Shiraz (Bendigo) $30. Right out of the bottle, this wine brims with blackberry and cassis aromas and flavors, but with air, it takes on more earthy, briary—even nutty, as is the case with the nose—notes. Has a chalky feel and medium body; restrained and food friendly. **89** —*D.T. (10/1/2005)*

Balgownie Estate 2000 Shiraz (Bendigo) $25. Bendigo is a subappellation of Victoria, approximately 100 miles north of Melbourne. This medium-bodied Shiraz is quaffable, even though its price may not encourage spontaneous purchase. Blueberries and sweet cream waft from the nose, while the fruit on the palate is redder, and more tart than sweet. **86** — *D.T. (3/1/2003)*

BALLANDEAN

Ballandean 2002 Cabernet Sauvignon (Granite Belt) $13. This wine is fragrant and concentrated, but its flavors are sour enough to make it almost difficult to drink. Has musky, men's cologne aromas, and sour plum plus stalky greenness on the palate. Tannins are thick and sawdusty. **82** —*D.T. (12/31/2005)*

Ballandean 2004 Semillon-Sauvignon Blanc (Granite Belt) $13. Comes from a vineyard in Queensland that is 850 meters above sea level. Smells like white chocolate and juicy peaches, with peach and lemon taking over on the palate. It's soft in the mouth, with the lemon contributing some sourness that lasts through the finish. **85** —*D.T. (12/1/2005)*

Ballandean 2002 Shiraz (Granite Belt) $13. One of the few Queensland offerings we see stateside; this one has cool plum and coconut-candy bar aromas, with plum flavors persisting through. Its pulpy, newsprint-y texture is a detraction. 1,200 cases produced. **83** —*D.T. (12/1/2005)*

BALLAST STONE ESTATE WINES

Ballast Stone Estate Wines NV Sparkling Blend (Currency Creek) $17. Coppery-yellow in color; has aromas of peach pit and orange peel. It's a basic, uncomplicated sparkler with steady but coarse bead. Despite grapefruit notes deep at its core, it just tastes like ginger ale to me, an impression that's only underscored by the mouthfeel. **84** —*D.T. (12/31/2003)*

BALNAVES OF COONAWARRA

Balnaves of Coonawarra 1998 The Blend Bordeaux Blend (Coonawarra) $15. This mix of Merlot, Cabernet Sauvignon, and Cab Franc is a bit earthy and brambly, with just a hint of sweaty leather adding character. Plum and cherry fruit offers some sweetness to the palate but there's also a hint of tomato. Mild oak and moderate persistence to the finish seal it. **85** —*M.S. (12/15/2002)*

Balnaves of Coonawarra 1997 The Blend Bordeaux Blend (Coonawarra) $26. A Bordeaux-style mix of 35% Cabernet Sauvignon, 35% Merlot, and 30% Cabernet Franc, this wine has a tangy, fruit-juicy style that's distinctly un–Bordeaux-like. Sour cherry, cranberry, and blackberry flavors and a hint of pipe tobacco carry through a soft and lingering, medium-bodied palate. Enjoy this crowd-pleaser now and over the next three years. **87** —*J.F. (9/1/2001)*

Balnaves of Coonawarra 1998 Cabernet Sauvignon (Coonawarra) $30. Black to the eye and loaded with aromas of black cherry, cassis, and toasted oak. There are ample berry, cherry, and coffee flavors, but they don't exactly shine beyond the basics. The full and aggressive acidity comes on late. This has some size and strength but you can't call it a thoroughbred. **85** —*M.S. (12/15/2002)*

Balnaves of Coonawarra 1997 Cabernet Sauvignon (Coonawarra) $37. Cream and blackberry fruit dominates this Cab's nose; on the palate, the cream explodes into a heavy oakiness that masks the ripe fruit, and even turns it a bit tart. Too much acid on the palate and on the back end. The finish is medium-long but tart. **82** —*D.T. (9/1/2001)*

Balnaves of Coonawarra 1998 The Tally Reserve Cabernet Sauvignon (Coonawarra) $75. On the nose, has cherry, eucalyptus, and chocolate aromas. Fruit on the palate is plummy, though stewy, and is accented by a little herb. Finishes with oak and nut. Enjoyable, if a little disjointed. **87** —*D.T. (12/31/2003)*

Balnaves of Coonawarra 1998 Cabernet Sauvignon-Merlot (Coonawarra) $20. Rich coffee and mocha aromas mixed with some grassiness start it off, followed by smoked meat, plum and cassis on the palate. While there isn't much complexity here, it's a good, forward wine with mostly healthy, chunky fruit. "Verve" could be its middle name, and it's fairly easy to drink. **86** —*M.S. (12/15/2002)*

Balnaves of Coonawarra 1997 Cabernet Sauvignon-Merlot (Coonawarra) $30. Racy yet refined, this blend of 76% Cabernet Sauvignon and 24% Merlot shows a good, restrained balance of acid and tannins. There are plenty of mint, plum, and black cherry flavors along with a hint of toast; it also has a nice, even mouthfeel and structure. Hints of cherry dot the finish. **89** —*J.F. (9/1/2001)*

Balnaves of Coonawarra 1999 Chardonnay (Coonawarra) $30. Feels rather full in the mouth, but the flavors aren't as big as its body. Dry, citrusy notes (lemon peel, lemonade) play on the palate and the finish. Nose offers lots of toast and butterscotch. **84** —*D.T. (8/1/2003)*

Balnaves of Coonawarra 1998 Shiraz (Coonawarra) $30. Nose of sawdust, light brown sugar, apple peel, leather, and grilled meat; palate of dry red fruit with an emphasis on meat and brown sugar. An attention-getting body and lasting finish make the mark. **88** —*K.F. (3/1/2003)*

BALTHASAR RESS

Balthasar Ress 2001 Balthazar of the Barossa Shiraz (Barossa Valley) $35. Nuanced and meek? Not so much. This is a full on, knock-you-out Shiraz, big in flavor and size. Meaty mixed plums are dusted with white

AUSTRALIA

flour; on the nose, there are deep blackberry and eucalyptus aromas. **89** —D.T. (9/1/2004)

BANNOCKBURN VINEYARDS

Bannockburn Vineyards 2001 Chardonnay (Geelong) $38. 87 (7/2/2004)

Bannockburn Vineyards 2001 Chardonnay by Farr Chardonnay (Geelong) $39. As the label says, this Chard is grown and made by Gerry Farr, hence the clever name. It's medium weight and balanced; fruit is oft peach, but there is a plethora of toast, nut and malt flavors as well. **86** (7/2/2004)

BANROCK STATION

Banrock Station 2004 Cabernet Sauvignon (South Eastern Australia) $7. Smells like beef bouillon and some mushroom, and tastes of plums and berries coated in an oaky veneer. A darkly flavored wine, but a hollow one. **82** —D.T. (12/31/2005)

Banrock Station 2005 Chardonnay (South Eastern Australia) $5. This Chardonnay is fragrant and flavorful, full of easy, bright pineapple and peach flavors. Round and full in the mouth, with a little sweetness. 80,000 cases produced. **84 Best Buy** —D.T. (4/1/2006)

Banrock Station 2004 Chardonnay (South Eastern Australia) $7. Peach fuzz is this Chard's main flavor, with grass and cream accents on the nose. Acids are a little tart. A simple, everyday white. **83** —D.T. (10/1/2005)

Banrock Station 2003 Chardonnay (South Eastern Australia) $7. Just what you want in a chilled, porch-sippin', beach-lyin' wine. It's straightforward, uncomplicated Chard, but one with fleshy white peach and Granny Smith apple flavors. Aromas are on the sweet side, though, with pineapple syrup and flowers taking the lead. **84** (7/2/2004)

Banrock Station 2001 Chardonnay (South Eastern Australia) $6. Good party Chard. Nothing too complex or subtle, just mixed tropical fruit with a hint of wood and sweet fruit-cocktail flavors. **83** —J.C. (7/1/2002)

Banrock Station 2005 Merlot (South Eastern Australia) $5. Just the thing you need if there are dozens of people on your deck, and burgers are on the grill. Cherry and red plum flavors have earthy, oaky accents. It's medium-bodied and easy to drink. **84 Best Buy** —D.T. (11/15/2006)

Banrock Station 2001 Merlot (South Eastern Australia) $6. Burnt rubber and yeasty bread aromas precede cherry flavors that are a bit briary. An awkward acidity, matched with a watery midpalate, makes for a wine that needs to be consumed now. **82** —C.S. (6/1/2002)

Banrock Station 2000 Merlot (South Eastern Australia) $6. A nose of nutmeg, clove and cranberry gives this uncomplicated Merlot some character. On the palate, it's extremely tart and soft with sour cherry and spicy oak flavors, but in a lightweight, unassertive way. **82** —J.F. (9/1/2001)

Banrock Station 2005 Riesling (South Eastern Australia) $5. Has a nice intensity of flavor—lemon, peach, and pineapple, mostly—and wide, fragrant lemon and mineral aromas. Does it taste like you'd expect Riesling to taste? Maybe not. But if this zesty but soft-around-the-edges wine turns more people on to the variety, let it flow. **85 Best Buy** —D.T. (8/1/2006)

Banrock Station 2004 Riesling (South Eastern Australia) $7. Finally, a Riesling at a truly introductory price. Green apple and pear aromas introduce a soft, sweetish, plump palate. It's a fresh and quaffable white, a simple rendition of the variety. **84 Best Buy** —D.T. (10/1/2005)

Banrock Station 2004 Semillon-Chardonnay (South Eastern Australia) $5. Offers up light mineral-talc aromas, with a similar feel on the palate. Peach-skin flavors don't really sing. Fine for casual gatherings. **83 Best Buy** —D.T. (4/1/2006)

Banrock Station 2003 Semillon-Chardonnay (South Eastern Australia) $6. Aromas are of ripe tropical fruit and nuts, and the palate follows suit with pear, melon, and oak flavors. Finishes soft and a little sweet, but still a fine quaffer. **84 Best Buy** —D.T. (3/1/2005)

Banrock Station 2000 Semillon-Chardonnay (South Eastern Australia) $6. This white blend has a decidedly floral, garden-y bouquet with honeysuckle, green-bean, and butterscotch notes. Though the wine is medium-full (and much bigger than you'd expect a Chardonnay to be), the apple, cream, and grapefruit flavors aren't over the top. Finishes

medium-long, with a pleasant citrusy tang. **88 Best Buy** —D.T. (9/1/2001)

Banrock Station 2003 Shiraz (South Eastern Australia) $7. Though the alcohol pokes out a bit in this wine, it's still a good, value-priced sipper. On the palate, it's all about chewy plum and blackberry fruit. The nose offers black pepper, chocolate, and coconut aromas. **84 Best Buy** —D.T. (12/31/2005)

Banrock Station 2000 Shiraz (South Eastern Australia) $8. An interesting spiciness adds interest, keeping this round, accessible wine from being just another bottle. The dark fruit shows tobacco, cumin, anise, and red pepper notes. It's soft, not fat, on the palate, and goes down easy with a tangy pepper-licorice close. **87 Best Buy** (10/1/2001)

Banrock Station 1999 Shiraz (South Eastern Australia) $7. 88 Best Buy —M.M. (10/1/2000)

Banrock Station 2004 White Shiraz (South Eastern Australia) $5. A fun, affordable pink wine. Dry cherry and toast aromas stat things off; it's soft-bodied and tropical-flavored on the palate, with floral accents. Finishes dry. 18,000 cases produced. **84 Best Buy** —D.T. (4/1/2006)

Banrock Station 2003 Shiraz-Cabernet Sauvignon (South Eastern Australia) $6. Easy-drinking and pleasing. Vanilla bean, cream, and musky aromas usher in red fruit (plum, cherry, you name it), a judicious amount of wood, and a streak of anise. 43,000 cases produced. **86 Best Buy** —D.T. (8/1/2005)

Banrock Station 2000 Shiraz-Cabernet Sauvignon (South Eastern Australia) $6. Ah, the great outdoors. On the nose, raspberry, blackberry and plum meet tobacco and hickory, campfire-like aromas. Palate smolders with smoke, oak and charcoal over fruit flavors; this is a big, but not too heavy, wine. Slightly hot finish is peppered with black fruit flavors. This will overshadow many dishes—try it with barbecue or s'mores. **87 Best Buy** (9/1/2001)

BARNADOWN RUN

Barnadown Run 1999 Heathcote Cabernet Sauvignon (Victoria) $28. Graves-like aromas of earth and tobacco laced with cassis are an instant hit; even the palate is Bordeaux-like, featuring a lean, chalky mouthfeel and drying tannins that demand cellaring. Age it one or two years and drink it over the next 3–5. **87** —J.C. (6/1/2002)

Barnadown Run 1999 Shiraz (Victoria) $25. Though this Oz Shiraz is woodier than a log cabin, it shows some pleasant cherry flavors, and menthol, smoked-meat, and smoke aromas. Otherwise, the nose is all oak; the palate and finish are tart and cedary. **85** (11/1/2001)

Barnadown Run 2000 Heathcote/Bendigo Winery Shiraz (Victoria) $30. Simple, with sweet, mixed fruit and oak, this Shiraz is acceptable in casual, drink-me-now circumstances. Its price, however, will probably prohibit such casual consumption. **84** —D.T. (1/28/2003)

BAROSSA VALLEY ESTATE

Barossa Valley Estate 2000 Ebenezer Cabernet Sauvignon-Merlot (Barossa Valley) $30. Chalky tannins dress up pretty basic cherry and plum flavors. This isn't a fat wine; on the contrary, the fruit's taut rather than fleshy. Nose is an interesting mélange of eucalyptus, barbecue, and anise. **86** —D.T. (12/31/2003)

Barossa Valley Estate 1999 Chardonnay (Barossa Valley) $10. 87 Best Buy —M.M. (10/1/2000)

Barossa Valley Estate 2000 Chardonnay (South Australia) $10. Aromas and flavors of pear and lemon. Neither fat nor flamboyant, it has appeal because of its poise and restraint—adjectives formerly not often associated with Australian Chardonnay. A fine choice for light foods or just to sip on its own. **85** (6/1/2001)

Barossa Valley Estate 2004 Spires Chardonnay (Barossa Valley) $12. Smells very nice. The wine deals vanilla bean, nutmeg, musk, and floral notes. This isn't a Chardonnay for the tropically inclined. There's fruit here, but it's taut (think unripe pear, sour apple, peach pit, that sort of thing). Sparse on the fluff overall. **86** —D.T. (12/1/2005)

Barossa Valley Estate 2003 Spires Chardonnay (Barossa Valley) $12. 84 (3/1/2005)

Barossa Valley Estate 2003 Spires Chardonnay (Barossa Valley) $12.
Smells and tastes appley, with a backbone of citrus. Light in body; the fruit doesn't sing loudly—we could only wish there were more of it. Finishes with tart citrus. **83** *(7/2/2004)*

Barossa Valley Estate 2002 Spires Chardonnay (Barossa Valley) $10.
There's a zippy citrus note on the nose, though the underlying aroma is of cracker, or flour; the citrusy streak resurfaces on the palate and carries through to the finish. A little creaminess rounds out the nose. Quite a value for Barossa Chardonnay. **86** *—D.T. (8/1/2003)*

Barossa Valley Estate 1998 Shiraz (Barossa Valley) $10. 89 Best Buy
(10/1/2000)

Barossa Valley Estate 2000 Shiraz (South Australia) $10. This unique, complex wine received mixed reviews. Some found the orange-pine-cardamom, sweet-and-sour plum package very appealing, while it was much less pleasurable (and too atypical) to others. Spice and orange elements play on the long finish. **86** *(10/1/2001)*

Barossa Valley Estate 1999 Black Pepper Sparkling Shiraz (Barossa Valley) $NA. There's not much of this sparkler made, because the winery has to make the difficult decision of parting with E&E-quality grapes to do it. Has spicy, fireplace-smoke and plum aromas, with meaty, plummy flavors. On the palate, it offers good mousse, and steady bead. Not currently available in the U.S. **90** *(3/1/2005)*

Barossa Valley Estate 2002 E&E Black Pepper Shiraz (Barossa Valley) $85. A puzzle. An excellent wine with an excellent reputation from an excellent vintage, but one that we felt didn't quite live up to some of its past incarnations. Has aromas of plum, raspberry, vanilla, and oak, with many of the same notes reprising on the palate. As good as it is, there's something missing this year. Tasted twice; note reflects the higher score. **90** *(6/1/2006)*

Barossa Valley Estate 2001 E&E Black Pepper Shiraz (Barossa Valley) $85. Dusty and pretty on the nose, with cassis, cedar, and black pepper aromas. On the palate, the fruit tastes as inky and purple as the wine shows in the glass, its crisp acids and lush tannins rounding out this rich, sumptuous Shiraz. Finishes bright and medium-long. Drink 2008+. **92** *—D.T. (12/31/2004)*

Barossa Valley Estate 2000 E&E Black Pepper Shiraz (Barossa Valley) $NA. Now showing unusual aromas of eucalyptus, roasted fruit and pickle barrel. It's supple in the mouth, with over-the-top stone fruit flavors and fresh herb accents. Finishes on a bitter-chocolate note. Drinking well now. **90** *(3/1/2005)*

Barossa Valley Estate 1999 E&E Black Pepper Shiraz (Barossa Valley) $NA. Fir tree, orange liqueur, and meaty aromas; the palate offers a veneer of vanilla enveloping raspberry, plum, and chocolate flavors. Not as lush as some of the older wines; feels crisp and lively in the mouth. Cranberry flavors punctuate a crisp finish. **92** *(3/1/2005)*

Barossa Valley Estate 1998 E&E Black Pepper Shiraz (Barossa Valley) $NA. From a terrific vintage, and still going strong. Smells great—like beef and leather, with black fruit underneath. In the mouth, it's structured and bright, its pure berry fruit operating in easy harmony with accents of pencil eraser and caramel. Finishes long. Drinking well now, but could easily go through 2015 or so. **93** *(3/1/2005)*

Barossa Valley Estate 1997 E&E Black Pepper Shiraz (Barossa Valley) $65. 90 *(10/1/2000)*

Barossa Valley Estate 1996 E&E Black Pepper Shiraz (Barossa Valley) $NA. Offers a compelling, unusual mix of Christmas spice, Worcestershire sauce, tawny Port, meat, and pepper on the nose. Bright acids and chewy tannins characterize the palate, which offers juicy, meaty flavors but not the full-throttle, over-the-top lushness that characterizes some other vintages. Finishes long, with dust and bacon notes. Drink now–2010. **94** *(3/1/2005)*

Barossa Valley Estate 1994 E&E Black Pepper Shiraz (Barossa Valley) $NA. What we liked best about this vintage is its lush, velvety grip on the mid-palate—its texture is just A-1. The panel had differing ideas about whether it should be drunk now or held even longer to see how its blackberry and dried spice flavors develop. In any case, it's drinking beautifully now. Smells of black pepper, smoke, toasted nuts, and all things smoldering and brooding. **92** *(3/1/2005)*

Barossa Valley Estate 1991 E&E Black Pepper Shiraz (Barossa Valley) $NA. One panelist thought this vintage the best of the bunch, but all agreed that the wine is at its prime now. It's rich and very supple on the palate, with notes of milk chocolate, nut, cola, and earth. Finishes long and focused; just hot stuff. **93** *(3/1/2005)*

Barossa Valley Estate 1998 E&E Sparkling Shiraz (Barossa Valley) $NA. Deep black-purple in color, and tastes as it looks, with black, stewed fruits that are just sweet enough to stand up to the bubbles. Finishes clean and dry, with some eucalyptus. Doesn't really taste like a sparkling version of their flagship wine, but a good drink nonetheless. **88** *—D.T. (2/1/2004)*

Barossa Valley Estate 2002 Ebenezer Shiraz (Barossa Valley) $35. Blackberry, maple, and smoke aromas lead to juicy blackberry and raspberry flavors on the palate. Offers up smooth tannins in a narrow pathway through the finish. **87** *—D.T. (8/1/2006)*

Barossa Valley Estate 2001 Ebenezer Shiraz (Barossa Valley) $30. With such rich blackberry and clove aromas, the wine's powerful berry and plum flavors should come as no surprise. There's spice on the palate, too, which is medium-sized, elegant—and maybe even a little lighter than you'd expect. **88** *(3/1/2005)*

Barossa Valley Estate 2000 Ebenezer Shiraz (Barossa Valley) $28. Assistant Winemaker Will Thompson calls it "a hug from the inside," and it's easy to see what he means: There's warming, concentrated cassis and mixed plums on the palate, with smoky barbecue aromas on the nose. But be forwarned that the fruit here is so rich that it is liable to suffocate folks who prefer pecks on the cheek to large-scale embraces. **90** *—D.T. (2/1/2004)*

Barossa Valley Estate 1999 Ebenezer Shiraz (Barossa Valley) $30. This isn't a wine to be held until the next century, but it's such a ringer that you probably wouldn't be able to save it that long, anyway. You'll recognize in Barossa Valley Estate's second wine E&E's trademark caramel, mocha, and plum flavors. It's medium-bodied though muscly, with an alluring bouquet of jammy blackberry, chocolate, and soil. Yum. **90** *—D.T. (3/1/2003)*

Barossa Valley Estate 1998 Ebenezer Shiraz (Barossa Valley) $32. This dense wine starts with aromas of smoke, leather, and game, then shows lush blackberry fruit on the palate. Hints of espresso, vanilla, and chocolate round out the midpalate; the finish shows some unintegrated toasty oak. Give it 3 to 5 years to develop. **89** *—J.C. (9/1/2002)*

Barossa Valley Estate 1997 Ebenezer Shiraz (Barossa Valley) $29. 90 *(10/1/2000)*

Barossa Valley Estate 1996 Ebenezer Shiraz (Barossa Valley) $25. 91 *(4/1/2000)*

Barossa Valley Estate 2003 Spires Shiraz (Barossa Valley) $12. 85 *—D.T. (12/1/2005)*

Barossa Valley Estate 2002 Spires Shiraz (Barossa Valley) $12. Aromas are a curious mix of hickory smoke, flowers, and pickle barrel. This Shiraz's mouthfeel is soft and dry, with flavors of red plum, earth, and oak. A good wine, at a good price. **84** *—D.T. (11/15/2004)*

Barossa Valley Estate 2001 Spires Shiraz (Barossa Valley) $10. From a winery that makes some top-flight Shiraz, I can only surmise that this entry-level bottling got its share of the picked-over grapes. It smells nice, of mixed, stewed plums, and starts off on the palate with dark fruit and tealike tannins. The mouthfeel needs some stuffing, though, and the finish is short. **84** *—D.T. (12/31/2003)*

BARRATT

Barratt 2001 Chardonnay (Piccadilly Valley) $40. Light stone fruit aromas on the nose; it's round in the mouth, with stone fruit, mineral, and citrus flavors. A good aperitif, and a solid choice if creamy, oaky Chards just aren't your style. **88** *—D.T. (8/1/2003)*

Barratt 2001 The Reserve Pinot Noir (Piccadilly Valley) $50. Not all that vibrant or fruity—this Pinot is all about earth. Smells like tree bark, dirt, and maybe a little leaf. There's definitive brownness to the palate, too, with mushroom and earth flavors prevailing. Could work well with mushroom or truffle dishes. **84** *—D.T. (12/31/2003)*

AUSTRALIA

AUSTRALIA

BARWANG

Barwang 1997 Regional Selection Cabernet Sauvignon (Coonawarra) $18. 90 (12/1/1999)

Barwang 1997 Vintage Select Cabernet Sauvignon (South Eastern Australia) $10. 86 (12/1/1999)

Barwang 1996 Winemaker's Reserve Cabernet Sauvignon (New South Wales) $25. 93 (12/1/1999)

Barwang 1998 Regional Selection Chardonnay (Yarra Valley) $14. A ripe and fruity Chard with a lavish overlay of sweet, smoky oak and spicy vanilla. It's very extracted and a little clumsy, with a rough, earthy finish. 84 —S.H. (9/1/2001)

Barwang 1997 Regional Selection Chardonnay (South Eastern Australia) $16. 88 (12/1/1999)

Barwang 1997 Vintage Select Chardonnay (South Eastern Australia) $10. 87 Best Buy (12/1/1999)

Barwang 1999 Merlot (South Eastern Australia) $9. Slight berry and carob notes compete with woody and herbaceous aromas on the nose of this light wine. The palate has decent balance and shows tart berry fruit, but here the herbaceous note turns more green and bell pepper-like, remaining through the finish. 83 —M.M. (9/1/2001)

Barwang 1998 Regional Selection Merlot (Coonawarra) $14. Forward fruit and a soft mouthfeel characterize this Merlot from a region famous for Cabernet Sauvignon. Nice blueberry, vanilla, and tobacco flavors emerge on the palate with medium intensity. Not a very structured wine, it's pleasurable with an easy, lingering finish of berry and mineral notes. 87 —J.F. (9/1/2001)

Barwang 1997 Regional Selection Merlot (Coonawarra) $20. 81 —S.H. (10/1/2000)

Barwang 1999 Shiraz (South Eastern Australia) $9. Dark cherry fruit wrangles with a lavish oaking on the nose and palate. The wine is light-weight considering its dark profile, and the fruit, with its cinnamon-clove accents, just can't compete with the dominant woodiness. Ends short with a bit of pepper. 83 (10/1/2001)

Barwang 1997 Regional Selection Shiraz (South Eastern Australia) $18. 90 (12/1/1999)

Barwang 1997 Vintage Select Shiraz (South Eastern Australia) $10. 87 Best Buy (12/1/1999)

Barwang 1997 Winemaker's Reserve Shiraz (Coonawarra) $20. 88 —S.H. (10/1/2000)

Barwang 1996 Winemaker's Reserve Shiraz (Coonawarra) $25. 91 (12/1/1999)

Barwang 1996 Winemaker's Reserve Shiraz (New South Wales) $25. 91 (12/1/1999)

BASEDOW

Basedow 1999 Chardonnay (Barossa Valley) $18. Big, nutty aromas and thick, heavy smoke let you know right away what to expect. Rich and weighty in the mouth, but the fruit is subdued and disappears quickly on the finish. 84 —J.C. (7/1/2002)

Basedow 1998 Shiraz (Barossa Valley) $20. Basedow's 1998 offering is black—no, blacker than black: Dark berry fruit, smoke, toasty oak, and black coffee aromas lead into similarly dark black cherry, black pepper, and oak flavors. Ends a little hot, with licorice, cedar, and pepper notes. 85 (10/1/2001)

Basedow 1996 Johannes Shiraz (Barossa Valley) $60. The overall impression here is candied—from molasses aromas to confected grape flavors, to a finish that pops with bright fruit, but leaves a gelatinous, manufactured fruit flavor in the throat. Saving graces here are a smooth mouthfeel, and dark earth flavors that partially mask the other flavors. 83 —D.T. (1/28/2003)

BATTLE OF BOSWORTH

Battle of Bosworth 2002 Cabernet Sauvignon (McLaren Vale) $28. Ballsy one moment and then suave the next, Joch Bosworth's Cabernet is an interesting wine for a number of reasons: his vineyards are organic, and a small percentage (which varies between 2 and 7%) of the fruit for this bottling is cordon cut on the vines and left to dry, Amarone-style. Plus, this Cab just flat-out tastes good: it's brawny and plummy, with the cordon-cut fruit adding extra richness. Finishes with chocolate-mocha flavors. Drink after 2006, as the nose is still pretty closed and the tannins still substantial. 90 —D.T. (3/1/2005)

Battle of Bosworth 2003 Shiraz (McLaren Vale) $28. This powerful Shiraz starts off purring softly, its volume eventually escalating to a roar. Cracked black pepper aromas open to reveal deep, rich fruit; on the palate, it seems linear at first but unfolds to show a velvety texture and clay, cranberry, cherry, plum, and chalk flavors. Finishes long. 92 —D.T. (2/1/2006)

BECKETT'S FLAT

Beckett's Flat 2002 Cabernet Sauvignon-Shiraz (Margaret River) $22. A wine with moderate body that serves up a blend of briary black cherry, herb, raspberry, smoke, and spice, all couched in moderate tannins. Kosher. 86 —J.M. (4/3/2004)

Beckett's Flat 2002 Reserve Chardonnay (Margaret River) $22. Apricot and citrus fruit is couched in oak on the nose. In the mouth, it's balanced, and shows mild yellow fruit, plus a malty note that continues through to the finish. This is not a Technicolor, loud wine, but that's why it may work with dinner. 87 —D.T. (10/1/2003)

Beckett's Flat 2004 Reserve Kosher Chardonnay (Margaret River) $20. Offers vanilla bean, pear, and herb aromas. On the palate, the wine is soft and a little sweet, with tropical fruit flavors dominating. Kosher. 84 —D.T. (4/1/2006)

Beckett's Flat 2003 Reserve Kosher Chardonnay (Margaret River) $18. Starts off smelling like vanilla bean, but quickly goes quite lactic. Heavy on the palate, with flavors of lemon and butterscotch candy. Kosher. 82 —D.T. (12/1/2005)

Beckett's Flat 2004 Cerise Kosher Rosé Blend (Margaret River) $17. Though the wine has the strawberry cheesecake flavors and aromas that this reviewer typically finds sweet and simple, they are countered here by some fresh berry fruit and a minerally feel. Good wine. Kosher. 86 —D.T. (4/1/2006)

Beckett's Flat 2002 Sauvignon Blanc-Semillon (Margaret River) $20. Quite herbal in the nose, with hints of hay, grass and herbs. That theme continues throughout, with a tart lemon edge on the finish. Kosher. 80 —J.M. (4/3/2004)

Beckett's Flat 2003 Kosher Late Harvest Semillon (Margaret River) $16. Has an odd green aroma, like capers. On the palate, this Sem offers soft peach and guava flavors, and a green, herbal note. Doesn't taste very late harvest, either—especially compared to other Oz sweeties. 83 —D.T. (8/1/2006)

Beckett's Flat 2002 Late Harvest Semillon (Margaret River) $18. 83 —D.T. (10/1/2003)

Beckett's Flat 2001 Semillon-Sauvignon Blanc (Margaret River) $15. 84 —D.T. (10/1/2003)

Beckett's Flat 2004 Kosher Semillon-Sauvignon Blanc (Margaret River) $17. This 80-20 Sem-Sauv isn't all that exciting on the nose at first, but reveals hints of vanilla and anise with time. On the palate, it's an approachable, slightly tropical wine, soft around the edges but with decent intensity. One of the better Kosher Aussies I've had lately. 86 —D.T. (4/1/2006)

Beckett's Flat 2002 Shiraz (Margaret River) $22. Juicy, ripe, and fun, with plenty of upfront raspberry, strawberry, cherry, toast, and vanilla notes. Soft tannins and moderate acidity make it easy to drink. Clean and fresh at the end. 87 —J.M. (4/3/2004)

Beckett's Flat 2001 Shiraz (Margaret River) $18. The first take on the bouquet is one of funk and green herbs, but then it turns to black pepper and candle wax, which may be unconventional but is still attractive. The palate, meanwhile, delivers typical raspberry and cherry flavors, while both the finish and mouthfeel are simple but positive. 87 —M.S. (3/1/2003)

Beckett's Flat 2000 Shiraz (Margaret River) $17. Tart cherry-blackberry fruit and loads of licorice-vanillin oak show immediately and play all the way through in this Western Australian example. Balanced, tart-sweet, and earthy, with good acidity, it could almost be mistaken for a modern-style Dolcetto from Italy's Piedmont. **86** *(10/1/2001)*

Beckett's Flat 2003 Kosher Shiraz (Margaret River) $20. Aromas are a metallic and jarring at first, but get meaty, almost saline, with air. Flavor is confected—think Pixie Stix. **81** *—D.T. (4/1/2006)*

BELLARINE ESTATE

Bellarine Estate 2000 James Paddock Chardonnay (South Eastern Australia) $15. Sure it's oaky, but it's good oak, contributing complex aromas of burnt sugar, smoke, and bacon fat to an otherwise straightforward peach-and-pear-flavored Chardonnay. The disparate elements converge in a harmonious finish that invites you back for another sip. **88** *—J.C. (7/1/2002)*

Bellarine Estate 2000 Portarlington Ridge Merlot (South Eastern Australia) $14. Green-bean notes on the nose blow off with aeration to reveal barbecuey, tomatoey aromas. Plum fruit on the palate is more plum skin than flesh, and sadly not as expressive as I'd like. Has a nice, medium body and chalky tannins, though. **83** *—D.T. (1/1/2002)*

Bellarine Estate 1999 Shiraz (Bellarine Peninsula) $15. Although one taster felt this wine was much better than this rating, majority rules. The meaty, peppery aromas and a sharp herbal edge to the flavors were too much for the rest of our panel, who found it chemical and vegetal. **81** *(10/1/2001)*

BENJAMIN

Benjamin NV Museum Reserve Muscat (Victoria) $16. Pours as viscous as motor oil, and has the most beautiful amber sheen. Smells explosive and fantastic, with white chocolate, nougat, crème brûlée, anisette, and Kahlúa, and turns classically rich in the mouth. The flavors are enormous, and very sweet, but what's most impressive is the texture—sheer velvet with perfect, bright acid. **95** *—S.H. (9/1/2002)*

Benjamin NV Museum Reserve Muscat (Victoria) $16. 91 *—L.W. (3/1/2000)*

Benjamin NV Tawny Port (South Eastern Australia) $10. 88 Best Buy *—L.W. (3/1/2000)*

Benjamin NV Museum Reserve Tokay (Victoria) $16. 92 *—L.W. (3/1/2000)*

BETHANY

Bethany 2003 Chardonnay (Barossa) $23. Very fragrant with tropical, peachy fruit. Ditto for the palate, where peaches and mangoes reign, couched in a soft, buttery feel. Over-the-top and soft. **84** *—D.T. (4/1/2006)*

Bethany 2002 Chardonnay (Barossa) $26. This wine's tropical-fruit aromas are overpowering, but settle down on the palate. Butter joins the mango-peach flavors to create a hard candy-like impression in the mouth. Feel is soft; finishes with anise notes. **84** *—D.T. (10/1/2005)*

Bethany 2004 Riesling (Barossa) $25. This Riesling's aromas are quite nice: stone, lime, and grapefruit, maybe even some almond. Flavors are delicate on the palate, with light pear and stone flavors picking up in intensity toward the finish. Approachable; it's rounder and softer in feel than Rieslings from Clare. **88** *—D.T. (4/1/2006)*

Bethany 2002 Shiraz (Barossa) $37. This Shriaz offers pickling spice and wood aromas. On the palate, it's more of the same—dull wood, and some roasted fruit. Simple and flat. **81** *—D.T. (10/1/2005)*

BILLABONG

Billabong 1999 Merlot (South Eastern Australia) $8. Some pretty red cherry notes and a lively tartness keep this simple wine afloat. There's a faint mineral character and a touch of mint to go along on a light, loose frame. **81** *—J.F. (9/1/2001)*

Billabong 1999 Shiraz (South Eastern Australia) $8. A red berry-cherry jamball with rhubarb and herb accents. Lighter-styled, it has a slick mouthfeel, although tart, even sharp, acidity comes up on the back end. This easy drinker closes sweet yet tart, with a slight peppery tang. **85 Best Buy** *(10/1/2001)*

BIMBADGEN

Bimbadgen 2001 Proprietary Estate Chardonnay (Hunter Valley) $11. An odd wine, in that the nose and finish is full of butterscotch, with green sour-apple or sweet pea accents. The palate, on the other hand, is pretty spry on flavor, with just some citrus and steel notes coming through. The parts are okay on their own, but don't work together as well as they could. **83** *(7/2/2004)*

Bimbadgen 2001 Proprietary Grand Ridge Chardonnay (Hunter Valley) $10. The Grand Ridge is soft and round in the mouth, and shows honey, peach, and lactic-cream flavors. Interesting aromas—resin, golden raisin, and peach. Toasty-orange flavors on the finish. **85** *(7/2/2004)*

Bimbadgen 2002 Grand Ridge Verdelho (Hunter Valley) $10. Aromas are of bread and something vaguely chemical, but its flavors are all fruit—apricot or nectarine, and maybe some sour plum. It's a mouthful, with that mouthcoating quality that you get from sucking on hard candy. Finishes crisp and smooth. **85** *—D.T. (5/1/2004)*

BIRD IN HAND

Bird in Hand 2001 Cabernet Sauvignon (Adelaide Hills) $28. A rustic-feeling wine with black cherries and plums at the fore; gummy, chewy tannins in the mouth and juicy plum and blackberry aromas complete the package. A very nice wine, and a good introduction to how nice Adelaide Hills reds can be. **88** *—D.T. (5/1/2004)*

Bird in Hand 2001 Nest Egg Cabernet Sauvignon (Adelaide Hills) $40. A feminine-boned, elegant style of Cab—you'll think "Old World" in body, but it's definitely New World in flavor. Black cherry, plum, and even a little raspberry show on the palate, and on through the finish, where there's some stayingpower. Offers compelling pastry dough, red fruit and eucalyptus on the nose. **89** *—D.T. (5/1/2004)*

Bird in Hand 2001 Merlot (Adelaide Hills) $28. A light, simple wine with red fruit and a body that's not unlike Beaujolais. Raspberry, plum, and oak flavor it; oak is what hangs around on the finish. Sweet vanilla-butterscotch aromas on the nose. **83** *—D.T. (1/1/2002)*

Bird in Hand 2001 Two in the Bush Merlot-Cabernet Sauvignon (Adelaide Hills) $16. Mixed plums, black cherries, and white pepper aromas are a good sign of what's to come on the palate: Fresh, powerful plum fruit, plus oak that grows more obvious toward the finish. Still, you won't be able to resist the yummy, bouncy fruit. Makes a good case for big reds in Adelaide Hills. **88** *—D.T. (9/1/2004)*

Bird in Hand NV Joy Pinot Noir (Adelaide Hills) $70. Aromas are of cherry and ginger; salmon-copper in color. What you get on the palate follows suit: light cherry and peach flavors, packaged in a medium-bodied sparkler that is soft on palate entry and grows crisper and more tangy toward the finish. Pleasantly perplexing in that it manages to feel both fragile and forceful. **88** *—D.T. (12/31/2004)*

Bird in Hand NV Sparkling Pinot Noir (Adelaide Hills) $25. What your preteen daughters would drink if they could: it's a light pink wine, ultrafeminine, with a frothy, moussey mouthfeel that will bring to mind stuffed animals and baby dolls—everything blush-colored and innocent. Cherry flavors and aromas, through and through. Firms up on the finish. **84** *—D.T. (12/31/2004)*

Bird in Hand 2001 Sparkling Pinot Noir (Adelaide Hills) $22. This rose-colored sparkler boasts alluring aromas of baking bread and strawberry jam on toast. The palate is fresh and lively, laced with strawberries and cream. Refreshing and satisfying. **87** *—C.S. (12/1/2002)*

Bird in Hand 2000 Shiraz (Fleurieu Peninsula) $26. The bouquet is deep, condensed and full of vanilla and berry syrup. The flavors, however, are a bit candied, and the finish offers just more of the same. And while it's thick and tasty, it is also loaded with lemony wood notes, most likely from American oak. **87** *—M.S. (3/1/2003)*

BLACK CREEK

Black Creek 1998 Verdelho (Hunter Valley) $10. 82 *—M.M. (10/1/2000)*

BLACK OPAL

Black Opal 2000 Cabernet Sauvignon (South Eastern Australia) $11. The nose starts out with bacon and toast. The palate is loaded with cranberry and cherry fruit, but that doesn't mean it's lean and mean. Quite the contrary; it's round and spicy, with some Zin-like character to the flavor profile. **85** —*M.S. (12/15/2002)*

Black Opal 1999 Cabernet Sauvignon (South Eastern Australia) $11. This is typically Australian in its rich, outgoing fruit. The density and concentration are all based around great black-fruit flavors, which give strength and power to the wine. Delicious, soft tannins underpin it, but hardly affect the ripeness of the fruit. **84** —*R.V. (11/15/2001)*

Black Opal 2002 Cabernet Sauvignon-Merlot (South Eastern Australia) $8. Most all of your friends will get on board this berries-and-caramel train, and at this price, you can afford to treat them. Has ripe fruity aromas and flavors, with a maple-caramel tinge that's a little sweet for this reviewer, but will find plenty of fans. 82% Cabernet, 18% Merlot. **85 Best Buy** —*D.T. (12/31/2004)*

Black Opal 2000 Cabernet Sauvignon-Merlot (South Eastern Australia) $11. Medium and round in the mouth, this Cab-Merlot reminded this reviewer a little of Carmenere, with its red-fruit core and loads of barbecue-like spices. There's plenty of clove on the nose, too; what it lacks in subtlety it makes up for with quaffability. You should have no trouble finding it in stores. **84** —*D.T. (6/1/2003)*

Black Opal 1998 Cabernet Sauvignon-Merlot (Barossa Valley) $16. The deep ruby/black color prepares us for more in this wine but it just doesn't come. There is little fruit on the nose, and mouth-searing tannins that just don't let up dominate the palate and finish. **83** —*M.N. (6/1/2001)*

Black Opal 2004 Chardonnay (South Eastern Australia) $10. Shows a dry, citrusy verve on the nose. Acids are in full force on the palate, which, with its citrus and gooseberry flavors, reminded me more of Sauvignon than of Chardonnay. Fattens up on the finish; a good, bargain-priced quaff. **85 Best Buy** —*D.T. (5/1/2005)*

Black Opal 2003 Chardonnay (South Eastern Australia) $8. Buttered-toast aromas and green apple flavors get a boost from a minerally mouthfeel. Finish is medium-length, with a dusty feel. **83** —*D.T. (11/15/2004)*

Black Opal 2002 Chardonnay (South Eastern Australia) $14. This medium-weight wine has sweet cream and toast aromas, with a hint of tar; in the mouth, toasty, almost charred wood prevails. Finish is to the point, with talc and herb flavors. **83** *(7/2/2004)*

Black Opal 2001 Chardonnay (South Eastern Australia) $11. A heavyweight wine, loaded with cooked pear and apple flavors and accented by mint and cream. Like a real-life heavyweight, it's a bit ponderous in this crowd, albeit packed with flavor. **83** —*J.C. (7/1/2002)*

Black Opal 1998 Chardonnay (South Australia) $11. **83** —*L.W. (12/31/1999)*

Black Opal 2003 Shiraz (South Eastern Australia) $10. Has a very rustic, outdoorsy quality to it overall. The wine tastes and smells like berries rolled in earth—even its texture is uneven and rustic. **82** —*D.T. (12/31/2005)*

Black Opal 2001 Shiraz (South Eastern Australia) $12. The wine's black plum fruit is firm but ripe; fruit on the nose and on the finish, though, is sweet and red—like strawberry jam. Still, the wine has nice clay-chalk notes on the finish that tries to keep that sweetness under wraps. **84** —*D.T. (12/31/2003)*

Black Opal 2000 Shiraz (South Eastern Australia) $11. Smooth and enticing aromas of warm black fruit and vanilla go a long way toward rolling out the welcome mat. Those scents get backing from a structured palate of cherry and pomegranate, while the straight-ahead finish is clean, even if it doesn't offer a whole lot of complexity or texture. **87 Best Buy** —*M.S. (3/1/2003)*

Black Opal 1999 Shiraz (South Eastern Australia) $11. One of several Aussie Shirazes we've tasted recently that combines cheesy lactic aromas with eucalyptus and sour berries. Some grapey, blackberry nuances on the finish and a smooth mouthfeel provide mass appeal. **83** *(10/1/2001)*

Black Opal 1996 Shiraz (Barossa Valley) $16. **84** —*L.W. (12/31/1999)*

Black Opal 2005 Shiraz-Cabernet Sauvignon (South Eastern Australia) $8. Shows simple, grapey aromas, plus a little chile spice on the nose. What follows on the palate is simple, straightforward fruit edged in a veneer of oak. A little bitter on the finish, but overall it's fine for large gatherings or casual parties. **83** —*D.T. (11/15/2006)*

Black Opal 2001 Shiraz-Cabernet Sauvignon (South Eastern Australia) $12. A surprisingly disappointing showing for this value brand that usually performs better. Though the nose overdelivers with eucalyptus, black pepper, earth, and meat aromas, the palate's sour black fruit and heavy oak is dark yet hollow in the mouth. A sour, acidic bite on the back doesn't help. **82** —*D.T. (1/1/2002)*

BLACK SWAN

Black Swan 2002 Cabernet Sauvignon (South Eastern Australia) $8. Sweet red fruit—think raspberry, plum, and strawberry—show on the nose and keeps going, on through the finish. Simple and sweet, like strawberry shortcake in a bottle. **82** —*D.T. (1/1/2002)*

Black Swan 2003 Chardonnay (South Eastern Australia) $8. Aromas are of buttered toast and pear; in the mouth, the pear, melon, and peach flavors are halfhearted, or not all that concentrated. A good pour if you need an inexpensive, cold quaff. **84** *(7/2/2004)*

Black Swan 2003 Chardonnay (South Eastern Australia) $8. Dusty floral notes on the nose. In the mouth, its texture is mealy—you want to bite into it, or chew it, rather than drink it. Finishes with a oil/resin flavor. **83** —*D.T. (11/15/2004)*

Black Swan 2002 Chardonnay (South Eastern Australia) $8. Nice floral, pear, and vanilla notes waft from the nose. Its body is on the soft side, but the sweetish, white stone fruit-and-citrus profile (and its bargain price) are surefire crowd pleasers. **85** —*D.T. (8/1/2003)*

Black Swan 2003 Merlot (South Eastern Australia) $8. Has some sweetness on the nose, like cherry candy. On the palate, it's a medium-sized red, with plum fruit accented by acorn and anise. Finishes with smooth, oaky tannins. A good, please-everyone bet for the neighborhood block party. **85 Best Buy** —*D.T. (12/31/2004)*

Black Swan 2004 Shiraz-Merlot Red Blend (South Eastern Australia) $9. Has a nice graham-crackery aroma, with a pulpy, woody feel and sour plum skin and rubber flavors. 155,000 cases produced. **82** —*D.T. (10/1/2005)*

Black Swan 2002 Shiraz (South Eastern Australia) $8. Complexity isn't at issue here—you'll be downing this wine, not thinking about it. There is simple but ripe red and purple fruit on the palate. Finishes with a slightly acidic bite. **83** —*D.T. (1/1/2002)*

Black Swan 2004 Shiraz-Cabernet Sauvignon (South Eastern Australia) $9. Smells like bread flour and tastes like black cherries. One-dimensional and simple; two-thirds Shiraz, and one-third Cab. 125,000 cases. **83** —*D.T. (10/1/2005)*

Black Swan 2003 Chardonnay & Semillon White Blend (South Eastern Australia) $9. Meaty and molassesy on the nose, which is an odd thing for a white wine, maybe. In the mouth, the wine is round with pear and molasses flavors, and passion fruit and peach on the finish. A fine, straightforward white for most occasions. **84** —*D.T. (11/15/2004)*

BLEASDALE

Bleasdale 2000 Mulberry Tree Cabernet Sauvignon (Langhorne Creek) $16. Smells great, with smoke, pie crust, and black pepper accenting rich blueberry fruit. But in the mouth, the nuances get muddled in the huge blackberry and blueberry fruit. Rich through the middle palate, it drops off a bit on the short, warm finish. **87** —*J.C. (6/1/2002)*

Bleasdale 1999 Cabernet Sauvignon-Shiraz (Langhorne Creek) $12. Despite this wine's heady 14.9% alcohol level, it comes across as only medium-bodied. But the alcohol does show in the warm, slightly boozy and liqueur-like blackberry and chocolate aromas and flavors. Hints of licorice and charcoal add interest. **86** —*J.C. (9/1/2002)*

Bleasdale 1999 Bremerview Shiraz (Langhorne Creek) $15. The mouthfeel on this Langhorne Creek Shiraz is full and slightly tart; the palate shows tart, rich blackberry, anise, and cedar. Sandwich that between a complex bouquet of plum, cocoa, and deep blackberry, and a lengthy, minerally finish, and, well, you've got some drinking to do tonight. **89 Best Buy** *(10/1/2001)*

BLUE MARLIN

Blue Marlin 2004 Chardonnay (South Eastern Australia) $10. This wine has bright tropical and citrus fruit on the palate, and caramelly aromas. Has an odd, fuzzy spritz on the palate that was a detraction. **83** —*D.T. (10/1/2005)*

BLUE PYRENEES

Blue Pyrenees 1999 Cabernet Sauvignon (Victoria) $15. The bouquet is basically nonexistent—it's that flat and mute. Weak but tart flavors of plum and strawberry lead into a finish that has sticky, overt tannins. This wine isn't offensive, but it has no real personality to speak of. **82** —*M.S. (12/15/2002)*

Blue Pyrenees 2004 Chardonnay (Pyrenees) $16. Has aromas of vanilla bean, apple, resin, and light toast. On the palate, peach is the dominant flavor, coupled with an undercurrent of olive oil and a white-peppery edge. A little soft on the palate, but quite charming nonetheless. **88** —*D.T. (6/1/2006)*

Blue Pyrenees 2001 Chardonnay (Victoria) $NA. **81** —*D.T. (8/1/2003)*

Blue Pyrenees 1999 Estate Reserve Chardonnay (Victoria) $20. This weighty California lookalike nevertheless comes across as balanced, thanks to a long, mouthwatering finish. Citrus and yellow-plum flavors stand up well to a hefty dose of vanilla and buttered toast. **87** —*J.C. (7/1/2002)*

Blue Pyrenees 2000 Shiraz (Pyrenees) $16. Opens with aromas of black soil, mint, and cola. Its acids are lively, its cherry fruit tight, and an undercurrent of eucalyptus ties it all together—all characters that you either love or you don't. The wine has a lot going for it, though, and is worth a look. **89** —*D.T. (6/1/2006)*

Blue Pyrenees 1999 Shiraz (Victoria) $15. Complex berry, vanillin oak, fig, and pepper aromas set up this round and flavorful wine. The palate, too, offers interesting notes—blueberry, cinnamon, licorice, and more. Yes, there's plenty of wood, but it's nicely integrated here. The velvety mouthfeel and mint and plum elements play out on the long finish. **87** **Editors' Choice** *(10/1/2001)*

Blue Pyrenees 1999 Estate Reserve Shiraz (Victoria) $20. This individual and exotic wine boasts aromas of sweet bay leaves, dried apricots, and crushed black pepper. The fruit flavors are tart, veering toward red cherries and apple skin, finishing with firm acids and tannins. Drink young with herbed roasts to help bring out the fruit. **85** —*J.C. (9/1/2002)*

BLUE TONGUE

Blue Tongue 2004 Chardonnay (South Eastern Australia) $10. Getting past the nose, with black pepper, pickle, and lactic aromas, takes some doing; but once you do, the flavors are fine. White stone fruit dominates, couched in a puffy, soft feel. Finishes with a lemon meringue note. **83** —*D.T. (8/1/2006)*

Blue Tongue 2002 Chardonnay (South Eastern Australia) $7. Though it's 100% Chardonnay, this wine doesn't taste particularly Chard-like: it has light floral and stone fruit notes more akin to a Riesling. It's a lightweight in the mouth, rounded out by a little creaminess. A decent, economical choice to quaff on a hot day. **84** —*D.T. (8/1/2003)*

Blue Tongue 2004 Shiraz (South Eastern Australia) $9. Roasted, sandy aromas set the wine off on a shaky start, but the palate delivers plum and mealy apple flavors that compensate. Medium sized, with an even texture. **83** —*D.T. (6/1/2006)*

Blue Tongue 2002 Shiraz (South Eastern Australia) $7. Easy to drink, and a sweet tooth's dream: maple syrup on the nose, with sweet raspberries and blackberries on the palate. Finishes with an interesting carob-mocha combination. **83** —*D.T. (1/1/2002)*

BOGGY CREEK

Boggy Creek 2003 Cabernet Sauvignon (King Valley) $15. Out of the chute, the aromas are sweet and cloying, but settle to reveal cured meat and leather notes. Purple fruit on the palate has its share of stably, briary accents, on through the finish. It's not the deepest, broadest wine on the block, but its unusual profile merits it a look, particularly with food. **87** —*D.T. (6/1/2006)*

Boggy Creek 2004 Chardonnay (King Valley) $19. Offers light toast and nut aromas, and modest peach and pear flavors on the palate. A middleweight in terms of size and intensity. **86** —*D.T. (4/1/2006)*

Boggy Creek 2004 Unwooded Chardonnay (King Valley) $15. This unwooded Chard is elegant and a little austere, but very nice. It has a sturdy spine with a dry, mineral texture and light pear and citrus flavors. The finish isn't tremendous at first, but lengthens and reveals citrus flavors with some time in the glass. **88** —*D.T. (4/1/2006)*

Boggy Creek 2003 Shiraz (King Valley) $21. Fragrant aromas of spice, clove, and hickory smoke continue through to the palate, where the same flavors hang on a wiry, black-cherry frame. It's a straightforward, medium-sized Shiraz, just the right weight to be served with dinner. **87** —*D.T. (4/1/2006)*

BOOKPURNONG HILL

Bookpurnong Hill 1999 Cabernet Sauvignon (Riverland) $40. This Cab takes a while to open and show some flavor, but when it does, it has subtle buttercream and blackberry aromas and a blackberry, grape jelly, and honey palate. It's smooth, round, and easy to drink, with a long, slightly sweet, blackberry-jam finish. **87** —*D.T. (9/1/2001)*

Bookpurnong Hill 1999 Petite Verdot (South Eastern Australia) $40. This tawny-black Riverland offering has a Port-like bouquet of stewed fruit, mulling spices, and smoked meat. Superripe (perhaps overripe) blackberry fruit stars in the mouth, with ancho chile and black pepper flavors in supporting roles. This chewy Petit Verdot is, as the song goes, a bit too "Hot Hot Hot," but is still an enjoyable drink. **85** —*D.T. (9/1/2001)*

Bookpurnong Hill 1999 Block 267 Rhône Red Blend (Riverland) $40. Though it has pleasing light blueberry aromas on the nose, and smoke and black grape flavors on the palate, this Cab-Petit Verdot-Merlot-Shiraz blend has a slightly offputting cream-cheese aroma as well. Mouthfeel is a little zingy, as if this blend has a few Zin genes, too. The finish is medium-long and more oaky than fruity. **84** —*D.T. (9/1/2001)*

Bookpurnong Hill 1999 Shiraz (Riverland) $43. Sweet-smelling oak, reminiscent of marshmallows around the campfire, blends nicely with cassis and black-cherry flavors. Finishes tart, with dried spice, cocoa, and coffee shadings. **87** *(11/1/2001)*

BOOLAROO

Boolaroo 2003 Chardonnay (Victoria) $14. A well-made Chardonnay, but one that follows a pretty familiar recipe: Yellow stone fruit aromas and flavors; liberally wooded, with a toasty finish. Good, textbook Chard, and pretty full on the palate. **86** —*D.T. (8/1/2005)*

BOUTÍQUE WILDFLOWER

Boutíque Wildflower 2003 Chardonnay (South Eastern Australia) $11. Darker gold in color; smells like baking apples, in a good way. Flavors of yellow stone fruit and oak want more snap on the palate. **84** —*D.T. (6/1/2006)*

BOUTIQUE WINES

Boutique Wines 1998 The Region Chardonnay (Adelaide Hills) $22. This Chardonnay comes from five different wineries in the Adelaide Hills. Each vinified their own juice and then sent it to one of the quintet for blending—ergo the Boutique Wines name. The final product displays their careful crafting, with apple, cinnamon, and well-integrated oak flavors. There's decent structure and a nicely textured mouthfeel. Grilled salmon would like this one, too. **88** *(6/1/2001)*

BOWEN ESTATE

Bowen Estate 2003 Shiraz (Coonawarra) $27. This couldn't be from anywhere but Coonawarra: its clay-earth texture is its hallmark. Flavors of plum, bramble, mint, and spice persist through the finish. A little closed now, and could benefit from decanting, or another year or two in the bottle. **89** —*D.T. (6/1/2006)*

BOX STALLION

Box Stallion 2001 Red Barn Chardonnay (Mornington Peninsula) $20. This wine's yellow fruit and soft mouthfeel are pleasant though simple. It's a good quaffer for the porch on a sunny afternoon—but that sort of casual enjoyment should come at about half this wine's price. **84** —*D.T.* (5/1/2005)

Box Stallion 2001 The Enclosure Chardonnay (Mornington Peninsula) $30. This Chardonnay is a glowing-gold color, and its further impressions live up to the expectation that you get from its appearance: buttery/nutty aromas, and a buttery texture. Structure and concentration are also not strengths here. Very expensive for what's in the bottle. 2,000 cases produced. **82** —*D.T.* (5/1/2005)

BRANSON COACH HOUSE

Branson Coach House 2004 Greenock Coach House Block Cabernet Sauvignon (Barossa Valley) $105. From the folks who bring you Two Hands comes this big Cab, which sticks to the glass and deals a chile-spiced nose right out of the gate. The front palate is loaded with chocolate, mocha, and forward fruit—all of the hedonistic sexiness your palate can handle. A hint of sour cherry is buried, suggesting that some of its assets may reveal themselves down the track. **91** —*D.T.* (11/15/2006)

Branson Coach House 2002 Rare Single Vineyard Coach House Block Shiraz (Barossa Valley) $75. Aromas are broad and profound, with very ripe fruit, and pretty biscuit and black pepper accents. The palate? Cassis, pepper, plum, and meat. Firm in the mouth, with fine tannins, and its flavors grow darker—olive, earth, pepper—through the long finish. Has substance, class, restraint, and perhaps best of all, holding power. Sexy as all get-out now, but we'll probably say the same thing in 2015. **93** —*D.T.* (12/31/2004)

Branson Coach House 2002 Single Vineyard Greenock Block Shiraz (Barossa Valley) $45. Has meaty, bacon aromas with creamy, peppery highlights. In the mouth, it's brawn in a glass—not a dumb jock, mind you, but the amiable linebacker who also wins "Mr. Congeniality." It has a rich, creamy feel on the front palate, good meaty heft in the middle, and zips up with a juicy plum and anise conclusion. Muscular, mobile and piquant, not fat and inert. **91** —*D.T.* (12/31/2004)

BREMERTON

Bremerton 1999 Tamblyn Rhône Red Blend (Langhorne Creek) $20. On the nose, fresh earth and dark blackberry notes are coated in a milky-calcium aroma. The wine will certainly have wide appeal, given its light-to-medium body and red berry-oak-leather profile. It's two-thirds Cabernet Sauvignon, with Merlot, Malbec, and Shiraz taking up the slack. **84** —*D.T.* (6/1/2002)

Bremerton 2000 Sauvignon Blanc (Langhorne Creek) $17. Sweet aromas on the nose don't carry through to the earthy palate. There are some pear notes and it is balanced, if rather soft and low in acidity. **81** —*J.F.* (9/1/2001)

Bremerton 2000 Selkirk Shiraz (Langhorne Creek) $18. Bright, mouthwatering acidity should be tempered with food. But the light aromas of brown sugar, mint, and raspberry don't show a lot of depth; the thin, green raspberry flavors may not hold up. **85** —*K.F.* (3/1/2003)

Bremerton 1999 Young Vine Shiraz (Langhorne Creek) $20. Unique cilantro and corn-husk scents on the nose accent sweet blackberry fruit. The herb notes continue on the palate, along with roasted fruit and nuts, but the highlights are the rich, chewy texture and snappy, peppery finish. **86** (10/1/2001)

BROKEN EARTH

Broken Earth 2004 Chardonnay (South Eastern Australia) $8. This wine will please bargain hunters who like their Chards soft and fruity. Honey, pineapple, and citrus aromas usher in even more overt peach, pineapple and mango flavors. An easy quaff. **84 Best Buy** —*D.T.* (8/1/2006)

Broken Earth 2004 Shiraz (South Eastern Australia) $8. "Wine for a new world" says the wine's tagline; it offers orange-y, berry aromas and flimsy cranberry-plum flavors. Not structured or deep. **81** —*D.T.* (10/1/2006)

BROKENWOOD

Brokenwood 2002 Cricket Pitch Cabernet Blend (McLaren Vale & Padthaway) $17. This is quite a hodgepodge of a red—one with Cab, Merlot, Cab Franc, and Shiraz—but boy, is it tasty. Svelte in size, there's a briary-earthy component (wheat toast, smooth wood, earth, you name

it) through and through, with firm red plum fruit flavors. With good hold on the midpalate, this reasonably priced red could easily go another couple of years. **90** —*D.T.* (8/1/2005)

Brokenwood 2004 Semillon (Hunter Valley) $22. The heart of this Semillon is bony and minerally; barely ripe peach flavors and a green-apple finish completes the flavor profile. Lightly petillant in the mouth, with a burst of Sweet Tart on palate entry. It's a pleasing, refreshing white. **87** —*D.T.* (8/1/2005)

Brokenwood 2001 Semillon (Hunter Valley) $17. Fresh, clean aromas of Asian pear and citrus lead the way, followed up by similar flavors on the palate. It's crisp and citrusy from start to long, tart finish. Not terribly complex at this young age, it should add layers of toast and spice with age. **87** —*J.C.* (2/1/2002)

Brokenwood 2002 Graveyard Vineyard Shiraz (Hunter Valley) $100. A gorgeous wine that defies the modern idea that wines have to be big and brash to be excellent. This one feels simultaneously fresh and old as the hills, with a meaty, merdy appeal. Red fruit aromas and flavors are concentrated and sprinkled in black pepper; the tannins are manageable now, but still substantial enough to age. A modest 13.5% alcohol, and, bless 'em, sealed en screwcap. Tastes good now, but probably even better around 2009. **95** —*D.T.* (8/1/2005)

Brokenwood 1999 Graveyard Vineyard Shiraz (Hunter Valley) $69. This Shiraz is medium-weight but feels lean and dry, due in large part to the toasty oak, smoke, and mineral flavors that have this wine under their spell. Add to the cauldron cherry and blackberry notes on the nose and in the mouth, and a long finish, and you have the makings of a fine wine. It may be even better after five or six years in the dungeon—ahem, we mean cellar. **88** (11/1/2001)

Brokenwood 2002 Rayner Vineyard Shiraz (McLaren Vale) $70. A spitfire of a Shiraz. High-toned blackberry and black cherry flavors have undertones of coffee and mocha. As nice as the flavors and aromas of fresh earth and cola are, the acids stick out some, giving the palate a prickly feel. Would easily have reached the next decile otherwise. **88** —*D.T.* (10/1/2005)

Brokenwood 2002 Wade Block 2 Shiraz (McLaren Vale) $46. Smells smoldering but sweetish, a combo of roasted meat and very ripe berries. The palate's texture is chalky, the tannins soft; the wine's berry fruit swathed in loads of bitter chocolate. Warm overall. Finishes with a nutty note. **89** —*D.T.* (10/1/2005)

Brokenwood 2001 Wade Block 2 Vineyard Selection Shiraz (McLaren Vale) $37. Obviously well pedigreed, but this wine is soft, and wants a little more acid. Its black fruit is just this side of sweet, backed up by mocha and marshmallow flavors. Medium-bodied and fruity, an easy-to-drink wine, but probably not much of an ager. Tasted twice. **86** —*D.T.* (5/1/2004)

BROOKLAND VALLEY

Brookland Valley 1999 Cabernet Sauvignon-Merlot (Margaret River) $27. There is a slight vegetal note, but there's enough pretty red plum fruit and smoky oak to distract you. Leaf, beef, putty, and eucalyptus waft from the nose. **87** —*D.T.* (10/1/2003)

Brookland Valley 2000 Estate Cabernet Sauvignon-Merlot (Margaret River) $33. Says Cabernet-Merlot on the label, but Merlot makes up a whopping 5% of the blend. This wine is excellent, but its cool-climate profile isn't for everyone. This reviewer found a lot to like about the sweet-and-tart black fruit and eucalyptus aromas; cool, red fruit on the palate and lovely, clay-chalk finish. But the wine is taut, and the eucalyptus persistent. **90** —*D.T.* (9/1/2004)

Brookland Valley 2002 Verse 1 Cabernet Sauvignon-Merlot (Margaret River) $15. Has earthy, brambly aromas, which follow through to give purple and red berries some luster. Has woody tannins, but also a narrow, hollow feel on the palate. A blend of 88% Cabernet Sauvignon, 12% Merlot. **85** —*D.T.* (12/1/2005)

Brookland Valley 2002 Verse 1 Cabernet Sauvignon-Merlot (Margaret River) $15. Briary, clay, fresh green aromas. It's straight down the line on the palate, with black cherry fruit, soft tannins, vanilla accents and a fair amount of flat wood on the palate. **87** —*D.T.* (6/1/2006)

Brookland Valley 2002 Chardonnay (Margaret River) $27. Smells toasty and musky, like roasted meat, even. On the palate, soft yellow fruit gives way to a buttery finish. Good, but straightforward. **86** —D.T. (5/1/2005)

Brookland Valley 2001 Estate Chardonnay (Margaret River) $27. Panel members had differing opinions about this wine. While one taster found it too woody and wrought with caramel and toasted marshmallow flavors, another found it quite elegant, with fresh herb and understated stone fruit flavors. Round in the mouth; try it and break our deadlock. **88** (7/2/2004)

Brookland Valley 2002 Verse 1 Chardonnay (Margaret River) $16. Straightforward, with bright yellow fruit and some mustard seed flavors in the mouth. Finishes with oak and nut flavors. **84** (1/1/2004)

Brookland Valley 2001 Verse 1 Chardonnay (Margaret River) $20. Straightforward, with bright yellow fruit and some mustard seed flavors in the mouth. Finishes with oak and nut flavors. **84** —D.T. (10/1/2003)

Brookland Valley 2004 Verse 1 Semillon-Sauvignon Blanc (Margaret River) $16. This is a lively Sem-Sauv in which the Sauvignon seems to steal the show. Semillon lends a hay-like aroma, but apart from that, zesty lime and grass flavors dominate. Tastes just as it smells, with a dry feel. Very nice. **88** —D.T. (10/1/2005)

Brookland Valley 2002 Verse 1 Semillon-Sauvignon Blanc (Margaret River) $16. A welcome addition to any raw bar, this lean, crisp wine might just be too crisp to drink on its own. It tastes and smells like fresh lemon pith; finishes with nice citrus-slate flavors. **85** —D.T. (10/1/2003)

Brookland Valley 2001 Verse 1 Shiraz (Margaret River) $18. Hugely concentrated and purple in color, with tight, deep aromas of black plum and match stick. Powerful, with cassis and cherry fruit, while the finish is oaky, delivering vanilla and coffee. The wine's heavy weight and sharp acidity don't exactly match, but the overall impression is still positive. **87** —M.S. (3/1/2003)

BROWN BROTHERS

Brown Brothers 2001 Estate Bottled Cabernet Sauvignon (Victoria) $13. Creamy, oaky flavors accent black fruit on the palate, with woodsy, ashy tannins on the follow-through. It's good, though a little dull around the edges, and with less stuffing than I'd like. **84** —D.T. (12/31/2003)

Brown Brothers 2000 Patricia Reserve Cabernet Sauvignon (Victoria) $30. Black as black in color, which may or may not have anything to do with the 7% Petit Verdot inside. It's a straight-up plum-and-oak combo, dense in the mouth with tealike tannins that linger on the finish. **88** (8/1/2004)

Brown Brothers 2003 Chardonnay (Victoria) $13. A food-friendly, drinkable Chard. On the nose, it is just a little nutty, with pear, peach, and resin, and it tastes just as it smells. Round and just a little alcoholic on the palate. **86** —D.T. (10/1/2005)

Brown Brothers 2001 Estate Bottled Chardonnay (Victoria) $11. A feminine Chardonnay, one that has scents and flavors of cream, talc powder, and flowers. In contrast, the wine's mouthfeel is a coarse accompaniment for what the palate and nose offer. **84** —D.T. (12/31/2003)

Brown Brothers 2001 Patricia Reserve Chardonnay (Victoria) $28. Round but restrained in the mouth, this Chardonnay's pear and apple fruit is clean and flavorful, and are accented by butter and oat. Picks up more oak, and a little heat, on the finish. **88** (8/1/2004)

Brown Brothers 2000 Patricia Reserve Merlot (Victoria) $30. Dust, dried herb, and pure black cherry aromas segue into black cherry, vanilla, and tree bark flavors on the palate. On the lighter side, as far as Merlot goes. Finishes with a bite of herb and coffee. **87** (8/1/2004)

Brown Brothers 1999 Patricia Late Harvested Noble Riesling (Australia) $33. Green-amber in color; the wine's very aromatic, with deep, apricot marmalade, nectarine, orange, and olive oil scents. In the mouth, there's a tremendous rush of flavor: honey, marmalade, nectarine, and a hint of petrol. A little rough on the medium-long finish, but that won't keep you from reaching for another glass. Only 100 6-bottle cases imported to the U.S. **91** (8/1/2004)

Brown Brothers 2000 Patricia Reserve Shiraz (Victoria) $33. Opens with peppery-smoky aromas. This is a supple, elegant Shiraz, easy to drink, with blackberry, vanilla, and dill flavors that fade into a smooth finish. **88** (8/1/2004)

BROWNS OF PADTHAWAY

Browns of Padthaway 2002 Estate Grown Verdelho (Padthaway) $13. Bright green-gold in color, with aromas as disparate as fresh green pea and chili spice. On the palate, there's more fresh green peas (odd flavor, but pleasant) swimming in a sea of bright yellow fruit. Medium in body; finish is somewhat abrupt. **86** —D.T. (11/15/2004)

BRUMBY CANYON

Brumby Canyon 2002 Jillaroo Red Red Blend (South Australia) $14. The name requires another Australian-to-American English translation: A "brumby" is a wild Australian horse; a "jillaroo," a farm worker. Thankfully, this wine doesn't taste like anything you'd find in a stable: it offers very ripe black cherry flavors, with some black soil joining in on the finish. Beaujolais-sized in body, this Shiraz (60%), Grenache (33%), Mataro (7%) blend is an inexpensive, easy quaffer. **87** —D.T. (12/31/2004)

BUCKELEY'S

Buckeley's 2002 Cabernet Sauvignon-Shiraz (South Australia) $10. A rich, thickly textured wine marked by furry tannins and big, jammy flavors of blackberries, plums, and an interesting cut of sour cherry. Drinks very dry and juicy, with good Aussie acidity. **88 Best Buy** —S.H. (10/1/2003)

Buckeley's 1999 Chardonnay (South Australia) $10. 84 —M.S. (10/1/2000)

Buckeley's 2002 Chardonnay (South Australia) $10. A solidly made Oz Chard, with those distinctly crisp, bright acids and big flavors of citrus, apples, and tropical fruits. Very clean and tasty. **89 Best Buy** —S.H. (10/1/2003)

Buckeley's 2001 Chardonnay (South Australia) $10. A light but pretty wine that showcases melon and tropical-fruit aromas and finishes with charming tangerine and citrus flavors that are fresh and clean. Try some on the patio or deck this summer. **85** —J.C. (7/1/2002)

Buckeley's 2000 Chardonnay (South Australia) $10. Nutty and buttery on the nose, with some pineapple notes. Light on the palate, just some faint pear and white peach flavors, finishing lemony and clean. **84** —J.C. (1/1/2004)

Buckeley's 2002 Merlot (South Australia) $10. Not a bad Merlot, with pleasant blackberry flavors, and quite dry. On the other hand, this wine possesses a rough texture that scours the palate, and there is an herbal finish. **85** —S.H. (10/1/2003)

Buckeley's 2002 Sauvignon Blanc (Currency Creek) $10. Aromas are of grapefruit and peach. In the mouth, it's varietally correct, though not very concentrated, with citrus and herb flavors. Finishes medium, with lemon flavors. **84** —D.T. (11/15/2004)

Buckeley's 2001 Shiraz (South Australia) $12. Opens with a quick burst of black currant jam, white pepper, and vanilla aromas. There's plenty of juicy cherry-berry flavors in the mouth, but the wine is also soft and a little sweet. **85** —S.H. (10/1/2003)

Buckeley's 2000 Shiraz (South Australia) $10. After a few minutes, the tight nose reveals hints of smoke, anise, and cream. Thin on the palate, with lemony-oak and lean fruit flavors. Finishes short and tangy, with some pepper and caramel. **81** (10/1/2001)

BULLETIN PLACE

Bulletin Place 2004 Cabernet Sauvignon (South Eastern Australia) $9. Wide, juicy plum fruit on the palate is no surprise, given the fat plum and blueberry notes that waft from the glass. It drops off a little sooner than I'd want on the finish, but it's still a good Cab pick at an attractive price. **85 Best Buy** —D.T. (11/15/2006)

Bulletin Place 1999 Cabernet Sauvignon (South Eastern Australia) $10. The nose is a bit medicinal with cedar and leather. There is a lack of fruit and a thin, hollow mouthfeel that finishes soft. **83** —C.S. (6/1/2002)

Bulletin Place 2005 Chardonnay (South Eastern Australia) $8. Very citrusy, from beginning to end. Its aromas and flavors run the gamut from lemon drop and grapefruit to citrus pulp. A little sour and broad, but still enjoyable. **84 Best Buy** —D.T. (11/15/2006)

AUSTRALIA

Bulletin Place 2004 Chardonnay (South Eastern Australia) $8. A delicate, feminine Chardonnay, exciting in that it has more nuance than you'd expect from an $8 wine. The nose offers pretty citrus and olive oil scents, and it tastes a little like lemon pannacotta, dusted with some chalk. Mouthfeel has a viscous, round texture. Way to go. **87 Best Buy** —D.T. (12/31/2004)

Bulletin Place 2001 Chardonnay (South Eastern Australia) $8. Crisp and refreshing in the mouth, with a light resin or fig note that is also detectable on the nose. Mellow yellow fruit rounds out the finish. This is one of Len Evans's wines, named for a restaurant he used to own. **85** —D.T. (11/15/2003)

Bulletin Place 1999 Chardonnay (South Eastern Australia) $8. Tropical fruits start this one off and on the palate, toasted oak and butterscotch join in. The structure is solid and the acid just right. This is a clean, decent Chardonnay. **85** —M.N. (6/1/2001)

Bulletin Place 2002 Merlot (South Eastern Australia) $10. Lots of vanilla and cream on the nose; it's a little sloppy on the palate, with sweet grape and blackberry fruit and mouthcoating caramel. Fine for casual circumstances, just don't think too hard about it. **83** —D.T. (1/1/2002)

Bulletin Place 1998 Shiraz (South Australia) $10. 85 (10/1/2000)

Bulletin Place 2003 Shiraz (South Eastern Australia) $8. Though this Shiraz smells somewhat sweet, you thankfully don't get the same impression on the palate. Instead, there is red berry and plum fruit, with lemony-oak accents. It's simple, but still a steal. **84 Best Buy** —D.T. (5/1/2005)

Bulletin Place 2000 Shiraz (South Eastern Australia) $10. Mint leaves and young sage do well to cover the aromas of wilted greens, with plenty of caramel, toast and grape jelly that extend to the palate. The finish is tinged with herbal qualities and white pepper. **86** —K.F. (3/1/2003)

Bulletin Place 1999 Shiraz (South Eastern Australia) $10. This bright, deep ruby-colored wine exhibits a deep cherry, black pepper, and smoke nose. On the palate, there's good balance, medium body, and a smooth mouthfeel that glides right into a long finish displaying the same flavors as the opening notes. This is good everyday wine for Shiraz lovers. **84** —M.N. (10/1/2001)

BUNDALEER

Bundaleer 2002 Shiraz (Heathcote) $40. Labeled a moderate 13,5% alcohol. Feels mouthfilling, yet delicate and feminine. Aromas evolve from muted cassis, to eucalyptus, bread flour, and animal. Tannins are smooth and dry, and the wine's blueberry, black cherry, and blackberry flavors are fruit-sweet, yet taut. A chocolate-biscuit richness and pretty plum flavors bring it to a pleasing close. **91** —D.T. (12/31/2004)

BURTON

Burton 1999 Cabernet Sauvignon (Coonawarra) $27. Aromas on the nose are compelling—there's beef, ink, caramel, black, and red cherry. What you get on the palate (red plum, and a fair bit of oak) is fine, but a little less interesting. The same flavors, plus a hint of eucalyptus, shows on the finish. **85** —D.T. (6/1/2003)

Burton 1998 Reserve Cabernet Sauvignon (Coonawarra) $40. Medium-bodied, with gummy tannins, this Cab's core is of red fruit that verges on tangy, with dark soil and oak notes to dress it up. Has nice blackberry, eucalyptus, and wheat notes on the nose; finishes with more oak and soil. **86** —D.T. (6/1/2003)

Burton 2000 Cabernet Sauvignon-Merlot (South Eastern Australia) $16. Aromas are of licorice, plum, and whole wheat. Merlot makes up just 10% of this blend, which has a smooth claylike texture and flavors of roasted meat and plum. It's approachable now, and very tasty. **88** —D.T. (8/1/2003)

BUSH BIKE

Bush Bike 2004 Chardonnay (Western Australia) $14. This unoaked Chard is floral, feminine, and a little soft, showing melon, citrus, talc powder, and apple aromas and flavors. A good warm-weather choice for picnics or parties. **86** —D.T. (12/1/2005)

Bush Bike 2003 Merlot-Shiraz (Western Australia) $14. A juicy, medium-bodied, focused blend of Merlot (70%) and Shiraz (30%). Shows notes

of fresh whipping cream and blackberry on the nose, and red plum, mocha, and coffee flavors, the latter persisting through the finish. **87** —D.T. (2/1/2006)

Bush Bike 2004 Riesling (Western Australia) $14. Offers fresh green produce and herb aromas. On the palate, the rocky-minerally feel is nice, but the weak lemon flavors don't quite live up to it. **83** —D.T. (12/1/2005)

Bush Bike 2003 Shiraz (Western Australia) $14. Just good, this wine's plum, cherry, cumin, and tangy oak aromas are pleasing enough, but the palate offers a jumble of leaf, earth, and soda pop-like raspberry and blackberry fruit underneath. Finishes with a tangy, sour streak. **83** —D.T. (12/31/2005)

CALEDONIA AUSTRALIS

Caledonia Australis 2001 Chardonnay (Gippsland) $30. Offers apple and butter aromas and flavors, with a very buttery—though blessedly not too oversized—mouthfeel. Aged in French oak; 1,000 cases produced. **85** —D.T. (8/1/2005)

Caledonia Australis 2003 Mount Macleod Chardonnay (Gippsland) $17. This is a pretty Chard, with a medium-long, dry finish. Rounded on the palate, with stone fruit and light toast flavors, it zips up tight, tall and dry on the back end. **88** —D.T. (8/1/2005)

Caledonia Australis 2003 Pinot Noir (Gippsland) $26. A fairly powerful Pinot, if somewhat sour and lacking harmony at this stage. Aromas are of plums and dates, while the palate's flavors are of plum skin, iced tea, and cheese rind. Black peppery on the finish. May just be dumb in its youth. Worth revisiting in 6 months. **86** —D.T. (10/1/2005)

Caledonia Australis 2003 Mount Macleod Pinot Noir (Gippsland) $17. Not a please-everyone style of Pinot—we found that out the hard way in the tasting room. I enjoyed this wine quite a bit: it's tight, sour, and leathery, both intense and delicate at the same time. The finish is long and juicy, and the nose shows cherry, earth, and tree-bark notes. Another taster found it just too wiry, even thin. If you're tired of Pinots that taste like Shirazes, this is a good place to start. **89 Editors' Choice** —D.T. (12/31/2005)

CALLAHAN

Callahan 1998 Shiraz (South Eastern Australia) $11. Ripe, maybe overripe, but still very flavorful and supple on the palate. Cherry fruit is accented by smoke, coffee, and meaty notes that add interest and depth. The lingering finish shows chalky tannins, vanillin notes, plus plenty of fruit. **88 Best Buy** (10/1/2001)

Callahan Hill 2000 Shiraz (South Eastern Australia) $9. Blackberry fruit and ample toasty oak mesh well here. Cinnamon, dark chocolate, and peppery notes show in the bouquet and on the palate. Even, medium weight, not complex, but offering decent length, it's a great find— a fully realized, very satisfying everyday wine. **87 Best Buy** (10/1/2001)

CALLARA ESTATE

Callara Estate 2000 Reserve Bin Shiraz (South Eastern Australia) $8. This pleasant sipper is complex enough to drink as an everyday wine without your getting bored halfway through a case purchase. Jammy blackberries and blueberries, along with dried cherries, are complemented by chocolate, cinnamon, vanilla, and toast nuances and a bit of meatiness on the finish. **86 Best Buy** (10/1/2001)

CAMPBELLS

Campbells 1995 The Barkly Durif (Rutherglen) $30. This Durif (a variety better known to Americans as Petite Sirah) has dark fruit, eucalyptus, and bready flavors, and some stewed fruit and slight stemminess on the nose. It finishes with the same dark fruit that it has on the palate, plus some brown earth. Somewhat of a lightweight for its variety. **86** —D.T. (6/1/2003)

Campbells 1993 The Barkly Durif (Rutherglen) $30. This wine has an uncertain future, hence the less-than-enthusiastic rating. On first opening, it's mute on the nose and simply earthy and dull on the palate, with a dry, dusty finish. Later on, it opened up some and showed some nice aged fruit as well, then shut down again. **84** —J.C. (9/1/2002)

Campbells NV Muscat (Rutherglen) $17. Smells alcoholic at first, but after a few minutes in the glass the aromas are of charred wood. Feels somewhat rough, or rustic, in the mouth—not the smooth unctuousness that other Oz dessert wines have—with burnt sugar/caramel and stewed fruit flavors. Smooths out on the finish. **87**—*D.T. (12/31/2004)*

Campbells NV Rutherglen Muscat (Rutherglen) $10. This wine is so intensely textured and flavored, you've got to brace yourself. Packed with ultra sweet honey, peach, dried apricot, toast, walnut, coffee, caramel, licorice, and sesame notes, it holds onto the palate with bright acidity and length. Massive. **94 Editors' Choice**—*J.M. (12/1/2002)*

Campbells 1998 Bobbie Burns Shiraz (Rutherglen) $20. If there's nothing special to recommend here, there's also nothing awry. Leather and earth join modest tart berry flavors. Finishes dry and tough; it's an austere wine that probably needs food to come alive. **83**—*J.C. (9/1/2002)*

Campbells NV Tokay (Rutherglen) $17. From one of Rutherglen's most noted producers, there are lovely apple, cinnamon, and peach flavors on the palate that fade into a buttery finish. There's more apple on the nose, plus pickling spices, prunes, and pickle-barrel. An odd mix, but still an enticing one. **88**—*D.T. (12/31/2004)*

CANONBAH BRIDGE

Canonbah Bridge 1999 Vintage Reserve Champagne Blend (Victoria) $20. Pale copper-salmon in color, with bacon aromas and blackberry and cherry flavors. Cream aromas and flavors are present from the start through the brief finish. In the mouth, the mousse is soft but the cherry tautness gives it some spine. 52% Chardonnay, 24% Pinot Noir, 24% Pinot Meunier. **85**—*D.T. (12/31/2004)*

Canonbah Bridge 2002 Rams Leap Chardonnay (New South Wales) $12. Soft and light in feel. Aromas are muted; only a hint of peach shows through. Yellow-fruit flavors are indistinct—maybe it's pineapple? Finishes with a mouthcoating butterscotch candy flavor. **83** *(7/2/2004)*

Canonbah Bridge 2002 Ram's Leap Merlot (Western Plains) $12. Has eucalyptus, earth, and red plum aromas. This is a straightforward wine, but one that has surprising finesse, particularly given its reasonable price. It shows firm, ripe red plum fruit on the palate, and takes on a little coffee with air. Medium-bodied, it finishes with a gummy, pencil-eraser feel. **86**—*D.T. (9/1/2004)*

Canonbah Bridge 2000 Ram's Leap Semillon-Sauvignon Blanc (New South Wales) $10. Hickory, pear skin, and herb aromas preface pear and toast flavors. Its smooth mouthfeel is a plus for this reviewer; another taster found green notes that weren't pleasing. Finishes with pear and citrus. Simple, but fine. **84**—*D.T. (12/31/2003)*

Canonbah Bridge 2002 Drought Reserve Shiraz (Western Plains) $30. Good wine, one that stays the brown-earthy-tobacco-y camp rather than the sweet, forward one. Moderate plum fruit is its base; not too long on the finish. **84**—*D.T. (10/1/2006)*

Canonbah Bridge 2000 Ram's Leap Shiraz (New South Wales) $10. A straightforward, bring-to-a-party wine, with plum fruit on the palate and spicy, stewed fruit on the nose. It is what it is—pretty ordinary. **84**—*D.T. (12/31/2003)*

Canonbah Bridge 2002 Rams Leap Shiraz (Mudgee) $12. Smells and tastes like the fruit juice blends that kids drink—those mixes of peach, pear, apple, and other non-grape fruits. Add in an industrial-chalk note and you get a Shiraz that doesn't much taste like a Shiraz, or any red wine, for that matter. **81**—*D.T. (11/15/2004)*

CAPE CLAIRAULT

Cape Clairault 1996 The Clairault Reserve Red Bordeaux Blend (Margaret River) $35. **92**—*M.S. (10/1/2000)*

CAPE JAFFA

Cape Jaffa 1999 Shiraz (Limestone Coast) $18. A strong cedar component dominates tart blueberries and blackberries on the nose and in the mouth. Still, the mouthfeel is plush and soft, the finish long and creamy, making the overall package a pleasant one. **84** *(10/1/2001)*

CAPE MENTELLE

AUSTRALIA

Cape Mentelle 1999 Cabernet Sauvignon (Margaret River) $42. Fine oaky tannins make for a sturdy frame; red-brown fruit fills in the picture, with mocha accents on the palate and finish. A very good, solid Cab. **88**—*D.T. (10/1/2003)*

Cape Mentelle 2001 Cabernet Sauvignon (Margaret River) $40. This is still quite dark in color, right to the rim, and it overflows with complex aromas of flowers, herbs, tobacco, cassis, and subtle oaking. Firmly structured, but the tannins are ripe, not hard, while the flavors bring waves of cassis, plum, tobacco, and vanilla without ever seeming overly rich or jammy. Drink this wonderfully harmonious offering from 2008–2015. **91** *(12/15/2005)*

Cape Mentelle 2002 Cabernet Sauvignon-Merlot (Margaret River) $19. Heavy Bourbon-barrel, toasty flavors distract from otherwise very pleasant mixed berry fruit on the palate, and sweet-fruit aromas also take on hints of green pepper. It's a well-built wine, but one that's not showing as well as it has in the past. **86**—*D.T. (12/31/2004)*

Cape Mentelle 2003 Trinders Cabernet Sauvignon-Merlot (Margaret River) $16. A bit plummy and chocolaty, but it also has herbal and floral notes to add complexity. What this wine lacks next to its big brother the Cabernet is weight and density; it's a charming, supple wine that closes with crisp acids. **87** *(12/15/2005)*

Cape Mentelle 2001 Trinders Cabernet Sauvignon-Merlot (Margaret River) $18. Meaty, peppery aromas accent sturdy black fruit on the nose. This is an excellent wine, elegant and restrained, with mixed black and red fruit at its core. Chalky tannins on the palate follow through to the finish, where they're joined by subtle mocha and herb notes. **90 Editors' Choice**—*D.T. (10/1/2003)*

Cape Mentelle 2003 Chardonnay (Margaret River) $26. Kicks off with nutty, meaty aromas that move easily into apple and pear flavors. Marked by ripe fruit—Golden Delicious apples—and spice, finishing with echoes of clove and cinnamon. **90 Editors' Choice** *(12/15/2005)*

Cape Mentelle 2002 Chardonnay (Margaret River) $25. Certainly a buttery, toasty wine, but there's enough peach fruit here to back it up. It's medium-full in the mouth, with a resinous feel; finishes with good length. Oaky, but enjoyable. **87** *(7/2/2004)*

Cape Mentelle 2001 Chardonnay (Margaret River) $25. Toasty, buttery, and round in the mouth, with yellow fruit underneath. Fruit, not toast, is the key player on the finish. The nose offers a strange mix of mustard, meat, and beef aromas. **86**—*D.T. (10/1/2003)*

Cape Mentelle 2005 Sauvignon Blanc-Semillon (Margaret River) $13. Pungently grassy and herbal, with hints of passion fruit and grapefruit on the nose. In the mouth, the lush fruit flavors are considerably tamer, finishing long, and balanced by crisp acids. **88 Best Buy** *(12/15/2005)*

Cape Mentelle 2003 Sauvignon Blanc-Semillon (Margaret River) $19. Piquant, grassy, and fresh, the Sauvignon really stands out in terms of flavor; Semillon lends the wine some heft. Flavors of citrus peel, mineral, and fresh green grass lead to a zesty, almost tart finish. **89**—*D.T. (9/1/2004)*

Cape Mentelle 2003 Shiraz (Western Australia) $23. Earthy and meaty, balanced by lifted hints of violets and peppery spice. Black plum and dark chocolate flavors evenly coat the palate, ending on a firm note that provides a sense of elegance. **90 Editors' Choice** *(12/15/2005)*

Cape Mentelle 2002 Shiraz (Margaret River) $19. There's a smoldering toast-blackberry-vanilla fiesta on the nose, which is just the way to usher in plums, cherries, and mocha, plum and toast on the finish. It's a rich, attractive wine, but not one you'd call elegant. **89**—*D.T. (11/15/2004)*

Cape Mentelle 2001 Shiraz (Margaret River) $19. Creamy-vanilla dominates the nose; after some aeration, it's joined by herb and caramel notes. Palate offers sweet black fruit and fine, chalky tannins that carry through to the finish. A sturdy and pleasing, if not lush, Shiraz. **88**—*D.T. (10/1/2003)*

Cape Mentelle 1999 Shiraz (Margaret River) $19. Opaque and full, with smoke, leather, and a bit of stable on the nose. This has complexity and style, and dark is the word—dark plum and berry, dark chocolate, dark coffee, dark spices. The palate is supple, the finish long and earthy. Maybe not tall, but, yes, dark and handsome. **88** *(10/1/2001)*

CARLEI

Carlei 2002 Green Vineyards Shiraz (Heathcote) $31. Has pleasing aromas of dust, earth, and black pepper, and a very nice surge of black berries and cherries on the palate. Wants a little more stuffing on the palate, and a little more length on the back, to catapult it into the next decile. Still, this is a very good wine with plenty to recommend it. **87** —*D.T. (12/31/2005)*

CARRAMAR ESTATE

Carramar Estate 1999 Chardonnay (South Eastern Australia) $9. Soft, sweet, and showing its age, it'd be best served colder than normal to accentuate its pineapple fruit and tone down the sweetness. **82** —*J.C. (9/10/2002)*

Carramar Estate 1999 Merlot (South Eastern Australia) $9. This tawny red-colored Merlot has aromas of red berry, barbecue sauce, and cedar. In the mouth, fresh-off-the-grill toasted red cherry and raspberry notes are clocked in ashy-dry tannins. Finishes with wood. Tastes older than its years. **83** —*D.T. (6/1/2002)*

Carramar Estate 2000 Shiraz (South Eastern Australia) $9. Ripe red raspberries and vanilla aromas and flavors mingle easily in this soft, slightly candied wine that's best used as a bar pour or party wine. It goes down easy, just the ticket for the dozen beer-drinking buddies you're introducing to decent wine. **83** *(10/1/2001)*

CASCABEL

Cascabel 1999 Shiraz (Fleurieu Peninsula) $19. Imagine wet tree bark—or even cedar—covered in maple syrup, and you've got a pretty good idea of this Shiraz's odd bouquet. Its mouthfeel is supple, with dark black fruit, black pepper, and caramel flavors. Finishes with tangy oak and a slight brininess—it's better in the middle than on either end. **84** *(10/1/2001)*

CEDAR CREEK

Cedar Creek 1999 Shiraz (South Eastern Australia) $13. Loads of burned licorice, smoke and petroleum aromas here—if you're a non-smoker, you should probably steer clear of the ashy bouquet. Ashy, sour cranberry and citrus notes dominate the palate, and the medium-length finish. **81** *(10/1/2001)*

CHAIN OF PONDS

Chain of Ponds 1998 Ledge Shiraz (Adelaide Hills) $36. Smoke, funk, and game aromas, plus a sprinkling of cracked black pepper, give this wine's bouquet an interesting twist. But opinions on this wine were divided; while some tasters praised its unique and structured style, others criticized it for being tart and lacking fruit. **88** *(11/1/2001)*

CHALICE BRIDGE

Chalice Bridge 1999 Cabernet Sauvignon (Margaret River) $20. The bouquet is sharp and muscular, with ample leather and spice. The flavors veer toward spicy and tangy red fruit, with undertones of cinnamon and chocolate. Vanilla and Asian spices dominate the warm finish. This wine emphasizes nuance and spice over bold, lush fruit, and therefore should work well at the table. **89** —*M.S. (12/15/2002)*

Chalice Bridge 2003 Cabernet Sauvignon-Shiraz (Margaret River) $16. Taut and twangy, this 65-35 Shiraz-Cab blend has black pepper in abundance, nose to finish, plus gumtree and black cherry flavors. Would have merited an even higher score had the alcohol (listed on the label at a modest 14%) not felt so evident. **87** —*D.T. (8/1/2005)*

Chalice Bridge 2003 Chardonnay (Margaret River) $16. Slightly reductive. Aromas are of butterscotch and sulphur, and flavors are awash in butterscotch hard candy and toast. **81** —*D.T. (10/1/2005)*

Chalice Bridge 2001 Chardonnay (Western Australia) $16. Light in weight and subtle in flavor, this Chard is a welcome change from some of its mega-mallowy Oz compatriots. There are citrus and peach flavors on the palate and floral, yellow fruit aromas; it starts to get toasty with aeration. **85** —*D.T. (8/1/2003)*

CHAPEL HILL

Chapel Hill 2000 Cabernet Sauvignon (South Eastern Australia) $25. Fruit is 79% McLaren Vale, 21% Coonawarra; the wine's flavor profile gives the impression that it's even leaner than it is: Tomato and herb aromas notes on the nose reappear on the palate. With air, the fruit tastes a little more like sour cherry, but it's still pretty lean on flavor. **82** —*D.T. (9/1/2004)*

Chapel Hill 2002 Unwooded Chardonnay (South Australia) $15. Has down-the-line, straightforward yellow fruit flavors on the palate, with a minerally, dry feel that makes this wine a good choice to go with seafood, or rich, butter-based sauces. Aromas are light—think hay, wheat, and a little anise. **85** *(7/2/2004)*

CHARLES CIMICKY

Charles Cimicky 1997 The Red Blend Bordeaux Blend (Barossa Valley) $30. 91 —*M.S. (3/1/2000)*

Charles Cimicky 1999 Daylight Chamber Shiraz (Barossa Valley) $19. An earthy, grilled-nut, stewed fruit nose is an accurate preview of what's to come. Deep black cocoa, smoke, blackberry, and pine-needle flavors smolder on the palate. Finishes with good length and cedar-plum flavors. **88** *(10/1/2001)*

Charles Cimicky 1998 Reserve Shiraz (Barossa Valley) $40. This big, broad-shouldered Shiraz is brimming with flavor and ready to drink now. The bright, deep ruby/black robe sets you up for the full, persistent blackberry fruit that follows, and the palate doesn't disappoint. This has very good balance, a chewy mouthfeel, and finishes long, with full but even tannins. **90** *(6/1/2001)*

Charles Cimicky 1998 Signature Shiraz (Barossa Valley) $30. Loads of oak adorn the blackberry and blueberry fruit in this big, suave charmer. Bitter chocolate and espresso flavors; full, structured mouthfeel. If slightly one-dimensional, it continues to offer pleasure right through the long tart, slightly lemony finish, and has the stuff to hold through mid-decade, at least. **89** *(11/1/2001)*

Charles Cimicky 1997 Signature Shiraz (Barossa Valley) $30. 92 *(3/1/2000)*

CHARLES MELTON

Charles Melton 2002 Cabernet Sauvignon (Barossa Valley) $35. Spicy, peppery oak aromas are presented on a backdrop of red berry fruit. This wine's texture is its centerpiece: It has a smooth, mouthcoating, milky-clay feel, and deals berry and subtle oak flavors. Very enjoyable. **90** —*D.T. (4/1/2006)*

Charles Melton 2001 Cabernet Sauvignon (Barossa Valley) $44. The hints of toast and crème brûlée that accent mixed plum on the palate come through with more force on the finish. Black and red plum fruit on the palate is solid and pure. A really smart package. **91** —*D.T. (2/1/2004)*

Charles Melton 2000 Cabernet Sauvignon-Shiraz (Barossa Valley) $44. Melton is a reliably good producer, which is why I'm puzzled by this offering. The palate fruit has meaty, caramelly accents, while the distinctive aroma is watermelon. The sum of its parts just doesn't yield a better than good wine. **84** —*D.T. (12/31/2003)*

Charles Melton 2000 Grenache (Barossa Valley) $37. This is a very good Grenache, with vivid violet and cherry aromas. "Vivid" is an appropriate word for what you get in the mouth, too—the wine's alcohol is noticeable, and its fruit fairly high toned. Cherry, earth, and red plum flavors meld on the palate and fade into an herb-tinged finish. **87** —*D.T. (9/1/2004)*

Charles Melton 2002 Nine Popes Red Blend (Barossa Valley) $37. A disappointing showing for a wine that is usually very good or excellent. Has aromas of cracker and cola, and a hefty dose of dusty bark and sour cherry on the palate. Lighter in weight than usual, too. Just isn't singing for me this year; tasted twice. **85** —*D.T. (10/1/2005)*

Charles Melton 2001 Nine Popes Red Blend (Barossa Valley) $39. Mint and bread flour on the nose, with raspberry and red plum flavors on the palate. Its smooth, oaky tannins continue through to the finish, where there's bread-flour and graham-cracker flavors. A terrific GSM. **90** —*D.T. (2/1/2004)*

Charles Melton 1999 Nine Popes Red Blend (Barossa Valley) $39. The name "Nine Popes," as the story goes, came about when Charlie just wanted to muck up the translation of "Châteauneuf-du-Pape." And appropriately enough, this is a blend of Grenache, Shiraz, and Mourvèdre, an excellent one, with sexy, stewed plum fruit and bready flavors, almost like fruitcake. Smells earthy, with the same sort of fruit; a dose of brown sugar coats the whole package. **89** —*D.T. (2/1/2004)*

Charles Melton 2005 Rosé Blend (Barossa Valley) $15. This is probably the best rosé that comes out of Australia, and I like it better every year. It has an underlying, piquant citrus note, and raspberry and black cherry flavors galore. Medium-full in the mouth, it's dry, chalky, refreshing. Darkens and deepens on the finish. A crazy blend of Grenache (47.2%), Shiraz (18%), Pinot Meunier (16%), Cab Sauv (15.5%), and Pinot Noir (3.3%) **91 Best Buy** —*D.T. (6/21/2006)*

Charles Melton 2004 Rosé Blend (Barossa Valley) $16. Stop and smell the rose and you'll get what I think a good rosé should smell like: a red wine with a slight chill. Deep plum, blackberry, and raspberry aromas are edged in flint, with like flavors on the palate and a finish where the flinty dryness is reprised. Deep pink-magenta in color—not shy. A curious blend of Shiraz, Grenache, Cab, and Pinot Meunier. **89** —*D.T. (12/31/2004)*

Charles Melton 2003 Rosé Blend (Barossa Valley) $18. This pinky, which is called "Rosé of Virginia" outside the U.S., is a very pretty, delicious wine. Don't let its bright-pink hue fool you into thinking that it's a saccharine sugar-bomb; this is a dry, elegant rosé with a minerally texture, and heaps of red berry fruit on the palate. With floral and vanilla aromas and a dry, chalky finish, it'll make a rosé lover out of every doubting Thomas. **90 Editors' Choice** —*D.T. (9/1/2004)*

Charles Melton 2003 Rose of Virginia Rosé Blend (Barossa Valley) $15. Melton says Rose, we say rosé—a Grenache, Shiraz, Cabernet, and Petit Verdot rosé, to be precise. Though the nose is all cherry and raspberry, the main palate impression is a floral one, with some raspberries hiding in the background and on through the finish. A very nice wine, and fairly dry as well. **88** —*D.T. (2/1/2004)*

Charles Melton 2002 Shiraz (Barossa Valley) $35. This Shiraz features light plum and caramel aromas, and plum and oak flavors. It's more straightforward than it usually is, but it is still very good. Drink now. 448 cases produced. **87** —*D.T. (4/1/2006)*

Charles Melton 2001 Shiraz (Barossa Valley) $39. Has great grip on the tongue—the chalky tannins hold on for dear life. Medium-bodied; its fruit shows graham cracker, powder, and wheat flour through and through. Quite enjoyable. **90** —*D.T. (2/1/2004)*

Charles Melton 2000 Shiraz (Barossa Valley) $39. Has eucalyptus and black fruit on the nose, but takes on hints of caramel with air; plum and berry fruit reads a little redder on the palate. A yummy, fiesty wine—energetic, yet cunning enough to act like a grownup, a serious Shiraz when it needs to. **91** —*D.T. (2/1/2004)*

Charles Melton 2000 Laura Shiraz (Barossa Valley) $39. There are beef, plum, and pencil eraser aromas on the nose. This wine's tannins have stick-to-your palate gumption, but the mouthfeel still manages to be fairly smooth. Flavors are mostly of mixed plums until the finish, where mocha takes over. **89** —*D.T. (5/1/2004)*

Charles Melton 2003 The Father in Law Shiraz (South Australia) $18. This is all about immediate drinking pleasure. Offers bright blue-, black-, and raspberries on the nose. It's more of the same on the palate, where there are some cherry and rhubarb notes mixed in. Wooly-textured at first but softens with time, as fathers-in-law tend to do. **89** —*D.T. (8/1/2006)*

Charles Melton NV Sparkling Red Sparkling Blend (Barossa) $60. With only 60 six-packs imported to the U.S., this will be a rare sight on retailer shelves, but it is a tasty wine. The aromas and flavors are harmonious and balanced, with no one element dominating among the raspberry fruit, chocolate sauce, and dried spices. The weight is kept under control, and the wine finishes with mouthwatering freshness and soft tannins. **88** —*J.C. (12/31/2006)*

CHATEAU REYNELLA

Chateau Reynella 2002 Cabernet Sauvignon (McLaren Vale) $NA. This Cabernet is drinkable now, and showing soft red fruit with coffee-mocha notes on both the nose and the palate. Very juicy on the finish. Enjoy through 2008. **88** —*D.T. (3/1/2005)*

Chateau Reynella 1996 Basket Pressed Cabernet Sauvignon-Merlot (McLaren Vale) $24. **88** —*M.S. (4/1/2000)*

Chateau Reynella 2002 Chardonnay (McLaren Vale) $14. Aromas are of apple turnover and minerals. Slim bodied and a little soft, but don't dismiss this Chard right off as simple: It has a tight, sour core with peach and oak flavors rounding it out in the mouth. **87** —*D.T. (12/1/2005)*

Chateau Reynella 2001 Chardonnay (McLaren Vale) $15. Has peach, banana, and vanilla aromas on the nose; palate shows light yellow fruit, plus a sour peach-pit note, both of which continue through to the finish. Body is medium, with some viscosity. **84** —*D.T. (8/1/2003)*

Chateau Reynella 1999 Chardonnay (McLaren Vale) $11. Harmony is the hallmark here. Apple, oak in the background, and closing butterscotch are the flavors. The supporting cast of crisp acidity, medium body, and velvety mouthfeel complete this well-knit package. **90 Best Buy** —*M.N. (6/1/2001)*

Chateau Reynella 1998 Chardonnay (McLaren Vale) $11. **90 Best Buy** *(3/1/2000)*

Chateau Reynella 2002 Basket Pressed Grenache (McLaren Vale) $24. Dark, smoky aromas have high-toned black cherry fruit underneath. On the palate, the smoke and black cherry continue, on a rather slight, feminine frame. A wine that will complement, not overpower, food. **87** —*D.T. (3/1/2005)*

Chateau Reynella 2002 Basket Pressed Shiraz (McLaren Vale) $28. Smells spicy, and similar smoke and spice flavors resurface on the palate. This is not a big, overdone style of Shiraz, but it's still a nice one. It has flavors of smoke and red fruit. Flashy and substantial on the midpalate—with good, gripping tannins and a smooth texture—but the palate entry and finish are not quite as impressive. **88** —*D.T. (3/1/2005)*

Chateau Reynella 2000 Basket pressed Shiraz (McLaren Vale) $28. Dried oak and barnyard aromas led to more juicy than fleshy flavors of red raspberries. Could have used more depth and structure, but an enjoyable wine nonetheless. **87** —*C.S. (3/1/2003)*

Chateau Reynella 1999 Basket Pressed Shiraz (McLaren Vale) $30. Most reviewers found this Shiraz a little run-of-the-mill, with oak and blackberry flavors in control from start to finish. Its proponents, though, found a lot to like about its coffee, leather, and meaty aromas, and its long, black-tea finish. **87** *(11/1/2001)*

Chateau Reynella 1996 Basket Pressed Shiraz (McLaren Vale) $24. **90** —*M.S. (4/1/2000)*

CHECKERED CAB

Checkered Cab 2003 Cabernet Sauvignon (South Australia) $10. Aromas of plum and woodspice lead to similar notes on the palate. Though the wine has a dusty-earthy feel, it's still on the tangy side, with some cherry and cranberry accents to the plum fruit. **86 Best Buy** —*D.T. (6/1/2006)*

CHEVIOT BRIDGE

Cheviot Bridge 2000 Cabernet Sauvignon-Merlot (South Eastern Australia) $16. Juicy fruit and tasty, overt American oak mark this lithe red. Like inexpensive Aussie Shiraz, this is about upfront flavor and smooth texture. Though comprised of the two major Bordeaux grapes, this is not complex or for cellaring, but will provide good easy drinking over the next year or two. **85** —*M.M. (12/15/2002)*

Cheviot Bridge 1999 Cabernet Sauvignon-Merlot (Yea Valley) $16. More and more Cab-Merlot blends from down under are hitting our shores. This tasty example shows good palate feel and an above average balance of fruit, wood, acidity, and tannins. Stylish almost all the way through, it turns just a bit tart and lemony on the finish. Should improve, evening out further over the next year. Drink through 2005. **87** —*M.M. (12/15/2002)*

Cheviot Bridge 2001 Chardonnay (South Eastern Australia) $16. Bouncy and full of ripe mixed fruit—mainly peaches and pears (think fruit cocktail)—this wine also has a creamy lactic note that doesn't quite mesh with the other elements. **83** —*J.C. (7/1/2002)*

AUSTRALIA

Cheviot Bridge 2000 Chardonnay (Victoria) $16. Reminiscent of good white Burgundy, this atypically (for Australia) flinty Chard has notes of gunmetal, intricately intertwined with white peach and toasted oatmeal. Finishes soft and round but long, with hints of lemon. **90** —*J.C. (7/1/2002)*

Cheviot Bridge 2001 Merlot (Yea Valley) $17. The nose offers lots of black pepper, and less cream; it's smooth in the mouth, with drying, oaky tannins that persist through the finish. Red plum is the main player on the palate. Good, but nothing out of the ordinary. **85** —*D.T. (6/1/2003)*

Cheviot Bridge 2001 Pinot Noir (Yea Valley) $17. Tastes commercial in the "being all things to all people" way, but it's still a well-made Pinot. Chalk envelops cherries and plums; there's a nice weight on the palate, where smoke and pine notes step in. The same pine-cone note comes through on the nose. **87** —*D.T. (10/1/2003)*

Cheviot Bridge 2000 Shiraz (South Eastern Australia) $16. Less overtly sweet than much modest Aussie Shiraz, this shows good fruit with a touch of earthiness and a hint of structure. The fairly high acidity and angular character makes this more food-friendly than many. It even shows some back-end edge. Drink now, with food rather than as a glugger. **84** —*M.M. (12/15/2002)*

CIGALE

Cigale 2004 Shiraz (Barossa Valley) $25. Soft in the middle with a tangy oak shell, this Shiraz offers up plenty of cushiony plum fruit and an easy feel. But it's not a simple wine—there are enough oak shadings here to give it some complexity. **88** —*D.T. (8/1/2006)*

CLARENDON HILLS

Clarendon Hills 2004 Brookman Cabernet Sauvignon (Clarendon) $65. Shows tons of beautiful red and black berries on the nose, which carry over to the palate in the form of juicy, perfectly ripe flavors tinged with just a hint of graham cracker. Acidity is lively; can be enjoyed now through 2011. **91** —*D.T. (10/1/2006)*

Clarendon Hills 2003 Brookman Cabernet Sauvignon (Clarendon) $75. This isn't an oversized Cab, but that's its appeal. It's excellent, with flavors of black cherry, cassis, and black grape that surge on the palate, and just don't let go. It's all swaddled tightly in young, smooth tannins, and gumtree and beef stock accents on the nose. Drink 2007 and beyond. **92** —*D.T. (8/1/2005)*

Clarendon Hills 2004 Hickinbotham Cabernet Sauvignon (Clarendon) $70. Of Clarendon Hills' three Cabs, this one is generally considered the flagship. This vintage, the Hickinbotham, is a darker, more brooding sort of Cab than the other two, with drying, tealike tannins in the mouth and bramble aromas. In spite of its dark profile, it's not oversized or overoaked. Shows good length on the finish. Drink now–2012. **91** — *D.T. (10/1/2006)*

Clarendon Hills 2003 Hickinbotham Cabernet Sauvignon (Clarendon) $75. This wine deserves plenty of adjectives: excellent and sexy among them. It's also a burly wine, somehow less classy and refined than the best of them. Its plum fruit has a stewy, barbecued spiciness to it, and it's big and brawny on the palate. Fans whose mantra is "bigger is better" will likely ratchet my score up a few points. **90** —*D.T. (8/1/2005)*

Clarendon Hills 2004 Sandown Cabernet Sauvignon (Clarendon) $65. Aromas are of red eraser, nut, and dry earth or sand. On the palate it takes quite a different tack, its juicy black, blue-, and raspberry fruit still tautly youthful. Powerful, though still so young; will probably show best in 5–8 years. **92 Cellar Selection** —*D.T. (10/1/2006)*

Clarendon Hills 2003 Sandown Cabernet Sauvignon (Clarendon) $70. This wine's flavors have a cooler-climate profile to them—think red and black cherry, rather than cassis or plum fruit. Blueberry and bread flour steps in midpalate, and march on through the long finish. Lifted, tight and very pretty. **91** —*D.T. (8/1/2005)*

Clarendon Hills 2004 Blewitt Springs Grenache (Clarendon) $70. This wine boasts fantastic spice-drop character on the nose, seamlessly blending bold blackberry and plum fruit with notes of anise and licorice. It's lush and richly textured in the mouth, with a long, spice-driven finish. A wine that's wonderfully exotic and approachable now, but one that should last up to 10 years. **93** —*J.C. (12/15/2006)*

Clarendon Hills 2003 Blewitt Springs Grenache (Clarendon) $80. Made from bushvines that are about 75 years old, this tremendous Grenache is a vibrant pink-purple color and has deep peppery, fruit-sweet aromas. On the palate it's massive but controlled, iike a rhinoceros behind a steel wall. Intense plum and cherry fruit warms the palate. Dry tannins persist through the long, minerally finish. Drink after 2010. **95 Cellar Selection** —*D.T. (3/1/2005)*

Clarendon Hills 2004 Clarendon Grenache (Clarendon) $61. From one of the cooler sites in Clarendon Hills' arsenal, this Grenache shows floral, slightly lifted aromas and hints of blueberry and strawberry. Yet it still shows the soft, lush texture of all of the CH Grenaches and a long, gently lingering finish. **90** —*J.C. (12/15/2006)*

Clarendon Hills 2003 Clarendon Grenache (Clarendon) $73. What a ride. On the palate, it comes and goes in waves, with cassis surging one moment, and violets and black pepper the next. Tannins are manageable but textured, and the finish brings a nutty, earthy flavor and another burst of berry fruit. Delicious now, and should age well through the decade. **93** —*D.T. (8/1/2005)*

Clarendon Hills 2003 Hickinbotham Grenache (Clarendon) $73. This is a thick, rich, delicious Grenache that has mocha, chocolate, and coconut aromas and a berry basket full of flavors on the palate. The feel is velvety, and it pushes all the right buttons, but it's built more for the near term than for the cellar. Drink now and over the next five years. **90** —*D.T. (8/1/2005)*

Clarendon Hills 2004 Kangarilla Grenache (Clarendon) $70. Winemaker Roman Bratasuik calls Kangarilla "quite a warm spot," and that character is evident in this wine's dark blackberry and plum flavors, soft, open-knit texture and warmth on the finish. It's a lush, sexy wine with tons of appeal in its youth—why wait? **92** —*J.C. (12/15/2006)*

Clarendon Hills 2003 Kangarilla Grenache (Clarendon) $80. Smells peppery and spicy, with meat, brown sugar, and red pencil eraser to boot. Very pretty, chewy red fruit on the midpalate, though it's still not at its peak. Finishes long, with chalky-woody tannins. Try after 2008. **92** — *D.T. (3/1/2005)*

Clarendon Hills 2004 Romas Grenache (Clarendon) $100. Cropped at a measly half ton per acre, this is Clarendon Hills' top Grenache bottling. It's tighter and denser than the other, more flamboyant offerings, needing time in the bottle to develop. For now, it's loaded with wonderfully pure blackberry and cassis fruit, but it promises to develop more complexity over the years; try from 2008–2020. Long and softly tannic on the finish. **95 Cellar Selection** —*J.C. (12/15/2006)*

Clarendon Hills 2003 Romas Grenache (Clarendon) $115. Aromas are fruit-sweet one minute, and dark and earthy the next. Offers thick, pulpy tannins on the tongue, with fruit that glows red, then purple. Medium-long on the finish; this is an excellent, very compelling Grenache. Will show its best in 2–3 years. **91** —*D.T. (8/1/2005)*

Clarendon Hills 2004 Brookman Merlot (Clarendon) $60. Perennially one of Australia's best Merlots, the 2004 version "shows the cool season," according to winemaker Roman Bratasiuk. Dried herbs and tobacco blend into pepper and cassis flavors. The tannins are supple, gradually fading on the finish into a smooth stream of mocha. Drink now–2012. **90** —*J.C. (12/15/2006)*

Clarendon Hills 2003 Brookman Merlot (Clarendon) $65. This is probably the best Merlot that I've had from the region. Aromas are fruit-sweet, with wide plum fruit and light caramel at the fore. There are green notes on the nose—fresh produce, and maybe some lima bean—but they are strangely appealing, and the wine boasts tremendous grip at midpalate. Finishes with dry wood and tealike tannins. **90** —*D.T. (3/1/2005)*

Clarendon Hills 1999 Moritz Shiraz (Clarendon) $49. The palate shows cocoa, red berries, black cherries, and eucalyptus flavors; the finish is medium-length, with green pepper and earth flavors. Is all this, plus a bouquet of deep black fruit, dark soil, and brined meat, a recipe for success? Almost. Though reviewers praised this Shiraz for being well made with a smooth mouthfeel, we couldn't get past the idea that there is something a little unfulfilling about it, or something that the winemakers might have done differently. **87** *(11/1/2001)*

Clarendon Hills 2004 Astralis Syrah (Clarendon) $325. The flagship of the Clarendon Hills line, this comes from a patch of 80-year-old vines that winemaker Bratasiuk claims routinely provides his best fruit. The 2004 is a stunner, yielding up scents of flowers and spice, framed by hints of vanillin oak. It's dense and amply textured in the mouth, packed with wonderfully expressive blackberry and blueberry fruit, then shows layers of rich tannins on the finish that leave no doubt this needs time in the cellar to show its best. This is a tour de force of Australian winemaking that should be consumed 2010–2025. **98 Cellar Selection** —*J.C. (12/15/2006)*

Clarendon Hills 2003 Astralis Syrah (Clarendon) $375. A fantastic wine, but so young that it would qualify better as "fetus" than as "infant." Still very closed on the nose, showing cassis and black cherry aromas after much airing. Its color is a powerful, almost glowing, purple and its flavors—a vibrant surge of pure black and blueberries—are just as intense. Very concentrated and tight, with a linear, minerally frame underneath its monstrous tannins. Winemaker Roman Bratasiuk recommends aging for a mimum of 6 years before drinking; if you are as foolish as I and insist on opening a bottle today, decant for a minimum of 6-8 hours. Rating may look stingy by the time Bush finishes his second term. **95 Cellar Selection** —*D.T. (3/1/2005)*

Clarendon Hills 2004 Bakers Gully Syrah (Clarendon) $65. Clarendon Hills' "entry-level" Syrah comes from vines that are only 12 years old, but it is still a very good effort. The bouquet includes graham cracker, sour red plum, and herbal notes, while the palate picks up some dusty, red-earth flavors. The finish is crisp. Minus the minerality, it's comparable to a good Crozes-Hermitage in a warm year. **89** —*J.C. (12/15/2006)*

Clarendon Hills 2003 Bakers Gully Syrah (Clarendon) $75. The palate of offers lifted black, red, and blueberries, mixed in with a hint of roasted tomato. A little of the same roasted-fruit quality on the nose, but the quibble is a minor one. Drink over the near term. **89** —*D.T. (8/1/2005)*

Clarendon Hills 2004 Brookman Syrah (Clarendon) $100. If the Liandra is Bratasiuk's Côte-Rôtie, this is the wine he calls "more Hermitage." And it does have some iron-like, minerally notes to it. But there's more New World suppleness and flesh as well, featuring lush plum and cassis fruit, some hickory-smoked bacon, and layers of coffee and cream on the lengthy finish. Approachable now, but should be even better in five years and will easily last for 10–15. **95** —*J.C. (12/15/2006)*

Clarendon Hills 2003 Brookman Syrah (Clarendon) $75. Smells indescribably good, but it's hard to pick out specific scents—think instead of farmers' market of the freshest fruit. It's no slouch on the palate, either, where the impression is similarly seamless: In the mix you might discern a rainbow of just-ripe fruit, earth, and wheat toast, for starters. It's balanced, restrained, and pretty, and should stay that way through at least 2010. **95 Cellar Selection** —*D.T. (8/1/2005)*

Clarendon Hills 2004 Hickinbotham Syrah (Clarendon) $100. One of the more obviously ageworthy offerings from Clarendon Hills, the 2004 Hickinbotham Syrah boasts a wonderfully perfumed bouquet of flowers, minerals, and spice. Then it backs up those captivating aromatics with rich blueberry fruit shaded with mint and cracked pepper and a long, firmly tannic and minerally finish. Drink 2010–2020. **96 Cellar Selection** —*J.C. (12/15/2006)*

Clarendon Hills 2003 Hickinbotham Syrah (Clarendon) $115. This Syrah—yes, Syrah, not Shiraz—has a mouthfeel that will make you swear, or call out to your deity of choice. Just velvety-smooth on the palate, with plump plum fruit that tightens up on the finish, which reprises the peppery-herb notes that first showed on the nose. It's certainly nothing you'd kick out of bed now, but will probably taste even better in five or six years. **94** —*D.T. (3/1/2005)*

Clarendon Hills 2004 Liandra Syrah (Clarendon) $78. This is sexy stuff that proprietor Roman Bratasiuk says is "more Côte-Rôtie" than his other Syrahs. Its perfumed nose offers up hints of violets and cracked pepper to go along with raspberry fruit, while it's supple in the mouth—almost too easy—with pretty mixed berry flavors and a nib of bitter chocolate. Long and elegant on the finish. Drink now–2015. **94 Editors' Choice** —*J.C. (12/15/2006)*

Clarendon Hills 2003 Liandra Syrah (Clarendon) $90. This Syrah is sexy and compelling, but in the company of Roman Bratasiuk's other wines, feels softer and not quite as intense. It packs bright red raspberry and blackberry fruit on the palate, and richly fruity aromas on the nose. Drink over the next 3 to 4 years. **90** —*D.T. (8/1/2005)*

Clarendon Hills 2004 Moritz Syrah (Clarendon) $78. This wine is stylistically somewhere between the Liandra and the Brookman. It's rich and dense, packed with authoritative flavors of dark fruits—blueberries and plums—accented by espresso and smoke. Long and powerful on the finish, with 10-plus years of ageability. **93** —*J.C. (12/15/2006)*

Clarendon Hills 2003 Moritz Syrah (Clarendon) $90. This Syrah is still a baby, but is already just a gorgeous expression of pure plum fruit. It's not lush yet—it will probably be drinking its best in around 2012. In the meanwhile deep, intoxicating whiffs of black peppercorns, wheat bread, dried fruit, and fresh plums and berries will just have to hold you over. **93** —*D.T. (3/1/2005)*

Clarendon Hills 2004 Piggott Range Syrah (Clarendon) $150. Boasts a slightly lifted character to the aromas, but also shadings of Asian spice and espresso. This is supple on the palate and dark-fruited, with bold flavors of prune-plum and coffee and a long, firm finish that demands cellaring. Drink 2008–2020. **94** —*J.C. (12/15/2006)*

Clarendon Hills 2003 Piggott Range Syrah (Clarendon) $175. Thick and textured—almost wooly—on the palate. A sip brings big blackberry and smoke on the front palate, which tightens up to blueberry by the finish. The nose is very pretty, too, showing bread flour, blueberry, fresh herb, and even some lavender. **92** —*D.T. (8/1/2005)*

CLASSIC MCLAREN

Classic McLaren 2000 La Testa Cabernet Sauvignon (McLaren Vale) $41. Gives an overall impression of redness, from tomato and red fruit aromas on the nose to red plum, cherry, and clay on the palate. Chewy in the mouth, it closes with more juicy fruit, clay, and some herb. **88** —*D.T. (12/31/2003)*

Classic McLaren 2000 Cabernet Sauvignon-Merlot (McLaren Vale) $19. There's a liberal dose of caramel, plus taut red plums, on the palate. Has smooth, oaky tannins; oak (in the form of Bourbon barrel and black pepper) is a key player on the palate as well. **86** —*D.T. (12/31/2003)*

Classic McLaren 2000 La Testa Merlot (McLaren Vale) $41. Medium-bodied with plum fruit that isn't quite gloppy, but doesn't seem to hang on a very structured frame. Tomato accents on the nose and palate suggest rather overtly that this Merlot may just be the wine that your arribiata sauce is looking for. **85** —*D.T. (6/1/2003)*

Classic McLaren 2000 La Testa Shiraz (McLaren Vale) $78. This Shiraz offers over-the-top blackberry, raspberry, and caramel flavors, with a chili-spicy kick, but doesn't quite have the plushness that such big flavors warrant. Stewy black and red berries on the nose have caramel nuances; heat (or is it jalapeño?) punctuates the finish. **89** —*D.T. (6/1/2003)*

CLIMBING

Climbing 2004 Cabernet Sauvignon (Orange) $17. Its aromas are quite nice—clay, black cherry, eraser, graham cracker—but the palate doesn't deliver the goods quite as prettily. Has a papery/wooly feel; fruit has a green, sourish edge. Not imported to the U.S. **84** —*D.T. (8/1/2006)*

Climbing 2005 Chardonnay (Orange) $17. Like other Philip Shaw wines, this one has an ethereal quality to it that could be understood as elegant by one person and just too delicate by another. Very light vanilla and butterscotch aromas start things off, bringing soft melon and pear on board in the mouth. Soft around the edges with fine acidity; finishes with a sour citric note. **87** —*D.T. (8/1/2006)*

Climbing 2004 Merlot (Orange) $17. From winemaker Philip Shaw, this Merlot is soft in the mouth, with raspberry and black plum fruit. A veneer of oak and spice adds interest on the palate. **86** —*D.T. (6/1/2006)*

CLONAKILLA

Clonakilla 1999 Shiraz (Langhorne Creek) $19. A very odd bouquet, yet we could not turn our noses away from Clonakilla's strong eucalyptus, yard mulch, and tobacco aromas. Dark coffee, earth, ash, and sour blackberry flavors comprise a "complex, but funky" palate, which, by the way, has just about the smoothest mouthfeel of any wine we've had in the past month. Bottom line? So strange that you're best off sampling this one for yourself. **85** *(10/1/2001)*

Clonakilla 2003 Hilltops Shiraz (New South Wales) $25. Though the aromas and flavors are really nice, this wine's flat, woody feel keeps it from being as excellent as it could be. It starts off with black olive and eucalyptus on the nose, and brings black cherry, plum, herb, and eucalyptus on the palate. Good acids; an even, balanced wine. **88** —*D.T.* *(12/1/2005)*

CLOVER HILL

Clover Hill 2001 Brut Champagne Blend (Tasmania) $30. From Taltarni's Tasmanian outpost, this is a plump, medium-bodied sparkler with ample complexity. Smoke, citrus, and eggy, brioche notes mark the nose, while the palate adds crisp appley flavors. Finishes long, picking up hints of grapefruit as well. **88** —*J.C.* *(12/31/2006)*

Clover Hill 2000 Brut Champagne Blend (Tasmania) $30. Dust, apple, mushroom, and toast aromas start things off, and reveal some stone fruit and talc on the palate. Its texture—moussey and frothy, rather than dry and crisp—reminds me of Cremant or Prosecco. 53% Chardonnay, 35% Pinot Noir, 12% Pinot Meunier. **87** —*D.T.* *(12/31/2004)*

Clover Hill 1998 Brut Champagne Blend (Tasmania) $29. Yellow peach fruit has underlying cured-meat flavors, which are hinted at on the nose. Mouthfeel is very foamy—it feels as though the wine dissolves when it hits your tongue. I like a little more substance in sparklers, but fans of superdelicate wines may feel differently. **85** —*D.T.* *(12/31/2003)*

Clover Hill 1996 Brut Champagne Blend (Tasmania) $29. 80 —*J.M.* *(1/1/2003)*

COCKATOO RIDGE

Cockatoo Ridge 2002 Cabernet Sauvignon-Merlot (South Australia) $7. An 80%–20% blend in favor of Cabernet, this is a simple, one-track wine with sweet fruit aromas and flavors. There's an underlying note of tartness—seeped tea, or herb—that is a out of joint with everything else, but it's still a good wine at a good price. **83** —*D.T.* *(9/1/2004)*

Cockatoo Ridge 2002 The Real Taste of Australia Cabernet Sauvignon-Merlot (South Australia) $7. Aromas are straight out of the ground—earth, with perhaps some stony mineral thrown in. It's plump in the mouth, with an earthy-rustic feel and red fruit that is taut, verging on sour. Finishes with plum and a sandy-earthy note. **83** —*D.T.* *(9/1/2004)*

Cockatoo Ridge 2000 The Real Taste of Australia Cabernet Sauvignon-Merlot (South Australia) $7. The nose is tight, with some tobacco, leather, and green bean poking through. Cherry and chocolate flavors lead into a dry palate. The early impression beats the lasting one, making it solid but unspectacular. **84** —*M.S.* *(12/15/2002)*

Cockatoo Ridge NV Brut Champagne Blend (South Australia) $10. Has a sulfury smell that doesn't blow off. The flavors are overly fruity, with a raspberry flavor, and the bubbles are rough. This sparkling wine scours the palate with acidity. It's acceptable, but just barely. **81** — *(12/1/2002)*

Cockatoo Ridge NV Brut Champagne Blend (South Eastern Australia) $7. In this price category, you're lucky to find a sparkler that won't give you a killer headache the morning after revelry—so it's just gravy that this wine tastes good, too. Slight coppery hue, with dusty cherry aromas and flavors. It's soft, foamy, and goes down easy. **85 Best Buy** —*D.T.* *(12/31/2004)*

Cockatoo Ridge 2003 Chardonnay (South Australia) $7. Shows aromas of dust, pineapple, and orange. In the mouth, it's slightly built with low-intensity yellow fruit and a woody, peach-pit bite. Finishes with more wood. **84** *(7/2/2004)*

Cockatoo Ridge 2001 Chardonnay (South Australia) $7. This Chard is smooth in the mouth, with white stone fruit on the palate, plus white pepper and mineral notes that extend through the finish. What's here is pleasant enough, but more of these good things wouldn't hurt. **83** — *D.T.* *(8/1/2003)*

Cockatoo Ridge 2000 Chardonnay (Australia) $7. Simple melon and vanilla aromas and flavors in a lightweight wine. It'll go fine with carryout

rotisserie chicken on a busy weeknight, when something else might be overkill. **83** —*J.C.* *(7/1/2002)*

Cockatoo Ridge 2004 Sauvignon Blanc (South Eastern Australia) $7. A very dry, lean, spare style of Sauvignon. Smells fresh—like fresh green pea—and a green herbaceousness continues on the palate. It's just the thing for an outdoor party or wedding, but its wiry profile won't appeal to everyone. **84 Best Buy** —*D.T.* *(12/1/2005)*

Cockatoo Ridge 2002 Shiraz (South Australia) $7. Grape jelly and graham cracker aromas suggest a cloying palate, but that's thankfully not what you get. Instead, there's a foundation of cherry fruit, and a whole lot of wood. **83** —*D.T.* *(11/15/2004)*

Cockatoo Ridge 2000 Shiraz (South Australia) $7. Lightweight and easy drinking, this opens with aromas of grilled meat, toast and raspberries. The balanced palate offers plenty of red fruit, while the finish tastes of buttered rum and meat juices. **86 Best Buy** —*K.F.* *(3/1/2003)*

COCKFIGHTER'S GHOST

Cockfighter's Ghost 2001 Cabernet Sauvignon (Langhorne Creek) $19. Red fruit is at its core, but the wine also has both flavors and aromas of celery. It's a light, slight-boned wine, with smooth tannins on the finish. **84** —*D.T.* *(5/1/2004)*

Cockfighter's Ghost 1998 Premium Reserve Cabernet Sauvignon (Coonawarra) $35. Bright herbal and black cherry aromas start things off; blackberry flavors are prevalent, but tinged with an oaky tang. Some tasters found minty notes to appreciate; others were turned off by the same flavor because they thought it too medicinal. **84** —*D.T.* *(6/1/2002)*

Cockfighter's Ghost 2004 Chardonnay (Hunter Valley) $19. This Chard's charms are its delicate feel and slim body. Peach flavors take a backseat to a dry, stony feel. Good pre-dinner selection, with a modest 12.7% alcohol. 3,500 cases produced. **87** —*D.T.* *(4/1/2006)*

Cockfighter's Ghost 2001 Chardonnay (Hunter Valley) $18. As spooky as the name may sound, the profile here is sunny as can be—peach, mango, sunflower, with light cream accents. Medium-weight and billowy in the mouth; the nose's funky cologne-meets-lead pencil aroma was the only downside for us. 3,500 cases produced. **87** *(7/2/2004)*

Cockfighter's Ghost 2004 Semillon (Hunter Valley) $17. A good, approachable white, this Semillon shows grass and hay aromas, and modest banana, peach, and cream flavors. Pretty hefty in feel; finishes short. **86** —*D.T.* *(4/1/2006)*

Cockfighter's Ghost 2001 Shiraz (McLaren Vale) $23. Straight out of the bottle, the wine tastes and smells quite a bit sweeter than it does after a few minutes in the glass. With air, the caramelly aromas and sweet fruit flavors settle nicely into an enjoyable, easy-drinking wine gussied up with a stony-chalky feel. Straightforward, but evolves nicely. **87** —*D.T.* *(9/1/2004)*

Cockfighter's Ghost 2004 Verdelho (Hunter Valley) $17. It's a good thing that the weather is warming up, because this is just the kind of wine that you want in a chiller out on the deck. Floral and light citrus aromas preface flavors of lemon meringue and river rocks. Smooth, dry, and refreshing. **88** —*D.T.* *(4/1/2006)*

COLDSTREAM HILLS

Coldstream Hills 2002 Chardonnay (Yarra Valley) $18. A straightforward, pleasurable wine, where intense vanilla and toast flavors and tropical fruity aromas reign. With a soft, medium-weight mouthfeel, it's an easy choice for novices and experts alike. **85** *(7/2/2004)*

Coldstream Hills 2000 Chardonnay (Yarra Valley) $18. Despite a full, rich texture and mouthfeel and aromas of lime and pear, the flavors contain a vegetal element of canned peas. **81** —*J.C.* *(9/10/2002)*

Coldstream Hills 1998 Chardonnay (Yarra Valley) $22. 91 —*J.M.* *(1/1/2003)*

Coldstream Hills 2002 Pinot Noir (Yarra Valley) $18. It's a just-right Pinot, not too tart, not too big, and not too fruity. Bing cherry flavors are wide in the midpalate, where there's just enough oak. Oak and earth show on the finish. Definitely food-friendly; try with a mushroom dish, or fleshy fish. **87** —*D.T.* *(10/1/2003)*

Coldstream Hills 1998 Sauvignon Blanc (Yarra Valley) $17. 88 —*S.H. (10/1/2000)*

Coldstream Hills 2005 Sauvignon Blanc (Yarra Valley) $17. Aromas are fresh and green: grass, kiwi, lime. On the palate, the wine has hints of citrus, green grape, and grass flavors. Soft and approachable in feel; doesn't feel as high in acid as many other SBs. **86** —*D.T. (4/1/2006)*

Coldstream Hills 2002 Sauvignon Blanc (Victoria) $18. Has youthful grapefruit, yellow peach, and hay aromas. Sweet fruit nectar—like yellow peach—greets you at palate entry. The wine is round in the mouth but finishes with an odd metallic note. Bring it to the beach, or to your next picnic. **86** —*D.T. (5/1/2004)*

Coldstream Hills 2001 Sauvignon Blanc (Yarra Valley) $NA. Grassy and herbal, with grapefruit and a sense of soft, brushed leather. Grapefruit and lime flavors finish long and tart. **86** *(2/1/2002)*

COOKOOTHAMA

Cookoothama 2001 Chardonnay (South Eastern Australia) $11. Starts off with warm, inviting aromas of peach and ripe pear, blending in some nutmeg and clove. But the palate doesn't deliver on the early promise, lacking flavor and finishing spicy but short. **83** —*J.C. (1/1/2004)*

Cookoothama 2000 Pigeage Limited Release Merlot (Darlington Point) $25. Pigeage is the old-fashioned method of using human feet to press the grapes. This will give you softer tannins because you won't get any bitterness from breaking the seeds. This wine is very smooth with a balanced mouthfeel. The aromas of green olives and black pepper contrast the flavors of red berries and a touch of stemmyness. Drink now till 2005. **85** —*C.S. (6/1/2002)*

Cookoothama 2002 Sauvignon Blanc (King Valley) $10. The nose carries cologny, sugary aromas. It starts off lively in the mouth, and feels weightier as it goes; has light flavors of yellow stone fruit, punctuated by flavors of the stone alone. **84** —*D.T. (1/1/2002)*

Cookoothama 2001 Botrytis Semillon (South Eastern Australia) $18. Flavors of orange marmalade and butterscotch are satisfying, and hang on a medium-sized, taut frame, but fade into a woody finish. Smells like a tropical cocktail—cream, vanilla, peach, and a hint of orange liqueur. A pretty tasty wine, particularly for its moderate price. **87** —*D.T. (9/1/2004)*

COORALOOK

Cooralook 2002 Cabernet Sauvignon (Strathbogie Range) $20. Ripe black cherry, blackberry, and eucalyptus aromas. It's pretty linear on the palate, with pretty plum fruit accented with caramel. **86** —*D.T. (4/1/2006)*

Cooralook 2004 Pinot Gris (Mornington Peninsula) $16. Peach, melon, and bread aromas lead to bread, hay, and peach skin flavors on the palate. Medium bodied, straightforward and fine for casual occasions. 500 cases produced. **84** —*D.T. (2/1/2006)*

Cooralook 2003 Pinot Noir (Mornington Peninsula) $20. You won't mistake this for a Burgundy. It smells big and plummy—not so Pinot-esque, really—with some violet aromas coming through with air. Black cherry flavors carry through to the finish. A little soft, but approachable and enjoyable now. **87** —*D.T. (4/1/2006)*

CORIOLE

Coriole 2004 Cabernet Sauvignon (McLaren Vale) $30. Smells of sweet blueberry and cumin and, with air, toasted marshmallows. The palate has lifted flavors of black cherry and blueberry, with a soft feel and a good helping of vanilla to round it out. On the sweet side, but an edge of oak saves it from being too lollied. **86** —*D.T. (12/31/2005)*

Coriole 2001 Cabernet Sauvignon (McLaren Vale) $29. Aromas are of eucalyptus, cherry, and a dash of sea salt. Offers black cherry fruit on the palate, and a soft, approachable mouthfeel. Drink now. **87** —*D.T. (12/31/2004)*

Coriole 2001 Mary Kathleen Reserve Cabernet Sauvignon-Merlot (McLaren Vale) $45. Aromas are of dark fruit and stable tack. Smooth tannins on the palate cushion fresh black cherry and plum flavors, tinged with a thread of fresh herb. Pretty now, but could go another five years easily. **89** —*D.T. (3/1/2005)*

Coriole 2004 Chenin Blanc (McLaren Vale) $16. Offers predominantly pear aromas and flavors, with a minerally feel that continues through the finish. It's a light, clean quaff that's just right for drinks on the veranda. The Chenin comes from 5 or 6 area growers, one of whom has 82-year-old Chenin bushvines. **87** —*D.T. (3/1/2005)*

Coriole 2003 Chenin Blanc (McLaren Vale) $15. This is a casual, porch-sippin' wine, lively and zippy, with prominent yellow peach flavors. Clean on the close, with dust or mineral flavors and feel. Bright, grassy, and floral on the nose. **86** —*D.T. (5/1/2004)*

Coriole 2006 Rosé Nebbiolo (McLaren Vale) $19. A rosé for the dinner table. This is a dry version—not superfruity, not sweet—with berry and orange peel aromas, and flavors of blackberry on the palate. The minerally texture is what drives this train. **87** —*D.T. (11/15/2006)*

Coriole 2003 Contour 4 Sangiovese-Shiraz Red Blend (McLaren Vale) $16. This Sangiovese (60%)-Shiraz (40%) blend has dried-spice aromas and plum flavors. There's a vanilla-mocha accent, as well as an interesting almost orange/citrus one. Tannins will easily cut through an extra-cheese pizza. **88** —*D.T. (4/1/2006)*

Coriole 2001 Lalla Rookh Old Vines Red Blend (McLaren Vale) $29. A sexy, goes-down-easy Grenache (55%) and Shiraz (45%) blend. Aromas and flavors are of black cherry fruit couched in dark, earthy accents. The nose has a deep, dusty-wheat note, too. Finishes with soil and toast. 700 cases produced. **89** —*D.T. (9/1/2004)*

Coriole 2003 Sangiovese (McLaren Vale) $NA. From vines planted in 1982 comes this sturdy red, which features cherry and plum flavors, smooth tannins, and an herb-anise finish. Fresh red fruit aromas are a nice beginning. **87** —*D.T. (3/1/2005)*

Coriole 2003 Semillon-Sauvignon Blanc (South Eastern Australia) $15. This wine shows light floral-talc aromas on the nose, and citrus and white stone fruit flavors on the palate. It's light and straightforward, with a likeable, crisp feel. **85** —*D.T. (9/1/2004)*

Coriole 2004 (McLaren Vale-Adelaide Hills) Semillon-Sauvignon Blanc (McLaren Vale) $16. Coriole's varietal Semillon is now only distributed at cellar door. Their American Sem fans will have to instead enjoy this blend, which has dusty attic and pear aromas, and an unusual but fresh palate full of stone and fresh greens. Clean and quaffable. **86** —*D.T. (3/1/2005)*

Coriole 2003 Shiraz (McLaren Vale) $27. A dark, textbook Shiraz with all the proper parts in place. Smells of fresh, fleshy plums and almonds, and tastes like the same purple fruit decked out with some earth and cream. Charming and very drinkable. **87** —*D.T. (12/31/2005)*

Coriole 2001 Lloyd Reserve Shiraz (McLaren Vale) $65. Estate-grown; Coriole's flagship wine is the only one of their line to go through malolactic fermentation in barrels, rather than in open fermenters. Dark and meaty on the nose, this quietly powerful, sexy Shiraz has plum fruit at its core; the same plummy chord resonates on the finish. **91** —*D.T. (3/1/2005)*

Coriole 2000 Lloyd Reserve Shiraz (McLaren Vale) $NA. Cocoa and mocha accent red fruit and a little eucalyptus on the nose. Black fruit on the palate falls into a vortex of the usual accoutrements—toffee, mocha, and caramel. Chewy but soft tannins complete the picture; though the flavors are dark, the wine isn't at all unapproachable. It's a teddy bear. **88** —*D.T. (5/1/2004)*

Coriole 2004 The Soloist Shiraz (McLaren Vale) $40. New to the American market, and worthy of a splashy debut. Plum fruit is deep and muscular on the nose, while the palate offers lifted berry flavors along with softer, more plush plums. Juicy and well structured, and probably not unlike your other favorite big South Australian Shirazes. **91** —*D.T. (11/15/2006)*

Coriole 2001 Redstone Shiraz-Cabernet Sauvignon (McLaren Vale) $20. Peppery oak and mixed plum aromas preface classy black-plum fruit in the mouth. It's a medium-sized wine, with a pleasing, chalky feel; on the finish, the chalk is punctuated by a green note. Still, it's very good overall, with a size and feel appropriate for pairing with food. 80% Shiraz; 20% Cabernet. 2,000 cases produced. **87** —*D.T. (9/1/2004)*

AUSTRALIA

AUSTRALIA

CRABTREE

Crabtree 1999 Watervale Riesling (Clare Valley) $16. Tastes quite mature, with characteristic diesel-petrol notes and ripe Golden Delicious apple aromas and flavors. The mouthfeel is round and the wine dry on the palate, turning very dry on the almost mineral-spirit finish. **86** —*M.M. (9/1/2001)*

CRAGG'S CREEK

Cragg's Creek 2003 Unwooded Chardonnay (Riverland) $15. The bottle may say Chardonnay, but blind, it smells more like Muscat. Orange blossoms and honey aromas and flavors reign here, as does a soft, oily texture. **80** —*D.T. (10/1/2005)*

CRANEFORD

Craneford NV Champagne Blend (Barossa Valley) $30. This is definitely an acquired taste. The aromas were true to the varieties, with spice rack, blackberries, and plums. Slightly sweet black plums and caramel on the palate mix with tannins and bubbles. Not for the meek. Drink now or give it some time to see what happens. **85** —*C.S. (12/1/2002)*

Craneford 2000 Chardonnay (Barossa Valley) $12. You need to like oak to enjoy this wine, but if you do, you'll revel in its aromas of toast, vanilla and wood smoke and thrill to its spicy, oaky finish. In between, you'll find simple peach and vanilla flavors. **85** —*J.C. (7/1/2002)*

Craneford 2002 97 Year Old Single Vineyard Grenache (Barossa Valley) $28. Blackberry and earth aromas open to flavors that settle into blackberry and black cherry with some air. It's medium-sized and a lovely drink, with caramel-toffee nuances and a bite of fresh herb on the back end. **88** —*D.T. (9/1/2004)*

Craneford 2003 John Zilm Merlot (Barossa Valley) $30. A focused, perhaps a little narrow, Merlot with paper-smooth tannins and flavors of grapes and plums. Offers up molasses and fig aromas, plus a fair helping of animal/stably notes. **87** —*D.T. (4/1/2006)*

Craneford 2003 John Zilm Petite Verdot (Barossa Valley) $33. Dense with roasted, grapy fruit on the nose. On the palate, grape and blueberry notes prevail. Somewhat sour, with pronounced acids. Finishes with black pepper. **86** —*D.T. (6/1/2006)*

Craneford 2000 Quartet Red Blend (Barossa Valley) $24. This kitchen-sink blend boasts a high percentage of Petit Verdot (38%), which may account for its dramatic floral aromatics. Aside from roses, cherries also play a role. In the mouth, complex floral-herbal elements have a solid underpinning of cherries and raspberries, finishing with just enough tannins to stand up to rare beef. **87** —*J.C. (9/1/2002)*

Craneford 2000 Riesling (Eden Valley) $12. 90 Editors' Choice —*M.M. (2/1/2002)*

Craneford 2000 Semillon (Barossa Valley) $12. Smoky and toasty at first, there's even a sense of meatiness to the aromas. With air, superripe nectarines emerge, combined with a mineral-graphite note. Finishes long and a bit hard; pair it with assertively flavored fish dishes, maybe something with a Moroccan influence. **90 Best Buy** —*J.C. (2/1/2002)*

Craneford 2000 Shiraz (Barossa Valley) $28. Lean and focused in the mouth, with red fruit and caramel flavors. Both the bouquet and the finish, however, show touches of plastic or resin. **85** —*D.T. (3/1/2003)*

Craneford 2004 Viognier (Adelaide Hills) $17. Smells like fresh whipping cream and melon, and the flavors are similar, but edged in some white pepper. This is a lithe Viognier, not a fat, alcoholic one, with a bony, dusty spine that stays the fresh-and-balanced course through the finish. **88** —*D.T. (12/31/2005)*

CULLEN

Cullen 2002 Diana Madeline Bordeaux Blend (Margaret River) $75. Cullen's signature red is 80% Cabernet, 12% Merlot, and 8% Petit Verdot this vintage, with a moderate 13% alcohol. Has aromas of black cherry and ink. The same fruit is showing (and is quite tangy) on the palate, moderated by tealike tannins. Full and round, but tough around the edges and not too giving quite yet. A few years in the cellar may turn that around. **88** —*D.T. (10/1/2006)*

Cullen 2000 Diana Madeline Bordeaux Blend (Margaret River) $50. The nose offers ink and chocolate and, with some aeration, caramel. Though the cherry, raspberry, and plum fruit is pretty nice on its own, it's the mouthfeel that makes it stand out—it has powdery tannins, plus good weight and grip in the midpalate. Cabernet Sauvignon (65%) provides a sturdy backbone; Merlot, Petit Verdot, Malbec ,and Cab Franc make up the balance. **90** —*D.T. (10/1/2003)*

Cullen 2003 Mangan Bordeaux Blend (Margaret River) $40. A blend of Malbec, Petit Verdot, and Merlot, dense and dark in color. There are ripe, juicy fruit aromas, with a light smokiness. Ripe, vibrant black fruits dominate with wood flavors in the background. This blend brings out the juiciness of the Merlot and balances it with the tannins of Malbec. **88** *(4/1/2005)*

Cullen 2001 Diana Madeline Cabernet Sauvignon-Merlot (Margaret River) $75. This is the flagship red from Cullen's Wilyabrup vineyards in Margaret River. A classic blend of Cabernet and Merlot, aged for 18 months in wood, it has huge, ripe fruit, along with elegance. Flavors of chocolate, mulberry, and spices come together with ripe tannins. This wine definitely needs aging—give it five years at least. **92 Cellar Selection** —*R.V. (4/1/2005)*

Cullen 2002 Chardonnay (Margaret River) $55. From the low-yielding 2002 vintage, this wood-aged Chardonnay has finely knit tropical fruits with creamy wood and ripe green plums. It is ripe and rich, with a light touch of pepper hinting at the 14% alcohol. **89** *(4/1/2005)*

Cullen 2003 Ephraim Clarke Semillon-Sauvignon Blanc (Margaret River) $30. Intense tropical fruit aromas, along with white currants. This blend of Semillon and Sauvignon Blanc is packed full of caramel and vanilla flavors, along with asparagus and ripe wood. Lovely acidity leaves a fresh aftertaste. **87** *(4/1/2005)*

Cullen 2001 Ephraim Clarke Semillon-Sauvignon Blanc (Margaret River) $30. Fruity? Not so much. This 65% Semillon, 35% Sauvignon Blanc blend is steely—it's a core of a wine, without much fluff. Flavors are of olive oil, biscuit, and some citrus pith; finishes medium-long with fruit-pit tartness. **89** —*D.T. (10/1/2003)*

CURLY FLAT

Curly Flat 1999 Pinot Noir (Victoria) $30. A straightforward Pinot, one with red cherry fruit wrapped in tree bark and tea notes. It's light to medium in body, and shows pretty earth and orange pekoe tea aromas. Will probably be at its best with food. **86** —*D.T. (9/1/2004)*

CURRENCY CREEK ESTATE

Currency Creek Estate 2003 The Black Swamp Cabernet Sauvignon (Currency Creek) $17. Smells like demiglace, earth, and tree. On the palate, it's twangy, and not very well integrated: A filmy layer of oak hovers over cursory plum fruit. Simple, one-dimensional. **83** —*D.T. (12/31/2005)*

Currency Creek Estate 2004 The Viaduct Unwooded Chardonnay (Currency Creek) $14. This wine has a nice feel—it tastes like it's coated in a thick layer of attic dust, the way some good Champagnes do—with apple and melon fruit below. What I can't get by is a strong lactic-buttery aroma (no really, it smells like a stick of butter), which lets up some on the palate. Finishes on a sour-apple lollipop note. **84** —*D.T. (12/1/2005)*

Currency Creek Estate 2005 Sedgeland Sauvignon Blanc (Currency Creek) $14. Has light aromas of soy or saline, coupled with dust and mineral flavors. Medium-weight and good, but there's not much verve here. **83** —*D.T. (6/1/2006)*

Currency Creek Estate 2003 Ostrich Hill Shiraz (Currency Creek) $17. A lighter-sized Shiraz, this one features red berry and cherry in abundance on the palate, but flattens out to a dusty, woody finish. Aromas run the gamut from black pepper and sweet raspberry to floral notes, then rhubarb and tomato. **86** —*D.T. (12/31/2005)*

CUTTAWAY HILL ESTATE

Cuttaway Hill Estate 2003 Merlot (Southern Highlands) $13. One of the better inexpensive Oz Merlots I've had lately. This wine offers spicy, fireplace-smoke aromas and cool-cherry undertones on the palate. It doesn't hit you over the head with tannins and it's not one for the cellar, but it's a good wine, and light enough, even, to enjoy with lunch. **87 Best Buy** —*D.T. (12/1/2005)*

Cuttaway Hill Estate 2004 Southern Highlands Pinot Gris (Australia) $16. A thick, fat Gris. This version offers abundant peaches and apricots, spiced with some ginger, on both the nose and the palate. Pleasing and sunny; a good, food-friendly choice. **86** —*D.T. (12/1/2005)*

Cuttaway Hill Estate 2004 Sauvignon Blanc (Australia) $13. Spice and herb aromas usher in grapefruit, then tropical fruit flavors on the palate. Soft in the mouth; a good casual quaffer. **84** —*D.T. (12/1/2005)*

D'ARENBERG

D'Arenberg 2001 The Galvo Garage Bordeaux Blend (South Australia) $35. There's a lot of oak here—the nose, particularly, shows wood-derived herb and white peppery notes. Red fruit on the palate fades into smooth, oaky tannins on the finish. **87** —*D.T. (12/31/2003)*

D'Arenberg 2003 The Coppermine Road Cabernet Sauvignon (McLaren Vale) $65. Aromas start sweet, then grow tomatoey and earthy with air. The palate offers lifted berry and cherry fruit countered by an herbal, almost sour, greenness that lasts through the finish. It's a well-made wine with a smooth, chalky feel, but its flavors are not all that harmonious. **86** —*D.T. (8/1/2006)*

D'Arenberg 2002 The Coppermine Road Cabernet Sauvignon (McLaren Vale) $65. Shows very nice, bright, red cherry aromas, while substantial red plum fruit drives the bass on the palate. My quibble here is with the dry, woody mouthfeel, which may resolve itself with 2–3 years of cellaring. Try after 2008. **89** —*D.T. (3/1/2005)*

D'Arenberg 1999 The Coppermine Road Cabernet Sauvignon (McLaren Vale) $65. Deep and inky up front, with notes of earth and bitter chocolate. Anyone thinking about trying this wine should be a fan of naturally sweet reds. It has an unmistakable sugar to it, but it's not a cloying or fake sweetness. Clearly it's ripe, and a bit unyielding. A few years in the cellar will do it some good. **90** —*M.S. (12/15/2002)*

D'Arenberg 2002 The High Trellis Cabernet Sauvignon (McLaren Vale) $19. Not a fruity, forward style of Cab—instead, earth and wood are prevalent, which gives the wine a wild, wooly feel in the mouth. Aromas reflect its earthiness; black cherry lingers underneath. A good match for grilled meat, or dishes with wild mushrooms. **87** —*D.T. (3/1/2005)*

D'Arenberg 2001 The High Trellis Cabernet Sauvignon (McLaren Vale) $18. Fruit on the nose is very stewy, and doused in licorice. Mixed plum fruit flavors on the palate take on an iced-tea flavor; the finish shows more of the same plus a little green herb. This is a low-acid wine, in need of more structure. **85** —*D.T. (5/1/2004)*

D'Arenberg 2000 The High Trellis Cabernet Sauvignon (McLaren Vale) $18. The wine is 80% from McLaren Vale vineyards, and it's chunky with mild hints of tomato both in the nose and on the palate. Otherwise it's full of red-berry fruit, and the finish features a hefty dose of oak-based vanillin and coffee. Aggressive and racy; probably best with food. **89** —*M.S. (12/15/2002)*

D'Arenberg 2004 The Olive Grove Chardonnay (McLaren Vale) $16. Pear, melon, and peach are foremost on the front and middle palate, with a zip of citrus and mineral creeping in through the finish. Dusty and minerally on the nose, with a Viognier-like viscous feel. **89** —*D.T. (8/1/2006)*

D'Arenberg 2003 The Olive Grove Chardonnay (McLaren Vale) $16. Hints of vanilla, or whipping cream, dress up clear, pretty aromas of pear, peach and apple. On the palate, it's not a fat wine, nor is it wiry—it's somewhere in the middle, with a dry feel and pear and mineral flavors. Has a flat woodiness on the finish, but overall it's a very nice Chardonnay. 2,000 cases produced. **89** —*D.T. (3/1/2005)*

D'Arenberg 2002 The Olive Grove Chardonnay (McLaren Vale) $15. Tastes and smells quite tropical, with pineapple and melon at the fore. The nose shows some butter, but on the palate that plump yellowness is more like honey. Finishes a little tart, but it's still a juicy wine. **85** *(7/2/2004)*

D'Arenberg 2001 The Olive Grove Chardonnay (McLaren Vale) $15. Aromas are musky and nutty at the same time, but also mix in some grapefruit notes. It tastes largely neutral, except for a dollop of baking spices that turn aggressively peppery on the lean finish. **83** —*J.C. (7/1/2002)*

D'Arenberg 2001 The Custodian Grenache (McLaren Vale) $19. Clay, earth, and smoke aromas are brightened by a flash of eucalyptus and cherry. In the mouth, a black-cherry core has pretty accents of dust and clay, but also bright hints of metal or herb. Quite nice overall, this Grenache has a dusty, medium-sized feel. 1,000 cases produced. **88** —*D.T. (3/1/2005)*

D'Arenberg 1999 The Custodian Grenache (McLaren Vale) $23. Varietally correct, with red cherry fruit taking center stage and herb and earth notes in supporting roles. Has some chalky tannins, with black and green pepper flavors on the finish. **85** —*D.T. (12/31/2003)*

D'Arenberg 2002 The Derelict Vineyard Grenache (McLaren Vale) $35. Though more expensive than d'Arenberg's The Custodian Grenache, I liked this one less. Brown sugar and maple syrup aromas dominate; the palate is mercifully not as sweet as the nose would suggest, showing mostly black plum and berry notes. Wooly tannins on the finish have staying power, but the feel on the palate is pretty straighforward. 500 cases produced. **86** —*D.T. (3/1/2005)*

D'Arenberg 2004 The Stump Jump G-S-M (McLaren Vale) $10. One heck of a nice GSM for $10, this wine has pretty tree bark and barbecue aromas, followed up by juicy plum and raspberry fruit on the palate. Light vanilla/oak accents add interest, as does a mouthfeel thick with dust/chalk. 15,000 cases produced. **88 Best Buy** —*D.T. (8/1/2006)*

D'Arenberg 2002 The Twentyeight Road Mourvèdre (McLaren Vale) $35. Classy, not sassy or brassy—think gallant older gentleman in a bowtie, not a shirtless, greased-up meathead. Aromas are of sturdy red fruit and get sweeter, like meat marinade, with air. Bramble, oak, and fresh herb nuances dress up the plum fruit on the palate; has some hold here on the tongue, and a chalk-claylike feel. **90** —*D.T. (3/1/2005)*

D'Arenberg 1999 The Twentyeight Road Mourvèdre (McLaren Vale) $30. One to bring to your next blind tasting, because it's just so puzzling. Nose has cranberry, eucalyptus, and some meat gravy; on the palate, red fruit takes a backseat to the oak. With aeration, smooth oaky tannins come through. Finishes a little sour. **85** —*D.T. (12/31/2003)*

D'Arenberg 2001 d'Arry's Original Shiraz Grenache Red Blend (McLaren Vale) $18. d'Arry's original shows the best of both varieties—it's fresh, fun, and middleweight, with meaty, plummy flavors more associated with Shiraz. An enjoyable, drink-now wine. **88** —*D.T. (5/1/2004)*

D'Arenberg 2002 The Galvo Garage Red Blend (McLaren Vale) $35. Its name is a nod to French garagiste wines, as is its composition (Cabernets Sauvignon and Franc, Merlot, and Petit Verdot). It tastes Old World, too, with drying tannins and wood on the palate, and red fruit in a supporting role. Aromas are of briar patch and roasted berries; finishes with a tangy lemon/tea bite. **86** —*D.T. (3/1/2005)*

D'Arenberg 2002 The Ironstone Pressings Red Blend (McLaren Vale) $65. Named for the ironstone deposits cleared from area vineyards, which—perhaps by power of suggestion—you can taste in the wine. What at first feels like a fistful of oak on the palate smooths out to an earthy, minerally impression with air. The texture is also quite nice; chewy tannins rule the roost here. Fans of forward, fruity wines should keep shopping. **89** —*D.T. (3/1/2005)*

D'Arenberg 2000 The Ironstone Pressings Red Blend (McLaren Vale) $65. Low in acid, with cherry flavors on the palate and a very dry, Bourbon-barrel finish. The nose has nice brown sugar, herb, and red fruit notes that are sweet, yet still alluring. **84** —*D.T. (12/31/2003)*

D'Arenberg 2003 The Laughing Magpie Shiraz Viognier Red Blend (McLaren Vale) $35. Meaty, peppery aromas give way to ones of cherry pie filling after airing. Rhône-styled, perhaps, on the palate, with a cracked-pepper quality accenting the black fruit; there's a lifted quality—the Viognier's floral notes—to the black cherry fruit, that feels overdone. This is a tasty wine, to be sure, but one whose 6% Viognier is about 3% too much. **88** —*D.T. (3/1/2005)*

D'Arenberg 2002 The Sticks & Stones Red Blend (McLaren Vale) $40. Mixed plum and a firm amount of wood on the nose and palate; an herb-metallic tinge shows on the latter. A very good, feminine-sized wine with eraser-like tannins, and not too many bells and whistles. 45% Tempranillo, 43% Grenache, 12% Souzao—what may be the strangest McLaren Vale blend ever. **88** —*D.T. (3/1/2005)*

AUSTRALIA

D'Arenberg 2003 The Stump Jump Red Blend (McLaren Vale) $10. Smells of sweet berries, apples and grapes. On the palate, it's a food-sized wine, but it's not very distinctive varietally (cut it some slack, it's a blended wine). Just the kind of no-brainer you want for pizza night. Grenache, Shiraz, and Mourvedre. 15,000 cases produced. **85 Best Buy** —*D.T.* (3/1/2005)

D'Arenberg 2001 The Stump Jump Red Blend (McLaren Vale) $11. Crowd-pleasing and agreeable, with black fruit rounded out with oak and caramel accents. Fruit turns redder on the finish, but the oak remains. Nose brims with marshmallow-vanilla fluffiness, plus cherry and earth. **86** —*D.T.* (12/31/2003)

D'Arenberg 2003 The Cadenzia Rhône Red Blend (McLaren Vale) $NA. 89 —*D.T.* (8/1/2005)

D'Arenberg 2003 The Money Spider Roussanne (McLaren Vale) $22. Honey, nut, and grape juice aromas. There's pretty yellow fruit and some floral nuances on the palate. Moderate in size and intensity; finishes dry. **87** —*D.T.* (3/1/2005)

D'Arenberg 2001 The Broken Fishplate Sauvignon Blanc (Adelaide Hills) $15. The nose here is flat as a board, offering next to nothing. Simple green apple and underripe pear flavors fail to rescue the wine, while a finish lacking definition and length seals its fate. For a producer that largely succeeds with Shiraz, the cute name of this wine is unfortunately the best thing that it has to offer. **82** (8/1/2002)

D'Arenberg 2003 The Dead Arm Shiraz (McLaren Vale) $65. Another top-flight Dead Arm, the 2003 boasts attractive scents of leather, spice, vanilla, and boysenberries. The palate is lush and creamy, carrying earthy dark-fruited flavors enlivened by a bright streak of acidity. Turns chewy on the finish, suggesting short-term cellaring is in order. Try after 2008. **90** —*J.C.* (12/15/2006)

D'Arenberg 2002 The Dead Arm Shiraz (McLaren Vale) $65. Impresses the hell out of you on the first look—it offers controlled, pretty plum, and berry fruit on the palate, with black pepper, cassis, and graham cracker aromas. Overexamine it, though, and you start to find things that you wish were different (for me, it wants more intensity midpalate), but that doesn't mean that this isn't delicious. Why not just sit back and enjoy the mocha-laden finish, and leave analysis to another day? **91** —*D.T.* (3/1/2005)

D'Arenberg 2000 The Dead Arm Shiraz (McLaren Vale) $65. This wine gets its name from a vine fungus that kills off part of the vine. The vine gets pruned back, which leads to small berries and low yields; this concentrates the intense, fleshy blue-black fruit flavors. There is a rich, juicy feel to the wine, which has firm but well-integrated tannins. **90** —*C.S.* (3/1/2003)

D'Arenberg 1998 The Dead Arm Shiraz (McLaren Vale) $60. An inky, dark candidate with blackberry and black pepper from stem to stern. Licorice, black, of course, accents and lots of toasty oak abound through the tangy finish. Has good depth, tart sweet fruit, and tangy acidity, but is a bit hard...will it blossom? Needs time, and may open, but the dark wrap is tight now. **87** (11/1/2001)

D'Arenberg 2002 The Footbolt Shiraz (McLaren Vale) $19. Smells like a blended fruit-box juice, and gives a similar impression on the palate. Distinct red raspberry, plum, apple, and grape flavors rides some rough wood on the palate. A straightforward Shiraz, but one that has not smoothed out yet. Give it six months or a year; maybe the wood will settle down. **86** —*D.T.* (3/1/2005)

D'Arenberg 2000 The Footbolt Shiraz (McLaren Vale) $18. The fruit here is fleshy and red, which gives the wine an unexpected softness. Easy earth, mocha, and oak notes round out this wine, The Dead Arm's baby sister. One to drink now rather than hold. **86** —*D.T.* (3/1/2003)

D'Arenberg 1999 The Footbolt Shiraz (McLaren Vale) $17. An almost medicinal salt-pepper-anise note opens onto a palate full of tart white pepper and black cherry, plus a shade of vanilla. Finish has a lot of sour fruit and pepper—some reviewers called it tangy, others harshly acidic. **85** (10/1/2001)

D'Arenberg 1997 The Footbolt Shiraz (McLaren Vale) $15. 91 (11/15/1999)

D'Arenberg 2002 The Laughing Magpie Shiraz (McLaren Vale) $35. The wine's scant 7% Viognier is really noticeable, particularly on the nose,

where feminine, floral aromas pretty up black-as-night oak and plum; this reviewer found violets among the wine's similarly dark flavors. The feel is chewy and substantial at midpalate, though a little too woody on the finish. **88** —*D.T.* (5/1/2004)

D'Arenberg 2002 d'Arry's Original Shiraz-Grenache (McLaren Vale) $19. A fun, youthful wine. Juicy, chewy fruit on the palate isn't overpowered by lots of oak. Ripe plum and blackberry on the nose; finishes with less verve than the palate has. **87** —*D.T.* (3/1/2005)

D'Arenberg 2004 The Hermit Crab White Blend (McLaren Vale) $16. Smells like fresh laundry, and has modest pear flavors on the palate. Fairly full in the mouth, and finishes with a sour peach-pit note. **86** —*D.T.* (10/1/2006)

D'Arenberg 2002 The Hermit Crab White Blend (McLaren Vale) $15. Starts off with a kick of white pepper on the palate, which segues into fleshy stone fruit and a citrus-like tang. It's round in the mouth and moderately zesty, finishing a little less so. **85** —*D.T.* (5/1/2004)

D'Arenberg 2005 The Stump Jump White Blend (McLaren Vale) $10. Blending Riesling, Sauvignon, Marsanne, and Roussanne in this case yields a white with cushy, soft aromas (like white chocolate), and light flavors of peach and olive oil. Not a lively, acidic wine, but fine for an everyday quaff. 15,000 cases produced. **84** —*D.T.* (10/1/2006)

D'Arenberg 2003 The Stump Jump White Blend (McLaren Vale) $10. This blend of Riesling, Marsanne, and Sauvignon Blanc is a good, all-purpose mutt of a white. With floral, gingery aromas ushering in a drier, herb-tinged palate, its parts may not come together gracefully, but it's still a good drink. **85 Best Buy** —*D.T.* (3/1/2005)

D'Arenberg 2002 The Stump Jump White Blend (McLaren Vale) $10. More known for his Grenaches, Syrahs, and Mourvèdres (and blends thereof), winemaker Chester Osbourn has a hit with this oddball white blend. Its composition changes yearly, but it's always unoaked. This vintage is fresh and lively, with zesty citrus, melon, and peach on the nose. Citrus and yellow fruit, plus some minerals, come through on the palate. **87** —*D.T.* (11/15/2003)

DALWHINNIE

Dalwhinnie 2002 Moonambel Cabernet Sauvignon (Victoria) $50. Smooth and inviting, with black plum fruit at its core. Aromas are deep and dark, yet aren't overt at this young stage. Feminine in style; not a wine for tannin or acid hounds, to be sure. **88** —*D.T.* (10/1/2006)

Dalwhinnie 2000 Chardonnay (Australia) $54. Where there's butterscotch and vanilla on the nose, you can bet that it will follow on the palate. There's quite a bit of it, too—toast and butter—with hints of yellow fruit losing its footing in the process. Fans of the style will find our rating conservative. **82** (7/2/2004)

Dalwhinnie 2001 Pyrenees Chardonnay (Australia) $40. This Chardonnay opens with fluffy, vanilla-like aromas that thicken to a custardlike density after a few minutes in the glass. As you'd expect, buttery, oaky accents are present on the palate, too, but its core is bright and citrusy. Folks who like a Chard with plenty of creamy fluff on its bones may find this score stingy. **87** —*D.T.* (5/1/2005)

Dalwhinnie 2001 Pyrenees Shiraz (Australia) $49. The Dalwhinnie offers sexy aromas of fresh whipping cream, anise, and blackberry. Wooly tannins, and flavors are of ripe blackberries. Warm on the finish, but still an alluring wine. **90** —*D.T.* (8/1/2005)

DAVID FRANZ

David Franz 2000 Georgie's Walk Cabernet Sauvignon (Barossa) $40. This wine gets 14 months oak aging, and two and a half years of bottle age; this is the current vintage. Hats off to Franz for making a completely different sort of Barossa Cabernet. That it's under 13% alcohol is just the tip of the iceberg; there's cola, black pepper, and plum flavors, and aromas of spice and leather. Feels fresh and spry, but its age has also given it hints of maturity. **92** —*D.T.* (10/1/2006)

David Franz 1999 Georgie's Walk Cabernet Sauvignon-Shiraz (Barossa-Langhorne Creek) $40. The packaging is great: a heavy bottle, with all the wine's details handwritten in what looks like White-Out on an otherwise unlabeled bottle. But for all that style, what's in the bottle is good, but not quite as exciting as the outside package: there's stewy plum fruit, heavy helping of wood, and caramel and cream aromas. **86** —*D. T. (11/15/2004)*

David Franz 2000 Benjamin's Promise Shiraz (Barossa) $40. Nicely complex, this offering combines cherry fruit with plenty of leathery, smoky, and herbal nuances. In fact, one might argue there's a touch too much leather, as it seems to dull the fruit slightly, smoothing out any rough edges, but also lessening the fruit's bite. The wine is medium-bodied, with a creamy mouthfeel that finishes on a leathery note. **87** —*J. C. (12/15/2006)*

David Franz 1999 Benjamin's Promise Shiraz (Barossa Valley) $40. There's a lot to like about this wine, including deep peppery aromas and interesting cedar-toffee accents on the palate. This reviewer, however, found the fruit a little stewy, and the acids a little low. Its chunky, fruity style will surely win fans, if the supercool bottle packaging doesn't do it first. **88** *(11/15/2004)*

DAVID HOOK WINES

David Hook Wines 2002 The Gorge Shiraz (Hunter Valley) $17. Fruit on the nose is very ripe, with nutty, coconutty, barbecue notes alongside. The same characters—nut, carob, ripe cherry—carry over on the palate. The wine's wooly texture is nice, finishing smooth and with a bite of tangy oak. **87** —*D. T. (4/1/2006)*

DAVID TRAEGER

David Traeger 1998 Shiraz (Victoria) $24. Tart candied fruit, similar to SweetTarts, with a toasty overlay of cedary oak. Lean; firmly structured by dusty tannins. **83** *(11/1/2001)*

DAVID WYNN

David Wynn 1996 Cabernet Sauvignon (Eden Valley) $15. **80** *(3/1/2000)*

David Wynn 1999 Chardonnay (Barossa Valley) $11. The label on this wine says "unwooded Chardonnay," and in this case that seems to be part of the problem. This is a case of just too little fruit—the wine could certainly use some wood for texture, even flavor. There's a taut framework, but there's not much on it. **82** —*M. N. (6/1/2001)*

David Wynn 1995 Patriarch Shiraz (Eden Valley) $30. **92** —*M. G. (11/15/1999)*

DE BORTOLI

De Bortoli 2001 Cabernet Sauvignon (Yarra Valley) $35. This lighter-style Cab smells like a basket of plums with a few dates thrown in. On the palate, the wine has a sweet grape flavor and smooth tannins. Finishes with pulpy wood. **85** —*D. T. (10/1/2005)*

De Bortoli 2000 Cabernet Sauvignon (Yarra Valley) $34. There's more Cab planted in Yarra Valley than Shiraz, so here's a real local treat. This is a leaner-style wine, with a rustic profile overall: Flavors are of taut plums, wood, and wheat; aromas are of earth, anise, and some tobacco. **86** *(11/1/2004)*

De Bortoli 1999 Melba Reserve Cabernet Sauvignon (Yarra Valley) $59. Though the wine contains fruit from the winery's oldest blocks, with only 1.5 tons harvested per acre, we didn't find it quite up to the quality of other De Bortoli wines. Nose shows hints of stewed fruit, molasses, and a leafy quality. In the mouth, it tastes similarly past its prime— dusty, slightly baked-tasting fruit. A bit of a disappointment, considering the wine's reputation. **84** *(11/1/2004)*

De Bortoli 1998 Melba Reserve Cabernet Sauvignon (Yarra Valley) $60. With such big, jammy, plums, oak and caramel notes on the nose and the palate, you'd expect it to have the heft to carry these bold flavors off. It doesn't. Medium-bodied, and drinkable now. **85** —*D. T. (12/31/2003)*

De Bortoli 2004 Willowglen Cabernet Sauvignon-Merlot (South Eastern Australia) $9. This wine has black cherry and cassis aromas that briefly go the way of tomato, then fade into a pretty, white-peppery note. On the palate, cool, black cherry fruit is juicy and couched in textured tannins. 100,000 cases produced. **86 Best Buy** —*D. T. (2/1/2006)*

De Bortoli 2003 Chardonnay (Yarra Valley) $27. Pleasant tropical-summery aromas have nut and toast accents. The wine is round and medium-bodied in the mouth, with understated yellow fruit flavors. Finishes soft, with a lingering leesy note. **87** *(11/1/2004)*

De Bortoli 2001 Chardonnay (Yarra Valley) $30. Toasty, nutty, and even eggy, there's apple and caramel on the palate, though the midpalate feels a little hollow. Sours up on the finish, with herb and anise. **82** *(7/2/2004)*

De Bortoli 2003 dB Chardonnay (Big Rivers) $9. This Chard is a good wine, but it's not the best De Bortoli can do. Aromas are of cream and petrol, and the yellow-fruit flavors are light and straightforward. Lean in the mouth; fine for big groups or casual outings. **83** —*D. T. (12/31/2004)*

De Bortoli 2002 dB Chardonnay (Riverina) $6. The kind of wine that should be served cold, at beachside getaways—it shows coconut and butterscotch aromas, and tastes like a tropical fruit cocktail. It's an easy quaffer, and a little sweet. It won't win the hearts of wine collectors, but will go over very well with the party crowd. **84** *(7/2/2004)*

De Bortoli 2001 Deen Vat 7 Chardonnay (South Eastern Australia) $10. There's a lot of toast on the nose, which is followed up by flavors of candied and sour apples on the palate. Like sucking on a hard candy—it's not flat-out sweet, but has that viscous, resiny impression in the mouth. Finishes with cream and anise. **84** —*D. T. (12/31/2003)*

De Bortoli 2003 Gulf Station Chardonnay (Yarra Valley) $20. **85** *(11/1/2004)*

De Bortoli 2003 Hunter Valley Chardonnay (Hunter Valley) $20. Very light yellow in the glass, with light floral/fresh meadow aromas to match. White meat and pear fruit is weighty on the front palate, and fades into a bright herbal-steeliness on the finish. Not hugely fat or mouthcoating. It's just the right size, and rather interesting at that. **87** —*D. T. (11/15/2004)*

De Bortoli 2003 dB Merlot (South Eastern Australia) $8. **84 Best Buy** —*D. T. (10/1/2005)*

De Bortoli 2005 dB Selection Petite Sirah (South Eastern Australia) $9. Aromas are of intense, ripe blackberry fruit heavily dosed with vanilla. The palate deals much of the same, but dialed down a notch in intensity. Feel is smooth; 10,000 cases produced. **87 Best Buy** —*D. T. (8/1/2006)*

De Bortoli 2003 dB Selection Petite Sirah (Big Rivers) $8. value case **85** —*D. T. (11/15/2005)*

De Bortoli 2004 Deen Vat 1 Petite Sirah (South Eastern Australia) $13. Easy and approachable for a Petite Sirah, the Vat 1 starts off with oak, black pepper, eucalyptus, and maple-syrup aromas; the syrupy component blessedly lets up after a few minutes in the glass. Has an interesting texture—tannins are almost furry—and would be just lovely with braised short ribs or other rich fare. **86** —*D. T. (11/15/2006)*

De Bortoli 2004 Deen Vat 4 Petite Verdot (South Eastern Australia) $13. Smells kind of confected, like blueberry fruit roll-up. There's intensity on the front palate, but it fades away as quickly as it came. Offers anise and berry flavors, and a metallic hint on the finish. **83** —*D. T. (11/15/2006)*

De Bortoli 2002 Deen Vat 4 Petite Verdot (South Eastern Australia) $10. This is one black, inky wine, but its blackberry and plum fruit is focused and concentrated, enveloped in a smooth, chalky bubble. Mocha and chalky tannins continue on the finish. Thick and rich, it's a wee bit low acid, and is not for the faint of heart. A sizeable wine, more appropriate solo than with dinner. **88 Best Buy** —*D. T. (5/1/2004)*

De Bortoli 2005 Windy Peak Pinot Grigio (Victoria) $17. Very fragrant, with banana notes most dominant. In the mouth, you get tropical fruit (banana again, plus peach) and a soft, almost flabby, feel. Fine, but runs contrary to what you might expect from the variety. **84** —*D. T. (2/1/2006)*

De Bortoli 2002 Pinot Noir (Yarra Valley) $34. Medium-lean in body, with a spicy-herb nose that also has medicinal, red-catsup hints. Tastes like a mix of fruits—plum and cranberry, surely, but also apple and even apricot. Taut cranberry flavors wind up the finish, where there's also chocolate, and some tea-like tannins. **86** *(11/1/2004)*

De Bortoli 2002 Gulf Station Pinot Noir (Yarra Valley) $20. **86** *(11/1/2004)*

De Bortoli 2003 Windy Peak Pinot Noir (Victoria) $15. Not a fat wine—on the contrary, one whose cherry, orange tea, and earth flavors make it feel slim and dry. Offers similar aromas (oak, plum, cherry) that grow sweeter with air. A good introduction to Pinot at a fair price; 800 cases produced. **85** —*D. T. (12/31/2004)*

De Bortoli 2004 Gulf Station Riesling (Yarra Valley) $20. This Riesling offers pretty white chocolate and floral aromas, but what you get on the palate isn't quite as expressive, or as unusual. Soft-bodied in the mouth, which is unusual for a Riesling, with honeysuckle and olive oil flavors on the end. Surely easy to drink, but not too deep. **85** —*D.T. (12/31/2004)*

De Bortoli 2003 Windy Peak Cabernet Rosé Blend (Yarra Valley) $15. A vibrant wine, but one whose flavors and aromas err on the side of strawberry shortcake, whipped cream, and cheese. Dessert in a glass. **82** —*D.T. (10/1/2005)*

De Bortoli 2002 Windy Peak Sangiovese (King Valley) $15. Aromas are somewhat stewed and Portlike, with some fireplace smoke thrown in. Has smooth, woodsy tannins and cherry and plum fruit. Dries out on the finish with tangy herb/citrus flavors. **86** —*D.T. (12/31/2004)*

De Bortoli 2005 Deen De Bortoli Vat 2 Sauvignon Blanc (South Eastern Australia) $12. Consistent on the palate, with red apple, white peach, and hay flavors in a round, food-friendly size. Has some unctuousness, and light resin aromas, that makes it feel more like a Sem-Sauv blend. **86** —*D.T. (6/1/2006)*

De Bortoli 2004 Deen Vat 2 Sauvignon Blanc (South Eastern Australia) $11. It smells like lemondrops, and has plenty of zesty acidity on palate entry. By midpalate, this high-strung Sauvignon settles down a bit, revealing melon in addition to the earlier citrus. It's less intense on the finish, but still a good buy. **86 Best Buy** —*D.T. (10/1/2005)*

De Bortoli 2003 Noble One Botrytis Semillon (New South Wales) $29. One of Australia's most noted dessert wines does not disappoint: It's medium-full in the mouth, with warming burnt sugar and meat aromas, which are followed up by apricot, peach, and butterscotch flavors and a dry finish. Definitely has a buttery, oily quality to it, through and through. Needs no accompaniment to end a meal well. **91** —*D.T. (8/1/2006)*

De Bortoli 2002 Noble One Botrytis Semillon (New South Wales) $29. This is a safe bet for people who aren't big on sweeties: It's balanced and round, and not too cloying. Tastes of apricot and a sweet hint of citrus, like lemon sorbet, and smells like dried pineapple fruit and lemon pudding. **88** *(11/1/2004)*

De Bortoli 2002 Shiraz (Yarra Valley) $34. Smells of leather, black olives, and dusty spice. On the palate, the wine has a dry, dusty, chalky feel, medium body, and flavors of wheat cracker and plum. Finishes with good structure, and a dusty-peppery flavor. **87** *(11/1/2004)*

De Bortoli 1998 Shiraz (Yarra Valley) $28. Though it's easily quaffed, one reviewer noted that this Shiraz's flavors are more like that of Chardonnay: It offers strong butterscotch, vanilla, and popcorn notes on the nose, and more creamy vanilla, burnt-sugar flavors in the mouth. There are raspberry and blackberry flavors here, but they're well hidden. Finishes short, with oak and licorice. **85** *(11/1/2001)*

De Bortoli 1999 GS Reserve Shiraz (Yarra Valley) $59. Though there are pleasant aromas of meat and Port-like fruit, this wine seems rustic, even mature, at this stage of the game. Broad in the mouth, it has meaty, savory flavors and a finish laden with wooly, tea-like tannins. **84** *(11/1/2004)*

De Bortoli 1997 GS Reserve Shiraz (Yarra Valley) $60. Blackberry fruit on the nose has a thick, almost molasses-like quality, and is accented by eucalyptus. Fruit on the palate feels dry—maybe it's the briary oak notes talking. Finishes with tealike tannins and smoldering meaty-black peppery flavors. **87** —*D.T. (12/31/2003)*

De Bortoli 2002 Gulf Station Shiraz (Yarra Valley) $20. **85** *(11/1/2004)*

De Bortoli 2004 Willowglen Shiraz (South Eastern Australia) $9. Tastes made for the masses, with sweet black cherry flavors and aromas. Simple; gets sweeter the longer it airs. Good for casual circumstances. **83** —*D.T. (10/1/2005)*

De Bortoli 2005 dB Selection Shiraz-Cabernet Sauvignon (South Eastern Australia) $9. This 80-20 Shiraz-dominant blend has nice aromas of wheat bread and oak, with lifted blueberry and raspberry fruit peeking through from underneath. The palate is solid in terms of texture and plum-blackberry flavor, but suffers from a green/citrus pith sourness. **83** —*D.T. (11/15/2006)*

De Bortoli 2004 Willowglen Shiraz-Cabernet Sauvignon (South Eastern Australia) $9. The aromas give a distinctly dessert-like impression: Think blackberry pie filling, cherry sorbet. Confected raspberry and black cher-

ry flavors follow on the palate. With air, takes on a hint of weediness on both nose and palate. **82** —*D.T. (10/1/2005)*

De Bortoli NV dB Brut Sparkling Blend (South Eastern Australia) $10. Tastes and smells like peach, with molasses and meat accents. Hollow and pedestrian on the palate, but brightens up with crisp citrus notes on the finish. **83** —*D.T. (12/31/2005)*

DE IULIIS

De Iuliis 1999 Show Reserve Verdelho (Hunter Valley) $9. Smells and tastes a bit like poached pear in a vanilla sauce. Rich and unctuous on the palate, with a tart, metallic finish. **83** —*J.C. (2/1/2002)*

DEAKIN ESTATE

Deakin Estate 2004 Cabernet Sauvignon (Victoria) $9. Follows a cooler-climate profile, offering light fresh herb aromas and tangy black and blueberry flavors. Its sturdy, chalky mouthfeel is pretty nice, too. **85 Best Buy** —*D.T. (11/15/2006)*

Deakin Estate 2001 Cabernet Sauvignon (Victoria) $9. Has an unusual note of grain or bran on both the nose and the palate. It's medium-bodied, with oaky tannins and stewed fruit notes that extend through the finish. **84** —*D.T. (6/1/2003)*

Deakin Estate 2005 Chardonnay (Victoria) $9. Very fragrant and tropical on the nose. In the mouth, this Chard offers the same pear, banana, and other tropical fruits spread broadly across the palate. Its texture is a little thick, but at this price, this wine more than does its job. **85 Best Buy** —*D.T. (8/1/2006)*

Deakin Estate 2004 Chardonnay (Victoria) $9. A good quaffing wine, this Chardonnay is showing yellow fruit aromas, accented by white pepper and a little vanilla. The palate has citrus flavors and a smooth, if a little bulky, body. **85 Best Buy** —*D.T. (5/1/2005)*

Deakin Estate 2003 Chardonnay (Victoria) $9. On the nose, melon meets oaky, meaty notes. On the palate, yellow melon flavors fall into a white peppery, fresh-herb finish. Not a powerfully concentrated wine, but just right for porch sipping. **84** —*D.T. (12/31/2004)*

Deakin Estate 2002 Chardonnay (Victoria) $8. Has smoke and pear aromas, with pear and anise following through on the palate. Its feel is lean and wiry; finishes with a bright herb or mint accent. **85 Best Buy** *(7/2/2004)*

Deakin Estate 2004 Sauvignon Blanc (Victoria) $9. What a bargain-priced Sauvignon. Its backbone is pure lemon—pith, peel, the whole fruit. It's pretty straightforward, but it has dryness and crispness on its side, all wrapped in a dusty envelope. **85 Best Buy** —*D.T. (8/1/2005)*

Deakin Estate 2002 Shiraz (Victoria) $9. Smells like wheat biscuit and grape jelly, with purple fruit and toasty wood following up on the palate. Good but straightforward. **84** —*D.T. (5/1/2005)*

Deakin Estate 2000 Shiraz (Australia) $11. It isn't the most complex wine in the world, but this Deakin Estate is a sure crowd-pleaser. Its mouthfeel is smooth, almost bright; the wine is creamy until the very end, when toast and licorice flavors coat the back palate. Cherry, dark berry, and vanilla flavors prevail in the mouth. **86** *(10/1/2001)*

Deakin Estate 1998 Shiraz (Victoria) $12. **89** *(11/15/1999)*

DEEN DE BORTOLI

Deen De Bortoli 2000 Vat 5 Botrytis Semillon (South Eastern Australia) $10. The aromas and flavors are altogether pleasant ones, but don't stray far from honey, honeysuckle, honeycomb—all the honey you could want—dotted with a light, plastic-rubber note. It's a simple, straightforward approach that yields a good, but pretty predictable, sticky wine. **84** —*D.T. (9/1/2004)*

Deen De Bortoli 1999 Vat 8 Shiraz (South Eastern Australia) $10. Here's a sweet, easy-drinking Shiraz that's made to please the masses. Candied red-berry fruit is laced with caramel and toasty oak. Hints of black pepper on the nose and finish remind you that you're drinking Shiraz. **86** *(10/1/2001)*

DELATITE

Delatite 2000 Devil's River Mansfield Cabernet Sauvignon-Merlot (Victoria) $18. Though there's some plum fruit and tea on the palate, there isn't as much structure here; there's not so much to hold on to. Fruit on the nose is stewy, with eucalyptus accents. **84** —*D.T. (12/31/2003)*

Delatite 1999 Mansfield Chardonnay (Victoria) $16. 83 —*D.T. (8/1/2003)*

Delatite 2004 Dead Man's Hill Gewürztraminer (Victoria) $19. Intriguing, in a way. The nose has a meaty-oily component, with pleasant coconut flakes and vanilla—it's almost a savory dessert, really. On the palate it is dry and angular, with fruit flavors that are not very generous (banana peel, peach skin). I like it for its singularity and its finish, but still find a disconnect between nose and palate. **85** —*D.T. (5/1/2005)*

Delatite 2004 Sauvignon Blanc (Victoria) $19. Briny and odd, with flavors akin to watermelon rind mixed with ginger ale. If that sounds strange, join the club. One of our tasters commented that it "hardly seems like wine." **82** —*D.T. (8/1/2005)*

Delatite 1998 Mansfield Limited Release Shiraz (Victoria) $17. This smooth wine has structure, spice, and a somewhat mature quality to the plain fruit. Although simple, the fleshy black plum flavor is complemented by notes of violets, brown sugar, and a hint of spicy pepper. **87** —*K.F. (12/31/2003)*

DEVIL'S LAIR

Devil's Lair 2001 Bordeaux Blend (Margaret River) $23. The best feature of this Bordeaux blend (nearly three-quarters Cabernet Sauvignon) is its cottony, furry tannins. Tobacco, wheat toast, and nutmeg flavors and aromas are compelling if fading a little already, but they also cover up the wine's tart, plummy core. An Old World-styled wine, not a bruising fruit bomb. **87** —*D.T. (10/1/2005)*

Devil's Lair 2000 Cabernet Sauvignon (Margaret River) $23. This wine has both its fans and its detractors: in other words, it's one to judge more by words than by score. It has a strong eucalyptus component on the nose and on the palate, plus substantial cherry fruit. It also offers up chalky, claylike tannins, but not enough to mask these very distinctive flavors. **84** —*D.T. (10/1/2003)*

Devil's Lair 2002 Cabernet Sauvignon-Merlot (Margaret River) $23. Very enjoyable flavors—plum, black cherry, and a fresh herb note that adds some crispness. Feel is flat and even, rather than multidimensional. **87** —*D.T. (6/1/2006)*

Devil's Lair 1999 Fifth Leg Cabernet Sauvignon-Merlot (Margaret River) $22. Very meaty in the nose, with an uncanny similarity to bacon. This wine is on the fat, soft side of the fence, and it doesn't have a lot of persistence or drive. But it does offer rich black fruit, ample oak, and some satisfying big-bodied flavor. A little more balance would help it along. **86** —*M.S. (12/15/2002)*

Devil's Lair 2003 Chardonnay (Margaret River) $23. This Margaret River Chard has a good spine, with textbook yellow stone fruit flavors and aromas. It straddles the line between creaminess and crispness well, but has an odd lactic quality that is a detraction. **86** —*D.T. (10/1/2005)*

Devil's Lair 2002 Chardonnay (Margaret River) $23. This balanced Chard has fresh stone fruit, vanilla, and pineapple flavors, and light talc, citrus, and floral aromas. Seems to unfold on the finish—it's fatter and rounder on the back half than it is on the front. Straightforward and satisfying. **87** *(7/2/2004)*

Devil's Lair 2001 Chardonnay (Margaret River) $23. 83 —*D.T. (8/1/2003)*

Devil's Lair 2004 Fifth Leg Red Blend (Western Australia) $12. A Bordeaux blend (plus 28% Shiraz, that is) with pretty blackberry and blueberry fruit flavors. Has earthy aromas, with an edge of Sweet Tart. Not a deep wine, but just fine for everyday consumption. **86** —*D.T. (8/1/2006)*

Devil's Lair 2003 Fifth Leg Red Blend (Western Australia) $12. Rich cassis aromas are tinged with a ribbon of green. The berry and plum fruit flavors are flat, rather than ripe and textured. Fine for casual gatherings. A blend of Cab, Merlot, Shiraz, and Cab Franc. **83** —*D.T. (8/1/2005)*

Devil's Lair 2001 Fifth Leg Red Red Blend (Margaret River) $12. It's not a big-boned wine, but its powdery tannins give it texture to spare. Mixed plums and cherries are out in full force on the palate. A blend of Cabernet, Shiraz, Merlot, and Cabernet Franc. **87** —*D.T. (10/1/2003)*

Devil's Lair 2004 Fifth Leg White Blend (Western Australia) $12. A refreshing, utlitarian white, just right for apéritifs on the deck and summer weddings. Dust and lemondrop aromas; lemondrop and white peach flavors are couched in a soft, dry mouthfeel. Has acids manageable enough for wine newcomers, and enough quaffing enjoyment for anyone. 57% Sauvignon, 26% Semillon, 17% Chardonnay. **86** —*D.T. (8/1/2005)*

Devil's Lair 2003 Fifth Leg White Blend (Margaret River) $12. Though this white is a blend of 48% Semillion, 40% Sauvignon, and 12% Chardonnay, the flavors and aromas—crisp lemon zest, fresh grass, and herb—say "Sauvignon." The weight that the other two varieties add to the mouthfeel is a kind of a disconnect from its fresh, lean flavors, but it's still a good wine whose size may recommend it more for dinner, than pre-dinner, drinks. **86** —*D.T. (12/31/2004)*

Devil's Lair 1999 Fifth Leg White White Blend (Margaret River) $11. This wine's not going to knock you out with bright, overpowering fruit, but that's what I like about it. It has yellow stone fruit and olive-oil notes on the palate, plus a nice minerally component. Smooth and viscous in the mouth; a blend of 54% Semillon, 36% Sauvignon Blanc, and 10% Chardonnay. **87 Best Buy** —*D.T. (10/1/2003)*

DEVIL'S MARBLES

Devil's Marbles 2003 Shiraz (Limestone Coast) $10. Has aromas of plums and Sweet Tarts, with tangy, chunky plum fruit on the palate. Soft tannins and a lively bite of acid on the finish complete the picture. **85 Best Buy** —*D.T. (6/1/2006)*

Devil's Marbles 2004 Chardonnay/Verdelho White Blend (Limestone Coast) $10. This 85-15 blend of Chardonnay and Verdelho isn't one you see every day—and neither is a low price on a quality wine. Forward peach and pineapple aromas are back for another round in the mouth, where the fruit is modulated by a liberal dusting of chalk and mineral. **87 Best Buy** —*D.T. (4/1/2006)*

DI GIORGIO FAMILY WINES

Di Giorgio Family Wines 2000 Lucindale Cabernet Sauvignon (Limestone Coast) $22. This middleweight Cab has taut, tightly wound red plum and berry fruit on the palate. High-toned medicinal-cherry-eucalyptus aromas lead to a very dry mouthfeel and woodsy finish. **86** —*D.T. (9/1/2004)*

Di Giorgio Family Wines 2001 Lucindale Merlot (Limestone Coast) $22. Medium-bodied; has lively blackberry and molasses flavors, yet it's dry in the mouth. Sweet only on the nose, which is its saving grace. **86** —*D.T. (12/31/2003)*

Di Giorgio Family Wines NV Lucindale Sparkling Blend (Coonawarra) $18. This pinkish-coppery sparkling wine tastes as it looks: on the sweet side, fun but simple, with ginger and raspberry flavors and a sugary finish. A good bet for a birthday party—it's both festive and perhaps sweet enough to stand up to cake. **84** —*D.T. (12/31/2003)*

DIAMOND RIDGE

Diamond Ridge 2000 Shiraz (South Eastern Australia) $8. This lightweight wine seems prematurely aged, with aromas and flavors of damp earth and cremini mushrooms. **81** —*J.C. (9/1/2002)*

DINGO'S DESIRE

dingo's desire 2003 Chardonnay (South Eastern Australia) $8. If you can get past the glowing purple-blue dingo on the label, you're in for a straight-shooting, soft-bodied party wine. Light pear, peach, and pineapple flavors pick up a little residual sugar on the finish. **86 Best Buy** *(7/2/2004)*

DOMINIQUE PORTET

Dominique Portet 2002 Cabernet Sauvignon (Heathcote) $35. Smells fairly intense, like blackberry and meat, but tastes cool and crisp. It's not a rich deep wine; some might even call it light bodied. Me? I think the cherry/black cherry characteristics on the palate will strike some as medicinal, but I liked them just fine. **87** —*D.T. (10/1/2005)*

Dominique Portet 2000 Cabernet Sauvignon (Yarra Valley) $30. Disappointing, because it's obvious that this Cab was made by people who know their stuff. Smells dirty; plum and cherry fruit on the palate is

AUSTRALIA

a little sour; the mouthfeel is both creamy and chalky. Finishes with chalk and an herbal bite. **84** —*D. T. (12/31/2003)*

Dominique Portet 2004 Fontaine Rosé Blend (Yarra Valley) $18. The wine's lactic/cheese aroma right out of the bottle was a turn off, but it blew with time to reveal rosy, raspberry prettiness on the nose. The same notes continue on the palate, where there's also black cherry in a supporting role, and a mineral-smooth feel. 41% Cab, 34% Shiraz, 25% Merlot. **87** —*D. T. (12/31/2005)*

Dominique Portet 2004 Sauvignon Blanc (Yarra Valley) $20. A stylistic wine in that it shows the Oceania region's telltale passion fruit aromas along with those of green pepper. Quite a lot of citrus to the palate, but also a touch of green bean and pith. Dry and stony on the finish, with light but cleansing acidity. **89** *(7/1/2005)*

Dominique Portet 2004 Handpicked Sauvignon Blanc (South Eastern Australia) $13. Aromas and flavors of almond and peanut shells dominate through the midpalate, at which point bright lemon notes rush in. Another reviewer found the wine a bit green, with asparagus or green bean accents. **84** —*D. T. (10/1/2005)*

Dominique Portet 2002 Shiraz (Heathcote) $35. Toast and black pepper aromas are deep and broad. This is a muscular wine, pretty burly but not overly rich, with flavors of cassis, raspberry, and toast balanced by black pepper and herb. Very nice; 350 cases produced. **89** —*D. T. (12/1/2005)*

DONNELLY RIVER

Donnelly River 1997 Shiraz (Currency Creek) $16. Full-flavored and fairly full-bodied, this black and blueberry-fruited wine has chocolate and eucalyptus accents. Smooth and viscous on the palate, it shows a strong vanilla-caramel quality in the mouth, and shows both cool mint and pepper on the back end. Mature, drink now. **87** *(10/1/2001)*

DOWNING ESTATE

Downing Estate 2002 Cabernet Sauvignon (Heathcote) $35. Aromas are of blackberry and earth. The best feature here is the wine's texture—it's nice and smooth, like river rocks, and the impression really sticks on the midpalate. Red fruit flavors hover underneath. **89** —*D. T. (10/1/2006)*

EARTHWORKS

Earthworks 2004 Shiraz (Barossa Valley) $15. Offers an odd mix of mushroom, beef, and purple fruit flavors on the nose. Blackberry and blueberry fruit flavors on the palate are sweet and straightforward. **83** —*D. T. (12/31/2005)*

EDEN SPRINGS

Eden Springs 1999 High-Eden Shiraz (Eden Valley) $25. The High Eden's jammy blackberry and vanilla flavors are at the same time tart and sweet; its equally fruity grape and blackberry aromas, though, are complicated a bit by caramel and leather undertones. It's a "jamfest" and a "fleshpot" that may not have much depth, but has plenty of drink-me-now appeal. **87** *(11/1/2001)*

ELDER VINE

Elder Vine 2002 Shiraz (Barossa Valley) $13. Though it's Barossa, the wine is showing the coolness of the vintage in the form of cherry and black cherry fruit flavors. It's pretty fragrant on the nose, too, the cherry bolstered by pine and nut aromas. Fine, minerally tannins complete the picture. **88 Best Buy** —*D. T. (11/15/2005)*

ELDERTON

Elderton 2001 Ashmead Single Vineyard Cabernet Sauvignon (Barossa) $73. Has an earthy, tree-bark aroma on the nose, followed on the palate by red plums, with a few cranberries and cherries thrown in. Wooly-textured, and layered, but approachable enough to enjoy with dinner. **88** —*D. T. (10/1/2006)*

Elderton 1999 Ashmead Single Vineyard Cabernet Sauvignon (Barossa Valley) $33. Elderton's single-vineyard Cab is much different from its regular bottling—this one has red fruit on the palate and the finish, but is a little low in acid. Smells of plums and maple syrup, and finishes with wood and an acidic bite. **86** —*D. T. (5/1/2004)*

Elderton 2000 Exclusive Estate Wine Cabernet Sauvignon (Barossa Valley) $27. Has aromas of dried spice, and red plum and cherries. Tastes Barossa, with a caramelly, oaky overlay melting into fleshy plum fruit on the palate. Finishes with toffee and caramel. A juicy, tasty wine. **89** —*D. T. (5/1/2004)*

Elderton 2004 Unwooded Chardonnay (South Australia) $14. A decent Chardonnay, but one that just isn't all that harmonious. There's burnt-matchstick on the nose, and twangy yellow flavors (mustard seed, citrus) lending tart flavors to the palate. 140 cases produced. **83** —*D. T. (10/1/2005)*

Elderton 2000 Merlot (Barossa Valley) $30. Though the fruit on the nose is a little stewy the flavors are not. On the contrary, juicy plum fruit unfolds on the palate, jazzed up with caramel and toast. Finishes with like flavors, and some mushroom. A nice, solid Merlot. **88** —*D. T. (9/1/2004)*

Elderton 2002 Riverina Botrytis Semillon (Barossa Valley) $17. The nose offers a pungent yet strangely alluring combination of petrol and honeysuckle. Butterscotch candy and apricot flavors dominate the palate, but the feel is thick. This is a good wine but one that wants grace, and a little more acidity. **86** —*D. T. (9/1/2004)*

Elderton 1997 Command Shiraz (Barossa Valley) $62. The gang went wild for the Command Shiraz—every reviewer called it "mouthfilling" (yes, really, they all wrote that very word). Though its trademark seems to be juicy, almost jammy blackberry fruit, this Shiraz also had a sweet graham-cracker-meets-chocolate note on the nose, and chocolate and caramel highlighting the berry-laden palate. Finishes long, with a little black pepper and soft tannins. **93** *(11/1/2001)*

Elderton 2003 The Ashmead Family Shiraz (Barossa) $30. Smells smoky sweet—like fruitcake, nut, and barbecue smoke. On the palate, the wine is narrow, rather than round and mouthfilling, with fresh herb, plum, and blackberry flavors dominating. It's a very good wine, but falls short of anything more. **87** —*D. T. (12/1/2005)*

ELDREDGE VINEYARDS

Eldredge Vineyards 2000 MSG Red Blend (Clare Valley) $19. Aromas are wide, and of cherry, chocolate, and eucalyptus. This wine takes a little time to unfold, but when it does, black cherry fruit joins the wine's more predominant flavors of green and black peppers. Round and smooth in the mouth, it's drinkable now. **87** —*D. T. (5/1/2004)*

Eldredge Vineyards 2002 Semillon-Sauvignon Blanc (Clare Valley) $14. A feminine, pretty wine, this white has Clare's minerally accents and mouthfeel dressing up white stone fruit flavors. Finishes medium-long with similar flavors, plus some citrus. **88** —*D. T. (12/31/2003)*

ELEMENT

Element 2001 Chardonnay (Western Australia) $14. Smells sweet and soft, with vanilla, peach, and caramel aromas. It's similar at first in the mouth; then it turns even sweeter on the finish, with caramel popcorn flavors. **85** *(7/1/2002)*

Element 2001 Shiraz-Cabernet Sauvignon (Western Australia) $14. Starts off with a big blast of black cherry and blackberry fruit that continues on the palate, picking up leather and vanilla nuances. It's full and flavorful, soft without being flabby—just what the doctor ordered for everyday drinking. **88** *(7/1/2002)*

Element 2001 Chenin/Verdelho White Blend (Western Australia) $8. Intense sweet pear aromas balance pungent herbaceous elements. The up-front fruit is big and ripe, but turns lean and grassy on the finish. It's an odd flavor dichotomy that may work better for some tasters than others. **85** *(7/1/2002)*

ELLEN LANDING

Ellen Landing 1999 Cabernet Sauvignon (Riverland) $19. This easy-to-drink Cabernet's black and white peppercorn aromas jazz up the berry-and-cream bouquet. The palate's bright red currant flavors are shadowed by a medium-length, spicy-hot finish with an almost ancho-chile quality. **86** —*D. T. (9/1/2001)*

Ellen Landing 1999 Petite Verdot (Riverland) $19. This is, perhaps, one of the strangest wines I have ever tasted. The aromas are of the sea—brine and seaweed—over a smidge of blackberry fruit. Ditto the palate. Medium-bodied, not too tannic, and ends with a black peppery note that evens out once the wine sits for a few minutes. Bizarre. **82** —D.T. (9/1/2001)

Ellen Landing 2000 Shiraz (Riverland) $19. Pleasing though simple, with red fruit, caramel-oak, and earth flavors, with earth and black pepper notes on the nose. Medium-weight and bouncy; one reviewer found it a little too lactic. **85** (3/1/2003)

Ellen Landing 1999 Shiraz (Riverland) $16. Though the nose has deep blackberry and blueberry aromas, some reviewers were turned off by what they describe as a lumbery-mallowy note. The palate shows loads of oak, plus Sweet Tart and cranberry flavors. Mouthfeel is even, though a tad acidic; finishes with a tart, lemon-white pepper edge. **83** (10/1/2001)

ELYSIAN FIELDS

Elysian Fields 2000 Chardonnay (Adelaide Hills) $23. Rather dry in the mouth, with a minerally feel; flavors are similarly dry—think red apple skin, plus some pear. Has clarified butter and a plastic- or resin-like note on the nose, and toffee and cream on the finish. **84** —D.T. (8/1/2003)

Elysian Fields 2001 Riesling (Clare Valley) $20. Has a nice citrus-pear core, but the fruit wears a strange faux-sweetness (really, it tastes like saccharine) that was a little offputting. Still, it's a nice wine, with medium body and nice resiny and creamy notes on the nose. **86** —D.T. (8/1/2003)

EPPALOCK RIDGE

Eppalock Ridge 2000 Shiraz (Victoria) $25. An easy-to-drink wine (though some reviewers think that it will get more complex in two or three years), the Eppalock Ridge has a full, rich mouthfeel rounded out by blackberry, licorice, and briary flavors. Black pepper and tart black fruit at the beginning, and on the finish. **88** (11/1/2001)

Eppalock Ridge 1999 Heathcote Shiraz (Heathcote) $25. The giveaway that this is Shiraz is the palate's caramelly accents. Otherwise, this wine is heavy on the cherry—and on the tart, lean side at that. Finishes with some fleshy plum and strawberry notes. **85** —D.T. (3/1/2003)

EPSILON

Epsilon 2004 Coalsack Shiraz (Barossa Valley) $23. This is a wine that hovers on the surface rather than getting too profound. Its fruit is lifted and sweet, accented by violet/floral notes. Finishes with black pepper. **85** —D.T. (12/1/2005)

EUROA CREEKS

Euroa Creeks 2002 Shiraz (Victoria) $60. This is one big, sexy mouthful —it even looks thick and opaque in the glass. There is a ton of mocha or cocoa here, as well as black plum, blackberry, and moist black soil. Smells rich, too, with fat black fruit, gingerbread, vanilla bean, and crushed black pepper. Finishes with a hint of mint. 300 cases produced. **92** —D.T. (5/1/2004)

EVANS & TATE

Evans & Tate 2002 Gnangara Cabernet Sauvignon (Western Australia) $11. Has tannins the texture of bread flour or chalk, and flavors of wheat, soil, and vibrant black plum. The nose smells like a forest (tree bark, earth, leaf) with a little eucalyptus and pepper thrown in. A very good value; Western Australian wines don't come cheap. **88 Best Buy** —D.T. (5/1/2004)

Evans & Tate 2001 Redbrook Cabernet Sauvignon (Margaret River) $49. Not showing much on the nose apart from some nut and biscuit aromas. In the mouth, there's a whisper of cool eucalyptus at palate entry, and the wine flattens and widens out on the palate. The fruit is not giving— like grape and plum skins rather than flesh. Very good. **87** —D.T. (10/1/2005)

Evans & Tate 1999 Redbrook Cabernet Sauvignon (Margaret River) $49. E&T's top red, the 1999 Redbrook Cabernet displays excellent depth, rich, slightly weedy cassis fruit, and sizable helpings of tobacco and vanilla. The finish is long, and somehow combines mouthwatering flavors with mouth-drying tannins. Drink 2005–2012. **91** (12/15/2002)

Evans & Tate 2003 Underground Series Cabernet Sauvignon (Western Australia) $11. Smells fat, like cherry liqueur and white pepper. In the

mouth, it's medium-sized and decent weight; it's a one-trick wine that gets the job done. Raspberry and plum fruit take on a hefty dose of oak through the finish. **85** —D.T. (12/31/2005)

Evans & Tate 2004 Chardonnay (Margaret River) $16. Offers sun-warmed, fresh golden apple and caramel aromas. Apple flavors come through as well but the texture is odd, like sawdust and mineral. I didn't enjoy this bottling quite as much as E&T's unwooded Chardonnay, but those who prefer caramel to fresh fruit and acidity will feel differently. **85** —D.T. (12/1/2005)

Evans & Tate 2002 Chardonnay (Margaret River) $15. Another good Chardonnay from one of Western Australia's biggest wineries, we liked this wine because it has flavors and aromas that were quite different from those of other wines we tried. It has a sultry cinnamon character on the nose, and stony, even limey flavors, along with some white peach, on the palate. It's a zesty, structured wine, and is just the thing if you need a change from tropical fruit and toast. **89** (7/2/2004)

Evans & Tate 2001 Chardonnay (Margaret River) $15. The winery's style of Chardonnay is to lean heavily on wood for flavor interest. This wine has plenty of vanilla, clove, and cinnamon flavors that dominate the lean, lemony, apple, and pear fruit. If you like wood, you'll like this wine. **86** (12/15/2002)

Evans & Tate 2003 Gnangara Unwooded Chardonnay (Western Australia) $11. The first "G" is silent. Taste it blind and you'll probably think that there's some Sauvignon Blanc in here, so prevalent are the fresh grass and garden-vegetable notes on the nose and palate. Still, melon and peach fruit shines through. A clean, lean, refreshing wine, and a good bargain from Western Australia. **87** —D.T. (11/15/2003)

Evans & Tate 2002 Gnangara Unwooded Chardonnay (Western Australia) $11. In contrast to the winery's other Chardonnays, this one sees no oak. The result is a musky, pear, and guava cocktail that's given focus by some pineapple and citrus nuances. Serve well chilled to avoid it becoming too sweet-tasting—the copious fruit can stand up to the fridge. **85** (12/15/2002)

Evans & Tate 2001 Redbrook Chardonnay (Margaret River) $39. An excellent, flavorful wine, with fragrant peach, nuts, and pencilly, toasty oak on the nose. These notes are all reprised (along with some apple) on the plump, medium-weight palate. Finishes long and toasty. 1,000 cases produced. **90** (7/2/2004)

Evans & Tate 2000 Redbrook Chardonnay (Margaret River) $39. Smoky and toasty, the main flavor elements of this ambitious Chard are oak-derived, with modest underpinnings of crisp pear fruit. Cinnamon and clove spice up the finish. **87** (12/15/2002)

Evans & Tate 2004 Underground Series Unwooded Chardonnay (Western Australia) $11. An unwooded Chardonnay for people who say they prefer Sauvignon Blanc; this one offers crisp green apple and citrus aromas, with green apple joining pineapple flavors on the palate. Medium weight, balanced, refreshing. 60,000 cases produced. **87 Best Buy** —D.T. (12/1/2005)

Evans & Tate 2003 Classic Red Red Blend (Margaret River) $15. This blend of Shiraz (66%), Cab (28%), and Merlot (5%) has pleasing aromas and flavors of plum, with Band Aid and oak in supporting roles. Acids are lively. Not a big, rich wine for the cellar but it certainly is a good, everyday bottle. **86** —D.T. (10/1/2005)

Evans & Tate 2001 Classic Red Red Blend (Margaret River) $14. This medium-weight blend of Shiraz, Cabernet Sauvignon, and Merlot boasts a richly textured mouthfeel and plush tannins that perfectly highlight the wine's dark plum, earth, and tobacco flavors. A bright beam of acidity provides lift to the finish. **88** (12/15/2002)

Evans & Tate 2005 Underground Series Sauvignon Blanc (Western Australia) $11. This is a pretty interesting Sauvignon Blanc. White stone fruit aromas lead into a brisk, lemon-and-hay-flavored palate. Shows some anise and wax on the finish. **86 Best Buy** —D.T. (11/15/2005)

Evans & Tate 2003 Margaret River Classic White Semillon-Sauvignon Blanc (Margaret River) $15. A surprisingly average performance, given the good showing that E&T's Chardonnays made this year. Its flavors are fairly dilute yet still a little sour—grass and herb greenness, plus a rocky, quarrylike edge. Finishes short. **82** —D.T. (9/1/2004)

AUSTRALIA

Evans & Tate 2001 Shiraz (Margaret River) $18. Some tasters may find the blatant American oak too much; others will love its soft, toasty qualities. Underneath all of the vanilla is solid briary fruit and a rough, rustic finish that needs six months of bottle age to smooth out. **89** *(12/15/2002)*

Evans & Tate 2001 Gnangara Shiraz (Western Australia) $11. A bouncy, fun Shiraz that's easy to warm up to. The aromas are jammy and juicy, the flavors crisp and crunchy. Lots of berries, with some herbal and chocolate notes creeping in on the finish. **85** *(12/15/2002)*

Evans & Tate 2004 Underground Series Shiraz (Western Australia) $11. Smells of earth and ink, with sweet berry fruit on the palate. Has a metallic note on the palate. **83** *—D.T. (12/31/2005)*

Evans & Tate 2002 Classic White White Blend (Margaret River) $14. Crisp and clean, with a bright, refreshing finish, this blend of Semillon, Sauvignon Blanc, and Verdelho would be a great accompaniment to raw oysters or clams. Lemon, quince, and lime flavors ring loudly on the finish. **86** *(12/15/2002)*

EVANS FAMILY

Evans Family 1998 Howard Shiraz (Hunter Valley) $20. Jammy blue and blackberry fruit that might have grounded a rich, balanced wine is overwhelmed by a cedary element that enters early and doesn't leave. The mouthfeel is even, and the sweet-sour finish shows leathery notes, but the flavor range in this overoaked wine is reduced and woody. **83** *(10/1/2001)*

EVANS WINE COMPANY

Evans Wine Company 1998 Cabernet Sauvignon (King Valley) $12. 87 Best Buy *—M.S. (10/1/2000)*

FAT CROC

Fat Croc 2002 Chardonnay (South Eastern Australia) $8. "Won't cost you an arm and a leg" is Fat Croc's motto. Made in the unoaked, ripe, and juicy Australian style, this nicely combines deliciously juicy, tropical fruit flavors with plenty of bracing acid. It avoids the hot, flabby, fake oak flavors that plague most cheap Chardonnays, and gives you a wine that will work better with many foods than a lot of the pricey stuff. **88 Best Buy** *—P.G. (11/15/2004)*

FEATHERTOP

Feathertop 2002 Merlot (Alpine Valleys) $16. Though the wine offers substantial blackberry and blueberry flavors and aromas, there's also heaps of tangy oak along with it. Finishes a little hot. **85** *—D.T. (8/1/2005)*

Feathertop 2004 Sauvignon Blanc (Alpine Valleys) $16. A wiry, acidic Sauvignon that's just round enough not to be bracing. Offers vibrant aromas and flavors of lime and white peach. It's pleasingly tart, and plumps up toward the medium-long finish. **90** *—D.T. (8/1/2005)*

FERN HILL

Fern Hill 1999 Shiraz (McLaren Vale) $22. There's lots of caramel and brown-sugar aromas and flavors in this Shiraz, but none of the reviewers were complaining. Outdoorsy leather, fresh-picked berries, and spice aromas lead into a palate with similar flavors. Supple in the mouth, it finishes long and a bit on the tart side. Top Value. **90** *(11/1/2001)*

FERNGROVE

Ferngrove 2003 Cabernet Sauvignon-Merlot (Frankland River) $13. Aromas are dark but delicate, and quite nice: clay, ink, charcoal. This is clearly a wine with promise, judging by its texture and tannins, yet this bottling just isn't singing for me. The midpalate wants more stuffing, and the fruit tastes not quite ripe. Keep your eyes on this wine in coming vintages, though. 8,000 cases produced. **86** *—D.T. (8/1/2006)*

Ferngrove 2004 Chardonnay (Frankland River) $13. Apple, nut, and pear aromas. All its flavor pieces are in place (yellow stone fruit, some vanilla); a good, basic commercial wine. **84** *—D.T. (4/1/2006)*

Ferngrove 2005 Cossack Riesling (Frankland River) $18. This is a fresh and appealing Riesling, with floral and mineral aromas. In the mouth, it's crisp and elegant, its stony, rocky notes overshadowing very light hints of fresh herb. 1,000 cases produced. **88** *—D.T. (4/1/2006)*

Ferngrove 2005 Sauvignon Blanc-Semillon (Frankland River) $13. Grass, hay, and peach aromas. Semillon gives it some weight and breadth, and the Sauvignon, a nice mineral and citrus quality. For the price, it wouldn't hurt to keep a bottle or two on hand to serve with a chicken salad, or other light meals. **86** *—D.T. (4/1/2006)*

Ferngrove 2004 Estate Shiraz (Frankland River) $15. Solid and angular, this Shiraz is all about plum and stone flavors; its disposition is one that would make it more an appropriate partner to charbroiled beef than a party sipper. Berry and plum aromas turn barbecued and ketchupy with air. **86** *—D.T. (11/15/2006)*

FIDDLERS CREEK

Fiddlers Creek 1999 Cabernet Sauvignon-Merlot (South Eastern Australia) $10. A short, simple wine with a basic mix of berries. Sweet raspberry and cherry make up the flavor profile, and the finish is ultrasweet but preserved by firm acids. It's a bit like candy, but not cloyingly so. **84** *—M.S. (12/15/2002)*

Fiddlers Creek 2000 Chardonnay (South Eastern Australia) $7. Has a hint of green vegetable mixed in with sweet yellow fruit—it's as though two or three green beans made it onto the sorting table and into the bottle. Oak steps in to give the wine (whose fruit is sourced from Victoria) an almost-resiny mouthfeel, and a super-woody finish. **83** *—D.T. (6/1/2003)*

FIRE BLOCK

Fire Block 2005 Dry Rosé Grenache (Clare Valley) $14. A rosé of free-run Grenache, medium-full on the palate, with smoky, pine-needle aromas. Its flavors are of flowers and fresh berries, with a fresh herbal note persisting through the finish. 400 cases produced. **87** *—D.T. (4/1/2006)*

Fire Block 2002 Old Vine Grenache (Clare Valley) $19. From vines planted in 1926. Though the wine's cherry flavors are a little sweet at first—imagine black cherry soda—it takes on deeper earthy notes with air. Aromas are a little too funky at first, but eventually go the way of black pepper. The message here? Give it some time in the glass to come around. **87** *—D.T. (10/1/2005)*

FIRE GULLY

Fire Gully 2000 Cabernet Sauvignon (Margaret River) $24. Medium-bodied with some richness in the mouth; meaty, stably notes on the nose return on the palate, where there is also a rich molasses flavor enveloping deep black fruit. A very nice wine; the molasses richness suggests judicious pairing, though. **90** *—D.T. (10/1/2003)*

Fire Gully 1999 Cabernet Sauvignon-Merlot (Margaret River) $23. Structured and elegant, with cherry and plum fruit at its core and oak underneath for support and texture. The fruit is sturdy and stiff on the palate, but softens up a bit on the back end. Nose offers strawberry and red fruit aromas. **89** *(10/1/2003)*

Fire Gully 1999 Merlot (Margaret River) $24. Fruit is more brown than vibrant and juicy, and is couched in dusty earth. Tannins are woodsy, maybe even tinged with a little amaretto. A flash of coffee or chocolate pops up before the finish. **86** *—D.T. (10/1/2003)*

Fire Gully 2002 White Blend (Margaret River) $19. Shows sweet, citrus flavors on the palate (think lemondrops) and a simple, sort of flat feel in the mouth. Finishes short. **82** *—D.T. (5/1/2004)*

FISHBONE

Fishbone 2003 Cabernet Sauvignon-Shiraz (Western Australia) $15. Get past the Sweet Tart-y aromas and you'll be knee-deep in juicy berry flavors and an ample helping of accenting toast. Pleasing and forward; meant to be drunk over the near term. **87** *—D.T. (8/1/2006)*

Fishbone 2005 Unwooded Chardonnay (Western Australia) $15. Though there are pretty tones of vanilla, grass, and cream throughout, this Chard is a little clumsy and without the acidity it needs. Brighter flashes of citrus and mineral come through on the finish. **83** *—D.T. (11/15/2006)*

Fishbone 2004 Merlot (Western Australia) $15. A really interesting, different style of Merlot for Australia. Bramble and black pepper accent berry fruit on the nose, and the palate has focused, taut berries with a claylike mouthfeel. **88** *—D.T. (6/1/2006)*

Fishbone 2005 Classic White White Blend (Western Australia) $15. This blend of Semillon, Chenin Blanc and Chardonnay smells like lime zest. The palate offers more lime and lemon, plus a slightly spritzy feel. **85** —D.T. (8/1/2006)

FIVE GEESE

Five Geese 2004 Grenache-Shiraz (McLaren Vale) $23. A pretty good Tuesday night pizza red. Purple fruit flavors are couched in an oaky, chocolaty veneer. Smells like coconut and chocolate. **84** —D.T. (11/15/2006)

FLINDER'S BAY

Flinder's Bay 2001 Shiraz (Margaret River) $18. You're going to have to get creative when pairing this excellent Shiraz with food—there's a lot of blueberry at its core. It offers a great limestone-chalk texture and restrained fruit; all in all the package may feel subdued, even lean, to folks used to South Austrlalian Shiraz. But give it, and its long, juicy finish, a chance. **90** —D.T. (9/1/2004)

Flinder's Bay 1999 Shiraz (Margaret River) $18. This wine boasts a lot of the horsey, leathery, and peppered-meat characteristics we found in many of the wines from Western Australia, but also a silky texture and enough blackberry fruit to hold everything together. **86** (10/1/2001)

FONTHILL

Fonthill 2002 Dust of Ages Grenache (McLaren Vale) $30. A pretty wine with black cherry fruit at the core, but with toasty oak ruling the roost. There's a lot of black pepper, chile pepper, and spice here, particularly for a Grenache. Could easily stand up to steak. **89** —D.T. (5/1/2004)

Fonthill 2001 Silk Shiraz (McLaren Vale) $32. Big fruit and wide-reaching eucalyptus aromas waft from the nose, while on the palate, blackberry and plum fruit flavors take on accents of bramble or fireplace. Dark but elegant; approachable now through 2008. **90** —D.T. (5/1/2004)

Fonthill 1999 Silk Shiraz (McLaren Vale) $23. This McLaren Vale beauty has sturdy, ripe blackberry, and plum fruit and big, chewy tannins, with both fruit and tannins lingering on the finish. Not one you'd ever call a jamball, or a fruit bomb—it's just pure, delicious, focused goodness. Aromas of anise, summer berries, earth, and eucalyptus are fabulous as well—but with what you get on the palate, they just feel like a bonus. **92 Editors' Choice** —D.T. (12/31/2003)

FONTY'S POOL

Fonty's Pool 2003 Chardonnay (Pemberton) $18. **88** —D.T. (4/1/2006)

Fonty's Pool 2003 Pinot Noir (Pemberton) $18. **85** —D.T. (4/1/2006)

Fonty's Pool 2003 Shiraz (Pemberton) $18. Broad on the nose with a pretty dried-spice aroma. Texture is pulpy and chewy, with tangy oak on the finish. A good wine, but one that is missing a deeper layer. **86** —D.T. (6/1/2006)

FOREFATHERS

Forefathers 2001 Shiraz (McLaren Vale) $18. **89** —J.M. (1/1/2003)

FOUR EMUS

Four Emus 2004 Cabernet Sauvignon Shiraz Merlot Cabernet Blend (Western Australia) $11. Smells of Salisbury steak and green pepper, with sour herbs and plums on the palate. Just acceptable. **80** —D.T. (12/31/2005)

Four Emus 2005 Chardonnay (Western Australia) $11. Has aromas of butter and cured meats. On the palate, it is fruit sweet, but modulated by a light oaky overlay. Finishes with pineapple flavors. **84** —D.T. (6/1/2006)

Four Emus 2005 Sauvignon Blanc-Semillon (Western Australia) $11. A 50-50 blend, with aromas and flavors of green pea, mineral, and citrus. It's a fresh, crisp wine, but don't let the Sauvignon component bring visions of puckery, zesty New Zealand editions to mind. Nope. The Sem is an equal partner, adding both heft and a musky, haylike accent. It's nice to see value-priced wines from somewhere other than South Eastern Australia, too. **86 Best Buy** —D.T. (11/15/2005)

FOUR SISTERS

Four Sisters 2004 Chardonnay (South Eastern Australia) $13. This Chard's aromas are of sour apple and dust, and preface similar flavors on the palate. Broad in the mouth; a good cocktail-party Chardonnay. **85** — D.T. (6/1/2006)

Four Sisters 2002 Chardonnay (Goulburn Valley) $12. White pepper and nut aromas on the nose are light, but the apple, citrus, and toast flavors in the mouth are present, in full force. Generously oaked on the finish; a straightforward, good wine. **86** (7/2/2004)

Four Sisters 2002 Trevor Mast 2002 Four Sisters Shiraz (South Eastern Australia) $12. Black plum fruit on the palate shares the spotlight with a meaty, stably flavor—the same note that I found on the nose. It's a straightforward wine, but a much different sort from other lollipop-styled ones that you'll find at this price point. **84** —D.T. (5/1/2005)

FOX CREEK

Fox Creek 2002 Reserve Cabernet Sauvignon (McLaren Vale) $30. The nose is beautiful, showing spice, meat, and bramble atop red plum fruit. This is an elegant wine on the palate, feminine-sized rather than brawny, with more spice and red plum flavors. Finish is subtle, with a surge of flavor at the very end. **91** —D.T. (3/1/2005)

Fox Creek 2001 Duet Cabernet Sauvignon-Merlot (McLaren Vale) $22. A 70% Cab–30% Merlot blend with very dark flavors—earth, oak, black plum. In spite of the flavors, it's a manageable, approachable size. Finishes quite lovely, with amaretto, cassis, and ink, and dry tannins. I only wish it would show a little more on the nose, which is pretty hard to read. **89** —D.T. (12/31/2003)

Fox Creek 2000 Duet Cabernet Sauvignon-Merlot (McLaren Vale) $15. Take a sniff and you'll say to yourself, "not bad." There's some grapiness along with smoke and flowers, and that mix is nice. The flavors and feel follow suit. You get some blueberry, blackberry, and vanilla and then a full fruity finish. If "balance" means it sits right on your tongue while offering a mix of sweet and spice, then this is well balanced. **87** —M.S. (12/15/2002)

Fox Creek 2005 Chardonnay (McLaren Vale) $13. Pear and green apple flavors dominate on the palate, with similar aromas. Clean, with a wide, chalk and mineral feel. **87** —D.T. (10/1/2006)

Fox Creek 2004 Chardonnay (McLaren Vale) $13. Light green pea and yellow fruit aromas; palate has peach and pear flavors, with just a hint of vanilla. This vintage, this Chard was barrel fermented for 3-4 weeks in what winemaker Chris Dix calls an "almost unwooded style." Future vintages, he says, will get more oak. **87** —D.T. (3/1/2005)

Fox Creek 2002 Chardonnay (South Australia) $15. Refreshing and straightforward, with crisp white peach flavors on the palate. Nose offers floral, vanilla, and citrus notes; finish offers a dash of mint or eucalyptus. There's toast here from start to finish, but it's subtle. **87** —D.T. (8/1/2003)

Fox Creek 2002 Chardonnay (South Australia) $15. This McLaren Vale winery makes reliable, good wines, and this Chard is no different. Bursts with pineapple and hickory aromas, with a similar pineapple-dried spice flavor profile. Medium-weight, with a fresh close. Straightforward and tasty. **87** (7/2/2004)

Fox Creek 2001 Reserve Merlot (McLaren Vale) $27. A classy, well-made wine, with pastry crust and red pencil-eraser aromas and a chalky, dusty mouthfeel. On the palate, there's ripe, juicy plum fruit and chewy tannins, all of which persists through the finish. That I don't mention auxiliary flavor nuances doesn't mean that the wine has nothing else going on—it just means that the fruit and the texture, really, is what you most notice. **89** —D.T. (9/1/2004)

Fox Creek 2001 Red Blend (McLaren Vale) $20. This is tasty if not complicated, with purple-red fruit and a hearty helping of oak. Smooth on the palate; drink now. **87** —D.T. (12/31/2003)

Fox Creek 2002 JSM Red Blend (McLaren Vale) $20. A blend of Shiraz (70%), Cabernet Franc (20%), and Cabernet Sauvignon (10%). The Cab Franc comes through loud and clear on the palate and the long finish, where the plum fruit is taut, even a little tart. The fleshy berries and plums on the nose, though, say Shiraz. Well-behaved, and a successful if unusual blend. **90** —D.T. (3/1/2005)

AUSTRALIA

Fox Creek 2005 Sauvignon Blanc (McLaren Vale) $13. Shows pear and citrus flavors, with a soft, minerally edge. Fresh and clean, and just the thing for summertime, al fresco meals. **87** —D.T. (10/1/2006)

Fox Creek 2004 Sauvignon Blanc (South Australia) $13. The fruit is all McLaren Vale fruit, though the label says South Australia. Mineral and citrus aromas. On the palate, fresh-cut grass envelopes a citrus-rind spine; floral notes surface on the finish. Fresh, zingy and enjoyable. **87** —D.T. (3/1/2005)

Fox Creek 2002 Sauvignon Blanc (South Australia) $15. This refreshing Sauvignon is clean, refreshing, though a little lean. Has soft aromas of trading-card bubblegum powder, and a streak of lemondrop that heads full-tilt into the finish. **87** —D.T. (11/15/2004)

Fox Creek 2001 Sauvignon Blanc (South Australia) $15. It's not that easy to find the fruit in this wine, yet persistence will uncover some peach and grapefruit as well as a little bit of melon and pear. The finish is also somewhat innocuous, with only mild amounts of fruit and verve. It's clean enough, just not very captivating. **86** (8/1/2002)

Fox Creek 2002 Semillon-Sauvignon Blanc (South Australia) $15. A zesty, pretty, medium-sized wine, one that shows nice acidity and a minerally feel. Tastes as though it's infused with quince, citrus, and white peach. Aromas are light, like talc powder. **88** —D.T. (11/15/2004)

Fox Creek 2002 Reserve Shiraz (McLaren Vale) $74. Meaty, burnt sugary aromas are deep. On the palate, tannins are chewy and red fruit is dressed up with coffee and mocha; coffee continues through the long finish. Bears some resemblance to the 1994 Reserve Shiraz, which is still going strong. Drink through 2012. **91** —D.T. (3/1/2005)

Fox Creek 2004 Short Row Shiraz (McLaren Vale) $27. It has legs, and it knows how to use them. This Shiraz just sticks to the glass, its blackberry, plum and oak flavors not revealing themselves fully just yet, but sure to impress in 3–5 years. The structure is pleasing—along with a smooth, clay-mineral feel, and a medium-long finish. **90** —D.T. (11/15/2006)

Fox Creek 2003 Short Row Shiraz (McLaren Vale) $27. Fox Creek made no 2003 Reserve Shiraz, so this Short Row is the year's top wine. It's plummy and elegant on the palate, with some red pencil eraser and bread flour accents, and a seeped-tea bite on the finish. Aromas—wheat flour, red fruit, licorice—are pretty, too. **90** —D.T. (3/1/2005)

Fox Creek 2001 Short Row Shiraz (McLaren Vale) $30. 89 —D.T. (6/1/2003)

Fox Creek 2000 Short Row Shiraz (McLaren Vale) $31. A delicious wine, a Shiraz that is neither sloppy nor overblown. Solid, strong plum fruit is at the core, shrouded in bacon fat and oak. Keep shopping if it's caramel and jammy fruit you want; this one's in it for the long haul, folks. Drink 2004–2007. **91** —D.T. (3/1/2003)

Fox Creek 2001 JSM Shiraz-Cabernet Sauvignon (McLaren Vale) $19. This wine is 70% Shiraz, with Cabernets Franc and Sauvignon filling out the rest of the blend. The JSM isn't quite as good this vintage as it has been in the past, owing largely to its stewy fruit flavors. But it does have its high points. The wine's smooth tannins and sturdy frame are admirable, as are its clay, sand, and mocha accents. **87** —D.T. (11/15/2004)

Fox Creek 2000 JSM Shiraz-Cabernet Sauvignon (McLaren Vale) $27. Another excellent wine from this dependable winery, the JSM is named for Captain James Stanley Malpas, who once lived in the cottage that's now Fox Creek's tasting room. This 70% Shiraz–20% Cab Franc–10% Cabernet Sauvignon has deep blackberry, blueberry, and plum flavors, and even some red-fruit accents. Eucalyptus brightens the palate; mouthfeel is smooth, even plush. Sturdy, but not hefty. An excellent wine. **90** —D.T. (12/31/2004)

Fox Creek 2001 Shiraz-Grenache (McLaren Vale) $17. I like this wine's chewy grip on the palate, and its red plum, berry, and wheat-flour flavors. Well-made, it's just the ticket for a potluck dinner with friends—it would probably stand up equally well to spicy sauces and roasted fowl or meats. **88** —D.T. (12/31/2004)

Fox Creek NV Vixen Sparkling Blend (McLaren Vale) $15. This is a blend of Shiraz (54%), Cabernet Franc (32%), and Cabernet Sauvignon (14%). And yes, it's a sparkling wine. The flavors are dark chocolate and blackberries with caramel and toast. The finish is semisweet, with good acidity and a nice layer of tannins. **86** —C.S. (12/1/2002)

Fox Creek NV Vixen Sparkling Blend (South Australia) $17. The winery's cellar door markets this sparkler's name on various clothing items (including a man's shirt that says "Nothing goes down like a Vixen"); if you know an appropriately saucy woman, break open this bubbly. Aromas are inky, and perhaps a little salty, wtih dark plum and ink flavors. Bead is a little coarse at palate entry but softens up soon after. A blend of Shiraz (55%), Cab Franc (30%), and Cab Sauvignon (15%), made nonvintage each year in a solera-like system. **88** —D.T. (3/1/2005)

Fox Creek NV Vixen Sparkling Shiraz-Cabernet Franc-Cabernet Sauvignon Sparkling Blend (McLaren Vale) $19. A reasonably good value in sparkling Shiraz, Fox Creek's Vixen is a dark, vibrant, purple hue and boasts a heady bouquet of blackberry liqueur, vanilla, and spice. This is a rich, oaky, full-on Shiraz, slightly enlivened by the presence of bubbles. Some soft, dusty tannins on the finish make it seem quite dry, and well-suited for its traditional pairing with grilled steak. **88** —J.C. (12/31/2006)

Fox Creek 2003 Verdelho (McLaren Vale) $13. Grassy on the nose, with a citrus base. Has a tiny bit of sweetness on the front palate, like a dot of confectioner's sugar, which is only a minor distraction. Stone fruit and a dusty-talc feel segues to a fresh, pretty finish that tastes like clean rain water and peach purée. Sound too fairytale and frou-frou to be true? Taste it. **88 Best Buy** —D.T. (11/15/2004)

Fox Creek 2002 Verdelho (South Australia) $15. Viscous in the mouth; the palate yields yellow stone fruit that's offset by nougat and mineral flavors. An interesting, refreshing wine with some weight, without flashy toast. One to sneak past Chard lovers. **88 Editors' Choice** —D.T. (12/31/2003)

Fox Creek 2004 Shadow's Run White Blend (South Australia) $10. Fox Creeks' entry-level white is a fresh, everyday drinking wine made mostly of Verdelho, with smaller shares of Chardonnay and Sauvignon. Medium-bodied, with peach and white melon flavors, it's an ideal poolside (or porchside) drink. **86 Best Buy** —D.T. (3/1/2005)

FRANKLAND ESTATE

Frankland Estate 2004 Isolation Ridge Vineyard Chardonnay (Frankland River) $21. Almond, white pepper, and citrus aromas start things off. In the mouth, it's soft and delicate in feel, narrow but not simple or lean, with sweet fruit and a resin overlay. **88** —D.T. (6/1/2006)

Frankland Estate 2001 Isolation Ridge Vineyard Chardonnay (Western Australia) $20. Has woodsy, hickory aromas, and yellow peach on the palate that tastes just shy of ripe. Wood flavors are also prominent; a good wine but not as impressive as the Frankland's Riesling, from this same vineyard. **84** (7/2/2004)

Frankland Estate 2000 Isolation Ridge Vineyard Chardonnay (Western Australia) $20. Starts off slowly, but opens considerably with air—so much so that it's probably worth decanting as you might a bottle of young white Burgundy. It's buttery and full, yet possesses a stony mineral quality that gives it balance. Initial peppery-spicy notes on the finish smooth out the longer it sits in the glass. **90 Editors' Choice** —J.C. (7/1/2002)

Frankland Estate 2000 Olmo's Reward Red Blend (Western Australia) $26. Named for Dr. Harold Olmo, a UC Davis viticulturalist, this red is 42% Cabernet Franc, with Merlot, Cab Sauvignon, Malbec, and Petit Verdot making up the balance. With such a makeup, its core of very taut red plum shouldn't come as a surprise. Also has top-to-bottom herbal accents and a tangy-oak finish—all told, a good, but rather tough, unfamiliar style of wine for most. **86** —D.T. (9/1/2004)

Frankland Estate 2002 Cooladerra Vineyard Riesling (Western Australia) $18. The pairing possibilities with this wine seem endless: seafood of all kinds, chicken, pasta salad, maybe pork, but it'd also make perfect sense to drink it as an aperitif. Clean and dry in the mouth, mineral and chalk are at the fore, with lime pith, soy, and grass underneath. Finishes medium-long, with more of the same. **89** —D.T. (8/1/2003)

Frankland Estate 2004 Isolation Ridge Vineyard Riesling (Frankland River) $20. Dry, stone, and hay notes on the nose are also present on the palate. The main flavor here is peach skin—it's almost sour, but pleasantly so. A little bulky, but has good length on the finish. **88** —D.T. (10/1/2005)

Frankland Estate 2001 Isolation Ridge Vineyard Riesling (Western Australia) $18. This Riesling is all about good acidity and a clean, racy mouthfeel. Flavors are fresh but don't speak volumes—think pear skin, plus some grass. Offers nice banana, pear, and dust aromas on the nose. **87** —D.T. (8/1/2003)

Frankland Estate 2002 Poison Hill Vineyard Riesling (Western Australia) $18. A straight-ahead Riesling, pleasant but uncomplicated. Minerals envelop white stone fruit on the palate; the fruit is more fruit skin than flesh. Nose is light and feminine, with citrus and confectioners' sugar notes. **85** —D.T. (8/1/2003)

Frankland Estate 1999 Isolation Ridge Vineyard Shiraz (Western Australia) $20. The Frankland's outdoorsy, leather-black cherry-eucalyptus amply prepares you for its earthy, medium-weight, tobacco-pepper-black cherry palate. Long finish smolders with smoke and pepper. **87** (10/1/2001)

FROG ROCK

Frog Rock 2003 Chardonnay (Mudgee) $24. This quaffer is soft in the mouth with peach fuzz and pear flavors, and a smoky, marinated-meat aroma. Pleasant but straightforward and a little light in terms of intensity. **84** —D.T. (4/1/2006)

Frog Rock 1999 Chardonnay (Mudgee) $20. 86 —M.S. (3/1/2003)

Frog Rock 1999 Shiraz (Mudgee) $24. The nose has a malty, mocha quality to it along with some root beer and cola. The mouthfeel is crisp, while flavors of cherry pop in fairly full force. The finish is pretty standard as it deviates very little from the palate. As a whole it's good and tasty but not overwhelming. **86** —M.S. (3/1/2003)

Frog Rock 1998 Shiraz (Mudgee) $25. This Shiraz's spicy aromas were identified as barbecue marinade by one reviewer, and black pepper by another. Add spiciness to leather, caramel, coffee, and earth—no one identified the bouquet as outwardly fruity—and you've got a winning opening to an excellent wine. Stably cedar palate, plus tart cherry, herb, and sweet caramel notes; a tad lean in the mouth, but smooth nonetheless. Finishes with firm tannins, hay, and cedar. Top Value. **91** (11/1/2001)

GEMTREE

Gemtree 2002 Chardonnay (McLaren Vale) $17. Fresh, lively, different—but not for everyone. We found peach on the nose, plus a distinct sweet-pea or fresh-vegetable aroma. The same characteristics recur on the palate: peach, with a fresh garden greenness. You'll either love it or hate it; this score reflects a panel divided in the same way. **85** (7/2/2004)

Gemtree 2003 Citrine Chardonnay (McLaren Vale) $15. This Chardonnay only gets three months in French oak, and it's no suprise—it's a fresh, clean rendition of the variety, with dust and melon flavors on the palate. Finishes fresh and minerally. **88** —D.T. (3/1/2005)

Gemtree 2003 Cinnabar Grenache-Tempranillo-Shiraz Red Blend (McLaren Vale) $25. Light white peppery aromas usher in peppery plum fruit on the palate. Has a nice, sturdy feel in the mouth, and firm tannins on the finish. A 60-20-20% blend of Grenache, Tempranillo, and Shiraz. **88** —D.T. (3/1/2005)

Gemtree 2003 Tatty Road CS-PV-MER Red Blend (McLaren Vale) $25. Roughly three quarters Cab Sauvignon and one quarter Petit Verdot, with a smidge of Merlot for good measure. Plums, cherries, and spices on the nose hint at what's under inside the palate's thick, tannic shell. Finishes with smooth tannins. **87** —D.T. (3/1/2005)

Gemtree 2002 Obsidian Shiraz (McLaren Vale) $40. A very good wine; though the fruit is the same as in the Uncut, this wine spends 10 months more in oak—all new French oak. And it shows. The nose is dusted with dry spices, and the palate has considerable wood-derived bells and whistles hiding the plum fruit underneath. Hold for five years, and dive in. **89** —D.T. (3/1/2005)

Gemtree 2003 Uncut Shiraz (McLaren Vale) $28. Gemtree's "regular" Shiraz bottling is just as good as its flagship, the Obsidian, though the latter is probably going to last longer in your cellar. This bottling has light fireplace-smoke aromas, and good intensity of fruit on the palate. Plum and black cherry flavors are the focus until black, smoky flavors pop up again midpalate. Medium-sized; appropriate with food. **89** —D.T. (3/1/2005)

GEOFF MERRILL

Geoff Merrill 2001 Cabernet Sauvignon (South Australia) $23. Very good, but the sort of Cabernet with rough, briary edges. Black plum and earth aromas come before the plum-skin and briary flavors. A little hard on the palate, but offers up bright red fruit (strawberry, raspberry) on the finish. **87** —D.T. (3/1/2005)

Geoff Merrill 1990 Cabernet Sauvignon (South Australia) $50. Handsomely dark and even, this shows a ripe sweetness to the fruit. Attractive licorice, mint, and pepper accents add interest, and the wine is medium weight, well-balanced and lively on the palate. Sturdy tannins, dark dry berry, toasty oak, and bitter chocolate notes close it nicely. **89** (2/1/2002)

Geoff Merrill 1985 Cabernet Sauvignon (South Australia) $60. This is a half-decade younger but a lot less lively than the 1980, showing caramel and very earthy aromas. Light dried fruit flavors show on the shallow palate. It's decidedly mature, and on its way out, but graciously. **85** (2/1/2002)

Geoff Merrill 1980 Cabernet Sauvignon (South Australia) $55. Mature and lovely, but still a quite tasty at 20 years, this displays a lovely range of complex aromas and flavors. Dried berries, tobacco, forest floor, smoke, mint, and mushroom notes all show in this light, even wine. A treat that finishes long and earthy, like an older Bordeaux, with more dried fruit and herb notes. **89** (2/1/2002)

Geoff Merrill 1998 Reserve Cabernet Sauvignon (Coonawarra) $35. Shows earthy, dark aromas, plum flavors, and lingering clay notes on the finish. "Reserve" is an apt descriptor here—this wine is stylish, and not over-done. **89** —D.T. (3/1/2005)

Geoff Merrill 1997 Reserve Cabernet Sauvignon (South Australia) $30. At nearly six years, this wine is still virtually undrinkable. It's tannic as heck, and the acidity scours the mouth. The palate searches for fruit, in vain. It's all about alcohol and heat. Forget about aging this untrained puppy. **82** —S.H. (1/1/2002)

Geoff Merrill 1996 Reserve Cabernet Sauvignon (South Australia) $40. Even and elegant, this is decidedly tart-sweet, with lots of aromatic and flavor interest. A full spectrum of earth, herbs, vanilla, pepper, and olive accents adorn the dark, plummy fruit. The wine turns quite dry, with firm but dusty tannins on the long back end. Perhaps this will open more in time, but though refined, it seems it will always be lean in manner. Drink now–2006. **88** (2/1/2002)

Geoff Merrill 1995 Reserve Cabernet Sauvignon (South Australia) $35. Layered, lovely, and admired by all, including Geoff, for its big, open bouquet of black and red berries, chocolate, and a cool menthol-eucalyptus note. Lovely tart-sweet fruit shows on the palate, offset by mineral notes and tangy oak. Again, a fine sense of balance shows, and the wine closes long with crisp acidity and full tannins, promising plenty of life. Drinks well now, best 2004-2009. **91 Cellar Selection** (2/1/2002)

Geoff Merrill 2003 Cabernet Sauvignon-Merlot (South Australia) $15. This red blend offers brambly-berry aromas and fruit-sweet plum and cranberry flavors. A good wine, but doesn't stand out from other Cab-Merlots in its category. **85** —D.T. (3/1/2005)

Geoff Merrill 2000 Pimpala Vineyard Estate Grown Cabernet Sauvignon-Merlot (McLaren Vale) $33. My favorite of the Geoff Merrill wines, and the only one with estate-grown fruit. A singular fresh-eucalyptus note pervades the wine; supplying its weighty core is mixed plum fruit. The eucalyptus note won't appeal to everyone, but it does me. It has its own character, like it or not, as a single-vineyard wine should. **91** —D.T. (3/1/2005)

Geoff Merrill 2002 Cabernet Sauvignon-Shiraz (South Australia) $20. In screwcap, and meant for near-term drinking. From the outset, though, seems pretty sophisticated for its class: dusty plums on both the nose and the palate are forward but taut. It's medium-bodied, but soft and approachable. Finishes with some tautness. A by-the-glass winner. **87** —D.T. (3/1/2005)

Geoff Merrill 2002 Chardonnay (McLaren Vale) $20. This Chardonnay is round and toasty, with green apple and melon notes dominating. A nice size and not overdone on the oak, but there's a slight metallic hint on the back end. **86** —D.T. (3/1/2005)

Geoff Merrill 1999 Reserve Chardonnay (McLaren Vale) $26. Tangy melon and citrus flavors and a steely backbone characterize Merrill's reserve Chardonnay. There's oak here—mostly present on the nutty, toasty nose—but there's not much of it rounding out the palate, which makes it feel a little disjointed. Still, a very good wine. **87** —D.T. (3/1/2005)

Geoff Merrill 1996 Reserve Chardonnay (South Eastern Australia) $25. Fruit, acid, and oak are handsomely balanced in this elegant wine. The toasty, almost matchstick, nose opens to a dry apple and lemon-fruited palate, but a dry, nutty— rather than an opulently fruited quality—prevails. Finishes long and reserved, drink now through 2006. **90 Editors' Choice** (2/1/2002)

Geoff Merrill 1995 Reserve Chardonnay (South Eastern Australia) $22. Caramel, toast and baked apple aromas open this ripe, spicy wine. Apple, pear and subdued tropical fruit flavors show on the even, medium-weight palate. The finish is long, tangy and oak-driven; avid fans of heavily wooded Chardonnays will rate this higher. Drink now–2004. **88** (2/1/2002)

Geoff Merrill 2004 Grenache Rose Grenache (McLaren Vale) $15. A bright, cheerful shade of pink, with aromas of fresh berries. It's round on the palate, with a dry, minerally feel, and berry and cream flavors. A fairly priced but serious rosé—not overtly sweet or forward, and a good companion for the table. **88** —D.T. (3/1/2005)

Geoff Merrill 2001 Merlot (South Australia) $23. Aromas are steely, like iron ore. The palate shows the same steely, irony edge—it's not a harsh, underripe, or jagged wine, but seems strong and wiry. Plum, berries, and well-integrated oak complete this medium-sized wine. Finishes juicy. **88** —D.T. (3/1/2005)

Geoff Merrill 2003 Liquid Asset SZ-Gren-Vio Red Blend (McLaren Vale) $19. One of Geoff Merrill's newest wines, the Liquid Asset's label is designed to look like a bank check. It's a pretty sophisticated blend for its intended, entry-level market, with black cherry notes dominating. It's an easy, enjoyable quaff and a red that I could even (gasp!) imagine chilling. 80% Shiraz, 15% Grenache, 5% Viognier. **86** —D.T. (3/1/2005)

Geoff Merrill 2001 Sz-Gren-M Rhône Red Blend (South Australia) $20. Another screwcapped Merrill wine that was once part of its Owen Estate label. This Shiraz (35%), Grenache (35%), Mourvedre (30%), offers plum and oak flavors, the latter of the fresh-cut pine sort. Still, the wine is forward, lively, and a good value, and sports a flourish of black cherry on the end. **87** —D.T. (3/1/2005)

Geoff Merrill 2004 Sauvignon Blanc (McLaren Vale) $20. Light citrus and stone aromas; has less freshness and verve than the Sem-Sauv blend. Still, it's a good, reliable white with mineral and citrus notes at the fore. **86** —D.T. (3/1/2005)

Geoff Merrill 2004 Sauvignon Blanc-Semillon (South Australia) $15. Fresh, grassy Sauvignon aromas start things off. On the palate, Semillon adds weight and texture to Sauvignon's citrus and grass flavors. Lovely, and would be just great at the table. 80% Sauvignon, 20% Semillon. **88** — D.T. (3/1/2005)

Geoff Merrill 2001 Shiraz (McLaren Vale) $23. Shows acorn/nut and mint aromas, and flavors of red plum and chalk that are still somewhat closed. Finishes with juicy plums. Still not at its peak; try in a year or two. **90** — D.T. (3/1/2005)

Geoff Merrill 1998 Henley Shiraz (McLaren Vale) $145. Geoff Merrill's flagship wine is an excellent one, featuring light maple and dusty black plum aromas, and a mountain of flavor on the palate. Peaks midpalate with understated plum, anise, and hazelnut flavors. Finishes juicy, with fine tannins. **91** —D.T. (3/1/2005)

Geoff Merrill 1996 Henley Shiraz (Australia) $100. Merrill's new flagship red enters the top tier of Australian Shiraz, coming on strong with a nose of sweet toasty oak, a hint of cumin, and peppery notes. The palate offers lots of dark, briary fruit, chocolate hints, and the fine balance characteristic of all his best wines. Finishing long, this forward and delicious wine is already drinkable. It should last a decade or more, peaking after 2004. **93 Cellar Selection** (2/1/2002)

Geoff Merrill 1998 Reserve Shiraz (McLaren Vale) $40. Like the 2001 Shiraz, this excellent wine isn't at its peak yet. It's an understated,

reserved style of wine, its tannins fine, its finish juicy and chalky. Aromas are of mineral and clay. Try in 2007. **90** —D.T. (3/1/2005)

Geoff Merrill 1998 Reserve Shiraz (McLaren Vale) $30. Pours dark as ink, and smells young and mute, with hints of white pepper and blackberry. Tastes young, too, with brash acids and brisk tannins framing jammy flavors. It would be a shame to drink this too early. Try cellaring it through 2005. **89** —S.H. (1/1/2002)

Geoff Merrill 1997 Reserve Shiraz (McLaren Vale) $45. Subdued black fruits, licorice, spices, and smoky notes hint at the rewards cellaring will bring to this deep, rather brooding wine. The palate feel is big, but even and smoothly textured, while the finish is long, with full, supple tannins. Large-scaled and still closed, this dark, toasty, and tasty wine needs a year or two to open. Best after 2003. **89** (2/1/2002)

Geoff Merrill 1996 Reserve Shiraz (McLaren Vale) $32. Leathery and cedary, with a liberal dusting of dried spices (clove and cinnamon). Mouthfeel is rich, but has fairly high acidity, making it finish tart. Mature; drink now with marinated steak or lamb to help bring out the fruit. **90** (11/1/2001)

Geoff Merrill 1995 Reserve Shiraz (South Australia) $40. Layered, supple fruit and a lovely mouthfeel—ripe, but not flabby—really shine in this wine. Rich blackberry and plum flavors, impressive integration of fruit and oak mark the finely balanced palate. Closes long with very smooth tannins, dark chocolate, and coffee flavors. It's less structured but more seductive than the 1994. Drink now through 2008. **91 Cellar Selection** (2/1/2002)

Geoff Merrill 1994 Reserve Shiraz (South Eastern Australia) $40. Big, solid, and substantial, with lots of dark berry fruit bearing meat, earth, and mineral accents. Well-structured, it still needs a little more time to come together completely. Even tannins, tangy fruit and oak play out on the smoky, long, dry finish. Drink now to 2008+. **90 Editors' Choice** (2/1/2002)

GHOST GUM

Ghost Gum 2000 Cabernet Sauvignon (South Eastern Australia) $9. Smooth and lean in the mouth, this Cab is easily drinkable, but it's probably nothing that you haven't had already. It's just blackberry, black cherry, peppery oak aromas, with black fruit on the palate and finish. **83** —D.T. (6/1/2002)

Ghost Gum 2003 Chardonnay (South Eastern Australia) $9. Has very strong aromas of peaches and baked apples. Tastes like apple juice and oak. **82** —D.T. (6/1/2006)

Ghost Gum 2000 Chardonnay (South Eastern Australia) $9. A simple, lemony style that would work best with shellfish but has just enough pear and quince fruit to lend it flesh. Finishes tart and clean. **84** —J.C. (7/1/2002)

Ghost Gum 2002 Shiraz (South Eastern Australia) $9. Straightforward and enjoyable, a no-brainer for a Tuesday in front of the TV. Aromas are of meat, blackberry, and talc, while the palate deals tangy plum and cherry fruit, with overtones of pulpy wood. **86 Best Buy** —D.T. (6/1/2006)

Ghost Gum 2000 Shiraz (South Eastern Australia) $9. Thin aromas of cranberry, meat, coffee, and toast are met in the mouth with thin, tart red fruit and green herbs. Finishes peppery, with a bit of acidity. **84** — K.F. (1/28/2003)

Ghost Gum 1998 Shiraz (South Eastern Australia) $9. Dark plum fruit with cedar, toast, slight meaty notes, and an herb accent comprise an attractive package. It turns a touch prickly and metallic on the finish, but not enough to turn off our tasters to this dependable quaff. **87 Best Buy** (10/1/2001)

GIACONDA

Giaconda 2001 Chardonnay (Victoria) $125. A Chardonnay that typically ranks among Australia's stratospheric best didn't do as well this year. Nose is rather mute, with only hints of peach and toast. Yellow fruit on the palate is bright, bolstered by vanilla and toast, but doesn't achieve the richness and body that it has in past vintages. Finishes with a full dose of oak. **86** (7/2/2004)

Giaconda 2000 Chardonnay (Victoria) $80. Medium-full but also lively in the mouth, the palate of this top-notch Chard offers has sumptuous pear, pineapple, and toast notes, and finishes long with nut and citrus flavors. Nose has mealy, nutty—even smoky—aromas, plus some citrus and pear. Excellent stuff. **92** *(6/1/2003)*

Giaconda 2005 Nantua Vineyard Chardonnay (Victoria) $50. Big, full, and lush, but beautifully balanced. Offers nutty aromas and persistent nut, white pepper, melon, and peach flavors. There's nothing not to love about this wine. Finishes long. **92** —*D.T.* *(11/15/2006)*

Giaconda 2004 Nantua Vineyard Pinot Noir (Victoria) $100. Dark garnet-black in color, but as dark as it is, this is not one of those explosive, overextracted types of New World Pinot. This one serves up cherry flavors that are juicy but just shy of tart, and they're coated in a hefty helping of chalk or mineral. Narrow but very nice; finishes with an old-school iron-ore flavor. **90** —*D.T.* *(11/15/2006)*

Giaconda 2005 Aeolia Roussanne (Victoria) $100. Buttery gold in color, with hay and peach flavors and a long, dry, persistent finish. Tasted blind, some mistook this Roussanne—a variety that isn't seen often on its own—for a Chardonnay. Very pretty, with good acidity. **90** —*D.T.* *(11/15/2006)*

Giaconda 2002 Aeolia Roussanne (Victoria) $75. Nose is an unusual mix of butter, bacon, and a hint of greenness that disappears after a few minutes in the glass. Its mouthfeel is minerally, with warm honey and pear skin flavors, and just a hint of herb. A very good wine, but not as good as it has been in recent vintages. **89** —*D.T.* *(11/15/2004)*

Giaconda 2001 Aeolia Roussanne (Victoria) $75. Just about the best white wine out of Australia this year, this Roussanne isn't a fleshy wine, but it has beauty, power, and structure in its corner. Full-bodied with powdery tannins, it has flavors of honeydew, peach fuzz, and mineral, and an herbal-peppery finish that lingers on the tongue. Nose is a tantalizing mix of marzipan, jasmine, and clover. Just excellent. **93** *(6/1/2003)*

Giaconda 2002 Nantua Les Deux White Blend (Victoria) $45. This Chardonnay (85%) and Roussanne (15%) blend has a pretty, though quiet, bouquet—think dust and pastry crust. In the mouth, the wine has a similar vibe: ethereal and fluffy, and full, like a cloud of feminine flavor. Melon, chalk, and some nut or toffee are the main flavors here, but mouthfeel and body are the main attractions. **88** *(7/2/2004)*

Giaconda 2001 Nantua Les Deux White Blend (Victoria) $45. Made by Giaconda, this white is excellent but doesn't quite live up to the winery's other top-notch offerings. (But at half the price, how can you go wrong?) It has a tropical-fruit core and a medium-bodied, viscous mouthfeel. Finishes with some length, and a buttery-resiny feel. **90** *(6/1/2003)*

GIANT STEPS

Giant Steps 2002 Merlot (Yarra Valley) $35. This is a good red wine, with aromas of bacon bits and vanilla bean, but it is not very interesting or varietally distinct. It has red-plum flavors and a medium body, and closes with smooth, woody tannins. **86** —*D.T.* *(5/1/2005)*

Giant Steps 2002 Pinot Noir (Yarra Valley) $35. Offers cherry, cola, and light caramel aromas, and taut red-fruit flavors, from plum to roasted tomato. It's smooth and restrained on the palate, and finishes with black cherry flavors. **86** —*D.T.* *(8/1/2005)*

GIBSON'S BAROSSAVALE

Gibson's BarossaVale 1999 Merlot (South Australia) $28. Flavors of cherry are a bit watery, but there is a pleasing dry earthiness on the nose with hints of black raspberry and sawdust. An easy-drinking non-offensive quaff. **83** —*C.S.* *(6/1/2002)*

Gibson's BarossaVale 2000 Sparkling Merlot (South Australia) $26. The nose is like a basket of fresh-picked strawberries, while the palate is deeper and richer, and fairly chewy. The flavors run toward cherry and chocolate, and the feel is smooth throughout. Yes, it's a bit like a cough drop at times, but mostly it's full, balanced, snappy, and pleasurable. Quite the find among red-grape sparklers. **88** —*M.S.* *(6/1/2003)*

Gibson's BarossaVale 2000 Shiraz (South Australia) $40. Hot, dark, and strong, much like a good coffee, this is a natural match for grilled fare. Focused cinnamon, black plums, molasses, and a hint of eucalyptus bear

well on the nose and palate. Well-balanced, with a long finish. **89** —*K.F.* *(3/1/2003)*

Gibson's BarossaVale 1999 Shiraz (Barossa Valley) $35. Fans of "bigger is better" won't be disappointed by this wine: There's big alcohol, bigger oak, biggest fruit. Blueberry, vanilla, and cinnamon lead the way, accented by licorice, clove, and cedar. Finishes long and smooth, with hints of dark chocolate and plum. **90** *(11/1/2001)*

Gibson's BarossaVale 2000 Australian Old Vine Collection Shiraz (Barossa Valley) $75. Toast, vanilla and a slight nuttiness to the aromas are well balanced by red plum and light cherry flavors on the palate. An accent of char continues through the toasty finish, turning slightly herbal. **87** —*K.F.* *(3/1/2003)*

GLEN ELDON

Glen Eldon 2003 Riesling (Eden Valley) $18. This Eden Valley white has a core of peach or pear skin, with a dusty overlay. It's a pretty, though not superconcentrated, wine with dusty, white peach aromas. Finishes with more intensity and concentration than you get on the palate. **86** —*D.T.* *(11/15/2004)*

Glen Eldon 2001 Dry Bore Shiraz (Barossa Valley) $25. The Dry Bore has an earthy, dusty-cocoa overlay, nose to tail, like it's just taken a tumble through the desert. A dry, earthy-woodsy feel keeps the impression going, but the juicy, fat fruit on the front palate brings technicolor to the wine's initial sepia-toned impression. **89** —*D.T.* *(12/31/2004)*

GLENDONBROOK

Glendonbrook 2001 Shiraz, Cabernet, Merlot Red Blend (Hunter Valley) $17. The nose is quite oaky, offering bacon and also some tomato. Raspberry fruit is dominant, that and some seriously drying oak. The finish has coffee notes and yet more woodiness. All in all this wine is adequate, but like the quiet kid in the corner, it makes no noise and is hard to notice. **84** —*M.S.* *(12/15/2002)*

GOLDING

Golding 2004 Billy Goat Hill Chardonnay (Lenswood) $22. Aromas are very pungent: yellow pineapple, peach, mustard seed—another reviewer even noted some corn notes. Coats the mouth with a butterscotch-toast flavor, with peach and apple to finish. Wants more stuffing midpalate. **85** —*D.T.* *(6/1/2006)*

Golding 2004 Sauvignon Blanc (Adelaide Hills) $15. Aromas are of fresh green peas, and flavors are of grass and limes. Medium-weight and just tart enough; a textbook, very good Sauvignon. **88** —*D.T.* *(8/1/2005)*

Golding 2002 Lenswood Sauvignon Blanc (Adelaide Hills) $17. Darren Golding's excellent Lenswood SB stood out in a flight of its peers—it toes the line between raciness and roundness. It has lime, passion fruit, and stone fruit on the palate and fresh green pea, grass, and floral aromas. Finishes with lime and fleshy yellow peach. **90** Editors' Choice —*D.T.* *(5/1/2004)*

Golding 2005 Western Branch Sauvignon Blanc (Lenswood) $20. Very fragrant meat and hickory notes waft from the nose. Palate offers yellow peach and pear flavors, but a flat, dull feel. Weighty, rather than nimble, as a SB should be. **85** —*D.T.* *(8/1/2006)*

GORGE

Gorge 2004 Pinot Grigio (Hunter Valley) $15. Smells of clarified butter. On the palate, it offers hints of citrus and white peach, and a medium body. Dry on the finish, with more citrus. **85** —*D.T.* *(12/1/2005)*

GOTHAM

Gotham 2004 Shiraz (Langhorne Creek) $19. It's beyond me why anyone would name an Australian wine "Gotham", and top it all off with a metropolis-at-night label that looks like something out of a Tim Burton movie. Has stably, Sweet Tart aromas and plum and rhubarb flavors. **82** —*D.T.* *(6/1/2006)*

GOUNDREY

Goundrey 2003 Offspring Cabernet Sauvignon (Western Australia) $16. Offers crisp wintergreen notes on the nose followed by plum and cherry flavors. A little light in terms of heft and concentration, but is certainly well made and pleasing. **86** —*D.T.* *(12/31/2005)*

Goundrey 2002 Offspring Cabernet Sauvignon (Western Australia) $15. Has rich coffee or capuccino notes on the nose, and reined-in mixed-berry fruit flavors that are juicy but blessedly not too sweet. Slim in body, this is the kind of Cab that will show best at the dinner table, with gravied meats and spaghetti alike. **88** —*D.T. (12/31/2004)*

Goundrey 2003 Offspring Chardonnay (Western Australia) $16. There's a fair amount of citrus and peach fruit in this Western Oz Chard. The oak flavors here are not overwhelming, but the texture does have a pulpy, woody character. Finishes short; most of the action here is on the palate. **85** —*D.T. (10/1/2005)*

Goundrey 2002 Offspring Chardonnay (Western Australia) $15. It's difficult to find many Western Australian wines at this price, and this Chard is a good introduction to how good the wines out there can be. White peach, citrus, and soy aromas preface peach and oak flavors on the palate. An easy-drinking wine, and one that's made to please everyone. **85** —*D.T. (12/31/2004)*

Goundrey 1999 Shiraz-Grenache Red Blend (South Eastern Australia) $13. The Grenache introduces an interesting stone-fruit influence to this 60-40 blend, something akin to peaches. There's also plenty of smoky, toasty oak, dried spices, and chocolate, ending on a liqueur-like note. Full and supple; drink now. **85** —*J.C. (9/1/2002)*

Goundrey 2005 Offspring Riesling (Western Australia) $13. Peachy from nose to palate, with melon in a supporting role. Medium-bodied and dry; an easy, enjoyable, apéritif-style white. **86** —*D.T. (10/1/2006)*

Goundrey 2002 Offspring Shiraz (Western Australia) $15. Blackberries and blueberries star on the palate; the nose, on the other hand, is all about black pepper. A slimmer-sized Shiraz rather than a huge, jammy one. **87** —*D.T. (5/1/2005)*

GRANDIS

Grandis 2000 Merlot (South Australia) $14. This red blend is on a one-track express train to the finish; it shows the same nice flavors plum fruit, eucalyptus, and earth flavors from beginning to end. Simple overall, and smooth on the palate. **84** —*D.T. (1/1/2002)*

GRANT BURGE

Grant Burge 2002 Cameron Vale Cabernet Sauvignon (Barossa) $19. Has aromas of crisp fruit, cola, and bramble. On the palate the wine's plum and earth flavors are more restrained than rambunctious. An elegant style with fine, tea-like tannins on the finish. **88** —*D.T. (4/1/2006)*

Grant Burge 2001 Cameron Vale Cabernet Sauvignon (Barossa Valley) $20. Fruit on the nose has a stewed quality, plus a hint of leafiness. On the palate, blackberry and plum fruit wears a cloak of woody tannins. Juicy, and an easy drinker. **87** —*D.T. (2/1/2004)*

Grant Burge 2000 Shadrach Cabernet Sauvignon (South Australia) $50. Tasted alongside other South Australian Cabs, this one is distinguished by its restraint and elegance. The nose has a nice briary quality; the palate has well-integrated tannins, and flavors of red fruit and eucalyptus. Medium in body, and very juicy through the long finish. Drink now–2013. **93** —*D.T. (10/1/2006)*

Grant Burge 1999 Shadrach Cabernet Sauvignon (Coonawarra) $70. Nose has fern, mint, black cherry, and earth aromas. Juicy black plum is on center stage, with the taut, red Coonawarra fruit in the background. Just the right size—bold, but not overpowering. An excellent Cab, though in short supply in the U.S. **91** —*D.T. (2/1/2004)*

Grant Burge 2002 Barossa Vines Cabernet Sauvignon-Merlot (Barossa Valley) $12. Smells like toast and plush plums. The palate has a cool-vintage tanginess offsetting, perhaps overshadowing, its berry fruit. Dry; finishes with tangy oak. **85** —*D.T. (12/1/2005)*

Grant Burge 2003 Barossa Vines Chardonnay (Barossa Valley) $11. Easy to drink, with focused green apple, passion fruit, and white peach flavors. Not terribly concentrated, but this wine, well chilled, would make a good picnic or beach drink. **85** —*D.T. (2/1/2004)*

Grant Burge 2002 Barossa Vines Chardonnay (Barossa Valley) $11. An unwooded Chard, one in which there's nothing to distract you from the bouncy, tropical yellow fruit on the palate. Smells nice, like fresh hay. A fun, easy-drinking white. **86** —*D.T. (2/1/2004)*

Grant Burge 2001 Barossa Vines Chardonnay (Barossa Valley) $13. More interesting to smell than to taste, the aromas burst with apple, nectarine, straw, and clover honey, but the flavors are simple apple and citrus. Finishes short and lemony. **83** —*J.C. (7/1/2002)*

Grant Burge 2003 Barossa Vines Unwooded Chardonnay (Barossa Valley) $11. This Barossa Chard has lime, floral, and butter notes on the nose. On the palate, there are yellow fruit flavors—think apples and bananas—and a mealy, weighty texture. Finishes with a little alcoholic warmth. Chill it and enjoy on the patio. **83** *(5/1/2004)*

Grant Burge 2003 Summers Chardonnay (South Australia) $19. Round and medium-sized on the palate, this Chard shows flavorful citrus and tropical fruit flavors, bolstered by oak-derived smoke and nut notes. Dry and crisp on the finish; a very good wine, with all its elements in balance. **89** —*D.T. (8/1/2005)*

Grant Burge 2002 Summers Chardonnay (Eden Valley) $17. Crisp and flavorful, with medium body and honey, pineapple, and toast aromatics. Its pineapple and nut flavors fade into a bright, citrus-pineapple finish. A very good wine, aptly named for the season in which it should be drunk. **87** *(7/2/2004)*

Grant Burge 2000 Summers Chardonnay (Eden Valley) $18. This Chardonnay is a little heavy-handed on the butterscotch or caramel, top to bottom, but its citrus and mineral accents keep the toastiness in check. Offers yellow fruit on the palate and on the nose. **87** —*D.T. (8/1/2003)*

Grant Burge 2003 Summers Eden Valley Chardonnay (Barossa Valley) $18. Aged in 40% new French oak, and most all is barrel fermented. The oak shows most on the nose, which has a little vanilla, and on the very back palate. Otherwise, the wine is crisp and minerally in the mouth, with pear and citrus fruit. **87** —*D.T. (2/1/2004)*

Grant Burge 2003 Hillcot Merlot (Barossa Valley) $19. Demonstrative aromas of jammy fruit and a touch of brown sugar usher in red cherry fruit flavors with an overlay of bread flour. Mouthfeel is quite nice; pleasingly slender in size, with a tangy zip on the finish. **88** —*D.T. (4/1/2006)*

Grant Burge 2000 The Holy Trinity Red Blend (Barossa Valley) $33. Wide, bread-flour aromas on the nose; behaves and weighs as a Pinot does, but with a completely different flavor profile. Focused black cherry fruit on the palate takes on a powdery texture that reminds this reviewer of Sweet Tarts. Just the right size and character to pair with dinner; its dominant black-cherry fruit would work well with game sauced in fruit-and-wine reduction. **88** —*D.T. (2/1/2004)*

Grant Burge 2001 Holy Trinity Rhône Red Blend (Barossa Valley) $33. Has a really fragrant, ripe berry bouquet. Feels quite thick on palate entry, full of red plum and black cherry flavors, but it lets up on the palate and finish, which are marked by smooth, soft tannins. **88** —*D.T. (5/1/2004)*

Grant Burge 2002 The Holy Trinity Rhône Red Blend (Barossa) $34. Red fruit aromas have a roasted edge, oddly balanced out by cooler eucalyptus notes. The palate bursts with berries, smoothed out by peppery, minerally nuances. A very good wine, but one that feels more like a solid Côtes-du-Rhône than a candidate for the cellar. **87** —*D.T. (8/1/2006)*

Grant Burge 1999 The Holy Trinity Rhône Red Blend (Barossa Valley) $33. A slight herbal or minty note on the palate keeps this GSM from falling into an abyss of blackness, albeit a pleasant blackness, of black berries, earth, and toast. Medium-bodied with chalky tannins, it finishes with juicy mixed plum fruit. **88** —*D.T. (6/1/2003)*

Grant Burge 1998 The Holy Trinity Rhône Red Blend (Barossa Valley) $35. This Châteauneuf-du-Pape lookalike (43% Grenache, 39% Shiraz, 18% Mourvèdre) tastes like one as well, boasting rustic, earthy aromas and flavors that combine country roads with dusty leather and exotic spices. The underlying fruit changes in the glass, switching from cherry to blueberry and back. Dry tannins and juicy acids suggest it will last until 2008 or beyond. **89** —*J.C. (9/1/2002)*

Grant Burge 1997 The Holy Trinity Rhône Red Blend (Barossa Valley) $33. Burge's allusion is to the trio of Grenache, Shiraz, and Mourvèdre that he blends together in this wine, not to the Father, Son, and Holy Ghost. Sweet, jammy aromas of crushed cherries laced with caramel pick up some creamy and cedary notes with airing, then cinnamon and red-earth and iron-mineral flavors spice up the palate. A bit tart on the finish, but this should smooth out over the next year. Will then drink well for five or more years. **88** —*J.C. (9/1/2001)*

Grant Burge 2005 Thorn Riesling (Eden Valley) $19. Offers up aromas of citrus peel and fresh whipping cream. On the palate, there's a clean scour of mouthwatering lemon and pink grapefruit flavors. Layered and smooth, finishing with a pucker of sour hard candy. **89** —*D.T. (8/1/2006)*

Grant Burge 2004 Thorn Riesling (Eden Valley) $19. Feminine on the nose, but a little broad on the palate. Pear and talc notes start things off, with heaps of stone fruit, white pepper, and citrus flavors. A very good wine, but doesn't quite have the kick of acidity that it has had in recent vintages. **88** —*D.T. (4/1/2006)*

Grant Burge 2002 Thorn Riesling (Eden Valley) $19. This excellent Riesling puts your salivary glands into overdrive: In the mouth it's refreshing, dry, and puckery, with vibrant grapefruit, lemon, and melon notes. Finishes long and mouthwatering, and smells much the way it tastes: sweet and sour citrus, with some mineral or dust. **90** —*D.T. (8/1/2005)*

Grant Burge 2005 Kraft Sauvignon Blanc (South Australia) $19. This Sauvignon Blanc is amped up on flavor: pear, citrus, flour, and even some floral notes peeking through on the nose. Dry and full on the mid-palate, with an acidic, almost sharp, finish. **88** —*D.T. (6/1/2006)*

Grant Burge 2004 Kraft Sauvignon Blanc (South Australia) $19. A fuller-styled Sauvignon, with resiny aromas and loads of yellow fruit on the palate. Citrus and mineral accents, though, keep this very good wine light on its feet. Grapes from this vintage are all from Adelaide Hills, though the wine's front label still bears a South Australia GI. **88** —*D.T. (8/1/2005)*

Grant Burge 2003 Kraft Sauvignon Blanc (Barossa Valley) $16. Clean and fresh in the mouth, with a taut, pear-fruit core that sticks it out through the finish. On the nose, there's green grass and fresh sweet peas. **87** —*D.T. (2/1/2004)*

Grant Burge 1998 Kraft Sauvignon Blanc (Barossa Valley) $16. 84 *(4/1/2000)*

Grant Burge 2003 Barossa Vines Shiraz (Barossa) $15. Bright red, bouncy berry aromas are buried underneath nut and vanilla on the nose. It tastes much the same—soft and approachable, with bright raspberry fruit. A good midweek wine. **86** —*D.T. (10/1/2005)*

Grant Burge 2002 Barossa Vines Shiraz (Barossa Valley) $11. A bouncy, goes-with-pizza wine with taut plum and cranberry fruit and a dry mouthfeel. Wheaty, bready aromas hide lively red berries underneath. **85** —*D.T. (2/1/2004)*

Grant Burge 2000 Barossa Vines Shiraz (Barossa Valley) $11. Packed with grapey, plummy fruit, smoke, and vanilla, this is solid entry-level stuff. It's not particularly rich or concentrated, but it is something that's uncommon at this price: balanced. That makes it an attractive by-the-glass option or barbecue companion. **85** —*J.C. (9/1/2002)*

Grant Burge 1999 Barossa Vines Shiraz (Barossa Valley) $11. Sweaty leather meets trail dust in this rustic version of Barossa's favorite grape. Dark-skinned berries tinged with anise and coffee round out the flavors. A bright beam of acidity provides focus to this otherwise brooding wine. **86** *(10/1/2001)*

Grant Burge 2003 Filsell Shiraz (Barossa) $30. Grant Burge's new Shiraz releases are looking very good, and more proof is in this mid-level bottling. It's smooth and silky on the palate, with dried spice accents and seeped tea-like tannins. Its red plum and raspberry fruit is juicy now, but will hang on just fine for the next 5 or so years. **90** —*D.T. (2/1/2006)*

Grant Burge 2002 Filsell Shiraz (Barossa Valley) $30. So well done, from beginning to end. The nose offers a good balance of beef, cherry, plum, and black pepper notes. On the palate, it's mouthwatering, medium sized, and moderately oaked—that is, there's no caramel or toast in sight. Focused; flavors of black cherry, blackberry, eucalyptus, and black pepper are mouthwatering, and the tannins smooth. **91** —*D.T. (10/1/2005)*

Grant Burge 2000 Filsell Shiraz (Barossa Valley) $25. Light to medium weight in feel with evenly distributed ripe plum, raspberry, char, and baking spice aromas and flavors. A twist of red licorice throughout adds

an interesting element. Finishes with a peppery zing. **87** —*K.F. (1/1/2004)*

Grant Burge 1998 Filsell Shiraz (Barossa Valley) $25. Nicely built on a solid red fruit core, the berry, cherry, and licorice aromas and flavors here wear a heavy wood cloak that holds the fruit in check a bit too much. It's hard not to feel that the full potential of the fruit has been stymied here. Still, the mouthfeel is good and it finishes with attractive, spicy dry cherry, anise, and wood notes. Will appeal more to lovers of lavish oak. **87** —*M.M. (6/1/2001)*

Grant Burge 1999 Meschach Shiraz (Barossa Valley) $145. Aged mostly in American oak, which lends the nose crème brûlée and caramel aromas. What's most prominent on the nose, though, is a dark meatiness —like beef jus. Black cherry fruit on the palate is juicy though restrained by a heap of chewy, gummy tannins that persist through the finish. Lip-smacking and delicious, but not at its best until after 2006. **91 Cellar Selection** —*D.T. (2/1/2004)*

Grant Burge 2001 Meshach Shiraz (Barossa) $82. Gorgeous on the nose: clove, tree bark, black pepper, and fruit that is still hibernating. On the palate, it's sexy and layered, with meat accents to the plum fruit and a silky texture that trails on through the long, nut-laden finish. Nice now, but it's still young. Drink 2007–2012. **92** —*D.T. (2/1/2006)*

Grant Burge 2000 Meshach Shiraz (Barossa Valley) $82. Right out of the gate, this Shiraz may not push your buttons. Give it a few minutes to open up, though, and it offers attractive but restrained plum, cherry, and iron-ore aromas and flavors. Smooth tannins have a firm grip on the midpalate, and follow through to a juicy, lasting finish. Drink now–2013. **91** —*D.T. (8/1/2005)*

Grant Burge 1996 Meschach Shiraz (Barossa Valley) $145. Seamless, rich, and intense are among the words tasters used to describe this complex wine with its tart-sweet fruit, cedar, smoke, coffee, and brown-sugar profile. The even, full mouthfeel is seductively lovely, as is the long, tangy, roasted fruit and toasted coconut finish. Already nicely evolved, this pleasure package is a keeper that will last ages. **94 Cellar Selection** *(11/1/2001)*

Grant Burge 2003 Miamba Shiraz (Barossa) $19. Most of the higher-tier Grant Burge Shirazes this vintage were excellent, so maybe it's not such a surprise that this one is just good. There's a kirsch-ish aspect to the plummy nose, plus tangy oak. Oak and plum are reprised on the palate; a little rough on the tongue, and finishes short. **85** —*D.T. (6/1/2006)*

Grant Burge 2002 Miamba Shiraz (Barossa Valley) $15. Medium-bodied, with very bright plum, raspberry, and blackberry fruit. Gets more dense toward the finish, with gummy, chunky tannins. Coffee, eucalyptus, and mocha aromas on the nose. **88** —*D.T. (5/1/2004)*

Grant Burge 2001 Miamba Shiraz (Barossa Valley) $15. A sturdy, curmudgeonly wine, rather than a sweet lively one; red fruit is staunch, with chalky, dusty tannins. Very good, reliable, and straightforward. **87** —*D.T. (2/1/2004)*

Grant Burge 2000 Miamba Shiraz (Barossa Valley) $15. Young and jammy, a brooding purple liquid that coats the palate with thick, glycerined honey, and ripe flavors of blueberry and blackberry marmalade. Very rich and delicious, with crisp youthful acidity. **89** —*S.H. (1/1/2002)*

Grant Burge 1999 Miamba Shiraz (Barossa Valley) $15. A young wine, dark purple in color, whose aromas are dominated now by oak. The sweet, sappy vanilla scents mask the grapes, but not in the mouth, where jammy berry fruit is powerfully ripe. Fortunately, the wine is dry, with lively acids. **87** —*S.H. (9/1/2002)*

Grant Burge 2002 Filsell Shiraz-Cabernet Sauvignon (Barossa Valley) $25. Has great weight in the midpalate, with chewy tannins and bright berry fruit that's tempered by a layer of chalk or talc. On the nose, berry fruit is buried under deep coffee, mocha, and mint aromas. Powerful, but has personality. **90** —*D.T. (5/1/2004)*

Grant Burge 2001 Filsell Shiraz-Cabernet Sauvignon (Barossa Valley) $25. From vines planted circa 1925, the wine feels thick and Portlike in the mouth at first, with bright berry fruit on the palate. The fruit lingers in the back of the throat but not so much on the palate. Nose offers yummy red clay and fruitcake aromas. **88** —*D.T. (2/1/2004)*

AUSTRALIA

Grant Burge 2003 Nebuchadnezzar Shiraz-Cabernet Sauvignon (Barossa) $34. This big red has smoky, barbecue-marinade aromas. On the palate, tangy oak and plums have a cool, herbaceous streak. Finish is tannic. **88** —*D.T. (2/1/2006)*

Grant Burge 2003 Balthasar Shiraz-Viognier (Barossa) $33. With just 4% Viognier, for better or worse it doesn't have that lifted-aroma quality that Viognier usually lends these kinds of blends. Feel is rough at first but smoothes out; there's a fair dose of wood here. With air, blueberry flavors come to the fore. Still this is not a deep wine. **88** —*D.T. (6/1/2006)*

Grant Burge 2002 Balthasar Shiraz-Viognier (Barossa Valley) $32. Apart from a slight floral character on the nose, the 7% Viognier doesn't seem to add much to this wine. But that doesn't mean it's not a very good one: It has sweetish plum and cherry aromas, with oak in a supporting role, and tastes just as the nose would lead you to believe. Soft tannins; drink now. **88** —*D.T. (10/1/2005)*

GREEN POINT

Green Point 2004 Cabernet Sauvignon-Shiraz (Victoria) $18. This Cab-Shiraz adheres to the idea of moderation in all things. Its size is just right for enjoying with food, and its black cherry and plum flavors, not oak or other shadings, are center stage. Would go well with game meats in fruit-based sauces. **88** —*D.T. (8/1/2006)*

Green Point 2003 Chardonnay (Yarra Valley) $16. They've toned down the new oak here, but it's still apparent on the nose, which gives up toasty, nutty scents in addition to ripe melon and pear aromas. Flavor-wise, there's plenty of citrus is this relatively lean, tightly focused Chard. It's clean and fresh on the finish, picking up some mineral notes. **87** *(12/15/2005)*

Green Point 2002 Chardonnay (Yarra Valley) $16. Shows light stone fruit and citrus flavors and aromas. It's zesty and lively on the palate, perhaps a little lean for some, but plumps up on the finish. A pre-dinner-or-raw bar sort of Chard. **86** —*D.T. (12/31/2004)*

Green Point 2004 Reserve Chardonnay (Yarra Valley) $27. Enjoyable, with a light-handed pencil-lead character on the nose. If you're looking for a forceful, overoaked, buttery wine, buy something else. This one has a slight dash of fresh vanilla, but deals mostly light pear and citrus flavors on a feminine body. **88** —*D.T. (11/15/2006)*

Green Point 2003 Reserve Chardonnay (Yarra Valley) $24. A bit fuller and richer than the regular Chardonnay, with nutty, spicy aromas and flavors of whie peaches and citrus. Long, with a toasty-nutty aftertaste that lingers elegantly on the finish. **89** *(12/15/2005)*

Green Point 2002 Reserve Chardonnay (Yarra Valley) $25. There's some loud and proud fruit in this Yarra Chard. The wine is very light—almost clear—in color, with intense citrus and stone fruit flavors on the palate. Finishes medium-long with fresh herb and sweet talc powder. A classy, feminine, slinky wine. You want a plump, tropical model? Look elsewhere. **90** —*D.T. (12/31/2004)*

Green Point 2003 Shiraz (Victoria) $18. Soft and silky, this is an approachable Shiraz meant for early consumption. Cola, plum, cherry, and blackberry flavors provide plenty of interest, while the finish adds hints of peppery spice. **89** *(12/15/2005)*

Green Point 2002 Shiraz (Victoria) $18. Big black and red fruit aromas have a barbecued smokiness. On the palate, mixed plums rest on a pillow of bread flour. Unfolds to juicy, ripe fruit on the finish, the floury texture holding on until the end. Very nice. **89** —*D.T. (12/31/2004)*

Green Point 2003 Reserve Shiraz (Yarra Valley) $24. Meaty yet floral at the same time, with distinct stone fruit notes mingling with darker plum and black cherry flavors. Medium- to full-bodied, with soft tannins, but crisp acids that define the wine's structure. Drink now. **90 Editors' Choice** *(12/15/2005)*

Green Point 2002 Reserve Shiraz (Yarra Valley) $25. On the nose, this Yarra Shiraz has smoldering, dried spice and barbecue-smoke notes that follow through to the palate, giving more pizazz to its red plum and berry flavors. Has decent grip on the midpalate. This reserve is very good, but no better than the winery's regular Shiraz. **88** —*D.T. (5/1/2005)*

GREENOCK CREEK

Greenock Creek 2003 Cabernet Sauvignon (Barossa Valley) $125. Just the thing if you like high-alcohol (15.5%) Barossa Cabs with lifted red cherry and blackberry flavors. Hints of wintergreen and black pepper add interest; another reviewer noticed hints of prune as well. This is a very good wine, but not as layered and rich as it could be. Drink over the near term. **88** —*D.T. (10/1/2006)*

GREG NORMAN ESTATES

Greg Norman Estates 2002 Cabernet Sauvignon-Merlot (Limestone Coast) $17. This is a good wine but one whose odd elements (soy-sauce and baked beans notes on the nose, and a little greenness on the palate) distract from its more pleasing attributes (smooth, dry tannins, hints of tea flavors). Just doesn't come together well enough to merit the higher scores that this producer routinely garners. **84** —*D.T. (12/31/2004)*

Greg Norman Estates NV Champagne Blend (Australia) $19. Traditional scents and aromas of hay and citrus blend with unexpected ones like durum flour, mango, and apricot. Frothy on the palate, with brisk acidity and a slightly chalky medium-length finish. Overall, an even package that will age well. **91** —*K.F. (12/1/2002)*

Greg Norman Estates NV Australian Sparkling Champagne Blend (South Eastern Australia) $19. Pale in color but with decent flavor and body, there a lot to like in this Oz sparkler with a famous name. It offers toast and vanilla aromas, flavors of melon, dried fruit, and earth, and a fine even bead. There's good length to the dry citrus-tinged finish. **87** —*M.M. (12/1/2001)*

Greg Norman Estates 2004 Chardonnay (Victoria) $14. A fine, food-friendly, medium-sized Chard whose nose and finish both show a fair amount of wood. Fruit in the center is not very demonstrative, some peach skin holding down the fort. **85** —*D.T. (12/1/2005)*

Greg Norman Estates 2003 Chardonnay (Victoria) $14. I like this wine's crispness and freshness. It's all Granny Smith apple, pear, and mineral, nose to tail. Has a pretty delicacy about it; try as a pre-dinner cocktail. **87** —*D.T. (10/1/2005)*

Greg Norman Estates 2002 Chardonnay (Victoria) $14. A solid wine with presence, not too big or overblown. The nose isn't all that expressive—we found subtle nut and chalk notes—but the palate offers up plenty of sturdy pear fruit, with shakes of nutmeg and chalk. Lingers on the close, with more nut flavors. **88** *(7/2/2004)*

Greg Norman Estates 2001 Chardonnay (Yarra Valley) $17. 81 —*D.T. (8/1/2003)*

Greg Norman Estates 2000 Chardonnay (Yarra Valley) $17. The lime, pear, and melon aromas and flavors are garnished with just a touch of vanilla. Picks up some vegetal lima bean notes on the palate, and the acids stick out a bit on the finish. Still, it's crisp and clean—and would go down easy after a hot round of golf. **84** —*J.C. (7/1/2002)*

Greg Norman Estates 1998 Chardonnay (Yarra Valley) $15. 88 *(12/31/1999)*

Greg Norman Estates 2003 Shiraz (Limestone Coast) $16. This Shiraz's black-pepper accent is its best feature; on the nose, it's joined by meaty notes. On the palate, it's taken over by a smooth, woody overlay and sour plums. **86** —*D.T. (2/1/2006)*

Greg Norman Estates 1999 Shiraz (Limestone Coast) $17. This wine seemed better a vintage or two ago. Fortunately, it's still a nice easy-drinking Shiraz with grape and blackberry fruit, some dried spices, and a hint of black pepper. **83** —*J.C. (9/1/2002)*

Greg Norman Estates 1998 Shiraz (Limestone Coast) $17. Full, dark berry aromas and a slight mint note open this very friendly, ready-to-drink-tonight Shiraz. The supple mouthfeel, ripe blackberry/cassis flavor package and dark, toasty oak accents make this as much of a crowd-pleaser as its namesake. Not tremendously complex, but a real winner, this finishes long with very even tannins. **87** *(6/1/2001)*

Greg Norman Estates 2000 Padthaway Reserve Shiraz (South Australia) $40. An okay vintage of a typically better wine. The wine is dominated by a nutty, amaretto or liqueurish note, with tangy oak on the finish.

There's firm plum fruit and a piquant sweet-tartness that grabs on mid-palate, though, that's quite nice. **88** —*D.T. (12/1/2005)*

Greg Norman Estates 1999 Reserve Shiraz (South Eastern Australia) $40. This Shiraz has medium body and chalky-chewy tannins. A dried spice, or clove, note that shows on the nose comes around again to accent the palate's bright, juicy plum fruit; brown sugar and caramel components are almost too hedonistic and rich, but toe the line nicely. The wine comes to a medium-long close, the chewy tannins hanging on after the flavor gives up. **90** —*D.T. (9/1/2004)*

Greg Norman Estates 1998 Reserve Shiraz (McLaren Vale) $40. Full-on fruit on the palate (blackberry jam, and a host of berries) plus eucalyptus and vanilla. It's big and rich in the mouth, with a medium-long finish that sings of eucalyptus and vanilla. It is what it is—big, fruity, alcoholic—and it's pretty darned good at that. **92** *(10/1/2003)*

Greg Norman Estates 2002 Shiraz-Cabernet Sauvignon (Limestone Coast) $16. This Shiraz-Cab has lively acidity on its side, and cool plum and black cherry flavors to back it up. Its tannins are manageable now, and soften and widen on the nutty finish. **88** —*D.T. (10/1/2005)*

Greg Norman Estates NV Sparkling Blend (Australia) $19. 85 —*D.T. (12/31/2003)*

Greg Norman Estates NV Sparkling Blend (South Eastern Australia) $19. Though it's a good, reasonably priced wine, appropriate any day of the week as an apéritif or party quaff, I was puzzled by a flavor profile of lime and fresh corn tortillas, with dusty, citrus flavors riding in the back seat. Dry in the mouth, though a little coarse. **85** —*D.T. (12/31/2003)*

Greg Norman Estates NV Sparkling Blend (South Eastern Australia) $16. A perennial favorite in the Australian sparklers arena, this wine balances pretty bread-flour and golden apple aromas and flavors with a crisp citrus cleanness. Blessedly dry on the palate; citrus, pear, and biscuit flavors bring it to a clean close. **88** —*D.T. (12/31/2004)*

GROOM

Groom 2005 Sauvignon Blanc (Adelaide Hills) $17. This Sauvignon starts off with a very pretty lemon meringue aroma, which translates on the palate as a dusty-citrus core. There's a helping of fresh green herbs and peas just at palate entry, with white peach and green apple flavors on the midpalate. Round and a shade less zesty than it has been in previous vintages, but still one of the prettier Hills SBs available in the U.S. **89** —*D.T. (6/1/2006)*

Groom 2004 Sauvignon Blanc (Adelaide Hills) $16. A fuller-sized, round SB, one that feels more Californian than from the Hills. Still, it's a very pleasing wine. It smells of pure peach nectar—a flavor that is echoed on the palate, along with fresh mango. It all hangs on a dry, minerally frame. **89** —*D.T. (8/1/2005)*

Groom 2003 Sauvignon Blanc (Adelaide Hills) $16. A sunny, lovely wine, the Groom smells of yellow fruit and vanilla bean (the latter note is strange, considering the wine's unoaked). On the palate, it's lively and crisp, with bright pineapple, citrus, and green grape flavors. Juicy and crisp on the finish, with chalk drawing the wine to its close. Delicious, and affordable to boot. **90 Editors' Choice** —*D.T. (5/1/2004)*

Groom 2002 Sauvignon Blanc (Adelaide Hills) $16. A bold wine, loaded with bright acidity but balanced with plenty of good body. It's redolent of grapefruit, gooseberry, fig, melon, fresh cut hay, lemon, and mandarine orange. Long and fresh on the finish. **91** —*J.M. (6/1/2003)*

Groom 2001 Shiraz (Barossa Valley) $40. Classic Aussie Shiraz from the vineyard that borders the backbone vineyard of Penfold's Grange. This one's made by ex-Grange winemaker Daryl Groom, who now lives in California's Sonoma County but owns his own Australia vineyard. Lush, deep, rich, and ripe, the wine fans out to reveal complex layers of black cherry, plum, licorice, spice, chocolate, blackberry, tar, vanilla, coconut, and herbs. Smooth and plush textured, with a finish that doesn't quit. **94** —*J.M. (6/1/2003)*

GROSSET

Grosset 2001 Gaia Cabernet Blend (Clare Valley) $40. Winemaker Jeffrey Grosset advises that you open this Bordeaux blend an hour before you drink it, and I am inclined to agree. Even after a couple of minutes in the glass, the nose won't show more than traces of clay and bread dough.

On the palate, the wine is just as hard to read, but the overall impression—great mouthfeel, smooth tannins, and tightly wound red fruit—means only good things for future enjoyment. Drink 2005+. **91 Cellar Selection** —*D.T. (2/1/2004)*

Grosset 2000 Picadilly Chardonnay (Adelaide Hills) $31. Toasty, mealy aromas combine with peach and smoke in a beguiling, complex nose that resembles a fine Chassagne-Montrachet. Flavors of peach and citrus coat the palate without ever seeming overly rich, heavy or oily, extending through the long ripe-citrus finish. **91** —*J.C. (7/1/2002)*

Grosset 2003 Piccadilly Chardonnay (Adelaide Hills) $37. Though better known for his Rieslings, Jeffrey Grosset also makes a mean Chardonnay, which is all the more special for a dinner date because it's not that easy to come by. If your evening is alfresco, you may mistake the wine's light aromas of fresh-cut grass and hay for the scents of your outdoor surroundings. On the palate, pear and lemon zest aromas are couched in a judiciously creamy pillow. As should be true of any romantic partner, this wine's best feature is its texture. In this case, it feels like a soft cloud of cotton and chalk dust, and lasts long. **91** —*D.T. (8/1/2005)*

Grosset 2002 Piccadilly Chardonnay (Clare Valley) $39. Aromas are super, like vanilla bean and fresh cream. The palate strikes a great balance of cream and clean, crisp citrus and stone fruit. The finish is long and zesty, and tastes of lime. Excellent overall. With only 90 cases imported to the U.S., you're more likely to find it on a restaurant list than on your retailer's shelf. **93** —*D.T. (9/1/2004)*

Grosset 2004 Polish Hill Riesling (Clare Valley) $34. This is a very enjoyable Riesling, and always one of Australia's best. This vintage, yellow stone fruit aromas come on strong, followed up by pear and citrus zest flavors. It is tangy and dry overall, with a very steely, very rigid spine. The first sip feels almost too rigid, but it grows on you. **90** —*D.T. (10/1/2005)*

Grosset 2003 Polish Hill Riesling (Clare Valley) $29. Has beautiful yellow stone fruit aromas and flavors. The mouthfeel is fairly full, but a thread of citrus fruit keeps it zesty and nimble on the tongue. **91** —*D.T. (2/1/2004)*

Grosset 2002 Polish Hill Riesling (Clare Valley) $30. Whether you ask me, God, or the lamp post, anyone who's ever had Australian Riesling will count this among the country's best versions of the variety. On the nose, it yields a little sweetness, plus some grapefruit and passion fruit; after a few minutes in the glass, the passion fruit aromas hold on and are joined by kiwi and other fresh tropical fruit. It's a very dry Riesling, with strong lime and a fresh herbal (perhaps cilantro?) flavors, which makes the mineral foundation seem that much drier and racier. Finishes medium-long with grapefruit and putty flavors. An excellent food wine…or an excellent last meal in itself. **91 Editors' Choice** —*D.T. (8/1/2003)*

Grosset 2001 Polish Hill Riesling (Clare Valley) $29. Penetrating aromas of apple blossom, peach, and tarragon burst from the glass. The flavors are even more intense: Granny Smith apples, with softer, warmer, stone-fruit undercurrents. The finish boasts searingly tart flavors that last and last. Should age gloriously. **92** —*J.C. (2/1/2002)*

Grosset 2003 Watervale Riesling (Clare Valley) $24. Not an overtly flavorful wine, the Watervale is wiry, with citrus and peach-skin flavors and not any fluff. Its mineral-chalk texture, which continues on through the finish, is what's most pleasing. Clean, crisp, and correct. **88** —*D.T. (9/1/2004)*

Grosset 2002 Watervale Riesling (Clare Valley) $25. This Riesling is smooth in the mouth, with yellow-fruit flavors and aromas—banana is particularly prevalent—and a fine dusting of chalk. Opens and closes with nice citrus accents. **87** —*D.T. (8/1/2003)*

GULLIN LANDSCAPE

Gullin Landscape 1999 Red Earth Cabernet Cabernet Sauvignon (Coonawarra) $11. The initial impression from the bouquet is that you are in the middle of a barnyard. Fruit just isn't part of the aromatic show. Cherry and leather dominate the palate, which has ample tannic grip and the full allotment of spiciness. Unfortunately, however, it doesn't sing as a whole. **84** —*M.S. (12/15/2002)*

Gullin Landscape 2000 Chardonnay (South Eastern Australia) $8. 83 —*D.T. (8/1/2003)*

AUSTRALIA

Gullin Landscape 1999 Red Earth Shiraz (McLaren Vale) $16. Considering this wine's flavor profile, it's easy to see how the words "landscape" and "earth" are part of its name. Meat, earth, and briary aromas segue into more earthy goodness, plus some blackberry fruit, on the palate. Medium-bodied, it's an easy choice for those who value a dose of terroir with their fruit. **88** —*D.T. (3/1/2003)*

HAAN

Haan 2002 Hanenhof Bordeaux Blend (Barossa Valley) $20. This is one pretty wine, with powdery tannins and a medium-sized body. The nose offers vanilla and blueberry-blackberry aromas. On the palate, there's a baseline of coffee, or cappuccino, with a fan of berry flavors. However sweet or cloying these descriptors make this wine sound, it really isn't. A blend of 78% Cabernet Sauvignon, 12% Merlot, and 10% Cabernet Franc. **90** —*D.T. (5/1/2005)*

Haan 2003 Estate Wine Viognier (Barossa Valley) $30. The nose is the best part: honeycomb, and some flowers. But flavors of butter, bitter herb, and flowers, and a very oily mouthfeel, make this marginal at best. **80** —*D.T. (11/15/2004)*

HAMELIN BAY

Hamelin Bay 1999 Cabernet Sauvignon (Margaret River) $29. Lemon and cream with dusty oak aromas turn to flavors of vanilla and blackberries. There is a very tannic finish in this wine; it needs a few years of bottle age before it will be approachable. **88** —*C.S. (6/1/2002)*

Hamelin Bay 2001 Chardonnay (Margaret River) $22. Opens with aromas of green pea, yellow fruit, and oak. This is a fairly big Chard, but one that's more focused on toast and butterscotch than it is fruit. Coats the mouth with a hard candy-esque feel, like green apple Jolly Ranchers. **85** *(7/2/2004)*

Hamelin Bay 2000 Chardonnay (Margaret River) $28. With a nose full of buttered popcorn and vanilla, it's clear that much if not all of this wine was barrel-fermented and aged, maybe a tad too much. The vanilla and toast flavors partially obscure pretty white peach fruit. **84** —*J.C. (7/1/2002)*

Hamelin Bay 2001 Sauvignon Blanc (Margaret River) $22. The bouquet starts off snappy and clean, but with time some pungent sea foam and green-bean aromas arise. Basic pear, melon, and green herbs make up the flavor profile, while the short finish, though offering ample pepper and mineral, is lacking in fruit. **87** *(8/1/2002)*

Hamelin Bay 2000 Sauvignon Blanc (Margaret River) $22. Seems a bit dull and watery at first, then develops some fennel and green-apple aromas with airing. Simple apple and anise flavors turn peppery on the finish. **82** —*J.C. (2/1/2002)*

Hamelin Bay 1999 Semillon-Sauvignon Blanc (Margaret River) $19. 90 — *S.H. (2/1/2002)*

Hamelin Bay 2004 Five Ashes Vineyard Semillon-Sauvignon Blanc (Margaret River) $19. Smells of hay, beeswax, and citrus peel. On the palate, almond, hay, and citrus flavors are pleasing, but the wine lacks stuffing. It is dry and clean, but would be even nicer if there were more here to appreciate. **85** —*D.T. (10/1/2005)*

HAMILTON'S BLUFF

Hamilton's Bluff 1999 Cowra Chardonnay (South Eastern Australia) $10. This simple wine has a juicy apple flavors and a tang that—given the whipping cream-meets-nutmeg bouquet—comes as a bit of a surprise. High acid and oak characterize the palate, and show up again on the back end. **82** —*D.T. (9/1/2001)*

HAMILTON'S EWELL VINEYARD

Hamilton's Ewell Vineyard 2000 Ewell Vineyard Cabernet Sauvignon (Barossa Valley) $18. The bramble-laden nose is tight and potent, with the essence of mint peeking through. Powerful berry and plum fruit follows on the stylish, smooth palate, and there's a good dose of mocha on the airy, svelte finish. It's young but not awkward, with a clean profile and a healthy mouthfeel. **90 Editors' Choice** —*M.S. (12/15/2002)*

Hamilton's Ewell Vineyard 2002 Sturt River Cabernet Sauvignon-Shiraz (South Australia) $14. Aromas are pruny and toasty, and on the palate

hard flavors of cherry and rhubarb take over. A stemmy-beany note persists through the finish. **83** —*D.T. (8/1/2005)*

Hamilton's Ewell Vineyard 2000 Railway Chardonnay (Barossa Valley) $13. The warm climate of the Barossa is reflected in the heavy, sweet fruit flavors. The melon, guava, and honey aromas and flavors lack zip and definition but certainly don't lack for ripeness. **83** —*J.C. (7/1/2002)*

Hamilton's Ewell Vineyard 2004 Sturt River Chardonnay (South Australia) $14. This is a refreshing Chard, but one whose flavors are hard to discern—there's some stone fruit, some drying citrus, maybe. Not complicated, but an easy quaff. **83** —*D.T. (10/1/2005)*

Hamilton's Ewell Vineyard 1999 Fuller's Barn Shiraz (Barossa Valley) $30. Black plums, faint char, vanilla, and rose stem aromas intensify on the palate, with the char taking on a more herbal note. Firm acidity is backed by fine, sandy tannins and dark fruit. Finishes with good length. **88** —*K.F. (3/1/2003)*

Hamilton's Ewell Vineyard 2002 Railway Shiraz (Barossa Valley) $25. Very ripe—overripe, maybe—berry fruit aromas are an appropriate prelude to dark, deep, ripe flavors. The thing is, the wine doesn't have a strong enough frame on which to hang such big flavors. Does the ripe Shiraz thing well, and will surely have hosts of fans. **87** —*D.T. (10/1/2005)*

HANDPICKED

Handpicked 2004 Chardonnay (South Eastern Australia) $13. This Chardonnay follows the same profile that many other please-everyone Chardonnays do: citrus and yellow stone fruit aromas and flavors, a dry mouthfeel, and a medium-sized body. It's a good wine, but it will be nothing new to regular Oz Chard drinkers. **84** —*D.T. (5/1/2005)*

HANGING ROCK

Hanging Rock 2002 Strathbogie Chardonnay (Victoria) $16. A feminine, almost sweet wine, with a perfumey, floral, bubblegum powder aroma and floral-fuzzy peach flavors. It's slim in build, with wood surfacing on the finish. **85** *(7/2/2004)*

HARDYS

Hardys 2001 Stamp of Australia Cabernet Sauvignon (South Eastern Australia) $6. Nose shows ripe plum fruit, plus a brown-gravy meatiness. Red and black fruit on the palate is confected. A straightforward, no-surprises wine. **82** —*D.T. (1/1/2002)*

Hardys 1994 Thomas Hardy Cabernet Sauvignon (Coonawarra) $50. 90 *(3/1/2000)*

Hardys 1999 Tintara Cabernet Sauvignon (South Australia) $18. Black and burnt. Coffee, caramel, charcoal, and a hint of roasted peppers make for a dark and distressingly fruitless wine. Finishes with some redeeming earth and tobacco nuances. **83** —*J.C. (6/1/2002)*

Hardys 2002 Nottage Hill Cabernet Sauvignon-Shiraz (South Eastern Australia) $8. I tasted this wine without knowing what it was, and my first thought was that more restaurants (okay, I think my musing was as specific as "tapas restaurants") should serve this wine by the glass. Though only the more progressive Spanish joints would serve an Aussie, it's really what a food-friendly, by-the-glass pour should be. It's soft and comfortable in the mouth, like broken-in loafers, with brambly, pretty plum, and raspberry fruit on both the nose and the palate. **86 Best Buy** —*D.T. (11/15/2004)*

Hardys 2000 Nottage Hill Cabernet Sauvignon-Shiraz (South Eastern Australia) $8. Sharp aromas, something similar to thistles on a hot day, start it off. The cherry and raspberry fruit that spreads across the acidic palate is sort of lackluster and light. Some bacon fat bulks up the light finish. **84** —*M.S. (12/15/2002)*

Hardys 2005 Nottage Hill Chardonnay (South Eastern Australia) $8. Fragrant aromas of peach, pineapple, and burnt sugar segue into more subdued apple and tropical fruit flavors on the palate. Has the advantages of being both approachable and affordable. **85 Best Buy** —*D.T. (6/1/2006)*

Hardys 2004 Nottage Hill Chardonnay (South Eastern Australia) $8. Smells like toasted marshmallows, but offers clean, bright peach, and citrus flavors on the palate. Simple and pleasant, and should be easy to find. 20,000 cases produced. **84 Best Buy** —*D.T. (10/1/2005)*

Hardys 2003 Nottage Hill Chardonnay (South Eastern Australia) $8. Hardys Nottage Hill line is almost always a good buy, and this Chard fits the bill quite right. It smells of roasted peanuts and stone fruit, and maybe a little pineapple. Plump and easy in the mouth, there's melon and toast flavors, with a little sorghum sweetness. **85 Best Buy** *(7/2/2004)*

Hardys 2002 Nottage Hill Chardonnay (South Eastern Australia) $8. A harmonious, balanced wine, with bright citrus and white stone fruit aromas, and vanilla and cream nicely balancing yellow fruit on the palate. At this price, it's a no-brainer. Drink now. **87 Best Buy** —*D.T. (8/1/2003)*

Hardys 2001 Nottage Hill Chardonnay (South Eastern Australia) $7. What sets this apart from dozens of other Australian Chardonnays clustered at the low end of the price scale? The finish—which is clean, fresh, and appealing, not syrupy or sweet-tasting. Aromas and flavors combine peach, citrus, and Asian pear with a dash of vanilla. **85 Best Buy** —*J.C. (7/1/2002)*

Hardys 2000 Nottage Hill Chardonnay (South Eastern Australia) $7. Apple, pear, and oak aromas and flavors prevail in this simple but not unattractive blend from several regions. Good acidity and a round mouthfeel help it along. Good for poolside or hors d'oeuvres. **83** —*M.N. (6/1/2001)*

Hardys 2005 Oomoo Unwooded Chardonnay (McLaren Vale) $15. Offers light aromas of banana and other tropical fruits, and segues into sour green apple and citrus flavors on the palate. Round in the mouth; a good, straightforward Chard. **84** —*D.T. (4/1/2006)*

Hardys 2005 Stamp of Australia Chardonnay (South Eastern Australia) $6. Pear and golden apple aromas lead to a fat, sweet palate. Shows some alcohol; finishes short. **82** —*D.T. (11/15/2006)*

Hardys 2002 Stamp of Australia Chardonnay (South Eastern Australia) $6. This Chard is a straightforward, good quaffer, with a light, pleasant sweetness more suited for late-summer picnics than dinner parties. Offers crisp yellow fruit, plus light citrus and mineral notes on the palate; on the nose, the fruit is tropical. Drink it before the weather gets too crisp. **85** —*D.T. (8/1/2003)*

Hardys 2001 Tintara Chardonnay (Adelaide Hills) $15. A well-balanced and straightforward wine, the Tintara is medium-bodied and creamy in the mouth, with stone fruit and vanilla flavors. Butterscotch, and maybe some nuttiness, wraps it up on the finish. **86** —*D.T. (8/1/2003)*

Hardys 2000 Tintara Chardonnay (South Australia) $15. New oak and ripe fruit blend together to yield complex aromas of baked apples and pears, complete with a pat of melted butter and a dash of cinnamon. Finishes clean, not cloying, with a distinct Granny Smith flavor. **87** —*J.C. (7/1/2002)*

Hardys 2003 Nottage Hill Merlot (South Eastern Australia) $8. This Merlot is full of black plum and bread flour, nose to finish. Tannins are soft and approachable, and the texture creamy. A good value. **85 Best Buy** —*D.T. (4/1/2006)*

Hardys 2002 Nottage Hill Merlot (South Eastern Australia) $8. Sand and red-plum flavors at the fore, and a prickly rather than smooth feel on the palate. Good and straightforward. **83** —*D.T. (8/1/2005)*

Hardys 2000 Nottage Hill Merlot (South Eastern Australia) $7. Woodsy, drying tannins put a bit of a damper on this Merlot's bright red-cherry fruit. Expect the same red berry-oak-herb profile on the nose, and plenty of woodiness on the back end. **84** —*D.T. (6/1/2002)*

Hardys 2005 Nottage Hill Pinot Noir (South Eastern Australia) $9. Lifted cherry, red eraser, and coconut aromas dominate. Medium sized; has a chunky, gravelly feel with grabby plum and raspberry fruit on the palate. Well priced for such an easy-drinking Pinot. **85 Best Buy** —*D.T. (11/15/2006)*

Hardys 2005 Stamp of Australia Riesling (South Eastern Australia) $6. This is a sweeter, softer, more approachable take on Riesling. Shows citrus and peach flavors, with a zip of acidity on the back end, and chalky aromas. **84 Best Buy** —*D.T. (4/1/2006)*

Hardys 2002 Botrytis Semillon (South Eastern Australia) $15. This sticky pulls out all the stops; where words like "ripe, full, rich, and sweet" are detriments to some wines they only explain this one's attractiveness. Apricot aromas are laid on thick, backed by some citrus and fig. Apricot, passion fruit, mango, and burnt sugar emerge on the palate and through

the finish. Would do your favorite apple pie or peach cobbler real justice. **90 Best Buy** —*D.T. (8/1/2006)*

Hardys 2000 Tintara Botrytis Semillon (South Eastern Australia) $17. Well balanced, smooth, sweet, and blessed with just the right touch of acidity, this honeyed wine also has a fine blend of orange, peach, melon, spice, and citrus flavors. Fresh at the end. **90** —*J.M. (12/1/2002)*

Hardys 2001 Eileen Hardy Shiraz (McLaren Vale) $90. Shows beefy, nutty notes on the nose, and black plum, berry, and pepper on the palate. Has interesting meaty, beefy undertones; feels built for near-term enjoyment. **88** —*D.T. (4/1/2006)*

Hardys 2000 Eileen Hardy Shiraz (South Australia) $90. On the nose, the sweet plum fruit is just this side of stewy; dark black and blueberry fruit on the palate is edged by caramel, toast, and maybe a little rubber. Medium-weight, with woodsy tannins on the finish. A solid, dark wine. **88** —*D.T. (5/1/2004)*

Hardys 1999 Eileen Hardy Shiraz (South Australia) $85. High-toned black-and blueberry fruit, with distinctive eucalyptus overtones, play on the bouquet. Ditto on the palate, where nice earthy notes thankfully keep the brightness in check. As a package, the wine tastes a little stylized, even confected, as though it's been manipulated to death. Even the stellar 1998 vintage didn't measure up to its hefty price tag, which makes the '99 even less of a bargain. **86** —*D.T. (3/1/2003)*

Hardys 1998 Eileen Hardy Shiraz (McLaren Vale & Padthaway) $70. Opens with an inky nose of tart black fruits, a spice-herb element, and saddle leather—with a definite horse-stable note some tasters found complex, others just rough. The dark toasty-earthy palate has a soft, even mouthfeel, and it finishes with espresso, earth, and an almost bitter note. **89** *(11/1/2001)*

Hardys 1996 Eileen Hardy Shiraz (McLaren Vale & Padthaway) $62. **93** *(3/1/2000)*

Hardys 2004 Nottage Hill Shiraz (South Eastern Australia) $9. Smells a little like fruitcake, with its thick wheat and dried-fruit aromas. On the palate, it's a medium-sized, linear wine with plum and blueberry in the starring roles. Finish is brief. **85 Best Buy** —*D.T. (11/15/2006)*

Hardys 2001 Nottage Hill Shiraz (South Eastern Australia) $8. A smooth, straightforward wine, medium-bodied in the mouth, with mixed plum and caramel flavors. Smells of oak and meat; a no-brainer for Tuesday nights or backyard barbecues. **86 Best Buy** —*D.T. (5/1/2004)*

Hardys 2000 Nottage Hill Shiraz (South Eastern Australia) $8. Good spice, briar, and smoke aromas go well with expressive, clean fruit. The wholesome palate features a fine dose of cherry and plum, while the finish is rich and chewy. For a value-priced wine, this has a lot to offer. With purity and verve, it can compete with higher-priced bottles. **88 Best Buy** —*M.S. (3/1/2003)*

Hardys 2001 Oomoo Shiraz (McLaren Vale) $12. A down-the-line, straight-forward Shiraz, not superlayered or nuanced, but enjoyable. Fresh plum fruit is forward, and takes on sweet-spice accents of clove and cinnamon on the nose. **86** —*D.T. (12/31/2005)*

Hardys NV Sparkling Shiraz (South Australia) $20. One of the better sparkling Shirazes available in the U.S. at the moment. It offers dusty, dry blackberry aromas and blackberry and clay flavors. Structured, with some complexity; some fruit sweetness appears on the finish, but it's pretty dry otherwise. **89** —*D.T. (12/31/2005)*

Hardys 2004 Stamp of Australia Shiraz (South Eastern Australia) $6. A good wine for wine newbies, featuring bouncy, fruit-ripe flavors and raspberry and smoke aromas. Has a Sweet Tart flavor and feel, and a graham-cracker finish. **84 Best Buy** —*D.T. (12/31/2005)*

Hardys 2002 Stamp of Australia Shiraz (South Eastern Australia) $6. Smells nice, like a fireplace in winter—smoldering, smoky, with maybe some pinecones thrown in. The palate, though, has sour black and red fruit, wtih a lactic or creamy note that's a little offputting. An unbeatable price, but the Stamp Shiraz isn't quite as good as the Chardonnay. **83** —*D.T. (1/1/2002)*

Hardys 2001 Stamp of Australia Shiraz (South Eastern Australia) $6. Smells like a fireplace, in the best sense of the word—it has nice pine cone, smoke, and oak aromas. But it's simple in mouth, with black and red fruit and a heavy dose of lactic-creaminess. Finishes with dried herbs. **83** —D.T. (1/1/2002)

Hardys 1999 Tintara Shiraz (South Australia) $18. Kirsch, licorice, earth, and dark black fruit make for a welcoming opening to this Hardys offering. Deep earth, mushroom, and smoke flavors over blackberry fruit give this Australian Shiraz flavors as dark as its color. Finishes with sharply acidic coffee and cocoa flavors. **87** (10/1/2001)

Hardys 2005 Stamp of Australia Shiraz-Grenache (South Eastern Australia) $6. Soft and sort of formless in terms of structure, this is a strawberry-centered rosé, with a creamy, sweet edge. Inexpensive, and just the thing for White Zin fans who want to try something new. **83** —D.T. (4/1/2006)

HARTZ BARN WINES

Hartz Barn Wines 2001 Mail Box Merlot (Barossa Valley) $30. Though there's oak, cherry, and herb flavors on the palate, the texture is a different story—meaning, until the finish, there isn't much texture at all. Finishes with killer oak and tealike tannins. **83** —D.T. (1/1/2002)

Hartz Barn Wines 2001 General Store Shiraz (Barossa Valley) $30. A puzzling wine, with fruit flavors that taste sort of manufactured or powdery. There's a nice smooth mouthfeel, but it turns milky on the finish. **84** —D.T. (5/1/2004)

HASTWELL & LIGHTFOOT

Hastwell & Lightfoot 2000 Shiraz (McLaren Vale) $28. This Shiraz's aromas change from caramel and stewed fruit to mineral and back to caramel; the palate offers up plenty of red plum and cherry, and a minerally feel. It's slight-bodied—not lean, but not a big wine, by any means—with caramel and gravelly-mineral on the finish. **87** —D.T. (9/1/2004)

Hastwell & Lightfoot 2002 Viognier (McLaren Vale) $22. Here's a wine that caused some debate among our editors. It's weighty in the mouth, with flavors that approach a cordial-filled white chocolate candy, finishing with passion fruit and more white chocolate. Your thoughts on the wine will hinge on whether you think it's lush and hedonistic, and practically fit for dessert, or just too heavy and low acid for its own good. **86** —D.T. (5/1/2004)

HAWKERS GATE

Hawkers Gate 2000 Shiraz (McLaren Vale) $21. The nose offers stewy, jammy fruit and pickling-spice aromas. This is a lighter-sized wine that wants to be a heavyweight, with such dark oak, caramel, and black cherry flavors. Finishes with similar flavors. **85** —D.T. (5/1/2004)

HEARTLAND

Heartland 2003 Director's Cut Shiraz (Langhorne Creek-Limestone Creek) $24. This is a crisp, focused Shiraz—not a killer in terms of richness or size, which is part of its draw (particularly if you're looking for something to drink with dinner). It has cool wintergreen and gingerbread aromas, and black cherry fruit on the palate. Finishes off with mint and tobacco flavors. **88** —D.T. (12/1/2005)

Heartland 2004 Stickleback White Blend (South Australia) $11. Here, 25% Verdelho is an unexpected component to a typical Sem-Chard blend, and the overall result is a very pleasing one. This is a fresh, clean white, with pear and Granny Smith apple flavors and a flinty-chalky feel. Great for the outdoors, and priced reasonably enough to keep a few extras around the house. **88 Best Buy** —D.T. (8/1/2005)

Heartland 2004 Viognier-Pinot Gris White Blend (Langhorne Creek) $12. Sounds like an odd blend, but you know what? This Ben Glaetzer wine works. It's a 75-25 Viognier dominant blend, with a fragrant bouquet of honeydew, flowers, and fresh cream. Its flavor profile (peach, some coconut, maybe some banana) may sound as upscale as a piña colada at a Cancún resort, but a wiry, dry citrus spine reins in the wine's more rambunctious notes. **89 Best Buy** —D.T. (8/1/2005)

HEATH WINES

Heath Wines 2002 Southern Roo Cabernet Sauvignon-Shiraz (South Australia) $14. Has aromas of anise gumdrop, chocolate, and coconut. On the palate, black plum and blackberry fruit tastes slightly underripe. Not a fleshy, generous red. 85% Cab, 15% Shiraz. **83** —D.T. (5/1/2005)

Heath Wines 2003 100 Year Old Vine Shiraz (Barossa Valley) $60. This wine has notable attributes, but also some drawbacks. Initial aromas are tarry and rubbery, although these temper with air into something more resembling tree bark. The bulk of the flavors are dark notes of coffee, earth, and prune, although a streak of tart berries stands out, becoming dominant on the tart, fresh finish. **86** —J.C. (12/15/2006)

HEATHCOTE ESTATE

Heathcote Estate 2003 Shiraz (Heathcote) $48. Glows purple in the glass. This is such an enjoyable wine, though young. Ripe berry fruit flavors are pure and focused, couched only in a light cushion of vanilla. Balanced, harmonious and very pretty; drink 2007–2011. **92** —D.T. (4/1/2006)

HEATHFIELD RIDGE

Heathfield Ridge 1998 Cabernet Sauvignon (Limestone Coast) $15. 83 (10/1/2000)

Heathfield Ridge 1999 Cabernet Sauvignon (Limestone Coast) $16. Piercing in the nose, with wood spice and herbal notes. The raspberry flavor is rather high toned, while the finish is a touch acidic and short, with overt oak that isn't fully integrated. The final impression is a touch hot and tart. **84** —M.S. (12/15/2002)

Heathfield Ridge 1997 Patrick Cabernet Sauvignon (Coonawarra) $40. The nose is oaky and a bit weedy—we'll call it minty to be nice. Raspberry and red currant comprise the flavors. While it's clean, it is not terribly impressive. The quick take is that it's zippy and nice. But further evaluation reveals some veggie notes. **85** —M.S. (12/15/2002)

Heathfield Ridge 2000 Reserve Chardonnay (Limestone Coast) $16. Fans of toast, butterscotch, and butter will gulp this down happily, but these reviewers are sad to see the wine's fruit get lost beneath it all. Finishes like caramel candy; smells like buttered whole wheat toast. Will certainly have its appeal, but we'd like to see the fruit center stage next vintage. **83** —D.T. (8/1/2003)

Heathfield Ridge 1999 Merlot (Limestone Coast) $16. Offers drying, tealike tannins from palate through to finish, plus red fruit, earth, and oak flavors. Pretty standard stuff, but that's not a bad thing. Fruit from this wine come from Heathfield Vineyard, near the Bool Lagoon. **85** —D.T. (6/1/2003)

Heathfield Ridge 1999 Shiraz (Limestone Coast) $16. The aromas, despite some chocolate qualities, are mostly sharp and woody, with just a hint of cola. Snappy red fruit controls the palate, followed by bright acidity on the finish. This has a racy quality but not a lot of fruit or depth backing that up. **84** —M.S. (1/28/2003)

Heathfield Ridge 1998 Jennifer Shiraz (Padthaway) $34. Rich aromas of blackberries, licorice, and toasted oak start it off, followed by cherry and plum flavors. This particular wine lacks that thick, oozing style common to Australian Shiraz; instead, it's fairly racy and agile, with lively acidity. As a result, it's probably best with food. **87** —M.S. (3/1/2003)

HEAVEN'S GATE

Heaven's Gate 2001 Shiraz (Barossa Valley) $15. From nose to palate and on through the finish, this wine has high-toned cherry and plum fruit. Straightforward and perfectly good, though not quite as interesting as some other Barossa offerings. **86** —D.T. (12/31/2003)

HEGGIE'S VINEYARD

Heggie's Vineyard 1998 Chardonnay (Eden Valley) $20. Light lemon and cream, plus heavy oak aromas lead into a slightly hot, apple-cidery palate. Feels weighty in the mouth—almost gummy—and finishes short, with citrusy accents (particularly lemon). Will please a wide audience. **85** —D.T. (9/1/2001)

Heggie's Vineyard 1996 Merlot (Eden Valley) $22. There's a smooth quality to the wood, berry, and caramel notes on the nose of this wine, but overall it's mostly about wood, as only faint fruit hints still show. Quite mature, it feels old and somewhat tired, albeit elegantly so. **82** —M.M. (9/1/2001)

Heggie's Vineyard 1998 Viognier (Eden Valley) $22. 82 (10/1/2000)

Heggie's Vineyard 1999 Viognier (Eden Valley) $22. Viognier is never this inexpensive, let alone this inexpensive and this good. On the nose, clean citrus notes balance brighter, richer tropical fruit and butter aromas. It's smooth in the mouth, where bright sunflower and chalk flavors play tug of war with underdog chalk and caramel notes, but it's so well integrated that it's hard to say who's winning. **85 Best Buy** —D.T. (2/1/2002)

Heggie's Vineyard 2004 Chardonnay (Eden Valley) $20. Has a pineapple-pear fruity aroma that, with air, takes on a toasted-nut note. The same pleasant notes hang on through the palate and finish. Enjoyable in its understatement, with a smooth, stony-minerally feel. **88** —D.T. (12/1/2005)

Heggie's Vineyard 2001 Chardonnay (Eden Valley) $20. Lovers of big, rich Chards will instantly fall in love with this lush wine, with its citrus and apple flavors and strong mineral component. Elaborate oak adds vanilla and toast complexities, while a great burst of bright, tingly acidity washes over and cleanses the mouth. **92** —S.H. (1/1/2002)

Heggie's Vineyard 2000 Chardonnay (Eden Valley) $20. A straightforward, moderately priced Chard, with characteristic golden apple and toast notes from start to finish. A good wine, but those averse to wood should steer clear. **84** —D.T. (8/1/2003)

Heggie's Vineyard 1998 Merlot (Eden Valley) $22. A very dark and young wine that opens with the aroma of blackberries and chocolate but also an odd note of cooked green vegetables. It's disjointed in the mouth, with ripe berry flavors and upfront tannins, and a jolt of sweetness through the finish. **84** —S.H. (12/15/2002)

Heggie's Vineyard 2004 Viognier (Eden Valley) $20. Smells like honey and talc powder, and shows Viognier's typical floral quality most in the mouth. It has the straw/hay quality that I associate more with Semillon, and a flourlike feel. Less weighty than you expect a Viognier to be, too, but shows how nice the variety can be when made with a lighter hand. **87** —D.T. (12/1/2005)

HENSCHKE

Henschke 2002 Cyril Henschke Bordeaux Blend (Eden Valley) $100. A blend of 75% Cab, with Cab Franc and Merlot making up the balance in equal parts. Its smooth, claylike texture is just excellent, and the fruit's mochalike accents are quite pretty. Feels warm on both the nose and the palate, though it's only 14.5% alcohol. **90** —D.T. (10/1/2006)

Henschke 2000 Cyril Henschke Cabernet Sauvignon-Merlot-Cabernet Franc Bordeaux Blend (Eden Valley) $100. A tribute to Stephen Henschke's father, this excellent Bordeaux-style blend is approachable even now, but could age through 2010, and maybe even beyond. The nose is just amazing, with mint, pepper, caraway seed, and cream, all over lush plum fruit. Plum fruit is juicy and ripe on the palate, swathed in smooth, chalky tannins that linger on the finish. **92** —D.T. (5/1/2004)

Henschke 2000 Lenswood Abbott's Prayer Bordeaux Blend (Adelaide Hills) $60. From Lenswood, in Adelaide Hills, this wine is named for the town's first settler. It's 75% Merlot, with Cabernet making up the balance. It smells like mulling spices and Macintosh apples, and tastes like a compote of cherries and plums, plus some caramel. Soft in the mouth; drinkable now. **90** —D.T. (2/1/2004)

Henschke 2002 Lenswood Abbotts Prayer Bordeaux Blend (Adelaide Hills) $70. This is an enjoyable wine, one with coffee and caramel accents on the nose, and plum, berry, and oak flavors. It's hard not to like, but at this price, shouldn't it be love at first sight? Merlot, with some Cab Sauvignon and Cab Franc. **87** —D.T. (8/1/2005)

Henschke 1996 Lenswood Abbotts Prayer Bordeaux Blend (Adelaide Hills) $55. **88** —M.S. (4/1/2000)

Henschke 2002 Cranes Chardonnay (Eden Valley) $38. This is a very good Chardonnay, but one with oak around every turn. Has aromas of caramel, brown sugar, and nut, plus baked apple and caramel flavors. Obviously well made with quality fruit—we'd just like to see a little less wood next vintage. **87** (7/2/2004)

Henschke 2000 Cranes Chardonnay (Eden Valley) $36. There's a distinct hardness to this wine, so that the fruit comes across more as a tough-skinned yellow-plum than as a soft, ripe peach. It's a little stingy on the midpalate, but there are plenty of other things to make up for it. Melon

and pineapple flavors add layers of interest, as does the toasty, nutty finish. **87** —J.C. (7/1/2002)

Henschke 2003 Lenswood Croft Chardonnay (Adelaide Hills) $45. An elegant style and size for Chardonnay, the Croft pleases again this vintage. Smells and tastes lightly nutty, like almonds and walnuts. Fuzzy peach flavors and feel complete the picture. **89** —D.T. (8/1/2005)

Henschke 2002 Lenswood Croft Chardonnay (Adelaide Hills) $40. Lenswood, in the Adelaide Hills, is apple-growing country; "Croft" refers to local apple-grower Frederick Croft. But it's peach and nectarine, not apples, that you get on the nose and palate of this amazing Chardonnay. Fruit tastes juicy and freshly cut on the palate, and is light and delicate on the nose. The cream and vanilla is subtle, despite full malolactic and 50% new French oak. Excellent, delicious, and exciting. **93 Editors' Choice** —D.T. (2/1/2004)

Henschke 1998 Lenswood Croft Chardonnay (Adelaide Hills) $40. **88** (3/1/2000)

Henschke 2001 Lenswood Abbotts Prayer Merlot (Adelaide Hills) $70. **89** —D.T. (8/1/2005)

Henschke 2005 Innes Vineyard Littlehampton Adelaide Hills Pinot Gris (Adelaide Hills) $30. Well balanced, refreshing, and pretty. This PG has intense citrus and pear undertones, with an overarching sweetness that some found to be in the fruity peach-melon camp, and others identified as burnt sugar. In any case, it would pair nicely with a pear, walnut, and mixed greens salad. **89** —D.T. (11/15/2006)

Henschke 2003 Little Hampton Innes Vineyard Pinot Gris (Adelaide Hills) $30. **87** —D.T. (8/1/2005)

Henschke 2002 Little Hampton Innes Vineyard Pinot Gris (Adelaide Hills) $28. Littlehampton is, as its name suggests, a tiny village in the Adelaide Hills. Has really nice fruit, this wine-sweet yellow pear that's been dusted in cake flour, or chalk. [Not exported to the U.S., unfortunately—look for it at Henschke's cellar door.] **89** —D.T. (2/1/2004)

Henschke 2004 Little Hamptons Innes Vineyard Pinot Gris (Adelaide Hills) $30. Smells pretty and feminine—yellow peach, pencil eraser, and a definitive floral quality you might first attribute to Viognier. On the palate, it's delicate and elegant, with yellow peach, honey, and straw flavors. Feels dry and stony, yet smooth. **89** —D.T. (8/1/2005)

Henschke 2002 Henry's Seven Red Blend (Barossa Valley) $30. A blend of 60% Shiraz, 35% Grenache, and 5% Viognier; I enjoyed this year's vintage much more than last year's. It's forward and approachable, with black and red cherry fruit wrapped in a black-earth blanket. **89** —D.T. (5/1/2004)

Henschke 2001 Henry's Seven Red Blend (Barossa Valley) $25. Disappointing, considering the wine's pedigree. Sweet black fruit on the nose follows through to the palate, where it's still sweet, but mighty dilute. Finishes with some oak. What happened? **82** —D.T. (1/1/2002)

Henschke 2000 Keyneton Estate Red Blend (Eden Valley) $40. This blend of Shiraz, Cabernet, and Merlot has bright cassis and raspberry aromas. Plum fruit on the palate is framed by fresh herb and chalk accents. Smooth tannins complete a pretty overall picture. Has wintery pine-needle, or fireplace, aromas on the nose. **89** —D.T. (2/1/2004)

Henschke 2002 Johann's Garden Rhône Red Blend (Eden Valley) $30. This medium-bodied wine features taut plum fruit on the palate, and lots of eucalyptus on the nose and the finish. A strange but very good wine; I picked up a bananalike flavor among the plums on the palate. **87** —D.T. (5/1/2004)

Henschke 2005 Julius Riesling (Eden Valley) $30. Very minerally on the nose, with a twist of fresh citrus. The palate follows suit, with minerality and vibrant citrus characters meshing beautifully through the finish. Acidity is just lively enough. A very pretty wine that relies more on texture than overt fruit to shine. **90** —D.T. (11/15/2006)

Henschke 2003 Julius Riesling (Eden Valley) $23. Named after Stephen Henschke's great uncle, this Riesling is a little chewy in the mouth, with tasty yellow fruit on the palate, and a clean citrus-grass finish. Shows fresh lime juice and sorghum notes on the nose. **88** —D.T. (2/1/2004)

Henschke 2001 Julius Riesling (Eden Valley) $25. For a Riesling, the Julius is no lightweight. It's medium-weight, with pretty flavors of yellow

AUSTRALIA

fruit, resin, honeysuckle, even olive oil. Petrol and minerally notes play on the nose. A very good wine, and one with enough range of flavor to keep you guessing. **89** —*D.T. (8/1/2003)*

Henschke 2003 Lenswood Green's Hill Riesling (Adelaide Hills) $NA. This Adelaide Hills vineyard faces Green's Orchard, and I don't know if it's the power of suggestion or something in the soil, but the wine truly does taste like fresh Granny Smith apples. Smells like green apples (and passion fruit), too. Pair those crisp flavors and aromas with a long finish and a nice, round mouthfeel and you've got an excellent wine. **92** —*D.T. (1/1/2002)*

Henschke 2005 Coralinga Sauvignon Blanc (Adelaide Hills) $27. Smells very pretty, like mineral, lemon meringue, and fresh produce. It's elegant and balanced on the palate, with floral, melon, and minerally notes working in harmony. Fairly long and persistent on the finish. **90** —*D.T. (11/15/2006)*

Henschke 2004 Lenswood Coralinga Sauvignon Blanc (Adelaide Hills) $27. Quite minerally on the nose, with flint and some pickled vegetable to boot. Grapefruit, green apple, and lemon-lime flavors carry the palate to a finish that is tart and tight. Seems to pick up speed along the way, thus it finishes better than it starts. **85** *(7/1/2005)*

Henschke 2003 Lenswood Coralinga Sauvignon Blanc (Adelaide Hills) $23. Not a zesty, zingy style of Sauvignon with searing acids; instead, it's more tempered, with delicate citrus, white peach, and medium body. Smells like fresh produce—the best kind of green. Finishes with good length and green apple flavors. **89** —*D.T. (2/1/2004)*

Henschke 2005 Louis Semillon (Eden Valley) $27. This delicate wine offers a minerally feel, high acidity, and persistent lemon and white pear flavors. Elegant but not overly demonstrative; beeswax candle is the main note on the nose. **88** —*D.T. (11/15/2006)*

Henschke 2002 Louis Semillon (Eden Valley) $25. Smells like a meadow, with fresh grass and flowers at the fore. Apricots and other yellow fruits flavor the mouth. Has good grip in the mouth; a gummy, resinous feel lingers on the tongue and through the finish. A fine wine. **89** —*D.T. (2/1/2004)*

Henschke 1999 Hill of Grace Shiraz (Eden Valley) $350. On the nose, the first aromas are of wheat bread, and a stably-animal character; after a few minutes in the glass, sweet plum and a little caramel steps in. I can't use the descriptors "subtle," "lovely, chalky tannins" and "gorgeous, juicy fruit" enough. Finishes long and juicy, with those lovely, chalky tannins, plus caramel, mocha, and mint flavors. **96 Cellar Selection** —*D.T. (5/1/2004)*

Henschke 1998 Hill of Grace Shiraz (Eden Valley) $300. "Hill of Grace has a smell that reminds me of my grandmother's handbag—cloth, with a wooden handle," says Stephen Henschke. Strange but understandable. I thought it smelled like an odd but nice mix of green olive, eucalyptus, and eggroll wrapper. It's a beautiful wine, with a base of red plums on the palate, dusted with mulling spices. Finishes with a flourish of clay and chalk. As excellent as this wine is, the '99 is even better. **94 Cellar Selection** —*D.T. (2/1/2004)*

Henschke 2001 Mt. Edelstone Shiraz (Eden Valley) $70. My resolution for 2004: To mount a campaign for Mt. Edelstone appreciation, as this excellent wine is always overshadowed in the U.S. by its better-known, smaller-production sibling, Hill of Grace. Mt. Edelstone is a consistent, fabulous wine at a fraction of HOG's price. This vintage shows penetrating spearmint, bread flour, and perfectly ripe red plums on the palate; In perfect balance; it finishes long and red. **94 Editors' Choice** —*D.T. (5/1/2004)*

Henschke 2003 Tilly's Vineyard White Blend (Eden Valley) $NA. A straight ahead, flavorful wine, this 60-40 blend has pleasant grass, hay, and white stone fruit flavors, and a viscous mouthfeel. Finishes with more white peach. Unfortunately not exported to U.S.; Stephen Henschke says that it is most prevalent in Australian cafés. **87** —*D.T. (1/1/2002)*

HENTLEY FARM

Hentley Farm 2002 Shiraz (Barossa Valley) $27. Though I liked this Shiraz's dry, minerally feel, I'm less enthused about its flavors and aromas, which are of the fruitcake/plum/yeast/date ilk. Those who

appreciate these flavors in a wine will like this much more than I did. **84** —*D.T. (10/1/2005)*

HERITAGE ROAD

Heritage Road 1999 Bethany Creek Vineyard Limited Reserve Cabernet Sauvignon (Barossa Valley) $30. Dense all the way, from the dark, almost black color, to the huge aromas of blackberry jam, smoke, and cassis, to the enormously fruity flavors. The texture is massive. This dry, complex wine coats the palate with all sorts of sensations, and the lush, sweet, fruity flavor lasts a full 30 seconds on the finish. **93** —*S.H. (6/1/2002)*

Heritage Road 2000 Old Saxonvale Vineyard Reserve Cabernet Sauvignon (Hunter Valley) $18. Oak and earth are heavy hitters in this wine— Heritage Road isn't paved, is it? If you're looking for fruit, take the road to Barossa. Here, oak suffocates blackberries in the mouth then the flavors drop off. A woody texture persists on the back end. **82** —*D.T. (6/1/2002)*

Heritage Road 1998 Reserve Cabernet Sauvignon (Limestone Coast) $16. **89** *(12/1/2000)*

Heritage Road 1999 Reserve Old Mundulla Vineyard Cabernet Sauvignon (Limestone Coast) $18. Dark and young, it impresses for sheer power. In its youth, it's packed with precocious aromas and flavors of sappy blackberry jam framed in oak, and with a hefty dose of tannins. This young, juicy wine needs time to soften and collect itself, but if the lengthy, elaborate finish is any indication, it will age just fine. **90 Editors' Choice** —*S.H. (9/1/2001)*

Heritage Road 1999 Chardonnay (Hunter Valley) $13. This is an interesting Chardonnay for what it's not: not a blockbuster in terms of fruit, not overwhelming in oak, not an overly sweet puppy, not cheesy and thick from massive lees contact. Instead, it's balanced, one might almost say refined. Don't look for nuances, just enjoy it for what it is. **87** —*S.H. (6/1/2001)*

Heritage Road 1998 Chardonnay (Hunter Valley) $13. **87** *(12/1/2000)*

Heritage Road 2001 Sandy Hollow Vineyard Chardonnay (Hunter Valley) $12. A wonderfully fruity, vibrant wine. Notable for its strong bite of crisp, green apple acidity, almost shocking. Feels young and fresh and delicious. The finish is long and spicy. **88** —*S.H. (1/1/2002)*

Heritage Road 2000 Merlot (South Australia) $12. Earthy aromas of bark and mulch, plus a hint of blackberry, turn sweet in the mouth. It tastes like berry cola with supple tannins, but the residual sugar makes it syrupy. **82** —*S.H. (9/1/2001)*

Heritage Road 2001 Shiraz (South Australia) $12. A big, bold wine that takes no hostages in the mouth. Rolls over the palate with thick but fine tannins and crisp acids that carry jammy blackberry fruit. One-dimensional, but fun to drink with rich foods. **85** —*S.H. (12/15/2002)*

Heritage Road 2000 Shiraz (South Australia) $12. Blackberry and blueberry aromas are accented by hints of chocolate, cream, and mint. Doesn't quite live up that promise in the mouth, where it turns simple and sweetly fruity. **83** *(10/1/2001)*

Heritage Road 1998 Shiraz (South Australia) $10. **88 Best Buy** *(12/1/2000)*

Heritage Road 2000 Mundulla Vineyard Reserve Shiraz (Limestone Coast) $18. **85** *(1/1/2004)*

Heritage Road 1998 Reserve Shiraz (Limestone Coast) $16. **91** *(12/1/2000)*

Heritage Road 1999 Vine Vale Vineyard Limited Release Reserve Shiraz (Barossa Valley) $30. Almost black in color, this big wine begins with impressive aromas of cedar, smoke, and oak, and fruitier notes of black stone fruits and berries. In the mouth, it's huge and assertive, with gigantically jammy fruit. Bone dry tannins and acids provide structural relief, and the finish lasts forever. Definitely a cellar candidate. **91** —*S.H. (1/1/2002)*

Heritage Road 1998 Chardonnay (Hunter Valley) $9. **85** *(10/1/1999)*

HEWITSON

Hewitson 2004 Miss Harry Dry Grown & Ancient G-S-M (Barossa Valley) $20. Serves up plum and red berry flavors and faint black currant aromas. Easygoing and tasty; one to drink over the near term. **87** —*D.T. (4/1/2006)*

Hewitson 2004 Old Garden Mourvèdre (Barossa Valley) $36. Drinkable and enjoyable, and a varietal wine that you just don't run across often. Aromas are of dried plums and dates, with peanut and eucalyptus. Juicy on palate entry, its plum, fruit round and pretty on the palate. Dry on the finish. **88** —*D.T. (8/1/2006)*

Hewitson 1999 Shiraz (Barossa Valley) $27. Red berries, cedar,and a dull red cabbage note open this Shiraz; earthy, red-berry, and burnt-sugar notes carry it through the herb-and-tree-bark finish. Medium to lean in the mouth. **88** *(11/1/2001)*

Hewitson 2001 L'Oizeau Shiraz (McLaren Vale) $27. Medium-bodied, with a soft mouthfeel, this wine is all about black cherry and eucalyptus, top to bottom. It's quite a nice wine, if one that doesn't have too many tricks up its sleeve. **87** —*D.T. (9/1/2004)*

Hewitson 2003 Ned & Henry's Shiraz (Barossa Valley) $20. A well-built but drink-now Shiraz, with all of its elements fitting together very nicely. It is spicy and plummy on the nose, with good acidity, deep plum fruit, and well integrated oak. A little woody on the finish, but overall, it's a very nice package. **89** —*D.T. (10/1/2005)*

HILL OF CONTENT

Hill of Content 2001 Grenache Shiraz Grenache-Syrah (Clare-McClaren Vale) $13. Has pretty aromas of cherry and mocha, and a chewy mouthfeel. Its plum and cherry fruit is bright, but tempered well by darker earth and oak notes. Finishes with tangy tea-oak flavors. The fruit is from Clare Valley (83%) and McLaren Vale (17%). **89** —*D.T. (9/1/2004)*

Hill of Content 2002 Pinot Noir (Victoria) $15. This Pinot is 78% Mornington Peninsula fruit, with the rest coming from the Adelaide Hills. Aromas are of herb and spice, finished off with a chalky, minerally overlay. Round and medium-bodied in the mouth, there's juicy red plum and cherry fruit, with a fresh-herb edge. Finishes with the same fine mineral-powder notes that you get on the nose. **89** —*D.T. (9/1/2004)*

Hill of Content 2004 Benjamin's Blend White Blend (Western Australia) $14. This is an unwooded blend of Chardonnay, Semillon and Sauvignon. Nose offers fresh green bean and grass aromas. Bulky in the mouth, with sour citrus and mineral flavors. **82** —*D.T. (10/1/2005)*

Hill of Content 2002 Benjamin's Blend White Blend (Western Australia) $12. Named for importer John Larchet's son, this wine is a 50% Chardonnay, 39% Sauvignon Blanc, and 11% Semillon., It's round in the mouth, and toes the line between crispness and viscosity. Aromas of hay and olive oil segue to white stone fruit and fresh herb on the palate. Finish is a little bulky, but it's a nice wine overall. **89** —*D.T. (9/1/2004)*

HILLSVIEW VINEYARDS

Hillsview Vineyards 1999 Blewitt Springs Cabernet Sauvignon (Fleurieu Peninsula) $15. The core of this Cab is red plum coated in chalky but smooth tannins that extend through the finish. Nut, toast, and Bourbon-liqueurish aromas emerge on the nose. (Thanks, French oak barrels!) An approachable, yummy Cab...and it won't break the bank, either. **88** —*D.T. (6/1/2003)*

HOFFMANN'S

Hoffmann's 2002 Shiraz (McLaren Vale) $24. Sweet plum fruit is the key component in this very pretty Shiraz; it's pure on the nose, and edged in moderate oak on the palate. Hints of black pepper and dried spice add interest, as do woodsy tannins. Drink 2007–2011. **90** —*D.T. (2/1/2006)*

HOLLICK

Hollick 1997 Bordeaux Blend (Coonawarra) $20. 87 —*M.S. (10/1/2000)*

Hollick 1998 Cabernet Sauvignon-Merlot (Coonawarra) $20. There's a strong green streak running through this wine, so if you enjoy a lot of eucalyptus and herb in your Cabernet, you'll rate it higher. There's some smoke on the nose and modest berry flavors, but overall it doesn't show a lot of fruit. **83** —*J.C. (6/1/2002)*

Hollick 2001 Chardonnay (Coonawarra) $15. We found pear and cinnamon at the core of this medium-weight wine, which is punctuated with a tangy finish. Quite a buttery chard, but a harmonious, very good one. **87** *(7/2/2004)*

Hollick 1999 Chardonnay (Coonawarra) $17. Slightly over the top and disjointed, the sweet honey, butterscotch, toast, and baked Golden Delicious aromas and flavors at war with powerful acids. The elements are all here, just not working together. **83** —*J.C. (7/1/2002)*

Hollick 1998 Reserve Chardonnay (Coonawarra) $17. 91 —*M.M. (10/1/2000)*

Hollick 1998 Wilgha Shiraz (Coonawarra) $34. It seems as if the emphasis is more on the oak than on the fruit. But the oak is darn tasty—toasty, vanillin, and bringing all sorts of dried-spice complexities to the table. The wine is creamy and full enough to support the oak, even if the cherry-berry flavors do take a back seat. **87** —*J.C. (9/1/2002)*

Hollick 1999 Shiraz-Cabernet Sauvignon (Limestone Coast) $17. At 93% Shiraz, many wineries would have just labeled it as Shiraz, but not Hollick. The wine itself has lots of tart, almost sour, cherry fruit that marries well with the earthy, bitter undercurrents. Very smooth and supple in the mouth. Only light tannins make this a wine to drink now. **87** —*J.C. (9/1/2002)*

HOPE ESTATE

Hope Estate 1999 Cabernet Sauvignon (Hunter Valley) $13. The nose of this Bordeaux-like Cabernet displays strong herb and earth tones. Cassis, earth, dried herb, and licorice flavors ride the even, medium-weight palate. The finish is dry, with tart berry and a slight citrus note. **86** *(7/1/2001)*

Hope Estate 1999 Cabernet Sauvignon-Merlot (Hunter Valley) $13. With its forward fruit and touch of toasty oak, this blend of 60% Cabernet Sauvignon and 40% Merlot is soft and easy to like. There's a sweetness to the cherry, vanilla, and cassis flavors, which are supported by bright acidity. The easy structure yields a juicy mouthfeel. **85** —*J.F. (9/1/2001)*

Hope Estate 2005 Chardonnay (Hunter Valley) $10. Only 25% malolactic, and made, as Hope explains, "in the Burgundian style. We don't kill it with oak." Showing white stone fruit, plantain, and just a hint of toast on the nose, with the same notes, and a ribbon of minerality, coming through on the palate. A fresh, easy drinker, and a good bet to keep around the house this summer. **86 Best Buy** *(6/1/2006)*

Hope Estate 2003 Chardonnay (Hunter Valley) $11. Smells like Brazil nuts and talc powder. On the palate, this minerally, dry wine has lingering peach-fuzz flavors. This bottling is not quite as good as last year's, but it's still a great value. 6,000 cases produced. **86 Best Buy** —*D.T. (5/1/2005)*

Hope Estate 2002 Chardonnay (Hunter Valley) $10. One of Hunter's best performers in this tasting. Aromas are racy and slight, like steel and pear, with some cinnamon. Medium-weight in the mouth, there's a nice spine of citrus fluffed up with white peach and very light butter flavors. Well-balanced; it finishes long and a little tart. **88 Best Buy** *(7/2/2004)*

Hope Estate 2000 Chardonnay (Hunter Valley) $10. Starts off with understated aromas of buttered whole-grain toast, pineapple, and tropical that gradually build in intensity, finishing with a blast of toasty American oak, vanilla, and spice. It's slightly unpolished, but flavorful and full of character. **87** —*J.C. (7/1/2002)*

Hope Estate 1999 Chardonnay (Hunter Valley) $10. Ripe and buttery with tropical fruit and oak on the nose, this Chardonnay has decent mouthfeel and an attractive sweet-tart profile. The apple-pear flavors wear lots of citrus and spicy oak on the back end. It's not complex, but it's as pleasant as a g'day. **86** *(7/1/2001)*

Hope Estate 2005 Merlot (Hunter Valley) $10. This Merlot has good acidity and none of the green, underripe notes that typically plague Merlots at this price point. Blueberry and graphite notes rule both the nose and palate, with some plummy fullness on the midpalate as well. **86 Best Buy** *(6/1/2006)*

Hope Estate 2003 Merlot (Hunter Valley) $11. It's hard to find good Merlots in Australia; it's even harder to find one that's such a bargain. Offers brambly, tangy oak aromas that carry through to the palate. The feel is dusty, the fruit treading the black-cherry and tangy plum track. **86 Best Buy** —*D.T. (4/1/2006)*

Hope Estate 1999 Merlot (Hunter Valley) $13. There's a nice, jammy, berry, and herb nose here with a touch of weediness among the fruit and cedar flavors on the palate. Light-to-medium-weight and smootly

AUSTRALIA

textured, it has balance, and berry and cocoa flavors. Singing on the nose, even on the palate, it's turns astringent on the back end. **85** *(7/1/2001)*

Hope Estate 2002 Estate Merlot (Hunter Valley) $15. Smells and tastes like sweet fruit plus tree bark and earth. Fruit on the palate tastes a little overripe and has a metallic tinge; finishes with a curry-like note. **83** —*D.T. (12/1/2005)*

Hope Estate 1998 Shiraz (Hunter Valley) $13. 83 *(4/1/2000)*

Hope Estate 2005 Shiraz (Hunter Valley) $10. Jam, bramble, and clay aromas usher in fresh grape, blackberry, and black pepper flavors. Medium bodied, closing with spicy purple fruit. Still very young when evaluated; by the time it hits stores this summer, this should be ready to drink. **87 Best Buy** *(6/1/2006)*

Hope Estate 2003 Shiraz (Hunter Valley) $10. Full and fleshy, almost stewed, on the nose, with brambly, peppery notes offsetting plum fruit on the palate. Smooth in the mouth, though a hair short on the finish. **85 Best Buy** *(6/1/2006)*

Hope Estate 2000 Shiraz (Hunter Valley) $14. Dark, brooding aromas (black cherry, leather, balsamic vinegar) open onto an equally dark—though tart—bitter chocolate/blackberry/grape palate. Medium-weight with decent structure, this Aussie finishes with coffee, sour plums, and leather. **85** *(10/1/2001)*

Hope Estate 1999 Shiraz (Hunter Valley) $13. Opens deep and inky with prune, licorice, chocolate, Asian spices, and a touch of leather. If you think that's a lot of nose for a $13 Shiraz, you're right. The almost full-bodied palate delivers nicely on the bouquet's promise, with a creamy feel and bright, Port-like flavors—nuts, chocolate, and prunes. Finishes with good length and more of the same delicious stuff. Grab a case for summer fun. **89 Best Buy** *(7/1/2001)*

Hope Estate 2003 The Ripper Shiraz (Western Australia) $16. Fragrant on the nose, with cool cherry and menthol undertones. On the palate, it's powerful but restrained, with fresh herb hints and crisp, red raspberry and cherry fruit and the barest hint of cranberry at the core. Wood is very well integrated; texture is suede-smooth. **90** —*D.T. (2/1/2006)*

Hope Estate 2004 The Ripper! Shiraz (Western Australia) $15. Deep inky-red in color, this Shiraz's name is an easy clue to how it behaves in the mouth. It's a wine to be reckoned with, full and round. It offers very ripe purple fruit, white pepper, and even some Porty notes on both the nose and the palate, and feels bigger than its modest (for Australia) 14.5% alcohol. Finishes warm and spicy. **89** *(6/1/2006)*

Hope Estate 2004 Verdelho (Hunter Valley) $9. Bravo to winemaker Michael Hope, bringing Verdelho to value hunters. Offers melon, mango, even curry aromas. Though it is a little heavy on the palate, its peach and pear flavors are pleasing and refreshing. And what a bargain! 3,000 cases produced. **85 Best Buy** —*D.T. (8/1/2005)*

Hope Estate 2002 Verdelho (Hunter Valley) $8. Medium-bodied and round, this Verdelho doesn't give up more than some light fruit-skin flavors on the palate. The nose yields traces of butter and yellow fruit but that, too, isn't talking much. What's here is a start, but it wants a little more oomph. **84** —*D.T. (12/31/2003)*

Hope Estate 2000 Verdelho (Hunter Valley) $9. A wax, hay, smoke, and even sandalwood nose opens to a sweet, grapey palate with nut accents. But very high acidity detracts from this bottle's pleasant front end. It closes very briskly, with citrus, spice, and a cutting feel. **84** —*M.M. (2/1/2002)*

Hope Estate 1998 Verdelho (Hunter Valley) $9. This pleasant, medium-weight white from an Iberian grape shows why it has caught on among our adventurous Aussie cousins. The nose of tangerine, hay, and a mild stony note opens to a mouth full of melon, citrus, and herb flavors. It sports a tangy citrus finish. **87 Best Buy** *(7/1/2001)*

Hope Estate 2005 Estate Verdelho (Hunter Valley) $10. Offers good structure and juicy stone fruit at a giveaway price. This dry white is medium-sized, with straw and nut accents to its ripe stone fruit flavors. Offers meaty, nutty accents on the nose, too. A fine introduction to a variety that is just making its way in the U.S. **86 Best Buy** —*D.T. (11/15/2005)*

HOUGHTON

Houghton 2005 Chardonnay (Western Australia) $15. Receives what Houghton calls a whisper of oak; indeed, most of its flavors—modest peach and citrus—are at a muted volume. Still, this is a good, dry, austere style of Chard, appropriate for the pre-dinner cocktail hour. **86** —*D.T. (4/1/2006)*

Houghton 2004 Red Blend (Western Australia) $15. Meaty aromas make way for a red blend that's light in the mouth with a nice, chalky-rocky grab on the midpalate. Simple and quaffable; reminiscent of a basic Côtes-du-Rhône in size and style. **86** —*D.T. (8/1/2006)*

Houghton 2005 Semillon-Sauvignon Blanc (Western Australia) $15. Offers up pretty white peach and floral aromas, while the palate deals some pink grapefruit and grass notes. Not very giving flavorwise; with more acidity, it would be just the thing for oysters. **84** —*D.T. (8/1/2006)*

Houghton 2005 Shiraz (Western Australia) $15. A juicy, drink-now Shiraz with some complexity. Meaty, olive-y aromas start it all off, and raspberry and chocolaty oak notes follow through on the palate. Drinkable, accessible, and enjoyable. **89** —*D.T. (8/1/2006)*

Houghton 2005 White Blend (Western Australia) $15. Two-thirds Chardonnay with Verdelho making up the balance, this is a pretty unique white. Has grassy notes on the nose, which join with pretty pungent notes of tangerine and peach on the palate. Soft and round in the mouth, it finishes with an orange-y note. **87** —*D.T. (8/1/2006)*

HOWARD PARK

Howard Park 2001 Mad Fish Bordeaux Blend (Western Australia) $16. This Bordeaux-style blend doesn't show much on the nose at first, but with air, you'll see very pretty red fruit and some dried spice. On the palate, the plum fruit is pure—not sweet, but nicely ripe. Medium in body with tealike tannins, it closes darker than it begins, with tea and oak flavors. A lovely wine. **89** —*D.T. (9/1/2004)*

Howard Park 2002 Cabernet Sauvignon (Western Australia) $37. This is a sleek, Old World kind of Cabernet Sauvignon with a crisp, black cherry focus and a dusty mouthfeel. Bramble and earth aromas go the way of tomato after some air, which was a detraction for me, but otherwise, a very enjoyable wine. **88** —*D.T. (4/1/2006)*

Howard Park 2001 Cabernet Sauvignon (Western Australia) $37. A taut, laced-up, good-acid wine with plenty of black pepper and high-toned cherry aromas and flavors. Comes together fairly well with some air, but the feel and complexity isn't quite up to some of the winery's previous offerings. **87** —*D.T. (8/1/2005)*

Howard Park 2003 Leston Cabernet Sauvignon (Margaret River) $21. This big, dark wine has blackberry jam and a little brown sugar on the nose, with anise and black cherry fruit taking over on the palate. The fruit's juicy but has a taut, sour edge that restrains it. Finishes with woodsy tannins. New World through and through; drink over the next four years. **89** —*D.T. (8/1/2006)*

Howard Park 2002 Leston Cabernet Sauvignon (Margaret River) $21. The Leston Cab is excellent again this year, with juicy, ripe black- and blueberries from start to finish. Has a smooth feel—like washed river rocks—and earthy, iron-ore nuances on the nose. Drinkable now, but will hold 3–5 years. **90** —*D.T. (12/1/2005)*

Howard Park 2001 Leston Cabernet Sauvignon (Margaret River) $30. Tastes like the essence of ripe blackberries but as with the best wines, texture is everything. It's velvety and rich in the mouth, with chewy tannins. On the finish, the blackberry plays on, leaving little room for the oak-nut accents that peek through. Nose has permeating menthol and black pepper notes. **91** —*D.T. (5/1/2004)*

Howard Park 2003 Scotsdale Cabernet Sauvignon (Great Southern) $21. Full but not overoaked nor overly rich, the Scotsdale Cab is a winner this vintage. The nose's black cherry, clay, and light herb notes get deeper the longer the wine sits. On the palate, smoldering, smoky notes envelope tight red cherry and berry flavors. Seems to have an almost Chianti-like, iron-ore core. Very nice. Probably best drunk after 2009. **91** —*D.T. (8/1/2006)*

Howard Park 2002 Scotsdale Cabernet Sauvignon (Great Southern) $21. Has a green asparagus or pepper streak on the nose, plus a dominant acorn note that continues through to the palate, where there's also some just-ripe plum buried under mounds of dust. Winemaker Mike Kerrigan thinks that this is the style of wine that shines better with food, rather than in a wine-by-wine lineup. He's probably right. **86**—*D.T. (10/1/2005)*

Howard Park 2001 Scotsdale Cabernet Sauvignon (Great Southern) $30. The Scotsdale has a straightforward plum-berry profile, with a creamy mouthfeel. Tannins cling nicely on the finish. Not as good in this reviewer's opinion as Howard Park's Leston Cab—but at least there is regional difference between the bottlings. **87**—*D.T. (5/1/2004)*

Howard Park 1999 Cabernet Sauvignon-Merlot (Western Australia) $48. Chalky, fine tannins coat black plum fruit in the mouth. Earthy notes on both the nose and the palate, and on through the finish, give the wine an even darker cloak. **88** *(10/1/2003)*

Howard Park 2004 Chardonnay (Great Southern) $26. Not tropical or woody; flavors stay the pear and citrus track (there's even a hint of SB-like grassiness), while a stony smoothness seals the deal. It's an acidic, food-friendly style, but not a terribly round one—and that's fine, particularly when ceviche or salads are on the menu. **88**—*D.T. (10/1/2006)*

Howard Park 2001 Chardonnay (Western Australia) $25. The fruit here is nice, bright, and peach—it's so nice, in fact, that I kind of wish that the toffee and butterscotch flavors would take a backseat and let the fruit through a little more. Round and a little oily in the mouth, it finishes with ample toast. **88** *(10/1/2003)*

Howard Park 2003 Mad Fish Chardonnay (Western Australia) $18. An unwooded Chardonnay, with a peach-and-citrus profile. Soft and smooth in the mouth, the wine finishes with pear. Enjoyable, and easy to drink. **88** *(7/2/2004)*

Howard Park 2002 Mad Fish Chardonnay (Western Australia) $16. The nose and the palate offer all kinds of tropical fruit—think pineapple, mango, and passion fruit. But the wine's not sweet or candied; a nice, minerally mouthfeel keeps the fruit in check. Finishes strong and sleek, with chalk and minerals. **89**—*D.T. (10/1/2003)*

Howard Park 2005 Riesling (Western Australia) $20. Acidic, refreshing, very dry, and very citrusy. Offers bright citrus, mineral, and melon aromas, along with lemon and grapefruit flavors. A good bet if seafood is on the menu, or if the temperature outside is soaring. **89**—*D.T. (10/1/2006)*

Howard Park 2003 Leston Shiraz (Margaret River) $21. Profoundly plum-my on the nose, with blueberry in the secondary role. On the palate, the Leston is broad, its black- and blueberry flavors a little tangy at first, but softening with air. Finishes with lively doses of black pepper and menthol. Very pretty. **90**—*D.T. (8/1/2006)*

Howard Park 2002 Leston Shiraz (Margaret River) $21. Such a juicy wine. Well-ripened plums, blackberries, and raspberries dominate the palate, though here and on the nose there are tea and earth accents, too. Takes on hints of anise with air. Drinking well now. **89**—*D.T. (10/1/2005)*

Howard Park 2001 Leston Shiraz (Margaret River) $30. All Margaret River fruit, from the same parcel of the Leston Vineyard. This is a very nicely done Shiraz, with black-as-night aromas, and, on the palate, chewy plum fruit dusted with earth and bread flour. Chewy tannins on the finish. **90**—*D.T. (11/15/2004)*

Howard Park 2000 Leston Shiraz (Margaret River) $30. A well-made, enjoyable Shiraz, with predictably pleasurable blackberry and toast flavors hanging on a woodsy-tannin frame. Offers mixed plum fruit on the nose, and vanilla on the finish. **89** *(10/1/2003)*

Howard Park 2002 Mad Fish Shiraz (Western Australia) $18. A quirky, crazy mix of black plum, acorns, fresh-cut grass, and a little pickle-barrel on the nose, but it settles down into something quite nice on the palate. Tannins are soft; no-nonsense plum fruit has undertones of brown-red clay. Finishes with a burst of mocha, coffee, and eucalyptus. **89**—*D.T. (11/15/2004)*

Howard Park 2001 Mad Fish Shiraz (Western Australia) $16. Medium-bodied and straightforward; fruit is mostly red with some blackberries. Red fruit is sweet on the nose—think strawberry and raspberry—and is joined with dusty tannins on the finish. **85**—*D.T. (10/1/2003)*

Howard Park 2004 Scotsdale Shiraz (Great Western) $20. Though the nose is really sexy, with cinnamon and lush berry aromas, the palate isn't revealing its best yet. Fruit is sturdy but still tight, and the oak unintegrated. In three years, this score could look stingy. **89**—*D.T. (11/15/2006)*

Howard Park 2003 Scotsdale Shiraz (Great Southern) $21. This vintage doesn't really gel with the wine's typically earthy character, but it is delicious, in any case. This year there's cherry and light spice on the nose, and a palate brimming with juicy plums and black cherries. The feel is excellent—like smooth stone or clay. **92 Editors' Choice**—*D.T. (8/1/2006)*

Howard Park 2002 Scotsdale Shiraz (Great Southern) $21. Crisp, racy, and minty; I liked this wine more than I generally like HP's very earthy Scotsdale bottlings. This Shiraz is probably just as earthy as the rest, but is balanced out by eucalyptus, black pepper, curry, black cherry, and plum flavors. Medium-sized, with a smooth feel. **90**—*D.T. (12/1/2005)*

Howard Park 2001 Scotsdale Shiraz (Margaret River) $30. I somehow always prefer HP's Leston Shiraz to the Scotsdale, but at least the two bottlings do have their own personalities. This wine has woodsy tannins, and a slight greenness mixed in with its black grape and plum fruit. Finishes woody and wooly, with that leaf-stem flavor again. The note that is offputting to this reviewer stems from terroir, not flawed winemaking; the wine may be more attractive to others. **86**—*D.T. (11/15/2004)*

Howard Park 2000 Scottsdale Shiraz (Margaret River) $30. Heavy on the herb-and-black pepper combination, which turns some people off, this reviewer included. Black fruit hides underneath, couched in smooth, woody tannins. If you can get past the pungent aromas and flavors, you'll like it even more. **86**—*D.T. (10/1/2003)*

HUGH HAMILTON

Hugh Hamilton 1998 Shiraz (McLaren Vale) $16. Dark, sour cherry, anise, and oak flavors make this already lean wine seem even leaner. Soy, mint, toasted grains and sour cherry aromas are more appealing than they sound. Finishes very dry with lemony-cola flavors. **86** *(10/1/2001)*

HUNTER VALLEY ELEMENTS

Hunter Valley Elements 1999 Shiraz (Hunter Valley) $20. Blends wood-derived elements of caramel, toast, and spice with blackberry and plum fruit in a well-balanced, medium-weight format. Bright acidity accents the cranberryish flavors before dry woody tannins take over on the finish. Short-term cellaring (six to nine months or so) should help smooth the rough edges. **86** *(10/1/2001)*

INDIS

Indis 2004 Chardonnay (Western Australia) $15. Smells spicy and tropical, like something that you would want to drink on a beach vacation. The palate deals pineapple and coconut flavors, and good acidity. (Disclaimer: This review makes this wine sound sweeter and simpler than it actually is, but that's because I can't play steel-drum music in the background, and throw some sand between your toes.) **87**—*D.T. (12/1/2005)*

INNOCENT BYSTANDER

Innocent Bystander 2004 Pinot Gris (Yarra Valley) $20. I really liked this white newcomer, and its fancy Bonny Doon-meets-film noir packaging. The wine displays light bread-flour and white-peach aromas, as well as yellow stone-fruit flavors and a lingering, minerally feel. A welcome addition to the few Oz Pinot Gris that we see here in the States. **88**—*D.T. (5/1/2005)*

Innocent Bystander 2004 Rose Pinot Noir (Yarra Valley) $16. I like this wine, though it is a little odd. The wine's cherry fruit also takes on an interesting orange character, through and through, plus accents of lavender. Closes taut, with sour cherries and citrus. Give it a go. 300 cases produced. **87**—*D.T. (10/1/2005)*

Innocent Bystander 2002 Sangiovese Merlot Red Blend (South Eastern Australia) $20. This 49% Sangiovese, 46% Merlot, 5% Cab smells of fresh black and red grapes. It tastes pretty darned good, proof to any naysayers that experimenting with unusual blends is working well in Oz.

AUSTRALIA

AUSTRALIA

Plum and blackberry fruit dominate on the full, round palate, with oak riding in the backseat. 300 cases produced. **87** —*D.T. (8/1/2005)*

IRONWOOD

Ironwood 2003 Chardonnay (South Eastern Australia) $6. A straightforward South Eastern Australian offering that won't ruffle any feathers. Aromas are of golden apples and toast, and it tastes as it smells. Citrus accents bring it to a dry close. **85 Best Buy** —*D.T. (12/31/2004)*

Ironwood 2002 Shiraz (South Eastern Australia) $6. Smells and tastes like red plums, top to bottom, with a moderate amount of oak. A simple quaffing wine, but oh, look at that price. **84 Best Buy** —*D.T. (5/1/2005)*

IRVINE

Irvine 2002 Unoaked Chardonnay (Eden Valley) $16. Unoaked though it may be, we picked up a lot of nut, plus dusty yellow fruit, on the nose. Tastes perfumey and talcy, like a lady's dressing room, with spicedrops, pear, and melon in the background. Finish is tangy. **84** *(7/2/2004)*

JACKAROO

JackaRoo 2003 Chardonnay (South Eastern Australia) $9. For those who don't know, a JackaRoo is sort of the Aussie equivalent of a cowboy. Has flavors of watermelon, apple, and citrus, with a candied, Jolly Rancher-esque finish. Simple, with a sweet style that will have its fans. **83** *(7/2/2004)*

Jackaroo 2001 Big Red Red Blend (South Eastern Australia) $7. A blend of Cabernet Sauvignon, Shiraz and Merlot. Carmel, red fruit, and herb aromas lead to a middle-weight palate that offers up plum and cherry fruit. Mouthfeel is soft; finishes with earth, plum, and orange-pekoe tea. An easy drinking wine, and a good choice if you're trying to sidestep the overly sweet and candied wines that are sometimes offered at this price point. **86 Best Buy** —*D.T. (12/31/2004)*

Jackaroo 2001 Shiraz (South Eastern Australia) $7. A straightforward, fruit-sweet wine, full of juicy red plums on the palate, and sweet berry fruit on the nose. A drying orange-tea flavor and feel wraps it up. Drink now. **86** —*D.T. (11/15/2004)*

JACOB'S CREEK

Jacob's Creek 2003 Cabernet Sauvignon (South Eastern Australia) $9. Straightforward and lacking stuffing, this Cab has some berry fruit tucked under a veneer of oak. Aromas of soy sauce, plum, and putty complete the picture. **83** —*D.T. (12/31/2005)*

Jacob's Creek 2002 Cabernet Sauvignon (South Eastern Australia) $9. Aromas are of black cherry and bramble. Plum fruit is couched in sawdusty tannins. Tastes like a wine made in the winery, with added bells and whistles. **83** —*D.T. (11/15/2004)*

Jacob's Creek 2001 Cabernet Sauvignon (South Eastern Australia) $10. With taut plum fruit and dry tannins, this is a good introductory Cabernet—nothing that veers off the course of predictable, which is understandable, considering how much of this hits the market. Briary, oaky notes and a dash of eucalyptus set off the fruit. **84** —*D.T. (6/1/2003)*

Jacob's Creek 1998 Cabernet Sauvignon (Barossa Valley) $11. Deep cassis aromas, a touch of licorice, and menthol notes on the nose open to a palate of black currant and cocoa flavors in this well-balanced, medium-weight wine. Nicely structured, it finishes with good length and moderate tannins; can be cellared a few years. **88 Best Buy** *(2/1/2001)*

Jacob's Creek 2002 Reserve Cabernet Sauvignon (South Australia) $13. Very dark in color. This wine's aromas are pretty straightforward, just red berry and wood. On the palate, there's red fruit and earth. The highlight here is the wine's velvety, wooly texture. It's mainstream, yes, but it's food-friendly and tasty. **88 Best Buy** —*D.T. (12/31/2005)*

Jacob's Creek 2001 Reserve Cabernet Sauvignon (South Australia) $13. Bouncy plum fruit revs up on the nose and just doesn't quit until the end. Its sweetness is more ripeness than sugar; it fades away with smooth tannins on the back. It may only have a few tricks up its sleeve, but they're amusing enough to keep you interested. **88 Best Buy** —*D.T. (2/1/2004)*

Jacob's Creek 2003 Cabernet Sauvignon-Merlot (South Eastern Australia) $9. Smells okay, but overdone and syrupy. Has a metallic note on the palate, plus sour berry and plum fruit. Tasted twice. **82** —*D.T. (8/1/2005)*

Jacob's Creek 2002 Cabernet Sauvignon-Merlot (South Australia) $9. This particular blend is only available on the U.S. market. Back by popular demand, there's sturdy red plums here, with just a few taut cranberries thrown in. Soft and straightforward in the mouth; drying herbs tie it up on the finish. Has a tautness that reminds me of Sangiovese. **86 Best Buy** —*D.T. (2/1/2004)*

Jacob's Creek NV Brut Cuvee Champagne Blend (South Eastern Australia) $12. Chief Winemaker Philip Laffer says that he wanted this wine to be of an "aperitif style…that once you count to five, it should all disappear." In both respects, the wine succeeds. It's 20% Pinot Noir, with very light stone fruit flavors and wide foamy mousse on the palate. Chalk and stone fruit flash on the finish. Only 3 or 4,000 cases on the U.S. market now, but many more are sure to follow. **85 Best Buy** —*D.T. (2/1/2004)*

Jacob's Creek 2005 Chardonnay (South Eastern Australia) $8. Smooth in the mouth, this Chard starts off with citrus and dust aromas with a light edging of cake frosting. In the mouth, it's tauter and more austere than it usually is. Clean and not a vibrant wine, but that's a matter of preference. **84 Best Buy** —*D.T. (8/1/2006)*

Jacob's Creek 2004 Chardonnay (South Eastern Australia) $8. Aromas are of hard cheese rind and butter. On the palate, the wine is dilute and shapeless, with little more taste than a flavored mineral water or club soda. **81** —*D.T. (5/1/2005)*

Jacob's Creek 2003 Chardonnay (South Eastern Australia) $8. Has feminine, talc, and floral aromas, and sour, citrusy yellow fruit flavors. Mouthfeel is wide and somewhat viscous. It grows leaner on the finish, with citrus peel and fresh green-produce flavors. **84** *(7/2/2004)*

Jacob's Creek 2002 Chardonnay (South Eastern Australia) $9. Pleasant but nothing out of the ordinary, this Chard has peach and nectarine flavors, with a noticeable underlay of oak. Nose is rather closed, giving not much more than a little oak. **84** —*D.T. (6/1/2003)*

Jacob's Creek 2001 Chardonnay (South Eastern Australia) $8. Slightly lean, the emphasis in this Chard is on Asian pear and citrus aromas and flavors. Picks up some tangy pineapple notes on the clean, zesty finish. **84** —*J.C. (7/1/2002)*

Jacob's Creek 2000 Chardonnay (Barossa Valley) $10. This defines mainstream, affordable Chardonnay via its soft apple, pear, and pineapple bouquet, pleasing mouthfeel, and nice, lightly sweet blend of fruit, butter, and spice elements on the palate and finish. **87 Best Buy** *(2/1/2001)*

Jacob's Creek 1999 Chardonnay (South Eastern Australia) $9. 85 —*J.C. (5/1/2000)*

Jacob's Creek 2002 Limited Release Chardonnay (Barossa Valley) $33. This is a solid wine—and one whose food-pairing possibilities could run into the dozens. In the mouth it's smooth, with subtle oak that's more nutty than it is toasty. Yellow fruit makes for a sturdy core, with peach and pear peel dryness on the finish. **89** —*D.T. (11/15/2004)*

Jacob's Creek 2000 Limited Release Chardonnay (Padthaway) $33. Medium and smooth in the mouth, Jacob's Creek's top Chard has stone and star fruits at its core, and a sleek mineral quality. Creamy on the nose, but with a lively lime streak that keeps it crisp. Finishes medium-long with drying minerals. **89** *(6/1/2003)*

Jacob's Creek 1997 Limited Release Chardonnay (Padthaway) $38. Nutty, toasty, and tropical-fruit elements are nicely balanced in this wine's appealing bouquet. Subdued tropical-fruit flavors, mineral notes, and a buttery, elegant mouthfeel with good acidity follow. The lengthy finish shows lingering, complex fruit flavors. **90** *(2/1/2001)*

Jacob's Creek 2004 Reserve Chardonnay (South Australia) $13. Though this is the reserve-tier Chard, it seems simpler than the other Jacob's Creek offering. This one deals confection on multiple levels: It smells like glazed donut, and has a flavor not unlike lemon pudding. Soft and full, but missing some heft in the middle. **83** —*D.T. (8/1/2006)*

Jacob's Creek 2003 Reserve Chardonnay (South Eastern Australia) $13. Peach, butter, and oak aromas and flavors make for a please-everyone style of wine. It's a medium-sized, food-friendly, reliably good Chardonnay. 444,000 cases produced. **86** —D.T. (10/1/2005)

Jacob's Creek 2002 Reserve Chardonnay (South Australia) $13. A refreshing, lighter-style Chard, with just a hint of buttercream from the 35% that goes through malolactic. Flavors are largely of white peach, with a swipe of oak on the back end. **88 Best Buy** —D.T. (2/1/2004)

Jacob's Creek 2001 Reserve Chardonnay (South Australia) $13. Taut yellow fruit laced with a bit of citrus peel—that's pretty much what you get here—make this Chard a potential match for seafood, particularly white fish or scallops. Medium-weight in the mouth, with only a hint of that butteriness that can be either a blessing or a curse. **84** —D.T. (6/1/2003)

Jacob's Creek 2000 Reserve Chardonnay (South Australia) $14. If you favor tropical flavors in your Chardonnay, here's one you'll love. Pineapple, coconut, and vanilla aromas blend together artfully on the palate in this surprisingly lightweight wine. Picks up lots of spicy oak on the citrus-flavored finish. **85** —J.C. (7/1/2002)

Jacob's Creek 1999 Reserve Chardonnay (Barossa Valley) $16. This strongly-oaked wine has apple, lemon, and toast aromas that open to a similar palate displaying pear elements and a buttery feel. Full on the nose and palate, this wine, 100% barrel fermented in French oak, finishes long with spicy notes. **88** (2/1/2001)

Jacob's Creek 1998 Reserve Chardonnay (Padthaway) $16. 88 (5/1/2000)

Jacob's Creek 1997 Reserve Chardonnay (Padthaway) $14. 85 (10/1/1999)

Jacob's Creek 2004 Merlot (South Eastern Australia) $9. Nose is hard to read, but shows a little toasted coconut. The palate offers some plum and cherry fruit; finish grows woody with air. A good, straight ahead Merlot. **83** —D.T. (10/1/2005)

Jacob's Creek 2003 Merlot (South Eastern Australia) $9. Has a nice gum-eraser aroma and texture that you don't typically get in wines at this price. There's also hints of nail polish remover in the midpalate. Finishes short. **83** —D.T. (3/1/2005)

Jacob's Creek 2002 Merlot (South Eastern Australia) $9. This Merlot doesn't taste as sweet as many others that you find at the price point, but it's also not a very concentrated wine. Sweet red plum and herb aromas take on beefy, coffee accents with air. Plum and berry flavors marry with chocolate, or mocha, on the palate. Finishes a bit metallic. **84** —D.T. (9/1/2004)

Jacob's Creek 2001 Merlot (South Eastern Australia) $10. Red cherry fruit is swathed in oaky tannins, which continue on through to the finish. A good entry-level Merlot for casual circumstances. **84** —D.T. (6/1/2003)

Jacob's Creek 2000 Merlot (South Eastern Australia) $10. Starts off slowly, then gradually adds grassy, smoky notes to simple strawberry aromas. Tart cherries, sour herbs, and a trace of cocoa on the palate. **82** —J.C. (6/1/2002)

Jacob's Creek 1998 Merlot (South Eastern Australia) $10. 84 (5/1/2000)

Jacob's Creek 2002 Red Blend (South Eastern Australia) $9. Purple in color, with syrupy aromas that carry a hint of cinnamon and spice. This youngster is meant to be drunk now—and probably without much analysis. It's a quaffer, one with a bulky, chewy body and full tannic grip. Almost certainly it went through carbonic maceration, a fermentation method that pumps up sweetness several times over. **83** —M.S. (12/15/2002)

Jacob's Creek 2005 Riesling (South Eastern Australia) $9. Floral and talc aromas return on the palate, which tastes of honeysuckle and some melon. Not much spine here, but it's a decent, value-priced quaff. **84** —D.T. (4/1/2006)

Jacob's Creek 2004 Riesling (South Eastern Australia) $9. Smells like dusty peaches. On the palate, it offers yellow gumdrop flavors that start off fairly flavorfully, but quickly go dilute, then flavorless, by the finish. **82** —D.T. (12/1/2005)

Jacob's Creek 2002 Riesling (Barossa Valley) $9. 84 —D.T. (2/1/2004)

Jacob's Creek 2004 Reserve Riesling (South Australia) $13. Offers perfumed floral/minerally notes on the nose. The palate deals citrus and dust flavors that aren't very detailed. A fine quaff. **84** —D.T. (8/1/2006)

Jacob's Creek 2003 Reserve Riesling (Clare Valley) $13. A pleasing powder puff of a wine, one that feels round and airy in the mouth, with a chalky flavor throughout. Finishes with fluffy lemon meringue. **88 Best Buy** —D.T. (2/1/2004)

Jacob's Creek 2002 Reserve Riesling (South Australia) $14. Whereas other Oz Rieslings can be described as having light chalky notes, this one's got rocks and boulders. It's dry in the mouth, with lime skin and a bold rocky-slatey sort of minerality. Has a slight spritz in the mouth, with star fruit on the finish and melon notes on the nose. **87** —D.T. (8/1/2003)

Jacob's Creek 2004 Semillon-Chardonnay (South Eastern Australia) $8. The nose is pretty fragrant—floral, honey, sour apple, and pear notes—but the sour apple and pear flavors on the palate are dilute. Wants more intensity. **83** —D.T. (4/1/2006)

Jacob's Creek 2003 Semillon-Chardonnay (South Eastern Australia) $8. Fragrances of talc, white stone fruit, and Silly Putty make for an interesting, eye-opening nose. On the palate, the wine feels round and minerally, but is not very demonstrative in terms of flavor, beyond some fresh citrus and herb notes. Easy-drinking and straightforward. **84 Best Buy** —D.T. (11/15/2004)

Jacob's Creek 2000 Semillon-Chardonnay (Barossa Valley) $8. The tangy grapefruit, lemon, and pear notes on the nose carry over nicely to the palate. Subtle underlying tropical fruit adds dimension, the mouthfeel has a creamy texture (from the Semillon), and it finishes dry and clean. **85** (2/1/2001)

Jacob's Creek 2005 Semillon-Sauvignon Blanc (South Eastern Australia) $8. This Semillon-Sauvignon is not a super flavorful or profound wine, but it gets the job done when a clean, workhouse white is in order. Offers notes of wet stone and citrus pith, from beginning to end. **84 Best Buy** —D.T. (8/1/2006)

Jacob's Creek 1998 Shiraz (South Eastern Australia) $10. 88 Best Buy (5/1/2000)

Jacob's Creek 2000 Shiraz (South Eastern Australia) $10. The bouquet is clean, offering a good mix of berries and oak. The palate drives forward with vital fruit and drying oak, while the finish is toasty, with vanilla coming on late. This wine is firm, balanced and tasty. At all check points it belies its value price. **87 Best Buy** —M.S. (3/1/2003)

Jacob's Creek 1999 Shiraz (South Eastern Australia) $11. With its restrained fruit, this wine is more food accompaniment than stand-alone quaff. The smoky, weedy aromas and flavors positively demand a juicy burger to bring out the underlying cassis and tobacco. **84** —J.C. (9/1/2002)

Jacob's Creek 1998 Shiraz (South Eastern Australia) $9. 87 Best Buy (3/1/2000)

Jacob's Creek 2001 Reserve Shiraz (South Australia) $13. Offers juicy, attractive plum fruit at a good price, and finishes with red clay flavors. It's forward and accessible, not complicated but still very good. **88 Best Buy** —D.T. (2/1/2004)

Jacob's Creek 1999 Reserve Shiraz (South Australia) $18. 87 (9/1/2002)

Jacob's Creek 1998 Reserve Shiraz (Barossa Valley) $18. The blackberry, vanilla, and toasty oak elements are nicely balanced on the nose and in the mouth. Deep fruit shines, and the supple mouthfeel is very appealing. Finishes long, with a compelling back-end bouquet that completes the package in fine style. **91** (2/1/2001)

Jacob's Creek 1997 Reserve Shiraz (Barossa Valley) $15. 89 (5/1/2000)

Jacob's Creek 2004 Shiraz-Cabernet Sauvignon (South Eastern Australia) $8. Shoots for a mouthfilling style, but misses the mark. Though the feel is halfhearted, this red has a pleasing mocha/oak shell and black berry and raspberry aromas. **83** —D.T. (11/1/2006)

Jacob's Creek 2002 Shiraz-Cabernet Sauvignon (South Eastern Australia) $8. Aromas are of sweet, dark fruit, roasted meat, and oak. Mouthfeel is somewhat dusty, with pedestrian red and black fruit, bolstered by just enough oak. **84 Best Buy** —D.T. (12/31/2004)

Jacob's Creek 2001 Shiraz-Cabernet Sauvignon (South Eastern Australia) $9. Red fruit, earth, and oak go the way of sweet and creamy in terms of flavor and aroma. Has gritty tannins in the mouth, and plenty of wood on the finish. **83** —D.T. (1/1/2002)

Jacob's Creek 2000 Shiraz-Cabernet Sauvignon (South Eastern Australia) $10. A light, smooth quaffer that'll get you through the summer, this blend of 71% Shiraz and 29% Cabernet Sauvignon boasts aromas and flavors of charcoal-grilled black cherries tinged with chocolate. **83** —J.C. (9/1/2002)

Jacob's Creek 1998 Shiraz-Cabernet Sauvignon (South Eastern Australia) $9. 87 Best Buy (5/1/2000)

Jacob's Creek 1999 Limited Release Shiraz-Cabernet Sauvignon (South Eastern Australia) $50. Shiraz from this well-tempered, pretty wine is from Barossa, and the Cab from Coonawarra. Aromas are crisp and racy—think black cherry and eucalyptus, plus some cinnamon or spice—and the same elements play out on the palate. Mouthfeel is dry and dusty, all the way through the medium-long finish. **89** —D.T. (12/31/2004)

Jacob's Creek 1998 Limited Release Shiraz-Cabernet Sauvignon (South Australia) $50. Jacob's Creek's top-end red is complex, dense, and supple. A seductive bouquet of cassis, Asian spice, leather, cocoa, and smoke pulls you in and the palate delivers with a thick, velvety feel and concentrated black fruit. Dry, but ripe, and even tannins on the long finish portend a good future for this already attractive wine. **92 Cellar Selection** (2/1/2001)

Jacob's Creek 1997 Limited Release Shiraz-Cabernet Sauvignon (South Australia) $50. A big, button-pushing concentrated wine, and so obviously Shiraz (75%, anyway) that you'd easily pick it out of a blind lineup. Caramel, butterscotch, and black pepper highlights run all the way through. New World and yummy, but if over-the-top ain't your thing, steer clear of it. **90** —D.T. (12/15/2002)

Jacob's Creek 1994 Limited Release 150th Annivers Shiraz-Cabernet Sauvignon (South Eastern Australia) $65. 91 (5/1/2000)

Jacob's Creek 2003 Syrah-Grenache (South Eastern Australia) $8. Sweet, light, and fruity from top to bottom: Coconut, cherry, and chocolate aromas kick it off, and segue to cherry and raspberry flavors on the palate. A simple, easy quaffer. **83** —D.T. (9/1/2004)

Jacob's Creek 1999 White Blend (South Eastern Australia) $8. 87 Best Buy (5/1/2000)

JAMES ESTATE

James Estate 2000 Cabernet Sauvignon (McLaren Vale) $13. Medium-weight, with creamy, black-currant flavors, this Cab has a touch of herbal or weedy greenness on the palate. On the nose, that greenness is eucalyptus, backed by graham cracker, cassis, and spice aromas. Finishes tart, with cocoa and herbal flavors. **86 Best Buy** (11/1/2002)

James Estate 1999 Cabernet Sauvignon (McLaren Vale) $13. The least successful of this fine winery's current offerings, it's an awkward wine that combines balanced flavors with overly sweet, raisined ones. There's a Port-like quality that persists through the finish. Some will relish it, but lovers of dry Cabernets won't. **82** —S.H. (6/1/2002)

James Estate 2001 Sundara Cabernet Sauvignon-Merlot (South Eastern Australia) $9. Our least favorite of the JE wines reviewed, this 70% Cab, 30% Merlot is thin in the mouth, with a sour strawberry-rhubarb-oak flavor profile. Bouquet offers graham crackers, smoke, high-toned date, plus some weedy aromas. **82** (11/1/2002)

James Estate 2000 Sundara Cabernet Sauvignon-Merlot (Hunter Valley) $9. Cabernet brings deep flavors of black currants and tannic structure, while Merlot contributes softer, richer notes. The result is good drinking. It's not complex or ageworthy, but it is clean and satisfying and won't break your budget. **85** —S.H. (6/1/2002)

James Estate 2000 Compass Chardonnay (Hunter Valley) $13. This beauty has it all. From Oz, a sinfully fruity wine, packed with tangerine, mango, guava, and spicy peach flavors, with a solid layer of oaky complexities. Beyond the flavors is a rich, creamy texture, lifted by very high acids. **90 Best Buy** —S.H. (6/1/2002)

James Estate 2001 Reserve Chardonnay (Hunter Valley) $20. The whole lot of this Chard did 9 to 10 months' time in French and American oak, which might explain why it tastes more of nuts, coconut, and vanilla

then it does of fruit. Hazelnut, hickory, and toasty on the nose; closes with lemon, oak, and vanilla. **84** (11/1/2002)

James Estate 2001 Sundara Chardonnay (South Eastern Australia) $9. Yellow fruit on the palate is cloaked in plenty of toasty vanilla and a thick, syrupy mouthfeel; yellow fruit (pineapple, pear) aromas have both buttered toast and citrus accents. Finishes bright, sweet, and a touch metallic. **84** (11/1/2002)

James Estate 2000 Merlot (South Eastern Australia) $13. Smells like a cozy night next to the fireplace, with smoke, ash, oak, and dried herb aromas. There's a green-herb streak laced through the black cherry flavors, but it's supersoft and easy in the mouth. Finishes short, with some burned oak and sour berry flavors. **84** (11/1/2002)

James Estate 2000 Reserve Merlot (Hunter Valley) $20. This Merlot's bouquet offers briary fruit with spicy, hickory, or marinade accents. It's fairly substantial and easydrinking, with well-oaked mixed berries and black cherry flavors. Tangy oak gives the finish a tart bite. **87** (11/1/2002)

James Estate 1995 Botrytis Semillon (Australia) $25. Hedonistic and delicious, this richly textured wine offers a seductive blend of apricot, peach, cinnamon, vanilla, Mandarin orange, and honey flavors. Thick and full on the finish. **92** —J.M. (12/1/2002)

James Estate 2000 Sundara Semillon-Chardonnay (Hunter Valley) $9. A classic white blend from Down Under, this lively, flavorful wine is filled with flavors of lime and juniper berry, tangerine zest, buttery smoke, and oriental spices. The fruit is accompanied by very high acidity, and it's dry. **88 Best Buy** —S.H. (6/1/2002)

James Estate 2000 Shiraz (South Eastern Australia) $13. Peter Orr told us that this was made to be a soft, easy-drinker—he succeeded. The mouthfeel is soft and zippy, with bright red fruit, cocoa, and just a hint of sour berry or herb. Brown sugar, cocoa, leather, and dried spice aromas start things off. **85 Best Buy** (11/1/2002)

James Estate 1999 Shiraz (Hunter Valley) $13. Good color, forward, peppery aromas, a solid burst of fruit and tannins in the mouth, and a rich, velvety texture that lasts through the finish—all that at a good price. Quibblers will notice a bit of residual sugar that makes it slightly sweet. **84** —S.H. (6/1/2002)

James Estate 2000 Reserve Shiraz (Frankland River) $20. Black pepper is the key player in this reserve offering—it partners with meaty, spicy notes on the nose, and bell pepper, spice, and red berry on the palate. Finishes with cocoa and oak notes, and another healthy dose of black pepper. **89** (11/1/2002)

James Estate 2000 Reserve Shiraz (McLaren Vale & Langhorne Creek) $20. This Reserve Shiraz is worth seeking out for its own reasons, though it isn't quite as subtle as the Frankland River offering. Smoldering oak and mixed berry fruit aromas are warmed up by some bacon and maple notes; it's bouncy and big in the mouth, with mixed berry fruit and vanilla flavors. Finishes dry, with herb and metallic hints, and some ripe tannins. **88** (11/1/2002)

James Estate 2000 Sundara Shiraz-Cabernet Sauvignon (Hunter Valley) $9. Dark berries and tree stone fruits from entry to finish. It's also very dry, with a scour of tannins. Don't look for softness, though. Exceptionally high acidity tingles the palate, which means this puppy needs rich foods. **84** —S.H. (6/1/2002)

James Estate 2001 Verdelho (Hunter Valley) $13. A dusty floral-and-spice bouquet opens this medium-weight, unoaked Verdelho. Pear and tropical fruit flavors are also dimmed by dustiness. Medium-weight, it closes with tart fruit-pit, herbal notes. **85** (11/1/2002)

JANSZ

Jansz NV Premium Non Vintage Cuvée Brut Chardonnay (Australia) $19. After pouring it into the glass, the bead dies down pretty quickly. Feels flat in the mouth, with pear notes coming through loudest. Simple, and a good quaff. **84** —D.T. (12/31/2005)

JCP MALTUS

JCP Maltus 2003 The Colonial Estate L'Étranger Cabernet Sauvignon (Barossa Valley) $27. L'Étranger is the most appropriately named wine I've come across in a while. This bottling offers raisiny, bready aromas (think cinnamon-raisin bagel), and earthy, sweet-and-sour notes on the palate (think Sweet Tart, tree, and raisin). A strange one, indeed. **84** —D.T. (8/1/2005)

JCP Maltus 2003 ÉMIGRÉ Red Blend (Barossa Valley) $100. Composed of such a hodgepodge of grapes (Shiraz, Grenache, Cabernet Sauvignon, Mourvèdre, Carignan, Muscadelle), it's no wonder that this wine sticks out of the pack. The nose offers an unusual spicy note—pickling spice or cumin?—which persists on the palate. Fruit flavors are overripe and overpower this modestly sized wine. Finishes with chocolate. **87** —D.T. (4/1/2006)

JCP Maltus 2003 EXILE Red Blend (Barossa Valley) $200. The '02 Exile had plenty of oak, and this '03 has its share as well (coffee, toast, spice, mocha—the works). This edition, though, has very juicy plum and raspberry fruit to back it up, along with smooth, suave tannins, and a tangy cranberry finish. Hedonistic? Yes. An ager? Maybe not. Drink up. **90** —D.T. (4/1/2006)

JCP Maltus 2002 EXILE Red Blend (Barossa Valley) $200. Aromas are stewy; if you're looking for subtlety, just keep on shopping. This wine isn't shy, and lays the wood, mocha, and cola flavors on thick. It's good, though low in acid, and will certainly have its followers. **86** —D.T. (8/1/2005)

JIM BARRY

Jim Barry 1997 McCrae Wood Bordeaux Blend (Clare & Eden Valleys) $30. Lots of berry fruit and oak aromas lead into this ruby-black Cab-Malbec's oak and peppery, nearly fruit-devoid palate. The wine is unbalanced, and has a bracingly acidic bite to the finish. **82** —D.T. (9/1/2001)

Jim Barry 2000 First Eleven XI Cabernet Sauvignon (Coonawarra) $17. The first vintage of Jim Barry's second Coonawarra Cabernet, this is an enjoyable, flavorful wine with mixed plum and oak notes pervading, and firm tannins on the palate. Superior to, but maybe not as charismatic as, Barry's Cover Drive Cabernet. Drink 2006 through 2008. **91** —D.T. (3/1/2005)

Jim Barry 2004 The Cover Drive Cabernet Sauvignon (South Australia) $17. A nice, enjoyable wine as it always is, but seems broader, rounder, and less from a single place than it has in the past. Black cherry comes back on the palate, enlaced with a rocky, minerally quality. Still a very good value for the money. **88** —D.T. (8/1/2006)

Jim Barry 2003 The Cover Drive Cabernet Sauvignon (South Australia) $17. Tastes a little more mainstream and crowd-pleasing than usual, the jaunty, pick-it-out-of-a-crowd eucalyptus character of vintages past toned down considerably. Still, there are very nice bitter chocolate and anise accents to the fruit on the palate, and tree bark or acorn notes on the nose. **88** —D.T. (12/31/2005)

Jim Barry 2002 The Cover Drive Cabernet Sauvignon (South Australia) $17. Wintergreen and mocha are a nice beginning, and blackberry and white pepper notes join in on the palate. The feel is smooth and claylike, with a milky-coffee finish. Quite enjoyable, particularly if you're attracted to minty-eucalyptus notes. **89** —D.T. (5/1/2005)

Jim Barry 2002 The Cover Drive Cabernet Sauvignon (Clare Valley-Coonawarra) $15. I very much like and admire this wine for many reasons, but primarily because it doesn't taste like any other wine. There's black cherry fruit at the center, with currant, olive and earthy flavors. It's a sizeable, though not overdone, wine with a nice chalk-clay texture, and aromas of eucalyptus, earth and cool-climate fruit. Only in its second vintage but already consistently good. **90 Editors' Choice** —D.T. (11/15/2004)

Jim Barry 2001 The Cover Drive Cabernet Sauvignon (Coonawarra) $15. Give this Cab a little time to open, and you'll be rewarded with blackberry and black pepper aromas, and big, smooth plum flavors on the palate. The best part is its chalky-claylike mouthfeel. This is Jim Barry Wines' first foray outside of Clare; the winery has bought a Coonawarra vineyard that's planted on a former cricket field, hence the label and the name. **90 Editors' Choice** —D.T. (5/1/2004)

Jim Barry 2003 Lodge Hill Riesling (Clare Valley) $15. Medium-full in the mouth; has a strong mineral backbone, and is dressed up with white peach and floral flavors. It's even more floral and perfumed on the nose,

with delicate jasmine and honey aromas. **89 Editors' Choice** —D.T. (2/1/2004)

Jim Barry 2005 The Florita Riesling (Clare Valley) $30. This second vintage of Barry's Florita Riesling is excellent. Its flour-like, dusty mouthfeel follows light floral, minerally aromatics. On the palate it's blissfully dry, with lively acidity and dusty citrus flavors. Finish is persistent; delicious throughout. **92** —D.T. (11/15/2006)

Jim Barry 2004 The Florita Riesling (Clare Valley) $30. Jim Barry's first Florita is a delicious wine with Meyer lemon aromas and a dry, smooth, austere feel. The first sip is an intense rush of green apple, pink grapefruit, and Meyer lemon flavors; the second sip, it's demure, almost coy, in its minerality and auserity. Ever-changing, with a kaleidoscope of flavors and sensations. Drink now through 2020. **93 Cellar Selection** —D.T. (4/1/2006)

Jim Barry 2004 The Lodge Hill Riesling (Clare Valley) $17. Oysters, porches, weddings—the Lodge Hill is just this type of wine. Citrus peel on the nose ushers in gooseberry and chalk flavors on the palate. It's clean and refreshing, with a medium-length finish. **85** —D.T. (10/1/2005)

Jim Barry 2002 The Lodge Hill Riesling (Clare Valley) $15. Though it's crisp and fresh in the mouth, this wine has some weight (and some oily viscosity) to it. Starts off in the mouth with a burst of sweetness, and a limey, grassy streak carries it through to the finish. Nose is fruity, with nectarine and mango highlights. **90 Best Buy** —D.T. (8/1/2003)

Jim Barry 2002 Armagh Shiraz (Clare Valley) $100. Abyss-black and adheres to the unwritten but well understood rule that Armagh must be big and bold, more appropriate for a passionate rendezvous than the dinner table. This vintage offers penetrating eucalyptus, white pepper, even meaty aromas. The palate is full and rich, dealing mixed berries, plum, eucalyptus, and a hint of caramel. There are lasting, grippy tannins on the back palate, with notes of wheat bread and licorice on the finish. Drink through 2014. **94** —D.T. (6/1/2006)

Jim Barry 2001 Armagh Shiraz (Clare Valley) $100. A warming, lusty wine, with tannins that are soft and supple enough that the wine can be drunk now. Tastes like plum, caramel, and coffee; smells like pure red grapes, plus walnuts and roasted meat. Will cure whatever ails you. Drink now–2010. **92** —D.T. (5/1/2004)

Jim Barry 1996 The Armagh Shiraz (Clare Valley) $75. 97 (11/15/1999)

Jim Barry 2001 Lodge Hill Shiraz (Clare Valley) $15. This is an easygoing, food-friendly Shiraz, with lightly jammy scents of red berries accented by smoke and graham cracker. Finishes tart and crisp, marked by coffee and chocolate. **87** (12/1/2003)

Jim Barry 2002 McRae Wood Shiraz (Clare Valley) $35. 92 —D.T. (1/1/2002)

Jim Barry 2001 McRae Wood Shiraz (Clare Valley) $35. Meat, plum, and penetrating menthol-eucalyptus aromas are assertive and complex. The red fruit on the palate isn't going anywhere—it's firm and ripe, and accompanied by a red-licorice flavor. Eucalyptus is wide and lasting on the finish. **90** —D.T. (5/1/2004)

Jim Barry 2000 McRae Wood Shiraz (Clare Valley) $35. Aromas of cured meat and bacon add punch to straightforward flavors of red plums and blackberries. Slightly creamy in the mouth, turning talc-like and showing some lovely soft tannins on the finish. **89** (12/1/2003)

Jim Barry 2000 The Armagh Shiraz (Clare Valley) $100. Monster stuff—thick, black, and oozy—yet with high-toned red fruit and mint scents that match the intensity of the smoke and toast of new oak. Maple syrup, black olive, and blackberry flavors pick up hints of pepper, particularly on the finish. **94** (12/1/2003)

Jim Barry 1999 The Armagh Shiraz (Clare Valley) $100. You could fill your pen with this stuff, it's that dark. Aromas of black cherry marmalade, cassis, and white chocolate, young and fresh. In the mouth, it's massive and ripe, yet balanced and harmonious, with perky acids and caressing tannins. Be forewarned: Big is not necessarily better. Despite the high score, this wine will drown many foods. **95 Cellar Selection** —S.H. (12/15/2002)

Jim Barry 1997 The Armagh Shiraz (Clare Valley) $100. This very impressive juice shows a rich, complex nose of blackberry, earth, saddle leather,

AUSTRALIA

cocoa, molasses, and a lovely mint element. The rich, syrupy mouthfeel supports similar ripe flavors. The long finish is deeply fruited, with handsome fig, smoke, and licorice notes. Solid stuff—can drink now, but it's built to last and will be best 2004–2012 and beyond. **93 Cellar Selection** *(11/1/2001)*

Jim Barry 2004 The Lodge Hill Shiraz (Clare Valley) $17. Blackberry and eucalyptus aromas with a coffeelike accent set the stage for a full, smooth wine. Vanilla bolsters bright blackberry flavors on the palate, and fades into a substantial finish. Very impressive for an under-$20 Shiraz. **88** —*D. T. (8/1/2006)*

Jim Barry 2003 The Lodge Hill Shiraz (Clare Valley) $17. Creamier and fuller than other Clare Shirazes at its price point, this bottling offers spice, plum, and sweet tart flavors. The drawback for me is a creamy-sweet lactic aroma—like a nose full of cheesecake—but that might be a turn-on for others. **85** —*D.T. (12/1/2005)*

Jim Barry 2002 The Lodge Hill Shiraz (Clare Valley) $15. This Shiraz is rich in fruit yet slender in body. There's eucalyptus on the nose, too, backed by limestone and plum aromas. The blackberry, and even blueberry, fruit is taut yet concentrated, and brightened by refreshing eucalyptus notes. The minty-eucalyptus crispness clings on through the finish, where it's moderated by a wheaty, pastry-crust close. At this price, and this quality, there's really no reason not to keep a few bottles around the house. **89 Editors' Choice** —*D.T. (9/1/2004)*

Jim Barry 1999 The Mcrae Wood Shiraz (Clare Valley) $35. Looks menacingly dark and young, with aromas of jammy primary fruit and the flavors of plums, blueberries, and white chocolate. This is a dense, yummy wine, with thick young tannins and juicy acidity. It's appealing now, and should develop in the bottle. **92 Editors' Choice** —*S.H. (12/15/2002)*

JINDALEE

Jindalee 2004 Cabernet Sauvignon (South Eastern Australia) $9. An odd Cabernet. Has aromas and flavors akin to a blended juice beverage—there's peach, apple, berries, some Sweet Tart. A simple quaff. **83** —*D. T. (12/31/2005)*

Jindalee 2004 Chardonnay (South Eastern Australia) $8. This fun, easy Chardonnay shows golden apple and white pepper aromas, along with tropical peach and pineapple flavors. Just what you'd expect from a $10 Chardonnay, delivered at $8. **84 Best Buy** —*D.T. (6/1/2006)*

Jindalee 2005 Sauvignon Blanc (South Eastern Australia) $8. Shows aromas of fresh-cut grass and white peach. Peach resurfaces on the palate, where it's joined by some green apple flavors. Straightforward and easy, but tasty enough. **84 Best Buy** —*D.T. (6/1/2006)*

JINKS CREEK

Jinks Creek 2002 Pinot Noir (Gippsland) $30. This Pinot's fruit hails from Gippsland, in Victoria—plum fruit is red and softer than you'll get on many other Pinots, with anise, spice, and pepper accents. Has a nice, chalky mouthfeel; finishes with more red plum fruit. Enjoyable and very good, and very New World in style. **88** —*D.T. (9/1/2004)*

Jinks Creek 2004 Sauvignon Blanc (Gippsland) $25. Plenty of cantaloupe, lime, and just a touch of vegetal sweat to the nose. Runs straight down the middle in that it offers melon and citrus flavors, easy acidity and good minerality. A smooth drink that aims to please. **87** *(7/1/2005)*

Jinks Creek 2002 Sauvignon Blanc (Gippsland) $20. More White Wine than Sauvignon, there's lightweight yellow fruit at its core, dressed up with confectioner's sugar and flour. Couple that with pineapple and passion fruit aromas on the nose, and meat-and-sugar flavors on the close, and you've just got a good but confused, varietally vague wine. **84** —*D.T. (5/1/2004)*

Jinks Creek 2002 Shiraz (Yarra Valley) $30. On the nose, the fruit is red red red—raspberry, even some tomato—and is sweetened up with caramel or butterscotch. Mouthfeel is smooth and chalky. Bright redness is the name of the game on the palate as well: The fruit is soft and sweet, but it's amped up with an anise-and-herb overlay. **85** —*D.T. (9/1/2004)*

JOHN DUVAL WINES

John Duval Wines 2003 Plexus S-G-M Red Blend (Barossa Valley) $35. The first solo endeavor from former Penfolds head winemaker John Duval is an admirable one, containing 46% Shiraz, 32% Grenache, and 22% Mourvèdre. Blackberries and plums take on a hearty helping of spice and black pepper, nose to finish. Chewy tannins and charred meats linger on the midpalate as well. **90** —*D.T. (8/1/2005)*

JOHN HONGELL

John Hongell 2001 Biscay Vineyard Shiraz (Barossa Valley) $25. Woodsy tannins have a firm grip on the palate, and hang on tight through the finish. Though oak lends this wine most of its charming creamy, leathery accents, it's still an enjoyable, rich offering—warm, yes, but still very attractive. **90** —*D.T. (8/1/2005)*

JOSEPH

Joseph 2002 Moda Cabernet Sauvignon-Merlot (McLaren Vale) $48. Meaty, with a sexy bass line of plum. Tannins are smooth; accents are of vanilla bean, and some easy toasty, woody notes. Broad but not abyss-deep, but still very enjoyable and drinkable. **90** —*D.T. (6/1/2006)*

Joseph 2005 D'Elena Pinot Grigio (McLaren Vale) $21. The fruit for this Pinot Grigio comes from a vineyard on a hill above Clarendon. The wine opens with citrus and pear aromas, moving on to flavors of golden apple and pink grapefruit. On the heavy side for a PG, but its fresh, straightforward style is appealing. **86** —*D.T. (10/1/2006)*

KAESLER

Kaesler 2001 Cabernet Sauvignon (Barossa Valley) $22. The smooth tannins on this wine are just stupendous; the black plum and white pepper flavors are also excellent, but definitely secondary to the wine's silky texture. Burnt brown sugar comes through on the nose, perhaps an indication of the 50% new French oak treatment. **92 Editors' Choice** —*D.T. (2/1/2004)*

Kaesler 2001 Stonehorse Chardonnay (Geelong) $NA. This wine's style will feel familiar to California Chard fans. Buttercream aromas preface tropical fruit on the palate and toast on the finish. An undercurrent of citrus keeps it crisp. **87** —*D.T. (2/1/2004)*

Kaesler 2002 Avignon Red Blend (Barossa Valley) $24. A GSM with a great, soft, milky-chalky mouthfeel, the Avignon has rich plum fruit layered with soil, and a shot of raspberry running through it. Keep this one in mind for next year's Thanksgiving—it would stand up superbly to turkey and roasted yams. **90** —*D.T. (2/1/2004)*

Kaesler 2003 Stonehorse Red Blend (Barossa Valley) $19. From a winery better known for its huge Shirazes, this is one of its comparatively entry-level wines. It offers red plum and blackberry aromas and flavors. Though it has a pleasing texture, it is pretty straightforward. Finishes with thick, toasty wood. **86** —*D.T. (5/1/2005)*

Kaesler 2002 Stonehorse Red Blend (Barossa Valley) $18. The cherry notes typical of Grenache are prevalent on the nose and on the palate, with Shiraz's darker plum fruit coming up quick behind. Lively in the mouth, with very bright fruit flavors. 2,000 cases produced. **86** —*D.T. (2/1/2004)*

Kaesler 2003 Old Vine Semillon (Barossa Valley) $17. A Semillon that wants to be a Sauvignon Blanc, with straightforward, crisp citrus, and Granny Smith apple flavors and a lean body. A nice everyday white. **87** —*D.T. (2/1/2004)*

Kaesler 2001 Old Bastard Shiraz (Barossa Valley) $110. Gets 100% new French oak for two years, and it shows. This is a big wine, with jammy berry and plum fruit that's doused in toasty, smoky flavors. Similar caramel-vanilla notes ring true on the nose. Finishes in a crescendo of caramel, and black plum and berry flavors. Excellent, to be sure, but also just massive. Don't try to drink this with anything other than a date and a bearskin rug—it's just not going to go with dinner. About 300 cases produced. **92** —*D.T. (2/1/2004)*

Kaesler 2001 Old Vine Shiraz (Barossa Valley) $45. This vintage, I preferred this wine to the flagship Old Bastard—it's more versatile, and at half the price of the Old Bastard, it feels like a steal. Opens with lovely coffee, mocha, and earth aromas, with only the slightest trace of barnyard. The fruit on the palate has tremendous staying power—it's a big basket of fresh-picked berries that just won't go away. **93 Editors' Choice** —*D.T. (2/1/2004)*

Kaesler 2000 Old Vine Shiraz (Barossa Valley) $NA. Gives an elegant but straightforward overall impression, with forward plum fruit and a subtle, claylike mouthfeel that overshadows all else. Wide bready, spicy aromas unfold on the nose. **89** —*D.T. (2/1/2004)*

Kaesler 2002 Stonehorse Shiraz (Barossa Valley) $28. A very good wine, with mixed plums and caramel on the palate. Contains 4% Viognier, which may well account for the floral quality that also shows in the mouth. Has a hearty helping of oak on the finish. **88** —*D.T. (2/1/2004)*

KALBARRI

Kalbarri 2003 Bin Select 667 Shiraz (South Eastern Australia) $7. Vanilla, plum, and a tangy, citrusy note dominate the palate, with brown sugar and red plum on the nose. Broad but not very deep; wants more stuffing in the midpalate. **83** —*D.T. (6/1/2006)*

KANGA RESERVE

Kanga Reserve 2004 Chardonnay (South Eastern Australia) $6. Pretty down-the-line as value-priced Chards go: Has buttery, creamy aromas, and peach, apple and oak flavors. No surprises here; good and correct. **84 Best Buy** —*D.T. (6/1/2006)*

KANGARILLA ROAD

Kangarilla Road 1997 Bordeaux Blend (McLaren Vale) $20. Already mature, with light red fruit, cedar, and a hint of green to the nose. The palate is refreshing and has a good feel; it's a bit thin in terms of fruit power, but the strawberry and cherry that's here is nice. The finish is smooth and crisp. A good wine, but one without much power. **86** —*M.S. (12/15/2002)*

Kangarilla Road 2000 Cabernet Sauvignon (McLaren Vale) $23. Black on the nose, with earth and deep black cherry and blackberry notes, this Cab has more of the same soil and fruit on the palate. Finishes acidic. **82** —*D.T. (6/1/2002)*

Kangarilla Road 1999 Cabernet Sauvignon (McLaren Vale) $23. The nose has beautiful green olive with fresh vegetables and burnt coffee. Flavors of juicy blackberries and bitter chocolate add to the complexity. This wine has a leaner style that is well put together and delicious. **90** —*C.S. (6/1/2002)*

Kangarilla Road 1998 Cabernet Sauvignon (McLaren Vale) $23. **83** —*M.S. (10/1/2000)*

Kangarilla Road 2002 Shiraz (McLaren Vale) $21. An unusual, enjoyable Shiraz. A mint-and-chocolate peppermint-patty quality pervades the wine, nose to tail, but the quality is an attracive one. Feels steely and linear on the palate, as though oak contributes to the wine's flavor, but not to its texture. Red and black plums, and some toasted oak flavors, persist through the finish. **89** —*D.T. (3/1/2005)*

Kangarilla Road 2001 Shiraz (McLaren Vale) $21. Almost a meal in itself, with a burst of blackberry and currant, ripe plum, Portabello mushrooms, soy sauce, and a flourish of cherry sauce. Despite this huge array of ripeness the wine is thoroughly dry. Way too soft in acids, though, which lowers the score. **86** —*S.H. (10/1/2003)*

Kangarilla Road 2000 Shiraz (McLaren Vale) $21. This full-bodied effort goes down surprisingly easy. Aromas of shoe polish, black plums, and a dash of black pepper presage flavors of blackberry, plum, and brandied spice cake. Finishes with warm notes of chocolate and spice. **87** —*J.C. (9/1/2002)*

Kangarilla Road 1999 Shiraz (McLaren Vale) $19. Some weedy, eucalyptus notes add a sour edge to what is otherwise a fine mix of berries and meats. The chewy mouthfeel is a treat, as is the dusty finish. Rare beef will help tame the wine's tannins and enhance its texture. **85** *(10/1/2001)*

Kangarilla Road 2003 Shiraz-Viognier (McLaren Vale) $21. The Viognier contributes beautiful floral aromatics to this wine, and the Shiraz, plenty of black pepper. The palate surges wtih berries and cherries—taut, fresh, and pure. Smooth and firm on the finish. Nicely done. **90** —*D.T. (3/1/2005)*

Kangarilla Road 2002 Zinfandel (McLaren Vale) $33. Spicy cherry aromas lead to similar flavors on the palate—cherries, spice, and plums. Finishes a little thick and portlike. Very enjoyable overall. How often do you find a very good Aussie Zin? **88** —*D.T. (3/1/2005)*

Kangarilla Road 2001 Zinfandel (McLaren Vale) $33. Australian Zin? Yes, and it's as hard to "get" Down Under as it is in California. Pours richly dark, and smells great, with loads of briary fruit, sweet earth, and chocolate. Good berry, cherry flavors wrapped in sturdy tannins are fine, but marred by residual sugar. **85** —*S.H. (12/31/2003)*

KANGAROO RIDGE

Kangaroo Ridge 2002 Cabernet Sauvignon (South Eastern Australia) $6. This sweet, fruit-driven wine has a note of burnt marshmallow on both the nose and the palate. Finishes wtih caramel, plum, and raspberry fruit. **82** —*D.T. (5/1/2004)*

Kangaroo Ridge 2002 Chardonnay (South Eastern Australia) $8. A Beringer Blass partner, and quite a success. Medium-soft in the mouth, with pineapple, pear, and apple aromas and flavors. It has good length on the finish, where it picks up some toast nuances. In spite of its fruit-driven profile, this isn't a sweet, insipid wine. Better than many wines we sampled that were twice the price. **87 Best Buy** *(7/2/2004)*

Kangaroo Ridge 2002 Merlot (South Eastern Australia) $8. This wine is very sweet and soft, and not at all my style, but I have no doubt that it a very large audience. Aromas are sweet, like a coconut candy bar; flavors are similarly candied—like chocolate and fruit ganache. **83** —*D.T. (9/1/2004)*

Kangaroo Ridge 2002 Shiraz (South Eastern Australia) $8. This brand's Chardonnay was a Best Buy, but its Merlot wasn't quite as enjoyable. Though the Merlot's style will surely have its fans, this reviewer found its flavors (chocolate-covered raisins, or cookies?) a little too sweet. Aromas are of scone dough and dried fruit. **83** —*D.T. (9/1/2004)*

KATHERINE HILLS

Katherine Hills 2000 Cabernet Sauvignon (South Australia) $10. Its aromas are interesting—I picked up fresh herbs and some chocolate-covered cherries—and what follows in the mouth is good, but it's nothing you haven't already tried. It's medium-bodied with sturdy red fruit, herb, and earth notes. **85** —*D.T. (12/31/2003)*

KATNOOK ESTATE

Katnook Estate 2000 Cabernet Sauvignon (Coonawarra) $22. This wine's a testament to how pretty, ripe New World fruit doesn't need to be overdone with toasty oak to be excellent. Nose is deep and earthy, and the earthy-dustiness carries over to the palate, where there's a surge of fruit-sweet, chewy plum, and berry fruit. Blackberry, plum, and clay linger on the finish. **90** —*D.T. (12/31/2004)*

Katnook Estate 1999 Cabernet Sauvignon (Coonawarra) $22. Medium-bodied but taut, this Coonawarra Cab has unyielding red cherry and plum fruit, with such a dose of oak that the fruit takes a backseat, anyway. Finishes with dry oak. **85** —*D.T. (6/1/2003)*

Katnook Estate 2000 Odyssey Cabernet Sauvignon (Coonawarra) $50. Aromas are of roasted meat and tobacco. It's just an excellent wine, the oak overlay giving just enough flavor and patina to deep, liquerish blackberry flavors. "Cigar box" is a descriptor I don't get to use often when talking about Oz wine, but it's appropriate here. Finishes long. Give the wood a little more time to integrate, then enjoy. Drink 2007–2013. **91 Cellar Selection** —*D.T. (10/1/2005)*

Katnook Estate 2002 Chardonnay (Coonawarra) $17. Though the nose is a pretty combination of almond, meat, and citrus, this Chard's steely, angular frame carries more than its share of buttered-toast flavors. Butter and wood punctuate the finish as well. Tasted twice, with consistent results. **84** —*D.T. (5/1/2005)*

Katnook Estate 2001 Chardonnay (Coonawarra) $20. Cologne, butter and brioche aromas are vibrant, and are backed up by overt caramel and cinammon-bun flavors. Soft and plump in the mouth, and goes down easy. **85** *(7/2/2004)*

Katnook Estate 2000 Chardonnay (Coonawarra) $17. Unusual nectarine and tangerine flavors are accented by some ginger, but make no

AUSTRALIA

AUSTRALIA

mistake—there's still lots of wood-derived cream and butter here, particularly on the nose and on the finish. 84 —D.T. (8/1/2003)

Katnook Estate 1999 Merlot (Coonawarra) $22. A strange wine; it tastes older than it is, with lots of oak, and over-the-hill red fruit. Mouthfeel is dry—like dry earth. Finishes with dry plum-skin, or plum-pit, notes. 83 —D.T. (1/1/2002)

Katnook Estate 2004 Sauvignon Blanc (Coonawarra) $15. Grass and gooseberry aromas have pleasing white pepper and vanilla accents, while the palate delivers clean grapefruit and lime flavors. A lot of zest coats the mouth, a little less as far as stuffing is concerned. 87 —D.T. (8/1/2005)

Katnook Estate 2002 Shiraz (Coonawarra) $22. I've come to like Katnook's wines quite a lot, but this one is a disappointment. Though the wine has cool cherry fruit and black pepper aromas, it feels tired and weak on the palate. The berry fruit starts showing through on the finish, but its cameo appearance just isn't enough. 85 —D.T. (12/1/2005)

Katnook Estate 2000 Shiraz (Coonawarra) $22. Salinity, charcoal, hickory smoke, leather, and brown sugar aromas blend well with the flavors of juicy, ripe red plums and raspberries. Overall, this is dark, spicy, full. Sure to please any Shiraz fan. 89 —K.F. (3/1/2003)

Katnook Estate 2002 Prodigy Shiraz (Coonawarra) $50. Excellent in large part for being quite different from other Shirazes: This one offers an overarching exotic quality, which manifests itself as spice on the palate, and as pipe tobacco, fireplace, and black licorice on the nose. Smooth tannins in the middle, with a little toast and black pepper toward the back end. 90 —D.T. (6/1/2006)

Katnook Estate 1999 Prodigy Shiraz (Coonawarra) $50. Bloody coloring portends the rich aromas of gamy meat, cayenne, currants, and golden raisins. The thick, jammy fruit extends to the palate, with the added nuance of brown sugar, which holds on the long finish. As satisfying as a slab of chocolate cheesecake, but will likely age longer. 90 —K.F. (3/1/2003)

KELLY'S PROMISE

Kelly's Promise 2002 Cabernet Sauvignon-Merlot (South Eastern Australia) $8. Smells like strawberries and cream, but the palate falls more in the plum-and-cherry camp, and isn't as sweet. A simple, bargain red. 84 Best Buy —D.T. (8/1/2005)

Kelly's Promise 2000 Cabernet Sauvignon-Merlot (South Eastern Australia) $9. Smooth and stylish, and all for a song. The mouth is loaded with tasty, high-quality cherry and cassis fruit, while the finish is lengthy and layered. What a solid wine for such a fair price. In fact, it would be nice at any price. 87 Best Buy —M.S. (12/15/2002)

Kelly's Promise 2003 Chardonnay (South Eastern Australia) $8. Aromas are of dusty tropical fruits. It's a soft-bodied wine, easy to drink, with fresh tropical fruit flavors on the palate. Enjoy on the patio. 86 Best Buy (7/2/2004)

Kelly's Promise 2002 Shiraz (South Eastern Australia) $8. Plum and cherry aromas and flavors, with cream and cheese on the nose and the finish. Straightforward and simple. 83 —D.T. (11/15/2004)

KELLY'S REVENGE

Kelly's Revenge 2004 Chardonnay (South Eastern Australia) $6. Actually has decent structure, which you can say of very few wines at this price. Sunny, peach, and mineral aromas are reprised on the palate, where the feel is just a little viscous. Has high enough acidity to pair well with food—chicken curry, maybe, or grilled shrimp? 84 Best Buy —D.T. (11/15/2005)

Kelly's Revenge 2003 Shiraz (South Eastern Australia) $6. Aromas are somewhat meaty, and the palate delivers generic red fruit flavors and a thin feel. 83 Best Buy —D.T. (12/31/2005)

KILDA

Kilda 2005 Chardonnay (South Eastern Australia) $7. This is an approachable, easy Chardonnay that won't break the bank. It offers light hay, cream, and spice aromas that usher in peach and citrus flavors on the palate. Soft around the edges, with a wiry core. 5,000 cases produced. 86 Best Buy —D.T. (8/1/2006)

KILLERBY

Killerby 2000 Cabernet Sauvignon (Western Australia) $30. A very good wine, though not a very fleshy one. It's medium-weight, with plum skin and tea accents on the palate, and a nose that takes a little while to open. There's a fair amount of oak here as well—if that bothers you, look elsewhere. 88 —D.T. (5/1/2004)

Killerby 1999 Cabernet Sauvignon (Western Australia) $30. In a style that nods more to Bordeaux than the New World, the cassis, tobacco, and herb bouquet shows class and style. Displays fine balance and good acidity, which supports the ripe black-currant fruit, cedar, and peppery notes. It's structured rather than plush, and finishes long, dry, and toasty. Drinkable now, it should improve further with a few years' aging. 88 (6/1/2001)

Killerby 2000 Chardonnay (Western Australia) $45. With its high-toned, herbal, and toasty style that sets it apart from the crowd, this distinctive Chardonnay may not be to everyone's taste. Shows lots of oak and powdered dry spices on the finish to accent the custardy-lemony fruit. Should age well and might surprise you in five years. 87 —J.C. (7/1/2002)

Killerby 2002 Sauvignon Blanc (Margaret River) $15. Shows pleasing, bright aromatics of citrus and fresh grass; on the palate, however, the yellow fruit is fairly dilute, and the mouthfeel a little heavy. 83 —D.T. (5/1/2004)

Killerby 1999 Semillon-Sauvignon Blanc (Western Australia) $15. From a newly delimited region in Western Australia, this odd but likable blend offers aromas of hot candle wax, quince, and pickled jalapeño peppers. Some pear fruit complements the spicy pepper notes. Finishes crisp. 86 —J.C. (9/1/2001)

Killerby 1999 Shiraz (Western Australia) $30. This oaky, opaque Shiraz from the new GI (appellation) of Geographe in Western Australia offers pepper, root-beer, even candy-bar aromas. Medium-weight, it has nice palate texture and good acidity to support the black fruit, caramel, and pepper. Powdery tannins, pepper, and oak flavors close it nicely. Drink now through 2007. It may open to show more fruit in a year or two. 87 (11/1/2001)

KISSING BRIDGE

Kissing Bridge 2002 Chardonnay (South Eastern Australia) $6. Simple; tropical fruit and buttered popcorn aromas lead the way to light pineapple flavors on the palate. Slight in body and richness; probably best as a pre-dinner drink. 83 (7/2/2004)

Kissing Bridge 2001 Chardonnay (South Eastern Australia) $8. Opens with soft talc aromas, which lead to a palate that's rife with flavors of pear skin than ripe, fleshy fruit. Mallowy oak makes the fruit that much more difficult to find, and lends a lactic note to the finish. 83 —D.T. (6/1/2003)

Kissing Bridge 2002 Merlot (South Eastern Australia) $10. Aromas are of dust and roasted plum. The wine feels light and insubstantial in the mouth, with a slight metallic edge. Finishes short. 81 —D.T. (12/1/2005)

Kissing Bridge 2001 Shiraz (South Eastern Australia) $6. A dark, dark Shiraz: The nose shows dark earth, blackberry, and eucalyptus aromas; the palate has plum, blackberry, and toast. An easy, straightforward wine. 84 —D.T. (9/1/2004)

Kissing Bridge 2000 Shiraz (South Eastern Australia) $8. Medium-weight and straightforward, with sweet red plum fruit on the palate that continues on through the finish, which is punctuated with an herbal bite. Nose offers cola, cream, and a little leafiness. 83 —D.T. (10/1/2003)

KNAPPSTEIN LENSWOOD VINEYARDS

Knappstein Lenswood Vineyards 2002 Lenswood Sauvignon Blanc (Adelaide Hills) $NA. Tastes of stone fruit and melon rind, but the stranger thing about this wine is its texture, which is powdery—almost like a dissolving sweet tart. The nose shows meat and a pronounced petrol note. 84 —D.T. (5/1/2004)

KOALA VALLEY

Koala Valley 2003 Chardonnay (Riverland) $8. A soft, round wine, full of pineapple and stone fruit flavors and aromas. Simple, and just right for parties or casual circumstances. 85 Best Buy (7/2/2004)

KOONOWLA

Koonowla 2000 Shiraz (Clare Valley) $20. This is an enjoyable, easy-to-drink Shiraz, medium-bodied and balanced. Offers soft red plum and cherry fruit, which is swathed in pleasing earth and oak flavors. An inviting bouquet of clay and sweet red and blueberry fruit kicks things off. **87** —D.T. (3/1/2003)

KOOYONG

Kooyong 2000 Pinot Noir (Mornington Peninsula) $28. From Mornington Peninsula, just south of Melbourne, comes a Pinot with pretty violet, earth, and meringue aromas. It has oaky, tealike tannins; red cherry fruit is at its core, but takes on a hint of rubber, or plastic. Finishes a little tart. **85** —D.T. (9/1/2004)

Kooyong 2001 Estate Pinot Noir (Mornington Peninsula) $31. What a nice wine. Garnet-colored; perfumed with violet, meat, black pepper, and cherry aromas. Tannins are wooly and textured, and the palate offers up a sturdy black cherry shell with molten bittersweet chocolate inside. Dry and woody on the finish. **90** —D.T. (10/1/2005)

KOPPAMURRA

Koppamurra 1998 Cabernet Blend (South Australia) $20. Smells sweet and jammy, full of blackberries and vanilla, almost like pancake syrup, but wow does it turn lemony on the palate, finishing with a powerful acidic edge. Almost half Cabernet Sauvignon, the balance split equally between Merlot and Cab Franc. **83** —J.C. (6/1/2002)

Koppamurra 1999 Red Blend (Limestone Coast) $20. Inky and black, with blueberry and intense tire rubber on the nose. The palate is dense, requiring a jackhammer to get at the black-fruit core. The finish is hard and tannic, and the wine has a sharp personality. Power and depth is all here, but balance and charm are nonexistent. **85** —M.S. (12/15/2002)

KOPPAROSSA

Kopparossa 1999 Shiraz (Coonawarra) $24. Mouthwatering aromas of black plums, cherries, dried figs, cocoa, oiled leather, redwood, and raw meat are matched in flavor. Rounding out the palate are coffee, blackberries, and a creosote note that follows through the finish. **89** —K.F. (3/1/2003)

KURTZ FAMILY

Kurtz Family 2000 Boundary Row Grenache (Barossa Valley) $18. Rich and intense but also round and soft. A horsey note adds complexity and rusticity to the dark chocolate, leather, and black cherry aromas and flavors. **88** —J.C. (9/1/2002)

Kurtz Family 1998 Boundary Row Shiraz (Barossa Valley) $25. The intensity and depth of this blockbuster from the Barossa Valley are noted right at the start. Blackberry, cassis, chocolate, and a touch of pepper roar off the nose and continue in full stride through the mid-palate and on to the long finish. There's an underpinning of even tannins, good acidity, a round supple body, and a texture like velvet. This is a wine for hearty fare or to contemplate with the cheese course. **90** (6/1/2001)

LABYRINTH

Labyrinth 2003 Valley Farm Vineyard Pinot Noir (Yarra Valley) $35. Loved it last vintage, so what happened here? Aromas are funky, horsey, almost saline. In the mouth, there's a smooth, minerally feel that falls off toward the back end, but it doesn't have the verve it has had. Black cherry flavors; lightly lollied on the finish. **85** —D.T. (12/1/2005)

Labyrinth 2002 Valley Farm Vineyard Pinot Noir (Yarra Valley) $38. This is a delicately sized Pinot, even by Burgundian standards. But boy, is it good. Starts off with bark and trading-card bubblegum powder aromas, and displays long, lasting tannins on the palate. Cherry and plum flavors are subtle at first, and grow juicier and more intense with air. Elegant and delicious. 100 cases produced. **92 Editors' Choice** —D.T. (8/1/2005)

Labyrinth 2003 Viggers Vineyard Pinot Noir (Yarra Valley) $42. This Pinot is texturally very interesting, its robust, wooly tannins well obscuring the cherry and cola flavors underneath. That will change in the short term, I expect; a more integrated wine would lead to an even more favorable review. 283 cases produced. **89** —D.T. (12/1/2005)

Labyrinth 2002 Viggers Vineyard Pinot Noir (Yarra Valley) $45. I liked this wine very much, but not quite as much as Labyrinth's Valley Farm Pinot. This one has aromas of amaretto and hard cheese rind, and more giving flavors of black cherry and toast. Tannins are nicely textured—furry, almost. Very good; 100 cases produced. **89** —D.T. (10/1/2005)

LAKE BREEZE

Lake Breeze 2002 Winemaker's Reserve Shiraz (Langhorne Creek) $36. A solid wine in every respect; there's nothing to complain about here. Acidity is lively, and fruit runs the crisp, cool spectrum of black cherry, raspberry, even a citric edge. Black pepper and clay hints complete the picture. 310 cases produced. **89** —D.T. (10/1/2006)

LANGHORNE CROSSING

Langhorne Crossing 2003 Red Blend (Langhorne Creek) $11. Aromas are of sweet fruit, with tangy tea and oak accents. On the palate, it's a case of now you see it, now you don't: The black pepper, Sweet Tart, and red berry flavors that this wine offers are fleeting, but were fine while they lasted. **82** —D.T. (12/1/2005)

LANGMEIL

Langmeil 2002 The Blacksmith Cabernet Sauvignon (Barossa Valley) $20. Certainly appropriately named, but so terribly charming, irresistible, and unusual. Smoldering, dark, briary, stably aromas are streaked with aromatic eucalyptus. On the palate, it's incredibly concentrated, with more smoldering aromas: black soil, black fruit, smoke, even walnut and hazelnut. Still, there's a shining core of red fruit deep in there, like a glowing ember in the forge. Not slammed with oak (only 20% is new); feel is dense, but not heavy. **93 Editors' Choice** —D.T. (3/1/2005)

Langmeil 1985 Liqueur Shiraz Tawny Shiraz (Barossa Valley) $56. This tawny Shiraz has a good backbone but positively melts in the mouth. It's warming and seductive on the palate, with hazelnut and honey flavors joining more expected plum and blackberry characters of Shiraz. Gorgeous. **92** —D.T. (3/1/2005)

Langmeil 2002 The Freedom Shiraz (Barossa Valley) $60. The first acre of this vineyard was planted in 1843, in pre-phylloxera days; the fruit is dry-grown, handpicked—treated with all the care that a winery's flagship bottling gets. Has an alluring putty note on the nose, and smooth, fine tannins on the palate. Concentration is excellent, and the plum and berry fruit pure and ripe. Finishes with a surge of tannins. Delicious. **93** —D.T. (3/1/2005)

Langmeil 2002 Valley Floor Shiraz (Barossa Valley) $23. Meaty, white peppery aromas bring you around to red plum, berry, and toast on the palate. Feels very firm on the palate, with dusty-clay tannins and cocoa on the finish. Very nice! Drink now–2009. **90** —D.T. (12/31/2004)

Langmeil 2003 Three Gardens SGM Shiraz-Grenache (Barossa Valley) $16. A 47%-45%-8% belnd of Shiraz, Grenache, and Mourvedre. Cherry aromas lie under a dusting of bread flour. It's forward on the palate, with typical GSM character: cherry and plum, with soil and eucalyptus accents. A very good, enjoyable wine. **87** —D.T. (3/1/2005)

LARK HILL

Lark Hill 1999 Canberra Yass Valley Cabernet Sauvignon-Merlot (New South Wales) $35. A simple, sweetish wine overall. Caramel and marshmallow aromas give way to bright plum and raspberry fruit on the nose and the palate. A seeped-tea flavor, and a twinge of unsweetened chocolate keep the wine from tasting too confected. **83** —D.T. (9/1/2004)

Lark Hill 2001 Canberra Yass Valley Chardonnay (New South Wales) $35. One reviewer found this wine fresh and clean, with prevalent acids, and pear and green apple flavors. Another thought it a little too toasty. Aromas are of smoke, and yellow fruit. **85** (7/2/2004)

LARRIKIN

Larrikin 2002 Shiraz (Barossa Valley) $28. This Shiraz is slender and feminine, its currant and black cherry fruit taking center stage. With air, bright eucalyptus and aloe aromas show through; black pepper seeps into the palate. Very enjoyable. 1,800 cases produced. **89** —D.T. (12/31/2004)

AUSTRALIA

LAWRENCE VICTOR ESTATE

Lawrence Victor Estate 1999 Shiraz (Coonawarra) $25. This is what folks mean when they say "food wine": A wine of moderate size, with pretty, smooth tannins and not a lot of oak or sweetness to muck it up. Red licorice and plum aromas on the nose lead to a focused, pure plum core. Finishes medium-long with wheaty, pastry-dough flavors. **89** —*D.T. (9/1/2004)*

LEASINGHAM

Leasingham 1999 Bin 56 Cabernet Sauvignon (Clare Valley) $19. Offers penetrating aromas of mint, black soil, and meat. The red fruit on the palate is a little tight, and is dressed in judicious oak and powdery tannins. A very nice wine; in a perfect world, it'd have a little more stuffing and a longer finish, but wouldn't they all? **88** —*D.T. (6/1/2003)*

Leasingham 1998 Classic Clare Cabernet Sauvignon (Clare Valley) $35. An opaque purple color with aromas of juicy black fruit, vanilla, and eucalyptus. The mouthfeel is lush with rich tannins that finish chewy and a little gritty. A very good wine from a quality house. **90** —*C.S. (6/1/2002)*

Leasingham 1997 Classic Clare Cabernet Sauvignon (Clare Valley) $35. This opaque Cab shows a sexy bouquet of black currants, cream, figs, and cinnamon. The palate's black-on-black berry-pepper flavors and cedar accents set up the spicy finish. It's hefty and chewy, but balanced and well-fruited. Can be enjoyed now, and should drink well for three to five years. **90** —*D.T. (9/1/2001)*

Leasingham 1996 Classic Clare Cabernet Sauvignon (Clare Valley) $28. **91** —*M.S. (4/1/2000)*

Leasingham 2001 Bin 56 Cabernet Sauvignon-Malbec (Clare Valley) $19. Not a burly wine, despite its components. There's juicy red fruit on the palate, though it's taut; cola, mocha, root beer, and big red fruit echo on nose and finish. Only 12% Malbec; only small amounts are exported to the U.S. **88** —*D.T. (2/1/2004)*

Leasingham 2004 Bin 7 Riesling (Clare Valley) $15. A soft and approachable, rather than bracing, Riesling—we probably have the vintage to thank for that. Smells of yellow stone fruit, flowers, and white chocolate, and tastes of green grass and stone fruit. Finishes minerally **86** —*D.T. (5/1/2005)*

Leasingham 2003 Bin 7 Riesling (Clare Valley) $16. Though the wine wasn't aged within sight of a barrel, the warm vintage lends it vanilla-cream aromas and flavors. Granny Smith apple makes up the rest of the flavor profile. Has lively acids and a hint of spritz on the finish. **89** —*D.T. (2/1/2004)*

Leasingham 2002 Bin 7 Riesling (Clare Valley) $16. What a combination—quality on par with some of Australia's top performers at a price point that doesn't put you on the bread line. Lively, with brisk acidity, the Bin 7 has lime, grass, and mineral notes and just enough viscosity to remind you that it's Riesling, not Sauvignon Blanc. Finishes long and fresh, with sour apple flavors. **90 Editors' Choice** —*D.T. (8/1/2003)*

Leasingham 2001 Bin 7 Riesling (Clare Valley) $9. Appealing apple, floral, and mineral aromas, open this young, racy wine. It's crisp, with a slightly spritzy citrus and slate palate, and it stays that way, closing long with chalky hints. It's not finely nuanced, but it's refreshing, lean, and angular, with the acidity to improve for a year or two. **87 Best Buy** —*M.M. (2/1/2002)*

Leasingham 2000 Bin 7 Riesling (Clare Valley) $8. Very classic Riesling in a Mosel style with green apple, hay, and herb and a hint of petrol on the nose. The mouth shows a slight spritz, brisk acidity, and more of the crisp Granny Smith apple that shows on the nose. Finishes with bright, almost sharp acidity. **88 Best Buy** —*M.M. (9/1/2001)*

Leasingham 2003 Classic Clare Riesling (Clare Valley) $NA. A museum release that won't be on the market, probably, until late 2004, but is worth the wait. It's elegant, with subdued slate, citrus, and bread flour notes; however nice the flavors, the finessed mouthfeel is even more impressive. Juicy lime and crisp acids show through on the finish. **92** —*D.T. (2/1/2004)*

Leasingham 2004 Magnus Riesling (Clare Valley) $12. This bottling doesn't taste much different from the Bin 7 Riesling, which costs a few

dollars more. It shows the same stone fruit and floral qualities, but there is a sour-appley edge to this wine. Soft and powdery on the palate. **86** —*D.T. (5/1/2005)*

Leasingham 2003 Magnus Riesling (Clare Valley) $12. This reasonably priced Riesling shows trading-card bubblegumpowder and white peach aromas. Firm white peach and citrus flavors are couched in a round, amply sized feel. A very good wine, from an always reliable producer. **87 Best Buy** —*D.T. (11/15/2004)*

Leasingham 2001 Bin 61 Shiraz (Clare Valley) $21. Although the price is creeping up, this is still a great value for Shiraz lovers. Mulberries, toast, and dried spices blend together in a creamy, full-boded wine whose supple tannins make it easy to drink now yet capable of aging several years. **90 Editors' Choice** *(11/15/2003)*

Leasingham 2000 Bin 61 Shiraz (Clare Valley) $21. There's lots of wood and cream on the nose. A bit of that creaminess follows through onto the palate, but really, the flavors veer more toward sour red cherry and plum. A little lacking, in terms of heft and concentration. **83** —*D.T. (2/1/2003)*

Leasingham 1999 Bin 61 Shiraz (Clare Valley) $17. Tastes bold, intense, and a bit rustic and rambunctious, the way a good young Shiraz should. Black pepper, earth, and leather notes draped over blackberry fruit. It's full and verging on syrupy in the mouth, finishing with a trace of heat and firm but ripe tannins. **90 Editors' Choice** —*J.C. (9/1/2002)*

Leasingham 1998 Bin 61 Shiraz (Clare Valley) $17. Though the nose of the Bin 61 has bright blackberry-jam, leather, and cinnamon aromas, the flavors and the finish are unanimously flagged as overoaked, with sour blackberry and blueberry flavors. Finishes short, dry, and tangy, with some cocoa and dry wood. **85** *(10/1/2001)*

Leasingham 1997 Bin 61 Shiraz (Clare Valley) $15. **88** *(3/1/2000)*

Leasingham 2001 Classic Clare Shiraz (Clare Valley) $45. Excellent. Flavors and aromas are taut and lifted: Raspberry and black cherry, mainly, wrapped around a core of iron ore and charred meats. Tightly wound, powerful and delicious. 4,000 cases produced. **92** —*D.T. (8/1/2005)*

Leasingham 1999 Classic Clare Shiraz (Clare Valley) $45. Big and black, with complex aromas and flavors of earth, tobacco, coffee, and dark plums that hit you hard and pump out the bass notes all the way through the finish. It's bold, dense, and stylish, ending on a bright, vanilla-tinged fruity note. Drink now–2015. **91** *(11/15/2003)*

Leasingham 1998 Classic Clare Shiraz (Clare Valley) $35. Some reviewers thought this wine's medium-full mouthfeel "tangy;" others called it "brisk acidity." In any case, the wine's aromas and flavors are dark, dark, dark: Look forward to leather, earth, and an almost matchstick note on the nose, and black fruit, bitter chocolate, and "old baseball glove" in the mouth. Finishes with tobacco, leather, and juicy berry fruit. **88** *(11/1/2001)*

Leasingham 1997 Classic Clare Shiraz (Clare Valley) $28. **87** *(10/1/2000)*

Leasingham 1994 Classic Clare Shiraz (Clare Valley) $NA. A new release, despite the vintage, but not available in the U.S. Another Leasingham with a deep, penetrating nose here, it's eucalyptus and black pepper. There's big berry and plum fruit on the front palate, and tobacco and oak on the back. Soft and lush, drinkable now. Quite good. **91** —*D.T. (2/1/2004)*

Leasingham 1995 Show Reserve Shiraz (Clare Valley) $NA. A current release, despite the vintage; these parcels were selected from some set aside for the Classic Clare bottling. Smells just great, with deep, penetrating menthol and dark plum fruit. Sorghum and licorice palate flavors are subtle on the palate and fatten up for a grand finale on the finish. **91** —*D.T. (2/1/2004)*

Leasingham 1994 Sparkling Shiraz (Clare Valley) $NA. Made in the méthode Champenoise style, of the same grapes that go into Classic Clare. Smells like Shiraz (which isn't always true of sparkling Shiraz), with full red plums that reappear on the palate. It's soft in the mouth, with fine mousse and bouncy red fruit. Finishes with steely-mineral dryness. Winemaker Kerri Thompson suggests that you drink it like the Aussies do, as an apéritif before the Thanksgiving turkey. **89** —*D.T. (2/1/2004)*

Leasingham 2002 Magnus Shiraz-Cabernet Sauvignon (Clare Valley) $12.
Though the Magnus errs on the taut, snappy side of big reds, there's a horse-stable quality to the lifted plum and cherry fruit, and a hollowness midpalate, that keeps it from measuring up to previous vintages. Finishes with a sour bite. **84** —*D.T. (8/1/2005)*

Leasingham 2001 Magnus Shiraz-Cabernet Sauvignon (Clare Valley) $10.
This 60-40 blend uses fruit from younger vines that doesn't get into the Leasingham's top wines. It's a sweetly oaked red that blends slightly candied red fruit with darker notes of earth and tobacco. **85** *(12/31/2003)*

LEEUWIN ESTATE

Leeuwin Estate 1999 Art Series Cabernet Sauvignon (Margaret River) $45.
This Cabernet's texture is what makes it so appealing: It has smooth, chewy tannins with some lingering chalkiness on the finish. Fruit here is black and stewy-sweet, like blackberry pie filling. **89** —*D.T. (10/1/2003)*

Leeuwin Estate 1998 Art Series Cabernet Sauvignon (Margaret River) $NA.
Boasts intense aromas and flavors of cassis and mulberry, with a firm underpinning of cedary, chocolaty oak. Full-bodied, it has a long, tart finish buoyed by soft tannins. **92** *(10/1/2002)*

Leeuwin Estate 1997 Art Series Cabernet Sauvignon (Margaret River) $NA.
From what must have been a cooler year, the 1997 folds in hints of black pepper, smoke, and dried herbs on top of cassis and blackberry fruit. Finishes slightly tough and hard. **88** *(10/1/2002)*

Leeuwin Estate 1996 Art Series Cabernet Sauvignon (Margaret River) $NA.
The '96 is in a fine drinking window right now, deliciously balancing primary fruit with secondary elements. Dried spices and herbs blend with cassis, cedar, and tobacco. **89** *(10/1/2002)*

Leeuwin Estate 1995 Art Series Cabernet Sauvignon (Margaret River) $NA.
Made in a quasi-Bordeaux style, the '95 has developed cedar, tobacco, and earth flavors but doesn't have the richness and completeness of the other vintages. The firm, drying tannins on the finish will likely never completely resolve. **87** *(10/1/2002)*

Leeuwin Estate 1994 Art Series Cabernet Sauvignon (Margaret River) $NA.
Our panel disagreed substantially on this wine. While some found it still youthful and promising, others found it already tiring. There's smoke, toast, cedar, and cassis flavors along with a firm structure—the question is whether it will improve from here. **88** *(10/1/2002)*

Leeuwin Estate 1993 Art Series Cabernet Sauvignon (Margaret River) $NA.
The rating reflects an average of the two bottles that were sampled, one of which was fresher than the other (both came from the winery). Both were mature, with vegetal accents to the cigar box and cassis aromas. Red fruit on the finish fades quickly, leaving creamy oak and a tangy, herbal aftertaste. **87** *(10/1/2002)*

Leeuwin Estate 1999 Prelude Cabernet Sauvignon-Merlot (Margaret River) $29. Straightforward but tasty, with chocolate, earth, and blackberry flavors. Similar notes are reprised on the nose. A pleasing wine, but doesn't have quite the depth or structure of some other top-notch Western Australian offerings. **85** —*D.T. (10/1/2003)*

Leeuwin Estate 1998 Prelude Vineyards Cabernet Sauvignon-Merlot (Margaret River) $NA. This starts off slightly vegetal, hinting at rotting compost, but quickly rights itself, delivering cassis, plum, leather ,and coffee aromas and flavors in a soft, creamy, full-bodied format. Finishes with some peppery spice. Meant for current enjoyment. **87** *(10/1/2002)*

Leeuwin Estate 2001 Art Series Chardonnay (Margaret River) $65.
Gingerbread and vanilla aromas are light, as are the vanilla accents on the palate. This wine's citrus core and soft, powdery feel are very nice. But it's still a lightweight, and somewhat of a disappointment, given its lofty reputation and past performance. **87** —*D.T. (5/1/2005)*

Leeuwin Estate 2000 Art Series Chardonnay (Margaret River) $65. Subtle and elegant. Yellow stone fruit is accented by cream and vanilla flavors but none of the ubermallowed toasty-butteriness that often accompanies them. Racy citrus plays on the nose, with vanilla bean and passion fruit on the long finish. **91** —*D.T. (10/1/2003)*

Leeuwin Estate 1999 Art Series Chardonnay (Margaret River) $65. Despite having one year of bottle-age prior to release, this youthful wine could use more to round off the hard, tart edge to its finish. It's a rich, full wine, loaded with mouthfilling peach, toast, and mealy flavors. **90 Cellar Selection** *(10/1/2002)*

Leeuwin Estate 2004 Prelude Vineyards Chardonnay (Margaret River) $29.
The Prelude Vineyards Chard typically seems a soft-edged, full wine to me—this year it's even more so. Floral and pear aromas lead to more tropical, toasty flavors of nut and plantain. Acid hounds will want more zing, but this will satisfy most everyone else. **87** —*D.T. (8/1/2006)*

Leeuwin Estate 2002 Prelude Vineyards Chardonnay (Margaret River) $29.
This Chard's aromas are very pleasing: there's some fragrant peach, accented by honeysuckle or jasmine notes. In the mouth, however, fresh-cut pine flavors hide the pretty peach and pear core. 1,000 cases produced. **87** —*D.T. (3/1/2005)*

Leeuwin Estate 2001 Prelude Vineyards Chardonnay (Margaret River) $29.
A zesty, crisp wine with verve—you'll need to have a few sips before the round, medium-full mouthfeel becomes apparent. Pear, pineapple—even orange—fluffs up a minerally spine. Light, pure yellow peach and nectarine notes are echoed on the medium-length finish. Smooth, harmonious, yummy. 1,000 cases produced. **89** *(7/2/2004)*

Leeuwin Estate 2000 Prelude Vineyards Chardonnay (Margaret River) $29.
An evolved and interesting, but spare, wine. The mouthfeel has grip and viscosity; as for flavors, there's white stone fruit aplenty, plus a black-peppery note that continues on through the finish. **90** —*D.T. (10/1/2003)*

Leeuwin Estate 1999 Prelude Vineyards Chardonnay (Margaret River) $29.
This subtle, delicate wine deftly combines toast and white peach aromas with flavors that include pear, toasted oatmeal, and citrus. Goes down almost too easily, the flavors building in intensity on the finish. **89** —*J.C. (9/10/2002)*

Leeuwin Estate 2004 Art Series Riesling (Margaret River) $22. Delicious, precise, and excellent, but this Riesling isn't built to satisfy the masses. Its acidity is scouring and it gives the wine a tartness that makes your mouth water. Aromas are dusty and delicate, and flavors stay the lime and green grape track. Worth seeking out, but don't judge it on that first mouthpuckering sip. **91 Editors' Choice** —*D.T. (8/1/2006)*

Leeuwin Estate 2003 Art Series Riesling (Margaret River) $22. It's sad that this pretty Art Series Riesling seems to get lost in the shadows of its Chardonnay sibling—there's plenty here to like. This is a fresh, pure, unctuous wine. Though there is citrus in every sip, it still feels fleshy, rather than tart. A stony, minerally dusting completes the picture. **89** —*D.T. (5/1/2005)*

Leeuwin Estate 2002 Art Series Riesling (Margaret River) $22. This Riesling is a beautiful rose-copper color. Fresh flavors of white stone fruit and straw on the palate, with more of the same, plus some custard or cream, on the nose. It's medium-bodied and is more elegant than it is zippy or fresh. Finishes clean, with hay and peach. **88** —*D.T. (8/1/2003)*

Leeuwin Estate 2001 Art Series Riesling (Margaret River) $NA. Softer and more approachable than some Oz Rieslings, this one still delivers plenty of size and weight. Aromas of pears and limes turn peachy and appley in the glass, balanced by racy acidity. **88** *(10/1/2002)*

Leeuwin Estate 2004 Siblings Sauvignon Blanc-Semillon (Margaret River) $20. Citrus, grass, and hay notes on the nose are echoed in the mouth, where they show as straw and citrus pith. Linear and smooth, though falls a little flat on the palate. **86** —*D.T. (8/1/2006)*

Leeuwin Estate 2001 Siblings Semillon-Sauvignon Blanc (Western Australia) $20. Dry and racy, Siblings combines asparagus with ripe melon in a blend that's intriguing but not entirely harmonious. It's rich and full, turning slightly chalky on the finish. **86** *(10/1/2002)*

Leeuwin Estate 2001 Art Series Shiraz (Margaret River) $30. This is not a demonstrative, fleshy wine; on the contrary, it doesn't show much richness or complexity at this stage. Maybe its backwardness has something to do with this being a current vintage; the flavors of red eraser, modest plum, and cherry, and tea tannins are fine, but slight. **86** —*D.T. (11/15/2006)*

Leeuwin Estate 2000 Art Series Shiraz (Margaret River) $30. Red fruit on the palate is understated, and takes a backseat to the wine's smooth tannins and black pepper-and-tea finish. Nose offers ginger, green pepper, and meaty notes. A very good wine, though maybe a little disjointed. **87** —*D.T. (12/31/2003)*

Leeuwin Estate 1999 Art Series Shiraz (Margaret River) $NA. Like all of the Leeuwin wines, the Art Series Shiraz is rich and full-bodied, but because of its cool-climate origins, it never feels jammy or heavy. Toast and smoke mingle with peppery, leathery scents, and ripe blackberries. Finishes with firm tannins and hints of coffee and black pepper. **89** *(10/1/2002)*

Leeuwin Estate 2002 Siblings Shiraz (Margaret River) $20. Aromas that start off as dense and fruitcake-y take on a candied grapiness with air. On the palate, moderate blackberry and plum flavors are masked by a flat woodiness. **84** —*D.T. (10/1/2006)*

Leeuwin Estate 2002 Siblings White Blend (Margaret River) $20. Clean and fresh, with bright citrus fruit and fresh grass on the palate. There's a slightly sweet note that surfaces on the midpalate, though, that counters the lemony-sourness. It smells like a New Zealand Sauvignon Blanc—all fresh gooseberry and grass. **87** —*D.T. (10/1/2003)*

LEN EVANS

Len Evans 1999 Shiraz (McLaren Vale) $30. Dark and elegant, this offering from veteran Oz winemaker Len Evans is full-bodied and velvety, with a restrained flavor profile. It shows tart black fruits with cedar, pepper, and herb accents, and is a bit creamy. Finishes long and reserved, with deeply wooded, dry tart fruit, and a tangy back end note. **89** *(11/1/2001)*

LEWINSBROOK CREEK

Lewinsbrook Creek 2000 Shiraz (South Eastern Australia) $8. A lighter style Shiraz, with delicate cranberry fruit perked up by allspice and black pepper. The tea-like notes from start to finish, combined with the tartness, make this wine seem almost like Pinot Noir. **85 Best Buy** *(10/1/2001)*

LIMB

Limb 2001 Patterson Hill Cabernet Sauvignon (Barossa Valley) $40. With such abyss-deep black aromas (steak, pepper, licorice) the palate, by not knocking you out with giant tannins and lots of charred oak, feels slender in comparison. This is a pleasing balance of smooth tannins, and pretty black plum and blueberry flavors. **87** —*D.T. (11/15/2004)*

Limb 2000 Patterson Hill Cabernet Sauvignon (Barossa Valley) $38. This wine smells much better than it tastes. The aromas are of toasted coconut, cassis, and a slight bubble gum like you might find in a pack of trading cards. Unfortunately, the mouth lacks richness for a good but boring Cabernet. **86** —*C.S. (6/1/2002)*

Limb 2001 Three Pillars Reds Red Blend (Barossa Valley) $20. A good wine; an unusual blend of Mourvèdre (50%), Cabernet Sauvignon (27%), and Shiraz (23%). Has a nice dusty texture, and an approachable, medium-weight size, but the plum fruit plays second fiddle to oak, dust, Sweet Tart, earth, and other flavors. I'd love to see the fruit show it stuff more next vintage. **86** —*D.T. (12/31/2004)*

Limb 2000 Patterson Hill Shiraz (Barossa Valley) $42. An odd animal note blows off quickly, leaving pleasurable molasses, blackberry, and black plums on the nose and palate. Acidity lifts the fruit out of darkness and a note of barrel char creeps in on the finish. **88** —*K.F. (3/1/2003)*

LIMELIGHT

Limelight 1999 Syrah (McLaren Vale) $50. This "top-flight Oz" Syrah has loads of big, jammy blackberries on the nose and on the palate, plus enough chocolate and earth to cover it from beginning to end. Hints of mint and bacon also surface on the nose; a full, rich mouthfeel, and a little maple and tea leaves on the back end will have you asking for another glass. **90** *(11/1/2001)*

LINDEMANS

Lindemans 1999 Pyrus Bordeaux Blend (Coonawarra) $30. Aromas are dark and stewy right out of the bottle, but unfold to reveal fresh herb and eucalyptus with air. Red fruit on the palate wears dusty, sweet-and-sour tannins, and a hint of the fresh mintiness. Not a huge, dense wine, but a robust one with chewy tannins. **89** —*D.T. (11/15/2004)*

Lindemans 1998 Pyrus Cabernet Blend (Coonawarra) $27. This mix of Cabernet Sauvignon, Merlot, and Cab Franc scores points for its deep and lush bouquet, which brings with it a healthy whack of oak that smells a lot like charred hamburger. The flavors veer toward cassis, cherry, and plum, almost as the nose indicates. A bright, flashy finish with some raciness is the curtain call. **90** —*M.S. (12/15/2002)*

Lindemans 2003 Bin 45 Cabernet Sauvignon (South Eastern Australia) $8. Very sweet, cloyingly so, on both the nose and the palate: juicy fruit, for certain, including some (banana?) that you may not expect to find in a Cab. Will have its fans, but it's a little too candied for this reviewer. **82** —*D.T. (11/15/2004)*

Lindemans 2002 Bin 45 Cabernet Sauvignon (South Eastern Australia) $8. Red berry fruit wears toasty oak. Has nice, smooth tannins that are uncommon in wines of this price. It's a little sweet, but I suppose that's part of its mass appeal. **85** —*D.T. (12/31/2003)*

Lindemans 2000 Bin 45 Cabernet Sauvignon (South Eastern Australia) $8. Fairly rich and ripe, with a charry, smoky edge that gives way to black cherry and plum flavors. **86 Best Buy** —*J.M. (12/15/2002)*

Lindemans 2000 St. George Cabernet Sauvignon (Coonawarra) $30. Chalk dust, bubblegum powder, and juicy, fleshy berry fruit is a lovely aromatic combination, and the mix expresses itself just as nicely on the palate. The feel is velvety, and the oak noticeable, but still works well in terms of the the big picture. Very nice, and shows the best of what Lindemans can do. **90** —*D.T. (11/15/2004)*

Lindemans 1998 St. George Cabernet Sauvignon (Coonawarra) $27. Like many other ripe Aussie Cabs, this has a pronounced sweetness to it. In the nose, it's much like American Zinfandel, as it shows blueberry aromas. The palate is acidic and juicy, while the finish is tighter, with heavy tannins and a touch of leather. This wine has a somewhat hard feel to it, but it's also very good in terms of power and raw flavor. **88** —*M.S. (12/15/2002)*

Lindemans 1998 Cabernet Sauvignon-Merlot (Padthaway) $15. You get a lot for your money with this one: The earthy, meaty aromas are very promising. The flavor profile, meanwhile, is downright complete, offering a full and wholesome dose of berries and chocolate. The smooth finish fades away in proper time, with touches of bitter chocolate and espresso. It's big, but not clumsy. And what a nice mouthfeel. **88 Best Buy** —*M.S. (12/15/2002)*

Lindemans 2004 Bin 80 Cabernet Sauvignon-Merlot (South Eastern Australia) $8. Smells first like cherry cough syrup, then turns earthy and salty with air. In the mouth, flavors are one-dimensional, like grape or plum skin rather than flesh. **82** —*D.T. (12/31/2005)*

Lindemans 2001 Chardonnay (Padthaway) $13. Smells great, mixing lemon meringue pie with pears, vanilla, and tropical fruit. So what happened? The midpalate is fat, the flavors are simpler, and the finish a touch metallic. **84** —*J.C. (7/1/2002)*

Lindemans 1998 Chardonnay (Padthaway) $15. **85** —*S.H. (10/1/2000)*

Lindemans 1997 Chardonnay (Padthaway) $13. **87** *(11/15/1999)*

Lindemans 2005 Bin 65 Chardonnay (South Eastern Australia) $8. Deep gold in color, with nut, peach, and overt floral aromas. Bright and tropical on the palate, with a soft, almost oily feel; shows its alcohol on the finish. **84 Best Buy** —*D.T. (8/1/2006)*

Lindemans 2003 Bin 65 Chardonnay (South Eastern Australia) $8. This perennial good value shows a lot of oak this vintage. Toast, vanilla, and butterscotch aromas preface buttery yellow fruit on the palate. Finishes with a hearty dose of toast and nut. **82** *(7/2/2004)*

Lindemans 2002 Bin 65 Chardonnay (South Eastern Australia) $8. This recommendation is more a reader reminder than breaking news, because the Bin 65 has been Australia's hallmark value-priced white since 1985. But it is still a reliable, inexpensive choice as well as Australia's most-exported white wine. Bouncy yellow fruit on the palate is accented by spicy, gingery notes that seem a little grown-up for a wine of this price. Fat, ripe nectarines and peaches, plus some nutmeg and cream, waft from the nose. The 2002 Bin 45 Cab (85 points, $8) is also a great buy. **87 Best Buy** —*D.T. (11/15/2003)*

Lindemans 2001 Bin 65 Chardonnay (South Eastern Australia) $9. Probably the wine that put Australian Chardonnay on American consumers' maps, the current vintage boasts aromas of creamery butter, tangerine, and lime, with a touch of movie-theater popcorn. Soft peach and vanilla flavors finish with spicy oak. **84** —*J.C. (7/1/2002)*

Lindemans 1999 Bin 65 Chardonnay (South Australia) $10. **86** *(10/1/2000)*

Lindemans 2003 Reserve Chardonnay (South Australia) $10. Smells vaguely like pina colada, and offers indistinct yellow fruit on the palate. Not particularly flavorful or structured. **82** —*D.T. (5/1/2005)*

Lindemans 2002 Reserve Chardonnay (South Australia) $10. **83** —*D.T. (8/1/2003)*

Lindemans 2005 Bin 40 Merlot (South Eastern Australia) $8. Aromas are of ash, with moderate black cherry. There's no depth or complexity here, and flavors of only earth and cherry, with a metallic edge. **81** —*D.T. (11/15/2006)*

Lindemans 2001 Bin 40 Merlot (Riverland) $8. Simple and straightforward, with cherry, spice, and toasty oak at the fore. **80** —*J.M. (12/15/2002)*

Lindemans 2002 Reserve Merlot (South Australia) $10. This is a slimmer-sized Merlot that features accents of seeped tea and mocha on the palate, with fruit playing second fiddle. Aromas are of baked fruit and cream. Good for casual gatherings. **84** —*D.T. (8/1/2005)*

Lindemans 2004 Bin 85 Pinot Grigio (South Eastern Australia) $8. Vibrant copper-yellow in color. There's not a lot of flavor on the palate—just some olive oil or butter, and a similar feel. Dries up on the finish, where it also shows some alcohol. **81** —*D.T. (12/1/2005)*

Lindemans 2005 Bin 99 Pinot Noir (South Eastern Australia) $8. A good, value-priced New World-style Pinot. Raspberry and cherry flavors are framed by faint caramel, while on the nose, cherry and plum notes dominate. Not complicated, but solid. **85 Best Buy** —*D.T. (11/15/2006)*

Lindemans 2001 Bin 99 Pinot Noir (South Eastern Australia) $9. The initially effusive nose of strawberries and caramel quiets rather quickly, replaced by cola and tree bark. There's more of the same in the mouth, finishing with a stemmy note. **84** —*J.C. (9/1/2002)*

Lindemans 2004 Bin 75 Riesling (South Eastern Australia) $8. Not very Riesling-like, but this is a good, inexpensive white nonetheless. Shows golden apple, pear, and some lanolin aromas and flavors. Fairly full in the mouth for the variety. **84 Best Buy** —*D.T. (8/1/2006)*

Lindemans 2002 Bin 75 Riesling (South Eastern Australia) $8. Aromatic, with interesting putty and powdered-sugar notes on the nose. The flavors are of pear, white peach, and a dash of fresh cilantro. Zips closed with a zesty, lime-and-rainwater freshness. Refreshing, flavorful and, best of all, a steal. **87 Best Buy** —*D.T. (11/15/2004)*

Lindemans 2003 Bin 75 Riesling (South Eastern Australia) $8. On the nose, has a confected, lemon soda-poppy aroma. Heavy on the palate, with a zip of citrus on the finish. **83** —*D.T. (12/1/2005)*

Lindemans 2004 Bin 95 Sauvignon Blanc (South Eastern Australia) $8. This Sauvignon is easy to drink, with soft peach aromas and flavors, and a zing of lemon on the nose. Simple, yes, but dry and fresh. **84 Best Buy** —*D.T. (10/1/2005)*

Lindemans 2003 Bin 95 Sauvignon Blanc (South Eastern Australia) $8. Aromas are light—citrus pith and peach skin. In the mouth, it's a fresh, springtime wine; clean but not too lean, and soft around the edges. Flavors run the gamut of citrus fruits. Finishes round and clean. **86 Best Buy** —*D.T. (11/15/2004)*

Lindemans 2001 Bin 95 Sauvignon Blanc (South Eastern Australia) $8. **81** —*J.M. (12/15/2002)*

Lindemans 2000 Bin 95 Sauvignon Blanc (South Australia) $9. Starts off almost sweet-smelling, blending passion fruit and strawberry or currant aromas, then it turns very green-peppery on the palate before finishing with decent acidity. **84** —*J.C. (2/1/2002)*

Lindemans 1998 Bin 9255 Semillon (Hunter Valley) $16. Lushly aromatic, with scents of cream, vanilla, smoke, and toast. Which might lead you to think it's been aged in oak—but it hasn't. Grapefruit, peach, and cream flavors lead into a mouthwatering, lemony finish. It's a bit austere on the palate yet; give it a few years in the cellar to round out **91 Best Buy** —*J.C. (2/1/2002)*

Lindemans 2002 Bin 77 Semillon-Chardonnay (South Eastern Australia) $8. Neither supple nor complicated; its tropical yellow fruit and light-to-medium weight made it a candidate for a summer picnic or other such casual circumstance. But it has a faux-sugar note on the finish (think Nutrasweet) that made me like it less than I wanted to. **82** —*D.T. (1/1/2002)*

Lindemans 2001 Bin 77 Semillon-Chardonnay (South Australia) $9. **80** —*J.M. (12/15/2002)*

Lindemans 2000 Cawarra Semillon-Chardonnay (South Eastern Australia) $NA. Dusty lemon and pear aromas open onto a clean, tangy palate where lemon, mineral, and metal are the key flavors. Finishes with more of the same. This white's aromas and flavors are very subtle—it's probably better as a food complement than on its own. **84** —*D.T. (2/1/2002)*

Lindemans 1998 Shiraz (Padthaway) $16. There's plenty of plush dark berry fruit in this steady performer, and a smooth—even cotton-soft—mouthfeel, too. The fruit core is accented by cocoa and pepper notes; spice shadings shows later. **87** *(10/1/2001)*

Lindemans 2001 Bin 50 Shiraz (South Eastern Australia) $9. Grapey and sappy, with almost candied cherry fruit, this is a young wine made to be consumed young. Try chilling it to give the cherry and chocolate flavors greater focus and quaff it with burgers this summer. **84** —*J.C. (9/1/2002)*

Lindemans 2003 Reserve Shiraz (South Australia) $10. A straightforward wine, meant for immediate drinking. Smells of pickling spices, tree bark, and vibrant red berries. On the palate, you get pedestrian red and purple berries, jazzed up with black pepper, and a tangy-oak finish. **84** —*D.T. (12/31/2005)*

Lindemans 2002 Reserve Shiraz (South Australia) $10. This is a good-value wine with broad appeal, and a pretty sophisticated, chalky texture for the price. Its blackberry-oak-amaretto profile has an interloping strawberry note that wasn't a high point for me, but adds an approachable streak of red to an otherwise dark Shiraz. **86 Best Buy** —*D.T. (5/1/2005)*

Lindemans 1999 Reserve Shiraz (Padthaway) $15. Jammy, sweet, and lush, just as it should be. This wine is one saturated, fruity monster, and while there are bigger, bolder ones out there, this one is still pretty rich. Yet while it offers plenty of Shiraz's natural chewy, yummy character, it does come up a little short on depth, which is why it falls shy of that elusive higher plateau. **89 Best Buy** —*M.S. (3/1/2003)*

Lindemans 2005 Bin 55 Shiraz-Cabernet Sauvignon (South Eastern Australia) $8. Soft in the mouth and pretty straightforward, but still a bargain. This Shiraz-Cab shows black pepper aromas, with purple plum and oak flavors. Its slightly sour, green edge is a minor detraction. **84 Best Buy** —*D.T. (11/15/2006)*

Lindemans 2000 Cawarra Shiraz-Cabernet Sauvignon (South Eastern Australia) $6. Fat aromas of caramel and mushy black fruit seem disjointed. Some plump strawberry fruit drives the oaky palate, and the finish is dry and sizable. It has the basics but it doesn't really shine or say much. **83** —*M.S. (12/15/2002)*

Lindemans 1999 Limestone Ridge Shiraz-Cabernet Sauvignon (Coonawarra) $30. Excellent. Has deep, pretty aromas of clay, eraser and ripe red plum. Its plum-fruit core has a crisp minty edge, and the package is all couched in a rich, claylike texture. The wine is well structured and sturdy, its red fruit tightening and retreating through the finish. Needs time; drink 2006+. **90 Cellar Selection** —*D.T. (11/15/2004)*

Lindemans 2004 Bin 70 White Blend (South Eastern Australia) $8. Not a blend that you see often, that's for sure—it's 70% Chardonnay, 30% Riesling. The wine offers light peach aromas and flavors, with moderate vanilla and cream to round it out. It's a broad-shouldered wine, particularly for one that contains Riesling. Good and inexpensive quaff. 5,400 cases produced. **84 Best Buy** —*D.T. (12/1/2005)*

LITTLE BOOMEY

Little Boomey 2004 Cabernet Sauvignon-Merlot (South Australia) $7. Two-thirds Cabernet with Merlot making up the balance, this straightforward red had some berry fruit on the nose that fades with air. Tastes made for the masses, with red berry flavors. **83** —*D.T. (12/31/2005)*

AUSTRALIA

Little Boomey 2004 Shiraz (South Australia) $7. Offers sweet black and raspberry aromas and flavors, with some earth accents. Gets simpler and softer with air. A quaffer. 82,800 cases produced. **83** —*D.T. (10/1/2005)*

Little Boomey 2004 Shiraz-Cabernet Sauvignon (South Australia) $7. Pink-purple in color. Smells and tastes of sweet fruit, with metallic hints on the palate and a stably note on the nose. **82** —*D.T. (10/1/2005)*

LITTLE PENGUIN

Little Penguin 2003 Cabernet Sauvignon (South Eastern Australia) $7. The dominant aroma here is raspberry, which is followed up on the palate by some sweet, concentrated berry fruit. A good casual quaffer. **82** —*D.T. (11/15/2004)*

Little Penguin 2005 Chardonnay (South Eastern Australia) $8. Smells of buttered toast, with flavors of unripe pineapple on the palate. Has an offputting plasticy texture and buttered popcorn flavors on the finish. **81** —*D.T. (11/15/2006)*

Little Penguin 2004 Chardonnay (South Eastern Australia) $8. Blooms with vibrant peach and nectarine notes on the nose, which persist in the mouth. The palate also has a slightly honeyed, or gingery character. Soft and slightly sweet, and just the thing for your next big gig. 200,000 cases produced. **84 Best Buy** —*D.T. (10/1/2005)*

Little Penguin 2003 Chardonnay (South Eastern Australia) $7. The first edition of Southcorp's new brand yields is a nice, easily likeable Chard. Aromas are light, like talc powder or baking flour, mixed with a few golden apples. The feel is soft and fresh, with soft peach and apple flavors and a juicy finish. **85 Best Buy** —*D.T. (11/15/2004)*

Little Penguin 2005 Merlot (South Eastern Australia) $8. Smells like flowers and ripe berries, and the palate delivers berry and maple flavors. One-dimensional, but will satisfy those who like forward, sweetish wines. **83** —*D.T. (11/15/2006)*

Little Penguin 2004 Merlot (South Eastern Australia) $8. Blackberry and plum aromas have mochalike accents, and it tastes just as it smells. A streak of mint saves this wine from being too cloying, but on the sweet side it certainly is. Will probably appeal most to newer wine drinkers. **83** —*D.T. (10/1/2005)*

Little Penguin 2003 Merlot (South Eastern Australia) $7. Smells and tastes like a confection: aromas are sweet and marshmallowy, and fruit on the palate is soft, sweet, and candied. Will please wine newbies, but may be too simple for others. **82** —*D.T. (3/1/2005)*

Little Penguin 2005 Pinot Noir (South Eastern Australia) $8. A good, introductory-level Pinot with decent intensity and a very approachable style. Offers cherry, cola, and modest oak shadings, and a soft mouthfeel. **83** —*D.T. (11/15/2006)*

Little Penguin 2003 Shiraz (South Eastern Australia) $7. Nose shows light, meaty, smoky aromas, and the palate offers up a soft-and-easy feel and plenty of mixed berry fruit. A safe, straightforward, please-almost-everyone Shiraz. **84 Best Buy** —*D.T. (12/31/2004)*

Little Penguin 2005 White Shiraz (South Eastern Australia) $8. Smells as rosy and pink as it looks. Just slightly off dry, this Shiraz tastes like flowers and peaches. Drink this quaff on the patio. **84 Best Buy** —*D.T. (12/1/2005)*

LITTLE'S

Little's 2000 Green Label Semillon-Chardonnay (Hunter Valley) $12. Its flavors are crisp and clean—think citrus and taut yellow fruit—but it's no sourpuss. This Sem-Chard has medium body and some viscosity, plus a little butter on the nose and the finish. One to try with a beurre blanc sauce, perhaps? Fresh and sunny; perfect as a summertime wine. **87** —*D.T. (12/31/2003)*

LOGAN AUSTRALIA

Logan Australia 1999 Chardonnay (Orange) $17. Shows promise in its lightly toasty and citrusy aromas and lemon and green-apple flavors, but tails off rapidly on the finish. It's lean and racy, obviously from a relatively cool-climate region, and should be served as you would basic Chablis, with oysters and the like. **84** —*J.C. (7/1/2002)*

Logan Australia 1999 Reserve Chardonnay (Orange) $21. Focused in the mouth with just a touch of creaminess, the Logan offers pear and nutmeg flavors, and a hint of green apple on the finish. It's not a mouth-filling, overly flashy wine, but this could be a good thing if you're pouring it with dinner. Try it with your first-course seafood dish. **86** —*D.T. (8/1/2003)*

Logan Australia 2000 Ripe Chardonnay (Hunter Valley) $10. 82 —*D.T. (8/1/2003)*

Logan Australia 1998 Ripe Red Blend (Orange) $10. The bouquet is sort of thin and odd, with herbal notes as well as molasses. Chocolate-covered strawberries is the flavor memory triggered by the oaky palate, and the finish veers toward bitter. With only modest acidity, this one comes off heavy and flat. **84** —*M.S. (12/15/2002)*

Logan Australia 2001 Logan Sauvignon Blanc (Orange) $13. Has a dryish, spritzy mouthfeel and flavors of unripe melon and stone fruits that vanish more quickly than we'd like. The nose has both light, feminine notes (apricot, honey) and more masculine scents of beef and musk. This Sauvignon was reviewed by two editors, with consistent notes. **84** —*D.T. (5/1/2004)*

LONG FLAT

Long Flat 2003 Cabernet Sauvignon (Coonawarra) $14. This medium-weight Cabernet shows true to its terroir, with hints of mint or eucalyptus adding a medicinal edge to the bright cherry fruit. Fully dry, but soft and rounded on the finish. **87** *(12/1/2005)*

Long Flat 2004 Chardonnay (Yarra Valley) $14. This fruit comes from Cheviot Bridge shareholders, with the wine made at Yering Station. Lightly toasty, with hints of vanilla and sweet corn to the Golden Delicious apple flavors. Turns citrusy on the finish. **86** *(12/1/2005)*

Long Flat 2002 Chardonnay (South Eastern Australia) $8. This wine's residual sugar is apparent, but it's still a pleasant, moderately priced offering. Smells like smoky vanilla, and is full and soft on the palate with peach, apple, and nectarine flavors. Closes with a snap of citrus. **85** *(7/2/2004)*

Long Flat 2002 Merlot (South Eastern Australia) $8. Soft and fruity in the mouth, the Long Flat has plum and coffee flavors, and a nose that sports black pepper, toast, and an orange-liqueur note. Finsihes with a sour herb, or metallic note, but it's fleeting. 5,000 cases imported to U.S. **84** —*D.T. (9/1/2004)*

Long Flat 2004 Pinot Noir (Yarra Valley) $14. Light in weight, but there's a creaminess to the texture so it doesn't come across as thin. Sour cherry and beet flavors add resiny, herbal, and charred notes on the finish. **85** *(12/1/2005)*

Long Flat 2002 Cabernet-Shiraz-Malbec Red Blend (South Eastern Australia) $8. Don't come looking for varietal character in this value-priced red—it's a blend of three varieties (55% Cab, 30% Shiraz, and 15% Malbec). What this wine delivers is red and black berry fruit with moderate oak and vanilla shadings. Tightens up on the finish, with a crisp blast of mint. **84** —*D.T. (11/15/2005)*

Long Flat 2004 Riesling (Eden Valley) $14. Floral and citrusy, with hints of lime sherbet and orange blossom on the nose and ripe pear and citrus flavors. Fairly full-bodied and soft, with a dry finish and more weight and texture than expected. **86** *(12/1/2005)*

Long Flat 2004 Sauvignon Blanc (Adelaide Hills) $14. Quite tropical and fruity, with estery notes of banana on the nose before passion fruit and herbal-grassy flavors take firmer hold. Plump on the midpalate, but turns hard and citrusy on the finish. **85** *(12/1/2005)*

Long Flat 2004 Semillon-Sauvignon Blanc (South Eastern Australia) $7. Weighty and full on the palate, this wine is nearing its "Best Before…" date, yet still carries enough interesting pear, honey, beeswax, and clove flavors to warrant a modest recommendation. An even better bet is to try the '05 when it arrives in February. **83** *(12/1/2005)*

Long Flat 2002 Semillon-Sauvignon Blanc (South Eastern Australia) $7. An 80-20 Semillon-Sauvignon blend, the wine's yellow fruit flavors are a little dilute, but its aromas of sweet yellow and citrus fruit are quite pleasant. Finishes with a mealy bananal-ike texture. **84** —*D.T. (5/1/2004)*

Long Flat 2004 Shiraz (Barossa) $14. Derived from Grant Burge's own Barossa plantings, this soft, enveloping wine boasts expressive black cherry and plum flavors and a subtle hit of vanilla. Not hugely complex, but satisfying. **87** *(12/1/2005)*

AUSTRALIA

LONGVIEW

Longview 2003 Devil's Elbow Cabernet Sauvignon (Adelaide Hills) $19. Has aromas of plum, berry, and spice. On the palate, surging, mouthwatering flavors of tart plums and eucalyptus follow, couched in furry, dusty tannins. Lively acidity completes a lovely package. 400 cases produced. **90 Editors' Choice** —*D.T. (8/1/2005)*

Longview 2005 Blue Cow Chardonnay (Adelaide Hills) $18. This delightful Chardonnay is both femininely styled and intense. The nose proffers dusty lemondrop aromas, and the palate, lemon-lime, chalk, and mineral notes. Fresh and clean, it's lively enough to work as an apéritif. **89** —*D.T. (10/1/2006)*

Longview 2004 Blue Cow Chardonnay (Adelaide Hills) $16. This Adelaide Hills wine offers pretty pear, melon, and apple aromas and flavors. It has a steely, minerally spine and a clean, mouth-watering feel. Not a flabby wine, and equally suited to the cocktail hour, and pairing with food. 1,500 cases produced. **89** —*D.T. (8/1/2005)*

Longview 2004 Black Crow Nebbiolo (Adelaide Hills) $21. Has aromas of licorice, cola, and briar, with much of the same being echoed on the palate. Moderately sized, and not too intense. 1,000 cases produced. **86** —*D.T. (8/1/2006)*

Longview 2003 Black Crow Nebbiolo (Adelaide Hills) $20. Has welcoming, plummy aromas, with hints of lemony oak. The palate has a sturdy nutty-oaky shell that is the wine's focus, and some creaminess to the feel, but not quite enough plum stuffing to fill it out. Still a good wine. **86** —*D.T. (8/1/2005)*

Longview 2005 Iron Knob Riesling (Adelaide Hills) $16. This is a Riesling for every day, not too intense or acidic to drive away those new to the variety. Lemon drop and fresh herb notes on the nose are echoed on the palate. Ends with a hearty squeeze of lime, lime, lime. **87** —*D.T. (8/1/2006)*

Longview 2005 Whippet Sauvignon Blanc (Adelaide Hills) $16. A surprising sort of Sauvignon in that it doesn't start out like much, but really deserves a second (or third) look. Mineral and melon aromas and a dilute, almost heavy feel is what you get right off. After a few sips, the intensity builds up, and flavors of citrus zest, mineral, and fresh herb emerge. 1,400 cases produced. **88** —*D.T. (8/1/2006)*

Longview 2004 Whippet Sauvignon Blanc (Adelaide Hills) $16. The nose is very pretty: white peach, a little resin, a little lychee. The flavors are nice—lemon peel, grapefruit pulp—but don't quite live up to the nose's offerings. **86** —*D.T. (8/1/2005)*

Longview 2004 Yakka Shiraz (Adelaide Hills) $20. Has chocolate fudge and barbecue aromas that go the way of black pepper and roast beef with air. Black pepper is the name of the game in the mouth, too, where dark berry fruit and eucalyptus character takes up the slack. Unique; drink over the near term. **87** —*D.T. (8/1/2006)*

Longview 2003 Yakka Shiraz-Viognier (Adelaide Hills) $19. Many will appreciate this restrained, pretty Shiraz; it is a food-friendly style and size, showing chalky-smooth tannins and flavors of cola and blackberry. This is evidence of how the Hills is having success with reds as well as its whites. **90** —*D.T. (8/1/2005)*

Longview 2005 Beau Sea Viognier (Adelaide Hills) $20. Medium, almost full, in weight but mildly flavored for its heft. Offers up delicate talc and lemondrop aromas, with pear skin flavors dominating on the palate. After a few sips, limey-citrus flavors step in and take over. 1,500 cases produced. **87** —*D.T. (10/1/2006)*

Longview 2004 Beau Sea Viognier (Adelaide Hills) $18. Offers pretty trading card bubblegum powder and floral aromas and flavors. Flavors of lemon and Granny Smith apple flavors are almost tart, but not unpleasantly so, but brighten on the juicy finish. **87** —*D.T. (8/1/2005)*

LONGWOOD

Longwood 1999 Shiraz (McLaren Vale) $28. This impressively dark and smooth Shiraz has a taut black fruit and licorice bouquet. Very smooth and supple on the palate, it offers rich black currant, cassis, and chocolate flavors. Fine, even tannins on the long finish close this very well structured, nicely integrated wine that should improve with two to four years cellaring. **89** —*M.M. (6/1/2001)*

LONSDALE RIDGE

Lonsdale Ridge 2002 Chardonnay (Victoria) $8. Soft apple and citrus fruit has a slighty oily mouthfeel, and finishes with a toasty, buttery flourish. Aromas are delicate, of flowers and pear. **85 Best Buy** *(7/2/2004)*

Lonsdale Ridge 2002 Merlot (Victoria) $8. This Merlot has some unusual characteristics, but it's still a compelling, value-priced offering. Both the aromas and flavors carry spice, bacon, straight-off-the-barbecue, rustic notes. There's mixed plums underneath it all, all of which is framed in a soft, easily accessible feel. **85 Best Buy** —*D.T. (9/1/2004)*

Lonsdale Ridge 2002 Shiraz (Victoria) $8. Somewhat thin and acidic in the mouth, with a rubbery note on the palate. Still, blue and blackberry aromas and flavors are nice. **83** —*D.T. (12/31/2004)*

LOOSE END

Loose End 2005 Rosé Grenache (Barossa) $15. Has a very pretty pink-garnet color, and fragrant rose and brown sugar aromas. Indeed, this rose shows some sugar on the palate, too—not unwarranted, but certainly not totally dry. The floral quality persists on the palate, as does a hint of orange liqueur. **85** —*D.T. (11/15/2006)*

Loose End 2004 G-S-M (Barossa) $17. Raspberry and red plum aromas are sweet and ripe, but not in a cloying kind of way. Oak shadings on the palate give this GSMM (39% Grenache, 35% Shiraz, 24% Merlot, and 2% Mataro) a nice texture. The mixed-berry flavors have a rustic quality to them that gives this wine the overall impression of an untamed field blend. A nice change of pace. 1,000 cases produced. **89** —*D.T. (8/1/2006)*

Loose End NV Sparkling MSM Red Blend (Barossa) $20. MSM stands for Merlot-Shiraz-Mataro, with Merlot accounting for 87% of the blend. It's a full-bodied, oaky red wine with bubbles, so if that appeals to you, this wine will too, featuring toasted coconut and vanilla shadings over blackberry liqueur flavors. **87** —*J.C. (12/31/2006)*

Loose End 2004 Shiraz-Viognier (Barossa) $18. Has aromas of wet concrete. It's medium weight, with modest blackberry and blueberry flavors. Even keel on the palate, but has a metallic edge to the finish. **84** —*D.T. (6/1/2006)*

LORIKEET

Lorikeet NV Brut Champagne Blend (South Eastern Australia) $10. Overall, the brut is pretty similar to Lorikeet's Extra Dry sparkler. Honeyed, tropical fruit, a medium body and light toasty aromas make for an easy, enjoyable value-priced bubbly. **86 Best Buy** —*D.T. (12/31/2005)*

Lorikeet NV Extra Dry Champagne Blend (South Eastern Australia) $10. Almost identical to the Lorikeet Brut. There's more peachy-tropical fruit here; it's off-dry, as it should be, with a brief finish. **86 Best Buy** —*D.T. (12/31/2005)*

Lorikeet NV Sparkling Shiraz (South Eastern Australia) $10. Has a bubblegum center, with a woody, almost metallic, shell. Aromas are of tea and toast; tannins are pretty dominant. **84** —*D.T. (12/31/2005)*

Lorikeet NV Sparkling Shiraz (South Eastern Australia) $9. Raspberry, blackberry and plum flavors and aromas rule the roost here, with oak and cream in supporting roles. It wants some length on the finish, but overall, it's a fine introduction to sparkling Shiraz, and one of the least expensive on the U.S. market. **84 Best Buy** —*D.T. (12/31/2004)*

Lorikeet NV Brut Sparkling Blend (South Eastern Australia) $9. Smells pretty yeasty—caramelly, even—and the palate's toasty graham-cracker quality follows suit. Cherry flavors pick up midpalate, and drive the wine through the finish. Will have wide appeal, particularly for those who like their still Chards and Pinots fat and toasty. **85 Best Buy** —*D.T. (12/31/2004)*

Lorikeet NV Extra Dry Sparkling Blend (South Eastern Australia) $9. This new brand's extra dry is a light-bodied apéritif-style wine with light peach and floral flavors, and powdered-sugar notes on the nose and the finish. The bead's a little coarse, but the wine is still a fine choice (and a good value) for holiday parties. **84 Best Buy** —*D.T. (12/31/2004)*

LOWE

Lowe 1997 Ashbourne Vineyard Chardonnay (Hunter Valley) $18. This is what happens to old Chards made with tropical fruit and lots of oak—the fruit fades away, leaving nothing but caramel and butterscotch flavors, hollow at the core. **81** —*J.C. (9/10/2002)*

M. CHAPOUTIER AUSTRALIA

M. Chapoutier Australia 2000 Mount Benson Shiraz (Australia) $30. What do you get when a Rhône master heads to the Southern Hemisphere? Has black fruit and a pickle-barrel note on the nose, and plenty more black fruit in the mouth. Intensity falls off a bit on the finish, where there's just some oak and plum skin. **84** —*D.T. (12/31/2003)*

M. Chapoutier Australia 1999 Mount Benson Shiraz (Australia) $30. Even and tangy, the quite dry, tart fruit sports white-pepper and tarragon accents in noted Rhône winemaker Michel Chapoutier's Australian project. Crisp and high in acidity, this is slightly atypical but attractive Shiraz from Down Under, with a lighter, almost claret-like weight and sour cherry, tobacco-tinged finish. **88** *(11/1/2001)*

M.BROWN

M.Brown 1998 Shiraz (Barossa Valley) $20. An overly woody almost sawdust-like nose yields to allow sweet-and-sour dark berry fruit to come forward. This raspberry-cedar tinged wine shows medium acidity and weight, closing with pepper and chalk notes and firm tannins. **85** *(10/1/2001)*

MACAW CREEK

Macaw Creek 2003 Grenache-Shiraz (South Australia) $17. Though this Grenache-Shiraz also contains some Cabernet Sauvignon and Petit Verdot, it still feels like a lightweight. The nose is pleasing, with fleshy plum and berry fruit, but the palate is sort of tart—think cranberry, veiled with a few ripe plums. 1,000 cases produced. **86** —*D.T. (5/1/2005)*

MACQUARIEDALE

Macquariedale 1999 Four Winds Vineyard Chardonnay (Hunter Valley) $17. A sweet, somewhat simple Chard that boasts melon and citrus aromas and flavors, gently couched in hints of buttered toast. Finishes short, with tangerine flavors. **85** —*J.C. (7/1/2002)*

Macquariedale 1999 Old Vine Semillon (Hunter Valley) $18. This richly textured blend of Anjou pears, beeswax, and lemon flavors finishes long and tangy, with hints of vanilla. Forward and delicious now, so why wait? Enjoy it over the next year. **87** —*J.C. (2/1/2002)*

Macquariedale 1999 Thomas Shiraz (Hunter Valley) $22. Smells dry and dusty, like a midwestern country lane in August. The fruit comes through in the mouth, filling it with bright red berries and cherries, while touches of ground black pepper and vanilla oak show up on the finish. **83** —*J.C. (9/1/2002)*

MAD FISH

Mad Fish 2005 Rosé Cabernet Sauvignon (Western Australia) $14. The meaty, fresh-herb notes that we like about Cab manifest themselves differently in a rosé version of the variety. Though there's some mixed-berry fruit here, it's not a giving, fruit-forward wine. Perhaps suffers by being evaluated without food; this one's meant for the table. **86** —*D.T. (4/1/2006)*

Mad Fish 2003 Cabernet Sauvignon-Shiraz (Western Australia) $15. It's not often that you find interesting wines, wines that have their own individual character, at this price. This red blend offers cool eucalyptus, earth, and nutmeg aromas, and a palate rife with mixed berries. It's dry (if you want sweet fruit, look elsewhere) and has soft, easy tannins—a wine suited for easy quaffing as it is to some contemplation. **87** —*D.T. (12/1/2005)*

Mad Fish 2004 Chardonnay (Western Australia) $15. Fragrant tropical fruit flavors waft from the nose, but the palate is more understated, relying on mineral and chalk notes for flavor and texture. A simple, good choice whenever chicken breast is on the menu. **85** —*D.T. (12/1/2005)*

Mad Fish 2005 Riesling (Western Australia) $14. Smells fresh and inviting, like lemon curd and freshly laundered sheets. Acidic but not overly tart; pear and peach flavors only get better and more intense as the wine opens. A very good wine at a fair price. 3,000 cases imported. **88** —*D.T. (4/1/2006)*

Mad Fish 2004 Sauvignon Blanc (Western Australia) $15. Has a little candle wax and citrus on the nose. The mouthfeel has a citrusy kick, but relies on its smooth, minerally feel. Offers lemon and lime flavors, but its understated, for sure. **87** —*D.T. (12/1/2005)*

Mad Fish 2004 Shiraz (Western Australia) $14. This Shiraz is all about black cherry and plum fruit, accented with a cool, minty crispness. A forward, drink-now wine, but not as simple as all that. 30,000 cases produced. **87** —*D.T. (4/1/2006)*

MAK

Mak 2003 Chardonnay (Adelaide Hills) $16. A solid wine with both presence and delicacy. It's not overpowering, but it has good length and staying power. Firm, clear peach and olive oil flavors complement similar aromas. There's also a nice spiciness on the palate that fades into the finish. Very tasty. 2,000 cases produced. **89 Editors' Choice** *(7/2/2004)*

Mak 2001 Chardonnay (Adelaide Hills) $16. This wine is packed with bright tropical fruit and citrus aromas and flavors, yet stays balanced and spritely through the long, citrusy finish. It's easy to like and easy to drink. **87** —*J.C. (7/1/2002)*

Mak 2000 Cabernet, Shiraz, Merlot Red Blend (Coonawarra) $18. Black fruit and some road tar comprise the potent, dark nose. Sweet black cherry flavors follow, with a long sultry finish closing the program. The feel is soft and dense, and the fruit quality is good but not stunning. **84** —*M.S. (12/15/2001)*

Mak 2002 Shiraz (Clare Valley) $18. An interesting Shiraz, this one's plummy aromas and flavors have one foot in the prune/raisin camp. Still, there are pretty flavors of Christmas spice, bread flour, tea, and tobacco here, too; the latter two leave a somewhat sour taste on the finish. **87** —*D.T. (10/1/2006)*

MANDU

Mandu 2003 Cabernet Sauvignon (Margaret River) $12. This narrow, value-priced wine is unusual in its category because its dominating notes are earthy, woodsy ones, rather than forwardly fruity ones. Has edgy, wooly tannins that would make it a ready partner for some charbroiled meats. **84** —*D.T. (8/1/2006)*

MARCUS JAMES

Marcus James 2000 Shiraz (South Eastern Australia) $6. Though some reviewers had trouble getting past the plum, cotton candy, mint, and bologna nose, all agreed that the palate and finish had the trappings of a true fruit-bomb. Easy-to-quaff, slightly sweet, red berry and vanilla palate flavors lasted through the red fruit-and-caramel finish. **84** *(10/1/2001)*

MARGAN

Margan 2003 Limited Release Single Vineyard Ceres Hill Barbera (Hunter Valley) $15. Straightforward but not simple, this Aussie Barbera has shadings of maple on the nose and plum-and-oak flavors on the palate. Finishes with lively acidity, but wants a little more stuffing on the palate to reach the next level. **86** —*D.T. (4/1/2006)*

Margan 2002 Cabernet Sauvignon (Hunter Valley) $17. This Cab seems narrow and kind of mainstream at first, but really blooms after a few minutes in the glass. Has menthol and carob accents on the nose, with a sweet-plum core of flavor. Blankets the tongue with textured tannins. **90** —*D.T. (4/1/2006)*

Margan 2000 Cabernet Sauvignon (Hunter Valley) $15. Faux-creaminess pervades nose and palate flavors, though I'm not convinced that what's underneath is necessarily worth fighting for. The bouquet offers soil, juicy berry, and watermelon aromas; tart black fruit peeks out from under the palate's creamy cloak. **82** —*D.T. (6/1/2002)*

Margan 2000 Chardonnay (Hunter Valley) $12. A boldly flavored wine that doesn't hold back, packed with sweet pears, powdered cinnamon, and clove. Smooth and supple in the mouth and leaves tangy, lingering flavors of lime on the finish. **87** —*J.C. (7/1/2002)*

Margan 2003 Merlot (Hunter Valley) $17. I like this wine for what it isn't—brash or sweet. Tannins are smooth and manageable, with mushroom and stable notes accenting firm plum and cherry flavors. A little soft on the palate, with a bite of herb at the finish, but it's nearly as enjoyable as the winery's excellent Cabernet. **88** —*D.T. (4/1/2006)*

Margan 2000 Semillon (Hunter Valley) $12. This is a lush, immediately approachable style of Semillon, one that puts the focus on vanilla, cream, and smoke aromas and sweet peach flavors, yet still finishes lemony and long. Drink now. **88 Best Buy** —*J.C. (2/1/2002)*

Margan 1999 Semillon (Hunter Valley) $13. A prickly cactus of a wine that may yet blossom, given enough time. Piney, resinous notes on the nose, along with aromas reminiscent of scrambled eggs. Then the attack is sweet—almost cloying—before a strong sour-lemon flavor takes over on the finish. Bury this in your cellar for 10 years in the hopes that it will improve as dramatically as many other Hunter Valley Semillons. **81** —*J.C. (9/1/2001)*

Margan 2004 Botrytis Semillon (Hunter Valley) $25. Orange-gold in color, this is a very good sweet wine but doesn't have quite the sophistication that Australia's top stickies do. This one is linear in the mouth at first, finally fleshing out with peach syup and mango toward the back palate. **87** —*D.T. (8/1/2006)*

Margan 2000 Shiraz (Hunter Valley) $16. Smoothly integrated aromas of blackberry, licorice, and toast leave your mouth watering, but the palate can't quite keep up, offering only simple grape and toast flavors that peter out all too quickly on the finish. A lighter Shiraz than we're accustomed to seeing from Australia. **85** *(10/1/2001)*

Margan 2005 Saignée Rosé Shiraz (Hunter Valley) $15. One of the better Oz rosés I've had lately. It's fairly dark in color, with deep black cherry and raspberry flavors and aromas. It's medium-full in size, with a dry, minerally feel. Perfect for those warm days that you spend on the deck grilling up a storm. **89** —*D.T. (4/1/2006)*

Margan 2001 Verdelho (Hunter Valley) $13. Floral aromas—particularly honeysuckle—are complemented by sweet peaches and pears. But it's not all about fruit, there's a minerally streak of lime or chalk that runs through the flavors. A laser-like beam of lemony acidity offsets a rich, thick mouthfeel. **89** *(2/1/2002)*

Margan 1999 Verdelho (Hunter Valley) $13. **89** —*M.M. (1/1/2004)*

MARIENBERG

Marienberg 1997 Reserve Shiraz (South Australia) $20. Though it's dry, tangy, and lean in profile, it's still smooth on the palate. This South Australian Shiraz has dark berry, cream, and cedar aromas followed by a mouth of licorice, soy, sour cherry, and menthol. Finishes with bitter coffee and tart berry notes. **86** *(10/1/2001)*

MARINDA PARK

Marinda Park 2001 Chardonnay (Mornington Peninsula) $19. **81** —*D.T. (8/1/2003)*

Marinda Park 2001 Pinot Noir (Mornington Peninsula) $26. The fruit is dark for a Pinot, and has a definite steeped-tea tang, thanks to the hearty oak. The mouthfeel is strangely powdery. **85** —*D.T. (10/1/2003)*

MARKTREE

Marktree 1999 Soldier's Block Vineyard Chardonnay (Australia) $9. Starts off decently, with menthol-toast aromas of new oak layered over apple and lime fruit. Then turns overly oaky on the palate, blending caramel, toast, and dill flavors with tart apple, finishing off with a slice of lemony acidity. **83** —*J.C. (7/1/2002)*

Marktree 1999 Soldier's Block Vineyard Shiraz (New South Wales) $9. The jammy grapiness of this decent quaff is offset by violet and clove, a leathery touch and even a tangy, citrus note. It's lithe, maybe even lean for the flavor profile, with some black tea accents. Turns woodier on the back end, showing a peppery note as well. **85** *(10/1/2001)*

Marktree 1999 White Blend (Australia) $7. This bright gold Aussie is medium-full in the mouth, with throat-coating golden apple and caramel flavors on the palate and on the finish. Its bouquet has similar butterballish flavors. Most of its fans will come from the California Chard-lovers camp. **83** —*D.T. (2/1/2002)*

MARQUEE

Marquee 2001 Selections Chain of Ponds Cabernet Sauvignon-Cabernet Franc-Merlot Cabernet Blend (Kangaroo Island) $30. Offers cherry and menthol aromas, and taut, almost sour, cherry and plum flavors. It's sturdy, smooth, and certainly not sweet. A blend of 50% Cabernet Sauvignon, 40% Cabernet Franc, and 10% Merlot. **88** —*D.T. (8/1/2005)*

Marquee 2001 Selections Cabernet Sauvignon (Adelaide Hills) $28. If you're expecting big and overblown, just keep walking. Made at Chain of Ponds, this Cab offers pretty taut, borderline tart, flavors with a heap of outdoorsy, rustic elements. Briary, tree-bark aromas on the nose preface taut red plum and cherry fruit, and the texture on the finish is really nice and velvety. The near-tart element is the only thing that's keeping me from launching this into the next decile. **89** —*D.T. (12/31/2004)*

Marquee 2001 Selections Classic Cabernet Sauvignon (South Eastern Australia) $10. Marquee Selections is an interesting outfit: They find dozens of lesser-known wineries from all parts of Australia, and bring them into the U.S. under the same Marquee label. (Information about the wineries that produce each bottling is on the back label.) This Cab has nuances of mocha or coffee, particularly on the finish, and a palate that stays on the plum-earth-oak track. It's a tried-and-true profile, but it succeeds here. **85 Best Buy** —*D.T. (11/15/2004)*

Marquee 2000 Selections Saddler's Creek Cabernet Sauvignon (South Eastern Australia) $20. Taste this blind with friends, and place big bets: This wine's not likely to be identified as Australian, or New World at all, for that matter. Smells earthy, with iron accents that reminded me of mature Chianti. Ditto for the flavors: Stout cherry fruit, brown earth, and some rustic oak. Very good, but not at all what you're expecting. 1,500 cases produced. **87** —*D.T. (12/31/2004)*

Marquee 2003 Signature Cabernet Sauvignon (Langhorne Creek) $20. A solid Cab for a fair price. Thick but smooth tannins dominate on the palate, where plum and berry fruit are pretty tight, almost sour. Woodspice and barbecue aromas on the nose; an even, constant wine overall. 475 cases produced. **89** —*D.T. (8/1/2006)*

Marquee 2004 Artisan Wines Classic Cabernet Sauvignon-Merlot (Victoria) $10. Smells almost cloying, like raspberries and strawberry preserves, with the barest hints of herb and earth. The same sweet fruit flavors appear on the palate, along with some Sweet Tart. **83** —*D.T. (12/31/2005)*

Marquee 2003 Classic Cabernet Sauvignon-Merlot (Victoria) $10. Sweetish and straightforward, this is a wine made for the masses: It offers juicy, peppery aromas and a boatload of black and blueberry fruit, edged with some earth. Good and affordable, too. **85 Best Buy** —*D.T. (8/1/2005)*

Marquee 2002 Chardonnay (South Eastern Australia) $12. Marquee's lowest-priced offering performed best in our tastings. This bottling is vibrant and tasty, medium weight, with pure peach fruit, and accents of vanilla, tropical fruit and grilled nuts. How's the bouquet? Just as nice as the palate. **88 Best Buy** *(7/2/2004)*

Marquee 2001 Adelaide Hills Chardonnay (Adelaide Hills) $27. A crisp wine, but not one with demonstrative fruit. There are pear, anise, and floral aromas, with firm pear fruit and a talc-powder presence that lends as much flavor as it does texture. **86** *(7/2/2004)*

Marquee 2004 Artisan Wines Classic Chardonnay (Victoria) $10. Smells of peach and creamy vanilla, and unfolds to reveal forward apple, pear, and oak flavors on the palate. Crisp in the mouth; enjoyable and uncomplicated overall. **85 Best Buy** —*D.T. (12/1/2005)*

Marquee 2003 Artisan Wines Classic Chardonnay (Victoria) $10. Smells like citrus and peach, with a cottony-vanilla overlay. Citrus stays the course on the palate, but the flavors are halfhearted, and the feel soft. But Marquee's sleek new packaging is quite nice. **83** —*D.T. (5/1/2005)*

Marquee 2001 Macedon Ranges Chardonnay (Victoria) $27. From Cleveland Winery in Victoria, this Chard shows butter and burnt sugar aromas. On the palate, there is light butter and talc flavors, and a powdery textured finish. Wants more stuffing in the middle. **83** *(7/2/2004)*

AUSTRALIA

AUSTRALIA

Marquee 2001 Selections Chardonnay (Mornington Peninsula) $20. At first, it's fairly buttery and mouthcoating, in that butterscotch-candy way, but the feeling cedes to a smooth, elegant minerality. Similarly, buttered popcorn and pretty, dusty aromas fight on the nose. The wine seems conflicted between two distinct Chard styles and, as such, I fear may not be the ideal wine for either camp. **85** —*D.T. (11/15/2004)*

Marquee 1999 Shoalhaven Coast Chardonnay (New South Wales) $17. This Marquee offering is from Camberwarra Estate, just south of Sydney. It's slim on pear and peach fruit but has a hearty helping of butter and butterscotch flavors. Finishes with buttered popcorn notes. A mouthcoating, well-balanced wine, but also one that doesn't quite feel stuffed. **85** *(7/2/2004)*

Marquee 2004 Signature Chardonnay (Yarra Valley) $15. Aromas run the gamut from light peach and flowers to corn, and the palate offers more of the same. A light, soft, enjoyable wine. Finishes with cream and vanilla. 370 cases imported. **84** —*D.T. (4/1/2006)*

Marquee 1999 Selections Pfeiffer Wines Marsanne (Victoria) $15. Medium-weight with honeyed Jolly Rancher and fresh green pea aromas. It's flat on the palate, and light on flavor, offering only light honey and butter notes. **83** —*D.T. (12/31/2004)*

Marquee 1999 Selections Pfeiffer Wines Merlot (South Eastern Australia) $25. This Merlot doesn't live up to Pfeiffer's excellent sweet wines. It does have a smooth, claylike feel, particularly on the finish, but the baked-fruitcake aromas and flavors aren't as enjoyable. **83** —*D.T. (5/1/2005)*

Marquee 2003 Signature Merlot (Rutherglen) $20. Starts off thick and molassesy on the nose, a weedy note revealing itself with air. Plum flavors are on the sour side, couched in woody tannins. **84** —*D.T. (4/1/2006)*

Marquee NV Selections Classic Muscat (Rutherglen) $25. Butterscotch and some noticeable alcohol on the nose; the palate has butterscotch, then a flash of peach and citrus, then chocolate-cherry candy. Smooth and unctuous, but not superrich. A nice-sized wine for folks who are afraid of big stickies. **89** —*D.T. (12/31/2004)*

Marquee 2000 Selections Pinot Noir (Macedon Ranges) $27. Sour and herbaceous. Smells very taut, like dry herbs, dill, green olive. Herb and cherry, top to bottom, through the finish. **81** —*D.T. (12/31/2004)*

Marquee 2001 Selections Port Phillip Estate Pinot Noir (Mornington Peninsula) $27. Round, overt aromas of plum fruit, cedar, and putty prepare you for a wine that's more brash than this one is. It's a slimmer-sized Pinot, the cedar and plum notes still present on the palate but taking second billing to a nice, rocky-minerally feel that lasts on the finish. **89** —*D.T. (8/1/2005)*

Marquee 2004 Signature Pinot Noir (Mornington Peninsula) $20. Medium-sized on the palate, this Pinot's red and black cherry flavors have a pleasing fresh-herb edge. Aromas are meaty; a moderate, balanced wine that will probably shine even more with food. **88** —*D.T. (4/1/2006)*

Marquee NV Tawny Port (Rutherglen) $25. There's a lot to like about this wine, including biscuit, earth, and fresh herb aromas and orange, biscuit, stone fruit, and meat flavors. Has a sturdy shell, but a little hollowness in the midpalate. Doesn't have the unctuousness, or stickiness, that you typically get from fortified wines—for this reviewer, something was missing from this very good wine. For others, this characteristic might be a boon. **87** —*D.T. (12/31/2004)*

Marquee 2004 Artisan Wines Classic Riesling (Victoria) $10. Smells and tastes like lemon pudding, or creamsicle. On the palate, the Riesling is heavy, with an odd artificial-sweetener flavor. **82** —*D.T. (12/1/2005)*

Marquee 2002 Selections Chain of Ponds Sauvignon Blanc (Adelaide Hills) $15. An apéritif-style wine. It's lean and crisp in the mouth, but not a flavor explosion. Aromas and flavors are understated, with hints of peach and pear. Finishes with a lingering unctuousness. **86** —*D.T. (11/15/2004)*

Marquee 2002 Hunter Valley Semillon-Chardonnay (New South Wales) $17. This is a wine of many personalities: The nose has nutty, cedary notes, but also some brininess. Fruit on the palate is just this side of ripe. A nice effort, but doesn't quite hit its stride. **83** —*D.T. (11/15/2004)*

Marquee 2004 Signature Semillon-Chardonnay (Hunter Valley) $15. The nose is odd but compelling in its own way (pear, peach, toasted marshmallow). The wine's texture is nice enough, too, but its tropical fruit flavors just need a little more oomph. Shows promise. **84** —*D.T. (4/1/2006)*

Marquee 2001 Selections Chain of Ponds Shiraz (McLaren Vale) $25. Wheat bread and black-olive aromas segue to a medium-weight wine on the palate. Shows a Rhônish, fresh herb-and-black pepper brightness, framing chewy plum fruit. Finish shows some wood, and is not as vibrant as the palate. **87** —*D.T. (3/1/2005)*

Marquee 2004 Signature Shiraz (McLaren Vale) $20. Very compelling aromas of fresh whipping cream and vanilla bean take on some black pepper notes with air. On the palate, you get textbook Shiraz, with nice graham cracker accents. **88** —*D.T. (6/1/2006)*

Marquee NV Selections Selections Cleveland Winery Brut Sparkling Blend (Macedon Ranges) $27. Gold-green in color, with yellow fruit, oak, and mustard-seed aromas. It's medium-full on the palate, with coarse bead and pear and peach flavors. One more suited for dinner than for an apéritif, due to its fuller size. **86** —*D.T. (12/31/2004)*

Marquee NV Selections Classic Tokay (Rutherglen) $25. Sticky, syrupy, and full-bodied, but still not cloying, by any means. Smells of orange peel, cardamom, and caraway seeds, and has more orange, plus honey, hay, and meat flavors on the palate. As busy as it sounds, it has some delicacy, too, with shortcake flavors taking over midpalate and running hand-in-hand with honey through the finish. **90** —*D.T. (12/31/2004)*

Marquee 2001 Selections Shoalhaven Coast Verdelho (New South Wales) $15. This medium-bodied, straightforward white has a candied quality to it—it's not overly sweet, but its pineapple aromas and flavors may remind you of the Jolly Ranchers you had as a kid. **83** —*D.T. (11/15/2004)*

MARQUIS PHILIPS

Marquis Philips 2000 Cabernet Sauvignon (South Eastern Australia) $15. Magnificently rich and decadent, a wine stuffed with complexity but one that manages balance and harmony. Name the fruit and it's in there, from blackberry to orange rind. Dry, crisp, and stylish, with soft but intricate tannins, this wine would cost two to three times as much in California. **92** —*S.H. (6/1/2002)*

Marquis Philips 2000 Merlot (South Eastern Australia) $15. Rich, dark, and plummy. Here's a big wine in every respect that combines fully ripened fruit with dry tannins and crisp acidity to produce a wonderfully drinkable wine. Lacks the extra dimensions to qualify as great, but it's a super mouthful, although it does require big rich foods. **87** —*S.H. (6/1/2002)*

Marquis Philips 2000 Sarah's Blend Red Blend (South Eastern Australia) $15. Writes the book on how to make a wine filled with gigantic jammy fruit that's nonetheless dry, balanced, and harmonious. The Cabernet contributes black currants and structural tannins. The Syrah brings a peppery richness, while Merlot adds soft fruitiness. You can actually taste each varietal, yet the wine hangs together, dry and rich. **93 Best Buy** —*S.H. (6/1/2002)*

Marquis Philips 2000 Shiraz (South Eastern Australia) $15. Dark, dark, dark purple. Big, rich, jammy, and intense, filled with blackberry, blueberry, and black cherry preserves and dark chocolate, but dry as dust. That sums up this muscular, heady wine. The tannins are soft, and it's fun to drink and delicious. **88** —*S.H. (6/1/2002)*

MATILDA PLAINS

Matilda Plains 2001 Red Blend (Langhorne Creek) $12. This 58% Cab, 28% Shiraz, 14% Merlot has an easy, simple feel and a palate chock-full of red plum, tomato, and tomato stem flavors. Fruit on the palate is sweet and stewy; all around, just an odd combination. **82** —*D.T. (9/1/2004)*

MCGUIGAN

McGuigan 1999 Genus 4 Cabernet Sauvignon (Hunter Valley) $20. Smooth and cool in the nose, with a touch of menthol topping off fragrant blackberry. The palate is searingly fresh, courtesy of bright acids and even brighter ripe grapes. Some tasty cocoa and coffee derived from well-integrated oak adds character the finish. Full-bodied but not even bordering on flabby. **91 Editors' Choice** —M.S. (12/15/2002)

McGuigan 2001 Bin 7000 Chardonnay (Hunter Valley) $10. A smooth, easy-drinking Chardonnay, with mild, understated aromas of green apple and toast, but also sweet tropical fruit flavors and a ripe pineapple-citrus finish that picks up hints of oranges. **88 Best Buy** —J.C. (7/1/2002)

McGuigan 2000 Black Label Chardonnay (South Eastern Australia) $8. Filled with bouncy aromas of melon, pear, and tropical fruit, this lightweight charmer even blends in notes of butter and anise on the finish. It's a fun wine with the accent on fruit. **86 Best Buy** —J.C. (7/1/2002)

McGuigan 2000 Genus 4 Chardonnay (Hunter Valley) $20. Though its standout aroma is of toasted campfire marshmallows on the palate, this wine is toasty without being too creamy, and offers pleasant toast, apple, and pear flavors that persist on the finish. It's a medium-weight, crowd-pleasing wine. **86** —D.T. (8/1/2003)

McGuigan 2001 Bin 3000 Merlot (Murray River Valley) $10. Offers a red-plum core with tea-like flavors and tannins, and bright cherry and oak aromas. Simple and straightforward Merlot. **84** —D.T. (6/1/2003)

McGuigan 1998 Bin 3000 Merlot (South Eastern Australia) $9. 89 Best Buy (11/15/1999)

McGuigan 2000 Black Label Merlot (South Eastern Australia) $8. Lima bean aromas largely obscure the modest cherry fruit. Soft and sweet; finishes short. **80** —J.C. (6/1/2002)

McGuigan 2000 Bin 2000 Shiraz (Murray River Valley) $10. Here's a value Shiraz that shows astonishing depth in the nose, with intriguing cedar, tobacco, and vanilla notes wafting through. Sweet fruit leads the palate, with an interesting, leafy mix of tobacco and herbs after. Soft, with well-managed tannins, it's ready to go and a perfect everyday "go-to" bottle. **86** —P.G. (10/1/2001)

McGuigan 1999 Bin 2000 Shiraz (South Eastern Australia) $10. From the outset to the long finish, there's a lot to like in this sweet jammy Shiraz. Berry, cherry, chocolate, and a touch of cassis abound. The structure is soft, the mouthfeel is even and joyous. A killer barbecue red, anything not too complicated on the grill would be a good match. **86** (6/1/2001)

McGuigan 2000 Black Label Shiraz (South Eastern Australia) $8. Offers jammy red-raspberry aromas, sweet red fruit flavors, and a juicy finish. A good, simple wine. **86 Best Buy** —C.S. (3/1/2003)

McGuigan 1999 Genus 4 Shiraz (Hunter Valley) $20. Yummy aromas of cola, plum pie, and smoked meats start off this well-priced, stately Shiraz. And nothing that follows disappoints. The palate is full yet balanced, with spicy plum-styled fruit and enough acidity to preserve the juicy feel. The finish is smooth and just about perfect. This is neither overdone nor wimpy. In a word, it's complete. **91 Editors' Choice** —M.S. (3/1/2003)

McGuigan 2001 The Black Label Shiraz (South Eastern Australia) $10. A nosing reveals charcoal, currants, and black cherry. As for taste, some bitter chocolate mixes nicely with plum and vanilla, while the finish is positively fresh and lean. A touch of rusticity and leather adds character to this red bubbly. Furthermore, it's something you don't come across every day. **86** —M.S. (6/1/2003)

MCLAREN VALE PREMIUM WINES

McLaren Vale Premium Wines 2004 III Associates Renaissance Bordeaux Blend (McLaren Vale) $20. A blend of 63% Merlot, 25% Cabernet Sauvignon, and 12% Petit Verdot, the wine is medium-full in the mouth, with a feel that's juicy and soft for the most part—there are some wooly, woody tannins here, too. It has a plum and red cherry core, with a slight sour bite at the finish. Enjoyable; drink over the next three years. **88** —D.T. (8/1/2006)

McLaren Vale Premium Wines 2002 Associates Chardonnay (McLaren Vale) $13. Opens with thick honey, butter, and mango-papaya aromas; the thickness doesn't let up on the palate, either, where there's bright peach flavors and a dense, heavy mouthfeel. It's pleasing though a little simple—its heavy fruitiness reminded us a little of lollipop, or canned tropical fruit. **85** (7/2/2004)

McLaren Vale Premium Wines 2003 III Associates Three Score & 10 Grenache (McLaren Vale) $20. Ultrasmooth, this is an easy-drinking rendition of Aussie Grenache that's not swamped by new oak. There's some vanilla, but it simply serves to support the red cherry and currant aromas and flavors. Hints of dill and mint keep it from being too confected, as does a mouth-watering tartness on the finish. Drink now. **87** —J.C. (12/15/2006)

McLaren Vale Premium Wines 2000 III Associates The Third Degree Red Blend (McLaren Vale) $17. A compelling wine from a marketing perspective: The label says that the Associates won't tell you what's in it, but fully expect "the third degree by our refusal to comment," hence the wine's name. From a taste perspective, though, this is an odd wine: It has both meaty, green pepper flavors and ripe, juicy plum fruit, with stewy, grapy aromas on the nose. **85** —D.T. (5/1/2004)

McLaren Vale Premium Wines 2005 III Associates Sabbatical Sauvignon Blanc (McLaren Vale) $20. Clean, correct, and refreshing; this is not a big wine by any means, but, for an SB, it does have some baby fat. Almond notes in the midpalate are bolstered by a narrow band of citrus flavor. Peach and grass aromas start it all off. **87** —D.T. (8/1/2006)

MCLAREN WINES

McLaren Wines 2001 Linchpin Shiraz (McLaren Vale) $45. A medium-sized, excellent wine, and a Shiraz that won't overwhelm your meal. Ripe, mixed berries and plums have well-integrated oak that only hints at caramel. Meaty, smoky aromas give way to dark fruit with some air. Typical Shiraz, but just done very well. **90** —D.T. (3/1/2005)

MCPHERSON

McPherson 2001 Cabernet Sauvignon (Murray-Darling) $8. Light, breezy aromas of plum, cherry, and rhubarb on the nose; the red fruit gets sweeter on the palate, where it tastes more like fresh raspberries. A good but simple wine with fine, powdery tannins on the finish, and small-boned for a Cabernet. **85** —D.T. (10/1/2003)

McPherson 2000 Cabernet Sauvignon (South Eastern Australia) $8. Sure to have widespread appeal, the McPherson has more of a red berry flavor profile than its compatriots. Bright red fruit shows up on the nose with molasses highlights; in the mouth, the fruit is doused in some chalk and dried spices. Chalk and bright berries linger on the finish. **85 Best Buy** —D.T. (6/1/2002)

McPherson 1999 Cabernet Sauvignon (South Eastern Australia) $8. There isn't much depth here, and the cassis flavor has a chemical aspect to it. The structure, however, is fine and the finish long. It's a lightweight but shouldn't be difficult to enjoy with some roast beef. **83** —M.N. (6/1/2001)

McPherson 1999 Cabernet Sauvignon-Shiraz (South Eastern Australia) $8. 87 Best Buy —S.H. (10/1/2000)

McPherson 2002 Chardonnay (Australia) $8. The bouquet is like a puffy cloud of confectioner's sugar, laced with a ribbon of tight citrus. Tropical, buttery fruit shows in the mouth, with an impression of residual powdered sugar that lingers from the nose. Well-balanced, if a little sweet for the panel's taste. **85 Best Buy** (7/2/2004)

McPherson 2001 Chardonnay (Murray-Darling) $8. 82 —D.T. (8/1/2003)

McPherson 1999 Chardonnay (South Eastern Australia) $7. 85 —S.H. (10/1/2000)

McPherson 2000 Murray-Darling Chardonnay (Australia) $7. Toasty and oaky, but in a warm and lovable way, all underpinned by lean citrusy fruit that helps maintain a sense of balance and proportion. There's even a bit of crème brûlée thrown into the mix. Finishes smoothly, with nary a rough edge. **87 Best Buy** —J.C. (7/1/2002)

McPherson 2001 Merlot (South Eastern Australia) $8. From Murray Darling, an area that straddles northern Victoria and New South Wales, this Merlot is an easy quaffer with bouncy plum fruit, earth, and just the right amount of oak. Just one of many great McPherson's buys; their Shiraz and Chardonnay (both 87 points, $7) are also worthwhile. **85** —D.T. (11/15/2003)

McPherson 2000 Merlot (South Eastern Australia) $8. It's black cherries all the way in this clean, dry wine. The fruit is ripe and polished, wrapped in chewy tannins, and set off by crisp acidity. Little evident oak, but the pretty flavors really don't need any. **84** —*S.H. (6/1/2002)*

McPherson 2002 Shiraz (Australia) $8. This dry wine has seeped tea and oak flavors riding in the front seat. Still, there's a nice core of taut red fruit, and dusty red fruit on the nose, that make it worth a look. **84** —*D.T. (9/1/2004)*

McPherson 2001 Shiraz (Murray-Darling) $8. Telltale oak is manifested in the scents of smoke and bacon fat aromas, though that oakiness over-shadows the black fruit. In the mouth, you get some black cherry and blackberry, but also plenty of vanilla and licorice. With decent depth and moderate complexity, this is a good, likable wine. **87** —*M.S. (3/1/2003)*

McPherson 2000 Shiraz (South Eastern Australia) $8. Anise-wintergreen shadings on the cherry fruit open to a flavorful, sweet, and sour palate. It's yet another example of the eminently drinkable, inexpensive wines that have spearheaded the Aussie invasion. The dry finish shows a hint of chalk and a nutty note. **88 Best Buy** *(10/1/2001)*

McPherson 1999 Shiraz (South Eastern Australia) $8. 86 Best Buy —*S.H. (11/1/2000)*

McPherson 2000 Reserve Shiraz (Goulburn Valley) $19. The bouquet is meaty, dense, and full of berry jam, but it is also rather generic and lacks any particular individual notes. That said, the wine is quite good, bor-dering on excellent. In the mouth, you get a full blast of black cherry and licorice, and the finish is typically full and chewy. Not that complex but very good in a straight-ahead way. **89** —*M.S. (3/1/2003)*

McPherson 1999 White Blend (South Eastern Australia) $7. 85 —*M.S. (10/1/2000)*

MCWILLIAM'S HANWOOD ESTATE

McWilliam's Hanwood Estate 2004 Cabernet Sauvignon (South Eastern Australia) $12. Has aromas and flavors of raspberries and Sweet Tart. The palate is accented with some oat and coconut flavors, too. Juicy, for-ward, and made to drink now. **86** —*D.T. (12/31/2005)*

McWilliam's Hanwood Estate 2003 Cabernet Sauvignon (South Eastern Australia) $11. Bear with the aromas—the caramel popcorn note will go away soon enough. Red fruit on the palate is taut, and the tannins smooth and dusty. The Cab's overall profile is a tried-and-true one (plum, earth, oak), but it is successful here. **87 Best Buy** —*D.T. (12/31/2004)*

McWilliam's Hanwood Estate 2002 Cabernet Sauvignon (South Eastern Australia) $12. A juicy, easy-to-drink Cabernet that shows clean cassis fruit tinged with notes of earth and tobacco. With components coming from Riverina, Coonawarra, Limestone Coast, Hilltops, and Yarra Valley, this well illustrates the Australian art of blending. **87 Best Buy** *(10/1/2003)*

McWilliam's Hanwood Estate 1998 1877 Cabernet Sauvignon-Shiraz (South Eastern Australia) $85. This blend (73% Cab, 20% Shiraz, 7% Merlot) receives "200 percent" new oak, spending a total of 24 months in cask. The oak shows, imparting deliciously creamy vanilla aromas and flavors; but there's plenty of depth and substance to the fruit as well. Cassis, tobacco, and richly earthy notes round out the wine, finishing with firm tannins. Drink 2005–2015. **92** *(10/1/2003)*

McWilliam's Hanwood Estate 2004 Chardonnay (South Eastern Australia) $12. A please-everyone style of wine, this Chardonnay is upbeat, easy to drink, and uncomplicated, and offers bright stone fruit and floral aromas. Maybe a wee bit soft, winding up with pineapple, peach, and lemon fla-vors. **87 Best Buy** —*D.T. (12/1/2005)*

McWilliam's Hanwood Estate 2003 Chardonnay (South Eastern Australia) $11. It's familiarly New World all the way—gold color, apple, and but-terscotch aromas, the toast-cream-yellow stone fruit trifecta in the mouth. But when it's done well, it's done well. Bonus when it's a value price. **86 Best Buy** —*D.T. (12/31/2004)*

McWilliam's Hanwood Estate 2001 Chardonnay (South Eastern Australia) $11. Tastes what you'd expect "yellow" to taste like, if colors had flavors. Medium-full in the mouth, with drying oak that turns into an herbal or fruit-pit note on the back end. Lots of wood and black pepper on the nose, too. **82** —*D.T. (1/1/2002)*

McWilliam's Hanwood Estate 2002 Hanwood Estate Chardonnay (South Eastern Australia) $12. Typical Australian Chardonnay, balancing hints of wood and butter against exuberant fruit. Pear, baked apple, and citrus flavors finish with surprising length. **88 Best Buy** *(10/1/2003)*

McWilliam's Hanwood Estate 2004 Merlot (South Eastern Australia) $12. A fine, casual sipper with bouncy berry fruit at its center, and aromas of earth and berry. Beaujolais-styled and sized, so much so that it might make sense to chill it for a few minutes in the fridge before taking it on a summer picnic. **85** —*D.T. (6/1/2006)*

McWilliam's Hanwood Estate 2003 Merlot (South Eastern Australia) $12. Though the aromas of silly putty, blackberry, vanilla, and dust are nice, what you get on the palate is pretty pedestrian: fresh berry flavors, and a lightish body. Straightforward but good. **84** —*D.T. (5/1/2005)*

McWilliam's Hanwood Estate 2002 Merlot (South Eastern Australia) $12. Bright black cherry fruit and some citrus and vanilla elements make this clean, snappy red food-friendly. Finishes with a hint of cocoa powder. **85** *(10/1/2003)*

McWilliam's Hanwood Estate 2004 Shiraz (South Eastern Australia) $12. Has talc and sweet fruit aromas. Round and approachable on the palate, with plum fruit and a tangy oak overlay. **84** —*D.T. (6/1/2006)*

McWilliam's Hanwood Estate 2002 Shiraz (South Eastern Australia) $12. There's a hint of black pepper, but this wine is all about big, juicy black-berries. The fruit is bold and clean, finishing with a tart edge to the flavors. **86** *(10/1/2003)*

McWilliam's Hanwood Estate 2001 Shiraz (South Eastern Australia) $11. A young, aggressively jammy wine with biting acidity that brings Beaujolais to mind. It's simple, with berry and fruit flavors, and very dry. **85** —*M.S. (12/15/2002)*

MCWILLIAM'S OF COONAWARRA

McWilliam's of Coonawarra 2000 Cabernet Sauvignon (Coonawarra) $25. Fruit on the nose has a pretty black-peppery finish, with just a hint of herbal brightness. Mocha, chocolate, and eucalyptus are accents on the palate, which fades into sweet red berries, white pepper, and oak on the finish. **88** —*D.T. (11/15/2004)*

McWilliam's of Coonawarra 1999 Cabernet Sauvignon (Coonawarra) $25. The classic Coonawarra flavors of mint and eucalyptus are present, but in balance with assertive black currants and chocolate. It's got soft tan-nins on the long finish, suggesting that the best is yet to come. Drink now–2010. [Sold as Brand's of Coonawarra outside the U.S.] **89** *(10/1/2003)*

McWilliam's of Coonawarra 2001 Brand's Laira Vineyards Cabernet Sauvignon (Coonawarra) $28. Out of the gate, it smells like hard-cheese rind, but opens to reveal cream and vanilla notes. On the palate, there's ripe red fruit and lively acidity. Narrow in the mouth with interesting, rustic, Old World nuances of iron ore. **89** —*D.T. (6/1/2006)*

McWilliam's of Coonawarra 2000 Shiraz (Coonawarra) $25. This is a mas-culine, big-boned Shiraz, one with a black cherry-and-plum core. You want sweet and toasty? Look elsewhere. This wine's dry, chewy tannins and earth-and-oak finish recommend it well for a grilled steak, and/or a couple years in the cellar. **88** —*D.T. (9/1/2004)*

McWilliam's of Coonawarra 2000 Brand's Laira Vineyards Shiraz (Coonawarra) $28. This feminine, well-made Shiraz has cool crispness, good acidity, and a chalky-smooth feel going for it. Taut cherry fruit is at its core, with an unusual mix of anise, talc, and acorn aromas wafting from the nose. Excellent, though with only 250 cases produced, may be a challenge to find. **90** —*D.T. (12/31/2004)*

McWilliam's of Coonawarra 1999 Laira Vineyard Shiraz (Coonawarra) $25. Smoke and toast aromas give almost a maple syrup quality to the aro-mas, which are rounded out by eucalyptus and blackberries. Shows a bit of a briary or herbal streak on the palate, finishing soft and sweetly wooded. Drink now–2010. [Sold as McWilliam's of Coonawarra outside the U.S.] **89** *(10/1/2003)*

McWilliam's of Coonawarra 2000 Stentiford's Reserve Old Vines Shiraz (Coonawarra) $55. Mocha, anise, and eucalyptus aromas are compelling, as are juicy, mixed berry and spice flavors. This is a very enjoyable, by-the-book kind of Shiraz, built to please far and wide. **89** —*D.T. (4/1/2006)*

McWilliam's of Coonawarra 1999 Stentiford's Reserve Old Vines Shiraz Shiraz (Coonawarra) $49. Made from vines said to be the oldest producing vines in Coonawarra (planted in 1893) and aged in French oak, this is a supple wine that caresses the palate with silky blackberries and spice. Hints of vanilla and chocolate echo on the finish. Drink now–2010. [Sold as Brand's of Coonawarra outside the U.S.] **90** *(10/1/2003)*

MEEREA PARK

Meerea Park 1999 Alexander Munro Shiraz (Hunter Valley) $38. The nose is intriguing, with some root beer and horsehide. The mouth offers a ton of plum fruit with tobacco nuances, and then the finish is smooth and of good length. The body is heavy and full, like many an Oz Shiraz, but it's also packed with the vital acidity needed to keep it fresh. **89** —*M.S. (3/1/2003)*

Meerea Park 2001 The Aunts Shiraz (Hunter Valley) $24. Nose shows soil and cherry aromas. Verges on lean in body, with slightly sour, stalky accents on the midpalate. **83** —*D.T. (11/15/2004)*

Meerea Park 2000 The Aunts Shiraz (Hunter Valley) $24. Very rich and extracted, with a bright purple hue and legs that could run. The nose is broad and overtly woody, with barnyard nuances adding an interesting and needed rustic touch. The palate offers some burnt or baked fruit and a jolt of espresso, while the finish is smooth and not unlike Port. Best for fans of the thick and rich. **88** —*M.S. (3/1/2003)*

Meerea Park 1999 The Aunts Shiraz (Hunter Valley) $24. A controversial wine among our panelists. The majority found it offered little more than sweet-sour fruit, licorice, and oak, but others called it rich and velvety, with creamy fruit and a long finish. **84** *(11/1/2001)*

MERMAID RIDGE

Mermaid Ridge 2004 Chardonnay (Great Southern) $15. A straightforward hitter, not superlayered and nuanced, but what is here is enjoyable. Pink grapefruit and peach flavors persist through the finish, where there are some nut and mineral accents. **87** —*D.T. (6/1/2006)*

Mermaid Ridge 2002 Shiraz (Great Southern) $15. Shows peanutty, brambly aromas, and a smooth texture on the palate. Sour cherry flavors dominate at first, but open to encompass plummy, wheaty notes, too. **87** —*D.T. (6/1/2006)*

MESH

Mesh 2004 Riesling (Eden Valley) $25. This Hill Smith-Grosset joint venture is a very good wine, but not quite up to the snuff of past vintages. It smells like whipping cream and citrus (and goes the way of petrol with a little time in the glass), and unfolds to a bracing, minerally, sourish wine on the palate. Not overtly flavorful, but still enjoyable. **87** —*D.T. (10/1/2005)*

MITCHELL

Mitchell 2002 Sevenhill Vineyard Cabernet Sauvignon (Clare Valley) $24. A delicate, feminine-sized Cabernet, this Clare offering has a round, creamy feel but not a lot of breadth. But once you take in the wine's harmonious aromas and flavors of Mexican cinnamon, blackberry, fresh cream and eucalyptus notes, you'll be sold, too. **89** —*D.T. (12/31/2005)*

Mitchell 2001 Sevenhill Vineyard Cabernet Sauvignon (Clare Valley) $25. Another Mitchell red that's drinkable even in its infancy, this Cab has soft but approachable tannins, and a great bouquet of pure plum and grape fruit. The palate shows black currant, mostly, dusted with pastry flour. Yum. **90** —*D.T. (2/1/2004)*

Mitchell 1999 Sevenhill Vineyard Cabernet Sauvignon (Clare Valley) $28. Dark and whole, the full package with nary a flaw. Very rich and spicy, but with enough plump black fruit to support all that spice, licorice, and espresso. It's tight now, almost unyielding, but for fans of masculine Cabs that still feature a sensationally sweet core of fruit, this is terrific stuff. **93 Editors' Choice** —*M.S. (12/15/2002)*

Mitchell 2001 Grenache (Clare Valley) $18. No longer called "The Growers," as it was in the past, because Mitchell's own fruit goes into this wine. Smells like cherries and cologne, with raspberry the most

prevalent note on the palate. Soft in the mouth, it finishes with anise, herb, and more red fruit. 7% Mataro. **88** —*D.T. (2/1/2004)*

Mitchell 2002 GSM Red Blend (Clare Valley) $15. A GSM, yes, but one with Sangiovese rather than Shiraz in that secondary position. It's dry grown, handpicked, and unoaked, the Sangiovese bringing a pleasant tanginess to complement Grenache's juicy, black-cherry fruit. Medium-sized, and finishes with black pepper. **91 Best Buy** —*D.T. (2/1/2006)*

Mitchell 2004 Watervale Riesling (Clare Valley) $16. What a nice wine. Very fragrant on the nose; it's an alluring blend of tropical fruit, citrus, and olive oil. Zesty, crisp, and mouthfilling, its citrus spine supporting white peach and talc flavors. Pleasingly tangy on the finish. **90 Editors' Choice** —*D.T. (4/1/2006)*

Mitchell 2003 Watervale Riesling (Clare Valley) $18. Fresh grass and hay lend a slight sweetness to wheat notes on the nose. As is the case with other area 2003 Rieslings, the mouthfeel on this one is full, not racy, as were last year's wines. The palate offers yellow stone fruit and citrus flavors buried under a heavy layer of rock. By the finish, fresh lemon flavors are back at the fore. **90 Editors' Choice** —*D.T. (2/1/2004)*

Mitchell 2001 Watervale Riesling (Clare Valley) $19. This is a lean, fresh Riesling with white stone fruit at its core. Grass and mineral—even waxy—flavors freshen up the palate, and floral and saffron notes waft from the nose. Lemon rind and viscous sour apple flavors linger on the finish. For this range of flavors to work in harmony, you surely must count elegance and subtlety among its virtues. **90** —*D.T. (8/1/2003)*

Mitchell 2000 Watervale Riesling (Clare Valley) $NA. **89** —*D.T. (2/1/2004)*

Mitchell 1992 Watervale Riesling (Clare Valley) $NA. **91** —*D.T. (2/1/2004)*

Mitchell 2004 Semillon (Clare Valley) $16. I really like most all of Andrew Mitchell's wines, but this one, while good, came up short for me. It has closed peach, pineapple, and apple flavors, and a slightly mealy texture. Aromas are meaty and appley, too. **84** —*D.T. (4/1/2006)*

Mitchell 2002 Semillon (Clare Valley) $18. Though there's a base of sweet, rich yellow fruit at this wine's heart, what's more prevalent here are garden-fresh grass, or pea shoot notes, from nose through to the palate. Medium-weight, with a viscous mouthfeel. **89** —*D.T. (2/1/2004)*

Mitchell 2001 The Growers Semillon (Clare Valley) $18. Though there's yellow fruit on the palate, it's hiding under a mountain of toast, toffee, and butter, which gets sweeter on the finish. Straightforward, and a little sweet for this reviewer's taste, though there are plenty of folks who appreciate this style. **85** —*D.T. (12/31/2003)*

Mitchell 2002 Peppertree Vineyard Shiraz (Clare Valley) $26. A soft, ripe, excellent Shiraz, and drinkable even at this early age. Licorice stands out on the palate, under which mixed plums forge a solid foundation. Finishes, appropriately enough, with black pepper. **91** —*D.T. (2/1/2004)*

Mitchell 2001 Peppertree Vineyard Shiraz (Clare Valley) $26. Restrained and medium-bodied in the mouth, this wine's always of reliably good quality, and this year's no exception. Plum fruit and chunky meat-and-molasses notes on the nose resurface on the palate, where they wear a heavy coat of chalky tannins. Tasty and elegant. **90 Editors' Choice** —*D.T. (2/1/2004)*

Mitchell 2000 Peppertree Vineyard Shiraz (Clare Valley) $26. Insubstantial in the mouth, as though it's a shell of a wine without much stuffing. What's here are earthy, generic, red fruit flavors. Finishes short. **82** —*D.T. (1/28/2003)*

Mitchell 1999 Peppertree Vineyard Shiraz (Clare Valley) $26. **85** —*J.C. (9/1/2002)*

Mitchell 1998 Peppertree Vineyard Shiraz (Clare Valley) $NA. **89** —*D.T. (2/1/2004)*

Mitchell 1997 Peppertree Vineyard Shiraz (Clare Valley) $NA. **87** —*D.T. (2/1/2004)*

MITCHELTON

Mitchelton 1998 Marsanne (Goulburn Valley) $18. **90** —*S.H. (10/1/2000)*

Mitchelton 2001 Crescent Red Blend (Central Victoria) $21. An appealing wine, composed of 40% Shiraz, 30% Mourvèdre, and 30% Grenache. Tannins are textured, and linger long and dry on the palate. Tastes cool

AUSTRALIA

AUSTRALIA

and taut, with blueberry and blackberry fruit at its core and barbecue smoke enveloping it. **90** —*D.T. (5/1/2005)*

Mitchelton 2000 Airstrip Rhône White Blend (Central Victoria) $20. This could be taken for a white Burgundy—or big white Rhône, which is closer to actuality. Mild tropical fruit notes underlie the subtle apple, caramel, and toast bouquet. It's full, dry, and rich, yet subdued, with nuanced pear, lemon, and mineral flavors. Finishes long and tangy, with elegant oak accents. Drinks well now and should keep nicely through 2005. **91 Editors' Choice** *(2/1/2002)*

Mitchelton 2002 Airstrip Marsanne Roussanne Viognier Rhône White Blend (South Australia/Victoria) $20. This white blend was reviewed by two editors, and this note reflects both opinions. The mouthfeel is slick and creamy; where one editor found tropical fruit on the palate, another saw more citrus and currants. Also up for debate are the aromas (honey and white chocolate, versus herbal greenness). The moral here? It's a very good wine, but one that is apparently different things to different people. **87** —*D.T. (5/1/2004)*

Mitchelton 1996 Print Shiraz (Victoria) $45. 92 *(10/1/2000)*

Mitchelton 1999 Print Shiraz (Central Victoria) $42. A pretty, feminine wine that's soft around the edges but has a good grip on the midpalate. Plush red plum, mocha, and coffee flavors fade into a chalk-clay finish. Black cherry, olive, and pencil eraser aromas grow more peppery and spicy with air. A class act. **90** —*D.T. (12/31/2004)*

Mitchelton 1999 Thomas Mitchell Shiraz (Victoria) $11. Combines rhubarb and sour cherries with tobacco, vanilla, and toast in a package that ultimately comes across as light, tart, and herbaceous. Might lose some of that sour edge with another six months in the bottle, but this isn't one for long-term cellaring. **83** *(10/1/2001)*

MITOLO

Mitolo 2004 Serpico Cabernet Sauvignon (McLaren Vale) $57. Made from grapes dried passito-style, this is an excellent Cab. Well-balanced with soft tannins, it shows earth and focused blackberry aromas, and very juicy blackberry and plum fruit. Pretty, unique, and worth seeking out. **90** —*D.T. (10/1/2006)*

Mitolo 2004 G. A. M. Shiraz (McLaren Vale) $45. Full-bodied and lush, this hedonistic Shiraz easily hides its elevated alcohol level (15%) behind layers of concentrated plummy fruit. Hints of coffee, herbs, and spices impart complexity, so this isn't a simple fruit bomb. Long and focused on the finish, with well-concealed structure that keeps the fruit from becoming jammy. Drink now–2015. **92** —*J.C. (12/15/2006)*

Mitolo 2002 Jester Shiraz (McLaren Vale) $20. Mitolo has the right idea here, delivering a suave, balanced, medium-sized Shiraz, en screwcap, for only 20 bucks. It has chalky, smooth tannins, and undrestated black fruit dusted with mocha. Sees a surge of clay, and a flash of eucalyptus, on the finish. There's a little alcoholic warmth on the nose, but it's a balls-on solid wine overall. **90 Editors' Choice** —*D.T. (12/31/2004)*

MONDAVI/ROSEMOUNT

Mondavi/Rosemount 2002 Kirralaa Cabernet Sauvignon (South Eastern Australia) $15. A very, very dark Cab, and not fluffed up by vanilla or cream. Blackberry aromas; sturdy black fruit feels even darker with drying tealike tannins that start midpalate and don't let up through the medium-long finish. A big slab of beef is the knee-jerk solution to making it more approachable; cellaring a year or two may also help. **88** —*D.T. (12/31/2004)*

Mondavi/Rosemount 2001 Kirralaa Cabernet Sauvignon (South Eastern Australia) $15. Medium-bodied and pretty black on the nose and palate, this Cab is chock-full of black fruit, toasty oak, and caramel. Smooth tannins show best on the finish. A solid choice, and moderately priced. **87** —*D.T. (10/1/2003)*

Mondavi/Rosemount 2003 Kirralaa Chardonnay (South Eastern Australia) $14. Nose is at once smoky and herbal, with a twist of lime. Feels lean and wiry in the mouth, its fruit flavors veering more toward peach fuzz and citrus peel than juicy fruit flesh. Finishes tangy and fresh, with a hint of butter. **86** *(7/2/2004)*

Mondavi/Rosemount 2002 Kirralaa Chardonnay (South Eastern Australia) $14. From the Rosemount Estate-Robert Mondavi partnership, a tart,

very citrusy Chard whose fruit is bright and vivid on the palate. High acids create a tingle from start to finish. The lemon and lime flavors drink bone dry, but there's a creamy richness on the palate that makes the wine round and full-bodied. **87** —*S.H. (12/31/2003)*

Mondavi/Rosemount 2001 Kirralaa Merlot (South Eastern Australia) $15. An easy-drinking wine with medium body and soft tannins, this Mondavi-Rosemount project has black and red fruit, earth, and oak, plus a caramel or molasses note that also shows on the nose. Eucalyptus is another aromatic standout. Finishes with juicy, bouncy fruit. **87** —*D.T. (10/1/2003)*

Mondavi/Rosemount 2002 Kirralaa Bushvine Shiraz (South Eastern Australia) $15. Bright cherry and herb aromas don't prepare you for the palate's darker characteristics. Chocolate sweetness is a major player here—think cordial candy. Straightforward and a little candied, but good. **86** —*D.T. (11/15/2004)*

Mondavi/Rosemount 2001 Kirralaa Bushvine Shiraz (South Eastern Australia) $15. Black fruit is fresh and bouncy in the mouth. There's also a floral or colognelike note on the nose and in the mouth that may interest some, but wasn't necessarily a bonus for me. Finishes with charry tannins. **86** —*D.T. (10/1/2003)*

Mondavi/Rosemount 2001 Kirralaa Indelible Reserve Shiraz (Victoria) $50. Has oak and pepper aromas, with juicy plum, ink and dry oaky tannins on the palate. Finishes with a little sourness—like herbs or seeped tea—but it's still a smooth, very good wine that can be enjoyed now. **88** —*D.T. (5/1/2004)*

MOON DOG ACRE

Moon Dog Acre 2004 Shiraz (South Eastern Australia) $8. An odd wine that can't decide whether it wants to be sweet (cotton candy aromas, lifted cassis flavors) or more rustic (mushroom aromas, earth flavors). Has some textured tannins but wants a little more heft midpalate. **83** —*D.T. (4/1/2006)*

MOONDARRA

Moondarra 2001 Conception Unfiltered Pinot Noir (Victoria) $50. Has pure, focused cherry and red plum flavors and fine, minerally tannins in the mouth; it finishes with the same broad wheat and biscuit notes that you'll find on the nose. It's New World in style, though it tastes like nothing out of Oregon or California. Total case production is 200; only 60 make it stateside. **91** —*D.T. (10/1/2003)*

MOOROOROO

Mooroooroo 2001 Limited Release Shiraz (Barossa Valley) $78. This winery makes them thick, soft, and woody, and this Limited Release Shiraz stays that path. The prevailing flavor is grape jam, with some toasty, picklespice notes on the nose. On the sweet side, at least for this reviewer, and built to drink now. **85** —*D.T. (4/1/2006)*

MORGAN SIMPSON

Morgan Simpson 2000 Cabernet Sauvignon (McLaren Vale) $17. With a nose of tomato and herbs and so little fruit, you immediately question this wine's ripeness. Sour cherry flavors are strong on the palate, which is quite green at its core. The wine has a good enough mouthfeel but neither the flavors nor richness to match. **82** —*M.S. (12/15/2002)*

Morgan Simpson 2002 Row 42 Cabernet Sauvignon (McLaren Vale) $25. This wine gets full credit for its smooth, eraser-like tannins—the feel is just lovely, as are eucalyptus and black pepper aromas. All of these signs point to excellence, but the palate is a little disappointing, with sourish fruit and a strange watermelon note continuing through the finish. Still very good, with great potential. **87** —*D.T. (5/1/2005)*

Morgan Simpson 2000 Chardonnay (McLaren Vale) $13. This medium-bodied Chard has nice oregano and thyme notes on the nose, with more fresh herbal accents on the palate. Cream and nutmeg flavors are most prevalent in the mouth; finishes with pleasant floury-nutmeg notes. **87** —*D.T. (8/1/2003)*

Morgan Simpson 2002 Shiraz (McLaren Vale) $25. Steady and sturdy wins the race for this Shiraz. The dusty-clay-chalk aromas preface a surge of blackberries on the palate, which are joined immediately with more rocks and dust. Shows class and restraint, with nary a lick of obvious toast. **89** —*D.T. (12/31/2005)*

Morgan Simpson 2000 Stone Hill Shiraz (McLaren Vale) $17. An excellent wine and an excellent value, though you may have trouble finding it in the U.S. There's juicy, jammy raspberry and blackberry fruit backed up by oak and caramel, with alluring black pepper, bacon, cherry and fresh garden aromas. It's what you want from an Aussie Shiraz. **90 Editors' Choice** —*D.T. (3/1/2003)*

MOSS WOOD

Moss Wood 2001 Cabernet Sauvignon (Margaret River) $60. Deep black fruit notes on the nose go a little raisiny with air, but there are enough pleasant tree/earth aromas to distract you. On the palate, hickory smoke flavors mesh nicely with sweet fruit; tannins are soft and plush. Finishes medium-long, with juicy berry and cherry flavors. **90** —*D.T. (12/31/2004)*

Moss Wood 2000 Glenmore Vineyard Cabernet Sauvignon (Margaret River) $31. You won't sip this wine and think about how long you should age it—it's ready to drink now, with sweet black fruit, creamy oak, and a medium-bodied, easy mouthfeel. Finishes with some nuttiness. **89** —*D.T. (10/1/2003)*

Moss Wood 2003 The Amy's Blend Cabernet Sauvignon (Margaret River) $26. The "blend" in the wine's name refers to the fact that the grapes come from two vineyards: Glenmore (66%) and Montgomery Brothers (34%). Fruit on the nose is very concentrated, borderline syrupy or pruny. Moderate in size; the palate offers black plum and blackberry flavors. Very good, though you'd more likely guess South Australia than Margaret River if you taste it blind. **89** —*D.T. (5/1/2005)*

Moss Wood 2002 Ribbon Vale Vineyard Cabernet Sauvignon-Merlot (Margaret River) $33. This 60-30-10 blend of Cab Sauv, Merlot, and Cab Franc has fleshy plum, oak, and cinnamon aromas. Flavors are much the same, but there's a hardness—a slight metallic quality, even—to the palate. **85** —*D.T. (5/1/2005)*

Moss Wood 2003 Chardonnay (Margaret River) $40. The palate announced loud and clear what this wine's color and aromas also suggest: There's just too much wood here. This is obviously a well-made wine, one with dry citrus and mineral components, and a surge of citrus on the medium-long finish. The toasty overlay, however, is overdone—without it, this wine would climb easily into the next decile. **87** —*D.T. (3/1/2005)*

Moss Wood 2002 Chardonnay (Margaret River) $48. We found a lot to like about this wine, from the passion fruit, mango, and ginger aromas to the yellow plum, ginger, and wheat flour flavors on the palate. A rich wine, it finishes with toast and a zing of grapefruit. **88** *(7/2/2004)*

Moss Wood 2001 Chardonnay (Margaret River) $45. Vibrantly caramelly on the nose, with ripe yellow fruit and floral notes underneath. The palate works the same way—fruit seems nice (in this case, it's white peach) though fights with toast for top billing. Smooth and oaky on the finish. **87** —*D.T. (10/1/2003)*

Moss Wood 2001 Pinot Noir (Margaret River) $35. Brambly earth/tree aromas vie with anise/gumdrop ones. Flavors are pleasant—dusty earth, taut cherry—but the palate wants more stuffing. Another panelist found it quite oaky, but I thought it very good. **87** —*D.T. (12/31/2004)*

Moss Wood 1999 Pinot Noir (Margaret River) $36. Taut red fruit is accented by some moist earth on the palate. The same fruit on the nose is couched in meaty and floral notes. The wine's quality is obviously good, but its depth and length aren't quite what they should be. **87** —*D.T. (10/1/2003)*

Moss Wood 2002 Semillon (Margaret River) $24. One wild wine. Its aromatics remind me of chile powder, and the palate is rife with more chiles, pear fruit, and leafy-greens accents. The mouthfeel is nice—medium-weight, with both zest and viscosity—but it's a little disjointed. **86** —*D.T. (11/15/2004)*

Moss Wood 2000 Semillon (Margaret River) $20. Smooth and slick in the mouth, with ripe yellow fruit and a viscous mouthfeel. Has a little caramel and a lot of roundness. **89** *(10/1/2003)*

MOUNT HORROCKS

Mount Horrocks 2004 Riesling (Clare Valley) $25. This vintage feels just slightly clumsy and big compared to the wine's usual performance, but it's still pretty good. Aromas and flavors of peach, white grape and nectarine are lightly dusted in chalk; finishes with a slight scouring spritz. **88** —*D.T. (10/1/2005)*

Mount Horrocks 2002 Riesling (Clare Valley) $21. Zippy and fresh in the mouth, well balanced, with eye-opening fresh green herb and lemon peel flavors. The same green herb, plus some petrol, shows on the nose. A gravelly, minerally finish brings it to a dry close. **88** —*D.T. (8/1/2003)*

Mount Horrocks 2002 Cordon Cut Riesling (Clare Valley) $26. As beautiful as it ever is. Minerally, nectarine and peach aromas lead to honey, apricot and chalk on the palate. Balanced, with good acidity, it finishes clean, with a lasting, minerally close. **91** —*D.T. (9/1/2004)*

Mount Horrocks 2001 Cordon Cut Riesling (Clare Valley) $27. A tremendous, sweet Riesling, unctuous but not cloying. Smells like ripe green apples; tastes like petrol at palate entry, but melts seamlessly into honey, floral, and sweet chalk flavors. Winemaker Stephanie Toole says that "actually goes with desserts…it doesn't fight with them." Amen, sister. **92** —*D.T. (2/1/2004)*

Mount Horrocks 2003 Watervale Riesling (Clare Valley) $20. The aromas are tremendous—trading-card powder, fresh river water, even some earth. Sweet dustiness sticks around on the palate, where there's also some delicate white stone fruit. Finishes very clean, with citrus and peach pit. At once feminine and powerful, it's a suprisingly nimble wine, considering the vintage. **91 Editors' Choice** —*D.T. (2/1/2004)*

Mount Horrocks 1999 Shiraz (Clare Valley) $28. Wide black plum fruit sprawls out on the palate; Clare's signature chalky-limestoney mouthfeel is in full effect here. There's a ribbon of rusticity—tobacco, peanut shells, or something—running throughout. Nose is an unusual mix of granola, blueberry, and blackberry. As lush as it sounds, don't forget, it's from Clare, and bears scant resemblance to a Barossa bruiser. **89** —*D.T. (5/1/2004)*

MOUNT LANGI GHIRAN

Mount Langi Ghiran 2004 Pinot Gris (Victoria) $20. Doesn't show much on the nose, but has modest mineral and peach pit flavors on the palate. Wide and round; this is a good wine, but not a particularly acidic or flavorful one. **84** —*D.T. (10/1/2006)*

Mount Langi Ghiran 2003 Pinot Gris (Victoria) $18. This Pinot Gris has apple and pear flavors, but they're dry and tart, like fruit skin rather than flesh. A good, apéritif-styled white, it's one to enjoy cold and on the balcony. 250 cases produced. **85** —*D.T. (8/1/2005)*

Mount Langi Ghiran 2004 Riesling (Victoria) $18. Citrus, chalk dust, and pear are this Riesling's main components, on both the nose and the palate. It's a very compelling wine, though spare and delicate in style. Finishes with a dusty-gumdrop note. Nicely done. **89** —*D.T. (10/1/2005)*

Mount Langi Ghiran 2003 Riesling (Victoria) $17. This wine has a lot of potential, with compelling jasmine and pencil-eraser aromas, but its flavors are not all that concentrated. There are nice lemon peel and Sweet Tart notes on the palate, but they fade away a little too quickly. Spritzy in the mouth, it finishes a little less so. **85** —*D.T. (5/1/2004)*

Mount Langi Ghiran 1999 Shiraz (Victoria) $36. A puzzling but still very good wine, because Oz Shiraz isn't supposed to taste like it's from the Rhône. There's a lot of black pepper and herbaceousness in this slim-bodied wine. Taut red plum and cherry is at its core, with all the pepper and fresh herb you could hope for. Bag it, and blind-taste it with some friends—not many will guess Australia. **88** —*D.T. (9/1/2004)*

Mount Langi Ghiran 2003 Billi Billi Shiraz (Victoria) $15. The 2003 Billi Billi Shiraz features slightly medicinal flavors of cherries and rhubarb accented by scorched chocolate notes and a hint of eucalyptus. The texture is creamy-smooth, while the finish lingers elegantly. It's a pleasant counterpoint to some of the heavyweight Shirazes from South Australia, at a bargain price. **90 Best Buy** —*J.C. (12/15/2006)*

Mount Langi Ghiran 2002 Billi Billi Shiraz (Victoria) $15. Crispness and lively acidity mark this Victorian Shiraz. Offers cherries and a hint of fresh herbs in the mouth. **88** —*D.T. (2/1/2006)*

AUSTRALIA

Mount Langi Ghiran 2000 Langi Shiraz (Victoria) $35. The sort of wine that really needs to be experienced, rather than written about, because comments about it don't do justice to how attractive it is. It smells like acorns and iron ore—metallic, yes, but powerfully so, and not at all shrill. In the mouth it offers thick, wooly tannins and an iron-steely spine, with juicy plum and black cherry flavors. Atypical and very enjoyable. **90** —*D.T. (8/1/2005)*

MOUNT MARY

Mount Mary 2001 Quintet Bordeaux Blend (Yarra Valley) $120. A very delicate wine. On the nose, it has focused berry fruit and a stably undercurrent that follows through on the palate. It's smooth in the mouth, subtle in that it shines with the impression of bright berry fruit, but its size doesn't knock you over. Pretty, feminine, and best of all, different. **90** *(8/1/2005)*

Mount Mary 2001 Chardonnay (Yarra Valley) $90. So delicate that it, at times, seems fleeting. There are pineapple and spice aromas, and white peach joins in on the palate. What's most remarkable is the feel—one minute it feels full, and the next, like dust blowing in the wind. Changing in the glass, and by the sip. Good for the soul. **90** —*D.T. (12/1/2005)*

MOUNTADAM

Mountadam 1997 Chardonnay (Eden Valley) $15. 89 *(10/1/1999)*

Mountadam 1996 Pinot Noir (Eden Valley) $16. 81 *(10/1/1999)*

MT. BILLY

Mt. Billy 2002 Harmony Rhône Red Blend (Barossa Valley) $36. This Rhône blend (half Shiraz, with Mataro and Grenache evenly split in the remainder) really does taste French, rather than Australian. This is a very good wine, one that offers sour but plump black plum fruit with a tobaccoey, herbaceous edge. It almost needs a "If you don't like Crozes-Hermitage, keep shopping" warning label; suits me just fine. **88** —*D.T. (12/31/2005)*

Mt. Billy 2001 Antiquity Shiraz (Barossa Valley) $49. Lifted blueberry and blackberry flavors are at the heart of this interesting Shiraz, and cherries and berries are on the nose. It's not mouthfilling and overly rich, but strong in its own right—like there's iron and charcoal at its core. Will show very well with a rare steak or Shiraz pie. **90** —*D.T. (8/1/2005)*

Mt. Billy 2002 Liqueur Shiraz (Barossa Valley) $26. So thick and so delicious. It is a deep, almost glowing, red-garnet color, and smells like fresh whipping cream and black pepper. Despite its almost 18% alcohol, this fortified Shiraz is very well-balanced. It floods the palate with sweet cassis and vanilla, then settles down to reveal smoky, charred wood flavors, smooth, gripping tannins, and a nutty, long finish. Torbreck winemaker Dave Powell is behind this sexy, must-try "late-night" dessert wine. **94** —*D.T. (12/31/2005)*

MT. JAGGED

Mt. Jagged 2003 Chardonnay (Southern Fleurieu) $15. The nose doesn't show much more than faint notes of peach skin, which continue on the palate to join jarring but crisp citrus flavors on the finish. Taste it again, and the citrus goes the way of green apple. A good, basic Chard—one in which wood isn't an intrusion. **85** —*D.T. (10/1/2005)*

Mt. Jagged 2001 Lightly Wooded Chardonnay (Southern Fleurieu) $18. Fruit on the palate is yellow but flat; you'll find more yellow fruit on the nose, where it shows a little more life. Finishes with some chalk and herb. **82** —*D.T. (8/1/2003)*

Mt. Jagged 2001 Merlot-Cabernet Sauvignon (McLaren Vale) $15. The nose offers dark aromas of black soil, black plum, and caramel, with some noticeable sweetness to the fruit. What you experience on the nose is larger on the palate: black plum, and rustic, outdoorsy flavors. It's ample in the mouth, a straight-shooting, easy-to-like wine. **87** —*D.T. (9/1/2004)*

Mt. Jagged NV Sparkling Red Red Blend (South Australia) $18. Porty, blackberry aromas lead to off-dry flavors of cassis and blackberry. A soft-bodied, frothy wine for post-dinner, rather than during-dinner, enjoyment—cheese course, anyone? **86** —*D.T. (12/31/2005)*

MURDOCK

Murdock 1999 Cabernet Sauvignon (Coonawarra) $50. A svelte and earthy Cab, but an excellent one. A sweet black-cherry core fades into a taut finish with plenty of juicy tannins. Tree bark, anise, and clove aromas complete the pretty picture. **90** —*D.T. (12/31/2004)*

Murdock 2003 Riesling (Coonawarra) $22. This wine's a tough mistress. Though there are some piquant yellow-fruit aromas under a hefty dose of chalk dust, there's something very reserved and cool about the palate's offerings. Dust and chalk coat firm, white stone fruit flavors that taste a day short of ripe. The flavors aren't green or unpleasant by any means—they just indicate a very good, firm, not tropical, not overdone Riesling. **87** —*D.T. (12/31/2004)*

NARDONE BAKER

Nardone Baker 2000 Cabernet Sauvignon (South Eastern Australia) $10. Graham crackers and citrus rind but no real fruit make up the nose. The flavors are sweet like a confection, as if residual sugar is present. The finish is oaky and overall the wine seems manipulated more than natural. **81** —*M.S. (12/15/2002)*

Nardone Baker 2001 Cabernet Sauvignon-Merlot (South Eastern Australia) $10. Grapey, sweet aromas send this one off, and then comes a palate of berries and plums. It's soft and plush in the mouth, but short on the finish. Tasty and simple; a more-than-decent blend from multiple appellations. **86** —*M.S. (12/15/2002)*

Nardone Baker 2001 Chardonnay (South Eastern Australia) $10. Made "without the influence of oak maturation," and it shows. A very good, clean, interesting wine with fresh peach and citrus flavors, medium body and pretty floral aromas. Not complicated, but pleasant. Finishes with chalk and a little sweetness. **87** —*D.T. (8/1/2003)*

NEIGHBOURS

Neighbours 1999 Shiraz (McLaren Vale) $20. Winemaker Chester Osbourn's second release is a promising Shiraz, with solid plum fruit at its core, and a dash of herb to keep things interesting. It's smooth, though perhaps not as concentrated as I'd like. Nice chalky notes characterize the start and the finish.. **87** —*D.T. (3/1/2003)*

NEPENTHE

Nepenthe 2000 The Fugue Bordeaux Blend (Adelaide Hills) $27. This Bordeaux blend isn't austere, exactly, but feels a little Old World. Maybe it's the wine's dryish tannins and modest size, or maybe it's that wines from the cool-climate Adelaide Hills just aren't oversized by definition. It's a very good wine, though, with a base of black plum and some meat and oak aromas on the nose. **88** —*D.T. (12/31/2003)*

Nepenthe 2003 Tryst Cabernet Blend (Adelaide Hills) $14. What's not to like about this wine's red and purple plum flavors, smooth tannins, and easy mouthfeel? It's an enjoyable, straightforward quaffer; one to drink now. A blend of 60% Cab, 25% Zinfandel, and 15% Tempranillo **86** —*D.T. (8/1/2005)*

Nepenthe 1998 The Fugue Cabernet Sauvignon (Adelaide Hills) $27. This Bordeaux-style blend is 81% Cabernet Sauvignon and it shows in the wine's tight structure. Plum and black cherry fruit is framed in toasty, smoky oak and finishes with drying tannins. Age it a few years for maximum enjoyment. **87** —*J.C. (6/1/2002)*

Nepenthe 2001 The Fugue Cabernet Sauvignon-Merlot (Adelaide Hills) $20. Winemaker Peter Leske's 70-30 Cab-Merlot has good spine, with black cherry and red plum fruit at the fore. Cool menthol and black cherry aromas are exhilarating; finishes medium-long and earthy. A classy, fly-under-the-radar-but-impress-the-heck-outta-you wine. **91 Editors' Choice** —*D.T. (8/1/2005)*

Nepenthe 2000 Zoes Chardonnay (Adelaide Hills) $15. A smooth, easy-to-drink wine made to the New World formula: Sweet caramel, vanilla and peach aromas and flavors, capped off by spicy oak on the finish. **86** —*J.C. (7/1/2002)*

Nepenthe 1999 Pinot Noir (South Australia) $25. The mouthfeel of this wine is just right—an airy, delicate lacework that glides the flavors over the tongue. But the flavors are just so-so, harkening back to the Kinks' famous line, "C-O-L-A cola." Finishes with some dry tannins and a touch of citrus. **85** —*J.C. (9/1/2002)*

Nepenthe 2002 Charleston Pinot Noir (Adelaide Hills) $20. This Pinot does not show particularly well right out of the bottle—it feels dull, with earth overshadowing all its other attributes—so give it time. With air, it peps up, and some black cherry fruit shows through. Juicy and enjoyable if you give it a few minutes to unfold. **87** —*D.T. (8/1/2005)*

Nepenthe 2002 Tryst Red Blend (Adelaide Hills) $14. A blend of Cabernet, Tempranillo, and Zinfandel; you've got to hand it to Nepenthe for experimenting with new varieties. Smells cool-climate, with nuances of eucalyptus/fresh herb, and taut, cherry fruit. Soft and dry in the mouth, where red plum and tangy oak flavors are the key players. It's a nice red wine, but one that just hasn't hit its stride yet. **86** —*D.T. (12/31/2004)*

Nepenthe 2004 Sauvignon Blanc (Adelaide Hills) $14. My first reaction to this wine was that it's made in a safe, please-everyone style. With some air, a pretty citrus-pulp flavor and texture also emerges. Very good. **87** —*D.T. (8/1/2005)*

Nepenthe 2001 Sauvignon Blanc (Adelaide Hills) $17. A decent stand-in for New Zealand Sauvignon Blanc, this medium-weight wine has some cat pee aromas mixed with celery and grapefruit. The passion fruit flavors finish long and tangy. **86** —*J.C. (2/1/2002)*

Nepenthe 2004 Tryst White Blend (Adelaide Hills) $14. Dusty, chalky aromas and flavors coat toned-down grapefruit and fresh herb notes underneath. Dry and understated overall, but enjoyable. A Sem-Sauv blend, with just 5% Pinot Gris thrown in. 162 cases produced. **87** —*D.T. (8/1/2005)*

Nepenthe 1999 Zinfandel (South Australia) $36. Winemaker Peter Leske has made only 80 cases of this 16% alcohol Zin, and, however unconvential a variety for Australia, it is a noble effort. Medium-bodied with a gummy, resiny texture, the palate offers sweet red fruit, plus a smooth mineral-woody overlay. Finishes a little hot, but with nice caramel and earth notes, and some drying tannins. **87** —*D.T. (6/1/2003)*

Nepenthe 2001 Charleston Zinfandel (Adelaide Hills) $39. Dry tannins on the palate, with blueberry and blackberry flavors that get lost beneath permeating citrus—more precisely, orange—flavors and aromas. It's a very unusual wine, but intriguing in its own way. Finishes dry, with leather and oak. **86** —*D.T. (12/31/2004)*

NINE STONES

Nine Stones 2003 Shiraz (McLaren Vale) $12. Aromas are of plum, meat, and a dash of caramel. In the mouth, it's medium-bodied, with pure mixed plums and a little vanilla on the palate. This Shiraz is not just a bargain, it's just the ticket for the dinner table. Try it with curries, jambalaya—anything that has a spicy kick. **88 Best Buy** —*D.T. (3/1/2005)*

Nine Stones 2003 Shiraz (Barossa) $12. A rustic-style, good-value Shiraz. Oak lends it a woodsy, dusty mouthfeel and aromas of coffee, oak, and black pepper. Purple and red plum and berry fruit on the palate is straightforward, yet tasty. **86** —*D.T. (5/1/2005)*

NINTH ISLAND

Ninth Island 2005 Pinot Noir (Tasmania) $19. Proof that Tasmania has what it takes to succeed on the export market. The wine's feel is wooly; it's not superfull on the palate, but it's an enjoyable New World-style Pinot with solid plum, black cherry, and mineral components. **88** —*D.T. (11/15/2006)*

Ninth Island 2001 Riesling (Tasmania) $16. Smooth on the palate, though perhaps not as crisp and dry as some of its countrymen. Still, it has fragrant thyme and rose notes on the nose, with white pepper and sweet yellow fruit flavors. A thread of white pepper from beginning to end holds it all together. **87** —*D.T. (8/1/2003)*

NIRVANA

Nirvana 2000 White Blend (Margaret River) $10. This wine's eclectic nose of cotton, butter—and, as one reviewer thought, tinned asparagus—will please few wine enthusiasts. Palate is high in acid and minerally, with tinges of citrus and cream. Add to the mix a tangy finish of fresh wood, light honey, and a green-apple Jolly Rancher. An enigma. **80** *(9/1/2001)*

NOON

Noon 2004 Reserve Cabernet Sauvignon (South Australia) $120. The wine now bears a South Australia appellation because the fruit is coming from Langhorne Creek. This vintage clocks in at 15.5% alcohol, with nutmeg and blackberry aromas. Blackberry fruit is encased in a pretty dark, char-barrel shell at this early stage; tannins are woody and textured. Optimal enjoyment likely 2008–2010. **90** —*D.T. (10/1/2006)*

Noon 2003 Reserve Cabernet Sauvignon (McLaren Vale) $55. Alluring aromas of black pepper, vanilla, chalk, and a streak of eucalyptus kick off this excellent wine. Tannins on the palate are still young and dominant, but the wine's attractive black plum and soil flavors will show through in a few years' time. Finishes long and smooth. Drink 2007+. **92** —*D.T. (3/1/2005)*

Noon 2002 Reserve Cabernet Sauvignon (McLaren Vale) $55. A feminine Cab, one that feels delicate and elegant in the mouth but has the power and intensity to beat the crap out of you, if only she were that kind of girl. On the palate, pure black-cherry fruit receives a judicious dose of smooth oak, which fades into chalk on the finish. Very classy, and quite excellent. **94** —*D.T. (5/1/2004)*

Noon 2003 Eclipse Grenache (McLaren Vale) $55. This Grenache has some dark, smoldering character but it's still a manageable size. Deep black cherry lurks beneath smoke, ash, and cream aromas and flavors. Finishes with fine, chalky tannins. Open a few hours before drinking. **91** —*D.T. (3/1/2005)*

Noon 2002 Eclipse Grenache-Shiraz (McLaren Vale) $55. 70% Grenache and 30% Shiraz, it absolutely needs to be decanted a few hours before drinking. (Straight out of the bottle it pulls that overpowering, cherry-and-alcohol trick that Grenache can play.) Once it settles down you'll find black cherry fruit and some charcoal-toast accents, which persist through the finish. Not a tannic wine, but packs a whollop with New World flavor. **90** —*D.T. (5/1/2004)*

Noon 2003 Reserve Shiraz (McLaren Vale) $55. Spice and black pepper is the name of the game on the nose, while youthful plum fruit on the palate is jazzed up with herb and earth. Finishes smooth and minerally; still closed overall, and probably not at its best until around 2008. **91** —*D.T. (3/1/2005)*

Noon 2002 Reserve Shiraz (McLaren Vale) $55. Aromas are of bright black plum and cassis; more of the same is delivered on the palate, where there are also smooth tannins and mocha accents. This is an excellent, medium-bodied, well-measured wine, where fruit and oak coexist peacefully and seamlessly. Finishes with a burst of black fruit and more mocha. **92** —*D.T. (5/1/2004)*

NORFOLK RISE

Norfolk Rise 2005 Noolook Pinot Gris (Mount Benson) $16. Has pretty floral aromas that go the way of honeysuckle and ripe pear flavors on the palate. It's a little light, but it's still a good, enjoyable everyday wine, just right for lunch on the patio. **86** —*D.T. (2/1/2006)*

NORMAN WINES, LTD.

Norman Wines, Ltd. 2001 Teal Lake Cabernet Sauvignon-Merlot (South Eastern Australia) $13. This kosher performer begins with a strong whiff of smoked meats and some unbridled grapey aromas. The palate is fairly complex, with plum, licorice, coffee, and mineral notes. The finish is rather spicy, bordering on hot. Despite a touch of bitterness on the back end, it's got a lot going for it. **86 Best Buy** —*M.S. (12/15/2002)*

Norman Wines, Ltd. 2001 Teal Lake Chardonnay (South Eastern Australia) $13. This Chard is somewhat viscous on the palate, though its fruit takes a backseat to mallowy, carmelly flavors that calm down with some aeration. Nose offers butterscotchy, carmel-coated tropical fruit aromas. **83** —*D.T. (6/1/2003)*

Norman Wines, Ltd. 2001 Teal Lake Pinot Noir (South Eastern Australia) $16. Fairly hollow, with lots of wood, woodsy tannins, and not too much in the way of fruit. The nose, with sweet, juicy red fruit, was a bit more promising than what the palate delivers. **82** —*D.T. (6/1/2003)*

NORMANS

Normans 2002 Chais Clarendon Cabernet Sauvignon (South Australia) $30. This is one good Cabernet with all its pieces in place: fruit-sweet and nutty on the nose, with a juicy blackberry and black cherry core and a gravelly, minerally texture. It's not as mouthfilling and plush as it has been in recent vintages, but it's still an enjoyable wine. **88** —D.T. (10/1/2005)

Normans 1999 Chais Clarendon Cabernet Sauvignon (Adelaide Hills) $30. Call it what you want—big-boned, broad-chested, varón—but this is a manly, sizeable wine, and laudable because it doesn't have some of the cloying, messy richness that big Cabs can sometimes have. Smells of black pepper, and cola or root beer. There's mixed plum fruit, lively acids, and gripping tannins on the palate and the finish. Does let up with air, but still probably best after 2007. **92** —D.T. (12/31/2004)

Normans 2001 Encounter Bay Cabernet Sauvignon (South Australia) $10. There's a sweet, candied whiff on the nose, plus a nice gumtree accent. In the mouth, earth and black cherry get a dusting of a Sweet Tart confection, which rides through the finish. **86 Best Buy** —D.T. (3/1/2005)

Normans 2002 Old Vine Cabernet Sauvignon (South Australia) $15. Opens with meaty, molassesy aromas that turn to tomato with air. On the palate, plum and oak are accented by minty flavors that come through in full force on the finish, along with some cherry cordial. Feminine-sized, with smooth tannins. **86** —D.T. (12/31/2005)

Normans 2003 Encounter Bay Chardonnay (South Eastern Australia) $10. A straight-shooting, easy-quaffing Chard. Offers yellow stone fruit and mustard seed aromas and flavors, with moderate oak on the palate. Medium-bodied; a good, please-everyone choice for large groups. **86 Best Buy** —D.T. (3/1/2005)

Normans 2002 Old Vine Grenache (McLaren Vale) $15. Vanilla and pepper aromas lead to sexy, vanilla, and black cherry flavors on the palate and finish. A very good effort and an enjoyable wine, though a little heavy on the vanilla. **87** —D.T. (3/1/2005)

Normans 2001 Chais Clarendon Shiraz (McLaren Vale) $30. Both 2001 Chais Claredons are excellent this vintage. This Shiraz's fluffy, soft tannins make it feel approachable but it's still a substantial wine. Juciy black cherry and plum fruit wears a dusty, chalky jacket. With air, toffee notes start coming on. Finishes with bold beefy, meaty flavors. Drink now and over the next three years. **90** —D.T. (12/31/2004)

Normans 2001 Encounter Bay Shiraz (South Australia) $10. A sweeter, more forward style of Shiraz, with jammy berry and peanut aromas, and ripe plum and cherries on the palate. Soft on the palate; finishes with a light grip of tannins. **86 Best Buy** —D.T. (3/1/2005)

Normans 2003 Old Vine Shiraz (South Australia) $15. A wine that feels warm in alcohol but cool in flavor, with minty, cedary notes and sour plums giving a crisp, narrow impression. Aromas are pretty—like blackberry and bramble—but the wine tastes somewhat sour and lean. **86** —D.T. (2/1/2006)

Normans 2002 Old Vine Shiraz (South Australia) $15. Starts off beautifully, with earthy-meaty aromas and vibrant, juicy fruit on palate entry. Midway through, someone drops a barrel on your tongue, which holds on until the last swallow. Very pretty at first; maybe next vintage won't be quite as woody. **87** —D.T. (3/1/2005)

NUGAN FAMILY ESTATES

Nugan Family Estates 2002 Alcira Vineyard Cabernet Sauvignon (Coonawarra) $23. Made to fit a standard mold, but made well. Aromas are of plum and cinnamon, with similar notes on the palate. Slender in body, with smooth tannins and a nut-laden finish. **89** —D.T. (6/1/2006)

Nugan Family Estates 2004 Chardonnay (South Eastern Australia) $12. This wine has a good helping of pleasing sour apple fruit, but along with that, a fair amount of oak. It's toasty around the edges, with a dry, woody finish. **84** —D.T. (6/1/2006)

Nugan Family Estates 2002 3rd Generation Chardonnay (South Eastern Australia) $12. Shows pineapple, peach, and toast on the nose. On the palate, there's yellow stone fruit and clove at its core but wood and alcohol stand out a bit more. Finish is brief, with bright herb and wood notes. **82** (7/2/2004)

Nugan Family Estates 2002 Alcira Vineyard Chardonnay (Coonawarra) $18. Nose gets more and more toasty with aeration; peach and pear fruit hides behind a curtain of butter and smoky, toasty oak that intensifies through the finish. **84** (7/2/2004)

Nugan Family Estates 2004 Frasca's Lane Vineyard Chardonnay (King Valley) $22. This Chardonnay's vanilla bean and smoky oak aromas are compelling, as are its flavors of citrus peel, white pepper, and cream. It's fresh and round on the palate, finishing with a zing of citrus. **88** —D.T. (6/1/2006)

Nugan Family Estates 2001 Third Generation Chardonnay (South Eastern Australia) $11. Takes sweet fruit and oak to an extreme for a dry table wine, with aromas and flavors of vanilla, coconut, honey, and tropical fruit. Try serving it ice-cold to lessen the sensation of sweetness. **82** —J.C. (7/1/2002)

Nugan Family Estates 2004 Manuka Grove Durif (South Eastern Australia) $23. Lifted but plush plum and blueberry fruit on the palate, with chocolate aromas. Tannins are moderate but textured; a good match for savory dishes with sweeter sauces (think braised rabbit or venison with a fruit-based accompaniment). **89** —D.T. (8/1/2006)

Nugan Family Estates 2002 Frasca's Lane Vineyard Sauvignon Blanc (King Valley) $16. Has pretty aromas of hay or straw, and cream. Though there is peach and pear fruit here, it's the citrusy core that stands out, and persists through the finish. **86** —D.T. (11/15/2004)

Nugan Family Estates 2002 KLN Vineyard Botrytis Semillon (Riverina) $22. The bouquet has a pleasing floral component, and the palate, an oily, though not clumsy, feel. Yellow peach fruit dominates in the mouth. It's a good wine, but not a vibrant, deep one. **84** —D.T. (9/1/2004)

Nugan Family Estates 2004 Shiraz (South Eastern Australia) $12. Not Nugan's finest effort; their single-vineyard wines are much better. This wine is hollow, with sweet, Bazooka gum-like aromas. **82** —D.T. (6/1/2006)

Nugan Family Estates 2004 McLaren Parish Vineyard Shiraz (McLaren Vale) $23. Crisp aromas of black pepper, root beer, and eucalyptus are unusual and appealing. On the palate, well-judged oak envelops plum and blackberry fruit. Very good, if a little short on the finish. **87** —D.T. (6/1/2006)

Nugan Family Estates 2002 Third Generation Shiraz (South Eastern Australia) $12. A middle-of-the-road Shiraz, moderately sized and easy in feel. Has sweet berry and caramel aromas, and generic berry and plum fruit in the mouth. **86** —D.T. (11/15/2004)

O'LEARY WALKER

O'Leary Walker 2002 Cabernet Sauvignon-Merlot (Clare-Adelaide Hills) $15. This is a cool-climate red, which means it's no fruit bomb. Plum fruit is taut in the mouth, with fern, earth, and tree-bark aromas. Soft in the mouth, and drinkable now. **87** —D.T. (2/1/2004)

O'Leary Walker 2001 Chardonnay (Adelaide Hills) $20. Nut and stone fruit notes vie for center stage on this wine, and the race is neck in neck. Smoky, nutty aromas smolder against a backdrop of pear on the nose, and on the palate, peach takes the lead with nuts, toast, and butter falling into the background. It's a medium-weight wine, straightforward and good. **86** (7/2/2004)

O'Leary Walker 2003 Watervale Riesling (Clare Valley) $15. Fragrant, with lovely honeysuckle aromas. Despite the vintage, still manages a lean, lithe mouthfeel and upbeat, citrus flavors. **87** —D.T. (2/1/2004)

O'Leary Walker 2002 Watervale Semillon (Clare Valley) $20. From Watervale, a Clare Valley area better known for its Rieslings. Aromas and flavors are light and pretty—think hay, olive oil, citrus peel, and light stone fruit. In the mouth the wine is round, with some viscosity. Would probably pair very well with scallops, or a seafood-based stew. **87** —D.T. (9/1/2004)

O'Leary Walker 2002 Shiraz (Clare-McClaren Vale) $15. Sweet blackberry and plum fruit is bouncy and fresh, though goes a little green on the finish. Approachable now. **86** —D.T. (2/1/2004)

OAKLEY ADAMS

Oakley Adams 1999 Merlot (South Eastern Australia) $10. A soft, light Merlot with aromas of earth and cedar. The palate brings flavors of strawberries and graham cracker crust; finishes showing only tannins and lacking fruit. **83** —*C.S. (6/1/2002)*

OAKRIDGE

Oakridge 2003 Pinot Noir (Yarra Valley) $21. An approachable Pinot: its feel is soft and round, and its cherry fruit falls squarely in the cherry cola camp, rather than the tart and rigid one. Starts to get serious on the finish, where firm tannins take hold. **86** —*D.T. (12/1/2005)*

OCCAM'S RAZOR

Occam's Razor 2001 Shiraz (Heathcote) $26. Full-bodied and tightly wound, this Shiraz probably won't show its best for another 2–3 years. It's a focused, solid wine, with a blackberry and blueberry core and a note of wheat or biscuit. Dry, smooth tannins come on strong in the midpalate and follow through to the finish. **90** —*D.T. (12/31/2003)*

OLD SCHOOL

Old School 2002 Cabernet Sauvignon (Barossa Valley) $34. A worthy sister wine to the Old School Shiraz. Both offer good value for the money. The vintage has given this Barossa Cab an undertone of cool crispness; plum and wheat bread flavors and textured tannins complement a spicy chile-powder note on the nose. One to watch in the future. **90** —*D.T. (10/1/2006)*

Old School 2002 Shiraz (Barossa Valley) $34. Winemaker Noel Heidenreich's Shiraz is compelling, not overwhelming, with some vanilla flavors framing juicy red plum and raspberry fruit. It's pleasing and textured, and gives the same impression on the nose: spice, curry, moist clay, red fruit. Very appealing overall, tiptoeing out on the finish with soft tannins. **90** —*D.T. (6/1/2006)*

OLIVERHILL

Oliverhill 2000 Bradey Block Grenache (McLaren Vale) $20. A soft, round wine that almost seems designed for glugging. Dusty earth and dried grass aromas give way to a sweet, alcoholic attack filled with red berries and cherries. The warm, spirity finish leaves you glowing and reaching for another sip. **87** —*J.C. (9/1/2002)*

Oliverhill 2003 Jimmy Section Shiraz (McLaren Vale) $33. This is one sexy, concentrated wine. Aromas are rich and perfumed, featuring purple fruit and black pepper at the fore. It's still fairly tannic and young, but in a few years' time the purple fruit and wheat flour flavors will be showing beautifully. **92** —*D.T. (3/1/2005)*

Oliverhill 2000 Jimmy Section Shiraz (McLaren Vale) $33. A complex bouquet of dark plummy fruit, bacon, wheat, leather, and eucalyptus opens this uniformly well-liked offering. It's full and even, with fine fruit-to-acid balance on the palate, good texture, and weight, and roasted fruit, licorice, earth, and mint flavors. More than one panelist described this seamless, smooth wine as sexy. It's a lovely, seductive example with a long, evenly tannic blackberry, cocoa, and caramel-tinged finish. **92 Editors' Choice** *(11/1/2001)*

ONE LEGGED DUCK

One Legged Duck 2000 Redhouse Red Blend (South Australia) $14. Smooth and supple on the palate, this 70-30 blend—whose grapes come from Barossa, McLaren Vale, and Limestone Coast, thus the broad "Australia" designation—offers chewy red fruit and earth flavors, with a little tomato thrown in. Fine tannins linger on the back end. **89 Editors' Choice** —*D.T. (12/31/2003)*

ORIGIN

Origin 2002 Reserve Series Shiraz (Barossa Valley) $19. A Pinot-weight Shiraz with pleasing flavors of black cherry, earth and eucalyptus. Cooler notes prevail on the nose. Ends with seeped-tea flavors. **87** —*D.T. (10/1/2005)*

ORMON HILL

Ormon Hill 2001 Shiraz (Heathcote) $20. From Heathcote, which is northwest of Yarra Valley in Victoria. Eighteen months in American oak give this wine spicy clove aromas, plus some blueberry and cereal notes. It's an enjoyable, moderately sized wine, with lively acidity and juicy black and red berry fruit on the palate and finish. **89** —*D.T. (12/31/2004)*

OUTBACK CHASE

Outback Chase 2003 Chardonnay (South Eastern Australia) $7. Tropical/yellow fruit on the palate, with decent concentration. It finishes with a generous dose of pulpy wood, but it is still a good, inexpensive quaffer. **84 Best Buy** —*D.T. (5/1/2005)*

Outback Chase 2003 Wobbly White White Blend (South Eastern Australia) $7. A simple, sweet wine. This blend of Riesling, Muscat, and Verdelho smells and tastes like floral perfume, with some pineapple-piña colada flavors for good measure. **83** —*D.T. (5/1/2005)*

OWEN'S ESTATE

Owen's Estate 1999 Cabernet Sauvignon-Shiraz (South Eastern Australia) $13. Clean, bright, and refreshing, this pretty wine is no blockbuster, but has lots of cherry fruit and spice in a dry, spicy, and balanced package. The tannins are lush and lend good structure. Might even improve with a year or so in the cellar. **86** —*S.H. (9/1/2001)*

Owen's Estate 1999 Chardonnay (South Eastern Australia) $15. Basic Chardonnay—pear, citrus, and green apple balanced by vanilla and wood. Lighter, leaner, and more food-friendly than many Aussie Chards, finishing with tart acidity. **84** —*J.C. (7/1/2002)*

Owen's Estate 1999 Merlot (South Eastern Australia) $15. American oak can smell like cloves, and this wine, which was aged in American oak, does, along with meat, chocolate, and blackberries. It's juicy in the mouth, with some numbing tannins. A little earthy and rough around the edges, and finishes with an almond-skin bitterness. **84** —*S.H. (9/1/2001)*

Owen's Estate 1999 Sauvignon Blanc (McLaren Vale) $13. Brilliant fruit powers this delightful wine, at such a great price. Aromas of kiwi and lime explode from the glass with herbal, smoky overtones. In the mouth, it's a lusty wine, filled with lime and grapefruit flavors and intense acidity. Scouringly clean and dry. **90 Best Buy** —*S.H. (9/1/2001)*

Owen's Estate 1998 Shiraz (South Australia) $15. 85 *(4/1/2000)*

Owen's Estate 1999 Shiraz (South Australia/Victoria) $14. Subtle aromas of infield dust, cedar, and red clay plus dark fruit were, to all reviewers, too mute. So dark that it's nearly opaque purple-black, it shows burned oak, raisin, and overripe berries on the palate. Finishes bland, with soy and mineral notes. **82** *(10/1/2001)*

OXFORD LANDING

Oxford Landing 1999 Limited Release Cabernet Sauvignon (South Australia) $10. Oxford Landing's garnet-colored Cab will please fans of simple, high-tannin wines. Oaky and peppery from beginning to end, the wine shows light blackberry and cherry flavors on the nose, and closes long and cedary. **84** —*D.T. (9/1/2001)*

Oxford Landing 1999 Cabernet Sauvignon-Shiraz (South Australia) $8. There's a lot going on in this simple Cab-Shiraz. Aromas of earth, cherry, and Sweet Tarts pave the way for white pepper, plum, and fresh cedar on the palate. Medium-full, with nice balance, the wine finishes with a zippy (but not too hot) black pepper note. An easy mainstream sell. **86 Best Buy** —*D.T. (9/1/2001)*

Oxford Landing 2005 Chardonnay (South Australia) $9. All you could want in a Chardonnay at this price point: A soft, approachable feel and easy flavors of apple and peach. Finishes with a zip of citrus zest. **85 Best Buy** —*D.T. (6/1/2006)*

Oxford Landing 2004 Chardonnay (South Australia) $9. Smells like it tastes—full of toast, pear, and peach notes, accented by a piquant yellow flavor. Tasty and easy to drink. **86 Best Buy** —*D.T. (8/1/2005)*

Oxford Landing 2002 Chardonnay (Eden Valley) $7. Big and mouthfilling, this Chard has honey and citrus flavors on the palate, and a nose that combines steely, floral-and-anise aromas. A little hot on the finish, but still a good value. **85** *(7/1/2004)*

Oxford Landing 2000 Chardonnay (South Australia) $8. The nose offers hot, fresh green-herbal scents, plus a bit of butter and pear. Oak shows on the mouth, as does the expected creaminess that comes with barrel fermentation. Finish is slightly oaky, with a hot, tingly sensation that's reminiscent of mouthwash. A simple, slightly antiseptic wine. **83** —*D.T. (9/1/2001)*

Oxford Landing 1998 Limited Release Grenache (South Australia) $10. Deceptively light in color, this wine nevertheless packs a wallop, with a hefty 14.5% alcohol. The delicate—almost Burgundian—cherries start off buried by oak and alcohol, but after some airing the flavors come together in a pleasant mélange of Bing cherries, maple syrup and caramel, accented on the finish by a touch of black pepper. **86 Best Buy** —*J.C. (9/1/2001)*

Oxford Landing 2003 Merlot (South Australia) $9. Just the right size to enjoy with a meal. This is one juicy Merlot, with a parade of plum, blackberry, and raspberry flavors and aromas. Feels smooth, with oak adding an acorn-like accent through the finish. **86 Best Buy** —*D.T. (5/1/2005)*

Oxford Landing 1999 Merlot (South Australia) $8. This decent entry-level Merlot has mild berry and cocoa aromas and flavors and just a hint of an herb note. The even mouthfeel and fairly smooth finish make it an attractive, easy to drink wine and it tastes like Merlot, rather than an indistinct red. **84 Best Buy** *(9/1/2001)*

Oxford Landing 2002 Shiraz (South Australia) $9. Flavors and aromas are red and a little tart—not cherry, exactly, maybe more along the lines of persimmon? A fair amount of oak joins the fruit on the palate, and hangs on for a drying, oaky finish. **83** —*D.T. (5/1/2005)*

Oxford Landing 1999 Limited Release Shiraz (South Australia) $10. A bland McIntosh apple-and-pistachio bouquet ushers you into a solid but uninspiring palate of dark black berry fruit, oak, and anise. Wintergreen and oak flavors dominate the finish. **84** *(10/1/2001)*

Oxford Landing 2005 Viognier (South Australia) $9. An overt, forward Viognier, this has flavors of white pepper, white chocolate, and fresh grass rounding out its medium-full palate. Also demonstrates the grape's characteristic slippery, oily character. **86 Best Buy** —*D.T. (10/1/2006)*

Oxford Landing 2004 Viognier (South Australia) $9. Typical with its floral and honey aromas. Medium-weight, with pear, melon, and floral notes. Its 14.5% alcohol is noticeable, but it's still a good wine at a good price. **86 Best Buy** —*D.T. (8/1/2005)*

Oxford Landing 1998 Limited Release Viognier (South Australia) $10. 85 *(10/1/2000)*

OZ ROZ

Oz Roz 2004 Rosé of Shiraz (South Eastern Australia) $7. Smells like strawberry, oak, herb, and plum. Tastes, however, like a strawberry short-cake. Simple, and a little sweet. **83** —*D.T. (12/1/2005)*

PAIKO

Paiko 2005 Chardonnay (Alpine Valleys) $10. Has some lemon meringue and nut on the nose, but the palate quickly loses steam after a punchy, acidic first impression. Flattens out on the finish. **82** —*D.T. (11/15/2006)*

Paiko 2004 Chardonnay (Alpine Valleys) $10. An odd wine altogether: Smells like candy (gumdrops, lollipops) and tastes like a different sort of candy: the dry, tart, hard lemon candy. Has an oily, hard-candy texture. **82** —*D.T. (5/1/2005)*

Paiko 2002 Merlot (Murray-Darling) $10. Solid, offering rustic bark-leaf-smoke-nut nuances top to bottom, with blackberry and plum flavors underneath. A Band-aid note on the nose resurfaces on the finish. **86 Best Buy** —*D.T. (8/1/2005)*

Paiko 2002 Shiraz (Murray-Darling) $10. The nose has penetrating euca-lyptus aromas, with purple fruit underneath. On the palate, sweet berry fruit and oak flavors are couched in a soft, easy feel. There's nothing too fancy about this $10 Shiraz, but for many, that will be part of its draw. **85 Best Buy** —*D.T. (5/1/2005)*

Paiko 2004 Viognier (Murray-Darling) $10. This is a good, medium-sized white wine, but apart from a little viscosity on the finish, doesn't really show much of what Viognier is capable of. Smells like heavy yellow stone fruit, and offers honey and butterscotch Lifesaver flavors. **84** —*D.T. (12/1/2005)*

PALANDRI

Palandri 2002 Cabernet Sauvignon (Western Australia) $15. Starts off with bouncy, juicy fruit on the palate, with almost Portlike aromas. With time a flattening, oaky veneer overtakes the fruit. Light- to medium-bodied; finish is brief. **85** —*D.T. (12/31/2005)*

Palandri 2001 Cabernet Sauvignon (Western Australia) $16. 87 *(8/1/2003)*

Palandri 2002 Cabernet Sauvignon-Merlot (Western Australia) $16. Roughly two-thirds Cab and one-third Merlot, this red wears a judicious amount of oak, and is drinking well now. At its core is black cherry and plum fruit. Its chalk-clay feel persists through the finish, as does a ribbon of fresh eucalyptus. It's a solid, well-made wine. 3,500 cases produced. **88** —*D.T. (9/1/2004)*

Palandri 2001 Cabernet Sauvignon-Merlot (Western Australia) $16. 87 *(8/1/2003)*

Palandri 2004 Chardonnay (Western Australia) $12. Has spicy aromas; on the palate, it has a pleasing, zesty spring in its step, like herbs and green apples. In the background, has a persistent butterscotch hard-candy fla-vor and feel. 5,000 cases produced. **86** —*D.T. (12/1/2005)*

Palandri 2002 Merlot (Western Australia) $15. Aromas are dark and inter-esting, including black pepper and tree bark notes. Red-fruit flavors are tangy but tempered by a sandy, earthy component and lively acids. Wooly tannins complete the picture. 4,000 cases produced. **87** —*D.T. (8/1/2005)*

Palandri 2001 Merlot (Western Australia) $16. 86 *(8/1/2003)*

Palandri 2004 Boundary Road Sauvignon Blanc (Western Australia) $11. Will appeal to fans of grassy, green New Zealand Sauvignons. This Western Australian version has intense grass and green pea aromas that are repeated, though with less pizazz, on the palate. Finishes flat. **84** —*D.T. (10/1/2005)*

Palandri 2001 Shiraz (Western Australia) $16. 88 *(8/1/2003)*

PARACOMBE

Paracombe 2002 Cabernet Franc (Adelaide Hills) $30. This wine's pretty green. There's celery seed and weed on the nose; red, tomato-y fruit on the palate gets a dose of green bean toward the finish. **83** —*D.T. (8/1/2005)*

Paracombe 2002 Cabernet Sauvignon (Adelaide Hills) $35. Weedy on the nose one moment, sweet the next. Feels halfhearted on the palate, and missing verve. Still, it offers black and purple berry fruit, and moderate tannins. **84** —*D.T. (8/1/2005)*

Paracombe 2002 The Reuben Red Blend (Adelaide Hills) $30. Aromas are of meat and tree bark; fruit flavors are more like plum skin than flesh. Not very giving. Tasted twice. **85** —*D.T. (8/1/2005)*

Paracombe 2001 The Reuben Red Blend (Adelaide Hills) $30. This is a stylish, feminine Cabernet, one that has plenty of blackberry and cassis fruit but dealt it with a delicate hand. Wood adds anise and mocha-like accents. A very good wine, and a good flag-bearer for the Hills. A blend of Cabernets, Malbec, Merlot, and Shiraz. 192 cases produced. **89** —*D.T. (5/1/2005)*

Paracombe 2004 Sauvignon Blanc (Adelaide Hills) $23. Fresh and lively bouquet, with aromas of grapefruit and green veggies, i.e. peas and beans. Pours on the citrus flavors, with accents of passion fruit and gin-ger. Spritzy feeling, with zesty acidity. Turns a bit lemony toward the back end. **87** *(7/1/2005)*

Paracombe 2002 Shiraz (Adelaide Hills) $35. A very good wine, with a smooth feel on its side. The nose has a stewy, figgy quality, and the fin-ish, a fair amount of char, but what's in between—taut plum fruit—is enjoyable. **87** —*D.T. (8/1/2005)*

Paracombe 1999 Shiraz (Adelaide Hills) $28. Aromas of cut flowers and cherry fruit hidden by a veneer of toast and a certain medicinal quality leave off at the palate, where pretty cherry fruit and a lean back end fore-tell of a slim cherry finish. Delicate, with firm acids.. **86** —*K.F. (3/1/2003)*

Paracombe 1998 Shiraz (Adelaide Hills) $28. This South Australian shows complexity from stem to stern, its deep, dark fruit accented by tobacco and anise. The fruit shines on the palate, but the finish really stands out, with tremendous length and an impressive cocoa, nut, plum, and caramel fade. The elements aren't unique; this just struts its fine stuff in perfect proportion, with great balance and style. Drink now and until 2006. Top Value. **91** *(11/1/2001)*

Paracombe 2001 Somerville Shiraz (Adelaide Hills) $80. A Shiraz with a Type A personality: Big and brash on the nose, with enthusiastic, forward flavors on the palate. Up front, it smells like marzipan, toast, raspberry, and blackberry, and similar notes ring true in the mouth. Finishes pretty long, with a biscuit or cracker-like flavor. Very tasty. **90** —D.T. *(8/1/2005)*

Paracombe 1997 Somerville Shiraz (Adelaide Hills) $70. This straight shooter opens with gamy meat and burned toast aromas. The palate shows solid red plum and cherry fruit. It is this honest fruit combined with such good acids that make the nose forgivable. **86** —K.F. *(3/1/2003)*

PARINGA

Paringa 2001 Individual Vineyard Shiraz (South Australia) $10. Aussie Shirazes have swept across the United States over the last decade, but many brands seem to have lost the quality edge that made them successful. Let's hope the same doesn't happen to this wine, which is only in its third vintage. It displays all the things we love about Shiraz—sweet blackberry fruit, lashings of vanilla oak, and a lush, velvety texture. Bottlings like this are proof that importer Dan Phillips isn't just about finding expensive microproduction wines, but that he also has an eye for value. **90 Best Buy** —J.C. *(11/15/2002)*

Paringa 2000 Individual Vineyard Shiraz (South Australia) $10. With its full-on blueberry and pie-crust aromas and plushly textured mouthfeel, this sexy effort comes on strong and keeps giving, all the way through to its finish of soft, ripe tannins that almost seem to caress the tongue, leaving behind hints of licorice and chalk. May be even better in 2003. **89 Best Buy** *(10/1/2001)*

PARKER

Parker 2001 Terra Rosa Cabernet Sauvignon (Coonawarra) $30. Though its aromas are a little rich (think cola, amaretto, vanilla), this wine's a workhorse, not a show pony. Its feels admirably sturdy to the core, with hearty red plum and cherry fruit and a rustic, earthy impression overall. An apt tribute to a wine bearing a "terra rossa" name. Drink through 2011. **90** —D.T. *(12/31/2004)*

Parker 2000 Terra Rosa First Growth Cabernet Sauvignon-Merlot (Coonawarra) $70. Aromas are nutty, but also have some stewiness. In the mouth, the wine's tannins are soft enough, perhaps uncharacteristically so, but its taut berry and plum skin flavors still give it an unapproachable pucker. It's a wine that can typically go some years in the cellar, which may help the flavors unfold some in this case. **87** —D.T. *(12/31/2004)*

Parker 2001 Terra Rossa First Growth Cabernet Sauvignon-Merlot (Coonawarra) $70. Wide, smooth, and dark on the palate, this blend offers a burst of flavorful, dark fruit at palate entry. The juicy fruit is well oaked, but not toasty; brambly aromas start it all off. A very pretty wine. **90** —D.T. *(10/1/2006)*

PASSING CLOUDS

Passing Clouds 1998 Shiraz (Bendigo) $25. Medium-full in the mouth, with a long, oaky finish, this Shiraz offers predictably oak-derived cream and vanilla notes on the nose and on the palate. Juicy fruit flavors were lauded by some, and compared by others to black cherry gelatin. An easy quaff, but nothing to ponder by the fireside. **85** *(11/1/2001)*

Passing Clouds 1997 Shiraz (Bendigo) $28. A product of organic viticulture and American oak, the wine's scent and flavor are mainly blackberry with touches of chocolate, smoke, and spice. The palate experience is good except for some unresolved coarse tannins. This is a solid Shiraz that needs just a little more time. **86** —M.N. *(6/1/2001)*

Passing Clouds 1998 Graeme's Blend Shiraz-Cabernet Sauvignon (Bendigo) $25. This big, rugged 60-40 blend may dry out if cellared too long, so drink it young with rare beef to help tame the substantial tannins. Smoke, dried-herb, and black currant flavors should mesh nicely with your next roast. **86** —J.C. *(9/1/2002)*

PATRITTI

Patritti NV Shargren Sparkling Red Wine Shiraz-Grenache (South Australia) $11. A blend of Shiraz and Grenache, this dark-purple sparkler is a bit herbal and underripe tasting, with an herb-laced bouquet and hints of green pepper on the palate. But for all that, it's not unpleasant, as there is adequate cassis fruit for balance and a crisp, reasonably fresh finish. **85** —J.C. *(12/31/2006)*

Patritti NV Shargren Sparkling Blend (South Australia) $12. A sparkling wine made of Shiraz and Grenache; very dark red-black in color. This wine is just too strange: The palate shows sweet fruit with a twist of balsamic vinegar. Smells like grape jelly and apple butter. Bizarre. **82** —D.T. *(12/31/2003)*

PEARSON VINEYARDS

Pearson Vineyards 1999 Cabernet Franc (Clare Valley) $30. Smells spicy, like Mexican cinnamon; plum fruit on the palate is austere, with oak, herb, and tobacco accents. A very good wine, but it might benefit from less wood. **87** —D.T. *(2/1/2004)*

Pearson Vineyards 2002 Cabernet Sauvignon (Clare Valley) $39. What's nice about this wine is that its cooler-climate origins are clear. Aromas are of cherry and gumtree, and the palate unfolds with crisp black cherry flavors. Its mouthfeel is very dry, but put it away for a few years and the issue will likely resolve. **88** —D.T. *(5/1/2005)*

Pearson Vineyards 1999 Cabernet Sauvignon (Clare Valley) $39. Though it spends three years in oak, it doesn't scream "wood" at all. There's dark black plum and berry fruit on the palate, but the dominating note here is one of deep, moist clay soil. That lovely clay shows on the nose, too, where there's also some licorice. A very good example of Clare Cab, with nice texture. **88** —D.T. *(2/1/2004)*

Pearson Vineyards 2003 Riesling (Clare Valley) $NA. Yellow-fruit aromas are light and fragrant, and become more focused and recognizable, as pear and citrus, on the palate. Feels clean from the moment you take your first sip. **87** —D.T. *(2/1/2004)*

PENFOLDS

Penfolds 1998 Bin 389 Cabernet Sauvignon (Australia) $19. Made for almost 40 years—since 1962—this edition of 389 sports lots of spicy American oak, and displays black fruit and tobacco aromas and flavors. The mouthfeel is big, the texture rich and the full, spicy finish is long and tannic. It's drinkable now, but really needs a few years to unwrap a bit, and the oak mantle will probably always be heavy. Satisfying, though somewhat one-dimensional. **89** *(3/1/2001)*

Penfolds 2002 Bin 407 Cabernet Sauvignon (South Australia) $25. On the nose, it shows a sticky-sweet fruit and an anise accent. On the palate, there's plum fruit buried under some polished wood. A disappointing showing for what is typically a reliably impressive, complex, better-than-everyday Cabernet. **84** —D.T. *(10/1/2005)*

Penfolds 2001 Bin 407 Cabernet Sauvignon (South Eastern Australia) $26. Shows deep plum aromas on the nose, with juicy, judiciously oaked fruit on the palate. Medium in body, and finishes with toasty oak. A very good wine, and unmistakably Cabernet. **89** —D.T. *(5/1/2004)*

Penfolds 1998 Bin 407 Cabernet Sauvignon (South Australia) $19. Attractive blackberry aromas with bright tobacco and herb accents open this well-balanced wine. The palate shows strong cassis, earth, and herb flavors, and an even mouthfeel. Finishes with dark cherry notes and full, fine tannins. This will age nicely and can use a little time. Quite flavorful and elegant. **90 Editors' Choice** *(3/1/2001)*

Penfolds 1996 Bin 407 Cabernet Sauvignon (South Australia) $25. 86 *(12/31/1999)*

Penfolds 2002 Bin 707 Cabernet Sauvignon (South Australia) $80. The 2002 is a very interesting rendition of the 707. On the palate, juicy plums and berries are doused in Indian spices—curry and the whole lot. Roasted meat, pen ink, and nut aromas complete an unusual, compelling, excellent package. **90** —D.T. *(10/1/2005)*

Penfolds 2001 Bin 707 Cabernet Sauvignon (South Australia) $80. Soft and supple in the mouth, with plum and oak the key flavor components. There are hints of sweetness here, from the brown-sugary aromas that

AUSTRALIA

appear with time in the glass, to the ripe, ripe fruit on the palate. Still, it's an excellent, delicious wine. Drink now–2008. **90** —*D.T.* *(11/15/2004)*

Penfolds 1999 Bin 707 Cabernet Sauvignon (South Australia) $80. Gas up the Porsche and step on the pedal; that's what this full-force racehorse is like. It's deep and flowery in the nose, with cocoa, bread dough, and peanut. The palate is so racy it's practically on fire. Tight and smooth, big and bold; this one has a lot going on. For best results try to age it for three to five years. **93 Cellar Selection** —*M.S. (12/15/2002)*

Penfolds 1998 Bin 707 Cabernet Sauvignon (South Australia) $90. The rich blackberry, vanilla, and toast nose sets you up for a lush, supple wine and this one does not disappoint. Full and dense, it offers rich black cherry and cassis flavors on the palate, and a huge finish with fine-grained tannins. Very well poised for its size, it's approachable now. Nevertheless, it will be much more nuanced and show more finesse in 5–8 years. Keep for a decade or two, maybe more. To be released 5/01. **93** *(3/1/2001)*

Penfolds 2003 Thomas Hyland Cabernet Sauvignon (South Australia) $15. Mixed berry fruit and vanilla on the nose lead to plum fruit and tealike tannins on the palate. Not so intense on the palate, but just fine for everyday drinking. **84** —*D.T. (8/1/2006)*

Penfolds 2002 Thomas Hyland Cabernet Sauvignon (South Australia) $15. Berry and cherry aromas lead to a palate profile that is just this side of ripe. Soft and round, with sour cherry fruit flavors, it finishes with an acidic bite. **85** —*D.T. (12/31/2005)*

Penfolds 2001 Thomas Hyland Cabernet Sauvignon (South Australia) $15. A medium-boned Cab with an ink-and-oak overlay to its dark-fruit core. The nose is even more expressive, showing ripe blackberries, fresh herb, and meat aromas. It's very good, and its moderate price makes it even more appealing. **87** —*D.T. (12/31/2003)*

Penfolds 2003 Koonunga Hill Cabernet Sauvignon-Merlot (South Eastern Australia) $12. Very dark in color, with plum flavors accented by a layer of tangy oak. Very narrow on the palate. **83** —*D.T. (12/31/2005)*

Penfolds 2001 Koonunga Hill Cabernet Sauvignon-Merlot (South Eastern Australia) $9. Sweet and perfumed, with additional aromas of bacon and baking spice. The palate is warm, chunky, and jam-packed with plum fruit and tasty spice. The tail end is meaty and toasty, with some chocolate notes adding richness. **88 Best Buy** —*M.S. (12/15/2002)*

Penfolds 2000 Bin 389 Cabernet Sauvignon-Shiraz (South Eastern Australia) $26. A sturdy, well-crafted wine, and a solid choice when a big-boned red is in order. Acids are lively, and the tannins are chewy. Nose has lots of vanilla, plus some mint, plum, and raspberry. **89** —*D.T. (10/1/2003)*

Penfolds 1999 Bin 389 Cabernet Sauvignon-Shiraz (South Australia) $26. Dense and woody in the nose, with a strong hint of charcoal and caramel. The power-packed palate has black cherry, blackberry, and chocolate on full offer, while it finishes slightly bitter, with a taste of espresso. Very hard and firm; not a cuddly wine. **87** —*M.S. (12/15/2002)*

Penfolds 1997 Adelaide Hills Chardonnay (Adelaide Hills) $27. **86** *(12/31/1999)*

Penfolds 2003 Koonunga Hill Chardonnay (South Eastern Australia) $11. Soft, easy, tropical, and sweet from beginning to end. This is just the no-brainer that people who want an inexpensive Aussie Chard are looking for. A good quaff. **83** —*D.T. (12/1/2005)*

Penfolds 2002 Koonunga Hill Chardonnay (South Eastern Australia) $10. Good for casual circumstances, this is a simple oak-and-yellow fruit Chard, with stone fruit and smoke on the nose, and oaky, malty flavors on the finish. **84** —*D.T. (10/1/2003)*

Penfolds 2001 Koonunga Hill Chardonnay (South Eastern Australia) $10. Manages to taste sweet and sour at the same time, blending lemon custard and caramel with tart grapefruit-like acids. Okay, just serve it thoroughly chilled. **82** —*J.C. (7/1/2002)*

Penfolds 1998 Koonunga Hill Chardonnay (South Australia) $10. **86** *(12/31/1999)*

Penfolds 2003 Rawson's Retreat Chardonnay (South Eastern Australia) $9. This value-priced Chard is on the lean side, with pear, melon, and peach flavors that are just this side of ripe and juicy. Pear, melon, and anise aromas complete the picture. Most appropriate as an apéritif. **83** *(7/2/2004)*

Penfolds 2002 Rawson's Retreat Chardonnay (South Australia) $9. This drink-now wine has plenty of yellow fruit on the palate, with bright, ripe tropical fruit on the nose. In the mouth, it has some viscosity, which is more than what you get from many other wines at this price. **86 Best Buy** —*D.T. (10/1/2003)*

Penfolds 2001 Rawson's Retreat Chardonnay (South Eastern Australia) $11. A decent introduction to Aussie Chardonnay, this new line from Penfolds boasts plenty of sweet vanilla and peach flavors in a full and somewhat syrupy package. **83** —*J.C. (7/1/2002)*

Penfolds 1998 The Valleys Chardonnay (Clare & Eden Valleys) $12. **83** *(3/1/2000)*

Penfolds 2003 Thomas Hyland Chardonnay (South Australia) $14. Tastes and feels just shy of juiciness and roundness, but that isn't a bad thing. There's minerality at its core, wrapped in unyielding flavors of apple peel and unripe peach. It's an austere, spry wine, but a clean, correct one as well. **85** *(7/2/2004)*

Penfolds 2002 Thomas Hyland Chardonnay (South Australia) $14. Oak on the palate is noticeable but not cumbersome, with some yellow fruit underneath. What's here is quaffable, though, particularly if you're not sensitive to wood and all its component flavors; more fruit would have merited it a better review. **84** —*D.T. (6/1/2003)*

Penfolds 2001 Thomas Hyland Chardonnay (Adelaide Hills) $18. Standard stuff, done right. Smoke and toast aromas add nuance to scents of citrus and peach. Hints of vanilla and baking spices buttress apple and pear flavors. The wine finishes with fresh, lemony notes. This is textbook Chardonnay. **87** —*J.C. (7/1/2002)*

Penfolds 2001 Yattarna Chardonnay (South Eastern Australia) $65. An excellent, feminine wine. Aromas (talc powder, flour, and caramel) are soft and pretty. In the mouth, it's round and mallowy, but just the right size; white stone fruit flavors have both floral and leesy nuances. Closes nicely. **91** —*D.T. (11/15/2004)*

Penfolds 2000 Yattarna Chardonnay (Adelaide Hills) $65. On the nose, mallowy, toasty notes with some citrus dominate; in the mouth, prim yellow fruit is swathed in mallowy, toasty, buttery flavors. The wine is balanced and very tasty, but not as good as it has been in past vintages. **89** —*D.T. (10/1/2003)*

Penfolds 1999 Yattarna Chardonnay (South Australia) $65. An elegant wine, and one that feels that it has a few years ahead of it, the Yattarna—Penfolds' flagship Chardonnay—has a core of citrus and melon, with hints of toast and vanilla. It's full, but by no means as creamy or fleshy a wine as some of its Oz compatriots, which, to us, makes it a top candidate for the dinner table. Finishes long and clean, with citrus and mineral notes. **92** *(6/1/2003)*

Penfolds 1998 Yattarna Chardonnay (South Eastern Australia) $65. This big wine presents a sophisticated bouquet of toasty, leesy, nutty aromas. Fine depth of fruit and plenty of quality oak show here, with butterscotch, pear, and apple flavors. Full-bodied and luscious, it shows the tremendous attention paid and importance assigned to this flagship white. The long, spicy finish sports complex lemon, leesy, and mineral accents. To be released 5/01. **92 Cellar Selection** *(3/1/2001)*

Penfolds 2004 Bin 138 Old Vine G-S-M (Barossa Valley) $22. Smells like whole wheat bread, bordering on dense fruitcake aromas. Plum and berry-basket flavors take over on the finish, edged with briar and mineral qualities. Texture is nice; built to drink over the near term. **88** —*D.T. (8/1/2006)*

Penfolds 2005 Rawson's Retreat Merlot (South Eastern Australia) $9. Has sweet cola, blueberry, and syrup aromas. The palate is dominated by a thick, pulpy texture with some sour fruit underneath. **81** —*D.T. (11/15/2006)*

Penfolds 2001 Rawson's Retreat Merlot (South Eastern Australia) $11. A light, almost candied style that features sweet strawberry and watermelon aromas and flavors. Try it slightly chilled as a party pour. **82** —*J.C. (6/1/2002)*

Penfolds 2002 Cellar Reserve Pinot Noir (Adelaide Hills) $35. One of Penfolds' few Adelaide Hills-designated wines, and the only one available in the States at the moment. This Pinot is very good, with lifted, tangy cherry and plum fruit at the fore, and admirable intensity and length. But it's not as good as I've seen it in past vintages; this one has a pervading pickling-spice or barrel note that was a detraction for me. **88** —*D.T. (8/1/2005)*

Penfolds 2003 Bin 138 Old Vine GSM Red Blend (Barossa Valley) $22. A good GSM, but one that tastes monotone, rather than in surround-sound stereo. Fruit on the nose is lifted and molassesy, and on the palate it's black cherry. And more black cherry. And maybe some molasses. **86** —*D.T. (10/1/2005)*

Penfolds 2000 Bin 2 Shiraz/Mourvedre Red Blend (South Eastern Australia) $11. Despite the Mourvèdre only comprising 26% of the blend, it plays a powerful role in this wine, giving horsey aromas of cassis and tree bark. Flavors of plum, leather, and earth also speak of the Mourvèdre component. The unique earthy nature of Mourvèdre is showcased without the grape variety's frequently heavy tannins. **90** —*J.C. (9/1/2002)*

Penfolds 2003 Bin 2 Shiraz-Mourvedre Red Blend (South Eastern Australia) $12. An odd wine. Caramelized sugar aromas and flavors are offset by herbaceous, borderline metallic, notes. The feel is soft and round, at least. **83** —*D.T. (12/1/2005)*

Penfolds 1996 Bin 389 Rhône Red Blend (South Australia) $25. 88 *(12/31/1999)*

Penfolds 2000 Reserve Riesling (Eden Valley) $18. A round, ripe pear and lemon nose opens this medium-weight, full-flavored white. Grapefruit, spice, and green apple coat the palate, the texture is fairly rich—maybe even fat for Riesling—but there's good acidity to support the fruit. Finishes long with white peach and mineral notes. **88** *(3/1/2001)*

Penfolds 1999 Reserve Riesling (Eden Valley) $15. Tasty mid-weight Riesling that opens with muted apple-hay aromas. The round, even palate shows apple and mineral flavors and just the slightest spritzy tang. It's not complex, but it's completely pleasing, and a perfect step off the Chardonnay train. All aboard. **87** —*M.M. (2/1/2002)*

Penfolds 2003 Reserve Bin Riesling (Eden Valley) $16. Offers yellow peach and mineral aromas, and citrus peel and pith flavors. It's a very dry style of Riesling, perhaps a little rounder than is typical and unfolds to reveal peach once more on the finish. 350 cases produced. **87** —*D.T. (8/1/2005)*

Penfolds 2002 Reserve Bin Riesling (Eden Valley) $19. Understated stone fruit and mineral flavors dominate the palate, with peach-pit and citrus notes on the finish. Round and resinous in the mouth; nose offers a white peppery, plasticy bite. **87** —*D.T. (8/1/2003)*

Penfolds 1998 Adelaide Hills Semillon (South Australia) $16. Smells a bit like New Zealand Sauvignon Blanc, with strong capsicum and grapefruit components; also some toast notes. Broad and fat in the mouth, yet there are more green pepper flavors and a harsh, woody finish. **82** —*J.C. (2/1/2002)*

Penfolds 1997 Adelaide Hills Semillon (Adelaide Hills) $27. 89 —*M.S. (4/1/2000)*

Penfolds 2003 Koonunga Hill Semillon-Chardonnay (South Eastern Australia) $11. Pear and dust flavors and aromas are pleasant, as is the wine's dry feel. However, the wine is showing a latex or epoxy-like note on the nose and the palate that is a detraction. **82** —*D.T. (12/1/2005)*

Penfolds 2001 Koonunga Hill Semillon-Chardonnay (South Australia) $9. A bouquet that smelled like bright citrus and fresh green produce to one taster translated to another taster as cheap perfume. Similar flavors show on the palate of this bright, greenish-gold blend. Mouthfeel is medium and chalky. **82** —*D.T. (2/1/2002)*

Penfolds 2001 Rawson's Retreat Semillon-Chardonnay (South Eastern Australia) $11. 83 —*J.C. (7/1/2002)*

Penfolds 2001 Bin 128 Shiraz (Coonawarra) $24. This is a medium-sized, drink-now Shiraz that's easy to like and hard to put down. Red and black plum fruit is dressed up with oak, toffee, and a hint of Grand Marnier. Finishes with smooth, chalky tannins. **87** —*D.T. (11/15/2004)*

Penfolds 2000 Bin 128 Shiraz (Coonawarra) $24. Understated, subtle— not words that you usually use in talking about Oz Shiraz, but it's appropriate here. Black plum fruit provides a base for nice floury-chalky tannins, which fade away by the wine's end to let the fruit shine through. There's just black pepper and earth on the nose, for now. Maybe a few more months in the bottle will yield more facets, but it's quite good as it is. **88** —*D.T. (12/31/2003)*

Penfolds 1999 Bin 128 Shiraz (Coonawarra) $24. Subtle black-pepper notes add an extra layer of complexity to smoke, earth, plum, blackberry, and dried spices. This full-bodied, sturdy wine finishes with firm tannins and some lingering coffee notes. Should improve over the next 2–3 years. **88** —*J.C. (9/1/2002)*

Penfolds 1998 Bin 128 Shiraz (Coonawarra) $22. Comes on full and lush from the opening, with blackberry, chocolate, menthol, and smoke aromas. In the mouth it delivers dark, dry flavors of plum, cassis, and toasty oak and has good acidity that keeps it from getting mushy. The solid finish offers more of the same, a nice spiciness and some substantial tannins. Drink now; should be even better in two years. **90** *(3/1/2001)*

Penfolds 1996 Bin 128 Shiraz (Coonawarra) $22. 89 *(10/1/1999)*

Penfolds 2000 Bin 28 Kalimna Shiraz (South Australia) $24. Though its fruit core is of mixed black and red plums, its dark soil, ink, and oak accents make this Shiraz feel a bit like a hefty, swarthy bruiser. Still, it's approachable now, and quite steak-appropriate with its medium-full mouthfeel, and charred oak on the finish. **87** —*D.T. (6/1/2003)*

Penfolds 1999 Bin 28 Kalimna Shiraz (South Australia) $24. Starts off pretty oaky, with smoke, cedar, and toast dominating the aromatics. Fortunately, with some time in the glass the berry fruit emerges, along with a hint of eucalyptus. Despite firm tannins, the juicy berries shine on the finish, which bodes well for cellaring. **89** —*J.C. (9/1/2002)*

Penfolds 2001 Grange Shiraz (South Australia) $225. Not great by Grange standards, but still a fabulous wine, the 2001 Grange boasts an intoxicating, heady bouquet of rich chocolate and coconut. It follows that up with deep, plummy fruit that's full-bodied and lush yet quite tannic, promising decades of ageability. Despite the dark chocolate and plum flavors, the wine is still fresh, with a long finish. Drink 2010–2025. **93** —*J.C. (12/15/2006)*

Penfolds 2000 Grange Shiraz (South Australia) $225. The nose offers date and cassis notes, while the palate deals more cassis, plus raspberry, earth, and oak as it opens. Its flavors are juicy, and its tannins, delicate and textured (one reviewer actually likened it to a Rhône wine). Not as full, powerful, or overwhelming as the wine can be, but enjoyable nonetheless. Drink through 2012. **90** *(10/1/2005)*

Penfolds 1999 Grange Shiraz (South Australia) $225. An excellent wine as it always is, but this vintage of Grange is one that isn't just built for aging, it requires it. Its flavors and aromas require a good 20 minutes in the glass to show themselves, but with time, pretty eucalyptus/mint and anise aromas come through. In the mouth, this vintage feels more feminine than other recent vintages. It's very tightly wound, with tea, biscuit, and plum notes peeking through; its tannins are powdery and pretty, and its finish long and juicy. Drink 2012+. **93 Cellar Selection** —*D.T. (11/15/2004)*

Penfolds 1997 Grange Shiraz (South Australia) $195. An excellent wine, but not an outstanding vintage for Grange, the 1997 seems a trifle loose-knit and less "packed" when compared to great vintages in the past. Black plums and blackberries are laced with dried spices and vanilla. Give it some time to knit together and drink from 2005–2015. **90** *(9/1/2002)*

Penfolds 1996 Grange Shiraz (South Australia) $185. As unevolved as they are, the dense and multilayered aromas and flavors are truly impressive here. Black currant, herb, tea, oak, vanilla, maple, anise, blueberries, and more—it could be an excercise in overkill, if all the parts weren't in such fine harmony. Really big, but with excellent balance, this reveals much less now than the RWT. It is everything a flagship wine in its infancy should be—immaculate component parts, superbly full on the palate, possessed of great length and incredible potential. An absolute keeper to visit in 7, 15, or 25 years. To be released 5/01. **96 Cellar Selection** *(3/1/2001)*

AUSTRALIA

AUSTRALIA

Penfolds 1994 Grange Shiraz (South Australia) $163. 96 *(10/1/1999)*

Penfolds 2001 Kalimna Bin 28 Shiraz (South Eastern Australia) $24. Smooth and nicely balanced, this wine is all about its lovely fruit. The palate's plum fruit are dense and mouthfilling, and go the distance through the finish. Nose is deep with concentrated fruit, soil, and eucalyptus notes. Drink after 2006. **89** —*D.T. (11/15/2004)*

Penfolds 1996 Kalimna Bin 28 Shiraz (South Australia) $25. 90 *(10/1/1999)*

Penfolds 1996 Kalimna Bin 285 Shiraz (South Australia) $25. 86 *(12/31/1999)*

Penfolds 2004 Koonunga Hill Shiraz (South Eastern Australia) $12. On the nose, there's very ripe berry fruit and some floral notes. The palate deals plum, and blueberry fruit, but take heed: This is not a forward, fruity style of wine. It's bound up and tight, and may or may not ever unfold. **85** —*D.T. (11/15/2006)*

Penfolds 2003 Koonunga Hill Shiraz (South Eastern Australia) $12. Round in the mouth, but with a sharp point in the middle. Offers cream, red plum and raspberry flavors and aromas, with a metallic note on the finish. **84** —*D.T. (6/1/2006)*

Penfolds 2000 Magill Estate Shiraz (Adelaide Hills) $50. Magill is a big, imposing, impressive wine, not drinkable for another few years but certainly worth the wait. This vintage, typical of this wine, is a black beauty—there's vibrant black fruit here, but also black pepper, char, and earth. Chewy tannins and chocolate and earth on the finish. Its size won't appeal to everyone, but you can't help but marvel, anyway. **92** — *D.T. (10/1/2003)*

Penfolds 1999 Magill Estate Shiraz (South Australia) $50. Complex and spicy, with cinnamon, clove, and vanilla notes that blend seamlessly with rich blackberry fruit and hints of cured meat. Coffee and caramel imparted by oak stick out a little at present; try after 2005. **91** *(9/1/2002)*

Penfolds 1996 Magill Estate Shiraz (South Australia) $47. 91 *(10/1/1999)*

Penfolds 2001 Magill Estate Shiraz Shiraz (South Australia) $50. Round, plush, and hedonistic, the Magill barely falls on the conservative side of "over the top" this year. Deep aromas of vanilla bean and meat segue to a blackberry-and-vanilla ride on the palate. Long and luscious on the finish; really quite sexy overall. **91** —*D.T. (11/15/2004)*

Penfolds 2003 RWT Shiraz (Barossa Valley) $75. Inky purple-black in color, this looks like a heavyweight, and lovers of big, rich wines likely won't be disappointed. It's full-bodied, verging on heavy, with chocolaty plum and prune flavors that nevertheless stay surprisingly fresh on the long finish. It's approachable now, but how long it will last is a tough call. **90** —*J.C. (12/15/2006)*

Penfolds 2002 RWT Shiraz (Barossa Valley) $70. Aromas of ripe, soft fruit and ink are compelling. On the palate, it's medium weight, with soft, wooly tannins, and fruit-sweet blackberry fruit in its center. Understated, but hedonistic. **90** *(10/1/2005)*

Penfolds 2001 RWT Shiraz (Barossa Valley) $80. This year, the RWT is tightly wound, masculine, and stately, but all in all, a pleasant walk in the dark. Smells like soil, meat and char/smoke and tastes likewise, with those flavors enveloping black plum fruit on the palate. Juicy but taut on the finish, like there's some blueberries thrown in for good measure. Drink after 2008. **91 Cellar Selection** —*D.T. (11/15/2004)*

Penfolds 2000 RWT Shiraz (Barossa Valley) $69. The nose is rather closed, but you can still detect sensational biscuit, mint, cumin, and cinnamon notes. Fruit on the palate is dense and super-ripe—one reviewer calls it plum cake, another sees more blackberry and cherry. Finishes long with coconut, chocolate, and toast. Its tannins feel smooth now, but this wine will reward long-term cellaring. Drink 2005–2015. **93** — *D.T. (10/1/2003)*

Penfolds 1999 RWT Shiraz (Barossa Valley) $70. Starts off tight, showing refined cedar aromas, then explodes with a few minutes' air to yield lush blackberries and vanilla. The lush, rich mouthfeel carries the blackberry, vanilla, and chocolate flavors effortlessly across the palate into a long, toasty finish. This thoroughly modern-style wine should drink well over the next 12 years or so. **93** *(9/1/2002)*

Penfolds 1998 RWT Shiraz (Barossa Valley) $70. Seamless luxury from stem to stern, this 'baby Grange' is impressive juice. Blackberry, menthol and smoke play unusually elegantly on the nose, the texture is velvet on the tongue with dark berry, coffee, licorice, and muted black pepper flavors. The superb, very long finish combines all the elements with wonderful finesse and a rare grace. Not inexpensive, but fairly priced; you could pay twice as much for half the wine, almost any day in any fine wine store in the country. To be released 5/01. **95 Editors' Choice** *(3/1/2001)*

Penfolds 2002 St. Henri Shiraz (South Australia) $40. All of the sexiest adjectives apply: forward, brash, lush. Flavors are of licorice and full-tilt blackberry. Does it taste like St. Henri usually does (low-dose oak, tight red fruit)? Not so much. In this vintage, it is almost like mocha. Drink now. **89** —*D.T. (11/15/2006)*

Penfolds 2001 St. Henri Shiraz (South Australia) $40. Grape and blackberry flavors hold the fort down on the palate, and cassis is the main player on the nose. Although it is a very good wine, the feel here is dry, thick, and woodsy—a curious thing considering that St. Henri is traditionally matured in old oak vats. Alcohol is also evident on both nose and palate. I love St. Henri in general, but this young one is looking a little awkward. **87** —*D.T. (10/1/2005)*

Penfolds 2000 St. Henri Shiraz (South Australia) $40. Red berry aromas and flavors have a tinge of stewiness to them, but the wine's smooth tannins and pencil-eraser aromas more than make up for it. A little more straightforward than St. Henri usually is, but it's still very tasty. **89** — *D.T. (11/15/2004)*

Penfolds 1999 St. Henri Shiraz (South Australia) $39. This Shiraz is aged in enormous old oak vats and so doesn't offer the toasty, caramelly flavors that we often associate with Oz Shiraz. Instead, the fruit speaks for itself—the palate is showing mostly black plum and black cherry, with chewy tannins and a little earthiness on the finish. Toast can sometimes be a good thing, but St. Henri is where I hide out when I've got the new-wood blues. **91** —*D.T. (10/1/2003)*

Penfolds 1998 St. Henri Shiraz (South Australia) $40. Put big, rich fruit in a tightly wound package without new oak influence and you have a very ageworthy wine that might not be ready until 2008, and should last through 2020. Blackberries, black pepper, earth, spice, and leather provide plenty of complexity without any oak embellishment. **90** *(9/1/2002)*

Penfolds 2003 Thomas Hyland Shiraz (South Australia) $15. A dark but not very mouth-filling wine. This Shiraz offers cherry and rhubarb aromas, and a sour plum-and-tree bark profile to the palate. With air, the fruit seems riper, and the wood nuances more noticeable. **84** —*D.T. (12/31/2005)*

Penfolds 2000 Thomas Hyland Shiraz (South Eastern Australia) $18. Nicely perfumed, with full-blast aromas of root beer and cola. The palate is a bit foresty, with tree bark and peppery notes. The finish is the first place you notice overt oak, and it's kind of buttery and unintegrated. In Penfolds' stable of Shiraz, this is meant to be round, friendly, and not too complicated. **85** —*M.S. (3/1/2003)*

Penfolds 1998 Grange Shiraz-Cabernet Sauvignon (South Australia) $205. Though the nose on this wine is still somewhat closed, it's still remarkable. Individual notes (apart from eucalyptus and toast) aren't discernible; instead, it's an intense, penetrating sensation that fills the nose. Vanilla and coffee flavors are sumptuous foils to rich blackberries on the palate, which is muscular and plush as all get-out. Finishes long, with big but soft tannins. We can't wait to revisit it in 10–15 years, when the gems that are locked up tight now will sparkle. **95** —*D.T. (10/1/2003)*

Penfolds 2003 Koonunga Hill Shiraz-Cabernet Sauvignon (South Eastern Australia) $12. Sweetish plum aromas lead to more plum fruit on the palate. It's a good, straightforward quaff, but feels simpler the longer it sits. Drink up. **84** —*D.T. (12/1/2005)*

Penfolds 2002 Koonunga Hill Shiraz-Cabernet Sauvignon (South Eastern Australia) $12. This is an approachable wine with plum and tobacco aromas and flavors. Soft and somewhat hollow in the mouth, but still a fine everyday wine. 84,000 cases produced. **84** —*D.T. (10/1/2005)*

TASTING REPORTS

Penfolds 2000 Koonunga Hill Shiraz-Cabernet Sauvignon (South Eastern Australia) $11. Shy is not how to describe this wine's bold, plump, grapey bouquet, which features a good dose of bacon. The palate is flavorful and fruity, but it's also one-dimensional in that it's all fruit and no nuance or layering. The smooth finish has coffee and black fruit in full quantities. **87 Best Buy**—*M.S. (12/15/2002)*

Penfolds 1999 Koonunga Hill Shiraz-Cabernet Sauvignon (South Eastern Australia) $15. This solid red has deep currant and toasty oak aromas. It opens to rich dark berry, plum, and leather flavors with Asian spice accents. The mouthfeel is creamy, almost syrupy, and it shows some vanilla, spice, and a tart-sweetness on the finish. **87** *(3/1/2001)*

Penfolds 1997 Koonunga Hill Shiraz-Cabernet Sauvignon (South Australia) $11. 88 Best Buy *(10/1/1999)*

Penfolds 2005 Rawson's Retreat Shiraz-Cabernet Sauvignon (South Eastern Australia) $9. Aromas run the gamut from earth to sweet grapiness. On the palate, the wine has sour plum fruit with a green, metallic edge. Not a giving, round wine. **82**—*D.T. (11/15/2006)*

Penfolds 1998 Koonunga Hill White Blend (South Australia) $8. 85 *(12/31/1999)*

PENLEY ESTATE

Penley Estate 2002 Phoenix Cabernet Sauvignon (Coonawarra) $25. This Cab has a pleasing, creamy-smooth feel, and nice integration of oak and plum fruit on the palate. Shows plum and berry on the nose, plus overt spice aromas. A very pretty wine. 1,000 cases produced. **89**—*D.T. (5/1/2005)*

Penley Estate 2001 Phoenix Cabernet Sauvignon (Coonawarra) $25. Smells of red fruit, caramel, ginger, and allspice, with black plum fruit and leafy flavors on the palate. Its alcohol is quite noticeable, though. Finishes dense and black. **86**—*D.T. (5/1/2004)*

Penley Estate 2000 Phoenix Cabernet Sauvignon (Coonawarra) $25. The entry is largely tomato and wet earth along with some spice. In the mouth, a bit of cherry and plum escapes, but still not enough to push the wine forward. While it seems solid and structured, what charms it has is mostly around the edges, meaning there isn't adequate depth. **85**—*M.S. (12/15/2002)*

Penley Estate 2002 Reserve Cabernet Sauvignon (Coonawarra) $65. Has a hint of black pepper and mustard seed on the nose. The palate is all about its smooth, claylike feel, its flavors of cola and bramble prettily supporting it. Finishes wooly and textured. **91**—*D.T. (10/1/2006)*

Penley Estate 1999 Reserve Cabernet Sauvignon (Coonawarra) $58. Darker, and with more nuance than many other Coonawarra Cabs, the Penley's black-plum fruit wears a dusting of wheat bran; it finishes (however sooner than I'd like) with similar flavors. On the nose, the fruit's redder—there may even be some tomato in there. A nice, medium-bodied Cab, this would pair nicely with black bean stew, or even hamburgers. **88**—*D.T. (6/1/2003)*

Penley Estate 1998 Vintage Blend Cabernet Sauvignon-Shiraz (South Australia) $30. Distinct black, earthy aromas cloak sweet caramel and pastry notes underneath. The palate offers a roller-coaster ride of high-toned jammy fruit at the front that settles into understated roasted fruit, mocha, and oak notes on the finish. The final impression is one of menthol and dry tannins. **89**—*D.T. (12/15/2002)*

Penley Estate 1994 Pinot Noir-Chardonnay Sparkling Wine Champagne Blend (Coonawarra) $30. Bananas, mineral, and cheese make for a less-than-appealing nose. The tart apple and citrus flavors on the palate are just acceptable as they lead into an adequately smooth finish that could be the wine's saving grace. Thin and lacking as a whole, but not offensive or poor. From Australia with age. **82**—*M.S. (1/1/2004)*

Penley Estate 2001 Chardonnay (Coonawarra) $25. Has waxy melon, tropical fruit, and coconut aromas, and pleasant stone fruit and citrus flavors. Finishes with juicy peach, and a hint of herb. **85** *(7/2/2004)*

Penley Estate 2002 Hyland Shiraz (Coonawarra) $25. This Coonawarra Shiraz has meaty, stably aromas. On the palate, red plum fruit is pure and fairly unadorned, with slight earth and oak nuances. Tannins are velvety, almost furry. Very enjoyable; 1,000 cases produced. **90**—*D.T. (10/1/2005)*

Penley Estate 2001 Hyland Shiraz (Coonawarra) $25. This medium-sized Shiraz has flavors of oak and tangy red plum, and a sweet barbecue-and-toffee nose. Its powdery tannins are pretty, but don't hide the fact that the palate is a little hollow. Finishes with smooth, oaky tannins. **86**—*D.T. (9/1/2004)*

Penley Estate 1999 Hyland Shiraz (Coonawarra) $25. Deep, dark toast aromas join fatty grilled meat, prunes, and molasses. All repeat on the palate with additions of sweet blackberries, black plums, leather, dark chocolate, and more molasses. Chocolate and pepper ride out a long, dark finish. This is a fantastic wine for the price. **91 Editors' Choice**—*K.F. (3/1/2003)*

Penley Estate 1998 Hyland Shiraz (Coonawarra) $25. Though it's a little on the tight side, the Penley's palate shows black cherry and smoked-meat flavors, and a red berry-and-spice finish. Reviewers were up in arms about whether it was smoked meat and mint, or marshmallow, hot pepper, and cake flour on the nose. In any case, an unusual bouquet. Give it two or three years. **87** *(11/1/2001)*

Penley Estate 2000 Special Select Shiraz (Coonawarra) $65. This wine has lots of nice flavors and aromas—cherry, raspberry, and graham cracker, among them—but feels disjointed and a little tart at this stage. A couple of years in the dark may do it some good; try after 2007. **88**—*D.T. (10/1/2005)*

PENMARA

Penmara 2000 Chardonnay (New South Wales) $8. This stylish lightweight has some tasty pear, quince, and citrus flavors, finishing with a hint of spice. Best as an apéritif or with a light fish course. **84**—*J.C. (7/1/2002)*

Penmara 2000 Reserve Chardonnay (New South Wales) $13. A big step up from the "regular" Chardonnay, this is riper, richer, and longer. Buttered toast and tropical-fruit flavors, a rich, textured mouthfeel and a smooth, easy finish make this a very enjoyable drink. **88**—*J.C. (7/1/2002)*

Penmara 2000 Five Families Shiraz (New South Wales) $9. Expect mainly red berries—cranberries and strawberries—from this medium-weight quaffer. Some orange and tea flavors, along with cedar and white pepper, blend in, but it's basically a simple fruity red. **85** *(10/1/2001)*

PENNA LANE

Penna Lane 2001 Cabernet Sauvignon (Clare Valley) $25. Smells like figs and dates rolled in bread flour. Fruit on the palate has the same stewy quality—more a sign of vintage conditions than anything, I guess. Easy on the palate, it finishes with molasses. **86**—*D.T. (2/1/2004)*

Penna Lane 2003 Riesling (Clare Valley) $21. Fragrant honeysuckle aromas preface generic yellow fruit on the palate. Medium-bodied; good but simple. **85**—*D.T. (2/1/2004)*

Penna Lane 2001 Shiraz (Clare Valley) $25. Has penetrating black pepper aromas, and soft red plum fruit on the palate. Goes down easy; drink now. **86**—*D.T. (2/1/2004)*

Penna Lane 2000 Shiraz (Clare Valley) $20. The cherry and dried herb flavors are bright, to say the least, and perhaps too piquant. Thankfully, a dash of earth brings these high-toned notes down a little. Offers cream, caramel, and dark fruit on the nose. **85**—*D.T. (3/1/2003)*

PENNY'S HILL

Penny's Hill 2002 Chardonnay (McLaren Vale) $18. Aromas are of sweet-smelling nectarines and melon. The panel was unanimous in describing this wine as harmonious—medium in body, but soft in demeanor, with all the parts in order. Flavors are of nectarine and mango, with toast and vanilla accents, and continue on through the finish. **87** *(7/2/2004)*

Penny's Hill 2004 Red Dot Chardonnay-Viognier (McLaren Vale) $20. Honey and hay accent flavors and aromas of white peach and pear. The two grape components complement each other well, with Viognier giving some lift on the nose, and some heft on the palate. Very good. **87**—*D.T. (12/31/2005)*

Penny's Hill 2003 Cadenzia Grenache (McLaren Vale) $30. Bright, red fruit on the nose. The palate is smooth, though the wood isn't shy; overlaid with briary, tobaccoey notes. A very good wine, though the lifted cherry-eucalyputs flavor combination may not be for everyone. **88**—*D.T. (8/1/2005)*

Penny's Hill 2003 Shiraz (McLaren Vale) $33. Has aromas of coffee and cola, sprinkled with black peppercorn. The palate offers smooth, dry tannins with juicy plum and stone-mineral flavors. A very pretty, enjoyable wine overall. **90** —*D.T. (12/1/2005)*

Penny's Hill 1999 Shiraz (McLaren Vale) $33. Blackberry, cream, and a doughy note on the nose open to attractive cherry-licorice and coffee flavors. This is medium-weight and complex, with olive, caramel, mineral, and earth notes, though not particularly deep. Closes with a tangy, peppery finish. A split-decision for our panel, but enjoyed by most tasters. **89** *(11/1/2001)*

Penny's Hill 2003 Red Dot Shiraz (McLaren Vale & Langhorne Creek) $18. The nose offers a host of red aromas, including stewy, almost tomatoey fruit, and pretty red pencil eraser. A medium-sized wine on the palate, this Shiraz reprises the familiar red berries-plum-earth-oak theme, but does it well. **87** —*D.T. (3/1/2005)*

PENNYFIELD WINES

Pennyfield Wines 2002 Basket Pressed Petite Verdot (Riverland) $19. The nose is very pretty: Graham cracker, vanilla bean, maybe some blueberry pie. On the palate, the wine deals straightforward plum fruit overlaid with oak. **86** —*D.T. (6/1/2006)*

Pennyfield Wines 2002 Basket Pressed Shiraz (Riverland) $22. Though this feminine-sized wine has a nice, dusty feel, its overall impression is a purple one. Smells sweet on the nose (think grape jam with some molasses), with grapy flavors returning on the palate. **86** —*D.T. (10/1/2005)*

PEPPER TREE

Pepper Tree 2000 Grand Reserve Cabernet Sauvignon (Coonawarra) $100. A steak lover's Cab made in an old-school style, sturdy but not brash. Has its share of oak, to be sure, but it's the "dry tannins and black pepper flavors" kind, not the toast-and-nut route. Red plum and cherry fruit are at its firm core. Enjoyable and traditional. **91** —*D.T. (8/1/2006)*

Pepper Tree 2003 Grand Reserve Chardonnay (Wrattonbully) $34. One of the most impressive white wines I've had this year. Its nose deals a different fragrance every time you go back to it: nut, focused yellow fruit, cola, then fresh baked pastry. It's multilayered on the palate, and pretty tight, with apricots dressed up in cream around the wide, soft edges, and a nucleus of tight, tart citrus. Zesty, consistent and compelling. **93 Editors' Choice** —*D.T. (6/1/2006)*

Pepper Tree 2003 Grand Reserve Shiraz (Wrattonbully) $55. A crisp, cool style of Shiraz—if you think "eucalyptus" equals "medicinal," this probably isn't your cup of tea. But there's a lot to like about this wine's gumtree, black pepper, and blackberry aromas, and the way that its earth-clay feel steals the show on the palate. Has blueberries and blackberries at its core, and a dusting of cinnamon arund the edges. Crisp and lasting on the finish. **90** —*D.T. (6/1/2006)*

Pepper Tree 2004 Grand Reserve Tannat (Wrattonbully) $58. Has aromas of eucalyptus and earth, with more of the same on the palate accenting very taut mixed fruit. Layered and complex with chenille-like tannins; not a massive-sized nor overly tannic version of Tannat. Would pair nicely with braised pork in sauce. **90** —*D.T. (8/1/2006)*

PERRINI

Perrini 1999 Meadows Shiraz (McLaren Vale) $18. An herbal-Chicklet note envelopes red berry and blueberry aromas on the nose; on the palate, expect a big, structured dark blackberry-and-oak powerhouse. Finishes with dark soy, blueberry, and anise notes. **88** *(10/1/2001)*

PETALUMA

Petaluma 2001 Cabernet Sauvignon-Merlot (Coonawarra) $35. Medium-bodied with chewy tannins, this 50-50 Cab-Merlot blend offers a sturdy foundation of plum and black cherry fruit. Anise, tree bark, and spearmint accent the palate; spice, caramel, and grilled meat aromas play on the nose. Excellent and very enjoyable. **90** —*D.T. (8/1/2005)*

Petaluma 2000 Unfiltered Cabernet Sauvignon-Merlot (Coonawarra) $36. The clay-and-chalk mouthfeel is a winner, as are the ink, bark, and eucalyptus aromas. On the palate, this 50-50 blend shows a definitive fresh-herb note over taut, unyielding red fruit. The result is something that tastes rustic, Old World, unexpected—yet still very good. **87** —*D.T. (9/1/2004)*

Petaluma 2001 Chardonnay (Piccadilly Valley) $28. One of this tasting's top performers—Adelaide Hills shines again. This is an elegant, harmonious Chardonnay, with white stone fruit at the core, and hazelnuts, vanilla, and talc flavors that accent rather than overwhelm the fruit. In the mouth it's round and pillowy; a hint of nut on the long finish is a satisfying close, just the mint on the pillow at turndown. **90 Editors' Choice** *(7/2/2004)*

Petaluma 1999 Chardonnay (Piccadilly Valley) $32. 82 —*J.C. (7/1/2002)*

Petaluma 2001 Tiers Chardonnay (Piccadilly Valley) $64. From a famed Adelaide Hills vineyard. Panelists agree that fruit gets shortshrift here—the focus is chalk, stone, or mineral. Pear and peach are most present on the finish. Austere in style; a wine that will shine more with food. **85** *(7/2/2004)*

Petaluma 1999 Tiers Vineyard Chardonnay (Piccadilly Valley) $120. At this price, it would be hard for this wine to live up to expectations—which is why we taste blind. But without any preconceptions, this wine was still delicious. The promising oaky aromas of honey drizzled over toast, coconut, and vanilla are backed by white peach. It's tightly wound and less giving on the palate. **89** —*J.C. (7/1/2002)*

Petaluma 2000 Riesling (Australia) $14. The spicy apple, pear, and quince notes are understated and elegant, rather than effusive or brash. Has a steely edge to the flavors that provides enough structure for a few years of aging, and finishes long and intense with notes of gray clay. **88** *(2/1/2002)*

Petaluma 2003 Hanlin Hill Vineyard Riesling (Clare Valley) $16. I'd buy the this wine just to smell it—the nose's fresh citrus, floral, marshmallow, and fresh meadow aromas are just lovely. On the palate are lemon-lime, chalk and floral notes, and the pretty chalk-powder texture that you find in many Clare whites. Finishes juicy, with bright gooseberry flavors. **89 Best Buy** —*D.T. (5/1/2004)*

Petaluma 2002 Shiraz (Adelaide Hills) $30. Pretty brick/purple in color. Mixed plum aromas are accented with anise and cola notes. This is one nice Shiraz, of manageable size—just right for the dinner table. There's a base of red plum fruit with smoky, meaty nuances that roll straight through the finish. **89** —*D.T. (3/1/2005)*

Petaluma 1999 Shiraz (Adelaide Hills) $36. Compost aromas blow off to reveal delicate, if thin, red cherry and toast. One-dimensional red fruit and a hint of green herb carry through the short, acidic finish. **85** —*K.F. (3/1/2003)*

Petaluma 1999 Bridgewater Mill Shiraz (Australia) $15. Unlike many an Australian Shiraz, this one sees only French oak barrels for aging. The result is a dense, blueberry-filled wine, supported by hints of toast and espresso. It's full-bodied but not tiring to drink, thanks to an enlivening burst of black pepper on the finish. **88 Best Buy** —*J.C. (9/1/2002)*

PETER LEHMANN

Peter Lehmann 1999 The Mentor Cabernet Blend (Barossa Valley) $50. Though it's named after Peter Lehmann, this is not an imposing, masculine wine. It has plum and cassis fruit at its core and fresh cream on the nose, with a moderate, appropriate-for-food weight. A blend of Cabernet Sauvignon, Merlot, Shiraz, and Malbec. **90** —*D.T. (2/1/2004)*

Peter Lehmann 2002 Cabernet Sauvignon (Barossa) $16. This wine is full of dark, earthy, stably, black olive-y aromas and flavors. Their predominance makes for an interesting wine, but also a wine that tastes mature beyond its years. Finishes with tree bark and leaf notes. Drink up. **86** —*D.T. (12/31/2005)*

Peter Lehmann 2001 The Barossa Cabernet Sauvignon (Barossa Valley) $16. Nose is closed, but does show some attic dust. Flavors of red plum and coffee are wrapped in a smooth-tannin coccoon on the palate, and persist through the finish. **88** —*D.T. (12/31/2004)*

Peter Lehmann 2005 Chardonnay (Barossa) $12. Offers fragrant pineapple, and pear aromas, its fruit turning sour and citric on the palate. Has an odd artificial-sweetener texture. Fine for casual get-togethers. **83** —*D.T. (11/15/2006)*

Peter Lehmann 2002 Chardonnay (Barossa Valley) $12. Shows clarified butter and a zing of lime or lemon peel on the nose. A fatter-style Chard, this Barossa offering successfully follows the straightahead, stone-fruit-and-oak recipe. A good wine, but a pretty run-of-the-mill one. **85** —*D.T. (12/31/2004)*

Peter Lehmann 2003 G-S-M (Barossa) $18. Offers straightforward red fruit flavors dressed up in a fair amount of vanilla and toast. Good and mainstream. **84** —*D.T. (4/1/2006)*

Peter Lehmann 2003 Clancy's Red Blend (Barossa) $16. A straightforward sort of wine: red berry, plum, oak on nose and palate, dressed up with some earthy aromas. Alcohol shows on the nose; finishes crisp, with a blast of tangy oak. 15,000 cases produced. **85** —*D.T. (2/1/2006)*

Peter Lehmann 2002 Clancy's Red Blend (Barossa Valley) $16. A straightforward wine in every way but for its intricate blend (54% Shiraz, 29% Cab Sauvignon, 12% Merlot, 5% Cab Franc). Aromas are of bitter herb and grape jelly; palate to finish offers plum, earth, and herb flavors. **84** —*D.T. (12/31/2004)*

Peter Lehmann 1998 Mentor Red Blend (Barossa Valley) $50. Has lifted aromas of raspberry and blueberry that turn almost pruny with air. Tree and earth flavors dominate the palate, which tastes a little sour and past its prime. This wine has been much better in other vintages. Tasted twice, with consistent results—could it be two bad bottles? **84** —*D.T. (8/1/2005)*

Peter Lehmann 2004 Riesling (Eden Valley) $16. Very fragrant, with white pepper and fuzzy ripe peach aromas. Peach continues on through the palate, with lemon and grapefruit accents, all couched in a softish, minerally feel. **87** —*D.T. (8/1/2005)*

Peter Lehmann 2003 Riesling (Eden Valley) $16. This Riesling stays the citrus track, with zesty lemon and lime flavors and aromas rising even above those of white peach. A slick, olive-oily feel tempers the zesty citrus acidity well, making for a whole whose parts work together quite nicely. **88** —*D.T. (12/31/2004)*

Peter Lehmann 1998 Reserve Riesling (Eden Valley) $NA. Austere in the mouth, but in the most complimentary way, with crisp pear and lemon fruit that last through a medium-long finish. Honeydew aromas among the more expected white pepper and pear ones are a pleasant surprise. **90** —*D.T. (2/1/2004)*

Peter Lehmann 2003 Semillon (Barossa Valley) $11. This enjoyable white has all the right elements: It's mouthwatering and juicy, crisp and clean, offering dust and lemondrop aromas, with intense flavors of grapefruit and green apple. At this price, you can afford to keep a few bottles around the house, too. 70,000 cases produced. **89 Best Buy** —*D.T. (8/1/2005)*

Peter Lehmann 2002 Semillon (Barossa Valley) $11. A wine that could ease Chardonnay or Pinot Gris lovers out of their comfort zones. Offers light grass and hay notes on the nose, with honey, hay, and lean citrus notes on the palate. **87 Best Buy** —*D.T. (2/1/2004)*

Peter Lehmann 1999 Eight Songs Shiraz (Barossa Valley) $45. Delicious Barossa, through and though: Chewy tannins, rich plum, and cassis flavors, and threads of soil, beef stock, and even some amaretto. Finishes long and rich; drinking well now. 600 cases produced. **90** —*D.T. (8/1/2005)*

Peter Lehmann 1999 Eight Songs Shiraz (Barossa Valley) $55. Feels big around the edges, but less so on the palate. Its plum and berry fruit is wonderfully juicy, and the bacon and stewed fruit aromas quite nice, but the Eight Songs needs a little more size-and-fruit harmony to hit the right notes. **89** —*D.T. (2/1/2004)*

Peter Lehmann 1999 Stonewell Shiraz (Barossa) $75. Despite what seems like a soft, easy finish, this wine could use another year or two in the cellar to allow better integration of oak and fruit. Right now, the vanilla notes are a little too obvious, sitting atop a wine of considerable substance. Marked by deep plum and mixed berry fruit, this is an impressive effort that should age at least 8–10 years. **90** —*J.C. (12/15/2006)*

Peter Lehmann 1998 Stonewell Shiraz (Barossa Valley) $75. Sturdy, masculine, and sexy. This excellent Shiraz's fruit core glows bright red (plum, cherry) but all of its bells and whistles—among them soil, black olive, blackberry—are dark as night. Unfolds with air to reveal streaks of cassis

and mint as well. Medium-long and juicy on the finish. Drink through 2010. **91** —*D.T. (8/1/2005)*

Peter Lehmann 1999 The Barossa Shiraz (Barossa Valley) $17. Cinnamon-sugar toast and creamy coffee nuances marry sweetly with blackberry liqueur. The thick, viscous mouthfeel is almost custard-like and silky smooth. Lest this sound too confectionary, it should be noted that the wine is dry and finishes with assertive notes of leather and espresso. **88 Editors' Choice** *(10/1/2001)*

Peter Lehmann 1997 The Barossa Shiraz (Barossa Valley) $15. 89 *(11/15/1999)*

Peter Lehmann 2001 The Futures Shiraz (Barossa Valley) $NA. What was once a cellar door-only wine finally makes its way Stateside. Fruit is juicy and chewy from palate to finish, dressed up with a hint of barbecue smoke. Nose is super creamy, with plum fruit in a supporting role. **89** —*D.T. (2/1/2004)*

PETERSONS

Petersons 1999 Shiraz (Mudgee) $20. A straightforward wine, even but rather thin, with the familiar dark berry-toast-licorice-espresso profile of so much heavily oaked Shiraz. Firm and tightly structured, with tangy tannins on the close. **84** *(10/1/2001)*

PETTAVEL

Pettavel 2001 Platina Cabernet Sauvignon-Cabernet Franc (Geelong) $25. This 50-50 Cab Sauv-Cab Franc is a good wine, but doesn't quite live up to the winery's whites. Smells sweet but pleasant—think berry basket and Sweet Tart—and offers similarly straightfoward flavors. 500 cases produced. **84** —*D.T. (8/1/2005)*

Pettavel 2003 Evening Star Chardonnay (Geelong) $17. This Chard has spice and white pepper aromas, and a warm but comfortable tropical fruit, nut and spice profile on the palate. Drink now. **87** —*D.T. (8/1/2005)*

Pettavel 2002 Platina Chardonnay (Geelong) $25. Wood weighs heavily on this wine, which means that you'll love it or you won't. Smells like baked apple pie, and on the palate, apple fruit has a tangy, sawdusty wooden feel to it. Didn't have the acidity that a wine like this needs. **83** —*D.T. (12/31/2005)*

Pettavel 2004 Evening Star Riesling (Geelong) $17. Though the style of this Riesling is juicier, more overtly fruity, and somewhat heavier than is typical, the unusual combination still works here. Its medium weight is tempered by good acidity, and the palate's peach, tangerine, and honeyed flavors are balanced nicely by lemon and orange peel. 200 cases produced. **88** —*D.T. (8/1/2005)*

Pettavel 2004 Evening Star Sauvignon Blanc-Semillon (Geelong) $17. This wine isn't too thick in the middle, but packs a wallop around the edges, coating the mouth with zingy lemon and lime flavors. Its chalk-dust texture is its best feature. **88** —*D.T. (8/1/2005)*

PEWSEY VALE

Pewsey Vale 2003 Riesling (Eden Valley) $15. Lovely acidity is this Riesling's hallmark; it's round but crisp in the mouth. Offers lovely lemon, lime, and white pepper flavors in the mouth, and smells just as it tastes. Finishes with some length, and a chalky feel. **90 Best Buy** —*D.T. (2/1/2004)*

PHILIP SHAW

Philip Shaw 2004 No 11 Chardonnay (Orange) $30. Delicate and kind of ethereal at first, but seems to grow a spine the longer it sits in the glass. Aromas are of talc, vanilla, and citrus; the palate feel reprises the dusty-talcy impression. A dry twist of lemon drop on the finish completes a very pretty picture. **90** —*D.T. (6/1/2006)*

Philip Shaw 2005 No 19 Sauvignon Blanc (Orange) $25. Smells like sand, gravel, and Meyer lemon zest. The feel is dry, smooth, and crisp, with some unctuousness—pretty different from most Aussie Sauvignons, to be sure. The texture is the salient feature here; if you're one who prefers bright SB fruit character, this wine's dust, citrus pith, and hay notes might not satisfy. **87** —*D.T. (6/1/2006)*

AUSTRALIA

PICARDY

Picardy 2002 Merlot-Cabernet Sauvignon-Cabernet Franc Bordeaux Blend (Pemberton) $18. Has roasted, ripe flavors of prune or date, plus a hint of volatility on the nose. Has a dusty feel on the palate, with coffee, leather, and blackberry flavors taking center stage. Finishes narrow and a little tart. **87** —*D.T. (6/1/2006)*

Picardy 2004 Chardonnay (Pemberton) $27. Though there are moderate doses of toast and nut adding interest to yellow peach and pineapple flavors, the wood manifests itself differently on the nose and the finish. Smells like pine, dried spice, and burned popcorn, with bacon, hickory, and some lactic notes coming through on the finish. Goes down easily, but could have fared even better. **87** —*D.T. (8/1/2006)*

Picardy 2004 Pinot Noir (Pemberton) $27. 84 —*D.T. (11/15/2006)*

Picardy 1999 Shiraz (Western Australia) $28. Lean in the mouth, with tart cranberry, pepper, and cedar flavors, the Picardy finishes tart, with lemon and pepper flavors. Bouquet à la Salisbury steak, with gravy. **84** *(11/1/2001)*

PIERRO

Pierro 2000 Red Table Wine Cabernet Sauvignon (Margaret River) $45. A Bordeaux blend, it's easier to drink than some of its hard-hitting ingredients might have you think. Fruit is soft and manageable, with tannins that are approachable now. **88** —*D.T. (10/1/2003)*

Pierro 2001 Chardonnay (Margaret River) $45. The palate's yellow fruit is tropical but not sweet. The wine is round and smooth in the mouth; wood doesn't play a major role until the finish, which is a little toasty. **90** *(10/1/2003)*

Pierro 2001 Semillon-Sauvignon Blanc (Margaret River) $25. Viscous in the mouth, but a little flighty with flavor. Lemon, peach, and floral flavors, with minerally sweetness on the finish. Still, the longer it sits, the better you like it; also recommends itself as a good pre-dinner choice. **86** —*D.T. (10/1/2003)*

PIKE & JOYCE

Pike & Joyce 2003 Lenswood Chardonnay (Adelaide Hills) $27. This Chard hails from one of the Adelaide Hills' better-known subregions. It's a very good wine, with enjoyable cream and nut aromas, and juicy, tropical yellow fruit flavors coming on the palate. Straightforward, and drinking well now. **87** —*D.T. (8/1/2005)*

Pike & Joyce 2004 Lenswood Pinot Gris (Adelaide Hills) $21. A lively wine, this wine is full of subtle red apple and pear flavors. The feel is dry; out of the bottle it's quite crisp but softens with air. At 180 cases made, might be hard to come by **87** —*D.T. (8/1/2005)*

Pike & Joyce 2002 Lenswood Pinot Noir (Adelaide Hills) $27. Shows sexy, intense aromas of lifted cherry, tree bark, and cola, and flavors of earth, tea, plum, and cherry. It's quite a ride on the palate—enjoyable and tasty, but meant for near-term drinking. **89** —*D.T. (8/1/2005)*

Pike & Joyce 2002 Sauvignon Blanc (Adelaide Hills) $20. This SB has fresh green pea and yellow fruit aromas, and trading-card powder and yellow fruit flavors. The texture is a little coarse, and the body bolder than many other SBs, but it's still a refreshing, food-friendly alternative to Chardonnay. **87** —*D.T. (5/1/2004)*

Pike & Joyce 2004 Lenswood Sauvignon Blanc (Adelaide Hills) $21. This steel-cored Sauvignon is zesty, dry and clean. It offers lifted grapefruit and banana aromas, and grapefruit, lemon and stone flavors on the palate. One to drink poolside, on the hottest day of the year. **88** —*D.T. (8/1/2005)*

PIKES

Pikes 2000 Shiraz-Grenache-Mourvedre Red Blend (Clare Valley) $20. Here's proof that Pikes can make more than just a good Riesling. This red is over half Shiraz, with equal parts Grenache and Mourvèdre. The cool-climate fruit has cherry and mint nuances; the body is feminine but sinewy, and quite classy, reserved but still flavorful. **90** —*D.T. (5/1/2004)*

Pikes 2003 Riesling (Clare Valley) $19. Smells clean, but doesn't show much more than cotton and kerosene on the nose. There's a slight spritz at palate entry, but the wine smooths out into lime and mineral flavors

afterward. A good-quality, pretty standard Riesling, and just the ticket with Thai food. **87** —*D.T. (5/1/2004)*

Pikes 2002 Riesling (Clare Valley) $18. Tastes and smells fresh and sweet, like freshly mown hay and nectarines. The overall impression here is one of freshness, really, from its crisp, summery flavors to its zippy mouthfeel. A very nice wine, and a fair price for a taste of a perennial Oz favorite. **89** —*D.T. (8/1/2003)*

Pikes 2004 Dry Riesling (Clare Valley) $19. Great for a noodle or pasta-based salad, or spicy ethnic dishes. The more sips you take of this Clare Riesling, the more intense it seems to get. Its starts off slow, with muted minerality, and blossoms in the glass to reveal peach, nectarine, and pink grapefruit flavors. Dry, but still unctuous, with a lingering, dusty mouthfeel that outlasts even the finish. **91** —*D.T. (8/1/2005)*

Pikes 2001 Reserve Riesling (Clare Valley) $23. This Reserve somehow didn't show quite as well as Pikes's regular bottling, though it's still a very good wine. It's a little viscous in the mouth, with straw, lemon rind, and mineral flavors that flow through the finish. **88** —*D.T. (8/1/2003)*

Pikes 2004 The Merle Reserve Riesling (Clare Valley) $38. Pikes' reserve-level Riesling is one to seek out. It has hints of fresh green herb interspersed with layers and layers of stony, minerally flavors. The wine is intense and has lively acidity and a long, smooth finish. 180 cases produced. **91 Editors' Choice** —*D.T. (4/1/2006)*

Pikes 2002 Luccio Sangiovese (Clare Valley) $15. Tasted twice with differing impressions; this score represents the average of the two. One look at the wine showed roasted aromas, and an orange-peel aroma, followed by sour red fruit on the palate. The second go revealed juicier fruit and pleasing, chalky tannins on the palate. Give it the benefit of the doubt. 600 cases produced. **86** —*D.T. (12/1/2005)*

Pikes 1999 Shiraz (Clare Valley) $19. Bright red fruit, cedar, and creamy aromas on the nose tricked one reviewer into thinking that this bouquet smelled a little like stewy, fake fruit. A smooth, even mouthfeel compensates for the tart mocha-wood-pepper notes that obscure fruit on the palate. Minerals, chalk, and tannins wrap it up. **84** *(10/1/2001)*

Pikes 1998 Reserve Shiraz (Clare Valley) $48. Smooth and medium in weight, this is a fine example of the lavishly oaked style, the deep sweet cherry fruit wrapped in a dark, toasty cocoon with leathery accents adding interest. Even tannins, black toast, and coffee accents show on the long finish. There's a lot of wood here, but it's better-utilized than in many other wines. **89** *(11/1/2001)*

PINK BY YELLOWGLEN

Pink by Yellowglen NV Champagne Blend (South Eastern Australia) $12. This wine is all about popular appeal, from its attractive pale rose color to its obvious, fruit-driven bouquet and its simple, tutti-frutti flavors. It's light and clean, with a short but pleasant finish. **84** —*J.C. (12/31/2006)*

PINK KNOT

Pink Knot 2005 Rosé Blend (McLaren Vale) $12. This rosé is a blend of Shiraz, Cabernet, and Sangiovese. It tastes like tangerine and peach, but suffers from a strange, mushroomy-meaty aroma. 10,000 cases produced. **83** —*D.T. (12/1/2005)*

PIPERS BROOK VINEYARD ESTATE

Pipers Brook Vineyard Estate 2002 Riesling (Tasmania) $19. A fresh and crisp, though unusual, wine. It has pleasing flavors yet tastes like it's made from flowers rather than fruit. There's jasmine, honeysuckle—you name it—on both the nose and the palate. Lean in the mouth, with a hint of apple skin toward the finish. **87** —*D.T. (8/1/2003)*

PIPING SHRIKE

Piping Shrike 2004 Shiraz (Barossa Valley) $14. Black cherry is the main component here, accented by plum flavors and earthy aromas. Down-the-line, basic, good Shiraz. **84** —*D.T. (10/1/2005)*

Piping Shrike 2003 Shiraz (Barossa Valley) $14. Made by Charles Cimicky, who apparently also had to join the "animals on labels" contest. Fanatics of the super-jammy, over-the-top style need look no further: Here is a package of vanilla and tea, dressing up vibrant blackberry-raspberry fruit. Still, it accomplishes its goal with class; you're not going to mistake this for an under-$10 wine. 5,000 cases produced. **87** —*D. T. (5/1/2005)*

PIRRAMIMMA

Pirramimma 1998 Shiraz (McLaren Vale) $20. Lushly textured if a bit over-oaked, this full, smooth wine displays a complex dark berry, smoke, bacon fat, and herb nose. A classically dark palate profile and the long, white pepper-eucalyptus finish with its chalky tannins close it nicely. **87** *(10/1/2001)*

PLANTAGENET

Plantagenet 1999 Mount Barker Chardonnay (Western Australia) $21. Leads off with dusty, nutty, sugary aromas, like the bottom of the bag of honey-roasted peanuts, but there's also hints of buttered toast, ripe pears, and black pepper. Flavors are simpler—caramel and pineapple—and it's heavy on the palate. **85** —*J.C. (7/11/2002)*

Plantagenet 2003 OMRAH unoaked Chardonnay (Western Australia) $15. Both the nose and the palate of this Chardonnay focus on peach, apple, and citrus notes; we also found some floral and citrus accents. Medium-weight and soft in the mouth, it's a good quaffing wine, and will show even better with a little chill on it. **85** *(7/2/2004)*

Plantagenet 2000 Unoaked Chardonnay (Western Australia) $14. Lack of oak makes this Chardonnay easier than most to pair with food, and its lean, tart style makes it a natural with fish or shellfish. Aromas and flavors of lemon, lime, and green plum finish clean and zesty. **84** —*J.C. (7/1/2002)*

Plantagenet 2001 Estate Shiraz (Mount Barker) $25. Not as good as the winery's less expensive bottling. The plum fruit in this Shiraz tastes a little sour, and finishes pretty woody. Fruit on the nose is high toned, with interesting ginger, soil, and plum accents. **85** —*D.T. (5/1/2004)*

Plantagenet 1998 Mount Barker Shiraz (Western Australia) $28. Strong cracked black pepper notes on the nose challenge red berry and cinnamon aromas underneath. Cherry, sour herb, and even more black pepper flavors fill out this full but well-structured wine. Peppery finish. **88** *(11/1/2001)*

Plantagenet 2001 Omrah Shiraz (Western Australia) $15. Nose is an outdoorsy mix of wood, earth, and leather aromas. On the palate, red plum fruit is angular, and almost liqueurish. Tannins are chewy on the mid-palate, and fade into a woody finish. **87** —*D.T. (5/1/2004)*

Plantagenet 2000 Omrah Shiraz (Western Australia) $17. Aged in French and American oak for 12 months, the wine's weight is more reminiscent of Beaujolais than Shiraz. In terms of flavor, earthy, meaty notes take charge on the palate. **84** —*D.T. (2/1/2003)*

Plantagenet 1998 Omrah Shiraz (Western Australia) $18. 88 —*M.S. (10/1/2000)*

Plantagenet 1997 Omrah Shiraz (Mount Barker) $17. 88 —*M.S. (4/1/2000)*

POOLES ROCK WINES

Pooles Rock Wines 2001 Chardonnay (Hunter Valley) $24. Bright gold in color, with waxy melon aromas. Waxy melon aromas on the nose lead to peach, toast, and beeswax in the mouth. Medium-bodied; a nice mineral-chalk note dries up the finish. **87** —*D.T. (8/1/2003)*

Pooles Rock Wines 2001 Firestick Chardonnay (Adelaide Hills) $14. This Chard offers a fair dose of oak (and the creamy-toasty goodness that goes with it), yet has tropical yellow fruit to back up the wood. Soft in the mouth; finishes dry and oaky. **85** —*D.T. (8/1/2003)*

PREECE

Preece 1998 Sauvignon Blanc (Victoria) $15. 87 —*S.H. (10/1/2000)*

PRETTY SALLY

Pretty Sally 2003 Single Vineyard Estate Cabernet Sauvignon (Victoria) $25. On the palate, black plum and cranberry fruit is couched in a smooth, clay-chalk feel. It's not sweet, overly oaky, nor is it extraordinarily nuanced or ageable. What it is is a very good wine, appropriately sized for drinking with food over the near term. **88** —*D.T. (10/1/2006)*

PRIMO ESTATE

Primo Estate 1999 Il Briccone Red Blend (Adelaide Hills) $18. 84 —*J.C. (9/1/2002)*

Primo Estate 2003 La Biondina White Blend (Adelaide Hills) $NA. "The little blonde," as its name translates, is made of Colombard. It's thick and round in the mouth, with peach, apricot, and grapefruit flavors that persist through the finish. A good choice if crispness isn't high on your list of priorities. **85** —*D.T. (5/1/2004)*

Primo Estate 2005 La Biondina White Blend (Adelaide) $15. This blend of Colombard, Riesling, and Sauvignon Blanc is an odd wine, giving straw/stable notes on the nose and lemon, pink grapefruit, and straw flavors on the palate. Goes peachy toward the finish. Light and soft. **84** —*D.T. (8/1/2006)*

Primo Estate 2004 La Biondina (Adelaide, not Adelaide Hills) White Blend (Adelaide Hills) $16. This is a mutt of a white, an unexpected blend of Colombard, Riesling, and Sauvignon that comes off like Gewürz at first blush. It offers honeyed, earthy aromas and nectarine, peach, floral, and orange flavors all front-loaded on the palate. Finishes dry. **87** —*D.T. (8/1/2005)*

PUNT ROAD

Punt Road 2003 Cabernet Sauvignon (Yarra Valley) $22. Winemaker Kate Goodman's Cab is very enjoyable. It offers brown meat and wood aromas. It's tight and racy on the palate, with good acidity and juicy fruit at its core. The fruit feels like it's not quite in full bloom yet; might be best to revisit this one next year. **90** —*D.T. (10/1/2006)*

Punt Road 2004 Chardonnay (Yarra Valley) $18. Vanilla and light butterscotch aromas on the nose preface yellow stone fruit flavors. Pretty straightforward, but good. **84** —*D.T. (4/1/2006)*

Punt Road 2004 Pinot Gris (Yarra Valley) $20. A lower-acid rendition of PG than you'll find in Oz, but it's also a pretty tart one. On the palate, peach pit and lemon pith flavors dominate, giving the wine a puckery flavor overall. A little cream on the finish makes it go down a little easier. **83** —*D.T. (2/1/2006)*

Punt Road 2003 Pinot Noir (Yarra Valley) $22. Though the red fruit smells a little overripe on the nose, the palate offers the opposite impression—one of tart, crisp fruit. Disjointed; flavors may go over easier with food. **84** —*D.T. (4/1/2006)*

Punt Road 2003 Shiraz (Yarra Valley) $22. This wine's winning feature is its cool, minty accent, which gives an otherwise fairly straightforward Shiraz a different twist. Finish is brief; 1,500 cases produced. **86** —*D.T. (4/1/2006)*

PUNTERS CORNER

Punters Corner 1999 Cabernet Sauvignon (Coonawarra) $25. Black as night in color, with coffee, _mocha, and heat emanating from the bouquet. Theirs is more than enough edgy cassis and cherry fruit on the palate, but also the slightest detectable note of green vegetable. The finish is a rush of coffee, toast, and charred meat. Plump and easygoing. **88** —*M.S. (12/15/2002)*

Punters Corner 1998 Cabernet Sauvignon (Coonawarra) $27. This 100% Cabernet Sauvignon wine shows why Cab is the grape that made Coonawarra famous. Dense and Port-like in color, the full nose displays cassis, fruit, leather, tobacco, green olive, and eucalyptus. Rich and supple on the palate, it still has plenty of backbone. The extracted black cherry flavors, accented by green olive, sun-dried tomato, and mint, sit atop some firm tannins. It finishes long, but a little hard, and could use a few years in the cellar. **89** *(9/1/2001)*

Punters Corner 1999 Cabernet Sauvignon-Merlot (Coonawarra) $27. This assertive, eucalyptus-scented blend is a spunky, personality-loaded blend of 91% Cabernet Sauvignon and 9% Merlot. It's elaborately endowed with sour cherry and cassis fruit, accented by mint, spice, smoke, and chocolate flavors on a generous, balanced framework. This big red's firm but not astringent tannins and balanced acidity promise long life to a wine that's forward and rewarding right now. **89** *(9/1/2001)*

Punters Corner 2000 Chardonnay (Coonawarra) $19. Carmel is the key player on the nose; it persists on the palate, where a hearty helping of zingy citrus flavors nicely balance the carmelly sweetness. Finishes with pear, citrus, and toast. **87** —D.T. (8/1/2003)

Punters Corner 2002 Triple Crown Red Blend (Coonawarra) $20. A blend of 56% Cab, 30% Merlot, and 14% Shiraz. This is an odd, disjointed wine. An impression of cotton-candy sweetness competes with a weedy, green streak on both the nose and the palate. Underneath it all is pleasant red plum fruit and anise flavors, and a fine feel, all caught in the cross-fire. **84** —D.T. (5/1/2005)

Punters Corner 2001 Triple Crown Red Blend (Coonawarra) $20. An unusual wine with bright red fruit, tea, oak, and pine needle flavors and dry, chewy tannins in the mouth. The nose has similar permeating green pine-needle aromas. A very good wine; a blend of 67% Cabernet, 24% Shiraz, and 9% Merlot. **88** —D.T. (5/1/2004)

Punters Corner 2002 Shiraz (Coonawarra) $28. This wine feels well-built and sturdy in the mouth, with smooth, integrated tannins. Its flavors and aromas, though, run the gamut from rhubarb to sour stone fruit to slight briary, stemmy notes. Tea-like tannins on the finish have a shrill edge. **86** —D.T. (10/1/2005)

Punters Corner 1998 Shiraz (Coonawarra) $26. The tart, sour cherry fruit merely serves to support the leathery, earthy, spicy elements; the fruit never really takes charge. That said, the wine does have plenty to offer. The dried-spice aromas are an attractive blend of cracked black pepper, cinnamon, and clove, the mouthfeel is smooth and rich. Finishs long, with hints of espresso. **87** —J.C. (9/1/2002)

Punters Corner 2000 Spartacus Reserve Shiraz (Coonawarra) $62. Disappointing, considering its price and the performance of some past vintages. Though the nose offers pleasing pastry crust and plum fruit aromas, fruit on the palate tastes flat, with a slight green bean note. Finishes dry, with sour plum fruit. Tasted twice. **84** —D.T. (9/1/2004)

Punters Corner 1999 Spartacus Reserve Shiraz (Coonawarra) $60. Not as wild and robust as you might expect from the name, this offering is instead a silky-smooth blend of mint and creamy chocolate layered over a base of pepper-dusted blackberries. Despite the richness, it never seems overly heavy. Drink now and over the next 10 years. **91** —J.C. (9/1/2002)

Punters Corner 1998 Spartacus Reserve Shiraz (Coonawarra) $46. It's lean, and some say it's a bit green. Leather, tobacco, and an herb-menthol note open onto a mouthful of tart cranberry, oak and fresh vegetal flavors. Finishes with bitter espresso flavors. **85** (11/1/2001)

QUARTETTO

Quartetto 2000 Shiraz (McLaren Vale) $20. The brown sugar-molasses-blackberry profile that entices many an enthusiast shows on this wine's bouquet, but in the mouth, a strange melange of red berry, herb, and resin takes over. A bitter herbacousness, plus some hard cheese, follows on the back end. **84** —D.T. (1/28/2003)

RAINMAKERS

RainMakers 2003 Shiraz-Grenache (McLaren Vale) $23. A 50-50 Shiraz-Grenache blend that has pretty black pepper and menthol accents on the nose. The palate offers up mixed berry and vanilla flavors, but lacks depth and stuffing. **84** —D.T. (4/1/2006)

RAM'S LEAP

Ram's Leap 2004 Shiraz (Western Plains) $11. Every other inhale, you'll smell either leather or sweet fruit. On the palate, taut plum and rhubarb flavors dominate. A closed, somewhat disjointed wine, but it has an interesting rocky texture and some complexity. **85** —D.T. (11/15/2006)

RANFURLYS WAY

Ranfurlys Way 2003 Cabernet Sauvignon (Clare Valley) $29. Big and dark but angular, this Cabernet sports plenty of oak and blackberry flavors, but also some sourish green wood and eucalyptus flavors. **86** —D.T. (10/1/2006)

Ranfurlys Way 2004 Chardonnay (Adelaide Hills) $25. This Chardonnay deals a tangy combo of golden apple and bright citrus against a toasty, lactic backdrop that was a detraction for me. Medium-full in the mouth, it shows more toast and apple notes on the nose. **85** —D.T. (12/1/2005)

Ranfurlys Way 2005 Riesling (Clare Valley) $29. Smells very nice, just lightly floral and minerally. Starts on the palate with a surge of white peach and citrus, then it lets up midpalate, and comes back for a rousing finish. I really liked this Riesling; without that intensity interruption in the middle, its score would have reached the next decile. **88** —D.T. (12/1/2005)

Ranfurlys Way 2001 Shiraz (Clare Valley) $29. This wine follows the "give the people what they want" formula to a T, and does it very well. It smells like blackberry jam and is moderate in size, with a core of plums and berries. Nut and toast nuances on the finish are the bow on the package. **88** —D.T. (12/31/2005)

RBJ

RBJ 2001 Vox Populi Grenache (Barossa Valley) $10. From winemaker Chris Ringland and viticulturalist Russell Johnstone; Ringland is the winemaker of the Rockford and Chris Ringland (née Three Rivers) wines. The Rockford wines cost about $40. The Chris Ringland wines? $400, if you're lucky. In any case, this Grenache is a bargain. It tastes like a well-done Rhône red, medium-slender in the mouth, with cherry/black cherry flavors and minimal wood. Aromas are of earth and cola, and the finish is clean. **87 Best Buy** —D.T. (11/15/2004)

RED BUCKET

Red Bucket 2005 Semillon-Sauvignon Blanc (Adelaide Hills) $13. Made by the folks at Longview, this Sem-Sauv is cottony-soft around the edges, with a clean feel overall. Smells like green grass, pea, and flowers. A good Saturday afternoon wine: Easy, uncomplicated, and fresh. **85** —D.T. (8/1/2006)

RED HILL ESTATE

Red Hill Estate 2001 Penguin's Kiss Chardonnay (Mornington Peninsula) $10. 83 —D.T. (8/1/2003)

RED KNOT

Red Knot 2003 Cabernet Sauvignon (Fleurieu Peninsula) $12. There's a nice grab of dry tannins in the midpalate, with mixed plum and earth flavors. The nose holds pencil eraser and some outdoorsy aromas: tree bark, earth, maybe a little leaf. A well-done wine, particularly for the price. Made by Shingleback's winemaker, John Davey. **87 Best Buy** — D.T. (11/15/2004)

RED KNOT

Red Knot 2004 Shiraz (McLaren Vale) $12. Smells syrupy-sweet, with toast and tea accents. On the palate, there's some nice black plum and cherry fruit. The finish reprises the tea and oak notes. Straightforward, but good. **86** —D.T. (10/1/2005)

Red Knot 2003 Shiraz (McLaren Vale) $12. Cinnamon-clove aromas on the nose. The wine has dry tannins in the mouth, and very solid, taut cherry and plum fruit, with dusty pencil-eraser accents. Would pair well with grilled food, or just about anything in barbecue sauce. **87 Best Buy** —D.T. (11/15/2004)

REDBANK

Redbank 2002 The Fugitive Cabernet Sauvignon (Victoria) $15. This surely is a good-quality wine, but it follows a tried-and-true recipe. It offers dusty blackberry aromas, and blackberry and red plum flavors. It's just the right size on the palate, with smooth tannins and a gummy hold on the midpalate. At this price, you can afford to keep a few on your drink-now rack. **89** —D.T. (5/1/2005)

Redbank 2000 Percydale Cabernet Sauvignon-Merlot (King Valley) $16. There's an herbal aroma that reminds me of eucalyptus trees, and the wine is very strongly flavored with menthol or, to use the winemaker's own word, mint. This is said to be a cool area, which may explain why it's not fruitier. That said, it's compelling. It's so structurally beautiful, so well balanced that you find yourself returning for a second sip. **91 Editors' Choice** —S.H. (12/15/2002)

Redbank 1999 Percydale Cabernet Sauvignon-Merlot (King Valley) $15. This wine reads like a sexy but aloof woman: Ruby-colored at the lips, on the thin side, and corset-tight. What little perfume she wears (this you only detect after a number of swirls, twirls, and minutes in the glass)

AUSTRALIA

has promising notes of cream and anise. Oak and black pepper in the mouth; medium-length black pepper and grape finish. **84** —*D. T. (9/1/2001)*

Redbank 1998 Long Paddock Cabernet Sauvignon-Shiraz (Victoria) $14. 88 —*M.M. (10/1/2000)*

Redbank 1998 Long Paddock Chardonnay (Victoria) $11. 85 —*M.M. (10/1/2000)*

Redbank 2003 The Long Paddock Chardonnay (Victoria) $10. I appreciated this Chardonnay's fruit focus, how its unadorned melon and stone fruit was not ruined by too much oak interference. Pure and naked, but tastes very good. **87 Best Buy** —*D. T. (5/1/2005)*

Redbank 2002 The Long Paddock Chardonnay (Victoria) $10. An interesting wine, at a good price: Has pastry dough, lime, and yellow fruit aromas, and a slightly viscous texture. In the mouth, stone fruit wears a minerally cloak. White pepper and herb flavors add zip to the finish. **87** —*D. T. (8/1/2003)*

Redbank 2001 The Long Paddock Chardonnay (Victoria) $10. In Australia, a paddock is an enclosed area, like a corral, where livestock graze. There's a story to the wine's name that's too long to tell here. It's incredibly rich, especially for this price, with tropical fruit, lime, vanilla, and peach flavors. The mouthfeel is creamy smooth, with a honeyed aftertaste. It's a brilliant value. **90** —*S.H. (1/1/2002)*

Redbank 2003 The Long Paddock Merlot (Victoria) $10. This is a nice, value-priced Merlot whose black peppery aromas and leathery, rustic flavors are welcome changes from the sweeter styled Merlots at this price point. Just the right addition to a family-style spaghetti dinner. **86 Best Buy** —*D. T. (10/1/2005)*

Redbank 2004 Goldmine Series Sunday Morning Pinot Gris (King Valley) $16. Smells fresh and clean, and has a stony mouthfeel. White stone fruit dominates the palate; elegant, though not quite as concentrated as it should be. Very good, and will be excellent in another vintage. 250 cases produced. **89** —*D. T. (8/1/2005)*

Redbank 2001 Sunday Morning Pinot Gris (King Valley) $16. Clever name, but apt. This would be nice with an omelet, warm biscuits, fresh fruit. It has flavors of peaches, a rich, honeyed texture, and is off-dry. Total acidity is refreshingly crisp. The wine was 80 percent steel fermented and 20 percent barrel fermented. **87** —*S.H. (1/1/2002)*

Redbank 2000 Sunday Morning Pinot Gris (King Valley) $15. This very pale, crisply flavorful white has great backbone and surprising presence. It cuts a lean profile with pear and herb aromas and flavors predominating, a touch of vanilla and mild spice for added interest. Showing character and length, this will pair well with veal, seafood…and maybe even smoked salmon on Sunday morning. **87** —*M.M. (9/1/2001)*

Redbank 2002 The Long Paddock Sauvignon Blanc (Victoria) $10. Starts with eye-opening lemon and lime fruit on the nose that is not quite as piquant when it resurfaces on the palate. Finishes comparatively weighty, with cream flavors. A promising, dead-on Sauvignon beginning; would have been even better with more citrus on the follow-through. **85** —*D. T. (12/31/2003)*

Redbank 1999 Fighting Flat Shiraz (King Valley) $15. Redbank? More like redwood. Though most reviewers found cedar and toast to be the predominant flavors and aromas in the Fighting Flat, others identified pleasing spice and coffee notes on the nose, and cherry and cocoa flavors on the palate. Finishes tart, with—you guessed it—dry, smoked-wood flavors. **82** *(10/1/2001)*

Redbank 2001 The Anvil Shiraz (Heathcote) $50. Almost impenetrable at first, but with 15 minutes of air, coffee, plum skin, and eucalyptus/mint aromas begin to unfold. On the palate, it's a very textured wine; it has a thick veil of clay-chalky tannins, yet stays on the conservative side of richness and fullness. Its flavors reprise the aromas, for the most part, with an added accent of sea-breeze salinity that lasts through the finish. Will be at its best after 2007. **91** —*D. T. (8/1/2005)*

Redbank 2000 The Fighting Flat Shiraz (King Valley) $16. This 100% Shiraz shows off the tension between the variety wild, savage quality and the elegance the winemaker tries to impose on it. Here, savage wins. The berry and herb flavors have a rough edge, and it's pretty tannic, too. Not

offering a lot of pleasure now. Try cellaring through 2005. **86** —*S.H. (12/15/2002)*

Redbank 2000 The Long Paddock Shiraz-Cabernet Sauvignon (Victoria) $10. This wine is a spectacular value. It's just delicious, filled with intense raspberry liqueur, chocolate, and tobacco flavors, richly dry, with super-velvety tannins. It coats the palate with sweet, ripe fruit. True, this is not a big wine and won't age, but on every other level, it's superb. **90 Best Buy** —*S.H. (12/15/2002)*

Redbank 2004 The Widow Jones Viognier (King Valley) $16. This very good wine is round and hefty in feel, with aromas and flavors of melon, pear, and straw. It doesn't show very much of Viognier's telltale floral notes on the nose, but the palate and finish don't disappoint. **87** —*D. T. (8/1/2005)*

REDHOUSE

Redhouse 2001 Shiraz-Grenache (McLaren Vale) $15. This 50-50 Shiraz-Grenache blend has pretty powerful cherry and earth flavors on the front of the palate, but it lightens up some on the latter half. The wine's moderate size won't bowl you over, but the flavor explosion just might. **87** —*D. T. (12/31/2004)*

REILLY'S

Reilly's 2002 Dry Land Cabernet Sauvignon (Clare Valley) $27. This is a narrow wine, just shy of a mouth-filling, va-va-voom element that would have catapulted it into the next decile. Still, I enjoyed it very much. It has fragrant cinnamon and eucalyptus notes on the nose that continue on the palate, where blackberry and blueberry fruit reigns. Finishes medium-long. **89** —*D. T. (12/31/2005)*

Reilly's 2003 Old Bushvine Grenache-Shiraz (Clare Valley) $17. It's nice to know that some Australian wineries and importers have kept a lid on prices. Reilly's 2003 Old Bushvine is a 75-25 blend that showcases Grenache's soft, caressing texture. It's full-bodied but silky, with sweetly ripe cherries matched by bold lashings of vanilla and spiced with hints of clove and cinnamon. Drink now. **92 Editors' Choice** —*J.C. (12/15/2006)*

Reilly's 2004 Barking Mad Riesling (Clare Valley) $13. Like Reilly's Watervale bottling, this will certainly inspire debate. The nose offers pineapple, resin, and waxy melon, and the palate deals a similar waxy, tart, Pixie Stix kind of profile. I admire its tanginess and intensity—less enamored with the bulky feel—but its flavors are certainly atypical. **84** —*D. T. (10/1/2005)*

Reilly's 2004 Watervale Riesling (Clare Valley) $15. You'll like or dislike this wine. I liked it. I read the flavors profile as honeysuckle/floral/powder-on-chewing-gum, and another taster found it not unlike hard candy. Clean citrus and bubblegum powder aromas; one to try for yourself. **85** —*D. T. (10/1/2005)*

Reilly's 1999 Watervale Riesling (Clare Valley) $12. Tart and tangy with tropical fruit and grapefruit aromas and flavors, this lively white provides good drinking now. The citrus and mango tango continues on the palate, and the wine finishes crisply, with good length and a touch of vanilla and spice. A great wine for grilled seafoods. **87** —*M.M. (2/1/2002)*

Reilly's 2002 Dry Land Shiraz (Clare Valley) $25. Nutty, almost Porty, aromas. On the palate, the wine offers plum and some vanilla cream. Straightforward, but good. **85** —*D. T. (12/1/2005)*

Reilly's 1999 Dry Land Shiraz (Clare Valley) $25. The sweet, caramel-vanilla aromas complement dark berries and earth on the palate. Lush, rich, and velvety, this wine is marked by lots of oak, but has the fruit to back it up, finishing with soft, supple tannins and hints of coffee and chocolate. Top Value. **90** *(11/1/2001)*

RESCHKE

Reschke 2002 Bos Cabernet Sauvignon (Coonawarra) $30. This is a very good Cab, but one that doesn't really show the hallmarks that typically say "Coonawarra." Black fruit, coffee, and vanilla bean aromas and flavors take on black-peppery accents on the palate. Underneath it all is a sturdy base of smooth wood. **88** —*D. T. (5/1/2005)*

Reschke 2002 Bos Cabernet Sauvignon (Coonawarra) $35. Bos (which means "bull" in Latin) is a big, black wine; but for the fact that it doesn't scream "oak" it could swallow you whole. Has smooth, chewy tannins and knockout juicy fruit and mocha on the finish. On the nose, shows earth, black pepper, and light vanilla or baked-goods aromas. Yum. **90** —*D.T. (5/1/2004)*

Reschke 2002 Vitulus Cabernet Sauvignon (Coonawarra) $20. This vintage of Reschke Bos's little-brother Cab, the Vitulus, is similiar to the Bos, though it is $10 cheaper. This wine's vanilla and caramel aromas usher in mixed plums and a woodsy, dry mouthfeel. A very good, though fairly predictable, Cab. **88** —*D.T. (5/1/2005)*

Reschke 2002 Vitulus Cabernet Sauvignon (Coonawarra) $26. Little brother to Reschke's "Bos" hence the name "Vitulus," which means "bull calf." This one's appropriately more jaunty and youthful, but unfolds nicely on the finish. Aromas are deep, mostly black cherry; flavors are of black cherry and mocha. **89** —*D.T. (5/1/2004)*

REYNOLDS

Reynolds 2002 Cabernet Sauvignon (New South Wales) $8. I tasted this wine beside $100 Napa Cabs, and while it obviously wasn't in the same league, it held up well. The fruit is ripe and flattering, suggesting black-berries and cherries enriched with oak, and the tannins are rich and smooth, with sharp acids. **85 Best Buy** —*S.H. (11/15/2004)*

Reynolds 2001 Cabernet Sauvignon (New South Wales) $10. There is some varietal character in this dark, dry red wine, notably the black currant taste. But it's thin in body, and marred by overripe notes of raisins and prunes. High acidity only adds to the impression of austerity and hardness in the mouth. **83** —*S.H. (12/15/2002)*

Reynolds 2001 Reserve Cabernet Sauvignon (Orange) $15. As you might expect, the cool climate has led to the development of weedy, tobacco aromas and flavors, backed by cassis. A bit broader and fleshier than the Merlot, but still crisply acidic on the finish. **86** *(9/1/2003)*

Reynolds 2002 Chardonnay (New South Wales) $10. A straightforward but solid Chardonnay, with pleasing honey and yellow pear flavors and a hearty helping of toasty oak. Its formula is one that might ring familiar to you, but it works, and it won't set you back too many bucks, either. **86** —*D.T. (12/31/2003)*

Reynolds 2001 Chardonnay (New South Wales) $10. These grapes are sourced from the relatively cooler region of Orange, and it shows in the wine's pear and citrus flavors. Hints of nuts (cashews, perhaps?) add complexity and style not often found in this price range. Crisp and clean on the finish, with refreshing citrus notes. **88 Best Buy** —*J.C. (7/1/2002)*

Reynolds 2002 Reserve Chardonnay (Orange) $15. Packs in plenty of plump, pineapple fruit framed by smoky, toasty oak. Maybe it's just the power of suggestion, but are there some orange scents in among the lightly buttered peach aromas? Could use more elegance, but it's rich, full-bodied, and flavorful. **87** *(9/1/2003)*

Reynolds 2001 Merlot (New South Wales) $10. Has a lot going for it, from the rich, dark color to the savory plum and tobacco flavors to the soft, detailed tannins. Dry and straightforward, a little too soft in acids, but a nice glass of red. **85** —*S.H. (12/15/2002)*

Reynolds 2001 Reserve Merlot (Orange) $15. Smells perfectly correct, with black cherries blending with milk chocolate, vanilla, and dried herbs on the nose. In the mouth, the acidity lends the wine a hard edge, and the flavors are slightly greener and harder than you might expect. Very tart; definitely better with food. **85** *(9/1/2003)*

Reynolds 2002 Sauvignon Blanc (New South Wales) $10. Dry, tart, and electric in its intense acidity, this wine features pure, bright flavors of limes, grapefruits, gooseberries, and vanilla. It's long on taste, and the acidic freshness carries the citrus flavors through a long finish. **87 Best Buy** —*S.H. (3/1/2003)*

Reynolds 2002 Reserve Sauvignon Blanc (Orange) $15. Slightly sweet tasting, with weighty peach and melon flavors that are counter-balanced by a finish that's quite tart. Hints of grassiness, jalapeño, and passion fruit jazz up the nose. **84** *(9/1/2003)*

Reynolds 2001 Shiraz (New South Wales) $10. Good, young Aussie Shiraz. What more needs to be said? It's jammy and fruity, stuffed with blackberry, loganberry, and black cherry flavors that come across dry and tannic. The tannins and considerable acidity make it a bit rough in the mouth—try it with rich foods. **85 Best Buy** —*S.H. (12/15/2002)*

Reynolds 2001 Reserve Shiraz (Orange) $15. This wine reveals its cool-climate origins in its aromas of black pepper and cranberries, then bolsters those credentials by adding berry flavors and bright acidity. Creamy vanilla notes help balance out the crunchy fruit. Doesn't appear to be an ager. **87** *(9/1/2003)*

RIBBONVALE

Ribbonvale 1998 Cabernet Sauvignon-Merlot (Margaret River) $18. An excellent and elegant wine—this is no blockbuster—with tea and unsweetened chocolate flavors accenting ripe red fruit on the palate. Nose shows dusty, herbaceous notes. **90** —*D.T. (10/1/2003)*

RIDDOCH ESTATE

Riddoch Estate 2002 Katnook Estate Cabernet Sauvignon-Merlot (Coonawarra) $45. It's a great thing to find a Coonawarra wine that's good and inexpensive. Its smooth texture is an asset. Its plum fruit is fairly taut, and has gumtree-earthy accents, rather than sweetish, caramelly ones. Though I detected greenness on the nose right out of the bottle, it dissipates with time in the glass. **88** —*D.T. (5/1/2005)*

Riddoch Estate 2000 Katnook Estate Cabernet Sauvignon-Merlot (Coonawarra) $11. Medium and smooth in the mouth, the Cab's so prevalent here you'd think there was more than 52% here. There's sturdy blackberry and black plum fruit on the palate, plus some eucalyptus and toast; dry, oaky tannins finish it off. A very good, though textbook, sort of wine. **87** —*D.T. (6/1/2003)*

Riddoch Estate 2001 Cabernet Sauvignon-Shiraz (Coonawarra) $11. This 60-40 Cab-Shiraz blend has aromas of black olive and eucalyptus and taut plum and black cherry flavors. Its chalky, claylike mouthfeel is Coonawarra, all the way. I'm glad this wine is as affordable as it is—it will help value seekers appreciate regional differences among Australian wines. **87 Best Buy** —*D.T. (12/31/2004)*

Riddoch Estate 2000 Katnook Estate Cabernet Sauvignon-Shiraz (Coonawarra) $11. When a wine's flavors are this vibrant, thoughts about texture and ageability may fall by the wayside. Juicy blackberry, blueberry, and plum is joined on the palate by mushroom, chocolate and oak. There's a lot going on in this tasty red. **88 Best Buy** —*D.T. (12/31/2003)*

Riddoch Estate 1996 Shiraz (Coonawarra) $18. 88 *(10/1/2000)*

RINGBOLT

Ringbolt 2002 Cabernet Sauvignon (Margaret River) $15. Smells meaty, with a streak of eucalyptus. Taut, cool black-plum fruit warms the palate, where there's also a substantial amount of oak. Very good—it's nice to find hallmarks of the region for a reasonable price. **87** —*D.T. (5/1/2005)*

Ringbolt 2001 Cabernet Sauvignon (Margaret River) $14. The first of Yalumba's forays into Western Australia, the Cab fruit is from a 27-year-old vineyard. It's high quality, particularly for the price, and full and lively in the mouth. Bright blackberry and plum fruit gets a dose of eucalyptus and black pepper on the palate; finishes up with bright plum fruit. **89 Best Buy** —*D.T. (2/1/2004)*

Ringbolt 2001 Cabernet Sauvignon (Margaret River) $15. Red fruit is accented with dark earth, oak, and caramel. Has smooth tannins on the palate, and wheaty, oaky notes on the back end. Easy to drink; standard, but very good. **88** —*D.T. (10/1/2003)*

RIPE

Ripe 1999 Chardonnay (Hunter Valley) $10. Lean and toasty at the same time, boasting aromas and flavors of toast and caramel, lemon, and tart pineapple. Despite the brand name, it tastes distinctly less than fully ripe, with a long, tart-citrus finish. **85** —*J.C. (7/1/2002)*

RIVERINA ESTATES

Riverina Estates 2002 Kanga's Leap Cabernet Sauvignon (South Eastern Australia) $8. The mixed plum fruit is unremarkable but fine. In terms of texture, there's not much, until some powdery-woody tannins pop up on the back end. **82** —*D.T. (8/1/2003)*

Riverina Estates 2002 Bushman's Gully Chardonnay (South Eastern Australia) $7. A soft wine, with flavors of peach, and banana flavors on the finish. Smells sweet, with more peach and a douse of confectioners' sugar. **83** *(7/2/2004)*

Riverina Estates 2001 Lizard Ridge Chardonnay (South Eastern Australia) $7. A soft and approachable Chardonnay, with meaty, yellow-fruit aromas and sour citrus and pear fruit at its core. A touch of honey or caramel makes it go down easier. **84** *(7/2/2004)*

Riverina Estates 2001 Lombard Station Premium Selection Chardonnay (South Eastern Australia) $10. As the '70s song went, "if you like piña coladas," this wine is for you. Has nice jasmine-talc perfume and a cream-and-tropical fruit flavor profile. A good introduction to Chardonnay. **84** *(7/2/2004)*

Riverina Estates 2001 Warburn Chardonnay (New South Wales) $10. Goes down so easy; if you can't get away to Cancun for vacation, this is the next best thing. This is a tropical Chardonnay if ever there was one, with pineapple and melon notes on the palate, and with pineapple and coconut on the nose. Finishes dry, with some citrus peel. **86** *—D. T. (8/1/2003)*

Riverina Estates 2001 Lombard Station Premium Selection Merlot (South Eastern Australia) $9. Burly wood, black pepper, and steak waft from the nose. Oak on the palate gives the otherwise pretty simple wine some texture; jammy black fruit lingers underneath. **85** *—D. T. (10/1/2003)*

Riverina Estates 2001 Warburn Semillon (South Eastern Australia) $10. **83** *—D. T. (9/1/2004)*

Riverina Estates 2001 Warburn Semillon (New South Wales) $10. The aromas may remind you a little of Chardonnay: butter, toast, yellow fruit. In the mouth, there's a spine of lemon-citrus acidity, fleshed out with peach and butter accents. Flavors intensify on the finish. **86 Best Buy** *—D. T. (11/15/2004)*

Riverina Estates 2003 Bushman's Gully Semillon-Chardonnay (South Eastern Australia) $7. Simple and steady wins the best buy race. Flavors are sunny and bright—yellow fruit with floral/honeysuckle accents—and the body is medium and approachable. Zesty aromas and a Sweet Tart finish complete a nice, affordable picture. **86 Best Buy** *—D. T. (11/15/2004)*

Riverina Estates 2001 Lombard Station Premium Selection Semillon-Chardonnay (South Eastern Australia) $9. This brand's Warburn and Lombard Station lines yield some good, and well-priced, selections. I like this white's minerally, powdery mouthfeel and flavors, and subtle yellow fruit. There's some cream here, which gives the wine some roundness in the mouth, plus nice vanilla and toffee aromas. It's pretty, talc-like, and feminine. **85** *—D. T. (11/15/2003)*

Riverina Estates 2000 1164 Family Reserve Shiraz (South Eastern Australia) $30. Black fruit is couched in fine tannins in the mouth, with tobacco and root beer flavors following up on the finish. The nose, too, is unusual, with soy, hickory, and anise aromas. What keeps this wine from showing a bit better than it did, however, is a sour note that hits at palate entry. **87** *—D. T. (12/31/2003)*

Riverina Estates 1998 1164 Family Reserve Shiraz (Riverina) $29. The first impression from the nose is that of raisins, but with time you get pound cake and some Port. As with the bouquet, the first taste reveals prunes and raisins, but behind that there's some coffee and character. While this is not a full-force, in-your-face wine, it does have weight, heft, and other calling cards of Aussie Shiraz. **88** *—M.S. (3/1/2003)*

Riverina Estates 2002 Bushman's Gully Shiraz (South Eastern Australia) $7. A peppy, red-all-over wine, with not a dark note to be found. Sweet raspberry and red plum aromas preface cherry, red plum, and pencil eraser flavors. Straightforward, with a slight metallic edge on the finish. **84 Best Buy** *—D.T. (12/31/2004)*

Riverina Estates 2002 Kanga's Leap Shiraz (South Eastern Australia) $7. This is a pretty straightforward Shiraz, with simple, sweet berries and plums on the nose, and bright cherry and raspberry fruit on the palate. **83** *—D. T. (9/1/2004)*

Riverina Estates 2001 Warburn Shiraz (New South Wales) $10. Though this wine is chock full of juicy, red-fruit flavors, there's something odd about its powdery texture. Fine for parties. 30,000 cases produced. **84** *—D. T. (5/1/2005)*

Riverina Estates 2000 Warburn Show Reserve Shiraz (Riverina) $15. Ink and offputting petroleum aromas dominate on the nose. Thin and dilute in the mouth, what fruit is here is probably black plum. **81** *—D. T. (1/28/2003)*

Riverina Estates 2001 Bushman's Gully Shiraz-Cabernet Sauvignon (South Eastern Australia) $6. This wine's tangy red fruit—raspberry, cherry, plum—and slim body will remind you more of Grenache than a Shiraz/Cab. The nose doesn't exactly say Shiraz, either, with its Asian-inspired aromas (is that rice paper?). Finishes with oak and herbs. **85** *—D.T. (10/1/2003)*

ROBINVALE

Robinvale 2003 Shiraz-Cabernet Sauvignon-Merlot Red Blend (Victoria) $20. A Demeter-certified wine, made with biodynamic grapes. Has fragrant aromas of ginger and cola going for it, though it's less of a powerhouse in terms of flavor. Smooth papery tannins give the wine structure, but the fruit on the palate is pretty pedestrian. **85** *—D.T. (12/31/2005)*

ROCKBARE

RockBare 2003 Chardonnay (McLaren Vale) $13. A light- to medium-weight wine, just the size and profile for a pre-dinner apéritif. Soft in the mouth; we found flavors and aromas of pear and pineapple. On the nose, there's a nutty-toasty accent. **86** *(7/2/2004)*

RockBare 2002 Chardonnay (McLaren Vale) $12. Lime, wildflower, and peach flavors are wrapped in decent acids; the finish is dry and clean. It fills the mouth with fruity flavors that carry through the spicy finish. **85** *—S.H. (10/1/2003)*

RockBare 2001 Chardonnay (McLaren Vale) $12. This powerful, intense wine starts with scents of lemon curd enriched by butter and hints of peach and vanilla. Flavors are similar, but incorporate a saltwater note and an extremely tangy finish, which impart a coarseness that the wine's intensity can't overcome. **85** *—J.C. (9/10/2002)*

RockBare 2002 Shiraz (McLaren Vale) $15. Rich, thick and juicy, bursting with plum, blackberry, cassis, chocolate, and sweetened espresso flavors. A bit soft in the mouth due to low acidity, so that the texture is syrupy. But acidity is high enough. **85** *—S.H. (10/1/2003)*

ROCKFORD

Rockford 2004 Alicante Bouschet (Barossa Valley) $NA. Meant to be served chilled and young, this peppy red has vibrant berry-basket aromas and flavors. It's a fresh, happy wine, very juicy with pure fruit. Goes well with crabcakes, and probably just as well with fiery curries. **89** *—D.T. (3/1/2005)*

Rockford 2001 Rod & Spur Cabernet Blend (Barossa Valley) $NA. A blend of two-thirds Cabernet and a third Shiraz, this is a wine with awesome balance and beautiful, pure plum fruit on the palate. Bouquet shows soft red plum and pine needles. **93** *—D.T. (2/1/2004)*

Rockford 2001 Rifle Ranch Cabernet Sauvignon (Barossa Valley) $40. A beautiful wine whose plum fruit is juicy and pure. Crème brûlée rounds the fruit out on the palate, and lingers on the nose, where there's also some cocoa. Balanced, restrained, and well-behaved, with the capacity to make some noise. Absolutely drinkable now, but one of those wines that you'll just be sad to see go. **94 Editors' Choice** *—D.T. (2/1/2004)*

Rockford 2002 Rifle Range Cabernet Sauvignon (Barossa Valley) $53. This Cabernet is a youthful wine, with tannins that are still grabby. There's a lot to like here—briary, earthy aromas; taut, tightly wound fruit and a fresh eucalyptus bite on the finish. Best to wait a couple of years to see it at its best. **93** *—D.T. (8/1/2005)*

Rockford 2000 Moppa Springs GSM Grenache-Shiraz (Barossa Valley) $40. Sweet red berry and plum aromas on the nose are forward and ripe. On the palate, it's a medium-sized wine with fine tannins and an attractive, chocolate-and-mocha finish. **90** *—D.T. (3/1/2005)*

Rockford 1999 Moppa Springs Red Blend (Barossa Valley) $30. A GSM with fireplace, foresty, wheaty aromas that echo on the palate, where the prime flavors are pine, earth, and red plum. A terrific wine, this wine shows the best of what Grenache can do. **92** *—D.T. (2/1/2004)*

Rockford 2001 Hand Picked Riesling (Eden Valley) $25. Perfume on the nose is beautiful, like light jasmine or honeysuckle. It's a feminine wine, delicately built, with more floral flavors bolstering white stone fruit on the palate. Finishes long. **92 Editors' Choice** —*D.T. (2/1/2004)*

Rockford 2000 Semillon (Barossa Valley) $25. An excellent wine, with smooth, chalky tannins in the mouth followed by a long finish. Resin and lanolin aromas come through on the nose; flavors on the palate are more of the white-peach kind. Just lovely. **90** —*D.T. (2/1/2004)*

Rockford 2001 Basket Press Shiraz (Barossa Valley) $55. Closed on the nose, with traces of mint and black pepper showing through. In the mouth, it's subtle, with juicy black plum flavors and a great, lasting grip on the palate. I could be crazy, but is there a Grand Marnier-esque orange liqueur note on the finish? Winemaker Chris Ringland calls this wine "a baby," and suggests aging for at least 4–5 years. **93** —*D.T. (2/1/2004)*

Rockford NV Black Shiraz (Barossa Valley) $NA. A hard-to-find wine outside of Rockford's mailing list and tasting room (only about 600 cases produced, and they go quickly), but certainly the standard-bearer as far as sparkling Shiraz goes. The average age of Rockford's nonvintage sparkling is 7 years; though it has 23 grams of residual sugar, it tastes just as I'd always envisioned a good sparking Shiraz would: like the still wine, but cold and with bubbles. Plums and juicy berries on the palate, with grape and violet aromas on the nose. Good luck finding it, but certainly grab it if you do. **92** —*D.T. (2/1/2004)*

ROCKY GULLY

Rocky Gully 2004 Dry Riesling (Frankland River) $14. Nimble and understated. Pear and citrus hold the fort down on the palate, surrounded by a cloud of dust and mineral. Just as dusty on the nose. Refreshing and classy; a good opening to an upscale dinner party. **88** —*D.T. (10/1/2005)*

Rocky Gully 2004 Shiraz (Frankland River) $14. Made by the folks at Frankland Estate, this Shiraz contains 5% Viognier, which didn't add the nuances that it typically does. Starts off on the nose with black and green pepper, which turns to toast and ink with some time in the glass. Inky on the palate, yes, but also a touch shrill. **85** —*D.T. (12/1/2005)*

ROLLING

Rolling 2005 Chardonnay (Central Ranges) $13. From vineyards 600 meters above sea level comes a Chard with white peach and mineral notes at its core. On the nose, they're dressed up in a subtle dose of burnt sugar; on the palate, they're backed up with vanilla and floral notes. Soft and even a little oily in feel. 20,000 cases produced. **86** —*D.T. (8/1/2006)*

Rolling 2005 Sauvignon Blanc-Semillon (Central Ranges) $13. Not impressive out of the gate—a pithy, stalky note dominates the palate. But after a few sips, these qualities subside and this very dry wine's gravelly texture starts to grow on you, its mouthwatering finish tempting you to another sip. Pear and melon notes on the nose start it all off. **87** —*D.T. (8/1/2006)*

Rolling 2004 Shiraz (Central Ranges) $13. Tastes more like a junior-varsity Barossa bomb than something out of NSW: The nose is forward and full of confected blueberry, like pie filling or Pop Tart. The fruit on the palate is also moderately forward, dosed with a fair helping of char and maple syrup characters. Made in a style that will likely have wide appeal, but falls on the sweet side. **84** —*D.T. (11/15/2006)*

ROSEMOUNT

Rosemount 1996 Traditional Bordeaux Blend (McLaren Vale) $21. **89** *(11/15/1999)*

Rosemount 2001 Traditional Cabernet Blend (McLaren Vale & Langhorne Creek) $30. Although this is a blend of Cabernet, Merlot, and Petit Verdot, the fruit tastes more red than black. Smells like soft, ripe, red fruit and trading-card bubblegum powder, and tastes quite the same. Fruit is juicy on the palate, with a chalky feel that continues through the finish. A feminine, juicy wine to be enjoyed through 2007. **89** —*D.T. (5/1/2004)*

Rosemount 1999 Traditional Cabernet Blend (McLaren Vale & Langhorne Creek) $7. **88** —*C.S. (12/15/2002)*

Rosemount 2002 Cabernet Sauvignon (South Eastern Australia) $12. Blackberry and bramble aromas on the nose; similar black fruit and oak

flavors on the palate. Tealike tannins on the finish. A good, gets-the-job-done Cab. **84** —*D.T. (3/1/2005)*

Rosemount 1996 Cabernet Sauvignon (South Eastern Australia) $11. **87** *(11/15/1999)*

Rosemount 2001 Diamond Label Cabernet Sauvignon (South Eastern Australia) $11. Medium-bodied and easy to drink, there's sweet plum fruit and oak front and center, with a bran or oak note on the follow-through. Nicely built, and a good value at $11. **86** —*D.T. (12/31/2003)*

Rosemount 2002 Hill of Gold Cabernet Sauvignon (Mudgee) $17. A classy, nice-sized Cab. The nose shows deep black pepper, dried spice, and mixed plums, and the palate—plums, oak, and blackberry—follows suit. Finishes with dry, woodsy tannins. **88** —*D.T. (9/1/2004)*

Rosemount 2000 Hill of Gold Cabernet Sauvignon (Mudgee) $19. Black fruit, spiced meats, and overt wood tones set the stage for a traditional Cabernet palate of cassis, blackberry, clove, and anise. The finish is fully tannic but not harsh, and tasty well-applied oak comes on late with the taste of coffee. This wine has plenty of merits, most of all its impeccable balance. **89** —*M.S. (12/15/2002)*

Rosemount 1999 Hill of Gold Cabernet Sauvignon (Mudgee) $19. Rosemount's new offering opens with a pleasant vanilla, oak, and dark berry fruit nose. On the palate, the fruit takes a backseat to dominant wood. Oak and cedar flavors reign here. It's a little high in acid and tannins to be an easy drinker, and it finishes long and dry with a tart edge. Try with grilled sausages. **85** —*D.T. (9/1/2001)*

Rosemount 1999 Orange Vineyard Cabernet Sauvignon (McLaren Vale & Langhorne Creek) $30. For a wine of this price, there is too much veggie action. In fact, there is far too much in the way of vegetal aromas and flavors for a wine of any price. Yes, it has ample structure and a smooth mouthfeel, but rarely do you encounter a Cabernet that's this underripe. **82** —*M.S. (12/15/2002)*

Rosemount 2002 Show Reserve Cabernet Sauvignon (Coonawarra) $24. Wood, it seems, is what gives this wine most of its character: has tea, spice, and smoke aromas, with tangy, seeped-tea tannins. Medium-bodied, it shows some of the classic Coonawarra clay-soil notes at its heart. **87** —*D.T. (12/1/2005)*

Rosemount 2001 Show Reserve Cabernet Sauvignon (Coonawarra) $24. Smells of black pepper, smoke, and pastry crust. On the palate, yes, it's woody—smoky rather than caramel-sweet, though—with tight plum and briary earth underneath. This score reflects my expectation that more of the fruit will come to the fore in a couple of years; try again in 2006. **90** —*D.T. (8/1/2005)*

Rosemount 2000 Show Reserve Cabernet Sauvignon (Coonawarra) $24. Has the claylike texture that shows the best of Coonawarra. Fruit is black and sturdy, tannins are chalky and smooth. Mocha and clay linger on the finish. An excellent Cabernet with nice texture and judicious oak. **90 Editors' Choice** —*D.T. (10/1/2003)*

Rosemount 1998 Show Reserve Cabernet Sauvignon (Coonawarra) $24. Dense, dark, and young, this beauty is brimming with thrillingly clean, upscale fruit, if you can find it under heavy tannins. It's a well-structured wine with a solid core of blackberry and cassis fruit. Oak is moderate, but noticeable. The overall result is a fancy, very good Cab. **90** —*S.H. (6/1/2001)*

Rosemount 2000 Cabernet Sauvignon-Merlot (South Eastern Australia) $8. Bright fruit, zesty acidity, and soft but adequate tannins mark this enjoyable wine. The aromas and flavors are jammy and young, suggesting heaps of newly picked blackberries. It's dry, and finishes a bit rough and strong. Might even improve with a year or two of age. **86** —*S.H. (6/1/2001)*

Rosemount 2001 Estate Bottled Cabernet Sauvignon-Merlot (South Eastern Australia) $9. For an under-$10 wine, this one delivers some oak, healthy black fruit, and bright acidity. One poke at the nose reveals some barrel char, which persists onto the fresh, tight, and juicy palate. Because it's so forward and bright, nobody will mistake it for flabby; it's really quite the opposite. **86 Best Buy** —*M.S. (12/15/2002)*

Rosemount 1997 Mountain Blue Cabernet Sauvignon-Shiraz (Mudgee) $40. **89** —*M.S. (10/1/2000)*

Rosemount 1999 Chardonnay (South Eastern Australia) $12. 85 —M.M. (10/1/2000)

Rosemount 2003 Chardonnay (South Eastern Australia) $10. A perennial value-priced favorite, and easy to find. The mouthfeel in this edition is odd—strangely chalky, or milky. But its zingy lemon zest and yellow peach aromas are nice, as is the stone fruit playing prominently on the palate. **84** —D.T. (12/31/2004)

Rosemount 2004 Diamond Label Chardonnay (South Eastern Australia) $10. Though the nose doesn't show much—just a little hay—the palate doles out plenty of soft peach-fuzz flavors, plus some anise. 150,000 cases produced. **84** —D.T. (10/1/2005)

Rosemount 2003 Diamond Label Chardonnay (South Eastern Australia) $10. Nose shows nougat, hickory smoke, nut, and light pear aromas. Pear is the big player on the palate, too, where it's accented by vanilla and couched in a full, almost viscous, mouthfeel. Finishes with smooth oak and chalk. **86 Best Buy** (7/2/2004)

Rosemount 2002 Diamond Label Chardonnay (South Eastern Australia) $10. Medium-bodied and soft in the mouth, this Chard has nice floral and pear aromas, and stone fruits dusted with a smidge of powdered sugar. A good large-gathering wine, but isn't that when you first tried it, too? **86** —D.T. (8/1/2003)

Rosemount 2000 Diamond Label Chardonnay (South Eastern Australia) $10. From one of Down Under's most dependable wineries, this rich, fragrant wine has lots to offer. There's plenty of ripe peach and tropical fruit and also a wallop of oak. It's full-flavored, and finishes spicy and a little sweet. **88 Best Buy** —S.H. (9/1/2001)

Rosemount 2000 Estate Bottled Chardonnay (South Eastern Australia) $10. Mainstream Chardonnay has been a mainstay for this dependable and recently-merged-with-Southcorp family enterprise. The orange and mild tropical fruit bouquet has just a kiss of oak, and some mild spice notes enter on the palate. The even mouthfeel and just slightly tangy finish keep this lightly sweet and sour, round—but not mushy—wine right on target. **86** —M.M. (6/1/2001)

Rosemount 1998 Giant's Creek Chardonnay (Hunter Valley) $17. Here's one of the bigger Chards of the year. Explodes with aromas of butterscotch, caramel, vanilla, and, oh yes, tropical fruits. The flavors are mouth-filling and rich, like a sweet, custardy, creamy, tangerine-flavored dessert, yet it's dry. However, it loses a few points for being too big and aggressive without the necessary balance. It's awkward. **87** —S.H. (6/1/2001)

Rosemount 2002 Giants Creek Chardonnay (Hunter Valley) $17. This is a medium-bodied wine, with not a lot of stuffing but some interesting flavors. Smolders with butterscotch, cinammon, and woodsmoke on the nose, against a backdrop of Golden Delicious apples. Palate flavors are similar, but not quite as pronounced—dried spices, honey, peach skin. Tasted twice. **85** (7/2/2004)

Rosemount 2001 Giants Creek Chardonnay (Hunter Valley) $17. Fermented with its natural yeasts, this Chardonnay has a honeysuckle nose accented by marshmallow. The peach and mango flavors have a trace of curry, and the creamy, nutty mouthfeel finishes with an even balance. **88** (2/1/2003)

Rosemount 1999 Giants Creek Chardonnay (Hunter Valley) $17. Big butterscotch—aromas and flavors—come close to drowning out some of the finer nuances of this wine, which include green apples, citrus fruits, and dried spices. Spicy oak and tart lemons linger on the finish. **84** — J.C. (7/1/2002)

Rosemount 2004 Hill of Gold Chardonnay (Mudgee) $13. Nutty, peachy aromas; similar flavors, plus flashes of white pepper, come through on the palate. Wide and soft but not full, easy but not profound. **86** —D.T. (8/1/2006)

Rosemount 2002 Hill of Gold Chardonnay (Mudgee) $17. Smoke and wood set off approachable yellow fruit on the palate, both of which follow through to the finish. Smoke, biscuit, and white pepper aromas don't make it to the palate, but were nice while they lasted. **87** —D.T. (10/1/2003)

Rosemount 2001 Hill of Gold Chardonnay (Mudgee) $17. A lean, toasty style that pairs dried spices—cinnamon and ginger—with zesty citrus fruits. The toast and vanilla battle green and lime flavors from the nose all the way through the finish. **85** —J.C. (7/1/2002)

Rosemount 2000 Hill of Gold Chardonnay (Mudgee) $17. Lemony and zingy are buzz words for this bouquet—expect the same citrusy tang on the palate as well. Mouthfeel, given the high acidity and citrusy notes, is best described as clean. Finish is medium-length, with apple and oak flavors, and acid that gives the back end another dash of unwelcome tartness. **82** —D.T. (9/1/2001)

Rosemount 2002 Orange Vineyard Chardonnay (Orange) $23. Has toasty, bready aromas backed up by green apple and pear. It's medium-weight, and not a very expressive wine, with some peach and buttered toast flavors peeking out on the palate. Finishes slightly herbal. **85** (7/2/2004)

Rosemount 2001 Orange Vineyard Chardonnay (Orange) $22. A cooler climate Chardonnay that has hints of white peach and orange peel in the nose. Nutmeg, ash, and stone fruit in the palate finish with lively acidity. **88** (2/1/2003)

Rosemount 1998 Orange Vyd Chardonnay (Hunter Valley) $22. 91 (11/15/1999)

Rosemount 1999 Rose Label Orange Vineyard Chardonnay (Orange) $23. Raciness, class, and breed mark this delicious wine. With its bright, tropical fruit and spice aromas and bold, rich flavors, it's a delight from start to finish. Crisp acidity carries waves of ripe extract through the long finish. **91 Editors' Choice** —S.H. (9/1/2001)

Rosemount 2002 Roxburgh Chardonnay (Hunter Valley) $25. Rosemount's most famous Chard is a success again, with ample nut, vanilla bean, hickory, grilled meat, and stone fruit flavors, coming to a lemony point on the finish. A flamboyant style of wine, its smokiness a fine complement to fresh-off-the-grill seafood. **89** —D.T. (4/1/2006)

Rosemount 2001 Roxburgh Chardonnay (Hunter Valley) $30. Lots of caramel, smoke, and vanilla aromas show the oak treatment on this wine. The spicy pink and green peppercorn flavors combine with a full, complex finish in a unique Chardonnay. **89** (2/1/2003)

Rosemount 1998 Roxburgh Chardonnay (Hunter Valley) $30. Lemon and lime are the aromas, mingled with the smoky vanillins of oak and a lot of leesy notes. It's a tight wine, lean in flavor, steely in texture. Don't look for enormous fruit. This is an angular, structured wine with high acidity, meant for aging. **86** —S.H. (9/1/2001)

Rosemount 2004 Show Reserve Chardonnay (Hunter Valley) $20. Light cream and vanilla aromas; the wine has light citrus flavors with modest stone fruit, floral, and sawdust accents. Linear on the palate, and finishes with a touch of oak. **87** —D.T. (4/1/2006)

Rosemount 2003 Show Reserve Chardonnay (Hunter Valley) $20. This is a very good Chard, featuring toast, citrus, and tropical fruit aromas, and yellow stone fruit and toast flavors. Its recipe may be predictable, but the wine follows it well. **87** —D.T. (10/1/2005)

Rosemount 2002 Show Reserve Chardonnay (Hunter Valley) $15. A taut, wound-up wine, and dry on the palate. Yellow stone fruit is dressed in heavy helpings of butter, caramel, and toast. Our rating is conservative, perhaps, if you like your wines well-wooded. **85** (7/2/2004)

Rosemount 2001 Show Reserve Chardonnay (Hunter Valley) $18. Aromas of butterscotch, toast, and anise combine with tropical fruit flavors. The finish is clean with a slight minerality that adds complexity. **86** (2/1/2003)

Rosemount 1999 Show Reserve Chardonnay (Hunter Valley) $18. Powerful and clean, this Chard opens with pronounced aromas of citrus and peaches, underscored by honey, smoke, and butter. The wine is tight and complex, seemingly wrapped in a minerally, iron straightjacket now, but with good aging possibilities; the long finish also supports this hypothesis. High acidity boosts the impression of strength and cleanliness. **92 Editors' Choice** —S.H. (6/1/2001)

Rosemount 2002 Giants Creek Chardonnay-Viognier (Hunter Valley) $17. This pretty Hunter white offers up citrus, vanilla, and nut aromas, with more nuttiness on the palate. Round and creamy, with firm pineapple and peach flavors dominating. **88** —D.T. (4/1/2006)

Rosemount 2002 Merlot (South Eastern Australia) $12. Cola aromas preface mixed berry fruit on the palate. A fine red quaffing wine at a good price; not very varietally distinct. **84** —D.T. (3/1/2005)

AUSTRALIA

Rosemount 2003 Diamond Label Merlot (South Eastern Australia) $12. Aromas are lactic and creamy out of the gate, and go sweet and candied with air. Fruit on the palate is lackluster, the smooth wood flavors and feel dominating. **83** —*D.T. (12/31/2005)*

Rosemount 2000 Diamond Label Merlot (South Eastern Australia) $11. An easy-drinkin' Merlot, medium-bodied, with plum fruit and earth flavors. Fruit gets fleshier and redder toward the back end. One to drink now, and share at the neighborhood block party. **86** —*D.T. (6/1/2003)*

Rosemount 1999 Diamond Label Merlot (South Eastern Australia) $11. A first-rate Merlot, this big-boned wine has juicy, rich flavors that explode out of the glass and last right through the rich, long finish. It's generous, but well-made, with nice oak shadings. This is the kind of wine to lug along to the beach. Everyone will like it. **87 Best Buy** —*S.H. (9/1/2001)*

Rosemount 1999 Orange Vineyard Merlot (Orange) $26. Sturdy and straightforward; a little tight, perhaps, but a well-made wine with firm red plum and cherry fruit on the palate. Dry soil and drying woody tannins make up the balance; the tannins get tea-like on the back end. **86** —*D.T. (6/1/2003)*

Rosemount 1998 Orange Vineyard Merlot (Orange) $26. Darkly colored and flavored, this Merlot shows lots of toasty oak wrapped around a core of berry and black plum flavors. The mouthfeel is even and smooth, but the spicy finish turns a bit woody, picking up a dry, tart edge as the oak takes over. Tastes rather like a Cabernet, with its dark hue and flavor range. **89** *(9/1/2001)*

Rosemount 2004 Pinot Noir (South Eastern Australia) $12. Tastes like it smells: like soft, sweetish plums and raspberries, touched up by toast and vanilla. It's not a powerhouse Pinot, but is a fine intro to the variety at a decent price. 23,500 cases produced. **84** —*D.T. (12/1/2005)*

Rosemount 2003 Pinot Noir (South Eastern Australia) $12. An easy-to-approach, entry-level Pinot that lacks that je ne sais quoi that make people love the variety, or detest it. Nose shows distinctly orange-citrus aromas. Fruit on the palate is red; has some cherry verve at its core and fades into a peppery finish. **84** —*D.T. (12/31/2004)*

Rosemount 2005 Diamond Label Pinot Noir (South Eastern Australia) $12. On the nose, this Pinot has a milky, minerally character that makes a textural re-appearance on the palate. Flavors flirt with black cherry and black pepper, with green herb on the finish. **84** —*D.T. (11/15/2006)*

Rosemount 2001 Diamond Label Pinot Noir (South Eastern Australia) $12. This is a bigger, more forceful wine than its Lindemans stablemate, but not quite as charming. The flavors are earthy and dark, featuring hints of cola and root beer. Finishes with drying tannins. **83** —*J.C. (9/1/2002)*

Rosemount 1999 Diamond Label Pinot Noir (South Eastern Australia) $12. A gentle fruitiness marks this approachable, drink-me-now wine. Offers pretty black cherry Pinot Noir character with tobacco and earth accents that follow right through the long, sweet fruit finish with its modest hint of tannins. This is not a complex Pinot, but it's a very appealing one. **87 Best Buy** —*S.H. (9/1/2001)*

Rosemount 2001 Grenache-Shiraz Red Blend (Australia) $9. Simple, sweet-tasting and slightly candied, this bouncy drink is best served slightly chilled. Think of it as an introduction to wine—something to explore after white Zinfandel. **83** —*J.C. (9/1/2002)*

Rosemount 1999 GSM Grenache Syrah Mourvedre Red Blend (McLaren Vale) $30. The small (10%) Mourvèdre component provides an interesting horsey nuance to the aromas, while the engine driving this blend is the Grenache (50%), which contributes rich, juicy cherries. It's full bodied and ultrasmooth—almost creamy—on the palate, finishing with supple tannins. Drink now–2006. **90** —*J.C. (9/1/2002)*

Rosemount 2000 GSM Grenache Syrah Mouvedre Red Blend (Barossa Valley) $30. This well-integrated blend boasts blueberry and black pepper aromas. The gamy flavors, reminiscent of barbecue, mesh with chocolate and dark fruits. The finish is toasty, spicy, and big. **89** *(2/1/2003)*

Rosemount 2000 Grenache-Shiraz Rhône Red Blend (South Eastern Australia) $8. Is this Australia's answer to Beaujolais? The sweet, black cherries are accented by tart red berries fore (on the nose) and aft (on the finish). Some sweet caramel flavors and negligible tannins make this easy to gulp. **87 Best Buy** —*J.C. (9/1/2001)*

Rosemount 2001 GSM Rhône Red Blend (McLaren Vale & Langhorne Creek) $30. Aromas are lovely, of cherries, berries, and pastry crust. Fruit on the palate is red and juicy, yet taut, though there's just a hint of cherry or rhubarb. A food-friendly wine, one that would work well with any number of dishes. **89** —*D.T. (5/1/2004)*

Rosemount 2003 Riesling (South Eastern Australia) $10. Light floral and honeysuckle aromas are very pretty and compelling, as is the wine's citrus-laden palate. What an introduction to the variety—it's a good value, it's correct, and it's dry. Worth keeping a few bottles around the house. **87 Best Buy** —*D.T. (3/1/2005)*

Rosemount 2005 Diamond Label Riesling (South Eastern Australia) $10. Honey, beeswax, and light banana cream aromas get this value-priced Riesling going. On the palate, it's round and has just a hint of sweetness couched in stone fruit and mineral flavors. **85 Best Buy** —*D.T. (4/1/2006)*

Rosemount 2004 Diamond Label Riesling (South Eastern Australia) $10. This is a good cocktail-party Riesling, medium-sized (maybe a little heavy?), without the bracing acidity that enthusiasts either love or don't about the variety. This bottling deals fresh cream aromas, with lemon and peach skin flavors. 14,000 cases produced. **85 Best Buy** —*D.T. (12/1/2005)*

Rosemount 2001 Estate Bottled Riesling (South Eastern Australia) $9. With banana and other tropical fruit flavors, though not exactly weighty, this Riesling's medium body feels heavy compared to zippier Clare Valley renditions. Still, it's a nice, easy-drinking wine, and just the sort of wine you need to win Chard fanatics over to a new white. **86** —*D.T. (8/1/2003)*

Rosemount 2002 Sauvignon Blanc (South Eastern Australia) $10. A straightforward Sauvignon Blanc, and one that just hints at the zest that Sauvignon Blanc can have. There's pineapple, lime, and citrus here; kicked up a few more notches, it could be even better. **85** —*D.T. (10/1/2003)*

Rosemount 2001 Sauvignon Blanc (South Eastern Australia) $10. Subtle fresh, green notes give this Sauvignon Blanc a clean, dry mouthfeel and make it a good accompaniment to rich foods. Lime and floral notes dominate the bouquet; fresh green herb, green apple, and a little passion fruit brighten the palate. Finishes dry, with tangy lime and mineral notes. **84** —*D.T. (2/1/2002)*

Rosemount 2000 Estate Bottled Sauvignon Blanc (South Eastern Australia) $10. This is a little soft and low–acid but the fruit aromas and flavors are quite pleasant, with pineapple and grapefruit predominating. There's some weight, even a succulent quality—to the fruit that keeps the flavor and texture lingering on the back end. **85** —*J.F. (9/1/2001)*

Rosemount 2003 Semillon (South Eastern Australia) $10. This is a fun, easily quaffed wine—a pretty overt version of Semillon, though, showing vibrant flavors and aromas of yellow peach, citrus, and banana. Softish in the mouth, but approachable, with a dry apple-skin flavor on the finish. **85 Best Buy** —*D.T. (8/1/2005)*

Rosemount 2000 Semillon (South Eastern Australia) $NA. Very green. Weedy, legumey notes on the nose are offset slightly by cream and flour. Lima bean and tart citrus notes prevail in the mouth; finishes with tart, lime-rind, stone and herb notes. **82** —*D.T. (2/1/2002)*

Rosemount 2000 Diamond Label Bottled Semillon (South Eastern Australia) $10. This dry and racy wine begins with a bang: grapefruit, passion fruit, pear, and fig scents burst from the glass. Turns tart on the palate, with lemon accents over fig, citrus, and hay flavors. The finish is tangy with a slightly bitter citrus-pith note. **85** —*J.C. (9/1/2001)*

Rosemount 2002 Semillon-Chardonnay (South Eastern Australia) $8. A tasty white, with wide yellow fruit (citrus, plus some tropical fruit) flavors that extend to the back end. It smells as it tastes—it's not complicated, but that doesn't mean that it's not good. **86 Best Buy** —*D.T. (10/1/2003)*

Rosemount 2003 Shiraz (South Eastern Australia) $12. A very good year for the Diamond Label Shiraz. It's a chunky, sturdy red with mixed plums and a ribbon of mocha or chocolate from the nose through to the finish. Not overdone, and very enjoyable. **87 Best Buy** —*D.T. (3/1/2005)*

Rosemount 2004 Diamond Label Shiraz (South Eastern Australia) $12. Nose shows a little brambly earthiness. The wine is quite dark in color, but lackluster in its body and plum flavors. **82** —*D.T. (10/1/2006)*

Rosemount 2002 Diamond Label Shiraz (South Eastern Australia) $12. This is Everyman's Shiraz, made to appeal to the masses—and appeal it does with bouncy mixed fruit, medium body, and judicious oak. The nose, too, will reel the crowds in, with its jammy grape and raspberry fruit. **85** —*D.T. (10/1/2003)*

Rosemount 2001 Diamond Label Shiraz (South Eastern Australia) $12. Filled with bright, bouncy cherry-berry fruit and imbued with a slightly viscous mouthfeel, this fun, gulpable Shiraz won't break the bank. Its easygoing nature makes it worth having on hand for your next barbecue. **87** —*J.C. (9/1/2002)*

Rosemount 1999 Diamond Label Shiraz (South Eastern Australia) $11. 87 Best Buy —*M.S. (10/1/2000)*

Rosemount 2001 Estate Bottled Shiraz (South Eastern Australia) $10. Deep aromas of baked black fruit and berry syrup come together on the hefty, very ripe nose. The palate is persistent and offers depth, but the fruit seems a tad overdone and murky. If richness and a soft texture are what you're after, then this wine will suffice. Just don't expect much acidity or complexity. **86** —*M.S. (3/1/2003)*

Rosemount 2003 Hill of Gold Shiraz (Mudgee) $17. Earthier, oakier notes prevail in this wine, with sour plums buried deep beneath. Aromas are of tea, bramble, and plum. A straightforward wine, not too nuanced. **85** —*D.T. (10/1/2005)*

Rosemount 2002 Hill of Gold Shiraz (Mudgee) $17. Earth and dried spice accents are in abundance here, as is cherry fruit. The combination makes an already dry mouthfeel feel even drier. A good candidate for the dinner table, particularly the next time you have a rich sauce or gravy on the menu. **86** —*D.T. (11/15/2004)*

Rosemount 2000 Hill of Gold Shiraz (Mudgee) $19. Bright yet deep blackberry aromas are a bit herbaceous. The flavors of ginger, brown earth, and black fruit finish with soft tannins and an even balance. **86** *(2/1/2003)*

Rosemount 1999 Hill of Gold Shiraz (Mudgee) $18. Though well-oaked, the wood used is beautifully integrated in this full, round, suave red. Plum, chocolate, and licorice elements accented by smoke and mint provide plenty of flavor. A touch soft on the palate, the sweet and sour finish firms up with dusty, even tannins. **89 Editors' Choice** *(10/1/2001)*

Rosemount 1999 Orange Vineyard Shiraz (Orange) $26. Smoky oak and licorice notes lead the way, backed by pretty cherry, blackberry, and herb flavors. Bright on the finish. **87** —*J.M. (12/15/2002)*

Rosemount 2001 Show Reserve Shiraz (South Australia) $24. Though the nose is dominated by dark fruit and some anise, with wood accents, what you get on the palate is the opposite. Ripe berry fruit is secondary to a flat, heavy veneer of oak. The wood isn't manifesting itself as toast; it's just wood, and a fair amount of it. Maybe it will integrate with time? **86** —*D.T. (12/31/2005)*

Rosemount 2000 Show Reserve Shiraz (McLaren Vale & Langhorne Creek) $24. Medium-bodied, borderline big, really; nice, dusty tannins swathe a core of ripe red plums and raspberries. Opens and closes with oak's signature spice and black peppery notes. **88** —*D.T. (6/1/2003)*

Rosemount 1999 Show Reserve Shiraz (McLaren Vale & Langhorne Creek) $24. Powerful aromatics feature cloves and black currants. Toasty black fruit flavors are medium-bodied, with drying tannins. **86** *(2/1/2003)*

Rosemount 2001 Estate Bottled Shiraz-Cabernet Sauvignon (South Australia/Victoria) $8. 87 Best Buy —*S.H. (11/15/2002)*

Rosemount 1999 Mountain Blue Shiraz-Cabernet Sauvignon (Mudgee) $50. Aromas of eucalyptus, mint, and wet clay signal a quality wine. The wine has blackberry fruit and a finish that combines sweet molasses and gravelly tannins. May be enjoyed now or will hold up to a few years in the cellar. **91** *(2/1/2003)*

Rosemount 2001 Balmoral Syrah (McLaren Vale) $50. Smells of black soot and barbecue spice. Fruit the palate is a liqueurish blackberry, but there is also loads of chunky wood framing it. The combination is a burly one,

but aging it might see the fruit fade before the oak. Drink now with a big, rich stew or like foods. **89** —*D.T. (11/15/2006)*

Rosemount 2000 Balmoral Syrah (McLaren Vale) $50. Solid and excellent, as it almost always is. Plum fruit dominates, with anise accents; tannins are smooth. Wood is present but subtle—mouthfeel is textured more like clay than oak. **90** —*D.T. (12/31/2003)*

Rosemount 1999 Balmoral Syrah (McLaren Vale) $50. This is what Syrah was meant to taste like. It has big blackberry flavors mixed with nutmeg and clove, which give it great complexity and depth. The finish is full and long. Drink 2004–2012. **92** *(2/1/2003)*

Rosemount 1998 Balmoral Syrah (McLaren Vale) $50. Super-black and super-dry—if you can handle the truth about the Balmoral, and you're still reading this review, you'll love it. Reviewers appreciated the wine's deep blackberry, toast, and chocolate aromas, as well as its blackberry and black pepper flavors (offset by a slight vanilla creaminess). Mouthfeel is full and well balanced, with tannins to spare. **90** *(11/1/2001)*

Rosemount 1997 Balmoral Syrah (McLaren Vale) $50. 93 —*M.S. (10/1/2000)*

Rosemount 2001 Chardonnay-Semillon White Blend (South Eastern Australia) $8. Though it's 51 percent Chardonnay, this blend still retains a clean, angular mouthfeel that speaks more of its Semillon component. Pear, buttercream frosting, and toast mark the bouquet; in the mouth, a bit of cream keeps the green apple and lemon-lime flavors from being too tangy. Citrus pith flavors brighten up the back end. **85 Best Buy** —*D.T. (2/1/2002)*

Rosemount 2002 Diamond Label White Blend (South Eastern Australia) $9. 86 —*D.T. (10/1/2003)*

Rosemount 2002 Diamond Label Chardonnay-Semillon White Blend (South Eastern Australia) $10. A straight-shooting, tasty white, with wide yellow fruit (citrus, plus some tropical fruit) flavors that extend to the back end. It smells as it tastes—it's not complicated, but that doesn't mean that it's not good. **86** —*D.T. (10/1/2003)*

Rosemount 2005 Diamond Label Traminer Riesling White Blend (South Eastern Australia) $10. Lemon candy and floral aromas are cloying. It's sweet and soft on the palate, and finishes watery. **81** —*D.T. (8/1/2006)*

Rosemount 2004 Diamond Label Traminer Riesling White Blend (South Eastern Australia) $8. Oy. I know this Gewürztraminer (56%)–Riesling (44%) is the sweetest wine in the Diamond Label series, but, having tasted it blind, it still managed to shock my palate. Offers aromas of canned peach juice and pineapple, with sweet, simple tropical fruit on the palate. Soft, with a little spritz. **80** —*D.T. (12/1/2005)*

Rosemount 2002 Estate Bottled Traminer-Riesling White Blend (South Eastern Australia) $9. 83 —*D.T. (10/1/2003)*

Rosemount 2001 Traminer-Riesling White Blend (South Eastern Australia) $8. Loads of peach and tropical fruit aromas make for a super-sweet nose—a sneak preview, really, of what's to come on the palate. Bright apple, peach, and honey flavors play in the mouth. Sweetness tapers off on the finish, where mineral notes take over. Will win fans among novice enthusiasts and white Zin fans. **83** —*D.T. (2/1/2002)*

ROSENBLUM

Rosenblum 2001 Feather Foot Man Jingalu Special Artist Series Shiraz (McLaren Vale) $31. Pure, unadulterated Aussie Shiraz, a big, rich wine exploding with jammy blackberry, black cherry, tobacco and sage flavors. Bone dry, with big bones. The tannins are negotiable and young, with vibrant acidity. Will benefit from midterm aging. **90** —*S.H. (1/1/2002)*

ROSS ESTATE

Ross Estate 1999 Bordeaux Blend (Barossa Valley) $20. Powerful oaking marks the aromas of this wine, which feature scents of toast, butter, cream, and dill; the finish is likewise woody and dry. In between is a big-boned, cherry-flavored wine that lacks a bit of flesh. Still, the oak provides a sexy if somewhat superficial mouthful. **85** —*J.C. (6/1/2002)*

Ross Estate 1999 Cabernet Sauvignon (Barossa Valley) $20. 89 —*C.S. (6/1/2002)*

Ross Estate 2001 Chardonnay (Barossa Valley) $12. Musky spiced pear and melon aromas lead off, backed up by lush ripe pear and melon fla-

■ WINE ENTHUSIAST ESSENTIAL BUYING GUIDE 2008 ■

vors. Finishes with a tasty blend of tart pineapple and peppery, clove-like spice. **87** —*J.C. (7/1/2002)*

Ross Estate 2003 Old Vine Grenache (Barossa Valley) $20. Barossa fans should be seeking out the well-priced offerings from Ross Estate. This Grenache, from vines more than 80 years old, starts off with dark notes of coffee and plum, then gradually reveals dried cherries accented by hints of spice. The texture is creamy and lush, the finish mouthwatering and long. Drink now–2012. **91 Editors' Choice** —*J.C. (12/15/2006)*

Ross Estate 1999 Old Vine Grenache (Barossa Valley) $18. Like many Aussie Grenaches, this is a soft, forward wine that's made for early consumption. But the alcohol is in balance with the juicy cherry fruit and the oak is well-integrated, adding dried spices and a hint of chocolate without becoming overpowering. **89** —*J.C. (9/1/2002)*

Ross Estate 2000 Semillon (Barossa Valley) $12. Despite its "unwooded" status, there are plenty of smoky, toasty notes—a hallmark of Oz Semillon. Anise and grapefruit scents add depth and complexity. Flavors are broad and ripe-feeling, but there's a persistent note of stewed peppers as well. **87** —*J.C. (2/1/2002)*

Ross Estate 2000 Shiraz (Barossa Valley) $20. A very good wine, though nothing out of the ordinary, in terms of quality, for Barossa. Offers toasty oak and plum fruit on both nose and palate; finishes with herb and a calcium-mineral note. **87** —*D.T. (3/1/2003)*

Ross Estate 2002 North Ridge Shiraz (Barossa Valley) $18. Ross Estate is only several years old, but winemaker Rod Chapman is a long-time veteran, and his North Ridge Shiraz is a knockout for the price. Dense aromas of fruitcake and spice ease out of the glass, while the flavors follow a similar trajectory—rich and a touch syrupy, with dried fruit and spice notes that are distinctly Barossa. Finishes with a dusty, layered feel to its tannins, suggesting a drinking window of 2008–2015. **91 Editors' Choice** —*J.C. (12/15/2006)*

ROTHBURY ESTATE

Rothbury Estate 2001 Cabernet Sauvignon (South Eastern Australia) $7. Round and creamy in the mouth, with fine tannins, this is a drink-now Cab that is just the right weight to be enjoyed with food. Plum and cherry fruit in the mouth dries out on the finish, with the help of some smooth tannins. **87 Best Buy** —*D.T. (10/1/2003)*

Rothbury Estate 2002 Chardonnay (South Eastern Australia) $8. Bright gold in color, this wine's all about sweet tropical fruit, particularly pineapple and passion fruit. An undercurrent of smokiness on both the nose and the palate adds interest and complexity. **85** —*D.T. (8/1/2003)*

Rothbury Estate 2001 Chardonnay (South Eastern Australia) $8. This deliciously full-bodied and rich Chardonnay is unabashedly New World in style. From its caramel and tropical fruit aromas through its flavors of Golden Delicious apples, mango, vanilla, and baking spices, it screams "Australia." **90 Best Buy** —*J.C. (7/1/2002)*

Rothbury Estate 1998 Chardonnay (South Eastern Australia) $8. 86 Best Buy —*M.S. (10/1/2000)*

Rothbury Estate 2002 Brokenback Chardonnay (Hunter Valley) $30. This Hunter wine shows light peach and citrus aromas and flavors. Its feel, though, is crystalline, unyielding and hard to warm up to. Finishes lemony and hard, with a little toasted wood. Tasted twice. **84** *(7/2/2004)*

Rothbury Estate 2001 Brokenback Chardonnay (Hunter Valley) $30. This Hunter wine shows light peach and citrus aromas and flavors. Its feel, though, is crystalline, unyielding, and hard to warm up to. Finishes lemony and hard, with a little toasted wood. **84** *(7/2/2004)*

Rothbury Estate 2001 Shiraz (South Eastern Australia) $7. Jammy and rich, this dry wine has some hefty tannins, but can be enjoyed now with big foods. It's simple and direct and tart and straightforward, a clean wine with flavors of blackberries. **85 Best Buy** —*S.H. (12/15/2002)*

Rothbury Estate 1999 Brokenback Shiraz (Hunter Valley) $34. The plum and cherry fruit on the palate is pretty bouncy, but is tempered by oak and earth. An interesting meaty-saltiness (like cured meat) shows on the nose and on the finish. This is a very good wine, with tannins that are approachable even now. **89** —*D.T. (12/31/2003)*

RUFUS STONE

Rufus Stone 1998 Shiraz (McLaren Vale) $30. Toast and matchstick notes on the nose are met with, depending who you talk to, either grape Hi-C aromas, or dark, musky ones. We had just as many arguments about what was happening on the palate, but if grapes, menthol, black-tea, or tart black-cherry flavors sound good to you, you're in luck. Medium-weight and well balanced, finishing with tart, peppery oak flavors. **88** *(11/1/2001)*

RUMBALL

Rumball NV M3 Coonawarra Cuvée Sparkling Merlot (Coonawarra) $28. Sparkling reds are a bit of an acquired taste, but this is a relatively easy introduction. Raspberry fruit is laced with chocolate and vanilla flavors that come across as reasonably balanced in weight, but with a touch of sweetness on the finish. **85** —*J.C. (12/31/2006)*

Rumball NV SB13 Sparkling Shiraz (South Eastern Australia) $26. Very dark and intense, this decidedly acquired taste is nonetheless very impressive. A serious Shiraz with bubbles, this shows deep black cherry, earth, soy, and coffee aromas and flavors. Medium-weight, with an even bead, it finishes long, dry, and complex. Recommended for the adventurous palate. **90 Editors' Choice** —*M.M. (12/1/2001)*

Rumball NV SB16 Coonawarra Cuvée Sparkling Shiraz (Coonawarra) $26. One of the best-known sparkling Shiraz makers in Australia, Peter Rumball's Coonawarra version offers some stewy fruit aromas and flavors, and caramel accents on the palate. However dark its flavors sound, it's still feels fresh on the palate. Finishes short. **84** —*D.T. (12/31/2004)*

Rumball NV SB17 Coonawarra Cuvée Sparkling Shiraz (Coonawarra) $27. Has some herbal, medicinal overtones to the bouquet, which is otherwise rather fruity and appealing, while the strawberry and cherry flavors are slightly piney or resinous. Medium in weight, it retains a sense of freshness on the finish that makes it drinkable on its own or with food. **86** —*J.C. (12/31/2006)*

RUTHERGLEN ESTATES

Rutherglen Estates 2004 Red Red Blend (Rutherglen) $12. Made of 85% Shiraz and 15% Petite Sirah, this red shows a lot of alcohol on the nose along with overripe plum flavors. Thin and short on the finish. **82** —*D.T. (11/15/2006)*

Rutherglen Estates 2004 The Reunion Red Blend (Rutherglen) $15. A blend of 40% Mourvèdre, 35% Shiraz, and 25% Grenache; it's a lighter-body wine, full of black cherry flavors and ready to drink now. Finishes with a smoky-char note. **87** —*D.T. (4/1/2006)*

Rutherglen Estates 2004 The Alliance White Blend (Rutherglen) $14. A 70-30 blend of Marsanne and Viognier, the Alliance is an interesting wine but is not one with a lot of concentrated flavor and verve. Offers aromas of wheat cracker and sour apple candy, and flavors of peach, flowers, and olive oil. Smooth and slightly oily on the palate; its texture thickens on the finish. 500 cases produced. **86** —*D.T. (10/1/2006)*

RYMILL

Rymill 1996 Shiraz (Coonawarra) $17. 90 *(4/1/2000)*

SAINT JOHN'S ROAD

Saint John's Road 2003 Old Vine Semillon (Barossa Valley) $20. Fans of fat Chards: this isn't much of a leap from what you're used to. Very bright green-gold in color, and very buttery from nose to finish. The palate has an oily, hard-candyish feel with decent length on the finish. Will have its fans. **84** —*D.T. (3/1/2005)*

SALENA ESTATE

Salena Estate 2001 Cabernet Sauvignon Cabernet Blend (South Australia) $10. Simple and fruity, with soft, cassis flavors. Alcohol shows through a bit on the finish. **84** *(9/2/2004)*

Salena Estate 2000 Ellen Landing Cabernet Sauvignon (Riverland) $18. 83 —*M.S. (12/15/2002)*

Salena Estate 1999 Ellen Landing Cabernet Sauvignon (South Eastern Australia) $18. Best for those who aren't sensitive to oak, the Ellen Landing offers hefty samplings of wood from nose to finish. In supporting roles are red berries on the nose, and blackberries in the mouth. Its rustic tannins may inspire a Survivor-like camping expedition. **84** —*D. T.* *(6/1/2002)*

Salena Estate 2003 Chardonnay (Riverland) $10. Jasmine, honey, and pear aromas lead to honey and pear flavors on the palate. Standard, and enjoyable—particularly if it's well chilled, and drunk with sand between your toes. **86 Best Buy** *(7/2/2004)*

Salena Estate 2001 Chardonnay (Riverland) $11. This warm-climate Chard shows its origins in its ripe, sweet peach-nectar aromas, kissed with caramel and smoke. Weighty in the mouth—close to syrupy—then it finishes cleanly in a burst of tart, lime-like acidity. **85** —*J.C.* *(7/1/2002)*

Salena Estate 2002 Merlot (South Australia) $10. Like all of the Salena reds, this offers a plump, juicy mouthfeel and simple, varietally correct flavors. In this case, there are hints of cherry and mocha and some tart acids on the finish. **84** *(9/2/2004)*

Salena Estate 2000 Merlot (Riverland) $11. Riverland is an appellation in South Australia known for inexpensive but quality wines and this is no exception. Aromas of raspberry are laced with cinnamon; bright cherry flavors accented with spice finish light and soft for a well-made, good-value Merlot. **86** —*C.S.* *(6/1/2002)*

Salena Estate 2001 Petite Verdot (South Australia) $10. Stands out for its olivey, peppery nose, followed by plump, grapey flavors and a dash of meaty complexity. Fire up the barbie and break out the lamb chops. **86 Best Buy** *(9/2/2004)*

Salena Estate 2001 Shiraz (South Australia) $10. Medium-weight Shiraz, with smoky leathery notes that play off against dark, pruny fruit. A solid farmhouse-style red for rustic dishes. **85** *(9/2/2004)*

Salena Estate 1999 Shiraz (Riverland) $12. There's so much going on in the '99 Salena Estate, that it can't help but please everyone: Juicy black-berries are front and center on the nose and in the mouth; cedar, tobacco, and dried herbs give the palate added complexity. Big, chewy mouthfeel? Check. Chocolate, vanilla, and truffle aromas will throw you for a loop; even tannins, and licorice and mineral flavors, tie this Shiraz up nicely. **89 Best Buy** *(10/1/2001)*

SALISBURY

Salisbury 1999 Shiraz (South Eastern Australia) $8. Jammy but not insubstantial, this straightforward wine delivers ripe, juicy berry flavors atop a light but lively mouthfeel. The finish of tangy bright fruit with cocoa shadings is a winner. A quintessential quaff—what easy drinking wine is all about. **87 Best Buy** *(10/1/2001)*

SANDALFORD

Sandalford 1999 Cabernet Sauvignon (Mount Barker & Margaret River) $22. It's toasty from 17 months in French oak, but the wood is well balanced by cassis and the nose picks up some lovely hints of anise with air. Straightforward black currant and vanilla flavors flow smoothly across the tongue. Soft tannins and low acidity make this a Cab that's meant to be enjoyed now. **90 Editors' Choice** *(7/1/2002)*

Sandalford 1998 Cabernet Sauvignon (Western Australia) $24. **88** *(1/1/2004)*

Sandalford 2001 Chardonnay (Western Australia) $21. A full, rich, woody style that emphasizes toast, vanilla, and butter. Imagine sliced peaches doused in melted butter and sprinkled with cinnamon-sugar. Finishes thick and oily. **88** *(7/1/2002)*

Sandalford 2000 Merlot (Western Australia) $24. Somewhat weedy on the nose; then shows a lot of overripe cherries on the palate, along with baking spices like clove and cinnamon. Soft and pleasantly chewy. **86** *(7/1/2002)*

Sandalford 2001 Riesling (Western Australia) $17. This peach- and pear-scented wine was bottled with screw caps so you needn't fear TCA. Baking spices accent simple peach and pear flavors in this medium-weight Riesling. Finishes dry and stony. **87** *(7/1/2002)*

Sandalford 2001 Semillon-Sauvignon Blanc (Western Australia) $16. Scents of smoke, green vegetables, and pungent grasses; flavors of pink grapefruit and green pepper. It's a little soft, yet green-tasting at the same time. **85** *(7/1/2002)*

Sandalford 1997 Shiraz (Mount Barker & Margaret River) $23. **85** *(4/1/2000)*

Sandalford 1998 Shiraz (Western Australia) $24. Sourced from the cool-climate regions of Margaret River and Mount Barker, this full-bodied Shiraz boasts plenty of peppery aromas, but also eucalyptus, sour cherry, and dill. Shows more leather and caramel on the palate, finishing with soft, dusty tannins. **90** *(7/1/2002)*

SANDHURST RIDGE

Sandhurst Ridge 2001 Cabernet Sauvignon (Bendigo) $50. The nose is an odd combination of Raisin Bran, Play Doh and licorice, but the palate offers more compelling notes of plums, anise and gumdrops. Thick, wooly tannins complete the picture. **87** —*D. T.* *(8/1/2005)*

SCHILD ESTATE

Schild Estate 2002 Cabernet Sauvignon (Barossa Valley) $24. Though other tasting panelists liked it better, I can't get on board with the Raisin Bran element that pervades this wine, nose to finish. Blackberry and oak flavors underneath are a little sweet, too; the whole package is good, though for the price, GI, and vintage, I had hoped for more. Tasted twice, with consistent results. **84** —*D. T.* *(5/1/2005)*

Schild Estate 2001 Cabernet Sauvignon (Barossa Valley) $19. Fruit is sweet and little stewy, but tangy oak plays first fiddle, anyway. The nose is quite nice, with a nice biscuit-pastry note, plus some candied cherries. **83** —*D. T.* *(1/1/2002)*

Schild Estate 2004 Frontignac Muscat Blanc à Petit Grain (Barossa) $14. A "wide appeal" kind of wine that's fun but not too complicated. Shows sweet melon and peach flavors and sour apple and pear aromas. Dry on the finish. **84** —*D. T.* *(11/15/2006)*

Schild Estate 2004 GMS Red Blend (Barossa Valley) $22. Tastes a lot less oaky than Schild's Shirazes—here, black pepper and spice flavors, and nutty aromas, are accents rather than principals. Soft tannins couch ripe black plums on the palate, and juicy cherry revs up on the finish. **88** —*D. T.* *(2/1/2006)*

Schild Estate 2003 Riesling (Barossa Valley) $15. Honeysuckle and white peach aromas; the palate shows some citrusy verve. The flavors are light and the mouthfeel and finish quite dry. Just the thing for an aperitif, or to be drunk outdoors. **86** —*D. T.* *(12/31/2004)*

Schild Estate 2004 Semillon (Barossa Valley) $18. This is a petite-sized Sem with some plumpness in the mouth. Flavors are of citrus and straw, but aren't as concentrated as I'd like. Aromas are peachy and musky. **85** —*D. T.* *(10/1/2005)*

Schild Estate 2002 Shiraz (Barossa) $24. Medium-sized, with deep fruit-cake, and stewed berry aromas. The same notes follow through on the palate, which is dominated by cassis but puckers up with tight plum fruit on the finish. **88** —*D. T.* *(12/1/2005)*

Schild Estate 2004 Ben Schild Reserve Shiraz (Barossa) $48. This is a big, lush, lavishly oaked wine that nonetheless pulls it all together with balance and elegance. Inky black in color, it leads with a blast of toasty, mentholated oak on the nose, backed by waves of blueberries and mint. Then the flavors call to mind dark chocolate and coconut, accented by almonds and the recurring blueberries. It's creamy-textured and finishes long, with supple tannins that deftly dry your palate; they're almost unnoticeable yet still provide structure. Drink now–2012, maybe longer. **94 Editors' Choice** —*J.C.* *(12/15/2006)*

Schild Estate 2003 Ben Schild Reserve Shiraz (Barossa Valley) $65. A lavishly oaked wine, with woody, coconutty flavors and aromas. There's fruit there—raspberry and cherry cordial on the nose, and some sour plum on the palate—but you're going to have to do some digging to get to it. Surely has its following, but is just too much for me. **86** —*D. T.* *(12/1/2005)*

Schild Estate 2004 Sparkling Shiraz (Barossa) $24. Schild Estate seems to have found its stride in 2004, fashioning a solid lineup of wines across the board. This inky purple sparkler bursts from the glass with assertive blackberry and blueberry fruit, but it's accented by vanilla, cinnamon, and crushed pepper, giving it uncommon complexity. Finishes long and powerful, framed by soft tannins. **90 Editors' Choice** —*J.C.* *(12/31/2006)*

AUSTRALIA

AUSTRALIA

SCREWED

Screwed 2005 Pink Red Blend (McLaren Vale) $10. Light orange-pink in color, this wine's aromas start off with plums and berries, but go south quickly. Peach and raspberry flavors are modest; simple, and will appeal most to fans of white Zin. **82** —D.T. (11/15/2006)

Screwed 2004 Red Red Blend (McLaren Vale) $10. From McLaren Vale's Davey family, this wine smells nice—fresh herb, fireplace, red fruit—and offers plum and black olive flavors on the palate. Soft and approachable in terms of feel; with such savory accents, this one is probably best enjoyed with dinner. **85 Best Buy** —D.T. (11/15/2006)

Screwed 2005 White Semillon-Chardonnay (McLaren Vale) $10. Made by the Davey family—the folks who make Shingleback—this Semillon-Chardonnay blend is a fun wine. On the palate it has a slight viscous quality and a soft feel; flavors are rooted in the honeysuckle and mango camp. Just the thing for summer. In screwcap. **85 Best Buy** —D.T. (8/1/2006)

SEAVIEW

Seaview 1997 Champagne Blend (South Eastern Australia) $10. 87 (11/15/1999)

Seaview 2000 Brut Champagne Blend (South Eastern Australia) $9. Here's a clean, vibrant sparkler that offers plenty of high-class character at a giveaway price. It has a kick of peach-fruit flavor, and the bubbles are a bit rough and jagged. But it's perfect for big gatherings that don't call for the expensive stuff. **85 Best Buy** —S.H. (12/1/2002)

Seaview 1999 Brut Champagne Blend (South Eastern Australia) $10. Enough complexity shows in this great-value sparkler's nut, plum, and ginger notes to keep the educated taster interested. It's medium-full with a hint of sweetness and an even, persistent bead. Soft, but not mushy, the pear-green herb finish is refreshing, with unexpected length for a wine in this price range. **88 Best Buy** (12/1/2001)

Seaview 1997 Chardonnay (McLaren Vale) $10. 83 (12/31/1999)

Seaview NV Brut Sparkling Blend (South Eastern Australia) $10. It's hard to quibble with the fact that this wine almost always over-delivers for the price: It's fairly widely available and is good alone, or in sparkling cocktails. This year's edition shows wheat flour, ginger, and a banana note—unexpected, maybe, but still gets the job done. **84** —D.T. (12/31/2004)

SERAFINO

Serafino 2001 Shiraz (McLaren Vale) $20. This is one spicy, sexy Shiraz. It tastes like a fruitstand exploded in the bottle—it shows vibrant, fresh plum, and berry fruit in abundance, with caramel and oak in a supporting role. Try at once; one to drink now rather than save for later. **89 Editors' Choice** —D.T. (3/1/2005)

SEXTON

Sexton 2002 Giant Steps Vineyard Chardonnay (Yarra Valley) $35. A toasty, mallowy, fun, tropical-fruity wine, from nose to finish. Round and full in the mouth; fits Americans' idea of a party-appropriate Oz Chard to a T. Its price tag, however, may prohibit you from inviting too many friends over. **86** (7/2/2004)

Sexton 2003 Giant Steps Vineyard, Bernard Clones Chardonnay (Yarra Valley) $40. For the number of times I wrote descriptors of butter, butterscotch, and vanilla for this wine, I normally wouldn't like it as much as I did. It works here, because the aforementioned notes are light on the citrus spine. Finishes with—guess what?—butterscotch. **87** —D.T. (5/1/2005)

SHADOWFAX WINES

Shadowfax Wines 2001 Chardonnay (Victoria) $9. 83 —D.T. (8/1/2003)

SHALLOW CREEK

Shallow Creek 2002 Shiraz (Victoria) $24. Has nice black plum fruit at its core, but it's obscured by strange, rubbery notes. The nose has even more unusual notes—catsup? Maybe aioli? A curiosity, from beginning to end. **84** —D.T. (5/1/2004)

SHAW AND SMITH

Shaw and Smith 2004 M3 Vineyard Chardonnay (Adelaide Hills) $29. There's a core of pear and melon fruit, which lends the wine its delicate aromatics and flavors. Toasted nut and smooth river rocks offer flavor and textural nuances on the palate, and through the persistent finish. Pretty, balanced, and very food-friendly. **90** —D.T. (11/15/2006)

Shaw and Smith 2003 M3 Vineyard Chardonnay (Adelaide Hills) $29. A pretty Chardonnay. It's piquant and interesting, with a buttery foundation that's buried deep beneath lemon peel and dry mineral flavors, and a nose that shows floral and kiwi notes. Surges with bright citrus on the finish. **90** —D.T. (8/1/2005)

Shaw and Smith 2004 Sauvignon Blanc (Adelaide Hills) $19. This Sauvignon is as crisp and zesty as the Marlborough Sauvignons that are so in vogue right now, minus the lime-green flavors. Fresh-cut grass aromas usher in a bright, lemon-centric palate. As dry as they come; very appealing, and very intense. Just delicious. **90 Editors' Choice** —D.T. (8/1/2005)

Shaw and Smith 2004 Shiraz (Adelaide Hills) $29. This Adelaide Hills Shiraz starts off with spicy, peppery aromas that are echoed again on the palate, which shows tangy plum and blackberry flavors. Quite nice, though the spicy, earthy finish could benefit from just a bit more depth. **88** —D.T. (11/15/2006)

Shaw and Smith 2003 Shiraz (Adelaide Hills) $29. Enjoyable, with likable flavors of raspberry and blackberry, and a smooth, medium-full mouthfeel. It's not quite as complex as some of S&S's other wines (the whites in particular), but it's still very good. **88** —D.T. (8/1/2005)

SHEEP'S BACK

Sheep's Back 2001 Old Vine Shiraz (Barossa Valley) $23. Has deep, pleasing aromas of eucalyptus, earth, and cream. It's a big wine in the mouth, not blowsy but pretty enthusiastic with oak—red cherry and raspberry flavors are trimmed with caramel and oak flavors that widen to a creamy-vanilla close. **88** —D.T. (12/31/2004)

Sheep's Back 2000 Old Vine Shiraz (Barossa Valley) $23. Fruit-forward, with mixed berry fruit and plums, which follow through on the finish. Fruit is particularly jammy on the nose; overall, there's not a lot of tannins here. A drink-now Shiraz. **86** —D.T. (12/31/2003)

SHINGLEBACK

Shingleback 2002 Cabernet Sauvignon (McLaren Vale) $19. This Cab feels tall: not round, not muscular, but lanky and vertical. It's a textured wine, though, with sandy-floury tannins and a plum-and-cherry core. Aromas of stewy, dusty fruit, and powdery tannins on the finish, complete the pretty picture. **89** —D.T. (12/31/2004)

Shingleback 2005 Chardonnay (McLaren Vale) $18. McLaren Vale is not renowned for its white wines, yet this Chardonnay is a very good, appealing sip. It's medium-sized with apple and pear aromas and flavors dominating. It's not noticeably oaky, either; a fresh, please-all style. 2,002 cases produced. **87** —D.T. (10/1/2006)

Shingleback 2005 Grenache (McLaren Vale) $22. Forward and very fruity, this Grenache shines from nose to tail with plum and blueberry flavors. Medium-bodied, and drinking well now. **87** —D.T. (11/15/2006)

Shingleback 2005 Rosé Grenache (McLaren Vale) $17. This rosé smells like flowers, particularly roses. It's soft and feels low in acid in the mouth, its berry fruit accented with a twist of orange. Refreshing and easy, it finishes dry and minerally **87** —D.T. (6/21/2006)

Shingleback 2003 Shiraz (McLaren Vale) $20. Though a young brand, Shingleback already has a track record of reliably good, reasonably priced wines. This one falls right in line: It's sturdy and medium-sized, with a rush of berry and plum fruit at palate entry that settles into the palate comfortably. Nose offers deep, ripe, plum, and blackberry aromas. **88** —D.T. (10/1/2005)

Shingleback 2002 Shiraz (McLaren Vale) $19. Smoke, pepper, red fruit, and vanilla aromas. Tastes dark and earthy, with powerful accents of earth, oak, and mushroom atop the plum fruit. Smooth, fine tannins on the palate; pure, taut plum fruit at the close. **89** (11/15/2004)

Shingleback NV Black Bubbles Sparkling Shiraz (McLaren Vale) $20. A good Oz sparkler, offering molasses and mixed-berry aromas, followed up by plum flavors on the palate. Tannins are notable, and persist through the finish. **86** —D.T. (12/31/2005)

Shingleback NV Black Bubbles Sparkling Shiraz (McLaren Vale) $22. Seems rather oaky, with cinnamon, clove, and cedar notes all taking the lead over modest black cherry fruit. It's on the lean side for sparkling Shiraz, but maybe you're looking for a touch of austerity, not full-blown fruit. **84** —J.C. (12/31/2006)

Shingleback 2002 D Block Reserve Shiraz (McLaren Vale) $50. Shingleback's signature Shiraz is heavy on the mocha, dried fruit, and liqueur aromas—really, it smells like fruitcake in a glass. Its flavors are similar: dried fruit, wheat, and nut, but more subdued than it is on the nose. Sweetish and forward; drink this one if it's just you, a partner, and the fireplace, and go for the regular Shingleback Shiraz if there's food on the table. **88** —D.T. (10/1/2005)

Shingleback 2001 D Block Reserve Shiraz (McLaren Vale) $40. From winemaker John Davey, a wine with jammy berries on the nose and a pleasing, round mouthfeel. Once you get through the juicy, ripe black berries on the palate, there's a tightly wound, bright red-cherry core that gives you hope that a couple of years in the cellar will do it more good than harm. Meaty on the back palate; finishes with chewy tannins. **90** (11/15/2004)

SHOOFLY

Shoofly 2004 Buzz Cut White Blend (South Eastern Australia) $14. Has golden aromas and flavors—think golden apples and raisins. It's not very lively in the mouth, but is a fine, everyday white. A blend of Verdelho, Viognier, Sauvignon, and Riesling. **84** —D.T. (10/1/2006)

SHOTTESBROOKE

Shottesbrooke 2000 Shiraz (South Australia) $17. Offers toasted caramel with root beer and tar; the palate displays sweet blackberries and blueberries. The tannins are smooth and the finish, juicy. Made to drink now. **88** —C.S. (3/1/2003)

Shottesbrooke 1998 Eliza Shiraz (McLaren Vale) $30. Complex aromas of bacon, blackberries, and toasted coconut lead into a smooth mouthful of smoked meats, dark chocolate, and black cherries. One taster referred to it as a Mounds bar. Finishes long, with juicy, tangy fruit flavors taking the lead. **90** (11/1/2001)

Shottesbrooke 2000 Eliza Reserve Shiraz (McLaren Vale) $30. The mint and eucalyptus aromas are always an indication that you are about to consume a quality wine. Along with the blackberry and cocoa flavors there is a rich, juicy mouthfeel with firm tannins, then bright acidity to clean everything up. Approachable now but will last until 2010. **91** — C.S. (3/1/2003)

SIDESHOW

Sideshow 2004 The Contortionist Red Blend (South Eastern Australia) $9. Both the nose and palate deliver bouncy red plum and cherry fruit. It's an easy-drinking, weekday-night wine, and a good introductory GSM. 45% Grenache, 35% Shiraz, 20% Mourvèdre. **86 Best Buy** —D.T. (2/1/2006)

Sideshow 2004 Queen Roma Riesling (South Eastern Australia) $9. Mouthfilling, with modest flavors of sour apple and pear. Citrus and white pepper aromas start things off. A good, introductory Riesling. **84** —D.T. (4/1/2006)

SILVERWING

Silverwing 2005 Cabernet Sauvignon-Shiraz (Margaret River) $10. Meaty, mushroomy aromas lead to berry-basket flavors with a tart edge. Smoky, toasty oak adds some dimension to this drink-now red. **86 Best Buy** — D.T. (8/1/2006)

Silverwing 2005 Chardonnay (Yarra Valley) $10. This is a linear Chardonnay that gets from point A (light white peach and pineapple aromas) to point B (peach and mineral flavors) without any difficulty or fanfare. Made in a lighter, feminine style and will appeal to the oak-averse. **84** —D.T. (8/1/2006)

Silverwing 2004 Pinot Noir (Yarra Valley) $10. It's something to get a Yarra-appellation wine at a price like this. Smells quite nice, with hints of orange peel and burnt sugar dressing up sturdy red fruit. On the palate, tea-like tannins put the wine's cherry fruit in the back seat. Lean and almost tart, with tea and lemon notes on the finish. **85 Best Buy** —D.T. (11/15/2006)

Silverwing 2004 Riesling (Adelaide Hills) $13. This Adelaide Hills Riesling has lively acidity and pretty talc-dust aromas. Its mineral and pannacotta flavors are delicate, and would ideally be a little more concentrated. Could be a factor of the '04 vintage, in which I've found flavor concentration to be an issue. **87** —D.T. (8/1/2006)

SIMON GILBERT

Simon Gilbert 2000 Semillon-Sauvignon Blanc (Hunter Valley) $10. Smells softer and rounder than it tastes, starting off with scents of pear, fig, and melon that turn herbal and a bit medicinal on the palate. Finishes with palate-cleansing lemony acidity. **85** —J.C. (9/1/2001)

Simon Gilbert 2004 Central Ranges Semillon-Sauvignon Blanc (New South Wales) $15. What we get of this Semillon-Sauvignon Blanc is nice, but there's just not enough of it to go around. Mineral and green grape flavors fade into fresh herbs on the palate, but the flavors are less than intense. Peach skin and grass aromas are joined by some rubber on the nose. Has potential; just wants to be dialed up a little louder. **85** —D.T. (8/1/2006)

Simon Gilbert 1999 Shiraz (Mudgee) $10. The whirl of conflicting aromas and flavors in this wine include lactic cream cheese and butter, medicinal menthol, eucalyptus, and sour stewed berries. Still, the even, smooth mouthfeel makes it a decent bar glug. **83** (10/1/2001)

Simon Gilbert 1998 Wongalere Shiraz (McLaren Vale) $35. Smooth and even, pleasantly creamy, this wine shows lots of toasty oak, chocolate, and cedar over the jammy yet tart blackberry fruit. Pepper, anise, and vanilla accents add interest, and though the fruit is dense and heavily oaked, the wine is mid-weight and even rather than monolithic. Good length, lemon, and cedar accents mark the close. Drink or hold through 2006 and beyond. **89** (11/1/2001)

Simon Gilbert 2004 Central Ranges Verdelho (New South Wales) $14. Nice wine—fresh, zesty, and enjoyable. It has a surge of passion fruit, white peach, and citrus on the palate, all of which press on through the crisp finish. Serve it at your next gathering; it's a wine with broad appeal. **88** —D.T. (10/1/2006)

SIMON HACKETT

Simon Hackett 2000 Cabernet Sauvignon (McLaren Vale) $18. Simple aromas of fresh fruit and oak do nothing to turn you away from this brambly, spicy Cabernet. Solid berry fruit flows across the palate, with super spicy oak forming the basis of the persistent finish, which gives off ample vanilla as well. More open than tight. Drink sooner than later. **89** —M.S. (12/15/2002)

Simon Hackett 1999 Cabernet Sauvignon (McLaren Vale) $18. The aromas alone are worth the price: black currants and plums, smoke and anise, vanilla and cocoa, and something herbaceous, like tapenade. There are also leathery nuances that give it an almost gamy character. Some mint flavors on the finish, with firm tannins that should allow this wine to age well. **90** (6/1/2001)

Simon Hackett 1997 Foggo Road Cabernet Sauvignon (McLaren Vale) $38. Loaded with ripe dark fruit, this expansive wine carries a lot of oak but wears it comfortably. Jammy blackberries are graced with leather and chocolate. The mouthfeel is plush and so rich it verges on syrupy. Finishes long, with enough soft tannins to taste good now yet age for another 5–10 years. **92** (6/1/2001)

Simon Hackett 1999 Foggo Road Limited Release Cabernet Sauvignon (McLaren Vale) $38. There's plenty of plum to be had here, from nose to finish. Aromas of soy, or rice noodles or something of the sort, add interest to the nose. Tannins are gummy in the mouth, and dry out on the back end, where a burst of fleshy fruit resurfaces. **87** —D.T. (6/1/2003)

Simon Hackett 2001 Chardonnay (Barossa Valley) $18. A flavorful Chardonnay, with a backbone of ripe, tropical fruit and apples. Toast and caramel notes sing loudly, though, from beginning to end (the wine

AUSTRALIA

was aged in French and American oak hogsheads)—steer clear if you're averse to wood. **85** —*D.T. (8/1/2003)*

Simon Hackett 1999 Chardonnay (Barossa Valley) $15. Ripe and pungent, this opens with a blast of oak-influenced melon and peach aromas, mixed with smoke, spices, and buttered toast. It's very rich and forward in the mouth, with tropical fruit flavors, some sweetness, and a thick, custardy texture. Of interest are the acids, which are very high and penetrating. **91 Best Buy** —*S.H. (6/1/2001)*

Simon Hackett 2004 Brightview Chardonnay (Barossa Valley) $15. An easy-drinking, overt wine, but an enjoyable one. Aromas are vibrant and springy—flowers, lemon-lime, mineral. The palate offers up fleshy yellow fruit and stony-mineral accents that carry through the finish. **87** —*D.T. (3/1/2005)*

Simon Hackett 2002 Brightview Chardonnay (Barossa Valley) $15. A good, standard-issue Chardonnay, with typical yellow fruit and cream, and a nice, round feel. Aromas are of pineapple and citrus; finish is brief. **85** *(7/2/2004)*

Simon Hackett 2002 Old Vine Grenache (McLaren Vale) $18. Bright, bouncy cherry and plum aromas; wood and earth are interspersed with mixed cherries on the palate. A straighforward, enjoyable Grenache. **87** —*D.T. (3/1/2005)*

Simon Hackett 2001 Old Vine Grenache (McLaren Vale) $18. This wine feels rustic and curmudgeonly, with mixed cherries, earth, oak, and not much fluff. Finishes medium-long, rife with juicy cherry and a dark, lingering oak-soil component. **89** —*D.T. (9/1/2004)*

Simon Hackett 2000 Old Vine Grenache (McLaren Vale) $18. Seems slightly hollow, and finishes with some coarse oak, but the fruit flavors of cherries and yellow-fleshed red plums are pretty and accented by a hint of smoke. Quaffable. **84** —*J.C. (9/1/2002)*

Simon Hackett 2004 Brightview Semillon (Barossa Valley) $15. Very pleasant and drinkable, this is an approachable Semillon that'll win Chard lovers over to the other side. Aromas are minerally, with hints of butter and vanilla. Hay, fresh herb, and yellow fruit flavors are clean, and linger through the finish. **88 Editors' Choice** —*D.T. (3/1/2005)*

Simon Hackett 2000 Brightview Semillon (Barossa Valley) $15. Brightly fruity on the nose, with notes of lemon, anise, or pine, and pear nectar. It's weighty on the palate—thick and almost syrupy—yet the flavors are lemon and beeswax. The long finish is tart and very resinous. This distinctive style of wine may not be for everyone. **90** —*J.C. (2/1/2002)*

Simon Hackett 2002 Shiraz (McLaren Vale) $18. On the nose, dark, stably-earth aromas are accented by a ribbon of eucalyptus that follows through on the palate. Fruit flavors are red, but all its accents are dark: think black cured olives and earth. Tea-like tannins fade though the finish. Enjoy with charcuterie. **87** —*D.T. (3/1/2005)*

Simon Hackett 2001 Shiraz (McLaren Vale) $18. A quaff-worthy Shiraz, starring plum, rhubarb, and Sweet Tart flavors; feels big, but not rich, in the mouth. Nose is an odd blend of potting soil, ink, and barnyard flavors. **85** —*D.T. (3/1/2003)*

Simon Hackett 2000 Shiraz (McLaren Vale) $18. An easy quaff if ever there was one, the Simon Hackett opens with cumin, cedar, leather, and earthy notes, and shows tangy red fruit and berry zinger tea on the palate. A couple of reviewers noted herbaceousness on the bouquet and the palate. Medium-weight, it finishes with toasty oak and ripe tannins. **85** *(10/1/2001)*

Simon Hackett 1999 Shiraz (McLaren Vale) $18. Dark and fragrant, this wine is a baby, full of fat, precocious fruit tinged with smoke and herbs. Blackberries, plums, and black cherries bounce along, buoyed by adequate acidity and chalky, dusty tannins. It's full and plush in the mouth, finishing a little fat. **89** *(6/1/2001)*

Simon Hackett 1998 Anthony's Reserve Shiraz (McLaren Vale) $38. The fruit aromas are pretty: plums and black cherries. Add fine oak aromas of smoke, cocoa, vanilla, toast, and menthol, and this has all the ingredients to please. The acidity is firm, preventing the wine from ever seeming flabby or over the top and giving strength to the long spicy finish. **92** *(6/1/2001)*

SIMPLICITY

Simplicity 2005 Pink Rosé Blend (McLaren Vale) $10. **82** —*D.T. (11/15/2006)*

Simplicity 2005 White Blend (McLaren Vale) $10. There's not much to this wine's nose, and the alcohol is quite noticeable on the palate. Modest citrus and mineral flavors are couched in a bulky, low-acid body. **82** —*D.T. (11/15/2006)*

SIRROMET

Sirromet 2002 Seven Scenes Chardonnay (Queensland) $30. Has a creamy quality on the palate due to its 12 months on lees, but it's still a light-handed, delicately-styled wine. Peach and pear nuances are at its core. Doesn't shout; it whispers. **87** —*D.T. (11/15/2006)*

SKILLOGALEE

Skillogalee 2003 Riesling (Clare Valley) $18. Smells big and oily, with some honeysuckle. In the mouth, it's smooth, with lemon and herb flavors. Clean on the back, with more citrus. **85** —*D.T. (5/1/2004)*

Skillogalee 2001 Shiraz (Clare Valley) $25. Aromas are of plum, eucalyptus and toast. This is a taut, classy Shiraz whose blackberry and plum fruit is quite tightly wound, and framed in a judicious amount of toasty oak. It really is a pretty wine—well behaved, too, not one to scream out at you—but it still feels young. Drink 2005+. **89** —*D.T. (9/1/2004)*

SMITH & HOOPER

Smith & Hooper 2000 Wrattonbully-Limited Edition Merlot (South Australia) $30. Medium-bodied with chalky tannins, this textbook Merlot offers blackberries and raspberries from palate to finish. Nice toasted-nut and caramel aromas, and a twinge of leafiness, complement the blackberries on the nose. **87** —*D.T. (6/1/2003)*

SONS OF EDEN

Sons of Eden 2001 Kennedy Grenache-Syrah (Barossa Valley) $20. Red raspberry peeks out from under toffee and mocha on the nose. Red plum, earth, and oak flavors hang on a frame that feels more Rhônish than New World in size. A flash. **87** —*D.T. (9/1/2004)*

Sons of Eden 2003 Kennedy G-S-M Rhône Red Blend (Barossa Valley) $23. An enjoyable wine, but one that tastes more built for the masses than for wine sophisticates. Fruit on the palate is juicy and bright, like purple fruit and raspberries; the nose is awash with vanilla bean and cream. **86** —*D.T. (5/1/2005)*

Sons of Eden 2000 Remus Old Vine Shiraz (Barossa Valley) $40. Robust, with ripe plum and cherry flavors, the palate is accented with pleasing briary, earthy notes, but also a hint of green stemminess. Medium-weight, with red fruit and caramel on the nose, it closes with dry oak and green tobacco notes. **88** —*D.T. (6/1/2003)*

SOUTHERN TRACKS

Southern Tracks 2001 Chardonnay (South Eastern Australia) $10. A leaner style of Chardonnay, particularly when you compare it to other offerings at this price point. Sour-ish yellow fruit takes on a bit of oak on the palate; finishes with an herbaceous streak. **84** —*D.T. (6/1/2003)*

Southern Tracks 2000 Red Blend (South Eastern Australia) $10. Brick-ish in color, with light and spicy aromas and more than a touch of tomato. The palate is thin and vegetal, and the finish provides the undisputed tang of tomato juice. Some spice and mild fruit is here, but it's pretty weak. **81** —*M.S. (12/15/2002)*

SPRINGWOOD PARK

Springwood Park 1998 Nicholas Shiraz (McLaren Vale) $35. In the mouth, the Nicholas is pretty soft and creamy—there are no killer tannins here; this is a wine that is as enjoyable now as it will be after a few years in the cellar. Has nice cherry and plum flavors, and a healthy dose of oak and vanilla that extends to the finish. The longer it sits, the more it grows on you. **89** —*D.T. (12/31/2003)*

ST. ANDREWS ESTATE

St. Andrews Estate 2000 Ceravolo Chardonnay (Adelaide Hills) $12. No oak means that the pear and melon flavors are front and center in this slightly syrupy wine that finishes unexpectedly hard and tart, with metallic notes. **83** —*J.C. (7/1/2002)*

St. Andrews Estate 2000 Adelaide Plains Shiraz (Adelaide Hills) $22. It's "obvious" Syrah according to a couple of tasters, but what's wrong with that? Vanilla-caramel, blackberry, and cocoa-coffee aromas and flavors; finishes long, with moderate tannins and stewed fruit flavors. Top Value. **89** *(11/1/2001)*

St. Andrews Estate 2000 Ceravolo Shiraz-Cabernet Sauvignon (Adelaide Hills) $20. Hailing from near Adelaide, the wine features lemony barrel-driven aromas and a full blast of toasty char. The flavor profile is sweet, with candied plum and cherry. On the finish you get some additional oak in the form of espresso and butter. Overall it's woody, teetering on medicinal. **88** —*M.S. (3/1/2003)*

ST. HALLETT

St. Hallett 1999 Cabernet Sauvignon (Barossa Valley) $21. A good by-the-glass, textbook New World Cabernet pour; offers stewy blackberry, buttercream, and oak flavors from bouquet to finish. Dried green herb gives the back end a little oomph. **85** —*D.T. (6/1/2002)*

St. Hallett 2002 Gamekeepers Reserve Red Blend (Barossa Valley) $NA. A blend of Grenache, Shiraz, Touriga, and Mourvedre; pair with foods that you'd ordinarily pair with Pinot. Spicy, with earth, clay, and bright plum fruit that should be taken seriously; dry in the mouth, with gummy, chalky tannins that give the wine very nice texture and length. More than you'd expect of a wine of this price. A pleasant surprise. **90 Editors' Choice** —*D.T. (2/1/2004)*

St. Hallett 1999 Gamekeeper's Reserve Rhône Red Blend (Barossa Valley) $10. 88 Best Buy —*M.M. (10/1/2000)*

St. Hallett 2002 Blackwell Shiraz (Barossa Valley) $39. Manages simultaneous youth, energy, and classy reserve. On the nose and palate, this Shiraz is a pretty cocktail of chewy plums and mixed berries, with a twist of caramel. Utterly addictive. Drink now–2008. **91** —*D.T. (3/1/2005)*

St. Hallett 2001 Blackwell Shiraz (Barossa Valley) $30. Fruit is black and big, as it typically is, framed in spicy oak and claylike, chewy tannins. This vintage is elegant compared to the more unrestrained 2000 vintage. A bull, to be sure, but one that's more likely to buy something in the china shop than to break something. Drink 2006+. **90** —*D.T. (2/1/2004)*

St. Hallett 2000 Blackwell Shiraz (Barossa Valley) $30. Winemaker Stuart Blackwell calls this Shiraz "noisy... the adolescent boy who says, 'Look at me!'" Calling it noisy, or boisterous, is a good call: It has pretty loud, dark, black cherry, and plum fruit without a lot of oak or earth to muck it up. Simple? No. Just hold on tight and let the bold fruit take you for a ride. **90** —*D.T. (5/1/2004)*

St. Hallett 1997 Blackwell Shiraz (Barossa Valley) $25. Now, five years after the harvest, this wine still seems incorrigibly young. It's still very primary, showing lots of blackberry fruit mingled with Nilla Wafer crumbs—like a rich berry-vanilla compote. Hold for another few years, unless you're looking only for primary fruit. **90 Cellar Selection** —*J.C. (9/1/2002)*

St. Hallett 1998 Blackwell Shiraz (Barossa Valley) $25. Very powerfully oaked, this old-vine wine opens with aromas of smoke and vanilla, and the beautiful perfume of young new wood. The flavors are oaky, too, but the underlying fruit flavors are so dramatically bold, they handle the wood well. Long in the middle palate and the finish, this wine is stuffed with fruit. **91** —*S.H. (12/15/2002)*

St. Hallett 2004 Faith Shiraz (Barossa) $20. Ripe plum and black soil aromas; offers soft tannins and lifted, bouncy flavors of blue-, black-, and raspberries. An enjoyable, drink-now younger sibling to St. Hallett's Old Block Shiraz. **88** —*D.T. (6/1/2006)*

St. Hallett 2002 Faith Shiraz (Barossa Valley) $20. St. Hallett's entry-level Shiraz is made from young-vine fruit. It's satisfying but simple, as it's meant to be, with plum and cherry flavors, and just a little burned sugar, on the palate. On the finish, black plum and cherry surfaces, with hints of eucalyptus and black pepper that are more pronounced in the winery's top bottlings. **88** —*D.T. (2/1/2004)*

St. Hallett 2000 Faith Shiraz (Barossa Valley) $19. From younger vines, a fresh and juicy wine notable for sheer succulence of flavor. It has youth-ful flavors of jam and immature, perky tannins and acids that feel lively on the palate. Yet there's a sense of harmony and elegance. **87** —*S.H. (12/15/2002)*

St. Hallett 1999 Faith Shiraz (Barossa Valley) $18. A ripe, dark cherry, bacon fat, leather, and American oak nose comes on strong, and the wine continues in that manner. The acids are bright, but the mouthfeel smooth (a little cough-syrupy to some tasters), which keeps it from getting sharp. Coffee and licorice flavors play out on the long, handsome finish. **88** *(10/1/2001)*

St. Hallett 2001 Gamekeepers Shiraz (South Australia) $11. A basic blend, super-juicy, and jammy. It fills the mouth with upfront wild berry, stone fruit, and pepper flavors that drink dry and crisp and richly textured with thick, dusty tannins. A blend of Grenache, Mourvedre, Shiraz and Touriga. **85** —*S.H. (12/15/2002)*

St. Hallett 2001 Gamekeepers Reserve Shiraz (Barossa Valley) $NA. A blend of Shiraz, Grenache, Touriga, Malbec, Cabernet Franc and Mourvèdre; winemaker Stuart Blackwell says that the biggest export market for this wine in the U.S. is Houston, of all places, but taste the earth, graham cracker, and spice that coats the cherry fruit, and Texas barbecue sounds like a darned good idea (though the wine's back label says to drink it with "vegetarian lunches and Friday pizza"). Hey, either way, y'all. **88** —*D.T. (2/1/2004)*

St. Hallett 2002 Old Block Shiraz (Barossa) $64. A wine that almost always lives up to its lofty expectations, this vintage being no different. Has aromas of pastry crust, blueberry, anise, and graham cracker. It's not as brawny as it is in some vintages but this is still a wine of class and pedigree, with smooth tannins, and lively black and blueberry fruit that lasts through a long finish. **92** —*D.T. (6/1/2006)*

St. Hallett 2001 Old Block Shiraz (Barossa Valley) $52. Nose shows deep eucalyptus or pine needles, plus a lot of caramel. Has excellent structure, and the plum and berry fruit regime to fill it out admirably. Big, yes, but will settle down in time. Drink 2007+. **91** —*D.T. (2/1/2004)*

St. Hallett 2000 Old Block Shiraz (Barossa Valley) $54. Nose has beautiful, permeating pine-needle, mocha, and meaty aromas. In the mouth it boasts chewy tannins, cassis fruit, and slatelike accents. Finishes long; a sexy wine overall, with a beautiful, mouthcoating feel. **93** —*D.T. (5/1/2004)*

St. Hallett 1997 Old Block Shiraz (Barossa Valley) $40. Liking it wasn't an issue for reviewers—we all dug this Barossa, but had a hard time agreeing on its aromas and flavors. Imagine a bright raspberry, licorice, toasted-coconut, and nutmeg bouquet coupled with big cherry, raspberry, and cream flavors and a licorice-coffee finish…well, go ahead and wake up from your dream now. **92 Editors' Choice** *(11/1/2001)*

St. Hallett 1998 Old Block Shiraz (Barossa Valley) $40. From vines over 70 years old, this delightful wine combines sheer size with the finesse of a great red. Powerful flavors of anise, blackberry jam, sweet cassis and dark chocolate cascade over the palate, stunning with richness and intensity. Yet the wine maintains a lilting grace and lightness, not to mention the near-perfect balance for aging. **95 Editors' Choice** —*S.H. (12/15/2002)*

St. Hallett 2003 Poacher's Blend White Blend (Barossa Valley) $NA. This blend of Semillon, Riesling, Colombard, and Sauvignon Blanc is not yet available in the States, which is a shame. It's a fruit cocktail in the glass, with fresh pineapple flavors at the fore, yet it's hardwired to taut citrus fruit underneath, which extends through the finish. **88** —*D.T. (2/1/2004)*

St. Hallett 2001 Poachers Blend White Blend (South Australia) $10. A crazy quilt blend of Chenin Blanc, Semillon, Sauvignon Blanc, and Chardonnay that combines tart citrus flavors with riper ones of tropical fruits. The wine is very dry and acidic, and fun to drink. Definitely a great value. **88** —*S.H. (1/1/2002)*

ST. MARYS

St. Marys 1999 House Block Cabernet Sauvignon (Coonawarra) $20. Aromas of mint, coconut, and eucalyptus tease you into thinking this will be a great wine. However, it has an awkward balance that is a letdown from the wonderful nose. Finishes lean and hard. **85** —*C.S. (6/1/2002)*

AUSTRALIA

St. Marys 1999 Shiraz (Coonawarra) $19. An understated, elegant sleeper, with a reserved, sweet black plum nose. The smooth palate shows more fruit with licorice, mild white pepper, and mint shadings. This firm wine could use two or three years to open, and while apparently densely-oaked, it shows good fruit-wood integration. **87** *(10/1/2001)*

St. Marys 2000 Shiraz (Limestone Coast) $20. At first some tank and barrel notes obscure the fruit, but with a few minutes of airing that blows off to reveal raspberry, plum, and cranberry fruit. Fruit is forward throughout, and the wine is never too heavy or sharp. Both the texture and tannic structure seem right for the body, which is about middle of the road. **88** *—M.S. (3/1/2003)*

STANLEY BROTHERS

Stanley Brothers 1998 Thoroughbred Cabernet Sauvignon (Barossa Valley) $22. Hot aromas of creamy vanilla and mint lead the way. Flavors of blackberries, fresh vegetables, and a potato-like starchiness are a little thin in the middle. This is a pleasing wine that should be drunk soon. **87** *—C.S. (6/1/2002)*

Stanley Brothers 1999 Pristine Chardonnay (Barossa Valley) $16. An interesting wine that shows some bottle evolution akin to Aussie Semillon in its development of dry toast and smoke aromas despite minimal wooding. Sweet apple and pear fruit on the palate turns citrusy on the finish, picking up hints of greengage plum. **85** *—J.C. (7/1/2002)*

Stanley Brothers 1998 Pristine Chardonnay (Barossa Valley) $15. 86 *— M.M. (10/1/2000)*

Stanley Brothers 1999 Black Sheep Red Blend (Barossa Valley) $18. Chunky and big in the nose, with a touch of sulfur and gas. The palate features black cherry fruit and a pleasant roundness, while the finish is full of fruit and licorice. For a quaffer, this fits the bill. But something about it, including the price, indicates that it's striving to be more than that. **85** *—M.S. (12/15/2002)*

Stanley Brothers 1998 Black Sheep Red Blend (Barossa Valley) $16. 86 *— M.S. (10/1/2000)*

Stanley Brothers 1999 John Hancock Shiraz (Barossa Valley) $24. This Shiraz is mouthfilling, but stops short of the lushness that characterizes top-tier Shiraz. It's all about plum, earth, and caramel from beginning to end; textbook Barossa Shiraz, yummy if not out of the ordinary. **88** *— D.T. (3/1/2003)*

STARVEDOG LANE

Starvedog Lane 1999 Cabernet Sauvignon (Adelaide Hills) $23. If eucalyptus is your thing, look no further, because there's plenty of it here, accenting cherry and plum fruit on the palate. Has interesting Indian spice aromas on the nose; finishes with tealike tannins. Could use more stuffing, too. **84** *—D.T. (6/1/2003)*

Starvedog Lane 2001 Chardonnay (Adelaide Hills) $17. Bright springtime-and-honey aromas are welcoming on the nose. The palate is one on which yellow fruit—everything from pears, apples, even lemon—takes the reins, with lactic-butter flavor underneath. Slick and round in the mouth, it closes with a prickly lemon-herb feel. **86** *(7/2/2004)*

Starvedog Lane 2000 Chardonnay (Adelaide Hills) $19. It tastes like it smells—like lots of toast and butterscotch. Palate also offers some yellow fruit and a fresh herbal streak (or maybe it's pine needles?). The same herbal note shows again on the finish. **84** *—D.T. (8/1/2003)*

Starvedog Lane 2004 No Oak Chardonnay (Adelaide Hills) $15. This is a straightforward Chard, one for those who prefer not to drink their butter and toast. This wine offers dusty lemon aromas and white stone fruit on the palate. 2,000 cases produced. **85** *—D.T. (8/1/2005)*

Starvedog Lane 2003 Shiraz-Viognier Rhône Red Blend (Adelaide Hills) $15. Has all the working parts that a good Oz red needs: fleshy plum fruit, judicious oak, and a please-all medium size. Smells earthy, and finishes with a taut smack of plum skin. Contains 6% Viognier, but its tell-tale floral qualities aren't so obvious here. **86** *—D.T. (8/1/2005)*

Starvedog Lane 2004 Sauvignon Blanc (Adelaide Hills) $15. A good SB, but not a lot of verve. Offers lime flavors, and a minerally feel. Lemon flavors bring the wine to a tart close. **86** *—D.T. (8/1/2005)*

Starvedog Lane 2003 Sauvignon Blanc (Adelaide Hills) $15. Tropical yellow fruit and fresh garden greens on the nose let you know exactly what you're in for: A crisp, zesty, summery wine. Tangy grapefruit, peach, and grassy flavors follow through on the clean finish. **87** *—D.T. (9/1/2004)*

Starvedog Lane 1999 Shiraz (Adelaide Hills) $23. Gaminess, thin cherry, and light toast aromas meet tart red fruit and woody flavors. The acidity is good and firm, while the finish is tinged with cranberry and red plum. **85** *—K.F. (3/1/2003)*

STEFANO LUBIANA

Stefano Lubiana NV Brut Champagne Blend (Tasmania) $34. Mild herb and ginger notes comprise the attractive side of this sparkler from Tasmania—Australias Down Under. However there's also a creamy, even cheese-like element that was much less appealing. Soft and frothy on the palate, it closes even and grassy, but still with the odd diary note. **84** *— M.M. (12/1/2001)*

Stefano Lubiana 1999 Pinot Noir (Tasmania) $39. Smells like Pinot, combining leather, smoke, and tart cherry aromas. In the mouth, this light-to-medium-weight wine doesn't show a lot of fruity flavors, but rather leather, dried spices, and dusty notes. Juicy cherries gradually emerge on the finish. **87** *—J.C. (9/1/2002)*

Stefano Lubiana 1999 Riesling (Tasmania) $27. Maybe an ambitious attempt gone awry, with the bouquet an ungainly grape-alcohol mix. The ripe grapey elements and brisk acidity hold it together—but barely—against earthy, vaguely musty notes. Finishes with intriguing spice and chalk notes, but also more hot vapors—almost like a much lighter grappa. Unusual and interesting, but lacks balance. **84** *—M.M. (2/1/2002)*

STEVE HOFF

Steve Hoff 2002 Cabernet Sauvignon (Barossa) $25. Smells nice—super-ripe blackberry, mineral, caramel—and the dark flavors continue on through the palate. But the wine's texture is simple, soft, maybe a little halfhearted. Good, with the potential for power in another vintage. **83** *—D.T. (10/1/2005)*

Steve Hoff 1999 Cabernet Sauvignon (Barossa Valley) $18. Fresh pine branches, smoke, and black cherries make for an inviting bouquet, but the palate is awkwardly metallic and tart. Citrus and orange peel flavors fight with the aromatics rather than complementing them. **83** *—J.C. (6/1/2002)*

Steve Hoff 2000 Shiraz (Barossa Valley) $20. A flat-out strange but good wine, and a good selection if you're trying to stump your friends in a blind tasting. Standing out on the bouquet are earth and lanolin; juicy, red-plum fruit is tinged with a little rhubarb in the mouth. Medium-bodied, and not what you'd expect from Barossa Shiraz. **86** *—D.T. (3/1/2003)*

Steve Hoff 2002 Rossco's Shiraz (Barossa) $40. Though this wine has the same cherry and plum fruit that many others in Barossa do this vintage, it is bolstered by mocha and toasty accents. A solid, food-weight wine, and one that would suit a burger or roast beef very well. **87** *—D.T. (10/1/2005)*

STICKS

Sticks 2002 Cabernet Sauvignon (Yarra Valley) $15. Though this wine grips the midpalate with some enthusiasm, the impact on palate entry and finish is less impressive. Red fruit rules here, including traces of roasted tomato. **84** *—D.T. (5/1/2005)*

Sticks 2003 Chardonnay (Yarra Valley) $16. Aromas are subtle; we detected some floral, citrus, and green apple aromas. Medium-weight with pear and melon flavors on the palate, it closes with a tart snap of lime. **85** *(7/2/2004)*

Sticks 2002 Chardonnay (Yarra Valley) $15. A classic Aussie Chard, big in that creamy lime way, with additional flavors of peaches, figs, and vanilla. It's all boosted by very bright, crisp acidity, and a steely structure. Fills the mouth with a honeyed juiciness. **91 Best Buy** *—S.H. (10/1/2003)*

Sticks 2002 Pinot Noir (Yarra Valley) $15. Seems like a hot-climate Pinot, with aromas of baked cherry pie and rich, jammy cherry flavors. A nice wine, and shows off this difficult varietal's soft, silky tannins, and gentle mouthfeel. **86** *—S.H. (10/1/2003)*

STONEHAVEN

Stonehaven 1999 Cabernet Sauvignon (Limestone Coast) $14. A very good wine, though more textbook than nuanced. It offers black plum and dry earthy flavors that extend through the finish; medium body and a nice blackberry-and-soil nose. **86** —*D.T. (6/1/2003)*

Stonehaven 1997 Cabernet Sauvignon (Limestone Coast) $18. 88 *(11/1/2000)*

Stonehaven 1998 Reserve Cabernet Sauvignon (Coonawarra) $46. Now this is Cabernet: big, burly, black fruit, serious tannins, and some black olive and oak flavors, with moist soil, ink, and black fruit aromas. Mouthfilling; drink now–2006. **91** —*D.T. (12/15/2002)*

Stonehaven 1996 Reserve Cabernet Sauvignon (McLaren Vale) $40. 88 *(11/1/2000)*

Stonehaven 2003 Winemaker's Selection Cabernet Sauvignon (South Australia) $12. There's some juicy cassis fruit here, accented by hints of chocolate, but also some green, herbal notes. Pleasant, easy-drinking wine, but a touch too green to rate higher. **85** *(11/1/2005)*

Stonehaven 2001 Chardonnay (Limestone Coast) $13. 83 *(7/2/2004)*

Stonehaven 2001 Chardonnay (South Eastern Australia) $8. This wine could be the poster boy for Australian Chardonnay. The nectarine and peach aromas and flavors are coddled by a touch of vanilla and the entire package is soft, juicy, and easy to drink. It's nothing fancy, just yummy weekday wine. **86** —*J.C. (7/1/2002)*

Stonehaven 2000 Chardonnay (Limestone Coast) $16. Features a complex nose of green apples, pears, and pineapples, accented by smoky notes. The flavors are similar, folding in more vanilla and toast nuances—the oak in this wine seems to build toward the finish, while the fruit does the reverse, turning fainter and more citrusy. **87** —*J.C. (7/1/2002)*

Stonehaven 1999 Chardonnay (Limestone Coast) $17. 89 *(11/1/2000)*

Stonehaven 1999 Chardonnay (South Eastern Australia) $9. 86 *(11/1/2000)*

Stonehaven 2003 Premium Chardonnay (South Eastern Australia) $6. From Banfi, a basic Chardonnay with bright yellow fruit and oak on both the nose and the palate. Finishes with a tart, citrus, and metal note. **83** *(7/2/2004)*

Stonehaven 1999 Reserve Chardonnay (Padthaway) $29. A richer, yet no better, style than the 2000 Limestone Coast bottling. Peach and vanilla aromas and flavors take the lead, with buttered popcorn and alcoholic warmth playing supporting roles. The finish is long, featuring a slightly bitter note akin to citrus rind. **87** —*J.C. (7/1/2002)*

Stonehaven 1997 Reserve Chardonnay (Australia) $29. 87 *(11/1/2000)*

Stonehaven 2004 Winemaker's Selection Chardonnay (South Australia) $12. A bit nutty (almonds) at first, married nicely to pineapple and citrus aromas. Plump in texture, with broad, mouthfilling flavors, but finishes a touch rustic, with some unintegrated wood. **85** *(11/1/2005)*

Stonehaven 2003 Merlot (South Eastern Australia) $6. Smells metallic at first, and goes the way of vanilla and toast with air. Flat and one-dimensional in the mouth, its red fruit flavors taking on a metallic tinge that lasts through the finish. **81** —*D.T. (12/1/2005)*

Stonehaven 2000 Merlot (Padthaway) $9. A good, crowd-pleasing quaffer that would go well with red-sauced pasta—a subliminal pairing, perhaps, given the tomato-y note that I picked up on the palate (though it's bolstered by plenty of red cherry, raspberry and cedar flavors). Opens with plum, toast and caramel aromas. **85 Best Buy** —*D.T. (6/1/2002)*

Stonehaven 1999 Merlot (South Eastern Australia) $9. 87 *(11/1/2000)*

Stonehaven 2004 Winemaker's Selection Riesling (South Australia) $12. Produced exclusively from estate grown fruit, this was our favorite of Stonehaven's new line. Soft, round, and honeyed in the mouth yet mostly dry, with piquant flavors of apples and pears. Mouthwatering on the finish. Good value. **86** *(11/1/2005)*

Stonehaven 2004 Shiraz (South Eastern Australia) $6. This Shiraz has sweet blackberry and raspberry aromas, but the same fruit on the palate is blessedly not as sweet as many other inexpensive, big-production wines. A good value and easy to drink; 50,000 cases produced. **84 Best Buy** —*D.T. (10/1/2005)*

Stonehaven 1999 Shiraz (South Eastern Australia) $9. Smoke, herb, olive, and menthol notes are carried on a lean frame of tart cherries and dark coffee that veers toward bitter chocolate and espresso. Finishes green and tannic; may improve slightly with short-term cellaring. **83** *(10/1/2001)*

Stonehaven 1999 Shiraz (Limestone Coast) $16. Dense and purple, with mocha, chocolate, and black fruit all mixing nicely on the nose. The mouth is full and corpulent, like Aussie Shiraz should be. And on the finish there's the essence of wood spice and vanilla, with some length. Really balanced and delivers a lot in proper proportions. **88** —*M.S. (3/1/2003)*

Stonehaven 1998 Shiraz (Limestone Coast) $17. 87 *(11/1/2000)*

Stonehaven 1998 Shiraz (South Eastern Australia) $9. 88 Best Buy *(11/1/2000)*

Stonehaven 1997 Reserve Shiraz (Padthaway) $46. We used plenty of adjectives to describe this wine's flavors, but few had anything to do with fruit. An unlikely flavor pairing, black olive and cinnamon, dominates the bouquet and the palate. Leather and meat aromas flesh out the nose, and clove and coffee (plus a little blackberry) spice up the palate. Medium-long tannin and mineral finish. **86** *(11/1/2001)*

Stonehaven 1996 Reserve Shiraz (Padthaway) $46. 88 *(11/1/2000)*

Stonehaven 2003 Winemaker's Selection Shiraz (South Australia) $12. Shows some roasted fruit character, with predominantly earthy flavors and notes of cooked meat, coffee, cinnamon, and brown sugar. Low acidity and decent concentration give it a fat mouthfeel. **85** *(11/1/2005)*

Stonehaven 1999 Shiraz-Cabernet Sauvignon (South Eastern Australia) $9. 86 *(11/1/2000)*

STONEY RISE

Stoney Rise 2002 Shiraz (Limestone Coast) $19. This is one dry Shiraz now, with tree-bark, black pepper, and high-toned black fruit aromas and flavors, and tea-like tannins firmly gripping the palate. Give it a year or two to settle down and smooth out. **87** —*D.T. (12/31/2004)*

STRINGY BRAE

Stringy Brae 1998 Cabernet Sauvignon (Clare Valley) $33. The palate is Swiss Miss cocoa meets Sweet Tarts and sour red berries; wood and mixed berry aromas have a slight chlorinated twinge on the nose. Finishes with tangy oak and dusty tannins. **84** —*D.T. (6/1/2002)*

Stringy Brae 1999 Shiraz (Clare Valley) $30. The impression here is more herbal and earthy than fruity; the mouthfeel is a little light, but strangely resinous. Finishes with stewed red fruit. **83** —*D.T. (1/28/2003)*

SYLVAN SPRINGS

Sylvan Springs 1999 Cabernet Sauvignon (McLaren Vale) $18. A little on the lean side, as far as Cabernet Sauvignons are concerned, but offers some nice, bright red berry fruit on the nose and palate. Splashes of dried spice and oak complete the picture. **84** —*D.T. (6/1/2002)*

Sylvan Springs 2000 Shiraz (McLaren Vale) $20. Get past the nose, and you're in for a lean, mean Shiraz machine. A whiff out of the glass, though, will get you a nose full of lactic, milky notes, plus some herb. Palate offers a sour cherry-cranberry mixed bag, with a distinctive herb-and-tree-bark component. **84** —*D.T. (1/28/2003)*

T'GALLANT

T'Gallant 2000 Chardonnay (Mornington Peninsula) $18. Seems almost Burgundian in this crowd, with its aromas of smoke and white peach and flavors of roasted hazelnuts and grilled peaches. Finishes clean and crisp, with tart, lime-like acidity and hints of smoke. **87** —*J.C. (7/1/2002)*

T'Gallant 2000 Imogen Pinot Gris (Mornington Peninsula) $18. Creamier and less spicy than their Tribute bottling, the Imogen offers gentle pear and vanilla aromas and flavors. Some people may like it better, as it's softer and milder on the palate, but the Tribute has a bolder attitude. Closes dry and even, with modest length. **86** —*M.M. (2/1/2002)*

T'Gallant 2000 Tribute Pinot Gris (Mornington Peninsula) $20. The full pear and spice bouquet of this wine pulls you right in. Similar appealing ripe flavors follow, offset by earthy notes on the rich, slightly viscous palate. The spicy close shows good length and texture, a pleasant back

AUSTRALIA

bouquet. It's close in manner to some Pinot Gris from Alsace. **88** —*M.M. (2/1/2002)*

T'Gallant 2000 Pinot Noir (Mornington Peninsula) $25. A pretty, light-weight wine that offers up smoky, herbal scents along with almost ephemeral wisps of red fruit. It's dry and delicate; a waif-like Pinot that could benefit from a little more flesh. **85** —*J.C. (9/1/2002)*

TAHBILK

Tahbilk 2002 Cabernet Sauvignon (Nagambie Lakes) $25. This wine's flavors are dark and interesting, but folks looking for a full-throttle, super-rich wine should just keep browsing. Lifted black and blueberry fruit on the nose. On the palate, smoke, chewy cherry, and bitter chocolate flavors are couched in a dusty feel. Lessens in intensity toward the back end, but it's still very attractive. **88** —*D.T. (12/31/2005)*

Tahbilk 1999 Cabernet Sauvignon (Nagambie Lakes) $20. This Cab is already turning somewhat brick in color. Its flavors and aromas are of red fruit, but they are less fleshy than they are like skin and seeds. The wine's pleasing, smooth mouthfeel is its best feature. **84** —*D.T. (5/1/2005)*

Tahbilk 1998 Cabernet Sauvignon (Australia) $18. The "legs" on this wine are thick and gluey, the visible sign of enormous extract. One sniff and taste confirm that. This is a big, sturdy wine, stuffed with wild berry flavors, and very dry. But beware, the tannins are outsized. Have it with red meat-based foods or age for up to a decade. **92** —*S.H. (6/1/2002)*

Tahbilk 2000 Reserve Cabernet Sauvignon (Nagambie Lakes) $59. The aromas are just beautiful: Inhale deeply and there's spice, nut, cassis, and gumtree notes. Has wooly, textured tannins that grip the midpalate firmly, along with plum and almond paste notes that carry on through the finish. A real pleasure; drink after 2008. **91** —*D.T. (6/1/2006)*

Tahbilk 1994 Reserve Cabernet Sauvignon (Goulburn Valley) $35. Opens with a taut but full bouquet of dense, black plum fruit and eucalyptus accents that blend into seductive licorice and dark cherry flavors and a fat chewy texture. Finishes long, with rich flavors and full even tannins. This wine is still just a baby, with a great life ahead of it. **93** *(6/1/2001)*

Tahbilk 2003 Chardonnay (Nagambie Lakes) $NA. Smoky, nutty aromas lead to textbook, commercial peach-and-oak flavors that finish a little short. Good; tastes like a basic, by-the-glass pour at your local boîte. **84** —*D.T. (4/1/2006)*

Tahbilk 2005 Marsanne (Nagambie Lakes) $18. This varietal Marsanne has pretty almond and coffee liqueur aromas, and a palate rife with grassy, citrusy tones. It sounds disjointed but actually works quite well. Acidity is lively and would be razor sharp, were it not saved by a moderating minerally overlay. Worth seeking out. **89** —*D.T. (10/1/2006)*

Tahbilk 1999 Marsanne (Victoria) $12. Opens with distinctive smoky and nutty aromas, but the flavors are of stone fruits—peaches and plums. Not a rich or overbearing wine, it's more about balance and restraint. Finishes long and tangy, with a nutty reprise. **88** *(2/1/2002)*

Tahbilk 2002 Shiraz (Nagambie Lakes) $25. Has flavors of blackberry and grape. At this stage of its young life, this Shiraz is dominated by a veneer of oak, and seems flat, rather than vibrant, because of it. A year or two in bottle may yield a plumper, rounder wine. **87** —*D.T. (6/1/2006)*

Tahbilk 1998 Shiraz (Victoria) $18. This Shiraz is a top-to-bottom berry bomb—it has bright, juicy black fruit aromas and flavors—but one reviewer thought it possibly overripe; another said that the berry fruit verged on the artificial. Finishes with red fruit, with a chalky overlay. A good starting place for novice wine enthusiasts. **85** *(10/1/2001)*

Tahbilk 1997 Shiraz (Goulburn Valley) $18. **89** —*S.H. (10/1/2000)*

Tahbilk 2000 1860 Vines Shiraz (Nagambie Lakes) $125. There's just 350 cases produced of this terrific wine, which has light tobaccoey aromas layered over cherry pie. It just floods the front palate with juicy fruit: raspberry, a hint of cranberry, even quince. It's pure, focused, juicy and sophisticated. Finishes medium-long. **92** —*D.T. (4/1/2006)*

Tahbilk 1996 1860 Vines Shiraz (Nagambie Lakes) $125. This is a wine that feels old-fashioned but still not ready to drink. It smells nutty and dusty, with black pepper and anise accents. Its plum fruit core is wound very tightly, and encased in a fair amount of good-quality oak. Tannins are thick and wooly, so much so that I'd forget that I even had this in the cellar until Bush is out of office, then drink through 2014 or so. **92** **Cellar Selection** —*D.T. (8/1/2005)*

Tahbilk 1994 1860 Vines Shiraz (Goulburn Valley) $60. **92** *(10/1/2000)*

Tahbilk 2000 Reserve Shiraz (Nagambie Lakes) $59. Plum and berry fruit on the palate are juicy but fairly mainstream; pretty notes of spice accent roasted blackberry aromas. Textured tannins add interest on the finish. **88** —*D.T. (4/1/2006)*

Tahbilk 2005 Viognier (Nagambie Lakes) $19. A very good, medium-bodied Vigonier, but one that may stump you if you taste it blind: it smells of yellow stone fruit and clarified butter, followed by flavors of fresh bread, trading card bubblegum powder and citrus. The pleasantly dry, citrus component continues on through the finish. **88** —*D.T. (10/1/2006)*

TAIT WINES

Tait Wines 2002 Basket Pressed Cabernet Sauvignon (Barossa Valley) $30. Anise and oak on the nose; winemaker Bruno Tait says, "Believe it or not, it's 15.5% alcohol," but I don't see why we're supposed to be so surprised. It's a sizeable wine, with woody tannins that linger on the palate, and mixed plum fruit underneath. A very nice wine, concentrated and intimidating. **91** —*D.T. (2/1/2004)*

Tait Wines 2002 The Ball Buster Red Blend (Barossa Valley) $17. Not as brutal on the palate as the name might suggest, this blend of 60% Shiraz, 20% Cabernet, and 20% Merlot is better called "the affable, easy-to-get-on-with chap." Juicy, sweet red berry fruit bounces around on the palate and on the nose. Finishes quite the same, but it's just so fun to drink, and goes down so easily, that you won't help but like it. **89** —*D.T. (2/1/2004)*

Tait Wines 2000 Basket Press Shiraz (Barossa Valley) $25. This Shiraz offers candied yet sour red fruit and herb flavors. It's less than lush in the mouth, verging on thin. Cheese and herb round out the finish. **84** —*D.T. (1/28/2003)*

Tait Wines 2002 Basket Pressed Shiraz (Barossa Valley) $33. This vintage, this Shiraz isn't filtered. It's elegant, and not an unruly blockbuster as many other '02s are, with juicy black fruit and a little buttercream for good measure. Its chalky tannins are lovely. Drinkable soon; give it six months to a year, at least, to settle down. **92** —*D.T. (2/1/2004)*

TALAGANDRA

Talagandra 2001 Chardonnay (Australia) $17. Pure sweet fruit stars in this show. Peaches and pears, mainly, with just a hint of vanilla and toast. Some clove and butter notes sneak in on the finish. It's a light, fruity wine to drink over the next few months. **85** —*J.C. (9/10/2001)*

Talagandra 2000 Canberra District Shiraz (Australia) $19. Aromas of sarsaparilla soda and dill hardly qualify as ordinary. Then the flavors don't much match the bouquet; they are tangy and sharp, veering toward cherry and sugared citrus rind. Below the surface there is some quality cherry fruit, but overall it seems to lack plushness. **83** —*M.S. (2/1/2003)*

TALTARNI

Taltarni 1995 Cabernet Sauvignon (Victoria) $16. **88** *(12/31/1999)*

Taltarni 2000 Cabernet Sauvignon-Merlot (Victoria) $14. Cherry and herb flavors are prefaced by black pepper and green pepper aromas. This is a tasty, very good wine, though a lean one—if "black beauty" is what you're looking for in a Cab–Merlot, keep looking. **87** —*D.T. (12/31/2003)*

Taltarni 2003 Three Monks Cabernet Sauvignon-Merlot (Victoria) $16. Almost three-quarters Cab, with Merlot rounding out the balance. Shows cola, wheat bread, and a hint of wintergreen on the nose, and tight red fruit and earth flavors on the palate. A smooth, clay-like feel completes the picture. Very nice, and more tight than plump. **89** —*D.T. (8/1/2006)*

Taltarni 2005 Sauvignon Blanc (Victoria) $16. An elegant style of Sauvignon, but one that's also pretty austere. Has aromas of lemon curd and flavors of pear; feel is minerally and the acidity is high. A very good wine and likely a good companion to food, but may not appeal to those looking for a ripe, fruity SB. **87** —*D.T. (4/1/2006)*

Taltarni 2004 Sauvignon Blanc (Victoria) $16. This is a very enjoyable Sauvignon, with a zesty profile that is green, but not in the typically

AUSTRALIA

limey, Kiwi-inspired way. Here you'll find pleasant aromas of fresh, leafy greens (lettuce, and even some mint), and flavors that reminded me of key lime or lemon meringue pie—citrusy, yes, but certainly not sour. A chalky, dusty feel completes the picture. 2,000 cases produced. **88** —*D. T. (12/1/2005)*

Taltarni 2000 Sauvignon Blanc (Victoria) $13. Distinctly uncharacteristic, this Sauvignon Blanc shows pear, banana, and vanilla aromas. There's some soft tropical fruit with hints of butter, pear, and apple, but as with so many Australian Sauvignon Blancs, not enough of an acid spine to keep it lively. **82** —*J.F. (9/1/2001)*

Taltarni 2004 Shiraz (Heathcote) $35. I've liked other Taltarni wines more than this, and many a fan will surely find this score stingy. If lifted berry fruit couched in maple syrup notes and soft tannins gets you going, this is right on the mark. This reviewer prefers more acid, and less sweetness. **85** —*D. T. (8/1/2006)*

Taltarni 2003 Shiraz (Heathcote) $35. Smells of raspberries, but tastes meaty, chalky, and a hint metallic, though the metallic edge isn't too much of a bother. Thick, dusty, very dry tannins complete the picture. **87** —*D. T. (12/1/2005)*

Taltarni 2002 Shiraz (Pyrenees) $20. Blackberry and vanilla flavors take on a maple character with air, but on the palate, it's all bouncy fruit, all the time. Finishes with sweet vanilla notes. Truly an enjoyable wine, but one that doesn't quite go deep enough to make it to the next decile. **89** —*D. T. (6/1/2006)*

Taltarni 1997 Estate Grown Shiraz (Victoria) $16. 89 *(12/31/1999)*

Taltarni 2000 Cephas Shiraz-Cabernet Sauvignon (Victoria) $30. Varietal components aside, this baby isn't big enough to stand up to grilled meat. There's some red fruit mixed in with the black; it all tastes like it's been rolled in red clay. The nose—an unusual mix of ginger, eucalyptus, and clay—may well be the best part. **88** —*D. T. (12/31/2003)*

Taltarni NV Brut Taché Sparkling Blend (Australia) $22. Brought to you by the folks at Clos Du Val, this "rosé-style" wine has a crisp cranberry and raspberry core couched in a fluffy pillow of biscuit flour. The same bready-biscuity note, plus some sour cherry, shows on the nose as well. Mouthfeel is fairly dry, with foamy mousse. **88** —*D. T. (12/31/2003)*

Taltarni NV Brut Taché Sparkling Blend (Victoria) $20. Light pink in color, with aromas of dust, earth, and cherry. It's medium-full in the mouth, cherry notes once again at the fore, but bolstered by earth, toast, and a racy, grapefruit edge through the finish. Very enjoyable; 1,600 cases produced. **89** —*D. T. (12/31/2005)*

Taltarni 2003 Brut Taché Sparkling Blend (Victoria) $20. Taltarni's Brut Taché is a coppery-pink rosé with a bouquet that combines toasty, yeasty notes with assertive citrus scents, then adds on some savory, mushroomy elements. It's even meatier and more savory on the palate, making it better suited than most sparklers to match with meat courses. Doesn't seem likely to age further, so drink up. **86** —*J.C. (12/31/2006)*

TAMAR RIDGE

Tamar Ridge 2004 Sauvignon Blanc (Tasmania) $20. Ultra fresh, with bright aromas of passion fruit, citrus, cucumber, bell pepper, and blanched asparagus. Then comes the fruit, which falls squarely into the tangy grapefruit realm, with notes of lime and pineapple. Razor sharp and wholesome. **89** *(7/1/2005)*

TAPESTRY

Tapestry 2003 Cabernet Sauvignon (McLaren Vale) $22. Briar and moist clay aromas lead to tannins that feel grabby at first, then smooth out with air. Aeration is key, too, in allowing flavors of blackberry and blueberry to emerge. Nice now, and probably better after another year in bottle. **89** —*D. T. (6/1/2006)*

Tapestry 2002 Cabernet Sauvignon (McLaren Vale) $21. This Cab has a smooth, milky texture. Its core is cherry, verging on rhubarb, and black pepper is the main player on the nose. Light in size for a Cab. **86** —*D. T. (10/1/2005)*

Tapestry 2001 Cabernet Sauvignon (McLaren Vale) $20. This Cab has smooth tannins in the mouth, wtih flavors of black plum and cherry fruit edged in brown sugar; the finish shows bright herb, nut, and oak

notes. A very nice, classy wine, and drinking well now. **89** —*D. T. (5/1/2004)*

Tapestry 1999 Bin 388 Cabernet Sauvignon (McLaren Vale) $25. Medium-weight with an overlying creaminess to the tart black fruit on the palate, this Cab's nose is awash with sweet, mixed-berry aromas. The wine wants more acidity to hold it all together and give it a little spine. **83** —*D. T. (6/1/2002)*

Tapestry 2001 Fifteen Barrels Cabernet Sauvignon (McLaren Vale) $36. Wood is so very prevalent here, in the forms of fresh-cut pine, caramel, oak, burnt sugar, and white pepper that the lovely plum fruit sadly takes a backseat. Folks who have more tolerance for wood may find this review conservative. **86** —*D. T. (5/1/2004)*

Tapestry 2004 Chardonnay (McLaren Vale) $16. A feminine-style Chardonnay, offering light floral aromas and a soft, approachable mouthfeel. Flavors of yellow stone fruit and chalk turn citrusy and tart toward the finish. **86** —*D. T. (4/1/2006)*

Tapestry 2002 Chardonnay (McLaren Vale) $15. A racy wine, with a tart streak: Aromas are of pear, green apple, and grapefruit. Feels clean in the mouth with citrus and peach fruit, and a hint of herb. Finishes with a peppery sourness. Bring a bottle to the raw bar. **85** *(7/2/2004)*

Tapestry 2005 Riesling (McLaren Vale) $16. Pear and floral aromas usher in lively acidity and modest pear skin flavors on the palate. A delicate, easy wine, just the sort for a spring picnic. **85** —*D. T. (4/1/2006)*

Tapestry 2002 Shiraz (McLaren Vale) $21. This is an easy-drinking Shiraz, with plums, blackberries, and oak at the fore. As good for red-sauced pastas as it is for red meats. Medium in weight; drink now and over the next two years. **87** —*D. T. (2/1/2006)*

Tapestry 2001 Shiraz (McLaren Vale) $19. Pretty plum fruit and pencil-eraser aromas lead to similar flavors, with a light underlay of fresh herb. Finishes a little brief, though with gummy tannins. **87** —*D. T. (3/1/2005)*

Tapestry 1999 Bin 338 Shiraz (McLaren Vale) $25. The nose on the Tapestry is a little subdued—but that's a good thing, if brett, garlic, and meaty gravy aren't what you're looking for in a Shiraz. Medium-weight and a little chewy in the mouth, the palate offers lots of blackberry plus earth, leather, and horsey flavors. Finishes medium-long with grape and oak flavors. **87** *(11/1/2001)*

Tapestry 2003 The Vincent Shiraz (McLaren Vale) $40. From the same Bakers Gully Vineyard as Clarendon Hills' Bakers Gully Shiraz, this is a full-bodied Shiraz with bold vanilla and saddle leather aromas and flavors of brambleberries. Rustic notes include hints of rubber or Band-Aid, but they're in the background, while warm berries, vanilla, and roasted coffee notes lead the way. Drink now. **89** —*J.C. (12/15/2006)*

Tapestry 2002 The Vincent Shiraz (McLaren Vale) $39. This Shiraz is sexy in its way but overdone, like a woman who's wearing entirely too much makeup. Aromas are alluring, but on the sweet side—blackberry, anise, creampuff, vanilla, Sweet Tart. Cocoa, caramel, and raspberry flavors follow suit. Not confected or manufactured-tasting by any means, but it's a New World, modern style that just won't appeal to everyone. **87** —*D. T. (3/1/2005)*

Tapestry 2001 The Vincent Shiraz (McLaren Vale) $36. From vines with a minimum age of 30 years, this is a pretty accessible style of Shiraz. The nose offers jammy, bright fruit with judicious oak accents, which deepen into nice hazelnut notes. In the mouth, smooth oak overlays mixed plum fruits. A feminine wine, rather than an overstuffed, burly one. **88** —*D. T. (11/15/2004)*

TATACHILLA

Tatachilla 2000 Cabernet Sauvignon (McLaren Vale) $20. Powdered sugar and blackberry preserves on the nose are promising; bitter green herb and flinty soil on the palate hold the place of where fruit should be. Finish is bitter, as though the wine might be acidified. **81** —*D. T. (6/1/2002)*

Tatachilla 1999 Cabernet Sauvignon (Padthaway) $20. Sweet berry aromas on the nose are cloaked in a creamy, cough-syrupy note. A distinct faux-herbaceous flavor (like a menthol cough drop) mars both palate and finish. **81** —*D. T. (6/1/2002)*

Tatachilla 1998 Cabernet Sauvignon (McLaren Vale) $20. Lots of cedary wood is wrapped around the red berry and dark cherry fruit in this smooth, medium-weight offering. It shows moderate acidity and a licorice and toast finish with some tangy tannins. It's quite woody, but likeable nonetheless. **86** —*M.M. (9/1/2001)*

Tatachilla 2000 Breakneck Creek Cabernet Sauvignon (South Australia) $12. Reminiscent of some Paso Cabernets in its warm blackberry and plum fruit combined with hints of sweet grass and alfalfa. Finishes a bit thin, with coffee flavors closing things out. **83** —*J.C. (6/1/2002)*

Tatachilla 1999 Wattle Park Cabernet Sauvignon (South Australia) $10. An overripe quality to the blackberry-liqueur fruit, especially on the nose, marks this lovable sweet jam-fest. The smooth palate has tea and clove accents that add enough interest to prevent a descent into sticky simplicity, and the package turns less sugary and a touch more rustic and earthy on the finish. **87** *(6/1/2001)*

Tatachilla 2000 Chardonnay (Padthaway) $15. Tropical aromas and flavors of coconut and pineapple are loaded up with vanilla and melted butter. A slight hint of varnish detracts from the package and most likely indicates that it needs to be consumed soon—the wine might have been better a few months back. **84** —*J.C. (7/1/2002)*

Tatachilla 2000 Chardonnay (McLaren Vale) $14. A bright, sunny, yellow Chard through and through—and the cream-and-tropcial fruit nose is just the beginning. Peach, banana, and vanilla flavors resurface on the palate; toasty-butterscotch flavors round out the back end. An instant mood-lifter. Drink now. **86** —*D.T. (8/1/2003)*

Tatachilla 2000 Chardonnay (Adelaide Hills) $25. **83** —*D.T. (8/1/2003)*

Tatachilla 1999 Chardonnay (Padthaway) $16. Don't let the youngsters get a hold of this pale-gold Chardonnay: The medium-bodied wine has easy-to-drink, apple-cidery flavors, with such low acidity that you might mistake it for a nonalcoholic cider. The sunny bouquet has lemongrass, apple, and date highlights. **84** —*D.T. (9/1/2001)*

Tatachilla 1999 Chardonnay (McLaren Vale) $14. The moral of this story? Drink your tropical fruit-and-oak Chards young, before the fruit disappears, leaving nothing but the hollow shell of an empty barrel. **80** —*J.C. (9/10/2002)*

Tatachilla 1998 Chardonnay (McLaren Vale) $12. Tropical fruit and tangy lemon aromas and flavors are nearly buried under dense oak here, but when they peek through they are bright and pleasing. The acids are sharp, but in here they seem to help the fruit cut through the wood veneer. Good, but a lighter hand letting the fruit shine more would be even better. **84** *(6/1/2001)*

Tatachilla 2001 Breakneck Creek Chardonnay (South Australia) $9. Toasty and thick in the mouth, it smells syrupy, like peach jelly and honey. The palate flavors reminded the panelists more of Gewürztraminer than Chardonnay. A puzzling wine. **82** *(7/2/2004)*

Tatachilla 1999 Wattle Park Chardonnay (South Australia) $10. A creamy but not mushy mouthfeel and nicely defined flavors mark this friendly, easy-to-enjoy bottling. It's mainstream, with mild tropical fruit and citrus aromas and flavors, but it has a bit more class than many similar wines, especially with its even feel and long finish. **88 Best Buy** —*M.M. (9/1/2001)*

Tatachilla 1998 Grenache-Shiraz (McLaren Vale) $14. This blend of 78% Grenache and 22% Shiraz shows surprisingly light fruit. Starts off with eucalyptus, horse saddle, and cedar aromas that morph into menthol and sauna flavors, with only brief glimpses of tart red currants. **84** —*J.C. (9/1/2001)*

Tatachilla 1999 Clarendon Vineyards Merlot (McLaren Vale) $35. The vineyard is located between the demarcated areas of McLaren Vale and the Adelaide Hills, hence the simple "Australia" appellation. Artfully combines spicy vanilla oak with juicy blackberry and cassis fruit in a simple but fun and satisfying wine perfect for casual dining. **87** —*J.C. (6/1/2002)*

Tatachilla 2000 Wattle Park Merlot (South Australia) $12. A trifle burlier and rougher than Tatachilla's Clarendon Vineyard Merlot, the Wattle Park offering adds hints of tobacco and earth to the cassis-and-vanilla mix. The somewhat tough finish could use a grilled steak to smooth it out. **86** —*J.C. (6/1/2002)*

Tatachilla 1999 Wattle Park Merlot (South Australia) $10. The red berry and cocoa aromas offer solid Merlot character in this soft, medium-weight wine. It's appealing, if not particularly deep, but there's no argument here with the stylish cocoa-coffee shadings on the red currant fruit. Finishes just as pleasurably, with a bit more spice than on the palate. **87 Best Buy** —*M.M. (9/1/2001)*

Tatachilla 2000 Grenache/Shiraz Red Blend (McLaren Vale) $15. A 70-30 blend, this wine shows loads of cherry fruit that's surprisingly tart given the wine's loose-knit nature. Finishes with a warm alcoholic glow and hints of damp earth, cinnamon, clove, and eucalyptus. **84** —*J.C. (9/1/2002)*

Tatachilla 1999 Grenache-Mourvedre Rhône Red Blend (South Australia) $9. At two-thirds Grenache and one-third Mourvèdre, this wine comes across full and rich, and a trifle alcoholic. The overall sensation is of a cherry-vanilla sundae smothered in toffee and chocolate—too much of a good thing for some tasters, heaven in a glass to others. **86** —*J.C. (9/1/2002)*

Tatachilla 2000 Shiraz (McLaren Vale) $20. Shows eucalyptus, cola, and thick black plum flavors on the nose. Black cherry, red plum, and clove flavors hit you at palate entry; by midpalate, a pleasing chalk-clay feel steps in. A very good red wine, but not one you'd immediately recognize as Shiraz. **87** —*D.T. (5/1/2004)*

Tatachilla 1999 Shiraz (McLaren Vale) $22. Shows nice complexity in its aromas of cherry, vanilla, soy sauce, leather, and meat, then fills the mouth with supple cherry fruit that carries a hints of medicinal herbs. Finishes with tart cherries and a slight lactic note. **87** —*J.C. (9/1/2002)*

Tatachilla 2002 Breakneck Creek Shiraz (South Australia) $9. Smells and tastes of light brown sugar and soft red fruit. It's a simple, easy-drinking, accessible wine, and priced accordingly. **85** —*D.T. (9/1/2004)*

Tatachilla 2000 Breakneck Creek Shiraz (South Australia) $9. This is a thick, ripe Aussie red in which you can stand up a fork. The bold blackberry, vanilla, black pepper, and dark earth flavors are not about finesse or elegance; this is stick-to-your-ribs stuff. **88 Best Buy** —*J.C. (9/1/2002)*

Tatachilla 1998 Foundation Shiraz (McLaren Vale) $45. The nose offers penetrating eucalypus notes, plus blackberry and stone aromas. Eucalyptus persists on the palate, enveloping bright red fruit flavors. Medium-bodied and smooth, it closes with smooth, slatelike minerality. **88** —*D.T. (3/1/2003)*

Tatachilla 1996 Foundation Shiraz (McLaren Vale) $40. This mature and ripe wine shows impressive complexity and a smooth, full mouthfeel. Deep dark-cherry fruit wears meaty, peppery accents and an almost Worcestershire/marinade quality noted by more than one taster. Mocha and earth, black pepper, leather, and herb all show on the long and even finish. Drink this handsome wine now through 2005. **91 Editors' Choice** *(11/1/2001)*

Tatachilla 2000 Chenin Blanc-Semillon-Sauvignon Blanc White Blend (South Australia) $9. This bright gold wine is tangy in the mouth, with lemon, green bean, and metallic flavors; its bouquet shows canned green bean flavors, with some bright yellow fruit and white pepper notes underneath. Finishes minerally, but also sweet. **80** —*D.T. (2/1/2002)*

Tatachilla 1999 Chenin Blanc-Semillon-Sauvignon Blanc White Blend (South Australia) $10. This wine's mouthfeel lends itself, it seems, to this wine's flavors: chalk and a light floral-gardeny note on the palate, and minerals on the finish. On the nose, a little cream and butter softens up clean, lime-mineral aromas. **84** —*D.T. (2/1/2002)*

TATIARRA

Tatiarra 2003 Cambrian Shiraz (Heathcote) $58. This Shiraz has a remarkable texture—like smooth river stones—and offers a berry-basket full of juicy flavors. On the nose, aromas of coconut, toast, and chocolate (no, it's not at all candied, as it may sound) mingle with fresh raspberries. **90** —*D.T. (12/1/2005)*

TEAL LAKE

Teal Lake 2002 Private Reserve Cabernet Sauvignon (South Eastern Australia) $19. Quite bright, with tangy acidity and blackberry, tar, smoke, and herb flavors at the fore. Tannins are moderate, while the finish has a citrus-like edge. Kosher. **83** —*J.M. (4/3/2004)*

Teal Lake 2002 Cabernet Sauvignon-Merlot (South Eastern Australia) $13. Boasts tobacco and dried-spice aromas, then turns a bit tart and cranberryish on the palate. Lean and herbal on the finish. **83** —*J.C. (4/1/2005)*

Teal Lake 2003 Chardonnay (South Eastern Australia) $13. Tropical fruit and sweet corn flavors, with a pat of butter for good measure. Shows some oak and alcohol on the finish. **84** —*J.C. (4/1/2005)*

Teal Lake 1999 Herzog Selection Chardonnay (South Eastern Australia) $12. Opens with ripe apple, honey, and herb aromas, and opens to apple and peach flavors and an even, almost velvety texture. It's a stylish Chardonnay for everyday drinking. **85** *(4/1/2001)*

Teal Lake 2002 Petit Verdot-Cabernet Red Blend (South Eastern Australia) $13. A bit grapey and unformed at first, but seems to develop a bit in the glass, adding cassis, roasted meat, and coffee notes. Crisp and smooth in the mouth. **85** —*J.C. (4/1/2005)*

Teal Lake 2001 Shiraz (South Eastern Australia) $13. Although mouthfilling, this comes off cool and smooth. Aromas of meat, dried Italian herbs, and black olives meet plenty of spice and fruit on the palate, and linger through the finish. Kosher.. **87** —*K.F. (3/1/2003)*

Teal Lake 2000 Shiraz (South Eastern Australia) $12. There's nothing subtle about this intensely fruity wine. It's ripe black cherries all the way, with hints of chocolate and wintergreen. The tannins are soft, the acids low, but the flavors are so pretty that the lack of structure isn't a big issue in this everyday drinker. **85** *(4/1/2001)*

Teal Lake 2002 Shiraz-Cabernet Sauvignon (South Eastern Australia) $12. Simple leather and plum aromas and flavors; a medium-weight wine that turns a little tart on the finish. **84** —*J.C. (4/1/2005)*

TEMPLE BRUER

Temple Bruer 1999 Cabernet Blend (Langhorne Creek) $20. Smells fine, with floral oak, cinnamon oak, and vanilla oak aromas backed up by blackberry fruit. But in the mouth, there's a resinous oak flavor that gets in the way more than complements. And the fruit (a blend of 72% Cabernet Sauvignon and 28% Petit Verdot) comes across as blowsy and a bit hot. **82** —*J.C. (6/1/2002)*

Temple Bruer 2001 Reserve Cabernet Blend (Langhorne Creek) $22. This is an interesting, pleasing blend of 81% Cabernet Sauvignon and 19% Petit Verdot, organically grown in Langhorne Creek. I like how unusual its characteristics are—aromas of menthol and blackberry, and flavors of clove, cinnamon, and black plums. Altogether it is a harmonious, medium-bodied wine worth a look. **89** —*D.T. (5/1/2005)*

Temple Bruer 1998 Reserve Cabernet Sauvignon (Langhorne Creek) $16. This lush, full-throttle Cab is organically grown and includes 14% Petite Verdot. Intense mint, chocolate, and blueberry aromas waft out of the glass. It's firm and tightly structured, but at once evenly textured and mouthfilling. Layers of tobacco, more mint, leather, chocolate, and blueberry flavors coat the palate. Hardy tannins will soften with cellaring, but the fruit/acid/tannin balance is very good. It finishes long and complex, with that blueberry note. **93 Editors' Choice** —*J.F. (9/1/2001)*

Temple Bruer 2001 Cabernet Sauvignon-Merlot (McLaren Vale & Langhorne Creek) $16. Has ripe blackberry and plum fruit from nose to finish. It's a subtle wine, medium-sized with chalky tannins—just the profile you want in a dinnertime quaff. **88** —*D.T. (12/31/2003)*

Temple Bruer 1999 Cabernet Sauvignon-Merlot (Langhorne Creek) $16. This blend of 54% Cabernet Sauvignon, 34% Merlot, and 12% Cabernet Franc spent 15 months in American oak, which is why I can't really account for why the aromas are confected and grapey (Maneschewitz comes to mind). Palate offers clove and earth; finish offers almost nothing. **81** —*D.T. (6/1/2002)*

Temple Bruer 2003 Chenin Blanc (Langhorne Creek) $15. If peach aromatherapy exists—that is, the purest, most concentrated smell of peach in a bottle—this nose is it. After a while, though, an acrylic-like aroma starts emerging, and the palate shows evidence of both acrylic and peach. Still, it's a worthwhile wine, but would have been better with the focus on the fruit. **84** —*D.T. (5/1/2005)*

Temple Bruer 1998 Cornucopia Grenache (Langhorne Creek) $13. This round, soft, alcoholic wine deserves praise for its spicy-peppery warmth and abundant cherry fruit. Those same qualities are also its biggest short-

coming: The low acidity and high alcohol make it seem a bit heavy. **85** —*J.C. (9/1/2002)*

Temple Bruer 1998 Reserve Merlot (Langhorne Creek) $20. Woodsy, rustic tannins in the mouth are appropriate accompaniments to oak, green herb, and mixed berry flavors. Ditto for the aromas. Finish is dry, with lots of oak. **84** —*D.T. (6/1/2002)*

Temple Bruer 2000 Shiraz-Malbec (Langhorne Creek) $16. Two-thirds Shiraz and one-third Malbec, this wine is surprisingly soft in the mouth, considering its near-black color and plum and cherry fruit. Big, burly tannins come in on the finish. A tasty wine, black but not at all oppressively so. **88** —*D.T. (5/1/2004)*

THE BLACK CHOOK

The Black Chook 2004 Shiraz-Viognier (South Australia) $18. This wine inspired some debate in the tasting room, others appreciating it more than I did. Made by Ben Riggs, a winemaker who certainly knows his way around Shiraz-Viogniers. The aromas are very sweet, with raspberry and blueberry holding court. The flavor? Blueberry jam. Tastes low in acid, but its 15% alcohol is no surprise. **84** —*D.T. (12/31/2005)*

THE COLONIAL ESTATE

The Colonial Estate 2004 Etranger Cabernet Sauvignon-Shiraz (Barossa Valley) $30. Aromas are of roasted fruits; on the palate, it has a dark, oaky underlay offset by sourish red fruit. Straightforward. 1,900 cases produced. **85** —*D.T. (10/1/2006)*

The Colonial Estate 2004 Évangéliste Reserve Chardonnay (Adelaide Hills) $30. Right out of the gate, there's a pungent aroma of cat pee, plus nuts and floral notes. With time, the pungency subsides, revealing pretty honeysuckle notes that usher in peach and Fuji apple on the palate. Has persistence, medium body, and holds fast on the finish. **90** —*D.T. (6/1/2006)*

The Colonial Estate 2005 Enchanteur Grenache (Barossa Valley) $20. This rosé offers sweet berry aromas and tangy, sour cherry and herb flavors. Disjointed, and wants concentration. **83** —*D.T. (4/1/2006)*

The Colonial Estate 2004 L'eclaireur Sauvignon Blanc (Adelaide Hills) $25. Sensationally clean on the nose, with freshwater stream minerality mixed with pure peach and pear. Not much to find issue with here; the grapefruit and tangerine flavors are nice, the mouthfeel is textured yet upright, and the finish is zippy and plenty long. **89** *(7/1/2005)*

The Colonial Estate 2004 Explorateur Shiraz (Barossa Valley) $30. A wine that evolves through a few phases while in the glass, each more odd than the last. Starts off with a sold berry-and cream profile, straightforward and accessible. With time, the nose turns tomato-y, and the palate bubblegum-sweet, then a little green. Well-made, but odd. **86** —*D.T. (6/1/2006)*

THE EDGE

The Edge 2002 Sauvignon Blanc (King Valley) $16. The primary flavors are of lime/lime pith and white peach, which hang on a clean frame. Fresh green accents are pleasant, but not for everyone. **86** —*D.T. (11/15/2004)*

The Edge 2001 Sauvignon Blanc (King Valley) $15. Ample aromas of toast and wood announce the oak treatment this wine received. Oak-inspired flavors like vanilla and nutmeg are further intermixed with lemon and other citrus flavors in the mouth. The finish is a touch flat, and it's a bit heavy on the back end with banana and coconut nuances—again from the oak. **87** *(1/1/2004)*

THE GATE

The Gate 2003 Shiraz (McLaren Vale) $32. An enjoyable Shiraz to drink now: Cream, vanilla, and sweet fruit on the nose, with a standard earth-plum-oak formula on the palate. Has a little herbal bitterness on the finish, but very good overall. **87** —*D.T. (6/1/2006)*

The Gate 2003 Shiraz (McLaren Vale) $32. Another label from Shingleback winemaker John Davey, this vintage of The Gate delivers a well-structured, tasty wine full of black and white pepper, plum, and blackberry flavors. The nose shows milk chocolate, blackberry, and cherry aromas. Very enjoyable; one to drink over the next 3 years. **89** —*D.T. (12/31/2005)*

AUSTRALIA

The Gate 2002 Shiraz (McLaren Vale) $32. Berry aromas on the nose are sweet and verge on overripe. The mouthfeel is soft, with flavors of mixed berries and wheat on the palate. The finish has nutmeg, herb, and heaps of oak and toffee. **86** —D.T. (12/31/2004)

THE GREEN VINEYARDS

The Green Vineyards 1999 The Forties Old Block Shiraz (Victoria) $30. Winemaker Sergio Carlei's Shiraz is heavy on herb (some say mint; others call it eucalyptus) from nose to palate. Cherry is the other dominant flavor here, so much so on the nose that the cherry-herb combination struck one reviewer as "cough syrupy." Mouthfeel is velvety; cedar and vanilla round out the palate and finish. **86** (11/1/2001)

THE LANE

The Lane 2001 19th Meeting Cabernet Sauvignon (Adelaide Hills) $44. A Cab from an area better known for its white wines, the 19th Meeting has bacon, eucalyptus, and cream on the nose. Similar oak and eucalyptus notes on the palate make the wine feel leaner than it is at first; with air, the mouthfeel smooths out and the flavors unfold. Not what Americans have in mind when they think of Oz Cabs; worth a look for that very reason. **88** —D.T. (5/1/2004)

The Lane 2002 Beginning Chardonnay (Adelaide Hills) $38. A new premium brand from the Starvedog Lane folks, this wine opens with pleasing mineral, chalk, and peach aromas. Close your eyes and you're drinking fruit nectar—the mango and peach flavors are that pure, and that ripe. A bright, sunny wine but also a firm one with good viscosity. Finish is medium-long and juicy. **89** (7/2/2004)

The Lane 2002 Gathering Semillon-Sauvignon Blanc (Adelaide Hills) $30. This new brand is the big brother of Starvedog Lane. This 80-20 Sauvignon-Semillon blend is zesty, wtih bright, interesting grass, lime, and white stone fruit flavors that come to a limey-chalky point on the finish. It's quite a fragrant wine as well, wtih pure peach, olive oil, and citrus notes. **90** —D.T. (5/1/2004)

The Lane 2001 Reunion Shiraz (Adelaide Hills) $44. The nose offers permeating black pepper aromas, and some maple sweetness. Black plum and cherry fruit on the palate is encased in a fairly dry, leathery mouthfeel; the finish brings more black cherry, leather, and oak flavors. It's very good, mouthcoating and big in size, but a little less so in richness. **87** —D.T. (9/1/2004)

THE LUCKY COUNTRY

The Lucky Country 2003 Grenache- Syrah- Mourvedre Grenache (Barossa Valley) $13. Cherry and earth aromas, with a hint of Sweet Tart. On the palate, it's a straightforward tea-and-cherry flavored wine with a slightly creamy fatness on the midpalate. 85% Grenache, 10% Shiraz, 5% Mourvedre. **86** —D.T. (3/1/2005)

THE WINNER'S TANK

The Winner's Tank 2004 Shiraz (Langhorne Creek) $16. A wine that was a contest entry, hence its name. It's rich, but a little hollow; as one taster says, it tries too hard. Aromas are of grape jelly, nutmeg, and wheat bread. In the mouth, it has similar flavors. **86** —D.T. (12/1/2005)

THE WISHING TREE

The Wishing Tree 2005 Unoaked Chardonnay (Western Australia) $10. This Chard is a good value again this vintage. It's crisp and clean, with lemon and grapefruit flavors and a dry, minerally feel. Delicate floral, grass, and talc aromas start things off. It's nice to see a Chardonnay at this price that doesn't taste like tropical fruit and buttered toast. **87 Best Buy** —D.T. (4/1/2006)

The Wishing Tree 2004 Unoaked Chardonnay (Western Australia) $11. "Unoaked" oftentimes means "light-bodied," but this Chard's no lightweight. It's actually pretty sizeable, all things considered, with red apple and white stone fruit flavors, and a dry mouthfeel. Its tangy, zippy finish makes the wine. 250 cases produced. **86 Best Buy** —D.T. (11/15/2005)

THIRSTY LIZARD

Thirsty Lizard 2002 Chardonnay (South Eastern Australia) $8. It performed a few points better straight out of the glass, but once it warms up and gets a little air, it just went downhill. Toast is a key player, as is yellow fruit that gets more and more tart. A simple, quaffworthy Chard. **83** —D.T. (1/1/2002)

Thirsty Lizard 2002 Shiraz (South Eastern Australia) $8. Has sweet but generic red fruit flavors, plus some leafiness. Pretty sour and acidic in the mouth; finishes with freshly cut wood. **81** —D.T. (1/1/2002)

Thirsty Lizard 2000 Shiraz (South Eastern Australia) $8. At once sweet and acidic; simple but sweet red fruit is the key player in the mouth. Definite leafiness surfaces on both the nose and the palate. **81** —D.T. (12/31/2003)

Thirsty Lizard 2004 White Shiraz (South Eastern Australia) $8. Dark pink-garnet in color. Raspberry and blackberry flavors are sweet; finishes with some residual sweetness. Drink cold. **82** —D.T. (12/1/2005)

THOMAS MITCHELL

Thomas Mitchell 1998 Marsanne (South Eastern Australia) $14. 86 Best Buy —S.H. (10/1/2000)

THORNY DEVIL

Thorny Devil 2003 Shiraz (Gundagai) $11. From Gundagai, an area southwest of Sydney. A linear, fine quaff, full of black cherry and plum fruit. Its cottony-tannic shell has more staying power than its stuffing. Finishes with more black cherry fruit. **86** —D.T. (12/1/2005)

THREE BRIDGES

Three Bridges 1999 Golden Mist Boytrytis Semillon (Riverina) $18. Lushly textured, with a heady blend of citrus and apricot notes that pair wonderfully. Honey, peach, toast, and herbs add character. The finish is long and velvety. A classy dessert. **91** —J.M. (12/1/2002)

TIM ADAMS

Tim Adams 2001 Cabernet Sauvignon (Clare Valley) $21. Tastes and feels liberally wooded, with tobacco on the nose and plenty of wood on the palate and finish. Fruit underneath it is taut and red. It's very good, but maybe a little out of joint. **88** —D.T. (2/1/2004)

Tim Adams 2000 Cabernet Sauvignon (Clare Valley) $23. There's solid plum fruit at the core of this Clare Cab that seems to take on a little eucalyptus (and maybe even a little sweetness) the longer it sits in the glass. Fruit has inky, oaky edges on the nose. This is just the sort of Cab that you'd need for dinner this weekend—it's big enough to stand up to a grilled steak, but not so big that it can't be drunk now. **89** —D.T. (12/31/2003)

Tim Adams 2003 The Benefit Cabernet Sauvignon (Clare Valley) $15. This medium-sized, food-friendly Cab isn't fancy, but it has a nice rustic, earthy quality to its red berry fruit. Clay-like smoothness on the palate ends with some light tea tannins. **87** —D.T. (8/1/2006)

Tim Adams 2004 The Fergus Grenache (Clare Valley) $18. This Clare offering shows Grenache in a much different light than what McLaren Vale or Barossa offers. Red berry fruit is offset with a red-eraser quality on the palate. Finish is modest, with shadings of burnt sugar. **87** —D.T. (11/15/2006)

Tim Adams 2001 The Fergus Grenache (Clare Valley) $20. Quite a mutt of a blend, with Grenache (85%), Shiraz, Cabernet Sauvignon, and Cabernet Franc. Honey, of all things, is a sweet overlay for tart cherry and plum aromas. It's taut in the mouth, where flavors of tobacco and herb make the wine feel leaner than it is. Named for a neighbor called Fergus, from whom they get some of these grapes. **88** —D.T. (2/1/2004)

Tim Adams 2006 Pinot Gris (Clare Valley) $18. A fine effort. This Clare Pinot Gris has a slight coppery tinge, and is dominated by apples and pears on both nose and palate. It's juicy at palate entry, but quickly moderated by a dry, fine minerally feel. Finishes with tart sour cherry and citrus flavors. Tastes, in a way, like a still version of a very nice Champagne. **90 Editors' Choice** —D.T. (10/1/2006)

Tim Adams 2005 Riesling (Clare Valley) $18. Its dry, dusty minerality is all Clare. There's a lemon-lime core here, too, that's very pretty. This isn't a snappy, super-acidic style of Riesling, which may disappoint some but please those who want a delicate white for the afternoon or just before dinner. **88** —D.T. (10/1/2006)

Tim Adams 2003 Riesling (Clare Valley) $15. It's unfortunate that it's not available in the U.S., because this is a very refreshing Riesling, with steel-mineral and citrus flavors. Finishes crisp, like running river water. **87** —D.T. (2/1/2004)

Tim Adams 1999 Riesling (Clare Valley) $NA. 90 —D.T. (2/1/2004)

Tim Adams 1994 Botrytis Riesling (Clare Valley) $NA. Fresh-sliced melon, mustard seed, and honey on the nose. Ripe peach, melon, honey, and hay flavors are dry rather than cloyingly sweet. Finishes clean, with a dry, slate-like feel. **90** —D.T. (2/1/2004)

Tim Adams 2005 The Benefit Riesling (Clare Valley) $15. This is a very delicately styled wine, with some citrus and mineral aromas and flavors. It's fine for everyday, but lacks the intensity and vibrant acidity that typify Clare Rieslings. **85** —D.T. (10/1/2006)

Tim Adams 2002 Semillon (Clare Valley) $15. Aromas are of honey and melon, and flavors are of hay and honey. What it lacks in concentration it makes up in crispness. **86** —D.T. (2/1/2004)

Tim Adams 2002 Shiraz (Clare Valley) $21. Yum. An excellent expression of Shiraz, with all its parts behaving as they should: Chalky tannins and good grip on the palate, and fresh herb and plum on the finish. Has a bright clay-epoxy note, plus brown sugar and beef, on the nose. Drink 2007–2010. **90 Editors' Choice** —D.T. (2/1/2004)

Tim Adams 2002 The Aberfeldy Shiraz (Clare Valley) $50. A little gum tree and blackberry on the nose leads to tangy tannins and red plum fruit on the palate. Very tight with angular oak shadings at this stage, though airing does coax those flavors out. One to try again in 2009. **89** —D.T. (11/15/2006)

Tim Adams 2001 The Aberfeldy Shiraz (Clare Valley) $45. A 100% Shiraz, from a vineyard established in 1904 by the Birks family, the same family that established Wendouree. Has toasty, meaty notes on the nose—an appropriate preamble to the grilled meat and black plum flavors on the palate. Chalky tannins are top-notch, but need 6–8 years to settle down. 1,000 cases produced, 200 of which come to the U.S. **92** —D.T. (2/1/2004)

Tim Adams 2004 The Benefit Shiraz (Southern Flinders Ranges) $NA. Penetrating eucalyptus aromas largely obscure the sweet berry fruit underneath. Berries rule the palate, too, which has soft tannins and tangy, tea-oak notes on the back. **86** —D.T. (8/1/2006)

TIM GRAMP

Tim Gramp 2001 Proprietary Grenache (Clare Valley) $17. Aromas are of coffee and oak; palate flavors are of taut plum and tea. The feel is smooth, with good, chunky weight in the midpalate. Red fruit persists on the finish. **88** —D.T. (9/1/2004)

Tim Gramp 2002 Watervale Riesling (Clare Valley) $18. Though supposedly the winery's current vintage, this wine is already showing signs of age. It is darkening in color, and somewhat reductive on the nose. On the palate, butterscotch and resin flavors stand where fresh citrus might once have been. Past its prime. **83** —D.T. (5/1/2005)

Tim Gramp 2000 Proprietary Shiraz (Clare Valley) $29. The nose offers dried spice, cigar box, and eucalyptus aromas, and the palate yields cool, taut, red fruit, including a hint of tomato. Has a nice, gummy texture and lithe size; finishes with more red fruit and eucalyptus. **87** —D.T. (9/1/2004)

TIN COWS

Tin Cows 2001 Chardonnay (Yarra Valley) $13. Here's one of those zippy Aussie Chards with those distinctly ripe tropical fruit flavors of mango, guava, and papaya. The flavors are given a boost by big acids, and there's even a rich streak of smoky oak. **88** —S.H. (1/1/2002)

Tin Cows 2000 Merlot (Yarra Valley) $13. Another wine well worth its price, and more, from Tin Cows. It's rich in succulent berry and stone fruit flavors, and dusty spices that linger well into the finish. The texture is smooth and fancy. Makes you want to lick your lips to get the last drops off your lips. How do they do it this good at this price? **90** —S.H. (1/1/2002)

Tin Cows 2001 Pinot Noir (Yarra Valley) $13. You'll like the true varietal character in this wine, with its silky tannins, crisp acids, light body, and full-throttle flavors. Cherries and raspberries, tobacco, sweet beet, peppery oriental spice, and smoky oak mingle to create a rich, textured

mouthfeel. In California, this would be a $25 wine, which makes this import a super value. **89** —S.H. (1/1/2002)

Tin Cows 2001 Shiraz (Yarra Valley) $13. Another great value from this winery, a wine with beautiful balance and integration. The ripe flavors of blackberries and pepper are folded into rich, velvety tannins, and the mouthfeel is as fancy as wines costing far more. Except for a certain hollowness in the middle palate, it is a great wine. **90** —S.H. (1/1/2002)

TINTARA

Tintara 2003 Cabernet Sauvignon (McLaren Vale) $18. Mocha and coffee aromas preface a palate full of dark, earthy-briary character. Medium-bodied; closes with tangy, tealike tannins. **87** —D.T. (3/1/2005)

Tintara 2004 Reserve Grenache (McLaren Vale) $50. The 2003 bottling was big, vibrant, and flavorful. This one is less so; it's juicy, berry fruit wearing a thick veneer of oak that hasn't yet integrated. Surely meant for midterm aging, but still it doesn't show the verve that the previous vintage did. Maybe this bottling is in a dumb phase? **88** —D.T. (11/15/2006)

Tintara 2003 Reserve Grenache (McLaren Vale) $49. This is Tintara's first varietal Grenache to be released in the U.S., and what a splash it'll make. Lifted cherry and violet aromas have a light wheat-biscuit accent. The palate follows suit with the same violet and black cherry notes. It's fresh and vibrant, with a chalky-mineral finish. "It's really hard to get people to notice it," laments winemaker Rob Mann of the variety. With this wine, Rob, your troubles are over. **90** —D.T. (3/1/2005)

Tintara 2003 Shiraz (McLaren Vale) $18. All basket-pressed, with 50-50 French and American oak. Aromas are meaty, with some toast and wheat biscuit thrown in. Plum and tart black cherry fruit on the palate show hints of mineral and herb; good length on the finish. **88** —D.T. (3/1/2005)

Tintara 2002 Reserve Shiraz (McLaren Vale) $49. Chewy on the palate, with vibrant plum, blueberry, and blackberry flavors that persist through the finish. Its aromas are similarly juicy and flavorful: plum and blackberry, and a dusting of bread flour. A pretty, concentrated, feminine-style Shiraz. 900 cases made, with 300 coming to the U.S. **90** —D.T. (3/1/2005)

TORBRECK

Torbreck 2002 The Bothie Muscat (Barossa Valley) $NA. Found only at Torbreck's cellar door and a few Australian restaurants, this is 100% Muscat a Petit Grains. It's fresh and springy, and tastes like buttercups, lemondrops, and other pretty things. Smells like perfume, and fresh-cut grass. A very good end to a very good evening. **88** —D.T. (2/1/2004)

Torbreck 2002 Juveniles Red Blend (Barossa Valley) $25. Named for a wine bar in Paris for which this wine was formulated, this is a GSM with 60% Grenache, and equal parts Shiraz and Mourvèdre. In past vintages, I've found it lean and herbal, but this vintage brings flavors of ripe plum and cherry fruit, and earth, in equal measure. Light- to medium-bodied in the mouth, it's 100% tank fermented, with bread flour and eucalyptus aromas. **90 Editors' Choice** —D.T. (2/1/2004)

Torbreck 2001 The Steading Red Blend (Barossa Valley) $35. This GSM is almost the same blend as the Juveniles (with "only a few parcels' difference," says winemaker Dan Standish), but it spends 18 months in oak. Me, I narrowly prefer the Juveniles' freshness—The Steading's palate shows oak and cedar, and the heavier tannins that go with it. Nose is pretty closed. Very good, and perhaps one to revisit in a year or two. **89** —D.T. (2/1/2004)

Torbreck 2002 Woodcutter's Red Red Blend (Barossa Valley) $20. Made from all young-vine fruit, Woodcutter's is aptly named in that the palate has earth and tree bark flavors that give black cherry fruit an even darker foil. Stewed fruit and pine needle aromas on the nose come back to clean up the finish. A fun, good, weeknight pizza wine. **88** —D.T. (2/1/2004)

Torbreck 2001 Run Rig Shiraz (Barossa Valley) $145. There are plenty of reasons the winery gives to account for this wine's hefty price: 125+-year-old vines; 70% new French oak; yields of a half-ton per acre; fruit costs about $7,400 (U.S.) per ton, and is all handpicked. Torbreck's investment pays off—the mixed-plum fruit is beautiful and rich, enveloped in smooth, chalky tannins. Mouthfeel is round and creamy; spicy black pepper aromas are subtle. 800 cases produced. **92** —D.T. (2/1/2004)

Torbreck 2001 The Descendant Shiraz (Barossa Valley) $85. A junior Run Rig, in more ways than one: The Descendant's grapes come from a single vineyard made from Run Rig cuttings. The wine is aged in two-year-old Run Rig barrels, and, like its big brother, contains a small percentage of Viognier. The Viognier lends floral aromas to the nose; it's big and syrupy in the mouth at first, but smooth, silky tannins step in thereafter. Fruit is a little stewy, but that's the vintage conditions talking. 800 cases produced. **90** —*D.T. (2/1/2004)*

Torbreck 2001 The Factor Shiraz (Barossa Valley) $85. On the nose, there's caramel, wheat, and pine aromas; fruit on the palate is juicy and fat, and doesn't pick up oak flavors until the finish. A very good, tasty wine, though straightforward. 1,500 cases produced. **89** —*D.T. (2/1/2004)*

Torbreck 2001 The Struie Shiraz (Barossa Valley) $50. A textbook Shiraz, with all its components in the right places: There's big plum fruit on the palate backed by oak and earth; aromas are of pine and wheat. Aged in 30% new French oak. **89** —*D.T. (2/1/2004)*

Torbreck 2002 White Blend (Barossa Valley) $35. There's not a great likelihood that you'll see much of this wine; only 200 cases are made and most of them stay in Australia. Still, it's worth looking for: it's fat in the mouth, with stone fruit and floral flavors, and a steely, flinty mouthfeel. Finishes with nectarine, white peach, and stone flavors. **88** —*D.T. (2/1/2004)*

Torbreck 2002 Woodcutter's White White Blend (Barossa Valley) $16. A 100% Semillon, with banana-cream aromas and honeysuckle and jasmine flavors. Light and fresh, with snappy white-pepper flavors on the finish. **85** —*D.T. (2/1/2004)*

TOWER ESTATE

Tower Estate 2002 Riesling (Clare Valley) $24. Though it starts with a burst of tropical yellow fruit and its accompanying sweetness, this is still a dry wine, with a strong mineral-and-citrus backbone. Finishes with more tropical fruit and some white pepper. Try it with Asian cuisine—this plus a ginger-based sauce makes for a good match. **88** —*D.T. (8/1/2003)*

TRENTHAM

Trentham 2000 Big Rivers Shiraz (Australia) $11. Dry, woodsy tannins rein in juicy red and black plum fruit on the palate; a wine with both solid fruit and a sense of restraint as this has is a good bet for a meal (and if I were cooking, that meal would be enchiladas). A very good wine that, had it more to the finish, could have been an excellent one. At this price, though, it's a minor complaint. **88 Best Buy** —*D.T. (12/31/2003)*

Trentham 2000 Murphy's Lore Big Rivers Shiraz-Cabernet Sauvignon (Australia) $8. Just the kind of wine that you want to keep around the house: inexpensive and uncomplicated. Red fruit is dusted with earth and some oak. It's medium-bodied in the mouth, with mushroomy, beefy aromas and closing flavors. **84** —*D.T. (12/31/2003)*

TREVOR MAST

Trevor Mast 2001 Four Sisters Merlot (South Eastern Australia) $12. This simple Merlot has cherry and plum flavors, and oak that shows up on the finish. Black pepper and sweet red fruit show on the nose. Straightforward and easy. **83** —*D.T. (1/1/2002)*

Trevor Mast 2000 Four Sisters Shiraz (South Eastern Australia) $15. The nose offers cola and sweet red raspberry aromas. In the mouth, the fruit is red but quite sour—think cranberry and rhubarb rather than raspberry. Finishes, tastes, and feels like artificial sweetener. **81** —*D.T. (1/1/2002)*

TURKEY FLAT

Turkey Flat 2001 Cabernet Sauvignon (Barossa Valley) $36. A very good, pleasing Cabernet with bouncy plum and blackberry fruit that verges on sweet. Nose has plum, eucalyptus, and mocha aromas; finishes a little woody, with more vivid plum. A straightahead, enjoyable wine. **87** —*D.T. (2/1/2004)*

Turkey Flat 2002 Grenache (Barossa Valley) $15. Red fruit is spicy on the nose, and segues to lush raspberry and cherry flavors on the palate.

Finishes full and dry, with red plums. Made from bush vines that were planted in the 1920s. **88** —*D.T. (2/1/2004)*

Turkey Flat 2002 Marsanne-Semillon Marsanne (Barossa Valley) $17. Fruit-driven and fresh, yellow fruit on the palate takes on honey accents as well. Dressed up with bright citrus notes. 10% barrel fermented in new French oak. **87** —*D.T. (2/1/2004)*

Turkey Flat 2002 The Turk Red Blend (Barossa Valley) $16. Turkey Flat's new introductory-level wine, The Turk is a blend of Shiraz, Grenache, Cabernet, and Mourvèdre. Very dry in the mouth, with taut plum and cranberry fruit. An angular wine; the opposite of many far-flung fruit-bombs at this price. **85** —*D.T. (2/1/2004)*

Turkey Flat 2001 Butchers Block Rhône Red Blend (Barossa Valley) $25. Tastes as its bouquet suggests, with soft, red plum and cherry fruit from beginning to end. Obvious and straightforward, but tasty. **87** —*D.T. (2/1/2004)*

Turkey Flat 2003 Rosé Blend (Barossa Valley) $16. A blend of Grenache (45%), Shiraz (25%), Cabernet Sauvignon (22%), and Dolcetto (8%), this quaffer shows bright raspberry and plum flavors on the palate, with just a hint of sweetness. Floral and raspberry aromas are bright and inviting on the nose. Finishes like a Cabernet, quite dry, with chalky tannins. A hit with spicy food, or as a summertime sipper. **87** —*D.T. (2/1/2004)*

Turkey Flat 2001 Shiraz (Barossa Valley) $36. Juicy and pleasurable on the palate—a great mix of berries and plums, caramel, and smooth tannins. The nose was a little closed when the wine was reviewed; aeration is probably in order if it's drunk now. **90** —*D.T. (2/1/2004)*

TURRAMURRA ESTATE

Turramurra Estate 1999 Proprietary Chardonnay (Mornington Peninsula) $23. Full-bodied, with all the love that an apple pie can give: a baked apple core and buttery, toasty, caramelly accents. Aromas are of butterscotch and coconut; finishes a little alcoholic. **85** *(7/2/2004)*

TWELVE STAVES

Twelve Staves 2000 Grenache (McLaren Vale) $18. Aptly named, for the oak influence here is strong—a dusty woodiness that's almost cedary. Fortunately, it's well integrated with the full-bodied cherry fruit. Finishes dry, but soft and ripe. **86** —*J.C. (9/1/2002)*

Twelve Staves 1999 Grenache (McLaren Vale) $20. Sweaty leather and cinnamon notes dress up sour cherry aromas and flavors. Shows nice complexity, folding in sweet spice and plum notes, but finishes with a tart, hard edge. **85** —*J.C. (9/1/2001)*

TWIN BEAKS

Twin Beaks 2002 Chardonnay (South Eastern Australia) $10. David Lynch fans aren't the only folks who will appreciate this Chard—those who like oak and all of its related flavors should queue up. It's golden in color, smells of nut and white pepper, and has flavors of cream, nuts, and peach fuzz. Smooth in the mouth and a little oily on the finish. A good wine, particularly for the price. **85 Best Buy** —*D.T. (12/31/2004)*

Twin Beaks 2002 Merlot (South Eastern Australia) $10. Soft red fruit and campfire-smoke aromas after a few minutes in the glass go the way of caramel popcorn. Has decent weight on the palate, though, and doesn't taste as sweet as it smells. Mixed red fruit and soft tannins make this a good by-the-glass pour with dinner. **84** —*D.T. (12/31/2004)*

TWO HANDS

Two Hands 2004 Aphrodite Cabernet Sauvignon (Barossa Valley) $159. A manageable 14.5% alcohol, Two Hands' flagship Cab has dark aromas with a ribbon of raspberry jam running through them. The palate is heavy on bitter chocolate and wood, again, with lifted red fruit peeking through. This is a very good wine overall, but not one that's long enough, or deep enough, to reach that next level. **89** —*D.T. (10/1/2006)*

Two Hands 2004 Aerope Grenache (Barossa Valley) $102. There's no doubting the quality of this wine, which exudes class and refinement. It's not as plush as some other Aussie Grenaches, but deftly marries kirsch, vanilla, and dried spices into an integrated and complex whole. Firm on the finish, with a bit of a tart edge. **90** —*J.C. (12/15/2006)*

Two Hands 2006 Brilliant Disguise 500ML Moscato (Barossa Valley) $19. Utterly enjoyable, and meant to be drunk now. This petillant Moscato has a pretty, moussey feel and flavors of flowers and white peaches. A great alternative for Prosecco fans, too. **89** —*D.T. (11/15/2006)*

Two Hands 2002 Brave Faces Red Blend (Barossa Valley) $27. Cassis, licorice, and caramel on the nose signal what's to come in the mouth: This wine's a big, bright fruit bomb, full of sweet blackberry and blueberry fruit with some caramel thrown in for good measure. Full-on fruit can be a good thing, but a little restraint in this case wouldn't hurt. **86** — *D.T. (12/31/2003)*

Two Hands 2004 The Wolf Riesling (Clare Valley) $24. The citrus component on this Riesling's palate really sings, and its floral/violet and minerally accents are just the right accompaniments. It's dry, clean, and very pretty, with good length on the finish. **89** —*D.T. (3/1/2005)*

Two Hands 2003 The Wolf Riesling (Clare Valley) $19. Stone fruit (particularly an alluring apricot-nectarine combination) dominates this viscous, fairly full Riesling, which has nice acidity and a finish that tastes like lemon drops. Breathe deeply enough and you're sure to find almonds. **90 Editors' Choice** —*D.T. (2/1/2004)*

Two Hands 2005 Angel's Share Shiraz (McLaren Vale) $30. Forward and youthful, this Shiraz shows lifted blueberry and blackberry jam flavors, plus accents of tangy oak and earth. An over-the-top, drink-now wine. **87** —*D.T. (10/1/2006)*

Two Hands 2002 Angel's Share Shiraz (McLaren Vale) $20. Nose is a sexy cocktail of pastry crust, black fruit, and caramel—palate flavors are similar but more subdued. Still, there's nice grip in the back palate. Finishes with fine, oaky tannins. **86** —*D.T. (12/31/2003)*

Two Hands 2003 Lily's Garden Shiraz (McLaren Vale) $60. The nose is fairly closed now, showing just herb and ink aromas, but gives the impression that it's a blackberry volcano about to erupt. With such menace and potential on the nose, the fact that the palate flavors don't knock me on the floor is almost a disappointment. This is still an excellent, flavorful wine, with reined-in plum, blackberry, raspberry, and red pencil eraser notes. **90** —*D.T. (3/1/2005)*

Two Hands 2004 The Bull and the Bear Shiraz-Cabernet Sauvignon (Barossa Valley) $59. Practically black in color; vanilla and plum aromas start it all off. In spite of its color, this is not a dense wine. It's very forward, its red fruit playing off a sawdusty-woody texture in the mouth. Not harmonious, with more sawdust on the finish. **86** —*D.T. (10/1/2006)*

Two Hands 2005 Brave Faces Shiraz-Grenache (Barossa Valley) $36. A burly blend of 65% Shiraz and 35% Grenache, the 2005 Brave Faces is a big, chunky monster that's difficult to judge at this stage. It's closed and inexpressive on the nose, but it has enough body and black cherry fruit to warrant confidence, supported by the long, spice-tinged finish. **89** — *J.C. (12/15/2006)*

TYRRELL'S

Tyrrell's 2001 Moore's Creek Cabernet Sauvignon (South Eastern Australia) $9. Medium-bodied and easy to drink, a hint of vanilla cream gives this Cab a roundness that makes its taut plum and cherry fruit rather approachable. Midpalate to finish, the fruit gets blacker, with bacon and oak accents. Though you're not going to mistake it for a $30 wine, it's a hell of a deal for $9. **86 Best Buy** —*D.T. (6/1/2003)*

Tyrrell's 2002 Old Winery Cabernet Sauvignon-Merlot (New South Wales) $10. Has an eye-opening, eucalyptus-cherry-plum profile, with just a few blackberries thrown in for good measure. Finishes with dark berries and more eucalyptus. A very good wine, if perhaps an acquired taste. **88 Best Buy** —*D.T. (12/31/2003)*

Tyrrell's 2001 Old Winery Cabernet Sauvignon-Merlot (New South Wales) $15. Its red cherry and plum fruit is unyielding, and perhaps a little on the sour side; there's plenty of oak and dusty earth notes, too, from beginning to end. A light acidic bite keeps it from going down as easily as it could. **83** —*D.T. (1/1/2002)*

Tyrrell's 2003 Lost Block Chardonnay (South Eastern Australia) $14. This is the kind of Chard you want to have on the table when you've ordered a scallop course, or white fish (and it would be no shame to enjoy it bare-

foot in the grass). It has pretty, summery aromas of citrus and yellow peach, streaked with just a hint of smoke. The palate reprises the yellow peaches, couched in a dusty-minerally feel. **88** —*D.T. (5/1/2005)*

Tyrrell's 1999 Moon Mountain Chardonnay (Hunter Valley) $21. Buttered toast and vanilla scents lead the way, buttressed by peach and citrus. It's medium-weight and smooth in the mouth, with a long finish that boasts echoes of orange and lemon. **88** —*J.C. (7/1/2002)*

Tyrrell's 2005 Moore's Creek Chardonnay (South Eastern Australia) $10. This Chard has good intensity and length for a wine of its price. It starts off with fresh cream, nut, and white peach aromas, followed by focused peach, pear, and chalk flavors. Not a heavyweight at all, but even and constant. **87 Best Buy** —*D.T. (8/1/2006)*

Tyrrell's 2002 Moore's Creek Chardonnay (South Eastern Australia) $9. Bring this Chardonnay straight to the raw bar: Its white stone fruit, mineral and pear flavors, and gravelly tannins offer just the right mix of zing and fleshiness in the mouth. Finishes with like flavors, but a bit more intensity. 25,000 cases produced. **87 Best Buy** —*D.T. (6/1/2003)*

Tyrrell's 2003 Old Winery Chardonnay (New South Wales) $12. The Old Winery tier always has reliably good wines, and this middle-weight Chardonnay is no different. It smells of pineapple and lemon meringue, with pineapple, plus pear and vanilla, following through on the palate. Finishes with tart lemon pith. **86** *(7/2/2004)*

Tyrrell's 2002 Old Winery Chardonnay (Hunter Valley) $14. A fresh, food-friendly wine and a good value, the Old Winery Chardonnay has passion fruit, papaya, and fresh herb flavors, with a light nougat aroma on the nose. On the palate, it's gravelly, and maybe a little spritzy. It's not a full, creamy, toasty blockbuster—but that's part of its charm. **88** —*D.T. (8/1/2003)*

Tyrrell's 2001 Old Winery Hunter Valley/McLaren Vale Chardonnay (Hunter Valley) $14. Understated and less ripe than many Australian Chardonnays, which makes for a nice change of pace when tasting, but also a leaner, more austere style dominated by citrus flavors. This atypical Aussie Chard could even be paired with shellfish. **87** —*J.C. (7/1/2002)*

Tyrrell's 2003 Reserve Chardonnay (Hunter Valley) $25. The nose shows well-restrained oak that manifests itself as musk, or sandalwood. It has a rich, oily texture—a little slippery, but nice—and powerful, unusual fruit (passion fruit, maybe?). A nice, unexpected style of Chard. **88** *(7/2/2004)*

Tyrrell's 2000 Reserve Chardonnay (Hunter Valley) $37. The pear, apple, and herb aromas and flavors here are almost swamped by the spicy oak. Bright acidity and the powerful wood presence give the wine a rather lean cast, but this ship rights itself, and keeps its balance nicely in the end. The lively finish and overall tangy personality will pair well with grilled shellfish or broiled seafood. **88** —*M.M. (6/1/2001)*

Tyrrell's 2003 Vat 47 Chardonnay (Hunter Valley) $40. This Chardonnay takes a little while to unfold in the glass, but when it does, fresh vanilla bean and cream aromas emerge. More of the same follows through on the palate, where there's also some almond and fresh white peach flavors. Zips shut with a burst of lemon. Suave, and will only improve with age. **89** —*D.T. (4/1/2006)*

Tyrrell's 2001 Vat 47 Chardonnay (Hunter Valley) $60. Tyrrell's flagship Chardonnay didn't show as well as some of their more inexpensive bottlings. This wine has a candied, slightly viscous mouthfeel, with fruit that tastes not quite ripe. Finishes with butterscotch candy and tropical fruit flavors. **84** *(7/2/2004)*

Tyrrell's 2000 Vat 47 Chardonnay (Hunter Valley) $50. A very nice wine that's zesty and fresh in the mouth, and deep gold in color, the Vat 47 offers bright yellow fruit flavors, with light vanilla, toast, and citrus accents. Nose is alternately perfumey and toasty. Tasted twice. **89** *(8/1/2003)*

Tyrrell's 1999 Reserve Merlot (McLaren Vale) $37. The nose on this wine is still very tight, showing only earth. However, the flavors explode with bright Bing cherries and spicy cedar. Mouthfeel is lush and velvety, leading to a lingering finish. A wine made to enjoy now, but will last another 5-7 years. **89** —*C.S. (6/1/2002)*

Tyrrell's 2003 Lost Block Pinot Noir (South Eastern Australia) $14. Plots the course of many more expensive European renditions: Stable meets plum and cherry on the nose, with the same red fruit taking a tart, sour-cherry turn on the palate. That tartness is not a bad thing. Soft in the mouth, with lemony oak on the finish. **85** —*D.T. (11/15/2005)*

Tyrrell's 2000 Old Winery Pinot Noir (South Eastern Australia) $15. A sturdy wine, sporting plenty of roasted cherries and caramel on a medium-weight frame. Turns strongly sour on the finish, where the flavor of charcoal dust also intrudes. **82** —*J.C. (9/1/2002)*

Tyrrell's 2000 Vat 6 Pinot Noir (Hunter Valley) $40. As good as this wine usually is, this bottling was a disappointment. It is already browning in color, and its fruit already starting to fade (though it's easy to see how the cherry and earth flavors were pretty and vibrant once upon a time). 2000 is the current vintage, though most other Oz Pinots are a year or two newer. **85** —*D.T. (10/1/2005)*

Tyrrell's 1999 Vat 6 Hunter Pinot Noir (Hunter Valley) $50. A lush Pinot, the Vat 6 smolders with mixed cherry and steeped tea flavors; the wood that shows on the medium-long finish is also smoky, and tastes more like hickory than oak. Has smooth, gummy tannins and spicy cumin and ginger aromas. Drink this with a duck dish—any duck dish. **90** —*D.T. (5/1/2004)*

Tyrrell's 2003 Lost Block Semillon (Hunter Valley) $18. Light on both flavors and aromas, this is just the style of wine you'll want as an apéritif or with seafood. Light citrus aromas are followed up by firm white stone fruit flavors and a crisp, lean mouthfeel. Plumps up a bit on the finish. **86** —*D.T. (9/1/2004)*

Tyrrell's 1994 Vat 1 Semillon (Hunter Valley) $50. Toasty, as you'd expect from an aged Semillon, but also boasts a bit of butter and some clove notes. Flavors are tart and citrusy—mainly lemon, with a hint of unripe pear. This big-boned wine could still age a while longer. **87** —*J.C. (2/1/2002)*

Tyrrell's 2004 Moore's Creek Semillon-Sauvignon Blanc (South Eastern Australia) $9. Melon, citrus, and mineral fragrances are feminine and pretty; the palate, on the other hand, is a zesty, wake-me-up of a white. It's dry in the mouth, with citrus and mineral flavors. A lively, economical choice for brunch, lunch, or outdoor sipping. 1,500 cases produced. **86 Best Buy** —*D.T. (3/1/2005)*

Tyrrell's 2003 Moore's Creek Semillon-Sauvignon Blanc (New South Wales) $9. Another good value from the Moore's Creek line, this white has flavorful tropical fruit on the palate, and a brisk, zippy mouthfeel. Clean hay, or fresh-cut grass, aromas complete the package. **86** —*D.T. (9/1/2004)*

Tyrrell's 2002 Moore's Creek Semillon-Sauvignon Blanc (Hunter Valley) $9. Fresh and citrusy, and just the ticket if a seafood dinner or prolonged porch-sitting is on your agenda. Piquant lemon-zest aromas brighten the nose, and similar flavors persist through the finish. A general word to the wise: All four of the wines in the Moore's Creek line have garnered Best Buys from Wine Enthusiast, with scores from 85 through 87 points. All retail for $9. How can you go wrong? **85** —*D.T. (11/15/2003)*

Tyrrell's 2003 Old Winery Semillon-Sauvignon Blanc (Western Australia) $7. Starts off with a kick of white pepper on the palate, which segues into fleshy stone fruit and a citrus-like tang. It's round in the mouth and moderately zesty, finishing a little less so. A pretty good value. **85** —*D.T. (5/1/2004)*

Tyrrell's 2002 The Long Flat Semillon-Sauvignon Blanc (South Eastern Australia) $7. An 80-20 Semillon-Sauvignon blend, the wine's yellow fruit flavors are a little dilute, but its aromas of sweet yellow and citrus fruit are quite pleasant. Finishes with a mealy banana-like texture. **84 Best Buy** —*D.T. (5/1/2004)*

Tyrrell's 1999 Brokenback Shiraz (Hunter Valley) $24. The bouquet is confusing: There's mushroom, peanut, root beer, and bramble bush—but hardly any fruit. Then in the mouth it goes fruity and snappy, offering the essence of cranberry and other red berries. The finish has length to it, but all in all it's basically a simple wine without a lot of individuality. **85** —*M.S. (3/1/2003)*

Tyrrell's 2003 DB24 Shiraz (McLaren Vale) $80. Tyrrell's new flagship Shiraz, the DB24 was matured in two sets of new oak barrels for a total of 24 months, yet remarkably isn't overoaked. Instead, it offers luscious aromas of blackberries and vanilla but also intriguing soy and grilled

meat notes. It's full-bodied and densely packed, like a coiled spring that needs some time to relax. Finishes with firm tannins; anticipated maturity: 2010–2020. **92 Cellar Selection** —*J.C. (12/15/2006)*

Tyrrell's 2004 Moore's Creek Shiraz (South Eastern Australia) $10. Adequate but disappointing; the Moore's Creek wines usually perform better than this. Offers some barnyard on the nose, and dilute plum and tea flavors on the palate. Finishes short. **82** —*D.T. (10/1/2006)*

Tyrrell's 2001 Moore's Creek Shiraz (South Eastern Australia) $9. On both the nose and palate are red plums, toasted pumpernickel, and grilled meat. Accents of caraway and white pepper lend spice to a medium-length finish. Seems a natural match for seared tuna or swordfish steaks. **86 Best Buy** —*K.F. (3/1/2003)*

Tyrrell's 2001 Old Winery Shiraz (Hunter Valley) $10. Aromas of meat, toasted bread, and molasses cover the prettier star anise and caraway wisps that accent thin strawberry and raspberry fruit. The red fruits and sweet spices show again on the palate. Tannins are smooth, if seemingly transparent. **85** —*K.F. (3/1/2003)*

Tyrrell's 2001 Reserve Shiraz (McLaren Vale) $12. Aromas are of black fruit and bread flour. On the palate, the alcohol is a little noticeable, but the plum and oak flavors are harmonious and tasty. A nice value. **87 Best Buy** —*D.T. (11/15/2004)*

Tyrrell's 1999 Reserve Shiraz (McLaren Vale) $37. Smells pretty—elegant dried spice aromas mingle with cedar, plum, and anise. Turns darker and earthier in the mouth, slowly revealing flavors of blackberry, earth, and coffee. A hint of citrus marks the warm finish. **88** *(11/1/2001)*

Tyrrell's 2002 Rufus Stone Shiraz (McLaren Vale) $30. This Shiraz is medium-bodied and full of black cherry aromas and flavors. Dry, tealike tannins complete the picture. An enjoyable pizza or pasta accompaniment, though its price may prohibit casual, everyday consumption. **87** —*D.T. (3/1/2005)*

Tyrrell's 2000 The Long Flat Vineyard Shiraz (South Australia) $9. The aromas and flavors of leather, baked mixed berries, and dried spices like cinnamon, clove, and white pepper provide a top-notch introduction to Australian Shiraz while offering enough complexity to assuage even jaded palates. Finishes with dusty cocoa notes that provide backbone. **87 Best Buy** *(10/1/2001)*

Tyrrell's 2002 Vat 8 Shiraz (Hunter Valley) $40. Tyrrell's wines are meant to be aged, which may be why this Shiraz isn't particularly singing right now. The nose offers an overt rubber/plastic note, backed by some blackberry underneath. Moderate amounts of cool, black cherry flavors characterize the palate. Would be worth a look in 2010 to see how it's changed. **86** —*D.T. (10/1/2006)*

Tyrrell's 1998 Vat 9 Shiraz (Hunter Valley) $50. This is an understated kind of Shiraz, without the caramel-and-blackberry typical of some of its countrymen. Instead, you get cherries, brown sugar, and stably flavors in the mouth and some drying, woody tannins on the finish. A tar/resin note persists on the nose. **88** *(12/31/2003)*

Tyrrell's 1997 Vat 9 Shiraz (Hunter Valley) $40. A leaner-style Shiraz with leathery, stably accents on both the nose and the palate. Plum and iron flavors are forceful at the outset, then soften up toward the spice-laden finish. Alcohol is a modest 13%. **88** —*D.T. (4/1/2006)*

Tyrrell's 2001 The Long Flat Vineyard White Blend (South Eastern Australia) $7. Lemon and chalk notes play on the even, almost elegant palate, and on the zesty finish. On the nose, I picked up an unusual damp-fog or cellary note—maybe it sounds strange, but I liked it. Sixty-five percent Semillon, 35 percent Sauvignon Blanc. **85 Best Buy** —*D.T. (2/1/2002)*

TYRRELL'S OLD WINERY

Tyrrell's Old Winery 2003 Chardonnay (Hunter Valley & McLaren Vale) $11. Round and mouth-coating, the Old Winery Chard pleases again this year. Offers up pretty floral aromas, followed by yellow peach and muted olive oil flavors. Smolders on the end with a little hickory, or smoked meat. **86 Best Buy** —*D.T. (12/31/2004)*

UBET

UBET 2001 Chardonnay (South Eastern Australia) $10. Offers ripe though unoriginal yellow fruit flavors, plus custardy-oaky notes on the nose and on the palate. It's medium-bodied and pleasant, but wouldn't suffer from a tad more concentration. **84** —*D.T. (6/1/2003)*

UBET 2001 Shiraz (South Eastern Australia) $10. The nose is flowery and quite out of the ordinary. Flavors of sweet blackberry make for a ripe palate, while the finish is heavier than most, with pronounced woody notes coming on late in the game. It's a thick wine that toes the line of balance. Yet amid all the richness there is some necessary nuance and complexity—just not very much. **86** —*M.S. (3/1/2003)*

VASSE FELIX

Vasse Felix 2003 Heytesbury Bordeaux Blend (Margaret River) $50. This is a wine that would benefit from further bottle aging: Just a little earth and anise come through on the nose. It's tightly wound all around—a little lean, even—but pleasantly so, its juicy, tangy black cherry flavors and lively acidity dominating at this stage. Supple and layered on the palate and through the finish. Drink 2008–2012. **93 Cellar Selection** —*D.T. (10/1/2006)*

Vasse Felix 2001 Heytesbury Bordeaux Blend (Margaret River) $40. Yum. This blend of 84% Cab, 8% Shiraz, 6% Malbec, and 2% Merlot has a silky, chalky feel and deftly acts both wild and reserved. There's an outdoorsy element to the palate, underneath which the fruit feels cool, crisp, and buttoned up—that is, until the finish, where there's a burst of ripe plum. As is the case with many Margaret River reds, the bow on this excellent package is the region's telltale mintiness. Drink now–2010. **91** —*D.T. (5/1/2005)*

Vasse Felix 2001 Cabernet Sauvignon (Margaret River) $30. Red and black plums build a strong core for this medium-bodied Cab. Clay-like texture and flavors show in the midpalate, and make for a fine close to a fine wine. Fruit comes from Mt. Barker and Margaret River; aged 18 months in French oak. **90** —*D.T. (10/1/2003)*

Vasse Felix 2000 Cabernet Sauvignon (Margaret River) $30. Almost black in color, an infant of a wine whose aromas are just beginning to emerge. Cassis and blackberry jam are joined to smoky, oaky scents. Huge, young, and tannic, with high acidity and a treasure chest of buried fruit, this wine needs at least three years in the cellar. **92 Editors' Choice** —*M.S. (12/15/2002)*

Vasse Felix 2000 Cabernet Sauvignon (Margaret River) $30. This is one pure, pretty, sturdy Cab. On the palate, black plum and berry fruit is front and center, with oak and caramel most evident on the finish and on the nose. Go ahead, show your guests some love and pour them something that won't overwhelm dinner. **89** —*D.T. (11/15/2004)*

Vasse Felix 1999 Cabernet Sauvignon (Western Australia) $30. Black-garnet Vasse Felix has aromas of fresh wood, mint, and blackberry that are muted somewhat by a cottony scent. Tart oak and blackberry flavors on the palate lead to a flash-in-the-pan, high-acid finish. **84** —*D.T. (9/1/2001)*

Vasse Felix 1998 Cabernet Sauvignon (Western Australia) $29. 92 —*M.S. (10/1/2000)*

Vasse Felix 2001 Cabernet Sauvignon-Merlot (Margaret River) $20. Fruit is distinctly red (plum, cherry, and raspberry); there's some tree bark on the palate as well. Has an unusual texture, like coarse earth. Oak is the key player on both the nose and the finish. **88** —*D.T. (10/1/2003)*

Vasse Felix 2002 Adam's Road Cabernet Sauvignon-Merlot (Margaret River) $15. This wine has a lot going for it—it has a black cherry core, is amply but not overly-sized, and has deep mint aromas. Finishes with smooth, chalky tannins. A blend of 53% Cab Sauvignon, 44% Merlot, and 3% Cabernet Franc. **87** —*D.T. (9/1/2004)*

Vasse Felix 2003 Adams Road Cabernet Sauvignon-Merlot (Margaret River) $15. Tastes and smells like sweet berry and plum fruit, with oak flavors rearing up toward the finish. A good, pedestrian red wine. **84** —*D.T. (12/31/2005)*

Vasse Felix 2002 Chardonnay (Margaret River) $20. From one of Margaret River's benchmark wineries, this Chard has aromas of nut, melon, and caramel, with a hint of petrol. Some of the fruit flavors are unusual—

nectarine, maybe, with more nuttiness—but the core is still sturdy and citrusy. Medium weight with firm acids, it finishes with a citrus bite. **87** *(7/2/2004)*

Vasse Felix 2001 Chardonnay (Margaret River) $24. A very good wine, but noticeably the Heytesbury's junior, this Chard offers taut yellow fruit and some caramel and toast. Woodsy tannins follow through on the finish. **88** —*D.T. (10/1/2003)*

Vasse Felix 1998 Chardonnay (Western Australia) $19. 90 *(10/1/2000)*

Vasse Felix 2004 Adams Road Chardonnay (Margaret River) $15. The nose offers manageable amounts of toast and vanilla, which segue into tangy peach and citrus flavors on the palate. Dry in the mouth, and not too long on the finish, this is a simple, easy-to-like Chard. 900 cases imported. **86** —*D.T. (10/1/2005)*

Vasse Felix 2003 Adams Road Chardonnay (Margaret River) $15. This Chard is a new addition to Vasse Felix's value-priced Adams Road line. Yellow fruit aromas are flattened out by woody notes. It's medium-full on the palate, wtih bright but somewhat sour peachy flavors, and a helping of mallowy vanilla. Sour peach stays the course on the finish. **85** —*D.T. (12/31/2004)*

Vasse Felix 2001 Heytesbury Chardonnay (Margaret River) $30. Balanced, elegant, and focused, the Heytesbury shows some noticeable wood, but it's subtle wood, and not mallowy. It's crisp in the mouth, with peach, pear, and nectarine flavors, and a medium-long finish. **92** —*D.T. (10/1/2003)*

Vasse Felix 2001 Heytesbury Chardonnay (Western Australia) $30. Full-bodied and creamy on the palate, this iconic Margaret River Chard has sturdy, ripe peach, and nectarine fruit, and nut and toast accents. Petrol and nut aromas, and a pear-apple finish, frame the wine nicely. **88** *(7/2/2004)*

Vasse Felix 2000 Heytesbury Chardonnay (Western Australia) $30. The aromas are so promising, redolent of toast and pears, butter and nectarines, that expectations are high. And make no mistake—this is very good wine. It's just that a slightly resinous veneer of spicy oak largely dominates the palate and finish. **87** —*J.C. (7/1/2002)*

Vasse Felix 2000 Heytesbury Red Blend (Margaret River) $40. Beautifully built—smooth and supple in the mouth, with long, fine tannins, which envelop blackberry and plum flavors. Its fine tannins continue through to the finish, where they turn tea-like and a bit oaky. Has earth, vanilla, and eucalyptus on the nose. **91** —*D.T. (10/1/2003)*

Vasse Felix 1999 Heytesbury Red Blend (Western Australia) $40. A monumental wine. Black-purple in color, with massive, but juvenile, aromas of cassis and white pepper. Huge and explosive in the mouth, coating the palate with blackberry flavors, but very tannic and acidic now. **93 Editors' Choice** —*S.H. (12/15/2002)*

Vasse Felix 2001 Shiraz (Margaret River) $30. You can identify a wine of quality by the way it evolves and improves in the glass. And that's exactly what happens with this wine, whose nose started rather woody, but eventually revealed deep eucalyptus, chalk, and earth notes. The palate, likewise, unfolded from unadorned black fruit to reveal nuances of carob, nut, and cinnamon. Has wild and wooly tannins, but is moderate enough in size to enjoy with food. Very enjoyable. **90** —*D.T. (11/15/2004)*

Vasse Felix 2001 Shiraz (Margaret River) $30. This is one dark wine, and the aromas are young and fresh, with a heap of blackberry and white chocolate and a hint of something herbal, like licorice. It's huge and concentrated now, but should soften and gain complexity in time. **91** —*S.H. (10/1/2003)*

Vasse Felix 2000 Shiraz (Margaret River) $30. This is one dark wine, and the aromas are young and fresh, with a heap of blackberry and white chocolate and a hint of something herbal, or licorice. It's a big, lusty wine, packed with berry flavors and with a solid grip of tannins. Huge and concentrated now, but should soften and gain complexity in time. **91 Editors' Choice** —*S.H. (12/15/2002)*

Vasse Felix 1999 Shiraz (Margaret River) $30. Though it could use two years in the cellar to integrate, the Vasse Felix shows blackberry and cedar from start to finish, and lots of cocoa and toast flavors along the

AUSTRALIA

AUSTRALIA

way. Bouquet has mint accents; finish is dry, with mineral and cedar notes. **89** *(11/1/2001)*

Vasse Felix 1998 Shiraz (Margaret River) $27. 91 —*M.S. (10/1/2000)*

Vasse Felix 2002 Adam's Road Shiraz (Margaret River) $15. A new lower-priced offering from Vasse Felix, and bargain as far as Margaret River offerings go. Don't pass judgment on this wine until it's been in the glass a few minutes—this one changes considerably with air. With patience, you'll see blackberry and black plum aromas, and ripe blackberries (and a hint of blueberry) on the palate. Tannins are smooth, and run through the finish, where oak and eucalyptus wrap it up. **89 Editors' Choice** —*D.T. (5/1/2004)*

Vasse Felix 2002 Adams Road Shiraz (Margaret River) $15. A new offering from Vasse Felix, and a bargain as far as Margaret River offerings go. Changes considerably with air; with patience, you'll find blackberry and black plum aromas, and ripe blackberries and a hint of blueberry on the palate. Tannins are smooth through the finish, where oak and eucalyptus wrap it up. **89 Editors' Choice** —*D.T. (5/1/2004)*

VIRGIN HILLS

Virgin Hills 1998 Red Blend (Victoria) $30. Attractive aromatics and plenty of complexity are the pluses; the minus is a healthy dose of bell pepper. Smoke, herbs, eucalyptus, and sour cherry hang on a claret-style frame. **86** —*J.C. (9/1/2002)*

VOYAGER ESTATE

Voyager Estate 2000 Chardonnay (Margaret River) $20. Brings together rich buttery aromas of Bananas Foster and spun sugar with citrus, green apple, and yellow plum. Surprisingly light in body, with a short, tart finish. **84** —*J.C. (7/1/2002)*

Voyager Estate 1999 Shiraz (Margaret River) $19. Complex, with horsey, leathery notes alongside roasted nuts, cedar, and coffee. But where's the fruit? It's like it got lost in an oak forest on the way to the bottle. Still, our more oak-tolerant panelist loved this wine, so if you're into Quercus maximus you may find our panel score stingy. **85** *(10/1/2001)*

WAKEFIELD ESTATE

Wakefield Estate 2002 Cabernet Sauvignon (Clare Valley) $16. So big that even the winemaker calls it "the monster." Feels like Port on palate entry, with high-toned red fruit and a little fresh herb. Tannins are dry, but the finish is even drier, with cranberry, oak, and herb flavors. **86** —*D.T. (2/1/2004)*

Wakefield Estate 2001 Cabernet Sauvignon (Clare Valley) $15. A very good, straightforward, drink-now Cab, with wide-reaching toffee and caramel aromas. It's just right size—medium-boned, with a pleasing, easy texture. Plum and maybe even some blueberry on the palate are oaked judiciously, and both the wood and the juicy fruit persist through the finish. **87** —*D.T. (5/1/2004)*

Wakefield Estate 1998 St. Andrews Cabernet Sauvignon (Clare Valley) $60. In the mouth, bold black fruit takes on lots of molasses, or brown sugar, and that sweetness carries through to the finish. The package is wrapped with a ribbon of eucalyptus that's deep on the nose, and gives the otherwise dark-and-sweet flavors a nice, unexpected tweak. One to drink with a beef roast, particularly if it's served with gravy or a reduced wine sauce. **89** —*D.T. (2/1/2004)*

Wakefield Estate 2002 Promised Land Cabernet Sauvignon-Merlot (South Australia) $13. Vibrant blackberry aromas and flavors are swathed in dark, earthy accents. Medium-bodied, with tea-like tannins, it finishes with nut and wood notes. **87** —*D.T. (11/15/2003)*

Wakefield Estate 2004 Chardonnay (Clare Valley) $17. The brand is Wakefield here in the U.S., but Taylors in Australia; Taylors is one of the biggest brands out of Clare. This Chard is round, soft, and medium-full, with a minerally feel and white stone fruit flavors at the fore. Will have wide appeal. **87** —*D.T. (10/1/2006)*

Wakefield Estate 2003 Chardonnay (South Australia) $18. From the Clare Valley winery Taylors, which is known in the States as Wakefield. This Chard shows concentrated pear, toast, and mineral aromas. Its flavor profile is both floral and caramelly, with pear fruit at its core. Medium-soft in body. **86** *(7/2/2004)*

Wakefield Estate 2003 Promised Land Chardonnay (South Australia) $13. Sunny, lively, and unique in that it's floral on both the nose and the palate, where the fruit is bright and tropical. A good white wine, though the floral bits may throw you off from guessing that it is Chardonnay. **85** *(7/2/2004)*

Wakefield Estate 2002 Promised Land Unwooded Chardonnay (South Australia) $10. Offers cracker and wheat aromas, and light white stone-fruit flavors that seem coated in confectioner's sugar, or talc. Perhaps it's the "unwooded" designation talking, but this wine seems a little light, and not much like Chardonnay. **82** —*D.T. (8/1/2003)*

Wakefield Estate 2005 Promised Land Unwooded Chardonnay (South Australia) $13. A full, weighty Chard, but one that doesn't come across as clumsy. It smells like almonds and olive oil, and tastes like white peaches layered with hay and herb. **86** —*D.T. (11/15/2006)*

Wakefield Estate 2000 St. Andrews Chardonnay (Clare Valley) $17. A thick, gooey wine, a triumph for fans of the butter-toast-candied fruit style. Aromas are of butterscotch, cocoa, and toasted coconut. Peach is at the core, but it's buried deep. **84** *(7/2/2004)*

Wakefield Estate 2005 Riesling (Clare Valley) $17. Moderately acidic with broad appeal, this Riesling deals light citrus, grass, and pear aromas and flavors. Zips to a close with an interesting, kiwi-like flavor. **86** —*D.T. (10/1/2006)*

Wakefield Estate 2002 Shiraz (Clare Valley) $16. Sweet raspberry and blackberry aromas; mixed plum fruit on the palate. The fruit's so jammy that it'd be at home with some peanut butter, between two slices of bread. Dries up on the finish, with taut red fruit. **86** —*D.T. (2/1/2004)*

Wakefield Estate 1999 St. Andrews Shiraz (Clare Valley) $60. Tastes like what we Americans expect a premium Australian Shiraz to taste like (and there's nothing wrong with that): Three parts ripe plum fruit, one part each oak and caramel. Fruit is sweet on the nose, and coupled with smoky grilled meats. It was "created to take on Grange," explained winemaker Adam Eggins. The wine is on its way, but still has a little farther to go. **90** —*D.T. (2/1/2004)*

Wakefield Estate 2001 Promised Land Shiraz-Cabernet Sauvignon (South Australia) $13. Molasses or burnt sugar is a big player on the nose. Blackberry fruit takes a turn for the tangy in the mouth, with the help of some oak. Falls off on the finish. **83** —*D.T. (1/1/2002)*

WALLABY CREEK

Wallaby Creek 2000 Chardonnay (South Eastern Australia) $7. Nose offers tropical fruit and caramel aromas, but that's not quite what you get in the mouth. Doesn't pack too much fruit flavor into the glass—there are only hints of white peach, plus some oak, on the palate. **82** —*D.T. (1/1/2002)*

Wallaby Creek 2001 Merlot (Big Rivers) $6. If the supermarket's out of wine coolers, Wallaby Creek should be your next choice. It tastes like raspberry cheesecake, with very sweet berry fruit and a definite lactic-cream presence. Ditto for the aromas. **81** —*D.T. (1/1/2002)*

Wallaby Creek 2000 Shiraz (South Eastern Australia) $7. Very light in color, with brick-tinged edges. That mature look is matched on the nose, which has clove and earth notes. But it is also a lot like sherry, indicating some oxidization. In the mouth, the cherry fruit is too thin and the finish is sharp. **82** —*M.S. (1/28/2003)*

WANDIN VALLEY

Wandin Valley 2000 Riley's Reserve Cabernet Sauvignon (Hunter Valley) $20. This Cab feels rustic and dry in the mouth, with tree bark and taut plum flavors. There are also hints of stem and dried spice, making for an outdoorsy impression all around. Chalky, smooth tannins complete the picture. **86** —*D.T. (9/1/2004)*

Wandin Valley 2002 Chardonnay (Hunter Valley) $13. Apple pastry in a glass, with bready, baked-apple aromas, and clove and mealy apple flavors. Soft and middleweight on the palate, it finishes a little dilute. 500 cases produced. **85** *(7/2/2004)*

Wandin Valley NV Muscat (South Eastern Australia) $15. Dark, almost coffee-colored. Smells like ash. Though there are pleasing ginger and root-beer flavors here, it seems past its prime. Drink now. **84** —*D.T.* *(12/31/2004)*

Wandin Valley 2002 Verdelho (Hunter Valley) $13. Pear and resin aromas are light. This wine's palate entry is really neat: you slide effortlessly into green-apple flavors and a nice, viscous texture, which clings through the dusty finish. Nice, unusual, and hey, what a bargain. **87** —*D.T.* *(11/15/2004)*

WARBURN

Warburn 2000 Show Reserve Cabernet Sauvignon-Merlot (Riverina) $15. At 90% Cabernet, this wine is pitch black in color, with mustard seed, leather, and violets making up the intriguing bouquet. Black cherry is the predominant flavor on the juicy, acid-packed palate. The finish is quite dry, with ample oak and beefy tannins. **85** —*M.S. (12/15/2002)*

Warburn 2000 Show Reserve Durif (Riverina) $15. Sturdy and ripe, with beautiful purple-brick color, this is a wine with great pairing potential for lamb or other grilled meats. Black fruit on the nose has interesting accents of water chestnuts, or maybe bamboo shoots. Juicy blackberry and tobacco flavors are front and center in the mouth, and continue on through the finish. **88** —*D.T. (6/1/2003)*

WARRABILLA

Warrabilla 2004 Parola's Limited Release Cabernet Sauvignon (Rutherglen) $60. Like the reserve Cab but from the Paola's block, this Cab is vibrant purple in color and positively sticks to the glass—its 16.1% alcohol is surprising, given the wine's overall balance. It has light chocolaty aromas on the nose (like pudding), with bouncy berry fruit and some vanilla on the palate. A nice wooly texture completes the picture. **90** —*D.T. (10/1/2006)*

Warrabilla 2004 Reserve Cabernet Sauvignon (Rutherglen) $45. Just a really enjoyable mouthful of wine: Dark earth, blackberry, piercing fruitiness and some oak and char shadings. Finish is thick and claylike. It's 15.5% alcohol, but wears its size quite well. **91** —*D.T. (10/1/2006)*

Warrabilla 1998 Chardonnay (Rutherglen) $18. **85** —*S.H. (10/1/2000)*

Warrabilla 2004 Parola's Limited Release Durif (Rutherglen) $55. A focused wine, with smooth tannins and ripe apricot, violet, and cassis flavors. There's a fair amount of spice, toast, and nut on the nose. Clocks in at a massive 17.5% alcohol, but it's balanced. **88** —*D.T. (6/1/2006)*

Warrabilla 2004 Reserve Durif (Rutherglen) $40. This wine's back label talks a big game: "If you can find a bigger wine, buy it!" At 16.5% alcohol, it's a big wine that wears its size well (but you don't have to go far to find a bigger wine—Warrabilla's Paola's bottling is a percent higher in alcohol). Medium-sized and flavorful, with dense purple fruit and soft tannins, this wine is moderate, not super-rich, and best that way. **88** —*D.T. (6/1/2006)*

Warrabilla 2000 Petite Sirah (Rutherglen) $27. This big and broodingly dark wine is packed with grapey fruit and vanilla. The tannins on the finish are dusty but ripe and should preserve the wine for up to 10 years in the cellar. Still, why not drink it now with barbecue and savor the youthfully lusty fruit? **88** —*J.C. (9/1/2002)*

Warrabilla 1999 Petite Sirah (Victoria) $29. If you've been inside a natural food store, you've already experienced this Petite Sirah. The nose has olive-y, earthy, green-produce notes; the palate shows similarly organic-tasting, fresh earthy elements. Finishes short, with a slight tang. Its uniqueness will either mesmerize you or puzzle you to no end. **83** —*D.T. (9/1/2001)*

Warrabilla 2000 Shiraz (Rutherglen) $27. A tart, chalky finish suggests a couple years of cellaring would help this flavorful wine blossom because the other ingredients are already in place: Black pepper and eucalyptus add complexity to the blackberry aromas and flavors. **87** —*J.C. (9/1/2002)*

WARREN MANG VINEYARDS

Warren Mang Vineyards 2002 Vinello Red Blend (King Valley) $20. A blend of Barbera, Nebbiolo, Sangiovese, and Dolcetto—not something that comes out of Australia every day. Tastes distinctly red, with eucalyptus accents—a profile that registers as medicinal to some. It's well made, with bouncy sweet plum aromas on the nose, until the cherries and herbs

take over again. Nice and unusual, if you like the component flavors. **85** —*D.T. (1/1/2002)*

WARRENMANG

Warrenmang 1999 Estate Shiraz (Victoria) $45. Offers powerful brown sugar aromas that are overcome by black pepper with air; black pepper accents plum and black cherry fruit flavors as well. Has some hold on the palate. It's not going to get any better than it is now. **89** —*D.T. (8/1/2005)*

WATER WHEEL

Water Wheel 1999 Cabernet Sauvignon (Bendigo) $15. Where's the fruit? It's buried under a pile of charred wood and mouth-starching tannins. The cassis and tobacco that poke through just aren't enough to carry this wine. **82** —*J.C. (6/1/2002)*

Water Wheel 2000 Chardonnay (Bendigo) $12. The palate has tropical and yellow fruit at the core, plus a powdery overlay akin to confectioner's sugar. Still, it's not as sweet as it sounds; woody tannins run from palate to finish. **84** —*D.T. (6/1/2003)*

WAYNE THOMAS

Wayne Thomas 2004 Petite Verdot (McLaren Vale) $24. Fruit flavors on the palate are focused and at the forefront; oak intervention is minimal but for a brambly, black-peppery accent. Medium and smooth on the palate, with deep plum, blackberry, and tea aromas. A very nice wine; 500 cases produced. **89** —*D.T. (8/1/2006)*

Wayne Thomas 2003 Shiraz (McLaren Vale) $21. Like many McLaren Vale Shirazes, this one seems to fall somewhere between the full-blown Barossa style and the herb- and spice-driven styles of cooler climates. There's a minty edge to the blackberry fruit, espresso notes similar to those found in the northern Rhône, and firm tannins on the finish. Try after 2008. **89** —*J.C. (12/15/2006)*

WEDGETAIL-ROSSETTO WINES

Wedgetail-Rossetto Wines 2001 Shiraz-Cabernet Sauvignon (Riverina) $8. Smells and tastes a little past its peak already. Red fruit is on its way downhill, and is joined with some meaty, earthy flavors on the palate. Finishes flat. **82** —*D.T. (12/31/2003)*

WEST CAPE HOWE

West Cape Howe 2003 Cabernet Sauvignon (Western Australia) $19. Has very nice spicy, smoky aromas and a hearty dose of red raspberry and plum flavors, and lively acidity. **87** —*D.T. (8/1/2006)*

West Cape Howe 2003 Chardonnay (Western Australia) $18. This Chard relies heavily on oak to get its message across. It's gold in color, with aromas of butterscotch and pickling spice. Hefty wood and a lactic note coats firm yellow peach fruit on the palate. Has a nice mouthfeel, though—it's the texture of smooth river rocks. **86** —*D.T. (8/1/2006)*

West Cape Howe 2005 Unwooded Chardonnay (Western Australia) $15. This Chard offers mealy Golden Delicious apple flavors hung on a narrow frame. Modest floral aromas and citrus peel flavors start and finish the wine. **83** —*D.T. (11/15/2006)*

West Cape Howe 2004 Riesling (Western Australia) $17. An accessibly styled Riesling, by which I mean that the mouthfeel is a little rounder and acidity is a little lower than it could be. Has fragrant lime and pink grapefruit notes on the nose, with plenty more lime and dust on the palate. **86** —*D.T. (8/1/2006)*

West Cape Howe 2004 Semillon-Sauvignon Blanc (Western Australia) $15. Smells like mango, plus a pickle-like note. On the palate it is mouth-puckeringly dry, like grapefruit juice, with nuances of apricot and orange. **83** —*D.T. (8/1/2006)*

WHITE KNOT

White Knot 2005 Chardonnay (McLaren Vale) $12. Nut and white stone fruit aromas start things off. Tastes like pineapples and fresh cream; broad, but not so deep. **84** —*D.T. (8/1/2006)*

WHITSEND ESTATE

Whitsend Estate 2002 Cabernet Sauvignon (Yarra Valley) $20. A well-made wine, one with a dryish mouthfeel and a Cab-typical flavor profile.

AUSTRALIA

Aromas are of dusty black fruit, pencil eraser, and orange, of all things. Black plums and earth flavors; a good, sturdy red overall. **87** —*D.T. (12/31/2004)*

WILLOW BRIDGE

Willow Bridge 2001 Estate Cabernet Sauvignon (Western Australia) $13. A straightforward, gets-the-job-done Cabernet, smooth and creamy in the mouth, with flavors of mixed plums and tree bark. Blackberry fruit is jammy on the nose, with plenty of vanilla. **87** —*D.T. (5/1/2004)*

Willow Bridge 2001 Winemaker's Reserve Cabernet Sauvignon-Merlot (Western Australia) $13. Yes, the wine is wooly, wild, and woody—it's dry in the mouth, with woody tannins and earthy, bark flavors framing its focused plum fruit. What's nice about it, though, is that the wood is present more in texture than in flavor. Aromas continue with the rustic theme: dried spice, fireplace, acorn. **87** —*D.T. (9/1/2004)*

WILLOW CREEK

Willow Creek 1998 Cabernet Sauvignon (Mornington Peninsula) $21. Smells young and elusive, with earthy, green aromas masking riper notes of blackberries and cassis. There's little oak evident here. The wine tastes riper than you'd expect, with sweet blackberry fruit, but high acidity keeps it on the austere side. A highly structured wine that is fine on its own and even better with the right foods. **87** —*S.H. (9/1/2001)*

Willow Creek 1999 Tulum Reserve Chardonnay (Mornington Peninsula) $26. High acid, austere fruit mark this cool-climate wine, with aromas and flavors of green apples and peaches. It would be rather lean and tart on its own, but they fattened it up with French Oak and aging on the lees. It's a terroir-driven wine. **86** —*S.H. (9/1/2001)*

Willow Creek 2001 Unoaked Chardonnay (Mornington Peninsula) $18. From a cool-weather region, this tangy, slightly sharp Chardonnay aims at a Chablis style and almost pulls it off. Smells ripe, with pear and guava notes, but the palate is less so—grapefruit and lima bean flavors prevail. **85** —*J.C. (7/1/2002)*

Willow Creek 2000 Unoaked Chardonnay (Mornington Peninsula) $18. Like the label says, no oak has touched this wine. All you get is pure fruit, and dry, high acid fruit, at that. The flavors veer toward citrus with a hint of peach, and the acidity is very high. Elegant, crisp, and refreshing, it finishes with a slight burn. **85** —*S.H. (9/1/2001)*

Willow Creek 2000 Sauvignon Blanc (Mornington Peninsula) $18. Grassy and bone dry, it has strong aromas of lemons and grapefruits, with no oak influence at all. The result is clean, fresh, and tart. A nice apéritif wine that would be good with fresh shellfish. **86** —*S.H. (9/1/2001)*

WILLOWGLEN

Willowglen 2001 Shiraz (South Eastern Australia) $6. A feast of mallowy caramel for the senses: ginger and spice aromas on the nose morph, with aeration, into what smells like butter pecan ice cream. The same candied, buttery-vanilla quality appears on the palate as well, where it steals the spotlight from red fruit. Others may like it better. **84 Best Buy** —*D.T. (12/31/2003)*

Willowglen 2003 De Bortoli Wines Shiraz-Cabernet Sauvignon (South Eastern Australia) $9. Plum and oak flavors and aromas, from top to bottom. Good red wine, built for the masses. Three-quarters Shiraz, with Cab making up the remainder. **84** —*D.T. (12/31/2004)*

WILSON VINEYARD (AUS)

Wilson Vineyard (AUS) 2000 Gallery Series Cabernet Sauvignon (Clare Valley) $22. Just the right weight, with the feel (and the flavor) of clay running throughout. The nose offers earth, bark, and curry spice aromas. The palate has red plum fruit that segues into leather and earth on the finish. Quite enjoyable. **89** —*D.T. (5/1/2004)*

Wilson Vineyard (AUS) 2002 Proprietary Riesling (Clare Valley) $18. Winemaker John Wilson has crafted a crisp, racy wine from the Polish Hill River area of Clare Valley. The nose is fragrant, feminine and floral, and the palate shows pear and pencil-eraser notes, with a snap of fresh lime and mineral on the finish. **90 Editors' Choice** —*D.T. (5/1/2004)*

WINDSHAKER RIDGE

Windshaker Ridge 2004 Carnelian (Western Australia) $14. Here's a variety you never see, let alone from Australia. The nose offers notes of bread, cracker, and forward berry. Ripe blackberry flavors are dusty and sandy around the edges, and close with soft tannins. Not a huge, overstuffed wine; fine for the dinner table. 1,000 cases imported. **87** —*D.T. (8/1/2006)*

WINDSHAKER RIDGE

Windshaker Ridge 2003 Carnelian (Western Australia) $13. An interesting, simple, but pleasing wine. Aromas are of blackberry and violet, and the palate offers up a mixed berry basket full of flavor. Has papery-smooth tannins, and softens with air. A good quaff. 25,000 cases produced. **86** —*D.T. (8/1/2005)*

Windshaker Ridge 2003 Chardonnay (Western Australia) $13. This straightforward Chardonnay is pretty soft and approachable in the mouth, with flavors of apple and citrus. Smells very appley, too, with a spritz of lemon. Good for casual affairs; 15,000 cases produced. **84** —*D.T. (10/1/2005)*

Windshaker Ridge 2003 Shiraz (Western Australia) $13. Tastes cool and crisp, just as it smells: think dried cherry fruit, with a minty streak. Feels thin at first, but give it some time in the glass to come around. 25,000 cases produced. **86** —*D.T. (12/1/2005)*

Windshaker Ridge 2005 Verdelho (Western Australia) $14. Just the right size; just acidic enough. Has olive-oil aromas, and floral, citrus, and grass flavors. Smooth on the palate, finishing with some peach. Will have many fans. **87** —*D.T. (10/1/2006)*

Windshaker Ridge 2003 Verdelho (Western Australia) $13. This very likable Verdelho offers straw and hay aromas, plus a little Band-aid, on the nose. The mouthfeel is smooth and dry, with flavors of yellow peach flesh and lavender. The longer it sits, the more toasty it seems to get, so adjust your drinking speed accordingly **87 Best Buy** —*D.T. (8/1/2005)*

WINDY PEAK

Windy Peak 2002 Chardonnay (Victoria) $13. Aromas are deep and unusual—like a mix of petrol, olive oil, and smoke. It's a medium-bodied, sunny wine, with melon and pear flavors that pick up some toast toward the finish. **86** *(7/2/2004)*

Windy Peak 2001 Pinot Noir (Victoria) $13. Cream, cinnamon and ginger aromas on the nose. The palate hides an underlying creamy-lactic note, but there's ample plum, cherry, and earth flavors. Has dry, powdery tannins that extend through the finish. **85** —*D.T. (10/1/2003)*

Windy Peak 2000 Shiraz (Victoria) $13. Sawdust and cardboard flavors obscure what simple fruit this wine shows. Bubble bath, grape Hi-C, and toast aromas open this thin offering. **81** *(10/1/2001)*

WINTER CREEK

Winter Creek 2000 Shiraz (Barossa Valley) $20. The pleasant nose features a hint of violets, rose petals and then some licorice and leather for rusticity. The palate is bold and flashy, and actually more fresh than heavy. The red fruit flows forth and doesn't quit. And the finish is snappy with nice weight. **89** —*M.S. (3/1/2003)*

WIRRA WIRRA

Wirra Wirra 2003 Scrubby Rise Chardonnay (McLaren Vale) $11. Medium-bodied, with light aromas and flavors of vanilla, cream, and stone fruit. Somewhat flabby; good, but not much different from many other Chardonnays at its price point. **84** —*D.T. (3/1/2005)*

Wirra Wirra 2003 Scrubby Rise Chardonnay (South Australia) $13. Has verve and freshness, with green apple, white stone fruit, grass, and lime flavors and aromas. Finishes a bit soft, with fresh herb and chalk notes. A nice wine at a nice price, it's just right for an alfresco lunch. **87 Best Buy** *(7/2/2004)*

Wirra Wirra 2004 Sexton's Acre Unwooded Chardonnay (McLaren Vale) $NA. Features talc, perfume, and citrus aromas and flavors. Simple and enjoyable. **84** —*D.T. (3/1/2005)*

Wirra Wirra 2002 Grenache (McLaren Vale) $27. Made from bushvine fruit in McLaren Flat, this Grenache shows lifted cherry aromas, and pretty black cherry and floral flavors. Minerally and dry on the finish; a very good, typical example of McLaren Grenache. **89** —*D.T. (3/1/2005)*

Wirra Wirra 2002 Church Block Red Blend (McLaren Vale) $17. Aromatic, with smoke, earth, and barbecue on the nose. Dry tannins in the mouth; black plum and oak are the principal flavors here. Would pair well with a broad range of foods, from pizzas to pastas and burgers. A blend of Cabernet Sauvignon, Shiraz, and Merlot. 4,000 cases imported. **88** —*D.T. (3/1/2005)*

Wirra Wirra 1999 Church Block Red Blend (McLaren Vale) $20. A disappointing effort from this normally reliable winery. There's some dark earth and fruit but it's hard to get at under a veil of charred oak, cellar dirt, and alcohol. The finish tastes of coffee grounds. The mouthfeel is fine, the flavors just don't come together. **81** —*J.C. (9/1/2002)*

Wirra Wirra 2000 Scrubby Rise Red Blend (Fleurieu Peninsula) $10. This easy-to-drink blend of 50% Shiraz, 35% Cabernet Sauvignon, and 15% Petit Verdot starts off jammy, with black cherry liqueur and clove notes before settling down and developing some interesting peach and mocha nuances. The persistent finish, lined with velvety tannins, makes it stand out from the crowd. **87 Best Buy** —*J.C. (9/1/2002)*

Wirra Wirra 2002 Scrubby Rise SZ-CS-PV Red Blend (McLaren Vale) $11. What's wrong with this picture? This wine is better than the Scrubby Rise Shiraz, but is only available in Florida and Texas (the latter locale is understandable, as this wine is probably a heavenly marriage wtih barbecue!). Contact your retailers and distributors and put up a fuss—there's nice cherry and plum fruit here, jazzed up with smoke and spice accents. An interesting blend, too, particularly for the price. **87 Best Buy** —*D.T. (3/1/2005)*

Wirra Wirra 2001 Hand Picked Riesling (Fleurieu Peninsula) $13. Only a little sweet, but very fruity, this shows why Riesling is the wine that can really taste most like grapes. It's soft, and though higher acidity would provide better spine and definition, it's generous and easy to like. Far beyond White Zin in quality, it's a perfect choice if you just want a fruitier wine, or for people who have grown out of the pink, simple stuff and are ready for a big step up. **86** —*M.M. (2/1/2002)*

Wirra Wirra 2000 Hand Picked Riesling (McLaren Vale) $13. 87 —*M.M. (1/1/2004)*

Wirra Wirra 2004 Mrs. Wigley Rosé Blend (South Australia) $19. 88 —*D.T. (2/1/2006)*

Wirra Wirra 2002 Shiraz (McLaren Vale) $27. A nice combination of earth, pencil eraser, and dried spice on the nose ushers in raspberry and black cherry flavors. It's a mid-sized Shiraz, accessible even now, with tannins that grip the midpalate and don't let up through the finish. 5,000 cases produced. **89** —*D.T. (3/1/2005)*

Wirra Wirra 2001 Shiraz (McLaren Vale) $26. A very nice Shiraz, with meaty, chocolaty flavors and a core of ripe black plums. The nose also takes on earthy-mushroom and molasses scents; from end to end, oak is present, but not overbearing. A natural match for beef roast and gravy. **88** —*D.T. (12/31/2003)*

Wirra Wirra 1999 Shiraz (McLaren Vale) $28. Loaded with earthy espresso and charred wood, this full-bodied Shiraz makes for a chunky mouthful of wine. Black pepper, leather and dried spices round out the flavors. **86** —*J.C. (9/1/2002)*

Wirra Wirra 1998 Chook Block Shiraz (McLaren Vale) $75. Complex aromas of mocha and milk chocolate, vanilla and black cherry lead into a full, viscous, creamy mouthful of blackberry and earth flavors. Powerful and intense, finishing with hints of tobacco and milk chocolate. **89** *(11/1/2001)*

Wirra Wirra 1998 R.S.W. Shiraz (McLaren Vale) $67. Its smooth, velvety mouthfeel is almost reason enough to buy this wine, but the river of ripe red fruit, nut, and cassis flavors on the palate make it a lock. The nose may be right in line with the "big Oz Shiraz" profile (caramel, big black fruit, a little herb and oak), but the eucalyptus and mocha flavors are all its glorious own. 300 cases produced. **92** —*D.T. (12/31/2003)*

Wirra Wirra 1997 R.S.W. Shiraz (McLaren Vale) $35. 90 *(10/1/2000)*

Wirra Wirra 2002 RSW Shiraz (McLaren Vale) $54. The nose is still fairly closed but shows some plum and bacon aromas. The palate is likewise not expressing much flavor, but the wine's formidable size, chewy tannins, and medium-long finish promise good things to come down the road. Drink 2007+. **91 Cellar Selection** —*D.T. (3/1/2005)*

Wirra Wirra 2003 Scrubby Rise Shiraz (South Australia) $12. Rhône-styled and slight in build, this Shiraz deals an abundance of black pepper, earth, and black cherry flavors. A cool and crisp style, and a relative bargain. **86** —*D.T. (12/1/2005)*

Wirra Wirra 2002 Scrubby Rise Shiraz (South Australia) $10. Blackberry and plum fruit is taut, accented by some exotic spice, and feels more dense on the front palate than on the toasty-oak finish. Still, it's a pleasing, easy-to-drink wine that's a safe bet for parties—particularly barbecues, as this seems just the ticket for a burger, or grilled meat. **86** —*D.T. (9/1/2004)*

Wirra Wirra 2001 Scrubby Rise White Blend (Fleurieu Peninsula) $10. Light floral, orange, and passion fruit aromas are pleasant, but from palate to finish this Oz white has very tangy, acidified grapefruit flavors, punctuated by a metallic bite on the back end. **81** —*D.T. (2/1/2002)*

Wirra Wirra 2000 Scrubby Rise White Blend (McLaren Vale) $13. 82 —*D.T. (1/1/2002)*

Wirra Wirra 1999 Scrubby Rise White Blend (McLaren Vale) $13. 90 Best Buy —*M.S. (10/1/2000)*

WISE

Wise 1997 Cabernet Sauvignon (Margaret River) $17. 86 —*M.S. (10/1/2000)*

Wise 1999 Aquercus Unwooded Chardonnay (Margaret River) $10. 85 *(10/1/2000)*

Wise 2003 Reserve Chardonnay (Pemberton) $35. Yum. The best of the Wise Chardonnays I tried, this bottling offers apple and pear aromas, and pear and mineral flavors. Very light in color, with only a hint of toast coming through on the finish. Dry, with good acidity. 500 cases produced. **89** —*D.T. (12/1/2005)*

Wise 2003 Single Vineyard Chardonnay (Western Australia) $25. Very toasty on the nose—with air, some fresh produce shows through. Wood dominates the palate, too, obscuring peach fruit underneath. **84** —*D.T. (12/1/2005)*

Wise 2004 Unwooded Chardonnay (Pemberton) $15. A blonde wine: soft, pretty, and light. It feels like soft peach fuzz and tastes like musk, its aromas brimming with brisk tropical fruit. Gets tighter and more floral toward the finish, where there's some Band-Aid. **86** —*D.T. (12/1/2005)*

Wise 2001 Unwooded Chardonnay (Western Australia) $13. 'Tis a noble pursuit, making Chardonnay that tastes like Chardonnay and not like oak, and Wise has succeeded in making a wine that exemplifies the peach, yellow-plum, and citrus flavors Chardonnay can display. But the flavors are fruit-cocktail-syrupy sweet, causing the wine to get muddled and lose focus on the finish. **83** —*J.C. (7/1/2002)*

Wise 2004 Classic White Semillon-Sauvignon Blanc (Western Australia) $16. Floral, peachy aromas are understated. The palate has a melony, peachy shell and a lightly creamy, almost oily, center. Goes down easy. **86** —*D.T. (12/1/2005)*

Wise 2002 Eagle Bay Shiraz (Margaret River) $28. Tight, cool, and feminine, this Shiraz shows some of its region's best hallmarks: eucalyptus, black pepper, and solid plum and blackberry fruit. Smooth and minerally on the palate, with a black-peppery finish. **88** —*D.T. (12/1/2005)*

Wise 1998 Eagle Bay Shiraz (Western Australia) $20. This wine has some pretty strawberry and red raspberry aromas and flavors, but the bulk of its interest lies in its oak-derived elements of clove, cinnamon, cedar, menthol, coffee, and chocolate. Wood-lovers will rate it higher. **85** *(10/1/2001)*

Wise 2002 Shiraz-Cabernet Sauvignon (Margaret River) $12. There's not much body or intensity to this Shiraz-Cab, and what's here is pretty odd. Aromas and flavors run the gamut from sautéed mushrooms in gravy to lifted fruit to Blow Pop. Confused. **82** —*D.T. (8/1/2006)*

AUSTRALIA

AUSTRALIA

WIT'S END

Wit's End 2002 Shiraz (McLaren Vale) $NA. 88 —D.T. (5/1/2005)

WOLF BLASS

Wolf Blass 2001 Gold Label Cabernet Sauvignon-Cabernet Franc Cabernet Blend (Adelaide Hills) $NA. A very good wine, and not a blend that you see often from South Australia. Has chewy, smooth tannins and serious black plum at its core, with fresh herb and soil notes on the palate. Finishes isn't a grand finale—it fades to black subtly. 23% Cabernet Franc. **89** —D.T. (2/1/2004)

Wolf Blass 2002 Gold Label Cabernet Sauvignon (Coonawarra) $24. Even tasted blind, this excellent Cab's smooth, velvety-clay feel says "Coonawarra." It's a restrained, balanced wine with pencil eraser and red plum fruit flavors, and cherry brightening the finish; even still, it's the texture you'll remember. **90** —D.T. (12/31/2004)

Wolf Blass 2000 Gold Label Cabernet Sauvignon (Coonawarra) $NA. A textbook Coonawarra Cab, with taut red fruit and dry, claylike tannins. A little herb shows on the nose and on the finish. Tasty, and classy. **88** —D.T. (5/1/2004)

Wolf Blass 2003 Grey Label Cabernet Sauvignon (Langhorne Creek) $32. The nose shows creamy vanilla aromas, plus some earthy, stemmy ones. Lifted berry fruit flavors are countered by smooth tannins on the palate. Has fine treble, but is missing bass notes that would give it more depth. **88** —D.T. (8/1/2006)

Wolf Blass 2002 Grey Label Cabernet Sauvignon (Langhorne Creek) $32. Tasty, sexy, well-built, and smooth. Not at all fat or flabby, the wine smells like mint and sweet fruit, but is, perhaps, a little nutty. Flavors are of beef, plum, and ripe raspberry, with little chips of coconut and toffee candy bar. **90** —D.T. (11/15/2004)

Wolf Blass 1998 Jimmy Watson Trophy Black Label` Cabernet Sauvignon (Barossa Valley) $50. The Real McCoy, from the standpoint of a massive, New World Cabernet. It's hard to tell which aroma prevails, the ultraripe cassis scent of grapes or massive oak. Ditto on the palate. Gigantic, huge mouthfeel, an Incredible Hulk of a wine, yet it's balanced. Too rich to drink now. Best to cellar for a decade and let it develop subtlety. **93 Cellar Selection** —S.H. (12/15/2002)

Wolf Blass 1998 Platinum Label Cabernet Sauvignon (Barossa Valley) $34. The fruit on the palate is the very picture of plum. The wine's not lean, nor is it sweet—it's a solid, medium- to full-bodied Cabernet that doesn't try to bowl you over with oak or caramel or, well, anything. It's balanced and well-behaved, with aromas that run the gamut from blackberry and plum to mocha to cherry to caramel. Very nice. **90** —D.T. (12/31/2003)

Wolf Blass 2001 Presidents Selection Cabernet Sauvignon (South Australia) $19. Smells sweet, like molasses, and the same quality reappears on the nose, mixed in with plum and wheat bread flavors. Medium-bodied and a little shrill. **85** —D.T. (8/1/2005)

Wolf Blass 2000 Presidents Selection Cabernet Sauvignon (South Australia) $20. Opens with fat red and black fruit, plus some chocolate and cinnamon. It's medium-bodied with red plum and raspberry fruit on the palate, this Cab has soft tannins and a fleshy, caramelly finish. It's got just the right body to drink tonight with dinner—have a glass with just about anything that you throw on the grill. **87** —D.T. (6/1/2003)

Wolf Blass 2002 Yellow Label Cabernet Sauvignon (South Australia) $12. There's a warming hint of chocolate caramel on the nose, followed up by ripe, feminine fruit on the palate. And "feminine" is the word I'd use to describe the wine's body, too: Slim-waisted and elegant, it's a sensible Cab—no rash, outlying flavors, and worth revisiting. **88 Best Buy** —D.T. (11/15/2004)

Wolf Blass 2001 Yellow Label Cabernet Sauvignon (South Australia) $14. Straightforward but quite nice, with bright raspberry and mixed plum fruit and smooth tannins in the mouth. The nose shows some meat and a cherry-candy note. **87** —D.T. (12/31/2003)

Wolf Blass 2000 Yellow Label Cabernet Sauvignon (South Australia) $12. Blueberry aromas open up this soft, easy, highly quaffable wine. It has an abundance of fruit and just the right amount of buttery oak to make things interesting. All throughout it steers clear of the dark stuff; i.e.,

burnt and toasty wood or heavy fruit. What it offers instead is some strawberry and a breath of fresh air. **87 Best Buy** —M.S. (12/15/2002)

Wolf Blass 1999 Yellow Label Cabernet Sauvignon (South Australia) $12. This solid mainstream offering sports plenty of cherry and tart berry aromas and flavors wrapped in a toasty cocoon. Medium weight, with an even mouthfeel, it has a spicy almost lemony element and a touch of licorice on the finish. Drink now. **86** (6/1/2001)

Wolf Blass 1997 Yellow Label Cabernet Sauvignon (South Australia) $12. 87 Best Buy (3/1/2000)

Wolf Blass 2000 Black Label Cabernet Sauvignon-Shiraz (Barossa-Langhorne Creek) $60. Wolf Blass's top-level blended wine, this is 51% Cabernet and 49% Shiraz with straight-shooting cassis and black plum fruit on the palate. Finishes with flair-with chocolate, liqueur, and coffee, like a savory after-dinner drink. **89** —D.T. (5/1/2004)

Wolf Blass 2001 Chardonnay (South Australia) $12. A simple but good wine, with toast and golden apple flavors. Has nice apple and olive oil aromas, and a mouth-puckering herb and white pepper finish. **84** —D.T. (8/1/2003)

Wolf Blass 1999 Chardonnay (South Australia) $12. 86 —L.W. (3/1/2000)

Wolf Blass 2000 Barrel Fermented Chardonnay (South Australia) $12. A bright pear and cinnamon nose opens this attractive, medium-weight wine. The palate shows peach and pear flavors, supported by brisk—some might say sharp—acidity, but flabby it isn't. Shows good balance and a nice long spicy finish, where the oak comes on strong. **86** (6/1/2001)

Wolf Blass 2004 Gold Label Chardonnay (Adelaide Hills) $21. A buttoned up, classy wine offering peach and fresh corn aromas and flavors. Medium-weight, the palate also has floral hints. 3,000 cases produced. **88** —D.T. (8/1/2005)

Wolf Blass 2003 Gold Label Chardonnay (Adelaide Hills) $20. Offers toast, cream, and yellow fruit on the nose and similar banana cream, toast and yellow peach flavors on the palate. Aged in French oak, with 50% malolactic fermentation; strikes the right balance between oak and fruit. **88** —D.T. (11/15/2004)

Wolf Blass 2003 Presidents Selection Chardonnay (South Australia) $14. Nice on the nose, with fresh herb, white plum flesh, and white pepper aromas. It's less striking on the palate, where a heavier feel and stony, woody flavors are at the fore, with yellow fruit in the background. **84** (7/2/2004)

Wolf Blass 2002 Presidents Selection Chardonnay (South Australia) $15. A slim-and-trim wine rather than an oversized one, with baked apple and toast flavors infused with a balancing shot of citrus. Yeasty, ginger, and apple aromas and a toasty finish complete the pretty picture. **87** (7/2/2004)

Wolf Blass 2001 Presidents Selection Chardonnay (South Australia) $15. There's taut yellow fruit at the core of this Chard, which doesn't taste as mallowy and toasty as the nose would led you to believe. It has a chalky mouthfeel, which extends through to the dry finish. **84** —D.T. (6/1/2003)

Wolf Blass 2005 Yellow Label Chardonnay (South Australia) $12. This is a lighter-style Chard that's pleasing and easy to drink. Light nut, floral and white stone fruit aromas lead to a palate that's full of chalk and almond-like flavors, finally finishing with some pear. **86** —D.T. (8/1/2006)

Wolf Blass 2004 Yellow Label Chardonnay (South Australia) $12. The nose doesn't offer much, but the palate is soft, with peach skin and oak flavors. Sours up on the finish. A fine casual quaff. **83** —D.T. (10/1/2005)

Wolf Blass 2003 Yellow Label Chardonnay (South Australia) $12. A good, straightforward wine, with mealy aromas and flavors of apple and pear. Finishes somewhat lackluster, wtih some oak and apple skin. **84** —D.T. (11/15/2004)

Wolf Blass 2001 Merlot (South Australia) $14. Black plum and cherry fruit on the palate is juicy, though not overblown or sweet, and wears a fair dose of oak and leather to boot. Wood persists on the finish, bothering one reviewer and interesting another. **85** (6/1/2003)

Wolf Blass 2004 Yellow Label Merlot (South Australia) $12. Has aromas of earth, mushroom, and berry; on the palate, the berry fruit is very ripe, with a citric, almost spritzy edge. Soft in the mouth otherwise, but wants a little more stuffing midpalate. **84** —*D.T. (6/1/2006)*

Wolf Blass 2003 Yellow Label Merlot (South Australia) $12. Oak is this Merlot's star—on the palate it outshines the cherry and plum fruit. Aromas are of tea and mocha. Good, but pretty basic. **84** —*D.T. (10/1/2005)*

Wolf Blass 2003 Gold Label Riesling (Clare & Eden Valleys) $14. Citrus is the name of the game here, from understated citrus-rind aromas to dry, zesty grapefruit and lemon flavors. It's bright and has the roundness in the mouth seen in a lot of 2003 Rieslings. Tiny spritz on the finish, plus citrus and stone fruit. **87** —*D.T. (2/1/2004)*

Wolf Blass 2001 Gold Label Riesling (Eden Valley) $12. Year in year out a winning Riesling, the 2001 sports a handsome new package. On par with the fine 2000, but a touch softer, especially on the muted hay and vanilla nose. Turns crisper in the mouth with fine green apple and grapefruit flavors. It's finely balanced and sports a long, clean finish. **89** —*M.M. (2/1/2002)*

Wolf Blass 2000 Gold Label Riesling (South Australia) $12. This even, fairly full Riesling has fragrant, grapey nose and lots of ripe apple-grape fruit. Nicely balanced, with modest acidity, it's mildly sweet on the palate but finishes dry and fairly long. Great drinking now, this would be a perfect step off the Chardonnay train for many enthusiasts. **89 Editors' Choice** —*M.M. (9/1/2001)*

Wolf Blass 1999 Gold Label Riesling (South Australia) $12. 86 —*M.S. (10/1/2000)*

Wolf Blass 2003 Gold Label Sauvignon Blanc (Adelaide Hills) $NA. Starts out beautifully, with grassy, sweet-pea aromas mixed in with some hay. Cleansing lemon-lime flavors in the mouth mellow out on the finish, where lemon pith lingers. Zingy half the time; understated for the remainder. **87** —*D.T. (2/1/2004)*

Wolf Blass 2000 Shiraz (South Australia) $12. The nose is herbal, bordering on piquant. There are also detectable notes of cherry and beet. The berry fruit that dominates the palate is mild, even slightly citrusy, at the edges. This isn't the most exciting wine you'll encounter, but it's beyond pedestrian and shouldn't disappoint by-the-glass drinkers and those with modest expectations. **85** —*M.S. (3/1/2003)*

Wolf Blass 2001 Gold Label Shiraz (Barossa Valley) $24. Big, jammy blackberry and plum fruit that you find on the nose and palate turns a little taut—like cranberry—on the finish. Still, a very good wine with forward, enjoyable fruit. **87** —*D.T. (2/1/2004)*

Wolf Blass 2002 Gold Label Shiraz-Viognier Shiraz (Barossa Valley) $NA. Only 6% Viognier, and only 1,000 cases produced, this wine won numerous trophies at Australian wine shows at the end of last year. An excellent wine, one in which black pepper flavors and aromas are so prevalent that drinking it with anything other than steak au poivre seems criminal. Smooth on palate entry; plum fruit and eucalyptus prevail through the finish. **90 Editors' Choice** —*D.T. (5/1/2004)*

Wolf Blass 2002 Platinum Label Shiraz (Barossa) $72. Light maple, grape jelly, and meaty aromas are succeeded by berry-basket flavors on the palate. A Shiraz with wide appeal, though it's young right now and not yet singing at full volume. Drink after 2007. **90** —*D.T. (4/1/2006)*

Wolf Blass 2001 Platinum Label Shiraz (Adelaide Hills) $72. An elegant Shiraz, rich in the mouth. Black pepper on the nose is followed by subdued black plum fruit enveloped by chalky tannins and fresh herb flavors. Cellar for a few years; it needs time to unwind. **90** —*D.T. (5/1/2004)*

Wolf Blass 1999 Platinum Label Shiraz (Barossa Valley) $72. Starts off with scents of caramel popcorn and oak; it feels mouthfilling, but its size is more about sweet fruit than it is about structure or tannins. Black plum fruit on the palate is just a little too sweet and syrupy for this reviewer's taste; others may think this rating too conservative. Past vintages have fared better. **87** —*D.T. (5/1/2004)*

Wolf Blass 2003 Presidents Selection Shiraz (South Australia) $17. Aromas of black pepper, bramble, and berries lead into similar flavors, interlaced with some bitter chocolate. It's crisp, medium-sized, and focused. **88** —*D.T. (2/1/2006)*

Wolf Blass 2001 Presidents Selection Shiraz (South Australia) $19. Anise notes sex up the nose, and the palate delivers red plum and oak flavors in a pack of chewy tannins. Finishes rich, with earth, meat, demiglace, and juicy fruit. **88** —*D.T. (5/1/2004)*

Wolf Blass 2000 Presidents Selection Shiraz (South Australia) $20. There is a heavy woody accent to this wine, from the nose all the way through the mouth and onto the finish. There is also plenty of healthy berry character and tangy acids. The core is rather sweet and pleasing, but complexity is not a factor. Ultimately those who like oak will be happy, while those who do not may be put off. **87** —*M.S. (3/1/2003)*

Wolf Blass 2003 Yellow Label Shiraz (South Australia) $12. This medium-bodied Shiraz offers black and green pepper aromas, and firm plum fruit on the palate. Hints of cream and herb add interest to the wine's flavors. A good, everyday red. 35,000 cases produced. **86** —*D.T. (12/31/2005)*

Wolf Blass 2002 Yellow Label Shiraz (South Australia) $12. Oak lends nutty, caroby aromas and big, woodsy tannins to this well-priced red; fleshy red plum and berry fruit makes up the balance. Has pretty good length on the finish, too. Well made, and, with 17,000 cases produced, should be relatively easy to find. **87 Best Buy** —*D.T. (5/1/2005)*

Wolf Blass 2001 Black Label Shiraz-Cabernet Sauvignon (South Australia) $62. This 71-29 Shriaz-Cab blend is heavy on meat and coffee aromas, and juicy blackberry and plum flavors. Vanilla and cream are the uniting factors here, making for a rich, luscious, drink now wine. **88** —*D.T. (4/1/2006)*

Wolf Blass 2002 Red Label Shiraz-Cabernet Sauvignon (South Australia) $12. A fruity, balanced red from an ever-reliable producer. Firm red plum and cherry fruit has grip on the palate; it's medium-bodied, with oak and nut flavors, and ginger-nut accents on the nose. It's noticeably more sophisticated—less sweetness, less vanilla, more heft—than most Shiraz-Cabs in the under-$10 category. **88** —*D.T. (11/15/2003)*

Wolf Blass 2001 Red Label Shiraz-Cabernet Sauvignon (South Australia) $12. Red plum and cherry flavors dominate on the palate, with some tangy oak hovering underneath. Nut, ginger, and herbal notes on the nose. A good example of how reasonably priced a reliably good Oz Cab can be. **87** —*D.T. (12/31/2003)*

Wolf Blass 2000 Red Label Shiraz-Cabernet Sauvignon (South Australia) $12. Some sweet cherry aromas lead into a tight and tart palate with simple but fresh cherry and raspberry fruit. The wine is mildly sour and acidic, but it is also impeccably fresh and inoffensive. **84** —*M.S. (12/15/2002)*

Wolf Blass 1999 Red Label Shiraz-Cabernet Sauvignon (South Australia) $12. It's the color of fake blood but (I'm guessing) this wine is much more palatable. There are light, airy aromas of cherry, cumin, and tobacco, and flavors of blackberries and concord grapes. The wine's a mouthful, with a long chalk-meets-chile-pepper finish. **87** —*D.T. (9/1/2001)*

Wolf Blass NV Brut NV Sparkling Blend (Australia) $10. This wine could be a challenge to find (1,000 cases produced), but it's a value worth seeking out. The nose shows just light biscuity aromas, and the palate, pear, peach, and bread flour flavors. it's dry, even minerally, in the mouth. Not profound, but enjoyable and easy to drink. **87 Best Buy** —*D.T. (12/31/2004)*

Wolf Blass NV Traditional Method Brut Sparkling Blend (South Australia) $11. The Australian equivalent of California's Chandon, or Mumm Napa: it's an inexpensive, please-everyone, enjoyable wine, with yellow fruit, dust and a dry mouthfeel. Middle of the road in the best sense—it's not "too" anything to be at all disagreeable. **86 Best Buy** —*D.T. (12/31/2003)*

WOMBAT GULLY

Wombat Gully 2000 Cabernet Sauvignon (South Eastern Australia) $10. Very light, with spicy green aromas and much more tomato than fruit. The flavors are sugary and sweet. It should not be hard to find better Cabs than this. **80** —*M.S. (12/15/2002)*

Wombat Gully 2001 Shiraz (South Eastern Australia) $10. Tight in the nose, with hints of tomato and black plum. The flavors veer toward plum and cherry, as there's quite a lot of fruit here. Furthermore, it's nice

AUSTRALIA

and easy on the palate. Some toasty oak appears on the finish, which is buttery and fairly long. **84** —*M.S. (1/28/2003)*

WOOD PARK

Wood Park 1999 Cabernet Sauvignon-Shiraz (King Valley) $25. Gamey, leathery aromas don't quite hide this wine's sweet cherry nuances. In the mouth, the leather, tobacco, cigar box, and oak notes are prominent, but some nice plum, berry, and cherry come through in medium-bodied style. There's good acidity and some firm tannins that need to soften. Enjoy from 2003 through 2006. **88** *(9/1/2001)*

Wood Park 1998 Cabernet Sauvignon-Shiraz (King Valley) $22. This wine's sweet edge will please those who haven't yet grown to appreciate complex Cabs. Aromas of mushrooms and wet soil burn off to reveal a sugary, grapey bouquet. Oak and an herbal, tarragon-like flavor dominate the palate; finishes with smoke and a sweet, Port-flavored candy taste. **84** —*D.T. (9/1/2001)*

Wood Park 1999 Meadow Creek Chardonnay (Victoria) $25. This Chard's nose has pleasing butterscotch and cream aromas (that were somehow light enough to almost smell like a Sauvignon Blanc); sadly, the rest of the wine couldn't live up to the promising bouquet. Oak is the dominant flavor on the tangy, hot palate; there's high acidity in the mouth and on the back end. Pucker, pucker. **82** —*D.T. (9/1/2001)*

WOOP WOOP

Woop Woop 2004 Chardonnay (South Eastern Australia) $11. This dusty, pineapple-and-peach wine has a common flavor profile, but its round mouthfeel, lively acids, and crisp finish give it a leg up on other value-priced offerings. (Though its name may sound like an indigenous, endangered Oz animal, "Woop Woop" is actually another term for "way the hell out in the middle of nowhere.") **87 Best Buy** —*D.T. (12/31/2004)*

WYNDHAM ESTATE

Wyndham Estate 2002 Bin 444 Cabernet Sauvignon (South Eastern Australia) $10. This is a straight-shooting Cab, solid in its rendition of the red plum-oak-earth profile. Has sweet fruit, pepper, and a helping of dust on the nose, and a woodsy feel on the back end. **86 Best Buy** —*D.T. (5/1/2005)*

Wyndham Estate 2001 Bin 444 Cabernet Sauvignon (South Eastern Australia) $10. Aromas change with aeration—look for olive, then tart red fruit and black pepper. Red cherry and plum, plus a creamy note, lend flavor; mouthfeel is smooth. **85** —*D.T. (10/1/2003)*

Wyndham Estate 2000 Bin 444 Cabernet Sauvignon (South Eastern Australia) $10. The nose begins a bit wet and dirty, but some of that funk blows off, leaving the scent of wintergreen and dried cherries. The mouthfeel is bulky, while the flavors are mostly driven by sweet cherry. The finish is woody, and slightly vegetal. **84** —*M.S. (12/15/2002)*

Wyndham Estate 1998 Bin 444 Cabernet Sauvignon (South Eastern Australia) $12. This full-bodied Cab has loads of grape and blackberry in the mouth, with just a shade of vanilla bean flavor. The bouquet is an odd but appealing mix of whipping cream, anise, stewed fruit, and Chiclets gum. Finishes slightly hot and supertangy. **84** *(9/1/2001)*

Wyndham Estate 1997 Bin 444 Cabernet Sauvignon (South Eastern Australia) $12. This light- to medium-weight wine features a bouquet of berry and earth aromas and mature Cabernet flavors. The wood doesn't overwhelm, but the mouthfeel is slightly prickly and astringent, and the fruit doesn't really sing. Closes with mild tobacco notes. **83** *(6/1/2001)*

Wyndham Estate 2002 Bin 888 Cabernet Sauvignon-Merlot (South Eastern Australia) $10. Dusty black cherry aromas preface a similar profile on the palate: Dark plums, black cherry, wheat bread, and an earthy/leafy hint. It's a nice, medium-full weight, not so rich or mouthfilling that drinking it with dinner is out of the question. Finishes smooth. **87 Best Buy** —*D.T. (11/15/2004)*

Wyndham Estate 2000 Bin 888 Cabernet Sauvignon-Merlot (South Eastern Australia) $10. Rustic in feel as well as flavor, this red has woodsy tannins and some briary, earthy notes on the nose and the palate. Red plum and cherry are at the core, where they compete with a slight lactic-cheesy note. **84** —*D.T. (12/31/2003)*

Wyndham Estate 1999 Bin 888 Cabernet Sauvignon-Merlot (South Eastern Australia) $10. In a leaner, more restrained style than we've become accustomed to from inexpensive Oz reds—a welcome change. Cherry fruit is layered with leather and chocolate, blending in dusty tannins on the tart finish. **86 Best Buy** —*J.C. (6/1/2002)*

Wyndham Estate 1997 Show Reserve Cabernet Sauvignon-Merlot (Hunter Valley) $25. A lovely nose with plum, cassis, and notes of roasted coffee is followed by a lush, chewy mouthfeel. The ripe fruit flavors are ample and soft with cherries, plums, berries, and roasted nuts blanketing the palate. Clearly this 1997 has benefited from extended aging. Enjoy it over the next two to five years. **90** *(9/1/2001)*

Wyndham Estate 2005 Bin 222 Chardonnay (South Eastern Australia) $9. This is a good casual sipper without a lot of kick, but one that gets the job done. Offers lemon drop aromas and faint pineapple and chalk flavors. **83** —*D.T. (8/1/2006)*

Wyndham Estate 2004 Bin 222 Chardonnay (South Eastern Australia) $9. Has lively acidity at the center and dominant citrus-pith flavors. Smells and tastes like it's been through a woodchipper, and finishes on a sweet note. **83** —*D.T. (12/1/2005)*

Wyndham Estate 2003 Bin 222 Chardonnay (New South Wales) $9. Light in both weight and concentration, the 222 is a good choice if it's an easy, cold quaff that you're looking for. It's tropical and creamy on the nose, but shows lighter, fresher notes of white stone fruit, particularly pear, and lime. Finishes with more lime. **85** *(7/2/2004)*

Wyndham Estate 2002 Bin 222 Chardonnay (South Eastern Australia) $9. Passion fruit dominates the nose, then segues into a palate with green apple and lemon peel flavors, with a hefty dose of oak. Its tangy flavors seemed at first to shock the palate; after a few minutes of aeration, the tang subsided and the wine seemed to close up. **83** —*D.T. (6/1/2003)*

Wyndham Estate 2000 Bin 222 Chardonnay (South Eastern Australia) $9. A pillowy and tropical Chard that doesn't get sloppy soft or overly tart and hard. Toasted marshmallow, pineapple, and banana aromas; lightly caramelized pineapple dusted with cinnamon flavors. Finishes with a smoky edge. **87 Best Buy** —*J.C. (7/1/2002)*

Wyndham Estate 2001 Show Reserve Chardonnay (South Eastern Australia) $19. Smells of sweet gumdrops, smoke, and earth. In the mouth, it's similarly smoldering, with toast rounding out peach and pear flavors. A pretty straightforward, good wine. **85** *(7/2/2004)*

Wyndham Estate 2004 Bin 999 Merlot (South Eastern Australia) $10. Raspberry and blackberry aromas usher in twangy, thin berry fruit on the palate. A good wine with mass-market appeal, finishing with Sweet Tart flavors. **83** —*D.T. (6/1/2006)*

Wyndham Estate 2002 Bin 999 Merlot (South Eastern Australia) $10. This value-priced Merlot has decent mouthfeel and heft, but its taut cherry and plum fruit is showing hints of green. A good wine; would be even better without the stemmy quality. **84** —*D.T. (9/1/2004)*

Wyndham Estate 2001 Bin 999 Merlot (South Eastern Australia) $10. Lean and on the dry side, this Merlot's core is warm and ironlike, like an old Chianti. Cherry fruit, plus some oak and eucalyptus, open and close it. A good wine, though not one that will immediately conjure up images of Oz. **85** —*D.T. (6/1/2003)*

Wyndham Estate 2000 Bin 999 Merlot (South Eastern Australia) $10. Hints of sweetness surround the berry and licorice flavors of this light-bodied wine. It's brightly tart and very soft; in short, an easy, unadorned quaff. **82** —*J.F. (9/1/2001)*

Wyndham Estate 2004 Bin 333 Pinot Noir (South Eastern Australia) $10. Has aromas of cherries and caraway seeds, which are followed up by straightforward cherry fruit flavors. Soft in the mouth; not much verve here. **83** —*D.T. (12/1/2005)*

Wyndham Estate 1999 Bin 333 Pinot Noir (South Eastern Australia) $10. **86 Best Buy** —*M.S. (10/1/2000)*

Wyndham Estate 2002 Bin 777 Semillon (South Eastern Australia) $9. This wine has definite dinner potential—clams or scallops, maybe, are in its future. Citrus fruit is dressed up with mineral and a fresh green vegetable note on the palate; hay and fresh herb play on the nose. Fades a little bit

AUSTRALIA

the longer it sits in the glass, but you can eat quickly, can't you? **84** — D.T. (12/31/2003)

Wyndham Estate 1999 Bin 777 Semillon (South Eastern Australia) $10. Almost seems wooded, with strong aromas of toast, caramel, and cinnamon that fight for prominence with tart lime fruit. The palate is sweet upfront, tart, and almost sharp on the finish. Give it a few months to settle down and integrate before trying it this winter with poultry. **85** — J.C. (9/1/2001)

Wyndham Estate 2005 Bin 777 Semillon-Sauvignon Blanc (South Eastern Australia) $9. Smells interesting and somewhat sophisticated, with notes of lime, chalk, and straw. Those same notes continue on the palate, which is lively and intense, albeit still pretty straight-forward. **85 Best Buy** —D.T. (11/15/2006)

Wyndham Estate 2004 Bin 777 Semillon-Sauvignon Blanc (South Eastern Australia) $9. A very dry wine that doesn't have much flavor to offset its minerally feel. Piquant green-herb aromas preface some dilute lemony flavors. 220,000 cases produced. **82** —D.T. (12/1/2005)

Wyndham Estate 2002 Bin 555 Shiraz (South Eastern Australia) $10. Black plum and berry fruit aromas and flavors are ripe and fairly deep, especially considering this wine's value price. A easy-drinking Shiraz with unexpected but pleasing tannins on the finish. A good by-the-glass pour, and a "I can't believe this is $10" conversation starter at your next large gathering. **86 Best Buy** —D.T. (12/31/2004)

Wyndham Estate 2001 Bin 555 Shiraz (South Eastern Australia) $10. This is one straightforward, easy-drinking Shiraz; its raspberry and plum fruit is bouncy and ripe. It's got a little sweetness on the palate as well; mouthfeel has fine, powdery tannins that show again on the finish. **84** — D.T. (10/1/2003)

Wyndham Estate 2000 Bin 555 Shiraz (South Eastern Australia) $10. Very basic aromas are probably the best part. The mouth is thick and syrupy, and the flavors run toward prune. On the finish, oak gives off a coffee flavor, but there's still a lot of sugar there. It seems a bit off the mark, with no real correlation between the aromas and flavors. **81** —M.S. (1/28/2003)

Wyndham Estate 1998 Bin 555 Shiraz (South Eastern Australia) $12. Even, dark, and not too sweet, this Shiraz is a very solid offering. The berry, chocolate, licorice nose doesn't get too jammy and the ripe even texture on the tongue bears full black cherry, tar, and toast flavors. Finishes long, with sweet and sour black currant and licorice flavors. Good now, and should improve for two to four years. **88** —M.M. (6/1/2001)

WYNNS COONAWARRA ESTATE

Wynns Coonawarra Estate 1956 Claret Bordeaux Blend (Coonawarra) $NA. Aromas are of cherry, mushroom, and roasted meat. Pleasing, dusty texture on the palate, with stably, leathery notes. Some tannins still hanging on. **88** —D.T. (2/1/2005)

Wynns Coonawarra Estate 2000 Cabernet Blend (Coonawarra) $13. Medium-bodied, with soft tannins, this is a good red wine but, by definition, generic in terms of varietal character. Earth, oak and mixed plums lead to juicy plums on the finish. A good party (or pizza) selection. **85** —D.T. (12/31/2003)

Wynns Coonawarra Estate 1999 Cabernet Blend (Coonawarra) $13. Pretty blackberry, cherry, herb, and smoke tones come to the fore, though the tannins are a bit rustic. Finish is short. **86 Best Buy** —J.M. (12/15/2002)

Wynns Coonawarra Estate 1998 Cabernet Blend (Coonawarra) $13. This even, accessible claret-like red opens with berry aromas and flavors offset by smoke and earth. Smooth, with round fruit on the palate that shows handsome earth notes and good fruit-acid balance and depth. It's smoothly put together and closes with even, gentle tannins. **87** (11/1/2001)

Wynns Coonawarra Estate 2001 Cabernet Shiraz Merlot Cabernet Blend (Coonawarra) $11. This red is soft and so easy to drink. Spice, black pepper, and clove aromas and flavors couch mixed plum fruit on the palate. Not intense, but just the ticket for everyday drinking. **86 Best Buy** — D.T. (12/1/2005)

Wynns Coonawarra Estate 2001 Cabernet Sauvignon (Coonawarra) $11. Has cool, deep cherry on the nose, bolstered by olive and chalk dust.

This is a dry, firm Cab with taut plum fruit at the center, plus some coconut/toffee accents. Reliably very good, and a very good value. **87 Best Buy** —D.T. (11/15/2004)

Wynns Coonawarra Estate 2000 Cabernet Sauvignon (Coonawarra) $15. Oak and plum fruit are the main players on both the nose and the palate. Finishes with more dry, oaky tannins. This is a straightforward, medium-sized Cab, and a good food- and guest-friendly option for your next dinner party. **85** —D.T. (12/31/2003)

Wynns Coonawarra Estate 1999 Cabernet Sauvignon (Coonawarra) $14. Chocolate and mint aromas lead the way, while black cherry, plum, coffee, herb, smoke, and spice flavors are framed by moderate tannins. **88** —J.M. (12/15/2002)

Wynns Coonawarra Estate 1998 Cabernet Sauvignon (Coonawarra) $NA. Offers ripe, mouthcoating tannins, with a core of blackberry fruit. Finishes with some length; can last a few more years but is drinking well now. **90** —D.T. (2/1/2005)

Wynns Coonawarra Estate 1998 Cabernet Sauvignon (Coonawarra) $15. An impressively balanced Cabernet with a dark cherry-cassis-herb-tobacco profile. Lithe and supple, it has fine fruit and elegance for a wine in this price range. It also has the potential to last surprisingly well. Finishes with good fruit and acidity and firm, even tannins. **91 Best Buy** (11/1/2001)

Wynns Coonawarra Estate 1996 Cabernet Sauvignon (Coonawarra) $NA. Taut plum fruit on the palate, with tannins that are hefty but still approachable. Offers pretty spice, carob, and cassis aromas. **89** —D.T. (2/1/2005)

Wynns Coonawarra Estate 1991 Cabernet Sauvignon (Coonawarra) $NA. Displays impressive flavors of dark berry, herb, and menthol, and an even, dry mouthfeel. It's balanced and probably at its best now—no mean feat for a Cabernet that was about $10 when released. The long, ripe finish shows dark fruit, complex spice, and forest-floor accents. **91** (11/1/2001)

Wynns Coonawarra Estate 1991 Cabernet Sauvignon (Coonawarra) $NA. More plush on the palate than the 1990, with sweet fruit flavors and a dusty overlay of bread flour. At its peak now. **91** —D.T. (2/1/2005)

Wynns Coonawarra Estate 1990 Cabernet Sauvignon (Coonawarra) $NA. Acids are lively, and tannins hold on through the finish. Nose still isn't revealing its all, but the palate is full of plums and cherries, which wear a pleasing, brambly overlay. **90** —D.T. (2/1/2005)

Wynns Coonawarra Estate 1988 Cabernet Sauvignon (Coonawarra) $NA. This is mature, with dried-cherry, mushroom, and forest-floor aromas and flavors. It's lean, with a strong herbaceous edge that shows on the berry fruit. Dry and even, it closes tart with modest length. **86** (11/1/2001)

Wynns Coonawarra Estate 1986 Cabernet Sauvignon (Coonawarra) $NA. Still kicking almost 20 years later, with good grip and fine tannins on the palate. Flavors are of black plum and earth; could still go another 5–10 years. **91** —D.T. (2/1/2005)

Wynns Coonawarra Estate 1965 Cabernet Sauvignon (Coonawarra) $NA. Bramble, plum, and eucalyptus on the nose. Smooth tannins still hanging on; feel is fresh, with flavors of red clay/earth and plum. **90** —D.T. (2/1/2005)

Wynns Coonawarra Estate 1962 Cabernet Sauvignon (Coonawarra) $NA. With air, shows cassis, meaty aromas. Smooth and medium-full on palate, with chewy tannins on the finish. **89** —D.T. (2/1/2005)

Wynns Coonawarra Estate 2003 John Riddoch Cabernet Sauvignon (Coonawarra) $45. Has whole wheat aromas. The palate deals juicy fruit and nicely textured, youthful tannins. Medium-sized and built for the long haul; aging John Riddoch for 20 years is common down under. **90** —D.T. (10/1/2006)

Wynns Coonawarra Estate 1994 John Riddoch Cabernet Sauvignon (Coonawarra) $NA. Still young, this cuts a dark, handsome profile, opening with blackberry, dark chocolate, and licorice. The mouthfeel is big and plummy, and though fatter in feel than the other Wynn's reds, it has the same fine balance that characterizes the line. Closes long, with

AUSTRALIA

well-integrated black fruit and oak. Can use two or three years to really strut its stuff. **93 Cellar Selection** *(11/1/2001)*

Wynns Coonawarra Estate 1990 John Riddoch Cabernet Sauvignon (Coonawarra) $NA. Spicy red and dark fruit, a bit of graphite, and an herb note—in a positively Bordeaux manner—mark this youthful wine. Bright acidity supports the fruit, and the mouthfeel is even and supple, not fat. The finish is lovely, with cassis, black-and white-pepper notes and even, smooth tannins. **92** *(11/1/2001)*

Wynns Coonawarra Estate 1988 John Riddoch Cabernet Sauvignon (Coonawarra) $NA. Deep aromas of berry, earth, and licorice open this mature red. Dried cherries, spice, and wood emerge on the lean and dry palate. Possesses an almost Spanish personality (dry and woody), finishing with good length. **88** *(11/1/2001)*

Wynns Coonawarra Estate 1998 John Riddoch Limited Release Cabernet Sauvignon (Coonawarra) $35. Deep, rich aromas give way to a plush-textured dollop of black cherry, plum, cassis, chocolate, herb, and spice flavors. Tannins are supple and the finish is generous. **90** —*J.M.* *(12/15/2002)*

Wynns Coonawarra Estate 2003 Chardonnay (Coonawarra) $11. With concentrated, nectar-like pear, melon, and floral aromas, it smells nice and feminine, yet more like a Muscat than a Chardonnay. On the palate you get no-frills fruit cocktail and a dry, crisp mouthfeel. Finishes spicy. Just the ticket for an apéritif. **85** *(7/2/2004)*

Wynns Coonawarra Estate 2002 Chardonnay (Coonawarra) $13. A well-balanced and medium-bodied offering; pear and other stone fruit flavors dominate the palate, while pear and lemon-lime aromas harmonize on the nose. Finishes with drying chalk and mineral notes. A solid, flavorful wine. **88** —*D.T.* *(8/1/2003)*

Wynns Coonawarra Estate 2001 Chardonnay (Coonawarra) $9. Yellow fruit nuances abound in this slightly sweet-tasting offering from an area better known for growing Cabernet. Pear, pineapple, and lemon aromas and flavors predominate, finishing with a bit of heat and slightly rough acids. **84** —*J.C.* *(7/1/2002)*

Wynns Coonawarra Estate 2000 Chardonnay (Coonawarra) $13. Restrained tropical fruit and mild coconut accents open this stylish white. The taut, bright fruit emerges on the palate, where tangy acidity keeps things very lively. No butterball, it finishes crisp and zingy, with a mineral accent to the tart-sweet pineapple fruit. **88** *(11/1/2001)*

Wynns Coonawarra Estate 1997 Chardonnay (Coonawarra) $13. **83** — *M.M.* *(10/1/2000)*

Wynns Coonawarra Estate 2002 Red Blend (Coonawarra) $11. There's a lot to like about this wine: It's a medium, food-friendly size; its plum base has compelling accents of bramble and herb; it isn't at all sweet and hey, look at the price. The wine will probably taste even better to you once you see what else $11 buys you. Nicely done. **87 Best Buy** —*D.T.* *(10/1/2005)*

Wynns Coonawarra Estate 2005 Riesling (Coonawarra) $14. Clean, with white stone fruit flavors and light grass and white pepper aromas. A good, everyday Riesling, but doesn't have quite the snap and verve that this value wine usually does. **85** —*D.T.* *(10/1/2006)*

Wynns Coonawarra Estate 2004 Riesling (Coonawarra) $15. Light floral and citrus aromas. On the palate, the feel is lively, with overtones of citrus dressing up a steely, minerally core. A good value in Oz Riesling. 2,000 cases imported. **88** —*D.T.* *(4/1/2006)*

Wynns Coonawarra Estate 2003 Riesling (Coonawarra) $11. Here's an understated Riesling, one with subdued flavors and a pretty mineral-flour feel to it. Smells pretty, like pastry dough and talc; flavors are minerally, with some light peach fuzz and citrus peel flavors. On the dinner table, it would complement just about any cream-based sauce. **86 Best Buy** —*D.T.* *(11/15/2004)*

Wynns Coonawarra Estate 2002 Riesling (Coonawarra) $12. Well balanced and medium bodied, this isn't a biting-acids, oyster-ready sort of Riesling. Instead, it's rather feminine, with pretty sunflower, honey, and peach fuzz flavors swathed in chalk. The nose has nice, waxy yellow melon and citrus notes. Delicate, easy to find, and a bargain, as are most all of Wynns' "Coonawarra"-labeled bottlings, which are all priced in the low-to-mid teens. **90 Best Buy** —*D.T.* *(11/15/2003)*

Wynns Coonawarra Estate 2004 Shiraz (Coonawarra) $16. Starts off with sturdy plum and fresh green character, but grows sweeter with air. Dominated by a dry chalk-earth flavor and feel; a good wine, but just not as giving as it can be. **85** —*D.T.* *(6/1/2006)*

Wynns Coonawarra Estate 2003 Shiraz (Coonawarra) $12. **85** —*D.T.* *(12/1/2005)*

Wynns Coonawarra Estate 2001 Shiraz (Coonawarra) $14. From the ever-reliable, value-priced Wynns tier, this Shiraz doesn't disappoint. It's a straightforward, please-everyone wine, with the blackberry-oak-earth combo in play. The finish and the nose yield similar notes. **86** —*D.T.* *(12/31/2003)*

Wynns Coonawarra Estate 2000 Shiraz (Coonawarra) $15. Seems heavy on the American oak, displaying lactic, dill-laden aromatics that partially mute the berry fruit underneath. Still, the tart berries come through on the finish—a good sign for the future. Give it a couple of years in the cellar to come together. **87** —*J.C.* *(9/1/2002)*

Wynns Coonawarra Estate 1999 Shiraz (Coonawarra) $15. This jammy, mid-weight Shiraz has very ripe, maybe a bit overripe, fruit. There's a herbaceous note here that doesn't snug up to the fat berry flavors. Still, the soft mouthfeel makes it a very friendly wine, and it closes with licorice notes and modest tannins. **85** *(10/1/2001)*

Wynns Coonawarra Estate 1998 Michael Shiraz (Coonawarra) $49. A hint of eucalyptus on the nose blossoms into a full-blown green streak in the mouth, but it balances nicely with the blueberry and cherry fruit. The '98 Michael is a more restrained, herbal, and even claret-style Shiraz than most from Oz, and should age well. Drink 2005–2015. **90** *(9/1/2002)*

Wynns Coonawarra Estate 1997 Michael Shiraz (Coonawarra) $49. Though by all accounts, the Wynn's is subject to tons of oak from start to finish, there is enough other stuff going on in this Shiraz that the oak didn't take center stage. Cinnamon, tobacco, and coconut perk up the bouquet; jammy blackberry and dark chocolate are the main players on the palate and on the finish. **91 Cellar Selection** *(11/1/2001)*

XANADU

Xanadu 1999 Cabernet Sauvignon (Margaret River) $18. All Margaret River fruit, and spends 18 months in barrique. There's a nostril-permeating, menthol-white pepper aroma on the nose, with cream and earth underneath. Palate has very nice, ripe plum, and blackberry fruit and a little herb for good measure. Finishes dry, with more white pepper. **87** *(10/1/2003)*

Xanadu 1998 Lagan Estate Reserve Cabernet Sauvignon (Margaret River) $32. A blend of 65% Cabernet, 20% Cab Franc, and 15% Merlot, this takes a while to unwind. Black pepper-coated plums fill the palate, and chalky, oaky tannins finish it off. Give it another year or two in the bottle —more surprises will probably emerge. **89** *(10/1/2003)*

Xanadu 2002 Chardonnay (Margaret River) $15. Gets full malolactic fermentation, which is most evident on the nose (in the form of crème brûlée, nut, and oak aromas) and in the round, somewhat viscous mouthfeel. White stone fruit is present, but controlled; finishes with oak and some green apple. **86** *(10/1/2003)*

Xanadu 2000 Chardonnay (Margaret River) $15. Boasts plenty of buttery tropical fruit set off by aromas of toast and smoke, then shines in the mouth, where the mouthfeel is custardy but not heavy and the fruit flavors shine. Finishes long and tart, seamlessly turning citrusy along the way. **90 Best Buy** —*J.C.* *(7/1/2002)*

Xanadu 2002 Merlot (Frankland River) $10. Xanadu's winemaker, Conor Lagan, says that this is "a $15 Merlot for $10," and it's true. It's medium-bodied with fine tannins, and a nice eucalyptus note enveloping tight mixed plum fruit. More plum, plus some oak, wraps it up. Mercifully lacks the weediness that many value-priced Merlots sport. **87 Best Buy** *(10/1/2003)*

Xanadu 2000 Merlot (Margaret River) $22. Margaret River wines are known for their finesse rather than their weight. This Merlot holds true, showing a well-balanced mouthfeel with flavors of fleshy black cherries and spicy toasted oak. The finish moves toward tart cherry, ending with an elegant softness. **88** —*C.S.* *(6/1/2002)*

Xanadu 2002 Sauvignon Blanc (Margaret River) $10. Medium and round in the mouth, there's a base of stone fruit flavors here, but what makes this wine interesting is a resiny-olive oil note on the palate. Finishes with citrus pith and grass flavors. **85** *(10/1/2003)*

Xanadu 2001 Shiraz (Frankland River) $18. This Shiraz has a one-track mind: Earth, wood, vanilla, and plum, from start to finish. Has medium body, and dry tannins on the finish. Sees 40% American oak. **85** *(10/1/2003)*

Xanadu 2000 Shiraz (Frankland River) $17. Tar and charcoal emerge from the dark, deep nose, which is also oaky and mildly lemony. This wine is from Western Australia, and it runs toward the rich, ripe, and syrupy side. The finish is quite smooth and lush, as it verges on creamy. All in all this offers the right mix of barrels and berries. And it seems fresh, not heavy. **89** *—M.S. (3/1/2003)*

Xanadu 2002 Shiraz-Cabernet Sauvignon (Frankland River) $10. This Shiraz has a one-track mind: Earth, wood, vanilla, and plum, from start to finish. Has medium body, and dry tannins on the finish. Sees 40% American oak. **86 Best Buy** *(10/1/2003)*

YABBY LAKE VINEYARD

Yabby Lake Vineyard 2004 Chardonnay (Mornington Peninsula) $38. This is not an oaky, or even a rich Chardonnay; instead it treads the understated mineral-and-pear line. Finishes with some sour citrus pith and a chalky, smooth feel. **87** *—D.T. (11/15/2006)*

Yabby Lake Vineyard 2004 Pinot Noir (Mornington Peninsula) $58. Out of the bottle, this Pinot feels as though it straddles Old and New World styles; it has a beautiful, minerally feel and dusty, meaty aromas. Let it sit for a while and it becomes a New World powerhouse—big, forward, and muscular. Watch this winery. **90** *—D.T. (11/15/2006)*

YACCA PADDOCK

Yacca Paddock 2002 Dolcetto (Adelaide Hills) $42. One to bring to a blind-tasting party—how many people will ever guess Australian Dolcetto? Aromas are of pen ink, vanilla bean, and wheat cracker. On the palate, it's medium-sized but sturdy, with vanilla and oak flavors in supporting roles. Very good, and a food-friendly red to boot. 250 cases produced. **88** *—D.T. (8/1/2005)*

Yacca Paddock 2003 Red Blend (Adelaide Hills) $65. This is an excellent red, and further evidence of the Hills' success with unusual grape varieties. Tannat (20%) gives this Shiraz more grip on the midpalate than most other regional Shirazes have. Good acids, plum, and blackberry fruit, and black pepper nuances make this classy wine a winner, however difficult it might be to rationalize paying this much for such an odd blend. 250 cases produced. **90** *—D.T. (8/1/2005)*

YALUMBA

Yalumba 2000 Cabernet Sauvignon (Barossa Valley) $17. An angular, oaky Cab, more red than black in flavor. A layer of chalky clay envelops red fruit on the palate; tangy wood and pepper aromas are bright on the nose. A good drink-me-now Cabernet. **87** *—D.T. (12/31/2003)*

Yalumba 1999 Cabernet Sauvignon (Barossa Valley) $17. What a study in contrasts. Smells gamy and leathery, even sour, but packs in lots of blackberry, vanilla, and mint flavors. Finishes long, tart, woody, and hard. Give it a couple years in the cellar to mellow and soften, then try with full-flavored meats. **87** *—J.C. (6/1/2002)*

Yalumba 1997 Cabernet Sauvignon (Clare Valley) $25. Opens with a stylized nose that displays cassis, mint, leather, and even toasted marshmallow notes. It's unique, and draws you in to the unusual, sweet caramel-spice and dark cherry flavor combination the palate offers. A long finish with good tannic structure closes this harmonious wine. Lots of oak, but it works well here. **91 Editors' Choice** *(6/1/2001)*

Yalumba 2002 The Menzies Cabernet Sauvignon (Coonawarra) $45. This is a young Cab, not meant to be drunk for another 3–5 years at least. At this stage, it takes a long time in the glass to reveal its black cherry, eucalyptus, and soil flavors; its tea-like tannins reign for now. Even, measured and pleasantly full, it just wants more richness and vibrance, which may or may not reveal themselves with time. **89** *—D.T. (6/1/2006)*

Yalumba 2000 The Menzies Cabernet Sauvignon (Coonawarra) $45. Big, dark, and cool is the name of the game here. The fine fruit, all the way through, is blackberry and boysenberry, with a minerally-earthy overlay. This excellent Cab has wooly, textured tannins that will last at least through the end of the decade. **90** *—D.T. (5/1/2005)*

Yalumba 1999 The Menzies Cabernet Sauvignon (Coonawarra) $40. This Cab is serious business, and could not be mistaken for any other variety. It's excellent but curmudgeonly, without any flavors that you'd ever call feminine. Fruit is big and black, ripe but not sweet, with smudges of dirt, as though it took a tumble in a fistfight. Oaky tannins through and through. May soften in its older age—drink after 2007. **90** *—D.T. (12/31/2003)*

Yalumba 1997 The Menzies Cabernet Sauvignon (Coonawarra) $30. This wine proves that too much of too many things isn't always a good thing. There are lots of super-ripe blackberry, fig, and plum aromas on the nose, but these ripe flavors are masked by loads of tannins and acid on the palate. Finishes so hot that it's almost medicinal. A steak dinner may tame this bad boy. **83** *—D.T. (9/1/2001)*

Yalumba 1996 The Menzies Cabernet Sauvignon (Coonawarra) $28. **86** *(4/1/2000)*

Yalumba 2001 Y Series Cabernet Sauvignon (South Australia) $10. With sweet earth and a little caramel on the nose, the Y Series Cab has red plum fruit and a plastic-like note on the palate. Closes wtih dry tannins and a briary note. It's medium-bodied, and a good quaffer. **84** *—D.T. (6/1/2003)*

Yalumba 2001 Cabernet Sauvignon-Shiraz (Barossa Valley) $17. Happy-go-lucky, sweetish plum, and raspberry aromas preface a mainstream-styled, plum-based palate. The wine feels angular, even taut, on the palate, however much the aromas might lead you to expect a soft, jammy style. **85** *—D.T. (5/1/2005)*

Yalumba 2000 The Signature Cabernet Sauvignon-Shiraz (Barossa Valley) $45. The nose is interesting—dusty but also piquant, similar to mustard seed. This red's flavors are of dusty stone fruit, accompanied by pleasing, chewy tannins. It's not an overly ripe, sweet wine, which is why it would be a welcome presence at the dinner table. **87** *—D.T. (5/1/2005)*

Yalumba 1998 The Signature Cabernet Sauvignon-Shiraz (Barossa Valley) $40. Most of the Shiraz goes into American oak, says Ferrari, and most of the Cab sees French oak. Oak, indeed, is the operative word for this wine, at least for now. Though the nice red plum and blackberry nuances are easy to find, wood plays a big role here, lending butterscotch and toast flavors from beginning to end, and rustic tannins to the mouthfeel. Ferrari advises us to uncork this vintage in honor of her 50th birthday (that's in 11 years!). **89 Cellar Selection** *(5/1/2003)*

Yalumba 1997 The Signature Cabernet Sauvignon-Shiraz (Barossa Valley) $44. There's tons of red fruit here, most of which is jammy plum and raspberry, with just a slight sour cranberry edge. Amaretto and pastry cream notes pervade from beginning to end, however, which turned some tasters on and proved a little too sweet for others. **88** *—D.T. (12/15/2002)*

Yalumba 1996 The Signature Cabernet Sauvignon-Shiraz (Barossa Valley) $40. Nicely balanced dark berry herb and tobacco bouquet opens this pleasing, supple red. Full and even in the mouth, it offers a lot of black cherry cassis and toasty oak flavors, good texture, and enough structure to be considered serious. This is a delicious Cabernet-Shiraz blend, already drinkable and capable of holding for the next two to four years, maybe longer. **91** *—M.M. (1/1/2004)*

Yalumba 2002 Chardonnay (Barossa Valley) $15. Nectarine and grapefruit aromas are bright and focused; yellow stone fruit is the palate focus. Medium in body, but leans up by the close, with citrus pith and peach skin flavors. A good wine. **85** *(7/2/2004)*

Yalumba 2000 Chardonnay (Barossa Valley) $16. This relatively lean wine focuses on pear and apple aromas and flavors. Some spearmint scents spice up the nose, while buttery nuances appear on the palate. Finishes a bit short, but with crisp and clean with herb notes, unencumbered by lots of oak. **85** *—J.C. (7/1/2002)*

Yalumba 2002 Heggies Vineyard Chardonnay (Eden Valley) $20. Round and more rustic than most Eden Valley Chards, it opens with mallowy, woody aromas that segue into vanilla, toast, and light yellow fruit on the palate. Finishes with a woody, wooly feel. **85** *(7/2/2004)*

Yalumba 1997 Reserve Chardonnay (Eden Valley) $15. 84 *(3/1/2000)*

Yalumba 2005 Wild Ferment Chardonnay (Eden Valley) $17. This Chard is smooth and medium-bodied, with aromas and flavors of vanilla bean, passion fruit, and pear. Welcoming and easy to drink, it shows some complexity yet is sure to please just about everyone. **88** —*D.T. (10/1/2006)*

Yalumba 2003 Wild Ferment Chardonnay (Eden Valley) $17. Whether due to the wild ferment, this is one of the more singular-tasting Chards we sampled. Aromas are of almond, banana cream pie, and green grapes. Green fruit—more green grapes, but also Granny Smith apples—reappear on the palate, and are refreshing. That's not to say that vanilla and oak aren't present—they are, but there's enough else going on. An interesting, very good wine. **87** *(7/2/2004)*

Yalumba 2002 Y Series Unwooded Chardonnay (South Australia) $10. Yalumba should call should this Chard "refreshingly unwooded"; its non-toasty flavor profile is clean and brisk. The palate offers plenty of gooseberry and stone fruit, plus lime and mineral notes. Minerally tannins extend through the finish. **86** —*D.T. (6/1/2003)*

Yalumba 2003 Y series Unwooded Chardonnay (Eden Valley) $9. A good wine at a good price: This unwooded Chard has fragrant floral, peach, pear, and pineapple aromas. Fruit-cocktail flavors on the palate are bold and assertive. A straightforward, fruity wine, and one that everyone in the room will enjoy. **86 Best Buy** *(7/2/2004)*

Yalumba 2004 Bush Vine Grenache (Barossa) $17. Yalumba doesn't mess around when it comes to Grenache, but this one doesn't quite hit the mark. The plum fruit is enjoyable, but the wine feels halfhearted on the palate. Needs more stuffing. **84** —*D.T. (11/15/2006)*

Yalumba 2002 Bush Vine Grenache (Barossa Valley) $15. Much better than last year's offering, the '02 is a bouncy, easy-drinking Grenache, with flavors that veer more toward plum and earth than high-toned cherry, as it sometimes does. Earth plays a major role on the nose, too. A fun, please-everyone wine. **87** —*D.T. (2/1/2004)*

Yalumba 2001 Bush Vine Grenache (Barossa Valley) $15. From 20-year-old vines, this Grenache isn't a lush wine—rather, its red fruit is heartily dosed in char, from the nose through the finish. The pleasant creamy-butterscotchy flavors only make the fruit that much harder to enjoy. **84** *(5/1/2003)*

Yalumba 2000 Bush Vine Grenache (Barossa Valley) $16. From old head-pruned vines, this full-bodied red wine satisfies despite a certain one-dimensionality. The flavors are rich in cherries, the tannins are thick but fine, and the wine is very dry. It has an attractive suppleness that feels good on the palate. **87** —*M.S. (12/15/2002)*

Yalumba 2001 Tricentenary Grenache (Barossa Valley) $15. Medium-bodied, with plum and cherry fruit that's quite bouncy until earth shows up midpalate and reins the fruit in. Begins and ends with earth, graham cracker, and oak. Drinkable now. **87** —*D.T. (12/31/2003)*

Yalumba 2000 Tricentenary Grenache (Barossa Valley) $30. They say the vines date to 1889. The color is inky black. The aromas are impressive and promising. White chocolate, blackberry, cassis, licorice, and white pepper begin to describe them. It's a hugely extracted wine, packed with berry flavors, very dry, with substantial tannins. It's far too big to describe as elegant—rustic does it more justice. The winemaker suggests aging until 2006. He may be short of the mark. **87** —*S.H. (12/15/2002)*

Yalumba 2003 Tricentenary Vines Grenache (Barossa Valley) $32. Offers rich, pretty aromas of molasses, tea, mixed cherries, and anise. On the palate, it has a Côtes-du-Rhônish style and weight, with plum, herb, and pepper flavors. A very good wine in the grand scheme of things but perhaps a disappointment for this particular bottling, considering what these old vines are usually capable of. Tasted twice. **87** —*D.T. (3/1/2005)*

Yalumba 2001 Y Series Merlot (South Australia) $10. Simple, and manages to be both tangy and sweet. Cherry and blackberry fruit characterizes the palate, though it tastes (and smells) a little over the hill already. Finishes with tangy oak. **82** —*D.T. (1/1/2002)*

Yalumba 2000 Y Series Merlot (South Australia) $10. This is the kind of wine that makes me feel charitable. I want to find excuses for its raw thinness. This wine is exceedingly tannic, and makes your palate feel like sandpaper. There's little or no fruity sweetness to offer relief. Beyond all that, it has enough acidity to eat through lead. **82** —*S.H. (6/1/2002)*

Yalumba 2005 Y Series Pinot Grigio (South Australia) $11. A pretty, clean, perhaps atypical PG—it's as light in color as a Sauvignon Blanc, and the first flavors that come through are crisp citrus and cilantro. Dig a little deeper and the wine starts to feel more familiar: apple is at the core, and the mouth feels like smooth, wet rocks. Finishes dry, with a fresh herb note. **87 Best Buy** —*D.T. (10/1/2006)*

Yalumba NV Antique Tawny Port (Barossa Valley) $17. I regret that I didn't rate this wine a point or two higher when I reviewed it for the February 2003 issue. Since last winter, I've purchased nearly a case of it. It's smooth and warming, with lovely nut, beef, and butterscotch flavors. I know what you're thinking: At $17, is it really such a value? Quality Port, my friends, doesn't come cheap. And when was the last time you had one from Australia? **89** —*D.T. (11/15/2003)*

Yalumba NV Antique Tawny Port (Barossa Valley) $17. Ferrari claims that this "Port" is good chilled, in shot glasses, and served alongside crème brûlée—and we'd be hard pressed to disagree, though it'd probably be just as nice next to a roaring fire on a cold winter night. The wine is aged in 60-gallon hogsheads, which give it a buttery, butterscotchy quality. It's warming and smooth, like a Bourbon-meets-Port love child. **89** *(5/1/2003)*

Yalumba 2004 Hand Picked t/g/v Tempranillo-Grenache-Viog Red Blend (Barossa) $32. This is a new addition to Yalumba's Hand Picked range. Blackberry, black cherry, and raspberry aromas and flavors dominate, from nose to tail. This is an enjoyable wine, but it's not quite as complex as the line's other offerings. **88** —*D.T. (2/1/2006)*

Yalumba 2003 m/g/s Red Blend (Barossa Valley) $32. Dry and grippy, as a colleague called it, on the palate—in other words, these tannins just aren't going anywhere. Fruit here is tight, taut stuff: like the skin of black plums and purply berries, quite like what you get on the nose. This wine will keep you on your blind-tasting toes, and will even hold up in the cellar. A blend of 60% Mourvèdre, 21% Grenache, and 19% Shiraz. **89** —*D.T. (5/1/2005)*

Yalumba 2000 Mawsons Red Blend (Limestone Coast) $20. The nose is foresty and reminded me a little of Carmenère. In the mouth, there's mixed plum fruit, but seeped tea and tangy wood flavors are in the driver's seat. Finishes with tea and earth and smooth, chalky tannins; a blend of Cabernet, Shiraz, and Merlot. **87** —*D.T. (5/1/2004)*

Yalumba 1999 Shiraz-Viognier Red Blend (Barossa Valley) $30. High hopes for complexity and intensity here. Syrah contributes basic red notes of blackberries and tannins, while Viognier adds upfront, pushy white fruit and flower notes. The result is awkward. Is it red or white? It's dry, but a puzzle. Frankly, the Viognier detracts. This wine would be better as a Shiraz. **85** —*S.H. (1/1/2002)*

Yalumba 2002 Rhône Red Blend (Barossa Valley) $30. Sixty percent Mourvèdre, with Grenache and Shiraz getting 30% and 10%, respectively. The texture's great—a little rough around the edges, but that's part of its charm. Juicy mixed plums on the palate get a strong kick of black pepper, which you'll also pick up on the nose. I see plenty of food-pairing potential here (lamb or rabbit, for starters), though winemaker Jane Ferrari says that cheese is the way to go. **91 Editors' Choice** —*D.T. (2/1/2004)*

Yalumba 2004 Hand Picked m/g/s Rhône Red Blend (Barossa) $32. On the nose, it's all black cherry. Black peppercorns rule the palate, which also offers a smooth, clay-like feel and hints of red plums. **90** —*D.T. (2/1/2006)*

Yalumba 2003 Riesling (South Eastern Australia) $11. Clean, correct, and enjoyable; this Riesling is well balanced, with a dry feel and citrus, olive oil and floral components through and through. At first blush, it smells a little like Viognier—a testament, maybe, to the winery's renown with that variety? **88 Best Buy** —*D.T. (3/1/2005)*

Yalumba 2002 Mesh Riesling (Eden Valley) $25. This Riesling's fruit is from a 70-year-old Eden Valley vineyard; half the wine was vinified by

Jeff Grosset at Polish Hill, the other half was vinified by Rob Hill Smith at Yalumba. Once the wine was all brought together, Grosset and Hill-Smith, as the story goes, took four days to decide on the final blend. The wine's at once viscous and very dry, with stone fruit, vanilla bean and some floral flavors. Green apple rounds out the long, dry finish. **89** *(8/1/2003)*

Yalumba 2001 Pewsey Vale Riesling (Eden Valley) $18. "Riesling [in Australia] is the Barbie doll," explains Ferrari. "It's the toy we've always had, and when we tire of the other toys, we go back to the Barbie." Taste this wine—with its dry, minerally mouthfeel, and mineral, lime, and olive-oil flavors—and you'll see why those Aussies keep coming back to it. Starts and ends with bright Granny Smith apple notes; it's the perfect pick for the raw bar. **88** *(5/1/2003)*

Yalumba 2002 Y Series Riesling (South Australia) $10. The Y Series is a good, simple introduction to Riesling that includes fruit from Eden and Barossa Valleys. Offers lively gooseberry, lime, and yellow fruit flavors, plus a mouthfeel that is almost viscous; finishes with some zip. **85** *(5/1/2003)*

Yalumba 2001 Y Series Riesling (South Australia) $10. You expected fruity, flowery flavors? A little sweetness? Then go someplace else. This wine is one of the driest of the year, and offers no relief at all from alcohol and other winey compounds. If there's a single, solitary flavor, it's watered down lemon juice. But it might be pretty good with clams on the half shell. **85** —*S.H. (9/1/2002)*

Yalumba 2005 Y Series Rosé Sangiovese (South Australia) $11. An envelope of chalk contains bright, fresh berry and orange flavors, ending in a dry, smooth, minerally finish. The nose reflects all of these components; just a delightful, easy summer wine. **87 Best Buy** —*D.T. (6/21/2006)*

Yalumba 2005 Y Series Sauvignon Blanc (South Australia) $11. This Sauvignon Blanc boasts lively acidity, and flavors of citrus peel and white pepper. Has a tiny bit of spritz on the palate, followed up by nectarine flavors on the finish. **86 Best Buy** —*D.T. (8/1/2006)*

Yalumba 2001 Shiraz (Barossa Valley) $17. From 20-year-old vines, and containing 5% Viognier, this is a simple, entry-level Shiraz with fresh berry-cherry-plum flavors. **85** —*D.T. (2/1/2004)*

Yalumba 2000 Shiraz (Barossa Valley) $17. An easy, drink-me-now Shiraz with cream and juicy red fruit on the palate. More creamy oak plays through the finish, and on the nose. **86** *(5/1/2003)*

Yalumba 1999 Shiraz (Barossa Valley) $16. Though deep, sour berries, stewed fruit, and amaretto aromas permeate the bouquet, some reviewers reacted negatively to a sulphury-green note. The palate's brisk acidity burns off after a few minutes, revealing leathery, dark chocolate, blackberry, and black pepper flavors. Finishes tangy and toasty with good length. **87** *(10/1/2001)*

Yalumba 2000 Handpicked Shiraz (Barossa Valley) $30. Medium-bodied, with meaty, peppery notes on the nose, this Shiraz (90%)-Viognier (10%) has loads of raspberry, plum, and blackberry fruit, and toasty oak notes that start at midpalate and just keep on going. Though it's built (and priced) to last for a few years, it's just as tempting to open it now. **89** *(5/1/2003)*

Yalumba 2000 The Octavius Shiraz (Barossa Valley) $85. The nose brings licorice in abundance, and the palate, a first-class package of blackberries and chocolate, delivered in a smoky-oak envelope. Drink through 2015. **91** —*D.T. (8/1/2005)*

Yalumba 1999 The Octavius Shiraz (Barossa Valley) $80. Mint, thyme, and maybe even some ginger peek through on the nose. It starts off on the palate with sweet fruit that suggests a bold, in-your-face wine, but it's more elegant than that: It has smooth tannins, mixed plums, and a snap of white pepper and rosemary at the finish. This wine (as it always does) shows some serious oak—more than other tasters could handle—but it's excellent nevertheless. **92 Cellar Selection** —*D.T. (2/1/2004)*

Yalumba 1995 The Octavius Shiraz (Barossa Valley) $80. 88 *(4/1/2000)*

Yalumba 1997 The Octavius Old Vine Shiraz (Barossa Valley) $80. The nose smolders with dried spices, toast, and earth aromas; Octavius's palate and finish are similarly deep, with delicious dark-chocolate, jammy blackberry, and licorice flavors. Dense and creamy in the mouth, with lots of oak from start to finish. **92 Cellar Selection** *(11/1/2001)*

Yalumba 2001 Y Series Shiraz (South Australia) $10. A Beaujolais-like, candied red berry nose promises easy drinking, but the palate delivers something altogether different. Imagine a single blackberry having lost its way in a forest. Yeah, it's that oaky. **82** —*D.T. (1/28/2003)*

Yalumba 2000 Y Series Shiraz (South Australia) $10. What, you expected Grange Hermitage? Raw and juicy, with earthy, berry flavors, and dry to the point of austerity. Doesn't offer much in the way of anything, except it's clean, acidic, and will wash down anything you care to put in your mouth. **84** —*S.H. (1/1/2002)*

Yalumba 2001 Shiraz-Viognier (Barossa Valley) $30. It's always interesting to see why some wineries will acknowledge small percentages of Viognier on the label and some won't—in this case, maybe it's because the Viognier clocks in at a whopping 9% of the wine's volume. In any case, it's just excellent, with sweet chalk or trading-gum powder on the nose, and dry tannins in the mouth. Plum fruit is beautiful, and framed by dry earth. Quite a classy wine. **90** —*D.T. (2/1/2004)*

Yalumba 2003 Hand Picked Shiraz-Viognier (Barossa) $32. Crisp and focused, with graham cracker on the nose. 5% Viognier imparts just a little of a floral, violet quality to the wine. It's still tight (it should be drinking very nicely in 2–3 years), but offers glimpses of black cherry and plum flavors, and a suave, silky feel. **91** —*D.T. (2/1/2006)*

Yalumba 2004 Viognier (Eden Valley) $17. Offers up some talc powder aromas, and the sensation carries through to the palate, where there are also light and feminine flavors of melon, pear, and white pepper. Hints of almond creep in on the finish. Pretty, light, and clean. **88** —*D.T. (10/1/2006)*

Yalumba 2004 Viognier (South Australia) $11. Has sweet, though not candied aromas—think coconut, truffle, white chocolate, maybe some honey. Yellow peach and lychee flavors have a powdery feel that continues on through the finish. Not a sizeable, fat Viognier, which isn't at all a bad thing. **87 Best Buy** —*D.T. (3/1/2005)*

Yalumba 2003 Viognier (Eden Valley) $17. Though aged in mature French barriques, this wine's toasty, leesy aromas are in line with Yalumba's liberal use of oak. On the palate, it's lively and enjoyable, wtih light floral and honey notes atop white stone fruit. Medium-bodied; finishes with some fresh herb and a slick hard-candy feel. **87** —*D.T. (12/31/2004)*

Yalumba 2001 Viognier (Eden Valley) $18. Viognier, according to Jane Ferrari, is Yalumba's "prime white varietal"; this bottling offers more toast and honey than anything that you'd see out of Condrieu. One whiff of the baked apple and pastry-crust aromas on the nose, and you'll be sucked in. It's medium-bodied and lively, with creamy, toasty oak and tropical fruit flavors that continue through the medium-length finish. **88** *(5/1/2003)*

Yalumba 2000 Viognier (Eden Valley) $17. The family-owned Yalumba winery has made something of a speciality of its Australian Viognier, including one of the top wines in its range, the Virgilius. This wine, more modestly priced, has ripe peachy fruit, almost tropical, with a finely judged toasty element, leaving a fresh, creamy green taste in the mouth. **88** —*R.V. (11/15/2001)*

Yalumba 1999 Viognier (Eden Valley) $16. The intense nose of this white Rhône varietal wine offers flower-shop and orange notes and an almost Gewürztraminer-like spiciness. Similar tart-sweet flavors prevail on the medium-weight palate, and high— almost cutting—acidity shows. The spicy finish has a bitter note and decent length. Unique and recommended for the adventurous palate. **85** —*M.M. (9/1/2001)*

Yalumba 2002 Heggies Vineyard Viognier (Eden Valley) $20. Floral on the nose, with jasmine, clover, and the whole nine yards. On the palate the floral sweetness is reprised, and couched in waxy yellow fruit and olive oil flavors. A very good wine, and one that brings the out of doors inside. **87** —*D.T. (5/1/2004)*

Yalumba 1998 Limited Release Viognier (Barossa Valley) $14. 86 *(10/1/2000)*

Yalumba 2003 The Virgilius Viognier (Eden Valley) $40. Opens with aromas of pastry flour, olive oi,l and honey. This is one beautifully textured wine; yellow fruit, floral, and olive oil flavors ride the wave of unctuousness, rather than outshine it. Finishes long. **92** —*D.T. (3/1/2005)*

AUSTRALIA

Yalumba 2002 The Virgilius Viognier (Eden Valley) $36. An excellent wine, a seamless one in which the overall impression is so pretty that it's hard to pick out individual flavors (though I'd say there were some apricots and apples in there). Mouthfeel is viscous; shows honey and white pepper on the nose. **91** —D.T. (2/1/2004)

Yalumba 2004 Virgilius Viognier (Eden Valley) $40. A classy, consistent wine of the first order. Starts off with delicate floral and melon aromas, the honeysuckle component persisting on through the long finish. It's the wine's minerality, rather than this floral sweetness, that is its highlight. Round and just viscous enough, closing with mineral and white pepper. **93 Editors' Choice** —D.T. (6/1/2006)

Yalumba 2005 Y Series Viognier (South Australia) $11. Sunny, summery, pretty: While this wine is almost always a good value, it's particularly good this vintage. Honeysuckle, melon, pear and other stone fruit flavors are delivered in a medium-sized package; the wine is pretty complex, too, especially considering its price point. A house pour for summer if ever there was one. **88 Best Buy** —D.T. (8/1/2006)

Yalumba 2003 Y Series Viognier (Eden Valley) $9. Aromas are of grass and tropical yellow fruit. Fresh pineapple and pear are the dominant flavors on the palate, and persist on through the finish. Medium-bodied, with nice weight; very good overall, particularly at this price. **87 Best Buy** —D.T. (2/1/2004)

Yalumba 2002 Y Series Viognier (South Australia) $10. Melon and honey flavors and aromas are lovely, but I wish those flavors were more concentrated than they are. Finishes with taut yellow-fruit skin and mineral flavors. **84** —D.T. (12/31/2003)

Yalumba 2000 Y Series Viognier (South Australia) $10. Sweet and simple, tastes like that syrup they pack canned peaches in, except of course it has good acidity. Make that super acidity, which is its saving grace. The acids get up under the fruit and push it, saving the wine from being insipid. **84** —S.H. (9/1/2002)

Yalumba 2000 Y Series Viognier (South Australia) $10. Viognier is never this inexpensive, let alone this inexpensive and this good. On the nose, clean citrus notes balance brighter, richer tropical fruit and butter aromas. It's smooth in the mouth, where bright sunflower and chalk flavors play tug of war with underdog chalk and caramel notes, but it's so well integrated that it's hard to say who's winning. **89 Best Buy** —D.T. (2/1/2002)

YANGARRA ESTATE VINEYARD

Yangarra Estate Vineyard 2004 Old Vine Grenache (McLaren Vale) $25. 90 — (8/1/2005)

Yangarra Estate Vineyard 2003 Old Vine Grenache (McLaren Vale) $20. This is some of the Vale's most sought-after Grenache; it was planted by the Smart family in 1946 and narrowly escaped being pulled up a few years back. Mint, fresh herb, and black pepper aromas are profound; on the palate, lifted black cherry and plum fruit is swathed in fine tannins. A wine worth seeking out, as it tends to sell out shortly after release. **91** —D.T. (3/1/2005)

Yangarra Estate Vineyard 2002 Old Vine Grenache (McLaren Vale) $20. The old-vine designation will make more sense when you see how black and extracted the wine appears in the glass. Aromas are abyss-deep, with dust and black soil over dark fruit. The palate holds nothing but the purest blackberry, dressed up with some toast. Finishes with taut cherry. A solid, masculine wine. **89 Editors' Choice** —D.T. (9/1/2004)

Yangarra Estate Vineyard 2005 Rosé Grenache-Shiraz (McLaren Vale) $12. This 70-30 Grenache-Shiraz blend is full but very dry. Yangarra's first rosé has a strong core of minerality, dressed up with blackberry and raspberry fruit, and a light orange-peel accent. Rosés have a reputation for being fun wines, and this is, too, but in this case "fun" and "serious" aren't mutually exclusive. **89 Best Buy** —D.T. (6/21/2006)

Yangarra Estate Vineyard 2002 Grenache Shiraz Mourvedre Rhône Red Blend (McLaren Vale) $20. Addictively tasty, and a good approachable size, this wine is a good mix of red berry, earth, and a hint of burnt sugar. Finessed; finishes with a warming amaretto note. Not sure how long it would go in the cellar, but there's no time like the present, if it is so pleasing now. **90** —D.T. (12/31/2004)

Yangarra Estate Vineyard 2003 GSM Rhône Red Blend (McLaren Vale) $20. An abyss of black pepper on the nose, with some whiffs of white cotton. Imagine strapping an eight-cylinder engine to a basket full of berries and black peppercorns and watching it go: That's what this wine tastes like. It's full-throttle and fruit-ripe, with lifted fruit, spice, and black pepper on the finish. **92** —D.T. (3/1/2005)

Yangarra Estate Vineyard 2004 Shiraz (McLaren Vale) $25. Good as ever, this vintage of the Yangarra Shiraz doles out plenty of juicy blackberry and blueberry fruit accented with fresh but subtle vanilla bean notes. Full and bouncy on the palate, and long on the finish. Winemaker Peter Fraser just doesn't know how to make bad wine. **92** —D.T. (8/1/2006)

Yangarra Estate Vineyard 2003 Shiraz (McLaren Vale) $20. It might be worth laying this down for six months or a year before giving this Shiraz a go, because it's still pretty closed. Only light meat aromas emerge, and some graham cracker and dark fruit on the palate. Finishes juicy. Will probably emerge as the elegant complement to the winery's full-throttle Grenache-based wines. **90** —D.T. (3/1/2005)

Yangarra Estate Vineyard 2002 Shiraz (McLaren Vale) $20. Yangarra is becoming synonymous with excellent wines at fair prices. Nose is a little hot at first, but later reveals pastry flour and black pepper aromas. Ripe, red plums and vanilla accents unfold in the mouth. Not a huge, rich wine, but certainly a classy one. **90 Editors' Choice** (11/15/2004)

YANGARRA PARK

Yangarra Park 2001 Cabernet Sauvignon (South Eastern Australia) $10. No question it's Cabernet, with black currant and cassis aromas and the detailed vanillins and smoky spice from oak that nearly always accompanies the varietal. Its weakness is in the mouth, where sharp acids accompany good berry flavors and green, herbal notes. **84** —S.H. (6/1/2002)

Yangarra Park 2000 Cabernet Sauvignon (South Eastern Australia) $10. Easy drinking and juicy, this wine shows black and red plum, plus vanilla and wood-pulp aromas and flavors. Finishes with herb and dull oak flavors, and another helping of black plum. **84** —D.T. (6/1/2002)

Yangarra Park 2001 Appelation Series Cabernet Sauvignon (Coonawarra) $17. So massive in fruity-berry flavor, so young and acidic now, it's practically undrinkable, although a greasy leg of lamb will work. The solid core of black currants and rich, thick tannins suggest cellaring for a couple years. **88** —S.H. (1/1/2002)

Yangarra Park 2001 Chardonnay (South Eastern Australia) $10. 87 Best Buy —S.H. (7/1/2002)

Yangarra Park 2000 Chardonnay (South Eastern Australia) $10. This wine from Kendall-Jackson's Australian outpost offers aromas of butter, clove, and tropical and citrus fruits. Dried spice flavors accent soft peach and-vanilla, finishing with a touch of tangerine. **87 Best Buy** —J.C. (7/1/2002)

Yangarra Park 2001 Merlot (South Eastern Australia) $10. Surprisingly true to its variety for this price, a lush, juicy, mouth-filling wine with smooth tannins and pretty flavors of berries and cherries. It's just what you think of in Merlot, an easy-drinking wine that's rich and full-bodied, yet silky and accessible. **87 Best Buy** —S.H. (6/1/2002)

Yangarra Park 2001 Appelation Series Merlot (McLaren Vale) $17. Young and vibrant now, with a great burst of fresh acidity, but with scads of fruit. Explodes on the palate with waves of sweet cherry, blackberry, and plum flavors. Tannins are thick and fancy. This is an ager but it would be a shame to miss the youthful vivacity. **90** —S.H. (1/1/2002)

Yangarra Park 2001 Shiraz (South Eastern Australia) $10. This baby has aromas of just-picked ripe plums, boysenberries, and a peppery-chocolatey note that shows up on the palate. It's dry, clean and sharp, and it's a lot of fun. **87 Best Buy** —S.H. (9/1/2002)

Yangarra Park 2001 Appelation Series Shiraz (McLaren Vale) $NA. Pours black, and smells backward now. Plenty of airing brings out hints of black cherry, cassis, white pepper, and sage, but it's still pretty mute. At the first sip the palate is flooded with rich flavors of the ripest summer blackberries. Better after 2004. **89** —S.H. (1/1/2002)

YARRA BURN

Yarra Burn 2000 Cabernet Sauvignon (Yarra Valley) $21. The best thing about this Cab is its texture, which is something between tea-like and clay-like. Fruit on the palate is juicy, both red and black, accented with a manageable amount of char. Finishes with dark clay notes. With dark earth, black olive, and a hint of herb on the nose, you might mistake it for a baby Bordeaux. **89** —*D.T. (6/1/2003)*

Yarra Burn 2003 Chardonnay (Yarra Valley) $15. Smells and tastes like a pleasing mix of white stone fruit, citrus, and rainwater. Feels fresh on the palate, though not as concentrated as I would like. **85** —*D.T. (5/1/2005)*

Yarra Burn 2002 Chardonnay (Yarra Valley) $15. This Yarra Valley mainstay has aromas of olive oil and herb framing tropical fruit. Its fruit-cocktail flavor profile is refreshing and clean, but, as one reviewer points out, finishes with a heavy dose of charred wood. **86** *(7/2/2004)*

Yarra Burn 2000 Chardonnay (Yarra Valley) $16. Palate offers sweet but simple yellow fruit flavors, particularly peach and banana. Finishes with peach pit and caramel flavors. What's here is fine, but better concentration would have merited it a better score. **84** —*D.T. (8/1/2003)*

Yarra Burn 1997 Bastard Hill Chardonnay (Yarra Valley) $27. The reviewers who tasted this wine were in agreement about one thing: This is an unusual wine (and yes, '97 is the current vintage). Bright gold color is only the first hint of the malo that this wine has seen, and an über-butterscotchy nose is the second hint. One reviewer describes the palate flavor as that of peach pit, and the other marvels that the wine can have this kind of weight without a lot of flavor. Yarra Burn says that the Bastard Hill Chard is made only in exceptional vintages, and has 10-15 years ahead of it; we would like to think that some time in the cellar would make it a little more comprehensible. **86** *(6/1/2003)*

Yarra Burn 2001 Pinot Noir (Yarra Valley) $19. Aromas are of chalk dust and dark earth. Chewy tannins mark the mouthfeel, where there are flavors of red plum, tea, and a little lemony oak. Finishes with the same oak-tea-lemon profile. Sturdy and straightforward. **86** —*D.T. (9/1/2004)*

Yarra Burn 2000 Pinot Noir (Yarra Valley) $19. Stably, rhubarb aromas may remind you of a villages-level Burgundy, but that's where the similarity ends. In the mouth, it's thin, with weak cherry fruit, and an herbaceousness that lingers on the finish. Could use more concentration. **82** *(1/1/2004)*

Yarra Burn 2000 Shiraz (Victoria) $21. This Shiraz aspires to be a big bruiser but just misses the mark. It's medium-bodied with plum flavors on the front palate. Finishes with a burst of sweetness and some anise. **84** —*D.T. (12/31/2003)*

YARRA YERING

Yarra Yering 2003 Dry Red Wine No.1 Cabernet Blend (Yarra Valley) $75. Doesn't taste like much of anything else out of Australia, and that's a good thing. Smells like smoke and pencil shavings, with wood dominating the palate in the form of tree bark or bramble. Has a bit of a citrusy tang midpalate, its plum fruit finally coming through on the finish. An oddball now, but will likely have a few surprises in store in 3–6 years. **89** —*D.T. (10/1/2006)*

YARRABANK

Yarrabank 1996 Cuvée Brut Champagne Blend (Australia) $32. New to us, this handsome Aussie sparkler made by a French duo offers full aromas and flavors, an even bead, and soft mousse. Green apple aromas and flavors predominate, with hay and bread accents. The back end displays a nice closing filled with limes. **90** —*M.M. (12/1/2001)*

Yarrabank 1999 Yering Station Cuvee Sparkling Blend (Victoria) $22. Very good. Starts off crisp and clean, with aromas of mineral and dust, and flavors of bright citrus. Midpalate, it unfolds and softens a little, revealing hints of toast and caramel that persist through the finish. **88** —*D.T. (12/31/2005)*

YELLOW BY YELLOWGLEN

Yellow by Yellowglen NV Chardonnay (South Eastern Australia) $12. This inexpensive sparkling wine features a slightly honeyed, floral bouquet that shows a touch of spicy complexity. The soft melon and pineapple flavors lack acidic cut and finish short. **82** —*J.C. (12/31/2006)*

YELLOW TAIL

Yellow Tail 2003 Cabernet Sauvignon (South Eastern Australia) $7. Smells like trail mix, barbecued over an open fire. On the palate, it's butterscotch central. Caramel and oak try to steal the spotlight from the chocolate-covered cherry core, and only narrowly miss. Its low-acid, sweet style has millions of fans, but it's too much for this reviewer to handle. **82** —*D.T. (11/15/2004)*

Yellow Tail 2003 Cabernet Sauvignon-Merlot (South Eastern Australia) $7. One-dimensional, sweet aromas are of raspberry, blackberry, and caramel. On the palate, the sweet fruit is soft and bulky, and enveloped in a filmy, faux-wood texture. **82** —*D.T. (9/1/2004)*

Yellow Tail 2003 Cabernet Sauvignon-Shiraz (South Eastern Australia) $7. Straight out of the bottle, without air, the Tail shows some restraint. After a few minutes, sweet cotton candy and caramel aromas emerge. In the mouth, the wine starts out tasting like juicy berries and cinnamon, but morphs rather rapidly into cherry Slurpee. **83** —*D.T. (12/31/2004)*

Yellow Tail 2003 Chardonnay (South Eastern Australia) $7. Has aromas of honey, flowers, and toast, and similarly feminine flavors. Sweet on the palate, with Sweet Tart, nectarine, and pear flavors. Finishes with candied fruit, ginger, and spice. **84** *(7/2/2004)*

Yellow Tail 2002 Chardonnay (South Eastern Australia) $7. Straightforward and soft-bodied, with lots of sweet yellow and tropical fruit; even oak and mallowy flavors take a backseat to the bright fruit. I'm not saying it's nuanced, but this is the easy, quaffable kind of wine that sucks novices into enophilia in the first place. **84** —*D.T. (6/1/2003)*

Yellow Tail 2000 Chardonnay (South Eastern Australia) $7. There are no complaints with this Chardonnay. Apple, pineapple, butter, and toasted oak load the flavor package. The perfect balance and velvety mouthfeel provide a solid background. The producer recommends kangaroo tail soup with this one—but why not? You get to go to Australia, and kangaroo is low in fat and cholesterol. **88 Best Buy** —*M.M. (6/1/2001)*

Yellow Tail 2003 Merlot (South Eastern Australia) $7. Nutty-brambly aromas and red fruit on the nose lead to plum and black raspberry fruit on the palate. There's some caramel flavor here, but it's not as prevalent as it has been in other wines by this brand. Flavors are a little bright overall, but it's still a good value. **84 Best Buy** —*D.T. (12/31/2004)*

Yellow Tail 2001 Merlot (Australia) $7. Simple and on the sweet side, with blackberry and raspberry fruit; it's less Merlot than it is a Generic Red Wine. Has an odd lactic-cheese note on the nose, under mounds of sweet red cherries. **82** —*D.T. (6/1/2003)*

Yellow Tail 2004 Pinot Grigio (South Eastern Australia) $7. Aromas of pear, melon, and white pepper are appealing enough. Offers very intense flavors of sour peach and citrus, and a slightly spritzy feel, on the palate. **83** —*D.T. (2/1/2006)*

Yellow Tail 2004 The Reserve Pinot Grigio (South Eastern Australia) $11. Cologny, haylike aromas lead to a dilute palate, offering weak yellow fruit and meat flavors. Finishes short. **82** —*D.T. (2/1/2006)*

Yellow Tail 2002 Shiraz (South Eastern Australia) $7. This wine offers grapey, dark fruit with a touch of dry earth and an aroma of buttered toast. The acidity and fruit are balanced, but lack the structure that more noticeable tannins would provide. **86 Best Buy** —*K.F. (3/1/2003)*

Yellow Tail 2001 Shiraz (South Eastern Australia) $7. Combines smoky, slightly acrid aromas with pretty strawberry scents and then piles juicy berries onto the palate. Finishes tart with hints of smoke and wood. For summer grilling at home, this is a pretty good choice. **86 Best Buy** —*J.C. (9/1/2002)*

Yellow Tail 2000 Shiraz (South Eastern Australia) $7. Dominated by blackberry notes, this is an easy rider that you can enjoy any night. The tannins are soft, the mouthfeel smooth and the finish long. Enjoy it with some pasta. **85 Best Buy** —*M.N. (6/1/2001)*

YERING STATION

Yering Station 2001 Cabernet Sauvignon (Yarra Valley) $17. Eucalyptus and asphalt aromas lead to blackberry, plum, and eucalyptus flavors on the palate. Mouthfeel is smooth; a very good wine. 1,000 cases produced. **88** —*D.T. (8/1/2005)*

AUSTRALIA

Yering Station 2000 Cabernet Sauvignon (Yarra Valley) $17. The nose is this wine's strongest suit. It evolves nicely, first showing eucalyptus and earth, and then mocha, anise, and dense, sweet fruit. The wine's feel and flavors are also very good—it's feminine in size, focused on plum fruit. Finishes a little flat, but still very good overall. **88** —*D.T. (12/31/2004)*

Yering Station 1999 Reserve Cabernet Sauvignon (Yarra Valley) $43. Classy, sexy, and certainly ageworthy. Dusty, meaty, peppery aromas lead to a palate rife with dark fruit and substantial oak. Supple in the mouth, with burly black fruit and wheat flour on the finish. Drink through 2012. **90** —*D.T. (11/15/2004)*

Yering Station 2004 Chardonnay (Yarra Valley) $18. If this isn't the thing to drink on the deck as the sun goes down, I don't know what is. Offers delicate mineral and nut aromas on the nose, and citrus, pear, and white peach flavors on the palate. It's all drawn in a delicate, feminine hand. 3,000 cases produced. **88** —*D.T. (8/1/2006)*

Yering Station 2003 Chardonnay (Yarra Valley) $17. A pretty, talc-mineral note pervades from nose to palate, bolstered by tangy peach and pear fruit. It's a lighter style of Chard, not an explosion of flavors; finishes with a buttery-lactic note. **86** —*D.T. (12/1/2005)*

Yering Station 2002 Chardonnay (Yarra Valley) $17. Grips the midpalate and doesn't let go, but overt flavor isn't this wine's strong suit. Yellow fruit and resin flavors are understated, and finish in a cheese rind-lemon zest medley. Texture is the main attraction here; fruit-bomb fanatics look elsewhere. **86** —*D.T. (12/31/2004)*

Yering Station 2001 Chardonnay (Yarra Valley) $20. Medium-weight, with nuances of pear on the palate; the fruit is fairly overwhelmed by nutty, smoky notes, which persist through the finish. The nose likewise offers a similar toast-and-oak tag team. A good wine, but one in which the pretty fruit doesn't get its moment in the spotlight. **85** *(7/2/2004)*

Yering Station 2000 Chardonnay (Yarra Valley) $20. This medium-bodied Chard has some butterscotch notes on the nose, but thankfully lacks similarly overpowering flavors on the palate. Some citrus flavors accent the wine's peachy core; finishes a little watery. **85** —*D.T. (8/1/2003)*

Yering Station 1999 Chardonnay (Yarra Valley) $20. This is the kind of wine that showcases just how distinctive and special Australia can be across so many varietals. It unites ripe, tropical-fruity characteristics with mineral and herbal ones, and yokes them together with smoky oak. There's very great fruity extract, but it's not over the top, and the acidity, as usual, is high and makes things shine. If you're tired of fat, flat Chards but demand fruit, try this one. **90** —*S.H. (6/1/2001)*

Yering Station 2001 Reserve Chardonnay (Yarra Valley) $39. We liked the deep aromas of nuts and smoke on the nose. Palate flavors are of white peach and wood; panelists were simply divided over whether oak flatters or flattens the fruit. Light to medium in body, with a mineral and smoke finish. Tasted twice. **87** *(7/2/2004)*

Yering Station 2001 Pinot Noir (Yarra Valley) $17. Shows a nice synthesis of juicy red plum, earth, and leather on the palate. A medium-sized wine, but feels pretty sizable for a Yarra Pinot; has a nice tannic grip in midpalate, and smooth tannins on the medium-length finish. **89** —*D.T. (12/31/2004)*

Yering Station 2000 Pinot Noir (Yarra Valley) $28. Fresh hay and caramel aromas lead to similar brown-sugary accents on the palate. Has promise, but it's a real lightweight, with whispers of tart red plum fruit that extends through the back end. **83** *(6/1/2003)*

Yering Station 1999 Pinot Noir (Yarra Valley) $22. A wine that combines pretty black cherry fruit with cinnamon, earth, and mushrooms. The fruit is pleasant enough, but the emphasis is on the earthier side of Pinot—soil and mulch and bark; some herbal flavors chime in on the finish. Might improve with mid-term cellaring. **88** *(6/1/2001)*

Yering Station 2004 Extra Dry Rosé Pinot Noir (Yarra Valley) $13. For once, "extra dry" on a label means just that: This isn't a sweet, or particularly fruit-forward, pink wine. It has the crispness of a dry white, but the versatility and flavor of a bigger red—just what you want to drink cold and outdoors, to wash down a bucket of fried chicken. Sturdy plum and plum skin flavors hold the fort down, but the real draw is its smooth feel. **89** —*D.T. (8/1/2005)*

Yering Station 2003 Reserve Pinot Noir (Yarra Valley) $36. This is not a Pinot you'd ever mistake for an Old World version—its palate is brimming with plums, berries, and noticeable wood, but it still retains some recognizable varietal character. Soft, dusty tannins give it a good feel. The nose, though, is trail-mix central: granola, dried fruit, dates. **88** —*D.T. (12/1/2005)*

Yering Station 2002 Reserve Pinot Noir (Yarra Valley) $36. This Burgundian-styled Oz Pinot is harmonious and sturdy, though a little tight and sour at this stage. Tree bark and meat aromas usher in mixed cherries, orange peel, and oak flavors. Medium-long and chewy on the finish. Could benefit from a few years in the cellar. **90** —*D.T. (10/1/2005)*

Yering Station 2000 Reserve Pinot Noir (Yarra Valley) $36. Medium-weight and smooth, this Pinot's calling card is its drying tannins, which last through to the very end. Red plums on the palate have a roasted quality—or maybe it's just the char and caramelized sugar talking. **86** *(6/1/2003)*

Yering Station 1998 Reserve Pinot Noir (Yarra Valley) $36. Perhaps the best Oz Pinot we've tasted, with smoky, meaty aromas that segue seamlessly into sour cherry, chocolate, and earth flavors. It's full and soft in the mouth before finishing long, with notes of leather, cedar, and cherries. **91** *(6/1/2001)*

Yering Station 2001 Shiraz (Yarra Valley) $17. Starts off with nutmeg and cinammon aromas, which grow sweeter and more grapy with air. Straightforward plum fruit on the palate, with a decent, medium-sized feel. A good wine, but a pretty ordinary one. **85** —*D.T. (12/31/2004)*

Yering Station 1999 Shiraz (Yarra Valley) $22. The Yarra Valley's relatively cool climate really shows through in this wine's smoky, herbal nuances, which sometimes threaten to take over from the primary cherry fruit. It's lean, more in the Rhône style, and finishes with tart cherries and hints of meaty portobello mushrooms. **86** —*J.C. (9/1/2002)*

Yering Station 2001 Reserve Shiraz (Yarra Valley) $36. Violet in both color and aroma, this is a huge but elegant, mouthfilling wine, and one built for the long haul. Tannins are lush but taut, and the finish is long, with chalk, mint, and smooth tannins. Drink 2006+. **91** —*D.T. (9/1/2004)*

Yering Station 1998 Reserve Shiraz (Yarra Valley) $36. Displays a winning combination of cool climate and low yields in its rich, earthy, peppery aromas. There's an undeniable herbal streak that adds complexity akin to some Northern Rhône Syrahs, supported by fleshy mulberry fruit. Finshes dusty and dry, but with a lush juiciness at the same time. **93 Editors' Choice** —*J.C. (9/1/2002)*

Yering Station 2002 Shiraz-Viognier (Yarra Valley) $17. Not as good as Yering's Shiraz-Viogniers have been, but still a good wine. This vintage offers a nose full of amaretto, green herb—and, with some time, black and green pepper. On the palate the wine is on the thin side, with high-toned cherry and herb flavors. The soily-smooth texture is its high point. **85** —*D.T. (12/1/2005)*

Yering Station 2003 Reserve Shiraz-Viognier (Yarra Valley) $36. Aromas are of violets and wheat bread, both of which unfold on the palate, too. Mocha, black cherry and plum flavors carry through to the smooth, meaty finish. A very nice wine, but Viognier's floral component is very dominant, a little too much so for this reviewer. **89** —*D.T. (4/1/2006)*

Yering Station 2004 M.V.R. White Blend (Yarra Valley) $17. Almost two-thirds Marsanne, wtih Viognier and Roussanne making up the balance. It is an intellectually interesting wine, a study of a Rhône composition, and I value it for that. But is just not a giving wine, or one that I could imagine going well with dinner. Notes of tree root, nut, and peach pit dominate, and the feel is a little viscous. **86** —*D.T. (8/1/2005)*

Yering Station 2003 M.V.R. White Blend (Yarra Valley) $17. The idea of this wine really intrigues me—a Rhône blend from Yarra, comprised of nearly three-quarters Marsanne, 5% Roussanne, and the balance Viognier. It's floral and aromatic on the nose, with whiffs even of dime-store bubble gum. The palate has a slight viscous oiliness, but the flavors—some floral notes, maybe some green grapes—are light and innocuous. If the flavors were as titillating as the aromas, and the whole package amped up a notch in intensity, I wouldn't be able to put this wine down. **86** —*D.T. (12/31/2004)*

YERINGBERG

Yeringberg 2002 Bordeaux Blend (Yarra Valley) $65. This delicately styled wine is a blend of Cabernet Sauvignon, Cabernet Franc, Merlot, and Malbec. Woodspice and earth aromas lead to cool plum and cherry notes, backed by lively acidity and woodsy tannins. Finishes with a citrusy tang. Will surely develop even more interesting nuances over the near to mid-term; try again in 2008. **90** —*D.T. (10/1/2006)*

YOU BET

You Bet 2002 Shiraz (South Eastern Australia) $10. Say the wine's name fast. Get it? Some may not get past the, ahem, rear view emblazoned on the front label and humorous references on the back label to this red being "a cheeky little number." For others, the packaging will be a draw. Offers confected black-cherry aromas. In the mouth, the flavors and texture feel like Sweet Tarts (a second reviewer likens it more to raspberry jam). Finishes short. Tasted twice. **82** —*D.T. (12/31/2004)*

YUNBAR

Yunbar 2000 Craig's Cabernet Sauvignon (Barossa Valley) $23. The aromas of this Cabernet are as intoxicating as the alcohol. Black olives, pine cones, and blackberry lull you to flavors of fresh herbs and red berries. The finish is long and mouthwatering for a wine that is delicious now. **89** —*C.S. (6/1/2002)*

Yunbar 2000 Chaste Chardonnay (Barossa Valley) $15. The sound you hear when you open the bottle is of chainsaws buzzing. Wood, wood, and more wood—on the nose, on the palate, on the finish. Some citrus pokes through, but drink soon before it's totally submerged. **82** —*J.C. (7/1/2002)*

Yunbar 2000 Miracle Merlot (Barossa Valley) $23. Earthy aromas of fresh compost and eucalyptus leave you wondering, where's the fruit? You have to wait until it reaches the palate, then you find the sweet dark fruit with caramel and toasted oak. The bright acids and soft tannins make for a short but pleasant finish. **86** —*C.S. (6/1/2002)*

Yunbar 2000 Eden Riesling (Barossa Valley) $15. Balanced and dry, this is a world away from too many Americans' idea of Riesling. This medium-weight wine's green apple and light peach aromas and flavors wear mineral and even classic diesel accents. A solid example from South Australia, a Riesling locale since the early German settlement there. **86** —*M.M. (2/1/2002)*

Yunbar 2000 Sinner's Shiraz (Barossa Valley) $23. How can a Barossa Shiraz be so green? Its flavors are herbal to the point of being close to cabbage or green bean, with just enough high-toned cherry fruit to be acceptable. **82** —*J.C. (9/1/2002)*

ZEEPAARD

Zeepaard 2005 Sauvignon Blanc (Western Australia) $10. Starts off with grassy, fresh herbal aromas and flavors of almond. After a second look, it's all lemon and grapefruit flavors, with an edge of sweetness—almost like a lemon tart. Slim in size, soft in feel. An easy quaff. **84** —*D.T. (8/1/2006)*

ZEMA ESTATE

Zema Estate 2001 Cluny Bordeaux Blend (Coonawarra) $25. Tight and taut from the get-go, time in the glass not resolving the thick woody tannins that envelop the plum and blackberry fruit that lies beneath. Anise, curry spice, and bread flour does come to the fore, though. Add a backbone of lively acidity to this picture and the result is a wine that'll shine much more in 2009 than it does now. 59% Cabernet, 19% Merlot, 15% Cab Franc, 7% Malbec. **90** —*D.T. (6/1/2006)*

Zema Estate 2001 Cabernet Sauvignon (Coonawarra) $25. Cabernet through and through, with interesting aromas of pepper, bacon, and sausage that take on cool menthol notes with air. Wide and juicy on the palate, its purple fruit taking a backseat to the wine's chenille-like texture. Drink 2007–2009. **89** —*D.T. (6/1/2006)*

ZILZIE

Zilzie 2002 Selection 23 Cabernet Sauvignon-Merlot (Victoria) $10. On the nose, fruit is sweet and jammy—rather like grape jelly. The fruit sours up on the palate, where rhubarb and plum notes take over.

Straightforward; finishes with a smooth, chalky feel. **83** —*D.T. (9/1/2004)*

Zilzie 2002 Selection 23 Chardonnay (Victoria) $10. A workhorse of a wine, one that will get the job done with ease but may not win any beauty contests. It's big and a little bulky in the mouth, with melon, pear, and danish pastry flavors and sour pear, matchstick, and lemon aromas. **85** *(7/2/2004)*

Zilzie 2003 Viognier (Victoria) $14. Has a certain crisp acidity that many Viogniers lack, which balances out honey and tropical yellow fruit flavors. Its concentration doesn't hit you with a whollop, but it's still good, with floral, apple, pear and honey aromas. **87** —*D.T. (5/1/2004)*

ZONTE'S FOOTSTEP

Zonte's Footstep 2003 Cabernet Sauvignon-Malbec (Langhorne Creek) $15. Sweet, plummy fruit wears heavy, lemon-tinged oak aromas. Tastes like wines half its price: simple plum and berry fruit, with a metallic edge. Finishes short. **82** —*D.T. (5/1/2005)*

AUSTRALIA

Austria

Thanks to two grapes and two wine styles, Austrian wine has an important presence on the international wine-making stage. One of these grapes is Riesling, of which Austrian wine producers are some of the greatest exponents. The other is Grüner Veltliner, of which Austrian wine producers have a virtual monopoly, but one they exploit with panache and stunning results.

The wine styles are both white, but otherwise completely different. There are beautifully crisp, balanced, dry whites; and there are some of the most impressive sweet, botrytis wines, rich, unctuous, and intense.

These are the traditional Austrian wine styles. In recent years, red wines have become increasingly important and of better quality. Using local as well as international grape varieties, Austrian reds now cover one third of the country's vineyards.

Austrian vineyards at Retz, Niederösterreich.

Austria's wine-making history goes back to ancient Roman days, with some of today's best vineyards planted at that time, Grape varieties—red and white—are found on Austrian labels, along with the geographic origin. Today's Austrian vineyards are found in the east of country, whereas classic areas are along the Danube Valley, north-west of Vienna, and in the far east in the province of Burgenland.

The Danube Valley offers superlatives, both in wine and in wine country. The beautiful Wachau vineyards, best known but also one of the smallest wine regions, are caught between steep mountain slopes and the wide Danube River. The purest, most elegant Rieslings and Grüner Veltliners are made by a succession of some of the best producers in Austria. Quality levels are specific to the region: the lightest style is Steinfeder, next is Federspiel, and the richest style is Smaragd.

Other Danube districts include the Kremstal and Kamptal. Both make great white wines: the Kamptal produces some of the most characteristic Grüner Veltliner, crisp, dry, and peppery, from vineyards that are generally cooler than those of Kremstal. One of Austria's most famed vineyard sites, Heiligenstein (rock of saints), is in Kremstal.

North of the Danube, stretching away to the north-east corner of the country, is the Weinviertel, the largest Austrian wine area. Great value wines come from here, mainly made with Grüner Veltliner. A new wine designation is DAC, modeled on the French AC or the Italian DOC: stressing geographic origin rather than grape variety, DAC wines are some of the best everyday dry white wines coming out of Austria.

The Burgenland is where the great dessert wines, and—increasingly—red wines come from. This is the hottest region of Austria, dominated by the marshy, shallow Neusiedlersee lake. Great sweet wines come from the villages all around the lake, while reds come from here as well as hillier vineyards further south.

Wines from Styria, a smaller area in the south east, are worth seeking out. The region has astonished the world with the quality of its Sauvignon Blanc and Chardonnay, and some great white wine makers are based there, as well.

AUSTRIA

ADOLF & HEINRICH FUCHS

Adolf & Heinrich Fuchs 2003 Chardonnay (Südsteiermark) $16. A creamy, ripe wine, with some vanilla aromas and flavors of plums and ripe peaches. In Styria, Chardonnay is also known, confusingly, as Morillon. **84** —*R.V. (5/1/2005)*

Adolf & Heinrich Fuchs 2001 Classik Trocken Chardonnay (Südsteiermark) $13. A fat style of Chardonnay, with creamy fruit on the nose and some acidity. Green, crisp, citrus fruit flavors and green plums contrast with a layer of fatness. **86** —*R.V. (11/1/2002)*

Adolf & Heinrich Fuchs 2003 Classic Gelber Muskateller (Südsteiermark) $NA. The Gelber Muskateller has a long tradition in Styria, where this wine comes from. It is a great apéritif drink, with its racy, fragrant character, and ripe, heady perfumes. This example is well-balanced, with a good touch of acidity to keep it fresh. **85** —*R.V. (5/1/2005)*

Adolf & Heinrich Fuchs 2003 Classic Halbtrocken Gewürztraminer (Burgenland) $NA. The term "Halbtrocken" means that the wine is semi-sweet. This increases the spicy character of the Gewürztraminer, but along the way some of the intensity is lost. Flavors of lychees make it powerful, but the sweetness makes this a simple wine. **84** —*R.V. (5/1/2005)*

Adolf & Heinrich Fuchs 2003 Libelich Gewürztraminer (Südsteiermark) $NA. A rich, sweet wine, with flavors of ripe oranges, lychees, and intense spice. It is very concentrated, and straightforward. **83** —*R.V. (5/1/2005)*

Adolf & Heinrich Fuchs 2003 Classic Grüner Veltliner (Neusiedlersee) $NA. This is full-bodied, much bigger than the Grüner Veltliner of the Weinviertel in northern Austria. From the hot Burgenland, this is rich, with pepper and white fruit flavors, but only a slight touch of acidity. The aftertaste has hints of caramel. **83** —*R.V. (5/1/2005)*

Adolf & Heinrich Fuchs 2001 Classik Trocken Grüner Veltliner (Burgenland) $13. The fruit on the nose is reminiscent of hedgerow fruits—blackberries, alpine strawberries, plums, and blueberries. The palate is very green with high acidity and light, fresh fruit flavors. The final impression is of a fresh, crisp wine, with just a touch of pepper. **87** —*R.V. (11/1/2002)*

Adolf & Heinrich Fuchs 2003 Reserve Grüner Veltliner (Burgenland) $NA. This is something of a curiosity, a Grüner Veltliner which has been matured in wood. It gives the wine extra spiciness and intensity of flavor, although some of the pepper character of the grape is lost in the process. This wine is big, ripe, and full. **86** —*R.V. (5/1/2005)*

Adolf & Heinrich Fuchs NV Landwein Muskat Ottonel (Burgenland) $NA. A clean, fresh wine, with perfumed fruit. It is spicy, aromatic, and soft, with layers of nutmeg and finishes with just a touch of sweetness. This is a pleasant, easy apéritif wine. Although it does not carry a vintage, the wine is from the 2003 vintage. **83** —*R.V. (5/1/2005)*

Adolf & Heinrich Fuchs 2003 Sauvignon Blanc (South Styria) $20. Smells much like a bowl of freshly made fruit cocktail: there's apple, pear, citrus, and kiwi. Spicy melon with hints of green herbs control the palate, while the mouthfeel is rich and chewy. Quite heavy and sweet, but good if you aren't looking for a lot of zest. **87** —*(7/1/2005)*

Adolf & Heinrich Fuchs 2001 Classik Trocken Sauvignon Blanc (Südsteiermark) $13. A simple, tank-fermented Sauvignon Blanc with crisp, grassy fruit and herbaceous aromas. The flavor is ripe fruit, structured with a layer of tannin and grassiness. Gooseberries and tropical fruit vie for attention on the finish. **86** —*R.V. (11/1/2002)*

Adolf & Heinrich Fuchs 2003 Classic Weissburgunder (Südsteiermark) $NA. From the southern Austrian region of Styria, this wine is marked by a touch of spice, and flavors of almonds and white fruits. It is clean, but quite fat, a sign of the warm vintage. **83** —*R.V. (5/1/2005)*

Adolf & Heinrich Fuchs 2003 Classic Welschriesling (Südsteiermark) $NA. A clean, fruity wine, with flavors of red currants, green plums, and a good layer of fresh acidity. This is attractive and easy-drinking, showing just what can be done with Welschriesling. **85** —*R.V. (5/1/2005)*

ALLRAM

Allram 2003 Gaisberg Grüner Veltliner (Kamptal) $25. Like many of the wines from Austria's hot 2003 vintage, this is really ripe. Weighty and slightly viscous on the palate, with scents of nectarine that merge easily into flavors of stone fruits, mineral oil, and a hint of white pepper. So rich on the finish it seems almost off dry. **90** —*J.C. (5/1/2005)*

Allram 2003 Strassertal Grüner Veltliner (Kamptal) $14. Another nice GV from Allram—and at an excellent price. Pear, pepper, and mineral scents and flavors; a bit oily in the mouth. A bit short on the finish, but a nice intro-level Grüner. **87** —*J.C. (5/1/2005)*

ANTON BAUER

Anton Bauer 2001 Wagram Reserve Cabernet Blend (Donauland) $28. Starts with clove, coffee, and plum on the nose, while the flavors follow in a similar vein: plum, coffee, and dried spices. Medium-weight, with a tangy finish filled with soft tannins. Ready to drink. A blend of Cabernet Sauvignon, Blaüfrankisch and Zweigelt, with tiny amounts of Syrah and Merlot. **84** —*J.C. (5/1/2005)*

Anton Bauer 2003 Reserve Grüner Veltliner (Donauland) $20. Reticent on the nose, yielding stony, waxy notes but little else. It's medium-bodied and a bit austere on the palate as well, but then the stone and melon flavors open out on the finish into lemon, hints of pepper, and celery leaf. **87** —*J.C. (3/1/2006)*

Anton Bauer 2003 Wagram Cuvée No. 9 Red Blend (Donauland) $20. The heat of 2003 figures in this wine, which boasts outsized flavors of super-ripe fruit, ranging from peaches and apricots to cherries. Then it finishes on notes of anise and pepper. It's all almost Grenache-like, despite being a blend of Blaufränkisch, Zweigelt, Cabernet Sauvignon, and Merlot. **86** —*J.C. (3/1/2006)*

Anton Bauer 2002 Reserve Riesling (Donauland) $18. There's a hint of apricot, maybe some tangerine on the nose, but this is a dry Riesling, filled with similar hints to its flavors and culminating in a long, spicy flourish. Shows some intriguing chalky-minerally notes on the finish. **88** —*J.C. (12/15/2004)*

BOCKFLIESS

Bockfliess 1999 Pinot Blanc (Weinviertel) $14. Aromas of ripe pears drizzled with canola oil turn a little dieselly in the mouth. But the mouthfeel is rich and full, the finish long and slightly peppery. Mature, so drink up. **86** —*J.C. (3/1/2002)*

BRAUNSTEIN

Braunstein 2003 Oxhoft Chardonnay (Burgenland) $18. This plump, medium-bodied Chardonnay would have scored higher had its aromas not been marred by a burnt, acrid note. Ripe melon and pear flavors are welcoming, while the finish lingers softly. **83** —*J.C. (11/15/2005)*

Braunstein 2002 Oxhoft Chardonnay (Burgenland) $18. Starts off with hints of honey and ripe melony scents, then adds toast and caramel accents to the melon and citrus fruit on the palate. Medium-bodied and balanced, with just a hint of burnt toast on the finish. **85** —*J.C. (11/15/2005)*

Braunstein 2003 Mitterjoch Zweigelt (Burgenland) $14. Slightly rubbery and herbal, with rustic tannins and acids framing blackberry fruit. **82** —*J.C. (3/1/2006)*

BRÜNDLMAYER

Bründlmayer 2000 Kamptaler Terrasssen Grüner Veltliner (Kamptal) $18. At first the aromas bursting forth are warm and inviting, turning harder and sterner with air, finally becoming almost crystalline in their apple and pear character. Flavors of honey and clove, with a long, dry talc-like finish. **87** —*J.C. (3/1/2002)*

Bründlmayer 2003 Langenloiser Spiegel Grau und Weissburgunder Pinot Gris (Kamptal) $NA. A blend of Pinot Gris and Pinot Blanc, this rich, complex wine brings out the best in both grapes. The fruit and the green flavors of the Blanc combine with the spice of the Gris to give a rich, deep, satisfying wine that has a fresh, but mature aftertaste. **91** —*R.V. (2/1/2006)*

Bründlmayer 2002 Langenloiser Spiegel Grau und Weissburgunder Pinot Gris (Kamptal) $NA. Compared with the 2003 version of this wine, this is more lively, fruitier and fresher, despite its extra year of age. There is great acidity as well as green and white fruit flavors in balance, delicious spice, pepper and complexity that develops as you taste it. **92** —*R.V. (2/1/2006)*

AUSTRIA

Bründlmayer 2005 Kamptaler Terrassen Riesling (Kamptal) $23. A blend of young vines from different vineyards, this has crisp fruit, apple, and grapefruit flavors. Bright, vibrant, easy to drink. Ready now. **88** —R.V. (10/1/2006)

Bründlmayer 2004 Langenloiser Kamptaler Terrassen Riesling (Kamptal) $25. A highly perfumed wine, with delicious green, grassy flavors. It has crispness, a layer of tannin, and great fresh fruits. Apples and grapefruit exist comfortably together with a firm structure, which suggests good aging. **90** —R.V. (8/1/2005)

Bründlmayer 2003 Langenloiser Kamptaler Terrassen Riesling (Kamptal) $25. A softer style than Bründlmayer's famed Heiligenstein wines, it has an immediate warmth and richness that goes with the ripe flavors of white currants and green fruits. There is freshness as well, which gives a great lift to the aftertaste. **89** —R.V. (8/1/2005)

Bründlmayer 2005 Langenloiser Steinmassel Riesling (Kamptal) $30. This wine is all about fruit: flavors of grapefruit, white currants, white peaches, and lychees. But it also has great minerality and a lift of acidity. **90** —R.V. (10/1/2006)

Bründlmayer 2003 Langenloiser Steinmassel Riesling (Kamptal) $34. A crisp, green wine, with flavors of grapefruit peel, and a lively character. Rieslings from the thin soil of the Steinmassel vineyard live indefinitely, and this wine, with its tannins and high minerality, is a baby. It could be enjoyed now for its freshness, but really 10 years of age would be a better starting point. **93** —R.V. (8/1/2005)

Bründlmayer 2000 Langenloiser Steinmassel Riesling (Kamptal) $25. Enormously complex, with aromas and flavors that run the gamut from oil shale and beeswax, to quince and Asian pear, baking spices and honey. Finishes long and spicy, with a dry mineral component. **90** —J.C. (3/1/2002)

Bründlmayer 2005 Zöbinger Heiligenstein Riesling (Kamptal) $36. A very intense, full-flavored wine, with structure and minerality the dominant characteristics. There's certainly acidity in this youthful wine, but it is the intensity of flavors that will eventually—give it four years—shine through. **93 Editors' Choice** —R.V. (10/1/2006)

Bründlmayer 2003 Zöbinger Heiligenstein Riesling (Kamptal) $39. A full-bodied wine with great minerality and steely flavors along with green, grapefruit flavors at this young stage. But it is just setting out, and within 2–3 years will soften, and open up into a ripe, intense wine with beautiful yellow fruits. **91** —R.V. (8/1/2005)

Bründlmayer 2005 Zöbinger Heiligenstein Alte Reben Riesling (Kamptal) $NA. The purest Riesling flavors are to be found in this great wine. At this stage, it is still very tight and closed up, but there is so much leashed power there, along with complex hints of fruits, minerals, and exotic perfumes. Give it at least five years, and it will begin to slowly evolve. **95 Editors' Choice** —R.V. (10/1/2006)

Bründlmayer 2001 Zöbinger Heiligenstein Alte Reben Riesling (Kamptal) $49. The nose is both deceptive and enticing, with its sweet fruit and honey aromas. But they lead to a stunningly rich wine from the great Heiligenstein vineyard, one that is dry with a fine mineral character. It has flavors of pink grapefruit, hedgerow fruit, white currants, and a layer of tannin to give structure. This great wine will age for a long time—10 to 15 years at least. **95 Cellar Selection** —R.V. (8/1/2005)

Bründlmayer 2000 Zöbinger Heiligenstein Beerenauslese 375ml Riesling (Kamptal) $95. This is a delicate wine, with intense sweetness. The dryness of the botrytis is there with apricot and honey flavors, along with great waves of piercing acidity. A wine to age. **92 Cellar Selection** —R.V. (10/1/2006)

Bründlmayer 2005 Zöbinger Heiligenstein Lyra Riesling (Kamptal) $60. Named after the lyre method of training vines, which Willi Bründlmayer uses on the Heiligenstein vineyard to open out the vine's canopy, this is a full-bodied, many-layered wine, with pink grapefruit, quince, and apricot flavors. Like other Rieslings from Heiligenstein, this will certainly age almost indefinitely. **94 Cellar Selection** —R.V. (10/1/2006)

Bründlmayer 2002 Zöbinger Heiligenstein Lyra Riesling (Kamptal) $66. The famed Heilingenstein vineyard is certainly the greatest in the Kamptal, a sandstone and volcanic ridge that radiates heat in the summer. The wine is full of yellow peach, tropical fruits, along with mineral flavors. This is a beautiful, intense wine, with weight as well as full acidity. **93 Editors' Choice** —R.V. (8/1/2005)

DINSTLGUT LOIBEN

Dinstlgut Loiben 2005 Loibenberg Grüner Veltliner (Wachau) $NA. An attractively spicy wine, with clean lemon and bitter orange flavors, fresh acidity, and a peppery aftertaste. **88** —R.V. (10/1/2006)

Dinstlgut Loiben 2005 Loibenberg Riesling (Wachau) $NA. Perfumed white currants are the dominant theme of this flavorful wine. It is fresh, lightly mineral, with layers of acidity. **88** —R.V. (10/1/2006)

Dinstlgut Loiben 2003 Loibenberg Trockenbeerenauslese Riesling (Wachau) $NA. Tiny quantities of this wine were produced in '03 and again in '04. It is an impressive wine, with intense sweet apricot and honey flavors, still giving fine, fresh acidity to balance the dense texture. **93** —R.V. (10/1/2006)

Dinstlgut Loiben 2005 Pfaffenberg Riesling (Kremstal) $NA. The Loiben cooperative also produces wines from the neighboring Kremstal, notably the Pfaffenberg vineyard. This is a heavily mineral wine, dry, crisp, with apple fruit flavors and delicious finishing acidity. **89** —R.V. (10/1/2006)

DOMAINE WACHAU

Domaine Wachau 2005 Achleiten Smaragd Grüner Veltliner (Wachau) $27. Smoky, peppery flavors, minerality, and a firm structure all show the poor slate soil of the Achleiten vineyard. Yes, quince and grapefruit flavors are there, but they come through only slightly on this still-young wine. **90** —R.V. (10/1/2006)

Domaine Wachau 2003 Dürnsteiner Kellerberg Smaragd Grüner Veltliner (Wachau) $23. Smaragd wines, the top category in the Wachau, are intended to be rich and powerful. And this wine from the Frei Weingärtner Wachau fits this profile well. It combines this power successfully with a racy character, some mineral flavors, and a good seasoning of pepper. **88** —R.V. (5/1/2005)

Domaine Wachau 2002 Federspiel Terrassen Grüner Veltliner (Wachau) $13. Grüner Veltliner is Austria's own special white—it's fresh, but peppery, aromatic, spicy, and flowery. This example has all those flavors, and is a bargain, too. It comes from one of the world's great cooperatives. The fruit comes from the terraced vineyards of the Wachau region in the Danube Valley. The term "Federspiel" is used in the Wachau to denote a good everyday wine, and this is exactly that. **87 Best Buy** —R.V. (11/15/2004)

Domaine Wachau 2003 Loibner Loibenberg Federspiel Grüner Veltliner (Wachau) $11. A breezy, fresh wine, packed with fruit, flavors of pepper, and spice that would work well as an apéritif, or with white fish. The wine comes from the Freie Weingärtner Wachau coop, probably the top cooperative in Austria. **87 Best Buy** —R.V. (5/1/2005)

Domaine Wachau 2005 Achleiten Smaragd Riesling (Wachau) $33. This very young wine is dominated at this stage by its piercing acidity, very green fruits, and minerality. But the future is there in the hints of ripe white fruit flavors and the racy aftertaste. **89** —R.V. (10/1/2006)

Domaine Wachau 2003 Dürnsteiner Kellerberg Smaragd Riesling (Wachau) $30. A classic Riesling from the Wachau, which combines intense, aromatic fruit with full flavors of white peaches and floral aromas. This is not as dry as most Wachau wines—it has a definite sweet aftertaste—but the whole wine is so well balanced that this sweeter character never dominates. **90** —R.V. (5/1/2005)

Domaine Wachau 2005 Loibenberg Smaragd Riesling (Wachau) $33. Richness and complete dryness go together in this impressive wine. It is very juicy, with some tropical fruit flavors, along with white fruits, but there is also a touch of minerality that gives the wine shape. **91** —R.V. (10/1/2006)

Domaine Wachau 2003 Terrassen Federspiel Riesling (Wachau) $12. A fairly big, round Riesling—reflective of the ripeness of the vintage—with aromas of ripe apple and pear and flavors of baked apple and dried spices. Yet despite the soft fruit flavors, the wine is dry and it retains a fine sense of minerality on the finish. Drink over the next 12–18 months. **90 Best Buy** —J.C. (5/1/2005)

DOMAINES SCHLUMBERGER

Domaines Schlumberger NV Cuvée Klimt Brut Welschriesling (Weinviertel) $18. Pleasant spiced pear and cinnamon aromas lead into pear and sour plum flavors. Medium-bodied, with a short finish, it's the only Austrian fizz we've ever tried—it makes us think the country has potential. **84** —J.C. (12/31/2001)

Domaines Schlumberger NV Cuvée Klimt Brut Welschriesling (Osterreichischer Sekt) $20. Tangerines and peaches on the nose, but much more citrusy in the mouth, with hints of apple and nectarine. Lemony and fresh on the finish, with a slightly coarse bead and a light, frothy mouthfeel. **85** —J.C. (12/31/2003)

DOMÄNE MÜLLER

Domäne Müller 1997 Ried Burgegg Fürstenstück Der Pinot Gris (Weststeiermark) $16. From the estate of the Prince of Liechtenstein, which is run by Eva and Gunter Müller, this mature wine shows plenty of fresh fruit flavors along with spice, toast, and acidity. Intense but balanced, this would go well with rich foods. **90** —R.V. (2/1/2006)

E. & M. BERGER

E. & M. Berger 2002 Grüner Veltliner (Kremstal) $11. It's difficult to find inexpensive Austrian wines in the United States; importers (somewhat justifiably) seem to think that the demand for Austrian wines is further up-market. So it was refreshing to find this lithesome gem. It's light and fresh, with a rainwater-mineral aspect to it and a dollop of Grüner character. Fine for a springtime picnic, or as an apéritif. **85** —M.S. (11/15/2003)

E. & M. Berger 2000 Zehetnerin Grüner Veltliner (Kremstal) $14. An easy-drinking GV with the emphasis on grapefruit and white peach flavors accented by peppery spice and minerals. It's light, clean, and crisp, but finishes short. **84** —J.C. (3/1/2002)

EICHINGER

Eichinger 2002 Strasser Gaisberg Grüner Veltliner (Kamptal) $25. A bit dark in color—polished brass—but shows lovely aromas of white peaches, corn oil and green peppercorns. Oily and viscous in the mouth, with flavors of peppered peaches. Pronounced pepperiness on the finish, along with a hint of alcohol. Drink now. **89** —J.C. (5/1/2005)

Eichinger 2002 Strasser Gaisberg Riesling (Kamptal) $25. The wonderfully citrusy, floral nose also carries hints of honey and melon; flavors are of mixed citrus, with floral, peppery notes akin to nasturtium. Less weighty than most 2003s, with a crisp, fresh finish that sets it apart; completely in vintage character. **90** —J.C. (5/1/2005)

Elfenhof 1999 Beerenauslese Chardonnay (Burgenland) $NA. Pale gold in color, this wine shows great, concentrated fruit, some of the botrytis dryness and flavors of toffee. Lacking acidity, it is ready to drink now. **87** —R.V. (5/1/2004)

ELFENHOF

Elfenhof 2001 Spatlese Lieblich Chardonnay (Burgenland) $NA. "Lieblich" is a term traditionally used to describe a sweet wine that has no noble rot. As expressed in this wine, the style is fresh and poised. Flavors of currants and ripe quince give both sweetness and acidity. **85** —R.V. (5/1/2004)

Elfenhof 1999 Eiswein Nebbiolo (Neusiedlersee-Hügelland) $NA. A fresh, delicate wine intense sweetness, this has flavors of crisp summer fruits along with a touch of honey and citrus acidity. It's beautifully balanced and light. **89 Editors' Choice** —R.V. (5/1/2004)

EMMERICH KNOLL

Emmerich Knoll 2005 Loibenberg Smaragd Grüner Veltliner (Wachau) $46. A perfumed, pure, light-bodied wine that has touches of fine acidity and crisp fruits. To finish, there are flavors of pepper, limes, and orange peel. This is a delicious, approachable wine that will age. **89** —R.V. (10/1/2006)

Emmerich Knoll 2004 Loibner Federspiel Grüner Veltliner (Wachau) $22. Light and fresh, but seems to lack a bit of intensity, offering modest melon and white pepper flavors. Finishes a bit short. **85** —J.C. (8/1/2006)

Emmerich Knoll 2003 Loibner Federspiel Trocken Grüner Veltliner (Wachau) $22. Light to medium in body, with subtle aromas of mineral smoke, apples, and pears, this Grüner won't wow, just artfully impress. Crisp tree fruit and melon flavors echo on the mineral-laden finish. **88** —J.C. (11/15/2005)

Emmerich Knoll 2004 Loibner Ried Kreutles Federspiel Grüner Veltliner (Wachau) $26. Starts off with an intense blast of white pepper and celery leaf, but that's buffered by layers of ripe nectarines. Like most Knoll wines, it leans toward the lighter-weight side of things, yet doesn't lack for flavor or concentration, finishing with a refreshing, minerally character. **90 Editors' Choice** —J.C. (8/1/2006)

Emmerich Knoll 2004 Ried Kreutles Loibner Smaragd Grüner Veltliner (Wachau) $35. To me, Knoll's wines are always among the lightest-bodied of the major Wachau producers, but they are exquisitely detailed, presenting their scents and flavors in a fine filigree. This one offers hints of celery and lettuce greens, melon, and white pepper edged with traces of honeyed richness. **89** —J.C. (3/1/2006)

Emmerich Knoll 2002 Ried Kreutles Smaragd Grüner Veltliner (Wachau) $33. A lovely, complex wine that starts with tangerines and dried spices, then opens up slowly to reveal layers of honey, citrus, and spice complexities. It's round in the mouth without being soft, finishing with good length. **90** —J.C. (5/1/2005)

Emmerich Knoll 2005 Loibenberg Smaragd Riesling (Wachau) $50. Knoll's wines tend to be delicate, expressing terroir rather than power. This is certainly the case with this crisp, clean, very fresh, and green wine. It's young, of course, and like other Knoll wines should age well. **91** —R.V. (10/1/2006)

Emmerich Knoll 2004 Loibner Federspiel Riesling (Wachau) $28. Lean, but not lacking for intensity, with green apple and lime flavors that pick up hints of wet stones. Tart and a bit unforgiving on the finish; try with shellfish. **86** —J.C. (8/1/2006)

Emmerich Knoll 2002 Loibner Ried Loibenberg Riesling Smaragd Riesling (Wachau) $45. From its explosive aromas of melon, spice, apricot, and herb to its intense flavors of peach, melon, and peppery spice, this wine's quality is obvious. Rich and viscous in the mouth, with a long, dried-spice and mineral-laden finish, this is world-class dry Riesling. **92** —J.C. (12/15/2004)

ERIC & WALTER POLZ

Eric & Walter Polz 2001 Grassnitzberg Grauburgunder (Südsteiermark) $NA. Dense and concentrated, with powerful fruit, and flavors of pepper, toast and mineral. It is dry, intense and rich. This impressive wine has the potential to age. **90** —R.V. (2/1/2006)

Eric & Walter Polz 2005 Hochgrassnitzberg Sauvignon Blanc (Südsteiermark) $47. A barrel-aged SB that shows some wood flavor, but this is dominated by the great fruit flavors—tropical fruits, pineapple. There is some chalky minerality as well as fine, fresh acidity. **90** —R.V. (10/1/2006)

Eric & Walter Polz 2003 Hochgrassnitzberg Reserve Sauvignon Blanc (Südsteiermark) $60. An impressive, barrique-aged wine. This is very rich and intense, full of flavors of spice, ripe melons and caramel. This is a wine for aging—try it again in 4 or 5 years. **91 Cellar Selection** —R.V. (10/1/2006)

Eric & Walter Polz 2000 Steirische Klassik Sauvignon Blanc (Südsteiermark) $27. Bright gooseberry aromas are accompanied by hints of pear, melon and anise. It's pleasant and easy to drink, with a lemony tang that brings a touch of bitterness to the finish. **85** —J.C. (3/1/2002)

Eric & Walter Polz 2005 Therese Sauvignon Blanc (Südsteiermark) $29. A classic, full-bodied, easy-drinking Styrian Sauvignon Blanc, packed with tropical fruits, ripeness, and just a touch of herbaceous character. There's a lively, fresh citrus aftertaste. **89** —R.V. (10/1/2006)

ERICH SALOMON

Erich Salomon 2000 Hochterrassen Grüner Veltliner (Kremstal) $11. A low-end Grüner that provides just enough lime fruit and green pea character to make a pleasant before-dinner drink. **83** —J.C. (3/1/2002)

AUSTRIA

ERNST TRIEBAUMER

Ernst Triebaumer 2004 Blaufränkisch (Neusiedlersee-Hügelland) $NA.
Aged for 8 months in large barrels, this wine relies on its simple, juicy fruit. It has red fruit flavors, soft, fresh, and ripe. **85** —*R.V. (10/1/2006)*

Ernst Triebaumer 2004 Gmärk Blaufränkisch (Neusiedlersee-Hügelland) $24. Herbs, spices, and dense, tannic fruit are balanced with elegant black fruits and layers of wood. It is solid, but overweight. **89** —*R.V. (10/1/2006)*

Ernst Triebaumer 2003 Mariental Blaufränkisch (Neusiedlersee-Hügelland) $NA. Famed as a cult wine in Austria, this lives up to its billing. It is powerful but elegant, with juicy, herbal flavors, blackberries, damsons, and a smooth, cocoa coating. But there is certainly structure here from the tannins. Like so many Triebaumer wines, this will age magnificently. **93 Editors' Choice** —*R.V. (10/1/2006)*

Ernst Triebaumer 2003 Oberer Wald Blaufränkisch (Neusiedlersee-Hügelland) $43. As smooth as a red wine can be. Eighteen months in barrels, of which 40% were new, have smoothed out any sharp edges. This is velvety in its texture, with its ripe fruit, sweet tannins, and red berry fruit flavors. **91** —*R.V. (10/1/2006)*

Ernst Triebaumer 2001 Sauvignon Blanc (Burgenland) $10. Stunningly rich and good, with the brilliantly pure and strong intensity of a Marlborough wine. Packed with lime, gooseberry, sweet nettle, and vanilla honey flavors that drink bone dry, with mouthwatering acidity. Outstanding and compelling and a world class value. **90** —*S.H. (10/1/2004)*

Ernst Triebaumer 2001 Auslese Sauvignon Blanc (Burgenland) $32. This is a crisp, fresh wine, bursting with flavors of apples and cream, and lively acidity. It has structure, depth, and balance. **86** —*R.V. (5/1/2004)*

Ernst Triebaumer 2001 Beerenauslese Traminer (Burgenland) $32. This is a finely balanced wine, not hugely sweet, but with structure as well as opulent fruit. The Traminer lends a touch of spice, but it is well restrained. This is a style that could certainly partner savory foods as well as desserts. **87** —*R.V. (5/1/2004)*

Ernst Triebaumer 1998 Ausbruch Essenz Weissburgunder (Burgenland) $81. As its name suggests, this is a wine which comes from shrivelled berries, full of concentrated sugar. Triebaumer specializes in these wines which are produced in limited quantities. This one has layers of golden botrytis flavors; it's intense and rich, and should be savored on its own. **90** —*R.V. (5/1/2004)*

Ernst Triebaumer 1999 Ausbruch Essenz White Blend (Burgenland) $135.
This blend of Welschriesling and Chardonnay, hugely sweet, but with balanced, intense acidity, was produced in tiny quantities. Flavors of intense crystallized orange peel dominate, balanced, with full, rich opulent fruit make this a wine to savor. **91** —*R.V. (5/1/2004)*

ERWIN SABATHI

Erwin Sabathi 2002 Merveilleux Morillon Chardonnay (Styria) $45.
Morillon is the local term for Chardonnay, while Merveilleux is Sabathi's term for their barrel-fermented wines. The result is top-flight Chardonnay, combining pear nectar with custardy notes and nutty, toasty goodness. The slightly oily mouthfeel carries the flavors through to a long, nutty finish. **89** —*J.C. (12/15/2004)*

Erwin Sabathi 2005 Klassic Sauvignon Blanc (Styria) $16. Sabathi's entry-level Sauvignon Blanc is a fresh, grapefruity rendition, with hints of gooseberry and a touch of smoky, fumé-style character. Lacks a bit of richness in the midpalate, but finishes with good verve. **85** —*J.C. (12/1/2006)*

Erwin Sabathi 2003 Klassik Sauvignon Blanc (Styria) $15. Modest apple, lime and melon flavors in this light, quaffable Sauvignon. Finishes with a blast of zippy lime flavors, but lacks intensity otherwise. **84** —*J.C. (12/15/2004)*

Erwin Sabathi 2002 Merviellieux Sauvignon Blanc (Styria) $50. A very ripe, barrel-fermented Sauvignon that comes close, but doesn't quite pull it off. Smells like Mandarin oranges, honey, and caramel, but tastes of buttered popcorn and citrus. Good raw materials, but trying too hard? **86** —*J.C. (12/15/2004)*

Erwin Sabathi 2005 Poharnig Sauvignon Blanc (Styria) $32. Pungent and herbal, with grassy notes that overlay bright lime fruit and a solid mineral base. Structured, this could age nicely over the next 5–8 years, much like a good Bordeaux blanc. **88** —*J.C. (12/1/2006)*

Erwin Sabathi 2004 Poharnig Sauvignon Blanc (Südsteiermark) $30.
Distinctive stuff, featuring scents of sweet corn and passion fruit accented by hints of resin and mint, then more standard melon and passion fruit flavors on the palate. Medium-bodied, but this wine seems to grow in intensity and pungency on the finish. **87** —*J.C. (8/1/2006)*

Erwin Sabathi 2003 Poharnig Sauvignon Blanc (Styria) $30. Certainly it's minerally, but beyond that the bouquet runs a touch mute. Clean on the palate, with green apple, lemon-lime, and that same minerality found on the nose. Light to medium in body, and easy to drink. **87** *(7/1/2005)*

Erwin Sabathi 2003 Possnitzberg Sauvignon Blanc (Styria) $35. An exciting Sauvignon Blanc from Styria, the Possnitzberg bottling is smoky and minerally, yet at the same time wonderfully ripe, boasting peach and citrus flavors and a full-bodied, concentrated mouthfeel. Finishes long. **90** —*J.C. (12/15/2004)*

Erwin Sabathi 2005 Pössnitzberg Sauvignon Blanc (Styria) $37. Not as attractive as the Poharnig, Sabathi's Pössnitzberg bottling shows some overtly vegetal aromas of bell pepper and crushed tomato leaf. It's plump and viscous, showing good sugar ripeness, but the flavors are just too green to garner a higher rating. **86** —*J.C. (12/1/2006)*

Erwin Sabathi 2004 Pössnitzberg Sauvignon Blanc (South Styria) $35.
Starts off with smoky-minerally notes that are quickly joined by green apple and lime aromas. In the mouth, it's fresh and crisp, with tangy citrus flavors balanced by more sedate apple notes. Could be more complex, but this is tasty stuff. **88** —*J.C. (8/1/2006)*

F X PICHLER

F X Pichler 2001 Dürnsteiner Kellerberg Smaragd Grüner Veltliner (Wachau) $NA. F.X. Pichler, one of the icons of Austrian wine, never shies away from power in his wines. This wine is seriously packed with concentration of fruit, rich spices, and pepper, and flavors of ripe apricots. But there is acidity there, along with a creamy vanilla character, which bring the wine to a harmonious finish. **92** —*R.V. (5/1/2005)*

FAMILIE ZULL

Familie Zull 2003 DAC Grüner Veltliner (Weinviertel) $23. The DAC, or Districtus Austriae Controllatus, is a new form of appellation applied to Grüner Veltliner in Weinviertel. This wine is typical of the taste profile of DAC wines: fresh and flowery, with crisp fruit and peppery spice. **86** —*R.V. (5/1/2005)*

FEILER-ARTINGER

Feiler-Artinger 2000 Umriss Blaufränkisch (Burgenland) $25. A deeply colored, rich, complex, juicy wine with generous fruit. Piles of ripe flavors and delicious acidity. Powerful, open red fruits with a touch of spice build up to a fine but simple wine. **85** —*R.V. (11/1/2002)*

Feiler-Artinger 2002 Umriss Trocken Blaufränkisch (Burgenland) $20.
Cranberry, orange zest, and clove aromas with leather and cherry flavors. This medium-weight wine is complex enough to hold a taster's interest over a full meal, yet bold enough to serve with full-flavored dishes. Finishes with hints of chocolate and clove. **87** —*J.C. (5/1/2005)*

Feiler-Artinger 2000 1006 Cabernet Sauvignon-Merlot (Burgenland) $60.
The 1006 refers to the year of the founding of Austria—not the vintage. This dark wine is a blend of 70% Cabernet Sauvignon and 30% Merlot. There are aromas of vanilla and ripe black fruits. On the palate, there is polished new wood and sweet tannins along with toast and spice. The whole effect is modern, rich, and smooth. **90** —*R.V. (11/1/2002)*

Feiler-Artinger 2002 Solitaire Red Blend (Burgenland) $50. This blend of Blaufränkisch, Cabernet Franc, and Zweigelt spent some time in oak, and it shows in the wine's caramel, cinnamon and vanilla aromas. But aside from the oak, there's also some lush fruit (brandied cherries) and a smooth mouthfeel. Seems ready to drink now, so why wait? **88** —*J.C. (3/1/2006)*

Feiler-Artinger 2000 Solitaire Red Blend (Burgenland) $60. An exotic blend of Blaufränkisch, Zweigelt, and Cabernet Franc. Huge new wood aromas dominate soft fruits. A sweet, rich wine with black tar, fruit flavors, and violets. Acidity and the red fruits of the Zweigelt and Blaufränkisch blend easily and successfully with the sophisticated flavors of the Cabernet. **91** —*R.V. (11/1/2002)*

Feiler-Artinger 2002 Beerenauslese Traminer (Burgenland) $NA. Aromas of lychees and spice follow through on the palate with ripe, spicy fruit, layering dry botrytis with richness. Light amounts of acidity suggest this is a wine which will age quickly. **88** —*R.V. (5/1/2004)*

Feiler-Artinger 1999 Ruster Ausbruch Welschriesling (Burgenland) $50. The initial aroma is curiously farmyardy and rustic. The palate, though, is fresher, with attractive fruit flavors along with sweetness and a touch of tropical fruit. The finish is sweet but balanced by good acidity. **88** —*R.V. (11/1/2002)*

Feiler-Artinger 1998 Ruster Ausbruch Welschriesling (Burgenland) $50. The Ausbruch style is typical of the Burgenland. It lies somewhere between Beerenauslese and TBA in sweetness, from the most shrivelled berries. This blend of Welschriesling and Weissburgunder has lovely acidity combined with sweet, poised fruit and powerful levels of dry botrytis. A complete wine, and still developing. **93 Editors' Choice** —*R.V. (11/1/2002)*

Feiler-Artinger 2000 White Blend (Burgenland) $NA. This wine is a 50/50 blend of Pinot Gris and Neuburger (but the composition changes vintage to vintage). Flavors of quince, pears, and a touch of spice give this beautifully sweet wine an exotic character. The wine finishes clean, fresh, and with great acidity. **90** —*R.V. (5/1/2004)*

Feiler-Artinger 2001 Ausbruch White Blend (Burgenland) $40. A rich, luxuriant wine, with smooth, ripe fruit balancing sweet honey, dry botrytis, and poised, fresh acidity. A toasty, vanilla flavor gives an exotic feel to this wine, which should last for many years. **93 Cellar Selection** —*R.V. (5/1/2004)*

Feiler-Artinger 2002 Auslese White Blend (Burgenland) $25. A fresh wine, intended by cellarmasters Hans and Kurt Feiler as a wine for food, with crisp acidity lying over layers of dry botrytis. This is delicious with savory foods and cheeses. **87** —*R.V. (5/1/2004)*

Feiler-Artinger 2002 Beerenauslese White Blend (Burgenland) $27. A blend of Welschriesling, Weissburgunder and Chardonnay, in a fresh style, with crisp but ripe fruits, flavors of apricots, and underlying honeyed botrytis. A deliciously fresh, lively wine. **89** —*R.V. (5/1/2004)*

Feiler-Artinger 1999 Ruster Ausbruch Essenz White Blend (Burgenland) $60. This beautifully stuctured wine is a blend of Chardonnay and Weissburgunder. Sweet, but with great acidity and lovely ripe fruit flavors, it is the delicious quintessence of sweet wines, balancing honeyed flavors with dry botrytis. **92** —*R.V. (11/1/2002)*

Feiler-Artinger 2004 Ruster Ausbruch Essenz 375ml White Blend (Burgenland) $50. Incredibly sweet and syrupy, this is an intense dessert wine from one of Austria's masters of the genre. Dried apricots dominate, but there are also complex notes of roasted coffee, orange marmalade, and dark honey. Long on the finish, with enough acidity to keep it from being cloying. For the quality, the price makes it a relative bargain. **92 Editors' Choice** —*J.C. (12/1/2006)*

Feiler-Artinger 1998 Ruster Ausbruch Pinot Cuvée White Blend (Burgenland) $60. A blend of Weissburgunder, Grauburgunder, Chardonnay, and Neuburger produces high levels of fresh acidity that give the intense sweetness a lift. A poised, elegant wine with strong apricot flavors. **92** —*R.V. (11/1/2002)*

Feiler-Artinger 2004 Ruster Ausbruch Pinot Cuvée 375ml White Blend (Burgenland) $38. Sweet and rich, but not as nuanced as Feiler-Artinger's more expensive Essenz bottling, this is still an excellent dessert wine. Dried apricot and pineapple flavors turn a bit caramelly on the finish. A blend of Pinot Blanc, Pinot Gris, Neuberger, and Chardonnay. **90** —*J.C. (12/1/2006)*

Feiler-Artinger 2001 Ruster Ausbruch Pinot Cuvée White Riesling (Burgenland) $37. This beautiful wine shows great elegance. It is not just sweet, it is sophisticated as well, bringing delicious acidity, dryness, and exotic fruits. To finish, there is a fruit salad of flavors, combined with spice and a lingering aftertaste. **94** —*R.V. (2/1/2006)*

Felsner 2005 Gedersdorfer Moosburgerin Grüner Veltliner (Kremstal) $20. Makes an interesting contrast to the spice-driven flavors of Felsner's Vordernberg bottling, by offering honeyed stones and peaches in a medium-bodied format. Finishes with bright notes of citrus zest. **88** —*J.C. (12/1/2006)*

Felsner 2004 Gedersdorfer Moosburgerin Grüner Veltliner (Kremstal) $15. Stony and minerally, with some nectarine and citrus scents that develop into grapefruit and stone fruit flavors on the palate. Clean and fresh without being hard or edgy, this is nicely balanced and nicely priced. **87** —*J.C. (11/15/2005)*

Felsner 2005 Gedersdorfer Vordernberg Grüner Veltliner (Kremstal) $26. A broad, mouthfilling Grüner Veltliner with distinctive scents of ginger and cinnamon backed by spice-drop flavors. This is satisfyingly warm and spice-driven, with a long, peppery finish. **88** —*J.C. (12/1/2006)*

Felsner 2004 Gedersdorfer Vordernberg Grüner Veltliner (Kremstal) $19. Smells and tastes like a combination of sun-warmed stones and white peaches. It's round and ripe, showing just a touch of alcoholic warmth on the finish. **86** —*J.C. (11/15/2005)*

Felsner 1999 Icon Eiswein 375 ml Grüner Veltliner (Kremstal) $35. This medium-bodied eiswein retains a strong sense of varietal character, layering white pepper aromas over sweet apricot and candied pineapple flavors. A bit short on the finish, but a solid effort overall. **87** —*J.C. (3/1/2006)*

Felsner 2004 Lössterrassen Grüner Veltliner (Kremstal) $10. The 2004 vintage didn't yield blockbuster Grüner Veltliners, but the lower-level wines seem particularly attractive. This offering boasts a pronounced leafiness, but also ripe, almost honeyed flavors and creamy texture. Some crisp acids on the finish give it the necessary edge to serve as an apéritif or alongside food. **87 Best Buy** —*J.C. (8/1/2006)*

Felsner 2004 Rohrendorfer Leithen Alte Reben Trocken Grüner Veltliner (Kremstal) $20. Round and plump in the mouth, with aromas of celery greens and flavors of white peaches, citrus, and herbs. Soft and a bit warming on the finish. **85** —*J.C. (11/15/2005)*

Felsner 2005 Rohrendorfer Gebling Riesling (Kremstal) $23. A bracingly acidic dry Riesling, this starts out with slatey, smoky aromas and hints of apple and clover, then adds crisp green-apple and grapefruit flavors. Finishes dry and tart, accented by grapefruit zest. **87** —*J.C. (12/1/2006)*

Felsner 2004 Rohrendorfer Gebling Riesling (Kremstal) $18. Starts off with hints of almond that quickly recede to reveal pear and lime scents. The apple, pear, and citrus flavors blend harmoniously, ending on a tart, racy note. A bit simply fruity, but elegant and well-made. **87** —*J.C. (3/1/2006)*

Felsner 2002 Gedersdorfer Weitgasse Zweigelt (Kremstal) $19. Opens with complex aromas of cranberry and cherry, but also dark chocolate, molasses, and barbecue sauce. A bit leaner in body than some of the other Zweigelts tasted for this issue, but also more interesting. Finishes with hints of game and citrus. **88** —*J.C. (5/1/2005)*

Fischer 2003 Pinot Noir (Thermenregion) $38. The mouthfeel of this Austrian Pinot Noir is supple and lush, but the aromas are a bit dull, filled with roasted fruit and charred oak. The plum and black cherry flavors seem lightly caramelized and lacking length. **84** —*J.C. (8/1/2006)*

Fischer 2004 Fasangarten Classic Zweigelt (Thermenregion) $17. Filled with blackberries and pepper on the nose, this is a bit Syrah-like in aromatic profile. Medium-bodied, it carries the flavors well, ending with tart berries and more pepper. Could stand more length and concentration, but this is tasty nonetheless. **87** —*J.C. (8/1/2006)*

Forstreiter 2003 Exclusiv Grüner Veltliner (Kremstal) $15. A youthful wine, quite rich but not yet integrated, with good fresh fruit and crisp acidity. It should develop into an elegant, fruit-driven wine that will be great as an apéritif. **88** —*R.V. (5/1/2005)*

Forstreiter 2003 Kremser Kogl Bergwein Grüner Veltliner (Kremstal) $11. Fine, crisp, fresh fruit from a sand and loam vineyard close to the

Danube, opposite Krems. It has is an attractive green streak, which gives the wine a lift and acidity. **89**—*R.V. (5/1/2005)*

Forstreiter 2003 Schiefer Grüner Veltliner (Kremstal) $18. A mineral character dominates this wine, a product of the terraced vineyards above the Danube. It is spicy and peppery, with pure white peach flavors and crisp, finishing acidity. It's still young, and should develop over four to five years. **90**—*R.V. (5/1/2005)*

FRANZ HIRTZBERGER

Franz Hirtzberger 1997 Grauburgunder (Austria) $37. 84 *(5/1/2004)*

Franz Hirtzberger 2003 Honivogl Smaragd Grüner Veltliner (Wachau) $70. Rich and full-bodied, with flamboyant aromas and flavors of honey, melon, and spice that cascade across the palate in a powerful wave. Long and intense on the finish. Tastes great now, but with its impeccable balance and concentration it should age wonderfully, too. **91**—*J.C. (5/1/2005)*

Franz Hirtzberger 2003 Rotes Tor Federspiel Grüner Veltliner (Wachau) $25. Classically proportioned GV, with good balance and a plump mouthfeel that fills out the wine's celery leaf, mineral, and apple flavors. Long and stony on the finish. **87**—*J.C. (11/15/2005)*

Franz Hirtzberger 2004 Rotes Tor Smaragd Grüner Veltliner (Wachau) $46. Rather herbal and peppery on the nose, instantly marking it as Grüner. Honey and green apple flavors merge easily on the weighty, slightly oily palate, finishing long and peppery. **90**—*J.C. (3/1/2006)*

Franz Hirtzberger 2003 Singerriedal Smaragd Riesling (Wachau) $80. I wanted to like this wine more than I did. It starts off with lovely aromas of tangerines, apples, and pineapples, as well as a delicate floral note. The mouthfeel is full, the stage is set. But the flavors seem a bit simple and fruity and the finish lacks the length expected of a wine of this pedigree. It's very good, but not the legend it should be. **88**—*J.C. (5/1/2005)*

Franz Hirtzberger 2004 Spitzer Hochrain Smaragd Riesling (Wachau) $66. Thickly textured in the mouth, serving only to amplify the initial impressions of minerals and crushed stones. Apple and citrus flavors add crispness, turning downright zesty on the finish. Drink now-2020. **90**—*J.C. (8/1/2006)*

Franz Hirtzberger 2004 Spitzer Singerriedel Smaragd Riesling (Wachau) $80. Classic, cellar-worthy Riesling, combining a ripe, creamy mouthfeel with great length and precision on the finish. Citrus and apple scents start it off, joined by riper pear flavors and hints of orange and bergamot. Long on the finish, picking up layers of peppery, minerally spice. Drink 2014-2020, or beyond. **91 Cellar Selection**—*J.C. (8/1/2006)*

Franz Hirtzberger 2001 Steinterrassen Federspiel Riesling (Wachau) $24. A beautifully elegant, focused wine, full of racy, steely fruit, managing to combine fullness with lightness and an intensely dry aftertaste. Hirtzberger's 29-acre vineyard is in the western Wachau village of Spitz, where the Rieslings are aged in large acacia wood barrels. **93**—*R.V. (8/1/2003)*

FRANZ LETH

Franz Leth 2005 Scheiben Grüner Veltliner (Donauland) $35. This is a style of wine that gives the lie to the belief that Grüner Veltliner does not age. With its pure, ripe fruit, its complex flavors of spice, red apples, backed by a firm structure, this will certainly improve over the next two to three years. **90 Cellar Selection**—*R.V. (10/1/2006)*

Franz Leth 2005 Scheiben Roter Veltliner (Donauland) $26. Franz Leth's Wagram vineyard contains some of the only 500 acres of Roter Veltliner in Austria. It makes a very fruity wine, with ripe apricot flavors. Full-bodied, fragrant, and spicy. **89**—*R.V. (10/1/2006)*

Franz Leth 2003 Selection Roter Veltliner (Donauland) $28. Roter Veltliner, despite its name, is a white wine grape, grown in small quantities in Kremstal and Donauland. It produces a crisp style of wine, like this special-selection wine. But the fruit is also ripe, and the wine has pepper, spice, and flavors of yellow fruits. **89**—*R.V. (5/1/2005)*

FRANZ MITTELBACH

Franz Mittelbach 2002 Tegernseerhof Bergdistel Dürnsteiner Grüner Veltliner (Wachau) $24. Solid Grüner, with hints of peach and pear fruit alongside notes of smoke and minerals. Soft, round mouthfeel, hints of

fresh green fruits and only a hint of pepper make this immediately approachable. **86**—*J.C. (12/15/2004)*

FREIE WEINGÄRTNER WACHAU

Freie Weingärtner Wachau 2004 Grüner Veltliner (Wachau) $9. A great value in Grüner Veltliner, this medium-bodied offering features a saliva-inducing blend of spices, garden herbs, and ripe fruit, shot through with a dose of dry minerality. True to the grape, and true to the terroir—all for less than $10. **88 Best Buy**—*J.C. (8/1/2006)*

Freie Weingärtner Wachau 2001 Domaine Wachau Achleiten Smaragd Grüner Veltliner (Wachau) $27. The intensely mineral, steely character of this wine is classic Wachau Grüner Veltliner. Hints of pepper, herbs, and spice act as a foil to the acidic and almost granite-like character of the wine. This should age well over 5 years. **88**—*R.V. (11/1/2002)*

Freie Weingärtner Wachau 2001 Domaine Wachau Terrassen Federspiel Grüner Veltliner (Wachau) $11. Herbs and spices dominate this wine, with citrus on the nose and elegant fruit and a mineral character on the palate. Attractive and fresh. **86** *(11/1/2002)*

Freie Weingärtner Wachau 2004 Riesling (Wachau) $11. Smells inviting, with notes of lime, fresh greens, and hints of peach that call to mind warm spring days. On the palate, it loses some of that grace, delivering chunky pear and citrus flavors in a medium-bodied package. Still good, especially for the price. **85**—*J.C. (3/1/2006)*

Freie Weingärtner Wachau 2001 Domäne Wachau Achleiten Smaragd Riesling (Wachau) $30. This bone-dry, poised wine is finely structured with floral aromas and flavors. It opens deliciously in the mouth, long-lasting and rich. **88**—*R.V. (8/1/2003)*

Freie Weingärtner Wachau 1995 Exceptional Reserve Riesling (Wachau) $35. **86**—*M.S. (5/1/2000)*

GRAF KOENIGSEGG

Graf Koenigsegg 2005 Velt 1 Grüner Veltliner (Burgenland) $11. Although the wine inside might not be the most complex GV you'll ever sample, it's light, clean, and fresh, with gingery, spicy nuances to the pear and apple flavors. Probably best as an apéritif, but it has enough intensity to match scallop or shrimp dishes. **87 Best Buy**—*J.C. (12/1/2006)*

GRITSCH MAURITIUSHOF

Gritsch Mauritiushof 2003 Singerriedel Grüner Veltliner (Wachau) $27. A riper, gentler style of Grüner, with trademark perfumy aromas of celery stalk and white pepper giving way to ripe peach and nectarine flavors. Soft and round in the mouth; there are no hard edges here. **87**—*J.C. (12/15/2004)*

Gritsch Mauritiushof 2003 1000 Eimerberg Select Neuburger (Wachau) $19. Neuburger is the grape variety, a cross between Weissburgunder (Pinot Blanc) and Sylvaner. The result is a richly textured white with lovely floral notes on the nose and flavors of honey, ripe peaches, and citrus. Finishes soft, with hints of dried spices. **88**—*J.C. (11/15/2005)*

Gritsch Mauritiushof 2003 1000 Eimerberg Smaragd Riesling (Wachau) $25. Terrific nearly-dry Riesling. Fruit-filled yet not simple at all, boasting a harmonious mix of apple, pear, and peach fruit, accented by honey and a hint of anise. It's large-scaled, unctuous on the palate, yet never seems heavy. A blend of botrytized and clean fruit. **92 Editors' Choice**—*J.C. (11/15/2005)*

Gritsch Mauritiushof 2005 Spitzer 1000-Eimerberg Smaragd Riesling (Wachau) $28. Given the prices for top Austrian Rieslings, this represents a bargain. It's rich and intense, with hints of honey, spice, and smoke that twine around a core of powerful mineral flavors. It's capped off by a long, mouthcoating finish. **92 Editors' Choice**—*J.C. (12/1/2006)*

GROSS

Gross 1997 Grauburgunder (Austria) $20. 84 *(5/1/2004)*

Gross 1998 Sauvignon Blanc (Styria) $37. 88—*M.S. (5/1/2000)*

GSELLMANN & GSELLMANN

Gsellmann & Gsellmann 2000 Gelber Muskateller Trockenbeerenauslese Muskateller (Burgenland) $35. Dried apricot and ripe pear aromas carry just a hint of volatile acidity, but once past that it reveals dusty, earthy flavors alongside orange marmalade and dried apricots. Sweet and viscous, it finishes with lingering spice notes. **87**—*J.C. (12/15/2004)*

Gsellmann & Gsellmann 2001 Blauburgunder Pinot Noir (Burgenland) $26. Seems past its peak already, with fading color and aromas, and flavors of sweaty leather and sour cherries. Candied and liqueur-like on the finish **81**—*J.C. (5/1/2005)*

Gsellmann & Gsellmann 2001 Pannobile Red Blend (Burgenland) $20. The unique combination of chocolate and spice in the aromas of this wine calls to mind chocolate Teddy Grahams, but its by no means a kiddie wine. It's full-bodied and soft, with flavors of tobacco, earth, and spice and a smoky, coffee-like note on the finish. A blend of Zweigelt, Blaüfrankisch, and Merlot. **86**—*J.C. (5/1/2005)*

Gsellmann & Gsellmann 2001 Eiswein White Blend (Burgenland) $25. This blend of Scheurebe and Welchsriesling boasts peppery notes atop sweet, concentrated fruit flavors. Apricot and dried citrus flavors lead the way, finishing with pepper and orange notes. **88**—*J.C. (12/15/2004)*

Gsellmann & Gsellmann 1998 Vom Goldberg Chardonnay-Weissburgunder Trockenbeerenauslese 375 ml White Blend (Burgenland) $25. Orange in color, with scents of toffee and burnt coffee, this is an oddly overdone TBA. Flavors of overcooked caramel deliver sweetness, lemony notes add a tart edge to the finish. **85**—*J.C. (12/15/2004)*

Gsellmann & Gsellmann 1999 Von Golser Goldberg Beerenauslese White Blend (Burgenland) $20. A relatively inexpensive beerenauslese, this blend of Scheurebe and Weissburgunder (Pinot Blanc) is medium in body and not overly sweet, its apricot and candied orange peel flavors balanced by a bitter marmalade note that persists through the finish. **87**—*J.C. (12/15/2004)*

HAFNER KOSHER

Hafner Kosher 2002 Pinot Gris (Burgenland) $8. A thin wine which has some freshness but loses intensity fading into light, green, fresh flavors. **83**—*R.V. (2/1/2006)*

HANS IGLER

Hans Igler 2003 Pinot Blanc (Burgenland) $15. Scents of honey and underripe melon are bolstered by sturdy pear and citrus flavors. Finishes clean and citrusy; refreshing. **85**—*J.C. (11/15/2005)*

Hans Igler 2002 Ab Ericio Red Blend (Burgenland) $62. Igler's top red is a blend of 40% Merlot, 40% Blaufränkisch, and 20% Zweigelt, aged in oak for 21 months. The result is a wine redolent of cherries, tobacco, and spice with a creamy, supple mouthfeel. Flavors lean toward cigar box and vanilla, with just enough cherry fruit in support. Drink now. **89**—*J.C. (3/1/2006)*

Hans Igler 2002 Vulcano Red Blend (Burgenland) $35. This blend of Blaüfrankisch, Cabernet Sauvignon, Zweigelt, and Merlot is very smooth and creamy on the palate, delivering cherry-berry and coffee flavors in a medium-bodied format. The long finish features soft, dusty tannins and accents of clove and menthol. Drink now and over the next few years. **88**—*J.C. (5/1/2005)*

Hans Igler 2003 Classic Zweigelt (Burgenland) $17. Broad and mouthfilling, with smoke and beet aromas and flavors. Finishes on a slightly tangy note, prolonging the finish and giving it a sense of liveliness. **85**—*J.C. (3/1/2006)*

HANS PITNAUER

Hans Pitnauer 2003 Franz-Josef Cabernet Blend (Carnuntum) $39. The wine is not named after Austria's emperor, but after a Pitnauer family member. The blend of Cabernet Sauvignon and Zweigelt works well, giving a powerful, dry, concentrated wine with big tannins. At this stage, the wood is rather too dominant, but that should soften over the next year. **91**—*R.V. (10/1/2006)*

Hans Pitnauer 2004 Quo Vadis Merlot-Cabernet Sauvignon (Carnuntum) $37. A complex blend of Merlot, Cabernet Sauvignon, and Zweigelt, this rich wine is smooth, with a structure that sits easily on the fruit. The small proportion of Zweigelt provides a pepper character, but the dominating Merlot gives ripe, juicy flavor. **90**—*R.V. (10/1/2006)*

Hans Pitnauer 2005 Ried Bildenspitz Sauvignon Blanc (Carnuntum) $18. A simple, fresh wine that has hints of tropical fruits as well as crisp acidity.

There is plenty of green fruit flavor to make this a fine food wine. **86**—*R.V. (10/1/2006)*

Hans Pitnauer 2004 Bienenfresser Zweigelt Bärnreiser Zweigelt (Carnuntum) $23. This red from the Bärnreiser vineyard, named after the Bienenfresser, or bee eater, is packed with great, ripe, chewy flavors and textures, very peppery, and with layers of wood for complexity. **89**—*R.V. (10/1/2006)*

HEIDI SCHROCK

Heidi Schrock 1999 Ausbruch Pinot Blanc (Burgenland) $78. A hugely sweet wine, almost the essence of botyrtis, made from 100% Pinot Blanc, with marmalade and orange peel flavors. There is a high level of acidity under all this sweetness, giving balance and complexity. This is as rich and concentrated as many TBAs. **91 Cellar Selection**—*R.V. (5/1/2004)*

Heidi Schrock 2002 Ruster Ausbruch White Blend (Burgenland) $65. This is a mélange of four grapes—Pinot Blanc, Pinot Gris, Yellow Muscat, and Sauvignon Blanc. Inevitably each lends its character to what is an impressive complex wine, with high levels of acidity masked by the sweet orange flavors and layers of botrytis. It should age over many years. **91**—*R.V. (5/1/2004)*

Heidi Schrock 2001 Ruster Ausbruch White Blend (Burgenland) $67. A rare blend of Sauvignon Blanc and Furmint, the grape used in Tokaji in Hungary, this is a concentrated, elegant wine, almost delicate yet giving great sweetness and balancing acidity. This is a sweet wine that demands rich food, like blue cheeses, smoked meats, fruit desserts. **90**—*R.V. (5/1/2004)*

HEINRICH

Heinrich 2004 Blaufränkisch (Burgenland) $19. Smells nice, with pure boysenberry and mulberry notes garnished with vanilla, but turns crisp and tart on the palate, adding hints of cocoa and a slightly lactic note on the finish. **86**—*J.C. (3/1/2006)*

Heinrich 2001 Pannobile Red Blend (Neusiedlersee) $34. "Pannobile" is a designation being used by Burgenland producers for the top blended reds, but this one is a bit of a disappointment. Coffee and cinnamon on the nose, with some green, herbal notes poking through the veneer of oak. Flavors are even more herbal and oregano-like, but supple and soft on the palate. Finishes with molasses and coffee notes. **83**—*J.C. (5/1/2005)*

Heinrich 1997 Red Red Blend (Burgenland) $16. **82**—*J.C. (5/1/2000)*

Heinrich 2004 Zweigelt (Burgenland) $19. A hint of vinyl on the nose detracts from this wine's otherwise positive impression. White pepper and blackberry-blueberry flavors are carried along on a smooth mouthfeel, while supple tannins and a cocoa note chime in on the finish. **83**—*J.C. (8/1/2006)*

Heinrich 2003 Zweigelt (Burgenland) $19. One of the better Austrian reds we've tried, with mouthwatering aromas of smoke, black cherry, cinnamon and clove. So ripe, it seems slightly creamy-textured on the palate. Very clean, with oak and fruit in nice balance. Fresh and long on the finish, without much tannin. Drink now and over the next few years. **89**—*J.C. (5/1/2005)*

HEISS

Heiss 1999 Trockenbeerenauslese Riesling (Burgenland) $50. There's a bit of VA to this wine, but also honeyed pear and pineapple fruit sweet enough to satisfy ardent sweet tooths. **86**—*J.C. (12/15/2004)*

Heiss 2001 Barrique Beerenauslese Sauvignon Blanc (Neusiedlersee) $35. Nicely done late-harvest Sauvignon Blanc, blending apricot and pineapple aromatics with flavors of honey and tangerines. It's medium in body, with a finish that's honeyed without being cloying. **90 Editors' Choice**—*J.C. (12/15/2004)*

Heiss 2001 Eiswein 375 ml Traminer (Neusiedlersee) $45. This is really sweet stuff, but it features some lovely dried spice notes that add complexity and balance out some of the residual sugar. Pears and honey on the nose, a slightly viscous mouthfeel and a long, honeyed finish. **91**—*J.C. (12/15/2004)*

AUSTRIA

Heiss 1998 Weissburgunder-Sauvignon Blanc Trockenbeerenauslese 375 ml White Blend (Neusiedlersee) $45. Impressive more for its over-the-top richness than its overall balance, with layers of honey, dried apricots, and orange marmalade all laid on thick and sweet. Persistent on the finish. 90 —J.C. (12/15/2004)

HELMUT LANG

Helmut Lang 1999 TBA Chardonnay (Neusiedlersee) $35. Very rich and sweet, with toasty elements and some spice. This Chardonnay is an exotic wine, with cinnamon flavors as well as sweetness. Just lacks the extra edge of acidity to give it distinction. 89 —R.V. (11/1/2002)

Helmut Lang 1997 TBA Chardonnay (Neusiedlersee) $35. There are aromas of vanilla and a touch of tropical fruits. The palate is soft and sweet, with some vanilla. There are hints of acidity underneath, but they are faint hints indeed. 85 —R.V. (11/1/2002)

Helmut Lang 1999 Beerenauslese Gewürztraminer (Neusiedlersee) $35. The aromas of this wine are dominated by rich spice, like Turkish Delight. The palate is soft and unctuous, with big spice flavors and a layer of dryness. This is an unusual wine, with rich spice rather than sweetness. 90 —R.V. (11/1/2002)

Helmut Lang 1998 TBA Rheinriesling Riesling (Neusiedlersee) $35. Hedgerow fruit is heavily aromatic with thick texture and layers of sweetness. This is a rich, concentrated, syrupy wine, with aromatic fruit, but it lacks acidity for balance. 84 —R.V. (11/1/2002)

Helmut Lang 2000 Beerenauslese Sauvignon Blanc (Neusiedlersee) $NA. Aromas of quince and a palate of sweet, toffee flavors make this a rich wine, with flavors of fig jelly. But it is unbalanced due to its almost total lack of acidity. 83 —R.V. (11/1/2002)

Helmut Lang 1999 Beerenauslese Samling 88 White Blend (Neusiedlersee) $35. Aromas of acidity and sweet fruits are immediately appealing. On the palate, there is a level of tension between tannins, sweetness, and acidity that gives it great attraction. It lacks complexity, but is delicious. 88 —R.V. (11/1/2002)

Helmut Lang 1997 Eiswein Cuvée White Blend (Neusiedlersee) $38. There are intense aromas of vanilla and sweet fruits, while the palate is light and rather undefined, with some caramel flavors. It is opulently sweet, but one-dimensional. 81 —R.V. (11/1/2002)

Helmut Lang 1999 TBA Samling 88 White Blend (Neusiedlersee) $NA. 86 —R.V. (11/1/2002)

HIEDLER

Hiedler 2003 Heiligenstein Riesling (Kamptal) $49. Ludwig Hiedler owns 2.5 acres in the Heiligenstein vineyard, planted to Riesling. This wine is typical of the vineyard, full of minerality as well as intense flavors of apricots and a touch of citrus. It is powerful and should age slowly over the next 10 years. 91 —R.V. (8/1/2005)

Hiedler 2003 Maximum Riesling (Kamptal) $59. An immediately attractive wine that still suggests great potential. With its aromas of summer flowers and its flavors of yellow peaches, citrus and a light layer of minerality, it is crisp yet full. 89 —R.V. (8/1/2005)

Hiedler 2003 Steinhaus Riesling (Kamptal) $34. A soft, full wine with attractive acidity and good green flavors. Still young, it has some intensity, but will develop early, giving a delicious flowery wine with tropical fruit flavors. 87 —R.V. (8/1/2005)

Hiedler 2005 Zöbinger Heiligenstein Riesling (Kamptal) $45. This hugely mineral wine boasts a great structure and full body. Its weight is balanced with peach, pear, and pineapple flavors that give it freshness, fruitiness, and also refreshing, crisp acidity. 91 —R.V. (10/1/2006)

HILLINGER

Hillinger 2003 St. Laurent (Burgenland) $27. No doubt this is a modernist's rendition of St. Laurent, with its notes of smoke, cinnamon, toast, and vanilla, but what stands out is this wine?s velvety mouthfeel, vibrant black cherry fruit, and long, mouthwatering finish. 90 Editors' Choice —J.C. (3/1/2006)

Hillinger 2004 Welschriesling (Burgenland) $9. This light, crisp white is the perfect counterpoint to a hot, lazy, summer afternoon. The slightly leafy, green apple and lime scents are a pick-me-up, followed by some delightfully pure and crystalline flavors ranging from rainwater to fresh greens, apple and pears to citrus. Clean and refreshing on the finish. 88 Best Buy —J.C. (8/1/2006)

Hillinger 2002 White Blend (Neusiedlersee) $55. The equivalent of a TBA, this blend of Chardonnay and Sauvignon Blanc is bottled without varietal indication. Inviting aromas of sweet toffee lead to flavors of ripe, fleshy apricots with layers of acidity to balance. This is a luscious, concentrated wine. 88 —R.V. (5/1/2004)

Hillinger 2004 Zweigelt (Burgenland) $18. A plump, juicy rendition of Zweigelt, with white pepper accenting blackberry and mulberry fruit. Long and succulent on the finish. 90 Editors' Choice —J.C. (8/1/2006)

Hillinger 2003 Trocken Zweigelt (Burgenland) $17. Gets off to a bit of a rough start, overwhelmed by charred, burnt coffee aromas—but don't give up on it. The flavors are much fruitier, featuring liqueur-like black cherry notes. The silky finish picks up hints of chocolate, but keeps pumping out the fruit. 87 —J.C. (5/1/2005)

HIRSCH

Hirsch 2000 Kammerner Heiligenstein Grüner Veltliner (Kamptal) $20. 88 —J.C. (3/1/2002)

Hirsch 2005 Zöbinger Heiligenstein Grüner Veltliner (Kamptal) $22. This big, opulent, and generous wine is one of the few Heiligenstein wines made of Grüner Veltliner. Its peppery character is tempered with fresh acidity and mineral flavors. 89 —R.V. (10/1/2006)

Hirsch 2005 Zöbinger Heiligenstein Riesling (Kamptal) $40. Spring blossom aromas and flavors of peach, white currants, and lychees are all in this finely balanced, delicate wine. The aftertaste is crisp and intense. 90 —R.V. (10/1/2006)

HOCHRIEGL

Hochriegl NV Extra Trocken Sekt Sparkling Blend (Austria) $19. Although this wine lacks cut and structure, it does display some soft minerality and citrus flavors. 83 —J.C. (6/1/2006)

HOGL

Hogl 2003 Grüner Veltliner (Wachau) $10. This medium-bodied GV is a textbook example, boasting hints of white pepper and anise on the nose, followed by flavors of apples, pears, and spice. Finishes on a minerally note, with an almost dusty quality. 88 Best Buy —J.C. (3/1/2006)

Hogl 2003 Ried Schon Smaragd Grüner Veltliner (Wachau) $22. Nicely balanced for such a big, full-bodied wine, with enough peppery spice, minerally intensity, and pink grapefruit to keep the bulk in check. Does have some baked-apple notes suggestive of a warm vintage, but also a long, peppery finish. Drink now. 91 Editors' Choice —J.C. (5/1/2005)

Hogl 2003 Stammliegenschaften Schön Smaragd Grüner Veltliner (Wachau) $24. Weighty (14% alcohol) yet crisp and peppery, giving it a refreshing feel. Starts with some leafy greens and ripe apples, then adds honey balanced by white pepper. 87 —J.C. (11/15/2005)

Hogl 2003 Terrassen-Spitzergraben Federspiel Grüner Veltliner (Wachau) $15. Based on our tastings, this winery fared well in the heat of 2003. Sure, this federspiel is full and lush—more like a smaragd, but if you put that aside, what is in the bottle excels. Hints of pepper, smoke, honey, melon, and nectarine give great complexity, while the long finish drives home with a firm edge honed in peppery spice. 90 Best Buy —J.C. (8/1/2006)

Hogl 2005 Loibner Vision Smaragd Riesling (Wachau) $30. This is a massive, brooding Riesling that seems to demand time in the cellar. Sweet corn, smoke, and peach kernel notes mark the bouquet, while the powerful mineral flavors are accented by apple and peach. Broad and palate-coating in texture, with a long, oily finish, this is undeniably impressive. 93 Cellar Selection —J.C. (12/1/2006)

Hogl 2003 Loibner Vision Smaragd Riesling (Wachau) $25. Starts with scents reminiscent of honey, ripe apples, and pears and even hints of peach, then gains complexity on the palate, picking up additional notes of spice and mineral. Verges on full-bodied, with the weight carrying over onto the long, slightly oily finish. 88 —J.C. (11/15/2005)

Hogl 2005 Ried Bruck Viessling Smaragd Riesling (Wachau) $38. I had a slight preference for Hogl's less expensive Loibner Vision Riesling

Smaragd, but you can't go wrong with this one either. Thick, viscous, and full-bodied, it's richly fruited but minerally as well, marrying diesel and smoke notes with orange and tangerine flavors. Long and spicy on the finish. **92** —*J.C. (12/1/2006)*

Hogl 2003 Terrassen Spitzergraben Federspiel Riesling (Wachau) $12. On the soft and full-bodied side for a federspiel, with scents of peaches, mineral oil, and ultra-ripe pears and apples. Broad and mouthfilling, with low acidity. **85** —*J.C. (8/1/2005)*

IBY

Iby 2005 Classic Zweigelt (Mittelburgenland) $14. The Mittelburgenland is Austria's red wine land. In the tiny village of Horitschon, the Iby family makes Zweigelt, Blaufränkisch, and a barrel-aged Pinot Noir. This Zweigelt is all about fruit, driving the wine with soft tannins, cranberries, and spice, leaving fresh, ripe acidity to finish. It's a great barbecue wine, and terrific with Mexican food. **86 Best Buy** —*R.V. (11/15/2006)*

ILSE MAZZA

Ilse Mazza 2002 Achleiten Smaragd Riesling (Wachau) $40. Bears a passing resemblance to Grüner Veltliner in its slightly leafy, peppery notes, but also shows apple and citrus flavors that are distinctively Riesling. Long and minerally on the finish. **87** —*J.C. (5/1/2005)*

JAUNEGG

Jaunegg 2002 Muri Chardonnay (Styria) $23. Starts off with apple, melon, and quince aromas, but shows more barrel influence in its flavors of cinnamon and toasted oats. The finish is even toastier, so I would opt for drinking this over the near term rather than aging it. **87** —*J.C. (12/15/2004)*

Jaunegg 2003 Knily Pinot Gris (Styria) $18. Heavily oaked but nice, with caramel, popcorn, and buttered toast comprising the nose. Equally toasty and warm in the mouth, where sweet, ripe white fruit takes on a toffee quality. **88** *(2/1/2006)*

Jaunegg 2002 Knily Pinot Gris (Styria) $20. Really thick and fading, with a heavy nose loaded down with corn and squash aromas. The palate features less than vibrant flavors that veer toward vegetal. Buttery and heavy; a wine that truly makes you wonder: what were the makers thinking? **83** *(2/1/2006)*

Jaunegg 2005 Klassik Sauvignon Blanc (Styria) $16. I prefer this to their pricier single-vineyard bottling, as it offers more assertive flavors and fresher, brighter fruit. It's slightly grassy, but also features passion fruit and currant scents and a minerally foundation. Plump and round without being flabby, with a long finish. **89 Editors' Choice** —*J.C. (12/1/2006)*

Jaunegg 2004 Klassik Sauvignon Blanc (Styria) $15. A bit musky and earthy, with hints of stone fruit and grapefruit that enliven the aromas. Honeyed peaches shine on the ripe, weighty palate, but the flavors fade a bit quickly on the finish.. **86** —*J.C. (11/15/2005)*

Jaunegg 2003 Klassik Sauvignon Blanc (Styria) $15. Not quite as nice as the 2004 version, but still a tasty, lightbodied, mouthful of Sauvignon, with stone and peach notes, a hint of jalapeño, and a chalky, tactile finish. **84** —*J.C. (11/15/2005)*

Jaunegg 2005 Knily Sauvignon Blanc (Styria) $26. Usually a better wine than this, the 2005 Knily shows modest quince and sour yellow plum aromas and rather anemic flavors. I had a substantial preference for the Jaunegg's Klassik bottling. **85** —*J.C. (12/1/2006)*

Jaunegg 2003 Knily Sauvignon Blanc (Styria) $25. Fairly pungent and different; this is no walk in the flower garden. The nose is green and carries a strong whiff of grass and/or alfalfa. In the mouth, it offers solid melon, nectarine, and mango. Better in the mouth than on the nose; it has a pleasantness and open-fruit quality that scores it some points. **87** *(7/1/2005)*

Jaunegg 2005 Daniel's White Blend (Styria) $11. A delightfully refreshing and mouth-watering drink that's light in body but heavy on crisp, citrusy flavors accented by just enough green apple. It's great for the price as an apéritif. A blend of Welschriesling, Weissburgunder (Pinot Blanc), and Sauvignon Blanc. **87 Best Buy** —*J.C. (12/1/2006)*

JOHANN DONABAUM

Johann Donabaum 2003 Berglage Loiben Smaragd Grüner Veltliner (Wachau) $27. Full-bodied, warm, and round in the mouth, this honeyed Grüner Veltliner shows nary a hard edge, marrying melon and pear flavors in a soft, easy-drinking wine that's simply delicious. Drink now. **88** —*J.C. (8/1/2006)*

Johann Donabaum 2002 Loibner Garten Grüner Veltliner Smaragd Grüner Veltliner (Wachau) $19. White pepper and celery leaf aromas are pure Grüner; this would be a good example to throw in a blind tasting. Peppery, minerally flavors are carried on a slightly oily mouthfeel that finishes with just a bit of heaviness. **87** —*J.C. (12/15/2004)*

Johann Donabaum 2003 Loibner Garten Smaragd Grüner Veltliner (Wachau) $19. Shows the ripeness of the vintage and its late-harvested style in its full weight and round, mouthfilling texture, but retains its essential Grüner-ness, combining spicy white pepper and celery leaf notes with just enough stone fruit. Long on the finish, where it adds a dose of minerality. **91** —*J.C. (8/1/2006)*

Johann Donabaum 2002 Spitzer Point Grüner Veltliner (Wachau) $22. As varietally true a GV as you'll find, with very peppery aromas alongside scents of celery leaf. On the palate, there's a blast of pepper, then some plump, slightly vegetal fruit. Not surprisingly, it's peppery on the finish. **87** —*J.C. (12/15/2004)*

Johann Donabaum 2003 Spitzer Point Federspiel Grüner Veltliner (Wachau) $13. Starts off well, with scents of honey and spice, broadening on the palate into ripe pears accented by anise and honeyed notes. Slightly oily in texture, this is a pretty wine that just falls short on the abbreviated finish. **86** —*J.C. (3/1/2006)*

Johann Donabaum 2001 Spitzer Point Reserve Grüner Veltliner (Wachau) $25. With its hints of honey on the nose and a rich, slightly viscous mouthfeel, it's immediately apparent that this is an ambitious effort. Melon and peach flavors are hung on a spine of black pepper, ending in a long, mouthwatering finish. It's dry, but lusciously ripe-tasting. **90** —*J.C. (12/15/2004)*

Johann Donabaum 2003 Bergterrassen Smaragd Riesling (Wachau) $25. This richly textured yet impeccably balanced Riesling features aromas that are just enough off the beaten path to intrigue: cinnamon, brown sugar, red berries, and fresh greens, all wrapped around a solid core of ripe apple and pear fruit. The long, fruit-driven finish fades away elegantly, putting an exclamation point on this wine's quality. **91 Editors' Choice** —*J.C. (11/15/2005)*

Johann Donabaum 2005 Spitzer Setzberg Smaragd Riesling (Wachau) $36. Bursts from the glass with terrific aromas of honey, nuts, and smoky grilled peaches, then adds apple and molten rock of minerality to go along with bold fruit. This round, full-bodied wine with a long, spicy finish should age easily over the next 10 years or more. **91** —*J.C. (12/1/2006)*

JOHANN SCHWARZ

Johann Schwarz 2004 White White Blend (Neusiedlersee) $45. An idiosyncratic wood-aged blend of Chardonnay, Welschriesling, and Semillon, full of ripe, toasty, sweet fruit, with an attractive citrus layer. It's intense, concentrated, and finely polished. **89** —*R.V. (10/1/2006)*

JOHANN TOPF

Johann Topf 2003 Strassertal Grüner Veltliner (Kamptal) $14. Good Grüner doesn't come this well priced very often. Although this rendition shows the rich, oily weight of the vintage, it also retains a strong sense of varietal identity—aromas and flavors of pepper, pear, and stone fruit, backed by a sense of minerality and depth. **88 Editors' Choice** —*J.C. (5/1/2005)*

JOSEF EHMOSER

Josef Ehmoser 2004 Aurum Grüner Veltliner (Donauland) $32. Slightly nutty-smelling at first, but that gives way to floral, fresh green notes alongside citrus and pear. It's on the full-bodied side, with pear and melon fruit accented by greens and a dusting of mineral. Long on the finish, seeming to build in intensity over time. **91 Editors' Choice** —*J.C. (3/1/2006)*

AUSTRIA

Josef Ehmoser 2005 Hohenberg Grüner Veltliner (Donauland) $23. Big, rich, and oily, with intense aromas of smoke and nut oil that build on the palate into flavors of peach kernel, spice, and layers of minerality. A long, mouth-coating finish cinches this wine's quality. The only catch is that of 800 cases produced, only 25 are scheduled to be imported to the U.S. **92 Editors' Choice** —*J.C.* (12/1/2006)

Josef Ehmoser 2004 Hohenberg Grüner Veltliner (Donauland) $22. Slightly nutty and a bit reductive at first, but it opens up to reveal flavors of citrus, peach, and mineral and a soft, tender mouthfeel. Ends on an orangey note. **86** —*J.C.* (11/15/2005)

Josef Ehmoser 2003 Hohenberg Grüner Veltliner (Donauland) $22. The loess slopes of the Hohenberg vineyard come through in the spicy character of this wine. It is still young, with grapefruit flavors, but should develop richness over the next two to three years. **86** —*R.V.* (5/1/2005)

Josef Ehmoser 2003 Hohenberg Grüner Veltliner (Donauland) $22. This medium-weight GV carries plenty of almost fat, ripe, peach flavors, but also a hard stony edge that sets it apart. Faint peppery notes chime in on the nose and palate, while the finish is long and minerally. **88** —*J.C.* (12/15/2004)

Josef Ehmoser 2005 Von Den Terrassen Grüner Veltliner (Donauland) $15. Could 2005 signal a new level of quality for Ehmoser? This entry-level Grüner augurs well, combining fresh citrus and tomato leaf with ripe stone fruits. Slightly creamy notes add textural interest, while the finish is crisp and clean. Good value. **88** —*J.C.* (8/1/2006)

Josef Ehmoser 2004 Von Den Terrassen Grüner Veltliner (Donauland) $15. Reasonably priced for the quality, this light, refreshing GV has aromas of wet stones and fresh greens, followed by crisp, minerally flavors and hints of lettuce leaf. A bit short on the finish, but that's a quibble. **85** —*J.C.* (3/1/2006)

Josef Ehmoser 2003 Von Den Terrassen Grüner Veltliner (Donauland) $15. Made in a lighter, less ripe, and less intense style, this is a typical quaffing Grüner, with modest pear and peach aromas and a hint of pepper. Under-ripe nectarine flavors join apple and herb on the palate before a tart, citrusy finish. **84** —*J.C.* (12/15/2004)

Josef Ehmoser 2003 Pinot Blanc (Donauland) $20. Plump and fruity, with pear, melon and citrus flavors that satisfy without inspiring. Tart and citrusy on the finish, so worth trying with seafood appetizers. **86** —*J.C.* (5/1/2005)

Josef Ehmoser 2005 Vom Gelben Löss Riesling (Donauland) $22. Pungent on the nose, offering up hints of grass and passion fruit. This medium-bodied Riesling shows solid fruit on the palate—melon and grapefruit come to mind—but it lacks a bit of intensity and length on the finish. **86** —*J.C.* (8/1/2006)

Josef Ehmoser 2004 Vom Gelben Löss Riesling (Donauland) $22. Features ripe fruit and citrus flavors, garnished by scents of apples, pears, peaches and a dusting of limestone. It's big and round in the mouth without being soft, ending on a lingering lemony note. **89** —*J.C.* (3/1/2006)

Josef Ehmoser 2003 Vom Gelben Löss Riesling (Donauland) $22. A lean, mineral-driven style, with austere pear and citrus fruit notes that take a back seat to flavors suggestive of graphite. Tart on the finish, picking up some grapefruity notes. **85** —*J.C.* (12/15/2004)

JOSEF HIRSCH

Josef Hirsch 2003 Gaisberg Zöbing Riesling (Kamptal) $45. A fresh, delicate style, with light acidity and flavors of white currants. The wine is round, with some good green flavors, but is also gentle and easy. Ready to drink now. Bottled with a screwcap. **87** —*R.V.* (8/1/2005)

JOSEF JAMEK

Josef Jamek 2000 Smaragd Ried Achleiten Grüner Veltliner (Wachau) $40. You can sense the extra ripeness in this wine's warm aromas of leather and spice. The scents are almost meaty. Dark and warm flavors of Moroccan spices burnish the palate. **86** —*J.C.* (3/1/2002)

Josef Jamek 2003 Ried Klaus Smaragd Riesling (Wachau) $70. This austere style of Riesling accurately reflects the mineral character that comes from the soil of the Ried Klaus vineyard. Lemon zest, white peach, and

spice flavors combine with a steely streak that suggests this wine will age well. **88** —*R.V.* (5/1/2005)

JOSEF SCHMID

Josef Schmid 2002 Alte Reben Priorissa Grüner Veltliner (Kremstal) $30. Schmid's cuvée of old vines exhibits exotic aromas that hints at bacon, pepper and citrus. Flavors continue the theme, with melon, citrus, and pepper flavors accented by a smoked-meat note. Full-bodied and rich, yet balanced, with a long finish that features mingled citrus and melon. **92 Editors' Choice** —*J.C.* (5/1/2005)

Josef Schmid 2002 Urgestein Bergterrassen Riesling (Kremstal) $23. This medium-weight Riesling is fruit-driven, but also boasts notable mineral and spice elements. Has ripe apples and dried spices on the nose, picking up oily, minerally notes on the palate. Finishes with lingering lime flavors. Drink now and over the next 10 years. **90 Editors' Choice** —*J.C.* (5/1/2005)

JURIS

Juris 2001 Altenberg Chardonnay (Burgenland) $13. This is Juris's unoaked, non-malalactic Chard. It's exceptionally intense in ripe, juicy peach, tangerine, and vanilla fruit, supported by extreme acidity, somewhat like an Oz Chard. Finishes lemony and prickly with acidity. Clean, zesty, and very foodworthy. **87** —*S.H.* (10/1/2004)

Juris 2000 Reserve Chardonnay (Burgenland) $25. This is the bells and whistles Chard. It opens with a strong aroma of buttered popcorn, and is very soft and oaky in the mouth. The chief flavor is a lemony, peachy custard, almost honey sweet, although the wine is totally dry. A bit over the top in terms of the winemaker interventions. **85** —*S.H.* (10/1/2004)

Juris 2001 TBA Chardonnay (Burgenland) $45. A round, smooth, creamy wine with a touch of toast and elegant fruit. It is opulent and elegant at the same time, with rich fruit and flavors of honey on the finish. **90** —*R.V.* (5/1/2004)

Juris 2001 TBA Welschriesling (Burgenland) $45. An enormously sweet wine, very intense, but manages to retain a feeling of structure and shape. Like drinking syrup, it has flavors of sweet apricots and still is able to bring acidity into the balance. **92** —*R.V.* (5/1/2004)

Juris 2001 Ausbruch White Blend (Burgenland) $40. This blend of the two unusual grapes of Semling and Bouvier gives an exotic wine with aromas of spice and herbs and wild flowers. The flavors are ripe, with intense honey, rich acidity, and soft acidity. **89** —*R.V.* (5/1/2004)

JURTSCHITSCH SONNHOF

Jurtschitsch Sonnhof 2001 Schenkenbichl Grüner Veltliner Langenlois Grüner Veltliner (Kamptal) $21. A crisp, fresh wine with light, fresh, open fruit. A touch of spice hints at the volcanic and granitic soil of the vineyard, while the fresh acidity highlights the fruit flavors and provides a crisp green aftertaste. **90** —*R.V.* (11/1/2002)

Jurtschitsch Sonnhof 2001 Spiegel Reserve Grüner Veltliner Langenlois Grüner Veltliner (Kamptal) $55. This is a sensational wine. Bright apple and cream aromas set the scene. It is rich and concentrated with a fat, oily texture, and spicy flavors. Spice and ripe fruit make it seem almost like an Alsatian Gewürztraminer. It is certainly powerful, but it has a layer of fine, elegant acidity as well. **94 Editors' Choice** —*R.V.* (11/1/2002)

Jurtschitsch Sonnhof 2001 Steinhaus Grüner Veltliner Langenlois Grüner Veltliner (Kamptal) $21. **89** —*R.V.* (11/1/2002)

Jurtschitsch Sonnhof 2001 Troken Gruve Grüner Veltliner (Kamptal) $16. Subtitled Mein Hausweine—my house wine—this is a light, fresh, slightly spritzy Grüner Veltliner. It has fresh and creamy apple aromas, crisp acidity, and a light, poised palate. **85** —*R.V.* (11/1/2002)

Jurtschitsch Sonnhof 2000 Rotspon Red Blend (Kamptal) $28. Here is a hugely dark purple-colored wine, with aromas of strawberries and plums that give way to spicy flavors, dry tannins, bitter fruits, and wood at the end. A young wine, firm, with great long-term potential. **86** —*R.V.* (11/1/2002)

Jurtschitsch Sonnhof 2005 Zöbinger Heiligenstein Alte Reben Riesling (Kamptal) $59. The Alte Reben (old vines) owned by Jurtschitsch Sonnhof on Heiligenstein give an impressively concentrated, very mineral wine. Bitter Seville orange flavors give the acidity and the juicy character. It is still very young—give it at least three years. **90** —*R.V. (10/1/2006)*

Jurtschitsch Sonnhof 2005 Zöbinger Heiligenstein Reserve Riesling (Kamptal) $83. Imagine sucking on pebbles, and you get some idea of the mineral character of this wine. It brings concentration from late harvest fruit, with ripeness and spice. **92** —*R.V. (10/1/2006)*

Jurtschitsch Sonnhof 2001 Zoebinger Heiligenstein Riesling Riesling (Kamptal) $NA. 90 —*R.V. (11/1/2002)*

KALMUCK

Kalmuck 2004 Grüner Veltliner (Wachau) $13. A joint venture between Johann Donabaum and Franz-Josef Gritsch, Kalmuck has produced a debut bottling that packs in substantial white pepper notes backed by melony underpinnings. Relatively light-bodied, with a refreshing lime and pepper finish. **88 Best Buy** —*J.C. (3/1/2006)*

KOLLWENTZ

Kollwentz 2002 Sauvignon Blanc Beerenauslese Sauvignon Blanc (Burgenland) $74. A stunning blend of the crispness of Sauvignon Blanc with smooth, honeyed fruit flavors. Aromas of ripe pears are balanced on the palate with some structure layers of dryness from the botrytis. With its acidity, this wine should hold up well over the next 10 years. **92** —*R.V. (5/1/2004)*

Kollwentz 1999 TBA Sauvignon Blanc (Burgenland) $121. For all its huge richness, its flavors of ripe pears, and its touch of honey, this is an impressively balanced, delicate wine, giving both a sense of depth as well as freshness. **92 Editors' Choice** —*R.V. (5/1/2004)*

Kollwentz 2002 TBA Scheurebe (Burgenland) $121. The advantage of this fat, ultrasweet wine is the streak of acidity which runs through it. The downside is the curious foxy aroma that is sometimes a character of this rare grape variety. **86** —*R.V. (5/1/2004)*

Kollwentz 2002 Beerenauslese Welschriesling (Burgenland) $74. Deliciously poised fresh fruits dominate this balanced wine. There is acidity, along with layers of honey, and flavors of apricots. To finish, there is lightness and a crisp acidity. **88** —*R.V. (5/1/2004)*

Kollwentz 1999 TBA Welschriesling (Burgenland) $121. A luxurious, opulent wine, deep gold in color, with ripe, luscious fruit. The wine has acidity, a fine sweet/dry botrytis structure, and great deep layers of apricots, figs, and almonds. It should last for 20 years or more. **92 Cellar Selection** —*R.V. (5/1/2004)*

KRACHER

Kracher 2001 Nummer 3 TBA Chardonnay (Burgenland) $74. This second Chardonnay in the Kracher 2001 TBAs may be the less successful than Nummer 7, but it is still impressive, concentrated, with intense liquorous flavors. The layers of toast in this wine—which Kracher describes as ìNouvelle Vagueî, new wave—are perhaps too dominant for the other elements in the wine. **88** —*R.V. (5/2/2004)*

Kracher 2001 Nummer 7 TBA Chardonnay (Burgenland) $84. This is the more successful of Kracher's two Chardonnays. It is both hugely rich and elegant, combining some toast flavors well with the smooth concentrated fruit. To finish, there is a hint of orange marmalade and a fine, delicate balancing acidity. **94** —*R.V. (5/2/2004)*

Kracher 2001 Nummer 2 TBA Muskat Ottonel (Burgenland) $74. An intensely perfumed wine, from its exotic aromas of orange zest and spice, to its liquorous, rich concentrated fruit. This is a barely-restrained wine which is just dying to break out, to give rein to its full richness. **90** —*R.V. (5/2/2004)*

Kracher 2005 Pinot Gris (Neusiedlersee) $14. Kracher, the king of sweet wines, also makes a few dry wines. While not in the same unique class as the sweet wines, this Pinot Gris is creamy, flavored with pears, green fruits, a touch of spice, and finishing with some delicate acidity. **87** —*R.V. (10/1/2006)*

Kracher 2003 Pinot Gris (Burgenland) $16. Best known for his numbered series of trockenbeerenauslesen, Kracher also shows a deft hand with dry wines, as evidenced by this tasty Pinot Gris. Opens with pineapple scents, then gives up plump, mouthfilling tropical and citrus flavors. Finishes in a rush of melon and orange. Yummy. **88** —*J.C. (5/1/2005)*

Kracher 2003 Blend One Red Blend (Neusiedlersee) $NA. A blend of Zweigelt and Merlot, using the best red grapes from the oldest of Kracher's Illmitz vineyards. It has ripe, concentrated fruit, showing some of the heat and alcohol of 2003, but also layering velvet tannins and smooth red fruits. **89** —*R.V. (10/1/2006)*

Kracher 2001 Nummer 4 TBA Scheurebe (Burgenland) $74. An astonishingly aromatic, richly flavored wine. Powerful layers of spice, of acidity, of fresh fruit, a touch of lemon zest, and flavors of lychees and apricots all mingle in a wine of enormous energy and power. **92 Cellar Selection** —*R.V. (5/2/2004)*

Kracher 2001 Nummer 9 TBA Scheurebe (Burgenland) $91. The most concentrated of the range of TBAs made by Kracher in 2001, this is almost too sweet, almost too concentrated. It is hugely liquorous, with very low alcohol because the sweetness of the grapes was too much for the yeasts, which gives it a character almost of intensely sweet, very pure grape juice. **91** —*R.V. (5/2/2004)*

Kracher 2001 Nummer 1 TBA Traminer (Burgenland) $69. An oak-aged wine, blending the hint of toast with spicy, sweet orange marmalade flavors. It is hugely ripe, but still surprisingly restrained letting the spicy fruit dominate. **89** —*R.V. (5/2/2004)*

Kracher 2001 Nummer 5 TBA Welschriesling (Burgenland) $74. A beautiful wine, structured, spicy, powered with flavors of apricots, intense layers of botrytis, and huge concentration. There is a hint of minerality typical of the grape which just counterpoints the richness and power of the wine. **94 Editors' Choice** —*R.V. (5/2/2004)*

Kracher 2001 Nummer 8 TBA Welschriesling (Burgenland) $91. Kracher describes this as a table selection, meaning that the berries were further selected on a sorting table before winemaking began. This gives a wine which is almost the essence of wine, just the richness, the sweetness, and the botrytis. The flavors run together, with touches of quince, of oranges, and white fruits. Flowery, mineral, this is a superb wine. **95 Cellar Selection** —*R.V. (5/2/2004)*

Kracher 2005 Beerenauslese Cuvée 375ml White Blend (Neusiedlersee) $29. The starting point for the series of Kracher's sweet wines. 2005 was a great year for sweet wines, but quantities of botrytis were 60% below normal. This blend of Chardonnay and Welschriesling shows elegance, freshness, honey, and apple flavors, and just a hint of caramel toffee. **90** —*R.V. (10/1/2006)*

Kracher 2003 Cuvée No 1. Nouvelle Vague Trockenbeerenauslese 375 ml White Blend (Neusiedlersee) $72. Kracher's fame rests on the series of cuvées he makes, which increases in intensity the higher the number. In 2003, the series was broken because of the dry year and the lack of botrytis, and only one wine was made. It certainly has exceptional power from the heat of the year, with raisins as much as botrytis on the palate, and relatively low acidity. **92** —*R.V. (10/1/2006)*

Kracher 2001 Eiswein Cuvée 375 ml White Blend (Burgenland) $38. Austria's master of dessert wines strikes again, this time with a sinful blend of Chardonnay and Welschriesling. Rich and sweet without being cloying, this wine combines dried apricots with floral notes on the nose, then adds honey and citrus (bergamot) on the palate. Finishes long and mouth-watering. **93 Editors' Choice** —*J.C. (3/1/2006)*

Kracher 2002 Kracher No. 12 375ml White Blend (Neusiedlersee) $110. The ultimate in the Kracher lineup of sweet wines, this is destined to become a legend. It is hugely liquorous, intensely flavored with botrytis, honey, acidity, and enticing aromas of honeysuckle and sweet cottage garden flowers. Because this essence couldn't ferment above 4% alcohol, it is not allowed to be called wine, so is described as partially fermented grape must. **94 Editors' Choice** —*R.V. (10/1/2006)*

Kracher 2001 Nummer 6 Grande Cuvée TBA White Blend (Burgenland) $81. The Grande Cuvée in Kracher's range is the blend that best typifies the vintage—in this case Welschriesling and Chardonnay. New oak aromas vie with toffee, while to taste the rich flavors of peaches and caramelized apples give the wine great intensity while still preserving some fresh acidity. **93 Editors' Choice** —*R.V. (5/2/2004)*

KRUTZLER

Krutzler 2004 Blaufränkisch (Burgenland) $23. This medium-weight wine smells rather nice, with plum and black cherry notes accented by

AUSTRIA

cinnamon and chocolate, but then the flavors pick up some green, herbaceous notes that turn bitter on the finish. **83** —*J.C. (3/1/2006)*

Krutzler 2003 Perwolff Red Blend (Burgenland) $93. It's creamy and soft—and frankly a bit formless—but this wine does feature bowls of ripe cherry fruit accented by lashings of vanilla and cream. Try putting a slight chill on it to tighten it up for a springtime picnic—an image admittedly a bit incongruous with the price. **85** —*J.C. (3/1/2006)*

LAURENZ AND SOPHIE

Laurenz and Sophie 2004 Singing Grüner Veltliner (Austria) $13. This well-priced wine boasts ripe aromas of nectarine and lime, then delivers more stone fruit on the palate. With its fresh, citrusy finish, this isn't a particularly peppery or complex Grüner, but one that provides a tasty introduction to the genre. **86** —*J.C. (8/1/2006)*

LAURENZ V.

Laurenz V. 2004 Charming Grüner Veltliner (Kamptal) $25. This easy-to-like wine offers a fullish, slightly oily mouthfeel to match with its peach-driven, mineral-tinged flavors. Grace notes of celery leaf and grapefruit provide focus and complexity on the long-lasting finish. **89** —*J.C. (8/1/2006)*

LEO ALZINGER

Leo Alzinger 2005 Loibenberg Grüner Veltliner Smaragd Grüner Veltliner (Wachau) $55. A full, fat style of wine that packs opulent flavors, ripe fruits, and smoky aromas. Lime, honey, and minerals balance with the crisp acidity. To finish, the wine is soft and rounded. **92** —*R.V. (10/1/2006)*

Leo Alzinger 2003 Loibner Loibenberg Smaragd Grüner Veltliner (Wachau) $NA. This wine, from the Loibner vineyard near Dürnstein, is rich, packed with pepper and spice flavors, and also shows some smoky mineral characters. It is powerful and concentrated, a good expression of the intensity that Grüner Veltliner can attain in the eastern end of the Wachau. **89** —*R.V. (5/1/2005)*

Leo Alzinger 2005 Loibenberg Smaragd Riesling (Wachau) $60. This is an intense, powerful wine, racy and fresh while also being full-flavored and opulent. Exotic perfumes reminiscent of honey and wild flowers waft from the glass. **90** —*R.V. (10/1/2006)*

LEOPLOLD & SILVANE SOMMER

Leoplold & Silvane Sommer 2003 Spätlese Gewürztraminer (Neusiedlersee-Hügelland) $15. This is a sweet style of Gewürztraminer, with a fine spice and lychee character that gives a heady accent to the sweetness. This is a good full-bodied wine, but without too high alcohol. When to drink it is a difficult call—the only probable answer is by itself. **88** —*R.V. (5/1/2005)*

Leoplold & Silvane Sommer 2001 M Grüner Veltliner Grüner Veltliner (Neusiedlersee) $13. 91 —*R.V. (11/1/2002)*

Leoplold & Silvane Sommer 2003 M Grüner Veltliner (Neusiedlersee-Hügelland) $15. A rich, spicy wine from a family winery near the Neusiedlersee, which has been in the wine biz since 1698. It's much richer than Grüner Veltliner usually is, but it has its own personality: it's spicy, with good acidity and plenty of varietal character. **87** —*R.V. (5/1/2005)*

Leoplold & Silvane Sommer 2003 Premium Reserve Grüner Veltliner (Neusiedlersee-Hügelland) $19. "Premium Reserve" to the Sommer winery means "wood aged," and this Grüner has plenty of wood-derived toast and spice, to complement the spiciness and pepperiness of the grape. The aftertaste is creamy and rich. **86** —*R.V. (5/1/2005)*

Leoplold & Silvane Sommer 2001 Premium Reserve Trocken Grüner Ventliner Grüner Veltliner (Neusiedlersee) $18. A taut, vibrant wine with green fruits and immediate acidity on the nose. The palate is crisp, with fresh fruit flavors along with some spicy wood. The aftertaste is completely refreshing. **88** —*R.V. (11/1/2002)*

LOIMER

Loimer 2003 Grüner Veltliner (Langenlois) $17. Pear, melon, and a hint of celery leaf mark the nose of Loimer entry-level GV. It's only 12.5% alcohol, yet comes across as honeyed and ripe; full-bodied yet tart and long

on the finish. Honey, melon, lime, and grapefruit flavors round out the package. **88** —*J.C. (5/1/2005)*

Loimer 2003 Käferberg Grüner Veltliner (Kamptal) $25. This plump, medium-weight Grüner doesn't have the weight and richness of many 2003s, but makes up for it with its juicy, fresh, lipsmacking finish. Apple, citrus, and mineral notes don't show a lot of typical spice, but still satisfy. **88** —*J.C. (5/1/2005)*

Loimer 2002 Lois Grüner Veltliner (Langenlois) $11. To avoid confusing American consumers, only the word "Lois" appears on the main label; the niggling details about grape variety, vintage, and origin are in small print on the back. It's an attempt at creating a branded Austrian wine, which should succeed if the quality of what's in the bottle remains this high. It's light and minerally, with hints of celery stalk, under-ripe honeydew, and green plums. Finishes tart and clean. **86** —*M.S. (11/15/2003)*

Loimer 2003 Riesling (Langenlois) $17. A nice package, but one that lacks intensity. Begins with hints of apple, pear, and honey, then delivers understated lime and mineral flavors. Tart and mouthwatering on the finish. **84** —*J.C. (8/1/2005)*

Loimer 2003 Seeberg Trocken Riesling (Kamptal) $25. Oily and minerally, but at the same time a bit sharp and light on the palate. It's stony, wrapped in a tight blanket of lemon and lime and finishes with zingy acids. **85** —*J.C. (8/1/2005)*

Loimer 2003 Steinmassl Riesling (Kamptal) $40. Starts off with hints of machine oil and grassy-herbal notes, then eases into melon and mineral flavors that finish clean and fresh. **88** —*J.C. (8/1/2005)*

LUDWIG EHN

Ludwig Ehn 2005 Zöbinger Heiligenstein Riesling (Kamptal) $22. A full-bodied, earthy wine that has tropical fruits, lychees, and juiciness around a core of minerality. Ehn's style is for food-friendly wines and this one is great with fish as well as lighter meats. **89** —*R.V. (10/1/2006)*

MACHHERNDL

Machherndl 2003 Kollmütz Federspiel Grüner Veltliner (Wachau) $15. Not quite in synch, with hard, stony aromas yet a round mouthfeel. Citrus, melon, and pepper aromas and flavors are solid, but finish a bit short. **85** —*J.C. (8/1/2006)*

Machherndl 2003 Kollmütz Federspiel Grüner Veltliner (Wachau) $15. Fairly big for a federspiel, with hints of honey and ripe apples on the nose, but then it turns less ripe on the palate, picking up intriguing spice drop flavors. Finishes crisp and clean. **86** —*J.C. (11/15/2005)*

Machherndl 2003 Smaragd Kollmitz Grüner Veltliner (Wachau) $25. A bit reticent on the nose, offering little more than hints of honey and peppery spice. It's much more expressive in the mouth, where it delivers melon, pear, and liquid minerals via a full, oily-textured mouthfeel.. **90 Editors' Choice** —*J.C. (3/1/2006)*

MALAT

Malat 2003 Dreigarten Grüner Veltliner (Kremstal) $29. Gerald Malat is a seminal figure in winemaking in Krems, the first to match grape variety to soil type in a region previously dominated by small holdings and tiny vineyards. So it's fitting that this Grüner Veltliner should power through with ripe, peppery fruit and flavors of apples, pears, and spice. It needs a year or two to age. **90** —*R.V. (5/1/2005)*

Malat 2004 Höhlgraben Grüner Veltliner (Kremstal) $22. Smells intriguing, with minerally, corn-oil scents dominating, but graced by hints of honeyed orange sections. In the mouth, it's firmly built without being hard—like a sharp-edged table that's been padded at the corners. Picks up a leafy note on the finish, but it's mostly minerally. **87** —*J.C. (8/1/2006)*

Malat 2004 Zistel Reserve Pinot Gris (Kremstal) $39. Despite its trocken (dry) indication, this wine is rich and has a touch of sweetness. There is a refreshing streak of crisp acidity and green fruit flavors. This wine is full of spice, lychees, and just a touch of pepper **89** —*R.V. (2/1/2006)*

Malat 2002 Das Beste Von Riesling Auslese Riesling (Kremstal) $60. An oily, viscous wine the color of polished brass, Malat's 2002 auslese boasts striking scents of honey, peaches, and orange marmalade. The ultra-ripe peach flavors pick up hints of spice and nuts on the finish. Bears a bit of similarity to a vendanges tardives Riesling from Alsace, and best paired with similar dishes, such as foie gras, or fish or chicken in cream sauce. **89** —*J.C. (8/1/2006)*

Malat 2004 Silberbühel Riesling (Kremstal) $38. A truly racy style of Riesling, which shows minerality, elegance, and fresh, crisp fruit. For the difficult 2003 vintage, this wine has great freshness, with delicious green plum flavors. It will age 5 years and more. **91** —*R.V. (8/1/2005)*

Malat 2003 Silberbühel Riesling (Kremstal) $36. A youthful Riesling, still bursting with energy and vitality but nowhere near ready to drink. It has flavors of white peach, currants, and minerality. It is full, but the acidity shows through, giving a deliciously crisp, fresh aftertaste. **89** —*R.V. (5/1/2005)*

Malat 2004 Steinbühel Riesling (Kremstal) $27. A bone-dry wine, with great green flavors, acidity, and fresh grapefruit. Gerald Malat is one of Austria's top award-winning winemakers, and this clean, clear wine shows why **89** —*R.V. (8/1/2005)*

Malat 2003 Brunnkreuz Reserve Sauvignon Blanc (Kremstal) $39. On the full-bodied side, with round, melon-scented fruit that picks up herbal and grapefruit notes on the finish. **88** —*J.C. (8/1/2006)*

Malat 2004 Reserve Sauvignon Blanc (Austria) $36. Unconventional, with some briny notes to the musky nose that also brings with it honey and lychee. Pretty solid across the palate, where tangerine and melon flavors are sweetened by a shot of guava. Not the easiest wine to wrap yourself around, but not without its virtues. **86** *(7/1/2005)*

MANFRED TEMENT

Manfred Tement 2001 Zieregg Sauvignon Blanc (Südsteiermark) $25. This single-vineyard wine comes from a southeast-facing vineyard planted in clay and limestone soils. This gives the wine a mineral character with powerful, peppery fruit and a touch of new wood spice to round it off. **91** —*R.V. (11/1/2002)*

MANFRED WEISS

Manfred Weiss 1999 Eiswein 375 ml Grüner Veltliner (Burgenland) $19. A fantastic value in eiswein, this brilliantly balanced offering blends intense dried apricot, quince, and bergamot aromas with flavors that are sweet but not cloying. Citrus and melon notes take charge of the midpalate. Because of its balancing acidity, serve this with foie gras rather than dessert. **91 Editors' Choice** —*J.C. (3/1/2006)*

MANTLERHOF

Mantlerhof 2003 Wieland Riesling (Kremstal) $45. A soft style of wine that has green acidity and flavors of pink grapefruit. This is a wine that shows its background rich ness slowly, and will need some years to develop. **87** —*R.V. (8/1/2005)*

Mantlerhof 2001 Wieland Riesling (Kremstal) $28. Josef Mantler's estate produces Rieslings from some of the best local vineyards in eastern Kremstal. This is a rich, soft wine, with exotic flavors of lychees and apricots. The aftertaste is just off-dry, but still has a good steely backbone. **89** —*R.V. (8/1/2003)*

Mantlerhof 2004 Zehetnerin Riesling (Kremstal) $25. While the 2003 Zehetnerin is big and opulent, 2004 is crisp, green, clean, and packed with green apple flavors. There is a steely intensity to this wine that shows it will age for many years. **90** —*R.V. (8/1/2005)*

Mantlerhof 2003 Zehetnerin Riesling (Kremstal) $25. A big, opulent, generous wine, with a touch of vanilla and toast. Rich, open-hearted, and powerful, there are touches of green fruit flavors underneath all this richness. **89** —*R.V. (8/1/2005)*

Mantlerhof 2000 Roter Veltliner (Kremser) $18. Warm, sun-ripened peaches and cool, stony notes blend together into a mélange of honey, apple, and pear flavors, finishing with spiced lemons. Made from a dark-skinned mutation of Grüner Veltliner, this would be an excellent choice as a discussion-provoking apéritif. **87** —*J.C. (3/1/2002)*

MARKOWITSCH

Markowitsch 2004 Reserve Chardonnay (Carnuntum) $NA. Having spent 16 months in oak, it is not unexpected that there are plenty of wood flavors to this wine. But after the initial toastiness, the wine opens out well,

with intense, ripe, creamy fruit and acidity. Polished, modern. **90** —*R.V. (10/1/2006)*

Markowitsch 2005 Alte Reben Grüner Veltliner (Carnuntum) $NA. The vines for this wine have an average age of 40–50 years, giving a great concentration of flavors from low-yielding plants. For a Grüner it is monumental in character, packed with flavors of lychees, sage, and pepper. With this intensity of flavor, this should be a wine for aging. **90** —*R.V. (10/1/2006)*

Markowitsch 2005 Schanzäcker Grüner Veltliner (Carnuntum) $13. Fresh, creamy aromas, crisp fruit, and layers of acidity and pepper create a very good wine. A great expression of Grüner in an area better known for red wines. **88 Best Buy** —*R.V. (10/1/2006)*

Markowitsch 2004 Schanzäcker Grüner Veltliner (Carnuntum) $13. Rated as one of the top Austrian red wine producers (look for his highly regarded Pinot Noir), Gerhard Markowitsch also seems to be at home with Austria's national grape. In the naturally warm climate of Carnuntum in the Danube valley east of Vienna, the Grüner can flourish into a ripe, full-bodied style while still keeping fresh acidity. This is a delicious wine, packed with citrus, pear, and quince flavors. Drink as an apéritif or with salads or cold appetizers. **89 Best Buy** —*R.V. (11/15/2005)*

Markowitsch 2003 Rosenberg Red Blend (Carnuntum) $NA. This is Markowitsch's flagship wine, from the Rosenberg vineyard. The blend varies from year to year, but always includes at least 50% Zweigelt, along with Merlot and Cabernet Sauvignon. This 2003 is as powerful and intense as is to be expected from a wine of this vintage, but is saved by its structure. It is rich, ripe, and very open, with damson, black currants, and creamy wood flavors blending well together. **93 Cellar Selection** —*R.V. (10/1/2006)*

Markowitsch 2004 Rothenberg St. Laurent (Carnuntum) $31. Bitter cherries and perfumed aromas mark this as a typical Saint Laurent wine. There are definite tannins, with power and dryness. It should age well, as shown by the layers of acidity that push all the way through from the palate to the finish. **89** —*R.V. (10/1/2006)*

MARTIN NIGL

Martin Nigl 2001 Privat Grüner Veltliner Grüner Veltliner (Kremstal) $39. **90** —*R.V. (11/1/2002)*

MARTIN PASLER

Martin Pasler 2001 Trockenbeerenauslese C Chardonnay (Burgenland) $35. A big step up from Pasler's BA, this Chardonnay-based TBA boasts rich pear and dried apricot aromas that carry a hint of volatility, followed by a wine that tastes like pear nectar, with nuances of apricot and tangerine. Mouthwatering acidity keeps the finish lively. **90** —*J.C. (12/15/2004)*

Martin Pasler 2001 Trockenbeerenauslese 375 ml Muskat Ottonel (Burgenland) $30. Muskat Ottonel seems to have an affinity for being made into unctuous late-harvest dessert wines that retain enough acidity to offset their enormous sweetness. This one has dried apricot, orange marmalade, and ripe melon flavors all balanced by mouthwatering acids on the long finish. **93 Editors' Choice** —*J.C. (12/15/2004)*

Martin Pasler 2001 Beerenauslese Welschriesling (Burgenland) $15. Dark gold color. Seems slightly volatile on the nose, with shoe polish aromas that turn acetic on the palate. It has a rich, viscous mouthfeel and decent flavors of caramelized fruit if you can get past the flaws. **84** —*J.C. (12/15/2004)*

MEINKLANG

Meinklang 2004 Pinot Gris (Burgenland) $15. Pure fruit, layers of pepper, and dry, concentrated flavors mark this wine. Fresh, clean, and finely crafted, with fine acidity. Very drinkable. **86** —*R.V. (2/1/2006)*

MELITTA & MATTHIAS LEITNER

Melitta & Matthias Leitner 2000 TBA Riesling (Neusiedlersee) $39. The Rhine Riesling, better known in the Danube vineyards further west, makes a rare appearance in the Burgenland with this sweet, ripe, spicy wine, which layers dryness within its honeyed flavors. **87** —*R.V. (5/1/2004)*

Melitta & Matthias Leitner 1999 TBA Riesling (Neusiedlersee) $39. A deliciously fresh wine, bursting with summer fruits which counterbalance

AUSTRIA

the sweetness. Acidity and sweetness are well-balanced, leaving a great, crisp aftertaste. **89** —*R.V. (5/1/2004)*

Melitta & Matthias Leitner 2000 Eiswein White Blend (Neusiedlersee) $NA. For an eiswein, this is impressively rich. A blend of Muskat Ottonel and Welschriesling, its opulence is tempered by a piercing layer of acidity. The grapes were picked on Christmas Eve 2000 by 24 members of the Leitner family. **90** —*R.V. (5/1/2004)*

METTERNICH-SALOMON

Metternich-Salomon 2005 Pfaffenberg Riesling (Kremstal) $NA. Salomon makes wines from the vineyards they have rented from the Metternich family on the Pfaffenberg. This is a beautiful floral wine, flinty and crisp. It also shows supple acidity, fruit flavors, and a long, intense aftertaste. Expect this to age well. **92 Editors' Choice** —*R.V. (10/1/2006)*

MICHLITS-STADLMANN

Michlits-Stadlmann 1999 Auslese Traminer (Neusiedlersee) $16. Not really sweet enough to be a full-fledged dessert wine, this pear- and honey-scented wine would make a nice accompaniment to seared foie gras. The ripe pear and melon flavors have enough acidity to balance the delicate sweetness. **85** —*J.C. (3/1/2002)*

NECKENMARKT

Neckenmarkt 2004 Blaufränkisch Classic Blaufränkisch (Burgenland) $12. This medium-bodied wine delivers aromas and flavors of plums, graham crackers, and vanilla, all rolled up in a crisp, harmonious package that finishes with a blast of peppery spice. **87 Best Buy** —*J.C. (3/1/2006)*

Neckenmarkt 2004 Classic Zweigelt (Burgenland) $12. Bold blackberry fruit is framed by notes of graham crackers or vanilla wafers. A bit crisp and lacking flesh, but showcases vibrant fruit, ending on a dry, dusty, tannic note. **85** —*J.C. (8/1/2006)*

NEUMEISTER WINERY

Neumeister Winery 2002 Grauburgunder Saziani Pinot Gris (Südsteiermark) $30. Packed with white fruit flavors, ripe pears, and a touch of spice. These fruit flavors combine with a dense but elegant structure and balancing acidity. This is a high-alcohol wine (14.5%) and it shows in the oily texture. **91** —*R.V. (2/1/2006)*

Neumeister Winery 2004 Grauburgunder Steirische Klassik Pinot Gris (Südsteiermark) $19. Albert Neumeister has made something of a specialty with his Grauburgunder (Pinot Gris), especially his Saziani range. This Klassik cuvée, while less exalted, is fresh, dry, crisp, and very pure, with spice and pepper along with light, poised acidity. **89** —*R.V. (2/1/2006)*

Neumeister Winery 2003 Moarfeitl Sauvignon Blanc (Styria) $37. Ripe and tropical, yet a bit over the top. This wine seems reflective of the hot 2003 vintage. It's sweet from start to finish, with a thick body that one reviewer labeled "cloying." If you like richness and size more than citrus and verve, this fits the bill. **86** *(7/1/2005)*

Neumeister Winery 2003 Steirische Klassik Sauvignon Blanc (Styria) $31. Musky, with aromas of lemon-lime, tonic water, and bubble gum. Downright spritzy in the mouth, where it almost seems to bubble up and impersonate a bottle of Sprite soda. Lacks sophistication, but pours on the citrus and green melon. **86** *(7/1/2005)*

NIGL

Nigl 2002 Privat Grüner Veltliner (Kremstal) $50. From his tiny valley above Krems, Martin Nigl seems to produce effortless wines with all the right intensity of flavor and richness. This Privat (which, for him, is the equivalent of a reserve wine), is intense, concentrated and packed with spice, pepper and yellow apples. **91** —*R.V. (5/1/2005)*

Nigl 2003 Kremsleiten Riesling (Kremstal) $44. A full-bodied wine, warm, spicy, and generous from the Kremsleiten vineyard. It radiates richness. Acidity is present, but subsumed into a powerful burst of generous fruit. **89** —*R.V. (8/1/2005)*

Nigl 2003 Privat Riesling (Kremstal) $71. Rich and concentrated, this wine comes from Martin Nigl's selection from old vines, which he bottles as his premium wines. It has denseness and concentration, but is still open and generous. There are flavors of green plums, lychees, other trop-

ical fruit, and herbs. A great open-hearted wine, it should age well over 5–10 years. **91** —*R.V. (8/1/2005)*

Nigl 2003 Senftenberger Piri Riesling (Kremstal) $47. This wine comes from Martin Nigl's top vineyard site, the Piri, which lies in the narrow valley by Senftenberg. The wine is full, rich, and generous. On the palate there is peach, green plum, a touch of thyme, and well-balanced acidity. It is already drinkable, but will develop over the next few years. **90** —*R.V. (8/1/2005)*

NIKOLAIHOF

Nikolaihof 1990 Smaragd Grüner Veltliner (Wachau) $NA. As Grüner Veltliner ages, it becomes more and more like mature Riesling. This wine has petrol flavors, along with light acidity, and a taste of vanilla and toast. Still lively, this has a bone dry aftertaste. It could certainly age longer. **89** —*R.V. (4/1/2005)*

Nikolaihof 2000 Im Weingebirge Smaragd Riesling (Wachau) $35. Nikolaihof produces intense, full-flavored Rieslings that age more quickly than Wachau Rieslings from further west. This is a silky, creamy wine, full of white fruit flavors, seared through with crisp acidity, enormously concentrated, with a bone-dry finish. **91** —*R.V. (8/1/2003)*

Nikolaihof 2000 Steiner Hund Premium Riesling (Wachau) $51. Nikolaihof has been farmed biodynamically since 1971, and the benefits show in a wine like this, whose fresh, hedgerow aromas just sing from the glass. The fruit is fresh, crisp, and intensely flavored, with currants and sweet pears alongside crafted acidity and just a touch of softness to finish. Not complex, but so drinkable. **90** —*R.V. (4/1/2005)*

Nikolaihof 2000 Vom Stein Federspiel Riesling (Wachau) $24. The intricate nose features head-turning scents of narcissus and ferns on one hand, and limes and green apples on the other. The flavors are all finely etched minerals, like liquid rock crystal or the most flavorful mountain stream. The long finish is mouthwatering, clean, and crisp. **90** —*J.C. (3/1/2002)*

NITTNAUS

Nittnaus 1999 Cabernet Sauvignon (Burgenland) $29. This wine's crunchy, cassis fruit carries more than a hint of green peppers, but still comes across as smooth and picks up some chocolate complexities on the abbreviated finish. **83** —*J.C. (3/1/2002)*

Nittnaus 1999 Von den Hugeln Red Blend (Burgenland) $21. Smells really interesting and unique, with scents of black pepper and cardamom, but doesn't follow through on the palate, which seems a bit hollow. **83** —*J.C. (3/1/2002)*

Nittnaus 1999 Selection St. Laurent (Burgenland) $25. The Saint Laurent grape is only rarely grown outside of Austria, where it is perceived to have great potential. This version verges on Port-like, with aromas of fruitcake and spice that seem a bit warm and overripe before picking up a citrus tang on the finish. **84** —*J.C. (3/1/2002)*

Nittnaus 2001 TBA White Blend (Burgenland) $47. Flavors of dried plums and prunes as well as honey and dry botrytis gives this blend of Weissburgunder, Chardonnay, and Neuburger a complex, balanced structure. It is not hugely sweet; instead it's rich with an element of crispness to make it both attractive and very drinkable. **89** —*R.V. (5/1/2004)*

Nittnaus 2000 Traminer White Blend (Burgenland) $NA. Harvested on December 24, 2000, this spicy wine has the classic eiswein freshness and acidity floating over the sweetness. There are aromas of fresh-cut flowers, flavors of fresh apricots, finishing with a touch of lychee. **89** —*R.V. (5/1/2004)*

OCHS

Ochs 1999 Eiswein Blaufränkisch (Weiden am See) $30. Some readers might be more familiar with one of this grape's other names, Lemberger. Taking a grape normally used for dry wines and making it as an ice wine results in a sweet but not overly treacly wine with flavors of cherries and citrus, with some tea-like notes on the finish. **85** —*J.C. (3/1/2002)*

Ochs 1998 Ungerberg & Zeiselberg & Satz Welschriesling (Weiden am See) $29. **86** —*J.C. (3/1/2002)*

ORIEL

Oriel 2004 Ortolan Falkenstein Grüner Veltliner (Weinviertel) $20. Although this wine starts well, with scents of lime, stone fruit, gunmetal, and mineral oil, it never really gets going on the palate, where the understated flavors of peach and pear end on a citrusy note. **84** —*J.C. (3/1/2006)*

PAUL ACHS

Paul Achs 2004 Blaufränkisch (Burgenland) $19. Seems reductive on the nose, with smoky, slightly acrid, sulfur notes that still don't obscure the ripe plums underneath. Tastes better, delivering plum and cherry flavors on a silky-smooth mouthfeel. Decant before serving, or hold another year or two before drinking. **87** —*J.C. (3/1/2006)*

PITNAUER

Pitnauer 2004 Hagelsberg Grüner Veltliner (Carnuntum) $16. Pungent and a bit tropical on the nose; a bit Sauvignon in character. Passion fruit flavors flow easily across the midweight palate, finishing tart but not that crisp. **85** —*J.C. (11/15/2005)*

Pitnauer 2002 Hagelsberg Ernte Pinot Blanc (Carnuntum) $20. This medium-weight white would be a fine accompaniment to almost any fish preparation. Its crisp apple and pear flavors carry a hint of liquid minerality that will enliven the dish's flavors without overwhelming them. **87** —*J.C. (12/15/2004)*

Pitnauer 2003 Hagelsberg St. Laurent (Carnuntum) $19. Whiffs of smoke, vanilla, grape preserves, and pastry dough set the stage for this big-boned wine that shows good size and structure but lacks a bit of midpalate richness to round out the mouthfeel. Vanilla and mixed berry flavors finish on a pleasant smoky note. **85** —*J.C. (3/1/2006)*

Pitnauer 2003 Classic Zweigelt (Carnuntum) $17. This creamy-textured wine combines low acids with plentiful fruit to come across as a bit soft, but the flavors are nice—a mix of plums, herbs, and brown sugar. **84** —*J.C. (3/1/2006)*

Pitnauer 2004 Klassik Blaufränkisch (Neusiedlersee) $22. Seemingly picked really ripe, this Blaufränkisch marries the aromas and flavors of prunes, plums, and black cherries with cedar and vanilla, then delivers them with fudge-like concentration and low acidity. Tannins are soft and supple, while the finish picks up a nice smoky note. **88** —*J.C. (3/1/2006)*

Pitnauer 2003 Klassik Blaufränkisch (Neusiedlersee) $23. Starts with layered aromas of leather, spice, and citrus, but doesn't deliver quite the same complexity on the palate, where the flavors are more reminiscent of brandied cherries. The creamy mouthfeel leads into a long, softly caressing finish that shows just a hint of alcoholic warmth. **88** —*J.C. (5/1/2005)*

Pitnauer 2003 Klassik Zweigelt (Burgenland) $18. Stumbles out of the blocks, with burnt rubber scents that take a while to recede, but then delivers crunchy black cherry flavors. Bold fruit and a crisp finish separate this Zweigelt from the rest of the pack. **89** —*J.C. (3/1/2006)*

PLODER-ROSENBERG

Ploder-Rosenberg 2003 Sauvignon Blanc (Styria) $8. The bouquet shows some hints of peach, but the aromas and flavors are largely dominated by stony, minerally notes. Relatively light in body, it fades quickly on the finish. Refreshing. **84 Best Buy** —*J.C. (11/15/2005)*

Ploder-Rosenberg 2002 Linea Sauvignon Blanc (Styria) $15. Full-bodied, even a touch oily in texture, this is a distinctive and very good Sauvignon. Grapefruit and passion fruit on the nose, tinged with honey and stone fruit, then honeyed peach flavors and a dusting of minerals. Honeyed but dry on the finish, and picks up a note of smoky complexity. Drink now. **88** —*J.C. (11/15/2005)*

PÖCKL

Pöckl 2004 Solo Rosso Red Blend (Burgenland) $22. Vibrant purple in color, this young, bouncy wine features bright cherry fruit accented by hints of smoke. Tannins are creamy and soft, while the acids are mouthwatering, especially on the finish, where the flavors pick up hints of coffee and cocoa. **87** —*J.C. (3/1/2006)*

Pöckl 2003 Zweigelt (Burgenland) $15. There are modest sour-cherry scents on the nose alongside mushroom and clean earth aromas. Cherry and marshmallow flavors are a bit candied, leading into a finish that lingers. **84** —*J.C. (5/1/2005)*

Pöckl 2004 Classique Zweigelt (Burgenland) $22. Herbal and tannic, this is one wine that smells better than it tastes. Smoke, pepper, and blueberry aromas set the stage, but the palate is lean, featuring some tea-like tannins that pick up a bitter edge on the finish. **82** —*J.C. (8/1/2006)*

PRAGER

Prager 2005 Achleiten Smaragd Grüner Veltliner (Wachau) $45. Citric flavors dominate this floral, very focused wine, from the steep Achleiten vineyard. It has some sweetness, or more precisely, richness, but this is only a small part of the vibrant, lively structure of a delicious wine. **95 Editors' Choice** —*R.V. (10/1/2006)*

Prager 2004 Achleiten Smaragd Grüner Veltliner (Wachau) $39. Lush and ripe, but it still retains that signature white pepper-celery leaf note that's a sure sign of the variety. Tastes like peaches and melons rolled in crushed stones, with a long, warm finish that retains a sense of minerality. **92 Editors' Choice** —*J.C. (8/1/2006)*

Prager 2004 Hinter Der Burg Federspiel Grüner Veltliner (Wachau) $22. Prager seemed to be a little inconsistent in 2004, or maybe I just had trouble understanding all of the wines. This one offers plenty of volume, combining passion fruit and pepper in a bold, loud cacophony that I didn't find find very harmonious. Bright and tangy on the finish. **86** —*J.C. (8/1/2006)*

Prager 2003 Hinter Der Burg Federspiel Grüner Veltliner (Wachau) $22. On the light side, but not lacking for concentration or flavor. Steely and minerally, with lime and tart cantaloupe flavors that finish with unusual freshness and zest for the vintage. **87** —*J.C. (5/1/2005)*

Prager 2004 Weitenberg Smaragd Grüner Veltliner (Wachau) $36. My reactions to the various 2004s in the Prager lineup were a bit mixed, and this bottling was no exception. It possesses a light mouthfeel that hints at oiliness appropriate to a smaragd designation, but the flavors seem a bit sour and slightly underripe, ranging from quince to gooseberry and finishing with a tart edge. **86** —*J.C. (8/1/2006)*

Prager 2004 Zwerithaler Smaragd Grüner Veltliner (Wachau) $39. Odd and jumbled on the nose, with apple and apricot scents, a hint of mint, and maybe even a bit of volatile acidity, then creamed corn flavors on the palate. Not my cup of tea; an unusual misstep from Prager. **82** —*J.C. (3/1/2006)*

Prager 2005 Achleiten Smaragd Riesling (Wachau) $48. This wine is going to age, and age magnificently. That's obvious from the taut, structured tannins and the curve of flavors that rise from the perfumes through peach and white fruits and finishing with fresh, juicy acidity. **95 Cellar Selection** —*R.V. (10/1/2006)*

Prager 2004 Achleiten Smaragd Riesling (Wachau) $48. A big, bold Riesling with a long, crisp finish, Prager's Achleiten Smaragd boasts stunning flavors of honey, apricot and stones. The bouquet isn't too shabby, either, presenting hints of mineral oil, honey, and fresh greens. A tour de force that will probably drink well until 2020. **93** —*J.C. (3/1/2006)*

Prager 2003 Durnstein Kaiserberg Smaragd Riesling (Wachau) $42. Can a wine be too minerally? This one's a candidate, with stony, minerally flavors that offer the merest hints of fresh greens or mint and crisp apple. It's a real mineral bath of flavor, backed by fresh limes; a tightly wound wine that needs a few years of age to open up. **89** —*J.C. (11/15/2005)*

Prager 2004 Hollerin Smaragd Riesling (Wachau) $42. The most flattering of Prager's 2004 smaragds to taste now, thanks to greater weight in the midpalate and riper fruit flavors that flirt with peach and melon while being firmly anchored by citrus and mineral. Hints of Earl Grey tea and stone dust garnish the nose. Drink now or hold. **89** —*J.C. (8/1/2006)*

Prager 2004 Kaiserberg Smaragd Riesling (Wachau) $42. Loaded with citrus, this Riesling is full in the mouth, yet not soft at all—possessed of a firm backbone of acids and minerals. Bergamot and cinnamon notes on the nose give way to lemony, orangey flavors that finish dry and tart. Hold at least five years. **88** —*J.C. (8/1/2006)*

Prager 2004 Klaus Smaragd Riesling (Wachau) $48. Flashier on the nose than on the palate, starting with traces of almond, melon, and dried spices but moving into flavors of herbs and citrus. A bold beam of acidity drives this wine, which finishes crisp and long. Worth cellaring to see if more richness develops on the midpalate. **89** —*J.C. (8/1/2006)*

Prager 2004 Steinriegl Federspiel Riesling (Wachau) $28. Seems a bit on the simple side, but still manages to pack in bright lime flavors and a steely, minerally intensity that lingers on the finish. Crisp and clean on the finish, ending with lemon-lime notes. **87** —*J.C. (8/1/2006)*

Prager 2003 Steinriegl Federspiel Riesling (Wachau) $28. Textbook federspiel-style, with fresh scents of lime and green apple reflective of less ripeness than many Rieslings from this sun-drenched vintage. Flavors echo the aromas, delivering green apple and citrus, and finish bright and fresh. **88** —*J.C. (5/1/2005)*

Prager 2003 Steinriegl Smaragd Riesling (Wachau) $56. Great Rieslings like this are world-class wines. In the hands of Prager's owner, Toni Bodenstein, the grape comes through with beautiful, rich fruit, flavors of white currants, and perfumes of hedgerow flowers. There is also a fine sense of the terroir, with a cool slate texture. **92** —*R.V. (5/1/2005)*

Prager 2004 Wachstum Bodenstein Smaragd Riesling (Wachau) $48. Racy, dry, and lean, with mineral, lime, and green apple notes giving this a rather hard mouthfeel. Tart green apple and citrus flavors finish crisp and refreshing, but this wine needs time (4-5 years?) to loosen up. **89** —*J.C. (8/1/2006)*

Prager 2003 Weissenkirchen Klaus Smaragd Riesling (Wachau) $47. So rich it almost seems syrupy, yet it's dry and full of minerally extract. Peppermint and apple aromas kick things off, followed up on the palate by that great weight and viscosity, along with hints of anise and pear. Shows a bit of alcohol on the finish, or this rating would have soared even higher. **90** —*J.C. (11/15/2005)*

Prager 2003 Weissenkirchen Smaragd Wachstum Bodenstein Riesling (Wachau) $47. Exotically perfumed, boasting scents of tangerines, grapefruit, honey, and apple blossoms—a real cornucopia of aromas. Flavors are more restrained at this stage of its evolution, focused on honey and apple, but this medium-weight Riesling should evolve effortlessly for 10–15 years at least. The long, mouthcoating, minerally finish is ample testament to that. **91** —*J.C. (5/1/2005)*

PROIDL

Proidl 2003 Senftenberg Grüner Veltliner (Kremstal) $29. The Senftenberg vineyard, which takes its name from the castle ruins above the village, is one of Kremstal's most illustrious sites. Franz Proidl makes a classically ripe, intense Grüner Veltliner from his vines. It is well balanced, with fine, crisp acidity. **89** —*R.V. (5/1/2005)*

R&A PFAFFL

R&A Pfaffl 2005 Exclusiv Chardonnay (Niederösterreich) $NA. The wood aging gives a smooth patina over ripe, generous, tropical fruit. To keep it all together, there is acidity and a fresh lift of citrus at the end. **89** —*R.V. (10/1/2006)*

R&A Pfaffl 2000 Exclusiv Trocken Chardonnay (Weinviertel) $18. This wine glorifies wood. There are huge spicy wood aromas, which also dominate the palate. There is also cinammon and vanilla, but not enough fruit. Generally the wood is too prominent. **87** —*R.V. (11/1/2002)*

R&A Pfaffl 2002 Rossern Chardonnay (Weinviertel) $45. Maybe this doesn't really say "Austria," but it is a great, creamy, fruity wine. Wood flavors are there, but don't dominate the tastes of ripe, green plums and peaches and some balancing mineral acidity. This is modern in style and delicious to drink. **90** —*R.V. (5/1/2005)*

R&A Pfaffl 2001 Goldjoch Grüner Veltliner Grüner Veltliner (Weinviertel) $18. 93 —*R.V. (11/1/2002)*

R&A Pfaffl 2003 Haidviertel DAC Grüner Veltliner (Weinviertel) $19. This wine, from the first vintage of DAC (Districtus Austriae Controllatus) wines, is packed with great, ripe fruit, fresh acidity, and delicious pepper and spice flavors. The aftertaste is crisp and vibrant. **88** —*R.V. (5/1/2005)*

R&A Pfaffl 2001 Hundsleien/Sandtal Trocken Grüner Ventliner Grüner Veltliner (Weinviertel) $18. There is a wonderful fresh-fruit salad of aro-

mas. The palate has a layer of acidity, plus full peppery flavors. The fruit is certainly ripe, but it has a firm sense of structure and a hint of greenness. **90** —*R.V. (11/1/2002)*

R&A Pfaffl 2005 Hundsleiten Grüner Veltliner (Niederösterreich) $NA. There is some wood here, particularly to smell, but it forms a seasoning for the intense concentrated flavors. Mandarin oranges and some smoky minerality are mixed in a creamy, rich blend. An impressive wine. **92** —*R.V. (10/1/2006)*

R&A Pfaffl 2004 Hundsleiten Grüner Veltliner (Niederösterreich) $NA. In keeping with a cool year, this '04 has layered acidity, pepper, and an intense lemon zest and light, poised flavors. It's vivid, fresh, and ready to drink. **89** —*R.V. (10/1/2006)*

R&A Pfaffl 2003 Hundsleiten/Sandtal Grüner Veltliner (Weinviertel) $21. A rich, creamy wine from a master of Grüner Veltliner. Packed with pepper and ripe fruit, it is full of character, but also reflects the heat of 2003. **89** —*R.V. (5/1/2005)*

R&A Pfaffl 2000 Hundsleiten/Sandtal Grüner Veltliner (Weinviertel) $18. Aromas of ripe apples and cream on the nose make this an immediately appealing wine. On the palate there are full peppery flavors and very ripe, aromatic fruit. The final touch of light acidity gives it a refreshing finish. **92** —*R.V. (11/1/2002)*

R&A Pfaffl 2005 Zeisneck Grüner Veltliner (Weinviertel) $13. Roman Pfaffl is the leader in the new Weinviertel DAC appellation, based around Grüner Veltliner. This wine is medium-bodied, but has typical spice, pepper, apple, and pear flavors. Demands instant pleasurable drinking. **88** —*R.V. (10/1/2006)*

R&A Pfaffl 1999 Excellant Reserve Red Blend (Weinviertel) $23. Jammy fruit on the nose is balanced by tannins, some acidity, and flavors of black plums. The result is slightly unbalanced, but could develop, especially as it has acidity at the end. **87** —*R.V. (11/1/2002)*

R&A Pfaffl 2001 Terrasen Sonnleiten Riesling (Weinviertel) $18. A wine full of fragrant alpine mountain aromas, of fresh air and open spaces. The palate has fresh acidity with a touch of pepper and fine, elegant fruit. At the finish there is the flavor of white currants. **94 Editors' Choice** —*R.V. (11/1/2002)*

R&A Pfaffl 2005 Terrassen Sonnleiten Riesling (Niederösterreich) $NA. Green, young, and firm, this wine is developing slowly. But it's obviously going to be a fine wine, with its mineral, steely character, intense dryness and flavors of ripe pears. **92** —*R.V. (10/1/2006)*

R&A Pfaffl 2004 Terrassen Sonnleiten Riesling (Niederösterreich) $NA. To say acidity dominates this wine is praise rather than condemnation. For this acidity comes from wonderful fresh fruits, intensely flavored white currants, and a steely poise that cuts right through. **92** —*R.V. (10/1/2006)*

R&A Pfaffl 2005 Altenberg Saint Laurent St. Laurent (Niederösterreich) $NA. From late harvest, superripe grapes, this is a firm, tannic, intensely flavored wine. There are some stalky bitter red fruits as well as dense bramble flavors. This is a wine that needs at least 3 or 4 years to develop. **90** —*R.V. (10/1/2006)*

R&A Pfaffl 2005 Saint Laurent St. Laurent (Niederösterreich) $NA. Raspberries and bitter cherries, fresh red fruits, great juicy flavors: this is a delicious, open red, which is friendly, generous, and ready for a barbecue. **87** —*R.V. (10/1/2006)*

R&A Pfaffl 2005 Nussern Weissburgunder (Niederösterreich) $NA. This Pinot Blanc is ripe and creamy, with some crisp acidity, green plums and full-bodied richness. It's a great food wine, smooth and rounded. **88** —*R.V. (10/1/2006)*

RAINER WESS

Rainer Wess 2005 Loibenberg Grüner Veltliner (Wachau) $32. Working mainly with purchased fruit, Rainer Wess has developed an enviable talent for wines from the Loibenberg vineyard. This is pure Grüner—with spicy, peppery, very pure fruit flavors—leaving understated elegance. **90** —*R.V. (10/1/2006)*

Rainer Wess 2004 Loibenberg Grüner Veltliner (Wachau) $33. Fresh and light, this wine reflects the relatively cool conditions of 2004. However, it still preserves much of the richness of the hot Loibenberg vineyard,

AUSTRIA

with spice and green fruits pushing through bright acidity. **89** —*R.V. (10/1/2006)*

Rainer Wess 2005 Pfaffenberg Grüner Veltliner (Kremstal) $33. Hugely ripe, this is a powerhouse of a wine, giving minerality as well as intense yellow fruit flavors. The pepper of the Grüner is discreet, leaving a soft, juicy, fruity aftertaste. **88** —*R.V. (10/1/2006)*

Rainer Wess 2004 Pfaffenberg Grüner Veltliner (Wachau) $33. Full-bodied, with a soft, round mouthfeel that fits well with the scents of white pepper and ripe peaches. Mineral and melon flavors ease across the palate, ending on a long, minerally, and subtly peppery note. **90** —*J.C. (3/1/2006)*

Rainer Wess 2004 Terrassen Grüner Veltliner (Wachau) $21. Rather full and round, this is a plump wine that offers white pepper notes amply buttressed by ripe peach and melon fruit. Firms and shows more pepper on the finish, suggesting at least a few years' of ageability. **90 Editors' Choice** —*J.C. (8/1/2006)*

Rainer Wess 2004 Wachauer Grüner Veltliner (Wachau) $17. Starts off with deep petrol and mineral notes on the nose before becoming more fruit-driven on the plump, medium-weight palate. Ripe peach and plum flavors add hints of red berries, then turn stony on the finish. **87** —*J.C. (8/1/2006)*

Rainer Wess 2003 Wachauer Trocken Grüner Veltliner (Wachau) $17. A bit fat, but still varietally correct, with aromas and flavors of celery leaf and white pepper. Subtle hints of stone fruits round out the midpalate. **85** — *J.C. (11/15/2005)*

Rainer Wess 2005 Loibenberg Riesling (Wachau) $32. Crisp, fresh, and poised, with delicious white currant fruits and pure, direct acidity piercing through. As befits a Riesling from this vineyard, this wine is just starting out. Give it 4 or 5 years at least. **89** —*R.V. (10/1/2006)*

Rainer Wess 2004 Loibenberg Riesling (Wachau) $33. Combines scents of peach pit and vegetable oil in an intriguing bouquet that seems to expand with airing. Rich and slightly oily-textured in the mouth, with flavors of peach, melon and liquified minerals, finishing long and refreshing. **91** —*J.C. (3/1/2006)*

Rainer Wess 2005 Pfaffenberg Riesling (Kremstal) $32. Hugely mineral, this wine rolls around the mouth, packed full of flavor. It still manages to be racy as well, with vibrant fresh fruits and a fine, firm structure. **90** —*R.V. (10/1/2006)*

Rainer Wess 2004 Pfaffenberg Riesling (Wachau) $33. Shows some exotic tropical nuances to its aromas and flavors, with hints of tangerine and other mixed citrus delivered via a plump, succulent mouthfeel. Long and crisply focused on the finish. **88** —*J.C. (8/1/2006)*

Rainer Wess 2004 Trocken Riesling (Wachau) $17. Plump and medium-weight, with hints of mineral oil and beef broth on the nose, followed by green apple, citrus, and some riper stone fruit flavors. The green apple notes linger on the finish. **88** —*J.C. (8/1/2006)*

Rainer Wess 2003 Trocken Riesling (Wachau) $26. Starts with lime and green-apple aromas, then delivers flavors of pineapple and minerals so intense they're like molten rock. Slightly oily-textured, and long on the finish. Fully dry. **89** —*J.C. (5/1/2005)*

REPOLUSK

Repolusk 2000 Morillon Chardonnay (Austria) $25. Smells terrific, even brilliant, with vibrant aromas of lemon-and-lime, vanilla and smoke, but there's an odd flavor that doesn't seem right, suggesting tapioca. If you can get past that, the enormous acidity is very cleansing. **84** —*S.H. (9/1/2002)*

Repolusk 2000 Gelber Muskateller (Austria) $23. Smells nice enough, with rich custardy aromas, freshly baked sweetened piecrust, and peaches and vanilla. It tastes much drier than you'd think, given the opening. Delicate peach and hazelnut flavors are offset by decent, not great, acidity. In fact, if the acids were higher, the wine would be better. **86** —*S.H. (9/1/2002)*

Repolusk 2000 Schilcher Red Blend (Austria) $22. A dry rose, the color of onion skins. The Austrians describe the aroma as "sweet tart" because it suggests freshly baked, butter-sweetened pastry crust. It drinks startlingly dry and rasping, with citrus flavors and acidity that will make your mouth water. **86** —*S.H. (9/1/2002)*

Repolusk 1999 Sweigelt Red Blend (Austria) $24. This medium-bodied, spicy wine, with a gorgeous ruby color, has tart, sour cherry flavors with rich acidity. It's extremely dry and racy, and turns almost sour on the finish because of the acids, but it's a pleasant sensation. **86** —*S.H. (9/1/2002)*

Repolusk 2000 Sauvignon Blanc (Austria) $26. Easy-drinking, this vibrantly crisp wine shines with well-etched lemon and grapefruit flavors and a grassy-herbal edge. Great acidity makes it clean and tart. Well-made, it's a pleasant sipper and would be good with shellfish. **88** —*S.H. (9/1/2002)*

Repolusk 2000 Roter Traminer Spatlese Traminer (Austria) $28. Lush, opulent scents of Kahlúa-soaked apricots and vanilla custard are inviting, but it drinks drier than it smells, with just a touch of off-dry sweetness compounding the peach and citrus flavors. Lively acidity makes it brisk. **86** —*S.H. (9/1/2002)*

Repolusk 2000 Welschriesling (Austria) $21. One of the drier wines I've had lately, it's pale in color and light in aromas, with a suggestion of lemon juice. Light in citrus flavors, with a big bite of acidity that makes it raspingly clean. **85** —*S.H. (9/1/2002)*

Repolusk 2000 Weissburgunder White Blend (Austria) $23. Vaguely Chardonnay-like, with peppery, peach aromas and flavors, bone dry, and a creamy mouthfeel. Not a lot of complexity, it's a country-style wine, with no flaws but kind of obvious. **83** —*S.H. (9/1/2002)*

RUDI PICHLER

Rudi Pichler 2004 Federspiel Grüner Veltliner (Wachau) $25. This wine packs plenty of varietal character into an elegant, lighter-bodied format. Leafy notes and white pepper aromas grace the nose, while the flavors add a slight foundation of melon and mineral. Drink now. **88** —*J.C. (8/1/2006)*

Rudi Pichler 2003 Federspiel Grüner Veltliner (Wachau) $24. Lots of fruit here, blending tangerine, pear, grapefruit, and melon. Missing are extra dimensions of richness and minerality. It's a clean, pleasant wine to drink over the next year or two. **86** —*J.C. (5/1/2005)*

Rudi Pichler 2003 Hochrain Smaragd Grüner Veltliner (Wachau) $57. Wines like this rich wine from Rudi Pichler are the best expression of the granite and slate soil of the Wachau. The wine has just the right peppery character of Grüner Veltliner combined with the crisp acidity of the region. This is an excellent food wine. **88** —*R.V. (5/1/2005)*

Rudi Pichler 2004 Terrassen Smaragd Grüner Veltliner (Wachau) $38. This nicely balanced GV features ripe pears and tropical fruit allied to citrus and white pepper, but just lacks that extra intensity and concentration of the best examples. **87** —*J.C. (3/1/2006)*

Rudi Pichler 2003 Wösendorfer Kollmütz Smaragd Grüner Veltliner (Wachau) $47. Very ripe and full-bodied, with baked apple and citrus aromas accented by oily-minerally notes reminiscent of corn oil and peppery spice. Shows superb concentration—enough to prolong the finish despite what seems to be pervilously low acidity. Drink now. **90** —*J.C. (5/1/2005)*

Rudi Pichler 2005 Achleiten Smaragd Riesling (Wachau) $62. Spicy and ripe with flavors of rich marmalade, orange, and red apple. The mineral character of the Achleiten vineyard is there as well, giving structure and length to this impressive wine. **90** —*R.V. (10/1/2006)*

Rudi Pichler 2003 Weissenkirchner Achleiten Smaragd Riesling (Wachau) $63. Fantastic stuff, even though it seems a bit closed at the moment. Nectarine and melon fruit on the nose; hints of greens as well. Full-bodied flavors are of ultra-ripe stone fruit and minerally diesel fuel, with peppery nasturtium blossoms on the finish. Approachable now. It may not be a 20-year wine, but should still hold easily through 2015. **93** — *J.C. (5/1/2005)*

SALOMON-UNDHOF

Salomon-Undhof 2003 Lindberg Reserve Grüner Veltliner (Kremstal) $35. In the Salomon-Undhof range, Reserve wines are late-harvest wines, but that means rich, with honey flavors, rather than sweet. This Grüner

AUSTRIA

Veltliner has all the right varietal character, pepper, spice, and pure, ripe fruit. Age it for three or four years to balance the richness with the fruit. **89** —*R.V. (5/1/2005)*

Salomon-Undhof 2001 Kremser Koegl Riesling (Kremstal) $23. This is a steely style of Riesling, poised and elegant, with crisp fruit flavors and tight, vivid fruit. It would be great with food, such as trout or chicken. **90** —*R.V. (11/1/2002)*

Salomon-Undhof 2001 Kremser Pfaffenberg Riesling (Kremstal) $18. 91 Editors' Choice —*R.V. (11/1/2002)*

Salomon-Undhof 2005 Pfaffenberg Riesling (Kremstal) $27. A lightly structured wine, but one that promises a firmer, steelier future. It is a crisp wine, pierced with green apple acidity and green plums. It is very fresh at this stage, but showing signs of rounding out. **90** —*R.V. (10/1/2006)*

Salomon-Undhof 2003 Pfaffenberg Riesling (Kremstal) $27. This is a single-vineyard wine from the rocky slopes above Krems. It is finely crafted, aiming at elegance rather than power. At this stage, it is lean, showing high mineral character. It has good primary green fruits and acidity that will soften out over the next few years. **89** —*R.V. (8/1/2005)*

Salomon-Undhof 2004 Steinterrassen Riesling (Kremstal) $18. This is delicious, lightweight, and fresh, and ready to drink now. Crisp, green, and lightly perfumed, it has a touch of sweetness and a fresh layer of tannins. **87** —*R.V. (8/1/2005)*

Salomon-Undhof 2003 Steinterrassen Riesling (Kremstal) $18. Leaner than the 2004 version of this wine, this 2003 has soft, fresh acidity, flavors of white peaches, and a touch of crispness. It is ready to drink now, and makes a great summer apéritif wine. **86** —*R.V. (8/1/2005)*

Salomon-Undhof 2003 Undhof Kögl Riesling (Kremstal) $24. There is a definite difference between this wine and its reserve counterpart. This boasts fresh acidity, and a perfumed layer with tannins and crispness. Without the same intensity as the reserve, it will certainly develop more quickly into a delicious, ripe wine. **89** —*R.V. (8/1/2005)*

Salomon-Undhof 2003 Undhof Kögl Reserve Riesling (Kremstal) $42. This is a great single-vineyard wine from the Kögl vineyard on the hill behind the streets of Krems. This wine is meant to be aged over many years, with its dense powerful character, its ripeness, and its big flavors of green plums, and long-lasting acidity. A great Riesling. **93 Cellar Selection** —*R.V. (8/1/2005)*

SCHINDLER

Schindler 2004 Sauvignon Blanc (Burgenland) $7. Unmistakably Sauvignon Blanc, with fresh, green, herbal aromas backed by hints of pineapple, grapefruit, and melon. Light in body and alcohol and crisply refreshing, this is the perfect antidote to oppressive heat and humidity. **85 Best Buy** —*J.C. (11/15/2005)*

SCHLOSS GOBELSBURG

Schloss Gobelsburg 2001 Altheiligenstiftung Grüner Ventliner Grüner Veltliner (Kamptal) $17. Fresh fruit, with light green-apple flavors and a refreshing streak of acidity give this wine lightness and poise. It shows the easy, simple side of Grüner Veltliner to great effect. **88** —*R.V. (11/1/2002)*

Schloss Gobelsburg 2000 Vom Urgestein Riesling (Kamptal) $19. Smoke and diesel aromas combine with honey and pear flavors in this rich yet dry wine. The flavors are complex and weighty without being heavy; the only nit-pick is that a trace of alcohol shows on the long, spicy finish. **87** —*J.C. (3/1/2002)*

Schloss Gobelsburg 2005 Zöbinger Heiligenstein Riesling (Kamptal) $36. Big, fat, and opulent as befits a wine produced in a winery owned by the Burgundian Cistercian order. The tropical fruit flavors are dominant, but still attractively balanced with lively, fresh acidity. **93** —*R.V. (10/1/2006)*

SCHLOSSWEINGUT GRAF HARDEGG

Schlossweingut Graf Hardegg 2003 Tethys Austrian White Blend (Weinviertel) $25. This is an innovative and unusual blend of Chardonnay, Pinot Blanc, and Grüner Veltliner that has been barrel fermented and aged. It is ripe, packed with vanilla flavors and intense fruit.

The Grüner Veltliner is hardly noticeable except by the fresh lift to finish. **90** —*R.V. (5/1/2005)*

Schlossweingut Graf Hardegg 2003 Drei Kruezen Grüner Veltliner (Weinviertel) $15. A crisp, fresh, youthful Grüner Veltliner, which has a young, grapefruit character, and fresh acidity. This shows all the earthy, peppery character of Weinviertel. **86** —*R.V. (5/1/2005)*

Schlossweingut Graf Hardegg 2003 Veltlinsky Grüner Veltliner (Weinviertel) $11. Maximilian Hardegg's branded Grüner Veltliner is a hit with the smart set in Vienna. It is an easy-drinking wine, full of soft fruit and freshness. A touch of soft sweetness at the end adds to its mainstream appeal. **84** —*R.V. (5/1/2005)*

SCHLUMBERGER

Schlumberger NV Cuvée Klimt Brut White Blend (Osterreichischer Sekt) $19. Light and frothy, but doesn't have that much flavor, yielding just hints of yeast and citrus. Ends crisp and lemony. **83** —*J.C. (6/1/2006)*

SCHUBERTH

Schuberth 2003 Hintaus Kabinett Grüner Veltliner (Kamptal) $16. Creamy-textured and more rounded than you might expect from a Grüner Veltliner, but mouth-filling and tasty. Hints of honey and melon are accented by ripe citrus, finally ending on a tangerine note. **86** —*J.C. (8/1/2006)*

SEPP MOSER

Sepp Moser 2003 Breiter Rain Grüner Veltliner (Kremstal) $NA. Nikolaus Moser, who currently runs this family winery, comes from one of Austria's most illustrious wine families. This is a fresh, clean style of Grüner Veltliner, but relatively light with some pleasant acidity. There is a good, racy, crisp undertone. **87** —*R.V. (5/1/2005)*

Sepp Moser 2002 Riesling Gebling Riesling (Kremstal) $30. Deliciously fresh, perfumed fruit, with layers of hedgerow fruits and soft, ripe acidity. Sepp Moser, son of the famed Lenz Moser, handed over control of the winemaking to his son, Nikolaus, who has crafted a smooth, polished wine. **89** —*R.V. (8/1/2005)*

Sepp Moser 2003 Schnabel Sauvignon Blanc (Kremstal) $25. Not a lot of zip or zest here. The nose is floral, with pineapple and peach accents. The body, however, is exceedingly soft and fleshy, with sweet, borderline mealy fruit. Finishes candied and sticky, yet harmonious. **84** *(7/1/2005)*

SONNHOF

Sonnhof 2000 Grüve Grüner Veltliner (Kamptal) $15. Sonnhof's entry-level GV is light, tasting of nothing more than lime and mineral water. It's clean and fresh, an apéritif wine without a lot of baggage. **83** —*J.C. (3/1/2002)*

SONNHOF

Sonnhof 2000 Schenkenbichl Trocken Grüner Veltliner (Kamptal) $37. This rich and full-bodied Grüner pulls no punches, hitting hard with smoke, green pear, honey, and peppery spice notes that score big on the long finish. Despite impressive ripeness and 14% alcohol, there's no apparent heat, just great depth. **91** —*J.C. (3/1/2002)*

Sonnhof 2000 Steinhaus Trocken Grüner Veltliner (Kamptal) $19. An interesting contrast to Sonnhof's Schenkenbichl bottling, this wine's alcohol content is about 2% lower, making it seem light in comparison. It's greener and less ripe-tasting as well, but still good, with pea and lime flavors layered over a base of white stone fruits. **86** —*J.C. (3/1/2002)*

Sonnhof 2000 Zobinger Heiligenstein Trocken Riesling (Kamptal) $28. Balanced for current drinking, the disparate aromas and flavors of clove, lime, quinine, ginger, and nectarine all come together harmoniously in this medium-weight wine. Everything—acids, fruit, alcohol—is well-proportioned and pleasing, maybe just a bit too polite and well-behaved. **88** —*J.C. (3/1/2002)*

SPAETROT GEBESHUBER

Spaetrot Gebeshuber 2001 Beerenauslese Pinot Gris (Thermenregion) $27. A soft, dusty flavored sweet wine, which has attractive currant fruit and a touch of citrus. It needs a couple of years to develop and bring together all its character. **87** —*R.V. (2/1/2006)*

STADT KREMS

Stadt Krems 2004 Sandgrube Grüner Veltliner (Kremstal) $14. If you wish you could afford to drink more Grüner Veltliner, load up on this gem, which features varietally correct aromas of white pepper and celery leaf layered over ripe stone fruit. It's full-bodied and seems soft at first, but then adds acidity and mineral notes on the finish that provide a firm backbone. Crisp and refreshing on the finish; perfect for summertime. **89 Best Buy** —*J.C. (8/1/2006)*

Stadt Krems 2004 Wachtberg Grüner Veltliner (Kremstal) $26. Ripe, fruity, and intense on the nose, with aromas of lime, orange zest, and peach. The palate develops more complexity, adding hints of pepper and dry minerals to bold tangerine flavors. Attractive and flashy, but just lacks a bit of length on the finish. **88** —*J.C. (3/1/2006)*

Stadt Krems 2004 Weinzierlberg Grüner Veltliner (Kremstal) $17. Smells fresh and citrusy, with hints of green apples, celery fronds, and white pepper. Medium-bodied, with no hard edges, this easy-to-drink Grüner develops flavors of stone fruit as well, ending with a nice balance of ripe peach and white pepper. **87** —*J.C. (3/1/2006)*

Stadt Krems 2004 Grillenparz Riesling (Kremstal) $27. This big, mouth-filling Riesling is loaded with tropical fruit and citrus flavors, although it starts off with more restrained aromas of peaches, mineral oil, and flow-ershop greens. As the fruit recedes, the mineral qualities should come to the fore, adding character to this fruity wine. **89** —*J.C. (3/1/2006)*

Stadt Krems 2003 Grillenparz Riesling (Kremstal) $27. Melon and herb notes on the nose give way to citrus-tinged fruit on the palate. As one might expect from the heat of the vintage, it's a plump rather than racy Riesling, but has a long, mineral-laden finish. **89** —*J.C. (8/1/2005)*

Stadt Krems 2004 Weinzierlberg Riesling (Kremstal) $21. Very fresh and citrusy on the nose, followed by lime and grapefruit flavors. They're backed by a bass note of apple. Creamy-textured on the palate, ending with more citrus and a hint of spice. **87** —*J.C. (8/1/2006)*

STEFAN HOFFMAN

Stefan Hoffman 1999 Ausbruch Chardonnay (Neusiedlersee) $38. Attractive aromas of ripe white peaches with a touch of dry honey make this wine very enticing. Although this is sweet, the sweetness is restrained by flavors of star fruit and high acidity in combination with a layer of dryness. **88** —*R.V. (11/1/2002)*

Stefan Hoffman 2001 Ausbruch Traminer Gewürztraminer (Neusiedlersee) $28. This wine oozes opulent, sweet, spicy fruit. The extravagantly sweet fruit is balanced by good acidity and a layer of dry botrytis. The texture is unctuous and sweet, leaving the palate almost shell-shocked with its richness. **90** —*R.V. (11/1/2002)*

STEINDORFER

Steindorfer 2001 Cuvée Klaus Eiswein 375 ml White Blend (Neusiedlersee) $30. A true eiswein, made from grapes frozen on the vine, with pear and honey aromas and flavors predominating. Picks up some hints of dried apricot, but doesn't show enormous complexity, just sweet viscosity and decent length. **90** —*J.C. (12/15/2004)*

STEININGER

Steininger 2004 Grand Grüner Veltliner (Kamptal) $22. Hints of jalapeño and stone fruits mingle easily on the nose of this intriguing wine. On the palate, big, mouth-filling flavors of mineral and peach end on a spicy-peppery note. True to the variety, and possessed of a distinct sense of harmony. **90 Editors' Choice** —*J.C. (3/1/2006)*

Steininger 2003 Kabinett Riesling (Kamptal) $NA. A finely layered Riesling, crisp, dry, and with fresh acidity. It has great lightness, poise, and elegance without huge intensity. Delicious summer drinking. Karl Steininger's winery now forms part of the impressive Loisium wine museum at Langenlois. **85** —*R.V. (8/1/2005)*

STIFT KLOSTERNEUBURG

Stift Klosterneuburg 2001 Ried Wiegen Trocken Grüner Veltliner (Donauland) $NA. Delightfully fresh, clean fruit on the nose, with aromas of green plums. This is a full, fat, slightly spicy wine, with good acidity as well. The palate is generous and rich, with touches of currants and spice. **87** —*R.V. (11/1/2002)*

Stift Klosterneuburg 2000 Ried Stiftsbreite, St. Laurent Ausstich Red Blend (Thermenregion) $NA. This is a soft, easy wine, with aromas of earth, vanilla, and caramel. To taste, it is soft, with light tannins, a touch of acidity, and rich chocolate flavors. With such slight tannins it could even be served slightly chilled. **86** —*R.V. (11/1/2002)*

Stift Klosterneuburg 2001 Ried Franzhauser Riesling (Donauland) $11. With its ripe acidity and green and perfumed fruit flavors, this wine is a little fat. A layer of boiled sweets spoils it at the end. **86** —*R.V. (11/1/2002)*

Stift Klosterneuburg 2000 Ried Stiftsbreite Ausstich Sankt Laurent Riesling (Thermenregion) $NA. 86 —*R.V. (11/1/2002)*

STRAUSS

Strauss 2003 Gamlitzberg Pinot Blanc Classic Pinot Blanc (Steiermark) $12. Chalky, minerally notes nicely offset the ripe pear and melon flavors in this ripe, slightly viscous Pinot Blanc. Picks up a bit of anise on the finish. **86 Best Buy** —*J.C. (12/15/2004)*

Strauss 2004 Classic Sauvignon Blanc (Steiermark) $16. Shows a grassy, almost fumé character to its aromas, then offers up tart grapefruit and unyielding minerally notes on the palate. Tart and crisp; very clean and refreshing on the finish. **86** —*J.C. (8/1/2006)*

TEGERNSEERHOF

Tegernseerhof 2003 Bergdistel Grüner Veltliner (Wachau) $20. Rather tropical and exotic, with peach and melon aromas and a creamy texture. Flavor-wise, it's fruit-forward, but still delivers enough spicy complexity to keep it interesting, finishing smoothly, elegantly, and long. **90 Editors' Choice** —*J.C. (3/1/2006)*

TERRA GOMELIZ

Terra Gomeliz 2003 Sauvignon Blanc (Südsteiermark) $17. A classic Styrian Sauvignon Blanc, with catty aromas, good flavors of acidity, and flavors of hedgerow fruits and minerals. This is a great food wine with river fish, such as trout. **87** —*R.V. (5/1/2005)*

Terra Gomeliz 2003 Welschriesling (Südsteiermark) $NA. A fine, simple wine with good fruit, flavors of pears, and a touch of creaminess. This is light, fresh and very drinkable. **84** —*R.V. (5/1/2005)*

TSCHEPPE

Tscheppe 2002 Czamillonberg Chardonnay (Styria) $22. A balanced and appealing Chardonnay with a slight floral cast to its aromas and a custardy texture. Pear, mineral, and citrus flavors round out the package. **86** —*J.C. (12/15/2004)*

Tscheppe 2002 Possnitzberg Pinot Gris (Styria) $18. This tasty, full-bodied white is a bit simple, but makes up for that with bold, assertive flavors of pear and melon. Try with simple fish or chicken dishes, or as an apéritif. **87** —*J.C. (5/1/2005)*

Tscheppe 2004 Pössnitzberg Pinot Gris (Südsteiermark) $19. Packed with direct, easy fruit, it is labeled Pinot Gris rather than Grauburgunder. It has light, almost fresh flavors, a crisp apéritif style. **88** —*R.V. (2/1/2006)*

Tscheppe 2001 Possnitzberg Reserve Pinot Gris (Styria) $33. Oakier than Tscheppe's regular bottling but ultimately not any more pleasurable. Toasty, mealy scents mask peach and melon flavors; the mouthfeel is thick and rich. Finishes with a hint of alcohol and a strong taste of nutty oak. **87** —*J.C. (5/1/2005)*

Tscheppe 2003 Pössnitzberg Reserve Pinot Gris (Südsteiermark) $33. As befits a reserve, this is a step up from Tscheppe's standard Pinot Gris. Full of white fruit flavors, with some toast from wood aging, and plenty of richness. **90** —*R.V. (2/1/2006)*

Tscheppe 2003 Czamillonberg Sauvignon Blanc (Styria) $25. Herbal and grapefruity on the nose, followed by melon flavors. A bit on the simple side, but shows nice plumpness in the midpalate and more grassy notes on the finish. **84** —*J.C. (12/15/2004)*

TSCHERMONEGG

Tschermonegg 2002 Grauburgunder (Styria) $15. Honeyed citrus fruits on the nose, followed by a plump, medium-weight wine with flavors of peach and tangerine. Finishes clean. A nice rendition of Pinot Gris. **87** —*J.C. (11/15/2005)*

AUSTRIA

AUSTRIA

Tschermonegg 2004 Grauburgunder Pinot Gris (Südsteiermark) $15. This clean, very pure, fruity wine is typical of the Tschermonegg style. With its acidity, dryness and delicious green fruit flavors, this may not be typical Pinot Gris, but the pepper and spice in the background give it away. **87** —R.V. (2/1/2006)

Tschermonegg 2002 Oberglanzberg Sauvignon Blanc (Styria) $29. This Austrian offering is very standard fare yet solid. The bouquet deals lemon, grapefruit, apricot and honey, while the palate is citrusy and full of plump, simple flavors of peach and grapefruit. Forceful yet drab; zesty but commonplace. **87** —(7/1/2005)

Tschermonegg 2003 Weissburgunder (Styria) $10. An easy quaffer, this Pinot Blanc boasts citrus and slate aromas backed by simple tangerine flavors that turn a little soft on the finish. **84** —J.C. (11/15/2005)

TÜRK

Türk 2005 Vom Urgestein Grüner Veltliner (Kremstal) $13. Packed with green fruit and citrus flavors, this finely crafted wine, smooth and crisp at the same time, is fruity, spicy, and immediately delicious to drink. A blend of grapes from two vineyards on the rolling plateau above the city of Krems, this wine is aged in stainless steel for eight months, and packed with freshness. The Türk family—vineyard owners since the 18th century—have changed their labels with this 2005 vintage, and the sunburst motif looks as elegant as the wine. **88 Best Buy** —R.V. (11/15/2006)

UMATHUM

Umathum 2001 Frauenkirchner Vom Stein St. Laurent (Burgenland) $67. This pretty, well-balanced wine starts off with scents of baked, jammy fruit and fresh cookie dough, while the flavors feature brighter, snappier cherry elements. Medium in weight, with almost sweet vanilla notes on the finish. Drink now, although it should hold for a few years because of its balance. **88** —J.C. (3/1/2006)

Umathum 2003 Zweigelt (Burgenland) $20. A bit Syrah-like, with smoke accents to its cherry and blackberry fruit, and a hint of pepper on the finish. Medium- to full-bodied, with a creamy, lush mouthfeel and little tannin. Drink over the near term. **88** —J.C. (3/1/2006)

VELICH

Velich 2002 Darscho Chardonnay (Burgenland) $25. Dominated by charred wood, with aromas of burnt marshmallow taking the lead. Has a decent texture and flavors of lemon and butter along with a short finish. **82** —J.C. (11/15/2005)

Velich 2001 Darscho Chardonnay (Burgenland) $25. Decent enough Chardonnay, but vaguely anonymous, with plump apple and pear fruit covered by smoky, leesy notes, toasted marshmallow, and charred oak. **85** —J.C. (12/15/2004)

Velich 2002 Tiglat Chardonnay (Burgenland) $55. Still a good wine, but not up to the fine quality of the 2001. Buttered toast seems to dominate, with nutty, melony notes more of an afterthought. **84** —J.C. (11/15/2005)

Velich 2001 Tiglat Chardonnay (Burgenland) $55. Top-notch Austrian Chardonnay, with lovely aromas of citrus and honey-nut Cheerios matched by lemon custard and toasted whole-grain flavors. Layered and rich, yet balanced by zesty acidity. **89** —J.C. (11/15/2005)

Velich 2001 Beerenauslese 375 ml Muskat Ottonel (Neusiedlersee) $30. Rich and viscous in the mouth, this is a sweet wine with some intriguing notes. Hints of thyme join orange marmalade scents on the nose, while the flavors bring in nuances of chocolate and herbs. Lasts a long time on the finish. **93 Editors' Choice** —J.C. (12/15/2004)

Velich 1999 Trockenbeerenauslese Welschriesling (Burgenland) $75. A golden-orange color with flecks of brown gives the (correct) impression of great ripeness. This is an unctuously sweet TBA, filled with layers of brown sugar, honey, caramel, and figs, accented by dried spices. Long and honeyed on the finish. **92** —J.C. (12/15/2004)

Velich 2001 Trockenbeerenauslese 375 ml Welschriesling (Burgenland) $70. Rich and syrupy yet not overly heavy, this unctuous dessert wine boasts aromas and flavors of honeyed nuts, dried apricots, and orange marmalade. Long and sweet on the finish, with enough sugar to stand up to fairly sweet desserts, although it might be at its best with blue cheese. **94** —J.C. (3/1/2006)

Velich 2000 Seewinkel Beerenauslese White Riesling (Burgenland) $21. Dark gold in color, this is a full-bodied dessert wine that fades quickly on the finish. Minty, peppery, wintergreen scents start it off, adding in caramel, honey, and cooked-fruit flavors on the palate. A bit strange, but good. **86** —J.C. (12/15/2004)

Walter Glatzer 2000 Kabinett Grüner Veltliner (Carnuntum) $11. Celery-leaf aromas mark the nose, and there's a strong green edge to the sugary flavors of roasted root vegetables. Low acidity leaves the wine feeling a bit heavy in the mouth. **82** —J.C. (3/1/2002)

WEINBAU SCHANDL

Weinbau Schandl 2002 Ruster Ausbruch Pinot Blanc (Burgenland) $55. The great sweet wines of Rust, known as Ausbruch, manage to combine the richness and intensity of botrytis berries with freshness. This wine from Peter Schandl fits the model, with honeyed, ripe flavors, layers of dry botrytis, and great acidity to finish. **88** —R.V. (3/1/2006)

WEINBAU ZAHEL

Weinbau Zahel 2001 Trocken Pinot Grigio (Weinviertel) $13. A wine full of spicy aromas, along with lemon sorbet. The palate is crisp, quite green, with high acidity. A crisply refreshing, simple wine that leaves a fine, clean aftertaste. **85** —R.V. (11/1/2002)

WEINBERGHOF FRITSCH

Weinberghof Fritsch 2003 Steinberg Grüner Veltliner (Donauland) $17. While the Steinberg does produce delicate wines, this is an exception. Powered and peppery, it is rich, ripe, and full-bodied. Karl Fritsch has developed almost an international style, emphasizing fruit intensity, but he has not lost all the fine balance of an Austrian Grüner Veltliner. **90** —R.V. (5/1/2005)

WEINGUT ALLRAM

Weingut Allram 2005 Zöbinger Heiligenstein Riesling (Kamptal) $38. Run by Michaela and Erich Hass, Weingut Allram has produced a full, ripe wine in which the fruit fronts layers of mineral and fresh, crisp acidity. The flavors are of white fruits, touched with citrus and almonds. This is a soft wine, but one that retains all the right structure. **90** —R.V. (10/1/2006)

Weingut Allram 2004 Zöbinger Heiligenstein Riesling (Kamptal) $38. Delicate, with delicious crisp fruit flavors of apples and white currants. Its mineral character is very obvious in the underlying dryness and tautness of structure. **89** —R.V. (10/1/2006)

WEINGUT RICHARD ZAHEL

Weingut Richard Zahel 2005 Nussberg Riesling (Vienna) $NA. This Nussberg wine has spice, citrus flavors, and great minerality. It's a full wine, perfumed and rich, but there's also a fine poise and delicacy to it. **88** —R.V. (10/1/2006)

Weingut Richard Zahel 2004 Nussberg Gemischter Satz Grande Reserve White Blend (Vienna) $NA. Gemischter Satz simply means, in Viennese dialect, a mixed vineyard, and this wine comes from a parcel of land that has eight different varieties and 50-year-old vines. The blend certainly gives complexity as well as richness, with currants and white fruits living together with crispness and a vivid aftertaste. **90 Editors' Choice** —R.V. (10/1/2006)

WEINGUT TFXT

Weingut TFXT 2000 Arachon Red Blend (Mittelburgenland) $32. A joint venture between F.X. Pichler in the Wachau, Manfred Tement in Styria and Illa Szemes in Burgenland. The wine, a blend of Blaufränkisch, Merlot, Zweigelt, and Cabernet Sauvignon, is produced in the Burgenland. The result is a hugely spicy wine, full of red berry fruits and firm but sweet tannins. **90** —R.V. (11/1/2002)

WEINKELLEREI TIEDL

Weinkellerei Tiedl 1999 Barrique Blaufränkisch (Neusiedlersee) $15. An easy-to-drink wine, dominated by aromas of juicy, sweet red fruits. There are firm tannins and some wood flavors but always sweet fruit underneath. A fruity, forward wine with some dry tannins at the end. **88** — *R.V. (11/1/2002)*

Weinkellerei Tiedl 2001 Trocken Pinot Blanc (Neusiedlersee) $13. There is bright green fruit on the nose. To taste, the wine is full-bodied with a soft, creamy texture and fat, ripe fruit. A highly drinkable, refreshing wine, oozing soft fruits, and crisp acids at the end. **90** — *R.V. (11/1/2002)*

Weinkellerei Tiedl 2000 Blauer Zweigelt Red Blend (Neusiedlersee) $15. An exotic if undemanding wine, with ripe raspberry fruit on the nose and a touch of vanilla. The palate has firm, dry tannins, with a rather stalky element, red fruit, paprika, and spice. The aftertaste is firm and dry. **85** — *R.V. (11/1/2002)*

WEINRIEDER

Weinrieder 2005 Grüner Veltliner (Weinviertel) $12. Intensely perfumed wine with concentrated, ripe flavors of bitter oranges and pepper. At the end, though, the primary taste is of freshness, with a lift of acidity. **87 Best Buy** — *R.V. (10/1/2006)*

Weinrieder 2004 Alte Reben Grüner Veltliner (Niederösterreich) $24. From 50-year-old vines, harvested at the end of November, this wine has definite late-harvest richness and intensity of flavor. Fruit tastes are less obvious than the perfumes, the flavors of almonds and complexity, what Friedrich Rieder calls a wine with character. **93 Editors' Choice** — *R.V. (10/1/2006)*

Weinrieder 2005 Schneiderberg Grüner Veltliner (Niederösterreich) $15. Weinrieder's hallmark purity of fruit is very evident with this wine's freshness and flavors of pears and green plums. It has good weight, great poise, and a deliciously light aftertaste. **90 Best Buy** — *R.V. (10/1/2006)*

Weinrieder 2001 Schneiderberg Grüner Veltliner (Austria) $12. Rich and fragrant, a wine that opens with a blast of wild honey, clove, key lime pie, toast, vanilla, and other spicy aromas. Mouth-filling and intense, with massive citrus, peach, and flower flavors that last through the honeyed finish. Dry, with high acidity, this gorgeous wine is a great value in a GV. **91** — *S.H. (10/1/2004)*

Weinrieder 2003 Schneidersberg DAC Grüner Veltliner (Weinviertel) $12. The DAC (Districtus Austriae Controllatus) wines, designed for easy drinking but with a good character of terroir and character, have found just the right expression in this wine. It is made from old vines which give it beautiful integration, concentration, and depth of fruit. **89 Best Buy** — *R.V. (5/1/2005)*

Weinrieder 2001 Bockgarten II Riesling (Austria) $25. Great Riesling, with its clean, pure aromas of buttercup flowers, smoky honey, and ripe citrus veering into tropical fruit. Enters very dry and crisp in acidity, with an intense, palate-searing taste of fresh lime and pineapple. Turns complex, unveiling tiers of flowers, white and yellow stone fruits and spice. **90** — *S.H. (10/1/2004)*

Weinrieder 2004 Bockgärten II Riesling (Niederösterreich) $29. The second harvesting pass through the vineyard in 2004 produced the grapes for this wine. The purity of the fruit flavors are the most striking thing about this delicious and impressive wine. Flavors of white currants vie with hedgerow fruits, lychees, and almonds. **92** — *R.V. (10/1/2006)*

Weinrieder 2005 Kugler Riesling (Niederösterreich) $19. From a vineyard that has 50% loess soil and 50% sandstone, this wine is open, generous, and opulent. The fruits are in the green spectrum, but they are rich and finely perfumed. **91 Editors' Choice** — *R.V. (10/1/2006)*

Weinrieder 2003 Schneiderberg Eiswein 375mL Riesling (Niederösterreich) $70. What a beautiful wine, with honey, perfumes, acidity, and delicate fruit. It is certainly ripe, with tropical fruits and a pure citric streak. But more than the parts is the sum: The acidity promises long bottle aging, but the pleasure is also there now. Treasure this wine—none was produced in 2004 or in 2005. **95 Cellar Selection** — *R.V. (10/1/2006)*

Weinrieder 2004 Hohenleiten Welschriesling Auslese Welschriesling (Niederösterreich) $38. This is one of those rare sweet wines that manages to tread the line between sweetness and acidity, combining the best of both worlds. The acidity is very present, but it doesn't overwhelm the delicate fruit flavors and the touch of honey. **90** — *R.V. (10/1/2006)*

Weinrieder 2005 Hohenleiten Welschriesling Eiswein 375mL Welschriesling (Niederösterreich) $40. Tropical fruits combine with honey to give a wine with both exotic flavors and considerable intensity and weight. Still, as befits an ice wine, there is some delicacy from pure, piercing acidity. **92** — *R.V. (10/1/2006)*

Weinrieder 2005 Hölzler Welschriesling Eiswein 375mL Welschriesling (Niederösterreich) $35. This intensely sweet wine, almost like nectar, is so fresh and poised, that it is both overwhelming and refreshing. Honey marches with acidity, smokiness, and perfumed fruit. **93** — *R.V. (10/1/2006)*

WENZEL

Wenzel 2001 Bandkraften Blaufränkisch (Burgenland) $25. This Burgenland producer has been a real discovery for us over the past year or so, excelling with sweet wines, dry whites, and reds. This spice-driven red relies on clove, cracked pepper, and tea notes for interest, layered against a backdrop of cherry-berry and plum fruit. Supple enough to drink now. **88** — *J.C. (5/1/2005)*

Wenzel 2003 Noble Selection 375ml Gelber Muskateller (Burgenland) $22. Very fragrant on the nose, with floral notes and peppery-spicy nuances as well as a solid backdrop of melon and apple. The flavors are almost Gewürz-like, with air freshener and rose petal notes accented by honeyed sweetness. Drink young. **88** — *J.C. (12/1/2006)*

Wenzel 2003 Pinot Gris (Burgenland) $19. From its intense, fruity flavors, it's obvious that there is a New World influence. Michael Wenzel worked in New Zealand, California, and Australia before coming back to the family winery. The spice of the grape is there, with toast and ripe fruit. **87** — *R.V. (2/1/2006)*

Wenzel 2001 Pinot Gris (Burgenland) $19. Does this sound old to be a current release Pinot Gris? Yes, but the quality makes it worth the wait. A rich, unctuous mouthfeel brings a cascade of stone fruit and mineral flavors, while the aromas boast hints of nectarine, pear, and spice. Has a long finish, too. A real find. **92 Editors' Choice** — *J.C. (5/1/2005)*

Wenzel 2002 Beerenauslese Riesling (Burgenland) $40. Smells like essence of superripe peach, blended with honey and dried apricots. Peach, apricot, and bergamot flavors in the mouth are sweet but not overly heavy; this wine finishes on a fresh, clean note, not a sticky-sweet one. **91 Editors' Choice** — *J.C. (12/15/2004)*

Wenzel 2002 Am Fusse des Berges Ruster Ausbruch 375 ml White Blend (Burgenland) $52. A bit of a letdown after the 2001 version, but still a pretty good dessert wine. Nut and citrus aromas give way to pineapple, orange, and melon flavors in this blend of Sauvignon Blanc, Pinot Gris, and Welschriesling that comes across as fruity and sweet but a bit simple. **86** — *J.C. (3/1/2006)*

Wenzel 2001 Am Fusse Des Berges Ruster Ausbruch 375 ml White Blend (Burgenland) $60. Despite being a blend of Welschriesling, Sauvignon Blanc, and Pinot Gris, this sticky-sweet dessert wine doesn't have the complexity of Wenzel's other Ruster Ausbruch (made from only two grape varieties). What you get here is pear, pineapple, and honey at impressive levels of sucrosity. **90** — *J.C. (12/15/2004)*

Wenzel 2003 Noble Selection 375ml White Blend (Burgenland) $20. Wenzel's least expensive sweet wine is a solid introductory effort. Light in body, it offers a distinct spice-drop set of aromas and flavors—ginger, white pepper, and anise—allied to moderate sweetness. Finishes fresh, with herb and spice notes. **86** — *J.C. (12/1/2006)*

Wenzel 2001 Saz Ruster Ausbruch White Blend (Burgenland) $120. Apricot and orange marmalade scents presage this wine's viscous sweetness, but the wine also boasts incredible precision and clarity to its flavors. Dried apricots, honey, and citrus all come together in a complex swirl that never seems too heavy or cloying. Finishes with a hint of bergamots (the flavoring in Earl Grey tea). A blend of Furmint and Gelber Muskateller. **95** — *J.C. (12/15/2004)*

Wenzel 2002 Saz Ruster Ausbruch 375 ml White Blend (Burgenland) $120. Wenzel's top cuvée is frighteningly expensive, but there's no denying the quality. Intensely botrytized aromas of dried apricots billow from the glass, accented by hints of toast, vanilla, and coconut from aging in new oak barrels. Round and mouthfilling, it is very sweet, but with just enough acid to provide a semblance of balance. Dried apricot flavors

AUSTRIA

dominate, but there's also super-ripe apple and melon flavors, while hints of spice and citrus emerge on the long finish. A worthy successor to the 2001. **94** —*J.C. (12/1/2006)*

WERNER DUSCHANEK

Werner Duschanek 2000 Image Barrique Cabernet Sauvignon (Mittelburgenland) $NA. A dark, almost black wine. High toast and vanilla on the nose, combine with black-currant fruit on the nose. This is a smooth, polished, ripe wine—fruit, wood, and tannins are in balance with acidity and black fruits. This should develop well over 5–10 years. **90** —*R.V. (11/1/2002)*

Werner Duschanek 2000 Spatlese Pinot Noir (Mittelburgenland) $NA. **86** —*R.V. (11/1/2002)*

Werner Duschanek 2000 Zweigelt Red Blend (Mittelburgenland) $NA. **84** —*R.V. (11/1/2002)*

WIENINGER

Wieninger 2005 Herrenholz Grüner Veltliner (Vienna) $14. From the sandy Herrenholz vineyard north of Vienna, this is a full, open, fruity style of Grüner, from 35-year-old vines. It is ripe, generous, and packed with fresh acidity. **89 Best Buy** —*R.V. (10/1/2006)*

Wieninger 2004 Herrenholz Grüner Veltliner (Vienna) $15. Hard to mistake this for any other grape variety, given its prominently white-pepper and celery-leaf aromas. A bit austere on the palate, with chalky-mineral notes and leafy flavors. A notch below the excellent 2003, which showed more stone-fruit character, but still very good—and very fairly priced. **88 Editors' Choice** —*J.C. (8/1/2006)*

Wieninger 2003 Herrenholz Grüner Veltliner (Vienna) $17. Shows good acidity for a 2003, with a crispness on the finish that belies the vintage. Peppery and a bit green-herbal-vegetal on the nose—classic GV. Then it delivers peach and mineral oil flavors on the palate and finish. Good value. **90 Editors' Choice** —*J.C. (5/1/2005)*

Wieninger 2005 Kaasgraben Grüner Veltliner (Vienna) $23. A vineyard high on the Nussberg hill gives this hugely concentrated wine perfumed flavors of ripe plums to go with its touch of pink grapefruit. Well structured and outstanding. **91** —*R.V. (10/1/2006)*

Wieninger 2004 Leicht & Trocken Grüner Veltliner (Vienna) $12. As the name suggests, this is light and dry, filled with modest aromas and flavors of citrus and mild salad greens. Finishes on a tart note. **84** —*J.C. (3/1/2006)*

Wieninger 2003 Leicht & Trocken Grüner Veltliner (Vienna) $12. A great buy in GV, this offering shows more minerality that most GVs at any price, delivering scents of powdered stone, apple, and citrus flavors. As the name suggests, it's light and dry, with a long, smoky, mouth-watering finish. If you like Grüner but think you can't afford to drink it every day, buy this one by the case. **89 Best Buy** —*J.C. (5/1/2005)*

Wieninger 2005 Nussberg Grüner Veltliner (Vienna) $15. From 30-year-old vines, this steely style of Grüner comes from the Nussberg vineyard in western Vienna, near the Vienna woods. It is fresh and concentrated, with flavors of quince and a backbone of mineral and pepper flavors. **90 Best Buy** —*R.V. (10/1/2006)*

Wieninger 2005 Preussen Grüner Veltliner (Vienna) $32. Grapes from a small parcel of vineyard on the Nussberg hill go into this 100-case production wine. It has some wood aging, but the main element is the rich and concentrated fruit. This will certainly repay some bottle age. 100 cases produced. **92 Cellar Selection** —*R.V. (10/1/2006)*

Wieninger 2004 Wiener Trilogie Red Blend (Vienna) $19. An easy, fresh blend of Zweigelt, Merlot, and Cab Sauvignon, Wiener Trilogie is an easy, fruity wine, with red fruit flavors, light acidity, and a soft aftertaste. Not for aging, but great for barbecues. **86** —*R.V. (10/1/2006)*

Wieninger 2003 Wiener Trilogie Red Blend (Austria) $19. This blend of Zweigelt, Merlot, and Cabernet Sauvignon is firmly structured. In fact, it's more a structural wine than a flavorful one, although it does boast scents of tar and cooked plum and modest, fruity notes on the palate. Drink it over the next few years before the fruit fades. **85** —*J.C. (3/1/2006)*

Wieninger 2005 Nussberg Riesling (Vienna) $25. Patches of limestone soil on the Nussberg hill allow Riesling to be fruity—with white peaches and apricots—and also mineral. There is a touch of spice as well as a long-lasting citric aftertaste. **91** —*R.V. (10/1/2006)*

Wieninger 2005 Preussen Riesling (Vienna) $32. A touch of botrytis gives this wine complexity, and underlines the sweet fruit, the flavors of white currants. Lively acidity lifts the wine; will age well. **89** —*R.V. (10/1/2006)*

Wieninger 2003 Riedencuvée Riesling (Vienna) $15. A good value in Austrian Riesling, this wine delivers bright green-apple aromas, then pear and citrus flavors in a medium-bodied format. Finishes clean and fresh, with a tactile quality suggestive of talc. **89** —*J.C. (5/1/2005)*

Wieninger 2004 Riedencuvée Riesling (Vienna) $14. Lean and focused, with crisp green apple and lime notes that add hints of ripe oranges on the finish. Its fresh, zesty character would work well with a simple poisson meunière. **87** —*J.C. (8/1/2006)*

Wieninger 2001 Riedencuvée Vienna Riesling (Austria) $NA. In a remote northern suburb of Vienna, Fritz Wieninger runs his cellar from a house that also doubles as a heurige (a wine bar that sells young wine). This young, racy Riesling is crisply steely, light, and fresh with a delicious tingle of acidity. **86** —*R.V. (8/1/2003)*

Wieninger 2004 Nussberg Alte Reben White Blend (Vienna) $25. From a blend of nine different grapes, all picked together in the traditional Gemischter Satz style, this is pure Vienna. For such a seemingly haphazard way of working, this is a stylish, complex wine, with flavors coming from all directions. Nuts, ripe fruits, and spice all contribute, as does good minerality. **92 Editors' Choice** —*R.V. (10/1/2006)*

Wieninger 2001 Nussberg Alte Reben White Blend (Vienna) $26. From a small parcel of mixed old vines (alte reben) in the Nussberg vineyard, this wine combines ripe pear and melon flavors with an intense stony minerality. The mouthfeel is slightly oily without being overly weighty or rich; the finish is long, long, long. **90 Editors' Choice** —*J.C. (12/15/2004)*

Wieninger 2003 Nußberg Alte Reben White Blend (Vienna) $25. Not as successful as other recent vintages, the 2003 offers hints of honey and peaches laid over a minerally foundation, then finishes on a spicy, peppery note. From old, mixed vines that include Neuburger, Weissburgunder, Welschriesling, Grüner Veltliner, and (in smaller amounts) Sylvaner, Rotgipfler, Zierfandler, Traminer, and Riesling. **86** —*J.C. (8/1/2006)*

Wieninger 2005 WB Wieninger Blend White Blend (Vienna) $11. There's no need to think about this delicious, crisp blend of Welschriesling, Sauvignon Blanc, and Grüner Veltliner—just drink it. It's a light, fresh and easy thirst quencher. **85** —*R.V. (10/1/2006)*

WILLI BRUNDLMAYER

Willi Brundlmayer 2001 Langenloiser Steinmassel Riesling (Kamptal) $25. A complete cocktail of fruits—pears, peaches, apricots—are mixed together with spices and a mineral character. This is a finely judged wine from a master winemaker, which will age well. It would be worth giving it five years before drinking. **93 Editors' Choice** —*R.V. (11/1/2002)*

Willi Brundlmayer 2001 Lyra Zöbinger Heiligenstein Riesling (Kamptal) $48. Bründlmayer, one of Austria's most famed winemakers, finds that the lyre method of training the vine gives significantly more concentration. That's certainly true of this rich, full, intense wine, with its powering acidity and flavors of almonds, white currants, and cranberries. **93** —*R.V. (8/1/2003)*

WILLI OPITZ

Willi Opitz 1998 Weisser Schilfmandl Muskat Ottonel Muscat (Burgenland) $50. A wine that combines sweetness and elegance in balance. Spice and cinnamon flavors give it an exotic perfumed appeal, while the crispness leaves a refreshing feel in the mouth. **90** —*R.V. (11/1/2002)*

Willi Opitz 2001 White Blend (Neusiedlersee) $18. An extravagantly perfumed wine, with acidity and flavors of lychees and melons. Fresh, crisp, and exotic. **88** —*R.V. (5/1/2004)*

Willi Opitz 2002 Goldackerl White Blend (Neusiedlersee) $18. A full-bodied, ripe wine, with honeyed sweetness, flavors of apricots, and crisp

AUSTRIA

acidity all in good balance. Even though it is rich, it is still impressively crisp, leaving a fresh aftertaste. **89** —*R.V. (5/1/2004)*

Willi Opitz 2001 Schilfwein Zweigelt (Neusiedlersee) $46. The Zweigelt is a red grape, and this wine, made from pressing dried grapes, has an attractive red/gold color. To taste, it has flavors of honey and marmalade, and lilting acidity. It's an unusual style, but very attractive. **87** —*R.V. (5/1/2004)*

WIMMER-CZERNY

Wimmer-Czerny 2003 Fumberg Grüner Veltliner (Donauland) $16. The Czerny family, who have 27 acres of vines on the terraces of the Wagram, make long-lived, bone-dry wines, produced from an organic vineyard. This wine has years to go. It is still fresh, but yielding only grapefruit and spice flavors at this stage. Power and elegance should come later. **87** —*R.V. (5/1/2005)*

WINZER KREMS

Winzer Krems 2005 Kremser Goldberg Grüner Veltliner (Kremstal) $16. Spice, tobacco, and pepper characterize this wine, with its floral aromas, full fruit, and just a touch of acidity. Not a wine for aging, but one to drink today. **88** —*R.V. (10/1/2006)*

Winzer Krems 2005 Kremser Wachtberg Grüner Veltliner (Kremstal) $22. A big, full-bodied wine, packed with spice, red currants, and very ripe fruits. It's open, generous, soft, and very pleasurable. **87** —*R.V. (10/1/2006)*

Winzer Krems 2003 Kellermeister Privat Kremser Kremsleiten Riesling (Kremstal) $15. A generous, rich, open style of Riesling from the excellent Krems cooperative. The wine is soft, full of fresh acidity and lively green fruit flavors. Well-balanced, and should be ready to drink within a year. **88** —*R.V. (8/1/2005)*

Winzer Krems 2005 Kremser Pfaffenberg Riesling (Kremstal) $24. There's just the right amount of structure with this wine to promise some good aging. But right now, the Krems coop has made a beautiful, green fruit-flavored wine that shows some mineral character as well as vibrant, racy acidity. **89** —*R.V. (10/1/2006)*

Winzer Krems 2003 Kremser Pfaffenberg Riesling (Kremstal) $17. The largest cooperative in Austria produces some great-value Rieslings and Grüner Veltliner, from the Kremstal region, just east of the Wachau. This Riesling is fresh, peachy, racy, and crisp, clean and delicious. **87** —*R.V. (5/1/2005)*

Winzer Krems 2004 Riesling von den Terrassen Riesling (Kremstal) $10. An initially gentle, easy wine opens out to give richness and generosity. It may not be complex, but it has great acidity, and good grapefruit flavors. The aftertaste is crisp and fresh. **86** —*R.V. (8/1/2005)*

WOHLMUTH

Wohlmuth 1999 Summus Cabernet Blend (South Styria) $25. This blend of Cabernet Sauvignon, Merlot, and Zweigelt isn't unlike a lightweight Merlot. Earth and black cherry aromas and flavors on a lithe frame are tinged with dried herbs. Finishes tart. **85** —*J.C. (3/1/2002)*

Wohlmuth 2001 Summus Chardonnay (Südsteiermark) $18. A clean, fresh-fruited Chardonnay, exhibiting ripe flavors and some softness. Flavors of melon and spices give it roundness, but the essence of the wine is the easy, soft fruit. **87** —*R.V. (11/1/2002)*

Wohlmuth 2000 Summus Gewürztraminer (South Styria) $16. A bit restrained, but identifiably Gewürz, with its trademark aromas of lychees and rose petals. Picks up some ripe melon nuances on the palate. A polite introduction to Gewürztraminer, virtually guaranteed to not offend. **86** —*J.C. (3/1/2002)*

Wohlmuth 2000 Summus Muskateller (South Styria) $16. Spicy, musky, and fruity, this Austrian Muscat is full-bodied, even a bit fat—a marked contrast to most Austrian wines. The peach and melon fruit finishes soft, accented by a spicy-peppery note. **84** —*J.C. (3/1/2002)*

Wohlmuth 2000 Summus Pinot Blanc (South Styria) $15. Very light, with only faint hints of pear and peppery spice. Pleasant, just insubstantial. **83** —*J.C. (3/1/2002)*

Wohlmuth 2004 Pinot Gris (Südsteiermark) $12. Especially attractive, with poised, elegant, fresh flavors. While not intense, there is great pleasure to be found in this fresh, green wine, with its layers of acidity and smooth, silky texture. **88** —*R.V. (2/1/2006)*

Wohlmuth 2000 Summus Pinot Gris (South Styria) $16. **84** —*J.C. (3/1/2002)*

Wohlmuth 2003 Sauvignon Blanc (South Styria) $27. Herbs, mineral, and grass along with some lime and melon create a modest bouquet. Round with ample structure; the flavor profile is reserved, with melon, orange, and doughy notes. Chalky is the best way to describe the mineral-laden finish. **86** —*J.C. (7/1/2005)*

Wohlmuth 2001 Summus Sauvignon Blanc (Südsteiermark) $20. The Wohlmuths make classic Styrian Sauvignon Blanc, with a balance between ripe tropical fruit and crispness. You'll find herbs and spices, and just a touch of wood from the 25% new barriques. **88** —*R.V. (11/1/2002)*

Wohlmuth 2000 Summus Sauvignon Blanc (South Styria) $18. Despite a rush of pungent herbaceousness and cat pee, the flavors are sweetly fruity and low in acid. Rich and a bit heavy. **83** —*J.C. (3/1/2002)*

ZANTHO

Zantho 2003 St. Laurent (Burgenland) $13. Smoky and herbal aromas support black cherry preserves—a nice enough effect. However, the wine is less attractive on the palate, where it picks up some stemmy notes and even a hint of bitterness on the finish. **84** —*J.C. (3/1/2006)*

Zantho 2002 St. Laurent (Burgenland) $13. Subtle spice and candied cherries on the nose give way to pure intense black cherries on the palate. Medium- to full-bodied, it does pick up a hint of heat on the finish, but also a spicy, cedary nuance. Drink now. **87** —*J.C. (5/1/2005)*

Zantho 2002 Zweigelt (Burgenland) $13. Zantho is a joint venture between Wolfgang Peck and Josef Umathum. Don't be put off by the colorful label with a the cute lizard—this is not an Australian wine. It's a young, fresh, vibrant red, filled with bouncy cherry fruit accented by just a bit of chocolate and spice. Drink now. **87** —*J.C. (5/1/2005)*

Zull 2000 Odfeld Grüner Veltliner (Weinviertel) $17. Oily and rich describe this GV's mouthfeel, while its aromas are all about gardenias, apples, and honey. Clove and cinnamon accent the ripe apple and pear fruit. Minerally and intense on the finish. **90** —*J.C. (3/1/2002)*

AUSTRIA

Chile

Chile saw its original grapevines arrive with sixteenth-century Spanish missionaries, but the first semblance of a modern winemaking industry dates back to the early part of the nineteenth century, when a naturalist by the name of Claudio Gay imported about sixty varieties of grapes from France. In turn, some of these grapes were planted in the Maipo Valley, which encompasses the city of Santiago, and by the 1850s commercial wine existed.

From an American's perspective, Chilean wine started to make its mark in the 1970s, when protectionist restrictions were lifted by the military dictatorship headed by Augusto Pinochet. Almost immediately, exports spiked, with value-priced wines pouring into America as well as other countries. Some thirty years later, Chile is one of the world's most aggressive exporters; its wines make it to nearly one hundred countries around the globe, with shipments to the United States leading the way.

In many ways, the climate, geology, and geography of Chile are like that of western North America, but turned upside-down. Chile's north is a bone-dry desert, roughly equal to Baja California, only drier. The middle of the country is verdant and river-fed, with soils perfect for all sorts of agriculture, not the least of which is grapes. So in that sense it's like California, Oregon, and Washington. And as one goes south it quickly gets colder and more rugged, not unlike British Columbia and eventually Alaska.

In the midsection of this 4,000-mile-long sliver of a country, there's a 500-mile chunk called the Central Valley, and within this valley there are a number of

Wine barrels in the cellars of Viña Luis Felipe Edwards, Chile.

prime wine-growing regions. The most historic is Maipo, in which just about all grapes are grown. But it's Cabernet Sauvignon that has always been king in Maipo. Whether it's a simple everyday Maipo Cabernet like Cousiño-Macul's Antiguas Reservas or one of the country's best premium offerings like Concha y Toro's Don Melchor, a Maipo Cabernet is well worth hailing.

Other prominent wine regions include Aconcagua and Limari, the two northern frontiers of premium grape growing. There aren't many wineries there, but the wines are solid and true. Bordering Maipo to the west is the Casablanca Valley, first planted by Pablo Morandé and his family in the early 1990s. Cool and coastal, Casablanca and neighboring Leyda and San Antonio are prime spots for Chardonnay and Sauvignon Blanc but have trouble when it comes to producing ripe red wines.

South of Maipo is Rapel and its two parallel valleys: Cachapoal and Colchagua. Here the weather is warm, and the majority of grapes are red. Colchagua is arguably the leading region in Chile for red wines, and there's a plethora of big, burly wines based on Syrah, Cabernet Sauvignon, Merlot, Malbec, and Carmenère coming from Colchagua wineries including Montes, Casa Lapostolle, Viu Manent, MontGras, and Los Vascos.

Further south are the regions of Curicó and Maule. It was in Curicó that Miguel Torres of Spain set up shop in 1979 and introduced the then-revolutionary concept of steel-tank fermentation to Chile. To borrow a well-used phrase and apply it to how wine is now being made throughout the country: the rest is history.

2 BROTHERS

2 Brothers 2003 Big Tattoo Syrah (Colchagua Valley) $9. A strong whiff of olive and leather carries the nose, which simply isn't that fruity. Berry fruit and some green notes on the palate. Oaky and drying late. **82** — *M.S. (11/1/2005)*

AGUSTINOS

Agustinos 2000 Estate Cabernet Sauvignon (Cachapoal Valley) $8. 83 — *D.T. (1/1/2002)*

Agustinos 2000 Reserve Cabernet Sauvignon (Cachapoal Valley) $13. 85 —*D.T. (7/1/2002)*

Agustinos 2001 Reserve Carmenère (Maipo Valley) $9. 82 —*D.T. (7/1/2002)*

Agustinos 2000 Reserve Carmenère (Maipo Valley) $13. There's brightness here, though the wine's flavors are a little strange. The nose is a mix of wet soil, caramel, and clarified butter; the palate offers the same wet-soil flavor, plus plum and wood. Not nuanced; closes with herb and metal. **83** —*D.T. (7/1/2002)*

Agustinos 2001 Estate Chardonnay (Cachapoal Valley) $8. Flamboyant, exotic aromas of oranges and mangoes emanate from the glass, but the tropical and citrus fruits are more muted in the mouth, finishing with earth and a spicy, clove-pepper note. **85** —*J.C. (7/1/2002)*

Agustinos 2000 Estate Chardonnay (Cachapoal Valley) $8. 84 —*M.S. (7/1/2002)*

Agustinos 2000 Reserve Chardonnay (Cachapoal Valley) $13. Bright gold in color, with a full, rich, woody nose. The pear and apple fruit to the palate is solid, even if it leans toward over-ripe. There's a touch of resin on the finish, and ultimately the final impression is of oak and toast. The bottom line is that definition of fruit just isn't there. **85** —*M.S. (7/1/2002)*

Agustinos 2000 Reserve Merlot (Cachapoal Valley) $13. Sweet chocolate flavors and a layer of toast pair well with the raspberry and earth aromas. The wine is made to be drunk now and enjoyed. **85** —*C.S. (12/1/2002)*

ALFASI

Alfasi 1998 Cabernet Sauvignon (Maule Valley) $8. It's nice to see an ever-increasing number of serviceable kosher wines like this one being made available to consumers from around the world. That said, this one isn't much more than adequate. There's a modest amount of cassis fruit dressed up with earthy chocolate and vaguely minty aromas, but it lacks depth. Still, it's better than the kosher stuff I remember from my friends' bar mitzvahs. **82** —*J.C. (2/1/2001)*

Alfasi 2000 Reserve Cabernet Sauvignon (Maule Valley) $10. Fairly supple, with moderate body, the wine is framed in soft tannins. Black cherry, blackberry, cassis, smoke, tar, and licorice flavors come to mind, ending in a finish of moderate length. Kosher. **87 Best Buy** —*J.M. (4/3/2004)*

Alfasi 1998 Reserve Cabernet Sauvignon (Maule Valley) $8. This kosher Cabernet has been on the market too long. It was once a ripe wine, but it has faded into an orange-tinged lightweight with just some dried cherry fruit and apple skins. This wine isn't dead, but it's tired. New vintage, please. **80** —*M.S. (7/1/2003)*

Alfasi 1999 Chardonnay (Maule Valley) $8. This Chilean wine displays two personalities. The nose offers aromas of ripe peaches and cream, with honey and buttered-toast accents. On the tongue it turns crisp and tart, with citrus and green-apple flavors and fairly sharp acidity. It finishes short and bright. **84** *(4/1/2001)*

Alfasi 2002 Reserve Chardonnay-Sauvignon (Maule Valley) $8. This 50-50 blend yields hints of diesel or kerosene on the nose, then adds honey and pear flavors. A bit rough and phenolic on the finish. **82** —*J.C. (4/1/2005)*

Alfasi 2002 Reserve Malbec-Syrah (Central Valley) $10. Kind of smoky and tangy, with powdery tannins and a hint of spice. Flavors range from bing cherry to citrus, framed in an oaky web. Not as enticing as the winery's Cabernet from 2000. Kosher. **81** —*J.M. (4/3/2004)*

Alfasi 1998 Merlot (Maule Valley) $7. The seemingly late-picked, almost over-ripe fruit veers from plum and blackberry aromas and flavors into sweet rhubarb and tomato preserves. This Chilean Merlot is flavorful, with light to medium body and a dry finish. **85** *(4/1/2001)*

Alfasi 2001 Estate Bottled Merlot (Maule Valley) $6. This kosher offering is light and leafy, with strong notes of vegetables and tomatoes. The raspberry and cherry flavors are thin. **80** —*M.S. (7/1/2003)*

Alfasi 2001 Reserve Merlot (Maule Valley) $10. Strong tobacco and olive scents emerge from the glass, followed by modest cherry flavors with an intensely herbaceous edge. Lean. **82** —*J.C. (4/1/2005)*

Alfasi 1998 Reserve Merlot (Maule Valley) $10. Rather dilute, it shows slight black cherry and blackberry aromas and flavors. The overall impression is really little more than alcohol and faint body. Finishes very dry, with innocuous tannins. **80** *(4/1/2001)*

Alfasi 1998 Flora Semi Dry Red Blend (Maule Valley) $10. There's a tanginess to the red cherry-berry fruit aromas and flavors; oaky heat makes the flavors less approachable. Cranberry, plum, and oak finish it up. **82** —*D.T. (7/1/2002)*

Alfasi 1999 Sauvignon Blanc (Maule Valley) $8. This light and lemony wine would make a good afternoon sipper, or a tasty match for grilled fish. The spicy, citrus fruit shows good intensity midpalate. Finishes clean, with moderate length and herb notes. **86** *(4/1/2001)*

Alfasi 2001 Late Harvest Sauvignon Blanc (Maule Valley) $15. Simple and sweet, with aromas and flavors of apricot jam. Medium-weight and low in acidity. **82** —*J.C. (4/1/2005)*

ALMAVIVA

Almaviva 1998 Bordeaux Blend (Puente Alto) $87. A dense bouquet of dark cherries, plum, earth, meat, and subtle tobacco pulls you in. It is big in the mouth, yet never brutish, with lovely depth of fruit flavor, earthy accents, and great texture. The fine, long finish has even, dry tannins. Seductively accessible, this world class wine will age well for 6–12 years or longer. **93 Cellar Selection** —*M.M. (2/1/2001)*

Almaviva 2003 Cabernet Blend (Puente Alto) $75. Impressive in every way. The color shines an irridescent ruby, while the bouquet is massive, an amalgamation of fresh-cut cedar, pencil lead, and lush berry fruit. Ripe as can be and balanced, with plushness and depth you don't normally find. Finishes round and creamy, with vanilla and liqueur notes. Does not require cellaring but should hold for up to 10 years. **94 Editors' Choice** —*M.S. (10/1/2006)*

Almaviva 2000 Cabernet Blend (Puente Alto) $91. Just the fifth vintage of this Concha y Toro/Baron Rothschild joint venture superbly blends the robust with the reserved. Despite a challenging millennium vintage, the wine is ripe, with cassis and licorice aromas and expressive currant and plum flavors. The tannins are mild, the finish deep with plum and coffee. While not a heavyweight Cabernet, it still packs punch. Drink now through 2007. **92 Cellar Selection** —*M.S. (12/1/2002)*

Almaviva 1999 Red Blend (Maipo Valley) $91. This joint venture between Concha y Toro and the owners of Château Mouton Rothschild is hitting its stride. The latest Almaviva showcases sweet, dark, plummy fruit, all wrapped in a cedary cloak of earth, tobacco, and cassis. Smooth and supple, framed with soft tannins, there's no need to cellar it, but it should last well. **92 Cellar Selection** —*J.C. (3/1/2002)*

ALTAÏR

Altaïr 2002 Sideral Cabernet Blend (Rapel Valley) $25. Solid and sweet, with a nose that's plum-filled, fresh, and intriguing. A blend of several grapes, but the base is Cabernet. Flavors of cherry, raspberry, and plum are bright, while the finish is fairly bold and carries a note of chocolate. Not super lush but rock solid, with a serious tannic foundation. **89** — *M.S. (11/1/2005)*

Altaïr 2002 Altair Cabernet Sauvignon (Cachapoal Valley) $55. Powerful and cranked up to another level, with a lot of natural purity. Gigantic on the palate, with berry syrup, earth, and extremely powerful tannins. Tight and built like a fort; not an easy wine to just pop and quaff. The jackhammer tannins see to that. **88** —*M.S. (11/1/2005)*

Altaïr 2003 Red Blend (Cachapoal Valley) $59. Terrific Chilean red wine; seductive and succulent, with a beautiful burgundy hue matched by pure, ripe Bordeaux-like flavors. Deep and satisfying, and smooth as silk.

CHILE

If ever a Chilean red ranked as world class, this is it. **94 Editors' Choice** —M.S. (11/1/2005)

Altaïr 2003 Sideral Red Blend (Rapel Valley) $29. Finely oaked, with lovely cedar scents accenting robust but smooth black cherry and dark plum aromas. Sings a pretty tune in the mouth, with ripe berry fruit, tobacco, toast, and a long finish. A significant step up from the first vintage. **91** —M.S. (11/1/2005)

ANTINORI-MATTE

Antinori-Matte 2001 Albis Cabernet Sauvignon (Maipo Valley) $53. The inaugural wine from the joint venture between Piero Antinori and Haras de Pirque owner Eduardo Matte is, as might be expected, a rich, bruising, forceful red. The blend is 85% Cabernet Sauvignon and 15% Carmenère and it exudes deep charcoal, smoke, and black-fruit aromas. Next in line is a smooth but heady palate of cassis and herbal notes. The finish is oaky with a hint of coconut. A worthy new entry into the high-end Chilean sweepstakes. **92** —M.S. (8/1/2004)

Antinori-Matte 2002 Albis Cabernet Sauvignon-Carmenère (Maipo Valley) $55. Bulky and big, with initial green oak that morphs into coffee and vanilla. Red fruit in the mouth, with good tannins that create a plush feel. Lots of wood and espresso on the finish, with persistence. Expect better in 2003 from this Antinori-Matte joint venture; the inaugural '01 was excellent. **87** —M.S. (7/1/2006)

ANTIYAL

Antiyal 2003 Red Blend (Maipo Valley) $50. Having very much liked previous vintages of this Carmenère-Cabernet-Syrah blend, the 2003, while perfectly good, seems a bit short on substance. The nose has a bit more beet and red plum than desirable, and the palate just doesn't have that much style or flair. Registers a bit hot and grabby on the finish. **86** —M.S. (3/1/2006)

Antiyal 1999 Red Blend (Maipo Valley) $30. A terrific wine, boasting exquisite class, texture, and suppleness. It's very fruity, opening with a burst of berries and stone fruits that have an herbal edge but maintain their sweetness through the long finish. Yet it's dry, with smooth tannins. A blend of Carmenère, Cabernet Sauvignon, and Syrah. **89** —S.H. (12/1/2002)

Antiyal 2004 Sons of the Sun Red Blend (Maipo Valley) $50. This small-production luxury red blends Carmenère, Cabernet Sauvignon, and Syrah, and the end result is excellent. Licorice and black fruit carry the masculine bouquet, and next up is a palate of ripe berries that explode in a fireball of flavor. Not oaky, but well oaked; shows the essence of Maipo fruit. **91 Editors' Choice** —M.S. (11/15/2006)

Antiyal 2000 Super Chilean Blend Red Blend (Maipo Valley) $32. 90 — C.S. (2/1/2003)

APALTAGUA

Apaltagua 2003 Cabernet Sauvignon (Colchagua Valley) $10. A bit rubbery and green, but still more solid than problematic. The red fruit on the palate is spunky, as it's driven by firm, grabby tannins and a lot of acid. Finishes with some buttery wood notes, but it weighs in more racy than heavy. **85 Best Buy** —M.S. (11/1/2005)

Apaltagua 2001 Cabernet Sauvignon (Colchagua Valley) $10. Very good, a Cab with big, rich tannins and enough stuffing to age for a couple years. The blackberry and currant flavors are ripe and pure, making this wine a terrific value. Easily as good as many wines at a much higher price. **87** — S.H. (1/1/2002)

Apaltagua 2005 Estate Cabernet Sauvignon (Colchagua Valley) $10. Coffee, leather, and toast are the opening aromas, and then comes black fruit. It runs a touch more red and racy in the mouth, with raspberry, strawberry, and light green flavors. Solid in its mouthfeel, with modest depth. Basic but nice. **85 Best Buy** —M.S. (11/15/2006)

Apaltagua 2003 Carmenère (Colchagua Valley) $10. Straight-ahead in style, with red cherry on the nose along with some saucy, marinated aromas. Runs a bit lemony and lean on the palate, but at the surface level it's solid. Peppery and upright on the finish, with a little bitterness. For the most part, it's spicy and right. **85 Best Buy** —M.S. (11/1/2005)

Apaltagua 2001 Carmenère (Colchagua Valley) $10. 88 Best Buy —S.H. (11/15/2002)

Apaltagua 2000 Envero Carmenère (Colchagua Valley) $15. Deep purplish-scarlet in color, with rich tobacco, cassis, and smoke aromas and an incredibly dense mouthfeel. The dry fruit and soft, luscious tannins make the wine weightless on the palate. **91 Best Buy** —S.H. (12/1/2002)

Apaltagua 2004 Estate Carmenère (Colchagua Valley) $10. The bouquet is classic Carmenère, meaning it's spicy and peppery, with balsam wood, chocolate, and wet leaves in the blend. The palate is a bit green, but not so much so that it doesn't taste good. Finishes a bit raw and hot, with lasting red-fruit flavors that help keep it afloat. **86** —M.S. (12/31/2006)

Apaltagua 2002 Estate Bottled Carmenère (Colchagua Valley) $10. Simple, with mild vegetal aromas, hints of tobacco, and lean red fruit. Typical beet and bramble define the palate, which is textured if not overly flavorful. Finishes dark and smoky, with a shock of green. **85 Best Buy** —M.S. (2/1/2005)

Apaltagua 2002 Grial Carmenère (Colchagua Valley) $40. Rock solid, with fully developed berry, plum, cola, and fine-oak aromas. Rich and fancy, with all the best attributes Carmenère has to offer, including red plum fruit, earth, herbs, and chocolate. Big on the finish, but kept afloat by healthy acidity. A model for extracted New World Carmenère. **91 Editors' Choice** —M.S. (2/1/2005)

Apaltagua 2000 Grial Carmenère (Colchagua Valley) $30. The top tier of Apaltagua's three Carmenères is softer and richer in fruity flavors, with extremely fine tannins. It's plump and sumptuous as velvet on the palate. Seems balanced enough for the cellar, but the Envero bottling, at half the price, is a better value. **91** —S.H. (12/1/2002)

Apaltagua 2003 Vineyard Selection Envero Carmenère (Colchagua Valley) $15. A Carmenère-based wine with dark blackberry aromas and a touch of cherry cough drop to the bouquet. This one veers toward juicy, with prime acidity pushing black plum and boysenberry flavors. Fairly long and moderately complex on the finish. With 15% Cabernet. **88** —M.S. (11/1/2005)

ARAUCO

Arauco 2004 Reserve Cabernet Sauvignon (Maule Valley) $16. Deep in color, with dense blueberry, coffee, and spice aromas. Very firm and dense, with extruding tannins that push cola, berry, and plum flavors. A touch of heat and glycerol on the finish frame berry essence. This wine kicks it up a notch. **86** —M.S. (7/1/2006)

Arauco 2004 Reserve Carmenère (Maule Valley) $16. Ripe and sturdy, with saturated, well-spiced aromas. Fairly ripe and rich on the palate, with ample oak. The fruit flavors are dark, a touch creamy, and only slightly herbal. Doesn't try to reach too far; should be good with meat. **87** —M.S. (3/1/2006)

Arauco 2003 Lagrimas de Luna Red Blend (Maule Valley) $55. Overoaked and hot, with sour raspberry fruit. Plain and simple, this wine has way too much wood, tannin, and fire to it. And the price is outlandish. **81** — M.S. (5/1/2006)

Arauco 2004 Reserve Shiraz (Maule Valley) $16. Heavy on the maple, menthol, and horsehide, meaning it's not that smooth of a wine. The palate is loud and loaded with hefty plum flavors. The finish comes up toasty and bitter. Has merits but the wood level isn't one of them. **83** — M.S. (3/1/2006)

ARBOLEDA

Arboleda 2001 Cabernet Sauvignon (Maipo Valley) $15. Big enough and herbal, with cassis and cherry to the nose. More currant and plum carry the palate, and things seem to be on a clear path until the finish goes medicinal and syrupy, leaving a touch too much cough medicine on the finish. **86** —M.S. (7/1/2005)

Arboleda 1999 Cabernet Sauvignon (Maipo Valley) $20. This wine doesn't come from Caliterra's Arboleda Estate, in Colchagua, and it seems a little tight and short of cheer. The palate is tannic, and there are flavors of cherry, tobacco, and wood. **86** —M.S. (3/1/2002)

Arboleda 1998 Cabernet Sauvignon (Maipo Valley) $20. This cedary Cab offers lots of flavor and texture for the price. A cigar-box, black olive, and cassis nose is very inviting; the sweet berry and tobacco flavors are appealing if not quite as deep and vibrant as the bouquet. Medium-weight and plush, it closes with chocolate-toast notes and dry, even tannins. **88** *(10/1/2001)*

Arboleda 2003 Carmenère (Colchagua Valley) $15. Very nicely made, with good balance. The nose offers olive, tree bark, coffee, and black plum, while the leathery palate is ripe and full as it oozes with chewy blackberry. Finishes warm and toasty, with a spot of herbaceousness. Not quite luxurious but fairly plush. **87** —*M.S. (12/15/2005)*

Arboleda 2002 Carmenère (Colchagua Valley) $15. Dull and herbal, with a lot of the bell pepper and rhubarb character that Carmenère is well known for. While it has decent body and seems balanced, the aromatic and flavor profiles are decidedly vegetal. **82** —*M.S. (7/1/2005)*

Arboleda 2000 Carmenère (Colchagua Valley) $20. The grapes were very ripe and jammy, offering up rich, thick flavors of blackberries, cherries, and plums, wrapped in thick, soft dry tannins and a hint of smoky oak. This is a big wine, not very complex, but direct and appealing. The finish is fruity and simple. **85** —*S.H. (12/1/2002)*

Arboleda 1999 Carmenère (Maipo Valley) $20. Very dark colors and meaty, road-tar notes in the nose put you on notice that the wine is big. But more than big, it's pure, with layers of plum and berry fruit mixed with a peppery, bacon quality. It has an almost late-harvest depth and softness throughout, so the best bet might be to drink it soon. **88** —*M.S. (3/1/2002)*

Arboleda 2005 Chardonnay (Casablanca Valley) $15. A big-time effort for Arboleda. The wine hits with copious but balanced wood, which creates a strong blast of popcorn on the nose. The mouthfeel is sturdy and intense, with nectarine, honey, and toast flavors. **90 Best Buy** —*M.S. (10/1/2006)*

Arboleda 2003 Chardonnay (Casablanca Valley) $15. Sort of an odd yellow in color, with chunky, hard-to-discern aromas. Pear and vanilla control the palate, followed by some banana on the heavy finish. A touch dull for Casablanca Chard. **83** —*M.S. (12/15/2005)*

Arboleda 2000 Chardonnay (Central Valley) $8. 86 —*M.S. (3/1/2002)*

Arboleda 2003 Merlot (Colchagua Valley) $15. Dark and moody, with olive, leather, and spice drawing in the nose. Good cherry and plum fruit appear on the palate, backed by noticeable coconut and chocolate. A structured wine with focus and ample acidity. **87** —*M.S. (7/1/2006)*

Arboleda 2002 Merlot (Colchagua Valley) $15. Somewhat minty and spicy to start, with round plum and blackberry flavors coming next. The wine shows admirable texture, full tannins, and overall balance. Nothing spectacular but very solid and likable. **86** —*M.S. (5/1/2006)*

Arboleda 2001 Merlot (Colchagua Valley) $15. This is Caliterra's single-estate wine from Colchagua, and like most other reds from this solid vintage, it works. The nose is a bit spicy and peppery, but there's plenty of cherry and plum fruit to support it. The finish is modest but spreads out nicely. **86** —*M.S. (3/1/2004)*

Arboleda 2000 Merlot (Colchagua Valley) $20. A certain level of tightness and structure in the nose hides the immensely ripe and clean cherry, plum, and toast flavors that come across on the firm, supported palate. With full tannins and noticeable oak, this is a good Merlot in all the departments that matter. **88** —*M.S. (3/1/2002)*

Arboleda 1999 Merlot (Colchagua Valley) $20. A solid and stylish wine with plenty of toast and a plush mouthfeel. Ripe black cherry-plum fruit keeps the lavish oak from being overwhelming. Finishes full, with well-dispersed tannins and cocoa notes on the persistent fruit foundation. **87** *(10/1/2001)*

Arboleda 2005 Sauvignon Blanc (Leyda Valley) $15. Light tropical aromas are inviting as they offer a bit of green pepper and herbs. Nice in the mouth, with distinct grapefruit, apple, and lime notes. Flush and bright; it's straight-ahead wine with positives. **86** —*M.S. (7/1/2006)*

Arboleda 2002 Syrah (Colchagua Valley) $15. Dark and tight, with sturdy plum and berry aromas along with some minty oak in support. Plump and chunky on the palate, but stand up, with a finish that runs peppery. A touch raw and oaky, but still better than most Chilean Syrah. **86** —*M.S. (2/1/2005)*

Arboleda 2001 Syrah (Colchagua Valley) $15. Ripe, rich, and rubbery, and seemingly just hitting its stride. The nose offers earth, tar, and lots of magnetic black fruit. Flavors of plum, blackberry, and sugar beet are sweet yet not candied, while the finish deals espresso, mocha, and wood dust. A very good Chilean Syrah, but one that should be judged among its Chilean brethren. **88** —*M.S. (6/1/2004)*

Arboleda 2000 Syrah (Colchagua Valley) $20. The wine features outsized jammy flavors of various berries, but it's not very nuanced. It's a sweet, gooey wine, although it's technically dry. Super-ripeness has made this wine excessively fruity. **84** —*S.H. (12/1/2002)*

Arboleda 1999 Syrah (Colchagua Valley) $20. Full, earthy notes and red berry fruit with leathery accents characterize this medium-weight, well-built wine. The cassis-tobacco profile pleases, there's a grainy texture, and the big back end shows firm, full tannins, earth, and black plum notes. Should improve over the next two years. **88 Editors' Choice** *(10/1/2001)*

ARESTI

Aresti 2004 Cabernet Sauvignon (Curicó Valley) $9. Good color and depth up front, with liqueur-like aromas. Rather intense, with full-throttle cherry, raspberry, and plum flavors. Generally speaking, this is perfectly good Cabernet. It's one of Aresti's better wines in recent years. **86 Best Buy** —*M.S. (7/1/2006)*

Aresti 2003 Cabernet Sauvignon (Chile) $8. Rubbery and green, with heavy, weedy flavors and some heat. Turns toward barnyard as it opens up. Lacks pizzazz and probably won't inspire. **80** —*M.S. (7/1/2005)*

Aresti 1999 Family Collection Cabernet Sauvignon (Curicó Valley) $30. Grabby and lean, with a strong herbal element to the mild plum flavors. Finishes sticky and woody, with leftover oak. Already past its prime. **81** —*M.S. (7/1/2005)*

Aresti 1999 Family Collection Cabernet Sauvignon (Rio Claro) $26. Toast and bacon from the new-oak aging compete with smoked meat and blackberry on the bountiful nose. Plum and cassis fruit dance on the palate, and ultimately there's a lot of power to this first-ever prestige bottling by Aresti. With 15% Merlot and Carmenère. **88** —*M.S. (3/1/2002)*

Aresti 2002 Montemar Cabernet Sauvignon (Curicó Valley) $8. Aromas of leather and spice are okay, but thrown in are some sweaty notes and a whiff of green. Flavors of apple skin and pie cherry are lean for Cabernet, while the tight, leathery finish is sharp. Shows flashes of quality but also flaws. **82** —*M.S. (8/1/2004)*

Aresti 2001 Montemar Cabernet Sauvignon (Curicó Valley) $8. The nose is mildly pickled, most likely a result of American oak barrels, but overall the wine is pretty and easygoing. The flavors of sugar beet and plum skin are good, and the tannic body ensures that it's not a lightweight eager to be knocked out in the early rounds. **85 Best Buy** —*M.S. (7/1/2003)*

Aresti 1999 Montemar Cabernet Sauvignon (Curicó Valley) $8. 87 Best Buy *(9/1/2000)*

Aresti 1999 Reserva Cabernet Sauvignon (Rio Claro) $11. 89 Best Buy *(9/1/2000)*

Aresti 2004 Reserve Cabernet Sauvignon (Rio Claro) $13. Well oaked, so there's bacon, smoke, and meaty berry aromas. The palate, however, is condensed, so there isn't much variety or layering going on. Heavy on the finish, with chocolate. Seems exceedingly weighty on the back end. **83** —*M.S. (7/1/2006)*

Aresti 2000 Reserve Cabernet Sauvignon (Rio Claro) $11. An initial aromatic check reveals some cheesy, funky smells, but they blow off to reveal a solid, everyday red wine. The palate is surprisingly rich, and it tastes of boysenberry fruit. The finish has some zip and length to it, and also some overt oaky flavor. Sure, it's thin and easy by big-wine standards, but within its class of value-priced reds it's sturdy and satisfying. **85** —*M.S. (7/1/2003)*

Aresti 2003 Carmenère (Curicó Valley) $8. Meaty up front, with soy and earth aromas. Rounds into better form on the palate, where cherry and blackberry flavors are modest but real. Round and chocolaty on the finish, with acidity that keeps it moving forward. **83** —*M.S. (11/1/2005)*

Aresti 2004 Reserve Carmenère (Curicó Valley) $13. A heavy wine with bacon and meaty berry aromas. Condensed and dark, with a weighty personality and some chocolate on the finish. Comes crashing down at the end under a blanket of extract. **83** —*M.S. (7/1/2006)*

CHILE

Aresti 2001 Reserve Carmenère (Rio Claro) $11. There is some green bean and ashtray aromas on the nose, but also some maple-like wood. The palate is also slightly green at its center, but surrounding that is a fair amount of plum and cranberry. The finish is smooth, properly textured and tannic enough to create a dry, cheek-gripping feel. There's definitely some character here. **85** —*M.S. (7/1/2003)*

Aresti 2005 Chardonnay (Curicó Valley) $9. Plump and ripe, that's for certain. Buttery peach aromas are what you'd call overt, while the warm, honeyed palate has punch now but seems on the big side, meaning it may not hold for long. A drink-now Chard in the easy Chilean style. **84** —*M.S. (7/1/2006)*

Aresti 2004 Chardonnay (Curicó Valley) $8. Smells like crushed vitamins, while the palate is crisp and lemony, with hints of green apple and spice. Not a bad wine in that it holds form all the way through. Seems just a bit resiny and grabby on the tongue. **84 Best Buy** —*M.S. (11/1/2005)*

Aresti 1999 Chardonnay (Curicó Valley) $8. 84 *(9/1/2000)*

Aresti 2005 Gewürztraminer (Curicó Valley) $9. Chunky in size as it shows mostly canned fruit on the nose. Full banana, melon, and citrus flavors are ripe but also kind of sticky. Light in color but not weak. **83** —*M.S. (7/1/2006)*

Aresti 2002 Montemar Gewürztraminer (Curicó Valley) $8. On the nose, it's floral and sweet, with a sticky quality to the fruit. In the mouth, it's like lemon-lime soda, with some bitter green melon thrown in. And the feel is thin and acidic. A tangy, lean rendition of this potentially interesting variety. **82** —*M.S. (7/1/2003)*

Aresti 2004 Merlot (Curicó Valley) $9. Starts with earth, leather, and basic berry aromas. Red fruits riding on a forceful wave of acidity carry the palate, while the finish is tart and lets go of any depth the wine may have had. **82** —*M.S. (7/1/2006)*

Aresti 2003 Merlot (Chile) $8. Initial burnt, harsh aromas transition to peanut and raisin if given time. The palate is tangy and lean, with base-level red fruit. Decent acidity and some chocolate on the finish. **82** —*M.S. (11/1/2005)*

Aresti 2000 Montemar Merlot (Curicó Valley) $8. Though the nose (with acorny-oak and red berry aromas) is okay, I was left wondering where the concentration is—the dried herb and berry fruit taste watered down. **81** —*D.T. (7/1/2002)*

Aresti 1999 Montemar Merlot (Curicó Valley) $8. 85 Best Buy *(9/1/2000)*

Aresti 1999 Reserva Merlot (Rio Claro) $11. 87 Best Buy *(9/1/2000)*

Aresti 2004 Reserve Merlot (Rio Claro) $13. Opening aromas of black olive, rubber, and spice vie for attention with herbal fruit. The plum and cherry flavors are present and accounted for but it's also slightly vegetal. Not a lot of meat on the bones. **83** —*M.S. (7/1/2006)*

Aresti 2001 Reserve Merlot (Rio Claro) $11. The nose is pickled and vegetal. Some cherry and raspberry fruit mix on the palate, while the finish is hot and spicy. In the mouth, this wine starts off better than it finishes, so it might be acceptable for low-care, quick consumption. **82** —*M.S. (7/1/2003)*

Aresti 2000 Reserve Merlot (Rio Claro) $11. This clean, crisp Merlot is smoky, with ample black fruit in the nose. The sweet, pure black-fruit palate is just as it ought to be, and the black cherry and coffee flavors work together on the finish. **86** —*M.S. (3/1/2002)*

Aresti 2006 Sauvignon Blanc (Curicó Valley) $9. A tiny bit stony on the nose, with touches of powdered sugar and green pepper. Citrus and green apple work the palate, followed by a snappy, generally clean finish. Fully charged and pretty good for under $10. **84** —*M.S. (11/15/2006)*

Aresti 2005 Sauvignon Blanc (Curicó Valley) $9. A blowsy, full-bodied version with round aromas of apple and melon and fairly similar flavors. Not a ton of acidity on this wine so it comes across easy, almost honeyed. Sweet and easy to drink. **84** —*M.S. (7/1/2006)*

Aresti 2004 Sauvignon Blanc (Curicó Valley) $8. A bit antiseptic but with some likable floral and green-apple aromas. Citrus carries the palate, especially grapefruit and orange. Dry and clean on the finish, with some peppery, bitter cleansing notes. **84 Best Buy** —*M.S. (11/1/2005)*

Aresti 2002 Montemar Sauvignon Blanc (Curicó Valley) $8. Pungent aromas of pineapple, passion fruit, and grapefruit are so untamed that they run wild. The mouth deals tangerine and other citrus, which broken down is a lot like chewable vitamins. Very racy and acid-packed, and more boisterous than subtle. **83** —*M.S. (7/1/2003)*

Aresti 2000 Montemar Sauvignon Blanc (Curicó Valley) $8. Grapefruit and lime aromas and flavors play nicely against melon and dry stone fruits here. Medium weight and well-balanced, this well put together package shows a nice nuttiness, some texture and a fairly full finish. **86 Best Buy** —*M.M. (8/1/2001)*

Aresti 1999 Reserva Sauvignon Blanc (Rio Claro) $11. 87 *(9/1/2000)*

Aresti 2001 Reserve Sauvignon Blanc (Rio Claro) $11. Lean and angular in the nose, with grapefruit and pine aromas. The palate offers some grapefruit and citrus pith, and the finish is tangy, sharp, and runs toward bitter. In addition, the mouthfeel is flat. **82** —*M.S. (7/1/2003)*

Aresti 2005 Winemakers' Sauvignon Blanc (Leyda Valley) $17. Lots of green characteristics rule, with lettuce, pepper, and grapefruit speaking up. Grassy on the palate, with hints of peach and melon. Lacks legitimate core fruit. **82** —*M.S. (7/1/2006)*

BALDUZZI

Balduzzi 1999 Reserva Cabernet Sauvignon (Maule Valley) $11. Tomato and herb aromas are followed by red fruit and peppery notes. The simple finish does nothing to hurt or improve the wine. It's very Average, but drinkable. **81** —*M.S. (7/1/2003)*

Balduzzi 2001 Reserva Chardonnay (Maule Valley) $9. The bouquet is a bit dusty and musty. Pear, banana, and white pepper can be pulled from the palate, but the feel is flat and the finish dull. Not totally dismissible, but hard to support. **80** —*M.S. (7/1/2003)*

BARON PHILIPPE DE ROTHSCHILD

Baron Philippe de Rothschild 2000 Escudo Rojo Bordeaux Blend (Chile) $15. It's easy to see Rothschild's Bordeaux influence in this one—it's more about chalky, minerally tannins than oak, and offers mixed berries on both palate and nose. An acorn nuttiness and some dried spices linger throughout. A blend of Cabernet Sauvignon, Cabernet Franc, and Carmenère. **88 Best Buy** —*D.T. (7/1/2002)*

Baron Philippe de Rothschild 2001 Reserva Cabernet Sauvignon (Maipo Valley) $10. A well-built Cabernet that should please the masses. Aromas of red berries, milk chocolate, and dry earth precede clean cherry, cassis, and blackberry on the palate. There is little nuance or subtlety to the wine, but it's ripe and satisfying. **86 Best Buy** —*M.S. (3/1/2004)*

Baron Philippe de Rothschild 2000 Reserva Cabernet Sauvignon (Maipo Valley) $10. Rich and ripe, although rough, with pronounced blackberry flavors and soft tannins. The mouthfeel is especially nice, and rolls over the palate like a velvet scarf. The finish is dry. **85** —*P.G. (12/1/2002)*

Baron Philippe de Rothschild 2001 Reserva Carmenère (Rapel Valley) $10. From a varietal similar to Cabernet Sauvignon that shares its profile of a full-bodied, dry red wine, with herbal and berry flavors and dusty tannins. Hard to tell the difference, except for a peppery, tobacco note. **87 Best Buy** —*P.G. (12/1/2002)*

Baron Philippe de Rothschild 2001 Reserva Chardonnay (Casablanca Valley) $10. A big, rich, and ripe wine, with a blast of tropical fruit flavors. It's also very oaky, with a thick overlay of vanilla, caramel, and char. Despite the size it's basically one-dimensional, and finishes fast and sweet. **85** —*P.G. (12/1/2002)*

Baron Philippe de Rothschild 2003 Escudo Rojo Red Blend (Maipo Valley) $15. A touch roasted and fiery on the nose, with a lot of earth and wood-based spice. The palate runs toward tart and snappy, with cherry skin and blackberry accounting for the fruit content. Bright in terms of flavor and profile, but on the leaner side when it comes to feel. **87** —*M.S. (5/1/2006)*

Baron Philippe de Rothschild 2001 Escudo Rojo Red Blend (Maipo Valley) $15. Dark and firm, a hard wine marked by aromas and flavors of nettles, earth, and tobacco. There's some fruit in there but it's buried under the enormous tannins. Yet the texture is polished and smooth, and the wine will work well against roasted beef or pork. **86** —*S.H. (1/1/2002)*

CHILE

Baron Philippe de Rothschild 1999 Escudo Rojo Red Blend (Maipo Valley) $15. Blackberry aromas start things off, but there's a vegetal note, like canned asparagus, that suggests unripe fruit. Those veggies continue in the mouth, along with riper berry notes. A blend of Cabernet Sauvignon, Carmenere, and Cabernet Franc. **81** —*S.H. (11/20/2002)*

BIG FAT LLAMA

Big Fat Llama 2005 Cabernet Sauvignon (Chile) $8. An okay little confection. A bit rubbery and lightly fruity on the nose, but also a touch funky. Decent cherry and strawberry flavors; more generic than anything. Totally inoffensive and fine if you like critter wines with goofy names. **83** —*M.S. (11/15/2006)*

Big Fat Llama 2005 Chardonnay (Chile) $8. Not bad, really! The name is corny but the wine is good enough. Pear, caramel, and walnut notes are quite acceptable, while the weight is bulky and the acidity low. Drink now. **83** —*M.S. (7/1/2006)*

BOTALCURA

Botalcura 2003 La Porfia Grand Reserve Cabernet Sauvignon (Rapel Valley) $20. Cedary and slightly herbal, but backed by ample cassis fruit, Botalcura's top Cabernet boasts a silky-smooth texture and nicely balanced acidity—its main drawback is its limited length on the finish. **86** *(10/1/2006)*

Botalcura 2002 La Porfia Grand Reserve Cabernet Sauvignon (Maule Valley) $18. Almost Port-like on the bouquet, with loud, saucy, sweet aromas that seem to weigh a ton, assuming aromas can be weighed. The palate is surprisingly lean, however, with thin raspberry fruit leading toward cranberry and pepper on the finish. A confusing wine that doesn't make sense as a whole. **84** —*M.S. (2/1/2005)*

Botalcura 2003 Reserve El Delirio Cabernet Sauvignon (Maule Valley) $11. Start with the bouquet of crushed violet petals, tar, black olive, and berry, and then move on to the forward, ripe palate that stays the course courtesy of firm tannins. Finishes a bit hollow, but with piercing coffee and dark chocolate accents. **87 Best Buy** —*M.S. (7/1/2006)*

Botalcura 2003 La Porfia Grand Reserve Carmenère (Curicó Valley) $20. From what may be Chile's trickiest grape to get just right, this is an admirable offering. Some of the variety's tomato leaf and herb notes are evident, but there's also plenty of plum and blackberry fruit to provide balance. Medium-bodied, framed by slightly rustic tannins on the finish. **85** *(10/1/2006)*

Botalcura 2002 La Porfia Grand Reserve Carmenère (Central Valley) $18. Muddled and chunky, with raspberry and leather on the nose. Not entirely fresh or forward; instead it sits on the palate in bland, heavy fashion. Shows pepper and red fruit flavors, but not much texture or variety. **83** —*M.S. (7/1/2005)*

Botalcura 2004 La Porfia Grand Reserve Chardonnay (Casablanca Valley) $20. An ambitious wine that's largely (70%) aged in barrel for seven or eight months, this shows plenty of oak flavor and ample weight, but lacks the freshness and vibrancy of the less expensive bottlings. Caramel, toast, and sweet corn notes make up the majority of the flavor profile. **84** *(10/1/2006)*

Botalcura 2005 El Delirio Chardonnay-Viognier (Central Valley) $12. Our favorite of the Botalcura white wines, there's only 20% Viognier, but it makes a strong impression, adding floral and orangey scents to this round, creamy wine. Peach and melon flavors show ripeness and class without seeming too sweet or flabby. **87 Best Buy** *(10/1/2006)*

Botalcura 2003 La Porfia Grand Reserve Malbec (Maipo Valley) $20. This Chilean stab at Malbec is clean and fresh, with bright fruit flavors that come across as a bit one-dimensional. Still, it's a solid, fruity dimension, one that many palates will enjoy, and framed by vanilla and oak-spice notes on the finish. **85** *(10/1/2006)*

Botalcura 2004 El Delirio Merlot (Central Valley) $12. Supple and round, this is an easy-drinking Merlot with defined varietal character. It's slightly herbal on the nose, then adds mocha notes to the black cherry and plum flavors that turn a bit crisp. **84** *(10/1/2006)*

Botalcura 2003 El Delirio Merlot (Central Valley) $13. Whole and fruity, with some inviting richness to the nose along with alcoholic heat. Driving plum and cherry fruit is ripe, although the feel of the wine is a touch hard. Not long or deep, but good in a front-loaded way. **86** —*M.S. (2/1/2005)*

Botalcura 2004 Reserve El Delirio Syrah-Malbec Red Blend (Central Valley) $11. Grassy and sweet to start, and it never gets darker or more precise. The palate is o.k. but scattershot in how it delivers candied raspberry and black cherry amid heat and tannin. Kind of aggressive in the final analysis. **84** —*M.S. (7/1/2006)*

Botalcura 2005 El Delirio Sauvignon Blanc (Casablanca Valley) $12. A clean, crisp Sauvignon Blanc that won't break the bank, combining bright gooseberry and passion fruit notes in a reasonable facsimile of the Marlborough style. Plump and fruity on the midpalate, then turns crisp on the relatively short finish. **85** *(10/1/2006)*

CALAMA

Calama 2001 Cabernet Sauvignon (Central Valley) $6. Mushroom and charcoal dot the nose, but with that comes just a modicum of fruit. The palate is a bit bland even if it's far from offensive, and so is the finish. Some wines don't offend while they fail to impress. This is an example of that type of wine. **83** —*M.S. (7/1/2003)*

Calama 2002 Chardonnay (Casablanca Valley) $9. A mild aromatic note of corn goes alongside basic pineapple, pear, and green apple on the nose. The flavors of melon, apple, and pear are standard and delivered in conformed, pedestrian style. And the finish has some girth and substance. Very ordinary but successful in achieving its assumed mass-appeal goals. **86** —*M.S. (7/1/2003)*

Calama 2001 Merlot (Casablanca Valley) $9. Briar patch, some green pepper, and a little sweet baking spice carry the nose. The plum and berry flavors are accented by brown sugar and caramel, but also some green characteristics. The finish is smooth, but too green. **83** —*M.S. (7/1/2003)*

Calama 2002 Sauvignon Blanc (Curicó Valley) $6. The nose smells a bit like corn. The wine is round, soft, and without much edge. The fruit seems a little pliable and ultimately it isn't all that structured. Finishes with a bit of banana. **82** —*M.S. (7/1/2003)*

CALIBORO ESTATE

Caliboro Estate 2002 Erasmo Bordeaux Blend (Maule Valley) $30. Still a new wine looking for its place, Erasmo from Caliboro Estate is once again crisp and tight, but unlike the inaugural 2001 the '02 shows a bit of green alongside racy, tannic red fruit. Hits like a bass drum on the tongue; expect better from the 2003, although this wine is still very good. **87** —*M.S. (3/1/2006)*

Caliboro Estate 2001 Erasmo Bordeaux Blend (Maule Valley) $30. Caliboro's first-ever release sports excellent aromatics. But like any serious red made from young grapes, it's not terribly concentrated. The mouthfeel is light, while the depth and texture are modest. Still, it offers a glimpse of what's to come, and the future looks bright. A blend of 60% Cabernet Sauvignon, 30% Merlot, and 10% Cabernet Franc. **88** —*M.S. (11/1/2005)*

CALINA

Calina 2001 Cabernet-Carmenere Cabernet Blend (Maule Valley) $14. Carmenère has a rude, rough character to it, but the addition of 60% Cabernet fancies things up a lot. This is a fascinating wine. It's big, rich, and dense. Glycerin coats the glass, and the flavors stick to the palate. Yet the thick tannins are fine and complex. Like a fine Cabernet, with an undercurrent of tobacco. **90 Best Buy** —*S.H. (12/1/2002)*

Calina 2000 Reserve-Cabernet Sauvignon/Carmenere Cabernet Blend (Maule Valley) $13. A straight shot down blackberry lane. The palate is all about the fruit; it's got lots of texture, and maybe even some tannins to shed. Finishes with gravel, herb, and a certain meatiness. The nose—wood and maybe a bit of mocha—is not its strength. **86** —*D.T. (7/1/2002)*

Calina 1999 Bravura Cabernet Sauvignon (Colchagua Valley) $50. Calina's first attempt at a super Chilean is successful. The wine, a multiappellation blend, really pops in the mouth. The fruit is ripe and the power is there. However, for someone looking for a reserved red made in the Bordeaux style, something that Chile can deliver, this could come across as aggressive, as the acidity is a bit sharp. **89** —*M.S. (7/1/2003)*

Calina 2002 Reserva Cabernet Sauvignon (Colchagua Valley) $9. Aromatically, it's light, with leafiness and citrus peel scents. Cherry, cassis, and olive flavors float on a bed of firm tannins, while the finish is toasty and slightly medicinal. 84 —*M.S. (10/1/2006)*

Calina 2000 Reserve Cabernet Sauvignon (Colchagua Valley) $8. Smells sharp and green, as though the grapes had been pushed into over-production. Yet there are pretty black currant flavors and richness in the mouth of this dry, balanced wine. The texture is nice and velvety smooth. 84 —*S.H. (6/1/2001)*

Calina 2001 Bravura Cabernet Sauvignon-Merlot (Maule Valley) $40. Bold and full of berry and plum aromas. The palate is a touch short of refined but it features nice cherry, cassis and blackberry flavors. Plush in the mouth and on the finish, with tannins to spare. At its center it shows the slightest hint of green. 88 —*M.S. (7/1/2006)*

Calina 1999 Carmenère (Maule Valley) $7. This appealing wine offers a very smooth mouthfeel and full berry cocoa and herb aromas and flavors, with a touch of earthiness that adds unexpected complexity. The finish is long with even tannins, a surprise at this price. A notable value worth pursuing, made of a grape varietal incorrectly thought to be Merlot for many years in Chile. 88 Best Buy —*M.M. (1/1/2004)*

Calina 2004 Alcance Carmenère (Maule Valley) $15. Round and burly, with a ton of color and plenty of berry fruit aromas. The mouth is equally big and forward, with cherry, berry, and herb flavors. Full and layered, with popping acidity. Not too refined but lively. 85 —*M.S. (7/1/2006)*

Calina 2004 Reserva Carmenère (Maule Valley) $9. Rustic and leathery, with horse, licorice, and black plum on the nose. Saturated but rough in the mouth, with giant crushed-fruit flavors that push hard tannins and bold acidity. An untamed wine. 84 —*M.S. (7/1/2006)*

Calina 2002 Reserve Carmenère (Maule Valley) $8. Made when Kendall-Jackson still owned this label, and it's a pretty decent legacy in terms of value-priced Carmenère. The bouquet features leather, cherry, caramel, and some foresty nuance, while the round palate is loaded with plum and dark berry. Some light oak and vanilla on the finish softens the back end. 85 Best Buy —*M.S. (6/1/2004)*

Calina 2001 Reserve Carmenère (Maule Valley) $8. Rich and full-bodied, a big wine packed with fruity, berry flavors. It's very dry, with noticeable tannins. Lacks subtlety and finesse, but has other things to recommend it. 85 —*S.H. (12/1/2002)*

Calina 2000 Reserve Carmenère (Maule Valley) $8. Carmenère is popular in Chile, less so in this country, although that's changing. This Cabernet-like wine is inky black, and opens with big gooey aromas of blackberry jam, dark honey, smoky vanilla, and a rich earthiness. It tastes simply grand, with enormously extracted blackberry flavors, hugely rich and complicated, but bone dry. Try it with rich foods like braised oxtails or barbecued ribs. 90 —*S.H. (11/15/2001)*

Calina 2001 Chardonnay (Casablanca Valley) $8. Made in a wildly popular style that emphasizes lush, ripe tropical fruit flavors and elaborate oak, with smoky, vanilla nuances. Feels lush and creamy in the mouth. Turns a bit earthy in the finish, but a very good wine for this price. 86 Best Buy —*S.H. (1/1/2002)*

Calina 2003 Reserva Chardonnay (Casablanca Valley) $9. Very good in the value vein, with light but balanced aromatics that show tropical fruit offset by honey and vanilla. The palate is ripe and on edge, with melon, pear, and a hint of banana. Nice from start to finish. A very good buy. 88 Best Buy —*M.S. (7/1/2006)*

Calina 2002 Reserve Chardonnay (Casablanca Valley) $8. This former Kendall-Jackson label produced a good, pedestrian Chard in 2002. It's fat, sweet, and goes heavy on the pear and apple. Finishes plump, lean, and clean. A simple yet confectionary white. 85 Best Buy —*M.S. (8/1/2004)*

Calina 2000 Reserve Chardonnay (Casablanca Valley) $8. Snappy and pure aromas grace the nose, with Bartlett pear, lees, and toasty oak most prominent. The palate is overt and fruity, featuring apple and citrus flavors accented by bright acidity. This seems like a fine appetizer, by-the-glass, or party-friendly wine, but the composite cork the winery is using is madness to get off the corkscrew. 86 Best Buy —*M.S. (7/1/2002)*

Calina 1996 Merlot (Maule Valley) $16. 90 *(11/15/1999)*

Calina 2003 Reserva Merlot (Maule Valley) $9. Buttery from the onset, with coconut, olive, and plum making up the bouquet. The fruit is jumpy and acidic, so it dances on the palate, supported by wood and tannin. Not a lot on the finish besides vanilla and butter. Seems more tart than it should be. 84 —*M.S. (7/1/2006)*

Calina 2002 Reserve Merlot (Maule Valley) $8. A perfectly nice, drinkable red that offers licorice and cherry on the nose, followed by wide-open raspberry and strawberry flavors. With its broad finish and round texture, this is textbook everyday Merlot. 87 Best Buy —*M.S. (8/1/2004)*

Calina 2001 Reserve Merlot (Maule Valley) $8. The nose is standard fare as it offers cherry, plum, and a hint of herbaceousness. Good plum and berry fruit carries the mouth, while the finish is round and smooth. The wine is balanced and entirely satisfying even if it is basic in its intent. As per usual, Calina delivers a good wine for the price. 86 —*M.S. (7/1/2003)*

Calina 2000 Reserve Merlot (Maule Valley) $8. There's a sharp, green, minty aroma along with riper notes of blackberries, and the wine drinks fruity and simple, but with some real richness. Structurally, the acids, tannins, and alcohol are in good balance. Another affordable winner from Chile. 85 —*S.H. (6/1/2001)*

CALITERRA

Caliterra 1998 Cabernet Sauvignon (Central Valley) $8. 84 —*M.S. (12/1/1999)*

Caliterra 2002 Cabernet Sauvignon (Central Valley) $8. Pretty nice for a basic Chilean Cab. The nose has typical cassis and cherry, but also a leafy, herbal quality reminiscent of black olive. It's spicy and herbal on the palate, too, with vanilla and clove picking up the rear. Finishes well, with warmth. 87 Best Buy —*M.S. (6/1/2004)*

Caliterra 2000 Cabernet Sauvignon (Colchagua Valley) $9. 87 —*M.S. (3/1/2002)*

Caliterra 1999 Cabernet Sauvignon (Central Valley) $8. What deep, supple flavors on this soft, delicious wine. The grapes obviously had no trouble ripening, and offer waves of blackberries, plums, and black currants, not to mention spices like fennel and pepper. Very dry and fancy, this wine could sit on the best tables and not hang its head. 87 Best Buy —*S.H. (2/1/2001)*

Caliterra 1998 Arboleda Cabernet Sauvignon (Maipo Valley) $20. There are pretty blackberry aromas, along with some sharp wintergreen, complexed with smoke and vanilla from oak barrels. In the mouth, it's velvety smooth and soft, with extracted blackberry flavors, and very dry. The texture is a little syrupy. 85 —*S.H. (2/1/2003)*

Caliterra 2002 Reserva Cabernet Sauvignon (Colchagua Valley) $15. A bit of earth and leather on the nose, but also some sour, gamy notes. In the mouth, it's lean and easy, with mild oak alongside strident strawberry and raspberry. Finishes a touch creamy, with level balance. 84 —*M.S. (11/1/2005)*

Caliterra 1997 Reserve Cabernet Sauvignon (Maipo Valley) $13. 88 Best Buy —*M.S. (12/1/1999)*

Caliterra 2004 Tribute Cabernet Sauvignon (Colchagua Valley) $17. Starts off showing crisp, almost burnt aromas; later comes committed plum, cherry, and cassis scents. The fruit on the palate seems a touch peppery and short, while the finish is snappy and forward, but a tad leafy in flavor. More of a lean, medium-bodied specimen than opulent. 86 —*M.S. (11/15/2006)*

Caliterra 2001 Carmenère (Colchagua Valley) $20. 86 —*M.S. (3/1/2002)*

Caliterra 1999 Arboleda Carmenère (Maipo Valley) $20. Starts with earthy, blackberry aromas and deeper notes of plum preserves and blueberry. Picks up some pretty blackberry and cherry notes in the chewy core, then turns rich and solidly tannic in the finish. Needs time. 85 —*S.H. (2/1/2003)*

Caliterra 2003 Chardonnay (Central Valley) $8. Fat apple and pear aromas are softened by almondy notes. More apple and spice follows on the palate, and while the depth of fruit is modest, the acidity is there and the mouthfeel is pretty good. A fresh wine to drink soon. 86 Best Buy —*M.S. (2/1/2005)*

Caliterra 2001 Chardonnay (Central Valley) $8. What's so nice about this wine is that it doesn't get in your face with an excess of everything. Modulated apple and peach flavors are treated with just the right dose of lees and oak, while bright acids provide needed crispness. It has an elegance that belies the giveaway price. **88 Best Buy** —*S.H. (12/1/2002)*

Caliterra 2000 Chardonnay (Central Valley) $10. Mild green apple flavors play off a creamy note in this neither flabby nor over-wooded, even, mainstream Chardonnay. An easy spiciness and modest toast notes add appeal. It closes dry, with moderate length. **85** *(10/1/2001)*

Caliterra 1999 Chardonnay (Central Valley) $8. At this price, you can expect an honest, workman-like everyday wine, and you get that here—along with other qualities that will surprise you. Not least is the fruit, nicely ripened and finely etched, and the spices that dance on the tongue. It's dry, of course, with fine acidity. What stands out is the depth of flavor. **86** —*S.H. (2/1/2001)*

Caliterra 2005 Reserva Chardonnay (Curicó Valley) $11. A perfectly good Chardonnay, one with lemon curd, butter, peach, and melon on the nose. The mouth offers apple and a hint of orange, while the finish is ripe, bordering on sweet, with a little bit of creaminess. Great for everyday drinking. **86 Best Buy** —*M.S. (10/1/2006)*

Caliterra 2003 Reserva Chardonnay (Casablanca Valley) $13. Smoky almost to the point of being a one-noter, but as it warms the heavy toast gives way to apple, orange, and coconut flavors. The savior is prime acidity, which creates a raciness that rivals the woodiness. **87** —*M.S. (7/1/2005)*

Caliterra 2005 Tribute Chardonnay (Casablanca Valley) $17. Heavily oaked, with pineapple and toast aromas. Very round in the mouth, and smooth, but ultimately it's not that lively or flavorful. The apple and spice flavors kind of lay flat on the palate, while the finish is rather oak-dominant. **85** —*M.S. (10/1/2006)*

Caliterra 2004 Tribute Malbec (Colchagua Valley) $17. Jammy blueberry aromas get it going in a good direction, and overall the wine is solid and friendly. Blackberry, plum, and cassis grace the palate, backed by toast and chocolate on the finish. With firm, lively acidity the wine almost jumps from the glass. **88** —*M.S. (10/1/2006)*

Caliterra 2003 Merlot (Rapel Valley) $7. Strawberry preserves, leather, and some funk create an adequate nose, while the palate offers cherry, plum and black olive. Seems salty and/or pickled on the finish. **83** —*M.S. (7/1/2005)*

Caliterra 2002 Merlot (Central Valley) $8. Peppery and grainy in the nose, with overt notes of leather. Basic cherry, raspberry, and vanilla create a simple, smooth palate that's generally clean. Not a thriller, but an o.k. quaffer. **83** —*M.S. (3/1/2004)*

Caliterra 2001 Merlot (Central Valley) $8. This joint Mondavi-Chadwick venture has a rustic, woodsy texture, but not as much fruit as it needs to back the texture up. Black-fruit and sweet soil aromas dominate; blackberries rolled in gravel show in the mouth and on the finish. **83** —*D.T. (7/1/2002)*

Caliterra 2000 Merlot (Rapel Valley) $8. Here's an everyday wine with pretty flavors of cherries and herbs. It's nicely dry and balanced, with soft but detailed tannins. Finishes with an elegant fruitiness. At this price, it's a bargain. **84** —*S.H. (6/1/2001)*

Caliterra 1999 Merlot (Central Valley) $10. A well-constructed value Merlot, serious and dry, with some structure. Honest varietal character shows with berry, cocoa, and herb notes on the nose and palate. Hints of licorice and mineral add interest. The finish is dry, with herb notes and modest tannins. Drink over the next two years. **85** *(10/1/2001)*

Caliterra 1998 Merlot (Central Valley) $8. With 19% Cabernet Sauvignon, this is a deeply flavored, youthful wine, precocious and sharp with acidity, and fresh as newly crushed grapes. The dominant fruits are blackberries and plums, with a hint of bitter chocolate. The tannins are soft and creamy. It's a bit rough around the edges but is well-made and gets the job done. **83** —*S.H. (2/1/2001)*

Caliterra 1999 Arboleda Merlot (Colchagua Valley) $20. Dark, with aromas of spiced plums, earth, bark, and a rich, chocolatey note. Heavy and dense, the syrupy texture carries plummy, peppery flavors through to a long, rich finish. It's a bit coarse and rough, and pretty tannic, too. Drink with well-marbled beef. **84** —*S.H. (5/1/2001)*

Caliterra 2004 Sauvignon Blanc (Central Valley) $7. A pungent wine, with overt citrus aromas and flavors. Easily identifiable as Sauvignon Blanc; the palate delivers smooth citrus, although the finish is lemony and a bit tart. **84 Best Buy** —*M.S. (7/1/2005)*

Caliterra 2003 Sauvignon Blanc (Central Valley) $8. Open on the bouquet, and very citrusy. This is one clean, lean wine. It's got forward lemon, lime, and orange flavors that ride nicely on the zippy, crisp palate. Good acids and modest depth make it a good bet for summer. **85 Best Buy** —*M.S. (6/1/2004)*

Caliterra 2001 Sauvignon Blanc (Central Valley) $7. Grapefruit aromas lead the fruit parade on this exceedingly refreshing white. Easy to drink and tasty, with just enough zip to keep you on your toes. Notes of banana and papaya add sweetness to the citrus. **86** —*M.S. (3/1/2002)*

Caliterra 2000 Sauvignon Blanc (Central Valley) $9. This pulls the taster in with an attractive bouquet of grapefruit and melon-peach elements. A grassy note accents the citrus flavors of the palate; the even mouthfeel is nicely poised between soft roundedness and adequate acidity. It's seen no oak, and closes with a hint of pepper. **86 Best Buy** *(10/1/2001)*

Caliterra 1999 Sauvignon Blanc (Central Valley) $8. Sometimes you just need a cheap, quaffable, crisp dry white wine to drink in copious amounts, and this one will do just fine, thank you. It's citrusy, spicy, and dry, and has enough acid to cleanse the palate. **84** —*S.H. (2/1/2001)*

Caliterra 2004 Tribute Shiraz (Colchagua Valley) $17. Bold and dark, with perfume galore on the nose. The palate is sweet and rich, a little bit creamy, and loaded with zest. For Chilean Shiraz this is quite good; the finish is flush and offers enough acidity to keep it dancing. **88** —*M.S. (10/1/2006)*

Caliterra 2001 Syrah (Central Valley) $NA. Scattered and gaseous at first, and only later does it show any true berry aromas. The palate offers mostly sour cherry and rhubarb, while the finish is raw and grippy. Not offputting, but could use more charm. **83** —*M.S. (6/1/2004)*

Caliterra 2000 Syrah (Central Valley) $8. Roasted red berry and tangy woodsy notes on both the nose and on the palate. Finishes with more oak, plus a tart metallic-herbal note that is softened by chalky tannins. **84** —*D.T. (7/1/2002)*

Caliterra 1999 Arboleda Syrah (Colchagua Valley) $20. There's something earthy, sharp, and green in the nose, and airing doesn't bring out hidden fruit. Sharp and thin. The spicy midpalate contains a trace of berry-cherry fruit, and then it turns dusty and tannic on the finish. Might soften with a year or so of cellaring. **83** —*S.H. (2/1/2003)*

CANEPA

Canepa 1997 Private Reserve Cabernet Sauvignon (Curicó Valley) $12. 85 —*M.S. (11/15/1999)*

Canepa 1998 Chardonnay (Rancagua) $10. Mild floral aromas and clean flavors. Too typical of central valley Chard. Kind of flat and vague. **80** — *M.S. (11/15/1999)*

Canepa 1999 Sauvignon Blanc (Cachapoal Valley) $8. 84 —*M.S. (11/15/1999)*

CARMEN

Carmen 1999 Reserve Cabernet Blend (Maipo Valley) $15. You can detect the Cabernet with its blackberry and cassis flavors, but the Carmenère adds a whole other dimension, and a wild one at that. Jammy, animal, smoky, and spicy, this is a big wine, and tannic too. Extreme dryness makes it a good food wine, but it will soften in a year or so. **89 Best Buy** —*S.H. (12/1/2002)*

Carmen 2002 Cabernet Sauvignon (Maipo Valley) $7. Cherry and berry flavors and aromas tend to get lost amid some heavier green bean and bell pepper characteristics. That herbal, vegetal streak is also prominent on the finish, where licorice and black pepper appear. Despite heft to the body, it's just too green to rate higher. **83** —*M.S. (3/1/2004)*

Carmen 1999 Cabernet Sauvignon (Central Valley) $8. Subtle cherry aromas are masked by deep oak and smoke aromas on the nose. Fruit isn't much more prevalent on the palate—instead, expect more oak and some

CHILE

earthy, minerally notes. Mouthfeel is chalky and tannic, the short finish a bit edgy. **84** —*D.T. (8/1/2001)*

Carmen 1998 Cabernet Sauvignon (Central Valley) $8. This is a light-bodied wine with berry and some rather pronounced vegetal notes on the nose. However these do not persist and the palate displays berry and and cocoa flavors. The finish is drily fruity with mild toast notes. **84** —*M.M. (1/1/2004)*

Carmen 2003 Classic Cabernet Sauvignon (Maipo Valley) $7. Solid Chilean Cab, with herbal notes and chewy cassis and chocolate flavors. Fine with burgers and the like. **84** *(12/15/2004)*

Carmen 2003 Estate Grown Reserve Cabernet Sauvignon (Maipo Valley) $13. Gets going in woody fashion, which unleashes cinnamon and coconut. Airing brings it into focus, and from then on it's all about cherry and cassis flavors, and a nice vanilla and mint finish. Classic Chilean Cabernet: fruit plus terroir plus wood equals a good result. **88 Best Buy** —*M.S. (7/1/2006)*

Carmen 2000 Estate Grown Reserve Cabernet Sauvignon (Maipo Valley) $15. With its herbal, traditional aromas, this New World Cabernet could impersonate and Old World model. The palate is tight and firm, with lively tannins and bracing acids. The flavors run toward plum and chocolate, and there's a bitter hint on the back palate. The finish is plummy and dark. **88** —*M.S. (7/1/2003)*

Carmen 2002 Gold Reserve Cabernet Sauvignon (Maipo Valley) $50. This Cabernet runs tight but herbal, with aromas of earth, tree bark, and leather but not much in the way of lively fruit. Flavors of plums and berries seem a touch stewy, while the finish is bulky and mildly tannic. In Carmen's defense, 2002 was a wet, cool year by Chilean standards. **86** —*M.S. (12/31/2006)*

Carmen 2001 Gold Reserve Cabernet Sauvignon (Maipo Valley) $70. With some rubber, prune, and earth, the nose is well put together. A second act of blackberry, cassis, and tobacco flavors is endearing, while the dark, woodsy finish is masculine, leaving a leftover espresso character. A touch heavy and awkward, but packs power. **88** —*M.S. (7/1/2005)*

Carmen 1997 Gold Reserve Cabernet Sauvignon (Maipo Valley) $65. This well-oaked offering has classic Cabernet aromas and flavors, with blackberry and cassis melding nicely with the heavy toast. The mouthfeel is full, even, and plush, and the dark cherry and densely oaked finish is smooth and pleasing. **88** *(2/1/2001)*

Carmen 1999 Gold reserve Estate Bottled Single Vineyard Cabernet Sauvignon (Maipo Valley) $65. Sweet dark fruit flavors accented with coffee are a bit cloying. There are heavy toast aromas with caramel, and the tannins are aggressive and gritty on the finish. This one needs to sit for a few years to come around. **88** —*C.S. (12/1/2002)*

Carmen 2003 Nativa Cabernet Sauvignon (Maipo Valley) $16. An organic wine with charred, coffee-heavy aromas. The mouth is bulky and tannic, with dark plum and black-fruit flavors. Quite roasted, on the cusp of burnt tasting, with prodding tannins. **83** —*M.S. (12/15/2005)*

Carmen 2002 Nativa Cabernet Sauvignon (Maipo Valley) $16. Aggressive all the way, with a heartily toasted nose that conceals leather and stable aromas. Quite tannic and bitter on the palate, but also loaded with coffee and background notes of coconut. **86** —*M.S. (7/1/2005)*

Carmen 2001 Nativa Cabernet Sauvignon (Maipo Valley) $16. Heavily smoked, with a grassy undercurrent to the nose. Seems to be on the downside, although raspberry and vanilla flavors are convincing. Textured enough, with good tannins. But still it seems to be searching for better balance and flavor clarity. **84** —*M.S. (7/1/2005)*

Carmen 1999 Nativa Cabernet Sauvignon (Maipo Valley) $15. It's all about red currants, rhubarb, and raspberries, with just a hint of mint. The tannins are on the large side, and thus the balance is a little awkward. Nonetheless it's a solid red wine, and it's organic. **85** —*M.S. (3/1/2002)*

Carmen 2000 Nativa Organic Wine Cabernet Sauvignon (Maipo Valley) $15. This wine comes from Carmen's organic vineyard, and it's full and hefty, a step up in size and quality from the average Chilean Cab. Aromas of marshmallow, spice, and pickle barrel indicate the possibility of American oak influence, while the cherry, blackberry, and chocolate palate is dense and chewy. A cool note of menthol graces the finish. **87** —*M.S. (12/1/2002)*

Carmen 2004 Reserve Cabernet Sauvignon (Maipo Valley) $15. Starts with a firm hint of green bean and tobacco, and later on plum and berry fruit enter the picture. The feel on this Cab is pretty good, with nice tannins and weight. But throughout you get touches of mint and pole beans that interfere with the fruit. Good to an extent, but green. **84** —*M.S. (11/15/2006)*

Carmen 2002 Reserve Cabernet Sauvignon (Maipo Valley) $14. Lots of wood influence (14 months; one-third new) gives this wine a cedary, vanilla-laden sheen layered atop a base of cassis-flavored fruit. Creamy and supple, with some drying tannis showing up on the finish. **87** *(12/15/2004)*

Carmen 2001 Reserve Cabernet Sauvignon (Maipo Valley) $15. Funky at first, with minor vegetal aromas that blow off and are replaced by notes of berry and red licorice. In the mouth, plum and red raspberry carry you to a dry but clean finish. Shows more late than early, and comes on strong toward the finish. **85** —*M.S. (3/1/2004)*

Carmen 1999 Reserve Cabernet Sauvignon (Maipo Valley) $15. Sweet cherries and lots of ripe plum make the nose very nice. A hint of smoked meat in the background adds complexity. Cherry and plum also define the flavors, and the body here is sizable but in balance. A pronounced oakiness and full tannins suggest that some aging might help it along. **87** —*M.S. (3/1/2002)*

Carmen 1998 Reserve Cabernet Sauvignon (Maipo Valley) $17. This solid offering hits all the right notes with a cassis and tobacco nose that shows nice depth, a mouthful of blackberry flavors. and an attractively smooth, supple mouthfeel. Finishes with a hint of tobacco and easy tannins. Altogether quite impressive, especaially for a wine from such a difficult vintage. **88** *(2/1/2001)*

Carmen 2004 Carmenère (Rapel Valley) $7. Ripe but still a touch herbal, with black cherry and cassis pushing along the rubbery bouquet. Blackberry and chocolate are the main flavors, while later on there is a bit of cough syrup and heft. **85 Best Buy** —*M.S. (3/1/2006)*

Carmen 2003 Carmenère (Rapel Valley) $7. Spicy and grassy, from nose to palate to finish. The feel is snappy and charged up, with jumpy acids and pie cherry flavors. Finishes tangy and saucy. **82** —*M.S. (11/1/2005)*

Carmen 2001 Carmenère (Rapel Valley) $7. Cranberry and raspberry comprise the red-fruit nose, and next is the aroma of horse hide and a heavy dose of oak. The fruity palate is all about plum and cassis, and on the finish everything is in place and the texture is firm. **85 Best Buy** —*M.S. (7/1/2003)*

Carmen 2004 Reserve Carmenère-Cabernet Sauvignon (Maipo Valley) $15. Deep and minty on the nose, with a slight foresty character that conjures scents of truffles or mushrooms. The palate, however, is bright; cherry, raspberry, and plum flavors carry the day. Finishes with vanilla and the essence of raspberry, and with good structure. A very nice blend of 60% Carmenère and 40% Cabernet Sauvignon. **89** —*M.S. (12/31/2006)*

Carmen 2002 Reserve Carmenère-Cabernet Sauvignon (Maipo Valley) $16. Quite leafy, with green olive but also some currant on the nose. Just when you think it might be too green, the Cab element rises up and to the fore come cassis, cherry, and herb flavors. Spicy and broad on the finish, with hints of spice and chocolate. **86** —*M.S. (11/1/2005)*

Carmen 1999 Chardonnay (Central Valley) $8. **84** —*M.S. (8/1/2000)*

Carmen 2004 Chardonnay (Casablanca Valley) $7. Fairly forward, with lively apple and nectarine aromas backed by a pungent shot of pine. Grapefruit and other citrus flavors carry this monotone but nice wine from attack to close. Basic yet affordable. **84 Best Buy** —*M.S. (5/1/2006)*

Carmen 2001 Chardonnay (Central Valley) $8. Some Chards have soft, fat noses because of overripe fruit and heavy oak. Not here! This is a no-oak wine that still boasts lush tropical fruit aromas followed up by bright orange and melon flavors. It also sports a defined lemony finish. **85** —*M.S. (3/1/2002)*

Carmen 2004 Classic Chardonnay (Casablanca Valley) $7. A plump, tropically fruity Chardonnay with hints of vanilla. Pear and melon flavors carry the weight, finishing with a touch of spicy oak. **85 Best Buy** *(12/15/2004)*

Carmen 2002 Classic Chardonnay (Central Valley) $8. Pear and apple aromas receive a kick from some creamy, vanilla-tinged oak. The palate is mostly tangerine and lime, with some rich baked-apple undertones. The lengthy finish is solid, as is the mouthfeel. **85 Best Buy** —*M.S. (7/1/2003)*

Carmen 2003 Nativa Chardonnay (Maipo Valley) $14. An organic wine with aromas akin to baked apple, melon, and vanilla. Features sweet apple and melon on the tongue, with a finish of white pepper, vanilla, and lasting sweetness. Upright and healthy if not entirely fascinating. **86** —*M.S. (7/1/2005)*

Carmen 2000 Nativa Chardonnay (Maipo Valley) $13. This is the white entry from Carmen's organic program, and it was 50% oak fermented, which yields some wood character and thickness. Flavors are balanced between sweet apples and sour lemons. The mouthfeel is correct, and lively acidity drives everything home. **87** —*M.S. (3/1/2002)*

Carmen 1999 Nativa Chardonnay (Maipo Valley) $15. Green apple and yeasty notes prevail in this organic, all-native-yeast Chardonnay. Still, it feels thin and has a vaguely oxidized quality, where one would perhaps expect rustic body and life. Soft and smoothly textured, it turns slightly tangy on the back end. **82** *(8/1/2001)*

Carmen 1997 Reserva Chardonnay (Maipo Valley) $11. A good everyday Chardonnay, this wine's apple and toasted oak notes are supported by brisk acidity and a smooth but lively mouthfeel. The finish is pleasing and displays a nice butterscotch note. **85** —*M.N. (2/1/2001)*

Carmen 2005 Reserve Chardonnay (Casablanca Valley) $12. Clean and nice, with a commendable blending of tropical fruit and light oak on the nose. Very nice across the palate, with sweet but balanced flavors of peach and melon sitting alongside appropriate acidity. Finishes cushy but upright. **88 Best Buy** —*M.S. (10/1/2006)*

Carmen 2004 Reserve Chardonnay (Casablanca Valley) $12. Starts with hay, peach, and a sprinkling of green pepper. The mouth offers mostly pineapple and nectarine flavors, and the finish holds onto that essence. A bit of Casablanca citrus appears later in the game to provide a tangy backdrop. **86** —*M.S. (7/1/2006)*

Carmen 2003 Reserve Chardonnay (Casablanca Valley) $13. Well-oaked and polished, but not overly expressive. The nose offers roast corn, lemon, and resin, which sets up a buttery palate that carries melon and papaya flavors. Pretty lengthy and smooth on the finish, with ample persistence. **85** —*M.S. (11/1/2005)*

Carmen 2001 Reserve Chardonnay (Maipo Valley) $13. Fifty percent barrel fermentation yields a roundness that Carmen's regular Chardonnay lacks. Its lemony flavors are offset by toasted coconut from the wood. Fairly intense throughout, with clear, defined fruit. **87** —*M.S. (3/1/2002)*

Carmen 2000 Reserve Chardonnay (Maipo Valley) $17. Opens with stylish lemon and cream notes, but a sweetness only hinted at on the nose takes over on the palate, and the wine loses focus. Really doesn't show the definition, spine, and structure for a reserve designation, ending up Lifesaver-sweet. **84** —*M.M. (8/1/2001)*

Carmen 2002 Winemaker's Reserve Chardonnay (Casablanca Valley) $45. Gold in color, and heavily oaked. The nose offers distant toast as well as oak and apple flavors. Quite chunky and soft, with a chalky, dry, rather flavor-free finish. Aging fast, with little zest. **83** —*M.S. (7/1/2005)*

Carmen 1999 Winemaker's Reserve Chardonnay (Casablanca Valley) $40. Dry and toasty, with some menthol and roasted nut aromas, there's not a lot of fruit to be found on the nose of this offering. Some orange and grapefruit flavors show through on the palate, but the overwhelming sense is of a wine that's more reliant on barrels than on fruit for its character. Still, not bad if you like the style. **85** —*J.C. (3/1/2002)*

Carmen 1997 Winemaker's Reserve Chardonnay (Casablanca Valley) $25. Handsomely constructed, this well-balanced Chardonnay is evidence of Chile's moving up in quality...and price. Attractive apple and tropical fruit aromas and flavors are supported by present, not overwhelming oak. The mouthfeel is round, the acidity adequate, and the finish nicely spicy. A solid Chilean competitor in this price range. **89** —*M.M. (1/1/2004)*

Carmen 2005 Gewürztraminer (Curicó Valley) $7. Sweet melon aromas mixed with mango are friendly and persistent. Full in the mouth, with a bit of creaminess accenting spice-infused melon and apple flavors. Meets the requirements of a solid Gewürz. **85 Best Buy** —*M.S. (7/1/2006)*

Carmen 2004 Merlot (Rapel Valley) $7. A bit sharp and vegetal, especially at first. Airing reveals cherry and raspberry flavors and some salty, woody notes. Tangy and fresh in terms of feel. Not that serious of a wine. **83** —*M.S. (3/1/2006)*

Carmen 2002 Merlot (Rapel Valley) $7. Chunky, with initial farm-like aromas of leather and green herbs. The chewy palate oozes with thick berry fruit that is a touch medicinal. Finishes large, but with that same green character that first appears on the nose. **85 Best Buy** —*M.S. (8/1/2004)*

Carmen 2003 Classic Merlot (Rapel Valley) $7. Slightly weedy and herbal, but it also boasts ripe plums and black cherries alongside mocha and caramel notes that make it easy to drink. **85 Best Buy** *(12/15/2004)*

Carmen 2004 Reserve Merlot (Casablanca Valley) $13. Light strawberry aromas work the not-too-heavy bouquet, while standard red fruit controls the palate. In the mouth, it's crisp and snappy, with a tiny touch of acidic scour. Finishes clean and right, and shows overall freshness. **86** —*M.S. (10/1/2006)*

Carmen 2003 Reserve Merlot (Casablanca Valley) $13. Lighter-weight red fruit aromas of raspberry and strawberry set the stage for plum and other snappy flavors. It's all reflective of being a red from Casablanca, hence there's a minute amount of herbal essence and fresh acidity **86** —*M.S. (12/15/2005)*

Carmen 2002 Reserve Merlot (Rapel Valley) $14. After a year in a combination of French and American oak, this medium-weight Merlot has acquired pleasant smoke and dried spice notes that accent its tobacco and black cherry flavors. Supple tannins, crisp acids on the finish. **87** *(12/15/2004)*

Carmen 2001 Reserve Merlot (Rapel Valley) $15. Simple and clean, with leathery plum aromas. Some cherry and red plum notes gather speed on the palate, while late in the game things turn more woody and dry. With plenty of tannin and clarity, this is a nice Merlot for everyday purposes. **87** —*M.S. (3/1/2004)*

Carmen 1999 Reserve Merlot (Rapel Valley) $15. 85 —*J.C. (3/1/2002)*

Carmen 1998 Reserve Merlot (Rapel Valley) $15. Merlot from Chile is coming up fast and this shows why. The aroma and flavor package is on target with plums, coffee, and chocolate predominating. The bell pepper note on the nose is not overbearing. The superb balance and long finish wrap it up nicely. **89** —*M.N. (2/1/2001)*

Carmen 2000 Reserve Estate Grown Merlot (Rapel Valley) $15. Dark and dramatically purple, a wine that looks like it has all the extracted fruit in the world. And in fact the flavors are enormous, filled with jammy berries and stone fruits. The wine is very soft in acids and tannins. It's a nice mouthful but could use more structure and finesse. **85** —*S.H. (12/1/2002)*

Carmen 2003 Reserve Petite Sirah (Maipo Valley) $15. Years have gone by since we last rated this novelty, and all signs indicate that it has vastly improved. The amalgamation of fruit, tannin, and acidity is quite impressive. The mocha and molasses that deck the finish is a rich, welcome touch. Big and unique; but beware of the rock-hard tannins. **88** —*M.S. (5/1/2006)*

Carmen 1997 Reserve Petite Sirah (Chile) $14. 84 —*M.S. (11/15/1999)*

Carmen 1999 Reserve Pinot Noir (Maipo Valley) $17. Flavors of tart cherries have been oaked to within an inch of their lives—what's left is cedar, toast, and dried spices and a dry, woody finish. **83** —*J.C. (3/1/2002)*

Carmen 1999 Reserve Carmenère/Cabernet Sauvignon Red Blend (Maipo Valley) $17. This Cab-Carmenère blend's more of the olive-earth-tree-bark kind than the blackberry-and-oak variety; still, there's enough black berry fruit underneath the outdoorsy aromas and flavors. Finishes with lots of green herb, and a vegetal note. **84** —*D.T. (7/1/2002)*

Carmen 2001 Wine Maker's Reserve Red Blend (Maipo Valley) $40. The bouquet displays saucy, savory aromas that are both earthy and rubbery but also sort of suave and stylish. The surface of the main body shows a bit of tartness on top of cassis and black plum, while the finish is round, with full tannins clamping down. A burly red with plenty of kick. **88** —*M.S. (10/1/2006)*

CHILE

Carmen 1999 Winemaker's Reserve Red Blend (Maipo Valley) $40. An interesting blend of 50% Cabernet Sauvignon, 20% Carmenère, and 10% each of Petite Sirah, Syrah, and Merlot. The seductive aromas of mint, eucalyptus, and orange peel are enchanting. Flavors of dill, blackberries, and tar lead to a rich, toasty mouthfeel that finishes with firm, well-integrated tannins. **90 Editors' Choice** —*C.S. (12/1/2002)*

Carmen 1997 Winemaker's Reserve Red Blend (Maipo Valley) $40. A blend of 50% Cabernet Sauvignon, 20% Grande Vidure, 20% Petite Syrah, and 10% Merlot, it is as if you can clearly account for each varietal's contribution. Ripe cassis, cherry, plum, and spice flavors are buttressed by well-integrated oak. Beautifully balanced, it has good acidity and mature tannins, and closes with a long, satisfying finish. Great wine for tonight's grilled T-bone, and worthy of mid-term cellaring. **91 Editors' Choice** —*M.N. (2/1/2001)*

Carmen 2000 Winemaker's Reserve Red Red Blend (Maipo Valley) $40. An excellent Bordeaux-style blend. The nose is deep and smoky, with a readiness that's exemplary. Rich, clean, and integrated on the palate, with layering and style. Sure, it's powerful and fruity, but there's also some mature subtlety to it. Really hits the spot. One of Carmen's best wines in years. **91 Editors' Choice** —*M.S. (11/1/2005)*

Carmen 2005 Sauvignon Blanc (Curicó Valley) $7. Get at this one right away and you'll likely enjoy the grassy, passion fruit aromas as well as the fresh, juicy tropical flavors. Shows medium-strength zest and citrus on the back palate, but doesn't scour. Tasty; a nice quaffer. **86 Best Buy** —*M.S. (3/1/2006)*

Carmen 2004 Classic Sauvignon Blanc (Curicó Valley) $7. Grassy and citrusy at first, picking up notes of green peas and bell pepper on the palate. Tart and tangy on the finish. **83** *(12/15/2004)*

Carmen 2002 Classic Sauvignon Blanc (Central Valley) $7. Initial aromas of vanilla and cream turn a bit sour upon deeper inspection. The citrusy palate is tart and sharp, and by no means is this a soft wine. Just the opposite: It's rather short and zingy. **85 Best Buy** —*M.S. (7/1/2003)*

Carmen 2005 Reserve Sauvignon Blanc (Casablanca Valley) $12. Tight as a drum, with less than ripe nectarine and green vegetables on the nose. Acidic, with tart citrus flavors and an extremely aggressive mouthfeel. Almost sour; Carmen's basic Sauvignon from Curico is easier to drink. **81** —*M.S. (7/1/2006)*

Carmen 2004 Reserve Sauvignon Blanc (Casablanca Valley) $12. The bouquet shows true S.B. aromas, including grapefruit and bitter greens. Properly acidic, so the palate delivers green apple and grapefruit flavors along with fresh veggies. Consistent on the finish, and largely on the mark. **86** —*M.S. (11/1/2005)*

Carmen 2003 Reserve Sauvignon Blanc (Casablanca Valley) $14. Smoky and a bit flinty, this wine does reveal a mineral aspect of Chilean Sauvignon Blanc. It's also very citrusy, with flavors that run toward grapefruit and lime. **84** *(12/15/2004)*

Carmen 2002 Reserve Sauvignon Blanc (Casablanca Valley) $13. Fresh and full, with a big nose of pineapple, peach and scallion. The palate is solid and whole, with ample orange, tangerine, and lime flavors. A smooth finish that's light but just deep enough ensures widespread appeal. **87** —*M.S. (6/1/2004)*

Carmen 2001 Reserve Sauvignon Blanc (Casablanca Valley) $13. 86 —*M.S. (3/1/2002)*

Carmen 2004 Shiraz (Maipo Valley) $7. Lots of crispness and red berry on the nose, with a touch of sugar beet. Tartness anchors the palate, but there's also flavorful red berry flavors mixed in. Good in a refreshing way; you could drink this with chips and salsa or Mexican food. **85 Best Buy** —*M.S. (3/1/2006)*

Carmen 2003 Reserve Shiraz (Maipo Valley) $14. Starts with woody aromas as well as leather, marzipan, and baked fruit. Runs on the rich, thick side of the fence, with chunky plum and blackberry flavors. The finish is creamy and sticky, with soft, plush tannins. A chewy yet not gooey New World Syrah. **87** —*M.S. (11/1/2005)*

Carmen 2002 Reserve Shiraz (Maipo Valley) $17. Dark and pruny, with molasses, chocolate, and beet juice on the nose. Semisweet raspberry and strawberry flavors set up a racy finish that carries live acidity and some serious tannins. **85** —*M.S. (2/1/2005)*

Carmen 2003 Reserve Shiraz-Cabernet Sauvignon (Maipo Valley) $15. Broad and bulky, with nothing feminine about it. The nose is a burly blend of olive, leather, and black fruit. Next up is a ripe palate with ample dark-berry flavors and a chocolate accent. Chunky and ripe all the way out the back door. **87** —*M.S. (3/1/2006)*

Carmen 1999 Reserve Syrah-Cabernet (Maipo Valley) $17. Not a by-the-book good wine, but I had trouble turning away from it. Date, caramel, peanut and juicy red-berry aromas usher in grape and plum fruit doused in gravel. Some chewy tannins give this wine a little heft and texture. Finishes with ash, char, and gravel. **85** —*D.T. (7/1/2002)*

Carmen 2005 Rosé Syrah-Cabernet (Maipo Valley) $10. Fairly fruity and fresh on the nose, while the round, soft palate runs easily with berry flavors. Quite big and cushioned, without much acidic punch. Pleasant in a bulky way, and based on Syrah and Cabernet Sauvignon. **84** —*M.S. (11/15/2006)*

CARTA VIEJA

Carta Vieja 2003 Chardonnay (Maule Valley) $8. Funky and lactic, with sweet, heavy fruit that falls into the canned pear and apple class. Heavy on the finish, with some green bean and asparagus poking through the mix. **81** —*M.S. (7/1/2005)*

Carta Vieja 2001 Estate Bottled Chardonnay (Maule Valley) $6. Simple but clean in the nose, with just a hint of cheesy pungency. The palate veers toward tangerine and pineapple. The finish is sharp and acidic. **84 Best Buy** —*M.S. (7/1/2003)*

Carta Vieja 2003 Sauvignon Blanc (Maule Valley) $8. Melon and crushed children's vitamins comprise the nose, while spiked tangerine and pineapple flavors carry the palate. Fairly solid, with an almost jazzy mouthfeel. **83** —*M.S. (7/1/2005)*

CASA JULIA

Casa Julia 2002 Cabernet Sauvignon (Maipo Valley) $8. The bouquet is closed, with only a touch of prune, plum, and cranberry aromas emerging. On the palate is raspberry fruit, a hint of veggies, and some tight tannins. The finish is lean, and here those tannins assert themselves again in a way that's more than the fruit calls for. Still, it's pretty solid Cab. **86 Best Buy** —*M.S. (7/1/2003)*

Casa Julia 2000 Cabernet Sauvignon (Maipo Valley) $9. There's too much flat-wood flavor here for this wine to be better than acceptable. On both the nose and the palate, flat-wood flavors obscure what fruit lies underneath. Medium-bodied, though appropriately dry, in the mouth. **82** *(7/1/2002)*

Casa Julia 2002 Reserve Cabernet Sauvignon (Maipo Valley) $15. Full oak results in aromas of BBQ beef, chocolate and licorice. The palate is more along the lines of red fruit, with an herbal twist. The finish keeps form and the wine is balanced. Likable and easy to grasp. **87** —*M.S. (2/1/2005)*

Casa Julia 2001 Reserve Cabernet Sauvignon (Maipo Valley) $12. Right off the bat this wine is pure and smooth. The nose is pretty, with cranberry and cassis. Next up is a palate of pure red fruit and only a light shading of oak. The finish draws applause for its clarity and buttery nuances. It's what a good Chilean Cabernet should be; it's ripe and easy to drink, yet fairly solid and impressive. **88 Best Buy** —*M.S. (7/1/2003)*

Casa Julia 2003 Merlot (Rapel Valley) $10. Starts murky and muddled, with a heavy jam-like consistency. With time it opens to offer plum, cherry, and a laudable mouthfeel. Yes, it's prickly on the finish, with some light green notes, but it's still good as a whole. **85 Best Buy** —*M.S. (2/1/2005)*

Casa Julia 2002 Merlot (Rapel Valley) $8. The nose is all black fruit and some cinnamon spice. Next up is a palate of cassis, plum, and cherry, while the finish is round and buttery. Taken as a whole the wine is fairly focused, with an easygoing character and nothing too out of whack. **85 Best Buy** —*M.S. (7/1/2003)*

Casa Julia 2001 Merlot (Chile) $9. 89 Best Buy —*C.S. (11/15/2002)*

Casa Julia 2000 Merlot (Rapel Valley) $9. Herb, black pepper, and wheat aromas lead to black plum and spicy oak flavors in the mouth. Some dusty tannins give this Merlot nice texture; finsihes with decent length and black plum and oak-derived flavors. **85** —*D.T. (7/1/2002)*

CHILE

Casa Julia 2000 Reserve Merlot (Maipo Valley) $12. Rustic and medium-bodied, this Merlot has a nice spiciness that would be a big hit at a backyard barbecue. There's some char on the nose, and a spicy-marinade note on the palate. Finishes with dryish tannins and outdoorsy, tree-bark flavors. **85** —D.T. (7/1/2002)

Casa Julia 2003 Sauvignon Blanc (Maule Valley) $10. Light peach, melon and orange aromas sit in front of mildly sour tangerine and grapefruit flavors. Acidic, with a sharp finish, but ultimately it's clean. **82** —M.S. (7/1/2005)

Casa Julia 2001 Sauvignon Blanc (Maule Valley) $8. Opens with lofty, airy aromas of flowers and pears, and then in the mouth comes a full rush of grapefruit and orange pith. Finishes nicely, tasting of tangerine with hints of licorice and tarragon. In terms of mouthfeel, it's a plump, medium-acid wine, so drink it now. **87 Best Buy** —M.S. (7/1/2003)

Casa Julia 2001 Syrah (Maipo Valley) $8. Plump and round on the nose, with some heavy oak and awkward plum/beet aromas. The palate is robust and forward, but a little confusing; the fruit is muddled. And the finish is grapey and thin, leaving a mildly sour lasting impression. **84** —M.S. (7/1/2003)

CASA LAPOSTOLLE

Casa Lapostolle 1997 Cabernet Sauvignon (Rapel Valley) $12. 91 Best Buy —M.S. (11/15/1999)

Casa Lapostolle 2004 Cabernet Sauvignon (Rapel Valley) $10. Full and a bit rough at first, with some heat on the nose. Swirling settles it down, and what comes up are brawny cherry, cassis, and chocolate flavors. Very sturdy and tannic, with energy. Significantly less lush and tasty than the benchmark 2003. **86 Best Buy** —M.S. (7/1/2006)

Casa Lapostolle 2003 Cabernet Sauvignon (Rapel Valley) $10. Intense and saturated, with dark aromas of pencil lead, tree bark, cola, and black fruits. In the mouth, it's full-force Cabernet. The blackberry and black cherry flavors are pure and satisfying, while the finish offers smoke, chocolate, and coffee. This wine features ripeness and an overall quality rarely achieved by others in the price range. **90 Best Buy** —M.S. (11/1/2005)

Casa Lapostolle 2002 Cabernet Sauvignon (Rapel Valley) $10. Bold and bright, with requisite cassis, leather, and toast aromas. A welcome mix of spices such as cinnamon and cola nut blend well with the currant-based fruit and vanilla on the palate. Extra creamy and rich, with soft, integrated tannins. Just right for the price. **88 Best Buy** (3/1/2005)

Casa Lapostolle 1999 Cabernet Sauvignon (Rapel Valley) $10. Starts off solid enough, with sweet oak and cassis aromas, before turning rustic and woody on the palate. **81** —J.C. (3/1/2002)

Casa Lapostolle 1999 Cuvée Alexandre Cabernet Sauvignon (Colchagua Valley) $20. For a taste of what a good Chilean winery can do with Cabernet, and not charge you an arm and a leg, this is a perennial best bet. Even better: the '99 might be the best Cuvée Al to date. The nose is deep, brambly, and inviting. The cassis and herb-tinged palate features tight tannins. Finally, it finishes with vanilla, coffee, and dark chocolate. Short-term cellaring will only improve it. **90** —M.S. (3/1/2002)

Casa Lapostolle 1998 Cuvée Alexandre Cabernet Sauvignon (Colchagua Valley) $25. Cab lovers who just love lavish oak on their bold fruit flavors will enjoy this wine. Medium-bodied, with fairly high tannins, the wine offers a little blackberry and cherry on the palate and aromas of oak, black pepper and alcohol. The finish is short and tannic. **85** —D.T. (8/1/2001)

Casa Lapostolle 2004 Cuvée Alexandre Apalta Vineyard Cabernet Sauvignon (Colchagua Valley) $22. Bright and bold, with forceful berry aromas in front of dark, saturated fruit flavors. Medium to full in weight, with a sturdy tannic structure. Shows a big spice, pepper and chocolate element on the finish. Typically large and satisfying. **90** —M.S. (5/1/2006)

Casa Lapostolle 2003 Cuvée Alexandre Apalta Vineyard Cabernet Sauvignon (Colchagua Valley) $21. As always, this wine exhibits power and intensity, with leather, earth, and beefy dark fruit making for an alluring bouquet. Round and ripe in the mouth, with big-time cherry and chocolate accents. A wine with true star power, and the lasting notes of smoke and charcoal are the real deal. **91 Editors' Choice** —M.S. (11/1/2005)

Casa Lapostolle 2001 Cuvée Alexandre Apalta Vineyard Cabernet Sauvignon (Colchagua Valley) $22. Excellent Cabernet at any price, and one of the best Lapostolle wines we've tasted. Pitch dark and layered, with pulsating berry, tobacco, earth, and charcoal aromas. Luscious on the palate, where plum, cherry, and cassis flow toward a classic finish of soft tannins and chocolate. Immensely ripe and tasty. **92 Editors' Choice** (3/1/2005)

Casa Lapostolle 2001 Estate Bottled Cabernet Sauvignon (Rapel Valley) $12. Lapostolle's basic Cab scores big in the fine '01 vintage. It features a deep nose of tire rubber, blackberry, and rusticity. The palate is high-octane and deep, with plenty of ripe, tannic black fruit. And the finish is round and lengthy. It should age well for a couple of years. **90 Editors' Choice** —M.S. (7/1/2003)

Casa Lapostolle 2003 Chardonnay (Casablanca Valley) $10. A touch creamy and fat on the bouquet, but backed by peach and tangerine flavors that sing of ripeness. Finishes scouring and tangy, but incredibly fresh. **87 Best Buy** (3/1/2005)

Casa Lapostolle 2002 Chardonnay (Casablanca Valley) $12. Starts off with peach, apple, and pear aromas, which are followed by flavors of candied pineapple slices drizzled with some anisette and cinnamon. And while it's sweet to begin with, the finish turns mildly dry and peppery. A good example of basic Chardonnay made well. **86** —M.S. (6/1/2004)

Casa Lapostolle 2001 Chardonnay (Casablanca Valley) $10. This round, fresh, and stylish Chardonnay from the Casablanca Valley is a step up from the middling 2000 version. The bouquet yields ample pear, almond, and coconut aromas, while the palate is loaded with pear fruit and a hint of oak-driven smoke. Classy and concise, and better made than almost every other similarly priced Chardonnay. **88 Best Buy** —M.S. (11/15/2003)

Casa Lapostolle 2000 Chardonnay (Casablanca Valley) $10. The house Chard from Casablanca is crisp, even lean. In the mouth, though, things warm up, where vanilla and smoke are both heavy compared to the more humble fruit. It's a bit racier in the finish, showing lemon. **85** —M.S. (3/1/2002)

Casa Lapostolle 2002 Cuvée Alexandre Chardonnay (Casablanca Valley) $17. A whiff of popcorn adds character to the nose, which is dominated by white stone fruits and apple. The palate offers pear, apple, and melon flavors, and then more popcorn-tinged oak. Even the finish is long and woody. If you like a ripe, well-crafted Chard with ample oak, this is for you. Fans of stripped down, natural Chards may find it too bolstered. **89** —M.S. (6/1/2004)

Casa Lapostolle 2000 Cuvée Alexandre Chardonnay (Casablanca Valley) $18. Heavy toast, butter, and vanilla aromas lead into a smooth, rich mouthfeel. Among the flavors, pear fruit seems to stick out the most. In the long run, however, whether intentional or not, the wine's weight seems to get the better of the taste, especially in the big, buttery finish. **87** —M.S. (3/1/2002)

Casa Lapostolle 2005 Cuvée Alexandre Atalayas Vineyard Chardonnay (Casablanca Valley) $20. As Chilean Chardonnays go, this single-vineyard bottling from Lapostolle is smooth and toasty, with plenty of vanilla, smoke, and tropical fruit aromas. The vintage was a good one, and that's reflected in the wine's body, which is hefty and broad but nicely balanced by freshening acids. If you like vanilla and toast accenting ripe New World flavors, this is for you. **89** —M.S. (12/31/2006)

Casa Lapostolle 2004 Cuvée Alexandre Atalayas Vineyard Chardonnay (Casablanca Valley) $18. Cuvée Alexandre is top-flight Chilean Chardonnay, year in and year out. The '04 is crisp and full of tightly wound fruit flavors. Offsetting things are nut and toast notes that fit the wine perfectly. Generous enough but not too big and not at all flabby. **89** —M.S. (3/1/2006)

Casa Lapostolle 2003 Cuvée Alexandre Atalayas Vineyard Chardonnay (Casablanca Valley) $18. Surely one of the finest Chardonnays in Chile. The balance, level of toast, and depth make it world class. Peach, buttered toast, and nuts make for a fine palate, while the finish is warm and dotted with the flavor of toasted almonds and walnuts. Pretty and defined. **90 Editors' Choice** (3/1/2005)

CHILE

Casa Lapostolle 2003 Merlot (Rapel Valley) $10. A touch of green tobacco and bell pepper on the nose, but not all-out weedy. Tobacco and mocha jab with black cherry and plum on the palate, while good length and overall suppleness bolster the finish. **86 Best Buy** (3/1/2005)

Casa Lapostolle 2000 Merlot (Rapel Valley) $11. Herbal, with aromas of rhubarb and stewed fruit, followed by sour herbs and a bitter, tannic finish. **81** —J.C. (3/1/2002)

Casa Lapostolle 1999 Merlot (Rapel Valley) $14. Toasty oak, oodles of sweet fruit, and supple tannins are hallmarks of superconsultant Michel Rolland, and he has managed to bring them to the masses in this gently constructed Merlot. Bing cherries and toast, with mocha and herb shadings, are brought together with a deft touch. **88** —J.C. (2/1/2001)

Casa Lapostolle 2001 Cuvée Alexandre Merlot (Colchagua Valley) $20. A meaty, smoky, leathery current flows through the ripe bouquet, followed by tons of blackberry, chocolate, and clove flavors. Finishing touches of coffee and burnt toast mostly mask the mild green note one detects on the back palate. **88** —M.S. (6/1/2004)

Casa Lapostolle 1999 Cuvée Alexandre Merlot (Colchagua Valley) $25. This meaty, rugged youngster is really purple in color, a sure sign of the extract and power to come. The structure is tight and it's immature now, maybe even harder than one might expect from Merlot. But given a little time (or simply some airing in a decanter), all the plum, oak, and other nuances should emerge. **89** —M.S. (3/1/2002)

Casa Lapostolle 1998 Cuvée Alexandre Merlot (Rapel Valley) $22. Lavish oak envelops the clove, black cherry, and coffee nose of this Michel Rolland-designed wine. The wood presence remains big on the palate, rivaling the ripe berry and mineral flavors. There's a softness to the structure but the mouthfeel is still chewy. Merlot fans who enjoy toasty oak will love this. **85** —J.F. (8/1/2001)

Casa Lapostolle 2004 Cuvée Alexandre Apalta Vineyard Merlot (Colchagua Valley) $20. Smoky and round, with big black fruit delivering a serious opening salvo. Like most from Lapostolle, this is a big-boned red with full plum and black cherry aromas and flavors. Plenty of oak yields vanilla and chocolate late. A solid, very nice Chilean Merlot. **87** —M.S. (7/1/2006)

Casa Lapostolle 2003 Cuvée Alexandre Apalta Vineyard Merlot (Colchagua Valley) $21. Black as night, with snazzy scents of marzipan, Bing cherry, and plum. Tight as nails in the mouth, and dead serious, with cherry, plum, mint, and black olive flavors. Now it's rather tannic, with coffee and bitter chocolate flowing off the finish; will be better in another eight to 12 months. **90 Editors' Choice** —M.S. (12/15/2005)

Casa Lapostolle 2002 Cuvée Alexandre Apalta Vineyard Merlot (Colchagua Valley) $19. Black cherry and mocha kick it off, while deep sniffers may uncover some eucalyptus and basil. Very supple and creamy, with seemingly edible plum and chocolate flavors gracing the full-bodied palate. Substantially complex for a wine this big and easy. **91 Editors' Choice** (3/1/2005)

Casa Lapostolle 2004 Estate Bottled Merlot (Rapel Valley) $12. Dark and fruity, with a lot of licorice, cola, tree bark, and plum aromas. Nicely balanced in the mouth, with dark plum flavors that feature a touch of smoked meat and earth. Chocolaty late, with enveloping tannins. Very respectable for the price. **88 Best Buy** —M.S. (3/1/2006)

Casa Lapostolle 2002 Estate Bottled Merlot (Rapel Valley) $12. At first this is aggressive, with an aromatic note of wet dog along with blueberries. But soon it finds its legs and opens to display chocolate, espresso, and a big batch of black plum and blackberry. The finish has full tannins and some coffee-like flavor. Currently it's wall-to-wall big, but it should settle down in no time and become a good red to drink on any occasion. **88 Best Buy** —M.S. (7/1/2003)

Casa Lapostolle 2001 Apalta Red Blend (Colchagua Valley) $55. Full and forceful, with aromas of green herbs piercing the cassis and cherry aromas that carry the bouquet. With molasses, cassis, and black plum flavors, it seems to have all that the wine is known for; however, there's also a green, tomato-like presence that may stem from the higher level of Carmenère that's going into the wine. **88** —M.S. (6/1/2004)

Casa Lapostolle 2001 Borobo Red Blend (Rapel Valley-Casablanca Valley) $65. Solid as a soldier and convincing despite its unconventional components, which include Pinot Noir Syrah, among others. It's probably more of a wine for now than for storing; the palate is ripe and supple, with a lot of extract, cola, and brown sugar. Tannic but not hard. **90** —M.S. (3/1/2006)

Casa Lapostolle 2003 Clos Apalta Red Blend (Colchagua Valley) $65. Dense as a brick, with deep blackberry, prune, earth, and chocolate aromas. Huge and multilayered, but already exhibiting perfect structure and integrated oak and spice flavors. Pure and exact; along with the 2001 this is Clos Apalta at its finest. **94 Editors' Choice** —M.S. (5/1/2006)

Casa Lapostolle 2002 Clos Apalta Red Blend (Colchagua Valley) $65. Saturated and rich, with meaty, forceful aromas of black fruit, molasses, and toasted marshmallow. A blend of Carmenère, Cabernet, and Merlot that's full of cassis, black cherry, and a light herbaceousness. Lush but structured; a real big boy. **92 Editors' Choice** (3/1/2005)

Casa Lapostolle 1999 Clos Apalta Red Blend (Chile) $60. Once again, arguably the best wine in Chile is this beauty from what may eventually become recognized as a world-class site for red wines—the dry-farmed, old-vines Apalta Vineyard. Fermentation involving big wood vats and the utmost in human attention yields a pure, stately wine that's equal parts power and finesse. Blendwise, it's mostly Merlot, and the flavors are all about kirsch, plum liqueur, and chocolate. Give it several years to fully blossom. **94 Editors' Choice** —M.S. (3/1/2002)

Casa Lapostolle 2005 Sauvignon Blanc (Rapel Valley) $10. This basic SB has never been a strong suit for Lapostolle, and two tastings of this vintage confirm flat melony aromas along with flavors of banana, papaya, and sugared almond. Finishes pithy and a touch bitter. Too high in alcohol as well. **83** —M.S. (3/1/2006)

Casa Lapostolle 2004 Sauvignon Blanc (Rapel Valley) $8. Classic citrus, grapefruit, and passion fruit on the nose, with more of the same in terms of flavors. Seems a touch warm and heavy at 14.5%, but no question about the ripeness. **86 Best Buy** (3/1/2005)

Casa Lapostolle 2001 Sauvignon Blanc (Casablanca Valley) $8. A piercing grapefruit aroma, the hallmark of Casablanca Sauvignon Blanc, is strong here, and there's a certain stony peachiness and some passion fruit as well. There's also a touch of green pepper and asparagus at the flavor core, and then some vanilla at the end. If that sounds like a lot to ponder, it is—probably too much, given the wine. **85** —M.S. (3/1/2002)

Casa Lapostolle 2000 Sauvignon Blanc (Rapel Valley) $9. Slightly fat, figgy aromas, with notes of thyme and mint, give way to a round palate and flavors of citrus and fig. The mouthfeel has just a touch of youthful fizz, and the finish is long and nutty, with a reprise of herbs. **86** —M.M. (2/1/2001)

Casa Lapostolle 2003 Estate Bottled Sauvignon Blanc (Rapel Valley) $9. Aromatic but slightly bland. This is a textbook "starter" Sauvignon that will go down well. The plain palate is round, with notes of bitter herbs, apple, banana and black pepper. The lasting mouthfeel is moderately thick and resiny. **85** —M.S. (6/1/2004)

Casa Lapostolle 2002 Cuvée Alexandre Syrah (Rapel Valley) $22. The first Cuvée Alexandre Syrah on record is better than adequate; it's exciting and intriguing, two huge virtues. The nose offers pepper, blackberry, and vanilla, while the palate is entirely ripe, meaty, and intensely spicy. A real comer amid Chile's new wave of Syrahs. **91 Editors' Choice** (3/1/2005)

Casa Lapostolle 2001 Cuvée Alexandre Syrah (Rapel Valley) $20. This is a new wine from one of Chile's most consistent producers, and it's quite the saturated bruiser. The color is deep purple, while the nose is raw and heavy, with deep fruit and plenty of bacon-like character. The mouth is like blackberry pie, while the feel is full and tannic, although not at all offensive or tough. The finish is dark, brooding, and just a little bitter. An interesting new entry to Chile's roster, and one that's very well oaked. **88** —M.S. (7/1/2003)

Casa Lapostolle 2003 Cuvée Alexandre Requinoa Vineyard Syrah (Rapel Valley) $23. Severely oaked with a roasted nose equal to baked plums mixed with crushed espresso beans. Ultra-rich in the mouth, with sweet, syrupy flavors that don't come across soft because the tannins are immense. This is not your average wine, and the nose is downright overwhelming. But it has some very impressive dark-berry flavors and it certainly should improve through 2006. **89** —M.S. (11/1/2005)

CHILE

CASA RIVAS

Casa Rivas 2001 Reserva Estate Bottled Cabernet Sauvignon (Maipo Valley) $10. Dark and grapey, with some strange candied aromas akin to bubble gum. Given time to air, it comes around to offer black plum flavors, but also a hint of green bean. The finish has a nice feel to it and some coffee-like flavor. Ample tannins leave a lasting impression. **84** —M.S. (12/1/2002)

Casa Rivas 2003 Carmenère (Maipo Valley) $7. Challenged Carmenère. It has a lot of vinegar, bell pepper, and green bean to it. Mouthfeel is fine; flavors of beet juice mixed with cola don't really cut it. **81** —M.S. (11/1/2005)

Casa Rivas 2002 Carmenère (Maipo Valley) $7. Quite herbal on the nose, with aromas of tomato and green peppers. In a word, it's basic Carmenère, with a fair amount of vegetal character. Under that, however, are pie cherry and raspberry flavors as well as piercing, razor-like acids. As a result, it's tangy and sharp. **83** —M.S. (6/1/2004)

Casa Rivas 2001 Estate Bottled Carmenère (Maipo Valley) $6. Tight and oaky in the nose, with some funky green notes. The palate is a bit herbal and mildly vegetal, but there's also some cherry fruit and spice. The texture on the finish is the high point, but the vegetal flavor at the wine's core is a sore point. **83** —M.S. (7/1/2003)

Casa Rivas 2002 Gran Reserva Carmenère (Maipo Valley) $22. Herbal and cool on the bouquet, with a dark, masculine color. The palate is sweet and plummy, with berry nuances. Tannins come up on the finish, which is ripe and pulsing. Overall, it's integrated and original, a decent bet within the Carmenère category. **86** —M.S. (6/1/2004)

Casa Rivas 2003 Chardonnay (Maipo Valley) $7. The scents of fireplace and matchstick hit you right away, while the flavor profile is made up of lemon, tangerine, and infused oak. Overall, it runs sharp and forceful, with intense citric notes. **81** —M.S. (6/1/2004)

Casa Rivas 2002 Estate Bottled Chardonnay (Maipo Valley) $6. The nose is oaky and grainy as it offers aromas of corn and wheat as well as some pear fruit. The apple, honeydew and oak flavors make for a robust palate, but one with a sweet, mildly artificial-tasting core. The finish is oaky and resiny, although there's some necessary balancing acidity and citrus flavors to keep it steady. **84** —M.S. (7/1/2003)

Casa Rivas 2001 Reserva Estate Bottled Chardonnay (Maipo Valley) $10. At first, the bouquet seems dense and tinged with a mild lactic note, but that moves on rather quickly. The flavor profile of banana, pear, and apple is perfectly fine, while the finish is a bit lean. **85** —M.S. (7/1/2003)

Casa Rivas 2003 Merlot (Maipo Valley) $7. Quite green and minty, and that unripe, herbal streak continues onto the palate, where bell pepper takes over. Lean and clean on the finish, however, to such a point that it simply disappears. **82** —M.S. (7/1/2005)

Casa Rivas 2002 Merlot (Maipo Valley) $7. Spicy and meaty, with olive and leather aromas. While somewhat herbal, there are ample plum, blackberry, and sugar-beet flavors. Definitely not your standard Merlot; this is a different breed, one that's generally good but strays off course. **85** —M.S. (6/1/2004)

Casa Rivas 2001 Estate Bottled Merlot (Maipo Valley) $6. Arugula, dark chocolate and faint cherry-vanilla aromas meld well with flavors of apple peel and a hint of white pepper. Red plum and dark chocolate repeat throughout. Light-bodied and fruity, with just enough acidity. **86** —K.F. (12/1/2002)

Casa Rivas 2002 Reserva Merlot (Maipo Valley) $11. A full dose of bell pepper and black pepper aromas raises questions about ripeness, but the wine saves itself on the palate, where berry fruit, black olive, and basil vie for attention. The finish is smooth and hangs around. **85** —M.S. (7/1/2005)

Casa Rivas 2003 Sauvignon Blanc (Maipo Valley) $7. Fresh and clean, as it should be. Round and full across the palate, with a forceful, direct orange flavor and little else getting in the way. Some lemon zest on the finish brings this easy drinker home. Not complex, but a nice quaff if properly chilled. **86 Best Buy** —M.S. (6/1/2004)

CASA SILVA

Casa Silva 1999 Altura Cabernet Blend (Colchagua Valley) $90. Casa Silva has entered the Super Chilean sweepstakes with this Cabernet/Merlot/Carmenère blend—and the winery scores some early points. From a fine vintage, this wine is minty, chocolaty, and full of red raspberry fruit. Some airing reveals graham cracker, caramel, and hidden fruit. It's definitely a big-time, well-made wine that reflects serious effort. And it's ageworthy, up to about five years. **91 Cellar Selection** —M.S. (3/1/2002)

Casa Silva 2000 Quinta Generacion Cabernet Blend (Colchagua Valley) $25. Very fragrant, with aromas of violets, charred meat, and ample black fruit. The flavor profile is uncommon but appealing, surely a result of the blend, which is Cabernet Sauvignon along with Carmenère and Petit Verdot. On the finish, you get a hint of charcoal in addition to espresso. If it were deeper and more complex it could potentially be a great wine. **88** —M.S. (7/1/2003)

Casa Silva 1999 Quinta Generacion Cabernet Blend (Colchagua Valley) $20. A sturdy, round, and pretty wine, with just a touch of grace, too. It's 52% Cabernet Sauvignon and 48% Carmenère, and the two seem happily married. Chocolate and raspberry aromas draw you in, and once in you'll find a soft mouthfeel and deep, true red-wine flavors. It's hearty and stylish enough to earn its "gran reserva" designation. **89** —M.S. (3/1/2002)

Casa Silva 2003 Los Lingues Gran Reserva Cabernet Sauvignon (Colchagua Valley) $17. Fleshy and full-bodied, with milk chocolate, raisin, cassis, char, and leather all making for a serious bouquet. Olive, prune, blackberry, and more coat the powerful, whole palate. Shows a lot of depth and color. An individual wine with character. **89** —M.S. (5/1/2006)

Casa Silva 2004 Reserva Cabernet Sauvignon (Colchagua Valley) $10. This winery has been getting things right lately, and the '04 Cabernet is deep and fruity, with a touch of oak and ripe, integrated tannins. Flavors of dark fruit are offset by chocolate and toast flavors, while the finish is rich but relaxed. Great for the money. **88 Best Buy** —M.S. (5/1/2006)

Casa Silva 2000 Classic Carmenère (Colchagua Valley) $10. If density is your thing, try this deep purple-colored offering from an up-and-coming Colchagua Valley producer—it's the perfect value-priced introduction to the upside of Carmenère. Sweet in the nose and mouth, with tons of almost overripe plums and chocolate. Still, the wild and spicy side of the grape is also here. **88 Best Buy** —M.S. (3/1/2002)

Casa Silva 2003 Los Lingues Gran Reserva Carmenère (Colchagua Valley) $17. Lots of toast, graphite, and coal on the masculine nose. It's slightly herbal and rustic, but in a good way. The fruit is solid and ripe, with black cherry and chocolate riding front and center. **88** —M.S. (3/1/2006)

Casa Silva 2002 Los Lingues Gran Reserva Carmenère (Colchagua Valley) $17. Ripe and meaty, with olive and herbs along with solid blackberry aromas. More of a full-bodied, heavier wine; there's substance and tannin along with beefy fruit and a fair dose of chocolate and roasted tomato. Quite dark on the finish. A successful reach for a higher level. **88** —M.S. (3/1/2006)

Casa Silva 2004 Reserva Carmenère (Colchagua Valley) $10. Ripe and a bit oily, with lots of leather and herbs. Shows mostly sweet fruit on a narrow body, with a touch of balsamic vinegar and earth. Feels fairly plush; a nice everyday rendition of the variety. **86 Best Buy** —M.S. (3/1/2006)

Casa Silva 2000 Reserve Carmenère (Colchagua Valley) $15. It's simply immense—like blackberry or plum pie. Dig in and there is grip, tannins, and acids, the signs of a real wine. Very pure Carmenère flavors are on display here: earthiness and smoked meat along with pulsating fruit. Big and burly for sure, but not clumsy. **89** —M.S. (3/1/2002)

Casa Silva 2001 Reserve Est Bottled Carmenère (Colchagua Valley) $15. At first take, the aromas are of barbecued meats, beets, and earth; later some lemony oak emerges. The fruit here is nice: It's a clean mix of cassis and cherry, with toasty oak-based undercurrents. Very solid and sturdy, and a bit charred at the edges. Try it for a positive look into modern Carmenère. **88** —M.S. (7/1/2003)

Casa Silva 2001 Classic Chardonnay (Colchagua Valley) $10. People who prefer a Mâcon-style Chard might like this a lot. It's lighter in color, while mild amounts of stone, petrol, and char define the nose. Solid pear and ripe apple flavors get some bump from the barreling the wine received. The tail end is smoky, with more apples showing through. **87 Best Buy** —*M.S. (3/1/2002)*

Casa Silva 2003 Angostura Gran Reserva Merlot (Colchagua Valley) $17. Deep and meaty, with a midnight hue and brooding aromatics. Ripe plum and blackberry dominate the chewy palate, while the finish is heady, with cola and espresso notes. Quite a powerball; nice but requires a bit more elegance and fruit definition to reach the next plateau. **87** — *M.S. (5/1/2006)*

Casa Silva 2000 Reserve Merlot (Colchagua Valley) $15. What a nice nose; quite deep and powerful. The palate is of the juicy kind, with all sorts of richness and power. Bold tannins give it structure. A big-bodied Merlot, quite in the house style of hefty red wines. **88** —*M.S. (3/1/2002)*

Casa Silva 2002 Quinta Generacion Red Blend (Colchagua Valley) $22. Big and ripe, with cotton candy, raspberry, and vanilla on the nose. The blend is 50% Cabernet, with smaller doses of Carmenère, Syrah, and Petit Verdot thrown in. Mouthfeel is an attribute in this case, as the fruit is plump, the tannins correct, and the acidity integrated. **88** —*M.S. (5/1/2006)*

Casa Silva 2003 Lolol Gran Reserva Shiraz (Colchagua Valley) $17. Heady and intense, with leather, graphite, and beef bouillon on the nose. Not at all jammy; it's tight at the core with plenty of acidity. Racy and aggressive for Shiraz. **88** —*M.S. (3/1/2006)*

Casa Silva 2003 Reserva Shiraz (Colchagua Valley) $10. Olive, warm leather, and heavy herbal fruit on the nose, with deep and powerful cherry, cola and pepper notes on the palate. It's pretty tannic and live-wire, with ample chocolate and herbal essence on the finish. **85 Best Buy** — *M.S. (3/1/2006)*

Casa Silva 2001 Quinta Generacion White Blend (Colchagua Valley) $23. The nose is barrel heavy, and it brings with it some mustard and cured-meat aromas that just don't cut it. This is a blend of Chardonnay, Viognier, and Sauvignon Gris, but frankly, it doesn't taste like much more than oaky white wine, though the texture and overall acidity are fine. **82** —*M.S. (7/1/2003)*

Casa Silva 2000 Quinta Generacion White Blend (Colchagua Valley) $20. This was one of the first attempts the Silvas made at a white blend (Chardonnay, Sauvignon Gris and Viognier), and it has some things going for it. The dry but pungent nose is intriguing, and the Sauvignon Gris is an unconventional Old World addition. Also, the full, creamy body makes it easy to drink. Overall, however, it's kind of nondescript. Expect more from the 2001 vintage. **86** —*M.S. (3/1/2002)*

Casa Silva 2003 Quinta Generación White Blend (Colchagua Valley) $17. Casa Silva is making this blend of Viognier, Chardonnay, and Sauvignon Gris in a soft, fully oaked manner. The nose deals heavy oak alongside melon and pear, while the palate is fleshy, with light apple, vanilla, and wood flavors. Plump for sure, with individuality. **86** —*M.S. (7/1/2006)*

CASA VERDI

Casa Verdi 2004 Aniceto Reserve Cabernet Sauvignon (Aconcagua Valley) $13. Not overly fruity on the nose; instead there's olive, tomato, and herbs as opposed to bulky berry or cherry notes. Seems snappy and tight in the mouth, where red fruit reigns. Largely in balance and highly respectable, but not complex. **86** —*M.S. (5/1/2006)*

CHÂTEAU LA JOYA

Château La Joya 2000 Gran Reserva Cabernet Sauvignon (Colchagua Valley) $16. A little lighter in body than many Colchagua Cabs, this one offers clean aromas of plum, cinnamon, and clove. Despite the Gran Reserva label, it's good but basic Cabernet. **86** —*M.S. (3/1/2002)*

Château La Joya 1998 Gran Reserva Cabernet Sauvignon (Colchagua Valley) $15. This Cabernet has a lean profile and is Bordeaux-like in weight and texture, but there's lots of dark raspberry and tobacco aromas and flavors. Hints of mint and licorice add a touch of complexity. Finishes with a slight herbal note and even tannins. **87** (6/1/2001)

Château La Joya 2000 Reserva Cabernet Sauvignon (Colchagua Valley) $12. The clean and rich aromatics here suggest chocolate and black berries. The palate is full and generally quite smooth, but as a whole it's not exactly exciting. For a wine with all the basics, this is it. But its over-all lack of complexity begs the question: what does "reserva" really mean? **85** —*M.S. (3/1/2002)*

Château La Joya 1999 Reserva Cabernet Sauvignon (Colchagua Valley) $10. This is less refined than the Gran Reserva, but not less pleasurable, and it delivers a lot for the price. The dark berry, tobacco, and spice aromas and flavors are solid. The palate shows nice texture, and full tannins mark the finish. This is a great barbeque red. **87 Best Buy** (6/1/2001)

Château La Joya 1998 Cuvée Premium Carmenère (Colchagua Valley) $28. This elegant wine opens with a bouquet of dark berry, toast, and mint. This example of Carmenère shows the variety can yield fruit for dark, suave, well-balanced reds. The oak is nicely integrated and there's a long reprise of the opening aromas on the finish. **90 Editors' Choice** (6/1/2001)

Château La Joya 2000 Gran Reserva Carmenère (Colchagua Valley) $20. Dense and chocolaty in the nose, and then even deeper in the body, with plum, black cherry, and coffee. This is one of many modern Carmenères that can only help carry the torch for the grape. It's a good wine worthy of discovery. **88** —*M.S. (3/1/2002)*

Château La Joya 2001 Estate Bottled Reserve Chardonnay (Colchagua Valley) $12. Smooth and richly aromatic, with pear and apple notes to go with the full allotment of oak and butter. This is Bisquertt's attempt at a top-shelf Chard, and it isn't a bad effort. The palate deals plenty of pear and mango flavors, while the finish is warm and oaky. Well-made, yet a bit flat. Drink this year for best results. **87 Best Buy** —*M.S. (7/1/2003)*

Château La Joya 1999 Gran Reserva Chardonnay (Colchagua Valley) $10. Mildly nutty aromas open to a palate of dry apple and oak flavors. This Chardonnay is a comfortable weight—it's neither too light nor too fat. Closes with good length, and a touch of nuttiness and spicy oak. **86** (6/1/2001)

Château La Joya 1998 Gran Reserva Chardonnay (Colchagua Valley) $15. Not unlike this producer's 1999 Chardonnay Selection, this Gran Reserva's delivery is all at the beginning. Apple and toasted oak start things off and are followed by crisp acidity and a smooth mouthfeel. However, the finish is short and the oak somewhat overbearing. **84** — *M.N. (2/1/2001)*

Château La Joya 2000 Reserva Chardonnay (Colchagua Valley) $10. This basic Chardonnay has a muted apple-earth nose and shows some tangy green apple flavors on the palate. The crisp acid spine keeps it lean, but it's even, not sharp—reminiscent of a decent Mâcon. Finishes with mild spices and moderate length. **84** (6/1/2001)

Château La Joya 1999 Selection Chardonnay (Colchagua Valley) $11. Everything is front end in this Chardonnay. The nose has plenty of tropical fruit, and with some toasted oak in the background. Decent acidity supports the fruit and the smooth mouthfeel is pleasing, but the wine cuts off abruptly with a somewhat short, resinous close. **83** —*M.N. (2/1/2001)*

Château La Joya 2001 Estate Bottled Reserve Malbec (Colchagua Valley) $12. This weighty Malbec is more rough than refined, but what's here is decent. The nose is round and full of plum and berry aromas, while there's a full blast of berry fruit along with detectable oak on the palate. The finish is basic and clean, with some buttery oak on the very back. **84** —*M.S. (7/1/2003)*

Château La Joya 2000 Reserva Malbec (Colchagua Valley) $NA. This is the winery's first-ever crack at Malbec, and the wine shows the grape's telltale blueberry and graham-cracker sweetness. But there's also some peanut and heavy earth in there, too, neither of which does much for what otherwise is a commendable wine. **84** —*M.S. (3/1/2002)*

Château La Joya 1999 Estate Bottled Gran Reserve Merlot (Colchagua Valley) $15. Soft acids and ripe tannins make this Chilean Merlot a consistent performer. Shows some weedy, herbal notes, but boasts enough berry, mocha, and leather to more than compensate. **87** —*C.S. (2/1/2003)*

Château La Joya 2000 Estate Bottled Reserve Merlot (Colchagua Valley) $12. This is a great house pour for fans of Chilean Merlot with its consistent fruit, soft acidity, and low tannins. On the nose and palate, a core of sweet, Red Delicious apple is accented by dry leather, toasty vanilla, and dried herbs. Simple, but well-crafted. **87 Best Buy** —*K.F. (7/1/2003)*

Château La Joya 2000 Gran Reserva Merlot (Colchagua Valley) $16. Enjoy this tasty, clean Merlot for it's roundness and well-applied lashing of oak. What you get here—without frills—is lots of plum and vanilla in the front and some smoke and coffee on the finish. **87** —*M.S. (3/1/2002)*

Château La Joya 1998 Gran Reserva Merlot (Colchagua Valley) $15. A notable lack of greenness makes this one of the best 1998 Chilean Merlots we've tasted. Classic varietal flavors of plum, cocoa, and dark berries are supported by good acidity and even tannins. This has structure, depth, and a touch of class. **89 Best Buy** *(6/1/2001)*

Château La Joya 1999 Reserva Merlot (Colchagua Valley) $10. The red berry aromas and flavors suffer from a tinge of bell peppers. The herb accents, decent fruit-to-acid balance, and nice earthiness on the finish are all positive, but the vegetal cast keeps this otherwise solid wine from being more than good. **84** *(6/1/2001)*

Château La Joya 2000 Reserva Sauvignon Blanc (Colchagua Valley) $10. Fairly rich and full, this wine offers good texture and ripe citrus, pineapple and herb aromas. There is a sour lemon-drop quality to the flavors, but they are neither unpleasantly tart, nor candy sweet. Good acidity provides lift and a fresh tang. **85** *(6/1/2001)*

CHÂTEAU LOS BOLDOS

Château Los Boldos 1998 Grand Cru Cabernet Sauvignon (Requinoa) $45. Pleasant aromas of earth and peanuts are tight on fruit, but the fruit comes through on the palate where you get potent plums and currants. The wine is very smooth, as all of its components are in balance, then finishes long. **89** —*C.S. (12/1/2002)*

Château Los Boldos 2003 Grand Reserve Cabernet Sauvignon (Requinoa) $11. Fairly saucy and earthy, with root beer and leather establishing a presence on the nose. Plump berry and plum flavors carry the palate, followed by toast, chocolate, and espresso on the finish. A touch grabby and tannic but overall it's more right than wrong. **86** —*M.S. (5/1/2006)*

Château Los Boldos 2003 Tradition Cabernet Sauvignon (Requinoa) $8. A bit dense, with prune and mint aromas. Limited in scope and depth; what's here is deep but monotone. Flavors of boysenberry and black plum are heavy and soft, while chocolate brings up the rear. Short in structure and tannins, but dense enough to match a rich weeknight dinner. **84 Best Buy** —*M.S. (7/1/2006)*

Château Los Boldos 2000 Vieilles Vignes Cabernet Sauvignon (Requinoa) $20. Solid and full-bodied, with thoroughness to the nose. Flavors of blackberry, cassis, pepper, and savory spice are totally convincing, while the finish is tight and right if not exactly effusive. This Cab is made from a vineyard that houses vines planted 150 years ago, so it has some serious terroir. **89** —*M.S. (5/1/2006)*

Château Los Boldos 1999 Vielles Vignes Cabernet Sauvignon (Requinoa) $20. Earthy and blackberry aromas are complemented by flavors of chocolate, tobacco, and leather. A nice balance of tannins and acidity makes for a pleasant-drinking Cab. **87** —*C.S. (12/1/2002)*

Château Los Boldos 1997 Grand Cru Cabernet Sauvignon-Merlot (Requinoa) $40. The Massenez family from Alsace is to thank for this Bordeaux blend, which offers fleshy, dusty, black plum and red berry fruit flavors, and a medium-long finish rife with oak and red berry. The nice nougaty-marscapone aromas are unfortunately overtaken by oak. **87** —*D.T. (7/1/2002)*

Château Los Boldos 2005 Grand Reserve Carmenère (Requinoa) $11. Massively jammy and purple; a true destroyer in terms of prune and heavy blackberry character. Also medicinal and full of brown sugar and maple. Seems over the top and overextracted. Can only get better with age. **83** —*M.S. (3/1/2006)*

Château Los Boldos 2005 Tradition Carmenère (Requinoa) $8. Soft and fruity, with a broad, grapy personality. Cherry, raspberry, and hard candy in the mouth, with carob and coconut from oak later on. Not many extra gears on this one. **83** —*M.S. (3/1/2006)*

Château Los Boldos 1999 CLB Reserve Chardonnay (Rapel Valley) $14. Pungent, grassy aromas seem off center for Chardonnay, while the mouthfeel is heavy and the flavors seem derived from overripe fruit. The finish is woody and has plenty of texture, but there's also a piercing bolt of acidity running through the middle. **82** —*M.S. (7/1/2003)*

Château Los Boldos 2001 Vielles Vignes Chardonnay (Requinoa) $16. The old-vine name is French, as are the estate owners, and the wine itself is pretty good despite being a bit thick, chewy, and aimless. The nose is full but nondescript, while apple and oak-driven flavors define the palate. The finish is textured and woody. Mouthfeel is its primary attribute while interesting or unusual tastes prove elusive. **86** —*M.S. (7/1/2003)*

Château Los Boldos 2003 Grand Reserve Merlot (Requinoa) $11. Dark berry, cassis, and some funky olive rate highest on the nose. The palate is firm and ripe, with dark plum and raspberry flavors. Kind of pruny on the back end, with bitter chocolate and blunt tannins. **83** —*M.S. (7/1/2006)*

Château Los Boldos 2004 Altitude Red Blend (Requinoa) $11. This three-piece band plays with Merlot, Cabernet, and Syrah, and the tune is a fruit fantasia with tons of ripe cherry and blackberry, but no base or treble monitor. It's warm, big and juicy. Not boring, but monotone. **86** —*M.S. (3/1/2006)*

Château Los Boldos 2005 Tradition Shiraz (Requinoa) $8. A big, young grapey mound of dark fruit is how best to describe this violet wine that's so candied and gummy it's like pressed black fruit and little more. Very dark but shows little to no character or depth. **82** —*M.S. (3/1/2006)*

CONCHA Y TORO

Concha y Toro 2004 Casillero del Diablo Cabernet Sauvignon (Central Valley) $9. Tar, leather, and smoke, all qualities of serious Cabernet, make themselves noticed on the nose. The palate delivers black cherry, plum, cassis, and all the usual suspects, while the mouthfeel is firm and solid. No complaints. **87 Best Buy** —*M.S. (11/1/2005)*

Concha y Toro 2003 Casillero del Diablo Cabernet Sauvignon (Central Valley) $9. Dark in the glass, with dense fruitcake aromas along with notes of molasses and dried cherry. The palate is round and big, and the finish deals a heavy blast of grilled beef and coffee. Almost at the next level, but still a little awkward and bulky. **86 Best Buy** —*M.S. (8/1/2004)*

Concha y Toro 2001 Casillero del Diablo Cabernet Sauvignon (Central Valley) $10. There is plenty of ripe black fruit on the tight, smoky, clean nose and then loads of cassis and raspberry flavors along with oak shadings on the palate. The body is just moderate in weight and there is a bit of weakness to the core, but it finishes nicely. **85** —*M.S. (12/1/2002)*

Concha y Toro 2000 Casillero del Diablo Cabernet Sauvignon (Maipo Valley) $10. The oak shows prominently on the nose and the blackberry and chocolate flavors here are darker, but drier and less plush than in the Merlot. The cedar and black toast over dark fruit profile plays out, with tobacco accents, on the dry, tannic finish. **85** *(12/31/2001)*

Concha y Toro 1999 Casillero del Diablo Cabernet Sauvignon (Maipo Valley) $11. Attractive aromas of berries with licorice and caramel accents promise pleasure, and on the palate the wine is round and smooth with dried cherry and herb flavors. The package is marred, however, by a dry, tart-even, bitter-espresso tinged finish, that comes on quite unexpectedly and unharmoniously. **84** *(1/1/2004)*

Concha y Toro 1998 Casillero del Diablo Cabernet Sauvignon (Maipo Valley) $10. **85** —*M.S. (12/1/1999)*

Concha y Toro 2002 Don Melchor Cabernet Sauvignon (Puente Alto) $47. Earthy and real, with strong hints of menthol, forest floor, cassis, and other concentrated berry notes. Ripe on the palate with a bit of berry candy balanced by cola, toast, and vanilla. Solid by any first-class standards, with firm tannins and acids providing structure. **91** —*M.S. (5/1/2006)*

Concha y Toro 1999 Don Melchor Cabernet Sauvignon (Puente Alto) $40. Flowery and fresh with bursting fruit. The texture is mildly jammy and bordering on syrupy, but that is as much a reflection of youth as it is extraction. The finish delivers toasty oak, vanilla, and some candied fruit. Very pleasing. **91** —*M.S. (6/1/2004)*

Concha y Toro 1998 Don Melchor Cabernet Sauvignon (Maipo Valley) $40. Given the El Niño-related difficulties of the '98 vintage, this version of Don Melchor is quite nice, and just right for immediate drinking. The bouquet is meaty, with strong leathery notes. Dark cherries and black plums on the palate are Bordeaux-like. Its soft tannins make it very approachable, especially with a lamb stew or something similar. **87** —*M.S. (3/1/2002)*

CHILE

Concha y Toro 2003 Don Melchor Vintage 17 Cabernet Sauvignon (Puente Alto) $47. Hard to believe that this Chilean icon is now in its 17th year. We recall back in the early '90s when it was just getting going at well under $20 a bottle. With this wine look for potent, almost buttery oak propping up ripe berry fruit. In the folds are notes of tobacco, earth, mineral, and mushroom. Tannic on the tail, with some overt wood that needs to find its place. Hold of at least a year. **90 Cellar Selection** —*M.S. (10/1/2006)*

Concha y Toro 2002 Marques de Casa Concha Cabernet Sauvignon (Puente Alto) $14. Ruby red in color, with a thick, modern nose that exudes aromas of mocha, caramel, ripe berry, burnt meat, and popcorn. To say it's offering quite a bit is an understatement. The mouth is creamy, with dark plum and berry fruit, while the back end is easygoing and sizable. Mouthfilling and likeable, and quite affordable for how much you get. **89 Best Buy** —*M.S. (8/1/2004)*

Concha y Toro 2001 Marques de Casa Concha Cabernet Sauvignon (Rapel Valley) $16. This sensational value has a range of flavors, structure, and other important characteristics that some wines costing five times more can't match. The nose is full of plum, black fruit, and coffee, while the palate is pure dynamite; it's a textbook modern Cabernet that hits the target squarely in the center. **91 Editors' Choice** —*M.S. (3/1/2004)*

Concha y Toro 2000 Marques de Casa Concha Cabernet Sauvignon (Maipo Valley) $14. Dark, dense, and saturated Cabernet is what's on offer here, the real deal for a steal. The nose is rich with cassis, plum, herbs, and tobacco. There's plenty of depth and density to the palate. The finish offers moderate tannins, tasty mocha and coffee flavors and vital berry fruit. **89 Best Buy** —*M.S. (12/1/2002)*

Concha y Toro 1999 Marques de Casa Concha Cabernet Sauvignon (Puente Alto) $15. The nose and palate of this medium-full, slightly burly red are darkly fruited, with sweet cedar, briar tobacco, and chocolate accents. A smooth, almost silky texture nearly belies the firm tannic structure beneath, which comes to the fore on the close. This should unfold nicely over the next two years. **87** *(12/31/2001)*

Concha y Toro 1997 Marques de Casa Concha Cabernet Sauvignon (Maipo Valley) $14. **86** —*M.S. (12/1/1999)*

Concha y Toro 1997 Private Reserve Don Melchor Cabernet Sauvignon (Maipo Valley) $40. Bacon and lavender are prominent on the meaty, slightly muddled nose, which unfolds gracefully if given lots and lots of time. Blackberry and some tannins up front, a fairly nice and buttery middle, and finally cola accents on the grapy, heavy, long finish. For years this was C&T's top effort, before Almaviva. **88** —*M.S. (2/1/2001)*

Concha y Toro 2003 Terrunyo Cabernet Sauvignon (Pirque) $28. A huge expression of Chilean Cab, which if you know the wine, is to be expected. Terrunyo pushes deep blackberry and violets on the nose, while the palate bursts with acidity that propels lasting dark flavors. On the spot, with a lot of heft and extraction. **91 Editors' Choice** —*M.S. (7/1/2006)*

Concha y Toro 2002 Terrunyo Cabernet Sauvignon (Pirque) $28. Full and leathery, with tobacco and lots of familiar dark fruit aromas. The palate seems almost jet-propelled in its forwardness, while the flavors of prune, black cherry, pepper, and chocolate are fine. Could stand for a bit more mouthfeel and plushness; the tannins run hard. **88** —*M.S. (11/1/2005)*

Concha y Toro 2001 Terrunyo Cabernet Sauvignon (Maipo Valley) $29. This luscious Cabernet makes you think that the Stags Leap District came to the Maipo Valley and dropped off a few secrets before heading home. Gorgeous leather and black fruit mix on the burly nose, which is backed up by lead pencil, tobacco and cassis. **92 Cellar Selection** —*M.S. (3/1/2004)*

Concha y Toro 1999 Terrunyo Cabernet Sauvignon (Pirque) $29. Coffee and burnt toast dominate the nose, courtesy of 50% aging in new French oak. But this is no woodman's delight. Quite the opposite: It's perfectly balanced and packed full of sweet cherries and plums. Best of all, the mouthfeel is undeniably creamy. Deeply extracted, with lots of muscle. **90** —*M.S. (3/1/2002)*

Concha y Toro 1997 Terrunyo Cabernet Sauvignon (Maipo Valley) $29. Concha y Toro is making an effort to upgrade its entire lineup. This offering boasts copious weedy, chocolaty, black currant aromas, followed by a soft, lush mouthfeel. It could use a bit more backbone, but this is a generously fruity wine ideal for early consumption. **87** —*J.C. (2/1/2001)*

Concha y Toro 1997 Trio Cabernet Sauvignon (Maipo Valley) $9. **84** —*M.S. (12/1/1999)*

Concha y Toro 2004 Xplorador Cabernet Sauvignon (Central Valley) $7. Kicks off with some balsamic and olive aromas, while the palate is full of black cherry and berry fruit. Round and clean, with a soft feel despite having real tannic backbone. Likable in a mainstream way. **86 Best Buy** —*M.S. (11/1/2005)*

Concha y Toro 2003 Xplorador Cabernet Sauvignon (Central Valley) $7. Incredibly saturated and lively for such an affordable Cabernet, with ripe aromas of leather, dried herbs, and a hint of pickle barrel. It whets the whistle with currant and berry flavors accented by spice and licorice. Xplorador Cab is almost always a solid buy, maybe more so in 2003 than usual. Think of it as the poster child for value reds from Chile. **87 Best Buy** —*M.S. (12/1/2004)*

Concha y Toro 2001 Xplorador Cabernet Sauvignon (Maipo Valley) $8. Ripe and ready, with powerful dark fruit. This is a fine "starter" Cab from Chile and Concha y Toro, one that will impress novices and satisfy the high end drinker as well. The palate is slightly sugary, but the black fruit is ripe and tasty. And the tannins are there, as they should be, although they're not overwhelming. **85 Best Buy** —*M.S. (7/1/2003)*

Concha y Toro 1999 Xplorador Cabernet Sauvignon (Maipo Valley) $8. Offers varietally correct flavors of black currants and hints of tobacco, but where's the structure and depth? A simple, fruity red for early drinking that would make a decent picnic wine or bar pour. **83** —*J.C. (2/1/2001)*

Concha y Toro 2004 Casillero del Diablo Carmenère (Central Valley) $9. Concha y Toro is getting Carmenère right. This affordable red is full bodied, with a fair amount of oak and bacon smothering plum and berry aromas. On the whole it's round, juicy and fresh, with lively flavors and good feel. **88 Best Buy** —*M.S. (3/1/2006)*

Concha y Toro 2003 Casillero del Diablo Carmenère (Rapel Valley) $10. Exuberant on the nose, with rich blackberry, rubber, and bacon. Generous and bright on the palate, where cherry and blackberry flavors start vividly and then are softened by creamy, chocolaty oak. Best of all, there's nothing vegetal about it. **87 Best Buy** —*M.S. (5/30/2005)*

Concha y Toro 2001 Casillero Del Diablo Carmenère (Rapel Valley) $10. Deep in color, with candied aromas of marshmallow and vanilla. The mouth is heavy and chewy, and a bit hot as well. Carmenère, which is on the rise in Chile, usually has a chocolaty quality, and this one does. But it doesn't have the charm and style that the best ones do. **84** —*M.S. (12/1/2002)*

Concha y Toro 2003 Frontera Carmenère (Central Valley) $11. It may have been abandoned in its Bordeaux home, but Carmenère has found a home and a new life in Chile. It makes red wines with good juicy fruit, freshness, flavors of ripe plums. This example, blended with 10% Cabernet Sauvignon and 5% Syrah, is a great wine just to drink, full of fruit, with a touch of toast, vanilla, and smooth tannins. **84 Best Buy** —*R.V. (11/15/2004)*

Concha y Toro 2003 Terrunyo Carmenère (Cachapoal Valley) $28. A lot of handiwork went into this wine; that much you can tell. The nose is loaded with heavy, oak-based aromas of coconut, butter and brown sugar. There's also intense dark fruit sitting beneath, and ultimately it all comes together in a modern, fruit-forward way. Not all that herbal or rugged; it's very polished and not terribly varietal. **90** —*M.S. (3/1/2006)*

Concha y Toro 2002 Terrunyo Carmenère (Cachapoal Valley) $28. Dark and saturated, with hefty aromas of toffee, toasted marshmallow, and berry syrup. Plenty of bulky dark fruit backs up the nose, while the body is full in every sense. Muscular, no-holds-barred stuff made in a modern way. Unique among Carmenère. **90** —*M.S. (7/1/2005)*

Concha y Toro 2001 Terrunyo Carmenère (Cachapoal Valley) $28. Saturated and dark, with intoxicating aromas of mint, cola, mushroom, herbs, and black fruit. Very rich and smooth, with a meaty, chewy texture. Fruity throughout, with an espresso-like bitterness to the finish. This is Carmenère made in a forward, modern style, with no vegetal flavors. **89** —*M.S. (8/1/2004)*

Concha y Toro 2000 Terrunyo Carmenère (Peumo) $29. Berry aromas are followed by a round wholesomeness that can't be criticized. The palate is unlike many a Carmenère because it eschews the herbal, green element that's inherent to the grape, and instead offers plum, blackberry, and all the richness one can conjure. A round finish of light oak and vanilla seals it all in fine fashion. Surely the most jammy, expressive, and pure Carmenère that Chile has to offer. **91** —*M.S. (7/1/2003)*

Concha y Toro 1999 Terrunyo Carmenère (Peumo) $29. If Carmenère is going to attract a global following, it's going to do it on the backs of wines like this. Made from grapes hailing predominantly from a subsection of the Rapel Valley, this is a thick, earthy, meaty wine with sweet and chewy black plums and ripe cherries at its core. The mouthfeel is a tad leathery, with a very firm grip. With about 15% Maipo Cabernet blended in, it's just about perfect, without any hint of green. **91** —*M.S. (3/1/2002)*

Concha y Toro 2004 Amelia Chardonnay (Casablanca Valley) $35. Bold melon and pear aromas to begin with, and alongside that there's a touch of toasted corn. Sweet enough to please, with pear and vanilla leading the flavor parade. Plump and smooth on the finish, with a sweet coconutty aftertaste. **88** —*M.S. (7/1/2006)*

Concha y Toro 2003 Amelia Chardonnay (Casablanca Valley) $34. One of Chile's highest-priced Chardonnays kicks off with ripe, creamy aromas of buttered corn along with baked apple and pear. Banana bread complete with walnuts and white raisins takes over on the palate, while a resiny, vanilla-dominated finish closes the show. Very good for Chilean Chardonnay, but undeniably fat and chewy in the grand scheme of things. **88** —*M.S. (7/1/2005)*

Concha y Toro 2002 Amelia Chardonnay (Casablanca Valley) $33. The winemakers at CyT intentionally lowered the oak level on this wine, and now it's a much better Amelia than what we tasted in the past. It's still a figgy, round wine with papaya, pear, and banana, but the transition from palate to finish is seamless. And without all that wood, you really taste the purity of the Casablanca fruit. **90** —*M.S. (3/1/2004)*

Concha y Toro 1997 Amelia Chardonnay (Casablanca Valley) $18. 88 —*M.S. (12/1/1999)*

Concha y Toro 2001 Amelia Limited Release Chardonnay (Casablanca Valley) $33. If you love overt oak, then add a couple of points to this plump, modern Chard that runs over with the aromas, flavors, and textures that stem from new-oak barrels. The bouquet is mostly popcorn atop apple and pear, while the flavor profile is ripe apple and banana. The finish is soft and creamy, with flavors of lemon and fresh-cut wood. Fine acidity and balance work in its favor. **88** —*M.S. (7/1/2003)*

Concha y Toro 2001 Block 25 Terrunyo Chardonnay (Casablanca Valley) $25. At first the nose is like caramelized popcorn, a forward combination of oak and toast. The flavors are of apple, pear, and citrus, and that well-blended package is carried by excellent acidity, the type you could call "bracing." The finish goes on for quite some time, proof that this is a ripe, healthy wine that's hitting its stride. **91** —*M.S. (7/1/2003)*

Concha y Toro 2004 Casillero del Diablo Chardonnay (Central Valley) $9. Nice and clean, with ample stone fruit and apple aromas. No, not a lot of nuance on display. But plenty of ripe, pure apple, and melon flavors followed by some length on the mildly creamy finish. Solid, with mass-market appeal. **87 Best Buy** —*M.S. (11/1/2005)*

Concha y Toro 2003 Casillero del Diablo Chardonnay (Casablanca Valley) $10. Creamy and plump; this is a fine bargain-priced Chard, one with character and balance. Sure, there are the telltale pear and banana flavors, but on the back it offers subtle apple notes prior to a light, casual finish. **87 Best Buy** —*M.S. (3/1/2004)*

Concha y Toro 2001 Casillero del Diablo Chardonnay (Casablanca Valley) $10. The nose is fruity, with hints of vanilla bean. In the mouth, peach and lemon flavors carry a note of cinnamon spice, although the finish veers toward asparagus and green beans. Acidity and balance; are both on the money. **86 Best Buy** —*M.S. (7/1/2003)*

Concha y Toro 2000 Casillero del Diablo Chardonnay (Casablanca Valley) $10. Ripe, even lush tropical fruit aromas mingle with apple-pear scents on the nose of this round, medium-weight Chardonnay. The full, slightly sweet fruit maintains on the palate, framed nicely by butter and toast accents. The okay notes linger on the finish, with its apple-pear reprise. **86 Best Buy** *(12/31/2001)*

Concha y Toro 1998 Casillero del Diablo Chardonnay (Casablanca Valley) $10. 85 —*M.S. (12/1/1999)*

Concha y Toro 2004 Marques de Casa Concha Chardonnay (Pirque) $16. This is a nice Chardonnay, especially from Maipo. It has fruit cocktail and peaches on the nose, followed by a mix of pink grapefruit, melon, and pineapple on the palate. Finishes with some oaky toast and citrus pith. Full-bodied within the category. **87** —*M.S. (5/1/2006)*

Concha y Toro 2002 Marques de Casa Concha Chardonnay (Casablanca Valley) $15. Packed with vanilla and oak this wine boasts a wonderful body and a great feel. It was 35% barrel fermented, and yet it still pops with acidity and fresh fruit. Touches of popcorn and creaminess are detectable, but neither detracts from the main act. **88** —*M.S. (3/1/2004)*

Concha y Toro 2000 Marques de Casa Concha Chardonnay (Pirque) $15. Opens with dry pear and almond-like, nutty, toasty oak notes, showing uncommon elegance for a wine in this price range. The fruit to acid balance is very good, and the core apple-pear flavors bear citrus, mango, and custard accents, as well as more of the refined oak. Finishes long and classy, again with fine style and integration of elements. **90 Editors' Choice** *(12/31/2001)*

Concha y Toro 1997 Marques de Casa Concha Chardonnay (Maipo Valley) $14. 87 —*M.S. (12/1/1999)*

Concha y Toro 2002 Terrunyo Chardonnay (Casablanca Valley) $25. Smooth, with more integrated oak than the other Chardonnays. Flavors of green apple, fresh pear and vanilla are tasty and supported by a touch of wood. Fine acids stop short of being harsh, creating lasting melon and nectarine notes. **89** —*M.S. (3/1/2004)*

Concha y Toro 2000 Terrunyo Chardonnay (Casablanca Valley) $25. Concha y Toro is making big, bold wines under its Terrunyo label, as evidenced by this powerhouse Chardonnay. The apple and pear fruit bursts from the glass, with mild oak and warm tropical undertones playing key supporting roles. **88** —*M.S. (3/1/2002)*

Concha y Toro 1998 Trio Chardonnay (Casablanca Valley) $9. 84 —*M.S. (12/1/1999)*

Concha y Toro 2004 Xplorador Chardonnay (Central Valley) $7. Clean and inoffensive, with light pear and apple aromas. This is usually one of the best inexpensive South American Chardonnays, and it's no different this go around. There's citrus, melon and structure. Tangy but not sour; sweet but not artificially so. **86 Best Buy** —*M.S. (11/1/2005)*

Concha y Toro 2003 Xplorador Chardonnay (Central Valley) $7. Given the price range at which this wine competes, it's something. The aromas are clean and pure: there's attractive honey, pineapple, and citrus. Cuddly flavors of orange, melon, and pear are harmonious, while the finish is clean and pure, albeit short. Medium-bodied and satisfying. **86 Best Buy** —*M.S. (6/1/2004)*

Concha y Toro 2002 Xplorador Chardonnay (Casablanca Valley) $7. Pretty nice in the nose, with pear, toffee, and vanilla. In the mouth, it's racy, probably bordering on shrill. The apple, lemon, and pear flavors do pack punch. However, it's ultimately a little sharp. **84** —*M.S. (3/1/2004)*

Concha y Toro 2001 Xplorador Chardonnay (Casablanca Valley) $7. Everything about this mass-market Chard works. The nose has some pleasant nectarine and apricot aromas, while the mouth is racy and lively, and loaded with mango, pear, and honeydew flavors. The finish is fruity, if a tad sweet. Nevertheless it's fresh and clean, and it leaves a good lasting impression. Anyone who likes a sweeter-styled white will fancy this. **86 Best Buy** —*M.S. (7/1/2003)*

Concha y Toro 2000 Xplorador Chardonnay (Casablanca Valley) $8. This has plenty of nuance and flavor, with apple and pear fruit and creamy, spicy accents. The supple mouthfeel has more texture than many more costly wines, and the dry, slightly nutty finish is a winner. Shows balance and restraint, even some depth. **88 Best Buy** —*M.M. (8/1/2001)*

Concha y Toro 1999 Xplorador Chardonnay (Casablanca Valley) $8. Ripe pear-pineapple fruit is layered with vanilla and tinged with citrus. This is a plump, slightly heavy Chard best served cold at parties and picnics. **84** —*J.C. (2/1/2001)*

Concha y Toro 2004 Casillero del Diablo Merlot (Central Valley) $9. Nice and full on the nose, with a bit of subtle oak that yields smoke, bacon,

CHILE

coffee, and mocha aromas. Red plum and sweet berry fruit lead to a smooth finish. Good and in proportion, if a touch raw and woody. **85 Best Buy** —*M.S. (11/1/2005)*

Concha y Toro 2003 Casillero del Diablo Merlot (Central Valley) $10. Huge and colorful, and very youthful. For density and lushness on what can best be described as basic Merlot, you're not going to find it much better than this. It's all blackberry, chocolate, and berries, but somehow they've squeezed some earth and spice in there as well. **88 Best Buy** —*M.S. (3/1/2004)*

Concha y Toro 2001 Casillero del Diablo Merlot (Rapel Valley) $10. Cedar and a touch of salinity on the nose. Stemmy flavors that are lean and green follow, finishing simple and quick. **83** —*C.S. (12/1/2002)*

Concha y Toro 2000 Casillero del Diablo Merlot (Rapel Valley) $10. An attractive bouquet of black plum, smoke, herbs, mocha—even a graphite note—opens this juicy but solidly built wine. Chocolate and herb accents add palate interest, the feel is comfortably plump, but with an underlying firmness and some slightly prickly back-end tannins. Good now, and will improve over the next year or two. **86** *(12/31/2001)*

Concha y Toro 2002 Marques de Casa Concha Merlot (Peumo) $14. Rich and stylish on one hand, and brawny and bold on the other. This saturated, meaty bruiser starts with dark plum, cassis, and eucalyptus aromas. Then comes a parade of chewy, high-powered fruit flavors: currant, cherry, and blackberry. Casual back notes of chocolate and caramel cement this generous offering. **89 Best Buy** —*M.S. (6/1/2004)*

Concha y Toro 2001 Marques de Casa Concha Merlot (Peumo) $14. Concha y Toro is making a big, burly Merlot for this line and it should have mass appeal given how rich, extracted, and oaky it is. The nose is dense as chocolate cake and deep as a well. The mouth is chewy and thick, with chocolate-covered berries and another whack of wood. **87** —*M.S. (7/1/2003)*

Concha y Toro 2000 Marques de Casa Concha Merlot (Rapel Valley) $14. A big and bursting combination of healthy black fruit and copious French oak is manifested in the nose as bitter chocolate and plum pie. The palate is lively and full-bodied, with mature fruit flavors and velvety tannins, while plenty more of that bitter chocolate echoes across the finish. **88 Best Buy** —*M.S. (12/1/2002)*

Concha y Toro 1999 Marques de Casa Concha Merlot (Peumo) $15. Big but supple, with a full vibrant bouquet of smoky, toasty oak over dark plum and cherry fruit. The palate shows more of the same, with coffee and chocolate accents. This tasty, likable oakster finishes with good length and a cocoa hint. **88** —*J.C. (12/31/2001)*

Concha y Toro 1997 Marques de Casa Concha Merlot (Rapel Valley) $14. **84** —*M.S. (12/1/1999)*

Concha y Toro 2004 Marqués de Casa Concha Merlot (Peumo) $19. Like always, this Merlot is a potent brew of dark fruit, molasses, peppery spice, and Chilean terroir. The plush palate is extremely ripe and forward, as it offers mounds of berries and chocolate. New World at every turn, and what's wrong with that? 38,000 cases produced, so it's available. **90 Editors' Choice** —*M.S. (10/1/2006)*

Concha y Toro 2003 Marqués de Casa Concha Merlot (Peumo) $14. A wine the band Deep Purple could get into, because it's just that color and it rocks. The bouquet is dusty and loaded with dark chocolate and ripe blackberry. In the mouth, there's nothing miserly about it: lush plum, blackberry, and licorice flavors are full and forward. Highly enjoyable, especially at this price. **89 Best Buy** —*M.S. (11/1/2005)*

Concha y Toro 1998 Trio Merlot (Rapel Valley) $9. **80** —*M.S. (12/1/1999)*

Concha y Toro 2004 Xplorador Merlot (Central Valley) $7. A bit hot and burnt, with wiry, raw fruit. But for the money it's a sturdy, drinkable red wine. Shows sticky black fruit and a bulky finish. Fits the bill at its price point. **83** —*M.S. (11/1/2005)*

Concha y Toro 2003 Xplorador Merlot (Central Valley) $7. Full-bodied and inarguably fruity. The nose is slightly stewed, while the mouthfeel is firm and acidic, with flavors of apple skin and black cherry. Fairly reduced and hard, so best if drunk with salty munchables. **85 Best Buy** —*M.S. (8/1/2004)*

Concha y Toro 2002 Xplorador Merlot (Rapel Valley) $7. This Merlot excels beyond its bargain classification by showing purity and a high level of fruit quality. The bouquet exudes plum, chocolate, and some creaminess, while the palate bursts with blackberry, bitter chocolate, and espresso. Round and satisfying, with enough structure to last a year or two—or until the next vintage comes around. **87 Best Buy** —*M.S. (7/1/2003)*

Concha y Toro 2000 Xplorador Merlot (Rapel Valley) $8. Slightly minty green herb notes and toasty oak offset the creamy, ripe fruit bouquet of this soft, accessible red. The mouth shows black cherry flavors, oregano, and cocoa accents, while mild tannins and a full fruitiness mark the close of this solid value. **85 Best Buy** *(12/31/2001)*

Concha y Toro 1999 Xplorador Merlot (Rapel Valley) $8. Richly fruity and soft, this wine boasts loads of black-cherry and plum flavors. Clearly made from very ripe fruit, it lacks the herbaceous-vegetal character so often found in Merlot, but also any sense of structure. Finishes with a bit of alcoholic heat. **85** —*J.C. (2/1/2001)*

Concha y Toro 2002 Block 30 Terrunyo Sauvignon Blanc (Casablanca Valley) $20. Passion fruit, tangerine, and fresh asparagus aromas are typical of this wine, which has been setting the pace for Chilean Sauvignon Blanc since its inception several years ago. The palate is snappy and busting loose with just-ripe banana and melon, while the finish is textured and long. **89** —*M.S. (7/1/2003)*

Concha y Toro 2005 Casillero del Diablo Sauvignon Blanc (Central Valley) $9. Sweet, clean, and melony to start, yet a bit tart and citrus-heavy to the taste. Definitely in balance, with solid if commonplace flavors of lemon, lime, and green melon. **84** —*M.S. (5/1/2006)*

Concha y Toro 2004 Casillero del Diablo Sauvignon Blanc (Central Valley) $10. Fresh, light and flowery, with a sweet, melon-driven palate. Finishes snappy yet a touch sugary. For the most part it serves its purpose, which is to prep the palate for better things to come. **85 Best Buy** —*M.S. (7/1/2005)*

Concha y Toro 2003 Casillero del Diablo Sauvignon Blanc (Central Valley) $10. One sniff reveals solid grapefruit and other textbook aromas. Then a sip delivers pink grapefruit and a consistent, acid-propped attack. Some tangerine appears on the finish before it slips away quietly. **86 Best Buy** —*M.S. (3/1/2004)*

Concha y Toro 1998 Casillero del Diablo Sauvignon Blanc (Maipo Valley) $10. **86** —*M.S. (12/1/1999)*

Concha y Toro 1999 Late Harvest Sauvignon Blanc (Maule Valley) $15. Peach, pear and apricot aromas lead off, with honeyed, toast, and peach flavors on the palate. This Chilean offering is long and lush at the end. **89** —*J.M. (12/1/2002)*

Concha y Toro 2001 Late Harvest Private Reserve Sauvignon Blanc (Maule Valley) $14. Gold and pretty, with apricot and butterscotch on the fruity nose. Thick melon dripping with honey is the primary flavor component, while the ripe finish is sweet and satisfying, and not at all cloying. If you like sweet orange marmalade, this wine is for you. **88** —*M.S. (5/1/2006)*

Concha y Toro 2005 Terrunyo Sauvignon Blanc (Casablanca Valley) $25. Starts out clean and neutral before unveiling hints of white peach and early season nectarine. The mouth is jolting in its acidity, creating a slightly tart flavor profile that drives home green apple and lemon. For some it will seem sharp; others will probably say it's Sauvignon Blanc in its best form. **89** —*M.S. (10/1/2006)*

Concha y Toro 2004 Terrunyo Sauvignon Blanc (Casablanca Valley) $21. Clean, fresh, and fruit-forward, with aromas of passion fruit, lemon-lime, and peach. It's all about the fruit here, but along the way there's good body and perfectly balanced acidity. Grapefruit and a tiny hint of mineral grace the long finish. A persistent, cheerful white; probably the best Sauvignon Blanc from Chile. **90 Editors' Choice** *(7/1/2005)*

Concha y Toro 2003 Terrunyo Sauvignon Blanc (Casablanca Valley) $20. This reserve-level bottling continues to set the bar for Chilean Sauvignon Blanc, and the credit goes to Ignacio Recabarren, the maestro behind CyT's Terrunyo line. It features intense nectarine, snap pea, and cucumber aromas followed by a sensational mouthful of citrus and minerals. **90** —*M.S. (3/1/2004)*

CHILE

Concha y Toro 2001 Terrunyo Sauvignon Blanc (Casablanca Valley) $20. With a no-oak wine like this it's all about the expression of fruit: bright green apple, pineapple, and lemon. Lip-smacking acids carry everything to a fine finale. If you like tasty, zippy Sauvignon Blanc that's full of pop, look no further. **88** —M.S. (3/1/2002)

Concha y Toro 1999 Terrunyo Sauvignon Blanc (Casablanca Valley) $29. Partial barrel-fermentation shows in this wine's hints of vanilla and cream, which marry smoothly with grapefruit and melon fruit. The grapefruit shades toward pink, particularly on the pleasantly crisp finish. **88** —J.C. (2/1/2001)

Concha y Toro 2004 Terrunyo Block 34 Shiraz (Cachapoal Valley) $28. The newest addition to the Terrunyo line is a single-vineyard Shiraz with high alcohol, ripe fruit, and varietal correctness. The nose has some wild game and spice alongside big black fruit aromas. The palate, meanwhile, is ripe as can be, with upbeat tannins and acidity. Huge but balanced. A winner. **92 Editors' Choice** —M.S. (7/1/2006)

Concha y Toro 2003 Marques de Casa Concha Syrah (Peumo) $16. Very modern and ripe, with syrupy black fruit crawling all over the beefy nose and onto the chewy palate. Flavors of black cherry and raspberry are live-wire and alert; they are supported by solid tannins and fine acidity. This wine gets better each time we try it. It has a lot of what most folks want in Syrah: flashy fruit and depth. **89 Editors' Choice** —M.S. (11/1/2005)

Concha y Toro 2004 Marqués de Casa Concha Syrah (Peumo) $19. Perfectly open and huge, with deep plum and black fruit smothering both the bouquet and palate. Over the past couple of years this wine has distinguished itself as a bruiser with charm. And while it may show very little in common with Rhône-style Syrah, for a Chilean version it rocks. Look for huge berry flavors and excellent balancing acids and tannins. **91 Editors' Choice** —M.S. (10/1/2006)

CONDE DE VELÁZQUEZ

Conde de Velàzquez 2001 El Conde Gran Reserva Cabernet Sauvignon (Aconcagua Valley) $10. Basic red plum, currant, and cough syrup are more than adequate aromas, while the palate offers tasty cherry and cassis. Very candied and won't be confused for a great wine, but serviceable. **84** —M.S. (7/1/2005)

Conde de Velàzquez 2001 Estate Vintage Cabernet Sauvignon (Aconcagua Valley) $13. Spicy up front, with aromas of tire rubber, forest and dried fruits. Decent levels of cherry and raspberry; while the finish has some mint. A touch green at the end, which brings it down. **85** —M.S. (7/1/2005)

Conde de Velàzquez 2001 Reserva Cabernet Sauvignon (Aconcagua Valley) $7. Rubbery, with harsh aromas that seem weedy. Better on the palate, where strawberry and raspberry flavors rise up. Finishes grassy and leathery. **81** —M.S. (7/1/2005)

Conde de Velàzquez 2002 Reserva Cabernet Sauvignon-Carmenère (Aconcagua Valley) $7. Saucy, with a ton of black olive and bell pepper to the nose and palate. Not much fruit and not much to latch onto. Base-level stuff. **80** —M.S. (7/1/2005)

Conde de Velàzquez 2003 El Conde Gran Reserva Chardonnay (Aconcagua Valley) $11. Yellow in color, and rather oaky. Spice and vanilla are the lead aromas and flavors, with peach, melon, and toast in the background. On the finish, the wood really rises up, creating cured ham and smoke aftertastes. Unusual for Chile. **84** —M.S. (11/1/2005)

Conde de Velàzquez 2003 Reserva Merlot (Aconcagua Valley) $7. Flat and chunky, but chewy and full of strawberry flavors. Somewhat lactic, with hints of sautéed mushroom—not a bad nuance. Nothing to get excited over as it shows decent quality for the price. **83** —M.S. (11/1/2005)

Conde de Velàzquez 2003 Sauvignon Blanc (Aconcagua Valley) $7. Tight and lemony, with sharp citrus aromas along with flavors of orange and other citrus fruits. Offers some texture and body, with freshness. **84 Best Buy** —M.S. (2/1/2005)

Conde de Velàzquez 2003 Syrah (Aconcagua Valley) $6. Weedy, with cinnamon and sweet aromas. Very soft and simple, with a touch of pepper to the marginal berry and plum flavors. **80** —M.S. (12/15/2005)

Conde de Velàzquez 2002 Reserva Syrah (Aconcagua Valley) $7. Candied up front, with unfocused, murky aromas. The palate is lean and hot, with thin fruit and not much feel. Nothing horrible but nothing to get excited about. **81** —M.S. (2/1/2005)

CONFIN

Confin 2004 Cabernet Sauvignon (Rapel Valley) $11. Firm, a touch rubbery, and quite full-bodied, with earthy aromas of coffee and black fruits. Cassis and berry are the primary flavors, while the saturated palate is chewy and dense. Runs a touch toward sweet and syrupy, but holds the line. **85** —M.S. (10/1/2006)

Confin 2004 Winemaker Reserve Cabernet Sauvignon (Rapel Valley) $14. Plum, blackberry, and other dark fruits coat the smooth bouquet. The palate is fairly intense, with saturated plum and berry flavors. Very solid and tight, with ripe tannins and a chewy feel. Good Cabernet that will please most. **86** —M.S. (10/1/2006)

Confin 2005 Carmenère (Rapel Valley) $12. Ripe and ready, although it is a little bit herbal. It runs sweet in the mouth, with berry flavors blended with chocolate. Tannic power builds on the palate, and it finishes firm but bearable. **85** —M.S. (11/15/2006)

Confin 2005 Chardonnay (Rapel Valley) $11. Citrus and mineral on the proportioned nose is a solid opening. Peach and green apple flavors are solid, while the feel is zesty if a bit narrow and acidic. Finishes with oomph and clarity. **84** —M.S. (10/1/2006)

Confin 2004 Merlot (Rapel Valley) $11. Sulfuric at first, and later it's strawberry and tomato that control the nose. In the mouth, it's sweet and a bit syrupy, with generic black fruit leading the way. Finishes with milk chocolate and a hint of burnt toast and grass. **83** —M.S. (10/1/2006)

Confin 2004 Winemaker Reserve Merlot (Rapel Valley) $14. More full and powerful than the regular Merlot, with berry compote, lemon peel and toast on the nose. Fairly full in body, while the red-fruit flavors are solid and familiar. Has good structure and a linear finish. Good in its class. **86** —M.S. (10/1/2006)

Confin 2004 Premium Reserve Red Blend (Rapel Valley) $20. Full, round, stocky, and ripe, with an aromatic foundation of tobacco, black fruit and rubber. The three grapes that comprise this wine are Cabernet Sauvignon, Carmenère, and Merlot, and together they form a full-bodied yet juicy triumverate that culminates with chocolate, pepper, and lush tannins. **88** —M.S. (11/15/2006)

CONO SUR

Cono Sur 2004 20 Barrels Limited Edition Cabernet Sauvignon (Maipo Valley) $25. Straightforward yet enticing berry, oak, and tar aromas get it off to a good start. The palate runs extremely juicy and racy, as lively acidity pushes angular cherry, cassis, berry, and plum flavors. Quite bright and jumpy for Chilean Cabernet, but also quite good. **88** —M.S. (11/15/2006)

Cono Sur 2005 The Southern Cone Cabernet Sauvignon (Central Valley) $10. All of the 2005 Cono Sur entry-level wines are showing nicely, including this Cabernet. The nose is fairly floral and touched up by lavender, while the palate is racy and defined by zesty red fruit. It's kind of a throwback in that it emphasizes light fruit and acidity over oak and heft. **87 Best Buy** —M.S. (11/15/2006)

Cono Sur 2005 The Southern Cone Carmenère (Colchagua Valley) $10. A good as well as interesting Carmenère. The berry and warm-earth aromas are welcoming, and the palate is savory and firmed up by serious tannic zap. Fairly bold and powerful as basic reds go, with elevated character. **87 Best Buy** —M.S. (11/15/2006)

Cono Sur 2005 20 Barrels Limited Edition Chardonnay (Casablanca Valley) $25. Very soft and plump up front, with strong aromatics akin to hard apple cider and baked corn. The mouth is welcoming, courtesy of good acidity, yet the flavor profile is dominated by a heavy dealing of oak and spice. Finishes a touch too resiny for my liking, but it's still a well-made wine. **85** —M.S. (12/31/2006)

Cono Sur 2005 Single Vineyard Visión Chardonnay (Casablanca Valley) $14. Soft, distant, and easy on the nose. The palate is defined by sweet banana, peach, and vanilla flavors, while the finish is sweet and simple. With a solid mouthfeel, this registers as a basic but good Chardonnay. **84** —M.S. (12/31/2006)

CHILE

Cono Sur 2001 20 Barrels Merlot (Colchagua Valley) $22. Jammy, with blackberry aromas as well as spice and tobacco. The palate is also jammy, but quickly you realize that it's equally reduced and hard. As the sipping continues, watch for jackhammer tannins, the total opposite of the "velvety" ones promised on the back label. **83** —*M.S. (6/1/2004)*

Cono Sur 2001 Reserve Merlot (Rapel Valley) $12. Bright violet in color and well-extracted, but also vegetal. You'd think from the hue and vintage that it would be seamlessly ripe, but it seems green at the core. Thus while it delivers texture, rich plum fruit and tannic structure, there's a gap in clarity of fruit flavor. **85** —*M.S. (7/1/2003)*

Cono Sur 2005 The Southern Cone Merlot (Central Valley) $10. Blackberry, mint, forest floor, and a touch of oak create a nice aromatic whole. Plum and berry flavors are full and ripe, while the mouthfeel is round and commendable. This is a Merlot that touches all the bases. **87 Best Buy** —*M.S. (11/15/2006)*

Cono Sur 2001 20 Barrels Pinot Noir (Casablanca Valley) $22. Sweet and round from start through finish. In between you'll find foresty aromas and sugary fruit with strong wood accents. The finish teeters on syrupy but with ample spicy berry fruit, coffee nuances, and healthy acidity, it's pretty good within its class. **86** —*M.S. (8/1/2004)*

Cono Sur 2001 Reserve Pinot Noir (Casablanca Valley) $12. When in Chile I heard a lot about Cono Sur Pinot, and how they're trendsetters and one of the country's best wineries. Well, not based on this sample. Yes, the texture is fine and it has some varietal character, but the nose is sour and funky, the wine, simple and tart. This reviewer found the Cono Sur o.k. to drink, but hardly a connoisseur's drink. **82** —*M.S. (7/1/2003)*

COUSIÑO-MACUL

Cousiño-Macul 1998 Cabernet Sauvignon (Maipo Valley) $11. This light to medium weight Cabernet has the right profile, but just doesn't seem to come alive. The nose shows blackberry and tobacco aromas and in the mouth there are dried black cherry and spice notes, but they never shine. A softly dry, slightly woody finish closes the package. **82** *(2/1/2001)*

Cousiño-Macul 2004 Antiguas Reservas Cabernet Sauvignon (Maipo Valley) $14. Rather heavy and condensed, with earthy, foresty notes and a touch of heat on the nose. The palate boasts full cassis and black cherry flavors, and there's additional dark cherry on the finish. Slightly medicinal. **86** —*M.S. (12/31/2006)*

Cousiño-Macul 2002 Antiguas Reservas Cabernet Sauvignon (Maipo Valley) $13. Starts out emitting the essence of tire rubber before settling down to show cooked fruit and tree bark. Remains stewy and deep throughout, with some grittiness to the mouthfeel. Not focused and fresh enough to rate higher. **83** —*M.S. (7/1/2005)*

Cousiño-Macul 2001 Antiguas Reservas Cabernet Sauvignon (Maipo Valley) $13. This boisterous young Cabernet really shows the new style at Cousiño-Macul. This Cab has maple, vanilla, and licorice to go with cassis, pepper, and a drop of cherry cough syrup. It's big, polished and shows integrated tannins. **89 Best Buy** —*M.S. (3/1/2004)*

Cousiño-Macul 1997 Antiguas Reservas Cabernet Sauvignon (Maipo Valley) $13. Juicy dark cherry and berry aromas with cedar and cola notes present a Pinot Noir-like profile for this wine. It continues the disguise with its cherry and oak flavors, rather light mouthfeel and lack of density for a Cabernet based wine. **83** *(2/1/2001)*

Cousiño-Macul 1999 Antiguas Reservas Estate Bottled Cabernet Sauvignon (Maipo Valley) $14. **87** —*C.S. (2/1/2003)*

Cousiño-Macul 2002 Finis Terrae Cabernet Sauvignon-Merlot (Maipo Valley) $30. It is 55% Cabernet and 45% Merlot, mostly from the winery's new Buin vineyards, and it features a heavily toasted, oaky nose but also some solid fruit. The fruit is riper and richer than anything the winery did at Macul, as proven by its dark chocolate and blackberry qualities. Some spice and a nip of green pepper carry the finish. **88** —*M.S. (3/1/2004)*

Cousiño-Macul 1997 Finis Terrae Cabernet Sauvignon-Merlot (Maipo Valley) $32. Lots of cedar is evident on the nose and palate of this red blend. The berry and cassis aromas and flavors are a bit hard to discern and also bear a too-prominent minty, slightly herbaceousness. This medium weight wine closes with a dry tart woodiness that lacks mass appeal. **83** *(2/1/2001)*

Cousiño-Macul 2004 Lota Cabernet Sauvignon-Merlot (Maipo Valley) $60. A little dense early on but airing unleashes cassis, cherry, and tobacco aromas. Next in line you'll find black cherry, chocolate, and vanilla. All in all it's a big, round, and nicely balanced red. Of note, it marks the winery's entry into the super-Chilean category, something timed to coincide with Cousiño-Macul's 150th anniversary. **90** —*M.S. (12/31/2006)*

Cousiño-Macul 2004 Chardonnay (Maipo Valley) $9. Too much scrambled egg and burnt, gaseous notes on the nose. Spritzy on the palate, with oak and banana flavors. Barely acceptable. **80** —*M.S. (7/1/2005)*

Cousiño-Macul 2001 Chardonnay (Maipo Valley) $9. Apple, pear, and melon aromas offer promise, but the palate doesn't deliver. Mostly it's banana-style fruit and a flat feel. The dry finish provides balance to the otherwise underwhelming performance in the mouth. **83** —*M.S. (7/1/2002)*

Cousiño-Macul 2004 Antiguas Reservas Chardonnay (Maipo Valley) $14. Quite round and chewy, but zesty enough to stay on balance. There's lemon custard and pineapple on the fresh nose, and apple, banana and vanilla flavors. Finishes slightly toasty; nicely oaked. **87** —*M.S. (3/1/2006)*

Cousiño-Macul 2003 Antiguas Reservas Chardonnay (Maipo Valley) $13. The opening aromas entail peach, pear, and some light oak—just what you'd hope for from a Chilean Chardonnay. Since only part of the wine was barrel aged, the body holds onto some snap and clarity. Still, some vanilla and lees character create richness and ultimately a good wine. **87** —*M.S. (3/1/2004)*

Cousiño-Macul 2004 Merlot (Maipo Valley) $9. Fairly tight and foresty, with more leather and herbal characteristics than full-force berry fruit. Sort of basic in a good way, with comfortable but run-of-the-mill red and black fruit flavors. Finishes with a hint of spice. **84** —*M.S. (3/1/2006)*

Cousiño-Macul 2002 Merlot (Maipo Valley) $9. Opens with raspberry, toast, and dusty earth aromas. On the palate, the fruit comes across as cranberries accented by toast and wisps of dried herbs. Finishes with toast and vanilla wrapped around a core of tart fruit and some chalky tannins. **87** —*K.F. (2/1/2003)*

Cousiño-Macul 2001 Merlot (Maipo Valley) $9. This old-school winery sticks to tradition, so if this new-release Merlot seems older than it is, that's by intention. The color is light, and the wine already carries fading edges. The nose is earthy and the flavors are spicy. **84** —*M.S. (7/1/2003)*

Cousiño-Macul 2000 Merlot (Maipo Valley) $9. **82** —*C.S. (12/1/2002)*

Cousiño-Macul 1998 Reserva Merlot (Maipo Valley) $15. Ripe berries, black cherries, earth, chocolate, and herbs all mark this nose of this solid Merlot. Fairly full on the palate, it has a supple feel and plum and berry flavors. The finish is reserved, maybe even a bit austere, with dry, semisweet chocolate notes on the tart plum fruit. **86** *(2/1/2001)*

Cousiño-Macul 2001 Finis Terrae Merlot-Cabernet Sauvignon (Maipo Valley) $20. In this vintage, the blend is 90% Merlot and 10% Cabernet, and the wine is nice in the mouth, where lush red fruit spreads out comfortably. It's a dry, full, lengthy wine that is on the heavy side now but should be perfect in another year or two. Twelve months in new French oak has provided just the right smoke and vanilla notes. **90 Editors' Choice** —*M.S. (3/1/2004)*

Cousiño-Macul 2003 Doña Isadora Riesling (Maipo Valley) $9. Lately, this rather unique Riesling seems to have found its calling. It's big and chewy, and very un-German. The bouquet deals melon, honey, and floral notes, which are capped by dry, minerally stone-fruit flavors that spread onto the long finish. A pleasant surprise. **88 Best Buy** —*M.S. (3/1/2004)*

Cousiño-Macul 2000 Dona Isidora Riesling (Maipo Valley) $8. Very particular yet still very Riesling. Oily, tight aromas signal intensity, which is delivered on the peach-like palate that turns creamy toward the finish as banana and papaya take over. There's a bitterness throughout, and at points it's interesting while at others it's too much. Also in abundance is the taste of pepper. A unique wine with attitude. **85** —*M.S. (8/1/2003)*

Cousiño-Macul 1999 Doña Isadora Riesling (Maipo Valley) $14. An attractive bouquet of pear, orange-lime, and floral notes opens this easy, round white. There's a hint of mint and plenty of citrus on the palate, but the fruit is touch too sweet low acid and the mouthfeel a bit fat. Lacks the spine we'd like to see in a top Riesling. **82** *(2/1/2001)*

Cousiño-Macul 2006 Sauvignon Gris (Maipo Valley) $12. A clean, correct, and fairly typical rendition of Chilean Sauvignon, but in this case the variety is Gris and not the more common Blanc. The result revolves around tropical aromas and flavors of green apple, pineapple and banana. Fairly flush and plump, with core sweetness. **87** —*M.S. (12/31/2006)*

CRUCERO

Crucero 2000 Syrah (Colchagua Valley) $8. Berry, chalk, and leather notes and a dry palate mark this interesting Chilean Syrah. There are earthy, and also tangy, almost citrus accents here. Tangy, with peppery notes on the blueberry fruit, it closes with moderate chalky tannins. **85 Best Buy** *(10/1/2001)*

D. BOSLER

D. Bosler 2002 Birdsnest Pinot Noir (Casablanca Valley) $10. From Casa Julia, this is one of the better, more varietally correct Pinot Noirs Chile is making. The nose is dry, leathery, and earthy, with a punch of cherry. The dried red fruit on the palate is intense and gritty, with racy acidity ensuring a brisk feel. **87 Best Buy** —*M.S. (7/1/2005)*

D. Bosler 2000 Birdsnest Pinot Noir (Casablanca Valley) $12. Bright but tart cherry and blackberry flavors are swathed in dusty tannins; the nose offers similar berry and plum aromas. It's a little acidic, but finishes with nice dusty-plum flavors. **86** —*D.T. (7/1/2002)*

DALLAS CONTÉ

Dallas Conté 2003 Cabernet Sauvignon (Maipo Valley) $10. A little bit pickled and prickly up front, with semi-tart fruit that veers toward raspberry and cherry. Fairly tannic and sharp, but not unfriendly. Finishes on the thin side, with wiry tannins. **83** —*M.S. (5/1/2006)*

Dallas Conté 2000 Cabernet Sauvignon (Rapel Valley) $10. Potent aromas of red fruit, rubber, and lemony oak kick things off, followed by a very typical mix of cherry and berry flavors. The finish is properly tannic and round, with an acid-driven freshness that secures the mouthfeel. This has more red than dark fruit, but it's still a perfectly quaffable Cabernet. **85** —*M.S. (7/1/2003)*

Dallas Conté 1999 Cabernet Sauvignon (Colchagua Valley) $9. Young and grapey, with plenty of heavily toasted oak, this is one Chilean red that could use a year or so to settle down. Right now the fruit is just too unformed and the charred oak too unintegrated, but the solid raw materials should knit together nicely in a relatively short time. **86** —*J.C. (2/1/2001)*

Dallas Conté 1997 Cabernet Sauvignon (Colchagua Valley) $10. 88 Best Buy —*M.S. (8/1/2000)*

Dallas Conté 1999 Reserve Cabernet Sauvignon-Merlot (Rapel Valley) $15. Pungent aromas of lemony oak, peanuts and maple are the opening act. The next act is a big, sweet palate with monster extraction and the flavors of brandied black cherries. For some it might be too sweet, especially when the acidity kicks in to create a juicy palate feel not unlike fruit juice. **85** —*M.S. (7/1/2003)*

Dallas Conté 2002 Chardonnay (Casablanca Valley) $10. Pungent aromas of pine needles and saw mill start it off. Next comes a juicy palate with flavors of orange and pineapple. The finish is fine, but it's kind of dull. The is a basic wine that veers toward flatness. But for now it's hanging in there. **84** —*M.S. (7/1/2003)*

Dallas Conté 1998 Chardonnay (Colchagua Valley) $10. Mild tropical fruit and citrus aromas draw you right in. Medium weight, with bright acidity that keeps the flavors lively, the wine displays pineapple and spice on the palate and finish and has an appealing chalky, leesy feel. **89 Best Buy** — *M.M. (2/1/2001)*

Dallas Conté 2001 Merlot (Rapel Valley) $10. Heavily oaked, with a strong essence of lemon on the nose and throughout. Flavors of tart cherry and bitter chocolate create a tangy, dark whole, while the overall feel is edgy and sharp. **84** —*M.S. (8/1/2004)*

Dallas Conté 2000 Merlot (Rapel Valley) $10. There's plenty of oak to this solid, peppery Merlot that's also a touch green. The cassis and cherry fruit that drives the palate is healthy and sturdy, while the finish features some tight-grained oak and firm enough tannins. Maybe too much oak given the fruit quality. **85** —*M.S. (7/1/2003)*

Dallas Conté 1997 Merlot (Colchagua Valley) $10. 87 Best Buy —*M.S. (5/1/2000)*

DE MARTINO

De Martino 1999 Cabernet Sauvignon (Maipo Valley) $10. A lot of Chilean Cabernets seem to have a distinct weediness to them; this is a perfect example of the style, boasting green hay and herb aromas over subdued—almost stewed—cassis fruit. Some tart acidity keeps things lively on the finish. **81** —*J.C. (2/1/2001)*

De Martino 1999 Estate Bottled Prima Reserva Cabernet Sauvignon (Maipo Valley) $13. Talk about wood spice! This has it in spades, and it covers up any fruit that might want to escape from the bouquet. But in the mouth some sweet cherry flavor emerges, followed by more cherry and ample woodiness on the finish. **84** —*M.S. (12/1/2002)*

De Martino 2002 Estate Bottled Gran Familia Cabernet Sauvignon (Maipo Valley) $45. Arguably not up to the De Martino standards, and definitely not up to the price. This full-bodied Cab is jam-packed with heavy mint and menthol aromas, which precede saturated but awkward plum and dark berry flavors. Steps on the accelerator with too much force; not ideally balanced. **85** —*M.S. (5/1/2006)*

De Martino 1998 Prima Reserva Cabernet Sauvignon (Maipo Valley) $13. Aromas of freshly cut lumber, complete with some hints of burning sawdust, are joined by caramel and cassis. Medium to full on the palate, where some sweet fruit and oak flavors make a decent impression. There's a hint of alcohol poking through on the finish, but little else. **81** —*J.C. (2/1/2001)*

De Martino 1997 Reserva de Familia Cabernet Sauvignon (Maipo Valley) $35. A bright berry bouquet with light herb and anise notes ushers in a palate of black currants and leather, with mega-doses of oak. It's a touch hot at first, but the smooth mouthfeel and a medium-length finish of black pepper, leather, and oak will please a wide audience. **85** —*D.T. (8/1/2001)*

De Martino 2003 Legada Reserva Carmenère (Maipo Valley) $15. Colorful, grapey, and rubbery, with chunky aromas. Jumpy and lively on the palate, with acidity, tannins and biting fruit. Licorice notes and citrus zest on the finish retain the wine's lively personality. Weighs in at 14.5%; some might find it too pumped up. **85** —*M.S. (1/1/2005)*

De Martino 2005 Legado Reserva Carmenère (Maipo Valley) $15. Standard but crisp red-fruit aromas are the greeting, while the main course is centered around bright raspberry and cherry flavors. It shows a touch of varietal character, meaning it's spicy and a touch saucy. But overall it registers well, with medium depth and length. **87** —*M.S. (10/1/2006)*

De Martino 1999 Prima Reserva Carmenère (Maipo Valley) $12. The nose is rustic, with horse hide, bramble bush and spicy, subdued black fruit. The palate is round and rich, with pure and ripe berry fruit along with some supporting oak. The finish is equally nice, with notes of licorice, coffee and spices. **89** —*M.S. (7/1/2003)*

De Martino 1999 Reserva de la Familia Carmenère (Maipo Valley) $10. Aromas of mint, berry, syrup and dense, lemony oak lay a good foundation for the heavy black fruit that comes on the palate atop a plush carpet of toasty, fresh-grained wood. The finish is round, tasty, and mouthfilling, while overall the wine seems to dance due to popping acidity. This is Carmenère with a vital streak. **88** —*M.S. (7/1/2003)*

De Martino 1999 Estate Bottled Chardonnay (Maipo Valley) $10. This medium weight Chardonnay offered aromas of over-ripe pineapple and citrus with an odd note somewhere between citrus and varnish. The apple and mild citrus flavors lack vitality, and turn overly tart on the finish. **81** *(2/1/2001)*

De Martino 2000 Estate Bottled Prima Reserva Chardonnay (Maipo Valley) $10. Creamy and lush, with pure peach and pear aromas along with nice vanilla accents. The palate is fairly rich and layered, but it's also properly acidic and, therefore, well-balanced. The flavors of pear and butter seem on the money, and the finish is solid and of moderate length. All in all, this is a very good Chardonnay with no overt faults. **89** —*M.S. (7/1/2003)*

De Martino 2004 Legada Reserva Chardonnay (Limarí Valley) $15. Big and broad, with 14.5% alcohol and a lot of butterscotch and baked apple character. The palate delivers toasty apple and lemon flavors, while the finish is solid. A bit of a chunkster but cleanly made and packed with flavor. **87** —*M.S. (3/1/2006)*

De Martino 2005 Legado Reserva Chardonnay (Limarí Valley) $15. Arguably a bit overwooded, but if you like a hefty wine (14.5%) with an oily feel, this is it. The mouthfeel is slick and a bit greasy, but with extract to spare that's the way it is. The flavors are big and typical, with peach, apple, and popcorn. A big boy from the Southern Hemisphere. **87** —*M.S. (10/1/2006)*

De Martino 1999 Prima Reserva Chardonnay (Maipo Valley) $13. The pineapple and lemon aromas and flavors in this wine just seem to lack the spark to make them come alive. There's a medium texture on the palate but the subdued, uninspired quality extends to the mouthfeel as well. A reserve label deserves more substance. **82** *(2/1/2001)*

De Martino 1999 Reserva de Familia Chardonnay (Casablanca Valley) $35. Dark gold color and buttery nose say that it was heavily oaked during its fermentation and afterward. The palate is flat and resiny. On the finish, buttered toast and some bitter, oaky leftovers hold it back. **84** —*M.S. (7/1/2003)*

De Martino 2000 Estate Bottled - Prima Reserva Merlot (Maipo Valley) $13. What a nice surprise. This full-bodied Merlot is of amazing quality. The dense aromas of coffee, mocha, earth and spice are unassailable. And the flavors are equally dynamite, with all the concentrated plum and blackberry on display. The finish is smoky, with obvious but welcome wood tones. As the saying goes, try it; you'll like it. **90 Editors' Choice** —*M.S. (12/1/2002)*

De Martino 1999 Prima Reserva Merlot (Maipo Valley) $13. There's not much point in making a reserve-style wine if the barrels are subpar. Aggressive menthol and sappy green-barrel aromas and flavors dominate this wine. There's good weight and texture, just not much in the way of vinous flavor. **80** —*J.C. (2/1/2001)*

De Martino 1998 Reserva de Familia Red Blend (Maipo Valley) $35. A taut, structured offering that emphasizes cocoa and coffee aromas and flavors, complemented by cedary underpinnings and just enough black cherries and black currants to keep things interesting. **85** —*J.C. (8/1/2001)*

De Martino 2001 Estate Bottled - Prima Reserva Sauvignon Blanc (Maipo Valley) $10. Creamy in the nose, with a hint of vanilla and Bartlett pear. The palate isn't boring; there's cantaloupe and nutmeg nuances along with some papaya and banana. The weakness: The wine turns soft almost immediately upon pouring. **84** —*M.S. (7/1/2003)*

De Martino 2004 Legado Reserva Sauvignon Blanc (Maipo Valley) $15. Grassy and fresh, with hints of cucumber, pickle and citrus. From start to finish the wine is pure S.B. The mouth offers tangerine, orange and lemon on an herbal base, and the feel is zesty, clean and fresh. **87** —*M.S. (7/1/2005)*

De Martino 2003 Legada Reserva Syrah (Colchagua Valley) $15. Starts out a touch raw and woody, then cherry, plum and popcorn flavors come out on the tongue. Fairly lean and driving, with a candied, firm finish. Forward and tannic, with quite a bit of snap. **86** —*M.S. (11/1/2005)*

DOMAINES BARONS DE ROTHSCHILD (LAFITE)

Domaines Barons de Rothschild (Lafite) 2000 Le Dix de Los Vascos Cabernet Sauvignon (Colchagua Valley) $40. Very Bordeaux-like up front, with minty, herbal aromas that lead into a palate defined by cherry, cola and chocolate. The finish mixes good fruit with sweet, oaky undertones. **89** —*M.S. (3/1/2004)*

Domaines Barons de Rothschild (Lafite) 2003 Los Vascos Cabernet Sauvignon (Colchagua Valley) $11. Overt and dark, with sweet, earthy aromas and plenty of tell-tale cassis. For a basic appellation Cabernet, this delivers the goods. The potent palate is packed full of plum, cherry, cassis, and more. The finish is so chocolaty and full that it almost seems chewable. Well done. **88 Best Buy** —*M.S. (12/1/2004)*

Domaines Barons de Rothschild (Lafite) 2002 Los Vascos Cabernet Sauvignon (Colchagua Valley) $10. Soft, thick and chewy. Red plums and raspberries define the palate, which is backed by a modest, oaky finish. A bit lactic and plump, but tasty. **86** —*M.S. (3/1/2004)*

Domaines Barons de Rothschild (Lafite) 2001 Los Vascos Grande Reserve Cabernet Sauvignon (Colchagua Valley) $17. More complex than the average Chilean red, with toasty oak, hard cheese and bacon on the nose. Full and meaty plum and berry fruit expands right before the finish, and overall there's adequate class and nuance in addition to full ripeness. **87** —*M.S. (3/1/2004)*

Domaines Barons de Rothschild (Lafite) 2004 Los Vascos Reserve Cabernet Sauvignon (Colchagua Valley) $21. A balanced specimen, from front to back and top to bottom. The nose deals smooth fruit touched up by chocolate and a whiff of mint, while the mouth is spicy and herbal but also saturated with dark berry notes and touches of the forest. Stout in terms of feel, with cheek-to-cheek depth. **90** —*M.S. (11/15/2006)*

Domaines Barons de Rothschild (Lafite) 2005 Los Vascos Chardonnay (Colchagua Valley) $12. A nicely sculpted white wine; fresh on the nose, with talcum powder, flowers, and citrus aromas. Shows little to zero oak, but lots of grapefruit that isn't sour at all—more like delicate and ripe. One of the better value Chards from Chile, and there are plenty of 'em. **88 Best Buy** —*M.S. (5/1/2006)*

Domaines Barons de Rothschild (Lafite) 2003 Los Vascos Chardonnay (Colchagua Valley) $10. This wine sees no oak, offering stony white peach and melon aromas as well as a whiff of celery. The acidity tends to play up the apple in the flavor profile, but there's also some banana. **86 Best Buy** —*M.S. (3/1/2004)*

Domaines Barons de Rothschild (Lafite) 2005 Los Vascos Sauvignon Blanc (Casablanca Valley) $12. Sharp and zesty, but in a racy, tropical way that works at all check points. Lime, kiwi, green melon, lemongrass, and a touch of bell pepper carry the textbook Casablanca palate, and the finish is fresh and on the mark. Yet another fine value from Los Vascos. **88 Best Buy** —*M.S. (7/1/2006)*

Domaines Barons de Rothschild (Lafite) 2004 Los Vascos Sauvignon Blanc (Central Valley) $11. Aromas of grapefruit, passion fruit, and citrus lead the way. The palate deals more citrus and a touch of banana. A bit thinner than many, with a peppery, clean finish. **85** —*M.S. (2/1/2005)*

Domaines Barons de Rothschild (Lafite) 2003 Los Vascos Sauvignon Blanc (Colchagua Valley) $10. Nearly translucent in color, with crisp aromas of passion fruit and orange. It's fresh, with lemon, lime, and grapefruit flavors. Sharp, but good if you enjoy the razor-like style. **87 Best Buy** —*M.S. (3/1/2004)*

DOMUS AUREA

Domus Aurea 2002 Cabernet Sauvignon (Maipo Valley) $45. Lots of leather and earthy spice start if off, and behind that there's black fruit and a hint of nuttiness. Solid and saturated on the palate, with sweet cherry, berry, and chocolate flavors. Fades a bit quick on the finish, with pepper. An achievement from what was a marginal year in Chile. **89** —*M.S. (10/1/2006)*

Domus Aurea 2001 Cabernet Sauvignon (Maipo Valley) $45. Quite funky, with roasted berry and earth aromas along with burnt grass, tar, and leather. Very sweet and syrupy, without a whole lot of zest. Is it losing steam or what? Seems to have core qualities and nicely integrated tannins but it lacks the overt fruit and purity of the best Chilean Cabs. **84** —*M.S. (12/15/2005)*

Domus Aurea 2001 Cabernet Sauvignon (Maipo Valley) $45. In tasting this vintage for the second time, we found better balance than originally but still we encountered dull fruit, a lot of earthiness and leather, and some pickle barrel. That said, we also see this as a more elegant expression of Chilean Cab, one that will do well with food. Not for everyone but has its virtues. **87** —*M.S. (5/1/2006)*

Domus Aurea 1999 Cabernet Sauvignon (Maipo Valley) $42. Seems a touch weedy at first, without much fruit. But that's more a reflection of the wine's age than any inherent under-ripeness. Still, it's starting to fade, and quickly. There's not a lot of zest left, and the finish seems chocolaty and syrupy. Was better a couple of years ago; now it's on the slide. **85** —*M.S. (11/1/2005)*

DON OSVALDO

Don Osvaldo 2004 Carmenère (Colchagua Valley) $10. Deep and leafy, with a rich, almost murky-mossy note. The palate, however, is raw and acidic. Thus the plum and berry flavors are in your face and short, with a peppery aftertaste. **82** —*M.S. (7/1/2006)*

Don Osvaldo 2003 Vina Bisquertt Reserve Carmenère (Colchagua Valley) $15. Dark and rubbery, with a heavyweight's presence. Nearly assaultive on the palate, with hard, acidic fruit that's jumpy and tight. A tough

CHILE

wine, no matter how many times you come back to it. **81** —*M.S.* *(7/1/2006)*

DUO

Duo 2003 Cabernet Sauvignon-Merlot (Maipo Valley) $14. This is a new entry from Chile, which blends three-quarters Cab with Merlot to fine results. There's a veneer of toasty oak on the solid nose, which features black cherry at the base. The fruit is bright and berry-driven, while chocolate and refreshing acids work the finish. A step up from the so-called "value blend." **88** —*M.S. (5/1/2006)*

Duo 2005 Sauvignon Blanc (Casablanca Valley) $14. Fresh and fruity, with a nice Casablanca green character that's much like good asparagus. Tangy and citrusy in the mouth, which is tight and zingy in terms of feel. Best if well chilled. **85** —*M.S. (5/1/2006)*

ECHEVERRIA

Echeverria 2002 Cabernet Sauvignon (Molina) $16. Rubbery red fruit carries the commonplace nose, followed by flavors of cherry, berry, and spice. And while it seems soft at first, time allows for the tannins to pile up and become hard. **84** —*M.S. (2/1/2005)*

Echeverria 1999 Family Reserve Cabernet Sauvignon (Molina) $29. Mature, with notes of raisin, leather, and tree bark. For an aged reserve-level Chilean Cab, it impresses. The palate still holds some cedary notes, but there's depth and nuance and fruit as well. A serious wine with warmth, structure, and just enough sly fruit to earn its mark. **90** —*M.S. (2/1/2005)*

Echeverria 2003 Limited Edition Cabernet Sauvignon (Central Valley) $28. Quite attractive in color and bouquet, with compact, deep aromas of leather, olive, black plum, and cassis. It's pure and powerful in the mouth, with tons of dark fruit and chocolate. Finishes long, with finely etched tannins. Very smooth and properly made in the New World style. **91** —*M.S. (12/31/2006)*

Echeverria 2000 Molina Cabernet Sauvignon (Chile) $8. Satisfying cedar, matchstick, and cherry-pie aromas; then equivalent flavors, with the addition of wet stone. The finish is earthy yet elegant. **87 Best Buy** — *C.S. (12/1/2002)*

Echeverria 2004 Reserva Cabernet Sauvignon (Molina) $18. A little wild and funky at first, but airing reveals smoky, round aromas of berries and rubber. The palate is quite bright and vibrant, as it shows solid berry flavors bolstered by pulsing acidity. Full, saturated and satisfying. Offers commendable depth. **88** —*M.S. (11/15/2006)*

Echeverria 2001 Reserva Cabernet Sauvignon-Merlot (Curicó Valley) $18. Sweet, condensed, and loaded with berry jam and lots of oak. The palate pitches the full assortment of dark fruits: plum, black cherry, and their buddies are all here. Finishes solid. The wine is 70% Cab and the rest Merlot. **88** —*M.S. (12/1/2004)*

Echeverria 2005 Carmenère (Central Valley) $12. Rubbery and funky, with menthol on the nose. Bold but amorphous in the mouth, with an almost salty finish. A rough ride for sure. **81** —*M.S. (11/15/2006)*

Echeverria 2002 Molina Carmenère (Curicó Valley) $9. Produced in a subsection of Curicó, this wine is hot and leathery, with some saline/chlorine notes on the brambly nose. The palate offers plum and cherry, while the finish is sweet and tannic. **83** —*M.S. (6/1/2004)*

Echeverria 2004 Reserva Carmenère (Central Valley) $18. If you like Chilean Carmenère, chances are you'll like this one. And if not, give it a try and it might help convert you to the variety. Echeverria's is dark, with lots of smoked meat, molasses, and cedary fruit on the nose. The palate is plump and bright, with spiced-plum flavors and plenty of nutmeg. Not harsh at all, and fairly well integrated. Tastes almost like Cabernet or Merlot. **88** —*M.S. (12/31/2006)*

Echeverria 2005 Reserva Chardonnay (Molina) $18. Perfumed but reticent, with simple apple and almond aromas and flavors. Feels a touch flat on the palate due to modest acidity, but for a basic New World Chardonnay it's good. Drink right away for best results. **85** —*M.S. (11/15/2006)*

Echeverria 2004 Reserva Chardonnay (Molina) $18. Rather flat, with cider and honey aromas. Thick and heavy on the palate, with butter and resin. Lacks sizzle and freshness. **82** —*M.S. (3/1/2006)*

Echeverria 2005 Unwooded Chardonnay (Molina) $13. Sweet and waxy, with aromas of honey and air freshener. Ultra sweet, with flavors of applesauce and candy. Soft and dilute on the finish. Quite simple stuff. **82** —*M.S. (3/1/2006)*

Echeverria 2003 Unwooded Chardonnay (Molina) $9. Aromas of fresh-squeezed orange juice and chewable children's vitamins attest to the fact there's no oak to be found. Along the way are soft citrus and melon flavors, and a chalky but thin finish. **82** —*M.S. (2/1/2005)*

Echeverria 2000 Merlot (Maule Valley) $12. Raspberry tea and black olive aromas are very appealing. The palate brings coffee and soft red berry flavors, yielding a smooth, easy-drinking wine. **88 Best Buy** —*C.S. (12/1/2002)*

Echeverria 1999 Reserva Merlot (Chile) $16. Strong-like-bull blackberry flavors follow dirt, oak and a little pepper on the nose—all of the above appear on the finish. It's not terribly lush or complex, but it gets the job done. **84** —*D.T. (7/1/2002)*

Echeverria 2002 Reserva Red Blend (Central Valley) $18. Ripe and pleasant, with red fruit aromas that tilt toward jammy. The palate features common but rewarding dark fruit, chocolate, and vanilla flavors. And the finish is tasty, albeit heady. Weighs in a touch heavy, but could use more kick. **86** —*M.S. (12/31/2006)*

Echeverria 2003 Sauvignon Blanc (Molina) $9. From a subsection of Curicó; sweet on the nose, with light vanilla. Heavy on the palate, with basic citrus and little else. Acceptable white wine in a field of thousands. **82** —*M.S. (2/1/2005)*

Echeverria 2004 Reserva Syrah (Colchagua Valley) $18. A powerball of a wine, with saucy fruit aromas mixed with oak and earth. If anything, it's extracted and big; the palate is like a rainbow of berry flavors. Finishes kind of sweet and sticky, with chocolate and vanilla notes. Rowdy, raw, and ripe as all get out. **88** —*M.S. (11/15/2006)*

EL GRANO

El Grano 2001 Carmenère (Rapel Valley) $10. A single sniff tells all; there's spicy pepper and funky red fruit. That's followed by sweet plum and clove flavors. It's soft, yet it has some blueberry and chocolate character, like Zin. **87** —*M.S. (11/15/2003)*

EL HUIQUE

El Huique 2002 Cabernet Sauvignon (Colchagua Valley) $8. Weedy and tight, with leather, forest floor, and leaf-like aromas. Shows some cherry and beet on the palate, while the finish grabs and doesn't let go. **82** —*M.S. (7/1/2005)*

El Huique 2002 Reserva Carmenère (Colchagua Valley) $12. Heavy on the nose, with aromas of leather, vegetables, and cheese. Better with air, displaying simple berry and plum before a light, easy finish. Straightforward in every sense. **83** —*M.S. (2/1/2005)*

El Huique 2001 Chardonnay (Colchagua Valley) $9. Sweet and syrupy up front, yet bitter and hollow later on. Low acidity creates a flat mouthfeel. Too old. **80** —*M.S. (2/1/2005)*

EL TOQUI

El Toqui 2002 Prestige Cabernet Sauvignon (Cachapoal Valley) $13. Cloudy in color, with aromas of tree bark, warm earth, and murky fruit. Very sweet, with overt yet totally basic berry flavors. Finishes haltingly sweet, with a screechy feel. **82** —*M.S. (10/1/2006)*

ENCIERRA

Encierra 2002 Vineyard Reserve Red Blend (Colchagua Valley) $25. Nice and meaty, with raisin, leather, and crystallized candy on the beefy bouquet. Blackberry and licorice dominate the palate on this blend of Cabernet, Syrah, Carmenère, and Merlot. With nice tannins and extract, you get a mouthful. It's also a little obtuse and oaky. **87** —*M.S. (12/1/2004)*

ERRAZURIZ

Errazuriz 1998 Don Maximiano Founder's Reserve Cabernet Blend (Aconcagua Valley) $30. This is a very distinctive, even eccentric, Cab that must reflect its single-vineyard terroir. The usual black currant and blackberry notes are there, but the aroma is sharply dominated by an herbal streak, somewhat stalky or green, as if some of the grapes didn't ripen. Tastes a little sharp. Purists might want to age it for 3-5 years to see if it softens up. **86** —*S.H. (2/1/2001)*

Errazuriz 2003 Viñedo Chadwick Cabernet Blend (Maipo Valley) $100. The Chadwicks have hit the big time with this superb Cabernet-dominated blend. The bouquet of black cherry, charcoal, plum, and tree bark is sensational, while the cassis, cherry, and tobacco flavors sing on the palate. Lots of fruit, power, and balance, with a touch of earthiness. **93 Editors' Choice** —*M.S. (10/1/2006)*

Errazuriz 2001 Cabernet Sauvignon (Aconcagua Valley) $12. The initial nosing reveals a char-broiled character along with maple. That nose turns even darker with airing, indicating that no barrel was spared in the making of this wine. The flavor profile is all dark berries and cream, with yet more wood at the heart. On the tail end, it's dry, broad, and full of tannins and extract that coat the mouth. **87 Best Buy** —*M.S. (7/1/2003)*

Errazuriz 2003 Don Maximiano Founder's Reserve Cabernet Sauvignon (Aconcagua Valley) $50. Yet another Don Max that pours on the olive and leather aromas alongside rustic plum and berry counterpoints. As in the past, the '03 shows a smidgen of bell pepper at the very center, and off that you get tight blueberry, black cherry and pepper notes. Expensive for what you're getting. **87** —*M.S. (7/1/2006)*

Errazuriz 2002 Don Maximiano Founder's Reserve Cabernet Sauvignon (Aconcagua Valley) $49. Solid as a rock, with its own unique set of characteristics. For starters, the wine blends overt new world fruit with some rustic old world touches. In addition, there's Carmenère in the blend, which offers an herbal edge. The only reason this wine doesn't rate higher is that it finishes a bit cloying and tannic. Seems that the vintage just didn't provide enough flesh and balance. **88** —*M.S. (11/1/2005)*

Errazuriz 2000 Don Maximiano Founder's Reserve Cabernet Sauvignon (Aconcagua Valley) $60. One of Chile's old-school, top-shelf Cabernets seems challenged in this vintage. The nose is herbal and mildly green, but underneath there's a sweet, meaty quality that serves it well. Black fruit and some creamy, chocolaty oak bring it around the bend; Bordeaux-like in its style. **88** —*M.S. (3/1/2004)*

Errazuriz 1999 Don Maximo Estate Reserva Cabernet Sauvignon (Aconcagua Valley) $25. Not much in the way of flavor on the palate, but the nose's blackberry-herb-white pepper-oak profile is decent. Finish offers drying, nutty-oak flavors with a bitter bite on the back end. **82** —*D.T. (7/1/2002)*

Errazuriz 1997 El Ceibo Estate Cabernet Sauvignon (Aconcagua Valley) $8. 88 *(11/15/1999)*

Errazuriz 2000 El Ceibo Estate Estate Cabernet Sauvignon (Aconcagua Valley) $10. The aromas shine with ripe berries, although there are some green notes, but it tastes fabulous. The texture is so softly silky and velvety, you don't want to swallow, while the flavors and ripe finish go on forever. Oaky nuances add to the pleasure. **87 Best Buy** —*S.H. (12/1/2002)*

Errazuriz 1999 El Ceibo Estate Cabernet Sauvignon (Aconcagua Valley) $10. Red and black wild berry aromas mingle with sharper notes of herbs and slightly green ones. The berry flavors are lean, framed by well-crafted tannins, and scored by good acidity. Finishes dry and and tart. **85** —*S.H. (6/1/2001)*

Errazuriz 2004 Estate Cabernet Sauvignon (Aconcagua Valley) $11. Right on the mark, with a likable nose full of cassis, blackberry, and spice. Super clean on the palate, with a flavor profile that's both juicy and round. Warm and extracted, with a hearty amount of chocolate. Balanced. **88 Best Buy** —*M.S. (11/1/2005)*

Errazuriz 2002 Estate Cabernet Sauvignon (Aconcagua Valley) $10. Broad and deep, with some rich, ripe aromatics some might called stewy. But the wine itself is balanced and healthy, with cassis, cherry, and tobacco flavors. The finish sports a liqueur-like sweetness, and the tannins are just right. **88 Best Buy** —*M.S. (6/1/2004)*

Errazuriz 2003 Max Reserva Cabernet Sauvignon (Aconcagua Valley) $21. Dark and full of tar, tree bark, smoke, and black fruit. This one sings a pretty tune, especially with its powerful berry, chocolate, and vanilla flavors. Finishes in smooth, mouth-filling form, with espresso and black cherry massing at the tape. **91 Editors' Choice** —*M.S. (11/1/2005)*

Errazuriz 2002 Max Reserva Cabernet Sauvignon (Aconcagua Valley) $19. Unconventional on the nose, with hints of leather, raisin, and corn chips. Mostly smooth from palate to finish, with flavors of berries, cherry, and chocolate. Holds form on the finish, which is solid, chewy, and fruity. **85** —*M.S. (7/1/2005)*

Errazuriz 2000 Max Reserva Cabernet Sauvignon (Aconcagua Valley) $60. Smoky and closed at first, with some peppery sharpness coming on late in the nose. A mouth filled with chewy plum and blackberry fruit is perfectly acceptable, while a thick and woody finish creates both the feel and flavor of chocolate. **85** —*M.S. (3/1/2004)*

Errazuriz 1999 Reserva Cabernet Sauvignon (Aconcagua Valley) $25. Ripe berry and coffee flavors and a solid dose of oak. The texture is seductive, all velvet and plush silk in the mouth. It finishes sweetly fruity, with good balance, but it's no better than the regular bottling. **87** —*S.H. (12/1/2002)*

Errazuriz 2002 Viñedo Chadwick Cabernet Sauvignon (Maipo Valley) $64. Dark and smoky, with a little bit of everything to the bouquet: cola, root beer, berry, and leather. More cherry and cola carry the palate, which clamps down in firm fashion. In fact, this wine has monster tannins that require a bit for body. In all, the wine is flavorful but lacks richness. **87** —*M.S. (11/1/2005)*

Errazuriz 2000 Viñedo Chadwick Cabernet Sauvignon (Maipo Valley) $70. Intense and dense, with campfire to the nose along with black fruit and tar. The palate is equally dark, with flavors of charcoal-studded cassis and plum. Bitter chocolate and espresso is what defines the powerful finish. A manly wine made entirely from the Chadwick family's home vineyard in Puente Alto. **91** —*M.S. (3/1/2004)*

Errazuriz 1999 Don Maximaino's Founder's Reserve Cabernet Sauvignon-Merlot (Aconcagua Valley) $60. There's a cut of acid tartness in this wine that might disappoint fans of fat, plush Bordeaux blends, but it feels lush and fancy in the mouth, framed with smoky oak. It's herbaceous and tannic now, but an ager. Try after 2005. A blend of Cabernet Sauvignon and Merlot. **87** —*S.H. (12/1/2002)*

Errazuriz 2003 Don Maximiano Estate Single Vineyard Carmenère (Aconcagua Valley) $25. A throwback wine to the days when nobody knew much about Carmenère. Why? Because it's natural and terroir-based. The result of which is raw bell pepper and herbal flavors along with zingy red plum and raspberry. At one moment it's green and leafy; at the next you taste Bordeaux and revel in its earthiness. **85** —*M.S. (11/1/2005)*

Errazuriz 2004 Single Vineyard Carmenère (Aconcagua Valley) $25. A well-oaked version, with ripe aromas touched up by plenty of aggressive resin and coconut. Also shows a lot of bright, zesty fruit, and spice. Could be less oaky and still succeed; but like it is get ready for vanilla and more. **89** —*M.S. (3/1/2006)*

Errazuriz 2002 Chardonnay (Casablanca Valley) $10. Fairly ripe, with body and big fruit. The nose is potent and carries the essence of pears in syrup. Flavors of lemon, pineapple, and green apple start strong and continue onto the finish. Bold from the get-go, with some chunkiness. **86 Best Buy** —*M.S. (6/1/2004)*

Errazuriz 2005 Estate Chardonnay (Casablanca Valley) $11. Light up front, with a whiff of fruit cocktail. Chalky apple and citrus control the palate, while the finish is bold yet dry, with a mild citrus pith note. Good feel and a touch of polish help it along. **86 Best Buy** —*M.S. (10/1/2006)*

Errazuriz 2004 Estate Chardonnay (Casablanca Valley) $11. Opens with peach, nectarine, and cinnamon notes. In the mouth, there are plump melon, apple, and banana flavors. Finishes a bit flat and flabby, but still wet enough to remain likable. Short on stuffing but better around the edges. **85** —*M.S. (7/1/2005)*

Errazuriz 2004 Estate Chardonnay (Casablanca Valley) $11. Neutral but clean, with easygoing pear and apple characteristics on both the bouquet and palate. Very much in the mainstream, with smooth vanilla, white-fruit, and toffee notes to the finish. Enjoyable and functional Chardonnay from Chile's best white-wine region. **87 Best Buy** —*M.S. (11/1/2005)*

Errazuriz 2000 Estate Chardonnay (Casablanca Valley) $10. A nosing reveals pineapple juice; it's a bit too forward and sharp. In the mouth,

CHILE

lemony flavors mix with buttery oak. It finishes heavier than it should, but still it's pretty clean. In total, it's simple, juicy, properly acidic white wine, but nothing more. **84** —*M.S. (7/1/2002)*

Errazuriz 1999 La Escultura Estate Chardonnay (Casablanca Valley) $10. A great price for a wine this rich and spicy. It's busting with ripe tropical fruit, peach, tangerine, and pear notes, and spices, too. And it's dry, with just a hint of residual sugar to make the fruit round and forward. Turns really pretty on the polished, spicy finish. **87 Best Buy** —*S.H. (2/1/2001)*

Errazuriz 2000 La Escultura Estate Reserva Chardonnay (Casablanca Valley) $10. Attractive aromas of pear and coconut set the stage for clean, fruity pear, and apple flavors. This wine is balanced, offering length on the palate and finish, but also defined flavors and freshness. By all indications it's well made, and best of all it tastes as it should. **86 Best Buy** —*M.S. (7/1/2002)*

Errazuriz 2004 Wild Ferment Chardonnay (Casablanca Valley) $21. A whole lot of oak and nuts hit you on the nose, but underneath there's good apple and melon aromas. The palate remains highly oak-infused, with wood at every corner. Finally, however, the wood fades, revealing heady pear, melon, and pineapple. A big wine with some awkwardness. **87** —*M.S. (7/1/2006)*

Errazuriz 2002 Wild Ferment Chardonnay (Casablanca Valley) $19. A moderately successful attempt at a serious, natural-yeast wine. The nose deals a full veneer of toast and popcorn along with baked apple and ripe melon. Flavors of dried apricot, apple, and corn are solid, leading to a long, rich finish. Plenty of body but not much acid. Soft and seemingly on the fade. **86** —*M.S. (11/1/2005)*

Errazuriz 2001 Wild Ferment Chardonnay (Casablanca Valley) $NA. A bit of popcorn and baked apple spice up the largely bland nose, while the palate deals lean apple and lemon flavors. All in all, it's a cleansing, easygoing wine, one with sharp, lemony notes and plenty of pure-acid zing. **85** —*M.S. (6/1/2004)*

Errazuriz 1999 Wild Ferment La Escultura Estate Chardonnay (Casablanca Valley) $22. This is what vineyard selection and winemaker intervention can do to enrich a wine. Everything here is on steroids. The fruit is deep and rich, the oak is smoky and spicy and the finish long and deep. Pretty fancy stuff that might even improve with a few years in the cellar. **90** — *S.H. (2/1/2001)*

Errazuriz 2000 Fumé Blanc (Casablanca Valley) $10. Opens with lemon and grapefruit aromas and a hint of butter and smoke, then turns dry and crisp in the mouth, with lemony flavors. High acidity is balanced by a nice, creamy texture. **85** —*S.H. (5/1/2001)*

Errazuriz 2001 Merlot (Curicó Valley) $10. Good solid drinking at a fair price. Northing fancy, but there's nice dark stone fruit and berry flavors, and the wine is dry and polished, with dusty tannins. **84** —*S.H. (1/1/2002)*

Errazuriz 1999 Don Maximiano Estate Reserva Merlot (Aconcagua Valley) $25. The nose is lovely, with sweet, jammy blackberries and plums, dried spices, and cedar tree bark notes. What follows is a little disappointing in comparison: dull wood, dry leaves, and herbs, over tart plum fruit. Same dried-out leaves, oak, and herbs follow on finish. **82** —*D.T. (7/1/2002)*

Errazuriz 1999 El Decanso Estate Merlot (Curicó Valley) $10. Hooray for the fruit on this beauty! Gobs of freshly crushed blackberries, blueberries, plums, espresso, black currants, and vanilla are charming, and the flavors are every bit as lush. Technically, it's bone dry, but it's one of those wines that tastes fruity sweet. It has elegance and style that belie the value price. Plus, the tannins are soft as velvet. **87 Best Buy** —*S.H. (2/1/2001)*

Errazuriz 2005 Estate Merlot (Curicó Valley) $11. Tar, char, and black fruit work the nose, but there's also a slight hint of wet dog thrown in. The palate is full and grabby, with black cherry, cassis, and plum flavors. Spicy late, with pronounced tannins. A typical big, bold, and slightly raw Chilean Merlot. **86 Best Buy** —*M.S. (11/15/2006)*

Errazuriz 2004 Estate Merlot (Curicó Valley) $11. A fair amount of coffee and mocha are present on the chunky nose, while the palate deals red plum fruit and only the mildest touch of green peppers. Snappy yet savory enough, with chocolate on the textured finish. **86 Best Buy** — *M.S. (11/1/2005)*

Errazuriz 2003 Estate Merlot (Curicó Valley) $11. Heavy and ripe, with some burnt, charred oak. Flavors of plum, berry, and rhubarb are soft and round, with coffee and chocolate notes to the finish. Fits the bill. **84** —*M.S. (2/1/2005)*

Errazuriz 2000 Max Reserva Merlot (Aconcagua Valley) $25. The early impression is that this wine is funky and a touch vegetal. The nose deals mostly pepper and leather, but not much ripe fruit. And while it never gets very rich or fruity, the mouthfeel is o.k. and it fans out and broadens on the slightly green finish. **83** —*M.N. (3/1/2004)*

Errazuriz 2000 Viñedo Chadwick Red Blend (Maipo Valley) $65. Eduardo Chadwick's signature wine is good, albeit a touch awkward on the nose. Aromas of cherry tomato and leather seem mildly sharp, yet there's no evidence of under-ripeness in the mouth. In fact, the cherry, blackberry, and vanilla flavors are lush, while the finish is sweet, oaky, and chocolaty. The blend is Cabernet, Cab Franc, and Carmenère. **87** —*M.S. (3/1/2004)*

Errazuriz 2005 Estate Sauvignon Blanc (Casablanca Valley) $11. Opens up with welcoming kiwi, green melon, and powdered sugar aromas, which are backed by melon and mild green pepper, flavors. The overall take is positive, as the body teeters toward full but doesn't go overboard. More than solid, with lots of mainstream potential. **87 Best Buy** —*M.S. (10/1/2006)*

Errazuriz 2004 Estate Sauvignon Blanc (Casablanca Valley) $11. Simple, fresh, and mainstream, with warm tropical fruit on the nose and palate. Full melon, citrus, and mineral flavors are integrated and satisfying. Finishes zesty and lively, with proper weight and texture. **87 Best Buy** — *M.S. (2/1/2005)*

Errazuriz 2000 Estate Sauvignon Blanc (Casablanca Valley) $10. This estate wine is light and tastes a bit like white grapefruit. The palate runs heavy, and the finish tastes like a blend of grapefruit and celery. **80** — *M.S. (7/1/2003)*

Errazuriz 1999 La Escultura Sauvignon Blanc (Casablanca Valley) $10. A refreshing wine, with nicely ripened fruit and exceptional balance, that's pleasant in every way and a super value, too. The fruit goes beyond citrus into more deeply flavored apricot and pear, and modest sur lie aging adds creamy, buttery notes. This is a lovely wine and one of the best values of the year in Sauvignon/Fume Blanc. **87** —*S.H. (2/1/2001)*

Errazuriz 2005 Late Harvest Sauvignon Blanc (Casablanca Valley) $13. Late-harvest Sauvignon isn't commonplace, and this wine shows both pungency and freshness. The nose is definitely a bit prickly and sweaty, but the palate is loaded with mango and melon. Ultimately tastes like spun fruit, mostly pineapple, sweet melon, and mango. **87** —*M.S. (10/1/2006)*

Errazuriz 1999 Late Harvest Sauvignon Blanc (Casablanca Valley) $11. Honey-like, with hints of apricot, melon, apple, and spice. A hint of earthiness pervades this Chilean dessert wine. **86** —*J.M. (12/1/2002)*

Errazuriz 2006 Single Vineyard Sauvignon Blanc (Casablanca Valley) $20. This Casablanca Valley Sauvignon starts out slowly and quietly before picking up speed and volume. The nose evolves toward piquant and stirring, while the palate deals a good mix of green apple, peppery Thai melon, and citrus zest. It finishes crisp, but with character, and overall it speaks well for the potential of Chilean Sauvignon Blanc. **89** —*M.S. (12/31/2006)*

Errazuriz 2004 La Cumbre Shiraz (Aconcagua Valley) $50. Plenty of oak and coconut grace the modern-styled bouquet, while the palate is round as a balloon, with tons of black cherry and mint flavors. Doubtless it's a chunky red, and the finish runs rich to the point of syrupy. For now the oak and tannins have things under wraps; best to revisit in a year's time. **88** —*M.S. (12/31/2006)*

Errazuriz 2003 La Cumbre Shiraz (Aconcagua Valley) $39. Heavily toasted on the nose, with tobacco, leather, and vanilla along with powerful dark fruit. Sweet and plump in the mouth, with a solid mouthfeel that doesn't falter. Tasty and long on the tail, with the essence of coffee and an inkling of popcorn. Oaky and expensive, but still very good. **88** —*M.S. (11/1/2005)*

Errazuriz 2003 Max Reserva Shiraz (Aconcagua Valley) $19. A lot of mocha and carob on the nose, but also slightly damp and woody. The palate is both sweet and spicy, and the feel is flush if not exactly lush.

CHILE

CHILE

Licorice and vanilla, both wood-driven, define the finish. **85** —*M.S. (11/1/2005)*

Errazuriz 1999 Don Maximiano Estate - Reserva Syrah (Aconcagua Valley) $25. Black fruit up front has an earthy, composty quality; the palate's mixed berries take a back seat to wood. Persistent herb and white-pepper flavors on the finish persist longer than I wanted them to. A rustic, rough-around-the-edges wine that begs for stew or black beans. **86** — *D.T. (7/1/2002)*

Errazuriz 2000 Max Reserva Syrah (Aconcagua Valley) $25. Opens with odd, tanky aromas of veggies and old sox, although the flavors are quite a bit better. If you can get past the smell, the blackberry and tobacco flavors are dry and rich. **83** —*S.H. (1/1/2002)*

Errazuriz Ovalle 2004 Veo Grande Cabernet Sauvignon (Colchagua Valley) $8. Savory at first, with roasted aromas of beets, prune, and raisin. Tastes fairly sweet for a dry Cabernet, as the mouthfeel is almost cloying and sugary. Inoffensive on the finish but flat. **83** —*M.S. (11/15/2006)*

ESTAMPA

Estampa 2003 Gold Assemblage Carménère Red Blend (Colchagua Valley) $18. This Carménère-based heavyweight also packs in Cabernet and Merlot. The aromatic result is of candy and spice, but also some reediness. The palate is powerful and a touch aggressive as bulky tannins and sharp acidity push cherry and plum flavors toward a tight, grabby finish. **86** —*M.S. (10/1/2006)*

Estampa 2004 Reserve Assemblage Cabernet Sauvignon Carménère Petit Verdot Red Blend (Colchagua Valley) $12. With its black olive aromas touched up by spice and subtle dark fruits, this wine performs at a level beyond its price range. The palate features cola, black cherry, and plum, while the finish offers cleansing acids and savory tannins. What a nice, affordable red for a meal off the grill. **89 Best Buy** —*M.S. (11/15/2006)*

Estampa 2004 Reserve Assemblage Carménère-Cabernet Sauvignon-Cabernet Franc Red Blend (Colchagua Valley) $12. A little funky and loud at first but time reveals dark fruit and roasted earth. Comes on big and ripe in the mouth, with cherry and plum leading the way. Maybe it's a bit common and chunky, like your average New World red, but it has its merits and goes down well. **86** —*M.S. (10/1/2006)*

Estampa 2005 Reserve Assemblage White Blend (Central Valley) $12. Predominantly Sauvignon Blanc, and you get those varietal grassy, citric aromas and flavors as the main package. Chardonnay and Viognier at 15% each add roundness and riper flavors, particularly peach and apple. And it's minimally oak-aged, which adds to the mouthfeel. An interesting Chilean blend. **88 Best Buy** —*M.S. (11/15/2006)*

FRANCISCO GILLMORE

Francisco Gillmore 1998 Cabernet Franc (Maule Valley) $27. Some say that wine is a cure-all; that saying rings true here, because this offering tastes like Cab Franc supplemented by a dose of herb-tinged medicine. Red berry, green tobacco, and dusty tannins manage to peek through, but not as much as I'd like. **83** —*D.T. (7/1/2002)*

Francisco Gillmore 2000 Concepcion Cabernet Sauvignon (Maule Valley) $7. This wine from Francisco Gillmore is earthy and full of tomato and leather aromas. The palate is also a bit like tomato and herbs. The finish is tangy, courtesy of healthy acids, while the finish is tannic and a touch hot. **81** —*M.S. (7/1/2003)*

Francisco Gillmore 1998 Concepcion Gran Reserva Cabernet Sauvignon (Maule Valley) $11. From a difficult vintage, this is a strong performance, blending woody notes from barrel aging with earth, cherries, and green herbs. **86** —*C.S. (2/1/2003)*

Francisco Gillmore 1998 Concepcion Reserva Cabernet Sauvignon (Maule Valley) $11. This is a clean, lightweight wine with gripping yet silky tannins. The nose of hickory smoke is wrapped in loam, which repeats on the palate with smoky cherry and fresh green herbs. On the finish, the semisweet herbal quality is a treat. **86** —*K.F. (7/1/2003)*

Francisco Gillmore 2001 Concepcion Chardonnay (Maule Valley) $7. The nose is flat and not very expressive. The flavors are of sweet fruit, but beyond that they are hard to describe. A midland wine with a simple, clean finish and a bit of a waxy mouthfeel. **83** —*M.S. (7/1/2003)*

Francisco Gillmore 1999 Concepcion Gran Reserva Chardonnay (Maule Valley) $19. Heavily oaked, with aromas of popcorn and sawdust. The palate is a touch resiny, but underneath the oak veneer you'll find some ripe apple flavors. The creamy, long finish leaves a somewhat thick and bulky impression, but there's enough vital acidity to save it. **85** —*M.S. (7/1/2003)*

Francisco Gillmore 1999 Concepcion Reserva Chardonnay (Maule Valley) $11. Dark gold in color and on the path toward retirement. There's a strong funk to the nose, one of corn and wood. The palate is thick and oaky, with flavors of vanilla and baked apples. On the finish you get toffee and more vanilla. Despite its age and viscosity, decent acidity keeps it drinkable. **83** —*M.S. (7/1/2003)*

Francisco Gillmore 2000 Concepcion Merlot (Maule Valley) $7. The color is weak and the nose is earthy and chunky, with some funky elements as well. The flavors are simple and uneven. There's some chocolate and berry fruit, but they don't mesh particularly well. And then it's gone, leaving a dull, oaky aftertaste. **81** —*M.S. (7/1/2003)*

Francisco Gillmore 1999 Concepcion Reserva Merlot (Maule Valley) $11. The color is rusty, while the nose is malty and overdone with dried, raisiny fruit. Raspberry and dried cherry flavors are detectable on the palate, but so is some unwelcome vinegar. This wine may have seen better days; now it's barely acceptable. **80** —*M.S. (7/1/2003)*

Francisco Gillmore 2000 Concepcion Gran Reserva Syrah (Maule Valley) $16. Cherry aromas and flavors commingle with earth and toast. Delicate dried herb accents carry through to the finish, which blooms light vanilla at the very end. Deceptively smooth overall, but dusty tannins provide a firm structure. **88** —*K.F. (2/1/2003)*

GRAN DOMINIO

Gran Dominio 1999 San Cayetano Vineyards Gran Reserva Cabernet Franc (Maule Valley) $19. Opens with aromas suggesting cured French olives, white chocolate, and cherry, with a tropical fruit note of banana. Flavors of black cherry aren't bad, and the wine has a nice, gentle but firm mouthfeel. **85** —*S.H. (1/1/2002)*

Gran Dominio 1999 Nueva Aldea Vineyard Gran Reserva Cabernet Sauvignon (Iata Valley) $17. Strong tannins, the kind that numb the palate, make for a bumpy ride. The flavors are young and tight, of barely ripe blackberries and sweet tobacco. Might soften and improve with a few years in the bottle. **84** —*S.H. (1/1/2002)*

Gran Dominio 1999 Nueva Aldea Vineyard Chardonnay (Iata Valley) $14. An interesting and different sort of Chard marked by aromas and flavors of green apples, guava, nectarine, butter, cream, and an elusive mineral quality. It's a bit prickly and sandpapery on the finish. **85** —*S.H. (1/1/2002)*

GRAN ROBLE

Gran Roble 2003 Cabernet Sauvignon (Curicó Valley) $11. Slightly mulchy and damp, with herbal red fruit reflecting plum and cherry. Mildly tannic with a simple finish. Never really finds a groove. **82** —*M.S. (11/1/2005)*

Gran Roble 2003 Carmenère (Curicó Valley) $11. Chunky, ripe, and meaty, with aromas of black cherry, raisin, cinnamon, and earth. One of this label's best offerings to date; the palate deals monotone but healthy plum flavors before a dark, espresso-tinged finish. No real depth or complexity, but good. **84** —*M.S. (11/1/2005)*

Gran Roble 2003 Chardonnay (Curicó Valley) $11. Burnt, chemical aromas almost render it not worth rating, but the mouthfeel isn't bad and the flavors of sweet pear and apple are acceptable. **80** —*M.S. (7/1/2005)*

GUELBENZU

Guelbenzu 2002 Jardin Cabernet Blend (Colchagua Valley) $9. At first this wine is a touch skunky and strange, but they say time heals all wounds, and such is the case here. As it unfolds in the glass the wine offers sweet berry fruit and some wood notes. The finish is a little like beets and spice, but in that there's intrigue and appeal. Good tannins and acids ensure a proper mouthfeel. **85** —*M.S. (7/1/2003)*

Guelbenzu 2003 Hoppe Cabernet Sauvignon-Carmenère (Colchagua Valley) $15. The blend is 50-50 Cabernet Sauvignon and Carmenère, and the end result seems a touch dull and reserved. There's coconut and blackberry on the nose, but the aromas are quiet. The palate, however, is loud, with grape, vanilla, and coconut flavors. Seems to be not in the best harmony. **84** —*M.S. (3/1/2006)*

Guelbenzu 2003 Jardin Cabernet Sauvignon-Carmenère (Colchagua Valley) $8. This Navarran winery is making wines in Chile that taste a lot like what they are making in Spain. The nose has some herbal character along with solid berry aromas. Chewy and full in the mouth, with cherry and medicinal flavors. Good mouthfeel. It's 90% Cab and 10% Carmenère. **85 Best Buy** —*M.S. (7/1/2006)*

Guelbenzu 2002 Jardin Chardonnay (Colchagua Valley) $9. Anise and mineral add character to the aggressive, starchy nose. Flavors of ripe apple and mustard create a heavier-than-usual palate, although there's ample acidity to keep it more or less balanced. The finish is dry, with just a touch of citrus flavor. And at the very end it turns thin and rough. **83** —*M.S. (7/1/2003)*

HARAS

Haras 2001 Elegance Cabernet Sauvignon (Maipo Valley) $40. Kicks off with some herbal, foresty notes but then finds its fruit in the form of ripe plum and blackberry. The palate offers all the black fruit you could ask for as well as a dollop of chocolate fudge. Comes up a bit short of the upper echelon but still it has a lot of positives. **89** —*M.S. (5/1/2006)*

Haras 2003 Chardonnay (Maipo Valley) $11. Haras de Pirque's basic Chard works because it doesn't try to do too much. Basic peach, pear, and pineapple aromas pave the way toward apple, coconut, and banana flavors. Good texture; solid at its core. **86 Best Buy** —*M.S. (2/1/2005)*

Haras 2003 Character Chardonnay (Maipo Valley) $14. A little bit of waxy cheese interferes with the apple and pear nose, while flavors of pineapple and orange are live-wire and forward, courtesy of piercing acids. Finishes in a style that's consistent with the rest of the wine. **85** —*M.S. (5/1/2006)*

Haras 2004 Elegance Chardonnay (Maipo Valley) $20. Spritzy in the mouth, with a ton of sweetness. There's white corn, caramel, honeydew, and apples on the palate, while the finish turns ultra-sweet, borders on cloying. Seems a bit on the over-ripe side. **84** —*M.S. (5/1/2006)*

HARAS DE PIRQUE

Haras de Pirque 2002 Character Cabernet Sauvignon (Maipo Valley) $14. Plenty of coffee and toast on the nose, which also pumps olive and some green bean. The palate is firm, with encoding tannins. Flavors of cassis and black cherry are convincing, but there's also some green to the package. Structured to age but probably won't improve much. **85** —*M.S. (7/1/2006)*

Haras de Pirque 2001 Character Cabernet Sauvignon (Maipo Valley) $20. Inky dark in the glass, with a dense, smoky nose that succeeds in setting up the wine's jacked-up, high-wattage palate. This wine needs more time in bottle to settle down. **89** —*M.S. (3/1/2004)*

Haras de Pirque 2001 Elegance Cabernet Sauvignon (Maipo Valley) $40. Soft yet firm, and sweet yet stylish. The nose is dark and loaded with coffee and mocha, while in the mouth the blackberry and cassis really flow forth. With length and size compounded by firm, integrated tannins, this is a very solid signature wine for this new winery. **91** —*M.S. (3/1/2004)*

Haras de Pirque 2002 Estate Cabernet Sauvignon (Maipo Valley) $10. Chilean Cabernet can barely be more typical than this. The nose is deep and earthy, with olive, tobacco, and blackberry. Fairly full-bodied, with medium-strength tannins and good acidity. Significantly more brawny than cerebral, but appealing. Good core fruit dictates the structure. **87 Best Buy** —*M.S. (7/1/2006)*

Haras de Pirque 2001 Estate Cabernet Sauvignon (Maipo Valley) $11. Forceful and earthy, with a racy black fruit and chocolate nose. It's quite aggressive in the mouth, with piercing acidity that pushes the flavors and berry quotient to another level. Shows a slight hint of herbaceousness at the center, but overall it's ripe and solid. **88** —*M.S. (3/1/2004)*

Haras de Pirque 2002 Estate Carmenère (Maipo Valley) $11. Spicy and alive in the nose, with a touch of herbal green but also plenty of deeper berry fruit. This one tastes good; the palate is long and substantial, with chocolate and pepper notes jazzing it up. **87** —*M.S. (3/1/2004)*

Haras de Pirque 2002 Character Chardonnay (Maipo Valley) $15. More smoky and yeasty on the nose than the Estate, with lemon, grapefruit, and mineral notes. This wine is much more citric and tight than many, yet there's a barrel influence and vanilla that manage to poke their way through. **87** —*M.S. (3/1/2004)*

Haras de Pirque 2003 Elegance Chardonnay (Maipo Valley) $25. Fairly smoky, with aromas of campfire and roasted corn. Woody on the palate, but also plenty of citrus in the form of lemon and orange. Consistent throughout, meaning the wood resin influence is primary. **85** —*M.S. (2/1/2005)*

Haras de Pirque 2002 Elegance Chardonnay (Maipo Valley) $25. The bouquet offers a strong blast of toasty oak along with apple, lemon, and mango. This is no weak wine; in fact, it hits maximum overdrive in terms of zesty fruit and raw power. A full-force experience, with subtlety not really coming into play. **88** —*M.S. (3/1/2004)*

Haras de Pirque 2005 Estate Chardonnay (Maipo Valley) $10. Toasty for sure, with a strong blast of popcorn. Ripe and intense across the full-bodied palate, with bold shots of honey, apple, and pear. Not deep or complex; winds up sort of sugary. **84** —*M.S. (7/1/2006)*

Haras de Pirque 2002 Estate Chardonnay (Maipo Valley) $11. Zesty and driving, but with a true barrel-fermented personality. Flavors veer toward the tropical side of things, so look for mango, pineapple, and citrus. Some citrus pith and bitterness appear on the finish. **86** —*M.S. (3/1/2004)*

Haras de Pirque 2004 Character Sauvignon Blanc (Maipo Valley) $14. Light peach and mineral aromas are subtle and chunky. The flavors veer toward juicy orange and pineapple, while the overall take is one of freshness. Not complex in the least; very zesty. **84** —*M.S. (3/1/2006)*

Haras de Pirque 2002 Character Sauvignon Blanc (Maipo Valley) $15. Round, chunky, and sturdy, with big citrus aromas along with bold flavors of melon and honey. The mouthfeel is huge, courtesy of the wine being one-third barrel fermented, but it's a little unusual and awkward, running a touch hot. **86** —*M.S. (3/1/2004)*

Haras de Pirque 2005 Estate Sauvignon Blanc (Maipo Valley) $10. Gritty and candied at first, with citrus and green herb taking control as it opens up. Slightly tart orange and lemon flavors are predominant, while the finish is simple and citrusy. Kind of bulky but still zesty. **84** —*M.S. (7/1/2006)*

Haras de Pirque 2002 Estate Sauvignon Blanc (Maipo Valley) $11. Citrus, lemon, and honey aromas are big and clumsy, while overall the wine runs very thick and mouth-filling for Sauvignon Blanc. Maybe that's because 10% was aged in oak. As for flavors, look primarily for orange and grapefruit. **85** —*M.S. (3/1/2004)*

Haras de Pirque 2003 Character Syrah (Maipo Valley) $14. Alluring on the nose, with herbs, spice, olive, and mocha accenting rugged berry aromas. Big and jammy in the mouth, with black plum circled by coffee and clove notes. Weighs in as large, and it's tannic as nails. But if you like yours ripe and ready, this should make the grade. **88** —*M.S. (7/1/2006)*

IN SITU

In Situ 2003 Gran Reserva Cabernet Sauvignon (Aconcagua Valley) $20. A bit minty and herbal, with plenty of oak along with non-descript red fruit. Chunky and simple, with overt wood notes that come across as resiny. **83** —*M.S. (11/1/2005)*

J. & F. LURTON

J. & F. Lurton 2002 Gran Araucano Cabernet Sauvignon (Colchagua Valley) $35. Cherry, cassis, and pipe tobacco on the nose set up flavors of candied red fruit. The feel is a bit thick and sticky at first, and then the mouthfeel gives way to pronounced acidity. Not quite at the upper level; there's a touch of artificiality to the wine. **85** —*M.S. (5/1/2006)*

J. & F. Lurton 2005 Hacienda Araucano Cabernet Sauvignon (Central Valley) $11. Dry and leathery, with grabby red fruit propped up by forward tannins and firm acidity. Tastes of raspberry and bramble, with some tea notes thrown in for complexity. **84** —*M.S. (11/15/2006)*

J. & F. Lurton 2004 Hacienda Araucano Cabernet Sauvignon (Central Valley) $11. Lightweight and fresh, with spicy, minty aromas accenting deeper cherry and berry scents. Medium on the palate, with cherry, chocolate, and peppery flavors. Finishes fresh, with a touch of tobacco and vanilla. **85** —*M.S. (5/1/2006)*

J. & F. Lurton 2003 Hacienda Araucano Cabernet Sauvignon (Colchagua Valley) $10. Lots of red fruit on the nose along with cherry tomato and plum. Juicy and lively on the tongue, with good strawberry and plum flavors. Finishes smooth and steady, with a spot of beet and green bean on the aftertaste. Positive as a whole. **87 Best Buy** —*M.S. (11/1/2005)*

J. & F. Lurton 2002 Araucano Clos de Lolol Cabernet Sauvignon-Carmenère (Colchagua Valley) $25. Round and ripe, with forward aromas and spice. Ripeness isn't an issue with this Cabernet-Carmenère blend; it's pretty jumpy and electric, with amplified red berry flavors. From a warm, dry subregion of Colchagua. **87** —*M.S. (3/1/2006)*

J. & F. Lurton 2003 Alka Carmenère (Colchagua Valley) $65. Intensely oaked, with lemon peel and charcoal on the nose, which also features tar and crude oil. Below the surface there's cherry, red plum, and concentration. Powerful, with tannin and grabby acids. Not the smoothest wine but commendable for its power. Should improve in the future; this was only the second vintage. **87** —*M.S. (3/1/2006)*

J. & F. Lurton 2002 Alka Carmenère (Colchagua Valley) $55. Nice on the nose, with subtle lavender, plum, chocolate, and green pepper notes. Extremely rich and creamy, maybe too much so; the palate is a heavyweight, with black plum, fudge, and vanilla. Very soft and low-acid, almost like dessert. Has its qualities and faults. **87** —*M.S. (2/1/2005)*

J. & F. Lurton 2004 Hacienda Araucano Carmenère (Colchagua Valley) $11. This wine makes up the bulk of the production at this fledgling winery in Lolol. It's pungent and leathery, with a certain lean freshness that isn't at all offensive but seems a bit raw. Shows a bit of the variety's sauciness. Snappy and tight. **85** —*M.S. (3/1/2006)*

J. & F. Lurton 2003 Hacienda Araucano Carmenère (Colchagua Valley) $10. Deeper and more syrupy than many, but still nice. Tar, blackberry, and warm earth aromas emanate from the bouquet, followed by a sweet, thick palate that feels heavy due to relatively low acidity. Fully ripe with a fine mouthfeel. Not vegetal in the least. **87 Best Buy** —*M.S. (12/1/2004)*

J. & F. Lurton 2002 Hacienda Araucano Carmenère (Colchagua Valley) $10. Spicy up front, with a nose of brandied fruit and herbs, the latter arguably a euphemistic term for "mildly vegetal." Flavors of cassis and plum carry the thin palate, while the finish is modest. **84** —*M.S. (8/1/2004)*

J. & F. Lurton 2003 Gran Araucano Chardonnay (Colchagua Valley) $19. A reserve-level Chardonnay that's soft, yeasty, and smooth, but carries enough zip and structure to avoid being flabby. The toasty palate offers fine apple and lemon notes, but the main thing here is the wavy body the coddles plenty of oak, vanilla, and buttered toast. **89** —*M.S. (2/1/2005)*

J. & F. Lurton 2002 Gran Araucano Chardonnay (Colchagua Valley) $18. Oaky but good, with plenty of toasted barrel notes, popcorn, and white chocolate. Without solid fruit for the foundation, this would be an overoaked, problematic wine. But with forward baked apple, mango and lemon flavors, the oak succeeds in adding a smoky, toasted edge. **86** —*M.S. (6/1/2004)*

J. & F. Lurton 2005 Hacienda Araucano Chardonnay (Colchagua Valley) $11. Rather toasty and buttery for a wine backed by simple pear fruit. Emphasizes smooth but limited pear flavors warmed by firm notes of popcorn and brown butter. Soft in style. **84** —*M.S. (5/1/2006)*

J. & F. Lurton 2004 Hacienda Araucano Chardonnay (Colchagua Valley) $10. Plump and leesy, with aromas of corn and vanilla. The plate shows additional vanilla as well as melon and pear. Warm and textured on the finish, with a bit of snap. **86 Best Buy** —*M.S. (11/1/2005)*

J. & F. Lurton 2005 Gran Araucano Sauvignon Blanc (Casablanca Valley) $20. Sharp and prickly on the nose, with heavy blasts of under-ripe pineapple and grapefruit. Celery and bell pepper flavors dance with acid-based citrus to create a wanting whole. Finishes with pickled flavors and oversized acidity. **82** —*M.S. (3/1/2006)*

J. & F. Lurton 2004 Gran Araucano Sauvignon Blanc (Casablanca Valley) $19. Heavy grapefruit and asparagus aromas create that grassy, herba-

ceous nose that some love and others dislike. In the mouth, there's additional apple and citrus but still a lot of pickle and grass. Zesty on the tongue, but too herbaceous for these taste buds. **85** —*M.S. (7/1/2005)*

J. & F. Lurton 2002 Gran Araucano Sauvignon Blanc (Casablanca Valley) $18. Very vegetal, with strong aromas of canned green beans and asparagus. Flat and heavy on the palate, with more green flavors. Lurton's basic '03 Sauvignon is a much better wine. **80** —*M.S. (6/1/2004)*

J. & F. Lurton 2006 Hacienda Araucano Sauvignon Blanc (Central Valley) $11. Fairly prickly and sharp, especially early on. Time allows it to open somewhat, and what comes out is a sweet, mildly sticky wine with pear and melon flavors. Finishes slightly peppery, with capsicum and citrusy bitterness. Not out of whack or poorly made, but not that thrilling either. **84** —*M.S. (12/31/2006)*

J. & F. Lurton 2005 Hacienda Araucano Sauvignon Blanc (Central Valley) $11. Fairly hard and peanutty at first, with a touch of burnt jet fuel. That sulfur-driven element fades to let loose pleasant apple, pear, and green herb flavors. Lasting on the tail end, but not complex. **84** —*M.S. (7/1/2006)*

J. & F. Lurton 2004 Hacienda Araucano Sauvignon Blanc (Central Valley) $9. Falls firmly into the herbaceous, grassy style that emphasizes pickle barrel, jalapeño, and asparagus. But underneath you'll also find apple, melon, and a smidge of alfalfa. Good feel throughout, and consistent. **85 Best Buy** —*M.S. (7/1/2005)*

J. & F. Lurton 2003 Hacienda Araucano Sauvignon Blanc (Central Valley) $10. Jacques and François Lurton's fledgling Chilean venture seems to be on the right track. This attractive Sauvignon Blanc features snappy grapefruit, citrus, and celery aromas, which are backed up by full and satisfying grapefruit, passion fruit, and lemon peel flavors. The finish is lengthy and pure. A winner in its class. **88 Best Buy** —*M.S. (6/1/2004)*

J. BOUCHON

J. Bouchon 2003 Reserva Especial Cabernet Sauvignon (Maule Valley) $14. Fairly herbal in its aromas: olive, pepper, and tomato run the show. More olive character leads the savory palate, with dark fruit running second. Tight but not tannic, with a medium to full mouthfeel. **84** —*M.S. (7/1/2006)*

J. Bouchon 2004 Reserva Especial Carmenère (Maule Valley) $14. Olive aromas greet you, followed by chocolate, plum, and basic berry flavors. A solid wine with body, but there isn't much in the way of depth or complexity. Full and medium in tannins. **84** —*M.S. (7/1/2006)*

J. Bouchon 2004 Reserva Especial Malbec (Maule Valley) $14. Unrefined, chunky, and reduced is how you'd best describe this compact Malbec that is packed too tight with unrelenting plum and berry fruit that also tastes of beets. Has its merits, but in the end it doesn't grow on your palate. **81** —*M.S. (5/1/2006)*

J. Bouchon 2004 Merlot (Maule Valley) $9. Murky at first, with emerging aromas of animal cookies and berries. Lean and choppy in the mouth, with red fruit softened by chocolate and marshmallow notes. Runs a bit sticky. **82** —*M.S. (5/1/2006)*

KINGSTON FAMILY

Kingston Family 2004 Alazan Pinot Noir (Casablanca Valley) $28. Hillside fruit yields a seductive wine with flowery aromas offset by black cherry. Settles on the meaty, earthy, brawny style, with vigorous bitter chocolate, caramel, and vanilla flavors stemming from the new oak. The real deal in Chilean Pinot Noir. **89** —*M.S. (11/1/2005)*

Kingston Family 2004 Tobiano Pinot Noir (Casablanca Valley) $18. A "second" wine, if you will, with warm, dusty cherry aromas along with mineral and spice notes. Runs a touch hot and aggressive, with medium depth and fairly high alcohol (14.5%). Still, it shows true-blue Pinot character and poise. **87** —*M.S. (11/1/2005)*

Kingston Family 2004 Cariblanco Sauvignon Blanc (Casablanca Valley) $15. The bouquet deals a fine mix of citrus, melon, bell pepper, and asparagus, yet it's not vegetal. Shows weight and sweetness on the palate, thus it will offset Asian foods like magic. Interestingly, it's fermented in stainless steel barrels, not tanks, and with natural yeasts. **90** —*M.S. (11/1/2005)*

CHILE

Kingston Family 2003 Bayo Oscuro Syrah (Casablanca Valley) $28. To get this wine ripe, the grapes were picked in May (the equivalent of November in the U.S.). And still it has a zesty persona. The bouquet offers distant, meaty notes along with shades of asphalt and violets, but it's fairly tart and juicy in the mouth, with sharp raspberry fruit. **85** — *M.S. (11/1/2005)*

KUYEN

Kuyen 2003 Syrah-Cabernet (Maipo Valley) $23. Spicy and dark, with deep aromas of plum and berry mixed with crude oil and red pepper flake. For sure this is a serious, well-crafted blend; the fruit is ripe and tasty, but there's also enveloping oak touches and finely managed tannins. Covers the mouth in a blanket of texture and flavor. **89** —*M.S. (3/1/2006)*

Kuyen 2002 Red Wine Syrah-Cabernet (Maipo Valley) $22. Alvaro Espinoza, owner of this label, has thrown a lot of hot, spicy oak at this tannic heavyweight, and it may need a few years to show its true identity. For now, it's dark and brooding, with black plum, blackberry, and bitter chocolate flavors. Finishes rather hard and acidic, which time may tame. Needs food to match the vise-grip tannins. It's 70% Syrah and 30% Cabernet. **88** —*M.S. (2/1/2005)*

LA CAPITANA

La Capitana 2002 Cabernet Sauvignon (Cachapoal Valley) $12. The nose is slightly rosy, while overall it's a clean and welcoming red. Flavors of berry fruit are of modest power, while the finish offers chocolate and coffee. **84** —*M.S. (3/1/2004)*

La Capitana 2002 Carmenère (Cachapoal Valley) $12. Clean and fruity, with a meaty character that conveys ripeness. More spicy and interesting than some of the other wines from La Rosa, with most of what you want: spice, size, and fruit. **87** —*M.S. (3/1/2004)*

La Capitana 2003 Chardonnay (Cachapoal Valley) $12. Creamier and bigger than the winery's regular Chard, but not necessarily better. Features good acids and plenty of vanilla along with tropical fruit flavors. **85** — *M.S. (3/1/2004)*

LA PALMA

La Palma 2003 Cabernet Sauvignon (Cachapoal Valley) $7. More deep and grapey than the Cab-Merlot blend, but ultimately it falls into the same general range of acceptability. Flavors of bubble gum seem less than pure. **83** —*M.S. (3/1/2004)*

La Palma 2002 Cabernet Sauvignon (Cachapoal Valley) $7. Saturated in color and quite big, with penetrating aromas that scream of youth and exuberance. There's sun-drenched ripe berry flavors and some big tannins that result in a grippy mouthfeel and ultimately a starched palate. Drink with cheeseburgers, London broil, and the like. **85 Best Buy** — *M.S. (7/1/2003)*

La Palma 2001 Cabernet Sauvignon (Rapel Valley) $10. Medium-weight (more Gamay than Cabernet in the heft department) with a soft, subtle dusty texture, this Rapel Valley Cab offers red berry and dried spice aromas, and red plum and cedar flavors. Goes down so easily that you just might forget that wine has alcohol in it. **87 Best Buy** —*D.T. (7/1/2002)*

La Palma 2000 Reserve Cabernet Sauvignon (Rapel Valley) $12. Tired red fruit lurks under the black pepper and charred oak flavors on the palate, though the woody, rustic mouthfeel is interesting. Nose is rather mute, with a little dried herb showing through. **83** —*D.T. (7/1/2002)*

La Palma 1999 Reserve Cabernet Sauvignon (Rapel Valley) $10. Starts off with reductive aromas of road tar and swamp mud, but has plenty of earthy black currant flavors to balance things out. Lead pencil and tobacco elements grace the palate and sturdy tannins frame the finish. A full, rugged and somewhat rustic expression of Cabernet. **89 Best Buy** —*J.C. (3/1/2002)*

La Palma 1998 Reserve Cabernet Sauvignon (Rapel Valley) $10. This wine displays good color and structure, but there is just not much in the way of aroma or flavor here. Except for some minimal cassis on the nose, the wine is rather thin and weedy. A disappointment. **81** —*M.N. (1/1/2004)*

La Palma 2001 Cabernet Sauvignon-Merlot (Rapel Valley) $10. There's not much to ponder here—just blackberry and oak, from beginning to end. Grapes from this medium-bodied, 60-40 Cab-Merlot blend come from the La Palmería Vineyard. **83** —*D.T. (7/1/2002)*

La Palma 2002 Estate Bottled Cabernet Sauvignon-Merlot (Cachapoal Valley) $10. Very forward and young, with an overt, grapey style. This wine doesn't walk lightly, as it starts out more positive than it finishes. The plum, cassis, and berry fruit is really ripe and active, but there's also some aggressive acidity that makes it more tangy and sharp than ideal. **86** —*M.S. (7/1/2003)*

La Palma 1999 Reserve Cabernet Sauvignon-Merlot (Rapel Valley) $10. Dark fruit, Japanese seaweed, and oak aromas open to black fruit, black pepper and green-herb flavors. Tannins are a rustic and a little drying; try with sauced beef. **85** —*D.T. (7/1/2002)*

La Palma 2001 Reserve Est Bottled Est Grown Carmenère (Cachapoal Valley) $10. Pickled aromas mix with the scents of a field or brier patch. All together the blend is funky and not too welcoming. A palate of lean raspberry fruit and the veggies won't win a lot of fans, but if you drink it quickly and without too much analysis, you might find it pleasant enough. **82** —*M.S. (7/1/2003)*

La Palma 2003 Chardonnay (Cachapoal Valley) $8. Fruity, with floral aromas that are ripe and clean. Flavors of pineapple and the local cherimoya are thin but nice. If properly chilled down, this one has "quaffable" written all over it. **86 Best Buy** —*M.S. (3/1/2004)*

La Palma 2001 Chardonnay (Rapel Valley) $10. The ultra-light color portends a light wine with pear and apple fruit, plenty of flowery sweetness, and a surprisingly full, fresh finish. It's not a bad little wine, given its modest aspirations. **83** —*M.S. (7/1/2003)*

La Palma 2000 Chardonnay (Rapel Valley) $6. The sweet-smelling aroma of vanilla dominates the nose of this wine, followed up on the palate by more vanilla and some indistinct fruit. Creamy and soft. **82** —*J.C. (3/1/2002)*

La Palma 1999 Chardonnay (Rapel Valley) $7. Mild hay and peachy aromas mark the nose and palate of this simple and light Chardonnay. The mouthfeel is pleasant but there isn't the weight, depth, or length of flavor to warrant a great deal of attention. **82** —*M.M. (1/1/2004)*

La Palma 2002 Estate Bottled Chardonnay (Cachapoal Valley) $8. Pineapple and other tropical fruits comprise the simple, straight-forward nose. Pear and tangerine flavors come across sharp, as does the finish. The wine is a bit edgy and lean on its own. **83** —*M.S. (7/1/2003)*

La Palma 2000 Reserve Chardonnay (Rapel Valley) $12. Straight-ahead apples and pears define the nose, which is entirely standard but clean. The same apple and pear fruit comes forward on the palate, but there's also a good edge to it that becomes the basis of a dry, decent finish. A bit flat, but very drinkable. **83** —*M.S. (7/1/2002)*

La Palma 1999 Reserve Chardonnay (Rapel Valley) $10. A real mainstream Chard, with appealing pineapple and apple notes. It's mid-weight, with lively acidity that supports the fruit and a pleasing, if slightly one-dimensional, flavor profile. **85** —*J.F. (8/1/2001)*

La Palma 2003 Merlot (Cachapoal Valley) $7. Micro-oxidation during the winemaking process has softened the tannins and body, but the flavors are vegetal, with only modest notes of chocolate adding character. **82** — *M.S. (3/1/2004)*

La Palma 2002 Merlot (Cachapoal Valley) $7. Aromas of graham cracker and chocolaty fruit yield something similar to berry pie. The mouth is grapey and full, with sizable tannins and not much finesse. With airing this wine grows more cumbersome and untamed. **84** —*M.S. (7/1/2003)*

La Palma 2001 Merlot (Rapel Valley) $10. Mouthfilling though not necessarily nuanced, this Merlot offers blackberry, oak, and earth flavors, and similar aromas. A great choice for casual circumstances or big gatherings. **84** —*D.T. (7/1/2002)*

La Palma 2000 Merlot (Rapel Valley) $6. This jammy, plump wine is packed with fruity flavors of black cherries and blackberries; also some chocolate and cola. Good quaffing wine or bar pour. **84 Best Buy** —*J.C. (3/1/2002)*

CHILE

La Palma 1999 Merlot (Rapel Valley) $8. Opening with a bouquet of red berries complemented by an earthy element, this Merlot offers more fruit on the palate, together with a spicy note. A medium-weight wine with decent acidity, it finishes dry, with more berry and earth notes. **85** —*M.M. (2/1/2001)*

La Palma 2000 Reserve Merlot (Rapel Valley) $12. Fans of dark oak will enjoy this Cab, which is big on char, green herb, and dry tannins. Though there is a little plum and black cherry fruit underneath the oak, the midpalate still wants a little more oomph, and more fruit. **83** —*D.T. (7/1/2002)*

La Palma 2003 Merlot-Cabernet Sauvignon (Rapel Valley) $8. Forward and a touch bitter, with round, grippy tannins pushing basic black fruit flavors and sweetness **83** —*M.S. (3/1/2004)*

La Palma 2003 Sauvignon Blanc (Rapel Valley) $8. Clean and pure, with aromas of green grass, mint and passion fruit. Crisp on the palate, and lean on the finish. It's snappy and tight, with a welcome lightness. **85** —*M.S. (3/1/2004)*

La Palma 2002 Estate Bottled Sauvignon Blanc (Cachapoal Valley) $8. Simple, open, and ready to drink. The nose is floral, with hints of fresh pear. The flavor profile turns to citrus in the form of orange and pineapple, and then comes a full-force but fairly collected finish. **86 Best Buy** —*M.S. (7/1/2003)*

LA PLAYA

La Playa 1994 Maxima Claret Bordeaux Blend (Maipo Valley) $21. Loads of toasty oak, some mild cherry, and plum mark this Bordeaux-style blend. The fruit is a bit lean, but the wine has appeal and is reminiscent of classic Rioja in weight and balance—not dense or extracted and maybe a touch woody, but still likeable. **85** *(2/1/2001)*

La Playa 2002 Axel Primero Cabernet Blend (Colchagua Valley) $30. Very sturdy and measured, with ripe cherry and berry aromas touched up by a blast of leather and black olive. The palate on this Cab-dominated blend shows familiar but likable cassis, black cherry, and cola flavors. Tannic and firm late, with a shot of chocolate to sweeten things up. **88** —*M.S. (7/1/2006)*

La Playa 1996 Claret Maxima Cabernet Blend (Maipo Valley) $23. Aged for one year in new French oak, this Claret (68% Cabernet Sauvignon, 25% Merlot, and 7% Cab Franc) has dusty tannins that make the strong blackberry and blueberry flavors that much more subtle. Roasted red and blueberries are subdued on the nose. Nothing about it is overt, but that'll probably make it that much more of a crowd-pleaser. **85** —*D.T. (7/1/2002)*

La Playa 2003 Axel Cabernet Sauvignon (Colchagua Valley) $20. The surprise of the moment from Chile has to be this full-throttle keg of dynamite Cabernet. It's a cellar wannabe with credentials. First off, it's brilliantly ripe, with forceful black cherry, cinnamon, and wood spice on the palate. Huge tannins, poking acids and a couple of floors' worth of depth make it praiseworthy. **92 Cellar Selection** —*M.S. (7/1/2006)*

La Playa 2003 Block Selection Cabernet Sauvignon (Colchagua Valley) $11. With hickory, coal, and spice to the dark nose, this ranks as a masculine Cab with nary a flaw. The palate is chunky and ripe, with sweet dark fruit flavors. And the finish is spicy and full, with meaty but suave tannins. A high watermark for the La Playa label. **88 Best Buy** —*M.S. (11/1/2005)*

La Playa 2003 Estate Cabernet Sauvignon (Colchagua Valley) $8. Starts with a nutty, earthy personality before shedding that for more recognizable plum and berry characteristics. Features jumpy red fruit with forward acidity. The nose and palate don't seem to be on the same page, but the whole is o.k. **83** —*M.S. (7/1/2006)*

La Playa 2004 Estate Rose Cabernet Sauvignon (Colchagua Valley) $8. Light fruit, muddled aromas, candied flavors and a heavy aftertaste don't really add up to a lot. Yes, it's acceptable. But it's also aging quickly and won't be improving. **81** —*M.S. (5/1/2006)*

La Playa 2005 Rosé Cabernet Sauvignon (Colchagua Valley) $7. Generally speaking, it smells nice. In the mouth, the palate is a touch sugary and swirled with applesauce and berry flavors. Finishes heavy, sweet, and round. Good, but unexciting. **83** —*M.S. (10/1/2006)*

La Playa 2001 Estate Reserve Carmenère (Colchagua Valley) $10. Pungent and borderline sharp at first, this wine ultimately finds its legs and comes together fairly nicely. The mouth is round and quite deep, with good plum, cherry, and spice elements. The finish is jammy and full, with good tannins and proper balance. This is Carmenère in a very mainstream, likable form. **87 Best Buy** —*M.S. (7/1/2003)*

La Playa 2005 Block Selection Estate Reserve Chardonnay (Casablanca Valley) $10. A touch loud and foxy, with gritty aromas along with apple, spice, and wood. The palate runs big and creamy, but not overtly flabby courtesy of spunky acidity. Finishes with smoke and a lot of wood resin. Aims for the pinnacle but does not quite get there. **85 Best Buy** —*M.S. (11/15/2006)*

La Playa 2000 Estate Bottled Chardonnay (Maipo Valley) $7. The ripe pineapple and orange aromas and flavors here have appeal and there's a barely perceptible fizziness—or is it bright acidity—on the palate. All in all, the wine pleases and the fairly sweet fruit flavors are nicely balanced and checked by a slight dry chalkiness on the finish. **85** —*M.M. (1/1/2004)*

La Playa 2002 Estate Reserve Chardonnay (Colchagua Valley) $10. Fresh and clean, with light, lemony aromas in addition to tropical fruit. The palate is textured and full, with fairly pure apple and pineapple flavors and some nuttiness. Everything works here, including the smooth, lengthy finish. **87 Best Buy** —*M.S. (7/1/2003)*

La Playa 2003 Estate Reserve Chardonnay (Maipo Valley) $11. Opens with a highly perfumed bouquet of lime, anise, and a hint of paraffin. Delicate and fresh apple, lime, and stone-fruit flavors follow. Off-beat and slightly lean, but has nice balance. **84** —*J.F. (8/1/2001)*

La Playa 2003 Reserve Chardonnay (Colchagua Valley) $10. Full and chunky, with a nose of corn cakes, melon and a touch of pickled oak. Banana, mango and melon flavors are sweet and candied, but just enough acidity keeps it on an even keel. Good, but with a sugary side to it. **85 Best Buy** —*M.S. (2/1/2005)*

La Playa 2004 Merlot (Colchagua Valley) $8. Firm and a bit toasty, with some rubber and dark fruit on the nose. Offers sweet berry fruit and kirsch flavors and manages to stay on form through the finish. Likable and on the money. **85 Best Buy** —*M.S. (11/1/2005)*

La Playa 2001 Estate Reserve Merlot (Colchagua Valley) $10. Rubbery, with hot cherry and blackberry aromas. Feels heavy and tastes of nondescript jammy fruit. **81** —*M.S. (7/1/2005)*

La Playa 1999 Estate Reserve Merlot (Colchagua Valley) $10. This is a late release, but it's in good shape. The nose is earthy and dense, with just a nip of wet fur and forest floor. The palate is all about sweet berries and ripeness, while the finish is warm and lengthy. It's solid and without any obvious flaws even if it doesn't thump its chest and overwhelm you. **87 Best Buy** —*M.S. (7/1/2003)*

La Playa 1998 Claret Red Blend (Maipo Valley) $10. This wine, like so many from the 1998 vintage in Chile, is very light in texture and displays little depth. The flavors are accurate for a claret—mild berry and a touch of earth—and there's even a decent finish. A light quaff; don't expect weight. **83** —*M.M. (2/1/2001)*

La Playa 2003 Estate Sauvignon Blanc (Colchagua Valley) $7. Flat and heavy smelling, with sugary apple and mango flavors, which are strange for S.B. Nonetheless, it's adequately fresh, with some lemon and pineapple thrown in to stir interest. On the negative side, it's overly sweet. **82** —*M.S. (8/1/2004)*

La Playa 2000 Estate Bottled Sauvignon Blanc (Maipo Valley) $8. Smells like Sauvignon Blanc, with characteristic pink grapefruit, gooseberry, and passion fruit aromas. Just lacks a little zip on the palate, where the medium-weight, low-acid flavors don't quite carry through. **83** —*J.C. (3/1/2002)*

La Playa 2003 Axel Syrah (Colchagua Valley) $20. A bit obtuse and cluttered to begin with but it opens nicely to show black olive, berry, and earth notes in front of plum, blackberry, and cherry flavors. Truth be told, it's a touch common and anonymous, but it's a good red wine that fits the bill. **87** —*M.S. (7/1/2006)*

CHILE

LAURA HARTWIG

Laura Hartwig 1999 Gran Reserva Cabernet Blend (Colchagua Valley) $23. At two-thirds Cabernet, 20% Merlot, and 15% Carmenère, this French oak-aged beauty features earth, rose petals, and some bread dough on its bouquet. The wine represents the top of the line for the boutique Santa Laura winery, and it competes favorably with the best Chile has to offer, but at a fraction of the price. It's layered, creamy, and large, with tannins that are as soft as silk. **90** —*M.S. (3/1/2002)*

Laura Hartwig 2001 Cabernet Sauvignon (Colchagua Valley) $12. Very ripe, bordering on overdone, with raisin and black cherry aromas. The mouth is soft and spicy, with cassis, black plum and dark chocolate flavors. The mouthfeel is a bit flat and the acidity isn't that noticeable. Drink now. **87** —*M.S. (6/1/2004)*

Laura Hartwig 2002 Carmenère (Colchagua Valley) $12. Dense and ripe, with aromas of licorice, tar, and cola. The mouthfeel is starchy, with grippy tannins propping up black cherry, plum, coffee, and brown sugar flavors. Fairly tight and firm on the finish, with a burnt closing note. **86** —*M.S. (6/1/2004)*

Laura Hartwig 1999 Carmenère (Colchagua Valley) $12. Like any textbook Carmenère, you'll encounter plenty of deep black berry fruit and a hint of green pepper in the nose. The mouth is supersoft yet full, with pepper and chocolate flavors mingling with mint and ripe plums. It's definitely an easy-drinking red wine made to consume now. **87 Best Buy** —*M.S. (3/1/2002)*

Laura Hartwig 2000 Chardonnay (Colchagua Valley) $11. Soft, almost plush apple and pear aromas invite you in, where you'll find round tropical fruit flavors dancing on a clean, smooth palate. If you prefer a polished Chardonnay with depth of fruit as opposed to loads of buttery oak, this one is firmly in that style. Made by Santa Laura. **87 Best Buy** —*M.S. (2/1/2002)*

Laura Hartwig 1999 Merlot (Colchagua Valley) $12. Why do folks so love Merlot? Taste this wine and you will see; it's luscious and overflowing with black cherry and plummy fruit. For sure, it's a big-boned wine, but nevertheless it's fully balanced. The finish is pleasant, moderately long and pretty much on the spot. **88 Best Buy** —*M.S. (3/1/2002)*

Laura Hartwig 2000 Gran Reserva Red Blend (Colchagua Valley) $20. Jammy, with strawberry aromas dominating the soft, meaty nose. In the mouth, you'll find round, mature fruit defined by red plum, cassis, and pepper. It ends with rich, ripe, saturated notes, but not much acidity and only modest tannins. **87** —*M.S. (6/1/2004)*

LAUREL GLEN

Laurel Glen 2001 Terra Rosa Cabernet Sauvignon (Central Valley) $10. A simple wine for its herbal flavors that just barely suggest slightly unripe blackberries. It is very dry, and while the acids are soft, it rubs the palate with hard-edged tannins. The finish is tart. **83** —*S.H. (1/1/2002)*

Laurel Glen 2000 Terra Rosa Cabernet Sauvignon (Central Valley) $10. Judged on the soft, ripe tannins alone, this wine could be from Napa, it's that rich and flattering to the palate. The fruit is a little dilute. Still, Cabernet fans will find plenty of blackberries and currants to shout about. **86** —*S.H. (2/1/2003)*

LAYLA

Layla 2000 Malbec (Maule Valley) $9. This is a thin, sharp kosher wine that smells like a fruit roll-up and tastes about the same. Some raspberry and plum skin define the palate, while the finish is tangy and thin. **81** —*M.S. (7/1/2003)*

LEYDA

Leyda 2003 Estación Reserve Carmenère (Colchagua Valley) $12. Shows good depth of fruit, with leather and other earthy characteristics. The fruit is a touch hot and spicy, but it's sweet at the core and the vegetal character common to the variety is largely missing. Chocolate and pepper mix with oak notes on the finish. **86** —*M.S. (12/1/2004)*

Leyda 2003 Falaris Hill Vineyard Reserve Chardonnay (Leyda Valley) $18. A clear attempt at a serious wine, given the heavy oak and ripeness. But maybe too toasty and touched up with popcorn and butter to meet the mark. Still, the mature apple character and inherent acidity keep it in the game. A winery to watch. **86** —*M.S. (7/1/2005)*

LEYENDA DEL TOQUI

Leyenda del Toqui 2001 Bordeaux Blend (Cachapoal Valley) $45. Fairly herbal on the nose, with strong aromas of tomato, leather, and vanilla. The palate runs raisiny, with a mild Porty quality along with a heaping of chocolate. Very full-bodied but short on depth and balance. It's a chunker to say the least. **85** —*M.S. (12/31/2006)*

LOICA

Loica 2004 Carmenère (Maipo Valley) $12. Leafy and herbal, with citric berry aromas balanced by some sweetness. Cherry and just adequate ripeness on the palate, but ultimately a little oaky and soft. **84** —*M.S. (3/1/2006)*

Loica 2004 Sauvignon Blanc (Maule Valley) $12. Mouthfilling, with plump citrus flavors. The body is sort of oily and round, but there isn't much cutting edge to speak of. Finishes a bit melony and soft. **82** —*M.S. (12/15/2005)*

LOS VASCOS

Los Vascos 2004 Cabernet Sauvignon (Colchagua Valley) $11. Wines like this helped Colchagua earn its Wine Region of the Year award for 2005. For not much cash you get a ripe, smoky Cabernet with black plum and cassis aromas as well as flavors of raspberry and cherry. Balanced and pure, with some vanilla and oak on the finish. **89 Best Buy** —*M.S. (5/1/2006)*

Los Vascos 2001 Cabernet Sauvignon (Colchagua Valley) $10. Lean and spicy in the nose, with a hint of pepper and some green vegetables. The palate is a continuation of the nose: there's mild red fruit but also some strong green bean and bell pepper flavors. The finish is dry and tannic, as it should be. **83** —*M.S. (7/1/2003)*

Los Vascos 2000 Cabernet Sauvignon (Colchagua Valley) $10. This soft, easy-drinking Cabernet boasts aromas and flavors of cherries and dried herbs, followed by a finish that folds in sweet milk-chocolate notes. An ideal cocktail Cabernet. **84** —*J.C. (3/1/2002)*

Los Vascos 1999 Cabernet Sauvignon (Colchagua Valley) $11. There's very juicy, jammy red berry fruit here and the round, even soft palate may lack a bit of structure, but this is a flavorful, very approachable wine. Slight tobacco and cocoa notes add interest and keep it from being just fruity. Cabernet flavors in a Beaujolais-weight package. **86** *(2/1/2001)*

Los Vascos 1999 Le Dix Cabernet Sauvignon (Colchagua Valley) $40. The nose is big and forward, a statement of modernity for this French-owned Chilean winery. Once you get to the wine itself, it's a bit boxed in and young, but with plenty of berry and cherry fruit. The finish is big and expansive, an indication that the wine should age nicely for at least four or five years. A good wine for fans of Chile's reds. **88** —*M.S. (7/1/2003)*

Los Vascos 2003 Reserve Cabernet Sauvignon (Colchagua Valley) $20. Los Vascos' wines have been on the upswing, evidenced by this serious, round, mainstream Cab that blends in some Carmenère and Syrah. The bouquet is lush and attractive, the palate full of ripe berry and chocolate. Not unique, but very good and mouth-filling. **89** —*M.S. (5/1/2006)*

Los Vascos 2002 Reserve Cabernet Sauvignon (Colchagua Valley) $20. The bouquet features a textbook mix of leather, oak, and black fruit. True plum, cherry, and cassis flavors are round and solid even if they don't blow you away. Makes the grade at every level without pushing any envelopes. One of the better Colchagua Cabs from 2002. **87** —*M.S. (11/1/2005)*

Los Vascos 2000 Reserve Cabernet Sauvignon (Colchagua Valley) $18. Simply put, this one is weedy and green. Just the basics in terms of plum fruit and chocolate rise from the depths. The finish is dry and oaky, with some vanilla flavor. Colchagua is known for ripe, vibrant fruit, but this has more asparagus than a vegetable garden. **80** —*M.S. (12/1/2002)*

Los Vascos 1999 Reserve Cabernet Sauvignon (Colchagua Valley) $15. Made in a lighter style, as befits an offspring of Lafite, with cedar, tobacco and cherry aromas that persist nicely on the palate. It's certainly elegant, and balanced for drinking over the near term. **86** —*J.C. (3/1/2002)*

CHILE

Los Vascos 1998 Reserve Cabernet Sauvignon (Colchagua Valley) $18. This evenly balanced Cabernet has a Bordeaux-like profile, with berry and cassis flavors, nicely integrated oak, and a mild herbal, bell pepper note. Shows good fruit for a 1998 wine and some attractive tobacco and earth shadings. Medium-weight, it finishes nicely with moderate tannins and some spice-pepper notes. Drinks well now and may improve over two or three years. **87** *(2/1/2001)*

Los Vascos 1997 Reserve Cabernet Sauvignon (Colchagua Valley) $15. 85 —*M.S. (5/1/2000)*

Los Vascos 2004 Chardonnay (Colchagua Valley) $10. Extra light and lean, with candied aromas that ultimately settle on passion fruit. Some sugary melon mixes with asparagus on the palate, while the finish is thin and sweet. **82** —*M.S. (2/1/2005)*

Los Vascos 2002 Chardonnay (Colchagua Valley) $10. Aromas of pineapple, lemon, and stone fruits lead into a palate that is ripe and round, with apple butter and pear flavors. The finish is dry and fairly simple, with banana-like richness and tropical fruit notes, but also some late bitterness. Just two things hold it back: The texture is a bit flat, and the acidity could use a jolt. **85** —*M.S. (7/1/2003)*

Los Vascos 2000 Chardonnay (Colchagua Valley) $11. A light and crisp Chardonnay that leans more to the style of Mâcon than Monterey. Mild apple, peach, tropical fruit, and citrus notes on the nose open to a dry, slightly reserved palate with orange and spice elements. Bright acidity keeps it lively and it finishes dry with a classy, slightly chalky note. **86** *(2/1/2001)*

Los Vascos 1997 Le Dix de Los Vascos Red Blend (Colchagua Valley) $40. **88** —*M.S. (5/1/2000)*

Los Vascos 1996 Le Dix de Los Vascos Red Blend (Colchagua Valley) $40. **91** —*M.S. (5/1/2000)*

LUIS FELIPE EDWARDS

Luis Felipe Edwards 2002 Doña Bernarda Bordeaux Blend (Colchagua Valley) $22. Too pricey to qualify as a bargain, but pretty good for the price. There's serious weight and malty qualities to this premium Cab, with cassis and wild blackberry on the palate. Slightly aggressive in the mouth, with firm tannins. Shows a spot of chocolate on the finish. **88** — *M.S. (3/1/2006)*

Luis Felipe Edwards 1997 Cabernet Sauvignon (Colchagua Valley) $10. 82 —*M.S. (11/15/1999)*

Luis Felipe Edwards 2001 Doña Bernarda Cabernet Sauvignon (Colchagua Valley) $24. Coconut, charcoal, plum, and cassis greet you, followed by somewhat raw plum and apple-skin flavors. Ends leathery, with a foreign briny flavor. Attacks well, but sharp acids hamper the balance. **85** —*M.S. (7/1/2005)*

Luis Felipe Edwards 1999 Doña Bernarda Cabernet Sauvignon (Colchagua Valley) $26. With 5% each of Carmenère and Malbec, this tight, aggressive Cabernet is smoky, meaty, and intense. Red fruit such as currants, cherry, and raspberry swim together on the palate. The tail-end is long and full, but the acidity is powerful throughout, maybe a little too much so. **87** —*M.S. (3/1/2002)*

Luis Felipe Edwards 2000 Estate Bottled Cabernet Sauvignon (Colchagua Valley) $8. The nose is flat, yielding only some strawberry aromas and little else. But it's not off or offensive. Simple flavors of cherry and plum come next, followed by a clean but short finish. **84** —*M.S. (12/1/2002)*

Luis Felipe Edwards 2002 Gran Reserva Cabernet Sauvignon (Colchagua Valley) $13. Fading in color, with sweet, raisiny aromas. Soft and sugary on the tongue, without much punch. Lacks zest and spunk while not tasting particularly bad. **82** —*M.S. (7/1/2005)*

Luis Felipe Edwards 2001 Gran Reserva Cabernet Sauvignon (Colchagua Valley) $13. Sweet and complete, with a nice aromatic mix of dark plum, chocolate, and Bordeaux-like herbs. The mouth offers a racy blend of cherry and raspberry, which is followed by chocolate and vanilla. Somewhat simple, but with such good acid-tannin balance, it's more than acceptable. **87** —*M.S. (8/1/2004)*

Luis Felipe Edwards 2000 Gran Reserva - Estate Bottled Cabernet Sauvignon (Colchagua Valley) $13. Sweet, rich and open: This Colchagua Cab offers much of what's good about Chilean red wine. It's fresh,

emphasizing ripe and big berry fruit with a streak of sweet strawberry. It's round in the mouth, wholesome, and finishes with length and finesse, as well as some bitter chocolate flavors. An easy drink with no flaws. **87** — *M.S. (12/1/2002)*

Luis Felipe Edwards 2003 Pupilla Cabernet Sauvignon (Colchagua Valley) $8. Simple and lean, with light red fruit and no detectable oak to speak of. Flavors of sweet cherry and raspberry sherbet leave a gritty, lean finish. Not artisan but good. **83** —*M.S. (8/1/2004)*

Luis Felipe Edwards 1999 Pupilla Cabernet Sauvignon (Colchagua Valley) $8. 85 —*M.S. (11/15/1999)*

Luis Felipe Edwards 1999 Reserva Cabernet Sauvignon (Colchagua Valley) $12. Big and chunky, with a full-fruit bouquet that seems reticent to offer anything more specific than berries. Bright acidity drives the fruitiness forward; the wispy finish features licorice and cherry. **85** —*M.S. (3/1/2002)*

Luis Felipe Edwards 1997 Reserva Cabernet Sauvignon (Colchagua Valley) $13. 86 —*M.S. (11/15/1999)*

Luis Felipe Edwards 2003 Carmenère (Colchagua Valley) $8. Ripe and spicy, with some game and herbs creating a forceful but still savory nose. The fruit is typically herb-infused as it shows olive and tomato alongside plum and berry. Good to the core; probably an easier wine to drink than LFE's more oaky gran reserva. **86 Best Buy** —*M.S. (3/1/2006)*

Luis Felipe Edwards 2001 Carmenère (Colchagua Valley) $8. Some overt wood and lemon peel accent red fruit on the nose, while raspberry and cherry flavors are carried on a peppy, lean frame. A bit scouring on the back end, but with enough fruit and balance to pull it off. **86** —*M.S. (8/1/2004)*

Luis Felipe Edwards 2002 Estate Carmenère (Colchagua Valley) $8. Not a heavyweight, but what's here is largely balanced and likable. Aromas of tree bark and red fruit are best early but lose focus with time. In the mouth, raspberry flavors over-ride some light bell pepper notes. **84** — *M.S. (8/1/2004)*

Luis Felipe Edwards 1999 Estate Bottled Carmenère (Colchagua Valley) $11. Pretty aromas of cedar, milk chocolate, and mint are the highlights of this light-weight quaffer that blends in flavors of black cherry and cocoa on the finish. **84** —*J.C. (8/1/2001)*

Luis Felipe Edwards 2003 Gran Reserva Carmenère (Colchagua Valley) $13. Strong-boned and herbal, with a fair amount of sawdust and vanilla making up the bouquet. Shows zesty black cherry flavors and seems healthy at the core. Decent texture; balanced. **85** —*M.S. (3/1/2006)*

Luis Felipe Edwards 2001 Gran Reserva Carmenère (Colchagua Valley) $13. Chunky and round up front, with an aromatic mix of red and black fruits. It runs sweet on the palate, with lots of oak and chocolate. Very soft and candied, and maybe too plump and simple for connoisseurs. But for main street tastes, it should do the trick. **86** —*M.S. (3/1/2004)*

Luis Felipe Edwards 1999 Chardonnay (Colchagua Valley) $10. 88 Best Buy —*M.S. (11/15/1999)*

Luis Felipe Edwards 2004 Chardonnay (Colchagua Valley) $8. Clean and 100% middle of the road. Peach, melon, and vanilla flavors are sweet, while the texture is a bit buttery. Bready and open, with mild oak and lees notes. Decent but regular. **84 Best Buy** —*M.S. (11/1/2005)*

Luis Felipe Edwards 2003 Chardonnay (Colchagua Valley) $8. Soft and simple, but clean and fresh, with pear, and apple aromas prior to papaya and yet more apple flavor. It's dry, lean, and a bit spicy on the finish, and overall it's a solid offering with a round, expansive mouthfeel. **85 Best Buy** —*M.S. (6/1/2004)*

Luis Felipe Edwards 2001 Chardonnay (Colchagua Valley) $8. Aged in 20% French oak, this Chard from a cool vineyard is fresh as a daisy and loaded with light tropical fruit. There's also a touch of citrus on the back palate and a creamy pound-cake flavor to the finish. **85** —*M.S. (3/1/2002)*

Luis Felipe Edwards 2005 Estate Chardonnay (Colchagua Valley) $8. Opens with butterscotch and toast, but the palate doesn't really hold up. It offers dull orange and citrus flavors that are stretched thin. Lastly, citrus rind on the finish makes the final act bitter and rough. **81** —*M.S. (12/31/2006)*

CHILE

Luis Felipe Edwards 2002 Malbec (Colchagua Valley) $8. Round, with lively berry aromas accented by hints of cinnamon and mint. A good effort for a simple wine, as light oak easily props up the forward red fruit. Finishes smooth and with proper flavors and balance. An example of a good value red with ripe fruit. **86 Best Buy** —M.S. (12/1/2003)

Luis Felipe Edwards 2002 Gran Reserva Malbec (Colchagua Valley) $13. Flavorful and ripe, with plenty of raspberry and cherry fruit. There's also an overt, fat oak element that rides over what can best be described as pedestrian fruit. Still, it's a likable soft wine, one with high-toned flavors accented by chocolate, pepper, and wood resin. **85** —M.S. (8/1/2004)

Luis Felipe Edwards 2001 Gran Reserva Malbec (Colchagua Valley) $13. Although "gran reserva" and $13 don't usually go together, that's what you get in this rich, thick rendition that pours on the blackberry flavor as if there's no tomorrow. Ripe and raisiny, with creamy oak. Very chocolaty and much like a confection. **86** —M.S. (12/1/2003)

Luis Felipe Edwards 2002 Merlot (Colchagua Valley) $8. A mixture of sugar beet and red cabbage is intertwined with plum and berry, creating a sweet, awkward nose. Blackberry and candy flavors, a leathery finish, and a firm mouthfeel are the remaining defining characteristics. **84** —M.S. (8/1/2004)

Luis Felipe Edwards 2001 Merlot (Colchagua Valley) $8. This wine is a typical Merlot, with black cherry and earth aromas. Tannins are soft and the flavors match the aromas. It's a straightforward, satisfying quaffer. **85 Best Buy** —C.S. (12/1/2002)

Luis Felipe Edwards 1999 Estate Bottled Merlot (Colchagua Valley) $10. Menthol and blackberry aromas are followed by a palate of soft and straightforward blackberry, vanilla, and anise flavors. It's an uncomplicated, pleasant package, nicely balanced and easy to enjoy now. **83** —J.F. (8/1/2001)

Luis Felipe Edwards 2001 Gran Reserva Merlot (Colchagua Valley) $13. This one veers a little toward the light side, but it's solid and well-crafted, with clear red fruit aromas, flavors of dried cherries and plums, and a fresh, acidic finish that supports the wine's simple structure. Some dark chocolate on the back end adds weight and masculinity. **86** —M.S. (3/1/2004)

Luis Felipe Edwards 2000 Gran Reserva Estate Bottled Merlot (Colchagua Valley) $13. Inky in color, and the big, full, toasty aromas of plums and currants will get you excited about this wine. Unfortunately, the palate doesn't quite deliver on the promise. Green olive and spicy flavors finish thin and dilute. **85** —C.S. (12/1/2002)

Luis Felipe Edwards 2002 Shiraz (Colchagua Valley) $7. Initial aromas of wet dog and swimming pool blow off to reveal plum, cherry, and generic spice. Lasting notes of raisin and pepper are good, while a shortage of depth and grip renders it middle of the road but drinkable. **84** —M.S. (8/1/2004)

Luis Felipe Edwards 2002 Gran Reserva Shiraz (Colchagua Valley) $13. Shockingly solid and rich, with very few flaws. Is it rustic, Rhône-style Syrah? Definitely not; it's a heavy, extracted Aussie-style Shiraz with cassis, black plum, and chocolate throughout. Even the finish is firm and sturdy, and despite 14% alcohol, it's balanced. **88** —M.S. (8/1/2004)

MANTA

Manta 2003 Sauvignon Blanc (Central Valley) $6. Appealing, with pure pineapple and stone fruit aromas followed by a pithy, peppery palate defined by apple and citrus. Some plumpness on the finish, however, overall it's fairly clean and of proper weight and balance. From Casa Julia. **86 Best Buy** —M.S. (2/1/2005)

MAQUIS

Maquis 2004 Lien Red Blend (Colchagua Valley) $18. Brightly tinted to purple, with black cherry, graphite, and surity to the nose. The palate pushes lively black cherry, cassis, plum, and licorice, while the finish is lush and persistent. With no Cab or Merlot in the mix, this tasty five-grape blend leans on Syrah for its foundation. **88** —M.S. (10/1/2006)

Maquis 2003 Lien Red Blend (Colchagua Valley) $15. Ripe and sweet, with hunky open-knit aromas. Shows plum and chocolate cake flavors, but there's core acidity backing things up. Finishes more tart and snappy. **85** —M.S. (3/1/2006)

MARQUÉS DE CASA CONCHA

Marqués de Casa Concha 2003 Chardonnay (Pirque) $15. Lots of popcorn and butter on the nose, with more butter along with lemon and apple on the palate. This is a soft, rich wine without a lot of driving acids to spunk things up. Turns increasingly creamy on the finish. **87** —M.S. (7/1/2005)

MATETIC

Matetic 2003 EQ Pinot Noir (San Antonio) $25. Not your average Pinot Noir; it's inky, with a nose of sugar beet, black fruit liqueur, and a touch of alfalfa. Further nosing reveals mineral and black currants, characteristics more akin to a Mediterranean red than textbook Pinot. In the mouth, it's a hulk, with berry and kirsch, pepper, and ultimately some heat. **86** —M.S. (11/1/2005)

Matetic 2004 EQ Sauvignon Blanc (San Antonio) $15. Laudable for its combination of size and balance. The melon, kiwi, and citrus flavors are fat yet tempered by classic grassiness, so even though it weighs in at 14.6% alcohol, it's palatable. Should be drunk with a solid white fish like halibut or cod. **88** —M.S. (11/1/2005)

Matetic 2003 EQ Syrah (San Antonio) $25. Opaque in color and dense throughout. Starts with a smoky, baked-plum personality before showing its true colors, which include a silky texture, soft tannins, and masculine coffee, mocha, and pepper qualities. Great mouthfeel and a lot of richness. **90** —M.S. (11/1/2005)

MCMANIS

McManis 2002 River Junction Chardonnay (Central Valley) $10. From a Central Valley AVA approved in 2001. Very fruity with peaches and pears, but also a curiously baked taste, like pie crust. There's also a dollop of residual sugar that's uncomfortable. **82** —S.H. (1/1/2002)

McManis 2002 River Junction Pinot Grigio (Central Valley) $10. A nice, savory little white wine, crisp and firm in texture, and very dry, with the flavors of tart green apples and lemons. It's ideal for picnics, fast food, or family gatherings. Another great value, courtesy of California's excess of grape supply. **86** —S.H. (1/1/2002)

MELANIA

Melania 2004 Colección Especial Chardonnay (Maule Valley) $11. Lime and slate on the nose, but then it opens and turns blowsy. Surprisingly tart to the taste, with citrus and green apple in front and banana in the rear. Finishes flat, with a soda-water quality. **83** —M.S. (11/1/2005)

Melania 2004 Colección Especial Merlot (Maule Valley) $11. Nice color, with candied, sweet-as-sugar aromas. Black cherry and chocolate carry the reduced palate. Finishes slightly weedy. **83** —M.S. (11/1/2005)

MICHEL LAROCHE/JORGE CODERCH

Michel Laroche/Jorge Coderch 2002 Rio Azul Chardonnay (Casablanca Valley) $13. A dramatic contrast to Laroche's French Chardonnays, this one is loaded with tropical fruit and honey, dressed up with coconut oil and vanilla. It's unabashedly New World, yet finishes with firm, lime-like acidity. **87** (2/1/2004)

Michel Laroche/Jorge Coderch 2002 Piedra Feliz Pinot Noir (Casablanca Valley) $NA. The first crop off young vines and not available yet in the U.S., Laroche's Chilean Pinot shows potential in its complex, slightly vegetal aromas but lacks stuffing and flavor intensity. **83** (2/1/2004)

MIGUEL TORRES

Miguel Torres 2001 Manso de Velasco Cabernet Sauvignon (Curicó Valley) $37. Tight at first, with almost confounding aromas of tar, black plum, and herbs. Airing, however, turns it plush, with a heavy dose of fine tannins pushing powerful plum and cassis. A baby now, as is evident by how the finish goes from short to lengthy in no time. A real bruiser from Torres' Chilean outpost. Hold through 2007. **91** —M.S. (7/1/2005)

Miguel Torres 2000 Manso de Velasco Cabernet Sauvignon (Curicó Valley) $35. This structured, old-vine Cabernet is always a leader among the Chilean pack, and the current version is typical in that it's built like a house, with cool, concentrated aromas of blackberry, cassis, earth, and black olive. Cola notes on the palate frame cherry and cassis flavors, while the finish is firm yet rewardingly luscious, with ample depth. Very

CHILE

solid and tasty, and packed deep with power. Can be drunk immediately. **90** —*M.S. (7/1/2003)*

Miguel Torres 1999 Manso de Velasco Cabernet Sauvignon (Curicó Valley) $33. The grapes for this muscled-up Cab were grown in one of the oldest vineyards in the country. The wine has old-school terroir in it—meatiness and nuts. It's a French oak recipient (18 months), with dark plummy fruit at the tannin-protected core. A soft and cuddly fruitball, it's not; but real Cabernet it is for sure. **90** —*M.S. (3/1/2002)*

Miguel Torres 2003 Manso de Velasco Viejas Viñas Cabernet Sauvignon (Curicó Valley) $32. One of the more legendary wines from Chile, one we look forward to reviewing. The '03 model is almost mossy and beet-based on the nose, but give that denseness a pass and head to the luscious black cherry and licorice that layers the palate. Heady stuff for certain; drink within a few years. **92 Editors' Choice** —*M.S. (7/1/2006)*

Miguel Torres 2003 Santa Digna Cabernet Sauvignon (Curicó Valley) $12. Violet in color, and smells funky at first. Airing releases plum, blackberry, and licorice flavors. A bit medicinal on the finish, but that combination of warm, sweet, and sticky works in this case. Bottom line: this is a ripe, fruity wine that requires some patience. **86** —*M.S. (11/1/2005)*

Miguel Torres 2002 Santa Digna Cabernet Sauvignon (Curicó Valley) $13. A bit spicy and murky at first, but with airing some cranberry and pepper notes come up strong. The fruit flavor falls squarely into the cherry category, yet it's sweet and a bit simple. Roundness and a nice body work in the wine's favor; overall it's fairly chewy and substantive. **85** —*M.S. (7/1/2003)*

Miguel Torres 2000 Santa Digna Cabernet Sauvignon (Curicó Valley) $13. You get a taste for Torres' European style in this chunky, thick, leathery Cab that's young, easy and chewy, like a wine from Priorat, Spain. A mix of black fruit and black olive stirs interest prior to the soft licorice-tinged finish. The aging is primarily in used American oak barrels. **86** —*M.S. (3/1/2002)*

Miguel Torres 1999 Santa Digna Cabernet Sauvignon (Curicó Valley) $12. Leafy cassis and cocoa aromas and flavors carry hints of almond paste, saddle leather, and ground cinnamon. The mouthfeel is full and plush, with ripe tannins that coat the mouth and let you know that this wine is about more than up-front fruit. Drink now or anytime over the next five years. **88 Best Buy** —*J.C. (2/1/2001)*

Miguel Torres 2006 Santa Digna Reserve Rosé Cabernet Sauvignon (Curicó Valley) $10. Reddish in color, and based entirely on Cabernet Sauvignon, this heavy rosado tastes too much like fruit punch and not enough like dry wine. With sweet and soft fruit it comes on like a cherry or berry fruit drink, and the finish is candied and monotone. **80** —*M.S. (11/15/2006)*

Miguel Torres 2003 Santa Digna Rose Cabernet Sauvignon (Curicó Valley) $9. Very sweet, with more sugar than most folks will want. The color is attractive, as is the concept of a Cab-based rosé. But one must wonder what the market is for a sweet-style wine like this from South America. As for specific flavors, it's hard to pinpoint anything beyond generic berry and sucking candy. **84** —*M.S. (8/1/2004)*

Miguel Torres 2005 Tormenta Cabernet Sauvignon (Central Valley) $13. Early aromatics are a bit reedy and funky, but with time it finds its way. The palate offers black fruit and chocolate, but also some integral green flavors. Short and stout on the finish, with another modest but evident blast of green. **84** —*M.S. (11/15/2006)*

Miguel Torres 2004 Tormenta Cabernet Sauvignon (Central Valley) $11. Comes out of the blocks with harsh, sulfuric aromas that settle with time. In addition, there's a bit of olive and green character to the nose. In the mouth, there's basic black plum and berry. Finishes creamy and sweet. Not a lot of harmony. **83** —*M.S. (5/1/2006)*

Miguel Torres 2003 Santa Digna Reserva Carmenère (Curicó Valley) $16. Give this wine as much airing time as possible, because she starts out with pickled, rustic Carmenère aromas that haven't been softened by oak or anything else. Oxygen tames the funk and allows cherry and plum flavors to emerge. As for mouthfeel, it's clearly the wine's calling card: the palate is racy but smooth, with proper tannins and lively acidity. **85** — *M.S. (11/1/2005)*

Miguel Torres 2005 Santa Digna Reserve Carmenère (Central Valley) $12. From the first warm and piercing whiff, you get a sense that the ride will be fun. Aromas of cherry cough drop and herbs are just part of the bouquet, and the juicy palate of ripe, bursting black fruit works. Big and rewarding wine, with chocolate and spice on the back side. **88 Best Buy** —*M.S. (11/15/2006)*

Miguel Torres 2004 Santa Digna Reserve Carmenère (Curicó Valley) $12. Black olive, herbs, and crude oil create an incredibly dark nose, while the ripe, meaty palate is loaded with berry fruit and chocolate. Finishes hefty and powerful, but where's the nuance? Where's the additional layers? They're not here. **85** —*M.S. (7/1/2006)*

Miguel Torres 2002 Santa Digna Carmenère-Cabernet Sauvignon (Curicó Valley) $25. Big and brooding, with bacon, blackberry, and butter aromas in addition to notes of lavender and violets. The thick palate offers blueberry fruit mixed with chocolate and sage. The finish is three-star large. Turns slightly herbal at the end. **88** —*M.S. (12/1/2004)*

Miguel Torres 2004 Maquehua Chardonnay (Curicó Valley) $18. Fairly fresh and fruity, with peach and cantaloupe on the nose. Next up is a plump palate with round melon flavors. A soft finish with creaminess indicates modest acidity. Shows toasty dryness in the middle. **87** —*M.S. (7/1/2006)*

Miguel Torres 2003 Maquehua Chardonnay (Curicó Valley) $16. A serious barrel-fermented Chard that offers fat fruit and enough subtleties and nuances to register highly. Citrus, banana, and toasted nuts on the palate, followed by a one-note but persistent finish. Creamy and integrated; made for near-term drinking. **89** —*M.S. (2/1/2005)*

Miguel Torres 2002 Maquehua Chardonnay (Curicó Valley) $19. Consistency is always a virtue, and once again this wine is creamy, fully-oaked and more European in style than most Chilean Chardonnays. The nose is like popcorn, with apple and peach in the background. Flavors of banana, coconut, melon, and apple carry the rich palate, while the finish is smooth and oaky. This is very good Chardonnay even if it lacks the extra elements required of a great wine. Drink now for its freshness. **88** —*M.S. (7/1/2003)*

Miguel Torres 2000 Maquehua Chardonnay (Curicó Valley) $19. After a shaky opening, where an herb-like note bears an almost chemical tang, this light and elegant wine offers vanilla-cream and citrus flavors. The mouthfeel is light, and appealing apple, citrus, and mineral notes show on the even finish. **85** —*M.M. (8/1/2001)*

Miguel Torres 1999 Maquehua Chardonnay (Curicó Valley) $19. Makes a strong statement for the potential of Chardonnay in Chile, with powerful toast and hazelnut aromas playing opposite fruit comprised of peaches and Granny Smith apples. It's barrel-fermented and aged, but stayed only a relatively short time in wood, so you can still taste the fruit and all of the nutty, leesy complexities. **90 Editors' Choice** —*J.C. (2/1/2001)*

Miguel Torres 2002 Santa Digna Chardonnay (Curicó Valley) $10. Aromas of pineapple, ripe melon, and lemon create a balanced bouquet, while the citrus and banana on the palate make for a ripe and ready offering. The finish is long, clean, and fresh, and the mouthfeel is good and lean, and overall quite crisp. Standard fare, but a good example of Chardonnay. **86** —*M.S. (7/1/2003)*

Miguel Torres 2005 Santa Digna Selection Chardonnay (Curicó Valley) $11. Yellow in color, with touches of passion fruit and grapefruit on the nose. Citrusy and round in the mouth, with a soft, chunky, pithy finish. Cleanly made, just not packed or powerful. **84** —*M.S. (3/1/2006)*

Miguel Torres 2000 Don Miguel Gewürztraminer-Riesling (Curicó Valley) $11. A 75-25 blend that showcases the exotic lychee and pear aromas of Gewürz, while the Riesling asserts itself on the finish in a rush of bracing lime-like acidity. A unique blend that offers plenty of food-pairing versatility. **88 Best Buy** —*J.C. (2/1/2001)*

Miguel Torres 2004 Santa Digna Merlot (Curicó Valley) $12. A little root beer, chocolate, and plum make for a nice bouquet. Fully ripe blackberry and plum flavors carry the palate, which doesn't have as much texture as would be ideal. Finishes smooth, with bitter chocolate. Shines early but fades late. **86** —*M.S. (11/1/2005)*

Miguel Torres 2003 Santa Digna Merlot (Curicó Valley) $10. Deep violet in color, almost to the point of over-saturation. The nose is chunky and youthful, with black fruit and iodine. More heavy black fruit follows on the sweet palate. Forward, but lacks detail and elegance. **83** —*M.S.* *(2/1/2005)*

Miguel Torres 2002 Santa Digna Merlot (Curicó Valley) $10. The nose is murky and overdone, seemingly a victim of the rainy 2002 harvest. The palate is heavy and dark, with sweet plum and berry fruit, but not the pulsating, pure type normally sought. **83** —*M.S.* *(7/1/2003)*

Miguel Torres 2000 Conde de Superunda Red Blend (Curicó Valley) $70. A new blend of Cabernet Sauvignon, Carmenère, Monastrell, and Tempranillo, which alone makes it unique for Chile. The nose delivers a blast of menthol and the color is downright huge. Very plump and fruity, with a softness that serves it well. A real mouthful that's not overpowering but still packs punch. **90** *(11/15/2005)*

Miguel Torres 2001 Cordillera Red Blend (Curicó Valley) $27. This wine is made largely from Carmenère, with Merlot and Syrah helping out. It's zesty and piquant, with barbecued aromas that jazz up the plum and berry fruit that dominates the palate. Fresh and firm from top to bottom. Even the finish is reaffirming. **88** —*M.S.* *(11/1/2005)*

Miguel Torres 2000 Cordillera Red Blend (Curicó Valley) $26. There's much to like about this big-boned blend that features about 65% old-vine Andean Cariñena as well as Syrah and Merlot. Given the players, the color is expectedly huge, and the nose is very intense, a pleasure. Seductive tannins allow for immediate drinkability. If you like a rich, burly berry-and-spice-packed red, this will do the trick. **90** —*M.S.* *(3/1/2002)*

Miguel Torres 1999 Cordillera Red Blend (Curicó Valley) $26. A blend of old-vine Cariñena (60%), Syrah (25%), and Merlot (15%). The color is impressively dark and so is the fruit—mainly plums and blackberries. Toast and dried spices from new oak give an additional impression of opulence. But even more impressive is the balance. This is no low-acid, fruit-and-oak wonder; the natural acidity of the Carignane shines through, giving lift and definition to the flavors. Easy to drink now, but should easily hold a few years. **91 Editors' Choice** —*J.C.* *(2/1/2001)*

Miguel Torres 2000 Rosé Blend (Curicó Valley) $8. Strawberry and pink grapefruit aromas mingle enticingly on the nose. But on the palate it seems a bit syrupy and heavy, finishing with a touch of cola. **82** —*J.C.* *(2/1/2001)*

Miguel Torres 2000 Copihue Sauvignon Blanc (Curicó Valley) $15. This white is partially barrel fermented, and that woodiness and the related round texture sit heavy on the citrus fruit. Grapefruit is most forward, with orange and lemon in the backdrop. Use it as a quaff with hors d'oeuvres. **85** —*M.S.* *(3/1/2002)*

Miguel Torres 2003 Santa Digna Sauvignon Blanc (Curicó Valley) $10. Harsh and weedy at first, and only later giving way to muddled fruit. Tart apple and citrus on the palate, and lemony late. Whets the whistle with piercing acids. **81** —*M.S.* *(2/1/2005)*

Miguel Torres 2000 Santa Digna Sauvignon Blanc (Curicó Valley) $12. Bright grapefruit and gooseberry aromas flesh out admirably in the mouth, with tart apple and citrus flavors moving to the fore. Finishes clean and crisp—a perfect partner for shellfish or fresh chèvre. **85** —*J.C.* *(2/1/2001)*

Miguel Torres 2005 Santa Digna Selection Sauvignon Blanc (Curicó Valley) $11. A hard wine that doesn't elicit a smile. The nose is peanutty and prickly, while the palate is pure lemon-lime extract. Finishes firm, almost sour. **82** —*M.S.* *(5/1/2006)*

Miguel Torres 2004 Santa Digna Reserve Shiraz (Curicó Valley) $12. Quite intense and deep, with prune and black cherry covering the lush nose. Sweet and full in the mouth, with berry fruit backed by coffee, toffee, and chocolate. If you like yours big and rich, this fits the bill. **87 Best Buy** —*M.S.* *(10/1/2006)*

MILLAMAN

Millaman 2000 Cabernet Sauvignon (Curicó Valley) $8. Some rusticity in the form of leather, spice, and bacon separate the aromas of this wine from the ordinary. The mouth comes across a bit juicy due to high acidity,

but that also keeps things fresh across the tongue. Flavors of black fruit and plums lead into a finish that's dark with coffee. **86 Best Buy** —*M.S.* *(12/1/2002)*

Millaman 2004 Old Vines Reserva Cabernet Sauvignon-Malbec (Curicó Valley) $NA. Nicely colored, with blueberry and raspberry fruit. Seems solid, and it is, but there's a gigantic wave of acidity that mills around the middle, and the more you sip it the more sour it gets. Really needs food to show its best. **85** —*M.S.* *(12/15/2005)*

Millaman 2000 Chardonnay (Curicó Valley) $8. This one has bland aromatics, with only a touch of oak to grasp at. The palate is almost spritzy, which it shouldn't be, and the flavor resembles Mott's applesauce. A bit weak and only qualifies for an acceptable rating on its best day. **80** —*M.S.* *(7/1/2002)*

Millaman 2000 Red Blend (Curicó Valley) $8. Chocolate-covered cherries and freshly fallen pine needles are very aromatic in this blend. The flavors of clove, leather, and earth finish soft and simple for a satisfying glass of wine. **85 Best Buy** —*C.S.* *(12/1/2002)*

Millaman 2000 Sauvignon Blanc (Curicó Valley) $8. Nectarine aromas along with a touch of mint kick it off. The second act is an apple and pear palate with a bit of licorice and an under-current of mineral. The palate remains solid and fruity, and the wine seems fresh and healthy despite being a few years old. **85** —*M.S.* *(7/1/2003)*

Millaman 2002 Reserva Zinfandel (Central Valley) $NA. For Chilean Zinfandel, which isn't something you see every day, it has its positives. The nose is a bit sheer, with grape skins, citrus peel, and coffee making their mark. Scratchy raspberry flavors seem sugary, while the finish is full of mocha and vanilla. Overt, creamy, sweet,, and pretty good as a whole. **85** —*M.S.* *(7/1/2006)*

MONTES

Montes 1999 Montes Alpha M Bordeaux Blend (Colchagua Valley) $72. Hand-picked fruit from La Finca Estate in this case equals a real black beauty—one taster imagined that this would be difficult to drink without a hefty grilled steak. Smoldering smoke, ash and black fruit aromas make way for similar char, tar, licorice and blackberry flavors on the palate and on the finish. Drink from 2004. **88** —*D.T.* *(7/1/2002)*

Montes 2000 Montes Alpha M Bordeaux Blend (Colchagua Valley) $72. The oak on this Cabernet-dominated wine is a bit lemony, while the palate is spicy and racy, not plump like it has been in the past. The flavors are dotted by wood resin and pepper, while the fruit is slightly shy. It's more reticent than the excellent 1999 version. **89** —*M.S.* *(3/1/2004)*

Montes 2000 Ltd. Selection-Apalta Vnyd-Carmenere/Cab Sauv Cabernet Blend (Colchagua Valley) $16. High-toned raspberry aromas mingle with mint and cedar notes in this stylish blend. Mixed berry flavors, vanilla, and toast finish a bit tart and lemony, with firm tannins and hints of chocolate. Try in 1–2 years. **82** —*D.T.* *(7/1/2002)*

Montes 1996 Cabernet Sauvignon (Curicó Valley) $7. 89 *(11/15/1999)*

Montes 2004 Montes Alpha Cabernet Sauvignon (Colchagua Valley) $25. Foresty and mossy at first, with black fruit at the bottom of the nose. There's a ton of chocolate and mint on this Cab, mixed with raspberry jam and firm, spiky tannins. Finishes minty and dark, with a touch of cough drop. Contains 15% Merlot but still seems harder and more medicinal than previous vintages. **86** —*M.S.* *(12/31/2006)*

Montes 2003 Montes Alpha Cabernet Sauvignon (Colchagua Valley) $23. Begins with a touch of sawdust, but that quickly morphs into cinnamon and spice. Of course, there's bulky dark fruit to offset it. In the mouth, we're talking black plum and berry fruit in spades, while the feel is tight and right, with serious tannins. A generous wine, one that represents Chile and Colchagua positively. **90 Editors' Choice** —*M.S.* *(11/1/2005)*

Montes 2002 Montes Alpha Cabernet Sauvignon (Colchagua Valley) $22. Aromas of earth, bacon fat, and toasty oak lead the wine toward a snappy, young palate that pours on the red fruit, spice, and tannins. The finish, however, is a bit more complex, as vanilla cookies and cocoa do an attractive little dance. **88** —*M.S.* *(3/1/2004)*

Montes 2001 Montes Alpha Cabernet Sauvignon (Curicó Valley) $20. Tight and oaky at first, with aromas of lemon rind, maple, and leather. Next up, cassis and black cherry appear in the mouth, which precedes a tight,

CHILE

chocolaty finish that features good length and manly tannins. Very tightly wound, and powerful. **88** —*M.S. (3/1/2004)*

Montes 2000 Montes Alpha Cabernet Sauvignon (Curicó Valley) $20. Big and ripe, with cola, root beer, and berry aromas along with rich oak. The palate is a high-wire act of bright red fruit combined with thick milk chocolate and malt. The tannins and acidity allow the wine to be aggressive, maybe too much so given that the fruit is somewhat tart and prickly. **86** —*M.S. (7/1/2003)*

Montes 1999 Montes Alpha Cabernet Sauvignon (Colchagua Valley) $22. Deep, ripe, and plummy up front, with a firm mouthfeel and pronounced tannins. In other words, it's structured for the long haul. The fruit is tight and lively, running toward plum and cherry. The black fruit and coffee on the finish make a statement. **90** —*M.S. (3/1/2002)*

Montes 2004 Reserve Cabernet Sauvignon (Colchagua Valley) $10. Ripe and ready, with a rich, syrupy nose. Just right on the palate, where bold dark fruit flavors are supported by lively tannins and just enough acid. Spice and coffee on the finish, with ample oak. **87 Best Buy** —*M.S. (11/1/2005)*

Montes 2002 Reserve Cabernet Sauvignon (Colchagua Valley) $10. Some Merlot added to the Cabernet creates a jammy, soft nose, and a round, easy mouthfeel. The fruit is pure throughout, with tasty cassis and plum lifted by light tannins. With chocolate and spice on the finish, this is a fine Cabernet for the price. **87 Best Buy** —*M.S. (3/1/2004)*

Montes 2001 Reserve Cabernet Sauvignon (Curicó Valley) $10. Spicy and woody, with a pungency on the nose. The round palate is full of red berry fruit and a fair amount of supporting oak. That wood is confirmed on the finish, where things turn a bit buttery and rich. Fortunately some lively tannins and cleansing acids keep things from getting bogged down. A good everyday Cab. **86 Best Buy** —*M.S. (7/1/2003)*

Montes 1999 Reserve Cabernet Sauvignon (Colchagua Valley) $10. A moderately complex but low-acid wine that some will find mouth-filling and rich, others a bit heavy. Still, it shows smoke, herb, and cassis aromatics and picks up earth and chocolate nuances on the palate. **85** —*J.C. (7/1/2002)*

Montes 2000 Reserve Oak Aged Cabernet Sauvignon (Colchagua Valley) $10. Herbal and spicy, with some rubbery notes to the nose and a bit of pickle to the flavors. The plum fruit on the palate is round and peppery, while the wine finishes warm and full. Decent fruit but not rich. **84** —*M.S. (7/1/2003)*

Montes 2002 Cabernet Sauvignon-Carmenère (Colchagua Valley) $16. Fairly refined and classy for the price. There's spice and herbal qualities courtesy of the Carmenère (30%), and full-fledged berry fruit and size from the Cabernet (70%). It goes the distance and comes across as harmonious. **88** —*M.S. (3/1/2004)*

Montes 2004 Limited Selection Cabernet Sauvignon-Carmenère (Leyda Valley) $16. Big and oaky, with aromas of coconut, bacon, and wood resin. Very sweet and borderline syrupy on the tongue, where cocoa and clove flavors accent chewy, dark fruit flavors. A touch green and minty in the middle, or is that the Carmenère? **86** —*M.S. (11/1/2005)*

Montes 2005 Montes Alpha Chardonnay (Casablanca Valley) $25. Starts out a bit short and flat, with a bouquet housing basic Chardonnay aromas of pear, apple, and oak. The palate is more or less similar, with apple and melon flavors spreading wide across the mouth. But where's the precision and zest? Those key qualities, which we've previously lauded in this wine, are not entirely on vacation but they're not fully evident either. **87** —*M.S. (12/31/2006)*

Montes 2004 Montes Alpha Chardonnay (Casablanca Valley) $23. Very ripe and tropical, with a candied core sweetness that is hard not to like. Pear, vanilla, and toast coast the new-age bouquet, while the palate oozes nectarine and cantaloupe. Clean and moderately deep. Features good natural acids. **88** —*M.S. (7/1/2006)*

Montes 2003 Montes Alpha Chardonnay (Casablanca Valley) $23. A little oaky at first, resulting in some slight varnish-like aromas. But airing tones it down, and then you get popcorn, baked apple, and fresh pear notes. Ample and quite pleasurable throughout, with apple and banana flavors in front of a big, round finish. **89** —*M.S. (11/1/2005)*

Montes 2003 Montes Alpha Chardonnay (Casablanca Valley) $23. Soft and round, but with structure and spine. The nose exudes pretty pear, apple, and butterscotch, while the full-bodied palate offers apple, citrus, melon, and honey. A wine that stands on its feet; one of Chile's better Chardonnays. **89 Editors' Choice** —*M.S. (2/1/2005)*

Montes 2002 Montes Alpha Chardonnay (Casablanca Valley) $20. Almost gold, with a bright yellow luster. The nose is round and full, with a clear smokiness that isn't too heavy. Quite modern in style, with rich pear and apple flavors. The '02 version is significantly less oaky than previous Alpha Chardonnays. **88** —*M.S. (3/1/2004)*

Montes 2001 Montes Alpha Chardonnay (Casablanca Valley) $20. Rich and aromatic, with a full blast of fragrant toasty oak and plenty of tropical fruit. The apple, mango, and pear fruit that coats your mouth is round and ripe but not too thick or grabby. And the finish is perfectly smooth. Sure, it's a bit buttery and full, so no one will confuse it for Chablis. But in its class it's one of the best out there. **90 Editors' Choice** —*M.S. (7/1/2003)*

Montes 2000 Montes Alpha Chardonnay (Curicó Valley) $20. Butter and more butter up front, but like all good doses of oak it's not masking anything. Right below that veneer of wood is banana, ripe pear, and macadamia nuts. This is overwhelmingly pleasant to drink. Critics, on the other hand, might find it fat and in need of some racier edges. **90** —*M.S. (2/1/2002)*

Montes 1998 Montes Alpha Special Cuvée Chardonnay (Curicó Valley) $20. **91** —*M.S. (5/1/2000)*

Montes 2004 Reserve Chardonnay (Curicó Valley) $10. Typically oaky, with aromas of baked apple but also some tropical notes. Not the most pure-fruited wine going, but there's ample lemon curd and almond to go with some citrus. Chunky on the finish, with oodles of oak. Good mouthfeel is a bonus. **86 Best Buy** —*M.S. (11/1/2005)*

Montes 2003 Reserve Chardonnay (Curicó Valley) $10. Round and sugary, with simple but welcome notes of lemon verbena, apple, and vanilla. Sweet like candy corn, but with texture. A floral component adds complexity to what is otherwise as standard a Chard as you'll find. **86 Best Buy** —*M.S. (2/1/2005)*

Montes 2001 Reserve Chardonnay (Curicó Valley) $10. Toasty aromas and nuts sit on top of light, buttery fruit—and that's just the nose. The mouth is full of butter and vanilla, but also apples and pears. This has softness to offer, and then some. A clean, smooth five-minute finish doesn't hurt the package in the least. **89 Best Buy** —*M.S. (3/1/2002)*

Montes 1999 Reserve Chardonnay (Curicó Valley) $NA. A ripe, almost sweet wine with loads of pineapple and pear aromas and flavors. The mouthfeel is full and easy but a slight tang keeps it from getting too mushy. This veritable pineapple bomb wraps up with tangy, spicy oak notes. Simple, but fun. **84** *(1/1/2004)*

Montes 2002 Reserve Barrel Fermented Chardonnay (Curicó Valley) $10. The nose is light and attractive, with peach and floral accents. The mouth is perfectly smooth, with apple, melon, and a hint of flint or steel. On the finish, some cinnamon spice adds character to the baked-apple flavors. With no flaws, this is the epitome of affordable, drinkable Chardonnay. **88 Best Buy** —*M.S. (7/1/2003)*

Montes 2002 Fumé Blanc (Curicó Valley) $10. The telltale passion fruit character of this wine may not be as pure as it was on the splendid 2001 vintage, but it's unmistakably there. What I love about this wine is the zesty acidity and depth of flavor. If other Chilean Sauvignon Blancs have seemed unexciting, this partially barrel-fermented example may change your opinion. **87** —*M.S. (11/15/2003)*

Montes 2001 Reserve Fumé Blanc (Curicó Valley) $10. Taking complexity a step further than the fruit-driven Sauvignon Blanc, this oak-aged pretty boy conjures thoughts of Pouilly-Fumé on a good day. Pungent green apple persists from the opening sip to the finish, which offers lemon and lime and a soft closing sensation. It has much in common with Loire Valley whites. **90 Best Buy** —*M.S. (3/1/2002)*

Montes 2004 Late Harvest Botrytised Gewürztraminer-Riesling (Curicó Valley) $24. A spectacular dessert wine from South America; probably the best we've had to date. Amber in color, with intoxicating aromas of baked pineapple and orange liqueur. Caramel, toffee, burnt vanilla, and more cruise on the palate, all pushed by perky acidity. Sensational flavor and balance. A hidden gem among the world's best sweeties. **92** —*M.S. (5/1/2006)*

Montes 2000 Malbec (Colchagua Valley) $10. This is a wine from 65-year-old vines and it's perfectly floral and rich, as good Malbec should be. In the mouth, there's blackberry, licorice, nutmeg, and cinnamon. A little acidity on the palate keeps it fresh and focused. Aging this wine for a short time will probably do it some good. **89 Best Buy** —*M.S. (3/1/2002)*

Montes 2001 Oak Aged Reserve Malbec (Colchagua Valley) $10. Simple and clean up front, with inviting aromas. The mouth on this wine is broad and satisfying, and the flavors of plum, blackberry, black olive, and buttery oak work in tandem. The finish is a bit aggressive, and here the oak is powerful as it leaves a bitter lasting sensation. But overall the wine impresses for its solidity and full fruit. **86 Best Buy** —*M.S. (7/1/2003)*

Montes 2004 Reserve Malbec (Colchagua Valley) $10. Round and open knit, with welcoming aromas. Very well-shaped and solid, with cassis and blackberry flavors sitting comfortably in front of a spicy, chocolate-loaded finish. No flab or superficiality; this is a fine wine for the price. **88 Best Buy** —*M.S. (11/1/2005)*

Montes 1999 Reserve Malbec (Colchagua Valley) $10. Very smoky and dark on the nose, with hints of charcoal, chocolate, and blackberries. Opens up nicely on the palate to display sour plums and tart cherries allied with coffee and black tea. The finish is filled with dusty tannins, counter-balanced by juicy acidity. Drink now or hold for up to five years. **87 Best Buy** *(8/1/2001)*

Montes 2002 Reserve Oak Aged Malbec (Colchagua Valley) $10. Rarely does one get celery from the nose of a Montes wine, but in this case it's there. The mouth, meanwhile, is expectedly sweet, with blackberry and a touch of rubber. The wine improves with airing, but it's not a prime-timer. **83** —*M.S. (12/1/2003)*

Montes 2000 Montes Alpha Merlot (Curicó Valley) $20. From the Apalta Vineyard in Colchagua, this robust, fruity Merlot is rich and sweet, and offers a fine mesh of blueberry and black raspberry fruit. The wine is warm and friendly, and overall it's quite easy to drink. The structure is there and so is the flavor and foundation. And it improves with airing, always a good sign of quality. **88** —*M.S. (7/1/2003)*

Montes 1999 Montes Alpha Apalta Vineyard Merlot (Colchagua Valley) $22. Montes' "special reserve" is aged in French oak, which might explain the creamy vanillin and dried spice flavors that lie under the dark berry fruit. Mouthfeel is creamy, too; an easy crowd pleaser. Tasted twice. **85** —*D.T. (7/1/2002)*

Montes 2004 Reserve Merlot (Colchagua Valley) $10. Solid plum and cassis with hints of rubber and smoked ham all make for an attractive nose. This wine is ripe with zero of the green quality that can mar Chilean Merlot; thus the palate pulsates with plum and cherry, and the overall take is one of balance and easy drinkability. **87 Best Buy** —*M.S. (11/1/2005)*

Montes 2003 Reserve Merlot (Colchagua Valley) $10. Ignore the "reserve" qualifier because that's what Montes calls all of its basic varietals. This one starts with strange horseradish and pickled-oak aromas, but time unveils better and cleaner cherry and plum fruit prior to a warm finish. Improves with time, but green throughout. **83** —*M.S. (2/1/2005)*

Montes 2001 Reserve Special Cuvée Merlot (Colchagua Valley) $10. Montes tosses quite a few qualifiers at the name of this wine; i.e. "special cuvée" and "reserve," but at the end of the day it's a basic Merlot with earthy notes and some obvious oak. The fruit flavors veer toward plum and blackberry, while below that there's a shot of woodiness. **84** —*M.S. (7/1/2003)*

Montes 2002 Reserve Special Cuvée Merlot (Colchagua Valley) $10. A bit earthy in color; it's not your average bright ruby. The nose is more refined and condensed than one might expect, with subdued scents of raspberry, plum, and cola. Suave in terms of texture, and long on the finish. **86** —*M.S. (3/1/2004)*

Montes 2000 Special Cuvée Merlot (Colchagua Valley) $10. What's most special about this cuvée is that it offers such a natural mixture of smoked meat, black fruit, and oak. It's a little chewy and rustic now, with mildly

hard tannins. If possible, give it some time for it to evolve and release its hidden plum, spice, and vanilla notes. **88 Best Buy** —*M.S. (3/1/2002)*

Montes 2002 Montes Alpha Merlot-Cabernet Franc (Colchagua Valley) $20. Big and forward, with spicy, pungent aromas and also a softening hint of bread dough. The palate features snappy red fruit with drying oak in support. The tannic structure holds its own but doesn't rise up too much. A weighty, driving wine. **88** —*M.S. (3/1/2004)*

Montes 2004 Limited Selection Pinot Noir (Casablanca Valley) $16. Gritty, raw, and lean, with jammy aromas of strawberry and cherry. Tastes very sweet initially, then fades quickly. Finishes mildly bitter. **82** —*M.S. (11/1/2005)*

Montes 2003 Limited Selection Pinot Noir (Casablanca Valley) $16. Not unattractive, with nice cinnamon, leafiness, and leather to the overriding strawberry nose. Fairly soft and meaty on the palate, and sweet at the core. Finishes creamy and thick, almost on the border of syrupy. **85** —*M.S. (7/1/2005)*

Montes 2000 Oak Aged Pinot Noir (Casablanca Valley) $16. Cream, plus jammy blackberry and blueberry aromas may trick you into believing that this wine's a Syrah, but the truth comes through on the palate, where sturdy, brambly blackberry flavors dominate. Finishes dry, with medium length. **87** —*D.T. (7/1/2002)*

Montes 2002 Oak Aged Limited Selection Pinot Noir (Casablanca Valley) $16. Lightweight raspberry and strawberry aromas waft upward, setting you up for a palate of candied cherry. The finish, like the front palate, is sweet, with raisin touches. The feel is a bit gritty, and while it tastes clean and racy, the flavor is unusual for Pinot Noir. **85** —*M.S. (8/1/2004)*

Montes 2002 Reserve Pinot Noir (Casablanca Valley) $10. Kicks off with rooty, cola aromas along with campfire and light berry notes. Fairly sweet and spicy across the palate, but lacking in true Pinot fruit expression. Put simply, you won't confuse this wine for Burgundy. **84** —*M.S. (3/1/2004)*

Montes 2003 Purple Angel Red Blend (Colchagua Valley) $48. Big, bold, and saturated, with dense aromas of baked fruit, spice, and licorice. This brand-new wine ranks as Chile's most pricey Carmenère, but it's surely one of the country's very best. It's ripe, packed with black fruit, and textured beyond ordinary. With oak, heft, and style, it's a winner. With 8% Petit Verdot. **90** —*M.S. (11/1/2005)*

Montes 2004 Limited Selection Leyda Vineyard Sauvignon Blanc (Leyda Valley) $16. For sure it shows intense green aromas of peas and celery, much more so than bright, spunky fruit. But that's the style, and within that style it's good. The palate blends fresh asparagus and apple, while the textured finish rises up with a layer of crispness and tropical fruit notes. **87** —*M.S. (11/1/2005)*

Montes 2001 Reserva Sauvignon Blanc (Curicó Valley) $10. The purity and power of the grapefruit and passion fruit aromas are uncharacteristically strong for a wine of this price. Vital acids drive the pineapple and passion fruit flavors across the lively palate. The tropical blast ends in a smooth, long finish. Who knew Chile could produce inexpensive Sauvignon Blanc like this? **89 Best Buy** —*M.S. (3/1/2002)*

Montes 2004 Reserve Sauvignon Blanc (Casablanca Valley) $10. Fairly piquant, with much of the so-called New Zealand character, including pickle, gooseberry, and snap pea. Long on the back palate and finish, with only semi-sharp acidity. Additional fruit comes on late. **86 Best Buy** —*M.S. (2/1/2005)*

Montes 2003 Reserve Sauvignon Blanc (Casablanca Valley) $10. Every year this Sauvignon Blanc manages to deliver fresh citrus aromas and flavors, a full blast of zest, and all the food-matching capabilities one could ask for. On the nose, it's mostly passion fruit, while flavors include green apple and kiwi. **88** —*M.S. (3/1/2004)*

Montes 2002 Reserve Sauvignon Blanc (Casablanca Valley) $10. This could very well be Chile's most expressive, interesting white Sauvignon. It's got all those prickly pineapple, passion fruit, scallion, and pepper notes that are typical, and also a lot of pure citrus flavors backing it all up. The mouthfeel is zesty and spirited, but there's natural roundness, too. Some licorice adds complexity to the finish. **89 Best Buy** —*M.S. (7/1/2003)*

Montes 2005 Cherub Rosé of Syrah (Colchagua Valley) $16. Smooth, clean, and succulent, with a pretty, rich color. The base grape is all Syrah, and the result is zesty and flavor-packed. It's a punchy wine with deep raspberry and nectarine flavors, and among Chilean rosé wines it is in a class by itself. **89** —*M.S. (11/15/2006)*

Montes 2003 Folly Syrah (Colchagua Valley) $NA. Super dark; almost black like night. This is big-boned New World Syrah from the Apalta Vineyard, and the aromas of violets and cherry are appealing. Big in the mouth, with bracing acidity and a lot of spare tannin. Very chewy and ripe, with vivid fruit. You won't find other wines like this; it's one of a kind. **92** —*M.S. (3/1/2006)*

Montes 2001 Folly Syrah (Colchagua Valley) $70. This is fast becoming Montes' signature wine. In only its second vintage, this 100% Syrah from the highest reaches of the Apalta vineyard is lush, refined, and exciting. The nose offers a delicate amalgam of cherry, mustard seed, chocolate, and horseradish notes. And while it's huge and extracted, it toes the line of balance. On the palate, lovely blackberry, licorice and syrup flavors take control and don't let go. **92** —*M.S. (3/1/2004)*

Montes 2004 Montes Alpha Syrah (Colchagua Valley) $25. Syrah seems to be the new signature grape at Montes, and this high-end example rocks due to round, roasted aromas of earth, coffee, and black fruit as well as blackberry, plum, and clove flavors. A firm, deep wine with a lot going on. For Chilean Syrah it's quite the mover and shaker. **91 Editors' Choice** —*M.S. (11/15/2006)*

Montes 2003 Montes Alpha Syrah (Colchagua Valley) $23. Rock solid and impressive in a very New World way. Prime aromas of earth, dark fruit, smoke, and more stir intrigue, and the palate delivers what it should: plump berry fruit, a good amount of oak, spice, and full but manageable tannins. The finish of toast and pepper is textured and full. A high-octane wine that hits you with the kitchen sink. **91 Editors' Choice** —*M.S. (11/1/2005)*

Montes 2002 Montes Alpha Syrah (Colchagua Valley) $22. Smells exotic, with piquant notes of cinnamon, tree bark, and citrus peel. The body, however, runs a bit rough and raw. There's a lot of spice and chunky plum, but not much of that funky Syrah essence that fans are likely seeking. **86** —*M.S. (3/1/2004)*

Montes 2001 Montes Alpha Syrah (Curicó Valley) $20. Solid and sturdy, and more big than small, this Syrah runs toward the red fruit spectrum. But the nose offers dried fruit, herbs, and clove, while there's more clove and fennel underneath the fruit on the palate. There's oak throughout, especially on the finish, but it's not overdone. And if many Syrah-based wines need time to settle, this one seems made for immediate drinking. **87** —*M.S. (7/1/2003)*

Montes 2000 Montes Alpha-Viñedo Apalta Syrah (Colchagua Valley) $22. Though there are bright blackberry, almost cassis, notes on the nose and in the mouth, they're enveloped in an unusual toast-meets-green herb combination that one taster called burning green tobacco and another described as marinated stuffed grape leaves. Finishes with dry leather, cedar, and cocoa flavors. Still in all, this medium-weight, soft wine contains some big, sweet fruit that will appeal to many. **87** *(11/1/2001)*

Montes 2000 Montes Folly Syrah (Colchagua Valley) $70. This inaugural high-end 100% Syrah from one of Chile's best wineries is thick, rich, concentrated, and everything else that makes a wine a true blockbuster. Smoked meat and deep, dark berries make up the nose. The palate is luscious and full of black fruit. The viscous mouthfeel is a showstopper. On a par with the world's best Syrahs. **91 Cellar Selection** —*S.H. (12/1/2002)*

Montes 2000 Late Harvest White Blend (Curicó Valley) $18. Gold in color, this blend of 50% Riesling and 50% Gewürztraminer is packed with apricot, peach, and honey notes along with walnut and peanut hints. It's rich and fruity, with marzipan and other sugary flavors. Modest acidity suggests it should be consumed soon. **88** —*M.S. (3/1/2004)*

MONTGRAS

MontGras 2002 Antu Cabernet Sauvignon (Colchagua Valley) $19. Rustic and hard, with leather and a lot of wood on the nose. But it should not be dismissed for that; the flavors are saturated and driving, with baked plum and berry plowing their way through to a finish of bitter chocolate and coffee. Fierce as it is in terms of tannin, it has a true mountain quality to it. **86** —*M.S. (12/15/2005)*

MontGras 2003 Antu Ninquén Cabernet Sauvignon (Colchagua Valley) $19. Very dark and oaky, with a tarry, black, crusty streak on the nose. Very ripe and tight, with cassis, black cherry, and tobacco flavors. More tannic than expected on the finish, with plenty of wood and chocolate. Needs a lot of air to show its best. A seriously intense wine. **87** —*M.S. (3/1/2006)*

MontGras 2002 Ninquén Mountain Vineyard Cabernet Sauvignon (Colchagua Valley) $31. Four years later and this is still a tannic beast. The nose shows a lot of wood, cinnamon, and leather alongside deep berry aromas, while the palate is just as woody, with firm cherry and plum fruit supported by killer tannins. Nothing soft or creamy here; it's all about grip, resin, and power. **87** —*M.S. (5/1/2006)*

MontGras 2000 Ninquén Mountain Vineyard Cabernet Sauvignon (Colchagua Valley) $30. Ninquén is 100% Cabernet Sauvignon, 80% of which is aged in new wood; the U.S. is only allocated 500 six-bottle cases. Numbers aside, this is an excellent wine, firmly structured, with powdery-smooth tannins. Cassis fruit is swathed in toast, earth, and nut flavors; the nose offers fragrant berry fruit, coconut, and hints of herb. To Hobbs's knowledge, it is the first mountain fruit grown (at 400 meters above the valley floor) in the region. **90** *(3/1/2003)*

MontGras 2004 Reserva Cabernet Sauvignon (Colchagua Valley) $11. This winery rarely fails with its basic Cabernet; in fact, it has establsihed the benchmark for South American value Cabs. The 2004 version is loaded with ripe berry flavors, a spot of earth and leather, and plenty of baking chocolate and tannin. Smooth and easy, but hearty and assured. **89 Best Buy** —*M.S. (5/1/2006)*

MontGras 2003 Reserva Cabernet Sauvignon (Colchagua Valley) $12. Fairly dark, with masculine aromas of burning brush, leather, and cassis. The palate is pure as crystal, with cherry, tobacco, and earth flavors along with black currant. Finishes full as a packed house, with chocolaty overtones. Excellent forthe price. **90 Best Buy** —*M.S. (11/1/2005)*

MontGras 2001 Reserva Cabernet Sauvignon (Colchagua Valley) $10. Excellent red fruit is on display from start to finish. The bouquet is a sweet and sly mix of chocolate, toast, earth, and caramel, and once you taste it, well, it's your basic berry cornucopia. Very good in terms of feel and balance, with some complexity to boot. **90 Best Buy** —*M.S. (6/1/2004)*

MontGras 1999 Reserve Cabernet Sauvignon (Colchagua Valley) $9. There's something to like about the smoky, earthy, meaty quality on the nose. There's also a hint of a clove scent. Full cassis and berry flavors make up the palate. Bright acids and full tannins keep the wine in balance from start to finish. **87 Best Buy** —*M.S. (3/1/2002)*

MontGras 2004 Reserva Cabernet Sauvignon-Syrah (Colchagua Valley) $10. Displays spicy cherry and just enough smoky oak to make a statement. Red fruit is clean and starchy, while the finish is firm and chocolaty, with some rubbery tannins protruding. Seems young; should soften through 2006. **87 Best Buy** —*M.S. (3/1/2006)*

MontGras 2003 Reserva Cabernet Sauvignon-Syrah (Colchagua Valley) $12. For those who like fruit over oak, this 50/50 blend, a marriage you don't see very often, is just what the doctor ordered. The Cab component sees a year in barrel; the Syrah no wood at all. The end result is a juicy, pure wine that sports blueberry and cassis as well as a touch of savory spice. Perfect for pizza or a barbecue. **88 Best Buy** —*M.S. (12/15/2005)*

MontGras 2000 Reserva Estate Bottled Cabernet Sauvignon-Syrah (Colchagua Valley) $10. One to bring to a party, or drink on a Tuesday night, this is an easy-drinking, bouncy wine that's a good value to boot. Earth and toast flavors envelope blackberry fruit on the palate. Finishes smooth, with herb and earth flavors. **87 Best Buy** *(3/1/2003)*

MontGras 2004 Reserva Carmenère (Colchagua Valley) $11. Forward and ripe, with olive, rubber, and tar on the dark nose. Black fruit and tannin make for a rather normal, straightforward palate. Which doesn't mean there isn't tasty fruit, spice, power, and some chocolate on the finish. A good but simple Chilean Carmenère. **86 Best Buy** —*M.S. (3/1/2006)*

MontGras 2000 Reserva Estate Bottled Carmenère (Colchagua Valley) $10. Has the foresty-brambly flavors that we love about Carmenère, but it's as lightweight as a Beaujolais. The nose offers caramel, tomato, smoke, and herb aromas. **84** *(3/1/2003)*

MontGras 2005 Reserva Chardonnay (Colchagua Valley) $10. Snappy and nice, with a touch of mineral. Otherwise it's all about ripe apple and pear up front and citrus on the back palate and finish. Zesty and clean, with the mildest amount of honeyed sweetness. **87 Best Buy** —*M.S.* *(5/1/2006)*

MontGras 2003 Reserva Chardonnay (Colchagua Valley) $11. Tropical fruit mixed with fairly heavy oak is the theme here. The nose offers melon, pineapple, and butter, while the palate is fat and creamy, with plenty of vanilla. Finishes with a lot of wood and just enough acid to keep things balanced. **85** —*M.S.* *(12/15/2005)*

MontGras 2000 Reserve Chardonnay (Colchagua Valley) $9. Clean and substantial, with coconut and banana aromas. Lemon and vanilla oak in the mouth reflect the ripe fruit and 40% barrel fermentation. It offers plenty for the price. **86** —*M.S.* *(3/1/2002)*

MontGras 2000 Merlot (Colchagua Valley) $6. For $6, you can't go wrong with this plum-packed fruitball that also offers defined cherry and raspberry. There's even enough body here to let you chew on it a little. Is it standard Merlot? Yes, but nobody should be complaining about this fine bargain. **85 Best Buy** —*M.S.* *(3/1/2002)*

MontGras 2004 Reserva Merlot (Colchagua Valley) $11. Well proportioned and solid, with pure cherry and berry characterisitcs alongside notes of tobacco and sugar beet. A bit tannic and firm, but not overly so; the finish offers mocha and plenty of berry extract. **87 Best Buy** —*M.S.* *(5/1/2006)*

MontGras 2003 Reserva Merlot (Colchagua Valley) $11. Not all that "reserve" in its style, but perfectly likable. Cherry, cola, rubber, and leather carry the nose toward a palate defined by tangy cherry. Close to full-force on the finish, which is flush and packed. Tannic and full; a winner in its class. **87 Best Buy** —*M.S.* *(11/1/2005)*

MontGras 1999 Reserva Estate Bottled Merlot (Colchagua Valley) $10. Fruit is mostly cherry and red berries; herbs accent the fruit from beginning to end. Mocha and briary notes add interest on the nose. **86** *(3/1/2003)*

MontGras 1999 Ninquén Red Blend (Colchagua Valley) $30. The '99 is the final Ninquén not from MontGras' Ninquén Hill vineyard. Future Ninquén vintages will be from that site. This, however, is from old valley-floor vineyards, and it's soft, round, and chocolaty, with raspberry flavors. The mouthfeel is suave and stylish. The finish offers some molasses and/or brown sugar. **89** —*M.S.* *(3/1/2002)*

MontGras 2004 Quatro Reserva Red Blend (Colchagua Valley) $15. Leather, earth, and bold fruit on the nose, and then sweet plum, berry, and chocolate on the palate. It's a blend of Cabernet, Malbec, Merlot and Carmenère that really couldn't have come together much better. It's rich, ripe, and tasty, and at 14.6% alcohol it's nothing if not a New World heavyweight. **90 Best Buy** —*M.S.* *(12/15/2005)*

MontGras 2003 Quatro Reserva Red Blend (Colchagua Valley) $16. This four-grape blend, hence the name, always manages to get it more right than wrong. The bouquet of plum, vanilla, and licorice is perfectly nice, while the black cherry and cassis flavors should draw fans. Tight, structured and flavorful, with ripe, mouthfilling tannins. **88** —*M.S.* *(11/1/2005)*

MontGras 1999 Quatro Reserva Estate Bottled Red Blend (Colchagua Valley) $13. This wine is mostly Cabernet, with Merlot, Carmenère, and Malbec making up the balance. (Useful factoid: The four colored stripes on the label represent each of the grapes—for example, Cabernet is red, Malbec is lavender—and the label stripes change every year, based on the amount of each grape that is used.) It offers black berry and cherry fruit on the palate and good length on the back end. **86** *(3/1/2003)*

MontGras 2001 Sauvignon Blanc (Colchagua Valley) $6. Peach, passion fruit, and a little cream make up the ultra-pleasant bouquet. Full citrus and tropical fruit flavors in the mouth make it easy to quaff. Delicious as an apéritif, and easy on the wallet. **86 Best Buy** —*M.S.* *(3/1/2002)*

MontGras 2002 Estate Sauvignon Blanc (Central Valley) $7. A fresh and racy wine, and a good choice for an apéritif. Clean, lemon, and grapefruit flavors are at its core, and are dusted with nice mineral notes. Fermented in stainless steel. **86 Best Buy** *(3/1/2003)*

MontGras 2005 Reserva Sauvignon Blanc (Casablanca Valley) $10. Slightly floral, with backing melon and apple aromas. Round and melony on the tongue, with some passion fruit, grapefruit, and spice peeking through. A bit soft but still fairly persistent. **85 Best Buy** —*M.S.* *(3/1/2006)*

MontGras 2002 Reserve Sauvignon Blanc (Casablanca Valley) $10. The panel was divided on their opinions about this wine—some liked it better than the Estate Sauvignon. Advocates found it ripe and round, with smoke and pink grapefruit aromas. Naysayers found a green bean note and a lackluster mouthfeel. One to try for yourself. 5,000 cases produced. **86** *(3/1/2003)*

MontGras 2003 Limited Edition Syrah (Colchagua Valley) $15. Ripe and seductive, and displaying raw power, pomp, and quite a bit of char-broiled, dark character. Very fruity and alive, with crusty black plum and berry flavors. Fully tannic but not mean. Modernin style; really good. **89** —*M.S.* *(11/1/2005)*

MontGras 2002 Limited Edition Syrah (Colchagua Valley) $16. Candied aromas kick start this meaty, plum-and-berry filled wine. After that, you draw some alfalfa and hay notes off the nose. The palate is sticky and big, with syrupy berry flavors preceding hot and spicy finishing notes. Unlike the average Syrah, but it has its merits. **86** —*M.S.* *(6/1/2004)*

MontGras 2004 Ninquén Antu Mountain Vineyard Syrah (Colchagua Valley) $19. Brooding and dark, with pencil lead, charcoal, and crude oil on the powerful bouquet. Quite fruity, with sweet plum and black cherry. Nice and weighty, but not particularly spicy. Emphasizes fruit and more fruit. **88** —*M.S.* *(3/1/2006)*

MontGras 2001 Limited Edition Zinfandel (Colchagua Valley) $15. Aromas of ripe raspberries, vanilla, and spice open this single-vineyard Zin, most of which, Hobbs admits, will be exported to the United Kingdom. Ripe black plum and raspberry flavors are accented by musky, earthy notes. Finishes with earth and juicy fruit. **88** *(3/1/2003)*

MORANDÉ

Morandé 2001 Edicion Limitada 66 Barricas Cabernet Franc (Maipo Valley) $NA. Some earthy, herbal cranberry scents are given life by a touch of smoky oak. The palate is sweet and wholesome, and very well balanced. The finish gives a hint of syrup and oak, but the fruit is ripe and succulent enough to handle that. **87** —*M.S.* *(7/1/2003)*

Morandé 2002 Edicion Limitada 66 Barricas Cabernet Franc (Maipo Valley) $20. A round wine with aromatics of tobacco, mint, black fruit, and coffee. In the mouth, there's a plethora of juicy black cherry and plum, followed by a wholesomeness that really earns the wine its stars. A very good Chilean red with its own identity. **88** —*M.S.* *(8/1/2004)*

Morandé 2004 Cabernet Sauvignon (Maipo Valley) $8. A touch sweet and syrupy, with a hint of molasses and raisin on the nose. The mouth deals big cassis, raspberry, and cherry flavors, while the solid finish offers chocolate and a whiff of toast. Yourthful and forward; drink now and enjoy. **86 Best Buy** —*M.S.* *(5/1/2006)*

Morandé 2002 Cabernet Sauvignon (Central Valley) $7. The nose is a tiny bit pickled, probably a sign of American oak, but there's also raspberry and garden-like freshness. The palate is ripe and juicy, with plenty of sweetness. As a whole it's tasty, balanced, and expressive. For a day-to-day Cabernet, this one is recommended. **87 Best Buy** —*M.S.* *(7/1/2003)*

Morandé 1999 Cabernet Sauvignon (Maipo Valley) $30. Fruit for this Bordeaux blend (it's only 80% Cab) is grown organically in Maipo Valley's San Bernardo Vineyard. Though the nose is a bit closed, black pepper, dried herb, and toast aromas still peek through. A long, tannin-and-char finish punctuates the blackberry, and oak palate flavors. It's a little tight now, and will be better in a year or two. **89** *(8/1/2002)*

Morandé 2001 Grand Reserve Vitisterra Cabernet Sauvignon (Maipo Valley) $13. Quite condensed and woody, with brier and sawdust aromas and some vivacious berry fruit. The palate is deep and pure, with cherry and cassis along with hints of coffee and earth. Yes, it's a bit hard due to firm tannins, but it's also a complete wine with a long, overt finish. **88 Best Buy** —*M.S.* *(7/1/2003)*

Morandé 2000 Grand Reserve Vitisterra Cabernet Sauvignon (Maipo Valley) $14. Appealing aromas of coffee, tobacco, and barnyard are complemented by the flavors of dark fruit and bitter chocolate. There is a pleasing balance of fruit and soft tannins that finish light, clean, and fresh. **89 Best Buy** —*C.S. (12/1/2002)*

Morandé 2000 House of Morande Cabernet Sauvignon (Maipo Valley) $30. Round and sweet, with some grapey, creamy aromas and a hint of oak sticking out. The palate is sweet, a bit candied, and firm, all courtesy of sharp but healthy tannins. A sweet, chewy finish is the lasting impression. **84** —*M.S. (7/1/2003)*

Morandé 2001 House of Morandé Cabernet Sauvignon (Maipo Valley) $35. This traditional Bordeaux blend is sweet, rich and fruity, with fine balance and true flavors. There's chocolate, plum, and oak on the nose, while licorice and vanilla notes tune up the quality Maipo fruit featured on the palate. Hands down it's the best wine in the Morandé stable. **90** —*M.S. (3/1/2004)*

Morandé 2002 Reserve Terrarum Cabernet Sauvignon (Maipo Valley) $10. The nose is slightly creamy due to overt oak, and it's also somewhat disjointed, what with both bold berry fruit and a strong whiff of wet dog. In the mouth, things quickly turn grapey, and then that overt fruitiness morphs into cherry and espresso. Meanwhile, bursting acidity throughout keeps it lively and fresh. **86 Best Buy** —*M.S. (7/1/2003)*

Morandé 1999 Terrarum Cabernet Sauvignon (Maipo Valley) $9. Ripe berry and black cherry aromas and flavors bear attractive herb, licorice, and tobacco accents. Shows good balance and structure, and the solid fruit plays out on the finish, with its even tannins and good length. Will hold year or two. Firm and flavorful. **88 Best Buy** (8/1/2001)

Morandé 2002 Vitisterra Grand Reserve Cabernet Sauvignon (Maipo Valley) $15. In the global Cabernet market, this stylish wine scores well. Aromas of coffee, mocha, and oak support plum and cassis. Additional currant flavors are thorough, although the finish is a touch gritty due to hard-packed tannins. Serious stuff, with depth and saturation. **88** —*M.S. (2/1/2005)*

Morandé 1999 Edicion Limitada Cabernet Sauvignon-Merlot (Cachapoal Valley) $18. Black cherry and plum fruit flavors are enveloped in chalky mocha notes in the mouth. Cedar, red berry, and a tomato-like note show on the nose. A little soft in the mouth, the wine closes with soft tannins and a bit of an herbal-lemony tang. **87** (8/1/2002)

Morandé 2001 Golden Reserve Carignane (Loncomilla Valley) $25. This is more of an experimental wine than a mainstream product. The blend is Carignan, Cab Franc, and Merlot, from one of Pablo Morandé's family vineyards. It smells of coconut and cotton candy—think Malibu rum and blackberry jam. The flavors are equally big and so is the acidity. It's a wine from another zone. **82** —*M.S. (3/1/2004)*

Morandé 2002 Edicion Limitada Carmenère (Maipo Valley) $20. The nose is almost salsa-like, with the pepper and tomato aromas that come up from the glass. But if you can get past the herbal gatekeeper, there's a nice mouthfeel and spicy fruit. A different path in Carmenère, one that requires a second, maybe a third taste to appreciate. **85** —*M.S. (3/1/2004)*

Morandé 2002 Reserve Terrarum Carmenère (Maipo Valley) $9. Dark in color, with powerful aromas that lean toward green peppers and green beans. Those vegetal notes are fairly well covered by some sweet oak, however, you can't escape the vegetal taste and smell. That said, the texture is perfect and the mouthfeel just right. **84** —*M.S. (7/1/2003)*

Morandé 2001 Terrarum Carmenère (Maipo Valley) $9. Rustic, as Carmenère should be, this single-valley offering is a good drink-with-barbecue bet. Bark, dark berries, and chocolatey aromas show on the nose; earth and black fruit dominate the full, low-acid palate. Woodsy, briary notes and ample spice give oomph to the juicy berry finish. **87 Best Buy** (8/1/2002)

Morandé 2003 Terrarum Reserva Carmenère (Maipo Valley) $11. Carmenère can veer into the land of green, and this wine has too much bell pepper and pepperoni going on to sway the jury. It's herbal throughout, with oregano and burnt coffee flavors overriding the fruit. It's also a bit tough in the mouth, with a jagged feel. **82** —*M.S. (3/1/2004)*

Morandé 2004 Terrarum Reserve Carmenère (Maipo Valley) $11. Dark and oaky, with coffee, olive, and beet-like aromas. Displays good black cherry character but also a lot of vanilla, coffee, and wood grain.

Feelwise, it's kind of hard and tannic; and bitterness on the finish can't be avoided. **84** —*M.S. (3/1/2006)*

Morandé 2005 Chardonnay (Maipo Valley) $8. Shows both pretty wild flower aromas as well as some pickle, but overall this no-oak wine distinguishes itself for its ripe grapefruit flavor touched up by some cucumber. A lot of fruit here; like fruit salad mixed in a bowl. **85 Best Buy** —*M.S. (5/1/2006)*

Morandé 2003 Chardonnay (Maipo Valley) $8. Opens with simple apple and pear aromas, while the mouth is full and chunky. Overall the flavor is lasting, courtesy of heady residual sugar that tilts the wine toward candied. Will appeal mostly to those fancying sweeter Chardonnays. **84** —*M.S. (3/1/2004)*

Morandé 2002 Grand Reserve Vitisterra Chardonnay (Casablanca Valley) $15. Here's one of the roundest, richest versions of Chardonnay coming out of Chile. It's full, honeyed, and loaded with pear and apple. That said, it's also borderline sticky and cloying. As for flavor, expect an explosion of orange, tangerine, pineapple, and baking spices. Subtle, it's not. **87** —*M.S. (12/1/2004)*

Morandé 2001 Morande Pionero Chardonnay (Central Valley) $7. The nose has some pine-based cleaner aromas to it, but not much luscious fruit. The palate has apple, pear, and melon flavors, but they are more vague than distinct. The finish is a continuation of what you get on the palate, but at the end you get a hint of toffee or caramel. Straightforward and basic; not nuanced or exotic. **84** —*M.S. (7/1/2003)*

Morandé 2003 Reserva Chardonnay (Casablanca Valley) $11. This unoaked wine seeks to showcase Casablanca fruit, which can be racy and pure in its best form. Here the characteristics are of pear and pineapple aromas, and then banana-like flavors. This wine, like the regular Chard, runs sweet with residual sugar, and there's a note of almond on the finish. **86** —*M.S. (3/1/2004)*

Morandé 2001 Terrarum Chardonnay (Maipo Valley) $10. A buttery, by-the-book Chardonnay that's heavier on oak than on fruit, this Maipo Valley offering has apple, toast, and cream flavors and oak, spice, and ripe pear aromas. More of the same flavors pop up on the back end. 5,000 cases produced. **84** (8/1/2002)

Morandé 2002 Terrarum Reserve Chardonnay (Maipo Valley) $10. Plump to the nose, with big aromas of apple, pear, wood resin, and mint. This wine delivers nothing but big-shouldered fruit, which is manifested in ripe, sugary apple, and pear flavors. The finish is thick and expansive. **85** —*M.S. (6/1/2004)*

Morandé 2001 Visiterra Chardonnay (Casablanca Valley) $15. Morandé's top Chardonnay is a single-vineyard offering from the oldest vineyard in Casablanca Valley, and is aged in French oak. Hearty buttery aromas give way to some mineral and banana notes underneath; toasty apple flavors in a rich, full mouthfeel are thankfully devoid of cloying creaminess. Oak is good, but still overshadows the fruit. **86** (8/1/2002)

Morandé 2002 Vitisterra Grand Reserve Chardonnay (Casablanca Valley) $15. Fairly forward, with aromas of lemon curd and the insides of many oak barrels. In the mouth are the full allotment of pear, apple, and lemon flavors, while the finish sits down and dries out rather nicely. Tasty and refreshing, with just enough heft. **86** —*M.S. (7/1/2003)*

Morandé 2005 Terrarum Reserve Gewürztraminer (Casablanca Valley) $11. A juicy, fairly intense white with natural sweet and spicy aromas that are typical of the variety. Tangy citrus, particularly pineapple, carries the palate along with green apple. From a cool climate so it stays balanced, clean, and interesting. **86 Best Buy** —*M.S. (7/1/2006)*

Morandé 2002 Edición Limitada 88 Barricas Malbec (Maipo Valley) $17. The nose is dominated by cranberry and rhubarb, with oak in the rear. Pretty to the eye, with weight and stuffing. Its virtues are its balance and spice. The detractions consist of slightly pickled aromas and flavors. Mostly a nice wine, minus the green character. **84** —*M.S. (12/1/2003)*

Morandé 1999 Morande Edicion Limitada Malbec 1999 Malbec (Maipo Valley) $17. The thin nose carries the scent of chlorine and a bit of pickle barrel. On the tongue, there's some vegetal character and pedestrian red fruit. Even the finish seems mildly pickled. Mouthfeel is the wine's best feature, but it can't overcome the odd flavors of pickle and the tang those flavors bring along. **82** —*M.S. (7/1/2003)*

Morandé 2003 Merlot (Central Valley) $8. Chunky and meaty, with a strong streak of green pepper running through the middle of the bouquet. Flavors lean toward berry syrup, with notes of sweet and sour. The finish is dry and a bit weak, while the mouthfeel is just okay. **83** —*M.S. (8/1/2004)*

Morandé 2002 Grand Reserve Vitisterra Merlot (Maipo Valley) $15. Rich boysenberry and plum aromas kick off this muscular, well-made Merlot. Flavors of dark berries and equally rich plum fruit are on the money, as is the full mouthfeel that's propped up by good tannins and a hint of oak. **88** —*M.S. (8/1/2004)*

Morandé 2001 Grand Reserve Vitisterra Merlot (Maipo Valley) $13. Despite not being overly dense or powerful, the nose features ample berry aromas and a hint of herbal essence. The mouth delivers plum, cherry, and berry fruit and then it goes spicy and oaky on the drying finish. Though not big and fat, there's substance and plenty of taste here. **85** —*M.S. (7/1/2003)*

Morandé 2000 Pionero Merlot (Central Valley) $7. Well-balanced and forward, with a supple mouthfeel, this pleasant Merlot shows cherry, toffee, and herbal aromas. The mouth offers good fruit with more cherry flavor, tobacco and green olive accents. It's easy to enjoy and drinks well right now. **86 Best Buy** —*J.F. (8/1/2001)*

Morandé 2003 Terrarum Reserva Merlot (Maipo Valley) $11. The nose is mildly grassy, with a hint of citrus peel. The mouth is fuller, with a creamy feel along with plum and berry flavors. Fairly smooth on the finish, with chocolate/carob notes and a blast of spice. **85** —*M.S. (3/1/2004)*

Morandé 2003 Pinot Noir (Casablanca Valley) $8. For not much cash, this is real Pinot Noir with all the correct leathery, leafy aromas and dry raspberry and cherry fruit you could ask for. Some fresh citrus peel and cured-meat notes offer a nod of complexity. **86 Best Buy** —*M.S. (7/1/2005)*

Morandé 2002 Pinot Noir (Casablanca Valley) $7. The bouquet is redolent of stewed tomato, dried spices, and lean red fruit, while the palate is thin and tastes like strawberries mixed with oak. The finish is the definition of light and easy, yet here a hint of pickled vegetable arises. **81** —*M.S. (7/1/2003)*

Morandé 2001 Pinot Noir (Casablanca Valley) $11. Smoke and a refreshing minty note open this Casablanca Valley Pinot. Black cherry and plum flavors are backed by smoke and syrupy molasses notes. Mouthfeel is on the rich side; finishes with modest tannins and spicy, briary flavors. **85** *(8/1/2002)*

Morandé 2001 Edicion Limitada Rosé de Pinot Noir Pinot Noir (Casablanca Valley) $13. For a rosé, this wine is hefty and bold, with strawberry and plum flavors, with a dash of earthiness. One reviewer found it too creamy; another found lots to like about its spicy, fresh-herb finish. With such diverse evaluations, this is a wine to try for yourself. **85** *(8/1/2002)*

Morandé 2001 Pionero Pinot Noir (Casablanca Valley) $7. Morande is the biggest producer of Pinot Noir in Casablanca Valley, and this entry-level bottling is a good value to boot. Earthy, forest-fire aromas coat black cherry notes in the bouquet; the palate's bark, oak, and bacon flavors come from time in old American oak barrels. Creamy and simple, but a steal. **84 Best Buy** *(8/1/2002)*

Morandé 2003 Reserva Organico Pinot Noir (Casablanca Valley) $11. This is a large, odd Pinot. It seems almost textbook at first, but then loses its focus upon extended airing. At 15.2% it has size on its side; flavors, meanwhile, include root beer, raspberry, chocolate, and tea. Finishes heavy, with coffee notes. **85** —*M.S. (3/1/2004)*

Morandé 2003 Terrarum Reserve Pinot Noir (Casablanca Valley) $10. Attractive leather, earth, and cherry aromas smell healthy. The wine itself has bright fruit, potent acidity, and enough smoke and spice to stir the Pinot faithful. Quite a good effort in Chilean Pinot Noir. **87 Best Buy** — *M.S. (7/1/2005)*

Morandé 2000 Late Harvest Riesling (Casablanca Valley) $13. Made from Riesling, this wine was mildly affected by botrytis, yet it's still lively and zippy. Honey, butterscotch, and banana notes on the nose play opening act to papaya and mango flavors. Full and flavorful, and fairly well balanced for the style. **87** —*M.S. (3/1/2004)*

Morandé 2005 Sauvignon Blanc (Curicó Valley) $8. Full and melony, and ultimately rather soft. Bulky grapefruit with a touch of orange and/or tangerine are the primary flavors, while the stout finish is short and a bit too round. Not much life here. **82** —*M.S. (7/1/2006)*

Morandé 2004 Sauvignon Blanc (Curicó Valley) $8. Applesauce dominates the nose, which frankly seems a touch mushy. The fruit, however, carries a lot of pop, so the flavors are pronounced and aggressive. And those flavors include melon, apple, and pickle. **83** —*M.S. (7/1/2005)*

Morandé 2003 Sauvignon Blanc (Central Valley) $20. Clean but bland, with flavors that run sweet and candied; you get dried and sugared citrus rind and also some carrot. The finish, meanwhile, is borderline medicinal. **84** —*M.S. (3/1/2004)*

Morandé 2002 Sauvignon Blanc (Central Valley) $7. The nose is like citrus candy and applesauce, but it doesn't sing or pop like it could. The mouth is easygoing, with melon and grapefruit, but there's also a bit of unwelcome green bean. This wine fails to excite . **83** —*M.S. (7/1/2003)*

Morandé 2001 Sauvignon Blanc (Casablanca Valley) $11. Grassy tropical fruit and melon aromas lead to chalk and lemon-lime rind flavors on the palate. It's lean in the mouth, for the most part. Stony-mineral flavors and a nice jalapeño note bat cleanup. 3,000 cases produced. **87** *(8/1/2002)*

Morandé 2000 Edicion Limitada Golden Harvest Sauvignon Blanc (Casablanca Valley) $25. This 100% Sauvignon Blanc dessert bottling is fermented in new French oak, and is aged one year on lees. Rich honey, peach, and nectarine fruit could have rendered this wine too sweet and sloppy; instead, its light, gravelly texture keeps it from being too cloying. Honey, mustard grains, and light talc on the nose, and a nutty, crème brulee-like finish add elegance where, again, candy could otherwise have reigned. **90** *(8/1/2002)*

Morandé 2000 Pionero Sauvignon Blanc (Central Valley) $7. Apricot aromas with flavors of green apple, cucumber, and green bean. The finish is clean and easy, but bland. This wine does nothing to offend, but it doesn't do much to impress, either. **83** —*M.S. (7/1/2003)*

Morandé 2005 Terrarum Reserve Sauvignon Blanc (Casablanca Valley) $11. Floral up front, with a bit of citrus blossom. More round than linear, with plump melon flavors and a hint of grapefruit. Full and easy on the finish. A very simple white wine. **83** —*M.S. (5/1/2006)*

Morandé 2003 Terrarum Reserve Sauvignon Blanc (Casablanca Valley) $10. Pungent and forward, with citrus and passion fruit emanating from the bouquet. Flavors of orange, lemon, and pink grapefruit push it squarely into the citrus class, while the finish is expectedly tangy and charged. The mouthfeel is lively and acidic. **86 Best Buy** —*M.S. (6/1/2004)*

Morandé 2003 Syrah (Maipo Valley) $8. Fat and funky aromas yield some spice and floral notes. Beneath is leathery, meaty fruit and a wine with a chewy mouthfeel. Seekers may find black cherry, black plum, and licorice prior to a smoky, mildly awkward finish. **84** —*M.S. (3/1/2004)*

Morandé 2002 Syrah (Central Valley) $7. This baby starts out like any child; it's awkward and clumsy. But it's also nicely extracted and chewy, with ripe plum fruit, hints of licorice, and a culminating toasty, slightly burnt note. The finish is tight and beefy, with good tannins, while overall it's enjoyable to drink even if it doesn't pretend to be highly sophisticated. **86 Best Buy** —*M.S. (7/1/2003)*

Morandé 2002 Grand Reserve Vitisterra Syrah (Maipo Valley) $15. Opaque and thick, yet despite its mammoth proportions the wine is lacking. It smells sweaty, while the flavor profile is sour at the core, with only modest surrounding fruit. Finishes starchy. **82** —*M.S. (8/1/2004)*

Morandé 2001 Pionero Syrah (Central Valley) $7. Tar, ink, and rubber aromas dominate this Syrah's nose. Mouthfeel is thin and the palate is a bit hollow, with generic mixed-berry flavors plus a little earth. Finishes tannic. **82** *(8/1/2002)*

Morandé 2001 Vitisterra Grand Reserve Syrah (Maipo Valley) $15. Mint and licorice aromas combine to give a medicinal impression that fortunately is not confirmed on the palate. In the mouth, it's ripe and mostly fresh, with flavors of plum, cassis, and blackberry. The finish is round and smooth, with more mint. Solid and racy if not overly stylish. **86** —*M.S. (7/1/2003)*

CHILE

Morandé 2002 Edicion Limitada Syrah-Cabernet (Maipo Valley) $20. Dark and meaty, with a fat nose full of oozing black fruit, coffee, and mocha. Quite muscular and ready, with plum, raspberry, and full tannins. Yes, it's a tiny bit overdone on the finish, where the acidity and tannins are potent. But it's got the depth and fruit quality to rate high. **87** —*M.S.* *(6/1/2004)*

Morandé 1999 Edicion Limitada Syrah-Cabernet (Maipo Valley) $18. Pepper and molasses aromas top concentrated black plum notes on the nose. The mouth is chewy and medium-weight, and offers bright but sturdy blackberry fruit, and some earth and oak notes. Finishes with good length, and tart berry and fresh-cut wood flavors. **88** *(8/1/2002)*

Morandé 2001 Edición Limitada 22 Barricas Syrah-Cabernet (Maipo Valley) $18. A very tight and meaty wine, with lots of vitality and plenty of rich liqueur-like characteristics. The juicy palate burst with cassis and black cherry, while the finish is equally full force. Clearly Pablo Morandé has found something by mixing Syrah and Cabernet. **89** —*M.S.* *(7/1/2003)*

NIDO DE AGUILA

Nido de Aguila 2002 Armonía Bordeaux Blend (Maipo Valley) $20. An excellent Bordeaux-style blend of Cabernet, Merlot, and Cab Franc that sings a pretty tune. Concentrated but pleasantly fruity, with cherry, raspberry, and chocolate aromas and flavors. A long, developed finish with a core of spice and smoke cements this wine's position as a winner and a fine bargain. From a 10,000-case, family-owned Maipo operation that's worth watching. **91 Editors' Choice** —*M.S.* *(2/1/2005)*

Nido de Aguila 2003 Armonía Reserva Bordeaux Blend (Maipo Valley) $15. This winery does its best with Bordeaux-style blends, which in fact are the pride of Maipo and what brings people back to Chile. This wine offers some traditional game and leather on the nose and then plum and berry flavors on the palate. Spice, toast, and vanilla all join nicely on the finish. Hold until 2007. **89** —*M.S.* *(5/1/2006)*

Nido de Aguila 2003 Reserva Cabernet Sauvignon (Maipo Valley) $15. Light berry aromas feature herb and leather accents. Basic raspberry and cherry fruit hold down the core, while green-pepper notes float about the edges. **83** —*M.S.* *(12/15/2005)*

Nido de Aguila 2003 Reserva Merlot (Maipo Valley) $15. Rusty in color, with tomato and light red fruit on the nose. Shows mostly roasted fruit flavors and leafiness. Not a lot of depth, but not offensive. **81** —*M.S.* *(12/15/2005)*

Nido de Aguila 2002 Reserva Merlot-Cabernet Sauvignon (Maipo Valley) $18. Rusty in color and a bit stewy, but sill quite enjoyable and well-made. Licorice, earth, and molasses aromas control the mature nose, while cinnamon spices up the cherry and boysenberry palate. A touch heavy and syrupy, but likable for its rustic, dark sweetness. The mix is 80/20 in favor of Merlot. **89** —*M.S.* *(2/1/2005)*

NUEVOMUNDO

Nuevomundo 2004 Cabernet Sauvignon-Malbec (Maipo Valley) $15. DeMartino's organic wine is dark and loaded with blackberry and other dark fruits, but with these flavors come some really hard tannins. Thus, the mouthfeel is like nails. That said, the hope and belief here is that it will soften over the next six months and will be ready to drink by late spring 2006. If not, then I've overrated it. **87** —*M.S.* *(12/15/2005)*

Nuevomundo 2005 Reserva Sauvignon Blanc (Maipo Valley) $15. Very light and mute smelling, but overtly aggressive, tart, and acidic in the mouth. Loads up on the green apple skins and tangerine in building a one-dimensional flavor profile. Teeters on being sour. **81** —*M.S.* *(3/1/2006)*

ODFJELL

Odfjell 2003 Orzada Cabernet Franc (Maule Valley) $18. Not a whole bunch of that typical leafy, French character; this is a South American rendition for sure. Ripe, with hard rubber and black cherry to the heady nose. Quite dense and saturated, with firm tannins and a lot of extract. **88** —*M.S.* *(11/1/2005)*

Odfjell 2004 Armador Cabernet Sauvignon (Maipo Valley) $10. Here's a nice and dark Cab with black licorice, clove, pepper, and blackberry aromas. The palate is ripe and sweet, with roundness and serious depth.

Finishes with chocolate and mint as well as some lushness. **87 Best Buy** —*M.S.* *(10/1/2006)*

Odfjell 2003 Armador Cabernet Sauvignon (Maipo Valley) $12. Earth, leather, and bell pepper aromas tangle with some fresher cherry and berry notes. Juicy and full in the mouth, with a red fruit core followed by chocolate and mint on the finish. Good texture, but overall it's a touch green and medicinal. **85** —*M.S.* *(11/1/2005)*

Odfjell 2002 Armador Cabernet Sauvignon (Central Valley) $10. Fairly potent, with notes of red berry, leather, and Tootsie Roll carrying the nose. In the mouth, flavors of raspberry, red licorice, and red pepper flake create an intriguing whole, while on the finish there's a smooth carryover from the palate. Quite tasty and easy to drink. **88 Best Buy** —*M.S.* *(8/1/2004)*

Odfjell 2003 Orzada Cabernet Sauvignon (Colchagua Valley) $18. Deep in color with mint, tobacco, licorice, and coconut shadings to the deeply fruited nose. Very well-tuned, with lush blackberry and cassis flavors in front of a moderately tannic, no-bull finish. **89** —*M.S.* *(11/1/2005)*

Odfjell 2002 Rojo Cabernet Sauvignon (Chile) $8. A hint of prune mixes with aromas of tree bark, pepper, and celery, while flavors of raspberry and plum are full, rich, and expressive. Finishing notes of chocolate and warm earth ensure that there's a lasting impression of richness. Overall, it's a masculine wine with an aggressive attack. **87 Best Buy** —*M.S.* *(8/1/2004)*

Odfjell 2003 Orzada Carignan (Maule Valley) $18. Colorful, with hints of mushroom to the cherry and raspberry nose. A very nice wine that is ripe but monotone. It's juicy and fruity, but ultimately simple. Chocolate and vanilla notes soften the finish. **87** —*M.S.* *(11/1/2005)*

Odfjell 2001 Orzada Cariñena (Chile) $15. An oddball wine, but one with nice raspberry, rhubarb, and floral aromas. The palate deals a fine mix of clean cherry, red plum, and currant, while the finish is smooth and elegant. Lots of fruit is on display here, and the Carignan is presented in fairly classy fashion. **87** —*M.S.* *(8/1/2004)*

Odfjell 2004 Armador Carmenère (Maule Valley) $12. Comes at you with a positive mix of herbal aromas and red fruit. The palate is spicy and savory, with crisp but simple fruit flavors forming a nice foundation. Shows good weight and flow, as it ultimately registers as fresh. **87 Best Buy** —*M.S.* *(10/1/2006)*

Odfjell 2003 Armador Carmenère (Maule Valley) $12. The Odfjell family, originally from Norway, understands the shipping business and they also understand how to make wines with deep flavors and smooth textures. And whereas Carmenère frequently tastes of bell peppers or worse, this has to be one of the best, most full versions we've come across. Black olive, herbs, and dried fruits carry the nose. Lush in the mouth; truly delicious. **90 Best Buy** —*M.S.* *(11/15/2005)*

Odfjell 2002 Armador Carmenère (Central Valley) $12. Smooth and racy, with more pronounced acids and a more perky mouthfeel than most. Aromas of mint accent blackberry fruit, while in the mouth it's straightforward berry and plum. Finishing notes of chocolate and light oak are supported by healthy tannins. **87** —*M.S.* *(8/1/2004)*

Odfjell 2004 Orzada Carmenère (Maule Valley) $18. Ripe as can be, with black plum, earth, and coffee on the seductive bouquet. Comes across as juicy, with vibrant fruit as opposed to anything you might call jammy. Finishes in a couple of layers, with spice, chocolate, and lasting lushness. **89** —*M.S.* *(10/1/2006)*

Odfjell 2003 Orzada Carmenère (Central Valley) $18. Black as night, with cola, mint, and very little herbaceousness. In fact, the whole package offers only the slightest note of Carmenère's notorious herbal character. Without that identity, it's pure and delivers unabridged ripeness. Finishes with bitter chocolate and vanilla. **90** —*M.S.* *(11/1/2005)*

Odfjell 2003 Orzada Malbec (Curicó Valley) $18. Exceedingly fruity, with graham cracker and jelly bean aromas. It's a berry lover's paradise, with bold, jammy flavors pushed by pulsating acidity. Very racy and nice, with purity and lots of depth. **91 Editors' Choice** —*M.S.* *(11/1/2005)*

Odfjell 2004 Armador Merlot (Central Valley) $12. Kicks off a touch loud and syrupy, with jammy berry aromas. The mouthfeel is full and round, while the flavors are deep and veer toward chocolate, plum, and blackberry. Finishes with notable caramel and carob flavors. **87 Best Buy —** *M.S. (10/1/2006)*

Odfjell 2003 Armador Merlot (Maipo Valley) $12. Ripe as fresh-picked fruit, but with a creamy mouthfeel and a lot of natural warmth. Unlike so many murky, insipid Chilean Merlots, this wine has spine and spunk. **87 Best Buy —***M.S. (11/1/2005)*

Odfjell 2002 Armador Merlot (Central Valley) $12. A clean nose starts things in the right direction. Aromas of blackberry and cola feature a slathering of oak, but not much beyond that. The bold, round palate is spicy and fruity, while the finish has coffee, mocha, and clove nuances. Lengthy and young; should improve over the next six months or so. **87** —*M.S. (8/1/2004)*

Odfjell 2002 Aliara Red Blend (Chile) $26. Hard and rubbery, with burnt coffee and mineral aromas. Very hard and tannic, with a borderline weedy, herbal note to the finish. Has its merits, but the feel is too hard and the love has gone on hiatus. **84** —*M.S. (11/1/2005)*

Odfjell 2000 Aliara Red Blend (Chile) $25. This mystery blend of several red grapes carries no specific region of origin, but suffice it to say that it's another good red from the Odfjell Vineyards stable. It's full-bodied, a bit heavy and murky, yet still lively. Flavors of cherry, plum, vanilla, and licorice are pushed by a healthy dash of oak. Modestly tannic, with full acidity. **88** —*M.S. (8/1/2004)*

Odfjell 2004 Armador Syrah (Maipo Valley) $12. Blueberry and a hint of bacon get it going. Next up is a dense palate that offers touches of mushroom, spice, and gentle black fruit. Not at all racy or loud; the wine lacks bold acidity but still registers as mostly balanced. **86** —*M.S. (10/1/2006)*

Odfjell 2003 Armador Syrah (Maipo Valley) $12. Rather gamy and savory, with aromas of black olive and cured meat followed by a creamy, baked-fruit palate that is simultaneously candied yet earthy. Don't judge it too quickly, it unleashes hidden pizzazz if given time. **86** —*M.S. (11/1/2005)*

ORIEL

Oriel 2000 VQM Cabernet Sauvignon (Maipo Valley) $17. Dilute and leafy, with slightly stewed red fruit flavors. Finishes with some toast and smoke, but not much body. Seems more lifeless than it should be; almost Old World in style. **82** —*M.S. (11/1/2005)*

ORIGIN

Origin 2004 Chardonnay (Central Valley) $10. Smooth, with a pleasant aromatic opening of toast blended with white fruits. Round apple, papaya, and banana work the palate, which shows perfect acidity and an even keel. Tropical as a whole, with commendable texture. **88 Best Buy** —*M.S. (7/1/2006)*

Origin 2004 Merlot (Central Valley) $10. Perfectly good in a mainstream way; the nose offers earth and leather with some roasted dark fruit aromas. Black cherry and raspberry on the palate are softened by some wood, while the finish starts with bold flavors and then veers toward tight tannins. A bit tough, but tasty. **85 Best Buy** —*M.S. (5/1/2006)*

Origin 2005 Rosé Blend (Rapel Valley) $10. Pretty interesting and solid as Chilean rose goes. The color is convincing and the bouquet shines and smells the way it should. Peach and red plum combine on the palate, creating a Provençal sensation. Finishes dry and crisp. **85** —*M.S. (5/1/2006)*

PASO DEL SOL

Paso del Sol 2001 Cabernet Sauvignon (Central Valley) $6. In this price range, you'll be hard pressed to find many better wines. It starts out with some malty aromas and a nice dose of violet-like flowers. In the mouth, vanilla sits underneath cassis, while on the finish, buttery oak does not seem out of place or overdone. **85 Best Buy** —*M.S. (12/1/2002)*

Paso del Sol 2004 Carmenère (Central Valley) $6. Giant and grapy, with awkward flavors of sweet blueberries and resin. Strange as a whole, with hints of green bean and coffee. **81** —*M.S. (7/1/2005)*

Paso del Sol 2004 Chardonnay (Central Valley) $6. Flat as a board, with vanilla, custard, and pear aromas. Nondescript white fruit carries everything to a sweet, bland finish. Mass market wine, no more no less. **81** —*M.S. (2/1/2005)*

Paso del Sol 2001 Chardonnay (Central Valley) $6. Flat, corn-like aromas kick it off, then deeper within there's a hint of butterscotch. The palate is surprisingly lean, with apricot, apple, and pineapple flavors. **83** —*M.S. (7/1/2003)*

Paso del Sol 2003 Merlot (Central Valley) $6. Jammy but dilute, with plum and red licorice flavors. A bit of caramel and toffee come on late, but that only works to create a thick, fudge-like mouthfeel. **82** —*M.S. (7/1/2005)*

Paso del Sol 2004 Sauvignon Blanc (Central Valley) $6. Apple, pear, and some mint on the nose stir interest, and the palate delivers more of the same. The orange flavors are tangy, while the finish is simple and direct. **83 Best Buy** —*M.S. (7/1/2005)*

PEÑALOLEN

Peñalolen 2004 Cabernet Sauvignon (Maipo Valley) $18. Deep and earthy, as the nose exhibits touches of warm dirt, stewed meat, fresh tomato and dark fruit. The palate is livelier than the bouquet, with cherry, cassis and other forward fruit flavors. Finishes smooth, with sweeping tannins. Very good overall; high in quality. **89** —*M.S. (11/15/2006)*

Peñalolen 2003 Cabernet Sauvignon (Maipo Valley) $18. Begins with roasted, smoky aromas that morph straight to deep black fruit. Cassis and black cherry form a solid flavor core, and there's plenty of tannin and toast on the finish. Very solid and one of the best efforts yet from this label. **88** —*M.S. (12/15/2005)*

Peñalolen 2002 Cabernet Sauvignon (Maipo Valley) $17. Starts raw and rugged, with overt sawdust aromas, but settles down to show spicy red fruit, licorice, leather, and earth. A bit oaky, with coconut flavors along with molasses, chocolate, and baked plum. Finishes on the sweet, syrupy side of the fence, but good in a meaty, modern, woody way. **87** —*M.S. (2/1/2005)*

Peñalolen 2001 Cabernet Sauvignon (Maipo Valley) $16. Opens with a blast of white pepper in the aroma and flavor, and the blackberry fruit struggles to rise above that spicy power. Still, the wine is distinctive, and feels polished and complex on the palate. **86** —*S.H. (11/1/2004)*

Peñalolen 2000 Cabernet Sauvignon (Maipo Valley) $15. Seemingly stewed and a touch burnt, this heavy wine manages to shed some of its girth as it opens, but even then it remains rather bulky. Thick, ripe, chewy fruit, and oak precede a grippy, spicy finish. Seems over-ripe and a bit weedy. **84** —*M.S. (8/1/2004)*

Peñalolen 2000 Cabernet Sauvignon (Maipo Valley) $15. Seemingly stewed and a touch burnt, this heavy wine manages to shed some of its girth as it opens, but even then it remains rather bulky. Thick, ripe, chewy fruit and oak precede a grippy, spicy finish. Seems over-ripe and a bit weedy. **84** —*M.S. (11/1/2005)*

Peñalolen 1999 Cabernet Sauvignon (Maipo Valley) $15. Here's yet another wine bearing the signature of winemaker Ignacio Recabarren, and it's a touch thinner and disjointed than one might expect. The nose features blanched raspberry and a strong note of pine or fern frond. The mouth is chunky and plummy, and it evolves with air. But it is also a touch vegetal and never really hits stride. **84** —*M.S. (7/1/2003)*

Peñalolen 2005 Sauvignon Blanc (Limarí Valley) $12. Slightly pickled, but with citrus as well. Seems a touch overdone, with peach flavors and some noticeable bitterness. Goes very light on the sweetness and weighs in less than friendly. **82** —*M.S. (3/1/2006)*

Peñalolen 2004 Sauvignon Blanc (Limarí Valley) $12. A little sweet to the nose but overall it's more crisp and minerally than fruity. Green apple and lemon-lime are the key flavor components, while the finish is light and crisp, with melon and citrus. Good basic white wine; nothing out of place. **85** —*M.S. (11/1/2005)*

Peñalolen 2003 Sauvignon Blanc (Limarí Valley) $12. How dry this wine is, and how tart! It has strong acids that frame lime and gooseberry flavors, and is very clean. Turns peppery-spicy on the finish. Good value in a refreshing cocktail or garden party wine. **84** —*S.H. (12/1/2004)*

Peñalolen 2002 Sauvignon Blanc (Casablanca Valley) $12. Terrific stuff, really a dynamic mouthful. True, it's simple in structure. But the grassy, lemon-and-lime flavors are extra rich, with fig [newton] and peach fla-

CHILE

vors that are so powerful, they last well into the finish of this bone dry, crisp wine. **87** —*S.H. (8/1/2004)*

PENGWINE

Pengwine 2003 Cabernet Sauvignon-Carmenère Cabernet Blend (Maipo Valley) $10. Burnt and leathery on the nose, with basic olive, saline, cherry, and plum flavors. Gritty and tannic, with some green qualities. Seems like a wine you've encountered many times before. **83** —*M.S. (11/1/2005)*

Pengwine 2003 Humboldt Reserve Cabernet Sauvignon (Maipo Valley) $16. Herbal and spicy, with leafy, red fruit aromas. The palate is weighty, with vanilla and brown sugar flavors along with ample oak. Shows good snap and pop once it opens. **84** —*M.S. (11/1/2005)*

Pengwine 2005 Magellan Reserve Chardonnay (Maipo Valley) $14. The nose mixes tropical fruit, banana, and also some sharp nettle. Orange, tangerine, and grapefruit flavors are only basically convincing, while more citrus runs wild on the untamed finish. Sort of sweet but also kind of sour. **82** —*M.S. (10/1/2006)*

Pengwine 2004 King Special Selection Red Blend (Maipo Valley) $30. This wine boasts boutique roots in the Maipo Valley, but the label doesn't tell us what roots exactly. In the glass, look for angular aromas and spice more than discernible fruit, followed by cherry and cola flavors that end in menthol and chocolate. Quite big and sweet; has its good as well as strange moments. **85** —*M.S. (10/1/2006)*

PORTA

Porta 2000 Reserve Cabernet Sauvignon/Carmenere Cabernet Blend (Chile) $14. Perfectly pleasant, particularly as a by-the-glass pour, the Porta is medium-bodied and easy to drink. Blackberries and plums compete with rustic oak flavors in the mouth; the bouquet offers a bizarre blend of anise, butter cookies, and apricots. **84** —*D.T. (7/1/2002)*

Porta 2000 Estates Cabernet Sauvignon (Aconcagua Valley) $10. Bold and fragrant, with aromas of cassis, cherry, and oak. The only flaw to the bouquet is a touch of weedy greenness, but it's slight. The flavor profile is all berries: black currant, cherry, raspberry, and strawberry. The finish is racy, with a healthy acidic streak. There's no shortage of pop and verve, although deepness and richness are absent. **86 Best Buy** —*M.S. (12/1/2002)*

Porta 2000 Grand Reserve Cabernet Sauvignon (Aconcagua Valley) $21. This wine needs some time to settle. The finish was course and gritty, but the pleasingly complex aromas were of dark sweet plums, fresh herbs, and dusty chocolate. Flavors of currants with a hint of tea lead into a chewy mouthfeel. **87** —*C.S. (12/1/2002)*

Porta 1999 Reserve Cabernet Sauvignon (Aconcagua Valley) $14. The forceful nose is somewhat awkward; it has leather and some interesting unidentifiable notes, but also a solid whiff of green. That same green element appears on the palate in the form of bell pepper, which doesn't really work with the candied fruit. Big tannins put it all over the map. **83** —*M.S. (12/1/2002)*

Porta 1999 Estates Carmenère (Maipo Valley) $10. Odd rubbery scents of asphalt and latex turn to bitter coffee grounds on the palate. There are some grapey, black cherry flavors but they are tough to get at. Shows a unique personality, which some tasters may find refreshing. **81** —*J.C. (8/1/2001)*

Porta 2000 Chardonnay (Cachapoal Valley) $9. The gold luster is eye grabbing, and the nose doesn't back off as it yields cream, vanilla, and toast atop tropical fruit. The mouth is full, with creamy pear and apple fruit and lots of oak. It's on the plus side in terms of power and weight, but it's largely balanced and clean. **86** —*M.S. (7/1/2002)*

Porta 2000 Grand Reserve Chardonnay (Cachapoal Valley) $21. This wine is even more oaky than the Porta Reserve. From my vantage point, Porta's Chardonnays benefit from the school of less is more. This one is dominated by wood and wood spice, much more so than its brothers. There's also some vanilla in the mix, but it tastes artificial. **82** —*M.S. (7/1/2002)*

Porta 2000 Reserve Chardonnay (Cachapoal Valley) $13. This wine, unlike the regular Porta bottling, comes across fat and bulky. It's overloaded with tropical fruit and combative oak. And while better qualities seem to be fighting to show themselves, they can't seem to fake it past the glaring oak. This is for barrel lovers only. **83** —*M.S. (7/1/2002)*

Porta 1999 Select Reserve Chardonnay (Cachapoal Valley) $13. This reserve offering opens with great aromas of toast, smoked bacon, caramel, baked apple, and pear. More of the same and pineapple notes are wrapped in toasty new oak and ride a ripe, buttery mouthfeel. The oak comes up strong on the finish, so be prepared, and oak lovers take note. **86** —*J.F. (8/1/2001)*

Porta 2000 Estates Merlot (Aconcagua Valley) $9. Smoked meat and flowers comprise the aromatics, with lots of oak and berry fruit to the palate. The finish is tannic but not too much so, and there's also some cherry, vanilla, and coffee. **86 Best Buy** —*M.S. (12/1/2002)*

Porta 2000 Grand Reserve Pinot Noir (Bío Bío Valley) $22. The nose is a little closed, but there's a lot to like about this Pinot, particularly its gravelly tannins. Blackberry, black plum, and metallic-mineral flavors are lovely, but really, it's all about the texture. **87** —*D.T. (7/1/2002)*

Porta 1999 Grand Reserve Pinot Noir (Bío Bío Valley) $22. This Pinot, from a vineyard region not commonly seen in the U.S., boasts aromas of root beer and sour malt backed up by blackberries, black cherries, and licorice. The black cherries persist all the way through the dry, toasty, slightly bitter finish. **85** *(8/1/2001)*

PORTAL DEL ALTO

Portal Del Alto 1999 Cabernet Sauvignon (Maule Valley) $7. Sweet caramel, a touch of mintiness, and some earth-tinged cassis grace the nose. That's followed up by simple fruit flavors and a corpulent mouthfeel held together by some light tannins on the finish. **84** —*J.C. (2/1/2001)*

Portal Del Alto 1999 Gran Reserva Cabernet Sauvignon (Maipo Valley) $12. Dark in color, with aromas of bacon and spice. The palate is tight-grained and woody, with ample berry fruit peeking through. Firm acids keep it fresh from start to finish, while the only thing holding it back is some hollowness to the midpalate. **87 Best Buy** —*C.S. (12/1/2002)*

Portal Del Alto 1998 Gran Reserva Alejandro Hernández Cabernet Sauvignon (Maipo Valley) $15. This Cabernet has nice red berry fruit and is well-balanced, but is light in body and bears the tell-tale herbaceousness present in so many of the 1998 wines. Some handsome smoke and earth accents add class, but there isn't the depth in this vintage's wine for the designation it bears of Gran Reserva. **84** —*M.M. (1/1/2004)*

Portal Del Alto 2000 Hand Picked Selection Cabernet Sauvignon (Central Valley) $7. Some brambly spice gets it going, with apple skin, cherry, and other high-toned fruits coming next. For a value-priced wine, it delivers all that can be expected and arguably a bit more. The finish is lengthy and clean, bordering on stylish. **86 Best Buy** —*M.S. (12/1/2002)*

Portal Del Alto 2000 Reserva Cabernet Sauvignon (Maule Valley) $10. The bouquet is murky, with oak and funk but no clarity. The flavors are on the thinner side, and the light berry fruit carries a reedy note. Vanilla is the most identifiable note on the finish. **82** —*M.S. (12/1/2002)*

Portal Del Alto 1998 Reserve Cabernet Sauvignon (Maipo Valley) $12. This is a well-made wine, correct in all respects but decidely light for a Cabernet Sauvignon, perhaps a reflection of the difficult 1998 (La Niña) vintage. However, its attractive flavor package and appraochable structure make for easy drinking with tonight's pasta or pizza. **85** —*M.N. (2/1/2001)*

Portal Del Alto 2000 Gran Reserva Carmenère (Maule Valley) $12. This medium-bodied Carmenère offers blackberry, oak, and white-pepper flavors and herb, wood, and blueberry aromas. Good for a group; will appeal to a wide audience. **84** —*D.T. (7/1/2002)*

Portal Del Alto 2000 Chardonnay (Maule Valley) $7. This individualistic Chardonnay has a lot to offer. The nose is ripe, with floral, honey, and even petrol notes and opens to a palate of tangerine and lychee nut-like flavors. The mouthfeel is round and smooth; the sweet and sour finish, dry and spicy. Reminiscent of some Alsatian whites and worthy of notice for its flavorful uniqueness. **87 Best Buy** —*M.M. (2/1/2001)*

Portal Del Alto 2000 Gran Reserva Chardonnay (Maipo Valley) $12. Another wine from Portal del Alto that's just on the cusp of drinkability.

CHILE

Potent butterscotch and cream aromas don't seem authentic. Resiny flavors mask the fruit, and it finishes flat. **80** —*M.S. (7/1/2002)*

Portal Del Alto 1999 Reserva Chardonnay (Central Valley) $12. Alejandro Hernandez, professor of viticulture and oenology at Chile's Catholic University, produced this attractive bottle of Chardonnay to drink tonight. Aromas of toasted oak, apple, and pineapple open. The viscous mouthfeel is supported by crisp acidity. Offers a long apple-pineapple finish with a butterscotch finale. **87** —*M.N. (2/1/2001)*

Portal Del Alto 1999 Pinot Noir (San Fernando) $7. A light Pinot Noir, this shows some dried cherry aromas and flavors with touch of barnyard, but also a fair amount of greenness showing. The mouthfeel is correctly light and dry, but the back end is a bit leathery and short. **83** —*M.M. (1/1/2004)*

PRIMUS

Primus 1998 Veramonte Red Blend (Casablanca Valley) $20. Red berry fruit with a heavy dose of herb and bell pepper marks this red blend from Augsutin Huneeus. The mouthfeel is smooth, but the acidity is high and the wine finishes slightly tart, with a green note. Another victim of this tough year, we'll look forward to the 1999. **83** —*M.M. (1/1/2004)*

RIO ALTO

Rio Alto 2002 Syrah (Aconcagua Valley) $8. Grassy and mildly weedy, with sweet edges to the nose. The palate features weak red berry fruit and syrupy sweetness. This wine just doesn't really have it. **81** —*M.S. (6/1/2004)*

ROOT:1

Root:1 2003 Cabernet Sauvignon (Maipo Valley) $12. A new wine for the American market, one with soft, pickled aromas and backing flavors of black plum and blackberry. Sort of soft and a bit green, with oak-propelled chocolate on the sweet and savory finish. **83** —*M.S. (5/1/2006)*

SAN NICOLAS

San Nicolas 2003 Cabernet Sauvignon (Curicó Valley) $8. Perfectly nice, with black cherry, leather, and some snap. Ripe and generally clean on the palate, with cola, black fruit, and easygoing tannins. Stays the course; quintessential basic Chilean Cabernet. **85 Best Buy** —*M.S. (11/1/2005)*

San Nicolas 2003 Sophia Gran Reserva Cabernet Sauvignon (Curicó Valley) $15. Starts out with aromas of wet leaves but the balancing element is solid red fruit. The palate pours on the cherries, bolstered by heavy tannins, while the finish deals raspberry tinges atop vanilla. Disjointed, but with positive touches. **84** —*M.S. (10/1/2006)*

San Nicolas 2001 Sophia Gran Reserva Cabernet Sauvignon (Curicó Valley) $14. Solid enough, with lightweight fruit, tobacco, and mushroom scents. Adequately balanced, with black cherry and plum flavors. Pepper and a touch of espresso carry the finish. A bit medicinal, with a balsamic character. **84** —*M.S. (8/1/2005)*

San Nicolas 2004 Chardonnay (Curicó Valley) $8. Sort of sweet on the bouquet, with hints of lemon-lime and candy. Natural tasting, and veering toward tropical. Moderate girth in terms of body, with a finish accented by toast and vanilla. **84 Best Buy** —*M.S. (11/1/2005)*

San Nicolas 2003 Chardonnay (Curicó Valley) $8. Pedestrian, with light pear and apple aromas as well as a whiff of chlorinated swimming pool. Slight flavors, not much snap, and little style or voice. **81** —*M.S. (11/1/2005)*

San Nicolas 2004 Sabrina Reserve Chardonnay (Curicó Valley) $11. Warm and a bit oaky, with aromas of vanilla and baked bread along with more standard apple and pear. Falls on the leesy side of the fence, with creamy, toasty flavors of butter, baked pear, and cream. From Santa Julia. **86 Best Buy** —*M.S. (11/1/2005)*

San Nicolas 2005 Merlot (Curicó Valley) $8. Bramble and standard redberry aromas are the opening act. Next in line is a mildly vegetal palate with blackberry as the offset. Shows pickled flavors and decent feel toward the finish. Lacks that fully ripe character. **82** —*M.S. (11/15/2006)*

San Nicolas 2003 Maigo Reserve Merlot (Curicó Valley) $11. Hard rubber, wood smoke, and tobacco along with dark fruit is what you draw from

the bouquet. Fairly standard fare raspberry and strawberry flavors work the palate, which is generally healthy and well-balanced. Shows a touch of green toward the finish, but not enough to significantly hurt it. **85** — *M.S. (10/1/2006)*

San Nicolas 2005 Sauvignon Blanc (Curicó Valley) $8. Not easily identifiable as Sauvignon Blanc, but not a bad wine, per se. The nose has a cake-like sweetness, while the palate is sugary, with apple and lime accents. A basic wine with a candied personality. **83** —*M.S. (10/1/2006)*

San Nicolas 2003 Sauvignon Blanc (Curicó Valley) $8. Flat and devoid of character. Banana and melon flavors are adequate but unexciting. Not offensive, but there's really nothing going on here. **80** —*M.S. (7/1/2005)*

SAN PEDRO

San Pedro 2001 1865 Reserva Cabernet Sauvignon (Maipo Valley) $19. Winemaker Irene Paiva describes Maipo Cabernets as often having a minty or eucalyptus character, and that's certainly evident in this wine, alongside plump, ripe berry notes. Long and finely textured on the finish. **87** *(11/1/2005)*

San Pedro 2002 Cabo de Hornos Cabernet Sauvignon (Lontué Valley) $35. On the young side, with briary, berry-scented fruit that should calm and settle in another year or two. Dried herbs add complexity, while the mouthfeel displays Cabo's trademark luxurious texture, extending right through the elegant finish. **90** *(11/1/2005)*

San Pedro 2001 Cabo de Hornos Cabernet Sauvignon (Lontué Valley) $35. Smells lovely, with cedar, tea, and cassis mingling effortlessly on the nose. In the mouth, it's bigger and fleshier than the '99 or '00, with a long finish filled with sweet fruit. **91 Editors' Choice** *(11/1/2005)*

San Pedro 2000 Cabo de Hornos Cabernet Sauvignon (Lontué Valley) $35. From a difficult vintage, this is an admirable effort that just can't stand up to those surrounding it. Chocolate and green tobacco aromas and flavors, a more angular mouthfeel and tougher, more rustic finish add up to fewer points on our scorecards. **85** *(11/1/2005)*

San Pedro 1999 Cabo de Hornos Cabernet Sauvignon (Lontué Valley) $35. Harvested from dry-farmed vines 50 years old or more, rigorously selected on the sorting table, fermented after a short cold maceration, then put into French oak for 18 months and aged in bottle for a year before release, this wine gets coddled from start to finish. The results speak for themselves: floral, leather, and dried fruit aromas; flavors of cedar, cassis, and molasses; soft, supple tannins and a long, elegant finish. **91 Editors' Choice** *(11/1/2005)*

San Pedro 1998 Cabo de Hornos Cabernet Sauvignon (Lontué Valley) $45. This meaty, earthy Cab hails from a special vineyard near San Pedro's Curicó winery. It receives 18 months in oak, 50% of it new. Blueberry and blackberry flavors are dominant but are somewhat held back by heavy tannins. The structure is solid, maybe too much so. Additional aging could soften it up, but that's not a guarantee. **86** —*M.S. (3/1/2002)*

San Pedro 2005 Castillo de Molina Reserva Cabernet Sauvignon (Lontué Valley) $10. A nice, simple, easy to handle Cabernet is what you're getting here. Root beer, blackberry, and spice aromas work the nose, followed by slightly medicinal but generally big and bold black fruit flavors. Generally speaking, this is a very good everyday Cab that won't hurt the wallet. **87 Best Buy** —*M.S. (11/15/2006)*

San Pedro 2004 Castillo de Molina Reserva Cabernet Sauvignon (Lontué Valley) $11. From a region winemaker Irene Paiva describes as cooler than Chile's other Cabernet growing regions, this wine shows some herbal notes on the nose, but also a wonderfully supple texture and finely wrought flavors of cherries, tobacco and chocolate. **86 Best Buy** *(11/1/2005)*

San Pedro 2003 Castillo de Molina Reserva Cabernet Sauvignon (Lontué Valley) $11. The nose deals a nice blast of smoky leather and pepper, with briary fruit resting below. Somewhat herbal and peppery on the palate, with dark shadings of coffee made only more potent by firm tannins. Not the softest wine, but powerful. **86 Best Buy** —*M.S. (11/1/2005)*

San Pedro 2002 Castillo De Molina Reserva Cabernet Sauvignon (Lontué Valley) $10. Lots of tobacco, green bean, and berry fruit work the nose, followed by syrupy but standard red fruit flavors on the tongue. Plum,

CHILE

fudge and astringent tannins make for a mouthfeel that's at once soft but also hard. **84** —*M.S. (2/1/2005)*

San Pedro 2001 Castillo de Molina Reserva Cabernet Sauvignon (Lontué Valley) $11. A bit of complexity dances across the bouquet: there's rubber, wood, anisette, and mute red fruit; there's also some minty green aromas, too. The palate is properly round and buttery, with ample red fruit flavors, while the finish is smooth and mostly satisfying. This is a basic Cabernet, but a good one. **86** —*M.S. (7/1/2003)*

San Pedro 2005 Gato Negro Cabernet Sauvignon (Central Valley) $5. Bright day-glo purple in color, this is a fresh, fruity, light-weight wine that delivers Cabernet flavors of cassis and chocolate without real weight or structure behind it. Serve it as you would a Beaujolais or light-bodied Côtes-du-Rhône. **83 Best Buy** *(11/1/2005)*

San Pedro 2002 Gato Negro Cabernet Sauvignon (Central Valley) $5. Dusty, peppery aromas carry little richness, but in the mouth things turn more fruity. You get cherry and plum, but also a salty edge. The texture is smooth and solid enough, but the finish is disproportionately buttery, salty, and mildly vegetal. **83** —*M.S. (7/1/2003)*

San Pedro 2000 Reserva 1865 Cabernet Sauvignon (Maipo Valley) $20. The aromas are a touch prickly and sharp, and there's some heavy oak on the nose. But in the mouth it's more harmonious, with sweet fruit and more than enough barrel spice. The finish is simple and clean, so it fades away nicely. The only problem is a lasting salty, wood-dominated essence. **85** —*M.S. (7/1/2003)*

San Pedro 2002 San Andrés Cabernet Sauvignon (Lontué Valley) $NA. Earth and berry aromas, and then thin, woody cherry flavors. The finish is buttery and rather bland, and the palate feel is lean and overwooded, especially given the basic pedigree of the wine. **82** —*M.S. (7/1/2003)*

San Pedro 2002 1865 Reserva Carmenère (Maule Valley) $19. Smoky and herbal on the nose; like the rest of the Viña San Pedro offerings, this one is typical of its variety. Sappy, resiny, green notes alongside riper black cherry flavors end on a coffee-like note. **85** *(11/1/2005)*

San Pedro 2002 Gato Negro Carmenère (Lontué Valley) $5. Strawberry aromas are covered by heavy oak and a green tobacco note. The palate is also green, although some strawberry and raspberry fruit fights its way through. The finish is full and textured, but the flavor falls decidedly toward weedy and green. A chalky feel closes the show. **81** —*M.S. (1/1/2004)*

San Pedro 2005 Castillo de Molina Reserva Chardonnay (Casablanca Valley) $10. Fresh pear and a touch of oak grace the nose, followed by a crisp, generally well-balanced palate that's toting punchy white-fruit flavors and noticeable oak. A very nice Chilean Chardonnay with snap. **87 Best Buy** —*M.S. (11/15/2006)*

San Pedro 2004 Castillo de Molina Reserva Chardonnay (Casablanca Valley) $11. Toasty and buttery smelling, but blends in enough pear, citrus, and anise flavor to retain interest. Crisp on the finish, where the oak become a bit aggressive. **84** *(11/1/2005)*

San Pedro 2003 Castillo De Molina Reserva Chardonnay (Casablanca Valley) $10. A sweet-styled Chard with uncluttered mango, melon, and apple aromas. The same sweet element comes on strong on the palate, where pear and banana take over. May be too candied for connoisseurs, but packing a lot. **86 Best Buy** —*M.S. (7/1/2005)*

San Pedro 2002 Castillo de Molina Reserva Chardonnay (Lontué Valley) $11. Strongly oaked, but fresh, young, and healthy in the nose. The smell of coconut and lemon curd is friendly and soft, while the palate is loaded with more lemon, coconut, pear, and nutmeg. The texture is rich, and, for now, the acidity is bright. A solid Chardonnay for current drinking. **87** —*M.S. (7/1/2003)*

San Pedro 2003 Gato Blanco Chardonnay (Central Valley) $5. Not very expressive, but not offensive either. Soft white fruits and wheat on the nose, with mild apple and pear flavors. A bit hefty and round, with low-level acidity. **83 Best Buy** —*M.S. (2/1/2005)*

San Pedro 2002 San Andrés Chardonnay (Lontué Valley) $NA. At first the nose is bland, offering what a Spanish speaker would call nada. But with time some dry, spicy flavors and modest yet clean tropical fruit rise up. The finish turns a bit heavy and oaky, but with a proper chilling, this

should go down smoothly. It has the basics in terms of banana and papaya-like fruit. **84** —*M.S. (7/1/2003)*

San Pedro 2002 1865 Reserva Malbec (Curicó Valley) $19. Starts with inviting but oaky aromas of toast and menthol, then moves into crisp black cherry flavors on the palate. Offers an intriguing combination of flesh and structure, picking up hints of bacon on the finish. From untrained and unirrigated old plantings of Côt. **87** *(11/1/2005)*

San Pedro 2002 35 South Land of Passion and Fantasy Merlot (Lontué Valley) $8. Full in the nose, with leather and muted red and black fruit. The palate is big and oaky, with flavors of black plum and milk chocolate, and the finish is of modest length, with size and some tannins. This wine has all the typical Merlot characteristics, but in short order. **84** —*M.S. (7/1/2003)*

San Pedro 2003 Castillo de Molina Reserva Merlot (Lontué Valley) $11. Starts out with strong aromas of open-cut wood, vanilla, and mild red fruit. The palate offers acid-driven red cherry and plum flavors, with buttery oak in the background. More of a lean, racy Merlot with a lot of scour to it. **83** —*M.S. (11/1/2005)*

San Pedro 2002 Gato Negro Merlot (Lontué Valley) $5. Big, awkward aromas of red fruit and oak are followed by simple berry and plum flavors and even more overt oak. The finish is big and warm, while late in the game the wine turns tangy. This is one of many mass-market Merlots with few glaring faults; but still it fights to rise above basic acceptability. **82** —*M.S. (7/1/2003)*

San Pedro 2002 San Andrés Merlot (Lontué Valley) $NA. Meaty, woody aromas carry along some cherry and cinnamon, but those scents are distant and slightly artificial. The mouth is chunky and big, with plenty of buttery oak along with nondistinct red fruit. The feel is sharp, courtesy of strong acids, so there's a tangy, astringent final impression. **82** —*M.S. (7/1/2003)*

San Pedro 2003 Gato Blanco Sauvignon Blanc (Central Valley) $5. Soft and creamy, with lactic pear and vanilla aromas. Mild peach and nectarine flavors, with a dilute finish. **82** —*M.S. (2/1/2005)*

San Pedro 2006 Gato Negro Sauvignon Blanc (Central Valley) $5. Chill this down and let it go, and you'll be surprised at how solid this white is. Citrus peel aromas lead toward pear and banana flavors that are supported by acidity and pop. A lightweight in the end, but it's ripe and tasty. Good by the glass or in a spritzer. **85 Best Buy** —*M.S. (11/15/2006)*

San Pedro 2005 Gato Negro Sauvignon Blanc (Central Valley) $5. Soft and round without much bite. But it is clean, with melon and guava aromas and adequate citrus flavors. Not bad at all, especially at the price. A true bargain-basement deal. **83 Best Buy** —*M.S. (12/15/2005)*

San Pedro 2002 San Andrés Sauvignon Blanc (Lontué Valley) $NA. Fresh and forward, with aromas of pine, lemon, and pear. The mouth is rather lush, but hardly fat. There's clean flavors of pineapple and banana, and then comes a sharp, tangy finish. This is proof that Chile can produce good Sauvignon Blanc for immediate consumption. **85** —*M.S. (7/1/2003)*

San Pedro 2005 Castillo de Molina Reserva Shiraz (Lontué Valley) $10. Sweet and rich, and in the long run it's nice for the money. There's some alluring fruit aromas that vie with more floral scents, and behind that is a palate of plum and dark berries. An easygoing but sturdy wine; it impresses with its big, broad shoulders and easy-to-like personality. **88 Best Buy** —*M.S. (11/15/2006)*

San Pedro 2004 Castillo de Molina Reserva Shiraz (Lontué Valley) $11. Bottled after one year in oak, this plump, fleshy Syrah doesn't really show overt wood influence. On the nose, you get some tar and blackberries, followed by more berries on the palate before they turn slightly herbal and stemmy on the finish. **84** *(11/1/2005)*

San Pedro 2003 Castillo de Molina Reserva Shiraz (Lontué Valley) $11. Bold and fruity, with a dark nose full of rubber and coffee. The fruit on the palate is sweet if a bit baked, while the mouthfeel scores via ripe tannins and chocolaty warmth. For the money this is good South American Shiraz. **86 Best Buy** —*M.S. (11/1/2005)*

CHILE

SANTA ALICIA

Santa Alicia 2002 Gran Reserva Cabernet Sauvignon (Maipo Valley) $13. Rugged at first, with a strong blast of shoe polish and pickle barrel. Runs toward simple despite having a lot of color. The palate shows oaky notes of vanilla, marshmallow, and cherry liqueur, while the finish is a bit medicinal. Not a congruent package. **84** —*M.S. (7/1/2006)*

Santa Alicia 2001 Gran Reserva Cabernet Sauvignon (Maipo Valley) $13. The aromas of oregano, green bean, and plum are slightly misleading; you expect an under-ripe wine, but it's not. There's a good berry profile along with a soft, chocolaty finish. The fruit is more meek than forceful, but it's still satisfying. **85** —*M.S. (3/1/2004)*

Santa Alicia 1998 Gran Reserva Cabernet Sauvignon (Maipo Valley) $14. Red plum and dry oak get top billing on the palate. What's off-putting here is a dry, gritty-woody mouthfeel that hangs on until the very end. **82** —*D.T. (7/1/2002)*

Santa Alicia 2003 Reserve Cabernet Sauvignon (Maipo Valley) $9. This well-made bargain delivers yummy raspberry and cherry aromas and flavors, with touches of licorice and clove. A winner in its price range; dense and dreamy. What well-priced Chilean Cab should be. **88 Best Buy** —*M.S. (7/1/2006)*

Santa Alicia 2001 Reserve Cabernet Sauvignon (Maipo Valley) $8. Weedy and pickled, with a pedestrian mix of red berry flavors, veggies, and creamy oak. It gets cleaner and better with airing, but how much breathing time does a basic Chilean Cab deserve? **81** —*M.S. (3/1/2004)*

Santa Alicia 2001 Estate Bottled Reserve Carmenère (Maipo Valley) $8. Spicy, earthy aromas are warm and fairly deep, while a snappy, acidic palate of berry fruit supported buy buttery oak does the trick. The finish is substantive and only mildly tannic, while the overall personality is fresh and clean. **85 Best Buy** —*M.S. (7/1/2003)*

Santa Alicia 2002 Reserve Carmenère (Maipo Valley) $8. Meaty and dark on the nose, but reserved. In the mouth, chocolate envelops sturdy plum fruit, yielding a coffee-tinged aftertaste. And with bitter chocolate and espresso on the finish, this wine holds its own all the way to the end. **87 Best Buy** —*M.S. (8/1/2004)*

Santa Alicia 2001 Estate Chardonnay (Maipo Valley) $6. The nose is sulphuric and a bit barnyardy, which screams "watch out," but in the mouth there's acceptable if unspectacular apple fruit. It's scratchy in the finish, and probably just this side of not being worth drinking. **80** —*M.S. (7/1/2002)*

Santa Alicia 2004 Reserve Chardonnay (Maipo Valley) $9. Plump and oaky, with a lot of butter running alongside apple and pear fruit. In many ways, it's a common profile, one you see all the time from Chile. The body of the wine is round and fruity, while the oak is forward and adds a lot of cream and vanilla. **86 Best Buy** —*M.S. (7/1/2006)*

Santa Alicia 2003 Reserve Chardonnay (Maipo Valley) $8. Thin in body and color, but that lighter weight serves the wine well. It's not overdone and heavy like so many of its cousins. But it is a touch oily, and the flavor profile of banana and sweet apples has become all too common among Southern Hemisphere value Chards. **85** —*M.S. (8/1/2004)*

Santa Alicia 2003 Reserve Malbec (Maipo Valley) $9. Unfortunately, this wine is a step down from previous vintages. The nose is pickled and herbal, and throughout there is a pounding vegetal quotient that can't be ignored. Good mouthfeel, but too much green bean for what should be an opulent, rich, full-fruit style of wine. **81** —*M.S. (10/1/2006)*

Santa Alicia 2001 Reserve Malbec (Maipo Valley) $8. Ripe and round, with a full blast of oak on the nose. For Malbec, it's rather light in weight, with cherry, raspberry, and plum flavors wrapped in a nicely textured package. Maybe not too much character, but what's here is just fine. **86** —*M.S. (8/1/2004)*

Santa Alicia 2000 Reserve Malbec (Maipo Valley) $8. Black cherry, plum, and a mild creamy note characterize the nose. The palate is a nice combination of huckleberries and black cherries, all doused in chalk, white pepper, and tree bark. Dry, woody tannins. **87 Best Buy** —*D.T. (7/1/2002)*

Santa Alicia 2000 Estate Bottled Reserve Merlot (Maipo Valley) $6. Hailing from the renowned Pirque subsection of the Maipo Valley, this has earth, leather, and smoked meat aromas. The palate is full and rock solid, with layered plum and tobacco flavors. On the finish there's ample mocha and coffee. **88 Best Buy** —*M.S. (12/1/2002)*

Santa Alicia 2002 Gran Reserva Merlot (Maipo Valley) $13. Hard leather, black olives, and spicy stewed fruits on the nose are backed by one-dimensional black fruit flavors. The finish offers some black licorice and burnt toast, while the overall take is that it's just too heavy and extracted. **84** —*M.S. (7/1/2006)*

Santa Alicia 2001 Gran Reserva Merlot (Maipo Valley) $13. A bit rusty in color, with briary aromas that veer in the direction of sour red fruit and celery. The palate is dark and spicy, with fruity flavors that are hard to define. Notes of liqueur and licorice add sweetness to the finish. **83** —*M.S. (8/1/2004)*

Santa Alicia 1999 Gran Reserva Merlot (Maipo Valley) $14. Char and blackberry flavors on the palate are as brooding as the dark soil, oak, and berry fruit on the nose. Tannins speak louder than flavors in this wine; it's black, and with a little more lushness, could be a beauty. **84** —*D.T. (7/1/2002)*

Santa Alicia 2002 Estate Bottled Reserve Sauvignon Blanc (Maipo Valley) $8. Vanilla and pear aromas begin this soft-bodied wine that is mouth-filling and easy, but not up to shocking anyone. The flavors of orange and pineapple are close to the real thing, and the finish is smooth and easy. A mellow white wine at its best. **84** —*M.S. (7/1/2003)*

Santa Alicia 2004 Reserve Sauvignon Blanc (Maipo Valley) $9. Fairly pickled and funky, with a stale nose. Not a prime-time performer; it's just at the level of accpetable. **80** —*M.S. (7/1/2006)*

Santa Alicia 2003 Reserve Sauvignon Blanc (Maipo Valley) $8. Grapefruit and other citrus aromas lead into a palate of yet more grapefruit and passion fruit. The zesty finish is long-lasting. **85 Best Buy** —*M.S. (3/1/2004)*

Santa Alicia 2001 Reserve Syrah (Maipo Valley) $8. Meaty and large, with aromas of bacon and leather. Starts off more confidently than it finishes, with early plum, butter, and cashew notes. Fairly bland on the finish, but still a nice wine with an easygoing personality and simple, clean flavor notes. **86 Best Buy** —*M.S. (8/1/2004)*

Santa Alicia 2004 Late Harvest Muscatel White Blend (Limarí Valley) $10. Smells like children's vitamins and apple cider. The palate is sugary and fine but rather nondescript; there's candied flavors and persistence, but what does it add up to? Adequate acidity, but overall it's simply plain and sweet. **84** —*M.S. (5/1/2006)*

SANTA AMELIA

Santa Amelia 1997 Reserve Selection Cabernet Sauvignon (Maule Valley) $8. 83 —*M.S. (11/15/1999)*

SANTA CAROLINA

Santa Carolina 2001 VSC Bordeaux Blend (Maipo Valley) $35. Red fruit and milk chocolate aromas do battle with green pepper, and while there's no clear winner, each makes its mark. The fruit seems solid and healthy, with the palate showing good tannins and acidity. But those bell pepper aromas and flavors are heavy and refuse to cease. **85** —*M.S. (11/1/2005)*

Santa Carolina 2003 Barrica Selection Cabernet Sauvignon (Maipo Valley) $13. Cherry and red plum aromas on the nose, with a restrained, tolerable medicinal note. Mostly raspberry and strawberry on the palate, then some sticky tannins and milk chocolate flavors on the back end. Shows a starchy grip. **86** —*M.S. (12/15/2005)*

Santa Carolina 2001 Barrica Selection Cabernet Sauvignon (Maipo Valley) $13. All of the reds in this tasting showed distinct varietal differences. The Cab is chocolaty and slightly herbal but boasts solid cassis fruit. Supple tannins impart a velvety mouthfeel, but the wine lacks true depth. **84** —*(11/15/2003)*

Santa Carolina 2003 Colección Especial Cabernet Sauvignon (Rapel Valley) $7. It's a challenge finding good value-priced Cabernet from anywhere, but this fruit-driven, clean version from one of Chile's old-guard wineries is tasty and ripe, without a hint of green or funk. The profile is one of simplicity and red fruit flavor. A touch of vanilla and a mouthfeel that's soft as a pillow ensure its rightful place in any mix-and-match value case. **85 Best Buy** —*M.S. (11/15/2005)*

CHILE

Santa Carolina 2004 Reserva Cabernet Sauvignon (Colchagua Valley) $10. More leafy and herbal than dense and lush. But in the middle somewhere there's raspberry, cherry, carob, and spice. Finishes with an equal mix of candy and green. Good mouthfeel is a plus. **84** —*M.S. (10/1/2006)*

Santa Carolina 1999 Reserva Cabernet Sauvignon (Colchagua Valley) $9. This lighter-style Cab offers berry fruit and black tea flavors, and nut and oak finish. It's an easy quaffer, but nothing to mull over. **84** —*D.T. (7/1/2002)*

Santa Carolina 1998 Reserva Cabernet Sauvignon (Colchagua Valley) $9. A gravelly, rustic mouthfeel gives this indistinct mixed berry and wood-flavored wine what character it has. There's not much to the finish, either. Blackberry and green herb, plus a little Band-Aid, on the nose. **82** —*D.T. (7/1/2002)*

Santa Carolina 1997 Reserva Cabernet Sauvignon (Maipo Valley) $9. 82 —*M.S. (11/15/1999)*

Santa Carolina 1997 Reserva de Familia Cabernet Sauvignon (Maipo Valley) $15. 88 Best Buy (8/1/2000)

Santa Carolina 2004 Barrica Selection Carmenère (Rapel Valley) $15. Quite green and grassy, with overt aromas of green bean and tobacco. Berry and milk chocolate lead the flavor profile, while the finish is hollow. Too green to rate higher. **81** —*M.S. (10/1/2006)*

Santa Carolina 2003 Barrica Selection Carmenère (Rapel Valley) $13. Slightly green, but overall its better qualities outweigh the weaker ones. Almond paste and sweet black fruit flavors carry the palate, backed by a finish of spice and herbs. **84** —*M.S. (12/15/2005)*

Santa Carolina 2001 Barrica Selection Carmenère (Rapel Valley) $13. Smoky, plummy, and herbal, turning greener as it sits in the glass. Black cherry, plum and herb flavors, medium-weight and dry, with soft tannins. **84** (11/15/2003)

Santa Carolina 2003 Barrica Selection Chardonnay (Maipo Valley) $13. Light up front, with canned peach and pear aromas. Not that vibrant but clean, with sweet apricot and peach flavors. Good enough in the mouth, with a hint of banana and citrus on the finish. Not that oaky despite its "barrica" classification. **84** —*M.S. (12/15/2005)*

Santa Carolina 2002 Barrica Selection Chardonnay (Casablanca Valley) $13. Seems like typical oaky Chardonnay at first, boasting plenty of vanilla, butter, and toast. Then it becomes more toasty and mealy, blending in modest pear and anise flavors. Fairly big and thick, yet doesn't show a lot of depth. **84** (11/15/2003)

Santa Carolina 1998 Reserva de la Familia Chardonnay (Maipo Valley) $15. Rich and complex from the start, the nose and palate of this wine feature a fruit melange of mango, melon, banana wrapped in nicely integrated oak. For some, the acid may be a touch high but this keeps the wine bright and crisp, and sustains this fairly full, barrel-fermented wine's long finish. **90 Best Buy** —*M.N. (2/1/2001)*

Santa Carolina 1999 Merlot (Maule Valley) $9. This lighter-style Merlot has little texture, and standard dark berry, oak, and vanillin flavors. Finishes with more of the same. **83** —*D.T. (7/1/2002)*

Santa Carolina 2002 Coleccion Especial Merlot (Rapel Valley) $7. Shows good varietal character on the nose: black cherry and mocha elements with a distinct herbal overtone. Yet it doesn't deliver as emphatically on the palate, turning thin on the finish. Decent Merlot for your next big crowd. **84** (11/15/2003)

Santa Carolina 1999 VSC Red Blend (Chile) $35. Made under the previous regime, this is the debut vintage of a high-end interregional blend. The wine's strong suit is its supple texture and elegant mouthfeel; its weakness: a persistent herbal edge to the berry flavors that suggests under-ripe fruit. **86** (11/15/2003)

Santa Carolina 2002 Coleccion Especial Sauvignon Blanc (Rapel Valley) $7. Displays a nice nose, with some grassy notes, passion fruit aromas, and riper peach scents, but seems less expressive in the glass, showing little but grapefruit and ending on a slightly sour note. **84** (11/15/2003)

Santa Carolina 2005 Barrica Selection Syrah (Maipo Valley) $15. Not the most Syrah-like wine you're likely to encounter, but as a generic red it's juicy, fruity, and tasty. The balance is fine and the fruit weighs in solid and proper. Complete but lacking individuality. **85** —*M.S. (10/1/2006)*

Santa Carolina 2003 Barrica Selection Syrah (Maipo Valley) $13. Dark and rubbery, with typical spice, berry, and enough oak to come across woody. Ripe and ample in the mouth, with black plum and cedary oak. Chocolate and a pinch of pepper work the finish. Quite saturated, with a lot of flavor. **86** —*M.S. (12/15/2005)*

Santa Carolina 2002 Barrica Selection Syrah (Maule Valley) $13. Winemaker Consuelo Marin feels Syrah has a good future in Chile, but to be convincing, she'll need to get more richness and texture into this wine. Wiry blackberry aromas and flavors are simple and lean. **84** (11/15/2003)

SANTA EMA

Santa Ema 1996 Catalina Bordeaux Blend (Rapel Valley) $28. Cedar, cassis, and blueberry aromas open this mid-weight Bordeaux-style red. An even, lean mouthfeel, red-berry, cocoa, and mineral flavors, and silky tannins round out the package. This blend of 78% Cabernet Sauvignon, 14% Merlot, and 8% Cabernet Franc finishes dry, with tart-sweet flavors. **85** (8/1/2001)

Santa Ema 2004 Amplus Cabernet Sauvignon (Cachapoal Valley) $19. Given the icon name and inspired packaging you'd expect more than what you get, which is a heavy, over-ripe lug that features grassy, alfalfa aromas in front of a raisiny palate. The feel is thick and cloying and the lasting impression is that of prunes. **82** —*M.S. (11/15/2006)*

Santa Ema 2000 Estate Bottled Cabernet Sauvignon (Maipo Valley) $9. Full and meaty, with plenty of mainstream black fruit. There is a good amount of plum and cherry aromas and flavors, and a ripe, satisfying finish. With good acidity and fresh flavors, it can please the masses. **85** —*M.S. (7/1/2003)*

Santa Ema 1998 Estate Bottled Cabernet Sauvignon (Maipo Valley) $9. Boasts a reasonably complex bouquet of chocolate, cedar, and weedy cassis, followed by a mellow, soft palate impression. The fruit is sweet and direct, just the kind of thing that would hit the spot with an impromptu meal of steak frites. No, there's not a lot of structure, but why age a wine that's so clearly made for immediate gratification? **86** —*J.C. (2/1/2001)*

Santa Ema 2002 Reserve Cabernet Sauvignon (Maipo Valley) $14. On the heavier, stewed side, but still balanced enough to score points. The nose is earthy and dark, while the palate deals cooked plum and blackberry along with a touch of soy sauce. Round and surprisingly airy on the finish. It doesn't end as densely as it begins. **87** —*M.S. (7/1/2005)*

Santa Ema 2001 Reserve Cabernet Sauvignon (Maipo Valley) $14. The bouquet kicks up hints of graham cracker, iodine, and earth. The mouth is fat and broad, with a good amount of typical plum and cherry flavors. The finish is simple yet clean, with tight tannins and moderate length. Good and well made; a wine for everyday consumption. **87** —*M.S. (7/1/2003)*

Santa Ema 1999 Reserve Cabernet Sauvignon (Maipo Valley) $14. The oak influence is obvious, meaning there are distinct aromas of sawdust and mocha on the nose. The palate is lively, with a decent amount of cherry and raspberry fruit. Some additional oak-based coffee and mocha comes up on the finish. All in all it's fresh and easy enough to drink. **86** —*M.S. (12/1/2002)*

Santa Ema 2003 60/40 Barrel Select Cabernet Sauvignon-Merlot (Maipo Valley) $11. A Cab/Merlot blend that's ripe and alluring, with easy-going but still power-packed aromatics. Flavors of cassis, black cherry and raisin are full-bore, and the chocolaty finish scores. Balanced and correct. **89 Best Buy** —*M.S. (12/15/2005)*

Santa Ema 2002 60/40 Barrel Select Cabernet Sauvignon-Merlot (Maipo Valley) $10. A blend of Cabernet Sauvignon and Merlot that's outright fruity, with earthy aromas of leather, forest floor, and barnyard. The palate, however, runs light, with red fruit and a hint of tomato. Healthy but lightweight on the finish. Laudable for its fresh qualities and undeniable brightness. **86 Best Buy** —*M.S. (2/1/2005)*

Santa Ema 2001 Barrel Select Cabernet Sauvignon-Merlot (Maipo Valley) $12. Fresh and forward. The nose is pure, ripe, and rubbery, with a deep level of black fruit. The mouthfeel shows zippy acidity and total ripeness

CHILE

of the grapes. The grippy finish is long and rock solid. The tannins make it a touch hard, but with food you can't really fail. **87** —*M.S. (7/1/2003)*

Santa Ema 1999 Barrel Select Cabernet Sauvignon-Merlot (Maipo Valley) $10. Bright, ripe fruit is the name of the game in the mouth, where blackberry and red plum are countered with a manageable amount of oak. Tannins are chalky; bouquet and finish are more subtle and a little oakier. **87** —*D.T. (7/1/2002)*

Santa Ema 2003 Carmenère (Cachapoal Valley) $10. Smells burnt and green. Lots of color but little balance or style. Has almost no stuffing or charm. Barely acceptable. **80** —*M.S. (2/1/2005)*

Santa Ema 2001 Carmenère (Rapel Valley) $10. Open-knit and herbal, and mostly pleasant if entirely underwhelming. There's nothing offensive here; just your basics as far as cherry fruit, modest tannins, and a hint of the veggies. **83** —*M.S. (3/1/2004)*

Santa Ema 2000 Estate Carmenère (Rapel Valley) $9. This wine has such nice hickory, dried spice, and red berry notes, it'd be a shame to drink it anywhere but outside on your deck, with some slow-cooked baby back ribs. Medium-weight, with some chalky tannins, it finishes with more of the same flavors, plus some char and green herb. Fire up the grill. **87 Best Buy** —*D.T. (7/1/2002)*

Santa Ema 2002 Gran Reserva Carmenère (Cachapoal Valley) $17. Plenty of oak, which must be why it's called "Gran Reserva." Along with the lumber you'll find chocolate, marinade, and pickle. Fat on the palate, with bulky black plum and blackberry flavors. Licorice, coffee, and green bean notes define the finish. **85** —*M.S. (2/1/2005)*

Santa Ema 2001 Reserve Carmenère (Maipo Valley) $16. Scattered and overoaked, and even that heavy wood veneer doesn't cover up the green quality. What it does provide is a serious sweetness that manifests itself as vanilla and carob. This is the type of wine where less oak would have been more. **82** —*M.S. (3/1/2004)*

Santa Ema 2000 Reserve Carmenère (Rapel Valley) $16. Sweet Tart candy and blackberry aromas, and sweet mixed berry flavors make this a good choice for wine enthusiasts who favor fruit above all else. Herb and anise flavors (and woody tannins) keep the berry flavors from being too mushy; more acid would have bought this Carmenère another point or two. **86** —*D.T. (7/1/2002)*

Santa Ema 2004 Chardonnay (Casablanca Valley) $9. Crisp, with aromas of grapefruit, citrus, and a touch of bitter greens. Citrus dominates the mouth as flavors of tangerine, grapefruit, and orange rise to the surface. Finishes racy and zesty, with firm acidity at the center. **85 Best Buy** —*M.S. (11/1/2005)*

Santa Ema 2003 Chardonnay (Casablanca Valley) $9. Soft pear and apple aromas are clean if unspectacular. The flavor profile is mostly sugary apple and pear, while good Casablanca acidity ensures that the wine feels right on the palate. **84** —*M.S. (6/1/2004)*

Santa Ema 2001 Estate Chardonnay (Maipo Valley) $9. The nose starts out herbal and rowdy, but then settles down to offer basic pear and apple aromas. The palate is all pineapple and other racy fruits, but it's also sweet and a bit discordant. The long, driving finish doesn't really hit the mark, and it's a bit heavy and drying right through the last impression. **83** —*M.S. (7/1/2002)*

Santa Ema 2003 Reserve Chardonnay (Casablanca Valley) $14. Fairly woody, but there's enough quality fruit supporting the oak to make it work. Butterscotch and apple aromas lead into a fruity, satisfying palate of melon, papaya, and apple. The persistent barrel influence yields vanilla and anisette on the chunky, creamy finish. **86** —*M.S. (2/1/2005)*

Santa Ema 1999 Reserve Chardonnay (Maipo Valley) $14. Orangey aromas wrapped in not very subtle oak open this light-to-medium weight wine. Simple and a bit one-dimensional, it offers light pear flavors and a dry finish. Acceptable as an easy quaff, but not the stuff worthy of reserve designation. **83** *(2/1/2001)*

Santa Ema 2003 Merlot (Cachapoal Valley) $9. Sweet and grapey, but with enough darkness and structure to rank. Blueberry and cherry aromas precede snappy cherry and raspberry fruit. Rock solid and ripe at the core, with no funk or green. What a bargain Chilean Merlot is supposed to be. **86 Best Buy** —*M.S. (2/1/2005)*

Santa Ema 2001 Merlot (Rapel Valley) $9. The aromas are meaty yet undefined. In the mouth, the fruit seems snappy and overly excited. The acidity is a bit out of control and it leads to questionable balance. Still the raspberry and cherry flavors are good, and the oak shadings seem about right. **81** —*M.S. (7/1/2003)*

Santa Ema 1998 Merlot (Maipo Valley) $9. A pleasant and cleanly made quaffing wine with plenty of berry and black cherry fruit and a strong menthol streak running right through to the finish. A bit rough around the edges; might show better with a country-style dish of stewed chicken. **83** —*J.C. (2/1/2001)*

Santa Ema 2003 Reserve Merlot (Maipo Valley) $14. Overly sweet and candied, with creamy aromas of cherry-filled doughnuts, marshmallow, and boiling jam. Comes across heavy and slightly medicinal on the palate, with lots of milk chocolate on the finish. Needs more balance and polish to rate better. **81** —*M.S. (5/1/2006)*

Santa Ema 2001 Reserve Merlot (Maipo Valley) $14. In this case, "reserve" means overoaked, and the result is coconut and carob aromas and flavors. The finish is cloying and the mouthfeel is heavy. **80** —*M.S. (7/1/2003)*

Santa Ema 1999 Reserve Merlot (Maipo Valley) $14. Light enough for one taster to call it "Beaujolais-Merlot," this Maipo Valley offering isn't very substantial. Dark soil, tree bark, and black fruit aromas preface weak mineral and black plum on the palate. Flavors drop off at midpalate, leaving you wondering where the rest of it went. **82** —*D.T. (7/1/2002)*

Santa Ema 1998 Reserve Merlot (Maipo Valley) $14. Sure, cedar and chocolate are the dominant aromas and flavors, but there's enough blueberry fruit to stand up to the oak rather nicely. It doesn't hurt that the oak is high-quality stuff either, as the elements blend together in a harmonious whole. A little oaky, but shows a degree of finesse not often found in Chilean wines at this level. **87** —*J.C. (2/1/2001)*

Santa Ema 2004 Amplus One Red Blend (Cachapoal Valley) $19. Very sweet and extracted, and in the end it weighs in a little over the limit. The nose is at once sweet and green, while the palate is medicinal as it pumps forth with syrupy black fruit and licorice. Nothing wrong with the color, depth, and extraction; but where's the balance? **84** —*M.S. (11/15/2006)*

Santa Ema 2002 Catalina Red Blend (Cachapoal Valley) $38. Headlines include a richly perfumed nose with pulsing plum and berry along with spicy black fruit in the mouth. Last but not least there's charcoal, cola, and melting vanilla on the finish. A really fine blend of Cabernet Sauvignon, Carmenère, and Cabernet Franc. **91** —*M.S. (3/1/2006)*

Santa Ema 2001 Catalina Red Blend (Rapel Valley) $28. Fruity and secure, with ripe, roasted aromas of coffee, black fruit, and leather. Some cherry cola and apple skin make for a lively, fresh palate, while the finish is smooth, warm, and full. Good acidity and body. A Cabernet-Cab Franc blend that ranks among Santa Ema's best wines to date. **90** —*M.S. (2/1/2005)*

Santa Ema 1998 Catalina Red Blend (Rapel Valley) $28. At first the nose is scattered, offering iodine and Italian herbs but little fruit. In the mouth, blackberries appear. The finish is a bit like coffee. This wine has some character and appeal but also some fading characteristics. Maybe this 1998, never a great year, is just too old. **85** —*M.S. (7/1/2003)*

Santa Ema 2003 Rivalta Red Blend (Cachapoal Valley) $72. Named after the home town of Santa Ema's Italian-born owner, Rivalta blends Cabernet Sauvignon with smaller doses of Carmenère and Syrah. The result is a warm, extracted, almost foresty wine with tobacco, spice, pepper, and dark fruit aromas and flavors. Comes on fiercely woody on the finish, with a hint of leafiness. Very modern and extracted; the positives comfortably outweigh any shortcomings. **88** —*M.S. (11/15/2006)*

Santa Ema 2004 Sauvignon Blanc (Maipo Valley) $8. Seems a bit over-ripe. The nose is soft, unctuous, and overtly fruity, with a heavy melon-meets-citrus smell. Equally soft and melony on the palate, with a thick finish. Perfectly acceptable but not as precise as it should be. **84 Best Buy** —*M.S. (7/1/2005)*

CHILE

Santa Ema 2002 Estate Bottled Sauvignon Blanc (Maipo Valley) $8. The aromas of apricot, flowers, and beeswax are like a welcome mat. The mouth is full and properly acidic; flavors of honey, ripe white fruits, and some mustard seed make for a wine that's got a lot of power working for it. **86 Best Buy** —*M.S. (7/1/2003)*

SANTA EMILIANA

Santa Emiliana 2002 Sincerity Merlot-Cabernet Sauvignon (Rapel Valley) $15. Alvaro Espinoza produced this wine from organically grown grapes in the vineyards of the giant Santa Emiliana winery. The plan is for the vineyard to become biodynamic. It is dark in color, almost black, very intense, with bitter chocolate and tarry fruit flavors. This is full of sweet tannins and fruit, ready to drink now. **88** —*R.V. (4/1/2005)*

SANTA HELENA

Santa Helena 2002 Notas De Guarda Cabernet Sauvignon (Colchagua Valley) $18. A big, flavor-packed Cabernet with a hard-hitting nose of black fruit and sweet oak. Monster blackberry, cherry, and cassis flavors are accented by chocolate and pepper, and only on the finish do the hard tannins get aggressive. Excellent flavor; a bit hard in terms of mouthfeel. **89** —*M.S. (2/1/2005)*

Santa Helena 2001 Seleccion del Directorio Reserva Cabernet Sauvignon (Central Valley) $11. Clean and rich, with a bouquet of ripe berry notes accented by soft oak. Flavors of plum and cherry are defined and rich, while the finish is of proper weight and style; it's chewy yet racy enough. As reds go, it's round and robust, and very satisfying. It's what Chilean Cabernet should be. **89** —*M.S. (8/1/2004)*

Santa Helena 2002 Siglo de oro Cabernet Sauvignon (Central Valley) $9. Give this wine a few minutes in the glass and it really shows its stuff. It's a pleasant surprise from a previously unknown producer, one that offers sweet plum, cassis, and cherry on a sturdy, defined frame. Basic but good, with ripeness and nary a flaw. **88 Best Buy** —*M.S. (8/1/2004)*

Santa Helena 2002 Vernus Cabernet Sauvignon (Colchagua Valley) $18. Way beyond satisfactory, with smoky leather to go with the red fruit and oak aromas. Typical cassis and plum carry the lively palate, which is tight and tannic but tasty and full of excitement. Not complex, but ripe and forward. Good Cab in the under-$20 category. **88** —*M.S. (2/1/2005)*

Santa Helena 2002 Seleccion del Directorio Reserva Carmenère (Central Valley) $11. The nose is piquant and sharp, and it turns barnyardy with air. Simple red fruit with mild tomato notes create a palate that's adequate yet far from special. Some dry, woody notes define the lightweight finish. **84** —*M.S. (8/1/2004)*

Santa Helena 2002 Siglo de Oro Carmenère (Central Valley) $9. Sour cherry notes on the nose are followed by mildly weedy flavors of plum and raspberry. Some oak flavor pumps up the bland finish. Lacking in complexity but serviceable. **83** —*M.S. (8/1/2004)*

Santa Helena 2003 Seleccion del Directorio Reserva Chardonnay (Casablanca Valley) $11. Broad pear, apple, and vanilla aromas arise from copious oak, yet a woody element really sticks out on the palate. Fortunately there's a good mouthfeel to the wine and ample acidity. For oak fans. **85** —*M.S. (2/1/2005)*

Santa Helena 2002 Seleccion del Directorio Reserva Chardonnay (Casablanca Valley) $11. Overtly oaky, but in an artificial, overdone way. It's thick and woody, with bland fruit and resiny, fat flavor notes. **81** —*M.S. (8/1/2004)*

Santa Helena 2003 Siglo de Oro Chardonnay (Casablanca Valley) $9. Some mild peach and banana on the dull nose lead to a palate of soda crackers and sugared pear. Finishes surprisingly bitter, with the essence of orange pith. **83** —*M.S. (8/1/2004)*

Santa Helena 2001 Seleccion del Directorio Reserva Merlot (Central Valley) $11. Modest aromas of cola, mint, and lemon peel are clean but hardly stellar. Flavors of cherry, plum, and blackberry carry some spice and oak, while the finish is equally oaky and lasting. A touch acidic, but that helps propel the flavors. **86** —*M.S. (8/1/2004)*

Santa Helena 2002 Siglo de Oro Merlot (Central Valley) $9. Murky and vegetal, without much concentration. The palate is chunky and green,

and it doesn't hold up to air. Decent at first but loses it as time passes. **83** —*M.S. (8/1/2004)*

Santa Helena 2001 Late Harvest Riesling (Curicó Valley) $11. Pungent and forward, with can't-miss aromas of dried apricot and sweat. Flavors of white raisins and dried mango are super sweet, while the finish is thick and mouth-coating. **83** —*M.S. (8/1/2004)*

Santa Helena 2002 Seleccion del Dierctorio Reserva Sauvignon Blanc (Central Valley) $11. The nose isn't as expressive as the '03, but there's enough green apple and under-ripe banana on the palate to keep it in shape. Finishing notes of vanilla are cut by healthy acidity, and while the wine seems thick, it's not cloying. **84** —*M.S. (8/1/2004)*

Santa Helena 2003 Siglo de Oro Sauvignon Blanc (Curicó Valley) $9. Fairly crisp and defined, with true passion fruit, grapefruit, and stone-fruit aromas. Flavors of oranges and mango are a bit sweet, but the finish offers just enough of a dry edge to keep the wine pushing forward. **85** —*M.S. (8/1/2004)*

SANTA INES

Santa Ines 1998 Enigma Reserva Cabernet Sauvignon (Maipo Valley) $20. There's a strong oak element to this Cab, one that should be a bit more integrated than it is given that it's a '98. Black cherry fruit dominates the palate, which throws off some bitter oak. The finish is equally toasty, with a hefty dose of bitter chocolate. The feel is hard and firm; maybe it still needs time. **85** —*M.S. (12/1/2002)*

Santa Ines 2001 Estate Bottled Cabernet Sauvignon (Maipo Valley) $11. Nicely extracted aromas of blackberry and cherry are offset by an unfortunate lactic note. But that's about the only downside to this otherwise nice and friendly wine. The palate is all cassis, and the finish is surprisingly substantial, offering chewy tannins and a burnt coffee flavor. This isn't a great wine, but for a basic Cab it delivers a lot without any flaws. **85** —*M.S. (12/1/2002)*

Santa Ines 2002 Chardonnay (Central Valley) $7. A nose of pears, lemon, gym bag, and cheese isn't the purest and most attractive, but there is some substance to this wine. The palate has papaya, banana, and apple flavors and the finish is clean. Good in a pedestrian way. **83** —*M.S. (7/1/2003)*

Santa Ines 1999 Enigma Reserva Chardonnay (Maipo Valley) $15. Aromas of pineapple, melon, and green apple start it off, followed by a modest dosage of apple and pear flavors. The finish is smooth and buttery, especially toward the back end, but without much robust flavor. **85** —*M.S. (7/1/2003)*

Santa Ines 2000 Legado de Armida Reserva Chardonnay (Maipo Valley) $6. Named after the matriarch of the De Martino family, this is a tropical-influenced wine with full banana, papaya, and melon flavors atop lighter-weight aromas. The finish is equally tropical in style, with creamy oak mixing with ripe banana to create a sundae-like whole. The palate is chewy and satisfying as the wine tips the scale toward full-bodied. **88 Best Buy** —*M.S. (7/1/2003)*

Santa Ines 2001 Estate Bottled Merlot (Maipo Valley) $8. Enticing aromas of dry peat, milk chocolate, and radicchio lead to cedar, cocoa, and sweet, juicy red plum flavors. Ends a bit tight with awkward tannins, but it's still worthy of exploration. **86** —*K.F. (12/1/2002)*

Santa Ines 1998 Legado de Armida Reserva Merlot (Maipo Valley) $6. **86 Best Buy** —*M.S. (5/1/2000)*

Santa Ines 2001 Legado de Armida Reserva Sauvignon Blanc (Maipo Valley) $10. Creamy aromas of vanilla and pears also carry some typical Sauvignon Blanc pungency. For a rounder style, which it is, it's quite refreshing. The mix across the palate of banana, grapefruit, and almonds is attractive, and so is the round, pretty finish. Drink it very soon. **87** —*M.S. (7/1/2003)*

SANTA MARVISTA

Santa Marvista 2003 Reserva Chardonnay (Central Valley) $6. Funky and unusual to the nose, with flavors of lemon, tangerine, and green pear. The finish is large and heavy, and while the wine has a good attack, it doesn't hold its shape as it fades away in scattered fashion. **82** —*M.S. (6/1/2004)*

Santa Marvista 2003 Reserva Merlot (Central Valley) $6. A touch dilute and broken up in the nose, but not bad or off. In the mouth, tangy strawberry and raspberry fruit leads into an easygoing finish. Despite a few signs of artificiality and manipulation, this is not a bummer of a wine. **83** —*M.S. (3/1/2004)*

SANTA MONICA

Santa Monica 2000 Chardonnay (Rapel Valley) $8. A sweet nose with banana, lemon-lime, and pipe tobacco elements opens to a straightforward, rather tart palate with light apple and lemon flavors. **82** —*J.F. (8/1/2001)*

SANTA RITA

Santa Rita 2000 Cabernet Sauvignon (Rapel Valley) $7. The nose is closed, with only slight earth and green herb aromas; there are some chalky tannins and some raspberry flavors on the palate, but there's not much other than some chalky bubble gum powder to the finish. **83** —*D.T. (7/1/2002)*

Santa Rita 2002 120 Cabernet Sauvignon (Rapel Valley) $8. A decent mouthfeel and grippy tannins secures the palate, which doesn't really have the flavor profile of a fine wine. A sip reveals pickle, bell pepper, and rhubarb along with chocolate and some weedy, sugar beet notes. The texture isn't weak, but it's undeniably thin. **83** —*M.S. (3/1/2004)*

Santa Rita 2001 120 Cabernet Sauvignon (Rapel Valley) $8. 84 *(8/1/2003)*

Santa Rita 1999 120 Cabernet Sauvignon (Rapel Valley) $7. Very light berry and mint aromas open this austere, dry Cabernet. The fruit is dark, but needs more depth and profile to carry the woody presence here. **81** —*M.M. (2/1/2001)*

Santa Rita 2005 120 Rosé Cabernet Sauvignon (Maipo Valley) $8. Great color; spicy and full of plum-based aromas. Lucid from start to finish, and a true over-achiever in this class of wine. Flavors of cherry and nectarine are fresh and full. Finishes clean as crystal. Perfect for a spring picnic. **87 Best Buy** —*M.S. (5/1/2006)*

Santa Rita 2002 Casa Real Cabernet Sauvignon (Maipo Valley) $50. Even if this isn't the best Casa Real in recent years, it stands out from the crowd and doesn't have to work hard to do so. The nose is tight and clean, with leather, spice, and cherry aromas. The palate is packed with cherry and cassis, and the finish is lively but balanced. Despite a down vintage, this is Chilean Cabernet at its finest. **91** —*M.S. (5/1/2006)*

Santa Rita 2001 Casa Real Cabernet Sauvignon (Maipo Valley) $65. Made from 30-year-old vines, this wine represents the pinnacle of Santa Rita's production. It's lush and rich, with vanilla, cedar, tobacco, and cassis aromas. The palate is layered and textured, displaying the perfect mix of concentration and softness. Finishes supple, with smooth tannins and some chocolate and marshmallow. One of Chile's best. **93 Editors' Choice** —*M.S. (11/15/2004)*

Santa Rita 1999 Casa Real Cabernet Sauvignon (Maipo Valley) $65. The 1997 Casa Real was royal, and the '99 is even better. It's rich, deep, and lavishly oaked. The concentration is intense but it's not overly tight or tannic. In every way it's a dead ringer for sweet, luscious fruit-forward Napa Cabernet. Plum, coffee, and cream share center stage on the stylish finish. **94** —*M.S. (3/1/2002)*

Santa Rita 1997 Casa Real Cabernet Sauvignon (Maipo Valley) $40. 92 —*M.S. (5/1/2000)*

Santa Rita 1999 Casa Real Old Vines Cabernet Sauvignon (Maipo Valley) $65. 92 *(8/1/2003)*

Santa Rita 1999 Floresta Apalta Estate Cabernet Sauvignon (Colchagua Valley) $30. 91 Editors' Choice *(8/1/2003)*

Santa Rita 2002 Floresta Apalta Vineyard Cabernet Sauvignon (Apalta) $28. Quite floral despite having spent 14 months in French oak. With 15% Maipo fruit in the blend, the wine veers toward raspberry and cherry, while the finish is darker, dealing licorice and some fudge. Has the right acid-tannin balance. Powerful enough without being tough. **89** —*M.S. (11/15/2004)*

Santa Rita 2003 Medalla Real Cabernet Sauvignon (Maipo Valley) $18. For the first time in a long time there's some herbal character to this wine, which usually pushes pure cassis and berry aromas and flavors. But this version, while zesty and healthy in terms of tannin and acidity, has some leather and leafiness to it. Still, it's well formed and ranks as one of Chile's benchmark upper- to medium-level Cabernets. **87** —*M.S. (5/1/2006)*

Santa Rita 2000 Medalla Real Cabernet Sauvignon (Maipo Valley) $18. 88 *(8/1/2003)*

Santa Rita 1999 Medalla Real Cabernet Sauvignon (Maipo Valley) $18. Here's a dense, brooding, rich Cab that's jam-packed with plum and chocolate aromas. In the mouth, there's plenty of structure, with full tannins to boot. Yet it's perfectly round, smooth, and easy to drink. Cabernets this big and tasty don't usually cost less than $20, so jump at this Maipo marvel if you get the chance. **89** —*M.S. (3/1/2002)*

Santa Rita 2002 Medalla Real Special Reserve Cabernet Sauvignon (Maipo Valley) $18. Pretty much on the money, with verve, sass, and class. Plenty of black fruit, coffee, earth and leather on the nose, followed by red plum, cassis, and vanilla-infused tobacco on the palate. Nice and tasty, with fine richness and a good mouthfeel. **88** —*M.S. (11/15/2004)*

Santa Rita 1998 Medalla Real Special Reserve Cabernet Sauvignon (Maipo Valley) $15. Basic Cabernet Sauvignon, with all its goods up front. Opens with some nice cassis aromatics but there's just not much on the palate. The finish is short and there's a greenness to the fruit that reflects the tremendous difficulty of the 1998 vintage. Not up to previous efforts. **82** —*M.N. (2/1/2001)*

Santa Rita 2002 Reserva Cabernet Sauvignon (Maipo Valley) $12. Aromas of dust, cassis, and cream cheese become more integrated with time. The flavor profile offers cassis, berry, and a touch of herbaceousness. Forward, tight and lively, with a shot of green running through the middle. **86** —*M.S. (11/15/2004)*

Santa Rita 2001 Reserva Cabernet Sauvignon (Maipo Valley) $12. 87 *(8/1/2003)*

Santa Rita 2000 Reserva Cabernet Sauvignon (Maipo Valley) $8. The nose recalls the barnyard, and even after some of those funky aromas blow off, there isn't much fruit to speak of. The palate is big and burly, with a modicum of plum fruit but also a strong green flavor. The mouthfeel is proper but the over-riding green core hinders rather than helps. Usually Santa Rita's Cabs are riper than this. **84** —*M.S. (12/1/2002)*

Santa Rita 1999 Reserva Cabernet Sauvignon (Maipo Valley) $11. Garnet colored, with light raspberry and cedar flavors on the palate, this has an overall earthy, smoky cast that's high on acid and low on fruit. Finishes short, with light cassis-flavored, and very evident tannins. **82** —*D.T. (8/1/2001)*

Santa Rita 1998 Reserve Cabernet Sauvignon (Maipo Valley) $13. A run-of-the-mill Cabernet Sauvignon, it's all up front. There are nice cassis aromatics but little on the palate. The finish is short and vegetal. **83** —*M.N. (2/1/2001)*

Santa Rita 2004 120 Carmenère (Rapel Valley) $8. Definitely a Carmenère, which you can tell from the olive and herb nose and the plump, jammy palate that contains red plum, olive, and chocolate flavors. Shows juicy acidity. Nothing wrong with this wine, just basic. **84** —*M.S. (3/1/2006)*

Santa Rita 2002 120 Carmenère (Colchagua Valley) $8. 86 Best Buy *(8/1/2003)*

Santa Rita 2000 120 Carmenère (Rapel Valley) $7. Brambly fruit aromas are framed nicely by woodsmoke, in a balanced mix of fruit and wood. A bit light on the palate, but that only serves to better display the juicy, tart-berry flavors. Picks up some coffee notes on the finish. **85 Editors' Choice** —*J.C. (8/1/2001)*

Santa Rita 1999 Reserva Carmenère (Rapel Valley) $11. The smoke and menthol-toast aromas from new oak run alongside grass and green hay. The fruit flavors are light, but tend toward black cherries. This may improve a bit once the dry woody tannins on the finish subside; try in six months with grilled steak. **83** —*J.C. (8/1/2001)*

Santa Rita 2005 120 Chardonnay (Maipo Valley) $8. It's not a stretch to say that this is the model for blue-plate value Chilean Chardonnay. The soft nose offers pear and hazelnut, while the open palate is geared toward apples, pears and toast. A known entity, but good in its category. **85 Best Buy** —M.S. (7/1/2006)

Santa Rita 2003 120 Chardonnay (Aconcagua Valley) $NA. Piquant yet fruity, with green melon, nectarine, and citrus aromas. Tart, unforgiving flavors of green apple and oranges mix with a hint of natural spice. Overall, it's sharp and firm, without the roundness required of a top-shelf Chardonnay. **83** —M.S. (6/1/2004)

Santa Rita 2002 120 Chardonnay (Maipo Valley) $8. 85 Best Buy (8/1/2003)

Santa Rita 2001 120 Chardonnay (Lontué Valley) $NA. Heavy pear and apple aromas pound the olfactory senses, prior to citrus and Bosc pear flavors. In its favor, the acids are bright, which keeps the wine's weight and feel in balance. There's also an appealing flinty nuance, which will make it go well with shellfish and salads. **83** —M.S. (7/1/2002)

Santa Rita 2000 120 Chardonnay (Lontué Valley) $7. A light Chardonnnay showing pineapple and pear aromas, and similar flavors that turn quite lemony on the palate. Turns slightly tart on the finish, but the bright feel and the light flavors make it a good candidate for a bar pour or party wine. **84** (2/1/2001)

Santa Rita 2001 Medalla Real Chardonnay (Casablanca Valley) $15. Pear fruit and sweet oak strike a nice balance up front. The soft, creamy body offers ample acidity so that it remains lively. A persistent buttered-toast characteristic dominates the weighty finish. **85** —M.S. (3/1/2002)

Santa Rita 1999 Medalla Real Special Reserve Chardonnay (Casablanca Valley) $13. From the opening whiff, this wine shows an off-putting lean, piney aroma. The apple and pineapple fruit are almost completely veiled by the green oak perfume that most tasters won't get past. **81** — M.M. (8/1/2001)

Santa Rita 2005 Reserva Chardonnay (Casablanca Valley) $12. Here's a wine that advertises the Casablanca formula: pink grapefruit and orange on the nose, followed by lemon fruit with a fair amount of bitter zest. Being so citrusy, the finish is lasting albeit monotone. Fails to offer any richness. **84** —M.S. (7/1/2006)

Santa Rita 2003 Reserva Chardonnay (Casablanca Valley) $12. Very smoky, with a lot of toast and popcorn aromas covering the apple and pear that lurk below. Light straw in color, with zesty apple flavors drizzled with some honey. A bold, weighty wine with a sharp finish. **85** —M.S. (11/15/2004)

Santa Rita 2002 Reserva Chardonnay (Casablanca Valley) $12. 87 (8/1/2003)

Santa Rita 2001 Reserva Chardonnay (Casablanca Valley) $11. Its sharp grassy and gooseberry aromas are the type normally associated with Sauvignon Blanc. On the palate, grapefruit and passion fruit flavors further drive home that impression, but it's labeled Chardonnay, and that's what it is. The acidity is nice so the mouthfeel is fresh. **85** —M.S. (7/1/2003)

Santa Rita 2000 Reserva Chardonnay (Casablanca Valley) $11. Has an almost textbook blend of pineapple, apple, and tropical fruit aromas and flavors. A touch of grapefruit in the mouth keeps it tangy, and the mouthfeel is even and smooth. Finishes dry with a slight tang. **85** — M.M. (8/1/2001)

Santa Rita 1999 Reserva Chardonnay (Maipo Valley) $13. Tropical fruit flavors abound throughout in this balanced, straightforward wine. Simple yet attractive, it can be used as an apértif or for casual dining. Spicy shellfish dishes, especially coconut shrimp, would pair well with this. **84** —M.N. (2/1/2001)

Santa Rita 2002 120 Merlot (Rapel Valley) $8. The nose doesn't show much, especially at first, when you get light whiffs of dill and toasted corn. However, more fruit is apparent on the palate, primarily cherry and raspberry. Finally, some peppery notes seal the finish. **84** —M.S. (3/1/2004)

Santa Rita 2001 120 Merlot (Lontué Valley) $9. Varietal character is displayed in the dark earth, dark chocolate, and gamy mushroom scents, as well as in the red plum, cherry, and vanilla flavors. Throughout there is a hint of green herbs that really come out on the midpalate. **85** —K.F. (12/1/2002)

Santa Rita 2000 120 Merlot (Lontué Valley) $7. Weedy and herbal, but there are also black cherries and mocha on the nose and bitter chocolate and coffee on the palate. Finishes with toffee, smoke, and herbs, offering surprising complexity in a wine of this genre. **86 Best Buy** —J.C. (3/1/2002)

Santa Rita 2004 Reserva Merlot (Maipo Valley) $12. Overly herbal, with olive and tomato beating out the black fruit in the wine. The palate shows some bulky plum and cherry, but also roasted and sauteed bell pepper. Finishes a bit salty/tannic. **82** —M.S. (7/1/2006)

Santa Rita 2003 Reserva Merlot (Maipo Valley) $12. Herbal on the nose, with mocha and black cherry in support. The palate features a heavy green streak dancing between the layers of plum and berry. Warm and heady on the finish. **84** —M.S. (11/15/2004)

Santa Rita 2002 Reserva Merlot (Maipo Valley) $12. Round and fat, with a deep color and some earthy, mushroom notes to the nose. Flavors of blackberry and plum dominate, and the finish has some smoky character and a touch of natural, espresso-like bitterness. **86** —M.S. (3/1/2004)

Santa Rita 2001 Reserva Merlot (Maipo Valley) $13. Black cherry and black plums are wrapped around stolid leather, cedar, and tobacco. All repeat on the palate with a hint of chocolate and silky tannins. The finish is a bit brusque and green. **84** —K.F. (12/1/2002)

Santa Rita 2000 Floresta Red Blend (Maipo Valley) $30. Dense and bold, with heavy oak, dark fruit, and brazen cedar and lemon notes. This is your prototype muscle wine; it has huge coffee, clove, and anise accents riding side by side with plum and berry fruit. It's a bit ponderous and chocolaty, but if you like yours sweet and saturated, you're in luck. **89** — M.S. (12/1/2004)

Santa Rita 1999 Floresta Red Blend (Maipo Valley) $30. 89 (8/1/2003)

Santa Rita 1999 Floresta Apalta Estate Red Blend (Colchagua Valley) $30. With 15% Merlot, this is a gorgeous new wine under the Floresta label. It shows all the prime pedigree of the famed Apalta vineyard and lots of style from 17 months in French oak. It's deep and purple, with tons of sweet extract (just watch those legs stick to the glass). Jammy black fruit, cassis notes, toasty wood nuances and super soft tannins—what more could you ask for? **92 Editors' Choice** —M.S. (3/1/2002)

Santa Rita 1999 Triple C Red Blend (Maipo Valley) $45. This is a new limited-production wine that's made from 55% Cabernet Franc, 30% Cabernet Sauvignon, and 15% Carmenère (hence the Triple C name). It's aged in 100% new oak, so the wood is strong. Yet everything comes together nicely, and there's an immense amount of spice and spirit here. In a year or two it should unfold into a landscape of dry red fruit, leather, and clove. **91** —M.S. (3/1/2002)

Santa Rita 2005 120 Sauvignon Blanc (Lontué Valley) $8. A challenged wine with harsh petrol aromas. The palate is limited in its delivery of citrus and little more. Quite lean and tart, with pop but what else? **81** — M.S. (7/1/2006)

Santa Rita 2003 120 Sauvignon Blanc (Lontué Valley) $8. Clean and nice, with an open yet crisp personality. The wine shows more than adequate lemon, green apple, and passion fruit notes, while the finish is surprisingly long. A winner in its class, with zest and pop. **85 Best Buy** —M.S. (6/1/2004)

Santa Rita 2000 120 Sauvignon Blanc (Curicó Valley) $8. 84 (8/1/2003)

Santa Rita 2001 Medalla Real Sauvignon Blanc (Rapel Valley) $18. Round and full in the nose, with a heavy aromatic emphasis on grapefruit. Soft lemon and other citrus fruits show up on the palate. For Sauvignon Blanc, the mouth is rather heavy and creamy; the finish seems mildly warm. **85** —M.S. (3/1/2002)

Santa Rita 2005 Reserva Sauvignon Blanc (Casablanca Valley) $12. Santa Rita's SB always exhibits the peppery, green side of the variety. And as in the past, this vintage veers perilously close to being vegetal. But amid the cucumber, bell pepper, and asparagus notes there's gooseberry and passion fruit. A zesty, green wine to be sure. **85** —M.S. (10/1/2006)

Santa Rita 2004 Reserva Sauvignon Blanc (Casablanca Valley) $12. Fresh off the boat, this youthful SB pitches a no-hitter's worth of pungent grapefruit, passion fruit, cucumber, and thistle. Seems to be shooting for

CHILE

the New Zealand style, but it's true-blue Casablanca Sauvignon. Crisp as stones and zesty, with a hint of pickle on the finish. **87 Best Buy** —*M.S. (11/15/2004)*

Santa Rita 2003 Reserva Sauvignon Blanc (Casablanca Valley) $12. The nose features pungent grapefruit, but it stops there. Flavors of cucumber, lime, and grapefruit make for a bold and forward palate. Overall, however, things seem sharp and oversized. **83** —*M.S. (3/1/2004)*

Santa Rita 2002 Reserva Sauvignon Blanc (Casablanca Valley) $12. 86 *(8/1/2003)*

Santa Rita 2003 120 Shiraz (Maipo Valley) $8. Fermented in stainless steel but aged briefly on heavily toasted oak staves; this is one big, fruity red. The nose is roasted, offering coffee and charbroiled beef. The palate is young but smooth, with pounds of berry fruit. It's heavily oaked, but the fruit can handle it. **85 Best Buy** —*M.S. (11/15/2004)*

Santa Rita 2002 Reserva Shiraz (Maipo Valley) $12. Saturated purple in color, with vanilla, mint, and tobacco aromas. The fruit is a bit herbal, but there's still enough blackberry and coffee character to keep things balanced. Some poke-through acidity creates a piqued mouthfeel. **85** —*M.S. (11/15/2004)*

SEÑA

Seña 2003 Bordeaux Blend (Aconcagua Valley) $70. When folks say "country style" you should think of this. It's a good wine but the nose is so leathery and sweaty that it's like a well-worn saddle. Once it opens and the heavy Carmenère character settles, what's left is some black fruit flavor, chocolate, and coffee. Not sure what the message is; it seems rather herbal for a so-called super Chilean. **87** —*M.S. (12/31/2006)*

Seña 2002 Bordeaux Blend (Aconcagua Valley) $70. Very round and stylish, especially for an '02 (not a memorable vintage in Chile). The nose offers full berry and tobacco aromas, which are backed up by ripe cassis and plum flavors. Stacked on the finish, with chocolaty depth that's worth exploring. Quite a successful world-class red. **91** —*M.S. (10/1/2006)*

Seña 2001 Bordeaux Blend (Aconcagua Valley) $70. Big and woody on first blush, but relaxes to show clove, cinnamon, and dry plum-like fruit. More spice and clove on the cedary palate, with a chewy, real-deal mouthfeel. Firm tannins and plenty of oak say lay this down for another couple of years. Not a monster fruit ball, but ample. **91** —*M.S. (2/1/2005)*

Seña 2000 Bordeaux Blend (Aconcagua Valley) $70. Hard to gauge at first; the aromas of wood grain, lemon juice, and coffee change radically and frequently with airing. The palate offers cherry, raspberry, and some wood-based coffee notes, while on the back end there's a full spread of spice and mocha. Good tannins and structure help it along. Definitely not the best Seña of all time, but not bad. **88** —*M.S. (6/1/2004)*

Seña 1999 Bordeaux Blend (Aconcagua Valley) $70. Opens with serious toasted oak aromas. The sappy wood and char assaults the nose, obscuring underlying black currant, tarry notes that show up in the well-ripened flavors. This is an extravagantly extracted wine, long on flavor, big in size, although it could use more in the finesse department. Mainly Cabernet Sauvignon, with Merlot and a little Carmenère. **88** —*S.H. (12/1/2002)*

Seña 1998 Bordeaux Blend (Aconcagua Valley) $66. In a strong performance for a weak vintage, the tobacco-leather-menthol nose of the '98 opens to a dry palate of berry, soy, subdued cassis flavors and leather accents. The feel is even and supple, and this drinks well now, closing with dry cherry fruit and fine tannins. Not a long-term keeper—drink through 2004. **89** *(10/1/2001)*

Seña 1997 Bordeaux Blend (Aconcagua Valley) $60. From Robert Mondavi and Eduardo Chadwick, a Chilean producer (Errázuriz), this wine is a blend of 84% Cabernet Sauvignon and 16% Carmenère. The color is inky dark, and it smells young and intense, almost fiery—there's a suggestion of charcoal and embers. Massive fruit explodes in the mouth, but it's not a fruit bomb; it's much too sophisticated for that. Oak is fancy but not pronounced. Its aging timeline should be similar to that of a great Bordeaux. **92** —*S.H. (2/1/2001)*

SIEGEL

Siegel 2001 Crucero Cabernet Sauvignon (Colchagua Valley) $9. The nose is forceful and bold, but somewhat nondescript. Plum fruit leaps from the palate, and so does chocolate. In fact, chocolate is the over-riding characteristic in this wine, so if that's your bag, then dig in. The finish is warm and expansive. **87** —*M.S. (12/1/2002)*

Siegel 2000 El Crucero Reserva Cabernet Sauvignon (Colchagua Valley) $13. Loads of mocha and toffee aromas come across on the nose along with some black olive and standard Cabernet fruit. Vivacious cherry, plum, and cassis flavors grace the tight, structured palate, and the well-oaked finish delivers a blast of chocolate and espresso. This young wine is solid and well made—a pure and positive expression of the Colchagua Valley. **89** —*M.S. (12/1/2002)*

SINCERITY

Sincerity 2004 Chardonnay (Casablanca Valley) $17. Plenty of power and style on this organic winner from heralded winemaker Alvaro Espinoza. Butterscotch, apple, and almond smother the bouquet, while exotic pear and banana flavors blend harmoniously with clean, toasty barrel notes. Quite impressive for Chilean Chardonnay. **90 Editors' Choice** —*M.S. (11/1/2005)*

Sincerity 2003 Merlot-Cabernet Sauvignon (Colchagua Valley) $17. Lavishly oaked, and that's just fine given that this wine shows more than adequate depth of fruit and lushness. Coffee, popcorn, and chocolate appear throughout its creamy, rich profile. Along the way berry and cassis flavors thrive. Quite lively and free of holes. It shows 21st-century Chile (and organic farming) in a positive light. **90** —*M.S. (12/15/2005)*

SOUTHERN WIND

Southern Wind 2002 Chardonnay (Rapel Valley) $6. The nose is lemony and offers green apple, while the palate is heavier, with sweet apple and pineapple flavors. It gets duller on the finish, where lower acidity results in a mild but persistent bitterness. **83** —*M.S. (3/1/2004)*

ST. EMILIANA

St. Emiliana 2002 Sincerity Organically Grown Merlot-Cabernet Sauvignon (Colchagua Valley) $15. Consultant supreme Alvaro Espinoza has made a winner in this organic blend of 75% Merlot and 25% Cabernet. The nose is nicely roasted, with big, creamy fruit and strong chocolate notes. The palate is thick and balanced, with smooth flavors of black fruit and milk chocolate. All told, it's meaty and huge, but not overdone. And the tannins are pure velvet. **91 Editors' Choice** —*M.S. (8/1/2004)*

STERLING

Sterling 2002 Vintner's Collection Chardonnay (Central Valley) $13. Here's a nice everyday sort of Chard. It has enough of a fruity flavor and a creamy texture to satisfy, with a jacket of smoky oak. Plus, it won't break your budget. **84** —*S.H. (9/1/2004)*

TARAPACA

Tarapaca 1997 Zavala Bordeaux Blend (Maipo Valley) $25. 87 *(8/1/2000)*

Tarapaca 1999 Cabernet Sauvignon (Maipo Valley) $9. Well-balanced, with plenty of dark fruit and toasty oak, this is a medium-to-full-bodied wine that offers vanilla and licorice accents. The finish boasts spicy black fruit, cedary notes, and even tannins. Has the stuff to improve for a year or two in bottle. **87 Best Buy** *(8/1/2001)*

Tarapaca 1999 Gran Reserva Cabernet Sauvignon (Maipo Valley) $15. It's strange to encounter a current release 1999 wine, and this offering is uneven. Some wet dog and pickle-barrel aromas wrestle on the spicy, lightly fruited nose. The palate is more than a touch green, while the finish is chewy and creamy, with ponderous, spicy oak. **82** —*M.S. (3/1/2004)*

Tarapaca 2002 Reserva Cabernet Sauvignon (Maipo Valley) $10. Pretty good overall, with some rubber and tree bark on the nose. Shows medium depth and intensity throughout, with cherry and apple skin flavors on the palate. Fairly tannic and hard, with some candied sweetness to offset things. Fine with burgers and barbecue. **84** —*M.S. (5/1/2006)*

CHILE

Tarapaca 1999 Reserva Cabernet Sauvignon (Maipo Valley) $12. Light in color, suggesting a certain lack of concentration, and this impression is immediately confirmed by smell and taste. Earthy flavors combine loosely with wood, cinnamon, and some cassis to yield an open-knit wine for current consumption. **84** —*J.C. (7/1/2002)*

Tarapaca 2003 Reserva Carmenère (Maipo Valley) $10. A front of charred beef and coffee grounds sit sentry over the bouquet, while the palate is short on fruit other than heavy black plum and berry jam. Turns more volatile and rough-edged as it opens. **82** —*M.S. (3/1/2006)*

Tarapaca 2003 Chardonnay (Maipo Valley) $8. Waxy oak, citrus, and apple kick it off, followed by almond, coconut, and apple flavors. A sharp beam of acidity makes it lively, but the flavors never really rise above basic. **83** —*M.S. (2/1/2005)*

Tarapaca 2000 Chardonnay (Maipo Valley) $9. This is a wine that shows how inflated California prices have become. It's rich, spicy, ripe, and oaky enough to satisfy anyone, and it's easily as good as many wines currently on the market that cost twice as much. It's an international style Chardonnay at a value price. **85** —*S.H. (2/1/2003)*

Tarapaca 2001 Reserva Chardonnay (Casablanca Valley) $11. Very oaky and standard, with low-level acids that cause the wine to come across heavy and flat. From a taste perspective, it's woody and drying, with modest apple and pear flavors. The heavy finish cements this wine as a modern effort that got lost along the way. **84** —*M.S. (6/1/2004)*

Tarapaca 2001 Merlot (Maipo Valley) $8. Bold and peppery, with a mild gassy note to the nose. Flavors of cassis and carob create a creamy sensation that carries through the finish. **85 Best Buy** —*M.S. (3/1/2004)*

Tarapaca 2002 Estate Bottled Merlot (Maipo Valley) $8. Aromas of earth, warm leather, and light red fruit are not what you'd call luscious, but overall the sweet berry fruit, modest spice, and forward personality make this a decent mid-level red. **84** —*M.S. (8/1/2004)*

Tarapaca 2001 Reserva Merlot (Casablanca Valley) $11. The purple luster may be the wine's strongest point, because the nose is over the top with wood, and below that it's weedy and sharp, with aromas of pickles and cabbage. In the mouth, modest plum and other red fruit flavors seem covered by oak, but what doesn't get smothered is that ubiquitous bell pepper character that comes with almost every Casablanca red. **82** —*M.S. (3/1/2004)*

Tarapaca 1999 Reserva Merlot (Maipo Valley) $12. One-dimensional, with not much in the way of texture, this Merlot has red berry, black-cherry, and wood flavors. Some bonus earth and cheese on the nose. **82** —*D.T. (7/1/2002)*

Tarapaca 2000 Sauvignon Blanc (Maipo Valley) $14. The soft melon and white peach nose has mint and grass accents but also a faint mustiness. In the mouth the mild lime and melon flavors display an odd, lemon candy-drop sweetness. This light wine is balanced, but the elements never really come together. **82** —*M.M. (8/1/2001)*

Tarapaca 2000 La Isla Vineyard Sauvignon Blanc (Maipo Valley) $14. Surprisingly fresh and vital despite having a few years under its belt. Here's a round SB with a sweet nose of pear, vanilla, and butter. The palate is forward and almondy sweet, with a hint of banana peeking in there. And the finish is round and soft. This wine is at its peak now. **86** —*M.S. (7/1/2003)*

Tarapaca 2004 Reserva Sauvignon Blanc (Maipo Valley) $10. This is a nice wine that shows the chunkier, smoother style of the grape. Starts with a touch of banana and toasty oak on the nose before shifting to apple, pear, banana, and vanilla in the mouth. Mixes lushness with acidity in an easy way. One of the better recent wines from this label. **87 Best Buy** —*M.S. (3/1/2006)*

TERRA ANDINA

Terra Andina 2001 Reserve Cabernet Blend (Rapel Valley) $15. Smooth and inviting, with attractive licorice and vanilla aromas to the core scents of blackberry and dark plum. Very ripe, with an outpouring of plum and black cherry flavors. This ripe bomber delivers a lot of guts and gusto, and the finish is full of staying power. A nice discovery. It's 70-30 in favor of Cab Franc. **89** —*M.S. (8/1/2004)*

Terra Andina 2004 Cabernet Sauvignon (Central Valley) $8. Varietally correct and ripe, with a lot of creamy oak that creates a slight lactic mouthfeel. Thus if you prefer a more acidic, crisp wine, this might not work for you. But if you like chunky cassis and berry flavors backed by soft tannins and vanilla, this is it. **85 Best Buy** —*M.S. (5/1/2006)*

Terra Andina 2002 Cabernet Sauvignon (Central Valley) $8. Even if the nose is fat and murky, this wine still delivers a lot for under $10. The palate is both spicy and sweet, as is the finish, which starts out candy-like and then offers additional spice and substance. Weighty and extracted. **85 Best Buy** —*M.S. (12/1/2004)*

Terra Andina 2003 Alto Reserve Cabernet Sauvignon (Maipo Valley) $13. Woody, with dill and buttery oak along with toast, char, and distant berry and plum. The palate offers raspberry, cherry, and a blast of lollipop sweetness. Finishes with medium tannins, milk chocolate and a snap of tang. Impressive but affordable for Maipo Cabernet. **88 Best Buy** —*M.S. (5/1/2006)*

Terra Andina 2002 Reserve Cabernet Sauvignon (Maipo Valley) $13. Brilliant violet in color, with a lush nose featuring meaty black fruit and plenty of smooth French oak. Flavors of cassis and blackberry are true to form and rock solid, while firm tannins and proper acidity bolster the mouthfeel. A fine, tightly wound Cab at a great price. **90 Best Buy** —*M.S. (8/1/2004)*

Terra Andina 2003 Carmenère (Central Valley) $8. Exhibits ripe black fruit aromas of plum and blackberry, with pleasant shadings of vanilla and marzipan. Raspberry and plum make for a ripe and fruity palate that's devoid of any herbal, under-ripe flavors. Textbook stuff, with a couple of layers of fruit and tannins. **88 Best Buy** —*M.S. (11/1/2005)*

Terra Andina 2001 Carmenère (Central Valley) $8. A touch stewy and bulky, but still a positive wine from a good if now old vintage. Plum and cherry fruit on the palate seems ripe, and the finish is properly dry. A bit high in acidity, but still good in terms of mouthfeel. **85 Best Buy** —*M.S. (12/1/2004)*

Terra Andina 2004 Chardonnay (Central Valley) $8. Oddly oily, with aromas of cotton candy. Heavy citrus and pineapple makes up the flavor profile, and the finish lacks intensity. Bland overall, and loses focus rapidly. **82** —*M.S. (11/1/2005)*

Terra Andina 2003 Chardonnay (Central Valley) $8. Plump and forward smelling, with mild toast aromas. Full and easy, with light apple and mango flavors. Finishes open and spicy, with a jolt of acidic verve. **86 Best Buy** —*M.S. (2/1/2005)*

Terra Andina 2003 Alto Reserve Chardonnay (Casablanca Valley) $13. The bouquet starts with soft white fruit aromas, particularly peach and nectarine. The palate is sweeter than that, showing mango, melon, and citrus zest. Not all that focused or precise; it's mostly a mishmosh of fruit and acid. Needs to deliver a clearer message. **84** —*M.S. (5/1/2006)*

Terra Andina 2002 Reserve Chardonnay (Casablanca Valley) $13. Waxy and honeyed in the nose, with an aftershock of butterscotch. Pear, apple, and coconut dominate the sweet, simple palate. Finishes heavy and round, as do so many Chilean Chardonnays. **85** —*M.S. (8/1/2004)*

Terra Andina 2004 Merlot (Central Valley) $8. Shows earth and leather as well as solid fruit. Runs slightly tart, with red cherry. But that means it's fresh and upright rather than lazy and dull. Pepper and tannin on the finish seem right. Straightforward, good red wine, simple as that. **86 Best Buy** —*M.S. (11/1/2005)*

Terra Andina 2003 Merlot (Central Valley) $8. Spearmint, blackberry and plum unfold on the juicy, easy nose. The palate spreads out with raspberry, red plum, and licorice flavors. Lengthy and textured on the finish, with a dose of spice. Easy to drink. **86 Best Buy** —*M.S. (2/1/2005)*

Terra Andina 2004 Sauvignon Blanc (Central Valley) $8. Very much as expected, with some sweet and snappy aromas followed by a full palate graced by orange and tangerine flavors. Citrus is the dominant force here, and there's texture to support it. Surely good with appetizers. **85 Best Buy** —*M.S. (11/1/2005)*

Terra Andina 2003 Sauvignon Blanc (Central Valley) $8. Clean but bland on the nose, with distant aromatics of pineapple, green apple, and cantaloupe. Tasty enough, with notes of kiwi, passion fruit, and pineapple.

CHILE

Not too racy or bracing, but pretty good along the way. **85 Best Buy** —*M.S. (8/1/2004)*

Terra Andina 2003 Shiraz (Central Valley) $8. Lots of berry and spice on the nose, with basic everyman berry and plum flavors. Juicy and solid, with some tang and jump. Plenty of potency but not a whole lot of Syrah character. Boiled down, it's your average red wine. **84 Best Buy** —*M.S. (12/15/2005)*

Terra Andina 2002 Shiraz (Central Valley) $8. Soft and flabby on the nose, with heavy berry syrup aromas. The palate is more red fruit dominant, with plum and raspberry. Good zip and acidity, with a hint of buttery oak on the finish. **84 Best Buy** —*M.S. (2/1/2005)*

Terra Andina 2002 Reserve Shiraz-Cabernet Sauvignon (Maipo Valley) $15. A huge wine with aromas of molasses, berry syrup, rubber, and smoke. Flavors of ripe blackberry and plum are big but unrefined, while the finishing notes of coffee and earth are good. As for mouthfeel, it's a bit starchy and lean. **86** —*M.S. (8/1/2004)*

TERRA NOVA

Terra Nova 2003 Chardonnay (Curicó Valley) $7. Light and easy, with vanilla and a hint of spice. Peach and apple flavors lead to a fresh, short finish. Watery in the center. **83** —*M.S. (7/1/2005)*

Terra Nova 2003 Sauvignon Blanc (Curicó Valley) $7. Soft and melony, with little edge. Sour apple and lemon flavors, with sherry on the finish. Doesn't expand at all on the palate. **80** —*M.S. (7/1/2005)*

TERRAMATER

TerraMater 2001 Altum Reserve Cabernet Sauvignon (Curicó Valley) $17. Dark and minty, with licorice and cassis aromas that are positive. In the mouth, it's got Cab's typical plum and cassis character, and the finish is round and spicy, with a little heat. If only the mouthfeel were less jumpy and more lush, this would be even better. **87** —*M.S. (7/1/2005)*

TerraMater 2002 Reserva Cabernet Sauvignon (Central Valley) $12. Quite woody and minty to begin with. The palate, meanwhile, delivers a shock of berry syrup, something akin to blueberry or boysenberry. Warm and oaky on the finish, but also sweet and cloying. Likable but medicinal. **84** —*M.S. (7/1/2005)*

TerraMater 2001 Single Vineyard Cabernet Sauvignon (Maipo Valley) $8. Aromas of cherries and flowers get it going, followed by sweet flavors of red and black fruit. Nothing in particular stands out in this wine other than its balance and freshness. Ample tannins coat the mouth and there's a hint of oak on the finish. This is a good Chilean Cab, one that represents the value class well. **85** —*M.S. (12/1/2002)*

TerraMater 2003 Merlot (Maipo Valley) $9. Smooth and supple, with magnetic aromas of mocha, leather, and blackberry. A standout among the world's countless inexpensive Merlots; it displays succulent dark fruits, ample coffee, and chocolate notes, and an even mouthfeel. Surprisingly complete, and handsome. **88 Best Buy** —*M.S. (7/1/2005)*

TerraMater 1999 Altum Reserve Single Vineyard Merlot (Maipo Valley) $20. Unusual and sweet in the nose, with something similar to cinnamon or all-spice aromas. There is quite a woody undertone here; you get it in the nose and again on the palate. This wine is the proverbial hare, not the tortoise. It starts fast, making a good impression, but it fades before the finish line. **83** —*M.S. (1/28/2004)*

TerraMater 1999 Altum Single Vineyard Reserve San Clemente Merlot (Maule Valley) $17. Seems like a holdover from a few years ago. A bouquet of hard spice, chemical, and tree bark is rustic and lacking in friendly fruit. In the mouth, sweet but cooked plum and cherry flavors are heavy and almost medicinal. Finishes with oaky, burnt marshmallow flavors. **83** —*M.S. (7/1/2005)*

TerraMater 2003 Reserva Merlot (Central Valley) $12. Nice and satisfying, but softer and less dynamic than the basic varietal bottling. Nonetheless, it packs spice, mocha, and earth aromas, all backed by ripe blackberry and plum. A blast of cough medicine and licorice on the finish is a sweet, almost cloying, touch. **87 Best Buy** —*M.S. (7/1/2005)*

TerraMater 2001 Single Vineyard Zinfandel-Shiraz Red Blend (Central Valley) $8. From the plant-it-and-blend-it category comes this earthy, chunky, plum-filled red that turns sharp and sour. The finish is gritty

and the body too tannic compared to the quality of the fruit. **80** —*M.S. (7/1/2003)*

TerraMater 2001 Unusual Cabernet, Zinfandel, Shiraz Red Blend (Maipo Valley) $22. Unusual indeed. The blend is Cabernet, Zinfandel, and Shiraz, and frankly it's a mish-mash of oak, espresso, and sour fruit. Extremely lemony, with a fair amount of green. In no way does the fruit stand up to the huge pounding of oak it takes. Out of whack. **81** —*M.S. (2/1/2005)*

TerraMater 2000 Unusual Carmenère-Shiraz Red Blend (Central Valley) $22. The blend of these two grapes is indeed unusual, as so is the nose of green bean, tobacco, and berries. Not sure if the combination really works; at moments it shows some juicy fruit and zip, while at other times it seems vegetal and mismatched. **84** —*M.S. (11/1/2005)*

TerraMater 2004 Sauvignon Blanc (Maipo Valley) $9. Not a lot on the nose besides distant melon and honey, but the palate is brighter. On offer is a peach, melon, and orange flavor profile sitting in front of a round, chunky finish. Ripe but a bit soft-edged. **86 Best Buy** —*M.S. (7/1/2005)*

TERRANOBLE

TerraNoble 2004 Gran Reserva Cabernet Sauvignon (Colchagua Valley) $14. This wine is the perfect model for mid-level Chilean Cabernet. It costs under $15 yet it overdelivers. The nose is firm and toasty, with serious berry and cassis aromas. In the mouth, it sings its way through wavy raspberry and vanilla flavors. Balanced and rich, with some creaminess and depth. **90 Best Buy** —*M.S. (11/15/2006)*

TerraNoble 2003 Gran Reserva Cabernet Sauvignon (Colchagua Valley) $17. Barnyard meets pickle at first, but airing gives more clarity to the nose. The palate is a bit murky but it's also loaded with meat, cola, and dark, almost baked fruit. The mouthfeel is tight and strong, with tannins that hit hard and then hang around for the finish. **86** —*M.S. (10/1/2006)*

TerraNoble 2002 Gran Reserva Cabernet Sauvignon (Colchagua Valley) $13. Starts out sharp but settles after a while. Chewy and more sweet on the palate, but unconvincing as serious Cab goes. Bits of chocolate and crusty fruit work the thick, heavy finish. Fails to impress. **82** —*M.S. (11/1/2005)*

TerraNoble 2001 Gran Reserva Cabernet Sauvignon (Maule Valley) $20. Clearly the producer is shooting for a rich, lavish style of Cab, and for the most part that's what you get. The bouquet is dense and full of bacon, mushroom, and black fruit, while the palate is thick with plum, raisin, and smoky, tangy, saucy notes. A firm, oaky, lengthy finish renders it consequential. **88** —*M.S. (3/1/2004)*

TerraNoble 1999 Gran Reserva Cabernet Sauvignon (Colchagua Valley) $14. Leather, toast, and dark fruit mark this supple wine. One tends to expect weight with inky color, but this is lithe. The flavors are tangy black plums and berries, with licorice accents. **86** *(8/1/2001)*

TerraNoble 2004 Reserva Cabernet Sauvignon (Colchagua Valley) $11. Nice and ripe, with expressive plum, cassis, tobacco, and asphalt aromas. The mouthfeel and flavor profile are both fairly full, as cassis and plum notes run the show. For a basic Cabernet that qualifies as affordable, you get plenty for your money. **87 Best Buy** —*M.S. (11/15/2006)*

TerraNoble 2003 Reserva Cabernet Sauvignon (Colchagua Valley) $11. Raw and salty at first, with some baked aromas and wet leather. More snappy than fat on the tongue, where plum and berry flavors are supported by stern tannins. A tiny bit green in the middle as well as on the finish. **85** —*M.S. (12/15/2005)*

TerraNoble 2003 Gran Reserva Carmenère (Maule Valley) $13. Loaded with ripe aromas of cola, dark fruit, and earth, and that's followed up by the full allotment of blackberry and black cherry flavors. Chocolaty and full on the palate and finish, with supreme juiciness and laudable balance. Makes the grade and then some. **90 Best Buy** —*M.S. (12/15/2005)*

TerraNoble 1999 Gran Reserva Carmenère (Maule Valley) $24. Sure it's woody; the dominant aromas and flavors are smoke, cedar, and toast. But there's enough depth of plummy, black cherry fruit underneath to stand up to the oak and it finishes well, with good length and slightly dry tannins. **86** —*J.C. (8/1/2001)*

CHILE

TerraNoble 2003 Reserva Carmenère (Maule Valley) $12. Fat and attractive, with ripe fruit that can best be described as bruising. Black plum, ink, and delicate herbs make for a lovely nose that leads to a lush palate of black cherry, plum, and cassis. Smooth and full-bodied; a pleasant, legitimate surprise. **89 Best Buy** —M.S. (2/1/2005)

TerraNoble 2001 Reserva Carmenère (Chile) $12. Nice, fresh, and on the money. This is Carmenère in its ripest, most balanced state, and it is a fine red wine with a lot of spunk and natural flavor. The bouquet is perfumed and meaty, while the palate deals bacon, cassis, and black cherry. A smoky, mildly charred finish really helps it along. **89 Best Buy** —M.S. (3/1/2004)

TerraNoble 2005 Chardonnay (Casablanca Valley) $7. Delivers a punch bowl's worth of floral aromas and fruity flavors. Tangy in the mouth, with all the citrus and green apple you can reasonably expect from a wine of this price. Long, fruity, and properly acidic on the finish. **86 Best Buy** —M.S. (3/1/2006)

TerraNoble 2004 Chardonnay (Casablanca Valley) $8. Quite standard, but therein lies its virtues. Nothing wild or funky here, just fresh aromas of peach and melon along with good pear and apple flavors. Proper acidity keeps it moving forward, and while it finishes sweet, it holds the line on balance. Admirable for the price. **87 Best Buy** —M.S. (7/1/2005)

TerraNoble 2003 Chardonnay (Casablanca Valley) $8. Light pear and apple aromas are clean and appealing. Look for a zesty palate with citrus and banana flavors, and then vanilla and spice on the finish. It's sweetly persistent and well-proportioned. **86 Best Buy** —M.S. (3/1/2004)

TerraNoble 2000 Chardonnay (Maule Valley) $9. The tart green apple fruit has a musty note that doesn't yield with time in the glass. The wine is dry, the flavors nondescript, and there's not much palate texture. **82** —M.M. (8/1/2001)

TerraNoble 2005 Vineyard Selection Chardonnay (Casablanca Valley) $9. Tropical fruit carries the bouquet, while the palate is citrusy and lively as it ranges from ripe grapefruit to pineapple and on to orange. Fresh on the tongue, with laudable balance and structure. Nothing outrageous but perfectly good. **86 Best Buy** —M.S. (10/1/2006)

TerraNoble 2000 Merlot (Maule Valley) $9. A contrast of sweet and bitter elements shows in the blueberry jam, vanilla, and balsam aromas and the plum, earth, and herb flavors. Firm, puckering tannins frame this light-bodied Merlot. **81** —J.F. (8/1/2001)

TerraNoble 2004 Gran Reserva Merlot (Maule Valley) $16. Chilean Merlot in fine form. The nose is subtle and lightly spiced, with ample dark fruit aromas. The palate bursts with tight, snappy cherry and raspberry flavors, while the back end is smoky and drying, with perfect tannins. Golfers would liken this to a drive right down the middle. **89** —M.S. (10/1/2006)

TerraNoble 2003 Gran Reserva Merlot (Maule Valley) $13. Smooth and stylish, with ripe, meaty aromas and a solid, not-too-aggressive personality. Fresh on the tongue, where blackberry and plum flavors blend nicely with dark chocolate and bacon. The chewy, round finish completes the canvas. **88 Best Buy** —M.S. (11/1/2005)

TerraNoble 2002 Gran Reserva Merlot (Maule Valley) $14. Very little difference exists between this and the so-called "reserva." This wine is oakier, with more powerful pickle and barrel notes. Otherwise it shows the same red fruit flavors along with lively tannins and acids. **83** —M.S. (7/1/2005)

TerraNoble 2002 Reserva Merlot (Maule Valley) $12. Kind of hot and jagged, with forward cherry and plum aromas softened by vanilla. Cherry and raspberry flavors are basic and racy, with some spice. Tight on the finish, with hard tannins. **84** —M.S. (7/1/2005)

TerraNoble 2006 Vineyard Selection Sauvignon Blanc (Maule Valley) $8. This is definitely a bright, zesty, citrusy wine, but one with structure, especially given that it's an affordable, everyday Sauvignon Blanc. Aromas of citrus are dominant, while flavors of lime and grapefruit are nicely balanced and tasty. **87 Best Buy** —M.S. (11/15/2006)

TRINCAO

Trincao 2001 Reserva Carmenère (Maipo Valley) $11. Leathery and rough at first, with a green element to the nose. Time opens it up, freeing milk chocolate, carob, and black pepper, all telltale flavors common to this grape variety. A medicinal edge to the flavor profile holds it back. **85** —M.S. (8/1/2004)

Trincao 2001 Reserva Syrah (Maipo Valley) $11. Strong and meaty, with a hint of barnyard to the nose. This wine turns dark in the middle, with a heavyweight's texture minus the piercing tannins. It has depth, and in many ways it's akin to liquid cake due to its richness. Good, expressive fruit at all checkpoints. **87 Best Buy** —M.S. (8/1/2004)

TWO BROTHERS

Two Brothers 2001 Big Tattoo Red Red Blend (Colchagua Valley) $9. This blend of Cabernet Sauvignon, Syrah, and Merlot starts off a bit murky and brooding but then displays raspberry and plum fruit, and some big-time heft. A tad oaky and simple, but with grilled meats it should more than do the trick. If you like 'em big and a touch funky, get tattooed. **87 Best Buy** —M.S. (7/1/2003)

UNDURRAGA

Undurraga 2001 Cabernet Sauvignon (Colchagua Valley) $7. This is an easy, smooth Cabernet, the perfect "just go and pop the cork" red. It's ripe and sweet, with a full cherry flavor and a clean finish. No oak aging makes it all about the fruit, which is just fine. **86 Best Buy** —M.S. (3/1/2002)

Undurraga 2000 Cabernet Sauvignon (Colchagua Valley) $7. Jammy, soft, and juicy, this Cabernet Sauvignon tastes almost like a California field blend. But that's not bad, if not particularly varietally focused. Easy, very drinkable, it's a kind of "Cab-jolais" that can work as a bar pour or party wine. **85 Best Buy** —M.M. (2/1/2001)

Undurraga 2002 Altazor Cabernet Sauvignon (Maipo Valley) $42. A bit Old World in style, with a touch of leafiness to the nose along with hints of earth, leather, olive, and dried red fruits. Shows ample cassis, strawberry and brown sugar on the palate, followed by a smooth, relatively long finish. Healthy and powerful, especially after breathing. **88** —M.S. (5/1/2006)

Undurraga 1999 Altazor Cabernet Sauvignon (Maipo Valley) $46. The debut vintage, and already sold out, according to Undurraga. It's inky in color, with earthy scents complemented by cassis and mint. The chewy texture is silky as well, finishing with firm tannins and juicy acids. The next vintage will be the 2001, which should be more available, as 1,000 cases were produced. **90 Cellar Selection** (2/1/2004)

Undurraga 2004 Founder's Collection Cabernet Sauvignon (Maipo Valley) $22. Undurraga's high-tier Cabernet is an austere wine with strength and hard tannins but very little elegance. The bouquet issues a strong blast of rubbery red fruit, which is backed by jammy but rough red fruit flavors. To this taster, this producer's standard premium wines offer better value. **84** —M.S. (12/31/2006)

Undurraga 2002 Founder's Collection Cabernet Sauvignon (Maipo Valley) $21. Seductive, with cherry, earth, and chocolate-covered raisin on the bouquet. Ripe black fruit coats the sticky palate, while background flavors of tobacco and molasses are both sweet and spicy. Finishes long and nice enough, even if there are some austere tannins in the final analysis. **88** —M.S. (5/1/2006)

Undurraga 1999 Founder's Collection Cabernet Sauvignon (Maipo Valley) $25. Mature already, with aromatic notes of berry, lemony oak, and root beer. The flavor profile is at first medicinal, but it opens to reveal cherry, chocolate, and cassis. The chewy finish is aggressive and forward, and all told the wine is round if a bit candied. **86** (7/1/2003)

Undurraga 1997 Founder's Collection Cabernet Sauvignon (Maipo Valley) $25. Dark berry, fig, plum, and licorice aromas and flavors show, but the understated fruit has to contend with a lot of oak. The palate's full, smooth texture and interesting bacony notes have appeal. **85** (8/1/2001)

Undurraga 2003 Reserva Cabernet Sauvignon (Maipo Valley) $11. Deep and earthy, with aromatic hints of forest, toast, and nicely baked fruit. Shows good body and balance, with cherry and raspberry flavors. Seems healthy and upright, with some acidity on the finish that offers boost. Clean and well built. **87 Best Buy** —M.S. (5/1/2006)

Undurraga 2001 Reserva Cabernet Sauvignon (Maipo Valley) $14. Crisp and smooth in the mouth, with clean, unblemished flavors of chocolate

CHILE

and cassis wrapped around a core of firm acidity. Lacks the herbal notes that seem to abound in Chilean Cabernet. **87** *(2/1/2004)*

Undurraga 1998 Reserva Cabernet Sauvignon (Maipo Valley) $12. With a vegetal note, some cocoa and berry on the nose and its simple, rather flat flavor profile, this Cabernet suffers from both vintage deficiencies and over-oaking. Dry and woody on the back end. **82** —*M.M. (2/1/2001)*

Undurraga 2004 Aliwen Reserva Cabernet Sauvignon-Carmenère (Central Valley) $10. Smoked meat, mocha, and ripe red fruit work the nose, followed by red berry flavors jostled by hints of rhubarb. A fresh, snappy red wine that hits the bull's eye on some of its targets. **85 Best Buy** —*M.S. (12/31/2006)*

Undurraga 2004 Reserva Carmenère (Colchagua Valley) $12. This wine pulls no punches as its aromas leap from the glass and hit you with a blast of spice, animal hide, and black plum. The palate is amply oaked, thus vanilla notes intermingle with cherry and plum flavors. The feel and finish are equally creamy and easy, as modest tannins keep things from going soft. **87 Best Buy** —*M.S. (12/31/2006)*

Undurraga 2003 Reserva Carmenère (Colchagua Valley) $11. Starts with a spicy, baked quality as well as cola and leafy notes. Medium in body, with a slick flavor profile that's one part cherry and berry and one part herbal. Turns a bit more herbaceous with airing, bordering on vegetal. But still it's good Carmenère. **85** —*M.S. (12/15/2005)*

Undurraga 2002 Reserva Carmenère (Colchagua Valley) $14. A medium-weight wine, with aromas of plum, cocoa, and tomato leaf complemented by flavors of black cherries and fresh herbs. Supple and smooth-textured, picking up hints of black tea leaves on the finish. **87** *(2/1/2004)*

Undurraga 2001 Reserva Carmenère (Colchagua Valley) $11. Spicy and peppery, with lots of body and richness. In a word, it's true Carmenère. The fruit here is ripe and lush, with plenty of herbal essence, and for every drop of plum or black cherry there's a balancing hint of green herb and bell pepper, which does not signal under-ripeness. The finish is tight and long, with some espresso flavor. If you're interested in trying a well-made Carmenère, give this a go. **87** —*M.S. (7/1/2003)*

Undurraga 1998 Reserva Carmenère (Colchagua Valley) $12. With a bouquet of dark plum and toasty oak, with an earthy barnyardy note, this wine from this older Bordeaux grape still cultivated in Chile has medium weight and some plum and caramel flavors. In the end, the wood is a bit much for the fruit, and it is not dissimilar to some Barberas from Italy's Piedmont that wear an overweight of oak. **84** *(2/1/2001)*

Undurraga 1999 Reserve Carmenère (Colchagua Valley) $11. For Carmenère, this one is sharper than most. The mouth is tight and lean, with red cherries and only some meaty, earthy character. The finish is basic. **84** —*M.S. (3/1/2002)*

Undurraga 2001 Chardonnay (Maipo Valley) $7. Very fruity, with clean, driving apple and pear aromas. Fine in the mouth, with expressive citrus and apple flavors. This good-bodied wine, although inexpensive, should satisfy almost any palate. **86 Best Buy** —*M.S. (3/1/2002)*

Undurraga 2000 Chardonnay (Maipo Valley) $7. An easy wine that opens with bright pineapple and citrus notes. Mild apple and pear flavors follow, and if the mouthfeel is a bit ethereal, it is a lively lightness. The dry subtly spicy finish has an interesting chalky note. **85** —*M.M. (1/1/2004)*

Undurraga 2005 Aliwen Reserva Chardonnay (Central Valley) $10. This new wine from a venerable Chilean producer scores points all over the map. The nose is a smooth ride of white fruits and cleanliness, while the mouth pulsates with pear, green banana, and toasted walnuts. Harmonious and sturdy, with fine balance. One of the best ten-buck, buy-and-drink Chards you'll find. **90 Best Buy** —*M.S. (11/15/2006)*

Undurraga 2005 Reserva Chardonnay (Maipo Valley) $12. The bouquet here sports popcorn and butter, but also zesty tropical fruit and apple blossom aromas. The palate is rich but balanced, with pear and toffee flavors. Warm and woody throughout, but with such firm acidity it's a winner. **89 Best Buy** —*M.S. (11/15/2006)*

Undurraga 2002 Reserva Chardonnay (Maipo Valley) $14. A relatively lean and restrained Chardonnay, with pencilly toast notes alongside tart, apple-y fruit. Has a silky mouthfeel and plenty of nutty, toasty nuances on the finish. **86** *(2/1/2004)*

Undurraga 2001 Reserva Chardonnay (Maipo Valley) $12. Lean and fresh, with pure apple and oak aromas. The palate runs a little sweet, but melon and pineapple flavors ride popping acidity and thus it never seem heavy or overripe. Like many current-release whites from Chile, this one delivers verve and ample fruit. **85** —*M.S. (7/1/2003)*

Undurraga 1998 Reserva Chardonnay (Maipo Valley) $12. Wearing a heavy mantle of rather green, not-too-subtle oak, the fruit in this wine struggles to be noticed. Faintly apple, with earthy notes, it is fairly buried, and the wine lacks the life and dimension on the palate one seeks in a wine with reserve status. **82** —*M.M. (2/1/2001)*

Undurraga 2002 Gewürztraminer (Maipo Valley) $9. One whiff and you know what you have. The nose offers wild flower, mustard seed, and tell-tale lychee fruit. The body is fairly rich, and there are flavors of custard, apple, banana, and nutmeg-like spice. The finish is simultaneously chewy and fresh, which is a testament to the wine's forward acidity. **84** —*M.S. (7/1/2003)*

Undurraga 2000 Merlot (Maipo Valley) $7. Attractive and correct berry, plum, and cocoa aromas open to a plummy palate, with a round mouth-feel. The cocoa and toast finish has easy tannins. Has all the right elements, but in a rather simple expression, wanting intensity. **83** *(2/1/2001)*

Undurraga 2003 Reserva Merlot (Maipo Valley) $11. Shows some bramble and pickle on the nose along with a heavy blast of molasses. The palate, however, is more sharp and piquant than expected. Finishes with overt oak and acidity, which creates a lean, tangy finishing sensation. **84** —*M.S. (5/1/2006)*

Undurraga 2001 Reserva Merlot (Maipo Valley) $12. Smooth smelling, with pure and fresh berry and plum aromas. Very young and a bit tangy on the palate, with cherry and berry flavors and an oaky, soft finish that goes sweet then sour, and lasts for a long time. In terms of structure, it's balanced, mildly tannic, yet meant for drinking now. **87** —*M.S. (7/1/2003)*

Undurraga 1999 Reserva Merlot (Maipo Valley) $12. Lavishly-oaked, the fruit here struggles to make itself acknowledged, and when it does it is light plum-cranberry in aroma and flavor. Quite dry on the palate, the wine finishes tart with woody tannins. **81** *(2/1/2001)*

Undurraga 2001 Pinot Noir (Maipo Valley) $7. Pinot drinkers will recognize that this highly affordable wine is pretty good stuff, and they will like the tight, sporty, smoky nose that leads into a dry, peppery palate with ample black cherry and sweet plums. With this wine, Undurraga is delivering nice Pinot Noir for the cash-strapped consumer. **86 Best Buy** —*M.S. (3/1/2002)*

Undurraga 2000 Pinot Noir (Maipo Valley) $7. A light and tart wine, with a bouquet of berry, tea, and a touch of barnyard. On the palate, there's more cherry, tea, and oak. The fundamental Pinot characteristics are here, but it turns drying and a bit sour on the finish. **82** —*M.S. (2/1/2001)*

Undurraga 2002 Reserva Pinot Noir (Maipo Valley) $14. Shows a slightly sour, herbal twang that upstages the chunky black cherry and cola flavors. **84** *(2/1/2004)*

Undurraga 2001 Reserva Pinot Noir (Maipo Valley) $12. Rough at first, with leathery aromas and hints of bitter chocolate. Which all goes to say: Where's the snappy cherry fruit? It just doesn't seem to be here. What you do get is light raspberry and tea notes, and then some oak and herbal character on the finish. **84** —*M.S. (7/1/2003)*

Undurraga 1999 Reserva Pinot Noir (Maipo Valley) $12. With its nose offering toasty oak and leather notes, this shows a bit of depth. Light but full-flavored, as Pinot may be, the dark cherry and oak flavors are simple and rustic. **84** —*M.M. (2/1/2001)*

Undurraga 2006 Sauvignon Blanc (Central Valley) $7. Light fruit on the nose, yet somewhat chunky and full in the mouth, as if some apple juice or orange juice got into the blend. Decent enough but mildly heavy and sticky. Could use more zest and balance. **82** —*M.S. (11/15/2006)*

Undurraga 2005 Sauvignon Blanc (Central Valley) $7. About as new as you can get, here's a fresh, simple '05 Sauvignon that may not rock your world but it won't rock your wallet, either. Melon and apple aromas get it started, followed by kiwi, honeydew, and pineapple flavors. There's

CHILE

medium zest from moderate acidity, and some citrus rind on the finish. To call it innocuous would be unfair, but harmless, even friendly, is appropriate. **84 Best Buy** —*M.S. (11/15/2005)*

Undurraga 2003 Sauvignon Blanc (Lontué Valley) $10. A refreshing, simple quaff, with passion fruit and red currant aromas and a tart, grape-fruity finish. Would make a fine apéritif or picnic wine. **85** *(12/31/2003)*

Undurraga 2001 Sauvignon Blanc (Lontué Valley) $7. Lots of lemon and pineapple at first, and even a touch of soda-like spritz. Piercing grape-fruit flavors and citrus-inspiring acids leave notes of tangerine and orange on the clean finish. **86 Best Buy** —*M.S. (3/1/2002)*

Undurraga 2006 Aliwen Reserva Sauvignon Blanc (Central Valley) $10. Bartlett pear, passion fruit, and peach aromas get it going. The palate is sound and tropical, with common citrus and mild green notes. Finishes clean and fairly large, with plenty of citrus zest and an ample amount of lushness. **87 Best Buy** —*M.S. (12/31/2006)*

Undurraga 2004 Reserva Syrah (Colchagua Valley) $12. Initially the wine gives off an earthy-crusty air, and then earth and leather aromas sneak in along with black fruit. Additional fruit is released on the palate, primarily raspberry and black plum. For a ripe wine with prune and molasses, it holds its line. **86** —*M.S. (12/31/2006)*

VALDIVIESO

Valdivieso 2004 Single Vineyard Reserve Cabernet Franc (Colchagua Valley) $17. The bouquet is basically a sweet berry blend with touches of char and heat. The palate offers good core fruit and a sturdy structure. Full tannins and some oaky vanilla and coconut notes show up on the finish. Nice for Cab Franc, especially Chilean Cab Franc. **87** —*M.S. (12/31/2006)*

Valdivieso 2003 Single Vineyard Reserve Cabernet Franc (Central Valley) $17. Structured, tight, and linear at first, and then air unveils good oak notes, red fruit, and tobacco. Ripe and loaded in the mouth, with bold cassis and cherry flavors. Good tannins, spice, warmth, and a pleasing outlook make this a winner. **90** —*M.S. (5/1/2006)*

Valdivieso 2001 Single Vineyard Reserve Cabernet Franc (Lontué Valley) $17. No issues of under-ripeness or herbaceousness here; this a meaty, sweet rendition of Cab Franc, one with sweet cherry and raspberry in spades. If you seek Loire-style leafiness or Bordeaux complexity, go else-where. This version is chewy, rich, ripe, and fleshy. **89** —*M.S. (8/1/2004)*

Valdivieso 2000 Single Vineyard Reserve Cabernet Franc (Lontué Valley) $17. You don't hear much about Cab Franc from Chile, but this is one that is worth seeking out. The aromas are spicy and attractive, even if there's some lemony oak masking the fruit. In the mouth, raspberry, red cherry, and red apple run the show, and then comes a fresh, lithe, bal-anced finish. Everything is generally in place here, including some bright, refreshing acidity. Only the heavy oak dulls it down a touch. **88 Best Buy** —*M.S. (7/1/2003)*

Valdivieso 2004 Cabernet Sauvignon (Central Valley) $7. Unfolds with soft, almost candied strawberry aromas before gathering its legs to show more committed red fruit flavors. An easygoing wine that snaps and pops on the palate. Hardly complex but satisfying in a no-thought way. **84 Best Buy** —*M.S. (7/1/2006)*

Valdivieso 2001 Cabernet Sauvignon (Central Valley) $8. A no-frills mass-appeal wine with a pretty color, ripe aromatics, and a hint of oak. The palate is solid and full-flavored, while the finish is smooth and easy. Ripe, clean, and round. **85 Best Buy** —*M.S. (7/1/2003)*

Valdivieso 2002 Barrel Selection Reserve Cabernet Sauvignon (Central Valley) $10. That's too much name for a run-of-the-mill Cab, but who's complaining? The wine is a seriously good bargain; the color is bright, the nose pure, and the palate downright pleasant. Throughout there's ample cherry, cassis, and plum character, and here and there come hints of chocolate and cola. Textbook everyday wine. **88 Best Buy** —*M.S. (7/1/2005)*

Valdivieso 2003 Reserve Cabernet Sauvignon (Central Valley) $13. Firm up front, with cherry and leather-based aromas. Full and fruity, with solid plum and blackberry flavors. Offers good depth, quality fruit, and some chocolate on the finish. Well balanced; it's one of those classic, value-priced Chilean Cabernets. **88 Best Buy** —*M.S. (7/1/2006)*

Valdivieso 2000 Reserve Cabernet Sauvignon (Central Valley) $13. Ultra-ripe but balanced, with beams of black plum and cherry driving through the bouquet. Totally mature berry fruit on the palate, and loud. Juicy and racy across the tongue. Good with a steak. **88** —*M.S. (2/1/2005)*

Valdivieso 2000 Reserve Cabernet Sauvignon (Central Valley) $20. Rich plum and blackberry aromas are mirrored with the same fruit in the fla-vors with the addition of cedar and toast. The wine finishes long with big but well integrated tannins. **89** —*C.S. (2/1/2003)*

Valdivieso 1998 Reserve Cabernet Sauvignon (Central Valley) $20. Like the other Valdivieso Reserve wines, this one is very oaky and cedary. Thankfully, there's some black cherry flavors to go along with the sweet wood and dried spices. Folds in coffee notes on the somewhat lemony finish. **87** —*J.C. (3/1/2002)*

Valdivieso 2002 Rosé Cabernet Sauvignon (Central Valley) $8. Light on the nose. The flavor profile leans toward cranberry, but there seems to be a faint pickled note, too. The feel is juicy and acidic, so it's fresh. **82** —*M.S. (7/1/2003)*

Valdivieso 2004 Chardonnay (Central Valley) $7. Quite sweet on the nose, with mango and cantaloupe. Sort of syrupy and soft, with plump but basic citrus flavors. Finishes heavy, with a fleshy freshness and medium acidity. **83** —*M.S. (5/1/2006)*

Valdivieso 2003 Chardonnay (Central Valley) $7. What a good, affordable Chard should be. It's soft and stable, with melon, apple, and cinnamon notes to the rich but balanced palate. The finish is soft and spreads out broadly, with just hint of acidic sharpness. Mouthfilling although not particularly complex. **87 Best Buy** —*M.S. (6/1/2004)*

Valdivieso 2000 Barrel Selection Chardonnay (Central Valley) $12. This is the essence of fresh, crisp, light Chilean Chardonnay. A very light and well-applied dose of oak supports pear and apple fruit, and the finish is smooth and nicely nutty. **86** —*M.S. (3/1/2002)*

Valdivieso 2003 Reserve Chardonnay (Casablanca Valley) $13. Heavy gold in color; a butterball of the first order. The nose is full of oak along with pear and apple. That's backed by a palate of sweet corn, mango, banana, and apple. Toasty on the finish, with a splinter of pithy bitter-ness. Good Casablanca acidity ensures pop on the tongue. **86** —*M.S. (12/15/2005)*

Valdivieso 2001 Reserve Chardonnay (Central Valley) $14. With full oak and pineapple aromas along with a big mouthful of spicy apple and pear fruit, this is no weakling. On the contrary, it's full and meaty, with a lot of texture and extract. The feel is healthy even if the acidity is on the low side. A very good wine to drink now; it probably won't age that well. **88** —*M.S. (7/1/2003)*

Valdivieso 2001 Reserve Chardonnay (Casablanca Valley) $13. Yellow in color, with a murky nose full of over-ripe fruit and corn. Heavy, with chunky melon and apple flavors. **81** —*M.S. (2/1/2005)*

Valdivieso 1999 Reserve Chardonnay (Central Valley) $20. With its rich tropical fruits, nutty vanilla overtones, and toasty, smoky finish, this is a dead-ringer for a top-notch California Chardonnay. Tangerine, peach, and pineapple flavors combine with a custardy mouthfeel to offer satis-faction in every sip. **90 Editors' Choice** —*J.C. (3/1/2002)*

Valdivieso 2004 Malbec (Central Valley) $7. Roasted fruit and coffee pro-vide a masculine edge to the red fruit nose. The palate pushes lean berry flavors that are saddled with a hint of green. Mint and menthol appear on the jumpy finish. **83** —*M.S. (5/1/2006)*

Valdivieso 2003 Malbec (Rapel Valley) $7. Full-bodied and loaded with sweet aromas of violets and graham cracker. Flavors of blueberry, plum, and sugar beets lead into an oozing, rich finish. Round and thick, with plenty of extract. **87 Best Buy** —*M.S. (12/1/2004)*

Valdivieso 2001 Malbec (Central Valley) $17. What raspberry fruit there is gets spread thin amid light, weedy aromas, and scattered flavors. Good color and fresh on the palate, but faulty. **82** —*M.S. (12/1/2003)*

Valdivieso 2003 Single Vineyard Reserve Malbec (Maule Valley) $17. Brilliant in color, with lots of oak and derivative aromas. The palate is sweet and rich, as if syrup and caramel had been infused into the pack-age. Turns fiercely tannic on the back end, where an espresso bitterness rises up and steals away the finish. A bumpy ride with highs and lows. **85** —*M.S. (5/1/2006)*

Valdivieso 2000 Single Vineyard Reserve Malbec (Maule Valley) $17. The nose deals a lemony, oak-driven covering atop berry fruit. Flavors of plum and berry start fast but fade a bit as the oaky character of the wine takes over. Healthy and acidic, with length. Maybe too old, and from an average vintage. Drink now. **87** —*M.S. (12/1/2004)*

Valdivieso 2000 Single Vineyard Reserve Malbec (Lontué Valley) $17. Compact and full in the nose, with a fine level of berry fruit and some attractive wood spice. The mouth offers sweet berry flavors and some toasty oak, while the finish is round and soft. There's little complexity or style—what you smell and taste at first is what you get. **85** —*M.S. (7/1/2003)*

Valdivieso 1999 Single Vineyard Reserve Malbec (Curicó Valley) $23. Typical of the grape, this rendition offers loads of blueberry fruit on a tight, dark, moderately tannic frame. A year in 50% new French and American oak has added plenty of toasty woodiness. Now it's a tad hard; a little aging could soften it into something very pretty. With 8% Cabernet Sauvignon. **88** —*M.S. (3/1/2002)*

Valdivieso 2005 Merlot (Central Valley) $6. Mildly charred on the nose, with a strong whiff of green mixed in. The palate is fruitier than the bouquet, with cherry, plum, and blackberry weighing in. A bit narrow and simple, but for the price it doesn't steer you wrong. **83 Best Buy** —*M.S. (11/15/2006)*

Valdivieso 2004 Merlot (Central Valley) $7. Plum, raisin, and a bit of bramble/leather make for a fairly classy nose. And given that this wine is relatively inexpensive, what you get on the bouquet and the palate is admirable. The flavor profile deals juicy raspberry and plum, with chocolate shadings. Easy and persistent on the fruity finish. **86 Best Buy** —*M.S. (5/1/2006)*

Valdivieso 2003 Merlot (Central Valley) $7. Big, bold, and broad, with lots of fruit and a masculine, rubbery quality to the nose. Round plum, chocolate, and almond candy on the palate, followed by an extracted finish. A touch green at the center, but largely solid. **85 Best Buy** —*M.S. (2/1/2005)*

Valdivieso 2002 Merlot (Central Valley) $7. Clean and fruity, with a hint of smoke to the nose. Flavors of raspberry and cherry lead into a creamy, oaky finish that's firm. Textbook and tasty. **86** —*M.S. (3/1/2004)*

Valdivieso 2002 Single Vineyard Reserve Merlot (Curicó Valley) $17. Clean and sweet-smelling, with berry, leather, and candied aromas. The mouth scores with its rich plum and berry flavors, while the finish is warm and only mildly tannic. Shows charm, power, and friendliness. **87** —*M.S. (5/1/2006)*

Valdivieso 2000 Single Vineyard Reserve Merlot (Central Valley) $17. The bouquet is fairly exotic as it kicks up some cinnamon and forest floor. But there's also some lemony oak that doesn't really fit in. The flavors of cherry and cassis are tasty but they carry an acidic tang, and that aggressive acidity continues all the way through to the back end, thus leaving a sharp impression on the palate. **85** —*M.S. (7/1/2003)*

Valdivieso 2000 Single Vineyard Reserve Merlot (Lontué Valley) $17. Ripe and ready, with a forward personality. Pungent and full on the nose, with in-your-face but scratchy cherry and raspberry fruit controlling the palate. Not complex, but fruity and structured. Clamps down late with tannins. Good for burgers and simple grills. **87** —*M.S. (7/1/2005)*

Valdivieso 1999 Single Vineyard Reserve Merlot (Central Valley) $19. An example of good value, but good quality, Merlot. From low-yielding vines producing rich fruit, spice, and tobacco flavors along with soft, dusty tannins. Pure acidity and ripe fruits at the end. **89** —*R.V. (9/1/2001)*

Valdivieso 2005 Reserve Pinot Noir (Casablanca Valley) $13. Bright and dominated by forceful aromas of sugar beets, plums, leather, and funk. The palate is generally bright as it pushes cherry flavors from front to back. Leftover red fruit and apple skins work the tight, almost grabby finish. **84** —*M.S. (12/31/2006)*

Valdivieso 2002 Reserve Pinot Noir (Lontué Valley) $13. Clean, pure, and sweet on the nose, yet shrill once it hits the palate. Look for juiced-up cherry and berry flavors followed by a scorching finish in which the acids

rear up. Oddly, there seems to be a peanut note to the flavor profile. **86** —*M.S. (8/1/2004)*

Valdivieso 1999 Reserve Pinot Noir (Maule Valley) $23. Finding true-to-the-grape Pinot Noir in Chile is no easy task, but this one is varietally correct. It's fairly smoky, earthy, and peppery, with ample red cherry fruit popping up. The acids are powerful and proper, and the vanilla in the finish adds a nice touch. **88** —*M.S. (3/1/2002)*

Valdivieso NV Caballo Loco - No. 4 Red Blend (Lontué Valley) $35. Smooth, rich, and inviting, just like a top-of-the-line effort should be. Mounds of sweet red and black fruit floats effortlessly on the palate, while cherry, coffee, and kirsch form the basis of what is a terrific finish. This unique wine is made using the so-called solera system, whereby older and newer vintages are blended in order to achieve a premium result. **91** —*M.S. (3/1/2002)*

Valdivieso NV Caballo Loco No 6 Red Blend (Central Valley) $35. Good complexity of fruit and soil qualities. The dark fruit flavors are balanced with earth and a touch of char. The finish is rich but soft and elegant at the same time. **89** —*C.S. (2/1/2003)*

Valdivieso NV Caballo Loco No. 5 Red Blend (Lontué Valley) $40. Few table wines are made in the solera style, whereby vintages are blended together to create a more harmonious whole. Here is that rare solera red, the fifth shot this winery has taken at the Crazy Horse. And it's a fine effort that features spicy and sweet aromas, ripe strawberry fruit, and lots of toasty, charred oak. Warning: Airing helps tame the overt oak, especially on the finish. **91** —*M.S. (1/1/2004)*

Valdivieso NV Caballo Loco Number 8 Red Blend (Central Valley) $35. Year in and year out we love this non-vintage table wine from Valdivieso. Version 8 is round, smooth, slightly herbal and jam-packed with savory spice aromas. The palate is bright, forward and flush with raspberry and other dark fruit flavors. Stocky and sturdy; it's Chilean red at its consistent best. **90** —*M.S. (12/31/2006)*

Valdivieso NV Caballo Loco Number Seven Red Blend (Lontué Valley) $35. Caballo Loco, now in its seventh edition, ranks as one of Chile's most consistent ultra-premium reds. It's spicy and deep on the nose, with dark berry and ripe cherry at its core. Shows the slightest hint of cappuccino on the pleasant finish. Woody but balanced. **91 Editors' Choice** —*M.S. (3/1/2006)*

Valdivieso 2002 Eclat Red Blend (Maule Valley) $25. Very pretty in color, and that makes sense: it's a Carignan/Syrah blend. Shows hard, rubbery aromas with plenty of black olive on the side. Sure in the mouth, with red plum flavors and healthy, if not heady, tannins. A serious wine that will show its true colors if aired out before drinking. **89** —*M.S. (3/1/2006)*

Valdivieso 2005 Sauvignon Blanc (Central Valley) $6. Slightly sweaty and prickly, but those are true Sauvignon characteristics and with time they settle to reveal orange and tangerine flavors and even more citrus on the finish. Not the most detailed wine, but at $5.99 it is what it is. **84 Best Buy** —*M.S. (7/1/2006)*

Valdivieso 2004 Sauvignon Blanc (Central Valley) $7. Neutral, with a moderate juicy character. Tastes of nondescript citrus, while the finishing notes veer toward orange and tangerine. **83** —*M.S. (12/15/2005)*

Valdivieso 2002 Sauvignon Blanc (Central Valley) $8. Lean and basic, with fairly ripe aromas and a decent helping of apple, peach, and grapefruit. The fruit is a touch soft and lacking in structure though. **84** —*M.S. (7/1/2003)*

Valdivieso 2004 Reserve Sauvignon Blanc (Casablanca Valley) $13. Slightly spunky and sharp-smelling, with distant mineral notes and not a ton of forward fruit on the bouquet. Melon, apple, kiwi, and green papaya flavors are solid but timid, while there's pretty nice mouthfeel to hold the line. **85** —*M.S. (3/1/2006)*

Valdivieso 2003 Reserve Shiraz (Lontué Valley) $13. Light and fragrant, with tangy fruit and one note's worth of flavor. Not that dense but fresh, with a tannic, woody finish. Runs quick from front to back, with a blast of red fruit and chocolaty oak. **85** —*M.S. (11/1/2005)*

Valdivieso 2000 Barrel Selection Reserve Syrah (Central Valley) $12. A distinctly menthol-herbaceousness dominates this bouquet; expect tart red berry and Sweet Tart aromas in supporting roles. Its mouthfeel is smooth and medium-weight, with espresso, blackberry, and a bit of stemminess on the palate. **84** *(10/1/2001)*

Valdivieso 2004 Reserva Syrah (Central Valley) $13. A stacked wine with bold, grapey aromas that settle into blackberry. The palate is rather basic but with baked berry, chocolate, and ripe raisin flavors, it's pleasing. Best for those who favor a jammy, easygoing style. **85** —*M.S. (12/31/2006)*

Valdivieso 2003 Reserve Viognier (Maule Valley) $13. Overloaded with resiny oak, so much so that the fruit is buried. What's left is vanilla and a whole lot of banana. In fact, this wine tastes like the liquid version of Jell-O brand banana pudding. **82** —*M.S. (11/1/2005)*

VALLETE FONTAINE

Vallete Fontaine 1999 Memorias Cabernet Sauvignon (Maipo Valley) $NA. **81** —*D.T. (11/15/2002)*

VENTISQUERO

Ventisquero 2003 Gran Reserva Cabernet Sauvignon (Maipo Valley) $16. Heavy and ripe, but also floral and rich, with satisfying, intriguing aromatics. Draws you in with smoky notes of boysenberry, black plum, and bitter chocolate, and then seals the deal with a firm, balanced, moderately tannic finish. **88** —*M.S. (5/1/2006)*

Ventisquero 2003 Grey Cabernet Sauvignon (Maipo Valley) $27. Ventisquero's top bottlings feature gray labels, hence the name. The Cabernet features some minty-eucalyptus scents alongside standard cassis and plum aromas. A bit fuller than the other wines in the range, and also more structured, ending with firm tannins and mouthwatering acids. **88** *(2/1/2006)*

Ventisquero 2003 Grey Carmenère (Maipo Valley) $27. Ventisquero's top Camenère avoids the green qualities that can sometimes plague this variety. Instead, it's soft and lush, marrying plum and dark chocolate flavors in a seamless package. Contains 10% Cabernet Sauvignon and 5% Syrah, so not a pure expression of Carmenère, but a very good one. **89** *(2/1/2006)*

Ventisquero 2003 Gran Reserva Merlot (Maipo Valley) $19. Slightly dusty on the nose, with some floral notes alongside plum fruit. Shows decent richness on the palate, ending on a note of tangy fruit backed by chocolate and coffee. **87** *(2/1/2006)*

Ventisquero 2003 Gran Reserva Syrah (Maipo Valley) $19. From young hillside plantings, this Syrah boasts intense blackberry and blueberry fruit accented by hints of vanilla and cinnamon. Soft and ready to drink, with well-managed tannins. **88** *(2/1/2006)*

VERAMONTE

Veramonte 2004 Primus Bordeaux Blend (Casablanca Valley) $17. A Merlot-dominant wine with Cabernet and Carmenère, Primus shows licorice and raisin on the nose with concentrated black fruit carrying the flavor profile. There's ample warmth and spice on the finish, and a tight tannic structure holding it all together. **88** —*M.S. (12/31/2006)*

Veramonte 2002 Primus Bordeaux Blend (Casablanca Valley) $16. This blend of Merlot (36%), Cabernet Sauvignon (34%), and Carmenère (30%) flows creamily across the palate, delviering black cherry, coffee, and chocolate flavors; scents of dried herbs and tea leaves add complexity. Tart and tobaccoey on the finish. **88** *(2/1/2005)*

Veramonte 2002 Cabernet Sauvignon (Maipo Valley) $10. Plump and soft, this easygoing Cab delivers slightly weedy, cassis-laden fruit in an accessible format. Finishes with some plum notes but also black tea leaves. A nice weekday wine that will pair perfectly with burgers or steak. **86 Best Buy** *(2/1/2005)*

Veramonte 2000 Cabernet Sauvignon (Maipo Valley) $10. This is one of the best $10 Cabs ever. It has a depth and complexity of tannins and acids that almost guarantee improvement in the bottle. Dry, rich, and stylish, its a smooth, voluptuous wine, despite a certain thinness of fruit. The overlay of oak is gorgeous. **91 Best Buy** —*S.H. (12/1/2002)*

Veramonte 2004 Reserva Cabernet Sauvignon (Maipo Valley) $10. After a number of years of experimenting with Cab from cooler Casablanca, Veramonte has turned to warmer Maipo for this nicely made wine that offers red licorice and cinnamon aromas in front of bright cassis and

raspberry flavors. Shows purity, spice, and character. **87 Best Buy** —*M.S. (10/1/2006)*

Veramonte 2002 Single Vineyard Cabernet Sauvignon (Maipo Valley) $35. Dense and chocolaty, with lots of cassis fruit flavors to back it up. The mouthfeel isn't quite as rich as the Merlot's, but it boasts the same soft tannins and crisp acidity on the finish. **89** *(2/1/2005)*

Veramonte 2003 Chardonnay (Casablanca Valley) $10. Peach, pear, and pineapple fruit, all done up in toasty, butterscotchy oak. Plump in the mouth and a little soft on the vanilla-laden finish. A crowd-pleaser. **85 Best Buy** *(2/1/2005)*

Veramonte 2000 Chardonnay (Casablanca Valley) $10. Bright and lemony on the nose, this Chilean white serves up a tangy blend of pear, apple, toast, and citrus flavors on the palate. It's clean and fresh. **85** —*J.M. (11/15/2001)*

Veramonte 2003 Single Vineyard Chardonnay (Casablanca Valley) $35. Smoky and a bit nutty, one can sense that winemaker Rafael Tirado is aiming at a Burgundian style. Grilled peaches and fresh limes blend with pineapple flavors. Despite its crisp acids, it shows nice richness in the mouth, with substantially more density and concentration than the regular Chardonnay. **88** *(2/1/2005)*

Veramonte 2002 Merlot (Casablanca Valley) $10. A bit herbal, and doesn't show the same level of flavor intensity or mouthfeel that the Cabernet does. It still delivers varietal black cherry and mocha flavors, but finishes with tart flavors and lots of fresh herbs. **84** *(2/1/2005)*

Veramonte 2002 Merlot (Casablanca Valley) $10. Bright in the glass, with a ruby tint. The nose offers good berry fruit and some plum, while the palate is basic and pure, with mild tannins and round fruit. Simple yet satisfying. **86 Best Buy** —*M.S. (3/1/2004)*

Veramonte 2000 Merlot (Maipo Valley) $10. An interesting wine, with a rich tobacco and clove streak that's distinctive. There are underlying flavors of blackberries and chocolate, and the acidity is just right. It has depth and substance, which are rare at this price. Try pulling this one out and serving it to your wine snob neighbor, blind. **90 Best Buy** —*S.H. (12/1/2002)*

Veramonte 1999 Merlot (Casablanca Valley) $10. Strawberry and wet hay aromas give way to a sweet berry-flavored attack, but the wine turns tart and almost shrill on the finish. A green, stemmy sensation lingers in the mouth, along with dark coffee flavors. **82** —*J.C. (2/1/2001)*

Veramonte 2004 Reserva Merlot (Casablanca Valley) $10. Smooth and ripe, with as much gusto as one could expect from a $10 red. The nose is full of ripe berries and chocolate, while the juicy palate breathes black cherry, plum, and a spot of raisin. Finishes nicely, with an emphasis on fudge and coffee. **88 Best Buy** —*M.S. (10/1/2006)*

Veramonte 2002 Single Vineyard Merlot (Casablanca Valley) $35. Even after 14 months in French oak, this wine shows a lot of fruit. Black cherries abound on the nose and palate, accented by mocha, dried spices and a just a hint of herbaceousness. The plush mouthfeel ends in a velvety, herbally complex finish. **90** *(2/1/2005)*

Veramonte 2002 Pinot Noir (Casablanca Valley) $10. Dark in color, but not huge or saturated. There's more meat on the bones of this Pinot than many Chilean efforts, and it smells of cherry, tree bark, and some chocolate. Overall it's fairly fresh, full, and pretty. **86** —*M.S. (3/1/2004)*

Veramonte 2001 Primus Red Blend (Casablanca Valley) $20. Deep, with a zesty nose that's a bit sharp. Flavors of cherry, cassis and toast are round and ripe, as are the tannins and finish. For a Casablanca red, one that mixes Carmenère with Merlot and Cabernet, it's on the spot. Best Primus to date? **89** —*M.S. (3/1/2004)*

Veramonte 2000 Primus Red Blend (Casablanca Valley) $20. This is Veramonte's top red. But frankly, it's green, herbal, and difficult to enjoy. The nose offers plenty of green olive, while the heart of the wine is herbal and only gift-wrapped with coatings of blackberry and currant. **82** —*M.S. (7/1/2003)*

Veramonte 1999 Primus Red Blend (Casablanca Valley) $20. The nose of this Augustin Huneeus-made wine shows soil, wood, and a algae-greenness; the palate, blackberry and oak. Medium-bodied; finishes with dry

CHILE

tannins. 60% Carmenère, 30% Cabernet Sauvignon, and 10% Merlot. 86 —D.T. (7/1/2002)

Veramonte 1998 Primus Red Blend (Casablanca Valley) $20. Red berry fruit with a heavy dose of herb and bell pepper marks this red blend. The mouthfeel is smooth, but the acidity is high and the wine finishes slightly tart, with a green note. Another victim of this tough year. (We'll look forward to the 1999.) **83** —M.M. (2/1/2001)

Veramonte 2004 Sauvignon Blanc (Casablanca Valley) $10. Highly aromatic, this explodes with bright passion fruit scents and herbal pungency. Lots of pink grapefruit flavor and a zesty, crisp finish make this eminently drinkable. Drink now, as an apéritif or with light appetizers. **88 Best Buy** (2/1/2005)

Veramonte 2003 Sauvignon Blanc (Casablanca Valley) $10. Light and clear, with pure passion fruit, grapefruit, and snap-pea aromas. Tasty and fresh in the mouth, delivering citrus, pineapple, and a cleansing burst of bright acidity. **87 Best Buy** —M.S. (3/1/2004)

Veramonte 2001 Sauvignon Blanc (Casablanca Valley) $10. A bit thin in fruit, but so clean, so zesty, and filled with fresh acidity, you hardly notice. Besides, a little citrus goes a long way. Turns figgy on the finish. From Agustin Huneeus of Franciscan. **85** —S.H. (12/1/2002)

VERANDA

Veranda 2002 Reserve Pinot Noir (Casablanca Valley) $15. Light, with an attractive set of aromas that include licorice, tea, wood smoke, and raspberry. Flavors of cola, tea, clove, cumin, and red fruit are vivid, and happen to be pretty good. And the spicy, round finish is a pleasant ending. Well made but different. Remember: This is Chilean Pinot, not Burgundy. **86** —M.S. (8/1/2004)

Veranda 2002 Founder's Reserve Red Blend (Aconcagua Valley) $50. Boisset, a Burgundian négociant, is involved in this Franco-Chilean joint venture, and this blend is smooth and clean, with driving berry fruit. In the mouth, cherry and raspberry notes come across as high-voltage, especially in the midpalate, but with ample spice there's more than enough to latch on to. **87** —M.S. (3/1/2004)

Veranda 2002 Reserve Red Blend (Maipo Valley) $20. This single-estate red has a flat but peppery nose. The mouth offers cherry, raspberry, and chocolate in solid, candied doses, while the finish runs sweet, with an acidic ripple keeping things lively. **85** —M.S. (3/1/2004)

VIÑA AQUITANIA

Viña Aquitania 2003 Agapanto Cabernet Sauvignon (Maipo Valley) $12. Fairly firm and leathery, with an herbal/green streak running through the bouquet. Tangy as a whole, with cherry fruit and a smack of bell pepper. Tart on the back end, with drying tannins. Not dissimilar to a weak-vintage Cru Bourgeois Bordeaux. **84** —M.S. (7/1/2006)

Viña Aquitania 2002 Agapanto Cabernet Sauvignon (Maipo Valley) $10. The nose offers leather, briar patch, and smoky cherry fruit, while the leafy palate has good berry flavors along with touches of earth and herbs. It's 85% Cab and the rest Carmenère and Merlot. **87 Best Buy** —M.S. (3/1/2004)

Viña Aquitania 2002 Lazuli Cabernet Sauvignon (Maipo Valley) $32. Shows complex aromas of leather, herbs, and chocolate. This is a sensual, handcrafted red, one with real-time cherry, plum, and cassis flavors, but also a suave mouthfeel and more than a few things in common with a good Bordeaux. Made by Aquitania and winemaker Felipe de Solminihac. **90** —M.S. (3/1/2004)

Viña Aquitania 2003 Sol de Sol Chardonnay (Malleco) $30. This is one of Chile's best Chardonnays. It's made in the deep south of the country, where it's very cool. The result is a zesty, acidic wine, but one with a lot of tropical flavors such as pineapple, lemon, and melon. Well-balanced and real, with a pleasant streak of oak running through the citrusy finish. **88** —M.S. (5/1/2006)

Viña Aquitania 2002 Sol de Sol Chardonnay (Malleco) $32. From deep in the south of Chile comes this small-lot Chardonnay, surely one of the country's most interesting white wines. Felipe de Solminihac gets fruit from his in-laws' vineyard to make this snappy, lemon-tinged wine, which also delivers apple, melon, and citrus. Balanced and unique. **89** — M.S. (3/1/2004)

VIÑA BISQUERTT

Viña Bisquertt 2002 Casa La Joya Gran Reserve Cabernet Sauvignon (Colchagua Valley) $13. Mildly toasty, with baked berry, olive, and jam-like aromas. More snappy and crisp than expected, with red plum flavors and very tight, protruding tannins. Chocolate and some sugar beet come together on the finish. A touch too firm in terms of mouthfeel. **85** — M.S. (12/15/2005)

Viña Bisquertt 2004 Casa La Joya Reserve Cabernet Sauvignon (Colchagua Valley) $9. Lively, rich, and complete. There's a lot of wine here for under $10, and the assumption in these parts is that it has everything the average consumer is looking for. Boysenberry, blackberry, and cassis flavors are lively yet round, while the finish is saturated and thorough. A full-strength red at a great price. **89 Best Buy** —M.S. (5/1/2006)

Viña Bisquertt 2003 Casa La Joya Reserve Cabernet Sauvignon (Colchagua Valley) $9. Smoky and saturated, with jammy, smooth aromas of plum and cassis. Lots of tannin and depth, and thus it spreads out all over your palate in mouth-filling fashion. Features loads of plum and chocolate, with a likable chewiness. **87 Best Buy** —M.S. (12/15/2005)

Viña Bisquertt 2003 Casa La Joya Gran Reserve Carmenère (Colchagua Valley) $13. Big and relaxed, with a nice perfume that includes spice and earth. Shows balance and firmness on the tongue, with hints of olive, toast and fudge. Exemplary Carmenère from a good vintage. **89 Best Buy** —M.S. (3/1/2006)

Viña Bisquertt 2002 Casa La Joya Gran Reserve Carmenère (Colchagua Valley) $13. From Bisquertt, this is a saturated, earthy, berry-packed version of Carmenère. The palate is ripe and fruity, with a ton of spunky berry fruit wrapped in a nice coating of smooth oak. Chocolate and raisin flavors are nice finishing notes. Complete stuff, with just a tiny bit of outlying acidity. **88 Best Buy** —M.S. (12/15/2005)

Viña Bisquertt 2004 Casa La Joya Reserve Carmenère (Colchagua Valley) $10. This Carmenère starts out a bit austere and full of varietal character, meaning there's olive, roast tomato, dill, and pickle on the nose. But there's also perfectly ripe plum to back it up, and excellent feel and balance to boot. Chewy enough but more racy. **87 Best Buy** —M.S. (3/1/2006)

Viña Bisquertt 2004 Casa La Joya Gran Reserve Chardonnay (Colchagua Valley) $14. A lot of oak greets you, while lemon and apple cider aromas dwell below the surface. The palate is fairly round and dominated by apple flavors touched up by wood-based cinnamon. Feels nice and has that creaminess that many folks are looking for. But 2004 is already an old vintage, so drink right away or wait for the '05. **87** —M.S. (12/31/2006)

Viña Bisquertt 2003 Casa La Joya Gran Reserve Chardonnay (Colchagua Valley) $13. Light melon and wax bean aromas are pretty solid, as is the melon and pear palate. It's a fairly plump, round wine with vanilla notes and a nice texture. Finishes a bit sweet, with a blast of banana. **85** —M.S. (12/15/2005)

Viña Bisquertt 2004 Casa La Joya Reserve Malbec (Colchagua Valley) $9. Dark and tight aromas, things like coffee and charred meat, make for a brooding bouquet. The mouth offers cassis and cherry bonbon, while the finish is condensed and juicy, but doesn't issue much breadth. Fairly tight and hard, but healthy. **85 Best Buy** —M.S. (5/1/2006)

Viña Bisquertt 2002 Casa La Joya Gran Reserve Merlot (Colchagua Valley) $13. Good from the start, with an aromatic mix of black olive, berry, and cherry. The palate offers more of the same: cherry, plum, and pimiento. Finishes long and touch oaky, and along the way you might find some saline or sauciness. **86** —M.S. (5/1/2006)

Viña Bisquertt 2003 Casa La Joya Reserve Merlot (Colchagua Valley) $9. Deep in color, with sweet, rich aromas that revolve around molasses and bacon but fold in plum, blackberry, and toast. For the price this is an excellent wine, and price notwithstanding it's very good. The black fruit is ripe, the feel just right. Just short of lush but full. **88 Best Buy** —M.S. (12/15/2005)

Viña Bisquertt 2004 Casa La Joya Reserve Sauvignon Blanc (Colchagua Valley) $9. A touch pickled at first, with apple and lemon carrying the palate. Pretty good balance and feel keep it moving ahead. Finishes with apple notes but beyond that it's kind of nondistinct. **84** —*M.S. (3/1/2006)*

Viña Bisquertt 2004 Casa La Joya Reserve Shiraz (Colchagua Valley) $9. Dense and dark, with a shot of raisin and black licorice up front. Flavors of ripe berry fruit are simple and easy, with adequate tannin and pepper. Good New World Syrah. **86 Best Buy** —*M.S. (3/1/2006)*

Viña Bisquertt 2003 Casa La Joya Reserve Shiraz (Colchagua Valley) $9. Slightly herbal, with hints of tree bark and chewing gum. Runs a touch hard and tannic, with cherry and little more carrying the flavor profile. Firm, even hard, in the mouth. **82** —*M.S. (12/15/2005)*

VIÑA CASA TAMAYA

Viña Casa Tamaya 2002 Estate Bottled Reserve Chardonnay (Limarí Valley) $15. Aromas of corn and wheat give way to butterscotch. The flavor profile is of pineapple juice and not much more. Flat on the finish, without much verve. **82** —*M.S. (8/1/2004)*

Viña Casa Tamaya 2001 Estate Bottled Reserve Red Blend (Limarí Valley) $15. A mix of three standard grapes with a pickled, marinated quality and a noticeable vegetal character. Light and simple, with tomato on the palate and bell pepper on the finish. **82** —*M.S. (8/1/2004)*

Viña Casa Tamaya 2001 Reserve Viognier-Chardonnay White Blend (Chile) $15. The flower and honey aromas of the Viognier, which accounts for 60% of the blend, are front and center. In the rear, flavors of lemon and tarragon are pronounced, while the finish is basically dull and watery, although clean. Overall, this wine runs thin on the palate, and the acids are overblown. **83** —*M.S. (6/1/2004)*

VIÑA CASAS DEL BOSQUE

Viña Casas del Bosque 2001 Cabernet Sauvignon (Rapel Valley) $11. At first the tight nose is a bit like tar and industrial cleaner, but once it fans out some black fruit emerges. The palate is tight and tannic, but fresh and ripe. And the finish is healthy but also rather tannic. Good with barbecued meats and the like. **84** —*M.S. (7/1/2003)*

Viña Casas del Bosque 2000 Cabernet Sauvignon (Rapel Valley) $10. So light that it borders on dilute, this Rapel Valley Cab offers funky earth aromas over sweet fruit. The palate doesn't offer much in the way of fruit flavors—instead, with such outdoorsy forest notes, it's easy to see why this wine is called "houses of the forest." **84** —*D.T. (7/1/2002)*

Viña Casas del Bosque 2000 Gran Bosque Cabernet Sauvignon (Rapel Valley) $17. More concentrated than the winery's other reds, with root beer, cassis, and toasty wood on the bouquet. Yet it's still a lightweight in the world of Cabernets. It's snappy and tea-like on the palate, with a clean finish. **86** —*M.S. (3/1/2004)*

Viña Casas del Bosque 2002 Gran Bosque Family Reserve Cabernet Sauvignon (Rapel Valley) $35. Dry red fruit along with coffee and toast create a nice nose. And while hopes run high before you get to the palate, what lies ahead is mostly lemony oak and tannic black fruit. Finishes extremely hard, with spiky, piercing tannins. **85** —*M.S. (11/1/2005)*

Viña Casas del Bosque 2002 Reserve Cabernet Sauvignon (Rapel Valley) $12. Pretty light, with tea and licorice aromas in front of lean raspberry and cherry fruit. Since it doesn't deal the force of your average Cabernet, it's more like Cab Light. **84** —*M.S. (3/1/2004)*

Viña Casas del Bosque 2001 Reserve Cabernet Sauvignon (Rapel Valley) $16. Woody aromas smell much like warm cedar, and that's backed up by some nice cherry and cassis. There's plenty of pleasant red fruit on the palate, and not a hint of green. Some chocolaty earthiness makes it all the more cheerful. It's an easy drinker that delivers solid Cab character without a lot of fuss and heavy extraction. **87** —*M.S. (7/1/2003)*

Viña Casas del Bosque 2000 Reserve Cabernet Sauvignon (Rapel Valley) $17. Aromas of cola, caramel, and blackberries shift into flavors of earth and mushroom. The rich mouthfeel bursts with fruit and balanced tannins that finish with a suede-like sensation. **88** —*C.S. (12/1/2002)*

Viña Casas del Bosque 2002 Chardonnay (Casablanca Valley) $10. Clean pear fruit on the nose and refreshing throughout. This wine works because it's straightforward and lightly oaked. The apple, melon, and

mineral flavors stand out, and the round body and solid finish carry it home. **85** —*M.S. (7/1/2003)*

Viña Casas del Bosque 2000 Chardonnay (Rapel Valley) $9. Has some pleasant aromas of papaya and mint mixed with butter and vanilla, but turns lean and hollow in the mouth; there's some mild pear fruit, but mostly it's just light—verging on watery. **82** —*J.C. (7/1/2002)*

Viña Casas del Bosque 1999 Gredas Negras Chardonnay (Casablanca Valley) $15. **80** —*M.S. (7/1/2002)*

Viña Casas del Bosque 2001 Reserve Chardonnay (Casablanca Valley) $15. Heavy and gold in color, with aromas of browned butter, wheat, and corn cakes. The bouquet and color are heavy, and so is the palate: There you get oak barrel and toast, but little to no fruit. Even the finish is woody, with just a hint of melon and banana. A good experimental wine for those eager to taste oak; otherwise steer clear. **82** —*M.S. (7/1/2003)*

Viña Casas del Bosque 2000 Reserve Chardonnay (Casablanca Valley) $NA. Over-buttered; picture big slabs of it sitting atop your breakfast toast. There's some modest pineapple and citrus fruit but it's overwhelmed on the finish by slick, buttered movie popcorn. **81** —*J.C. (7/1/2002)*

Viña Casas del Bosque 2003 Reserva Merlot (Casablanca Valley) $12. Heavily toasted, with lemon and burnt-toast aromas. The palate is extremely lemony and short of any lushness normally associated with Merlot. Has color but no ripeness. Proof that Casablanca is not great for Bordeaux varieties. **80** —*M.S. (11/1/2005)*

Viña Casas del Bosque 2000 Reserva Merlot (Casablanca Valley) $10. Butterscotch, molasses, and capuccino notes bookend nut and ripe mixed-berry flavors. Medium-bodied; has widespread appeal. **86** —*D.T. (7/1/2002)*

Viña Casas del Bosque 2002 Reserve Merlot (Casablanca Valley) $12. Fairly herbal at first, with sharp currant and cherry aromas. Airing, however, exposes hidden qualities and more flesh; after about 10 minutes you get full plum and raspberry notes along with soft tannins. **85** —*M.S. (3/1/2004)*

Viña Casas del Bosque 2004 Reserva Pinot Noir (Casablanca Valley) $12. Dark and ripe; very Californian in style. Deep plum and black cherry aromas set the stage for spicy dark fruit flavors. The balance is good, the acidity just right, and the finish toasty and upright. With an underlay of warming oak, this is commendable Chilean Pinot. **87 Best Buy** —*M.S. (11/1/2005)*

Viña Casas del Bosque 2002 Reserve Pinot Noir (Casablanca Valley) $12. Brick red in color, with leathery aromas surrounding cherry and mint. The palate is lean and dry, with smoky flavors to the berry notes. With pulsing acidity, it's fresh and ripe on the finish. **85** —*M.S. (3/1/2004)*

Viña Casas del Bosque 2001 Reserve Pinot Noir (Casablanca Valley) $16. The cherry and cinnamon aromas are true and inviting, and they stand up to the oak that's been thrown at this Pinot. The flavor profile deals raspberry and cherry amid oaky shadings. The finish is toasty and warm, with some coffee popping up late in the game. Fresh, fruity and true. **85** —*M.S. (7/1/2003)*

Viña Casas del Bosque 2004 Sauvignon Blanc (Casablanca Valley) $10. Passion fruit and citrus aromas carry the nose, but they run alongside some strong vegetal aromas. Flavorwise, we're talking green apple and celery, while the finish is crisp. Has its strong points but also a bold vegetal underbelly. **83** —*M.S. (11/1/2005)*

Viña Casas del Bosque 2003 Sauvignon Blanc (Casablanca Valley) $9. Spritzy, with a stand-up mouthfeel that sports notes of fresh green peas and minerals. The fruit is mostly lemon-lime, with a touch of green bell pepper onto the midpalate. Herbaceous but nice. **86** —*M.S. (3/1/2004)*

Viña Casas del Bosque 2002 Sauvignon Blanc (Casablanca Valley) $10. Pungent, with grapefruit and grassy aromas that are true to the variety. The palate is fresh, the flavors good and fruity. There's mango and tangerine, and also some garden-fresh asparagus in the mix. The finish, too, is perfectly fresh; it's there one moment and gone the next. **85** —*M.S. (7/1/2003)*

Viña Casas del Bosque 2000 Sauvignon Blanc (Casablanca Valley) $9. Seemingly old, with heavy herbal and field-green aromas and a thick, heavy palate. It tastes like mature apples, and there's plenty of weight to it. A bit of honey sneaks onto the thick, grippy finish, while some healthy acidity keeps it ticking. **80** —*M.S. (7/1/2003)*

Viña Casas del Bosque 2003 Casa Viva Sauvignon Blanc (Casablanca Valley) $7. Pale in color, with light straw aromas and powerful scents of cucumber and grapefruit. Not too aggressive in the mouth, with a softer, lower-acid profile. Flavors of banana and pineapple suggest very ripe fruit. **85 Best Buy** —*M.S. (3/1/2004)*

Viña Casas del Bosque 2004 Reserva Sauvignon Blanc (Casablanca Valley) $12. Pungent and prickly, with a promise of sass to come. Solid citrus dominates the mouth, as grapefruit, snap pea, and lime flavors add nuance. Fresh and chalky in terms of feel, with spotless varietal character. Good Casablanca Sauvignon. **87 Best Buy** —*M.S. (11/1/2005)*

Viña Casas del Bosque 2002 Reserve Sauvignon Blanc (Casablanca Valley) $15. Lightly fruity in the nose, yet sharp on the palate. For a reserve wine, it's noticeably thinner and more linear than the regular Sauvignon Blanc. The flavors are of green apple and under-ripe citrus, while the finish, as the palate suggests, is lean and fresh, but lightweight. **83** —*M.S. (7/1/2003)*

Viña Casas del Bosque 2001 Reserve Sauvignon Blanc (Casablanca Valley) $15. Peach, melon and mineral waft from the nose, followed by melon and grapefruit flavors. The finish is surprisingly tropical, a mix of bananas and coconut. Starts off better than it finishes, leading one to believe that if served quickly and chilled it will do well with seafood and appetizers. **84** —*M.S. (7/1/2003)*

Viña Casas del Bosque 2003 Reserva Syrah (Casablanca Valley) $12. Good color, but mossy and rooty, with lemon-cola aromas. Shrill and tangy, with heat. Fails to turn the corner toward ripeness. **80** —*M.S. (11/1/2005)*

Viña Casas del Bosque 2002 Reserve Syrah (Casablanca Valley) $12. Spicy and lean, with aromas of basil, oregano, and distant raspberry. A bit acidic and short across the palate, yet clean on the finish. Lacks the fruit normally associated with Syrah. **83** —*M.S. (3/1/2004)*

VIÑA EL AROMO

Viña el Aromo 2001 Private Reserve Cabernet Sauvignon (Maule Valley) $10. Nice and open-knit, with touches of coffee, eucalyptus, and earth on the nose, and lots of textbook cassis, cherry, and raspberry on the palate. Powerful and flavorful, with a slight herbal streak through the center. **87** —*M.S. (6/1/2004)*

Viña el Aromo 2002 Private Reserve Carmenère (Maule Valley) $10. A bit funky and sweaty on the nose, with cherry, raspberry, and cola flavors. The feel is live-wired and racy, and the finish is warm, almost hot. Not bad, but with powerful herbal notes. **84** —*M.S. (6/1/2004)*

Viña el Aromo 2003 Chardonnay (Maule Valley) $10. A big enough Chard, with pear, apple, and citrus blossom aromas on the nose. The hefty palate gives sweet white fruit, while the finish is basic and sugary, and borderline cloying. **83** —*M.S. (6/1/2004)*

VIÑA LA ROSA

Viña La Rosa 2002 Don Reca Cabernet Sauvignon (Cachapoal Valley) $30. Chewy and oaky, with a round mouthfeel and big tannins. The finish is long, with a chocolate streak and a firm coffee-like bitterness. **85** —*M.S. (3/1/2004)*

Viña La Rosa 2004 La Capitana Barrel Reserve Cabernet Sauvignon (Cachapoal Valley) $14. Aromas of cherry and strawberry are alluring, but the mouth is rock hard and very tannic. Flavors of raspberry and cassis are lively and drill deep, but you have to have a brick layer's tolerance for tannins to get the most of this wine. Should be served with meat or other big foods. **85** —*M.S. (10/1/2006)*

Viña La Rosa 2004 La Palma Cabernet Sauvignon (Cachapoal Valley) $7. It's hard to take issue with this bargain-priced Cabernet; the nose is mildly oaky, with plenty of fruit and coffee scents. The mouth is equally fruity, with creamy chocolate as the prime accent. Plenty here for less than 10 bucks. **86 Best Buy** —*M.S. (11/1/2005)*

Viña La Rosa 2003 La Capitana Carmenère (Cachapoal Valley) $12. Quite deep and dark, with integrated scents of oak, bacon, cinnamon, and earth. Admirable and rich, with lush plum and sugar beet flavors in front of a warm, full-bodied finish. Shows a tiny touch of green, but generally it's a positive take on the grape. **87 Best Buy** —*M.S. (2/1/2005)*

Viña La Rosa 2004 La Capitana Barrel Reserve Carmenère (Cachapoal Valley) $14. Fairly pickled on the nose, backed by a wayward sweetness in the form of burnt brown sugar and nutmeg. Adequate mouthfeel, arguably a touch thick, but in the end it's less than exciting in terms of flavor. **82** —*M.S. (3/1/2006)*

Viña La Rosa 2002 La Palma Reserve Carmenère (Cachapoal Valley) $12. Dark and purple, with heavy aromas of prune, leather, and red cabbage. The palate is jammy and dark, with chocolate in addition to grapey fruit. Turns sweet and overweight with time. **82** —*M.S. (6/1/2004)*

Viña La Rosa 2003 Don Reca Chardonnay (Cachapoal Valley) $30. The nose yields banana and floral aromas, while in the mouth it's chunky and round, with apple, pear, and some wood spice. Decent but subdued given that it's the winery's top Chardonnay. **85** —*M.S. (3/1/2004)*

Viña La Rosa 2004 La Capitana Chardonnay (Cachapoal Valley) $15. Crisp and refreshing, with little to no oak character. By no means is it overpowering, but instead it features light citrus and flower aromas followed by apple, fresh scallion, and spice. A touch tangy, but smooth enough. Zesty. **85** —*M.S. (11/1/2005)*

Viña La Rosa 2005 La Palma Chardonnay (Cachapoal Valley) $8. On the soft, plump side, but with more than enough pineapple and other sweet fruits to make the grade. Nectarine and peach flavors are easy and inoffensive. A little bit creamy in terms of feel. **85 Best Buy** —*M.S. (3/1/2006)*

Viña La Rosa 2001 Sparkling Chardonnay (Cachapoal Valley) $15. Lightweight, however drilled full of piercing acidity. Emphasizes floral lime aromas and green-apple flavors. Acidic and bubbly. A rough ride. **80** —*M.S. (12/31/2004)*

Viña La Rosa 2002 Don Reca Merlot (Cachapoal Valley) $30. Fairly piquant and oaky to the nose, with an admirable drinkability level. Shows pure fruit, good flavors, and some vanilla notes. Mild tannins bulk up the finish. **86** —*M.S. (3/1/2004)*

Viña La Rosa 2003 La Capitana Merlot (Cachapoal Valley) $12. Great color but a bit green on the nose. Amid the timid bell pepper and green bean accents—and they're just that, accents—there's dark fruit and espresso. Very good in terms of mouthfeel, with structure and balance. Lots of positives here; but alas, some of the veggies as well. **85** —*M.S. (11/1/2005)*

Viña La Rosa 2004 La Capitana Barrel Reserve Merlot (Cachapoal Valley) $14. Full and chunky, with deep color and plenty of heft. Smells as if it might have some Carmenère in the blend, and it does (10%). There's an herbal quality to the wine, but that doesn't overshadow the plum and black cherry flavors nor the light oak touches. Good for Chilean Merlot. **86** —*M.S. (3/1/2006)*

Viña La Rosa 2004 La Palma Merlot (Cachapoal Valley) $7. Sort of stewy, with balsamic aromatics alongside coffee notes. Basic plum, blackberry, and mocha flavors on a flat, syrupy palate. No verve here; it's too innocuous. **82** —*M.S. (11/1/2005)*

Viña La Rosa 2003 La Palma Merlot (Cachapoal Valley) $7. Spunky and spicy, but vegetal. In the mouth, green bean and bell pepper gang up on the fat berry fruit, creating a mixed palate that doesn't register on the ripeness meter. Finishes big, with the taste of carob. **83** —*M.S. (2/1/2005)*

Viña La Rosa 2002 Don Reca Merlot-Cabernet Sauvignon (Cachapoal Valley) $30. After spending 12 months in French oak, there doesn't seem to be as much fruit present as wood. Still, the wine manages to come together in the middle to create a good final impression. **85** —*M.S. (3/1/2004)*

Viña La Rosa 2004 Don Reca Limited Release Merlot-Cabernet Sauvignon (Cachapoal Valley) $20. At 60% Merlot and 40% Cabernet, this signature blend from La Rosa exhibits touches of green on the nose but mostly deep black fruit. The palate runs thick and sticky courtesy of extract and tannin, however, the flavors of plum, chocolate, and bacon are satisfying. Quite a big, meaty red. Powerful if a bit clumsy. **87** —*M.S. (10/1/2006)*

CHILE

Viña La Rosa 2006 La Palma Rosé Merlot-Cabernet Sauvignon (Cachapoal Valley) $8. Begins rough and funky, with aromatic notes of red cabbage and syrupy berries. The palate on this Merlot-Cabernet rosé is less about berry flavors and more about plump, soft peach and citrus. Adequate in the mouth, but not very zesty. **83** —*M.S. (11/15/2006)*

Viña La Rosa 2005 La Palma Rosé Merlot-Cabernet Sauvignon (Cachapoal Valley) $9. This is mostly Merlot-based, with 30% Cabernet. The nose offers full cherry and plum aromas. In the mouth, there's pink grapefruit in the lead, with citrus pith coming on later. Fairly acidic and fresh. Food-friendly stuff. **85 Best Buy** —*M.S. (5/1/2006)*

Viña La Rosa 2006 La Palma Sauvignon Blanc (Cachapoal Valley) $8. Pear and a touch of candied almond set this light-bodied white in motion. The palate is solid if a bit monotone, with notes of citrus, green herbs, and fresh celery. Finishes chalky and sturdy, with adequate acidity. **84 Best Buy** —*M.S. (11/15/2006)*

Viña La Rosa 2005 La Palma Sauvignon Blanc (Cachapoal Valley) $9. Crisp and correct, with a nice mix of orange, tangerine, and fresh green vegetables. Tangy and light-bodied, with snap and just enough mouthfeel to make it worthwhile. **85 Best Buy** —*M.S. (12/15/2005)*

Viña La Rosa 2004 La Palma Sauvignon Blanc (Cachapoal Valley) $7. Quite nice, and decidedly full of fruit. Plump apple and peach flavors carry some mineral and adequate cleansing acids. Feels right on the tongue, with clean, fresh, simple flavors. **86 Best Buy** —*M.S. (2/1/2005)*

Viña La Rosa 2004 La Capitana Shiraz (Cachapoal Valley) $17. Smooth and inviting; one of La Rosa's better wines of late. It's classic New World Shiraz with ripe, black fruit that floats toward black cherry cassis. The mouthfeel is extracted and rich, with soft-styled tannins and a fair amount of jam. Drink soon; not an ager. **87** —*M.S. (3/1/2006)*

VIÑA LEYDA

Viña Leyda 2001 Vintage Selection Bordeaux Blend (Chile) $20. This blend of Cabernet Sauvignon, Cab Franc, and Merlot is lively and forward, with sweet, round cherry, plum, and berry fruit. The finish is mild and a touch earthy. **88** —*M.S. (3/1/2004)*

Viña Leyda 2002 Estación Cabernet Sauvignon (Maipo Valley) $NA. Fairly green and lacking in expression. A bit sharp and tart, too. Amid a sea of Cabernet, your best bet is to keep on fishing. **83** —*M.S. (3/1/2004)*

Viña Leyda 2001 Reserve Cabernet Sauvignon (Maipo Valley) $17. The bouquet is open and nice as it deals cherry, cassis, mocha, and cinnamon. While not too heavy, the body is solid and structured. This wine tastes of true Maipo fruit, and the tannins are mild. It's the type of Cab for which Chile has become famous. **87** —*M.S. (3/1/2004)*

Viña Leyda 2002 Reserve Carmenère (Colchagua Valley) $18. Starts out with plum, cherry, and red cabbage aromas, which lead to a palate of light red fruit and mild vegetal flavors. Broad and starchy on the finish, with some thickness. Has its moments but doesn't really strike up the band. **83** —*M.S. (11/1/2005)*

Viña Leyda 2001 Reserve Carmenère (Colchagua Valley) $17. Ripe and perfectly sweet, with aromas of black olive, leather, and pepper to go with plum and berry. With a full blast of cherry, raspberry, and plum in the mouth, the bases are well covered. **88** —*M.S. (3/1/2004)*

Viña Leyda 2003 Estación Chardonnay (Chile) $NA. Slight melon and peach aromas create a soft, mild nose. Basic apple and melon flavors follow, and the finish is bumped forward by some driving acidity. Almost Sauvignon Blanc-like due to some unusual grassy notes. **85** —*M.S. (3/1/2004)*

Viña Leyda 2002 Falaris Hill Vineyard Reserve Chardonnay (Chile) $17. Plump, with melon and butterscotch aromas. Barrel fermentation shows in its slightly buttery feel, with tons of body. The fruit in the midpalate, however, isn't as vivid as it could be. The finish is creamy and a bit peppery. **87** —*M.S. (3/1/2004)*

Viña Leyda 2001 Falaris Hill Vineyard Reserve Chardonnay (Leyda Valley) $17. This is one of the first Leyda wines in the United States. It's well toasted, with crystallized mango and pineapple fruit. The finish is long, yet rather sugary. The wine shows bold flavors, but it needs more stuffing. **85** —*M.S. (3/1/2004)*

Viña Leyda 2002 Estación Merlot (Maipo Valley) $NA. Briary and pickled, with under-ripe green notes affecting the flavors and nose. Not flawed, but not friendly enough to warrant much attention. **82** —*M.S. (3/1/2004)*

Viña Leyda 2003 Cahuil Vineyard Reserve Pinot Noir (Leyda Valley) $22. Plenty of kick to this wine, but not necessarily in the best spots. The nose deals leather, horseradish, and dark fruits, while the palate sends up beet and pepper flavors with an almost nutty aftertaste. Gets better with airing, but still a touch funky. **84** —*M.S. (11/1/2005)*

Viña Leyda 2002 Cahuil Vineyard Reserve Pinot Noir (Leyda Valley) $20. A bit sharp, with cola, spice, and persistent vanilla oak. Comes on ripe and intense, with tight cherry fruit at the center and finally a long, spicy finish. **86** —*M.S. (3/1/2004)*

Viña Leyda 2002 Las Brisas Vineyard Reserve Pinot Noir (Chile) $NA. The Leyda Valley, with its resemblance to the Sonoma Coast, could someday become Pinot country for Chile. This youngster gives an inkling of what might be the future via its ripe, rooty nose along with black cherry and cola flavors. Seems very Leyda, for what that's worth at this early point in the game. **87** —*M.S. (3/1/2004)*

Viña Leyda 2003 Las Brisas Vineyars Reserve Pinot Noir (Leyda Valley) $15. Overtly funky, and then syrupy. A full-out heavyweight, as if it were extracted from a punch bowl. Not sure what the point is. **80** —*M.S. (7/1/2005)*

Viña Leyda 2003 Lot 21 Pinot Noir (Leyda Valley) $32. Cranberry and spice on the nose, with a hint of herbal mint. The mouth is a bit jumpy and shrill, which yields a fresh feel. In the glass, there's candied cherry and raspberry flavors and then finishing notes of tomato and carob. **86** —*M.S. (11/1/2005)*

Viña Leyda 2002 Lot 21 Pinot Noir (Chile) $NA. One of the best Chilean Pinot Noirs we've tried is this lot-selected wine. It's loaded with briar and bramble aromas, and you can almost smell the sea air amid the fragrant cola and raspberry notes. It tastes of natural fruit with proper oak shadings. Quite serious, and only 250 cases made. **89** —*M.S. (3/1/2004)*

Viña Leyda 2002 Vintage Selection Red Blend (Central Valley) $22. Aromas are of leather, tomato, and stewed berry, followed by a hard, almost nutty palate. Tight and tannic, with a rubbery mouthfeel. **83** —*M.S. (11/1/2005)*

Viña Leyda 2003 Estación Sauvignon Blanc (Chile) $NA. Pungent and fresh, with grapefruit on the nose. This represents Viña Leyda's first Sauvignon Blanc, and it's pretty good. Flavors of melon, pineapple, and tarragon get lean in the center, but overall there's enough fruit and zest to keep it on the proper track. **86** —*M.S. (3/1/2004)*

Viña Leyda 2004 Estación Reserve Sauvignon Blanc (Leyda Valley) $12. Ocean fresh, with melon and tropical aromas. Fairly full and rich in the mouth, where melon and pineapple flavors dominate. Delivers enough zest and power to please. Shows what this emerging coastal region can do with Sauvignon Blanc. **86** —*M.S. (11/1/2005)*

VIÑA MORANDE

Viña Morande 2000 Morande Terrarum 2000 Cabernet Sauvignon (Maipo Valley) $9. 86 Best Buy —*M.S. (12/1/2002)*

Viña Morande 2000 Pionero Cabernet Sauvignon (Central Valley) $7. Herbal notes mingle with lavender and hints of wood on the bouquet. Wild berry flavors along with a touch of bacon follow on the palate. The finish is light and a tad woody, and the finishing note is one of chocolate. The midpalate isn't terribly full, but it's far from a vacuous wine. For the price, it delivers. **85 Best Buy** —*M.S. (12/1/2002)*

Viña Morande 2000 Terrarum Cabernet Sauvignon (Maipo Valley) $9. Clean, fresh, and welcoming, with a complex hint of bacon and spice. The mouth is full of plum, cherry, and other berry notes, making for a satisfying palate. The finish is smooth and adequately long, and while it's a touch weak at the core, it's still a nice wine. **86 Best Buy** —*M.S. (12/1/2002)*

Viña Morande 2001 Edicion Limitada Golden Reserve Red Blend (Loncomilla Valley) $80. Aged in new American oak for 20 months, this wine has intense aromas of vanilla and toast, but that's backed by ample blackberry, black cherry, and raspberry scents. It's a juicy, medium-

CHILE

weight wine, not overly rich, but packed with raspberries, dried herbs, and brown sugar. Finishes long and toasty—and might be more reminiscent of some Riojas than most Chilean wines. A blend of Carignan, Merlot, and Cabernet Franc. **90** *(11/1/2005)*

VIÑA PÉREZ CRUZ

Viña Pérez Cruz 2005 Reserva Cabernet Sauvignon (Maipo Valley) $11. Here's a full-force Maipo red that's ready to run. The black cherry aromas and flavors are dark and chocolaty, while the feel is solid and the finish long and minty warm. Big but not plush; loaded but not opulent. A commendable large-production wine (45,000 cases). **88 Best Buy** — *M.S. (12/31/2006)*

Viña Pérez Cruz 2004 Reserva Limited Edition Carmenère (Maipo Valley) $19. Complete as can be, with smooth, refined aromas of black fruit and tight-grained oak. This is an elevated varietal wine that hits firmly with ripe plum, berry, and herb flavors. The mouthfeel is ripe and lush, while the finish sports forward vanilla and more hidden cedar. A definite winner. **91 Editors' Choice** —*M.S. (12/31/2006)*

Viña Pérez Cruz 2003 Liguai Red Blend (Maipo Valley) $35. It seems that each year at least one noteworthy Chilean producer arrives on the U.S. market, and this year we're taking notice of Pérez Cruz, a Maipo Valley winery that started in the 2002 vintage and whose wines are made by the talented Alvaro Espinoza. All that said, this flagship blend is compact and jammy, with huge berry flavors and racy tannins. It showcases the winery's ability to match size with style. **91 Editors' Choice** —*M.S. (12/31/2006)*

Viña Pérez Cruz 2004 Reserva Limited Edition Syrah (Maipo Valley) $19. Shocked! That's hopefully how you'll feel after taking your first sip of this extraordinary Chilean Syrah. Potent is the nose; equally packed with plum, berry, and chocolate is the mouth. And with mouthcoating tannins, extract, and just enough cocoa acidity, the finish lasts for minutes on end. One of the best Chilean Syrahs you'll find, and it's under $20. **92 Editors' Choice** —*M.S. (12/31/2006)*

VIÑA REQUINGUA

Viña Requingua 2002 Potro de Piedra Family Reserve Bordeaux Blend (Curicó Valley) $20. Round and fruity, with a full nose of big fruit and leather. Smells solid, but hits the palate with tremendous tannic force, to the point that it's overdone. The mouthfeel is gritty, but the flavors of fudge, black cherry, and spice save it. **86** —*M.S. (11/1/2005)*

Viña Requingua 2001 Potro de Piedra Family Reserve Cabernet Blend (Curicó Valley) $18. This Cabernet Sauvignon/Cab Franc blend is potent and deep, with syrupy berry aromas touched up by hints of mint, green herbs, and coffee. The palate is rich and rewarding, with sweet plum, berry, and brown sugar flavors. It finishes plump and big, with chewy extract and meaty tannins. **88** —*M.S. (6/1/2004)*

Viña Requingua 2002 Puerto Viejo Cabernet Sauvignon (Curicó Valley) $10. A touch scattered and sour on the nose, with aromas of rhubarb pie and red raspberries. More round and meaty on the palate, with flavors of plum and sugared berries. Finishes short but clean. Overall it's a decent, meaty red with mass appeal. **86 Best Buy** —*M.S. (8/1/2004)*

Viña Requingua 2003 Toro de Piedra Reserva Cabernet Sauvignon (Curicó Valley) $14. Warm and spicy, with plenty of ripe black fruit backing things up. Along the path you'll find tree bark and fresh-turned earth. By no means a lightweight, as it offers plum, blackberry, clove, and the works. Concentrated and tight; a brawny, firm Cabernet. **88** —*M.S. (11/1/2005)*

Viña Requingua 2001 Toro de Pierdra Reserve Cabernet Sauvignon (Curicó Valley) $13. Tight and smoky on the nose. In the mouth, there's a jammy, juicy blast of plum and berry, while on the finish it's chewy and round, leaving extract and residue. A full-bodied Cab that's tasty and satisfying. **88 Best Buy** —*M.S. (8/1/2004)*

Viña Requingua 2003 Potro de Piedra Family Reserve Cabernet Sauvignon-Cabernet Franc (Curicó Valley) $25. Dark on the nose, with olive, rubber, plum, and black cherry scents. The mouth is deep and saturated; there's fairly lush plum, coffee, and mocha flavors to ponder. Shows some espresso-like bitterness on the back end, which adds to the complexity. A definite contender. **89** —*M.S. (7/1/2006)*

Viña Requingua 2003 Puerto Viejo Carmenère (Curicó Valley) $9. Overloaded with Middle Eastern spice aromas and a chewy, meaty, quality that submerges any fruit that might be present. A total oddball with hefty oak; it tastes like cumin-infused syrup. **81** —*M.S. (11/1/2005)*

Viña Requingua 2004 Puerto Viejo Chardonnay (Curicó Valley) $9. Pineapple, pear, and applesauce aromas are more encouraging that what follows. The palate is simply too oaky and cloying. What you get in the end is a sticky product with overly powerful vanilla and caramel candy notes. **82** —*M.S. (7/1/2005)*

Viña Requingua 2003 Puerto Viejo Chardonnay (Curicó Valley) $10. A touch oaky on the nose, with nuances of cream, banana, and coconut. Flavors of apple and pear are supported by nutmeg and other sweet spices. Quite soft and round on the tongue, with finishing notes of vanilla and white pepper, both courtesy of the forceful oaking. **86 Best Buy** —*M.S. (6/1/2004)*

Viña Requingua 2003 Puerto Viejo Merlot (Curicó Valley) $9. Heavy and unfocused, with unconvincing flavors of carob and coconut running roughshod on the palate. A hulk that's out of joint. **80** —*M.S. (7/1/2005)*

Viña Requingua 2002 Puerto Viejo Merlot (Curicó Valley) $10. Ripe and chunky, with pickled aromas to the plum and berry nose. In the mouth, look for dried cherry, herb, and carob flavors, then milk chocolate on the finish. Not boring, but strange. **84** —*M.S. (6/1/2004)*

VIÑA SAN ESTEBAN

Viña San Esteban 2003 President's Select Cabernet Sauvignon (Aconcagua Valley) $13. Here you'll find aromatics including rubber, cherry, and leather; however, the flavors run high and dry, meaning there's piercing red fruit and not much love. Turns medicinal near the finish, with hints of root beer and butter. **84** —*M.S. (11/1/2005)*

Viña San Esteban 2002 Reserva Carmenère (Aconcagua Valley) $8. Quite pickled, with rough vegetal notes making for a difficult bouquet. Flavors of beets, pepper, and clove lead into a lean finish that's both sugary and spicy, much like sweet-and-sour sauce. On the plus side, the mouthfeel is pretty good. **82** —*M.S. (6/1/2004)*

Viña San Esteban 2003 Reserva Merlot (Aconcagua Valley) $10. Stewy, with aromas of black olive and raisins. Tastes a bit herbal; but there's sweet red fruit as well. Kind of candied on the finish, with some chewiness. **83** —*M.S. (11/1/2005)*

Viña San Esteban 2001 Reserva Merlot (Aconcagua Valley) $8. Aromas of chili powder, cherry, and wild berries create a pleasant-smelling bouquet. Flavors of berries and cream lead into a lengthy, solid finish that's both soft and easy due to fine-grained tannins. **85 Best Buy** —*M.S. (3/1/2004)*

Viña San Esteban 2003 Reserva Shiraz (Aconcagua Valley) $10. Raisiny, with aromas of stewed fruit and sweet almond candy. Basic but blunted on the palate, with a dull feel and non-existent tannins. Adequate on a good day; a bit weedy. **83** —*M.S. (11/1/2005)*

VIÑA SANTA MONICA

Viña Santa Monica 1999 Cabernet Sauvignon (Rapel Valley) $8. Piercing aromas, but not very fruity. It's a bit like wasabe at the sushi joint. The palate has some cassis, cherry, and spice, while the finish is also spicy. At first it shows some power but things fade fast as opposed to improving. **83** —*M.S. (7/1/2003)*

Viña Santa Monica 2001 Chardonnay (Rapel Valley) $8. Heavy and gold in color, with aromas of browned butter, wheat, and corn cakes. The bouquet and color are heavy, and so is the palate: There you get oak barrel and toast, but little to no fruit. Even the finish is woody, with just a hint of melon and banana. A good experimental wine for those eager to taste oak; otherwise steer clear. **87 Best Buy** —*M.S. (7/1/2003)*

Viña Santa Monica 2001 Riesling (Rapel Valley) $8. Zippy, with natural rubbery aromas. This is quite tart and has a personality defined by lemon. There's lemon torte up front, while at the end it's purely tangy and sharp. Not an astringent, scouring wine, but high acidity comes into play. **84** —*M.S. (8/1/2003)*

Viña Santa Monica 2002 Sauvignon Blanc (Rapel Valley) $8. Varietally typical aromas of grapefruit and green onion start it off, but the palate is more citrusy, as it emphasizes flavors of orange, grapefruit, passion fruit,

CHILE

and some pickle. The finish is fresh and clean, and the mouthfeel is juicy. However, dilution of flavors and a failure to improve once opened hold it back. **84** —*M.S. (7/1/2003)*

VIÑA TABALÍ

Viña Tabalí 2003 Reserva Cabernet Sauvignon (Limarí Valley) $14. The bouquet enters into the land of exotic, with aromas of sandalwood and cinnamon. But from there the wine loses steam, offering only basic plum and berry flavors followed by an earthy, almost murky finish. Doesn't show enough in the middle and late stages to rate better. **83** —*M.S. (5/1/2006)*

Viña Tabalí 2003 Reserva Carmenère (Limarí Valley) $14. More than enough buttery oak and dill powers the nose, but there isn't a whole lot of body to back it up. The palate runs tight, with raspberry and cherry flavors teetering on citric. Spice and a spot of bell pepper define the finish. Not bad but a touch acidic in feel. **84** —*M.S. (3/1/2006)*

Viña Tabalí 2004 Reserva Especial Chardonnay (Limarí Valley) $17. Gets going like a buttercup, with toast gracing ripe peach and pear aromas. Racy and full in the mouth, with pineapple, apple, and mango flavors. A clean wine with good mouthfeel and texture. Shows plenty of oak but not the overdone type. **88** —*M.S. (7/1/2006)*

Viña Tabalí 2003 Reserva Merlot (Limarí Valley) $14. Very oaky; on the border of smelling like sawdust. Also brambly, with plum and cherry in the background. So much wood you get maple and pepper; not too convincing. **82** —*M.S. (3/1/2006)*

Viña Tabalí 2004 Reserva Pinot Noir (Limarí Valley) $18. The nose provides spicy cherry and tea aromas but also some sweaty leather. Leafy and lean on the palate, with strange fruit flavors. A real weird cat; not the Pinot most Americans are used to. **81** —*M.S. (7/1/2006)*

Viña Tabalí 2003 Reserva Especial Red Blend (Limarí Valley) $19. Warm and earthy, with a mild touch of stewiness to the nose. Sweet and candied in the mouth, with chocolate accents. Quite full through the middle with a meaty, big finish. Not a ton of complexity, however. The blend is Cabernet Sauvignon with a quarter each of Merlot and Syrah. **85** —*M.S. (3/1/2006)*

Viña Tabalí 2005 Sauvignon Blanc (Limarí Valley) $10. Starts with mild citrus aromas. Zesty in the mouth, with pineapple, grapefruit, and apple flavors. Short and compact, with nothing out of the ordinary. Drinkable and fresh. **84** —*M.S. (5/1/2006)*

Viña Tabalí 2004 Reserva Shiraz (Limarí Valley) $15. Quite the heavyweight in terms of its roasted, leathery nose. The palate runs a touch salty, with a lot of smoked and/or cured meat running through the middle of the palate. On the edges lie olive and dried plum flavors. Not that fruity or integrated; seems a bit cooked. **84** —*M.S. (3/1/2006)*

VIÑEDOS DE CANATA

Viñedos de Canata 2001 Paso Hondo Reserva Cabernet Sauvignon (Bío Bío Valley) $12. Murky and damp smelling, with buttery strawberry flavors. Peppery and dry, with a raw, thin mouthfeel. Acceptable at a base level. **80** —*M.S. (11/1/2005)*

Viñedos de Canata 2002 Carmenère (Bío Bío Valley) $9. Features some ripe and heavy aromas, with a touch of barnyard and rubber thrown in. More rustic than refined, but ultimately good, with cherry and raspberry flavors. Dry and smoky on the finish, with tannin offsetting any fatness. **85 Best Buy** —*M.S. (3/1/2006)*

Viñedos de Canata 2001 Paso Hondo Reserva Carmenère (Bío Bío Valley) $12. Light-bodied and tight, with bramble, raspberry, and burnt, reedy notes. Shows a snappiness and red cherry on the palate, with tight, crisp acidity. A touch hard on the back end. **83** —*M.S. (3/1/2006)*

Viñedos de Canata 2004 Chardonnay (Bío Bío Valley) $9. A touch waxy and oily, with flower blossom and butterscotch scents but no overt, identifiable fruit. Lively and acidic, a trait of the chilly, emerging southern Bío Bío area. Finishes spry but short on flavor. **84** —*M.S. (11/1/2005)*

Viñedos de Canata 2003 Paso Hondo Reserva Chardonnay (Bío Bío Valley) $12. Strikes a pleasing opening chord with its pear and vanilla aromas along with a splinter of oak. The palate is a bit toasty, with smooth apple

and pineapple flavors. Becomes more lemony as it opens, with woody, resiny notes peeking through. **86** —*M.S. (11/1/2005)*

Viñedos de Canata 2003 Paso Hondo Alto Selección Malbec (Bío Bío Valley) $16. Interesting on the nose, where flower petal, cola, and grape extract blend nicely. But that quality doesn't really make it to the palate, where the flavor profile is narrow. Grabby and scouring in terms of feel, but the aromas are really good. Too bad it's so limited to the smell. **84** —*M.S. (11/1/2005)*

Viñedos de Canata 2003 Merlot (Curicó Valley) $9. Vinegar and horseradish mar the plum notes on the nose, while the palate is exceedingly lean and snappy. Raspberry flavors fade as fast they arrive, and overall it's devoid of richness. **81** —*M.S. (11/1/2005)*

Viñedos de Canata 2003 Paso Hondo Alta Selección Merlot (Bío Bío Valley) $16. A bit sharp and raw from the beginning, and the palate features a jolt of bracing acids that turn the raspberry and plum flavors sharp. Far more raw than pulpy, so it's Merlot on the thin side. Which makes sense given that it comes from the very cool, southern Bío Bío Valley. **84** —*M.S. (11/1/2005)*

Viñedos de Canata 2003 Paso Hondo Alta Seleccion Winemaker's Cuvée Red Blend (Bío Bío Valley) $16. Takes off a bit dirty, with a lot of earth and green tobacco. Finds its stride later on, as it displays red fruit but also some clamping tannins. Sort of herbal in character as it struggles for adequate ripeness. **83** —*M.S. (11/1/2005)*

Viñedos de Canata 2004 Sauvignon Blanc (Bío Bío Valley) $9. Sort of sweet, with aromas of jelly beans and Easter candies. That sweetness carries to the palate, where apple and lime accents join the fray. Finishes short and kind of empty. **82** —*M.S. (11/1/2005)*

VIÑEDOS ORGANICOS EMILIANA

Viñedos Organicos Emiliana 2004 Adobe Carmenère (Colchagua Valley) $NA. Ripe and rubbery, with a little bit of jump. Blackberry and sweet plum flavors are not herbal, while background oak offers vanilla, pepper and a light creaminess. Finishes clean. **87** —*M.S. (3/1/2006)*

Viñedos Organicos Emiliana 2004 Adobe Syrah (Colchagua Valley) $NA. Full and ripe, with zero funk. It's juicy and tight, with a blast of pepper, on the nose. Potent and structured, with moderate tannins. Features 15% Carmenère for softening purposes. **88** —*M.S. (3/1/2006)*

VIÑEDOS TORREÓN

Viñedos Torreón 2003 Torreon de Paredes Sauvignon Blanc (Chile) $11. Not too much fruit comes off the nose, and the palate seems dilute and mildly watery. In between, there's some citrus, particularly lemon. Still, it is rather bland in the final analysis. **83** —*M.S. (6/1/2004)*

VINO DE EYZAGUIRRE

Vino de Eyzaguirre 2001 Cabernet Sauvignon (Colchagua Valley) $8. Some leather and horsehide aromas dance with burnt toast and red fruit on the nose. Flavors of vanilla-accented plum are standard, while the finish is a touch hot and spicy. It's weighty and thick in terms of body, a bit like a heavy blanket on a warm night. **85 Best Buy** —*M.S. (8/1/2004)*

Vino de Eyzaguirre 2001 San Francisco de Mostazal Reserva Especial Merlot (Colchagua Valley) $8. Burnt and smoky on the nose, with a meaty, earthy undercurrent. Flavors of plum and berry are best at first but lose clarity with each passing minute. Fairly plump but unfocused, thus not even the catchy blue burlap bag the bottle comes in is of much help. **84** —*M.S. (8/1/2004)*

Vino de Eyzaguirre 2002 Shiraz (Colchagua Valley) $8. Stewy, with a rough nose. Better in the mouth, with raspberry touched up by some spicy pepper. Underdeveloped, with light red fruit and some green character. **82** —*M.S. (2/1/2005)*

Vino de Eyzaguirre 2001 San Francisco de Mostazal Reserva Especial Syrah (Colchagua Valley) $8. Early aromas of sea water, mushroom, and rubber integrate into a more pleasant whole. The flavors are sweet and candied, while on the finish a mild vegetal hint comes on. That said, the wine is decent in the mouth, where the texture is pleasant. **82** —*M.S. (7/1/2003)*

CHILE

VIU MANENT 2005 CABERNET SAUVIGNON

Viu Manent 2005 Cabernet Sauvignon (Colchagua Valley) $8. Purple in hue, with jumpy, unsettled, grapey aromas. Fairly hard and firm in the mouth, where cherry and plum flavors careen about on the jets of bulky tannins and tangy acids. Plenty of fruit, but not much polish on the stone. **84 Best Buy** —*M.S. (7/1/2006)*

Viu Manent 2002 Cabernet Sauvignon (Colchagua Valley) $8. Berry jam and a distant hint of bell pepper define the bouquet. Next in line is a respectable mix of raspberry, vanilla, and chocolate flavors. It finishes charred, but easy and round. **85 Best Buy** —*M.S. (3/1/2004)*

Viu Manent 2004 Estate Cabernet Sauvignon (Colchagua Valley) $8. Not that packed or forward, but still quite good in its territory. The nose shows light cherry, while the palate is fairly savory, with berry flavors touched up by a shot of vanilla. A bit short on the finish and not that full in the middle, but for $8 what more do you want? **86 Best Buy** —*M.S. (5/1/2006)*

Viu Manent 2003 Estate Bottled Cabernet Sauvignon (Colchagua Valley) $8. Brawny and colorful, with big black fruit aromas along with scents of olive and green bean. Not vegetal, but the wine does show a green streak in addition to fine black cherry and cassis flavors. Powerful and full-bodied. Easy to enjoy. **87 Best Buy** —*M.S. (11/1/2005)*

Viu Manent 2004 La Capilla Estate Single Vineyard Cabernet Sauvignon (Colchagua Valley) $19. Rather deep and dense, with powerful black fruit aromas of menthol, berry, and pepper. Ripe and rich throughout, with a ton of lush plum flavor and extra servings of chocolate and vanilla. This is what Colchagua Cabernet is all about. **89** —*M.S. (10/1/2006)*

Viu Manent 2004 Oak Aged Reserve Cabernet Sauvignon (Colchagua Valley) $13. Round, chewy, and full-bodied, with cherry as well as mint and fresh herbs on the bouquet. Fairly saturated, with sweet, sappy red fruit flavors shading licorice and bitter chocolate notes. Not complex but quite pleasant. **86** —*M.S. (10/1/2006)*

Viu Manent 2003 Oak Aged Reserve Cabernet Sauvignon (Colchagua Valley) $12. Rather big, with earth, olive, forest, and coffee notes running side by side with black plum and berry. A ripe-styled wine, with full cherry and berry flavors. Feels good on the tongue and finish, with a slight herbal quality. Good in a mass-market way. **86** —*M.S. (7/1/2006)*

Viu Manent 2001 Oak Aged Reserve Cabernet Sauvignon (Colchagua Valley) $12. Aromas of raspberry jam are light yet nice, while a palate containing soft berry fruit is friendly and not overpowering. At first the wine seems zingy and tart, and while the body remains lean throughout, there's adequate berry fruit and a perfectly acceptable structure. **85** —*M.S. (3/1/2004)*

Viu Manent 2002 Reserve Cabernet Sauvignon (Colchagua Valley) $12. Lean and spicy, with some green in the middle of the nose that's similar to celery. Additional bell pepper hangs heavily on the palate, but there's just enough berry to offset it. Tight in terms of feel, with well-integrated tannins. Feels nice; tastes more herbal than ideal. **85** —*M.S. (2/1/2005)*

Viu Manent 1999 Reserve Cabernet Sauvignon (Colchagua Valley) $12. Sweet, oaky aromas draw you in, and below that is nothing but an easy-drinking red wine that's full of cherry, proper tannins, mild woody tones, and ample power. It's not overly complex; but it is immensely satisfying. **87 Best Buy** —*M.S. (3/1/2002)*

Viu Manent 2000 Special Selection Cabernet Sauvignon (Colchagua Valley) $20. This single-vineyard Cab has slight vegetal aromas and a flat mouthfeel. The nose is largely balanced, with just a hint of green bean and lemon. The palate is chunky and dark, with candied fruit, chocolate, and soft tannins. Not likely to improve; drink now or wait for the 2001. **85** —*M.S. (3/1/2004)*

Viu Manent 1998 Special Selection Cabernet Sauvignon (Colchagua Valley) $20. In this difficult vintage, Viu Manent has turned out a stylish, loosely knit wine that blends graham-cracker aromas with flavors of berry compote, vanilla, and dried spices. Finishes soft, with a refreshing minty note. **85** —*J.C. (7/1/2002)*

Viu Manent 2001 Special Selection La Capilla Vineyard Cabernet Sauvignon (Colchagua Valley) $20. Good and tight, especially at first. Some airing and swirling reveals finely scripted black plum and a good

deal of oak-driven coffee and chocolate. Neither heavy nor light; it toes the line of balance. If there's anything to take issue with, it's that the acidity seems on the high side. **89** —*M.S. (7/1/2005)*

Viu Manent 2002 Carmenère (Colchagua Valley) $8. Leathery and rustic, with a hint of bramble and leather on the bouquet. The palate is full-throttle, with lively plum, blackberry, and chocolate notes, with sweet accents of cola and wood. A substantive wine, one that turns creamy on the finish. **87 Best Buy** —*M.S. (8/1/2004)*

Viu Manent 2005 Estate Carmenère (Colchagua Valley) $8. Starts out a touch brambly, with tart-fruit aromas. The body is big and the tannins lively and hard, but the flavors work out in the end as the wine settles on berries and rusticity. **84 Best Buy** —*M.S. (11/15/2006)*

Viu Manent 2004 Estate Carmenère (Colchagua Valley) $8. Savory and a little leafy, but it blends the right amounts of salty olive and herbs with perky, red fruit notes. Almost crisp on the palate, with fairly precise olive, plum and cherry flavors. Good and fresh; varietally correct. **87 Best Buy** —*M.S. (3/1/2006)*

Viu Manent 2003 Estate Bottled Carmenère (Colchagua Valley) $8. Sweet and saucy, as if it had been marinated. The fruit tastes ultra sweet at first, but then it veers quickly toward vegetal. More grabby and sticky on the finish than desirable. **82** —*M.S. (2/1/2005)*

Viu Manent 2003 Oak Aged Reserve Carmenère (Colchagua Valley) $12. Stewed and heavy, with bulky fruit that mixes in hints of green. Slightly volatile on the nose, with a round, meaty mouthfeel. Probably not this winery's best effort, yet still it has some richness, sweetness, and commendable flavors. **83** —*M.S. (12/15/2005)*

Viu Manent 2002 Oak Aged Reserve Carmenère (Colchagua Valley) $12. Well-oaked and generous, with aromas of root beer, tree bark, licorice, and black cherry. A flavorful mix of plum, blackberry, and cherry defines the palate, which is sleek and juicy, with spice and size. A very drinkable, clearly defined red. **88 Best Buy** —*M.S. (6/1/2004)*

Viu Manent 2004 Reserva Carmenère (Colchagua Valley) $12. A solid wine from 10-year-old vines; it is bright and fruity, with round, complete aromas and flavors that range from leather and mint to plum and toast. Nicely oaked and well-made. **88 Best Buy** —*M.S. (3/1/2006)*

Viu Manent 2005 Secreto Carmenère (Colchagua Valley) $13. Fun to drink and a bit different than the rest. The nose is peppery and spicy, with berry and chocolate shading. Jammy raspberry coats the palate, infused with a blast of black pepper. Finish is persistent, with a hint of chili. **87** —*M.S. (10/1/2006)*

Viu Manent 2004 Secreto Carmenère (Colchagua Valley) $12. Dark and smoky, but also non-distinct. The rubbery nose is packed full of berry fruit and tar, but it's also a touch hard and unfocused. Pie-like fruit and chocolate control the palate; heavily toasted, with coffee on the finish. **85** —*M.S. (3/1/2006)*

Viu Manent 2003 Secreto Carmenère (Colchagua Valley) $12. Firm and tight, with dark aromatic shadings along with mint and fallen leaves. Stays hard and herbal on the palate, but underneath there's solid berry and plum flavors. Opens with airing and gains ground; has merits but requires patience. **86** —*M.S. (11/1/2005)*

Viu Manent 2004 Barrel Fermented Reserve Chardonnay (Casablanca Valley) $12. A lot of corn and butter, but with a strong infusion of vegetal notes like celery and squash. Buttery and bland on the palate, with mealy flavors and a resiny finish. Not one of this winery's better moments. **81** —*M.S. (3/1/2006)*

Viu Manent 2003 Barrel Fermented Reserve Chardonnay (Colchagua Valley) $12. A lively barrel-fermented wine with vanilla, pear, and apple aromas. Hefty but balanced, with a palate full of pear, buttered toast, and proper acidity. A very good wine in the South American mode. **88 Best Buy** —*M.S. (2/1/2005)*

Viu Manent 2004 Estate Bottled Chardonnay (Colchagua Valley) $8. Starts with banana and spiced meat on the nose, which are backed by apple, pear, and banana flavors. Ripe and rich, bordering on thick and syrupy, but with enough spine and flash to make the grade. **86 Best Buy** —*M.S. (7/1/2005)*

Viu Manent 1999 Reserve Chardonnay (Colchagua Valley) $12. Flat and dull in the nose, with only a touch of apple along with plenty of leftover wood. The palate is thick and woody, and there just isn't ample fruit to offset the oakiness. **83** —*M.S. (7/1/2003)*

Viu Manent 2004 Malbec (Colchagua Valley) $8. Gets off the mark with some maple aromas, then shifts toward ripe fruit. The palate offers sweet, likable berry flavors and the finish is appropriately woody, with a creamy feel. Very nice and well-made. **87 Best Buy** —*M.S. (11/1/2005)*

Viu Manent 2002 Malbec (Colchagua Valley) $8. Pretty good for the price; the wine has a forward blackberry flavor, toasty edges, and plenty of size. It's big in the nose, and given time in the glass it sheds its awkwardness. Meaty, masculine, and fine with hamburgers. Similar in style to a modest Montepulciano d'Abruzzo. **85 Best Buy** —*M.S. (12/1/2003)*

Viu Manent 2000 Malbec (Colchagua Valley) $8. This basic red gives an inkling of what Viu can do with Malbec. This is perfectly juicy, with a tight core of blueberry fruit. There's a nice roundness and balance to the wine, which is exactly the type that should be opened and enjoyed without a lot of thought and analysis. **87 Best Buy** —*M.S. (3/1/2002)*

Viu Manent 2003 Los Carlos Estate Single Vineyard Malbec (Colchagua Valley) $18. Exemplary Chilean Malbec from the winery that does it better than the rest. This is a purple fury of inky, rich quality. The nose is harmonious and the palate both juicy and big, with snappy black cherry and tons of chocolate. Tight and secure all the way through. Hits the spot. **91 Editors' Choice** —*M.S. (11/1/2005)*

Viu Manent 2004 Oak Aged Reserve Malbec (Colchagua Valley) $13. It's easy to size up this high-quality bargain. The nose is deep and dark, with crude oil, violet petal, and earth along with a stout package of mixed black fruits. The palate is impressively fruity and rich, with density. A very satisfying wine given the price. **89 Best Buy** —*M.S. (10/1/2006)*

Viu Manent 2003 Oak Aged Reserve Malbec (Colchagua Valley) $12. A strong-willed wine, with mint, leather, and oak aromas in front of a juicy flavor profile that emphasizes plum and raspberry. Nice color and zest, with some snap and tartness to the palate. Not an overweight wine but solid. Perfect for ribs or burgers. **87 Best Buy** —*M.S. (12/15/2005)*

Viu Manent 2001 Oak Aged Reserve Malbec (Colchagua Valley) $12. Great color, but what at first comes across as mint turns to and remains vegetal. Along the way there's snappy cherry fruit enlivened by bold acidity, and at the end there's some mocha flavor. But there's still too much green pepper. **84** —*P.G. (12/1/2003)*

Viu Manent 2004 San Carlos Estate Single Vineyard Malbec (Colchagua Valley) $19. Purple as midnight, with mint, cola, herbs, crushed slate and huge black fruit aromas. Quite bold, with a mountain of dark fruit flavor, while the tannins show up late on the finish and make their mark. Special not for its complexity but for its density and purity. **90 Editors' Choice** —*M.S. (10/1/2006)*

Viu Manent 2005 Secreto Malbec (Colchagua Valley) $13. Purple in color, with blackberry and leather aromas. Black cherry and plum lead the flavor profile, while coffee, toast, and black pepper carry the finish. Has good acidity but seems a touch short on depth and complexity. **87** —*M.S. (10/1/2006)*

Viu Manent 2004 Secreto Malbec (Colchagua Valley) $12. A true purple haze, with big, sort of clumsy aromas of blackberry and marzipan. Call it size over-precision. The palate is sweet and borderline sugary, but there's just enough acid to balance it off. Chocolate and tannin carry the finish. **86** —*M.S. (11/1/2005)*

Viu Manent 2001 Special Selection Malbec (Colchagua Valley) $16. A rich, well-made middleweight with exotic aromas of citrus peel, leather, and toasted wood sitting atop ripe, luscious fruit. More elegant than many, with cocoa and coffee coming on late. Doesn't have the depth of the very best in the field, but what's on display is admirable. **88** —*M.S. (12/1/2003)*

Viu Manent 2000 Special Selection Malbec (Colchagua Valley) $16. This serious Malbec comes with 15% Cabernet in the mix, and that bit of Cab offers just the boost the wine needs. It's sincerely jammy and grapey, but there's also depth and layers to the black fruit. Tannins, licorice, and vanilla all come on late. As the name implies, this has a lot of the character you'd expect from a so-called special selection. **89** —*M.S. (3/1/2002)*

Viu Manent 2001 Viu 1 Malbec (Colchagua Valley) $50. The second version of this world-class Chilean Malbec (with some Cabernet blended in) is on a par with the inaugural '99. If you like a rich, fully-oaked, corpulent red, one with ripe plum and berry fruit, oozing chocolate, and just enough spice to ward away boredom, this is it. Needs another year or so in bottle. **92** —*M.S. (12/1/2003)*

Viu Manent 1999 Viu I Malbec (Colchagua Valley) $39. This is 90% old-vine Malbec with 10% Cabernet thrown in. The best one-word description is "awesome." The 80-year-old Malbecvines are full of clove, licorice, and marzipan nuances. The flavor profile offers berries, sweetmeat pie, and maple syrup. The finish is huge but soft. The body is massive and concentrated, but entirely friendly. This is indeed a super Chilean in all senses of the word. **93 Editors' Choice** —*M.S. (3/1/2002)*

Viu Manent 2004 Merlot (Colchagua Valley) $8. Green bean and bell pepper aromas, then red pepper and more green pepper to the palate, which does offer some plum and berry. Finishes with red pepper flake. Not impressive. **80** —*M.S. (11/1/2005)*

Viu Manent 2002 Merlot (Colchagua Valley) $8. Floral on the nose, with a note of meatiness as well as light cherry and raspberry aromas. Has full cherry and plum flavors and a tight, firm body with no real faults. **86 Best Buy** —*M.S. (3/1/2004)*

Viu Manent 1999 Merlot (Colchagua Valley) $8. Lots of wood from beginning to end, but some nice cherry and leather notes keep it interesting. The wine has gritty, woodsy tannins, yet still left me feeling as though it was on the light side of medium-bodied. **83** —*D.T. (7/1/2002)*

Viu Manent 2005 Estate Merlot (Colchagua Valley) $8. Shows bold, sassy fruit aromas, but you wouldn't call it refined. The palate is mild in flavor and racy in feel, with red fruit showing the way. Chocolate notes and rugged tannins finish the deal. **85 Best Buy** —*M.S. (11/15/2006)*

Viu Manent 2003 Estate Bottled Merlot (Colchagua Valley) $8. The nose offers raisin, prune, and raspberry aromas that indicate a bit of over-ripeness. Molasses mixes with black fruit to create a creamy, thick palate. Finishes with chocolate and vanilla. **84 Best Buy** —*M.S. (11/1/2005)*

Viu Manent 2003 Oak Aged Reserve Merlot (Colchagua Valley) $12. Blends raspberry aromas with horseradish, and after that there are flavors of cherry, toast, coffee, and lingering oak. Turns lemony upon airing, with coffee and spiky tannins on the finish. **83** —*M.S. (12/15/2005)*

Viu Manent 2002 Oak Aged Reserve Merlot (Colchagua Valley) $12. Dark and muscular, with molasses, black licorice, plum, and road tar draped across the bouquet. In the mouth, the fruit is lush and ripe, yet the plum and berry notes are exact and satisfying. The finish is sweet and pure, as it should be. And there's even a layer or two of complexity. A wine that exceeds expectations. **89 Best Buy** —*M.S. (8/1/2004)*

Viu Manent 1999 Reserve Merlot (Colchagua Valley) $13. With such a dark flavor profile—blackberry, black grape, earth, oak—this wine needs a little more weight and concentration than it has. The nose's grape and plum notes are nice, but take some time to open. **83** —*D.T. (7/1/2002)*

Viu Manent 2003 Viu 1 Red Blend (Colchagua Valley) $50. A wine that's made only in top years, Viu 1 represents the best that Chile can do with Malbec. It's an old-vines heavyweight with a purple color, sweet coconut-tinged aromas, and luscious black cherry and baked plum flavors. It's rich, heady, and wide. Moderately tannic but not so much that you can't drink it now. **92 Editors' Choice** —*M.S. (7/1/2006)*

Viu Manent 2003 Sauvignon Blanc (Colchagua Valley) $8. Fresh and lightly minty, with citrus as the main flavor component. It's wet, zesty, and refreshing, with some chunk to the body and ample acidity. **86 Best Buy** —*M.S. (3/1/2004)*

Viu Manent 2001 Sauvignon Blanc (Colchagua Valley) $8. This is Viu's high-production wine (15,000 cases), yet it has the qualities of something made on a smaller scale. It's very grapefruity, with passion fruit subtleties. The palate is crisp and clean, and there's a sweetness to the finish that balances the pungency of the fruit. **87** —*M.S. (3/1/2002)*

Viu Manent 2004 Estate Bottled Sauvignon Blanc (Colchagua Valley) $8. The citrus and grapefruit aromas are pretty standard, but the wine really comes to life on the palate, delivering zesty citrus, fresh-cut asparagus, and even some minerality. Anisette, grapefruit, and tangerine notes cre-

CHILE

ate an interesting finish. For the money, one of the best Sauvignons in Chile. **88 Best Buy** —*M.S. (7/1/2005)*

Viu Manent 2004 Reserve Sauvignon Blanc (Colchagua Valley) $12. Easy and fruity, with sweet aromas preceding tangy orange on the palate. Finishes solid, with citrus all the way. Medium in weight, with a slight salty edge. **86** —*M.S. (2/1/2005)*

Viu Manent 2006 Secreto Sauvignon Blanc (Colchagua Valley) $13. Starts with a lot of green, crisp aromas such as fresh-cut grass, bell peppers, and asparagus. But it's not vegetal; to the contrary, the wine shows bright passion fruit and capsicum notes along with hints of lettuce. The acidity and balance are both correct, and the feel is wet and lively. One of the better Secreto SBs in recent years. **88** —*M.S. (12/31/2006)*

Viu Manent 2004 Secreto Sauvignon Blanc (Colchagua Valley) $12. Chunky, with citrus and asparagus on the nose. Flavors of orange, melon, and bell pepper carry the palate. Finishes with some lemon extract even though it registers more full-bodied than light. **84** —*M.S. (12/15/2005)*

Viu Manent 2003 Secreto Sauvignon Blanc (Colchagua Valley) $12. Tropical fruit mixes with tarragon and pickle on the nose, a clear take on the so-called New Zealand style. Flavors of lemon and orange are tangy and sharp, while the body holds onto some welcome roundness. A good one for sushi and pre-meal salads. **87 Best Buy** —*M.S. (7/1/2005)*

Viu Manent 2003 Semillon (Colchagua Valley) $8. This unusual white wine borders on being flat and stale. The aromas are of candy corn, while the palate doesn't come through with much sweetness or fruit; it's mostly mild citrus and sour apple. The finish, as could be expected for Semillon, is sizable and weighty. **83** —*M.S. (6/1/2004)*

Viu Manent 2005 Secreto Syrah (Colchagua Valley) $13. Deep and smoky, with a distinct earthy, leathery, almost animal element to the nose. The palate is thorough and round, with cassis, berry, and mild herbal flavors. Ends with solid fruit and chocolate notes. Funky and herbal, but interesting. **87** —*M.S. (11/15/2006)*

Viu Manent 2004 Secreto Syrah (Colchagua Valley) $12. With spiced meat, earth, and bright fruit on the nose, this shouldn't remain a secret forever. The wine is super easy to drink because the tannins are reserved. As for flavor, it features lively dark fruits and enough chocolate to satisfy a cocoa hound. Fine texture and balance are the finishing touches. **88 Best Buy** —*M.S. (11/1/2005)*

Viu Manent 2004 Secreto Viognier (Colchagua Valley) $12. As funky a white wine as you're likely to find in Chile, with lean flavors that veer toward pickles and veggies. Maybe it's already losing it because it seems lost. Mouthfeel, however, is an attribute that keeps it afloat. **82** —*M.S. (7/1/2006)*

Viu Manent 2003 Secreto Viognier (Colchagua Valley) $12. Sweaty on the nose, with pickle and wax bean along with peach and melon. The palate has some kick, and that supports the citrus and apple flavors. Not a lot of acid, so it feels a bit oily and rich. Probably best to drink as soon as possible; it's not made for the long haul. **85** —*M.S. (11/1/2005)*

WALNUT CREST

Walnut Crest 2003 Cabernet Sauvignon (Rapel Valley) $5. It's hard to imagine getting a better red wine for five bucks, which makes this one of the best Best Buys out there. On the mark at all check points, with ripe cherry and plum flavors and a clean, smooth finish. Surprisingly solid. **86 Best Buy** —*M.S. (11/1/2005)*

Walnut Crest 2001 Cabernet Sauvignon (Rapel Valley) $6. Dusty cherry and chocolate aromas are uplifted by some flowery notes. Flavors of cassis, raspberry, and mild buttery oak make for a correct, pleasant palate. Some additional butter and vanilla flavors are detectable on the finish. Given its price, this wine is fresh and tasty enough, with staying power. **85 Best Buy** —*M.S. (12/1/2002)*

Walnut Crest 2003 Chardonnay (Casablanca Valley) $5. Fruity and ripe, with the full blast of banana, melon, and peach aromas. In the mouth, ripe melon and candied apple get a boost from modest acids. Finishes mild and adequately smooth. **84 Best Buy** —*M.S. (6/1/2004)*

Walnut Crest 2001 Chardonnay (Casablanca Valley) $6. Here's a good example of a value Chardonnay. It's clean and fruity, with spicy apple fla-

vors, a focused and lengthy finish, and proper acidity. The whole is better than its parts. **86 Best Buy** —*M.S. (7/1/2003)*

Walnut Crest 2003 Merlot (Rapel Valley) $5. Jammy and funky on the nose, with aromas of raspberry candy and some vinegar. Flavors of apple skin and grape juice are acceptable but not developed. Finishes with a starchy mouthfeel and notes of burnt espresso. **83** —*M.S. (8/1/2004)*

Walnut Crest 2004 Sauvignon Blanc (Central Valley) $5. Clean up front, with peach and melon aromas. The body is round and smooth, with apple and other ripe flavors. Some lemon essence on the finish keeps things framed. Nice for the price. **84 Best Buy** —*M.S. (11/1/2005)*

Walnut Crest 2001 Shiraz (Rapel Valley) $6. Floral and creamy, with lively fruit and fairly powerful oak. Without having read the label you'd be hard pressed to peg this as Shiraz, but it does taste like a perfectly acceptable everyday red with clean red fruit, some spice and pepper, and even some woody notes and tannins. **83** —*M.S. (7/1/2003)*

WILLIAM COLE

William Cole 2004 Alto Vuelo Cabernet Sauvignon-Carmenère (Casablanca Valley) $13. Heavily roasted aromas of popcorn and hot earth eventually yield to coffee but never unmask much fruit. The palate does carry some plum and berry, but the acid level seems elevated. Aloof and hard to process. Seventy percent Cabernet Sauvignon with 30% Carmenère. **83** —*M.S. (10/1/2006)*

YALI

Yali 2001 Cabernet Sauvignon (Maipo Valley) $6. Cassis, cherry, and plum fruit gets a boost from the leathery, mouth-coating tannins, while ancillary notes of vanilla, tomato, and chocolate stir interest. Among basic Cabs, this is a good one. **86 Best Buy** —*M.S. (3/1/2004)*

Yali 2002 Chardonnay (Rapel Valley) $6. Soft honeysuckle, pear and apple aromas are nice enough, and the mouth is fairly full, with zesty fruit supported by oak that turns a bit coconutty. Tasty and fleshy. **85 Best Buy** —*M.S. (3/1/2004)*

Yali 2001 Merlot (Maipo Valley) $6. The nose isn't great at first: There are green tobacco notes and a mild sourness. Things improve with time, however, and the wine deals adequate to good plum, berry and chocolate flavors. Fairly racy and weighty, yet not refined. **84** —*M.S. (8/1/2004)*

Yali 2001 Syrah (Maipo Valley) $6. The strawberry notes on the nose are sweet and candied more so than refined or classy. Flavors of plum and cassis are good enough, while the finish is heavy and round. It falls off at the end, however, failing to hold its grip. **84** —*M.S. (8/1/2004)*

YELCHO

Yelcho 2003 Reserva Carmenère (Maipo Valley) $12. Blends herbal notes with super-ripe plum and carob flavors in an easy-drinking, medium-bodied wine. Falls off a bit on the finish, but as a weekday burger wine, it's fine. **85** *(2/1/2006)*

Yelcho 2005 Chardonnay (Rapel Valley) $7. Chunky citrus and grapefruit aromas greet you. The palate offers basic but heavy pink grapefruit flavors, while the finish is sweet and ponderous. Not much acidity and flat in terms of feel. **81** —*M.S. (10/1/2006)*

Yelcho 2003 Reserva Merlot (Maipo Valley) $11. Quite herbal, bordering on out-right vegetal. Yes, there's black plum and carob flavors mixed in, but overall it seems a bit stewy and rooty. Not Merlot in its best form. **81** —*M.S. (7/1/2006)*

Yelcho 2005 Reserva Sauvignon Blanc (Casablanca Valley) $12. Loaded with fruit, this grassy, grapefruity version of Sauvignon Blanc has plenty of spine and brightness, without ever getting overly acidic. A blend of four clones that's made entirely in stainless steel. **87** *(2/1/2006)*

CHILE

France

France is the source of some of the greatest wines in the world, but has also been the source of some of the worst. Despite a labeling system that is often confusing to many outside of France, French wine still gives the greatest pleasure of any wine-producing region. The style of French wine echoes that of the French themselves—elegant, well-dressed, showing an appreciation for the good things of life but never to excess. French wines go best with food, never overpowering either in flavor or in alcohol, always well-mannered, often beautiful.

The fact that, today, the quality of even the least-expensive French wine has improved impressively, means that there is a whole new range of wines open to wine drinkers.

All these qualities make it worthwhile to spend some time to get to know French wine and to appreciate its many facets. The country produces all styles of wine, from the cool wines of the Loire Valley, to the stylish whites of Alsace, through the classics of Bordeaux and Burgundy, to the more powerful, muscular offerings of the Rhône, to the warm wines of Languedoc and Roussillon, suffused with sun. And, of course, there are the great Champagnes.

In a world of international brands, where origin doesn't matter, France offers an alternative ethos. There is much talk of terroir, of the place and the culture from which a wine comes. It makes every wine different, makes many of them special. There is no homogeneity here.

France is an ordered country, and despite the seeming chaos of French wine, there is order in the system. Wines come from places, and these places are designated appellations. An appellation—*appellation contrôlée* on a wine label—is not a guarantee of quality. It is a guarantee of origin, and a guarantee that the wine has

Cabernet Sauvignon grapes in a vineyard at Château Pichon-Longueville-Baron, Pauillac, Gironde, France.

been made following certain rules specifying grape varieties, soil, planting, yields, and winemaking. The wine has also passed a sensory test which approves its style and its typicity for the appellation.

There are nearly 280 appellations in France, ranging from the huge—Bordeaux appellation, or Champagne—to the tiny, single-vineyard appellations of Coulée de Serrant in the Loire Valley and Romanée-Conti in Burgundy. There are regional appellations, there are district appellations, and there are appellations which cover only one commune.

A good example of this hierarchy is in Burgundy. The main appellation of the region is plain and simple: red and white, Bourgogne Rouge or Bourgogne Blanc. Climbing up the hierarchy are district appellations such as Chablis, for white wines, Mâcon for white and red wines, Côte de Beaune for reds, and so on.

Rising again in quality while the area of the appellation gets smaller are village appellations: Vougeot, Auxey-Duresse, Pommard, Nuits-St-Georges. In these villages, certain superior vineyards are designated premier cru—and you will find the name of the vineyard on the label. At the top of the quality heap are the single-vineyard appellations, the Grand Cru: Clos de Vougeot being perhaps the most famous.

There is one other category of wine which is in some ways the most interesting and exciting: Vin de Pays. These are everyday, ready-to-drink wines that offer some of the best values in the world. The labels, unlike appellation wines, will show grape varieties. Coming generally from the warm south of France, the wines will be warm, ripe, and fruity. The best-known example is Vin de Pays d'Oc.

FRANCE

Having established some of the ground rules for French wine, let's examine the fascinations of the different regions in more detail.

By far the largest, the most important, and one of the best regions, both for great wines and for bargains, is Bordeaux. Great reds from the great chateaus are what make the headlines, but Bordeaux is so big, that there is plenty of choice. Appellations with the name Côtes in the title are always worth seeking out, as are the white wines (yes, Bordeaux makes whites, both dry and sweet). And the general level of quality has improved dramatically. The reds are fruity, but never over-alcoholic, always with a layer of tannin that makes them great food wines. The whites are fresh, the best with wood flavors to give complexity. They may all be called "chateau this," "chateau that," but that's simply a way of saying that many Bordeaux wines come from one individual property.

Cabernet Sauvignon, Merlot, and Cabernet Franc are the main red grapes; Sauvignon Blanc and Sémillon are the main whites. But most Bordeaux is not a single varietal wine—it is more often a blend, which makes these wines more than the sum of their individual parts.

Burgundy is the other big French wine. It is a fifth the size of the Bordeaux region, and produces correspondingly more expensive wines, with fewer bargains, and more disappointments. The best way to buy Burgundy is to follow the best producers, and reliable reviews from buying guides or wine magazines. If you take that advice, the most seductive wines (red from Pinot Noir, white from Chardonnay, always 100 percent) are in your glass. It's not just chance that the Burgundy bottle has rounded sides, the Bordeaux bottle has straight: Burgundy appeals to the senses, Bordeaux to the intellect.

Much larger in scale than Burgundy is the Rhône valley. From the alcoholic and powerful highs of Châteauneuf-du-Pape, through the dense elegance of the Syrah wines of appellations like Côte-Rôtie and Hermitage, this is red wine country. Rich and generous, these wines appeal to wine drinkers used to California reds. And, just like Bordeaux, there is also great value to be found in this region: wines labeled Côtes du Rhône. If they have a village name attached (Rasteau and Seguret are among the best), they will be that much better, even if more expensive.

Bordeaux, Burgundy, and the Rhône are the best-known wine regions of France except for Champagne.

This sparkling wine from the chalk slopes east of Paris is France's best answer to a global brand. It is the drink of celebration, of success, and the best way to drown sorrows. And, unlike the still French wines, which have been successfully copied around the world, Champagne remains inimitable, despite thousands of attempts. The combination of cool climate, chalk soil and—there's no other word for it—terroir are just so special.

As a complete contrast, there are the hot, sun-drenched vineyards of the south. Languedoc and Roussillon don't just produce tanker loads of inexpensive wine. Some areas such as Corbières, Minervois, Coteaux du Languedoc, and Côtes de Roussillon offer a magic mix of great value, history, and some fascinating herbal and fruity flavors.

After these greats, come the Loire and Alsace regions, which produce some of the greatest and most fascinating wines in France. Bordeaux and the Rhône are known for reds, Burgundy for reds and whites. The two cool-climate areas of Loire and Alsace are where the whites shine.

Alsace is unique in France in that producers are allowed to put the grape variety on the label of an appellation wine. It is also unique in that the grapes are a mix of German and French: Riesling and Gewürztraminer, Muscat and Pinot Gris. These are not light wines, but they have a fruitiness and a richness that is quite different from the German models just across the Rhine river. At the top of this list are the Alsace Grand Cru vineyards, single vineyards that can produce astonishing quality and longevity.

The Loire Valley is a complete mix. Every style of wine can be found along its six-hundred-mile length. The greatest styles are the Sauvignon Blanc of Sancerre and Pouilly-Fumé, the models for Sauvignon Blanc around the world. And the Chenin Blancs of the central Loire—the sweet wines of Vouvray and Anjou—have a poise and acidity which allows them to age for decades, yet be fresh when young. The dry Chenins of Savennières are the purest expression of their granite soil to be found. Finally, to complete the mix are the reds of Chinon and Bourgueil and the fresh, easy whites of Muscadet.

It's obvious from this brief list that France has variety, in profusion perhaps, but it does mean that there is never a dull moment when reaching for a bottle of French wine. If your wish is to have the same, safe bottle of wine every day, then non-European brands are the better option.

FRANCE

A. SOUTIRAN

A. Soutiran NV Grande Cru Blanc de Blancs Champagne Blend (Champagne) $45. 91 —*P.G. (12/1/2000)*

A. Soutiran 1995 Grande Cru Brut Champagne Blend (Champagne) $60. 90 *(12/1/2000)*

ABARBANEL

Abarbanel 2001 Estate Bottled Chardonnay (Vin de Pays de L'Aude) $14. Melon and peach aromas start out fine but lose clarity. Citrus flavors that aren't quite full precede mild lemon and banana on the tail end. Nondescript and turns hot at the end. Kosher. **81** —*M.S. (9/1/2003)*

Abarbanel 1999 Estate Bottled Merlot (Languedoc) $10. Once the sulfur note blows off this young wine, the tart berry and cherry aromas and flavors wear cocoa and tobacco accents. On the tongue an even palate-feel and smooth texture please, and decent acidity supports the fruit. **84** *(4/1/2001)*

Abarbanel 2002 Old Vines Red Blend (Beaujolais-Villages) $12. Fruity and fun, with plum, cherry, raspberry, and herb flavors that go down easily. Soft, supple, and light textured, the wine shows its terroir well, finishing with a bright edge. **87** —*J.M. (4/3/2004)*

Abarbanel 2002 White Shiraz Shiraz (Vin de Pays de L'Aude) $9. Abarbanel sells itself short by calling this "White Shiraz," which would imply it's like White Zin—simple and sweet. But it's not. In fact, it tastes bone dry, bright, and fresh, with zippy lemon, herb, grapefruit, and cherry notes. Quite mineral-like on the finish. The back label reveals it's really Syrah rosé from France, but the front label implies it's from Australia. Clearly the marketing folks are confused. Kosher. **86** —*J.M. (4/3/2004)*

Abarbanel 2002 Syrah (Vin de Pays de L'Aude) $13. Somewhat smoky upfront, with a blend of black cherry, blackberry, licorice, and herb flavors. It's fairly herbaceous as well, finishing with moderate length. Kosher. **84** —*J.M. (4/3/2004)*

Abarbanel 2001 Estate Bottled Syrah (Vin de Pays de L'Aude) $13. Fat and pumped up, with raw berry fruit that's rough and ready. Black plum and cherry flavors seem to pick up some mint character, and there's coffee on the finish. There's also some fierce, grippy tannins that grab and don't let go. And for that, it takes a large step backward. A kosher offering. **83** —*M.S. (9/1/2003)*

Abarbanel 2003 Kosher Syrah Syrah (Vin de Pays de L'Aude) $14. This medium-bodied wine boasts aromas of leather and sour cherries, then adds grape and dried-fruit flavors. Finishes short. **83** —*J.C. (4/1/2006)*

ABBOTTS

Abbotts 2002 Zephyr Chardonnay (Limoux) $36. This Chardonnay from the coolest vineyards in the Languedoc has New World wood flavors without quite enough weight of fruit. The spice and toast are great, and the wine certainly is finely structured, but the fruit is lost somewhere along the way. **86** —*R.V. (12/31/2006)*

Abbotts 2000 Boreas Rhône Red Blend (Coteaux du Languedoc) $27. It's rare to find a Languedoc wine that is being released after six years. So it's worth relishing the ripe but mature flavors, meaty and full-bodied. The primary fruits have gone, leaving a mellifluous, velvety wine, finishing with vanilla and cream. **91 Editors' Choice** —*R.V. (12/31/2006)*

Abbotts 1999 Cumulo Nimbus Rhône Red Blend (Minervois) $36. An impressively concentrated wine, now maturing well, with flavors of herbs, lavender, and chocolate, very ripe tannins and spice from the American wood aging. Think of this as Cornas in Languedoc—the power is similar. **91** —*R.V. (12/31/2006)*

Abbotts 2005 Orthis Rhône White Blend (Coteaux du Languedoc) $13. A white blend dominated by Grenachem, this is soft and open, oily in texture, with white pear flavors. It is a full-bodied wine layered with some wood flavors, from vineyards near the Mediterranean. **86** —*R.V. (12/31/2006)*

Abbotts 1998 Cumulo Nimbus Shiraz (Minervois) $35. 91 —*M.M. (11/1/2000)*

Abbotts 2000 Cumulus Syrah (Minervois) $17. After the complex, varietally true bouquet of smoked meat, plum, and herbal-floral notes, this wine doesn't deliver quite the same wealth of flavor. Lean and high in acidity,

it finishes with tea-like tannins. Pretty on the nose, but lacks charm on the palate. **85** —*J.C. (11/15/2005)*

AGRAPART & FILS

Agrapart & Fils NV Blanc de Blancs Brut Champagne Blend (Champagne) $23. This wine is made from grapes harvested from grand cru vineyards in Avize, Oger, Cramant, and Oiry at the northern end of the Côte des Blancs. It has weight and richness along with acidity and crisp fruit. The aftertaste is almost sweet from the relatively high dosage. **88** —*R.V. (12/1/2002)*

Agrapart & Fils 1995 L'Avizoise Blanc de Blancs Brut Champagne Blend (Champagne) $53. This is made from old vines with an average age of 55 years, growing in Avize. The 100% wood aging gives it richness and complexity. But it is still young, and this is the style of Champagne, balancing ripeness, white fruits, toast, and acidity, that will age well for the next 10 years and beyond. **92** —*R.V. (12/1/2002)*

Agrapart & Fils 2000 Minéral Blanc de Blancs Brut Chardonnay (Champagne) $50. A richly soft, creamy wine, dominated by flavors of white currants and chives, this is full-bodied and still young. There is enough ripe acidity and full-flavored fruit to see it develop well over five years. **90** —*R.V. (11/1/2006)*

AILE D'ARGENT

Aile d'Argent 2005 Barrel Sample Bordeaux White Blend (Bordeaux Blanc) $NA. The white of Château Mouton-Rothschild, this is a fresh, lemony wine that veers to fat, but has attractive acidity that lifts it. **87** —*R.V. (6/21/2006)*

ALAIN GRAILLOT

Alain Graillot 1999 La Guiraude Syrah (Crozes-Hermitage) $NA. Alain Graillot, chemical industry executive turned farmer, is showing how good Crozes-Hermitage really can be. The 1999 vintage of his special cuvée, La Guiraude, is a powerful, but bright wine, full of red fruits and firm tannins and balancing acidity. Raisins and rich fruit join the mixture that goes to make an immediately enticing wine, but one that should age over the next 10 years. **92** —*R.V. (6/1/2002)*

ALAIN POULET

Alain Poulet NV Sparkling Blend (Clairette de Die Méthode Dioise Ancestrale) $12. 84 —*S.H. (12/15/2000)*

ALAIN VOGE

Alain Voge 2003 Fleur de Crussol Rhône White Blend (Saint-Péray) $51. Voge has a sure touch with the red wines, but this white is evidently a work in progress. On the plus side, it's broad in the mouth and reasonably rich. The downside is that it's perilously low in acidity. Flavors similarly divide, with pear and lemon notes but also a warm, buttery finish. **84** —*J.C. (11/15/2006)*

ALBERT BICHOT

Albert Bichot 2002 Chardonnay (Criots-Bâtard-Montrachet) $250. A beautifully proportioned wine, which is full of ethereal flowery aromas, crisp, fresh fruit, and just a touch of toast. It is so delicious to drink now that it is easy to forget it could age well over 7 years or more. **92** —*R.V. (9/1/2004)*

Albert Bichot 2003 Domaine du Pavillon Les Charmes Premier Cru Chardonnay (Meursault) $76. A blockbuster of a wine, with plenty of toast and flavors of sweet green plums. There is lively acidity at the end, which leaves a crisp, green aftertaste. **92** —*R.V. (9/1/2005)*

Albert Bichot 2003 Domaine Long-Depaquit Grand Cru Les Vaudésirs Chardonnay (Chablis) $NA. For a Chablis, this is no lightweight. But it does have a great flavor of green plums and layers of minerality to go with its richness. And it has great acidity to give it a lift and a fresh aftertaste. **90** —*R.V. (12/31/2006)*

Albert Bichot 2003 Domaine Long-Depaquit Les Vaucopins Premier Cru Chardonnay (Chablis) $NA. This full-flavored wine still has a fine crispness and fresh acidity. There are layers of toast on the pure green fruits. The aftertaste is delicious, fresh and crisp. **88** —*R.V. (12/31/2006)*

Albert Bichot 2003 Domaine du Clos Frantin Pinot Noir (Clos Vougeot) $NA.

This fine wine combines the new wood and modern fruit style of Bichot with the classic power of Clos de Vougeot. Toast and black fruits combine to make a wine which will develop slowly, giving ripe and powerful flavors along the way. **90** —*R.V. (12/31/2006)*

Albert Bichot 2003 Domaine du Clos Frantin Pinot Noir (Echezeaux) $130. From one of the greatest Pinot Noir vineyards in Burgundy, this is a huge, rich wine, finely structured and with great aging potential. Powerful black fruit dominates this wine, supported by dry tannins and a layer of new wood. Very firm and complex. **93** —*R.V. (9/1/2005)*

Albert Bichot 2002 Domaine du Clos Frantin Echézeaux Pinot Noir (Echezeaux) $125. A lean, serious wine with firm tannins but which has a slight hollowness at the center. Fresh fruit make it a pleasant, but not intense drink. **84** —*R.V. (9/1/2004)*

Albert Bichot 2002 Domaine du Pavillon Aloxe-Corton Clos des Maréchaudes Premier Cru Pinot Noir (Aloxe-Corton) $52. A light, fresh wine with soft, raspberry flavors and gentle tannins. Well-made but it is not for the long term **84** —*R.V. (9/1/2004)*

Albert Bichot 2003 Domaine du Pavillon Clos des Maréchaudes Pinot Noir (Corton) $100. Part of the Les Maréchaudes vineyard is grand cru Corton, while the rest is simply premier cru—go figure. It just means terroir. This wine, from the grand cru portion, is dense and tannic, typical of the wine and the vineyard. There is great juicy fruit under the tannins. An ager. **92** —*R.V. (9/1/2005)*

Albert Bichot 1996 Millennium Cuvée Pinot Noir (Gevrey-Chambertin) $29. 93 *(11/15/1999)*

ALBERT MANN

Albert Mann NV Brut Sparkling Blend (Crémant d'Alsace) $22. From this quality producer, known for his grand cru wines from Schlossberg and Hengst, this is a crisp, beautiful wine that shines with fruit, structure and liveliness. It is delicate, elegant, and a great apéritif wine. **90** —*R.V. (6/1/2006)*

ALBERT PIC

Albert Pic 1997 Montmains Premier Cru White Blend (Chablis) $33. 87 —*M.S. (10/1/1999)*

ALFRED GRATIEN

Alfred Gratien NV Brut Champagne Blend (Champagne) $50. A very lean, dry style that focuses on its acidity and green fruits. This makes it a style that needs good bottle aging—the sample tasted was too young. But for those who like dry, crisp Champagnes, this is beautifully made. **88** —*R.V. (12/1/2005)*

Alfred Gratien NV Cuvée Paradis Brut Rosé Champagne Blend (Champagne) $110. Onion-skin color leads to a wine that is packed with deep fruit flavors. Considerably dry but a great food wine, with good acidity and ability to age well in bottle. The sample tasted was too young, and needed at least a year's aging. **90 Cellar Selection** —*R.V. (12/1/2005)*

ALPHONSE MELLOT

Alphonse Mellot 2002 Edmond Sauvignon Blanc (Sancerre) $50. Named after Alphonse Mellot's son, this beautifully crafted top cuvée is produced from old vines, yielding a full body with a touch of wood that doesn't mask the fresh acidity, just softens it. And still the fruit remains taut with fine, intense grapefruit flavors. **91** —*R.V. (8/1/2006)*

ALTER EGO DE PALMER

Alter Ego de Palmer 2005 Barrel Sample Bordeaux Blend (Margaux) $NA. The other wine produced at Château Palmer is appropriately named. While the chateau wine has the opulence, this has delicacy and a grace that is immensely attractive. **91** —*R.V. (6/1/2006)*

ANDRÉ ET EDMOND FIGEAT

André et Edmond Figeat 2005 Les Chaumiennes Sauvignon Blanc (Pouilly-Fumé) $18. A very minerally wine, with white flower aromas and grapefruit flavors. This is such pure Sauvignon, it's just a joy to taste the ripe fruits, the freshness, and bubbling flavors. **90** —*R.V. (8/1/2006)*

ANDRE ET MIREILLE TISSOT

Andre et Mireille Tissot 1995 Brut Sparkling Blend (Crémant de Jura) $24. A ripe, creamy, toasty wine which has some mature oxidation that enhances the wine. Shows that Jura's sparkling wines have the ability to age. But do enjoy it this year—it won't age further. **89** —*R.V. (6/1/2006)*

Andre et Mireille Tissot 1996 Extra Brut Sparkling Blend (Crémant de Jura) $NA. A bone dry, very crisp wine that certainly needed the bottle aging to soften the acidity. This is definitely a food-friendly sparkling wine; needs some fresh asparagus or shellfish to balance the powerful layers of acidity. **87** —*R.V. (6/1/2006)*

ANDRE LORENTZ

Andre Lorentz 2003 Cuvée Particuliere Riesling (Alsace) $11. Another excellent value in Alsace Riesling. Lorentz's wine offers floral, citrus, and clove aromas to go with flavors of citrus and powdered stone. It's crisp and clean versus large and mouthfilling, with a refreshing acidity to the finish. **87 Best Buy** —*J.C. (11/1/2005)*

ANTONIN RODET

Antonin Rodet 2004 Chardonnay (Meursault) $43. A lively, rich, very fresh and crisp wine that has some of the buttery character of Meursault. This is open, easy, and generous. **88** —*R.V. (12/1/2006)*

Antonin Rodet 2001 Chardonnay (Bourgogne) $11. Subtle peach and toast scents on the nose, with pretty peach shadings on the palate that seems a little light and diffuse. Finishes short. **84** —*J.C. (10/1/2003)*

Antonin Rodet 1999 Chardonnay (Chassagne-Montrachet) $40. Apples, earth, and tangy oak are prominent in this spicy Chardonnay. Medium weight and tasty, with both a gentle creaminess and a grainy note on the tongue, it has considerable size, though not great depth. Finishes with caramel and spice notes. Drink now through 2005. **87** *(12/31/2001)*

Antonin Rodet 1999 Pinot Noir (Gevrey-Chambertin) $34. 89 *(1/1/2004)*

Antonin Rodet 1999 Pinot Noir (Nuits-St.-Georges) $37. Velvety yet sturdy, showing nuance and complexity, even though still youthfully tight. The dark cherry, cinnamon, and violet bouquet, and the more plummy, even mouth with its semisweet chocolate accents are solid and pleasing. Time is needed, though, to smooth out some tart notes and still-edgy tannins. The dusty cocoa and sour cherry close is dry, long, and tight. Drink 2003-2007. **88** *(12/31/2001)*

Antonin Rodet 1998 Pinot Noir (Nuits-St.-Georges) $37. This is a wine that you will either find exciting and exotic or overbearing and odd. Sensuous, musky, and redolent of Asian spicebox scents, it hits you like a blast of heavy perfume. The tannins, too, are a bit overwrought, and at the moment fall quickly into a hard, dry finish. But time may unlock the secrets of this wine and reveal something spectacular. **88** —*P.G. (11/1/2002)*

Antonin Rodet 2002 Les Porêts Pinot Noir (Nuits-St.-Georges) $44. A modern, spicy style of wine, which has toast and new wood aromas. It is dark and smoky, with new wood and ripe black fruit on the palate. **89** —*R.V. (9/1/2004)*

Antonin Rodet 2002 Rue de Chaux Premier Cru Pinot Noir (Nuits-St. Georges) $57. Powerful and dark, this wine has toasty, woody flavors as well as fine, ripe tannins. It's a powerful, smooth, well-structured wine. **88** —*R.V. (9/1/2004)*

ARNOUX & FILS

Arnoux & Fils 2003 1717 Grenache-Syrah (Vacqueyras) $39. Shows a bit more suppleness and fruity intensity than Arnoux's other wines, adding hints of clove to the leather and raspberry flavors. Drink now-2012. **87** —*J.C. (11/15/2006)*

Arnoux & Fils 2003 Seigneur de Lauris Rhône Red Blend (Côtes-du-Rhône) $10. Light in color and body, with modest cherry aromas and flavors. Picks up hints of tea leaves on the finish. Drink now. **83** —*J.C. (11/15/2006)*

Arnoux & Fils 2003 Vieux Clocher Rhône Red Blend (Vacqueyras) $NA. Starts with seemingly supple leather and cherry notes, but they build to powerful tannins on the finish. A bit too drying to be completely balanced, but the tannins would cut nicely through a fatty steak. Drink now. **85** —J.C. (11/15/2006)

Arnoux & Fils 2005 Vieux Clocher Rhône White Blend (Vacqueyras) $17. A pleasant surprise, Arnoux's 2005 blanc turned out very well, boasting floral scents and rich, mouth-filling heft. A solid, chunky wine with enough nuance to keep it interesting; try with roast chicken. Drink now. **87** —J.C. (11/15/2006)

ARTHUR METZ

Arthur Metz 2003 Cuvée Anne-Laure Gewürztraminer (Alsace) $11. Drier and crisper than many Gewürzes, with grapefruit and citrus blossom aromatics that flow easily into apple and pear flavors. Clean and citrusy on the finish, picking up hints of chalk dust. **86 Best Buy** —J.C. (11/1/2005)

AUGUSTIN FLORENT

Augustin Florent NV Syrah (Vin de Pays d'Oc) $9. What flavors could be discerned on the closed, mute nose were akin to wet socks, flea powder, curry, and tomato. Flavors are spicy, cherry, and peppery, though somewhat green. Some called it "exotic"; others said "two percent fruit." Finish fades fast. **82** (10/1/2001)

BAILLY-LAPIERRE

Bailly-Lapierre 2004 Chardonnay Brut Chardonnay (Crémant de Bourgogne) $19. Herb tea and white flower aromas give this wine a fine start. The Chardonnay flavors are all there: a touch of vanilla, some almonds, and pears. Fresh and rich. Could age for a couple of years. **90** —R.V. (6/1/2006)

Bailly-Lapierre 2004 Blanc de Blancs Brut Sparkling Blend (Crémant de Bourgogne) $20. A very pure, almost linear wine with plenty of fresh acidity. There is some structure of young tannins, but the main flavors are the gooseberries, kiwis and very green apples. A fine apéritif wine. **88** —R.V. (6/1/2006)

Bailly-Lapierre NV Rosé Brut Sparkling Blend (Crémant de Bourgogne) $20. A soft, strawberry-flavored wine with an attractive salmon-pink color. The wine is fresh, clean, and easy with a light vanilla character to add complexity. The aftertaste is crisp and lively. **86** —R.V. (6/1/2006)

BALLOT MILLOT ET FILS

Ballot Millot et Fils 2004 Les Criots Chardonnay (Meursault) $49. Soft and open, this wine has the generosity and drinkability of a good village Meursault. There are flavors of quince, spice, a touch of citrus, and some vanilla. **88** —R.V. (12/1/2006)

BALMA VENITIA

Balma Venitia 2005 Des Toques Rhône Red Blend (Côtes-du-Rhône) $NA. From Les Vignerons de Beaumes de Venise, this is a cheery, light-bodied Côtes-du-Rhône. Pretty cherry flavors lack much substance but do quench a thirst. Try serving it chilled with light meals, like you might a simple Beaujolais. **83** —J.C. (11/15/2006)

Balma Venitia 2005 Terre des Farisiens Rhône Red Blend (Beaumes-de-Venise) $NA. This attempt at a more serious, ageworthy Beaumes-de-Venise rouge has resulted in a wine that's a bit hard and unyielding, with firm tannins that seem out of character for the appellation. Try after 2008, but it's a gamble. **83** —J.C. (11/15/2006)

Balma Venitia 2004 Terres du Trias Rhône Red Blend (Beaumes-de-Venise) $NA. From the local co-op, the Cave de Vignerons de Beaumes-de-Venise, this is a soft, very ripe wine filled with flavors of licorice and prune, but without any sense of heaviness. Easy to drink. **84** —J.C. (11/15/2006)

BARNAUT

Barnaut 1998 Champagne Blend (Champagne) $58. This mature, toasty wine is made by the Secondé family, grandchildren of Edmond Barnaut. It is developing attractive, roasted almond and very ripe flavors. Drink now. **86** —R.V. (11/1/2006)

BARON GASSIER

Baron Gassier 2003 Rosé Blend (Côtes de Provence) $9. A decent quaffing rosé, with a bright strawberry hue and aromas and flavors of bubblegum, cherries, and red plums. Turns herbal and slightly drying on the finish. **84** —J.C. (12/1/2004)

BARON PHILIPPE DE ROTHSCHILD

Baron Philippe de Rothschild 2000 Baron'arques Bordeaux Blend (Vin de Pays de L'Aude) $40. Very modern, with overt maple notes and plenty of black fruit aromas. The toasty, tight bouquet oozes bitter chocolate and cassis, while the firm palate yields nothing but oak-enveloped plum and cherry. Needs two years to soften. From Baron Philippe de Rothschild and several Limoux-area growers known as the Vignerons du Sieur d'Arques. **89** —M.S. (1/1/2004)

Baron Philippe de Rothschild 2002 Mouton Cadet Rouge Bordeaux Blend (Bordeaux) $8. Branded Bordeaux has a deservedly spotty reputation, but this year's Mouton Cadet aims to start turning that around. Cherries and chocolate on the nose, followed by smoky, earthy tobacco and black cherry flavors. A silky texture makes it ready to drink now. **86 Best Buy** —J.C. (6/1/2005)

Baron Philippe de Rothschild 2003 Mouton Cadet Bordeaux White Blend (Bordeaux) $8. Yes, that Mouton Cadet has been transformed into a clean fresh wine featuring notes of apple and citrus and touches of earth and herb. A blend of 50% Sémillon, 40% Sauvignon Blanc, and 10% Muscadelle. **84 Best Buy** —J.C. (6/1/2005)

Baron Philippe de Rothschild 1999 Merlot (Vin de Pays d'Oc) $10. Nice earth and whole-wheat aromas open onto subtle dark berry fruit flavors, accented by a little wood. Even on the palate; hope that your neighborhood haunt pours it. **85** —D.T. (2/1/2002)

Baron Philippe de Rothschild 1998 Baron'Arques Rhône Red Blend (Vin de Pays d'Oc) $45. The cedar, cinnamon, and cigar box aromas of this beautifully balanced red are a tell-tale mark of its Mouton heritage. It has a depth and complexity not often seen from France's south. Dried cherry, tobacco, and earth flavors flow into a long and elegant, if a bit woody, finish. This can use two years in the cellar, and joins the upper echelon of wines setting the standard for this region. **88** —M.M. (2/1/2002)

Baron Philippe de Rothschild 2000 Viognier (Vin de Pays d'Oc) $10. This is a nice sipping wine. It has pretty fruit flavors of apricots and nectarines, with a floral note, and it's dry and clean, although soft. This would be nice with fresh fruit. **85** —S.H. (10/1/2001)

Baron Philippe de Rothschild 1999 Mouton Cadet White Blend (Bordeaux) $11. A famous old brand that seems to be living off past glory, this year's edition is quite neutral in aroma and flavor; you have to work to pick out some mild herb and citrus, but it does show a nice spicy, green-peppercorn character on the finish. **81** —J.C. (3/1/2001)

BARONS EDMUND BENJAMIN DE ROTHSCHILD

Barons Edmund Benjamin de Rothschild 1998 Haut-Medoc Bordeaux Blend (Haut-Médoc) $27. This solid Bordeaux achieves a nice balance between ripe fruit and a more austere earthiness. There's a solid core of blackberry flavor and firm, broad tannins that suggest it will develop more depth with near-term cellaring. **88** —J.C. (4/1/2001)

BARTH RENÉ

Barth René 2002 Vignoble de Bennwihr Pinot Blanc (Alsace) $13. Unusually rich for a Pinot Blanc, with scents of honey, dried apricots, peaches, and dried spices giving an impression of sweetness that's balanced on the palate by bright acidity that imparts a pineapple flavor. Finishes dry, fresh, and minerally. **88 Best Buy** —J.C. (8/1/2006)

Barth René 2003 Vignoble de Bennwihr Pinot Gris (Alsace) $17. Ginger and tonic water on the nose, with pear, apple, and sweet melon flavors. Seems a touch off-dry, with licorice and candy on the finish. Spunky but feminine in style. **85** (2/1/2006)

Barth René 2003 Rebgarten Riesling (Alsace) $19. Smells and tastes a bit confected, with lime sherbet aromas vying with hints of spring flowers and talcum powder, turning a little sweet and flabby in the mouth. **83** —J.C. (8/1/2006)

BARTON & GUESTIER

Barton & Guestier 2000 Bordeaux Blend (Médoc) $10. From the great 2000 vintage, this is suitably deep, impressive wine. Wood and vanilla aromas show through to taste with sweet black currants, some sweet jelly flavors, balanced with a big, long-term aging structure. Magnol is a property in the southern Médoc, owned by Barton & Guestier. **87** —*R.V. (12/1/2004)*

Barton & Guestier 2002 Cabernet Sauvignon (Vin de Pays d'Oc) $6. This is a well-structured juicy, fruity wine. Aromas of red currants, and flavors of fresh black fruits, are balanced by firm, dry tannins and some acidity. **83** —*R.V. (12/1/2004)*

Barton & Guestier 2000 French Tom Private Collection Cabernet Sauvignon (Vin de Pays d'Oc) $14. Easy does it with this pleasantly sippable Cab, which has lots to like. It's smooth and velvety in the mouth, and the soft texture carries nice flavors of blackberries that have been pureed into a creamy pulp. Finishes dry and a little tannic. **85** —*S.H. (1/1/2002)*

Barton & Guestier 2002 Chardonnay (Vin de Pays d'Oc) $6. There are sweet vanilla aromas, along with aromas of green plums. This is a soft, creamy wine, with just a touch of greeness, and a full, creamy texture. **82** —*R.V. (12/1/2004)*

Barton & Guestier 2002 Chardonnay (Mâcon-Villages) $9. A fresh, but full-bodied wine, which has aromas of citrus and sawn wood. It is ripe, smooth, with vanilla layers sandwiched between green fruits and white currants. This makes an attractive food wine for fish and white meat dishes. **84** —*R.V. (12/1/2004)*

Barton & Guestier 2000 Chardonnay Saint-Louis Tradition 2000 Chardonnay (Mâcon-Villages) $13. A simple, pretty little Chardonnay, brimming with sweet apple and peach flavors. Drinks dry and crisp, with a pleasant mouthfeel and a good finish. Not complex, but a good dry wine for the price. **86** —*S.H. (1/1/2002)*

Barton & Guestier 1998 Reserve Chardonnay (Vin de Pays d'Oc) $10. 86 Best Buy *(5/1/2000)*

Barton & Guestier 2001 Tradition Chardonnay (Pouilly-Fuissé) $9. This is a good price for a wine from this appellation. It's drier and earthier than the typical New World Chard, with peach flavors and crisp acidity. **85 Best Buy** —*S.H. (12/1/2004)*

Barton & Guestier 1999 Tradition Saint-Louis Chardonnay (Mâcon-Villages) $8. 82 —*D.T. (2/1/2002)*

Barton & Guestier 2001 Tradition Chenin Blanc (Vouvray) $NA. This is a pleasing wine that is simple and refreshing. The stone fruit flavors have an oiliness that is cleansed by the acidity on the finish. A nice picnic wine. **84** *(11/15/2002)*

Barton & Guestier 2001 Tradition Gamay (Beaujolais-Villages) $8. This wine is fading a bit, but still offers some pleasure. It's plump and supple in the mouth, with flavors of raisined black cherries and leather. **83** —*J.C. (11/15/2003)*

Barton & Guestier 2002 Gamay Noir (Beaujolais) $9. Aromas of sweet strawberries make this an immediately attractive wine. It is lightly colored, with flavors of fresh fruit and just a hint of dryness. Soft and easy, it is almost like alcoholic strawberry juice. **82** —*R.V. (12/1/2004)*

Barton & Guestier 2002 Melon (Muscadet Sèvre Et Maine) $9. Typical crisp, appley aromas set the scene for a wine with fresh, light, lively fruit and crisp acidity. **81** —*R.V. (12/1/2004)*

Barton & Guestier 2002 Merlot (Vin de Pays d'Oc) $7. Smells a bit funky and meaty, and turns watery in the mouth, with thin flavors of cherries. **82** —*S.H. (9/1/2004)*

Barton & Guestier 1999 Merlot (Vin de Pays d'Oc) $7. This Merlot's nose shows stewed fruit, plus some oak and metallic notes. In the mouth and on the finish, expect lots of green herb-tobacco, plus a little mineral dust. **82** —*D.T. (2/1/2002)*

Barton & Guestier 2000 French Tom Private Collection Merlot (Vin de Pays d'Oc) $14. Not as rich as B&G's Cabernet, which was co-released at the same time. This wine is dark, with earthy aromas, and turns tough and tannic in the mouth, with watered down flavors. **83** —*S.H. (1/1/2002)*

Barton & Guestier 1998 Reserve Merlot (Vin de Pays d'Oc) $10. 86 *(5/1/2000)*

Barton & Guestier 2000 Saint-Louis Beaujolais Tradition Red Blend (Beaujolais) $13. Simple and direct, a bubble-gummy wine with Lifesaver fruity flavors and a great big burst of fresh acidity. Dry, with soft, easy tannins and a direct appeal, which is what Beaujolais is all about. **84** —*S.H. (1/1/2002)*

Barton & Guestier 2001 Rhône Red Blend (Côtes-du-Rhône) $9. This is an earthy, perfumed style of wine, full of sweet, juicy fruit and layers of dry tannins. For a basic Côtes du Rhône, this is a full-bodied rich wine. **84** —*R.V. (12/1/2004)*

Barton & Guestier 2001 Tradition Rhône Red Blend (Châteauneuf-du-Pape) $9. Attractive, lightweight wine with flavors of red plums and damsons. The tannins are soft, easy, and the wine is ready to drink. **83** —*R.V. (3/1/2004)*

Barton & Guestier 2000 Tradition Rhône Red Blend (Côtes-du-Rhône) $NA. The aromas of white pepper and blackberry fruit are simple but enjoyable. The black plum flavors mix with char and more spice to finish juicy and pleasant. A good by-the-glass red. **85** *(11/15/2002)*

Barton & Guestier 2001 Founder's Collection Sauvignon Blanc (Bordeaux) $10. Aromas of sweet fresh peas accentuate the slightly herbal minerality of the nose. The finish is crisp and light with grassy, herbal flavors. **84** *(11/15/2002)*

Barton & Guestier 2002 Shiraz (Vin de Pays d'Oc) $6. A deep purple colored wine, with violet and lavender perfumes. There are firm tannins, and flavors of sweet, black fruits, balanced with acidity. The wine is just spoilt by a touch of leaness to finish. **82** —*R.V. (12/1/2004)*

Barton & Guestier 2001 Syrah (Vin de Pays d'Oc) $7. 83 *(11/15/2002)*

Barton & Guestier 1998 Tradition White Blend (Pouilly-Fuissé) $17. 86 *(5/1/2000)*

BAUCHET PÈRE ET FILS

Bauchet Père et Fils NV Brut Sélection Champagne Blend (Champagne) $NA. Cheesy aromas create a bouquet that lacks clarity. Quite sharp and citrusy in the mouth, with orange peel and an excessive tang. Satisfactory, but with serious holes in its fiber. **81** —*M.S. (12/15/2003)*

Bauchet Père et Fils NV Premier Cru Brut Sélection Champagne Blend (Champagne) $35. Toasty and dry, with notes of lemon meringue. Lean, clean, and tart, with some apple flavors and a bit of caramel to sweeten things up. Turns slightly mushroomy toward the end, where it begins to show some cracks in its veneer. **89** —*M.S. (12/15/2003)*

Bauchet Père et Fils NV Premier Cru Reserve Brut Champagne Blend (Champagne) $40. Unique bubble gum, anise, and butter scents on the nose, followed by a wine that tastes reminiscent of white gumdrops. Still, it's frothy, crisp, and clean on the finish and while different, pretty good. **85** —*J.C. (12/1/2004)*

Bauchet Père et Fils NV Sélection Roland Bouchet Champagne Blend (Champagne) $33. Waxy on the nose, with hints of wild flower that turn the bouquet mildly sweet. Pink grapefruit and tangerine flavors lead toward a light, easy, low-voltage finish. Tangy and juice-like, with little heft. **83** —*M.S. (12/15/2003)*

BEAUMONT DES CRAYÈRES

Beaumont des Crayères 1997 Fleur de Prestige Champagne Blend (Champagne) $45. A fine, mature, light, and poised wine which is great for an apéritif. The blend of 60% Chardonnay and 40% Pinot Noir is fresh, floral, just a touch toasty. Great balance from one of the top wines from this excellent cooperative. **90** —*R.V. (12/1/2004)*

Beaumont des Crayères 1998 Nostalgie Brut Champagne Blend (Champagne) $NA. This Chardonnay-dominated wine (70% to just 30% Pinot Noir) is the top cuvée from the quality-conscious Beaumont des Crayères cooperative. It is a well-balanced wine, with some toast from barrique vinification. It's ripe, already quite soft, and ready to drink. Not available in the U.S. **90** —*R.V. (11/1/2006)*

BELLEFONTAINE

Bellefontaine 1999 Cabernet Sauvignon (Vin de Pays d'Oc) $7. Medium-weight and balanced, this Cabernet opens with aromas of earth and mixed berries, complicated by a little unsweetened chocolate. Oak and red berries round out the palate. On the finish, more oak, plus a green wood-herb note. **83** —*D. T. (2/1/2002)*

BERNARD CHAVE

Bernard Chave 1999 Tête de Cuvée Syrah (Crozes-Hermitage) $21. Tart fruit, pine, rose, tar, and nuts are among the descriptors used for this lean, taut wine's complex bouquet. A chalky element and cedar notes surround the blueberry fruit core, and it finishes with prickly tannins, leather, and pepper. Drink 2003-2008. **88** *(11/1/2001)*

BESSERAT DE BELLEFON

Besserat de Bellefon NV Cuvée des Moines Blanc de Blancs Brut Champagne Blend (Champagne) $NA. 83 *(1/1/2004)*

Besserat de Bellefon NV Cuvée des Moines Brut Champagne Blend (Champagne) $32. 82 *(1/1/2004)*

Besserat de Bellefon NV Cuvée des Moines Brut Rosé Champagne Blend (Champagne) $45. 84 *(1/1/2004)*

BILLECART-SALMON

Billecart-Salmon NV Brut Rosé Champagne Blend (Champagne) $68. A bone-dry but delicious wine, with red fruits and a beautiful onion-skin color that just hints at rosé. Lovely acidity completes the serious and highly enjoyable wine. **92 Editors' Choice** —*R. V. (12/1/2005)*

Billecart-Salmon NV Réserve Brut Champagne Blend (Champagne) $45. The tiny mousse tells a lot about the quality of this impressive Champagne. It is quite full in style, with flavors of white currants and a rich, but still bone-dry aftertaste. It is a perfect food Champagne, with structure and a good tension between richness and elegance. **92** —*R. V. (12/1/2005)*

BLANC DE LYNCH-BAGES

Blanc de Lynch-Bages 2003 Bordeaux White Blend (Bordeaux) $35. A powerfully ripe wine, packed with flavors of honeyed fruit, layers of vanilla, and delicious richness. This white, from a small parcel in the Lynch-Bages vineyard, is beautifully made in a modern style. **92** —*R. V. (6/1/2005)*

BLASON DE BOURGOGNE

Blason de Bourgogne NV Cuvée Brut Champagne Blend (Crémant de Bourgogne) $10. This is ripe, smooth, and toasty, with caramel and green fruit flavors. There is some sweetness, coming from the ripeness of the fruit, but the acidity gives the wine a fine balance. **87** —*R. V. (6/1/2006)*

BOIZEL

Boizel 1998 Brut Champagne Blend (Champagne) $85. This is ripe, open wine with layers of Pinot Noir showing richness and lively acidity. It is soft, with white fruit and a pure, straightforward character. Maturing fast. **89** —*R. V. (11/1/2006)*

Boizel 1995 Joyau de France Champagne Blend (Champagne) $140. The special cuvée of Boizel, first made in 1961, is a Pinot Noir-dominant wine, giving an extra richness to the smooth, creamy, lightly toasty, flavors. It is powerful and rich, but with a touch of softness that leaves a flavor of orange peel in the mouth. **88** —*R. V. (11/1/2006)*

BOLLINGER

Bollinger 1996 La Grande Année Brut Champagne Blend (Champagne) $90. True to the Bolly style, this is a large-scaled Champagne, with outsized aromas and flavors of mushrooms and toast layered over a rich baked-apple core. The mouthfeel is lush; the finish long. Decadent enough that there's no need for additional age. **93** —*J.C. (12/15/2003)*

Bollinger 1992 La Grande Année Brut Champagne Blend (Champagne) $90. Mature caramel, soy sauce, meat, and apple butter notes open this medium-full, creamy, rich Champagne. In the mouth, tasters were quick to identify the earth, leather, and red plum flavors that come from this wine's healthy dose of Pinot Noir. Finishes long and dry, with hints of cherry and yeast. **89** *(12/15/2001)*

Bollinger 1996 R.D. Extra Brut Champagne Blend (Champagne) $190. The Bollinger R.D. (recently disgorged) is Bollinger's answer to a prestige cuvée. Keeping the wine long on its lees (this was disgorged in June 2006) yields a wine that is very much in the rich Bollinger style. This is a beautifully balanced wine, with acidity, intensity, and structure in perfect harmony. It is still so young, and certainly could age for years. **97 Cellar Selection** —*R. V. (11/1/2006)*

Bollinger 1990 R.D. Extra Brut Champagne Blend (Champagne) $150. An excellent balance of earthy, meaty flavors and bright, racy acidity. Its bead is fine; its mousse, creamy. Tangy lemon and grapefruit flavors liven up the finish. **90** *(12/15/2002)*

Bollinger 1988 R.D. Extra Brut Champagne Blend (Champagne) $150. This mature wine opens with rich apple and caramel aromas. The bead is excellent, the mouthfeel still taut and bracingly dry, showing the high acidity seen in many 1988s. Displays bitter-citrus, herb, and apple-skin flavors and a long lemon and spice finish with a burnt matchstick element. Tasters noted the dichotomy between the seductive, ripe nose and lean palate. This may need even more time. **89** *(12/15/2001)*

Bollinger NV Special Cuvée Brut Champagne Blend (Champagne) $45. Dusty and chalky on the nose, this opens up on the palate into a full-bodied style, rich and creamy yet packed with minerality. Despite the heft, there's enough crispness to the finish to keep it beautifully balanced. **90 Editors' Choice** —*J.C. (12/1/2004)*

Bollinger NV Special Cuvée Brut Champagne Blend (Champagne) $45. Yeasty and layered with streaks of citrus and stone, saturated with fresh bread-dough scents and bursting with fresh fruit, it hits the palate like a middle linebacker and holds it in a bulldog's grip. Flavor flavor flavor, through a confident, exceptionally long finish. **92 Editors' Choice** —*P.G. (12/15/2002)*

Bollinger NV Special Cuvée Brut Champagne Blend (Champagne) $50. The Bollinger style is always rich, food-friendly, and impressive. This wine is all of those things, with power and intensity of flavor along with ripe fruit, a layer of toastiness, and a dry aftertaste. This is a style of wine that can take even more bottle aging. **94 Editors' Choice** —*R. V. (12/1/2005)*

BONNAIRE

Bonnaire 1997 Blanc de Blancs Brut Champagne Blend (Champagne) $48. A great, pure-flavored wine, full of soft, toasty flavors, layers of honey and nuts, and a fine citrus streak. This is a delicious example of good Chardonnay that marries structure and acidity with richness and elegance. **93 Cellar Selection** —*R. V. (12/1/2002)*

BONNY DOON

Bonny Doon 2001 Heart of Darkness Red Blend (Madiran) $18. Dark indeed, of color and soul. This brooding, sensual wine has cherries, plums, black pepper, and Provencal herbs flowing through its veins. To say it's fruity, tannic, and dry misses the point, which is Latin complexity. This Mediterranean red runs deep. **91** —*S.H. (2/1/2004)*

BORIE LA VITARELLE

Borie la Vitarelle 2004 Les Terres Blanches Grenache-Syrah (Saint-Chinian) $15. A blend of Grenache and Syrah from the biodynamic Borie la Vitarelle estate. It's a typically ripe southern wine, but with a good tannic structure that underlies the raisin and blackberry flavors. **86** —*R. V. (12/31/2006)*

Borie la Vitarelle 2005 Cuvée des Cigales Rhône Red Blend (Saint-Chinian) $11. A very southern rosé, warm and ripe, with caramel and red fruit flavors as well as a crisp burst of acidity. A blend of Syrah, Grenache, and Mourvèdre, it's a great food wine for the Mediterranean diet. Like most rosés it's a drink-now wine, as it won't improve with age. **87 Best Buy** — *R. V. (12/31/2006)*

BOSQUET DES PAPES

Bosquet des Papes 2003 Chante le Merle Vieilles Vignes Rhône Red Blend (Châteauneuf-du-Pape) $50. Named after a corner of the vineyard where blackbirds (merles) sing, this is a wine made from old vines, 80–90 years old. It is huge, dry, and very tannic at this young stage. But just wait for it to open out into its full glory of packed black fruits, and superb concentration. **94** —*R. V. (12/31/2005)*

BOUCHARD AÎNÉ & FILS

Bouchard Aîné & Fils 2001 Chardonnay (Pouilly-Fuissé) $18. Lean and focused, with a smooth texture and tart, citrusy flavors, this is a cleanly made Chardonnay built to take on the role of an apéritif. You might also try it as an accompaniment to light shellfish preparations. **86** —*J.C. (10/1/2003)*

Bouchard Aîné & Fils 2000 Chardonnay (Meursault) $35. A simple, clean, fruity wine, with apples, citrus, and herb flavors. Not complex, but clean, crisp, and showing modest oak. **85** —*J.C. (10/1/2003)*

Bouchard Aîné & Fils 1999 Chardonnay (Meursault) $35. Round and a touch creamy, this is clean and shows just enough structure to keep its butter-toast, tropical fruit, and citrus personality from getting mushy. There's plenty of oak and mineral-earth notes as well. Finishes with good length and a bit more grip thatn expected from the overall soft mouthfeel. Still, drink this sooner rather than later, now through 2004. **89** *(11/15/2001)*

Bouchard Aîné & Fils 2004 Champ Gain Premier Cru Chardonnay (Puligny-Montrachet) $67. A fresh, light, crisp wine with some good mineral overtones layered with toast. While it doesn't have great complexity, this is an attractive, citrusy wine that's ready to drink now. **88** —*R.V. (12/1/2006)*

Bouchard Aîné & Fils 2004 Le Porusot Premier Cru Chardonnay (Meursault) $63. Full and fat, this wine has pleasant white-fruit flavors. It is fresh, but rather unfocused, with toast coming through the fruit to dominate the aftertaste. **87** —*R.V. (12/1/2006)*

Bouchard Aîné & Fils 2001 Gamay (Beaujolais-Villages) $8. This fairly big, extracted Beaujolais has held up remarkably well. Cherries and rasp-berries are beginning to fade into earth and bracken, so drink up. **85 Best Buy** —*J.C. (11/15/2003)*

Bouchard Aîné & Fils 2000 Pinot Noir (Bourgogne) $11. Leafy and sour, with tart, grapefruity flavors. **80** —*J.C. (10/1/2003)*

Bouchard Aîné & Fils 1999 Pinot Noir (Pommard) $NA. There is a light hint of volatility in the nose, along with scents of cracker and cocoa. The fruit tastes of strawberries and cherries, and it is a delicate, rather frail wine, but nonetheless pleasant and nuanced. **86** —*P.G. (11/11/2002)*

Bouchard Aîné & Fils 1999 Pinot Noir (Chambolle-Musigny) $45. A fresh, generous wine, with soft fruits, good acidity, and some fine strawberry flavors and a layer of dry tannins. It may not be complex, but it is finely made, with good fruit at the end. **88** —*R.V. (11/1/2002)*

Bouchard Aîné & Fils 2002 Clos du Roi Premier Cru Pinot Noir (Beaune) $32. Flavors of ripe blackberries make this premier cru immediately attractive. It is ripe and soft, with a good sense of background tannins. **87** —*R.V. (9/1/2004)*

Bouchard Aîné & Fils 2000 Cuvée Signature Pinot Noir (Savigny-lès-Beaune) $25. A pleasant surprise from an unheralded appellation, this Savigny boasts aromas of beets and cherries but folds in added complexity in the form of leather, toast, and bacon fat. Smooth and supple in the mouth, this is ready to drink tonight. **88** —*J.C. (10/1/2003)*

Bouchard Aîné & Fils 2000 Cuvée Signature La Maziere (Fixin) Pinot Noir (Burgundy) $24. Light and lean, with meager lemon and rhubarb flavors overshadowed by dusty wood. **82** —*J.C. (10/1/2003)*

BOUCHARD PÈRE & FILS

Bouchard Père & Fils 1998 Chardonnay (Chassagne-Montrachet) $39. 87 —*P.G. (7/1/2000)*

Bouchard Père & Fils 2005 Chardonnay (Chassagne-Montrachet) $48. A wood-dominated wine, with spice and toast. The citrus and white fruit element is very much subdued. The aftertaste continues on the same theme—dry tannins from the wood. Give it a few months and the balance should be better. **88** —*R.V. (12/1/2006)*

Bouchard Père & Fils 2004 Chardonnay (Meursault) $30. Open, ripe, and generous, this sums up what is so enjoyable about Meursault, without losing sight of a more serious, structured side. But drink now; it's ready. **88** —*R.V. (12/1/2006)*

Bouchard Père & Fils 2004 Chardonnay (Montrachet) $600. This wine is deceptive. At first smell and taste, it doesn't show much—its spice and green fruit aromas are not at all obvious. It's when you roll it around your mouth, that all the layers of flavor emerge. It is powerful, rounded, but with a fine line of minerality that holds the whole wine on a knife edge. The wood is beautifully judged, the fruit just beginning to develop secondary aromas. Hold for several years. **95 Cellar Selection** —*R.V. (12/1/2006)*

Bouchard Père & Fils 2003 Beaune du Château Premier Cru Chardonnay (Beaune) $75. A blend of premier cru vineyards, this wine is fresh, with plenty of lively white fruit flavors. But there's enough richness there to balance the green flavors. **88** —*R.V. (9/1/2005)*

Bouchard Père & Fils 2003 Charmes Premier Cru Chardonnay (Meursault) $75. A rich but very fresh wine that sings of green and yellow fruit, vibrant acidity, and just a hint of wood. Charmes vineyard is one of the best-known in Meursault, and this wine certainly lives up to the meaning of the name. **90** —*R.V. (9/1/2005)*

Bouchard Père & Fils 2002 Chevalier Montrachet Chardonnay (Puligny-Montrachet) $165. A floral wine that is more attractive than powerful. The fruit floats out of acidity and crispness with hardly a sign of wood. This is going to be delicious to drink soon, within 5 years. **89** —*R.V. (9/1/2004)*

Bouchard Père & Fils 2003 Corton-Charlemagne Chardonnay (Corton-Charlemagne) $115. A wine that has the structure, freshness, and green tannins of a 2002, but the richness of a 2003. There is a great mineral character to the flavors, which gives it a steely, piercing profile that suggests great aging potential. **94** —*R.V. (9/1/2005)*

Bouchard Père & Fils 2004 La Cabotte Chardonnay (Chevalier-Montrachet) $500. This comes from high up in the Chevalier-Montrachet vineyard, from vines surrounding a small workers shed, the "cabotte." It is the better of the two bottlings from this vineyard by Bouchard, although "better" here is like differentiating between two stars on top form. It has great poise, so although the richness is there, it is shot through with acidity and citric flavors that underline the huge, ripe fruit. Age for 10 years for best results. **96** —*R.V. (12/1/2006)*

Bouchard Père & Fils 2004 Les Clous Chardonnay (Meursault) $36. This is a great Meursault that's full of round, ripe, generous fruit. It's packed with yellow fruit and kiwi flavors. Revel in its richness. This wine comes from Bouchard's own vines. **90 Editors' Choice** —*R.V. (12/1/2006)*

Bouchard Père & Fils 2004 Les Gouttes d'Or Premier Cru Chardonnay (Meursault) $84. From the Bouchard domaine, this wine is soft and ripe. There is some structure and firm acidity, but that's secondary to the luscious flavors that roll around the mouth. The wood broadens but also gives extra complexity to the wine. **92** —*R.V. (12/1/2006)*

Bouchard Père & Fils 2004 Perrières Premier Cru Chardonnay (Meursault) $90. Perrières is often described as the greatest of the premier crus of Meursault. Wines like this certainly need aging, with their structure overlying the typical opulence of Meursault. It's possible to enjoy this now, but it would be worth waiting 3–4 years at least. **91** —*R.V. (12/1/2006)*

Bouchard Père & Fils 2000 Pinot Noir (Bonnes-Mares) $120. A deliciously concentrated and powerful wine from the domaine of négociant Bouchard Père et Fils. Rich chocolate aromas and intense concentrated black fruits give a strong sense of power and richness. The fruit is rich enough to dominate the tannins. This should age magnificently—10 years at least. **96 Editors' Choice** —*R.V. (11/1/2002)*

Bouchard Père & Fils 1998 Pinot Noir (Pommard) $45. 87 —*P.G. (7/1/2000)*

Bouchard Père & Fils 2003 Beaune du Château Premier Cru Pinot Noir (Beaune) $35. Bouchard makes a blend of premier crus for this proprietary wine. It's a juicy wine packed with sweet flavors. It's very generous, ripe, and rich. **89** —*R.V. (9/1/2005)*

Bouchard Père & Fils 2003 Beaune Marconnets Premier Cru Pinot Noir (Beaune) $50. This is a big wine, powered by dusty, ripe tannins, and dense black fruit flavors. The power doesn't take away from the wine's freshness and its rich perfumes. **91** —*R.V. (9/1/2005)*

Bouchard Père & Fils 2003 Caillerets Ancienne Cuvée Carnot Premier Cru Pinot Noir (Volnay) $70. A big-hearted, big-fruited wine, which has hints of vanilla. It is hugely ripe, jammy, and powerful, but still preserves a touch of freshness. **91** —*R.V. (9/1/2005)*

Bouchard Père & Fils 2003 Clos des Chenes Premier Cru Pinot Noir (Volnay) $70. A wine from one of the best vineyards in Volnay, it offers great definition, solid tannins, and dense fruit. It is both structured and fresh, fleshed out with juicy Pinot Noir flavors. Give it time; this is going to be one delicious wine. **93** —*R.V. (9/1/2005)*

Bouchard Père & Fils 2002 Echézeaux Pinot Noir (Echezeaux) $115. A powerful wine, filled with rich, solid fruit, high tannins, and shot through with dark plums, flavors of toast, and a layer of acidity. **94** —*R.V. (9/1/2004)*

Bouchard Père & Fils 1998 La Vignee Pinot Noir (Bourgogne) $10. 86 Best Buy —*P.G. (7/1/2000)*

Bouchard Père & Fils 2002 Le Corton Pinot Noir (Corton) $67. Solid, rich wine, which is piled with tannins and beautifully crafted black fruits, acidity, and firm tannins. **94** —*R.V. (9/1/2004)*

Bouchard Père & Fils 2002 Les Cailles Premier Cru Pinot Noir (Nuits-St.-Georges) $60. A very good, elegant wine, this premier cru has beautifully ripe plum fruit accented with spice. Firm tannins suggest mid-term aging. **88** —*R.V. (9/1/2004)*

Bouchard Père & Fils 2002 Rugiens Premier Cru Pinot Noir (Pommard) $58. Huge, solid tannins give this wine great power. Concentrated ripe fruit and acidity drive through the tannins. A firm, solid wine. **90** —*R.V. (9/1/2004)*

Bouchard Père & Fils 2002 Volnay Clos des Chênes Pinot Noir (Volnay) $46. Big, firm tannins dominate this wine, which has powerful fruit and wood flavors. This is a wine that will age well—give it at least 10 years for maturity. **91** —*R.V. (9/1/2004)*

BOUVET-LADUBAY

Bouvet-Ladubay NV Trésor Rosé Cabernet Franc (Saumur) $20. Made from Cabernet Franc, this is not as good as the Blanc de Blancs version of Trésor (not available in the United States). But it still has a good onion-skin color, a fresh raspberry character, and a good poise and lightness. **87** —*R.V. (6/1/2006)*

Bouvet-Ladubay NV Signature Brut Champagne Blend (Saumur) $13. Mostly Chenin, with 10% Chardonnay, this delicious bubbly mixes spicy yeast with clove and herb scents, inviting repeated sips. Full-bodied fruit flavors follow, with a slightly candied appeal, and the finish wraps you in hints of vanilla and light toast. **88 Best Buy** —*P.G. (12/15/2002)*

Bouvet-Ladubay NV Brut Signature Chenin Blanc (Saumur) $13. An attractive, fresh wine, with apple flavors, balancing acidity and a touch of softness to finish. This is just the thing for the summer. **86** —*R.V. (6/1/2006)*

Bouvet-Ladubay NV Excellence Brut Rosé Sparkling Blend (Vin Mousseux) $15. Salmon-colored, with nice scents of strawberry and leafy red berry, this sparkler has big, zesty bubbles and flavors of lime and citrus touched with red berry. Crisp on the finish, with citrusy-apple flavors. **86** —*M.D. (12/15/2006)*

Bouvet-Ladubay 1998 Saphir Brut Vintage Sparkling Blend (Saumur) $85. Right off the bat you'll detect that this Loire Valley sparkler is not Chardonnay; it's Chenin Blanc—you can tell from the yellow color and the unusual nose that's both meaty and toasty. Interesting across the palate, with notes of papaya, pear, and green herbs. Hefty and smoky at the end, with a fat mouthfeel. **87** —*M.S. (12/15/2003)*

BROTTE

Brotte 2005 *Barrel Sample* Château de Bord Croix de Frégère Laudun Rhône Red Blend (Côtes-du-Rhône Villages) $22. 87 —*J.C. (11/15/2006)*

Brotte 2003 Château de Bord Laudun Rhône Red Blend (Côtes-du-Rhône Villages) $16. Youthfully exuberant and filled with fruit, but also a bit tannic and drying on the finish. Leathery fruit seems a bit overdone, and there's a hint of volatility as well. Tough call, and this may well settle down and be better than it is now given a couple of years in the cellar. **84** —*J.C. (2/1/2005)*

Brotte 2003 Domaine Bouvencourt Rhône Red Blend (Vacqueyras) $25. A nice, easy-drinking Côtes-du-Rhône, with dark plum and blackberry aromas and flavors and hints of smoke and anise. It's neither too big nor too light—if Goldilocks were a wine drinker, she'd say the weight on the palate is just right. **86** —*J.C. (2/1/2005)*

Brotte 2003 Vieilles Vignes Rhône Red Blend (Châteauneuf-du-Pape) $45. A soft style of wine, with some oak, licorice, and pepper flavors. The wine is smooth, fresh, and fruity, although the presence of some concentrated tannins does give it the potential of aging. **87** —*R.V. (12/31/2005)*

Brotte 2003 Domaine du Versant Doré Viognier (Condrieu) $48. Odd stuff, with vegetal notes appearing in place of the ripe floral aromas expected of Viognier. Corn, lime, and green tomatoes all show up on the nose or in the mouth, along with a slightly oily mouthfeel. **82** —*J.C. (2/1/2005)*

Brotte 2003 Les Brottiers White Blend (Côtes-du-Rhône) $10. This full-bodied white boasts layers of mouthfilling pears, melons, and dried spices, and it finishes long. With its richness it would be a fine accompaniment to cream-sauced fish or chicken dishes. **89** —*J.C. (2/1/2005)*

BRUNO HUNOLD

Bruno Hunold 2004 Pinot Gris (Alsace) $19. A lot of vegetal character is draped on the nose of this rather heavy, chunky offering. Green bean, sauerkraut, and pickles all make a play for the lead, while the palate is full of pickled melon, pear, and a touch of nuttiness. Fairly aggressive acidity keeps it alive and kicking. **84** *(2/1/2006)*

BRUNO PAILLARD

Bruno Paillard 1995 Brut Champagne Blend (Champagne) $85. A densely aromatic nose offers caramel, floral, coconut, and lime scents. Soft and even in the mouth, the wine's yeasty-toasty flavors are offset by bright citrus accents that come forward on the long finish. Delicious now, this youthful wine should develop further over the next few years. **90** *(12/1/2001)*

Bruno Paillard 1990 N.P.U. Champagne Blend (Champagne) $185. A touch oxidized and mushroomy, but still fairly regal and full of vanilla and baked apple. Those same components carry onto the palate, where cinnamon enters the fray. Finishes lemony, with some tart apple along with sweeter caramel. **92** —*M.S. (12/31/2005)*

Bruno Paillard NV Première Cuvée Brut Rosé Champagne Blend (Champagne) $56. I applaud the fact that Paillard clearly labels his wines with the date of disgorgement—this one was August 2005. The wine immediately offers up enticing scents of peaches, apricots, and cherries. It's a full, fruit-powered Champagne that's round and rich and unusually ripe. It delivers a lot of flavor up front, and holds there through a clean finish. **90** —*P.G. (12/1/2006)*

Bruno Paillard NV Première Cuvée Brut Champagne Blend (Champagne) $44. Since he created his company in 1981, Bruno Paillard has become an important force in Champagne, owning a number of other brands. But his top wines are made under his own name; they go for finesse and elegance. This bottling also has a touch of mature, toasty acid flavors. The bottles carry the year of disgorgement—an excellent idea. **92** —*R.V. (12/1/2005)*

Bruno Paillard NV Premiere Cuvée Brut Rosé Champagne Blend (Champagne) $50. This handsome rosé opens with full strawberry, floral, and hay aromas, and even a decidedly Pinot, gamy hint. The palate shows very good depth of tart cherry and baked goods flavors and a fine mousse-soft, rich, and creamy texture. Closes with more berry fruit, a cinnamon note, and light tannins. **90** *(12/1/2001)*

Bruno Paillard 1995 Blanc de Blancs Brut Chardonnay (Champagne) $66. This is fresh and lively with great citrus flavors and a firm structure. On the dry side, it shows crispness, apple skin flavors, and a light, poised, elegant character. Will age over the mid term. **89** —*R.V. (11/1/2006)*

Bruno Paillard NV Réserve Privée Brut Chardonnay (Champagne) $60. This wine's wonderful nose of apple, sourdough, caramel, and ginger aromas gives way to a light, dry palate. The spice, pear, and lemon flavors are subtle and seductive, the mouthfeel soft and fairly full. Finishes long and refined, with citrus and green apple notes. **91 Editors' Choice** *(12/1/2001)*

BRUT DARGENT

Brut Dargent NV Blanc de Blancs Brut Sparkling Blend (Jura) $11. Light apple and powdered sugar make for a less than powerful nose, while the palate offers fresh orange. Quite light and simple, but generally speaking it's clean and easy. Finishes slightly sweet. **84** —*M.S. (12/31/2005)*

FRANCE

CALVET

Calvet 1998 Bordeaux Blend (Bordeaux) $7. 84 *(12/1/2000)*

Calvet 1996 Reserve Bordeaux Blend (Bordeaux) $10. 87 *(12/1/2000)*

Calvet 1998 Cabernet Sauvignon (Vin de Pays d'Oc) $7. 85 *(12/1/2000)*

Calvet 1998 Calvet Premiere Chardonnay (Bourgogne) $17. 89 *(12/1/2000)*

Calvet 2002 Calvet Reserve Merlot-Cabernet Sauvignon (Bordeaux) $15. Turns citrusy and tart on the finish, but this is a decent little claret nonetheless. Smells just right, with cedar, vanilla, and cherries combining on the nose, then delivers a light, satiny-smooth mouthful of tart berries and vanilla flavor. 84 —*J.C. (6/1/2005)*

Calvet 1999 Pinot Noir (Bourgogne) $39. 83 —*P.G. (11/1/2002)*

Calvet 1999 Pinot Noir (Nuits-St.-Georges) $39. The nose promises a bit of texture and flesh, and there are some slightly sweet, slightly caramelized flavors hinting at over-ripe fruit. A suggestion of green onion and fresh garlic creeps into the finish. 84 —*P.G. (11/1/2002)*

Calvet 1998 Calvet Premiere Pinot Noir (Bourgogne) $17. 85 *(12/1/2000)*

Calvet 2004 Extra Fruit XF Sauvignon Blanc (Bordeaux) $10. Middle of the road white wine, with a nose dictated by pink grapefruit, peach, and pear. Not the most exciting painting in the museum, but nothing wrong either. Good but sort of flat. 85 Best Buy *(7/1/2005)*

Calvet 1998 Reserve White Blend (Bordeaux) $10. 88 Best Buy *(12/1/2000)*

CAMILLE GIROUD

Camille Giroud 2003 Beaune Premier Cru Les Avaux Pinot Noir (Beaune) $51. A ripe, juicy wine, one that has a good balance between new wood, acidity, and fresh red fruit flavors. Its dry tannins suggest aging potential. It's a good, solid wine, already delicious but will develop well. 89 —*R.V. (9/1/2005)*

CASTEL MONTPLAISIR

Castel Montplaisir 1997 Red Blend (Cahors) $11. Another Cahors from the stable of Alain-Dominque Perrin, this one is the entry-level wine, made to be more accessible than his flagship wine from Château Lagrezette or the luxury cuvée. There's still plenty of toasty oak, but also some raspberry-cherry fruit and green tobacco on the finish. 84 —*J.C. (3/1/2001)*

CASTEL ROUBINE

Castel Roubine 1996 Cru Classe Rhône Red Blend (Côtes de Provence) $12. A light, toffee-and-caramel-tinged red that seems to be fading. Some earth and cherry flavors provide for acceptable drinking now, but this wine is headed south. Get to it soon. 82 —*J.C. (3/1/2001)*

CATHERINE DE SAINT-JUERY

Catherine de Saint-Juery 1998 Syrah (Coteaux du Languedoc) $8. Whoever this Catherine is, she doesn't say very much, and what she does say, she doesn't say very loudly. More than one reviewer called this Syrah mute—but what flavors and aromas we could discern were nice. Grape, mulling-spice and pencil eraser notes whisper from the bouquet; black tea, blackberry fruit, and leather resonate on the palate. Finishes short, dry and minerally. 84 *(10/1/2001)*

CATTIER

Cattier 1998 Cuvée Renaissance Champagne Blend (Champagne) $NA. This is Cattier's best wine, a fine blend of 60% red grapes and 40% Chardonnay, very refined, sophisticated. It has an element of toast, ripe fruits, with green fruit flavors and almonds. It could well age over the next 5 years, but at this stage it is already well integrated, and delicious as a food wine. 89 —*R.V. (12/1/2004)*

CAVE DE LUGNY

Cave de Lugny 2001 Les Charmes Chardonnay (Mâcon-Lugny) $9. A thick, gluey wine with the most curious texture, very soft and flaccid. Low in acidity, with Chardonnay flavors of apples. Not much to recommend this clumsy wine. 82 —*S.H. (1/1/2002)*

CAVE DE RIBEAUVILLÉ

Cave de Ribeauvillé 2004 Grand Cru Kirchberg de Ribeauvillé Riesling (Alsace) $22. A rich, sweet wine. Its main impression is of balance between that sweetness and the fresh, clean, white fruits, and spice. A touch of toastiness adds complexity. The aftertaste is fresh, rather than sweet. 88 —*R.V. (2/1/2006)*

Cave de Ribeauvillé 2002 Grand Cru Rosacker Riesling (Alsace) $22. Attractively priced for a grand cru wine, but not better than some producers' blended wines. A whiff of diesel adds nuance to the baked apple aromas, then spice and apple flavors take over on the palate. Sounds good up to then, but the finish strikes a discordant note, adding chalky, almost bitter, flavors. 85 —*J.C. (8/1/2006)*

Cave de Ribeauvillé 2004 Réserve Silberberg Riesling (Alsace) $21. Full marks to the co-op of Ribeauvillé for indicating on the label that this is a medium-dry wine. This is a fresh, very clean, full-bodied wine, which doesn't go for complexity, but does go for ripeness and softness. There is just a touch of spice to complete the wine. 85 —*R.V. (2/1/2006)*

Cave de Ribeauvillé 2004 Prestige Demi-Sec Tokay Pinot Gris (Alsace) $17. This wine has good, fresh fruit, and is attractive and soft. It layers acidity, white fruits, a touch of spice and thyme, over a core of dryness. The aftertaste is also dry, making this a good accompaniment to food. 85 —*R.V. (2/1/2006)*

Cave de Ribeauvillé 2000 Vendanges Tardives Tokay Pinot Gris (Alsace) $40. This fresh and delicate wine has some great botrytis, which gives richness to its ripe fruit. Also offers good acidity and flavors of spice and lychees. 89 —*R.V. (2/1/2006)*

CAVE DE SARRAS

Cave de Sarras 1998 Cuvée Champtenaud Syrah (Saint-Joseph) $19. Dense, deep, and darkly knit, but not saturated and black like some. The fruit element is all red; cherry, raspberry, and apple skins from start to finish. Speaking of the finish, it's nice and complete, with vanilla and chocolate notes adding a welcome richness. Good acids and overall balance carry it home. 87 —*M.S. (9/1/2003)*

CAVE DE TAIN L'HERMITAGE

Cave de Tain l'Hermitage 2005 Marsanne (Crozes-Hermitage) $15. A crisp, fresh style evidently meant for early consumption. Melon and pear flavors are a bit neutral, with a hint of bitterness on the finish. 83 —*J.C. (11/15/2006)*

Cave de Tain L'Hermitage 2003 Marsanne (Hermitage) $39. Shows what a quality-conscious co-op can achieve. This is mainly Marsanne, femented in barrel on its indigenous yeasts. The result is rich and viscous, plump with orange-tangerine and honey flavors, and marked by strong fennel notes. Adds a white pepper note on the finish. 89 —*J.C. (11/15/2006)*

Cave de Tain L'Hermitage 1999 Nobles Rives Marsanne (Hermitage) $NA. A modern, rich, almost new-world style of wine in its open fruit and generous new wood flavors. Ripe peaches and nectarines give the wine great richness. At this stage, the wood is still too dominant, but over the next four or five years, the opulent fruit will certainly balance out. 90 —*R.V. (6/1/2002)*

Cave de Tain L'Hermitage 2001 Rhône White Blend (Hermitage) $35. A ripe, spicy wood flavored wine, with tastes of fresh peaches and apricots. It is rich, with a balance that has come together well. This is 100 percent Marsanne, and that shows in the wine's full-body and dried fruit and spice. A great performance from the Tain cooperative. 90 Editors' Choice —*R.V. (2/1/2005)*

Cave de Tain L'Hermitage 2004 Syrah (Saint-Joseph) $18. Darker than the co-op's Crozes-Hermitage, with prune and coffee aromas and flavors. It's dark and sturdy, but still marked by firm acidity on the finish. Drink now. 86 —*J.C. (11/15/2006)*

Cave de Tain L'Hermitage 2003 Syrah (Hermitage) $52. Interestingly, the co-op (as a business entity) owns 55 acres in Hermitage, while its growers individually only own 23 acres. In general, bright raspberries accent cassis fruit, and while a bit of wood is evident, it's nicely integrated and balanced. Shows decent length, peppery spice, and supple tannins on the finish. Drink now–2015. 88 —*J.C. (11/15/2006)*

Cave de Tain L'Hermitage 2001 Syrah (Cornas) $25. For lovers of Syrah, Cornas is the purest expression, with its dark, brooding tannins and heady fruit. This wine, from the Tain cooperative, is a classic Cornas, which just misses the intensity of some examples, but still has fine, dry tannins and long-lasting acidity. 88 —*R.V. (2/1/2005)*

FRANCE

Cave de Tain L'Hermitage 1999 Cuvée Gambert de Loche Syrah (Hermitage) $70. Named after the first president of the Tain cooperative back in the 1930s, this wine comes from the 50 acres of vineyards controlled by the co-op on the Hermitage hill. It is a big, brooding wine with classic tannins and appetizing rich, juicy black fruits. Wood flavors are very apparent, but not dominant, with fruit tannins getting the upper edge. It could age well for 12–15 years before maturity. **90** —*R.V. (6/1/2002)*

Cave de Tain L'Hermitage 2002 Esprit de Granit Syrah (Saint-Joseph) $18. There is perfumed fruit, with aromas of red currants. This wine, named after the granite soil which forms the base of Saint-Joseph, is earthy, ripe, and firmly tannic, but with plenty of red fruit flavors. It should develop quickly, over the next 2-3 years. **87** —*R.V. (2/1/2005)*

Cave de Tain L'Hermitage 2003 Gambert de Loche Syrah (Hermitage) $85. Lacks the haunting fragrance of the best Hermitage wines, but shows plenty of concentrated dark fruit and toasty oak. Supple and vanilla-laden at first, it firms up and shows more plum fruit and pepper on the finish. **90** —*J.C. (11/15/2006)*

Cave de Tain L'Hermitage 2003 Les Hauts du Fief Syrah (Crozes-Hermitage) $20. The Tain co-op's Les Hauts du Fief bottling sees some smaller oak, marked by cedary, slightly meaty notes, to go with its cassis fruit. It's medium- to full-bodied, with supple tannins and a good balance of fruit and wood. Drink now. **88** —*J.C. (11/15/2006)*

Cave de Tain L'Hermitage 1999 Les Hauts du Fief Syrah (Crozes-Hermitage) $15. A finely soft wine, with concentrated ripe fruit that just demands to be drunk now. Red fruits, sweet jelly flavors, and soft tannins come together into an enticing blend. **88** —*R.V. (6/1/2002)*

CAVE DE VIGNERONS DE BEAUMES-DE-VENISE

Cave de Vignerons de Beaumes-de-Venise 2004 Rosexclusif Muscat (Muscat de Beaumes de Venise) $NA. **88** —*J.C. (11/15/2006)*

Cave de Vignerons de Beaumes-de-Venise 2004 Carte Or Muscat Blanc à Petit Grain (Muscat de Beaumes de Venise) $NA. **84** —*J.C. (11/15/2006)*

CAVE DES VIGNERONS DE MONTFRIN

Cave des Vignerons de Montfrin 2005 Domaine de Barrelle Rhône Red Blend (Côtes-du-Rhône) $NA. Recently bottled, some initial hints of sulfur give way to bold cherry and apricot notes; the blend is 80% Grenache, 20% Syrah. It's round and full in the mouth, with ample tannins. This youthful wine could use another 1–2 years of cellaring—that, or some red meat. **87** —*J.C. (11/15/2006)*

CAVE DES VIGNERONS DE PRISSE

Cave des Vignerons de Prisse 2004 Terres Secrets Chardonnay (Mâcon-Villages) $15. A good, fresh, green wine with attractive, ripe fruit. This is an easy, drinkable Chardonnay, that comes from the southern half of Burgundy. **87** —*R.V. (12/1/2006)*

CAVE FAYOLLE FILS ET FILLE

Cave Fayolle Fils et Fille 2004 Les Pontaix Syrah (Crozes-Hermitage) $NA. This is a simple, fruity quaff. There's plenty of cherries and some floral notes reminiscent of violets, but where's the peppery spice? Drink now. **85** —*J.C. (11/15/2006)*

CAVES DES PAPES

Caves des Papes 2001 Les Closiers Red Blend (Châteauneuf-du-Pape) $24. Shows slight browning at the rim and seems to be drying out a bit on the palate, yet still retains some charm. Dried cherries and apricots sport a leathery overlay and a dusting of dried spices. Drink up. **83** —*J.C. (3/1/2004)*

Caves des Papes 2000 Reserve des Fustiers Red Blend (Gigondas) $18. Crisply acidic, with scents of leather, dark chocolate, and cranberry. **83** —*J.C. (3/1/2004)*

Caves des Papes 2002 Heritage Rouge Rhône Red Blend (Côtes-du-Rhône) $11. Light and crisp, but pleasant, with cherry and black pepper flavors on a lean frame. **83** —*J.C. (2/1/2005)*

Caves des Papes 2001 Oratorio Rhône Red Blend (Gigondas) $28. From a large producer, this prestige cuvée was a pleasant surprise, with lovely aromas of dried flowers, leather, and cherries and a creamy, supple mouthfeel. Finishes long and softly tannic. Doesn't seem to have the stuffing to make old bones, so drink it now–2010. **89** —*J.C. (2/1/2005)*

Caves des Papes 2004 Heritage Rosé Blend (Côtes-du-Rhône) $10. Dark pink in color, close to red. This is a simple, assertively fruity rosé, loaded with cherries and berries, and finishing on a fresh, slightly rustic note. **83** —*J.C. (11/15/2005)*

CELLIER DES DAUPHINS

Cellier des Dauphins 2001 Réserve Les Dorinnes Rouge Rhône Red Blend (Côtes-du-Rhône) $14. A light, simple wine, with modest black cherry flavors partially obscured by rubbery notes. **83** —*J.C. (2/1/2005)*

Cellier des Dauphins 2003 Prestige Blanc Rhône White Blend (Côtes-du-Rhône) $8. This fat, slightly alcoholic white shows the warmth of the vintage, with scents of pears tinged with beeswax and honey suggestive of very ripe fruit. Yet there's enough stony, minerally flavors to redeem it. **84 Best Buy** —*J.C. (2/1/2005)*

Cellier des Dauphins 2005 Prestige Rosé Blend (Côtes-du-Rhône) $9. From the Rhône's biggest co-op, this is a simple, fruity concoction with hints of strawberry and cherry. A bit soft on the finish, so serve it well-chilled to give it a little more grip. **83** —*J.C. (11/15/2006)*

CHAMPAGNE CATTIER

Champagne Cattier NV Chigny-Les-Rosés Premier Cru Champagne Blend (Champagne) $30. A blend of 90% Pinot Noir and Pinot Meunier, and 10% Chardonnay has produced a light, attractive salmon pink-colored wine. It has crisp, poised acidity and ripe red currants, along with a layer of fresh tannins. To finish, there is just a touch of sweetness to balance. **87** —*R.V. (12/15/2003)*

CHANSON PÈRE ET FILS

Chanson Père et Fils 2003 Clos des Mouches Premier Cru Chardonnay (Beaune) $83. This is a delicious wine. It offers first aromas of fresh, green fruit, powerfully fruity, toasty flavors, and a fresh vibrant finish. It is not powerful, but it is very enjoyable. **91** —*R.V. (9/1/2005)*

Chanson Père et Fils 2003 Hauts Marconnets Premier Cru Chardonnay (Savigny-lès-Beaune) $34. A big, ripe, toasty wine that has peach and apricot flavors at its core. It will need little time to develop, but it is already showing generosity and style. **89** —*R.V. (9/1/2005)*

Chanson Père et Fils 2002 Vergennes Chardonnay (Corton) $115. White fruits, toast, and balancing acidity give this wine both a great, crisp freshness and complexity. It is also a wine which could age well—five years or more. **90** —*R.V. (9/1/2004)*

Chanson Père et Fils 2003 Clos de Mouches Premier Cru Pinot Noir (Beaune) $66. A finely structured wine, whose dark, dry tannins are supporting rich fruit and a layer of new wood. This is dense and solid, promising good aging. The dryness goes hand in hand with richness. **89** —*R.V. (9/1/2005)*

Chanson Père et Fils 2003 Clos des Fêves Premier Cru Pinot Noir (Beaune) $70. Chanson owns all of this 11-acre vineyard in the heart of the Côte de Beaune. This is a beautiful, opulent wine that still packs a punch of dry tannin at its heart. Red fruits, a touch of chocolate, and toast point to the richness of this finely structured wine. **92** —*R.V. (9/1/2005)*

Chanson Père et Fils 2002 Dominode Premier Cru Pinot Noir (Savigny-lès-Beaune) $35. A fine, sophisticated wine. Layers of refined wood, sweet black fruits, acidity, and ripeness come together in harmony. **87** —*R.V. (9/1/2004)*

Chanson Père et Fils 2003 Les Vergelesses Premier Cru Pinot Noir (Pernand-Vergelesses) $36. This wine is packed with new wood and woody tannins, but still reveals plenty of ripe fruit. It's firm now, but should soften into a much more seductive wine. **88** —*R.V. (9/1/2005)*

Chanson Père et Fils 2002 Premier Cru Les Boudots Pinot Noir (Nuits-St.-Georges) $80. A huge, rich wine that is full of sweet tannins and fruit. There are strawberries on the nose. The palate offers very firm but opulent fruit and lovely acidity. **91** —*R.V. (9/1/2004)*

CHARLES DE CAZANOVE

Charles de Cazanove NV Classique Brut Champagne Blend (Champagne) $26. Smooth and yeasty, with clean and pleasant pear aromas. The palate deals apple and pear fruit, and a hint of sweet, ripe banana. The finish is short, but what's there is pure and smooth. A solid, tasty Champagne that hits nearly all the right chords. **87** —*M.S. (6/1/2003)*

CHARLES DE FERE

Charles de Fere NV Grande Cuvée Champagne Blend (Crémant de Bourgogne) $15. A classic Champagne blend of Chard and Pinot Noir gives this wine some good depth and ripe flavors. Has flavors of toast, spices, and pears as well as some good tannin structure. The finish is dry, with just a hint of softness. **88** —*R.V. (6/1/2006)*

Charles de Fere NV Tradition Brut Chardonnay (France) $10. Forward and fruity, with a nice blend of light floral and apple aromas. This is a good, round, pleasant wine, clean, and mouthfilling. For its price it offers well-balanced flavors and surprising length. **87 Best Buy** —*P.G. (12/15/2002)*

Charles de Fere NV Tradition Chardonnay Brut Chardonnay (Vin Mousseux) $12. A fresh, simple fruity wine with honey and apple flavors. It's light, easy, and crisp to finish. Made from 100% Chardonnay. **84** —*R.V. (6/1/2006)*

Charles de Fere NV Réserve French Shiraz Shiraz (Vin Mousseux) $NA. This is one for the Australians, with their fine tradition of red sparkling wines made from Shiraz. For people of other nationalities, it's more of a curiosity, with firm tannins, some sweetness from ripe fruit, and finishing acidity. When to drink it? Probably with a red fruit dessert. **86** —*R.V. (6/1/2006)*

Charles de Fere NV Brut Tradition Sparkling Blend (France) $12. Sizable, in fact, almost chunky. The nose shows some pear and honey balanced by a shot of green herb. The palate is big, with ripe apple and tangerine notes. Tight and focused on the finish, with a mildly chalky, sticky mouthfeel. **87 Best Buy** —*M.S. (12/31/2005)*

Charles de Fere NV Cuvée Jean-Louis Blanc de Blancs Brut Sparkling Blend (Vin Mousseux) $10. Toasted English muffin greets the nose, while the palate embraces ripe, almost tropical white fruit flavors. There's acidity but it's low, making this seem more like a still wine with bubbles than a Mousseux. **83** —*M.D. (12/15/2006)*

Charles de Fere NV Réserve Blanc de Blancs Brut Sparkling Blend (Vin Mousseux) $11. Crisp grapefruit and kiwi flavors give this wine a green but elegant flavor. It is dry, fresh, and lively, finishing with layers of acidity. **85** —*R.V. (6/1/2006)*

CHARLES HEIDSIECK

Charles Heidsieck 1982 Blanc de Blancs des Chardonnay Champagne Blend (Champagne) $185. Bright gold in color, with saffron, butter, and toffee aromas. This is an elegant Champagne, with butter—even Sherry—flavors, and dried apricot fruit on the palate. Finishes a little shorter than we'd like, with mature cheese rind and dust flavors. Rendall recommends that you drink this with roasted, stuffed turkey at Thanksgiving, though, she admits, you won't have much opportunity to do so—at the time of this review, there were only 77 bottles of it left in the Heidsieck cellars. **91** *(12/15/2003)*

Charles Heidsieck 1995 Blanc des Millénaires Champagne Blend (Champagne) $95. Nice aromatics: there's honey, vanilla cream, and ripe pear. Quite forward and zesty on the palate, where tangy lemon dances with apple and mineral. Lots of snap on the finish, and overall it's pretty classy. **90** —*M.S. (12/31/2005)*

Charles Heidsieck 1983 Blanc des Millénaires Champagne Blend (Champagne) $170. This was the first cuvée of Blanc des Millenaires; Rendall is quick to clarify that the idea behind it was "not because of the millennium…it was to have a wine that you'll age for at least 10 years." If the key to Heidsieck's Pinot-Chard blends is "richness," it's "crispness" for this blanc des blancs. It has a sprightly, fresh mouthfeel with ginger, pear, and stone flavors, and a dusting of powdered sugar on the finish. **91** *(12/15/2003)*

Charles Heidsieck 1995 Brut Champagne Blend (Champagne) $65. A very nice wine, fairly full in the mouth, but a little stand-offish and closed at this age. Wide minerally aromas are all that showed on the nose, even after an hour of aeration. The butterscotch richness that seems to be Heidsieck's trademark is present here, too, with white peach flavors hiding underneath. Needs 8–10 years at the least; in the next decade, this evaluation may prove

conservative. A blend of 60% Pinot Noir and 40% Chardonnay; only the second vintaged wine of the 1990s. **90** *(12/15/2003)*

Charles Heidsieck 1995 Brut Champagne Blend (Champagne) $65. A lighter style, with a creamy texture and a crisp, youthful feel. Lemon and toast dominate, but there's a deep apple and mineral core lurking below. **90** —*J.C. (12/1/2005)*

Charles Heidsieck 1999 Brut Rosé Champagne Blend (Champagne) $80. Charles Heidsieck's rosé has a reputation for aging well—but 1999 seems to be an exception, since it is already mature. It shows some good biscuit and baked cookie flavors, but still retains its strawberry jam fruits. It is rich, soft, and very fruity, with the acidity only showing from the background. **90** —*R.V. (11/1/2006)*

Charles Heidsieck 1996 Brut Rosé Champagne Blend (Champagne) $70. Not a saigné, but made instead by blending in 5–7% red wine, this rosé is Heidsieck's first since 1985. With its beautiful salmon-copper color and dried cherry aromas, it was worth the wait. Earthy, dusty flavors envelop its sturdy white cherry frame, which holds on tight through the lingering finish. Still young, and a little closed; will show its best after 2008. **90** *(12/15/2003)*

Charles Heidsieck 1985 Champagne Charlie Brut Champagne Blend (Champagne) $125. One of the most famous brand names in Champagne gets its name from an exceptional salesman in the 19th century who had a music hall song written in his honor. He would have been proud to have sold this wine which, despite its age, is still impressively fresh and fruity. Flavors of almonds and toast blend well with green fruits, well-proportioned to go with food rather than as an apéritif. **91** —*R.V. (12/1/2004)*

Charles Heidsieck 1981 Champagne Charlie Brut Champagne Blend (Champagne) $150. Unusual, in that not many houses declared 1981 a vintage year. This is a supple, beautiful wine, virtually orange in color, a fact that hints at its earthy, autumnal palate impression. Shows hints of mushroom, clarified butter, and demi-glace notes on the nose, with baked apple and earth flavors in the mouth. Mature and sexy; drink now. **92** *(12/15/2003)*

Charles Heidsieck NV Réserve Brut Champagne Blend (Champagne) $40. This four-year-old bottling (indicated on the back label) is a rich Champagne, with some toasty maturity but also flavors of almonds, white currants and citrus peel. It is an intense, full-bodied food wine. **89** —*R.V. (12/1/2005)*

Charles Heidsieck NV Réserve Brut Champagne Blend (Champagne) $35. Medium-full and frothy in the mouth, the wine offers mouth-coating butterscotch and Macintosh apple flavors, and dust and light citrus aromas. Has richness and character, particularly for a non-vintage offering. Mis en cave in 1997 and disgorged in 2002, it is composed of 40% reserve wine and 60% wine from the 1996 harvest. **89** *(12/15/2003)*

Charles Heidsieck 1995 Blanc des Millénaires Chardonnay (Champagne) $95. Toasty aromas are the first hints that this is now a mature wine. Its layers of acidity mingle with toast, walnuts, and rich, mature fruit. Definitely a wine for those who prefer their bubblies with some age. **89** —*R.V. (11/1/2006)*

CHARLES HOURS

Charles Hours 2001 Cuvée Marie White Blend (Jurançon Sec) $18. Fresh—almost sea-air fresh—with intriguing floral notes. In the mouth, it's honeyed yet dry, with citrus and white peach flavors. Medium-weight, with a crisp finish. **88** *(10/1/2003)*

CHARLES LAFITTE

Charles Lafitte NV 1834 Cuvée Spéciale Brut Champagne Blend (Champagne) $32. Starts with sweet scents of bread dough, light herb, and green apple. Well-made, with lean, fresh flavors of apple and pear. The bubbles are extra fine, and the wine is crisp and balanced. For all its poise, it is a bit one-dimensional. A bracing style best-suited for salty, briny foods. **87** —*P.G. (12/1/2006)*

Charles Lafitte NV Brut Rosé Champagne Blend (Champagne) $43. Earthy and spicy, blending cinnamon and mushroom nuances with meaty, dark-berried flavors. Yet despite the rich-sounding flavors, the mouthfeel is fresh and lively. Try it with red meats and surprise your guests. **88** —*J.C. (12/1/2004)*

Charles Lafitte NV Grand Cuvée Brut Champagne Blend (Champagne) $27. Very pretty, with applesauce, bread, and cinnamon aromas. The palate sports green apple and papaya flavors, which are followed nicely by a finish that's dry and smooth. With good size, spirit and substance, this wine hits the right chords. **88** —*M.S. (12/15/2003)*

Charles Lafitte NV Grande Cuvée Brut Champagne Blend (Champagne) $21. Salty, even briny scents dominate, along with a slightly resinous character. In the mouth this is a flavorful, rather heavy wine which carries its weight and power in the dead center of the palate. Nothing elegant here, but it's a good mouthful of fruit, finishing with an herbal-metallic note. **87** —*P.G. (12/15/2002)*

Charles Lafitte NV Grande Cuvée Brut Champagne Blend (Champagne) $27. Pineapple and other tropical fruit flavors, plus a little custard, play on the palate; they're there, but not all intense. Lively in the mouth and on the medium finish, where tart citrus and slate notes keep the fruitiness in check. Bouquet shows mineral, orange peel and starchy, white rice aromas. **85** —*D.T. (12/15/2001)*

Charles Lafitte 1989 Orgueil de France Brut Champagne Blend (Champagne) $50. If this is the current release, it is showing its age. The color is noticeably tilted to the gold side; and a sweaty, musty scent overrides the oxidized Sherry-cask character. Tangy, even salty in the mouth, with some bitterness in the finish. **86** —*P.G. (12/15/2002)*

CHARLES MIGNON & FILS

Charles Mignon & Fils 2003 Rhône Red Blend (Côtes-du-Rhône) $8. A Beaujolais-style Côtes-du-Rhône, light and fresh on the palate, with pure cherry-scented fruit. Not much complexity, but it brings plenty of juicy, mouth-watering fruit to the table. Drink now. **84 Best Buy** —*J.C. (11/15/2006)*

CHARLES VIENOT

Charles Vienot 1996 Pinot Noir (Burgundy) $11. **82** *(5/1/2000)*

CHARTOGNE-TAILLET

Chartogne-Taillet NV Cuvée Sainte-Anne Blanc de Blancs Brut Champagne Blend (Champagne) $41. Philippe Chartogne's non-vintage Blanc de Blancs comes from 25-year-old vines in his family's Merfy vineyard. With its apple and green fruit aromas and soft, creamy mousse, it manages to balance richness, softness, and acidity. The aftertaste is light and crisp. **90** —*R.V. (12/1/2002)*

Chartogne-Taillet 1996 Cuvée Sainte-Anne Brut Champagne Blend (Champagne) $44. A blend of 60% Pinot Noir and 40% Chardonnay, this has the same style of mature fruit as all the Chartogne-Taillet wines. It's finely balanced, with a good structure and elegance. Finishes with flavors of almonds and quince. **91 Editors' Choice** —*R.V. (12/1/2002)*

CHARTRON ET TRÉBUCHET

Chartron et Trébuchet 2004 Chardonnay (Chablis) $20. **88** —*J.C. (11/15/2005)*

Chartron et Trébuchet 2003 Chardonnay (Meursault) $38. **87** —*J.C. (11/15/2005)*

Chartron et Trébuchet 2001 White Blend (Mâcon-Villages) $11. It's hard to find value Burgundy. The Mâcon region, in the south of Burgundy, is the only real source. Chartron et Trebuchet are négociants specializing in Chardonnay, and here they have come up with a typically soft, creamy wine, with floral aromas and flavors of white fruits with a touch of honey. Drink with fish or chicken. **86** —*R.V. (11/15/2003)*

CHÂTEAU DE PARAZA

Château de Paraza 2002 Red Blend (Minervois) $9. This flagship wine from the Minervois is disappointing. It is light-weight, dominated by acidity. Maybe the vintage did not help, but this is has an under-nourished feel to it which demands more in the way of richness. **83** —*R.V. (12/1/2004)*

CHÂTEAU PHÉLAN-SÈGUR

Château Phélan-Sègur 2000 Bordeaux Blend (Saint-Estèphe) $35. This is initially a somewhat austere wine, but that derives from the tannins of Saint-Estèphe. Underneath those tannins are solid, chunky fruits and a great generosity and richness. **92** —*R.V. (6/1/2003)*

CHÂTEAU PICHON LONGUEVILLE

Château Pichon Longueville 2000 Bordeaux Blend (Pauillac) $100. This is a powerful statement of ripe Cabernet Sauvignon. It has rich concentrated fruit, with ripe but dry tannins and considerable wood flavors. It is stylish, with layers of acidity and wood complementing the fruit. **92** —*R.V. (6/1/2003)*

CHÂTEAU ANGELUS

Château Angelus 2005 Barrel Sample Bordeaux Blend (Saint-Emilion Grand Cru) $NA. A spicy, densely sweet wine, all ripe purple fruits bursting out of a straitjacket of tannins, with the wood flavors quite dominant at this stage. The wine is firm, but the fruit is so big that the dryness is lost. **94** —*R.V. (6/20/2006)*

CHÂTEAU ANTHONIC

Château Anthonic 2003 Bordeaux Blend (Moulis-en-Médoc) $NA. A powerful, opulent wine that is packed with the ripe fruit of 2003. Its structure is dense, showing relatively soft but dry tannins. The high proportion of Merlot (59%) shows in the jammy fruits, and in the generosity of the finish. **90** —*R.V. (5/1/2006)*

CHÂTEAU AUSONE

Château Ausone 2000 Bordeaux Blend (Saint-Emilion) $600. Forget all those garage wines, forget the upstarts of Saint-Emilion. When you want real class, you have to turn to Ausone. What a wine—magnificently dense and opaque, hugely rich and sensual. Yet it doesn't seem in the least decadent—for deep inside the wine is a huge backbone of ripe tannins. Keep for at least 10 years. **98** —*R.V. (6/1/2003)*

CHÂTEAU BALESTARD LA TONNELLE

Château Balestard la Tonnelle 2005 Barrel Sample Bordeaux Blend (Saint-Emilion Grand Cru) $NA. Minty aromas and smooth wood show a New World character. The fruit is so ripe it borders on warm. There are tannins there, but not enough to structure the boundless fruit at this stage. **88** —*R.V. (6/21/2006)*

CHÂTEAU BASTOR LAMONTAGNE

Château Bastor Lamontagne 2004 Barrel Sample Bordeaux White Blend (Sauternes) $NA. Not much botrytis here, but a powerful wine which shows quite firm fruit, and some tannic structure. There is a layer of acidity, but it is rather sharp than balancing. **86** —*R.V. (6/1/2005)*

CHÂTEAU BATAILLEY

Château Batailley 2004 Barrel Sample Bordeaux Blend (Pauillac) $NA. The aromas of powerful new wood follow through on this wine with dark tannins and a feeling of brooding power. Acidity gives the wine a lift to finish. **92** —*R.V. (6/1/2005)*

CHÂTEAU BEAUCHÊNE

Château Beauchêne 2003 Grande Réserve Rhône Red Blend (Côtes-du-Rhône) $NA. A classic blend of southern Rhône grapes—Grenache, Syrah, Cinsault, and Carignan—this reflects the hot 2003 vintage but still manages to keep some restraint. The tannins hold the juicy, red berry fruit flavors together, while dry wood notes add complexity. **87** —*R.V. (12/31/2006)*

Château Beauchêne 2003 Premier Terroir Rhône Red Blend (Côtes-du-Rhône) $11. From the oldest of the Bernard family's vineyards, using vines planted in 1905, this is a seriously dense, concentrated wine, smooth and fruity. Sweet and rich, with fig and black fruit flavors, this wine can age well over the next 3–4 years. **89 Best Buy** —*R.V. (12/31/2006)*

CHÂTEAU BEAUMONT

Château Beaumont 2005 Barrel Sample Bordeaux Blend (Haut-Médoc) $NA. Very ripe, almost sweet fruit gives this wine a delicious, open, generous feel. Red fruits are the dominant character, layered with some spicy new wood that develops at the end. **88** —*R.V. (6/21/2006)*

CHÂTEAU BEAUREGARD

Château Beauregard 2005 Barrel Sample Bordeaux Blend (Pomerol) $NA. Hugely rich, very spicy, this wine is powered by huge Merlot flavors.

FRANCE

There is some fine acidity, which gives the wine a lift, but essentially it's all about unsubtle power. **86** —*R.V. (6/21/2006)*

CHÂTEAU BEAUSÉJOUR-BECOT

Château Beauséjour-Becot 2005 Barrel Sample Bordeaux Blend (Saint-Emilion Grand Cru) $NA. Very ripe, very soft at first taste, but there's a good punch of tannins and a dense, intense palate. This has the ripeness of some New World wines. **93** —*R.V. (6/20/2006)*

Château Beauséjour-Becot 2003 Barrel Sample Bordeaux Blend (Saint-Emilion) $NA. An exotic, smoky, tarry wine which has great ripe tannins and subtle flavors of new wood. It is smooth, polished but with the promise of power. **90** —*R.V. (6/3/2004)*

CHÂTEAU BEL AIR

Château Bel Air 1999 Perponcher Grande Cuvée Bordeaux Blend (Bordeaux Supérieur) $13. Another of the properties of Jean-Louis Despagne. This wine is rich and intense with flavors of mint and eucalyptus which give it an exotic element. It is powerful and concentrated, with soft tannins. It will be ready to drink in two or three years. **90** —*R.V. (12/1/2002)*

Château Bel Air 2005 Barrel Sample Bordeaux Blend (Saint-Emilion Grand Cru) $NA. Full of tannins, this wine is big and spicy, with a certain grandeur to it. It's likely to be a very fine wine, the pure acidity and black fruits pushing through. **95** —*R.V. (6/20/2006)*

Château Bel Air 2003 Barrel Sample Bordeaux Blend (Saint-Emilion) $NA. Pascal Dalbeck has fashioned a beautiful wine, all exotic fruits, dusty tannins, and power. This will age over a very long term. **91** —*R.V. (6/3/2004)*

CHÂTEAU BELGRAVE

Château Belgrave 2004 Barrel Sample Bordeaux Blend (Haut-Médoc) $NA. There are attractive mint aromas, which lead to a wine which has new wood, richness, and powerful fruit alongside the ripe tannins. **89** —*R.V. (6/1/2005)*

CHÂTEAU BELON

Château Belon 2002 Bordeaux White Blend (Graves) $12. Zesty and clean, with scents of green apple and fresh straw that give way to flavors of grapefruit and herbs. Citrusy and fresh on the finish, but ultimately a little simple. Try with oysters or other simple seafood items. **84** —*J.C. (6/1/2005)*

CHÂTEAU BERLIQUET

Château Berliquet 2005 Barrel Sample Bordeaux Blend (Saint-Emilion Grand Cru) $NA. Large-scale renovations to the vineyard and the advice of Patrick Valette as consultant have paid great dividends at this ancient vineyard. The wine is ripely opulent but balanced, with new wood that supports rather than dominates, and a structure that promises long aging. **91** —*R.V. (6/1/2006)*

CHÂTEAU BERTINERIE

Château Bertinerie 2004 Bordeaux White Blend (Premieres Côtes de Blaye) $12. A crisp, grassy, pure Sauvignon Blanc, which is fresh, acidic, and offers great grapefruit flavors. There's a lightness that balances the fine depth of flavor from this leading Blaye property. **88** —*R.V. (6/1/2005)*

CHÂTEAU BEYCHEVELLE

Château Beychevelle 2000 Bordeaux Blend (Saint-Julien) $500. If any wine could be described as beautiful, then Beychevelle is beautiful. Its flavors of licquorice and black currant are smooth and opulent, well-proportioned. The texture is rich, ripe, and generous. **92** —*R.V. (6/1/2003)*

Château Beychevelle 2004 Barrel Sample Bordeaux Blend (Saint-Julien) $NA. While the sample has reductive aromas, it has enough dry fruits and dense tannins to show a wine which has good potential. The acidity and freshness come through. **90** —*R.V. (6/1/2005)*

CHÂTEAU BONNET

Château Bonnet 2000 Bordeaux Rouge Bordeaux Blend (Bordeaux) $12. There are aromas of ripe, juicy fruit. To taste, the wine is soft, juicy, and easy, perhaps slightly dilute. A very approachable wine, but in the end lightweight. **83** —*R.V. (12/1/2002)*

Château Bonnet 2004 Bordeaux White Blend (Entre-Deux-Mers) $10. One of the most familiar Entre-deux-Mers chateaus, and certainly the largest, this is the home of master vigneron André Lurton. With its fresh, grapefruit flavors and aromas of white flowers and hedgerows, this is a great summer wine. **88 Best Buy** —*R.V. (6/1/2005)*

Château Bonnet 2001 Vinifie en Futs de Chene Entre deux Mers White Blend (Bordeaux) $14. To prove that white Bordeaux can age as well as white Burgundy, here comes André Lurton with his wood-aged Château Bonnet. It's a finely made wine, with well-judged wood and ripe, but crisp, fruit. It's certainly young at the moment and will repay aging for five years. **90 Best Buy** —*R.V. (12/1/2002)*

CHÂTEAU BOUSCAUT

Château Bouscaut 2003 Barrel Sample Bordeaux Blend (Pessac-Léognan) $NA. A relative unknown estate has done great things this year. The wine is finely structured with ripe fruit, balancing acidity and dusty tannins. **88** —*R.V. (6/3/2004)*

CHÂTEAU BRANAIRE-DUCRU

Château Branaire-Ducru 2003 Bordeaux Blend (Saint-Julien) $40. One of the great estates of southern Saint-Julien, producing wines whose regularity in succeeding vintages is remarkable. For 2003, Branaire has produced a dark wine, with dry, powerful tannins coming from very ripe fruit. The wood is dry and toasty, leaving a general impression of a wine that will age at a stately pace. **91** —*R.V. (5/1/2006)*

Château Branaire-Ducru 2005 Barrel Sample Bordeaux Blend (Saint-Julien) $NA. A huge, generous, opulent wine, with cedar aromas, a touch of toast, and immense black fruits. And it still keeps a delicacy and elegance: very Saint-Julien. **94** —*R.V. (6/20/2006)*

Château Branaire-Ducru 2003 Barrel Sample Bordeaux Blend (Saint-Julien) $NA. There are ripe fruit aromas, followed by spicy fruit, some new wood flavors by not too much. A well-balanced wine which has good potential. **89** —*R.V. (6/3/2004)*

CHÂTEAU BRANE-CANTENAC

Château Brane-Cantenac 2001 Bordeaux Blend (Margaux) $40. A great, rich wine from what owner Henri Lurton calls a classic year. There are huge, sweet tannins, solid black fruit flavors, and ripeness, without losing sight of balance between richness, dryness, and acidity. This is a wine that will age over many years. **92** —*R.V. (6/1/2005)*

Château Brane-Cantenac 2005 Barrel Sample Bordeaux Blend (Margaux) $NA. Initially this wine seems soft, but then it becomes obvious that the tannins are very present, dry, and massive. But they are already well-integrated, going together with the herbs, the spice, and pure black fruit flavors. Impressive wine. **95** —*R.V. (6/20/2006)*

Château Brane-Cantenac 2003 Barrel Sample Bordeaux Blend (Margaux) $NA. A stunning wine from this Lurton-owned estate. Pure black fruits give sweetness, richn ess and a long-lasting aftertaste. One of the best wines from the Margaux appellation. **93** —*R.V. (6/3/2004)*

CHÂTEAU BROWN

Château Brown 2003 Bordeaux White Blend (Pessac-Léognan) $50. A fine, elegant white wine, rich with wood and toast flavors overlying the white peaches and pink grapefruit. **89** —*R.V. (6/1/2005)*

CHÂTEAU CAILLOU

Château Caillou 2004 Barrel Sample Bordeaux White Blend (Sauternes) $NA. Quite soft, unfocused, but also quite full-bodied, this seems to have strayed from the hot 2003. Good botrytis shows through. **88** —*R.V. (6/1/2005)*

CHÂTEAU CALON-SÉGUR

Château Calon-Ségur 2000 Bordeaux Blend (Saint-Estèphe) $90. This is a solid, huge wine, with rich but very dry tannins. With its dense, almost black color, and its sense of brooding power, it promises long aging. It will never be in the opulent Bordeaux camp, despite its prominent new wood flavors, but will probably outlive all but a handful top wines. **93** —*R.V. (6/1/2003)*

CHÂTEAU CAMENSAC

Château Camensac 2004 Barrel Sample Bordeaux Blend (Haut-Médoc) $NA. There are mint and new wood aromas, new wood tannins, and good flavors of blackberries. The acidity is present, and gives the wine good balance. **90** —*R.V. (6/1/2005)*

CHÂTEAU CAMPLAZENS

Château Camplazens 1999 La Clape Rhône Red Blend (Coteaux du Languedoc) $17. This is the kind of wine a beaver would like. It's over-wooded, and that's a fact. Yes, there's hidden black fruit, but it would take a miner to dig for it. What most of us will get is vanilla, butter, and too little wine. **83** —*M.S. (2/1/2003)*

Château Camplazens 2001 Viognier (Vin de Pays d'Oc) $22. Quite meaty and spicy, with mustard and cured-meat aromatics. This wine is a quick starter but a slow finisher. The banana and pear flavors charm at first but slip away quickly and without much noise. Nonetheless, it's rich and mouth-filling enough to satisfy. **84** —*M.S. (9/1/2003)*

CHÂTEAU CANON

Château Canon 2005 Barrel Sample Bordeaux Blend (Saint-Emilion Grand Cru) $NA. An impressively minty wine, with eucalyptus showing through. But fruit is the thing here, a storm of flavors pierced through with high perfumes and powered by some fine, dense tannins. **93** —*R.V. (6/20/2006)*

CHÂTEAU CANON LA GAFFELIÈRE

Château Canon la Gaffelière 2000 Bordeaux Blend (Saint-Emilion) $50. This is the flagship wine from the mini-empire (now comprising five properties) that is controlled by Comte Stephan von Niepperg. He has made a modern, wood-dominated wine, with rich, concentrated black fruits. It is powerful, perhaps too powerful, lacking a sense of the usual grace of this estate, although the ripeness of the wine does compensate. **93** —*R.V. (6/1/2003)*

Château Canon la Gaffelière 2004 Barrel Sample Bordeaux Blend (Saint-Emilion Grand Cru) $NA. An intensely flavored wine, which still keeps elegance, ripe tannins and sweet, fresh acidity as its core. This will develop well. **94** —*R.V. (6/1/2005)*

CHÂTEAU CANTEMERLE

Château Cantemerle 2005 Barrel Sample Bordeaux Blend (Haut-Médoc) $NA. With its rather earthy, rustic aromas, this wine is old-fashioned, showing hard tannins and not much else at this stage. In time, if the fruit appears, this may be a nice wine. **88** —*R.V. (6/21/2006)*

Château Cantemerle 2003 Barrel Sample Bordeaux Blend (Haut-Médoc) $NA. This is a ripe, complete wine, full of black fruits, spicy wood and solid tannins. Over five-10 years, it will develop into a very satisfying wine. **89** —*R.V. (6/3/2004)*

CHÂTEAU CANTENAC-BROWN

Château Cantenac-Brown 2001 Bordeaux Blend (Margaux) $37. The style of Cantenac-Brown is generally softer, richer than other Margaux, and this 2001 is no exception. It has a perfumed character, which has sweet, meaty flavors over ripe fruit. It has exotic spices, layered with dark wood and red fruits. To finish, there are dark tarry flavors and a blackberry-jelly freshness. **90** —*R.V. (6/1/2005)*

Château Cantenac-Brown 2005 Barrel Sample Bordeaux Blend (Margaux) $NA. A finely balanced wine that will develop well, showing every aspect—fruit, tannin, wood, density—in harmony. **89** —*R.V. (6/21/2006)*

CHÂTEAU CANUET

Château Canuet 1998 Bordeaux Blend (Margaux) $30. Spicy, foresty aromas dominate what subdued fruit there is. The palate is tight and grippy, with full-on tannins that really get after your cheeks. Amid those tannins is some grapey fruit and a bit of toastiness. **83** —*M.S. (1/1/2004)*

CHÂTEAU CARBONNIEUX

Château Carbonnieux 2005 Barrel Sample Bordeaux Blend (Pessac-Léognan) $NA. Big and bold, this wine may lack grace, but it has many other attractive elements, like its ripe fruits, its Technicolor tannins, and its dark flavors. **93** —*R.V. (6/20/2006)*

Château Carbonnieux 2002 Bordeaux White Blend (Pessac-Léognan) $33. Toasty and nutty at first, but with aeration the fruit emerges—first as pungent passion fruit, then more elegantly as nectarine and limes. Finishes long, fresh, and clean—a wine that can be drunk now and over the next five years, possibly longer. **90 Editors' Choice** —*J.C. (6/1/2005)*

CHÂTEAU CARONNE SAINTE-GEMME

Château Caronne Sainte-Gemme 2003 Bordeaux Blend (Haut-Médoc) $17. The Nony-Borie family is one group of families at the heart of the Bordeaux wine trade, and with this château they show a belief in the classic characters of Bordeaux. The wine is firm, tannic, with true black currant flavors and some solid layers of wood. A very good benchmark Bordeaux. **86** —*R.V. (5/1/2006)*

CHÂTEAU CHASSE-SPLEEN

Château Chasse-Spleen 2003 Bordeaux Blend (Moulis-en-Médoc) $24. Always one of the star crus bourgeois, Chasse-Spleen has produced a 2003 that manages to combine the rich, ripe fruits of the year with the right tannins and sweetness, along with blackberry fruits. It has the elegance and delicacy of Moulis, as well as some good intensity of flavor. A wine that will certainly age for 10 years or more. **91** —*R.V. (5/1/2006)*

Château Chasse-Spleen 2000 Bordeaux Blend (Moulis) $35. Under any new classification, this should certainly be a classed growth. Today it is among the leaders of the crus bourgeois. The 2000 is opulent, generous, stylish. The tannins are ripe and sweet, the fruit is finely balanced. It will develop well over the next 10-15 years. **91** —*R.V. (6/1/2003)*

Château Chasse-Spleen 2004 Barrel Sample Bordeaux Blend (Haut-Médoc) $NA. A finely made wine, which shows softness as well as density of fruit. This will develop well, and relatively quickly. **89** —*R.V. (6/1/2005)*

CHÂTEAU CHEVAL BLANC

Château Cheval Blanc 2005 Barrel Sample Bordeaux Blend (Saint-Emilion Grand Cru) $NA. A hugely dark wine, packed with very dry tannins. Initially a little hot from alcohol, later it shows layers of sweet acidity. An example of the power of the vintage without losing grace. An impressive wine. **96** —*R.V. (6/20/2006)*

Château Cheval Blanc 2003 Barrel Sample Bordeaux Blend (Saint-Emilion) $NA. There have been more complete Cheval Blancs than this, but this 2003 does have power. Huge fruit, huge solid tannins, concentration—maybe some charm would create a better wine. **93** —*R.V. (6/3/2004)*

CHÂTEAU CITRAN

Château Citran 2002 Bordeaux Blend (Haut-Médoc) $NA. The beautiful château at Citran has been renovated, as has the vineyard. As a result, the wines are worth looking out for, even in a lesser vintage. The wine has tannins, but the fruit is also fresh, with red fruit flavors. This is not a heavyweight, but will be attractive in 3–5 years. **87** —*R.V. (6/1/2005)*

Château Citran 2004 Barrel Sample Bordeaux Blend (Haut-Médoc) $NA. A fresh wine, which has good acidity, and firm fruit tannins. It seems to be a typical wine of the year, fresh and fruity. **88** —*R.V. (6/1/2005)*

CHÂTEAU CLARKE

Château Clarke 2003 Bordeaux Blend (Listrac-Médoc) $30. With the huge investment of the Edmond de Rothschild family, it is no surprise that this is the most powerful Listrac wine. This is rich, hugely dense, and very ripe. The tannins are more dusty and soft than usual Bordeaux, but that is the year. Vanilla and grilled almonds show through as the wine finishes. A successful wine that should age well. **90** —*R.V. (5/1/2006)*

Château Clarke 2005 Barrel Sample Bordeaux Blend (Listrac-Médoc) $NA. A ripe wine, heavily dominated by new wood, spice, herbs, and dry tannins. The fruit tannins are somewhat harsh and tough, but the ripe fruit will certainly develop. **90** —*R.V. (6/21/2006)*

CHÂTEAU CLERC-MILON

Château Clerc-Milon 2003 Bordeaux Blend (Pauillac) $55. This Clerc-Milon, under the same winemaking team as Mouton Rothschild, is an attractive wine, not heavy, already quite soft. It seems to have been heavily extracted, in a New World style, with new wood aromas and flavors, losing something of Pauillac, but a winner in that it's immediately attractive. **89** —*R.V. (5/1/2006)*

Château Clerc-Milon 2003 Barrel Sample Bordeaux Blend (Pauillac) $NA. Dusty tannins indicate how ripe the fruit was in this wine. There are oak flavors, plus spice and toast, but the dominant character is black currant fruit. **88** —*R.V. (6/3/2004)*

Château Clerc-Milon 2005 Barrel Sample Bordeaux Blend (Pauillac) $NA. This is a finely crafted wine, packed with all the right tannins that blend easily into the wood and blackberry flavors. The fruit is very pure, intense, and finely layered. **91** —*R.V. (6/1/2006)*

CHÂTEAU CLOS HAUT PEYRAGUEY
Château Clos Haut Peyraguey 2005 Barrel Sample Bordeaux White Blend (Sauternes) $NA. A ripe, creamy wine, which has great poise and freshness. There's just a touch of caramel, but the fruit—sweet apples and crisp pears—is dominant. A pure pleasure to taste. **91** —*R.V. (6/1/2006)*

CHÂTEAU CLOS LABORY
Château Clos Labory 2005 Barrel Sample Bordeaux Blend (Saint-Estèphe) $NA. Hugely tannic, and somewhat rustic, this is dark, dense, and very tough. Its tannins are totally dominant, giving the wine a hard edge. **87** —*R.V. (6/21/2006)*

CHÂTEAU COMTE SAINT MARTIN
Château Comte Saint Martin 2000 Bordeaux Blend (Bordeaux) $8. Mushroom and plum aromas followed by coffee and black plum flavors. Hot, heavy, and over the top. **80** —*M.S. (6/1/2003)*

CHÂTEAU COS D'ESTOURNEL
Château Cos d'Estournel 2000 Bordeaux Blend (Saint-Estèphe) $130. For a Saint-Estèphe this is surprisingly supple at this stage. The density is all in the exotic fruit, while the tannins are more of a background. That suggests this is a wine that will develop relatively fast, but it is going to give great pleasure along the way. **94** —*R.V. (6/1/2003)*

CHÂTEAU COUFRAN
Château Coufran 2005 Barrel Sample Bordeaux Blend (Haut-Médoc) $NA. If you're looking for great, ripe black currant fruits, this is where to come. The wine is full and hugely fruity, but it still manages a good Bordeaux sense of proportion. **92** —*R.V. (6/1/2006)*

CHÂTEAU COUHINS-LURTON
Château Couhins-Lurton 2002 Bordeaux White Blend (Pessac-Léognan) $32. When Andre Lurton bought Couhins in 1970, he followed a long-established Bordeaux tradition and added his name to the name of the property. This is a delicious, grassy wine, 100% Sauvignon Blanc, with flavors of pink grapefruit, along with some spice from wood aging. There is firm acidity to the finish. **90** —*R.V. (6/1/2005)*

CHÂTEAU COUTET
Château Coutet 2005 Barrel Sample Bordeaux White Blend (Barsac) $NA. Spice and dry botrytis are what this wine is about. There's a wood element as well, which dominates the fruit and the flavors of baked apples and cinnamon. Like all the drier styles, this will be a good food wine. **91** —*R.V. (6/1/2006)*

CHÂTEAU CROIZET-BAGES
Château Croizet-Bages 2004 Barrel Sample Bordeaux Blend (Pauillac) $NA. The aromas are somewhat reductive, but the palate is dense, with caramel and blackberry jelly flavors which don't blend happily. **86** —*R.V. (6/1/2005)*

CHÂTEAU D'AGASSAC
Château d'Agassac 2003 Bordeaux Blend (Haut-Médoc) $NA. This château has recently been purchased by an insurance company. Money has been no object in restructuring the property, and the results for the past 4 or 5 vintages have been impressive. It's a ripe wine, almost opulent, with ripe cherry and blueberry flavors, lending sweetness and tannins. Flattering now, it will mature quickly. **90** —*R.V. (5/1/2006)*

CHÂTEAU D'ANGLUDET
Château d'Angludet 2003 Bordeaux Blend (Margaux) $NA. Delicacy and charm often seem to be the hallmarks of Angludet—positive virtues in a world full of alcoholic, powerful wines. This 2003 has perhaps more tannins than usual from small berries, but it retains the property's elegance. Can be drunk relatively young, but certainly improves over 5–10 years. **89** —*R.V. (5/1/2006)*

Château d'Angludet 2005 Barrel Sample Bordeaux Blend (Margaux) $NA. Here's a big bruiser of a wine, almost northern Médoc, not Margaux, and surprising for d'Angludet. The dark tannins fight the huge fruit and, for now, it's hard to know which will win. One thing's for sure—this is immense. **88** —*R.V. (6/21/2006)*

CHÂTEAU D'AQUERIA
Château d'Aqueria 2003 Rhône Red Blend (Lirac) $19. Much more famous for its Tavel rosé, this estate also turns out an attractive, easy-to-drink red from Lirac. The 2003 shows plenty of bright, fresh fruit married to complex briar and herb notes. Supple tannins make it approachable now. **88** —*J.C. (11/15/2006)*

Château d'Aqueria 2004 Rosé Blend (Tavel) $16. A lovely, fruit-filled rosé, yet one that manages to tie in notes of mineral and spice to complement cherry pie and peach flavors. Medium-bodied, with a long, complex finish. **90 Editors' Choice** —*J.C. (6/21/2006)*

CHÂTEAU D'ARCHE
Château d'Arche 2005 Barrel Sample Bordeaux White Blend (Sauternes) $NA. A well-balanced, concentrated wine, full of botrytis flavors: richness, poised honey, and lemon. This is going to be an impressive wine for a second growth—in about 10 years—but already shows signs of greatness. **91** —*R.V. (6/1/2006)*

CHÂTEAU D'ARMAILHAC
Château d'Armailhac 2005 Barrel Sample Bordeaux Blend (Pauillac) $NA. Very pure black currant fruits pour out of the glass with this wine. Yes, there are tannins, but the fruit is uplifting, fresh, and very vibrant. Delicious, and likely to remain so. **92** —*R.V. (6/20/2006)*

CHÂTEAU D'ARSAC
Château d'Arsac 2003 Cuvée le Colombier Bordeaux Blend (Margaux) $30. Arsac has become the artistic center of the Médoc, rivaling Mouton-Rothschild's museum. Since buying Arsac in 1986, owner Philippe Rauox has achieved a big turnaround in quality: this 2003 Cuvée Le Colombier, the top wine from the property, shows great dusty tannins, hearty fruit, and considerable richness. **90** —*R.V. (5/1/2006)*

CHÂTEAU D'OR ET DE GUEULES
Château d'Or et de Gueules 1998 Rhône Red Blend (Costières de Nimes) $8. Bears a striking resemblance to blueberry pie in its aromas. Lighter than expected on the palate, before fading on the finish. A pleasant lunch mate to pâté or charcouterie. **84** —*J.C. (3/1/2001)*

CHÂTEAU D'YQUEM
Château d'Yquem 2005 Barrel Sample Bordeaux White Blend (Sauternes) $NA. So pure, it is almost a straight line of ripe, honeyed fruit and dense spices. There are flavors of marmalade and ripe pear, and steely, tight acidity. As always, the best. **95** —*R.V. (6/20/2006)*

CHÂTEAU DASSAULT
Château Dassault 2005 Barrel Sample Bordeaux Blend (Saint-Emilion Grand Cru) $NA. Too spicy, without compensating fruit, this property, owned by the French aircraft-making family, is performing below high expectations. **87** —*R.V. (6/21/2006)*

CHÂTEAU DAUZAC
Château Dauzac 2004 Barrel Sample Bordeaux Blend (Margaux) $NA. The wine has acidity, fresh fruit flavors, and some dark tannins. It is full of life, the tannins showing as a counterbalance to the fresh fruit. **91** —*R.V. (6/1/2005)*

CHÂTEAU DE BASTET
Château de Bastet 2003 Cuvée Speciale Rhône Red Blend (Côtes-du-Rhône) $18. A fresh, fruity wine, with red fruit flavors and soft, juicy tannins. It has a youthfulness at this stage that suggests it will age well over the next 4–5 years. The large 138-acre vineyard is surrounded by

FRANCE

open land protecting it from chemicals from neighboring properties. **88** —*R.V. (4/1/2005)*

CHÂTEAU DE BEAUCASTEL

Château de Beaucastel 1998 Cuvée Hommage à Jacques Perrin Red Blend (Châteauneuf-du-Pape) $240. A wine made with a high quantity of Mourvèdre (60%), and produced only in the best years, in memory of François and Jean-Pierre's father. Superripe, with huge fruit, it's jammy, gamy, and rich. Dusty tannins and excellent black-fruit flavors. The final effect is a wine that epitomizes the potential elegance and the power of Châteauneuf-du-Pape in one glass. A great wine with a distinguished future—at least 20 years. **98** *(12/31/2001)*

Château de Beaucastel 1998 Rhône Red Blend (Châteauneuf-du-Pape) $62. A big, rich wine with huge amounts of fruit oozing out of the glass. Great concentration and intensity, with licorice flavors from the Mourvèdre, finishing with chewy tannins. A great year for this wine, which should age well for 15 to 20 years. **96** *(12/31/2001)*

CHÂTEAU DE CAMARSAC

Château de Camarsac 2000 Bordeaux Blend (Bordeaux Supérieur) $8. The fairy-tale castle of Camarsac, all turrets and grey stone, dominates its vineyard. The wine has a bright purple color. Aromas of black currants and herbs follow through to flavors that have a woody, stalky element along with the soft fruit. This is traditional red Bordeaux, and in a ripe year like 2000 it works. **86** —*R.V. (12/1/2002)*

CHÂTEAU DE CAMPUGET

Château de Campuget 1998 Cuvée Prestige Rhône Red Blend (Costières de Nimes) $14. Cocoa and cedar aromas dominate the bouquet, but then some dark fruit emerges on the palate. It's dense, rich, and flavorful, but lacks the elegance and finesse to score higher. **87** —*J.C. (3/1/2001)*

CHÂTEAU DE CAPITANS

Château de Capitans 2004 Gamay (Juliénas) $16. 86 —*J.C. (11/15/2005)*

CHÂTEAU DE CHAMIREY

Château de Chamirey 2001 La Mission Premier Cru Chardonnay (Mercurey) $24. This fairly rich Chardonnay is a fine introduction to white Burgundy, boasting plump pear and pineapple fruit yet blending in enough mineral and hazelnut nuance to mark it as something different. **88** —*J.C. (10/1/2003)*

Château de Chamirey 1995 Pinot Noir (Rully) $19. 87 *(11/15/1999)*

CHÂTEAU DE CRUZEAU

Château de Cruzeau 2000 Bordeaux White Blend (Pessac-Léognan) $17. One of the many Pessac-Léognan properties owned by Andre Lurton, Cruzeau has a long history dating back to the 18th century. This 2000 vintage, now totally mature, has great vanilla flavors that balance well with the intense grapefruit flavors and toasty aromas. **90** —*R.V. (6/1/2005)*

CHÂTEAU DE FARGUES

Château de Fargues 2005 Barrel Sample Bordeaux White Blend (Sauternes) $NA. Almonds, some spice, and dryness are the dominant impressions of this wine. It is concentrated, very rich with layers of dense botrytis and flavors of oak and sweet fruit. A success for this lesser-known property. **88** —*R.V. (6/21/2006)*

CHÂTEAU DE FESLES

Château de Fesles 1999 Cabernet Franc (Anjou) $12. 86 —*M.M. (1/1/2004)*

CHÂTEAU DE FIEUZAL

Château de Fieuzal 2005 Barrel Sample Bordeaux Blend (Pessac-Léognan) $NA. Lovely, delicious sweet fruit leads a ripe and generous wine, showing deliciously black, almost raisiny flavors. There's a pile of richness, with acidity acting as a seasoning. **92** —*R.V. (6/1/2006)*

CHÂTEAU DE FONSALETTE

Château de Fonsalette 1998 Réservé Syrah (Côtes-du-Rhône) $50. If this Syrah could sing, its song would probably be "It Isn't Easy Being Green."

(We'd probably want it to add a verse about loads of black pepper, through and through, too.) Edamame, mint, wintergreen, and herbal aromas set the stage for a largely green pepper and green-oak palate. It's tart, lean, and needs time but, as one reviewer noted, it will probably "always be hard." Finishes long, with dry tannins. **85** *(11/1/2001)*

CHÂTEAU DE FRANCE

Château de France 2003 Bordeaux White Blend (Pessac-Léognan) $24. Château de France has improved dramatically in recent years, especially its white wines. With the 2003, packed with wood toast flavors and full of ripe fruit from the warm vintage, there is richness and dense citrus and tropical fruit flavors. With its spice it should develop well over the next few years. **92** —*R.V. (6/1/2005)*

CHÂTEAU DE JAU

Château de Jau 2002 Jaja Red Blend (Vin de Pays d'Oc) $9. This blend of Syrah and Grenache has minty, wet-plaster aromas, but also some pure Grenache notes. The palate runs tart, with cranberry and cherry. And the finish is tight and bitter, with more acids than tannin. A viable bistro wine but go no further. **82** —*M.S. (9/1/2003)*

Château de Jau 2001 Talon Rouge Syrah (Côtes du Roussillon) $20. Young and boisterous, with a bright purple tint. This is sweet, jammy, and grapy stuff, but firm tannins and lively acids keep it largely in balance. The palate is huge, with tarry, smoky edges surrounding rich plum fruit. A strapping middleweight for near-term drinking. **88** —*M.S. (1/1/2004)*

CHÂTEAU DE LA CHAIZE

Château de la Chaize 2001 Gamay (Brouilly) $12. This is a lightweight, cheerful wine, boasting earthy, herbal aromas offset by cherry fruit. A hint of chocolate creeps in on the finish. **85** —*J.C. (11/15/2003)*

CHÂTEAU DE LA GARDINE

Château de la Gardine 2001 Rhône Red Blend (Châteauneuf-du-Pape) $40. Made with a not-so-subtle whack of wood, this Châteauneuf features aromas of toasted marshmallows to go along with ripe cherry flavors. Crisp and medium-bodied, with flavors of vanilla, toffee, or caramel and the recurring cherries. Doesn't seem like a long ager, but worth holding a few years to see if additional complexities develop. **87** —*J.C. (11/15/2005)*

Château de la Gardine 2003 Cuvée Tradition Rhône Red Blend (Châteauneuf-du-Pape) $40. This large, 132-acre estate is making great wines today. This 2003 is up with the best, full of flavor, fruit, richness, and layers of sweet licorice, black plums, and wood. Spice, coffee, and chocolate flavors complete a complex blend. With its dense, dusty tannins, it is certainly ageworthy. **93 Cellar Selection** —*R.V. (12/31/2005)*

CHÂTEAU DE LA RAGOTIERE

Château de la Ragotiere 2005 Terra Vitis Sur Lie Black Label Muscadet (Muscadet Sèvre Et Maine) $14. A fresh crisp wine that demands seafood. It is light, poised, dancing on acidity and grapefruit flavors. It could be a fresh apéritif if the holiday season gives you warm weather. The quality of this wine shows how far Muscadet has progressed, and how wine lovers are in for a treat when they revisit this much-maligned style. **87 Best Buy** —*R.V. (11/15/2006)*

CHÂTEAU DE LA ROCHE-AUX-MOINES

Château de la Roche-Aux-Moines 1996 Clos de la Bergerie Chenin Blanc (Loire) $32. 91 —*L.W. (12/31/1999)*

Château de la Roche-Aux-Moines 1996 Becherelle Coulée de Serrant White Blend (Savennières) $26. 86 —*L.W. (10/1/1999)*

CHÂTEAU DE LA TERRIERE

Château de la Terriere 2002 Vieilles Vignes Gamay (Beaujolais-Villages) $12. This wine has an earthy edge to it, which gives it something more to offer than simple fruity flavors. The boisterous black cherry aromas combine with scents of damp clay. This light-bodied wine finishes with loads of red berries and a hint of licorice. **86** —*J.C. (11/15/2003)*

CHÂTEAU DE LAMARQUE

Château de Lamarque 2004 Barrel Sample Bordeaux Blend (Haut-Médoc) $NA. A dark, solid tannic wine, which has dryness rather than fruit. It is dense and firm, dominated by wood. **86** —*R.V. (6/1/2005)*

CHÂTEAU DE LANCYRE

Château de Lancyre 2005 Pic Saint-Loup Rosé Blend (Coteaux du Languedoc) $NA. Plump and round, this is a soft, simply fruity wine imbued with modest cherry-berry flavors. The blend is 50% Syrah, 40% Grenache and 10% Cinsault. **83** —*J.C. (6/19/2006)*

CHÂTEAU DE LUSSAC

Château de Lussac 2000 Le Libertin de Lussac Bordeaux Blend (Lussac Saint-Emilion) $25. With its aromas and flavors of plum and leather and subtle hints of vanila, this is a supple, medium-weight Bordeaux that's ready to drink. No, it's not that intense or complex, it's just a pleasing mouthful of claret. **87** —*J.C. (11/15/2005)*

CHÂTEAU DE MALLE

Château de Malle 2004 Barrel Sample Bordeaux White Blend (Sauternes) $NA. This could work as a rich wine, because there is good structure and piles of botrytis. It could be delicious, with its lovely dry finish, but that's for the future. **87** —*R.V. (6/1/2005)*

Château de Malle 2004 Barrel Sample Bordeaux White Blend (Sauternes) $NA. This could work as a rich wine, because there is good structure and piles of botrytis. It could be delicious, with its lovely dry finish, but that's for the future. **87** —*R.V. (6/1/2005)*

CHÂTEAU DE MARSANNAY

Château de Marsannay 2003 Chardonnay (Marsannay) $20. Big and rich, this wine just oozes rich, creamy caramel flavors. The fruit is super-ripe but still with good acidity and tastes of white peaches, toast, and cinnamon. Give this wine another year and it will be delicious. **90** —*R.V. (9/1/2005)*

Château de Marsannay 2003 Pinot Noir (Marsannay) $20. The wine is packed with jammy red fruits that give it juiciness and softness. Tannins are subdued, giving just enough structure to an otherwise forward wine. **88** —*R.V. (9/1/2005)*

CHÂTEAU DE MAUVANNE

Château de Mauvanne 1999 Cuvée 1 Red Blend (Côtes de Provence) $14. Dried fruit and a light leafiness define the fresh, earthy nose that truly rings of the region. This tasty, balanced blend of Grenache, Syrah, and Carignan is crisp and loaded with cherry character and flavor. It's smooth but just rugged enough to excite. A sure thing with grilled steak or chops. **87** —*M.S. (1/1/2004)*

CHÂTEAU DE MEURSAULT

Château de Meursault 2003 Chardonnay (Meursault) $42. A rich and ripe, but very soft wine. For lovers of ripe New World Chardonnay, this is a treat. Lovers of white Burgundy, though, may feel that there is something missing. **87** —*R.V. (9/1/2005)*

Château de Meursault 2002 Clos du Château Chardonnay (Bourgogne) $19. **86** —*J.C. (11/15/2005)*

Château de Meursault 2003 Clos du Château Chardonnay (Bourgogne) $21. This wine comes from the walled vineyard in front of Patriarche's Château de Meursault. Although it is simply Bourgogne Blanc, it is treated as a showpiece vineyard. That explains the richness, the weight, and the layers of well-judged new wood. This is as ripe as many Meursaults but will develop more quickly. **89** —*R.V. (9/1/2005)*

Château de Meursault 2003 Premier Cru Chardonnay (Meursault) $58. Château de Meursault almost always produces powerful wines. That fact plus the ripe 2003 vintage has yielded a huge premier cru. White stone fruits dominate, but the toast isn't far behind. Has good structure, too, promising development over 5 years. **90** —*R.V. (9/1/2005)*

Château de Meursault 2003 Pinot Noir (Bourgogne) $20. This is good, simple Pinot Noir with tannins layered over its red fruits. This attractive wine shows how good 2003 is for some of the lesser red Burgundies. **85** —*R.V. (9/1/2005)*

Château de Meursault 2000 Pinot Noir (Bourgogne) $16. The trials of the 2000 vintage show in this wine's pale color and lean mouthfeel. It's pretty cherry and chocolate flavors are light, the finish tart. **83** *(4/1/2003)*

Château de Meursault 1999 Cent-Vignes Premier Cru Pinot Noir (Beaune) $31. Shows "redder" fruit than the Grèves; brighter and sweeter—more like strawberries than cherries. Soft and supple, there's no aging necessary. Picks up coffee and chocolate notes on the finish. **87** *(4/1/2003)*

Château de Meursault 2001 Clos de Epenots Premier Cru Pinot Noir (Pommard) $43. **82** —*J.C. (11/15/2005)*

Château de Meursault 2002 Clos des Chênes Premier Cru Pinot Noir (Volnay) $45. This is a smooth, opulent wine with very good acidity. It's taut on the palate, with ripe fruit and a dry finish. **88** —*R.V. (9/1/2004)*

Château de Meursault 1999 Clos des Epenots Premier Cru Pinot Noir (Pommard) $40. Dried spices, leather, and toast add complexity to the black cherry fruit. The flavors are slightly tarry and roasted; sturdy yet spicy. Best of all, the mouthfeel is lush and enveloping. **88** *(4/1/2003)*

CHÂTEAU DE MEURSAULT

Château de Meursault 2003 Premier Cru Pinot Noir (Beaune) $32. Red, juicy fruit merges with some dry tannins in this structured wine. The wine is dry, with some herbal character. At this stage, it is very closed up, and needs at least 3-4 years before the fruit really comes through. **88** —*R.V. (9/1/2005)*

CHÂTEAU DE MONTFAUCON

Château de Montfaucon 2005 Comtesse Madeleine Rhône White Blend (Côtes-du-Rhône) $15. An impressive white Rhône, this blend of Viognier, Marsanne, Clairette, Bourboulenc, and Picpoul offers expressive aromas of spring flowers, apricots, and pears. It's fresh and medium-bodied, with plenty of minerality and lingering spice on the finish. **87** —*J.C. (11/15/2006)*

CHÂTEAU DE MYRAT

Château de Myrat 2004 Barrel Sample Bordeaux White Blend (Barsac) $NA. A rather lean wine, which has the acidity, but not the full botrytis effect. Quite delicate and rather austere. **88** —*R.V. (6/1/2005)*

CHÂTEAU DE PENNAUTIER

Château de Pennautier 2000 Cabernet Sauvignon (Vin de Pays d'Oc) $9. The color is nice and the aromas are sweet with the essence of graham crackers. The palate is a bit leathery, with blackberry and coffee flavors emerging. Then on the back of the palate the wine gets tighter and more gritty. Here the tannins bite, although for an inexpensive drink with food it's up to the task. **86 Best Buy** —*M.S. (2/1/2003)*

Château de Pennautier 2000 L'Orangerie Rhône Red Blend (Languedoc) $9. Dark in the glass, with tight leathery aromas. The starching palate features licorice and black coffee along with plum fruit and spice. In a word, it's peppery, and a tad bit bitter. But it also delivers a decent punch, some puckery red fruit, and adequate complexity well within the Provençal style. Drink with food for best results. **85** —*M.S. (2/1/2003)*

Château de Pennautier 2001 Syrah (Vin de Pays d'Oc) $8. This is like a well-fed youngster. It's purple and offers mineral, lavender, and peppery black fruit aromas. But things go a bit south on the palate. The fruit is super-charged by piercing acidity. And there's also a jolting bolt of sugar on the back palate. Ripe, modern, but clumsy, without the balance and harmony to score better. **82** —*M.S. (1/1/2004)*

CHÂTEAU DE PEZ

Château de Pez 1995 Bordeaux Blend (Saint-Estèphe) $30. **87** *(5/1/2000)*

Château de Pez 2003 Barrel Sample Bordeaux Blend (Saint-Estèphe) $NA. Very much in the mold of Saint-Estèphe tannins, this wine still has room for power, huge dark fruits, and concentration. **88** —*R.V. (6/3/2004)*

CHÂTEAU DE PIBARNON

Château de Pibarnon 2005 Rosé Blend (Bandol) $NA. This pale copper rosé has enough richness to pair with such grilled summer fare as ribs or burgers. Hints of raspberry on the nose give way to stone fruit and citrus, backed by sturdy cocoa bass notes. Finishes with more chocolate and a silky texture. **87** —*J.C. (6/21/2006)*

CHÂTEAU DE POURCIEUX

Château de Pourcieux 2001 Rosé Blend (Côtes de Provence) $9. Sweet and musky smelling, which in its own way is appealing. The palate is a mix of grapefruit, melon, and other citrus, and lively acids keep it kicking while your tongue does a double take. Good, but a bit too tangy and jumpy. **83** —*M.S. (9/1/2003)*

FRANCE

CHÂTEAU DE ROUANNE

Château de Rouanne 2005 Rhône Red Blend (Vinsobres) $20. This has an intriguing bouquet that smoothly marries slightly herbal-spicy Syrah with ripe, plummy Grenache (the blend is 70% Grenache, 25% Syrah and 5% Mourvèdre). Plum and spice flavors are reasonably rich on the palate, ending with supple tannins. A promising early release that shows the fine quality of the 2005 vintage. **88** *—J.C. (11/15/2006)*

CHÂTEAU DE RULLY

Château de Rully 2003 Pinot Noir (Rully) $NA. Vinified and bottled by Antonin Rodet, this wine comes from a vineyard owned by the counts de Ternay. It is a fresh, simple, juicy wine with pleasant, light red raspberry flavors. It should develop quickly **85** *—R.V. (9/1/2005)*

CHÂTEAU DE SAINT-COSME

Château de Saint-Cosme 2004 Hominus Fides Rhône Red Blend (Gigondas) $50. A bit closed on the nose, but the potential of this wine is obvious. Crafted from 110-year-old Grenache, the flavors are intense, bathing the palate in layers of plum pudding, anise, and chocolate. A huge wine in need of at least five years. Owner Louis Barruol suggests 15 years may be a better bet. **93 Cellar Selection** *—J.C. (11/15/2006)*

CHÂTEAU DE SAINT-ROCH

Château de Saint-Roch 2004 Brunel Rhône Red Blend (Lirac) $13. Finely structured, with dark fruits and dry tannins, there's plenty going on here. The classic Rhône blend (including Mourvèdre) gives the wine fine perfumes as well as great ripe fruits. There is a delicious juicy element that rounds everything out. **89** *—R.V. (12/31/2006)*

CHÂTEAU DE SANCERRE

Château de Sancerre 1997 Sauvignon Blanc (Sancerre) $18. 87 *—M.S. (10/1/1999)*

CHÂTEAU DE SÉGRIÈS

Château de Ségriès 2004 Rhône Red Blend (Lirac) $14. Selected entirely from clay-and-limestone soils (other parcels go into the estate's Côtes-du-Rhône), this is a rich, plummy wine. Dark fruit carries an undercurrent of savory mushrooms backed by firm structure. Drink now–2010+. **89** *—J.C. (11/15/2006)*

Château de Ségriès 1999 Cuvée Reservée Rhône Red Blend (Lirac) $12. 87 *—J.C. (12/31/2000)*

Château de Ségriès 2005 Rosé Blend (Tavel) $15. Really fresh and lively, this Tavel balances ripe berry flavors with citrusy lime notes and a dry, minerally finish. Easy to drink on its own, but also versatile at the table. **88** *—J.C. (11/15/2006)*

CHÂTEAU DE SEGUIN

Château de Seguin 1999 Cuvée Carl Bordeaux Blend (Bordeaux Supérieur) $25. This wine has a deep purple color. The aromas are of attractive ripe fruit, wood, and black fruits. To taste, there is sweet, juicy black fruit, with some wood, which is well in balance. A fine wine, still young, this will age well. **89** *—R.V. (12/1/2002)*

CHÂTEAU DE SÉRAME

Château de Sérame 2001 Rhône Red Blend (Corbières) $10. Boasts some interesting aromas of clove and black pepper, balanced by blackberry and cherry flavors. Nicely proportioned and well-structured, with mild tannins and decent acidity; it's not a blockbuster—just a satisfying accompaniment to simply prepared red meats. With a butterflied leg of lamb off the grill, no one will guess you're serving a $10 wine. **86 Best Buy** *—J.C. (11/15/2004)*

CHÂTEAU DE SOURS

Château de Sours 2000 Bordeaux Blanc White Blend (Bordeaux) $8. With his almost half-and-half blend of Sauvignon Blanc and Sémillon, Scotsman Esme Johnstone has produced a ripe, modern, fruity wine, with a light touch of oak to round out the fruit and its balancing acidity. **87** *—R.V. (12/1/2002)*

CHÂTEAU DE TRACY

Château de Tracy 2004 Sauvignon Blanc (Pouilly-Fumé) $35. There aren't many aristocratic estates in the largely peasant-based culture of Pouilly. But this is one, and it's old, dating back to 1396. The Estutt d'Assay family makes one wine, an estate wine: This 2004 has great elegance, not hugely rich, but with fine, pure fruit flavors that are already well balanced. There's roundness from the terroir of Tract-sur-Loire as well as a streak of fine acidity. **91** *—R.V. (8/1/2006)*

Château de Tracy 2002 Sauvignon Blanc (Pouilly-Fumé) $30. Just enough chalk and mineral is present on the bouquet to complement the melon, citrus, and green herb notes. Very much of a streamlined, tight wine on the palate, where melon, lemon, and citrus pith come together. Refreshing, dry and firm; the perfect shellfish accompaniment. **89** *(7/1/2005)*

CHÂTEAU DE VALCOMB

Château de Valcomb 2001 Prestige Rhône Red Blend (Costières de Nimes) $12. A bit overdone, with aromas of leather and prune and flavors of molasses. Still, it's not as heavy as it sounds, and it finishes with some chalky tannins, so it does have some structure. Try with beef stew. **84** *—J.C. (2/1/2005)*

CHÂTEAU DE VAUX

Château de Vaux 2002 Les Gryphées White Blend (Moselle VDQS) $13. While the German wines down river get all the press, few consumers even know of this tiny French wine region. More should, as wines like this are perfect accompaniments to today's light cuisine. This wine, a blend of 30% Auxerrois, 30% Müller-Thurgau, 30% Pinot Gris, and 10% Gewürztraminer, layers elegant flavors of peach, melon, and green apple over an earthy, minerally core. Its modest alcohol level and lively acidity make it a natural as an apéritif, and versatile at the table. **89 Best Buy** *—J.C. (11/15/2004)*

CHÂTEAU DES ALBIÈRES

Château des Albières 2001 Cuvée Georges Dardé Red Blend (Saint-Chinian) $NA. Named after the founder of the local cooperative, this wine has fine, ripe juicy flavors and a layer of wood. This is a wine for early drinking, great with barbecues, and offering easy pleasure. **84** *—R.V. (12/1/2004)*

CHÂTEAU DES MILLE ANGES

Château des Mille Anges 1996 Bordeaux Blend (Premieres Côtes de Bordeaux) $13. 80 *—M.S. (7/1/2000)*

CHÂTEAU DES ROQUES

Château des Roques 2003 Rhône Red Blend (Vacqueyras) $8. Tastes pretty oaky—chocolate and coffee aromas partially obscure the modest berry fruit flavors. Still, it's reasonably supple, so if you don't mind wood this could be just the ticket. Picks up additional oaky notes of vanilla and caramel on the finish. **85 Best Buy** *—J.C. (11/15/2006)*

CHÂTEAU DES TOURS

Château des Tours 2000 Réserve Red Blend (Côtes-du-Rhône) $14. Has the silky, caressing mouthfeel of ripe Grenache (85%), along with wild, gamy aromas and bright flavors of cherries and spice. The long, tangy finish folds in enough dusty tannins to suggest that holding this for a few years wouldn't be a bad idea. **90 Best Buy** *(10/1/2003)*

CHÂTEAU DEYREM VALENTIN

Château Deyrem Valentin 2001 Bordeaux Blend (Margaux) $NA. This Soussans estate has produced a well-structured 2001, filled with black fruit, underscored by tannins. It has flavors of spice, some herbs, and dark, dry tastes. The layers of wood are there, but do not dominate. **87** *—R.V. (6/1/2005)*

CHÂTEAU DOISY VÉDRINES

Château Doisy Védrines 2004 Barrel Sample Bordeaux White Blend (Sauternes) $NA. Perfumed, with layers of dry botrytis, this is powerful and potentially hugely rich. It has solidity, depth, and great structure, but remains fresh. **91** *—R.V. (6/1/2005)*

FRANCE

CHÂTEAU DOISY-DAËNE

Château Doisy-Daëne 2005 Barrel Sample Bordeaux White Blend (Barsac) $NA. This has all the flavors of an Asian kitchen, spices dominant and, underneath, some attractive lemon and honey botrytis. This should be a great apéritif style of wine. **91** —*R.V. (6/1/2006)*

CHÂTEAU DU BASTY

Château du Basty 2001 Lantignié Gamay (Beaujolais-Villages) $13. Damp leather and black cherry aromas lead the way, then sweet, candied fruit takes over on the palate, backed by tart acidity. **83** —*J.C. (11/15/2003)*

CHÂTEAU DU CLUZEAU

Château du Cluzeau 2005 Barrel Sample Bordeaux Blend (Listrac-Médoc) $NA. Made by the same team as at Château Ducru Beaucaillou, this is pleasantly ripe, with fresh fruit and a delicious juiciness. **86** —*R.V. (6/21/2006)*

CHÂTEAU DU DONJON

Château du Donjon 2005 Rosé Blend (Minervois) $NA. The soft peach and berry flavors in this wine come across as slightly confected, but clean and fresh. It's on the full side, with a mouth-filling texture that could use just a touch more crispness to enliven it. **84** —*J.C. (6/19/2006)*

CHÂTEAU DU QUINT

Château du Quint 1999 Red Blend (Pomerol) $25. Green and under-ripe, with tobacco and rhubarb aromas. The flavors are too weedy and burnt for the wine to merit higher, and that's despite a perfectly good mouthfeel. Kosher. **80** —*M.S. (1/1/2004)*

CHÂTEAU DU TERTRE

Château du Tertre 2001 Bordeaux Blend (Margaux) $31. Under the same ownership as Giscours, and benefiting from big investment in recent years, this is an estate at the top of its form. The wine has aromas of sweet, new wood, while the palate is packed with tarry fruits and spicy wood and herbs. Flavors of ripe black currants give a rich, satisfying feel. This is a wine that is well-structured, dense and, given another five years, will be delicious. **92** —*R.V. (6/1/2005)*

CHÂTEAU DU TRIGNON

Château du Trignon 2000 Sablet Rouge Grenache-Syrah (Côtes-du-Rhône) $15. 91 Best Buy —*S.H. (11/15/2002)*

Château du Trignon 2004 Classic Rhône Red Blend (Côtes-du-Rhône) $15. Shows plenty of leather and spice on the nose, but seems to lack some concentration and fruit. It's a bit of a lightweight, with pretty aromas and plenty of spice and persistence on the finish. **85** —*J.C. (11/15/2006)*

CHÂTEAU DUCLA

Château Ducla 2002 Bordeaux Blend (Bordeaux Supérieur) $13. 81 —*J.C. (6/1/2005)*

Château Ducla 1998 Bordeaux Blend (Bordeaux) $10. I know Bordeaux isn't known for being fruit-driven, but this paucity of fruit in a wine that's 50% Merlot (from a vintage that favored this variety's development) is hard to fathom. Leather and old wood combine with earth and mushrooms. There's decent weight and intensity here, so if these are flavors you look for this is an example to seek out. **82** —*J.C. (3/1/2001)*

CHÂTEAU DUCRU BEAUCAILLOU

Château Ducru Beaucaillou 2003 Barrel Sample Bordeaux Blend (Saint-Julien) $NA. The tannins are so sweet with this wine, that they only just avoid tipping over into Napa Cabernet. But the structure saves the wine and propels it into classic, powerful Saint-Julien. **91** —*R.V. (6/3/2004)*

CHÂTEAU DUHART-MILON

Château Duhart-Milon 2003 Bordeaux Blend (Pauillac) $55. Under the control of the winemaking team of Lafite, this estate is on a roll. This is a beautifully balanced wine, with complexity, richness, and cassis, figs and black plums. It is developing relatively quickly, and will be ready to drink in two to three years. **89** —*R.V. (5/1/2006)*

Château Duhart-Milon 2005 Barrel Sample Bordeaux Blend (Pauillac) $NA. A ripe, fruity, very juicy wine, with delicious blackberry fruits and freshness. Attractive for its drinkability in the near term. **89** —*R.V. (6/21/2006)*

CHÂTEAU DUPLESSIS

Château Duplessis 2003 Bordeaux Blend (Moulis-en-Médoc) $NA. One of the three crus bourgeois Medoc properties under the control of Marie-Laure Lurton, Duplessis has produced an attractive, fruity wine in 2003, which shows good tannic structure under its black currant and herb flavors. It is fine and elegant, with a deliciously lively aftertaste, and should develop well. **88** —*R.V. (5/1/2006)*

CHÂTEAU DURFORT-VIVENS

Château Durfort-Vivens 2000 Bordeaux Blend (Margaux) $31. Animal and bell pepper aromas mask a soft, relatively lightweight wine, which has fine acidity and fresh red fruit flavors. **85** —*R.V. (6/1/2003)*

Château Durfort-Vivens 2004 Barrel Sample Bordeaux Blend (Margaux) $NA. This is powered by fruit tannins that dominate the fruit. But the typical acidity of this vintage shows through, giving the wine both potential and the likelihood of good fruit later. **93** —*R.V. (6/1/2005)*

CHÂTEAU FAUGERES

Château Faugeres 2000 Bordeaux Blend (Saint-Emilion) $40. Corinne Guisez scored a great success with her 2000. The wine is finely polished, shining, with its generous, deeply concentrated fruits and fine perfumes. The tannins show through the fruit, while the wood flavors hide much more discreetly in the background. **90** —*R.V. (6/1/2003)*

CHÂTEAU FERRANDE

Château Ferrande 2005 Barrel Sample Bordeaux Blend (Graves) $NA. This is rich, full of sweet-and-sour acidity, layers of sweet tannins and big, ripe fruit. It's powerful, intense, and full of pure black currant fruit flavors. Ends with great acidity. **91** —*R.V. (6/1/2006)*

CHÂTEAU FERRIÈRE

Château Ferrière 2005 Barrel Sample Bordeaux Blend (Margaux) $NA. Dark, dry, and tannic this wine currently offers little in the way of fruit. The tannins are firm, solidly based, and only hinting at the fruit underneath. It's a tough wine at the moment, but the structure will certainly see it into a good maturity. **91** —*R.V. (6/1/2006)*

CHÂTEAU FEYTIT-CLINET

Château Feytit-Clinet 2005 Barrel Sample Bordeaux Blend (Pomerol) $NA. An impressive wine with lovely, sweet, ripe fruit, a touch of new wood spice, and delicious acidity. **90** —*R.V. (6/21/2006)*

CHÂTEAU FIGEAC

Château Figeac 2005 Barrel Sample Bordeaux Blend (Saint-Emilion Grand Cru) $NA. A very ripe, soft wine, and a real pleasure to imbibe. There is perfumed fruit, while the tannins themselves are gentle, sweet, with only a touch of dryness to give the wine power. The acidity to finish gives the wine an attractive lift. **92** —*R.V. (6/1/2006)*

CHÂTEAU FILHOT

Château Filhot 2004 Barrel Sample Bordeaux White Blend (Sauternes) $NA. This is straight down the line, with dry botrytis and acidity, touched with richness. It has freshness, very much in keeping with the year. **88** —*R.V. (6/1/2005)*

CHÂTEAU FLAUGERGUES

Château Flaugergues 2003 Rosé Blend (Coteaux du Languedoc) $12. Soft flavors along with a burst of alcohol make this a powerful wine. It is peppery and full-bodied and not for the faint-hearted. **83** —*R.V. (12/1/2004)*

CHÂTEAU FOMBRAUGE

Château Fombrauge 2002 Bordeaux Blend (Saint-Emilion Grand Cru) $NA. Under the control of Bernard Magrez, this has become the largest of the Saint-Emilion grand cru vineyards. The wines are in a modern, dense style, with power-packed fruit, high extract, and huge, solid tannins. For a 2002, this is a big wine. **88** —*R.V. (6/1/2005)*

Château Fombrauge 2004 Barrel Sample Bordeaux Blend (Saint-Emilion Grand Cru) $NA. Packed with ripe Merlot, this wine has a darker side of black tannins, with flavors of toast and exotic spices. **90** —*R.V. (6/1/2005)*

FRANCE

CHÂTEAU FONBADET

Château Fonbadet 2000 Bordeaux Blend (Pauillac) $50. This wine has a distinctly herbal aroma and flavor. Sage, thyme, and broccoli come to mind. The tannins are firm and frame secondary flavors redolent of coffee, plum, and charry toast. Finishes with moderate length. Kosher. **89** —*J.M. (4/3/2004)*

CHÂTEAU FONRÉAUD

Château Fonréaud 2000 Bordeaux Blend (Listrac) $15. One of the stars in Listrac, Fonréaud is producing a modern style of wine, with plenty of new wood. The flavors are ripe, black, generous, while allowing a sense of elegance as well. **88** —*R.V. (6/1/2003)*

Château Fonréaud 1999 Red Blend (Listrac) $17. Jean Chanfreau's family, which owns Châteaux Fonréaud and Lestage in Listrac, produces this blend of 52% Cabernet Sauvignon, 45% Merlot, and 3% Petit Verdot, giving a wine with plenty of Cabernet cassis flavors, but also a roundness and spiciness that sit well with firm tannins. Lovers of young Bordeaux will find it ready to drink now, but it has a good five years before complete maturity. **88** —*R.V. (11/15/2003)*

CHÂTEAU FORTIA

Château Fortia 2003 Cuvée du Baron Rhône Red Blend (Châteauneuf-du-Pape) $32. This is hallowed territory, the home of Baron Roy, who created the Châteauneuf-du-Pape appellation, the first in France. His family still possesses the 25-acre property, and makes great wines. This 2003 is traditional in style, with dark tannins over spicy, jammy fruit and ripeness. This, as is usual from Fortia, is a wine that will age well. **92** —*R.V. (12/31/2005)*

CHÂTEAU FOURCAS DUPRÉ

Château Fourcas Dupré 2005 Barrel Sample Bordeaux Blend (Listrac-Médoc) $NA. Ripe, fruity black currant aromas and a fine, ripe element of new wood and dusty tannins give this wine a polished and elegant appeal. There's great depth of flavor as well as excellent aging potential. **89** —*R.V. (6/21/2006)*

CHÂTEAU FOURCAS-HOSTEN

Château Fourcas-Hosten 2002 Bordeaux Blend (Listrac-Médoc) $NA. This estate, long a positive bastion of traditional Bordeaux, has undergone quite a change with this wine. Packed with dark tannins, new wood flavors, and fresh, polished fruit. **88** —*R.V. (6/1/2005)*

Château Fourcas-Hosten 2005 Barrel Sample Bordeaux Blend (Listrac-Médoc) $NA. A delicious wine, packed with black currant juice aromas and flavors. The fruit is balanced with deliciously ripe tannins and just a touch of new wood. **90** —*R.V. (6/21/2006)*

CHÂTEAU FRANC-MAYNE

Château Franc-Mayne 2005 Barrel Sample Bordeaux Blend (Saint-Emilion Grand Cru) $NA. Balance is the key to this wine, as it shows off ripe fruits and then dry tannins, black plum, herbs, and finally finishing acidity. **91** —*R.V. (6/1/2006)*

CHÂTEAU FUISSÉ

Château Fuissé 2003 Chardonnay (Pouilly-Fuissé) $35. From the earliest harvest in memory, the appellation's landmark château has turned in an admirable effort. Slightly nutty and honeyed on the nose, with spiced baked apple flavors and a soft, easy finish. Drink now and over the next few years. **87** —*J.C. (11/15/2005)*

Château Fuissé 2003 Les Brûlés Chardonnay (Pouilly-Fuissé) $45. Shows more obvious oak than the other cuvées from this producer, with smoke and caramel notes layered over rich, baked apple fruit. A bit low in acidity, but powerful on the finish. Drink now–2010. **89** —*J.C. (11/15/2005)*

Château Fuissé 2003 Les Clos Chardonnay (Pouilly-Fuissé) $45. Produced from yields that were under 2 tons per acre, this wine is highly concentrated and rich, with exotic tropical fruit notes layered with orange marmalade. The only quibble is that the finish could be a little longer, but this is still a lovely mouthful. Drink now–2010. **90** —*J.C. (11/15/2005)*

Château Fuissé 2003 Les Combettes Chardonnay (Pouilly-Fuissé) $NA. In the warm style of the vintage, this wine is framed by nutty, honeyed aromas, but features a core of wonderfully elegant pear fruit. Finishes long, with chalk and mineral notes that provide structural support in lieu of crisp acidity. Drink now–2010. **90 Editors' Choice** —*J.C. (11/15/2005)*

Château Fuissé 2003 Vieilles Vignes Chardonnay (Pouilly-Fuissé) $50. Blended from 10 plots of vines, all over 30 years of age, with most planted in 1929, this is Château Fuissé's ultimate cuvée, and the one intended to have the most longevity. In 2003, it's incredibly rich and honeyed, with notes of grilled nuts balanced by fresh peach and melon flavors. Long on the finish. Drink now–2015. **92 Cellar Selection** —*J.C. (11/15/2005)*

CHÂTEAU GAUDRELLE

Château Gaudrelle 2002 Brut Chenin Blanc (Vouvray) $18. With its total dominance by Chenin Blanc, this is a classic Loire wine, fresh and crisp, with great acidity and apple and nut flavors. It is light and easy, with a soft mousse. **88** —*R.V. (6/1/2006)*

CHÂTEAU GÉNOT-BOULANGER

Château Génot-Boulanger 2000 Pinot Noir (Chambolle-Musigny) $NA. Earthy aromas, with ripe plums and bitter cherries give way on the palate to a rather lean wine, dominated by tannins that cover dry fruit. This could develop, but it seems to lack intensity of flavor. **86** —*R.V. (11/1/2002)*

Château Génot-Boulanger 2002 Clos Blanc Premier Cru Pinot Noir (Pommard) $30. A huge brooding wine. Dark black fruits and big tannins complete this powerhouse. **88** —*R.V. (9/1/2004)*

Château Génot-Boulanger 2002 Les Aussy Pinot Noir (Volnay) $25. Firm tannins give this wine great structure. It has richness and ripe coffee flavors along with spice. Dry tannins at the end suggest good aging potential. **88** —*R.V. (9/1/2004)*

CHÂTEAU GISCOURS

Château Giscours 2003 Bordeaux Blend (Margaux) $42. In normal vintages it's velvety and rich, but Giscours seems to have gone over the top in 2003. The fruit is certainly there, generally fresh, but there is an underlying sense of over-ripeness, which needs to be better integrated: Hopefully this will happen as time goes on. For the moment, it's a question mark. **90** —*R.V. (5/1/2006)*

Château Giscours 2000 Bordeaux Blend (Margaux) $45. This is a big, powerful, firm wine, with a top layer of ripe, glamorous fruit flavors. Black currant jelly fruits are shot through with ripe acidity and soft tannins. It should develop relatively fast, but then last well. **92** —*R.V. (6/1/2003)*

Château Giscours 2004 Barrel Sample Bordeaux Blend (Margaux) $NA. A delicious, fresh wine, with some new wood, good red, and black fruits, ripe tannins, and some dense character. The aftertaste leaves fresh acidity. **93** —*R.V. (6/1/2005)*

CHÂTEAU GLORIA

Château Gloria 2000 Bordeaux Blend (Saint-Julien) $30. Untypical of Saint-Julien, this wine is solid, chunky, quite foursquare. But it has good punch, richness, and depth, along with concentrated black fruits. **87** —*R.V. (6/1/2003)*

CHÂTEAU GRAND CORBIN-DESPAGNE

Château Grand Corbin-Despagne 2000 Bordeaux Blend (Saint-Emilion) $25. François Despagne has certainly pulled this property together after it lost Grand Cru Classé status in 1996. The 2000 shows real class and style. It has plenty of new wood flavors, but they are well-judged and have been used to support the solid fruit and black tannins. It is developing fast, but the tannins are there to allow it to age. **90** —*R.V. (6/1/2003)*

Château Grand Corbin-Despagne 2004 Barrel Sample Bordeaux Blend (Saint-Emilion Grand Cru) $NA. A finely crafted wine. Balanced between new wood and caramel flavors, and dark, ripe fruits. **90** —*R.V. (6/1/2005)*

CHÂTEAU GRAND MAYNE

Château Grand Mayne 2000 Bordeaux Blend (Saint-Emilion) $59. A modern, smooth wine, with polished fruit and a dark purple color. The wine is full of new wood, but still dominated by Licorice and dark chocolate flavors. It should develop relatively quickly, over the next 10 years. **91** —*R.V. (6/1/2003)*

CHÂTEAU GRAND-PUY-DUCASSE

Château Grand-Puy-Ducasse 2003 Bordeaux Blend (Pauillac) $30. One of the best vintages for many years from this rather forgotten property. The wine is developing fast, already well-integrated, powerful, and dense, but dominated by attractive, ripe fruit. **88** —*R.V. (5/1/2006)*

Château Grand-Puy-Ducasse 2005 Barrel Sample Bordeaux Blend (Pauillac) $NA. Rather simple, juicy fruits make a stand, but green flavors spoil this wine. It needs more richness to reflect the vintage. **86** —*R.V. (6/21/2006)*

CHÂTEAU GRANDE CASSAGNE

Château Grande Cassagne 2001 Les Rameaux "S" Syrah (Costières de Nimes) $10. The "S" stands for Syrah, a word prohibited from appearing on the label thanks to arcane French regulations. But one whiff erases any doubt on that point. The effusive blueberry aromas feature grace notes of pepper and spring flowers; the mouthfeel is rich and layered. Supple tannins coat the crevices of the mouth without turning bitter or astringent, and the licorice-tinged finish lingers a long time. **90 Best Buy** —*J.C. (11/15/2002)*

CHÂTEAU GRENOUILLE

Château Grenouille 2003 Grenouille Grand Cru Chardonnay (Chablis) $90. Richly honeyed on the nose, with layers of mineral that lure you in. Tastes like honey-drizzled wet riverstones with a squeeze of citrus— mouth-filling yet precise. Long and intense on the finish. **92** —*J.C. (4/1/2006)*

CHÂTEAU GREYSAC

Château Greysac 2005 Barrel Sample Bordeaux Blend (Médoc) $NA. There are very ripe, red fruit aromas in this wine, layered with acidity. The palate is also ripe, but with tannins that are dry, solid, and dominant in the aftertaste. A wine that is pretty tough at this stage. **86** —*R.V. (6/21/2006)*

CHÂTEAU GRUAUD-LAROSE

Château Gruaud-Larose 2003 Bordeaux Blend (Saint-Julien) $60. Under the management of Jean Merlaut, this estate has lost some of the super-opulence of the wines of the 90s, and gained finesse and elegance. That has stood the 2003 in good stead, emphasizing solidity and dry tannins to balance the wood and cranberry flavors of the fruit. **90** —*R.V. (5/1/2006)*

Château Gruaud-Larose 2005 Barrel Sample Bordeaux Blend (Saint-Julien) $NA. Acidity, black currant fruits, dry tannins: all the hallmarks of young Cabernet Sauvignon in a ripe, layered complex wine that will develop into something extraordinary. A great wine. **95** —*R.V. (6/20/2006)*

Château Gruaud-Larose 2003 Barrel Sample Bordeaux Blend (Saint-Julien) $NA. This is a very firm, direct wine, balancing wood with dry fruit tannins. It lacks fruit at this stage, but there is enough power to suggest the fruit will come through later. **88** —*R.V. (6/3/2004)*

CHÂTEAU GUIRAUD

Château Guiraud 2005 Barrel Sample Bordeaux White Blend (Sauternes) $NA. Already, this wine is developing a golden color. Typical of Guiraud, to taste it is big and powerful and full of complexity and ripeness. Currently missing freshness, but that will come later. **91** —*R.V. (6/1/2006)*

CHÂTEAU HANTEILLAN

Château Hanteillan 2003 Bordeaux Blend (Haut-Médoc) $NA. Always reliable, Hanteillan has reflected the hot summer of 2003 without losing its toasty, tannic quality. There are plenty of black currant fruits, a solid structure, and a good layer of acidity. **85** —*R.V. (5/1/2006)*

CHÂTEAU HAUT BAGES LIBÉRAL

Château Haut Bages Libéral 2005 Barrel Sample Bordeaux Blend (Pauillac) $NA. Very opulent, generous, and rich. It shows all the glories of the vintage, with huge but sufficiently restrained fruit, and exuberant tannins. **93** —*R.V. (6/20/2006)*

CHÂTEAU HAUT BAILLY

Château Haut Bailly 2005 Barrel Sample Bordeaux Blend (Pessac-Léognan) $NA. Dark, very tough, this wine certainly lacks charm at this stage, with the fruit completely hidden by tannins. But it will come round, because the weight is there, even if the pleasure isn't at the moment. **92** —*R.V. (6/1/2006)*

CHÂTEAU HAUT BATAILLEY

Château Haut Batailley 2003 Bordeaux Blend (Pauillac) $30. This château, owned by one of the old Bordeaux families, the Bories, has only recently begun to gain the stature its vineyard, in the south of Pauillac, demands. This '03 is still very tight, packed with dark, tannic fruits, and dominated by a dense layer of wood. The price is still reasonable, which makes this a great wine for drinking after 10 years. **89** —*R.V. (5/1/2006)*

CHÂTEAU HAUT BERTINERIE

Château Haut Bertinerie 2002 Bordeaux White Blend (Premieres Côtes de Blaye) $20. Wood gives complexity to the wine's rich, soft fruit. Flavors of quince, honey, and grapefruit blend well with the vanilla of the wood. This is the top white cuvée from Bertinerie, produced from old vines. **90 Editors' Choice** —*R.V. (6/1/2005)*

CHÂTEAU HAUT BRETON LARIGAUDIERE

Château Haut Breton Larigaudiere 1999 Bordeaux Blend (Margaux) $45. A soft, ready-to-drink Margaux, with scents of damp clay and leather followed by black cherry and vanilla flavors. Boasts a pleasant creaminess on the palate and complicating hints of leather and earth on the finish. **86** —*J.C. (6/1/2005)*

CHÂTEAU HAUT-BEAUSEJOUR

Château Haut-Beausejour 1997 Cru Bourgeois Bordeaux Blend (Saint-Estèphe) $23. **85** *(5/1/2000)*

CHÂTEAU HAUT-BERGEY

Château Haut-Bergey 2005 Barrel Sample Bordeaux Blend (Pessac-Léognan) $NA. This wine is tough, but there are also fine black flavors. The dryness is very dominant at this stage, but this is a firmly powerful wine, with perhaps too much extract. **89** —*R.V. (6/21/2006)*

CHÂTEAU HAUT-BRION

Château Haut-Brion 2004 Barrel Sample Bordeaux Blend (Pessac-Léognan) $NA. Intense perfumes of black fruits dominate this concentrated but always stylish wine. It has the acidity of 2004, but the main impression is of balanced, ripe fruit. **95** —*R.V. (6/1/2005)*

Château Haut-Brion 2000 Pessac-Léognan Bordeaux Blend (Bordeaux) $400. For a Haut-Brion, this is huge. Every characteristic suggests power, from the dark color, through the knock-out perfumes, full of dark, brooding fruits. The flavors are black, intense, and ripe. It is a delicious wine, surprisingly ready to drink. And yes, just at the end, there is a small hint of the delicacy and elegance that is true Haut-Brion. **96** —*R.V. (6/1/2003)*

Château Haut-Brion 2005 Blanc-Barrel Sample Bordeaux White Blend (Pessac-Léognan) $NA. Rich, hugely ripe, intense fruit flavors, with layers of spice and acidity, but also full-bodied, well-integrated fruit. As always, Haut-Brion's white is at the top. **94** —*R.V. (6/20/2006)*

CHÂTEAU HAUT-MARBUZET

Château Haut-Marbuzet 2002 Bordeaux Blend (Saint-Estèphe) $NA. Always a star turn, Haut-Marbuzet hasn't failed in 2002. It is a modern style of wine, dominated by toast and wood tannins. But there is plenty of rich, black fruit to balance, and the spices and vanilla flavors are already blending well together. **91** —*R.V. (6/1/2005)*

Château Haut-Marbuzet 2004 Barrel Sample Bordeaux Blend (Saint-Estèphe) $NA. A huge, tannin-packed wine which shows how the wines of St.-Estèphe are exhibiting their classic dryness and power. It will develop slowly, but surely. **92** —*R.V. (6/1/2005)*

CHÂTEAU HOSANNA

Château Hosanna 2000 Bordeaux Blend (Pomerol) $179. It is the power that is so evident in this wine—a full, up-front expression of Merlot at its most powerful. It is somewhat closed up at this stage, but it is going to continue its development as an enormous wine which still manages to keep its power under firm control. **94** —*R.V. (6/1/2003)*

Château Hosanna 2004 Barrel Sample Bordeaux Blend (Pomerol) $NA. One of the properties owned by the Moueix family in Pomerol, this is rich, intense, dark, and very firm. The fruit is certainly ripe, but it is also very dry. **94** —*R.V. (6/1/2005)*

CHÂTEAU KIRWAN

Château Kirwan 2001 Bordeaux Blend (Margaux) $40. To call Kirwan a rising star is no longer true, since this property, owned by the Schyler family, and with Michel Rolland as consultant, is now firmly back in its right quality place among classed growths. It is modern in style, as is expected, but the dark, black currant, extracted fruits, new wood, and structure don't detract from its elegance. **94 Editors' Choice** —*R.V. (6/1/2005)*

Château Kirwan 2005 Barrel Sample Bordeaux Blend (Margaux) $NA. There is excellent balance here: the fruit is dark and opulent, but also fresh from acidity, piled with firm but generous tannins. A wine with excellent potential. **93** —*R.V. (6/20/2006)*

Château Kirwan 2003 Barrel Sample Bordeaux Blend (Margaux) $NA. Kirwan has been transformed in the past decade or so. Today, as with this 2003, it produces smooth, rich polished wines, with firm wood but never too much. Acidity completes the balance. **89** —*R.V. (6/3/2004)*

CHÂTEAU L'HOSTE-BLANC

Château l'Hoste-Blanc 1999 Bordeaux Blend (Bordeaux Supérieur) $15. A dark colored wine, with aromas of wood and black fruits. Dense, concentrated, quite dry, but powerful and ripe at the same time, it is a very complete wine with good complex acidity as well as dry tannins and rich fruit. The effect is traditional in style, but the tradition has been modernized. **91** —*R.V. (11/15/2002)*

CHÂTEAU LA BESSANE

Château la Bessane 2001 Bordeaux Blend (Margaux) $NA. Under the same ownership as Château La Paloumey in the Haut-Médoc, this is rich, with well-integrated flavors of blackberry and figs. There are fruit tannins that lie easily over the wood and the acidity. **87** —*R.V. (6/1/2005)*

CHÂTEAU LA BOUTIGNANE

Château La Boutignane 2001 Grande Reserve Blanc Red Blend (Corbières) $13. A delightful and complex wine made from the Macabeu grape. It has dry flavors that range from citrus to fig to fennel, and is kind of a cross between Sauvignon Blanc and Roussanne. The smooth, velvety texture is great. **90 Best Buy** —*S.H. (12/31/2002)*

Château La Boutignane 1998 Grande Reserve Rouge Red Blend (Corbières) $18. An amazing wine, especially considering that the dominant grape is Carignan; the rest is Syrah. Just shows what old vines can do in the right soil. Rich, thick, complex, and noble, it's filled with grilled meat, white pepper, tobacco, cassis, violets, and sage. The depth of flavor is thrilling, the texture splendid. **94 Editors' Choice** —*S.H. (12/31/2002)*

Château La Boutignane 2005 Rosé Blend (Corbières) $12. Slightly confected on the nose, with hints of bubble gum that give way to herbal cherry-berry flavors. This plump, medium-bodied rosé finishes smoothly, making it all too easy to down more than one intended. **85** —*J.C. (6/21/2006)*

Château La Boutignane 2003 Rosé de Saignée Rosé Blend (Corbières) $12. Primarily Syrah and Grenache, this coppery, orange-colored wine is delicious. It has complex, richly textured flavors of strawberries, peaches, herbs, roasted hazelnuts, and vanilla. Hard to imagine a more versatile wine at the table, and an incredible value in something different for a change. **90 Best Buy** —*S.H. (10/1/2004)*

CHÂTEAU LA CANORGUE

Château la Canorgue 2001 Rhône Red Blend (Côtes du Luberon) $15. Nice clean nose, with scents of cherries and white pepper. But what are the green, stemmy flavors doing on the palate? Modest cherry fruit, but this medium-bodied wine finishes herbal and astringent. **83** —*J.C. (2/1/2005)*

CHÂTEAU LA CAUSSADE

Château La Caussade 2002 Sauvignon Blanc (Bordeaux) $10. This is the label under which Château La Rame—a sweet wine producer in Saint Croix du Mont—commercializes its dry white, made from Sauvignon Blanc. No, it is not a profound wine, but it should be an example to other producers of humble Bordeaux blanc of what can be achieved through care and dedication. It's concentrated and intense, with a rich mouthfeel and bold grapefruit flavors that linger a long time on the finish. **86 Best Buy** —*J.C. (11/15/2004)*

CHÂTEAU LA CONSEILLANTE

Château La Conseillante 2003 Barrel Sample Bordeaux Blend (Pomerol) $NA. There is plenty of fruit here, black and brooding. But the wine does suffer from excessive dry tannins. **88** —*R.V. (6/3/2004)*

CHÂTEAU LA CROIX DE GAY

Château la Croix de Gay 2005 Barrel Sample Bordeaux Blend (Pomerol) $NA. A ripe, smooth, almost velvety wine that has big depths of flavor and solid tannins, but seems one-dimensional in its profile. **89** —*R.V. (6/21/2006)*

CHÂTEAU LA CROIX MARTELLE

Château La Croix Martelle 2001 La Réserve du Sirus Red Blend (Minervois) $16. Produced from biodynamically grown grapes, this wine certainly has pure fruit. It also has fine tannins and a subtle mix of red fruit flavors, and juicy acidity. The tannins dominate the aftertaste. **87** —*R.V. (12/1/2004)*

CHÂTEAU LA DOMINIQUE

Château la Dominique 2005 Barrel Sample Bordeaux Blend (Saint-Emilion Grand Cru) $NA. This property has really improved, and the modern, new wood flavors are great testimony to that. The fruit is ripe, almost New World in style, but keeps the proper Bordeaux sense of proportion. **90** —*R.V. (6/21/2006)*

CHÂTEAU LA FLEUR DE GAY

Château La Fleur de Gay 2004 Barrel Sample Bordeaux Blend (Pomerol) $NA. A big, solid effort with spicy fruit, exotic herbs, and denseness. But the fruit is still fresh to give the wine a final lift. **91** —*R.V. (6/1/2005)*

CHÂTEAU LA FLEUR PEYRABON

Château la Fleur Peyrabon 2003 Bordeaux Blend (Pauillac) $27. A small proportion of Patrick Bernard's Haut-Médoc estate of Peyrabon is in Pauillac, and he uses the fruit to make a top cuvée. This wine is suitably powered by dark Pauillac tannins, laced with some new wood and black currant fruits. It's powerful and dense, with considerable aging potential. **91 Cellar Selection** —*R.V. (5/1/2006)*

CHÂTEAU LA FLEUR PTRUS

Château La Fleur Ptrus 2005 Barrel Sample Bordeaux Blend (Pomerol) $NA. A powerfully ripe wine, velvety smooth, with layers of wood, acidity, and dark, firm tannins. **93** —*R.V. (6/20/2006)*

CHÂTEAU LA GAFFELIÈRE

Château la Gaffelière 2000 Bordeaux Blend (Saint-Emilion) $120. Opulence and richness, with all the generosity of Merlot, are the hallmarks of this superb wine. It is huge and powerful and has enormous potential. What is so exceptional about this wine is that all its power is still to be revealed. In 10 years time, it will prove to be one of the stars of the vintage in Saint-Emilion. **94** —*R.V. (6/1/2003)*

Château la Gaffelière 2004 Barrel Sample Bordeaux Blend (Saint-Emilion Grand Cru) $NA. This wine has achieved a near-perfect balance between its rich fruit and exotic wood. Offers black currant flavors and finely judged extraction. **95** —*R.V. (6/1/2005)*

CHÂTEAU LA GRAVE À POMEROL

Château La Grave à Pomerol 2000 Bordeaux Blend (Pomerol) $46. Dense, sweet fruit, offering as much elegance as richness. It is poised, with pure, elegant fruit flavors. As it develops, the fruit is going to become more and more delicious, while the dusty tannins will soften to reveal great opulence. **89** —*R.V. (6/1/2003)*

FRANCE

CHÂTEAU LA GURGUE

Château la Gurgue 2001 Bordeaux Blend (Margaux) $21. Under the same control as Château Ferrière, this wine reveals the same sense of power, style, and elegance. It is polished, packed with ripe fruit and dense tannins. Tobacco and cedar aromas make this an immediately enticing wine that still offers great potential for aging. **90** —*R.V. (6/1/2005)*

CHÂTEAU LA LAGUNE

Château La Lagune 2004 Barrel Sample Bordeaux Blend (Haut-Médoc) $NA. Good, fresh, spicy fruit make this wine very attractive. There are firm fruit tannins. **90** —*R.V. (6/1/2005)*

CHÂTEAU LA LOUVIÈRE

Château la Louvière 2005 Barrel Sample Bordeaux Blend (Pessac-Léognan) $NA. Ripe, juicy fruit flavors of packed jelly and black fruit give this wine an initial lift. Tense tannins give the wine a dry feel, which comes through on finish. **90** —*R.V. (6/21/2006)*

Château la Louvière 2002 Bordeaux White Blend (Pessac-Léognan) $34. One of the great estates of the Graves, this vintage of La Louvière certainly fits into the classic whites of Bordeaux, packing impressive complexity into a wine dominated by Sauvignon Blanc. Intensity has been increased by the use of lees stirring following the Burgundy methods introduced by Denis Dubordieu. **93 Cellar Selection** —*R.V. (6/1/2005)*

CHÂTEAU LA MISSION HAUT-BRION

Château La Mission Haut-Brion 2005 Barrel Sample Bordeaux Blend (Pessac-Léognan) $NA. A surprisingly gentle wine, almost delicate, with smooth flavors, a texture like deep velvet curtains and, dominating at the end, acidity. **94** —*R.V. (6/20/2006)*

Château La Mission Haut-Brion 2003 Barrel Sample Bordeaux Blend (Pessac-Léognan) $NA. Every year, this estate turns in a wine which closely rivals the neighboring Haut-Brion. This year, the rivalry is just as intense. This has sweet, ripe, beautiful fruit, delicious acidity already. But wait for the tannins to kick in. **94** —*R.V. (6/3/2004)*

CHÂTEAU LA MOUTÈTE

Château la Moutète 2004 Rosé Blend (Côtes de Provence) $13. A typical blend of Cinsault, Mourvèdre, Grenache, and Syrah, this fresh, tangy rosé features hints of cherries and berries layered over peach and canteloupe. White chocolate adds a creamy note to the palate, completing this refreshing wine. **87** —*J.C. (6/21/2006)*

Château la Moutète 2004 Vieilles Vignes Rosé Blend (Côtes de Provence) $17. Slightly richer in texture than Moutète's regular bottling, but not any better overall. Smells a bit like fresh cantaloupe with hints of peach and raspberry, then adds some chalky notes on the fresh, clean finish. **87** —*J.C. (6/21/2006)*

CHÂTEAU LA NERTHE

Château La Nerthe 2000 Rouge Rhône Red Blend (Châteauneuf-du-Pape) $40. This is slightly oaky, with buttery aromas mixing with hard spices to create a somewhat jumbled but interesting bouquet. The fat fruit falls into the plum and berry category, while the finish is firm and fruity, but rather basic and one-dimensional. As with any good red, it softens and grows more whole and complex with time. In this case, patience will be rewarded. **89** —*M.S. (9/1/2003)*

CHÂTEAU LA POINTE

Château la Pointe 2005 Barrel Sample Bordeaux Blend (Pomerol) $NA. This is impressive—a ripe, open wine, but showing some lovely, polished new wood flavors, vanilla, and just a touch of spice. **92** —*R.V. (6/20/2006)*

CHÂTEAU LA ROSE BELLEVUE

Château la Rose Bellevue 2000 Cuvée Prestige Bordeaux Blend (Premières Côtes de Blaye) $13. This has pure, black currant fruit aromas and flavors, and wood and acidity on the palate. It is packed with fresh, vibrant fruit. **87** —*R.V. (4/1/2005)*

Château la Rose Bellevue 2002 Cuvée Prestige Blanc Bordeaux White Blend (Premières Côtes de Blaye) $12. Enticing aromas of green plums

lead to a rich, ripe, and intense wine packed with wood and fruit flavors. This wine, a blend of Sauvignon Blanc and the more aromatic Muscadelle, is a fine wine full of fresh fruits and spice. **88 Best Buy** —*R.V. (4/1/2005)*

CHÂTEAU LA TOUR BLANCHE

Château la Tour Blanche 2004 Barrel Sample Bordeaux White Blend (Sauternes) $NA. Apples and cream, richness and sweetness, this wine is almost ready to drink. There is acidity and freshness, as well as fine botrytis. **91** —*R.V. (6/1/2005)*

CHÂTEAU LA TOUR CARNET

Château La Tour Carnet 2004 Barrel Sample Bordeaux Blend (Haut-Médoc) $NA. Big dark fruit, with tannins and ripe flavors. It's dark, woody, and pretty tannic. But there is good acidity. **87** —*R.V. (6/1/2005)*

CHÂTEAU LA TOUR DE BESSAN

Château la Tour de Bessan 2003 Bordeaux Blend (Margaux) $NA. A stunning modern cellar has been constructed at this property owned by Marie-Laure Lurton. The wine has some modern polish and richness, but it is still very Margaux, showing elegant fruit to go with the ripe tannins and black jelly flavors. This is an attractively restrained wine, which should age well over the next 5–7 years. **89** —*R.V. (5/1/2006)*

CHÂTEAU LA TOUR DE PIN FIGEAC MOUEIX

Château la Tour de Pin Figeac Moueix 2005 Barrel Sample Bordeaux Blend (Saint-Emilion Grand Cru) $NA. A very dry, rather hard wine, redeemed by its solid structure that promises fruit to come. **86** —*R.V. (6/21/2006)*

CHÂTEAU LA TOUR FIGEAC

Château La Tour Figeac 2002 Bordeaux Blend (Saint-Emilion Grand Cru) $NA. Otto Rettenmaier's estate has succeeded in enticing ripe flavors out of a lightweight vintage. This wine has rich, dry tannins alongside firm flavors of black currants, dark plums, and spices. There is balancing acidity which brings out the youthful tannins. There is a fine, lingering aftertaste. **90** —*R.V. (4/1/2005)*

Château La Tour Figeac 2000 Bordeaux Blend (Saint-Emilion Grand Cru) $NA. This is an impressive wine from a great Bordeaux year. It is beginning to develop its tannins and the huge, pure, rich, black fruit is coming up. But with its acidity, its layers of wood flavors and its structure, this is a wine which has years ahead of it. Just don't drink it yet, however tempting that may be. **94 Cellar Selection** —*R.V. (4/1/2005)*

Château La Tour Figeac 2004 Barrel Sample Bordeaux Blend (Saint-Emilion Grand Cru) $NA. The purity of the fruit is the prime quality of this exemplary wine. It shows intensity, ripe, open tannins, and generosity, finishing both fresh and firm. **91** —*R.V. (6/1/2005)*

CHÂTEAU LA TOUR HAUT-BRION

Château La Tour Haut-Brion 2000 Bordeaux Blend (Pessac-Léognan) $60. From the same stable as Haut-Brion, La Tour Haut-Brion reveals a fruity, almost frivolous character that makes it immediately charming. But there is no question that the soft, rich, black jelly fruits are the mask for a more concentrated, tannic structure. Give it 5-10 years. **89** —*R.V. (6/1/2003)*

Château La Tour Haut-Brion 2004 Barrel Sample Bordeaux Blend (Pessac-Léognan) $NA. Big and chunky, this has good acidity, dusty tannins and dryness. It leaves the mouth deliciously fresh. **91** —*R.V. (6/1/2005)*

CHÂTEAU LABAT

Château Labat 2003 Bordeaux Blend (Haut-Médoc) $14. Under the same ownership as Château Caronne-Saint-Gemme, this, too, is in a soft, ripe style, which would benefit from early drinking. It's attractive, lightly toasty, and with good black fruits and acidity. **84** —*R.V. (5/1/2006)*

CHÂTEAU LABEGORCE MARGAUX

Château Labegorce Margaux 2001 Bordeaux Blend (Margaux) $50. Huge investment is paying off at Labegorce. And it has not resulted in a wine that is simply modern in style. For here the new wood is well-integrated, the fruit is structured, and never too extracted, and the ripeness also has layers of Bordeaux dryness. **89** —*R.V. (6/1/2005)*

FRANCE

Château Labegorce Margaux 2005 Barrel Sample Bordeaux Blend (Margaux) $NA. Rich, ripe, elegant fruit is balanced with spice, ripe tannins, and some new wood. For a young wine, this is already well-balanced, but that's a positive, considering the density of the flavors. **93** —*R.V. (6/20/2006)*

CHÂTEAU LABEGORCE ZÉDÉ

Château Labegorce Zédé 2001 Bordeaux Blend (Margaux) $NA. Owner Luc Thienpont, whose family also owns Vieux Château Certan and Le Pin in Pomerol, has crafted a classic Margaux with a modern face. Its solid tannins, dry flavors, and spice combine with some sweetness, fresh fruits, and great balance to give a hugely satisfying, and very food-friendly wine. **90** —*R.V. (6/1/2005)*

CHÂTEAU LACOMBE NOAILLAC

Château Lacombe Noaillac 2003 Bordeaux Blend (Listrac-Médoc) $26. A smooth, vanilla-flavored wine that shows good black currant flavors. There are soft tannins, some wood notes, but there is also a stalky dryness in the background. The aftertaste leaves wood and dry fruit in equal proportions. **84** —*R.V. (5/1/2006)*

CHÂTEAU LAFAURIE PEYRAGUEY

Château Lafaurie Peyraguey 2004 Barrel Sample Bordeaux White Blend (Sauternes) $NA. Dryness and structure dominate this wine. But there is good potential, it has layers of botrytis, which are good, and there is richness under the structure. **90** —*R.V. (6/1/2005)*

CHÂTEAU LAFITE ROTHSCHILD

Château Lafite Rothschild 2000 Bordeaux Blend (Pauillac) $400. Perhaps of all the first growths in the totally un-classic 2000, this retains most of the classic Bordeaux. It is certainly almost black in color, while the new wood flavors are very present. But it shows an impressive restraint, leaving the power of the wine to be revealed over the years rather than immediately. This could well be the longest-lived of the Pauillac first growths. **99** —*R.V. (6/1/2003)*

Château Lafite Rothschild 2004 Barrel Sample Bordeaux Blend (Pauillac) $NA. A beautiful wine, concentrated and intense without tasting in any way extracted or forced. It has tannins, certainly, very dark and concentrated, but the fruit is black, powerful, rich, yet still maintaining purity and a sense of minerality from the vineyard. **97** —*R.V. (6/1/2005)*

CHÂTEAU LAFLEUR PÉTRUS

Château Lafleur Pétrus 2003 Barrel Sample Bordeaux Blend (Pomerol) $NA. This is a wine which risks being dominated by dry tannins, but narrowly avoids this fate because the fruit is so sweet and ripe. The tannins should soften and the wine will be delicious. **87** —*R.V. (6/3/2004)*

CHÂTEAU LAFON ROCHET

Château Lafon Rochet 2005 Barrel Sample Bordeaux Blend (Saint-Estèphe) $NA. While there are super-ripe fruit aromas, the structure of this wine is totally solid. Somewhere lurking under the shell is huge black fruit, but now it is dark and very dry. **90** —*R.V. (6/1/2006)*

CHÂTEAU LAFONT MENAUT

Château Lafont Menaut 2003 Bordeaux White Blend (Pessac-Léognan) $NA. The Perrin family, proprietors of Château Carbonnieux, also owns this small Pessac-Leognan property in Martillac. It is fresh, soft, easy with good citrus and crisp, green-apple flavors. This is a forward style, ready to drink and very enjoyable. **86** —*R.V. (6/1/2005)*

CHÂTEAU LAGRANGE

Château Lagrange 2003 Bordeaux Blend (Saint-Julien) $30. A dark, dry, brooding wine, which has flavors of blackberries and red plum skins, which is not at all dominated by wood. This is a classic wine, with Saint-Julien's elegance and 2003's power. **92** —*R.V. (5/1/2006)*

Château Lagrange 2004 Barrel Sample Bordeaux Blend (Saint-Julien) $NA. A wine with great ripe fruit, delicious acidity, and freshness. It is firm, but the almost jammy sweetness makes it very appealing. **91** —*R.V. (6/1/2005)*

CHÂTEAU LAGREZETTE

Château Lagrezette 1997 Le Pigeonnier Malbec (Cahors) $60. A voluptuous blockbuster in the style we are becoming accustomed to from über-consultant Michel Rolland: big, deeply fruited (black cherries), and plush, with elegantly etched spice shadings from new oak. The tannins are supple but substantial; it should age for a long time. Made entirely from old-vine Malbec and named after the pigeon coop in the Château's courtyard. **93** —*J.C. (3/1/2001)*

Château Lagrezette 1996 Red Blend (Cahors) $20. 90 *(11/15/1999)*

CHÂTEAU LALANDE-BORIE

Château Lalande-Borie 2000 Bordeaux Blend (Saint-Julien) $25. This is an excellent wine, full of ripe fruit and black currant flavors, showing style and elegance in its balancing tannins. It is typical of this property in already showing signs of developing fast. Give it five years. **89** —*R.V. (6/1/2003)*

CHÂTEAU LAMOTHE

Château Lamothe 2005 Barrel Sample Bordeaux White Blend (Sauternes) $NA. This wine is fresh, layered with some attractive lightweight botrytis and delicate fruit. What it offers in accessibility it lacks in concentration, and will age fairly quickly. **87** —*R.V. (6/21/2006)*

CHÂTEAU LAMOTHE GUIGNARD

Château Lamothe Guignard 2005 Barrel Sample Bordeaux White Blend (Sauternes) $NA. This is hugely rich and powerful, with attractively ripe, intense fruit. Delicious layers of fresh fruits combine with concentrated botrytis and lemon flavors. A perfect foie gras partner. **91** —*R.V. (6/1/2006)*

CHÂTEAU LANGOA-BARTON

Château Langoa-Barton 2000 Bordeaux Blend (Saint-Julien) $NA. The junior of the two wines produced by the Barton family, this is a subtle, classic wine. Structure and firm tannins sit alongside the perfectly formed, under-stated red and black fruits. **90** —*R.V. (6/1/2003)*

CHÂTEAU LAPELLETRIE

Château Lapelletrie 1997 Bordeaux Blend (Saint-Emilion) $20. From a vintage known for its readily-approachable wines, this grand cru Saint-Emilion shows surprising structure. Some toasty oak frames delicate black-cherry fruit. Black tea notes on the finish carry more tannins than the fruit can handle in the long run, so catch this one soon before it heads south. **84** —*J.C. (3/1/2001)*

CHÂTEAU LARMANDE

Château Larmande 2000 Bordeaux Blend (Saint-Emilion) $25. This château shows continual improvement, and 2000 is a triumph. The wine is in a modern style, although at this stage its tannins are still firm and dry. Red fruit flavors and black currants promise huge drinking pleasure to come. **89** —*R.V. (6/1/2003)*

CHÂTEAU LAROQUE

Château Laroque 2000 Bordeaux Blend (Saint-Emilion Grand Cru) $45. Gems like this from the stellar 2000 vintage are still available to consumers willing to explore lesser-known châteaux. Concentrated scents of black cherries and cassis emerge from the glass, followed by admirably pure flavors of black cherries and vanilla. It's supple enough to drink now, but appears to have the stuffing to go another 5–10 years. A long, berry-filled finish caps off this find. **90** —*J.C. (6/1/2005)*

Château Laroque 2002 Grand Cru Classe Bordeaux Blend (Saint-Emilion Grand Cru) $45. 87 —*J.C. (11/15/2005)*

CHÂTEAU LAROZE

Château Laroze 2005 Barrel Sample Bordeaux Blend (Saint-Emilion Grand Cru) $NA. The style is spicy and modern, dominated by 50% new wood aging. But there is certainly enough fruit to show through once the wood effect eases off. **88** —*R.V. (6/21/2006)*

CHÂTEAU LARRIVET HAUT-BRION

Château Larrivet Haut-Brion 2005 Barrel Sample Bordeaux White Blend

FRANCE

(Pessac-Léognan) $NA. Attractive rosemary and thyme aromas lead to a very fresh wine with a herbal element. Excellent, with delicious fruit. **91** —*R.V. (6/1/2006)*

CHÂTEAU LASCOMBES

Château Lascombes 2003 Bordeaux Blend (Margaux) $50. Finally it looks as if Lascombes is back on form. With its huge vineyard, a good selection of the best fruit has been the issue, and this has happened with 2003. It's not a huge wine, but there is smooth, polished fruit, layered with wood and dusty tannins. **90** —*R.V. (5/1/2006)*

Château Lascombes 2003 Barrel Sample Bordeaux Blend (Margaux) $NA. This second growth has shown a renaissance since new owners took over three years ago. With its balanced fruit and very ripe tannins, it promises well. **90** —*R.V. (6/3/2004)*

CHÂTEAU LATOUR

Château Latour 2005 Barrel Sample Bordeaux Blend (Pauillac) $NA. This has to be the wine of the vintage. It sums up all the positives of a great year: glorious fruit, power, elegance, and acidity to balance. The tannins are enormous but they are still brooding rather than extracted. 87% of Cabernet Sauvignon. **99** —*R.V. (6/20/2006)*

Château Latour 2003 Barrel Sample Bordeaux Blend (Pauillac) $NA. What makes a great Latour is a sense of completeness, of restrained power, and of levels of complexity which the other first growths rarely achieve. That's why Latour 2003 is a great wine. **97** —*R.V. (6/3/2004)*

Château Latour à Pomerol 2005 Barrel Sample Bordeaux Blend (Pomerol) $NA. Another huge Pomerol. But like other wines vinified by Christian Moueix, this has a fine sense of balance, its softly extracted tannins and dry fruits paired with deliciously fresh blueberry flavors. **91** —*R.V. (6/1/2006)*

Château Latour à Pomerol 2003 Barrel Sample Bordeaux Blend (Pomerol) $NA. A very sweet fruity wine, full of attractive spice and ripe, not too heavy, tannins. This will develop over the medium-term. **88** —*R.V. (6/3/2004)*

CHÂTEAU LATOUR-MARTILLAC

Château Latour-Martillac 2002 Bordeaux White Blend (Pessac-Léognan) $NA. The Kressmann family produces a classic white at its Martillac estate. It is powered with fresh apples and cream flavors. A delicate layer of wood gives a fine lift to this Sauvignon Blanc-dominated the blend. There is a streak of minerality the wine more than just deliciously fruity. **91** —*R.V. (6/1/2005)*

CHÂTEAU LAVILLE HAUT-BRION

Château Laville Haut-Brion 2005 Blanc-Barrel Sample Bordeaux White Blend (Pessac-Léognan) $NA. Hugely citrusy in character, this delicious wine has layers of wood, spice, and intense acidity. A powerful wine, but on that retains its delicacy. **93** —*R.V. (6/20/2006)*

CHÂTEAU LE BON PASTEUR

Château le Bon Pasteur 2004 Barrel Sample Bordeaux Blend (Pomerol) $NA. New wood pushes through the fruit and acidity. Michel Rolland's family property has produced a fresh rather than extracted wine. **89** —*R.V. (6/1/2005)*

CHÂTEAU LE BREUIL RENAISSANCE

Château Le Breuil Renaissance 2001 Bordeaux Blend (Médoc) $25. Starts off with an herbal note that carries throughout. Blackberry, cassis, tar, spice and citrus flavors are in evidence as well. Tannins are a bit rustic. Kosher. **83** —*J.M. (4/3/2004)*

CHÂTEAU LE DEVOY MARTINE

Château le Devoy Martine 2003 Rhône Red Blend (Lirac) $20. Shows the baked quality some of the 2003 wines have, with dried fruit notes of dates and prunes but also lots of complex leather and spice flavors. Very supple, almost creamy in texture, this is supremely ripe and probably needs to be consumed in the next year or two. **90 Editors' Choice** —*J.C. (11/15/2006)*

Château le Devoy Martine 2004 Rhône White Blend (Lirac) $14. This is a rather minerally and crisp rendition of a southern white Rhône, with cit-

rus and orange peel aromas and flavors. Less broad than most, and more precise and focused. **86** —*J.C. (11/15/2006)*

CHÂTEAU LE DROT

Château Le Drot 1998 Bordeaux Blend (Bordeaux) $6. **85 Best Buy** —*D.T. (11/15/2002)*

CHÂTEAU LEBOSCQ

Château Leboscq 2003 Bordeaux Blend (Médoc) $NA. A fresh, but dry wine, with stalky black fruits and acidity. Light and crisp, this is a pleasant fruity mouthful that demands hearty winter dishes as an accompaniment. **84** —*R.V. (5/1/2006)*

CHÂTEAU LÉOVILLE LAS CASES

Château Léoville Las Cases 2004 Barrel Sample Bordeaux Blend (Saint-Julien) $NA. At first taste, this seems to be an overwhelmingly huge wine. But that is deceptive: it has dense fruit, but it is layered with great blackberry and currant fruits, and very attractive freshness. **94** —*R.V. (6/1/2005)*

CHÂTEAU LEOVILLE POYFERRE

Château Leoville Poyferre 2003 Bordeaux Blend (Saint-Julien) $75. A huge, opulent wine that packs sweet, rich tannins and spicy fruit. In the midst of all this decadence, though, is a kernel of tannic dryness. This estate, long the weakest of the three Lèoville wines, is now back in top form. **93** —*R.V. (5/1/2006)*

Château Leoville Poyferre 2005 Barrel Sample Bordeaux Blend (Saint-Julien) $NA. A beautiful, fruity wine with great black flavors, rich acidity, the tannins playing the essential bass counterpoint. The dryness from the structure only comes through right at the end. **93** —*R.V. (6/20/2006)*

Château Leoville Poyferre 2003 Barrel Sample Bordeaux Blend (Saint-Julien) $NA. This is certainly a big, tannic wine, but there are also huge dark-plum flavors, spices, and a fine long-term structure. **92** —*R.V. (6/3/2004)*

CHÂTEAU LÉOVILLE-BARTON

Château Léoville-Barton 2003 Bordeaux Blend (Saint-Julien) $115. Somehow Barton has overcome the heat of the 2003 vintage and has come out with a new wine that is rich and elegant. There are generous tannins, ripe black currant fruits, balancing acidity, all in an ensemble that is so much more than the sum of its parts. **95** —*R.V. (5/1/2006)*

Château Léoville-Barton 2005 Barrel Sample Bordeaux Blend (Saint-Julien) $NA. A solid, very firm wine that initially lacks charm. But it just needs time to knit together; as it is now, its huge, dry tannins completely hide the fruit, just giving hints of greatness to come. **96** —*R.V. (6/20/2006)*

Château Léoville-Barton 2003 Barrel Sample Bordeaux Blend (Saint-Julien) $NA. As always, this property turns in an excellent performance. Perhaps it lacks the true excitement of some years, but with its solid, chunky fruit, its restrained wood, and its dark fruit flavors, it will certainly be a wine to keep. **93** —*R.V. (6/3/2004)*

CHÂTEAU LES CARMES HAUT-BRION

Château Les Carmes Haut-Brion 2005 Barrel Sample Bordeaux Blend (Pessac-Léognan) $NA. A complete wine, rich and opulent. It has all the right balances of acidity, sweet fruits, black flavors, and underlying dry tannins. Excellent. **93** —*R.V. (6/20/2006)*

CHÂTEAU LES ORMES DE PEZ

Château les Ormes de Pez 2002 Bordeaux Blend (Saint-Estèphe) $27. Under the ownership of the Cazes family (also owners of Lynch-Bages), this estate produces richly satisfying wines, even in lighter years like 2002. This is finely constructed, with acidity along with the tannins and dense black fruits. It certainly has power, but there is also great elegance. **90** —*R.V. (6/1/2005)*

Château les Ormes de Pez 2005 Barrel Sample Bordeaux Blend (Saint-Estèphe) $NA. Rich, packed with super-ripe fruit and huge tannins, this wine still manages to keep elegance, power tempered with velvet: an impressive combination. **92** —*R.V. (6/20/2006)*

Château les Ormes de Pez 2003 Barrel Sample Bordeaux Blend (Saint-

Estèphe) **$NA.** This exemplary estate, under the same ownership as Lynch Bages, has made a classic, richly tanninc Saint Estèphe, powering solid blackberry flavors through the tannins and leaving a fresh acidity to finish. 88 —*R.V. (6/3/2004)*

CHÂTEAU LES ROCHERS MIRANDE

Château Les Rochers Mirande 2000 Red Blend (Montagne-St.-Èmilion) $18. Aromas of maple, black pepper, and cherry cough drop get it going in a fair to midland direction. The palate is basic, with only some standard berry fruit and oak, while the finish is lengthy and easy, but also kind of mute. In terms of mouthfeel, some hard tannins prevent it from falling into the "friendly" category. 83 —*M.S. (9/1/2003)*

CHÂTEAU LESTRILLE CAPMARTIN

Château Lestrille Capmartin 2000 Prestige Bordeaux Blend (Bordeaux) $17. Currently this wine is much too dominated by wood. There is some dark, tarry fruit, but the wood is ever-present. Buy this wine if you like wood flavors, the question is whether the fruit is powerful enough to come through. 84 —*R.V. (12/1/2002)*

CHÂTEAU LILIAN LADOUYS

Château Lilian Ladouys 2003 Bordeaux Blend (Saint-Estèphe) $17. From a mosaic of 90 different scattered parcels, oenologue Georges Pauli has constructed a firm style of wine, with Saint-Estèphe's characteristic tannins and fresh black currant fruits. This is a structured wine, which should certainly age well. 88 —*R.V. (5/1/2006)*

CHÂTEAU LOUDENNE

Château Loudenne 1995 Bordeaux Blend (Médoc) $15. 86 —*M.S. (12/31/1999)*

CHÂTEAU LYNCH-BAGES

Château Lynch-Bages 2000 Bordeaux Blend (Pauillac) $100. Typical of Lynch-Bages in its sumptuous rich style, this is a resounding success for the team of Jean-Michel Cazes. With its sweet fruit, opulent but balanced wood, and red and black fruit flavors, it is a wine that will develop relatively quickly but will certainly age. 95 —*R.V. (6/1/2003)*

Château Lynch-Bages 2004 Barrel Sample Bordeaux Blend (Pauillac) $NA. The wine is dominated by the aromas of new wood. It is rich, sweet, and packed with new-wood tannins. These dominate the fruit, but also give sweetness. 93 —*R.V. (6/1/2005)*

CHÂTEAU LYNCH-MOUSSAS

Château Lynch-Moussas 2005 Barrel Sample Bordeaux Blend (Pauillac) $NA. Very firm and dry, perhaps missing the exuberant fruit of other Pauillacs. But it has good restraint that shows serious tannins and a firm, solid character. 90 —*R.V. (6/21/2006)*

CHÂTEAU MAGDELAINE

Château Magdelaine 2000 Bordeaux Blend (Saint-Emilion) $87. This Moueix-owned premier grand cru classé property quietly goes about producing great wines. The 2000 is a complete success, with its aromas of red berry fruits and sweet wood, its flavors cedar and truffles alongside the fine, elegant tannins. It will age slowly and reveal layers of complexity over the years. 93 —*R.V. (6/1/2003)*

Château Magdelaine 2003 Barrel Sample Bordeaux Blend (Saint-Emilion) $NA. A sophisticated wine which has dusty tannins balancing fresh black fruits. With its lightening acidity and its rich, spicy flavors, this is a very polished wine. 89 —*R.V. (6/3/2004)*

CHÂTEAU MAINE-GAZIN

Château Maine-Gazin 1997 Bordeaux Blend (Bordeaux) $17. This is very light, in both flavor and body. The aromas are earthy, with a faint suggestion of blackberries, and the mouthfeel is thin. These aren't terrible flaws, but the wine just lacks substance. 81 —*J.C. (4/1/2001)*

CHÂTEAU MALARTIC-LAGRAVIERE

Château Malartic-Lagraviere 2005 Barrel Sample Bordeaux Blend (Pessac-Léognan) $NA. A firmly tannic wine, but one that lets the intense fruit flavors peep through. It's certainly dark, but also has a pleasurable liveliness to finish. 90 —*R.V. (6/21/2006)*

Château Malartic-Lagraviere 2002 Bordeaux White Blend (Pessac-Léognan) $37. A big wine from this classed-growth Graves estate, it has both oak and ripe fruit integrated well with quince and grapefruit flavors. To finish, there is a great lift of acidity. 90 —*R.V. (6/1/2005)*

CHÂTEAU MALESCASSE

Château Malescasse 2005 Barrel Sample Bordeaux Blend (Haut-Médoc) $NA. This wine is delicate, with dusty tannins and easy fruit flavors. It seems pretty closed up, as it hasn't much depth at the moment. 87 —*R.V. (6/21/2006)*

CHÂTEAU MALESCOT SAINT-EXUPERY

Château Malescot Saint-Exupery 2005 Barrel Sample Bordeaux Blend (Margaux) $NA. Big, ripe, and juicy—a Dolly Parton wine. With exuberant fruitiness this is attractive now, but there are solid, firm tannins, so the wine will perhaps grow up. 92 —*R.V. (6/1/2006)*

Château Malescot Saint-Exupery 2003 Barrel Sample Bordeaux Blend (Margaux) $NA. A surprising success from a lesser known château. This third growth has produced a finely balanced wine with black fruits and wood flavors. 90 —*R.V. (6/3/2004)*

CHÂTEAU MARBUZET

Château Marbuzet 2005 Barrel Sample Bordeaux Blend (Saint-Estèphe) $NA. A fine, smooth wine, showing great tannins over big, solid fruit, and very dark, chocolate flavors. There is acidity, but this is dominated by wood tannins. 92 —*R.V. (6/20/2006)*

CHÂTEAU MARGAUX

Château Margaux 2001 Bordeaux Blend (Margaux) $300. "For me, this vintage is what makes Margaux special," says Margaux winemaker Paul Pontallier. He is right: With its denseness, spice, flavors of black currants layered with dryness, and fresh acidity, this is a huge and impressive wine that never forgets that it is Margaux. It is still young, and the dry tannic aftertaste, which lasts for many minutes, shows this. 97 —*R.V. (6/1/2005)*

Château Margaux 2004 Barrel Sample Bordeaux Blend (Margaux) $NA. While this wine certainly has power, it is its almost other-worldly floating character that is most striking. The fruit glides over the palate, leaving freshness with layers of intense acidity and wood to finish. 96 —*R.V. (6/1/2005)*

Château Margaux 2002 Pavillon Blanc de Château Margaux Bordeaux White Blend (Bordeaux) $58. A powerful and weighty wine, even from the lighter 2002 vintage. Château Margaux's white is made with the same attention to detail as the reds, balancing fresh acidity, richness, layers of wood, and great sophistication. It will age over 5–10 years. 91 —*R.V. (6/1/2005)*

CHÂTEAU MARIS

Château Maris 1999 Rhône Red Blend (Minervois La Liviniere) $16. The nose of this Syrah-Grenache-Carignan blend has mineral and weedy notes at first; after a few minutes in the glass, the greenness fades, and spicy paprika notes show through. Taut but bright, blackberries and earth flavors lead into a toasty, dark, medium-length finish. 86 —*M.M. (2/1/2002)*

CHÂTEAU MAROUÏNE

Château Marouïne 2005 Rosé Blend (Côtes de Provence) $13. A blend of Grenache, Cinsault, Mourvèdre, and Carignan, this wine from organically grown grapes boasts aromas of crushed stone and fresh limes that set the mouth watering. It's medium-bodied, not as heavy or rich as some Provence rosés, but complex and refreshing. 88 Best Buy —*J.C. (6/21/2006)*

CHÂTEAU MARQUIS DE TERME

Château Marquis de Terme 2005 Barrel Sample Bordeaux Blend (Margaux) $NA. There's too much wood here, obvious on the nose and with dominant flavors of pine shavings. But there is fruit there, even if, at this stage, not rich enough to balance out the wood. 87 —*R.V. (6/21/2006)*

CHÂTEAU MAS NEUF

Château Mas Neuf 1998 Rhône Red Blend (Costières de Nimes) $9. 84 —*J.C. (12/31/2000)*

FRANCE

Château Mas Neuf 2003 Syrah (Costières de Nimes) $10. Wow. This classy, ripe château-bottled rosé is from the eastern Langeudoc, sometimes called Chateâuneuf-du-Pape South. Mainly Syrah with a little Grenache, it was fermented in steel to preserve freshness, and oak-aged. Smooth and ripe in cherries, with fresh Provençal herbs and a hint of flowers, it has minerally acids and tons of finesse. Full enough to drink with red meats. **88 Best Buy** —*S.H. (11/15/2004)*

CHÂTEAU MASSAMIER LA MIGNARDE

Château Massamier la Mignarde 2004 Domus Maximus Rhône Red Blend (Minervois La Liviniere) $34. Named after a Roman legionary who was given a grant of the land on which the estate of Massamier la Mignarde now stands, this wine is a blend of low-yielding Syrah and old-vine Grenache. It's become a classic since its launch with the 2000 vintage. This 2004, made of beautiful, ripe, densely packed fruit and layered with dry, perfumed tannins, is delicious now but should certainly age. **91 Editors' Choice** —*R.V. (12/31/2006)*

Château Massamier la Mignarde 2004 Tradition Rhône Red Blend (Minervois) $12. This is the classic style of Minervois, with herbal fruits, and strawberry and black plum flavors. The key to this wine is the dry, tannic structure, which roots it firmly in the style of the region. **88 Best Buy** —*R.V. (12/31/2006)*

CHÂTEAU MAUCOIL

Château Maucoil 2003 Rhône Red Blend (Châteauneuf-du-Pape) $NA. A soft style of wine that has earthy characters. There are layers of dryness, but the plum-flavored fruit shows every sign of maturing quickly over 2–3 years. **85** —*R.V. (12/31/2005)*

CHÂTEAU MAZEYRES

Château Mazeyres 2002 Bordeaux Blend (Pomerol) $33. A ripe wine that is polished almost as bright as a diamond. Big, chocolaty flavors are balanced by some acidity and soft tannins. This is a seductive wine that belies the quality of the vintage, showing concentration and sweet, dense fruit. **90** —*R.V. (6/1/2005)*

CHÂTEAU MEYNEY

Château Meyney 2000 Bordeaux Blend (Saint-Estèphe) $30. Typical of Saint-Estèphe, this wine is totally closed up. It is more tannins than fruit at this stage of its development. But it is obvious that there is fruit there, and that it will develop. But for now, it's a case of watch this space. **89** —*R.V. (6/1/2003)*

CHÂTEAU MEZAIN

Château Mezain 2003 Bordeaux White Blend (Bordeaux) $12. Grass and herb aromas vie with earthier, chalky nuances in this lithe little sipper. Lime and green apple fruit dominate the palate, which finishes crisp and clean, if a bit short. **84** —*J.C. (6/1/2005)*

CHÂTEAU MONBOUSQUET

Château Monbousquet 2000 Bordeaux Blend (Saint-Emilion) $160. This is Gérard Perse's home, and he has done wonders for a vineyard on the sandy plain of Saint-Emilion. With 2000, the property has shone, producing a serious, complex wine that boasts black fruits and solid tannins. The acidity and wood flavors give it shape and leave a delicious, lingering taste. **88** —*R.V. (6/1/2003)*

CHÂTEAU MONBRISON

Château Monbrison 2003 Bordeaux Blend (Margaux) $25. This château has a fine and deserved reputation, as this powerful but elegant 2003 shows. It has all the sophistication of Margaux, along with some lightness that balances the dry tannins. **89** —*R.V. (5/1/2006)*

Château Monbrison 2000 Bordeaux Blend (Margaux) $30. Thanks to the total dedication of owner Jean-Luc Vonderheyden, Monbrison continued to perform outside its class in 2000. Fragrant, perfumed aromas with suggestions of vanilla and lavender make this wine immediately attractive. It is soft, which suggests its aging will be fast, but the Licorice fruit flavors and ripeness will give pleasure after five years. **90** —*R.V. (6/1/2003)*

Château Monbrison 2003 Barrel Sample Bordeaux Blend (Margaux) $NA. This is a well balanced wine, classic in its blending of acidity firm fruit.

The vintage shows through in the sweetness of the tannins. **89** —*R.V. (6/3/2004)*

CHÂTEAU MONCONTOUR

Château Moncontour 2003 Cuvée Prédilection Chenin Blanc (Vouvray) $NA. A curious connection here: the wine is called "Prédilection" because apparently novelist Balzac's mistress loved Vouvray. Whatever the reason, the wine itself is fine and complex, with aromas of hazelnuts, layers of acidity, a touch of toast, but still retaining great fresh fruit. **90** —*R.V. (6/1/2006)*

CHÂTEAU MONGRAVEY

Château Mongravey 2001 Bordeaux Blend (Margaux) $30. This wine has pleasant, fresh fruit, some good tannins, and ripe fruit. It is soft, with forward fruits, and a simplicity that makes it ready to drink now. **86** —*R.V. (6/1/2005)*

CHÂTEAU MONT-REDON

Château Mont-Redon 2005 Rhône Red Blend (Côtes-du-Rhône) $15. A step up from the solid 2004, this year's version packs in riper Grenache flavors, ranging from cherries to peach or apricot. The texture is more supple as well, yet the wine is still fresh, picking up hints of spice on the finish. **88** —*J.C. (11/15/2006)*

Château Mont-Redon 2003 Rhône Red Blend (Châteauneuf-du-Pape) $45. Famed for its use of all 13 Châteauneuf grape varieties, Mont-Redon is also one of the great estates of the region. This 2003 captures the essence of Châteauneuf, with its herbal and warm, southern fruits, along with a power of black fruits and dark, brooding tannins. This will age magnificently. **92** —*R.V. (12/31/2005)*

CHÂTEAU MONTNER

Château Montner 2000 Rhône Red Blend (Côtes du Roussillon) $8. The bouquet is full of summer bramble, earth, and cherries. The mouthfeel is textured and hearty; a tasty, well-made wine that's a splendid example of affordable Syrah, Grenache, and Carignan. **87 Best Buy** —*M.S. (2/1/2003)*

CHÂTEAU MOULIN DE TRICOT

Château Moulin de Tricot 2001 Bordeaux Blend (Margaux) $NA. This is a great food wine, with sweet, soft fruit, cigar-box aromas, and classic flavors of black currants and red hedgerow fruits. Enjoy the fresh tannins and the way the fruit is brought out with red meat dishes. **86** —*R.V. (6/1/2005)*

CHÂTEAU MOURGUES DU GRES

Château Mourgues du Gres 2002 Les Galets Rouges Rhône Red Blend (Costières de Nimes) $12. Floral and violetty on the nose, blending smoothly into vibrant blackberry notes. It's relatively light-bodied, with a Burgundian weight and mouthfeel that make it seem alternately fragile and elegant. Drink over the next year or two. **89 Best Buy** —*J.C. (2/1/2005)*

CHÂTEAU MOUTON ROTHSCHILD

Château Mouton Rothschild 2000 Bordeaux Blend (Pauillac) $450. With its distinctive antique bottle and gold etched label dominated by a sheep, this is definitely a move away from classic Bordeaux bottling. It is good that the wine can support the presentation. The fruit is so ripe, it almost tastes of raisins, but that sweetness is finely balanced by the dry tannins and concentrated texture. To finish, there are exotic spices, giving an almost oriental character to the long aftertaste. **97** —*R.V. (6/1/2003)*

CHÂTEAU MOUTON ROTHSCHILD

Château Mouton Rothschild 2004 Barrel Sample Bordeaux Blend (Pauillac) $NA. A wine that is powerful, highly extracted, and intense. The chocolate flavors and serious, dry tannins go with big, fat blackberry fruits and finishing acidity. **93** —*R.V. (6/1/2005)*

Château Mouton Rothschild 2001 Aile d'Argent Bordeaux White Blend (Bordeaux) $50. The rare white wine from Château Mouton Rothschild is a creamy, full-bodied blend of 48% Sémillon, 38% Sauvignon Blanc, and 14% Muscadelle. Toast and mushroom scents merge easily into buttered stone-fruit flavors on the palate, finishing on a weighty note. **87** —*J.C. (6/1/2005)*

FRANCE

CHÂTEAU NAIRAC

Château Nairac 2005 Barrel Sample Bordeaux White Blend (Barsac) $NA. A deliciously fresh, vibrant wine with good ripe fruits, flavors of orange marmalade, and a light, citrus kick. Lovely, with just a touch of spice. **91** —R.V. (6/1/2006)

CHÂTEAU NENIN

Château Nenin 2005 Barrel Sample Bordeaux Blend (Pomerol) $NA. A very smooth, rich wine, with a slight touch of pepper from the alcohol. The tannins are huge but submerged by ripe fruit. There's almost Napa-like ripeness, but also delicious acidity. **91** —R.V. (6/1/2006)

CHÂTEAU NOTRE DAME DE SALAGOU

Château Notre Dame de Salagou 2002 Red Blend (Coteaux du Languedoc) $NA. High toast aromas and fresh, red currant fruits show the effect of the lighter vintage of 2002. The fruit is pleasant, but shot through with acidity. A wine for early drinking. **84** —R.V. (12/1/2004)

CHÂTEAU OLIVIER

Château Olivier 2002 Bordeaux White Blend (Pessac-Léognan) $NA. A rich, smooth wine, with flavors of grapefruit and toast, and grassy, herbaceous aromas. Attractive and fresh on the finish. **87** —R.V. (6/1/2005)

CHÂTEAU PALMER

Château Palmer 2003 Bordeaux Blend (Margaux) $120. With its usual high proportion of Merlot, Palmer 2003 was always going to be a generous, very ripe wine. And so it is proving, but what is so satisfying about the wine at this stage is that the great sweet fruit, which comes right out of the glass. Underneath, of course, there are tannins, so this wine could be drunk soon, and then aged for another 15 years. **94** —R.V. (5/1/2006)

Château Palmer 2000 Bordeaux Blend (Margaux) $120. At this stage, this is very closed, very tight, giving little. But it is possible to discern that this is going to be a beautiful wine. There are flavors of sweet raisins and the fruit has a new world richness, but the structure of dry tannins is always present. It looks as though it has a good, long life. **94** —R.V. (6/1/2003)

Château Palmer 2004 Barrel Sample Bordeaux Blend (Margaux) $NA. An opulent Palmer, which exhibits the richness of the Merlot. It has velvety tannins and sweetness. The wood is there, but does not dominate. **93** —R.V. (6/1/2005)

CHÂTEAU PAPE-CLEMENT

Château Pape-Clement 2004 Barrel Sample Bordeaux Blend (Pessac-Léognan) $NA. The fruit is packed full of intense black currants, while the acidity shows through the dark, dry tannins. A powerful wine. **93** —R.V. (6/1/2005)

Château Pape-Clement 2000 Pessac-Léognan Bordeaux Blend (Bordeaux) $80. A rich, open modern style of wine, full of new wood flavors. The fruit is solid, chunky, and square, while the tannins are ripe and generous. This will develop relatively quickly, over the next 10 years. **94** —R.V. (6/1/2003)

Château Pape-Clement 2005 Barrel Sample Bordeaux White Blend (Pessac-Léognan) $NA. Lemon flavors give a lift to a wine that is otherwise rather fat and heavy. There is nice spice from oak, but overall the wine is a little hot. **89** —R.V. (6/21/2006)

CHÂTEAU PATACHE D'AUX

Château Patache d'Aux 2002 Bordeaux Blend (Médoc) $22. A usually reliable performer, Patache d'Aux produced a solid wine in the difficult 2002 vintage. A whiff of mint carries through on the palate, which blends herbs, berries, and vanilla in a straightforward claret. Fruit shows through the firm tannins on the finish, suggesting this will improve over the next few years. Drink 2008–2012. **85** —J.C. (6/1/2005)

CHÂTEAU PAVIE

Château Pavie 2000 Bordeaux Blend (Saint-Emilion) $250. Under the regime of Gérard Perse, Pavie seems to have become more opulent, more extracted, and, dare I say it, more simplistic. The richness of the 2000 vintage lends itself to this technique. While it is a wonderful, immediately appealing wine, with its intense dark fruits, it seem to lack the complexity of other wines of similar status. **93** —R.V. (6/1/2003)

Château Pavie Macquin 2005 Barrel Sample Bordeaux Blend (Saint-Emilion Grand Cru) $NA. Juicy, fresh fruit, powerful black currant flavors and layers of obvious acidity. But there's more here: underlying, dark, brooding tannins, and vibrant fruits on top. **92** —R.V. (6/20/2006)

Château Pavie-Decesse 2000 Bordeaux Blend (Saint-Emilion) $NA. While Pavie itself goes for super-opulence, Pavie-Decesse is more restrained, more classic. It has harmony and balance, allowing the deep, black fruits to rest easily with the dense tannins. This is a wine which will age well, gracefully over 10 years and more. **90** —R.V. (6/1/2003)

CHÂTEAU PECH-REDON

Château Pech-Redon 2001 La Centaurée Red Blend (Coteaux du Languedoc) $NA. A hugely powerful wine which wears its high alcohol (14%) lightly. That's because the fruit is tempered with fine acidity and dark black, wood-flavored fruits. This is a wine that needs aging, with its power-packed tar and tannins. **91** —R.V. (12/1/2004)

CHÂTEAU PÉRIER

Château Périer 2003 Bordeaux Blend (Médoc) $17. A small, 17-acre property near Saint-Laurent in the north of Medoc, this is a classic Bordeaux, with its tight tannins, layers of dryness, and acidity. But these are not negatives because this is a delicious food wine, one that also has great black fruits. **87** —R.V. (5/1/2006)

CHÂTEAU PETIT VILLAGE

Château Petit Village 2004 Barrel Sample Bordeaux Blend (Pomerol) $NA. This has solid, modern, polished fruit that is taking on new-wood flavors. But that fruit is rich enough to power through the wood and give freshness and ripeness when mature. **92** —R.V. (6/1/2005)

CHÂTEAU PÉTRUS

Château Pétrus 2000 Bordeaux Blend (Pomerol) $1500. While the first impression with Pétrus is the wood, it is the fruit which gradually shows itself. It is extraordinary, this dense fruit, which simultaneously manages to float with elegance. There is layer after layer of fruit, sometime black, sometimes smoky, sometimes spicy. The wine is not yet totally integrated, still intensely young, with decades to go. But what a development it will be. **98** —R.V. (6/1/2003)

Château Pétrus 2004 Barrel Sample Bordeaux Blend (Pomerol) $NA. Always the star of Pomerol, this wine lives up to its reputation, with power but also a great sense of elegance to counterpoint the richness. This is classic Merlot at its best. **95** —R.V. (6/1/2005)

CHÂTEAU PEYRABON

Château Peyrabon 2003 Bordeaux Blend (Haut-Médoc) $NA. Under the ownership of Patrick Bernard (same family as the owners of Domaine de Chevalier), this is an up-and-coming estate that makes fine wines. This 2003 is particularly rich, a solid, generously tannic wine that has excellent ripe black fruits, sweet tannins, and tarry flavors. **89** —R.V. (5/1/2006)

CHÂTEAU PHÉLAN-SÉGUR

Château Phélan-Ségur 2003 Bordeaux Blend (Saint-Estèphe) $38. Under the ownership of the Gardinier family, this château now rivals some of the classed growths, and deserves its crus bourgeois exceptionnel classification. It is certainly full of new wood flavors, but these are not allowed to dominate dense tannins, flavors of black plums, and fine layers of acidity. Will certainly age for 10+ years. **93 Cellar Selection** —R.V. (5/1/2006)

Château Phélan-Ségur 2005 Barrel Sample Bordeaux Blend (Saint-Estèphe) $NA. A finely balanced wine, with the steel and tannins of Saint-Estèphe tempered with hugely ripe, concentrated black plum and dark fig flavors. This is elegant while also being powerful. **92** —R.V. (6/20/2006)

Château Phélan-Ségur 2003 Barrel Sample Bordeaux Blend (Saint-Estèphe) $NA. A black, dense wine which shows how ripe the tannins were in Saint-Estèphe in 2003. Powerful and intense, it reveals layers of wood and spicy fruits. **90** —R.V. (6/3/2004)

FRANCE

CHÂTEAU PICHON LONGUEVILLE

Château Pichon Longueville 2003 Bordeaux Blend (Pauillac) $100. Powerfully structured, with great depth and huge, ripe fruit, along with a muscular freshness of both fruit and tannins. **93** —*R.V. (5/1/2006)*

Château Pichon Longueville 2003 Barrel Sample Bordeaux Blend (Pauillac) $NA. Tar and licorice aromas make this an immediately enticing wine. It is rich, dense, with power supported by rich fruit. There is just a risk that high alcohol will spoil the balance. **91** —*R.V. (6/3/2004)*

Château Pichon Longueville Comtesse de Lalande 2005 Barrel Sample Bordeaux Blend (Pauillac) $NA. A superbly elegant wine that hides its power well. There are dry tannins, blackberry fruits, elevated acidity, and just a hint of raisins. **95** —*R.V. (6/20/2006)*

CHÂTEAU PIQUE-CAILLOU

Château Pique-Caillou 2005 Barrel Sample Bordeaux Blend (Pessac-Léognan) $NA. A smoothly rich wine, layering ripe red fruits with some poised acidity. The tannins are dry, but well integrated into the generous fruits. **91** —*R.V. (6/1/2006)*

CHÂTEAU PONTET-CANET

Château Pontet-Canet 2003 Bordeaux Blend (Pauillac) $55. A closed, austere wine; more solid than fruity, showing very firm tannins. There is a pronounced smoky character as well, with cigar box aromas and toasty flavors. What is certain is that this wine—racy and not too heavy—will develop slowly. **91** —*R.V. (5/1/2006)*

Château Pontet-Canet 2005 Barrel Sample Bordeaux Blend (Pauillac) $NA. A beautiful, aromatic, minty wine that has dusty, warm tannins, still within the Bordeaux structure. It's very dry, but the fruit is already enjoyable. This is going to be a delicious wine. **93** —*R.V. (6/20/2006)*

Château Pontet-Canet 2002 Kosher Bordeaux Blend (Pauillac) $100. On first whiff, it shows big fruit and vanilla, but it settles down on the palate to deliver cedary plum- and cassis-flavored fruit. Finishes long, with some dusty tannins. It's bulky and lacks a bit of grace, but it still makes for a satisfying mouthful of Bordeaux that should improve with time. **89** —*J.C. (4/1/2006)*

CHÂTEAU POTENSAC

Château Potensac 2005 Barrel Sample Bordeaux Blend (Médoc) $NA. This wine has fine tannins that are relatively soft, with good acidity and dryness. It's not powerful, but with its fine black currant flavor and ripe fruit it shows great style. **92** —*R.V. (6/1/2006)*

CHÂTEAU POUJEAUX

Château Poujeaux 2003 Bordeaux Blend (Moulis-en-Médoc) $25. Undoubtedly one of the two star properties in Moulis. Its quality is impeccable: a Cabernet-dominated wine, with superrich black currant flavors that retain great structure and aging ability. Enjoy this wine in 5–10 years. **92 Editors' Choice** —*R.V. (5/1/2006)*

Château Poujeaux 2000 Bordeaux Blend (Moulis) $34. A fruit-dominated wine, full of sweet, ripe, juicy flavors. It is not complex, but its richness in this vintage is going to make it very drinkable in five years. **87** —*R.V. (6/1/2003)*

Château Poujeaux 2004 Barrel Sample Bordeaux Blend (Haut-Médoc) $NA. Château Poujeaux. It may be powerful, but this wine has great layers of wood and acidity, flavors of blackberries, and a juicy, fresh aftertaste. **91** —*R.V. (6/1/2005)*

CHÂTEAU PREUILLAC

Château Preuillac 2003 Bordeaux Blend (Médoc) $NA. The Mau family, who also run négociants Yvon Mau, have poured money into this Médoc château, bringing it back to life. It has paid off in this powerful, rich 2003, which packs blackberry flavors alongside new wood, polished tannins, and impressive aging potential. **90** —*R.V. (5/1/2006)*

CHÂTEAU PRIEURÉ-LES-TOURS

Château Prieuré-les-Tours 2000 Cuveé Clara Bordeaux White Blend (Graves) $16. A finely balanced Graves that shows wood, rich spice, and toast as well as honey and smooth fruit flavors. It's an elegant, food-friendly wine. The release of this nearly 5-year-old wine shows just how well Graves wines can age. **88** —*R.V. (6/1/2005)*

CHÂTEAU PRIEURÉ-LICHINE

Château Prieuré-Lichine 2000 Bordeaux Blend (Margaux) $35. Under new ownership, Prieuré-Lichine continues its rapid quality improvement. The wine is concentrated, with dark tannins and brooding fruit, dominated by new wood. It is rich, but also structured for a steady development over 10-15 years. **91** —*R.V. (6/1/2003)*

Château Prieuré-Lichine 2004 Barrel Sample Bordeaux Blend (Margaux) $NA. The wine is packed with wood, but there is also firm, solid dense fruit, which pushes it to a higher level. There is great structure here. **92** —*R.V. (6/1/2005)*

CHÂTEAU PUECH-HAUT

Château Puech-Haut 2001 Red Blend (Coteaux du Languedoc) $NA. Eucalyptus aromas give this wine an almost Australian feel. It has has herbal flavors, alongside dark black fruits. It is powerful, tarry, medicinal flavors and very concentrated, young fruit. **88** —*R.V. (12/1/2004)*

Château Puech-Haut 2002 Les Complices de Puech-Haut Red Blend (Coteaux du Languedoc) $NA. A wine made from purchased grapes, this is fresh, juicy, and youthful. This is a great barbecue wine, made from a blend of Grenache and Syrah. Soft tannins balancing acidity give a great, easy-drinking wine. **85** —*R.V. (12/1/2004)*

Château Puech-Haut 2003 Rosé Blend (Coteaux du Languedoc) $NA. It's packed in a stylish frosted bottle. And luckily the wine inside echoes the outside in its full, but elegant character, it's crisp and flavored with light tannins, cherries, and a layer of acidity. **90** —*R.V. (12/1/2004)*

CHÂTEAU RABAUD PROMIS

Château Rabaud Promis 2005 Barrel Sample Bordeaux White Blend (Sauternes) $NA. The botrytis is amazingly perfumed, smelling like a Paris perfume shop. The fruit is lost in a crazy range of exotic flavors. Fun, but very different. **91** —*R.V. (6/1/2006)*

CHÂTEAU RAHOUL

Château Rahoul 2005 Barrel Sample Bordeaux Blend (Graves) $NA. Very soft and rather fat, this overextracted wine lacks the lively acidity that seems to mark 2005. The fruit is therefore heavy in the mouth, without needed structure. **88** —*R.V. (6/21/2006)*

CHÂTEAU RAUZAN DESPAGNE

Château Rauzan Despagne 2004 Cuvée de Landereau Bordeaux White Blend (Bordeaux) $12. A crisp, fresh wine, ready to drink now, with no wood aging, but with great ripe white-fruit flavors, and mouth-watering acidity. A great apéritif wine for the summer. **87** —*R.V. (6/1/2005)*

CHÂTEAU RAUZAN-GASSIES

Château Rauzan-Gassies 2005 Barrel Sample Bordeaux Blend (Margaux) $NA. Solid, dry tannins, very firm and hard, but they are also ripe. The wine has high extraction, very dark fruit flavors, but resists being too huge. This could well turn out to be a very elegant wine. **92** —*R.V. (6/20/2006)*

CHÂTEAU RAUZAN-SÉGLA

Château Rauzan-Ségla 2001 Bordeaux Blend (Margaux) $57. A huge, powerful, dense wine, which layers pure black fruits over dusty tannins. This is an impressive wine, proof of Rauzan-Ségla's improvements since Chanel took over ownership. It is packed with fruits, like an intense jelly, but also has dryness, acidity, and good aging potential. **94** —*R.V. (6/1/2005)*

Château Rauzan-Ségla 2005 Barrel Sample Bordeaux Blend (Margaux) $NA. A hard, powerfully dry wine that packs big tannins over the fruit. The wood element is certainly there, but it's the almost Napa-like fruit tannins that drive this wine. **94** —*R.V. (6/20/2006)*

CHÂTEAU RAYNE VIGNEAU

Château Rayne Vigneau 2005 Barrel Sample Bordeaux White Blend (Sauternes) $NA. A very pure, citrus-dominated wine with great intensity, spice, fresh fruits, and crisp, almost apple-like flavors. Very clean and fresh. **90** —*R.V. (6/1/2006)*

FRANCE

CHÂTEAU RÉAL MARTIN

Château Réal Martin 2004 Rhône Red Blend (Côtes de Provence) $10. Comes out of the chute a little stinky and reductive, so give it a good decanting before serving. Once it comes around, the flavors are bold and fresh: watermelon and strawberry held together by a crisp, citrusy backbone. **85 Best Buy** —*J.C. (11/15/2005)*

Château Réal Martin 2001 Syrah-Grenache (Côtes de Provence) $13. A 50-50 blend of Syrah and Grenache that's marred by sulfury notes on the nose that come across as garlicky on the palate. Seems to have decent weight and texture, so may be worth a try if you are less sensitive to these compounds.. **81** —*J.C. (11/15/2005)*

CHÂTEAU REDORTIER

Château Redortier 2004 Rhône Red Blend (Beaumes-de-Venise) $NA. A supple, elegant wine—the qualities that are alleged to be typical of Beaumes-de-Venise wines. It also has plenty of bright, crunchy cherry fruit and a hefty dash of peppery spice. Nicely balanced, and ready to drink now but capable of a few years' of development. **88** —*J.C. (11/15/2006)*

CHÂTEAU REYNON

Château Reynon 2003 Vieilles Vignes Bordeaux White Blend (Bordeaux) $17. This 2003, fat and full, shows skilled winemaking, extracting intensity of flavor, and a fine balance from a hot, super-ripe year. Toast and cream flavors at the fore, along with a light touch of acidity. **88** —*R.V. (6/1/2005)*

CHÂTEAU RIEUSSEC

Château Rieussec 2004 Barrel Sample Bordeaux White Blend (Sauternes) $NA. This is dry, firm, the botrytis giving richness rather than sweetness. Quite toasty, as well. **89** —*R.V. (6/1/2005)*

CHÂTEAU ROLLAN DE BY

Château Rollan de By 2002 Bordeaux Blend (Médoc) $32. A fine effort from this reliable cru bourgeois, the 2002 Rollan de By boasts hints of toast and vanilla in its bouquet, but mostly offers up solid cassis fruit, with just a whiff of dried herbs. A velvety, supple texture and lush tannins suggest early drinkability. Try now—2010. **88** —*J.C. (6/1/2005)*

CHÂTEAU ROMER DU HAYOT

Château Romer du Hayot 2005 Barrel Sample Bordeaux White Blend (Sauternes) $NA. As dry as this is, it is obviously going to be a dense, very powerful wine that will show both great breeding and concentration. Those who like their sweet wines with food will admire and enjoy this wine. **89** —*R.V. (6/21/2006)*

CHÂTEAU ROQUEFORT

Château Roquefort 2001 Roquefortissime Bordeaux White Blend (Bordeaux) $26. Some tropical fruit on the nose, but also sulfur and a distracting tarry note. Rubbery and artificial tasting, with a short peach-pit finish. Seems faux in the way it comes across. **82** *(7/1/2005)*

CHÂTEAU ROUBAUD

Château Roubaud 1998 Tradition Rhône Red Blend (Costières de Nimes) $13. **87** —*M.S. (11/1/2000)*

CHÂTEAU ROUBINE

Château Roubine 1998 Merlot (Côtes de Provence) $12. Deep blackberry and oak notes permeate this Merlot from start to finish. It's a little tangy in the mouth, and has mineral notes on the finish. Good, ordinary. **83** —*D.T. (2/1/2002)*

Château Roubine 2000 Cru Classe Rosé Blend (Côtes de Provence) $12. This pale but lively rosé is dryly fruited with light cherry aromas and flavors, anise and mineral accents. Even and lithe in the mouth, this has the qualities that make a good Provençal rosé so delightful. Perfect to drink now, this is a good value if found on sale. **85** —*M.M. (2/1/2002)*

CHÂTEAU ROUTAS

Château Routas 2003 Rouviere Rosé Blend (Coteaux Varois) $10. When my wife, normally no great fan of rosé, says, "I really like this wine," that's an endorsement you can take to the bank. Aromas of wild berries and melon are reserved, the punch solid, and the color a lovely light salmon. This Provençal wine is good year in and year out, so there's no reason not to expect the same from the upcoming 2004. A great summertime refresher that goes down fast and easy. Excellent with salads topped with vinaigrettes. **87 Best Buy** —*M.S. (11/15/2004)*

Château Routas 2005 Rouvière Rosé Blend (Coteaux Varois) $10. This medium-bodied blend of 40% Grenache, 30% Syrah, and 30% Cinsault offers simple, fruity flavors suggestive of peaches, red plums, and citrus fruit. Crisp and clean on the finish; a nice picnic rosé. **85 Best Buy** —*J.C. (6/21/2006)*

Château Routas 2000 Coquelicot White Blend (Vin de Pays Var) $16. This tasty Southern French white has an orange-tangerine profile and an even, faintly creamy mouthfeel. Cuts a fine line between citrus tang and softness—and succeeds. Respected Santa Barbara County vintner Bob Lindquist of Qupé consults, and has crafted a wine that closes with good length and a touch of pepper and spice. Drink through 2002. **87** —*M.M. (2/1/2002)*

CHÂTEAU RUSSOL GARDEY

Château Russol Gardey 1999 Grande Réserve Syrah (Minervois) $20. There's quite a bouquet in this Minervois: black fruits, clove, olive, cinnamon, bitter chocolate, and slight volatile acidity provide quite an aromatic spectrum. This compact, tart wine is taut, with a compressed complexity and a rather hard palate feel. Works now with complex foods—and will be even better after a few years in the cellar. **87** *(10/1/2001)*

CHÂTEAU SAINT ESTEVE D'UCHAUX

Château Saint Esteve d'Uchaux 2001 Vieilles Vignes Rhône Red Blend (Côtes-du-Rhône Villages) $30. Fully mature and ready to drink now, this is a thrilling Côtes-du-Rhône. Delicate cherry, chocolate, and tobacco scents provide a sense of elegance rare in the region, complemented by a velvety mouthfeel and anise and pepper notes on the finish. A knockout, with elegance and style. Tasted twice, with consistent notes. **91 Editors' Choice** —*J.C. (11/15/2006)*

Château Saint Esteve d'Uchaux 2005 Jeunes Vignes Viognier (Côtes-du-Rhône) $17. This 100% Viognier is a slightly floral, easy-to-drink apéritif. Pear and spice notes dominate, and there's plenty of body, but the acidity is still quite fresh. Drink now. **87** —*J.C. (11/15/2006)*

CHÂTEAU SAINT-COSMÉ

Château Saint-Cosmé 2001 Côtes du Rhône Les Deux Albions Rhône Red Blend (Côtes-du-Rhône) $18. A finely crafted wine, with elegant fruit balancing the perfumed tannins and sweet red fruit flavors. A light edge of acidity gives the wine poise, and that it may age well. **87** —*R.V. (3/1/2004)*

Château Saint-Cosmé 2001 Cuvée Valbelle Rhône Red Blend (Gigondas) $53. This wine is all about potential. At present, with the powerful tannins and layers of wood, the fruit is only showing early signs of richness. But over time, this is going to develop into a superb wine, powering through from the tannins to enormous, concentrated dark fruits and layers of herbal flavors. **94** —*R.V. (3/1/2004)*

CHÂTEAU SAINT-LAURENT

Château Saint-Laurent 1999 Cabernet Sauvignon-Merlot (Haut-Médoc) $32. This Kosher Bordeaux has woody, maple-like aromas along with some smoky, rubbery accents. The palate offers some cherry and cola flavors, while the finish is smooth enough, with pronounced woody notes. **83** —*M.S. (1/1/2004)*

CHÂTEAU SAINT-ROCH

Château Saint-Roch 2004 Brunel Rhône Red Blend (Lirac) $18. Perfumed on the nose, with attractive shadings of dried flowers and spice layered over a base of black cherries. It's ripe for a 2004, showing a hint of alcoholic warmth and supple tannins. Yet it stays just this side of balanced. Drink now. **88** —*J.C. (11/15/2006)*

CHÂTEAU SAINTE ROSELINE

Château Sainte Roseline 2004 Cru Classe Lampe de Meduse Rosé Blend

FRANCE

(Côtes de Provence) $20. A nice summer rosé, if only it weren't quite so expensive. The color is a pretty light copper hue, the aromas fresh and minerally, with touches of watermelon rind and strawberry. It's fairly full-bodied, with flavors that hint at berries and anise, then finish with a hint of fennel. 85 —*J.C. (6/21/2006)*

CHÂTEAU SIGALAS RABAUD

Château Sigalas Rabaud 2005 Barrel Sample Bordeaux White Blend (Sauternes) $NA. Caramel aromas spoil this otherwise beautiful wine. It is big and powerful, with nice spice and intense flavors. Even the wood seems in accord, except for the nose. 87 —*R.V. (6/21/2006)*

CHÂTEAU SIGNAC

Château Signac 2000 Melodie d'Amour Red Blend (Côtes-du-Rhône) $17. Jammy berry notes kick it off, and below that there are intriguing meaty aromas. All told, the nose is packed and sensual. The palate is juicy and healthy, with raspberry, cherry, and rhubarb all mixed together into one long, pure package. The finish, too, is right on the money. In a word, it's fresh. And that quality bears repeating. 89 —*M.S. (9/1/2003)*

Château Signac 2003 Cuvée Terra Amata Chusclan Rhône Red Blend (Côtes-du-Rhône Villages) $21. A bit sappy or resinous on the nose, but later that element seems to recede a bit, revealing herbal accents layered over rich black cherry scents. The ripe black cherry flavors are flawless, while the rich, supple mouthfeel displays lovely structure and balance. Ends with a hint of French roast; ready to drink now and over the next several years. 90 Editors' Choice —*J.C. (11/15/2006)*

Château Signac 2004 Tradition Chusclan Rhône Red Blend (Côtes-du-Rhône Villages) $16. Doesn't have nearly the spice and haunting aromatics as Signac's Cuvée Terra Amata, but this is still a smooth, supple, easy-to-drink Chusclan. Creamy textured, with flavors of plum and spice and good persistence on the palate. 87 —*J.C. (11/15/2006)*

CHÂTEAU SIRAN

Château Siran 2001 Bordeaux Blend (Margaux) $22. The 2001 is rich, dense, concentrated, with dusty tannins and solid black fruits. The palate is rich and spicy, with new wood flavors supporting firm, ripe fruit. The wine is still young, with dry fruit tannins and a layer of acidity, and excellent potential. 91 Editors' Choice —*R.V. (6/1/2005)*

Château Siran 2005 Barrel Sample Bordeaux Blend (Margaux) $NA. A delightful wine, with its delicate fruits, ripe tannins and fine, black plums. This is going to mature with grace and ease—a pleasure to drink. 93 —*R.V. (6/20/2006)*

CHÂTEAU SMITH HAUT-LAFITTE

Château Smith Haut-Lafitte 2005 Barrel Sample Bordeaux Blend (Pessac-Léognan) $NA. There are very ripe fruit aromas in this wine, with big, soft jelly-like fruit flavors and soft, sweet tannins. This doesn't seem to have the structure to age well, but will be perfectly enjoyable in the short run. 88 —*R.V. (6/21/2006)*

Château Smith Haut-Lafitte 2005 Barrel Sample Bordeaux White Blend (Pessac-Léognan) $NA. Very citrusy fruits, with spice, new wood, and delicious, almost tropical flavors. This wine has great poise and acidity. 91 —*R.V. (6/1/2006)*

CHÂTEAU SOCIANDO MALLET

Château Sociando Mallet 2002 Bordeaux Blend (Haut-Médoc) $35. This wine is fresh, with hints of ripe fruit and aromas of tobacco. It has some darkness, good black fruits, and dark tannins, along with some good smoky wood. 88 —*R.V. (6/1/2005)*

CHÂTEAU SUAU

Château Suau 2005 Barrel Sample Bordeaux White Blend (Barsac) $NA. This is a finely balanced, poised wine, with fresh fruits, ripeness, and a touch of lemon all coming together in potential harmony. There is wood, but it is laced with botrytis and fine, fresh flavors. 90 —*R.V. (6/21/2006)*

CHÂTEAU SUDUIRAUT

Château Suduiraut 2005 Barrel Sample Bordeaux White Blend (Sauternes) $NA. This is a hugely ripe wine dominated by concentrated, ripe fruits,

and flavors of pure sweet oranges. A powerful wine, surprising because of its weight in a year that seems more about freshness, but still good. 91 —*R.V. (6/1/2006)*

CHÂTEAU TALBOT

Château Talbot 2003 Bordeaux Blend (Saint-Julien) $32. For a young wine, this is remarkably balanced. With fine but not powerful tannins and sweet black fruit flavors, it is polished, with vanilla accents and good acidity. It is already well-integrated and should develop relatively quickly. 90 —*R.V. (5/1/2006)*

Château Talbot 2005 Barrel Sample Bordeaux Blend (Saint-Julien) $NA. Huge black currant flavors, very ripe fruit, but also a great sense of balance, of proportion, that give this wine both charm and impressiveness. It's going to age seriously, and well. 94 —*R.V. (6/20/2006)*

Château Talbot 2003 Barrel Sample Bordeaux Blend (Saint-Julien) $NA. This is one of the best-balanced wines from Saint-Julien, which may mean its future is medium-term. It has great fruit, generous tannins and a touch of spice. 91 —*R.V. (6/3/2004)*

CHÂTEAU TAYAC

Château Tayac 1995 Cuvée Prestige Bordeaux Blend (Côtes de Bourg) $30. 87 —*J.C. (5/1/2000)*

CHÂTEAU TEYSSIER

Château Teyssier 2005 Barrel Sample Bordeaux Blend (Saint-Emilion Grand Cru) $NA. This is a good value in Saint-Emilion, with the same wine-making team as Le Dôme. It is ripe, dense, with high acidity and firm black fruit. 88 —*R.V. (6/21/2006)*

CHÂTEAU THIEULEY

Château Thieuley 2003 Bordeaux White Blend (Bordeaux) $13. One of the top producers in the Entre-deux-Mers, Francis Courselle's white has a freshness, lift, and crispness that is not always apparent in 2003 whites. But there are also wood flavors to add complexity, and to produce a beautifully balanced wine. 91 Best Buy —*R.V. (6/1/2005)*

Château Thieuley 2000 Bordeaux Rouge Bordeaux Blend (Bordeaux) $76. A dense, concentrated fruit with a good balance of wood and fruit. There is a slight touch of stalkiness but the fruit is also rich, with flavors of fruitcake and good structure. 88 —*R.V. (12/1/2002)*

Château Thieuly 2001 Bordeaux Blanc White Blend (Bordeaux) $6. A delicious up-front style of wine, brimming with refreshing crisp, green fruit. Winemaker Francis Courselle believes the future of his part of Bordeaux (the Entre-deux-Mers) is in whites—and this easy wine proves the point. 87 —*R.V. (12/1/2002)*

CHÂTEAU TOUR DE MIRAMBEAU

Château Tour de Mirambeau 2000 Cuvée Passion Bordeaux Rouge Bordeaux Blend (Bordeaux) $19. Jean-Louis Despagne has made a deep, dark-colored wine from his flagship property. It is polished and smooth, with rich fruit that is still dominated by wood at this stage, but with powerful dark fruit flavors underneath. This is a wine with great intensity and the chance to age for at least 10 years. 91 —*R.V. (12/1/2002)*

Château Tour de Mirambeau 2002 Cuvée Passion Bordeaux White Blend (Bordeaux) $19. Old vines, low yields, and fermentation in wood give great complexity to this top cuvée from the Despagne family. There is a touch of wood flavor to this wine, but the main impression is of delicious, fresh fruit that has gained maturity from bottle age. It is in balance, with good acidity to give it a final lift. 90 Editors' Choice —*R.V. (6/1/2005)*

CHÂTEAU TOUR LÉOGNAN

Château Tour Léognan 2003 Bordeaux White Blend (Pessac-Léognan) $NA. This is the second-label white wine from Château Carbonnieux. It's a fresh, uncomplicated wine, which is given richness from the wood flavors and softness from the superripe year. 87 —*R.V. (6/1/2005)*

CHÂTEAU TOUR SIMARD

Château Tour Simard 1999 Bordeaux Blend (Saint-Emilion Grand Cru) $40. Already showing some bricking at the rim, this St.-Emilion from the owner of Château Pavie is altogether different from that storied wine. Starts with scents of raisins, smoke, and leather, and continues in that

FRANCE

vein on the palate, where the flavors run toward dried fruit and vanilla. Supple, soft tannins on the finish suggest early drinkability. 86 —J.C. (6/1/2005)

CHÂTEAU TRIMOULET

Château Trimoulet 1996 Bordeaux Blend (Saint-Emilion) $35. Dark earth and tobacco spice the aromas of this grand cru, followed by flavors of black cherries and herbs. The Cabernet Franc portion shines clearly through as a distinctive weediness, but it's somewhat balanced by roasted black cherries and only a hint of espresso-like oak. 86 —J.C. (3/1/2001)

CHÂTEAU TROPLONG-MONDOT

Château Troplong-Mondot 2000 Bordeaux Blend (Saint-Emilion) $85. A soft, rich wine that bears all the classic qualities of the Valette family's winery—a strength of line along and complexity. The fruit is ripe, ultra-generous, but is still tempered with layers of acidity and soft tannins. 92 —R.V. (6/1/2003)

CHÂTEAU TROTANOY

Château Trotanoy 2005 Barrel Sample Bordeaux Blend (Saint-Emilion Grand Cru) $NA. An immensely powerful wine with hugely ripe tannins. This is enormous, but is there a sense of balance? Yes, just at the end, as freshness and acidity play their roles. 94 —R.V. (6/20/2006)

Château Trotanoy 2003 Barrel Sample Bordeaux Blend (Pomerol) $NA. A wine which is dominated by sweet fruit, the sheer exuberance of the fruit dominating the huge, dark tannins. This will be a wonderful, intensely fruity wine. 92 —R.V. (6/3/2004)

CHÂTEAU VAL JOANIS

Château Val Joanis 1999 Cuvée Reserve Les Griottes Red Blend (Côtes du Luberon) $20. Deep and pretty, with pronounced bacon, violet, earth, and black fruit aromas. The palate is stylish and refined, a clear cut above the average Rhône red. In terms of flavor, there's ample cherry, plum, and chocolate. The finish eases off some, as it turns easy and slightly one-dimensional. But with such a great bouquet, tannic structure, and richness, the complaints are few. 89 —M.S. (9/1/2003)

Château Val Joanis 2001 Rouge Red Blend (Côtes du Luberon) $13. Hints of cinnamon and clove reflect a small amount of new oak aging, but the dominant flavors are of plum and dusty earth. Not a powerhouse, it's a balanced, food-friendly wine at a reasonable price—the kind of wine that wins friends, not ratings competitions. 85 —J.C. (2/1/2005)

Château Val Joanis 2001 Vigne du Chanoine Trouillet Red Blend (Côtes du Luberon) $30. Scents of buttered popcorn lead the way, followed by waves of oak-derived flavors: cedar, vanilla, and chocolate, backed up by some black cherry notes. The mouthfeel is supple and creamy, the finish moderately tannic. Drink this lavishly oaked wine from 2007-2015, once the wood has integrated a little better with its fruit substrate. 88 —J.C. (2/1/2005)

Château Val Joanis 1998 Estate Bottled Rhône Red Blend (Côtes du Luberon) $10. With its bold, jammy blackberries and a hint of black pepper on the nose, this wine is all about delivering a flavor punch. Straightforward berry fruit is tinged with licorice in a bulky but satisfying package. 87 —J.C. (3/1/2001)

Château Val Joanis 2004 Rosé Blend (Côtes du Luberon) $12. This salmon-colored wine isn't your typical cotton-candy rosé. Instead, it boasts wisps of delicate cherry-berry flavors wrapped around a core of minerality, finishing clean and citrusy. Just right for the picnic hamper. 84 —J.C. (11/15/2005)

Château Val Joanis 2002 Blanc White Blend (Côtes du Luberon) $13. A fruit salad white, with aromas and flavors that run the gamut from Asian pear to ripe apples and Hawaiian pineapple. Plump and medium-weight, picks up hints of honey and citrus on the lingering finish. 86 —J.C. (3/1/2004)

CHÂTEAU VALANDRAUD

Château Valandraud 2005 Barrel Sample Bordeaux Blend (Saint-Emilion Grand Cru) $NA. One of the likely candidates for promotion to Grand Cru Classé status, this is Jean-Luc Thunevin's original estate. This year there is considerable restraint in what is normally an immensely opulent wine: it is elegant, rather than having a no-holds-barred attitude, that will make this wine a classic. 91 —R.V. (6/1/2006)

Château Valandraud 2002 Kosher Mevushal Bordeaux Blend (Saint-Emilion) $260. A slight step down from the nonmevushal bottling, with less plumpness on the midpalate and slightly roasted, but similar, flavors of chocolate, mocha, cedar, and bacon. Supple on the finish, this is a blend of 70% Merlot, 30% Cabernet Franc. 88 (4/1/2006)

CHÂTEAU VILLA BEL AIR

Château Villa Bel Air 2003 Bordeaux White Blend (Graves) $20. This property, owned by the Cazes family of Château Lynch-Bages, has produced a really stylish, fresh, full-bodied wine. The fruit is rich, with a well-judged layer of wood and flavors of ripe green plums. 89 —R.V. (6/1/2005)

CHÂTEAU YON FIGEAC

Château Yon Figeac 1995 Bordeaux Blend (Saint-Emilion) $40. An elegant grand cru whose tannic structure is just beginning to resolve. Has a nose of berry aromas, earthy accents, and even meaty notes. The palate displays developed ripe cassis and earth flavors. Still youthful, it drinks well, but should evolve further over the next few years. 91 Editors' Choice (4/1/2001)

CHEVALIER DE GRUAUD

Chevalier de Gruaud 1999 Bordeaux Blend (Saint-Julien) $45. A subsidiary label of Château Gruaud Larose, obviously destined for earlier drinking than the grand vin. Supple tannins frame cedar, tobacco and earth notes, while the light frame holds just enough flesh to avoid leanness. 84 —J.C. (6/1/2005)

CIRCUS BY L'OSTAL CAZES

Circus by L'Ostal Cazes 2004 Viognier (Vin de Pays d'Oc) $13. Mint and mineral notes are layered delicately over honeyed baked apple aromas in this full-bodied Viognier. Flavors of anise and honeyed stones show a touch of alcohol on the finish, but this is a solid first effort. 86 —J.C. (11/15/2005)

CLAUDE CHEVALIER

Claude Chevalier 2003 Les Gréchons Premier Cru Chardonnay (Ladoix) $45. A light, fresh wine with crisp green apple flavors. It is clean, and rounded out, with a touch of vanilla. Finishes with lively acidity. 86 —R.V. (9/1/2005)

CLOS DE L'ORATOIRE DES PAPES

Clos de L'Oratoire des Papes 2000 Red Blend (Châteauneuf-du-Pape) $28. More harmonious at this stage than the property's Les Choregies luxury cuvée, this wine's supple black cherry and dark chocolate flavors are framed by earthy, leathery notes that culiminate in a complex finish of coffee, earth, and juicy fruit. 88 —J.C. (3/1/2004)

Clos de L'Oratoire des Papes 2003 Rhône Red Blend (Châteauneuf-du-Pape) $35. This reasonably priced Châteauneuf is intense and flavorful, yet holds onto a sense of elegance and proportion, something that's not always easy in a sun-baked vintage like 2003. Cherries and black cherries come rushing across the palate in waves, garnished by little curls of cinnamon and clove. Long on the finish, picking up subtle hints of bacon or wood smoke. 90 —J.C. (11/15/2005)

CLOS DE LA COULÉE DE SERRANT

Clos de la Coulée de Serrant 2002 Clos de la Coulée de Serrant Chenin Blanc (Savennières-Coulée de Serrant) $79. Nicolas Joly and his mother are possessors of the smallest appellation in France: Coulée de Serrant. This almost vertical vineyard, dropping down to the Loire, facing due south, makes a mythical wine that is powerful and laden with exotic fruit flavors: oranges, lemon, apricots, accented with spices and the tannins of a youthful white wine. This will last for decades. 95 Cellar Selection —R.V. (4/1/2005)

CLOS DES BRUSQUIÈRES

Clos des Brusquières 2003 Rhône Red Blend (Châteauneuf-du-Pape) $32. This is a solid performance. The wine is dense, with dark, dry tannins, but overlying this is very direct, juicy fruit, with flavors of raspberries and dark cherries. It is not initially as generous as some 2003s, but the tannins and acidity suggest it is ageworthy. 91 —R.V. (12/31/2005)

CLOS FOURTET

Clos Fourtet 2000 Bordeaux Blend (Saint-Emilion) $51. This was the last vintage at Clos Fourtet under the ownership of the Lurtons. They made fine wine, but the potential of the property was never quite realized. The wine just fails to excite: it is rich and concentrated with ripe tannins and some sweetness, but at the same time, there is a layer of acidity and structure which gives the wine a firm, solid shape. **90** —R.V. (6/1/2003)

Clos Fourtet 2004 Barrel Sample Bordeaux Blend (Saint-Emilion Grand Cru) $NA. Under new management, this estate has improved dramatically. There are freshness and fragrant aromas from the black currant fruits. To finish, it is dry, but poised. **92** —R.V. (6/1/2005)

CLOS LA COUTALE

Clos la Coutale 1999 Malbec (Cahors) $12. 86 Best Buy —D.T. (11/15/2002)

COMMANDERIE DE LA BARGEMONE

Commanderie de la Bargemone 2005 Rosé Blend (Coteaux d'Aix en Provence) $NA. This medium-hued rosé drinks more like a white wine, with stony, mineral scents, light body, melon, and citrus flavors and a tart, stony finish. Worth trying this summer as an apéritif or with fish. **86** —J.C. (6/19/2006)

COMTE AUDOIN DE DAMPIERRE

Comte Audoin de Dampierre NV Grande Cuvée Brut Champagne Blend (Champagne) $39. This starts out on the right foot, hitting you with a whiff of toasted nuts and crème caramel. The maturity of the blend seems well-calculated; there's a very nice mix of crisp green fruit, spicy clove, and more mature, slightly oxidized, nutty flavors. This is not a big wine, but it fills the palate evenly and persists with a core of pleasing, lightly salty, somewhat oily roasted almond. **90** —P.G. (12/1/2006)

COMTE CATHARE

Comte Cathare 1999 Syrvedre Rhône Red Blend (Vin de Pays d'Oc) $15. A Syrah-Mourvèdre wine, one of a family of similar blends, all with Syrah as the common element. This sibling offers a flattering dark berry earth and toast bouquet. A palate loaded with ripe berry fruit follows, the plush, even feel adding to the pleasure quotient. Finishes with good length, slightly drier, anise-tinged flavors, and subtle, even tannins. Worth hunting for. **88 Editors' Choice** —M.M. (2/1/2002)

COMTE DE LANTAGE

Comte de Lantage 1995 Premier Cru Blanc de Blancs Brut Champagne Blend (Champagne) $40. Forward from the get go, but not exactly a refined product. Melon, apple, and almonds on palate, with a heavy, creamy, lactic finish. Has its virtues but also its faults, primarily some oxidized sherry notes and a certain heaviness. **84** —M.S. (6/1/2003)

COMTE LAFOND

Comte LaFond 2002 Sauvignon Blanc (Sancerre) $32. Flinty and lean, with mineral and citrus aromas. An "oyster wine" in that it's ultra tart. Flavors of sour apple, lemon, and pineapple will show best if it's served chilled. And remember those oysters; this one needs them as much as the other way around. **84** (7/1/2005)

Comte LaFond 2000 Grand Cuvée Sauvignon Blanc (Sancerre) $48. Offers a lot of what makes Sauvignon a good pairing partner. The nose is minerally and bright, with nectarine, melon, and light smoke aromas. Not overwhelming in terms of flavor, as grapefruit and lemon carry the palate. Finishes lean, even, and crisp. A perfect wine for oysters. **90** (7/1/2005)

COUDERT PÈRE ET FILS

Coudert Père et Fils 2002 Clos de la Roilette Gamay (Fleurie) $18. Unlike the candied aromas exhibited by some Beaujolais, this boasts a seriously vinous nose, with cherries and herbs and a hint of smoke or rock dust. To further distinguish it from ordinary Beaujolais, it's fairly full-bodied and shows tea-like tannins on the finish. **90 Editors' Choice** —J.C. (11/15/2003)

CUVÉE MYTHIQUE

Cuvée Mythique 2001 Rhône Red Blend (Vin de Pays d'Oc) $17. Big, ripe, modern fresh berry fruits give this wine an immediate appeal. But there's more to it. With layers of wood, soft tannins, and flavors of herbs and acidity, this wine has complexity as well. Drink now, but age for five years. **89** —R.V. (12/1/2004)

DANIEL CHOTARD

Daniel Chotard 2003 Sauvignon Blanc (Sancerre) $22. Veers into the mineral, spiced-apple realm before displaying citrus in the form of grapefruit, melon, and peach. Quite minerally and dry, with a citrus and melon influence to the finish. Mainstream and healthy; perfect restaurant Sancerre. **89** (7/1/2005)

DANIEL RION

Daniel Rion 1999 Les Beaux-Monts Pinot Noir (Vosne-Romanée) $52. Rion holds back on the new oak, letting the pure, supple fruit speak for itself. This is a muscular Vosne, young and firm, showing excellent focus and structure. Already the finish lingers beautifully, with layers of texture and tightly wrapped fruit. Should cellar well for a decade or more. **92** —P.G. (1/7/2001)

DAUVERGNE & RANVIER

Dauvergne & Ranvier 2004 Rhône Red Blend (Côtes-du-Rhône) $13. A 50-50 blend of Grenache and Syrah, this offering boasts a lovely bouquet of chocolate and plum, but turns a bit firm and drying on the palate. Lacks lushness, but its structure might make it work well with rare beef or lamb. **84** —J.C. (11/15/2006)

Dauvergne & Ranvier 2005 *Barrel Sample* François Arnaud Rhône Red Blend (Côtes-du-Rhône) $NA. 88 Best Buy —J.C. (11/15/2006)

DE LADOUCETTE

De Ladoucette 2000 Baron de L Sauvignon Blanc (Pouilly-Fumé) $78. Fairly fragrant and creamy, with orange, pineapple, and other attractive tropical fruits. Remains restrained on the palate despite the fact that it displays some heavyweight attributes. Nuances of vanilla bean sweeten the soft, rather zipless finish. Ultimately it registers as an easy drinker. **88** (7/1/2005)

DE SAINT GALL

De Saint Gall NV Bouzy Brut Champagne Blend (Champagne) $32. 86 —M.S. (12/1/2000)

De Saint Gall 1995 Premier Cru Blanc de Blancs Brut Champagne Blend (Champagne) $48. 89 (12/1/2000)

De Saint Gall NV Blanc de Blancs Premier Cru Brut Chardonnay (Champagne) $35. Sweet at first, with aromas of corn, hay, and minty alfalfa. Quite nice across the palate, with a fine mouthfeel. In the mouth, flavors of apple and lemon soda are full, smooth, and clean. Fades fast on the finish, yet you can't gripe about the overall quality. **88** —M.S. (12/15/2003)

De Saint Gall 1998 Blanc de Blancs Premier Cru Brut Chardonnay (Champagne) $49. Light and airy on the bouquet, with lovely rosemary and other green herb notes. Zippy acids deliver flavors of pear and candied apple right to the precipice of one's palate. And even if it finishes a bit tangy and shrill, it's got great feel and purity. **90** —M.S. (12/15/2003)

De Saint Gall 1995 Cuvée Orpale Blanc de Blancs Chardonnay (Champagne) $95. Round, yeasty, and rich, with apple and lemon flavors that are perfectly bolstered by almond and butterscotch. Once in the mouth you notice some weight and drive. It's a persistent wine, with plenty of body and a solid acidic core. **90** —M.S. (12/15/2003)

De Saint Gall NV Grand Cru Blanc de Blancs Extra Brut Chardonnay (Champagne) $65. Biscuit aromas are a good starter for this bone-dry Champagne, which works because of bottle aging. It is crisp, full of biscuit tastes with some green fruits. It also has a tannic structure; piercingly dry overall. **89** —R.V. (12/1/2005)

De Saint Gall 1995 Premier Cru Blanc de Blancs Brut Chardonnay (Champagne) $48. This little-known house is turning out some fine bubbly. This is an intense, brooding wine, filled with dark toast and meat, earth, and soy complexities. It's a big, mouth-filling wine, creamy and

FRANCE

rich, finishing long. Seems mature already, so drink up. **92** —*J.C. (12/15/2001)*

DE SOUSA & FILS

De Sousa & Fils NV Brut Rosé Champagne Blend (Champagne) $60. A pleasant, fresh wine, with flavors of strawberries and a crisp, poised, and elegant aftertaste. **86** —*R.V. (12/15/2006)*

De Sousa & Fils NV Cuvée des Caudalies Blanc de Blancs Vielles Vignes Brut Champagne Blend (Champagne) $60. Erick de Sousa blends wines from six different years for this cuvée, which comes from old vines in the village of Avize. It has aromas of crisp green fruit and yeast. There is a light toast character on the palate along with lively acidity, which persists through the finish. This bottle had a disgorgement date of 4/19/2002. **87** —*R.V. (12/1/2002)*

De Sousa & Fils 1996 Extra Brut Champagne Blend (Champagne) $130. Impressively young, this wine shows both the open, tropical side of De Sousa's Champagnes and the firm, closed nature of 1996 bottlings. There is some toasty character and lively acidity along with flavors of pineapple. Has great aging potential. **96** —*R.V. (11/1/2006)*

De Sousa & Fils 2000 Cuvée des Caudalies Grand Cru Brut Chardonnay (Champagne) $120. A blanc de blancs, vinified in wood (15% new). It is rich, creamy, and still young with citrus and tropical fruits vying for dominance at this early stage. Wait for this wine to develop over the next five years—it will be magnificent. **94** —*R.V. (11/1/2006)*

DE VENOGE

De Venoge 1995 Brut Champagne Blend (Champagne) $NA. A ripe, balanced wine which is showing some good, toasty bottle age. De Venoge Vintage has a Pinot-dominated blend which ages the wine, but also gives elegance. The wine has flavors of white fruits, crisp apples, and fresh croissants to give good complexity and richness. **89** —*R.V. (12/1/2004)*

DEHOURS

Dehours 2002 Collection Les Genevraux Pinot Meunier (Champagne) $42. Named after a parcel of vines, this superripe wine is made exclusively of Pinot Meunier—it's rare to taste a wine entirely from this grape. Besides being full-bodied, it is also very minerally in character, it has a steely quality which suggests the ability to age well. Applause to Dehours for indicating the disgorgement date on the back label. **92** —*R.V. (11/1/2006)*

Dehours 2000 Collection Blanc de Pinot Noir Pinot Noir (Champagne) $NA. Dehours makes a range of single cépage Champagnes from specific parcels of old vines. This parcel of Pinot Noir in Mareuil-le-Port was aged in wood before blending, giving a superbly ripe, quite toasty, spicy character. It does need time, and is obviously a wine for aging, but even now it has great, ripe peach, and lemongrass flavors. **94 Editors' Choice** —*R.V. (11/1/2006)*

DELAMOTTE

Delamotte 1992 Blanc de Blancs Brut Champagne Blend (Champagne) $63. **90** *(12/1/2000)*

Delamotte NV Brut Champagne Blend (Champagne) $46. **85** —*S.H. (12/1/1999)*

Delamotte NV Brut Champagne Blend (Champagne) $34. Here is a Pinot-dominated blend (50% Pinot Noir, 30% Chardonnay, and 20% Meunier) which offers elegant, textural, and expansive flavors. Multi-dimensional and poised, it pushes the Pinot to the fore, which brings extra fruit intensity and hints of fresh red berries. The finish is crisp and lingering. **92 Editors' Choice** —*P.G. (12/15/2002)*

Delamotte NV Brut Champagne Blend (Champagne) $44. Owned by Laurent-Perrier, this small house makes a great, toasty Chardonnay-dominated nonvintage blend. Rich, full bodied and elegant; an impressive wine. **93** —*R.V. (12/1/2005)*

Delamotte NV Brut Champagne Blend (Champagne) $42. **88** —*S.H. (12/15/2000)*

Delamotte 1999 Blanc de Blancs Brut Chardonnay (Champagne) $79. A delicious apéritif style of Champagne, with nutty aromas, crisp, creamy fruit, and a delicate aftertaste. It should age attractively, over the next five years. **88** —*R.V. (11/1/2006)*

DELAS FRERES

Delas Freres 1999 Haute Pierre Grenache-Syrah (Châteauneuf-du-Pape) $40. While the color is just turning rusty, this wine is more alive than fading. The dusty, pungent nose carries lots of red berry fruit, and also some pickled character. Flavors of plum, blackberry, and char lead into a buttery, full-oak finish that has texture yet may be overly charred for some. Good and solid, but also a bit short on purity and complexity. **85** —*M.S. (9/1/2003)*

Delas Freres 1998 Les Launes Marsanne (Crozes-Hermitage) $10. Yellow in color, with heavy popcorn oak and aromas of burnt almonds. The flavors are of melon rind and buttered toast, and while the finish isn't exactly cloying, it's definitely thick and grabbing. Seemingly 1998 is just too old for a white wine with a pedestrian pedigree. **83** —*M.S. (9/1/2003)*

Delas Freres 2001 Les Launes Blanc Marsanne (Crozes-Hermitage) $19. This bone dry, delicate wine has scents and flavors of limes and grapefruit, roasted hazelnuts, and a touch of white peach, compounded by pretty notes of smoky oak. It is young and lean in the mouth, marked by citrus flavors and high acidity. **88** —*S.H. (1/1/2002)*

Delas Freres 2001 Selection Delas Merlot (Vin de Pays d'Oc) $8. Ripe and filled out, with some herbal, earthy aromas that contribute character. Raspberry fruit on a fresh frame, and a light chocolate-laced finish is what you get from this solid, lean performer. Would be good with steak frites and a green salad. **85** —*M.S. (9/1/2003)*

Delas Freres 2002 Red Blend (Côtes-du-Ventoux) $9. Smells o.k., with soft Bing cherry aromas and hints of peppery spice. But the flavors don't quite measure up, turning excessively tart and lemony on the finish. **81** —*J.C. (3/1/2004)*

Delas Freres 2003 Rhône Red Blend (Côtes-du-Ventoux) $10. After a tough 2002 vintage, Delas has bounced back nicely with this wine, which shows uncommon depth and intensity for a humble Côtes du Ventoux. Bold scents of black cherries, blackberries, and earth rise from the glass and there's plenty of richness on the palate, even some slightly rustic tannins to help rein in all that fruit. Notes of licorice, tar and earth on the finish make it more than a simple fruit bomb. **88 Best Buy** —*J.C. (11/15/2004)*

Delas Freres 2000 Domaine des Genets Rhône Red Blend (Vacqueyras) $19. Delas has made a Vacqueyras from the 61-acre Domaine des Genets since 1990, and the alluvial soil of the estate gives deep, plummy fruit with rich tannins and a fine layer of acidity. It is not a heavyweight, but is fine and elegant. **88** —*R.V. (3/1/2004)*

Delas Freres 1999 La Landonne Rhône Red Blend (Côte Rôtie) $105. Only 6,000 bottles and 300 magnums have been made of this wine, from a parcel in the famed La Landonne vineyard. This is a beautifully crafted wine, with vanilla and polished violet perfumes. To taste, the ripeness of the tannins and the richness of the fruit give both complexity and elegance. It should age for at least 15 years. **94** —*R.V. (6/1/2002)*

Delas Freres 1998 Les Calcerniers Rhône Red Blend (Châteauneuf-du-Pape) $29. A flavorful, tangy wine with spice, meat, and chalk notes offsetting the excellent vintage's ripe, chewy fruit. Has a lively palate texture and the slight herb-metallic overtones typical of many Rhône blends. Full without being weighty, this is well-structured with modest tannins to lose. Drinkable now with hearty fare, it will benefit from a another year of aging and be at its best from 2003 to 2007 and beyond. **91 Editors' Choice** *(3/1/2002)*

Delas Freres 2002 Saint-Esprit Rhône Red Blend (Côtes-du-Rhône) $13. Quite respectable for the 2002 vintage (a difficult one), Delas has turned out a crisp wine, filled with tart cherry fruit and a helping of characterful stable-y notes. **84** —*J.C. (2/1/2005)*

Delas Freres 1999 St. Espirit Rhône Red Blend (Côtes-du-Rhône) $10. This straight ahead Rhône red opens with a lively nose of faintly sweet red berries offset by earth, pepper, and anise accents. The dry palate follows suit, although perhaps with not the depth or intensity promised. Still, it's a good mid-weight red and a fine party or bar pour, closing with moderate tannins and length. **85 Best Buy** *(3/1/2002)*

Delas Freres 2004 Les Challeys Rhône White Blend (Saint-Joseph) $NA. Reflecting the house style, this Delas white is spare and minerally, a bit austere, but crisp and clean. There's a spicy note to this one that elevates it above Delas' Crozes or basic Côtes-du-Rhône. **87** —*J.C. (11/15/2006)*

Delas Freres 2005 Saint-Esprit Rhône White Blend (Côtes-du-Rhône) $13. Crisp and floral (the blend contains 18% Viognier) but also rather austere and minerally, with just hints of pineapple fruit. Best as an apéritif. Drink now. **85** —*J.C. (11/15/2006)*

Delas Freres 1999 Saint-Esprit Rhône White Blend (Côtes-du-Rhône) $9. It's one thing to hear about wine being statements of terroir, but one whiff of this chalky-minerally-earthy white Rhône wine, and you'll be transported back to the motherland. Minerally from start to finish, it also shows light citrus-apple aromas on the nose, and lime rind and bath soap flavors on the palate. Dry, with a decent fruit-to acid balance, the finish is a continuation of what you get in the mouth, punctuated with a lemony tang and some green herb. **85** *(11/15/2001)*

Delas Freres 1996 Francois de Tournon Syrah (Saint-Joseph) $21. 87 — *M.S. (5/1/2000)*

Delas Freres 2001 François de Tournon Syrah (Saint-Joseph) $27. An easy-drinking syrah from the northern Rhône, this medium-weight wine boasts aromas of horse sweat, black pepper, and roasted cherries, backed by flavors of black cherries and dried spices. It's plump and juicy. with a mouth-watering finish. Drink now–2010. **87** *(2/1/2005)*

Delas Freres 2003 Les Bessards Syrah (Hermitage) $146. Incredibly rich, velvety-textured, and long, this is a great example of Hermitage from a super-ripe vintage. It's dense like fruitcake without being excessively heavy, and boasts such a panoply of nuance as to be spellbinding, ranging from spice and herb to black olive and espresso. Wow! Drink now–2025. **95 Cellar Selection** —*J.C. (11/15/2006)*

Delas Freres 2000 Les Challeys Syrah (Saint-Joseph) $20. A ripe, perfumed, relatively soft wine, which is going to give great pleasure with its juicy fruit, ripe jelly flavors, and balancing acidity. You could enjoy this wine within a year, but it should age well over the next five or six. **89** — *R.V. (6/1/2002)*

Delas Freres 2002 Les Launes Syrah (Crozes-Hermitage) $19. Modest cherry and herbal-stemmy aromas give way to lean cherry flavors on the palate. It seems a little dilute and under-ripe, which could be a result of the vintage. Decent, but leaves one wishing for more power. **84** —*J.C. (2/1/2005)*

Delas Freres 1998 Les Launes Syrah (Crozes-Hermitage) $15. This Crozes is lean and herbal, but is nonetheless compelling. Sweet berry fruit, resin, and olive aromas lead into a palate highlighted by minerals, white pepper, and dried spices. Mouthfeel is dry but structured; finishes with white pepper and minerals. **88 Editors' Choice** *(10/1/2001)*

Delas Freres 2001 Marquise de la Tourette Syrah (Hermitage) $71. This is a blend from three of the top Hermitage vineyards—L'Ermite, le Sabot, and Les Bessards. It is powerful and rich, with black fruits, spices, and leather aromas. To taste, there are barnyard flavors, acidity, and dense tannins. It will certainly age, probably over 10 years. **90** —*R.V. (2/1/2005)*

Delas Freres 1997 Marquise de la Tourette Syrah (Hermitage) $58. Earth, barbecued meat, and fresh green clover aromas and flavors characterize this medium-weight, brisk Hermitage. Finish is angular and tannic, with black pepper, smoked meat, and cocoa flavors. **87** *(11/1/2001)*

Delas Freres 2004 Sainte-Épine Syrah (Saint-Joseph) $64. Bursts with bold pepper and raspberry aromas and flavors, but they're elegant as much as they're potent. Powerful fruit, supple tannins, and a long, structured finish make this one of the top Saint-Josephs. Drink now–2015. **92 Editors' Choice** —*J.C. (11/15/2006)*

Delas Freres 1998 Seigneur de Maugiron Syrah (Côte Rôtie) $25. The policy of Delas selling this particular cuvée at an older age than its competitors', Côte Rôtie certainly gives this wine a headstart in tasting. With its perfumed berry flavors and ripe but structured fruit, it is already showing signs of being ready to drink. Violets, toast, and flavors of dark coffee add to its complexity. **91** —*R.V. (6/1/2002)*

Delas Freres 2002 La Galopine Viognier (Condrieu) $51. 87 *(12/1/2004)*

Delas Freres 2001 La Galopine Blanc White Blend (Condrieu) $47. A dry, citrusy wine, and very youthful. Fresh young acids scour the palate, carrying flavors of lime and tobacco, although there are richer stone fruit notes buried deep. Not a big wine, but elegant. The acids will preserve it if you choose to cellar for five years. **89** —*S.H. (1/1/2002)*

Delas Freres 2000 Saint-Espirit Blanc White Blend (Côtes-du-Rhône) $9. As the name suggests, there's plenty of spirit in this dry, crisp wine. It has impressively deep flavors of minerals and flint and a long, penetrating note of raspberry liqueur. This is a delightful, complex wine and a very nice value. **87** —*S.H. (1/1/2002)*

DELBECK

Delbeck 1999 Brut Champagne Blend (Champagne) $60. An elegant, medium-weight Champagne with a persistent bead, this is young but already beautiful to drink. Citrus and chalk notes dominate, buttressed by apple, mineral, and toast. Finishes long. **92** —*J.C. (12/1/2004)*

Delbeck NV Cramant Brut Champagne Blend (Champagne) $48. 84 *(12/31/2000)*

Delbeck NV Rosé Heritage Brut Champagne Blend (Champagne) $42. 92 — *M.M. (12/15/2000)*

DEUTZ

Deutz 1995 Blanc de Blancs Champagne Blend (France) $72. A thrilling wine that picks up bottle bouquet of baked bread, smoke, and roasted meringue, in addition to underlying citrus. Incredibly rich and fine, yet powerful, with complex flavors and a light, refined elegance on the palate. A touch of sweetness rounds and softens. **94 Editors' Choice** — *S.H. (12/15/2002)*

Deutz 1999 Brut Champagne Blend (Champagne) $72. A blend of 60% Pinot Noir, 30% Chardonnay, and 10% Pinot Meunier, this is a light, fresh wine, well-developed already, with ripe fruit from a classic Champagne year. The acidity is already moving toward toastiness. **90** — *R.V. (11/1/2006)*

Deutz 1995 Brut Champagne Blend (Champagne) $52. Deutz is one of the great names of Champagne, and this vintage Brut from an excellent, ripe year, delivers rich, round, toasty flavors, buoyed by cascading fountains of fine, tiny bubbles. There is a precisely tuned balance to the wine, which shows off its full fruit without sacrificing its typical elegance and crisp authority. A pleasing toastiness, and a faint hint of honey completes the experience. **92** —*P.G. (6/1/2001)*

Deutz NV Brut Classic Champagne Blend (Champagne) $37. Year in and year out, Deutz manages to put out a fine, eminently drinkable nonvintage brut. This one projects vanilla, pear, and coconut via the bouquet, and apple, pear, and cinnamon through the palate. With lively citrus afternotes, it finishes tight and sure. The acidity is appley and moves everything along. **89** —*M.S. (12/15/2003)*

Deutz NV Brut Classic Champagne Blend (Champagne) $51. This is baseline Deutz, but still a standout. Sniff it and you sense the complexity, definition, and elegance. Good, tiny bubbles stream up steadily, bringing notes of chalk, candied fruit, and caramel. In the mouth, it fills out across the palate with mixed flavors that show stone fruits, caramel, and oily, slightly buttery nuts. Very approachable yet complex, refined, and aristocratic. **90** —*P.G. (12/1/2006)*

Deutz NV Brut Classic Champagne Blend (Champagne) $37. Limpid and refined, defining the elegance and finesse you expect from good Champagne. It's a bit on the sweet side, with a hefty dosage softening the high acidity and rounding off the peach and citrus flavors. Feels almost weightless, all the way through the young, yeasty finish. **92** — *S.H. (12/15/2002)*

Deutz 2000 Brut Rosé Champagne Blend (Champagne) $77. A wine that is still young and still developing. It shows great raspberry fruit flavors, as well as black cherries. Has a delicate mineral character; this is going to be a fine, mature wine. For now, it is just delicious. **90** —*R.V. (11/1/2006)*

Deutz 1998 Cuvée William Deutz Brut Champagne Blend (Champagne) $184. This Deutz prestige cuvée has a blend of red and white grapes (as contrasted with the blanc de blancs Amour de Deutz). It is beautifully balanced, the super-ripe Chardonnay giving richness to the structured red grapes. Great with spicy foods, this is a wine that has developed relatively quickly and is ready to drink now. **93** —*R.V. (11/1/2006)*

Deutz 1996 Cuvée William Deutz Brut Champagne Blend (Champagne) $158. This is one of the most satisfying of the prestige cuvées, following the vintages closely. But this 1996 is exceptional, reflecting the exceptional character of the vintage. It is elegant, finely crafted, with acidity and structure, very pure in its flavors of gooseberries and white currants. This will develop well over the 5-10 years. The wine is named after the 19th century founder of Deutz. **93** —R.V. (12/1/2004)

Deutz 1995 Cuvée William Deutz Brut Champagne Blend (Champagne) $115. A dry, bready bouquet with subtle herb notes opens this impressive bottling. The palate expands with full apple, herb, and lemon flavors, and shows a fine bead and an even, fairly structured mouthfeel. Finishes complex and toasty, with great length and style. **93** —M.M. (12/15/2001)

Deutz 1997 Cuvée William Deutz Brut Rosé Champagne Blend (Champagne) $115. Deutz seems to be on a roll. This Cuvée William Deutz has a seductive pale onion-skin color and aromas of crushed strawberries. It is richly mature but crisp and full-bodied, with layered toasty flavors, fine balance, and a deliciously soft aftertaste. **92** —R.V. (12/15/2003)

Deutz 1999 Amour de Deutz Blanc de Blancs Brut Chardonnay (Champagne) $206. Certainly an apéritif style, this is still a rich Chardonnay, toasty, developed, with white flower aromas and honey and citrus flavors, that hint at tropical fruits. This is a beautifully balanced wine, flowing through its development towards maturity, but still with good aging potential. **94** —R.V. (11/1/2006)

Deutz 1995 Amour de Deutz Blanc de Blancs Brut Chardonnay (Champagne) $149. Unlike some of the other '95s, this one seems more open and developed, with sexy aromas of vanilla and toasted coconut giving way to tropical fruit flavors. A smooth, creamy mouthfeel adds to the impression of voluptuousness, while the citrusy finish lingers delicately on the palate. **91** —J.C. (12/15/2003)

Deutz 1996 Blanc de Blancs Brut Chardonnay (Champagne) $78. Blasts off with warm, enveloping aromas of toasted brioche, evolving into baked apple and spice flavors. Lush, creamy, and rich on the palate, with a long, mouthwatering finish. Perfectly balanced for near-term consumption. **93** —J.C. (12/15/2003)

Deutz 1997 Brut Rosé Pinot Noir (Champagne) $60. Unusually, this wine is made entirely with Pinot Noir (most rosé Champagne has some Chardonnay). The result is a wine with some weight, combined with a light touch of crisp acidity. Poised, balanced fruit, and toast flavors make it a fine food wine. **90** —R.V. (12/15/2003)

DEVAUX

Devaux NV Grande Réserve Brut Champagne Blend (Champagne) $35. Devaux makes a yeasty, bubbly, straight ahead style of Champagne. It's tart and tastes mostly of green apples, with just a faint hint of toast in the finish. There's nothing particularly distinctive here, but it is well-made, refreshing, and crisp through a clean finish. **87** (6/1/2001)

DIDIER DAGUENEAU

Didier Dagueneau 2003 Pur Sang Sauvignon Blanc (Pouilly-Fumé) $60. A little pretentious with the appellation (it could be Pouilly-Fumé), but nothing but great wine in the bottle. Aromas of grapefruit, apple, mustard, and wet stones are framed by gentle notes of cinnamon and toast. The palate is louder as it sizzles with razor-crisp orange, apple, peach, and grapefruit, all with a proper mineral, herbal edge. Rock solid, but cheerful and universally likable. **92** (7/1/2005)

DIDIER MONTCHOVET

Didier Montchovet 2002 Hautes Côtes de Beaune Pinot Noir (Bourgogne) $29. Reductive and faintly smelling of merde at first, this seems to lessen with aeration to reveal modest cherry fruit carried along on a rather pinched and lean palate. Dusty tannins on the finish suggest another year or two of cellaring might help, although it will never be charming. **82** —J.C. (9/1/2006)

DIEBOLT VALLOIS

Diebolt Vallois 1999 Fleur de Passion à Cramant Blanc de Blancs Champagne Blend (Champagne) $75. A rare wine, which has no malolactic fermentation leaving acidity. It has very floral aromas, with intense ripe white fruits and power. This is very structured, with layers of wood flavors, it is more wine than Champagne. This is a great wine. **93** —R.V. (12/1/2004)

DOMAINE A. CAILBOURDIN

Domaine A. Cailbourdin 2000 Le Cris Sauvignon Blanc (Pouilly-Fumé) $20. This wine is so typical of the area. It's defined by a stony, dry nose, citrus, and tropical fruit flavors, a lean, tight finish, and mouth-cleaning acids. It's hardly the deepest, most complex wine you'll find, but not all good wines have to be complicated. **87** (8/1/2002)

DOMAINE A. MAZURD & FILS

Domaine A. Mazurd & Fils 1995 L'Or du Rhône Cuvée Exceptionnelle Grenache (Côtes-du-Rhône) $23. Like the other Mazurd wines, this is mature—maybe even a little past mature—but still very enjoyable. This cuvée is slightly floral, with delicate leather, dried fig, and spice aromas, and a silky-smooth mouthfeel. Folds in a touch of peppery spice on the finish. Drink now. **88** —J.C. (11/15/2006)

Domaine A. Mazurd & Fils 1995 Cuvée Mazurka Rhône Red Blend (Côtes-du-Rhône) $20. A luxury cuvée aged in oak, this is a rather mature wine, browning at the edges, yet still offering plenty of interest. Dates, tobacco, and slightly horsey elements give it a fair degree of complexity, while time has softened any rough edges, leaving it smooth and velvety on the finish. **87** —J.C. (11/15/2006)

DOMAINE ALAIN DELAYE

Domaine Alain Delaye 2000 Chardonnay (Pouilly-Loche) $15. A rich, softly fruity Chardonnay, with pear and acacia blossom on the nose and flavors of honey, ripe apples, and clove. Additional spice notes enliven the finish. **87** (10/1/2003)

DOMAINE ALBERT MANN

Domaine Albert Mann 2002 Grand Cru Schlossberg Riesling (Alsace) $28. A big, rich wine, full of aromas of apples and ripe fruits, this comes from the Schlossberg vineyard beneath the ruins of the Kaysersberg castle. It is powerful, concentrated, favoring currants and generous fruit flavors. It certainly has good aging potential—five years or more. **89** —R.V. (11/1/2005)

DOMAINE AMIOT-SERVELLE

Domaine Amiot-Servelle 2000 Pinot Noir (Chambolle-Musigny) $46. The real attraction of this wine is its delicious, perfumed fruit, which sings above the firm tannins. It is immediately enticing, with pure flavors and soft aftertaste. **87** —R.V. (11/1/2002)

Domaine Amiot-Servelle 2000 Les Amoureuses Premier Cru Pinot Noir (Chambolle-Musigny) $100. A rich, generous wine that seduces with pure berry flavors and velvety texture. Ripe plums flavors give it roundness, while the tannins are almost muted at the end. **91** —R.V. (11/1/2002)

DOMAINE ANDRE BRUNEL

Domaine Andre Brunel 1999 Cuvée Sommelongue Rhône Red Blend (Côtes-du-Rhône) $10. A delightful blend of cracked black pepper, blackberries, and hung game aromas lead into a surprisingly plush mouthfeel that's laden with cherry and berry fruit. The finish blends in some dark coffee flavors for extra complexity. **88 Best Buy** —J.C. (3/1/2001)

DOMAINE ANTONIN GUYON

Domaine Antonin Guyon 2002 Clos du Village Pinot Noir (Chambolle-Musigny) $48. A beautiful, silky wine that has smooth fruit and acidity. There are tannins and good aging potential, but at the moment it is vibrating with raspberry fruits. **90** —R.V. (9/1/2004)

Domaine Antonin Guyon 2002 Corton Bressandes Pinot Noir (Corton) $60. Gorgeous aromas of strawberry fruits lead to a palate of firm tannic fruit, balanced by luscious acidity and strawberry jelly flavors. It is rich, ethereal, and opulent all at the same time. **93** —R.V. (9/1/2004)

DOMAINE AUCHÈRE

Domaine Auchère 2004 Cuvée Calcaire Sauvignon Blanc (Sancerre) $21. Gritty and sweaty to start, although it finds a better groove with time. Shows basic citrus and herb on the palate, followed by lemon. Seems a bit salty on the finish. **84** (7/1/2005)

DOMAINE AUTHER

Domaine Auther 2003 Kirchweg Riesling (Alsace) $NA. With its tiny holdings scattered over many different vineyards, Domaine Auther is able to produce a bewildering array of wines. This from the Kirchweg vineyard is ripe, full of the ripe, condensed flavors that come from a maceration of the whole fruits before fermentation, and just plain delicious. It will benefit from two more years' aging. **89** —*R.V. (5/1/2005)*

DOMAINE BARRAUD

Domaine Barraud 2003 En Buland Chardonnay (Pouilly-Fuissé) $NA. From 70-year-old vines at the base of Solutré, this is an exceptionally elegant, precise, and minerally rendering of Pouilly-Fuissé, especially so when seen in the context of the vintage. There's ample richness and length, with pear and spice notes, but the lingering impression is one of great minerality and finesse. **88** —*J.C. (11/15/2005)*

DOMAINE BASTIDE SAINT VINCENT

Domaine Bastide Saint Vincent 2004 Cuvée Pavane Rhône Red Blend (Vacqueyras) $18. Basic Vacqueyras, with modest raspberry fruit accented by leather and spice. Lacks a bit of depth and intensity. Drink now. **83** —*J.C. (11/15/2006)*

DOMAINE BEAUMONT

Domaine Beaumont 2005 Saint Pierre Aux Liens Rhône White Blend (Lirac) $NA. A relatively light-bodied Lirac blanc that comes across as crisp and clean. Simple and citrusy, it lacks the ripeness and expansive mouthfeel of the best examples. Would be fine as an apéritif. **85** —*J.C. (11/15/2006)*

DOMAINE BEGUDE

Domaine Begude 2000 Chardonnay (Vin de Pays d'Oc) $10. An impressive Chard and an impressive value, the Begude is light, with an elegant, mineral-citrus-soy palate. Out of the bottle, it shows clean, bright lemon-citrus flavors on the nose; after a few minutes in the glass, the bouquet takes on peach, earth, and soy notes. In the mouth and on the finish, it manages to be at once smooth and minerally textured. Buy a case now. **88 Best Buy** —*D.T. (2/1/2002)*

DOMAINE BELLE

Domaine Belle 2004 Rhône White Blend (Crozes-Hermitage) $29. This stellar 2004 may be even richer than a tank sample of the 2005, with lovely pear and pepper aromas and honeyed flavors married to great minerality and freshness. A blend of 70% Marsanne and 30% Roussanne, with 60% of the total fermented in oak, the rest in stainless steel. Drink now–2012. **91 Editors' Choice** —*J.C. (11/15/2006)*

Domaine Belle 2004 Les Pierrelles Syrah (Crozes-Hermitage) $27. Very ripe-smelling, but without going over the edge into over-ripeness. There's plenty of cassis and blackberry flavor, not a lot of spice or complexity, but lovely, mouth-filling fruit. Supple and easy to drink now and over the next few years. **87** —*J.C. (11/15/2006)*

DOMAINE BERNARD MOREAU ET FILS

Domaine Bernard Moreau et Fils 2004 Chardonnay (Chassagne-Montrachet) $50. Steely and minerally, but also has fresh white and yellow fruit flavors. Bright acidity finishes this highly drinkable wine. **89** —*R.V. (12/1/2006)*

Domaine Bernard Moreau et Fils 2004 Grandes Ruchottes Premier Cru Chardonnay (Chassagne-Montrachet) $85. Made from 60-year-old vines, evidenced by its concentration and serious ageability. It is structured, firm, and relatively dry at this young stage. It's a wine that needs at least 5 years. Today, if you do open a bottle, watch for the mineral, stony character that pushes the fruit and demands attention. **93 Editors' Choice** —*R.V. (12/1/2006)*

Domaine Bernard Moreau et Fils 2004 Les Chenevottes Premier Cru Chardonnay (Chassagne-Montrachet) $70. In the fat, buttery style of white Burgundy, this wine, with its malolactic flavors and its vanilla flavors, would appeal immediately to California Chardonnay lovers. Except that it also has elegance: a hint of steel and a touch of acidity to temper the tropical fruits. **92** —*R.V. (12/1/2006)*

DOMAINE BERTAGNA

Domaine Bertagna 1998 Clos St. Denis Bordeaux Blend (France) $85. **91** —*P.G. (11/1/2002)*

Domaine Bertagna 1998 Premier Cru Chardonnay (Nuits-St.-Georges) $27. **89** —*P.G. (11/1/2002)*

Domaine Bertagna 1998 Pinot Noir (Clos Vougeot) $100. **90** —*P.G. (11/1/2002)*

Domaine Bertagna 1998 Pinot Noir (Marsannay) $17. **87** —*P.G. (11/1/2002)*

Domaine Bertagna 1998 Clos de la Perrière Premier Cru Pinot Noir (Vougeot) $60. **90** *(1/1/2004)*

Domaine Bertagna 1998 Clos St Denis Pinot Noir (Clos Vougeot) $96. Rich and fragrant, it immediately shows the depth and texture befitting a grand cru bottling. Exotic spices add interest, and the wine slowly unfolds with layers of berry, cinnamon, and red meat. **91** —*P.G. (11/1/2002)*

Domaine Bertagna 1998 Les Cras Premier Cru Pinot Noir (Vougeot) $55. Some mustiness cloaked the nose, which held hints of pretty black cherry fruit once the wine aired out a bit. The aromas expanded to include whiffs of meat, game, and seaweed; still, the wine is tannic and a bit stingy on the palate. **87** —*P.G. (11/1/2002)*

Domaine Bertagna 2000 Les Plantes Premier Cru Pinot Noir (Chambolle-Musigny) $75. There is a fine balance on the nose between modern new wood aromas and pure raspberry fruits. On the palate, the wood is sweet and is nicely balanced with a helping of chunky fruits and some elegant ripe flavors. Lovely acidity comes through toward the finish. This is a fine wine, both concentrated and yet elegant. **94 Editors' Choice** —*R.V. (11/1/2002)*

DOMAINE BERTHET-RAYNE

Domaine Berthet-Rayne 2003 Rhône Red Blend (Châteauneuf-du-Pape) $32. A ripe, earthy, animal wine, which shows good, juicy fruit, but moves more to herbal flavors. There are herbes de Provence aromas, dry tannins, and powerful, dry, black flavors. This is a well-made, traditional wine. **87** —*R.V. (12/31/2005)*

DOMAINE BERTRAND STEHELIN

Domaine Bertrand Stehelin 2004 Rhône Red Blend (Gigondas) $24. A new discovery, this is a darkly colored Gigondas with lovely ripe Grenache flavors. Blackberry and pepper notes also carry a hint of stone fruit. The tannins are supple, the finish long. Drink now–2012. **88** —*J.C. (11/15/2006)*

DOMAINE BORIE DE MAUREL

Domaine Borie de Maurel 1999 Syrah (Minervois) $9. This Minervois offering is on the thin side, but it offers comforting blackberry cobbler, chocolate, and barbecue sauce aromas. The palate shows tangy oak, sour red berry and metallic notes; coffee and cedar round out the dry finish. **84** *(10/1/2001)*

DOMAINE BOTT-GEYL

Domaine Bott-Geyl 2002 Burgreben de Zellenberg Riesling (Alsace) $20. The clay soil of the Burgreben produces a heavy style of Riesling, with some earthy flavors. But this wine also has fresh fruit, flavors of red apples and pears, along with a mineral streak that gives it a great lift on the finish. Leave it 3–4 years before drinking. **88** —*R.V. (11/1/2005)*

DOMAINE BRESSY-MASSON

Domaine Bressy-Masson 2003 A La Gloire de Mon Père Rasteau Rhône Red Blend (Côtes-du-Rhône Villages) $NA. Bressy-Masson's top cuvée reflects the heat of the vintage, but it's kept lively by adequate acidity and a sense of dusty minerality. Spice, plum and dried cherry notes finish long, framed by supple tannins. Drink now through 2013. **89** —*J.C. (11/15/2006)*

DOMAINE BRUNO COLIN

Domaine Bruno Colin 2004 Chardonnay (Chassagne-Montrachet) $NA. Although this wine is initially unfocused, the palate does show some pleasing rounded fruits and a touch of citrus and wood. Drink now. **87** —*R.V. (12/1/2006)*

Domaine Bruno Colin 2004 Les Chaumées Premier Cru Chardonnay (Chassagne-Montrachet) $NA. A ripe, open, generous wine, the opulent side of white Burgundy. This wine revels in its fruit, full flavors, and touch of wood. This wine opens well and is ready to drink now, but should age over 4–5 years. **93** —*R.V. (12/1/2006)*

FRANCE

DOMAINE BRUSSET

Domaine Brusset 2005 Laurent B Rhône Red Blend (Côtes-du-Rhône) $16. Dense and intense, this wine has a packed bouquet that's hard to read at first because of its sheer intensity. In the mouth, it's loaded with cherry and plum fruit, with a snappy, fresh character. Mouth-filling, it also offers considerable length on the finish. **88** —*J.C. (11/15/2006)*

Domaine Brusset 2004 Tradition Le Grand Montmirail Rhône Red Blend (Gigondas) $27. Brusset pushes the envelope, and my notes on this bottling make reference to its volatility, albeit in varying amounts. On one occasion I found it elevated, masking much of the wine's charms, while on another it lent an intriguing element to the super-ripe blackberry and chocolate flavors. **87** —*J.C. (11/15/2006)*

Domaine Brusset 2005 Les Clavelles Viognier (Côtes-du-Rhône) $20. This 100% Viognier is fermented part in barrel and part in vat, yielding a spicy, fresh, and floral bouquet that reflects its varietal character. Medium-bodied, it has a healthy sense of minerality to go with its spice and stone fruit flavors. **87** —*J.C. (11/15/2006)*

DOMAINE CALVET-THUNEVIN

Domaine Calvet-Thunevin 2004 Présidial Bordeaux Blend (Bordeaux) $12. When Jean-Luc Thunevin, master garagiste and creator of Saint-Emilion Château Valandraud, gets his hands on making a branded Bordeaux wine, it's worth taking notice. And this Merlot-dominated wine, distributed jointly with Bordeaux négociant Calvet, is the sort of wine that simple Bordeaux should taste like. It is smooth, ripe, concentrated, packed with red berries and attractive, forward fruit flavors, and yet with just the right layer of tannin to make a fine food partner. There is nothing complicated—leave that to the grand châteaux. This is just a great drink. **86 Best Buy** —*R.V. (11/15/2006)*

DOMAINE CASTEL OUALOU

Domaine Castel Oualou 2005 Rosé Blend (Lirac) $NA. Tons of berries here, very clean and pure in nature, which might be this wine's only shortcoming—is it too clean and pristine? Offers fresh, mouth-watering berry fruit and a long finish. Ideal picnic juice. **89** —*J.C. (11/15/2006)*

DOMAINE CAZES

Domaine Cazes 2003 Le Canon du Maréchal Rosé Grenache (Vin de Pays d'Oc) $16. A fresh, fruity style of rosé, with intense raspberry flavors, a touch of caramel, and just a touch of acidity. It's fresh enough to last until the next sunshine hits in the spring. **86** —*R.V. (4/1/2005)*

Domaine Cazes 2003 Le Canon du Maréchal Muscat-Viognier (Vin de Pays d'Oc) $15. In a white wine as young as this, it's the Muscat that dominates the aromas. The Viognier is much more present to taste, with its apricot flavors that shine through the Muscat perfumes and bring a sense of depth and richness to the wine. **87** —*R.V. (4/1/2005)*

Domaine Cazes 2000 Ego Rhône Red Blend (Côtes du Roussillon Villages) $16. One of a pair of blends of Syrah, Grenache, and Mourvèdre (the other is called Alter), this is soft, with fine red fruits, and a touch of wood. It is layered with red plums, acidity, and ripe tannins. **87** —*R.V. (12/31/2006)*

Domaine Cazes 2003 Le Canon du Maréchal Syrah Merlot (Vin de Pays d'Oc) $13. The Cazes estate is the largest in Roussillon, in the driest area of France. This blend of Syrah and Merlot, dominated by spicy, peppery Syrah, is full of rich fruit, with just a hint of jammy Merlot to bring out the fruit. Great fruit flavors and a delicious juicy finish. **87** —*R.V. (4/1/2005)*

DOMAINE CHANTAL LESCURE

Domaine Chantal Lescure 2002 Clos de Vougeot Pinot Noir (Clos Vougeot) $100. A wine that reveals all the possibilities of great Clos de Vougeot. It is rich, spicy, packed with new wood but also with great fresh fruit. Underneath, there are huge, dense tannins. **94** —*R.V. (9/1/2004)*

DOMAINE CHANTE-PERDRIX

Domaine Chante-Perdrix 2003 Rhône Red Blend (Châteauneuf-du-Pape) $32. This great, solid, tannic wine is a huge statement of black fruits, pepper, and enormous ripe flavors. With its high alcohol (marked on the label as 15.5%), this is almost too much. It impresses, but is it drinkable? **88** —*R.V. (12/31/2005)*

DOMAINE CHARLES THOMAS

Domaine Charles Thomas 2002 Clos du Roi Pinot Noir (Corton) $66. Firm, solid fruit, layers of concentrated black fruits, and a touch of acidity. A firm, serious wine, which has good potential. **89** —*R.V. (9/1/2004)*

DOMAINE CHAUME-ARNAUD

Domaine Chaume-Arnaud 2004 Rhône Red Blend (Côtes-du-Rhône) $NA. This wine displays a nicely balanced bouquet that melds dried cherries and dried spices. On the palate, those same elements persist, joined by dusty minerality and a chalky note on the finish. **86** —*J.C. (11/15/2006)*

Domaine Chaume-Arnaud 2005 Vinsobres Rhône White Blend (Côtes-du-Rhône Villages) $22. Ample pear fruit and a helping of peppery spice on the finish gives this medium-bodied white a little interest, amplified by a plump mouthfeel. Drink now. **84** —*J.C. (11/15/2006)*

DOMAINE CHEVALIER PÈRE ET FILS

Domaine Chevalier Père et Fils 2003 Pinot Noir (Ladoix) $29. An intensely perfumed wine that shows freshness and light tannins along with vibrant red flavors and acidity. This is a fast-developing wine, and is ready to drink now. **86** —*R.V. (9/1/2005)*

Domaine Chevalier Père et Fils 2003 Ladoix Premier Cru Les Corvées Pinot Noir (Ladoix) $35. An attractive, juicy wine with fresh strawberry flavors. Ladoix is a lesser-known commune, and the wines offer good value. Expect this to mature relatively quickly, to give open, generous drinking pleasure. **88** —*R.V. (9/1/2005)*

Domaine Christian Moreau Père et Fils 2000 Les Clos Chardonnay (Chablis) $64. Starts off promising, with aromas of apple slices spiced with cinnamon. Yet the palate offers an austere collection of flavors: liquid metal, powdered mineral, and a trace of green apple. Hold for a few years to see if the flavors unfold. **88** —*J.C. (10/1/2003)*

DOMAINE CLUSEL-ROCH

Domaine Clusel-Roch 2002 Syrah (Côte Rôtie) $52. Great ripe fruit is just beginning to show through this huge, dense wine. It's big, and dark and, obviously, still very young. But it is going to develop into a fine, solid dark wine which will age over many years. Buy now, start to enjoy in 5 years. **90** —*R.V. (2/1/2005)*

DOMAINE COLLIN

Domaine Collin 2000 Sparkling Blend (Blanquette de Limoux) $12. Smells like sourdough—emphasis on sour—and citrus. Very light and lean, with strong flavors of lemon and a finish reminiscent of unripe apples. **81** —*J.C. (12/15/2003)*

DOMAINE COMTE DE LAUZE

Domaine Comte de Lauze 2003 Rhône Red Blend (Châteauneuf-du-Pape) $40. An earthy style of wine, dominated by perfumed Grenache. The wine is rich, solid, and quite structured, with fine acidity penetrating through the dense tannins and rough Grenache flavors. **87** —*R.V. (12/31/2005)*

DOMAINE COMTE GEORGES DE VOGÜE

Domaine Comte Georges de Vogüé 2000 Pinot Noir (Chambolle-Musigny) $100. Made from the estate's young vines and from a tiny parcel in the premier cru Les Baudes, this is still a wine with great presence. The aromas of new wood and sweet fruit show through as flavors of vanilla and rich, dark plums and raspberry jelly. The finishing acidity leaves a clean, fresh taste. **90** —*R.V. (11/1/2002)*

Domaine Comte Georges de Vogüé 2000 Premier Cru Pinot Noir (Chevalier-Montrachet) $NA. This wine is made from vines in the Le Musigny Grand Cru vineyard that are less than 40 years old, and are therefore not included in the estate's Grand Cru wine. But it is more than just an adolescent Le Musigny, with aromas of red berries and vanilla and a rich, silky texture, giving way to ripe, sweet tannins on the finish. **91** —*R.V. (11/1/2002)*

DOMAINE CONFURON-COTETIDOT

Domaine Confuron-Cotetidot 2002 Pinot Noir (Chambolle-Musigny) $NA. An intensely perfumed wine, with a smoky character. It is big and rich, but there is also sweet, juicy fruit, a hint of new wood and piercing, acidity to finish. 88 —R.V. (9/1/2004)

Domaine Confuron-Cotetidot 1999 Pinot Noir (Chambolle-Musigny) $35. Confuron-Cotetidot was one of the pioneers of cold maceration before fermentation, giving extra color and extract to the wine. Intensely powerful coffee flavors and dry tannins support black fruits and just a touch of orange zest. Wood and fruit tannins are dry but generous, suggesting that this wine has good aging ability. 88 —R.V. (11/1/2002)

Domaine Confuron-Cotetidot 2002 Les Suchots Premier Cru Pinot Noir (Vosne-Romanée) $NA. Raspberry fruit aromas and smoky wood give this wine an immediately appealing character. It is intense, too, and finishes with loads of toasty wood. 89 —R.V. (9/1/2004)

DOMAINE COURBIS

Domaine Courbis 2004 Marsanne (Saint-Joseph) $23. A blend of barrel-fermented and tank-fermented wines, this is a fresh, crisp rendition of Saint-Joseph, combining pear fruit with stony minerality. Yet it also has a pleasant mealy texture and obvious substance. A blend of 95% Marsanne and 5% Roussanne. Drink now–2010. 88 —J.C. (11/15/2006)

Domaine Courbis 2004 Champelrose Syrah (Cornas) $45. From old vines dating back to before World War II (in a warm portion of the appellation), this is a wonderfully fruity and supple Cornas. Loads of fresh raspberries burst from the glass, but give it some time and spice and mineral complexities begin to emerge. Drink now–2015. 89 —J.C. (11/15/2006)

Domaine Courbis 2004 Les Royes Syrah (Saint-Joseph) $35. This is Courbis's luxury cuvée, but this reviewer preferred the regular bottling for its floral freshness. This seems to be verging on over-ripe, with prune notes. It's rich and creamy on the palate, but lacks zip. Drink now. 84 —J.C. (11/15/2006)

DOMAINE COURSODON

Domaine Coursodon 2004 Syrah (Saint-Joseph) $28. Dominated by horse blanket aromas. Modest cherry fruit turns metallic and thin on the finish. 83 —J.C. (11/15/2006)

Domaine Coursodon 2004 Le Paradis Saint-Pierre Syrah (Saint-Joseph) $35. A bit horsey and Brett-ridden, but it still shows a round mouthfeel and supple texture. Drink now. 86 —J.C. (11/15/2006)

DOMAINE D'ANDEZON

Domaine d'Andezon 2004 Vieilles Vignes Rhône Red Blend (Côtes-du-Rhône) $10. From the co-op in Estézargues, this cuvée boasts an elegant bouquet of smoke and blueberries. Less lush and intense than some other recent vintages (most notably the 2005), it still boasts crisp, well-defined flavors and good length. 87 Best Buy —J.C. (11/15/2006)

DOMAINE D'AUPILHAC

Domaine d'Aupilhac 1996 Montpeyroux Red Blend (Coteaux du Languedoc) $15. 92 —L.W. (10/1/1999)

DOMAINE DANIEL ET DENIS ALARY

Domaine Daniel et Denis Alary 2005 La Gerbaude Rhône Red Blend (Côtes-du-Rhône) $NA. Everything about this wine screams quality, from its impressively dark color to its precise aromas of dark fruit and spice. Plum, blueberry, and blackberry flavors glide across the palate, buoyed by a creamy, rich texture. Sure, it could be more complex, but this is an immensely likeable wine; a real find. 88 —J.C. (11/15/2006)

DOMAINE DE BEAURENARD

Domaine de Beaurenard 2004 Rhône Red Blend (Côtes-du-Rhône) $14. Lightweight, but the aromas are clean and reasonably complex, and the flavors follow suit. Bright raspberry and cherry fruit is accented by peppery spice and a hint of leather. Drink now. 85 —J.C. (11/15/2006)

Domaine de Beaurenard 2000 Rhône Red Blend (Châteauneuf-du-Pape) $27. Starts off with an unfortunate aroma of uncleanness, suggesting yesterday's gym sox. The flavor is better, with red and black stone fruits and berries, and the wine is very dry, with good, rich tannins. 82 —S.H. (1/1/2002)

Domaine de Beaurenard 2003 Rasteau Rhône Red Blend (Côtes-du-Rhône Villages) $23. From a producer better known for Châteauneuf-du-Pape,

this has a beautiful bouquet of crushed spices, violets, and black cherries followed by lush, deep flavors of plums, black cherries, and peppery spice. It's round and mouthfilling without being overwhelming, and it's framed by soft tannins. Complexity is raised a notch on the finish via the folding in of espresso and black olive notes. Drink now–2010. 91 —J.C. (11/15/2006)

DOMAINE DE CASSAN

Domaine de Cassan 2004 Rhône Red Blend (Gigondas) $27. A new discovery for me, this estate is turning out some very good wines from its vineyards in Gigondas and Beaumes-de-Venise. Perhaps its biggest 2004 is this richly warm Gigondas, which is filled with dried fruit and spices. It finishes with supple tannins and layers of spicy intensity. 90 —J.C. (11/15/2006)

Domaine de Cassan 2004 Cuvée Tradition Rhône Red Blend (Beaumes-de-Venise) $15. You know a producer is on a hot streak when this very good wine is the "weak link" in its lineup. Ripe black cherries and plums are dusted with a fine coating of anise and dried spices. Creamy and quite ripe, with a trace of warmth on the finish. Drink now. Jack Siler Selections. 88 —J.C. (11/15/2006)

DOMAINE DE CHAMPAGA

Domaine de Champaga 2000 Cuvée Reserve Rhône Red Blend (Côtes-du-Ventoux) $8. Rubber, beets, and root beer aromas lead into a sharp, cherry filled palate. The wine has a nice enough flavor profile but it's tight and hard—hard as a rock. The flavors are solid, but it's too hard to fully enjoy. 84 —M.S. (2/1/2003)

DOMAINE DE CHAMPAL

Domaine de Champal 2004 Chaubayou Syrah (Crozes-Hermitage) $28. Proprietor Eric Rocher has fashioned a pleasantly fruit-forward red Crozes that features black cherry fruit and a bit of peppery spice. It seems rather easy and supple at first, but then picks up sturdier, earthier notes of tapenade. 86 —J.C. (11/15/2006)

DOMAINE DE CHEVALIER

Domaine de Chevalier 2004 Barrel Sample Bordeaux Blend (Pessac-Léognan) $NA. Freshness and lightness are the hallmarks of this ripe but very poised wine. Blackberry fruit flavors shine through the underlying tannins. 93 —R.V. (6/1/2005)

Domaine de Chevalier 2000 Pessac-Léognan Bordeaux Blend (Bordeaux) $60. Huge, deep purple-black color, and aromas of rich, spicy fruit give a sense of great power to this superbly intense wine. Licorice and rich tannins suggest complexity, while subtle acidity adds refinement. 94 —R.V. (6/1/2003)

Domaine de Chevalier 2001 Bordeaux White Blend (Pessac-Léognan) $100. This is one of the legendary whites of Bordeaux. It lives up to its reputation. The 2001 vintage of the Domaine de Chevalier white (tasted from half bottle) is well-evolved, packed with flavors of almonds, toast, spice, fresh grapefruits, white fruits, and an impressive layer of acidity. It will age for a good 20 years or more. Expect a full bottle to be less evolved at this stage. 97 Cellar Selection —R.V. (6/1/2005)

DOMAINE DE COSTE CHAUDE

Domaine de Coste Chaude 2005 Les 4 Saisons Rosé Visan Grenache (Côtes-du-Rhône Villages) $NA. Produced from 100% Grenache, this is a citrusy, refreshing rosé that's aged in old barrels. Floral and berryish aromas mark the bouquet, while the flavors run toward lime and mineral. Juicy berry notes star on the mouthwatering finish. Drink now. 87 —J.C. (11/15/2006)

Domaine de Coste Chaude 2003 Jupiter Visan Rhône Red Blend (Côtes-du-Rhône Villages) $NA. A blend of wines matured in vat and barrel, adding subtle vanilla and woodspice shadings the bold Coste Chaude fruit. It's lush and soft on the palate, broad and expansive on the finish, picking up hints of chocolate and mocha. 90 —J.C. (11/15/2006)

Domaine de Coste Chaude 2004 La Rocaille Visan Rhône Red Blend (Côtes-du-Rhône Villages) $NA. Aged entirely in vat, this old-vines cuvée from selected parcels features a rich, creamy texture but also great peppery spice. Cassis and mulberry flavors provide power and length on the finish. Drink 2007–2012. 89 —J.C. (11/15/2006)

DOMAINE DE COURON

Domaine de Couron 2003 Cuvée Marie Dubois Syrah (Côtes-du-Rhône) $12. Overtly oaky, brimming with cedar, vanilla, and wood spice. Has a creamy-textured, vanilla-laden midpalate but finishes with enough dry wood to build a log cabin. **83** —*J.C. (11/15/2006)*

DOMAINE DE COURTEILLAC

Domaine de Courteillac 2001 Bordeaux Blanc White Blend (Bordeaux) $11. A fresh, full-bodied wine that stays on its lees after fermentation to give it a creamy broadness to go with the layer of acidity and ripe, crisp fruit. **88** —*R.V. (12/1/2002)*

DOMAINE DE CRISTIA

Domaine de Cristia 2003 Renaissance Rhône Red Blend (Châteauneuf-du-Pape) $70. Alain and Baptiste Grangeon make this wine from a small, 3.7-acre plot of old vines. Aged in wood for 2–3 years, it shows definite vanilla characters, with intense, ripe black flavors, great concentration, and richness and flavors of cassis and spice. There is a delicious juicy aftertaste to this impressive wine. **95 Editors' Choice** —*R.V. (12/31/2005)*

DOMAINE DE DEURRE

Domaine de Deurre 2004 Les Rabasses Grenache (Vinsobres) $22. A distinct step up from the domaine's regular cuvée, Les Rabasses boasts a richly fruity bouquet of super-ripe Grenache fruit. Raspberry, peach, and apricot notes cascade over the palate, framed by supple tannins. Drink now–2010. **87** —*J.C. (11/15/2006)*

DOMAINE DE DURBAN

Domaine de Durban 2004 Rhône Red Blend (Beaumes-de-Venise) $NA. From a domaine famous for its sweet Muscat, this is a rather dark, dusty expression of Beaumes-de-Venise rouge. Cocoa and coffee notes frame modest fruit. Drink now. **84** —*J.C. (11/15/2006)*

DOMAINE DE FAUTERIE

Domaine de Fauterie 2004 Les Combaud Syrah (Saint-Joseph) $22. Overoaked, with cedary notes obscuring the lean cherry fruit. Astringently woody on the vanilla-laden finish. **82** —*J.C. (11/15/2006)*

DOMAINE DE FENOUILLET

Domaine de Fenouillet 2005 Muscat Blanc à Petit Grain (Muscat de Beaumes de Venise) $NA. **84** —*J.C. (11/15/2006)*

DOMAINE DE FONTAVIN

Domaine de Fontavin 2004 Rhône Red Blend (Vacqueyras) $NA. It's an unusual blend of 75% Grenache (typical) and 25% Mourvèdre (atypical), which may account for some of its individuality. There's some cola and treebark murkiness to the aromas, but then the Grenache shines through on the palate, adding bright raspberry and a creamy texture. Supple and maybe a little delicate, but pretty. Drink now. **87** —*J.C. (11/15/2006)*

Domaine de Fontavin 2003 Rhône Red Blend (Côtes-du-Rhône) $NA. Rather light in hue, and already showing some browning. This is fully mature, maybe even a little past it, but still holds onto some attractive peach notes to go with leather and tea flavors. **83** —*J.C. (11/15/2006)*

Domaine de Fontavin 1999 Rhône Red Blend (Vacqueyras) $17. The nose is a blend of bramble, earth, smoke, and leather. It seems to have a slight floral note, too. Meanwhile, raspberry, vanilla and chocolate flavors dominate prior to a thick but not overly tannic finish. **87** —*M.S. (2/1/2003)*

DOMAINE DE FONTENILLE

Domaine de Fontenille 2000 Rhône Red Blend (Côtes du Luberon) $13. Fontenille is almost always a great value, and this 2000 is no exception, boasting concentrated raspberry aromas that leap from the glass. The intense fruit is nicely balanced by structure, and made complex by the addition of leather and dark chocolate notes on the lengthy finish. Drink now–2010. **90 Best Buy** —*J.C. (2/1/2005)*

DOMAINE DE GOURNIER

Domaine de Gournier 2005 Rosé Blend (Vin de Pays des Cévennes) $9. Washington D.C.-based importer Bobby Kacher has a veritable stable of bargain-priced rosés, but this one is among the least expensive. Although only a Vin de Pays, it's located in prime south-of-France rosé country, between Avignon and Nîmes. This blend of Merlot (35 percent), Syrah (25 percent), Grenache (20 percent), Mourvèdre, Carignana, and Cabernet Sauvignon offers slightly floral scents alongside hints of crushed stone, while the flavors lean toward rose petals and raspberries with a squirt of lime juice. Silky on the finish, with tangy acids for refreshment. **88 Best Buy** —*J.C. (6/21/2006)*

DOMAINE DE L'AMEILLAUD

Domaine de L'Ameillaud 2005 Rhône Red Blend (Côtes-du-Rhône) $14. Although the bouquet does include a rather odd nutskin component, it's also filled with enough bold cherry scents to compensate. The slightly creamy texture shows plenty of ripe fruit character, while picking up complex spice notes on the finish. **87** —*J.C. (11/15/2006)*

DOMAINE DE L'ESPIGOUETTE

Domaine de L'Espigouette 2004 Rhône Red Blend (Vacqueyras) $24. A fine effort from a relatively unknown estate, the 2004 Vacqueyras from Domaine de L'Espigouette boasts plenty of dusty, dried spice notes, perfumed red fruit and black pepper. It's nicely complex, and although it's not an overly rich wine, it's well-balanced and finishes long. Drink now–2010. **89** —*J.C. (11/15/2006)*

DOMAINE DE L'HERMITAGE

Domaine de L'Hermitage 2004 Rosé Blend (Bandol) $20. This blend of Cinsault, Mourvèdre, and Grenache shows plenty of stony minerality and even a suggestion of salinity, but also enough peach and lemon fruit to help balance that out. Creamy in the mouth, it finishes on the full side. **87** —*J.C. (6/21/2006)*

DOMAINE DE L'OLIVIER

Domaine de L'Olivier 2001 Chardonnay (Vin de Pays d'Oc) $6. **87 Best Buy** —*D.T. (11/15/2002)*

DOMAINE DE L'ORATOIRE SAINT-MARTIN

Domaine de L'Oratoire Saint-Martin 2004 Cuvée Prestige Cairanne Rhône Red Blend (Côtes-du-Rhône Villages) $27. From a parcel planted in 1905, this is a blend of Grenache (60%) and an unusually high proportion of Mourvèdre (40%). From the start the Mourvèdre is apparent, imparting hints of cola and treebark and dark fruit flavors—even a hint of espresso. Yet there's also peppery spice from the Grenache, and the wine avoids any sense of heaviness or rusticity. The tannins are supple and velvety, the finish long. Drink now–2014. **90** —*J.C. (11/15/2006)*

Domaine de L'Oratoire Saint-Martin 2004 Haut-Coustias Cairanne Rhône White Blend (Côtes-du-Rhône Villages) $17. A Marsanne- and Roussanne-dominated blend, this is ripe and honeyed—almost to the point of raising questions about its residual sugar levels. But co-proprietor François Alary says it's only 3g/L. Tastes like a mostly dry rendition of super-ripe oranges drizzled with honey, balanced by decent acidity and a sense of minerality. Spicy on the finish. **90** —*J.C. (11/15/2006)*

DOMAINE DE LA BOISSIERE

Domaine de la Boissiere 1999 Syrah (Costières de Nimes) $19. Ripe berry fruit, smoke, and cream aromas top off a cherry-and-herb palate. Brisk acidity gives it a tart mouthfeel, and a dry, toasty finish. A blend of 80% Syrah and 20% Grenache. **87** *(10/1/2001)*

Domaine de la Bouissiere 2001 Cuvée Classique Rhône Red Blend (Gigondas) $24. A brooding, intense wine that layers powerful tannins over new wood and black, heavy fruit flavors. Give this wine at least five years before drinking. **91 Editors' Choice** —*R.V. (3/1/2004)*

DOMAINE DE LA BRUNE

Domaine de la Brune 2004 Beaumes-de-Venise Rhône Red Blend (Côtes-du-Rhône Villages) $NA. A bit of matchstick on the nose, but that should clear up in time, and there's ample cherry fruit waiting to emerge. Earthy, chestnut notes add a subtle note of complexity, while the tannins are a bit dusty rather than completely supple. Drink 2007–2010. **86** —*J.C. (11/15/2006)*

DOMAINE DE LA CHARBONNIÈRE

Domaine de la Charbonnière 2003 Cuvée Mourre de Perdrix Rhône Red Blend (Châteauneuf-du-Pape) $30. This intense, sweet, jammy wine comes from 50-year-old vines on the Mourre de Perdrix plateau above the village of Courthezon. Hugely rich, high in alcohol, it is akin to drinking Port, with its smooth, dry tannins and peppery aftertaste. **91** —*R.V. (12/31/2005)*

DOMAINE DE LA CHEZATTE

Domaine de la Chezatte 2000 Sauvignon Blanc (Sancerre) $20. Despite the intense green aromas and flavors this wine possesses, it has its strong points. Namely, nice balance, a good mouthfeel, and a certain cleanliness that shouldn't be overlooked. But be warned: If green flavors like bell pepper and jalapeño are not for you, you might want to steer clear of this offering. Green is the dominant characteristic, from front to back. **86** *(8/1/2002)*

DOMAINE DE LA CÔTE DE L'ANGE

Domaine de la Côte de l'Ange 2003 Vieilles Vignes Rhône Red Blend (Châteauneuf-du-Pape) $NA. Tradition relates that an angel rested briefly on the slopes of the vineyard owned now by Monique Mestre and Yannick Gasparri. The wine from these 80-year-old vines certainly has a heavenly length to it, full of hugely ripe Grenache which bursts out of the glass. There are also big, tough tannins which promise long aging. **93 Cellar Selection** —*R.V. (12/31/2005)*

DOMAINE DE LA CROZE

Domaine de la Croze 2004 Bel Air Rhône Red Blend (Lirac) $12. Rather herbal on the nose, with a distinct note of fennel that sets it apart from other 2004 Liracs. Lean and red-fruited, leaning toward raspberry and herb rather than dark fruits and dried spices. **85** —*J.C. (11/15/2006)*

DOMAINE DE LA GASQUI

Domaine de la Gasqui 2000 Le Vallat des Taches Red Blend (Vin de Pays de Vaucluse) $10. Old Carignan and Grenache vines go into this wine, produced from a vineyard just south of Avignon in the Rhône Valley. No wood was used in aging this wine, which allows the full herbal character of the fruit to shine through. It is sweet and intense, with ripe acidity and soft, velvety tannins. Drink with cheeses or rich meat dishes. **85** —*R.V. (11/15/2003)*

DOMAINE DE LA GENESTIÈRE

Domaine de la Genestière 2005 Cuvée Raphaël Rosé Blend (Tavel) $14. Clean aromas of strawberries and cherries. This Tavel is on the heavier side, with white chocolate notes weighing down the berry fruit. But it's still reasonably balanced, thus it presents itself as being rich rather than heavy. **87** —*J.C. (11/15/2006)*

DOMAINE DE LA GUICHARDE

Domaine de la Guicharde 2003 Cuvée Genest Rhône Red Blend (Côtes-du-Rhône Villages) $14. In many ways, this wine reflects the spirit of France's new vignerons. Isabelle and Arnaud Guicharde started the domaine only 18 years ago. The husband and wife team, with no prior winemaking experience, admit that at the beginning, "We made all the mistakes we could." They've certainly come a long way. This wine is fragrant and spicy, filled with scents of garrigue, baking spices, and anise, yet at the same time showing plenty of ripe, mouth-filling fruit. Elegant, complex, and a fantastic value. **91 Best Buy** —*J.C. (11/15/2006)*

DOMAINE DE LA JANASSE

Domaine de la Janasse 2001 Les Garrigues Grenache (Côtes-du-Rhône Villages) $30. A wine that is made from 100% Grenache, giving intense herbal aromas and concentrated, solid fruit. For a Côtes-du-Rhône, this is a big, powerful wine. **88** —*R.V. (3/1/2004)*

Domaine de la Janasse 2000 Terre de Buissière Red Blend (Vin de Pays de la Principauté d'Orange) $12. The Domaine de la Janasse has 50 different parcels of vines scattered between Châteauneuf-du-Pape, Côtes du Rhône, and Vin de Pays. This blended wine introduces Merlot into the local Syrah and Grenache, giving an exotic mix of southern French perfumes and herbs, with a lift of freshness and lightness from the Merlot. **86** —*R.V. (11/15/2003)*

Domaine de la Janasse 2003 Rhône Red Blend (Châteauneuf-du-Pape) $45. The Sabons have carved a great reputation for their wines over the past 20 years, and this wine continues that in fine style. Rich and per-

fumed, it manages to combine weight with a finesse that belies the hugeness of the 2003 vintage. There are fine tannins, ripe black fruits, hints of wood, and a great sense of ageworthiness. A wine to savor in 10 years. **94 Editors' Choice** —*R.V. (12/31/2005)*

Domaine de la Janasse 2001 Terre d'Argile Rhône Red Blend (Côtes-du-Rhône Villages) $20. The name refers to the very dry, stony vineyard which gives intense, small-berried fruit. The tannins are ripe, the fruit has sweet jelly flavors, and vibrant fresh acidiy to balance. **85** —*R.V. (3/1/2004)*

Domaine de la Janasse 2001 Vieilles Vignes Rhône Red Blend (Châteauneuf-du-Pape) $110. Here is a wine that shows the serious side of Châteauneuf. While the fruit is certainly huge, what is equally apparent is the restrained power and the rich, concentrated tannins. This is a style of wine that would appeal to a Zinfandel lover. **94** —*R.V. (3/1/2004)*

DOMAINE DE LA LOUVETRIE

Domaine de la Louvetrie 2003 Sur Lie Muscadet (Muscadet Sèvre Et Maine) $11. Muscadet has changed since we all rejected it in favor of New World whites. This French region at the mouth of the Loire river now makes clean, fresh, light wines which are almost certainly the best accompaniment to shellfish there is. This estate wine is full-bodied, with a touch of toast and soft, ripe fruit. Finely focused, it is complex with green fruits and ripeness combined. **89 Best Buy** —*R.V. (11/15/2004)*

DOMAINE DE LA MAVETTE

Domaine de la Mavette 2003 Rhône Red Blend (Côtes-du-Rhône) $11. What a big difference between this wine and the same domaine's Côtes-du-Rhône Villages Sablet bottling. That one is round and supple, while this wine is rather astringent and tart, marrying sour cherry flavors with chocolate and herbal notes. **83** —*J.C. (11/15/2006)*

Domaine de la Mavette 2003 Sablet Rhône Red Blend (Côtes-du-Rhône Villages) $13. Smells like a horse that's been ridden hard and put away wet, but underneath the brett is a round, mouth-filling wine with hints of cherries and spice. Lovely texture and balance, with some dusty tannins on the finish; a bargain-priced pleasure for those who aren't put off by horse blanket. **89 Best Buy** —*J.C. (11/15/2006)*

DOMAINE DE LA MORDORÉE

Domaine de la Mordorée 2003 La Reine des Bois Rhône Red Blend (Lirac) $39. A blend of one-third each Grenache, Mourvèdre, and Syrah, year-in and year-out this is among Lirac's top wines, if not the top. In 2003, it's rich, ripe, and a touch alcoholic, but still boasts well-defined aromas of plum and spice. In the mouth, it's like liquid chocolate fudge—velvety, yet never ponderous or heavy. Ready to drink now, but should last up to 10 years. **93 Editors' Choice** —*J.C. (11/15/2006)*

Domaine de la Mordorée 2005 La Reine des Bois Rhône White Blend (Lirac) $30. A bit pricey for Lirac, but this is very good wine—easily the equal of most white Châteauneuf-du-Pape. Exotic tropical fruit comes through on the nose and palate, including hints of papaya and guava. It's creamy-textured, accented by spicy, peppery nuances. Drink now–2008. **88** —*J.C. (11/15/2006)*

DOMAINE DE LA PEPIÈRE

Domaine de la Pepière 2003 Muscadet (Muscadet Sèvre Et Maine) $10. The heat-drenched 2003 vintage has given this wine far more weight and flesh than is typical. Although this may turn off some Muscadet fans, it gives folks who haven't yet discovered Muscadet a relatively easy introduction to the genre. It's filled with soft stone fruit and melon flavors, but it still retains the briny, minerally soul of its appellation and a lingering finish. **87 Best Buy** —*J.C. (11/15/2004)*

DOMAINE DE LA POUSSE D'OR

Domaine de la Pousse d'Or 2002 Volnay Premier Cru Clos de la Bousse d'Or Pinot Noir (Volnay) $NA. Delicious structured fruit with aromas of ripe dark plums. The big tannins are well-balanced with acidity and solid black fruits. Coffee and acidity give complexity. **93** —*R.V. (9/1/2004)*

DOMAINE DE LA PRÉSIDENTE

Domaine de la Présidente 2004 Grands Classiques Cairanne Rhône Red Blend (Côtes-du-Rhône Villages) $NA. Nicely done, balancing raspberry

FRANCE

fruit with peppery spice and a hint of stone fruit. It could still use more complexity, but this is still very good. Drink now-2010. 87 —J.C. (11/15/2006)

Domaine de la Présidente 2005 Grands Classiques Rhône White Blend (Côtes-du-Rhône) $NA. Performs well above what its modest appellation would have you believe, delivering a perfumed bouquet of stone fruit and nasturtium blossom, with a hint of anise. On the palate, it's rich, mouth-coating and spicy, with a lingering finish. 89 —J.C. (11/15/2006)

DOMAINE DE LA RENJARDE

Domaine de la Renjarde 2002 Rhône Red Blend (Côtes-du-Rhône Villages) $13. There's a lifted, herbal element to this wine's aromas of cherries and dusty earth, but it serves to add complexity, not detract from the fruit. In the mouth, the flavors include hints of pepper and meat alongside oodles of ripe cherries. It's all balanced and harmonious even if it's not a blockbuster. A fine effort from a difficult vintage. 87 —J.C. (2/1/2005)

DOMAINE DE LA RONCIÈRE

Domaine de la Roncière 2003 Flor de Ronce Rhône Red Blend (Châteauneuf-du-Pape) $70. This is a modern, smooth style of wine, already easy to drink with its cooked black currant fruits and soft, open tannins. There are touches of herbs, as well as a Port-like richness and opulence. 89 —R.V. (12/31/2005)

DOMAINE DE LA ROYERE

Domaine de la Royere 1999 Cuvée Speciale L'Oppidum Syrah-Grenache (Côtes du Luberon) $11. A bit lean and ungenerous, with leather and horsey scents balanced by cherry aromas. Cherry, leather and clove flavors, finishing a bit hard and tannic. 83 —J.C. (2/1/2005)

DOMAINE DE LA SAUVEUSE

Domaine de la Sauveuse 2005 Cuvée Carolle Rosé Rhône Red Blend (Côtes de Provence) $10. This wine ambitiously blends organically grown Cinsault, Grenache, and Syrah, but the result is a light, modestly fruited wine that's ultimately a bit innocuous. 82 —J.C. (6/21/2006)

DOMAINE DE LA SOLITUDE

Domaine de la Solitude 2003 Rhône Red Blend (Châteauneuf-du-Pape) $33. A rather leathery, lean character, with heavy tannins indicate this is a wine made in the old style. For those who like this style, however, this is a fine example, packed with dense dryness and austere fruit. It is likely to age well, over 10 years. 85 —R.V. (12/31/2005)

Domaine de la Solitude 1998 Rhône Red Blend (Côtes-du-Rhône) $10. 88 —M.M. (12/31/2000)

DOMAINE DE LA TOURADE

Domaine de la Tourade 2003 Rhône Red Blend (Vacqueyras) $NA. A bit light in color, showing strawberry fruit tinged with streaks of milk chocolate. Pleasant, and potentially elegant, but a touch of alcoholic warmth shows through on the finish. 84 —J.C. (11/15/2006)

DOMAINE DE LA VOUGERAIE

Domaine de la Vougeraie 2003 Chardonnay (Beaune) $50. With its 25% new wood, this wine has hints of toast flavor. What is more evident is ripe, juicy fruit flavors of white peaches. A touch of acidity gives the wine shape. 88 —R.V. (9/1/2005)

Domaine de la Vougeraie 2002 Clos du Prieuré Chardonnay (Vougeot) $NA. A rare white from the Côte de Nuits, this white Vougeot is ripe, tropical, and packed with huge sweet fruits. It is exotic and intense, but still keeps a place for some acidity. 90 —R.V. (9/1/2004)

Domaine de la Vougeraie 2004 La Corvée des Vignes Chardonnay (Puligny-Montrachet) $NA. From a small parcel of village vines in Puligny-Montrachet, Domaine de la Vougeraie has fashioned an intense wine that balances ripe but crisp green plum and toast flavors. It is concentrated and already well-integrated. 90 —R.V. (12/1/2006)

Domaine de la Vougeraie 2002 Pinot Noir (Gevrey-Chambertin) $NA. A well-integrated wine that combines spice and black fruits in fine proportions. It is solid, but has delicious, approachable sweet fruit flavors. 89 —R.V. (9/1/2004)

Domaine de la Vougeraie 2003 Les Petits Noizons Pinot Noir (Pommard) $80. A very dark, spicy wine with generous, rich fruit. This is powerful

and concentrated, showing sweetness and openness. The structure is dry, a product of the stony soil of the vineyard. This will develop well over many years. 90 —R.V. (9/1/2005)

Domaine de la Vougeraie 1999 Le Clos Blanc de Vougeot White Blend (Vougeot) $79. This tiny 5.6 acre white vineyard in the heart of the red wine village of Vougeot is owned entirely by the Boisset family's Domaine de la Vougeraie. The wine is deliciously ripe and open, with spice and nutmeg. There is a balancing touch of acidity, and sweet, almost tropical fruit. Smoky, spicy aftertaste. 91 —R.V. (11/1/2001)

DOMAINE DE LALANDE

Domaine de Lalande 2000 Les Chevrières Chardonnay (Pouilly-Fuissé) $27. This toasty wine glides across the palate in waves of Golden Delicious apples and spicy oak, finishing with enough lemon-lime acidity to stay focused. 89 (10/1/2003)

DOMAINE DE LONGVAL

Domaine de Longval 2005 Rosé Blend (Tavel) $14. Slightly lighter in hue than others, with more of a coppery tinge. But it's still impressively pink. Strawberry aromas pick up floral hints with airing, while the red-berry flavors seem a touch syrupy and indistinct. Drink now. 85 —J.C. (11/15/2006)

DOMAINE DE MARCOUX

Domaine de Marcoux 2000 Cuvée Classique Rhône Red Blend (Châteauneuf-du-Pape) $50. This beautiful, mouth-wateringly ripe wine has huge fruit, flavors of raspberries, soft tannins, and a rounded sweet tarry aftertaste. A gorgeous wine, it will age magnificently over the next 10 years. 90 —R.V. (3/1/2004)

DOMAINE DE MONTVAC

Domaine de Montvac 2001 Cuvée Vincila Grenache-Syrah (Vacqueyras) $20. Seems to be already moving past its peak, with a bit of browning at the rim and advanced tobacco and dried-fruit aromas and flavors. Drink up. 84 —J.C. (11/15/2006)

Domaine de Montvac 2004 Rhône Red Blend (Vacqueyras) $13. An easy style dominated by red berry fruit, but not simple thanks to complex notes of herbs and dusty mineral notes on the finish. Supple, fresh, and easy to drink. Drink now–2009. 87 —J.C. (11/15/2006)

DOMAINE DE MOURCHON

Domaine de Mourchon 2003 Grande Reserve Séguret Rhône Red Blend (Côtes-du-Rhône Villages) $23. Matured in barrique for 9 months, this blend of Grenache and Syrah features intense cherry aromas accented by red plum notes—maybe even a hint of peach. Yet despite the evident ripeness it's still on the firm side, with some tea-like tannins on the finish. Drink 2008–2013. 89 —J.C. (11/15/2006)

DOMAINE DE NIZAS

Domaine de Nizas 2003 Carignan (Coteaux du Languedoc) $16. The pale oyster pink color gives a freshness and liveliness to the wine. A blend of Grenache, Mourvedre, and Syrah, it has freshness along with a soft, strawberry-flavored finish. 85 —R.V. (12/1/2004)

Domaine de Nizas 2001 Red Blend (Coteaux du Languedoc) $20. Rich fruit with a eucalyptus, herbal character gives this wine an intense exotic Mediterranean feel. Dark black fruits are there, but are dominated by the tannins and the brooding intensity. 88 —R.V. (12/1/2004)

Domaine de Nizas 2001 Mas Sallèles Red Blend (Vin de Pays d'Oc) $13. A Cabernet-Merlot-Syrah blend from the Nizas estate owned by John Goelet of Clos du Val in Napa, the wine is tannic, dry, and very firm. It's intense, though dominated by the austere Cabernet. Good wood flavors underline the fruit. 88 Best Buy —R.V. (12/31/2006)

Domaine de Nizas 2002 Rhône Red Blend (Coteaux du Languedoc) $16. This is a delicious wine, full of ripe southern perfumes, layered with black figs, dark acidity, and blackberry jelly. It is powerful, sweetly fruited (although the tannins keep it dry), and solidly ripe. 92 Editors' Choice —R.V. (12/31/2006)

Domaine de Nizas 2005 Sauvignon Blanc (Vin de Pays d'Oc) $13. A properly tropical fruited wine from the warm south, this is a simple, refreshing, well-made, clean wine with good ripe fruit, a light structure, and crisp ripe apples to finish. 85 —R.V. (12/31/2006)

DOMAINE DE PIAUGIER

Domaine de Piaugier 2004 Rhône Red Blend (Gigondas) $19. This has a remarkably herbal, garrigue-laced bouquet and a ton of space. It seems less fruity than many other Gigondas, instead relying on peppery spice and sour cherry flavors. It's a less ripe style but the complexity is really something. Drink 2008–2014. **89** —*J.C. (11/15/2006)*

DOMAINE DE POUY

Domaine de Pouy 2003 White Blend (Vin de Pays des Côtes de Gascogne) $8. Normally Ugni Blanc and Colombard grapes are distilled into Cognac or Armagnac, but owner Yves Grassa has chosen to turn these pedestrian varieties into a clean, crisp, dry wine that exudes grapefruit and green apple characteristics along with a nice smack of herbaceousness. In addition, there are aromatic notes of pine and weighty flavors of mango and banana. Not a long ager, however, as the 2002 version I also tried had lost its steam. **87 Best Buy** —*M.S. (11/15/2004)*

DOMAINE DE SERVANS

Domaine de Servans 1999 Cuvée Exceptionnelle Grenache (Côtes-du-Rhône) $16. Potent in the nose, with stylish cola and licorice aromas. The palate is super sweet, lush, and tasty, with a full blast of black plum, black cherry, and chocolate flavors. The tannins are drying and strong, but they intermix with the powerful fruit to create a coffee-like taste and mouthfeel. Very good and gets better with airing. **91 Editors' Choice** —*M.S. (9/1/2003)*

DOMAINE DE VAUGONDY

Domaine de Vaugondy NV Ph. Perdriaux Brut Chenin Blanc (Vouvray) $12. Not many sparklers have anise aromas to match white stone fruits, but this 100% Chenin Blanc has just that, and more. Crisp and lively with citrus fruits flavors, especially lemon and lime, the wine has firm mineral and some stemmy notes to add character. Goes to show you can still find good French sparklers for bargain prices. **88 Best Buy** —*M.D. (12/15/2006)*

DOMAINE DE VERQUIERE

Domaine de Verquiere 2004 Sablet Rhône Red Blend (Côtes-du-Rhône Villages) $11. Sturdy and solid. Nothing flashy here, just burly cherry fruit aromas and flavors with a modicum of spice. Drink now—maybe with something similarly styled, like a beef stew. **86** —*J.C. (11/15/2006)*

DOMAINE DE VIEUX TELEGRAPHE

Domaine de Vieux Telegraphe 1998 Red Blend (Châteauneuf-du-Pape) $42. Very complex, this is a major-league red with a tight but deep nose of black fruits, spice, and tar. The deep yet closed fruit on the palate is accented by pronounced clove, tarragon, and anise notes. Beautifully structured, with a velvety texture and fine fruit-to-acid balance. This impressive bottling finishes long, with dark fruit and cocoa notes. It virtually demands aging for three to five years. **94** —*M.M. (12/31/2001)*

DOMAINE DE VILLENEUVE

Domaine de Villeneuve 2001 Vieilles Vignes Rhône Red Blend (Châteauneuf-du-Pape) $32. From a biodynamic vineyard, this wine has pure, beautifully perfumed fruit. Aromas of herbs and wild flowers counterpoint the firm, huge, rich flavors, and ripe, black fruits. It is seductively ready to drink, but should age for at least 10 years. **93** —*R.V. (3/1/2004)*

DOMAINE DENIS GAUDRY

Domaine Denis Gaudry 2000 Pouilly-Fumé White Blend (Pouilly-Fumé) $20. Bulky, chunky lemony aromas come with a touch of green hay, or is it alfalfa? The mouth is entirely grapefruit and orange, making it citrus all the way. A stony, gravelly quality to the finish could be interpreted as mineral. The weight is on the heavy side, which costs the wine some style points. **84** *(8/1/2002)*

DOMAINE DES BAUMARD

Domaine des Baumard NV Carte Corail Rosé Cabernet Franc (Crémant de Loire) $19. A wine that is packed with delicious, fresh strawberry and red currant flavors. There is some structure, dryness, and some tannins, but it's really all about easy fruit flavors. **87** —*R.V. (6/1/2006)*

Domaine des Baumard 2002 Tirage Brut Chenin Blanc-Chardonnay (Crémant de Loire) $20. Mainly made of Chardonnay, with just a touch of Chenin Blanc, this is a big, fat rich wine that also has great poise. Tastes of apples and rich cream, with a layer of toast and light acidity to finish. **89** —*R.V. (6/1/2006)*

DOMAINE DES BERNARDINS

Domaine des Bernardins 2004 Rhône Red Blend (Beaumes-de-Venise) $NA. Grenache and 25% Syrah, this is a wonderfully supple wine—so easy to drink—yet with just enough lightly dusty tannins on the finish to give it structure. Raspberry and peach fruit is accented by hints of leather and clove. Drink now and over the next few years. **87** —*J.C. (11/15/2006)*

DOMAINE DES BERTHIERS

Domaine des Berthiers 2000 Sauvignon Blanc (Pouilly-Fumé) $24. Blends honeyed citrus and rasping jalapeño juice in a bouquet that's enticing, but the wine seems to thin out a bit on the palate, showing simple green pepper and lime flavors. Best with shellfish or vegetable appetizers. **85** *(8/1/2002)*

DOMAINE DES BLAGUEURS

Domaine des Blagueurs 2000 Syrah (Vin de Pays d'Oc) $9. From the Midi, a wine with a rich, tangy, animal earthiness to the blackberry flavors, and as dry as can be. It's complex but wild, untamed. It doesn't flatter on its own, but needs food. There's a quality a chef will appreciate and exploit. From Bonny Doon. **89 Best Buy** —*S.H. (2/28/2003)*

DOMAINE DES COCCINELLES

Domaine des Coccinelles 2002 Red Blend (Côtes-du-Rhône) $10. Coccinelles are ladybugs, a reference to this domaine's use of organic farming. This light, simple wine should be consumed over the next six months while it still holds on to its delicate red plum and cherry fruit. **84** —*J.C. (3/1/2004)*

Domaine des Coccinelles 2005 Rhône White Blend (Côtes-du-Rhône) $11. Slightly floral on the nose, then adds apple, mineral, and anise on the broad, mouth-filling palate. Tails off a bit on the finish, so catch this wine in its youth, while it's still fresh. **86 Best Buy** —*J.C. (11/15/2006)*

DOMAINE DES COMTES LAFON

Domaine des Comtes Lafon 2004 Charmes Premier Cru Chardonnay (Meursault) $NA. A structured wine that is going to need 4 or 5 years to really open up. Already there is power and intense green fruit flavors, but at the moment new-wood flavors are dominant. Don't drink now. **93** —*R.V. (12/1/2006)*

Domaine des Comtes Lafon 2004 Les Genevrières Premier Cru Chardonnay (Meursault) $NA. A wine that caresses the palate with initial silky, ripe-fruit flavors and then comes on with structure and acidity. The wood shows through but certainly doesn't dominate. A wine that has power, but also great charm. **92 Editors' Choice** —*R.V. (12/1/2006)*

DOMAINE DES DEUX ROCHES

Domaine des Deux Roches 2001 Chardonnay (St.-Véran) $19. A very nice, clean Chardonnay, and wait until the citrus, butter, and mineral flavors explode on your palate. They're intense, supported by high acidity in this bone dry, food friendly wine. Oak plays little or no part. **86** —*S.H. (1/1/2002)*

DOMAINE DES ENTREFAUX

Domaine des Entrefaux 1999 Syrah (Crozes-Hermitage) $13. **88** —*J.C. (12/31/2000)*

DOMAINE DES ESCARAVAILLES

Domaine des Escaravailles 2003 Vin Doux Natural (Rasteau) Grenache (Côtes-du-Rhône Villages) $44. Escaravailles makes two sweet wines, this one from Grenache Noir, as well as a white from Grenache Blanc. While both are impressive, the red is a touch more impressive. Dried black cherries and cinnamon mingle easily in this unctuously textured wine. The tannins give it a richer, more velvety mouthfeel. **92** —*J.C. (11/15/2006)*

FRANCE

Domaine des Escaravailles 2000 Côtes du Rhône Les Antimagne Rhône Red Blend (Côtes-du-Rhône) $NA. Ripe and soft, this wine has a warm, southern open feel that makes it immediately attractive. Drink it now, but it will age for up to five years. **86** —R.V. (3/1/2004)

Domaine des Escaravailles 2001 Côtes du Rhône Villages Rasteau La Ponce Rhône Red Blend (Côtes-du-Rhône Villages) $NA. Black herbal and dense, this is an impressive wine, showing dense tannins and rich, powerful but juicy fruit flavors. Good to drink in two to three years. **89** —R.V. (3/1/2004)

Domaine des Escaravailles 2002 Rhône White Blend (Côtes-du-Rhône) $NA. A 50/50 blend of Marsanne and Rousanne, this wine has a mineral character from the high elevation of the vineyard. This cool character give ripe, creamy fruit but also great acidity. **85** —R.V. (3/1/2004)

DOMAINE DES HAUTS CHASSIS

Domaine des Hauts Chassis 2004 Les Chassis Syrah (Crozes-Hermitage) $NA. Marked by some tarry, charred-barrel notes, but there's also plenty of sweet, ripe cherry fruit upfront, with roasted coffee notes chiming in on the finish. Supple, round, and easy to drink. Drink now–2012. **87** —J.C. (11/15/2006)

DOMAINE DES MURETTES

Domaine des Murettes 1998 Le Clos de l'Olivier Syrah (Minervois) $12. Grape and blackberry fruit is joined by notes of sur-maturité that call to mind tropical fruits. There's even a distinct papaya nuance. And strong licorice and black coffee flavors that seem a bit rough around the edges—but it's nothing that a couple of years in a cold cellar won't cure. **87 Best Buy** (10/1/2001)

DOMAINE DES OLIVIERS

Domaine des Oliviers 2005 Chardonnay (Vin de Pays d'Oc) $8. From a 50-acre property owned by the Roux family of Saint-Aubin in Burgundy, this Chardonnay is obviously made by specialists in the art of vinifying this grape. It has tropical flavors, ripe and full-bodied, with some touches of vanilla. Drink now and over the next year. **88 Best Buy** —R.V. (12/31/2006)

DOMAINE DES PERDRIX

Domaine des Perdrix 2003 Pinot Noir (Vosne-Romanée) $80. The Domaine des Perdrix belongs to the Devillard family, which also runs Antonin Rodet. This seriously rich, dark wine is packed with tannins and some new wood, plus ripe red fruits. There are layers of caramel and vanilla which, at this young stage, are masking the fruit. **90** —R.V. (9/1/2005)

Domaine des Perdrix 2003 Pinot Noir (Echezeaux) $200. An opulent wine, full of very ripe fruit. The fruit is so big that the tannins seem to be overshadowed by them, until the finish, when acidity and fresh black fruit emerge. Structured yet open. **89** —R.V. (9/1/2005)

Domaine des Perdrix 2001 Pinot Noir (Nuits-St.-Georges) $51. An intriguing nose blends herbs with smoke and toast, then yields to wonderfully ripe cherries on the palate. The wine is satiny smooth in the mouth, picking up spice notes on the lingering finish. **90** —J.C. (10/1/2003)

Domaine des Perdrix 2001 Pinot Noir (Bourgogne) $16. This wine is a bit of a fruit bomb, with jammy, super-ripe plums and black cherries crammed into a medium-weight wine. A pruny scent hints at the ripeness of the fruit, while a broad swath of vanilla speaks of oak aging. **85** —J.C. (10/1/2003)

Domaine des Perdrix 2002 Aux Perdrix Premier Cru Pinot Noir (Nuits-St.-Georges) $93. An impressive peformance, this wine has pure flavors of ripe blackberries and bitter cherries along with dark tannins and solid, chunky fruit. **90** —R.V. (9/1/2004)

Domaine des Perdrix 1999 aux Perdrix Premier Cru Pinot Noir (Nuits-St.-Georges) $61. 91 Cellar Selection (1/1/2004)

DOMAINE DES RELAGNES

Domaine des Relagnes 2003 Les Petits Pieds d'Armand Rhône Red Blend (Châteauneuf-du-Pape) $68. These pieds are the 100-year-old vines whose fruit goes into this wine. And Armand is the father of the present owner, Henri Boiron. With all that said, this is a fine wine, smooth, rich, generous and full of juicy black plum and wood flavors as well as pepper. **94** —R.V. (12/31/2005)

DOMAINE DES REMIZIÈRES

Domaine des Remizières 2000 Cuvée Emilie Rhône Red Blend (Hermitage) $NA. Philippe Desmeure has two small parcels of the Hermitage hill, near Jaboulet's La Chapelle vineyard. With malolactic fermentation in the barrel, and 100% new wood, this wine, named after his daughter, has sweetness, richness, black fruits, and firm, dry tannins. This sample was spoiled by an animal rusticity that may fade as the wine ages. **87** —R.V. (6/1/2002)

Domaine des Remizières 2004 Syrah (Saint-Joseph) $NA. Impressively dark in color and flavor, with bold plum and pepper notes leading the way. It's crisp and youthfully tight, and although it lacks flesh now, it should blossom in 2–3 years. Drink 2008–2012. **88** —J.C. (11/15/2006)

Domaine des Remizières 2000 Cuvée Christophe Syrah (Crozes-Hermitage) $30. Named after owner Philippe Desmeure's son, this has a new wood dominated wine, but also with dusty tannins and ripe, black fruit flavors. It was aged in small 225-liter barriques and this has given the wine a polished, ripe perfume of spices and new wood. **88** —R.V. (6/1/2002)

Domaine des Remizières 2000 Cuvée Particulière Syrah (Crozes-Hermitage) $NA. A long maceration and aging on large 600-liter barrels has given this wine a dominance of fruit flavors. Aromas of violets and ripe fruits follow on the palate with red fruits, fine tannins, spices, and a good twist of acidity. **87** —R.V. (6/1/2002)

DOMAINE DES SÉNÉCHAUX

Domaine des Sénéchaux 2003 Rhône Red Blend (Châteauneuf-du-Pape) $37. A ripely perfumed wine that shows power, but also delicious fresh, red fruits. There is a purity to the fruit character which, with the acidity, gives a vibrancy and lift to the wine. Already drinkable, it should develop well over the medium term of 5 years. **88** —R.V. (12/31/2005)

DOMAINE DU BERNIER

Domaine du Bernier 2005 Chardonnay (Vin de Pays du Jardin de la France) $8. A deliciously poised wine, layered with the honey flavors of malolactic fermentation, giving soft, open acidity and white nectarine flavors. It's a wine with the softness of ripe Chardonnay and the lightness and freshness that comes from cool-climate western Loire vineyards. Drink this holiday season, it will go great with the turkey. **87** —R.V. (12/31/2006)

DOMAINE DU CAYRON

Domaine du Cayron 2004 Rhône Red Blend (Gigondas) $NA. Thanks to trail-blazing importer Kermit Lynch, this is one Gigondas that's been available in the U.S. for years. The 2004 boasts an intriguing blend of spices that ranges from clove and coffee to pepper and celery seed, while the fruit lurks underneath. Tannins are supple, gently supporting the wine's weight and complexity. Drink now–2015. **88** —J.C. (11/15/2006)

DOMAINE DU CHÂTEAU VIEUX

Domaine du Château Vieux 2004 Les Hauts Syrah (Saint-Joseph) $36. This is a straightforward, easy-to-drink Saint-Joseph that leans toward the darker side of the Syrah spectrum. Black cherry and plum notes hint at tar and espresso. Although there's not much peppery spice, this is still a rich mouthful of northern Rhône Syrah. **87** —J.C. (11/15/2006)

DOMAINE DU CHÊNE

Domaine du Chêne 2003 Anais Syrah (Saint-Joseph) $37. A rich, weighty northern Rhône Syrah, with pepper and black plum flavors crammed into a big round wine. Structured and powerful; just lacks a bit of nuance. Drink now-2015. **88** —J.C. (11/15/2006)

DOMAINE DU CORIANÇON

Domaine du Coriançon 2004 Rhône Red Blend (Vinsobres) $NA. Marked by bright cherry fruit, this is a crisp, fruity quaff that turns a bit hard on the finish. **84** —J.C. (11/15/2006)

DOMAINE DU GRAND BOUQUETEAU

Domaine du Grand Bouqueteau 2005 Rosé Cabernet Franc (Chinon) $12. This rosé of Cabernet Franc shows hints of bubble gum and candied cherries on the nose, but settles down on the palate to offer more grownup notes of citrus, herb, and mineral. It's light and fresh, finishing with a hint of anise. Best on its own or with seafood. **86** —*J.C.* *(6/21/2006)*

DOMAINE DU GRAND TINEL

Domaine du Grand Tinel 2003 Rhône Red Blend (Châteauneuf-du-Pape) $34. Rough, earthy aromas give this wine a decidedly old-fashioned character, which is repeated on the palate. With its dominance of Grenache, this is a powerful wine, packed with herbs and tannins, and farmyard flavors. Great with equally powerful food. **85** —*R.V.* *(12/31/2005)*

DOMAINE DU GROS NORE

Domaine du Gros Nore 1999 Rosé Blend (Bandol) $20. Very pale, with inviting aromas of peaches and strawberries, vanilla and smoke. Delicate flavors of peaches, white chocolate, vanilla, strawberry, and minty sorbet. It's dry and crisp, with high acidity. Despite the lightness of body, this wine has interest and depth. **87** —*S.H.* *(2/1/2003)*

DOMAINE DU JONCIER

Domaine du Joncier 2003 Rhône Red Blend (Lirac) $18. A lifted, slightly volatile note on the nose, then plenty of spice and prune aromas. this is a big, velvety-textured wine that's also a bit ponderous. Packs in heavyweight power, but lacks a little finesse. **86** —*J.C.* *(11/15/2006)*

DOMAINE DU MAS BLANC

Domaine du Mas Blanc 1996 Cuvée La Coume Red Blend (Banyuls) $55. 93 *(11/15/1999)*

DOMAINE DU MONT SAINT-JEAN

Domaine du Mont Saint-Jean 1999 Merlot (Vin de Pays de L'ile de Beaute) $9. Plenty of barnyard-earth aromas, plus spices and tree bark, on the nose—a good thing—but the palate and finish shows nothing but wood and wood-derived flavors. **83** —*D.T.* *(2/1/2002)*

DOMAINE DU MOULIN

Domaine du Moulin 2004 Vieilles Vignes Rhône Red Blend (Vinsobres) $NA. Call it international if you must, but it's really just a ripe, supple style with a kiss of oak. Vanilla and dried spices work the nose, but there's also balanced raspberry fruit and eminent drinkability. Drink now. **87** —*J.C.* *(11/15/2006)*

DOMAINE DU MURINAIS

Domaine du Murinais 2004 Vieilles Vignes Syrah (Crozes-Hermitage) $22. Has a pretty bouquet of smoke, cracked pepper, and herb, but only modest levels of fruit. Seems a bit light or dilute on the midpalate and on the finish. Charming; drink now. **84** —*J.C.* *(11/15/2006)*

DOMAINE DU PESQUIER

Domaine du Pesquier 2004 Rhône Red Blend (Gigondas) $28. Dense and chocolaty, with plum and date flavors that verge on prune and fudge. Yet it's not overly heavy or tannic, showing solid balance and length on the finish. Drink now. **86** —*J.C.* *(11/15/2006)*

DOMAINE DU ROCHOY

Domaine du Rochoy 2004 Sauvignon Blanc (Sancerre) $25. Produced by Domaine Laporte (itself owned by Henri Bourgeois), this wine is firmly in the modernist camp of Sancerre. But I also has some complexity, with light, poised flavors of currants and crisp acidity. This is more of a food wine than an apéritif, and would also work well with Asian dishes. **88** — *R.V.* *(8/1/2006)*

DOMAINE DU TARIQUET

Domaine du Tariquet 2001 Vinifie Et Eleve En Fut De Chene Chardonnay (Vin de Pays des Côtes de Gascogne) $12. Toasty for certain, with smoky notes that grow bigger and bigger. Lemon and pineapple flavors dominate the snappy body, which is slightly lean but still possesses good balance. Best if you like oak and citrus. **85** —*M.S.* *(9/1/2003)*

Domaine du Tariquet 2005 Les Premières Grives Gros Manseng (Vin de Pays des Côtes de Gascogne) $15. Tariquet's answer to late harvest wines, this fine, ripe wine, with its layers of sweetness and intense acidity, would be a great accompaniment to pâté and terrines. Made from the southwest's Gros Manseng grape, which many locals claim is the unsung white

grape of the future, this is a pure, fruity, but complex wine. **90 Best Buy** —*R.V.* *(12/31/2006)*

Domaine du Tariquet 2005 Sauvignon (Vin de Pays des Côtes de Gascogne) $10. For those who prefer the ripe, fuller style of Sauvignon Blanc, this wine is just right. It's a great comfort wine, with its soft aftertaste. From the deep south-west of France, it is packed with floral aromas, fresh tropical flavors, and layers of minerals for structure. The Grassa family, owners of Tariquet, are major landowners in the Gascony region, with 2,100 acres under vine. **86 Best Buy** —*R.V.* *(12/31/2006)*

Domaine du Tariquet 2005 Chenin Chardonnay White Blend (Vin de Pays des Côtes de Gascogne) $10. What a fascinating blend, this combination of Chenin Blanc and Chardonnay. The natural acidity of the Chenin gives a great, fresh mouthfeel, while the fat Chardonnay broadens out the palate. This wine is full, rich, and packed with ripe grapes, yet with only 12% alcohol, there is still a light, fresh, and white fruit-flavored aftertaste. The Grassa family, owners of Tariquet, are major landowners in this Gascony region of southwest France, with 2,100 acres under vine. **89 Best Buy** —*R.V.* *(11/15/2006)*

DOMAINE DU TRAPADIS

Domaine du Trapadis 2005 Blovac Grenache (Côtes-du-Rhône) $12. This 100% Grenache shows impressive ripeness, as evidenced by its super-ripe scents of white cherries and a plump, supple texture. It's mouth-filling and round; maybe a little simple and lacking spice but ultimately very satisfying. **87 Best Buy** —*J.C.* *(11/15/2006)*

Domaine du Trapadis 2001 Rhône Red Blend (Côtes-du-Rhône) $13. Vibrant raspberry flavors give this wine a delicious, refreshing lift. At the same time, the tannins are solid and firm, showing a good, easy structure. **85** —*R.V.* *(3/1/2004)*

Domaine du Trapadis 2001 Côtes du Rhône Villages Rasteau Rhône Red Blend (Côtes-du-Rhône Villages) $18. Serious tannins and dense black fruits make this anything but a simple Côtes-du-Rhône. It has long-lived flavors of dark fruits and intense herbs, alongside considerable elegance. **88** —*R.V.* *(3/1/2004)*

Domaine du Trapadis 2003 Les Adrès Rasteau Rhône Red Blend (Côtes-du-Rhône Villages) $32. Really dark and savory in character, with scents and flavors that turn toward meat, soy sauce, mushroom, coffee, and prune. Tart and firmly tannic on the finish. Save the extra money and buy the regular bottling, which shows better balance. **82** —*J.C.* *(11/15/2006)*

Domaine du Trapadis 2003 Rasteau Rhône Red Blend (Côtes-du-Rhône Villages) $19. Shows better balance than Trapadis's Les Adrès luxury cuvée, with dried cherries, leather, and a lush, warming mouthfeel. The flavors are of super-ripe cherries, but there's still fresh acidity, that results in a long, mouthwatering finish. Drink now. **89** —*J.C.* *(11/15/2006)*

DOMAINE DU VIEUX TÉLÉGRAPHE

Domaine du Vieux Télégraphe 2003 La Crau Rhône Red Blend (Châteauneuf-du-Pape) $40. This classic wine from the Brunier family is certainly one of the best known names in Château-neuf-du-Pape. It is also a very fine wine, full of perfumed fruit, dark, dry but rich tannins, flavors of oak, pepper, and herbs, made in quite a traditional style. The name "La Crau" refers to the plateau on which the vines are planted. **92** —*R.V.* *(12/31/2005)*

DOMAINE DUSEIGNEUR

Domaine Duseigneur 2003 Angelique Rhône Red Blend (Lirac) $15. With its baked fruit aromas and high alcohol, this wine is very 2003. Will appeal to those who admire size and dried fruit; less so for those looking for freshness and spice. **83** —*J.C.* *(11/15/2006)*

DOMAINE EHRHART

Domaine Ehrhart 2004 Im Berg Pinot Gris (Alsace) $19. Starts with hints of roasted nuts, dusty minerals, and ripe melon, all carried aboard a rich, nearly unctuous mouthfeel. The vibrant finish reverberates with nuts, minerals and just a touch of sweet fruit. **91 Editors' Choice** —*J.C.* *(2/1/2006)*

DOMAINE FERME SAINT-MARTIN

Domaine Ferme Saint-Martin 2004 Cuvée Saint Martin Rhône Red Blend (Beaumes-de-Venise) $17. This is darker and richer than the domaine's

FRANCE

Les Terres Jaunes bottling, but also less precisely perfumed. Creamy black cherry fruit washes across the palate in waves carried by supple tannins. It may lack a little nuance—although that may emerge with another year or two in the cellar—but it's full, rich, and satisfying. **90** —J.C. (11/15/2006)

DOMAINE FOND CROZE

Domaine Fond Croze 2004 Cuvée Confidence Rhône Red Blend (Côtes-du-Rhône) $10. A pretty typical 70-30 blend of Grenache and Syrah, this is a solid, sturdy Côtes-du-Rhône, a bit rustic and spicy, but also boasting a fair amount of black cherry fruit. A good burger wine at a reasonable price. **84** —J.C. (11/15/2006)

Domaine Fond Croze 2004 Cuvée Vincent de Catari Rhône Red Blend (Côtes-du-Rhône Villages) $12. Almost 80% Grenache, with the rest largely Syrah, this is a solid, well-made wine at a great price. Red fruit flavors flow easily across the palate aboard a creamy mouthfeel, while complex spice notes chime in on the long, supple finish. **88 Best Buy** —J.C. (11/15/2006)

DOMAINE FONT DE MICHELLE

Domaine Font de Michelle 2003 Rhône Red Blend (Châteauneuf-du-Pape) $35. This is a dusty, softly tannic wine that brings together very ripe fruit with some elegance. Flavors of wood, strawberries, cherries, spice, and a hint of tobacco all give a sense of complexity. The tannins become dry in the mouth, hinting at ageworthiness. **89** —R.V. (12/31/2005)

DOMAINE FOUASSIER

Domaine Fouassier 2004 Domaine les Grands Groux Sauvignon Blanc (Sancerre) $17. Made from old vines, this ripe, intensely fruity wine has flavors of green plums and gooseberries to go with a firm, tight structure that promises a couple of years aging. **90** —R.V. (8/1/2006)

Domaine Fouassier 2004 Les Grands Champs Sauvignon Blanc (Sancerre) $NA. From mainly chalky soil, this wine, made from 15-year-old vines, has an immediately attractive mineral character. There are notes of pear skin and green apples, and a pure, fresh, crisp streak. The fruit shows a great clean, fresh aftertaste. **87** —R.V. (8/1/2006)

DOMAINE FRANÇOIS VILLARD

Domaine François Villard 2005 Fruit d'Avilleran Marsanne (Saint-Joseph) $NA. An interesting take on Marsanne, with 15% Roussanne to lighten it, and also a touch of unreleased CO2 to give it more life. The result is a honeyed but basically neutral wine with a chalky texture. Drink 2007–2010 after it's smoothed out a little. **84** —J.C. (11/15/2006)

Domaine François Villard 2004 Mairlant Syrah (Saint-Joseph) $40. Peppery and dense, with ample concentration and muscular cassis flavors. Not as nuanced, deep, or long as Villard's Reflet bottling, but still very good stuff, as it is framed by supple tannins. **87** —J.C. (11/15/2006)

DOMAINE GALÉVAN

Domaine Galévan 2004 Rhône Red Blend (Côtes-du-Rhône) $NA. Sports some interesting scents of clove and white pepper, but then adds rubbery Band-Aid notes and doesn't have the richness of fruit or texture to overcome them. **82** —J.C. (11/15/2006)

DOMAINE GEORGES ROUMIER

Domaine Georges Roumier 2000 Pinot Noir (Chambolle-Musigny) $45. This is a straightforward, deliciously fruity wine with rich, juicy fruit flavors. Fresh raspberry flavors provide a sweetness to dominate the soft tannins. Already drinkable, it should continue to mature well over the next five years. **87** —R.V. (11/1/2002)

Domaine Georges Roumier 2000 Les Amoureuses Premier Cru Pinot Noir (Chambolle-Musigny) $100. A deeply colored wine, generous and opulent, full of rich, silky fruit. Aromas of wild strawberries show through on the palate with ripe, sweet fruit and fine but dense tannins. This is a wine that lives up to its name vineyard—a wine for lovers, indeed. **91** —R.V. (11/1/2002)

DOMAINE GEORGES VERNAY

Domaine Georges Vernay 2002 Blonde de Seigneur Syrah (Côte Rôtie) $55. Blonde de Seigneur was first produced by Georges Vernay in 2000. It is a

wine which shows up elegance rather than power, great black fruit expression with fine tannins. It has some dry tannic structure, but there is plenty of fruit here, perfumed and with layers of smoky wood. A really great wine from a medium vintage. **94 Cellar Selection** —R.V. (2/1/2005)

Domaine Georges Vernay 1999 Maison Rouge Syrah (Côte Rôtie) $45. Bright purple-colored wine, with huge aromas of new wood and a smooth, ripe, polished palate. Chocolate and fine acidity give flavor and structure to the wine. A very modern style of wine, which seems to have left the taste of Rhône Syrah a long way away. **88** —R.V. (6/1/2002)

Domaine Georges Vernay 2000 Les Terrasses de l'Empire Viognier (Condrieu) $57. Georges Vernay is certainly the master of Condrieu. He takes Viognier to extremes and then makes drinkable wines. This evocatively named wine is ripe and creamy, flavored with delicious peaches, apricots, and nectarines. The new wood gives an underlayer of spice and vanilla. This wine, from the master of Condrieu, may be low in acidity, but it is wonderfully high in richness. **93** —R.V. (6/1/2002)

DOMAINE GERARD TREMBLAY

Domaine Gerard Tremblay 1998 Chardonnay (Chablis) $NA. Tropical, honeyed fruit on the nose. Sweet, but rather dilute fruit. A pleasant, easy wine, with wood flavors. Soft aftertaste. **84** —R.V. (6/1/2001)

DOMAINE GIRARD

Domaine Girard 2003 La Garenne Sauvignon Blanc (Sancerre) $20. Ripe and round, with aromas of almond, talcum powder, and plenty of melon and citrus. Quite standard but good, with full, attractive flavors of melon, orange, and custard. Not too racy, like almost every 2003 Sancerre we tried. **87** (7/1/2005)

DOMAINE GRAMENON

Domaine Gramenon 1998 Les Laurentides Rhône Red Blend (Côtes-du-Rhône) $16. 88 —M.M. (12/31/2000)

DOMAINE GRAND VENEUR

Domaine Grand Veneur 1998 Rhône Red Blend (Côtes-du-Rhône) $9. 86 —J.C. (12/31/2000)

DOMAINE GROS FRÈRE ET SOEUR

Domaine Gros Frère et Soeur 2002 Pinot Noir (Echezeaux) $NA. A fine, perfumed wine, full of tannins, meaty flavors, and black fruit. A complex wine, which layers acidity, fruits, toast, and sweetness. **91** —R.V. (9/1/2004)

Domaine Gros Frère et Soeur 2002 Premier Cru Pinot Noir (Vosne-Romanée) $NA. Aromas are of dark plums and tobacco. New wood gives a spicy, concentrated flavor to the wine, accenting its firm, solid fruit. **89** —R.V. (9/1/2004)

DOMAINE GROSSET

Domaine Grosset 2003 Cairanne Rhône Red Blend (Côtes-du-Rhône Villages) $16. With its dry, dusty mouthfeel and moderate tannins, this wine clearly calls for some cellaring, but the ingredients for a successful evolution are there: balanced measures of tannins, alcohol, fruit, and acidity. Leather, dried frruit, and chocolate notes lead the way, followed by ripe black cherries and a hint of anise on the finish. Drink 2007–2012. **87** —J.C. (2/1/2005)

DOMAINE HENRI PERROT-MINOT

Domaine Henri Perrot-Minot 2000 Vieilles Vignes Pinot Noir (Mazoyeres-Chambertin) $109. This is a rich, full-bodied grand cru that's loaded with dark fruit flavors. Blackberries and black cherries flow evenly across the palate, accented by notes of strong coffee and black tea. Anticipated maturity: 2006–2015. **93 Cellar Selection** (10/1/2003)

DOMAINE HENRY PELLÉ

Domaine Henry Pellé 2003 Morogues Sauvignon Blanc (Menetou-Salon) $23. Rounder and fuller than in previous years. The color is a bit gold and the nose offers aromas of lemon and peach touched up by some toast. Plump on the palate, with bergamot, melon, and peach flavors. Finishes with almondy, minerally notes. **86** (7/1/2005)

FRANCE

DOMAINE HOUCHART

Domaine Houchart 2000 Red Blend (Côtes de Provence) $11. The funky nose kicks up leather, iodine, and malted chocolate prior to a lean, muscular palate of condensed plum and berry. Pretty tannic stuff, with lots of grab across the cheeks. **83** —*M.S. (9/1/2003)*

DOMAINE HUET L'ECHANSONNE

Domaine Huet l'Echansonne 2003 Le Haut-Lieu Demi-Sec Chenin Blanc (Vouvray) $40. Flavors of fresh fruits, peaches, and layers of acidity dominate this wine from the 22-acre Haut-Lieu vineyard. This elegant wine is ripe, with a light sweetness. Try it with rich fish sauces or ripe blue cheese. **89** —*R.V. (4/1/2005)*

DOMAINE J-F MUGNIER

Domaine J-F Mugnier 1999 Pinot Noir (Musigny) $179. Jacques-Frédéric Mugnier, whose family owns the Château de Chambolle, has made a huge, deeply colored wine with aromas of roses and truffles. To taste, it is rich, opulent, and oozing fruit, with generous tannins and fresh acidity coming together in fine balance. It has all the seductive character of Musigny. **94 Editors' Choice** —*R.V. (11/1/2002)*

Domaine J-F Mugnier 1999 Les Fuées Premier Cru Pinot Noir (Chambolle-Musigny) $NA. A deeply colored wine that reveals flavors of raspberries and firm wood. It is broad and rich, with dark tannins, leaving a clean, fresh, poised taste of acidity and sweet fruits. The wine is still coming together, but promises to age well—give it at least five years. **91** —*R.V. (11/1/2002)*

DOMAINE JACQUES PRIEUR

Domaine Jacques Prieur 2004 Clos de Mazeray Chardonnay (Meursault) $69. Very rich, ripe, and packed with new-wood flavors, this is somewhat flashy, but it's still delicious to drink. Sit back and enjoy. **90** —*R.V. (12/1/2006)*

Domaine Jacques Prieur 2004 Les Combettes Premier Cru Chardonnay (Puligny-Montrachet) $110. The reputation of Les Combettes for charm is borne out by this deliciously ripe wine. It has layers of fresh fruit flavors, a touch of spice from the wood, and a long aftertaste. And, for the future, the acidity and the underlying structure promise at least 5 years of evolution. **93 Editors' Choice** —*R.V. (12/1/2006)*

Domaine Jacques Prieur 2002 Chambertin Pinot Noir (Gevrey-Chambertin) $192. Sweet fruit and layers of currants and berries give this wine an intense flavor. A touch of herbs adds complexity. Dry tannins and acidity finish a powerful, satisfying wine. **93** —*R.V. (9/1/2004)*

Domaine Jacques Prieur 1999 Champs Pimont Premier Cru Pinot Noir (Beaune) $48. **92** *(1/1/2004)*

Domaine Jacques Prieur 2002 Clos Vougeot Pinot Noir (Clos Vougeot) $135. Huge and serious wine with firm but very ripe tannins. This is wonderful and powerful, oozing rich black fruits and seduction. **94** —*R.V. (9/1/2004)*

Domaine Jacques Prieur 2002 Greves Premier Cru Pinot Noir (Beaune) $61. A huge, sweet, silky wine with lovely acidity and firm tannins on the finish. It's big, rich, and seductive. **91** —*R.V. (9/1/2004)*

DOMAINE JACQUES PRIEUR & ANTONIN RODET

Domaine Jacques Prieur & Antonin Rodet 1999 Clos de las Feguine Premier Cru Bordeaux Blend (Beaune) $50. Here is a big, bold, full-throttle wine that might almost have come from one of the top Yamhill County wineries. Jammy and ripe, the fruit is loaded with extract, and the nose augmented with scents of resin and spice. Young, edgy, and tannic, it seems designed for immediate pleasure more than long-term cellaring. **89** —*P.G. (11/1/2002)*

DOMAINE JAMET

Domaine Jamet 2002 Syrah (Côte Rôtie) $88. This is old-style winemaking, but in the best sense. It is big, dominated at this stage by tannins. The fruit is dark, brooding, and intense. It has layers of wood (of which 20 percent was new), while the acidity still needs to soften out. This will age, maybe 10-12 years. **90** —*R.V. (2/1/2005)*

DOMAINE JAUME

Domaine Jaume 2004 Génération Rhône Red Blend (Côtes-du-Rhône) $10. Already seems a bit oxidized, with hints of almond and chestnut. Dried fruit flavors on the palate. **82** —*J.C. (11/15/2006)*

DOMAINE JEAN ROYER

Domaine Jean Royer 2003 Cuvée Prestige Rhône Red Blend (Châteauneuf-du-Pape) $70. A superb, very traditional wine, with big, brooding tannins and very dark flavors. Tastes of southern herbs come through the intense Grenache, while the dryness persists right to the end. This is a wine that just needs aging. **91** —*R.V. (12/31/2005)*

DOMAINE JEAN-MICHEL GERIN

Domaine Jean-Michel Gerin 1999 Champin le Seigneur Rhône Red Blend (Côte Rôtie) $27. For Jean-Michel Gerin, the blending of the different lots which make up this wine was "the most complex of my career." He has created a wine of great concentration, piercing balanced acidity, and ripe, strawberry jelly fruit flavors. It is already attractive to drink, but there is a firm layer of tannin for aging. **92** —*R.V. (6/1/2002)*

Domaine Jean-Michel Gerin 2000 La Loye White Blend (Condrieu) $24. With its crisp fresh fruit and deliciously refreshing acidity, this wine from a small parcel of Condrieu owned by Domaine Gerin has a well-judged touch of wood, but is full of ripe white peach and spice flavors. When it has aged for a couple of years, it will be in peak condition. **91** —*R.V. (6/1/2002)*

DOMAINE LA BOUISSIERE

Domaine la Bouissiere 2004 Tradition Rhône Red Blend (Gigondas) $28. From a consistently excellent producer, this is excellent juice. It's not obvious, but instead is lush, richly fruited, and velvety in texture, with plum and blackberry fruit. There is also a complex interplay of spices on the finish. Drink now–2014. **90** —*J.C. (11/15/2006)*

DOMAINE LA CABOTTE

Domaine la Cabotte 2004 Gabriel Rhône Red Blend (Côtes-du-Rhône) $14. Although La Cabotte's basic Côtes-du-Rhône left me unmoved, this cuvée is worth commenting on. It's impressively dark in color, and marked by floral aromas that reflect its relatively large proportion (65%) of Syrah. Yet it's also a bit tough and unyielding on the palate, making me wonder about its future evolution. **86** —*J.C. (11/15/2006)*

DOMAINE LA COSTE

Domaine la Coste 2000 Ultra Red Blend (Coteaux d'Aix en Provence) $28. This wine is mostly Syrah—from old vines—and it really delivers the goods. The nose is deep and earthy, with a hint of minerals. The big plum-filled mouth is meaty and saturated, but not tannic or harsh. And the finish is tasty and fruity, with nuances of vanilla and spice. Overall it's a rock-solid winner with length, complexity, and muscle. **90** —*M.S. (2/1/2003)*

DOMAINE LA GARRIGUE

Domaine la Garrigue 2004 Traditional Reserve Rhône Red Blend (Vacqueyras) $19. Nicely perfumed, with cherry and raspberry fruit leading the way. A hint of coffee adds darkness and depth, while peach shadings bring a brighter note. A bit light in body, but pretty and elegant, gaining tannic strength on the finish. Drink now–2012. **87** —*J.C. (11/15/2006)*

DOMAINE LA HITAIRE

Domaine la Hitaire 2005 Hors Saison Sémillon -Sauvignon Blanc (Vin de Pays des Côtes de Gascogne) $11. A pleasant blend of Sauvignon Blanc and Sémillon, this wine from the Grassa family in Gascony, south-west France, is in an easy-drinking style. There are soft flavors of almonds, green plums, nice light, poised fruit. **84** —*R.V. (12/31/2006)*

DOMAINE LA MILLIÈRE

Domaine la Millière 2003 Vieilles Vignes Rhône Red Blend (Côtes-du-Rhône) $NA. An interesting wine that appears to be at its peak maturity, the 2003 Millière features elegant leather and spice notes on the nose, followed by plenty of dried fruit flavors. It's supple, but seems a bit light on the midpalate. Drink now. **84** —*J.C. (11/15/2006)*

FRANCE

DOMAINE LA MONTAGNETTE

Domaine la Montagnette 2004 Rhône Red Blend (Côtes-du-Rhône Villages) $12. A big step up from the regular Côtes-du-Rhône bottling, this villages wine is brimming with ripe stone fruits—peaches and cherries—accented by chocolate and spice. Silky flavors ease the flavors effortlessly across the palate, while the finish lingers elegantly. A winner from the co-op at Estézargues. **90 Best Buy** —*J.C. (11/15/2006)*

DOMAINE LA REMEJEANNE

Domaine la Remejeanne 2004 Les Arbousiers Rhône Red Blend (Côtes-du-Rhône) $NA. This blend of 70% Grenache and 30% Syrah starts off a bit slow, with hints of cabbage on the nose, but boasts a lovely creamy mouthfeel and bold cherry flavors. Finishes strong, loaded with spice and herbes de Provence. **87** —*J.C. (11/15/2006)*

DOMAINE LA ROQUÈTE

Domaine la Roquète 2003 Rhône Red Blend (Châteauneuf-du-Pape) $40. The 79-acre Domaine la Roquète was acquired by the Brunier family of Vieux Telegraphe in 1986. Its modern labeling belies its dense, huge, packed fruit and tannins that suggest classic Châteauneuf-du-Pape. But there are also great perfumes in the wood and herbal characters. Will age over many years. **93 Cellar Selection** —*R.V. (12/31/2005)*

DOMAINE LA ROUBINE

Domaine la Roubine 2004 Rhône Red Blend (Gigondas) $24. An excellent effort, La Roubine's 2004 Gigondas takes blackberry and pepper notes and combines them in a lovely bouquet that's more than the sum of its parts. There's a lushly textured, creamy mouthfeel that makes for even more hedonistic delight. Like a repeating decimal, it's long on the finish. Drink now–2012, maybe longer. **91** —*J.C. (11/15/2006)*

DOMAINE LAFLAIVE

Domaine Laflaive 2001 Chardonnay (Bourgogne) $NA. A young, crisp Chardonnay with some sharp elbows of acidity. The peach, apple, and citrus flavors are very dry. Offers plenty of polish and length for a regional wine. **88** —*S.H. (1/1/2002)*

Domaine Laflaive 1997 White Blend (Bâtard-Montrachet) $NA. An extremely complex wine. At five-plus years, the peach, lime, and tart apple flavors are picking up mineral, mushroom, earth, and medicinal overtones. Drinks soft, lush, and creamy, yet with crisp acidity. This multi-layered wine changes with each sniff and swirl, and finishes with astonishing length. **93** —*S.H. (1/1/2002)*

Domaine Laflaive 1998 Les Pucelles Premier Cru White Blend (Puligny-Montrachet) $NA. Completely different from neighboring Les Folatieres, this is a wine that is going over the hill. It has aromas of freshly baked peach bread, but in the mouth a maderized flavor like Sherry. **85** —*S.H. (1/1/2002)*

DOMAINE LAFOND

Domaine Lafond 2004 Roc-Epine Rhône Red Blend (Côtes-du-Rhône) $9. This blend of 70% Grenache and 30% Syrah features a wonderfully pure nose of ripe fruit. Black cherry and plum flavors continue this theme, washing across the palate with a lushly textured feel. Finishes reasonably long, picking up some spice notes. Drink now. **87 Best Buy** —*J.C. (11/15/2006)*

Domaine Lafond 2003 Roc-Epine La Ferme Romaine Rhône Red Blend (Lirac) $28. This domaine's luxury cuvée shines in 2003, offering a lovely bouquet that balances spice, leather, and dried fruits. Shows the plus side of the 2003 vintage in its great concentration, yet it doesn't seem overdone at all. Plum, black cherry, and spice: this wine has it all. Drink now–2015. Tasted twice, with consistent notes. **92 Editors' Choice** —*J.C. (11/15/2006)*

Domaine Lafond 2005 Roc-Epine Rosé Rosé Blend (Tavel) $17. Tavel is famous for its rosés, and wines like this are the reason. First, there's the beautiful red rose color. Then the complex, inviting bouquet of cherries, peaches, and herbs. Stone fruit flavors are bolstered on the finish by refreshingly cool herb and mineral shadings. A complete package. **89** —*J.C. (6/21/2006)*

DOMAINE LAMARGUE

Domaine Lamargue 2000 Merlot (Vin de Pays d'Oc) $13. The Lamargue offers mixed berries, oak, and sturdy tannins in the mouth, and more of the same (plus a metallic note) on the medium-length finish. The bouquet—chalk and a smoked meatiness, over bright mixed berries—is my favorite part. **85** —*D.T. (2/1/2002)*

DOMAINE LAMY-PILLOT

Domaine Lamy-Pillot 2004 Chardonnay (Chassagne-Montrachet) $49. A fruit-driven wine that balances a flinty character with flavors of green plums. It is fresh, light, poised, crisp, and green. **88** —*R.V. (12/1/2006)*

Domaine Lamy-Pillot 2004 Morgeot Premier Cru Chardonnay (Chassagne-Montrachet) $56. Rich and spiced with wood flavors, this is a rounded, powerful wine. The flavors suggest kiwis and pears leading to vanilla and caramel. It is developing well and is ready to drink. **92** —*R.V. (12/1/2006)*

DOMAINE LAROCHE

Domaine Laroche 1997 Les Blanchots Chardonnay (Chablis) $85. **92** *(11/15/2000)*

Domaine Laroche 2003 Les Clos Grand Cru Chardonnay (Chablis) $75. A big, fat, rich wine with great white currant and white peach flavors. This delicious wine still has fine acidity and just a touch of austerity to give it structure, depth, and potental longevity. **91** —*R.V. (9/1/2005)*

Domaine Laroche 1997 Les Vaillons Viellies Vignes Premier Cru Chardonnay (Chablis) $46. **88** —*J.C. (11/1/2000)*

Domaine Laroche 2003 Premier Cru Les Fourchaumes Chardonnay (Chablis) $40. This is a complex, structured wine. With its rich white stone fruit flavors and touch of chalky minerality, this is going to be a great, complete Chablis. **90** —*R.V. (9/1/2005)*

Domaine Laroche 2003 Reserve de l'Obédience Grand Cru Chardonnay (Chablis) $100. A seductive wine, full of sweet peach and mirabelle flavors, which just hints at acidity. It has certainly gained richness and softness from the weather of 2003: It's round and generous, leaving just a streak of mineral acidity to remind us of its origins. **92** —*R.V. (9/1/2005)*

Domaine Laroche 2003 St. Martin Chardonnay (Chablis) $25. A bit fatter and softer than usual for this wine. Ripe apple and pear flavors dominate, but you still get hints of Chablisian minerality. **86** —*J.C. (9/1/2005)*

DOMAINE LE CLOS DE CAVEAU

Domaine le Clos de Caveau 2003 Clos de Caveau Rhône Red Blend (Vacqueyras) $23. Stunning wine that's among the standard-bearers of the appellation, seamlessly blending bright, raspberry fruit with dried spices into a wonderfully complex whole. Then it pairs the complexity of the bouquet with a creamy, full mouthfeel and a long, satisfying finish. Drink now–2015. **91** —*J.C. (11/15/2006)*

DOMAINE LE CLOS DU CAILLOU

Domaine le Clos du Caillou 2003 Les Quartz Rhône Red Blend (Châteauneuf-du-Pape) $90. The top cuvée from the Domaine le Clos de Caillou takes its name from the stones of quartz which make up the vineyard. This is a deliciously rich wine, which shines with very ripe red fruits and layers of modern tannins. Although the aftertaste is dry, the fruit is already attractive. **90** —*R.V. (12/31/2005)*

DOMAINE LE COLOMBIER

Domaine le Colombier 2004 Vieilles Vignes Rhône Red Blend (Vacqueyras) $15. This impressive blend of 80% Grenache and 20% Syrah admirably showcases the attributes of Vacqueyras, featuring bold red fruit scents accented by clove spice. It's creamy and full-bodied, with raspberry and strawberry fruit buttressed by firm tannins on the finish. Drink now–2012. **90 Best Buy** —*J.C. (11/15/2006)*

DOMAINE LE COUROULU

Domaine le Couroulu 2003 Vieilles Vignes Grenache-Syrah (Vacqueyras) $30. Lovely stuff, boasting knockout aromas of herbal strawberries layered over ripe stone fruit. Flavors follow suit, carried aboard a lush, creamy mouthfeel. Then it finishes long and supple, gliding easily away on supremely ripe tannins. Drink now–2015. **90** —*J.C. (11/15/2006)*

Domaine le Couroulu 2000 Rhône Red Blend (Côtes-du-Rhône) $12. A solid, finely crafted wine, with fleshy ripe fruit, sweet raspberry flavors, and ripe tannins. Ready to drink now. 86 —*R.V. (3/1/2004)*

Domaine le Couroulu 2000 Cuvée Classique Rhône Red Blend (Vacqueyras) $13. Young, ripe fruit with good acidity reveal a promising, solid, tannic wine which will develop well over the next four to five years. 87 —*R.V. (3/1/2004)*

Domaine le Couroulu 2002 Rhône White Blend (Vacqueyras) $12. A soft, fat wine that shows attractive tropical fruits and flavors of sweet herbs, balanced with light acidity. 83 —*R.V. (3/1/2004)*

DOMAINE LEFLAIVE

Domaine Leflaive 2003 Chardonnay (Puligny-Montrachet) $80. For a village wine, this is impressive. The richness and ripeness of the grapes translates into a full wine with white fruit and spice flavors. But quite properly, there is a fine, poised mineral streak from the chalk soil that gives the wine shape and balance. 90 —*R.V. (12/1/2006)*

Domaine Leflaive 2003 Les Pucelles Premier Cru Chardonnay (Puligny-Montrachet) $175. As Anne-Claude Leflaive describes it, this wine is all about the complexity of the vineyard's soil. There is minerality and finesse from the chalk, which gives a structure. And at the same time the ripe fruit seems opulent, with vanilla and spice flavors adding something exotic. Age this wine for at least 5 years. 96 Editors' Choice —*R.V. (12/1/2006)*

DOMAINE LES AMOURIERS

Domaine les Amouriers 2004 Signature Rhône Red Blend (Vacqueyras) $25. Full-bodied, with a creamy texture and bright raspberry fruit that help to balance out the considerable tannic heft. Long on the finish, where it picks up lovely spice nuances. Drink 2009–2015. 91 —*J.C. (11/15/2006)*

DOMAINE LES APHILLANTHES

Domaine les Aphillanthes 2003 Le Cros Rhône Red Blend (Côtes-du-Rhône Villages) $NA. This 100% Syrah from Les Aphillanthes is smoky and slightly herbal, offering wonderfully complex hints to go along with bold blueberry flavors. A bit chunky, but full-bodied and winsome, with fruit flavors that pump out through the long finish. Drink now–2012. 90 Editors' Choice —*J.C. (11/15/2006)*

DOMAINE LES BRUYERES

Domaine les Bruyeres 2004 Syrah (Crozes-Hermitage) $22. Starts with some tarry, almost cola-like notes on the nose, then adds espresso and caramel flavors and a touch of red fruit. Smooth—almost creamy—in texture, but lacks the depth and complexity of the Domaine's Les Croix bottling. 85 —*J.C. (11/15/2006)*

DOMAINE LES GOUBERT

Domaine les Goubert 2000 Cuvée Florence Grenache-Syrah (Gigondas) $50. This prestige cuvée gets the full barrel treatment, and it shows in its aromas of smoke, cedar, tobacco, and molasses. Some plum and earth flavors do poke through on the palate, giving us hope that its evolution will put it into a more balanced place. Hold 4–5 years. 88 —*J.C. (11/15/2005)*

DOMAINE LES HERITIERS DU COMTE LAFON

Domaine les Heritiers du Comte Lafon 2003 Clos de la Crochette Chardonnay (Mâcon-Chardonnay) $29. Features an intriguing nose of honey, musky spice, and clove, balanced on the palate by layers of pear fruit and solid minerality. 86 —*J.C. (11/15/2005)*

DOMAINE LES PALLIÈRES

Domaine les Pallières 2003 Rhône Red Blend (Gigondas) $35. Shows the hot character of the vintage in its extreme ripeness and dense, fudge-like texture. Chocolate and date flavors dominate, but there's also a leavening of leather and spice to provide complexity as well as plentiful but supple tannins. Could use more freshness, but still has great appeal. Drink now–2015. 89 —*J.C. (11/15/2006)*

DOMAINE LONG-DEPAQUIT

Domaine Long-Depaquit 1998 Vaudsir Chardonnay (Chablis) $NA. Beautifully structured, ripe, concentrated wine with fine wood and pure acidity. There's a great sense of structure, giving firmness and a hint of tannins to the wine. Delicious, clean aftertaste. 91 —*R.V. (6/1/2001)*

DOMAINE LOUIS CARILLON

Domaine Louis Carillon 2004 Les Perrières Premier Cru Chardonnay (Puligny-Montrachet) $95. Wood and sweet fruit work together in this ripe, creamy wine. Floral aromas presage vanilla and white fruit flavors with a touch of spice, leaving a full, but still fresh, aftertaste. 92 —*R.V. (12/31/2006)*

DOMAINE MACHARD DE GRAMONT

Domaine Machard de Gramont 2000 Les Nazoires Pinot Noir (Chambolle-Musigny) $NA. Bertrand Machard de Gramont's Chambolle-Musigny is modern in style, with dominating aromas of new wood, spice, and toast. To taste, the fruit is rich, with layers of acidity and flavors of green figs. The pure fruit flavors are supported by the wood. 91 —*R.V. (11/1/2002)*

DOMAINE MARCEL DEISS

Domaine Marcel Deiss 2002 Altenberg de Bergheim Grand Cru Alsace white blend (Alsace) $95. Not labeled as late-harvest, but this wine is noticeably sweet, rich, and mouth-coating. Honey, baked apple, and cinnamon flavors easily glide across the palate, buttressed by just enough acidity to keep it from becoming cloying. Might be best with foie gras or cheese. Drinkable now, but should age effortlessly. 92 —*J.C. (8/1/2006)*

Domaine Marcel Deiss 2001 Grasberg Alsace White Blend (Alsace) $58. An intense, sweet wine, this is packed full of orange flavors, citrus fruits, and a touch of smokiness. A great wine, it's a delicious mix of fruits and mineral characters from the limestone soil of the Grasberg vineyard. 91 —*R.V. (4/1/2005)*

Domaine Marcel Deiss 2000 Huebuhl Alsace White Blend (Alsace) $47. A wine packed with noble rot, giving richness rather than sweetness. An intoxicating blend of smokiness and almonds mixes with flavors of citrus zest and toast in this complex, concentrated wine. From the tiny Huebuhl vineyard in Bergheim. Impressive. 96 Editors' Choice —*R.V. (4/1/2005)*

Domaine Marcel Deiss 2001 Rotenberg Alsace White Blend (Alsace) $47. The 12-acre Rotenberg vineyard in Wintzenheim produces vibrant, racy wines, like this blend of Riesling and Pinot Gris. It is fresh and intense, with concentrated flavors of sweet white currants. 95 —*R.V. (4/1/2005)*

Domaine Marcel Deiss 2002 Schoffweg Alsace White Blend (Alsace) $47. A fine, poised wine, fresh and vibrant, which just demands to be drunk. Flavors of orange zest and white currants are balanced by layers of tannin and acidity. A delicious wine, packed with flavor. 92 —*R.V. (4/1/2005)*

Domaine Marcel Deiss 2001 Bergheim Gewürztraminer (Alsace) $36. Bergheim is particularly noted for its Gewürztraminer, and it is not hard to see why with this concentrated, spicy example. The lychees and smoke aromas set the scene, and the flavors of spice, toast, and exotic spices continue the story. It is relatively restrained at the moment, because it is young, but this will develop impressively over the next five years. 90 —*R.V. (4/1/2005)*

Domaine Marcel Deiss 2001 Saint Hippolyte Gewürztraminer (Alsace) $30. Saint-Hippolyte's vineyards have produced a fresh, light style of Gewürztraminer, which has simple spice and a soft, oily texture that sits well for early drinking. Well-crafted and very drinkable. 87 —*R.V. (4/1/2005)*

Domaine Marcel Deiss 2002 Bennwihr Pinot Blanc (Alsace) $17. A smooth, creamy wine, almost like Chardonnay in its rich butteriness. It has very ripe fruit and toasty accents. This is a delicious, full-bodied expression of Pinot Blanc. 88 —*R.V. (4/1/2005)*

Domaine Marcel Deiss 2002 Bergheim Pinot Blanc (Alsace) $20. Intense vanilla and cream aromas set the scene for a wine that is the apotheosis of Pinot Blanc. It is rich, toasty, full of green plums, and acidity. This concentration of flavor pushes the wine forward to a final explosive, dry finish. 91 Editors' Choice —*R.V. (4/1/2005)*

FRANCE

Domaine Marcel Deiss 2002 Beblenheim Pinot Gris (Alsace) $NA. Very toasty aromas with softness and sweetness to parallel the structure and intensity of this fine Pinot Gris. Big, plump fruits and flavors show in this powerful, concentrated wine that leaves a clean, fresh taste. **90** —*R.V. (2/1/2006)*

Domaine Marcel Deiss 2000 Bergheim Pinot Gris (Alsace) $35. This is ripe, lightly sweet, and very rich. Pepper and exotic spices mingle with the toasty, smoky character of the wine. The fruit is intense, powerful, and very concentrated. **87** —*R.V. (4/1/2005)*

Domaine Marcel Deiss 2001 Sélection de Grains Nobles Pinot Gris (Alsace) $NA. This is not so much a sweet wine (although there is plenty of marmalade flavor here) as it is hugely rich and concentrated. It is like drinking drops of nectar, with honey, dryness, and ripe fruit. At this early stage in its development the richness dominates—it needs time to develop. **95** —*R.V. (2/1/2006)*

Domaine Marcel Deiss 2000 Burlenberg Pinot Noir (Alsace) $34. This pure Pinot Noir is ripe, smoky, toasty, and with a touch of earthiness. Fresh acidity shows through the flavors of ripe strawberries and leaves vibrant red fruits on the palate. **89** —*R.V. (4/1/2005)*

Domaine Marcel Deiss 2002 Beblenheim Riesling (Alsace) $22. This is a perfumed style of Riesling, full of hedgerow aromas and great, fresh acidity. It has a fine structure to go with its delicious fruit, which suggests it will age well. Bone dry, and an excellent food wine. **91** —*R.V. (11/1/2005)*

Domaine Marcel Deiss 2002 Saint-Hippolyte Riesling (Alsace) $25. A wonderful, minerally wine with delicious acidity and crisp apple flavors. This fits well into a scenario of Riesling as great food wine. Its green fruits, light tannic structure, and freshness all make this a fine, drinkable wine. **88** —*R.V. (11/1/2005)*

DOMAINE MARECHAL-CAILLOT

Domaine Marechal-Caillot 1999 Ladoix Cote de Beaune Bordeaux Blend (France) $18. This lovely wine is rich in color, inviting in its blueberry/raspberry scented nose and balanced throughout. Lively fruit is joined by subtle hints of mocha and cocoa, and it makes for an appealing, youthful wine that, nonetheless, has some years ahead of it. **88** —*P.G. (11/1/2002)*

DOMAINE MARECHAL-CAILLOT

Domaine Marechal-Caillot 1999 Pinot Noir (Bourgogne) $15. Simple Bourgogne though it may be, this wine has some stuffing! It sports plump, plummy fruit, soft tannins, and an overall roundness. **87** —*P.G. (11/1/2002)*

DOMAINE MASSAMIER LA MIGNARDE

Domaine Massamier la Mignarde 2005 Cuvée des Oliviers Rhône Red Blend (Vin de Pays des Coteaux de Peyriac) $10. Owned by the Venes family for 300 years, Massamier la Mignarde is an immaculate estate in the Aude department of France. This fresh rosé is a blend of Cinsault, Syrah, and Grenache. It is crisp, light and airy, with a delicious strawberry flavor. Drink now, it won't keep. **87 Best Buy** —*R.V. (12/31/2006)*

DOMAINE MASSON-BLONDELET

Domaine Masson-Blondelet 2004 Les Angelots Sauvignon Blanc (Pouilly-Fumé) $18. This is one of two terroir-based wines from Masson-Blondelet, coming from very minerally soil. It is fresh, taut, tight, and packed with poised fruit. The acidity, green fruit flavors, and the structure all suggest a wine which will age well. **91** —*R.V. (8/1/2006)*

Domaine Masson-Blondelet 2004 Villa Paulus Sauvignon Blanc (Pouilly-Fumé) $18. Masson-Blondelet has produced a sumptuous wine from the softer soils of Pouilly. It is ripe and rich, showing good concentration of green and yellow fruits, along with fine supporting acidity. There's a great depth, and certainly good aging ability. **92 Editors' Choice** —*R.V. (8/1/2006)*

DOMAINE MATHIEU

Domaine Mathieu 2003 Marquis Anselme Mathieu Rhône Red Blend (Châteauneuf-du-Pape) $35. A soft, fresh wine that is almost ready to drink. There are tannins, but the ripe red fruits, the fleshy richness, and the dusty flavors suggest a wine that will develop quickly over the next 3-4 years. **87** —*R.V. (12/31/2005)*

DOMAINE MICHEL BROCK

Domaine Michel Brock 2003 Le Coteau Sauvignon Blanc (Sancerre) $20. Quite fruity, with tropical aromas of pineapple and citrus. Not much mineral or flint, but plenty of soft fruit like pink grapefruit, peach, and melon. A round, warming wine that may not have a ton of verve; yet another softie from 2003. **87** *(7/1/2005)*

DOMAINE MICHEL THOMAS ET FILS

Domaine Michel Thomas et Fils 2005 Sauvignon Blanc (Sancerre) $19. A round, very ripe wine with concentrated, exuberant fruit flavors that leap out of the glass. This is a delicious, attractive wine, but one that should also age well, softening and taming the fresh, fruity acidity. **90** —*R.V. (8/1/2006)*

DOMAINE MICHELAS ST JEMM

Domaine Michelas St Jemm 2003 Syrah (Crozes-Hermitage) $18. Black olives and blackberries here, with the somewhat rustic flavors smoothed out by a full, round mouthfeel. Lacks a little spice and nuance, but shows good power and length on the finish. Drink 2007-2015. **89** —*J.C. (11/15/2006)*

DOMAINE MIQUEL

Domaine Miquel 2000 Merlot (Vin de Pays d'Oc) $9. The nose is a bit smoky, with nuances of pepper and pine needles. A shock of oak forges through the center of the palate, and it wrestles with the light, fading berry flavors. The body and feel seem right, but there's a lack of purity and power that holds it back. **83** —*M.S. (9/1/2003)*

DOMAINE MOILLARD

Domaine Moillard 2003 Corton Charlemagne Chardonnay (Corton-Charlemagne) $120. A huge, rich wine that exudes honey, spice, and cream notes. The wood, though, is more subtle and is a satisfying support to the fruit. **90** —*R.V. (9/1/2005)*

Domaine Moillard 2003 Pinot Noir (Chorey-lès-Beaune) $25. A fresh, perfumed wine with generous amounts of acidity along with red fruit flavors and dry tannins on the finish. **87** —*R.V. (9/1/2005)*

Domaine Moillard 2003 Pinot Noir (Nuits-St.-Georges) $45. This is solid, dark, and dense, with a firm layer of dry tannins balancing the acidity and the dark structure. **87** —*R.V. (9/1/2005)*

Domaine Moillard 2002 Pinot Noir (Savigny-lès-Beaune) $25. Lean and light, with tart cherries and cranberries that race to a crisply acidic finish. **82** —*J.C. (11/15/2005)*

Domaine Moillard 2003 Clos des Grandes Vignes Premier Cru Pinot Noir (Nuits-St.-Georges) $55. A dark, brooding wine that is structured, firm, and dry. Offers black fruit flavors, good acidity, and a very dry, tough finish which should soften out in time. **89** —*R.V. (9/1/2005)*

Domaine Moillard 2003 Epenots Premier Cru Pinot Noir (Pommard) $65. All the power of a ripe, intense Pommard is in this wine. It is well-structured, dense, and rich, balanced with juicy fruit and a solid, dry aftertaste. This is obviously a wine that will age well. **90** —*R.V. (9/1/2005)*

Domaine Moillard 2003 Rouge Pinot Noir (Côte de Nuits-Villages) $28. A firm, dry style of wine with strong tannins and solid, dense fruits. Dark flavors of black plums and damsons are balanced with good acidity. **88** —*R.V. (9/1/2005)*

DOMAINE MONTHELIE-DOUHAIRET

Domaine Monthelie-Douhairet 1999 Clos Le Meix Garnier Monopole Red Blend (Monthelie) $26. Firmly structured, with a smooth mouthfeel and a long finish, this wine needs a few years to relax its tightly wound core of black cherries. Right now, what's showing is mostly spicy, briary notes. **87** *(10/1/2003)*

DOMAINE MOREY COFFINET

Domaine Morey Coffinet 2000 Les Caillerets Premier Cru Chardonnay (Chassagne-Montrachet) $51. Starts off a bit nutty and leesy, with those aromas balanced by white peaches. But once on the palate, lime and mineral flavors surge to the fore, ending long and citrusy. **90** *(10/1/2003)*

FRANCE

DOMAINE OLIVIER MERLIN

Domaine Olivier Merlin 2003 Chardonnay (Saint-Véran) $23. A bit oaky, layered with vanilla and dried spices, but there's also ample richness and weight of fruit to help carry the wine forward. Spices intensify on the long, elegant finish. **88** —*J.C. (11/15/2005)*

DOMAINE OSTERTAG

Domaine Ostertag 2002 Fronholz Riesling (Alsace) $35. A fine, smooth wine, packed with mineral character and power. It also has fine acicity, but that's hard to find under the richness of the fruit. A fresh citric character gives a fine lift to the aftertaste. **89** —*R.V. (11/1/2005)*

Domaine Ostertag 2002 Heissenberg Riesling (Alsace) $39. A smooth, opulent Riesling, from a vineyard whose name literally means "hot mountain." It is hugely ripe, but still has some fine mineral character. The acidity is a little more in question; this could well be a wine that develops relatively quickly. **89** —*R.V. (11/1/2005)*

DOMAINE PASCAL BOUCHARD

Domaine Pascal Bouchard 2002 Special Reserve Bokobsa Chardonnay (Chablis) $32. What happened here? Smells and tastes like butterscotch Life Savers, minus the weight-providing and pleasure-giving sugar. Hollow at the center, too. **80** —*J.C. (4/1/2005)*

DOMAINE PATRICK JAVILLIER

Domaine Patrick Javillier 2004 Cuvée Tête de Murger Chardonnay (Meursault) $78. Blending grapes from two vineyards—Les Case-Têtes (broken heads, so called from the steepness of the slope) and Les Murgers de Monthelie—Patrick Javillier has created a big, bold, ripe wine that keeps a mineral, crisp center. The toast from 11 months in wood is beginning to calm down, and this will age magnificently. **93** —*R.V. (12/1/2006)*

DOMAINE PAUL AUTARD

Domaine Paul Autard 2004 Rhône Red Blend (Côtes-du-Rhône) $14. On the nose, hints of clove accent modest cherry and melon aromas; on the palate, it could use more fruit intensity, but it finishes well, with vibrant leather and spice. **85** —*J.C. (11/15/2006)*

DOMAINE PÉLAQUIÉ

Domaine Pélaquié 2005 Rosé Blend (Tavel) $NA. Slightly lighter in color than the other 2005 Tavels but no less flavorful, this is a balanced, classy wine with cherry and white chocolate notes that harmonize nicely on the nose and the palate. Not too complex; it's like getting comfortable in a familiar chair. **88** —*J.C. (11/15/2006)*

DOMAINE PHILIPPE FAURY

Domaine Philippe Faury 2004 Syrah (Côte Rôtie) $47. This contains a fairly high proportion (10–15%) of Viognier, but still seems more tightly packed than Faury's 100% Syrah Saint-Joseph. It's riper, with more cherry-berry fruit and less meatiness, but still has great floral aromas and hints of pepper on the finish. Drink now–2015. **91** —*J.C. (11/15/2006)*

Domaine Philippe Faury 2004 Vieilles Vignes Syrah (Saint-Joseph) $26. Floral and meaty, yet also filled with rich cassis fruit. Wonderfully complex, with silky—dare I say Burgundian?—tannins. Great complexity; from 40-year-old vines. **90** —*J.C. (11/15/2006)*

DOMAINE PIERRE ANDRÉ

Domaine Pierre André 2003 Chardonnay (Corton-Charlemagne) $NA. A fresh style of wine that seems to miss the portentous weight of a Corton-Charlemagne. It is pleasant and fresh, with some toast, but is really all about green apples and a light feel. **86** —*R.V. (9/1/2005)*

Domaine Pierre André 2003 Pinot Noir (Ladoix) $NA. A softly perfumed wine that has fresh, clean fruit, a lovely silky texture, and just a touch of tannin. Will be ready to drink within two years. **87** —*R.V. (9/1/2005)*

Domaine Pierre André 2003 Château Corton André Clos du Château Pinot Noir (Corton) $NA. A firm, ripe, smoky wine, from the vineyard surrounding the spectacular château of Corton. Dark, brooding, and rich tannins. Big-hearted and powerful, this wine will age well over many years, giving a dense mouthful of fine, juicy fruit. **91** —*R.V. (9/1/2005)*

Domaine Pierre André 2003 Corton-Renardes Pinot Noir (Corton) $NA. A big and dense wine, packed with tannins and black, chocolate flavors. The fruit is huge and generous, while the wood and herbal flavors give complexity. This is a wine to age. **90** —*R.V. (9/1/2005)*

DOMAINE PIERRE USSEGLIO ET FILS

Domaine Pierre Usseglio et Fils 2003 Cuvée de Mon Aïeul Rhône Red Blend (Châteauneuf-du-Pape) $79. Using Aïeul, an old word for grandfather, Thierry and Jean-Pierre Usseglio pay homage to grandpa Pierre. They have made a ripe and juicy wine, with red fruits, some touch of wood, and a light hint of dry tannins to finish. **86** —*R.V. (12/31/2005)*

DOMAINE PINSON

Domaine Pinson 1999 Les Clos Chardonnay (Chablis) $NA. Powerfully ripe wine, with honey and spicy wood aromas. Acidity combines with a smooth, creamy, toast character. Underneath the attractive fruit, there are also tannins and structure. Everything is in perfect harmony and balance. **92** —*R.V. (6/1/2001)*

DOMAINE RAOUL GAUTHERIN ET FILS

Domaine Raoul Gautherin et Fils 1998 Grenouilles Chardonnay (Chablis) $NA. Big, fat, rather clumsy wine, heavy and brash. The wine lacks structure and goes for broad strokes. Drink now. **81** —*R.V. (6/1/2001)*

DOMAINE RAYMOND USSEGLIO ET FILS

Domaine Raymond Usseglio et Fils 2003 Cuvée Impériale Rhône Red Blend (Châteauneuf-du-Pape) $56. Century-old vines are the source of this top cuvée from a 5-acre parcel owned by Raymond Usseglio. It is ripe, with tarry and black fig flavors, along with thyme and herbes de Provence. The tannins are hugely dense, almost impenetrable at this stage, but this will develop into a great wine in 10 years. **93 Cellar Selection** —*R.V. (12/31/2005)*

DOMAINE RENÉ MONNIER

Domaine René Monnier 2004 Chardonnay (Chassagne-Montrachet) $50. Sweet, full fruit flavors and elegance mark this friendly wine. The wood flavors blend effortlessly with the citrus and kiwi fruit, leaving a fresh, lifted aftertaste. The 2004 marks a good return to form after the less successful 2003s from this domaine. **90** —*R.V. (12/1/2006)*

Domaine René Monnier 2004 Les Chevalières Chardonnay (Meursault) $45. More steely than some Meursault, this layers wood and mineral flavors with a fine structure and tastes of apple skins and nutmeg. This wine could age 3–4 years, but it is already delicious. **91** —*R.V. (12/1/2006)*

DOMAINE ROBERT-DENOGENT

Domaine Robert-Denogent 2002 Cuvée Claude Denogent Chardonnay (Pouilly-Fuissé) $38. Very closed after its recent bottling, but shows even more length, minerality, and finesse than Robert-Denogent's other bottlings. I've no doubt it will emerge in several years even better. An incredible Pouilly-Fuissé. **92 Cellar Selection** —*J.C. (11/15/2005)*

Domaine Robert-Denogent 2002 Les Pommards Chardonnay (Saint-Véran) $28. From 45-year-old vines, this spent 20 months in second-use barrels, which imparted a delicate toastiness and vanilla to the concentrated fruit. Honey, apple, and citrus notes blend harmoniously with the ample oak. **89** —*J.C. (11/15/2005)*

Domaine Robert-Denogent 2002 Les Taches Chardonnay (Mâcon-Fuissé) $24. Despite 18 months in wood, the oak isn't that obvious. Instead, there's honey and pineapple, good richness for the Mâcon, and a long, crisp finish. **88** —*J.C. (11/15/2005)*

DOMAINE ROGER SABON

Domaine Roger Sabon 2005 Chapelle de Maillac Rhône Red Blend (Lirac) $20. Better known for his Châteauneuf-du-Pape, Domaine Roger Sabon actually owns more acreage on the Lirac side of the river. This cuvée, made from 40-50-year-old vines, is a big, muscular Lirac marked by hints of tree bark and dark, plummy fruit. Powerful and long on the finish; drink from 2008–2015. **90** —*J.C. (11/15/2006)*

FRANCE

DOMAINE ROMANÉE CONTI

Domaine Romanée Conti 2000 Le Montrachet Chardonnay (Burgundy) $1000. Supple, rich, and elegant, with a silky-rich texture that's backed by a classy core of balanced acidity. Explosive aromas of toast, grilled nuts, and caramelized peaches burst from the glass, while the palate is more about charm and finesse than raw power in this vintage. **93** *(10/1/2003)*

Domaine Romanée Conti 2000 Grands Echezeaux Pinot Noir (Burgundy) $250. Floral, spice, and cinnamon notes are evident up front. Smooth, silky tannins frame an elegant array of tangy cherry, strawberry, pepper, sage, and earth notes. At its core, there is an herbal note suggestive of cluster stems, adding depth and interest. A big step up from the Echézeaux. **93** *(10/1/2003)*

Domaine Romanée Conti 2000 Richebourg Pinot Noir (Burgundy) $375. Exquisitely perfumed. The wine starts off with cherry and spice, including a strong cinnamon component. It's packed with elegance and finesse, yet reveals a rich panoply of flavors: raspberries, bing cherries, spice, plum, allspice, vanilla, and thyme come to mind, all beautifully integrated into a classy, seamless whole. **95** *(10/1/2003)*

Domaine Romanée Conti 2000 Romanee-St.-Vivant Pinot Noir (Burgundy) $350. Mild cherry and herb aromas are followed by a touch of vanilla and chocolate. Somewhat reserved and lean, the wine is nonetheless silky textured, with firm tannins that could use a few years to come into balance. Flavors extend to raspberry, cherry, smoke, herb, and spice, with sweet oak and black tea at the end. **90** *(10/1/2003)*

DOMAINE SAINT AMANT

Domaine Saint Amant 2004 La Borry Viognier (Côtes-du-Rhône) $12. This blend of 95% Viognier and 5% Roussanne is fat and broad on the palate but not particularly floral or spicy. It's a big, neutral white to serve as an apéritif or with fish. **84** —*J.C. (11/15/2006)*

DOMAINE SAINT GAYAN

Domaine Saint Gayan 2001 Rhône Red Blend (Côtes-du-Rhône) $12. This is very superior Côtes-du-Rhône, since the vines are actually in Côtes-du-Rhône-Villages. But winemaker Jean-Pierre Meffre prefers to keep the name simple and the wine uncomplicated. Sweet, ripe fruit, solid tannins, and red fruit flavors make this very attractive. **87** —*R.V. (3/1/2004)*

Domaine Saint Gayan 2000 Rhône Red Blend (Gigondas) $23. A beautifully perfumed wine showing aromas of herbs and wild thyme. Rich, soft, with layers of ripe flavors, black fruits, and solid tannins. Open and soft, and ready to drink in three to five years. **89** —*R.V. (3/1/2004)*

Domaine Saint Gayan 2000 Rhône Red Blend (Châteauneuf-du-Pape) $28. A tiny production of 3,000 bottles makes this a particularly rare wine, but one worth seeking out for its rich, sweet, strawberry flavors and its finely perfumed aromas. **91** —*R.V. (3/1/2004)*

DOMAINE SAINT SIFFREIN

Domaine Saint Siffrein 2005 Rhône Red Blend (Côtes-du-Rhône Villages) $15. Starts with scents of exotic spices, then adds full, rounded flavors of dried fruit and a rich, velvety mouthfeel. Packed with tannins, but they're soft and ripe; try in 1–2 years. **87** —*J.C. (11/15/2006)*

DOMAINE SAINT-PRÉFERT

Domaine Saint-Préfert 2003 Collection Charles Giraud Rhône Red Blend (Châteauneuf-du-Pape) $52. A supremely powerful special cuvée that shows intense, rich, sweet fruit over layers of dark, brooding tannins. Black fruit, dried figs, and quince flavors combine with spice and pepper and wood tastes to produce a huge, long-lasting wine. **93** —*R.V. (12/31/2005)*

DOMAINE SAINTE BARBE

Domaine Sainte Barbe 2003 L'Épinet Chardonnay (Viré-Clessé) $19. Proprietor Jean-Marie Chaland crafts this cuvée from 50-year-old vines that are being transitioned to biodynamie. Smells like honey and spice, then delivers incredible ripe pear flavors and great richness balanced by minerality. Long on the finish. **89** —*J.C. (11/15/2005)*

DOMAINE SALVAT

Domaine Salvat 2000 Rhône Red Blend (Vin de Pays des Côtes Catalanes) $8. From the base of the Pyrenées comes this blend of Merlot, Syrah, and Grenache. The nose offers fresh ripe berries and a hint of citrus rind, but the palate is more dilute and scattered. It also carries a slight pickled taste, probably courtesy of the barrels it was aged in. The texture is good and the tannins are tame, but all in all it just doesn't rise to the occasion. **84** —*M.S. (2/1/2003)*

DOMAINE SANTA DUC

Domaine Santa Duc 2004 Rhône Red Blend (Gigondas) $37. This is one wine I could sit and smell all day, with its incredible black pepper nose and lovely blackberry fruit. May not have quite the richness and density of the 2003 version, but instead displays impeccable balance, freshness, and length. **91** —*J.C. (11/15/2006)*

DOMAINE SANTA DUC

Domaine Santa Duc 2002 Rhône Red Blend (Gigondas) $33. Poured to show it was possible to make good wine in this miserable vintage, this wine doesn't have a lot of stuffing, but is pleasant to drink now. Cedar and vanilla notes frame peppery, spiced cherries. **86** —*J.C. (11/15/2006)*

Domaine Santa Duc 2003 Prestige des Hautes Garrigues Rhône Red Blend (Gigondas) $54. Even though this tips the scales at close to 16% alcohol, there's no trace of heat, just an incredible lush, creamy texture and layers of rich raspberry and blackberry fruit. Hints of coffee and cocoa from two years aging in oak impart nuance, but the old-vine fruit comfortably carries the day. Drink now–2015+. **92** —*J.C. (11/15/2006)*

DOMAINE SERVIN

Domaine Servin 1998 Les Clos Chardonnay (Chablis) $NA. A seriously structured wine, revealing wood and honey flavors currently dominating ripe fruit. A powerful wine which needs time to develop. **89** —*R.V. (6/1/2001)*

DOMAINE SIMONNET

Domaine Simonnet 1999 Les Preuses Chardonnay (Chablis) $NA. Toasty, poised wine with delicious, ripe, and elegant fruit. There is structure which shows right through the wine, forming the base for flavors of vanilla and citrus fruits. **91** —*R.V. (6/1/2001)*

DOMAINE ST. DAMIEN

Domaine St. Damien 2003 Vieilles Vignes Rhône Red Blend (Gigondas) $NA. Features a creamy mouthfeel and supple tannins, but also entirely too much brett influence. Smells and tastes like a well-worn Band Aid. **82** —*J.C. (11/15/2006)*

DOMAINE TINEL-BLONDELET

Domaine Tinel-Blondelet 2004 Genetin Sauvignon Blanc (Pouilly-Fumé) $22. Named after the old word for Sauvignon Blanc, this is a fresh, still young wine, but one that already has complexity. Annick Tinel has produced a wine that has an herbal character as well as one which peels away layer after layer of concentrated fruit. **89** —*R.V. (8/1/2006)*

DOMAINE VACHERON

Domaine Vacheron 2004 Sauvignon Blanc (Sancerre) $27. Creamy aromas and layers of almonds, toast, and spice make this a fascinating wine that continues to reveal new characters. This is the main white from Vacheron, and the intensity of its fruit comes from the almost biodynamic way in which the family's 98-acre vineyard is cultivated. **87** —*R.V. (8/1/2006)*

DOMAINE VALETTE

Domaine Valette 2002 Vieilles Vignes Chardonnay (Mâcon Chaintré) $25. Despite rich aromas of honey and oak, this wine is clean and crisp, with bright pear and citrus flavors and mouthwatering acids. Finishes long and lemony; the perfect foil to fish or poultry. **88** —*J.C. (11/15/2005)*

Domaine Valette 2004 Cuvée des Muletiers Syrah (Saint-Joseph) $28. Rather earthy, with dark flavors of tapenade that never really shine. It's a more somber look at Saint-Joseph that needs herb-roasted meat to make it shine. **84** —*J.C. (11/15/2006)*

FRANCE

DOMAINE VINCENT BOUZEREAU

Domaine Vincent Bouzereau 2004 Chardonnay (Meursault) $49. A clean, fresh, attractively rounded wine that's rich, buttery, and demanding to be drunk. Vincent Bouzereau is one of the many Bouzereaus in Meursault with a tradition of grape growing over many generations. **87** —*R.V. (12/1/2006)*

DOMAINE VINCENT DANCER

Domaine Vincent Dancer 2004 La Romanée Premier Cru Chardonnay (Chassagne-Montrachet) $85. This delicious, crisp wine reveals the more delicate side of Chardonnay. Coming from one of the high vineyards in La Grande Montagne of Chassagne, it has pure, elegant freshness, supplemented by a touch of vanilla. **93** —*R.V. (12/1/2006)*

DOMAINE VINCENT GIRARDIN

Domaine Vincent Girardin 2004 Abbaye de Morgeot Premier Cru Chardonnay (Chassagne-Montrachet) $60. This wine shows crisp citric fruit allied to layers of spicy wood. Then it opens with some ripe white fruits and thirst-quenching acidity. It should age well over 3–4 years. The Abbaye de Morgeot vineyard is in the southern part of the appellation. **89** —*R.V. (12/1/2006)*

Domaine Vincent Girardin 2004 Les Charmes-Dessus Premier Cru Chardonnay (Meursault) $69. The complexities of Burgundy! This is the vineyard next to the more familiar Les Charmes, just up the slope—hence dessus, meaning above. This vineyard gives a mineral character, hinting at Chablis, but with some Meursault richness as well. Hold this wine, with its delicious vanilla flavors, and it will be ready in a year. **93** —*R.V. (12/1/2006)*

Domaine Vincent Girardin 2001 Les Vermots Dessus Chardonnay (Savigny-lès-Beaune) $23. Smoky and toasty up front, this is an attractive wine that ultimately lacks depth. Tart apple and pear fruit finishes lean and grapefruity, providing zip and a nice counterpoint to the heavy-handed oak. **86** —*J.C. (10/1/2003)*

Domaine Vincent Girardin 1999 Vieilles Vignes Les Chanlins Premier Cru Pinot Noir (Pommard) $42. There's plenty of wood influence here, but also a big, burly wine to support it. Plum and coffee, earth and bacon fat and a ruggedly tannic finish give this wine a feel that's akin to New World Pinot or Syrah. **89** —*J.C. (10/1/2003)*

DOMAINE VINCENT SAUVESTRE

Domaine Vincent Sauvestre 2003 Chablis Premier Cru Beauroy Chardonnay (Chablis) $23. **87** —*J.C. (11/15/2005)*

Domaine Vincent Sauvestre 2003 Pinot Noir (Bourgogne) $15. **84** —*J.C. (11/15/2005)*

Domaine Vincent Sauvestre 2002 Bourgogne Pinot Noir (Bourgogne) $11. A bit ruggedly tannic for basic Bourgogne, but with enough stuffing to last the two or three years until it comes around, this is a dark-fruited Pinot. Hints of spice top black cherries, then finish with black tea notes. **86 Best Buy** —*J.C. (11/15/2005)*

Domaine Vincent Sauvestre 2002 Pommard Clos de la Platière Pinot Noir (Pommard) $29. Light and fresh, with cherry-chocolate aromas and flavors that come across slightly confected. Does show some pretty vanilla and cinnamon shadings, and finishes with tart, lingering acidity. **86** —*J.C. (11/15/2005)*

DOMAINE VIRET

Domaine Viret 2003 Emergence Saint-Maurice Rhône Red Blend (Côtes-du-Rhône Villages) $40. Very ripe; it shows a touch of alcoholic warmth, but it's also richly textured, velvety, and supple. Hints of mint and chocolate accent the lush cassis flavors that glide across the palate. A blend of 50% Grenache, 25% Mourvèdre, and 25% Syrah. **91 Editors' Choice** —*J.C. (11/15/2006)*

Domaine Viret 2004 Maréotis Saint-Maurice Rhône Red Blend (Côtes-du-Rhône Villages) $33. This blend of 60% Grenache and 40% Syrah is more structured than the Renaissance bottling. Starts with almond and smoke aromas, then features plenty of plum and blackberry fruit. A bit tough to warm up to, marked by firm tannins and crisp acidity on the finish. **87** —*J.C. (11/15/2006)*

Domaine Viret 2003 Renaissance Saint-Maurice Rhône Red Blend (Côtes-du-Rhône Villages) $22. A blend of 80% Grenache and the rest Syrah and Mourvèdre that matured in vat for close to two years, this is a tremendously spice-driven wine, offering plenty of clove and cinnamon aromatics. Yet it's also round and supple in the mouth, marked by cherry and leather flavors that form a solid base for the spicy complexities. **87** —*J.C. (11/15/2006)*

DOMAINE WEINBACH

Domaine Weinbach 2002 Grand Cru Cuvée Ste Catherine Riesling (Alsace) $68. This wine pairs exceptionally with the Cuvée Ste Catherine L'Inédit. While that wine is at the top of Alsace Rieslings, this is not far behind. It is fatter, less austere, which means it will develop more quickly. But it still has a great pure streak of steely acidity, fresh apples, and a fine, citric and tannic structure. It is, simply, pure Riesling. **93** —*R.V. (5/1/2005)*

Domaine Weinbach 2001 Reserve Personelle Riesling (Alsace) $18. Even Weinbach's simplest Rieslings are full of intense flavors. This wine is floral, with flavors of white fruits along with a racy, crisp acidity. It is complex, concentrated, but essentially dry. **89** —*R.V. (8/1/2003)*

DOMAINE WILLIAM FEVRE

Domaine William Fevre 1999 Les Clos Chardonnay (Chablis) $NA. Ripe, earthy fruit aromas. Balanced wood and ripe, luscious fruit is underlined by a solid, serious structure which suggests excellent aging potential. This has power but also great elegance. Enjoy in five years. **90** —*R.V. (6/1/2001)*

DOMAINE ZIND-HUMBRECHT

Domaine Zind-Humbrecht 2002 Clos Windsbuhl Hunawihr Gewürztraminer (Alsace) $70. A smooth, rich, unctuous wine from the 13-acre Windsbuhl vineyard. It oozes charm, and hides its power underneath its seductive exterior. There is great fruit here, with some hints of acidity as well as flavors of lychees and pepper. **90** —*R.V. (4/1/2005)*

Domaine Zind-Humbrecht 2002 Grand Cru Goldert Gueberschwihr Vendange Tardive Gewürztraminer (Alsace) $123. An intensely sweet wine with layers of dry spice that give it balance. From the rich, fertile Goldert vineyard. This soil character gives it a richness and ripeness already, at this early stage in its development. Still the wine is structured and should age well over 10 years. **93** —*R.V. (4/1/2005)*

Domaine Zind-Humbrecht 2000 Grand Cru Hengst Gewürztraminer (Alsace) $68. **96** —*R.V. (10/1/2002)*

Domaine Zind-Humbrecht 2000 Heimbourg Gewürztraminer (Alsace) $54. **92** —*R.V. (10/1/2002)*

Domaine Zind-Humbrecht 2002 Herrenweg de Turckheim Gewürztraminer (Alsace) $43. A meaty, full-bodied style of wine, with concentrated, spicy flavors. It offers layers of tropical fruits, but the essence is pepper, bergamot, and some tannins. Finishes pleasantly fresh. This could certainly improve with age. **89** —*R.V. (4/1/2005)*

Domaine Zind-Humbrecht 2000 Turckheim Gewürztraminer (Alsace) $320. **88** —*R.V. (10/1/2002)*

Domaine Zind-Humbrecht 2000 Vendange Tardive Grand Cru Clos Saint Urbain Gewürztraminer (Alsace) $NA. **98** —*R.V. (10/1/2002)*

Domaine Zind-Humbrecht 2000 Wintzheim Gewürztraminer (Alsace) $32. **90** —*R.V. (10/1/2002)*

Domaine Zind-Humbrecht 2001 Clos Jebsal Sélection des Grains Nobles Pinot Gris (Alsace) $214. Smoky aromas followed by the explosion of sweet fruits, with flavors of ripe oranges, of wild flower honey, and acidity. This is gorgeous now, but its sweetness should be tamed with aging. A fantastic wine. **96 Editors' Choice** —*R.V. (4/1/2005)*

Domaine Zind-Humbrecht 2000 Clos Windsbuhl Pinot Gris (Alsace) $58. **94** —*R.V. (10/1/2002)*

Domaine Zind-Humbrecht 2002 Clos Windsbuhl Hunawihr Vendange Tardive Pinot Gris (Alsace) $68. A huge, opulent wine that oozes botrytis flavors, yet is not overtly sweet; it's a fine package of richness, dryness, and sweetness. Balancing acidity shows through on the fresh finish. **94** —*R.V. (4/1/2005)*

FRANCE

Domaine Zind-Humbrecht 2002 Grand Cru Clos Saint-Urbain Rangen de Thann Pinot Gris (Alsace) $102. This is a wonderful wine, which comes from the vineyard in the south of Alsace that the Humbrechts brought back from obscurity. It has both intensity and also great elegance. It has flavors of currants, layers of orange zest, and some fresh acidity. But it also has spice which lies gently with the fruit flavors. The taste just goes on forever. **96** —R.V. (4/1/2005)

Domaine Zind-Humbrecht 2002 Heimbourg Turckheim Vendange Tardive Pinot Gris (Alsace) $123. Orange marmalade aromas set the scene for a fresh, intensely sweet wine. It has rich flavors of tropical fruit and coconut, but the acidity still ensures that the wine is in balance. However, it will continue to develop. Try again in 2015. **91** —R.V. (4/1/2005)

Domaine Zind-Humbrecht 2001 Rotenberg Pinot Gris (Alsace) $42. A smooth, fresh wine, with some sweetness but also great, easy flavors of spice, acidity, and tropical fruits. This is one of the less intense of Humbrecht's wines, which lets you enjoy it now. **88** —R.V. (4/1/2005)

Domaine Zind-Humbrecht 2002 Rotenberg Wintzenheim Vendange Tardive Pinot Gris (Alsace) $123. It may not be a Sélection des Grains Nobles, but this still has the intoxicating orange zest and honey aromas. Similiar notes echo on the palate; will need many years to develop. **90** —R.V. (4/1/2005)

Domaine Zind-Humbrecht 2000 Selection des Grains Nobles Heimbourg Pinot Gris (Alsace) $NA. **97** —R.V. (10/1/2002)

Domaine Zind-Humbrecht 2000 Vendange Tardive Clos Jebsal Pinot Gris (Alsace) $75. **96** —R.V. (10/1/2002)

Domaine Zind-Humbrecht 2000 Vendange Tardive Herrenweg de Turckheim Pinot Gris (Alsace) $37. **92** —R.V. (10/1/2002)

Domaine Zind-Humbrecht 2000 Clos Hauserer Riesling (Alsace) $44. **93** —R.V. (10/1/2002)

Domaine Zind-Humbrecht 2000 Grand Cru Brand Riesling (Alsace) $85. **96** —R.V. (10/1/2002)

Domaine Zind-Humbrecht 2000 Grand Cru Brand Vendange Tardive Riesling (Alsace) $NA. **95** —R.V. (10/1/2002)

Domaine Zind-Humbrecht 2002 Grand Cru Clos Saint Urbain Rangen de Thann Riesling (Alsace) $103. With its tiny chapel, the Clos Saint Urbain is one of the great Alsace landmarks. On possibly the steepest vineyard in the region, the Humbrechts are able to make some of the greatest wines. It may be labeled Riesling, but the spiciness of this wine makes it almost like a Pinot Gris. It is so hugely rich that it is easy to lose track of its dryness and its fine structure, its acidity and its intense flavors of exotic fruits. **94** —R.V. (11/1/2005)

Domaine Zind-Humbrecht 2002 Heimbourg Riesling (Alsace) $57. From this Turckheim vineyard, close to the Brand grand cru vines, this is a big, rich wine, packed with great honeysuckle aromas, good acidity and spice accents. It is huge, but should age well. **90** —R.V. (11/1/2005)

Domaine Zind-Humbrecht 2000 Herrenweg de Turckheim Riesling (Alsace) $37. **92** —R.V. (10/1/2002)

Domaine Zind-Humbrecht 2000 Vendange Tardive Clos Windsbuhl Riesling (Alsace) $90. **93** —R.V. (10/1/2002)

Domaine Zind-Humbrecht NV Zind White Blend (Vin de Table Francais) $29. A blend of Chardonnay, Pinot Blanc, and Pinot Auxerrois which, under French law, is a Vin de Table because the Chardonnay is not permitted in Alsace. But Humbrecht makes sure you know the vintage by labeling it Z002 (get it?). It's a ripe wine, with very pure, concentrated fruit, a touch of spice, and finishing acidity. **87** —R.V. (4/1/2005)

DOMAINES GRASSA

Domaines Grassa 2005 Sauvignon Sauvignon Blanc (Vin de Pays des Côtes de Gascogne) $6. A fresh, creamy style of Sauvignon Blanc, with tropical fruits combining with apple skins and leading to a ripe but crisp finish. A great apéritif. **84** —R.V. (12/31/2006)

DOMAINES OTT

Domaines Ott 1997 Château De Selle Rouge Rhône Red Blend (Côtes de Provence) $34. **84** —M.S. (5/1/2000)

Domaines Ott 1998 Les Domaniers de Calignade Rhône Red Blend (Côtes de Provence) $11. **84** —M.S. (5/1/2000)

Domaines Ott 1998 Château De Selle Clair de Noir Rosé Blend (Côtes de Provence) $29. **89** —M.S. (5/1/2000)

Domaines Ott 2004 Clos Mireille Blanc de Blancs White Blend (Côtes de Provence) $20. Purchased by the Roederer Champagne group last year, this venerable Provence estate produces a fresh and crisp white that belies its hot origins. This 2004, a blend of Sémillon and Ugni Blanc, is in a lightly wooded style with fresh acidity and full flavors of melons and pears. **88** —R.V. (12/31/2006)

DOMAINES POCHON

Domaines Pochon 2004 Etienne Pochon Syrah (Crozes-Hermitage) $17. Starts off rather dark, marked by smoke, charred wood, espresso, and black olive notes. But there's a core of fruit and spice as well. Feels plump and round in the mouth, but lacks great depth or structure. Drink now for its pretty finish filled with spice and tea leaves. **87** —J.C. (11/15/2006)

DOMAINES SCHLUMBERGER

Domaines Schlumberger 1998 Cuvée Christine Vendange Tardive Gewürztraminer (Alsace) $72. An atypically elegant Gewürztraminer, one that achieves great delicacy without sacrificing varietal typicity or flavor. Honeyed pineapples and pears are graced by notes of spice and rose petals. Finishes without any trace of bitterness. Quite sweet, so best with foie gras or cheeses. Drink now-2010, possibly beyond. **91** —J.C. (1/1/2005)

Domaines Schlumberger 2003 Fleur Gewürztraminer (Alsace) $28. Soft, verging on flabby, with decent honey and pear flavors that finish without much lift or vibrancy. Good, but nothing more. **83** —J.C. (11/1/2005)

Domaines Schlumberger 2001 Fleur Gewürztraminer (Alsace) $22. Pungent but scattered aromas lead to spicy melon and banana flavors. In terms of feel, it's soft and a touch lazy on the palate. It doesn't hold up to heavy scrutiny. **85** —M.S. (12/31/2003)

Domaines Schlumberger 2002 Grand Cru Kessler Gewürztraminer (Alsace) $40. Oily and musky on the nose, giving the impression of great concentration and ripeness—an impression that's borne out by the impressively rich pear and honey flavors. Slightly sweet, but balanced by good minerality. **90** —J.C. (11/1/2005)

Domaines Schlumberger 2001 Grand Cru Kessler Gewürztraminer (Alsace) $32. Mineral and floral aromas waft on the nose. The mouthfeel is lively and silky, with a light dressing of menthol over buttery tropical fruit. Finishes with a hint of peppery spice. **89** (6/1/2004)

Domaines Schlumberger 2002 Grand Cru Kitterlé Gewürztraminer (Alsace) $54. Fat almost to the point of being flabby, this is an intensely aromatic Gewürztraminer loaded with slightly chemical, peppery scents and overtones of honey. Melon fruit gives the roundness on the palate, then finishes soft and easy. **87** —J.C. (8/1/2006)

Domaines Schlumberger 2000 Grand Cru Saering Gewürztraminer (Alsace) $32. Light, lemony, and fairly simple, but all the time fresh and friendly. Tart apple along with honey and lychee carry the palate into a balanced, mouth-filling finish that delivers more texture than flavor. Shows true Gewürz character but not full-force flavor. **86** —M.S. (12/31/2003)

Domaines Schlumberger 2000 Pinot Blanc (Alsace) $14. A delightful wine that makes you think of springtime, green apples, and baklava! I mean the nutty, cinnamon, and honey flavors. Vibrant acidity sets it off, and it's just the tiniest bit sweet. **87** —S.H. (1/1/2002)

Domaines Schlumberger 2002 Les Princes Abbés Pinot Blanc (Alsace) $14. Plump in the mouth, this is a straightforward wine but a clean, fresh, enjoyable one. Aromas are of yellow stone fruit and citrus. It offers core flavors of grapefruit and orange, couched in a soft cloud of honey. **86** (6/1/2004)

Domaines Schlumberger 1998 Cuvée Clarisse Sélection de Grains Nobles Pinot Gris (Alsace) $72. Burnt sugar notes cover up the densely packed apricot and peach that's lurking at the core. The palate is an amalgam of stone fruits and syrups, and the layered finish has a fine feel. It lacks some harmony, depth, and complexity, but it's a rich, creamy wine. **87** —M.S. (10/1/2003)

FRANCE

Domaines Schlumberger 2002 Grand Cru Kitterlé Pinot Gris (Alsace) $44. A beautiful wine, balancing acidity, spice, and fresh peach flavors with structure and ageability. This brings out all the characters of great Pinot Gris, elegance and power combining in harmony. 94 —R.V. (2/1/2006)

Domaines Schlumberger 2000 Grand Cru Kitterlé Pinot Gris (Alsace) $38. Stumbles a little coming out of the gate, revealing hints of shoe polish and burnt rubber, but gathers itself midpalate with intense flavors of muskmelon and orange marmalade and finishes strong, ending on a hint of Earl Grey tea. 87 —J.C. (2/1/2005)

Domaines Schlumberger 1998 Grand Cru Kitterlé Pinot Gris (Alsace) $37. Ripe, but with no evidence of botrytis. There's some baked apple to the nose, but otherwise it's simple and clean. Tasty peach, apricot, and cinnamon control the pure palate, and then on the back end it's light and smooth. 90 —M.S. (10/1/2003)

Domaines Schlumberger 2002 Grand Cru Spiegel Pinot Gris (Alsace) $26. A full, fresh wine, with very ripe, apricot fruit. This is generous, packed with spice and lychee flavors and with fine balancing acidity. 91 —R.V. (2/1/2006)

Domaines Schlumberger 2002 Les Princes Abbés Pinot Gris (Alsace) $21. Fat and flamboyant on the palate, with tropical fruit and floral flavors and a rich feel. One to try when you think Gewürz is the answer—bring on the pad thai. 87 (6/1/2004)

Domaines Schlumberger 1999 Spiegel Pinot Gris (Alsace) $32. Smells of sunflowers and nuts, and tastes like flowers and honey in a glass, with peach fruit at the core. Finishes firm, with apricot flavors. 89 (6/1/2004)

Domaines Schlumberger 1998 Vendange Tardive Pinot Gris (Alsace) $52. Honey, toast, and marmalade combine in this delicately sweet wine. There are currant flavors, acidity, herbs, and some spice. A fine wine that remains fresh and crisp. 89 —R.V. (2/1/2006)

Domaines Schlumberger 1999 Cuvée Ernest Sélection de Grains Nobles Riesling (Alsace) $72. In short supply; only 1,000 bottles were produced from 40-year-old vines that are about to be replanted, so you better grab it if you find it. As Beydon-Schlumberger tells it, 80 people picked grapes for this wine over two days. Has the most singular aroma—a combination of resin, tulips or violets, bergamot, and clarified butter. Taut and moderately sweet in the mouth, there's hay and grapefruit flavors at palate entry that explode into fleshy nectarine and peaches. Firm and long on the finish. 91 Cellar Selection (6/1/2004)

Domaines Schlumberger 1999 Grand Cru Kitterlé Riesling (Alsace) $38. Renowned for its Riesling, the Kitterlé vineyard in Guebwiller benefits from southern exposure, meaning the fruit is generally able to ripen. This 1999 is impressive in its developing complexity, showing layers of petrol, fine acidity, minerality, and elegance. Give it another three or four years. 91 —R.V. (11/1/2005)

Domaines Schlumberger 2002 Grand Cru Saering Riesling (Alsace) $23. Blasts from the glass with intense apple and mineral aromas, followed by full-bodied (but not heavy) flavors on the palate. Picks up a hint of anise in the mouth, then finishes long, with lingering notes of fruit and mineral oil. This explosive wine is drinking well already, but should age gracefully over at least the next 5–7 years. 91 Editors' Choice —J.C. (11/1/2005)

Domaines Schlumberger 2000 Grand Cru Saering Riesling (Alsace) $18. Beydon-Schlumberger calls this grand cru "democratic" and says that "people who don't know Riesling will like it." People who know Riesling will like it just the same. Flavors are of pear, with hints of pistachio, olive oil, and peach skin. It's medium-weight and finishes with some length. 89 (6/1/2004)

Domaines Schlumberger 2003 Les Princes Abbés Riesling (Alsace) $20. In 2003, Schlumberger only bottled one grand cru Riesling, leaving the fruit from Saering and Kessler to help beef up this wine. It's a plump yet minerally take on Riesling, with lime, apple, and melon aromas and flavors accented by a dry, minerally feel. Picks up a hint of anise on the finish. 87 —J.C. (8/1/2006)

Domaines Schlumberger 2002 Les Princes Abbés Riesling (Alsace) $20. For its relatively lowly status in the hierarchy of Domaines Schlumberger's wines, this is an excellent, fresh, floral wine with great acidity and lemon zest flavors. Bone dry, it is ready to drink now, but should improve over the short term. 88 —R.V. (11/1/2005)

Domaines Schlumberger 1998 Princes Abbes Riesling (Alsace) $16. So pure, so Riesling. Pine nuts, wild forest flowers, baked custard (botrytis?), lemon and lime, mineral (slate, granite). Richly textured, very dry with real tartness in the finish, and great acid that bites into the palate. A joy to drink. 91 —S.H. (1/1/2002)

DOPFF & IRION

Dopff & Irion 2000 Grand Cru Vorbourg Gewürztraminer (Alsace) $32. Here's a Gewürztraminer that's slightly viscous in the mouth, plump but not heavy, with a mouth-watering, refreshing finish. Pear and melon aromas lead into textbook lychee flavors. 88 —J.C. (2/1/2005)

Dopff & Irion 1998 Les Tonnelles Pinot Noir (Alsace) $19. 86 —M.S. (11/1/2000)

Dopff & Irion 2001 Grand Cru Schoenenbourg Riesling (Alsace) $32. There's a hint of kerosene to this wine's ripe, yet minerally, aromas. Shows a muscular, sturdy structure in the mouth, which should allow it age gracefully, slowly evolving from melon and pear fruit to exhibit the more mineral aspects it displays on the finish. 91 Editors' Choice —J.C. (2/1/2005)

Dopff & Irion 1995 Schoenenbourg Riesling (Alsace) $30. 81 —J.C. (12/31/1999)

Dopff & Irion 1997 Tokay Pinot Gris (Alsace) $16. 84 (8/1/1999)

Dopff & Irion 2002 Les Maquisards Tokay Pinot Gris (Alsace) $25. From the domaine of Dopff et Irion in Riquewihr, this wine is pleasantly soft and clean, with some good acidity and a touch of toastiness. It's ripe and easy to drink. 85 —R.V. (2/1/2006)

Dopff & Irion 2003 Crustaces White Blend (Alsace) $11. As the name suggests, this would be a solid option with shellfish. Green apple and pear scents carry just a whiff of honey, while the body is light and the flavors spare and minerally, finishing with a touch of grapefruit. 85 —J.C. (2/1/2005)

DOPFF AU MOULIN

Dopff Au Moulin 1996 Reserve Tokay Pinot Gris (Alsace) $19. 86 (8/1/1999)

DOURTHE

Dourthe 2003 Numéro 1 Bordeaux White Blend (Bordeaux) $10. Dourthe's branded Bordeaux is one of the best around, and this white from vintage 2003 is no exception. With its ripe, honeyed fruit, it is delicious both as an apéritif and as a food wine. Layers of soft creaminess are backed by fine crisp acidity. 88 Best Buy —R.V. (6/1/2005)

DUJAC FILS & PÈRE

Dujac Fils & Père 2001 Chardonnay (Meursault) $44. Nutty and toasty, but even those notes are muted and modest. Not much going on here—a real disappointment from a big name in Burgundy. 82 —J.C. (12/1/2005)

DULONG

Dulong 1999 Merlot (Vin de Pays d'Oc) $8. Medium-bodied and even, this Merlot's blackberry, black olive, and oak aromas follow through on the palate. Dark and brooding, a good everyday choice. 84 —D.T. (2/1/2002)

DUVAL-LEROY

Duval-Leroy 1990 Blanc de Chardonnay Champagne Blend (Champagne) $42. A young wine, still very green and crisp, this shows great potential. When its acidity and the dosage have blended together, this will be a rich, but elegant wine, with flavors of crisp white currants, and a touch of almonds. Great acidity gives this a fine, clean aftertaste. 87 —R.V. (12/1/2004)

Duval-Leroy NV Brut Champagne Blend (Champagne) $24. Run today by Carol Duval, one of the Champagne "widows" who seem to appear at critical moments in the history of Champagne houses, the quality of Duval-Leroy gets better every year. The fruit of this nonvintage wine is dominated by Chardonnay, pure, fresh, and crisp, with lovely refreshing acidity at the end. 88 —R.V. (12/1/2001)

FRANCE

Duval-Leroy 1995 Brut Champagne Blend (Champagne) $42. About two-thirds Chardonnay and one-third Pinot Noir, this is a soft, round, and fruity wine, with supple, silky flavors that lay out broadly across the palate. Lush and creamy, it seduces with big, forward fruit, rich enough to pair with salmon. **90** —*P.G. (12/15/2002)*

Duval-Leroy 1995 Femme Brut Champagne Blend (Champagne) $120. Fresh and toasty, with a medium-strength nose that pushes some aged notes, a touch of hard cheese, and more. Spicy apple and pear flavors are true and satisfying, and the finish deals a pleasing mix of vanilla, spice, and texture. Elevated and lasting. Should be good through 2013. **95** —*M.S. (12/31/2005)*

Duval-Leroy NV Paris Brut Champagne Blend (Champagne) $28. New in America, Duval-Leroy is set to make a splash with its bold, artistic "Paris" bottle, silk-screened by artist Leroy Neiman. A 40/60 Chardonnay/Pinot blend, it carries scents of honeysuckle, hazelnut, and vanilla into a fresh, flavorful, and persistent middle. Hints of mint and even mint julep roll around the tongue, keeping the flavors lively and interesting. **92 Editors' Choice** —*P.G. (12/15/2002)*

Duval-Leroy NV Rosé de Saignée Brut Champagne Blend (Champagne) $40. A very pretty copper color, just faintly tinged with pink. It's a sensuous, spicy wine with forward, pretty aromas of strawberry, raspberry, and sweet cherry. It doesn't fade in the mouth; there is real concentration here all the way through. It actually seems to build intensity as it sails into the long, graceful finish. **91** —*P.G. (12/1/2006)*

Duval-Leroy 1996 Blanc de Chardonnay Chardonnay (Champagne) $32. Some gunmetal scents are followed by flavors of ripe fruit, just bordering on over-ripe. Definitely a California style, with early signs of oxidation making for a fleshy, forward, succulently fruity wine. Ready to go right now. **90** —*P.G. (12/15/2002)*

Duval-Leroy NV Brut Rosé Pinot Noir (Champagne) $32. A wonderful discovery, spicy and pungent, with forward, very fresh, and pretty aromas of strawberry, raspberry and light cherry fruit. Vivid, vivaciou,s and very nicely balanced, this wine invites sip after delicious sip with its lively, crisp finish. **90** —*P.G. (12/15/2002)*

E. BARNAUT

E. Barnaut NV Blanc de Noirs Brut Champagne Blend (Champagne) $27. A rich wine with yeasty aromas; also tart, raspberry acidity that balances the almost chunky, full-bodied character of the palate. It could do with some more subtlety, but it's still a fine match for food. **86** —*R.V. (12/1/2002)*

E. GUIGAL

E. Guigal 2005 Marsanne (Crozes-Hermitage) $20. The 2005 vintage produced whites in the Rhône that are more immediately accessible, though probably shorter-lived, than the 2004s. Guigal's 2005 Crozes features open, slightly floral aromas backed by some deeper bass notes. Delicate apricot and melon flavors spread elegantly across the palate, while there's a mineral edge to the persistent finish. Reasonably priced. **88** —*J.C. (11/15/2006)*

E. Guigal 2001 Marsanne (Saint-Joseph) $28. This nondescript Marsanne boasts waxy, paraffin-like aromas alongside hints of lemon rind and smoke. Opens up to reveal some melon and citrus on the palate before finishing with hints of anise and beeswax. Might develop in time, might not. **85** *(2/1/2005)*

E. Guigal 2000 Lieu-dit Saint-Joseph Marsanne (Saint-Joseph) $28. From a small vineyard which was the original heart of the Saint-Joseph appellation, Guigal can now make what it jokingly calls the Saint-Joseph de Saint-Joseph. This rich, concentrated wine, with 50% new wood aging, is dominated by ripe apricot and new wood flavors. The wood should soften, but the apricots should become even more generous. **90** —*R.V. (6/1/2002)*

E. Guigal 2003 Rhône Red Blend (Gigondas) $25. Mature, but in no danger of senility, Guigal's 2003 Gigondas is a full-bodied, creamy-textured wine that reflects the ripeness of the vintage. Garrigue and leather notes accent black cherries, while the long, spicy finish adds hints of coffee and caramel. Drink now–2010. **90 Editors' Choice** —*J.C. (11/15/2006)*

E. Guigal 2001 Rhône Red Blend (Châteauneuf-du-Pape) $45. Smells leathery and a bit over-ripe, with scents of dried fruit outweighing fresh-ness. The leather and dried cherry flavors linger enticingly on the finish, but show a trace of alcoholic warmth as well. A solid wine, but a disappointing effort from the Rhône's most famous and reliable négociant. **86** —*J.C. (2/1/2005)*

E. Guigal 1999 Rhône Red Blend (Hermitage) $55. A massive wine, with its opaque, dense purple color, its huge tannins and its tight, powerful structure. When it develops—maybe in 10 or 15 years' time—the perfumed, juicy Syrah fruits that are just suggested for the moment are going to be as dominant as the tannins are now. What a wine it will be then. **95** —*R.V. (6/1/2002)*

E. Guigal 1999 Brune et Blonde Rhône Red Blend (Côte Rôtie) $40. The perfect combination of elegance and purity of fruit give this famous wine, a blend of fruit from both slopes of the hills above Ampuis, a great sense of style as well as power. The Syrah perfumes, at their richest and coolest, combine with black fruits to give an overwhelming impression of immense fruit flavors. **94** —*R.V. (6/1/2002)*

E. Guigal 1998 Château d'Ampuis Rhône Red Blend (Côte Rôtie) $90. This wine spends 38 months in new wood, and the question is whether the fruit can support it. Yes, but barely, since the spice, tannins, and dryness all come from the wood, not the fruit. Maybe in 10 years' time there will be a chance for black fruits and the perfumed flavors to come through. **91** —*R.V. (6/1/2002)*

E. Guigal 1998 La Mouline Rhône Red Blend (Côte Rôtie) $175. Even though the 42 months this wine has spent in new wood give it an intensely toasty character, the enormously soft, perfumed fruits and ripe, sweet flavors that go along with the wood produce a finely tuned, balanced wine that should age well over many years. As an expression of pure Syrah, there are few better. **96** —*R.V. (6/1/2002)*

E. Guigal 2004 Rhône White Blend (Côtes-du-Rhône) $12. Guigal has turned in a fine Côtes-du-Rhône blanc in 2004, with crisp acids that provide focus and verve to the pear and citrus flavors. It's not a heavyweight, but still boasts a slightly creamy texture and a hint of peppery spice on the finish. **86** —*J.C. (11/15/2006)*

E. Guigal 2000 Rhône White Blend (Condrieu) $35. A big, ripe, oily wine with apricots and overpowering perfumes of exotic spices. Unusual for a Condrieu, this is completely dry, and the sweetness comes from super-ripe, almost botrytised grapes which give it a hint of honey. Spice and new wood complete the package. **90** —*R.V. (6/1/2002)*

E. Guigal 2000 La Doriane Rhône White Blend (Condrieu) $60. Unlike so many Condrieus, this is a wine that needs to be aged. From a parcel of land in the south end of the Condrieu appellation, this vintage is currently dominated by new wood. But under that, there is elegant, spicy fruit with delicious flavors of ripe pears and peaches. Just a hint of acidity gives it structure and considerable potential for aging. **92** —*R.V. (6/1/2002)*

E. Guigal 2003 Syrah (Crozes-Hermitage) $22. This wine seems to have evolved quickly, going from dark and sturdily tannic in June to more perfumed and lighter-bodied in August. I'm happy to report that the changes have been largely for the better, although I have mild concerns about the wine's potential longevity. It now has a bouquet of fresh flowers, herbs, and flavors to match. Harmoniously blends amounts of florality, meatiness, spice, and fruit. Drink now–2010. **90 Editors' Choice** —*J.C. (11/15/2006)*

E. Guigal 2002 Syrah (Hermitage) $75. Big black fruit aromas on this serious, intense, and concentrated wine, which is a blend from different Hermitage vineyards. It shows acidity and firm structure, with some leathery character. Great, solid dark fruits, and prominent wood flavors show how this wine has potential—aging for 10 years at least. **90** —*R.V. (2/1/2005)*

E. Guigal 2001 Syrah (Crozes-Hermitage) $20. From its aromas of black pepper and cured meats, this wine screams Syrah. Of course, it tastes like syrah too, yielding flavors of blackberries, black pepper, and air-dried beef. A bit leaner and less generous on the palate than Guigal's Saint-Joseph, but still an impressive effort, with a firm structure and modest tannins on the finish. Drink 2006–2012. **87** *(2/1/2005)*

E. Guigal 1999 Syrah (Crozes-Hermitage) $15. Surprisingly, considering the importance of Guigal in the region, this is the first time the producer

FRANCE

has made a Crozes-Hermitage. But they have certainly started with a fine bang, with this finely perfumed wine, bringing together ripe fruit, acidity and sweet, jelly flavors. There are even tannins to give it structure and concentration. **89** —*R.V. (6/1/2002)*

E. Guigal 1999 Lieu-dit Saint-Joseph Syrah (Saint-Joseph) $28. Apart from the fact that this wine comes from a small parcel that is itself called Saint-Joseph, the other curiosity of this wine is its label, which is designed like a banknote, by the man who used to design French francs (now, of course, out of a job). The wine inside the bottle is powerful and concentrated, flavored heavily with new wood, vanilla, and spicy fruits. Guigal believes it is possible to make great Saint-Joseph, and this wine certainly proves the point. **93** —*R.V. (6/1/2002)*

E. Guigal 2003 Viognier (Condrieu) $45. Lovely soft, easy fruit, show up the fresh, fragrant style of Condrieu, despite coming from the hot 2003 vintage. Spice and wood show through the flavors of apricots and honey, leaving a smooth, oily texture to finish. This would be great with Asian food. **90** —*R.V. (2/1/2005)*

EMMANUEL DARNAUD

Emmanuel Darnaud 2004 Les Trois Chênes Syrah (Crozes-Hermitage) $25. An excellent effort from young Emmanuel Darnaud, offering good richness and texture to go with pepper-laden cherry aromas. It's plump and mouth-filling—especially for a 2004—with silky tannins on the lingering finish. Drink now–2015. **90** —*J.C. (11/15/2006)*

ERIC & JOEL DURAND

Eric & Joel Durand 1999 Empreintes Rhône Red Blend (Cornas) $37. A huge, ink-black wine with all the brooding majesty that gives Cornas its reputation. A blockbuster with enormous rich, sweet tannins. At the end it is the quality of the super-ripe fruit from old vines that dominates, but it is certainly a wine to keep for generations. **95** —*R.V. (6/1/2002)*

Eric & Joel Durand 2004 Les Coteaux Syrah (Saint-Joseph) $NA. Black cherries are subtly perfumed with ground black pepper, and then carried across the palate aboard a round, mouth-filling wine bolstered by creamy-textured tannins. Nothing at all to dislike here. Drink now. **90** —*J.C. (11/15/2006)*

Eric Rocher 2004 Terroir de Champal Syrah (Saint-Joseph) $28. Marked by slightly green flavors, that range from unroasted coffee beans to *poivre vert*. Crisp blackberry fruit is tart and a bit hard. Hold until 2008 and hope for positive evolution. **84** —*J.C. (11/15/2006)*

ERIC TEXIER

Eric Texier 1999 Syrah (Côtes-du-Rhône) $15. 82 *(1/1/2004)*

ERNST BURN

Ernst Burn 1997 Tokay Pinot Gris (Alsace) $18. 88 *(8/1/1999)*

ESPRIT DE CHEVALIER

Esprit de Chevalier 2000 Bordeaux Blend (Pessac-Léognan) $35. 83 —*J.C. (6/1/2005)*

ETIENNE SAUZET

Etienne Sauzet 2004 Chardonnay (Chassagne-Montrachet) $53. This is a lively, fresh wine with good acidity, a touch of toast under the fruit, and a great burst of energy and zing in the aftertaste. **89** —*R.V. (12/1/2006)*

Etienne Sauzet 2004 Chardonnay (Puligny-Montrachet) $57. Rich, buttery, and forward, but with a fine streak of minerality to give structure and interest. The wood gives a spicy character to the wine, but it doesn't dominate the rich burst of fruit. **90** —*R.V. (12/1/2006)*

Etienne Sauzet 2004 Chardonnay (Bâtard-Montrachet) $228. A wine of promise, but still in its infancy. This grand cru, structured and still waiting to open to its full opulence, is packed with concentrated flavors. It's a powerhouse that needs at least five years to even begin to show its structure, ripe fruit, and richness. **95** —*R.V. (12/1/2006)*

Etienne Sauzet 2004 Les Combettes Premier Cru Chardonnay (Puligny-Montrachet) $119. The most well-known of Puligny's premier cru vineyards, Les Combettes is at the very heart of the slope. This central position shows in this dense and concentrated wine that's big, powerful, and marked by fresh fruit salad flavors of green figs, green apple, and

spice. The whole is borne up by a fine, solid structure of wood and tannins. **94** —*R.V. (12/1/2006)*

Etienne Sauzet 2004 Les Perrières Premier Cru Chardonnay (Puligny-Montrachet) $89. Elegance is the hallmark of this wine, which flows round the mouth with generous flavors but still leaves a fresh, crisp aftertaste. Green apples, spice, and wood all balance well. **91** —*R.V. (12/1/2006)*

EUGÈNE KLIPFEL

Eugène Klipfel 2004 Grand Cru Kirchberg Tokay Pinot Gris (Alsace) $NA. Meaty, smoky aromas dominate the first approach to this wine. At this stage, it still needs to come together, with white fruits sitting apart from the spice. It is a dry wine, fresh, and rather lightweight. **84** —*R.V. (2/1/2006)*

F. CHAUVENET

F. Chauvenet 2000 Les Jumelles Chardonnay (Mâcon-Villages) $10. Tired, and acquiring a smoky, petrolly note to show for it. There's still some lemon and green apple flavors at the core, finishing with juicy acidity. **83** —*J.C. (10/1/2003)*

FAIVELEY

Faiveley 2004 Chardonnay (Mâcon-Prissé) $15. Plump and honeyed, this is a solid offering from a region in which Faiveley can't fall back on its vineyards. Pear, apple, and honey flavors finish soft, with gentle chalky nuances. Drink now. **86** *(11/1/2006)*

Faiveley 2001 Chardonnay (Puligny-Montrachet) $NA. Rather lean and sharp, a young Chardonnay marked by high acidity and even some tannins. Below all that is lemon and grapefruit, slightly softened with honey. Seems thin for the vintage, although it could pick up additional charm with age. **87** —*S.H. (1/1/2002)*

Faiveley 2004 Clos Rochette Chardonnay (Mercurey) $24. Notes of toast and smoky quartz show on the nose, then add pear and apple flavors on the palate. From a Faiveley monopole in Mercurey, this shows a fair amount of minerality on the finish and a plump palate presence. Drink now and over the next few years. **88** *(11/1/2006)*

Faiveley 2001 Georges Faiveley Chardonnay (Bourgogne) $NA. A sweetly limpid wine, a bit simple but with charm. Ripe peach and lemon flavors are framed in zesty acids, ending with a rich, honeyed flourish. **86** —*S.H. (1/1/2002)*

Faiveley 2003 Pinot Noir (Nuits-St.-Georges) $53. The wines of Faiveley avoid the raisiny notes found in many 2003 red Burgundies. This wine shows plenty of ripe Pinot character—dark cherries. plums, and chocolate—but also astringent tannins that give it a tough exterior. If these integrate better with time, this rating may look conservative, but there's no guarantee here. **86** —*J.C. (9/1/2006)*

Faiveley 2004 Domaine de la Croix Jacquelet Pinot Noir (Mercurey) $21. Shows some rustic spicy and herbal notes, along with strawberry and herbal tea flavors. Light in body, and a bit tart and tannic on the finish, this lacks the generosity shown by the other 2004 reds in the lineup. **84** *(11/1/2006)*

Faiveley 2003 Joseph Faiveley Pinot Noir (Bourgogne) $17. A bit herbal on the nose, but unlike some 2003s, it retains a sense of freshness, avoiding any baked character. It's crisp and tart in the mouth, too, with snappy cherry flavors that carry a fair amount of tannic grip. Maybe a bit too stern, but structure is part of the house style at Faiveley. **84** —*J.C. (9/1/2006)*

Faiveley 1996 Red Blend (Vosne-Romanée) $40. 87 —*S.H. (12/31/1999)*

Faiveley 1995 Red Blend (Pommard) $48. 92 —*S.H. (12/31/1999)*

Faiveley 1995 Clos des Myglands Red Blend (Mercurey) $24. 87 —*S.H. (12/31/1999)*

Faiveley 1995 Blanc Clos Rochette White Blend (Mercurey) $24. 86 —*S.H. (12/31/1999)*

FAT BASTARD

Fat Bastard 2004 Limited Release Cabernet Sauvignon (Vin de Pays d'Oc) $12. The story is simply told. A tasting session between Thierry Boudinaud of Rhône producers Gabriel Meffre and British wine merchant Guy Anderson produced a wine that Anderson, using an affectionate British term to describe a big wine, called "a fat bastard." A range of wines and a memorable name were born. This dry, firm Cabernet is packed with black currant and wood flavors and ripe fruits. "Limited Release" refers to the rarity of releases of this wine—the previous vintage was in 1998. **85 Best Buy** —*R.V. (11/15/2006)*

Fat Bastard 2005 Merlot (Vin de Pays d'Oc) $12. A ripe, chunky wine with smooth red fruits, light tannins, and a light, fresh finish marked by acidity, but also some softness. The name "Fat Bastard" is a British expression of praise for a big wine. **84** —*R.V. (12/31/2006)*

Fat Bastard 2005 Shiraz (Vin de Pays d'Oc) $12. A big, fruity wine with spicy, dry fruits, flavors of blackberries, and ripe plums, and a warm, ripe feel. This is big stuff, with solid, dark tannins and a toasty wood finish. It demands big food. **83** —*R.V. (12/31/2006)*

FÉRAUD-BRUNEL

Féraud-Brunel 2003 Rhône Red Blend (Gigondas) $33. Even if you're not a fan of the super-ripe 2003 vintage, it's hard to deny how lush and velvety this wine is. Plums, chocolate, and spice elements weave seamlessly in and out, finishing long, with soft tannins. Drink now–2012. **91 Editors' Choice** —*J.C. (11/15/2006)*

FERRATON PÈRE ET FILS

Ferraton Père et Fils 2005 La Source Marsanne (Saint-Joseph) $24. Neutral to the point of blandness. It's wet and fresh, but uninteresting. **82** —*J.C. (11/15/2006)*

Ferraton Père et Fils 2003 Les Oliviers Marsanne (Saint-Joseph) $NA. Honey and apricot aromas make this wine immediately enticing. This blend of Marsanne and Roussanne is rich, full-bodied, with attractive honey flavors. There are creamy layers from the wood fermentation and 10 month aging on lees. It's fat, food friendly, and ready to drink. **88** —*R.V. (2/1/2005)*

Ferraton Père et Fils 2004 Samorëns Rhône Red Blend (Côtes-du-Rhône) $12. Cleanly made, with modest black cherry and spice elements. A pleasant wine, just one that lacks intensity and length. **83** —*J.C. (11/15/2006)*

Ferraton Père et Fils 2004 La Source Syrah (Saint-Joseph) $24. Decently made but light, with modest fruit and a drying, astringent finish. Drink now. **83** —*J.C. (11/15/2006)*

Ferraton Père et Fils 2001 Le Grand Courtil Syrah (Crozes-Hermitage) $23. Ferraton is partly owned by Chapoutier, and affect to call their Crozes-Hermitage and Hermitage by the older spelling of Ermitage. But the important thing is the wine, and this Crozes is deliciously accessible with good acidity and some dry, but juicy fruit. The tannins and the wood play a good balancing role. **89** —*R.V. (2/1/2005)*

Ferraton Père et Fils 2000 Les Dionnières Syrah (Hermitage) $76. A powerful, dark, and tannic wine which reflects the power of this wine from 30-year old vines. It has great intense fruits, with some austerity at this young stage, but will ripen and richen over the next 5 years. Ferraton is partly owned by Chapoutier, and affect to call their Crozes-Hermitage and Hermitage by the older spelling of Ermitage. **90** —*R.V. (2/1/2005)*

FORTANT

Fortant 2003 Cabernet Sauvignon (Vin de Pays d'Oc) $6. A well-made wine which exhibits just the right amount of firm, dry tannic Cabernet structure to go with powerful black fruits. Good acidity gives balance, but the main impression is of great, ripe fruit. **88 Best Buy** —*R.V. (12/1/2004)*

Fortant 2003 Chardonnay (Vin de Pays d'Oc) $6. Smooth and soft, this wine has a touch of vanilla and apples and cream flavors. At the back, a freshness of acidity stops it being too rich or fat. It is well-made, well balanced, and slips down easily. **85 Best Buy** —*R.V. (12/1/2004)*

Fortant 1999 Chardonnay (Vin de Pays d'Oc) $10. It's hard to find any noticeable fruit on the nose, and there isn't much more in the mouth, except for a smidgen of citrus and green apple. It finishes mild and short. **81** —*M.S. (4/1/2002)*

Fortant 2003 Merlot (Vin de Pays d'Oc) $6. Soft fruit, with a light jammy character characterizes this easy, fresh wine. It has light tannins and a

firm, dry element which balanced the freshness. With some richness, it even manages a southern warmth **85 Best Buy** —*R.V. (12/1/2004)*

Fortant 2003 Sauvignon Blanc (Vin de Pays d'Oc) $6. There is lightweight, fresh fruit flavors of crisp apples and grapefruit, along with a refreshing touch of acidity. The only downside is that it seems unfocussed in its fruit flavors **82** —*R.V. (12/1/2004)*

FOURNIER PÈRE ET FILS

Fournier Père et Fils 2003 Grand Cuvée Fournier Sauvignon Blanc (Pouilly-Fumé) $25. As befits the hot, sultry summer of 2003, this is a big, fat wine. It's also maturing well, showing a soft acidity as well as tropical fruits, lychees, and some almond flavors. The structure is still there, with some fresh currants, giving crispness as well richness. **89** —*R.V. (8/1/2006)*

Fournier Père et Fils 2003 Les Chardouillonne Sauvignon Blanc (Sancerre) $25. With two years of aging, this wine has developed delicious nutty aromas and flavors; they have tamed the great, crisp fruit that still underlies what is a complex, intense wine. There is good depth to the white fruits and the aromas of white spring flowers. **90** —*R.V. (8/1/2006)*

FRANÇOIS CHIDAINE

François Chidaine 2004 Chenin Blanc (Montlouis-sur-Loire) $17. This is a great, concentrated wine, which packs clean, almond, kiwi, and apple flavors along with a creamy, rich mousse and delicious acidity. This is a wine that can age well—a 1996 was still fresh when tasted early in 2006 **91 Cellar Selection** —*R.V. (6/1/2006)*

FRANÇOIS COTAT

François Cotat 2003 Les Monts Damnés Sauvignon Blanc (Sancerre) $28. Fairly heavy and floral, with buttery, sweet aromas. That same bouquet weight carries onto the palate, where the ripe green melon and spiced fruit flavors are meaty and broad. Finishes warm and chunky. **86** *(7/1/2005)*

FRANCOIS LABET

Francois Labet NV Champagne Blend (Crémant de Bourgogne) $19. Based in Vougeot in the heart of the Côte d'Or, Labet makes a delicious Crémant, appley, crisp, and fresh. Offers pretty flavors of kiwis, green plums, and a touch of toast. **90** —*R.V. (6/1/2006)*

Francois Labet 2002 Clos du Domaine Chardonnay (Meursault) $120. Starts with a whiff of sulfur, then rolls on, delivering crisp apple and citrus aromas and flavors. Finishes on a long note of pink grapefruit. **87** —*J.C. (4/1/2005)*

Francois Labet 2002 Les Nosroyes Chardonnay (Puligny-Montrachet) $110. Smoky, minerally, and citrusy on the nose, followed on the palate by waves of lemon-lime and orange fruit. Plump yet minerally, with a long, citrusy finish. One of the best kosher Burgundies we've come across. **87** —*J.C. (4/1/2005)*

FRANÇOISE CHAUVENET

Françoise Chauvenet NV Silver Cap Grande Cuvée Blanc de Blancs Brut Sparkling Blend (Vin Moelleux) $10. Yellowish in color, with baked corn and yeast on the bouquet but very little oomph or zest. Heavy in the mouth, with spiced yellow fruits and banana. Soft, heavy, and creamy on the finish, with a spot of white pepper. **83** —*M.S. (12/31/2005)*

FRENCH RABBIT

French Rabbit 2005 Cabernet Sauvignon Cabernet Sauvignon (Vin de Pays d'Oc) $10. The most successful of the French Rabbit wines. This has some good, dense tannins, flavors of black currants, and a solid, dry finish. **83** —*R.V. (12/31/2006)*

French Rabbit 2005 Merlot (Vin de Pays d'Oc) $10. One of the range of wines in Tetrapak launched by the Boisset group, this is firm, rather green, with herbal flavors and a dry tannic aftertaste. **82** —*R.V. (12/31/2006)*

FRENCH REVOLUTION

French Revolution 1999 Le Rouge Red Blend (Côtes-du-Ventoux) $9. This 60% Grenache-40% Syrah blend is a tasty easy drinker. A soft mouthfeel, juicy red and blackberry aromas and flavors, and some chocolate and licorice accents make this affordable red a good value. Finishes a touch drier, with modest tannins. Drink now. **85** —*M.M. (2/1/2002)*

G. H. MUMM

G. H. Mumm NV Brut Rosé Champagne Blend (Champagne) $43. This blend of 60% Pinot Noir, 22% Chardonnay, and 18% Pinot Meunier is given color by the addition of red wine from Bouzy. It has a fresh pink color; soft, well-balanced fruit, with a good layer of forward, fresh strawberry flavors and balanced acidity. This is a well-judged wine that performs beautifully. **88** —*R.V. (12/15/2003)*

G. H. Mumm NV Carte Classique Extra Dry Champagne Blend (Champagne) $35. Good everyday bubbly. Dry, crisp, and clean, with subtle dough and citrus flavors and a lively mouthfeel. A bit rough around the edges, and finishes with a scour of acidity. **85** —*S.H. (12/15/2002)*

G. H. Mumm NV Carte Classique Extra Dry Champagne Blend (Champagne) $35. A blend of sweetness and tangy citrus flavors form the core of this wine, with apple and pear notes at the fringes. The finish is long, though a bit cloying. **85** —*J.M. (12/15/2001)*

G. H. Mumm NV Cordon Rouge Brut Champagne Blend (Champagne) $30. **88** *(12/1/2000)*

G. H. Mumm NV Cordon Rouge Brut Champagne Blend (Champagne) $45. Aromas of bread box, toast, and green herbs are simple, if a little short. The palate features apple, lemon curd, and anise, while it finishes tight and full. Easy to drink and well-made. A good basic Champagne. **86** — *M.S. (12/15/2003)*

G. H. Mumm NV Cordon Rouge Brut Champagne Blend (Champagne) $30. Mumm's ever-popular best seller is very dry and rough this year. It feels scouring on the palate, like steel wool. The flavors are austere and lemony, and the finish is bitter and acidic. **84** —*S.H. (12/15/2002)*

G. H. Mumm NV Cordon Rouge Brut Champagne Blend (Champagne) $45. The aromas are fresh and floral; combined with undertones of toast, they get this wine off to a fast start. The bead is fine and the mouthfeel creamy, but the solid flavors of tart citrus and green apple lack drama. **86** —*J.C. (12/15/2001)*

G. H. Mumm NV Grand Cru Brut Champagne Blend (Champagne) $60. Using only grapes from Mumm's own grand cru vineyards, winemaker Dominique Demarville has produced this impressive new cuvée. With a high proportion of reserve wines (from previous vintages), this is a well-integrated, elegant wine, with citrus characters and just a light touch of honey. **93** —*R.V. (12/1/2005)*

G. H. Mumm NV Joyesse Demi-Sec Champagne Blend (Champagne) $41. This demi-sec is sweet enough to try with dessert, featuring honeyed apple and pear flavors garnished with modest toast and citrus. Sweet but not cloying, thanks to a chalky note on the finish. **85** —*J.C. (12/1/2004)*

G. H. Mumm NV Mumm de Cramant Brut Chardonnay (Champagne) $70. This, the driest of Mumm's lineup, is also the leanest in flavor, a 100% Chardonnay that is very minerally and lime-citrusy. It's not very round in the mouth, with harsh acidity that scours the palate through the short finish. Could be a cellar candidate, if you're a gambler. **88** —*S.H. (12/15/2003)*

GABRIEL MEFFRE

Gabriel Meffre 2001 Domaine de Longue Toque Rhône Red Blend (Gigondas) $18. This 44-acre vineyard is situated in the heart of the rocky Dentelles de Montmirail. A blend of 75% Grenache, with Syrah, Mourvèdre, and Cinsault, it is big, brooding, and powerful with young, sweet tannins and solid spicy flavors. The texture is flowing and opulent, but the tannins remain at the end, offering good aging potential. **90** — *R.V. (3/1/2004)*

Gabriel Meffre 2005 La Chasse du Pape Prestige Rhône Red Blend (Côtes-du-Rhône) $10. A quaffable if somewhat innocuous Côtes-du-Rhône with modest cherry fruit. The blend of 60% Grenache, 30% Syrah, and the remainder Cinsault and Mourvèdre is medium-bodied, then thins out a bit on the finish. **83** —*J.C. (11/15/2006)*

Gabriel Meffre 2003 La Chasse du Pape Prestige Rhône Red Blend (Côtes-du-Rhône) $10. Slightly pruny and heavy, but this is still a solid wine, reflective of the vintage. Black cherry and plum scents carry the nose, accented by hints of marzipan, while the finish boasts a dusting of tan-

nins. Drink now. **84** —*J.C. (11/15/2006)*

Gabriel Meffre 2000 Laurus Rhône Red Blend (Vacqueyras) $17. Strawberry flavors dominate this big, hearty, fruity wine. It may not be hugely powerful, but the fruit is generous, spoilt by just a touch of alcoholic pepperiness. **86** —*R.V. (3/1/2004)*

Gabriel Meffre 2000 Laurus Rhône Red Blend (Gigondas) $20. Black, brooding wine, dominated by tannins and sweet fruit. The heady perfumes are dominant at this stage, but in time should balance the acidity and ripe fruit. **87** —*R.V. (3/1/2004)*

Gabriel Meffre 2003 La Chasse du Pape Prestige Rhône White Blend (Côtes-du-Rhône) $10. Still reasonably fresh and blalanced, this relatively simple quaff combines apple and citrus fruit with a hint of minerality on the finish. **84** —*J.C. (11/15/2006)*

Gabriel Meffre 2002 Laurus Rhône White Blend (Hermitage) $NA. Huge, spicy wood dominates this powerful wine. It also has good acidity, which gives it a lift and liveliness. At the moment, though, wood is right up front, leaving the apricot fruit flavors stuck in the background. Give it three or four years to develop. **87** —*R.V. (2/1/2005)*

Gabriel Meffre 2002 Laurus Syrah (Hermitage) $NA. A fine, well-made wine. It brings out the serious character of fine Hermitage, as well as emphasizing its great black fruits and acidity. There are leather aromas, spice and herb flavors, and huge, solid tannins. The only taste that spoils is the oxidative character that comes through. **88** —*R.V. (2/1/2005)*

Gabriel Meffre 2001 Laurus Syrah (Saint-Joseph) $NA. This is a wine that brings out the earthy character of Syrah. It has flavors of spice, herbs, and some black fruits. But it also has serious, dry tannins and acidity, which both suggest it needs time to develop. Over the next four years, it should soften and grow richer. **87** —*R.V. (2/1/2005)*

Gabriel Meffre 2000 Laurus Syrah (Cornas) $NA. A surprisingly light Cornas, with fresh, juicy fruit, flavors of red currants, and acidity. There is some wood, but the fruit is what makes this wine attractive, but developing fast. **85** —*R.V. (2/1/2005)*

GASTON CHIQUET

Gaston Chiquet 1997 Or Premier Cru Champagne Blend (Champagne) $52. A powerful, intense wine with ripe fruits and a good structure. Red fruit flavors are there, but the soft center with the crisp grapefruit aftertaste. Pinot Noir dominates this blend. **88** —*R.V. (12/1/2004)*

GEORGES DUBOEUF

Georges Duboeuf 2001 Cuvée Prestige Reserve Cabernet Sauvignon (Vin de Pays d'Oc) $10. Early aromas of clove and spice give way to chunky berry fruit and some grassy notes. The palate bursts forward with juicy fruit and full tannins, and the finish is reasonably long. Snappy and simple, with a forward attitude. **84** —*M.S. (9/1/2003)*

Georges Duboeuf 2001 Prestige Cabernet Sauvignon (Vin de Pays d'Oc) $10. Earthy, farmyard aromas suggest the youth of this wine. The taste is much better, rich and full of black fruits with ripe flavors and a touch of pepper. **87 Best Buy** —*R.V. (12/1/2004)*

Georges Duboeuf 2004 Chardonnay (Saint-Véran) $11. Yes, there are bargains to be had in white Burgundy, especially in the Mâcon region. Saint-Véran is close to Pouilly-Fuissé, with whose wines it shares some of the attractive mineral character. This wine, from Georges Duboeuf, is a partner to some of his Beaujolais, with the same flower presentation bottle as well as open, fresh fruit. Red apple and white fruit flavors, a touch of minerality, and a light, gentle aftertaste. This is easy, drinkable Chardonnay. **87 Best Buy** —*R.V. (11/15/2006)*

Georges Duboeuf 2001 Chardonnay (Pouilly-Fuissé) $19. A well-made Chard, combining peaches and toasty oak in a medium-weight wine. It's toasty more than fruity or minerally, but plump and flavorful. **85** —*J.C. (10/1/2003)*

Georges Duboeuf 1999 Chardonnay (St.-Véran) $11. 86 Best Buy —*M.S. (11/1/2000)*

Georges Duboeuf 2005 Chardonnay Chardonnay (Vin de Pays d'Oc) $7. With its distinctive enameled, flowered bottle, this sets out to be a fun party wine. It succeeds with its fresh, flowery, open fruit, enhanced by vanilla, spice, and green apple flavors. **84** —*R.V. (12/31/2006)*

Georges Duboeuf 2001 Cuvée Prestige Reserve Chardonnay (Vin de Pays d'Oc) $10. Lots of oak on the nose, and for that matter, throughout. The wine tastes of lemon, vanilla, and wood resin, while the creamy finish deals even more oak. Texture and richness are not a problem, but the wood runs roughshod over the mild, base-level fruit. **83** —M.S. (9/1/2003)

Georges Duboeuf 1999 Les Mures Chardonnay (Pouilly-Loche) $12. 87 — M.M. (11/1/2000)

Georges Duboeuf 1999 Milenage Chardonnay (Vin de Pays d'Oc) $9. 83 — M.S. (11/1/2000)

Georges Duboeuf 2002 Reserve Chardonnay (Vin de Pays d'Oc) $8. With its brighly colored bottle, this sure stands out on the shelf. The fruit is soft, lively with a touch of oak, to give it extra complexity. Tropical flavors complete the package. **85 Best Buy** —R.V. (12/1/2004)

Georges Duboeuf 2003 Gamay (Juliénas) $12. As we brace ourselves for the crush of this year's Beaujolais Nouveau, it's worth remembering that last year was the year that the region's most famous négociant described as "the vintage [that] may turn out to be the greatest vintage of my career." It's not the nouveau that turns the "may" into a "will"—it's cru wines like this fragrant, intensely concentrated Juliénas. Here, sweet berry fruit fleshes out into a long, vibrant, and persistent wine, one that lingers on the palate for an impossibly long time. **90 Best Buy** —P.G. (11/15/2004)

Georges Duboeuf 2001 Gamay (Régnié) $9. Tasty, tangy, and dark, with lively fruit-to-acid balance and vibrant tart-sweet raspberry flavors. Régnié only received cru status (allowed to bottle using the village name) about a decade ago, but the promotion was deserved. The wines have consistently performed on par with the best of the other communes. The smooth finish shows good length, herb, licorice, and dark berry notes. **86 Best Buy** —M.M. (11/15/2002)

Georges Duboeuf 2001 Gamay (Juliénas) $12. Solid cru Beaujolais as it should be, with good Gamay fruit, tangy acidity, and plenty of tart-sweet berry flavor accented by attractive herb notes. Medium-weight and even on the tongue, with a mild chalkiness, this has life and a bit of elegance. Closes dry, with surprisingly good length for an uncomplicated wine. **86** —M.M. (11/15/2002)

Georges Duboeuf 2001 Gamay (Chiroubles) $12. Ample, flavorful Gamay elements show from the nose through the finish, offering appealing tart red berry and herb aromas and flavors plus a good, tangy palate texture. Finishes tart and dry, with surprising body. **85** —M.M. (11/15/2002)

Georges Duboeuf 2000 Château de Nervers Gamay (Brouilly) $12. 85 (1/1/2004)

Georges Duboeuf 2001 Domaine des Quatre Vents Gamay (Fleurie) $14. A bit sterner stuff than we're accustomed to seeing from Duboeuf, with cedar and leather layered over black cherry and vanilla. Still firm on the finish, this uncommonly long-lived Beaujolais could use another 12 months in the cellar. **87** —J.C. (11/15/2003)

Georges Duboeuf 2001 Domaine des Rosiers Gamay (Moulin-à-Vent) $14. A bit raisiny and leathery on the nose, as if the fruit is drying out. Offers some black cherry and anise flavors, with caramel notes on the finish. **83** —J.C. (11/15/2003)

Georges Duboeuf 2002 Flower label Gamay (Juliénas) $12. Maybe the only disappointment in Duboeuf's 2002 lineup, this wine offers leathery aromas married to ripe black cherries, yet finishes with hints of Play-Doh and bubble gum. Still, the midpalate is fresh and light, offering bounteous red berries. **84** —J.C. (11/15/2003)

Georges Duboeuf 2002 Grand Cuvée Flower Label Gamay (Brouilly) $11. Filled to near-overflowing with bouncy, fresh, exuberant fruit, this fine Brouilly is a winner. Cherries and mixed berries cascade over the palate, finishing with crisp acidity. **87 Best Buy** —J.C. (11/15/2003)

Georges Duboeuf 2001 Grande Cuvée Gamay (Brouilly) $11. Medium-weight and even, with strong berry aromas and flavors but a pronounced tartness—some would call it sourness—to the fruit. The fairly rich, almost creamy texture doesn't fit well with the flavor profile. Closes with decent length, but the parts still aren't harmonious. **84** —M.M. (11/15/2002)

Georges Duboeuf 2001 Jean Descombes Gamay (Morgon) $12. A disappointing effort from this normally reliable estate, the 2001 shows hints of raisin and leather on the nose and slightly cooked black cherry flavors along with a supple mouthfeel. **84** —J.C. (11/15/2003)

Georges Duboeuf 1997 Pisse Vieille Gamay (Brouilly) $11. 88 —J.C. (11/15/1999)

Georges Duboeuf 2000 Prestige Gamay (Moulin-à-Vent) $20. 87 (1/1/2004)

Georges Duboeuf 2002 Merlot (Vin de Pays d'Oc) $7. Here is a wine packed with light, fresh, juicy red fruits. It has some dry tannins, flavors of herbs, and a layer of acidity. This is a good wine for summer drinking. **82** —R.V. (12/1/2004)

Georges Duboeuf 1998 Domaine de Bordeneuve Merlot (Vin de Pays d'Oc) $8. 85 —M.S. (12/31/1999)

Georges Duboeuf 2001 Prestige Merlot (Vin de Pays d'Oc) $10. Ripe, juicy fruit with gentle tannins make this wine well-rounded. It has acidity and flavors of cranberry jelly along with herbs and young fruits. **86 Best Buy** —R.V. (12/1/2004)

Georges Duboeuf 1999 Red Blend (St.-Amour) $14. 86 —M.M. (11/1/2000)

Georges Duboeuf NV GD Red Blend (Vin de Pays du Torgan) $5. A Beaujolais-style wine that smells young and fresh. The grapes are Rhône varietals, and they have that right-out-of-the-fermenter flavor, rich and juicy and rude. This simple country wine is very dry. **84** —S.H. (1/1/2002)

Georges Duboeuf 2000 Syrah (Vin de Pays d'Oc) $7. An example of the new style of wines that are beginning to emerge from the Languedoc: Rather than the sour, earthy wines of the past, the focus is on the fruit, which is bouncy and sweet. Flavors of grapes, bananas, and bubble gum mark this as a Beaujolais-style Syrah, best consumed slightly chilled. **82** (10/1/2001)

Georges Duboeuf 1999 Viognier (Vin de Pays d'Oc) $15. 87 —M.S. (11/1/2000)

GERARD BERTRAND

Gerard Bertrand 2003 Classic Chardonnay (Vin de Pays d'Oc) $10. No lack of weight here, but the heaviness isn't well-balanced by big fruit or crisp acids. Instead you get modest pear and peach flavors and a short finish. **82** —J.C. (12/1/2004)

Gerard Bertrand 2003 La Forge Rhône Red Blend (Corbières) $NA. Made from 80-year-old vines, this blend of Carignan and Syrah is an intense, concentrated wine, with mint and black fruit flavors and a velvety texture from the wood aging. Made in a limited edition of 6,000 bottles, the wine is worthy of aging, a fine example of southern flavors allied to modern winemaking. **91** —R.V. (12/31/2006)

Gerard Bertrand 2005 Le Blanc de Villemajou Rhône White Blend (Corbières) $NA. A rare white from Corbières, this blend of southern French white varieties is minerally, attractively lean, and fresh, with just a hint of wood. Its delicious fresh lemon and herb flavors lead to a crisp, green finish. **88** —R.V. (12/31/2006)

Gerard Bertrand 2003 Syrah (Vin de Pays d'Oc) $10. This youthful, vibrant purple wine is miles ahead of most insipid Vin de Pays d'Oc Syrahs. Scents of smoke and black pepper accent blackberry fruit, while supple tannins provide a smooth mouthfeel. It's a steak wine for a casual evening, uncomplicated but satisfying, with the requisite tannins and acids to handle red meat. **86 Best Buy** —J.C. (12/1/2004)

Gerard Bertrand 2005 Terroir Syrah (Coteaux du Languedoc) $NA. Firm but generous black fruits dominate this powerful wine. There are dry tannins, solid chunky fruits, and ripe acidity. From clay and chalk soil in the Coteaux du Languedoc, this is part of a line of wines designed to bring grape varieties and the local terroir together. **85** —R.V. (12/31/2006)

Gerard Bertrand 2005 Viognier Collection Viognier (Vin de Pays d'Oc) $NA. Full-bodied in style, this is an example of a Viognier that needs food. Its structure and acidity move away from the white fruits and perfumes, and more to coolness and dryness. There's just a touch of wood, but the fruit dominates. **86** —R.V. (12/31/2006)

FRANCE

GIGONDAS LA CAVE

Gigondas la Cave 2004 Beaumirail Rhône Red Blend (Vacqueyras) $NA. This is a bit herbal and light. But it's an easy-drinking quaff bursting with strawberry fruit and peppery spice. Drink now-2008. **85** —*J.C. (11/15/2006)*

GILLES ROBIN

Gilles Robin 1999 Cuvée Albéric Bouvet Syrah (Crozes-Hermitage) $20. The nose is a smoked meat, sandlewood, leather, and blackberry joyride; a cool, metallic note rides sidesaddle and keeps quiet for the most part. Bacon is the leader on the palate; juicy berry, plum, and mineral notes round out this medium-weight pleasure bomb. The finish is long and mouth-watering, and bolstered by soft tannins. Will be even better after two years in the cellar. **89 Cellar Selection** *(10/1/2001)*

GINESTET

Ginestet 2004 Bordeaux Bordeaux Blend (Bordeaux) $8. A blend of Merlot, Cabernet Sauvignon, and Cabernet Franc, this has some good density of structure. It's a firm, tannic wine but one that is sustained by some fresh red fruit flavors. A good example of a branded Bordeaux. **88** —*R.V. (12/31/2006)*

Ginestet 2005 Marquis de Chasse Bordeaux White Blend (Bordeaux Blanc) $9. The bust of a fictitious Marquis adorns the label of this wine, an indication that it is being presented as a luxury brand, according to the publicity. It's a blend of Sauvignon Blanc and Sémillon, fresh, unwooded, with ripe melon and pear flavors. **85 Best Buy** —*R.V. (12/31/2006)*

Ginestet 2005 French RootsCabernet Sauvignon (Vin de Pays d'Oc) $8. There is plenty of the firm tannins of Cabernet Sauvignon, but this wine, one of the more successful in the French Roots range, is also fully charged with Languedoc denseness and ripeness. It has a proper stalky, black currant finish. **86** —*R.V. (12/31/2006)*

Ginestet 2004 French Roots Merlot (Vin de Pays d'Oc) $8. This wine emphasizes the jammy, ripe fruited side of Merlot. It is big and bold, with some good dense black fruit flavors alongside the considerable layer of tannins. Not a Merlot to be drunk on its own: it needs food. **86** —*R.V. (12/31/2006)*

Ginestet 2005 French Roots Sauvignon Blanc (Vin de Pays des Côtes de Gascogne) $8. The famous comparison of Sauvignon Blanc to cats is certainly correct with this wine. It is flavored with gooseberries as well, a highly acid, green wine, very fresh, very crisp. **82** —*R.V. (12/31/2006)*

Ginestet 2005 French Roots Shiraz (Vin de Pays d'Oc) $8. Perfumed wood dominates this wine. There is softness, some attractive food-friendly acidity, and hints of red fruits, but otherwise it is spice and toast all the way. **84 Best Buy** —*R.V. (12/31/2006)*

GOSSET

Gosset NV Brut Excellence Champagne Blend (Champagne) $40. Pale, crisp, and very fresh, like biting into a tart green apple. Lively, with a slight beeriness, just beginning to round out the sharp edges into hints of spice. Quite dry and clean, it goes well with fried seafood. **87** —*P.G. (12/15/2003)*

Gosset NV Brut Grande Rosé Champagne Blend (Champagne) $70. Gosset comes in a stunningly beautiful antique-style bottle, but the wine inside must overcome the sulfurous scents of rotten egg before it can reveal its strengths, which are considerable. There is a definite Pinot Noir profile to the fruit flavors, which combine cherry and berry with light milk-chocolate flavors. **87** —*P.G. (12/15/2002)*

Gosset 1995 Celebris Brut Champagne Blend (Champagne) $150. Claiming to be the oldest Champagne house, founded in 1584, Gosset celebrates its antiquity with its traditional bottle, with a squat bulb and long neck. This Celebris is mature, toasty, honeyed, and very rich, almost too much. It certainly makes it a great food wine. **87** —*R.V. (12/1/2004)*

Gosset 1998 Celebris Brut Rosé Champagne Blend (Champagne) $135. The style of the Celebris bottle echoes the ancient Champagne bottles, with its tall neck and squat body. The rosé inside is light orange pink in color, appearing mature, with soft, toasty flavors and some rich fruit. The acidity is light, with the sweet strawberry flavors more dominant. **88** —*R.V. (12/1/2004)*

Gosset NV Excellence Brut Champagne Blend (Champagne) $40. Has some pleasant aromas of ginger and rising dough, followed by modest apple and citrus flavors. Medium-bodied, with a burst of lemon on the finish. **84** —*J.C. (12/1/2005)*

Gosset NV Excéllence Brut Champagne Blend (Champagne) $43. The latest edition of the Excéllence is the best in years. The crisp young flavors—like a tart green apple—are focused and unusually intense. The acids are lively and nuanced with lime, and the wine avoids the beery, yeasty excesses of previous bottlings. Dry, fresh, and clean, it's a cava-style Champagne; it seems made for fried seafoods. **89** —*P.G. (12/1/2006)*

Gosset 1999 Grand Brut Champagne Blend (Champagne) $85. An attractively perfumed wine, with white flowers, cut grass, and thyme. To taste, it is soft, with the delicacy of Chardonnay giving an elegance to the intense green, crisp flavors. This should be a long-lived wine—at least 10 years. **94** —*R.V. (11/1/2006)*

Gosset 1996 Grand Brut Champagne Blend (Champagne) $75. All Gosset bottles, copies of ancient designs, are so elegant. It is appropriate that this Millésime should equal the elegance of the bottle. It is soft, full, and ripe, flavored with green plums and kiwi fruits and with a touch of spice. It could still age, but is fresh and delicious now. **90** —*R.V. (12/1/2004)*

Gosset NV Grand Brut Rosé Champagne Blend (Champagne) $70. A lot of vanilla and cotton candy on the nose, and that's backed by sweet melon and strawberry flavors. Sweetness is a recurring theme, and although it's lively and has good mouthfeel, it's not as dry as we'd like. Best if you prefer a sweet-dosage style. **87** —*M.S. (12/15/2005)*

Gosset NV Grand Brut Rosé Champagne Blend (Champagne) $69. Sweet-tart cherry aromas and flavors, licorice, charcoal, and slightly meaty accents characterize this supple rose. Very soft and frothy on the palate, it has a slight candied note that is not unattractive, but a firmer acid backbone could elevate it to excellence. **87** —*M.M. (12/15/2001)*

Gosset NV Grande Réserve Brut Champagne Blend (Champagne) $60. Gosset's reserve bottling is always a rich, textured wine packed with an appealing flavor parade of fruits, toast, nuts, and vanilla. Ripe and doughy, it's not what you would call subtle or particularly elegant. But if it's big, ripe flavors you want, with plenty of fruit, here you go. **90** —*P.G. (12/1/2006)*

Gosset NV Grande Réserve Brut Champagne Blend (Champagne) $60. Richly colored in hues of amber and gold, with a toasty, full-bodied nose that offers maturity and depth. This Champagne is totally on the money, with ripe but reserved apple and citrus flavors, and then the slightest bit of mushroom and baked bread on the finish. **92** —*M.S. (12/15/2005)*

Gosset NV Grande Réserve Brut Champagne Blend (Champagne) $52. 90 *(12/31/2000)*

GRANDES SERRES

Grandes Serres 2004 La Combe des Marchands Rhône Red Blend (Gigondas) $NA. A well-made, mid-level Gigondas, the 2004 La Combe des Marchands boasts aromas of leather, red fruits, and spice, and attractively balanced alcohol and tannins. Medium-bodied, it does show some youthful astringency on the finish. Drink from 2007–2012. **86** —*J.C. (11/15/2006)*

GRANDIN

Grandin NV Brut Sparkling Blend (Vin Mousseux) $11. A floral nose and a very soft mouthfeel characterize this easy bubbly. With somewhat sweet, flowery flavors, it's really a demi-sec, and will have wide appeal. Finishes modestly and a little drier than the palate. It's a touch simple but makes no pretense, and is a decent, inexpensive pour. **84** —*M.M. (12/15/2001)*

Grandin NV Brut Sparkling Blend (Vin Mousseux) $11. 83 —*M.M. (12/31/2000)*

GRATIEN ET MEYER

Gratien et Meyer NV Cuvée Flamme Rosé Cabernet Franc (Saumur) $27. An attractive onion skin-colored wine with flavors of raspberries and a smooth, full mousse. This blend of Cabernet Franc and Grolleau is more than just fruity, with a fine structure and good finishing dryness. **88** —*R.V. (6/1/2006)*

Gratien et Meyer NV Cuvée Flamme Brut White Blend (Saumur) $27. With three years of bottle age, this is a sophisticated wine, ripe and soft, with a creamy mousse. The 30% Cab Franc (blended with Chenin Blanc and

FRANCE

Chardonnay) gives flavors of raspberry fruits. Gratien et Meyer's Champagne connection (the firm is linked with Alfred Gratien) shows in the depth of flavor and complexity. **89** —*R.V. (6/1/2006)*

GUILLEMOT-MICHEL

Guillemot-Michel 2002 Quintaine Chardonnay (Mâcon-Villages) $30. Tasted at a closed stage in its evolution, the fruit was very much quiescent, showing merely hints of peach and citrus. More mineral than the richer 2003, with a long, mineral-and-grapefruit finish. Drink 2008–2015, maybe longer. A 1986 tasted at the domaine late in 2004 was still delicious (90 points). **88** —*J.C. (11/15/2005)*

GUSTAVE LORENTZ

Gustave Lorentz 2000 Grand Cru Kanzlerberg Riesling (Alsace) $39. The Gustave Lorentz style with its emphasis on pure fruit flavors really shines through with this wine. There is some petrol character, but the main impression is of pure grapefruit flavors, streaked through with acidity, with crisp, green fruits and a great refreshing bone dry aftertaste. **91** —*R.V. (5/1/2005)*

GUY CHARLEMAGNE

Guy Charlemagne NV Blanc de Blancs Réserve Brut Champagne Blend (Champagne) $35. Made from grand cru vineyards in Mesnil, Oger, and Avize, this is 100% Chardonnay. It has delicious apple and creamy yeast and toast flavors, finishing with green fruits, fresh acidity, and lightness. **89** —*R.V. (12/1/2002)*

Guy Charlemagne 1996 Mesnillesimé Brut Champagne Blend (Champagne) $50. The combination of the name of Le Mesnil and the word for vintage, Mesnillesimé is hardly subtle. Nor is the bottle, with its Belle Epoque design. But the wine is great: Full-bodied, piled with ripe green plums and crisp freshness, it finishes with a lingering toasty, creamy note. **92 Editors' Choice** —*R.V. (12/1/2002)*

GUY-PIERRE JEAN & FILS

Guy-Pierre Jean & Fils 2003 Hautes-Côtes de Nuits Les Dames Huguettes Pinot Noir (Bourgogne) $22. A bit tarry and reductive, but the underlying fruit seems sound, with cherry flavors buttressed by a plump, velvety texture. Hints of coffee and chocolate creep in on the finish. **85** —*J.C. (9/1/2006)*

H.GERMAIN

H.Germain NV Cuvée President Champagne Blend (Champagne) $37. 91 *(12/31/2000)*

HEART OF DARKNESS

Heart of Darkness 2001 Tannat (Madiran) $18. Bonny Doon vineyard has gone in search of something unusual from France, and found it in this dark, seriously tannic Tannat-based Madiran. Heart of Darkness certainly describes the almost black color, but in fact the fruit is fresher than with many Madirans, and the tannins are beginning to soften. This wine is more than a curiosity, and gives a fine glimpse of this under-rated red wine area in the south-west of France. **87** —*R.V. (3/1/2006)*

HECHT & BANNIER

Hecht & Bannier 2003 Rhône Red Blend (Minervois) $NA. Packed with bramble, black plums, and leathery, dense tannins, this is strong stuff. Bitter cocoa flavors and pepper show the ripeness and firmness of the wine, which, at 14.5% alcohol, is no lightweight. **88** —*R.V. (8/1/2006)*

Hecht & Bannier 2003 Rhône Red Blend (Côtes du Roussillon Villages) $NA. This is big in all senses. It has dense, very rich, very powerful fruit and as a consequence of that, it has 14.5% alcohol. It's finely perfumed, with black and violet flavors and aromas, and some good, spicy flavors. **87** —*R.V. (8/1/2006)*

Hecht & Bannier 2002 Rhône Red Blend (Minervois) $21. A simple, fresh, fruity wine. Ripe Cinsault gives it some weight, but Syrah's dark fruits spiced with pepper and herbal notes prevail. **86** —*R.V. (3/1/2006)*

Hecht & Bannier 2002 Rhône Red Blend (Côtes du Roussillon Villages) $22. A sophisticated, elegant wine with dusty tannins and flavors of new wood and dark plum fruit. Fresh rather than powerful; drink now and over the next 18 months. **87** —*R.V. (3/1/2006)*

Hecht & Bannier 2005 Syrah Rosé Syrah (Vin de Pays des Côtes de Thau) $10. The Thau lake is in Herault, near Montpellier, where Hecht & Bannier also have their winery. They have made a fresh, candy explosion of a rosé, with just a touch of sweetness and open fruit. **84** —*R.V. (8/1/2006)*

HEIDSIECK & CO MONOPOLE

Heidsieck & Co Monopole NV Blue Top Brut Champagne Blend (Champagne) $28. Earthy and dusty on the nose, and this impression continues on the palate, where flavors of powdered limestone emerge. Medium-weight, with a finish that turns slightly sour. Lacks fruit, but gets the job done. **85** —*J.C. (12/1/2004)*

Heidsieck & Co Monopole NV Blue Top Brut Champagne Blend (Champagne) $32. Fresh and zesty, this clean, lemony sparkler would make a fine partner for oysters on the half shell. The mousse is a bit aggressive, revealing the wine's youthful edge and scouring the palate clean just in time for your next kumimoto. **86** —*J.C. (12/15/2003)*

Heidsieck & Co Monopole NV Blue Top Premier Cru Champagne Blend (Champagne) $39. Impressively fine bubbles cascade up from the bottom of the glass, suggesting richness and elegance. There's a lush creaminess in the mouth, packed with flavors of candied orange, apricot, and pineapple. The wine scores a flavor bulls eye in every possible way, from the textured, enticing bouquet to the rich, mouth-filling fruit and on through the lingering, precise, and powerful finish. **93** —*P.G. (12/1/2006)*

Heidsieck & Co Monopole NV Blue Top Premiers Crus Champagne Blend (Champagne) $40. Boasts hints of sauteed mushrooms on toast, followed by savory, meaty flavors that might sound heavy but are nicely balanced by bright acidity. Finishes long and citrusy. **88** —*J.C. (12/1/2004)*

Heidsieck & Co Monopole NV Diamant Blanc Champagne Blend (Champagne) $100. Strong-willed and forward, with a mild sherry note but mostly fresh apple fruit as its driving force. Green apple and citrus dominate the palate, which is a bit aggressive and soda-like. Big and toasty late, with even more spunk. A rambunctious wine. **88** —*M.S. (12/31/2005)*

Heidsieck & Co Monopole NV Diamant Blanc de Blancs Champagne Blend (Champagne) $50. 87 —*S.H. (12/15/2000)*

Heidsieck & Co Monopole 1995 Diamant Bleu Champagne Blend (Champagne) $70. Rich and toasty, with fully integrated flavors, this wine seems well on its way to matching the glories of the 1985. Alluring bread dough scents lead into a somewhat lean palate, laced with cinnamon spice. **91** —*P.G. (12/15/2002)*

Heidsieck & Co Monopole 1998 Diamant Rosé Champagne Blend (Champagne) $130. Overt and round, with chunky aromas of berries and stone fruits. Quite lively and zesty, with purity of flavors. Is it a touch limited in scope and complexity? Yes. But the nectarine and orange flavors are crystalline and the mouthfeel rocks. **90** —*M.S. (12/15/2005)*

Heidsieck & Co Monopole 1988 Diamant Rosé Champagne Blend (Champagne) $70. Perhaps past its peak, the wine is a pleasure nonetheless in so many ways. An amazingly deep rust hue, it smells distinctly of Sherry cask, with the complexity of old yeast. Elegant styling and a precise focus carry the appealing though certainly oxidized flavors all the way through a lingering finish. **89** —*P.G. (12/15/2002)*

Heidsieck & Co Monopole 1988 Diamant Rosé Champagne Blend (Champagne) $70. Maybe this wine is an acquired taste, but for lovers of older Champagne, this 15-year-old wine is fascinating. Its mature orange-pink color, closer to the color of sunrise than sunset, and aromas of ripe, toasty fruit set the scene. To taste, it is toasty, woody with layers of rich fruit, and flavors of vanilla and spices. **92** —*R.V. (12/15/2003)*

Heidsieck & Co Monopole NV Extra Dry Champagne Blend (Champagne) $37. Yeasty and a touch flat, but it spreads out nicely across the bouquet if you allow it to. Round through the mouth, with cinnamon-apple as the main flavor component. Overall it's fairly large, but it's also a bit awkward and sugary. **87** —*M.S. (12/15/2003)*

Heidsieck & Co Monopole 2002 Gold Top Champagne Blend (Champagne) $45. A ripe, easy soft style that allows some acidity to give the wine backbone. It is well-integrated, ready to drink now, and is a rare example from one of the worst vintages on record. **86** —*R.V. (11/1/2006)*

Heidsieck & Co Monopole NV Monopole Brut Champagne Blend (Champagne) $30. 85 *(12/15/1999)*

FRANCE

Heidsieck & Co Monopole NV Red Top Champagne Blend (Champagne)
$27. Creamy and full-bodied, maybe even a little heavy, but shows solid aromas and flavors of toast, roasted-caramelized meat, soy, and wild mushrooms. A main-course Champagne. **87** —*J.C. (12/1/2004)*

Heidsieck & Co Monopole NV Red Top Champagne Blend (Champagne)
$26. Lemony and fresh at first, but also has notes of green apples and fresh herbs. Creamy on the palate, like it's losing steam, but has some pretty green apple and citrus flavors that finish soft and short. **85** —*J.C. (12/15/2003)*

Heidsieck & Co Monopole NV Rosé Top Champagne Blend (Champagne)
$43. Like a big red wine, this is full-bodied and powerful, boasting scents of meat and leather and picking up berry and tobacco nuances on the palate. Its largish bead and lack of elegance hold it back, but this is one flavorful Champagne. **89** —*J.C. (12/1/2004)*

Heidsieck & Co Monopole NV Rosé Top Champagne Blend (Champagne)
$36. This is a rich, full-bodied wine, which has a slight sweetness and softness. Quite full, it has flavors of crushed strawberries, which are balanced with some finishing acidity. **85** —*R.V. (12/15/2003)*

Heidsieck & Co Monopole NV Diamant Blanc Grands Crus Chardonnay (Champagne) $65. Smoky and toasty at first, then broadens out to encompass scents of caramelized apples. On the palate, appley flavors start sweet and sugary, then finished tart and malic. **87** —*J.C. (12/15/2003)*

Heidsieck & Co Monopole 1995 Diamant Bleu Pinot-Chardonnay (Champagne) $130. This is Heidsieck Monopole's apéritif Champagne. Still young, it is light, crisp, dry, and fruity, with flavors of the maturing Pinot Noir and the fresh, yeasty Chardonnay. It is in great balance now, a lively eager wine, ready to please. **91** —*R.V. (12/1/2004)*

HENRI ABELÉ

Henri Abelé NV 1757 Brut Champagne Blend (Champagne) $28. A good value in Champagne, this nonvintage cuvée boasts delicate toast and citrus aromas followed up by tightly focused flavors of green apple, lemons, and limes. It's very different from Abelé's vintage offering but delicious in a different way. Finishes with a crisp, youthful edge to its flavors. **89** —*J.C. (12/31/2004)*

Henri Abelé NV Brut Champagne Blend (Champagne) $30. Abelé claims to be the third oldest Champagne house in Reims, and makes a very stylish, sophisticated wine for the price. A big, plush, yeasty nose sends sweet notes of cracker and toast above lime and mineral; the flavors that follow are forward, round, and rich. Hints of mango and papaya fruit lead into a sensuous, lightly spicy, thoroughly satisfying finish. **91 Editors' Choice** —*P.G. (12/15/2002)*

HENRI BOURGEOIS

Henri Bourgeois 2005 Sauvignon Blanc (Pouilly-Fumé) $18. There's great fruit here, lots of white currants, crisp green apples, and fresh pears. At the moment, it's all fruit, a result of the vintage and the fact that it's a young wine. But there will be more because the fruit is so concentrated it will give roundness and depth in a year or two. **89** —*R.V. (8/1/2006)*

Henri Bourgeois 2005 Le MD de Bourgeois Sauvignon Blanc (Sancerre) $24. Gorgeous, concentrated, ripe fruit show both the quality of this wine and the extra warmth of 2005. The MD is the top cuvée from the Bourgeois vineyard. It's dense and ripe, with almost exotic fruit flavors, and finishes generous and fruity. **93** —*R.V. (8/1/2006)*

Henri Bourgeois 2005 Les Bonnes Bouches Sauvignon Blanc (Sancerre) $20. This wine is packed with open, fresh, succulent fruit that zings in the mouth. There are flavors of green apple skins, lychees, and tropical fruits that last and last. Delicious and fresh; a wine for this summer. **89** —*R.V. (8/1/2006)*

HENRI DE VILLAMONT

Henri de Villamont 2003 Clos des Guettes Pinot Noir (Savigny-lès-Beaune) $NA. A big, toasty wine that shows deep, almost black color, and generous fruit. The wood spice just avoids being too dominant, leaving room for fresh red fruit flavors and a layer of acidity. **89** —*R.V. (9/1/2005)*

Henri de Villamont 2002 Grands Pinot Noir (Echezeaux) $80. A firm, tannic wine that hides ripe black fruit behind a severe exterior. Needs

extended cellaring. Big, solid tannns and dry fruits give it complexity. **90** —*R.V. (9/1/2004)*

Henri de Villamont 2002 Les Baudes Premier Cru Pinot Noir (Chambolle-Musigny) $45. A ripe, voluptuous wine with layers of new wood and dry tannins which offset the richness. Although the wood is strong, it is an overall well-balanced wine. **88** —*R.V. (9/1/2004)*

Henri de Villamont 2003 Les Groseilles Premier Cru Pinot Noir (Chambolle-Musigny) $NA. A round, generous wine which has soft tannins built around a core of toast and ripe, red fruit flavors. In the end, it is the fruit which dominates, juicy, super-ripe, and opulent. This wine will age over 5 years, but it gives great pleasure now. **90** —*R.V. (9/1/2005)*

Henri de Villamont 2002 Premier Cru Pinot Noir (Chambolle-Musigny) $40. Spice and toast notes give this wine an exotic luscious feel that balances the firm tannins. It is well-made, ripe, and sweet to the finish. **88** —*R.V. (9/1/2004)*

HENRIOT

Henriot 1996 Brut Champagne Blend (Champagne) $78. Flavors of ripe, crisp apples, white fruits, and cinnamon dominate this long-lasting, concentrated wine. There is a touch of toastiness in the aroma, but it is still young, with a firm, mineral character to finish. **92** —*R.V. (11/1/2006)*

Henriot NV Brut Rosé Champagne Blend (Champagne) $60. This excellent producer makes a lovely, copper-colored rosé, which sends up fresh and inviting aromas that suggest fresh-baked apple pastries. Baking spices, cinnamon in particular, liven up the scents and flavors, and the wine seems crisp, balanced, and full in the mouth. It's a complete, nicely evolved wine, which seems to be at the peak of flavor. **91** —*P.G. (12/1/2006)*

Henriot 1990 Cuvée des Enchanteleurs Brut Champagne Blend (Champagne) $149. Dominated by Chardonnay, this wine has great depth of flavor, benefiting from the 13 years-aging on lees before disgorging. It is now a fine, balanced, mature wine, dominated by grilled almond and toast flavors, leaving a pure trail of acidity to finish. **94** —*R.V. (11/1/2006)*

Henriot NV Souverain Brut Champagne Blend (Champagne) $40. There is great intensity to this finely crafted Champagne. It's rich and toasty, with flavors of ripe gooseberries and, in this example, some good bottle age. Henriot, which also owns Bouchard Père et Fils in Burgundy, is obviously on a good streak at the moment. **92** —*R.V. (12/1/2005)*

HENRY NATTER

Henry Natter 2004 Sauvignon Blanc (Sancerre) $23. This is a soft, rich Sancerre, coming from the warm vineyards of Montigny. There is also just a touch of wood and oxidation, which opens and softens the underlying citrus fruit flavors. With its weight, this is certainly more of a food wine than an apéritif. **88** —*R.V. (8/1/2006)*

HERON

Heron 1996 Red Blend (Vin de Pays d'Oc) $9. 85 *(11/15/1999)*

HERZOG SELECTION

Herzog Selection 1999 Chardonnay (Vin de Pays du Jardin de la France) $8. So light, dry, and taut, you might mistake this for a Sauvignon Blanc with its grapefruit profile and high acidity. Still, the cleansing tartness is likeable, if not entirely expected. This will work as an apéritif or paired with lighter foods. **84** *(4/1/2001)*

HIPPOLYTE REVERDY

Hippolyte Reverdy 2003 Sauvignon Blanc (Sancerre) $22. Full and fresh. Lots of mineral along with almond, white peach, and citrus on the nose. Zesty enough, with roundness as well. Flavors of melon, apple, peach, and more mix well together. Shows a bit of heat late, which folds into pithy bitterness at the very end. **90** *(7/1/2005)*

HUGEL

Hugel 2002 Gewürztraminer (Alsace) $20. Firmly in the house style, this Gewürz is restrained and minerally rather than dramatically flamboyant. Ripe melon and pear flavors are delivered in a medium-bodied format, finishing a bit short. **84** —*J.C. (2/1/2005)*

Hugel 1999 Gewürztraminer (Alsace) $19. An aromatic, dense bouquet of tangerine and lychee nut opens this textbook Gewürz. The spiciness really shows in the mouth, where pepper and dry-rub flavors accent the sweet, exotic fruit. Not particularly long, but it has the flavor and mouthfeel to complement complex or intensely flavored foods. **87** *(11/1/2001)*

Hugel 1997 Vendange Tardive Gewürztraminer (Alsace) $55. Dense rose and tangerine aromas open to a rich, sweet, but not over-the-top palate. Thick and smooth, the mouthfeel is very sexy, with lychee and grapefruit flavors. The long, spicy finish is ripe and seductive. **91** *(11/1/2001)*

Hugel 1999 Cuvée Les Amours Pinot Blanc (Alsace) $12. The nose is almost fat, with an attractive peach-pear-tangerine bouquet. This attractive medium-to-full-bodied white shows spicy accents on the peachy, creamy palate, as well as a touch of earth and citrus. Finishes with modest length, citrus, and mineral notes. **86** *(11/1/2001)*

Hugel 2001 Vendange Tardive Pinot Gris (Alsace) $92. This 2001 Vendange Tardive has richness and sweetness, with some dry botrytis character. It also shows sophistication and delicacy, with lovely acidity as well as yellow fruits. There is a delicious fresh aftertaste. **92** —*R.V.* *(2/1/2006)*

Hugel 2000 Riesling (Alsace) $17. This Riesling has refinement, elegance and freshness without huge complexity. It is a wine to drink now and over the next four or five years. **85** —*R.V. (8/1/2003)*

Hugel 1998 Hommage à Jean Hugel Riesling (Alsace) $50. A wine that has been created to celebrate the continuing life of Jean Hugel, one of the great ambassadors for Alsace, this has fine petrol aromas, with a dry palate and great flavors of currants, toast, and some spice. It has structure, dryness, and fine perfumed flavors. **91** —*R.V. (5/1/2005)*

Hugel 1998 Jubilee Reserve Personelle Riesling (Alsace) $35. Though not labeled as such, this wine is sourced entirely from the Schoenenbourg grand cru. The complex aromas and flavors of mineral oil, kerosene, ripe plum, apple, and spice are deep and impressive. There's good acidity, yet the wine is even and round on the palate. Finishes long, with ripe grapefruit and mineral notes. **89** *(11/1/2001)*

Hugel 1995 Vendage Tardive Riesling (Alsace) $65. There's very little of this delicious VT sourced from the Schoenenbourg grand cru, but it's worth the hunt. The botrytis nose is fat, as is the palate, wtih opulent honey, apricot, diesel, and Golden Delicious apple aromas and flavors. Though full, the wine is well-structured; though rich, it's more complex than overtly sweet. The lime-accented nut-and-honey finish is impressively long. **93 Cellar Selection** *(11/1/2001)*

Hugel 1997 Reserve Personelle Tokay Pinot Gris (Alsace) $35. **85** — *(8/1/1999)*

Hugel 2003 Gentil White Blend (Alsace) $11. This blended white combines fresh apple and pear fruit notes with minerally, petrolly nuances to give a surprisingly complex result. Finshes with a burst of lime. Drink now and over the next several months; this isn't built to age. **86 Best Buy** —*J.C. (2/1/2005)*

J. & F. LURTON

J. & F. Lurton 2005 Les Salices Pinot Noir Pinot Noir (Vin de Pays d'Oc) $9. Soft and ripe, with polished, dense red fruit flavors, soft tannins and richness from well-balanced wood. The wine comes from vineyards in the Minervois region. **86 Best Buy** —*R.V. (12/31/2006)*

J. & F. Lurton 2003 Château des Erles Cuvée des Ardoises Rhône Red Blend (Fitou) $12. This is a classy wine from the warm south of France. It has ripe, raisiny fruit aromas, flavors of fresh fruit, black figs, and herbs. Its dry tannins are balanced with a good layer of acidity. **89 Best Buy** — *R.V. (12/31/2006)*

J. & F. Lurton 2003 Les Fumées Blanches Sauvignon Blanc (Vin de Pays de Côtes du Tarn) $9. This simple acidic quaff blends grapefruit and gooseberry flavors in a tart, cleansing wine best served as an apéritif. **83** —*J.C. (12/1/2004)*

J. & F. Lurton 2003 Les Salices Viognier (Vin de Pays d'Oc) $10. Smells like a flower garden on a hot, humid day, when the aromas just lay there heavy and thick, like honey. It's a big, flowery wine, expressive of its variety

and the warm vintage conditions. It's a trifle short on the finish, but the price makes it a steal. **86 Best Buy** —*J.C. (12/1/2004)*

J. & F. Lurton 2005 Terra Sana White Blend (Vin de Pays Charentais) $10. The healthy earth in the wine's name refers to the organic viticulture which was used to grow the grapes in the Charentes region (better known for Cognac). The wine has some good pure, intense fruit flavors, with green apples and fresh, crisp acidity as well as some spice to broaden out the flavor spectrum. Lovely, clean finish. **88 Best Buy** —*R.V. (12/31/2006)*

J. DE TELMONT

J. de Telmont 1993 Consécration Champagne Blend (Champagne) $NA. A soft, mature, but unfocused wine which has acidity and toast without the weight and richness to sustain it. It is enjoyable as an old wine, yes, but it's missed something along the way. **83** —*R.V. (12/1/2004)*

J. de Telmont 2000 Grand Champagne Blend (Champagne) $NA. This is one of the youngest vintages on the market currently, and it tastes like it. It is fresh and fruity, but isn't balanced yet between the sweetness of the dosage and the fruit and acidity of the Champagne. This could change, but it would certainly need four or five years' aging. **84** —*R.V. (12/1/2004)*

J. de Telmont 1990 Consécration du Siècle Brut Champagne Blend (Champagne) $80. This lovely tete de cuvée shows off a mature, sweet bready nose with light citrus accents. It hits the palate with assertive, full green apple, and bright citrus fruit complemented by strong leesy notes. Quite young and lively despite its age, it closes long with complex lemon and yeast flavors, and should even improve with a few more years in the bottle. **89** *(6/1/2001)*

J. D. LAURENT

J. D. Laurent 2003 Sauvignon Blanc-Sémillon (Bordeaux) $10. Begins with modest apple and nectarine scents, then delivers bland stone fruit flavors in a plump, low-acid format that's easy to drink, as long as it's well chilled. Shows the ripeness of the 2003 vintage, but lacks concentration. **84** —*J.C. (6/1/2005)*

J. MOREAU & FILS

J. Moreau & Fils 2000 Chardonnay (Chablis) $14. This crisp wine, like the other Moreau Chablis, sees no oak and opens with green apple and mineral spirits aromas. Lemon and grapefruit flavors play on the tongue. The palate is very dry and flinty. It's correct Chablis, with a steely austere close, though without much nuance. **86** *(11/15/2001)*

J. Moreau & Fils 1999 Bougros Chardonnay (Chablis) $45. Starts off nutty, with hints of cinnamon toast, but also a strong sense of hard-to-describe cool stoniness. Peach fruit is merely an accent to dusty earth and chalk flavors. A bit lighter-weight than the other grand crus in this tasting. **88** *(6/1/2002)*

J. Moreau & Fils 2000 Cuvée Joyau Premier Cru Chardonnay (Chablis) $45. Showy aromas of vanilla cream, almond, and ripe peach blend in flavors of oranges and tangerines in the mouth. This medium-weight wine finishes gently, with soft underpinnings of toasted nuts and chalk. The best Joyau of the trio. **91** *(6/1/2002)*

J. Moreau & Fils 1997 Cuvée Joyeaux Premier Cru Chardonnay (Chablis) $45. The tight structure of this wine influenced Moreau to hold back its release until May 2002. Now that it's available, expect a full-bodied, powerful Chablis that combines aromas and flavors of butter, peach, apple, and nuts in a ready-to-drink package. **90** *(6/1/2002)*

J. Moreau & Fils 1999 Les Clos Chardonnay (Chablis) $45. A big, forceful, buttery wine that boasts loads of slippery river stones, along with spicy clove notes. Full-bodied and very ripe, showing more mineral than fruit, this grand cru should be approachable in 2–3 years and last up to 10. **91** *(6/1/2002)*

J. Moreau & Fils 1999 Vaillon Premier Cru Chardonnay (Chablis) $30. Thias premier cru has deep hay and mineral aromas and flavors with a touch of caramel cream. The mouthfeel is soft, and lower in acidity than anticipated; the wine seems too mature for a 1999. Flavorful, if already long in the tooth for its relatively youthful age. Drink now. **88** *(11/15/2001)*

J. Moreau & Fils 2001 Vaillons Premier Cru Chardonnay (Chablis) $29.

This is a taut, structured wine, it's tough, rocky-minerally aspect only slightly softened by a glaze of ripe pears. Picks up tangy lemon and lime notes on the finish. **88** —*J.C. (10/1/2003)*

J. Moreau & Fils 1999 Vaucoupin Chardonnay (Chablis) $28. Perhaps the most classically styled of these Chablis from Moreau is the Vaucopin, which features zesty lemon and lime aromas allied to crisp pear and green apple flavors. Finishes tangy, with hints of anise and toast. Try with oysters or soft chèvres. **88** *(6/1/2002)*

J. Moreau & Fils 2000 Vaucoupin Premier Cru Chardonnay (Chablis) $29. This is an odd but interesting duck, with some contrasting aromas and flavors. Aromas are slightly buttery but backed by powerful scents of flint and quince. In the mouth, there's a soft, slightly furry texture, yet the flavors are hard and unyielding. **87** —*J.C. (10/1/2003)*

J. Moreau & Fils 2000 Sauvignon Blanc (Sauvignon de St-Bris) $10. A handsome bouquet of nutmeg, grapefruit, melon, and cilantro marks this value white. The dry grapefruit and green apple palate allows plenty of chalkiness and medium acidity; the wine finishes medium-long with white pepper, lemon, and mineral notes. Tastes Chablis-like, though made of Sauvignon Blanc and not from the appelation. **87 Best Buy** *(11/15/2001)*

J. VIDAL FLEURY

J. Vidal Fleury 1999 Red Blend (Vacqueyras) $13. Earthy at first, and there's also a peanut-like scent to the concentrated bouquet. The palate is on the softer side, but ripe plum and pepper flavors drive it forward, and the final act is a finish of coffee and raisins. **87** —*M.S. (2/1/2003)*

J. Vidal Fleury 2001 Rhône Red Blend (Vacqueyras) $20. A little rustic, featuring leather and dried fruit aromas and some astringent tannins on the finish. But it shows some pleasing spice and prune flavors on the round midpalate. Drink now. **85** —*J.C. (11/15/2006)*

J. Vidal Fleury 2000 Rhône Red Blend (Côtes-du-Rhône) $10. This wine is a fine example of all that's good about the appellation. It has a complete nose of bold berries. The palate is open and welcoming, with cherry and raspberry fruit framed by a light shade of oak. Even the finish, which is round and nicely textured, works. And with light but healthy tannins, it's a breeze to drink. **88 Best Buy** —*M.S. (2/1/2003)*

J. Vidal Fleury 2004 Syrah (Crozes-Hermitage) $20. Light to medium in body, with a correspondingly light color and modest fruit. Instead, there's meaty complexity and more than a hint of Band-Aid. Drink now. **84** —*J.C. (11/15/2006)*

J. Vidal Fleury 2000 Syrah (Crozes-Hermitage) $16. Black plum, blackberry, and mineral notes comprise the nose, which leads into a palate of light, snappy red fruit with fine tannins and an overall good mouthfeel. The finish is soft, clean, and a bit simple, and in general, the attitude of the wine is reverent yet sufficiently wild. Clean and svelte; not much is out of place here. **87** —*M.S. (9/1/2003)*

J. Vidal Fleury 2004 Blanc Viognier (Côtes-du-Rhône) $11. This floral, spice-filled white is Viognier; it just can't advertise that fact on the bottle. It's plump and medium-bodied, with ample peach and melon fruit to support its flowery aromatics. Mouthwatering on the finish, where the slightest touch of pleasant bitterness creeps in. **87 Best Buy** —*J.C. (11/15/2006)*

J.J. VINCENT

J.J. Vincent 2001 Domaine Le Cotoyon Gamay (Juliénas) $17. Better known for its whites from the Maconnais, Vincent has crafted a successful wine from the difficult 2001 vintage. Sappy, briary, and herbal notes impart complexity to the ripe cherry flavors. Long finish. **87** —*J.C. (11/15/2003)*

J.L. CHAVE

J.L. Chave 1999 Rhône Red Blend (Hermitage) $125. Jean-Louis, the son of Gérard Chave, is now in charge of the family business, as well as being president of the Hermitage wine producers. He is continuing the family tradition of making powerful statements of Syrah from Hermitage, combining massive structure and over-powering perfumes. This 1999 seems to have the best of the traditional world of tannic immensity and the modern world of beautiful, ripe fruit. A wine that will age for a very long time. **97** —*R.V. (6/1/2002)*

J.L. Chave 1998 Syrah (Hermitage) $100. Opens with a vibrant berry, chocolate, Asian-spice, rosemary, olive, and bacon-fat nose so good you linger before tasting. Sour cherry, licorice, brush, leather, and a meaty note show on the palate. The wine is lean yet velvety, with powerful, deep structure. It closes with full, ripe tannins, notes of black tea and pepper. Cellar this keeper until 2004, drink through 2015+. **95 Cellar Selection** *(11/1/2001)*

J.P. CHENET

J.P. Chenet 2000 Founder's Reserve Chardonnay (Vin de Pays d'Oc) $8. Light oak-cream flavors plus a little nuttiness dominate the palate; less oak, plus dusty sour-apple flavors linger on the bouquet. Finishes with terroir-rific chalk-mineral notes. **85 Best Buy** —*D.T. (2/1/2002)*

JACQUART

Jacquart 1997 Blanc de Blancs Brut Champagne Blend (Champagne) $36. Great acidity is the hallmark of this crisp, green Chardonnay. It has good green fruit flavors, Granny Smith's apples and a touch of toast. This has blended well and is now approaching peak maturity. There is freshness, crispness, and a delicious lively aftertaste. **90** —*R.V. (12/1/2004)*

Jacquart 1992 Blanc de Blancs Brut Mosaïque Champagne Blend (Champagne) $38. **91** —*S.H. (12/31/2000)*

Jacquart NV Brut de Nominée Champagne Blend (Champagne) $57. Although Jacquart suggests most of the wine in this blend is from the 1996 vintage, it is labelled as Non-Vintage. The distinction makes little difference to the great fresh fruit that enhances this Champagne. It is fresh, lively, with green fruit flavors and good crispness. It should age well over 5 years. **88** —*R.V. (12/1/2004)*

Jacquart NV Brut Mosaïque Champagne Blend (Champagne) $30. **90** —*P.G. (12/15/2002)*

Jacquart NV Brut Mosaïque Champagne Blend (Champagne) $35. A rich, full-bodied style of wine, which has some caramel flavors as well as white peach flavors. Jacquart is a great value brand from one of the big cooperatives, and this style is immediately attractive and easy. **88** —*R.V. (12/1/2005)*

Jacquart 1996 Brut Mosaïque Champagne Blend (Champagne) $36. A ripe, creamy blend of 50% Chardonnay with 50% of the two Pinots. There are spice, cinammon, and flavors of black currants, mingled together in a full-bodied blend. The freshness is laced with mature toastiness to give a wine of great complexity. **91** —*R.V. (12/1/2004)*

Jacquart NV Brut Mosaïque Rosé Champagne Blend (Champagne) $40. A simple, fresh rosé, which has some attractive toasty bottle age. There is also a yeasty character, which leaves the fruit submerged in the more autolytic flavors. This is a fine rosé for food. **86** —*R.V. (12/1/2005)*

Jacquart 1998 Brut Mosaïque Rosé Champagne Blend (Champagne) $NA. An attractive pale salmon pink color and fresh strawberry aromas make this wine immediately appealing. To taste, it is crisp, light, with a touch of toast and flavors of red currants and fine, fresh fruit. **88** —*R.V. (12/1/2004)*

Jacquart 1999 Cuvée Allegra Champagne Blend (Champagne) $65. This is the first vintage of a cuvée named, so the advertising has it, after a figure who is both romantic and modern. It is certainly a fine blend that shows ripe fruit, some layers of toast to go with some honey, and fresh white fruits. It should age, but, as an apéritif wine, it's ready to drink now. **91** —*R.V. (11/1/2006)*

Jacquart NV Demi-Sec Champagne Blend (Champagne) $30. **91** *(12/31/2000)*

Jacquart 1999 Blanc de Blancs Brut Chardonnay (Champagne) $44. White fruits, almonds, and soft, crisp acidity are the hallmarks of this lightweight, fresh wine. **87** —*R.V. (11/1/2006)*

JACQUES PRIEUR

Jacques Prieur 1999 Clos de la Feguine Pinot Noir (Beaune) $50. **89** —*P.G. (11/1/2002)*

FRANCE

JACQUESSON ET FILS

Jacquesson et Fils NV Brut Rosé Champagne Blend (Champagne) $51. Pale salmon-pink color, with soft fruit, caramel, and vanilla flavors and sweet strawberries at its core. A well-balanced, simple, and attractive wine. **86** —R.V. (12/15/2003)

Jacquesson et Fils 2000 Dizy Corne Bautray Champagne Blend (Champagne) $125. This single-vineyard Champagne is one of the range produced by Jacquesson, and all are superb. This shows elegance, with ripe, almost toasty, flavors and a lovely, lingering acid and toast finish, which leaves freshness and intensity at the same time. **93 Editors' Choice** —R.V. (12/31/2006)

Jacquesson et Fils 1995 Grand Vin Signature Extra Brut Rosé Champagne Blend (Champagne) $110. An attractive onion skin colored wine with considerable acidity and maturity. This is very crisp, with flavors of red currants and hedgerow fruits, with a touch of mature toastiness. A fine fresh wine from this medium-sized family company. **89** —R.V. (12/1/2004)

Jacquesson et Fils 1995 Signature Extra Brut Champagne Blend (Champagne) $90. This Pinot Noir-dominated wine is rich and structured with waves of acidity passing through the white currant, toast, and a developing maturity. Extra richness comes from the oak fermentation, but, because of the low dosage, there is also an austerity and minerality about this wine that will find its best expression with food. **95** —R.V. (12/1/2005)

JAILLANCE

Jaillance 1999 Grande Réserve Brut Clairette (Crémant de Die) $20. A hint of sulfur blows off to reveal muted cookie and chalk, but the palate opens up with lemon-lime flavors and a smokey edge. Crisp and steely in the mouth, it hints at roundness and sweetness without taking the plunge. **87** —M.D. (12/15/2006)

Jaillance NV Brut Sparkling Blend (Crémant de Bourgogne) $16. This wine shows a richer, smoother mouthfeel than others of its ilk. The nose is nicely toasty, with tropical fruit aromas and mint. Flavors are similar, dealing out nicely oaked fruit that goes down easily. **87** —M.D. (12/15/2006)

JEAN ASTIER

Jean Astier 2002 Rhône Red Blend (Côtes-du-Rhône) $10. A decent effort from a rain-soaked vintage, Astier's 2002 Côtes-du-Rhône displays aromas of strawberries and red plums, picking up notes of cocoa and bitter coffee on the palate. It's light but pretty, finishing with peppery, herbal nuances. **85** —J.C. (12/11/2003)

JEAN PABIOT ET FILS

Jean Pabiot et Fils 2004 Domaine des Fines Caillottes Sauvignon Blanc (Pouilly-Fumé) $NA. The 20 different parcels that go to make up Fines Caillottes add up to 52 acres, a large estate for the region. Alain Pabiot makes an impressively classic Pouilly-Fumé, with the pure fruit of the Sauvignon made more subtle with flavors of herbs and a fine, poised structure. An excellent wine, and one that will certainly age well. **92** —R.V. (8/1/2006)

JEAN-BAPTISTE ADAM

Jean-Baptiste Adam NV Brut Pinot Blanc (Crémant d'Alsace) $20. A pleasant, easy Crémant, Adam has produced a balanced, fruity wine, with crisp acidity. Made from Pinot Blanc, there is some weight to the wine, but its main impression is of lightness and softness. **86** —R.V. (6/1/2006)

Jean-Baptiste Adam 2002 Grand Cru Wineck-Schlossberg Riesling (Alsace) $40. This wine is finely perfumed, with flavors of almonds, currants, and white berries. There is good intensity and the wine should age well over the next five years or more. **89** —R.V. (11/1/2005)

Jean-Baptiste Adam 2003 Cuvée Jean-Baptiste Tokay Pinot Gris (Alsace) $23. A dry, intensely spicy style, which layers acidity with freshness. The flavors are ripe, packed with white fruits, but the main impression is of lightness and elegance. The aftertaste is clean, fresh, and easy. **88** —R.V. (2/1/2006)

Jean-Baptiste Adam 2004 Réserve Tokay Pinot Gris (Alsace) $15. This was the first vintage in which the Adam vineyards were operated biodynamically. The fruit certainly is intense and very clean, with flavors of toast and spice and aromas of white flowers. There is some residual sugar, leaving a soft, rich aftertaste. **87** —R.V. (2/1/2006)

JEAN-CLAUDE BOISSET

Jean-Claude Boisset 2003 Pinot Noir (Bourgogne) $16. This blend of Pinots from Aloxe-Corton, Chorey, Savigny, and Marsannay is slightly lean and herbal. Has some nice black cherry fruit, then finishes on a teal-like note with some drying tannins. Try with rare beef or lamb. **84** (12/31/2005)

Jean-Claude Boisset 2003 Pinot Noir (Chambolle-Musigny) $50. Smoky and cedary, gradually opening to reveal bright cherries and some meaty nuances. It's medium-bodied and delicate in texture, with fine tannins on the well-balanced finish. **88** —J.C. (12/31/2005)

Jean-Claude Boisset 2003 Chaînes Carteaux Premier Cru Pinot Noir (Nuits-St.-Georges) $69. More obviously structured than many of these 2003s, with black cherry, plum, earth, and vanilla framed by ample tannins. Tobacco and black tea flavors linger on the long, intense finish. **88** —J.C. (12/31/2005)

Jean-Claude Boisset 2002 Clos de Verger Premier cru Pinot Noir (Pommard) $NA. A concentrated, structured wine that marries dusty tannins and rich, ripe fruit. The fruit is certainly intense at this stage, but watch it develop over 10–15 years. **91** —R.V. (9/1/2004)

Jean-Claude Boisset 2003 Grand Cru Pinot Noir (Clos Vougeot) $150. Cedary and meaty at first, with lush fruit aromas of black cherries and plum gradually taking over. Rich and creamy in the mouth, adding nuances of meat and vanilla on the long, textured finish. **91** —J.C. (12/31/2005)

Jean-Claude Boisset 2002 Les Charmes Premier Cru Pinot Noir (Chambolle-Musigny) $80. Minerality and structure combine with Chambolle opulence in this finely balanced wine. Its fruit is certainly firm, but it still manages to exude immense charm and attraction. **92** —R.V. (9/1/2004)

JEAN-LOUIS TROCARD

Jean-Louis Trocard 2001 Clos de la Vieille Eglise Merlot-Cabernet Sauvignon (Pomerol) $55. 85 —J.C. (11/15/2005)

JEAN-LUC COLOMBO

Jean-Luc Colombo 1999 Cote Bleue Les Pins Couches Red Blend (Coteaux d'Aix en Provence) $30. Like the proverbial hare, this wine fires out of the blocks but then runs out of steam before the finish line. Along the way, there are deep and pure aromas, potent cherry and raspberry fruit and some chocolaty warmth to the finish. **87** —M.S. (2/1/2003)

Jean-Luc Colombo 1997 Les Abeilles Rhône Red Blend (Côtes-du-Rhône) $9. 90 (11/15/1999)

Jean-Luc Colombo 2005 Les Abeilles Rhône White Blend (Côtes-du-Rhône) $12. A blend of the typical southern Rhône white grapes, along with some Viognier, this is a full, fat wine, but one which is leavened with delicious fruit flavors and an enticing floral aroma. Drink now. **86** —R.V. (12/31/2006)

Jean-Luc Colombo 2004 Rosé de Cote Bleue Rosé Blend (Coteaux d'Aix en Provence) $10. Herbal and fresh, with strawberry aromas and flavors that take on an earthy edge. Medium-bodied, it's ideal for picnics, where you never know what foods might turn up. Ends on a grapefruity note. **84** —J.C. (11/15/2005)

Jean-Luc Colombo 2005 La Violette Syrah (Vin de Pays d'Oc) $12. Pure Syrah, with its perfumed aromas, earthy ripe fruit flavors and dense texture, packed with tannins under the fruit. This is a great barbecue wine. **85** —R.V. (12/31/2006)

Jean-Luc Colombo 2001 Les Lauves Syrah (Saint-Joseph) $25. Here's a great juicy wine, with rich fruit flavors. It has flavors of black currant and other black fruits, with spices and bitter chocolate. There are dry tannins from the 12 months' wood aging. From the single vineyard Les Lauves, it leaves a great spicy, toasty aftertaste. **91** —R.V. (2/1/2005)

Jean-Luc Colombo 2002 Les Ruchets Syrah (Cornas) $64. It's a bit tart and thin on cherry flavor, but is an admirable success for this challenging

FRANCE

vintage. The vanilla and oak-spice notes are flattering, there just isn't enough material underneath. **86** —*J.C. (11/15/2006)*

Jean-Luc Colombo 2001 Les Ruchets Syrah (Cornas) $80. True to Colombo's style, this is rather oaky, but with a few years of aging the oak has turned cedary, blending easily with iron and cassis. Long on the finish, with strong cinnamon notes. Drink now–2015. **90** —*J.C. (11/15/2006)*

Jean-Luc Colombo 2003 La Violette Viognier (Vin de Pays d'Oc) $13. This full-bodied, muscular wine seems a bit strange for Viognier, which often has a more feminine, floral quality. This is firmly mineral, with notes of chalk and earth and only a hint of melon. Still decent wine, just not very Viognier-like to my tastes. **83** —*J.C. (11/15/2005)*

JEAN-LUC JOILLOT

Jean-Luc Joillot NV Champagne Blend (Crémant de Bourgogne) $24. An impressive wine, packed with concentrated white and green fruits. It has good structure, fresh acidity, and a touch of toastiness. It's a dry wine, but full and rich, and likely to age well over the next couple of years. **91** —*R.V. (6/1/2006)*

JEAN-MARC BROCARD

Jean-Marc Brocard 2002 Domaine Sainte Claire Chardonnay (Petit Chablis) $13. Smoky and minerally on the nose—like when you strike two pieces of flint together. But there are also ripe fruit flavors of honey and pink grapefruit and a richness of texture that's usually lacking in Petit Chablis. Such a vivid expression of minerality is hard to find at this price. **87** —*J.C. (2/1/2005)*

JEAN-MARIE HAAG

Jean-Marie Haag 2003 Vallée Noble Pinot Gris (Alsace) $24. Ripe and bulky, but also flinty and full of talc and almond. The palate is oily, with sweet apple and baked-pear flavors. Ends with some bitterness but also a sweet wave. **86** *(2/1/2006)*

JEAN-PAUL BRUN

Jean-Paul Brun 2002 Terres Dorees L'Ancien Vieilles Vignes Gamay (Beaujolais) $13. Brun packs a lot of complexity into this wine. Briary, stemmy aromas add a wild touch to the crystalline black fruit, and those same elements re-emerge on the long finish. Crisp and clean, and with enough weight that it's hard to believe the label's stated 11% alcohol. **88 Best Buy** —*J.C. (11/15/2003)*

JEAN-PHILIPPE MARCHAND

Jean-Philippe Marchand 2004 Vieilles Vignes Pinot Noir (Gevrey-Chambertin) $30. Reasonably priced for Gevrey, and this has plenty of Gevrey character as well, offering herbal, meaty, somewhat *sauvage* notes, firm structure, and crisp berry and tea-leaf flavors. Give it another year or two and drink until 2015. **87** —*J.C. (11/15/2006)*

JEANJEAN

Jeanjean 2003 Petit Devois Syrah-Grenache (Coteaux du Languedoc) $13. This blend of Syrah and Grenache comes from vineyards owned by the Jeanjean family. It is soft and gentle, although there are some tannins hiding in the background. The fruits are clean, somewhat jammy, easy to drink. **84** —*R.V. (12/31/2006)*

JOSEPH BURRIER

Joseph Burrier 2003 Château de Beauregard Gamay (Fleurie) $22. **83** —*J.C. (11/15/2005)*

JOSEPH DROUHIN

Joseph Drouhin 2004 Chardonnay (Chablis) $20. Light, crisp, and lean, this is prototypical Chablis, with steely lime and chalk aromas followed by tart apple and lemon flavors. Strident and citrusy on the finish. **86** *(3/1/2006)*

Joseph Drouhin 2004 Chardonnay (Puligny-Montrachet) $46. Rich and accessible, this is a rounded, buttery wine with fine, sweet acidity and delicious open fruit. It just demands to be enjoyed. **89** —*R.V. (12/1/2006)*

Joseph Drouhin 2003 Chardonnay (Rully) $18. From its aromas—which combine toasted nuts and ripe peach scents—to its flavors of peach,

apple, and a bit of cedar pencil shaving, everything about this wine is easy to like. It's not profound, but it's simple satisfying, finishing on a juicy, mouth-watering note that's a bit surprising for the vintage. **86** —*J.C. (11/15/2005)*

Joseph Drouhin 2003 Chardonnay (Chassagne-Montrachet) $38. Pineapple, mineral, and smoke notes mingle on the nose of this medium-bodied wine. On the palate, there's more pineapple, additional citrus, and some flinty notes. A bit simple, but well-made and tasty. **86** —*J.C. (4/1/2006)*

Joseph Drouhin 2001 Chardonnay (Chassagne-Montrachet) $41. Racy and tart, with lemon and green apple aromas and flavors marked by a dash of toasty oak. A bit lean right now, maybe it will fill out by 2005, when it should be hitting its peak drinking window. **85** —*J.C. (10/1/2003)*

Joseph Drouhin 2001 Chardonnay (Meursault) $38. This villages Meursault shows a greater degree of elegance and harmony than Drouhin's 2001 Perrieres, blending honey, citrus, and toast aromas into a seamless bouquet. Flavors consist of lightly grilled peaches and plums, finishing with a zesty blast of limes. **90** —*J.C. (10/1/2003)*

Joseph Drouhin 2001 Chardonnay (Puligny-Montrachet) $42. The nose is a little shy, showing only hints of honey, cream, and toast. The wine becomes more assertive on the palate, adding layers of apple, pear, and citrus, and gradually showing ample richness and depth. Finishes with hints of lemon and toast. **89** —*J.C. (10/1/2003)*

Joseph Drouhin 2002 Clos des Mouches Chardonnay (Beaune) $86. In a bit of an awkward stage now, the fruit seems to have closed in on itself, while the toasty, caramelly oak sits on the surface. Swirling brings out ripe peaches, and roasted nuts and develops a slightly tannic feel on the finish, so cellar a few years until the wine emerges from hibernation. At that time, it may deserve an even higher score. **88** *(3/1/2006)*

Joseph Drouhin 2004 Domaine de Vaudon Chardonnay (Chablis) $23. From an unclassified parcel between the premier crus of Montée de Tonnerre and Mont de Milieu, this is a step up from the regular Chablis, showing more ripeness and mineral character. Apple, citrus, and flint notes mingle harmoniously in this medium-bodied wine. **88** *(3/1/2006)*

Joseph Drouhin 2004 Folatières Premier Cru Chardonnay (Puligny-Montrachet) $65. Like so many Drouhin wines, this is beautifully balanced. The wood, green fruit, spice, and acidity already in fine harmony. There is a richness coming from the deep soils of the vineyard. Can it age? Probably, because of the firm structure. **91** —*R.V. (12/1/2006)*

Joseph Drouhin 2003 Laforet Chardonnay (Bourgogne) $12. Light in body, with apple, peach, and citrus notes on the nose and in the mouth. Very cleanly made, this is a solid introduction to white Burgundy at a good price. **84** —*J.C. (11/15/2005)*

Joseph Drouhin 2004 Marquis de Laguiche Chardonnay (Montrachet) $596. This is a beautifully shaped wine that rises from a quiet opening. Muted and slightly closed up at this stage, it opens opulently but with balanced acidity and crispness, as well as richness and restrained power. **96 Editors' Choice** —*R.V. (12/1/2006)*

Joseph Drouhin 2004 Montmains Premier Cru Chardonnay (Chablis) $33. Befitting a premier cru, there's a hint of honeyed ripeness to this wine's aromas and flavors. Sweetened lime notes accent apples and pears on the palate, ending in a rush of ripe fruit and minerals. **90** *(3/1/2006)*

Joseph Drouhin 2004 Perrières Premier Cru Chardonnay (Meursault) $68. Full, but structured, this is a wine that shows a serious side to Meursault. It layers fine stone fruit flavors with crisp apple skins and some fresh toast and butter. It should improve over 5 years. **93 Cellar Selection** —*R.V. (12/1/2006)*

Joseph Drouhin 2004 Premier Cru Chardonnay (Chablis) $29. A blend of lots from Montmains, Sécher, and Vaillons, this is a crisp, minerally, chalky rendition of Chablis that adds just a touch of honey to the tart apple and citrus fruit flavors. **89** *(3/1/2006)*

Joseph Drouhin 2001 Vaudesir Chardonnay (Chablis) $51. A big, ripe, rich Chablis, loaded with honey, melon, and pear. Subtle clove and cinnamon notes appear on the nose and linger delicately on the finish. **90** —*J.C. (10/1/2003)*

FRANCE

Joseph Drouhin 2003 Véro Chardonnay (Bourgogne) $20. Starts off perfumy and floral, then develops into a perfectly drinkable Chardonnay, with hints of toasted almond and vanilla but also pleasant peach, pear, and apple fruit. Not very mineral, but easy to like. **87** —*J.C. (11/15/2005)*

Joseph Drouhin 2001 Gamay (Morgon) $14. Earthy and dusty, with these elements leaving a more lasting impression that the wine's modest cherry and plum fruit. Tart, with some dusty tannins on the finish, but not enough stuffing to age. Drink up. **85** —*J.C. (11/15/2003)*

Joseph Drouhin 2001 Gamay (Brouilly) $15. Understated cherry aromas carry a slight medicinal edge that deepens and broadens on the palate, leaving a cherry cough syrup impression that's a bit cloying on the finish. **83** —*J.C. (11/15/2003)*

Joseph Drouhin 2000 Pinot Noir (Bonnes-Mares) $119. A powerful wine with aromas of coffee, spice, and smoked meats. With its huge rich red fruit flavors and dense sweet tannins, it manages to combine a sense of structure with piercing pure fruit. It will age well, and a corkscrew shouldn't even go near this bottle for another three to five years. **94 Editors' Choice** —*R.V. (11/1/2002)*

Joseph Drouhin 2003 Pinot Noir (Chorey-lès-Beaune) $21. Chorey is known for its relatively light, cherry-scented wines, but in the drought vintage of 2003, this is an impressively dark effort, loaded with plums, black cherries, and even a bit of chocolate fudge. It's full-bodied and a bit chunky, but nicely textured and shows good concentration and length. **87** *(3/1/2006)*

Joseph Drouhin 2003 Pinot Noir (Gevrey-Chambertin) $43. A big, solid wine, full of strawberry fruit flavors and solid tannins. Ripe and generous; earthy and juicy fruit flavors, and a layer of acidity, complete this delicious wine. **89** —*R.V. (9/1/2005)*

Joseph Drouhin 2003 Pinot Noir (Chambolle-Musigny) $73. A soft, seductive wine that oozes ripe Pinot Noir. There are tannins there, but they are subsumed into the beautiful red fruit flavors. Will mature well, over 5 years at least. **88** —*R.V. (9/1/2005)*

Joseph Drouhin 2001 Pinot Noir (Nuits-St.-Georges) $45. This wine seems to depart somewhat from the Drouhin house style, offering more size than usual while simultaneously lacking a little flesh. Outsized plum and black cherry fruit finishes firm, with drying tannins. **85** —*J.C. (10/1/2003)*

Joseph Drouhin 2001 Pinot Noir (Côte de Beaune) $23. Lean and tart but nicely textured, this lightweight Pinot offers understated cherry and leather aromas and flavors. Picks up some chocolate and a layered texture on the finish. **84** —*J.C. (10/1/2003)*

Joseph Drouhin 2001 Pinot Noir (Savigny-lès-Beaune) $20. Fruity and forward, with pretty but delicate flavors of red cherries. It's lightweight, yet turns a bit heavier and chocolaty on the finish. **84** —*J.C. (10/1/2003)*

Joseph Drouhin 2000 Pinot Noir (Chambolle-Musigny) $39. An attractively perfumed wine, with aromas of bold, charming fruit. Fruit flavors dominate the palate, showing ripe red fruits and dark cherries. Buried deep inside the wine are some tannins and dryness. **88** —*R.V. (11/1/2002)*

Joseph Drouhin 2002 Chambertin Clos de Bèze Pinot Noir (Gevrey-Chambertin) $NA. Power and tannins mark this smoky flavored wine. Chocolate and black fruit show through the dry flavors. This is a wine that needs at least 10 years in the bottle. **92** —*R.V. (9/1/2004)*

Joseph Drouhin 2001 Charmes-Chambertin Pinot Noir (Burgundy) $118. Big and fairly burly, this bruising effort contrasts with Drouhin's typically elegant style. Sturdy black cherry and plum fruit finishes on a tannic, spicy note and echoes of black tea. Should develop nicely over the next 4-5 years. **90** —*J.C. (10/1/2003)*

Joseph Drouhin 2002 Clos des Mouches Pinot Noir (Beaune) $57. This was the first Drouhin vineyard to become fully biodynamic, a process which now covers the entire domaine. The wine is full of rich, smoky plum fruit, cherries, and a touch of wood. **89** —*R.V. (9/1/2004)*

Joseph Drouhin 2002 Clos des Mouches Premier Cru Pinot Noir (Beaune) $91. Drouhin owns more than 75% of this vineyard, which they've made famous around the globe. Slightly stinky when first poured, this opens into a beautiful glass of Burgundy, delivering black cherries, minerals, and exotic spice notes in waves of wonderfully silky fruit. Great length

on the finish. Drink now–2015, or beyond, depending on your preferences. **93** *(3/1/2006)*

Joseph Drouhin 2002 Grands Echézeaux Pinot Noir (Echezeaux) $179. A dark, immensely tannic wine at this stage, this has firm, powerful dry fruit. It is still just feeling its way at this stage, a wine that can last 15–20 years at least. **96** —*R.V. (9/1/2004)*

Joseph Drouhin 2002 Les Amoureuses Premier Cru Pinot Noir (Chambolle-Musigny) $139. This is such an intense, seductive wine, packed with sweet fruit, rich with balancing acidity. There are certainly tannins, and it will age, but it is beautiful now. **93** —*R.V. (9/1/2004)*

Joseph Drouhin 2000 Les Baudes Premier Cru Pinot Noir (Chambolle-Musigny) $53. Drouhin owns 0.8 acres of this vineyard close to the grand cru of Bonnes Mares. This is a toasty, structured wine, expressing the firmer side of Chambolle-Musigny wines. Ripe, red fruits lend an open, fresh aspect, but the overall impression is of restrained power. **92** —*R.V. (11/1/2002)*

Joseph Drouhin 2000 Premier Cru Pinot Noir (Chambolle-Musigny) $46. This is a blend of wines from three small parcels in the premier cru vineyards of Les Plantes, Aux Combottes, and Noirots. A complex wine, bringing together spices, new wood, and rich red fruits, it is evolving well and should be drinkable by next spring. But its dry tannins and fresh acidity suggest it should age well for a good 5–10 years. **90** —*R.V. (11/1/2002)*

JOSEPH LANDRON

Joseph Landron 2003 Amphibolite Nature Melon (Muscadet Sèvre Et Maine) $NA. Named after the subsoil of granite which gives the wine a fine mineral intensity and very rich flavors of the terroir. A powerful statement of the potential of the Melon grape. **90** —*R.V. (1/1/2004)*

JOSEPH MELLOT

Joseph Mellot 2004 Le Troncsec Sauvignon Blanc (Pouilly-Fumé) $25. A fresh, currant- and green plum-flavored wine that is clean, full of fruit, and will develop soon. This is enjoyable already and will make great drinking this summer. **86** —*R.V. (8/1/2006)*

JOSEPH PERRIER

Joseph Perrier 1998 Cuvée Royale Champagne Blend (Champagne) $52. How soft and creamy this is! With its aromas of pears, its generous, open character, and its flavors of ripe white fruits, this is what 1998 is all about. Drink now; it's delicious, but it won't age much longer. **89** —*R.V. (11/1/2006)*

Joseph Perrier 1996 Cuvée Royale Champagne Blend (Champagne) $65. A full-bodied style, dominated by flavors of almonds, which indicate that this is moving from fruity youth to maturity. But there is still plenty of acidity there. Has a few years of life yet, but it is a pleasure to drink now. **90** —*R.V. (11/1/2006)*

JOSMEYER

Josmeyer 2000 Gewürztraminer (Alsace) $21. Lemon and wild flowers make for a pretty, lithe bouquet. The palate is richer, as it deals banana, litchi, and vanilla. The finish seems creamy, but it's also slightly bitter and fades fast. **84** —*M.S. (6/1/2003)*

Josmeyer 2004 Les Folastries Gewürztraminer (Alsace) $31. Rather reined-in on the nose, this wine lacks Gewürz's over-the-top aromatics, instead showing restrained pear and spice scents. Combined with the wine's lack of residual sugar, this aspect of the wine will make it more versatile with food, as it pumps out apple, citrus, and spice flavors that turn peppery on the finish. **90** —*J.C. (8/1/2006)*

Josmeyer 2001 Pinot Blanc (Alsace) $15. Starts with cotton candy, brown sugar, and apple aromas. But it's not rich, over-ripe, or even close to late-harvest in style. Just the opposite: It's lean in the mouth, with apple, papaya, and gooseberry flavors. Banana and melon notes along with nice acids mark the finish. **87** —*M.S. (10/1/2003)*

Josmeyer 2002 Mise du Printemps Pinot Blanc (Alsace) $28. Starts off with pretty pear, apple, and honey scents, then moves into flavors of green apple, citrus, and crushed stones. It's medium-bodied, plump without being too soft, with a crisp finish. **87** —*J.C. (2/1/2005)*

Josmeyer 2001 Pinot Gris (Alsace) $21. Here's a basic Alsatian Pinot Gris with grainy, mineral aromas and some pear scents. The palate yields orange and apricot flavors, but because the acids are very modest, the wine lacks pop and depth. **83** —*M.S. (1/1/2004)*

Josmeyer 2004 Fondation Vieilles Vignes Pinot Gris (Alsace) $NA. It's dry and elegant in the mouth, with a fusion of white fruits and almond flavors. This stylish wine, named after the company founder, Jos Meyer, is delicious and balanced. **91** —*R.V. (2/1/2006)*

Josmeyer 2002 Grand Cru Brand Pinot Gris (Alsace) $80. A dry style, but rich. The wine has intensity and clean fruit, along with fine flavors of white berry fruits, a touch of toast, and some roasted chestnuts. A great food wine, this would go with patés or fish with sauces. **92** —*R.V. (2/1/2006)*

Josmeyer 2004 Le Fromenteau Pinot Gris (Alsace) $30. An easy, fresh, elegant wine with flavors of crisp, green fruits, good acidity, and very pure fruit flavors. There is just a touch of spice, but the main character of this wine is its delicious, poised fruit. **87** —*R.V. (2/1/2006)*

Josmeyer 1996 Cuvée Reservée Alsace Pinot Noir (Alsace) $28. 84 —*M.S. (10/1/1999)*

Josmeyer 2001 Grand Cru Hengst Riesling (Alsace) $67. This is not an intensely sweet wine, more one that is rich. It has great floral aromas, flavors of peaches and apricots, balanced with a great freshness, acidity, and delicacy. Give it 3–4 years before drinking. **89** —*R.V. (2/1/2006)*

Josmeyer 2004 Le Dragon Riesling (Alsace) $38. Starts off stony and minerally on the nose, but offers more fruit on the palate, where its tart apple and citrus flavors come to the fore. On the full-bodied side for Riesling, with a slight creaminess to the mouthfeel and plush apple and citrus notes on the finish. **88** —*J.C. (8/1/2006)*

Josmeyer 2004 Le Kottabe Riesling (Alsace) $27. Lacks the breadth and expansiveness on the palate of Josmeyer's Le Dragon bottling, but features crisp lime and green apple flavors wrapped in a shroud of wet-stone minerality. Picks up a faint anise note on the finish. **87** —*J.C. (8/1/2006)*

Josmeyer 1996 Tokay Pinot Gris (Alsace) $20. 85 — *(8/1/1999)*

Josmeyer 2001 Collection Rare Tokay Pinot Gris (Alsace) $NA. A deep, concentrated, spicy wine. It is rich, intensely perfumed with Asian spices and a lift of fresh fruit coming through on the finish. A finely made wine, which is sure to age well. **90** —*R.V. (2/1/2006)*

Josmeyer 1997 Le Fromenteau Tokay Pinot Gris (Alsace) $18. 88 *(8/1/1999)*

KRITER

Kriter NV Blanc de Blancs Champagne Blend (Côte d'Or) $8. The aromas of lilacs and yeast are nice, but there's also an oily note there that doesn't work. The palate has grapefruit, apple, and pepper, but there's also a slight meaty note, too. Get the picture? The wine has both good and bad points, so it isn't the full package. **85** —*M.S. (6/1/2003)*

Kriter NV Brut de Brut Champagne Blend (France) $9. This soft and slightly green sparkler has redeeming mild spice notes. The bouquet's hint of anise and tarragon add interest, and the even, smooth palate shows more licorice notes and even light feel with a soft mousse. Green herbs show on the finish of this easy drinker. **84** —*M.M. (12/15/2001)*

Kriter 2000 Brut Prestige Chardonnay (Côte d'Or) $9. This Chardonnay sparkler is clean and fresh, with plenty of apple on the nose and palate. It's wholesome and well-crafted; the bouquet brings you in and the flavors, feel, and finish all follow suit. Robust and forward; a good young bubbly for when Champagne isn't in the cards. **86 Best Buy** —*M.S. (6/1/2003)*

Kriter NV Brut Blanc de Blancs Sparkling Blend (Vin Mousseux) $11. Clean and soft with some good citrus flavors, this well-known brand is reliable, fresh, and fruity. In a light, apéritif style, it finishes crisp, clean, and just off dry. **84** —*R.V. (6/1/2006)*

Kriter NV Eclat Carmin Rosé Sparkling Blend (Vin Mousseux) $11. Made from 80% Pinot Noir, this simple, fresh rosé has good raspberry aromas and tastes. It is a fruit salad of flavors, red fruits, peaches, and acidity all combining well. A good summer apéritif. **85** —*R.V. (6/1/2006)*

KRUG

Krug 1990 Brut Champagne Blend (Champagne) $224. A bit dark in color and lacking in bubbles, but when it comes to aromas and flavors it's out of this world. Vanilla, cinnamon, almond, and apple scents are ethereal and mature as can be, while the palate deals layered apple and spice in multiple layers. Runs a mile long but soft on the finish. Unique in style; not the least bit zesty. **95** —*M.S. (12/31/2005)*

Krug 1989 Brut Champagne Blend (Champagne) $500. This is a classic food Champagne, hugely rich, toasty, generous. Yes, there is acidity and minerality, but these individual factors are less important than the overall opulence of this intense wine. It is still amazingly young, fresh and vibrant, but also so powerful. **95** —*R.V. (11/1/2006)*

Krug 1988 Brut Champagne Blend (Champagne) $210. Incredibly sophisticated from the bouquet's first full toast, apple, thyme, meal, orange, even meaty notes. The fine steady bead, mouth-coating, creamy feel, and deep vanilla, apple, and earth flavors comprise a very complete statement about age-worthy Champagne. It's mature, and shows subtleties youthful wines can not, but it's still lively, and displays a wealth of life and spirit through the tangy flavored but smoothly textured finish. Drink now-2012. **93** *(12/15/2001)*

Krug NV Brut Rosé Champagne Blend (Champagne) $293. Beautifully toasted, with impressive apricot and orange peel on the nose. Crisp, dry, and delicate, but still forceful enough to make a statement. The flavors run toward citrus, and at this point in time they're a bit lean and restrained; will age well for a number of years. **93 Cellar Selection** —*M.S. (12/31/2005)*

Krug 1981 Collection Champagne Blend (Champagne) $500. This is the current vintage of the limited-release Collection series, in which wines are held in stock, in bottle, by Krug for later release. This fabulous 1981 is mature, but still evolving. Gold in color, it is toasty, integrating flavors of nuts, cocoa, and toffee, along with still fresh acidity. **98** —*R.V. (11/1/2005)*

Krug NV Grande Cuvée Brut Champagne Blend (Champagne) $150. On the nose, dried apples and yeast notes are drenched in the rich aromas of clarified butter and malt; in the mouth, expect tons of mousse and a full mouthfeel, plus concentrated, dry fruit flavors (especially pear). Finishes long, with smoldering toast and vanilla flavors. "Very solid stuff," wrote one taster. Worthy of a very special occasion. **91** —*J.C. (12/15/2001)*

Krug NV Grande Cuvée Brut Champagne Blend (Champagne) $172. This multivintage blend nails the essence of Krug, intense richness of fruit and flavor without weight. Meaty mushroom and soy aromas are balanced by rich red fruits, citrus, toast, and mineral notes. Long finish. **94** —*J.C. (12/1/2005)*

KUENTZ-BAS

Kuentz-Bas 2002 Collection Riesling (Alsace) $26. Earthy, hedgerow aromas and some floral character set the scene for a soft, delicate wine that is still very young. Offers acidity, good structure, and flavors of almonds. **87** —*R.V. (11/1/2005)*

Kuentz-Bas 2000 Collection Rare Riesling (Alsace) $28. A fresh, crisp Riesling, with just a touch of sweetness. It is light, fresh, and easy to drink, but also has good intensity of flavor to give it depth and some complexity. A selection from Kuentz-Bas hillside vineyards. **87** —*R.V. (11/1/2005)*

Kuentz-Bas 2000 Grand Cru Eichberg Riesling (Alsace) $42. This grand cru vineyard, renowned for its Gewürztraminer, is also able to produce elegant Riesling. This wine is rich and dry, with fresh acidity and a lovely steely, mineral character. There is green fruit, and crispness, with a fine structure. This should develop well over the next 5 years. **90** —*R.V. (11/1/2005)*

Kuentz-Bas 2000 Grand Cru Rangen Riesling (Alsace) $65. The suntrap of the terraced slopes of the Rangen vineyard makes a great place for late-ripening varieties such as Riesling. That's why this wine is so full of ripe white peaches and currants. But it also has fine structure and intensity, which promise long aging. **90** —*R.V. (11/1/2005)*

Kuentz-Bas 2000 Tradition Sylvaner (Alsace) $10. Sylvaner doesn't make the finest Alsace wines, but it can make some of the most drinkable. As an apéritif, this is delicious: fresh and crisp, with citrus and green plum flavors and a hint of almonds. Kuentz-Bas is a family-owned négociant making a full range of Alsace wines in Husseren-les-Châteaux, named after the three ruined castles that dominate the hill behind the village. **85** —*R.V. (11/15/2003)*

Kuentz-Bas 2003 Tradition Tokay Pinot Gris (Alsace) $22. A full-bodied, dry style, which emphasizes spice rather than richness. This is a good apéritif wine, with a touch of acidity. No need to age this wine, drink now. **86** —*R.V. (2/1/2006)*

L'ORVAL

L'Orval 1999 Merlot (Vin de Pays d'Oc) $6. Fresh green herbs, Sweet Tarts, and dried spices play on the nose, while more spice, tree bark, and earthy flavors round out the palate. Only after a few minutes does soft red fruit peek out. Medium-weight with a tangy oak finish, this Merlot only wants a little more fruit. **84 Best Buy** —*D.T. (2/1/2002)*

L'OSTAL CAZES

L'Ostal Cazes 2003 Circus Shiraz-Cabernet Sauvignon (Vin de Pays d'Oc) $13. Fully ripe and New World clean, this 60-40 blend from the Languedoc is part of a new venture from the Bordeaux-based Cazes family. Vanilla and black cherry flavors seem a bit simple, but will amply satisfy basic burger needs. **86** —*J.C. (11/15/2005)*

LA BASTIDE SAINT VINCENT

La Bastide Saint Vincent 2004 Rhône Red Blend (Gigondas) $23. A bit light in color—and while that isn't always a bad sign—in this case, the wine seems to follow suit, lacking bouquet and flavor intensity. Modest cherry fruit with some leathery notes; although it's perfectly drinkable, for a cru it's a disappointment. **83** —*J.C. (11/15/2006)*

LA BAUME

La Baume 2003 Chardonnay (Vin de Pays d'Oc) $8. Nectarines and melons are the dominant flavors in this rich, powerful, full-bodied Chardonnay. There aren't many punches pulled in this flavorful wine. A touch of wood completes the impact. The bottle has a screw cap. **87 Best Buy** —*R.V. (12/1/2004)*

La Baume 1999 Merlot (Vin de Pays d'Oc) $7. Earthy aromas, plus a twinge of fruity sweetness and a slight plastic note. A little thin in both texture and flavor, this Merlot offers more oak and green herb than fruit on the palate, and more of the same on the back end. **82** —*D.T. (2/1/2002)*

La Baume 1998 Syrah (Vin de Pays d'Oc) $7. On the earthy side, with aromas of damp wood and toast that far outweigh the modest blackberry fruit. It's medium weight, with a tart finish. **82** *(10/1/2001)*

LA CHABLISIENNE

La Chablisienne 2004 Chardonnay (Bourgogne) $14. Light and lean, with aromas of grapefruit pith giving way to flavors of grapefruit and pineapple. Finishes on a slightly bitter note that might make it just fine with cassis in a Kir. **83** —*J.C. (11/15/2005)*

La Chablisienne 2001 Chardonnay (Petit Chablis) $13. Tart, clean, and fresh, with fruit reminiscent of under-ripe pineapple. With its lingering acidic finish, it's probably best served with raw oysters or clams. **84** — *J.C. (10/1/2003)*

La Chablisienne 2003 Côte de Léchet Premier Cru Chardonnay (Chablis) $28. 84 —*J.C. (11/15/2005)*

La Chablisienne 2001 Cuvée LC Chardonnay (Chablis) $16. Prototypical oyster Chablis, with a lean, steely mouthfeel and tart, citrusy flavors. Green apples and limes provide plenty of zest to go with raw shellfish. **85** —*J.C. (10/1/2003)*

La Chablisienne 1999 Grenouille Chardonnay (Chablis) $NA. Lovely pure fruit aromas. This is a firm wine with excellent structure and rich fruit. The flavors are almost tropical, blending well with just a hint of wood, which becomes more obvious at the end. **88** —*R.V. (1/1/2004)*

La Chablisienne 2001 Le Chablis Premier Cru Chardonnay (Chablis) $24. Flinty and lemony on the nose, with minerally flavors and hints of honey, peaches, and apples. It's a trifle open-knit, but that only serves to

make the wine more accessible. Finishes long, with lemons and stones. **89** —*J.C. (10/1/2003)*

La Chablisienne 2003 Les Preuses Grand Cru Chardonnay (Chablis) $66. The dominant pear and melon notes actually come across as a bit austere despite the wine not being hugely mineral upfront. Where this wine shows its pedigree is on the long finish, which picks up anise and flint notes and a rich, plush texture. **91** —*J.C. (4/1/2006)*

La Chablisienne 2001 Montmain Premier Cru Chardonnay (Chablis) $27. Shows a softer side of Chablis, with ripe pear fruit joined by hints of melon and peach. It's still structured, just riper and fleshier than you might expect. **87** —*J.C. (10/1/2003)*

La Chablisienne 2003 Vaudesir Grand Cru Chardonnay (Chablis) $66. Flinty yet honeyed at the same time, this full-bodied wine delivers concentrated flavors of pear, melon, dried spices, and honey. Easy enough to drink now, yet should hold for at least five years despite relatively low acids. Long and silky-textured on the finish. **90** —*J.C. (4/1/2006)*

La Chablisienne 1997 Cuvée Brut Sparkling Blend (Chablis) $16. Dull and earthy, it reveals hints of terroir in traces of chalk dust found on the nose. But the flavors are of sour apple and earth, finishing short. **80** — *J.C. (12/15/2003)*

LA CRAU DE MA MÈRE

La Crau de Ma Mère 2004 Grenache (Côtes-du-Rhône) $35. From an estate based in Châteauneuf-du-Pape, this is a wine with a soft touch. Lovely aromas of raspberries and spice waft from the glass, while the texture is so silky it's positively Burgundian. Light, but still very flavorful and long; a real pleasure. **88** —*J.C. (11/15/2006)*

LA CROIX MARTELLE

La Croix Martelle 2001 Petit Frère Pinot Noir (Vin de Pays d'Oc) $24. From the Boisset-owned Château la Croix Martelle, this Pinot Noir is something of a rarity for Languedoc. It is firm with dense wood tannins which cover the varietal character. The end is a fine, well-made wine which seems to have little varietal character. **84** —*R.V. (12/1/2004)*

LA FORGE ESTATE

La Forge Estate 1999 Syrah (Vin de Pays d'Oc) $12. Veers toward the dark, earthy side of the Syrah spectrum, with aromas and flavors of black plum, cocoa, cinnamon, clove, and black coffee. The sensation of dried spices and cocoa persists through the finish, where the tannins seem almost powdery on the tongue. **85** *(10/1/2001)*

LA NOBLE

La Noble 2004 Merlot (Vin de Pays d'Oc) $9. A wine specially blended for importer Hand Picked Selections. It shows delightful easy juicy fruit with ripe flavors and soft tannins. The grapes come from the vineyards of grower Yves Delmas just to the west of Carcassonne. New packaging on this brand, which has been produced since 1989, has a bright yellow label, with a knight on horseback (the Noble of the wine's title) and a screw cap bottle. **85 Best Buy** —*R.V. (11/15/2005)*

LA POUSSIE

La Poussie 2002 Sauvignon Blanc (Sancerre) $30. This mass-market Sancerre offers nothing but tart citrus and acid. Lean on the palate but clean, with more than enough orange and lemon. A one-noter. **83** *(7/1/2005)*

LA SAUVAGEONNE

La Sauvageonne 2003 Les Ruffes Red Blend (Coteaux du Languedoc) $11. The young wine from this estate is principally a blend of Syrah and Grenache. Ripe soft fruit, easy to drink and full of black fruits, this is a delicious, early drinking wine. **84** —*R.V. (12/1/2004)*

La Sauvageonne 2001 Puech de Glen Red Blend (Coteaux du Languedoc) $40. This is the first vintage from new owners Gavin and Amanda Crisfield. This top cuvée, Puech de Guen is a blend of Syrah and Grenache. Big, but elegant fruit combines with dark tannins and big, black fruit. Great dense blackberry jam flavors are layered with wood and tannins. **90** —*R.V. (12/1/2004)*

LA SOUFRANDIÈRE

La Soufrandière 2003 Climat Les Quarts Chardonnay (Pouilly-Vinzelles) $44. Loads of floral and mineral notes, especially for a 2003. Layers of ripe pears and honey cascade across the palate, followed by a mineral reprise on the finish. Elegant and complete. **90** —*J.C. (11/15/2005)*

LA VIEILLE FERME

La Vieille Ferme 2003 Red Blend (Côtes-du-Ventoux) $8. Smells really nice, with bubbly Grenache fruit making a strong statement on the nose, but falls off a bit on the palate. Ripe and pleasant, bursting with black cherry fruit, just lacking concentration and length. **84 Best Buy** —*J.C. (2/1/2005)*

La Vieille Ferme 2001 Rhône Red Blend (Côtes-du-Ventoux) $7. Herbal and peppery, with tart cherry flavors that seem to lack the flesh of the Perrin family's better efforts—the wine is lean and wiry in the mouth, finishing on a cranberry note. **84** —*J.C. (3/1/2004)*

La Vieille Ferme 1997 Rhône Red Blend (Côtes-du-Ventoux) $8. 85 *(11/15/1999)*

La Vieille Ferme 2000 Rhône White Blend (Côtes du Luberon) $8. A faintly floral bouquet with tropical fruit notes opens this light white blend of Grenache, Roussanne, and Ugni Blanc. It's appealing, with similar flavors, but needs more substance. Yet another example of a straightforward wine with good elements, but just not enough there there. **82** —*M.M. (2/1/2002)*

La Vieille Ferme 2002 Rosé Blend (Côtes-du-Ventoux) $7. 84 —*J.C. (3/1/2004)*

La Vieille Ferme 2003 White Blend (Côtes du Luberon) $8. This clean, neutral white wine features modest aromas of apples and limes, a plump mouthfeel, and a stony, citrusy finish. Try it with fish stew, sometime during the next several months. **84 Best Buy** —*J.C. (2/1/2005)*

LABOURE-ROI

Laboure-Roi 2003 Fourchaume Premier Cru Chardonnay (Chablis) $25. 84 —*J.C. (11/15/2005)*

Laboure-Roi 2003 Premier Cru Chardonnay (Montagny) $16. A crisp, fresh, medium-weight wine that starts off a little stinky and sulfurous before righting itself. Decant in advance to enjoy the apple and smoke aromas and flavors and refreshing finish. **85** —*J.C. (11/15/2005)*

Laboure-Roi 2002 Pinot Noir (Corton) $52. Highly aromatic wine; fresh and very attractive at this stage, with fresh strawberry fruits. Has some good tannins, but will probably not age well. **87** —*R.V. (9/1/2004)*

Laboure-Roi 1998 Pinot Noir (Gevrey-Chambertin) $28. Port-like, spicy cherry flavors show on the nose and in the mouth—on the palate, though, they mingle with leather, mineral, and strong cedar notes. Medium-bodied with racy tannins, the Gevrey Chambertin finishes a little short, with more cherry and spice. **87** *(10/1/2001)*

Laboure-Roi 2002 Chassagne Montrachet Pinot Noir (Chassagne-Montrachet) $23. Dusty and herbal on the nose, with modest cherry fruit carrying peppery spice on the palate. Light and tart. **83** —*J.C. (11/15/2005)*

Laboure-Roi 2002 Echézeaux Pinot Noir (Echezeaux) $65. Hollow, rather soft wine, which lacks definition. It has some pleasant, soft, raspberry fruits and light hints of tannin. **82** —*R.V. (9/1/2004)*

Laboure-Roi 2002 Pommard Pinot Noir (Pommard) $32. Smells of dried spices and earth, but also shows hints of alcoholic warmth and sun-baked blackberries. Earth and tobacco flavors predominate on the palate, with a dried-fruit finish and some astringent tannins. Seems to be past peak already. **82** —*J.C. (11/15/2005)*

Laboure-Roi 1998 Red Blend (Pommard) $28. The nose takes a little while to unwind, but when it does, violet, coffee, blackberry, and honeysuckle notes shine through. Firm tannins in the mouth give the Pommard plenty of structure and a fleshy mouthfeel full of blackberry, leather, and earthy flavors. 10,000 cases produced. **88** *(10/1/2001)*

Laboure-Roi 1998 Domaine Sirugue Clos La Belle Marguerite Red Blend (Côte de Nuits-Villages) $19. What a nose. La Belle Marguerite's the color of ruby Port, so we shouldn't have been surprised at the luscious black currant, plum, black pepper and membrillo-paste aromas it showed. Cracked black pepper, and curry notes spice up the palate's cherry, fresh

red pepper, and mineral flavors. Racy and medium-bodied, it finishes with more spice, plus some dried cherry notes. **89 Editors' Choice** *(10/1/2001)*

Laboure-Roi 1998 White Blend (Chassagne-Montrachet) $28. No shrinking violet, this Chassagne-Montrachet has a medium-bodied, hearty mouthfeel that we'd almost call zingy. Pear, cinnamon, and nutmeg flavors are rounded out with some bacon-fat and peeled apple notes. Opens with Bartlett pear, mustard grain, and floral notes; finish is short, but characteristically zesty. **89** *(10/1/2001)*

Laboure-Roi 1999 Domaine Rene Manuel Clos des Bouches Cheres Premier Cru White Blend (Meursault) $43. This big, firm Meursault opens with a big bouquet of fresh butter, macadamia nut, vanilla and apple peel. Apple shows up again on the palate, where it is bolstered with light mineral, honeysuckle and pear flavors. Light floral accents on the finish and a firm acid backbone make this a good choice to drink with broiled fish or grilled shrimp. **90** *(10/1/2001)*

LACHETEAU

Lacheteau 2000 Sauvignon Blanc (Vin de Pays du Jardin de la France) $6. Very crisp and green, this offering from the broadest Loire area appellation comes off like a Kiwi more than a Frenchie. It's brisk, with almost sharp green herb notes and a touch of the (oh, yes) cat pee note that so many have. It's tangy and light, a very good example of that style (if that's your cup of tea). **85 Best Buy** —*M.M. (2/1/2002)*

LACOUR PAVILLON

LaCour Pavillon 1996 Bordeaux Blend (Bordeaux) $9. 86 *(11/15/1999)*

LALANDE

Lalande 2005 Chardonnay (Vin de Pays des Côtes de Gascogne) $12. Rich in vanilla and green plum flavors, this ripe Chardonnay from the Gascony region in south-west France comes from the Grassa family, the largest vineyard owners by far in the Gers department. This is a full, concentrated but easy drinking wine, just ready for lovers of a less woody style of Chardonnay. **86** —*R.V. (12/31/2006)*

LAMBLIN & FILS

Lamblin & Fils 2001 Chardonnay (Chablis) $13. Candied and floral, with strong aromas of pear nectar and a dull, disjointed finish. **82** —*J.C. (10/1/2003)*

Lamblin & Fils 2001 Fourchaumes Premier Cru Chardonnay (Chablis) $23. The best of this company's 2001s, the Fouchaumes shows flinty notes on the nose, but also ripe pear and melon. It's medium-weight, with pear and apple joining mineral flavors and a mouthwatering finish that folds in some riper, peachy notes. **88** —*J.C. (10/1/2003)*

Lamblin & Fils 2001 Vieilles Vignes Chardonnay (Chablis) $14. On the soft side for Chablis, but still very clean and fresh. A hint of honey complements pear and citrus, with a pleasant sensation of rainwater on the finish. **85** —*J.C. (10/1/2003)*

LANGLOIS-CHÂTEAU

Langlois-Château 2001 Vieilles Vignes Chenin Blanc (Saumur) $18. A distinctive and somewhat mature effort, with honey and nut aromas giving way to flavors that don't show much fruit yet manage to be rich—something akin to mineral or nut oil. Richly textured on the palate, the wine finishes reasonably long, despite not showing much freshness. **86** —*J.C. (8/1/2006)*

Langlois-Château 2004 Château de Fontaine-Audon Terroir Silex Sauvignon Blanc (Sancerre) $25. Well-known as a Saumur-based producer of Cremant de Loire, this winery, owned by Bollinger Champagne, also makes this soft, flowery Sancerre. It is ripe and fresh, with layers of citrus fruits and some full, mouth-watering acidity. **86** —*R.V. (8/1/2006)*

Langlois-Château NV Brut Sparkling Blend (Crémant de Loire) $17. Fresh and citrusy on the nose, with only the faintest hint of toasty, autolytic character. Lemon and grapefruit flavors come across as slightly coarse and rustic before a burnt note creeps in on the finish. **83** —*J.C. (12/1/2004)*

Langlois-Château NV Brut Rosé Sparkling Blend (Crémant de Loire) $16. Quite fruity, with aromatics of orange, crushed stone, and mustard.

Runs dry on the palate, with only a touch of sugar to the simple, baked fruit flavors. Fairly mainstream yet flavorful, with a dry, toasty, lasting impression. **87** —*M.S. (12/15/2003)*

Langlois-Château 1996 Quadrille Brut Sparkling Blend (Crémant de Loire) $24. Fresh and fruity, with a hint of sugared doughnut. Bright pear and apple fruit makes for a nice wine, and interestingly, it closes with an earthiness that is much like amontillado and/or mushroom. Powerful and poised, and quite nice for a Loire Valley sparkler. **88** —*M.S. (12/15/2003)*

Langlois-Château NV Brut White Blend (Crémant de Loire) $21. This is a ripe, creamy blend of Chenin Blanc, with 20% Chardonnay and 20% Cabernet Franc. Aged on its lees for 20 months, it has a smooth, open mousse, fine, full pear fruit flavors, and a touch of mature toast. It is delicious, ripe, and elegant. **90 Editors' Choice** —*R.V. (6/1/2006)*

LANSON

Lanson NV Black Label Brut Champagne Blend (Champagne) $28. Beery and soapy, with big, effusive bubbles and a sugary sweetness to the finish. Pleasant enough, broad, and almost hoppy, but without the texture and elegance of the best Champagne. **84** —*P.G. (12/15/2003)*

Lanson NV Brut Rosé Champagne Blend (Champagne) $50. This has a pleasing, pale cherry-fruit core; it's tart and tangy, but not much complexity beyond that. Full in the middle, with lasting flavors that smooth into vanilla and very light spice. **85** —*P.G. (12/15/2003)*

Lanson 1995 Gold Label Brut Champagne Blend (Champagne) $45. Citrus and Golden Delicious apple aromas, plus some notes of hay and Wheat Thins on the nose. Medium-weight, with good acidity, the palate offers more tart green apple and citrus notes. Close with good balance and length, plus more citrus. **87** *(12/15/2001)*

Lanson 1995 Noble Cuvée Blanc de Blancs Champagne Blend (Champagne) $110. A fine-beaded, rich, and toasty wine, with flavors of roasted nuts and vanilla dominating. It tastes like what you would expect of bubbly Chardonnay—tart and appley, but with good length and persistence. **90** —*P.G. (12/15/2003)*

LARMANDIER-BERNIER

Larmandier-Bernier NV Blanc de Blancs Premier Cru Brut Champagne Blend (Champagne) $58. This wine is a blend of fruit from Vertus and grand cru vineyards in Cramant, Avize, and Oger. It is a dry style with hints of almonds and vanilla, along with some toast. It is certainly a full wine, but the strongest feature is its elegance and balance. **88** —*R.V. (12/1/2002)*

Larmandier-Bernier 1997 Special Club Brut Champagne Blend (Champagne) $51. The Special Club is a grouping of around 30 vignerons who taste each other's wines before allowing the member to make a Special Club bottling. This 1997 vintage wine is almost completely dry to taste, allowing the rich fruit to dominate. Mineral and lemon flavors work with the attractive fruit. This is a wine that will develop well over the next few years. **91** —*R.V. (12/1/2002)*

Larmandier-Bernier NV Blanc de Blancs Premier Cru Brut Chardonnay (Champagne) $48. One of the top producers in Champagne's Côte des Blancs, the Larmandier and Bernier families own 30 acres of Chardonnay vineyards. This premier cru is fresh and crisp, with a light touch of toastiness and lively acidity. Flavors of ripe apples give the wine fine intensity. **89** —*R.V. (4/1/2005)*

Larmandier-Bernier NV Terre de Vertus Premier Cru Brut Chardonnay (Champagne) $55. A 100% Chardonnay blanc de blancs that is presented without any dosage to soften the acidity. Yet it doesn't seem to matter, because this Champagne is deliciously ripe, packed with mature fruit flavors, a touch of almonds to go with the white currant tastes, and a layer of toastiness. **94** —*R.V. (12/1/2005)*

Larmandier-Bernier 2002 Vieille Vigne de Cramant Chardonnay (Champagne) $70. This is certainly Chardonnay, full of green apple and white fruit creaminess that is still suspended in acidity and needs time to soften and open. Lovely flavors of spiced pears give the wine a great future. **92** —*R.V. (11/1/2006)*

LAROCHE

Laroche 2005 Chardonnay Chardonnay (Vin de Pays d'Oc) $10. A wine made from purchased grapes at Michel Laroche's Mas la Chevaliere. As a Chablis producer, Laroche knows a thing or two about Chardonnay, and this is a rich, creamy wine, but with elegance, the wood only a hint behind the ripe green plums and acidity. **87 Best Buy** —*R.V. (12/31/2006)*

Laroche 2005 Merlot (Vin de Pays d'Oc) $10. A friendly wine, with attractive, juicy, red berry flavors, this is soft and spicy with a touch of pepper. It is one in the branded range of wines produced at Chablis producer Michel Laroche's Mas la Chevaliere in the Languedoc. **86** —*R.V. (12/31/2006)*

Laroche 2003 Mas la Chevalière Red Blend (Vin de Pays d'Oc) $20. From the Michel Laroche estate of Mas la Chevalière north of Béziers, this is an intensely ripe, deep-fruited wine, powerful and elegant. Vanilla and soft spice add to the red fruit flavors that come from a blend of Syrah, Merlot, and Cabernet Sauvignon. **89** —*R.V. (12/31/2006)*

LAURENS

Laurens 1996 Clos des Demoiselles Brut Chenin Blanc (Crémant de Limoux) $15. **89 Best Buy** —*P.G. (12/15/2000)*

LAURENT CHARLES BROTTE

Laurent Charles Brotte 2001 Bouvencourt Rhône Red Blend (Vacqueyras) $20. A light, fresh wine with just a hint of dusty tannins. The flavors of red fruits give it poise but no particular depth. **81** —*R.V. (3/1/2004)*

LAURENT MIQUEL

Laurent Miquel 2005 Cabernet-Syrah Cabernet Sauvignon-Syrah (Vin de Pays d'Oc) $10. This Australian blend comes across as something altogether leaner in the hands of Laurent Miquel. The fruit is fresh and lively, with some dark tannins, but the essence of the wine is in the black currant and spice that form its backbone. **86** —*R.V. (12/31/2006)*

Laurent Miquel 2005 Cinsault-Syrah Rosé Blend (Vin de Pays d'Oc) $10. An attractive, onion-skin colored rosé, with fresh fruits, a fine lightness of touch and crisp, strawberry acidity to finish, which is soft, but still dry. **85** —*R.V. (12/31/2006)*

Laurent Miquel 2005 Nord Sud Viognier (Vin de Pays d'Oc) $13. The rows in Laurent Miquel's Viognier vineyard run north-south (Nord Sud), avoiding the midday sun but getting the gentler morning and evening heat. The wine has balance, with elegance and a good touch of acidity to lift full white and yellow fruit flavors. **87** —*R.V. (12/31/2006)*

LAURENT-PERRIER

Laurent-Perrier 1997 Brut Champagne Blend (Champagne) $60. This wine is all about finesse and elegance. Aromas of grapefruit and other citrus fruits are enticing. On the palate, the wine is toasty, with orange marmalade and honey flavors, and fresh acidity. **90** —*R.V. (11/1/2006)*

Laurent-Perrier 1996 Brut Champagne Blend (Champagne) $60. A dry, toasty wine that shows maturity now. It has a good structure, though, with hints of red apples and green plums. Ready to drink now; better with food than as an apéritif. **90** —*R.V. (11/1/2006)*

Laurent-Perrier 1995 Brut Champagne Blend (Champagne) $53. Serious apple and pear aromas show excellent depth and density, and that sense of power is confirmed on the palate, where green apple and citrus fruit is supported by a nip of celery and anise. Ultimately, this seems more a feminine Champagne, one that floats lightly and confidently across the palate. **91** —*M.S. (12/15/2003)*

Laurent-Perrier 1993 Brut Champagne Blend (Champagne) $50. Here's a young vintage Champagne in need of cellaring. It has classic dry citrus flavors, with a tart, crisp mouthfeel, fine bubbles, and a lengthy finish. It's elegantly structured, a full-bodied wine whose rough edges will soften in a few years. **90** —*S.H. (12/15/2001)*

Laurent-Perrier NV Cuvée Brut Rosé Champagne Blend (Champagne) $60. With its bottle shape dating from the late 16th century, this is a traditionally made rosé, using color from macerating Pinot Noir grapes. It is full, ripe, flavored with strawberries and other sweet red fruits, with a layer of dryness. The wine finishes fresh and crisp. **90** —*R.V. (12/1/2005)*

Laurent-Perrier NV Cuvée Brut Rosé Champagne Blend (Champagne) $50. **83** —*J.C. (12/15/2000)*

Laurent-Perrier NV Cuvée Ultra Brut Champagne Blend (Champagne) $65. 91 —*P.G. (12/1/2000)*

Laurent-Perrier NV Cuvée Ultra Brut Champagne Blend (Champagne) $39. This no-dosage sparkler is immensely crisp and appley, with aromas of mint and licorice. If you're not expecting an austere, dry style, the green apple and lemon flavors might seem sour. It's 100% tangy and sharp, but it's precise for what it is. Not a cocktail party wine, but something like sushi will help it along. **86** —*M.S. (12/15/2003)*

Laurent-Perrier NV Demi-Sec Champagne Blend (Champagne) $30. Smells slightly sweet, with apple and tropical fruit aromas that show flecks of coconut. Flavors are similar, emphasizing apple and pear. Sweet but not cloying (it contains a dosage of 45g/l); try it with light, fruit-based desserts. **87** *(12/31/2002)*

Laurent-Perrier 1997 Grand Siècle Champagne Blend (Champagne) $95. Crisp and refreshing, this is a young vintage Champagne with a good future ahead of it. Toast and ripe fruit notes on the nose give way to apple, cherry, and herbal flavors on the palate. Zippy and clean on the finish. **89** —*J.C. (12/1/2004)*

Laurent-Perrier 1990 Grand Siecle Alexandra Rosé Champagne Blend (Champagne) $260. It's a pale wine, on the rose side of gold, a beautiful visual introduction to a stunning wine. The strawberry flavors are wrapped in a silvery texture, crisply dry, and despite the intensity of fruit, the wine seems weightless on the palate. It's gorgeous now, but, amazingly, just a baby. It's long-term future is assured. Twenty years from now, this will be heavenly. **94** —*S.H. (12/15/2001)*

Laurent-Perrier NV Grand Siècle Brut Champagne Blend (Champagne) $110. Though very ripe, the wine's richness is somewhat hidden by a blast of SO2 until you have given it some good aeration. Then the true nose emerges, and if you like fresh-baked pastries and a creamy style of Champagne, this is your bottle. The fruit is peachy/tropical, and an unusual spice note—wintergreen?—adds some lift through the long finish. **91** —*P.G. (12/1/2006)*

Laurent-Perrier NV Grand Siècle La Cuvée Brut Champagne Blend (Champagne) $140. 95 —*P.G. (12/15/2000)*

Laurent-Perrier NV Grand Siècle La Cuvée Brut Champagne Blend (Champagne) $75. From the first sniff you know this is a refined and arrestingly complex wine, with a bouquet of subtly entwined layers mixing ripe fruits, mineral, leesy-cheesy accents, vanilla, and even a bit of metal in the steely center. Three-dimensional flavors and a wonderful lightness on the palate make for an exceptional bottle. **94 Editors' Choice** —*P.G. (12/15/2002)*

Laurent-Perrier NV Grand Siècle La Cuvée Brut Champagne Blend (Champagne) $90. Mature, with a touch of scrambled egg and burnt sulfur on the dry bouquet. This one runs lean and crisp, with green apple and a hint of lemon on the palate. That said, there's still laudable depth of flavor and complexity. Overall the impression is largely of citrus. **90** —*M.S. (12/15/2005)*

Laurent-Perrier NV L-P Brut Champagne Blend (Champagne) $30. A good value in Champagne, Laurent-Perrier's basic cuvée boasts scents of ginger, soy, and mixed citrus fruits. It's medium in body and a little soft on the finish, but carries a complex flavor melange of spice, citrus, yeast, and minerals. **89 Editors' Choice** —*J.C. (12/1/2004)*

Laurent-Perrier NV L-P Brut Champagne Blend (Champagne) $30. The emphasis is on sweet fruit, with a citrus tang—grapefruit, skin of lime, and nectarine. Fruit dominates the mid-palate, and the flavors are subtly delineated by a slightly chalky, mineral backdrop. Leads into a long, lime, and wet stone finish. **91** —*P.G. (12/15/2002)*

Laurent-Perrier NV L-P Brut Champagne Blend (Champagne) $40. Shines with elegance and class right from the start of the toasty, yeasty, appley bouquet with vanilla hints. It's a joy to taste, with its full, complex flavors, ripe mouthfeel, and long finish. A great example of how far wines designated Kosher have come, and what is possible in this category. **91 Editors' Choice** *(4/1/2001)*

Laurent-Perrier NV L-P Brut Champagne Blend (Champagne) $34. A full, creamy wine with a big mousse that fills the mouth. The fruit is more restrained, but the structure firm. This bottling was too young when tasted—another year of aging would have been an improvement. **87** —*R.V. (12/1/2005)*

Laurent-Perrier NV Ultra Brut Nature Champagne Blend (Champagne) $49. Almost bone dry, this Champagne can be difficult to appreciate, layered with acidity and green fruit. But get beneath its dryness and the fruit is surprisingly ripe, with pink grapefruit flavors. This is a wine that demands bottle aging to soften the acidity, so an indication of disgorgement would be helpful. **89** —*R.V. (12/1/2005)*

Laurent-Perrier NV Cuvée Brut Rosé Pinot Noir (Champagne) $48. Starts off toasty and citrusy, then seems to add weight and size in the glass, adding layers of cherry-berry fruit and a hint of dark chocolate. It ends up being a big, broad-shouldered wine you could pair with main course meats. **90** —*J.C. (12/1/2004)*

LE CELLIER DE MARRENON

Le Cellier de Marrenon 2001 Grand Luberon Rhône Red Blend (Côtes du Luberon) $10. Starts off with a hint of rubber on the nose, but also herbs and black cherries that deepen on the palate into flavors of plum, chocolate, and licorice. It's medium-weight and also quite sturdy and tannic, finishing with notes of black tea. **86** —*J.C. (3/1/2004)*

Le Cellier de Marrenon 2000 Terre de Levant Rhône Red Blend (Côtes-du-Ventoux) $8. Take a whiff and you'll get a combination of sweet and spicy fruit done up with notes of sandalwood and incense. The palate is mostly raspberry with a hint of chocolate, and although the feel is fairly lean, tangy, and edgy, there's enough smoothness and girth here to register some positive points. **85 Best Buy** —*M.S. (9/1/2003)*

LE CLOS DES CAZAUX

Le Clos des Cazaux 2003 Cuvée Prestige Grenache-Syrah (Vacqueyras) $18. Impressively full-bodied and tannic, but maybe too much so, with notes of torrefaction and cedar that run headlong into dried fruit flavors. **84** —*J.C. (11/15/2006)*

Le Clos des Cazaux 2004 La Tour Sarrazine Rhône Red Blend (Gigondas) $23. Named for a ruined Moorish tower on the property, this is a rather dark, brooding Gigondas with notes of coffee and molasses only partly enlivened by bright raspberry flavors. **85** —*J.C. (11/15/2006)*

LE DÔME

Le Dôme 2004 Barrel Sample Bordeaux Blend (Saint-Emilion Grand Cru) $NA. This single-vineyard wine has benefited immensely from the quality of the Cabernet Franc in 2004. The perfumes are immediate and enticing, while the ripe fruit just pushes out over the layers of new wood. **95** —*R.V. (6/1/2005)*

Le Dôme 2005 Barrel Sample Bordeaux Blend (Saint-Emilion Grand Cru) $NA. A fine, perfumed, Cabernet Franc-dominated wine that builds layers of rich, intense fruit. This is solid, powerful, but also shows potential charm. The dry aftertaste suggests good aging. **93** —*R.V. (6/20/2006)*

LE FONT DE PAPIER

Le Font de Papier 2001 La Fontaine des Papes Rhône Red Blend (Vacqueyras) $NA. Leathery and horsey on the nose, but the tannins are supple and the dried fruit flavors pick up a pleasant coffee note on the finish. **84** —*J.C. (11/15/2006)*

LE GRAND NOIR

Le Grand Noir 2004 Black Sheep Chardonnay-Viognier (Vin de Pays d'Oc) $10. This unusual blend of Chardonnay and Viognier combines apple and pear fruit aromas with scents of honey and crushed stones. Plump and medium-bodied, with pear and mineral flavors that add a hint of butter on the finish. **85 Best Buy** —*J.C. (11/15/2005)*

LE MAS DU CÈDRE

Le Mas du Cèdre 2002 Rhône White Blend (Côtes-du-Rhône Brézème) $14. Given this wine's inviting aromas of tropical fruit and peaches, it finishes surprisingly hard and tart. Candied anise notes add complexity. **85** —*J.C. (3/1/2004)*

LE VIEUX DONJON

Le Vieux Donjon 1998 Rhône Red Blend (Châteauneuf-du-Pape) $30. 94 —*M.M. (12/31/2000)*

FRANCE

LEON BEYER

Leon Beyer 2001 Réserve Pinot Gris (Alsace) $33. Spicy and full-bodied, but, in the house style of Léon Beyer, also elegant, dry, and poised. There is fine, ripe, spicy, slightly toasty fruit that floats over the concentration and richness. **90** —R.V. (2/1/2006)

Leon Beyer 2001 Riesling (Alsace) $9. Marc Beyer has succeeded well, with a crisp, mineral style of wine that can marry well with so many fish and seafood dishes. **85** —R.V. (8/1/2003)

Leon Beyer 2001 Les Ecaillers Riesling (Alsace) $37. A great, fresh, clean Riesling that just demands to be drunk. The wine has freshness, crispness, green fruits, and balancing acidity. Not very complex, but still delicious. **88** —R.V. (11/1/2005)

Leon Beyer 1997 Tokay Pinot Gris (Alsace) $35. 80 (8/1/1999)

Leon Beyer 2000 Cuvée des Comtes d'Eguisheim Tokay Pinot Gris (Alsace) $46. A rich, dry style, packed with spice and deep, almost brooding, fruit. From vines in the grand cru vineyards of Eichberg and Pfersigberg, this wine bears complex flavors of toast, nutmeg, and pepper, along with white fruits. Still young, this wine will evolve over the next 5–10 years. **94** —R.V. (2/1/2006)

Leon Beyer 1997 Sélection de Grains Nobles Tokay Pinot Gris (Alsace) $52. There is a hint of the maturity of a great botrytis wine, but it is lost in the old, toasty acidity. Three years ago, this would have been a great, but delicate wine. **86** —R.V. (2/1/2006)

LÉONCE BOCQUET

Léonce Bocquet 2003 Brut Champagne Blend (Crémant de Bourgogne) $17. A fine apple-and-cream wine that bounces with freshness and liveliness. There might not be complexity, but this is definitely a wine that gives great, fruity pleasure. **88** —R.V. (6/1/2006)

Léonce Bocquet NV Brut Rosé Champagne Blend (Crémant de Bourgogne) $17. Red fruit and apricot aromas show this fresh, crisp wine off to advantage. Made from a blend of Chard and Pinot Noir, it has ripeness along with a dry, lingering aftertaste. **87** —R.V. (6/1/2006)

LES AMIS DES HOSPICES DE DIJON

Les Amis des Hospices de Dijon NV Champagne Blend (Crémant de Bourgogne) $NA. Mostly Chardonnay, and quite crisp and well-made. Apple, pear and toasted bread aromas lead you straight to apple and cinnamon flavors, which then yield to a dryness on the finish that holds your attention. Zesty and forthright. An interesting sparkler for certain, and one from Burgundy. **87** —M.S. (6/1/2003)

LES CAVES DE BAILLY

Les Caves de Bailly NV Brut de Charvis Rosé Sparkling Blend (Vin Mousseux) $12. A taut, red currant flavored wine, with some tannic structure and clean, fresh acidity. It's lively, crisp, and clean, leaving a light, delicate aftertaste. **84** —R.V. (6/1/2006)

LES CLOS DE PAULILLES

Les Clos de Paulilles 2005 Rosé Blend (Collioure) $15. A bit heavy for a rosé, with slightly jammy scents of cooked cherries and berries. Picks up some hints of chocolate on the palate and finish. Best just cooler than room temperature, not ice-bucket cold. **84** —J.C. (6/21/2006)

LES DOMANIERS

Les Domaniers 2003 Rosé Blend (Côtes de Provence) $17. Citrusy, minerally, and dropping fruit at a rapid rate, this light-bodied rosé should have been consumed already. Modest peach and citrus flavors are pleasant, but fading. **83** —J.C. (11/15/2005)

LES FORTS DE LATOUR

Les Forts de Latour 2005 Barrel Sample Bordeaux Blend (Pauillac) $NA. Effectively a grand cru in its own right, Latour's second wine is superb, ripe with hugely strong tannins, and great, ripe acidity. **92** —R.V. (6/1/2006)

LES HERETIQUES

Les Heretiques 2001 Red Blend (Vin de Pays de L'Herault) $8. André Iché, who owns one of the best-known Minervois estates, Château d'Oupia, has expanded his family's production with this bottling of Carignan, Syrah, and Grenache. It's a chunky, satisfying wine brimming with berries, spice, and a hint of chocolate. No, it's not especially complex or long, but it's forward and delicious—everything you'd want in a hamburger red. **87 Best Buy** —J.C. (11/15/2002)

LES JAMELLES

Les Jamelles 2001 Badet Clement & Cie Cabernet Sauvignon (Vin de Pays d'Oc) $9. Aromas of red licorice, smoke, and rubber create an attractive nose, which is followed by ripe, moderately rich cherry fruit that's clearly a grade up in this category. The smoky, textured finish is the final stamp earning approval. Nicely done. **86 Best Buy** —M.S. (9/1/2003)

Les Jamelles 2005 Chardonnay (Vin de Pays d'Oc) $8. A cool, green style of wine, that shows freshness, lightness, and just a touch of spice. Good acidity gives the finish a lift. **84** —R.V. (12/31/2006)

Les Jamelles 1997 Chardonnay (Vin de Pays d'Oc) $8. 86 (11/15/1999)

Les Jamelles 2005 Cinsault (Vin de Pays d'Oc) $8. A perennial Best Buy, this juicy, fruit-filled rosé offers the ultimate in outdoor consumption, with simple, direct watermelon flavors bold enough to stand up to bbq smoke, pool chlorine, and cut grass. The mouthwatering finish is a bonus. **87 Best Buy** —J.C. (6/21/2006)

Les Jamelles 2001 Badet Clement & Cie Cinsault (Vin de Pays d'Oc) $9. The color is bright, almost red, and the wine keeps some of its red roots, so to speak. The nose offers fragrant crushed berries and spice, while there's cherry along with citrus on the palate. Full yet not ponderous or flat. But also not especially sharp or fresh. **85** —M.S. (9/1/2003)

Les Jamelles 2000 Rose Cinsault (Vin de Pays d'Oc) $8. There's more going on here than meets the eye in this rosé from this dependable producer of value wines. The very pale color of this rosé belies its crisp berry nose and dry flavors with chalky and even faint, gamy accents. Light-to-medium weight and evenly textured, it closes with decent length and a hint of sour cherry and spice. **86** —M.M. (2/1/2002)

Les Jamelles 2000 Merlot (Vin de Pays d'Oc) $8. There's substantial oak on the palate, but it's perfectly palatable because it's got lots of berries (plus a little caramel sweetness) to tone the wood down. Slightly tangy mouthfeel leads into a tangy, oak, and red berry finish. Its spicy-earthy nose is yummy. **85** —D.T. (2/1/2002)

Les Jamelles 2005 Merlot (Vin de Pays d'Oc) $9. Lean, slightly green fruit gives this wine's firm, tannic character center stage, with black currant acidity and some freshness. Light and ready to drink. **82** —R.V. (12/31/2006)

Les Jamelles 2000 Sauvignon Blanc (Vin de Pays d'Oc) $8. Lime and grapefruit characterize this citrus ball Sauvignon Blanc. There's enough melon in there to keep it from being overly sharp on the palate, and the wine has a decent finish with more tangy grapefruit notes. Another successful offering from Les Jamelles, who just seem to know what to do-and that it can be done well in the Pays D'Oc—at the right price. **85** —M.M. (2/1/2002)

Les Jamelles 1999 Syrah (Vin de Pays d'Oc) $8. Yet another tart red fruit-flavored Syrah from France's south. Touches of rhubarb and anise add a bit of interest. Balanced, but a touch dumb, it doesn't really go anywhere. Wood and licorice mark the close. **83** (10/1/2001)

Les Jamelles 2003 Special Reserve Viognier-Marsanne White Blend (Vin de Pays d'Oc) $15. The Les Jamelles line is pretty reliable, and even in the torrid conditions of 2003 this white is still pretty good. Smoke, honey, and mint notes on the nose turn floral and spicy on the palate, where the wine is full, softly textured, and a little alcoholic. **84** —J.C. (11/15/2005)

LES MARIONETTES

Les Marionettes 2003 Sauvignon Blanc (Vin de Pays d'Oc) $NA. A crisp, grassy style of wine, light and fresh, it is great as an apéritif style. It is low in alcohol at 12% which gives it a lift and greenness which is very attractive and drinkable. **85** —R.V. (12/1/2004)

LES ROCHETTES

Les Rochettes 2001 Sauvignon Blanc (Sancerre) $16. Citrus and white flowers comprise the nose, with a touch of melon underneath the top tier of scents. Flavors of orange, citrus pith, and green herbs lead into a juicy finish that at first offers roasted nuts and then fades away smoothly. Its major fault is high acidity, which leaves a somewhat sour overall impression. **85** *(8/1/2002)*

LES VIGNERONS DE CASES DE PÉNE

Les Vignerons de Cases de Péne 2003 Château de Peña Réserve S Rhône Red Blend (Côtes du Roussillon Villages) $20. A Syrah-dominant blend (hence the S in the name) from volcanic soil. The wine has a juicy character, but retains a fine sense of structure that comes from old vines. There's a wood element underlining the black fig and blackberry flavors. **87** —*R.V. (12/31/2006)*

Les Vignerons de Cases de Péne 2005 Ninet de Peña Viognier (Vin de Pays d'Oc) $10. Heady, perfumed aromas give this wine an exotic character. The fruit is rich, well concentrated, touched by apricots, but perfumed and soft. **86 Best Buy** —*R.V. (12/31/2006)*

LES VIGNERONS DE CHUSCLAN

Les Vignerons de Chusclan 2001 La Ferme de Gicon Rhône Red Blend (Côtes-du-Rhône) $9. With a fading, rather light color, it's hard to believe that this is only a few years old. In the nose, there's a slight burnt character, one of matchsticks and red pepper flakes. The palate, like the color, seems mature; it's soft and round, with a mix of oak and berry fruit. This wine is fine, if a little weak, but the real fault is that it has no signature feature. It's decent but just there. **84** —*M.S. (9/1/2003)*

Les Vignerons de Chusclan 2004 Les Genets Chusclan Rhône Red Blend (Côtes-du-Rhône Villages) $15. This is 50% Grenache, with the balance a blend of Syrah, Mourvèdre, Cinsault, and Carignan from vines averaging 40 years of age. The result showcases cherry and plum aromas and a velvety, creamy texture. Peppery spice comes in on the finish, completing the package. Just lacks a little depth or it would have scored higher. **86** —*J.C. (11/15/2006)*

Les Vignerons de Chusclan 2000 Les Monticauts Rhône Red Blend (Côtes-du-Rhône) $14. Not quite on a par with Les Ribières, but darn good nonetheless. It's jammy and fruity, with purity throughout. This is 70% Syrah, and it's focused and powerful, but still graceful and pleasant. The finish is properly tannic and slightly buttery. And the body is just right as it spreads across your palate as you drink it down. **89 Best Buy** —*M.S. (9/1/2003)*

Les Vignerons de Chusclan 2003 Les Ribières Chusclan Rhône Red Blend (Côtes-du-Rhône Villages) $15. This blend is 50-50 Grenache and Syrah, boasting a complex bouquet that encompasses scents of leather, prune, and meat, all of which make it a dark and stewy wine. Still, it has a nicely supple—verging on creamy—texture and some chewy tannins on the finish that give it welcome grip. **87** —*J.C. (11/15/2006)*

LES VIGNERONS DE L'ENCLAVE DES PAPES

Les Vignerons de l'Enclave des Papes 2004 Croix de Chêne Rhône Red Blend (Côtes-du-Rhône) $9. This smooth, medium-weight Côtes-du-Rhône is another solid, weekday drinker. Red plum flavors are clean and fresh without offering a lot of depth or complexity. Drink now. **84** —*J.C. (11/15/2006)*

LES VIGNERONS DE TAVEL

Les Vignerons de Tavel 2003 Richesse des Lauzeraies Rhône Red Blend (Lirac) $14. Starts with scents of spice and leather, but in the mouth the concentrated dark fruit comes through, powering its way with black cherries and plums while picking up a hint of licorice on the supple finish. Drink now. **88** —*J.C. (11/15/2006)*

Les Vignerons de Tavel 2005 Terre des Lauzeraies Rhône White Blend (Côtes-du-Rhône) $9. At the bottom end of the Tavel co-op's hierarchy, this white Côtes-du-Rhône is neutral and bland but still shows adequate weight and clean winemaking. **82** —*J.C. (11/15/2006)*

Les Vignerons de Tavel 2005 Cuvée Tableau Rosé Blend (Tavel) $14. From its potent strawberry and watermelon nose to its candied fruit flavors, everything about this wine tries a little too hard, like a strident voice that says pay attention to me. It's well made, tasty, and some will like the volume turned up. **86** —*J.C. (11/15/2006)*

Les Vignerons de Tavel 2005 Les Cigaliérs Rosé Blend (Tavel) $14. Has a

Mourvèdre-ish quality to its aromas, sort of like tree bark and briary fruit with a touch of muscularity. Blackberry, plum, and mushroom flavors stand out as being different from the rest of the Tavel crowd, but not necessarily better or worse. **88** —*J.C. (11/15/2006)*

LES VIGNERONS DU MONT-VENTOUX

Les Vignerons du Mont-Ventoux 2001 Grange des Dames Rhône Red Blend (Côtes-du-Ventoux) $10. This is a gulpable, satisfying wine that shows plenty of ripeness. Full, soft flavors of ripe black cherries are balanced by notes of coffee and chocolate. Long and harmonious finish. **88 Best Buy** —*J.C. (3/1/2004)*

LES VINS DE VIENNE

Les Vins de Vienne 2000 Les Pimpignoles Rhône Red Blend (Côtes-du-Rhône) $40. A big wine, but with many complex aromas, of vanilla, of black plums, of tar, and violets. The flavors are equally varied, showing concentration and tannins, as well as new wood. **90** —*R.V. (3/1/2004)*

Les Vins de Vienne 2004 L'Arzelle Syrah (Saint-Joseph) $28. Les Vins de Vienne is a négociant business jointly owned by Gaillard, Villard, and Cuilleron. This Saint-Joseph is smooth and well-rounded, with no rough edges. Pepper, cedar, and plum aromas and flavors are balanced and flavorful, finishing easy. Drink now. **87** —*J.C. (11/15/2006)*

Les Vins de Vienne 2004 Les Escartailles Syrah (Côte Rôtie) $46. Like many of the northern Rhône wines I tried from 2004, this has a wonderfully perfumed bouquet, with crisply defined scents of violets, raspberries, and pepper. It just needs a little more substance and richness on the palate. Drink over the next few years. **87** —*J.C. (11/15/2006)*

Les Vins de Vienne 2004 La Chambée Viognier (Condrieu) $42. A wonderful mélange of honey, orange, apricot, and spice; there's a lot of complexity to this wine, all carried by a plump, mouth-coating texture and ample freshness. Delicious now, so why hold it any longer? **90** —*J.C. (11/15/2006)*

LES VINS SKALLI

Les Vins Skalli 1998 Edition Limitée Cabernet Sauvignon (Vin de Pays d'Oc) $17. Dark fruit dominates the wine. A ripe, dark, and brooding texture gives this wine a fine sense of power. But it is also full of upfront fruit that powers through the sweet tannins, finishing with a touch of acidity. **89** —*R.V. (11/15/2002)*

Les Vins Skalli 2000 Oak Aged Chardonnay (Vin de Pays d'Oc) $10. The overall impression is of ripe, creamy fruit, with aromas of Granny Smith apples. On the palate, there are flavors of spicy wood, crisp acidity, and layers of apples and cream. A classic "apple pie" Chardonnay, delicious, but not heavy. **87** —*R.V. (11/15/2002)*

Les Vins Skalli 1999 Oak Aged Syrah (Vin de Pays d'Oc) $10. Soft wine, with ripe tannins, dry fruit at the end, and flavors of southern herbs and wild fruits. A rich wine, with a streak of power under the sophisticated exterior. At this stage, the southern flavors and modern sophistication clash. This could come around in 2–3 years, although it is hard to predict with confidence. **85** —*R.V. (11/15/2002)*

LOMBARD ET CIE

Lombard et Cie NV Brut Champagne Blend (Champagne) $NA. A small, family-owned producer based in Epernay, Lombard makes a fresh style of Champagne, dominated by Pinot Noir and Pinot Meunier, that has white currant and a delicious touch of lightness. The dosage seems to be out of balance with the rest of the wine, which is a shame, considering the good fruit. **85** —*R.V. (12/1/2005)*

LOUIS BERNARD

Louis Bernard 2001 Grenache-Syrah (Côtes-du-Rhône Villages) $11. **81** —*J.C. (3/1/2004)*

Louis Bernard 1999 Grenache-Syrah (Châteauneuf-du-Pape) $28. A complex bouquet of mint, meat, earth, and tobacco opens this reserved wine. A blend of approximately 60% Grenache and 40% Syrah, with small amounts of Carignane and Mourvedre, it's dry and fairly tart on the palate with a chalky overlay to the licorice and dried fruit flavors. Firmly structured and a bit hard now, it needs a few years to show fully. It closes with a meaty, herb-metallic, and black pepper finish. **88** *(11/15/2001)*

FRANCE

Louis Bernard 2001 Grande Reserve Grenache-Syrah (Châteauneuf-du-Pape) $37. A blend of Grenache and Syrah, this wine is packed with black fruits and with spice. It is tarry, dense, and concentrated. Layers of licorice give complexity to the powerful fruit. **88** —*R.V. (3/1/2004)*

Louis Bernard 2004 Rhône Red Blend (Gigondas) $NA. Has some sturdy plum and prune fruit accented by coffee and spice, but comes across a bit low in acidity and with some drying tannins that may not completely resolve, even if given time. Drink now. **84** —*J.C. (11/15/2006)*

Louis Bernard 2003 Rhône Red Blend (Châteauneuf-du-Pape) $35. A dark-hued wine, with bramble fruits, dry tannins, and some stalky fruits. But, as befits a 2003, there is also sweet fruit, solid flesh, and a layer of acidity to balance. Well-made and enjoyable, with a potential to age for 5+ years. **87** —*R.V. (12/31/2005)*

Louis Bernard 2003 Rhône Red Blend (Côtes-du-Rhône Villages) $9. The Boisset family's recent improvements at this négociant house were just beginning to take hold in 2003, a maddeningly inconsistent vintage in the Rhône. This is a relatively straightforward effort, combining modest cherry, leather, and chocolate flavors in a smooth, easy-to-drink wine. Drink now. **84** —*J.C. (11/15/2006)*

Louis Bernard 2001 Rhône Red Blend (Gigondas) $18. This is a big, dense wine, and full-bodied. It spares few punches, but delivers hugely on solid, dense, black fruits. It will be ready to drink in three to four years. **86** —*R.V. (3/1/2004)*

Louis Bernard 1999 Rhône Red Blend (Côtes-du-Rhône) $9. This straightforward Côtes-du-Rhône, about 70% Grenache, offers ripe, even-roasted, fruit aromas, earth, and leather accents. The mouth is full and chewy, fairly high in acidity, with black-plum, spice, and white pepper flavors. Closes with modest length and dusty cocoa notes. **85** *(11/15/2001)*

Louis Bernard 2005 Rouge Rhône Red Blend (Côtes-du-Rhône Villages) $12. A slight step up from Louis Bernard's simple Côtes-du-Rhône, showing greater intensity and darker fruit flavors that veer toward black cherry and plum. Drink now. **85** —*J.C. (11/15/2006)*

Louis Bernard 2003 Syrah (Crozes-Hermitage) $20. A good showing for this négociant Crozes, with dense black fruit on the nose followed by flavors of plum and black cherries over a firm, minerally core. It's full-bodied yet crisp in acidity, with a long, juicy finish and supple tannins. **89 Editors' Choice** —*J.C. (11/15/2005)*

Louis Bernard 1999 Syrah (Crozes-Hermitage) $13. Stewed dark fruit with leather and spice accents show on the nose of this angular, narrow wine. Very dry on the tongue, it offers black coffee and smoke flavors and high acidity. A taut finish closes this lean machine. **81** *(10/1/2001)*

LOUIS BOUILLOT

Louis Bouillot NV Grand Reserve Brut Champagne Blend (Bourgogne) $12. This is a crisp, bracing bubbly, with tight fruit tasting of green apples, outlined in lightly defined toast. Iron and mineral dominate the precise finish. **87** —*P.G. (12/15/2002)*

Louis Bouillot NV Grande Réserve Perle de Vigne Brut Champagne Blend (Crémant de Bourgogne) $15. A ripe, fresh, appley wine, with attractive grapefruit accents. It is soft and crisp, with just a touch of softness to finish. Simple and great for as apéritif wine. **85** —*R.V. (6/1/2006)*

Louis Bouillot NV Perle de Nuit Blanc de Noirs Brut Champagne Blend (Crémant de Bourgogne) $15. This deep-golden sparkler has some pleasantly toasty, faintly eggy aromas, medium body, and a relatively large bead. Finishes a little rough. **84** —*J.C. (12/1/2004)*

Louis Bouillot 2003 Perle Rare Brut Champagne Blend (Crémant de Bourgogne) $16. By far the best wine in the Louis Bouillot range, this is full, crisp, and layered with toastiness. It has taken on flavors of honey, spices, and vanilla from its wood aging. A fine wine, dry to taste, and finishing crisp and full-bodied. **90** —*R.V. (6/1/2006)*

Louis Bouillot NV Perle d'Aurore Rosé Brut Pinot Noir (Crémant de Bourgogne) $15. Made entirely from Pinot Noir from the heartland of Burgundy, this wine has an attractive light-pink color. The taste is very delicate—red currants and crisp raspberries, with just a touch of softness—but leaves a fresh, uplifting taste. **88** —*R.V. (6/1/2006)*

Louis Bouillot NV Perle d'Ivoire Blanc de Blancs Brut Sparkling Blend (Crémant de Bourgogne) $15. A rich yellow color, this wine shows prominent oak flavors and aromas. Toasty vanilla dominates the nose while butter and toast wrap around Chardonnay's flavors of yellow fruits. A bigger style, with big bubbles and a round feel. **84** —*M.D. (12/15/2006)*

Louis Bouillot NV Perle Noire Blanc de Noirs Sparkling Blend (France) $15. A salmon-infused slate color, this wine starts off gently with a nice yeast aroma. Citrus flavors interact with light boysenberry, again with a soft overlay of yeast. Crisp, with nice body and good bubbles, this is balanced and delicious. **87** —*M.D. (12/15/2006)*

LOUIS DE SACY

Louis de Sacy NV Brut Rosé Champagne Blend (Champagne) $39. The color of a new copper penny, this very attractive rosé shows bready, yeasty aromas, with tart rhubarb fruit. In the mouth the flavors are more ripe, with tart pie cherry and vanilla cookie. Very tasty, though not particularly complex. **89** —*P.G. (12/15/2003)*

Louis de Sacy NV Cuvée Brut Champagne Blend (Champagne) $35. Every one of the tasters mentioned soy as the dominant aroma on this "complex, but tired" wine's nose, backed by ginger, malt, and briny notes. Its flavor profile is unusual: Reviewers noted dried fruit, red plum, apple cider, and cream soda as its dominant flavors. Finishes long and a little sweet. **87** *(12/15/2001)*

LOUIS JADOT

Louis Jadot 2004 Chardonnay (Bâtard-Montrachet) $203. Bâtard-Montrachet is the largest of the white grand crus, yielding archetypal fat, open, generous white Burgundies. Louis Jadot's wine does not disappoint. It's a powerfully ripe, opulent wine that's generous and packed with delicious fruit balanced with a judicious touch of wood. **94** —*R.V. (12/1/2006)*

Louis Jadot 2002 Chardonnay (Corton-Charlemagne) $70. While this wine shows huge amounts of toasty wood at this stage, its potential for balancing out is all there. The fruit under the wood is hugely ripe, combining sweetness with lemony acidity in a fine balance. Give it 10 years. **94** —*R.V. (9/1/2004)*

Louis Jadot 2000 Chardonnay (Mâcon-Villages) $12. 82 —*D.T. (2/1/2002)*

Louis Jadot 1998 Chardonnay (Pouilly-Fuissé) $22. 88 —*M.S. (7/1/2000)*

Louis Jadot 2004 Champ Gain Premier Cru Chardonnay (Puligny-Montrachet) $61. An intense, complex wine that flows unctuously with rich white fruits, spice, vanilla, some toast, and a great depth of flavor. At this stage, the toast is quite dominant, but the rich fruit is on its way up. Like many great white Burgundies, this wine needs to be opened well in advance of drinking. **94 Cellar Selection** —*R.V. (12/1/2006)*

Louis Jadot 2000 Château des Jacques Grand Clos de Loyse Chardonnay (Beaujolais-Villages) $15. A pretty Chardonnay that's lean and steely, a refreshing counterpoint to the current sweet, oaky style. You can taste the flavor of crisp green apples, and the tart acidity is mouthwatering. This is a lovely cocktail wine, balanced, and refreshing. **87 Best Buy** —*S.H. (11/15/2002)*

Louis Jadot 2003 Corton Charlemagne Chardonnay (Corton-Charlemagne) $145. A hugely powerful wine that exudes dense, packed tropical fruit flavors. Yet, it is surprisingly delicate, its power tempered by a cocktail of green fruits, nuts, spice, and toasty new wood. Almost in balance already, it should still age well over many years. **95** —*R.V. (9/1/2005)*

Louis Jadot 2003 Le Clos Blanc Beaune Grèves Premier Cru Chardonnay (Beaune) $65. Le Clos Blanc is a rarity in the mainly red vineyards of Beaune, a patch of chalky soil that has long been planted with Chardonnay. This 2003 is an open wine, with touches of almond and toast flavors, leaving a fresh aftertaste of acidity and green plums. **90** —*R.V. (9/1/2005)*

Louis Jadot 2003 Gamay (Beaujolais) $10. Yes, I know Beaujolais Nouveau is out of favor, it's yesterday's wine. But this isn't Nouveau, this is the real stuff, the original up-front fruity wine. Made from the Gamay grape, it's packed with strawberries, cherries, and soft, generous fruit. There's a slight earthy, mineral touch to it that stops it just being a fruit bomb, and turns it into an easy food wine, especially with salamis, sausages, or burgers. **85 Best Buy** —*R.V. (11/15/2004)*

Louis Jadot 2000 Château de Bellevue Gamay (Morgon) $16. Big and sappy, this wine is filled with ripe berry flavors, and is very fresh and jammy. It also has some sturdy tannins and mouthwatering acids. It's a big Beaujolais but also a gentle one, easy to sip and a good, dry companion for French onion soup. **88** —S.H. (11/15/2002)

Louis Jadot 2000 Château des Jacques Gamay (Moulin-à-Vent) $20. Robust and full-bodied, this is a big Beaujolais, with sweet black raspberry and even cassis fruit, and a syrupy, honeyed-berry finish. Despite the size and dark color, it has a silky smooth texture and good acidity. Could develop with a few years of age. **87** —S.H. (11/15/2002)

Louis Jadot 2000 Domaine du Monnet Gamay (Brouilly) $16. Light-bodied and soft, this wine seduces with flavors of raspberries and sour cherries. Dry and tart, with a silky texture. The acid creates interesting heat and sting on the palate, which makes it a natural for food. **86** —S.H. (11/15/2002)

Louis Jadot 2004 Pinot Noir (Bourgogne) $17. A clean, fresh expression of Burgundian Pinot Noir, with slightly herbal tones laid over a base of tart cherries. It's a bit thin and lacking texture, but shows bright, crisp fruit dusted with a hint of cocoa on the finish. **84** —J.C. (11/15/2006)

Louis Jadot 2003 Pinot Noir (Chambertin Clos de Bèze) $200. Huge, dusty tannins and ripe fruit black plum flavors make for an opulent, rich wine. This is a magnificent, power-packed combination of fruit and structure, and a superb wine, that will develop over many years. **96** —R.V. (9/1/2005)

Louis Jadot 1999 Pinot Noir (Chambolle-Musigny) $37. This is a dry style of wine, with light, fresh red fruit and some dry tannins. The wine lacks concentration, but is perfectly pleasant. **84** —R.V. (11/1/2002)

Louis Jadot 1995 Pinot Noir (Marsannay) $20. **87** (11/15/1999)

Louis Jadot 2003 Beaune Theurons Premier Cru Pinot Noir (Beaune) $42. Packed with toast and roasted coffee flavors, this is an exotic wine that is only just beginning to develop. This wine will mature slowly, revealing its huge red fruits and perfumes over many years. **91** —R.V. (9/1/2005)

Louis Jadot 2002 Chambertin Clos de Bèze Pinot Noir (Gevrey-Chambertin) $140. This is one of the great Burgundies of 2002. It shows the power of the year, with huge black fruits and dense tannins. But it also shows the charm, with ripeness that promises a precocious development as well as long aging. **97** —R.V. (9/1/2004)

Louis Jadot 2002 Corton Greves Premier Cru Pinot Noir (Aloxe-Corton) $70. Black fruit flavors and ripe sweetness give this wine great character as well as richness. The acidity streaks through the rich fruit, leaving dark tannins to finish. **93** —R.V. (9/1/2004)

Louis Jadot 2002 Gevrey Chambertin Clos Saint-Jacques Premier cru Pinot Noir (Gevrey-Chambertin) $85. As so often with wines from Gevrey, this is huge and structured. It is packed with firm, dense, solid fruit, but tempered with ripe tannins. **94** —R.V. (9/1/2004)

Louis Jadot 1999 Les Baudes Premier Cru Pinot Noir (Chambolle-Musigny) $61. This vineyard is owned by the Gagey family that runs Louis Jadot. The wine is ripe and rich with deliciously generous fruit. A touch of wood gives it depth of flavor. At the end, there are sweet red-fruit flavors. **92** —R.V. (11/1/2002)

Louis Jadot 1999 Les Fuées Premier Cru Pinot Noir (Chambolle-Musigny) $61. A rich, concentrated wine that has solid black fruit flavors, fine dry tannins, and acidity. At this stage, there is a curious taste from the bottling that should fade as it ages. Then it will develop into a fine, solid wine. **89** —R.V. (11/1/2002)

Louis Jadot 2002 Volnay Clos des Chênes Premier Cru Pinot Noir (Volnay) $29. This Volnay is so intense, so seductive. It has great structure, too, deeply flavored and rich, with pure, sweet fruits. **92** —R.V. (9/1/2004)

Louis Jadot 2003 Château des Jacques Red Blend (Moulin-à-Vent) $22. **89** —J.C. (11/15/2005)

Louis Jadot 2001 Domaine du Monnet Red Blend (Brouilly) $16. With modest cherry and leather aromas, this Beaujolais doesn't offer a lot of charm or fruit. Tart cherries finish a bit astringent and green. **83** —J.C. (11/15/2003)

Louis Jadot 1998 Les Demoiselles White Blend (Chevalier-Montrachet) $NA. Light and poised fruit, with a brightly perfumed aroma and a touch of fresh bread. There is a hint of grilled nuts along with fresh acidity and a fine structure. **91** —R.V. (11/1/2001)

LOUIS LATOUR

Louis Latour 2000 Chardonnay (Bâtard-Montrachet) $220. Not for the faint-hearted, this is a huge, mouth-filling wine bursting with yellow plum, hazel-nut and peach aromas, and accented by smoke, butter, and toast. Yet for all its size, it manages to marry that power with a sense of mineral elegance. Drink now–2010. **92** (8/1/2002)

Louis Latour 2004 Chardonnay (Bâtard-Montrachet) $280. Rich and ample, this is an impressive wine. The fruit and wood flavors work together to give a feeling of seriousness and great ageability. With its spice, toast notes, and dark-hued structure, this will age well over the next five to 10 years. **94** —R.V. (12/1/2006)

Louis Latour 2004 Chardonnay (Bienvenues Bâtard-Montrachet) $250. This is the smallest of the grand crus of Puligny-Montrachet, a mere 8.6 acres. This wine shows the vineyard's typical elegance, with delicious flavors of pears, almonds, and vanilla, hovering on the palate for minutes, leaving a dancing freshness. **94** —R.V. (12/1/2006)

Louis Latour 2000 Chardonnay (Meursault) $34. It's plump and juicy, yet not devoid of structure, blending Asian pear and citrus aromas and flavors with nectarine skin and bitter almond. There's a softness to the finish that causes it to lose a little definition but helps it go down easy. **87** (8/1/2002)

Louis Latour 2000 Chardonnay (Beaune) $26. Without big oak or big fruit to make it ungainly, this is a real food-friendly Chardonnay. The delicate floral aromas and understated yet finely etched pear and almond flavors almost seem designed to show off that special weekend dish you just spent hours making. **86** (8/1/2002)

Louis Latour 1998 Chardonnay (Meursault) $34. **87** —P.G. (11/1/2000)

Louis Latour 1998 Chardonnay (Chassagne-Montrachet) $40. **88** —P.G. (11/1/2000)

Louis Latour 2004 Cailleret Premier Cru Chardonnay (Chassagne-Montrachet) $65. Ripe, open, and packed with melon and tropical fruit flavors, this wine is already showing enticing drinkability. Its fresh, ripe fruits are layered with some mineral character and an under-cushion of wood. **90** —R.V. (12/1/2006)

Louis Latour 1998 Charmes Premier Cru Chardonnay (Meursault) $55. **90** —P.G. (11/1/2000)

Louis Latour 2000 Château De Blagny Premier Cru Chardonnay (Meursault) $40. In contrast to many of the other wines, this one starts off tight, with only faint lime and mineral notes on the nose. But it blossoms with air, stubbornly yielding up taut citrus flavors that flow over the palate with an almost gritty, powdered-rock texture. **89** (8/1/2002)

Louis Latour 2003 Corton Charlemagne Chardonnay (Corton-Charlemagne) $140. Latour's signature wine is huge in 2003—certainly less subtle and less grand than the 2002, but still a great wine. It is rich, ripe, and creamy, with toast and wood nuances. The power is dominant, but there is still the recognizable elegance of a fine Corton-Charlemagne. **93** —R.V. (9/1/2005)

Louis Latour 2004 Goutte d'Or Premier Cru Chardonnay (Meursault) $65. A soft, open wine with some vanilla flavors emphasizing the opulence of Meursault. The wine is ready to drink now. **89** —R.V. (12/1/2006)

Louis Latour 1998 La Grande Roche Chardonnay (Montagny) $15. **86** —J.C. (7/1/2000)

Louis Latour 2000 Les Chenevottes Chardonnay (Chassagne-Montrachet) $47. This is a big, bold wine with scents of ripe pear and a hint of anise. The fruit seems to grow and add dimension in the mouth, featuring pears and peaches that are topped off with a dollop of spicy oak and butter. **88** (8/1/2002)

Louis Latour 2003 Les Demoiselles Chardonnay (Chevalier-Montrachet) $470. What a powerhouse of flavors: white and yellow fruit, herbs, and spicy wood, but still exhibiting some of the finesse and elegance for which this grand cru vineyard is noted. Ripe fruit means that this is not a wine for long aging, but it will certainly give pleasure over the next several years. **94** —R.V. (9/1/2005)

FRANCE

Louis Latour 2004 Les Folatières Premier Cru Chardonnay (Puligny-Montrachet) $79. This wine is soft and ripe, but seems to lack structure. Don't expect it to age. **87** —R.V. (12/1/2006)

Louis Latour 1998 Les Referts Premier Cru Chardonnay (Puligny-Montrachet) $55. 92 —P.G. (11/1/2000)

Louis Latour 2000 Morgeot Chardonnay (Chassagne-Montrachet) $50. Butter, *pain grillé* and roasted nut aromas expand on the palate into honey, peach and tangerine flavors, accented by citrus and mineral notes. Spicy (white peppery) on the finish. **89** (8/1/2002)

Louis Latour 1998 Morgeot Premier Cru Chardonnay (Chassagne-Montrachet) $48. 89 —P.G. (11/1/2000)

Louis Latour 2002 Puligny-Montrachet Chardonnay (Puligny-Montrachet) $37. Sweet, vanilla notes balance the pure green plums and delicious acidity. This is immediately attractive, and will also develop over the next five years. **89** —R.V. (9/1/2004)

Louis Latour 2004 Sous le Puits Premier Cru Chardonnay (Puligny-Montrachet) $49. High up on the slope, the Sous le Puits vineyard has produced a ripe, open, buttery wine that is full of generous, opulent fruit. It is packed with pineapple, tropical fruit, and lime flavors, along with a hint of caramel and almonds. Ready to drink now. **90** —R.V. (12/1/2006)

Louis Latour 2003 Pinot Noir (Aloxe-Corton) $45. A pleasingly ripe, rich wine that has very sweet fruit flavors. Red jelly is the dominant character, with some light tannic structure to hold it together. **87** —R.V. (9/1/2005)

Louis Latour 2003 Chambertin les Heritiers Latour Pinot Noir (Chambertin) $220. A wine that explodes with powerful, ripe flavors. It offers complex black fruit flavors, and tons of spice plus ample acidity. This great wine should develop over many years. **93** —R.V. (9/1/2005)

Louis Latour 2002 Corton Grancy Pinot Noir (Corton) $NA. A lovely, juicy wine with black tannins and immense fruits. Watch this wine develop over 10 years. **91** —R.V. (9/1/2004)

Louis Latour 1996 Domaine Latour Aloxe-Corton Pinot Noir (Burgundy) $29. 90 (11/15/1999)

Louis Latour 2002 Le Chaillots Premier Cru Pinot Noir (Aloxe-Corton) $NA. This wine has intense jammy fruit flavors and some tannins to give structure. It is powerful, but restrained. **89** —R.V. (9/1/2004)

Louis Latour 1995 Savigny-les-Beaune Pinot Noir (Burgundy) $20. 88 (11/15/1999)

LOUIS MOUSSET

Louis Mousset 1999 Prestige Syrah (Côtes-du-Rhône) $10. Grassy, hay-like aromas vie with scents of sweaty gym clothes in this light, tart Syrah. Barely acceptable. **80** (10/1/2001)

LOUIS PERDRIER

Louis Perdrier NV Brut Rosé Sparkling Blend (Vin Mousseux) $8. Orange pink in color, this is a soft, medium-dry wine that has pleasant raspberry flavors. It is fresh, made for those who like their sparkling wines without much acidity. **83** —R.V. (6/1/2006)

LOUIS ROEDERER

Louis Roederer 1995 Blanc de Blancs Brut Champagne Blend (Champagne) $55. Aromas of apples and hay open this stately and somewhat mature bubbly. In the mouth, it's richly and darkly fruited, with dried plum and pear flavors and soft mineral-chalk accents. The wine is not that effervescent, but closes with good length, lemon, and more mineral notes. It's not as nuanced or subtle as Roederer's Cristal, but it's nearly as enjoyable. **91 Editors' Choice** —M.M. (12/15/2001)

Louis Roederer 1993 Blanc de Blancs Brut Champagne Blend (Champagne) $55. 91 —M.S. (12/1/1999)

Louis Roederer 1997 Brut Champagne Blend (Champagne) $63. If you think Champagne is not just bubbles, but is also wine, then this vintage is for you. It is rounded, rich, powerful, with a fine sense of the red fruits of Pinot Noir. To add further flavors, there are almonds, creaminess or and warmth. There is a touch of austere minerality from the low dosage and the lack of malolactic which means it will age well over 10 years or more. **95** —R.V. (12/1/2004)

Louis Roederer 1996 Brut Champagne Blend (Champagne) $63. Bold and toasty, but also boasts plenty of subtleties: mushrooms, a hint of butter, ripe apples. It's full-bodied, rich, and creamy; intensely flavored yet retains a sense of elegance throughout its long, vinous finish. It's a good value in vintage Champagne. **93 Editors' Choice** —J.C. (12/1/2004)

Louis Roederer NV Brut Premier Champagne Blend (France) $41. A nice, dry Champagne, with very subtle citrus flavors and plenty of yeast and bread throughout. Acids are high, and scour the palate. The bubbles are pretty rough, and require rich, salty foods for balance. **87** —S.H. (12/15/2002)

Louis Roederer 1999 Brut Rosé Champagne Blend (Champagne) $71. Chalk and mineral aromas are backed by hints of wheat and orange peel. Lively and young in the mouth, almost to the point of being jumpy, with nice orange flavors. Subtle on the finish, with some spiced apple and zest. **89** —M.S. (12/31/2005)

Louis Roederer 1998 Brut Rosé Champagne Blend (Champagne) $63. A rich, smooth, very pale rosé, with intense, concentrated raspberry and red currant flavors and layers of crispness over the rich fruit. This wine is beautifully blended showing elegance as well as richness, the ability to be an apéritif wine, but just as important, the ability to go with food. **92** —R.V. (12/1/2004)

Louis Roederer 1994 Brut Rosé Champagne Blend (Champagne) $55. 86 —J.C. (12/15/2000)

Louis Roederer 1995 Brut Vintage Champagne Blend (France) $59. An astonishingly good wine, fine and complex, yet fun to drink. It's heady and rich and feels as fine as silk on the palate, but it's a serious, layered wine that will age. Dry and citrusy, with pronounced yeast and bread dough on the finish, it's as smooth as they get. **93 Editors' Choice** —S.H. (12/15/2002)

Louis Roederer 1999 Cristal Brut Champagne Blend (Champagne) $188. A powerful Cristal, which has all the richness of the 1999 vintage. The aromas of white flowers and cocoa lead to a palate that is rich, intense, concentrated, but restrained. It is already drinkable, but should mature well. **95** —R.V. (11/1/2006)

Louis Roederer 1996 Cristal Brut Champagne Blend (Champagne) $175. Still delicious, but not quite as impressive as a bottle tasted last year. Rich and full, with aromas and flavors of baked apples and citrus and an easygoing finish. **91** —J.C. (12/15/2003)

Louis Roederer 1995 Cristal Brut Champagne Blend (Champagne) $180. Great refinement shows in the subtle hazelnut, fruit, hay, and vanilla aromas of this famous luxury cuvée. The palate is flavorful with lovely dry grape, peaches and cream, toasted nut, and plum flavors, and the mouthfeel is soft, lightly and gently frothy. Finishes long and leaner, but not hard, with mineral and citrus notes. Drink now through 2007. **92** (12/15/2001)

Louis Roederer 1996 Cristal Rosé Champagne Blend (Champagne) $295. Perhaps this extravagantly priced bubbly just needs more time to fill out, because right now it's lean and light in body, strongly citrusy and tart on the finish. Toast and mushroom notes on the nose add complexity and hope for the future. **90** —J.C. (12/1/2004)

Louis Roederer NV Premier Brut Champagne Blend (Champagne) $52. A classic nonvintage Champagne, Brut Premier is also a yardstick by which others are measured. In the case of this bottle, that yardstick is working well: the palate is rich and creamy, there is maturity along with great fruit and elegance. Best as an apéritif wine, this could also go with light foods. **92** —R.V. (12/1/2005)

Louis Roederer NV Premier Brut Champagne Blend (Champagne) $45. Basic Champagne, but done exceedingly well, with toasty, yeasty aromas that dominate the nose, joined only by fleeting scents of lime. Medium in body, slightly creamy in the mouth, with more toast and citrus and even some chalky mineral notes on the finish. **89** —J.C. (12/1/2004)

Louis Roederer NV Premier Brut Champagne Blend (Champagne) $51. A solid choice, though perhaps not especially inspiring, the nonvintage Roederer Brut has a crisp apple-floral-toast nose and a light, even mouthfeel with lively bead. More apple appears on the palate, plus tart lemon and chalk notes. Finishes long and crisp, with similar flavors. A bit young—consider aging for 2-3 years. **87** (12/15/2001)

FRANCE

Louis Roederer 1996 Vintage Rose Champagne Blend (France) $55. What a wonderful wine. You could sniff it all day, with the beautiful raspberry, vanilla, and peach flavors, and their nuances of coconut, white chocolate, hazelnut, and yeast. In the mouth it's delicate and rich, very dry, with subtle flavors. **92** —*S.H. (12/15/2002)*

Louis Roederer 1999 Blanc de Blancs Brut Chardonnay (Champagne) $74. Better known for its blends dominated by Pinot Noir, Roederer is following the fashion for blanc de blancs in this very dry, but ripely toasty, full-bodied Chardonnay. It has super-rich fruit, but still keeps a sense of proportion in its acidity and green plum flavors. **93** —*R.V. (11/1/2006)*

Louis Roederer 1997 Blanc de Blancs Brut Chardonnay (Champagne) $59. Dry, almost dusty scents lead into a full, ripe, flavorful blanc de blancs with a lot of rich, round fruit flavors. It's a complete wine, full and quite tasty, with a good balance to the finish that includes toast, caramel, vanilla, and enough acid to prop up the big fruit. **90** —*P.G. (12/15/2003)*

LOUIS SIPP

Louis Sipp 2001 Grand Cru Kirchberg de Ribeauvillé Riesling (Alsace) $28. This is a firm, closed wine, which shows how well the Rieslings from this grand cru vineyard can age. It is powerful, with a tight structure and green fruits. There are fine, green flavors as well as some hints of green plums. Wait 5 years before drinking. **90** —*R.V. (11/1/2005)*

LOUIS TÊTE

Louis Tête 2003 Gamay (Moulin-à-Vent) $18. **86** —*J.C. (11/15/2005)*

LUCIEN ALBRECHT

Lucien Albrecht 2002 Cuvée Marie Gewürztraminer (Alsace) $27. A medium-bodied to full Gewürz, with floral aromas that carry attractive lychee notes. But bubble gum flavors seem slightly confected on the palate, and the wine finishes short. **84** —*J.C. (8/1/2006)*

Lucien Albrecht 2004 Reserve Gewürztraminer (Alsace) $18. Waxy, spiced pear aromas give way to musky, spicy notes alongside peach and melon flavors. Not as full or rich as some Gewürzes, but nicely structured on the palate. Finishes soft and easy to drink. **88** —*J.C. (11/1/2005)*

Lucien Albrecht 2000 Vendanges Tardives 375 ml Gewürztraminer (Alsace) $41. This lightly sweet VT goes down deceptively easily, blending ripe citrus and pear flavors with hints of clove and allspice. A hint of shoe polish detracts slightly from the nose, but the wine finishes soft and without any hint of bitterness. **88** —*J.C. (2/1/2005)*

Lucien Albrecht 2003 Cuvée Balthazar Pinot Blanc (Alsace) $12. This full-bodied Pinot Blanc is ripe and soft, boasting lots of round, melony fruit. Likeable and zaftig, but lacking nuance. Drink now. **86** —*J.C. (2/1/2005)*

Lucien Albrecht 2001 Clos des Récollets Pinot Gris (Alsace) $86. Starts off a little rocky, with rubbery, reductive notes that give way to flavors of ripe pears and melons, accented by dried spices. Medium-bodied and dry, with a slightly oily texture and a spicy, persistent finish. A natural with trout or salmon. **89** —*J.C. (2/1/2005)*

Lucien Albrecht 2002 Cuvée Cécile Pinot Gris (Alsace) $42. Aromas of honey and almonds lead to a palate that boasts a ripe, soft fruity character. This is rich and sweet, showing caramelized peaches and apricots and fresh acidity on the finish. **89** —*R.V. (2/1/2006)*

Lucien Albrecht 2003 Cuvée Romanus Pinot Gris (Alsace) $16. Surprisingly dry and steely for a 2003, with lime and green apples married to hints of almond and peach. Crisp acids and a dry, clean finish. **86** —*J.C. (2/1/2005)*

Lucien Albrecht 2001 Grand Cru Pfingstberg Pinot Gris (Alsace) $36. Pear and honey scents presage luscious flavors of ripe pears, melon, and dried spices. It's medium-bodied and dry with a long finish that shows a touch of alcoholic warmth, so opt for drinking it over the next few years. **90 Editors' Choice** —*J.C. (2/1/2005)*

Lucien Albrecht 2000 Sélection de Grains Nobles Pinot Gris (Alsace) $65. Intense orange marmalade and botrytis notes on the nose also come through on the palate. This wine is concentrated and intense, with layers of acidity balancing its intense sweetness. Give this wine 10 years. **92** —*R.V. (2/1/2006)*

Lucien Albrecht 2000 Vendages Tardives 375 ml Pinot Gris (Alsace) $46. With its slightly oily and sweet flavors of honeyed pears and melons, this

speaks plainly of late-picked Pinot Gris. Finishes on the short side, but there's no doubt that it's clean and varietally correct. **88** —*J.C. (2/1/2005)*

Lucien Albrecht 2001 Amplus Pinot Noir (Alsace) $44. Undoubtedly an ambitious effort, Albrecht's Amplus is an impressively extracted Pinot that ends up coming across as too woody and too tannic for its modest cherry fruit. Lots of vanilla, cedar, and caramel if you like that sort of thing. **84** —*J.C. (2/1/2005)*

Lucien Albrecht 2002 Clos Himmelreich Riesling (Alsace) $95. Clos Himmelreich has been owned by the Albrechts for four generations. This is a rich, full, bone-dry wine, with floral aromas. It is elegant, intense, and refreshing. **89** —*R.V. (2/1/2006)*

Lucien Albrecht 2004 Cuvée Henri Riesling (Alsace) $25. Solid, mainstream Riesling, combining apple and citrus aromas and flavors in a medium-bodied format. Tangerines and limes accent green apples in this simple, fresh wine. **85** —*J.C. (8/1/2006)*

Lucien Albrecht 2001 Grand Cru Clos Schild Pfingstberg Riesling (Alsace) $96. Not a blockbuster, but a medium-weight Riesling that should age almost indefinitely on its taut spine of acidity. Smoke and mineral aromas add complexity to bold, peach-accented apples and a broad streak of lime. **90 Cellar Selection** —*J.C. (2/1/2005)*

Lucien Albrecht 2001 Grand Cru Pfingstberg Riesling (Alsace) $35. A bit severe for present consumption, this is a lean, stony wine, enlivened by hints of green apple and lime. It's crisp and clean, making it possible to drink now, but its austerity suggests patience; try in 2010, when its angular minerals might be softened somewhat. **87** —*J.C. (2/1/2005)*

Lucien Albrecht 2003 Reserve Riesling (Alsace) $15. This is a ripe wine that accurately reflects the heat of the 2003 summer. Apple, peach, and honey aromas and flavors and a big, slightly oily mouthfeel overwhelm any mineral elements—at least now, in its boisterous, fun youth. **87** —*J.C. (2/1/2005)*

Lucien Albrecht 2000 Vendanges Tardives 375 ml Riesling (Alsace) $41. Scents of dried apricots and candied citrus leap from the glass, followed by flavors of honey, pear, and melon. This is slightly sweet, with a robust 13% alcohol that gives it heft on the palate. Try with rich appetizers or with the cheese course. **88** —*J.C. (2/1/2005)*

Lucien Albrecht 1997 Tokay Pinot Gris (Alsace) $19. **88** *(8/1/1999)*

LUCIEN CROCHET

Lucien Crochet 2000 La Croix du Roy Sauvignon Blanc (Sancerre) $20. The catch-all nose offers grass, grapefruit, flint, vanilla, and baking spices. What follows is a tasty blend of citrus, green herbs, Granny Smith apples, and a welcome chalkiness. Round yet structured, this bottling offers most of what's great about Loire Valley white wine. **90 Editors' Choice** *(8/1/2002)*

LUCIEN LE MOINE

Lucien Le Moine 2003 Chardonnay (Corton-Charlemagne) $150. Tasted twice, two months apart. This wine was fabulous on both occasions, combining the fat, fleshy ripeness and honeyed fruit of the vintage with the minerality of its grand cru site. Smoke, citrus, and toasted nuts round out the flavors, which finish long and complex. Delicious now, but should hold several years at least. **93** —*J.C. (4/1/2006)*

Lucien Le Moine 2003 Les Folatiéres Premier Cru Chardonnay (Puligny-Montrachet) $100. Rich and ripe, with buttery, toasty aromas that are also reminiscent of bacon fat. Full-bodied, with ample apple and citrus fruit flavors that come to a climax in the long, hazelnut-tinged finish. Lovely, but with its rather low acidity, it looks to be a Burgundy to drink rather than to cellar. **92** —*J.C. (4/1/2006)*

Lucien Le Moine 2003 Pinot Noir (Clos Saint-Denis) $130. Complex from the first sniff, where it seems herbal, briary, and even a bit peppery but simultaneously bacony, spicy, and laced with red cherries. On the palate, it's mostly about sous-bois and spice, with just enough cherry fruit for balance. Briary and a bit drying on the finish, but the bet here is that this wine will age superbly. Try after 2010. **92** —*J.C. (4/1/2006)*

Lucien Le Moine 2003 Les Charmes Premier Cru Pinot Noir (Chambolle-Musigny) $150. Full-bodied and deliciously supple, with layers of black cherries, plum, tea, and exotic spices that gently caress the palate. Long and silky on the finish, making it approachable now, but it should only improve over the next several years. **93** —*J.C. (4/1/2006)*

Lucien Le Moine 2003 Les Suchots Premier Cru Pinot Noir (Vosne-Romanée) $100. Firm and tannic, with a slightly worrisome astringency. If this comes into balance, this rating may look a couple points stingy in time. Shows an underbrush, briary side to its black cherry and plum flavors, then picks up coffee and spice notes on the finish. **90** —*J.C. (4/1/2006)*

LULU B.

Lulu B. 2005 Pinot Noir (Vin de Pays d'Oc) $10. From the cool hills of Limoux in the Aude, this well-structured wine has good raspberry flavors, cherries, and a layer of wood. It is firm and dry initially, but the finish mingles fruit and acidity. **84** —*R.V. (12/31/2006)*

M ET F LAMARIE

M et F Lamarie 1999 Château Aiguilloux Cuvée des Trois Seigneurs Red Blend (Corbières) $11. Solid and spicy right from the start, with a saturated palate of red country-style fruit, pepper, and cinnamon. The finish is round and satisfying, offering a healthy but restrained dose of tannins. The acidity is just right, yielding a wine of balance. For the price it has a lot to give. **87 Best Buy** —*M.S. (2/1/2003)*

M. CHAPOUTIER

M. Chapoutier 2000 Beaurevoir Grenache (Tavel) $23. Dark and rather weighty, more of a light red in color and texture. After a rather mute nose, the even-yet gently grainy-palate shows wood over dry, mineral-tinged Grenache fruit, and the flavors extend to the medium long finish. It's an interesting exercise, but the wood and weight don't sing as lightness and liveliness might. **84** —*M.M. (2/1/2002)*

M. Chapoutier 2004 Chante-Alouette Marsanne (Hermitage) $70. Like many of Chapoutier's whites, this wine doesn't show all that much fruit. There's honey and anise, good freshness, and a strong mouthfeel and texture capped off by tactile minerality on the finish. Hold 5–8 years. **87** —*J.C. (11/15/2006)*

M. Chapoutier 2005 Deschant Marsanne (Saint-Joseph) $35. Starts off with some modest melon and mineral scents, but this largely neutral wine is more about texture than flavor. It's softly stony in the mouth, like finely crushed stone or even powdered rock. Drink now–2008. **86** —*J.C. (11/15/2006)*

M. Chapoutier 2001 Le Méal Marsanne (Hermitage) $134. At five years of age, this is still a young wine, keeping much of its appeal firmly under wraps. The tight aromas and flavors only gradually reveal hints of their future grandeur in tantalizing glimpses of honey, anise, orange peel, and pineapple. Yet the never-ending length and pronounced minerality to this wine's finish leaves no doubt of its ultimate quality. Try after 2010? **94 Cellar Selection** —*J.C. (11/15/2006)*

M. Chapoutier 2000 Les Granits Blanc Marsanne (Saint-Joseph) $88. Fragrant, with honeyed, creamy aromas that alert you to the richness to come. Flavors of melon and spiced apple precede a dry, light finish that fades away surprisingly quietly. At the end there's a gap in continuity and then some bitterness. **88** —*M.S. (9/1/2003)*

M. Chapoutier 2001 Les Meysonniers Marsanne (Crozes-Hermitage) $26. Somewhat meaty, with chunky apricot and pear aromas as well as apple, lemon, and herb flavors. There's good power here, more so than poise, so while it's short on complexity, it's full-flavored and forward. **86** —*M.S. (9/1/2003)*

M. Chapoutier 1998 Domaine des Béates Red Blend (Coteaux d'Aix en Provence) $29. Dark cherry fruit and lots of toasty oak mark this midweight red from Provence. But it's rather hemmed-in and one-dimensional, and also bears some drying, prickly back-end tannins. This may come into better balance with time, but one doubts if the fruit will ever shine. Could be a decent match for grilled foods. **84** —*M.M. (2/1/2002)*

M. Chapoutier 2004 Rhône Red Blend (Gigondas) $40. Seems a bit unexpressive on the nose, like many of the Chapoutier wines, but also boasts admirable flavors of plum and spice. Not that tannic or long, just an enjoyable quaff with a pleasant mouthfeel. Drink now. **86** —*J.C. (11/15/2006)*

M. Chapoutier 2000 Rhône Red Blend (Gigondas) $39. Muscular and full

in the nose, with plum, earth, and mineral aromas. Gigondas can deliver hearty country-style reds, and this fits the bill. The palate is dense and loaded with plum and cherry, but also some chocolaty richness. A full, toasty finish deals hints of coffee and pepper. Well-balanced and satisfying. **88** —*M.S. (9/1/2003)*

M. Chapoutier 1999 Barbe Rac Récolte Rhône Red Blend (Châteauneuf-du-Pape) $141. Round and full, but not a heavy wine. The nose has ample cherry and spice, and later some floral aromas that instill interest. The palate is correct and medium in terms of power and size, while flavors of spicy berry fruit interact with chocolate to create a pleasant package. As for feel, the tannins are medium to big, but not overpowering. **88** —*M.S. (9/1/2003)*

M. Chapoutier 2003 Belleruche Rouge Rhône Red Blend (Côtes-du-Rhône) $14. A simple, straightforward quaffer, with light red fruit scents and flavors and an herbal tinge—like cherries and strawberry compote. Turns a bit dusty and drying on the finish, so best with rare beef. **84** —*J.C. (11/15/2006)*

M. Chapoutier 2000 Belleruche Rouge Rhône Red Blend (Côtes-du-Rhône) $14. Good concentrated fruit with fine, ripe, dusty southern herbs and spices. A slight hint of animal muskiness mars an otherwise solid, well-made and ripe wine. Drink now, or age over three or four years. **84** —*R.V. (6/1/2002)*

M. Chapoutier 2001 La Bernardine Rhône Red Blend (Châteauneuf-du-Pape) $37. This wine doesn't reveal that much of itself on the nose, showing just teasing hints of leather and cherries. But it oozes across the palate with dense, chocolate fudge flavors that carry cherry and dried spice notes. Drink now-2010+. **90** —*J.C. (2/1/2005)*

M. Chapoutier 1999 Le Méal Ermitage Rhône Red Blend (Hermitage) $150. Chapoutier's selections of the best parcels of vines in Hermitage are set to become legendary. Sold under the ancient spelling of the appellation name (Ermitage), they represent the epitome of the power and concentration that lies behind the reputation of the appellation. This cuvée is the best of the collection, with its brooding, opaque character, suggesting rather than revealing power at this stage. Age it until your new born baby is old enough to drink, and it will be just about ready. **98** —*R.V. (6/1/2002)*

M. Chapoutier 2001 Rhône White Blend (Condrieu) $83. Round and lush, with plenty of gardenia, stone fruit, mineral, and citrus peel. The mouth is emboldened with tangerine and lemon, and also just a hint of softening butter. And the finish is equally soft, dry, and easy. This Northern Rhône white comes out smooth and fades away quickly and quietly, much as it should. With personality and defined flavors, this is a pretty solid Viognier. And it's hardly over the top. **88** —*M.S. (9/1/2003)*

M. Chapoutier 2005 Belleruche Blanc Rhône White Blend (Côtes-du-Rhône) $14. This is a broad, mouth-filling wine that just isn't that expressive from a flavor perspective. There are hints of spice and minerality, including anise tinges, and hints of melon and pineapple fruit. But there's just not that much intensity. More of a textural experience than a flavorful one. **85** —*J.C. (11/15/2006)*

M. Chapoutier 1998 Belleruche Blanc Rhône White Blend (Côtes-du-Rhône) $11. 84 —*M.M. (11/1/2000)*

M. Chapoutier 2000 Chante-Alouette Rhône White Blend (Hermitage) $84. More forward and modern than De L'Orée, this bottling is clean, overtly fruity, and ultimately very stylish. Butterscotch notes start it off, followed by peach, melon, and apple flavors. Overall there's undeniable fruit quality here. The finish is round, substantive, and long, and here you'll find notes of honey and white pepper. For a Northern Rhône white, it's accessible and not too bitter or tight. **91** —*M.S. (9/1/2003)*

M. Chapoutier 1999 De l'Orée Ermitage Rhône White Blend (Hermitage) $253. The name refers as much to the brilliant green-gold color of this wine as to its richness. A tiny production from selected parcels of old Marsanne vines, this is a beautifully rich, creamy wine with a touch of honey and flavors of ripe pears. **93** —*R.V. (6/1/2002)*

M. Chapoutier 2001 La Bernardine Rhône White Blend (Châteauneuf-du-Pape) $44. Basic and clean, but fairly nondescript in terms of aromas. The flavor profile is mostly pear and melon, but once again, nothing on the palate is terribly defined or exciting. The finish is smooth and dry, and there's some citrus thrown in for excitement. But overall this wine seems neither here nor there. It's good, but that's about the most you can say. **85** —*M.S. (9/1/2003)*

M. Chapoutier 2000 Les Beatines Rosé Blend (Coteaux d'Aix en Provence) $13. Fairly full, with dark cherry, leather, and anise aromas and flavors, this is a scaled-down version of the Béates, and it may actually have broader appeal. There's a touch of heat, but plenty of texture, with palate-tingling tart cherry fruit and spice notes that linger on the back end. **85** —*M.M. (2/1/2002)*

M. Chapoutier 1999 Deschants Syrah (Saint-Joseph) $34. Get past the animal, rustic aromas of this wine, and it shows very fine paces. It is bursting with Syrah perfumes and ripe fruit. Solid, powerful, concentrated, with spice and fine tannins, it will develop over the next five years. **91** —*R.V. (6/1/2002)*

M. Chapoutier 2000 L'Ermite Syrah (Hermitage) $368. Harmonious, with plenty of spicy oak accenting the bruising black fruit that builds and builds as the bouquet unfolds. The palate isn't overly complex, but it is loaded with black cherry and plum. Then mounds of bitter chocolate take over on the finish. Forward and in your face; a linear, powerful monotone wine but one of unquestionable quality. **91** —*M.S. (9/1/2003)*

M. Chapoutier 2000 La Sizeranne Syrah (Hermitage) $110. Supple and silky in the mouth, with blackberry and cherry flavors bolstered by black olive and floral notes. What you get on the nose is similar—flowers, plus deep earth and berry flavors. Finishes long, with soft tannins and punctuated by a peppery-herb note. Drink 2005–2008. **92** *(9/1/2003)*

M. Chapoutier 2000 Le Méal Syrah (Hermitage) $317. If the gorgeous notes of brown sugar, graham cracker, and black pepper on the nose don't reel you in, what's in the mouth will. Its blackberry core is juicy without being overblown; black olives, earth, leather, and even a little raspberry flesh out the flavor profile. Has a velour-like texture in the mouth; its tannins are soft enough to age well, but age it certainly needs—it's showing restraint, and will need about 10 years to reach full bloom. **96 Cellar Selection** *(9/1/2003)*

M. Chapoutier 1999 Les Bécasses Syrah (Côte Rôtie) $79. You couldn't mistake this Côte-Rôtie for anything else: Floral-herb aromas are bolstered by smoky green tobacco, white pepper, and cranberry. It's ultrastructured, with a strong iron-mineral core that needs at least two, but as many as 10, years of cellaring to soften. Tart red-berry, even animal, flavors cushion the steely core flavors and round out the finish. **94 Cellar Selection** *(11/1/2001)*

M. Chapoutier 2000 Les Granits Syrah (Saint-Joseph) $95. Seemingly at its peak of maturity, although it should stay there for several years, this is a masterful Saint-Joseph, showing great complexity (flowers, pepper, smoke, cherries), ripe fruit, and satin-textured tannins. Drink now-2012. **92** —*J.C. (11/15/2006)*

M. Chapoutier 2004 Les Meysonniers Syrah (Crozes-Hermitage) $25. Peppery and herbal upfront, then come deeper notes of coffee, black olive, and sour plum. Rather fleshy for an '04, with ample mouthfeel and supple tannins. Turns peppery and tart on the finish. A good effort for the vintage. **89** —*J.C. (11/15/2006)*

M. Chapoutier 1997 Les Meysonniers Syrah (Crozes-Hermitage) $24. 86 — *J.C. (7/1/2000)*

M. Chapoutier 2001 Petite Ruche Syrah (Crozes-Hermitage) $23. Green pepper and tobacco aromas signal some of the sour fruit that appears on the palate. Tastes of beets and pie cherries and an oaky, disparate finish doesn't do much to shape things up. Too sour and scattered. **82** —*M.S. (9/1/2003)*

M. Chapoutier 1999 Petite Ruche Syrah (Crozes-Hermitage) $19. This Crozes-Hermitage caused some dissention among our panelists. While some reviewers found the nose "handsome and complex," with dark chocolate, licorice, plum, and hickory smoke aromas, one panelist criticized it as having a sour, manufactured Pixy Stix quality. Comments on the mouthfeel ran the gamut from lean to full; most agreed, at least, that the palate showed tart blackberry, leather, and licorice flavors. **86** *(10/1/2001)*

M. Chapoutier 2005 Invitare Viognier (Condrieu) $68. Made entirely in stainless steel, so the apricot and floral scents of Viognier really stand out

in this wine, adding orange and spice elements. But on the palate there's a bit of a disconnect, as the lush fruit vanishes, replaced by chalky, minerally notes. **87** —*J.C. (11/15/2006)*

MAILLY

Mailly NV Brut Rosé Champagne Blend (Champagne) $46. A pretty salmon-pink-colored wine, which is soft and dominated by easy flavors of pink grapefruit and crisp acidity. This is fresh, and fine as an apéritif. **87** —*R.V. (12/1/2005)*

Mailly 1997 Grand Cru Champagne Blend (Champagne) $40. A fine choice as an apéritif, this is a delicately flavored, light-bodied Champagne with enough toasty, yeasty nuances to keep its citrus and apple flavors from coming across as simple. **87** —*J.C. (12/1/2004)*

Mailly 1998 Grand Cru Brut Champagne Blend (Champagne) $49. Very soft and open, this wine seems to be all froth and apples-and-cream flavors. It has a light touch of acidity, which comes through as the froth subsides. **88** —*R.V. (11/1/2006)*

Mailly NV Grand Cru Réserve Brut Champagne Blend (Champagne) $30. Seems very fruity and simple at first—offering little more than hints of peach and strawberry. But it picks up on the midpalate, turning toastier and more savory. Plump, yet finishes with a crisp burst of citrus. **87** — *J.C. (12/1/2004)*

Mailly 1999 L'Intemporelle Grand Cru Brut Champagne Blend (Champagne) $69. The name means "timeless," and this wine is a definite apéritif wine, maybe for when time matters little. It is soft but still crisp, layering attractive apple acidity over a creamy texture and a light, fresh aftertaste. **89** —*R.V. (11/1/2006)*

Mailly 1996 Les Echansons Champagne Blend (Champagne) $89. A tour de force from this cooperative, whose vines are concentrated in the grand cru vineyards of Mailly. This is a big, bold wine, dominated by Pinot Noir, but with layers of creamy Chardonnay showing through. This is still young, and will certainly age. **93** —*R.V. (11/1/2006)*

MAISON BOUACHON

Maison Bouachon 2004 Duc de Montfort Rhône Red Blend (Gigondas) $NA. Despite some dark flavors of chocolate fudge and dates that often connote richness and depth, this wine isn't particularly rich or deep. The 2003 vintage looks to have been more successful at Bouachon. Drink now. **84** —*J.C. (11/15/2006)*

Maison Bouachon 2004 Les Rabassières Rhône Red Blend (Côtes-du-Rhône) $15. A bit lean and lacking fruit; the main flavor elements in this wine consist of leather and clove. Dries out on the finish. **82** —*J.C. (11/15/2006)*

Maison Bouachon 2003 Pierrelongue Rhône Red Blend (Vacqueyras) $18. Nicely balanced, with no elements overpowering any of the others, just a nice mix of black cherries, chocolate, and spice cake in a mouth-filling, yet firmly structured wine. Ends with some silky tannins, suggesting that holding another 2-3 years may smooth it out even more. **87** —*J.C. (11/15/2006)*

Maison Bouachon 2003 Roguebrussane Syrah (Saint-Joseph) $30. Has some attractive anise and cinnamon aromas, but turns tannic and drying on the finish, with no prospects for improvement over time. Drink now. **82** —*J.C. (11/15/2006)*

MAISON CHAMPY

Maison Champy 2003 Chardonnay (Corton-Charlemagne) $145. At this stage, this wine is fresh and lemony, but what lies beneath has huge power and richness and layers of toast and vanilla. Has great potential. **90** —*R.V. (9/1/2005)*

Maison Champy 2003 Pinot Noir (Savigny-lès-Beaune) $32. A ripe, soft wine that is already well-developed. With just a touch of caramel, this generous wine has attractive red fruits and a light layer of tannins. **87** — *R.V. (9/1/2005)*

Maison Champy 2002 Beaune Premier Cru Aux Cras Pinot Noir (Beaune) $29. A ripe, sweet wine which has aromas of crushed red fruits and dense flavors of ripe plums. A slight bitterness spoils the general effect. **84** — *R.V. (9/1/2004)*

Maison Champy 2002 Champs Pimont Premier Cru Pinot Noir (Beaune)

$41. There is good deep color with aromas of wood, dry tannins, and red berries. A firm, solid wine, it has layers of acidity with a soft sweet aftertaste. **85** —*R.V. (9/1/2004)*

Maison Champy 2002 Pommard Premier Cru Les Charmots Pinot Noir (Pommard) $55. A woody wine with some acidity. The fruit is firm, and with layers of earthy, black fruit. **83** —*R.V. (9/1/2004)*

MAISON JAFFELIN

Maison Jaffelin 2001 Chardonnay (Pouilly-Fuissé) $16. Light and fresh, with delicate notes of pear, cinnamon, and clove that linger elegantly on the finish. **86** —*J.C. (10/1/2003)*

Maison Jaffelin 2001 Les Villages de Jaffelin Chardonnay (Saint-Véran) $13. A clean, midweight expression of Chardonnay fruit, with white nectarine and melon aromas and flavors that turn lemony and tart on the finish. **85** —*J.C. (10/1/2003)*

MAISON SICHEL

Maison Sichel 2004 Sirius Bordeaux White Blend (Bordeaux) $NA. The branded wine from négociants Maison Sichel, this has freshness and wood accents, as well as plenty of new, clean acidity. Grassy flavors, a touch of citrus, and pink grapefruit all come well together in the end. **87** —*R.V. (6/1/2005)*

MALESAN

Malesan 1999 Château Prieure Malesan Bordeaux Blend (Premieres Côtes de Blaye) $16. For a solid mouthful of Merlot at a great price, there's no need to look further. Spicy blackberry and toast aromas add vanilla on the palate, before finishing with soft, ripe tannins and leathery notes. Drink now–2008. **89 Editors' Choice** *(9/1/2002)*

Malesan 1999 Reserve de Malesan Bordeaux Blend (Bordeaux) $15. Black cherries and chocolate combine on the palate, but there's also a certain weediness to the aromas. This blend of approximately 60% Merlot, 40% Cabernet Sauvignon finishes strong, with tart fruit and a dose of chocolate. **87** *(9/1/2002)*

Malesan 2000 Rouge Bordeaux Blend (Bordeaux) $9. Despite coming from a universally hailed vintage, this generic Bordeaux is still weedy, herbal, and lean. But it also has decent cassis and cherry fruit, some tasty vanilla and cinnamon notes from oak aging, and a tart, dry finish. It's light, but it hasn't been dumbed down for the mass market. **85 Best Buy** *(9/1/2002)*

Malesan 1999 Vielles Vignes Bordeaux Blend (Bordeaux) $13. "Old vines" means different things to different people. In this case, the fruit comes from vines that average 25–30 years old in the Côtes du Bourg and the Côtes du Blaye. The wine is fruit-focused (black cherries and cassis) but relatively light-bodied, finishing with lemony acids. **86** *(9/1/2002)*

MARC BREDIF

Marc Bredif 1999 Cabernet Franc (Chinon) $16. 88 Editors' Choice —*M.M. (1/1/2004)*

MARC DESCHAMPS

Marc Deschamps 1999 Les Vignes de Berge / Les Loges Sauvignon Blanc (Pouilly-Fumé) $19. Wild flowers and a touch of rubber make for a bouquet that at first is hard to appreciate. With air things improve, and the palate that follows is full of tart gooseberry and citrus. Racy acidity really drives the citrus onto the finish, so much so that the wine leaves you with a one-dimensional impression: that of citrus and acidity. **85** *(8/1/2002)*

MARC KREYDENWEISS

Marc Kreydenweiss 1997 Kritt Gewürztraminer (Alsace) $23. 90 —*S.H. (12/31/1999)*

Marc Kreydenweiss 2001 Les Charmes Pinot Blanc (Alsace) $NA. Rich, thick, and unctuous, a superb wine whose acidity makes it ideal for cellaring, if you wish. In its youth, it drinks tight and steely, with intense, nervy flavors of citrus fruits and roasted hazelnut. The finish is long and honeyed. **90** —*S.H. (1/1/2002)*

Marc Kreydenweiss 1997 Moenchberg Pinot Gris (Alsace) $35. 88 —*S.H. (12/31/1999)*

Marc Kreydenweiss 2003 Andlau Riesling (Alsace) $21. A big, ripe wine that is packed with flavors of white currants. It is full-sized, courtesy of

the hot 2003 vintage, but it has pure, mineral flavors that are developing well. **87** —*R.V. (11/1/2005)*

Marc Kreydenweiss 2003 Clos Rebberg Aux Vignes Riesling (Alsace) $89. A big, fat, ripe wine, but it still shows great Riesling character from one of Kreydenweiss's many fine vineyard holdings. There is crispness, acidity, and great toasty flavors. It is racy and intense, with good structure and vibrant fresh fruits to finish. **89** —*R.V. (11/1/2005)*

Marc Kreydenweiss 2003 Grand Cru Kastelberg Riesling (Alsace) $69. This Andlau vineyard has been planted since Roman times, making it one of the oldest vineyards in Alsace. It's famed for Rieslings, and this wine shows why. It is full-bodied, but still, shows some raciness and ripe acidity. At this stage, this great wine is still very young, but it has the potential to age for up to 20 years. **93 Cellar Selection** —*R.V. (11/1/2005)*

Marc Kreydenweiss 2003 La Dame Wiebelsberg Grand Cru Riesling (Alsace) $38. Intriguing—but strange—stuff, with herbal-grassy aromas and a smoky note, then more weird herbal notes on the palate, including dill and pine resin. Seems a touch sweet, then turns drying on the finish. An adventure in biodynamic winemaking. **85** —*J.C. (8/1/2006)*

Marc Kreydenweiss 2001 Grand Cru Moenchberg Le Moine Tokay Pinot Gris (Alsace) $NA. Stunningly beautiful. Decadently rich and flamboyant, with its peach, honeysuckle, apricot, wildflower, vanilla, and smoke aromas and flavors. Rich and sweet as honey, yet this wine is fully dry and quite crisp with acidity. Exquisite concentration, with the weight and density of a Grand Cru. **93** —*S.H. (1/1/2002)*

MARCEL HEMARD

Marcel Hemard NV Premier Cru Brut Champagne Blend (Champagne) $NA. A brand of the Union Champagne, one of the largest cooperatives in Champagne, this particular wine is produced in a limited release of 5,480 cases. It has some good bottle age, and ripe fruit, spoiled at the end by the relatively high dosage that is not well-integrated. **86** —*R.V. (12/15/2005)*

MARQUIS DE BELON

Marquis de Belon NV Brut Sémillon (Crémant de Bordeaux) $20. A 100% Sémillon wine, this crémant has a rich yellow color, aroma of crème brûlée, vanilla, and charred oak, and plenty of toast on the palate. Behind the oak veneer are lemon-lime flavors powered by zesty acidity. **86** —*M.D. (12/15/2006)*

MARQUIS DE CHASSE

Marquis de Chasse 1999 Reserve White Blend (Bordeaux) $9. With a nose of spicy green herbs—notably tarragon—and flavors of lemon and pink grapefruit, this no-nonsense blend of 50% Sauvignon Blanc and 50% Sémillon goes down easy and clean. The crisp finish is a good palate-cleanser. **84** —*J.C. (3/1/2001)*

MARQUIS DE LA TOUR

Marquis de la Tour NV Brut Collection Privee Sparkling Blend (France) $8. Creamy-textured in the mouth, this is an easy-to-drink bubbly that will satisfy the demands of any informal summer garden gathering. Flavors are of apples and pears, berries and cream; dry enough to serve with food, soft enough to serve on its own. **85 Best Buy** —*J.C. (6/1/2005)*

MARQUIS DE PERLADE

Marquis de Perlade NV Blanc de Blancs Brut Champagne Blend (France) $11. Strong burnt match aromas (too much SO2 at bottling?) mar the nose. With enough swirling, some simple, broadly fruity flavors emerge. The wine is clean and straightforward but generic. **83** —*P.G. (12/15/2002)*

MARTIN SCHAETZEL

Martin Schaetzel 2003 Kaefferkopf Ammerschwihr Pinot Gris (Alsace) $NA. This dry wine has fresh, crisp aromas and flavors. Concentration and intense flavors show this wine will age well. **90** —*R.V. (2/1/2006)*

Martin Schaetzel 2003 Grand Cru Marckrain Tokay Pinot Gris (Alsace) $NA. A richly sweet, intense wine, with almost botrytis-like sweetness and concentration. Honey and sweet fruit dominate this wine, beautifully made and balanced, leaving freshness and elegance at the end. **93** —*R.V. (2/1/2006)*

MAS DE DAUMAS GASSAC

Mas de Daumas Gassac 2002 Red Blend (Vin de Pays de L'Herault) $50. The big wine, the grand vin from Daumas Gassac is a blend of 80% Cabernet Sauvignon with more typical Languedoc varietals. It shows structure and impressive elegance to go along with its power. Flavors of dark plums and black fruits go along with the layer of wood. Considering the poor vintage, this doesn't miss a moment of richness. Ideally age for 10 years or more, but will be drinkable after 5. **93** —R.V. (12/1/2004)

Mas de Daumas Gassac 2004 Rhône Red Blend (Vin de Pays de L'Herault) $38. When Aimé Guibert set up the Mas de Daumas Gassac vineyard, he aimed to show it was possible to make top-quality wines in the Languedoc region of France. He succeeded, and continues to succeed, as this 2004 vintage estate wine shows. It is packed with generous, ripe, very dark, dense fruit, herbs, and an almost intangible layer of wood. **92** —R.V. (12/31/2006)

Mas de Daumas Gassac 2003 Rhône White Blend (Vin de Pays de L'Herault) $50. This southern classic is full of ripe fruit, but tempèred with complexities of herbal flavors, citrus, and ripe fruit hanging on a summer day. It is beautifully integrated, and should age over 10 years. **90** —R.V. (12/1/2004)

MAS DE GOURGONNIER

Mas de Gourgonnier 2005 Rosé Blend (Les Baux de Provence) $NA. Just from its bold, rosy color, you can tell this isn't a namby-pamby rosé, and the wine's assertive flavors confirm that impression. Pomegranate and ripe berry flavors pick up hints of smoke and cocoa. Probably better with meats than fish, and bold enough to stand up to the outdoors. **88** —J.C. (6/21/2006)

MAS DE LA BARBEN

Mas de la Barben 1998 Syrah (Coteaux du Languedoc) $12. Cedar, cherry cola, chamomile tea and sour cherry notes on the nose make for a piquant, unusual bouquet. The wine's flavors (black oak, spice, leather, and cherry) are more Chianti-like than Syrah-like. A short woody finish left us wishing for more. **85** (10/1/2001)

MAS DES CHIMÈRES

Mas des Chimères 2001 Red Blend (Coteaux du Languedoc) $18. An intense, dark colored wine with aromas of sweet black cherries. The fruit is deliciously juicy, powering through the fine, elegant tannins. A touch of wood from the 12 months barrel aging doesn't dominate, just adds an extra layer. **88** —R.V. (12/1/2004)

MATHILDE ET YVES GANGLOFF

Mathilde et Yves Gangloff 1999 Rhône White Blend (Condrieu) $65. Yves Gangloff is from Alsace, and the estate was created in 1983. He makes an enormously ripe Condrieu, with aromas of apricots and almonds. The fruit is super-ripe, with hints of noble rot giving a delicious character of honey and peaches. With its oily, condensed texture and a light touch of wood, this is beautifully smooth. **90** —R.V. (6/1/2002)

MICHEL GONET

Michel Gonet 1996 Brut Champagne Blend (Champagne) $36. A blend of 80% Chardonnay and 20% Pinot Noir, this is the sort of weighty wine you would expect from the 1996 vintage, with powerful toasty aromas. Flavors of vanilla and honey come from partial wood fermentation. The aftertaste is rich, powerful, and concentrated, though a little unbalanced from the dosage. **88** —R.V. (12/1/2002)

MICHEL GROS

Michel Gros 1999 Pinot Noir (Chambolle-Musigny) $38. Scents of graham cracker and malted milk chocolate tickle the nose, while the tart fruit slowly unwinds to reveal cherry and beet root scents and flavors. Tannic and hard, without immediately showing much sweetness, it seems to put the emphasis on mineral and soil, root and leaf, but may evolve into a very interesting wine. **89** —P.G. (1/7/2001)

Michel Gros 1999 Clos des Reas Pinot Noir (Vosne-Romanée) $65. This lovely wine, a Monopole, is already showing complex, forward fruit with flavors of plum, cherry, and cranberry. Soft and fulsome, it shows a light hand with the oak, allowing nuances of tobacco and leather to emerge. Good weight and texture, it seems bound for early glory. **93** —P.G. (1/7/2001)

MICHEL LAROCHE

Michel Laroche 2002 Chardonnay (Vin de Pays d'Oc) $8. Slightly Muscatty, a light spice note accents apple and pear fruit aromas and flavors. Medium-weight, crisp finish, a solid bargain Chardonnay. **85 Best Buy** (2/1/2004)

Michel Laroche 2001 Merlot (Vin de Pays d'Oc) $7. Michel Laroche has been branching out of Chablis in recent years and his southern French effort has some chlorine notes along with aromas of mint and sweet wood. The power is up there, but there isn't suppleness to match. The palate pulsates while the finish is dark and sharp, with a burnt flavor. **82** —M.S. (9/1/2003)

Michel Laroche 2001 Syrah (Vin de Pays d'Oc) $7. Fruity, slightly gummy aromas signal black raspberry, plum, and cherry. Indeed, there's plenty of berry fruit on the palate, that and some pepper. The finish is lively and tasty, with hints of coffee and mocha toward the very end. **84** —M.S. (9/1/2003)

MICHEL LYNCH

Michel Lynch 2003 Bordeaux White Blend (Bordeaux) $10. Named after the 18th-century founder of Château Lynch-Bages, this branded white Bordeaux has attractive, simple grapefruit and white-peach flavors. It is full, but crisp, a good example of well-made white Bordeaux. **86 Best Buy** —R.V. (6/1/2005)

Michel Lynch 1998 Sauvignon Blanc (Bordeaux) $9. Eye-opening lemon, green herb, and mineral aromas lead into a palate that's sweetened by nectarine, and powdered sugar flavors—don't worry, there's enough citrus in the mouth to keep the sweetness in check. Angular and somewhat steely in the mouth, it ends on a similarly metallic note. It's dry—what you'd expect from Bordeaux—and should be consumed with food. I had it with (and, well, in) cheese fondue, but it would be just as good with fish or pasta. **85** —D.T. (11/15/2001)

MICHEL PICARD

Michel Picard 1997 Chardonnay (Pouilly-Fuissé) $24. **84** —M.P. (6/1/2000)

Michel Picard 2001 Chardonnay (Vin de Pays d'Oc) $9. Apple aromas along with hints of celery, bread dough, and mint lead off. In the second spot are snappy lemon and apple flavors carried by healthy acids. A light, warm, and layered finish caps off the show. **86 Best Buy** —M.S. (9/1/2003)

Michel Picard 2001 Chardonnay (Chablis) $20. This is fairly big and full-bodied for Chablis, with a golden hue and aromas of dried spices that suggest it might have seen a little time in oak. The fruit takes a back seat to notes of earth and spice. **84** —J.C. (10/1/2003)

Michel Picard 1995 Domaine Champs Perdix Chardonnay (Rully) $16. **84** (6/1/2000)

Michel Picard 1997 Vouvray Chenin Blanc (Vouvray) $12. **81** —M.P. (6/1/2000)

Michel Picard 1996 Grenache (Châteauneuf-du-Pape) $23. **83** —M.P. (6/1/2000)

Michel Picard 1996 Pinot Noir (Bourgogne) $12. **82** —M.P. (6/1/2000)

Michel Picard 2000 Pinot Noir (Bourgogne) $12. Candied and sweet-tasting, yet with herbal notes intruding on the caramelized cherries. Finishes dry and astringent. **82** —J.C. (10/1/2003)

Michel Picard 2003 Clos des Fiètres Grand Cru Pinot Noir (Corton) $80. Dominated by wood from start to finish, from scents of vanilla, toast, and dried spices, to flavors of cinnamon-dusted toast and a dry, cedary finish. There's enough fruit to support the wood, but not to shine through. **85** —J.C. (9/1/2006)

Michel Picard 2003 Récolte du Château de Chassagne-Montrachet Le Charmois Premier Cru Pinot Noir (St.-Aubin) $30. Has Picard's signature oak treatment in spades, with cedar, cinnamon, and clove notes, but also strident cherry flavors that show enough promise to warrant cellaring 5–8 years. Long on the finish, which seems oaky right now, but the fruit wins out in the end. **89** —J.C. (9/1/2006)

FRANCE

Michel Picard 2000 Rhône Red Blend (Côtes-du-Rhône) $10. Dense, solid, and clean. Quite the full package of earthy berry fruit, healthy tannins and a supple mouthfeel. For a négociant wine, this is the real deal, a Rhône red with nary a flaw, delicious black plum flavors and plenty of length on the finish. Consider this wine an affordable find and stock up. **88 Best Buy** —*M.S. (9/1/2003)*

Michel Picard 2001 Syrah (Languedoc) $9. Fully oaked, but it works. The big, snappy black fruit absorbs the wood with help from healthy acids that coarse through the wine. The whole exceeds the parts; no one thing really stands out but taken all together the wine has some appeal. **84** —*M.S. (1/1/2004)*

MICHEL REDDE

Michel Redde 2001 La Moynerie Sauvignon Blanc (Pouilly-Fumé) $21. A total barrel buster with a heavily roasted nose along with waxy, slightly horsey aromas. Fails to excite on the palate; there's mostly baked fruit and pepper. Big and heavy on the finish. **84** *(7/1/2005)*

MICHEL REDDE ET FILS

Michel Redde et Fils 1999 Cuvée Majorum Sauvignon Blanc (Pouilly-Fumé) $35. Gold in color, with round, honeyed aromas of peach and mango. Not steely at all; in fact, it's all about ripe fruit, softness, and sun-drenched apricot and other stone fruit flavors. Not a ton of depth behind the curtain, but weighty and warm throughout. **86** *(7/1/2005)*

Michel Redde et Fils 2004 Les Tuilières Sauvignon Blanc (Sancerre) $24. This is a classic, fresh, straightforward, instantly enjoyable Sauvignon. It has crisp acidity, flavors of green peas, and just enough structure to allow it to age for another year. But it's great now, a delicious summer wine. **86** —*R.V. (8/1/2006)*

MOËT & CHANDON

Moët & Chandon 1996 Blanc Brut Champagne Blend (Champagne) $50. Fairly youthful and fresh, with lively apple and floral notes alongside deeper, toastier aromas and flavors. Creamy in the mouth, and finishes with a hint of bitter grapefruit. **89** —*J.C. (12/15/2003)*

Moët & Chandon 1998 Brut Champagne Blend (Champagne) $52. Very opulent, from the ripeness of fruit in 1998, this still seems drier than other Moët vintages. It layers acidity with almost tropical flavors, tempered with a citrus element. The aftertaste is round, soft, and appealing. **90** —*R.V. (11/1/2006)*

Moët & Chandon NV Brut Impérial Champagne Blend (Champagne) $38. Probably the best-selling Champagne brand in the world, with a production of over 30 million bottles a year, Moët's quality is consistent. It has a ripeness and richness, and in this bottle, some bottle age. This bottling is not hugely fruity, but it has more to offer than just fruit. **89** —*R.V. (12/1/2005)*

Moët & Chandon NV Brut Impérial Champagne Blend (Champagne) $38. Somewhat orangey citrus notes shown throughout in this popular, medium-weight, balanced mainstay. Good bead and decent texture mark the palate. Flavorful, with a core of ripe apple flavor and orange accents that put it towards the sweet end of the Brut range. **87** *(12/15/2001)*

Moët & Chandon 1995 Brut Impérial Champagne Blend (Champagne) $55. A bready, yeasty, mushroomy bouquet announces this handsome, fairly mature vintage offering. Quite effervescent, it displays apple and toast flavors, herb, and mineral accents. It's an elegant wine fairly low in acidity and not for long-term keeping, but perfect for drinking over the next two years. **90 Editors' Choice** —*S.H. (12/15/2001)*

Moët & Chandon NV Brut Impérial Rosé Champagne Blend (Champagne) $40. At first blush, the bouquet is rich and impenetrable, but when it opens citrus comes on strong. Chewy apple fruit with some Pinot heft define the palate, while licorice and anise add character to the finish. Plump, round, and a pleasure to drink. Very substantive. **90** —*M.S. (12/15/2003)*

Moët & Chandon 1995 Brut Impérial Rosé Champagne Blend (Champagne) $65. The color is a bright coppery onion skin; the scent pleasantly doughy, with plenty of tart, zippy citrus fruit. A core of light cherry anchors a wine with good focus and medium length; a noticeable sweetness lifts the finish. **88** —*P.G. (12/15/2002)*

Moët & Chandon NV Brut Rosé Champagne Blend (Champagne) $44. **88** *(12/1/2000)*

Moët & Chandon 1999 Brut Rosé Champagne Blend (Champagne) $65. Ripe and forward, with a bit of sweetness in the form of root beer and nutmeg. The palate is equally ripe, as it shows melon and red-apple flavors. Long on the back end, with a blend of cinnamon and vanilla. Fairly simple but classy. **89** —*M.S. (12/15/2005)*

Moët & Chandon 1996 Brut Rosé Champagne Blend (Champagne) $55. Rubbery and earthy in the nose, with a smoky Pinot Noir quality that can't be missed. Very tight and masculine, with grapefruit, melon, and pepper. Lots of licorice, pepper, and snappy fruit make for a tasty, complex whole. Full-bodied, lovely, and bold despite just-right acidity. **92** —*M.S. (12/15/2003)*

Moët & Chandon 1995 Dom Pérignon Champagne Blend (Champagne) $150. With a tight flow of bubbles and toasty Golden Delicious aromas, it's another high-quality sparkler from this consistent producer. The tart citrus flavors and crisp acidity are clean and fresh now, but will also age well. **92** *(12/15/2002)*

Moët & Chandon 1998 Dom Pérignon Champagne Blend (Champagne) $130. Robust and ripe, but also streamlined and precise. The palate is lean and properly framed, with flavors of apple and green melon poking through a light, penetrable veneer of toast. Finishes with green apple and lime, which creates a crisp lasting impression. Better to drink earlier than later. **91** —*M.S. (12/31/2005)*

Moët & Chandon 1996 Dom Pérignon Champagne Blend (Champagne) $140. This minerally, toasty wine has flavors of almonds and white stone fruits, and a long finish. It is still young, and is just coming into great balance. Elegant and ethereal. **96** —*R.V. (11/1/2006)*

Moët & Chandon 1996 Dom Pérignon Rosé Champagne Blend (Champagne) $425. This is going to be a great wine: going to be, because it is still firm, dry, serious, and very pure with structure over the red fruits and acidity. Give this wine another five years at least—and then it will be both impressive and delicious. **95 Editors' Choice** —*R.V. (11/1/2006)*

Moët & Chandon 1995 Dom Pérignon Rosé Champagne Blend (Champagne) $300. This is a full-blown, opulent, decadent wine that is packed with wonderful strawberry and ripe fruit flavors. It's at its peak now; it's a generous, delicious glass of wine that overflows with ripe flavors. **94** —*R.V. (11/1/2006)*

Moët & Chandon 1990 Dom Perignon Rosé Champagne Blend (Champagne) $290. This shows a beautiful, mature, burnished copper color and a plum, toast, earth, and smoke bouquet with that 'funky-in-a-great-way' complex Pinot edge. It's creamy and full on the palate, with a lovely mousse and near perfect acidity, and dried cherry, berry, and plum flavors bearing sweet hay and earthy notes. Finishes with incredible length and intensity, dusty rose, and kirsch notes. Great juice, delicious now and for a long time. **94 Editors' Choice** *(12/15/2001)*

Moët & Chandon NV Les Champs de Romont Sillery Champagne Blend (Champagne) $85. Fragrant peach aromas open this gently perfumed and flavored wine. Soft mousse, moderate acidity, mild citrus flavors and liqueur accents make this the most ready to drink of Moet's recently introduced vineyard-designate offerings. It finishes light-footedly, with good length, easy floral notes, and lemon accents. **90** —*M.N. (12/15/2001)*

Moët & Chandon NV Les Vignes de Saran Chouilly Champagne Blend (Champagne) $85. Medium-weight, pale-colored, yet mature-tasting, this Champagne offers supple, buttery caramel, and nut aromas. A smooth palate follows with subtle dried apples and pear flavors, an even mousse and moderate acidity. Balanced and even, it finished long with mild yeasty and leesy notes. **91** *(12/15/2001)*

Moët & Chandon NV Nectar Impérial Champagne Blend (Champagne) $48. A sweet, dessert-styled Champagne that might have wowed the czars, but now comes across as slightly blowsy and dull. Still, it's clearly made with care and could ably partner moderately sweet desserts. **83** —*J.C. (12/15/2003)*

Moët & Chandon NV White Star Champagne Blend (Champagne) $35. A new blend of this best-selling Champagne is soft, creamy, and openly fruity. There is acidity, but it is kept in place by the intensity of sweet fruit, which trails off to a soft, gentle finish. **87** —*R.V. (12/15/2006)*

Moët & Chandon 1995 Dom Pérignon Sparkling Blend (Champagne) $150. Intense and toasty on the nose, picking up scents of green apple and lime. Seems very young and fresh—capable of extended aging, but precocious for Dom, with enough fruit to make it pleasurable now. Supple and creamy in the mouth, this wine shows no sharp edges, yet boasts an extraordinarily long finish. **93** —*J.C. (12/15/2003)*

MOILLARD

Moillard 2002 Reserve Pinot Noir (Bourgogne) $28. Pricy for generic Bourgogne, but pretty good for the appellation, with earthy scents of cola vying with black cherries and coffee. Tannins are supple and the fruit ultimately carries the day. Turns a bit tangy on the finish. **86** —*J.C. (11/15/2005)*

Moillard 1997 Les Violettes Rhône Red Blend (Côtes-du-Rhône) $7. **83** —*M.S. (10/1/1999)*

MOMMESSIN

Mommessin 2002 Chardonnay (Pouilly-Fuissé) $19. A medium-weight Pouilly-Fuissé, with aromas of fresh greens, citrus fruits, and green apples joined on the palate by flavors of peach and melon. Finishes clean and fresh. **87** —*J.C. (10/1/2003)*

Mommessin 2001 La Clé Saint Pierre Chardonnay (Bourgogne) $12. While the aromas and flavors offer similar notes of under-ripe peaches and pencilly oak, the finish turns tart and grapefruity. It's pleasant enough, just a bit austere on its own; lean fish with a citrus preparation could help soften it. **84** —*J.C. (10/1/2003)*

Mommessin 2003 Nid D'Abeille Chardonnay (Vin de Pays d'Oc) $8. Decently made but modest Chardonnay, with melon flavors that turn tart and earthy, veering toward grapefruit on the finish. **83** —*J.C. (12/1/2004)*

Mommessin 2002 Old Vines Chardonnay (Mâcon-Villages) $10. Fresh greens delicately garnish notes of plump, ripe pears. This satisfying wine even folds in a note of white peach. The finish is clean and refreshing. Like most Mâcons, this is best consumed over the next year. **86 Best Buy** —*J.C. (10/1/2003)*

Mommessin 2003 6 Terroirs Gamay (St.-Amour) $21. **87** —*J.C. (11/15/2005)*

Mommessin 2001 Domaine de Champ de Cour Gamay (Moulin-à-Vent) $13. This is all about the wood—from the clove and cinnamon aromas to the dry, baking spice flavors and the toasty finish. Some faint cherry notes linger in the background. **83** —*J.C. (11/15/2003)*

Mommessin 2001 Les Grumières Gamay (Brouilly) $12. Sweet and dusty aromas of Bing cherries rise up from the glass, followed by a nice dose of fresh strawberry fruit. The mouth is properly acidic, so it seems juicy and ripe. While it's totally fruit-forward and young, the wine carries a mild but welcome dark edge and a hint of smoke. The mouthfeel is warm and substantial. **86** —*M.S. (11/15/2002)*

Mommessin 2000 Reserve Gamay (Fleurie) $15. The nose is a bit heavy, bordering on weedy and murky but not quite succumbing to that. However, the earthiness that such aromas portend does come through on the palate along with black plum and chocolate flavors. The wine feels right on the tongue, but it's missing clarity and pop. **83** —*M.S. (11/15/2002)*

Mommessin 2003 Le Montagne Bleue Gamay Noir (Côte de Brouilly) $19. **87** —*J.C. (11/15/2005)*

Mommessin 2001 Pinot Noir (Clos de Tart) $138. The wonderfully complex nose combines such disparate elements as mint, strawberries, pastry crust, and bacon fat into a harmonious whole that sings from the glass. Simultaneously lush yet focused and firm, it finishes long, with an herbal tinge. Anticipated maturity: 2008–2015. **92** —*J.C. (10/1/2003)*

Mommessin 2001 Charmes-Chambertin Pinot Noir (Burgundy) $90. A big, forceful wine, packed with oversized cherry and vanilla flavors. Herb and smoke aromas add complexity, delicately framing the powerful fruit. Finishes long and softly tannic. Drink 2005–2015. **92** —*J.C. (10/1/2003)*

Mommessin 2001 Clos Sainte Anne des Teurons Les Grèves Premier Cru Pinot Noir (Beaune) $34. This is an elegant, "feminine" Burgundy, with a supple, smooth texture supporting pretty hints of smoke, leather, cher-

ries, and milk chocolate. Shows very little tannin, but nicely balanced for near-term consumption. **87** —*J.C. (10/1/2003)*

Mommessin 2001 Les Suchots Premier Cru Pinot Noir (Vosne-Romanée) $67. Shows some attractive notes of cranberries and leather along with hints of chocolate and toast, but this wine is lean and just too astringent to think it will ever be hugely pleasurable. Drink now with rich dishes before the fruit fades. **83** —*J.C. (10/1/2003)*

Mommessin 2000 Oak Aged Pinot Noir (Bourgogne) $13. Strong, penetrating scents of spice and resin power the nose. The fruit tastes of tart berries and plums, with just a tiny suggestion of cocoa in the finish. Though this wine is light and short, it is still flavorful. **84** —*P.G. (11/1/2002)*

Mommessin 2000 Premier Cru Les Charmes Pinot Noir (Chambolle-Musigny) $57. Both color and scent suggest a wine with some stuffing; it is vertically structured, and still quite compact. The color and tannins and impression of alcohol in the finish reflect the power of the vintage, but at this point in time the fruit is not up to the challenge of the other components. **86** —*P.G. (11/1/2002)*

Mommessin 2000 Premier Cru Santenots Pinot Noir (Volnay) $65. A burst of ripe fruit suggests fresh raspberries, with a whiff of black pepper as well. The mouthfeel is soft and feminine, with plenty of forward fruit and interesting spices. But nothing follows; where is the next piece of the puzzle? **87** —*P.G. (11/1/2002)*

Mommessin 2002 Red Blend (Brouilly) $12. Brouilly is the largest of the Beaujolais crus (the individual villages in the northern part of the Beaujolais region). Its wines are the softest and least demanding of the crus, and this wine is typical. It has an enticing purple color, aromas of cherries and red currants, and open, generous flavors of strawberries. In the month when Beaujolais Nouveau 2003 will be launched, it is worth remembering that some Beaujolais is better drunk after a year's aging. **86** —*R.V. (11/15/2003)*

Mommessin 1999 Château De Domazan Rhône Red Blend (Côtes-du-Rhône) $8. This well-known Burgundy négociant has branched out into the Rhône, like so many others have before. The good news is that the wine is bursting with bright cherry flavors—tart and juicy. Would make a nice burger or sandwich accompaniment. **84** *(3/1/2001)*

Mommessin 1998 Les Epices Rhône Red Blend (Châteauneuf-du-Pape) $26. An undercurrent of green herb and black pepper dominates the nose (with some date and stewed fruit aromas), and liven up the black fruit and chalk flavors on the palate. **85** —*D.T. (2/1/2002)*

MONMOUSSEAU

Monmousseau NV Chenin Blanc (Vouvray) $12. This is classic Chenin Blanc, with flavors of almonds and layers of acidity. It needs some bottle age—maybe 2–3 years. **85** —*R.V. (6/1/2006)*

Monmousseau NV Clos du Château de Mosny Chenin Blanc (Montlouis-sur-Loire) $NA. Shows earth and almond flavors. Underneath this, though, there is some interesting complexity with acidity and apple flavors. **86** —*R.V. (6/1/2006)*

Monmousseau NV White Blend (Crémant de Loire) $NA. A ripe, complex wine, packed with great fruit and acidity. It is rich, almost opulent, made from Chenin Blanc, Chardonnay, and Cabernet Franc. There is great acidity to finish this delicious wine. **90 Editors' Choice** —*R.V. (6/1/2006)*

MONT SAINT-VINCENT

Mont Saint-Vincent 2000 Syrah (Vin de Pays d'Oc) $7. The dilute, grapey flavors are candied, and a pile of charred lumber doesn't make them go down any easier. A simple wood-and-juice quaff. **81** *(10/1/2001)*

MONTAUDON

Montaudon NV Brut Champagne Blend (Champagne) $30. **84** —*P.G. (12/15/2000)*

Montaudon NV Brut Champagne Blend (Champagne) $27. Very fragrant, this floral bottling shows bright green herb and lime aromas and flavors. Good acidity and a brisk mouthfeel give it a lively, refreshing character. Finishes with moderate length, more tangy flavors. **87** *(12/15/2001)*

Montaudon 1995 Brut Champagne Blend (Champagne) $36. **88** *(12/15/1999)*

FRANCE

Montaudon NV Chardonnay Premier Cru Brut Champagne Blend (Champagne) $34. Is that breakfast in the nose? The scrambled eggs and toast aromas leave you asking for the bacon and coffee. this bubbly is bulky and full-bodied, with a sugary center of ripe red apple and pear. Good in a simple way, but not exciting. **85** —*M.S. (12/15/2001)*

Montaudon NV Grande Brut Rosé Champagne Blend (Champagne) $31. The pretty salmon-pink color of this sparkler perfectly presages the strawberry fruit on the nose and in the mouth. Bits of leather and toast add a dose of complexity, but the wine turns very tart on the finish, verging on sour. **86** —*J.C. (12/15/2001)*

Montaudon NV Grande Brut Rosé Champagne Blend (Champagne) $35. A pretty, salmon-colored wine, it starts off with scents of strawberry, hay, and earth, with just a whiff of cinnamon spice as well. There's a good focus to the mid-palate, with rich cherry flavors mingled with tobacco and spice. Surprising length and concentration follow through into an unmistakable cherry tobacco flavor in the finish. Distinctive and good. **88** —*P.G. (6/1/2001)*

Montaudon NV Prestige Cuvée Classe M Champagne Blend (Champagne) $50. 82 —*P.G. (12/15/2000)*

MONTIRIUS

Montirius 2004 Grenache-Syrah (Vacqueyras) $20. A big, somewhat bulky wine dominated by drying tannins and leathery notes. There's enough raspberry fruit to provide short-term balance, so drink it soon with meats that can tame the tannic clout. **85** —*J.C. (11/15/2006)*

Montirius 2000 Grenache-Syrah (Vacqueyras) $23. This 50-50 blend of Syrah and Grenache is a ripe, sweet-fruited wine, with rich jelly flavors and enough acidity to give it balance. Give it at least five years in the cellar. **90** —*R.V. (3/1/2004)*

Montirius 2003 Clos Montirius Grenache-Syrah (Vacqueyras) $22. Still youthfully purple in color, possibly in part because of the elevated proportion of Syrah in the blend (50%). Deeply fruited and complex, mixing raspberry flavors with notes of coffee, tobacco, and spice. Drink now-2012. **90** —*J.C. (11/15/2006)*

Montirius 2002 Rhône Red Blend (Vin de Pays de Vaucluse) $NA. A blend of 50 percent Grenache, 30 percent Syrah, and 20 percent Cinsault from a portion of the Montirius vineyard close to the river Ouvèze. The wine is fresh, earthy, with spicy flavors and dark plum fruits. It is ready to drink now. **85 Best Buy** —*R.V. (4/1/2005)*

Montirius 2001 Rhône Red Blend (Vacqueyras) $22. A full-bodied wine with delicious flavors of perfumed fruits from the 30% Syrah and intense, brooding tannins from the 70% Grenache. This is a complex, minerally wine, which has intense concentration and purity of fruit. **89** —*R.V. (4/1/2005)*

Montirius 2000 Rhône Red Blend (Gigondas) $28. A hugely rich wine, from a biodynamic vineyard; it will be immensely long-lived. Its sweet fruit contrasts with brooding tannins and intense herbal essences. Drink this in 10 years. **91** —*R.V. (3/1/2004)*

Montirius 2002 Rhône White Blend (Vacqueyras) $21. Ripe quince and green plum flavors blend with crisp acidity. This is an excellent, well-structured wine with ripe but fresh fruit. **87** —*R.V. (3/1/2004)*

MOREY BLANC

Morey Blanc 2002 Clos du Chapitre Premier Cru Pinot Noir (Aloxe-Corton) $77. This is a finely crafted wine, with firm, solid tannins that balance ripe flavors of spice, acidity and black cherries. **90** —*R.V. (9/1/2004)*

Morey Blanc 2004 Chardonnay (Meursault) $54. This is an enjoyable wine, open and soft, with crisp white and yellow fruits, a touch of citrus and a touch of wood to give it all shape. Drink now. **88** —*R.V. (12/1/2006)*

Morey Blanc 2004 Charmes Premier Cru Chardonnay (Meursault) $92. It's not a bad name for this vineyard—Charmes. This wine, which expresses the nature of the vineyard, is certainly approachable, friendly almost. But there's also a steel fist there that demands time. And if you can't wait, it's a great wine to drink now. **93** —*R.V. (12/1/2006)*

Morey Blanc 2004 Gouttes d'Or Premier Cru Chardonnay (Meursault) $120. Pierre Morey also runs a small negociant business, Morey Blanc, specializing in whites from Meursault. This is one of the wines, a delicious,

fresh, crisp wine that's packed with light, airy flavors of green apples and citrus. **92** —*R.V. (12/1/2006)*

Morey Blanc 2002 Les Vercots Premier Cru Pinot Noir (Aloxe-Corton) $77. Firm tannins alongside wood and spice make this quite a dry wine. The fruit is way behind at this stage, though flavors of cranberries come through. **87** —*R.V. (9/1/2004)*

MOULIN DE GASSAC

Moulin de Gassac 2003 Le Mazet Old World Red Blend (Vin de Pays de L'Herault) $11. This is a blend of all the typical varieties of Languedoc—Syrah, Grenache, Carignan, Alicante, and Cinsault. A rich, generous wine it is marked by a dusty tannic structure by flavors of blackberries and bitter cherries, and by a completeness from a well-judged blending. **89** —*R.V. (12/1/2004)*

Moulin de Gassac 2005 Le Mazet Old World White Rhône White Blend (Vin de Pays de L'Herault) $10. A blend of many white grapes, this is a lovely crisp wine, fresh as can be but with an exotic herbal character. Dry to taste, it is also rich and rounded. **86** —*R.V. (12/31/2006)*

Moulin de Gassac 2002 Le Mazet Rosé Blend (Vin de Pays de L'Herault) $10. Clean and fruity, with pleasant notes of cherry, watermelon, and a strawberry. It's medium-bodied and makes for a fine late-summer quaff on the patio. By the time this gets into print, you'll probably want to look for the 2003, which should be arriving soon. **84** —*J.C. (12/1/2004)*

Moulin de Gassac 2003 Sauvignon Blanc (Vin de Pays de L'Herault) $11. The second label of Mas de Daumas Gassac produces a range of wines from un-cloned vines. This fresh, grassy Sauvignon Blanc is deliciously fresh, but has a fine depth of flavor, with a touch of herbs and pink grapefruit flavors. **87** —*R.V. (12/1/2004)*

Moulin de Gassac 2003 Le Mazet Old World White Blend (Vin de Pays de L'Herault) $11. A fascinating and eccentric blend of Sauvignon Blanc, Grenache Blanc, Vermentino, Clairette, and Terret Bourret, grown in small plots of uncloned vines. This is opulent, luxurious wine that preserves a great sense of the Mediterranean sun in its nut, green plums, and crisp flavors. **89** —*R.V. (12/1/2004)*

MOULIN DE LA GARDETTE

Moulin de la Gardette 2003 La Cuvée Tradition Rhône Red Blend (Gigondas) $19. Nicely balanced, with bright notes of raspberries and peppery spice playing off against darker flavors of chocolate and cassis. Easily approachable, with supple tannins that frame the fruit and provide support without overwhelming. Drink now–2011. **87** —*J.C. (11/15/2006)*

MOUTARD PÈRE ET FILS

Moutard Père et Fils 1999 Brut Chardonnay (Champagne) $50. With vineyards in the Côte des Bar, in the south of Champagne, the Moutard-Diligent family can trace its origins in the region back to the 17th century. This is a soft wine, a blanc de blancs (although only the back label indicates this). It is very ripe and creamy, benefiting from the warm conditions of the 1999 harvest, and just showing a touch of acidity to finish. **87** —*R.V. (11/1/2006)*

MOUTON-CADET

Mouton-Cadet 2000 Rouge Bordeaux Blend (Bordeaux) $14. Quite herbal, with some green beans and anise up front. Black fruit takes a back seat but is there if you look for it. Blackberry and beach plums come to mind. The tannins are a bit rustic. Kosher. **84** —*J.M. (4/3/2004)*

NICOLAS FEUILLATTE

Nicolas Feuillatte NV Blanc de Blancs Premier Cru Brut Champagne Blend (Champagne) $43. Zesty lime and ginger aromas deepen on the palate, where this wine develops mellower umami notes of meat and mushroom. It's harmonious and round in the mouth, finishing long and citrusy. **88** —*J.C. (12/1/2004)*

Nicolas Feuillatte NV Blue Label Brut Champagne Blend (Champagne) $28. A coconut streak stands out immediately, then there's a vertical wall of stone, citrus, and licorice. I like the intensity and the definitive spices that layer this wine; it's not shy or pedestrian. The style may or may not suit you, but it's well worth exploring. It finishes up crisp, with a green, citrusy lift. **90** —*P.G. (12/1/2006)*

Nicolas Feuillatte NV Brut Champagne Blend (Champagne) $40. The muted nose offers faint hay and floral aromas, but this wine opens up in the mouth with bread flavors accented by toast and citrus. The texture is dry and full, and the finish moderately long with attractive grapefruit and mineral flavors. 87 *(4/1/2001)*

Nicolas Feuillatte NV Brut Kosher Champagne Blend (Champagne) $47. A fruity brut, with Mandarin orange, pineapple, lemon, apple, and melon flavors, framed in a toasty edge. The finish ends on a tart note. 86 —*J.M. (4/3/2004)*

Nicolas Feuillatte NV Brut Kosher Mevushal Champagne Blend (Champagne) $45. If it has to be kosher, this cuvée is a solid choice. The bead is reticent, but earth and apple flavors pick up welcome notes of sautéed mushrooms. Turns clean and citrusy on the finish. 86 —*J.C. (12/1/2004)*

Nicolas Feuillatte NV Brut Rosé Champagne Blend (Champagne) $40. A light, frothy style of Champagne, fresh and crisp with a high proportion of Pinot Noir in the blend, giving quite tight acidity in the aftertaste. 85 —*R.V. (12/1/2005)*

Nicolas Feuillatte 1996 Cuvée Palmes d'Or Brut Champagne Blend (Champagne) $110. Rather yeasty, with sweet, candied citrus aromas. To the eye, it bubbles like a fountain, and in the mouth it's foamy. The flavor profile is apple and tart berries, while the finish is fairly mute but clean. Very good on its own but in the realm of top-flight vintage Champagne, it doesn't make the penthouse grade. 88 —*M.S. (12/31/2005)*

Nicolas Feuillatte 1992 Cuvée Palmes d'Or Brut Champagne Blend (Champagne) $125. 90 *(12/31/2000)*

Nicolas Feuillatte 1996 Cuvée Palmes d'Or Brut Rosé Champagne Blend (Champagne) $125. More orange than salmon in color, with impressively smooth aromas of melon, orange peel, and brown sugar. The palate deals a full hand of citrus, and there's a sweet quince-like undertone. The finish is bold, fruity, and long, like a couple of minutes long. This is a pure wine; it would be nearly impossible not to enjoy it. 91 —*M.S. (1/1/2004)*

Nicolas Feuillatte 1995 Cuvée Speciale Premier Cru Brut Champagne Blend (Champagne) $65. Rich and toasty, this has vanilla and soft ripe fruit flavors. Sweet white and yellow fruits dominate the palate, which has a butter layer from the malolactic fermentation of the Chardonnay in the blend. Good, well-balanced. 90 *(12/1/2004)*

Nicolas Feuillatte NV Premier Cru Brut Champagne Blend (Champagne) $30. 90 —*P.G. (12/15/2000)*

Nicolas Feuillatte NV Premier Cru Brut Champagne Blend (Champagne) $33. Hints of vanilla and white chocolate on the nose; modest toast, herb, and citrus flavors. Creamy mouthfeel and a clean, fresh finish. This is solid Champagne at a good price. 87 —*J.C. (12/1/2004)*

Nicolas Feuillatte NV Premier Cru Brut Rosé Champagne Blend (Champagne) $38. Solid and flavorful, this opens with dry, rose-petal aromas, and is medium-full in body with good texture and acidity, berry and consomme flavors. Good complexity; just the faintest hint of sweetness appears on the long finish. 90 **Editors' Choice** —*M.M. (12/15/2001)*

Nicolas Feuillatte NV Premier Cru Brut Rosé Champagne Blend (Champagne) $43. A solid value in rosé Champagnes, this wine offers delicate toasty scents alongside hints of chocolate and caramel—the impression is one of understated elegance. Adds some apple and berry flavors on the palate, finishing with note of coffee. 90 —*J.C. (12/1/2004)*

Nicolas Feuillatte NV Réserve Particulière Brut Champagne Blend (Champagne) $28. The cooperative that makes Nicolas Feuillatte is doing good things with this brand. This Réserve Particulière is elegantly made, with fine white fruit flavors along with a touch of toast. It is light, poised, and makes a good apéritif. 88 —*R.V. (12/1/2005)*

Nicolas Feuillatte 1998 Blanc de Blancs Brut Chardonnay (Champagne) $40. Light and grassy, with simple, bland flavors of apples and grain. Very bubbly in the mouth, more so than ideal. You could even call it foamy. Tastes fairly good but has its issues. Not great for the money. 84 —*M.S. (12/31/2005)*

Nicolas Feuillatte NV Blanc de Blancs Premier Cru Brut Chardonnay (Champagne) $35. In addition to typical citrus, stone fruit, toast, and butter notes, there are delicate ginger and oshinko notes. With such

bright acidity, this may well be a good match to spicy Pan-Asian cuisine. The finish falls too short for this taster. 85 —*K.F. (12/15/2002)*

Nicolas Feuillatte 1996 Cuvée Palmes d'Or Brut Rosé Pinot Noir (Champagne) $175. Kicks off with toast, citrus, and hints of red berries, then develops lots of berry and orange character on the somewhat youthful and aggressive palate. It's a bold, assertive wine that seems a bit simple for the price. Try aging it a few years to see what emerges. 88 —*J.C. (12/15/2003)*

NICOLAS JOLY

Nicolas Joly 2003 Coulee de Serrant Chenin Blanc (Savennières-Coulée de Serrant) $79. 93 **Cellar Selection** —*J.C. (11/15/2005)*

Nicolas Joly 2003 Les Clos Sacres Chenin Blanc (Savennières) $29. 91 **Editors' Choice** —*J.C. (11/15/2005)*

NICOLAS POTEL

Nicolas Potel 2003 Pinot Noir (Savigny-lès-Beaune) $32. 86 —*J.C. (11/15/2005)*

Nicolas Potel 2001 Pinot Noir (Vosne-Romanée) $40. This plump wine boasts sexy aromas of vanilla and cinnamon layered over plums and black cherries. Finishes with fine intensity and persistence of flavor, showing more oak than Potel's other offerings. 88 —*J.C. (10/1/2003)*

Nicolas Potel 2000 Pinot Noir (Volnay) $30. 87 —*C.S. (11/1/2002)*

Nicolas Potel 2000 Maison Dieu Vielles Vignes Pinot Noir (Bourgogne) $17. House of God it may be, but it is a thin and uninteresting style of wine. One searches for some old-vine character without success; instead it seems like generic Burgundy. 83 —*P.G. (11/1/2002)*

Nicolas Potel 2001 Vieilles Vignes Pinot Noir (Côte de Nuits-Villages) $18. Slightly horsey aromas layered over tart cherries and berries give this Potel offering a little something not found in the other wines tasted. Some tasters might find this level of brett objectionable, but here it adds character to an otherwise light, acidic wine. 86 —*J.C. (10/1/2003)*

Nicolas Potel 2000 Vieilles Vignes Pinot Noir (Volnay) $17. Scents of watermelon, strawberry, and pale red fruits lead into a light-bodied wine with pleasant, simple flavors. There is a good silkiness to this wine, and though it is a lightweight, it has its charms. 86 —*P.G. (11/1/2002)*

NOTRE DAME DE COUSIGNAC

Notre Dame de Cousignac 2005 Rhône Red Blend (Côtes-du-Rhône) $11. Some post-bottling sulfur should dissipate over the next several months, by which time this firmly structured, crisp wine should be slightly more approachable. Cherry flavors are clean and direct, but lack concentration and nuance. 83 —*J.C. (11/15/2006)*

OGIER

Ogier 2001 Les Allegories d'Antoine Rhône Red Blend (Gigondas) $34. Shows traces of under-ripe fruit in its herbal scents and bell-pepper flavors, but there are also bright cherry notes and a pleasant dusty earthiness. Tangy on the finish, blending chocolate and citrus. 84 —*J.C. (11/15/2005)*

Ogier 2004 Les Chaillés Syrah (Saint-Joseph) $21. Cherry and cinnamon notes on the nose, with a round, supple mouthfeel and simple but satisfying flavors. Picks up some slightly astringent tannins on the finish, but still a better bet to drink now instead of aging. 86 —*J.C. (11/15/2006)*

OLIVIER LEFLAIVE

Olivier Leflaive 2004 Chardonnay (Meursault) $40. A spicy, nutty wine that shows some of the Meursault broadness but also offers some subtlety, with ripe fruits layered with more complex wood and herb flavors. This could age well over the next 2–3 years. 90 —*R.V. (12/1/2006)*

Olivier Leflaive 2001 Chardonnay (Puligny-Montrachet) $42. This big, mouth-filling wine combines apples and pears with floral, mineral notes of smoky quartz and graphite. It's firm enough to age up to 10 years, yet approachable now. 90 —*J.C. (10/1/2003)*

Olivier Leflaive 2001 Chardonnay (Chablis) $18. Plump, yet with a firm core of acidity, this is a fairly easy-drinking Chablis that boasts riper notes of peach and pear to go with steely green apple and lemon. 86 —*J.C. (10/1/2003)*

FRANCE

Olivier Leflaive 1998 Chardonnay (Puligny-Montrachet) $39. A full masculine nose of lime and hazelnut opens this solid offering. Restrained orange, peach, and toasty oak flavors are displayed elegantly on the full, richly textured palate. Feels mature and ready to drink. Finishes with mineral, peach, and oak notes. **88** *(6/1/2001)*

Olivier Leflaive 1998 1 er Cru Les Champs Gains Chardonnay (Puligny-Montrachet) $50. This sleek, elegant wine opens with a crisp bouquet of limes, nuts, and toast. Subtle orange and stony mineral flavors sit atop a taut structure, making this archetypal Puligny. Firm acidity and a long, complex mineral finish make this young thoroughbred a champion. **93 Editors' Choice** *(6/1/2001)*

Olivier Leflaive 2004 Champ Gain Premier Cru Chardonnay (Puligny-Montrachet) $62. This is a dense structured wine with some herbal flavors as well as kiwi and green plums. Fruit dominates, leaving the wood with a walk-on part. It is developing slowly and needs another 2–3 years to open fully. **90 Cellar Selection** *—R.V. (12/1/2006)*

Olivier Leflaive 2003 Clos St. Marc Premier Cru Chardonnay (Chassagne-Montrachet) $58. A sophisticated, elegant wine, which shows white fruit, subtle wood flavors and a structure that promises good aging. It has acidity, and some fresh apples at this young age. The whole is much greater than the sum of its parts. **93** *—R.V. (9/1/2005)*

Olivier Leflaive 2001 En Remilly Premier Cru Chardonnay (St.-Aubin) $30. Tight, with restrained fruit aromas and flavors of pear and pineapple that stay lean and focused all the way through the fully dry finish. Citrusy and minerally, with an austere structure. **86** *—J.C. (10/1/2003)*

Olivier Leflaive 1999 Les Sétilles Chardonnay (Bourgogne) $15. This introduction to white Burgundy derives from sources in Puligny and Meursault. A bouquet of hay, earth, liqueur, and even some green tobacco aromas opens to a palate of ripe pear and mineral flavors. Evenly textured, the wine is round but not fat. Finishes crisp and dry, with decent length. Drink now. **86** *(6/1/2001)*

Olivier Leflaive 1998 Pinot Noir (Pommard) $42. Very good depth and intensity of fruit show in this rich and masculine bottling. A ripe black cherry foundation bears cocoa, herb, earth, and tobacco accents, yielding a complex range of aromas and flavors. The finish is taut and quite dry, dressed up with tart cherries and leather. Hold for 2–3 years. **89** *(6/1/2001)*

Olivier Leflaive 1998 White Blend (Criots-Bâtard-Montrachet) $150. Refinement and balance are this wine's hallmarks, with white peach and tropical-fruit aromas and flavors beautifully enmeshed by honeyed hazelnuts and toast. Despite its obvious richness, this wine is rather unevolved. The expansive, nuanced finish shows superb length and definition. This still needs three or four years for the component parts to fully integrate. **94 Cellar Selection** *(12/31/2001)*

ORIGIN

Origin 2003 Collection Series Pinot Noir (Santenay) $38. Shows some cedary oak on the nose, then slightly Port-like, raisin, and chocolate flavors emblematic of the vintage. It's chunky and full in the mouth, finishing with dusty notes and a hint of bacon fat. **84** *—J.C. (9/1/2006)*

PANNIER

Pannier 2000 Brut Champagne Blend (Champagne) $52. Crisp and fresh, this is a light wine, dominated by acidity and slightly unripe grapefruit flavors. It's pleasant, if too acidic, but could soften with age. Keep a couple of years and try again. **87** *—R.V. (11/1/2006)*

Pannier NV Brut Rosé Champagne Blend (Champagne) $40. An attractive, salmon-pink-colored wine, which has flavors of ripe strawberries and a touch of caramel. The acidity is relatively light, and the impression is of a ripe wine. **87** *—R.V. (12/1/2005)*

Pannier NV Brut Sélection Champagne Blend (Champagne) $26. 90 *(12/31/2000)*

Pannier 1999 Cuvée Louis Eugène Blanc de Noirs Brut Champagne Blend (Champagne) $56. From Pinot Noir, with just a touch of Pinot Meunier, this is a powerful, full-bodied wine, with aromas of dried flowers and flavors of stewed fruits, balanced with honey and fresh, crisp acidity. Weighty; this is definitely a food-friendly Champagne. **89** *—R.V. (11/1/2006)*

Pannier 1999 Egérie de Pannier Brut Champagne Blend (Champagne) $77. This top wine from Pannier is beautifully crafted and balanced, a credit to the cooperative. It has intense flavors of grapefruit, livened with lemon zest and fresh, crisp acidity. But there is also a weight to it, and a layer of acidity that suggests good aging potential. **93 Editors' Choice** *—R.V. (11/1/2006)*

Pannier 1998 Blanc de Blancs Brut Chardonnay (Champagne) $60. A very soft wine, dominated by a creamy character and fresh acidity. Very lively, very light, great as an apéritif. **87** *—R.V. (11/1/2006)*

PASCAL & NICOLAS REVERDY

Pascal & Nicolas Reverdy 2003 Cuvée Les Coûtes Sauvignon Blanc (Sancerre) $21. Ripe apple and peach aromas are numbed by a heavy mineral note. Generic but very pleasant flavors of citrus, melon and white pepper do the trick. Stony and crisp, and clear as polished glass on the finish. Just not terribly complex, however. **88** *(7/1/2005)*

Pascal & Nicolas Reverdy 2004 Vieilles Vignes Sauvignon Blanc (Sancerre) $27. This is a great, intense, apples-and-cream style of wine. The acidity is certainly there, but the richness and the ripeness of the fruit dominate. With its concentration and freshness, this will be delicious to drink this summer, but will age for a couple more years. **90** *—R.V. (8/1/2006)*

PASCAL DOQUET

Pascal Doquet 1997 Grand Cru Le Mesnil-sur-Oger Chardonnay (Champagne) $69. From a 6-acre parcel of grand cru vines, this blanc de blancs is still very young. Its pink grapefruit and mineral characters accent a core of lively acidity. It needs time, another five years at least, but is already an impressive wine. **93** *—R.V. (11/1/2006)*

PASCAL JOLIVET

Pascal Jolivet 1998 Sauvignon Blanc (Sancerre) $19. 83 *—M.S. (7/1/2000)*

Pascal Jolivet 2003 Sauvignon Blanc (Pouilly-Fumé) $20. Tart and grassy, with definition to the nose. Gentle lime, grass, stone fruits, and apple flavors make for a perfectly fresh and tasty palate, while the finish is dry, crisp, borderline tart and racy. Very good for everyday, no-frills Loire Sauvignon. **89** *(7/1/2005)*

Pascal Jolivet 2000 Sauvignon Blanc (Sancerre) $19. Pungent aromas of field greens and citrus lead into a palate defined by racy lime, grapefruit, and passion fruit. The finish is a bit watery, which is a disappointing drop off from the solid citrus flavors present on the front palate. Overall it's a nice wine, nothing more, nothing less. **86** *(8/1/2002)*

Pascal Jolivet 2000 Château du Nozay Sauvignon Blanc (Sancerre) $21. Mustard-seed aromas pierce the nose, which otherwise is mostly apple and pineapple. Lemon, green apple, and passion fruit flavors are accented by the lightest touch of oregano and basil. For a cru, it's rather simple, with extremely light fruit on the finish and very little length or substance to the back end. **86** *(8/1/2002)*

Pascal Jolivet 2000 Clos Du Roy Sauvignon Blanc (Sancerre) $22. Aromas of spiced apples, lemon, mustard seed and mineral make for an attractive nose, but the palate is a tad tart, featuring mostly lemon, green apple, and citrus rind. In general, it's light, lean, and probably better as an apéritif than as an accompaniment to fine food. **86** *(8/1/2002)*

Pascal Jolivet 2003 Le Château du Nozay Sauvignon Blanc (Sancerre) $26. Lively, full, tangy, and precise. Our tasting panel was unanimous in its support for this minerally, citrusy wine; we very much liked its fresh green apple, grapefruit and white peach flavors, and we're sure it would be an excellent food wine, especially with fish. **89** *(7/1/2005)*

Pascal Jolivet 2000 Les Caillottes Sauvignon Blanc (Sancerre) $22. Among the range of Jolivet's 2000 Sancerres, Les Cailottes, is the winner, hands down. It's zesty, with chalk and mineral qualities. The nose is clean, stony, and pungent, while the flavors that come next are pure and ripe citrus and melon, with just a nip of honey. It closes out firm, round and full, and with elegance. **90 Editors' Choice** *(8/1/2002)*

PATRIARCHE PÈRE & FILS

Patriarche Père & Fils 2004 Chardonnay (Mâcon-Villages) $13. Slightly doughy or nutty on the nose, this wine then opens up on the palate to reveal more citrus and tropical fruit flavors. Medium-bodied, with a finish that's short but fresh. **84** *—J.C. (11/15/2005)*

Patriarche Père & Fils 2003 Chardonnay (Vin de Pays d'Oc) $8. Has buttery, baked-apple aromas, but lacks that same sense of richness on the palate, with tart apple and lemon flavors following. Citrusy and fresh on the finish. **83** —*J.C. (11/15/2005)*

Patriarche Père & Fils 2001 Chardonnay (Pouilly-Fuissé) $25. Lacks concentration, but boasts modest apple and citrus flavors leavened by a touch of buttered sweet corn. **83** —*J.C. (11/15/2005)*

Patriarche Père & Fils 2005 Merlot Merlot (Vin de Pays d'Oc) $10. This simple wine is soft and juicy, with some fresh raspberry flavors. The tannins are light, round and fruity, leading to an easy, soft finish. **84** —*R.V. (12/31/2006)*

Patriarche Père & Fils 2003 Pinot Noir (Bourgogne) $10. 84 —*J.C. (11/15/2005)*

Patriarche Père & Fils 2000 Pinot Noir (Nuits-St.-Georges) $40. 83 —*J.C. (11/15/2005)*

Patriarche Pèrevv & Fils 2005 Syrah Syrah (Vin de Pays d'Oc) $10. A densely packed wine, with dark color, dusty tannins and ripe dark plum flavors. There is some edginess to the aftertaste, with acidity and some greenness. **85 Best Buy** —*R.V. (12/31/2006)*

PAUL BLANCK

Paul Blanck 2001 Pinot Blanc (Alsace) $11. 90 Best Buy —*C.S. (11/15/2002)*

Paul Blanck 2001 Grand Cru Schlossberg Riesling (Alsace) $33. This is one super-rich wine, with some light toast character and already a touch of petrol. It has freshness and spice, plus intense acidity and elegance. A Peter Vezan Selection, various U.S. importers. **92** —*R.V. (11/1/2005)*

Paul Blanck 2002 Patergarten Riesling (Alsace) $23. Situated in floor of the Kaysersberg valley, this vineyard produces great ripe Rieslings. The 2002 from the Blanck family is a deliciously rich wine, with exotic fruits, flavors of star fruit and green plums, along with fine aromatic spices. This will be a short-term wine: drink over the next five years. **88** —*R.V. (5/1/2005)*

PAUL DELANE

Paul Delane NV Brut Rosé Champagne Blend (Crémant de Bourgogne) $19. Attractive salmon pink color, fresh raspberry flavor, and lively acidity: it's all there with this deliciously, crisp, summertime rosé. There is just a touch of toastiness to give it some complexity, but freshness and openness are the main characters of this wine. **89 Editors' Choice** —*R.V. (6/1/2006)*

Paul Delane NV Brut Réserve Sparkling Blend (Crémant de Bourgogne) $18. A soft, ripe, creamy wine that has a richness from Pinot Noir along with some good crisp Chardonnay and Aligoté. There are great flavors of white currants, green apples, a touch of toast, and fine soft, finishing acidity. **90** —*R.V. (6/1/2006)*

PAUL GOERG

Paul Goerg NV Premier Cru Blanc de Blancs Champagne Blend (Champagne) $28. An attractive nose proffers fresh, yeasty scents with lemon wax highlights. Elegant and crisp, it loses some steam in the late going, and picks up some metallic bitterness which unfortunately lingers through the finish. **86** —*P.G. (12/15/2002)*

PAUL JABOULET AÎNÉ

Paul Jaboulet Aîné 1998 Domaine Raymond Roure Marsanne (Crozes-Hermitage) $33. This estate, with its small production from low-yielding old vines, is Jaboulet's latest pride. The white Crozes-Hermitage has great richness. There are aromas of honey from the ripe fruit, while the flavors mix exotic fruits and hints of mushrooms. Although it is rich, there is a firmer, more mineral streak, which adds to the complexity. **90** —*R.V. (6/1/2002)*

Paul Jaboulet Aîné 2001 Beaumes-de-Venise Red Blend (Côtes-du-Rhône Villages) $14. This gets off to a rough start, with hints of sulfur, herbs, and treebark that aren't very promising. But the wine pulls itself together with some time in the glass, and the flavors and mouthfeel are much more satisfying, offering bold black cherry and prune balanced by soft tannins, adequate acidity, and plenty of chocolaty nuances. **87** —*J.C. (3/1/2004)*

Paul Jaboulet Aîné 1999 Domaine de Saint-Pierre Rhône Red Blend (Cornas) $40. Jaboulet bought this 7.3-acre estate in 1998, and this is the first full vintage. It is a huge wine, with all the true inky blackness and density of a Cornas. Firm, dry, and concentrated, it also has generous ripe black plums, a hint of sweet jelly. It makes an excellent mix of the traditional foursquare Cornas style, with modern sophistication. **93** —*R.V. (6/1/2002)*

Paul Jaboulet Aîné 1997 La Chapelle Rhône Red Blend (Hermitage) $100. 96 *(11/15/1999)*

Paul Jaboulet Aîné 2003 Le Paradou Rhône Red Blend (Beaumes-de-Venise) $16. Not that effusive on the nose, but the flavors sing on the palate, revealing black cherry, earth and coffee flavors carried along on a supple, velvety mouthfeel. The fruit really comes through on the finish. Drink now, or anytime before 2012. **88** —*J.C. (2/1/2005)*

Paul Jaboulet Aîné 1998 Les Traverses Rhône Red Blend (Côtes-du-Ventoux) $9. 88 Best Buy —*M.S. (11/1/2000)*

Paul Jaboulet Aîné 1999 Chevalier de Sterimberg Rhône White Blend (Hermitage) $75. Jaboulet's white Hermitage is named after the crusading knight who built and settled in the small chapel on the Hermitage hill. The wine itself is powerful, rich, and concentrated, with heady perfumes of wild flowers and nuts. The palate combines a hint of wood, a full-bodied, oily texture, and a stunning burst of acidity that leaves a crisp aftertaste. **94** —*R.V. (6/1/2002)*

Paul Jaboulet Aîné 2000 Parallèle 45 Rhône White Blend (Côtes-du-Rhône) $9. A blend of Grenache Blanc, Roussanne, and Marsanne, this wine is flavored with new wood and ripe fruits. Apricots and spices give it a full character, with just enough acidity to make it refreshing. **86** —*R.V. (6/1/2002)*

Paul Jaboulet Aîné 2003 Domaine de Thalabert Syrah (Crozes-Hermitage) $33. A fine example of Jaboulet's Thalabert, the 2003 features plenty of ripeness without becoming jammy or overdone. It's round and mouth-filling, with supple tannins and a creamy texture, while the flavors are herbal and peppery but also meaty and dark, featuring notes of black olive and espresso. Drink now–2015. **90** —*J.C. (11/15/2006)*

Paul Jaboulet Aîné 2001 Domaine de Thalabert Syrah (Crozes-Hermitage) $30. Seems a little disjointed at this stage of its development, with components that don't seem completely integrated: caramel, cherries, pepper, and dusty earth notes. Supple mouthfeel bodes well, and if the pieces here come together, this rating may look stingy five years from now. **85** —*J.C. (2/1/2005)*

Paul Jaboulet Aîné 1999 Domaine de Thalabert Syrah (Crozes-Hermitage) $25. Jaboulet Aîné has the best-known estate in Crozes-Hermitage, on the flat land to the south of the hill of Hermitage. The 1999, a top year for Crozes, is deep, dark, almost black in color. It is a generous, rounded wine, smooth, rich, with a cocktail of spices, new wood flavors, and black fruits. The tannins are there, but are soft, ripe and already accessible. **89** —*R.V. (6/1/2002)*

Paul Jaboulet Aîné 1999 Domaine Raymond Roure Syrah (Crozes-Hermitage) $33. A densely colored wine from this small estate, bought by Jaboulet Aîné in 1995. It is a great expression of Syrah, with aromas of ripe, concentrated fruits, dense tannins and flavors of new wood, spices, and hedgerow fruits. It is a wine of great complexity, showing enormous aging potential. **92** —*R.V. (6/1/2002)*

Paul Jaboulet Aîné 1999 Le Grand Pompée Syrah (Saint-Joseph) $23. A huge, black, concentrated wine, full of Syrah perfumes of violets and herbs. To taste, there are firm, generous tannins along with acidity and raspberry jelly-fruit flavors. Powerful, but generous, and already ready to drink. **90** —*R.V. (6/1/2002)*

Paul Jaboulet Aîné 2001 Les Jalets Syrah (Crozes-Hermitage) $14. The nose is plump, fruity, and bursting with red licorice and cherry tomato, but the palate is leaner and thinner than expected. If you like snap and pop, it should do the trick. But most wines from this notable Northern Rhône region have more substance and body than this. **85** —*M.S. (9/1/2003)*

Paul Jaboulet Aîné 1999 Les Jumelles Syrah (Côte Rôtie) $68. Strong, bright fruit (red berry, black plum, and black cherry) rounds out the mouth of this medium-full Côte-Rotie. More earth berries, herb, and hickory smoke on the nose; tart pepper flavors dominate the medium-long, juicy finish. Cellar for 2–3 years. **91 Cellar Selection** *(11/1/2001)*

PAUL MAS

Paul Mas 2003 Que Serah Sirah Syrah (Vin de Pays d'Oc) $11. A simple, fruit-driven Syrah aimed squarely at the middle of the market, this wine's plum and black cherry flavors finish clean and fresh. It's a solid effort at an everyday price. **85** —*J.C. (11/15/2005)*

PAVILLON ROUGE DE CHÂTEAU MARGAUX

Pavillon Rouge de Château Margaux 2003 Bordeaux Blend (Margaux) $65. The second wine of Château Margaux is certainly as good as many crus bourgeois. This vintage is ripe and elegant. For fruit that is so ripe what is fascinating is the way the wine finishes with acidity and a great lift. Delicious in three to five years. **90** —*R.V. (5/1/2006)*

PERRIER JOUËT

Perrier Jouët NV Blason Brut Rosé Champagne Blend (Champagne) $76. Salmon to onion-skin pink in color, this is a rosé with a relatively high level of dosage and a soft finish. There are red fruits, but also nuts and a citrus kick on the finish. A very smooth Champagne. **87** —*R.V. (12/1/2005)*

Perrier Jouët NV Blason Brut Rosé Champagne Blend (Champagne) $76. A grand bottle of pink Champagne, round and luscious. The flavors come on like a cherry cordial, with exceptional Pinot Noir character and finesse. It is a seductive, elegant, and textured wine that shows a level of detail and length that only the finest examples achieve. Subtle but very rewarding. **93** —*P.G. (12/1/2006)*

Perrier Jouët 1993 Fleur de Champagne Blanc de Blancs Brut Champagne Blend (Champagne) $125. Rich ripe bread dough, toast, and almond biscuit aromas lead the way. The enticing bouquet is followed by a complex, beautifully balanced baked apple, plum, lemon, and orange peel and vanilla palate. This finely tuned wine is bright, yet also warm and smooth with a supple, honey-floral robe. Finishes with tangy spice notes and excellent length. **93** *(12/15/2001)*

Perrier Jouët 1996 Fleur de Champagne Brut Champagne Blend (Champagne) $120. The famous Belle Epoque bottle design is based on a 1902 bottle of Emile Gallé. Today's blend of this prestige cuvée is a fine balance between Chardonnay and Pinot Noir, crisp and fresh in a ripe, mature apéritif style. It is lively but complex, showing some toasty flavors to complement the rich, ripe green fruit tastes. Great balance and elegace. **93** —*R.V. (12/1/2004)*

Perrier Jouët 1995 Fleur de Champagne Brut Champagne Blend (Champagne) $120. 90 —*M.M. (12/1/2000)*

Perrier Jouët 1997 Fleur de Champagne Brut Rosé Champagne Blend (Champagne) $140. The familiar Belle Epoque bottle, based on the design of Emile Gallé, is accented in pink for this mature, balanced rosé, with a layer of crisp raspberry fruits and rich, elegant acidity. Aromas of caramel and strawberries are matched with honey and yeast. **91** —*R.V. (12/15/2003)*

Perrier Jouët 1995 Fleur de Champagne Brut Rosé Champagne Blend (Champagne) $150. Dried cherry, tarragon, and anise aromas open this medium-weight, brisk rosé. Brisk citrus accents adorn the plum and cherry fruit core. The mouthfeel has weight and edge; the bead is fine and steady here. Finishes very crisply, with a hint of bitter plum skin and mineral-herb accents. **90** *(12/15/2001)*

Perrier Jouët NV Grand Brut Champagne Blend (Champagne) $35. 88 —*S.H. (12/15/2000)*

Perrier Jouët NV Grand Brut Champagne Blend (Champagne) $40. Clean, if a bit flat, with toasty pear and apple aromas. More apple appears on the palate, and that crisp fruit is supported by sweet caramel, butterscotch, and cinnamon. Solid and perfectly acceptable; a good by-the-glass pour. **87** —*M.S. (12/15/2003)*

Perrier Jouët NV Grand Brut Champagne Blend (Champagne) $40. Frothy, vigorous, and youthful, with chalky-minerally nuances to its vibrant green apple and lime flavors. Finishes a bit softer than expected, but the chalky notes persist, giving a strong identity to the wine. **88** —*J.C. (12/1/2004)*

PERRIN

Perrin 2004 Réserve Rhône Red Blend (Côtes-du-Rhône) $11. This light, fun wine starts off with aromas of bright, bouncy cherries and peaches. Then it continues that theme in the mouth, with crunchy fresh fruit flavors of stone fruit, picking up some spice and mineral nuances on the finish. Drink now–2008. **87 Best Buy** —*J.C. (11/15/2006)*

PERRIN & FILS

Perrin & Fils 2004 Grenache-Syrah (Côtes-du-Rhône Villages) $15. A blend of 50% Grenache and 50% Syrah, this bold, assertively fruity wine is still very primary, showing a floral, almost confected, bouquet of cherries and plums. Picks up hints of chocolate and spice on the solidly built palate, then adds a juicy squirt of acidity on the finish. **87** —*J.C. (11/15/2006)*

Perrin & Fils 2003 L'Andéol Rasteau Grenache-Syrah (Côtes-du-Rhône Villages) $23. Impressively sized and full-bodied, but doesn't show the flesh or richness needed to rate higher. Roasted fruit, leather, and chocolate flavors finish on a slightly alcoholic note. Hold 2–3 years and hope it comes around. **85** —*J.C. (11/15/2005)*

Perrin & Fils 2003 La Gille Grenache-Syrah (Gigondas) $22. Full and lush, made with 80% Grenache whose ripeness clearly shows. Brandied cherries and well-integrated wood spice on the nose, then super-ripe stone fruits on the palate, cherries especially, but also including hints of apricot and peach. A dusting of cocoa and dried spices add nuance, while it all comes together in a velvety finish. **90 Editors' Choice** —*J.C. (11/15/2005)*

Perrin & Fils 2004 Les Christins Grenache-Syrah (Vacqueyras) $22. A blend of roughly 80% Grenache and 20% Syrah, this bottling from Perrin & Fils is dense and firm, with enough structure to suggest aging through 2010 at least. Yet it's also wonderfully perfumed, featuring floral and spice notes as well as dark berries that are almost liqueur-like in their intensity. **90 Editors' Choice** —*J.C. (11/15/2006)*

Perrin & Fils 1999 Red Blend (Vacqueyras) $19. Fairly powerful and extracted, with a dark hue, black fruit aromas, and scents of tar and rubber. The flavors are pure and pronounced—a hefty handful of plum, cassis, baking spices, and black pepper. And the finish is great, what with its length, plush texture, and rich chocolate and coffee flavors. Very warming and satisfying, with liveliness and zip. **90** —*M.S. (2/1/2003)*

Perrin & Fils 1996 Rhône Red Blend (Gigondas) $22. 86 —*J.C. (7/1/2000)*

Perrin & Fils 2000 Perrin L'Andéol Rasteau Rhône Red Blend (Côtes-du-Rhône Villages) $16. Muscled up and powerful, with graham cracker aromas and deep, saturated black fruit. For a Southern Rhône red, this has all you could ask for. The palate is sweet, ripe and meaty, with oozing black plum and berries framed perfectly by simple yet tasty oak. And the finish is snappy and lively, yet tannic and rich. The full package, with size and stature. **91 Editors' Choice** —*M.S. (9/1/2003)*

Perrin & Fils 2000 Vinsobres Rhône Red Blend (Côtes-du-Rhône Villages) $16. The bouquet is hard, tight and full of tobacco and green beans. Right away you get the impression that maybe the fruit for this wine wasn't quite at its ripest. How else to explain the strong green character at the core and the lack of sweetness? That said, the feel across the palate is good, as is the color and tannins. **84** —*M.S. (9/1/2003)*

Perrin & Fils 2002 Réserve Rhône White Blend (Côtes-du-Rhône) $10. 83 —*J.C. (3/1/2004)*

Perrin & Fils 2003 Les Cornuds Vinsobres Syrah-Grenache (Côtes-du-Rhône Villages) $23. The Perrin négociant business is now bottling a number of individual cuvées from the Côtes-du-Rhône. This one, a 50-50 blend of Syrah and Grenache, features plum and cherry fruit, with complex earth, spice, and leather notes. Firmly structured, look for it to be at its peak from 2008–2012. **88** —*J.C. (11/15/2005)*

PHILIPPE GONET

Philippe Gonet NV Le Mesnil sur Oger Réserve Brut Champagne Blend (Champagne) $33. Toasty aromas follow through to a soft, creamy wine that has light acidity, ripeness, and full Chardonnay flavors. This is a delicious, full-bodied wine, produced by a small family-owned firm in Le Mesnil sur Oger. **90** —*R.V. (12/1/2005)*

Philippe Gonet NV Roy Soleil Grand Cru Blanc de Blancs Chardonnay (Champagne) $41. No doubt Le Roi Soleil (Louis XIV, the Sun King) would have downed plenty of Champagne given half a chance, so I'm

FRANCE

surprised this is the first wine I have come across named after one of history's great hedonists. This is actually quite a delicate wine, crisp, and fresh, with a deliciously clean streak of acidity. **91** —*R.V. (12/1/2005)*

PHILIPPONNAT

Philipponnat 2000 Cuvée 1522 Grand Cru Champagne Blend (Champagne) $85. Philipponnat's 1522 cuvée is a reference to the date of the first record of Philipponnat as grape growers in Ay. It's one of their top wines, and shows off the food-friendly, rich style typical of this producer. It's ripe, rounded, full-bodied, and dominated by Pinot Noir giving it great depth of flavor. It's also a wine meant for aging. **94** —*R.V. (11/1/2006)*

Philipponnat 1997 Réserve Brut Champagne Blend (Champagne) $63. A blend of 70% Pinot Noir and 30% Chardonnay, this is a true food Champagne. "Our objective was to show how powerful Pinot Noir can get in our wines," says Charles Philipponnat, and he is right. It is rich but dry, concentrated, slightly spicy, with weight and intensity without losing freshness from the acidity. **93** —*R.V. (12/1/2005)*

Philipponnat NV Royale Réserve Brut Champagne Blend (Champagne) $40. The dry style of Philipponnat, with its Pinot Noir dominance, demands bottle aging, which the bottle tasted had. It has good structure, and intense grapefruit and orange peel flavors. A finely made wine, which is also a good value. **91** —*R.V. (12/1/2005)*

PIERRE AMADIEU

Pierre Amadieu 2003 Domaine Grand Romane Cuvée Prestige Rhône Red Blend (Gigondas) $25. Pierre Amadieu's flagship Gigondas is this luxury cuvée from old vines. Yet despite its quality raw materials, I found his 2004 Romane-Machotte more interesting. This bottling features entirely too much cedary, vanilla-laden, barrel-induced seasoning. Sometimes less is more. **84** —*J.C. (11/15/2006)*

Pierre Amadieu 2005 Roulepierre Rhône Red Blend (Côtes-du-Rhône) $10. A little light in body, but this is a charmer of a wine featuring fully ripe Grenache scents and flavors of cherries and apricots. Drink now. **87 Best Buy** —*J.C. (11/15/2006)*

PIERRE ANDRE

Pierre Andre 2001 Reserve Vieilles Vignes Pinot Noir (Bourgogne) $14. Pale in color, with aromas of cranberry tea, lean, lemony flavors, and drying tannins. **81** —*J.C. (10/1/2003)*

PIERRE BESINET

Pierre Besinet 2003 Le Bosc Chardonnay-Sauvignon (Vin de Pays d'Oc) $NA. This wine is certainly fresh, but it has an artificial boiled sweets and banana flavor which gives a tartness. **80** —*R.V. (12/1/2004)*

Pierre Besinet 2003 Le Bosc Rosé Blend (Vin de Pays d'Oc) $NA. A blend of Cabernet Franc and Syrah, here is a delicious, soft wine which finishes with a little sweetness. It lacks acidity but makes up for that by its attractive fruit. **86** —*R.V. (12/1/2004)*

PIERRE COURSODON

Pierre Coursodon 2000 Le Paradis Saint-Pierre Marsanne (Saint-Joseph) $23. A ripely concentrated wine, from super-ripe late-harvest grapes. The aromas of peach stones and caramel are very inviting. Initially it seems almost sweet, but then as its flavors of nuts and exotic fruits develop on the palate, it becomes hugely rich. **91** —*R.V. (6/1/2002)*

PIERRE FRICK

Pierre Frick 2001 Grand Cru Steinert Gewürztraminer (Alsace) $43. Aromas of intense spice leave little to the imagination. This has to be Gewürz, and it comes from the Grand Cru Steinert in Pfaffenheim. It's concentrated and rich flavors of lychees, pepper and a touch of honey are also intense. **88** —*R.V. (4/1/2005)*

Pierre Frick 2002 Cuvée Precieuse Tokay Pinot Gris (Alsace) $NA. A fresh style of Pinot Gris, with aromas of toast and chestnuts and flavors of ripe, juicy fruit. There is some acidity, but this is still rich, with some pepper and softness at the end. **86** —*R.V. (4/1/2005)*

PIERRE GAILLARD

Pierre Gaillard 2004 Clos de Cuminaille Syrah (Saint-Joseph) $30. Gaillard's Clos de Cuminaille shows substantial new oak, but it's reason-

ably balanced by dark fruit and pepper. It's round in the mouth, with a supple, velvety feel—it may be a touch modern or international, but it still retains a sense of place. Drink now. **87** —*J.C. (11/15/2006)*

PIERRE GIMMONET ET FILS

Pierre Gimmonet et Fils NV Cuis Premier Cru Blanc de Blancs Brut Champagne Blend (Champagne) $34. This is a light, poised wine, very fruity, with a fresh, lightly green flavor. The freshness makes this an attractive wine, made from fruit grown in the village of Cuis near the Gimmonet winery. **88** —*R.V. (12/1/2002)*

Pierre Gimmonet et Fils 1997 Special Club Brut Champagne Blend (Champagne) $53. This is a finely balanced wine, with a touch of toast and smooth, creamy fruit. For a Chardonnay, it is weighty, full-bodied, well-balanced and certainly a wine to go with food. **90** —*R.V. (12/1/2002)*

Pierre Gimmonet et Fils 1999 Fleuron Premier Cru Blanc de Blancs Brut Chardonnay (Champagne) $55. The aromas are almost honeyed, the palate is poised, elegant, crisply green. Despite its youth, this blanc de blancs shows delicious white fruit and crisp green flavors. Great as an apéritif, as it develops and ages, it should also be a good food wine. **93 Editors' Choice** —*R.V. (11/1/2006)*

Pierre Gimmonet et Fils 1998 Oenophile Extra Brut Chardonnay (Champagne) $55. A lively, crisp blanc de blancs that comes from Chouilly in the Côtes des Blancs. It is green, flavored with cinnamon, baked apples, along with some good, steely fruit. **90** —*R.V. (11/1/2006)*

PIERRE GONON

Pierre Gonon 2004 Syrah (Saint-Joseph) $32. Cherries and black olives on the nose, followed by a wine that's less concentrated than the 2003 but still boasts plenty of matière. Supple, with good length on the finish. Drink now. **87** —*J.C. (11/15/2006)*

PIERRE JEAN

Pierre Jean 2000 Cabernet Sauvignon (Vin de Pays de L'Aude) $7. Oak and greenish flavors—perhaps unripe fruit—on the palate; red berries and a metallic note characterize the bouquet. Finishes with berry, oak, and something green. **83** —*D.T. (2/1/2002)*

PIERRE MOREY

Pierre Morey 2004 Chardonnay (Meursault) $68. A village Meursault, but one which has been treated like a cru, with layers of ripe wood balancing the pure green- and white-fruit flavors. This is ready to drink now as it is well-balanced and deliciously fresh. **89** —*R.V. (12/1/2006)*

Pierre Morey 2004 Les Tessons Chardonnay (Meursault) $80. From the domaine of Pierre Morey, who is also cellarmaster at Domaine Leflaive. Like at Leflaive, he works his vines biodynamically. This is a layered wine; the pure, crisp fruit partnering with light toast flavors and a poised and structured apple-skin aftertaste. **91** —*R.V. (12/1/2006)*

PIERRE SPARR

Pierre Sparr 2001 Gewürztraminer (Alsace) $13. Fresh and pure, with pineapple and pine needle aromas. The apple, pear, and honey flavors are accented by some nutmeg, while the smooth finish has a hint of butterscotch. Good acidity and a fine texture make it pleasant to drink. **88** —*M.S. (6/1/2003)*

Pierre Sparr 2003 Reserve Gewürztraminer (Alsace) $17. This is a broad, mouth-filling Gewürz, one that leans heavily on spice to make its statement. Not a flowery, fruity model, but one that emphasizes cinnamon, clove, and allspice, leavened by a helping of citrus. Finishes with a hint of orange peel. **87** —*J.C. (2/1/2005)*

Pierre Sparr 2004 Réserve Gewürztraminer (Alsace) $16. This plump, easygoing wine starts of with voluminous floral and pear scents, then folds in peach notes on the palate. Decidedly low in acidity, but round and satisfying, and priced right. **88 Editors' Choice** —*J.C. (11/1/2005)*

Pierre Sparr 2001 Reserve Pinot Blanc (Alsace) $10. Airy and light, with lemongrass and pear aromas. A palate full of apple, peach, and cinnamon leads you to a textured, full finish. Has good feel and body, but never does it become rich or cumbersome. **89 Best Buy** —*M.S. (10/1/2003)*

Pierre Sparr NV Brut Réserve Pinot Blanc-Pinot Noir (Crémant d'Alsace) $18. A fresh, crisp wine, with refreshing citrus flavors and a touch of

FRANCE

minerality. Has great delicacy and poise. A blend of Pinot Blanc and Pinot Noir. **86** —*R.V. (6/1/2006)*

Pierre Sparr 2003 Pinot Gris (Alsace) $15. Pear, honey, and pineapple notes on the nose give way to more melony flavors on the palate. Mouthfeel is slightly oily, leaving behind the suggestion of quince and honey on the finish. Not complex, but mouth-.filling and well-balanced. **85** —*J.C. (2/1/2005)*

Pierre Sparr 2002 Grand Cru Mambourg Pinot Gris (Alsace) $30. Peaches and honey dominate the flavors of this full wine. It has some sweetness, with acidity and a touch of smokiness. Likely to age for five years. **90** — *R.V. (2/1/2006)*

Pierre Sparr 2003 Reserve Pinot Gris (Alsace) $17. Adds an extra level of richness compared to Sparr's regular Pinot Gris, but the flavors are similar: poached pears and ripe melons tinged with honey and pineapple. A smooth, harmonious expression of Pinot Gris that won't set you back a fortune. **87** —*J.C. (2/1/2005)*

Pierre Sparr 2004 Réserve Pinot Gris (Alsace) $17. A medium-bodied, food-friendly version of Pinot Gris, without the high residual sugar levels of some. Still, it is off-dry, with apple, pear and honey notes buttressed on the finish by fresh acidity and a hint of minerality. **86** —*J.C. (11/1/2005)*

Pierre Sparr 2000 Vendanges Tardives Pinot Gris (Alsace) $NA. A wine that balances sweetness with currant fruit flavors. It is fresh and crisp, but also has a depth of concentration. It should age well, but is ready to drink now. **88** —*R.V. (2/1/2006)*

Pierre Sparr 2003 Riesling (Alsace) $14. Seems a little sour and earthy at first, but it just needs some time in the glass to come around. It's a reasonably plump Riesling, with lemon custard and lemon rind flavors and a lingering finish. Easy to drink. **85** —*J.C. (2/1/2005)*

Pierre Sparr 2001 Altenbourg Riesling (Alsace) $25. This Kientzheim vineyard is surrounded by Grand Cru vineyards and gives attractively fruity wines. With its aromas of tropical fruits, this is quite an exotic wine, but has plenty of acidity to balance. There are great layers of structure, flavors of grapefruits and mangoes, and plenty of indication that this will age for 5 years or more. **89** —*R.V. (5/1/2005)*

Pierre Sparr 2000 Grand Cru Schoenenbourg Riesling (Alsace) $35. This wine shows finesse, quality, and at the same time power. There are fine flavors of mint and grapefruit, with long-lasting acidity. **90** —*R.V. (11/1/2005)*

Pierre Sparr 2001 Reserve Riesling (Alsace) $13. Not sure what the "reserve" qualifier means here, because the wine tastes everything like your garden-variety Alsace Riesling. There's stone fruit aromas touched up by mineral, but also some funky, meaty notes akin to sausage or hot dogs. The palate delivers green apple and melon, while spice and warmth rise up on the finish. **85** —*M.S. (12/1/2003)*

Pierre Sparr 2003 Réserve Riesling (Alsace) $16. A full-bodied wine, with aromas of apples and pears. It's dry, lively, and fresh, with great crisp fruit, flavors of grapefruits, and long-lasting acidity. It needs two years to develop. **87** —*R.V. (5/1/2005)*

Pierre Sparr 2000 Dynastie Brut Sparkling Blend (Crémant d'Alsace) $20. This is a fine, mature wine, showing delicious toasty characters, mature fruit, and a long, fine line of bubbles. Full-bodied but crisp, it has complex flavors of pears and almonds, plus some minerality. Good as an apéritif wine, but even better with food. **90** —*R.V. (6/1/2006)*

Pierre Sparr 1997 Brand Tokay Pinot Gris (Alsace) $25. 89 *(8/1/1999)*

Pierre Sparr 1997 Reserve Tokay Pinot Gris (Alsace) $13. 91 Best Buy *(8/1/1999)*

Pierre Sparr 2003 One White Blend (Alsace) $12. Despite the name, this is a blend of five of Alsace's white varieties: Riesling, Pinot Blanc, Gewürztraminer, Muscat, and Pinot Gris. The result is a simple sipper destined for the apéritif course or perhaps a casual picnic. Pear and melon flavors finish with a spicy, grapefruity edge. **84** —*J.C. (2/1/2005)*

PINK FLAMINGO

Pink Flamingo NV Gris de Gris Rosé Blend (Vin de Pays des Sables du Golfe du Lion) $9. It's cute critter wine with a name that colorfully relates to what's in the bottle. Peach, sun-warmed stone, and anise scents and flavors impart a sense of summer, finishing clean and fresh. **85 Best Buy**

—*J.C. (6/21/2006)*

PIPER-HEIDSIECK

Piper-Heidsieck NV Brut Champagne Blend (Champagne) $35. Very crisp and somewhat metallic, with a mineral or iron-ore core. On the palate, it opens up with somewhat rounder fruit flavors of tangerine and citrus, but it retains an austere, tightly delineated structure: Elegant and refined. **90 Editors' Choice** —*P.G. (12/15/2003)*

Piper-Heidsieck NV Brut Champagne Blend (Champagne) $35. Toasty aromas leap from the glass in this deliciously mature wine. It is soft but still very dry, with acidity tamed by both fine, mature fruit, and a creamy texture that sits well in the mouth. This is a very fine, tasty wine. **92 Editors' Choice** —*R.V. (12/1/2005)*

Piper-Heidsieck 1998 Brut Champagne Blend (Champagne) $65. Round and mildly yeasty, with vanilla, pear, and toast all wrapped into a welcoming whole. The palate is full and complex, with additional vanilla coating crisp apple. This is a fuller, mouth-filling style of Champagne, one with a broad, classy finish. That said, vital acidity should ensure a full lifespan. **92 Cellar Selection** —*M.S. (12/31/2005)*

Piper-Heidsieck 1995 Brut Champagne Blend (Champagne) $50. 89 *(12/31/2000)*

Piper-Heidsieck 1990 Brut Champagne Blend (Champagne) $50. 89 —*M.S. (12/1/1999)*

Piper-Heidsieck NV Brut Rosé Champagne Blend (Champagne) $44. A glorious russet-copper color, this seductive rosé sets the stage with a lush, sweet nose of spicy cranberries and baked apple pie. Perfectly integrated flavors fill the midpalate, cascading fruits and light spices, gently leading to a lingering, polished fade-away. **91** —*P.G. (1/1/2004)*

Piper-Heidsieck NV Cuvée Jean-Paul Gaultier Brut Champagne Blend (Champagne) $98. Thank goodness we tasted it blind—it's hard to take Champagne seriously when it's packaged in a ridiculous red-leather-and-black-laces bottle wrap, courtesy of Jean-Paul Gaultier. Well, the fashionista magazines dig it for its "style," but we dig it for what's in the bottle: intense aromas white grapes, toasted coconut and white peach, backed by sweet apple notes. In the mouth, dark toast and caramel notes are offset by a slight nectarine-fruity tang. It's so ful land frothy on the palate that the bead makes it way to the back of the throat. Finishes with peach and mineral flavors. **90** —*R.V. (12/15/2001)*

Piper-Heidsieck NV Cuvée Jean-Paul Gaultier Brut Champagne Blend (Champagne) $100. Perhaps this wine is the ultimate in Champagne packaging—a leather outer sleeve around the bottle designed by couturier Jean-Paul Gaultier. Does the wine justify the hype? If you like very mature tasting wine, yes, because this is all toast and not much fruit. But it does work, with good acidity to crispen it at the end. **90** —*R.V. (12/1/2004)*

Piper-Heidsieck NV Cuvée Rare Brut Champagne Blend (Champagne) $120. This is styled in a relatively mature, slightly oxidized fashion. It's round and full-bodied, with lots of oily, buttered-nut flavors. But it is not at all tired or tiring; an underpinning of crisp apple keeps it lively and fresh in the mouth. It drinks very well right now, as if it had been cellared for four or five years. **92** —*P.G. (12/1/2006)*

Piper-Heidsieck 1990 Cuvée Rare Réservée Brut Champagne Blend (Champagne) $70. Round and full-bodied style, with lots of smooth, well-integrated toasted, nutty and slightly oily flavors; the fruit plays hide-and-seek in the background, behind scents of black olive and Sherry. **91** —*P.G. (12/15/2003)*

Piper-Heidsieck 1988 Cuvée Rare Réservée Brut Champagne Blend (Champagne) $65. 94 —*E.M. (11/15/1999)*

Piper-Heidsieck NV Extra Dry Champagne Blend (Champagne) $35. More boldly yeasty than the brut, this has an intriguing note of coconut in the nose, and the beginning hints of an oily, toasty richness. The extra dollop of sweetness still leaves it tasting fairly dry, but in a more approachable, less austere, style. **89** —*P.G. (12/15/2003)*

Piper-Heidsieck NV Sauvage Brut Rosé Champagne Blend (Champagne) $45. This is Piper's style of making extra dry wines. Its pale raspberry color suggests a party wine, but to taste it is more raw than pretty, with high acids and light green flavors. It doesn't hang together, with the fruit struggling to get through the acidity. **83** —*R.V. (12/1/2004)*

FRANCE

Piper-Heidsieck NV Special Cuvée Brut Champagne Blend (Champagne) $100. **91** —*P.G. (12/15/2000)*

POL ROGER

Pol Roger 1995 Brut Champagne Blend (Champagne) $59. Spicy clove introduces this fairly tight, compact bottling. Firm fruit flavors of white peach and light pear are here, along with that streak of peppery spice leading into a well-rounded finish. **89** —*P.G. (12/15/2002)*

Pol Roger 1995 Cuvée Sir Winston Churchill Brut Champagne Blend (Champagne) $194. True to the house style, this is a rich, savory Champagne, with notes of ginger, soy sauce, and meat gravy mingling with earth, toast, and citrus. Smooth and creamy in the mouth, with an orangey finish. **90** —*J.C. (12/15/2003)*

Pol Roger 1993 Cuvée Sir Winston Churchill Brut Champagne Blend (Champagne) $166. Dusty, bready aromas are somewhat mute, and the mouthfeel on the sharp side—this Champagne is just not ready to come out of the cellar. Still, it has nice pineapple, ginger and brioche flavors and a lingering finish. Revisit it in 5 or 10 years. **89** *(12/15/2002)*

Pol Roger NV Extra Cuvée de Réserve Brut Champagne Blend (Champagne) $35. Pol Roger has hit the bull's eye with this year's release, which boasts smoky, toasty, spicy aromas and rich, mouth-filling flavors of red berries, citrus, and minerals. Creamy and mouthfilling, with a long, luscious finish. **92 Editors' Choice** —*J.C. (12/1/2004)*

Pol Roger 1996 Extra Cuvée de Réserve Brut Champagne Blend (Champagne) $67. An intensely complex wine which brings together 18 of the greatest vineyards in Champagne. This vintage combines richness with a relatively high level of acidity. This means it has already a fine balance, with a touch of toast, great power, and concentration and flavors of white currants and red fruits.The wine shouldn't be touched until 2005 and then will age for many years. **94** —*R.V. (12/1/2004)*

Pol Roger 1996 Extra Cuvée de Reserve Brut Rosé Champagne Blend (Champagne) $70. An enticing onion pink color draws you into this lively, full bodied rosé, which just demands a bowl of strawberries or a pair of star-struck lovers. It is packed with fresh red fruits and balancing acidity, not too dry, with a fresh raspberry element which fleshes out the flavors. **90** —*R.V. (12/1/2004)*

Pol Roger 1996 Réserve Brut Rosé Champagne Blend (Champagne) $71. A wonderfully balanced wine, with elegance and style from its pure red fruits and acidity. Pol Roger makes some of the most stylish Champagnes around, and this wine, with a color that bubbles from pale orange to beautiful onion-skin pink, is no exception. It goes well with food, even red meat. **94** —*R.V. (1/1/2004)*

Pol Roger 1996 Blanc de Chardonnay Brut Chardonnay (Champagne) $83. The bouquet offers aromas of fresh cream cheese, peach, and pear. Flavors of apple and Bartlett pear get a push from tarragon accents and a bit of earthy mushroom. Finishes fresh and powdery, with a crispness that's akin to perfectly fresh lettuce. Classy and stylish; made entirely from Chardonnay. **91** —*M.S. (12/15/2003)*

Pol Roger 1998 Extra Cuvée de Réserve Blanc de Chardonnay Brut Chardonnay (Champagne) $99. Gorgeous, delicious fruit, with flavors of crisp apples and lemon zest underlined by an intensity of structure and flavor. There is just great depth to this impressive wine. The only flaw is that it is too young—wait another five years. **94 Cellar Selection** —*R.V. (11/1/2006)*

POMMERY

Pommery 1995 Champagne Blend (Champagne) $55. 90 Editors' Choice *(12/1/2000)*

Pommery 1998 Brut Champagne Blend (Champagne) $70. A dry, serious wine, but with a delicious poise and elegance to it. Flavors hint at green apples; it glides in to the mouth, just giving a shape from its acidity. **92** —*R.V. (11/1/2006)*

Pommery NV Brut Apanage Champagne Blend (Champagne) $38. Warm, homey scents of honey, bacon, and toast lead into a citrusy palate that stays toasty. The finish is a little rough and coarse; like Pommery's Brut Royal, this wine could use 2-3 years to settle down. **87** —*J.C. (12/15/2001)*

Pommery NV Brut Rosé Champagne Blend (Champagne) $50. Pommery's rosé has a odd, yellowish cast to it, and a heavy, musky scent suggesting that it is a bit over the hill. Fat, fruity flavors send up broad vanilla and bread dough flavors. The wine is open and expansive, but definitely starting to tire. Drink up. **86** —*P.G. (12/15/2002)*

Pommery NV Brut Rosé Champagne Blend (Champagne) $60. Don't be misled by the pale copper color—this is a big, full-bodied rose, with scents and flavors of roasted meat, toast and a bit of mushroom. Yet it retains a sense of elegance, finishing with delicate citrus notes. **90** —*J.C. (12/1/2004)*

Pommery NV Brut Rosé Champagne Blend (Champagne) $45. Despite a finish that tails off a little, this sparkler packs a welcome degree of complexity into its aromas of suede, strawberries, anise, and toast to more than make up for it. And even though it's a lighter style, the flavors are rich, boasting elements of bread dough, toast and leather. **88** —*J.C. (12/15/2001)*

Pommery NV Brut Royal Champagne Blend (Champagne) $33. Pommery acknowledges the Royal as the synthesis of the house style; it is blended equally of Chardonnay, Pinot Noir, and Pinot Meunier, and has a distinct pungency that suggests a whiff of a sea breeze. The fruit stays close to the citrus-lemon axis, and the mouthfeel opens up with a pleasing creaminess. **89** —*P.G. (12/15/2002)*

Pommery NV Brut Royal Champagne Blend (Champagne) $34. A ripe, fruity Champagne that lacks complexity. There's some yeasty, rising-bread notes, but mainly peachy fruit in this medium-weight wine. Finishes short. **85** —*J.C. (12/1/2004)*

Pommery NV Brut Royal Champagne Blend (Champagne) $33. Aromas of toast and pear compete on the nose; mature pear and citrus flavors play on the palate. Its beads are even and strong; its mouthfeel, zippy, and crisp. Finishes with angular but clean lemon and mineral flavors. A bit young; hold for 2-3 years. **87** —*J.C. (12/15/2001)*

Pommery 1998 Louise Champagne Blend (Champagne) $180. This is a delicate style of wine, very classic Pommery. But it does have delicious, crisp fruit, apples, and cream flavors. It is still young, very fresh, and green—needs more time in the bottle. **91** —*R.V. (11/1/2006)*

Pommery 1990 Louise Champagne Blend (Champagne) $140. 93 Cellar Selection *(12/1/2000)*

Pommery 1989 Louise Champagne Blend (Champagne) $NA. A very toasty wine, with maturity but without the balancing elegance. Somehow the fruit seems to have been sidelined by the toastiness and the wine doesn't quite hold together. Pommery is supposed to be back on form now, so more recent vintage releases of Louise should be less disappointing than this. **83** —*R.V. (12/15/2004)*

Pommery 1992 Louise Rosé Champagne Blend (Champagne) $240. The brilliant, yet subtle anise, sandalwood, cherry, cocoa, vanilla, and almond bouquet that opens this delicious, elegant wine seems hard to follow. However, the full, creamy palate, with its dry cherry, chalk, toast, and mineral flavors and lively effervescence doesn't disappoint. Delicious and long, the clean and tangy finish has a winning blend of vinous, citrus, and caramel notes that show tremendous persistence. **92** *(12/15/2001)*

Pommery NV Pop Champagne Blend (Champagne) $11. In an attempt to lighten the image of Champagne, Pommery has gone for a light style of wine and an equally light name, which harks back to the 1930s description of Champagne. Luckily, it is not all marketing, and the wine is good, with some bottle age, along with a poise and charm, which certainly works. **89** —*R.V. (12/1/2005)*

POTEL-AVIRON

Potel-Aviron 2001 Château Gaillard Vieilles Vignes Gamay (Morgon) $19. Despite some pleasant scents of warm, dusty earth, this wine fails to deliver a lot of complexity. The black cherry fruit is supple in the mouth and offers ample flavor, finishing with tart acids. **85** —*J.C. (11/15/2003)*

Potel-Aviron 2001 Vieilles Vignes Gamay (Moulin-à-Vent) $19. Under a veneer of cedary wood you'll find some simple black cherry fruit. Shows good purity and concentration, finishing short and clean. **85** —*J.C. (11/15/2003)*

FRANCE

Potel-Aviron 2000 Vieilles Vignes Gamay (Fleurie) $17. A supple mouthfeel is the best part of this overtly oaky wine. The overbearing wood so obscures the slightly roasted quality of the fruit that it's hard to make much of it. Some interesting coffee and cola notes show on the back end, but the wood still reigns supreme. **84** —*M.M. (11/15/2002)*

Potel-Aviron 2001 Pinot Noir (Juliénas) $17. Cinnamon, clove, and hickory smoke mark the nose of this well-wooded Beaujolais. Mouthfeel is supple, but the fruit is subdued underneath its veil of oak. **85** —*J.C. (11/15/2003)*

PREMIÈRE

Première 2004 Chenin Blanc (Vouvray) $13. Sweet and a bit low in acidity, this Vouvray features thick, pear-flavored fruit and a short finish. Serve well chilled. **83** —*J.C. (8/1/2006)*

PREMIUS

Premius 1998 Bordeaux Blend (Bordeaux) $10. A négociant bottling from the ubiquitous Yvon Mau, this wine proudly boasts élevé en futs du chene on the label. You can certainly notice it in the cedary aromas and flavors, but it's adequately balanced by cassis and tobacco flavors. The fruit tastes a touch over-ripe, but it seems to work well here. **86 Best Buy** —*J.C. (3/1/2001)*

PRIEURE SAINT-HIPPOLYTE

Prieure Saint-Hippolyte 2004 Rosé Blend (Coteaux du Languedoc) $13. This relatively dark-colored rosé features nicely perfumed aromas of fruit blossoms and black cherries, then adds a hint of dark chocolate to the palate. It's fullish, but not heavy, balanced by some lemony notes on the finish. **86** —*J.C. (6/19/2006)*

PRIEURÉ SAINT-SIXTE

Prieuré Saint-Sixte 2005 Cuvée des Premices Rhône Red Blend (Lirac) $NA. A blend of 50% Syrah, 30% Carignan, and 20% Grenache, this cuvée is soft and supple, filled with blackberry and black cherry fruit. Finishes with crisp acids and plenty of vivacity. **87** —*J.C. (11/15/2006)*

PROSPER MAUFOUX

Prosper Maufoux 1999 Aligoté (Bourgogne) $11. A crisp nose of stone, lemon, and grass opens this clean white made from Burgundy's other legal white grape. It shows nice lemon flavors, a touch of spice and a straightforward finish. Aligoté is drier and leaner than Chardonnay, an alternative white worth a try. **84** *(7/1/2001)*

Prosper Maufoux 2005 Chardonnay (Viré-Clessé) $16. This early release gives a sense of the improvements made at Prosper Maufoux, as well as a taste of the potential quality of the 2005 vintage. Spiced pears and minerals add enough honeyed notes on the palate to seem rich, then finish long. This is all from a single grower, according to Fairchild. **88** *(11/15/2006)*

Prosper Maufoux 2004 Chardonnay (Bourgogne) $12. A fresh and fruity simple Bourgogne blanc, with hints of honey layered atop pear and apple fruit. Crisp on the finish; try as an apéritif. **84** *(11/15/2006)*

Prosper Maufoux 1998 Chardonnay (Puligny-Montrachet) $55. Very toasty and closed, it was hard now to get beyond this wine's wood veneer. Faint honey and earth flavors accompany a rich mouthfeel, but this wears an almost impenetrable oak shell. **88** *(7/1/2001)*

Prosper Maufoux 2003 Comme Dessus Chardonnay (Santenay) $24. Baked apple and cinnamon notes on the nose fail to carry all the way through, as the wine turns crisp and a bit metallic on the finish. Atypically austere for a wine from such a warm vintage. **85** *(11/15/2006)*

Prosper Maufoux 1999 Domaine des Combelières Chardonnay (Viré-Clessé) $14. Nice tension shows in the floral, peach, and stony aromas of this estate wine. It has a lean frame and taut spine, but good fruit, too, with the gentle peachy notes balancing the crisp edge. Closes clean, with citrus and spice. Viré-Clessé is a new appellation replacing the Macon-Villages, -Viré or -Clessé formerly mandated. **86** *(7/1/2001)*

Prosper Maufoux 2002 Les Folatieres Premier Cru Chardonnay (Puligny-Montrachet) $72. **87** *(11/15/2006)*

Prosper Maufoux 1999 Mont de Milieu Premier Cru Chardonnay (Chablis) $29. A nice perfume and crisp, well-defined stony and green apple flavors are attributes of this classified Chablis. Medium-weight, it has a good texture and structure. It finishes tight, with classic Chablis citrus and chalk notes. Appealing now, it should be even better in a year or two. **89 Editors' Choice** *(7/1/2001)*

Prosper Maufoux 2004 Pinot Noir (Bourgogne) $12. Nicely perfumed, with unusual structure for a Bourgogne rouge. Herbal notes wrap around a core of cherry fruit, finishing fresh and crisp. **84** *(11/15/2006)*

Prosper Maufoux 1997 Pinot Noir (Gevrey-Chambertin) $40. Solid and lean, this wine shows a bouquet of dried fruits and leaves, dark berries, and leather. The mouth is earthy and masculine in a traditional Gevrey manner, with spicy, dark cherry fruit and cocoa notes. It finishes with medium length and even, fairly resolved tannins. **87** *(7/1/2001)*

Prosper Maufoux 1997 Bourgogne Pinot Noir (Burgundy) $14. **85** *(11/15/1999)*

Prosper Maufoux 2004 Clos Paradis Premier Cru Pinot Noir (Mercurey) $23. A bit of a step down from the 2005 version of this wine. Tart cherries are accented by herbal notes that come perilously close to green bean. Not much texture or richness here, finishing crisp. **82** *(11/15/2006)*

Prosper Maufoux 2003 Les Gravieres Premier Cru Pinot Noir (Santenay) $36. **89** *(11/15/2006)*

Prosper Maufoux 2003 Les Gravières Premier Cru Pinot Noir (Santenay) $36. Complex from the start, marrying floral aromas, with hints of stemminess, herbs, and spice, all supported by lush black-cherry fruit. Picks up notes of black tea on the finish, so while this tastes good now, it may even improve in another year or two. **89** *(11/15/2006)*

Prosper Maufoux 1997 Premier Cru Beaumonts Pinot Noir (Vosne-Romanée) $57. This shows class and style immediately in its dry black cherry and soft leather aromas with chalk nuances on the nose. Opens with even, elegant cherry fruit; spice and leather accents atop a supple palate follow. The wine finishes gracefully, with good length and a sweet back-bouquet. **90** *(7/1/2001)*

Prosper Maufoux 1998 Sauvignon Blanc (Sancerre) $18. **84** *(5/1/2000)*

RAYMOND BECK

Raymond Beck NV Cuvée Prestige Sparkling Blend (Clairette de Die Méthode Dioise Ancestrale) $12. **87** —*P.G. (12/15/2000)*

RAYMOND HENRIOT

Raymond Henriot NV Brut Champagne Blend (France) $21. There is just a suggestion of color—a pale onion-skin blush. It's very sensuous, and the wine bursts immediately into a complex play of scents. Dusty pollen, fresh-cut flowers, and sweet fruits mingle invitingly, leading you into flavors of pomegranate, cranberry, and spice. Big and polished, this sensual feast of a wine delivers an extra dimension of flavor, power and length. **94 Editors' Choice** —*P.G. (12/15/2002)*

RED BERET

Red Beret 2004 Rosé Blend (Côtes-du-Rhône) $11. Surprisingly good for its name, packaging, and price, but that's why we taste the wines blind. On the dark side of copper, this wine shows floral and berry aromas and a touch of tree bark as well. Cherry-berry flavors are fresh and fruity, with a moderately long finish. **86 Best Buy** —*J.C. (6/19/2006)*

RED BICYCLETTE

Red Bicyclette 2003 Merlot (Vin de Pays d'Oc) $12. Different from many inexpensive Merlots in that it offers a fair amount of acid and tannin structure to go along with plummy, coffee-tinged fruit. Crisp and dry on the finish, giving it the edge to pair successfully with grilled steaks or burgers. **84** *(12/1/2004)*

Red Bicyclette 2003 Syrah (Vin de Pays d'Oc) $12. This is a riper, plummier style of Syrah, with dark, chocolaty notes and only the slightest hint of peppery meatiness. With its Syrah-wildness tamed and medium-weight style, this would be a solid choice as a cocktail-party red, and a Best Buy at its frequently quoted retail of $10. **85 Best Buy** *(12/1/2004)*

RÉGNARD

Régnard 1999 Pinot Noir (Bourgogne) $15. For funk lovers, this wine is slathered in horse sweat and old leather, yet underneath is a reasonably supple wine. **80** —*J.C. (10/1/2003)*

Régnard 1998 Pinot Noir (Chambolle-Musigny) $57. Portabello mushroom and borscht aromas show the complexity of the nose. One sip is like taking a bite out of a chocolate-covered cherry. This Pinot is silky, rich and a definite pleasure to drink. **89** —C.S. (11/1/2002)

Reignac 2001 Blanc Bordeaux White Blend (Bordeaux) $NA. Smoky and toasty on the nose, then opens up on the palate to deliver waves of honeyed stone fruits and hints of caramel, all while being totally dry. It's a nice, rich package, yet ends up finishing a little short. **86** —J.C. (6/1/2005)

REMY-PANNIER

Remy-Pannier 2000 Cabernet Franc (Chinon) $9. Here's a great expression of Cabernet Franc. Smells as juicy and fruity as Beaujolais, with that just-out-of-the-vat freshness, and drinks exuberantly young and fruity, with ultra-soft tannins. But dryness and acidity keep this charming wine balanced and pert. **87** —S.H. (9/12/2002)

Remy-Pannier 2000 Chardonnay (Vin de Pays du Jardin de la France) $6. You won't pick up any oak here, but the fruit is interesting and vibrant, smacking of ripe green apples and even more opulent peaches. It's springtime fresh in the mouth, nice, and round with a suggestion of fruity sweetness. **87** —S.H. (9/12/2002)

Remy-Pannier 2000 Chenin Blanc (Vouvray) $8. This pale, light Chenin Blanc drinks on the sweet side. It's like a bite of ripe peach, with the crisp attack of acidity so high, it makes your mouth water. Strikes a nice balance between the overt sugar and tartness. **85** —S.H. (9/12/2002)

Remy-Pannier 2000 Melon (Muscadet Sèvre Et Maine) $6. Very young and fragrant with the scent of grapefruits, this wine is bone dry and light-bodied and delicate. It's so fresh and clean, a perfect apéritif wine, or the acidic tartness would be nice with shellfish. **85** —S.H. (9/12/2002)

Remy-Pannier 2005 Sauvignon Blanc (Sancerre) $22. Crisp and light, with flavors of fresh cantaloupe and lychees. The aftertaste is soft, and just slightly sweet. **83** —R.V. (8/1/2006)

Remy-Pannier 2000 Sauvignon Blanc (Sancerre) $13. Sauvignon Blanc from the Loire, in all its light, crisp glory. The lemony flavors are weightless, accompanied by a chalky richness, while metallic acidity adds a refreshing counterpoint. This is a fun sipper all the way through the tart, clean finish. **86** —S.H. (9/12/2002)

RENE GEOFFROY

Rene Geoffroy NV Cuvée Prestige Premier Cru Brut Champagne Blend (Champagne) $51. Certainly this wine, a blend of two-thirds Chardonnay and one-third Pinot Noir, has fine acidity and flavors of toast, but it is somewhat unbalanced by a mix of crisp fruit and sweetness from the dosage, which has not fully integrated. **84** —R.V. (12/1/2002)

RENÉ MURÉ

René Muré NV Champagne Blend (Crémant d'Alsace) $20. Very fresh and crisp, with some good structure, this fine wine has apple and kiwi flavors and a touch of toast, caramel, and lively acidity. Muré also owns Clos Saint-Landelin in Rouffach, one of the top Alsace vineyards. **89** —R.V. (6/1/2006)

René Muré 2000 Domaine du Clos St Landelin Vendanges Tardives Grand Cru Vorbourg Gewürztraminer (Alsace) $45. The name is quite a mouthful, and so is this rich, yellow wine made from late-harvested grapes from the commune of Vorbourg. Aromas of apricot, honey, and botrytis are pure and regal, while the layered palate features baked apples, cinnamon, and toffee. The finish is layered and powerful; it's almost like a liqueur. Excellent weight and extract from start to end. **91** —M.S. (6/1/2003)

René Muré 2002 Clos de Rouffach Riesling (Alsace) $17. Sheltered by some of the highest Vosges mountains, the Clos Rouffach, with its chalk soil, is great for Riesling. This wood-aged wine, from Riesling master René Muré, is big, ripe, and powerful. It's a great wine, very modern and polished, with a nice mineral character. **91 Editors' Choice** —R.V. (11/1/2005)

René Muré 2002 Grand Cru Clos Saint Landelin Riesling (Alsace) $50. Within the grand cru vineyard of Vorbourg is this 54-acre vineyard, owned by René Muré. This is one of the great Rieslings of Alsace. It's elegant and layered with huge, ripe peaches and apricots, along with toast and caramel. It should age well over the next 10 years or more. **94 Cellar Selection** —R.V. (11/1/2005)

RESERVE ST. MARTIN

Reserve St. Martin 2002 Cabernet Sauvignon (Vin de Pays d'Oc) $8. This is a soft, easy wine which lacks focus but makes up for that with its fresh, light fruit and juicy tannins. Drink now and for another year. **82** —R.V. (12/1/2004)

Reserve St. Martin 2003 Merlot (Vin de Pays d'Oc) $8. An attractive wine with spicy fruitcake flavors. It is simple, easy to drink, and well-made. A touch of acidity lends it balance, the dried fruits give it some heat. **84 Best Buy** —R.V. (12/1/2004)

Reserve St. Martin 2005 Rosé Syrah (Vin de Pays d'Oc) $7. Nearly always a decent value, this vintage has turned out even better than usual, offering berry and milk chocolate aromas and flavors that are fresh and fruit, driven. Nicely textured on the finish, with soft tannins that make it easy to drink. **86 Best Buy** —J.C. (6/21/2006)

RICHARD BOURGEOIS

Richard Bourgeois 2005 Sauvignon Blanc (Sancerre) $19. This blending for the American market is softer than some Sancerre, but has some good fresh currant and light lemon flavors. It's ready to drink, with its soft, clean acidity **84** —R.V. (8/1/2006)

RIEFLÉ

Rieflé 2004 Classique Pinot Gris (Alsace) $25. Exotic aromas of smoke and fresh white fruits make this wine immediately attractive. On the palate, fresh fruits dominate, with some full flavors to round the wine out. An easy style of wine, just pushed forward by spice. **85** —R.V. (2/1/2006)

Rieflé 2003 Grand Cru Steinert Pinot Gris (Alsace) $40. This wine has power and concentration rather than sweetness. Velvet-smooth, it shows some spice, acidity, and lychees and just a touch of toastiness. It's a delicious food wine, ready to develop over three to five years. **91** —R.V. (2/1/2006)

Rieflé 1997 Côte de Rouffach Tokay Pinot Gris (Alsace) $19. 88 —M.M. (11/1/2000)

Rieflé 1996 Steinert Tokay Pinot Gris (Alsace) $30. 89 —J.C. (11/1/2000)

RIVEFORT DE FRANCE

Rivefort de France 1997 Viognier (Vin de Pays d'Oc) $10. 81 —J.C. (10/1/1999)

ROBERT GIRAUD

Robert Giraud 2000 Cepages Cabernet Sauvignon (Vin de Pays d'Oc) $7. Spicy, peppery aromas yield to tomato but not much fruit. The palate is sour, with tart plum and cherry. And the finish is equally lean and tart. High acids and not much fruit equals a lower-end wine. **81** —M.S. (9/1/2003)

ROC DE CAMBES

Roc de Cambes 1996 Bordeaux Blend (Côtes de Bourg) $29. 90 —M.S. (12/31/1999)

ROPITEAU

Ropiteau 2000 Les Perrieres Chardonnay (Meursault) $49. Intense, feminine aromas such as talc, vanilla, mineral, and pear waft from the nose. Lots of pear bursts from the palate, with an overlay of stone and nougat flavors. Finishes long with a glycerine-like texture and lean pear-skin and mineral flavors. If this sounds good to you, better hurry—only 100 cases were made. **90** (10/1/2002)

Ropiteau 2000 Les Tillets Chardonnay (Meursault) $37. It's medium-bodied but on the dry side, courtesy of the citrus (namely, grapefruit) and toast flavors on the palate. The bouquet smolders with toasty smokehouse and cashew notes over melon aromas. Finishes with lemon and more cashew. **88** (10/1/2002)

Ropiteau 2000 Meursault de Ropiteau Chardonnay (Meursault) $32. Roptieau produces 1,500 cases of this "flagship" white, which is light- to medium-bodied, with slightly buttery pear, melon, and banana aromas. Nutty, ripe melon flavors hang on a solidly citrus core, and it finishes short, marked by almond and mineral notes. **85** (10/1/2002)

Ropiteau 2000 Premier Cru Chardonnay (Rully) $18. A slightly creamy note adds a sweet foil to lemon, pear, and white peach aromas. A hint of minerals on the palate (thanks to the clay in the area's soil) keeps the pear, apple, and peach flavors lean. Medium-bodied, with lemon notes and good length on the finish. A full-of-fruit, easy drinker. **86** *(10/1/2002)*

Ropiteau 2000 Pinot Noir (Chassagne-Montrachet) $18. This red Chassagne is tart on the palate, which isn't surprising, given its plum-skin, cherry, leather, and tree bark flavors. Similar warm, cherry and earth notes play on the nose. Finishes chalky and dry, with a bitter note. **84** *(10/1/2002)*

ROUX PÈRE ET FILS

Roux Père et Fils 2005 Chardonnay (Chablis) $19. Citrus aromas and grapefruit flavors make this fresh, simple wine pleasing and attractive. This wine shows a style that has made Chablis so popular around the world. **85** —*R.V. (12/1/2006)*

Roux Père et Fils 2004 Chardonnay (Meursault) $39. The typical fat, buttery flavors are balanced here by elegance and freshness. With its honey, melon, and pear tastes, come fresh acidity and a underlying layer of vanilla from the wood. **89** —*R.V. (12/1/2006)*

Roux Père et Fils 2004 La Pucelle Chardonnay (St.-Aubin) $28. Roux Père et Fils, based in Saint-Aubin, has done much to enhance the reputation of the appellation. This wine shows the potential of the ripe fruit that can be produced in a year such as 2004. Perhaps the winemaker was carried away by new wood, but that should tone down in a year. **88** —*R.V. (12/1/2006)*

Roux Père et Fils 2004 Les Cortons Premier Cru Chardonnay (St.-Aubin) $42. Beautiful green plum flavored fruit shows how good Saint-Aubin can be. The vanilla flavors from wood fermentation and aging simply underline the pure, vivid flavors. Drink in three to 10 years. **90** —*R.V. (12/1/2006)*

Roux Père et Fils 2005 Les Murelles Chardonnay (Bourgogne) $12. Aromas of nuts and honey, with smooth, soft flavors. This wine has ripeness along with crisp acidity. It is pure in fruit, without a hint of wood. **85** —*R.V. (12/1/2006)*

RUINART

Ruinart NV Brut Champagne Blend (Champagne) $48. This is a blend of Pinot Noir (60%) and Chardonnay (40%), drawn largely from the 1999 vintage, with some '98 and '96 added. It's fresh and light, very delicate, with a creamy, soft mousse and flavors of pineapple and yellow plum. Finishes soft, picking up hints of green apple. **88** *(12/1/2003)*

Ruinart NV Brut Champagne Blend (Champagne) $48. With its light, snappy aromas of ginger, Anjou pears and green apples, this is an ideal apéritif-style Champagne: It won't overshadow what is to come, but its fresh, crisp finish whets the appetite and refreshes the palate. Drink now for its freshness and vitality. **87** —*J.C. (12/15/2001)*

Ruinart NV Brut Rosé Champagne Blend (Champagne) $83. The Ruinart house style leans towards producing elegant lightweight Champagnes and even it's rosé follows suit. Strawberry and citrus aromas give way to berry, toast, and mushroom flavors. It's dry and light—a pink bubbly perfect as a Valentine's Day apéritif. **87** —*J.C. (12/15/2001)*

Ruinart NV Brut Rosé Champagne Blend (Champagne) $83. Like the NV brut, this is based on wines from the 1999 vintage, but from only premier cru vineyards. It's 45% Chardonnay, the balance Pinot Noir, with almost 20% of the Pinot made as red. The Chardonnay adds a lively, lime-like quality to the soft, berry-fruited Pinot Noir. A plump, easy-to-like rosé. **87** *(12/1/2003)*

Ruinart 1993 Dom Ruinart Champagne Blend (Champagne) $130. Although not labeled blanc de blancs, this is 100% Chardonnay, bottled in 1994 and disgorged in 2002. The bouquet is intense and youthfully vigorous, carrying scents of toast and fresh limes, along with notes of ash and earth. It's creamy and delicate in the mouth, with assertive flavors of yellow fruits and toast, culminating in a long, citrusy finish. Drinkable now, but capable of aging another 10 years or more. **92 Cellar Selection** *(12/31/2003)*

Ruinart 1990 Dom Ruinart Brut Rosé Champagne Blend (Champagne) $NA. The palest of onion skin pink colors is certainly the freshest part of this mature wine. The flavors are full of mature toast and will certainly appeal to those who like their Champagnes with bottle age. With the fruit less prominent, it is left to the richness and great style of the wine to carry the day. **91** —*R.V. (12/1/2004)*

Ruinart 1993 R de Ruinart Brut Champagne Blend (Champagne) $72. 82 *(12/15/1999)*

Ruinart 1990 Dom Ruinart Blanc de Blancs Brut Chardonnay (Champagne) $130. Smells rich and heavy, with scents of candied Play-Doh wrapped around rosemary and anise upon first opening; later, aromas of sweet pastry dough and custard move to the fore. Despite the weighty aromas, the palate is lighter than you might expect, featuring lime and vanilla flavors. **86** —*J.C. (12/15/2001)*

SAINT COSME

Saint Cosme 2005 Les Deux Albion Rhône Red Blend (Côtes-du-Rhône) $20. From a vineyard near Cairanne, this is a young, muscular wine not necessarily intended for early consumption. Recently bottled prior to tasting, it showed some slightly reductive, rubbery notes at first, and then opened to reveal rich blackberry fruit and firm tannins. Drink 2008–2015. **89** —*J.C. (11/15/2006)*

Saint Cosme 2005 Syrah (Côtes-du-Rhône) $15. Made from 100% Syrah off a terroir rich in clay, this has very peppery aromas but also notes of violet and cassis. On the palate, it's quite firm but packed with crunchy dark berry fruit. Drink now with foods that will tame the tannins, or hold up to 2013. **88** —*J.C. (11/15/2006)*

Saint Cosme 2004 Syrah (Saint-Joseph) $35. Crisp and slightly herbal, with powerful cassis flavors that lack that extra bit of spice and nuance. Still, it's clean and well-made, with a long finish. Drink now–2012. **88** —*J.C. (11/15/2006)*

SAINT SAVIN

Saint Savin 2003 Bordeaux White Blend (Bordeaux) $11. 83 —*J.C. (6/1/2005)*

SAINT-HILAIRE

Saint-Hilaire 2002 Blanc de Blancs Brut Sparkling Blend (Blanquette de Limoux) $12. Dry, toasty, smooth, and clean; this is a textbook non-Champagne bubbly that will work as an apéritif or at parties. The palate is light and crisp, with citrus and apple flavors. And the body is just hefty enough. **87 Best Buy** —*M.S. (12/31/2005)*

SALON LE MESNIL

Salon Le Mesnil 1996 Blanc de Blancs Brut Chardonnay (Champagne) $300. Bone dry, this is a stunning wine that shows the aging qualities of the 1996 vintage as well as the intensity of Salon. It is packed with acidity and firm green fruits, leaving a twist of lemon and nuts on the finish. **95 Editors' Choice** —*R.V. (11/1/2006)*

Salon Le Mesnil 1995 Blanc de Blancs Brut Chardonnay (Champagne) $225. A thorough classic, with soda and mineral on the nose along with pineapple, apple, and other white fruits. The flavor profile is as pure and ethereal as it comes, with luscious apple, melon, and citrus. Lively and persistent on the finish, with a touch of toast. Feels just right; has great purity; will age nicely for another decade. **97** —*M.S. (12/31/2005)*

Salon Le Mesnil 1990 Blanc de Blancs Brut Chardonnay (Champagne) $200. Full and elegant, even plush, from the sexy butter, caramel, smoke, and vanilla bouquet through the plum, tropical fruit and dried peach flavors and chalk and mineral accents on the palate. There's great nuance here, as there always is with Salon. Though it's younger, this seems already softer and more forward than the 1985 and 1988 tasted last year. Drink now through 2010. **91** *(12/15/2001)*

Salon Le Mesnil 1985 Blanc de Blancs Brut Chardonnay (Champagne) $216. 96 *(12/1/2000)*

SANTA DUC

Santa Duc 2003 Les Buissons Cairanne Rhône Red Blend (Côtes-du-Rhône Villages) $17. Lots of spice—particularly anise, but also clove and cinnamon—with wonderfully supple tannins to carry the flavors through a long finish. Ready to drink now. **90 Editors' Choice** —*J.C. (11/15/2006)*

SAUVION

Sauvion 2003 Baronne du Cléray Melon (Muscadet Sèvre Et Maine) $NA. Good green fruits, with some ripe acidity. A little fat, but it has some good green flavors at the back. **86** —*R.V. (1/1/2004)*

Sauvion 2001 Sauvignon Blanc (Sancerre) $15. Its citrus and melon aromas unfortunately also take on the added and unwanted scent of cleaning solution. The mouth is tart and lean, with lots of lemon. It finishes on the sour side. Properly chilled and with the right food, however, it could be refreshing. **83** *(8/1/2002)*

SCHRÖDER ET SCHYLER

Schröder et Schyler 2003 Signatures en White Blend (Bordeaux) $NA. A soft wine which maybe lacks acidity but makes up for it with its rich flavors of tropical fruits and a generous food-friendly character. Serve it like a white Burgundy, not too cold. **84** *—R.V. (6/1/2005)*

SEIGNEURS DE BERGERAC

Seigneurs de Bergerac 2002 White Blend (Bergerac Sec) $8. Slightly grassy on the nose, along with hints of lime and green bean. On the palate, it's light in body, offering only watery green bean flavors. **80** — *J.C. (12/1/2004)*

SERGE MATHIEU

Serge Mathieu NV Blanc de Noirs Cuvée Tradition Brut Champagne Blend (Champagne) $30. A full-bodied Champagne, with ripe yellow peach and toast flavors, finishing with ripe currants. A 100% Pinot Noir, it has good weight on the palate and distinct acids on the finish. **89** *—R.V. (12/1/2002)*

Serge Mathieu NV Cuvée Prestige Brut Champagne Blend (Champagne) $34. From his 30-acre vineyard in the Aube, Serge Mathieu makes a complex, honeyed blend of two-thirds Pinot Noir and one-third Chardonnay. Flavors of hazelnuts and quince go with fresh balanced toast and yeast. The wine practically floats across the palate, leaving a light, fresh feel. This is a great apéritif wine. **91** *—R.V. (12/1/2002)*

SIEUR D'ARQUES

Sieur d'Arques 2001 Vichon Mediterranean Chardonnay (Vin de Pays d'Oc) $7. 85 Best Buy *—R.V. (11/15/2002)*

Sieur d'Arques 2000 Grande Cuvée Millénaire Sparkling Blend (Crémant de Limoux) $NA. With the local Mauzac grape as the predominant variety in this blend, there are aromas of white flowers and grapefruit. To taste, it is spicy, with toast and honey and some fresh acidity. A fine, balanced wine. **89** *—R.V. (6/1/2006)*

Sieur d'Arques NV Toques et Clochers Sparkling Blend (Crémant de Limoux) $16. This light-bodied sparkler from the south of France is clean and refreshing because of its lightness, rather than any great crispness. Delicate toast scents accent mushroom, apple, and pear flavors. **86** *—J.C. (12/31/2004)*

SIMONNET-FEBVRE

Simonnet-Febvre 1999 Chevaliere (Vin de Table) Bordeaux Blend (France) $8. 86 *—P.G. (11/1/2002)*

Simonnet-Febvre 1999 Red Blend (Bourgogne) $15. Here the scents are on the weedy side of Pinot, with stemmy, earthy notes prevailing. There is also some high-toned, candied fruit on the palate, but overall it just doesn't gel. **85** *—P.G. (11/1/2002)*

TAITTINGER

Taittinger 1999 Brut Champagne Blend (Champagne) $65. A powerful, intense wine. The fruit is green and crisp, but the wine is full-bodied, with flavors of toast and almonds over ripe grapefruit and gooseberries. This wine is still very young, only just beginning to integrate the fruit and the acidity—give it 10 years. **92** *—R.V. (11/1/2006)*

Taittinger 1998 Brut Champagne Blend (Champagne) $70. A fine, soft wine, which shows all the Taittinger elegance. It has richness and ripe fruit, flavors of white currants, and good freshness. It is beautifully poised, still fresh, and likely to age well. **88** *—R.V. (12/1/2004)*

Taittinger 1995 Brut Champagne Blend (Champagne) $56. 92 *—P.G. (12/1/2000)*

Taittinger 1996 Comtes de Champagne Blanc de Blancs Brut Champagne Blend (Champagne) $130. Subtle, complex scents open with evocative layers of cinnamon, mace, vanilla, and even a hint of chocolate. This is still quite tight and youthful, with a small but concentrated core of Pinot flavors that seems to need more time to unwrap. **90** *—P.G. (12/15/2003)*

Taittinger 1995 Comtes de Champagne Blanc de Blancs Brut Champagne Blend (Champagne) $130. A subtle, textured, and fascinating nose suggests layers of spice (cinnamon, mace), lemongrass and light citrus. But in the mouth it trails off quickly, showing a medium body and little persistence. Well-made but a little disappointing given the price and reputation. **90** *—P.G. (12/15/2002)*

Taittinger 1994 Comtes de Champagne Blanc de Blancs Brut Champagne Blend (Champagne) $170. 89 *(12/31/2000)*

Taittinger 1999 Comtes de Champagne Brut Rosé Champagne Blend (Champagne) $210. Very airy, light, and floating, this is a typical fresh, elegant wine in the Taittinger style. It has delicious, open raspberry, and citrusy flavors, with a great finishing pizzazz of freshness. **92** *—R.V. (11/1/2006)*

Taittinger 1995 Comtes de Champagne Brut Rosé Champagne Blend (Champagne) $204. 95 *—M.S. (12/15/2000)*

Taittinger NV La Française Brut Champagne Blend (Champagne) $35. Pale straw in color with a fine bead. As always, this is an elegant, distinctive, and impeccably crisp Champagne. It is the epitome of stylish; tightly focused, it gently unwraps itself into a graceful, immaculately clean finish that's lightly toasty and hints at coconut and vanilla wafer. **91** *—P.G. (12/1/2006)*

Taittinger NV La Française Brut Champagne Blend (Champagne) $43. 92 *—S.H. (12/1/2000)*

Taittinger NV La Française Brut Champagne Blend (Champagne) $35. A pleasing, distinctly spicy bouquet strongly suggests clove and perhaps hints of fresh ham. Young, yeasty, and tightly focused, this is a classy, assertive wine, still quite green, but extending itself through a lingering, immaculately clean finish. **91** *—P.G. (12/15/2002)*

Taittinger NV La Française Brut Champagne Blend (Champagne) $45. 85 *(12/15/1999)*

Taittinger NV Prélude Grands Crus Brut Champagne Blend (Champagne) $70. A blend made entirely from grand cru vineyards, this is a superbly ripe, full wine; a very different, richer one from the normally light Taittinger style. A great Champagne, impressive and worth aging. **94 Cellar Selection** *—R.V. (12/1/2005)*

Taittinger NV Prélude Grands Crus Brut Champagne Blend (Champagne) $65. Pretty big and tight at first, with burnt match, pepper, and mustard aromas. Full and layered, with citrus, apple, grapefruit, and spice flavors. Quite round and chewy, and a little off the beaten path. Seems to improve the more you get to know it. **88** *—M.S. (12/15/2003)*

Taittinger NV Prestige Brut Rosé Champagne Blend (Champagne) $70. This deep rose-colored Champagne is full-bodied with ripe, fresh fruit flavors. There is acidity but with the very fruity character of this wine, it is one which can be drunk relatively young and fresh. **89** *—R.V. (12/1/2005)*

Taittinger NV Prestige Brut Rosé Champagne Blend (Champagne) $52. 88 — *J.C. (12/15/2000)*

Taittinger 1998 Comtes de Champagne Blanc de Blancs Brut Chardonnay (Champagne) $150. A delicious, welcoming, generous wine that also manages to keep the pure, mineral character of Chardonnay. It has a very direct, linear, steely taste. Great acidity plays a part, as do ripe, fruity flavors and fine balance. This wine should develop well, but it's delicious now. **94** *—R.V. (11/1/2006)*

TARDIEU-LAURENT

Tardieu-Laurent 2004 Guy-Louis Rhône Red Blend (Côtes-du-Rhône) $24. Not a wine for the oak-averse, as it's slathered with cinnamon, vanilla, and other baking spices from aging in special barriques. Exotic, but built on a solid foundation of cherry fruit. Drink now–2010. **87** *—J.C. (11/15/2006)*

Tardieu-Laurent 2004 Vieilles Vignes Rhône Red Blend (Gigondas) $34. My only gripe with the Tardieu-Laurent wines is not their overall quality—I found every one I tasted to be very good—but that the use of oak obscures some of their more delicate characteristics, at least at this young stage. This Gigondas is wonderfully perfumed with vanilla and a vast array of dried spices, and it shows richly supple fruit notes of cherry and apricot. It's delicious now—in its own way—but maybe the wood will be more effectively integrated in a couple of years. **88** *—J.C. (11/15/2006)*

TERRE DE MISTRAL

Terre de Mistral 2004 Red Blend (Côtes-du-Rhône) $11. A bit floral and herbal on the nose, but there are also peach and berry fruit flavors that end up carrying the day. Finishes a little short, picking up hints of Earl Grey tea amid a dusting of light tannins. From the co-op at Estézargues. **85** —*J.C. (11/15/2006)*

TERRES NOIRES

Terres Noires 2003 Chardonnay (Vin de Pays d'Oc) $NA. Full-bodied flavors of tropical fruits give this wine richness and ripeness. It is simple, straightforward, with immediately attractive depth of flavor. No complexity here. **83** —*R.V. (12/1/2004)*

THIERRY & GUY

Thierry & Guy 2003 Fat Bastard Chardonnay (Vin de Pays d'Oc) $11. Despite pleasant aromas of apple tinged with cinnamon, vanilla, and honey, the palate is hard, with grapefruit and sour apple flavors. **83** —*J.C. (11/15/2005)*

Thierry & Guy 2000 Fat Bastard Shiraz (Vin de Pays d'Oc) $10. This lightweight, tart-cherry flavored wine displays some coffee and game notes on the nose. The aromas and flavors are correct, but it's a bit hollow. It lacks the body (and shows more sourness) that most enthusiasts would want from an inexpensive quaff. **83** *(10/1/2001)*

TOQUES ET CLOCHERS

Toques et Clochers 2003 Clocher D'Ajac Reserve Jean-Pierre Bourret Vigneron Chardonnay (Limoux) $33. Slathered with spicy oak, sweet caramel, and blatant buttery notes, which largely overwhelm the modest apple and citrus fruit. If you like heavy oaking, you'll like this more than we did. **83** —*J.C. (11/15/2005)*

Toques et Clochers 2003 Merlot-Syrah-Grenache Red Blend (Limoux) $15. Half Merlot, with the balance a blend of 35% Syrah and 15% Grenache, this wine yields slightly baked fruit aromas, then delivers plenty of dried cherry and chocolate flavors. Shows good texture and length on the finish, so this large producer may be on to something special if they could just freshen up the aromatics. **86** —*J.C. (11/15/2005)*

TORTOISE CREEK

Tortoise Creek 2004 Chardonnay (Vin de Pays d'Oc) $9. A lightweight Chardonnay, with scents of apple, earth, and flinty minerality. Flavors run along the same lines, picking up riper pear notes before finishing with hints of quince. **84** —*J.C. (11/15/2005)*

Tortoise Creek 2004 Chardonnay-Viognier (Vin de Pays d'Oc) $8. Broad and mouth-filling, with apple, melon, and mineral flavors that fan out nicely across the palate. A nicely balanced table wine that could easily partner with fish or poultry. **85 Best Buy** —*J.C. (11/15/2005)*

Tortoise Creek 2003 Merlot (Vin de Pays d'Oc) $8. Medium-weight, with just enough supple tannins to provide a modicum of structure, this soft, easygoing Merlot boasts plummy fruit and notes of coffee and brown sugar. Finishes with hints of dried herbs and tea leaves. **86 Best Buy** —*J.C. (12/1/2004)*

Tortoise Creek 2000 Les Ámoureux Red Blend (Vin de Pays d'Oc) $8. This Rhône blend (70% Syrah-30% Mourvèdre) just doesn't come together. A sour edge shows early and prevails throughout. Thin, it shows less body and texture than other value reds tasted, as well. **80** —*M.M. (2/1/2002)*

Tortoise Creek 2003 Sauvignon Blanc (Vin de Pays d'Oc) $8. Ripe- and fresh-smelling—peach-like, with overtones of pink grapefruit. Plump and slightly viscous in the mouth, offering pink grapefruit and melon flavors. A bit low in acid, likely a result of the tremendously hot vintage, but still tasty. **84 Best Buy** *J.C. (12/1/2004)*

Tortoise Creek 2000 Les Ámoureux Sauvignon Blanc (Vin de Pays d'Oc) $8. This offering displays some of the fuller fig and nut side of Sauvignon Blanc, as well as the lime and melon seen more often in the less expensive bottlings. Even and medium weight, it's full, but not intense, with a chalky note on the back end. Drink now. **83** —*M.M. (2/1/2002)*

Tortoise Creek 2000 Les Ámoureux White Blend (Vin de Pays d'Oc) $8. A nicely balanced simple white blend with a melon and white peach bouquet. It's light in weight with an even mouthfeel. Honey and vanilla

notes add interest, as does a touch of white pepper on the finish. Best consumed now. **84** —*M.M. (2/1/2002)*

TRIENNES

Triennes 1996 Syrah (Vin de Pays Var) $15. 89 *(11/15/1999)*

TRIMBACH

Trimbach 2000 Gewürztraminer (Alsace) $18. 86 *(1/1/2004)*

Trimbach 1994 Selection de Grains Nobles Gewürztraminer (Alsace) $130. 92 *(1/1/2004)*

Trimbach 2001 Pinot Blanc (Alsace) $11. Trimbach may be famed for its superb (and expensive) Rieslings, but for a great value, this Pinot Blanc is a well-made, ripe, rounded wine, which is just now completely ready to drink. With flavors of white peaches and an impressive richness, this could be drunk as an apéritif, but could equally partner cold cuts or fish. **85** —*R.V. (11/15/2003)*

Trimbach 2000 Hommage à Jeanne Pinot Gris (Alsace) $60. Named in memory of Jeanne Trimbach, this cuvée celebrates the centenary of her birth. It is packed with toast aromas, just a touch of honey and is layered with green fruits, with fresh acidity on the finish. **92** —*R.V. (2/1/2006)*

Trimbach 2002 Réserve Pinot Gris (Alsace) $20. Very dry, this is the perfect food wine, a partner for fish or salads. It has green fruits, soft, easy flavors, structured with acidity and toasty spices. A straightforward, finely made wine. **87** —*R.V. (2/1/2006)*

Trimbach 1997 Reserve Personnelle Pinot Gris (Alsace) $40. 90 *(1/1/2004)*

Trimbach 2000 Sélection de Grains Nobles Pinot Gris (Alsace) $150. Already developing a depth of orange-gold color, this wine is maturing beautifully. It is more rich than overwhelmingly sweet, showing structure, acidity, and a toasty character. A finely crafted wine, packed with intense flavors and a fresh aftertaste. **94** —*R.V. (2/1/2006)*

Trimbach 2002 Riesling (Alsace) $17. This is a fresh and soft, but dry style of wine. It is the least expensive in the range of Trimbach Rieslings, but it still shows a great, crisp character, some good intensity of flavor, and, at this stage, youthful structure and tannins. Even this level of wine from Trimbach needs 3–4 years of aging. **88** —*R.V. (11/1/2005)*

Trimbach 1998 Clos Ste Hune Riesling (Alsace) $100. 93 *(1/1/2004)*

Trimbach 2000 Cuvée Frédéric Emile Riesling (Alsace) $42. This is one of Alsace's greatest Rieslings, a wine from the grand cru vineyard of Osterberg. It is bone dry, a style that remains a passion for the Trimbachs. With its steely, mineral character, and its grapefruit flavors, it can seem too austere. But just wait 10 years—the wine will be transformed. This is superb Riesling by any standard. **95** —*R.V. (11/1/2005)*

Trimbach 2002 Réserve Riesling (Alsace) $20. This is a great, steely, dry wine, which shows fine acidity and flavors of currants. It also offers crisp apple flavors, hedgerow aromas, and a great, fresh finish. It should develop well over the next 4–5 years. **90 Editors' Choice** —*R.V. (11/1/2005)*

VAL D'ORBIEU

Val d'Orbieu 2001 Reserve St. Martin Cabernet Sauvignon (Languedoc) $8. Cherry, plum, and earth aromas lead into a tart, lean palate that struggles to offer more than a modicum of cherry and cassis flavors. The finish is sweet and spicy, which makes for an odd, not terribly appealing combination. **82** —*M.S. (9/1/2003)*

Val d'Orbieu 2001 Reserve St. Martin Merlot (Languedoc) $8. Quite nondescript, with spicy chili aromas and other hard-to-peg piquant smells. The palate is sweet, awkward, and deals cinnamon and clove along with weak berry fruit. It's almost there, but throughout it lacks a certain something. **83** —*M.S. (9/1/2003)*

Val d'Orbieu 2001 Les Deux Rives Rouge Red Blend (Corbières) $8. Spicy, with raspberry and spearmint aromas. Shows cranberry and plum skin on the palate, which is lean and lacking in the texture category. Gets better with airing, but still shows some bitterness on the finish and not much in the middle. **84** —*M.S. (9/1/2003)*

Val d'Orbieu 2001 Reserve St. Martin Syrah (Languedoc) $8. Sweet aromas of leather and caramel seem murky and tired. The palate comes without snap, and that's despite some plum and raspberry flavors. The finish is lean and basic, and overall it's a simple wine that doesn't really taste much like Syrah. **82** —*M.S. (9/1/2003)*

FRANCE

Val d'Orbieu 2001 Les Deux Rives Blanc White Blend (Corbières) $8. Spicy, with raspberry and spearmint aromas. Shows cranberry and plum skin on the palate, which is lean and lacking in the texture category. Gets better with airing, but still shows some bitterness on the finish and not much in the middle. **84** —*M.S. (9/1/2003)*

VERBAU

Verbau 2000 Cabernet Sauvignon (Bordeaux) $12. Lean and earthy, but clean, and with an appealing freshness. Cherry and berry fruit dominates, and the finish is true. And there's even some patented Bordeaux herbaceousness, but in a good way. Kosher. **83** —*M.S. (6/1/2003)*

Verbau 2001 Grand Cru Gewürztraminer (Alsace) $12. This semi-sweet Kosher Gewürz is clean and well-made. The nose offers pear and butterscotch, while the sweet and spicy palate provides some litchi and white chocolate. It's round and sweet, but easy to drink. An easy wine that shouldn't disappoint. **87 Best Buy** —*M.S. (6/1/2003)*

VEUVE AMBAL

Veuve Ambal NV Blanc de Blancs Brut Sparkling Blend (Vin Mousseux) $13. A simple, crisp apéritif style of wine, with flavors of green apples, plums, and a touch of pine nuts. The wine, a blend of Airen and Ugni Blanc, is dry, and fresh. **85** —*R.V. (6/1/2006)*

VEUVE CLICQUOT PONSARDIN

Veuve Clicquot Ponsardin NV Brut Champagne Blend (Champagne) $50. Creamy and soft in the mouth, yet well-balanced, this is an easy-to-down Champagne that would be a good party choice. Toast, anise, and citrus notes are joined by riper nectarine and apple flavors. **87** —*J.C. (12/1/2004)*

Veuve Clicquot Ponsardin NV Brut Champagne Blend (Champagne) $50. Round, ripe, and lemony, it's more like a very good California sparkler than fine Champagne. Tasty, fruity, and approachable, but missing the refinement and the texture that elevates the very top Champagnes. **88** —*P.G. (12/1/2006)*

Veuve Clicquot Ponsardin 1998 Brut Champagne Blend (Champagne) $76. The current release of the vintage wine, the 1998 seems a touch richer than the '99, with hints of brioche, mushroom, and ginger to its citrusy flavors. Round and soft in the mouth, but also a little short on the finish. **89** *(12/1/2005)*

Veuve Clicquot Ponsardin NV Brut Rosé Champagne Blend (Champagne) $50. Bold, vivacious, and forward, this appealing wine is true to the house style, with plenty of sweet, pretty fruit. There are unchallenging but undeniably enjoyable flavors of ripe stone fruits, hints of grapefruit and citrus zest, and a smack of wet stone in the back of the throat. Young and fresh, without the toasty finesse of the vintage rosés. **88** —*P.G. (12/1/2006)*

Veuve Clicquot Ponsardin 1985 Brut Rosé Champagne Blend (Champagne) $250. Tasted from a magnum disgorged in '97, this provides ample evidence that '85 was a great year for Clicquot. Toasty, but seems less evolved than the '85 Brut, with a deep copper color, meaty, savory aromas, berry flavors, and a full, creamy texture. Long on the finish. It's made from the same base as the '85 Brut, but with 14.5% red from Bouzy added. **93** *(12/1/2005)*

Veuve Clicquot Ponsardin NV Demi-Sec Champagne Blend (Champagne) $50. The dosage level is 45g/l, which makes this wine a bit sweet, but not cloying. Toast and candied citron aromas and some honeyed apple and lemon flavors. Decanting reduces the apparent acidity, thereby raising the perception of sweetness. **87** *(12/1/2005)*

Veuve Clicquot Ponsardin 1998 La Grande Dame Brut Champagne Blend (Champagne) $120. A superbly ripe Champagne that has all the open generosity of the 1998 vintage. Peach and apricot aromas are followed by flavors of hazelnuts, honey, and spices. Of course, it is still very young, and, like all vintages of La Grande Dame, it will age for many years. **92** —*R.V. (11/1/2006)*

Veuve Clicquot Ponsardin 1996 La Grande Dame Brut Champagne Blend (Champagne) $150. In five years, this rating may look conservative, as this wine seems to have the building blocks upon which to age well. Right now, it's tight and citrusy, with some riper pear notes and a creamy midpalate. Expect this to develop richer toast and nut nuances, and for

the grapefruity finish to soften and become more harmonious. **91 Cellar Selection** —*J.C. (12/1/2004)*

Veuve Clicquot Ponsardin 1993 La Grande Dame Brut Champagne Blend (Champagne) $150. Young, with a taut citrus, ginger, mineral, soice, and floral bouquet, this bright and light-on-its-feet wine has lots of dimension. Yellow fruit flavors, anise accents, and fine fruit-to-acid balance mark the cream, yet airy palate. The mineral-chalk and the citrus-peel finish is long, with brisk acidity. High-strung, like fine white Burgundy; though delicious now, it will benefit from aging for three to six plus years. **91 Cellar Selection** *(12/15/2001)*

Veuve Clicquot Ponsardin 1989 La Grande Dame Brut Champagne Blend (Champagne) $NA. The richest and ripest of the 1988–1990 trilogy, with notes of brioche and berry flavors. Round and full in the mouth, but without the same degree of elegance exhibited by the other two years. **90** *(12/1/2005)*

Veuve Clicquot Ponsardin 1995 La Grande Dame Brut Rosé Champagne Blend (Champagne) $200. Like the regular Grande Dame, the aim here is finesse. It's softer and more elegant than Clicquot's vintage rosé, with delicate hints of cherry, toast, mushroom, and citrus. Long, tight, and tannic on the finish, this wine is worth cellaring. **92** *(12/1/2005)*

Veuve Clicquot Ponsardin 1995 La Grande Dame Brut Rosé Champagne Blend (Champagne) $230. Big, big, big—did I say big—flavors, with lush, full red fruits and a mouth-filling, almost juicy and long-lasting impression of ripe cherries. There's plenty of vanilla and toast as well, rounding out a voluptuous finish. The fruit comes from top vineyards, and it's exceptional all the way. **92** —*P.G. (12/15/2003)*

Veuve Clicquot Ponsardin 1998 Réserve Brut Champagne Blend (Champagne) $75. Just lightly toasty, with hints of green apple and lime also appearing on the nose. Vividly fresh fruit on the palate, with crisp acidity to give it bite on the finish. Tighter-knit and seemingly drier than the nonvintage stuff from Clicquot, this could use a little time in the cellar to plump up and gain richness. Try in 2008. **90** —*J.C. (12/1/2004)*

Veuve Clicquot Ponsardin 1995 Réserve Brut Champagne Blend (Champagne) $68. Herbal, grassy aromas waft from its nose, accented by traces of lemon-lime and toast. Toast, pear, and citrus flavors show both the palate and the finish. One reviewer called it, "ordinary, but done well," but we think that there is nothing wrong, in this case, with getting what you expect when you imagine what good Champagne should taste like. **88** *(12/15/2001)*

Veuve Clicquot Ponsardin 1999 Réserve Brut Rosé Champagne Blend (Champagne) $86. Floral and fruity on the nose, with lots of forward cherry aromas. It's 15% Bouzy, but not tannic at all, with an elegant mouthfeel and a long, silky finish. **89** *(12/1/2005)*

Veuve Clicquot Ponsardin 1996 Réserve Brut Rosé Champagne Blend (Champagne) $75. Very forward, with pretty strawberry/cherry fruit, and some earthy tannin in the finish. Like chocolate-covered cherries, with an unusual bittersweet character running through the finish. **89** —*P.G. (12/15/2003)*

Veuve Clicquot Ponsardin 1993 Réserve Brut Rosé Champagne Blend (Champagne) $75. 92 —*M.S. (12/1/1999)*

Veuve Clicquot Ponsardin NV Yellow Label Brut Champagne Blend (Champagne) $50. The standard-bearer, which, for many people, defines the classic taste of Champagne. Rich, round, lemony fruit fills the mouth, and there is a refreshing, lightly bitter, yeasty finish of citrus rind. **88** —*P.G. (12/15/2003)*

VEUVE DU VERNAY

Veuve du Vernay NV Blanc de Blancs Brut Champagne Blend (Bordeaux) $10. 86 Best Buy —*M.M. (12/31/2000)*

Veuve du Vernay NV Brut Blanc de Blancs Champagne Blend (France) $10. Extremely light and yeasty, there are subtle whiffs of baked apple and sweet cracker in the nose, but no real weight in the mouth. Neutral green apple fruit and a pleasantly beery finish, with just a hint of bitterness. **84** —*P.G. (12/15/2002)*

VF

VF 2002 Lasira Red Wine Rhône Red Blend (Costières de Nimes) $9. The new VF line from Beaucastel's Perrin family is a stunning statement of affordable quality. Screw-capped and plainly packaged, Lasira delivers the goods where it counts: in the bottle. The blend is three-quarters Syrah, one-quarter Grenache, and as the label points out, 0% cork. Bright, spicy, and showing sharp berry flavors, this fruit and acid-driven bottling is a classy new wine for a new generation of wine drinkers. **88 Best Buy** —*P.G. (11/15/2004)*

VICHON

Vichon 1997 Mediterranean Chardonnay (Vin de Pays d'Oc) $10. 82 —*S.H. (7/1/2000)*

Vichon 1998 Mediterranean Sauvignon Blanc (Vin de Pays d'Oc) $10. 82 —*S.H. (7/1/2000)*

VIEUX CHÂTEAU GAUBERT

Vieux Château Gaubert 2003 Benjamin Bordeaux White Blend (Graves) $14. Named after a low-lying vineyard in alluvial soil, his white is soft and very ripe, with quince flavors and a light touch of wood. **87** —*R.V. (6/1/2005)*

VIGNERONS DE BUZET

Vignerons de Buzet 2000 Baron d'Ardeuil Bordeaux Blend (Buzet) $15. Made from a selection of vineyard plots and aged in new wood, this is a blend of Merlot, Cabernet Franc, and Cabernet Sauvignon. There are soft tannins and fresh acidity along with some ripe but soft fruit. Ready to drink now, but could go another three or four years. **88** —*R.V. (3/1/2006)*

Vignerons de Buzet 2003 Château de Padère Bordeaux Blend (Buzet) $NA. One of the single estate wines produced by the Buzet cooperative, this is a dense, rich, but tannic wine with big raisin and black fruit flavors. It is a solid wine, with hints of wood, and will certainly age over several years. **89** —*R.V. (9/1/2005)*

Vignerons de Buzet 2004 Le Lys Bordeaux Blend (Buzet) $NA. A simple, soft red with flavors of red berries and light tannins. This is a easy wine, which can be served slightly chilled, as well as working well with light meat dishes. **85** —*R.V. (9/1/2005)*

VIGNERONS DE CARACTERE

Vignerons de Caractere 2001 Bois du Ménestral Rhône Red Blend (Vacqueyras) $16. A special cuvée from the local co-op, this Vacqueyras is showing all the signs of being mature, from its lightening color to its aromas and flavors of coffee, tobacco, and dried fruit and its resolved tannins. Drink up. **84** —*J.C. (11/15/2006)*

Vignerons de Caractere 2004 Domaine Mas du Bouquet Rhône Red Blend (Vacqueyras) $16. Starts with some matchstick scents, then adds aromas and flavors of coffee and prune. Good if you're looking for dark flavors and dried fruits. Just don't expect something racy or fresh. **83** —*J.C. (11/15/2006)*

Vignerons de Caractere 2004 Les Hautes Restangues Rhône Red Blend (Gigondas) $18. A reliable but unexceptional source of Gigondas and Vacqueyras, this co-op has turned out a decent 2004 Gigondas with plenty of heavy plum and fruitcake flavor but low acidity. Drink now. **84** —*J.C. (11/15/2006)*

Vignerons de Caractere 2004 Privilege des Vignerons Rhône Red Blend (Côtes-du-Rhône) $NA. Just another competently made but ultimately innocuous wine with understated cherry flavors and a thin finish. Good but not exciting. **83** —*J.C. (11/15/2006)*

VIGNOBLES ALAIN JAUME & FILS

Vignobles Alain Jaume & Fils 2005 Clos de Sixte Rhône Red Blend (Lirac) $23. Dense and richly fruited on the nose, but not jammy or simple—there's a healthy dose of spice to add nuance to the plum and black cherry flavors. Ripe tannins impart a creamy texture to the midpalate, while the finish is long and fresh. Nuanced yet powerful; supple yet structured. This is top-notch stuff from a vintage that's looking extremely promising. **92 Editors' Choice** —*J.C. (11/15/2006)*

Vignobles Alain Jaume & Fils 2004 Grande Garrigue Rhône Red Blend (Vacqueyras) $19. All of the Jaume wines emphasize mouthfeel and texture, and this offering is no exception. It's full-bodied, with a creamy texture and supple tannins that highlight raspberry fruit. It's definitely modern in execution, but satisfying rather than superficial. **89** —*J.C. (11/15/2006)*

Vignobles Alain Jaume & Fils 2004 Clos de Sixte Rosé Blend (Lirac) $23.

Pale in color, tending toward copper, with a bright, fruit-driven bouquet of fresh limes and strawberries. Sounds promising? You bet. Then it turns a bit heavy and syrupy on the palate, picking up chalky notes on the finish. Solid, and the extracted style will appeal more to some tasters than others. **86** —*J.C. (11/15/2006)*

VIGNOBLES COSTE

Vignobles Coste 2004 Domaine de la Charité Rhône Red Blend (Côtes-du-Rhône) $13. A bit light, but this modest Côtes-du-Rhône features ample leather, spice, and dried fruit. Supple, with mild tannins on the finish. Drink now. **84** —*J.C. (11/15/2006)*

VIGNOBLES DE FRANCE

Vignobles de France 2000 Cabernet Sauvignon (Vin de Pays d'Oc) $6. Light in body and flavor, this southern France everyday wine has slight aromas of berries, and drinks thin, tasting mostly of alcohol and acids. There's not much to recommend, beyond affordability. **80** —*S.H. (7/1/2001)*

Vignobles de France 2000 Merlot (Vin de Pays d'Oc) $6. Smells earthy and sharp, with a blast of anise and oak. In the mouth, it's tart and rough, with some berry flavors. The finish is tart and scoury. **82** —*S.H. (7/1/2001)*

Vignobles de France 2000 Sauvignon Blanc (Entre-Deux-Mers) $7. Here's everyday drinking at an okay price. Lemony and grapefruity aromas and flavors, with very high acid that scours the palate. It's rough around the edges, and the tartness lasts through the finish. **83** —*S.H. (7/1/2001)*

VILLA SYMPOSIA

Villa Symposia 2003 Red Blend (Coteaux du Languedoc) $NA. Made by Eric Prisette of Château Rol Valentin in Saint-Emilion, this wine is powered with intense fruit, dusty tannins, and sweet, jammy flavors. Big and rich, it is designed for lovers of cult wines, of forward fruit, and powerful tannins. **92** —*R.V. (12/1/2004)*

Villa Symposia 2003 White Blend (Coteaux du Languedoc) $10. A wine made by Eric Prissette of Ch Rol Valentin in Saint-Emilion, this blend of Grenache and Clairette has a distinctly herbal wine with green fruits and a very southern, Mediterranean feel. Reminiscences of the wild rock bushes that litter the landscape make it hot and aromatic. **88 Best Buy** —*R.V. (12/1/2004)*

VINCENT DELAPORTE

Vincent Delaporte 2003 Chavignol Sauvignon Blanc (Sancerre) $26. Talcum powder, orange peel, and a bit of fresh-cut grass make for a pleasant bouquet. Quite forward and fully charged on the palate; there's melon, apple, and lemon as well as some softer peach flavors. Good and lively. **89** *(7/1/2005)*

VINSOBRAISE

Vinsobraise 2005 Cuvée Ambre Rhône Red Blend (Vinsobres) $NA. This is the co-op's entry-level wine, a blend of 60% Grenache and 40% Syrah. The bright raspberry fruit is pretty on the nose, but a bit tart and hard on the finish. **83** —*J.C. (11/15/2006)*

Vinsobraise 2005 Cuvée Grenat Rhône Red Blend (Vinsobres) $NA. Crisp black cherry and raspberry aromas and flavors show a bit of richness and some slightly creamy tannins, but turn a bit hard on the finish. **84** —*J.C. (11/15/2006)*

VITTEAUT-ALBERTI

Vitteaut-Alberti NV Blanc de Blancs Sparkling Blend (Crémant de Bourgogne) $19. A delicious apple and cream-flavored fresh wine with good acidity. Has touches of nuttiness and kiwi fruits, and a fresh, easy finish. **87** —*R.V. (6/1/2006)*

VRANKEN

Vranken 2000 Demoiselle Brut Champagne Blend (Champagne) $100. With its aromas of fresh hay, this is strangely mature for such a young wine. It seems to already have reached the toast and butter stage, leaving most of its fresh fruit behind. It's drinkable, but won't keep. **85** —*R.V. (11/1/2006)*

Vranken NV Demoiselle Brut Rosé Champagne Blend (Champagne) $38. Shaded a light salmon-orange, scented with fresh-cut apple and a hint of green onion, herb, and grass, this wine shows its Pinot side with pretty cherry candy fruit, and a simple, lightly candied finish. **86** —*P.G. (12/15/2002)*

FRANCE

Vranken NV Demoiselle Cuvée 2000 Blanc de Blancs Champagne Blend (Champagne) $30. 88 *(12/15/1999)*

Vranken 1995 Demoiselle Cuvée 21 Champagne Blend (Champagne) $80. With an extra year in bottle, the Cuvée 21 is losing some of its yeastiness and adding suggestions of lemon meringue. It seems rather austere for a '95, a year in which many Champagnes were quite ripe and tropical. The finish seems to fall off quickly. **86** —*P.G. (12/15/2003)*

Vranken NV Demoiselle E.O. Tête de Cuvée Brut Champagne Blend (Champagne) $35. Light in body, but flavorful, with ginger and soy aromas yielding to mixed citrus and berry fruits and dark, meaty notes in the mouth. Crisp and vibrant on the finish. **87** —*J.C. (12/1/2004)*

Vranken NV Demoiselle E.O. Tête de Cuvée Brut Champagne Blend (Champagne) $33. A pleasant Champagne, but not one that sets the world alight. The fruit has a touch of apples, some toast, and a slight sweetness to finish that verges on clumsy. **84** —*R.V. (12/1/2005)*

Vranken NV Demoiselle Grande Cuvée Brut Rosé Champagne Blend (Champagne) $45. A light-boded rosé, but one with a fair amount of complexity. Toasty, autolytic notes run alongside leather, apples, and berries. Good stuff, but with a large bead and short finish. **86** —*J.C. (12/1/2004)*

Vranken NV Demoiselle Grande Cuvée Brut Rosé Champagne Blend (Champagne) $43. Shaded a very pale salmon, scented with fresh apple and herb. It's a very light, elegant wine, with flavors of wild strawberry and tart cherry. **86** —*P.G. (12/15/2003)*

Vranken NV Demoiselle Premier Choix de Cuvées Brut Champagne Blend (Champagne) $30. Much improved over previous efforts, this wine is scented with citrus fruit and rind, and fills the mouth with firm, well-balanced fruit flavors. It does a slow, elegant fade into a crisp, refreshing finish of apple, melon, and kiwi. **88** —*P.G. (12/15/2002)*

Vranken 1996 Demoiselle Tête de Cuvée Champagne Blend (Champagne) $90. With its beautiful white frosted glass bottle, this cuvée stands out, at least in its appearance. To taste, it is full, soft, and certainly mature, with acidity and flavors of ripe quince blending well. Named after a small dragonfly, Demoiselles originated in the vineyard of the Château des Castaignes. It is dominated by Chardonnay, a fine, well-balanced blend. **87** —*R.V. (12/1/2004)*

Vranken 1994 Demoiselle Tête de Cuvée Grand Reserve Brut Champagne Blend (Champagne) $30. Flavors are plain-jane green apple and the barest suggestion of spice. Not much to hang your hat on. **85** —*P.G. (12/15/2002)*

Vranken 1999 Diamant Blanc Champagne Blend (Champagne) $120. This is soft, with ripe peach flavors and some toasty acidity. It's an easy style, perfumed and ready to drink. **88** —*R.V. (11/1/2006)*

Vranken 1998 Diamant Rosé Champagne Blend (Champagne) $135. A very soft, creamy wine that seems to miss the fruit flavors, but still delivers an attractive if somewhat unfocused taste. Drink now. **85** —*R.V. (11/1/2006)*

Vranken NV Tête de Cuvée Tradition Grande Reserve Champagne Blend (Champagne) $22. Crisp and refreshing, with showers of tiny bubbles and a lingering citrus and apple core. Not a big, toasty style, but very clean and bracing. **88 Editors' Choice** —*P.G. (12/15/2003)*

W. GISSELBRECHT

W. Gisselbrecht 2002 Franstein Grand Cru Gewürztraminer (Alsace) $25. After a somewhat understated bouquet that only hints at lychee and floral notes, this wine grows more assertive on the palate, broadening out and adding ripe pear flavors. Finishes a bit soft, with more lychee flavors. **87** —*J.C. (8/1/2006)*

W. Gisselbrecht 2004 Pinot Blanc (Alsace) $11. Starts off slightly nutty, but also boasts pear and honeysuckle scents. It's smooth and easy to drink, with dried spices accenting ripe pears alongside a hint of cashew. Clean, elegant, and citrusy on the finish, even if not overly concentrated. **87 Best Buy** —*J.C. (8/1/2006)*

W. Gisselbrecht 2002 Grand Cru Muenchberg Riesling (Alsace) $21. Minty, herbal notes mark the nose, layered over a base of apples and minerals. Lean and a bit ungenerous at first, the herbal, stony, stridently citrusy flavors open up in time to show a touch of honey on the finish. **85** —*J.C. (8/1/2006)*

WILLM

Willm 2004 Pinot Blanc (Alsace) $12. A plump, medium-bodied white with ripe pear and melon aromas, this is standard fare among Alsace Pinot Blancs. Crisp pear and citrus flavors pick up a hint of anise on the finish. A simple quaffer destined for weeknight dinners at the corner bistro. **85** —*J.C. (8/1/2006)*

Willm 2004 Pinot Gris (Alsace) $15. Attractive white fruits and spice dominate the aromas of this fresh, soft, clean wine. There is a considerable amount of residual sugar to go with the spice and the tropical fruits. Acidity is less evident, but there is a firmness that holds the wine together. **86** —*R.V. (2/1/2006)*

Willm NV Blanc de Noirs Pinot Noir (Crémant d'Alsace) $15. What a solid Alsatian sparkler this is. Some banana and caramel notes richen the nose, while flavors of grapefruit, licorice, and lemon zest dot the palate. The finish is dry and toasty, with quite a bit of the essence of citrus rind and pepper. **87** —*M.S. (6/1/2003)*

WOLFBERGER

Wolfberger NV Sparkling Blend (Crémant d'Alsace) $19. Made by the Eguisheim cooperative, this brut Crémant is soft and creamy, with a mouth-filling mousse. There are flavors of pears and almonds but also a touch of bitterness which spoils the aftertaste. **84** —*R.V. (6/1/2006)*

YANN CHAVE

Yann Chave 2005 Cuvée Traditionnelle Syrah (Crozes-Hermitage) $NA. Nicely balanced and ready for near-term consumption, this dark-purple wine features smoke, herb, and cassis notes. Picks up a bit of charred meat and coffee on the supple, easy-going finish. Drink now. **86** —*J.C. (11/15/2006)*

YVES CUILLERON

Yves Cuilleron 2003 Cuvée Saint-Pierre Marsanne (Saint-Joseph) $44. Cuilleron's use of wood is subtle, leaving just a hint of caramel on this smooth, opulent wine. It is rich, fat, and full-bodied, with flavors more of apricots and white fruits. There's a light touch of acidity, but spices and ripe fruits dominate. **89** —*R.V. (2/1/2005)*

Yves Cuilleron 2003 Le Lombard Marsanne (Saint-Joseph) $40. The ever increasing range of Yves Cuilleron's wines includes a number of single parcel wines, especially from his Saint-Joseph holdings. This wine, from the Lombard vineyard, is typically rich and opulent, packed with spice and ripe fruits. It is full-bodied, and at this young stage still dominated by toast and wood flavors. **90** —*R.V. (2/1/2005)*

Yves Cuilleron 2005 Saint-Pierre Roussanne (Saint-Joseph) $48. Honeyed orange aromas easily handle the oak that's been placed over them. On the palate, this is a rich, round wine that fills the mouth without being heavy, ending with a lengthy flourish of toasty oak. Drink now–2008. **88** —*J.C. (11/15/2006)*

Yves Cuilleron 2004 L'Amarybelle Syrah (Saint-Joseph) $40. Yves Cuilleron's style is not aimed at blockbuster levels of extract. The 2004 L'Amarybelle exemplifies his balanced approach, yielding ample blackberries and spice couched in a medium-weight wine that is very supple, elegant, and persistent. Drink now–2012. **90** —*J.C. (11/15/2006)*

Yves Cuilleron 2002 Les Pierres Sèches Syrah (Saint-Joseph) $32. Hugely perfumed pure Syrah and flavors of black currants and smoky wood, this is a power-packed wine, which shows a great purity of fruit. It has solid, dark tannins as well, which suggest it should age well over 5-10 years. **89** —*R.V. (2/1/2005)*

Yves Cuilleron 2002 Les Serines Syrah (Saint-Joseph) $58. A serious style, big with tannins and dry fruit, this is still packed with perfumed Syrah flavors. It has a dark, brooding structure, with acidity, and pure fruits. This is the pair to the more exuberant L'Amarybelle. **90** —*R.V. (2/1/2005)*

Yves Cuilleron 1999 Terres Sombres Syrah (Côte Rôtie) $65. A bright, modern, deep purple color immediately shows the approach with this wine. The brightness continues to the aromas of red berry fruits and new wood. To taste, it is dominated by sweet new-wood flavors, but has also some deep black currant fruit and big, firm, perfumed tannins. Give it five years and it will be delicious. **91** —*R.V. (6/1/2002)*

FRANCE

Yves Cuilleron 2003 La Petite Côte Viognier (Condrieu) $58. A ripe, spicy wine flavored with spicy wood, honey, and apricots, favoring elegance rather than opulence. It comes from a slope outside the village of Chavanay in the heart of Condrieu. **87** —*R.V. (2/1/2005)*

Yves Cuilleron 2000 Les Chaillets Viognier (Condrieu) $65. This is a balanced, not over-rich Condrieu, with enticing cooked wood flavors. The big attraction, a result partly of the fresh 2000 vintage, is its refreshing acidity, which cuts through the weight and richness and makes it very drinkable. **90** —*R.V. (6/1/2002)*

YVON MAU

Yvon Mau 2002 Yvecourt Bordeaux Blend (Médoc) $15. Quite minty and herbal, but balanced, somewhat by cherry, blackberry and vanilla flavors. A medium-weight quaffer with a fresh, cinnamon note to the finish. **84** —*J.C. (6/1/2005)*

Yvon Mau 2004 Yvecourt Bordeaux White Blend (Bordeaux) $10. This 100% Sauvignon Blanc is a fresh, delicious summer wine. It is light and clean, with flavors of mango and citrus and a flowery feel. Acidity gives it a great lift to the finish. **85** —*R.V. (6/1/2005)*

Yvon Mau 2004 Premius Sauvignon Blanc (Bordeaux) $10. Yvon Mau's branded white Bordeaux is a soft, full-bodied wine, with great citrus flavors. It has a good grassy character, freshness and a long, crisp acidic finish. **85 Best Buy** —*R.V. (6/1/2005)*

ZOÉMIE DE SOUSA

Zoémie De Sousa NV Précieuse Grand Cru Brut Champagne Blend (Champagne) $NA. Zoémie De Sousa is a négociant brand created by Erick de Sousa in 2004 to satisfy world demand for his wines. A 100% Chardonnay from the Côte des Blancs, this deliciously creamy Champagne has lightness, freshness, and great flavors of crisp apples and grapefruit. A bonus with De Sousa Champagnes is the disgorgement date indication—the older, the better. **92** —*R.V. (12/1/2005)*

Germany

German wine labels can be intimidating: long foreign words and ornate gothic script are enough to make many consumers head for a different section of the wine shop. But for the initiated—and you'll qualify after reading this quick primer—German wine labels are among the most descriptive out there.

As on any wine label, you'll find the name of the producer, the vintage, the region, and sometimes the name of the grape.

In addition to the grape-growing region (see below), most labels will show the names of the town and the vineyard in large type, such as Graacher Himmelreich (the town of Graach, Himmelreich vineyard). In much smaller type will be the terms *Qualitätswein bestimmter Anbaugebiete* (often just Qualitätswein, or QbA), indicating a "quality wine," or *Qualitätswein mit Prädikat (QmP)*, denoting a quality wine picked at designated minimum ripeness levels that vary by grape variety and growing region. These ripeness levels will be indicated on the label as follows:

Label on a bottle of Zimmermann-Graeff.

Kabinett The least ripe of the *prädikat* levels, and typically the lightest of a grower's offerings. With their low alcohol levels and touch of sweetness, these wines make ideal picnic quaffs and mouth-watering apéritifs. Most often consumed in their youth, they can last for ten years or more.

Spätlese Literally, "late picked." These grapes are generally only late-picked with respect to those grapes that go into Kabinett or QbA wines. If vinified dry (an increasingly popular style), they can still seem less than optimally ripe. Traditionally made, with some residual sugar left in, they are extremely food friendly. Try them with anything from Asian food to baked ham and roast fowl. Most should be consumed before age twenty.

Auslese Made from "select" bunches of grapes left on the vine until they achieve high sugar readings, these wines often carry a hint or more of botrytis (see Glossary). While some are sweet enough to serve with simple fruit desserts, others are best sipped alone. With age, some of the sugar seems to melt away, yielding wines that can ably partner with roast pork or goose. Thirty-year-old auslesen can smell heavenly, but sometimes fall flat on the palate. Enjoy them on release for their luscious sweet fruit, or cellar for ten to twenty years.

Beerenauslese "Berry select" wines are harvested berry by berry, taking only botrytis-affected fruit. While auslesen are usually sweet, this level of ripeness elevates the wine to the dessert-only category. Hold up to 50 years.

Trockenbeerenauslese These "dried berry select" wines are made from individually harvested, shriveled grapes that have been heavily affected by botrytis. Profoundly sweet and honeyed, their over-the-top viscosity and sweetness can turn off some tasters, while others revel in the complex aromas and flavors.

Eiswein Made from frozen grapes that are at least equivalent in sugar levels to beerenauslese, but which produce wines with much racier levels of acidity. The intense sugars and acids enable these wines to easily endure for decades.

Aside from the ripeness levels denoted by the QmP system, you can expect to see the terms *trocken* ans *halbtrocken* on some labels (their use is optional). *Trocken*, or dry, may be used on wines with fewer than 9g/L residual sugar (less than 0.9 percent); *halbtrocken* (half-dry) refers to wines with between 9 and 18g/L. Given the allowable ranges, these wines may be truly dry or verging on sweet, depending on acid-sugar balance.

In an effort to simplify German labels, a few relatively new terms have cropped up that supplement, replace, or partially replace the traditional labeling system. *Erstes Gewächs* wines, or "first growths," come only from designated sites in the Rheingau. Classic wines must be "harmoniously dry" and must omit references to specific villages or vineyards. Selection wines bear a single-vineyard designation on the label and must be dry.

GERMAN WINE REGIONS

Most of the classic German wine regions are closely identified with river valleys, the slopes of which provide the proper exposure for ripening grapes at this norther latitude. Virtually all of Germany's best wines come from the Riesling grape, but there are several exceptions, like the fine Gewürztraminers from Fitz-Ritter in the Pfalz and Valckenberg in Rheinhessen and the exquisite Rieslaners and Scheurebes from Müeller-Catoir in the Pfalz.

Mosel-Saar-Ruwer The coolest of the German growing regions, and home to Germany's crispest, raciest, and most delicate Rieslings. Green apples, floral notes, and citrus are all likely descriptors, but the best wines also display fine mineral notes that express their slate-driven terroirs.

Rheingau Steep slate slopes and slightly warmer temperatures than found in the Mosel-Saar-Ruwer yield powerful, sturdy wines, with ripe fruit flavors underscored by deep minerality.

Rheinhessen Source for much of Germany's production, quality here can vary from generic *liebfraumilch* to fine single-estate wines.

Nahe This small side valley is the only rival to the Mosel-Saar-Ruwer for elegance and finesse, with Rieslings that balance lightness of body with mineral-based tensile strength.

Pfalz One of Germany's warmest winegrowing regions, with a great diversity of soils, microclimates, and grape varieties. Dry styles, whether made from Riesling or other white grapes, are more common here, and show better balance than those from cooler regions. Spätburgunder (Pinot Noir) is also more successful here than elsewhere.

Wines from other German winegrowing regions, such as the Ahr, Baden, Franken, and Württemberg, are infrequently seen in the United States.

2 BROTHERS

2 Brothers 2003 Big Tattoo White QbA White Blend (Nahe) $9. This bargain-priced white is a blend of two-thirds Riesling and one-third Pinot Blanc. The result is a somewhat simple but clean and tasty wine that mixes apple and pear with citrus. Feels biggish in the mouth but without a lot of depth. Good party option. **84** —*J.C. (5/1/2005)*

A. CHRISTMANN

A. Christmann 1997 Konigsbacher Idig Spätburgunder Pinot Noir (Pfalz) $50. This is an astonishing wine, a German Pinot Noir with power, breed, elegance, and depth. The fruit is varietal and true, firm and velvety, with layers of bacon, smoke, leather, and earth. It is built to age, but already showing great stuff. Thrown into a premier cru Burgundy tasting, this would turn some heads. **93** *(12/31/2001)*

A. Christmann 1999 Konigsbacher Idig Spätlese Trocken Riesling (Pfalz) $40. I dig the vineyard, highlighted in big capital letters on the label, which puts the focus on the terroir. The intense spice in this wine literally seems to explode from the glass, accenting the tart fruit. Intense, concentrated, and strongly chalky/minerally at its core, this is a thrilling wine of great concentration and power. **93 Editors' Choice** —*P.G. (12/31/2001)*

A. Christmann 2004 Königsbacher Idig Spätlese Trocken Riesling (Pfalz) $54. Even if it's a bit weighty, this Riesling remains balanced, thanks to intense minerality and crisp acids. Apricot and peach scents on the nose mingle with wet stones and hints of cinnamon, turning slightly oily and viscous on the palate. Finishes dry and clean. **90** —*J.C. (5/1/2006)*

A. Christmann 2002 Königsbacher Idig Spätlese Trocken Riesling (Pfalz) $48. Heavy and a bit dull, with muted fruit flavors and a short finish. A major disappointment from this normally reliable producer. **83** —*J.C. (11/1/2004)*

A. Christmann 2003 Konigsbacher Idig Trocken Riesling (Pfalz) $60. Quick out of the gate, with vibrant pear, pineapple, and apple aromas, then picks up speed, delivering full-throttle apple and citrus flavors all wrapped around a sturdy mineral core. Nicely balanced and long on the finish, leaving a trail of spice and minerals in its wake. **90** —*J.C. (5/1/2005)*

A. Christmann 2004 QbA Riesling (Pfalz) $21. Light and very crisp, this wine even boasts hints of retained carbon dioxide to further enliven its mouthfeel. Lime and flint-smoke scents yield to citrusy, stony flavors. Would work well as an apéritif. **84** —*J.C. (5/1/2006)*

A. Christmann 2001 QbA Riesling (Pfalz) $17. Lighter and racier than many Pfalz Rieslings, this one leans toward lime and green apple flavors, with a long, minerally finish. **88** —*J.C. (3/1/2003)*

A. Christmann 2002 Qualitätswein Riesling (Pfalz) $20. This dry, minerally wine is medium weight and a bit plump in the mouth, with understated acidity. Hints of apple and lime rear up on the finish, but the focus flavors are mineral oil and earth. **85** —*J.C. (11/1/2004)*

A. Christmann 2003 Ruppertsberger Reiterpfad Auslese Riesling (Pfalz) $40. Rich, unctuous, and low-acid, this Auslese impresses for its weight and sucrosity. Aromas and flavors of marmalade, honey, dried apricot, and baked apple finish long and sweet. Despite the relatively low acids, it should age easily for at least the next decade. **91** —*J.C. (5/1/2005)*

A. Christmann 2001 Ruppertsberger Reiterpfad Auslese Riesling (Pfalz) $32. Starts off funky and stinky, like sweaty socks plus a little pineapple. Thankfully, it's much more enjoyable in the mouth, providing rich sweet fruit balanced by bright acidity. If the initial off-putting aromas go away in time, this could rate as many as three points higher. **89** —*J.C. (3/1/2003)*

A. Christmann 1999 Ruppertsberger Reiterpfad Auslese Riesling (Pfalz) $50. This spectacular boutique estate swings for the fences with this unctuous, botrytised, intensely concentrated auslese. Exceptionally clean, with brilliantly vivid tropical fruit, it's perfectly balanced—powerful yet still elegant. Young and rich, it shows layers of concentrated, ripe fruit that lead to a tightly focused finish. Grab it up while you can. **94 Editors' Choice** —*P.G. (12/31/2001)*

A. Christmann 2003 Trocken Riesling (Pfalz) $20. Light, fresh, and dry, this is one Riesling that avoids the excess weight present in some of the wines from 2003. Smoke, mineral, and cucumber aromas glide easily

into flavors of apple, pear and citrus. Finishes with a lime streak that stands a little apart from the rest of the wine. **85** —*J.C. (5/1/2005)*

ADELSECK

Adelseck NV Juwel Brut Riesling (Nahe) $15. This is very fizzy, with broad, fairly flat flavors, beery and kind of clunky. It's lean, and shows a bit of light citrus and not much else. **84** —*P.G. (12/31/2002)*

ALFRED MERKELBACH

Alfred Merkelbach 2001 Ürziger Würzgarten Auslese Fuder 15 Riesling (Mosel-Saar-Ruwer) $23. Würzgarten translates as "spice garden," and this example displays the powdered cinnamon and clove nuances befitting its name. The fruit is fleshy, almost berry-like, finishing with a citrus tang. Sweet yet lithe, and a steal at the price. **91 Editors' Choice** —*J.C. (3/1/2003)*

Alfred Merkelbach 2001 Ürziger Würzgarten Spätlese Fuder 11 Riesling (Mosel-Saar-Ruwer) $17. Classic apple blossom and dried spice aromas are backed by a core of steely citrus fruits and Granny Smith apples. The tart, lemony finish imbues the wine with great zip and verve, making it seem only lightly sweet, despite what is undoubtedly considerable residual sugar. **90 Editors' Choice** —*J.C. (3/1/2003)*

AM TURM

Am Turm NV Turm-Exquisit Brut Sekt Chardonnay (Pfalz) $25. An elegant Chardonnay-based sekt, with mineral notes accented by a fine bead and apple, citrus, and spice components in pleasant balance. Creamy and smooth in the mouth, with a lingering finish. **88** —*J.C. (6/1/2006)*

Am Turm NV Turm-Exquisit Brut Sekt Pinot Blanc de Noir Pinot Noir (Pfalz) $25. Perfumy on the nose, with scents of lilacs and bubble gum. Light and frothy on the palate, offering soft, slightly sweet flavors reminscent of cotton candy. **82** —*J.C. (6/1/2006)*

Am Turm NV Trocken Sekt Riesling (Pfalz) $21. Clean and freshly fruity, with apple and citrus aromas and flavors leading the way. This is clearly off-dry, but not cloying, instead coming across as soft and easy. **85** —*J.C. (6/1/2006)*

Am Turm NV Turm-Exquisit Brut Sekt Weissburgunder (Pfalz) $23. Light and frothy, this isn't quite as vinous as the Chardonnay sekt from Am-Turm. Instead, there's ginger, lime, and cilantro aromas and wet stone and lime flavors that finish clean and dry. **84** —*J.C. (6/1/2006)*

ARTUR STEINMANN

Artur Steinmann 2004 Sommerhäuser Steinbach Riesling (Franken) $29. Although somewhat pricey, this is a very good wine, marrying a minerally, crushed stone character with ripe tree fruits. Round and slightly honeyed peach and apple flavors are a treat, backed by citrusy notes that extend through the finish. **88** —*J.C. (12/1/2006)*

BALDUIN VON HOVEL

Balduin von Hovel 2002 Estate QbA Riesling (Mosel-Saar-Ruwer) $14. This well-priced offering runs slightly sweet, but the sugar is well-balanced by lime-like acids. Modest apple and pear aromas and flavors are spiced up by hints of cinnamon and citrus. Finishes clean and long. **87** —*J.C. (8/1/2004)*

BALTHASAR RESS

Balthasar Ress 2001 Hattenheimer Engelmannsberg Eiswein Riesling (Rheingau) $160. Something of a disappointment from a top producer. The wine has rustic aromas and flavors which hide the obvious potential. There are hints of quince flavors and acidity, which could well make the wine come good. **85** —*R.V. (1/1/2004)*

Balthasar Ress 2001 Hattenheimer Nussbrunnen Auslese Riesling (Rheingau) $25. This shows the Ress touch, with its freshness and lightness. But the fruit flavors are attractively forward. There are flavors of red currants and white peaches. The texture is crisp, with layers of acidity and with the sweetness of fresh apricots. The aftertaste is fresh and refreshing, despite the sweetness. **89** —*R.V. (1/1/2004)*

Balthasar Ress 2001 Hattenheimer Nussbrunnen Beerenauslese Riesling (Rheingau) $120. From one of the top Hattenheim vineyards, this stunning wine has flavors of sweet apricots and ripe summer fruits overlay botrytis and dryness. The freshness and ripeness of the fruit is what gives this wine its flavor and attraction. **91** —*R.V. (4/1/2003)*

Balthasar Ress 2001 Hattenheimer Nussbrunnen Spätlese Riesling (Rheingau) $18. Aromas of apples and cream make this an instantly enticing wine. It is finely polished, ripe, with some acidity along with flavors of baked apples. A touch of currants completes the entrancing fruit salad flavors of the wine. **91** —*R.V. (1/1/2004)*

Balthasar Ress 2001 Hattenheimer Nussbrunnen Trockenbeerenauslese Riesling (Rheingau) $170. A blockbuster wine, hugely sweet and rich wine with powerful botrytis and honey. There are flavors of honey and acacia and an opulent layer of rich dryness. The underlying acidity gives the wine an enormous potential. **94** —*R.V. (1/1/2004)*

Balthasar Ress 2001 Hattenheimer Schützenhaus Kabinett Riesling (Rheingau) $12. This is the epitome of thirst-quenching fine German wine. It fills your mouth with ripe, crisp apples, with balancing rich sweetness. The aftertaste just goes on and on. **89** —*R.V. (3/1/2003)*

Balthasar Ress 2001 Rüdesheimer Berg Roseneck Auslese Riesling (Rheingau) $23. The Ress wines are made for early drinking, as this fragrant wine shows. It has aromas of cherry blossom, a light, fresh palate with layers of light sweetness overlaying fresh, spring fruit flavors. **90** —*R.V. (1/1/2004)*

Balthasar Ress 2001 Rüdesheimer Berg Rottland Beerenauslese Riesling (Rheingau) $120. Powerful aromas of honeyed botrytis come leaping from the glass. This is a concentrated wine, with layers of dry botrytis flavors and fresh, floral honey. There's plenty of richness, but also a lightness of touch which makes it appealing. **92** —*R.V. (1/1/2004)*

Balthasar Ress 2001 Rüdesheimer Berg Rottland Spätlese Riesling (Rheingau) $19. Surprisingly light on its feet, with a spritely mouthfeel that complements tart lemon-lime and green apple flavors. Finishes long and crisp, wonderfully refreshing. **89** —*J.C. (8/1/2004)*

Balthasar Ress 2001 Rüdesheimer Berg Rottland Trockenbeerenauslese Riesling (Rheingau) $170. This is pure rich botrytis sweetness. The wine is concentrated, hugely rich with enormous power of intense ripeness. There is acidity and a sense of dry structure. Just amazing. **93** —*R.V. (1/1/2004)*

Balthasar Ress 2001 Schloss Reichartshausen Kabinett Riesling (Rheingau) $14. A famed name in German vineyards, the Reichartshausen vineyard is close to the banks of the Rhine. Poised, light, and fresh, with a touch of yeastiness at present, this is a lovely, light wine that will develop with age. **88** —*R.V. (3/1/2003)*

Balthasar Ress 2001 Schloss Reichartshausen Spätlese Riesling (Rheingau) $14. This vineyard, a Balthasar Ress monopoly, has produced wine that balances some dryness with the richness. It is powerful, ripe, and intense, with rich flavors of green plums. **91** —*R.V. (1/1/2004)*

BARON ZU KNYPHAUSEN

Baron zu Knyphausen 2004 Baron K Riesling Kabinett Riesling (Rheingau) $15. Aside from vaguely mineral aromas, this wine is devoid of interest. Slightly pickle-y notes on the palate combine with subdued melon and apple flavors. **80** —*J.C. (7/1/2006)*

Baron zu Knyphausen 2005 Kiedricher Sandgrub Spätlese Riesling (Rheingau) $23. This delicate wine is waif-like and virtually ephemeral on the nose, with subtle scents of mineral, fresh greens, citrus, and apple. In the mouth, it shows similar finesse, striking a fine balance between sweetness and tart green apple and lime flavors. Finishes long, accented by bright citrus notes. **91 Editors' Choice** —*J.C. (12/1/2006)*

Baron zu Knyphausen 2004 Kiedricher Sandgrub Spätlese Riesling (Rheingau) $23. Starts with slate and lime aromas, adding in modest apple notes on the medium-weight palate. Clean and crisp, just lacks a bit of distinction. **85** —*J.C. (5/1/2006)*

Baron zu Knyphausen 2004 QbA Riesling (Rheingau) $14. A soft, fruity wine, Knyphausen's entry-level Riesling has hints of flowers on the nose, then delivers weighty pear and melon flavors. Off-dry. **84** —*J.C. (5/1/2006)*

Baron zu Knyphausen 2001 Charta Kabinett Riesling (Rheingau) $18. This was probably not the best time to be sampling this wine, as it appeared lean and closed at this stage of its evolution. Lime and powdered mineral aromas and flavors finish extremely crisp and unforgiving. Give it another few years to loosen up and this rating may look downright stingy. **85** —*J.C. (5/1/2005)*

Baron zu Knyphausen 2003 Erbacher Steinmorgen Kabinett Riesling (Rheingau) $24. Much better than a bottle previously reviewed, this medium-bodied kabinett bears hints of kerosene and slate on the nose, then opens to reveal lime, apple, and honey flavors. Good length on the finish, but also a hint of bitterness. **87** —*J.C. (5/1/2005)*

Baron zu Knyphausen 2001 Erbacher Steinmorgen Kabinett Riesling (Rheingau) $14. Although interesting and ultimately a good wine, this one's a little tough to warm up to. Start with the slightly musky aromas, then the slightly sour flavors. Finish with tart, malic acidity. But put these pieces all together and the result is a focused, crisp wine that would cut wonderfully through the fat of a pork roast. **86** —*J.C. (3/1/2003)*

Baron zu Knyphausen 2003 Erbacher Steinmorgen Riesling Kabinett Riesling (Rheingau) $17. A minerally wine that gives the impression of wet sand and grapefruit, but there's also a disconcerting edge of volatile acidity. Slightly acetic on the finish. **82** —*J.C. (12/15/2004)*

Baron zu Knyphausen 2001 Erbacher Steinmorgen Spätlese Riesling (Rheingau) $22. Tons of stuff in here: waxy, paraffin-like scents, peach, citrus, and tarragon. Ripe pears and peaches, graced by hints of anise and mint, combine elegantly in this surprisingly light-bodied wine. Racy acidity frames the mouthwatering finish. **91 Editors' Choice** —*J.C. (3/1/2003)*

Baron zu Knyphausen 2001 Hattenheimer Wisselbrunnen Erstes Gewächs Riesling (Rheingau) $28. This dry Riesling is very brisk and clean in the mouth, racing past in a blur of smoky liquid minerals, fresh limes, and ginger. With its impressive cut and firm finish, it would be a fine accompaniment to roast fowl or pork. **89** —*J.C. (3/1/2003)*

Baron zu Knyphausen 2003 Hattenheimer Wisselbrunnen Riesling Auslese Riesling (Rheingau) $51. A bit discordant at this early stage of its evolution, combining rich, oily, minerally flavors with baked apples and pears and picking up bitter, peppery notes on the finish. Love the minerals, hate the finish, and it's not clear where this will go in the future. **85** —*J.C. (12/15/2004)*

Baron zu Knyphausen 2003 Kiedricher Sandgrub Spätlese Riesling (Rheingau) $23. Very floral and lilac-like—almost a little artificial-flower smelling. Lightweight and on the lean side, with apple and lime flavors that finish tart and clean. **84** —*J.C. (5/1/2005)*

Baron zu Knyphausen 2003 QbA Riesling (Rheingau) $13. This is a big, relatively high-alcohol Riesling, tipping the scales at 11.5%. Pear and pineapple flavors are bold, and still sweet enough to stand up to modestly spicy dishes, but it might work best with something substantial like roasted pork. **87** —*J.C. (12/15/2004)*

Baron zu Knyphausen 2001 QbA Riesling (Rheingau) $12. Fresh citrus—grapefruit and lemon—combine with powdered cinnamon and brown slate in this light, pleasantly tart offering that folds in peach and apple flavors on the finish. **86** —*J.C. (3/1/2003)*

BEND IN THE RIVER

Bend In The River 2001 QbA Riesling (Rheinhessen) $10. Basically a négociant-style blend, this is solid stuff, if a bit simple. Soft melon and lemon-lime flavors turn tangy on the finish. **83** —*J.C. (3/1/2003)*

BERNHARD EIFEL

Bernhard Eifel 2003 Longuicher Maximiner Herrenberg Spätlese Riesling (Mosel-Saar-Ruwer) $25. Complex and minerally, with hints of honey and powdered stone layered over ripe apples and peaches. It's medium-weight yet powerfully structured—ample acidity offsets the honeyed fruit. Picks up nuances of allspice and cinnamon on the lingering finish. **90** —*J.C. (11/1/2004)*

Bernhard Eifel 2004 Maximilian E Trocken Riesling (Mosel-Saar-Ruwer) $23. On the full-bodied side, with pear, melon, and white peach aromas and flavors that finish in a flurry of spice and mineral. Has the weight to stand up to roast chicken with Indian seasonings, just don't go too spicy, as this dry wine lacks the sugar to combat the heat. **86** —*J.C. (7/1/2006)*

Bernhard Eifel 2003 Maximillian Classic Qualitätswein Riesling (Mosel-Saar-Ruwer) $16. An intriguing wine, one that balances aromas of peaches and spring flowers with minerally, oily flavors. It's fairly full-bodied, with a suggestion of oiliness to its texture as well. Finishes long and close to dry. **88** —J.C. (11/1/2004)

Bernhard Eifel 2004 Trittenheimer Apotheke Kabinett Halbtrocken Riesling (Mosel-Saar-Ruwer) $22. Starts off with an over-powering scent of burnt matchstick, but with determined swirling, some lemon curd and green apple aromas emerge. It's light to medium in body and rounded rather than crisp, with citrus and apple flavors that turn minerally on the finish. **86** —J.C. (7/1/2006)

BLACK TOWER

Black Tower 2004 Pinot Grigio (Rheinhessen) $8. Clean, with pear, cucumber, and a touch of diesel on the nose. Slightly candied but largely pleasant, with citrus and apple. Finishes with enough zest to make the grade. Lasting notes of grapefruit and lemon-lime are tasty. **86 Best Buy** (2/1/2006)

Black Tower 2003 QbA Riesling (Pfalz) $8. Like its rivals, Black Tower has had to improve its quality to remain competitive. The 2003 Riesling offers scents of ripe pears and anise allied to a honeyed, concentrated mouthfeel. It's a soft, user-friendly introduction to Riesling. **84 Best Buy** —J.C. (12/15/2004)

BLOOM

Bloom 2004 Petals Müller-Thurgau (Mosel-Saar-Ruwer) $7. Broad and sweet on the palate, with peppery aromas and simple melon and citrus flavors. Short, clean finish. **83** —J.C. (7/1/2006)

Bloom 2004 Pinot Gris (Nahe) $7. Rather full-bodied, this inexpensive Pinot Gris is spiked with scents of flowershop greens. Herbal notes accent the off-dry, citrusy fruit. Cleanly made, but short on the finish. **83** —J.C. (7/1/2006)

Bloom 2004 Riesling (Mosel-Saar-Ruwer) $7. This colorfully packaged wine is a little on the sweet side, which creates a broad, mouth-filling texture while at the same time it lacks real depth or complexity. Instead, you get soft pear and melon flavors that finish short. **83** —J.C. (7/1/2006)

Bloom 2005 QbA Riesling (Mosel-Saar-Ruwer) $8. A plump, off-dry Riesling imported in relatively large quantities (30,000 cases), this is a notable re-introduction to the grape variety. Has basic Mosel characteristics of green apple and lime aromas and flavors. There's even a soft, slightly mineral finish. **84 Best Buy** —J.C. (12/1/2006)

BLUE FISH

Blue Fish 2004 Estate Riesling (Pfalz) $10. From a Pfalz cooperative, this is a strong effort at a bargain price. It's not the most complex Riesling, but its aromas of cinnamon-dusted apples are followed by refreshing off-dry flavors of apple and melon. **86 Best Buy** —J.C. (10/1/2005)

BLUE NUN

Blue Nun 2002 Eiswein Riesling (Rheinhessen) $36. This bargain-priced eiswein from a well-known brand fared surprisingly well in our blind tastings, with dense aromas of marmalade and ripe melons and sweet, candied-citrus flavors. A bit big and bulky, but it satisfies the sweet tooth. **88** —J.C. (12/15/2004)

Blue Nun 2001 QbA Riesling (Pfalz) $7. This ain't your father's Blue Nun. This is recognizably a Riesling, boasting modest green apple and pear flavors and a close-to-dry finish. A quantum leap beyond what Blue Nun used to be back in the 1970s and '80s. **84** —J.C. (8/1/2004)

Blue Nun 2003 Qualitätswein Riesling (Rheinhessen) $7. The recent quality improvements at this producer are praiseworthy. There's a brief whiff of sulfur in this wine, but it gives way to lots of fresh, apple-scented fruit. It's light to medium in body and much less sweet than it used to be, picking up hints of red berries on the finish. **85 Best Buy** —J.C. (11/1/2004)

C.H. BERRES

C.H. Berres 1990 Erdener Treppchen Beerenauslese Riesling (Mosel-Saar-Ruwer) $80. It's rare to see older vintages of German wines released straight from the estate cellars, so if you haven't had the chance to sample older German dessert wines, this may be worth a try. It's pretty darn good, too, with lovely clover blossom and honey scents leading into dried apricot and juicy pineapple flavors. Don't expect a thick, syrupy wine—this has a light touch and impeccable balance that might best be paired with foie gras, fresh fruit, or mild cheeses rather than full-blown dessert. Reasonably priced, considering the prädikat and age. **91 Editors' Choice** —J.C. (9/1/2006)

C.H. Berres 2004 Erdener Treppchen Kabinett Riesling (Mosel-Saar-Ruwer) $21. A very good kabinett, one that effortlessly combines aromas of fresh greens, mixed citrus, and green apples in a relatively lightweight package. Apple, citrus, and melon flavors turn slightly honeyed on the finish, while remaining crisp enough to be refreshing. **88** —J.C. (7/1/2006)

C.H. Berres 2004 Impulse (Gold) QbA Riesling (Mosel-Saar-Ruwer) $14. This fresh, medium-bodied Riesling is clean and fruity, combining flavors of ripe pears and white peaches with hints of apple and slate. **86** —J.C. (5/1/2006)

C.H. Berres 2004 Impulse (Sapphire) QbA Riesling (Mosel-Saar-Ruwer) $14. A touch drier than the Gold label Impulse Riesling previously reviewed, this wine has a fine, almost filigreed bouquet of finely intertwined lime and mineral notes accented by green plum. Lean and elegant, with a crisp finish and good length. **87** —J.C. (12/1/2006)

C.H. Berres 2004 Ürziger Goldwingert Auslese Riesling (Mosel-Saar-Ruwer) $48. A nicely balanced auslese that's not too rich or sweet, marrying ripe apples and pears with floral notes, tropical fruit, and a healthy dose of crushed stone minerality. Finishes with flourishes of pineapple and citrus. **90** —J.C. (5/1/2006)

CARL EHRHARD

Carl Ehrhard 2004 Rüdesheimer Kabinett Feinherb Riesling (Rheingau) $14. Although not an officially defined label term, feinherb seems to be gaining in usage to describe a wine that's drier than the traditional fruchtig style, but not as severe as a halbtrocken or trocken. This one is light and fresh, with minerally, spicy notes layered over green apple and citrus. Finishes crisp and nearly dry. **86** —J.C. (7/1/2006)

CARL GRAFF

Carl Graff 2003 Erdener Pralat Auslese Riesling (Mosel-Saar-Ruwer) $25. Light in body but intense in flavor, with delicately floral aromas but bold pineapple, brown sugar, and cinnamon flavors. Ermst Loosen is now consulting for this label, and the positive results show. **89** —J.C. (5/1/2005)

Carl Graff 2001 Erdener Prälat Auslese Riesling (Mosel-Saar-Ruwer) $14. A light, racy auslese that coasts on taut, citrusy flavors, finishing long and juicy. It's lighter than most auslesen, but very focused and pretty. A pleasant surprise from this producer, and at a great price. **88 Best Buy** —J.C. (3/1/2003)

Carl Graff 2001 Erdener Treppchen Spätlese Riesling (Mosel-Saar-Ruwer) $11. Once past some sulfur on the nose, this wine opens up to show some delicate lime and green apple flavors. Finishes a bit short and lacking intensity, but very pretty, even if not terribly concentrated. **85** —J.C. (3/1/2003)

Carl Graff 2003 Graacher Himmelreich Spätlese Riesling (Mosel-Saar-Ruwer) $15. Abundant apple and peach aromas presage the rush of fleshy fruit that cascades across the palate. There's a hint of unreleased CO2 to help enliven the relatively low-acid mouthfeel, and a bit of lime on the finish to help balance things out further. **86** —J.C. (5/1/2005)

Carl Graff 2001 Graacher Himmelreich Spätlese Riesling (Mosel-Saar-Ruwer) $12. If you love the deep, earthy petroleum notes that Riesling can sometimes develop, you'll like this wine a lot. There's so much of that here—like the aroma of home heating oil—that it overwhelms the baked Golden Delicious apples that should have been the core of this wine. Still, if you like that style…. **85** —J.C. (3/1/2003)

Carl Graff 2001 Kabinett Riesling (Mosel-Saar-Ruwer) $8. A regional blend that has much of its character overwhelmed by matchstick aromas. Faint green apple and citrus flavors are pleasant, but extremely light and lacking intensity. **83** —J.C. (1/1/2004)

Carl Graff 2001 Piesporter Goldtropfchen Kabinett Riesling (Mosel-Saar-Ruwer) $12. Lean and tart, showing solid lime and green apple aromas and flavors underneath a mild sulfur funk that should dissipate with additional bottle age. Give it some time in a decanter before serving if you open it in the next few months. **85** —*J.C. (3/1/2003)*

Carl Graff 2001 Piesporter Goldtropfchen Spätlese Riesling (Mosel-Saar-Ruwer) $15. Like many of the Graff wines, this one is on the light side, but does feature some pretty aromas of talcum powder, chalk dust, and fresh limes. Citrusy flavors turn to grapefruit on the mildly peppery finish. **86** —*J.C. (3/1/2003)*

Carl Graff 2001 Piesporter Michelsberg Auslese Riesling (Mosel-Saar-Ruwer) $14. Fairly soft and sweet, featuring Golden Delicious apples and cinnamon. Could use more cut and focus, but it's still an enjoyable drink for those who like them sweet. **86** —*J.C. (3/1/2003)*

Carl Graff 2001 QbA Riesling (Mosel-Saar-Ruwer) $7. Smells tart and slightly underripe, like grapefruit, with a bit of sulfur mixed in for good measure, then turns sweet and dull on the palate, finishing short. Standard stuff. **82** —*J.C. (1/1/2004)*

Carl Graff 2003 Riesling Kabinett Riesling (Mosel-Saar-Ruwer) $11. A simple, lightweight Riesling that starts off a bit sulfury, then reveals tart flavors of green apples and grapefruit. Decent value, worth trying as an apéritif. **85** —*J.C. (12/15/2004)*

Carl Graff 2001 Urziger Wurzgarten Auslese Riesling (Mosel-Saar-Ruwer) $17. Hey, the price is right for this serviceable auslese that smells a bit diesely and delivers plenty of ripe pear and fruit cocktail flavors. Blends in some green apple and citrus as well, but seems a bit hollow in the midpalate. **84** —*J.C. (3/1/2003)*

Carl Graff 2003 Ürziger Würzgarten Auslese Riesling (Mosel-Saar-Ruwer) $22. Lean and a bit ungenerous, especially for a 2003. Tart apple and citrus aromas and flavors shed some early sulfur but never really blossom, finishing hard. **84** —*J.C. (5/1/2005)*

Carl Graff 2003 Ürziger Würzgarten Spätlese Riesling (Mosel-Saar-Ruwer) $19. Sweet and light-weight, with typical floral, green apple, and peach aromas and flavors. Lime flavors kick in on the finish, which seem a bit insubstantial and lacking depth. A superficial charmer that's easy to drink over the next few years—just don't expect a long-term relationship. **85** —*J.C. (5/1/2005)*

Carl Graff 2001 Wehlener Sonnenuhr Spätlese Riesling (Mosel-Saar-Ruwer) $12. Verges on being overly light, but in the end it delivers enough finely wrought flavor to be worthy of recommendation. Combines sweet sugary notes with leafy greens and floral elements, underlined by modest lime accents. **87 Best Buy** —*J.C. (3/1/2003)*

CARL LOEWEN

Carl Loewen 2004 Leiwener Klostergarten Kabinett Riesling (Mosel-Saar-Ruwer) $19. In what could prove to be a breakout vintage for Loewen, the Leiwener Klostergarten Kabinett is a star. Heavily mineral on the nose, with some characteristic leesy notes, it then bursts on the palate with concentrated flavors of apple, pear, and lime, all underscored by cool minerality. Finishes long and citrusy. **91 Editors' Choice** —*J.C. (10/1/2005)*

Carl Loewen 2001 Thörnicher Ritsch Spätlese Riesling (Mosel-Saar-Ruwer) $20. The vineyard site's black slate speaks loudly in this wine, blaring forth smoky, mineral notes layered over yellow plums, peaches and citrus fruits. Folds in honey notes on the long, lingering finish. **90 Editors' Choice** —*J.C. (3/1/2003)*

CARL SCHMITT-WAGNER

Carl Schmitt-Wagner 2001 Longuicher Maximiner Herrenberg Auslese Riesling (Mosel-Saar-Ruwer) $26. For such a ripe wine, with its heaping bowls of tropical fruit, it is surprisingly light-bodied and elegant—not an easy trick to turn. The long, chalky-mineral finish adds an intellectual note to this hedonistic offering. **90** —*J.C. (3/1/2003)*

Carl Schmitt-Wagner 2001 Longuicher Maximiner Herrenberg Spätlese Riesling (Mosel-Saar-Ruwer) $19. This delicate wine showcases Riesling's feminine, floral side. Could those be lilacs? Green apple and citrus flavors linger seductively on the finish. **89** —*J.C. (3/1/2003)*

CASTELL

Castell 2004 Frenzy Müller-Thurgau Trocken Müller-Thurgau (Franken) $12. One of the better M-T's to come our way, this offering from Castell is virtually dry, with exotic orange-blossom and spice notes that give it plenty of character. It's plump and fleshy, yet still fresh on the finish. **86** —*J.C. (7/1/2006)*

Castell 2003 Riesling QbA Trocken Riesling (Franken) $14. Starts with smoky quartz notes that beautifully accent pear and cinnamon scents, then reveals dried spices and powdered minerals on the palate, enveloped in honeyed fruit. Despite the sweet-sounding descriptors, this wine is clean, crisp, and refreshingly dry on the finish. Drink now–2007. **89 Best Buy** —*J.C. (12/15/2004)*

CLUSSERATH-WEILER

Clusserath-Weiler 2004 HC Riesling QbA Riesling (Mosel-Saar-Ruwer) $21. Smells lovely, sending images of cinnamon-dusted baked apples strengthened by a minerally backbone through my mind. Yet if it's not fully dry, then it's close, a jolt of dissonance from what's expected. Ends on a note of under-ripe melon. **86** —*J.C. (2/1/2006)*

Clusserath-Weiler 2004 Trittenheimer Apotheke Auslese 375 ml Riesling (Mosel-Saar-Ruwer) $42. A step up from the 2003 offerings from this estate, with clean, vibrant aromas of vanilla, melons, and white peaches. Flavors are similar, with just enough citrus to balance the sweetness. It's plump, yet spry and light on its feet—an attractive combination. **90** —*J.C. (9/1/2006)*

Clusserath-Weiler 2003 Trittenheimer Apotheke Spätlese Riesling (Mosel-Saar-Ruwer) $25. Most of the Clüsserath-Weiler wines had elevated levels of sulfur (burnt matchstick aromas) on the nose, which depressed their ratings. A shame, as otherwise the wines seemed to be of generally high quality. This one was no exception, with modest apple and pear scents partially overpowered, while the sulfur also seemed to detract from the finish, muting it. **85** —*J.C. (11/1/2004)*

Clusserath-Weiler 2003 Trittenheimer Apotheke Spätlese Riesling (Mosel-Saar-Ruwer) $33. This wine is impenetrably stinky at first, giving off lots of funky matchstick aromas. It does come around in time, with viscous, sweet nectarine flavors that finish soft. There's a hint of grapefruit, but not enough to give this wine a racy edge. **86** —*J.C. (11/1/2004)*

Clusserath-Weiler 2003 Trittenheimer Apotheke Spätlese Trocken Riesling (Mosel-Saar-Ruwer) $24. Smoke, pear, and quince aromas on the nose, then the wine shows less fruit on the palate. It's a sip of liquid rocks—a bit hard to get at—without the normal friendliness of young Riesling, yet possessed of a certain intellectual pleasure. **86** —*J.C. (11/1/2004)*

Clusserath-Weiler 2005 Trittenheimer Apotheke Spätlese Riesling (Mosel-Saar-Ruwer) $31. Sweet and full-bodied, this is packed with apple, pear, and quince flavors. Initial leesy notes slowly blow off, so decant prior to serving, or age 5–7 years. This is lush rather than classically racy, but still very enjoyable. **89** —*J.C. (12/1/2006)*

DEINHARD

Deinhard 2002 Hanns Christof Liebfraumilch (Rheinhessen) $6. Smells good, with fresh lime zest notes playing a leading role, then turns floral and almost insubstantial in the mouth. Finishes with more citrusy flavors of tangerine and grapefruit. **83** —*J.C. (8/1/2004)*

Deinhard 2003 Classic Pinot Blanc (Pfalz) $8. Although this doesn't exhibit the orange and tangerine notes often characteristic of Pinot Blanc, it is a lightweight, refreshing wine. Starts off with scents of earth and clay, then shows flavors of green apples and under-ripe melons before finishing with some zesty grapefruit. Probably best as an apéritif. **84 Best Buy** —*J.C. (11/1/2004)*

Deinhard 2003 Classic Riesling (Rheinhessen) $8. Fresh and slightly gingery on the nose, but dominated by lemons and limes. Simple citrus and earth flavors are light, tart, and refreshing. **84 Best Buy** —*J.C. (11/1/2004)*

Deinhard 2002 Classic Riesling (Rheinhessen) $8. Earthy and tart, with modest citrus fruit competing with damp clay and hints of chalk dust. **82** —*J.C. (8/1/2004)*

Deinhard 2002 Green Label QbA Riesling (Mosel-Saar-Ruwer) $6. This crisp lightweight is a perfect patio sipper for this summer—tart, mouthwatering, and refreshing. Green apple and grapefruit flavors finish short, but look at the price. **84 Best Buy** —*J.C. (8/1/2004)*

Deinhard 2003 Green Label Qualitätswein Riesling (Mosel-Saar-Ruwer) $6. Rieslings drawn from Bereich Bernkastel, as this one is, are often floral, but this one is oddly floral, with a plasticy note to the flavors of apple and pear. **82** —*J.C. (11/1/2004)*

Deinhard 2004 Piesporter QbA Riesling (Mosel-Saar-Ruwer) $8. Founded in 1794, Deinhard is an old merchant house—what the French would call a négociant—that markets a wide array of wines. The company's 1808 price list offered 89 different Rhine and Mosel wines, but that's been at least somewhat shortened in recent years. No, it's not that intense, nor does it show a lot of minerality, but this wine ably shows off Mosel Riesling's array of fruity, off-dry flavors, ranging from peach and pear to apple, pineapple, and lime. Crisp and clean on the finish. **86 Best Buy** —*J.C. (5/1/2006)*

Deinhard 2002 Piesporter QbA Riesling (Mosel-Saar-Ruwer) $9. Snappy and fresh, this is a large-production German Riesling that manages to rise above mediocrity. You'll find green apple and lime flavors, while a touch of red berries make an interesting counterpoint. Firm acidity on the finish makes the wine seem almost dry, despite some residual sugar. **86 Best Buy** —*J.C. (8/1/2004)*

Deinhard 2003 Piesporter Qualitätswein Riesling (Mosel-Saar-Ruwer) $9. Classic lime, slate, and green apple aromas and flavors signal this budget-priced offering's origin. It's light and delicate, just as it should be; the only knock on this wine is its soft, short finish. Still, it's a fine example of how good some of the lower-priced wines can be in 2003. **85 Best Buy** —*J.C. (11/1/2004)*

Deinhard NV Cabinet Traditions-Cuvée Sekt Trocken Sparkling Blend (Germany) $8. Fruity and berryish on the nose, with an exuberant, almost aggressive mouthfeel. There's a hint of toast as well, plus some fruity flavors that make this a decent party pour. **84 Best Buy** —*J.C. (12/31/2004)*

Deinhard NV Feiner Fruchtiger Sekt Halbtrocken Sparkling Blend (Germany) $9. A bit sweet, with large bubbles and floral and toast aromas and flavors. Cleanly made. **83** —*J.C. (12/31/2004)*

Deinhard NV Lila Riesling Brut Sekt Sparkling Blend (Germany) $11. Green apples and limes mark the nose, while the palate shows its Riesling roots in hints of diesel; fresh fruit flavors just peek through. The mouthfeel is slightly creamy, while the wine's finish is crisp and fresh. **86 Best Buy** —*J.C. (12/31/2004)*

Deinhard NV Rose de Blanc et Noir Feiner Fruchtiger Sekt Halbtrocken Sparkling Blend (Germany) $8. Hints of toast and citrus on the nose give way to frankly sweet strawberry flavors. Yes, it's meant to be somewhat sweet, but this is verging on being unbalanced. **82** —*J.C. (12/31/2004)*

DES GRAFEN NEIPPERG

Des Grafen Neipperg 2001 Neipperger Schlossberg Kabinett Trocken Riesling (Württemberg) $14. Simple green apple and citrus flavors finish short and crisp, picking up some chalky notes. Light and dry, with a slightly bitter edge. **83** —*J.C. (1/1/2004)*

Des Grafen Neipperg 2001 Hemma QbA White Blend (Württemberg) $17. Oyster wine from Germany? That's the appropriate pairing for this lean, green wine that ends slightly bitter and pithy. **82** —*J.C. (1/1/2004)*

DOMDECHANT WERNER

Domdechant Werner 2002 Hochheim Classic Riesling (Rheingau) $17. Classic is a relatively new term being adopted by some German producers to describe harmoniously dry wines from traditional grape varieties. It's also supposed to have a quality connotation, and this wine bears that out. Smoky, minerally aromas presage flavors of green apples layered over a foundation of minerals. Finishes tart, crisp, and refreshing. **89** —*J.C. (8/1/2004)*

Domdechant Werner 2002 Hochheim Domdechaney QbA Erstes Gewachs Riesling (Rheingau) $44. This remarkable (almost) dry Riesling is big and broad-shouldered, with intense, oily aromas paired with hints of Golden Delicious apples. It seems to expand in the mouth, flooding the senses with oily, minerally flavors that linger on the finish. **91** —*J.C. (8/1/2004)*

Domdechant Werner 2002 Hochheimer Domdechaney Auslese Riesling (Rheingau) $49. This is a solid wine, offering hints of honeyed richness to go with sweet flavors of dried fruits (pineapple, apricot). Its brassy color is darker than that of most young auslesen, so it might be best to drink this over the next few years rather than laying it down for an extended length of time. **88** —*J.C. (8/1/2004)*

Domdechant Werner 1999 Hochheimer Domdechaney Auslese Riesling (Rheingau) $35. Delicious and bold, the bouquet of this Auslese is a melange of orange blossom, honey, cinnamon—even banana aromas. Rich, but not cloyingly sweet, orange, honey, and mango flavors show on the palate, and the velvety smooth texture wears them well. Turns a bit drier and towards mild citrus flavors on the finish. Best now through 2004. **90** *(8/1/2001)*

Domdechant Werner 1999 Hochheimer Domdechaney Beerenauslese Riesling (Rheingau) $126. Simply gorgeous aromas of honey, apricots, and tangerines are echoed on the palate, where the wine is full, rich, and sweet without seeming overly heavy. The moderate levels of acidity provide adequate balance now, but may prove too low for extended aging; that's okay, because it's so good now. Probably best over the next 5–10 years. **92** *(8/1/2001)*

Domdechant Werner 2004 Hochheimer Domdechaney Spätlese Riesling (Rheingau) $27. Shows the bright, vibrant character of the vintage, marrying zesty lime notes with hints of minerals, sweet pineapple, and green apple. Fresh and clean, with a mouth-watering finish that leaves you wanting another sip. **90** —*J.C. (9/1/2006)*

Domdechant Werner 2003 Hochheimer Domdechaney Spätlese Riesling (Rheingau) $29. There's a bit of sulfur stink still lurking in the background of this wine, looming over the apple and citrus scents that should emerge more strongly in another six months or so. Lightweight and fresh, with surprising energy and drive. **86** —*J.C. (5/1/2005)*

Domdechant Werner 2001 Hochheimer Domdechaney Spätlese Riesling (Rheingau) $21. A stunningly intense wine, with ripe fruit with perfectly balanced crisp acidity. At the moment, it is certainly young, but Werner estate, long-established in Hochheim, has made a wine that will develop slowly and beautifully over many years. **92** —*R.V. (1/1/2004)*

Domdechant Werner 1999 Hochheimer Domdechaney Spätlese Riesling (Rheingau) $24. Floral and pineapple aromas and a touch of musky spice on the nose open this medium-weight Riesling. Shows a slightly lean profile, pear/apple and lemon flavors and a decent acid spine. Turns sharper on the back end with pepper, spice, and very tart citrus and green apple notes. **87** *(8/1/2001)*

Domdechant Werner 2001 Hochheimer Domdechaney Spätlese Trocken Riesling (Rheingau) $23. The dryness gives this wine a hard edge which makes it difficult to enjoy. But there is concentrated fruit with flavors of almonds and green fruits and a layer of yeastiness and pepperiness. It should develop over the next few years. **85** —*R.V. (1/1/2004)*

Domdechant Werner 1999 Hochheimer Domdechaney Trockenbeerenauslese Riesling (Rheingau) $227. Similar in aromatics and flavor to Werner's slightly less weighty BA, the TBA features musky scents reminiscent of tropical flowers as well as tremendous weight and texture. Molasses and caramel notes reverberate on the long finish. **91** *(8/1/2001)*

Domdechant Werner 2004 Hochheimer Hölle Kabinett Riesling (Rheingau) $17. Seems sweet beyond the normal bounds of kabinett, but despite the high sugar levels, there's also a dry, dusty stoniness to the finish that provides a sense of balance. Crushed stone, green apple, and lime scents lead the way, followed by riper apple, pear, and honey flavors on the medium-weight palate. A candidate to match with spicy or slightly sweet Asian dishes. **88** —*J.C. (7/1/2006)*

Domdechant Werner 2003 Hochheimer Hölle Kabinett Riesling (Rheingau) $19. Typical in some ways for 2003, this is a soft, cuddly Riesling that boasts modest pear, apple, and melon flavors. Plump and easy to drink over the short term. **86** —*J.C. (5/1/2005)*

Domdechant Werner 2002 Hochheimer Hölle Kabinett Riesling (Rheingau) $19. A solid kabinett with bright scents of pineapple that seem to peter out a bit in the glass, replaced by melon and apple flavors that carry this medium-weight wine across the palate. **85** —*J.C. (8/1/2004)*

Domdechant Werner 2001 Hochheimer Hölle Kabinett Riesling (Rheingau) $12. A wine with sweet, soft fruit, with rich, creamy flavors and delicious light acidity. The wine has already developed, and it looks as though it will age fast. For now, though, it is a delicious wine. **88** —R.V. (1/1/2004)

Domdechant Werner 1999 Hochheimer Hölle Kabinett Riesling (Rheingau) $14. Smells crisp and steely, full of limes and green apples, then turns softer on the palate where ripe pears and MacIntosh apples take over. It's delicately off-dry, balanced by adequate acidity that extends through the finish. **88** (8/1/2001)

Domdechant Werner 2003 Hochheimer Hölle Kabinett Trocken Riesling (Rheingau) $19. Light and very crisp, with modest apple and citrus flavors. A whiff of sulfur on the nose distracts a bit, but the overall emphasis is on zesty limes. **84** —J.C. (5/1/2005)

Domdechant Werner 1999 Hochheimer Hölle Kabinett trocken Riesling (Rheingau) $14. A full bouquet with tropical fruit, floral notes, and vanilla accents opens this very friendly and lively Riesling. This offers a lot—bright and pretty orange and lime flavors and a brisk, zingy mouthfeel from the citrusy fruit and the underlying acidity. The full finish features spicy tarragon notes on top of the fruit. More Americans should try with wines like this. **89 Best Buy** (8/1/2001)

Domdechant Werner 2003 Hochheimer Kirchenstück Auslese Riesling (Rheingau) $46. This sweet wine even smells honeyed, with notes of clover blossom and bergamot adding complexity. Citrus, melon, and peach flavors are carried across the palate by a fairly full-bodied wine that finishes long, but a little sticky-sweet. **89** —J.C. (2/1/2006)

Domdechant Werner 2002 Hochheimer Kirchenstück Auslese Riesling (Rheingau) $49. Filled with aromas and flavors of pineapple and strawberries, this slightly viscous offering is fairly rich and mouth-coating, plump and satisfying. **89** —J.C. (8/1/2004)

Domdechant Werner 2003 Hochheimer Kirchenstück Beerenauslese 375 ml Riesling (Rheingau) $300. Wines like this are why 2003 has generated such buzz across Germany. Thick and oily-textured, and filled with flavors of super-ripe pears, peaches, and dried apricots, this is a monumental dessert wine. Yes, it's decadently rich, but it also boasts sufficient acidity to keep it from becoming cloying. Finishes long, with lingering notes of tropical fruit and citrus. One for the ages. **96 Cellar Selection** —J.C. (5/1/2005)

Domdechant Werner 2002 Hochheimer Kirchenstück Eiswein Riesling (Rheingau) $149. This thick, viscous wine boasts hints of dried apricot and orange marmalade surrounding a core of crunchy pineapple. Lush, rich, and sweet, picking up notes of honey on the long finish. **91** —J.C. (8/1/2004)

Domdechant Werner 2001 Hochheimer Kirchenstück Eiswein Riesling (Rheingau) $126. In keeping with this estate's reputation for elegance, this eiswein is finely poised, with some delicious acidity alongside the flavors of ripe quince jelly. It is certainly intense, but this is balanced by the complex layers of crisp, dry honey and acidity. **92** —R.V. (1/1/2004)

Domdechant Werner 1999 Hochheimer Kirchenstück Eiswein Riesling (Rheingau) $126. Vanilla and crème brûlée aromas add complexity to intensely sweet orange-marmalade and apricot aromas and flavors. Focused, with good balancing acidity that leaves a clean citrusy finish. **89** (8/1/2001)

Domdechant Werner 2002 Hochheimer Kirchenstück QbA Erstes Gewachs Riesling (Rheingau) $44. Hints of smoke and powdered quartz add nuance to aromas of rainwater and green apple. It's an austere, aristocratic blend of hard minerals and tart apples barely softened by notes of softer, rounder fruits—peaches come to mind. **89** —J.C. (8/1/2004)

Domdechant Werner 2003 Hochheimer Kirchenstück Spätlese Riesling (Rheingau) $29. Soft, lush, and voluptuous, this is not the raciest German Riesling you're likely to find, but it is easy to like. Dried apricot, apple, and pineapple scents pick up additional citrus notes on the mid-palate. Drink now. **88** —J.C. (5/1/2005)

Domdechant Werner 2002 Hochheimer Kirchenstück Spätlese Riesling (Rheingau) $30. Sweet and relatively low in acidity, this spätlese boasts a lilac-like, perfumy nose followed by simple, fruit-juicy flavors. **84** —J.C. (8/1/2004)

Domdechant Werner 1999 Hochheimer Kirchenstück Spätlese Riesling (Rheingau) $22. Smells ripe, with honey and pear aromas that fold in apples and tangerines. The apples and pears continue on the palate, accented by baking spices—cinnamon, clove, and allspice or nutmeg. The acidity is low, making this a candidate to drink now with your favorite Asian cuisine. **87** (8/1/2001)

Domdechant Werner 2003 Hochheimer Kirchenstuck Spätlese Trocken Riesling (Rheingau) $29. Subdued on the nose, where the sulfur is still very much in evidence. Pear and lemon fruit on the palate, gliding into a finish that seems a bit hard, with acids that jut out, interrupting the smooth flow of the wine. **84** —J.C. (5/1/2005)

Domdechant Werner 1999 Hochheimer Kirchenstück Spätlese Trocken Riesling (Rheingau) $20. Scents of soft ripe pears are complemented by citrus and floral nuances. Turns spicy and lean on the palate, with flavors of cinnamon and clove making for an almost dusty mouthful that's even a bit austere. **87** (8/1/2001)

Domdechant Werner 2004 Hochheimer Stein Kabinett Halbtrocken Riesling (Rheingau) $17. A very good halbtrocken, with fruit aromas and flavors reminiscent of tangerines and peaches layered over a minerally bedrock. Its medium weight and long, mouth-watering finish give it extra appeal. **87** —J.C. (7/1/2006)

DÖNNHOFF

Dönnhoff 2001 Schlossböckelheimer Kupfergrube Spätlese Riesling (Nahe) $42. Helmut Dönnhoff is at the top of his game. From its explosive nose of powdered quartz and fresh apple skin through the flavors of apple, peach, melon, and mineral, this wine has it all. It's medium-weight—even a bit full-bodied for Riesling—but impeccably balanced. Great length completes the package. Simply put, a tour de force. **93** —J.C. (3/1/2003)

DR. BÜRKLIN-WOLF

Dr. Bürklin-Wolf 1999 Bürklin Estate Red Blend (Pfalz) $20. This is a proprietary blend of grapes that may include Lemberger, Dornfelder, Cabernet, Merlot, and Sangiovese. It surprises, with handsome and ripe loganberry and black cherry fruit offset by dark, tarry, smoky barrel flavors with a chocolatey under-current. There's brisk acidity, but the fruit is ripe, clean, and interesting, and proves that in the right hands red grapes can work in Germany's warmer Pfalz region. **88** —P.G. (8/1/2001)

Dr. Bürklin-Wolf 2001 Bürklin Estate Riesling (Pfalz) $16. Rich and a bit sweet, this is an atypically powerful wine. Full-bodied, powerful flavors of ripe apples and green plums are balanced by citrusy acids; complexity is added by notes of menthol and floral greens. **90 Editors' Choice** —J.C. (3/1/2003)

Dr. Bürklin-Wolf 1999 Bürklin Estate Riesling (Pfalz) $15. This has good, juicy fruit, with green apples, green berries, and limes leading the way. There's just a hint of white peaches too, and a full, spicy mouthfeel. It gathers strength in the finish, with hints of anise and herb. **87** —P.G. (8/1/2001)

Dr. Bürklin-Wolf 2002 Bürklin Estate Qualitätswein Riesling (Pfalz) $20. Smoky and earthy, with flavors of damp clay and just hints of pear and apple fruit. Lacks the acidity to make the flavors sing. **83** —J.C. (11/1/2004)

Dr. Bürklin-Wolf 2004 Deidesheimer Hohenmorgen GC Fass 23 QbA Riesling (Pfalz) $50. Starts slow, gradually ramping up its complexity and concentration as it warms in the glass, eventually opening up to show scents of diesel and peach pit alongside flavors of lime, peach, and melon. Throughout, there's a strong sensation of minerality, ending on a crisp, mouth-watering note. **91** —J.C. (5/1/2006)

Dr. Bürklin-Wolf 2003 Estate QbA Riesling (Pfalz) $19. Starts with ripe apple and white peach scents that gravitate toward green apple and vanilla flavors on the palate. Medium- to full-bodied, with a mildly spicy-peppery finish. **85** —J.C. (5/1/2005)

Dr. Bürklin-Wolf 2004 Forster Kirchenstück GC Riesling QbA Trocken Riesling (Pfalz) $80. Unique and idiosyncratic, this extravagantly priced wine certainly makes a statement. Smoky, mineral, and spice scents are layered over tropical fruits that range from mango to lychee. Clean and crisp on the finish, without the same length as Bürklin-Wolf's Deidesheimer Hohenmorgen. **88** —*J.C. (5/1/2006)*

Dr. Bürklin-Wolf 2004 Old Vines Estate Riesling (Pfalz) $19. Rather big and full-bodied (13% alcohol), but also full-flavored, combining honey-eyed orange peel with ripe melon notes and a dry-ish, spicy finish. **86** —*J.C. (7/1/2006)*

Dr. Bürklin-Wolf 2002 Qualitätswein Riesling (Pfalz) $12. Starts with sparkling aromas of fresh limes, hints of ripe apple, and honey, but loses it on the palate, where it's fat and lacking in acidity. Finishes short. **83** —*J.C. (11/1/2004)*

Dr. Bürklin-Wolf 2002 Ruppertsberger Gaisbohl Qualitätswein Trocken Riesling (Pfalz) $48. Plump and concentrated, but it doesn't have the same raw power as Bürklin-Wolf's Rechbächel bottling. What it does have is finely defined fruit that ranges from Anjou pears to Golden Delicious apples, all tinged with honey and spice. **88** —*J.C. (11/1/2004)*

Dr. Bürklin-Wolf 1998 Ruppertsberger Gaisbohl Spätlese Trocken Riesling (Pfalz) $37. This 14-acre monopole is Dr. B-W's top property. The wine has big fruit, but is still tight, with interlaced layers of pineapple, lime, and mineral with a waxy note. Extremely concentrated and rich, with a slightly viscous mouthfeel, it's a baby that's impressive for its vigor, density and superbly-balanced weight. Talk about structure—after two days, it showed even more vigor, power and depth than when it was first tasted. **92 Cellar Selection** *(8/1/2001)*

Dr. Bürklin-Wolf 2003 Ruppertsberger Gaisböhl Trocken Riesling (Pfalz) $50. Rich and thickly textured, showing impressive concentration but also a heavy, plodding feel. Pear and apple flavors struggle alongside hints of unripe melon and quince. Unclear how this one will evolve, hence the conservative rating. **84** —*J.C. (5/1/2005)*

Dr. Bürklin-Wolf 2001 Ruppertsberger Gaisböhl Trocken Riesling (Pfalz) $37. Just enough pear fruit pokes through the sheen of kerosene and other oily flavors to provide ample pleasure. It's still an intellectual exercise in mineral and petroleum more than a hedonistic thrill, but it's well made and worth seeking out if you like that sort of thing. **87** —*J.C. (3/1/2003)*

Dr. Bürklin-Wolf 1998 Ruppertsberger Hoheburg Spätlese Trocken Riesling (Pfalz) $23. Explosive ripe, luscious fruit bursts from the glass in the pungent nose and expands full throttle on the palate. The flavors, complex and layered, include honeysuckle, lime, mineral, and some lovely, tropical fruit—especially mango and pineapple. Long and seamless. **91 Editors' Choice** —*P.G. (8/1/2001)*

Dr. Bürklin-Wolf 1990 Wachenheimer Rechbächel 'R' Riesling (Pfalz) $44. Yes, this is the current release. The "R" series of Dr. B-W has a minimum of 5 years in bottle; in this case it's 10. The concentrated and intense super-ripe aromas and flavors are not too sweet, show no botrytis, and are still quite lively at this age. Tropical fruit, orange, and pure grape flavors mingle sensuously with spice and vanilla. They play out on a long, ripe, almost unctuous finish that blends in hints of diesel. A perfect foil for foie gras. **91** *(8/1/2001)*

Dr. Bürklin-Wolf 2002 Wachenheimer Rechbächel Qualitätswein Trocken Riesling (Pfalz) $26. This is a big, broad-shouldered Riesling that for all its size stays soft and friendly in the middle. Smoky, leesy aromas give way to flavors of mineral oil ladled over spiced pears. There's a sense of custardy richness that lingers on the finish. **90** —*J.C. (11/1/2004)*

Dr. Bürklin-Wolf 1998 Wachenheimer Rechbächel Spätlese Trocken Riesling (Pfalz) $28. The soft, spicy scents of the bouquet mix grapes, flowers, talcum powder, and a faint petrol note to create an almost Gewürz-like symphony. It's lovely and impressively complex, as layers of grape flavor, flowers, minerals, and citrus rind gain power in the mouth. The mineral elements come up on the tangy finish. Exotic and smooth, it is immediately appealing but also built to age for 6–8 years. **90** *(8/1/2001)*

DR. FISCHER

Dr. Fischer 2005 Classic Riesling (Mosel-Saar-Ruwer) $14. From the family's estate holdings in the Saar, this is a steely, minerally wine, but the ripeness of the vintage has given it a saber's heft rather than the more typical rapier-like weight. A bit austere, but long, dry, and minerally on the finish. **89 Best Buy** —*J.C. (12/1/2006)*

Dr. Fischer 2003 Classic QbA Riesling (Mosel-Saar-Ruwer) $14. Burnt match aromas don't get this wine off on the right foot, nor do the aggressive acids on the finish. In between is a medium-weight wine with modest pear and grapefruit flavors. **82** —*J.C. (11/1/2004)*

Dr. Fischer 2003 Ockfener Bockstein Kabinett Riesling (Mosel-Saar-Ruwer) $17. Slightly green aromas of fern fronds and citrus fruits start things off, and this wine stays light, lean, and tart throughout. Mixed citrus fruits—tangerine, lime and grapefruit—finish clean but short. **84** —*J.C. (11/1/2004)*

Dr. Fischer 2003 Ockfener Bockstein Spätlese Riesling (Mosel-Saar-Ruwer) $20. Strong matchstick aromas can't hide over-ripe melon flavors and a heavy, dull mouthfeel. This wine tastes as if the fruit was baked, and as a result it lacks zip and vitality. **82** —*J.C. (11/1/2004)*

Dr. Fischer 2002 Wawerner Herrenberger Spätlese Riesling (Mosel-Saar-Ruwer) $20. Under-stated on the nose, with modest scents of petrol and apples. Medium-sweet on the palate, with flavors of corn oil layered over apples and pears. Finishes with a burst of citrus. **85** —*J.C. (11/1/2004)*

DR. H. THANISCH (ERBEN MÜLLER-BURGGRAEF)

Dr. H. Thanisch (Erben Müller-Burggraef) 2002 Berncasteler Doctor Auslese Riesling (Mosel-Saar-Ruwer) $42. Sweet and fruity, loaded with melon, peach, grapefruit, apricot, and pineapple. There's also a hint of honey. It's a pretty, well-made wine that ultimately just doesn't seem to have the concentration needed to score higher. **87** —*J.C. (11/1/2004)*

Dr. H. Thanisch (Erben Müller-Burggraef) 2002 Berncasteler Doctor Kabinett Riesling (Mosel-Saar-Ruwer) $29. Shows the wonderful mineral aromas of the Doctor site, along with apple, nectarine, and lime scents, but lacks the fine edge of racy acidity and lingering finish that can make this wine truly special. Plump, with sweet, oily flavors just balanced out by tart green apple notes. **86** —*J.C. (8/1/2004)*

Dr. H. Thanisch (Erben Müller-Burggraef) 2001 Berncasteler Doctor Kabinett Riesling (Mosel-Saar-Ruwer) $27. This is expensive for a kabinett, but it comes from perhaps the most famous vineyard on the middle Mosel. That pedigree shows through in its polished mineral core. There's a slight citrusy tang to the green apples and crushed stones, and a delicacy and lightness of weight that belie the wine's intensity. **90** —*J.C. (3/1/2003)*

Dr. H. Thanisch (Erben Müller-Burggraef) 2002 Berncasteler Doctor Spätlese Riesling (Mosel-Saar-Ruwer) $46. Rich and sweet, but a trifle low in acidity, this is a plump, succulent wine from a vineyard renowned for its raciness and delicacy. Apple, peach, and honey aromas and flavors dominate, melding together in a pleasant whole. **88** —*J.C. (8/1/2004)*

Dr. H. Thanisch (Erben Müller-Burggraef) 2004 Bernkasteler Badstube Kabinett Riesling (Mosel-Saar-Ruwer) $19. A bit of a letdown after the past couple of vintages, this wine boasts slightly spicy and floral aromatics, but doesn't quite follow through on the palate, where there's ample weight but less flavor. Pleasant, but not special this year. **84** —*J.C. (7/1/2006)*

Dr. H. Thanisch (Erben Müller-Burggraef) 2003 Bernkasteler Badstube Kabinett Riesling (Mosel-Saar-Ruwer) $19. Soft and mouth-filling, with apple, pear, citrus and mineral elements all elegantly intertwined. Finishes with hints of grapefruit and fuel oil. Drink over the next few years. **87** —*J.C. (5/1/2005)*

Dr. H. Thanisch (Erben Müller-Burggraef) 2002 Bernkasteler Badstube Kabinett Riesling (Mosel-Saar-Ruwer) $17. Light and a bit green, with fresh scents of green apples and limes followed by similar flavors and hints of mint and green plums. Fresh and clean on the finish. **86** —*J.C. (8/1/2004)*

Dr. H. Thanisch (Erben Müller-Burggraef) 2001 Bernkasteler Graben Spätlese Riesling (Mosel-Saar-Ruwer) $18. Smells slightly waxy, with yellow-skinned fruits pre-dominating; think lemons and pears. Sweeter in the mouth, the flavors open up to include pineapple as well, all under-scored by citrus. The bright finish folds in notes of chalk dust. **89** —*J.C. (3/1/2003)*

Dr. H. Thanisch (Erben Müller-Burggraef) 2005 Bernkasteler Lay Spätlese Riesling (Mosel-Saar-Ruwer) $26. Rather fruit-driven and sweet, with dried fruit and apple shadings on the nose, and apple, melon, and citrus flavors. It's medium-bodied, and ends with more melon flavors and a hint of slate. **88** —J.C. (12/1/2006)

Dr. H. Thanisch (Erben Müller-Burggraef) 2005 Brauneberger Juffer-Sonnenuhr Auslese Riesling (Mosel-Saar-Ruwer) $35. Seems a bit simple at first, mounding up fruity scents of apple, pineapple, and pear. But give it some time to develop and it adds complex mineral and spice nuances. The wine is fairly rich and full-bodied, but the sweetness is balanced by crisp acids. Long in the finish and packed with dry mineral notes. **93 Editors' Choice** —J.C. (12/1/2006)

Dr. H. Thanisch (Erben Müller-Burggraef) 2005 Brauneberger Juffer-Sonnenuhr Spätlese Riesling (Mosel-Saar-Ruwer) $26. Plump and succulent, this is a deceptively easy wine. Ripe apple, pear, and melon flavors make it seem simple, but underneath the flesh is a spine of bright acids and slatey minerality. Zesty lime and ripe orange notes give length to the crisp, lingering finish. Both this wine and the auslese are great. **92 Editors' Choice** —J.C. (12/1/2006)

Dr. H. Thanisch (Erben Müller-Burggraef) 2003 Brauneberger Juffer-Sonnenuhr Spätlese Riesling (Mosel-Saar-Ruwer) $24. Smells like ultra-ripe nectarines or peaches, flesh practically oozing from the skins. In the mouth, it's big, rich, and enveloping, yet it finishes with a trace of bitter peach pit. **87** —J.C. (5/1/2005)

Dr. H. Thanisch (Erben Müller-Burggraef) 2002 Brauneberger Juffer-Sonnenuhr Spätlese Riesling (Mosel-Saar-Ruwer) $21. Nicely balanced, blending tart green apples with hints of pear and peach. Light in body, with a fresh, clean finish. Drink now–2015. **88** —J.C. (8/1/2004)

Dr. H. Thanisch (Erben Müller-Burggraef) 2004 Classic Riesling (Mosel-Saar-Ruwer) $17. Aromas of lime sherbet, pear, and quince are slightly dampened by hints of sulfur and lees, but this should be only transitory. It is light in body, with flavors of green apple and lime that end on a racy note, if a little short. **85** —J.C. (2/1/2006)

Dr. H. Thanisch (Erben Müller-Burggraef) 2005 Classic QbA Riesling (Mosel-Saar-Ruwer) $17. Considerably heftier than the light-bodied 2004 version, and a better wine for the extra weight, with baked apple, melon, and spice notes amply filling out this wine's medium body. Finishes long, picking up a dusting of cinnamon and crushed stone. **88** —J.C. (12/1/2006)

Dr. H. Thanisch (Erben Müller-Burggraef) 2004 Graacher Himmelreich Spätlese Riesling (Mosel-Saar-Ruwer) $26. Intensely petrolly on the nose, with a rather full mouthfeel and dense, minerally flavors. This is stolid and sullen right now, but undeniably intense. Hints of spice on the finish bode well for the future, so stow it away for 3–4 years before trying it with something substantial, like roast pork. **87** —J.C. (9/1/2006)

Dr. H. Thanisch (Erben Müller-Burggraef) 2004 Wehlener Sonnenuhr Kabinett Riesling (Mosel-Saar-Ruwer) $19. Broad and mouth-filling, this sweet kabinett starts with muted honey and tangerine aromas, then blossoms on the palate into ripe peach flavors. Verges on tropical before being reined in on the finish by bright lime notes. **87** —J.C. (7/1/2006)

Dr. H. Thanisch (Erben Müller-Burggraef) 2002 Wehlener Sonnenuhr Kabinett Riesling (Mosel-Saar-Ruwer) $17. This large-scaled, fully ripe Riesling boasts aromas of mineral oil and baked apple backed by expansive, mouth-filling flavors of the same. It's certainly rounder and riper than a traditional kabinett, but it doesn't seem at all flabby. **89** —J.C. (8/1/2004)

DR. H. THANISCH (ERBEN THANISCH)

Dr. H. Thanisch (Erben Thanisch) 2004 Berncasteler Doctor Auslese Riesling (Mosel-Saar-Ruwer) $64. What balance! This wine's considerable sweetness is admirably buffered by ample acidity, while low alcohol adds to the impression of lightness and ease. This structural balance is complemented by the way slaty-minerally aromas play off bright tangerine and peach flavors, ending seamlessly, crisp, and long. Delicious now, but should easily age 20 years. **94 Editors' Choice** —J.C. (9/1/2006)

Dr. H. Thanisch (Erben Thanisch) 2003 Berncasteler Doctor Kabinett Riesling (Mosel-Saar-Ruwer) $47. An odd wine, with some favorable elements, but also a strange sourness on the nose and a mouthfeel that's a bit syrupy and sweet. In between, there are appealing dusty-minerally notes, and pineapple and pear flavors. **84** —J.C. (5/1/2005)

Dr. H. Thanisch (Erben Thanisch) 2003 Bernkasteler Badstube Kabinett Riesling (Mosel-Saar-Ruwer) $23. Limes, minerals, and green apples dance on the nose of this lithe yet flavorful kabinett. Flavors lean heavily toward green apples and citrus, yet the acids are ripe on the finish, giving an impression of softness and early approachability. **88** —J.C. (12/15/2004)

Dr. H. Thanisch (Erben Thanisch) 2001 Bernkasteler Badstube Kabinett Riesling (Mosel-Saar-Ruwer) $30. This is a rich wine, with red currant flavors and a touch of yeastiness. The sweetness and the weight make it unusual among normally lightly flavored kabinetts. **87** —R.V. (3/1/2003)

Dr. H. Thanisch (Erben Thanisch) 2001 Bernkasteler Doctor Auslese Riesling (Mosel-Saar-Ruwer) $60. The legendary Thanisch estates has produced an auslese which is almost beerenauslese in its richness and color. There are layers of botrytis, flavors of honey, and rich lemon zest and a long lingering aftertaste. **93** —R.V. (3/1/2003)

Dr. H. Thanisch (Erben Thanisch) 2004 QbA Riesling (Mosel-Saar-Ruwer) $21. Slatey, minerally, and oily scents on the nose are followed by apple, mineral, and melon flavors. Medium-bodied, this off-dry wine finishes long, with fresh acidity that leaves the mouth watering. **88** —J.C. (2/1/2006)

Dr. H. Thanisch (Erben Thanisch) 2003 QbA Riesling (Mosel-Saar-Ruwer) $19. A lusciously fruity wine, showing better acids than many 2003s yet remaining soft and friendly. Apples and pears on the nose blend with tropical and citrus fruit on the palate. Finishes sweet and long, balanced by ripe acidity. **90** —J.C. (12/15/2004)

Dr. H. Thanisch (Erben Thanisch) 2001 QbA Riesling (Mosel-Saar-Ruwer) $16. This regional blend is a solid quaff. Starts off with peach and pear aromatics, then turns less-ripe-tasting in the mouth, emphasizing fresh limes and green apples. Light, tart, and clean, probably best as an apéritif. **86** —J.C. (3/1/2003)

DR. LOOSEN

Dr. Loosen 2004 Villa Wolf Pinot Gris (Pfalz) $11. As a simple summer quaffer, this wine fits the bill. It's off-dry and slightly plump in the mouth, with citrusy flavors that range from grapefruit through orange to tangerine. Short on the finish. **84** —J.C. (7/1/2006)

Dr. Loosen 1999 Riesling (Mosel-Saar-Ruwer) $10. This straight ahead bottling from the Loosen brothers is simply labeled Riesling. It has a surprisingly rich nose with hints of hay, diesel, and citrus, while the palate shows ripe, concentrated yellow fruits. Low in alcohol (8.5%) and modest in price, this is a perfect introduction to Mosel Riesling and a great everyday wine for our Chardonnay-obsessed land. **86 Best Buy** (8/1/2001)

Dr. Loosen 1999 Bernkasteler Lay Riesling (Mosel-Saar-Ruwer) $17. 84 —C.S. (5/1/2002)

Dr. Loosen 2003 Bernkasteler Lay Kabinett Riesling (Mosel-Saar-Ruwer) $20. Pungently grassy and grapefruity on the nose, with strange apple and pink grapefruit flavors on the soft, sweet palate. A rare mis-step from Ernie Loosen? **82** —J.C. (5/1/2005)

Dr. Loosen 2002 Bernkasteler Lay Kabinett Riesling (Mosel-Saar-Ruwer) $17. Light in weight and possessed of a fine balance between sweetness and acidity, this is an ideal apéritif wine. Pungent lime and green apple aromas combine with green gage plum notes in a mouth-watering ensemble. **88** —J.C. (8/1/2004)

Dr. Loosen 2001 Bernkasteler Lay Kabinett Riesling (Mosel-Saar-Ruwer) $17. If the hallmark of the Mosel is delicacy combined with intense flavors, then this wine from the great Dr. Loosen estate hits the mark perfectly. It has green floral notes, and aromas of summer flowers. Lightly sweet flavors and a touch of green tannins give way to intense tastes of ripe peaches. **90** —R.V. (3/1/2003)

Dr. Loosen 1999 Bernkasteler Lay Kabinett Riesling (Mosel-Saar-Ruwer) $12. The name translates as "the slate of Bernkastel" and this wine lives up to its name. Peachy-tropical ripe fruit is offset nicely by the pronounced mineral scent and texture, and a slight spritz. The stony side of its nature glides into a chalk-tinged, palate-cleansing finish with sweet pear flavors. **87** (8/1/2001)

Dr. Loosen 2002 Dr. L QbA Riesling (Mosel-Saar-Ruwer) $11. Ernst Loosen's big-production wine is a smashing success in 2002, a bit shy on the nose, but possessing a well-balanced blend of apples, pears, and citrus fruits on the palate. Its soft, talcum powder-like texture and touch of sweetness make it easy to like, the balancing acidity makes it easy to drink. **87 Best Buy** —*J.C. (8/1/2004)*

Dr. Loosen 2001 Dr. L QbA Riesling (Mosel-Saar-Ruwer) $10. Good solid stuff with a bit of funk to keep things interesting. A cheesy note on the nose gives way to melon and sweet corn flavors and a tangy finish. **85** — *J.C. (3/1/2003)*

Dr. Loosen 2003 Dr. L Qualitätswein Riesling (Mosel-Saar-Ruwer) $10. Seems a bit sweeter than it has been in other recent vintages, but still hits the right notes. Green apple and grapefruit aromas segue into apple and citrus flavors tinged with a bit of red berry fruit. A bit of unreleased CO2 helps to balance the sugar levels; drink over the next six months or so while it remains fresh. **86 Best Buy** —*J.C. (11/1/2004)*

Dr. Loosen 2002 Erdener Prälat Auslese Riesling (Mosel-Saar-Ruwer) $48. In contrast to the delicate, ethereal nature of Loosen's '02 Ürziger Würzgarten auslese, this is a plump, rich wine filled with nectarine, honey and lime flavors. Despite a modest finish, this wine has loads of up-front appeal. **90** —*J.C. (8/1/2004)*

Dr. Loosen 2001 Erdener Prälat Auslese Gold Capsule Riesling (Mosel-Saar-Ruwer) $48. A bit of a let down, this is big, rich, and oily, redolent of honeyed apples, but lacks the precision and clarity of some of Loosen's other 2001s. It's still very good, close to a beerenauslese in ripeness and weight, just somewhat monolithic and weighty, picking up some lemon and apricot notes on the finish. Tasted twice, with consistent notes. **88** —*J.C. (3/1/2003)*

Dr. Loosen 2003 Erdener Treppchen Auslese Riesling (Mosel-Saar-Ruwer) $40. Wonderfully clean and precise aromas of pear and honeydew give way to apple and lime flavors. This avoids excess weight or sugar, revealing a more classical structure than many of the 2003s. Long and fresh on the finish. **90** —*J.C. (5/1/2005)*

Dr. Loosen 2001 Erdener Treppchen Eiswein Riesling (Mosel-Saar-Ruwer) $200. Dr. Loosen is one of the great estates of Germany, able to produce wonderfully expressive wines. Here is a hugely sweet wine, delicate and fresh, with flavors of maple syrup and mangos. Enormously complex wine in flavor, but there is nothing—a mere 6.5%—in alcohol. **94** — *R.V. (3/1/2003)*

Dr. Loosen 2002 Erdener Treppchen Kabinett Riesling (Mosel-Saar-Ruwer) $18. A light-bodied, delicately flavored wine, filled with notes of flower-shop greens, ripe apples, and citrus. Finishes crisp and clean, with just a touch of sweetness, making it perfect to sip on its own as an apéritif. **87** —*J.C. (8/1/2004)*

Dr. Loosen 2001 Erdener Treppchen Kabinett Riesling (Mosel-Saar-Ruwer) $18. Strike flint on flint and you'll get a smoky aroma remarkably similar to the bouquet of this wine. Too bad flint on flint won't generate this kind of sweet pear nectar, pineapple, and stone fruit flavors. It's sweet, but there's sufficient acidity to carry the sugar. **89** —*J.C. (3/1/2003)*

Dr. Loosen 1999 Erdener Treppchen Kabinett Riesling (Mosel-Saar-Ruwer) $18. A sinuous wine with lots of lime and mineral elements beautifully entwined. The bouquet is attractive but taut with lime and mineral notes. In the mouth the wine really opens up, with peach, tangerine, lime, and green apple fruit with a faintly spritzy feel. The sweet fruit is supported by good acidity and balanced nicely by the strong, stony mineral element. The fruit, minerals, and good grip, must come from the amazingly steep rocky vineyard source. Just 400 cases made. **90 Editors' Choice** *(8/1/2001)*

Dr. Loosen 2001 Erdener Treppchen Spätlese Riesling (Mosel-Saar-Ruwer) $25. Packed with vibrant ripe fruit and flavors of white currants, this big, sweet wine has enormous depth of flavor, showing intensity with tannins over sweet fruit. **89** —*R.V. (3/1/2003)*

Dr. Loosen 1999 Ürziger Würzgarten Riesling (Mosel-Saar-Ruwer) $25. Dr. Loosen's Kabinett wines sometimes approach the Spätlese level of concentration and flavor; this Spätlese could be someone's Auslese. It's decadently ripe, a rich mouthful of peaches, apricots, orange, and pineapple, almost viscous and floral-honey sweet. Which is not to say it lacks acidity, structure, or balance. Wonderful, spicy-sweet cinnamon

and nutmeg accents offset the fruit, there's a somewhat grainy palate texture, like ultraripe pears. Finishes long. **89** *(8/1/2001)*

Dr. Loosen 2001 Urziger Wurzgarten Auslese Riesling (Mosel-Saar-Ruwer) $42. Musky hedgerow flavors lie alongside high acidity and crisp sweet pineapple flavors. Possesses fine structure and enormous aging ability. **90** —*R.V. (3/1/2003)*

Dr. Loosen 2003 Ürziger Würzgarten Auslese Riesling (Mosel-Saar-Ruwer) $40. Fresh and crisp, but it lacks a bit of intensity. An initial blast of sulfur fades readily enough, revealing simple apple and citrus flavors, but that's as far as this usually stellar bottling goes this year. **85** —*J.C. (5/1/2005)*

Dr. Loosen 2002 Ürziger Würzgarten Auslese Riesling (Mosel-Saar-Ruwer) $42. May have even more finesse than Loosen's UW spätlese, but packs a little less power; it's a delicate wine, with powdered quartz and fresh citrus aromas backed by quince and pink grapefruit flavors. Malic notes linger on the finish. **90** —*J.C. (8/1/2004)*

Dr. Loosen 2004 Ürziger Würzgarten Kabinett Riesling (Mosel-Saar-Ruwer) $20. Befitting its namesake Würzgarten vineyard, this wine starts off with musky-spicy notes layered over ripe pear and apple fruit and smoky, slate-driven aromas. It's light in body, yet it doesn't lack for strength or intensity at all, finishing long, with cleansing, lime-like acids. **90** —*J.C. (5/1/2006)*

Dr. Loosen 2001 Urziger Wurzgarten Spätlese Riesling (Mosel-Saar-Ruwer) $25. A deliciously sweet wine that's not at all heavy; its spice-laden aromas mirror those of a dry rub for roast pork, folding in flavors of ripe Granny Smith apples and Anjou pears. The mouthwatering finish persists admirably, bringing back echoes of dry spices. **90** —*J.C. (3/1/2003)*

Dr. Loosen 2003 Ürziger Würzgarten Spätlese Riesling (Mosel-Saar-Ruwer) $28. Starts with some lime and grapefruity notes, but seems to get softer as it moves toward the finish, ending with ripe flavors of apples, pears, and even some stone fruit. Light in body, a tough trick in this sunbaked vintage. **85** —*J.C. (5/1/2005)*

Dr. Loosen 2002 Ürziger Würzgarten Spätlese Riesling (Mosel-Saar-Ruwer) $25. Great Spätlese from Loosen, combining apple, citrus, pear, pineapple, and lime flavors into a seamless whole that defies such deconstructionist description. And while it has great aromatics and midpalate flavor, it's also lively, fresh, and long on the finish. **91 Editors' Choice** — *J.C. (8/1/2004)*

Dr. Loosen 1999 Wehlener Sonnenuhr Riesling (Mosel-Saar-Ruwer) $17. A lovely bouquet of ripe peach, apricot, and lemon notes. Fairly round peach, tart apple, and earth flavors play on the palate and linger through the clean finish with its green apple and crisp mineral elements. From a well-regarded vineyard on a heart-stopping vertical slope, known for its elegant wines, everything here is beautifully defined. This will age well. **88** *(8/1/2001)*

Dr. Loosen 1999 Wehlener Sonnenuhr Riesling (Mosel-Saar-Ruwer) $30. This is a lovely wine, impeccably balanced between sweet and crisp, with concentrated fruit that retains its elegance. Honeysuckle, apricot, jasmine tea, and every kind of citrus fruit you can conjure up. Young, hard, and fruity, it barely shows the depth and layers of flavor that will develop. It will be hard to keep your hands off it. **93** —*P.G. (8/1/2001)*

Dr. Loosen 2001 Wehlener Sonnenuhr Auslese Riesling (Mosel-Saar-Ruwer) $38. This lean, racy auslese has plenty of sweetness and ripe apple and pear fruit, but those elements play a secondary role to the intense mineral notes. Bright acidity gives great life and verve to this wine, which should age beautifully. **90** —*J.C. (3/1/2003)*

Dr. Loosen 2001 Wehlener Sonnenuhr Goldkapsel Auslese Riesling (Mosel-Saar-Ruwer) $33. The wine has a sweet honeyed nose with a fragrance of tea roses. The fresh and sweet combines great acidity with a layer of soft honey, finishing with flavors of fresh ripe apricots. **92** —*R.V. (3/1/2003)*

Dr. Loosen 2001 Wehlener Sonnenuhr Kabinett Riesling (Mosel-Saar-Ruwer) $35. The wine has an attractive pale green color, suggesting lightness as well as softness. But there is also a fine, steely backbone of rich fruit, with flavors of baked apples and white currants. **89** —*R.V. (1/1/2004)*

Dr. Loosen 2003 Wehlener Sonnenuhr Spätlese Riesling (Mosel-Saar-Ruwer) $28. Features apple, pear, and citrus flavors on a lithe, sweet frame. It would score higher, but for a slight note of grapefruit-pith bitterness on the honey-laden finish. **86** —*J.C. (5/1/2005)*

Dr. Loosen 2002 Wehlener Sonnenuhr Spätlese Riesling (Mosel-Saar-Ruwer) $25. This offering from Loosen manages to combine great minerality—an almost palpable sense of rock dust—with terrific fruit. Ripe apples and candied pineapple are sweet, but nicely balanced by crisp acids. **91 Editors' Choice** —*J.C. (8/1/2004)*

Dr. Loosen 2001 Wehlener Sonnenuhr Spätlese Riesling (Mosel-Saar-Ruwer) $25. This is ripe and sweet fruit, with a yeasty overtone and flavors of soft, white peaches. It is an immediately attractive wine with a well-judged touch of acidity to balance. **88** —*R.V. (3/1/2003)*

DR. PAULY BERGWEILER

Dr. Pauly Bergweiler 2000 Berkasteler Badstube Spätlese Riesling (Mosel-Saar-Ruwer) $21. 85 —*D.T. (5/1/2002)*

Dr. Pauly Bergweiler 2003 Bernkasteler alte Badstube am Doctorberg Auslese Riesling (Mosel-Saar-Ruwer) $50. Full-bodied, sweet, and thick in the mouth, this is more like a beerenauslese than a true auslese. But evaluated on its own merits, it is a special wine: pear and honey scents give way to apricot preserves that finish sweet and lingering on the finish. **92** —*J.C. (11/1/2004)*

Dr. Pauly Bergweiler 2002 Bernkasteler alte Badstube am Doctorberg Auslese Riesling (Mosel-Saar-Ruwer) $46. One of Pauly Bergweiler's best efforts in 2002, this auslese is a plump, sweet offering loaded with attractive peachy fruit. Pineapple and citrus notes keep the sweetness in check, leaving behind a long, honeyed, mouth-coating finish. **92** —*J.C. (8/1/2004)*

Dr. Pauly Bergweiler 2001 Bernkasteler alte Badstube am Doctorberg Auslese Riesling (Mosel-Saar-Ruwer) $36. This sweet, almost candied, auslese packs in plenty of bright pineapple fruit that turns citrusy. Picks up some hard, metallic-mineral notes on the finish that will please some tasters but turn others off. "Obvious" now, should show better in a few years when the puppy fat of sugar is more integrated. **87** —*J.C. (3/1/2003)*

Dr. Pauly Bergweiler 2003 Bernkasteler alte Badstube am Doctorberg Beerenauslese Riesling (Mosel-Saar-Ruwer) $150. This wine's honeyed apple and pear flavors seem to represent the concentrated essence of fruit. This is intensely sweet, perhaps a bit low in acidity, but winemaker Edmund Licht has crafted a wine that shows amazing purity and extract. 0ct. **93** —*J.C. (12/15/2004)*

Dr. Pauly Bergweiler 2004 Bernkasteler alte Badstube am Doctorberg Beerenauslese 375 ml Riesling (Mosel-Saar-Ruwer) $90. Shows a bit of minerality in its smoky scents, but the Pauly-Bergweiler emphasis is always on sweet, luscious fruit, which plays to this wine's strengths. Candied apples and oranges finish gently, neither overly sweet nor overly acidic. Drink now–2020. **93** —*J.C. (2/1/2006)*

Dr. Pauly Bergweiler 2005 Bernkasteler alte Badstube am Doctorberg Kabinett Riesling (Mosel-Saar-Ruwer) $21. Relatively high in alcohol and dark in color, this is a kabinett that doesn't quite fit the mold, yet still provides a pleasurable experience. Minerally, diesely notes on the nose are matched by baked apple scents, while the flavors turn toward honeyed stones and sweet corn. It's creamy in texture, rich, and off-dry. **89** —*J.C. (12/1/2006)*

Dr. Pauly Bergweiler 2004 Bernkasteler alte Badstube am Doctorberg Kabinett Riesling (Mosel-Saar-Ruwer) $23. Firmly in the house style, with soft, fully ripe fruit flavors that caress the palate rather than awaken it. Peach and pear lead the way, backed by melon notes. **87** —*J.C. (10/1/2005)*

Dr. Pauly Bergweiler 2003 Bernkasteler alte Badstube am Doctorberg Kabinett Riesling (Mosel-Saar-Ruwer) $21. Like all of the 2003s from Dr. Pauly-Bergweiler, this is quite sweet-tasting for its prädikat: Honey, cinnamon, and lush peaches give the impression of great ripeness, yet it retains a sense of minerality and even picks up some citrus notes on the finish. **89** —*J.C. (11/1/2004)*

Dr. Pauly Bergweiler 2002 Bernkasteler alte Badstube am Doctorberg Kabinett Riesling (Mosel-Saar-Ruwer) $20. Like most of this producer's 2002s, this is a plump, succulent wine, amply endowed with fruit. What sets this one apart is its combination of baked apple, ripe peach, dried spices, and dusty minerality. **88** —*J.C. (8/1/2004)*

Dr. Pauly Bergweiler 2001 Bernkasteler alte Badstube am Doctorberg Kabinett Riesling (Mosel-Saar-Ruwer) $16. Loaded with tropical fruit, this kabinett surely includes a portion of declassified spätlese or even auslese-level fruit. Don't expect a razor-edged, tart wine, but a mellow, sweet, viscous rendering of Riesling that's probably best served on its own. **88** —*J.C. (3/1/2003)*

Dr. Pauly Bergweiler 2005 Bernkasteler alte Badstube am Doctorberg Spätlese Riesling (Mosel-Saar-Ruwer) $27. In the house style, this is rather lush and sweet for its prädikat. Candied pineapple notes anchor the bouquet, lightly garnished with hints of crushed stone. Flavors continue along the same theme, adding notes of tropical fruit and super-ripe pears. Approachable now; it should firm up a little with age. **89** —*J.C. (12/1/2006)*

Dr. Pauly Bergweiler 2004 Bernkasteler alte Badstube am Doctorberg Spätlese Riesling (Mosel-Saar-Ruwer) $30. Big and sweet; broad and mouth-filling. It has decent complexity (pear, peach, dried spices and fuel oil) but lacks delicacy and raciness. If you like your Rieslings on the heavy side, you'll rate this even higher. **87** —*J.C. (10/1/2005)*

Dr. Pauly Bergweiler 2003 Bernkasteler alte Badstube am Doctorberg Spätlese Riesling (Mosel-Saar-Ruwer) $28. The raciest of Pauly Bergweiler's 2003 offerings, this spätlese boasts notable lightness allied to plenty of flavor intensity. Vanilla and pears, apple and citrus are all set off by delicate floral nuances. Doesn't seem to show the effects of the hot vintage nearly as much as some of the other wines. **90** —*J.C. (11/1/2004)*

Dr. Pauly Bergweiler 2002 Bernkasteler alte Badstube am Doctorberg Spätlese Riesling (Mosel-Saar-Ruwer) $26. Nicely balanced, if a little on the sweet side, with aromas of lime and stone dust rounded out in the mouth by flavors of honey, pineapple, and apricot. Plump and easy to drink. **90** —*J.C. (8/1/2004)*

Dr. Pauly Bergweiler 2001 Bernkasteler alte Badstube am Doctorberg Spätlese Riesling (Mosel-Saar-Ruwer) $20. Rich and sweet, packed with weighty peach and ripe apple fruit that picks up nuances of diesel fuel and spice. Despite the sweetness, there's enough acidity to hold it in check, making it deceptively easy to drink. **87** —*J.C. (3/1/2003)*

Dr. Pauly Bergweiler 2001 Bernkasteler alte Badstube am Doctorberg Trockenbeerenauslese Riesling (Mosel-Saar-Ruwer) $150. Smells spicy, redolent of apricots poached in honey, cinnamon, and cloves. Baked apples come through on the palate, which is mouthcoatingly viscous and luxuriously rich. A trifle low in acidity, so drink sooner rather than later. **92** —*J.C. (3/1/2003)*

Dr. Pauly Bergweiler 2000 Bernkasteler alte Badtube am Doctobergretail Kabinett Riesling (Mosel-Saar-Ruwer) $21. 85 —*J.C. (5/1/2002)*

Dr. Pauly Bergweiler 2000 Bernkasteler alte Badtube am Doctorberg Auslese Riesling (Mosel-Saar-Ruwer) $42. 86 —*D.T. (5/1/2002)*

Dr. Pauly Bergweiler 2003 Bernkasteler Badstube Auslese Riesling (Mosel-Saar-Ruwer) $30. Begins with scents of clover-blossom honey drizzled over supremely ripe apples and pears, then opens to show a dizzying array of fruits ranging from apricot to pineapple. Sweet, luscious, and soft; don't expect a razor edge of acidity, just all-enveloping fruit. **91 Editors' Choice** —*J.C. (11/1/2004)*

Dr. Pauly Bergweiler 2001 Bernkasteler Badstube Beerenauslese Riesling (Mosel-Saar-Ruwer) $115. The beauty of this stunning wine is its intensity. Rich layers of botrytis pile on top of each other, with flavors of orange marmalade and piercing, balancing acidity. The pleasure also is that it has a great lightness of touch. **92** —*R.V. (3/1/2003)*

Dr. Pauly Bergweiler 2003 Bernkasteler Badstube Eiswein Riesling (Mosel-Saar-Ruwer) $175. Absolutely incredible eiswein, with finely etched flavors of pear and pineapple that flow across the palate like fruit syrup borne on light-footed acids. Stunningly sweet, but with great balancing acidity and a finish that lingers for minutes. **96** —*J.C. (12/15/2004)*

Dr. Pauly Bergweiler 2002 Bernkasteler Badstube Eiswein Riesling (Mosel-Saar-Ruwer) $75. Sweet but also very high in acidity. The pineapple and Granny Smith notes never broaden out much, remaining tight and reined in. No evidence of botrytis, just sweetness balanced by tart, acids on the finish. **90** —*J.C. (8/1/2004)*

Dr. Pauly Bergweiler 2001 Bernkasteler Badstube Eiswein Riesling (Mosel-Saar-Ruwer) $115. Features crisp pears and a honeyed quality but no sign of botrytis. It's so clean that its floral complexities show through the high ripeness and huge sugar levels. Despite the intense sweetness, it's relatively light in body; the finish picks up a distracting chalky note that dries the palate. **89** —*J.C. (3/1/2003)*

Dr. Pauly Bergweiler 2004 Bernkasteler Badstube Eiswein 375 ml Riesling (Mosel-Saar-Ruwer) $90. Reasonably priced for an eiswein, this immensely thick, oily offering coats the palate with intense sweetness, but also succulent flavors of flower syrup, ultra-ripe pears, and apricots. Candied orange notes linger forever on the finish. **96 Editors' Choice** —*J.C. (9/1/2006)*

Dr. Pauly Bergweiler 2004 Bernkasteler Badstube Kabinett Riesling (Mosel-Saar-Ruwer) $23. Racier than the other Pauly-Bergweiler kabinetts, but maybe not quite as complex, with ripe apple and citrus flavors that pack more verve but less nuance. **86** —*J.C. (10/1/2005)*

Dr. Pauly Bergweiler 2003 Bernkasteler Badstube Kabinett Riesling (Mosel-Saar-Ruwer) $19. Sweet and plump, with ripe apple and pear flavors that glide easily across the palate, then finish tart and pineappley. Very fruity, not showing a lot of mineral character. **86** —*J.C. (11/1/2004)*

Dr. Pauly Bergweiler 2002 Bernkasteler Badstube Kabinett Riesling (Mosel-Saar-Ruwer) $18. Starts off with lush pineapple and stone fruit aromas, then develops almost floral, perfumy, candied flavors. A tart edge on the finish provides good balance. Refreshing, and easy to drink. **87** —*J.C. (8/1/2004)*

Dr. Pauly Bergweiler 2001 Bernkasteler Badstube Kabinett Riesling (Mosel-Saar-Ruwer) $14. Green apple and lime aromas are partialy disguised by a moderate sulfur funk (think burnt matchstick). The flavors are clean but frankly sweet, showing notes of strawberries and candied apples. Soft on the finish. **84** —*J.C. (1/1/2004)*

Dr. Pauly Bergweiler 2005 Bernkasteler Badstube Spätlese Riesling (Mosel-Saar-Ruwer) $24. The style at Pauly Bergweiler leans toward ultra-ripe, and this wine is no exception, boasting sweet, lush flavors of honeyed melons and pears that verge on fatness. Thankfully, there's a touch of unreleased CO2 to help provide freshness and a just a hint of grapefruit on the finish—enough to give the wine some focus. **89** —*J.C. (12/1/2006)*

Dr. Pauly Bergweiler 2004 Bernkasteler Badstube Spätlese Riesling (Mosel-Saar-Ruwer) $30. True to the style at Pauly-Bergweiler, this is a sweet, rich wine, with super-ripe apple, pear, and even tropical fruit notes. There's also a bit of diesel and slate and good acidity for balance. Finishes long and mouthwatering. **89** —*J.C. (10/1/2005)*

Dr. Pauly Bergweiler 2003 Bernkasteler Badstube Spätlese Riesling (Mosel-Saar-Ruwer) $24. Completely different from P-B's other Bernkasteler spätlese, this one is ripe and rich. Pear and melon aromas boast a hint of spice; spice and mineral flavors highlight ripe peaches and pears. Long, textured finish. **90** —*J.C. (11/1/2004)*

Dr. Pauly Bergweiler 2002 Bernkasteler Badstube Spätlese Riesling (Mosel-Saar-Ruwer) $23. In a vintage that doesn't show a lot of minerality, this wine adds a firm, slate-like edge to plump flavors of apples, pears, and pineapples. This would pair beautifully with roast pork. **89** —*J.C. (8/1/2004)*

Dr. Pauly Bergweiler 2001 Bernkasteler Badstube Spätlese Riesling (Mosel-Saar-Ruwer) $18. Baked Golden Delicious apples spiked with clove and traces of vegetable oil are backed up by firm citrusy acids. Shows more delineation and focus than some of the other 2001 Pauly Bergwiler efforts, but also less weight and a shorter finish. **87** —*J.C. (3/1/2003)*

Dr. Pauly Bergweiler 2002 Erdener Prälat Auslese Riesling (Mosel-Saar-Ruwer) $48. This is sweet even for an auslese, blending flavors of apples and pears with honey and citrus fruits. A bit of tangerine on the finish keeps the wine from registering as cloying. **89** —*J.C. (8/1/2004)*

Dr. Pauly Bergweiler 2002 Erdener Treppchen Spätlese Riesling (Mosel-Saar-Ruwer) $25. Possesses a very clean, almost crystalline quality on the nose, highlighting apple and citrus notes that broaden out on the palate to include peach and pear. **87** —*J.C. (8/1/2004)*

Dr. Pauly Bergweiler 2001 Graacher Himmelreich Eiswein Riesling (Mosel-Saar-Ruwer) $100. Acidity combined with sweetness dominate this wine, whose freshness contrasts nicely with its intense sweetness and overwhelming acidity. It should age indefinitely. **94** —*R.V. (3/1/2003)*

Dr. Pauly Bergweiler 2001 Graacher Himmelreich Kabinett Riesling (Mosel-Saar-Ruwer) $14. Relatively rich and easy-drinking for a kabinett, this wine is full of apple and berry flavors, balanced by mild citrus fruits and a trace of apricot-kernel bitterness. A bit on the sweet side for kabinett, but yummy nonetheless. **88** —*J.C. (3/1/2003)*

Dr. Pauly Bergweiler 2002 Noble House QbA Riesling (Mosel-Saar-Ruwer) $11. Smells dieselly and minerally, offering flavors of poached pear that finish with a hint of bitterness. Not the wine the 2001 was—and the price has gone up as well. **84** —*J.C. (8/1/2004)*

Dr. Pauly Bergweiler 2001 Noble House QbA Riesling (Mosel-Saar-Ruwer) $8. A dusty, minerally nose gives way to tart green apples on the palate. It's light but flavorful, finishing with juicy lime notes. Would make a perfect house pour this summer. **88 Best Buy** —*J.C. (3/1/2003)*

Dr. Pauly Bergweiler 2004 Noble House Qualitatswein Riesling (Mosel-Saar-Ruwer) $12. Smells like honey, tangerines, and pears, then folds in some minerally notes on the palate. Pleasantly weighty without being heavy, finishing dry and clean. **87 Best Buy** —*J.C. (10/1/2005)*

Dr. Pauly Bergweiler 2003 Noble House Qualitätswein Riesling (Mosel-Saar-Ruwer) $11. Green apple and pear aromas, along with a bit of stone dust, but the flavors seem a little bland and understated, and the wine finishes short. Good, well-made wine at a reasonable price, just seems to lack a bit of intensity. **84** —*J.C. (11/1/2004)*

Dr. Pauly Bergweiler 2000 Urziger Wurzgarten Spätlese Riesling (Mosel-Saar-Ruwer) $23. 83 —*D.T. (5/1/2002)*

Dr. Pauly Bergweiler 2001 Urziger Wurzgarten Trockenbeerenauslese Riesling (Mosel-Saar-Ruwer) $265. The color of polished brass, this extraordinary dessert wine boasts delicate floral scents layered over intense aromas of dried apricots and orange-blossom honey. It's immensely sweet and viscous, yet balanced, thanks to a lime edge to the flavors of honey and apricots. The finish lingers, coating the mouth in a web of complex flavors. **94 Cellar Selection** —*J.C. (3/1/2003)*

Dr. Pauly Bergweiler 2002 Ürziger Würzgarten Trockenbeernauslese Riesling (Mosel-Saar-Ruwer) $175. Not the stunning wine that the 2001 was, but still impressive, with pineapple and Granny Smith aromas yielding to riper, sweeter flavors of peach and citrus on the palate. Finishes with a lime-like tang that keeps it from seeming overly sweet. Ten cases made. **92** —*J.C. (8/1/2004)*

Dr. Pauly Bergweiler 2000 Wehlener Sonnehur Spätlese Riesling (Mosel-Saar-Ruwer) $23. 85 —*D.T. (5/1/2002)*

Dr. Pauly Bergweiler 2005 Wehlener Sonnenuhr Auslese Riesling (Mosel-Saar-Ruwer) $37. A rich, unctuous style of auslese, with broad, sweet flavors of poached apple and pear, accented by hints of dried apricots and spice. This is a bit on the sticky side but may come into better balance over time. **90** —*J.C. (12/1/2006)*

Dr. Pauly Bergweiler 2004 Wehlener Sonnenuhr Auslese Riesling (Mosel-Saar-Ruwer) $40. Starts off really promising, with scents of honey, spiced pears, slaty-minerally notes, and a touch of diesel. Flavors follow suit, cleaned up on the finish by mild citrusy notes. The only problem area for this wine is its mouthfeel, which lacks the lightness and grace to score higher, instead coming across as slightly round and bulky. **89** —*J.C. (9/1/2006)*

Dr. Pauly Bergweiler 2003 Wehlener Sonnenuhr Auslese Riesling (Mosel-Saar-Ruwer) $37. The tautest of Pauly Bergweiler's auslese-level offerings, with aromas of stone dust, lime and green apple, balanced on the palate by candied pineapple dusted with minerals. Long finish shows more acidity than many ausleses this vintage. **90** —*J.C. (11/1/2004)*

GERMANY

Dr. Pauly Bergweiler 2001 Wehlener Sonnenuhr Auslese Riesling (Mosel-Saar-Ruwer) $26. If the components meld more harmoniously with age, this rating may seem stingy, but for now there's a disconnect between the sweet flavors of baked pineapple and brown sugar and the hard, ungenerous mouthfeel. Perhaps it's just going though a tough stage in its evolution? **87** —*J.C. (3/1/2003)*

Dr. Pauly Bergweiler 2004 Wehlener Sonnenuhr Kabinett Riesling (Mosel-Saar-Ruwer) $23. Starts off really promising, loaded with vibrant scents of green apples, powdered minerals, and hints of peaches and pears. But while it's nice enough on the palate, it doesn't quite follow through. Off-dry flavors pick up hints of petrol and kerosene and finish short. **86** —*J.C. (10/1/2005)*

Dr. Pauly Bergweiler 2003 Wehlener Sonnenuhr Kabinett Riesling (Mosel-Saar-Ruwer) $22. A bit simple and sweet, offering pineapple fruit, a bit of smoke, and a hint of flowers. Easy drinking, to be sure, but lacks acidity to give the flavors crispness and definition. **84** —*J.C. (11/1/2004)*

Dr. Pauly Bergweiler 2001 Wehlener Sonnenuhr Kabinett Riesling (Mosel-Saar-Ruwer) $10. This is quite a bargain of a wine. With its yeasty aromas and soft flavors of ripe apples and sweet acidity, the wine is full and straightforward with just a touch of currants. **86 Best Buy** —*R.V. (1/1/2004)*

Dr. Pauly Bergweiler 2004 Wehlener Sonnenuhr Spätlese Riesling (Mosel-Saar-Ruwer) $30. A bit simple for a spätlese from such a storied site, but still an enjoyable wine. Sweet apple and pear flavors are paired with relatively low acids. It's mouth-filling; satisfying rather than refreshing. **86** —*J.C. (10/1/2005)*

Dr. Pauly Bergweiler 2003 Wehlener Sonnenuhr Spätlese Riesling (Mosel-Saar-Ruwer) $28. This is very sweet for a spätlese, yet possesses just enough acidity to keep it from seeming too rich or too heavy. Ripe pears and tropical fruits glide across the palate, finishing soft, cushioned in plush, baby fat. Drink now for a sweet, fruity quaff or hold 10 years until it develops more complexity. **90** —*J.C. (11/1/2004)*

Dr. Pauly Bergweiler 2002 Wehlener Sonnenuhr Spätlese Riesling (Mosel-Saar-Ruwer) $25. This light- to medium-bodied wine seems a little low in acidity, but offers a pleasant mouthful of baked apple flavors. A piney, resinous note persists throughout, extending onto the off-dry finish. **85** —*J.C. (8/1/2004)*

Dr. Pauly Bergweiler 2001 Wehlener Sonnenuhr Spätlese Riesling (Mosel-Saar-Ruwer) $20. In 2001, the Pauly Bergweiler wines are sweet for their prädikats across the board. This spätlese shows rich baked pear flavors that play off against oily-stony notes. Finishes a little soft and lacking precision, but it is still very enjoyable. **88** —*J.C. (3/1/2003)*

Dr. Pauly Bergweiler 2002 Wehlener Sonnenuhr Kabinett Riesling (Mosel-Saar-Ruwer) $21. Plump and fruit-filled, this kabinett comes across more like a typical spätlese, with ample sugar and alcohol giving a distinct impression of richness. Baked apple and pear flavors are balanced by just a hint of lime. **88** —*J.C. (8/1/2004)*

DR. WAGNER

Dr. Wagner 2004 Ockfener Bockstein Kabinett Riesling (Mosel-Saar-Ruwer) $19. Light and fresh, this spritely kabinett won't bowl you over, but it just may charm you off your feet. Scents of lime and fresh greens lead the charge, backed by crisp apple and citrus flavors. Lively and mouth-watering on the finish. **89** —*J.C. (5/1/2006)*

Dr. Wagner 2001 Ockfener Bockstein Kabinett Riesling (Mosel-Saar-Ruwer) $17. Light and easy. Clean and refreshing. How else to describe this perfect apéritif wine? There's some crisp green apple and grapefruit flavors and yeasty scents of sour dough that will stimulate the appetite. **87** —*J.C. (3/1/2003)*

Dr. Wagner 2003 Ockfener Bockstein Riesling Kabinett Riesling (Mosel-Saar-Ruwer) $18. This is textbook M-S-R Riesling, light-bodied and elegant, with green apple and lime flavors. It's slightly sweet yet refreshingly acidic, adding pear and citrus on the finish. **87** —*J.C. (12/15/2004)*

Dr. Wagner 2004 Ockfener Bockstein Spätlese Riesling (Mosel-Saar-Ruwer) $22. Juicy and crisp, like a nicely ripened apple or still-hard pear, this medium-bodied spätlese lacks the complexity to push its rating

higher, but it's still a well-balanced, easy-to-drink wine. **86** —*J.C. (2/1/2006)*

Dr. Wagner 2001 Ockfener Bockstein Spätlese Riesling (Mosel-Saar-Ruwer) $20. Smoky and sulfury at first, with just a tiny bit of orange blossom coming through. But the flavors are better, pairing pears and lemons with notes of paraffin. Finishes tart; green apples make a brief appearance before fading. **85** —*J.C. (3/1/2003)*

DUIJN

Duijn 2003 Jannin Trocken Spätburgunder (Baden) $45. Starts off promising, with an elegant bouquet that evokes just-ripe cherries and delicate herbal notes. Turns chocolaty on the palate, offering a smooth, polished mouthfeel and tangy acids on the finish. **84** —*J.C. (7/1/2006)*

EGON MULLER

Egon Muller 2002 Scharzhof QbA Riesling (Mosel-Saar-Ruwer) $17. Light and zesty—but maybe a little too light, as the lemon-lime and gingery flavors don't come across with the strength and precision expected at this estate. Fresh, tart, and cleansing on the finish—a Riesling for shellfish. **84** —*J.C. (11/1/2004)*

Egon Muller 2002 Scharzhofberger Kabinett Riesling (Mosel-Saar-Ruwer) $40. Give this wine a vigorous decanting if you are going to drink it young, as it does have some sulfury, leesy notes that initially detract from its light floral aromas. Light-bodied, with apple, citrus, and earth flavors and a long finish. Gets a lot better with air, so this rating may seem conservative in five or ten years. **87** —*J.C. (11/1/2004)*

EGON MÜLLER-SCHARZHOF

Egon Müller-Scharzhof 2001 Kabinett Riesling (Mosel-Saar-Ruwer) $34. A classic from a great vineyard site, the 2001 kabinett boasts grassy, lime aromas and plenty of tart, citrusy, green apple fruit. It's an S&M wine— the piercing acidity almost painful, while the fresh, sweet fruit provides intense pleasure. Rare is the kabinett that will improve over 20 years, but this one's a shoo-in. Cellar Selection. **92 Cellar Selection** —*J.C. (3/1/2003)*

Egon Müller-Scharzhof 2001 Scharzhof QbA Riesling (Mosel-Saar-Ruwer) $17. The least of Egon Muller's offerings, it's nevertheless a fine wine, featuring crisp Asian pears blended with a dusty brown-mineral-spice component. Slightly sweet, but balanced by just enough grapefruit to keep it together, this would be a good match with many Asian dishes. **89** —*J.C. (3/1/2003)*

EILENZ

Eilenz 2001 Ayler Kupp Kabinett Riesling (Mosel-Saar-Ruwer) $12. Refreshingly close to dry, this wine also layers earth and mineral notes atop crisp green apples and grapefuits. It's light, juicy, and long, with a finish that leaves you thirsting for more. A fine apéritif. **88 Best Buy** —*J.C. (3/1/2003)*

Eilenz 2001 Ayler Kupp QbA Riesling (Mosel-Saar-Ruwer) $12. Thin and sour, a bit too much like lemon water, but does blend in some diesel notes. **81** —*J.C. (1/1/2004)*

Eilenz 2001 Ayler Kupp Spätlese Riesling (Mosel-Saar-Ruwer) $16. The tart, lemony flavors pack a petrol edge, but not a lot of weight or intensity. Pineapple and a hint of kerosene round out the package. **83** —*J.C. (1/1/2004)*

EMRICH-SCHONLEBER

Emrich-Schonleber 2003 Monzinger Frühlingsplätzchen Kabinett Riesling (Nahe) $25. Starts off with some mild sweaty-sock scents that quickly give way to cleaner aromas of pear, apple, and lime. Elegantly wrought and balanced, with off-dry apple and citrus flavors that finish on a tart, lime-driven note. **86** —*J.C. (5/1/2005)*

Emrich-Schonleber 2003 Monzinger Halenberg Auslese Riesling (Nahe) $35. This sweet, full-bodied auslese starts off a little shaky, offering up lots of smoke, diesel, lees, and traces of sulfur, then rights itself in the mouth, where the ripe melon and pear flavors are nicely complemented by smoke and minerals. The long finish picks up a trace of bitterness, which actually helps to balance the sweetness. **90** —*J.C. (2/1/2006)*

ERICH BENDER

Erich Bender 2004 Trockenbeerenauslese 375 ml Huxelrebe (Pfalz) $37. This rather obscure grape variety has produced a medium-bodied TBA complete with scents of dried apricots and a dieselly component. Candied pineapple and citron-like flavors end with hints of peppery spice and sourness. **88** —*J.C. (9/1/2006)*

EUGEN WEHRHEIM

Eugen Wehrheim 2001 Niersteiner Bildstock Kabinett Riesling (Rheinhessen) $13. Raw oysters might be just the ticket to match with this lean, lemony kabinett. There's a bit of plumpness in the midpalate that comes across as a custardy quality, but the lengthy finish is extremely tart. **84** —*J.C. (1/1/2004)*

Eugen Wehrheim 2003 Niersteiner Bildstock Riesling Kabinett Riesling (Rheinhessen) $13. A decent value, Wehrheim's Bildstock kabinett features standard German Riesling aromas and flavors—apple, pear, and citrus—but at a slightly low intensity. Soft textured, with a short finish, but all in proportion and good overall. **86** —*J.C. (12/15/2004)*

Eugen Wehrheim 2003 Niersteiner Oelberg Auslese Riesling (Rheinhessen) $24. Honeyed apples and pears mark the nose of this sweet but balanced auslese. Tasting it reveals hints of dried apricots, cool mint, and an earthy minerality, all tied up in a clean, crisp finish. **89** —*J.C. (5/1/2006)*

Eugen Wehrheim 2003 Niersteiner Orbel Riesling Spätlese Riesling (Rheinhessen) $16. Slightly rubbery at first, with notes of slate, diesel, and lime, then develops apple, pear, and citrus flavors on the palate. Light and spry; well-balanced. Finishes with hints of pith. **87** —*J.C. (12/15/2004)*

Eugen Wehrheim 2001 Niersteiner Orbel Spätlese Riesling (Rheinhessen) $15. Nicely balanced, this wine walks the fine edge between sweet and tart. It brings together apple and pear aromas with pineapple and peach flavors, complementing them with zesty acidity. **89** —*J.C. (3/1/2003)*

EYMANN

Eymann 2003 Classic Riesling (Pfalz) $12. Light, dry, and crisp, this is the perfect Riesling to enjoy with food. It has structure, acidity, flavors of green apples, and a lively, fresh finish. **87 Best Buy** —*R.V. (4/1/2005)*

Eymann 1999 Gönnheimer Mandelgarten Eiswein Riesling (Pfalz) $74. The Toreye is the ancient name of the Eymann family and is used to designate the top wines from this third-generation family estate. As so often with eiswein, this wine distills the essence of Riesling into a few drops of sweetness, honey, and piercing acidity. Will develop over many years. A beautiful wine. **91** —*R.V. (4/1/2005)*

Eymann 2001 Selektion Toreye Gönnheimer Sonnenberg Trocken Spätburgunder (Pfalz) $26. This is a very dry red wine, with flavors of fresh strawberries and just a touch of toast. It is lean and austere but there is still a lively juiciness to the fruit. Drink now. **86** —*R.V. (4/1/2005)*

FALCON HILL

Falcon Hill 2005 Dry Riesling (Rheinhessen) $9. Light and dry, with scents of limes, fresh ferns, and green apple. Flavors of green apple and citrus finish crisp and clean. **83** —*J.C. (12/1/2006)*

FISCHER

Fischer 2004 Kabinett Trocken Riesling (Baden) $18. This hard, stony-textured wine will be tough to warm up to for some, while rock-heads will extol its minerally virtues. Hints of lime and green plum keep it from being too austere, while it finishes cool and long. **86** —*J.C. (12/1/2006)*

FITZ-RITTER

Fitz-Ritter 2003 Spätlese Gewürztraminer (Pfalz) $18. Nice Gewürz, for those consumers looking for something outside of Alsace. Exaggerated floral aromas are typical, so are the lychee and spice flavors. There's a modest sweetness to this wine, so it should work well with spicy Asian foods. **88** —*J.C. (12/15/2004)*

Fitz-Ritter 2005 Dürkheimer Abtsfronhof Kabinett Trocken Riesling (Pfalz) $16. Perfumed and floral on the nose, but there's also a fair degree of crushed stone buffered by hints of green apple and citrus. Flavors are strongly floral and mineral, then finish stony and dry. **86** —*J.C. (12/1/2006)*

Fitz-Ritter 2003 Dürkheimer Abtsfronhof Riesling Spätlese Halbtrocken Riesling (Pfalz) $18. For a halbtrocken, this is pretty darn dry. Grapefruit and green apple aromas give way to flavors of wet stone and lime, finishing tart and stony. There's just enough fruit to balance the elevated acids and low residual sugar. Probably best with seafood. **87** —*J.C. (12/15/2004)*

Fitz-Ritter NV Extra Trocken Sekt Riesling (Pfalz) $15. Slightly toasty on the nose, but there's plenty of fresh fruit as well, ranging from apple to pineapple and tangerine. Clean, fresh, and easy to drink and enjoy. **87** —*J.C. (6/1/2006)*

FORSTMEISTER GELTZ ZILLIKEN

Forstmeister Geltz Zilliken 2001 Ockfener Bockstein Kabinett Riesling (Mosel-Saar-Ruwer) $NA. This is an attractively poised wine with crisp, fresh fruit and flavors of white currants and green apples. Good acidity shows through, giving the wine lightness and poise. **88** —*R.V. (1/1/2004)*

Forstmeister Geltz Zilliken 2001 Saarburger Rausch Kabinett Riesling (Mosel-Saar-Ruwer) $NA. The 24 acre vineyard of Hans-Joachim Zilliken is in one of the best vineyard sites of the Saar. The style combines pleasing soft fruit with fresh, refreshing crisp, appley fruit flavors. It is finely poised, shot through with steel and acidity. **89** —*R.V. (1/1/2004)*

FRANZ KÜNSTLER

Franz Künstler 2001 Hochheimer Holle Auslese Riesling (Rheingau) $60. It's the glorious pale gold color which sets this wine as a star. That color is the forerunner of the rich botrytis and honey aromas, touched with flavors of tropical fruits and mangos. It is rich, balanced, and intense. **92** —*R.V. (1/1/2004)*

Franz Künstler 2001 Hochheimer Hölle Eiswein Riesling (Rheingau) $140. The intense sweetness of this may be one-dimensional, but what a dimension. With its deep gold color, the richness is overpowering and intensely opulent. A wine to savor in sips rather than gulps. **90** —*R.V. (1/1/2004)*

Franz Künstler 2001 Hochheimer Holle Spätlese Trocken Riesling (Rheingau) $40. These Trocken Spätlese with their high (12.5%) alcohol are strange. They lack the grace of the lighter wines. But they pack punch and power which lies oddly with freshly ripe grapes. Peppery characters are uncomfortable to drink. **84** —*R.V. (1/1/2004)*

Franz Künstler 2001 Hochheimer Kirchenstück Eiswein Riesling (Rheingau) $150. This wine is the perfect example of the difference between the huge richness of a TBA and the relative delicacy of an Eiswein. Like pure syrup, it trickles through the palate, leaving flavors of ripe apricots, orange marmalade, and intense honey. The intensity of the fruit flavors masks the high acidity but does show up the lightness that stays in the mouth. **94** —*R.V. (1/1/2004)*

Franz Künstler 2002 Hochheimer Reichestal Kabinett Riesling (Rheingau) $20. This is sweet and rich for a kabinett, with smoky, minerally scents that accent bright apple-juice flavors. Finishes a bit soft. **85** —*J.C. (8/1/2004)*

Franz Künstler 2001 Hochheimer Reichestal Kabinett Riesling (Rheingau) $20. Caramel and warm straw aromas are not what makes this wine attractive. But the yeasty fruit, and full fat flavors with a touch of acidity certainly make it immediately drinkable. **84** —*R.V. (1/1/2004)*

FRED PRINZ

Fred Prinz 2003 Hallgartener Jungfer Kabinett Riesling (Rheingau) $21. Plump and round in the mouth yet not fat or heavy, this is what 2003 can deliver when the wines are well-made—easy to like, easy to drink Rieslings of great mass appeal. Ripe stone fruit blends with apple and citrus, picking up hints of melon on the finish. **87** —*J.C. (5/1/2005)*

Fred Prinz 2001 Hallgartner Jungfer Spätlese Riesling (Rheingau) $NA. There is crisp acidity with a nice concentration of fruit salad flavors. The wine still tastes young and fresh, but could develop. **87** —*R.V. (1/1/2004)*

Fred Prinz 2001 Hallgartner Schonhell Spätlese Trocken Riesling (Rheingau) $NA. This is a rare Trocken that works, and finishes by tasting like an Alsace. Rich, concentrated, and powerful, there are flavors of spice and exotic fruits. It should develop well. **89** —*R.V. (1/1/2004)*

Fred Prinz 2001 Hallgartner Jungfer Kabinett White Blend (Rheingau) $NA. Fred Prinz makes the most of his small Hallgarten vineyards. This wine, with its full, pure fruit and delicious acidity has intense piercing vibrant flavors of currants. It is delicious and intense. **92** —*R.V. (1/1/2004)*

FREIHERR HEYL ZU HERRNSHEIM

Freiherr Heyl zu Herrnsheim 2003 Baron Heyl Estate Riesling QbA Riesling (Rheinhessen) $15. Modest melon and baked apple notes are offset by earthier, slatier nuances, wrapped around a core of grapefruity acids. A bit tart, but well-made and deserving of a place at the table. **86** —*J.C. (12/15/2004)*

Freiherr Heyl zu Herrnsheim 2005 Baron Heyl Kabinett Riesling (Rheinhessen) $19. A fairly big, broad-shouldered wine that displays ripe baked apple and spice scents, but also intense minerality. The slightly oily texture comes off like creamy molten rock, finishing long and mostly dry, with lingering slatey notes. **91 Editors' Choice** —*J.C. (12/1/2006)*

Freiherr Heyl zu Herrnsheim 2004 Baron Heyl Nierstein Kabinett Riesling (Rheinhessen) $19. On the big (12% alcohol) and dry side, with weighty flavors of minerals and spice undergirding ripe apple and pineapple notes. Not a traditional fruchtig kabinett, but one that should go well with rich fish dishes and roast chicken. Long on the finish. **90 Editors' Choice** —*J.C. (7/1/2006)*

Freiherr Heyl zu Herrnsheim 2003 Baron Heyl Nierstein Kabinett Riesling (Rheinhessen) $16. Herrnsheim tends toward a drier style of wine without labeling it as such, so this kabinett is crisp and almost dry-tasting. Apple blossoms and limes on the nose are complemented by hints of diesel and a tart, steely finish. **86** —*J.C. (12/15/2004)*

Freiherr Heyl zu Herrnsheim 2003 Baron Heyl Nierstein Riesling Spätlese Riesling (Rheinhessen) $24. Starts with slightly floral apple and pear aromas, developing tons of tropical fruit flavors on the palate; soft and inviting yet full-flavored. Not a simple fruit bomb, as it reveals smoky, minerally nuances on the long finish. **91 Editors' Choice** —*J.C. (12/15/2004)*

Freiherr Heyl zu Herrnsheim 2001 Baron Heyl Nierstein Spätlese Riesling (Rheinhessen) $11. Straightforward baked apple and dried spice aromas and flavors combine pleasantly in this value-priced regional blend. It's weighty enough to work with food, sweetly balanced enough to work on its own, with a peppery bite to the finish. **87 Best Buy** —*J.C. (3/1/2003)*

Freiherr Heyl zu Herrnsheim 2001 Nierstein Kabinett Riesling (Rheinhessen) $14. Light and dry, with aromas of citrus and honey, and flavors reminiscent of nasturtium blossoms—floral and peppery. Grapefruit takes charge on the tart, clean finish. **86** —*J.C. (3/1/2003)*

Freiherr Heyl zu Herrnsheim 2001 Nierstein Pettental QbA Trocken Riesling (Rheinhessen) $30. A bit pricey, but it's a fine dry Riesling, filled with green apples, limes, and hints of slate. The slightly powdery texture in the mouth speaks of crushed rock and minerals, while the zesty lime flavors linger on the finish. **88** —*J.C. (3/1/2003)*

Freiherr Heyl zu Herrnsheim 2001 Red Slate Spätlese Trocken Riesling (Rheinhessen) $25. This wine shows the perils in producing trocken-style wines. There's no sugar to hide the wine's apparent under-ripeness. It tastes lean and citrusy, screaming of grapefruit on the finish. Try with raw oysters or clams. It's a Riesling that could stand in for Chablis or Muscadet. **84** —*J.C. (3/1/2003)*

FRIEDRICH-WILHELM-GYMNASIUM

Friedrich-Wilhelm-Gymnasium 2004 Bernkasteler Badstube Kabinett Halbtrocken Riesling (Mosel-Saar-Ruwer) $14. This medium-bodied halbtrocken features open aromas of blended apples, pears, and melons, infused with just enough spicy complexity. Finishes off-dry, finely representative of its classification. **87** —*J.C. (7/1/2006)*

Friedrich-Wilhelm-Gymnasium 2001 Graacher Himmelreich Auslese Riesling (Mosel-Saar-Ruwer) $24. The school vineyards of this high school (whose more famous alumni include Karl Marx) produce wines which are typically light. This wine is still very young, showing yeasty aromas, but the palate is creamy, with some yeast flavors on top of sweet

acidity and flavors of green grapes. The aftertaste leaves a touch of citrus. **92** —*R.V. (1/1/2004)*

Friedrich-Wilhelm-Gymnasium 2001 Graacher Himmelreich Kabinett Riesling (Mosel-Saar-Ruwer) $18. With its poised, sweet, but delicate fruit, this is a fine, fresh wine from the top vineyard in Graach, next to Bernkastel. Acidity shows through at the end, leaving a fine purity and tastes of red currants. **90** —*R.V. (1/1/2004)*

Friedrich-Wilhelm-Gymnasium 2004 Graacher Himmelreich Spätlese Riesling (Mosel-Saar-Ruwer) $19. Plump in the mouth but backed by strong acidity, this spätlese offers impressive value. Pineapple, green apple, and citrus flavors are joined by a streak of dusty minerals that give this a drier-than-expected finish. **90 Editors' Choice** —*J.C. (9/1/2006)*

Friedrich-Wilhelm-Gymnasium 2001 Graacher Himmelreich Spätlese Riesling (Mosel-Saar-Ruwer) $18. The light, poised delicate character of this wine, with delicious fruit shows a fine, crisp style. With its fresh acidity, and flavors of apricots, it already makes an appealing glass of summer wine. **91** —*R.V. (1/1/2004)*

Friedrich-Wilhelm-Gymnasium 2000 Graacher Himmelreich Spätlese Riesling (Mosel-Saar-Ruwer) $18. **83** —*D.T. (5/1/2002)*

Friedrich-Wilhelm-Gymnasium 2001 Trittenheimer Apotheke Ausles Riesling (Mosel-Saar-Ruwer) $20. The wine has immediately attractive aromas of almonds, followed by full, nutty fruit with layers of acidity and sweet fruit. It is intense, immediately appealing, showing flavors of almond cakes. **90** —*R.V. (1/1/2004)*

Friedrich-Wilhelm-Gymnasium 2000 Trittenheimer Apotheke Kabinett Riesling (Mosel-Saar-Ruwer) $14. **84** —*J.C. (5/1/2002)*

Friedrich-Wilhelm-Gymnasium 2001 Trittenheimer Apotheke Spätlese Riesling (Mosel-Saar-Ruwer) $18. The minerally wines of the Trittenheim Apotheke vineyard have gained enormously in reputation in recent years. The character shows well in this creamy ripe wine, with its soft, delicate fruit flavors shot through with a crisp layer of tannin, which shows how young the wine is. Yeasty flavors show through. This will develop well over 5-10 years. **92** —*R.V. (1/1/2004)*

Friedrich-Wilhelm-Gymnasium 2000 Trittenheimer Apothke Spätlese Riesling (Mosel-Saar-Ruwer) $18. **86** —*C.S. (5/1/2002)*

FÜRST VON METTERNICH

Fürst von Metternich NV Brut Riesling Sekt Riesling (Germany) $23. Fresh and apple-y from start to finish, with even a hint of spring flowers. Creamy and a bit soft in the mouth. This isn't complex, but is clean and tasty, easy-to-drink bubbly. **86** —*J.C. (12/31/2004)*

Fürst von Metternich NV Cuvée Trocken Riesling Sekt Riesling (Germany) $15. Lilac-scented, this wine develops hints of apples and pears on the nose, while the flavors gravitate toward melon and peach. Light-bodied and a bit soft, but easy to drink. Not as dry as expected, given the trocken designation. **85** —*J.C. (12/31/2004)*

FURST ZU HOHENLOHE

Furst zu Hohenlohe 2002 Verrenberger Verrenberg Butzen QbA Trocken Riesling (Württemberg) $13. Shows complexity and freshness, with scents of apple blossoms and citrus blending into flavors of pear and lime. Nicely balanced, dry without being austere, yet crisp and refreshing on the finish. **87** —*J.C. (8/1/2004)*

Furst zu Hohenlohe 2002 Verrenberger Verrenberg Butzen Spätlese Riesling (Oehringen) $24. Lacks the sweetness expected of a spätlese—much of the sugar has been converted to alcohol, which is a substantial 12.5%. Pleasant green apple aromas are backed by similar flavors and a touch of lemon. **84** —*J.C. (8/1/2004)*

G. DICKENSHEID

G. Dickensheid 2003 Riesling Kabinett Riesling (Rheinhessen) $10. Apricot and tangerine aromas lead into flavors of ripe peaches and nectarines. This is a bit heavy and low in acid, but the richness is not so much from sugar as it is from high alcohol. **84 Best Buy** —*J.C. (12/15/2004)*

GEH. RAT DR. VON BASSERMANN-JORDAN

Geh. Rat Dr. von Bassermann-Jordan 2004 Deidesheimer Paradiesgarten Kabinett Riesling (Pfalz) $19. On first glance, this wine comes across as too simple and sweet. But give it some time and a spicy, slatey-minerally component emerges, providing balance and complexity to the ripe pear flavors. An estate that seems to be undergoing a bit of a resurgence. **86** —J.C. (5/1/2006)

Geh. Rat Dr. von Bassermann-Jordan 2001 Deidesheimer Paradiesgarten Kabinett Riesling (Pfalz) $16. A disappointing effort from a usually reliable producer, the 2001 Paradiesgarten kabinett is tart and citric, lacking in depth but not for acidity. Because of this, it would make a nice match with raw shellfish. **83** —J.C. (1/1/2004)

Geh. Rat Dr. von Bassermann-Jordan 2003 Deidesheimer Paradiesgarten Riesling Kabinett Riesling (Pfalz) $19. Intriguing notes of smoke and mineral on the nose raise hopes, but this medium-weight wine's soft, sweet pear fruit turns tart and sour on the finish. **84** —J.C. (12/15/2004)

Geh. Rat Dr. von Bassermann-Jordan NV Deutscher Sekt Brut Riesling (Pfalz) $NA. Crisp and assertive, with boldly fruity aromas of apple, pear, pineapple and melon. No yeastiness to speak of, just bright fruit and froth in a dry, fresh format. **87** —J.C. (6/1/2006)

Geh. Rat Dr. von Bassermann-Jordan 2003 Forster Jesuitengarten Riesling Spätlese Riesling (Pfalz) $29. Features lots of ripe apple and peach flavors, made more interesting by a mineral note that's lurking beneath the surface (it should emerge more fully in a few years' time). Slightly viscous and quite sweet, but with firm acids on the finish to provide balance. **89** —J.C. (12/15/2004)

Geh. Rat Dr. von Bassermann-Jordan 2004 Forster Jesuitengarten Spätlese Riesling (Pfalz) $28. With a nose marked by poached pears, dried spices, and mineral inflections, this gets off to a good start. Add in flavors of melon, mineral, and spice, a racy mouthfeel and a long mineral-dusted finish, and it's a true winner. **90** —J.C. (2/1/2006)

Geh. Rat Dr. von Bassermann-Jordan 2001 Forster Jesuitengarten Spätlese Riesling (Pfalz) $26. Some sulfurous aromatics dampen the nose, but you can still pick up high-toned scents of green apple, citrus, and mint. The flavors are crystal-clear, but a bit simple, revolving around lime candy. Lighter and cleaner than some other spätlesen this vintage, it should age better as a result. **86** —J.C. (3/1/2003)

Geh. Rat Dr. von Bassermann-Jordan 2003 Forster Ungeheuer Riesling Spätlese Trocken Riesling (Pfalz) $27. An intriguing wine, one that starts with scents of slate and under-ripe melon. The palate is full of melon and peach, but also sharp, citrusy acids that provide balance and a racy mouthfeel. Crisp on the finish. **87** —J.C. (12/15/2004)

Geh. Rat Dr. von Bassermann-Jordan 2001 QbA Riesling (Pfalz) $14. Starts off just fine, with pear and quince aromas alongside a warm cinnamon note. Then in the mouth it's rich and soft upfront, yet overly tangy on the finish—a disconnect that never quite resolves. **83** —J.C. (1/1/2004)

Geh. Rat Dr. von Bassermann-Jordan 2004 QbA Trocken Riesling (Pfalz) $17. Smoky and leesy on the nose, this big, broad-shouldered trocken boasts bold flavors of apple and clove, yet finishes dry, stony and long. Could work nicely with not-too-sweet, not-too-hot Asian dishes. **88** —J.C. (10/1/2005)

Geh. Rat Dr. von Bassermann-Jordan 2001 QbA Trocken Riesling (Pfalz) $14. While the aromas hint at peaches and cinnamon, the flavors lean toward baked apples, with a backbone of grapefruity acidity. Finishes long and tart—maybe a trifle too tart for some tasters. **85** —J.C. (3/1/2003)

Geh. Rat Dr. von Bassermann-Jordan 2005 Trocken QbA Riesling (Pfalz) $16. Starts off with beautiful scents of minerals, dried spices, and a hint of peach, but not quite as attractive on the palate, where it seems heavy at times despite some unreleased CO2. Then it turns tangy-tart on the finish. This youthful wine comes across as a bit disjointed; hopefully, that will improve over the next few months in bottle and this rating will look conservative. **85** —J.C. (12/1/2006)

GEORG BREUER

Georg Breuer 2004 Spätburgunder Rouge Pinot Noir (Rheingau) $20. Light and fresh, marked by flavors of pie cherries, cranberries, and fresh herbs or grasses. Crisp and tart on the finish. **83** —J.C. (7/1/2006)

Georg Breuer 2004 Berg Schlossberg Auslese 375 ml Riesling (Rheingau) $95. On the full-bodied side, but the combined weight of sugar and alcohol is ably balanced by bountiful acids. Floral notes lead off the nose, followed by hints of pineapple and spice, then dried apricots and candied fruit kick in on the palate. Clean on the finish, not overly sweet or cloying. **92** —J.C. (9/1/2006)

Georg Breuer 2003 Berg Schlossberg Auslese 375 ml Riesling (Rheingau) $80. Thick and oily, showing impressive levels of sugar. Starts with honeyed peaches, then shows off marmalade and dried fruit notes on the palate. Definitely big and sweet, but also a bit heavy at this stage. Drink now for the sweetness, or try holding 10 years and see what happens. **88** —J.C. (5/1/2005)

Georg Breuer 2003 Berg Schlossberg Trockenbeerenauslese Riesling (Rheingau) $250. There's a hint of volatility to the otherwise heady aromas of dried apricot and candied pineapple, but the flavors seem unaffected, delivering loads of sweet stone fruit and citrus. Thick and viscous on the palate, finishing long and sweet, if somewhat low in acidity. Approachable now, but should easily age for 20–30 years. **91** —J.C. (5/1/2005)

Georg Breuer 2002 Charm Riesling (Rheingau) $14. Smells like warm sandstone and cinnamon, turning crisp and racy on the palate. It's a bit lean, but offers fine flavors of peach, spice, and plenty of mineral notes. Finishes bright and clean. A good value in Rheingau Riesling. **87** —J.C. (11/1/2004)

Georg Breuer 2004 Estate Rüdesheim QbA Riesling (Rheingau) $20. Breuer's entry-level wine isn't cheap, but it's also pretty good, marrying stony, minty scents with flavors of lime, fresh herbs, and wet stones. It's light in body for such an alcoholic Rheingau Riesling, with a clean, fresh finish. **85** —J.C. (5/1/2006)

Georg Breuer 1999 GB Riesling (Rheingau) $13. A floral and lightly citric nose introduces this dry, crisply elegant Riesling. The wine cleanses the palate with compact and detailed flavors and leaves you reaching quickly for the next sip. This brand new wine for Breuer is designed especially for early consumption and wine-by-the-glass programs, and fulfills its mission beautifully. **88 Best Buy** —P.G. (8/1/2001)

Georg Breuer 1999 Montosa Riesling (Rheingau) $23. Montosa is a proprietary wine from Breuer's vineyards. Attractively aromatic it displays ripe pear, kiwi, and tangerine scents wiht a hint of petrol. On the palate it's like a crisp green apple, offset by stony accents and showing bright acidity. The crisp finish shows good length. **88** (8/1/2001)

Georg Breuer 1998 Rauenthal Nonnenberg Riesling (Rheingau) $36. Solid and well-rounded, this very tasty wine has lively spice and apple aromas. The juice has nice texture on the tongue, well-defined apple, and peach flavors, and again the spice, which may be characteristic of the Nonnenberg vineyard. The long, even finish shows the tangy spice elements well. Will drink well for the next five years, maybe more. **89** (8/1/2001)

Georg Breuer 2004 Rauenthal Nonnenberg QbA Riesling (Rheingau) $50. My colleagues tell me I'm being too harsh on this wine, but I just don't get it. It's good, but rather austere and unyielding, despite having ripe citrus flavors. There's also a grassy, herbal note that detracts from the purity of the Riesling fruit. **85** —J.C. (7/1/2006)

Georg Breuer 2002 Rauenthal Nonnenberg QbA Riesling (Rheingau) $46. Seems a bit muted and unexpressive, offering up hints of citrus accompanied by rich earth and spice components. A bit full-bodied, almost heavy. Close to dry. **85** —J.C. (11/1/2004)

Georg Breuer 2003 Rauenthaler Nonnenberg Auslese 375 ml Riesling (Rheingau) $79. Very sweet and unctuous, this thick, honeyed wine tastes more like a beerenauslese (or more), but without much if any botrytis. Candied pineapple and penetrating orange flavors coat the palate. Despite low acidity, this wine seems more balanced than a couple of Breuer's earlier 2003 releases. Hold 10–15 years, unless you like drinking marmalade. **93** —J.C. (2/1/2006)

GERMANY

Georg Breuer 2003 Rauenthaler Nonnenberg Riesling Trockenbeerenauslese 375 ml Riesling (Rheingau) $283. Insanely priced, but if you love ultra-sticky dessert wines, this is one you'll want to try at least once. Shows the merest hint of volatility on the nose, but also striking floral and mineral components. Broad and viscous on the palate, with intensely honeyed flavors of dried apricots and orange marmalade that last a long, long time. Should age virtually forever. **94** —*J.C. (9/1/2006)*

Georg Breuer 2002 Rudesheim Berg Schlossberg QbA Riesling (Rheingau) $50. Slightly floral, with apple blossom notes gracing pear and lime fruit, but a bit low acid and even heavy, showing a trace of sweetness. Good wine, but disappointing for this bottling. Tasted twice, with consistent results. **85** —*J.C. (11/1/2004)*

Georg Breuer 1998 Rüdeshemier Berg Schlossberg Riesling (Rheingau) $40. Slate, smoke, and tart and tropical fruit scents mix in the beguiling nose. This concentrated wine is still young and tight, but it already shows rich, full fruit flavors that broaden into a full, generous finish as it breathes. The brisk acidity and mineral-slate elements add depth and complexity. Can use a few years to show all its best stuff. **92** *(8/1/2001)*

Georg Breuer 2001 Terra Montosa Riesling (Rheingau) $20. Dusty and smoky, the emphasis is on dried earth and spices, with mere hints of baked apple. It's a full-bodied, muscular Riesling that shows the essence of the earth from which it comes, enlivened by a bracing, lemony finish. **90 Editors' Choice** —*J.C. (3/1/2003)*

Georg Breuer 2002 Terra Montosa Qualitätswein Riesling (Rheingau) $22. This big, muscular Riesling is practically dry and features very little overt fruitiness. Instead, it's loaded with minerals: the aromas are of diesel fuel and vegetable oil, the flavors are liquid stone. Finishes long. **89** —*J.C. (11/1/2004)*

GRAFF

Graff 2004 Wehlener Sonnenuhr Kabinett Riesling (Mosel-Saar-Ruwer) $12. Star winemaker Ernie Loosen is now consulting for Graff, and the wines have taken a step up in quality. Leesy and a bit sulfury on the nose, but underneath are some wonderfully pure flavors of melon and mineral, finishing with a dusting of dried spices and powdered mineral over poached apple. Could be racier, but the broad, mouth-filling flavors are satisfying in a different way. **89 Best Buy** —*J.C. (10/1/2005)*

GRANS-FASSIAN

Grans-Fassian 2003 QbA Riesling (Mosel-Saar-Ruwer) $17. Shows more delicacy than many 2003s, with flowery, green fruit aromas and a light, ethereal mouthfeel. Pear and melon flavors are easy to enjoy now, finishing soft. **86** —*J.C. (5/1/2005)*

Grans-Fassian 2001 Trittenheimer Apotheke Riesling (Mosel-Saar-Ruwer) $21. Thick, rich, and sweet, this is not what you'd typically expect in a kabinett, but put the labeling prejudices aside, and it's an enjoyable wine, filled with stone fruits and smoky quartz dust. Unlike most kabinetts, it's probably best served at the end of the meal. **87** —*J.C. (3/1/2003)*

Grans-Fassian 2005 Trittenheimer Apotheke Auslese Riesling (Mosel-Saar-Ruwer) $40. This estate has been turning out better and better wines nearly every year, and this may be its best yet. A fabulous bouquet of honeyed slate, green apples, and limes is followed by flavors that are sweet yet balanced, with great freshness and racy acidity. Finishes long and mouth-watering. Not only about power, there's also elegance to spare. **94 Editors' Choice** —*J.C. (12/1/2006)*

Grans-Fassian 2004 Trittenheimer Apotheke Auslese Riesling (Mosel-Saar-Ruwer) $40. This winery seems to be moving from strength to strength, turning out thickly concentrated yet precise wines in 2003 and now offering this lithe, succulent 2004 auslese. Lime and green apple aromas even smell refreshing, while the sweet apple and pineapple flavors are balanced by ample, yet soft, acids. A mouth-watering finish just adds to the package. **90** —*J.C. (9/1/2006)*

Grans-Fassian 2004 Trittenheimer Apotheke Spätlese Riesling (Mosel-Saar-Ruwer) $31. Lacks the layered intensity that the 2003 version of this wine showed at this stage, but still delivers stony, minerally aromas and prototypical flavors of green apples and fresh limes. Light in body, but clean and wonderfuly refreshing on the finish. **86** —*J.C. (5/1/2006)*

Grans-Fassian 2003 Trittenheimer Apotheke Spätlese Riesling (Mosel-Saar-Ruwer) $30. Boasts plenty of bright springtime aromas—rainwater and apple blossoms—but adds deep bass notes of mineral and earth. Honeyed tree fruits on the palate are sweet, but balanced by plentiful acids (not tart, malic acidity, but riper, tartaric acids). Thickly concentrated, yet light-bodied and fresh. Another 2003 that is drinkable now, yet should age for 10–15 years. **91** —*J.C. (12/15/2004)*

Grans-Fassian 2005 Trittenheimer Kabinett Riesling (Mosel-Saar-Ruwer) $21. It's stony and minerally on the nose, but also boasts vivid pear, melon, and green apple scents. The flavors verge on tropical, mixing ripe pear and melon notes with underpinnings of tangerine. It's all wrapped in a plump, succulent texture and features a long, lipsmacking finish. **91 Editors' Choice** —*J.C. (12/1/2006)*

Grans-Fassian 2004 Trittenheimer Kabinett Riesling (Mosel-Saar-Ruwer) $21. Light, clean, and refreshing—all the qualities you might expect from a Mosel kabinett—and this wine has them. Pear, apple, and melon aromas and flavors even bring hints of spice and minerality with them, elevating this wine above the rest of the pack. **88** —*J.C. (7/1/2006)*

Grans-Fassian 2001 Trittenheimer Kabinett Riesling (Mosel-Saar-Ruwer) $14. This is an atypically big, mouth-filling kabinett, full of stone fruits, such as peach and nectarine, as well as some red fruits—perhaps cherries. Despite its richness and kaleidoscopic waves of fruit, it never seems heavy, coming elegantly to a long and mouth-watering close. **91 Best Buy** —*J.C. (3/1/2003)*

GROEBE

Groebe 2003 Westhofener Kabinett Trocken Riesling (Rheinhessen) $17. Starts off sulfury and earthy, and stays in that sullen funk for a while. It's plump on the palate, just doesn't give up that much in the way of fruit flavors, finishing tart. **84** —*J.C. (11/1/2004)*

Groebe 2003 Westhofener Kirchspiel Spätlese Riesling (Rheinhessen) $26. Nicely balanced, yet still reflects the vintage's hot character in its rounded acids and sweet finish. Rainwater, green apples, and limes provide a counterweight to the sugar and give the wine a light, airy feel. **87** —*J.C. (11/1/2004)*

Groebe 2004 Westhofener Riesling Kabinett Riesling (Rheinhessen) $18. Flagrantly floral on the nose, with lilac scents layered over pineapple fruit. Despite fresh apple and pear flavors over a minerally foundation, this wine comes across as a bit heavy, only partially balanced by some tangy acids on the finish. **84** —*J.C. (7/1/2006)*

GUNDERLOCH

Gunderloch 2004 Diva Spätlese Riesling (Rheinhessen) $21. This light-bodied, relatively dry spätlese starts off with some slightly rubbery scents, then moves into green apple and citrus. Picks up some spice and melon notes on the medium-length finish. **86** —*J.C. (10/1/2005)*

Gunderloch 2002 Diva Spätlese Riesling (Rheinhessen) $20. Seems lacking in acidity, with slightly baked or cooked apple aromas and flavors that aren't unpleasant, just lacking an extra dimension of verve or stuffing. **85** —*J.C. (8/1/2004)*

Gunderloch 2004 Dry Qualitätswein Riesling (Rheinhessen) $19. A bit leesy and reduced on the nose, but that should clear up within another few months (maybe even by the time you read this). Underneath is a plump, custardy wine that's marked by citrus and mineral flavors. Finishes peppery, chalky, and dry. Serve with anything from shellfish to poultry. **87** —*J.C. (10/1/2005)*

Gunderloch 2002 Jean Baptiste Kabinett Riesling (Rheingau) $18. If not for a sulfury-yeasty note on the nose, this wine would have scored higher. Its citrus and mineral elements bring to mind limes and riverstones, picking up luscious peach notes on the finish while staying fresh and lively. Try decanting, or hold another year or two before opening. **86** —*J.C. (8/1/2004)*

Gunderloch 2004 Jean-Baptiste Kabinett Riesling (Rheinhessen) $20. Smoky, stony, and minerally, but there's also a solid core of melon and nectarine fruit in this medium-bodied, fairly dry kabinett. Crisp on the finish, where it picks up a hint of citrus pith. **87** —*J.C. (10/1/2005)*

GYSLER

Gysler 2004 Weinheimer Kabinett Riesling (Rheinhessen) $17. Starts off a bit tarry and rubbery—downright stinky, in fact. Just be patient, or decant vigorously, and you'll be amply rewarded by pineapple fruit so pure it seems almost crystalline in both flavor and structure. It's fleshy, yet sharply delineated and focused, ending in a laserbeam of vibrant citrus. **89** —*J.C. (10/1/2005)*

H. & R. LINGENFELDER

H. & R. Lingenfelder 2001 Freinsheimer Goldberg Spätlese Scheurebe (Pfalz) $26. Whoa, is this a different animal from the Rieslings. Smells slightly cheesy and funky, but delivers fresh pineapple flavors. A well-made example from a variety that's a bit of an acquired taste. **85** —*J.C. (1/1/2004)*

HANS LANG

Hans Lang 2001 Hallgartner Jungfer Eiswein Riesling (Rheingau) $NA. A deliciously fresh wine, with springtime ripeness and a vibrancy and life. Flavors of orange marmalade and crisp honey come with the lightness and freshness. **91** —*R.V. (1/1/2004)*

Hans Lang 2001 Hattenheimer Wisselbrunnen Auslese Riesling (Rheingau) $NA. Crisp currant flavors and a touch of sweet acidity play with fine ripe fruit to make an attractive, early drinking style of wine. **85** —*R.V. (1/1/2004)*

Hans Lang 2001 Hattenheimer Wisselbrunnen Beerenauslese Riesling (Rheingau) $NA. The 45-acre Hans Lang estate is run by Johann Maximilian Lang from the winery in Hattenheim. With this Beerenauslese, he has been able to extract all the best elements of botrytis. It is beautifully intense, full of ripe, sweet fruit, with tangible flavors of raisins and honey. The palate is silky smooth, voluptuous, opulent. There is enormous intensity. **94** —*R.V. (1/1/2004)*

Hans Lang 2001 Hattenheimer Wisselbrunnen Spätlese Riesling (Rheingau) $NA. Balanced fruit between sweetness and dryness shows some acidity over flavors of quince and baking apples. The wine has a creamy texture, but also full, sweet and dry fruit. **88** —*R.V. (1/1/2004)*

Hans Lang 2001 Kabinett Riesling (Rheingau) $NA. This is a classic, but it just misses greatness. There is sweetness at the start and the fruit is very ripe, balanced by a layer of tannin. Very pure fruit with thirst quenching acidity. **88** —*R.V. (1/1/2004)*

Hans Lang 2001 Spätlese Riesling (Rheingau) $NA. A touch of sulfur on the nose spoils the wine, but there is also attractive simple fruit with some pleasant sweetness. **83** —*R.V. (1/1/2004)*

HEINRICH SEEBRICH

Heinrich Seebrich 2001 Niersteiner Hipping Spätlese Riesling (Rheinhessen) $13. Simple apple and citrus fruit in a snappy, fresh package. The sugar is a little high for use as an apéritif, so chill it down and serve it at your next picnic. **85** —*J.C. (3/1/2003)*

HEINZ SCHMITT

Heinz Schmitt 2004 Halbtrocken Riesling (Mosel-Saar-Ruwer) $13. Seems a bit too big and bulky in the mouth, with a touch of warmth on the finish, but has plenty of pluses as well, showing more minerality and complexity than many wines in this price range. Hints of honey, petrol, and smoke intertwine with melon and pineapple fruit. **86** —*J.C. (7/1/2006)*

HELMUT HEXAMER

Helmut Hexamer 2001 Meddersheimer Rheingrafenberg Spätlese S Riesling (Nahe) $26. New World enthusiasts may ask, "Where's the fruit?" This wine is all about the earth, and fans of terroir should jump at it. Smoky and earthy on the nose, the palate delivers deep, rich notes of honeyed stones and dried spices. **90** —*J.C. (3/1/2003)*

HELMUT HEXAMER

Helmut Hexamer 2004 Quarzit Meddersheimer Rheingrafenberg Qualitätswein Riesling (Nahe) $22. Racy and crisp, this wine showcases the balance that is a hallmark of the best '04s. Green apple and lime aromas segue easily into similar flavors, graced with touches of spring flowers and leafy greens, while the vibrant apple notes linger elegantly on the finish. **91 Editors' Choice** —*J.C. (10/1/2005)*

HENKELL

Henkell 2000 Chardonnay Brut Sekt Chardonnay (Germany) $23. An ambitious bottling, but one that reveals dominating burnt toast aromas and flavors. A hollow midpalate doesn't help. **80** —*J.C. (12/31/2004)*

Henkell NV Rosé Feiner Sekt Trocken Rosé Blend (Germany) $11. Pale rose color. Really light-bodied, with modest lemon-lime flavors and a short finish. **83** —*J.C. (12/31/2004)*

Henkell 2002 Gamay Rose Brut Sekt Sparkling Blend (Germany) $25. Pale peach in color—and it even smells a bit like peaches or other stone fruits, plus lots of lime aromas. Light and dry, with a crisp, citrusy finish. **84** —*J.C. (12/31/2004)*

Henkell NV Trocken Sekt White Blend (Germany) $12. Pleasantly off-dry, with simple, fruity aromas and flavors reminiscent of apple and citrus. A solid choice for an outdoor gathering this summer. **84** —*J.C. (6/1/2006)*

HESS. STAATSWEINGÜTER

Hess. Staatsweingüter 2001 Rauenthaler Baiken Kabinett Riesling (Rheingau) $17. Tastes richer than it smells: the aromas are of limes, crushed granite, and under-ripe melon, but the mouth-filling flavors are ripe melon and peach. The mouthfeel is thick and viscous yet not cloying, finishing with just a touch of fresh fruit sweetness. **88** —*J.C. (3/1/2003)*

Hess. Staatsweingüter 2001 Steinberg QbA Riesling (Rheingau) $14. Seems likely to be lean, given its opening aromas of flint and grapefruit, but fleshes out nicely on the palate, folding in peach and nectarine flavors along with a hint of sweetness. Has enough weight to be versatile with food, finishing just off-dry. **88 Best Buy** —*J.C. (3/1/2003)*

Hess. Staatsweingüter 2001 Steinberger Spätlese Riesling (Rheingau) $34. From one of Germany's best sites (the vineyard name is allowed to stand alone on the label, without reference to village), this is an outstanding effort. Aromas of lime, stone, and wet sand convey an intense minerality, then flavors of honeydew, peach, and apricot bring home the fruit. Light and zippy in the mouth, tart and clean on the finish. **90** —*J.C. (3/1/2003)*

I.Q.

I.Q. 2002 QbA Riesling (Rheinhessen) $9. Burnt match on the nose is followed by lime and mineral flavors that never really blossom into complexity. Light to medium in body, with a mouth-watering finish. **83** —*J.C. (11/1/2004)*

IMMICH-BATTERIEBERG

Immich-Batterieberg 2004 Blauschiefer QbA Riesling (Mosel-Saar-Ruwer) $23. Full-bodied for a Mosel wine, at 12% alcohol, but tasty, offering rather bland apple or melon flavors but dusted with enough spice and mineral notes to add considerable complexity. Long, spice-driven finish. **88** —*J.C. (7/1/2006)*

Immich-Batterieberg 2005 Detonation Riesling (Rhein-Mosel) $11. It's an intriguing idea to blend fruit from the Rhine and the Mosel, theoretically balancing the best qualities of each. Astute tasters will catch a little bit of that in this wine, with darker spice notes playing against brighter floral nuances. The result is a pleasant if rather generic Riesling that finishes with soft pear and melon fruit. **84** —*J.C. (12/1/2006)*

Immich-Batterieberg 2004 Enkircher Batterieberg Spätlese Riesling (Mosel-Saar-Ruwer) $38. Starts with beautifully defined aromas of green apple and lime, then adds tangerine flavors to the mix on the palate. It's not heavy, but it's not light, either, deftly balancing acid, alcohol, and sugar. Long and minerally on the finish. **90** —*J.C. (9/1/2006)*

Immich-Batterieberg 2003 Kabinett Riesling (Mosel-Saar-Ruwer) $20. Starts with pineapple and apricot scents, then delivers mint and vanilla flavors to go along with citrus custard. Long on the finish, with soft acids, just lacks a bit of raciness. **89** —*J.C. (5/1/2005)*

Immich-Batterieberg 2004 Rotschiefer Trocken Riesling (Mosel-Saar-Ruwer) $20. This bursts out of the chute in a blaze of fruit—pineapple, pear, green apple, even a trace of banana. Honestly, it's a bit disconcerting. But give it some time in the glass and it really changes, going from simply fruity to complex and minerally. Rather full-bodied for a Mosel wine; it does show a touch of alcohol warmth on the finish. **90 Editors' Choice** —*J.C. (7/1/2006)*

Immich-Batterieberg 2003 Rotschiefer Trocken Riesling (Mosel-Saar-Ruwer) $20. "Rotschiefer" means "red slate," a reference to the soils underlying the vineyard parcel from which this wine is made. The wine itself is thick and rich, with pure scents of fresh-picked apples, and flavors of applesauce and minerals. Lacks the bit of zip that would put it over the top, ratings-wise, but still a very attractive wine for casual sipping. **87** —*J.C. (5/1/2005)*

IRONSTONE

Ironstone 2005 QbA Riesling (Pfalz) $10. Smells like Riesling, with scents of green apples, citrus, and some vaguely floral notes, but turns a bit fat and dull on the palate. Soft and short on the finish. **82** —*J.C. (7/1/2006)*

J. & H.A. STRUB

J. & H.A. Strub 2004 Niersteiner Brückchen Kabinett Riesling (Rheinhessen) $20. A slightly smoky, rock-dust component adds a layer of minerality to this wine's spiced pear and melon aromas. On the palate, it's off-dry, zesty, and refreshing, with green apple and citrus flavors that end on a tangy note. One of the more lithe examples from the Rheinhessen. **89** —*J.C. (7/1/2006)*

J.L. WOLF

J.L. Wolf 2000 Forster Jesuitengarten Spätlese Trocken Riesling (Pfalz) $30. Smells of ripe apples but tastes more like unripe peaches, with apple and citrus playing supporting roles. The lime-dominated finish is long, crisp, and clean. **87** —*J.C. (3/1/2003)*

J.L. Wolf 2003 Forster Pechstein Spätlese Riesling (Pfalz) $28. The peach and pineapple scents seem almost candied—or maybe crystalline is a better descriptor—hard yet fragile. Melon and spice at the core are pleasant enough, but the wine seems to lack a bit of depth and length. **84** —*J.C. (5/1/2005)*

J.L. Wolf 2001 Wachenheimer Riesling (Pfalz) $14. Smoky and pungent, this wine features hints of diesel fumes and apricot in the bouquet. It's less flamboyant on the palate, where the flavors favor green apples, hard stone fruits, and mint. **86** —*J.C. (3/1/2003)*

J.L. Wolf 2002 Wachenheimer Belz QbA Riesling (Pfalz) $18. This is relatively rich and close to dry, with apple and stone fruit flavors complemented by floral aromas and a weighty finish. **86** —*J.C. (8/1/2004)*

J.L. Wolf 2003 Wachenheimer Belz Spätlese Riesling (Pfalz) $20. Citrusy and leaner than most spätlesen in this vintage of unremitting heat, with candied lime and green apple aromas and flavors, and a prickle of CO2 on the palate. Turns a bit metallic and hard on the finish. **85** —*J.C. (5/1/2005)*

J.L. Wolf 2001 Wachenheimer Gerumpel QbA Riesling (Pfalz) $18. Lean and citrusy, this is a hard, severe style of trocken that is difficult to drink without food. There's admirable concentration to be found in the long, tart finish. Try with shellfish. **84** —*J.C. (1/1/2004)*

J.L. Wolf 2003 Wachenheimer Kabinett Riesling (Pfalz) $13. This wine features an unflattering dichotomy: soft, stewy fruit on one hand, and a hard, slightly metallic finish on the other. Passable, but lacks harmony. **82** —*J.C. (5/1/2005)*

J.L. Wolf 2002 Wachenheimer QbA Riesling (Pfalz) $14. Apple and crystallized honey notes on the nose move gently into apple, peach, and vanilla notes on the palate. The slightly creamy mouthfeel is pleasant, but could use a bit more raciness. **86** —*J.C. (8/1/2004)*

J.u.H.A. STRUB

J.u.H.A. Strub 2001 Niersteiner Kabinett Riesling (Rheinhessen) $13. Almost dry-seeming (a conscious effort on the part of the importer), this wine is a great bargain. (Keep in mind you're getting 33% more than in a 750-ml bottle.) Although a bit quiet on the nose, the flavors are zippy and pure, blending limes and peaches with a minerally, graphite note and a chalky finish. **87 Best Buy** —*J.C. (3/1/2003)*

J.u.H.A. Strub 2001 Niersteiner Paterberg Spätlese Three-Star Riesling (Rheinhessen) $27. Strub was successful across the board in 2001, and this three-star spätlese is one of its best efforts. Hints of minerals and diesel mark the nose, while the flavors are more fruit-driven, featuring apple and pineapple. The mouthfeel is lush; the finish long and chalky. **91** —*J.C. (3/1/2003)*

JOH. HAART

Joh. Haart 2003 Piersporter Riesling (Mosel-Saar-Ruwer) $15. Nicely done for an entry-level wine, with lovely fresh notes of green apple, spring flowers, and lime on the nose, followed by apple, pear, and pineapple flavors. It's light in body, with a soft finish that maintains its focus without being excessively tart. **87** —*J.C. (5/1/2005)*

Joh. Haart 2003 Piersporter Goldtröpfchen Riesling Auslese Riesling (Mosel-Saar-Ruwer) $31. Pineapple and pear fruit combine with floral elements in this richly sweet auslese. Despite appearing soft and sweet it's not unstructured, it's just that the acids are so round and ripe. Great now, but should last as well. **92 Editors' Choice** —*J.C. (12/15/2004)*

JOH. JOS. CHRISTOFFEL

Joh. Jos. Christoffel 2001 Erdener Treppchen Kabinett Riesling (Mosel-Saar-Ruwer) $23. Rather sweet for a kabinett, but remarkably balanced and pure. Starts with lovely spring flowers, lime, and chalky, mineral notes, then develops peach and green apple flavors, finishing with a touch of vanilla. **91 Editors' Choice** —*J.C. (3/1/2003)*

Joh. Jos. Christoffel 2001 Ürziger Würzgarten Auslese Two-Star Riesling (Mosel-Saar-Ruwer) $48. There's a hint of botrytis on the nose in the dried apricot and lime scents, but everything else about this wine is crystalline. The fruit flavors of apricot and peach are the freshest, ripest imaginable, balanced by lively, racy acidity, while intense mineral notes grace the lengthy finish. **92** —*J.C. (3/1/2003)*

Joh. Jos. Christoffel 2004 Ürziger Würzgarten Kabinett Riesling (Mosel-Saar-Ruwer) $27. A bit tarry and rubbery on the nose, this plump kabinett boasts plenty of leesy pear and apple flavors allied to a slightly custardy texture. Not as impressive as in other recent vintages. **86** —*J.C. (10/1/2005)*

JOH. JOS. PRÜM

Joh. Jos. Prüm 2001 Graacher Himmelreich Spätlese Riesling (Mosel-Saar-Ruwer) $35. J.J. Prüm remains one of the masters. The complexity built into this wine is astounding: white peaches, melon, green apples, grapefruit, traces of minerals and nuts—all on a lithe frame that beautifully supports the fruit. **91** —*J.C. (3/1/2003)*

Joh. Jos. Prüm 2001 Wehlener Sonnenuhr Kabinett Riesling (Mosel-Saar-Ruwer) $25. Something about this wine speaks "pink." Pink grapefruit aromas. A hint of cranberry or red currants. Rose quartz. It's light but by no means delicate, showing a firm backbone and a long, mouth-watering finish. **90** —*J.C. (3/1/2003)*

Joh. Jos. Prüm 2001 Wehlener Sonnenuhr Spätlese Riesling (Mosel-Saar-Ruwer) $37. Like many of the J.J. Prum wines when young, this one was difficult to taste because of the elevated sulfur levels. Yet in time, this rating may look stingy, as they tend to evolve beautifully in the bottle. For now, there's some pineapple and citrus showing, but the bulk of the score stems from the wine's rich, honeyed texture that's perfectly enlivened by just a trace of spritz. Try in 2010 or beyond. **90 Cellar Selection** —*J.C. (3/1/2003)*

JOHANN HAART

Johann Haart 2001 Piersporter Goldtropfchen Kabinett Riesling (Mosel-Saar-Ruwer) $17. Typical Mosel Riesling aromas, flavors, and textures, but with an elegance and harmony that raises it above ordinary. Flowery, ginger-like, and green apple aromas; pear, melon and even some berry flavors; and an almost weightless mouthfeel, add up to a winning combination. **89** —*J.C. (3/1/2003)*

Johann Haart 2001 Piersporter Goldtropfchen QbA Riesling (Mosel-Saar-Ruwer) $13. The understated bouquet doesn't offer much of a clue to this wine's identity, but in the mouth, it's all juicy melons and peaches—a fat, easy drinker that finishes slightly soft. Ice it down and enjoy with a picnic lunch this summer. **84** —*J.C. (1/1/2004)*

Johann Haart 2001 Piersporter Goldtropfchen Spätlese Riesling (Mosel-Saar-Ruwer) $20. Citrusy-sweet, this spätlese epitomizes the strengths of the 2001 vintage: good ripeness allied to firm acids. Lime and quince aromas develop into green plum flavors, finishing long and juicy, sweet but balanced. **91 Editors' Choice** —*J.C. (3/1/2003)*

JOHANN RUCK IPHOFEN

Johann Ruck Iphofen 2002 Iphöfer Julius-Echter-Berg Kabinett trocken Riesling (Franken) $24. Light in weight, with crisp flavors of lime, apple, and earth that turn a bit grapefruity on the finish. A simple but enjoyable quaff. **84** —*J.C. (8/1/2004)*

Johann Ruck Iphofen 2002 Iphofer Julius-Echter-Berg Spätlese Trocken Riesling (Franken) $36. Shows a rich, earthy note that runs through the wine, backed up by tart lime and grapefruit. Some green apple flavors add additional interest to this light-bodied, slightly off-dry offering. **85** —*J.C. (8/1/2004)*

JOHANNISHOF

Johannishof 2002 Charta Riesling (Rheingau) $14. Smoky and intense, with peach, melon, and floral aromas that burst from the glass. In line with the Charta designation, it's made in a trocken, or dry, style, yet doesn't lack for fruit or flesh. It's fairly rich and full (12% alcohol), yet boasts racy acidity for near-perfect balance. **90** *(11/15/2003)*

Johannishof 2001 Charta QbA Riesling (Rheingau) $14. Charta Rieslings are dry, and this one is no exception. Imagine tart pineapple sprinkled with rock dust—more specifically, powdered quartz. It's that mineral-filled, with a rich mouthfeel that avoids heaviness and shows real character. **90 Best Buy** —*J.C. (3/1/2003)*

Johannishof 2005 Johannisberg G Kabinett Riesling (Rheingau) $19. Fresh and minty on the nose, with restrained pear and melon notes, this medium-bodied kabinett is firmly tart and acidic on the palate, with balanced sweet-sour flavors. Turns slightly chalky on the finish. **88** —*J.C. (12/1/2006)*

Johannishof 2004 Johannisberg V Kabinett Riesling (Rheingau) $18. This luscious, easy-to-drink Riesling starts off with perfumed, floral notes layered over ripe Winesaps, then moves smoothly into a midpalate laden with more apples and citrus. The long, succulent finish ends on a dry, minerally note, giving this rather sweet wine a fine sense of balance. **88** —*J.C. (7/1/2006)*

Johannishof 2003 Johannisberg V Kabinett Riesling (Rheingau) $17. You might expect a wine that smells like baked apples and poached pears to be soft and mushy, yet this wine finishes stony and crisp—in fine balance with its 10% alcohol and slightly viscous mouthfeel. **88** —*J.C. (12/15/2004)*

Johannishof 2001 Johannisberger Goldatzel Kabinett Riesling (Rheingau) $11. Oily and rich—verging on creamy—this is a textural oddity (although not an unpleasant one), but the pear and lime flavors are classic. Tangy citrus flavors linger delicately on the finish. **88 Best Buy** —*J.C. (3/1/2003)*

Johannishof 2003 Johannisberger Hölle Beerenauslese 375 ml Riesling (Rheingau) $132. Wonderfully rich and sweet, yet while this completely coats the palate with super ripe apples and honey flavors, it never seems like too much. Despite low acidity, the sweetness is balanced by powerful minerality on the long finish. **95** —*J.C. (2/1/2006)*

Johannishof 2004 Johannisberger Klaus Spätlese Riesling (Rheingau) $24. A bit straightforward and simple for what we've come to expect from this producer, with wet slate and honeyed pear aromas that add apple flavors on the palate. It's still very good Riesling, medium-bodied, and clean on the finish. **88** —*J.C. (5/1/2006)*

Johannishof 2001 Johannisberger Vogelsang Kabinett Riesling (Rheingau) $11. Liquid minerals pour from this rich, oily, and dense offering. There's enough peach nuance to remind you of the summer's ripe fruit, but the core of the wine is all about smoke and rocks. A hint of sweetness on the finish is balanced by a zing of grapefruit-like acidity. **90 Best Buy** —*J.C. (3/1/2003)*

Johannishof 2003 Rudesheimer Berg Rottland Spätlese Riesling (Rheingau) $26. Stony and minerally on the nose, followed by gentler whiffs of honey, then finally broad, sweet flavors of ripe apples and pineapples. Mouth filling and soft, but with balanced acidity and a long, complex finish. **92 Editors' Choice** —*J.C. (12/15/2004)*

Johannishof 2005 Rüdesheimer Berg Rottland Spätlese Riesling (Rheingau) $27. If there is any complaint at all to be made about this wine, it's that it is too easy to drink. Succulent, ripe, honeyed fruit balanced by just enough acidity slips down without any edginess, yet the flavors still linger nicely on the finish. **90** —*J.C. (12/1/2006)*

JOSEF BIFFAR

Josef Biffar 2001 Deidesheimer Kieselberg Kabinett Riesling (Pfalz) $16. This fairly large-scaled kabinett is also fairly dry. A stony, minerally nose leads into flavors that hint at stone fruit (plums?) but veer toward river stones. More intellectual than hedonistic. **87** —*J.C. (3/1/2003)*

Josef Biffar 2001 Wachenheimer Altenburg Spätlese Riesling (Pfalz) $32. If you are a fan of oily, dieselly character in your Riesling, you'll like this more than I've rated it here. It's intensely mineral, like you've sprinkled powdered rock over Macintosh apples, and has an oily texture that contrasts with the crispness and delineation in so many other Rieslings from this vintage. **86** —*J.C. (3/1/2003)*

JOSEF LEITZ

Josef Leitz 2004 Dragonstone Qualitätswein Riesling (Rheingau) $18. Named for its source, the Rüdesheimer Drachenstein, Leitz's entry-level wine is a perennial favorite. Unfortunately, the price has crept up over the past few vintages to the point that it is no longer the screaming bargain as it once was, but it is still a lovely wine, with citrusy, bergamot flavors and riper hints of apple. Long, clean, and refreshing on the finish. **88 Editors' Choice** —*J.C. (10/1/2005)*

Josef Leitz 2001 Rüdesheimer Berg Rottland Spätlese Trocken Riesling (Rheingau) $33. For a vineyard the importer characterizes as "adamant," this wine is surprisingly showy. There's a strong backbone of lime and green apple, but also sweet hints of apricot and peach. Finishes tart and long, dry enough to appeal to folks who "don't care for sweet wine." **90** —*J.C. (3/1/2003)*

Josef Leitz 2001 Rüdesheimer Drachenstein Riesling (Rheingau) $12. To steal a phrase from Terry Thiese's 2002 catalogue: "insane quality." Instead of lamenting the fact that more consumers aren't drinking German wines, maybe those of us who are should be grateful, for only lack of interest keeps wine that's this good, this affordable. A touch of sweetness admirably balances the wine's penetrating acidity, which frames taut apple, red berry, and citrus fruit. The Sweet Tart finish lingers delicately in the mouth long after you've taken the last swallow. **89 Best Buy** —*J.C. (11/15/2002)*

Josef Leitz 2002 Rudesheimer Drachenstein Riesling QbA Riesling (Rheingau) $12. Johannes Leitz is rightfully proud of his 2002s. This is his entry-level wine, and it's gorgeous, with a touch of sweetness and slightly rounder acidity than last year's version (which, incidentally, is still going strong). It boasts copious apple, red berry, and citrus flavors and a forceful, lingering finish. Sinfully easy to drink. **90 Best Buy** —*J.C. (11/15/2003)*

JOSEPH MÜLLER

Joseph Müller 2003 Qualitätswein Riesling (Pfalz) $6. Earthy and a bit sour, with sweet pineapple flavors that war with a mouth-puckering earthiness. **82** —*J.C. (11/1/2004)*

JUL. FERD. KIMICH

Jul. Ferd. Kimich 2001 Deidecheimer Paradiesgarten Kabinett Halbtrocken Riesling (Pfalz) $15. Yellow fruit aromas burst from the glass, followed by sweet pineapple and pear flavors. A slightly custardy mouthfeel adds plumpness to the midpalate, while a tangy edge of lemony acids keeps the fruit fresh and lively. **87** —*J.C. (1/1/2004)*

JULIUSSPITAL

Juliusspital 2001 Iphofer Julius-Echter-Berg Auslese Riesling (Franken) $24. This light but intense auslese offers up aromas of honey, malt, and dried pineapple. It's very sweet and has a compelling finish that blends sour cherries with citrus and sugar. **89** —*J.C. (3/1/2003)*

GERMANY

KARL ERBES

Karl Erbes 2004 Ürziger Würzgarten Auslese Gold Capsule 375 ml Riesling (Mosel-Saar-Ruwer) $40. This is a buxom, charming fleshpot of a wine, round and mouth-filling—even a bit fat—but amiable and pleasing. Apple, pear, and honey notes are accented by spice, minerals, and citrus, with a lusciously peachy finish. **89** —J.C. (9/1/2006)

Karl Erbes 2001 Ürziger Würzgarten Kabinett Riesling (Mosel-Saar-Ruwer) $12. The "spice garden" was one of the more favored vineyard sites in 2001, and Erbes's kabinett is very successful, offering some apple blossom and quince elements in a light, tart, well-balanced package. **88 Best Buy** —J.C. (3/1/2003)

Karl Erbes 2003 Ürziger Würzgarten Riesling Auslese Riesling (Mosel-Saar-Ruwer) $29. Smoky and minerally on the nose, gradually opening up to reveal candied pineapple and pink grapefruit notes. It's sweet yet light-bodied on the palate, with flavors of red berries and quince that are refreshing on the finish. **88** —J.C. (12/15/2004)

Karl Erbes 2003 Ürziger Würzgarten Riesling Spätlese Riesling (Mosel-Saar-Ruwer) $18. Nicely done spätlese—slightly sweet, yet well-balanced by acidity. Delicately etched pear and pineapple fruit carries hints of apple blossoms and vanilla. More length on the finish would have pushed the score higher. **88** —J.C. (12/15/2004)

Karl Erbes 2004 Ürziger Würzgarten Spätlese Riesling (Mosel-Saar-Ruwer) $19. Lithe, with delicate tendrils of apple, nectarine, and melon flavors that deftly infiltrate the palate. Sweetness is nicely balanced by acidity, but the flavors fall off a little quickly on the finish. **87** —J.C. (2/1/2006)

Karl Erbes 2001 Ürziger Würzgarten Spätlese Riesling (Mosel-Saar-Ruwer) $14. Smells minty fresh, with sweet apples and pears forming the core of the wine. There's just enough acidity to balance the wine; although it tastes sweet now, it should firm up in a few years. Tasted twice, this score reflects the better bottle; another showed some volatile acidity and would have rated 82 points. **89 Best Buy** —J.C. (3/1/2003)

KARTHAUSERHOF

Karthauserhof 2002 Kabinett Riesling (Mosel-Saar-Ruwer) $20. Rather full-bodied and slightly sweet, with mouth-filling mineral and tree fruit flavors of apples and pears. Powdered quartz imparts a dusty quality to the nose, picking up lime notes on the finish. **88** —J.C. (8/1/2004)

KASSNER SIMON

Kassner Simon 1998 Brut Riesling (Pfalz) $17. Full-bodied, this wine shows typical Riesling aromas of flowers, with hints of peach and lemon furniture polish. Seems to be a relatively ripe vintage, and the wine carries a noticeable hint of residual sugar. Good solid weight leads into a big, flavorful finish. **87** —P.G. (12/31/2002)

Kassner Simon 2001 Freinsheimer Oschelkopf Spätlese Scheurebe (Pfalz) $16. Very aromatic, with aromas reminiscent of vanilla and spice. It's so aromatic, it even tastes floral, which may put off some tasters, but it's also ripe, full, and concentrated. The only quibble is an abbreviated finish, characteristic of the variety. **87** —J.C. (1/1/2004)

KELLER

Keller 2003 Kabinett Riesling (Rheinhessen) $33. Part of a growing trend among German wines, the front label omits the vineyard name, but this is from the Westhofener Kirchspiel. Starts off a bit sulfury, but the fruit flavors come through on the palate, delivering lime and apple flavors. Light in body, with a hint of spritz to help keep it fresh on the finish. **87** —J.C. (5/1/2005)

Keller 2003 Pius Beerenauslese Riesling (Rheinhessen) $36. Sweet and full-bodied—a little chunky to be honest—but with its seductive aromas of orange marmalade and super-ripe apples it makes the grade. Flavors are slightly roasted, leaning toward caramel and sweet corn, but it hangs together pretty well on the finish, ending without cloying sweetness. **90** —J.C. (2/1/2006)

KENDERMANNS

Kendermanns 2004 Kalkstein Dry QbA Riesling (Pfalz) $21. Serve this crisp, citrusy dry Riesling as an apéritif or with simple seafood dishes, where its simple lemon-lime and green apple flavors will refresh the palate. **85** —J.C. (7/1/2006)

Kendermanns 2004 Schiefer Riesling QbA Trocken Riesling (Mosel-Saar-Ruwer) $21. This slate selection from Kendermanns is a pleasant surprise, speaking of its origins in the smoky, wet slate aromas and stony flavors couched in layers of white peach, melon, and hints of honey. Despite a considerable 12.5% alcohol, it seems light and fresh, ending on notes of citrus and melon. **88** —J.C. (5/1/2006)

KIRSTEN

Kirsten 1998 Brut Riesling (Mosel-Saar-Ruwer) $16. A quick whiff of sulfur blows off, and then some inviting toasty scents, redolent of fresh bread dough, jump-start a sparkling wine that evokes real French bubbly. Kirsten shows good body and balance, with a delicately floral, peachy finish that hints at some sugar. **88** —P.G. (12/31/2002)

KNIPSER

Knipser 2003 Auslese Gewürztraminer-Riesling (Pfalz) $30. This unique blend of 51% Gewürz and 49% Riesling boasts an expressive and flowery bouquet of spice, baked apples, and pears, and hints of lychee fruit. Full-bodied without being heavy, it finishes off-dry, with impressive notes of bergamot. **90** —J.C. (5/1/2006)

Knipser 2004 Steinbuckel Grosses Gewächs Spätlese Trocken Riesling (Pfalz) $46. Relatively round and lush for a dry German Riesling, with pronounced ripeness and texture. A hint of diesel marks the bouquet, followed by scents of super-ripe apples, honey, and dried apricot, while the flavors add notes of mineral and spice. A long, spice-driven finish completes the package. **90** —J.C. (12/1/2006)

Knipser 2003 Chardonnay & Weissburgunder Trocken White Blend (Pfalz) $27. It's roughly two-thirds Chardonnay, one-third Pinot Blanc, made in a dry style. Smells like vanilla and pears, but there's also a persistent vinegary note that creeps in and doesn't fade. Tasters less sensitive to this character will no doubt find more to like. **83** —J.C. (5/1/2005)

KÖSTER-WOLF

Köster-Wolf 2004 Müller-Thurgau Halbtrocken 1 Liter Müller-Thurgau (Rheinhessen) $12. Lacks expressiveness on the nose, but offers a broad, sweetish swathe of melon and citrus flavor. Garden party material. **83** —J.C. (7/1/2006)

Köster-Wolf 2004 Riesling QbA Trocken 1 Liter Riesling (Rheinhessen) $12. A good buy in dry Riesling, this light to medium-bodied wine boasts nicely balanced flavors of citrus, green apple, and herbs and a zesty, lemony finish that will perk up jaded palates this summer. **85 Best Buy** —J.C. (7/1/2006)

Köster-Wolf 2003 Trocken 1 Liter Riesling (Rheinhessen) $11. A solid value in dry Riesling (keep in mind that the bottle is one-third larger than standard). The ripe apple scents lead into dry minerally flavors that boast rounded, smooth edges. Purists may gripe that it lacks a certain precision because of this, but others will find it more accessible and easier to drink for precisely the same reason. **86** —J.C. (5/1/2005)

KOWERICH LUDWIG VON BEETHOVEN

Kowerich Ludwig von Beethoven 1998 Brut Riesling (Mosel-Saar-Ruwer) $17. A fancy package boasts of some distant connection to the family of the famous composer. The juice in the bottle delivers firm and resilient flavors, with plenty of yeastiness. Citrus and grapefruit rind dominate, in a true brut style. How about naming it "Beethoven's other fifth"? **87 Best Buy** —P.G. (12/31/2002)

KRUGER-RUMPF

Kruger-Rumpf 2001 Münsterer Rheinberg Kabinett Riesling (Nahe) $17. With 24 hectares of vineyard holdings, Kruger-Rumpf is the largest landholder in Terry Thiese's impressive portfolio. The 2001 Rheinberg kabinett smells smoky, showing plenty of mineral notes atop a base a Golden Delicious apples. A lively tartness carries the finish. **88** —J.C. (3/1/2003)

KÜHL

Kühl 2003 Kabinett Riesling (Mosel-Saar-Ruwer) $9. Dusty and earthy on the nose, followed by pear and melon flavors that seem a bit flabby and broad, lacking sharp definition. Picks up a canned sweet corn note on the finish. **83** —J.C. (12/15/2004)

KÜNSTLER

Künstler 2004 Estate Qualitatswein Riesling (Rheingau) $18. Lovely, delicate aromas of fern fronds, green apples, and limes set the stage for crisp flavors of pineapple and lime. Yet despite the high acidity, the mouthfeel is somewhat plump. Finishes long, tart, and mouth-watering. **88** —*J.C. (10/1/2005)*

Künstler 2004 Hochheimer Reichestal Kabinett Riesling (Rheingau) $25. A broad, mouth-filling kabinett that's filled with green apple and plum fruit, with some riper peach notes sprinkled in as well. Plump and sweet, maybe a bit soft for some palates, but clean and very well made. **88** —*J.C. (10/1/2005)*

KURT HAIN

Kurt Hain 2003 Piesporter Goldtröpfchen Spätlese Riesling (Mosel-Saar-Ruwer) $23. This wine's light, airy mouthfeel belies its sweetness and intensity of flavor. Honeyed pineapple aromas; similar flavors on the palate, adding gentle citrus notes toward the long, sweet finish. **89** —*J.C. (5/1/2005)*

LANDSHUT

Landshut 2004 QbA Riesling (Mosel-Saar-Ruwer) $5. Cleanly made, this plump, sweet wine offers simple pear flavors at an bargain price. **82** —*J.C. (7/1/2006)*

Landshut 2002 Qualitätswein Riesling (Mosel-Saar-Ruwer) $5. No, this is not a great, classic single-vineyard wine. But it is a clean, well-made blended Riesling that sells for a song. With its blend of melon, peach, cinnamon, and stone dust, you could do a lot worse for a fiver. **83 Best Buy** —*J.C. (11/1/2004)*

LOOSEN BROS.

Loosen Bros. 2000 DR. L Riesling (Mosel-Saar-Ruwer) $10. 83 —*C.S. (5/1/2002)*

LOSEN-BOCKSTANZ

Losen-Bockstanz 2001 Wittlicher Lay Spätlese Riesling (Mosel-Saar-Ruwer) $18. An attractive wine with a sense of youth and freshness. Aromas of fresh hay, flavors of green fruits, and a restrained sweetness suggest this will go well with food. **86** —*R.V. (1/1/2004)*

Losen-Bockstanz 2001 Wittlicher Portnersberg Kabinett Riesling (Mosel-Saar-Ruwer) $10. There is something about the age of German wine houses. Losen Bockstanz has been in the same family since 1590, a mere 400 plus years. They have made aromas of pears lead to a palate of sweet apples and ripe currants, with an soft acidity. Just showing through is a layer of intense very pure fruit flavors. **87** —*R.V. (1/1/2004)*

LOTHAR FRANZ

Lothar Franz 2001 Hattenheimer Pfaffenberg Spätlese Riesling (Rheingau) $NA. Rich fruit with flavors of toffee apples and simple, but attractive, ripeness. A layer of acidity gives balance, but this is not a complex wine. **86** —*R.V. (1/1/2004)*

LOUIS GUNTRUM

Louis Guntrum 2004 Dry Riesling (Rheinhessen) $11. Smells solid, showing hints of honey and melon layered over some stony notes, but turns dull and earthy on the palate, then roughly acidic on the finish. **82** —*J.C. (12/1/2006)*

Louis Guntrum 2005 Niersteiner Rehbach Spätlese Riesling (Rheinhessen) $23. This wine pleases from start to finish, beginning with mouth-watering aromas of zesty limes and green apples and then adding plump, mouth-filling flavors of melon. Ends long, with pepper, spice, and mineral notes. **91** —*J.C. (12/1/2006)*

Louis Guntrum 2003 Niersteiner Rehbach Spätlese Riesling (Rheinhessen) $19. Nicely balanced for the vintage, this Riesling is only slightly sweet, boasting moderately intense aromas of apple and pear. Flavors are bolder, building on apple and reaching toward white nectarine and chalk. Finishes clean and refreshing. **87** —*J.C. (11/1/2004)*

Louis Guntrum 2005 Oppenheimer Herrenberg Auslese Riesling (Rheinhessen) $28. Unique in character, this wine features powerful white pepper and spice drop notes layered over white peach and melon flavors. It's rather big and round in the mouth, but it also has a bit of a hole in the midpalate. Turns peppery and spicy on the finish. **87** —*J.C. (12/1/2006)*

Louis Guntrum 2002 Oppenheimer Herrenberg Auslese Riesling (Rheinhessen) $23. This medium-bodied auslese has a rich, concentrated mouthfeel that perfectly suits its flavors of ripe apples, pears, and melons. Some slate notes on the nose add interest, while the finish is firmer than you might expect, suggesting decent ageability. Try now or in five years. **88** —*J.C. (12/15/2004)*

Louis Guntrum 2002 Oppenheimer Sackträger Riesling Auslese Riesling (Rheinhessen) $23. Bit of an odd nose, with hints of butter and volatility layered over dried apricots. Viscous texture in the mouth, where the wine seems to regather itself, featuring fine flavors of candied pineapple and dried spices. Picks up dieselly notes on the finish. **87** —*J.C. (12/15/2004)*

Louis Guntrum 2002 Oppenheimer Sackträger Riesling Spätlese Trocken Riesling (Rheinhessen) $19. Flint and mineral notes accent pineapple and lime aromas, while on the palate, the wine shows plenty of ripe, citrusy fruit flavors. Note that trocken wines can still have some residual sugar and this seems to have some, or perhaps it's just the very ripe-tasting fruit. Tangy acids on the long finish provide balance. **87** —*J.C. (12/15/2004)*

Louis Guntrum 2002 Penguin Eiswein Silvaner (Rheinhessen) $52. Smells and tastes like scorched creamed corn laced with honey and marmalade. Sweet but not very harmonious. **81** —*J.C. (5/1/2005)*

LUCASOF

Lucasof 2002 QbA Riesling (Pfalz) $11. Tart, lemony, and earthy, but could be just the ticket on a hot summer day, when you're looking for something more complex than lemonade yet similarly refreshing. **84** —*J.C. (8/1/2004)*

LUDWIG NEUHAUS

Ludwig Neuhaus 2000 Piesporter Michelsberg Riesling (Mosel-Saar-Ruwer) $5. 82 —*J.C. (5/1/2002)*

MARKUS MOLITOR

Markus Molitor 2002 Bernkasteler Badstube Spätlese Feinherb Riesling (Mosel-Saar-Ruwer) $18. Sulfury on the nose, but behind that there's plenty of zesty lemon-lime fruit in a lean, dry format. Try with oysters and the like. **86** —*J.C. (12/15/2004)*

Markus Molitor 2002 Bernkasteler Bratenhöfchen Kabinett Riesling (Mosel-Saar-Ruwer) $13. Interesting stuff, starting with aromas of kerosene and corn oil and moving into flavors of pears and sweet corn. Light to medium in weight, with a crisp, malic note on the finish. **86** —*J.C. (12/15/2004)*

Markus Molitor 2003 Erdener Treppchen Auslese Riesling (Mosel-Saar-Ruwer) $45. A disappointment from this producer, or maybe the wine is just in a closed phase. Poached apple and citrus aromas are light and balanced, picking up orange, tangerine, and lime notes on the crisp finish. Right now, it's a bit simple and short. **86** —*J.C. (2/1/2006)*

Markus Molitor 2001 Graacher Himmelreich Spätlese Riesling (Mosel-Saar-Ruwer) $16. Another mineral-laden wine from Markus Molitor, with a rich, oily texture balanced by a firm spine of acidity. Green apples, peaches, and citrus combine with stones and vegetable oil on the palate. Finishes long and crisp, like a good 2001 should. Good now, better in five years. **91** —*J.C. (12/15/2004)*

Markus Molitor 2002 QbA Feinherb Riesling (Mosel-Saar-Ruwer) $12. Lots of sulfury, leesy notes on the nose lead into a lean, citrusy, earthy wine that finishes with a tart, grapefruity edge. **84** —*J.C. (12/15/2004)*

Markus Molitor 2002 QbA Trocken Riesling (Mosel-Saar-Ruwer) $12. Slightly sulfury and leesy on the nose, then lean and tart flavors of lemon curd and green apple on the palate. Light in body, very tart, and close to sour on the finish. **84** —*J.C. (12/15/2004)*

Markus Molitor 2001 Wehlener Klosterberg Eiswein Riesling (Mosel-Saar-Ruwer) $46. Starts with some smoky, dieselly notes, then moves on to simple pineapple and pear fruit. Only 6.5% alcohol, yet it doesn't seem overly sweet. **89** —*J.C. (12/15/2004)*

Markus Molitor 2002 Zeltinger Sonnenuhr Auslese Feinherb Riesling (Mosel-Saar-Ruwer) $28. Aromas dominated by slate and diesel allow only a vague notion of fruit to show through, but the flavors are more apparent on the palate, where ripe peach emerges to complement the sense of slaty, minerally strength. Crisp acids turn a little grapefruity on the finish. **90** —*J.C. (12/15/2004)*

Markus Molitor 2002 Zeltinger Sonnenuhr Kabinett Riesling (Mosel-Saar-Ruwer) $15. Honey and diesel aromas, along with a hint of botrytis. In the mouth, this is surprisingly dry-tasting, with apricot and orange flavors that finish stony and tart. Seems to be evolving quite fast; drink now–2010. **87** —*J.C. (12/15/2004)*

Markus Molitor 2002 Zeltinger Sonnenuhr Spätlese Riesling (Mosel-Saar-Ruwer) $20. Intensely minerally, this wine features an avalanche of stony flavors supported by baked apple notes for softness, and fresh-squeezed limes for backbone. Hints of diesel and oil shale dominate the nose. It's richly textured—almost chewy—yet crisp on the finish. Drink now–2010. **91** —*J.C. (12/15/2004)*

MAX FERD. RICHTER

Max Ferd. Richter 2001 Braueneberger Juffer Auslese Riesling (Mosel-Saar-Ruwer) $40. As with many of these ausleses, this wine is still young, as its yeasty flavors show. The sweetness is balanced with high acidity. It is fresh, with flavors of ripe sweet apples and crisp oranges. **91** —*R.V. (1/1/2004)*

Max Ferd. Richter 2001 Braueneberger Juffer Kabinett Riesling (Mosel-Saar-Ruwer) $20. Wonderful floral aromas of white spring flowers, and soft, lightly sweet fruit, with a balancing layer of crispness, make this a wine that is more ready to drink than 2001s, but with the other side that it has less aging ability. **88** —*R.V. (4/1/2003)*

Max Ferd. Richter 2001 Braueneberger Juffer Spätlese Riesling (Mosel-Saar-Ruwer) $28. This is surprisingly ready to drink for a 2001. Its rich, sweet fruit has some acidity balancing the ripeness. Flavors of honey and a touch of ripe peaches are alongside green plums. **89** —*R.V. (1/1/2004)*

Max Ferd. Richter 2001 Braueneberger Juffer-Sonnenuhr Auslese Riesling (Mosel-Saar-Ruwer) $55. Dirk Richter makes wonderful, pure wines at this estate, which has been in his family for 300 years. Aromas of sweet honey and botrytis lead to an intensely flavored wine, filled with vibrant tastes of wild fruits and sweet apricots. **92** —*R.V. (1/1/2004)*

Max Ferd. Richter 2001 Braueneberger Juffer-Sonnenuhr Spätlese Riesling (Mosel-Saar-Ruwer) $30. Yeasty aromas. Ripe, full flavors with layers of green plums and pears. A delicious, fresh wine buy with power and full flavors. **87** —*R.V. (1/1/2004)*

Max Ferd. Richter 2001 Graacher Himmelreich Kabinett Riesling (Mosel-Saar-Ruwer) $20. The palate of this wine is fresh, light, and green, with dry, yeasty notes. Flavors of gooseberries and aromas of hedgerow fruits add a refreshing attractiveness. **87** —*R.V. (1/1/2004)*

Max Ferd. Richter 2001 Graacher Himmelreich Spätlese Riesling (Mosel-Saar-Ruwer) $28. An intoxicating floral, aromatic nose sets off this light, delicate wine, with its delicious acidity balancing the sweet flavors of wild fruits. A touch of tannins gives the wine fine promise for the future, with maturity in 10 years or more. **90** —*R.V. (1/1/2004)*

Max Ferd. Richter 2001 Veldenzer Eisenberg Auslese Riesling (Mosel-Saar-Ruwer) $40. The light yeasty character is overlain with crisply sweet apple flavors and touches of orange peel. It is a wine which shows youth at this stage, but has a sense of great aging ability. **90** —*R.V. (1/1/2004)*

Max Ferd. Richter 2001 Veldenzer Eisenberg Spätlese Riesling (Mosel-Saar-Ruwer) $28. Pure and balanced, this wine with its lovely crisp fruit and fine acidity, shows all the delicacy of the Mosel. Green fruits give it a depth of flavor, but to finish, all is sweetness and light. **91** —*R.V. (1/1/2004)*

MAXIMIN GRÜNHÄUSER

Maximin Grünhäuser 2005 Abstberg Auslese Riesling (Mosel-Saar-Ruwer) $40. Rock hounds will adore this wine, which shows off the dry mineral-ity of the Abstberg. Crushed stone, spice, and melon scents are fleshed out and embellished on the palate by honeyed notes of pineapple and dried fruit. Persistent citrus, honey and mineral notes linger elegantly on the finish. **92 Editors' Choice** —*J.C. (12/1/2006)*

Maximin Grünhäuser 2004 Abstberg Auslese Riesling (Mosel-Saar-Ruwer) $40. Surprisingly big and full-bodied for a Grünhäus wine, with hints of diesel and baked apple on the nose followed by a panopoly of flavors that ranges from apple and lime to honey, and mineral. The finish is powerful and lingers a long time. **92** —*J.C. (2/1/2006)*

Maximin Grünhäuser 2004 Abstberg Beerenauslese Riesling (Mosel-Saar-Ruwer) $167. A dramatic contrast to the sticky-sweet nature of the 2003 Abstberg BA, this vintage boasts piercing, mouth-watering acids to bal-ance the super-ripe pineapple flavors. If wines age on their acidity, this one will last a good, long time. **93** —*J.C. (2/1/2006)*

Maximin Grünhäuser 2005 Abstberg Spätlese Riesling (Mosel-Saar-Ruwer) $28. A bit sulfury on the nose, but even through that veil it's possible to discern greatness. Citrus, melon and pear notes shine through, picking up mineral notes on the long finish, while the texture is plump but with elegant underlying structure. Drink 2010–2020. **92 Editors' Choice** —*J.C. (12/1/2006)*

Maximin Grünhäuser 2004 Abstberg Spätlese Riesling (Mosel-Saar-Ruwer) $28. A bit reticent on the nose, but hints of honeyed fruit and powdered stone emerge after some coaxing. In the mouth, the flavors explode into strident notes of green apple, honey, and lime zest, carried easily by only 8% alcohol. Long, tart, and refreshing on the finish; a wine that can be consumed in its exuberant youth or aged into something more refined and complex. **91 Editors' Choice** —*J.C. (5/1/2006)*

Maximin Grünhäuser 2003 Abtsberg Auslese 122 375 ml Riesling (Mosel-Saar-Ruwer) $32. Unlike some 2003s, this auslese is big without being gloppy. The sweet apricot, peach, and citrus flavors are balanced by ade-quate acidity and strong sense of minerality that really emerges on the finish. **91** —*J.C. (2/1/2006)*

Maximin Grünhäuser 2003 Abtsberg Beerenauslese Riesling (Mosel-Saar-Ruwer) $167. Heavily botrytized, this thick, unctuous wine virtually oozes with dried apricots and spiced applesauce aromas and flavors. So much going on it's hard to adequately describe, with a long, sticky finish. **95** —*J.C. (12/15/2004)*

Maximin Grünhäuser 2003 Abtsberg Riesling Auslese Riesling (Mosel-Saar-Ruwer) $40. The regular Abtsberg auslese is as impressive as the fuder-designated bottlings, showing extremely floral aromatics akin to gardenia blossoms. Lightbodied and quite sweet, with harmonious apple, pear, and spice elements. Long, sugary finish. **90** —*J.C. (12/15/2004)*

Maximin Grünhäuser 2003 Abtsberg Riesling Auslese 155 Riesling (Mosel-Saar-Ruwer) $38. A mild disappointment, given the strong showing of so many of Von Schubert's other bottlings, the 2003 Auslese 155 is pleas-antly light-bodied and nicely balances sugar and acidity. But unless I missed it, it doesn't show the same compelling complexity and minerality, instead relying on fruity-sweet flavors of ripe apples and pears. Hold 5–10 years, hoping for more detail to emerge with time. **88** —*J.C. (12/15/2004)*

Maximin Grünhäuser 2003 Abtsberg Riesling Auslese 70 Riesling (Mosel-Saar-Ruwer) $36. Shows wonderfully clean, pure fruit aromas and flavors ranging from ripe peaches and pears to oranges and white grapes. Light in body, a bit sweet, but balanced by zesty acidity. **91** —*J.C. (12/15/2004)*

Maximin Grünhäuser 2003 Abtsberg Spätlese Riesling (Mosel-Saar-Ruwer) $28. Good depth and richness here, yet balanced by soft acids, minerali-ty and spice. Hints of kerosene spark the aromas, which also boast ripe apple and pear notes. Baked tree fruit on the palate, wrapped in minerals and spice, yet not overly heavy. **90** —*J.C. (5/1/2005)*

Maximin Grünhäuser 2001 Herrenberg QbA Trocken Riesling (Mosel-Saar-Ruwer) $12. Crisp and refreshingly tart, the dominant element is pink grapefruit, graced with notes of apple and pear. Light and lean, use as an aperitif or with delicate seafood preparations. **85** —*J.C. (1/1/2004)*

Maximin Grünhäuser 2003 Herrenberg Riesling Kabinett Riesling (Mosel-Saar-Ruwer) $22. A bit sulfury at the moment, so give it some time in a decanter if opened in the next year or so. Once past that, it delivers apple, pear and orange-scented fruit in a plump, medium-weight pack-age. Finishes long and a little soft, making it easy to drink now. **89** —*J.C. (12/15/2004)*

Maximin Grünhäuser 2003 Herrenberg Riesling Spätlese Riesling (Mosel-Saar-Ruwer) $28. Wonderfully blends apple, pear, and peach flavors, picking up mixed citrus fruits on the finish. Yet there's also a deep undercurrent of earth and mineral that provides a strong backbone. It's plump and concentrated on the palate, yet light on its feet. Great spätlese. **92** —J.C. (12/15/2004)

Maximin Grünhäuser 2004 QbA Riesling (Mosel-Saar-Ruwer) $19. Crisp and light, this off-dry wine features lovely aromas of flowershop greens, apples, citrus fruit, and pineapple. Apple, pear, and citrus flavors mingle on the tongue before ending on notes of limes and berries. **88** —J.C. (2/1/2006)

Maximin Grünhäuser 2003 QbA Riesling (Mosel-Saar-Ruwer) $19. Light in weight and crisper than many 2003s, with plenty of citrusy elements to support the ripe apple and pear flavors. There's also plenty of smoke and mineral notes to add complexity and a long finish that folds in touches of tangerine. **90** —J.C. (12/15/2004)

MEILEN 2003 KABINETT

Meilen 2003 Kabinett Riesling (Mosel-Saar-Ruwer) $9. A big, broad-shouldered kabinett, filled with ripe apple and poached pear flavors. Seems a bit high in alcohol (10%), but that's the extraordinary nature of the vintage making itself known. **86 Best Buy** —J.C. (12/15/2004)

MÖNCHHOF

Mönchhof 2002 Astor Kabinett Riesling (Mosel-Saar-Ruwer) $18. The aromas burst from the glass, a bold kaleidoscope of limes, peaches, and minerals, but it's sweet and a bit soft on the palate, lacking cut and precision. Hold a few years, hoping it will emerge from this babyfat stage into a sleeker, more refined bottling. **85** —J.C. (8/1/2004)

Mönchhof 2003 Estate QbA Riesling (Mosel-Saar-Ruwer) $14. It's an impressive achievement to be able to make 10,000 cases of Mosel Riesling this good and this representative. Apple blossoms and citrus fruits are hallmarks of the region and this wine is true to type, with slightly sweet flavors enlivened by a touch of unreleased carbon dioxide. **86** —J.C. (8/1/2004)

Mönchhof 2004 Estate Qualitatswein Riesling (Mosel-Saar-Ruwer) $16. A delicate, racy wine, with attractive aromas of flint smoke, lime, and Granny Smith apple. Flavors are a bit simpler, reminiscent of crisp apples—tart but not hard-edged. Only quibble is that it finishes a bit short. **86** —J.C. (10/1/2005)

Mönchhof 2004 Mosel Slate Spätlese Riesling (Mosel-Saar-Ruwer) $21. Selected from the Erdener Treppchen vineyard, this racy, elegant spätlese is sweet, yet artfully balanced by lime-like acids and stony, mineral tones. Piercing notes of Granny Smith apples, limes, and pineapple reprise on the crisp, long finish. **90 Editors' Choice** —J.C. (10/1/2005)

P.J. VALCKENBERG

P.J. Valckenberg 2001 QBA Gewürztraminer (Pfalz) $10. Next time you're looking for a solid Gewurz at a rock-bottom price, think twice before going straight for Alsace. This Pfalz version has all of the requisite elements—rose petals, lychee fruit, spice, and pears—in a round but not flabby package. **87 Best Buy** —J.C. (1/1/2004)

P.J. Valckenberg 2003 QbA Pinot Grigio (Pfalz) $11. This medium-bodied wine would give many Italian Pinot Grigios a run for their money. Honeyed peaches with a trace of minerality and a dry, clean finish at a reasonable price. Sure, labeling it Grigio is a pure marketing ploy, but the quality is in the bottle. **85** —J.C. (5/1/2005)

P.J. Valckenberg 2003 1808 Wormser Liebfrauenstift-Kirchenstück Riesling Spätlese Trocken Riesling (Rheinhessen) $27. Combines peach and lime scents with flavors that are more earthy and chalky. Medium-bodied and dry on the palate. Alternative closure fans will want to check out this bottling's cool Vino-Lok glass stopper from Alcoa. **85** —J.C. (12/15/2004)

P.J. Valckenberg 2004 Estate Dry Riesling (Rheinhessen) $12. Modest green apple and lime scents on the nose translate directly onto the palate, where they pick up a bit of minerality. Medium-weight, with a dry, short finish. **84** —J.C. (10/1/2005)

P.J. Valckenberg 2004 Estate Kabinett Riesling (Rheinhessen) $18. Medium in body—and even a bit oily in texture—this amply ripened wine boasts smoky, pungent aromas that veer toward green apple and lime after some airing. It's a bit heavy, but flavorful. **86** —J.C. (5/1/2006)

P.J. Valckenberg 2004 Estate Spätlese Riesling (Rheinhessen) $22. From the Liebfrauenstift-Kirchenstück vineyard near Worms, Valckenberg's estate Riesling boasts smoky, minerally aromas and understated fruit this vintage. It's on the full-bodied side, balanced by stony notes and a burst of quince on the finish. **86** —J.C. (9/1/2006)

P.J. Valckenberg 2001 Liebfrauenstift-Kirchenstück Kabinett Riesling (Rheinhessen) $14. Shows some real similarities to Valckenberg's spätlese from the same vineyard, particularly the finish, which is long and stony. The aromas are slightly creamy and nutty, while the flavors ring with tangerine and honey without being terribly sweet. **87** —J.C. (3/1/2003)

P.J. Valckenberg 2001 Liebfrauenstift-Kirchenstück Spätlese Riesling (Rheinhessen) $18. After a bit of sulfur and mint on the nose, this wine creates tension and interest through its juxtaposition of warm, soft flavors (baked apple, vegetable oil) with a hard, edgy mouthfeel and a stony, mineral-tinged finish. **87** —J.C. (3/1/2003)

P.J. Valckenberg 2003 Liebfrauenstift-Kirchenstück Spätlese Riesling (Rheinhessen) $22. This is the flagship vineyard for the large Valckenberg firm, and one of their best wines, year in and year out. The 2003 shows yeasty, leesy, minerally aromas and flavors of pear, pineapple, and talc, finishing on tart, grapefruity notes. Light in body; try as an apéritif. **87** —J.C. (5/1/2005)

P.J. Valckenberg 2001 Liebfrauenstift-Kirchenstück Spätlese Trocken Riesling (Rheinhessen) $18. Nutty and stony, this is a lean, dry wine built for the table, not for casual sipping. Limes and stone fruits finish with a quartz-like edge. **86** —J.C. (3/1/2003)

P.J. Valckenberg 2003 QbA Riesling (Rheinhessen) $11. A bit floral on the nose, picking up green apple and grapefruit scents as well. Soft, pillowy fruit flavors are balanced by acidity that seems to build in strength on the finish. **84** —J.C. (12/15/2004)

P.J. Valckenberg 2001 QbA Riesling (Rheinhessen) $7. A touch austere, you have to work a bit to ferret out the green apple and citrus aromas and flavors. But it's crisp and clean, finishing with a hit of fresh lime. **84 Best Buy** —J.C. (3/1/2003)

P.J. Valckenberg 2001 QbA Trocken Riesling (Rheinhessen) $10. Surprisingly complex and good, blending clove and ginger complexities with pear and peach fruit. Finishes long and vibrant, ending on a slight bitter note. **89 Best Buy** —J.C. (3/1/2003)

P.J. Valckenberg 2003 Riesling QbA Trocken Riesling (Rheinhessen) $14. Standard apple and pear aromas, but there's also a weird hint of peanut butter. Flavors are leaner and tart, focusing on under-ripe fruit and limes. This is lightweight yet intense, with a tactile, chalky quality to the finish. **84** —J.C. (12/15/2004)

P.J. Valckenberg 2005 Spätlese Trocken Riesling (Rheinhessen) $22. From the Wormser Liebfrauenstift-Kirchenstück, this dry Riesling boasts a clean, crystalline quality to its pear, apple, and melon flavors. Scents of stone dust enhance that aspect of the wine, which follows through on the minerally finish. **88** —J.C. (12/1/2006)

P.J. Valckenberg 2005 Trocken Riesling (Rheinhessen) $14. This citrusy wine is a bit of a one-note wonder, but it performs that note well, featuring strident lime aromas and a zippy, dry finish. **84** —J.C. (12/1/2006)

P.J. Valckenberg 2003 Wormser Liebfrauenstift Kirchenstück Sekt Brut Riesling (Rheinhessen) $25. Tart and very dry, this sparkler appears cleanly made, just somewhat meagerly endowed. Monochromatic—and that's a sour shade of citrus. **82** —J.C. (6/1/2006)

P.J. Valckenberg 2003 Wormser Liebfrauenstift-Kirchenstück Kabinett Riesling (Rheinhessen) $16. Redolent with fresh, vibrant fruit aromas, but not nearly as exciting in the mouth, where the plump baked apple and pear flavors finish short. **84** —J.C. (12/15/2004)

P.J. Valckenberg 2003 Wormser Liebfrauenstift-Kirchenstück Riesling Spätlese Trocken Riesling (Rheinhessen) $22. Starts off with honey, peach, and grapefruit aromas, and this creative tension between sweetly ripe flavors and tart acids continues across the palate. Shows good concentration and density, and finishes long and dry. **88** —J.C. (12/15/2004)

PAZEN

Pazen 2001 Zeltinger Himmelreich Kabinett Riesling (Mosel-Saar-Ruwer) $14. What a beauty. It's packed with tropical fruits (mangos) and ripe

GERMANY

apples, yet beautifully balanced by bracing acidity, like a squeeze of fresh lime juice on the finish. Pulls off the amazing trick of tasting rich, while feeling lightweight at the same time. **91 Best Buy** —*J.C. (3/1/2003)*

Pazen 2001 Zeltinger Himmelreich Spätlese Riesling (Mosel-Saar-Ruwer) $18. So if this is the spätlese, shouldn't it be better than Pazen's kabinett from the same site? No, it doesn't always work that way. It's still very good, though, and worth seeking out for its ripe melon and pear fruit graced with notes of mint and fresh greens. **88** —*J.C. (3/1/2003)*

PETER JAKOB KUHN

Peter Jakob Kuhn 1999 Oestricher Lenchen Kabinett Riesling (Rheingau) $12. Here's a racy Riesling that won't break your budget. Has everything you look for: pretty apple, peach, and honey aromas, with a distinct trace of sun-warmed slate, and long, rich, fruity, flowery flavors. Just a bit off-dry, it's balanced with crisp acidity. **87** —*S.H. (6/1/2001)*

PETER NICOLAY

Peter Nicolay 2001 Berkasteler Badstube Kabinett Riesling (Mosel-Saar-Ruwer) $15. This is a light, fresh wine. Fresh, crisp appley aromas, light sweetness, and pure, fresh fruit, are balanced with greenness. **88** —*R.V. (3/1/2003)*

Peter Nicolay 2001 Bernkasteler alte Badstube am Doctorberg Auslese Riesling (Mosel-Saar-Ruwer) $47. Flavors of ripe sweet currants along with delicate, poised perfumed fruits, show a wine that has all the makings of a fresh, sweet wine. Currently, the yeasty flavors dominate. **87** —*R.V. (3/1/2003)*

Peter Nicolay 2001 Bernkasteler alte Badstube am Doctorberg Spätlese Riesling (Mosel-Saar-Ruwer) $27. A fruit sorbet of a wine, with rich flavors of intense currants, white peaches, and citrus. Fine and crisp, it nicely balances fresh concentrated pure fruit flavors with sweetness. **90** —*R.V. (3/1/2003)*

Peter Nicolay 2001 Bernkasteler Badstube Spätlese Riesling (Mosel-Saar-Ruwer) $21. Soft fruit, aromas of fresh nuts, flavors of red currants, and sweet blackberries all give this wine richness and softness. The acidity is attractive but needs a shot in the arm to give it real balance. **87** —*R.V. (3/1/2003)*

Peter Nicolay 2004 Erderner Prälat Auslese Riesling (Mosel-Saar-Ruwer) $48. Rich and unctuous, mixing peach, melon, and apple aromas and flavors into a creamy fruit blend that wraps around the palate and won't let go, finishing long and elegantly. **92** —*J.C. (2/1/2006)*

Peter Nicolay 2004 Estate QbA Riesling (Mosel-Saar-Ruwer) $14. Medium-bodied, somewhat full, in fact, with a fair amount of sweetness that comes across as ripe melon and apple flavors, partly balanced by citrus on the finish. **84** —*J.C. (7/1/2006)*

Peter Nicolay 2001 Urziger Goldwingert Auslese Riesling (Mosel-Saar-Ruwer) $32. The Peter Nicolay estate belongs to the wife of Peter Pauly of Pauly-Bergweiler, and the two properties are run together. The wine is young, with yeasty aromas. The palate is hugely rich, with lovely ripeness and great sweetness. This is a big, rich intense wine, with flavors of botrytis and crisp honey. **92** —*R.V. (3/1/2003)*

Peter Nicolay 2001 Urziger Goldwingert Spätlese Riesling (Mosel-Saar-Ruwer) $26. A wine that is going to show great elegance and style, produced from the tiny, steep Goldwingert vineyard in Ürzig. At the moment, the yeastiness is prominent, but it doesn't hide the beautiful black currant flavors, intense acidity, and pure fruit. **92** —*R.V. (3/1/2003)*

Peter Nicolay 2004 Ürziger Würzgarten Auslese Riesling (Mosel-Saar-Ruwer) $40. This medium-bodied auslese even smells sweet, offering up notes of tangerine and honey. On the palate, there are hints of petrol and mineral to counter-balance all of the ripe melon and citrus flavors, while the finish lingers elegantly. **90** —*J.C. (2/1/2006)*

Peter Nicolay 2004 Ürziger Würzgarten Eiswein 375 ml Riesling (Mosel-Saar-Ruwer) $125. This wine's intense aromas of honey, oranges, and tea seem almost a little roasted or caramelized, but on the palate the flavors are brilliantly defined and focused by vibrant acidity that brighten the bold citrus and honey notes. A rich and viscous mouthfeel, yet miraculously crisp at the same time; the acids keep the finish echoing in your mouth for a long, long time. **95 Cellar Selection** —*J.C. (9/1/2006)*

Peter Nicolay 2004 Ürziger Würzgarten Kabinett Riesling (Mosel-Saar-Ruwer) $16. Light, crisp, and fresh, with bright citrus notes leading the way. Aromas of fresh lime and grated orange peel mark the nose, while the palate adds green apples and a touch of mint. Refreshing on its own, or with modestly spicy cuisine. **87** —*J.C. (7/1/2006)*

Peter Nicolay 2004 Ürziger Würzgarten Spätlese Riesling (Mosel-Saar-Ruwer) $23. Starts with lacy floral aromas layered over a bed of pear and pineapple fruit, then develops more weight in the mouth, adding honey and tangerine notes. Long and mouth-watering on the finish. **90** —*J.C. (2/1/2006)*

PFEFFINGEN

Pfeffingen 2002 Pfeffo Kabinett Riesling (Pfalz) $18. Starts off a bit fat, with warm, baked fruit flavors of apple pear crisp and spice, but firms up nicely on the finish, folding in additional spice notes and a pleasant tang that keeps things lively. **87** —*J.C. (8/1/2004)*

PRINZ

Prinz 2004 Hallgartener Jungfer Auslese Riesling (Rheingau) $43. Crushed pineapple, dried apricots, and fresh hay scents all mingle on the nose of this creamy-textured auslese. Flavors follow a similar path, ending elegantly. It doesn't have the racy balance of a Mosel wine, but instead has a smooth harmony and richness. **91** —*J.C. (2/1/2006)*

Prinz 2004 Hallgartener Jungfer Spätlese 375 ml Riesling (Rheingau) $19. Medium- to full-bodied, this sweet spätlese features lively aromas of green apple layered over scents of diesel oil. Pineapple flavors add citrusy brightness to the midpalate, finishing with milder notes of tangerine. **88** —*J.C. (9/1/2006)*

Prinz 2004 Riesling Trocken Riesling (Rheingau) $14. Floral and apple-y on the nose, providing textbook Riesling aromas. Crisp green apple and lime flavors continue the theme, accented on the finish by racy acids. With its modest weight on the palate, this is a dry, refreshing summer drink. **86** —*J.C. (7/1/2006)*

PRINZ ZU SALM-DALBERG

Prinz zu Salm-Dalberg 2003 Johannisberg Wallhausen Auslese Riesling (Nahe) $50. Intensely minerally, with hints of fuel oil on the nose, then crushed stones and ripe melon flavors on the palate. This shows unusual balance and precision for a 2003, culminating in a long, mouth-watering finish. **90** —*J.C. (5/1/2005)*

Prinz zu Salm-Dalberg 2001 Roxheimer Berg Spätlese Riesling (Nahe) $26. Grapefruit and earth combine in this hard, difficult wine that needs to be paired with the right dishes to succeed. There's no doubting its intensity and earthy concentration or its long, minerally finish, it's just not as open and friendly as so many of the other wines from this vintage. **86** —*J.C. (3/1/2003)*

Prinz zu Salm-Dalberg 2003 Schloss Wallhausen Berg Roxheim Spätlese Riesling (Nahe) $29. If German wine labels are confusing to Americans, labels like this one are one reason why. Traditionally this wine would be written as Roxheimer Berg, but for some reason this producer has written it Berg Roxheim. Green apple and diesel fuel aromas lead the way, followed by simple, fruity, apple flavors. Sweet and low in acidity, with a finish that's close to cloying. Try this as a dessert sipper with fresh fruit. **85** —*J.C. (5/1/2005)*

Prinz zu Salm-Dalberg 2001 Schloss Wallhausen Kabinett Riesling (Nahe) $16. Starts off peppery and herbal on the nose, then settles down and displays tropical fruit on the palate, including nuances of mango and melon. An off-dry style that seems a bit light. **85** —*J.C. (3/1/2003)*

Prinz zu Salm-Dalberg 2001 Wallhäuser Johannisberg QbA Riesling (Nahe) $31. This is a big, sturdy, dry Riesling, made to be matched with rich dishes. Limes combine with green floral notes on the nose to give a sense of freshness, then apple and peach flavors take over. The finish is long and intense, folding in hints of fresh mint. **90** —*J.C. (3/1/2003)*

RATZENBERGER

Ratzenberger 1998 Bacharacher Kloster Furstenal Riesling (Mittelrhein) $17. Despite the unfortunate name, this is a very pleasant sparkling wine, offering a concentrated apricot nose. The flavors carry plenty of fruit, along with some earthy, ashy flesh. Some ashy bitterness is the only off note. **87** —*P.G. (12/31/2002)*

REICHSGRAF VON KESSELSTATT

Reichsgraf von Kesselstatt 2001 Graacher QbA Trocken Riesling (Mosel-Saar-Ruwer) $NA. Von Kesselstatt's dry wine is a solid offering, but lacks the extra dimensions found in their more traditional bottlings. It's light, lean, and clean, combining green apples, Bartlett pears, and fresh lemons. **86** —*J.C. (1/1/2004)*

Reichsgraf von Kesselstatt 2004 Josephshöfer Spätlese Riesling (Mosel-Saar-Ruwer) $33. This medium-bodied spätlese has a firm spine of acidity to help keep its shape through potentially decades of aging. Apple, clove, and melon fruit is buttressed by layers of minerals and spice and a long, crisp finish. **91** —*J.C. (9/1/2006)*

Reichsgraf von Kesselstatt 2001 Josephshöfer Spätlese Monopol Riesling (Mosel-Saar-Ruwer) $20. Has all of the things you expect in a Mosel Riesling: floral notes, citrus, apple, peach, and pear fruit, all in a zippy, harmonious package. In 2001, the Josephshöfer spätlese seems very much like an auslese, with rich, honeyed flavors and a hint of apricot. **90 Editors' Choice** —*J.C. (3/1/2003)*

Reichsgraf von Kesselstatt 2001 Kaseler Nies'chen Kabinett Riesling (Mosel-Saar-Ruwer) $19. At 86 points, this wine may be underrated. It has those sorts of nuances and indescribable properties that often get overlooked in blind tastings, like balance, finesse, and elegance. The flavors of nectarine and dried spices are supremely harmonious; nothing sticks out, which hurts it in a blind-tasting format, but should help it with a meal. **86** —*J.C. (3/1/2003)*

Reichsgraf von Kesselstatt 2001 Piesporter Goldtropfchen Kabinett Riesling (Mosel-Saar-Ruwer) $19. The 2001s from von Kesselstatt turned out well across the board, including this delicate yet intense offering. Strongly citric, there's also a honeyed component to the tangerine flavors and a long, finely wrought finish that balances sweetness with grapefruit-like acids. **89** —*J.C. (3/1/2003)*

Reichsgraf von Kesselstatt 2005 Piesporter Goldtröpfchen Kabinett Riesling (Mosel-Saar-Ruwer) $22. Qualitatively on a par with the fine 2001, but in a plumper, sweeter style, with honeyed apple and pineapple aromas and flavors. A hint of bitter citrus pith on the finish provides a counterweight to all of the sweet fruit. **89** —*J.C. (12/1/2006)*

Reichsgraf von Kesselstatt 2003 Piesporter Goldtröpfchen Riesling Kabinett Riesling (Mosel-Saar-Ruwer) $22. Smells great, with expansive floral notes that are reminiscent of roses. Yet that promise isn't fully fulfilled on the palate, where its relatively high (9.5%) alcohol levels make for an awkward balance with the guava and citrus flavors. Cellar it and hope for positive evolution, or drink up in the short term. **86** —*J.C. (12/15/2004)*

Reichsgraf von Kesselstatt 2001 Piesporter Goldtropfchen Spätlese Riesling (Mosel-Saar-Ruwer) $24. Crisp, clean, and fresh, this is a little less weighty than many of the other spätlesen tasted for this report, but none the worse for that. The off-dry flavors of lemons and limes, quince, and green apples are in fine balance, blending in some pretty floral notes. **88** —*J.C. (3/1/2003)*

Reichsgraf von Kesselstatt 2004 RK QbA Riesling (Mosel-Saar-Ruwer) $13. This wine boasts intense and pure aromas of pear and pineapple, then adds notes of melon and dried spices on the palate. Medium in body and slightly sweet, with a short, crisp finish. **87** —*J.C. (5/1/2006)*

Reichsgraf von Kesselstatt 2003 RK QbA Riesling (Mosel-Saar-Ruwer) $13. A pleasant, lightweight Riesling, but one without a lot of intensity. Modest pear, melon, and apple flavors finish soft and easy. **84** —*J.C. (5/1/2005)*

Reichsgraf von Kesselstatt 2001 RK QbA Riesling (Mosel-Saar-Ruwer) $9. A bargain-priced Riesling that should be a mandatory house pour this summer. Warm hints of guava and tropical fruit are offset by cool, green notes. Crisp and clean, light and zesty; a perfect summertime refresher. **88 Best Buy** —*J.C. (3/1/2003)*

Reichsgraf von Kesselstatt 2002 Scharzhofberger Auslese Riesling (Mosel-Saar-Ruwer) $84. Smells like a mix of apricots, pineapples, and pears, with a judicious sprinkling of cinnamon. On the palate, the spice and earth components really kick in, adding richness to the fruit and honey flavors. Finishes with lingering sweetness. Approachable now, but should age beautifully. **92** —*J.C. (12/15/2004)*

Reichsgraf von Kesselstatt 2004 Scharzhofberger Auslese Fuder 4 Riesling (Mosel-Saar-Ruwer) $46. This lovely auslese starts with scents of bergamot, apple, and slate, then delivers full-bore pineapple and supersweet apple flavors on the plate. Despite the intense sweetness, the wine is wonderfully balanced, thanks to zippy, pink grapefruit-like acids. **92** —*J.C. (2/1/2006)*

Reichsgraf von Kesselstatt 2004 Scharzhofberger Kabinett Riesling (Mosel-Saar-Ruwer) $22. Smells ripe and rich, with scents of baked apples and pineapples and a trace of honey, and the wine is plump in the mouth, full of citrus and melon flavors. Yet for some reason this sample lacked zip and verve to balance the fruit, ending somewhat short. **85** —*J.C. (7/1/2006)*

Reichsgraf von Kesselstatt 2003 Scharzhofberger Kabinett Riesling (Mosel-Saar-Ruwer) $22. Starts with scents of smoke, apples, and pears, veering toward tropical fruit on the palate. It's appropriately light-bodied, its flamboyant fruit flavors reined in by ripe acids and a spicy, minerally note to the finish. **88** —*J.C. (12/15/2004)*

Reichsgraf von Kesselstatt 2001 Scharzhofberger Spätlese Riesling (Mosel-Saar-Ruwer) $25. Does a great job walking the knife's edge—it's ripe, yet racy. The apple and pear flavors are crisp and inviting, so fresh that they transport you to an apple orchard at the instant the fruit was picked. Great balance. **90** —*J.C. (3/1/2003)*

ROBERT WEIL

Robert Weil 2004 Estate Dry QbA Riesling (Rheingau) $25. This is a big, mouth-filling, dry Riesling, a bit austere on the nose, but ample in the mouth, where crunchy rocks dominate. Hints of under-ripe peach and crisp apple peek through, but this wine is all about the minerals and stony dryness. **89** —*J.C. (10/1/2005)*

Robert Weil 2002 QbA Trocken Riesling (Rheingau) $20. This is a fun, fresh, juicy wine, redolent of mixed citrus fruits. Lime, orange, and tangerine flavors bounce across the palate, finishing clean and refreshing. **86** —*J.C. (8/1/2004)*

RUDI WIEST

Rudi Wiest 2001 Mosel River QbA Riesling (Mosel-Saar-Ruwer) $9. Despite a lightness that verges on insubstantialness, this clean, fresh wine is flowery and citrusy, picking up green apple flavors on the finish. A good patio wine. **84** —*J.C. (8/1/2004)*

Rudi Wiest 2002 Rhein River QbA Riesling (Rheingau) $10. Importer Rudi Wiest has taken to selecting wines to bottle under his own label that offer fine quality for the price. This Rhine bottling blends peach and anise flavors in a medium-weight, off-dry wine that finishes strong. **85** —*J.C. (8/1/2004)*

RUDOLF EILENZ

Rudolf Eilenz 2004 Ayler Kupp Kabinett Riesling (Mosel-Saar-Ruwer) $15. Textbook Saar kabinett, still wearing a some youthful leesy accents on the nose, but crisp and pure on the palate. Citrus and green apple aromas broaden ever so slightly into melon and pear flavors in the mouth, then return to crystal clear focus on the finish. **89** —*J.C. (7/1/2006)*

Rudolf Eilenz 2004 Ayler Kupp Spätlese Feinherb Riesling (Mosel-Saar-Ruwer) $18. Feinherb suggests a style part way between fruchtig and full-blown trocken, and this wine matches the description, finishing almost dry. Slightly minty notes on the nose combine with flavors of citrus and melon in this lean, crisp Riesling. May be best with seafood dishes. **86** —*J.C. (9/1/2006)*

Rudolf Eilenz 2003 Ayler Kupp Spätlese Feinherb Riesling (Mosel-Saar-Ruwer) $17. The term "feinherb" is only rarely seen on German wine labels, but it indicates a dry-ish version of whatever prädikat is in question, sort of a halbtrocken. This version is nicely balanced, and yes, on the dry side, with apple and melon aromas and flavors that finish dry and minerally. **87** —*J.C. (5/1/2005)*

RUDOLF MÜLLER

Rudolf Müller 2004 Eiswein 375 ml Riesling (Pfalz) $19. Bargain-priced eiswein doesn't grow on trees (it's picked from frozen vines), but this offering is excellent. Honey and baked apple scents lead into flavors of poached or baked apple and pears, touched with a hint of bergamot. Clean and focused on the finish, so it doesn't end up sticky and cloying. **90 Editors' Choice** —*J.C. (9/1/2006)*

S.A. PRÜM

S.A. Prüm 2003 Blue Slate Kabinett Riesling (Mosel-Saar-Ruwer) $16. Shows off the tropical nature of the vintage in impressive style, with mango, melon, and nectarine fruit overflowing the glass. It's big, relatively dry, and full-bodied, but it all works, capped off by super-ripe grapefruit on the finish. **88** —*J.C. (5/1/2005)*

S.A. Prüm 2005 Essence Riesling (Mosel-Saar-Ruwer) $10. Light and fresh, this is a friendly fruitball of a Riesling. Riper peach and melon notes accent green apples and limes, then end on a crisp, refreshing note. A solid choice for the picnic hamper. **85 Best Buy** —*J.C. (7/1/2006)*

S.A. Prüm 2004 Essence Riesling (Mosel-Saar-Ruwer) $10. Raimond Prüm's 2004 Essence is better than his successful 2003. It's a big, forceful mouthful of Riesling, filled with ripe apple and pear flavors that ends on a harmonious off-dry note of citrus. **86 Best Buy** —*J.C. (2/1/2006)*

S.A. Prüm 2003 Essence QbA Riesling (Mosel-Saar-Ruwer) $10. Not a lot of depth or length, but what's here is pretty enough, blending peach and pear nectar. Full and soft; easy to drink. **84** —*J.C. (5/1/2005)*

S.A. Prüm 2001 Graacher Domprobst Eiswein Riesling (Mosel-Saar-Ruwer) $175. A hint of white pepper accents reined-in green apple and citrus aromas. Ultrasweet on the palate, picking up hints of caramel and honey on the finish, but balanced by some lime-like acidity. This is an eiswein with 40 years or more of aging potential. **90** —*J.C. (3/1/2003)*

S.A. Prüm 2002 Graacher Domprobst Trockenbeerenauslese Fass 61 Riesling (Mosel-Saar-Ruwer) $360. Powerful aromas of dried apricots signal concentrated botrytis, but there is more complexity as well: honey, peach, and bergamot flavors are all layered artfully over a deep foundation of apricot preserves. And yet the wine, intensely sweet, isn't at all cloying. Amazing, but probably impossible to find: 8 cases made. **95 Cellar Selection** —*J.C. (8/1/2004)*

S.A. Prüm 2001 Graacher Hammelreich Eiswein Riesling (Mosel-Saar-Ruwer) $165. Thanks to formidable acid levels, this eiswein doesn't seem that sweet at all, making it easier to drink than many others. Green apple, citrus, and ginger close long and tart—a refreshing dessert wine rather than a sticky one. **89** —*J.C. (3/1/2003)*

S.A. Prüm 2002 Graacher Himmelreich Eiswein Fass 56 Riesling (Mosel-Saar-Ruwer) $195. Layers of sweet mango, pineapple, and citrus fruits are beautifully balanced on a razor's edge of bright acidity. Hints of apricot add complexity to the aromas, while the finish extends for what seems like minutes. **94** —*J.C. (8/1/2004)*

S.A. Prüm 1998 Graacher Himmelreich Eiswein Vat 28 Riesling (Mosel-Saar-Ruwer) $140. Dark in color for an eiswein, with intense, caramelized sugar, golden raisin, and dried-spice aromas. Tastes intensely sweet and sour, with sky-high acids and sugars that can't quite keep up. And it finishes with tart, quince-like notes. **84** —*J.C. (5/1/2005)*

S.A. Prüm 2003 Graacher Himmelreich Spätlese Riesling (Mosel-Saar-Ruwer) $26. Plump and soft on the midpalate, but tangy on the finish, resulting in a slightly discordant impression. Still, the raw material seems to be in place, with quince and lime custard aromas and baked apple and pear flavors. Give this another 3–6 months to settle down and it should be fine. **86** —*J.C. (5/1/2005)*

S.A. Prüm 2001 Kabinett Halbtrocken Riesling (Mosel-Saar-Ruwer) $20. With aromas of smoke, quartz dust, and ripe apples, you'd expect mineral-laden flavors, but they're more crunchy, more fresh fruity, with the emphasis on apple and lemon. Finishes long and tart. **89** —*J.C. (3/1/2003)*

S.A. Prüm 2001 QbA trocken Riesling (Mosel-Saar-Ruwer) $19. Fairly full-bodied for a Mosel Riesling, this dry wine starts off with peach, graphite,

and smoke aromas, but the flavors are peppery, finishing with tangy grapefruit and stone fruits. **88** —*J.C. (3/1/2003)*

S.A. Prüm 2001 Spätlese trocken Riesling (Mosel-Saar-Ruwer) $23. Standard apple and citrus aromas and flavors join here in a wine that would be largely unremarkable except for its plump, custardy texture and racy, zippy finish, both of which add appeal. **87** —*J.C. (3/1/2003)*

S.A. Prüm 2002 Wehlener Sonnenuhr Auslese Riesling (Mosel-Saar-Ruwer) $65. Despite this wine's remarkable sweetness and viscosity, it never seems unbalanced or heavy. Aromas of ripe apples, pears, and melons give way to waves of tropical fruit flavors on the palate, buoyed by dried apricots and cinnamon. Finishes long, echoing of golden raisins and apricot. **93 Editors' Choice** —*J.C. (8/1/2004)*

S.A. Prüm 2001 Wehlener Sonnenuhr Auslese Riesling (Mosel-Saar-Ruwer) $53. Smells wonderful, like the most perfectly tree-ripened peaches. But the flavors are harder and less giving, with green apple and only a hint of peaches. Further aging may smooth it out. **87** —*J.C. (3/1/2003)*

S.A. Prüm 2005 Wehlener Sonnenuhr Kabinett Riesling (Mosel-Saar-Ruwer) $20. Floral and citrusy on the nose, then picking up white peach, melon, and pineapple flavors on the palate. Off-dry, but crisp and clean on the finish, where there's also a slight bitter-pith note. **87** —*J.C. (7/1/2006)*

S.A. Prüm 2003 Wehlener Sonnenuhr Kabinett Riesling (Mosel-Saar-Ruwer) $20. Still a bit sulfury, but otherwise correct, with melon, pear, and spice flavors, lithe body, and a clean, short finish. Should be better in another year or two. **85** —*J.C. (5/1/2006)*

S.A. Prüm 2001 Wehlener Sonnenuhr Kabinett Riesling (Mosel-Saar-Ruwer) $23. Minty and grassy at first, it develops peach and pear aromas as it sits in the glass. The sweet stone-fruit flavors are balanced by a stony, minerally hardness that persists through the finish. **88** —*J.C. (3/1/2003)*

S.A. Prüm 2001 Wehlener Sonnenuhr Spätlese Riesling (Mosel-Saar-Ruwer) $24. Is that gardenia in the bouquet? It's floral in any event, combined with green apples and a hint of dried apricots. Flavors are pear and over-ripe peach; finishes soft. **86** —*J.C. (3/1/2003)*

S.A. Prüm 2001 Wehlener Sonnenuhr Spätlese Halbtrocken Riesling (Mosel-Saar-Ruwer) $35. A sturdy, strong-boned wine with apple and grapefruit aromas that give way to flavors suggestive of unripe melons and peaches. Tastes dry, ending on a mild citrus note. **86** —*J.C. (3/1/2003)*

S.A. Prüm 2001 Wehlener Sonnenuhr Spätlese Trocken Riesling (Mosel-Saar-Ruwer) $35. A long, grapefruity tang elegantly finishes out this dry offering, which starts off with damp earth and green apples before developing some spicy complexity on the midpalate. Lively acidity makes it a good apéritif candidate. **87** —*J.C. (3/1/2003)*

SAINT M

Saint M 2004 Qualitatswein Riesling (Pfalz) $12. Bottled by Villa Wolf (Ernie Loosen's Pfalz winery) for Chateau Ste. Michelle, this broad, mouth-filling Riesling features decent earthy, diesel fuel flavors in place of vibrant fruit. **83** —*J.C. (10/1/2005)*

SANDER

Sander 2002 Terravita Dornfelder (Rheinhessen) $18. A fresh, structured wine, with a touch of acidity, some wood, and bitter chocolate flavors and a juicy, ripe aftertaste. This is a light red, very fresh, and would work best at a cool cellar temperature. Like all Sander wines, the fruit was treated as gently as possible, with only small amounts of sulfites added. **85** —*R.V. (4/1/2005)*

Sander 2003 Kabinett Halbtrocken Terravita Riesling (Rheinhessen) $13. Clean, fresh Riesling which has light fruit, flavors of ripe pears, and a lively, racy aftertaste. This is a delicious apéritif wine with good crispness, acidity, and a soft, easy aftertaste. **84** —*R.V. (4/1/2005)*

Sander 2002 QbA Riesling (Rheinhessen) $13. Waxy and citrusy, this wine, made from organically grown grapes, is virtually dry, although not labeled as trocken. It's relatively heavy for a Riesling, finishing short. **84** —*J.C. (8/1/2004)*

Sander 2003 Terravita Riesling (Rheinhessen) $13. An enticingly aromatic Riesling, which is full of flowers and white currants. It is fresh, light and attractively crisp with flavors of fresh apples and currants. The acidity gives the whole wine lift and liveliness. **87** —*R.V. (4/1/2005)*

Sander 2004 Metterheimer Sauvignon Blanc (Rheinhessen) $28. You don't find too many German Sauvignons, and maybe this wine tells us why. It's spritzy and artificially sweet, almost like lemon-lime soda pop. Could be better in the summer if served nicely chilled. **83** *(7/1/2005)*

Sander 2003 Trocken Spätburgunder (Rheinhessen) $15. Full of dry tannins and rich, juicy fruit. Flavors of dark plums, coffee, and toast come through the firm structure, which suggests the wine needs aging for two to three years. **86** —*R.V. (4/1/2005)*

Sander 2003 Trocken Weissburgunder (Rheinhessen) $13. A full-bodied, ripe wine with soft Pinot Blanc fruit and a touch of vanilla and caramel flavors. There are flavors of currants and a good layer of acidity with a full, but fresh aftertaste. **85** —*R.V. (4/1/2005)*

Sander 2004 Mettenheimer Sauvignon Blanc-Riesling White Blend (Rheinhessen) $25. Lots of pure peach on the nose, with notes of lemon and ginger. Open-knit and sweet on the palate, with hints of custard, mango, and baked pineapple. Spritzy and zesty, yet sweet. An interesting wine that isn't commonplace. **87** *(7/1/2005)*

Sander 2003 Trio Terravita White Blend (Rheinhessen) $11. A fresh, uncomplicated light wine, with good clean and ripe fruit. This is a perfect apéritif wine, with good crisp pear and apple flavors. There is a touch of sweetness just to give it a lift. **84** —*R.V. (4/1/2005)*

SCHLOSS JOHANNISBERGER

Schloss Johannisberger 2004 Kabinett Riesling (Rheingau) $28. Artfully shows the majesty of the Rheingau, combining a rich, full mouthfeel with enough acidity to keep it from seeming at all heavy. Slate, melon, and lime flavors turn crisp and refreshing on the finish. **88** —*J.C. (7/1/2006)*

Schloss Johannisberger 2001 Kabinett Riesling (Rheingau) $18. This is a decent if unspectacular Riesling from what should be one of the greatest sites in the Rheingau. Lean pear and apple fruit is mentholly, tart, and ungenerous. Admire it for its structure. **84** —*J.C. (1/1/2004)*

Schloss Johannisberger 2004 QbA Riesling (Rheingau) $23. Light and dry, with floral, minty scents that morph into apple and citrus flavors on the palate. Ends a bit hard and crystalline—brilliantly clear, yet slightly unwelcoming. May be better in another year or two. **84** —*J.C. (2/1/2006)*

Schloss Johannisberger 2003 QbA Riesling (Rheingau) $23. This is nicely balanced, with a relatively light body and sweet fruit, yet enough grapefruity acids on the finish to offset the residual sugar. Bright apple and pear flavors sing loudly, alongside hints of honey and citrus. **86** —*J.C. (12/15/2004)*

Schloss Johannisberger 2001 QbA Riesling (Rheingau) $15. Smells lush and tropical, offering up hints of banana, pear, and pineapple, then turns crisper and cleaner, showing some sour apple notes. Light and fresher than the nose suggests, with a long, tangy finish. **87** —*J.C. (3/1/2003)*

Schloss Johannisberger 2003 Riesling Kabinett Riesling (Rheingau) $28. Fairly full-bodied and quite dry, with low residual sugar levels and high alcohol (12%), this is an atypically muscular kabinett. Smoke and earth flavors are minerally and complex, backed by hints of peach and grapefruit, finishing tart. **86** —*J.C. (12/15/2004)*

Schloss Johannisberger 2003 Spätlese Riesling (Rheingau) $34. Lime and mineral flavors are pleasant enough, nicely carried on a sweet, low-alcohol frame, but the aromas and finish are marred by a slightly vinegary note of volatile acidity. **84** —*J.C. (12/15/2004)*

SCHLOSS KOBLENZ

Schloss Koblenz NV Weisslack Trocken Sekt Sparkling Blend (Germany) $12. A decent value in sparkling wine, with pronounced yeasty notes and some green apple flavors delivered via a creamy, medium-bodied wine. Labeled trocken, but tastes slightly off-dry. **85** —*J.C. (6/1/2006)*

SCHLOSS SAARSTEIN

Schloss Saarstein 2001 QbA Trocken Riesling (Mosel-Saar-Ruwer) $11. While the bouquet mixes exotic aromas of tropical fruit (guava?) with vanilla, the flavors are lean and focused, ranging from green apple to lemon and lime. It's dry, crisp and refreshing, a great apéritif wine at a great price. **88 Best Buy** —*J.C. (3/1/2003)*

Schloss Saarstein 2003 Riesling QbA Trocken Riesling (Mosel-Saar-Ruwer) $17. Schloss Saarstein has made trocken wines a bit of a specialty, and this 2003 is one of their best efforts. Ripe pear scents cannot overtake an intense graphite or slate minerality on the nose, while on the palate, green apple and pear flavors are enlivened by lime-like acidity. Light and refreshing. **88** —*J.C. (12/15/2004)*

Schloss Saarstein 2003 Riesling Spätlese Trocken Riesling (Mosel-Saar-Ruwer) $26. This wine is for folks who bemoan the lack of acidity in the 2003s. Here's your acid fix: zippy, zesty lime-like acids are cushioned by just enough ripe peaches to make it enjoyable. Crisp and stone-dry on the finish. **87** —*J.C. (12/15/2004)*

Schloss Saarstein 2003 Serriger Schloss Saarsteiner Auslese Riesling (Mosel-Saar-Ruwer) $39. Delicate and lacy, with finely etched flavors of green apples, dried spices, and limes. This is light in body and relatively low in alcohol and sugar for the vintage, finishing on a crisp note. **89** —*J.C. (12/15/2004)*

Schloss Saarstein 2004 Serriger Schloss Saarsteiner Kabinett Riesling (Mosel-Saar-Ruwer) $20. Light and fresh, this tart, strident wine is a poster-child for cool-climate Riesling. Lime, green apple, and pineapple aromas and flavors are bold and crisp, tinged with enough slatey minerality to mark its Saar origins. **89** —*J.C. (5/1/2006)*

Schloss Saarstein 2003 Serriger Schloss Saarsteiner Kabinett Riesling (Mosel-Saar-Ruwer) $20. Decently balanced for short-term drinking, this wine has managed to retain a sense of freshness to its finish that some 2003s are lacking. Apricot and pineapple aromas give way to apple and pear flavors and a lively, citrusy finish. **88** —*J.C. (5/1/2005)*

Schloss Saarstein 2003 Serriger Schloss Saarsteiner Spätlese Riesling (Mosel-Saar-Ruwer) $26. The 2003s from Schloss Saarstein all share a certain delicacy and lightness—this wine is no exception. Lime, honey, and stone aromas give way to similar flavors, plus green apple. The wine is slightly sweet, yet not expansive in the mouth, with a crisp finish. **88** —*J.C. (12/15/2004)*

Schloss Saarstein 2003 Weisser Burgunder QbA Weissburgunder (Mosel-Saar-Ruwer) $17. This is a dramatic contrast to the Rieslings from Schloss Saarstein, which tend to be delicate and racy. This Pinot Blanc is fat, with modest melon and baked apple flavors and a soft, short finish. **84** —*J.C. (12/15/2004)*

SCHLOSS SCHÖNBORN

Schloss Schönborn 2001 Domanenweingut Hattenheimer Pfaffenberg Spätlese Riesling (Rheingau) $28. A wine from the old domaine of Schloss Schörnborn. It is ripe, with some toffee flavors. Layers of sweetness and baked apple tastes show through the intense, underlying acidity. It is a little out of balance at present, but the structural tannins on the wine suggest it will age well. **90** —*R.V. (3/1/2003)*

Schloss Schönborn 2001 Erbacher Marcobrunn Kabinett Riesling (Rheingau) $14. Intense flavors of crisp apples and pears open in the mouth to reveal freshness, ripeness, and currant fruits. A well-poised, balanced wine, full of fruit flavors. **90** —*R.V. (3/1/2003)*

Schloss Schönborn 2001 Erbacher Marcobrunn Spätlese Riesling (Rheingau) $23. A perfume maker would kill for this intoxicating perfume of summer fruits. Flavors of ripe quince come with the poise of light acidity and freshness. To finish, this lightness and the ripeness come together in fine balance. **92** —*R.V. (3/1/2003)*

Schloss Schönborn 2001 Hattenheimer Pfaffenberg Kabinett Riesling (Rheingau) $12. Rich and intense, with power and concentration, this is a blockbuster wine, full of Riesling ripeness and intensity, along with flavors of crisp, juicy apples. **90** —*R.V. (3/1/2003)*

Schloss Schönborn 2001 Hattenheimer Pfaffenberg Spätlese Riesling (Rheingau) $17. Intoxicating acidity is the main character of this wine. It is certainly ripe, there is crisp fruit, but at the end it is always this acidity that pierces through the sweetness like a rapier. At the end, there is great balance. **91** —*R.V. (3/1/2003)*

Schloss Schönborn 2001 Johannisberger Klaus Spätlese Riesling (Rheingau) $16. Rich, toffee aromas balance a touch of ripe, crisp acidity. The wine is soft, very rich initially with some toffee apple flavors. Intense acidity comes through to give it balance and poise. **87** —*R.V. (3/1/2003)*

Schloss Schönborn 2001 Kabinett Riesling (Rheingau) $10. A lively, vibrant wine with balanced acidity and delicious crisp fruit. Flavors of lychees and hedgerow fruits leave a clean, refreshing aftertaste. **88** —*R.V. (3/1/2003)*

Schloss Schönborn 2000 Rudesheimer Berg Rottland Auslese Riesling (Rheingau) $43. Graf Schönborn has aimed for a fine delicacy of flavor in this sweet wine. Lovely acidity and elegant fruits balance the flavors of cranberries and sweet pears. This is poised, delicate, and certainly age-worthy. **93** —*R.V. (3/1/2003)*

SCHLOSS THORN

Schloss Thorn 2001 Spätlese Riesling (Mosel-Saar-Ruwer) $20. An attractive floral wine, with fine, ripe fruit. Flavors of white peaches show through the crispness and fresh sweetness. The perfumes linger right through the wine. **89** —*R.V. (1/1/2004)*

SCHLOSS VOLLRADS

Schloss Vollrads 2003 Auslese Riesling (Rheingau) $50. Despite the inclusion of 25% botrytized fruit, this wine remains well-balanced; fresh, not heavy. Melon and green apple flavors offset riper notes of honey and orange marmalade. **90** *(8/1/2004)*

Schloss Vollrads 2001 Auslese Riesling (Rheingau) $46. The ancient estate of Schloss Vollrads dates at least from 1211, when it was already producing wine. The general style of the wine today is uncomplex. This example has powerful aromas of botrytis, flavors of baked apples, with a touch of spice. But there's good acidity to balance. **88** —*R.V. (3/1/2003)*

Schloss Vollrads 2004 Auslese 375 ml Riesling (Rheingau) $50. Rich and unctuous, but not a simple fruit-bomb of concentrated fruit, there's also great minerality and some kerosene. Apple, peach kernel, and baking spice flavors end on a honeyed note. **91** —*J.C. (9/1/2006)*

Schloss Vollrads 2003 Beerenauslese Riesling (Rheingau) $180. Orange marmalade and dried apricots run rampant on the nose, joined by spicy notes reminiscent of nutmeg or cinnamon. Flavors are mouthcoating and rich, yet never seem heavy, and last a long, long time. **93** *(8/1/2004)*

Schloss Vollrads 2004 Beerenauslese (375ml) Riesling (Rheingau) $170. A bit of a disappointment after the stellar 2004 auslese, Vollrads's BA is thick and syrupy, but also has a slightly acetic edge to its aromas and flavors. Dried fruit and honey marry with melon notes that tail off a bit on the finish. **87** —*J.C. (9/1/2006)*

Schloss Vollrads 2002 Eiswein Riesling (Rheingau) $160. This wine's high acidity provides balance for the wine's intense sweetness, imparting a racy quality to the long, lemony finish. Aromas and flavors of "yellow" fruits—pineapple, citrus, and quince—predominate. **91** *(8/1/2004)*

Schloss Vollrads 2001 Eiswein Riesling (Rheingau) $119. This is typical of the lighter style of Schloss Vollrads' sweet wines. It has as much dryness and acidity as sweetness, with flavors of quince and white figs. The delicate wine leaves a crisp, fresh aftertaste. **90** —*R.V. (3/1/2003)*

Schloss Vollrads 2004 Kabinett Riesling (Rheingau) $19. Seems slightly disjointed, with pungent diesel aromas on one hand and Sweet Tart melon and pear flavors on the other. It's atypically broad in the mouth for Riesling, almost fat, yet closes on a tangy, earthy note. **84** —*J.C. (5/1/2006)*

Schloss Vollrads 2003 Kabinett Riesling (Rheingau) $17. Plump, medium-weight kabinett that features aromas of peach and apple blossom and flavors of peach and mango. Finishes a bit tart, giving it a nice sense of balance. **86** *(8/1/2004)*

Schloss Vollrads 2001 Kabinett Riesling (Rheingau) $15. A delicate wine, with crisp, light, pure fruit. It is fresh, vibrant and ready to drink now, without much suggestion of ageability. **87** —*R.V. (3/1/2003)*

Schloss Vollrads 2004 Kabinett Halbtrocken Riesling (Rheingau) $19. This halbtrocken is light and crisp, featuring an almost dry finish that shows just a bit of honey at the end. Green apple, lime, and pineapple aromas and flavors are fresh and inviting, just lack a little complexity. **85** —*J.C. (7/1/2006)*

Schloss Vollrads 2002 Kabinett Halbtrocken Riesling (Rheingau) $17. Starts off with a hint of diesel fuel, then merges seamlessly into green apples, pears, honey, and mineral notes. Finishes crisp and clean, picking up additional mineral flavors. **87** *(8/1/2004)*

Schloss Vollrads 2001 Kabinett Halbtrocken Riesling (Rheingau) $15. The dryness of the wine is somewhat shocking. It is full-bodied with prominent, dry, appley acidity and crisp, fresh green flavors. A layer of tannin gives the wine a slight tartness. **87** —*R.V. (3/1/2003)*

Schloss Vollrads 2003 Kabinett Trocken Riesling (Rheingau) $17. Seems a bit disjointed right now, with aromas of ripe stone fruit and mineral that aren't obvious on the palate, where the flavors are grapefruity and sharp. Give it another six months to come into balance. **85** *(8/1/2004)*

Schloss Vollrads 2004 QbA Riesling (Rheingau) $16. A soft, easygoing Riesling that's a nice introduction to the sterner stuff of the Rheingau, this medium-bodied wine offers mouth-filling baked apple and spice flavors to match its broad melon, spice, and mineral aromas. **88** —*J.C. (5/1/2006)*

Schloss Vollrads 2003 QbA Riesling (Rheingau) $17. A soft, fruity, easy-to-drink wine, with notes of peach, tropical fruit, and melon that make for a simple, satisfying drink, not an intellectually stimulating one. **85** *(8/1/2004)*

Schloss Vollrads 2004 QbA Trocken Riesling (Rheingau) $16. Relatively light in weight for the Rheingau, with modest pineapple and fern aromas on the nose. Tart and flavorful on the palate, marrying pineapple and green apple flavors that finish crisp and dry. **86** —*J.C. (5/1/2006)*

Schloss Vollrads 2003 QbA Trocken Riesling (Rheingau) $15. Smells fresh and a bit yeasty and minerally, then follows through with rich fruit and grapefruity acids that finish on a razor-sharp edge. Try with shellfish. **86** *(8/1/2004)*

Schloss Vollrads 2003 Spätlese Riesling (Rheingau) $26. In an interesting twist, this wine actually seems lighter and crisper than the kabinett, pairing peach, apple, and pear flavors with a minerally finish that still retains the vintage's inherent softness. **89** *(8/1/2004)*

Schloss Vollrads 2001 Spätlese Riesling (Rheingau) $25. Creamy aromas. The fruit is fresh but light, with flavors of white currants and baked apples. High acidity suggests some ageability. **86** —*R.V. (3/1/2003)*

Schloss Vollrads 2003 Spätlese Halbtrocken Riesling (Rheingau) $26. This full-bodied, mostly dry Riesling features a rich, layered texture and a spicy finish. Slightly floral notes add nuance to solid pear, melon, and mineral flavors. **88** *(8/1/2004)*

Schloss Vollrads 2002 Trockenbeerenauslese Riesling (Rheingau) $300. Hugely rich and syrupy, with enormous aromas and flavors of dried apricots and pineapple. Mineral and honey notes linger forever on the finish. **92** *(8/1/2004)*

SCHLOSS WALLHAUSEN

Schloss Wallhausen 2004 Kabinett Riesling (Nahe) $17. Plump, yet buttressed by firm acidity, Wallhausen's kabinett features strong minerality this year. My original notes on its aromas read: powdered mineral, apple, pear, mineral. Tastes like liquid rocks, with hints of green herbs. Finishes with a grapefruity flourish. **88** —*J.C. (10/1/2005)*

Schloss Wallhausen 2005 Spätlese Riesling (Nahe) $23. Fairly priced for a Nahe Riesling, the Schloss Wallhausen spätlese offers penetrating scents of lime and minerals, garnished with touches of flowers and green apple. Despite its plumpness in the mouth, there's an almost austere quality to the minerality, which is only slightly buffered by sweet apple and citrus flavors. Picks up the slightest hint of bitterness on the finish. **89** —*J.C. (12/1/2006)*

SCHMITGES

Schmitges 2004 Erdener Prälat Spätlese Alte Reben Riesling (Mosel-Saar-Ruwer) $41. This old-vine parcel of Erdener Prälat has yielded an impressively minerally and spicy spätlese, buffered by ripe apples and pears. A slightly oily texture suggests ample concentration, but the wine doesn't fully flesh out in the midpalate, leaving a slight hollowness that kept me from being more enthusiastic. **87** —*J.C. (9/1/2006)*

Schmitges 2004 Erdener Treppchen Kabinett No. 11 Riesling (Mosel-Saar-Ruwer) $18. Scents of fresh greens—perhaps fern fronds—quickly give way to flavors of super-ripe apples and honey. Yet the wine retains a light, feathery mouthfeel, turning drier on the finish, with a slight sense of sourness at the end. **86** —*J.C. (7/1/2006)*

Schmitges 2003 Erdener Treppchen Kabinett No. 7 Riesling (Mosel-Saar-Ruwer) $17. Citrusy and leesy on the nose, followed by pretty much textbook apple, pear, and citrus flavors. It's lightly sweet, medium in body, with tingly acids that keep everything balanced. Picks up some lovely bergamot notes on the finish. **88** —*J.C. (11/1/2004)*

Schmitges 2004 Erdener Treppchen Spätlese No. 14 Riesling (Mosel-Saar-Ruwer) $25. Has some hints of wild greens on the nose to go with more standard notes of pineapple and melon. But it's on the palate that this wine really shines, adding flavors of apple, citrus and edible flowers, and culminating in a long, balanced finish. **89** —*J.C. (2/1/2006)*

Schmitges 2005 Grauschiefer Dry Riesling (Mosel-Saar-Ruwer) $15. Relatively plump and succulent for a "Dry Riesling," with honeyed, musky notes that accent ripe peach and dusty mineral flavors. Not quite dry on the finish, but powered by crisp acidity. **87** —*J.C. (12/1/2006)*

Schmitges 2003 Grauschiefer Qualitätswein Trocken Riesling (Mosel-Saar-Ruwer) $15. Smells fruity, with scents of apple, lime, pineapple, and pear that are echoed on the palate. Doesn't offer a lot of mineral complexity, but plenty of tart, light-bodied, almost completely dry fruit. **86** —*J.C. (11/1/2004)*

Schmitges 2004 Grauschiefer Trocken Riesling (Mosel-Saar-Ruwer) $15. Easily mixes melon and slate scents on the nose, then blends in pear flavors on the palate. Just off-dry ("trocken" doesn't necessarily mean bone-dry), with weight and body provided by relatively high (12.5%) alcohol. Turns pleasantly spicy on the finish. **89 Editors' Choice** —*J.C. (10/1/2005)*

Schmitges 2003 QbA Riesling (Mosel-Saar-Ruwer) $17. Apple and pineapple on the nose, bolstered by scents of spring flowers. It's medium-bodied on the palate, with mineral-accented apple flavors and a long, crisply acidic finish. **88** —*J.C. (11/1/2004)*

Schmitges 2004 Qualitatswein Riesling (Mosel-Saar-Ruwer) $15. A simple, crisp Riesling that will work well as an apéritif. Green apple and lime aromas and flavors finish on the dry side. Tart and mouthwatering. **85** —*J.C. (10/1/2005)*

SCHMITT SCHENK

Schmitt Schenk 2001 Ayler Kupp Auslese Riesling (Mosel-Saar-Ruwer) $14. Flavors of grapefruit and crisp green fruits lie above sweet, soft acidity. This is a clean wine, with a touch of lightness and delicacy. **86** —*R.V. (3/1/2003)*

SCHMITT SOHNE

Schmitt Sohne 2001 Piesporter Michelsberg Auslese Riesling (Mosel-Saar-Ruwer) $12. Aromas of fruit candies lead to a light, fresh crisp wine with some pleasing acidity and fresh fruits. **84** —*R.V. (3/1/2003)*

Schmitt Sohne 2004 Relax QbA Riesling (Mosel-Saar-Ruwer) $8. This light-bodied Riesling is true to its roots in the Mosel, offering slatey complexity that's surprising for the price, balanced by citrus and pineapple flavors. **84 Best Buy** —*J.C. (7/1/2006)*

Schmitt Sohne 2001 Spätlese Riesling (Mosel-Saar-Ruwer) $9. A soft, yeasty, simple fresh wine, which comes packed in a blue bottle. Has some pleasant, light fruit. **83** —*R.V. (3/1/2003)*

Schmitt Sohne 2001 Wehlener Sonnenuhr Auslese Riesling (Mosel-Saar-Ruwer) $14. Ripe, simple fruits with some nice acidity and flavors of white currants from ungrafted vines in the famed Sonnenuhr vineyard. The wine is soft and sweet, light and fresh. **86** —*R.V. (3/1/2003)*

Schmitt Sohne 2001 Wehlener Sonnenuhr Kabinett Riesling (Mosel-Saar-Ruwer) $18. A rich, easy wine with ripe currants and a touch of cranberries which give a good balance and easy drinkability. Soft acidity goes along with the easy, soft fruit. **86** —*R.V. (3/1/2003)*

Schmitt Sohne 2001 Wehlener Sonnenuhr Spätlese Riesling (Mosel-Saar-Ruwer) $11. Flavors of candy and sweet fruits mark this rather one-dimensional wine. There is some acidity, but it is masked by sweetness. **85** —*R.V. (3/1/2003)*

SCHUMANN-NÄGLER

Schumann-Nägler 2004 Christopher Philipp QbA Riesling (Rheingau) $13. The fruit seems rather restrained in this medium-bodied Riesling. Instead, the emphasis is on slatey, minerally scents, backed by soft apple and citrus flavors. **83** —*J.C. (5/1/2006)*

Schumann-Nägler 2001 Christopher Philipp QbA Riesling (Rheingau) $10. Simple apple and citrus aromas and flavors in a weightier-than-expected package. The lingering finish turns slightly sour at the end. **83** —*J.C. (1/1/2004)*

Schumann-Nägler 2003 Christopher Philipp Riesling QbA Riesling (Rheingau) $12. Like your neighbor's Saint Bernard, this is a big, friendly fellow that's eager to please. Spiced pear and dusty sandstone aromas provide pleasure to fruit and mineral lovers alike, while the moderately sweet, low-acid flavors are easygoing and practically gulpable. **87 Best Buy** —*J.C. (12/15/2004)*

Schumann-Nägler 2001 Johannisberger Ertenbringer Riesling (Rheingau) $15. Petroleum product complexities abound in this fairly dry offering. Smells a bit like diesel oil—maybe even home heating oil—then takes on mineral notes akin to oil-shale deposits. It's relatively full-bodied and viscous, a far cry (as it should be) from its Mosel Riesling cousins. **86** —*J.C. (3/1/2003)*

SEEBRICH

Seebrich 2004 Niersteiner Hipping Auslese Riesling (Rheinhessen) $24. Reasonably priced for an auslese, this medium-weight Riesling offers perfumes of clover blossom and poached apples and pears. On the palate, there's a pronounced quince or citrus edge that provides balance, but also a slight hint of bitterness. **88** —*J.C. (9/1/2006)*

Seebrich 2003 Niersteiner Hipping Spätlese Riesling (Rheinhessen) $17. Slightly sweet and low in acidity, Seebrich's spätlese perfectly reflects the challenges of the vintage. Very ripe apples carry notes of cinnamon and clove, but finish a little soft. Drink now. **86** —*J.C. (12/15/2004)*

SELBACH

Selbach 2001 Piesporter Michelsberg Riesling Kabinett Riesling (Mosel-Saar-Ruwer) $11. 87 Best Buy —*D.T. (11/15/2002)*

Selbach 2004 Qba Dry Riesling (Mosel-Saar-Ruwer) $14. Lightly floral on the nose, with modest green apple scents as well. This light, dry Riesling is clean and refreshing, but lacks the flavor intensity to warrant a higher rating. **83** —*J.C. (2/1/2006)*

SELBACH SÖHNE

Selbach Söhne NV Blau-Gold Mild Schaumwein Sparkling Blend (Germany) $13. A bit heavy and sweet, with modest pear and melon flavors that fall flat. **81** —*J.C. (6/1/2006)*

SELBACH-OSTER

Selbach-Oster 2004 Kabinett Riesling (Mosel-Saar-Ruwer) $23. Crisp and clean, without quite the depth or minerality of the Zeltinger Sonnenuhr bottling but still imbued with impressive purity and fruit. The pineapple and muskmelon flavors, with touches of peach and citrus, finish long and citrusy. **87** —*J.C. (10/1/2005)*

Selbach-Oster 2001 Zeltinger Sonnenuhr Auslese Riesling (Mosel-Saar-Ruwer) $33. As it should be, this wine is riper-tasting than Selbach-Oster's one-star spätlese, but not any better from a qualitative perspective. It shows more yellow plum aromatics and features a lush mouthfeel that partially masks a steel backbone of acidity. Expect this to close down for a few years before blossoming around age eight. **91** —*J.C. (3/1/2003)*

Selbach-Oster 2004 Zeltinger Sonnenuhr Kabinett Riesling (Mosel-Saar-Ruwer) $26. Very primary and fruity, with excellent purity of flavor. Pineapple, pear, and apple scents start it off, then add strawberry nuances on the palate. It's graceful yet powerful; lithe like a feline huntress. Finishes long, with hints of mineral and spice. **88** —*J.C. (10/1/2005)*

Selbach-Oster 2001 Zeltinger Sonnenuuhr Spätlese One Star Riesling (Mosel-Saar-Ruwer) $27. This wine is a classic expression of Riesling, boasting green apples and limes on the nose, and peach and dried spices on the palate. The mouthfeel is lively, zesty, and clean; the finish long. It's hard to imagine anyone mistaking this wine's Mosel pedigree, even when tasted blind. **91** —*J.C. (3/1/2003)*

SOMMERAU CASTLE

Sommerau Castle 2004 QbA Riesling (Mosel-Saar-Ruwer) $7. Plump and sweet, this simple summer quaff features ripe pear and pineapple flavors offset by hints of lime. Zesty acids on the finish provide more refreshment value than other wines in this class. **83** —*J.C. (7/1/2006)*

SPREITZER

Spreitzer 2001 Oestricher Lenchen Spätlese Riesling (Rheingau) $27. Limes and green apples cast a decidedly green hue over this wine's aromas and flavors, which also incorporate green plums. It's light and elegant, a focused effort with finely etched flavors. **89** —*J.C. (3/1/2003)*

ST. GABRIEL

St. Gabriel 2002 Auslese Riesling (Mosel-Saar-Ruwer) $9. Light-bodied, with sweet apple, lime, and peach fruit. Hints of kerosene mark the nose, while the finish is sweet but simultaneously crisp and grapefruity. **86 Best Buy** —*J.C. (12/15/2004)*

St. Gabriel 2002 Kabinett Riesling (Mosel-Saar-Ruwer) $7. Matchstick and earth on the nose, along with hints of green apples and limes. Lean and crisp, with earthy flavors that lean toward lemon and Granny Smith apples. **83** —*J.C. (11/1/2004)*

St. Gabriel 2002 Qualitätswein Riesling (Pfalz) $6. Simple lime and apple flavors, lightly sweet and low in acidity, but supple, easy to drink, and generally harmonious. A good by-the-glass choice at your local German restaurant. **84 Best Buy** —*J.C. (11/1/2004)*

St. Gabriel 2002 Spätlese Riesling (Mosel-Saar-Ruwer) $8. The price might indicate a mass-produced wine, but only 4,000 cases of this bargain-priced spätlese were made. After a bit of burnt matchstick on the nose, melon, peach, and chalk flavors give way to pink grapefruit on the finish. **84 Best Buy** —*J.C. (11/1/2004)*

ST. URBANS-HOF

St. Urbans-Hof 2001 Ockfener Bockstein Auslese Riesling (Mosel-Saar-Ruwer) $16. The palate is clean, fresh, softly sweet rather than intense. Flavors of ripe plums and currants give it an attractive directness and simplicity. It could age, but only in the medium-term. **87** —*R.V. (1/1/2004)*

St. Urbans-Hof 2001 Ockfener Bockstein Kabinett Riesling (Mosel-Saar-Ruwer) $14. There is light, easily sweet fruit, but it is spoiled by clumsy flavors and sulphur. **80** —*R.V. (1/1/2004)*

St. Urbans-Hof 2000 Ockfener Bockstein Kabinett Riesling (Mosel-Saar-Ruwer) $14. **86** —*J.C. (5/1/2002)*

St. Urbans-Hof 2004 Ockfener Bockstein Spätlese Riesling (Mosel-Saar-Ruwer) $20. Is this a breakout year for Nik Weis? Never before have I found his range of wines so compelling, and this spätlese is just one example. Yes, it's still marked by heavy leesy notes on the nose, but the fruit is plump and succulent on the palate, mixing melon and apple notes with a heavy dose of spice and mineral. **92 Editors' Choice** —*J.C. (9/1/2006)*

St. Urbans-Hof 2001 Ockfener Bockstein Spätlese Riesling (Mosel-Saar-Ruwer) $16. The palate is dominated by yeast, but there is also some dusty fruit flavors. Meaty flavors spoil the wine. **84** —*R.V. (1/1/2004)*

St. Urbans-Hof 2000 Ockfener Bockstein Spätlese Riesling (Mosel-Saar-Ruwer) $18. **86** —*C.S. (5/1/2002)*

St. Urbans-Hof 2001 Piesporter Goldtropfchen Auslese Riesling (Mosel-Saar-Ruwer) $12. A very young, yeasty, bready wine with rich, fat fruit with only light balancing acidity. It shows youth, but doesn't have great potential for development. **85** —*R.V. (1/1/2004)*

St. Urbans-Hof 2004 Piesporter Goldtröpfchen Auslese Riesling (Mosel-Saar-Ruwer) $45. Like virtually all St. Urbans-Hof wines, this one starts off a bit sulfury, but the quality of the wine underneath is readily apparent, from its scents of slate and apple to flavors of white peach and melon. It's generous in fruit, yet restrained in texture, featuring an almost austere minerality that balances the wine's residual sugar. Cool and stony on the finish, this wine has a long future ahead of it. **91 Cellar Selection** —*J.C. (9/1/2006)*

St. Urbans-Hof 2004 Piesporter Goldtröpfchen Kabinett Riesling (Mosel-Saar-Ruwer) $18. Still in need of cellaring or decanting to rid itself of some sulfury scents, but underneath that are some strident lime and green apple notes struggling to emerge. But have no doubt they will, blossoming into a wine that's crisp and light without lacking in intensity or flavor. Even now, it's long and racy on the finish. **89** —*J.C. (7/1/2006)*

St. Urbans-Hof 2001 Piesporter Goldtröpfchen Kabinett Riesling (Mosel-Saar-Ruwer) $16. The fresh, lively mouthfeel and crisp lemon, grapefruit, and green apple flavors more than make up for an offputting sulfur smell when the bottle is first opened. Airing it before tasting, or aging it another six months or more should be all the help it needs. **88** —*J.C. (3/1/2003)*

St. Urbans-Hof 2001 Piesporter Goldtropfchen Spätlese Riesling (Mosel-Saar-Ruwer) $20. It's hard to get past a lingering burnt matchstick quality on the nose, but once you do, there's a light, well-balanced wine with typical lime and green apple flavors. Picks up some minty overtones and a slight bitterness on the finish. **86** —*J.C. (3/1/2003)*

St. Urbans-Hof 2000 Piesporter Goldtropfchen Spätlese Riesling (Mosel-Saar-Ruwer) $21. **86** —*C.S. (5/1/2002)*

St. Urbans-Hof 2005 QbA Riesling (Mosel-Saar-Ruwer) $12. Given the steep slopes of the region and resulting high production costs, it's a mystery to me how proprietor Nik Weis has managed to keep his wines so affordable. The least expensive of his 2005s is a great introduction to the wines of the Mosel, with surprising minerality and precision for a wine that savvy shoppers can find for as little as $10. It's crisp and clean, lightly sweet, but balanced by fine acidity. It's delicate, yet full of flavor. **89 Best Buy** —*J.C. (11/15/2006)*

STAATSWEINGÜTER KLOSTER EBERBACH

Staatsweingüter Kloster Eberbach 2001 Erbacher Marcobrunn Kabinett Riesling (Rheingau) $19. Another classic from Kloster Eberbach, which seems to be on form after some dull years. There is fresh fruit, with a yeasty touch showing youth. Ripe and full, it is dominated by flavors of green plums and white currants. This is a wine for aging. **91** —*R.V. (3/1/2003)*

Staatsweingüter Kloster Eberbach 1998 Rauenthaler Baiken Brut Riesling (Rheingau) $17. Pale to the point of looking almost watery, this subtle wine smells of rosewater and light peaches. Wan but elegant, balanced and dry, it is refreshing and a bit lower in alcohol (11.5%) than most of the rest. If you want restrained styling, which is fine for sipping, this is a good bet. **86** —*P.G. (12/31/2002)*

Staatsweingüter Kloster Eberbach 2001 Steinberger Kabinett Riesling (Rheingau) $18. Just what a kabinett should be, from the state wine estate based in the monastery of Kloster Eberbach. There are crisp, lightly sweet fruit flavors, delicious acidity, and flavors of ripe plums. This is a finely balanced wine, with acidity supporting the ripe fruit. **92** —*R.V. (3/1/2003)*

Staatsweingüter Kloster Eberbach 2001 Steinberger Spätlese Riesling (Rheingau) $34. **89** —*R.V. (3/1/2003)*

STARLING CASTLE

Starling Castle 2004 QbA Riesling (Mosel-Saar-Ruwer) $11. Garish packaging aside, this is a decent introductory Riesling, with lightly floral and apple aromas and apple, peach, and pear flavors. Off-dry, it finishes with a slightly stony sensation. **84** —*J.C. (2/1/2006)*

STEPHAN EHLEN

Stephan Ehlen 2004 Erdener Treppchen Spätlese Riesling (Mosel-Saar-Ruwer) $20. Ripe apples meet oily terpenes in this medium-bodied spätlese. Baked apple and sweet melon notes pick up hints of spice and

GERMANY

kerosene on the palate, finishing long and clean. **90 Editors' Choice** — *J.C. (5/1/2006)*

Stephan Ehlen 2003 Erdener Treppchen Spätlese Riesling (Mosel-Saar-Ruwer) $20. Starts off with delicate scents of lime, green apple, and talcum powder. Restrained apple flavors make room for minerally notes to shine through in this sweet, but decently balanced, wine. Finishes short. Drink now–2008. **86** —*J.C. (5/1/2005)*

STICH DEN BUBEN

Stich den Buben 1999 Kabinett Riesling (Baden) $13. A nicely complex nose of apple, lemon, and herbs gives way to a dry, smooth mouth full of grape flavor. An even, if slightly thin mouthfeel and smooth finish wrap it up nicely. It strikes one that Riesling is the only variety—certainly the variety that most often—does taste like grapes, as opposed to other fruits. **84** *(8/1/2001)*

Stich den Buben 1999 Qualitätswein Riesling (Baden) $12. This rather rustic wine in a round wide "bock" bottle has a round mouthfeel, simple and earthy aromas and flavors. But a ripe, fermenting-hay note begins on the nose, continues into the mid-palate where it becomes a musty mature element on the straightforward grape flavors. Still, it might work with sausages or other country fare. **82** *(8/1/2001)*

STUDERT-PRÜM

Studert-Prüm 2002 Maximiner Cabinet Trocken Sekt Riesling (Mosel-Saar-Ruwer) $20. Starts off slowly, with sulfurous notes that blow off in under an hour to reveal a soft, gentle sekt with mineral and ripe apple flavors. **84** —*J.C. (6/1/2006)*

SUN GARDEN

Sun Garden 2004 QbA Riesling (Mosel-Saar-Ruwer) $10. Comes out of the chute with hints of smoke and minerals layered over ripe melon and citrus. Round and mouth-filling in its sweetness, yet with enough acidity to give it some length and freshness on the finish. **84** —*J.C. (7/1/2006)*

SYBILLE KUNTZ

Sybille Kuntz 2001 Dreistern Lieser Niederberg-Helden Spätlese Trocken Riesling (Mosel-Saar-Ruwer) $NA. The dry style of this wine emphasizes the flavors of green plums and hedgerow fruits. Crisp, but full-bodied with its almond aromas, it is peppery and spicy and has some weight. **89** —*R.V. (1/1/2004)*

Sybille Kuntz 2001 Wehlen Sonnenuhr Spätlese Trocken Riesling (Mosel-Saar-Ruwer) $NA. A dry style from this winery which specializes in drier wines. Nuts and aromas of fruit pits lead to a rich, concentrated wine with 14% alcohol, with dry, crisp, piercing acidity and flavors apples and sharp pears. **88** —*R.V. (1/1/2004)*

TESCH

Tesch 2001 Langenlonsheimer Lohrer Berg Auslese Riesling (Nahe) $30. Quite sweet, even for an auslese, with ample evidence of botrytis in its dried apricot and orange blossom aromas. Tastes of honey and orange marmalade, with just enough acidity to keep it drinkable. Finishes long and sweet. **90** —*J.C. (3/1/2003)*

Tesch 2001 Langenlonsheimer Lohrer Berg Eiswein Riesling (Nahe) $68. There might be a hint of botrytis, but this is largely clean, delivering sweet pineapple, peach, melon, and citrus flavors. Fat and unctuous for an eiswein, and finishes soft, but is still delicious. **91** —*J.C. (3/1/2003)*

Tesch 2001 Langenlonsheimer Löhrer Berg Kabinett Halbtrocken Riesling (Nahe) $15. In some wines, the juxtaposition of soft, flowery aromas against a backbone of steely acidity might not work. In this case it does, matching lilacs with quince and minerals in a harmonious whole. The result smells like spring, but finishes firm and long. **89** —*J.C. (3/1/2003)*

Tesch 2001 Langenlonsheimer Lohrer Berg Spätlese Riesling (Nahe) $21. Starts off with tart, lemony aromas of quince and unripe apples, but tastes sweeter and riper, with bold apple flavors and considerable sugar kept in check by zippy, grapefruit-like acidity. **89** —*J.C. (3/1/2003)*

Tesch 2001 Laubenheimer St. Remigiusberg Spätlese Trocken Riesling (Nahe) $23. Seems tough and ungenerous at first. Take some time to get to know this wine, and its prickly exterior melts away to yield the crisp,

stony flavors of hard white peaches and a long, mouth-watering finish. **88** —*J.C. (3/1/2003)*

Tesch 2001 QbA Halbtrocken Riesling (Nahe) $10. This halbtrocken tastes drier than some trockens. That's because there's a sharp, sour apple note to the acidity that conceals any residual sugar. The citrus and green apple flavors are light, tart, and dry, finishing crisp and clean. **84** —*J.C. (1/1/2004)*

TWO PRINCES

Two Princes 2004 P2 Qualitatswein Riesling (Nahe) $10. Solid Riesling from the zu Salm family. Pear, pineapple, and melon scents waft from the glass, while the flavors take all of those and add dried spice notes. Not the most intense or longest wine, but an enjoyable quaff. **85 Best Buy** —*J.C. (10/1/2005)*

ULRICH LANGGUTH

Ulrich Langguth 2001 Piesporter Goldtropfchen Auslese Riesling (Mosel-Saar-Ruwer) $28. This is a light, uncomplex wine with some fresh fruit flavors. Touches of honey and white peaches make it pleasant and clean. **84** —*R.V. (1/1/2004)*

Ulrich Langguth 2001 Piesporter Goldtropfchen Spätlese Riesling (Mosel-Saar-Ruwer) $20. Full, and fat, with a layer of meaty flavors on top of light acidity and flavors of ripe green plums. **82** —*R.V. (1/1/2004)*

VAN VOLXEM

Van Volxem 2001 Scharzhofberger Spätlese Riesling (Mosel-Saar-Ruwer) $30. The only "sweet" wine this producer made in 2001, this spätlese is still fairly dry, showing diesel and oil shale aromas. Mineral and lime-citrus flavors provide cut and focus, but this is a wine for lovers of mineral flavors, not for fans of fruit. **86** —*J.C. (3/1/2003)*

VILLA WOLF

Villa Wolf 2003 Kabinett Riesling (Pfalz) $12. This light-bodied wine shows impressive balance, it's just not that expressive at this early stage of its evolution. There's some lime and green apple notes, but also lots of beery, yeasty, leesy notes, with the true flavors still unformed. Try in six months. **87 Best Buy** —*J.C. (5/1/2005)*

Villa Wolf 2004 QbA Riesling (Pfalz) $11. Round and medium-bodied, this relatively low-acid Riesling is soft and easy to drink. Mineral and spice notes accent ripe pear and melon flavors. Drink now. **86 Best Buy** —*J.C. (5/1/2006)*

Villa Wolf 2003 Saint M Riesling (Pfalz) $12. This is a great budget sipper, hitting all the bases you expect from German Riesling: bright fruit flavors of pear and pineapple combined with minerality reminiscent of stone dust. Even finishes with decent length. **87 Best Buy** —*J.C. (11/1/2004)*

VON BEULWITZ

Von Beulwitz 1999 Kaseler Nies'chen Spätlese Riesling (Mosel-Saar-Ruwer) $12. This fruit-forward, honeyed wine is irresistibly drinkable. Has pronounced aromas of baked custard and creme caramel and wildflowers at their scented peak, and drinks vibrantly fruity and rich. Beautiful acidity creates balance. **89** —*S.H. (6/1/2001)*

VON BUHL

Von Buhl 2002 Maria Schneider QbA Medium-Dry Riesling (Pfalz) $14. Muted on the nose, yet the flavors are minerally and appley. A slight prickle keeps the wine from seeming overly weighty on the palate, while the tart finish is a bit austere. **84** —*J.C. (8/1/2004)*

VON OTHEGRAVEN

Von Othegraven 2004 Kanzem Altenberg Auslese Riesling (Mosel-Saar-Ruwer) $55. This is a knockout, from the floral and apricot-laced aromas right through the lingering notes of honey and fruit. It's rich and unctuous on the palate, balancing its considerable residual sugar with only 7% alcohol and crisp, mouth-watering acids. Blends a mélange of fruit—apricots, peaches, pears, and apples—with nuances of spice and mineral that no other country in the wine-producing world has yet matched. Like many top German Rieslings, you can drink this now, or enjoy it 20 years from now, and it should last well beyond that. **94 Cellar Selection** —*J.C. (5/1/2006)*

Von Othegraven 2003 Kanzem Altenberg Auslese Riesling (Mosel-Saar-Ruwer) $50. A soft, mouth-filling wine that boasts impressive ripeness, Von Othegraven's Kanzem Altenberg Auslese oozes with spiced poached pear aromas and flavors that spread out across the palate to encompass cinnamon and vanilla in addition to the sweet fruit. Drink now–2010, but it may surprise you and last even longer. **88** —*J.C. (5/1/2005)*

Von Othegraven 2004 Kanzem Altenberg Eiswein First Growth 375 ml Riesling (Mosel-Saar-Ruwer) $250. Words hardly do this wine justice. It's unctuous almost beyond the point of being wine—offering a mélange of dried fruits and honey that ooze over every taste bud, filling the pores of your mouth and then releasing sugar and flavor for minutes afterward. And the aromas aren't too shabby either, giving up intense scents of dried apricots and orange marmalade, tinged with tea-like notes that add a sense of lightness and complexity. **97 Cellar Selection** —*J.C. (9/1/2006)*

Von Othegraven 2004 Kanzem Altenberg First Growth Riesling Kabinett Riesling (Mosel-Saar-Ruwer) $21. More powerfully built than most Saar wines, with a weighty 10% alcohol providing a solid core. Its dense, slate-driven aromas glide into a richly textured, creamy mouthfeel filled with smoke, petrol, and peach-pear flavors that turn slightly oily on the finish. A bit different, but worth trying. **88** —*J.C. (7/1/2006)*

Von Othegraven 2004 Kanzem Altenberg QbA First Growth Riesling (Mosel-Saar-Ruwer) $35. Starts off a bit sulfury, but it's manageable, lifting in a few minutes to reveal bright citrus and green apple notes. The wine is light and dry, with modest pear and citrus fruit flavors, but its focus is on minerality, which persists through the long finish. **87** —*J.C. (7/1/2006)*

Von Othegraven 1999 Kanzemer Altenberg Riesling (Mosel-Saar-Ruwer) $25. This is a big, slatey, mouth-filling Saar wine, bone dry, with depth and dimension, the kind of wine one can savor with or without food. The forward, effusive nose suggests flowers, fruit, and stone, and the wine has a tight, confident focus in the mid-palate. Still hard and young in the finish; this is a cellar candidate at a good price. **89** —*P.G. (8/1/2001)*

Von Othegraven 2001 Kanzemer Altenberg Auslese Riesling (Mosel-Saar-Ruwer) $32. In 15 years, this will still be an amazing wine. Currently young, meaty, yeasty aromas, mask a rich, full-flavored fruit, with fine, fresh flavors of ripe apples. There is a fine balance between acidity and sweetness. **90** —*R.V. (3/1/2003)*

Von Othegraven 1999 Kanzem Altenberg Auslese Riesling (Mosel-Saar-Ruwer) $50. The juice here comes from old vines from the steepest portion of the Altenberg slope. Still quite young, showing a hint of diesel with some botrytis as well. Clean, slatey, unbelievably intense bouquet with dense floral, citrus rind, and mineral scents. The fruit is ripe, full, perfectly harmonious, and long. It finishes with just a kiss of honey. Delicious right now, but built for the long haul. **94 Cellar Selection** *(8/1/2001)*

Von Othegraven 2001 Kanzemer Altenberg QbA Riesling (Mosel-Saar-Ruwer) $27. Tight at first, the aromas gradually open up to offer delicate floral notes, green apples, and limes. It's light and elegant but intensely flavored at the same time; green flowershop nuances with a firm underpinning of steely green apples and citrus. The explosive finish brings waves of minerals and bracing acidity. **91 Editors' Choice** —*J.C. (3/1/2003)*

Von Othegraven 2001 Kanzemer Altenberg Spätlese Riesling (Mosel-Saar-Ruwer) $27. This is still a very young wine. The fruit is there, with its flavors of cantaloupe and melons, but it is currently dominated by young, yeasty flavors. Rich, full, and intense, the wine lasts forever in the mouth. **88** —*R.V. (3/1/2003)*

Von Othegraven 2001 Maria V. O. Riesling (Mosel-Saar-Ruwer) $15. This must be the best way to experience Saar Riesling on a budget. The high-strung acidity, a sense of nervosité, as the French would say, epitomizes the balancing act performed by estates in this coldest of German growing regions. Apple and pineapple flavors race along the edge of mouthwatering acids. **90 Best Buy** —*J.C. (3/1/2003)*

Von Othegraven 2003 Maria V.O. Riesling (Mosel-Saar-Ruwer) $17. This sturdy, medium-weight wine begins with scents of pears and peaches alongside delicate floral notes; on the palate, the wine takes on more

minerality—like wet river stones warming in the summer sun while still showcasing ripe fruit. Finishes firm, with bright acids. **89** —*J.C. (11/1/2004)*

Von Othegraven 1999 Maximus Riesling (Mosel-Saar-Ruwer) $18. The smooth, citrus-scented nose that opens this wine shows an interesting, faint candlewax-like note. Vivid, focused fruit follows—kiwi and green berries dominate—with bracing acids and a crisp slatey bottom. Fine balance keeps it light and lively despite the ripe fruit, and it extends into a clean finish of medium length. **87** *(8/1/2001)*

Von Othegraven 2003 Ockfen Bockstein Riesling (Mosel-Saar-Ruwer) $33. Disappointing. Has some nice lime and mineral scents and flavors, but finishes very tart and citrusy, without the expected depth. **84** —*J.C. (5/1/2005)*

Von Othegraven 2001 Ockfen Bockstein Riesling (Mosel-Saar-Ruwer) $25. Like slices of fresh-cut Macintosh at first, but then folds in lime and mineral notes. Tart, zesty limes and powdered minerals are packed together in a refreshing wine that tastes almost dry. **90** —*J.C. (3/1/2003)*

Von Othegraven 2004 Ockfen Bockstein QbA Riesling (Mosel-Saar-Ruwer) $30. Slightly spicy and musky on the nose, but there's also plenty of apple and melon to balance out the ledger. Cinnamon and baked apple flavors finish a trifle soft, but there's good persistence and minerality as well. Made in a fuller style, but avoids clumsiness. **88** —*J.C. (7/1/2006)*

Von Othegraven 2003 Ungrafted Vines Kanzemer Altenberg Riesling Spätlese Riesling (Mosel-Saar-Ruwer) $45. Lovely Riesling. Starts gently, with scents of poached pear and floral, spicy hints, then reveals more layers of fruit and spice on the palate. It's plump but balanced, albeit by extract and spice, and not the crisp acids of a more normal harvest. **90** —*J.C. (5/1/2005)*

Von Othegraven 2000 Kanzemer Berg Brut Sekt Sparkling Blend (Mosel-Saar-Ruwer) $35. An interesting sparkler, one that tastes like aged Riesling with a soft, creamy mousse. Sound excellent? It is, but the layers of toast and yeast piled on top don't fully mesh with the rest of the wine, making it merely good. **85** —*J.C. (12/31/2004)*

WILHELMSHOF

Wilhelmshof 1999 Siebeldingen Brut Riesling (Pfalz) $17. Beery Riesling scents send up whiffs of green apples and perhaps a hint of citrus. This has searingly high acid; it's truly like sucking on a lemon. If ever a wine needed an oyster, this is that wine. **83** —*P.G. (12/31/2002)*

WILLI HAAG

Willi Haag 2004 Brauneberger Juffer Kabinett Riesling (Mosel-Saar-Ruwer) $20. Starts off with sulfury notes reminiscent of burnt matchstick; slightly rubbery. But with airing, subtle citrus and floral notes emerge, unfolding into baked apple, pear, and melon flavors on the palate. This shows balance, elegance, and finesse on the crisp, long finish—just give it some time in a decanter if you're going to be drinking it soon. **88** —*J.C. (5/1/2006)*

Willi Haag 2003 Brauneberger Juffer Riesling Kabinett Riesling (Mosel-Saar-Ruwer) $18. Hints of ripe apples and pears are largely submerged under lots of dieselly aromas. On the palate, once past the cloud of terpenes, there is some lively ripe fruit, but it finishes a little soft. Drink now. **87** —*J.C. (12/15/2004)*

Willi Haag 2003 Brauneberger Juffer Riesling Spätlese Riesling (Mosel-Saar-Ruwer) $21. Nicely balanced and light in body yet assertively flavored. Reveals notes of slate and diesel fuel, buffered by ripe apples, pears, and citrus fruits. Finishes long, with ample sucrosity. **91 Editors' Choice** —*J.C. (12/15/2004)*

Willi Haag 2004 QbA Riesling (Mosel-Saar-Ruwer) $15. Despite this wine's lightweight feel, it packs in plenty of authority and flavor, ranging from the suggestion of honeyed apples to hints of petrol and ripe peaches. A firm, minerally edge to the finish provides balance to the sweetness. **87** —*J.C. (7/1/2006)*

WITTMANN

Wittmann 2003 Trocken Riesling (Rheinhessen) $23. A light fresh style of wine, which is fruity, lively, and easy drinking. There is a touch of tannic structure and flavors of green fruits, apples, and gooseberries. This is a good food style of Riesling. **85** —*R.V. (4/1/2005)*

Wittmann 2003 Westhofen Aulerde Trocken Riesling (Rheinhessen) $NA. A single-vineyard wine packed with flavors of sweet currants, apricots and nuts. Offers fresh acidity, minerally accents, and great elegance. It is still so youthful, and with its richness it is likely to age for at least 10 years. **90** —*R.V. (4/1/2005)*

Wittmann 2003 Westhofen Morstein Trocken Riesling (Rheinhessen) $NA. A lively, crisp Riesling with enough rich fruit to give it weight as well as freshness. An intense wine, with floral aromas, and flavors of white currants, pears, and fresh herbs. **88** —*R.V. (4/1/2005)*

Wittmann 2002 Westhofener Kirchspiel Auslese S Riesling (Rheinhessen) $66. A fresh, ripe wine that tastes rich enough to be a beerenauslese. It is packed with honey flavors, baked apples, mulberries, and light acidity. At 7.5% alcohol, you can give into the temptation to drink a second glass. **90** —*R.V. (4/1/2005)*

Wittmann 2003 Westhofener Morstein Auslese S Riesling (Rheinhessen) $NA. Full of sweet fruit and balancing acidity, this is a light, fresh style of Auslese, with lively fruit and flavors of honey and quince jelly. **87** —*R.V. (4/1/2005)*

Wittmann 2001 Westhofener Morstein Spätlese Riesling (Rheinhessen) $31. Starts off by showing a bit of sulfur, but underneath is a plump, juicy wine that tastes of sweetened kumquats, firming up on the finish, where limes and apple skin make appearances. **89** —*J.C. (3/1/2003)*

Wittmann 2003 Westhofener Morstein Trockenbeerenauslese Riesling (Rheinhessen) $NA. Aromas of pure, sweet, dry botrytis follow through to a wine of great richness, sweetness, and acidity on the palate. Offers orange marmalade flavors and concentrated super-ripe fruit; at this stage, it is just beginning to come together—give it 10 years or more. **91** —*R.V. (4/1/2005)*

YBURG

Yburg 1999 Riesling (Baden) $12. This is solid, journeyman Riesling offering a full grapey bouquet with diesel and earth accents. Grape and mild citrus flavors play on the easy mouthfeel and the decently long, slightly mineral finish. **86** *(8/1/2001)*

ZILLIKEN

Zilliken 2004 Butterfly Riesling (Mosel-Saar-Ruwer) $17. As a basic Riesling from the Mosel-Saar-Ruwer, this carries it off better than some, conveying steely, slatey notes suggestive of its origins alongside apple and lime flavors. Off-dry, balanced by mouthwatering acids. **85** —*J.C. (2/1/2006)*

Italy

In ancient times, the Italian peninsula was commonly referred to as enotria, or "land of wine," because of its rich diversity of grape varieties and many acres dedicated to cultivated vines. In more ways than one, Italy became a gigantic nursery and a commercial hub fortuitously positioned at the heart of the Mediterranean for what would become western civilization's first "globally" traded product: wine.

Italy's prominence in the global wine industry has in no way diminished despite millennia of history. The sun-drenched North-South peninsula that extends from the thirty-sixth to the forty-sixth parallel embodies pockets of geographical, geological, and climatic perfection between the Upper Adige and the island of Pantelleria for the production of quality wine. Italian tradition is so closely grafted to the vine that the good cheer and easy attitudes associated with wine culture are mirrored in the nation's temperament.

Tenuta la Volta, near Barolo, Piemonte, Italy.

Despite Italy's long affinity with *Vitis vinifera*, the Italian wine industry has experienced an invigorating rebirth over the past three decades that truly sets it apart from other European wine nations. American baby boomers may still recall watery Valpolicella or Chianti Classico in hay-wrapped flasks at neighborhood New York eateries, or the generic "white" and "red" wines of Sicily's Corvo. Wines like those cemented Italy's reputation as a quantity (as opposed to quality, like in France) producer of wines sold at attractive prices. But as Italy gained confidence during the prosperous post-war years in the areas of design, fashion, and gastronomy, it demonstrated renewed attention to wine. Thanks to a small band of primarily Tuscan vintners, Italy launched itself with aggressive determination onto the world stage as a producer of some of the best wines ever produced anywhere: Amarone, Barolo, Brunello di Montalcino, and Passito di Pantelleria.

Like a happy epidemic, modern viticulture and enological techniques swept across the Italian peninsula throughout the 1980s and 1990s: Vertical shoot positioning and bilateral cordon trellising in vineyards; stainless steel, temperature-controlled fermentation, and barrique wood aging in wineries. As profits soared, producers reinvested in technology, personnel, and high-priced consultants, and a modern Italian wine revolution had suddenly taken place.

As it stands, Italy is the world's second-largest producer of wine after France. Each year, one in fifty Italians is involved with the grape harvest. And like France, Italy has adopted a rigorously controlled appellation system that imposes strict controls, with regulations governing vineyard quality, yields per acre, and aging practices among other things. There are over three hundred DOC (Denominazioni di Origine Controllata) and DOCG (Denominazioni di Origine Controllata e Garantita) wines today, and the classifications increase to over five hundred when IGT (Indicazioni Geografica Tipica) wines are factored in. Thanks to this system, Italy's fifty thousand wineries enjoy a competitive advantage when it comes to the production and sales of quality wines.

Interestingly, there is a second wine revolution underway that promises to unlock potential uniquely associated with Italy. It is the re-evaluation and celebration of Italy's rich patrimony of "indigenous" grapes. (Because some varieties actually originated outside Italy, producers often refer to them as "traditional" varieties instead.) These are grapes—like Nero d'Avola, Fiano, Sagrantino, and Teroldego—that only modern enotria can offer to world consumers. As a result, a rapidly increasing number of vintners from Italy's twenty wine-making regions are banking on "traditional" varieties to distinguish themselves in a market dominated by "international" varieties, such as Merlot, Cabernet Sauvignon, and Chardonnay.

NORTH

The Italian Alps butt against the long expanses of the Po River plains leaving tiny pockets and microclimates along the foot of the mountains that are each linked to their own special wine. Starting in northwestern Piedmont, Nebbiolo grapes form two tall pillars of Italy's wine legacy: Barolo and Barbaresco, named in the French tradition after the hilltop hamlets where the wines were born. Like in Burgundy, the exclusivity of these wines has a lot to do with the winemakers' battle against nature and the wine's extraordinary ability to age. Rare vintages like the stellar 1985 or 1990 Barolos are the darlings of serious wine collectors.

Further east, in the Veneto region, vintners follow an ancient formula in which wine is made from raisins dried on straw mats. With its higher concentration and alcohol, silky Amarone is Italy's most distinctive wine and can command record prices for new releases. The Veneto Trentino, Alto Adige, and Friuli-Venezia Giulia are celebrated for their white wines—such as the phenomenally successful Pinot Grigio. Italy's best sparkling wine is made in Trentino and the Franciacorta area of Lombardy (known as the "Champagne of Italy") under strict regulation with Pinot Noir and Chardonnay grapes.

CENTER

With its cypress-crested hills and beautiful stone farmhouses, Tuscany is the pin-up queen of Italian enology. The region's iconic dreamscape has helped promote the image of Italian wine abroad like no other. Within Tuscany's borders is a treasure-trove of excellent wines:

Chianti Classico, Brunello di Montalcino, Vino Nobile di Montepulciano, San Gimignano whites, Bolgheri and Maremma reds. Italy's wine revolution started here when storied producers like Piero Antinori worked outside appellation regulations to make wines blended with international varieties such as Cabernet Sauvignon. These wines are known as Super Tuscans and are considered on par with the top crus of Bordeaux and California.

Central Italy delivers many more exciting wines, such as Sagrantino from the Umbrian town of Montefalco, dense and dark Montepulciano from Abruzzo, and white Verdicchio from Le Marche.

SOUTH AND ISLANDS

The regions of southern Italy, and the island of Sicily in particular, are regarded as Italy's enological frontier: Relaxed regulation and increased experimentation promise a bright future for vintners and investors alike. In many ways, Italy's south is a "new world" wine region locked within the confines of an "old world" wine reality. This unique duality has many betting on its enological promise.

Campania boasts wonderful whites, such as Fiano and Greco di Tufo that embody crisp, mineral characteristics from volcanic soils. Its red is Taurasi ("the Barolo of the south"), made from Aglianico. That same grape makes Basilicata's much-hyped Aglianico del Vulture. Puglia, the "heel" of the boot of Italy, was mostly a producer of bulk wine, but holds its own today among nascent wine regions with its powerhouse Primitivo and Negroamaro grapes.

Sicily has shown keen marketing savvy in bringing media attention to its native grapes like Nero d'Avola (red) and Grillo (a white once used in the production of fortified wine Marsala) and has done a great job of promoting the south of Italy in general. Some of Europe's most sensuous dessert wines, like the honey-rich Passito di Pantelleria, come from Sicily's satellite islands. The Mediterranean's other big island, Sardinia, is steadily working on its Cannonau and Vermentino grapes to raise the bar on quality there.

ITALY

A-MANO

A-Mano 2003 Primitivo (Puglia) $11. A-Mano's solid, well made Pimitivo has yet again delivered a winning hand despite the hot vintage. Ripe black cherry, cigar box, nutmeg, clove, and fruit roll-ups seem to dance in a circle right under your nose. There is slight jamminess that gets mopped up by the wine's fierce power and structure. **87 Best Buy** —*M.L. (9/1/2005)*

A-Mano 2002 Primitivo (Puglia) $11. A model of consistency is this New World-style wine, which delivers red licorice, fruit pie, raisin and clove on the nose. It's a bit more tart on the palate, with cherry and raspberry taking over. Finishes in the red fruit spectrum, with a gritty, tannic mouthfeel. **87 Best Buy** —*M.S. (2/1/2005)*

A-Mano 2001 Primitivo (Puglia) $10. Mark Shannon of California has made his name on the back of this perennial Southern Italian value, a dead-ringer for friendly Golden State Zinfandel—as it should be, considering that Primitivo and Zin are genetically identical. This vintage is sweet, chewy, and packed with chocolate and cinnamon flavors. You get the essence of natural sugar on the palate, yet ample acids and tannin keep it lively. A perfect wine for the winter. **88** —*M.S. (11/15/2003)*

A-Mano 2000 Primitivo (Puglia) $10. One of the most Zinfandel-like Primitivos we've tried (the grapes are alleged to be identical). Perhaps it's the result of California-trained winemaker Mark Shannon's influence. Bright raspberry fruit is intertwined seamlessly with darker berries and a touch of black tea and herbs. The velvety texture is a special treat. **88 Best Buy** *(5/1/2002)*

A-Mano 2003 Prima Mano Primitivo (Puglia) $28. California's Mark Shannon flexes his winemaking muscles in Puglia with this barrique-aged reserve wine. He pumps out dried rosemary, thyme, and smells that resemble those fish-shaped crackers backed by plenty of rich fruit. Tannins are forceful and the wine's alcohol and thick concentration might make it hard to pair with anything other than a thick slab of red meat. **88** —*M.L. (9/1/2005)*

A-Mano 1999 Prima Mano Primitivo (Puglia) $22. If you enjoy a big Californian Zinfandel you will love this wine. It's got ripe, zesty black fruits with a juicy mouthfeel. It's big but not overblown—the acidity balances well with the fruit and oak to make this another winner from the A-Mano line. **90** —*C.S. (5/1/2002)*

AAA

AAA NV Montenisa Brut Satèn Chardonnay (Franciacorta) $46. The Antinori daughters have teamed up to make wine in Franciacorta, Italy's most exciting sparkling wine zone. This 100% Chardonnay offers aromas of citrus, peaches, some raspberry, and freshly cut grass. In the mouth it follows up with roasted nuts. **88** —*M.L. (12/15/2004)*

AAA NV Montenisa Brut Sparkling Blend (Franciacorta) $30. Here is a wine that knows it shines. The confidence of its creators, Piero Antinori's three daughters, comes through with toasty aromas and touches of creamy apricot and melon on the bouquet. The mouth is treated to a meringue finish and those tenacious little bubbles don't ever give up. Engineered to be easily drinkable. **91** —*M.L. (12/15/2004)*

ABBAZIA DI NOVACELLA

Abbazia di Novacella 2004 Pinot Grigio (Alto Adige) $21. Greets the nose with kiwi, lime, pineapple, and a large dose of candied, sweet aromas. Well-integrated acidity and a medium-weight body round off a very food-friendly wine. **88** —*M.L. (2/1/2006)*

ABBAZIA MONTE OLIVETO

Abbazia Monte Oliveto 2000 Vernaccia (San Gimignano) $10. The slightly nutty nose is touched with melon and pineapple. The flavors are citrus and lemon peel; the mouthfeel is rich and textured. **87 Best Buy** *(12/31/2002)*

ABBAZIA SANTA ANASTASIA

Abbazia Santa Anastasia 2003 Litra Cabernet Sauvignon (Sicilia) $70. A deep, brooding, and penetrating wine with licorice, fruit preserves, red rose, and toasted notes applied in lavish layers. You might want to keep this bottle in the cellar for a few more years to let the tightly-weaved tannins relax. **91** —*M.L. (7/1/2006)*

Abbazia Santa Anastasia 2002 Litra Cabernet Sauvignon (Sicilia) $70. Sandwiched between Cefala's postcard perfect beaches and western Sicily's Madonie Mountains, this estate benefits from cool and hot temperature extremes and frequent winds. Its flagship Cabernet Sauvignon is big and brawny, concentrated and inky with dark berry, charred meat, and notes of deeply shaved cedar. Penetrating tannins add a dusty but firm quality. **91** —*M.L. (7/1/2006)*

Abbazia Santa Anastasia 2000 Litra Cabernet Sauvignon (Sicilia) $40. You'd think the warmth and terroir of Sicily would ensure a ripe, fruity, forward wine, but this 100% Cabernet tastes like a St.-Estephe without sweetness. At first it's all green pepper and green bean. But it builds steam with time, and ultimately fruit emerges. **86** —*M.S. (10/1/2003)*

Abbazia Santa Anastasia 1998 Litra Cabernet Sauvignon (Sicilia) $40. A predominately Cabernet-based wine (90%), this has a likable floral and medicinal nose, accented with char and toast. The tannins are huge and suck the moisture out of your mouth. Premium drinkablity is an additional 2–3 years away. **88** —*C.S. (5/1/2002)*

Abbazia Santa Anastasia 2001 Baccante Chardonnay (Sicilia) $37. A fine blend of tropical fruit flavors and new wood give this wine a real vibrancy and lift. **88** —*R.V. (10/1/2003)*

Abbazia Santa Anastasia 2005 Contempo Grillo (Sicilia) $12. Not as intense as other Sicilian white varieties, this Grillo slowly doses out measured aromas of stone fruit and white stone. In the mouth, it is both fresh and slightly tart. **86** —*M.L. (7/1/2006)*

Abbazia Santa Anastasia 2005 Contempo Inzolia (Sicilia) $12. A neutral white with measured almond, stone fruit, and green, clover-like notes. It's easy to drink and an easy match for finger foods or appetizers. **85** —*M.L. (7/1/2006)*

Abbazia Santa Anastasia 2002 Nero d'Avola (Sicilia) $13. Good raisin and cherry aromas give way to chocolate and earth scents. Fairly snappy and lean in terms of fruit, but incredibly fresh and lively. Some bitter chocolate and coffee on the finish add character. Fine as an everyday offering. **87** —*M.S. (2/1/2005)*

Abbazia Santa Anastasia 2001 Nero d'Avola (Sicilia) $11. Leathery and nice on the nose, with warm earth, light red fruit, and mineral. Flavors of plum and berry jam mix with some graham cracker sweetness and grit, then a finish of strawberry flows forth. **89 Best Buy** —*M.S. (10/1/2003)*

Abbazia Santa Anastasia 2004 Contempo Nero d'Avola (Sicilia) $12. You'll encounter mild rose and floral aromas on the nose of this cheerful Nero d'Avola, with cherry and blackberry notes and plenty of almond. There's some tartness in the mouth but the rest gives way to spice and black peppercorn. **88 Best Buy** —*M.L. (7/1/2006)*

Abbazia Santa Anastasia 1998 Montenero (Sicilia) $34. This New Wave wine from Sicily is a blend of 70% Nero d'Avola, 20% Syrah, and 10% Merlot. Aromas of vanilla buttercream, cedar, cinnamon, and clove make one wonder if the fruit has been oaked into submission, but the bright cherry fruit shines on the palate and lingers through the tart, smooth finish. Soft enough to drink now, but should get better through at least 2005 and drink well until 2010. **90 Cellar Selection** *(5/1/2002)*

Abbazia Santa Anastasia 2002 Montenero Red Blend (Sicilia) $40. Montenero is a Nero d'Avola, Cabernet Sauvignon, and Merlot blend that underlines Sicily's winemaking potential. It is ripe with pungent aromas of plum, cherry, wet earth, cigar box, and slate; it's soft and velvety in the mouth with dusty tannins. Drink now. **90** —*M.L. (7/1/2006)*

Abbazia Santa Anastasia 2002 Passomaggio Red Blend (Sicilia) $19. Always a good red blend; this vintage offers smooth, saucy aromas of soy, tree bark, and berry fruit. Flavors of raspberry and black cherry are straight ahead pure and tasty, while the mouthfeel is bulky yet firm. Affordable and ripe; just what most folks are looking for. **89** —*M.S. (2/1/2005)*

Abbazia Santa Anastasia 2001 Passomaggio Red Blend (Sicilia) $14. Quite the seductive modern-style wine, with deep black cherry aromas. It's all fruit all the time on the palate, as blackberry and cherry vie for the front row. Rich, round, and pretty, with lusty smoke and chocolate nuances toward the back end. It's 80% Nero d'Avola and 20% Merlot. **92 Best Buy** —*M.S. (10/1/2003)*

Abbazia Santa Anastasia 1998 Passomaggio Red Blend (Sicilia) $14. Two of Italy's greatest wine consultants have worked their genius at this property: first Giacomo Tachis and, starting in 2000, Riccardo Cotarella. A blend of 80% Nero d'Avola and 20% Merlot, Passomaggio boasts lush cherry and berry fruit married elegantly to cedar and vanilla accented by mocha and dried spices. **89 Best Buy** *(5/1/2002)*

Abbazia Santa Anastasia 2003 Rosso di Passomaggio Red Blend (Sicilia) $18. An 80-20 Nero d'Avola-Merlot blend from north of Palermo, this is a ruby-colored wine that delivers rich notes of prune, tobacco, leather, and wild sage. The tannins are soft and the wine would pair well with game meats or roast lamb. **89** *—M.L. (7/1/2006)*

Abbazia Santa Anastasia 2004 Baccante White Blend (Sicilia) $39. This is a successful blend of Grillo and Chardonnay that delivers Golden Delicious apple, banana, vanilla, and tomato leaf. It's smooth and creamy in the mouth with notes of cracked white peppercorn on the finish. **88** *—M.L. (7/1/2006)*

Abbazia Santa Anastasia 2005 Bianco di Passomaggio White Blend (Sicilia) $14. Here is a 60-40% Insolia-Chardonnay blend that appears rather neutral on the nose. Distant stone fruit and mineral notes carry forward a lean mouthfeel. **85** *—M.L. (7/1/2006)*

Abbazia Santa Anastasia 2002 Bianco di Passomaggio White Blend (Sicilia) $14. A refreshing yet substantive white from the island of Sicily. The blend is 20% Chardonnay, 20% Sauvignon Blanc, and 60% Inzolia. With dry, focused aromas and ripe citrus flavors, it's the quintessential wine to pair with Mediterranean classics such as olives, salads, and seafood. The estate, which spans nearly 1,000 acres including olive groves, is named after a 12th-century abbey. This wine is a winner. **88** *—M.S. (11/15/2003)*

Abbazia Santa Anastasia 2005 Sinestesìa White Blend (Sicilia) $27. This Sauvignon Blanc-Insolia blend offers a wide range of unique aromas, from chopped herbs to scrambled egg. The nicest thing about this wine is how easily it glides down the palate, leaving a cool trail of freshness behind. **86** *—M.L. (7/1/2006)*

ABBONA

Abbona 1998 Barbera (Barbera d'Alba) $19. The up-and-coming Abbonas of Dogliani have another winner in this dense, deeply extracted wine that flawlessly exhibits the best of the modern Barbera style. The grape's inherent high acidity is controlled. Chocolate, cherries, and spice, plus a leathery touch continue across the palate and through the lingering finish. Enjoy now. **90** *—M.N. (9/1/2001)*

Abbona 1997 Papa Celso Dolcetto (Dolcetto di Dogliani) $16. 89 *(4/1/2000)*

ADAMI

Adami NV Bosco di Gica Prosecco (Prosecco di Valdobbiadene) $15. A thick and frothy bubbly that tickles your nose with its effervescence, lemon-lime acidity, grass, and gravel tones. Stone fruit rides smooth over a bone dry, mouth-cleansing finish. **87** *—M.L. (6/1/2006)*

Adami NV Dei Casel Extra Dry Prosecco (Prosecco di Valdobbiadene) $15. Simple, clean, and linear with lime, stone fruit, green apple, and kiwi flavors. That trademark Prosecco minerality and acidity comes through nicely as well. Drink as an apéritif. **86** *—M.L. (6/1/2006)*

Adami 2005 Vigneto Giardino Dry Prosecco (Prosecco di Valdobbiadene) $18. Simple and straightforward. Has banana, peach, and citrus flavors over a crisp but sweet finish (this has the highest sugar content of the estate's three wines). From a steep-sloped, amphitheater-shaped vineyard that faces south. **86** *—M.L. (6/1/2006)*

ADRIANO MARCO & VITTORIO

Adriano Marco & Vittorio 2000 Nebbiolo (Barbaresco) $35. Dried fruit, subtle spices, and understated chocolate notes provide a lovely bouquet, which eases into a big, fruit-filled presence on the palate. Richly textured with velvety tannins on the finish, this is an excellent value in Barbaresco. **90** *(4/2/2004)*

Adriano Marco & Vittorio 1999 Nebbiolo (Barbaresco) $35. 88 *(4/2/2004)*

Adriano Marco & Vittorio 1999 Nebbiolo (Barbaresco) $40. Mildly floral on the nose, with hints of cherry, leather, and chocolate that roll gently into supple cherry flavors. This wine's on the lighter side, but very pretty, and its modest tannins suggest early drinkability. Try 2005–2015. **88** *(4/2/2004)*

Adriano Marco & Vittorio 2000 Basarin Nebbiolo (Barbaresco) $40. Big, chewy, and expansive, with a blend of dark and milk chocolates, black cherries, and plums. Picks up intriguing hints of anise and leather on the extended, finely textured finish. **92** *(4/2/2004)*

AGOSTINA PIERI

Agostina Pieri 2001 Brunello (Brunello di Montalcino) $50. Our panelists had issues with initial lactic and rhubarb notes but warmed up to the wine as it opened. Violets, blueberry, pencil shavings, spicy wood, tealeaf, and tobacco are carried forth by bright acids and drying tannins. **90** *(4/1/2006)*

AGOSTINO PAVIA & FIGLI

Agostino Pavia & Figli 2000 Bricco Blina Barbera (Barbera d'Asti) $12. Simple and dark, with plum and grape skins carrying the nose. A note of plum skin adds snap to the already snappy cherry fruit that runs through the palate. A hint bitter and lean, but very natural and unadulterated as far as Barbera goes. **85** *—M.S. (12/15/2003)*

Agostino Pavia & Figli 2000 Moliss Barbera (Barbera d'Asti) $14. Fairly spicy and sharp, with aromas of leather, red fruit, and earth. Raspberry and cherry make for a traditional flavor profile, but that fruit fails to sing and dance. Instead, it's rather lean, tight, and short on expression. Good and solid, but borderline boring. **84** *—M.S. (12/15/2003)*

AGRICOLA ARANO

Agricola Arano 1997 Red Blend (Amarone della Valpolicella Classico) $67. Brandied cherry aromas along with leather, cocoa, and raisins make for an attractive nose. The palate is all cherry and leather, with a hint of tobacco and toffee. The finish is powdery smooth and pleasant, with some firm tannins and strong acids. **91** *(5/1/2003)*

AGRICOLA QUERCIABELLA

Agricola Querciabella 2001 Camartina Sangiovese (Toscana) $104. Zesty and woody at first, but later balsamic notes blend with jammier aromas to create a solid but oak-influenced bouquet. The palate features berry and vanilla flavors while the finish is creamy and a touch chewy. Very nice, with no serious faults. But very expensive, or what you get. **88** *—M.S. (9/1/2006)*

Agricola Querciabella 2003 Querciabella Sangiovese (Chianti Classico) $31. Ripe and earthy, with foresty aromas that trigger memories of oregano-based tomato sauce and dried fruits. The palate is round and chewy, with red fruit propelled by forceful tannins and ample acids. Shows vanilla and oak late. Grabby and starchy, but good. **87** *—M.S. (10/1/2006)*

Agricola Querciabella 2003 Batàr White Blend (Toscana) $78. Yellow in color, which announces richness and weight to come. Aromas of lemon curd, orange, and vanilla are nice, while the melon and honey flavors are soft. Interesting and stylish, but low in acid courtesy of a blazing vintage. Drink this Chard-Pinot Bianco blend now. **88** *—M.S. (9/1/2006)*

AGRICOLE VALLONE

Agricole Vallone 1997 Riserva Vigna Flaminio Red Blend (Salice Salentino) $10. This Southern Italian wine fits more into the mold of traditional than modern. By that we mean it's lean, elegant, and not overly extracted. The fruit is earthy and mildly stewed, but good acidity keeps it fresh on the palate. Look for flavors of rhubarb, cranberry, and cherry along with hints of raisin and earth. **88 Best Buy** *—M.S. (11/15/2003)*

AGRICOLTORI DEL CHIANTI GEOGRAFICO

Agricoltori del Chianti Geografico 1998 Riserva Montegiachi Sangiovese (Chianti Classico) $20. 88 *—R.V. (8/1/2002)*

AL BANO CARRISI

Al Bano Carrisi 1997 Negroamaro (Salice Salentino) $9. Dried sage, herbal, and mint aromas give way to oak and dried cherry with a dusty mouthfeel. It'll work fine with a slice of pepperoni pizza. **83** *—C.S. (5/1/2002)*

Al Bano Carrisi 1997 Nostalgìa Negroamaro (Salento) $10. Light and pretty, this Southern Italian shows spicy cola and cherry notes on the nose and palate. It's a bit unfocused as the spicy flavors overtake rather than mesh with the fruity ones, but it has soft tannins and a good overall balance. **85** —*C.S. (5/1/2002)*

AL VERDI

Al Verdi 2004 Pinot Grigio (Terra degli Osci) $7. Fresh and somewhat herbal on the nose, with hints of green papaya and under-ripe melon. Apple, anise, and almond notes work the palate, backed by a clean, citrusy finish. **84 Best Buy** *(2/1/2006)*

ALBERTO LOI

Alberto Loi 1995 Grenache (Sardinia) $15. Somewhat vegetal, featuring sun-dried tomatoes, this wine is definitely more soil- than fruit-driven, reflecting classic Old World style. The finish is light but smooth. **84** —*C.S. (5/1/2002)*

Alberto Loi 1995 Tuvara Red Blend (Sardinia) $35. On the first satisfying whiff, close your eyes and you're in a stable, full of sweaty and leather tack. The impression continues in the mouth, joined by mature flavors of dried fruit. This is a terrific, brawny dinner wine. Pair it with roasted meats. **88** —*C.S. (5/1/2002)*

ALBINO ARMANI

Albino Armani 2001 Pinot Grigio (Veneto) $17. Herbal and citrusy, this is a cleanly made Pinot Grigio that offers a modicum of complexity. Pear and citrus flavors mingle with notes of bitter herbs. Finishes with a hint of bitter grapefruit pith but also lingering apple notes. **86** —*J.C. (7/1/2003)*

Albino Armani 1998 Corvara Red Blend (Veneto) $28. Spearmint and chocolate aromas add character to the raspberry on the nose. Berries, cocoa powder, pepper, and herbs create an exciting palate, one that leads nicely into a smooth, lengthy finish that's graced by mint and solid but forgiving tannins. One reviewer found it dusty and lean while still liking the wine. **88** *(5/1/2003)*

ALBINO ROCCA

Albino Rocca 1999 Vigneto Brich Ronchi Nebbiolo (Barbaresco) $65. Long and firmly tannic, the only question is whether it has enough fruit. Our money says it does—the hints of black cherries, leather, and citrus peel currently walled off by a veil of cedar and tannin should emerge by 2010. **91** *(4/2/2004)*

ALBOLA

Albola 2005 Pinot Grigio (Friuli Aquileia) $12. Round and full aromas with some toasted notes, almonds, grapefruit, and tangerine, but thinner in the mouth, with more flavors and a crisp, short close. **85** —*M.L. (6/1/2006)*

Albola 2004 Pinot Grigio (Friuli Aquileia) $13. A solid Grigio with a flattering bouquet of ripe fruit rounded off by mineral tones. Lean in the mouth with soft acidity and a sour note at the back. **85** —*M.L. (2/1/2006)*

ALDEGHERI

Aldegheri 2004 Pinot Grigio (Veneto) $10. This copper-colored stainless, steel-fermented Pinot Grigio has a unique and interesting nose: yellow roses, vinous notes, and something along the lines of sweet green peapods. It's not hugely structured but has elegance and charm. **85 Best Buy** —*M.L. (2/1/2006)*

ALDO CONTERNO

Aldo Conterno 1999 Barbera (Barbera d'Alba) $40. Leather, earth, and oak scents define the nose. The palate is razor sharp, featuring a blast of pie cherry and bitter chocolate. If red fruit is your bag, then by all means dig in. But the feeling here is that most folks will find this to be overly tart, almost sour. The acidity is piercing and the wine just isn't that friendly. **84** —*M.S. (11/15/2002)*

Aldo Conterno 1996 Conco Tre Pile Barbera (Barbera d'Alba) $37. **91** *(4/1/2000)*

Aldo Conterno 1998 Bussia Soprana Dolcetto (Dolcetto d'Alba) $22. **83** *(4/1/2000)*

Aldo Conterno 1998 Colonello Nebbiolo (Barolo) $116. Decidedly not a powerhouse this vintage, the '98 Colonnello is a pretty, relatively lightweight wine, displaying a range of aromas and flavors from cherries to cigarbox and dried spices. Drink now–2015. **89** *(4/2/2004)*

ALESSANDRO DI CAMPOREALE

Alessandro di Camporeale 2003 Kaid Syrah (Sicilia) $8. The nose is slightly muddled or blurred, but you can get through to exotic spice, coffee, and blackberry. A simple, linear wine that performs well in the mouth thanks to a solid structure; there's a slightly sour note on the close. **86 Best Buy** —*M.L. (7/1/2006)*

ALLEGRINI

Allegrini 1998 La Poja Corvina (Veronese) $85. Never mind the fanciful name: It's basically Corvina from the Verona area made in an ultra-modern, international style. The color is dark, the nose extracted and sweet, and the mouthfeel thick and creamy. There's a pile of black fruit and chocolate on the palate and some cheek-grabbing tannins to the finish. **90** *(5/1/2003)*

Allegrini 2004 Garganega (Soave) $15. This is a pleasantly fresh and fragrant white, seemingly designed with summertime drinking in mind. Pear and peach scents give way to plump, melony fruit in the mouth, with a slightly confected note to the finish. **85** —*J.C. (10/1/2006)*

Allegrini 2001 Red Blend (Valpolicella Classico) $12. A young wine with aromas of blackberry, bitter chocolate, and espresso. The flavors veer toward plum, apple skins, and more chocolate. The finish is full and round, with firm tannins. **87 Best Buy** *(5/1/2003)*

Allegrini 2000 Red Blend (Amarone della Valpolicella Classico) $75. Dark and smoky, with a dab of charcoal along with prune, chocolate, and herbs on the nose. Runs zesty and fast, with lively black cherry flavors and a touch of pepper. Definitely well-made, with chewy richness. **90** *(11/1/2005)*

Allegrini 1998 Red Blend (Amarone della Valpolicella Classico) $65. Black as coal and a true powerhouse. The nose dishes out tons of bacon, chocolate, caramel, and prune-like fruit. Then comes the regal but complex palate that is much like the liquid version of fruitcake: there's liqueur, raisins, and dark chocolate in abundance. A rich, smooth mouthfeel solidifies it as a dynamite wine. **93 Cellar Selection** *(5/1/2003)*

Allegrini 1999 La Grola Red Blend (Veneto) $20. Dark in the glass, with deep, inky aromas that carry hints of toast, wet earth, and smoked meat. The palate bursts with healthy, ripe plum and black cherry, while the easygoing finish is full of coffee and rusticity. Very smooth and solid; a good wine with guaranteed mass appeal. **88** *(5/1/2003)*

Allegrini 1999 Palazzo della Torre Red Blend (Veronese) $19. This blend is grapy and ripe, with aromas of earth and tree bark mixing nicely with the scent of sweet fruit. The mouthfeel and balance are strong points; the wine seems well-structured, with modest tannins and firm acids. Length and drive on the finish confirm its stature and indicate that it will go well with most foods. **88** *(5/1/2003)*

Allegrini 1993 Recioto Superiore Red Blend (Amarone della Valpolicella Classico) $40. **94** *(11/15/1999)*

ALOIS LAGEDER

Alois Lageder 2004 Pinot Grigio (Vigneti delle Dolomiti) $15. Nice and fruity with banana, pear, and Golden Delicious apple aromas and flavors. But there are fresher, green notes buried within as well. Try it with Chinese dumplings. **85** —*M.L. (6/1/2006)*

Alois Lageder 1999 Pinot Grigio (Alto Adige) $15. **90 Best Buy** —*M.N. (12/31/2000)*

Alois Lageder 1998 Pinot Grigio (Alto Adige) $11. **87** —*M.S. (4/1/2000)*

Alois Lageder 2004 Riff Pinot Grigio (Delle Venezie) $10. The wine opens with the fruity intensity typical of Pinot Grigio, but remains one dimensional and stops short of delivering intricate aromas. The same can be said of the wine's impact in the mouth. **84** —*M.L. (6/1/2006)*

ALTEMASI

Altemasi 1995 Graal Riserva Sparkling Blend (Trento) $30. Vanilla and pear aromas are neither exciting nor a turn-off, while the palate is solid, if a bit tangy and weighty. Overall this is a modest wine that's on the downturn. It's not bad but it is flat-edged and bulky. **84** —*M.S.* *(12/15/2005)*

Altemasi 1996 Riserva Graal Sparkling Blend (Trento) $30. Fresh-baked apple pie or peach cobbler notes are intense on the nose. The mouthfeel is creamy, accented by attractive toasted notes followed by a bitter twist at the close. **86** —*M.L. (6/1/2006)*

ALTESINO

Altesino 2001 Brunello (Brunello di Montalcino) $70. Strawberry, cherry, apple cider, almond paste, caramel, hints of mint, and deeper notes of chocolate and espresso make for an engaging and complex nose. Pronounced acidity is backed by firm tannins and a smooth, spicy finish. **91 Cellar Selection** *(4/1/2006)*

Altesino 2000 Brunello (Brunello di Montalcino) $55. Strangely this one has a nose of Italian bitters, anise, and pine. It's not a warm, ripe wine. What it does give is tight, dry cherry and berry flavors with layers of complexity and intrigue. Not very woody or chewy. More old school and an enigma among so many forward, fruity compatriots. **89** —*M.S. (7/1/2005)*

Altesino 1999 Brunello (Brunello di Montalcino) $60. Splendid from the gun, and classy. Early aromas of hard spices, mineral, and matchstick announce some young oak, but that shortly dissipates, revealing a tight cherry and dark chocolate bouquet. This model Brunello is impeccably balanced through the palate and onto the finish, which features a huge mix of pepper, licorice, baked fruit, and vanilla. Hold at least until 2006. **93** —*M.S. (6/1/2004)*

Altesino 2001 Montosoli Brunello (Brunello di Montalcino) $106. This is a wine that never won consensus despite multiple tastings. One panelist noted a strong dislike for a garlicky, skunky aroma that the others did not pick up. They lauded its herbal, wet clay, blueberry, cherry, and violet tones. **89** *(4/1/2006)*

Altesino 1999 Riserva Brunello (Brunello di Montalcino) $90. Begins with a light touch of raisin, while the mouth feels soft, albeit a touch tannic. Further inspection unveils a deeper, meatier side, but also a touch of stewed fruit. Finishes solid, with coffee and chocolate as well as a medicinal hint. **90** —*M.S. (7/1/2005)*

AMBRA DELLE TORRI

Ambra Delle Torri 2002 Vernaccia (Vernaccia di San Gimignano) $10. From Casa Rossa di Alessandro Chiti, this is a citrus-and-chalk Vernaccia. It's tight, lean, and citric, with a narrow flavor profile along with some spice and apple-like fruit. It gets bigger and bigger as you drink it, but it never reaches the highest level. **85** —*M.S. (8/1/2004)*

AMINEA

Aminea 2004 Fiano (Fiano di Avellino) $19. Slightly reductive at the start, this lightly golden Fiano carries through with exotic fruit and dough-like notes. Ripe and viscous in the mouth with medium persistence. **84** — *M.L. (9/1/2005)*

Aminea 2004 Greco (Greco di Tufo) $19. Three young friends joined forces to make wines 1,500 feet above sea level near the hamlet of Montemarano. Thanks to mineral-rich soils, Italians would praise this white wine as sapido, or pleasantly "salty." Marine tones with veiled fruit and flower notes make for an elegant apéritif wine. **87** —*M.L. (9/1/2005)*

ANERI

Aneri NV Brut Prosecco (Prosecco di Valdobbiadene) $20. Fairly plump and wayward on the bouquet, with chalky, tart, green apple flavors. A bit sulfuric and bitter toward the end, with dry lemon notes. Good enough in the mouth, but sort of short on fruit. **84** —*M.S. (12/15/2005)*

ANIME

Anime 1998 Pinot Grigio (Alto Adige) $11. 83 *(8/1/1999)*

ANNA SPINATO

Anna Spinato 2004 i Vini Pinot Grigio (Marca Trevigiana) $8. Floral and understated, with open but light pear, almond and peach aromas. Fresh in the mouth, with simple citrus, melon and pear flavors. Fresh but short, with some cleansing tang. **84** *(2/1/2006)*

ANSELMA

Anselma 1996 Barbera (Barbera d'Alba) $15. 86 *(4/1/2000)*

Anselma 1997 Vigna Rionda Nebbiolo (Barolo) $48. This traditional-style Barolo spends three years in Slavonian oak. This brings aromas of cured meats and ocean breeze. There are flavors of field greens and charred oak, with a rich, ample mouthfeel. Drink 2005–2010. **87** —*C.S. (11/15/2002)*

ANSELMI

Anselmi 2001 Capitel Croce White Blend (Delle Venezie) $18. Roberto Anselmi has quit the Soave DOC, but continues to make some of the best wines in the area. This is full of ripe and light acidity, aromas of spring flowers and fresh garden scents and a finish of aniseed and almonds. **91** —*R.V. (7/1/2003)*

Anselmi 2002 San Vincenzo White Blend (Delle Venezie) $11. This huge, ripe wine is packed with sweet fruit and a sense of structure. It is concentrated and intense and has good aging potential for the next four or five years. **89** —*R.V. (7/1/2003)*

Anselmi 2001 San Vincenzo White Blend (Veneto) $10. Tropically fruity and plump, with some banana and custard aromas and flavors—also some tapioca and vanilla. Finishes with a refreshing citrus edge. **84** —*J.C. (7/1/2003)*

ANTINORI

Antinori 2004 Fattoria Aldobrandesca Aleatico (Toscana) $35. Not many U.S. wine drinkers will be familiar with red dessert wines made from the little-known Aleatico grape. The wines recall the characteristics of Port with rose petal, black cherry, and a robust structure making them a perfect pairing partner to fudge cake or brownies. Very few dessert wines can stand up to chocolate as beautifully as Aleatico. **87 Editors' Choice** — *M.L. (10/1/2006)*

Antinori 2001 Pian delle Vigne Brunello (Brunello di Montalcino) $65. Blockbuster Brunello that is welcoming and inviting no matter how you cut it. The aromatic portfolio is luscious and intense with sweet bread, cinnamon, chewy cherry, raspberry roll-up, dried oregano, cassis, and blueberry. Concentrated and creamy, this brand is easy to find at retail. **94** *(4/1/2006)*

Antinori 2000 Pian delle Vigne Brunello (Brunello di Montalcino) $65. Looks good, smells good, and tastes good, too. Displays a dark ruby luster, while the nose is full of oak, leather, black cherry, marzipan, and citrus peel. And the palate is sweet and rich as it pours on chocolate, liqueur, and ultra-mild tannins. At more than 12,000 cases of production, this Antinori wine should be relatively easy to find. **91** —*M.S. (7/1/2005)*

Antinori 1999 Pian delle Vigne Brunello (Brunello di Montalcino) $80. Lovely, with its own version of perfume exuding from the glass. Additional rose and berry notes lead to a silky palate featuring prune, flourless chocolate torte, and coffee. The back end is tighter and heavier than the front, which bodes well for its future. Made in the modern style. **93** —*M.S. (6/1/2004)*

Antinori 1997 Pian Delle Vigne Brunello (Brunello di Montalcino) $70. The work of award-winning winemaker Renzo Cotarella shows through in this wine's modern, bright purple color, its new wood and ripe fruit aromas and in the juicy blackberry and berry fruit flavors. Yet it is certainly not just modern glitz: Lurking behind is the real heart of a tough, age-worthy, tannic Brunello, which promises a good 10 years at least before being ready to drink. **93** —*M.S. (8/1/2002)*

Antinori 1995 Pian delle Vigne Brunello (Brunello di Montalcino) $60. 89 —*M.S. (9/1/2000)*

Antinori 1998 Castello della Sala Chardonnay (Umbria) $10. 84 —*M.S. (4/1/2000)*

Antinori 1999 Guado Al Tasso Red Blend (Bolgheri) $80. Fast becoming one of the world's top luxury cuvées, this blend of 60% Cabernet Sauvignon, 30% Merlot, and 10% Syrah is a complex amalgam of dry, classy fruit, herbal notes, smoked meat, black pepper, and baking spices. Its calling card is its perfect body weight. It isn't heavy or jammy, but it manages to offer tons of stuffing and a graceful finish loaded with the

ITALY

ITALY

essences of cola, coffee, and chocolate. If possible, it should be cellared for several more years. **95** —*M.S. (8/1/2002)*

Antinori 1997 Guado al Tasso Red Blend (Bolgheri) $80. Antinori turns an impressive hat trick with another winning offering. Full cherry-plum and chocolate flavors display an intriguing olive-herb note. It's plush on the tongue, with round, supple tannins; the black fruit and tobacco flavors flow effortlessly into the long finish with its full, mouth-coating tannins. **91** *(9/1/2001)*

Antinori 2004 Santa Cristina Red Blend (Toscana) $11. Fruity, fun, and fresh, this young 90% Sangiovese and 10% Merlot blend is flexible, accommodating, and easy to drink. Plum, cherry, toast, and menthol notes emerge from the glass, while in the mouth this wine is clean, juicy, and smooth, with a spicy finish. **86 Best Buy** *(9/1/2006)*

Antinori 1997 Solaia Red Blend (Toscana) $115. Top-echelon, with a stunning purity and depth of layered fruit both sensuous and intellectually appealing. The dark cherry and plum core is oak-enveloped with rarely seen seamlessness, while the big but supple mouthfeel belies the wine's profound power and structure. A classic effort marked by perfect fruit-to-acid balance, firm, refined tannins and a seemingly endless finish. **97 Editors' Choice** *(9/1/2001)*

Antinori 1996 Badia A Passignano Riserva Sangiovese (Chianti Classico) $38. Plum, caramel, tobacco, and glove-leather aromas show fine depth. Creamy and elegant, the mouthfeel supports the black plum fruit and toasty, earthy overtones nicely. Finishes with refined tannins and very dark flavors. In its prime now, this is a perfect restaurant wine through 2004. The bank-note label is fun. **90** *(4/1/2001)*

Antinori 2000 Guado al Tasso Sangiovese (Bolgheri) $80. Probably not what you'd expect from this wine. It's a fair amount gamy, with caramel, warm earth, and some bacon on the nose. There's sweet berry fruit and licorice notes, but also a dry, peppery, woody character. Shows a young, willing attitude, but it's not the best "Guado" of the past few vintages. **89** —*M.S. (10/1/2004)*

Antinori 2001 Pèppoli Sangiovese (Chianti Classico) $21. A perfectly solid, well-made Chianti in every sense. The nose is spicy, with hints of wood smoke, barbecue sauce, cedar, and coconut. The palate delivers requisite berry, plum, cherry, and tea in a fine wrapping, while the finish is harmonious, with bits of espresso and chocolate. Not in-your-face, but still fairly forward. **89** *(4/1/2005)*

Antinori 1999 Pèppoli Sangiovese (Chianti Classico) $23. Ripe and juicy, and overall quite tasty. It begins with a lot of red fruit, and in the mouth it's more of the same with no rough edges. It's a seamless Chianti, a sure hit in the trattorias. And there's nothing wrong with the smooth raspberry finish that features some creamy vanilla oak. **87** —*M.S. (8/1/2002)*

Antinori 1998 Pèppoli Sangiovese (Chianti Classico) $22. Opens with rich, dense fruitcake and spice aromas followed by dark plum, chocolate, and licorice flavors. The texture is supple, even, and dry, and the fine powdery tannins on the finish give it great immediate appeal. **89** *(4/1/2001)*

Antinori 1999 Riserva Sangiovese (Chianti Classico) $36. Sweet and meaty, with caramel, cedar, and root beer on the ripe, modern bouquet. Still kicking after several years in bottle, with black plum, cherry, and a shot of lemony oak. Finishes with black coffee and bitter chocolate. Vacillates between traditional and modern. **88** *(4/1/2005)*

Antinori 2001 Santa Cristina Sangiovese (Toscana) $11. This fruity, made-to-quaff Sangiovese has some earthy, mineral notes along with black fruit and full but nonaggressive tannins. Hints of cocoa and licorice add some complexity to what is otherwise a simple, fruity wine. In most ways it's similar to Beaujolais. **86 Best Buy** —*M.S. (12/31/2002)*

Antinori 1999 Santa Cristina Sangiovese (Toscana) $11. This wine boasts aromas of saddle leather and black cherries, with just a hint of medical tape. On the palate, the flavors remain true, with cherries and leather predominating, and a slight creaminess. Finishes tart and a bit one-dimensionally fruity, but this is a nice entry-level Sangiovese with good varietal character. **86** —*J.C. (9/1/2001)*

Antinori 1998 Tenuta Marchese Antinori Riserva Sangiovese (Chianti Classico) $23. A classically powerful Riserva from Antinori, produced from the three family estates at Tignanello, Pèppoli, and Badia a Passignano. Aromas of violets and cherries are followed by tobacco and spice flavors from the wood, as well as concentrated black fruits. Rich and full-bodied, it should age well over the next 10 years. **92** —*R.V. (8/1/2002)*

Antinori 1997 Tenute Marchese Antinori Riserva Sangiovese (Chianti Classico) $38. This medium weight wine shows complex dark plum, toast, tar, and cocoa notes, but there is also a decidedly sauvage element, and this gamy note won't appeal to all tasters. Dense black cherry, plum, and licorice flavors, brisk acidity, and full, ripe tannins round out the package. Has impressive qualities, but also controversial ones. Cellar until 2005. **87** *(4/1/2001)*

Antinori 2000 Tignanello Sangiovese (Toscana) $70. Clearly not the greatest of Tignanellos, but still a fine wine in its own right. One of the founding super Tuscans, this rendition features chunky, grapy, flowery aromas backed by blackberry and black cherry flavors. It's plump, maybe a bit heavy and oaky, but still worthy of its reputation. **90** —*M.S. (10/1/2004)*

Antinori 1997 Tignanello Sangiovese (Toscana) $80. Reticent at first, the elements show their complexity and depth with time. Full and very dark, this offers plenty of black cherry and cedar aromas and flavors offset by impressive licorice and Mouton-like pencil-lead notes. Smooth on the palate, showing great balance and integration, the ripe fruit here sings through the long finish with its soft tannins, good grip, and tobacco-nut-mineral-dust accents. **93 Cellar Selection** *(9/1/2001)*

Antinori 2001 Villa Antinori Sangiovese (Toscana) $23. An excellent blend of Sangiovese, Cabernet Sauvignon, Merlot, and Syrah. The bouquet is loaded with sweet fruit, lushness, and a deft dollop of oak. A masculine yet bright wine, with cassis, cherry, and the works. Finishes fresh, with chocolate notes. A value in its price range. **91 Editors' Choice** —*M.S. (10/1/2004)*

Antinori 1998 Villa Antinori Riserva Sangiovese (Chianti Classico) $65. Minty in the nose, with deep aromatics. As a whole, the bouquet is assuring. Wild blackberry and dark plum fruit create a tasty palate, while the finish is more subtle. It's a bit tannic and starching, and probably too heavy and forceful to drink today. Some time will soften it up. **89** —*M.S. (12/31/2002)*

Antinori 1997 Villa Antinori Riserva Sangiovese (Chianti Classico) $21. A bouquet of saddle leather, cherry, and rhubarb opens to a richly textured palate of sour cherries and dry spice accents. The sprightly, tannic finish offers notes of tart cherry and leather in this solid offering. Drinking well now; can hold through 2005. **87** *(4/1/2001)*

Antinori 2001 Conte delle Vipera Sauvignon (Umbria) $24. Sweet and tropical on the nose, but ultimately not terribly expressive. Simple orange and pineapple flavors amount to a rudimentary palate, while some yellow wax bean works its way into the equation. Good but fails to reach greater heights. **85** *(7/1/2005)*

Antinori 2001 Guado al Tasso Vermentino (Bolgheri) $18. In only its second vintage in the U.S., this nutty, mineral-rich, immensely fruity wine from Antinori's coastal estate is a great example of the heights that Vermentino can achieve. This version is full of lime, stone, citrus, and marzipan, and is focused from beginning to end. **91** —*M.S. (8/1/2002)*

Antinori 2002 Tenuta Guado al Tasso Vermentino (Bolgheri) $18. Talk about a white wine with shine. This aromatic slugger offers a pretty luster, lovely almond, and wildflower aromas and also touches of sea air and honey. Flavors of pineapple, lime, and banana are unadulterated, and the finish is clean. **90** —*M.S. (8/1/2004)*

Antinori 2002 Campogrande White Blend (Orvieto Classico) $11. Like lightning, this wine hits you with a bolt of power. (Except this zap is acid-driven and exhilarating, not fatal.) Orvieto, made in Umbria, is often seen as a pedestrian white wine one step up from water. But not in this case. Made from early ripening grapes such as Trebbiano, Grechetto, and Verdello, the wine has a nice pineapple and green apple character. If you like your whites crisp and clean, this is for you. **86** —*M.S. (11/15/2003)*

Antinori 1999 Villa Antinori White Blend (Toscana) $11. A mix of Trebbiano and Chardonnay, this pale, almost water-clear, wine features nutty aromas that blend seamlessly with those of white stone fruits. The flavors are similar, with blanched almonds and white peaches predominating. Finishes with a lively, zippy finish of lemons and limes. **87 Best Buy** (9/1/2001)

ANTONELLI

Antonelli 1998 Estate Bottled Red Blend (Montefalco) $15. Another solid, rustic red from Umbria, with dark berry, cumin earth aromas. The four grapes in the blend—Sangiovese, Sagrantino, Cannaiolo, and Ciliegiolo—are vinified separately, then blended prior to cask aging. The result is a big, chewy wine with tart black cherry flavors and a long but tannic finish. Best with stews or braises. **86** (4/1/2001)

Antonelli 2000 Rosso Red Blend (Montefalco) $14. Warm and bit stewy, with molasses and blackberry on the nose. Surprisingly, things go tangy on the palate. And that tartness remains throughout the finish. Nevertheless this is a good, solid Umbrian red for casual occasions. Needs food to show its stuff. **86** —M.S. (10/1/2004)

Antonelli 1999 Rosso Red Blend (Montefalco) $14. 88 Best Buy —M.S. (2/1/2003)

Antonelli 2001 Sagrantino (Sagrantino di Montefalco) $40. Filippo Antonelli is one of the forces that helped push Sagrantino into the international spotlight. His wine is ripe with black currant, cherry, cassis, vanilla, and a sweet and sour note that tastes like orange peel. Tannins are hefty. **88** —M.L. (9/1/2005)

Antonelli 1995 Sagrantino (Sagrantino) $16. 86 (9/1/2000)

Antonelli 1999 Estate Bottled Sagrantino (Sagrantino di Montefalco) $34. A heavy wine with youthful tobacco, plum, and berry aromas. The bold plum and blackberry flavors are bruising, but the fruit is a kitten compared to the tannic structure of this wine, which hits like a sledgehammer. A very young and willing red, maybe not perfectly refined but powerful. **89** —M.S. (10/1/2004)

Antonelli 1998 Estate Bottled Sagrantino (Sagrantino di Montefalco) $33. A big, bold red with vanilla cream and game aromas. Blueberry, dark chocolate, and earth flavors carry big tannins. Great with grilled meats. Drink 2004–2010. **90** —C.S. (2/1/2003)

Antonelli 1997 Estate Bottled Sagrantino (Sagrantino di Montefalco) $30. Deep and sweet and aromas of dark cherry, leather, and spice open this big red. Full-flavored and dry, it has good depth of fruit and acidity to balance. Long and powerful, the finish bears full tannins and a blackberry-prune note. This wine is built to last; try it in two or three years—or now with hearty fare. **90 Editors' Choice** (4/1/2001)

ANTONIO CAGGIANO

Antonio Caggiano 1999 Aglianico (Aglianico d'Irpinia) $32. There is a lot going on here, starting with the wonderful floral nose supported by vanilla, toast, and black cherries. The fruit continues on the palate, joined by coffee, tobacco and earth. The wine is big, full, and rich, yet at the same time elegant. **92** —C.S. (5/1/2002)

Antonio Caggiano 1997 Vigna Dei Gotti Aglianico (Taurasi) $42. We loved this wine's complex and distinctive aromas of black olive, mushrooms, smoked meat, and black pepper. We didn't love the ponderous, low-acid mouthfeel and intense tannins. The result? A middle-of-the-road rating for a wine that consumers may either love or hate. **84** (5/1/2002)

APOLLONIO

Apollonio 1997 Red Blend (Copertino) $10. 95 Best Buy (11/15/1999)

ARAGOSTA

Aragosta 2003 Vermentino (Vermentino di Sardegna) $13. Light and flowery, with aromas of gardenia, air freshener, and simple white fruits. Runs sweet and easy on the palate, if a bit watery. Flavors of apple and nectarine aren't dilute but they are thin. With a big lobster on the label, it seems targeted for waterside fish joints. **84** —M.S. (7/1/2005)

ARANO

Arano 2000 Estate Amarone (Amarone della Valpolicella Classico) $50. A touch of early sulfur leaves quickly, and what's left on the bouquet is coffee, cola, smoke, and a bit of apple skin. Black cherry and licorice flavors meet on the palate, which sports a tiny bit of acrid campfire. Finishes rather long and peppery, with a solid, largely supple feel. **90** (11/1/2005)

ARCANO

Arcano 2004 Pinot Grigio (Veneto) $9. Cornflakes, apple, and anise on the nose, followed by a meaty, almost nutty palate that's full but lacks spirit. Peach and heavy apple flavors carry the soft, billowy finish. Sort of bulky; not that precise. **83** (2/1/2006)

ARÈLE

Arèle 1994 Vin Santo Nosiola grape White Blend (Trentino) $42. Made from the native Nosiola grape, which are dried on mats for several months before crushing, this golden wine is nicely balanced and not overly sweet. Apricot, candied oranges, and nuts are honeyed and rich, lightly sugary, yet balanced by crisp acids. Try with cheese or lightly sweetened biscotti. **90** (4/1/2004)

ARGENTIERA

Argentiera 2003 Bordeaux Blend (Bolgheri Superiore) $78. Smoky and dark, with blackberry as the main fruit-based aroma. This is one deep, ripe, plump red wine; it shows plum, berry, and chocolate on the palate, and that's followed by toast, vanilla, and fudge. In the end it's a lot like dessert, albeit a tiny bit medicinal and clumsy. **89** —M.S. (9/1/2006)

Argentiera 2003 Villa Donoratico Bordeaux Blend (Bolgheri) $30. Cherry, citrus rind, and oak make for a short, stout nose. It seems more precise on the palate, with pure cherry and coffee flavors poking through a veil of tight tannins. Gets even firmer on the finish, with a smack of raisin. A wine that requires airing; or more cellar time. **88** —M.S. (9/1/2006)

ARGIANO

Argiano 2001 Brunello (Brunello di Montalcino) $61. A crowd-pleaser that starts in fifth gear with generous smoky, cedar-like notes, vanilla, cherry, dill, and white mushroom. Equally complex and creamy in the mouth with a lush, berry-filled finish. **92** (4/1/2006)

Argiano 2000 Brunello (Brunello di Montalcino) $57. Tobacco, earth, and tree bark make for a bouquet that doesn't hit you over the head. Still, it has red fruit galore. The palate is tight, ripe, and chock-full of proper acidity and tannins. A lively wine with vanilla and oak coming on late. Solid stuff. **90** —M.S. (7/1/2005)

Argiano 1999 Brunello (Brunello di Montalcino) $66. Full and open on the nose, showing fresh herbs, crushed berries, and damp earth. A fruity wine, with plum and cherry carried on a chewy, clean frame. Good and generous, with just enough complexity. **90** —M.S. (6/1/2004)

ARGIOLAS

Argiolas 1997 Turriga Grenache (Sardinia) $50. Caramel, floral, and dried herb on the nose fuses elegantly with what follows in the mouth—juicy raspberry, plum, and spice. Finishes in a crescendo of fruit and tannins that will only get better with time. **94 Cellar Selection** —C.S. (5/1/2002)

Argiolas 1996 Isola dei Nuraghi Red Blend (Sardinia) $9. 90 (11/15/1999)

Argiolas 1999 Korem Red Blend (Sardinia) $34. Red raspberry, spice, and clove on the nose blends well with large amounts of juicy, rich berry and spice on the palate. Finishes long and luscious with soft tannins. **91** —C.S. (5/1/2002)

Argiolas 2001 Perdera Red Blend (Isola dei Nuraghi) $12. This wine is a bit special. It's made mostly of the native Monica grape, which gives off unbridled aromas to go with leathery nuances and wild raspberry flavors. Owner Antonio Argiolas's winemaking team ferments the wine in glass-lined cement tanks for purity, then ages it for 16 months in French oak. Perdera is spicy, precocious, and out of the ordinary; best of all, it improves with each minute it's open. **89** —M.S. (11/15/2003)

Argiolas 2003 Costamolino Vermentino (Vermentino di Sardegna) $14. Round, fruity, and fleshy, like Vermentino from Sardinia should be. It also has that telltale spiced-meat aroma. As a whole this is totally pleasant, a touch hefty but with proper acids and balance. Flavorwise, the mix offers apple, pear, and herbs. Easy to drink and versatile. **87** —M.S. (8/1/2004)

Argiolas 2000 Costamolino Vermentino (Vermentino di Sardegna) $9. Right now, the slight spritz that gives this wine its zip is just a little too prominent. The pear and peach fruit tinged with bitter almond is fresh enough to stand on its own; this wine should taste broader and smoother

ITALY

in another six months. Drink now with raw shellfish or as a patio wine; pair it with delicate chicken and fish dishes down the road. **86** —*J.C. (9/1/2001)*

ARMILLA

Armilla 2001 Brunello (Brunello di Montalcino) $65. A medium-bodied wine with finesse and elegance that delivers cedar, Graham cracker, floral notes, stone fruit, and fresh herbs. Velvety smooth with mixed berries and vanilla in the mouth, a lush finish and overall drinkability. **91** *(4/1/2006)*

ARNALDO CAPRAI

Arnaldo Caprai 2000 Red Blend (Montefalco) $22. The color is dark and youthful, while the nose is at first earthy and dusty before opening to reveal a deep plum core. Dark cherry and plum fruit mixes with coffee on the palate, while the finish is perfectly broad and smooth, an appropriate epilogue to a fine, extracted, modern Sangiovese-based wine. **91 Editors' Choice** —*M.S. (2/1/2003)*

Arnaldo Caprai 2000 Poggio Belvedere Red Blend (Umbria) $14. Floral and barnyard aromas start showing fruit on the palate with juicy blackberries and cedar. The tannins are soft and well-integrated for a wine that is meant to be drunk soon. **88 Best Buy** —*C.S. (2/1/2003)*

Arnaldo Caprai 2003 Rosso Red Blend (Montefalco) $22. Ruby-red with fresh forest berries and distant floral aromas. Medium structure and finish for a solid, easy-to-drink Sangiovese-Sagrantino blend that sees 12 month in Slovenian casks. **85** —*M.L. (9/1/2005)*

Arnaldo Caprai 2001 25 Anni Sagrantino (Sagrantino di Montefalco) $110. Not a wine you will easily forget. Marketing-savvy Marco Caprai has taken a difficult, little-known variety and turned it into an international superstar. A made-to-please wine—meaning all nuts and bolts are screwed tight in terms of color, aromatics, and structure—it has tar, coffee, leather, and velvety fullness in the mouth. **93 Cellar Selection** —*M.L. (9/1/2005)*

Arnaldo Caprai 1999 25 Anni Sagrantino (Sagrantino di Montefalco) $100. This might be the quintessential Sagrantino. It's jammed full of tobacco, cola, plum, and blackberry aromas. Nothing disappoints after that; the palate is a blast of black fruit and cherry, while the finish hits squarely with rock-hard tannins as well as a delicious buttery oak note. Hold for more than five years for best results. **92 Cellar Selection** —*M.S. (10/1/2004)*

Arnaldo Caprai 2001 Collepiano Sagrantino (Sagrantino di Montefalco) $55. There's no mistaking that Caprai touch. Resin, dark chocolate, coffee bean, and new oak in layer after layer from the man who put Montefalco on the enological map. Big on tannins but carefully structured, balanced, and lacking the alcoholic burn of some of its contemporaries. **90** —*M.L. (9/1/2005)*

Arnaldo Caprai 1999 Collepiano Sagrantino (Sagrantino di Montefalco) $50. Sweet and spicy on the nose, with floral notes, perfume and then a blast of buttery oak. This wine pours on the black cherry and plum. On the finish a current of wood rips on through without so much as an "excuse me." Oaky at first, but improves as it absorbs some air. Hold until 2005. **90** —*M.S. (10/1/2004)*

Arnaldo Caprai 1998 Collepiano Sagrantino (Sagrantino di Montefalco) $48. This Sagrantino is made in a New World style with fresh cedar, ripe blackberry, and blueberry fruit. A rich, intense mouthfeel touched off with dark chocolate makes for a truly delicious wine. **92** —*C.S. (2/1/2003)*

Arnaldo Caprai 1998 Venticinque Anni 25 Sagrantino (Sagrantino di Montefalco) $88. Wonderful aromas are of cedar, earth, and leather. The flavors are intense black plums and dark chocolate. The tannins are huge but the fruit and complexity will still be there when they soften. This wine needs some time: drink 2005-2015. **93 Cellar Selection** —*C.S. (2/1/2003)*

ARUNDA

Arunda 1995 Riserva Brut Sparkling Blend (Alto Adige) $27. Lean and dominated by tart apple aromas and flavors. Lemon and acid on the palate ensures a fresh, snappy feel, but with so much tang it's on the sour side. **82** —*M.S. (12/31/2004)*

ASTORIA

Astoria 2004 Cabernet Sauvignon (Piave) $14. Astoria's wines are typically fairly priced for the quality, and this pleasant Cabernet is no exception. It's plump and well-rounded for an Italian Cab, with ripe cassis flavors that finish a bit tart but juicy and fresh. Drink now. **86** *(11/15/2006)*

Astoria 2003 Il Puro Merlot (Piave) $11. An ambitious effort, featuring a lush, supple mouthfeel and chocolate, vanilla and cream flavors layered over fruit that seems just a little overdone. Black cherries veer toward the raisiny side of ripe, picking up hints of black tea on the finish. **84** —*J.C. (12/31/2004)*

Astoria 2004 Pinot Grigio (Delle Venezie) $12. Textbook Grigio with pretty, clean aromas of pear, yellow rose, and vanilla bean. But it is the intensity and clarity of each smell that makes this wine stand apart. **87 Best Buy** —*M.L. (2/1/2006)*

Astoria 2001 Pinot Grigio (Delle Venezie) $11. An interesting Grigio that blends nutty, herbal aromas with fleshier flavors of honey and tangerines. The weight in the mouth is reminiscent of some Alsatian Pinot Gris, while the tangy citrus on the finish is strong enough to cut through fatty appetizers. **85** —*J.C. (1/1/2004)*

Astoria NV Prosecco (Prosecco del Veneto) $9. Fresh and uncomplicated, which is the true DNA of basic Prosecco. It's a cocktail-apéritif wine par supreme, a bit sweet but not overwhelmingly so. The flavors of apple and pear are pure and likable. And the wine shows a touch of creaminess as it sits on your tongue. **86 Best Buy** —*M.S. (12/15/2006)*

Astoria 2001 Prosecco (Prosecco di Conegliano e Valdobbiadene) $13. Talk about fresh and flowery. This lightweight sprinter is the epitome of style and zest. It's sweet yet statuesque, with pungent gardenia aromas and pure tangerine, lime, and tarragon flavors. It's racy and graceful, a tasty surprise awaiting anyone uninitiated in good Prosecco. **89** —*M.S. (12/31/2002)*

Astoria 2004 18 Dry Prosecco (Prosecco di Conegliano) $15. Lightly mineral, with lime on the nose along with sugared pastry. Mostly it's about ripe apple flavors along with lemon-lime, but along the way there's some wayward bitterness that wrestles with overt sweetness. Still, it's good overall. **86** —*M.S. (12/15/2005)*

Astoria NV Casa Vittorino Diciasette Anniversario Dry Prosecco (Prosecco di Conegliano) $15. A dry bubbly with soft applesauce aromas preceding sweet peach and melon flavors. The finish is long and citrusy; and the acidity creates a juicy mouthfeel. Very nice and easy to quaff. **87** —*M.S. (12/15/2004)*

Astoria NV Cuvée Lounge Prosecco (Prosecco) $10. Smooth and chummy, with a light but fragrant nose featuring the slightest hint of yeast. Tasty in the mouth, with clean flavors of apple and mineral. A secure, long-on-the-finish bubbly with a good mouthfeel and more than adequate density. **87 Best Buy** —*M.S. (12/15/2006)*

Astoria 2004 Cuvée Tenuta Val de Brun Prosecco (Prosecco di Valdobbiadene) $13. No surprises here; just good, clean fun. The nose is fresh as a spring garden and the palate delivers nothing but pure lemon-lime. The feel and bubble bead are lively and friendly, while the finish is crisp, smooth, and somewhat long. Mildly sweet but not at all cloying. **88 Best Buy** —*M.S. (12/15/2005)*

Astoria 2002 Cuvée Tenuta Val de Brun Prosecco (Prosecco di Valdobbiadene) $15. Fresh greens give this light and elegant sparkler a touch of grassiness that highlights its lime and green apple flavors. Finishes with soft, melon-pear-citrus flavors. **86** —*J.C. (12/31/2003)*

Astoria 2005 Cuvée Tenuta Val de Brun Extra Dry Prosecco (Prosecco di Valdobbiadene) $18. Made in a fuller style than is customary with Prosecco, with granular aromas of baked apple and peaches. The palate sports white peach and apple flavors, and the feel is one of roundness. Some may find this wine too amped up or thick, but we like its power, especially on the finish, where scallion and pepper enter the mix. **88** —*M.S. (12/15/2006)*

Astoria 2003 Cuvée Tenuta Val de Brun Extra Dry Prosecco (Prosecco di Valdobbiadene) $15. This extra dry offering is very nice. The bouquet is warm and full of apple, cinnamon, and a distant whiff of anise/black

ITALY

licorice. The palate offers sweet stone fruits and some zest. A bit of lemony citrus on the finish is rock solid. **88** —*M.S. (12/15/2004)*

Astoria NV Extra Dry Prosecco (Prosecco di Valdobbiadene) $16. A moderately intense Prosecco that wins points for its elegance and refined floral tones. Flavors are of lemon-lime crispness with dried sage and pink grapefruit. On the sweet side, but refreshing nonetheless. **86** —*M.L. (6/1/2006)*

Astoria 2001 Extra Dry Prosecco (Prosecco di Valdobbiadene) $9. Smartly packaged and well-executed, this is Prosecco on the sweet edge, but with the balance to pull it off. Its orange and green herb aromas are attractive. So are the bright tangerine and lime flavors. The finish is slick at first, then mildly tart. Yes, it's sweet, but it's also very, very tasty. **90 Best Buy** —*M.S. (12/31/2002)*

Astoria 2005 Millesimato Prosecco (Prosecco di Valdobbiadene) $19. Sharp citrus tones are embellished by floral intensity, stone fruit, and lemonade. Snappy and lip-smackingly fresh on the palate, with acidity that comes to the fore over a long finish. **87** —*M.L. (6/1/2006)*

Astoria 2002 Sedici Anni Dry Prosecco (Prosecco di Conegliano) $15. This soft, creamy Prosecco boasts plump, easy-to-understand flavors of tangerines and melons. Finishes just slightly sweet, balanced by modest orange-citrus notes. **87** —*J.C. (12/31/2003)*

Astoria NV Superiore di Cartizze Prosecco (Prosecco Superiore di Cartizze) $20. A well-executed Prosecco from the first-rate Cartizze cru, with refined floral and mineral notes. Banana fruit, apricot, and tart apple brushstrokes are lightly applied over a deliciously tart finish. **88** —*M.L. (6/1/2006)*

Astoria NV Val de Brun Extra Dry Prosecco (Prosecco del Veneto) $9. This sweet Prosecco almost reaches the land of "exotic," but not quite. Yet along the way you'll find ripe apricot and peach flavors, a grabby, medium-weight body, and a sizable, zesty finish. Shows orange and tangerine notes between the stone fruits. **87 Best Buy** —*M.S. (12/15/2004)*

Astoria 1998 Rosso Croder Red Blend (Colli di Conegliano) $18. Deep and dark, with rubber, toast, and smoke aromas on the complex, layered nose. Defined dried red fruit flavors along with hints of chocolate and tobacco make for a pleasurable palate. It finishes subtle and warm. Drink now or hold through 2010. **89** *(5/1/2003)*

Astoria 2004 Sauvignon Blanc (Delle Venezie) $20. Blends aromas of blanched nuts, field greens, and snappy fruit into a very nice whole. The palate is sharp and clean, with grassy notes along with apple and lime. Sort of New Zealand-like in its approach, with a finish that is precise and crisp. And there's just enough texture to the wine so that it isn't lean. **90** *(7/1/2005)*

Astoria 2005 Suade Sauvignon Blanc (Delle Venezie) $14. Made entirely in stainless steel to preserve its freshness and fruit, this isn't lean or sharp at all, rather, it's bursting with bold passion fruit and grapefruit flavors. Lacks subtlety, but satisfies the Sauvignon craving. **86** *(11/15/2006)*

Astoria 2000 White Blend (Colli di Conegliano) $17. Buttery and richly oaked, with some apple and pear flavors underneath, this wine is okay—if you're okay with oaky wines. Finishes with a torrent of vanilla flavors. **85** —*J.C. (7/1/2003)*

ATTEMS

Attems 2003 Pinot Grigio (Collio) $20. There's a hint of copper to the color of this wine, but its flavors are white all the way, from melon and pear, to apple and hints of spice. Slightly viscous in the mouth, it finishes on a tangy note of anise. **84** —*J.C. (12/31/2004)*

Attems 2001 Pinot Grigio (Collio) $20. **81** —*J.C. (7/1/2003)*

Attems 2001 Sauvignon Blanc (Collio) $20. Grassy and grapefruity, with sour, close to vegetal, flavors and a touch of sweetness on the finish. **84** —*J.C. (7/1/2003)*

Attems 2003 Sauvignon Sauvignon Blanc (Collio) $20. Very ripe Sauvignon for Collio, with only a hint of grassiness gracing a full-bodied, well-fruited wine. Bold notes of pink grapefruit and fig wrap around a sturdy melon core, and is that a hint of warmth on the finish? **88** —*J.C. (12/31/2004)*

ATTILIO GHISOLFI

Attilio Ghisolfi 1998 Barbera (Barbera d'Alba) $20. The nose is toasty and smooth, with lots of spiced fruit showing. In the mouth, things turn a touch heavy; the fruit is mature and full, but it's heavier than ideal. A finish of black pepper, exotic nuances, and ripe flavors keep it firmly positive; some mushiness is the lone drawback. **87** —*M.S. (12/15/2003)*

Attilio Ghisolfi 1997 Barbera (Barbera d'Alba) $14. **91 Best Buy** *(4/1/2000)*

Attilio Ghisolfi 1996 Vigna Lisi Barbera (Barbera d'Alba) $17. **88** *(4/1/2000)*

Attilio Ghisolfi 1997 Dolcetto (Dolcetto d'Alba) $13. **86 Best Buy** *(4/1/2000)*

Attilio Ghisolfi 1998 Bricco Visette Nebbiolo (Barolo) $37. This large-scaled wine shows plenty of tannins to match its concentrated black cherry fruit. Complexity comes in the form of tobacco, earth, and understated cedar and vanilla notes. Try after 2010. **89** *(4/2/2004)*

Attilio Ghisolfi 1995 Bricco Visette Nebbiolo (Barolo) $42. **89** *(9/1/2000)*

AURELIO SETTIMO

Aurelio Settimo 1999 Nebbiolo (Barolo) $38. A fine example of old-school Barolo, with Nebbiolo character in spades. Dried cherries, leather, and spice combine in this meaty, chewy, tannic mouthful. Thankfully, the tannins are ripe and forgiving, not hard and astringent. Finishes long, with lovely hints of roasted meat. **91 Editors' Choice** —*J.C. (11/15/2004)*

Aurelio Settimo 1999 Rocche Nebbiolo (Barolo) $45. Artfully combines enormous power, complexity, and finesse. Aromas and flavors include tar, roses, orange peel, cherries, anise, dried spices, and earth, all in a rich, chewy wine that reveals the beginnings of elegance. Finishes long, with ripe tannins that need time to resolve. Try in 2015. **93 Cellar Selection** —*J.C. (11/15/2004)*

AVANTI

Avanti 2004 Pinot Grigio (Delle Venezie) $8. A wine that delivers everything expected from good Grigio: fresh fruit aromas such as peach with crisper mineral notes. This wine has a delicate nose with loads of white field flowers and a light touch in the mouth. **87 Best Buy** —*M.L. (2/1/2006)*

AVIDE

Avide 2000 Cerasuolo di Vittoria Red Blend (Sicilia) $14. Heavily roasted, pruny notes combine with unmistakable sulfuric aromas to create a funky nose that takes too long to come around. In the mouth, stewed black fruit and licorice flavors come in front of a rich, thick finish that's dark and long. With time, this wine improves, but it never really rolls out the red carpet. **83** —*M.S. (12/15/2003)*

AVIGNONESI

Avignonesi 2002 Sangiovese (Vino Nobile di Montepulciano) $25. New-oak and raw fruit aromas create a sharp, somewhat angular bouquet holding the slightest hint of vinegar. Airing reveals smoky notes and more richness. Plenty of cherry and berry on the palate mixed with cedar and vanilla. The mouthfeel, meanwhile, seems a little heavy. **86** —*M.S. (7/1/2005)*

AVIGNONESI-CAPANNELLE

Avignonesi-Capannelle 1998 50 & 50 Sangiovese (Toscana) $112. First things first, the wine is from Avignonesi, and it's a 50-50 blend of Sangiovese and Merlot. In terms of power, the Sangiovese drives the boat, while the Merlot navigates. Aromas of tar, bacon, plum, and oak are strong. In the mouth, zingy cherry and plum flavors are supported by gritty tannins. Lots of fruit and power; firm as a rock. **89** —*M.S. (12/15/2003)*

AZELIA

Azelia 1998 Bricco dell'Oriolo Dolcetto (Dolcetto d'Alba) $15. **90** *(4/1/2000)*

Azelia 1999 San Rocco Nebbiolo (Barolo) $71. Modern, but it still tastes like Barolo underneath its veneer of toast, coffee, and coconut. Under the wood beats a heart of tar, molasses, and dates nestled in soft, supple tannins and finishing with juicy acidity. **91** *(4/2/2004)*

ITALY

AZIENDA AGRARIA SCACCIADIAVOLI

Azienda Agraria Scacciadiavoli 2000 Red Blend (Montefalco) $12. 88 Best Buy —*M.S. (2/1/2003)*

Azienda Agraria Scacciadiavoli 1998 Red Blend (Sagrantino di Montefalco) $34. Earth driven aromas of leather and wet hay touched with berries.The flavors are a little more fruit driven showing juicy blackberries with anise and spice.There is rich acidity to clean up the tannins for a lingering finish. **88** —*C.S. (2/1/2002)*

Azienda Agraria Scacciadiavoli 2001 Sagrantino (Sagrantino di Montefalco) $29. Local legend says a young damsel was possessed by a demon and cured by an exorcist who forced her to drink red wine. Scacciadiavoli, or "chase away devils," is owned by the Pambuffetti family and is one of the area's most established wineries. The nose is less intense and the structure is not as large, but you can't go wrong with a story like that on a first date. **86** —*M.L. (9/1/2005)*

AZIENDA AGRICOLA ADANTI

Azienda Agricola Adanti 2000 Arquata Sagrantino (Sagrantino di Montefalco) $40. This beautiful, 30-hectare vineyard surrounding a convent near Bevagna produces seven wines. This Sagrantino delivers whiffs of beef jerky, leather, and barnyard and is aged for three years. Sagrantino is not for everyone, although it works wonders with barbecued meats and cold weather. **87** —*M.L. (9/1/2005)*

AZIENDA AGRICOLA BORGNOT/VIRNA

Azienda Agricola Borgnot/Virna 1998 Nebbiolo (Barolo) $NA. Sumptuous aromas of fine leather—or is it suede, burst from the glass, accompanied by cherries, underbrush, and dusty earth. Thick and tarry on the finish, with chewy tannins and hints of anise. Drink 2008–2020. **90** *(4/2/2004)*

Azienda Agricola Borgnot/Virna 1998 Cannubi Boschis Nebbiolo (Barolo) $35. This is a great value in Barolo. It's a big, somewhat rustic wine, with scents of horse sweat and leather inter-mingling with black cherries. anise and intense, meaty flavors chime in on the long, firm finish. Try in 2008 or beyond. **92 Editors' Choice** *(4/2/2004)*

AZIENDA AGRICOLA COGNO

Azienda Agricola Cogno 1998 Ravera Nebbiolo (Barolo) $58. Everything about this Barolo is sensational, from the aromatic notes of eucalyptus and wintergreen to the bright cherries on the palate to the smooth, spicy finish. There's nothing tired or off about this approachable middle-weight. The spicy, drying tannins seem right, as do the rooty undernotes and overall balance. It's not overwhelming or too demanding, so it can be drunk in the near future. But holding it for 10 years is also an option. **93 Editors' Choice** —*M.S. (11/15/2002)*

Azienda Agricola Cogno 1997 Vigna Elena Nebbiolo (Barolo) $75. This wine already seems mature. The color is fading and the aromas are dusty and raisiny. All in all it seems a bit ungenerous for a '97. The tannins are kind of starching and it lacks lushness. With all that said, if offers ample cherry, spice, and plenty of tannic fodder for rich foods like osso buco or lamb shanks. **86** —*M.S. (11/15/2002)*

AZIENDA AGRICOLA LUISA

Azienda Agricola Luisa 2004 Tenuta Luisa Pinot Grigio (Isonzo del Friuli) $23. Toasted nut, sage, exotic fruit, and earthy-musty aromas preface what later reveals itself as a wine of unexpected width and character. **88** —*M.L. (2/1/2006)*

AZIENDA AGRICOLA PALOMBO

Azienda Agricola Palombo 1999 Cabernet Atina Red Blend (Lazio) $21. Cranberry aromas lack some depth, while in the mouth, tart cherry notes turn a touch sour upon inspection. A decent mouthfeel, but lean in terms of fruit and density. **84** —*M.S. (11/15/2003)*

Azienda Agricola Palombo 1998 Cabernet Duca Cantelmi Red Blend (Lazio) $34. Aromas of burnt wood, tobacco, and dense fruit, but not exactly opulent. Raspberry and currant control the palate of this blend of Cabernet Sauvignon, Cab Franc, and Syrah. The finish is earthy, with notes of cocoa. Big enough but not overdone; toasty, with adequate fruit. **85** —*M.S. (11/15/2003)*

AZIENDA AGRICOLA PIRA LUIGI

Azienda Agricola Pira Luigi 1999 Vigneto Margheria Nebbiolo (Barolo) $60. It's oaky, marked by aromas of buttercream and coffee, but it's oh so sexy too, possessed of a lush, captivating mouthfeel. Hints of anise accent the black cherry fruit that forms a solid base for the wood-imparted flavors above. Drink now–2010. **91** *(4/2/2004)*

AZIENDA AGRICOLA PUGNANE

Azienda Agricola Pugnane 1996 Vigna Villero Barolo Nebbiolo (Barolo) $39. Boasts a plethora of great aromas, including cabbage, beet, caramel, and cola. A whiff of sawdust and creosote lead into similar flavors on the palate, combining with tea, earth, hard salami, and raspberry. Smooth, firm tannins point to good aging potential, which may give the sharp acidity time to integrate. **89** *(11/15/2002)*

AZIENDA AGRICOLA RESSIA

Azienda Agricola Ressia 2000 Canova Nebbiolo (Barbaresco) $50. Boasts intricately complex aromatics, combining leather, balsamic notes, mushrooms, citrus peel, and dried cherries. Plump in the mouth, but loses a bit of steam, finishing shorter than expected and lacking acidic verve. **89** *(4/2/2004)*

AZIENDA AGRICOLA ROBERTO CERAUDO STRONGOLI

Azienda Agricola Roberto Ceraudo Strongoli 2003 Imyr Chardonnay (Val di Neto) $36. Off the charts in almost every way. First, it's a Calabrian Chardonnay with tons of hangtime and oak. Second, it hardly resembles Chardonnay as we know it. The nose is oily, with lemon, baked corn, and quince. The palate is custardy, ultra-ripe and borderline over the top. Finishes in complex ways, with peach, apricot, and nutmeg along with white pepper. More of a sommelier/explorer's wine. **89** —*M.S. (7/1/2005)*

Azienda Agricola Roberto Ceraudo Strongoli 2001 Petraro Red Blend (Val di Neto) $39. Rusty in color and stripped of fruit; what this wine does offer in abundance is leathery aromas and flavors, piercing tannins, and lots of tobacco-tinged citrusy flavors. But the wine is ultimately just too much of a stretch American palate. **84** —*M.S. (7/1/2005)*

Azienda Agricola Roberto Ceraudo Strongoli 2000 Petraro Red Blend (Val di Neto) $37. Rusty, with aromas of tar, sweet rubber, petrol, and dark chocolate. Call it funky, call it cooked, call it classic, call it Calabrian. Flavors of dried cherry, raisin, and toffee are sly; so is the spicy, sweet finish. There's a bit of Barbaresco spirit in this wine, but the real fuel is Gaglioppo and Cabernet. **91** —*M.S. (10/1/2004)*

AZIENDA AGRICOLA SUAVIA

Azienda Agricola Suavia 2002 White Blend (Soave Classico) $15. Pretty peach, melon, almond, and mineral notes lead off. The palate is fresh, with an open and pleasant mix of orange, tangerine, and cantaloupe. The wine transitions nicely from palate to long finish. **88** —*M.S. (10/1/2004)*

Azienda Agricola Suavia 2001 Le Rive White Blend (Soave Classico) $37. Dark and gold, so you just know something's up. And that's the fact that this is over-the-top Soave, a heavyweight tipping the scale at 14%. Thus, there's butterscotch, honey, baked fruit, and a whole lot of extract and sweetness. Not for everyone, but maybe worth trying. **87** —*M.S. (10/1/2004)*

AZIENDA AGRICOLA TABARRINI

Azienda Agricola Tabarrini 2001 Colle Grimaldesco Sagrantino (Montefalco) $NA. A surprise hit from newcomer Giampaolo Tabarrini. This Sagrantino offers fresh red fruit and earthy, mushroom flavors in the mouth. The tannins are colossal, so pair it with succulent red meat. **90** —*M.L. (9/1/2005)*

AZIENDA VINICOLA FRATELLI FABIANO

Azienda Vinicola Fratelli Fabiano 2004 Pinot Grigio (Terra degli Osci) $6. This Pinot Grigio is etched with nice mineral tones. But there's also a broad, almost flat, quality to the mouth that holds a lot of the potential fruitiness back. **85 Best Buy** —*M.L. (6/1/2006)*

ITALY

BADIA A COLTIBUONO

Badia a Coltibuono 1998 Sangiovese (Chianti Classico) $20. The traditional flavor profile shows ripe cherries, herbs, dried tomatoes, and a touch of chocolate. Good acidity supports the fruit and contributes to the overall brisk, lively feel. Closes with tart fruit and medium, firm tannins that show a little bite. This will work well with tomato-based pasta sauces. **87** *(4/1/2001)*

Badia a Coltibuono 1999 Cetamura Sangiovese (Chianti) $11. Light, but elegant and flavorful, this spry 1999 shows creamy cherry and light toast aromas, tart dried cherry, and chalk notes on the palate. Bright acidity keeps the fruit lively, and mild tarragon notes add interest. **88 Best Buy** *(4/1/2001)*

Badia a Coltibuono 1997 Cetamura Sangiovese (Chianti) $11. 90 Best Buy —*M.S. (3/1/2000)*

Badia a Coltibuono 2001 Estate Sangiovese (Chianti Classico) $23. What starts out fresh and fancy takes on a burnt, slightly vegetal character after airing. The flavor profile offers standard plum and berry, but also some charred bell pepper. Tannic at the end, although not devastatingly so. **85** *(4/1/2005)*

Badia a Coltibuono 1999 Riserva Sangiovese (Chianti Classico) $31. Sweet and simple on the nose, with caramel and red licorice. Black cherry, raisin, and tobacco flavors don't carry much pop. Seems tired and empty, which it shouldn't be at this age. **83** *(4/1/2005)*

Badia a Coltibuono 2001 Roberto Stucchi Sangiovese (Chianti Classico) $19. Jammy, with sweet raspberry and sappy black cherry aromas. Medium in weight and largely in balance; the flavor profile consists of tea, strawberry, and tobacco. A touch leathery and stretched thin on the finish, but mostly it fits the bill. **86** *(4/1/2005)*

Badia a Coltibuono 1999 Roberto Stucchi Sangiovese (Chianti Classico) $20. Plenty of menthol-toasty oak surrounds the dark cherry fruit in a wine of ample size and fairly soft mouthfeel. Cedar, cocoa, and mild spices mark the finish, with its even, powdery tannins. **86** *(4/1/2001)*

BADIA A PASSIGNANO

Badia a Passignano 1999 Riserva Sangiovese (Chianti Classico) $45. A bit charred and foresty, with dry, earthy notes of leather and mushroom. Tea, root beer, and spice darken up the cherry flavors, but the feel is rough, with hammering tannins that don't make it friendly. Somewhat disappointing given that it's from Antinori. **86** *(4/1/2005)*

BADIA DI MORRONA

Badia di Morrona 2002 I Sodi Del Paretaio Sangiovese (Chianti) $14. Sharp and volatile, with vegetal aromas mixed with candied fruit. Finishes salty and dull, with a blast of asparagus. **80** *(4/1/2005)*

Badia di Morrona 1998 I Sodi del Paretaio Sangiovese (Chianti) $11. There's some interesting game and slate accents on the nose here, but also a candied quality to the cherry fruit. The acidity is fairly high and the tannins tense and somewhat drying on the finish. **83** *(4/1/2001)*

Badia di Morrona 1997 N'Antia Sangiovese (Toscana) $30. A serious and structured wine, N'Antia shows spicy black cherry and tobacco aromas, and plenty of toasty new oak as well. It's firm and somewhat tight right now, with bitter chocolate, cherry, and mineral flavors peeking through the oaky frame. More of the delicate cherry fruit starts to emerge on the finish. A year or two of bottle age will bring this beauty around. **91** —*J.F. (9/1/2001)*

BADIOLO

Badiolo 2000 Sangiovese (Chianti) $9. Light aromas of raspberry and clove. There are dried cherry, and plum flavors, but it's also rather hard in terms of tannins. Should be perfectly good with food, but sipped alone the acid-tannin combination is harsh. **84** —*M.S. (11/15/2003)*

Badiolo 1998 Reserva Sangiovese (Chianti) $13. Thick across the nose, with caramel, dried cherry and vanilla bean aromas. Fairly tight, tart, and somewhat raisiny. There's more of a lean quality to this wine than anything else; it tastes of cherries, tomato, and some oak. **84** —*M.S. (11/15/2003)*

Badiolo 2000 Riserva Sangiovese (Chianti) $14. Light and dilute, with strawberry aromas and then tangy fruit on the palate. Finishes clean, with more citrus and acids than meaty red-fruit notes. Made by Trambusti. **83** —*M.S. (10/1/2004)*

BAGLIO DI PIANETTO

Baglio di Pianetto 2002 Piana dei Salici Merlot (Sicilia) $26. A dark ruby Merlot with generous and well-defined notes of cherry, strawberry roll-up, chocolate, soy sauce, toast, and a spicy, succulent quality that is pleasantly complex and round on the palate. **90** —*M.L. (7/1/2006)*

Baglio di Pianetto 2002 Piana dei Cembali Nero d'Avola (Sicilia) $32. A very luscious, ripe—any more ripeness would bring it over the top—and muscular Nero d'Avola redolent of cherry, prune, cigar box, and toasted notes. It's soft and smooth in the mouth with dusty tannins. **88** —*M.L. (7/1/2006)*

Baglio di Pianetto 2002 Ramione Red Blend (Sicilia) $20. A 50-50 blend of Nero d'Avola and Merlot that suffers from an initial pungent smell reminiscent of garlic but that blows off later and yields wet earth, pipe tobacco and tea leaf. **85** —*M.L. (7/1/2006)*

Baglio di Pianetto 2004 Piana del Ginolfo Viognier (Sicilia) $24. Toasted walnut and woodshop notes conceal many of the exotic fruit aromas. Despite the strong oak-derived aromas here, this is cleansing and fresh in the mouth. **85** —*M.L. (7/1/2006)*

Baglio di Pianetto 2004 Ficiligno White Blend (Sicilia) $17. It's great to see more Sicilian producers work with Viognier and although this Insolia-Viognier blend is an interesting concept, it fundamentally lacks poise. Notes of stone fruit and grass on a hot day also carry a slightly musty quality. **85** —*M.L. (7/1/2006)*

BANEAR

Banear 2001 Rosso Merlot (Colli Orientali del Friuli) $15. Candied in the nose, with the aromatic essence of powdered fruit drink. The palate doesn't exactly agree with the nose; it's more about olives and overripe raspberry. In the end, a sweet, semicloying finish that carries high-toned flavors makes it more confusing than it should be. **83** —*M.S. (12/15/2003)*

Banear 1997 Pinot Grigio (Grave del Friuli) $10. 84 *(8/1/1999)*

Banear 2004 Pinot Grigio (Friuli Grave) $14. Very floral, with kiwi, exotic fruit, chamomile, and dried rose petal aromas, this is a delicate and elegant wine. It's also an easy-to-drink wine that is somewhat neutral in the mouth. **86** —*M.L. (2/1/2006)*

Banear 2001 Pinot Grigio (Friuli Grave) $13. Starts off with fresh but simple aromas of apple wedges, greens, and limes, but shows altogether more interesting flavors—the apple and citrus are complemented by hints of oil or shale. Turns minerally on the finish. **87** —*J.C. (7/1/2003)*

BANFI

Banfi 2005 Rosa Regale Brachetto (Brachetto d'Acqui) $23. A berry cornucopia with bursting raspberry, strawberry, and blueberry—just like a good Brachetto d'Acqui should be. Also typical of this style of sweet, sparkling wine with low alcohol is its soda pop fizz in the mouth and spicy finish. **86** —*M.L. (6/1/2006)*

Banfi 2002 Rosa Regale Brachetto (Brachetto d'Acqui) $23. Displays a pleasing array of earth, spring flowers, and red berries on the nose, but seems simple and sweet in the mouth. **84** —*J.C. (12/31/2003)*

Banfi 2001 Rosa Regale Brachetto (Brachetto d'Acqui) $23. Distinct notes of cranberry and raspberry on the nose and palate are accented by wisps of toast and rolled oats. The acidity is elegantly wrapped in juicy fruit. As in previous vintages, this is a clean, classic and delicious treat. **87** —*K.F. (12/31/2002)*

Banfi 2000 Rosa Regale Brachetto (Brachetto d'Acqui) $23. This rosé sparkler is very sweet, as it's meant to be, with cherry and strawberry aromas and flavors. The sweetness would be more palatable if it were supported by higher acidity, but here it's like the juice in frozen strawberries. Still, many people will just love it—maybe as a Bracchetto float with vanilla ice cream. **82** —*M.M. (12/31/2001)*

Banfi 2004 Col Di Sasso Cabernet Sauvignon-Sangiovese (Toscana) $9. Not a bad entry-level Tuscan red; it shows sweet bubble gum and Life

Saver aromas with just enough darkness to make it nice. Very young and cheeky in the mouth, meaning it's kind of hard, tannic, and scratchy. But it's also fully ripe, thus with pizza or spaghetti it won't hurt at all. **84** —*M.S. (9/1/2006)*

Banfi 2004 Le Rime Chardonnay-Pinot Grigio (Toscana) $9. This innocuous, large-volume (60,000 cases) Chadonnay-Pinot Grigio blend deals orange and apple cider on the nose, followed by chunky melon, peach, and apple flavors. Short but good enough; inoffensive and not difficult to quaff. **84** —*M.S. (9/1/2006)*

Banfi 2000 Pinot Grigio (Toscana) $14. There's a violet note to the nose and palate that makes you wonder if there's some Viognier in this wine. Flowery and delicately fruity with mild peach, apple, and ginger flavors, this wine is soft and light-bodied, with a slight tongue prickle, but the bold, perfumed flavors bring character and appeal. **86** —*J.F. (9/1/2001)*

Banfi 2001 Centine Red Blend (Toscana) $11. This trattoria wine has it going on. The nose offers bacon and smoke at first, and then lots of red berry fruit and a bit of light wood. Snappy red fruit dominates the palate, while the zesty finish is lean and tight, with freshness and length. Great for pastas and pizza. **87 Best Buy** —*M.S. (10/1/2004)*

Banfi 2000 Col di Sasso Red Blend (Toscana) $9. 86 Best Buy —*R.V. (11/15/2002)*

Banfi 2003 Rosa Regale Rosé Blend (Brachetto d'Acqui) $23. Heavy on the rose petal and raspberry compote aromas, and also heavy on the palate. Yes, there's definitely a touch of cherry cough syrup to this red sparkler. To enjoy this you have to like yours sweet; maybe best with a custard dessert or vanilla ice cream. It's too sweet and candied for chocolate. **84** —*M.S. (12/15/2004)*

Banfi 2003 Sangiovese (Chianti Classico) $9. A basic wine that's in proportion. The bouquet offers bacon, menthol, and rubber along with nuances of espresso and modest complexity. Boysenberry and blackberry flavors carry notes of cinnamon and vanilla, while the feel is soft yet substantive. Not a thriller, but eminently drinkable. **87 Best Buy** —*(4/1/2005)*

Banfi 1999 Sangiovese (Brachetto d'Acqui) $23. This unique red sparkler from Piedmont offers cherry and earth aromas before turning lighter on the palate, with slightly sweet strawberry flavors and a soft mousse. A unique wine, the finish has nice length and appealingly full fruit flavors that have appeal even to serious wine drinkers. **87** —*(2/1/2001)*

Banfi 2003 Centine Sangiovese (Toscana) $11. A succulent, chewy Sangiovese, Merlot and Cabernet Sauvignon blend with a pretty ruby color and intense aromas of coffee, tar, leather, and toasted wood. The tannins are still a bit raw and beg for hearty meat. Tightly packed cherry and blackberry linger over a long finish. Castello Banfi performs the extraordinary vintage after vintage: It's almost a one million case per year winery and it continues to offer excellent quality on its lowest priced products. **87 Best Buy** —*M.L. (11/15/2005)*

Banfi 2002 Centine Sangiovese (Toscana) $11. A good little blend of Sangiovese, Cabernet, and Merlot, probably best for a lunchtime pasta or pizza in the evening. The body is plump and sweet, with candied fruit. Firm on the palate, but maybe a tad too sugary. **85** —*M.S. (11/15/2004)*

Banfi 2002 Col di Sasso Sangiovese (Toscana) $9. Purple in the middle and light on the edges. A candied, sweet, simple red with plum, raisin, and chocolate flavors. Bold and basic. **83** —*M.S. (11/15/2004)*

Banfi 2001 Riserva Sangiovese (Chianti Classico) $18. A fair amount of sweet character comes off the nose, primarily chocolate, berry jam, and sugar beet. In the mouth, there's additional milk chocolate alongside dried fruit, herbs, and a hint of citrus. Finishes solid but with starchy tannins. There's also some marshmallow sweetness to the aftertaste. **87** *(4/1/2005)*

Banfi 1998 Riserva Sangiovese (Chianti Classico) $17. Toasted wheat bread, bacon, and clove add interest to the nose, which is robust and loaded with black fruit. The palate is complex enough to trigger some intrigue: Cinnamon, butter, and licorice support the dark fruit nicely. The finish is smoothly textured, and there's an airy quality to it. Quite meaty and solid, with a firm core. **88** —*M.S. (12/31/2002)*

Banfi 1997 Riserva Sangiovese (Chianti Classico) $16. Tobacco and herb accents play off cherry fruit on the slightly muted nose of this medium-

weight wine. Plum, chocolate, and wood flavors mark the slightly lean palate. Finishes dry, with cocoa and tea notes. **87** *(4/1/2001)*

Banfi NV Brut Sparkling Blend (Piedmont) $24. Made with Chardonnay, Pinot Nero, and Pinot Bianco grapes from the Vigne di Strevi in Piedmont, this is a linear, genuine sparkler with lemon-lime flavors and toasted bread notes that come through loud and clear. Easy to drink and easy to like. **89** —*M.L. (6/1/2006)*

BANOLIS

Banolis 1998 Merlot (Grave del Friuli) $11. **84** *(3/1/2000)*

Banolis 1998 Pinot Grigio (Grave del Friuli) $13. **87** *(8/1/1999)*

BARBERANI

Barberani 2004 Grechetto (Umbria) $22. Grechetto is one of the most important elements in the Orvieto Classico blend and this expression of the variety offers fresh sage, thyme, and ripe apple. Most elements jive well, although high alcohol and bitterness are distractions. **86** —*M.L. (9/1/2005)*

Barberani 2003 Villa Monticelli Grechetto (Umbria) $28. Fresh cut timber and woodshop aromas are distracting and ultimately leave a bitter taste that overpowers the wine's lean consistency in the mouth. But lovers of oak-aged whites will have success matching this wine with cream-based dishes or smoked foods. **82** —*M.L. (9/1/2005)*

Barberani 2004 Castagnolo Grechetto, Chardonnay, Trebiano (Orvieto Classico Superiore) $15. Dried grass and ripe melon come after initial rubber boots and pine resin aromas blow off. A likable wine with a full feel in the mouth and a backdrop of bitterness. The blend consists of Trebbiano and Grechetto, with a smaller component of Chardonnay. **85** —*M.L. (9/1/2005)*

Barberani 2003 Villa Monticelli 500ml Moscato (Umbria) $40. A dessert wine densely packed with aromatic intensity, flavor, and texture. Deeply perfumed Moscato Bianco grapes are left to dry on the vine or on mats to concentrate intensity and notes of almond, honey, and dried fruits. **91** —*M.L. (10/1/2006)*

Barberani 2002 Calcaia Muffa Nobile 500ml White Blend (Orvieto Classico Superiore) $40. An opulent, honey-rich dessert wine that is sticky and chewy in the mouth with apricot jam, raisin, toasted almond, and a long and satisfying finish. Morning fogs in the fall months create the perfect conditions for muffa nobile, or noble rot, that produces densely concentrated flavors. **90** —*M.L. (10/1/2006)*

BARBI

Barbi 2001 Brunello (Brunello di Montalcino) $50. Initial sulfur notes blow off quickly, leaving attractive aromas of tobacco, ripe cherry, nutmeg, vanilla, anise, and a hint of fresh dill. Medium structure with firm tannins and a long, tea-like finish. **89** *(4/1/2006)*

Barbi 2000 Brunello (Brunello di Montalcino) $50. Earthy on the nose, with hints of coffee. Tastes a bit sweet and candied, with cherry, plum, and berry flavors—your standard three-pack. Not terribly deep, but tasty. Finishes smooth, if a bit simple. **88** —*M.S. (7/1/2005)*

Barbi 2000 Riserva Brunello (Brunello di Montalcino) $100. A normally strong contender, this reserve wine left us unconvinced. There were blue flowers and stone fruit-peachy notes but also band-aid, barnyard, orange peel, and astringent tannins for an unsynchronized whole and an oily exterior. **86** *(4/1/2006)*

BARBOLINI

Barbolini NV Lambrusco Grasparossa di Castelvetro Lambrusco (Emilia-Romagna) $11. Real Lambrusco is a rarity in this country, but here it is, purple hued, with just enough fizz to help cut through the fattiness of fine salume. It's grapy and dry, with hints of anise and herbs that prevent it from being too simple. **86 Best Buy** —*J.C. (12/31/2003)*

BARICCI

Baricci 2001 Brunello (Brunello di Montalcino) $49. Brimstone notes blow off quickly to reveal smooth vanilla, coffee, chocolate, toast, cherry and eucalyptus. A wine with a long, spicy finish, firmly-built body and drying tannins. **90** *(4/1/2006)*

BARONCINI

Baroncini 1999 Sangiovese (Chianti Colli Senesi) $9. Shows poise and balance in its nicely melded herb, licorice, cherry, and bitter chocolate elements. There's good texture on the palate and some complexity on the finish, where a mineral note accents the dry cherry and tea flavors. **89 Best Buy** *(4/1/2001)*

Baroncini 1999 Sangiovese (Toscana) $10. Aromas of strawberries and milk chocolate gradually turn a bit grassy with air until a green-hay note takes hold. Light and tart, the bouncy red berries and cream flavors persist through the finish. Nice pasta red. **85** *—J.C. (9/1/2001)*

Baroncini 1999 Sangiovese (Chianti) $8. Like a mouthful of sour cherries, this is classic lean and tart Chianti garnished with flourishes of tobacco and earth. The even-textured palate and medium tannins on the finish complete a package that delivers more than expected at the price. **86 Best Buy** *(4/1/2001)*

Baroncini 1998 Casina Del Giglio Sangiovese (Chianti Classico) $14. Slightly muted nose with tobacco elements. Shows tart cherry fruit, medium-weight, and decent balance. A good basic Chianti, but also features a funky earthiness that's not for everyone. Finishes dry, with decent length. **85** *(4/1/2001)*

Baroncini 2001 Chianti Sangiovese (San Gimignano) $10. Dried cherry and strawberry aromatics, but little else. Those simple fruits carry onto the light-bodied palate. Finishes simple, with bright acidity. **83** *—M.S. (11/15/2003)*

Baroncini 2002 La Mandorlae Sangiovese (Morellino di Scansano) $17. A bit weak and horsey in the nose, with saline and saddle leather. Some time in the glass allows it to shed its awkward aromas, and later it reveals flavors of cherry and rhubarb, but also some misplaced butter. Full tannins and some acidic tartness create an aggressive mouthfeel. **84** *—M.S. (11/15/2003)*

Baroncini 1998 Le Mandorlae Sangiovese (Morellino di Scansano) $11. Thin brambly aromas and wet rubber don't bode well for the mouth, which is thin, tart, and dominated by pie cherries and apple skins. A long, starching finish sends it on its way without much charm. **80** *— M.S. (8/1/2002)*

Baroncini 1997 Le Mandorlae Riserva Sangiovese (Morellino di Scansano) $23. Starts off with rustic, horsey aromas of sweaty tack, which fade somewhat with airing. Sour cherries vie with dark, earthy flavors in the mouth and the wine finishes with almost lemony acidity coupled with dark coffee flavors. A complex, individualistic effort that takes some contemplation to appreciate. **86** *—J.C. (9/1/2001)*

Baroncini 1999 White Blend (Vernaccia di San Gimignano) $10. The fresh peaches and pears tinged with citrus develop a slight bitterness on the finish that's something like the skin of an under-ripe peach. In this context, it's a pleasant flavor that gives structure and crispness to this bouncy, refreshing quaff. **86** *—J.C. (9/1/2001)*

BARONE

Barone 1998 Pinot Grigio (Del Veneto) $6. 86 Best Buy *(8/1/1999)*

BARONE FINI

Barone Fini 2002 Merlot (Trentino) $14. Straightforward, varietally correct Merlot, with aromas of black cherries, chocolate, tobacco, and a hint of vanilla. It's medium-weight, with soft tannins and crisp acids that leave your mouth watering. Solid stuff. **86** *—J.C. (12/31/2004)*

Barone Fini 1998 Pinot Grigio (Valdadige) $10. 87 Best Buy *(8/1/1999)*

Barone Fini 2003 Pinot Grigio (Valdadige) $12. Plump in the mouth, with scents of blanched almonds and apple butter. Picks up dried spices on the palate to go along with apple-y fruit. It's low-acid nature correctly reflects the heat of the vintage. **84** *—J.C. (12/31/2004)*

Barone Fini 2002 Pinot Grigio (Valdadige) $11. Light and easy to drink, with just enough apple and lime to keep things interesting. Makes a fine apéritif. **84** *—J.C. (7/1/2003)*

Barone Fini 2001 Pinot Grigio (Valdadige) $10. A lightweight Pinot Grigio marked by dried spices and delicately-flavored apple fruit. **83** *—J.C. (1/1/2004)*

Barone Fini 2000 Pinot Grigio (Valdadige) $11. Apple and pear notes predominate in this straightforward, pleasant wine. The palate feel is good, and the finish is reasonably long. It's a perfect picnic quaff. **83** *—M.N. (9/1/2001)*

BARONE RICASOLI

Barone Ricasoli 2001 1141 Sangiovese (Chianti Classico) $15. Initially, this light-framed Chianti seems scattered and unrefined. With time in the glass it yields fresh red fruit. A slightly woody and tannic finish is borderline astringent. It needs some basic food to carry it, i.e. pizza or spaghetti. **84** *—M.S. (11/15/2003)*

Barone Ricasoli 2000 1141 Sangiovese (Chianti Classico) $13. Young and snappy, from the brambly nose right into the core of healthy fruit. There's warmth to the palate, maybe even some heat, and then plenty of spice to the finish. It's well balanced, and overall it's pretty easy to drink. **86 Best Buy** *—M.S. (12/31/2002)*

Barone Ricasoli 1998 1141 Sangiovese (Chianti Classico) $18. The tart cherry and toasty oak aspects of this medium-weight wine are nicely balanced. It's dry, with straightforward cherry flavors and dusty cocoa accents on the back end. **86** *(4/1/2001)*

Barone Ricasoli 2002 Brolio Sangiovese (Chianti Classico) $22. The difficult vintage of 2002 prompted Ricasoli to forgo releasing a Castello di Brolio or Casalferro, instead blending those lots into his Brolio bottling to improve its quality. Production is still down 15% from 2001 because of severe selection. The efforts have paid off in this fine Chianti, which boasts layers of earth, tobacco, and black olive flavors and soft tannins. **88** *(12/15/2004)*

Barone Ricasoli 2002 Brolio Sangiovese (Chianti Classico) $22. Straight from the sawmill, this is one heavily oaked Chianti. The nose oozes espresso, burnt toast, marinade, and more. But do the depth of fruit and the level of flavor deserve such wood? We liked the size, texture, and pillowy tannins, but in giving this positive rating we still question the fruit at the foundation. You be the judge. **89** *(4/1/2005)*

Barone Ricasoli 2001 Brolio Sangiovese (Chianti Classico) $17. Fairly deep, dark, and concentrated, with aromas of black plum, raw oak, and mushroom. A pure and ripe Chianti; the flavors are full, emphasizing plum and black cherry. A touch of butter and wood graces the black-cherry finish. Tight and entirely dry. **87** *—M.S. (11/15/2003)*

Barone Ricasoli 2002 Campo Ceni Sangiovese (Toscana) $20. Ricasoli's easy-to-drink, "international" bottling blends cherry, tobacco, earth, and vanilla flavors in a soft, supple package that admirably achieves its goal. **87** *(12/15/2004)*

Barone Ricasoli 2000 Casalferro Sangiovese (Toscana) $40. Dark and deep, with massive oak throughout. In the nose, a lemony quality is powerful and persistent. In the mouth, saturated plum and blackberry amplify copious wood. The finish is tannic and mouth-filling, and the structure is firm and mostly unforgiving. Needs time to come around. Best for fans of modern, oaky reds. **88** *—M.S. (11/15/2003)*

Barone Ricasoli 2000 Casalferro Sangiovese (Toscana) $40. This modern-styled blend is 25% Merlot, with the balance being Sangiovese. Lots of vanilla oak on the nose, but also hints of cinnamon, mocha, and dried herbs. Bright berry flavors ride atop a darker base of earth, plum, and tobacco, all couched in plush tannins. **89** *(12/15/2004)*

Barone Ricasoli 2000 Castello di Brolio Sangiovese (Chianti Classico) $50. Ricasoli calls this the "grand cru" of the estate. It's a blend of the estate's best lots, consisting of approximately 90% Sangiovese, 10% Cabernet Sauvignon, and Merlot. Aromas of tobacco and earth, with hints of cedar and vanilla, lead into flavors of black cherries and plums. It's got a rich, supple mouthfeel and a long, softly tannic finish. **90** *(12/15/2004)*

Barone Ricasoli 2000 Castello di Brolio Sangiovese (Chianti Classico) $55. Inky and raw, but in the best way. This is an unbridled, unchained monster of a Chianti, one with impeccable depth and extraction but also one that doesn't sit on your palate like dead weight. Racy acids and firm tannins work in tandem to prop up the bulky dark fruit, creating a structured, delicious mass. Drink from 2007 through 2015. **92 Cellar Selection** *(4/1/2005)*

ITALY

ITALY

Barone Ricasoli 1999 Castello di Brolio Sangiovese (Chianti Classico) $45. Smooth and luscious, with a fragrant nose of bold red fruit, polished oak, and earth. The palate comes together with rich cherry and berry fruit, toast, coffee, and tannin. The finish is rich, smoky, and long, with a delightful texture. Quite the showpiece wine, courtesy of extra-ripe fruit and 18 months in oak. **92** —*M.S. (11/15/2003)*

Barone Ricasoli 2000 Formulae Sangiovese (Toscana) $10. Forward and broad, with plum and blackberry aromas. The palate, however, is a bit raw and not terribly refined, with jammy flavors and coffee and chocolate on the finish. It's a meaty mouthful with all the standard components, but doesn't offer much style or flair. **85 Best Buy** —*M.S. (12/31/2002)*

Barone Ricasoli 2001 Formulæ Sangiovese (Toscana) $10. Simple and smooth, and true to the old Chianti formula that called for Sangiovese, Canaiolo, and some white grapes. The palate is eminently bold and fresh, featuring plum and berry fruit with oak shadings. The finish is fairly developed and moderately long, with a note of milk chocolate. **87 Best Buy** —*M.S. (11/15/2003)*

Barone Ricasoli 1998 Rocca Guicciarda Riserva Sangiovese (Chianti Classico) $18. Intensely aromatic full of earth, leather and rhubarb. The palate seems to want to offer more, but it's missing some charm and depth. Despite that, there's length to the finish and complexity to the red-fruit palate. **87** —*M.S. (12/31/2002)*

Barone Ricasoli 1999 Rocca Guicciarda Riserva Sangiovese (Chianti Classico) $20. Powerful. The nose is loaded with black fruit, mineral and leather, while the flavor profile is a pure blend of cherry, black pepper, and leather. A mellow but substantive finish cements what is ultimately a wholesome, balanced Chianti that serves its region well. **90 Editors' Choice** —*M.S. (11/15/2003)*

Barone Ricasoli 1997 Rocca Guicciarda Riserva Sangiovese (Chianti Classico) $22. Despite its heft, shows finesse in its black cherry, licorice, and cedar aromas and flavors. Even, balanced, and supple in the mouth. Boasts very dark espresso and chocolate flavors, with full tannins and good structure. Hold for two or three years. **89** *(4/1/2001)*

Barone Ricasoli 1999 San Ripolo Sangiovese (Chianti) $13. Quite bright, with herb-and-leather-tinged tart cherry fruit on the nose and palate. High acidity keeps the fruit racy, while licorice notes and peppery tannins mark the finish. Has youthful, good fruit; give it six to 12 months to settle down. **86** *(4/1/2001)*

BARTENURA

Bartenura 1998 Barbera (Barbera d'Asti) $10. 87 Best Buy *(4/1/2000)*

Bartenura 2003 Moscato (Moscato d'Asti) $12. Gingery sweet, with tiny bubbles and a racy melon, lychee, and herb finish. Only 5% alcohol. Quite nice, if you like this style. Kosher. **85** —*J.M. (4/3/2004)*

Bartenura 2000 Moscato (Moscato d'Asti) $10. The inviting apricot preserves, honey, butter, and roasted almond aromas of this semi-sparkler pull you right in. It's on the sweet side, with stone fruit flavors kept alive by the decent acidity. The palate bubbles and tingles and maintains its balance. Fine as an apéritif or with dessert. **90 Best Buy** *(4/1/2001)*

Bartenura NV Spumante Moscato (Asti) $15. Bright and fresh, though sweet and spicy. A wonderful apéritif or dessert wine—low in alcohol (7%), but high in flavor, with hints of ginger, peach, apricot, pear, and vanilla notes. Kosher. **86** —*J.M. (4/3/2004)*

Bartenura NV Spumante Kosher Moscato (Asti) $15. Lime and gardenia are dominant on the nose, with ample powdered sugar as well. Runs toward ripe nectarine and cantaloupe on the palate, with a sweet finish of dried mango. Shows pure Moscato flavors with only a hint of sugary artificiality. **86** —*M.S. (6/1/2005)*

Bartenura 1998 Pinot Grigio (Veneto) $10. 86 —*S.H. (9/1/2000)*

Bartenura 2002 Pinot Grigio (Pavia) $12. A bit oily in texture, with hints of lemon and melon flavors. Fairly simple. Kosher. **82** —*J.M. (4/3/2004)*

Bartenura 2000 Pinot Grigio (Veneto) $10. A deep gold color sends up warning flags, and the flavors bear that out. Has simple apple flavors with a touch of shellac and no depth. Kosher. **82** —*J.C. (7/1/2003)*

Bartenura 1999 Pinot Grigio (Veneto) $7. Refreshing, and zesty, this is a good afternoon sipper or predinner drink. It's light, dry, and crisp, with tangy lemon-grapefruit aromas and flavors that may be too sharp for some, but we like the kick. **85 Best Buy** *(4/1/2001)*

Bartenura NV Prosecco (Prosecco di Valdobbiadene) $12. Crisp and clean, with a lemon and grapefruit core. Not complex, but dry and refreshing. Kosher. **85** —*J.M. (4/3/2004)*

Bartenura 1998 Sangiovese (Chianti) $11. Pale in color, this light wine makes up in flavor for its thin feel. The tart cherry and wild berry fruit is expansive, and the flavors are supported by bright, but not sharp acidity. It's soft and easy, a very likeable house red. **86** *(4/1/2001)*

Bartenura NV Prosecco Brut Kosher Sparkling Blend (Italy) $12. Clean and encouraging even if it lacks that true Prosecco nose of lime and slate. Here you get apple and vanilla aromas before fresh apple, pear, and cinnamon flavors. Easygoing and perfectly good. Even a touch rich and creamy. **87 Best Buy** —*M.S. (6/1/2005)*

BASTÍA

Bastía 1998 Chardonnay (Langhe) $34. There's oak galore in this medium-weight apple-fruited Piedmont wine. The palate is slightly tart, with tangy oak splayed over a Granny Smith green apple base. Finishes with decent length, but again propelled more by wood than fruit. Oak lovers will gush over this, and will find more to like about it than this reviewer did. **86** —*M.M. (9/1/2001)*

BATASIOLO

Batasiolo 1997 Barbera (Barbera d'Alba) $11. 87 Best Buy *(4/1/2000)*

Batasiolo 2003 Barbera (Barbera d'Alba) $15. Modern-style Barbera right from the start, with vibrant color and scents of cedar, vanilla, and black cherry on the nose. Dried spices and vanilla buttress crisp cherry flavors on the palate, ending long and tangy. Drink now. **87** —*J.C. (3/1/2006)*

Batasiolo 2001 Barbera (Barbera d'Alba) $12. Barbera raised in stainless steel can sometimes be too tart; this one is done in large wood vats. Plenty of ripe fruit balances healthy natural acidity. Floral aromas and a crisp, clean finish make this a solid choice for a busy weeknight. **86 Best Buy** *(4/1/2003)*

Batasiolo 2001 Sabri Barbera (Barbera d'Asti) $13. Basic and meaty, but pretty nice once you delve into this dense, well-oaked wine that runs fast with snappy, cheerful red fruit. Cherry and cassis are the main players, with chocolate making a cameo appearance. Not complex, but tasty and flavorful. **86** —*M.S. (12/15/2003)*

Batasiolo 2004 Sovrana Barbera (Barbera d'Alba) $18. This is a medium-bodied, crisp Barbera that cuts a swath midway between traditional and New Wave, aged in one-third stainless steel, one-third old American oak, and one-third large botti, it has some smoky, barbecue-sauce aromatics, then layers on slightly tangy tomato and black cherry flavors. **86** *(12/1/2006)*

Batasiolo 2001 Sovrana Barbera (Barbera d'Alba) $18. This is Batasiolo's "New Wave" Barbera, matured in barrique to add a layer of toast and softness to Barbera's naturally crunchy fruit. It's a big, mouth-filling wine, filled with red plums and finishing with a hint of chocolate. **89 Editors' Choice** *(4/1/2003)*

Batasiolo 1996 Sovrana Barbera (Barbera d'Alba) $18. 85 *(4/1/2000)*

Batasiolo 2002 Serbato Chardonnay (Langhe) $12. Heavily oaked, thus it hits hard with aromas of toast, popcorn, and papaya. It's basic, but balanced, with plenty of oak-based push on the finish. Mouthfeel is an attribute; the feel is lush and round. However, the flavors lean a bit toward the dull side. **85** —*M.S. (12/15/2003)*

Batasiolo 2000 Vigneto Morino Chardonnay (Langhe) $17. Partial barrel fermentation shows in the wine's aromas of smoke and cashew. Modest pear and citrus flavors turn mealy on the finish, picking up hints of anise and resin. **86** *(4/1/2003)*

Batasiolo 2005 Granée Cortese (Gavi) $14. Fermented and aged only in stainless steel to preserve freshness, this is a crisp Gavi with scents of green apples and limes and a dose of chalk-like minerality. Crystalline clean, but with a slightly creamy texture. **87** *(12/1/2006)*

Batasiolo 2004 Granée Cortese (Gavi di Gavi) $15. Nicely balanced, this Gavi artfully mixes ripe pears and oranges with tarter citrus notes and dry, chalky minerality. Light to medium in body, this crisp, clean wine is an ideal palate refresher. **87** —*J.C. (3/1/2006)*

Batasiolo 2002 Granée Gavi del Comune di Gavi Cortese (Gavi) $15. Clean on the nose, with aromas of pear and nectarine. Turns racy and fruity the minute it hits your tongue; pink grapefruit and tangerine flavors prevail. Snappy and tight on the tail end, with a high-voltage, piquant mouthfeel. **87** —*M.S. (12/15/2003)*

Batasiolo 1998 Dolcetto (Dolcetto d'Alba) $11. 86 Best Buy *(4/1/2000)*

Batasiolo 2001 Bricco di Vergne Dolcetto (Dolcetto d'Alba) $14. A dark, earthy wine, this single-vineyard Dolcetto doesn't have the exuberant fruit of the variety, substituting size, density, and tannins. It all adds up to a sturdy, plummy wine that would go well with simply grilled beef. **86** *(4/1/2003)*

Batasiolo 2002 Vigneto Bricco di Vergne Dolcetto (Dolcetto d'Alba) $14. Plum and cherry aromas with a touch of leather. Quite snappy in the mouth, with cherry flavors and accents of black coffee. A smooth, expansive finish with firm tannins and ample fruit make it more solid than many. **87** —*M.S. (12/15/2003)*

Batasiolo 2005 Bosc Dla Rei Moscato (Moscato d'Asti) $12. A lush, fruity style of Moscato, imbued with lovely floral scents and notes of peach, melon, and spice. Lacks the acidity and zip of the best examples, but still quite enjoyable. **86** *(12/1/2006)*

Batasiolo 2004 Bosc Dla Rei Moscato (Moscato d'Asti) $12. This Moscato d'Asti gives a strong performance thanks to notes of dried herbs, soapsuds, rose petal, and a very clean and crisp impression in the mouth. Try it as an afternoon aperitivo. **89 Best Buy** —*M.L. (12/15/2005)*

Batasiolo 2001 Bosc Dla Rei Moscato (Moscato d'Asti) $12. This light, slightly fizzante wine displays a variety of floral aromas that range from apple blossom to gardenia wrapped around a core of oranges and lemons. Finish is short and sweet. **85** *(4/1/2003)*

Batasiolo 2000 Muscatel Tardi Moscato (Piedmont) $40. This late-harvest Muscat is made much like a Sauternes, using botrytized grapes and small oak barrels. Honeyed apricot and orange flavors are not overly sweet, while a toasted grain note on the finish suggests pairing with seared foie gras or grilled fruit. **86** *(4/1/2003)*

Batasiolo 2003 Nebbiolo (Barbaresco) $35. The extreme heat led to an early harvest, and the result is this big, ripe wine that's not particularly lush or textured. Slightly dusty or floral notes accent the dried fruit flavors and the finsh stops a little abruptly. **87** *(12/1/2006)*

Batasiolo 2001 Nebbiolo (Barbaresco) $40. Herbal and cherry aromas emerge with airing, but this medium-bodied Barbaresco isn't all that aromatic. Cherry and cola flavors finish on a firm note, but the fruit holds up. Try in 5–8 years. **88** —*J.C. (3/1/2006)*

Batasiolo 2001 Nebbiolo (Barolo) $38. Features slightly floral notes, but the dominant aromas are of plum and spice cake, and those repeat on the palate, adding hints of anise. It's plump and ample, but firmly structured and should easily last 10 years or more. Aged exclusively in botti, so no intrusive oak mars the Nebbiolo flavors. **89** *(12/1/2006)*

Batasiolo 2001 Nebbiolo (Barolo) $37. Reasonably priced, Batasiolo's 2001 Barolo features a knockout bouquet of roses, cherries, and white chocolate, followed up by flavors of cherries and chocolate. It's relatively light in body for Barolo, yet despite a certain delicacy also shows great tensile strength in its long, tannic finish. **90 Editors' Choice** —*J.C. (3/1/2006)*

Batasiolo 2000 Nebbiolo (Barbaresco) $33. Everything is harmonious about this wine, from the aromas of cedar and cherries to the flavors of ripe fruit and vanilla. The mouthfeel is supple and round, making for an exceptionally easy-to-drink Barbaresco. Drink now–2010. **89** *(4/2/2004)*

Batasiolo 1999 Nebbiolo (Barbaresco) $27. Among the myriad of tight Barbarescos out there, this one is overt and friendly, a ball of cheer amid a tough crowd. The cherry aromas are soft and inviting, while the mouth offers a nice blend of dried red fruit and spice. Vanilla and chocolate as well as some fading raspberry grace the smooth finish. This is one to drink sooner rather than later. **89** —*M.S. (11/15/2002)*

Batasiolo 1999 Nebbiolo (Barolo) $33. Tarry, with plum and black cherry notes that combine with dusty flavors to give a lasting impression of dark earth. It seems plump and round on first impression, then the tannins clamp down on the finish, ending with slightly bitter black tea leaves. **85** *(4/2/2004)*

Batasiolo 1998 Nebbiolo (Barolo) $32. This soft, easy-drinking Barolo is already approachable. Delicate aromas of roses, leather, and anise draw you in; cherry and earth flavors fill your mouth, before a chocolate note emerges on the finish. Good restaurant choice, where more tannic examples are often served too young. **88** *(4/1/2003)*

Batasiolo 2002 Arsigà Nebbiolo (Dolcetto d'Alba) $15. Meaty and dense, but like many of the '02s, it's not what you'd call rich. Plenty of plum, cherry, chocolate, and espresso run through the wine, while the finish is clean and features perfectly ripe flavors. Round, tasty, and firm, like a Dolcetto should be. **88** —*M.S. (12/15/2003)*

Batasiolo 1997 Vigneto Bofani Nebbiolo (Piedmont) $52. The wine may be powerful, with initial chunky dark plum flavors and acidity. But at the same time, there is a degree of elegance from mint and dry grass aromas and red fruit flavors at the finish. **89** —*R.V. (11/15/2002)*

Batasiolo 1997 Vigneto Boscarecto Nebbiolo (Piedmont) $52. This is the most earthy and rustic of the wines produced by Batasiolo. The fruit is firm, solid, and tannic, with flavors of parsnips and crisp acidity. Already coming into balance, it should develop relatively fast, over the next five to 10 years. **87** —*R.V. (11/15/2002)*

Batasiolo 1998 Vigneto Cerequio Nebbiolo (Barolo) $63. Like the other Batasiolo Barolos we tasted, the tannins in this wine are soft, making it approachable within the next few years. Leather and red earth notes are layered over a base of red plums, finishing with a touch of anise. **90** *(4/1/2003)*

Batasiolo 1997 Vigneto Cerequio Nebbiolo (Piedmont) $52. A dense, black wine with high acidity. The fruit, though, has a very ripe, juicy character, with flavors of black figs and truffles. The main impression is of an older style of wine, with concentration and dry tannins overlying the fruit, giving the wine the ability to develop well. **90** —*R.V. (11/15/2002)*

Batasiolo 2001 Vigneto Corda della Briccolina Nebbiolo (Barolo) $NA. This comes from a 1.6-hectare (4-acre) vineyard in Serralunga solely owned by the Doglianis. Floral notes grace the nose, picking up leather and plum flavors. Rich, deep, and supple on the palate, this was by far the most impressive of the Batasiolo wines we recently sampled. Aged in barrique. **92** *(12/1/2006)*

Batasiolo 1998 Vigneto Corda della Briccolina Nebbiolo (Barolo) $70. The ample tannins of this wine are deceptively soft—but don't let that fool you. This one should age gracefully through 2015. For now, it's dominated by earth, tar, and tobacco, but shows glimpses of plum, particularly on the finish. Aged in barrique, but not particularly oaky. **91 Cellar Selection** *(4/1/2003)*

Batasiolo 1997 Vingna Corda della Briccolini Nebbiolo (Piedmont) $60. This flagship wine from Batasiolo comes from a southwest-facing vineyard in Serralunga d'Alba. It is already developing a brick-red color and soft, velvety tannins. Flavors of pomegranates and black plums give it a sweet-and-sour character, leaving balancing acidity to finish. **91** —*R.V. (11/15/2002)*

BAVA

Bava 1996 Piano Alto Vigneti Bava d'Agl Barbera D'Asti Superiore Barbera (Barbera d'Asti) $38. 84 *(4/1/2000)*

Bava 1995 Stradivario Barbera D'Asti Superiore Barbera (Barbera d'Asti) $38. 85 *(4/1/2000)*

Bava 2003 Thou Bianc Chardonnay (Piedmont) $15. Unoaked Chardonnay from Piemonte isn't something we run across every day, but this example is a tasty, minerally counterpoint to oaky Chards. Medium-bodied apple and peach flavors are tinged with dry almond skin and chalk notes. **86** —*J.C. (3/1/2006)*

Bava 1998 Controvento Dolcetto (Dolcetto d'Asti) $13. 87 Best Buy *(4/1/2000)*

Bava 2004 Bass Tuba Moscato (Moscato d'Asti) $25. Tightly packed with mineral notes, white flowers, dried grass, sage, and beeswax. Seductively sweet in the mouth with good foam and bubble persistency; a good companion to cookies or panettone. **87** —*M.L. (12/15/2005)*

Bava 1997 Barolo di Castiglione Falletto Nebbiolo (Barolo) $60. Bava's Barolo is solid and tannic, with concentrated dried fruit aromas showing the character of the powerful 1997 vintage. There are flavors of sundried tomatoes as well as black fruits. This is a serious wine that will age slowly. **89** —*R.V. (11/15/2002)*

BEGALI

Begali 1999 Red Blend (Amarone della Valpolicella Classico) $55. Cola is one of the dominant aromatics, and there's also some cedar emanating from the nose. Super-ripe in the mouth, with near-perfect acidity and tannins pushing plum, spice and a touch of licorice and cola. With its lively finish and excellent balance, this wine should age nicely. **91** *(11/1/2005)*

Begali 1999 Monte Ca'Bianca Red Blend (Amarone della Valpolicella Classico) $75. Nice and sturdy on the bouquet, where dainty cedar notes blend perfectly with cola, gingerbread, and tree bark. Healthy and muscular, with intense cherry, plum, and raspberry flavors. Throughout there's power and pizzazz, and just enough sweet chocolaty notes to make it friendly. A winner with some kick. **91** *(11/1/2005)*

BELLA ROSA

Bella Rosa 2003 Pinot Grigio (Veneto) $8. Starts off slightly smoky and nutty, with sweet, peachy fruit and some almond and citrus to enliven the finish. A bit viscous and heavy and it tastes like it might have a bit of residual sugar, but shows decent character. **84 Best Buy** —*J.C. (12/31/2004)*

Bella Rosa 2002 Sangiovese (Chianti) $13. Plum and berry fruit, but in candied form. The nose is like a hard sucking candy, while the palate is grapey and endowed with black cherry. Tangy and high-ended on the back end, but decently textured. **84** *(4/1/2005)*

BELLA SERA

Bella Sera 2003 Pinot Grigio (Delle Venezie) $7. Shows decent fruit, with floral hints giving way to peach and nectarine flavors tinged with honey and tangerines. Light in weight and not very concentrated, but a pleasant little sipper that finishes on a grapefruity note. **84 Best Buy** —*J.C. (12/31/2004)*

Bella Sera 2002 Tre Venezie Pinot Grigio (Delle Venezie) $7. Lime and green apples on the nose, with a floral note as well. It's medium-bodied, featuring a sharp, citrusy edge to the finish. **84** —*J.C. (7/1/2003)*

BELLAVISTA

Bellavista NV Brut Champagne Blend (Franciacorta) $30. This popular northern Italian shows a good bead and a nice gingery quality. It's round on the palate and, having tasted it before, seems a little sweeter than remembered. Closes with good length, but surprisingly soft. **85** —*M.M. (12/31/2001)*

Bellavista NV Cuvée Brut Champagne Blend (Franciacorta) $26. The yeasty vanilla and mushroom notes on the nose are typical and correct. Nectarine, apple, and some resiny flavors make for an interesting palate. The finish is warm and spicy even if it's short and simple. Not the most hearty bubbly out there, but what's here is solid. **86** —*M.S. (6/1/2003)*

Bellavista NV Cuvée Brut Champagne Blend (Franciacorta) $26. 87 *(12/31/2000)*

Bellavista 1991 Vittorio Moretti Reserve Cuvée Champagne Blend (Franciacorta) $100. 83 *(12/31/2000)*

Bellavista NV Gran Cuvée Satén Chardonnay (Franciacorta) $58. Satén sparklers are made with slightly less carbonization, which helps render a creamier, silkier mouthfeel. This wine is a beautiful example of this winemaking methodology and delivers omelet, custard, and nutmeg-like aromas. **90** —*M.L. (6/1/2006)*

Bellavista NV Cuvée Brut Sparkling Blend (Franciacorta) $37. Full and yeasty, with popcorn, white pepper, and baker's yeast on the mature, stately bouquet. Everything hits the spot, from the baked apple and peach palate to the smooth, toasty, and entirely tasty finish. Champagne lovers will find this up their alley. **90** —*M.S. (12/15/2004)*

Bellavista NV Cuvée Brut Sparkling Blend (Franciacorta) $34. Here's a sparkling wine with all its many facets beautifully fitted together to form an incredibly seductive and inviting whole. The aromas span the exotic fruit spectrum from banana to kiwi, but leave room for butter and yeast notes. Very creamy and silky in the mouth, with lively perlage. **92** —*M.L. (6/1/2006)*

Bellavista NV Cuvée Brut Sparkling Blend (Franciacorta) $36. Snappy yet smooth, with subtle apple, toast, and vanilla aromas. Very good in terms of feel, with dry, spicy flavors of baked apple, white pepper, and herbs. Slightly mature notes of mushroom and Sherry rise up on the finish, lending this bubbly added complexity. **91 Editors' Choice** —*M.S. (12/15/2005)*

Bellavista 1999 Gran Cuvée Brut Sparkling Blend (Franciacorta) $53. Fresh and lively, with citrus and mild yeast aromas. Crisp, dealing primarily green apple and orange flavors. Fruity and clean, with a light body. Jumpy and not too complex. **87** —*M.S. (12/15/2004)*

Bellavista 1998 Gran Cuvée Brut Sparkling Blend (Franciacorta) $39. Bellavista's house style favors lightness and elegance over power. This vintage offers understated toast and apple aromas followed up by delicate flavors of cinnamon, apple, toast, and citrus. Airy and light. **89** —*J.C. (12/31/2003)*

Bellavista 2001 Gran Cuvée Brut Sparkling Blend (Franciacorta) $53. Brilliantly luminous with generous and intense aromas of yellow rose, exotic fruit, almond, and melted butter. The wine is creamy and smooth, with sharp points of acidity that keep the mouth lively. The overall effect is a carefully crafted balance between creaminess and crispness. **90** —*M.L. (6/1/2006)*

Bellavista 2000 Gran Cuvée Brut Sparkling Blend (Franciacorta) $54. Straightforward and easygoing, with pure apple and pear aromas. Sort of jumpy and youthful, with a fresh but foamy mouthfeel that is as much Sprite/7-Up as it is classic-method spumante. Forward apple and citrus flavors are clean and light, and if complexity is a bit lacking there's enough forward, tasty fruit to more than make up for it. **89** —*M.S. (12/15/2005)*

Bellavista 1999 Gran Cuvée Brut Rose Sparkling Blend (Franciacorta) $59. Firm on the nose, with mineral and under-ripe peach aromas. The palate is more plump, with riper peach flavors accenting cantaloupe. Shows good verve, but remains tame on the palate. Very dry and food-friendly. **88** —*M.S. (12/15/2004)*

Bellavista 2000 Gran Cuvée Brut Rosé Sparkling Blend (Franciacorta) $59. Amber/salmon in color, with earthy, complex aromas of dried leaves, cherry, and toast. More spicy and sly than overtly fruity, with dried plum and apricot flavors. Nice and smooth in the mouth and persistent on the finish. Gets better with airing, as it opens to show a smoky and nuanced alter ego. **89** —*M.S. (12/15/2005)*

Bellavista 2001 Gran Cuvée Rosé Sparkling Blend (Franciacorta) $58. A beautiful wine with a pale rose color that shines with golden and reddish highlights, just like the skin of a ripe peach. The nose is a pretty mélange of raspberry, cranberry, white cherry, and fresh baked bread. The mouthfeel is deep and penetrating. **89** —*M.L. (6/1/2006)*

Bellavista NV Gran Cuvée Satèn Sparkling Blend (Franciacorta) $59. Starts with austere scents of toast and rising bread dough, but turns rich and creamy on the palate, showcasing flavors of toasted coconut, ripe fruit, and a hint of butter. Finishes long, with an almost chewy textural component. **90** —*J.C. (12/15/2004)*

Bellavista NV Gran Cuvée Satèn Sparkling Blend (Franciacorta) $59. Lightly scrambled egg, vanilla, and apple fruit all total a seductive, classy nose that's one part Champagne and one part Italian. Crisp but deep, with lovely apple and peach flavors. Quite zesty yet smooth, with serious aging potential; in fact, cellaring for a few years should really bring it to its peak. **93 Editors' Choice** —*M.S. (12/15/2005)*

Bellavista 1998 Grand Cuvée Brut Rosé Sparkling Blend (Franciacorta) $45. This is a pretty, light wine that seems almost airy in the mouth. Aromas of toast and hints of cherries and berries develop into fresh herb and citrus flavors, finishing with a feeling of evanescence. **88** —*J.C. (12/31/2003)*

Bellavista 1999 Pas Operé Gran Cuvée Sparkling Blend (Franciacorta) $62. Plump and yeasty, with apple, lemon, and green banana flavors. Very restrained and lithe, with a clear but distant character. The mouthfeel is supple and easy but it doesn't pack much punch. Finishing notes of mushroom and mineral are light. **87** —*M.S. (12/15/2005)*

BELLUSSI

Bellussi NV Belcanto Cartizze Prosecco (Prosecco Superiore di Cartizze) $24. A fresh and bright bubbly with grass, almond paste, peach, and apricot aromas. Grapefruit and tart citrus glide clear over the palate in a straight and direct manner. Packaged in beautifully printed bottles. **89** —*M.L. (6/1/2006)*

Bellussi NV Belcanto Extra Dry Prosecco (Prosecco di Valdobbiadene) $18. A fruit-driven bubbly with distinct honeydew, stone fruit, citrus, mineral, and floral notes. There's a soda pop quality in the mouth thanks to biting effervescence and forward acidity. **87** —*M.L. (6/1/2006)*

Bellussi NV Dry Prosecco (Prosecco di Valdobbiadene) $16. This Prosecco boasts a very attractive combination of fresh, lively, and concentrated floral notes opposite complex toasted notes. Medium bodied, which is big for Prosecco, with good acidity and a spicy finish. **87** —*M.L. (6/1/2006)*

Bellussi NV Extra Dry Prosecco (Prosecco di Valdobbiadene) $16. Orange blossom, tangerine skin, almond, stone fruit—the list goes on. This is very aromatic with plush, sweet notes on the nose. Has dimension and texture in the mouth, and a crisp close. **86** —*M.L. (6/1/2006)*

BELMONDO

Belmondo 2004 Pinot Grigio (Pavia) $6. Here's a Pinot Grigio made not far from the bright lights of fashion capitol Milan. There's a whiff of burnt matchstick, musk, and peanut skin; clean and crisp in the mouth. **83** —*M.L. (6/1/2006)*

Belmondo 1999 Pinot Grigio (Oltrepò Pavese) $5. 81 —*M.N. (12/31/2000)*

BELTRAME

Beltrame 1997 Pinot Grigio (Friuli Aquileia) $15. 84 *(8/1/1999)*

BENANTI

Benanti 2001 Il Monovitigno Nerello Mascalese (Sicilia) $34. It takes a certain amount of courage to import an obscure indigenous grape like Nerello Mascalese and expect a foreign market to appreciate it. If you're up for tasting something new, prepare yourself for deep mineral, currant, and toasted almond flavors. Although this wine is less complex than the estate's blended wines, it does paint a clear picture of the variety. **87** —*M.L. (7/1/2006)*

Benanti 2000 Il Monovitigno Nerello Mascalese (Sicilia) $30. A leaner, meaner red with plush under-currents of cigar smoke, ash, granite rock, and bright red fruit in the background. This is unmistakably a wine from the volcanic soils of the mighty Mount Etna. It has medium body, and firm, dusty tannins. **87** —*M.L. (7/1/2006)*

Benanti 2000 Il Monovitigno Nero d'Avola (Sicilia) $30. Made from twisted old vines from Pachino, in the province of Syracuse, this luscious red delivers an ample dosage of mineral tones upfront with background black berry fruit and dried cassis. You'll pick up notes of resin and black tar, too. **88** —*M.L. (7/1/2006)*

Benanti 2000 Lamorémio Red Blend (Sicilia) $32. This is a carefully crafted volcanic wine (1/3 each Nerello Mascalese, Nero d'Avola, and Cab Sauvignon) with bright red fruit and cherry embellished by notes of forest floor, charcoal, and some Band-Aid. Good fruit flavors and firm tannins create a very nice overall effect. Aged 18 months in French oak. **89** —*M.L. (7/1/2006)*

Benanti 2001 Rosso di Verzella Red Blend (Etna) $15. Espresso rinds, leather, black soil, pencil shavings, and blackberry are firmly etched on the nose; the wine has a pretty, dusty finish that reflects toasted highlights. **89** —*M.L. (7/1/2006)*

Benanti 2000 Rovittello Red Blend (Etna) $33. Rolling out the hits, Benanti delivers yet another Nerello Mascalese and Nerello Cappuccio blend (80-20%) that tops the charts of Sicilian indigenous reds. You can't get enough of those polished berry and volcanic notes or of its

incredible depth and dimension in the mouth. Aged for one year in oak. **90** —*M.L. (7/1/2006)*

Benanti 2000 Serra della Contessa Red Blend (Etna) $38. A must-try blend of two indigenous grapes, Nerello Mascalese and Nerello Cappuccio. Red cherry and plum is backed by delicate almond-paste, licorice and toast notes. Has a solid structure with drying tannins over a long finish, thanks to steel fermentation and 18 months of aging in French oak. A very unique and special wine, and a standard-bearer among Sicilian indigenous varieties. **93 Editors' Choice** —*M.L. (7/1/2006)*

Benanti 2004 Bianco di Caselle White Blend (Etna) $15. This is a particular wine that might not appeal to everyone. The Carricante grapes are harvested very late (the second half of October) and only see stainless steel. The results bring strongly fragrant, incense-like floral and sweet candy notes, backed by very noticeable minerality. **86** —*M.L. (7/1/2006)*

Benanti 2003 Edélmio White Blend (Sicilia) $22. Benanti's unique Etna whites are distinguished by a candy-like, almost bubble gum note. This blend of Carricante and Chardonnay exhibits citrus candy, mineral, and floral notes that are also **87** —*M.L. (7/1/2006)*

Benanti 2001 Pietramarina White Blend (Etna) $33. Fruit for this crisp and mineral-rich white wine comes from 80-year-old bush-like vines and one of the most extreme viticulture spots on the planet (950 meters in altitude on the volcano). It is rich with exotic fruit, delicate floral, and peach lollipop notes, and a firm, compact structure. **89** —*M.L. (7/1/2006)*

BENINCASA

Benincasa 2000 Sagrantino (Sagrantino di Montefalco) $NA. The aromas are dominated by monotone vibrant cherry lollipop and candied strawberry. Moderately intense in the mouth with solid structure but less power than your standard Sagrantino. **85** —*M.L. (9/1/2005)*

BERLUCCHI

Berlucchi 2002 Cellarius Brut Sparkling Blend (Franciacorta) $NA. One notch up on the aromatic intensity ladder but slightly muddled in its complexity. The aromas are fresh, but lie somewhere between flowers and fruit. Silky, rich, and smooth on the palate. **87** —*M.L. (6/1/2006)*

Berlucchi 2002 Cellarius Rose Sparkling Blend (Franciacorta) $NA. One of the most successful rosé sparklers out of this part of Italy, this wine offers a beautifully delicate ensemble of forest berry, rose petal, violets, white cherry, and peach. Tangy and crisp in the mouth; this is a special sparkler with a feminine touch. **90 Editors' Choice** —*M.L. (6/1/2006)*

Berlucchi NV Cuvée Imperiale Brut Sparkling Blend (Franciacorta) $NA. Redolent of lighter aromas like melon, white peach, and almond skin, this is a polished and linear sparkler that delivers nice acidity and long persistence after an initial carbonization sting. **88** —*M.L. (6/1/2006)*

Berlucchi NV Cuvée Storica Brut Sparkling Blend (Franciacorta) $32. Made from Chardonnay with 5% Pinot Nero, this festive sparkler delivers Golden Delicious apple, roasted nut, water chestnut, banana, and a slight note of green grass. Clearly etched and polished in the mouth, with a slightly hefty body. **89** —*M.L. (6/1/2006)*

BERSANO

Bersano 1997 Costalunga Barbera (Barbera d'Asti) $12. 89 Best Buy *(4/1/2000)*

Bersano 1997 Cremosina Barbera (Barbera d'Asti) $17. 86 *(4/1/2000)*

Bersano 1997 Generala Barbera (Barbera d'Asti) $34. 91 *(4/1/2000)*

Bersano 2001 Cortese (Gavi) $12. Full aromas of melon and peach that are clear and focused distinguish this wine. It's citrusy, emphasizing orange and grapefruit, but under that a core of green apple provides a firm foundation. Tight on the finish, but then it spreads out. Squarely on the money for the style, and likely up to fine food, say grilled branzino. **88 Best Buy** —*M.S. (12/15/2003)*

Bersano 2001 Raggio Cortese (Gavi) $23. Very lean in the nose, and beyond that there isn't much to the wine. Basic orange and lemon flavors lead into a modestly sharp finish. Not sour or aggressive, but definitely sharp and less than friendly. **82** —*M.S. (12/15/2003)*

ITALY

ITALY

Bersano 2004 Moscato (Moscato d'Asti) $8. Not an intense nose, but an attractive one with floral and fruity layers. There's chalk, peach, and generous cream in the mouth, which beg for all kinds of cream or custard-based desserts. **88 Best Buy** —*M.L. (12/15/2005)*

Bersano 2003 San Michele Moscato (Moscato d'Asti) $10. This Moscato underwent natural fermentation, and boasts loads of apple skin and minerality but is a little flat on the nose. A good wine to pair with raw fruit. **84** —*M.L. (12/15/2005)*

Bersano 1997 Badarina Nebbiolo (Barolo) $49. Tight and traditional, which doesn't mean harsh. The nose melds raisin, leather, and cedar, while on the palate you get a fine mix of plum, cherry, and raspberry. A modicum of layering on the smooth finish completes the package. **88** — *M.S. (12/15/2003)*

Bersano 1998 Nirvasco Nebbiolo (Barolo) $35. Smells a bit like Grandma's sun-warmed attic, with dry, dusty scents tinged with leather. Sweet, dried fruit flavors softly fill the mouth, accented by enough spice to keep things lively. Ruggedly tannic on the finish, but there should be enough fruit in the end. Drink 2010–2020. **88** *(4/2/2004)*

BERTANI

Bertani 2004 Velante Pinot Grigio (Veneto) $12. Opens with peach and pineapple but has a dab of nuttiness that helps complete a rich and interesting nose. It is crisp and simple in the mouth and would make a good match to curry chicken or light pasta dishes. **87 Best Buy** —*M.L. (2/1/2006)*

Bertani 1997 Red Blend (Amarone della Valpolicella Classico) $90. Dry and maturing, with aromatic notes of tea, toast, cherry, and earth. Not a ton of complexity or layering here. Instead it's straightforward and lean, with a hint of saline to the finish. **85** *(11/1/2005)*

Bertani 1995 Red Blend (Amarone della Valpolicella Classico) $75. Quite likable, with a viscous body and firm tannins. The aromas are perfumed and sweet, with hints of licorice, chocolate, and raisins. This is textbook Amarone. **87** *(5/1/2003)*

Bertani 2000 Villa Arvedi Red Blend (Amarone della Valpolicella Valpantena) $54. Smooth, toasty, and solid even if it doesn't offer any one particular thing that will sear into your memory. The bouquet is toasty and fruity, with a bit of cedar. The mouth offers cherry, berry, and chocolate, the standard three of Amarone. Finishes steady, with some size. **88** *(11/1/2005)*

Bertani 2002 White Blend (Soave Classico Superiore) $14. A soft, almond-flavored wine that has fresh, green, and ripe fruit. The blend, with small amounts of Chardonnay and Trebbiano, gives a feeling of fullness and roundness and is already ready for drinking. **86** —*R.V. (7/1/2003)*

Bertani 2002 Due Uve White Blend (Delle Venezie) $13. A 50-50 blend of Pinot Grigio and Sauvignon Blanc that's crisp and ripe, and offers a touch of spice. A lovely, fresh, green wine. **85** —*R.V. (7/1/2003)*

Bertani 2001 Le Lave White Blend (Delle Venezie) $23. This blend of 65% Chardonnay and 35% of the Soave grape Garganega is aged in French oak for 10 months. The result is rich, spicy, and toasty, with soft vanilla flavors and concentrated green plum and almond flavors from the fruit. **89** —*R.V. (7/1/2003)*

BERTELLI

Bertelli 1995 Montetusa Barbera (Barbera d'Alba) $13. 83 *(4/1/2000)*

BIAGINI MANRICO

Biagini Manrico 2000 Signano Sangiovese (Chianti Colli Senesi) $11. Light, smooth, and pretty upfront, with appropriately light strawberry and cherry flavors. The finish is clean, broad, and pleasant. Even the mouthfeel is smooth and airy. This is a genuinely easygoing wine, sort of a liquid version of a strawberry parfait. **86** —*M.S. (12/31/2002)*

BIGI

Bigi 2003 Amabile White Blend (Orvieto Classico) $9. High in residual sugar this is a sweet white that is almost too generous with its notes of exotic fruit and candied peach. Beyond those obvious tones is an interesting aromatic layer of vanilla and crème caramel. **84** —*M.L. (10/1/2006)*

BIONDI-SANTI

Biondi-Santi 1997 Il Greppo Brunello (Brunello di Montalcino) $120. Little changes at Biondi-Santi. The tannins on this huge 1997 are dense, almost impenetrable. The flavors are of cherry, tobacco, old wood, and solid, black fruits. The aftertaste is all tannin at this stage. Despite this rigorous adherence to tradition, the 1997 seems a touch less overwhelming than previous vintages of this classic wine. Nevertheless, age for at least 15 years before drinking. **93 Cellar Selection** —*R.V. (8/1/2002)*

Biondi-Santi 2000 Sassoalloro Sangiovese (Toscana) $30. This Sangiovese has a lot going for it: a sweet maple-tinged aroma, a pretty ruby color, round but snappy plum and raspberry flavors, and a long, layered finish. But in the end it doesn't really sing, it's a bit hollow at the core, and there's an oak-driven, buttered popcorn note on the finish that leaves a heavy, lasting flavor. **87** —*M.S. (8/1/2002)*

Biondi-Santi 1995 Sassoalloro Sangiovese (Toscana) $25. 91 —*M.G. (5/1/1999)*

BISOL

Bisol NV Cartizze Prosecco (Prosecco di Valdobbiadene Superiore) $44. Clean and attractive, with seductive honey, melon, and ripe peach flavors. Not as lively or aggressive as some, but that can be construed as a virtue. Sweet in that likable extra dry sense. **88** —*M.S. (12/15/2005)*

Bisol NV Crede Prosecco (Prosecco di Valdobbiadene) $12. Pretty aromas of citrus and vanilla smell almost like a scented candle. But all subtlety ends there; the palate delivers a blast of fruit. From the time you taste it, it's in your face, providing the essence of Prosecco's sweet side with soft but healthy acidity. **90 Best Buy** —*M.S. (12/31/2002)*

Bisol NV Crede Prosecco (Prosecco di Valdobbiadene) $18. Not cheap by Prosecco standards, and that extra level of quality is evident at every checkpoint. The bouquet is exceedingly snappy, with pure lemon-lime aromas. Citrus, green apple, and white pepper flavors create a near-perfect palate, while the mouthfeel is excellent. About as good as Prosecco gets. **90 Editors' Choice** —*M.S. (6/1/2005)*

Bisol 2005 Crede Prosecco (Prosecco di Valdobbiadene) $15. This is as good as Prosecco gets. Bisol blends 85 percent Prosecco with Verdiso and Pinot Bianco to produce a luminous and delicately sublime sparkler with distinct lemon-lime and mineral notes weaved within fruity, fresh whole. The wine's overall presentation is clean, genuine, and delicious: Persistent perlage makes it creamy and frothy in the mouth with lively accents of acidity at the close. A perfect pair to cocktail and finger foods. **89 Best Buy** —*M.L. (6/1/2006)*

Bisol NV Crede Brut Prosecco (Prosecco di Valdobbiadene) $18. Interesting from the start, where crushed vitamin, orange pulp, and some warm dust make for an atypical but solid bouquet. As always, the palate is forward and fresh, with nectarine and citrus pith. Solid on the back end, with a bit of lemony heft. **88** —*M.S. (12/15/2005)*

Bisol NV Desiderio Jeio Brut Prosecco (Veneto) $15. Hints of citrus and yeasty bread define the nose. Next in line is a simple, clean pear-and-white grapefruit palate. As for feel, it's a bit thick and creamy, while the finish is open and clean. Not overpowering but solid. **87** —*M.S. (6/1/2005)*

Bisol NV Jeio Brut Prosecco (Prosecco) $15. Crisp, clean, and correct—nothing more or less. The palate pumps pure tangerine and apple flavors on the heels of fine, inoffensive bubbles. Balanced and tasty, but nothing fancy. **87** —*M.S. (12/15/2005)*

Bisol 2004 Superiore di Cartizze Dry Prosecco (Prosecco Superiore di Cartizze) $44. Aromas of Golden Delicious apple, exotic fruit, and kiwi seem very ripe and sweet—almost too much of a good thing. There's a saccharine quality to the mouthfeel too that is countered by a crisp close. This is a slightly aged Prosecco, so you should expect the bigger, bolder style. **88** —*M.L. (6/1/2006)*

Bisol NV Vigneti del Fol Extra Dry Prosecco (Prosecco di Valdobbiadene) $NA. With white peach, honeydew, dried sage, and green herb notes, this is light and refreshing with attractive luminosity and effervescence. **87** — *M.L. (6/1/2006)*

BIXIO

Bixio 2000 Ripasso Red Blend (Valpolicella Classico Superiore) $17. A medium-weight wine, with flavors of dried fruit and coffee. Pleasant cherry and prune aromas also hint at lactic notes, while modest tannins and a slight chalkiness accent the finish. **86** —*J.C. (12/31/2004)*

BOCCADIGABBIA

Boccadigabbia 2001 Akronte Cabernet Sauvignon (Marche) $52. This is a delightfully chewy, extracted, and penetrating wine that oozes blackness: Black licorice, black fruit, resin, slate, charcoal, and chalkboard grow in intensity with each swirl. A very intense, modern wine that sees 18 months of oak aging for taut tannins and a supple, velvety mouthfeel. Would pair well with aged cheeses or grilled meats. **93 Editors' Choice** —*M.L. (9/1/2006)*

Boccadigabbia 2004 La Castelletta Pinot Grigio (Marche) $17. Elvidio Alessandri's 2004 Grigio has melon and poached pear over a nicely structured body. **87** —*M.L. (2/1/2006)*

Boccadigabbia 2003 La Castelletta Pinot Grigio (Marche) $17. One extra year of bottle aging has replaced the fruity aromas with rich honey, banana, and vanilla bean. If you are looking for freshness, go for the 2004 vintage; and the 2003 if you want a complex, creamier wine. **86** —*M.L. (2/1/2006)*

BOLLA

Bolla 2001 Cabernet Sauvignon (Delle Venezie) $9. The overall profile here is heavy, probably too heavy given the pedigree of fruit. The nose is a potent mix of herbal-influenced black fruit and leather, while the palate is equally overblown, offering only some nondescript bulky fruit. Modest tannins on the finish make it feel soft. **82** *(5/1/2003)*

Bolla 1999 Creso Cabernet Sauvignon (Delle Venezie) $27. The oak is so aggressive it's as if a tree trunk had been put through a chipper. That pounding wood is clearly masking average Cabernet fruit, fruit that's challenged to begin with in this region of Italy. If you like the side effects of oak, i.e., resin, clove, and vanilla, or if you're curious what oak tastes like on certain types of wine, then you can check it out here. **83** —*M.S. (12/15/2003)*

Bolla 1998 Creso Cabernet Sauvignon (Delle Venezie) $27. Modest cherry and earth aromas mingle with a strong oaky note. The wine feels good across the palate, although the fruit is a bit light for Cabernet. It's more dry and tart than you'd expect. The solid mouthfeel is its best attribute. **84** *(5/1/2003)*

Bolla 2001 Corvina (Amarone della Valpolicella Classico) $45. Fairly toasty, with charcoal, coconut, tobacco, and other firm, wood-driven aromas. Racy and tight on the palate, with cedar, raspberry, and chocolate flavors. Lean and clean would be the best way to describe it, and it seems as though it would go well with food, even now. **88** *(11/1/2005)*

Bolla 2002 Merlot (Delle Venezie) $9. Round and meaty, with brazen cherry, and raspberry flavors. It runs tart and lean, but it's largely a clean, lightly managed wine that flies comfortably below the fine-wine radar. **83** —*M.S. (12/15/2003)*

Bolla 2001 Merlot (Delle Venezie) $9. Light and vague aromas of leather, cherry, and wet rubber give way to flavors of sour cherries, plums, and bitter chocolate. The finish is like a confection; at one point it's tangy and tart, and then it veers toward the overly sweet. Fairly tart and hollow as a whole. **82** *(5/1/2003)*

Bolla 2000 Colforte Merlot (Delle Venezie) $15. More substantive than Bolla's standard Merlot, this wine starts off with meaty, soy aromas as well as notes of wood and milk chocolate. The palate is round, bordering on heavy. In terms of taste, coffee and chocolate surround and overwhelm what nondescript fruit there is. **83** *(5/1/2003)*

Bolla 2004 Nero d'Avola (Sicilia) $9. This wine has sweet cherry flavors, accented with toast and bacon fat notes. Tannins are soft, and there's an herbal note on the finish. Bring on the pasta. **87 Best Buy** —*M.L. (7/1/2006)*

Bolla 2004 Pinot Grigio (Delle Venezie) $9. One of Italy's most recognized names in wine delivers an easy, everyday wine with intense floral aromas and tutti-frutti cheer. In the mouth it is on the simple side, but it's totally quaffable. **85 Best Buy** —*M.L. (6/1/2006)*

Bolla 2001 Pinot Grigio (Delle Venezie) $8. Tired and fading, this wine's better days are already behind it. Stewed apples turn lemony on the finish. **81** —*J.C. (7/1/2003)*

Bolla 2001 Arcale Pinot Grigio (Collio) $10. Boasts some interesting flavors of graphite or slate, and mineral oil, which complement its pear and kumquat aromas. Could use more focus and length, but certainly pleasant; chilling it well will make it seem firmer. **84** —*J.C. (7/1/2003)*

Bolla 2002 Red Blend (Bardolino) $10. Very light and spread thin, with raspberry and burnt-sugar aromas, cranberry driven flavors, and nonexistent tannins. A flyweight from the shores of Lake Garda. **81** —*M.S. (12/15/2003)*

Bolla 2001 Red Blend (Bardolino) $10. This wine smells wet and rubbery, and there's a raw leathery aroma, too. Cherry and plum fruit tastes a bit musty. The finish is big and chewy, with some pop to it. **82** *(5/1/2003)*

Bolla 2001 Red Blend (Valpolicella) $9. Heavy tomato sauce aromas with some plum and cherry on the side. The palate is sweet and tastes of root beer and tomato. A round, earthy finish is what you're left with. **81** *(5/1/2003)*

Bolla 1999 Red Blend (Bardolino) $8. Light, lean, and leathery is how to best describe the nose. Some dried cherry and leafiness is front and center on the palate, and while the finish is clean and minty, it's also rather thin and acidic. **82** *(5/1/2003)*

Bolla 1999 Red Blend (Valpolicella) $9. 84 —*J.C. (12/31/2000)*

Bolla 1998 Red Blend (Valpolicella) $8. The brown/orange color and oxidized aromas do little to draw you in. The wine's consistency is watery while the fruit flavors are very light. What it does have is some dried cherry notes and decent acidity. **80** *(5/1/2003)*

Bolla 1997 Red Blend (Amarone della Valpolicella Classico) $50. Some almondy sweet scents are followed by leather and dry fruit. The feel across the palate is a bit sharp because of strong acidity, but some leathery, raisiny flavors provide balance. Then a bit of burnt sugar and chocolate add sweetness to the tannic finish. A good Amarone, but not seemingly for long-term keeping. **88** *(5/1/2003)*

Bolla 1996 Red Blend (Amarone della Valpolicella Classico) $50. 86 —*M.N. (12/31/2000)*

Bolla 1998 Le Poiane Red Blend (Valpolicella Classico) $15. Raisins, bacon, and pickle brine comprise the nose, which comes before a palate full of leathery dried cherry, anise, and tannins. This wine is thinner than many, with a fairly sharp and angular mouthfeel. **83** *(5/1/2003)*

Bolla 2002 White Blend (Soave) $9. Lime, citrus peel, and apricot aromas are nice. The apple, pineapple, and mango fruit is on the sweet side. Finishes gritty, ultra-sweet and heavy. **83** —*M.S. (10/1/2004)*

Bolla 2001 White Blend (Soave) $9. Light, with simple pineapple flavors. Hints of green tea enliven the nose, while the finish is clean and citrusy. **82** —*J.C. (7/1/2003)*

Bolla 2004 Grillo White Blend (Sicilia) $9. Bolla's Sicilian wines hit the right marks and this white version (85% Grillo and 15% Chard) is informal and easy to drink with a thick consistency, and loads of banana, pineapple, and exotic fruit. **86 Best Buy** —*M.L. (7/1/2006)*

Bolla 2000 Tufaie White Blend (Soave Classico Superiore) $8. A reasonably full-bodied Soave, with delicate aromas of acacia blossoms and limes giving way to sturdy pear flavors. The lemony finish will seem shrill to some, pleasantly cleansing to others. **84** —*J.C. (7/1/2003)*

BOLLINI

Bollini 2005 Pinot Grigio (Trentino) $14. Fresh, crisp mineral tones greet the nose, followed by floral notes and lush exotic fruit. The mineral tones are almost brackish in their intensity, which underlines this wine's excellent food pairing potential. Try with stir-fry. **88** —*M.L. (6/1/2006)*

Bollini 2004 Pinot Grigio (Trentino) $13. A gorgeous and opulent nose with honey, vanilla bean, ripe pineapple, and yellow roses. The mouth is unusually silky for the variety with baked apple and cinnamon over a medium finish. **89 Best Buy** —*M.L. (6/1/2006)*

ITALY

Bollini 1999 Pinot Grigio (Trentino) $11. There's not a lot of wine behind the mildly buttery, faint peach flavors and aromas. Tastes extremely soft and dilute. **80** —*J.F. (9/1/2001)*

Bollini 1998 Pinot Grigio (Trentino) $11. 87 *(8/1/1999)*

Bollini 2004 Reserve Selection Pinot Grigio (Friuli Grave) $18. A fuller, richer texture is embellished with mineral, stone fruit, melon, and some rubber notes. This is a solid, consistent Grigio with very tasty fruit flavors that could easily accompany a full meal from start to finish. **87** —*M.L. (6/1/2006)*

Bollini 2003 Reserve Selection Pinot Grigio (Friuli Grave) $13. Loaded with yellow fruit, dried herbs, almonds, and honey. But 2003 was a scorching hot vintage and you can detect a hint of jamminess buried beneath the surface. **86** —*M.L. (2/1/2006)*

BONFIGLIO

Bonfiglio 2001 Cabernet Sauvignon (Colli Bolognesi) $24. Imagine a spot of green, such as a fava bean, wrapped tight with aromas of leafy spinach, Indian spice, tree bark, tobacco, and plum and that's what is delivered beautifully to the nose. There is also a delicate balance of flavors in the mouth followed by dry, dusty tannins. **91 Editors' Choice** —*M.L. (9/1/2006)*

BOOTLEG

Bootleg 2004 Pinot Grigio (Venezie) $15. Citrus and lemon zest are a recurring theme on this pulpy, grapefruit-driven new release from Click Wines. It's light, fresh, and tangy, with only a modicum of depth. Inoffensive and snappy. **83** *(2/1/2006)*

Bootleg 2004 Sangiovese (Chianti) $15. More round and chunky than its same-class brethren, with earthy plum aromas. The palate leads with cherry and plum before dispensing cola. Very standard for Chianti but made well. **85** —*M.S. (10/1/2006)*

Bootleg 2003 Grande Tuscan Sangiovese (Tuscany) $20. Nice color and richness, but a bit over the top given that the bouquet is pure raisin and chocolate. Tilts the scale a bit to the heavy side, with black plum and berry flavors along with soft, wide tannins. Brushes the frontier of Port with its thickness. Ripeness is not lacking. **85** —*M.S. (9/1/2006)*

BORGO AL CASTELLO

Borgo al Castello 1999 Mother Zin Primitivo (Apulia) $11. Not a lot of structure, just sweet, dark cherry fruit for this Americanized wine. A good choice for a party or get-together with friends. **82** —*C.S. (5/1/2002)*

BORGO CONVENTI

Borgo Conventi 1997 Pinot Grigio (Collio) $22. 87 *(8/1/1999)*

Borgo Conventi 2002 I Fiori del Borgo Pinot Grigio (Collio) $NA. A fresh, ripe style of wine, with spice and roundness. It has crisp citrus flavors to give it a lively aftertaste. **86** —*R.V. (7/1/2003)*

Borgo Conventi 2002 Sauvignon Blanc (Collio) $15. The top cuvée of Sauvignon Blanc from the Borgo Conventi estate, now owned by Ruffino but still run by the Vescovo family. This is a huge, rich, forward style of Sauvignon, very ripe and tropical. Yet it has a layer of crisp, grassy fruit that gives it balance and poise. **91** —*R.V. (7/1/2003)*

Borgo Conventi 2002 I Fiori del Borgo Sauvignon Blanc (Collio) $15. Crisp, green, grassy wine with fresh acidity and herbeceous character. It is very New World with its tropical flavors and open, forward fruit. **88** —*R.V. (7/1/2003)*

BORGO DEI VASSALLI

Borgo dei Vassalli 2004 Pinot Grigio (Venezia Giulia) $10. A very pretty aromatic package with melon, pineapple, apple, and pear. Good, and not hugely complex, but definitely casual and approachable. **87 Best Buy** —*M.L. (6/1/2006)*

BORGO PRETALE

Borgo Pretale 1999 Sangiovese (Chianti Classico) $17. Long gone; nothing here but acid and tannin. Think old Rioja, but without any sweet, leathery complexity. **81** *(4/1/2005)*

Borgo Pretale 1998 Borgato Sangiovese (Colli della Toscana Centrale) $50. Surprising to see a '98 coming onto the market now, but the wine is fine, raring and ready to go. Cola, charcoal, and sliced lemon carry the nose into a tangy, cherry-laden palate. The finish is long and liqueur-like. Some gritty tannins call out for food. **89** —*M.S. (11/15/2004)*

Borgo Pretale 1999 Riserva Sangiovese (Chianti Classico) $22. Weedy and sour, with grapefruit-like aromas and flavors. Out of whack. **81** *(4/1/2005)*

Borgo Pretale 1998 Riserva Sangiovese (Chianti Classico) $22. Not sure why this wine outperforms the '99, but it does. The nose has some caramel and toffee, but also some leather and dried fruit. Snappy on the tongue, with light cherry and raspberry flavors. Drying but clean on the finish. **86** *(4/1/2005)*

BORGO SALCETINO

Borgo Salcetino 1998 Lucarello Riserva Red Blend (Chianti) $32. You had better be prepared for a blast of aromatic oak or this will disappoint. It's very woody, so much so that it smells of popcorn. Beneath the heavy veneer of wood is an intense, berry-packed palate. As might be expected, the finish is all vanilla and burnt nuts. Over time the stomping oak should calm down some, but probably never enough to become fully integrated. **85** —*M.S. (12/31/2002)*

Borgo Salcetino 2000 Sangiovese (Chianti Classico) $22. Aromas of leather and tar override the spicy fruit. In the mouth, raspberry and cherry flavors are forward and tight, propelled by generous acids and ample tannins. Ultimately kind of tart, hard, and basic. **84** —*M.S. (10/1/2004)*

Borgo Salcetino 1999 Sangiovese (Chianti Classico) $18. Lots of sulfur and gas at first. That's followed by grainy aromatic notes and modest raspberry and cherry fruit. Grippy tannins, a medium-weight palate, and some green notes keep it down. At moments it strives to impress, but at other times it simply fails to cut the mustard. **83** —*M.S. (11/15/2003)*

Borgo Salcetino 1998 Sangiovese (Chianti Classico) $17. After some rough front-end sulfur blew off, nice cherry fruit with dried spice accents showed. The profile is lean and dry, and there's length to the finish; also some biting tannins. **84** *(4/1/2001)*

Borgo Salcetino 1999 Lucarello Riserva Sangiovese (Chianti Classico) $40. Quite funky at first, with leather, earth, and a certain murkiness that blows off after airing. Features ample black plum and chocolate on the palate, with minty, herbal notes to the finish. Seems mildly overoaked. **87** —*M.S. (10/1/2004)*

Borgo Salcetino 1997 Lucarello Riserva Sangiovese (Chianti Classico) $33. This wine spends two years in barrique, and it shows in its strong cedar and coconut aromas. On the palate, there's sufficient fruit to stand up to the oak, with intense sour black cherries and leafy tobacco and mushroom flavors. Much better than a bottle reviewed in the April 2001 issue. **88** *(10/1/2001)*

Borgo Salcetino 1999 RosSole Sangiovese (Chianti) $28. The nose of this Sangiovese-Merlot is muscular and broad, with a hint of earth and mushroom sneaking in between the folds of deep red fruit. More robust fruit fills out the palate, while it finishes long and chocolaty, with notes of coffee. Quite sturdy and eminently satisfying. **91** —*M.S. (11/15/2003)*

Borgo Salcetino 1998 RosSole Sangiovese (Chianti) $16. The nose is charred and mildly funky. Even with time to air out it's still very oaky. The palate, meanwhile, is a bit bland despite the fact that it's packed with the flavor of wild berries. The finish is drying due to heavy tannins, and while it delivers a punch, there aren't any of the balancing nuances that could potentially make it more pleasing. **84** —*M.S. (12/31/2002)*

BORGO SAN DANIELE

Borgo San Daniele 2004 Pinot Grigio (Isonzo del Friuli) $24. Hold tight for a blast of peach, honeysuckle, and acacia. Fresh and compact in the mouth with both tartness and sweetness on the finish. **87** —*M.L. (2/1/2006)*

BORGO SCOPETO

Borgo Scopeto 1998 Red Blend (Chianti Classico) $20. The solid dark cherry fruit here bears a heavy mantle of oak, but the fruit core is dense

ITALY

and can handle it. Black cherry, plum, licorice, and toast work well on the full palate. Finishes tart and dry with good length and firm tannins. The oak works better here than in many examples. Drink now through 2004. **87** *(4/1/2001)*

Borgo Scopeto 2003 Sangiovese (Chianti Classico) $18. Round and ripe, with hints of almond candy, raisin, earth, and leather. The palate runs more savory than expected, with marinated notes to the cherry flavors that dominate. Finishes warm and a bit herbal, with medium tannins. Makes you smile more than sing. **87** —*M.S. (10/1/2006)*

Borgo Scopeto 2000 Sangiovese (Chianti Classico) $15. This is a supple, medium-weight wine filled with the flavors of Chianti: cherries, earth, and tobacco. If the tannins are suppler than most and the fruit a shade darker and riper, it's probably because of the heat of this vintage, but the wine retains a crisply acidic bite on the finish. **86** *(3/1/2005)*

Borgo Scopeto 2001 Borgonero Sangiovese (Toscana) $35. Leather, earth, and dried red fruits comprise a classic nose, while the meaty palate is both heavy and loaded with plum and raspberry. Quite chewy, with firm tannins, extract, and chocolaty accents. Mainstream qualities give it mass appeal. **89** —*M.S. (9/1/2006)*

Borgo Scopeto 1999 Borgonero Sangiovese (Toscana) $35. A blend of 60% Sangiovese, with the balance split evenly between Cabernet Sauvignon and Syrah, this is a smoky, meaty wine that's balanced by bright, red raspberry fruit. Tobacco notes take over on the long finish. Supple enough to drink now. **89** *(3/1/2005)*

Borgo Scopeto 1998 Borgonero Sangiovese (Toscana) $35. This nuovo mondo Super Tuscan represents the first vintage of Borgo Scopeto under the management of Tenuta Caparzo, and it has a tremendous jammy, extracted quality to it, from the smooth, deep plum and blackberry nose to the soft, rich palate that exudes tons of black cherry fruit along with coffee and licorice. It's a mix of 60% Sangiovese, 20% Cabernet Sauvignon, and 20% Syrah, and everything is working in unison. **93** —*M.S. (8/1/2002)*

Borgo Scopeto 1998 Misciano Riserva Sangiovese (Chianti Classico) $35. The label reads Chianti, but this is more about deep, driving black fruit than typically racy Sangiovese. It kicks off with the purest scent of smashed berries, and then offers up a super-charged black cherry-laden palate with far more hedonistic weight than starching acids. The wine finishes with power and warmth. **93** —*M.S. (8/1/2002)*

Borgo Scopeto 1999 Misciano Riserva Sangiovese (Chianti Classico) $35. A lush, medium-weight wine that shows some barrique influence in its aromas of vanilla, tobacco, smoke, and bacon. Soft and chewy on the finish, this is approachable now, but should be more food-friendly in a year or two. **90** *(3/1/2005)*

Borgo Scopeto 2001 Riserva Sangiovese (Chianti Classico) $29. Potent up front, with aromas of Boston baked beans, dry red fruit, leather, and charcoal. Medium in the mouth, with cherry and plum floating on a classic structure of bright acids and robust tannins. Finishes lithe and fresh, with a shot of tomato and leather. **88** —*M.S. (10/1/2006)*

Borgo Scopeto 1999 Riserva Sangiovese (Chianti Classico) $21. Combines tobacco and earth aromas and flavors in a smooth, supple package. Black cherry fruit dominates the midpalate, while firm acids, tannins, and iron-like minerality grab the finish. Try again in two years. **88** *(3/1/2005)*

Borgo Scopeto 1998 Riserva Sangiovese (Chianti Classico) $28. Fantastic modern Chianti! Young but already exuding powerful berry fruit along with loads of cigar box and other attractive spices. The present tense of this wine is all about layered, climbing complexity. Its future is all but ensured, with its tight core, solid wall of tannins, and a deep, black cherry finish that lasts a good two minutes. **92** —*M.S. (8/1/2002)*

BORGOGNO
Borgogno 1993 Sangiovese (Barolo) $29. 90 —*M.G. (5/1/1999)*

BOROLI
Boroli 1998 Nebbiolo (Barolo) $38. This well-priced offering got off to a slow start in our tasting. Gradually it opened up to reveal lots of oak influence—toast, vanilla, maple syrup, and even some dill. But what really impressed were flavors of black cherries and tar that glided across the palate upon masses of soft, enveloping tannins. **91** *(4/2/2004)*

BORTOLOMIOL
Bortolomiol NV Alta Badia Riserva Speciale Extra Dry Prosecco (Veneto) $12. Honeysuckle and a cinnamon-cookie dough quality on the nose is accented by peach, pear, and apricot. A touch sour in the mouth, with soothing silk finesse. This is a special anniversary bottling that may be hard to find. **89** —*M.L. (6/1/2006)*

Bortolomiol 2005 Cartizze Prosecco (Prosecco Superiore di Cartizze) $33. Seductively feminine and floral, laced with jasmine and field flowers, with notes of banana nut bread, almond, and refined mineral tones. Creamy, fluffy, and filling in the mouth, with fruit flavors and a crisp close. **91** —*M.L. (6/1/2006)*

Bortolomiol 2005 Millesimato Selezione Banda Rossa Prosecco (Prosecco di Valdobbiadene) $19. A vintage-dated Prosecco with a festive, bubbly character and lemon-lime, peach juice, and melon overtones. Loads of zest in the mouth backed by a polished mineral flavor and more stone fruit. **89** —*M.L. (6/1/2006)*

Bortolomiol NV Prior Brut Prosecco (Prosecco di Valdobbiadene) $17. Very frothy, with thick, creamy mousse and aromas that include wildflower, fresh grass, mineral, and new rubber. Fresh and smooth in the mouth. **86** —*M.L. (6/1/2006)*

Bortolomiol NV Senior Extra Dry Prosecco (Prosecco di Valdobbiadene) $17. Full and floral, with good intensity and a very friendly and approachable style. This is what Prosecco is all about: a fun, quaffable wine that leaves your palate clean and revitalized. **87** —*M.L. (6/1/2006)*

BORTOLOTTI
Bortolotti NV Cartizze Dry Prosecco (Prosecco Superiore di Cartizze) $28. Green notes such as Granny Smith apple, lime, and even fresh pea pods are emphasized by a lingering, dusty-chalk quality. Full and creamy in the mouth with a distant hint of sweetness, this is a flavorful, satisfying and highly recommended Prosecco. A by Marc de Grazia Selection, various U.S. importers. **89** —*M.L. (6/1/2006)*

Bortolotti NV Brut Sparkling Blend (Prosecco di Valdobbiadene) $16. Here's a wine with loads of citrus, yellow fruit, pineapple, and Granny Smith apple. Rich banana and peach compliment a clean mouthfeel with snappy acidity and a dry finish. **87** —*M.L. (6/1/2006)*

Bortolotti NV Extra Dry Selezione Sparkling Blend (Prosecco di Valdobbiadene) $19. A different Prosecco with unexpected aromas of yellow rose, honeysuckle, and beeswax. Intense and persuasive with a frothy, creamy feel and tart acidity at the close. Made from 90% Prosecco and 10% Chardonnay. **87** —*M.L. (6/1/2006)*

BORTOLUSSO
Bortolusso 2004 Pinot Grigio (Friuli) $15. Banana, pineapple, and honeysuckle are vivid and expressive and follow through to the mouth, where the wine exhibits a lean, crisp consistency. **89** —*M.L. (2/1/2006)*

BORTOLUZZI
Bortoluzzi 2002 Chardonnay (Isonzo del Friuli) $17. Buttery and lactic on the nose, but lean and focused on the palate, this is an interesting study in contrasts between lemon and pear fruit on one hand and toasty, popcorn-like notes on the other. **85** —*J.C. (12/31/2004)*

Bortoluzzi 2001 Chardonnay (Isonzo del Friuli) $15. The peach flavors are pleasant enough, but even a slight spritz can't save this wine from seeming heavy and clumsy. **82** —*J.C. (7/1/2003)*

Bortoluzzi 2005 Pinot Grigio (Venezia Giulia) $17. Deep floral aromas are enhanced by traces of minerality and lavender-scented candle. This is a very likeable, clean, and polished Grigio with full apricot and peach flavors. **87** —*M.L. (6/1/2006)*

Bortoluzzi 2004 Pinot Grigio (Venezia Giulia) $17. Here's a Pinot Grigio with fruit selected from five different vineyards in Friuli's Gradisca d'Isonzo area. Three of the sites render fruit used as the wine's backbone and the remaining sites render fruit with more delicate aromas of dried hay, vanilla bean, and dried lemon rind. **87** —*M.L. (6/1/2006)*

Bortoluzzi 2001 Pinot Grigio (Isonzo del Friuli) $15. An open-knit, friendly nose features lots of nectarine and ripe apple scents. Medium-weight,

ITALY

with plenty of stone fruit on the palate, it finishes with a cleansing burst of peppery spice. Try as an apéritif. **87** —*J.C. (7/1/2003)*

Bortoluzzi 1997 Pinot Grigio (Isonzo del Friuli) $13. 82 *(8/1/1999)*

BOSCAINI

Boscaini 1996 Amarone Marano Corvina (Valpolicella) $35. 87 —*J.C. (9/1/2000)*

Boscaini 1999 La Cros Pinot Grigio (Valdadige) $12. 86 —*J.C. (9/1/2000)*

Boscaini 1993 Ca' de Loi Red Blend (Amarone della Valpolicella Classico) $52. Rich texture and extraction mark this full-bodied red. There are cherry, brown sugar, and chocolate flavors, along with a smoky note and a heady dose of alcohol. It stays in balance, though, and the whole thing comes together in a long, sweet finish. **90** —*J.F. (9/1/2001)*

BOSCARELLI

Boscarelli 2002 Sangiovese (Vino Nobile di Montepulciano) $33. Sharp on the nose, with background aromas of cola, cedar, and plum. Fairly tight and oaky on the palate, with a shot of lemon supporting plum and berry flavors. Sizable and solid, with some spice and red pepper on the finish. **86** —*M.S. (7/1/2005)*

Boscarelli 1999 Sangiovese (Vino Nobile di Montepulciano) $68. Lush and deep to the nose, with clove, chocolate, and pure potting soil. Elaborate in the mouth, with plum and coffee flavors. It's a touch hard at the end, but also intense. Tight, firm, tannic, yet aromatic and tasty. **90** —*M.S. (11/15/2003)*

Boscarelli 1994 Sangiovese (Vino Nobile di Montepulciano) $18. 87 — *M.M. (5/1/1999)*

Boscarelli 1999 35 Anni Sangiovese (Toscana) $51. Round and beautifully fragrant, with smoky nuances atop defined, elegant black fruit. What a stud this wine is; the palate is perfectly ripe, with a touch of oaky vanilla supporting first-class red and black fruits. The finish is clean, smooth, and pleasant. It's a stellar Super Tuscan, a leader in its field for sure. And it gets better every minute the bottle is open. **94 Editors' Choice** —*M.S. (11/15/2003)*

Boscarelli 2001 Nocio dei Boscarelli Sangiovese (Vino Nobile di Montepulciano) $69. Tight and pure, with mineral and charred oak dominating the pulsating nose. From a great vintage, this is like a baby just out of diapers. Now it's oaky, but there's also a boatload of raspberry, cherry, and plum waiting to take over. Best to cellar until 2008 so that the fruit and wood will be perfectly integrated. **92 Cellar Selection** — *M.S. (7/1/2005)*

Boscarelli 1999 Rosso Sangiovese (Toscana) $67. Intensely aromatic, this wine boasts strong hints of leather, smoke, and herbs. The palate is extremely tight and tannic, with cherry, raspberry and smoked meat flavors. Talk about a full and tannic finish; this has that and more as it almost seems to be bearing teeth. This muscular red surely needs some cellar time. Revisit it in about three years. **89** —*M.S. (12/31/2002)*

Boscarelli 1996 Vino Nobile Di Montepulciano Sangiovese (Toscana) $27. 85 —*M.S. (7/1/2000)*

BOSCO DEL MERLO

Bosco del Merlo 2004 Pinot Grigio (Lison-Pramaggiore) $16. There's a touch of something earthy, like straw or dried herbs, that underscores the overall dryness of this wine. In the mouth, there's a touch of sudden sourness with exotic fruit on the finish. **86** —*M.L. (2/1/2006)*

BOTROMAGNO

Botromagno 1999 Apulian Zinfandel Primitivo (Puglia) $10. The label says "Apulian Zinfandel" for American enthusiasts who don't know that Primitivo is Zin's cousin. Though a good quaffer, this bears little resemblance to big West Coast-style Zins. Black berry fruit comes through, albeit with little intensity, on the nose. Black plum and chalky, gritty tannins in the mouth lead to more plum-skin flavors, plus a metallic streak, on the finish. **84** —*C.S. (5/1/2002)*

Botromagno 2004 Gravina White Blend (Puglia) $10. A 60% Greco and 40% Malvasia blend from a surreal part of Puglia with long horizons and whole towns buried within deep ravines. Offers some buttery popcorn and peach and lots of yellow floral tones, like acacia. Nice tart finish. **87 Best Buy** —*M.L. (9/1/2005)*

Botromagno 2000 Gravina White Blend (Apulia) $9. Named for the town in Apulia from which it comes, this wine mixes Greco di Tufo and Malvasia. Apple, pear, cinnamon, and floral elements combine on the nose. On the palate, there is solid weight, tangy acidity, and a velvety texture. The finish persists with apple and cinnamon presiding. Would go well with shellfish. **88 Best Buy** —*M.N. (9/1/2001)*

Botromagno 2000 Passito di Malvasia Gravisano White Blend (Puglia) $30. Toasted walnuts, almond paste, and dried fruit merge nicely, leaving a velvety smooth trail in the mouth. This wine is a powerhouse despite the higher sugar content, which should soften the effects of 15% alcohol. **88** —*M.L. (10/1/2006)*

BOTTEGA VINAIA

Bottega Vinaia 2001 Chardonnay (Trentino) $20. Only 30% is barrel-fermented in French oak, the rest in stainless steel, so the wood component is understated, allowing lush pineapple and pear fruit to shine on the midpalate. Dried spices (clove and cinnamon) become more apparent on the finish, while the fruit fades away. **87** *(4/1/2004)*

Bottega Vinaia 2003 Lagrein (Trentino) $19. True to the variety, this wine opens with forest, anise, and menthol-infused freshness backed by more subtle nutmeg and vanilla coffee. A bit shallow in the mouth, but the spice lingers for a long time. **86** —*M.L. (9/1/2005)*

Bottega Vinaia 2002 Lagrein (Trentino) $21. This is a big comedown after the stellar 2000 (we never received samples of the 2001), but still a solid effort. It shows earth and cassis flavors, relatively light weight on the palate, and a crisp, herbal finish. **85** —*J.C. (12/31/2004)*

Bottega Vinaia 2000 Lagrein (Trentino) $21. The pick of the litter is this offering from the indigenous Lagrein grape, which is sometimes compared to Syrah. Floral notes add elegance to lush blackberry and blueberry fruit, finishing long and spicy, with a touch of vanilla. **90 Editors' Choice** *(4/1/2004)*

Bottega Vinaia 2000 Merlot (Trentino) $21. Plummy and chocolaty on the nose, with herbal notes that seem to grow stronger the longer the wine sits in the glass. It's structured and quite firm in the mouth, picking up increasing amounts of dried basil on the finish. **87** *(4/1/2004)*

Bottega Vinaia 2005 Pinot Grigio (Trentino) $18. Smooth, silky, and suggestively redolent of banana, yellow fruit, and white stone. There's a unique roundness or velvetiness to this wine, but also fruity freshness and playful youthfulness. Very food friendly. **88** —*M.L. (6/1/2006)*

Bottega Vinaia 2004 Pinot Grigio (Trentino) $18. A landmark Italian Grigio that has set the bar for dozens of other imports, and for good reason: This wine is packed tight with pear, peach, almond skin, and a touch of lemon zest. Compact and consistent in the mouth, and a great match for bouillabaisse. **87** —*M.L. (6/1/2006)*

Bottega Vinaia 2003 Pinot Grigio (Trentino) $20. This fruity and admittedly somewhat simple wine is nevertheless very clean and fresh, with finely etched flavors of pear and pineapple sharpened on the finish by a touch of citrus. A versatile white, made to stand alone or pair with white meats or fish. **86** —*J.C. (12/31/2004)*

Bottega Vinaia 2002 Pinot Grigio (Trentino) $20. A distinct step up from many Pinot Grigios, with floral and herbal nuances layered over a fresh-fruit core of peaches, pears, and white-fleshed melons. Tangerine and anise notes give a lift to the finish. **87** *(4/1/2004)*

Bottega Vinaia 2001 Pinot Noir (Trentino) $21. Boasts attractive aromas of cinnamon and clove, cherry and beet root, but comes across as light and lacking concentration on the palate. Winemaker Martini reports that experiments with open-top fermenters "are encouraging," which bodes well for future vintages. **84** *(4/1/2004)*

Bottega Vinaia 2002 Teroldego (Rotaliano) $21. This exuberantly fruity wine boasts super-ripe, candied fruit aromas, smoke and vanilla from oak aging and a fun, bouncy personality. Blackberry and black cherry fruit finishes tart and "crunchy," showing great freshness. **86** —*J.C. (12/31/2004)*

Bottega Vinaia 2003 Teroldego Rotaliano (Trentino) $19. The torrid 2003 heat helped shape a generously fruity wine with wild berry, red rose petal, and lots of nut, leather, and vanilla from six months of oak aging. Has rock-solid tannic structure and a zesty finish. Grapes come from a tiny triangle of land at the foot of the Dolomites. **88** —*M.L. (9/1/2005)*

BRAIDA DI GIACOMO BOLOGNA

Braida di Giacomo Bologna 2004 Vigna Senza Nome Moscato (Moscato d'Asti) $16. Honey and peach fills the mouth and is backed by lemon blossom, mineral, and chalky notes, apricot and a distant dairy smell that blows off after a few swirls. A pleasant touch of acidity at the rear keeps the wine's floral freshness intact in the mouth. **88** —*M.L. (12/15/2005)*

BRANCAIA

Brancaia 2002 Sangiovese (Chianti Classico) $32. Seriously well-made, with a few years of cellar potential. The nose is rich and full, displaying molasses, coffee, bacon, and cedar. Fine fruit on the palate, especially black plum. Long on the finish, with vanilla, marzipan, espresso, and earth notes. Excellent balance, with tannins that show themselves before disappearing into the woodwork. **91 Editors' Choice** *(4/1/2005)*

Brancaia 2001 Sangiovese (Chianti Classico) $32. Big, bold, and boisterous, with deep fruit, lots of oak, and plenty of heft. The palate is loaded with black cherry and chocolate, while the finish settles down and fades away with subtlety and smoothness. Quite evolved and forward. A fine modern-style Chianti. **90** —*M.S. (10/1/2004)*

Brancaia 2000 Sangiovese (Chianti Classico) $30. Big and bold, with overt barrique qualities manifested on the nose and palate. Aromas of ink, leather, maple, and leather draw you in, and once in you'll find cassis, prune, blackberry, and bitter chocolate. Heavy tannins create a starchy mouthfeel that begs for food. **90** —*M.S. (11/15/2003)*

Brancaia 2001 Il Blu Sangiovese (Toscana) $72. This wine has great potential among casual drinkers. It's inky black, with a deep, charred nose that frames dark fruit and new oak. The palate is forward and lively, with blackberry and cola. Finishes clean and fairly short despite its immense color and size. **88** —*M.S. (10/1/2004)*

BRESSAN

Bressan 2003 Pinot Grigio (Venezia Giulia) $40. Amidst the sea of copycat Grigios one exception stands out. It starts with a deep golden color and a nose ripe with toasted almond, pine box, caramel, and maple syrup. Compactly structured, smooth and silky with lingering spice from barrel aging. **93 Editors' Choice** —*M.L. (2/1/2006)*

BRIGALDARA

Brigaldara 2000 Red Blend (Amarone della Valpolicella Classico) $65. Two of our reviewers zeroed in on the wine's volatility, noting apple skin and nail polish aromas. But our third sampler found sweet, almondy scents and easygoing cherry and plum characteristics. A wine of no consensus: two-thirds of the camp found it lean and just acceptable; the other third liked it significantly more. **85** *(11/1/2005)*

BROGAL VINI

Brogal Vini 2001 Antigniano Sagrantino (Montefalco) $16. A dark, brooding beast with tar, coffee, and some barnyard. You can tell this is a big wine by the way it sits determined in your glass. The tannins will rip through your mouth like an 18-wheeler in the fast lane. Matured,18 months in French oak, a few more years of cellar aging should soften it up. **87** —*M.L. (9/1/2005)*

BRUNO FRANCO

Bruno Franco 2000 Barbera (Barbera d'Alba) $NA. Stale and lacking charm. Peppery and loaded with mid-level fruit. A bit green as well. **80** —*M.S. (12/15/2003)*

Bruno Franco 2000 Nebbiolo (Nebbiolo d'Alba) $NA. Leathery and funky at first, with mute dried fruit. When it opens, cherry and raspberry appear along with chunky tannins that turn bitter. A bit fatter than some; it has modest berry richness, but it's unfocused. **83** —*M.S. (12/15/2003)*

BRUNO GIACOSA

Bruno Giacosa 1997 Barbera (Barbera d'Alba) $20. 87 *(4/1/2000)*

Bruno Giacosa 1996 Dino Nero Spumante Champagne Blend (Piedmont) $36. 90 —*P.G. (12/15/2000)*

Bruno Giacosa 1994 Extra Champagne Blend (Piedmont) $38. 91 —*E.M. (11/15/1999)*

Bruno Giacosa 1997 Falletto di Serralunga Dolcetto (Dolcetto d'Alba) $19. 80 *(4/1/2000)*

Bruno Giacosa 1999 Nebbiolo (Barbaresco) $95. Starts off with leather and dried fruit aromas, but they are unusually delicate and floral as well. The feel of the wine is lacy, yet firm, a spider's web that lures you in to explore the depths of its complexity. Overall, it's a little light, but wonderfully complex and fragrant. 90 *(4/2/2004)*

Bruno Giacosa 1999 Falletto Nebbiolo (Barolo) $155. Big-boned but not showing much flesh, this wine didn't appear to be at its best when we tasted it, yet it was still impressive. Scents of rubber, tar, and prunes, flavors of red berries and cherry tomatoes. Long finish that builds in intensity is a positive sign for aging. Anticipated maturity: 2012–2020. 88 *(4/2/2004)*

Bruno Giacosa 1999 Le Rocche del Falletto Nebbiolo (Barolo) $175. It seems Giacosa's wines are often difficult to taste young, which leads us to wonder later whether we haven't underestimated them. Relatively unexpressive on the nose, this wine reveals only hints of leather, cherries, and citrus peel. But in the mouth, the quality is evidenced by a gradual building of intensity to a crescendo on the finish, where dried cherries, underbrush, mushroom, leather, and citrus explode into dazzling length and intensity. **93 Cellar Selection** *(4/2/2004)*

Bruno Giacosa 1999 Santo Stefano Nebbiolo (Barbaresco) $160. After this wine's identity was revealed, we naturally wondered if we hadn't underrated it. It ranks among the best of the Barbarescos, but not at the very top as we had expected. Leather, Asian spices, and citrus peel, anise and dried cherries provide remarkable complexity and mouth-filling flavors without ever seeming overdone. Tannins cut short the finish, but they're chewy and rich, and will support this wine's growth for decades to come. 91 *(4/2/2004)*

Bruno Giacosa 2000 Extra Brut Pinot Nero (Piedmont) $38. Known for his prize-winning Barbaresco and Barolo, Giacosa pulls off a surprise hit with his Pinot Noir-based sparkler. The aromas are more floral and a citrus backbone yields an overall sensation of freshness. A little-known wine definitely worth discovering. 90 —*M.L. (12/15/2004)*

BRUNO NICODEMI

Bruno Nicodemi 1998 Colline Teramane Riserva Montepulciano (Abruzzo) $23. Saturated and inky, with smoky, rustic notes that go green with airing. The palate kicks at first, delivering berry and plum fruit. But the flavors fade as the wine opens. What's left is a touch of green and a lack of persistence. Still, with a toasty, warm finish, it's quite adequate. 85 —*M.S. (11/15/2003)*

Bruno Nicodemi 1997 Dei Colli Venia Red Blend (Montepulciano d'Abruzzo) $11. Green peppercorn and olive along with black cherry, soy, and licorice aromas offer unexpected complexity on the nose of this Italian red. Also a nice surprise is the roundness and balance of this good value wine that shows cassis, green olive, and anise flavors. **87 Best Buy** —*J.F. (9/1/2001)*

BRUNO ROCCA

Bruno Rocca 1997 Barbera (Barbera d'Alba) $32. 85 *(4/1/2000)*

Bruno Rocca 2000 Barbera (Barbera d'Alba) $45. Ripe and rocking, with huge extract and aromas of bacon, black cherry and fine-grained oak. What a specimen this is; the palate blasts with blackberry and spiced meat, while the finish comes on like a freight train. Notes of jerky, leather, and bitter chocolate add grit to the pure fruit that defines this wine. 91 —*M.S. (12/15/2003)*

Bruno Rocca 1999 Estate Bottled Barbera (Barbera d'Alba) $40. The cherry, leather and nut aromas are soft, steady, and attractive. Bright cherry flavors with leathery undertones and a hint of coffee grace the palate. The finish is warm and spicy, with ample late-hitting power. It's refined and

ITALY

ITALY

confident at all points, a winner that's on target and one that will go well with pasta and meat dishes. **90** —*M.S. (11/15/2002)*

Bruno Rocca 1999 Coparossa Nebbiolo (Barbaresco) $85. 90 *(4/2/2003)*

Bruno Rocca 1996 Coparossa Nebbiolo (Barbaresco) $60. 89 —*J.C. (9/1/2000)*

Bruno Rocca 1998 Coparossa Estate Bottled Nebbiolo (Barbaresco) $42. The sweet nose offers a mix of cola, root beer, and orange peel, while the palate is quite ripe—there's a layer of rich black plum before a drying apple skin finish. This seems like the type of wine to drink now as your more structured reds age. For Barbaresco, it's actually rather soft, chunky, and easy going. **90** —*M.S. (11/15/2002)*

Bruno Rocca 1999 Rabajà Nebbiolo (Barbaresco) $85. Extraordinary stuff. The aromas practically defy description, packed with smoke, tobacco, cigar box, and cured meat, all wrapped around a deep, rich core of black cherries. Picks up even more complexity in the mouth, adding vanilla, plums, and dates in an expansive, mouth-filling experience, then— wham—the tannins hit home, sending you reeling and wondering when this wine will finally blossom. Great now, great 20 years from now. **95** Editors' Choice *(4/2/2004)*

Bruno Rocca 1996 Rabaja Red Blend (Barbaresco) $62. 88 —*M.S. (7/1/2000)*

BUCCI

Bucci 2003 Pongelli Red Blend (Rosso Piceno) $21. This 50-50 blend of Montepulciano and Sangiovese shows some Middle Eastern spice aromas as well as a leafy side that conjures aromas of lettuce and spinach. Fruity enough, with cherry, red licorice candy, and carob on the palate. Gets better as it opens; drink earlier rather than later. **86** —*M.S. (10/1/2006)*

Bucci 2002 Pongelli Red Blend (Rosso Piceno) $19. This 50-50 blend of Montepulciano and Sangiovese is fresh like sorbet but also sweet like a lollipop. Open red fruit greets you, followed by candied cherry and raspberry flavors. Zesty but a little sugary on the finish. **84** —*M.S. (6/1/2005)*

Bucci 2004 Verdicchio (Verdicchio dei Castelli di Jesi Classico Superiore) $21. After a couple of tough vintages, this Verdicchio is back in form in 2004. Apple, melon, almond, and vanilla work the nose, followed by a balanced but acidic palate pushing cider and orange peel. Finishes a touch pithy, with cleansing sharpness. **87** —*M.S. (10/1/2006)*

Bucci 2002 Verdicchio (Verdicchio dei Castelli di Jesi Classico Superiore) $19. Young and simple, with basic mineral and citrus notes. The taste profile is tangy, with good but pedestrian pineapple and orange flavors. The finish is long and solid, but again, pedestrian. **86** —*M.S. (8/1/2004)*

Bucci 1997 Verdicchio (Verdicchio dei Castelli di Jesi Classico) $16. 85 *(11/1/1999)*

Bucci 2000 Villa Bucci Riserva Verdicchio (Verdicchio dei Castelli di Jesi) $35. While it seems a bit mute and distant at first, time opens it, allowing clean, refined citrus and vanilla flavors to pour forth. This is a reserved riserva, a wine that charms but doesn't overwhelm. It's focused and dishes light but refreshing lemon-lime and mineral. **87** —*M.S. (8/1/2004)*

Bucci 1994 Villa Bucci Riserva Verdicchio (Verdicchio dei Castelli di Jesi Classico) $22. 88 *(11/1/1999)*

BURCHINO

Burchino 2002 Sangiovese (Chianti Superiore) $13. It has been years since we reviewed Burchino, and it's more or less the same wine now that it was in 1997. The nose offers light fruit and cinnamon shadings, which sit in front of strawberry and plum flavors. The finish may be a touch raw and grabby, but as a whole it's snappy enough to stay the course. **86** —*M.S. (10/1/2006)*

Burchino 2001 Sangiovese (Chianti Superiore) $13. Tart if not fully sharp. A lot of citrus and red fruit on the palate, which may be good for some and too raw for others. One of our panelists even called this a "sourball." Another liked the snappy berry character. **84** *(4/1/2005)*

Burchino 1999 Sangiovese (Chianti Superiore) $13. The opening aromas are not terribly concentrated or rich; they're more like field scents backed by mild red fruit. Thin raspberry flavors run the palate prior to a dry,

light finish with some dried and bitter cherry flavors. Simple. **84** —*M.S. (12/31/2002)*

Burchino 1997 Sangiovese (Chianti Superiore) $15. This smooth, balanced offering shows plenty of cherry, leather, and cedar flavors. The round mouthfeel and the licorice and toast flavors on the palate are wrapped around ripe, almost candied fruit. Oak is present but there's enough fruit to support it. A likeable wine to drink now. **87** *(4/1/2001)*

Burchino 2003 Genius Loci Sangiovese (Toscana) $26. Dark and tight, with toasted, masculine aromas that hint at barrique aging. The palate is serious and firm as it houses dark berry and plum flavors along with chocolate and smoke. A forward wine that should please most fans of Tuscan Sangiovese. **90** —*M.S. (9/1/2006)*

Burchino 1999 Genius Loci Sangiovese (Toscana) $17. The charred aromas are much like sniffing a match stick. That same piercing woodiness rides high on the palate along with cherries, berries, and licorice. The finish is plowed over with buttery oak—you can taste it clear as day. The texture, meanwhile, is firm and not easily penetrable. **85** —*M.S. (12/31/2002)*

BUSSIA SOPRANA

Bussia Soprana 2000 Dolcetto (Dolcetto d'Alba) $18. Aromas of tobacco, burnt toast, and roasted sesame seeds make it hard to peg, and nothing on the palate brings this wine into clearer focus. It's chewy and dry, but with fairly thin rhubarb fruit. Not overly bad but not terribly charming. **83** —*M.S. (12/15/2003)*

Bussia Soprana 1998 Nebbiolo (Barolo) $55. This medium-weight wine exhibits a ripe, creamy texture and fine aromatics of smoke, citrus rind, and tea. Dried cherries and peaches chime in on the palate, but the wine finishes too swiftly to rate higher. Drink now–2015. **88** *(4/2/2004)*

Bussia Soprana 1997 Bussia Nebbiolo (Barolo) $70. Dryness is the dominant character of this wine. Aromas of charred wood, toast, and sandalwood are more prominent than plum tomatoes. To taste, it is tough and slightly lean, but there are also red berries and herbs. Wood comes back to dominate the aftertaste, along with acidity. Will this age? It should, but it needs at least 10 years. **87** —*R.V. (11/15/2002)*

Bussia Soprana 1997 Moscani Nebbiolo (Barolo) $76. Solid and chunky, this wine is extra dry at this stage in its life. Tannins pile upon tannins, submerging the fruit flavors of strawberries and cherries as well as those of tobacco and spice. The aftertaste is slightly astringent, but if those tannins soften, it should be a serious long-term wine. **88** —*R.V. (11/15/2002)*

Bussia Soprana 1998 Mosconi Nebbiolo (Barolo) $68. This Barolo is a bit light in weight, but elegant and complex, prettily combining leather, dried orange peel, cured meat, and floral notes. Finishes dry and tannic, so revisit it in 10 years. **89** *(4/2/2004)*

Bussia Soprana 1998 Vigna Colonnello Nebbiolo (Barolo) $68. Complex on the nose, with leafy, herbal notes mixing with the sweetness of dried fruit and caramel, and turning horsey and leathery, after a short time in the glass. Flavors focus on prunes, leather and tar, picking up hints of orange peel on the relatively short finish. **87** *(4/2/2004)*

Bussia Soprana 2001 Vigne del Rio White Blend (Piedmont) $23. A little soft, but on the whole, it's a pretty nice wine. Applesauce and ripe melon aromas precede a palate that features full pear and honeydew flavors. Quite smooth and succulent on the finish, although maybe a touch mushy and low on acidity. Drink immediately for best results. **87** —*M.S. (12/15/2003)*

CÀ DEL SARTO

Cà del Sarto 2004 Pinot Grigio (Friuli Grave) $13. The nose certainly doesn't grab out at you but it does deliver delicate floral notes, almond paste, and ladies' hand cream-like aromas. Because it appears a bit heavy in the mouth, it calls for tart foods such as endive salad with mustard-balsamic vinegar vinaigrette. **84** —*M.L. (6/1/2006)*

CA' BERTOLDI

Ca' Bertoldi 1998 Red Blend (Amarone della Valpolicella) $30. More red than brick in color, with light, distant fruit aromas and touches of citrus peel, leather, and a smidgen of acetone. Black cherry, fairly sweet in stature, carries the palate, while the tail end is based on dark chocolate, coffee, and roasted meats. Sturdy and structured. **89** *(11/1/2005)*

CA' BIANCA

Ca' Bianca 2002 Barbera (Barbera d'Asti) $14. This oak-influenced Barbera manages to nicely integrate the tartness of fresh fruit with the vanilla and spices imparted by oak aging. Cherries mingle with cinnamon, clove, and vanilla, with a proper amount of acidity on the finish. Decent value, too. **88** —*J.C. (11/15/2004)*

Ca' Bianca 2001 Barbera (Barbera d'Asti) $15. Aromas of leather, oregano, and barnyard along with sour red fruit flavors are not impressive. Barely makes the cut. **80** —*M.S. (12/15/2003)*

Ca' Bianca 2000 Cortese (Gavi) $13. Gold in color, and rich in the nose, with apple and custard. More apple appears on the palate, where it's joined by lemon. A warm and big finish with ample spice pushes the wine toward chunky and high strung. **84** —*M.S. (12/15/2003)*

Ca' Bianca 1995 Nebbiolo (Barolo) $35. **92** *(7/1/2000)*

Ca' Bianca 1999 Nebbiolo (Barolo) $36. Scents of mint and sweet hay give this wine's flavors a slightly greenish cast, without obliterating the sturdy dried fig and cherry flavors. Features a supple, evolved mouthfeel that makes it approachable now. Anticipated maturity: 2006–2012. **86** *(4/2/2004)*

Ca' Bianca 1998 Nebbiolo (Barolo) $42. Lush and already approachable, this wine blends cherries, chocolate, and nougat into a supple whole that's more than the sum of its parts. Drink now–2010. **90** *(4/2/2004)*

Ca' Bianca 1997 Nebbiolo (Barbaresco) $33. Very ripe, with aromas of milk chocolate and molasses. The palate seems heavy, but despite such weight it offers some nice plum and berry flavors. The only problem here is mouthfeel: The wine seems on the heavy side, possibly a bit over-ripe in what was a very ripe and forward vintage. And ultimately the finish has no staying power. **86** —*M.S. (11/15/2002)*

CA' BOLANI

Ca' Bolani 2005 Pinot Grigio (Friuli Aquileia) $10. A mineral-driven, crisp white with crushed stone and talc powder backed by garden greens, stone fruit, and melon. Zesty and palate-cleansing, with sour grapefruit on the finale. **86 Best Buy** —*M.L. (6/1/2006)*

Ca' Bolani 2004 Pinot Grigio (Friuli Aquileia) $11. An uncomplicated and easy wine with lemon candy drops, pineapple, lemongrass, and a generally crisp and clean nose. There's a fat feeling in the mouth. **86 Best Buy** —*M.L. (2/1/2006)*

Ca' Bolani 2002 Pinot Grigio (Friuli Aquileia) $10. Simple, attractive, crisp wine, with a pleasant depth of flavor. It has fresh fruit, a light toast touch, and soft acidity. **85** —*R.V. (7/1/2003)*

Ca' Bolani 2000 Aquileia Pinot Grigio (Friuli Aquileia) $15. **86** *(12/31/2002)*

Ca' Bolani 2002 Traminer (Friuli Aquileia) $NA. This property, owned by the Zonin family, is improving with each vintage. The Traminer has ripe, intensely spicy fruit, with a fine, crisp layer to give it poise and shape. The aftertaste is exotic, flavors of oriental spices blending with lychees. **87** —*R.V. (1/1/2004)*

CA' BRUZZO

Ca' Bruzzo 2000 La Sperugola Merlot (Veneto) $15. The dark, saturated color is a fine indicator of this wine's power and drive. It's full of berry and mocha aromas, which are followed by plum, berry, and chocolaty flavors. This organic wine is finely textured and clean, an everyday drink that should please even sophisticated drinkers. **89 Editors' Choice** *(5/1/2003)*

CA' DEL BOSCO

Ca' del Bosco NV Champagne Blend (Franciacorta) $44. Comes out of the chute a little stinky—like used socks, but quickly rights itself with flavors of sour yellow cherries and tart lemon. Finishes crisply dry, with a hint of citrus pith. Open next holiday season, when it should be cleaner and less bitter. **85** —*J.C. (12/31/2001)*

Ca' del Bosco NV Champagne Blend (Franciacorta) $44. Aromas of lemon meringue and orange peel are pleasing. This sparkler is fresh, lively and

very well balanced. A great alternative to Champagne. **88** —*C.S. (12/31/2002)*

Ca' del Bosco 1993 Cuvée Annamaria Clementi Champagne Blend (Franciacorta) $120. Ripe Golden Delicious apples and mature fruit flavors blend with a creamy mouthfeel and great acidity. A distinct style—and if it happens to be your style, you'll love it. **90 Editors' Choice** —*C.S. (12/31/2002)*

Ca' del Bosco NV Carmenero Red Blend (Italy) $126. This unusual table wine is a Carmenère, the aloof Bordeaux variety found almost exclusively in Chile. That it comes from an Italian sparkling wine producer is odd. As for the wine, it's got color and body along with strong vegetal aromas and flavors. Looks and feels right; smells and tastes not as good. **85** —*M.S. (11/15/2004)*

Ca' del Bosco 1998 Maurizio Zanella Red Blend (Sebino) $87. A northern Italian red that delivers earthy aromas as well as mineral and barrel notes. Cherry and raspberry flavors are light, while the mouthfeel is a touch raw and peppery. A different breed of rosso from Franciacorta. **86** —*M.S. (10/1/2006)*

Ca' del Bosco NV Brut Sparkling Blend (Franciacorta) $39. Plump and a bit gassy on the nose, but it settles to display firm flavors. Quite single-layered, with a crisp but monotone personality. Good mouthfeel, nothing out of whack, but rather basic in the final analysis. **86** —*M.S. (12/15/2005)*

Ca' del Bosco NV Brut Sparkling Blend (Franciacorta) $44. A crystalline appearance is a preface for polished aromas of citrus, pineapple, and tangerine. This is a fresh and fruity sparkler that stands out thanks to the zesty and cleansing impression it leaves in the mouth. An excellent match to neutral fatty foods such as ricotta-stuffed puff pastry, gratin dauphinoise, or cheese soufflé. **91** —*M.L. (6/1/2006)*

Ca' del Bosco NV Brut Sparkling Blend (Franciacorta) $32. Fresh and snappy, with some grassy aromas and citrus notes. Medium-weight, with apple and lime on the palate; not quite as lively or long on the finish as Ca' del Bosco's vintage offerings. **86** —*J.C. (12/31/2003)*

Ca' del Bosco 1999 Brut Sparkling Blend (Franciacorta) $65. Rich and yeasty, with aromas of breakfast cereal, confectioner's sugar, and toasted bread. Shows complexity and regal characteristics such as buttered toast, crystalline apple fruit, and a touch of mineral. Finishes light, right and juicy, but with substance. **89** —*M.S. (12/15/2004)*

Ca' del Bosco 1997 Brut Sparkling Blend (Franciacorta) $65. Earthy—with some aromas and flavors reminiscent of damp clay—but shows pleasant notes of sourdough, vanilla, and cream as well, gliding gently into a citrusy palate and buttery, slightly soft finish. Drink now. **87** —*J.C. (12/31/2003)*

Ca' del Bosco 2001 Brut Millesimato Sparkling Blend (Franciacorta) $88. A strong show from one of Italy's most regarded sparkling producers. Offers rich aromas of baked apple, graham crackers, and buttered biscuits. Exotic fruit flavors highlight a mouthfeel that is crisp and persistent. **91** —*M.L. (6/1/2006)*

Ca' del Bosco 1994 Cuvée Annamaria Clementi Sparkling Blend (Franciacorta) $99. Mature, with aged aromas of biscuits, powdered sugar, toast, and mushroom. Baked apple with spice dominates the palate, while the finish, and for that matter the flavor profile, is one-note. Round and toasty. Drink now. **88** —*M.S. (12/15/2004)*

Ca' del Bosco 1999 Cuvée Annamaria Clementi Sparkling Blend (Franciacorta) $157. A standout sparkler, this wine delivers an intense and complex bouquet ripe with peach, pineapple, toasted almond, and egg custard. A brilliantly crystalline appearance underscores the acidity and crisp freshness on the palate. The wine's full, textured feel is most impressive. **93** —*M.L. (6/1/2006)*

Ca' del Bosco 1994 Cuvée Annamaria Clementi Sparkling Blend (Franciacorta) $120. Very fine wine, showing all of the complexity you expect from a great sparkler combined with delicacy and elegance. Toasted almonds, pears, and dried spices on the nose, with tangerine and apple notes chiming in on the palate. The mouthfeel is creamy and rich; the finish lingering and citrusy. **91** —*J.C. (12/31/2003)*

Ca' del Bosco 1998 Dosage Zero Sparkling Blend (Franciacorta) $65. Fairly firm and tight, with aromas of mineral and mushroom. The tight citrusy palate is alive and dancing, while the finish lasts and lasts. A bit tangy on the tail, and maybe a touch flat in terms of feel. Still, it has its virtues. **87** —M.S. (12/15/2004)

Ca' del Bosco 1998 Dosage Zero Sparkling Blend (Franciacorta) $65. Elegant, well-balanced, and fresh, this extremely dry Franciacorta has all the ingredients you could want in a sparkling wine: a complex bouquet of buttered toast, peaches, smoke, and dried spices; mouth-filling flavors of peach and apple; and a long, zesty finish. **91 Editors' Choice** —J.C. (12/31/2003)

Ca' del Bosco 2001 Dosage Zéro Sparkling Blend (Franciacorta) $90. "Dosage Zéro" means no sweetness has been added to this sparkler and the result is an intensely nutty wine with aromas of toasted almonds and walnuts, fresh apple, and peach cobbler. Those toasty, nutty notes spread evenly throughout the mouth thanks to the wine's smooth creaminess. **90** —M.L. (6/1/2006)

Ca' del Bosco 1998 Rosé Sparkling Blend (Franciacorta) $67. Soft and yeasty, with an open personality that emphasizes mature, biscuity aromas along with dried apricot. Flavors of orange, papaya, and melon are subtle rather than live-wire, while the finish is stylish. **88** —M.S. (12/15/2004)

Ca' del Bosco 1998 Rosé Sparkling Blend (Franciacorta) $67. Offers faint aromas of cherries and roasted meat that blossom on the palate into lush, juicy flavors of cherries and plums. Ultimately a bit simple but satisfying, with a fresh, lively finish. **88** —J.C. (12/31/2003)

Ca' del Bosco 1997 Rosé Sparkling Blend (Franciacorta) $67. Assertive toasty, yeasty aromas give way to peach and hints of game, followed on the palate by meaty flavors alongside hints of anise and stone fruits. It's rich enough to handle red meat at the table, finishing long and intense. **88** —J.C. (12/31/2003)

Ca' del Bosco 1993 Satèn Sparkling Blend (Franciacorta) $68. Toasty and vinous, with aromas that hint at soy sauce, roasted meats, and fresh apples. Turns slightly nutty on the palate, picking up notes of caramel and Golden Delicious apples displayed against a rich, supple texture. **90** —J.C. (12/31/2003)

Ca' del Bosco 1993 Satèn Sparkling Blend (Franciacorta) $68. Round and nicely balanced, but the flavor profile falls short of thrilling. The nose deals yeasty cornflake and toast aromas that veer toward vanilla liqueur when given air time, but the finish is spiky and lemony. An "intellectual" wine that should strike different folks differently. **89** —M.S. (12/15/2004)

Ca' del Bosco 2001 Satén Sparkling Blend (Franciacorta) $68. A truly beautiful wine with peach and pear aromas, Golden Delicious apple, toast, and and flavors of kiwi. A genuine, straight shooter wine that caresses the mouth with custard-like silkiness. **91** —M.L. (6/1/2006)

CA' DEL MONTE

Ca' del Monte 1994 Corvina (Amarone della Valpolicella Classico) $35. 84 —J.C. (9/1/2000)

Ca' del Monte 1993 Vigneto Scaiso Corvina (Valpolicella Classico Superiore) $18. 87 —J.C. (9/1/2000)

Ca' del Monte 1995 Vigneto Scaiso Red Blend (Valpolicella Classico Superiore) $19. For a ripasso, this wine delivers what it should: raisin, vanilla and cola aromas in front of spicy cherry, black plum and apple skin flavors. The finish is smooth and layered, but at the very end some tannins rear up. **86** (5/1/2003)

CA' DEL VISPO

Ca' del Vispo 2003 Sangiovese (Chianti Colli Senesi) $16. Lots of oak, but with tons of fruit and excellent balance the total package is extremely likable. There's smoke, rubber, and bacon on the bouquet, and then comes a deep offering of black plum, berry, and vanilla. With second and third layers of depth and complexity, this is a wine that exudes quality. **90 Editors' Choice** (4/1/2005)

Ca' del Vispo 2002 Sangiovese (Chianti Colli Senesi) $12. Lightweight, with innocuous aromas of pie cherry, tobacco, and earth. Mostly dried fruits on the palate, including cherry and red plum. Tangy and thin on the finish, but with a puncher's chance. **83** (4/1/2005)

Ca' del Vispo 2001 Sangiovese (Chianti Colli Senesi) $15. A bit weedy, with lean cherry fruit and borderline medicinal flavors. Finishes rubbery,

with moderate fruit flavors and some artificiality. Not a prime-timer. **82** —M.S. (10/1/2004)

CA' MARCANDA

Ca' Marcanda 2001 Magari Sangiovese (Toscana) $70. A silky, medium-weight wine that bears more than a slight resemblance to Right-Bank Bordeaux. Dried herbs, chocolate, and plum aromas and flavors finish long. Half Merlot, the rest evenly divided between Cabernet Sauvignon and Cabernet Franc. **88** (7/1/2005)

CA' MONTINI

Ca' Montini 2004 L'Aristocratico Pinot Grigio (Trentino) $16. Correct and attractive with fragrant honey, almond skin, pine nut, and dandelion. Coats the mouth evenly but appears a trifle heavy in the mouth. **86** —M.L. (2/1/2006)

Ca' Montini 2001 L'Aristocratico Sauvignon Blanc (Trentino) $15. This solid Sauvignon is lean and focused, yet manages to show some ripe melon (specifically cantaloupe) flavors to go with its core of tart limes. **85** —J.C. (7/1/2003)

CA' RUGATE

Ca' Rugate 1999 Monte Fiorntine Soave Classico White Blend (Soave) $13. This Superiore lives up to its designation, with more structure and weight than typically seen in Soave. The apple, herb, and stone fruit aromas and flavors have good intensity. The mouthfeel is full and round—yet there's good acidity—making this attractive for drinking on its own. Finishes with a mild spice note. **89 Best Buy** —M.M. (9/1/2001)

Ca' Rugate 2000 Soave Classico White Blend (Soave) $12. A clean, crisp nose of green apples with just a hint of almond opens this even, nicely balanced white. It's what a classic Soave is supposed to be—light, dry and refreshing. Slightly brisk. The long finish takes on a mineral, stony note. **86** (9/1/2001)

CA' VIOLA

Ca' Viola 2003 Brichet Barbera (Barbera d'Alba) $38. A bit of a disappointment, with modest red fruit flavors accented by hints of rhubarb and pepper. It's still a solid drink, but doesn't show the full ripeness of the vintage's best Barberas, finishing crisp and lemony. **84** —J.C. (3/1/2006)

CA'NTELE

Ca'ntele 1999 Riserva Negroamaro (Salice Salentino) $11. Meaty and solid, with mineral, and raisin aromas. Fresh more than stewed, with cherry and apple-skin flavors followed by a free flow of red fruits and acidity. It's almost a mouthwash with substance, something perfect for saucy pastas or chewy calzoni. **87 Best Buy** —M.S. (2/1/2005)

Ca'ntele 2002 Primitivo (Salento) $11. Excellent Southern Italian Primitivo. The sweet nose bursts with freshness, plums, berries, and dry earth. It's neither heavy nor lean, with ripe plum, watermelon, and chocolate flavors. Undoubtedly superb with pasta or pizza. **90 Best Buy** —M.S. (2/1/2005)

Ca'ntele 2001 Amativo Red Blend (Salento) $32. Ripe, with a sturdy, stand-up nose. Beyond the aromatic door awaits brown sugar, black cherry, and licorice flavors. Chocolate on the finish as well as lightly juicy acids make for a pleasant finale. It's 60% Primitivo and 40% Negroamaro. **88** —M.S. (10/1/2006)

CA'ROME

Ca'Rome 2003 La Gamberaja Barbera (Barbera d'Alba) $33. Lifted—verging on volatile—scents of sour cherries on the nose are followed by slightly pickle-y flavors of cherries and green herbs. It's a bit simple, and some might even say flawed, but the full mouthfeel and crisp cherry flavors put it back on the winning side. **84** —J.C. (3/1/2006)

Ca'Rome 1998 Nebbiolo (Barbaresco) $50. Solid and tight. Leathery and a touch sour at first, it opens to show handsome licorice, black chocolate, and creamy oak elements. Even on the palate, this closes long, dark, and dry with substantial tannins. Drink 2004–2010. **88** —M.M. (11/15/2002)

Ca'Rome 1999 Barbaresco Sori Rio Sordo Nebbiolo (Barbaresco) $60. Though this wine is overtly woody, the elements are very impressive. It's enticing and tasty—if unevolved—even now. Lovely black cherry, tar, coffee, and sweet spice notes play on the nose and palate. But the wood expands much more than expected, progressively veiling the fine component parts. Closes long with full, solid but even tannins. This needs time and has the stuff to be a knockout if the wood recedes sufficiently. Best 2005–2012. **90** —*M.M. (11/15/2002)*

Ca'Rome 2001 Maria di Brun Nebbiolo (Barbaresco) $83. Once past some funky burnt matchstick scents, this wine really shines, mixing cherry, leather, and dried spices together in a richly textured, creamy wine that finishes with masses of soft tannins. Should be approachable by 2008, and mature gracefully until 2016 or beyond. **90** —*J.C. (11/15/2004)*

Ca'Rome 2001 Rapet Nebbiolo (Barolo) $42. This powerfully built 2001 boasts a complex palate of aromas and flavors, ranging from tea and cocoa to leather, spice, and cherries. The finish bodes well for the future, combining mouth-watering length and firm tannins with great fruit intensity. Drink 2010–2020. **90 Editors' Choice** —*J.C. (3/1/2006)*

Ca'Rome 1998 Rapet Romano Morengo Nebbiolo (Barolo) $59. The Rapet is much softer than the Vigna Cerretta, with aromas of tomato and burnt match. Flavors of plum skin and char are satisfying and straightforward. The wine finishes soft; it's a nice simple Barolo. **88** —*C.S. (11/15/2002)*

Ca'Rome 2001 Söri Rio Sordo Nebbiolo (Barbaresco) $76. Having heard some promising buzz about the 2001 vintage, this wine—one of the first 2001 Barbarescos tasted—was a bit of a disappointment. The mint, citrus, and rhubarb aromas do open up and gain some chocolaty richness with air, but the finish remains tart, crisp, and astringent. **86** —*J.C. (11/15/2004)*

Ca'Rome 2000 Söri Rio Sordo Nebbiolo (Barbaresco) $76. The oak is well-judged and well-integrated, seamlessly joining layers of ripe red cherries, leather, and tar on the nose and palate. The wine is large-scaled and lush, offering ealry drinkability. Drink now–2010. **91** *(4/2/2004)*

Ca'Rome 2001 Vigna Cerretta Nebbiolo (Barolo) $78. A modern, creamy-textured Barolo, layered with new wood that needs some time to integrate with the fine underlying material. Tobacco, vanilla, and cedar dominate right now, but with time those scents should subside and make way for cherry and spice nuances. Try in 2010. **91** —*J.C. (3/1/2006)*

Ca'Rome 2000 Vigna Cerretta Nebbiolo (Barolo) $81. Oh baby. This wine has it all, from alluring scents of toast, black cherries, and cola to flavors of exotic spices and a big, plush, tannic framework that promises well for the future. Combines great power with a sense of proportion. Should reach its peak around 2015. **92 Cellar Selection** —*J.C. (11/15/2004)*

Ca'Rome 1998 Vigna Cerretta Nebbiolo (Barolo) $62. This is a delicious Barolo, with aromas of beets, cherries and a touch of toast. The flavors of soy, rhubarb, and leather are well balanced, with the tannins and acids leading to a satiny finish. Drinkable now, but has the staying power to last for 10-plus years. **92** —*C.S. (11/15/2002)*

CABREO

Cabreo 2003 La Pietra Chardonnay (Toscana) $26. Waxy melon and citrus aromas start it off. In the mouth, honeyed apple and nutmeg come on fairly strongly, while the finish has both sugar and spice. Quite full and soft, with a lot of sweetness. **85** —*M.S. (9/1/2006)*

Cabreo 2001 Il Borgo Sangiovese (Toscana) $47. The first aroma of this wine is like a good cigar; it's pure tobacco with a touch of background plum and berry. Lively, pure, and snappy in the mouth, where raspberry, cherry, and other red fruits mix with coffee and oak-based toast. Nicely textured for food; a touch zesty and raw by itself. The mix is 70% Sangiovese and 30% Cabernet. **90** —*M.S. (9/1/2006)*

CADIS-CANTINA DI SOAVE

Cadis-Cantina di Soave 1997 Pinot Grigio (Veneto) $6. 83 *(8/1/1999)*

CAIREL

Cairel 1996 Vigneto Caveia Barbera (Barbera d'Alba) $15. 87 *(4/1/2000)*
Cairel 1998 Vigneto del Mandorlo Dolcetto (Dolcetto d'Alba) $15. 83 *(4/1/2000)*

CALA SILENTE

Cala Silente 2000 White Blend (Vermentino di Sardegna) $13. On the nose, it begins with a complex, intoxicating mix of bright floral notes and a little banana. After a few minutes, citrusy aromas sneak in. Banana and red grapefruit notes on the palate lead to a lingering white-peppery finish. So sexy that a friend of mine grabbed the bottle and ran straight home to her boyfriend—believe me now? **89** —*D.T. (9/1/2001)*

CALATRASI

Calatrasi 2003 Accademia del Sole Cabernet Sauvignon (Sicilia) $15. A new world style Cabernet Sauvignon with deeply tasted notes of coffee, nut, vanilla, and moderate cherry and blackberry fruit. The power is there suggesting a pairing possibility with grilled meat, although the tannins are soft thus broadening its appeal to hearty pasta dishes too. **87** —*M.L. (7/1/2006)*

Calatrasi 2003 D'Istinto Magnifico Cabernet Sauvignon-Merlot (Sicilia) $31. The blend is 70% Cab Sauvignon and 30% Merlot and the resulting wine is ripe with blackberry, resin, tobacco, cigar box, and prune. There's a round, plush quality derived from oak use and the tannins are tight and smoky. **90** —*M.L. (7/1/2006)*

Calatrasi 2003 Terre di Ginestra Catarratto (Sicilia) $19. Floral and deeply aromatic; delivers lactic or rubber-like notes typical of the variety plus lemon pie, toasted almond, and stone fruit. Distant herb notes round off a simple, fresh white. **86** —*M.L. (7/1/2006)*

Calatrasi 2003 D'Istinto Chardonnay (Sicilia) $13. A golden, straw-colored wine that strikes the middle of the intensity meter but does deliver clean notes of exotic fruit, kiwi, talc powder, and dried hay. Three months of oak aging render a unique wine with pleasant notes of dried flowers. **87** —*M.L. (7/1/2006)*

Calatrasi 2004 TDG 651 Chardonnay (Sicilia) $29. The fruit for this wine is selected from different vineyard parcels that reach up to 651 meters above sea level. Despite the Sicilian sun, higher altitudes help shape a fresh, floral-driven white; fermentation in oak adds a creamy, textured quality. **87** —*M.L. (7/1/2006)*

Calatrasi 2003 Accademia del Sole Merlot (Sicilia) $15. A red fruit driven wine that appears more linear and less jammy than other Sicilian Merlots. Aromas of tobacco leaf, pencil shaving, and cedar wood back a spicy, medium texture in the mouth. **87** —*M.L. (7/1/2006)*

Calatrasi 2003 Terre di Ginestra Nero d'Avola (Sicilia) $19. This is a heavily toasted Nero d'Avola that puts blackberry and plum on equal footing with vanilla, roasted nuts, and wood notes. It's a New World-style wine made with an Old World grape. Ends with dusty tannins. **88** —*M.L. (7/1/2006)*

Calatrasi 2004 Solese Red Blend (Sicilia) $17. Dark and beautiful, this Sicilian 70-30% Cabernet Sauvignon and Shiraz blend lavishes deep cherry fruit and layered earth and leather tones. It's a ripe and round wine that definitely needs to be consumed with a hearty meal. **89** —*M.L. (7/1/2006)*

Calatrasi 2003 TDG 651 Red Blend (Sicilia) $29. A real crowd pleaser, this 55-45% Nero d'Avola-Shiraz blend is concentrated and redolent of toast, cherry wood, and plum. Wood is the driving theme here, yet the wine follows a precise winemaking philosophy. **90** —*M.L. (7/1/2006)*

Calatrasi 2003 D'Istinto Shiraz (Sicilia) $13. This Shiraz has generous servings of berry fruit, leather, and charred meat that appears spicy, long lasting, and smoky in the mouth thanks to its medium structure and persistence. **89 Best Buy** —*M.L. (7/1/2006)*

Calatrasi 2004 Accademia del Sole Viognier (Sicilia) $15. Minimal wood aging does not interfere with Viognier's natural floral aromas. There are plenty of sweet-smelling spring flowers with layers of citrus and cracked white pepper. Don't pair this wine with a neutral food: go with aromatic dishes, like fish in a basil pesto sauce. **87 Editors' Choice** —*M.L. (7/1/2006)*

Calatrasi 2004 Baglio Badami Vioca White Blend (Sicilia) $17. This is an 85-15 Viognier-Chard blend that will appeal to those who prefer toasted whites. Woodshop notes and vanilla bean overwhelm Viognier's floral qualities but emphasize Chardonnay's butter and exotic fruit. **85** —*M.L. (7/1/2006)*

ITALY

CALDARO

Caldaro 2004 Pinot Grigio (Alto Adige) $15. There's a smoky characteristic to this Grigio that wraps around the fruit aromas. A nicely made wine with elegance; would partner well with smoked salmon appetizers. **87** —M.L. (2/1/2006)

Caldaro 2004 Söll Pinot Grigio (Alto Adige) $28. The high 14% alcohol seems well-integrated. Pear, Golden Delicious apple, honeysuckle, floral notes, and some soda pop elements emerge on the nose. It is thick and viscous in the mouth with tangy spice on the finish. **86** —M.L. (2/1/2006)

CAMIGLIANO

Camigliano 2001 Brunello (Brunello di Montalcino) $57. A delicious, crafted Brunello that celebrates Montalcino tradition. One panelist was especially fond of its cola berry, forest underbrush, plum, charcoal, granite and vanilla notes. Medium structure, but very well distributed throughout the palate with rich tannins and a long berry finish. **91** (4/1/2006)

Camigliano 2000 Brunello (Brunello di Montalcino) $53. Ripe, snappy, alert, and forward, with aromas of toast and dried cherries. If you like a bit more red fruit than black in your Brunello, give this a shot. Cranberry, cherry, and red plum flavors dominate, while the finish is crisp, with hints of pepper and spice. Lively but not terribly deep. **90** —M.S. (7/1/2005)

Camigliano 1997 Estate Bottled Brunello (Brunello di Montalcino) $48. A nose of tree bark, leather, and spiced cherries kick it off, followed by a clean palate of pie cherry that's snappy and tangy. Hardly rich, this Brunello emphasizes acidic red fruit, some chocolaty nuances, and a bit of earthiness. **84** —M.S. (11/15/2003)

Camigliano 2000 Red Blend (Rosso di Montalcino) $19. Breaks the ice with saddle leather, mineral, and toast aromas. The palate deals enough racy cherry and chocolate to grab one's attention, while the back end is long, firm, yet not hard. **88** —M.S. (11/15/2003)

CAMPANILE

Campanile 1998 Pinot Grigio (Grave del Friuli) $11. 87 (8/1/1999)

Campanile 2004 Pinot Grigio (Delle Venezie) $10. This is run of the mill PG, but its low pricing makes for an attractive ensemble: You'll get honey-suckle, exotic fruit, citrus and some soapy tone, too. **86 Best Buy** —M.L. (10/1/2006)

Campanile 2003 Pinot Grigio (Delle Venezie) $10. Light in body, fresh, and imbued with fruit, this offering from Beringer Blass boasts pear, apple, and almond notes alongside enough lemony acidity to keep it crisp and refreshing. **85 Best Buy** —J.C. (12/31/2004)

Campanile 2002 Pinot Grigio (Delle Venezie) $12. A light, lemony, refreshing quaff. Zippy, citrusy, and clean, with a tart, malic finish, this is made to whet your summertime appetite. **85** —J.C. (7/1/2003)

Campanile 2001 Pinot Grigio (Friuli Grave) $10. Here's a fresh, fruity, and vibrantly alive wine brimming with juicy acids and ripe flavors of citrus fruits and apples. It's clean as a whistle and dry enough for shellfish. Great value. **87** —S.H. (1/1/2002)

Campanile 2000 Pinot Grigio (Friuli) $10. This wine has pure apple and pear fruit that's reminiscent of an unoaked Chardonnay. It's well balanced and the mouthfeel is round and more ample than the delicate color and aromas would suggest. A mild citrus-peel bite on the finish makes it fresh and appealing. **85** —J.F. (9/1/2001)

CAMPO AL MARE

Campo al Mare 2003 Bordeaux Blend (Bolgheri) $30. Dark in color, with very dense and sweet aromas of plum veering into prune. The palate is reduced and lacks the breadth and balance of a great wine. What you get instead is a jammy, simple specimen with modest flavors and even less complexity. **84** —M.S. (9/1/2006)

Campo al Mare 2004 Vermentino (Vermentino di Toscana) $17. Nice and mildly creamy up front, with aromas of pear, melon, and vanilla. It runs rather tangy and zesty across the palate, showing apple, kiwi, and peach flavors. Finishes long but monotone, with almond extract as the lasting impression. **86** —M.S. (10/1/2006)

CAMPO VERDE

Campo Verde 1996 Barrel Aged Barbera (Barbera d'Asti) $14. 84 (4/1/2000)

Campo Verde 1997 Dolcetto (Dolcetto d'Alba) $12. 83 (4/1/2000)

Campo Verde 1999 Nebbiolo (Barbaresco) $44. Starts off unexpressively yet reasonably complex, revealing only modest aromas of tobacco, earth, mushroom, and anise. Flavors are high acid, featuring tangy cherry, tar, and coffee. This is a difficult wine to figure, with its high acids and low tannins, yet the panel liked it for its earthy notes and complexity. Drink 2008–2020. **88** (4/2/2004)

CAMPOBELLO

Campobello 2004 Villa di Campobello Sangiovese (Chianti) $10. After scoring big in 2003, this vintage seems heavy and candied, with a bit too much red licorice and raisin. Throughout it seems weighty and dull, as if the acidity got lost in transit. Not bad but more clumsy and chunky than desirable. **83** —M.S. (10/1/2006)

Campobello 2003 Villa di Campobello Sangiovese (Chianti) $10. Sweet and intoxicating, with caramel, baked fruit, and cotton candy to the nose. Meaty on the palate, with full plum, boysenberry, and cherry flavors. Best of all, the balance is just where it should be. As a whole there's nothing not to like about it. **90 Best Buy** (4/1/2005)

CAMPOGIOVANNI

Campogiovanni 2000 Brunello (Brunello di Montalcino) $65. Fully charred, with a lot of leather and campfire to the nose. More dark and obscure than forward and fruity, with heavy plum flavors and a shot of pepper on the tail end. Smoky and brooding throughout. **88** —M.S. (7/1/2005)

Campogiovanni 1999 Brunello (Brunello di Montalcino) $NA. Smells great, with toasty, burnt edges to the nose that really work. The palate offers plenty of fresh, happy fruit spread across a broad canvas. It's not boisterous or loud, but it is a high-quality red that's balanced, lengthy, and just mildly oaky and contemporary. **91** —M.S. (6/1/2004)

CAMPOMAGGIO

Campomaggio 2003 Red Blend (Toscana) $20. Mildly minty and raisiny on the nose, with a jammy, heavy personality. Which makes it surprising that it's so tart and cherry-driven in the mouth. Yet on the finish milk chocolate and coffee come into play. Too scattered and all over the map. Doesn't have a defined personality. **84** —M.S. (9/1/2006)

Campomaggio 2000 Sangiovese (Chianti Classico) $14. A good deal for a 100% Sangiovese estate-bottled wine. The bouquet has nice baking-spice aromas, primarily cinnamon and nutmeg, while the flavor profile stocks foresty cherry-berry fruit. Smooth enough late, with vanilla and dried spices. High acidity prevailing in the center is the only fault. **87** (4/1/2005)

Campomaggio 1999 Sangiovese (Toscana) $18. An estate Sangiovese-based blend with leather, dried fruit, and cedar aromas. Flavors of tight red fruit hit forcefully, propelled by zesty acidity. Definitely tangy and racy on the finish, but the strawberry and raspberry flavors are solid enough. With food it will do just fine. **86** —M.S. (10/1/2004)

Campomaggio 1998 Sangiovese (Chianti Classico) $16. Just swamped by oak, the slight fruit here is a platform for the wood, yielding heavy cedar and prune flavors. It looks a bit old—odd at this age—and although even on the palate, it doesn't offer much in the way of mouthfeel or finish. Perhaps in the barrel too long, this wine is gone before its time. **82** (4/1/2001)

Campomaggio 1999 Riserva Sangiovese (Chianti Classico) $22. Ripe and fruity, with earth, leather, and plum aromas. The flavors drive toward strawberry and raspberry, while the finish is round and pleasant. Good quality; easy to drink. **88** —M.S. (10/1/2004)

Campomaggio 1999 Riserva Sangiovese (Chianti Classico) $18. Cigar box and sweet fruit aromas are encouraging, but the follow up is not there. There's only tart red fruit and vanilla aromas, and after that a whole lot of acid and oak. **83** (4/1/2005)

Campomaggio 1997 Riserva Sangiovese (Chianti Classico) $24. A distinctive offering marked by a beautiful seamless quality, some exotic aromatic notes, and a unique bottle design. Cedar, sandalwood, and a sweet dustiness on the nose open to a cherry and toasty oak palate. Dry and even in the mouth. The finish has fine-grained tannins and a lovely back end bouquet. Drink now through 2007. **91** *(4/1/2001)*

Campomaggio 1995 Riserva Sangiovese (Chianti Classico) $19. 87 *(9/1/2000)*

CAMPRIANO

Campriano 2003 Sangiovese (Chianti Colli Senesi) $16. This very nice, zesty wine blends aromatics of leather, charcoal, tire rubber, and pure black fruit into a full, masculine bouquet. The palate is equal to the task, offering ripe and rugged cherry, plum, and cedar. Yes, it's tannic, but it's also fairly young. So drink now with pasta or meats, or hold for a while. **89** *(4/1/2005)*

CANALETTO

Canaletto 2000 Winemaker's Collection Chardonnay (Puglia) $9. Quite round and fruity, this easy drinker is almost sweet. Displaying tropical fruit, honey, and pear nectar aromas and flavors, it turns warmly spicy on the finish. A simple wine, but with great potential appeal as a "transitional varietal" for drinkers moving up from jugs. Also indicates that Puglia can produce competitive everyday wines, especially if they further elevate acidity for a bit more spine. **84** *(5/1/2001)*

Canaletto 1999 Winemaker's Collection Montepulciano (Abruzzo) $9. Ripe cherry and dark plum fruit, light tobacco, and cedar accents mark this pleasant, medium-weight wine. It's a good basic red and will have wide appeal with its round, supple mouthfeel. Generally a workaday, inexpensive Italian red, Montepulciano d'Abruzzo is a good pizza/pasta choice. It's not to be confused with the Tuscan Montepulciano. In Tuscany, Montepulciano is a place; here, it's a grape. Here, the place (Abruzzo) is the province on Italy's east central coast. **85** *(5/1/2001)*

Canaletto 1998 Pinot Grigio (Venezie) $7. 87 Best Buy *(8/1/1999)*

Canaletto 2004 Winemaker's Selection Pinot Grigio (Delle Venezie) $10. Big minerality makes for an extremely food-friendly wine with candy-like lemon-lime powder and mouth-puckering tartness. **86 Best Buy** —*M.L. (2/1/2006)*

Canaletto 2003 Winemaker's Collection Primitivo (Puglia) $10. For a meatier, heavier bargain red, head south to the sun-drenched Puglia region. Canaletto sources fruit to make a wine that delivers bold fruit, black cherry, roasted espresso bean, and moist earth. The wine is aged 12 months in oak to shape a softer wine accented by exotic spice, cinnamon, and sandalwood. This is the kind of wine you want on a chilly winter evening at home in front of a roaring fire. **85 Best Buy** —*M.L. (11/15/2006)*

Canaletto 1999 Winemaker's Collection Primitivo (Puglia) $9. Primitivo is Zinfandel, according to University of California at Davis ampelographers (students of grape DNA), but that doesn't mean they taste the same, as this medium-weight southern Italian version proves. Dark cherry, leather, coffee, and cocoa predominate here, with some nice spice, tar, and a slight black pepperiness (maybe that's the Zin gene) on the finish. **85** *(5/1/2001)*

Canaletto 2000 Winemaker's Collection Red Blend (Sicilia) $9. This easy-to-drink, supple, jammy cherry bomb is a fine, inexpensive choice to accompany spring and summer grilling. The very ripe cherry fruit shows a slightly tart, earthy element on the back end that adds a bit of complexity, and will stand up to charcoal-broiled foods. **85** *(5/1/2002)*

CANALICCHIO

Canalicchio 2001 Brunello (Brunello di Montalcino) $51. This wine's intense nose boasts coffee, nutmeg, Indian curry, leather, and apple-cranberry. The mouthfeel is leaner with tangy spice, caramel, cocoa, and a lively, perky quality to the finish. **90** *(4/1/2006)*

Canalicchio 2000 Brunello (Brunello di Montalcino) $60. A ripe, oaky wine, with coffee, toast, tobacco, and berry on the nose. Truly delicious, with everything you might want in a modern-style rendition of Brunello: chocolate, silky tannins, supporting acidity, balance, you name it. Classy. **92** —*M.S. (7/1/2005)*

Canalicchio 1999 Brunello (Brunello di Montalcino) $75. Rock solid, with a pure nose that exudes leather, coffee, charred beef, and lots of prime red fruit. From the plum and cherry flavors riding the surface to the wine's deepest depths, there's nothing not to like. As a whole, this one is Brunello like it should be: lively, racy, and fun. Hold for several years for best results. **94** —*M.S. (6/1/2004)*

Canalicchio di Sopra 2001 Brunello (Brunello di Montalcino) $74. This wine takes its sweet time to open but once it does, you'll get tart cherry, cedar, tobacco, coffee bean, violet, and vanilla. Firm, chewy tannins back a bitter note and dusty minerality in the mouth. **88** *(4/1/2006)*

CANDIDO

Candido 1997 Capello Di Prette Negroamaro (Salento) $8. An opaque wine with much more on the palate than on the nose. Toasted cherries and cola combined with bountiful tannins make this an acceptable sipper, with a dry, pleasant finish. **83** —*C.S. (5/1/2002)*

Candido 1995 Duca D'Aragona Negroamaro (Salento) $25. Warm, inviting aromas of mocha, chocolate, fleshy black cherries, and ground cinnamon spice continue on the palate and through the finish, to create a light, simple wine with soft, drying tannins. **84** —*C.S. (5/1/2002)*

Candido 1998 Immensum Negroamaro (Salento) $18. The nose is a bit closed, showing some soil and menthol qualities with little fruit. The herbal and briny flavors are simple, pleasant, and uncomplicated, but a bit hollow in the midpalate. A rugged wine, best to drink in 2–3 years. **86** —*C.S. (5/1/2002)*

Candido 2000 Red Blend (Salice Salentino) $10. Here's a wine from Puglia that tastes like the sun-drenched southern region thanks to an aromatic assortment of Mediterranean oregano and sage, mint tea, dried hay, and ripe red fruit. Not a gigantically structured wine, but a lighter-hued blend of Negroamaro and Malvasia Nera that would bring out the best in pork or roasted chicken. **87 Best Buy** —*M.L. (11/15/2005)*

Candido 1997 Riserva Red Blend (Salice Salentino) $8. 84 —*M.N. (12/31/2000)*

CANDONI

Candoni 2001 Pinot Grigio (Friuli Venezia Giulia) $13. How can a wine that smells so citrusy seem so low in acidity? Some pleasantly zesty aromas of lemons and unripe pears turn into fat, low-acid flavors. **81** —*J.C. (7/1/2003)*

Candoni NV Prosecco (Veneto) $13. Aromas of vanilla bean and candied almonds get it going, however, there isn't a lot of fruit to the nose. The palate deals some tangerine as well as lemon-lime, but also a bit of obvious sugar. On the tail end there's a slight burnt almond note that comes across bitter, but for the most part it delivers what it should. In addition, the etched label is attractive and really catches the eye. **86** —*M.S. (6/1/2003)*

CANELLA

Canella NV Champagne Blend (Prosecco di Conegliano e Valdobbiadene) $11. Here's an extra dry (meaning slightly sweet) **87 Best Buy** —*P.G. (12/15/2000)*

Canella NV Extra Dry Champagne Blend (Prosecco di Conegliano e Valdobbiadene) $11. This Prosecco offers toasty, bready notes on the nose that combine with hay and a little cheese on the palate. The mouthfeel is medium-full, but minerally; the finish holds powdered sugar and mineral flavors, with an odd cheese aftertaste. **83** —*D.T. (12/31/2001)*

Canella NV Extra Dry Champagne Blend (Prosecco di Conegliano) $11. Very smooth on the nose, with fragrant, fresh aromas of flowers, lemon, and lime. The dry citrusy palate and soft mouthfeel work perfectly together, while the finish is long, fruity, and very pleasant. Quite a tasty sparkler with pure fruit. Its quality is obvious. **90 Best Buy** —*M.S. (6/1/2003)*

Canella NV Prosecco (Prosecco di Conegliano) $11. Floral, with dandelions, white rose, and jasmine. There's also a bit of fruit in the form of white peach, honeydew melon, and green apple. Tart, almost bitter, and very refreshing. **89 Best Buy** —*M.L. (6/1/2006)*

ITALY

Canella NV Prosecco (Prosecco di Conegliano) $15. Crisp and stylish; definitely a flag-bearer for the wine type and region. The palate rushes with zesty apple, peach and melon flavors, accented by a hint of bitter almond. The mouthfeel is excellent, a bit round and weighty but not too much so. The essence of fresh garden greens and wet slate add character. **89 Editors' Choice** —*M.S. (12/15/2004)*

CANEVELE

Canevele NV Brut Prosecco (Prosecco di Valdobbiadene) $13. Crisp and precise; entirely clean and refreshing. Plenty of fruit throughout, with no interference. The palate pumps apple fruit in droves, with hints of apricot and white pepper. Finish notes of citrus and talc work like a charm. **89 Best Buy** —*M.S. (12/15/2004)*

CANNETA

Canneta 2000 Brunello (Brunello di Montalcino) $NA. Light in color and dry on the nose, with leafy, leathery aromas. The palate seems a touch tannic and tight, almost like Nebbiolo in color and mouthfeel. Not a blockbuster; this is much more subtle and reserved. **86** —*M.S. (7/1/2005)*

CANNETO

Canneto 2002 Sangiovese (Vino Nobile di Montepulciano) $22. Raspberry and plum aromas are forward yet softened by a thick block of sweet oak. In the mouth, the wine shows serious ripeness, a bold cherry flavor, and raw but healthy tannins. With char and zest throughout, this is one of the better '02s you'll encounter. **88** —*M.S. (7/1/2005)*

Canneto 2001 Riserva Sangiovese (Vino Nobile di Montepulciano) $22. Burly, saucy, and ultimately quite attractive on the nose, with leather and herbs in addition to more standard berry fruit and oak aromas. Not as chewy and soft as you might expect from a wine made by consultant du jour Carlo Ferrini; it's tannic and tight now, but exciting nonetheless. Hold through 2006. **89** —*M.S. (7/1/2005)*

CÁNTELE

Cántele 2003 Chardonnay (Salento) $11. This medium-bodied Chardonnay is nutty and pear-scented, with plump, ripe pear fruit balanced by a grapefruity under-current that turns a bit metallic on the finish. **83** —*J.C. (12/31/2004)*

Cántele 1998 Primitivo (Salento) $6. A slight funk, reminiscent of rhubarb or sauerkraut, detracts from the otherwise pleasant red berry aromas. A creamy mouthfeel complements milk chocolate and lactic flavors that turn tart and thin on the finish. **82** —*C.S. (5/1/2002)*

Cántele 1996 Primitivo (Salice Salentino) $12. 89 *(11/15/1999)*

Cántele 1998 Riserva Red Blend (Salice Salentino) $10. Some wines are modern in style; others more traditional. Put this aromatic Puglian blend of 85% Negroamaro and 15% Malvasia Nera in the latter category. There's no bulk, heavy extract, or pounding oak; just aromas of lavender, flower petals, and citrus rind accompanying racy raspberry fruit accentuated by sharp acids. Any rawness will be tamed by pizza, pasta, or a chunk of hard cheese. **88** —*M.S. (11/15/2003)*

CANTINA BEATO BARTOLOMEO

Cantina Beato Bartolomeo 2004 Savardo Pinot Grigio (Breganze) $10. Fresh, exotic fruit, kiwi and grapefruit are interweaved with honey, soapy notes, and a touch of dried basil. The mouth is a bit hollow with chalkiness and sourness riding over a medium finish. **85 Best Buy** —*M.L. (2/1/2006)*

Cantina Beato Bartolomeo 2004 Superiore Pinot Grigio (Breganze) $11. Aromas of field flowers, lemon rind, pear, and wet slate are understated. There's good persistency and fruit essence on the finish. **85** —*M.L. (6/1/2006)*

Cantina Beato Bartolomeo 2004 Savardo Vespaiolo (Breganze) $10. Made from a little-known grape that delivers tomato leaf, chopped parsley, ripe melon, and generous honey on the nose. It's not a structured or complex wine but does leave a soothing trail of melted honey at the back of the mouth. **84** —*M.L. (10/1/2006)*

CANTINA BERA

Cantina Bera 2001 Moscato (Moscato d'Asti) $10. 90 Best Buy —*S.H. (11/15/2002)*

CANTINA DEL VERMENTINO

Cantina del Vermentino 2004 Aghilóia Vermentino (Vermentino di Gallura) $NA. Although the wine's intensity could overpower many foods, it remains an intriguing and penetrating white thanks to its notes of almond paste, melon, Golden Delicious apple, caramel, and tiny tones of Marsala that add depth; snappy and full of flavor in the mouth. **87** —*M.L. (10/1/2006)*

Cantina del Vermentino 2003 Arakena Vermentino (Vermentino di Gallura) $NA. Has amber and gold brilliance with lavish notes of pineapple, honey, oak, and pine nut. The nose has an almost sweet quality and the mouthfeel is rich with nutty flavors and is somewhat viscous. **87** —*M.L. (10/1/2006)*

Cantina del Vermentino 2004 Funtanaliras Vermentino (Vermentino di Gallura) $19. This wine falls somewhat flat in terms of intensity and delivers an apple cider aroma that overshadows other more delicate fruit notes. Zesty and lean in the mouth. **84** —*M.L. (10/1/2006)*

Cantina del Vermentino 2004 S'Éleme Vermentino (Vermentino di Gallura) $NA. A brilliantly luminous wine with an oddball aromatic offering that is lively and very interesting. There's freshly chopped parsley, honey, goat cheese, and almond. It feels great and crisp in the mouth where it is less complex but very refreshing. **87** —*M.L. (10/1/2006)*

CANTINA DELLA PORTA ROSSA

Cantina della Porta Rossa 1997 Vigna Bruni Dolcetto (Dolcetto d'Alba) $20. 87 *(4/1/2000)*

CANTINA DI CUSTOZA

Cantina di Custoza 2003 Trebbiano (Lugana) $12. Peach, kiwi, mango, grapefruit, and apricot merge with spring flowers and orange blossoms to accent a brilliantly colored wine with crisp tartness and concentrated flavor. It also has a unique consistency that is both chewy and sticky and promotes a long, polished finish. A wonderful leisurely lunch on the patio wine. **86 Best Buy** —*M.L. (11/15/2005)*

CANTINA DI MONTALCINO

Cantina di Montalcino 2000 Brunello (Brunello di Montalcino) $48. Fresh but bland, with plum, cherry, and leather aromas. Not bad but not sophisticated; call it a quaffing Brunello if such a category exists. Finishes tannic, with crisp, peppery flavors. **85** —*M.S. (7/1/2005)*

Cantina di Montalcino 2000 Riserva Brunello (Brunello di Montalcino) $50. Concentrated and ripe with cherry cola and freshly minced mint on the nose. Ripe, red, and meaty in the mouth with lush tannins and maple syrup consistency. Easy to drink. **91** *(4/1/2006)*

Cantina di Montalcino 2000 Villa di Corsano Red Blend (Toscana) $39. A super Tuscan that's not, dare we say, super. The nose is fine but the palate is overly acidic and heavily slanted toward tart. Has the color and nose going for it, however the palate is discordantly sharp. Not pleasant on the tongue. **81** —*M.S. (9/1/2006)*

Cantina di Montalcino 2003 Sangiovese (Chianti) $10. Smoky and masculine, with initial aromas of black cherry and coffee. Talk about perfect balance; this has it. The cherry and berry flavors glide on a wave of crisp acids and modest tannins. And while not velvety, the mouthfeel is lush. Worth more than a look. **90 Best Buy** *(4/1/2005)*

Cantina di Montalcino 2001 Sangiovese (Chianti Classico) $17. Green tobacco, bubble gum and a pungent whiff of vinegar-based salad dressing form a nose that never really draws you in. In the mouth, cherry and plum flavors are of medium intensity. Reasonably fresh and forward, however, but still short on charm. **84** *(4/1/2005)*

Cantina di Montalcino 2001 Riserva Sangiovese (Chianti) $15. Soy sauce is a major component of the aged, mature nose, while in the mouth you're looking at black cherry, leather, and vanilla, all with a slight citrusy kick. Short and somewhat tomato-based on the finish, with a tart, crisp feel. **85** *(4/1/2005)*

CANTINA DI MONTEFIASCONE

Cantina di Montefiascone 2004 Secco White Blend (Est! Est!! Est!!!) $10. This is a simple, lean white but one done well. The flavors run toward citrus and pineapple and the finish is crisp, almost sharp, with scouring acidity. Best by the glass, nicely chilled, with an oyster or chunk of cala-mari. **85 Best Buy** —*M.S. (10/1/2006)*

CANTINA DI VENOSA

Cantina di Venosa 1997 Carato Venusio Aglianico (Aglianico del Vulture) $18. For an older wine, this is fresh, lively, and isn't even close to fold-ing. In fact, it's coming along perfectly and still requires either sturdy food or another few years on its side. That said, it features a pristine black-fruit nose, delicious berry fruit, and a hard, starching finish with dynamite tannins. It's a touch like nails at the very back end, but like we said, with food it'll be great. **90 Editors' Choice** —*M.S. (12/15/2003)*

CANTINA PRODUTTORI S. PAOLO

Cantina Produttori S. Paolo 2004 Eggleiten Pinot Grigio (Alto Adige) $NA. The nose is Granny Smith apple in as pure a form you can get in wine-making. But there's also a distant note of rubber balloon that, to be honest, I rather liked. The wine shows good personality in the mouth, too, where it is flavorful and smooth. **85** —*M.L. (6/1/2006)*

CANTINA SANTADI

Cantina Santadi 2003 Grotta Rossa Carignano (Carignano del Sulcis) $14. Wild sage, myrtle, charred meat, white mushroom, dried figs, and ash are elements of a surprisingly complex nose from this Sardinian classic. The tannins are tame and a medium finish tops medium body. Cantina Santadi is a cooperative with some 300 mem-bers who have worked together to raise the level of the island's wines thanks to a focus on native grapes such as Carignano. **86 Best Buy** —*M.L. (11/15/2005)*

Cantina Santadi 2002 Grotta Rossa Carignano (Carignano del Sulcis) $11. Chunky and ripe, with red fruit defining the nose. The palate is intense and tannic, with a reduced cherry-powder flavor. Finishes firm, with leather and drying tannins. Ideal for everyday drinking; best with food. **87 Best Buy** —*M.S. (2/1/2005)*

Cantina Santadi 2002 Rocca Rubia Riserva Carignano (Carignano del Sulcis) $24. More sharp and tight than in previous vintages, with orange peel, cherry, and dried spices. Shows condensed, limited berry flavors, while the finish moves toward dark fruit and raisin. A bit rubbery and tannic, but still a good wine. In its defense, '02 was not a stellar year. **86** —*M.S. (10/1/2006)*

Cantina Santadi 2001 Rocca Rubia Riserva Carignano (Carignano del Sulcis) $28. Who knew Carignan could be this nice? After an initial blast of earth and alcohol subside, what's left is a model Sardinian red with intoxicating cola, lemon peel, herb, and deep fruit aromas. The mouth-feel is ideal and the flavor profile is like a dynamite keg full of blackberry, chocolate, and vanilla. Intense and interwoven. **92 Editors' Choice** —*M.S. (2/1/2005)*

Cantina Santadi 2000 Rocca Rubia Riserva Carignano (Carignano del Sulcis) $25. Tight and a touch grassy on the nose, with hints of licorice, clove, and forest floor. The palate hits firmly with berry fruit and buttery oak, and that overt, creamy, woody flavor holds on into the finish, where it mixes with cola. Fairly rich and smooth, but the oak is heavy. **87** —*M.S. (11/15/2004)*

Cantina Santadi 2000 Shardana Carignano (Valli di Porto Pino) $32. Lush and subtle on the nose, with moss and marzipan accenting raspberry, black cherry, and pepper flavors. That is maintained on the finish, where chocolate enters the fray. More cushy than precise; serious nonetheless. **90** —*M.S. (10/1/2006)*

Cantina Santadi 1999 Shardana Carignano (Valli di Porto Pino) $31. A Sardinian red with beautiful violet, root beer, and dark fruit across the bouquet. Quite racy on the palate, where red fruit and spice combine in a forceful, full-flavor way. Melted chocolate and coffee flavors make for a fine finish. A touch hard, however, due to firm, unyielding tannins. **90** —*M.S. (2/1/2005)*

Cantina Santadi 2001 Terre Brune Superiore Carignano (Carignano del Sulcis) $66. Rugged and aggressive, but that's just fine considering how big, broad, and tannic this Carignan is. Look for fiery licorice aromas with notes of citrus peel and black cherry. The palate offers tons of weight, richness, and spice. **92 Editors' Choice** —*M.S. (10/1/2006)*

Cantina Santadi 1999 Terre Brune Superiore Carignano (Carignano del Sulcis) $63. This Sardinian red is a bit rough and raw despite its age, yet it's also quite masculine and enjoyable, a traditional wine in a field of newcomers. The fruit is candied and ripe, veering toward sugary. A fin-ish full of raisin, butter, and carob offers a lot to chew on. Needs time to breathe; consider decanting. **88** —*M.S. (11/15/2004)*

Cantina Santadi 2004 Cala Silente Vermentino (Vermentino di Sardegna) $18. Nice white wine with some individuality; the nose hints at mustard seed, butterscotch, and mineral while folding in wildflower and apricot. The palate is big-boned but right, with nutty apple flavors. Full and waxy on the finish, with a few beams of lemony acidity. Drink now. **88** —*M.S. (7/1/2006)*

Cantina Santadi 2003 Cala Silente Vermentino (Vermentino di Sardegna) $18. Solid but more flat than normal, probably due to the scalding 2003 vintage. Somewhat buttery and cheesy on the nose, again a reflection of heat. But there's a good, thick feel to the mouth, with apple and banana flavors followed by a textured finish. **85** —*M.S. (2/1/2005)*

Cantina Santadi 2002 Cala Silente Vermentino (Vermentino di Sardegna) $16. Off-gold in color, but not overdone. This is a near-perfect rendition of Vermentino; it's powerful but restrained, with warm aromas that con-jure memories of baked apple and spice. The palate is sly and dry, with cinnamon notes supporting lemon and pineapple. A rich, creamy finish cements this wine's reputation as a leader in its class. **91 Editors' Choice** —*M.S. (8/1/2006)*

CANTINA SOCIALE COOPERATIVA

Cantina Sociale Cooperativa 2002 PIRAS Vermentino (Vermentino di Gallura) $16. A bit musty, with aromas of hay and creamed corn. Tastes grassy, without much fruit. It's also low on acid. Not horrible, just not up to the competition. **82** —*M.S. (8/1/2004)*

CANTINA TAVAGNACCO

Cantina Tavagnacco 2004 Pinot Grigio (Colli Orientali del Friuli) $10. The alcohol seems very prominent and translates into notes of Marsala, marzipan, rum spongecake, or ripe fruit doused with liquor. Those aro-mas seem to suggest slight oxidation. **82** —*M.L. (2/1/2006)*

CANTINA TERLANO

Cantina Terlano 2001 Lunare Gewürztraminer (Alto Adige) $43. From one sniff, you know this is Gewürz, its rose petal and lychee aromas erupting out of the glass. But the flavors are less expansive, picking up notes of peppery spice on the finish. **87** —*J.C. (7/1/2003)*

Cantina Terlano 2002 Pinot Bianco (Alto Adige) $16. Imagine aromas of the ripest pink grapefruit combined with beautiful floral notes. Then tropical fruit flavors chime in on the palate, which is satisfyingly full, yet not heavy. This is an intense and individualistic wine possibly best served as an apéritif. **91 Editors' Choice** —*J.C. (7/1/2003)*

Cantina Terlano 2000 Vorberg Pinot Bianco (Alto Adige) $21. This spends 12 months in oak and it shows: It offers aromas of liquid smoke and flavors of brown sugar, honey, and caramel. The fruit is subdued, leaving the emphasis on the oak and mineral components. Try with rich but delicately flavored fish dishes or mild chèvres. **88** —*J.C. (7/1/2003)*

Cantina Terlano 2004 Pinot Grigio (Alto Adige) $19. A first sniff, the nose is attractive with vanilla bean and a strong nutty component that borders on almond pastry. But later the wine doesn't seem to open up completely and fruity notes seem distant. **85 Best Buy** —*M.L. (6/1/2006)*

Cantina Terlano 2002 Pinot Grigio (Alto Adige) $17. The apple and citrus aromas are tinged with warmer, fuzzier, riper fruit, and the hints of peach carry over onto the palate. The finish is beautifully clean and pure, tingling with fruity acidity without being overly tart. A wonderful bal-ancing act. **90** —*J.C. (1/1/2004)*

Cantina Terlano 2001 Quarz Sauvignon Blanc (Alto Adige) $43. Pungent and smoky, filled with minerals and grapefruit, this is top-flight Sauvignon Blanc. The mouthfeel is smooth, silky, and slightly creamy; the finish, long and delicate. **90** —*J.C. (7/1/2003)*

ITALY

Cantina Terlano 1992 Riserva Sauvignon Blanc (Alto Adige) $95. There's smoke, pink grapefruit, graphite, and just a hint of asparagus on the nose, but virtually nothing to indicate this wine is over 10 years old. Honeyed grapefruit flavors feature a liberal dusting of minerals on the long finish. **90** —*J.C. (7/1/2003)*

Cantina Terlano 2001 Winkl Sauvignon Blanc (Alto Adige) $22. Intensely aromatic, with gooseberries, cat pee, and a strong dose of flint smoke all rounded out by pink grapefruit flavors that persist on the finish. **89** —*J.C. (7/1/2003)*

Cantina Terlano 2000 Winkle Sauvignon Blanc (Alto Adige) $18. In northeast Italy (in this case Alto Adige) they don't use the "Blanc" qualifier, but this is definitely SB. Lemon and mineral qualities are strong on the nose and in the mouth, while driving acids create a mouth-watering feel. While citrus rind and a touch of toast offer nice secondary qualities, the main flavors are apple and something akin to tangerine. A distant almond marzipan note comes on as a lasting final impression. **89** *(8/1/2002)*

Cantina Terlano 2000 Classico White Blend (Alto Adige) $15. A surprisingly poor showing from this normally reliable winery, the 2000 Classico, a blend of Pinot Bianco, Chardonnay, and Sauvignon Blanc, shows some lemony aromas, a plump, custardy mouthfeel, and a tangy finish. **83** —*J.C. (7/1/2003)*

Cantina Terlano 1997 Classico White Blend (Alto Adige) $12. 87 —*M.S. (4/1/2000)*

Cantina Terlano 2002 Terlano Classico White Blend (Alto Adige) $15. A blend of grapes, so maybe it is not surprising that the aromas and flavors are a blend: melons, pears, and limes, all presented with great freshness and verve alongside a rich texture. **88 Editors' Choice** —*J.C. (7/1/2003)*

CANTINA TOLLO

Cantina Tollo 1999 Villa Diana Red Blend (Montepulciano d'Abruzzo) $7. This is the product of a winery that has 1,300 members cultivating 6,670 primarily mountainous acres. The nose has a lovely bouquet of cherry, plum, and a touch of tobacco. On the palate, the wine is round and well-balanced. The finish is long and filled with cherry. Enjoy this with pizza Margherita. **86 Best Buy** —*M.N. (9/1/2001)*

CANTINA TRAMIN

Cantina Tramin 2004 Lagrein (Alto Adige) $33. A ruby-colored, purist take on Lagrein with a charming medley of forest berries, anise, violet, and menthol. Already expansive and expressive at a young age, this medium-bodied wine ends on a sour note. This could definitely use a few years in the cellar. **85** —*M.L. (9/1/2005)*

Cantina Tramin 2002 Pinot Bianco (Alto Adige) $13. A full, rich, concentrated wine, with fat, ripe fruit, and a touch of acidity. Big and powerful, it has a fresh, clean aftertaste. **87** —*R.V. (7/1/2003)*

Cantina Tramin 2002 Pinot Grigio (Alto Adige) $13. A full-bodied, rounded wine with some good crisp acidity to balance. It has flavors of pears and some spice, leaving an attractive fresh feel in the mouth. **86** —*R.V. (7/1/2003)*

CANTINA VALLE ISARCO

Cantina Valle Isarco 2004 Aristos Pinot Grigio (Alto Adige) $25. More floral than most Pinot Grigios, with alpine freshness and crisp, grassy notes. There's an unexpected rush of exotic spice on the finish and you'll feel the heat. Try it with artichoke and parmigiano risotto. **86** —*M.L. (6/1/2006)*

CANTINE BARBERA

Cantine Barbera 2004 Nero d'Avola (Sicilia) $13. We have high hopes for these two young Sicilian sisters who are enthusiastically carrying out their winemaking dream. Although this un-oaked red hits the right spots, there is room for improvement. The aromas are young and sharp with cherry preserves, wet earth, and white mushroom, but the mouthfeel is sticky. **87** —*M.L. (7/1/2006)*

CANTINE DEL NOTAIO

Cantine del Notaio 2003 Il Rogito Rosato Aglianico (Basilicata) $21. A rosé so red it could pass as a Pinot Noir. The nose has cassis, cherry, strawberry, and toasted notes and a prominent balsam tail. Aglianico is naturally high in malic acid and you can taste that crispness here. Not unbalanced, but not tightly knit, either. A Marc De Grazia Selection, various importers. **84** —*M.L. (9/1/2005)*

Cantine del Notaio 2003 L'Autentica 500mL White Blend (Basilicata) $25. An amber dessert wine with dried apricot and plump raisins followed by candied lemon drops and orange marmalade. Thick and commanding with good acidity to achieve balance. A blend of Moscato and Malvasia grapes. **88** —*M.L. (10/1/2006)*

CANTINE FLORIO

Cantine Florio 2003 Malvasia Bianca (Malvasia delle Lipari) $NA. A beautifully amber wine with generous notes of dried apricot, raisin, and melted honey that slide down silky smooth. Thick, syrupy, and sticky, this passito delivers that much needed sugar rush at the end of a satisfying meal. **91** —*M.L. (2/1/2006)*

Cantine Florio 1992 Baglio Florio White Blend (Marsala) $NA. Textbook Marsala with caramel, candied fruits, citrus peel, and lots of toasted, nutty notes. A good opportunity to consider Marsala on its own and not as a cooking ingredient for sauces. **89** —*M.L. (2/1/2006)*

Cantine Florio NV Vino Marsala Fine Ambra Dry White Blend (Marsala) $12. This dry version of Sicily's most famous fortified wine boasts lingering tones of pine cone, walnut, and custard for a more austere and powerful style. This Marsala is deep brown in color and very spicy on the close. **88** —*M.L. (7/1/2006)*

Cantine Florio NV Vino Marsala Fine Ambra Sweet White Blend (Marsala) $12. Dark amber in color with golden reflections, this is a sweet Marsala redolent of maple syrup, brown sugar, almond, pine resin, and dried fruit. There's a prominent vein of exotic spice that carries over to the mouth and rides over a long finish. **88** —*M.L. (7/1/2006)*

Cantine Florio 2002 Zibibbo (Passito di Pantelleria) $NA. A precious golden color and rich, flavorful consistency make this Moscato passito a real crowd pleaser. The complex nose is accented by a delicate but unyielding rush of fresh apricot, peach cobbler, toasted almonds, and honeysuckle. **93 Editors' Choice** —*M.L. (2/1/2006)*

Cantine Florio 2002 Morsi di Luce Zibibbo (Sicilia) $NA. You'll detect toast, caramel, and crème brûlée backed by dried fruits and honey and a dense, viscous consistency in the mouth. It represents what Italians refer to as a "meditation wine" because you'll want to let it linger in your glass. **92** —*M.L. (2/1/2006)*

CANTINE GEMMA

Cantine Gemma 1997 Bricco Angelini Barbera (Barbera d'Alba) $14. 85 *(4/1/2000)*

Cantine Gemma 1998 Madonna Della Neve Dolcetto (Dolcetto d'Alba) $11. 90 *(4/1/2000)*

CANTINE LUCIANI

Cantine Luciani 1997 Brunello (Brunello di Montalcino) $32. This Brunello hits the olfactory senses with a thud. It's rather horsey and raw as far as aromatics go, and upon tasting it's a touch shrill, with snappy cherry and raspberry fruit that's tart in the middle. **84** —*M.S. (11/15/2003)*

CANTINE PICHIERI

Cantine Pichieri 1999 Traditione del Nonno Primitivo (Primitivo Di Manduria) $24. As the name suggests, this is traditional southern Italian winemaking: high alcohol, roasted fruit with a pruny-raisiny note, and a full mouthfeel. Dried spices, chocolate, and coffee notes round out the flavors. Serve at the end of the meal with assertive cheeses. **85** —*C.S. (5/1/2002)*

CANTINE RIUNITE

Cantine Riunite NV Lambrusco (Emilia-Romagna) $5. This well-recognized Italian brand offers a vibrant, fizzy wine with strawberry, sour cranberry, and blueberry aromas. Sweet and simple in the mouth, it has a refreshing soda pop-like appeal. **82** —*M.L. (12/15/2006)*

Cantine Riunite NV Vivante Lambrusco (Emilia-Romagna) $10. Made from Lambrusco Salamino and Grasparossa varieties, this is a simple, fun, clean, and dry wine with bright raspberry, blackberry, and strawberry aromas, but a bittersweet note in the mouth. **83** —*M.L. (12/15/2006)*

CANTININO

Cantinino 2000 Cantinino de Renzis Sonnino Sangiovese (Tuscany) $30. This Sangiovese is potent, with dark plum and a meaty aromatic streak. The palate is pure blueberry, plum, and chocolate, while the finish deals size and some layering, although it's admittedly a touch dull. This is a chewy, rich, pleasant wine, albeit one without a lot of nuance and complexity. **86** —*M.S. (11/15/2003)*

CAPANNA

Capanna 2001 Brunello (Brunello di Montalcino) $50. Anise seed, cherry cola, balsam notes, bacon fat, sandalwood, and mint liquor are nicely stitched together. The wine renders a warm sensation in the mouth with exotic spice over a persistent finish. **90** *(4/1/2006)*

Capanna 2000 Riserva Brunello (Brunello di Montalcino) $70. We loved the menthol freshness of this wine with mineral notes, eucalyptus, candied cherry, tea leaf, or moist tobacco and leather. Warm, inviting, and lush and tightly packed by rock-hard tannins. A very persistent finish. **91** *(4/1/2006)*

CAPANNELLE

Capannelle 1998 Solare Vino di Tavola Red Blend (Toscana) $95. Seductively layered on the bouquet, where dried fruits, leather, and earth create an Old World welcome party. Plenty of solid red fruit flavors carry the palate of this Sangiovese/Malvasia Nera blend, and there are background notes of coffee, pepper, and chocolate that add complexity. Will go great with meat or pasta. **91** —*M.S. (9/1/2006)*

Capannelle 2000 Riserva Sangiovese (Chianti Classico) $42. Fresh and pure, if a tad light in weight and concentration. Fine plum and berry aromas and flavors convey ripeness, which is confirmed on the smooth, medium-bodied palate. Should go well with milder foods, things like roast pork loin or poultry. Supple and well-made. **87** *(4/1/2005)*

Capannelle 1999 Solare Sangiovese (Toscana) $85. Full and forward, yet it's not at all jammy or overdone. The nose is stately while the palate features electro-charged plum and cherry flavors softened ever so slightly by chocolate. Finishes toasty and warm, with oak and pepper. The total package in maturing Tuscan wine; drink now through 2009. **92** —*M.S. (9/1/2006)*

Capannelle 1997 Solare Sangiovese (Toscana) $83. Tasted for the first time in nearly three years, this Sangiovese-dominated super Tuscan seems to have improved, as now it shows a seductive, dry earthiness along with cinnamon and tree bark. Fairly Old World in style, with red fruit, little oak, acidity, and length. Some might find it thin, but with food it will be excellent. **89** —*M.S. (9/1/2006)*

Capannelle 1997 Solare Sangiovese (Toscana) $74. A hint of rust to the color indicates aging, and that perception is confirmed on the dried-fruit nose. Flavors of cherry tomato and plum lead toward a thick, chunky finish that has power but little polish. Falls flat at the end, but still has enough going for it to make it worthwhile. **85** — *M.S. (11/15/2003)*

Capannelle 1998 Vino di Tavola Rosso Sangiovese (Toscana) $78. A healthy wine with cherry, plum, earth, and chocolate on the nose. The fruit is racy, bordering on searing. But on that wave of acidity you'll encounter prime and pure cherry and raspberry flavors. Arguably a bit skinny and one-dimensional, but still it's worthy of praise. **89** —*M.S. (9/1/2006)*

CAPARZO

Caparzo 2000 Brunello (Brunello di Montalcino) $48. Stylish smoke and leather aromas combine with plum, cherry, and berry to create a fresh but monotone nose that is true Brunello. Snappy cherry and raspberry flavors appear on the palate along with accents of clove and spice. Upright on the finish. Forward and well-made, but hardly complex. **89** —*M.S. (7/1/2005)*

Caparzo 2000 La Casa Brunello (Brunello di Montalcino) $75. Shows lovely, complex aromas of plum and cedar, accented with hints of brown sugar, chocolate, and spice. It's medium in weight, developing flavors of fresh herbs and cherry on the palate before ending with lingering notes of cherry and soft, gentle tannins. **90** *(4/1/2006)*

Caparzo 1994 La Casa Brunello di Montalcino Brunello (Brunello di Montalcino) $76. **93** —*M.S. (11/15/1999)*

Caparzo 1999 La Vigna Brunello (Brunello di Montalcino) $66. Floral and round, and eminently approachable at this early stage. The bouquet is rosy and sweet, while the palate is easygoing and fresh. Yet once you think its aging potential might be short, the finish drives on for a long distance, tossing up coffee and earth notes. Drinkable now, but can last for at least a decade. **91** —*M.S. (6/1/2004)*

Caparzo 2003 Red Blend (Toscana) $15. Features rubbery red fruit and a lot of spunk. This is rosso in its freshest, most fruity form. Yet it's properly balanced by zesty acidity and noticeable but moderate tannins. With a lot of raspberry and strawberry in the mouth and a lifted, deep finish, you can't go wrong with this red and a plate of pasta and sauce. **88** — *M.S. (9/1/2006)*

Caparzo 1997 Cà del Pazzo Sangiovese (Toscana) $33. This is a full-bodied, bracing tart-cherry bomb with very attractive cedar, tobacco, and graphite accents. Though it has a creamy texture, the wine sports high acidity that keeps the fruit very bright and provides a great edge for food pairings. Closes long with some tannic bite and dry cherry cedar-toast notes. **88** *(9/1/2001)*

CAPESTRANO

Capestrano 2001 Red Blend (Montepulciano d'Abruzzo) $10. This is what this wine style is all about. You get a sweet, syrupy, deep nose and then lots of fruit on the palate followed by an incredibly dense, dark, chocolaty finish. It's a full-force express, bold, zippy, and solid. **89 Best Buy** —*M.S. (10/1/2004)*

CAPEZZANA

Capezzana 2001 Barco Reale Red Blend (Carmignano) $15. Leather and bacon aromas along with lavish oak create a plush bouquet. The fruit is powerful and makes an excellent first impression, though the wine seems to crumble a bit toward the finish. Nevertheless, a fruit-to-the-max red. **87** —*M.S. (11/15/2003)*

Capezzana 2000 Ghiaie dell Furba Red Blend (Rosso di Toscana) $50. Black as night, with heavy aromatics that range from soy and tobacco to prune and tar. Blackberry, cassis, and fudge dominate the flavor profile on this blend of Cabernet Sauvignon, Merlot, and Syrah, while the overall take is one of size, integration, and lushness. A wine made for early consumption. **91** —*M.S. (9/1/2006)*

Capezzana 1999 Ghiaie Della Furba Red Blend (Tuscany) $49. Very much a baby, this is one big, bold, burly Cab-Merlot-Syrah blend that's filled to the brim with extracted plum fruit, bitter chocolate, and earth. It takes a long time in the glass for it to lose its youthful, funky aromatics, and on the palate things are still a bit scattered. But in due time things will settle and integrate. **90** —*M.S. (8/1/2002)*

Capezzana 1998 Ghiaie della Furba Red Blend (Toscana) $52. The ultra-ripe tannins of this wine are so soft, it would be no shame to think, for a moment, that it is a '97. Leather and bitter dark chocolate aromas lead into flavors of sour black plums, cocoa, and coffee grounds. Despite this wine's softness, it should age well on its level of fruit concentration and firm acidity. Drink now through 2010. **88** —*J.C. (9/1/2001)*

Capezzana 2002 Sangiovese (Barco Reale di Carmignano) $14. Big and funky, and smelling a bit like Syrah. But it's actually a blend of Sangiovese, Cabernet, and Canaiolo, and the result is a tad sharp, leathery and spicy. More than decent in terms of fruit quality and mouthfeel. **86** —*M.S. (11/15/2003)*

Capezzana 1999 Sangiovese (Carmignano) $21. In 1998 Capezzana eliminated its "reserve" wine, thereby bumping up the quality of its DOC Carmignano by leaps and bounds. And the '99 is something to behold. Rich, extracted and jammy it is, with nuances throughout of crème de cassis, coffee, maple and most of all, chocolate. With a finish that coats every corner of your mouth, this Sangiovese (with 20% Cabernet) scores big. **91** —M.S. (8/1/2002)

Capezzana 1998 Sangiovese (Carmignano) $23. A woody Carmignano that relies too much on oak for its flavors. Smells a bit like new plywood, complete with adhesive residues, and the sour cherry fruit cuts a lean profile. Tannins are bitter, like a cup of oversteeped breakfast tea. Drink soon, before the fragile fruit disappears. **83** —J.C. (9/1/2001)

Capezzana 1997 Sangiovese (Carmignano) $23. 91 —M.S. (9/1/2000)

Capezzana 2000 Barco Reale Sangiovese (Carmignano) $14. Made from 70% Sangiovese and other red grapes, including Cabernet Sauvignon, this is a little rustic and wild. The palate is rich, full, and offers plenty to chew on. Bold plum and black cherry flavors dominate. A nice woody accent graces the finish. **86** —M.S. (8/1/2002)

Capezzana 2004 Conti Contini Sangiovese (Toscana) $10. This is a very attractive Sangiovese that is elegant without being too thin, and intense without being too powerful. The nose is ripe with aromas of forest berry, pressed violet flowers, and spice (the wine is aged in oak barrels for six months). But what makes it particularly well-suited to informal foods is its acidity, which cleanses the palate and leaves an almost menthol-like freshness in the mouth. Those qualities help give the wine a tasty, long finish as well. **85 Best Buy** —M.L. (11/15/2006)

Capezzana 2000 Conti Contini Sangiovese (Carmignano) $10. Chewy, chunky, a little buttery and full of milk chocolate, this crowd pleaser is a good introduction to Tuscan Sangiovese. It will work well with simple dishes like pizza and pasta. It's young and gawky, like a teenager going through adolescence. **85** —M.S. (8/1/2002)

Capezzana 1995 Ghiaie della Furba Sangiovese (Toscana) $53. 95 —M.S. (11/15/1999)

Capezzana 1995 Riserva Sangiovese (Carmignano) $41. 91 —M.S. (11/15/1999)

CAPICHERA

Capichera 2002 Assajé Carignano (Isola dei Nuraghi) $42. Flush on the nose and loaded with leather, earth, and spicy plum fruit. The palate is warm and saturated with all sorts of berries framed by genuine, appropriate tannins. Then on the finish it turns smoky and coffee-like. Simply an excellent, juicy, satisfying red wine. **91 Editors' Choice** —M.S. (2/1/2005)

Capichera 2001 Mantenghja Carignano (Isola dei Nuraghi) $91. Dark as night, with licorice, lavender, and blackberry aromas that are truly impressive. The palate is beyond deep, with over-the-top flavors of wild berry marmalade and chocolate. No surprise that it manages to finish in massive fashion. A total stud of a Carignan from Sardegna. Good 2010 and beyond. **94 Editors' Choice** —M.S. (10/1/2006)

Capichera 2003 Vermentino (Isola dei Nuraghi) $50. This Sardinian white is a ripe, sun-baked heavyweight, but in a good way. Plump, with lemon-curd aromas; the flavors are sweet and sugary at first, but later turn to complex apple, citrus, pineapple, and star anise. Great body, but on the low-acid, soft side. Drink now. **88** —M.S. (2/1/2005)

CAPPELLANO

Cappellano 1996 Barbera (Barbera d'Alba) $17. 89 (4/1/2000)

Cappellano 1994 Nebbiolo (Barolo) $40. 85 —M.S. (7/1/2000)

CAPRILI

Caprili 1997 Brunello (Brunello di Montalcino) $54. If you prefer older-style Brunello with its firm tannins and solid backbone of dry fruit, then this is the one for you. Aromas of wild cherries and chocolate are followed on the palate by powerful, brooding fruit and a solid structure on the palate. It leaves a dry aftertaste that should pair well with rich foods. Cellar for at least 10 years. **90** —R.V. (8/1/2002)

CAPUTO

Caputo 1999 Sannio Aglianico (Campania) $13. Fresh vegetable aromas and bright blackberry fruit greet you on the nose, and continue on the palate—a very pleasant start. The flavor of sautéed mushrooms blended with spice and juicy blackberries make for a long, seductive finish. Drink in 3-5 years. **85** —C.S. (5/1/2002)

Caputo 1999 Zicorra Aglianico (Campania) $20. Bright fruit, with herbal and metallic notes, make for a warm start, but the chewy tannins dissipate quickly on the short finish. **84** —C.S. (5/1/2002)

Caputo 2000 Piedirosso (Lacryma Christi del Vesuvio) $13. A simple wine with grapey and caramel notes on the nose, which transform into sage and soy on the palate. The finish is soft. Where's the pizzazz? **83** —C.S. (5/1/2002)

Caputo 2002 Rosso Red Blend (Lacryma Christi del Vesuvio) $11. Burnt and raw, with lean, tart red fruit on the nose. Equally tart raspberry in the mouth is pushed by fiery acidity. Call it a red-cherry snapper without much softness or character. **82** —M.S. (11/15/2004)

Caputo 2002 White Blend (Lacryma Christi del Vesuvio) $11. Heavy and full-bodied, but still nice despite being so plump. The nose is focused on pear and vanilla, while the flavors lean toward apricot, mango, and pineapple. **85** —M.S. (10/1/2004)

CARLO DI PRADIS

Carlo di Pradis 2004 Pinot Grigio (Isonzo del Friuli) $15. The first impression is of flint and minerals, but plenty of room is left for peach and white flower aromas. Tingling acidity in the mouth with a satisfying, well-integrated consistency. **87** —M.L. (6/1/2006)

CARMINA

Carmina NV Brut Prosecco (Prosecco di Conegliano) $NA. Delicate and elegant with wild flowers and loads of mineral-like layers. Zesty and cool in the mouth, with spicy acidity and good persistence. A real appetite-enhancing apéritif wine. **88** —M.L. (6/1/2006)

Carmina NV Cartizze Prosecco (Prosecco Superiore di Cartizze) $NA. White peach, exotic fruit, yellow rose, and fragrant flowers yield a generally sweet sensation on the nose and palate. Refreshing, with a finish strongly driven by dusty-mineral sensations. **87** —M.L. (6/1/2006)

Carmina NV Extra Dry Prosecco (Prosecco di Conegliano) $13. Textbook Prosecco with clean citrus notes, peach, apricot, and white flowers. There's also a smooth, creamier texture to this wine that yields depth and a longer finish. **87** —M.L. (6/1/2006)

CARPARZO

Carparzo 1993 Brunello di Montalcino Brunello (Brunello di Montalcino) $52. 90 —M.S. (11/15/1999)

Carparzo 1997 Le Grance Sant'Antimo White Blend (Tuscany) $25. This mostly Chardonnay white is from Tuscany; Sant'Antimo is the DOC for non-traditional wines from the village of Montalcino. Dry apple flavors are deftly melded with toasty oak, while Sauvignon Blanc and Traminer in the blend add character and interesting flavor accents. Finishes long and spicy, with elegant oak notes. **91** —M.M. (9/1/2001)

CARPENÈ MALVOLTI

Carpenè Malvolti NV Prosecco (Prosecco di Conegliano) $12. Malt, vanilla and citrus aromas lead into a full-force palate loaded with flavors of orange, grapefruit, and lime. The finish is smooth and pure, while the feel is good and light. This fresh bubbly is immensely easy to drink and satisfying. **88 Best Buy** —M.S. (6/1/2003)

Carpenè Malvolti NV Cuvée Brut Prosecco (Prosecco) $15. There's an initial harshness on the nose due to the carbonation, but it is quickly subdued by tender notes of honeydew melon and kiwi. Light and crisp on the palate, with lingering mineral notes. **87** —M.L. (6/1/2006)

Carpenè Malvolti NV Extra Dry Prosecco (Prosecco) $15. Sweet, round aromas and a slight herbal note blend well in this lemon-lime and mineral-driven bubbly. Those mineral tones help achieve a very fresh and clean sensation in the mouth. **86** —M.L. (6/1/2006)

CARPINETO

Carpineto 2000 Farnito Cabernet Sauvignon (Toscana) $30. Dark-fruited, but shows some slightly vegetal, green-peppery overtones. In the hot summer, one wonders whether the skins/seeds ripened before sugar levels pushed the limits. Big and round in the mouth, with recurring capsicum notes on the thick, tannic finish. **86** (8/1/2006)

Carpineto 1999 Farnito Cabernet Sauvignon (Toscana) $35. Although the aromas carry more than a hint of bell pepper, this green element takes a back seat on the palate to rich currant and earth flavors and just a hint of toasty oak. "We're in the ripe fruit business, not the lumber business," jokes Zaccheo. Firmly structured, with good grip on the finish. Drink 2005-2010. **89** *(11/1/2003)*

Carpineto NV Farnito Brut Chardonnay (Tuscany) $35. The nose offers celery seed, bread dough, vanilla, and pear. In the mouth, this Chardonnay-based sparkler is taught and tangy, with orange and pineapple flavors. That tang carries out to the end, where the bright acidity really shines. For fans of cool bottles; the tall, thin vessel is unique and should grace any table. **84** *—M.S. (6/1/2003)*

Carpineto NV Dolce Moscato (Tuscany) $17. Like the name indicates, this is a supremely sweet sparkler. And the bet here is that it is probably too sweet and sticky for the average bubbly drinker. The palate is loaded with over-ripe melon, citrus, peach, and lots of sugar. The finish is fairly clean given the wine's heavyweight stature, while the overall take is one of sugar and candy. **83** *—M.S. (6/1/2003)*

Carpineto 2002 Sangiovese (Chianti Classico) $20. Fairly classic in structure and character, with aromas of ground pepper, coffee, leather, and snappy red fruit. Moderately deep and ripe, with cherry and pepper on the palate. Not overly textured, but big and bulky enough to register as a full-bodied wine. Has more virtues than faults. **87** *(4/1/2005)*

Carpineto 2001 Sangiovese (Chianti Classico) $20. A bit sparse in terms of fruit, but still jammy and ripe enough to please. Look for raspberry and black cherry flavors, and a fresh, fairly acidic finish. A snappy, crisp Chianti. **86** *—M.S. (10/1/2004)*

Carpineto 2000 Sangiovese (Chianti Classico) $20. Rich, smoky, pure, and encouraging from the first take all the way to the back end. There's lots of zest and spunk to this racy yet round Chianti. The palate is full of blackberry and the feel is supple. It's totally ripe and tannic, with notes of vanilla, chocolate, and espresso forming the base. Oaky but integrated; modern but traditional enough. **91 Editors' Choice** *—M.S. (11/15/2003)*

Carpineto 1999 Sangiovese (Chianti Classico) $19. Plenty of cherries and a large dose of not-so-toasty oak are the core of this medium-weight red. A slight earthiness on the nose and woody tannins on the back end frame a solid palate that's full of cherry and vanilla flavors. **85** *(4/1/2001)*

Carpineto 2004 Dogajolo Sangiovese (Tuscany) $10. Where Vino Nobile grapes that don't make the cut for the Riserva go, as the estate doesn't produce a regular Vino Nobile, just a riserva. This perennial Best Buy combines crunchy, fresh cherry fruit with hints of caramel, coffee, and chocolate. It's a cheerful wine that should win Tuscany plenty of fans, at a great price. **85 Best Buy** *(8/1/2006)*

Carpineto 2001 Dogajolo Sangiovese (Toscana) $10. Here's a tasty, compact Sangiovese-Cabernet blend from the excellent 2001 vintage that gives pure fruit and varietal character. It's chewy and textured, definitely more so than your average Chianti, and there's some meaty rusticity and light oak to punch things up a notch. Good with grilled meats and vegetables, or with pizza. Pronounced doga-yolo. **86** *—M.S. (11/15/2003)*

Carpineto 2000 Dogajolo Sangiovese (Tuscany) $11. This country-style wine seems over-ripe. It has raisiny aromas, a heavy color, and flavors of molasses, cocoa, and baked fruit. The finish is chunky and a touch burnt, while overall it's tannic and falls flat. Previous vintages of this wine seemed better. **82** *—M.S. (11/15/2003)*

Carpineto 1986 Farnito Vin Santo Sangiovese (Toscana) $55. This is the winery's first release of vin santo and is just coming to market (according to Zaccheo, the next vintage will be the 1993). The aromas are of honey, apricot, and caramel, while the flavors turn nutty and peachy. It's not very sweet, and finishes very cleanly—not cloying at all. **90** *(11/1/2003)*

Carpineto 1999 Molin Vecchio Sangiovese (Toscana) $75. Richly oaked, with smoke and vanilla notes dominating at this young age. But there's also a firm core of blackberry flavors that grows in intensity and bodes well for cellaring. The mouthfeel is lush and creamy, finishing with chewy tannins. Try this blend of Sangiovese, Syrah, and Cabernet Sauvignon in 2008. **92** *(11/1/2003)*

Carpineto 1999 Poggio Sant'Enrico Sangiovese (Toscana) $70. Aromas of super-ripe cherries burst from the glass, folding in notes of chocolate and pain grillé. The Sangiovese (100%) was clearly harvested very ripe, with an almost Port-like character to it and creamy tannins, but it still retains good acidity. **91** *(11/1/2003)*

Carpineto 2001 Riserva Sangiovese (Vino Nobile di Montepulciano) $30. Despite an initial touch of coconut, the nose is seductive, especially when the leather and cedar elements take over. Fine fruit carries the palate, with an emphasis on blackberry, cherry, and plum flavors. Rich and internationally styled, with soft tannins and impeccable mouthfeel. Drinkable now through 2010. **90** *—M.S. (7/1/2005)*

Carpineto 2000 Riserva Sangiovese (Vino Nobile di Montepulciano) $30. Smoky, toasty, and earthy, this still needs a little time to fully integrate its two years in oak. In the mouth, it's big, creamy, and thick with tannins that provide a drying counterpoint to plum and prune flavors, while coffee and molasses notes play supporting roles. **90** *(8/1/2006)*

Carpineto 2000 Riserva Sangiovese (Chianti Classico) $25. Smooth and seductive, with leather, graham cracker, and vanilla on the nose in addition to smoke and plum. The palate shows modest spice accenting cherry, plum, and chocolate. A well-rounded, tasty wine. The tannins are chewy, the feel is correct, and the grip is tight but forgiving. **90** *(4/1/2005)*

Carpineto 1999 Riserva Sangiovese (Chianti Classico) $26. Floral, ripe, and full of red fruit and lavender. It's big and tight on the tongue, with raspberry, plum, and cassis flavors. Very juicy and solid. Not showy, but defined and correct for Chianti. **88** *—M.S. (10/1/2004)*

Carpineto 1998 Riserva Sangiovese (Vino Nobile di Montepulciano) $33. Carpineto doesn't bottle a normale from its Montepulciano vineyards, bottling only this riserva. Loaded with dark fruit, earth, and tobacco, it picks up notes of plum and chocolate on the finish. **88** *(11/1/2003)*

Carpineto 1998 Riserva Sangiovese (Chianti Classico) $22. Like many wines from this producer, it excels because of its sheer drinkability. They are using more new wood flavors than in the past, but the beautifully perfumed, vibrant fruit, deep acidity, and light elegance reveal a wine that will age well, as well as being drinkable now. **90** *—R.V. (8/1/2002)*

Carpineto 1998 Riserva Sangiovese (Chianti Classico) $28. For a 100% Sangiovese, this wine shows a remarkably smooth mouthfeel, the only quibble being a hard, unyielding finish. Red cherries, leather, earth, and tobacco aromas and flavors add in a dash of vanilla oak to give it a modern touch. Dessert Wine. **87** *(11/1/2003)*

Carpineto 1997 Riserva Sangiovese (Vino Nobile di Montepulciano) $69. Still needs 3–5 years to reach its peak, but approachable now for its smooth, supple texture and plush finish. Tar, leather, and cherry scents add notes of fig and tobacco on the palate. Shows the ripeness of the vintage without turning flabby. **91** *(8/1/2006)*

Carpineto 1996 Riserva Sangiovese (Chianti Classico) $24. The dark fruit and toasty oak are well meshed on the nose, with a rich, creamy-floral character. Full and rich blackberry and toast flavors are bold and appealing on the palate, and licorice, toast, and dark plum elements play out on the finish of this satisfying offering. Drink now through 2005. **90** *(4/1/2001)*

Carpineto 1995 Riserva Sangiovese (Vino Nobile di Montepulciano) $55. Drinking beautifully now, balancing vibrant fruit against an interesting array of secondary flavors. Leather, dusty minerals, and black cherry scents pick up plum, tobacco, and earth shadings on the palate. Silky and long on the still-firm finish. **90** *(8/1/2006)*

Carpineto 1990 Riserva Sangiovese (Vino Nobile di Montepulciano) $95. Still dark in color, albeit with some bricking evident, and still a bit tannic on the finish. Still, this is very good, combining earth and tobacco with plums and cherries. Big in the mouth, with a velvety feel, but also a touch of warmth from alcohol. Drink now or hold. **89** *(8/1/2006)*

Carpineto 1988 Riserva Sangiovese (Vino Nobile di Montepulciano) $99. Of the wines tasted, this is the one to drink now. It still shows some chewiness to its texture, but melds that with a smooth, satiny finish and flavors of earth, tobacco, and soy. Just enough cherry fruit remains, but this needs to be drunk up. **90** *(8/1/2006)*

Carpineto 1999 Sillano Sangiovese (Toscana) $75. The first vintage for this wine, a 60-40 blend of Sangiovese and Cabernet, has yielded a rich, currant-laden wine that picks up plenty of earthy and tobacco nuances on the nose. Again, the texture is creamy-smooth, the finish chewy and firm. **91** *(11/1/2003)*

Carpineto 2002 Vernaccia (Vernaccia di San Gimignano) $17. Pretty wild-flower and honey aromas grace the bouquet of this yellow-gold wine, which tosses up flavors of citrus, under-ripe pineapple, and peach. Finishes dry and clean, and not too heavy. It's medium-bodied at best, however, and loses intensity with airing. **86** *—M.S. (8/1/2004)*

CASA ALLE VACCHE

Casa alle Vacche 2001 Sangiovese (Chianti Colli Senesi) $11. Funky at first, with a nose of leather, rubber, and barnyard. It clears up after a while, and in the mouth you'll find some red plum. Spicy and oaky on the finish, with a good mouthfeel and thick tannins. Alas, there's also a burnt lasting impression. **84** *—M.S. (11/15/2003)*

Casa alle Vacche 1999 Cinabro Sangiovese (Chianti Colli Senesi) $20. Dark and powerful, with plenty of tight-grained oaky notes, hickory, and black fruit on the nose. Apple skin and black fruit flavors give way to a tannic, chocolaty finish that's as firm as a buttress. Some juicy acidity rounds out the package, which is substantive and rock solid. **88** *—M.S. (11/15/2003)*

CASA BALOCCA

Casa Balocca 1998 Dolcetto (Dolcetto d'Alba) $13. 89 Best Buy *(4/1/2000)*

Casa Balocca 1997 Nebbiolo (Barbaresco) $64. Shows a bit of the vintage's hot character in its aromas of roasted, caramelized fruit; also a touch of smoked meat. Flavors veer toward stone fruits, evidencing a touch of sur-maturité. Drinkable now and over the next 5–10 years. **88** *—J.C. (11/15/2004)*

CASA CONTINI

Casa Contini 2001 Red Blend (Salice Salentino) $7. Starts off with burnt aromas courtesy of full-force oak, and that scent never really loosens its grip. Apple skin and raspberry flavors come in front of a clean but somewhat innocuous finish. As for mouthfeel, bracing acids ensure that this wine doesn't feel flabby, which can sometimes be the case with Puglian reds of lesser quality. **86 Best Buy** *—M.S. (1/1/2004)*

CASA DI ROCCO

Casa di Rocco 2005 Pinot Grigio (Delle Venezie) $10. Lemongrass aromas are reminiscent of Prosecco and make this a crisp, informal wine to be enjoyed on hot afternoons. The mouthfeel is a tad watery, but the wine glides over the palate nonetheless thanks to good acidity. **86 Best Buy** —*M.L. (6/1/2006)*

Casa di Rocco 2004 Pinot Grigio (Venezie) $10. A little out of the ordinary with spicy, smoked meat aromas mixed with baked pear and melon. Shows a strong almondy note to the palate, which rides alongside melon and peach. Crisp and citrusy on the finish. **86 Best Buy** *(2/1/2006)*

Casa di Rocco 2004 Sangiovese (Chianti) $10. Exhibits touches of grilled meat, burnt grass, and red fruits on the nose. Next in line is a snappy palate of crisp cherry and red plum. Not hard and sour, but it is austere. Good in its own way. **84** *—M.S. (10/1/2006)*

CASA GIRELLI

Casa Girelli 1998 Fontella Chianti Red Blend (Tuscany) $8. Nicely balanced in a lighter style, this shows some barnyard and earth notes on the nose, coupled with cherry, cedar, and tea aromas. Cherry fruit and a chalky feel mark the palate and moderately long finish. **85 Best Buy** *(4/1/2001)*

Casa Girelli 2001 Virtuoso Syrah (Sicilia) $20. Powerful wine, with richly perfumed fruit and firm, dry tannins. Wood aging (12 months in French and American) produces smoky flavors of blackberries and vanilla. **87** —*R.V. (10/1/2003)*

CASA VINO

Casa Vino 2003 Nero d'Avola (Sicilia) $9. Fresh and fragrant, with a jumble of cherry, plum, and raspberry aromas. The palate is tight and snappy, with raspberry along with a sure fire dose of lemon-based acidity. Quite tight and scouring, due to that aforementioned acidity. **85 Best Buy** *—M.S. (7/1/2005)*

Casa Vino 2002 Sangiovese (Chianti) $10. Warm and fruity, with herbal cherry aromas. On the palate there's raspberry as well as an all-too-familiar lemony streak to the middle. Citrus peel and milk chocolate carry the finish. Too tart and zesty to be taken more seriously. **83** *(4/1/2005)*

Casa Vino 2000 Riserva Sangiovese (Chianti) $13. Grapey and jammy on the nose, with blackberry and vanilla aromas. Hits firmly with cherry flavors, but the feel is a touch coarse, courtesy of hard tannins. At times the wine even throws off an artificial flavor, but it's hard to retrieve, so we've discounted it. **86** *(4/1/2005)*

CASA ZULIANI

Casa Zuliani 2004 Pinot Grigio (Collio) $18. Of the two Pinot Grigios submitted by this producer, the Collio version was silkier, soother, and generally more satisfying. The nose opens with butterscotch, almonds, and ripe melon. Thick and fulfilling, with a zesty finish that leaves a long-lasting, tingling sensation. **87** *—M.L. (2/1/2006)*

Casa Zuliani 2004 Pinot Grigio (Isonzo del Friuli) $15. A notch below this producer's Collio version in terms of aromatic intensity, with green notes replacing nutty ones. Clean minerality is delivered on the back of dried grass or basil. **86** *—M.L. (2/1/2006)*

CASABIANCA

Casabianca NV Brut Prosecco (Montello e Colli Asolani) $14. A little inconsistent on the nose, with initial mustard seed and scallion notes giving way to cookie dough and saline. Apple, baking spices, and green herb flavors dominate the palate, while the finish is juicy, sweet, and straightforward. **85** *—M.S. (12/15/2004)*

CASALE DELLO SPARVIERO

Casale dello Sparviero 1997 Sangiovese (Chianti Classico) $16. This medium-weight wine displays ripe cherry fruit, heavy cedar accents, and an easy, balanced mouthfeel. The fruit turns a bit pruny, but it also shows richness, even a touch of viscosity. The oak is cranked up on the fairly long, dry dark finish. Good now, better in a year. **85** *(4/1/2001)*

Casale dello Sparviero 1997 Riserva Sangiovese (Chianti Classico) $27. This dark wine has ripe black cherry and plum fruit complemented by cinnamon, clove, and heavy-toast oak. The suavely smooth palate displays more black fruit, licorice, and olive accents. Espresso and semisweet chocolate flavors accompany the dusty tannins on the long finish. Cellar for two to four years. **88** *(4/1/2001)*

CASALE TRIOCCO

Casale Triocco 2001 Sagrantino (Sagrantino di Montefalco) $NA. One notch down in aromatic intensity compared to the others, yet unbashful with ripe cherry, prunes, and blackberry. More cherry in the mouth and pucker-time tannins. **85** *—M.L. (9/1/2005)*

CASALFARNETO

Casalfarneto 2002 Fontevecchia Verdicchio (Verdicchio dei Castelli di Jesi Classico Superiore) $14. Aromas of almond, flower blossoms, and sea air seem encouraging, but the palate disappoints. It's too sharp and citrusy, with harsher than ideal lemon and orange flavors. Not much complexity or nuance with this one; it attacks forcefully with sharp acidity. **83** —M.S. (8/1/2004)

Casalfarneto 2001 Grancasale Verdicchio (Verdicchio dei Castelli di Jesi Classico Superiore) $22. Bright gold in color, which is unusual for the variety. Aromas of ripe peach, apricot, and salty air are mature and chunky. The palate is equally ripe and forward, with flavors of honey, nuts and corn flakes. Turns sweet and mildly cloying on the midpalate, with vanilla on the finish. Not for everyone, but has merits. **86** —M.S. (8/1/2004)

CASALI DI BIBBIANO

Casali di Bibbiano 2000 Argante Sangiovese (Toscana) $32. Damp and dank smelling, with some caramel and fat fruit. Flavors of prune and carob are milky and full. Big and sweet. Not too charming. **82** —M.S. (10/1/2004)

Casali di Bibbiano 2001 Capannino Riserva Sangiovese (Chianti Classico) $30. Plump and ever so ripe, with hedonistic cinnamon, caramel and coffee aromas atop jammy black plum and prune. A tiny bit soft on the palate, but with enough racy kirsch, cassis, and nutmeg to rank it as a showstopper. Port-like at the end, where you finally feel some tannic weight. **91 Editors' Choice** *(4/1/2005)*

Casali di Bibbiano 2002 Montornello Sangiovese (Chianti Classico) $18. Dark and dense, with medicinal aromas of jerky, molasses and fresh-cut wood. Runs bold and sweet on the palate, with candied plum and black cherry. Quite a lot of burnt sugar on the finish renders it moody and chewy. **86** *(4/1/2005)*

CASALNOVA

Casalnova NV Extra Dry Prosecco (Prosecco del Veneto) $15. Apple and fresh celery aromas define the nose. The palate offers equal doses of apple, lees, and mineral notes, while the finish is a touch chalky and very slightly bitter. Not flawed but a bit less than generous in Prosecco's normal zest and clarity. **86** *—M.S. (12/15/2006)*

CASALOSTE

Casaloste 2000 Sangiovese (Chianti Classico) $30. The nose is grainy and dense, with short fruit aromas and iodine. The palate is grippy and loaded with dark, rubbery plum notes. Sharp and lean on the finish. **82** *—M.S. (10/1/2004)*

Casaloste 1999 Sangiovese (Chianti Classico) $28. Muscular, with earth and mineral notes to the cherry and currant aromas. The palate is more open and less dark than the bouquet, with raspberry and plum fruit. The finish is drying and hard, with a bitter chocolate note. This wine is definitely firm and structured, nicely done, but rather tough. **87** *—M.S. (12/31/2002)*

Casaloste 1998 Sangiovese (Chianti Classico) $26. The nose of this organically grown Chianti has attractive and balanced dark berry, violet, and saddle-leather elements, along with a lavish dose of toasty oak. In the mouth the wine is full but carries a bit of an edge, and the heavy char of the oak really takes over on the palate and into the long finish. **85** *(4/1/2001)*

Casaloste 1999 Don Vincenzo Riserva Sangiovese (Chianti Classico) $80. Friendly for a Chianti, with open aromas topped off by bacon, leather, and bitter chocolate. Masculine enough, but not hard. The palate is bulky and filled with berry and plum flavors. Lasting, long, and juicy toward the end, with firm tannins that act as pillars for the wine. **91** *(4/1/2005)*

Casaloste 1999 Riserva Sangiovese (Chianti Classico) $38. What begins as cheesy and astringent gains clarity with time. The nose ultimately turns toward bacon and cedar, while the toasty palate offers red plum and plenty of lemony oak. Intense and brightly fruity, but arguably a touch too zesty for its own good. **87** *(4/1/2005)*

Casaloste 1998 Riserva Sangiovese (Chianti Classico) $45. Oaky for sure, with a strong whiff of coconut and butter on the nose. The palate is fairly pure, with bursting cherry fruit pouring it on prior to a layered finish of tannins, wood, vanilla, and licorice. This could make for a good fireside wine, given its fullness. **87** *—M.S. (12/31/2002)*

Casaloste 1997 Riserva Sangiovese (Chianti Classico) $44. A finely rendered barrique-style wine, with an elegant menthol-cedar-toast nose. Medium-weight and smooth, it displays black cherry, chocolate, and licorice flavors, and velvety tannins on the long sweet-and-sour finish. The overall profile is dark, but the fine fruit holds its own against the heavy oak. One of the few certified organic Chiantis, this tastes good now and should improve over the next two to four years. **88** *(4/1/2001)*

CASANOVA DI NERI

Casanova di Neri 2000 Brunello (Brunello di Montalcino) $56. Almost opaque in color, with more smoke and leather than opulent fruit. The palate shows excellent depth and intensity, even if the blackberry and plum fruit flavors are currently blanketed by oak. Big tannins and a sturdy feel indicate that some aging is necessary. Finishes with masculine coffee, chocolate, and earth notes. **91** *—M.S. (7/1/2005)*

Casanova di Neri 1999 Brunello (Brunello di Montalcino) $70. Rich almost to the point of chunky; aromas of coffee and new oak announce its New World style, and then come blackberry, chocolate, and smoked-meat flavors. This wine is probably shocking to the old guard, but if tastes this good, drink it. **93** *—M.S. (6/1/2004)*

Casanova di Neri 2000 Cerretalto Brunello (Brunello di Montalcino) $130. Bravo Giacomo Neri! This wine raises the bar on modern Brunello and offers a peek view into the future and potential of this incredibly expressive wine. Super concentrated and intense, whiffs of roasted espresso bean, tannery, summer-ripe black cherries, and porcini mushrooms peel back layer after layer. A firmly tannic touch is there to remind you to drink this wine anytime after ten years. **96** *(4/1/2006)*

Casanova di Neri 2001 Tenuta Nuova Brunello (Brunello di Montalcino) $65. A beautiful showing thanks to rich red fruit, pomegranate, blackberry, plum, menthol, and heavy toasted notes such as clove, vanilla, almond, and coconut. Rich, supple, and inky, this is a big, bold wine that should be opened 5–10 years from now. **91** *(4/1/2006)*

Casanova di Neri 1994 Tenuta Nuova Brunello (Brunello di Montalcino) $50. 87 *—M.S. (3/1/2000)*

CASANUOVA DELLE CERBAIE

Casanuova delle Cerbaie 2001 Brunello (Brunello di Montalcino) $65. Delicate and subdued, there's an attractive herbal or menthol quality to this wine that is reinforced by cracked black pepper, tobacconists' shop, and mint tea. Candy-like cherry in the mouth with a clean, crisp finish make this an immediately approachable, casual Brunello. **88** *(4/1/2006)*

Casanuova delle Cerbaie 1999 Brunello (Brunello di Montalcino) $NA. Rich, lush, and Port-like, with tons of sweet fruit. The rush of dark plum and berry carried on the wavy, dense palate is hedonistic, and while it won't age forever, the bet here is that it'll prove irresistible to anyone who tries it. **92** *—M.S. (6/1/2004)*

CASANUOVA DI NITTARDI

Casanuova di Nittardi 2001 Sangiovese (Chianti Classico) $26. Entirely gaseous and funky, with persistent sulfuric aromas. Better in the mouth, but still pruny and aggressive. Not pleasurable enough to recommend. **81** *(4/1/2005)*

Casanuova di Nittardi 1999 Riserva Sangiovese (Chianti Classico) $48. Roasted as if Starbucks got a hold of the grapes, and that charred character lasts from the deep nose, to the chewy palate, and finally through the smoky finish. Does it have the stuffing to support such copious oak? That's the million-dollar question, and some may say yes and others no. We liked the coffee and black fruit characteristics but were less fond of the lemon-pushing wood. **88** *(4/1/2005)*

CASCINA BALLARIN

Cascina Ballarin 1996 Giuli Barbera (Barbera d'Alba) $16. 83 *(4/1/2000)*

Cascina Ballarin 1995 Nebbiolo (Barolo) $45. 85 *(9/1/2000)*

CASCINA BONGIOVANNI

Cascina Bongiovanni 1998 Dolcetto (Dolcetto d'Alba) $18. 89 *(4/1/2000)*

Cascina Bongiovanni 2002 Dolcetto (Dolcetto d'Alba) $31. Crisp and sappy in the mouth, with tart cherry fruit and hints of bubble gum on the nose. Medium-weight and a bit simple, but certainly well-made. **86** *—J.C. (11/15/2004)*

Cascina Bongiovanni 2000 Nebbiolo (Barolo) $60. Tight and tannic, showing just glimpses of cherries, leather, and citrus peel, but gradually opens with air. It's a bit burly and rustic, and mouth-drying on the finish, but should show greater balance with several years' age. **89** *—J.C. (11/15/2004)*

Cascina Bongiovanni 1998 Nebbiolo (Barolo) $45. A supple, easy-to-drink Barolo that should please consumers looking for immediate gratification. Dried strawberries, cherries, and brown sugar aromas and flavors mingle elegantly, finishing soft. Drink now–2010. **88** *(4/2/2004)*

Cascina Bongiovanni 1997 Nebbiolo (Barolo) $59. At first rubber and tar obscure the dried cherry fruit, but given time, things begin to emerge. There's firmness and grip, and a meaty flavor throughout. Some salt and chocolate appear on the finish, which is linear and tight. **88** *—M.S. (12/15/2003)*

Cascina Bongiovanni 1998 Pernanno Nebbiolo (Barolo) $57. The tannins are full and aggressive. Flavors of Bing cherry, toast, and tar lead to a finish that does not have the fruit or complexity to hold up to the tannins, which will outlive everything else. **88** *—C.S. (11/15/2002)*

ITALY

Cascina Bongiovanni 2001 Faletto Red Blend (Langhe) $46. This intriguing wine is a blend of approximately 50% Barbera, 25% Nebbiolo, and 25% Cabernet Sauvignon, aged in barriques. A slight acetic note gives way to hints of pepper and sturdy blackberry and cassis fruit. It's dry and tannic, but possesses decent depth so it could develop into something interesting with 3–4 years of bottle age. **86** —*J.C. (11/15/2004)*

CASCINA CHICCO

Cascina Chicco 1999 Bric Loira Barbera (Barbera d'Alba) $28. Piercing aromas of damp earth, cocoa, and leather tell you most of what you need to know: This is the real deal. A mouth full of cherry and currant may not push finesse, but the fruit is merciless in its intensity. Juicy and full, with gas in the tank. **89** —*M.S. (12/15/2003)*

Cascina Chicco 1997 Bric Loira Barbera (Barbera d'Alba) $26. 93 *(4/1/2000)*

Cascina Chicco 1997 Valmaggiore Nebbiolo (Roero) $25. 89 —*M.M. (9/1/2000)*

CASCINA CUCCO

Cascina Cucco 1998 Cerrati Nebbiolo (Barolo) $64. Notes of truffle and flowers dominate the nose. There are some black cherry flavors but more prominent is a dried meat, quality. Tannins were a little aggressive on the finish, but should settle with time. **87** —*C.S. (11/15/2002)*

Cascina Cucco 1998 Vigna Cucco Nebbiolo (Barolo) $64. Mint, spice, red chilies, and even some charcoal are apparent on the bouquet. Flavors of dried cherries and apple skin follow on the leathery palate. The ending impression is a bit light, but that's o.k. Not every Barolo need be a tannic bomb, and this one is quite pleasant in its youth. That said, another three or four years of aging is probably in order. **90** —*M.S. (11/15/2002)*

CASCINA LA GHERSA

Cascina La Ghersa 1999 Camparo-Superiore Barbera (Barbera d'Asti) $14. Chunky red plum aromas get this one cooking, and there is plenty more plum and cherry backing up the lively bouquet. The finish is clean, if a bit basic. Overall it's a tight, structured, textbook modern Barbera, one that'll be ideal at the dinner table. **88 Best Buy** —*M.S. (11/15/2002)*

Cascina La Ghersa 1999 Vignassa Barbera D'Asti Superiore Barbera (Barbera d'Asti) $40. The bouquet is a bit earthy at first, but then it hits stride, offering a nice mix of muscular plum and mocha-scented oak. The palate features classy red cherry flavors and ample spice, while the core is wound tight as a ball. The finish reveals solid tannins and healthy acids. **89** —*M.S. (11/15/2002)*

Cascina La Ghersa 2004 Giorgia Moscato (Moscato d'Asti) $15. Here's a gem of a family-run winery and a refreshing discovery in the Asti area. Following a selection of international and local varieties in the producer's portfolio, the Giorgia Moscato d'Asti is thick with spring flowers, mimosa, and jasmine. Apricot and kiwi are tightly packed around a dessert wine with just enough acidity to keep it perky and interesting. **88** —*M.L. (12/15/2005)*

CASCINA LUISIN

Cascina Luisin 1999 Rabaja Nebbiolo (Barbaresco) $65. Complex notes of leather, herbs and spice bolster decadent aromas of strawberries and cream in this luscious wine. The mouthfeel is soft, with ripe tannins so silky smooth they feel creamy without making the wine seem heavy. Dried spices and elegant hints of tea linger on the finish. **88** *(4/2/2004)*

Cascina Luisin 1998 Rabaja Nebbiolo (Barbaresco) $50. Hefty and earthy, with black cherry fruit, rubbing spice, creamy oak and ample horsey notes. This fairly weighty wine from Barbaresco's respected Rabajà vineyard is dark and lively on the tongue, offering deep espresso and leather accents over tart fruit. Closes with substantial, structured tannins. This will reward cellaring. Drink 2005–2012. **91** —*M.M. (11/15/2002)*

Cascina Luisin 1999 Sori Paolin Nebbiolo (Barbaresco) $65. Slightly minty on the nose, but there's also solid fruit backing it up in the form of ripe cherries. Fairly full-bodied, and firmly tannic on the finish, this wine could use some time in the cellar; try after 2008. **90** *(4/2/2004)*

Cascina Luisin 1998 Sori Paolin Nebbiolo (Barbaresco) $56. Some mineral and smoke aromas carry a hint of hay or grass. The palate is tight knit, with the full allotment of cherry and red currant flavors. The finish is

properly smoky and tight, with ample tannins. Nuances of dried cherries, cinnamon, and tea add character. Give it until 2005. **88** —*M.S. (11/15/2002)*

CASCINA PIAN D'OR

Cascina Pian d'Or 2004 Bricco Riella Moscato (Moscato d'Asti) $12. Winemaker Valter Barbero has produced a wine that is distinguished by amazingly persistent foam and intense herbal, almost menthol-like aromas. You'll also get flowers, exotic fruit, suds, and long-lasting mineral notes. **87** —*M.L. (12/15/2005)*

CASCINACASTLE'T

Cascinacastle't 2004 Moscato (Moscato d'Asti) $13. Producer Maria Borio and her family have crafted an elegant Moscato d'Asti ripe with sticky white flowers, grapefruit, earthy tones, green herbs, and fresh-cut grass. That green theme continues in the mouth. A delightful wine with a colorful, child-painted label, it would be great for outdoor events like picnics and barbecues. **87** —*M.L. (12/15/2005)*

CASCINETTA VIETTI

Cascinetta Vietti 2004 Moscato (Moscato d'Asti) $14. With less lively mousse than some, this Moscato d'Asti delivers an elegant and refined nose pinpointed on garden flowers, white roses, and hints of jasmine. These aromas are further accented by the polished mineral note that tightly frames this wine. **86** —*M.L. (12/15/2005)*

CASISANO COLOMBAIO

Casisano Colombaio 2001 Brunello (Brunello di Montalcino) $40. This wine had loads of toast, coffee bean, moist earth, spice, and stable. There's fudge and spiced chocolate in the mouth with a pinch of sour cherry over a black velvety finish. A solid, broad wine for guaranteed gratification but no hidden surprises. **91 Editors' Choice** *(4/1/2006)*

Casisano Colombaio 1999 Brunello (Brunello di Montalcino) $NA. Arguably a touch sugary and overdone, but still a good utility-level Brunello. The aromas of caramel and marshmallow suggest plenty of barrel influence, while on the palate the fruit veers toward candied cherry and raspberry. Good enough on the finish, and largely satisfying as a whole. **87** —*M.S. (6/1/2004)*

CASTELCOSA

Castelcosa 1997 Pinot Grigio (Venezia Giulia) $NA. 83 *(8/1/1999)*

CASTELGIOCONDO

Castelgiocondo 2001 Brunello (Brunello di Montalcino) $56. Vibrant black cherry is backed by chocolate, spice, cedar, herbal notes and vanilla. Dry and extracted in the mouth with pine and sour cherry flavors and solid tannins. **89** *(4/1/2006)*

Castelgiocondo 1999 Brunello (Brunello di Montalcino) $NA. Frescobaldi's Montalcino estate produces this nicely extracted, fairly sweet and modern wine. The style is refined and highly polished, with fleshy cherry fruit and a smooth texture. Maybe too simple for the cognoscenti but possesses sure-fire restaurant and mass appeal. **90** —*M.S. (6/1/2004)*

Castelgiocondo 2000 Riserva Ripe al Convento Brunello (Brunello di Montalcino) $95. Very bold and big with charred meat, sausage, and wild mushroom like aromas backed by fruit and delicate menthol freshness. A complex yet easy to interpret wine with a straightforward, velvety plushness in the mouth. A wine that calls out for grilled meats. **94** *(4/1/2006)*

CASTELL'IN VILLA

Castell'In Villa 1998 Sangiovese (Chianti Classico) $30. Browning to the eye, with orange peel, leather, and a leafy spiciness to the bouquet. Doesn't deliver as much in the mouth, where tight berry and cherry flavors are lean and just a wee bit elegant. Good but not thrilling. **86** *(4/1/2005)*

Castell'In Villa 1998 Poggio Delle Rose Riserva Sangiovese (Chianti Classico) $75. After six plus years this wine still carries a huge whack of oak, so much so that the nose exudes menthol, cedar, and fir bark along with black cherry. Quite fresh and vertical on the palate, with clean cherry and vanilla flavors. Tannic for sure, but with enough cushion to handle it. **89** *(4/1/2005)*

Castell'In Villa 1996 Poggio delle Rose Riserva Sangiovese (Chianti Classico) $63. Opaque and ultra-toasty, this very international-style Chianti has "black" aromas and flavors, nice texture, and a long espresso-and-dark-chocolate finish. It's solid, but really reads deep only in one dimension—the heavy oak regime. Pleasurable, but one has to wonder if the fruit will ever really shine through the woody veil. **87** *(4/1/2001)*

Castell'In Villa 1997 Riserva Sangiovese (Chianti Classico) $48. Overall it's lovely on the nose, assuming you like cedary notes of tobacco, cinnamon, and wintergreen. Inordinately zesty on the tongue, with fiery tannins and live-wire acidity churning away. A little jagged and rough in terms of texture, but very much alive and kicking. **88** *(4/1/2005)*

CASTELLANI

Castellani 2005 Pinot Grigio (Delle Venezie) $9. A correct and clean Grigio that lacks snap but delivers clear floral and peach aromas. Fresh and thin in the mouth, this is a casual, weeknight dinner wine. **84** —*M.L. (6/1/2006)*

Castellani 2005 Biagio Pinot Grigio (Venezie) $8. A standard fruit and citrus-driven Grigio, but wants a little more intensity. Thin and lean in the mouth, with a grapefruit-driven close that could match spicy Chinese takeout. **84** —*M.L. (6/1/2006)*

Castellani 2000 Arbos Primitivo (Puglia) $10. Soft tannins bolster stewy blackberry and black plum flavors on the palate of this good-by-the-glass bar quaff. A bouquet of sweet mixed berries, fresh-cut pine, and anise start things off. **84** —*C.S. (5/1/2002)*

Castellani 2000 Essenza Primitivo (Puglia) $9. This blend of 80% Primitivo and 20% Sangiovese has widespread appeal, particularly for those who like their wines smoldering and dark. One reviewer described the bouquet of blackberries and smoky wood as "a sweet forest fire"; the same dark fruit and charred oak flavors follow through on the palate and on the back end. **85 Best Buy** —*C.S. (5/1/2002)*

Castellani 2000 Red Blend (Monteregio di Massa Maritima) $17. Hailing from a relatively unknown section of Tuscany, near Grosetto, this wine is definitely sun-baked and stewy, but it also has brazen blackberry and plum fruit and a forceful, ripe finish. It's not the kind of wine you come across daily, so remember the name: Monteregio di Massa Marittima. **88** —*M.S. (10/1/2004)*

Castellani 2003 Sangiovese (Chianti) $7. Mildly sweet and grapey, with an herbal, almost spiced gumdrop character to the nose. Comes across a bit green on the palate, with a light-bodied crispness. Tangy and fresh on the finish. **84 Best Buy** *(4/1/2005)*

Castellani 1999 Sangiovese (Chianti) $7. Although the nose is a little hard to read, the supple mouthfeel and focused tart cherry flavors make this a pleasing and quite affordable red. Has enough depth to keep it engaging and a clean finish; a great choice for everyday drinking. **85 Best Buy** *(4/1/2001)*

Castellani 1998 Sangiovese (Chianti Classico) $12. Quite fruit-driven, even a touch candied, there's still much appeal in this wine's fruitcake and plum aromas and the palate's sweet-and-sour fruit with mild oak shadings. The balanced mouthfeel and easy tannins on the finish wrap up this ready-to-drink package. **87 Best Buy** *(4/1/2001)*

Castellani 1997 Beni Duilio Castellani Riserva Sangiovese (Chianti Classico) $18. There's lots of toast on the nose and palate of this very New Worldish Chianti, but there's no denying the appeal of the blackberry, espresso, and bitter chocolate elements. Gracefully broad-shouldered, it packs in a lot of flavor. The long, black licorice-tinged finish bears full, but smooth, tannins. Drink now through 2004. **90** *(4/1/2001)*

Castellani 2004 Biagio Sangiovese (Chianti) $8. Begins as a toasty, earthy number yet the palate is exceedingly tart. It's slim pickings on the palate, especially if you're seeking depth and richness. Instead there's a lot of acidity and monotony. Adequate but unexciting. **82** —*M.S. (10/1/2006)*

Castellani 2000 Biagio Sangiovese (Toscana) $11. Dark and meaty, with a strong oak element. Cherry and plum flavors are full and roasted; the finish is spiky before going flat and heavy. Hammering tannins. **84** —*M.S. (10/1/2004)*

Castellani 1999 Biagio Sangiovese (Toscana) $11. The bouquet is tight, with cherry and cranberry fruit and a touch of milk chocolate poking through. The mouth has a chalky feel along with plum and currant flavors. There really isn't much more to say about this wine. It has a dry oakiness at its base and only modest richness. **85** —*M.S. (12/31/2002)*

Castellani 2001 Biagio Riserva Sangiovese (Chianti) $12. A lot of wood results in a bouquet that's heavy on the spice, sandalwood, and clove but short on fruit. The palate offers medium-weight plum and tomato flavors, while the finish is chocolaty and clumsy, with a bit too much cream and thickness. As a whole it's awkward. **84** —*M.S. (10/1/2006)*

Castellani 2002 Biagio Sangiovese-Cabernet Sauvignon Sangiovese (Toscana) $12. Berry and bacon aromas are marred by a strong pickled overtone. The tangy palate is thin and full of ripping berry notes that are surfing on wiry acidity. Almost citrusy on the finish. **82** —*M.S. (9/1/2006)*

Castellani 1998 Riserva Sangiovese (Chianti Classico) $18. The bouquet is a bit dull, with grapey aromas, some hay, and some leather. The palate isn't that intense, with apple skin and plum flavors, and the finish is simple. **84** —*M.S. (12/31/2002)*

Castellani 1997 Riserva Sangiovese (Chianti) $12. The cherry aromas and flavors here already have an aged quality. Some nice spicy accents conspire to keep it alive, but it closes rather tart and woody. Doesn't show the depth expected in a riserva. **83** *(4/1/2001)*

Castellani 1997 Villa Teseo Sangiovese (Toscana) $13. There's a lot of earthy, meaty qualities to the nose and a lot of cedar as well. The flavors of black cherry and red licorice carry the mildest tartness. Overall it's lean, tight, and still a bit tannic. Give it a few more years. **87 Best Buy** *(8/1/2002)*

CASTELLARE

Castellare 1999 Poggio ai Merli Merlot (Colli della Toscana Centrale) $89. The name is a play on words. Merli is the plural of "blackbirds," and this wine is 100% Merlot. But it isn't for the birds. Black as night in the glass, with a brooding power that's confirmed on the palate. What's special about it is that unlike so many flabby Merlots, it carries Chianti-like acidity and an unbridled raciness. Excellent now with food, and it will age well, too. **91** —*M.S. (8/1/2002)*

Castellare 2002 Sangiovese (Chianti Classico) $22. Wiry and tight, with leathery aromas sitting in front of tangy red fruit. Seems a bit vinegary and sharp, but not overwhelmingly so. Pumped up acidity means it's juicy and mouth-watering. **84** *(4/1/2005)*

Castellare 1998 Sangiovese (Chianti Classico) $19. The sour cherry fruit and cedar accents here are in balance, right down the middle of the divide between the old and new styles. This wine cuts a fairly lean profile, as do more than few of the 1998s, and finishes dry with moderate tannins. **85** *(4/1/2001)*

Castellare 2000 Il Poggiale Riserva Sangiovese (Chianti Classico) $36. Soft on the nose, where you get mostly peanut brittle and graham cracker. Underneath you'll find a bit of green along with plum and berry. The wine has power, but it's also rather flat and alcoholic. Likely better in a more balanced vintage like 2001. **85** *(4/1/2005)*

Castellare 1996 Riserva Sangiovese (Chianti Classico) $26. Shows unexpected age, with brown around the edges and mature prune and orange peel aromas. The flavors are more alive, but are not vibrant. Rather dull on the finish, this isn't bad wine but tastes like something four or five years older. **83** *(4/1/2001)*

CASTELLARE DI CASTELLINA

Castellare di Castellina 2002 Coniale Cabernet Sauvignon (Toscana) $50. Spicy wood aromas are in the center ring although they do allow for compelling notes of black cherry, plum, white mushroom, and Indian spice. There's an odd bit of coffee-flavored yogurt in there as well. The firm tannins are drying to the point of being almost astringent. Drink in 2007. **88** —*M.L. (9/1/2006)*

CASTELLARIN

Castellarin 2001 Cabernet Sauvignon (Delle Venezie) $10. The nose is highly perfumed with the essence of black fruit and burnt sugar. The palate keeps with that theme, offering over-ripe blackberry and cherry but little balance. A heavy shot of residual sugar to the finish puts it into the "cocktail party" class. **82** *(5/1/2003)*

Castellarin 2004 Pinot Grigio (Delle Venezie) $7. Very floral in an almost exaggerated way, with jasmine, sticky summer flowers, and orange blossom aromas. Offers a cleansing mouthfeel, one of lively acidity and a lean body. **86 Best Buy** —*M.L. (6/1/2006)*

Castellarin 2001 Pinot Grigio (Delle Venezie) $8. A slight spritz brightens the mouthfeel of this lemony wine. Aromas are a bit musky, but flavors of peach and lemon are correct, and the finish is harmoniously tart; mouth-watering and with a hint of almond. **86 Best Buy** —*J.C. (7/1/2003)*

Castellarin 1998 Pinot Grigio (Venezia Giulia) $8. 86 Best Buy *(8/1/1999)*

CASTELLO BANFI

Castello Banfi 1998 Excelsus Bordeaux Blend (Sant'Antimo) $73. Fans of full-bodied reds should like this Cabernet/Merlot blend for its pure berry and mint aromas, its ruby luster, and dry, clean raspberry, and chocolate flavors. There are full tannins now, indicating that it will age well for about five years, maybe more. And it finishes nicely. **90** —*M.S. (8/1/2002)*

Castello Banfi 1994 Brunello (Brunello di Montalcino) $43. 88 —*M.S. (3/1/2000)*

Castello Banfi 2001 Brunello (Brunello di Montalcino) $68. Beautiful layers of cherry-berry, anise, menthol, cedar, minerality, and damp clay form an intense and elegant whole. Medium structure with earth, tea-like flavors, and a mélange of berries preface a smoky, spicy finish. **91** *(4/1/2006)*

Castello Banfi 2000 Brunello (Brunello di Montalcino) $68. At 50,000 cases plus, this is as mass-market a wine as Brunello goes. But it's a darn good one, with tobacco, citrus, and herbs on the nose. Runs a bit simple and grapey on the palate, but it's overwhelmingly ripe, healthy, and full-force. Nothing tricky here, just clean cherry, plum, and chocolate flavors sitting comfortably on a medium-to-full frame. **90** —*M.S. (7/1/2005)*

Castello Banfi 1999 Brunello (Brunello di Montalcino) $66. Rich, dark, and muscular, with deep, jammy aromas of plum and blackberry. Banfi toes the line between modern and traditional, and this wine fits their model perfectly. It's a ripe, sizable mouthful, yet it has some true-life edges to it. Drink now through 2009. **91** —*M.S. (6/1/2004)*

Castello Banfi 1998 Brunello (Brunello di Montalcino) $59. Smoke, leather, and cedar on the nose, with tart cherries and dry tree bark to follow. Finishes long and juicy, with rugged tannins and some chocolaty oak. **89** *(11/15/2003)*

Castello Banfi 1997 Brunello (Brunello di Montalcino) $59. The Mariani family has produced a hugely concentrated, wood-dominated wine with powerful smoky aromas and concentrated black, ripe, chunky fruit. It's heavy on the berries, both in the rustic, brambly nose and on the deep, tight, classy palate. Toasty flavors come through the fruit, but these will soften and blend in with aging. Unlike many Brunellos, this one is drinkable right now, but could be cellared for 10 years or more. **92** —*R.V. (8/1/2002)*

Castello Banfi 1995 Brunello (Brunello di Montalcino) $54. Dense aromatics with black plum, game, leather, menthol, oak, and anise notes open this full-throttle red. The plate shows impressive depth of flavor with tart plum and bitter chocolate notes, as well as fine fruit to acid balance. The long, dry, even finish wraps it up beautifully with black fruit and bitter chocolate notes. **92 Cellar Selection** *(2/1/2001)*

Castello Banfi 1997 Poggio all'Oro Riserva Brunello (Brunello di Montalcino) $125. Rock solid and compact. This wine is true-blue Brunello, meant to be cellared for 10 or more years. Flavors of plum, cherry, and currant are pure, and there's far more fruit here than wood. But the tannins are like nails and they get harder and harder with each sip. Yes, it's a top-flight Brunello, but hold, for best results, until 2010. **93 Cellar Selection** —*M.S. (11/15/2003)*

Castello Banfi 1993 Poggio all'Oro Riserva Brunello (Brunello di Montalcino) $125. 92 —*J.C. (3/1/2000)*

Castello Banfi 1999 Poggio All'Oro Riserva Brunello (Brunello di Montalcino) $150. Smooth and lush, with a ton of berry, cherry, and smoke character. Supremely ripe and full, with chocolate and spice mixed into the prime cherry/berry palate. This is a wine for anyone who simply loves wine; maybe it isn't ultra-complex but there's no arguing about its polish and style. It's incredibly round and likable. **94 Cellar Selection** —*M.S. (7/1/2005)*

Castello Banfi 1999 Poggio alla Mura Brunello (Brunello di Montalcino) $75. Banfi's single-vineyard Brunello shines in '99. It's ruby/purple in color, with lush black-fruit aromas accented by vanilla, violets, and licorice. Made in the so-called modern style, but with fine tannins and body. Some firm oak pops up late in the game, but if given a few years, that should be integrated. Good teeth on the finish suggest ageability. **93** —*M.S. (6/1/2004)*

Castello Banfi 2001 Poggio Alle Mura Brunello (Brunello di Montalcino) $75. Year after year, Banfi delivers the goods with confidence and character. It's a vibrant, ruby-colored wine with cherry, plum, vanilla, coffee, wet slate, and a strong mineral component offset by hints of green bean or rhubarb. A full, round wine with silky tannins that will flesh out further in 5–10 years. **91** *(4/1/2006)*

Castello Banfi 2000 Poggio Alle Mura Brunello (Brunello di Montalcino) $75. Quite the fruit bomb with little to no vestiges of Old World red wine. It hits with broad, meaty aromas of black fruits and keeps that tone through the round, rich palate. Everything here is black and ripe, but there's enough acid to produce a juicy mouthfeel. Finishes with licorice, fudge, and mineral notes. **92** —*M.S. (7/1/2005)*

Castello Banfi 1998 Poggio Alle Mura Brunello (Brunello di Montalcino) $70. Round and smoky, with more modern touches than many riserva-level Brunelli. The bouquet offers sweet fruit, while the palate delivers a full-court press of cherry and raspberry along with firm, hard-hitting tannins. Lively acids and a bit sharp. Not one-dimensional, but not overly complex, either. **89** —*M.S. (11/15/2003)*

Castello Banfi 2000 Tavernelle Cabernet Sauvignon (Sant'Antimo) $41. Smooth and stylish enough, with hints of bold black fruit, earth, and dill. The flavor profile runs a touch candied, with ripe but sweet berry and plum. A cool, chocolaty finish closes it out. Juicy, flavorful, and properly oaked, but a bit short on structure and foundation. **88** —*M.S. (11/15/2003)*

Castello Banfi 1998 Tavernelle Cabernet Sauvignon (Sant'Antimo) $41. This 100% Cabernet Sauvignon from near Montalcino shows plenty of youthful character. It has deep earth, tobacco, and tar notes on a black-fruit nose, expansive cassis and blackberry flavors, and a tight, structured mouthfeel that should relax if given the three or so years it deserves. Very New World in style. **89** —*M.S. (8/1/2002)*

Castello Banfi 1996 Tavernelle Cabernet Sauvignon (Montalcino) $38. 87 —*M.S. (7/1/2000)*

Castello Banfi 2000 Excelsus Cabernet Sauvignon-Merlot (Sant'Antimo) $78. As usual, this blend of Cabernet Sauvignon and Merlot has weight and color but not a lot of richness or sweetness. The berry flavors are snappy and juicy, with tight, focused acidity. Less New World than most Banfi wines, yet for an off vintage it has its good points. **87** —*M.S. (9/1/2006)*

Castello Banfi 1999 Excelsus Cabernet Sauvignon-Merlot (Sant'Antimo) $73. Smooth and inviting on the nose, with cassis and ripe plum aromas. Very modern and international, as evidenced by the blend, which is Cabernet and Merlot. Regardless, it's ripe, exotic, and features tons of black fruit, coffee, and chocolate. So modern and rich it might be best on its own rather than with food. Drink soon. **92** —*M.S. (11/15/2003)*

Castello Banfi 1997 Excelsus Cabernet Sauvignon-Merlot (Montalcino) $73. Very supple on the palate, this Cabernet Sauvignon-Merlot blend has dense black cherry aromas and flavors framed by dill oak. Earth notes add a touch of complexity and the finish is full, with tobacco-earth accents. Attractive and easy-to-like as it is, but the wine seems to have the potential for more nuance and dimension than it presently shows. **89** *(2/1/2001)*

Castello Banfi 1995 Excelsus Cabernet Sauvignon-Merlot (Toscana) $50. 93 —*M.S. (3/1/2000)*

Castello Banfi 2002 Fontanelle Chardonnay (Montalcino) $19. Aromas of lemon drop, butter, dust, and fresh-cut wood are sizable, as is the palate, which pushes mango, peach, and pineapple. It's a fairly big mouthful overall, with somewhat of a waxy feel. Good but only reaches modest heights. **85** —*M.S. (10/1/2004)*

Castello Banfi 2002 Mandrielle Merlot (Sant'Antimo) $35. Soft on the bouquet, with an undeniable green, lightly, pickled quality. That holds true on the palate, where green notes infuse darker, riper blackberry and black plum flavors. Oak provides chocolate and espresso on the finish, but there's no escaping the vegetal undertones. **85** —*M.S. (9/1/2006)*

Castello Banfi 1999 Mandrielle Merlot (Sant'Antimo) $35. Fragrant and meaty, with aromatic hints of graham cracker, violets, and cool earth. But while the nose excites, the palate gets over-run with hard tannins that interfere with the blast of black cherry and cassis that's fighting to make it through. Good nose, nice flavors, but a tough mouthfeel. **86** —*M.S. (11/15/2003)*

Castello Banfi 2005 San Angelo Pinot Grigio (Toscana) $18. Creamy, rich, and sun-drenched Tuscan fruit always makes this Grigio stand out in a crowd. The differences between this and cooler-climate wines include generous summertime aromas such as yellow rose, ripe melon, tropical fruit, jasmine, and a fuller body. But you forego that extra crispness of northern regions. **87** —*M.L. (6/1/2006)*

Castello Banfi 2004 San Angelo Pinot Grigio (Toscana) $18. Most Italian Pinot Grigio is made in the northern part of the peninsula, and consequently a Tuscan version comes as a pleasant surprise. This is a very fresh wine redolent of apple, pear, exotic star fruit, and white grapes. The nose is clean as a whistle, and the mouth is spicy and crisp. **87** —*M.L. (6/1/2006)*

Castello Banfi 2004 San Angelo Pinot Grigio (Toscana) $18. Floral and a bit different, with a meaty, almost spicy character. Flavors of pear and citrus are modest, while the balance is good and the body light to medium in weight. Fresh and easy; borders on stylish. **84** *(2/1/2006)*

Castello Banfi 1999 San Angelo Pinot Grigio (Toscana) $13. Pinot Grigio is more commonly associated with northern Italian regions, but Banfi's Tuscan entry is a solid and fairly full-bodied contender. Lime and herb notes underlay the melon and pineapple fruit, and the mouthfeel is supple, almost rich—unusual for this varietal. The wine finishes positively, with herb and subdued tropical fruit notes. **88 Best Buy** *(2/1/2001)*

Castello Banfi 2003 Centine Red Blend (Tuscany) $NA. A succulent, chewy Sangiovese, Merlot, and Cabernet Sauvignon blend with a pretty ruby color and intense aromas of coffee, tar, leather, and toasted wood. The tannins are still a bit raw and beg for hearty meat. Tightly packed cherry and blackberry linger over a long finish. Castello Banfi performs the extraordinary vintage after vintage: It's almost a one million case per year winery and it continues to offer excellent quality on its lowest priced products. **87 Best Buy** —*M.L. (11/15/2005)*

Castello Banfi 2001 Summus Red Blend (Sant'Antimo) $66. Berry jam, open oak, and earth aromas come together after airing, and in the mouth there's blackberry, dark plum, and chocolate flavors. The finish is a bit reserved and toasty, and while the wine may not deliver the most complex secondary characteristics, it's on the money and exceedingly likable. A blend of Sangiovese, Cabernet Sauvignon, and Syrah. **90** —*M.S. (9/1/2006)*

Castello Banfi 1998 Sangiovese (Rosso di Montalcino) $22. This is a large-scaled rosso, and oak is used here lavishly but gracefully. Aromas of game, leather, and dill open to dark plum and licorice flavors and a dense feel on the palate. Moderate tannins show up on the long finish, accompanied by lots of toasty oak and licorice notes. **89** *(2/1/2001)*

Castello Banfi 2000 Cum Laude Sangiovese (Sant'Antimo) $36. Quite candied, with aromas of red licorice, cassis, and boysenberry syrup. A true berry ball, with forward fruit, a sweet and easy finish, and mild tannins. Laudable for its zippy qualities, but could use more structure. **86** —*M.S. (11/15/2003)*

Castello Banfi 1999 Cum Laude Sangiovese (Sant'Antimo) $35. This is a new kitchen sink offering from Banfi, featuring Cabernet, Merlot, Sangiovese, and Syrah. It goes full bore on the red fruit and oak, with spicy berry aromas and cherry flavors. The tannins are pretty hard, and with ample acids, this young wine currently starches the cheeks. But in

three years it should become a good to very good table wine. **87** —*M.S. (8/1/2002)*

Castello Banfi 2000 Summus Sangiovese (Montalcino) $63. Dark violet in color, and thick like syrup. Aromas of blueberries, graham cracker, and Coca-Cola seem sweet, while the palate is soft and one-dimensional, offering mostly muscular berry fruit but not much complexity or balancing characteristics. Has its merits, but given its track record it seems off form. **87** —*M.S. (10/1/2004)*

Castello Banfi 1999 Summus Sangiovese (Sant'Antimo) $63. Luscious and bold, with a round, masculine bouquet of blackberry, bitter chocolate and a whiff of coconut. The palate sports perfect harmony; it's full of cola, cherry, plum, and espresso. The finish is tight and right on the money. Lovely stuff from a fine vintage; a wine made in the rich, sweet, modern style. The blend is Sangiovese, Cabernet, and Syrah. **94 Editors' Choice** —*M.S. (11/15/2003)*

Castello Banfi 1997 Summus Sangiovese (Sant'Antimo) $63. This very internationally-styled blend of Sangiovese, Cabernet Sauvignon, and Syrah displays dense fruit, brisk acidity, and the lavish use of oak. Extremely dark aromas and flavors predominate, with firm black plum, tobacco, and earth elements. The long and even finish of this weighty offering shows tart blackberry flavors and full tannins. **91** *(2/1/2001)*

Castello Banfi 1998 Colvecchio Syrah (Sant'Antimo) $36. Syrah from central Tuscany? Sure. The '98 version of Colvecchio, an offering from a hot year, is leaner than might be expected and short on dimension. It has lots of oak up front and an abundance of spicy, tart red fruit in the middle. The oak kicks up on the finish as well. The effort is there and the fruit seems sound, but tartness is the over-riding impression it leaves. **86** —*M.S. (8/1/2002)*

Castello Banfi 1997 Colvecchio Single Vyd Syrah (Sant'Antimo) $35. **88** *(11/1/2001)*

CASTELLO D'ALBOLA

Castello d'Albola 2002 Sangiovese (Chianti Classico) $15. Candied and jammy, with reduced aromas. Black cherry flavors are moderately fresh, but the acids are spiky and the feel is a bit scouring. Not a ton of depth on offer. **84** *(4/1/2005)*

Castello d'Albola 2000 Sangiovese (Chianti Classico) $14. A solid, typical Chianti, with cherry, leather, and tobacco flavors. Largely supple, yet finishes with a tart, herbal edge. A blend of 95% Sangiovese and 5% Canaiolo. **86** *(3/1/2004)*

Castello d'Albola 1998 Sangiovese (Chianti Classico) $15. The aromas and flavors of black cherry, raspberry, cocoa, and toast are ripe and full in this medium-weight offering. There's a supple mouthfeel, and the finish displays even tannins and decent length, with caramel and coffee notes. Drinks well now, will be better in one or two years. **87** *(4/1/2001)*

Castello d'Albola 2000 Acciaiolo Sangiovese (Toscana) $50. This 60-40 blend of Sangiovese and Cabernet Sauvignon flaunts a dark purple robe and long legs. Floral, toasty notes complement black cherry flavors that come across the palate in supple, velvety waves. But this wine isn't just a sexpot. The finish is crisply tart, with a hint of orange pekoe. Anticipated release date: October 2004. **90** *(3/1/2004)*

Castello d'Albola 1997 Acciaiolo Sangiovese (Chianti Classico) $40. The black cherry fruit is accented by soy, menthol, and olive notes on the nose in this polished but reserved wine. Medium- weight and evenly balanced, it's very dark on the palate, with espresso, chocolate, and even a toasted sesame note showing. Closes quite dry with black licorice and mineral-chalk elements. **87** *(9/1/2001)*

Castello d'Albola 1995 Acciaiolo Sangiovese (Toscana) $44. **92** —*M.S. (3/1/2000)*

Castello d'Albola 1993 Acciaiolo Sangiovese (Toscana) $33. **92** —*M.G. (5/1/1999)*

Castello d'Albola 1999 Le Ellere Sangiovese (Chianti Classico) $20. Tobacco and black cherry aromas move into a dry, lean palate, where there are long, plush tannins and an earthy finish. Drink 2004–2010. **88** *(12/31/2002)*

Castello d'Albola 2000 Riserva Sangiovese (Chianti Classico) $25. Exhibits respectable clarity and focus, with aromas of bramble, hard spice, leather, and herbs. Strident on the palate, with potent lemon accents to the mainstream cherry and blackberry. Overall it's a little bit rustic and aggressive, as it seems more youthful than it is. **86** *(4/1/2005)*

Castello d'Albola 1999 Riserva Sangiovese (Chianti Classico) $23. Shows some obvious oak influence on the nose, in hints of coffee, toast, and chocolate. These elements smooth out and integrate nicely with the rest of the wine on the palate, joined by bright cherries and an underlying note of finely tanned leather. Boasts a chewy, rich mouthfeel and a long, tart finish, anchored by black tea notes. **91 Editors' Choice** *(3/1/2004)*

Castello d'Albola 1996 Trebbiano-Malvasia (Vin Santo del Chianti Classico) $62. Tuscany's flagship dessert wine is rigorously aged in wax-sealed miniaure oak barrels over many years in carefully ventilated rooms. The golden and delightfully sweet (but not too sweet) results are worth the long wait: dried apricot, almonds, honey, and roasted chestnut hit the palate. **90** —*M.L. (10/1/2006)*

Castello d'Albola 1992 Trebbiano-Malvasia (Vin Santo del Chianti Classico) $50. A beautifully balanced vin santo—not too sweet and not too alcoholic. Combines hints of nuts and stone fruits on the nose, develops apricot, almond paste, and chestnut honey flavors on the palate, finishing with notes of candied orange peel. Yes, the 1992 is the current vintage of this delicious dessert wine. **91** *(3/1/2004)*

CASTELLO DE CAMIGLIANO

Castello de Camigliano 1999 Brunello (Brunello di Montalcino) $58. Stately and complex, with fabulous structure and purity of fruit. The nose builds to an alluring peak, offering leather, cherry tomato, and plum along the way. In the mouth, the wine is strong and balanced, while at the end thick legs cling to your glass as it fades away like silk. **94** —*M.S. (6/1/2004)*

CASTELLO DEI RAMPOLLA

Castello dei Rampolla 2000 Sangiovese (Chianti Classico) $29. Medium-weight and medium-intensity, with aromas of cherry tomato, flowers, leather, and bramble. Firm and simple, with dried cherry and a touch of sweet chocolate. Hardly exciting but clean and much better than bland. **86** *(4/1/2005)*

Castello dei Rampolla 1998 Sangiovese (Chianti Classico) $26. Very dark plum and toasty oak aromas, deep espresso flavors, and a dense chewy texture are the hallmarks of this wine. Displays good structure: moderate acidity and ripe tannins. A bit one-dimensional now, it may show more nuance in a year or two. **86** *(4/1/2001)*

Castello dei Rampolla 1997 Riserva Sangiovese (Chianti Classico) $43. This wine pushes the oak regime to the max, and the cherry fruit is totally cloaked in menthol, toast, and leather aromas. Beneath the veil lie black cherry, licorice,, and black pepper flavors, and the texture is full and supple. The very dry finish is tannic, in a manner more woody than fruity. It has style and class, but only time will show if the fruit will ever come forward. Cellar for four to six years. **88** *(4/1/2001)*

Castello dei Rampolla 2000 Sammarco Sangiovese (Toscana) $116. Potent and alive, kind of rubbery and leathery, with a shot of barnyard thrown in for good measure. Shows solid cherry and berry at the core, but that fruit is offset by hard tannins and overt firmness. Not a lush, modern playboy; more of classic with old-world appeal. Needs time in the glass to unravel. **89** —*M.S. (9/1/2006)*

CASTELLO DEL POGGIO

Castello del Poggio 2000 Barbera (Barbera d'Asti) $13. Fresh herbs and arugula combine with bright cherry fruit and a little tar to make a Barbera that straddles the line between traditional and modern styles. **87** *(12/31/2002)*

Castello del Poggio NV Brachetto (Piedmont) $18. Bracchetto, especially made in this sweet, almost syrupy style, is not for everyone. But it is a little-known raspberry-colored wine with low alcohol that makes a perfect fit at outdoor barbecues or informal parties. The flavors and aromas are straightforward and direct: Raspberry, cranberry, and plum. **85** —*M.L. (11/15/2006)*

Castello del Poggio 2003 Dolcetto (Dolcetto di Monferrato) $12. This appealingly tender Dolcetto boasts floral aromas backed by ripe plums

and black cherries. Medium-bodied, it shows good length on the velvety-supple finish. **89 Best Buy** —*J.C. (3/1/2006)*

Castello del Poggio NV Moscato (Asti) $12. Flowery and spicy on the nose, this Asti boasts gobs of tropical fruit flavors and a short, clean finish. **84** —*J.C. (12/15/2004)*

Castello del Poggio 2004 Moscato (Moscato d'Asti) $12. Textbook appearance for a Moscato d'Asti with a thick layer of foam and a pale straw color. The nose is not super-intense but apricot, white blossoms, and fresh fruit are direct and clean as a whistle. Equally fresh and straightforward in the mouth. **87 Best Buy** —*M.L. (12/15/2005)*

Castello del Poggio NV Dolce Moscato (Asti) $15. If you can get past the intense lemon-lime aromas, this is a simple, easy-to-drink sparkler with loads of sweet citrus and pleasant tartness on the close. **84** —*M.L. (11/15/2006)*

Castello del Poggio NV Brachetto Sparkling Blend (Piedmont) $12. A bit heavy for Bracchetto, with slightly medicinal flavors of black cherries and sour herbs. Decent, just lacks finesse. **83** —*J.C. (12/15/2004)*

CASTELLO DEL TERRICCIO

Castello del Terriccio 2003 Lupicaia Cabernet Sauvignon (Toscana) $134. This is a first-class interpretation of Cabernet Sauvignon with a fine point of chopped parsley embellished by contrasting aromas of leather, dark chocolate, and plum. It's compact and composed on the palate with a refined smoky quality, dusty tannins, and lingering menthol freshness. **92** —*M.L. (9/1/2006)*

Castello del Terriccio 2001 Lupicaia Cabernet Sauvignon (Toscana) $140. A very exciting wine with amazing elegance and linearity that delivers intense aromas of licorice, menthol, toast, and pressed blackberry. It boasts a penetrating intensity in terms of its ruby color and in the mouth where firm tannins are followed by lingering freshness on the finish. **93** —*M.L. (9/1/2006)*

Castello del Terriccio 1998 Lupicaia Cabernet Sauvignon (Toscana) $90. A Type-A wine if ever there was one. It's high-voltage Cabernet, with just a touch of Merlot, and it's layered with cassis, buttery oak, and some toast. The mouthfeel is full but elegant, with mint and clove nuances poking through to impact the bold currant-laden palate. A smooth, well-oaked, persistent finish is the encore. Can easily be aged for a decade. **93** —*M.S. (8/1/2002)*

Castello del Terriccio 2002 Tassinaia Red Blend (Toscana) $43. This is a 40-30-30% blend of Sangiovese, Cabernet Sauvignon, and Merlot that is rich in floral and herbal notes. Rosemary, sage, violets, figs, plum, and licorice aromas are harmonious and well-integrated thanks to 14 months of oak aging. Allow the wine a few minutes to open in the glass. **91** —*M.L. (11/15/2006)*

Castello del Terriccio 2001 Tassinaia Red Blend (Toscana) $45. Always a fine choice among super Tuscans, Tassinaia blends one-third each of Sangiovese, Merlot, and Cabernet to a rousing result. The big nose takes a while to unwind, revealing deep black fruit and leather. Big and firm in the mouth, with unwavering structure and full boysenberry and other dark fruit flavors. Drinkable now but will hold nicely for another few years. **92 Editors' Choice** —*M.S. (9/1/2006)*

Castello del Terriccio 1999 Tassinaia Red Blend (Toscana) $35. Lively aromas of plum, cherry, and vanilla are on the mark and inviting. Flavors of blackberry, cherry and mineral are solid and complex. Finishes clean and proper. Simply a well-made, international-style red; round, ripe, and ready. **90** —*M.S. (10/1/2004)*

Castello del Terriccio 2000 Rondinaia Sangiovese (Toscana) $18. Rondinaia means "swallow's refuge," but you're going to want to swallow lots of this unoaked wine as proof that great Chard does come from Italy, and that it can be terrific without wood. Emphasizing fragrant apple and pear aromas, it has a wonderful natural texture and a smooth, stony finish. **91** —*M.S. (8/1/2002)*

Castello del Terriccio 1998 Tassinaia Sangiovese (Toscana) $55. Featuring Cabernet, Sangiovese, and Merlot, this New World red is big and powerful, with beautiful aromas of berry fruit, smoke, orange rind, and spice. The mouth is fully enveloping and downright delicious. It finishes with a blast of black coffee and toast. Big-boned and aggressive, but still fairly friendly. Drink now or hold for up to six years. **92** —*M.S. (8/1/2002)*

Castello del Terriccio 2003 Con Vento Sauvignon Blanc (Toscana) $36. This wine hails from the Maremma region of Tuscany, and frankly, it did not really excite us. The aromas are a bit harsh and astringent, while the palate is jumbled, offering tart fruit in front of heavy, bitter finishing notes. **83** *(7/1/2005)*

CASTELLO DI AMA

Castello di Ama 1997 Al Poggio Chardonnay (Toscana) $27. 88 —*J.C. (11/15/1999)*

Castello di Ama 1995 L' Apparita Merlot (Toscana) $150. 93 —*J.C. (11/15/1999)*

Castello di Ama 2000 Sangiovese (Chianti Classico) $38. Classy and precise. This is a wine that sooths and satisfies, but also is capable of playing at a pretty fast pace. The nose offers crisp red fruit, hints of orange, and plenty of dry leather. Snappy and secure on the palate, with structured cherry and raspberry. Proportion could be its middle name. **90 Editors' Choice** *(4/1/2005)*

Castello di Ama 1998 Sangiovese (Chianti Classico) $42. Plummy fruit supported by cocoa and herb notes and a decadent, over-ripe quality seen in no other 1998s. The ripe, supple mouthfeel provides sweet, if not overly nuanced, fruit. Finishes long, with even tannins and Sweet Tart chocolate and licorice flavors. Hold a year; drink through 2006. **87** *(4/1/2001)*

Castello di Ama 1997 Chianti Classico Sangiovese (Chianti Classico) $39. 90 —*J.C. (11/15/1999)*

Castello di Ama 1995 Cru Bellavista Sangiovese (Chianti Classico) $150. 93 —*J.C. (11/15/1999)*

Castello di Ama 1995 Cru La Casuccia Sangiovese (Chianti Classico) $150. 91 —*J.C. (11/15/1999)*

Castello di Ama 1995 Il Chiuso Pinot Nero Sangiovese (Toscana) $47. 87 —*J.C. (11/15/1999)*

Castello di Ama 1998 Rosato Sangiovese (Toscana) $16. 87 —*J.C. (11/15/1999)*

CASTELLO DI BOLGHERI

Castello di Bolgheri 2001 Superiore Sangiovese (Bolgheri) $79. From Contessa Franca Spalletti Trivelli, this wine goes back and forth. At one moment it shows light but clean red fruit but at other points it seems a touch weedy, pickled, and green. Raspberry, strawberry, and cola control the flavor profile, while the finish is soft and surprisingly light. **86** —*M.S. (10/1/2004)*

CASTELLO DI BOSSI

Castello di Bossi 2000 Girolamo Merlot (Toscana) $50. A varietal Merlot that is dark, masculine, and pure, even if it stumbles toward raisiny and syrupy. What keeps it in motion is the brightness of the palate, where cherry, plum, and chocolate dance in harmony. Probably best to drink soon, which will maximize vibrancy. **89** —*M.S. (9/1/2006)*

Castello di Bossi 2001 Sangiovese (Chianti Classico) $25. Dusty and moderately rich, with aromas of blackberry and a distant note of green bean. The mouthfeel is entirely on the mark, while the flavor profile consists of oak, plum, currant, and chocolate. Finishes tight and warm, with some bulk. A good food wine due to its correct balance. **88** *(4/1/2005)*

Castello di Bossi 2000 Berardo Riserva Sangiovese (Chianti Classico) $38. No bargain here, but it is a an excellent wine, made evident by the spicy, minty nose that's packed with attractive nutty nuances, coffee, and earth. Ripe and full, with fine structure, this Chianti is fresh, seductive, and round. The cherry and leather flavors are on the money, and the tannins are right there. **91 Editors' Choice** *(4/1/2005)*

Castello di Bossi 2000 Corbaia Sangiovese (Toscana) $50. A suave Sangiovese-Cabernet Sauvignon blend with dark, minty, cola aromas that mix with serious red fruit notes to create a character-packed bouquet. The palate is as ripe and aggressive as you want, but with good balance. Throughout the oak is present but integrated. Can hold

through 2010 without much effort. **91** —*M.S. (9/1/2006)*

CASTELLO DI BROLIO

Castello di Brolio 1999 Sangiovese (Chianti Classico) $16. This is rock-solid Chianti. Sharp, piercing aromas of cherry and red currant open the show, while intense red raspberry flavors make for a tantalizing wine that drives at full speed across the palate. A solid body and several layers of textures and flavors on the finish seal the deal. **88** —*M.S. (12/31/2002)*

Castello di Brolio 1998 Sangiovese (Chianti Classico) $50. Muscular and a bit raw in the nose; this is ripe Chianti, with a full dose of bursting berry fruit and an added element of earthy terroir. Firm tannins provide structure, and the cherry-berry flavor rides strong on the finish. **90** —*M.S. (12/31/2002)*

Castello di Brolio 1997 Sangiovese (Chianti Classico) $17. The cherry fruit shows mature earth and mushroom accents. Some coffee and leather notes on the palate add interest, and mild tannins on the finish wrap up the package. It's graceful, but also seems advanced for its age. **85** *(4/1/2001)*

Castello di Brolio 1997 Sangiovese (Chianti Classico) $40. Medium in weight but big on flavor, this is strong and stylish juice with plenty of plum, dark cherry, licorice, and toasty oak on the nose and in the mouth. Dusty tannins and ripe cherry fruit on the long finish close it nicely. Big and relatively unevolved; best held for two to four years. **89** *(4/1/2001)*

CASTELLO DI CACCHIANO

Castello di Cacchiano 1998 Sangiovese (Chianti Classico) $21. A bouquet of bright cherries, herbs, and cocoa opens this solid wine. The palate is big, with a creamy texture; tart cherry, tobacco, and toast flavors prevail. Tempered tannins and lots of oak flavors show through on the dry finish. Attractive, and should improve over next year or two. **88** *(4/1/2001)*

CASTELLO DI FARNETELLA

Castello di Farnetella 2002 Sangiovese (Chianti Colli Senesi) $14. Fresh and pure, if a tad light in weight and concentration. Fine plum and berry aromas and flavors convey ripeness, which is confirmed on the smooth, medium-bodied palate. Should go well with milder foods, things like roast pork loin or poultry. Supple and well-made. **88** *(4/1/2005)*

CASTELLO DI FONTERUTOLI

Castello di Fonterutoli 2001 Sangiovese (Chianti Classico) $26. Deep, lush, and enchanting for what amounts to a basic Chianti Classico. The nose offers licorice, black plum, wild berry, and clove. The palate is equally nice, with cherry, plum, and oozing berry all rolled into one. Fine texture; good tannic grip; good balance; just what the doctor ordered. From Mazzei. **91** —*M.S. (10/1/2004)*

Castello di Fonterutoli 1998 Riserva Sangiovese (Chianti Classico) $NA. The Mazzei family, along with consultant Carlo Ferrini, have produced another classic. It is immediately arresting, with aromas of dark chocolate, herbs, and new wood. On the palate, it is big, ripe, serious, with black cherry fruits and new wood flavors, combined with acidity and dry tannins. **91 Cellar Selection** —*R.V. (8/1/2002)*

Castello di Fonterutoli 1997 Riserva Sangiovese (Chianti Classico) $49. The great depth of dark cherry fruit in this suave, seamless wine is somewhat obscured now by the menthol-toast oak notes. But even now the supple mouthfeel is seductive, the blackberry and herb flavors compelling, as are the espresso and licorice notes on the smooth, lengthy finish. Fine fruit and structure will prevail in this keeper. Cellar for two to four years. **90** *(4/1/2001)*

CASTELLO DI GABBIANO

Castello di Gabbiano 2004 Pinot Grigio (Delle Venezie) $10. Slight lemon and almond aromas are freshened by a hint of the garden. Citrus and pear flavors show a bit of herb on the side, while the finish is tart and zippy. A bit dilute but better than simply decent. **84** *(2/1/2006)*

Castello di Gabbiano 1997 Sangiovese (Chianti Classico) $13. 84 —*M.S. (3/1/2000)*

Castello di Gabbiano 2003 Sangiovese (Chianti) $10. Jagged cherry and leather aromas carry some egg scents as well, followed by light red fruit flavors with a citrusy edge. Tart and tannic, but cleansing and fresh. Simple Chianti in its most main-stream form. **84** *(4/1/2005)*

Castello di Gabbiano 2001 Sangiovese (Chianti) $14. Leather mixes with the scent of dried fruits and smoke to make for an interesting bouquet. Ripe and snappy raspberry notes lead to a dry, precise finish that offers a shot of oak late in the game. Very lean and easy; quite the easy drinker. **86** *—M.S. (11/15/2003)*

Castello di Gabbiano 2000 Sangiovese (Chianti) $10. Earthy and dense, but somewhat brooding. Flavors of cherry and coffee mingle on the palate prior to a finish that shows some holes but nothing too radical. Tasty and more than satisfactory. **85** *—M.S. (11/15/2003)*

Castello di Gabbiano 2000 Sangiovese (Chianti Classico) $12. Simple and earthy, with aromas of sweet pipe tobacco and black cherries, and similar flavors. There's some sharp acidity in this very dry wine, so drink it with rich foods with plenty of butter, olive oil, and animal fat. **85** *—S.H. (1/1/2002)*

Castello di Gabbiano 1999 Sangiovese (Chianti Classico) $12. This affordable wine begins with aromas of tobacco, dried leather, meat, and cranberry, but it drinks fruitier than it smells. There's a burst of spicy black cherry on the palate, with soft tannins, and the high acidity was born to cut through heaps of olive oil and butter. **86** *—S.H. (9/1/2002)*

Castello di Gabbiano 1999 Alleanza Sangiovese (Toscana) $35. Leather, mint, and raisin aromas define the bouquet, which is backed by a ripe palate full of tree fruits. Feels rather heavy on the tongue, with grabby, hard tannins. The blend is Sangiovese, Merlot, and Cab. **85** *—M.S. (10/1/2004)*

Castello di Gabbiano 1997 Alleanza Sangiovese (Toscana) $40. The people at Beringer, which owns Gabbiano, had a lot to do with this super Tuscan, which explains the heavy dose of oak on the nose and palate. Nonetheless, it's full, expressive, and earthy, with an easy mouthfeel and ample cherry and berry flavors. Spicy, tannic, and still kicking—but maturing fast. **88** *—M.S. (11/15/2003)*

Castello di Gabbiano 1999 Bellezza Sangiovese (Toscana) $30. Hints of mint, licorice, and cedar precede grassy, leathery aromas. The palate on this Sangiovese is simple and slightly woody, with raspberry and strawberry notes. Finishes a bit thin and drying, with notes of oak and vanilla. **86** *—M.S. (10/1/2004)*

Castello di Gabbiano 1997 Bellezza Sangiovese (Toscana) $35. This 100% Sangiovese has sharp berry, leather, and chocolate aromas, raspberry and strawberry flavors, and a lean, oaky, yet fresh finish. Modest tannins work to spread the wine out, and the fruit, while thin and fading, seems ripe and not green. **85** *—M.S. (11/15/2003)*

Castello di Gabbiano 1999 Riserva Sangiovese (Chianti Classico) $17. Nice young Chianti with lots of black cherry fruit and brisk, sour acids that make your cheeks pucker. The wine is dry and balanced, and cries out for rich, decadent Italian food. **90** *—S.H. (12/31/2002)*

Castello di Gabbiano 1997 Riserva Sangiovese (Chianti Classico) $16. Lean and focused, this wine offers dark berry and plum aromas with cedary accents. Chocolate and cocoa notes add interest on the palate. The acids are a touch high—but they keep the flavors and mouthfeel lively and will make the wine work well with food. Drink now through 2005. **87** *(4/1/2001)*

Castello di Gabbiano 1995 Riserva Sangiovese (Chianti Classico) $16. 86 *—M.S. (3/1/2000)*

Castello di Gabbiano 2000 Bellezza Sangiovese Grosso (Toscana) $30. A lot of sawmill is present up front, but behind the loud oak there's plum, raisin, and some herbal leafiness. Attentive red fruit carries the palate, backed by a quick but clean finish that splits out the side doors. A bit gritty but will work with food. **86** *—M.S. (9/1/2006)*

CASTELLO DI LISPIDA

Castello di Lispida 1999 Terraforte Red Blend (Veneto) $40. Quite potent aromas of leather, berries, and smoked meat. Next comes a fruity plum and grape palate with pepper and plenty of wood underneath. The finish is forward, oaky, and dry, but not terribly complex or layered. Some might call it overoaked, but for most the fruit will come across as more than sufficient. **89** *(5/1/2003)*

CASTELLO DI MELETO

Castello di Meleto 2001 Sangiovese (Chianti Classico) $21. New age in style, with ultra-sweet aromas of berry preserves blended with pancetta and basil. One of the thickest, creamiest wines we encountered, with maple and bacon on the palate as well as candied cherry and plum. Could be perfect for some but sticky and cloyingly sweet to others. **87** *(4/1/2005)*

Castello di Meleto 2000 Sangiovese (Chianti Classico) $20. Pure and expressive up front, with aromas of leather, cherry, and earth. The palate deals standard but clean cherry and cranberry, while the finish runs tight and proper. Quite the textbook, traditional wine, but still rewarding due to its purity, snap, and pop. **88** *—M.S. (11/15/2003)*

Castello di Meleto 1999 Sangiovese (Chianti Classico) $17. Spice, clove, black pepper, and rhubarb make up the aromas, while the flavors are sharp and lean. There's a piercing red fruit quality to the palate that isn't overly generous. The finish, meanwhile, is fresh and mildly fruity, but again it's underwhelming. Overall this wine is rather thin, sharp, and angular. **83** *—M.S. (12/31/2002)*

Castello di Meleto 1998 Sangiovese (Chianti Classico) $23. Slightly candied cherry aromas accented by carob, cocoa, and herb give way to a smooth, fairly full palate with chocolate and Bing cherry flavors. This elegant wine finishes dark and dry, with full ripe tannins. Hold for two to four years; it should only improve. **89** *(4/1/2001)*

Castello di Meleto 1998 Fiore Sangiovese (Toscana) $36. Smooth and inviting aromas of spiced plums lay out the welcome mat, and that's followed by a bright, edgy palate with popping cherry fruit. On the finish, more of that cherry fruit comes on strong. The only weakness is that the plate is slightly hollow in the middle; thus the wine lacks the depth required to push it to the next level. **88** *—M.S. (12/31/2002)*

Castello di Meleto 2001 Rainero Sangiovese (Toscana) $39. Fairly ripe and round, with earth, fruit, and oak wrapped into a well-wrapped package. Medium-strength in the mouth, with good but not stellar blackberry and raspberry flavors. Finishes a touch sharp and short. Solid overall. **87** *—M.S. (9/1/2006)*

Castello di Meleto 1997 Riserva Sangiovese (Chianti Classico) $36. Chocolate, cinnamon, and plum aromas, a richly textured palate, and a lovely fruit-acid balance are all in play. Mint, dried spice, and leather notes accent the rich, plummy fruit. Well-dispersed tannins, tart plum, and cocoa flavors characterize the long finish. Drinks well now; will improve through 2004. **90** *(4/1/2001)*

Castello di Meleto 1999 Vigna Casi Riserva Sangiovese (Chianti Classico) $34. Tree bark and rubber combine with red fruit to create a sweet, woody bouquet. The cranberry and cherry flavors are dry and linear, while the finish is a medium-weight mix of baked red fruit and tannin. **85** *—M.S. (10/1/2004)*

CASTELLO DI MONASTERO

Castello di Monastero 2001 Sangiovese (Chianti Classico) $17. Smooth and likable, with a touch of candy, licorice, and cedar on the nose. More cedar on the palate along with plum, chocolate, and leather. And finally you get tannins and some acid. Sound textbook? It is exactly that. And it's good. **89** *(4/1/2005)*

Castello di Monastero 1998 Sangiovese (Chianti Classico) $16. It's black cherries and oak galore in this rich and very dark offering. Chocolate, espresso, and sour plum flavors keep on coming and the mouthfeel is big but not bulky. The fruit is solid enough to make its presence felt through the intense toast on the long finish. Drinks nicely now; better in one or two years. **89** *(4/1/2001)*

Castello di Monastero 2001 Montetondo Sangiovese (Chianti Superiore) $15. The real deal with a firm mouthfeel. From the start, where root beer and soy notes attach themselves to dry plum aromas, the mood is meaty. On the palate, it's almost hard. Tannin is in the lead, and it creates a gritty sensation on the tongue and cheeks. Best with food. **88** *(4/1/2005)*

Castello di Monastero 1998 Montetondo Sangiovese (Chianti Superiore) $13. Dark and alluring, with tobacco, toast, and mineral notes accenting the deep cherry fruit, this wine may not have the depth of this producer's 1996 Riserva, but is still pleasurable and more forward. Balanced and even, it's ripe and complete. Closes with interesting black tea notes and broad tannins. **88** *(4/1/2001)*

Castello di Monastero 1999 Riserva Sangiovese (Chianti Classico) $30. Round and full-bodied, with a touch of prune to the otherwise foresty nose. Tastes a bit cooked, but not enough to be a detractor. Beyond that, the plum, raisin, and black cherry flavors are deep and satisfying. Finishes expectedly rich, but with structure. Drink by the end of 2006. **90** *(4/1/2005)*

Castello di Monastero 1996 Riserva Sangiovese (Chianti Classico) $24. Deep cherry, cocoa, and cedar aromas, and flavors of plum, black cherry and chocolate are in full play here. The even, medium-weight mouthfeel is well-balanced and the long finish has fine, dusty tannins. A handsome example of the new, well-oaked style that will improve over the next three years. **88** *(4/1/2001)*

CASTELLO DI MONSANTO

Castello di Monsanto 2001 Nemo Cabernet Sauvignon (Toscana) $50. This wine is deeply toasted, boasting almost campfire-like notes lavished over aromas of prune, blackberry, tobacco, leather, and a hint of cherry liqueur. Roasted peanuts are another immediately recognizable aromatic component. Velvety in the mouth with firm tannins and a nice acid-to-fruit balance. **90** *—M.L. (9/1/2006)*

Castello di Monsanto 1999 Nemo Cabernet Sauvignon (Tuscany) $44. Earth, bacon, maple, and mushroom comprise the nose on this Tuscan Cabernet, which for reasons still unknown never seems to get to that optimum level of ripeness. Hence, there's a streak of green running through the heart of the palate. In addition, hard tannins make it tough to swallow. Time could help that, but it won't do much for the bell pepper flavor. **87** *—M.S. (12/31/2002)*

Castello di Monsanto 1998 Nemo Cabernet Sauvignon (Toscana) $38. Made entirely from Cabernet Sauvignon, Nemo is hard to analyze. It has typical Cabernet plum and cassis aromas, but also the scent of pickles. The palate is very soft, especially compared to the estate's Chianti. Flavors of soy sauce, licorice, and green pepper make for a confusing palate. It has its virtues, but also some faults. Hence the rating. **87** *—M.S. (8/1/2002)*

Castello di Monsanto 2003 Fabrizio Bianchi Collection Chardonnay (Toscana) $22. Here's a creamy Chardonnay with toasted nut, cheese rind, and even something that resembles bacon fat. It's clean and refreshing in the mouth, and promises to pair well with baked pasta or spicy chicken. **87** *—M.L. (10/1/2006)*

Castello di Monsanto 2005 Monrosso Red Blend (Chianti) $10. Stay-at-home pasta or pizza dinners call out for a simple but solid Chianti, and Monrosso fits the bill beautifully. The ruby-colored wine (80 percent Sangiovese with smaller components of Canaiolo and Merlot) is fermented in steel and aged six months in oak casks for fresh, fruit-forward results. It is redolent of cherry, plum, milk chocolate, and has distant hints of spice and licorice. Its lightweight consistency and subtle tannins make it an excellent, no-brainer match for most foods. **85 Best Buy** *—M.L. (11/15/2006)*

Castello di Monsanto 2002 Alaura Sangiovese (Chianti) $11. Normally a solid but unspectacular performer, Castello di Monsanto's "starter" Chianti struts its stuff in this down vintage (maybe some pedigreed grapes were declassified, thus making Alaura better). Regardless, it delivers spicy cola, leather, and tobacco aromas along with forward plum and berry fruit. The balance is correct and the feel is deeper than what we recall. **89 Best Buy** *(4/1/2005)*

Castello di Monsanto 1995 Chianti Classico Riserva Sangiovese (Chianti Classico) $22. **86** *—M.S. (11/15/1999)*

Castello di Monsanto 2001 Fabrizio Bianchi Sangiovese (Toscana) $35. Aromas of ruby berry, violets, and exotic spice identify this wine as 100% Sangiovese. Floral and fruity notes are followed by cookie dough, peach, almond paste, and toasted nuts with similar flavors in the mouth and a smoky, spicy finish. **90** *—M.L. (11/15/2006)*

Castello di Monsanto 1999 Fabrizio Bianchi Sangiovese (Tuscany) $39. More open and liberal than Il Poggio, this wine has damp earth, leather, and black coffee aromas. The flavors lean toward cherry and berry, with leathery accents providing a balancing offset. The finish is dark and chewy; it's something to mull, ponder, and enjoy. The structure and perfect balance say give it three or four years before it peaks. Editors' Choice. **92 Editors' Choice** *—M.S. (12/31/2002)*

Castello di Monsanto 1995 Il Poggio Chianti Classico Sangiovese (Chianti Classico) $45. **88** *—M.S. (11/15/1999)*

Castello di Monsanto 1999 Il Poggio Riserva Sangiovese (Chianti Classico) $55. Kirsch, smoke, and a hint of alcohol emerge from this muscle-bound, highly traditional Chianti. Cherry, spice, and pepper dominate the palate, which leads into a tight-grained, heavily tannic finish. The balance is impeccable, as is the purity, but if what you are looking for is a wide-open, fruit-forward wine, this may not be your bag. Give it at least five or six years before opening. **92** *—M.S. (12/31/2002)*

Castello di Monsanto 1997 Il Poggio Riserva Sangiovese (Chianti Classico) $44. This inky wine is large and very dark in flavor as well as color, with toast, fennel, black cherry, and tea on the nose and palate. Full and smooth in the mouth, it shows some attractive spice and good acidity. Finishes long, with full, mouth-coating tannins that need three or more years to resolve. **87** *(4/1/2001)*

Castello di Monsanto 2000 Riserva Sangiovese (Chianti Classico) $22. A touch stewy and brambly on the nose, with hints of plum and tree bark. Not overly packed or full, but with sturdy cherry and raspberry fruit. Finishes peppery, with soft oak; also fairly zesty, with live acids. **86** *—M.S. (10/1/2004)*

Castello di Monsanto 1999 Riserva Sangiovese (Chianti Classico) $23. Intense in the nose, with sharp leathery notes. Pure and clear cherry fruit forms the basis of what is a splendidly clean palate. The finish is tannic and tight, but it provides excellent support for the wine and indicates that it will age well. This is a leaner, traditional wine. Fanatics of fat, rich fruit bombs may not be impressed. **90** *—M.S. (12/31/2002)*

Castello di Monsanto 1998 Riserva Sangiovese (Chianti Classico) $23. Tight and closed right now, with a touch of sulfur and scrambled eggs on the nose. It's classic Chianti, meaning it's hard in its youth, with racy tannins and not much overt richness. Some caramel appears on the finish, courtesy of the oak. If given time, this wine will certainly open up more than it does currently. **87** *—M.S. (8/1/2002)*

Castello di Monsanto 1997 Riserva Sangiovese (Chianti Classico) $22. Elegant and cedary, toasty oak and tart black plums mark the nose and palate of this elegant medium-weight wine. Oak-derived dark chocolate and espresso flavors carry over onto the finish. Has appeal, but in a narrow range. **86** *(4/1/2001)*

Castello di Monsanto 1999 Tinscvil Sangiovese (Toscana) $35. At 75% Sangioveto (a particular Sangiovese clone) and 25% Cabernet Sauvignon, this beauty really pops both in the nose and in the mouth. It's quite international in style, meaning the Cabernet softens the Sangiovese, yielding a sweet and ripe product that has both character and proper balance. Despite 18 months in oak, the ripe fruit of the '99 vintage remains front and center. **91** *—M.S. (8/1/2002)*

Castello di Monsanto 1997 Tinscvil Sangiovese (Toscana) $34. This 75% Sangiovese-25% Cabernet Sauvignon wine's tangy dried cherry fruit shows herb, tobacco, and leather accents. The use of wood is quite apparent here—and the wine reads tart and somewhat cedary on the palate. Finishes with sour cherry and plum notes, showing good grip and brisk tannins. **87** *(9/1/2001)*

Castello di Monsanto 1998 Il Poggio Riserva Sangiovese Grosso (Chianti Classico) $50. In this vintage, Monsanto's flagship wine, made from 90% Sangiovese Grosso, is a prime example of traditional Chianti. It features racy, dry cherry fruit, hard edges, and structure galore. Whether it will evolve into a more open and friendly wine remains to be seen; normally Il Poggio ages well and improves in the bottle. **88** *—M.S. (8/1/2002)*

CASTELLO DI MONTEPÒ

Castello di Montepò 1997 Montepaone Cabernet Sauvignon (Toscana) $45. This 100% Cabernet Sauvignon from Jacopo Biondi Santi's Maremma estate is open-knit and sweet. Some creamy oak and loads of red raspberry make for an extremely cheerful wine, but one that doesn't have the tight grip and structure generally associated with varietal Cabernet. **89** —*M.S. (8/1/2002)*

Castello di Montepò 1998 Schidione Sangiovese (Toscana) $125. Despite a veneer of toasty French oak, this wine shines with complex layers of fruit. Black cherries lead the way, accented by hints of bacon, dried herbs, and spices. This is as graceful a medium-weight wine as we've tasted, satiny-smooth and filled with finesse. **93** *(11/15/2003)*

CASTELLO DI NEIVE

Castello di Neive 2000 Mattarello Barbera (Barbera d'Alba) $18. Great Barbera, perfectly matured and bargain-priced. Intense blackberry fruit sports accents of vanilla on the nose, but the flavors show hardly any trace of oak, instead emphasizing cherry and plum. Lushly textured, with a long, tangy finish. **90 Editors' Choice** —*J.C. (3/1/2006)*

Castello di Neive 1998 Basarin Dolcetto (Dolcetto d'Alba) $12. 91 Best Buy *(4/1/2000)*

Castello di Neive 1998 Messoirano Dolcetto (Dolcetto d'Alba) $12. 89 Best Buy *(4/1/2000)*

Castello di Neive 2005 Moscato (Moscato d'Asti) $16. Best enjoyed with fruit desserts, this wine is intensely floral with tones of cut grass and the variety's characteristic muskiness. Lusciously creamy and frothy in the mouth. **85** —*M.L. (12/15/2006)*

Castello di Neive 2001 Santo Stefano Nebbiolo (Barbaresco) $40. Crisp cherry and leather notes mark this medium-bodied Barbaresco. It's not particularly complex, but features the twin attributes of tasty flavors and early accessibility. A bit tart on the long finish, so likely to fare better with food than without. **88** —*J.C. (3/1/2006)*

Castello di Neive 2000 Santo Stefano Nebbiolo (Barbaresco) $38. Features delicate cherry and herbal notes on the nose, then intensifies on the palate, adding complex spice touches to the mix. Medium-bodied, with a fresh, mouth-watering finish. Drink now–2015. **90 Editors' Choice** —*J.C. (3/1/2006)*

Castello di Neive 2002 Metodo Classico Pinot Nero (Piedmont) $37. This is a well-balanced and pretty sparkling wine made from Pinot Noir grapes with brilliant amber reflections and notes of mature pineapple, toasted nut, and melon. It's frothy and creamy in the mouth with refreshing crispness on the close. The wine ages three years in the bottle on the lees. **88** —*M.L. (12/15/2006)*

Castello di Neive 2001 Metodo Classico Pinot Nero (Piedmont) $37. Vanilla, melon, stone fruit, honeysuckle, and lemon pie characterize this bottle-fermented (metodo classico), Pinot Noir-based sparkling wine. Rich and persuasive in the mouth thanks to two years of bottle aging on the lees, it makes an excellent alternative to Champagne. **88** —*M.L. (12/15/2006)*

CASTELLO DI POPPIANO

Castello di Poppiano 1998 Riserva Red Blend (Chianti Colli Fiorentini) $18. Deep and lush aromas of bacon, black plums, and leather make for a pretty bouquet. The mouth is like a full smorgasbord of cherries, plums, and chocolate. A warm and spicy finish that comes in several layers finishes it off. **87** —*M.S. (12/31/2002)*

Castello di Poppiano 2003 Il Cortile Sangiovese (Chianti Colli Fiorentini) $14. Sweet and creamy on the nose, with both caramel and vanilla accents. A touch candied on the palate, but chewy and wholesome. Maybe a little green if examined under a microscope, but if casually drunk with spaghetti or pizza it'll do the job. **86** *(4/1/2005)*

Castello di Poppiano 2001 Il Cortile Sangiovese (Chianti Colli Fiorentini) $12. Fairly dense on the nose, with balsamic, black olive, and tree bark aromas. The palate features cherry, plum, and pepper notes, while the finish is dark and herbal, with a noticeable amount of black pepper and other firm spices. Picks up complexity on the finish. **87 Best Buy** —*M.S. (10/1/2004)*

Castello di Poppiano 2000 Riserva Sangiovese (Chianti Colli Fiorentini) $22. This wine delivers bang for the buck as well as fine characteristics. On the bouquet, there's leather, black cherry, and so much depth it's as if you're looking down a well. Juicy yet firm on the palate, with

plum, raspberry, and chocolate flavors. Soft tannins don't mean it's flabby; rather they offer early drinkability. **90 Editors' Choice** *(4/1/2005)*

Castello di Poppiano 2000 Tosco Forte Sangiovese (Colli della Toscana Centrale) $18. It seems like this 100% Sangiovese has just missed the ripeness target because while it has a solid structure and a nice mouth-feel, it also has an unwanted green streak in the nose and throughout the palate and finish. So while there's modest cassis and plum fruit, there's also strong flavors and aromas of green tobacco and pole beans. **84** —*M.S. (12/31/2002)*

Castello di Poppiano 2000 Tricorno Sangiovese (Colli della Toscana Centrale) $50. You're going to love this minty, ultra-stylish red from Ferdinando Guicciardini, which boasts a nose of sage, cardamom, chocolate, and pure fruit. The mouth is deep and ripe, with delicious blackberry and boysenberry flavors. Finishes woody but satisfying. Drink after 2005. **92** —*M.S. (11/15/2004)*

Castello di Poppiano 1999 Tricorno Sangiovese (Colli della Toscana Centrale) $35. Smoky, rich, and pure, with potent aromas of black fruit and coffee. This is thick, extracted stuff, but it's beautifully balanced by grippy tannins that spread out rather than punish. The creamy finish is the coup de grace. **92 Editors' Choice** —*M.S. (11/15/2003)*

Castello di Poppiano 1998 Tricorno Sangiovese (Colli della Toscana Centrale) $35. Deep and dark, with extracted black fruit aromas as well as bacon and grilled meat. The flavor profile runs toward beets and blackberry, while there is plentiful sweet oak on the finish. The mix of tannins, acidity, and oak seems just about perfect, but the flavors don't seem entirely pure or integrated. Maybe time will bring it together. **86** —*M.S. (12/31/2002)*

Castello di Poppiano 2000 Conte Ferdinando Guicciardini Syrah (Colli della Toscana Centrale) $19. This wine just doesn't have it. It mixes tobacco and green bean aromas and the result is something akin to clove. Which doesn't sound bad, but is it Syrah? The mouth features pickled fruit and the finish tosses up some burnt coffee. Even the feel is hard and unfriendly. **81** —*M.S. (12/31/2002)*

CASTELLO DI QUERCETO

Castello di Querceto 2003 Cignale Cabernet Sauvignon (Colli della Toscana Centrale) $68. This lovely Tuscan Cabernet is blended with 10% Merlot and aged two years in French oak to render a softer, velvet-like wine that is an absolute joy to drink. The aromas are deep and penetrating and include sweet milk chocolate, cherry berry, leather, coffee, and tobacco. The wine makes an excellent impression in the mouth with a long tail of roasted espresso bean and candied cherry. **91** —*M.L. (9/1/2006)*

Castello di Querceto 2001 Cignale Cabernet Sauvignon-Merlot (Colli della Toscana Centrale) $69. You can't help but fall in love at first sniff: Here is a gorgeous nose with cherry and blackberry preserves, crushed clove, incense, black licorice, espresso bean, vanilla, and toasted wood notes. At the back of it all is a sweet touch of clover. The 10% Merlot helps render softer, rounder tannins and backs Cab's structure and firmness. **93** —*M.L. (9/1/2006)*

Castello di Querceto 1999 Il Picchio Riserva Sangiovese (Chianti Classico) $33. Smooth and deep, with cherry, chocolate, and earth aromas. Quite typical and traditional, with maturity as well as verve. Plum, cherry, and raspberry flavors create a fruity but basic palate, while the zingy finish is propelled by a wash of refreshing acidity. **88** *(4/1/2005)*

CASTELLO DI SPESSA

Castello di Spessa 1997 Pinot Grigio (Collio) $20. 86 *(11/1/1999)*

Castello di Spessa 1997 Tocai (Collio) $22. 87 *(11/1/1999)*

CASTELLO DI TASSAROLO

Castello di Tassarolo 2001 S Cortese (Gavi) $18. Not sure what the S signifies, but the wine is bland and low-impact. Some pear fruit finds its way onto the palate, and the finish manages to carry on, although it doesn't really say much. A bit of celery and tarragon flavor doesn't help. **82** —*M.S. (12/15/2003)*

Castello di Tassarolo 2005 Tassarolo S. Cortese (Cortese di Gavi) $13. Castello di Tassarolo is a medium-sized winery at the heart of Piedmont's

Gavi area with 20 hectares planted to the native Cortese grape. The entry-level Tassarolo S is an intensely fruity and refreshing wine that washes over the palate in a direct and determined manner. This is exactly the kind of wine you want to serve at picnics or outdoor lunches. White flowers, citrus peel, and exotic fruit emerge from the nose and the wine leaves a trail of zest and crispness in the mouth. **86 Best Buy** —*M.L. (11/15/2006)*

Castello di Tassarolo 2002 Villa Rosa Cortese (Gavi) $17. Rich in hue, with flowery aromas that turn creamy upon airing. This Gavi pours on the ripe apricot and nectarine, almost to the point of going overboard. While the fruit succeeds in exploding, there's some balance missing as it veers toward sticky sweet. **84** —*M.S. (12/15/2003)*

CASTELLO DI VALIANO

Castello di Valiano 1999 Sangiovese (Chianti Classico) $15. This spicy mainstream Chianti pours on the cherry fruit and plenty of tangy accents. Made from 100% Sangiovese, it eschews the blending of French grapes made legal in the 1990s. Medium-to-full-bodied, it has fine fruit to acid balance and a dry, even finish. It will pair well with grilled foods or tomato sauces. **88 Best Buy** —*M.M. (11/15/2001)*

Castello di Valiano 1998 Poggio Teo Riserva Sangiovese (Chianti Classico) $24. This 100% Sangiovese wine is from a single vineyard at about 400 meters elevation and made of hand-harvested fruit. The ripe nose and solid, masculine palate display power and class, showing brawny, dark, sour cherry flavors with tobacco and leather accents. Large-scale and well-structured, it is built to age. It should improve through 2004 and keep well for another decade or more. **91 Editors' Choice** *(11/15/2001)*

Castello di Valiano 1998 Riserva Sangiovese (Chianti Classico) $24. Full and dry, with excellent deep cherry fruit, the Riserva is impressive, and slightly less dense and intense than the Poggio Teo. It is also (at least now) a decidedly more refined wine. With its fine mouthfeel and even tannins, it shows more evolution, but will still benefit from a year or two of cellaring and hold well into the decade. **90** *(11/15/2001)*

CASTELLO DI VERRAZZANO

Castello di Verrazzano 1998 Sangiovese (Chianti Classico) $21. The nose here is appealing, with cinnamon and chocolate over black cherries. The wine has dry cedar and blackberry flavors and a lean profile. Finishes with moderate length and even tannins, and a slight bitter note. **85** *(4/1/2001)*

Castello di Verrazzano 1999 Riserva Sangiovese (Chianti Classico) $40. Leather, plum, berry, and chocolate aromas are standard, while the palate is citrusy and acidic. A touch too much acid-based zest and not enough fruit make it lean. Not unpleasant but lacking. **84** *(4/1/2005)*

Castello di Verrazzano 1997 Riserva Sangiovese (Chianti Classico) $38. Creamy berry and cherry aromas with glove-leather accents open into a tart cherry palate. Strikes a lean profile, with cedar and leather notes and even tannins on the dry finish. Best cellared a year or two; if it evolves well, it may merit a higher score. **87** *(4/1/2001)*

Castello di Verrazzano 2000 Sassello Sangiovese (Toscana) $60. Depth and richness are hinted at by berry aromas with a touch of liqueur. The palate runs snappy and snazzy, with racy but tasty cherry and raspberry fruit. This is a solid, medium-oak Sangiovese that shows modern touches as well as traditional purity. **89** —*M.S. (9/1/2006)*

CASTELLO DI VOLPAIA

Castello di Volpaia 1995 Sangiovese (Chianti Classico) $15. **88** —*M.M. (5/1/1999)*

Castello di Volpaia 2002 Sangiovese (Chianti Classico) $17. Red fruit carries this one, from the raw, leathery nose, through the cherry and red-plum palate, to the racy finish. Along the way are softening nuances of chocolate and cream. Modest tannins keep it from feeling too rough, so it should do well at the dinner table. **87** *(4/1/2005)*

Castello di Volpaia 2000 Sangiovese (Chianti Classico) $19. This purple, saturated middle-weight features aromas of soy, ink, violets, and mushroom, while the palate pours on blackberry and black currant. The lengthy, tasty finish provides layers of pleasure. This is a true mouth-filler that's thick and chewy. **90 Editors' Choice** —*M.S. (11/15/2003)*

Castello di Volpaia 1999 Balifico Sangiovese (Toscana) $46. Round and ripe, with woody hints, a note of bramble patch, and plenty of saturated red fruit. Flavors of plum, berry, pepper, and espresso drive the palate, followed by light oak and butter on the finish. Well-structured and well-made, it's another fine super Tuscan from the top-shelf 1999 vintage. **91** —*M.S. (11/15/2003)*

Castello di Volpaia 1995 Balifico Sangiovese (Toscana) $40. **90** *(2/1/2000)*

Castello di Volpaia 2002 Borgianni Sangiovese (Chianti) $10. Not very clean, with a murky nose of caramel and wet dog. Once things clear a bit, you get jammy fruit, some pepper, and a bit of earth. **82** *(4/1/2005)*

Castello di Volpaia 2001 Borgianni Sangiovese (Chianti) $10. Tight and muscular, with earthy, leathery aromas. Rich plum and berry fruit carries the palate, followed by a full-bodied finish. A well-balanced wine that's spry on the tongue and forceful, but not overdone. **88 Best Buy** —*M.S. (11/15/2003)*

Castello di Volpaia 1997 Classico Sangiovese (Toscana) $17. **87** *(2/1/2000)*

Castello di Volpaia 1996 Classico Sangiovese (Toscana) $17. **84** *(2/1/2000)*

Castello di Volpaia 1995 Classico Riserva Sangiovese (Toscana) $24. **88** *(2/1/2000)*

Castello di Volpaia 1995 Coltassala Sangiovese (Toscana) $40. **91** *(2/1/2000)*

Castello di Volpaia 2000 Coltassala Riserva Sangiovese (Chianti Classico) $36. Begins granular, with intense aromas of iodine and leather. Gets its feet underneath it with time, showing plum and black cherry flavors prior to a long, mildly bitter finish. If one word describes the palate, it's tannic. This is a wine that drills hard, leaving the cheeks exhausted. **87** *(4/1/2005)*

Castello di Volpaia 1999 Coltassala Riserva Sangiovese (Chianti Classico) $46. Spicy and bold at first, and then it evolves to display earth, trail dust, and flower petal aromas. Juicy in the mouth due to bright acids that prop up healthy fruit. The tannins are mammoth, but with a fine steak or breast of duck, they'll sing. Quite a nice surprise from a property in the midst of a renaissance. **91** —*M.S. (11/15/2003)*

Castello di Volpaia 2000 Riserva Sangiovese (Chianti Classico) $26. A bit bulky and roasted, but that brings with it tobacco, earth, and chocolate aromas. Expressive on the palate; the plum and berry fruit is exciting and braced by serious tannins. Those tannins are also a bit drying, so the finish seems tight as nails. Deserves air and time after opening. **90** *(4/1/2005)*

Castello di Volpaia 1999 Riserva Sangiovese (Chianti Classico) $29. Dense to the nose, with spice, mineral, plum, and chocolate poking through a veil of lightly applied oak. Roasted stone fruits carry the palate prior to a smooth, chocolaty finish. With full tannins and good acidity, this wine is pure and balanced. **89** —*M.S. (11/15/2003)*

Castello di Volpaia 1996 Riserva Sangiovese (Chianti Classico) $26. A nose of cherry, herbs, and chocolate opens to a mouthful of sour black cherries, licorice, and leather in this elegant offering. A well-balanced wine with nicely defined flavors, enough acidity to support the fruit, and solid tannins on the back end. Best held for two or more years. **89** *(4/1/2001)*

CASTELLO MONTAÚTO

Castello Montaúto 2004 Vernaccia (Vernaccia di San Gimignano) $13. A lighter, shimmying style of Vernaccia, complete with tropical aromas of pineapple, mango, and acacia. Stays light and crystallized through the palate, with fresh cantaloupe and mango flavors. Good but short on stuffing. **85** —*M.S. (10/1/2006)*

Castello Montaúto 2003 Vernaccia (Vernaccia di San Gimignano) $13. Sincerely aromatic, with scents of lilac, wild flower, and almond candy. All in all, the bouquet is anything but subtle, but it's still pretty. In the mouth, there's a ripe core of melon, papaya and spice, while the finish is big and smooth. Seems like the warm '03 summer helped this wine out. **87** —*M.S. (8/1/2004)*

CASTELLO ROMITORIO

Castello Romitorio 2001 Brunello (Brunello di Montalcino) $55. We can enthusiastically attest to this wine's top-notch quality across the board.

Rich and intense with cherry, leather, and a thick, syrupy nose followed by spice and power in the mouth. The estate is owned by one of Italy's most celebrated artists, Sandro Chia, and the winery is managed by Carlo Vittori. 92 *(4/1/2006)*

Castello Romitorio 2000 Brunello (Brunello di Montalcino) $50. Almost foresty on the nose, with an attractive, slightly sweet aromatic undercurrent. Quite tight and compact across the palate, with touches of black cherry, plum, and chocolate. Well-crafted, and with all the necessary components. 91 —*M.S. (7/1/2005)*

Castello Romitorio 1999 Brunello (Brunello di Montalcino) $59. A glorious Brunello, one overflowing with the scents of leather, tree bark, cherry tomato, and black cherry. One taste confirms the nose, and at every checkpoint it's full and rewarding. With its huge wingspan, there's flavor and texture at every turn. Hold for 3–10 years before drinking. 94 —*M.S. (6/1/2004)*

Castello Romitorio 1997 Brunello (Brunello di Montalcino) $55. Sandro Chia's winery is known not only for its reliable and enjoyable wines, but also for the art series labels—work from his New York and Montalcino studios—for each vintage. In 1997, the estate has produced an intense wine, skillfully managing the sweet wood and rich, dark, and concentrated fruit. The wine will age well—coming to maturity in 10 years or more—but will surely be drinkable in five. 92 —*R.V. (8/1/2002)*

Castello Romitorio 1999 Riserva Brunello (Brunello di Montalcino) $65. Surprisingly sweet but lovable just the same. The nose offers sugared doughnut and marzipan aromas yet the bracing acidity that ensures that the wine is neither flabby nor dull. Big-time cherry and plum flavors are pure and exciting; all in all there isn't much more to ask for. 93 —*M.S. (7/1/2005)*

Castello Romitorio 2002 Sangiovese (Rosso di Montalcino) $23. When you're seeking the perfect no-frills red but still want something that's made well, try this. It's a middle-weight with a hint of oak, raspberry, and a good, tannic finish. Brilliant with pasta topped in a meat sauce. 89 —*M.S. (6/1/2004)*

Castello Romitorio 1998 Sangiovese (Chianti Colli Senesi) $10. The solid core of cherry fruit bears herb, cocoa, licorice, and chalk accents. It's even a bit viscous, displaying a density on the palate not often seen at this price. Well-ripened tannins play on the smooth, moderately long finish. 88 Best Buy *(4/1/2001)*

CASTELLO VICCHIOMAGGIO

Castello Vicchiomaggio 2001 La Prima Riserva Sangiovese (Chianti Classico) $39. Expensive for what you get. The nose delivers cherries and mint, but also a shot of lacquer and/or chemical. Very sweet and bulky, with cotton candy, cherry, and cola flavors. Creamy in terms of feel, with a long finish. Of note: Our panel was not in agreement on this wine, thus the upper-midlevel score. 87 *(4/1/2005)*

Castello Vicchiomaggio 2001 Ripa Delle More Sangiovese (Toscana) $44. Rich and ripe, with a bit of prune, mincemeat, and tobacco. Very well put together, with blackberry and dark plum flavors floating on wide tannins that are present but not piercing. Finishes smooth and full, with likable notes of dark chocolate. 91 —*M.S. (9/1/2006)*

Castello Vicchiomaggio 1998 Riserva La Prima Sangiovese (Chianti Classico) $25. Produced from vines that are up to 80 years old (hence the name "The First"), this firmly concentrated wine is solid, rich, and powerful. The fruit has sweet black cherry flavors and layers of integrated wood to give balance. An impressive wine, this should age well over 10 years or more. 92 Editors' Choice —*R.V. (12/31/2002)*

Castello Vicchiomaggio 2001 Riserva Petri Sangiovese (Chianti Classico) $30. Highly complex and intriguing, given that it's also quite rich, extracted, and modern. The color is violet, while the nose is bloated with cured meat, vanilla, and dark cherry fruit. Rather thick and chewy, but balanced by proper acidity. A gem of wine, with a luscious mouthfeel. 91 Editors' Choice *(4/1/2005)*

Castello Vicchiomaggio 1998 Riserva Petri Sangiovese (Chianti Classico) $24. An elegant, balanced wine produced at the 10-year-old castle belonging to the Matta family. Fruit dominates, black and sweet with

soft tannins and perfumes of violets. A delicious wine that should age well over the next five years. 90 —*R.V. (12/31/2002)*

CASTELVERO

Castelvero 1996 Barbera (Barbera d'Asti) $12. 87 Best Buy *(4/1/2000)*

Castelvero 2003 Barbera (Piedmont) $9. From the region of Monferrato, this joyous wine just oozes youth, from its vivid purple hue to its fruity-perfumey aromas and bright flavors of cherries and plums. Sure, it's a little on the simple side, but it's fun to drink and would make a great pizza wine. 87 Best Buy —*J.C. (11/15/2004)*

Castelvero 2001 Barbera (Piedmont) $10. This regional Barbera is sweet and sugary, with thin fruit at the base. Seems false, although it doesn't taste truly bad. 80 —*M.S. (12/15/2003)*

Castelvero 1998 Barbera (Barbera di Piemonte) $8. 88 Best Buy *(4/1/2000)*

Castelvero 2001 Cortese (Piedmont) $9. The nose is akin to sweet pear, while the plate is mostly orange and apple. Despite it being low on acids, and consequently low on zip, the citrus flavors are good and the wine is round and pleasant. Some sweet pineapple works its way onto the finish. 84 —*M.S. (12/15/2003)*

CASTIGLION DEL BOSCO

Castiglion del Bosco 2001 Brunello (Brunello di Montalcino) $45. Engineered as modern Brunello and deliciously successful as such. Owned by the Ferragamo family. This is a wild card, new winery with little in the way of a track record and a lot to prove. But you can count on it becoming a pivotal force in a few years. Full, rich, ripe, dense, and fruit-forward with feathery softness in the mouth. 93 *(4/1/2006)*

Castiglion del Bosco 1997 Brunello (Brunello di Montalcino) $NA. As an expression of pure power, this wine is hard to beat. It has the classic Brunello color—red with edges of brick. The aromas are of bitter coffee, herbs, and mature, ripe fruit. On the palate, the concentration is enormous, the tannins pack a serious punch and the super-mature fruit is black and bright. All this gives it a one-dimensional, if impressive, quality. 89 —*R.V. (8/1/2002)*

Castiglion del Bosco 2000 Campo del Drago Brunello (Brunello di Montalcino) $75. Intense, rich, full-bodied: this wine has all the makings of Big Brunello with two capital Bs. Chewy fruit, incense-like sassiness, and an extra smooth ride over a panoramic finish. Nothing is out of place and no one element overpowers the others. Drink 2010–2020. 93 *(4/1/2006)*

CAVALIER BARTOLOMEO

Cavalier Bartolomeo 1998 Vigneti Solanotto Altinasso Nebbiolo (Barolo) $65. Nicely complex, blending such varied elements as smoke, vanilla, cured meat, tar, tobacco, plums and cherries in a pretty, lush package. Chewy tannins on the finish impart a hint of black tea. Try after 2010, when the tannins should have melted away. 90 *(4/2/2004)*

CAVALLERI

Cavalleri NV Brut Blanc de Blancs Champagne Blend (Franciacorta) $15. Here's a value in sparkling wine that boasts distinctive aromas, mainly scrambled eggs and toast. Chalk and mineral water flavors and a long, dusty-textured finish back them up. It's smooth and supple, yet also fresh. 86 —*J.C. (12/31/2001)*

Cavalleri 1995 Collezione Blanc de Blancs Champagne Blend (Franciacorta) $22. This sparkler got a major split decision from our panelists who either found it full and rich, loving it for its buttery, smoky, dense qualities, or disliked it for being heavy and simple because of its weighty, buttery, overly toasty personality. Either way, it's full-bodied and finishes dry and tart (or maybe bitter), with good length. 84 —*J.C. (12/31/2001)*

Cavalleri NV Satèn Blanc de Blancs Champagne Blend (Franciacorta) $18. Seems to be showing its age already—the aromas are of Emmenthal rinds and old moss. Toasty and vanilla-oaky, it's full and creamy in the mouth, with some subtle hints of plum. Finishes short. 84 *(12/31/2001)*

CAVIT

Cavit 1999 Merlot (Trentino) $9. This is a very dry, very acidic wine with thin flavors and a scoury roughness from entry to finish. It's acceptable for everyday drinking purposes, but doesn't offer a whole lot of pleasure. **81** —*S.H. (9/1/2001)*

Cavit 2000 Pinot Grigio (Trentino) $8. Sometimes all you need is a fresh, fruity wine that goes down easy and leaves your mouth feeling clean and zesty. This is that kind of wine. The flavors are citrusy and floral, and the acids are so high that there's a dry sourness in the finish. Perfect for grilled veggies. **84** —*S.H. (9/1/2001)*

Cavit 1998 Pinot Grigio (Trentino) $8. 86 Best Buy *(8/1/1999)*

Cavit 2005 Cavit Collection Pinot Grigio (Delle Venezie) $9. Nice banana nut, ripe peach, grapefruit, and mineral tones render a wine with caressing roundness and fullness. There's some citrus and spice on the finish, and a touch of sourness at the end. **86 Best Buy** —*M.L. (6/1/2006)*

Cavit 2004 Collection Pinot Grigio (Delle Venezie) $9. An enjoyable and quaffable wine that can be relied upon in spontaneous situations. Peach, ripe melon, lemon zest, and a dash of herbs create an interesting ensemble. Solid and smooth in the mouth, and very food-friendly. **86 Best Buy** —*M.L. (6/1/2006)*

Cavit 1999 Pinot Noir (Delle Venezie) $9. Atypical for this normally delicate varietal, here's a big, sturdy wine with aromas of black raspberries, licorice, and plums, and the fruity flavors are big and full-bodied, although those Pinot Noir silky tannins are here. There are some disagreeable raisiny, pruny notes in the finish. **82** —*S.H. (9/1/2001)*

Cavit 2004 Teroldego (Vigneti delle Dolomiti) $10. A very approachable wine for informal occasions. Has fruity forest berries, cherry, some herbaceous notes, a thin tannic veil, and refreshing crispness. There's nothing invasive or aggressive about this wine. **84** —*M.L. (9/1/2005)*

Cavit 1995 Arèle Vin Santo White Blend (Trentino) $42. A brilliant amber vin santo from the northern Trentino region with 10 years of age (six in oak) that flaunts toasted biscuits, rich nutty notes, and chestnut honey. Nosiola grapes are dried on mats, or settimana santa, from which the wine gets its name. **90** —*M.L. (10/1/2006)*

CCHIA

Cchia 2001 Corvina, Rondinella, Molinara (Amarone della Valpolicella) $30. Dry and balanced, this is a solid entry-level Amarone—not too big or rich, but still featuring plenty of Amarone character. Prune and fudge aromas and flavors are joined by a touch of almond skin on the finish. **87** —*J.C. (10/1/2006)*

Cchia 2004 Garganega (Soave Colli Scaligeri) $10. Floral on the nose, with confected scents of bubble gum and white gumdrop. Light in weight, with tart flavors of citrus and spice. Finishes crisp. Decent, just don't ask me how to pronounce it. **82** —*J.C. (10/1/2006)*

CECCHETTO

Cecchetto 2004 Pinot Grigio (Piave) $9. Offers Golden Delicious apple, pineapple, dried field hay, and jasmine aromas. A generous serving of baked apple comes through on the palate, backed by refreshing acidity. **87 Best Buy** —*M.L. (2/1/2006)*

CECCHI

Cecchi 2002 Sangiovese (Chianti Classico) $12. Herbal and leafy, with aromatics of damp earth, cherry, and leather. Snappy on the tongue, where apple skins and fresh red berries mix. Short on the finish, with mild tannins. Satisfactory, with no major bumps or dips. **85** *(4/1/2005)*

Cecchi 1999 Sangiovese (Chianti) $9. This is decent, basic Chianti with a tart cherry and spice profile. It took a little time for some sulfur on the nose to blow off, but when it did, the flavors were solid and the mouthfeel decent. Shows some tobacco and leather on the modest finish. Not complex, but good for every day. **85 Best Buy** *(4/1/2001)*

Cecchi 1998 Sangiovese (Toscana) $9. Seems old before its time, sporting aromas of baked fruit and worn glove leather. It's supple and aromatic but lacks the vibrancy and energy you'd expect from a young Sangiovese. Fading, but still holds some appeal. **83** —*J.C. (9/1/2001)*

Cecchi 1998 Sangiovese (Vino Nobile di Montepulciano) $27. The tight, foresty red berry nose opens with airing, setting the stage for a distinct plum flavor underscored by coffee and toasty oak. The fruit here is a little lean, but it's a nice, tasty wine sure to work well with food. Despite

being simple and straightforward, it should please most consumers. **87** —*M.S. (5/1/2002)*

Cecchi 1998 Sangiovese (Chianti Classico) $12. The cherries and dark plums on the nose and palate are accented by herbs and cinnamon. This light and dry wine is mildly astringent and closes with tart raspberry and cedar notes. **84** *(4/1/2001)*

Cecchi 2002 Arcano Sangiovese (Chianti Classico) $14. The nose leaks hard cheese and barnyard aromas at first, which are backed by notes of candied fruit and mint. Flavors veer toward cherry and raspberry, with finishing notes that are somewhat medicinal. **84** —*M.S. (10/1/2004)*

Cecchi 1999 Arcano Sangiovese (Chianti Colli Senesi) $12. The ripe fruit here bears lots of oak, yielding a black plum and licorice flavor profile, but it's pleasing and balanced on the palate. Sweet wood and cherry aromas play out on the fairly tannic finish. Good now, better in a year, but you have to have a taste for wood. **87 Best Buy** *(4/1/2001)*

Cecchi 1997 Messr Pietro di Teuzzo Riserva Sangiovese (Chianti Classico) $28. Dark fruit and menthol toast aromas set the tone, and the wine follows through in new-wave, deeply toasted style. Plum and cherry flavors, medium-weight. Closes with a tart, tangy finish offering dark chocolate notes. Hold for two or three years. **88** *(4/1/2001)*

Cecchi 2001 Spargolo Sangiovese (Toscana) $38. Big and boisterous, with cola, root beer, and raisin on the nose. The palate offers a ton of ripeness and hefty fruit, particularly cherry, plum, and currant. Finishes toasty, maybe slightly burnt, with some cookie dough sweetness. Mildly tannic in the long run. **89** —*M.S. (9/1/2006)*

Cecchi 2000 Spargolo Sangiovese (Toscana) $38. Very pretty on the nose, with warm plum, vanilla, and mint aromas. The palate is hearty and lively, arguably a bit acidic, but still very nice. Look for flavors of cherry, red plum, and light, balanced oak. The mouthfeel is good and the finish is smooth. Overall it's a winner. **89** —*M.S. (10/1/2004)*

Cecchi 2000 Teuzzo Riserva Sangiovese (Chianti Classico) $32. Cherry and raspberry aromas are sweet and easy, as is the palate, which sports black cherry, plum, and some kirsch. Finishes round, arguably a bit flat, with tannins that go thud. That said, aging isn't the ticket. Drink now with red meats. **87** —*M.S. (10/1/2004)*

Cecchi 1999 Teuzzo Riserva Sangiovese (Chianti Classico) $31. Named after the original owner of some of the Cecchi family's prime vineyards, this is a touch over-ripe but still offers a lot of sweet, rich fruit. Heavy prune and tar aromas announce the soft, saturated black plum flavor profile. The finish is also soft. It doesn't seem very ageworthy. **86** —*M.S. (8/1/2002)*

Cecchi 2002 Toscana Sangiovese (Sangiovese di Toscana) $9. Light and smelling of cherry Kool-Aid. Candied on the palate and finish. **81** — *M.S. (11/15/2004)*

Cecchi 2004 Trebbiano (Orvieto Classico) $11. There's a soapy-floral quality to this wine that is reminiscent of honeycomb, honeysuckle, and ripe peach. Thick and consistent in the glass, the wine has a creamy feel and some sourness on the finale. **85** —*M.L. (10/1/2006)*

Cecchi 2004 Litorale Vermentino (Maremma) $17. Firm but still a bit fleshy, with clean lemon and melon aromas. The palate is spunky and balanced, with tangy citrus and melon flavors. Finishes adequately long and fairly crisp, with lasting notes of passion fruit and grapefruit. **87** — *M.S. (10/1/2006)*

Cecchi 2003 Litorale Vermentino (Maremma) $17. Hugely aromatic, with sweet scents of flowers and candied licorice. Very big for a Tuscan white, a reflection of the warm region from which it hails as well as the warm summer in which it was born. On the back end, the finish pushes ripe apple and pear flavors. **88** —*M.S. (8/1/2004)*

Cecchi 1999 Vernaccia (Vernaccia di San Gimignano) $11. Musky aromas and flavors of melon and nectarine turn tart and lemony on the palate. The perfect setting for this wine: New York's San Gennaro festival, washing down clams from a mobile raw bar. **84** —*J.C. (9/1/2001)*

Cecchi 2003 White Blend (Orvieto Classico) $10. Soft, with vanilla cream and pear aromas. Lemon and melon flavors create a zesty wash across the palate, while the finish is chunky, round and mildly spicy. **85 Best Buy** — *M.S. (11/15/2004)*

ITALY

CECILIA BERETTA

Cecilia Beretta 1998 Terre di Cariano Red Blend (Amarone della Valpolicella Classico) $30. Anyone who says the 1998 vintage is a step down from 1997 hasn't tasted this excellent wine. The nose is rich and simultaneously complex: soy, marzipan, leather, and poached cherries are all there. The palate is quite a treat: There's snappy, acid-driven fruit as well as hints of orange peel, brown sugar, and coffee. **93 Editors' Choice** *(5/1/2003)*

CENNATOIO

Cennatoio 1997 Sangiovese (Chianti Classico) $22. Aromas of cherries, herbs, leather, and dried tomatoes on the nose open to a mouthful of cherry fruit accented by licorice and coffee notes. The texture is smooth, even, and dry. The full but ripe tannins on the finish have just the right amount of bite. **87** *(4/1/2001)*

Cennatoio 1995 O'Leandro Riserva Sangiovese (Chianti Classico) $43. Tart berries, a touch of maple syrup, and some orange peel on the nose open into a dry black cherry palate and lean mouthfeel. Sharply austere. **84** *(4/1/2001)*

Cennatoio 1996 Riserva Sangiovese (Chianti Classico) $37. Aromas of sour plum, chocolate, and wood give way to a mouthful of licorice-accented sour cherry fruit accented by cedar and caramel. Has good acidity and decent length, but the tannins on the back end are somewhat drying. **85** *(4/1/2001)*

Cennatoio 1998 Riserva O'leandro Sangiovese (Chianti Classico) $NA. **88** —*R.V. (8/1/2002)*

CERBAIA

Cerbaia 2001 Brunello (Brunello di Montalcino) $55. Chocolate cover cherries with interesting herbal, menthol like notes and a touch of earthy barnyard. Tannins are tightly bundled and need to relax, but there's enough fruit and structure to ensure graceful longevity. **90** *(4/1/2006)*

Cerbaia 2000 Brunello (Brunello di Montalcino) $55. Charred; almost tastes as if you came across a field or briar patch on fire. In the mouth it holds on to that burnt character, and the tannins seem exceedingly hard. More age should soften it up, but in its relative youth it's a raw, tough wine with screeching tannins. **85** —*M.S. (7/1/2005)*

CERBAIONA

Cerbaiona 2001 Brunello (Brunello di Montalcino) $135. Modern and smooth thanks to generous wood and toasted notes. Dusty cedar, lush vanilla, with blueberry and mineral tones. Oak smoothness translates well in the mouth and is helped by mellow tannins. Any more oak would bring it over the top. **91** *(4/1/2006)*

CERETTO

Ceretto 2002 Blangé Arneis (Piedmont) $20. Forward and fruity, with a nose of peach, pear, and subdued mineral. Flavors of lemon and green apple come with tang and zest, while the finish is sharp and precise, but not sour. The wine is a Piedmont white blend, one based largely on Arneis. **86** —*M.S. (12/15/2003)*

Ceretto 2000 Blangé Arneis (Piedmont) $30. So pale that it's almost colorless, the Blangé—made from Arneis grapes in Piedmont—has the oak-meets-citrus nose you'd expect of a Chardonnay. The lemon, grapefruit, and pear flavors, coupled with a super-spritzy, Asti-like mouthfeel, make this a good Sunday brunch eye-opener. Its slightly high acidity could cut through any French toast or waffle that you throw its way. Finishes medium-long, with herbal notes. **87** —*D.T. (9/1/2001)*

Ceretto 1999 Piana Barbera (Barbera d'Alba) $27. Super smooth and supple, with very ripe fruit and tasty oak galore. This is neo-New-World juice. It has rather low acidity for Barbera, and dense dark berry and prune flavors atop a plush, round mouthfeel. Finishes a touch shorter than expected, but it's a pleasure cruise all the way. Drink now–2005. **89** —*M.M. (11/15/2002)*

Ceretto 1998 Monsordo Rosso Cabernet Blend (Langhe) $38. This Cabernet Sauvignon-based blend is big, burly, and very young, showing some rough aromas of burnt rubber or asphalt at first, but later evolving to reveal firm black cherry fruit and licorice. The weight of the wine shows admirable extraction and richness, and the powdery tannins hint at a long and positive evolution. **89** —*J.C. (9/1/2001)*

Ceretto 2003 Rossana Dolcetto (Dolcetto d'Alba) $21. Well-made, but this Dolcetto from Ceretto offers nothing out of the ordinary. Cherry and spice notes on the nose add cedar nuances on the palate. Dry and lacking much charm on the finish. **84** —*J.C. (3/1/2006)*

Ceretto 2002 Rossana Dolcetto (Dolcetto d'Alba) $19. Shows decent complexity on the nose in its aromas of leather, rhubarb, and fresh herbs, but comes across as light and lacking ripeness in the mouth. Modest cherry flavors carry a hint of weediness through the finish. **84** —*J.C. (11/15/2004)*

Ceretto 2001 Rossana Dolcetto (Dolcetto d'Alba) $18. Overtly gassy and meaty at first, and requiring too long to lose that offputting quality. Once that funkiness passes, however, firm and rich plum and cherry fruit rises up. The tannins are tight and the drive is there. This is major league Dolcetto, but there is simply too much challenging the wine; it's not friendly like it should be. **84** —*M.S. (12/15/2003)*

Ceretto 1999 Rossana Dolcetto (Dolcetto d'Alba) $19. Earth dominates the nose, the tannins are still rough and the chocolate-cherry notes only appear on the medium-length finish. All in all, a disappointment from a producer from whom we have come to expect more. **82** —*M.N. (9/1/2001)*

Ceretto 1998 Rossana Dolcetto (Dolcetto d'Alba) $17. **90** *(4/1/2000)*

Ceretto 2005 I Vignaioli di Santo Stefano Moscato (Moscato d'Asti) $20. Very fragrant and fresh, this fizzy wine is redolent of melon, honey, and loads of mature peach. It has a particularly creamy mouthfeel yet is light and delicate in all respects. **87** —*M.L. (12/15/2006)*

Ceretto 2003 I Vignaioli di Santo Stefano Moscato (Moscato d'Asti) $19. Shows some nice floral, almost lilacy aromas; on the palate there is restrained pineapple and orange fruit in a soft, low-acid format that's reflective of the hot vintage. **85** —*J.C. (11/15/2004)*

Ceretto 2002 I Vignaioli di Santo Stefano Moscato D'Asti Muscat Canelli (Piedmont) $20. Clean and delicate, with a bouquet of pear, flowers, and vanilla cream. Intense flavors of apple and citrus, with an underscore of nutmeg and clove. Compact and engaging, with a tight body and firm core. **89** —*M.S. (12/15/2003)*

Ceretto 1998 Nebbiolo (Barbaresco) $111. The complex aromas of rhubarb, coffee, black cherries, tar, anise, cedar, and green tobacco evolve in the glass. Firm acids and tannins give this wine great structure; this should be a very long-lived Barbaresco despite its forward charms. From Ceretto. Cellar Selection. **91 Cellar Selection** *(9/1/2001)*

Ceretto 1999 Asij Nebbiolo (Barbaresco) $37. This solid effort blends cherries with darker notes of asphalt, prune, and molasses. Medium-weight in the mouth, the wine finishes with tart fruit, tarry notes, and good length. Drink 2008–2015. **88** *(4/2/2004)*

Ceretto 1998 Asij Nebbiolo (Barbaresco) $44. First up is a hint of citrus peel to the cherry driven nose. The fruit on the palate is light and clean, emphasizing red plum and dried cherry. Some earth and cola appear on the modest, astringent finish. Overall it's expectedly tight, but it's of good quality and offers some fine Piedmontese qualities. **88** —*M.S. (11/15/2002)*

Ceretto 1997 Barbaresco Asij Nebbiolo (Barbaresco) $44. **92** —*M.S. (9/1/2000)*

Ceretto 2001 Bernardot Nebbiolo (Barbaresco) $62. Shows some hints of vanilla on the nose and palate, but there's plenty of other stuff going on as well: brandied cherries and ginger on the nose add even more dried spices on the richly textured palate. Slowly unfolds into a long, layered finish. Drink 2008–2018. **92** —*J.C. (3/1/2006)*

Ceretto 2000 Bernardot Nebbiolo (Barbaresco) $67. Somewhat confusingly, Ceretto's estate wines from Barbaresco are now bottled under the name Bricco Asili, with Ceretto only in small letters. But the quality is in the bottle. Smoky, meaty aromas give way with air to dried cherries, leather, and a touch of citrus. Darker notes of asphalt and chocolate join in on the palate, which is big, muscular, and chewy without being overdone. Finishes long, picking up flavors and a texture akin to cocoa powder. **93 Editors' Choice** *(4/2/2004)*

Ceretto 1999 Bernardot Nebbiolo (Piedmont) $87. With brooding aromas, subdued fruit, and plenty of tannins, this is one for the cellar. Things kick off with some earthy, mildly sulfuric scents—you could even say that it's tough to like at first. But with time, classic leather and dried-cherry fruit emerge, followed by a perfect smokiness to the grip-galore finish. It's a traditional wine, one that could use several years to lose its clumsy youth and reveal its true character. And even then you should serve it with food. **91** —*M.S. (11/15/2002)*

Ceretto 1998 Bernardot Nebbiolo (Piedmont) $74. Ceretto's weakest Barbaresco in 1998 is still very good, with aromas of Asian spice, tea, and roses that turn slightly grassy with airing. Licorice and earth flavors are accented by black cherries and strong breakfast tea. Firm acidity and tough tannins crack the whip on the finish. **87** *(9/1/2001)*

Ceretto 1997 Bernardot Nebbiolo (Barbaresco) $74. **89** *(9/1/2000)*

Ceretto 2001 Bricco Asili Nebbiolo (Barbaresco) $116. Features plenty of bold cherry aromas tinged with dried spices, but there's also a hint of elevated alcohol on the nose. Big, full-bodied, and tannic, with dried fruit flavors that show a hint of overripeness. Long and powerful on the finish. **90** —*J.C. (3/1/2006)*

Ceretto 2000 Bricco Asili Nebbiolo (Barbaresco) $122. Beautifully balanced and fragrant Barbaresco, with floral notes joining scents of leather and fresh cherries. Hints of milk chocolate and vanilla sneak in on the palate, but the emphasis remains on the fruit. The mouth-watering finish boasts supple tannins, suggesting midterm ageability; try 2008–2015. **91** *(4/2/2004)*

Ceretto 1997 Bricco Asili Nebbiolo (Barbaresco) $111. **92** —*J.C. (9/1/2000)*

Ceretto 1995 Bricco Asili Nebbiolo (Barbaresco) $105. **90** —*M.S. (11/15/1999)*

Ceretto 2001 Bricco Rocche Nebbiolo (Barolo) $200. Shows great precision in its aromas and flavors, delivering ripe cherries, floral, and herbal notes in a swirl of complexity that never seems muddled or cluttered. Medium-bodied—despite great intensity of flavor it never feels weighty or heavy. Finishes with dusty tannins, so although its approachable now, it should easily go 20 years. **94** —*J.C. (3/1/2006)*

Ceretto 1999 Bricco Rocche Nebbiolo (Barolo) $200. The fruit here is of the dried variety, focusing on dates and prunes, but blending in notes of coffee, molasses, and smoked meats. The fruit barely peeks through the wall of chewy tannins on the finish, but it's there—enjoyment of this wine just requires patience. Try in 2010 or beyond. **90** *(4/2/2004)*

Ceretto 1998 Bricco Rocche Nebbiolo (Piedmont) $221. From Ceretto's Bricco Rocche winery, this is an impressive wine. Perfumed hedgerow aromas and, on the palate, big, dusty tannins, give tremendous power and richness. Tarry, black fruit flavors blend with layers of acidity and wood. **94 Editors' Choice** —*R.V. (11/15/2002)*

Ceretto 1997 Bricco Rocche Nebbiolo (Barolo) $147. Already complex, this cru Barolo from Ceretto is packed with exotic aromas and flavors that range from pipe tobacco, cedar, and cherries to tar, earth, and mushrooms. A licorice or tarragon note pulls it all together. This is a full yet balanced wine that should age well for a couple of decades. **92** *(9/1/2001)*

Ceretto 1995 Bricco Rocche Nebbiolo (Piedmont) $140. **96 Cellar Selection** *(3/1/2000)*

Ceretto 1998 Bricco Rocche Brunate Nebbiolo (Piedmont) $90. The 14-acre Brunate vineyard produces a more delicate style of Barolo. Aromas of ripe figs and flavors of super-ripe fruit give a sense of a sweet wine, but with huge tannins masking the sweetness. To finish, the acidity gives the wine shape and good potential—allow 10 years or more before drinking. **91** —*R.V. (11/15/2002)*

Ceretto 1998 Bricco Rocche Prapo Barolo Nebbiolo (Barolo) $90. A rustic style of Barolo from the six-acre Prapò vineyard. Farmyard aromas show through on the palate with soft fruit and flavors of bacon and acidity. It is certainly a distinctive style with a good sense of elegance and presence, but the flavors make it somewhat unusual. **88** —*R.V. (11/15/2002)*

Ceretto 2001 Brunate Nebbiolo (Barolo) $75. An intriguing wine, with aromas of smoke, cherries, dried spices, and root beer. On the palate, a shroud of cedar, vanilla, and spice surrounds a bright, flavorful core of cherries that should emerge in time. Finishes with mouth-watering fruit along supple tannins. Anticipated maturity: 2008–2018. **92** —*J.C. (3/1/2006)*

Ceretto 1999 Brunate Nebbiolo (Barolo) $80. Full-bodied yet supple, this Ceretto offering boasts charry, meaty notes layered over dried fruit and dried spices. The long finish features chewy tannins (drink 2008–2015) and hints of anise. **91** *(4/2/2004)*

Ceretto 1997 Brunate Nebbiolo (Barolo) $74. This wine from Ceretto shows the hallmarks of the 1997 vintage in Piedmont: ultra-ripe fruit and ample alcohol. Starts off with leathery, cedary aromas that quickly recede beneath huge, mouth-filling flavors of brandied fruitcake, candied fruit, and dried spices. Firm tannins mark this as age worthy, but the nearly overblown quality of the fruit makes it approachable now. **90** *(9/1/2001)*

Ceretto 2000 Fasêt Nebbiolo (Barbaresco) $67. Quit light in color, showing an amber-orange tinge at the rim and modest cherry, tobacco, and citrus aromas and flavors. Medium-weight, this is an atypically easy offering from Ceretto. Drink now–2010. **88** *(4/2/2004)*

Ceretto 1998 Fasêt Nebbiolo (Barbaresco) $74. This lithe, feminine rendition from Ceretto shows delicate floral and dried cherry notes deftly accented by cedar and leather. The various parts come together in an elegant, harmonious whole. This is not a bruising, tough Nebbiolo, but one that should prove versatile at the table. **90** *(9/1/2001)*

Ceretto 1996 Fasêt Nebbiolo (Barbaresco) $70. **93** —*M.S. (11/15/1999)*

Ceretto 1995 Prapo Nebbiolo (Barolo) $70. **92** —*M.S. (7/1/2000)*

Ceretto 2001 Prapó Nebbiolo (Barolo) $75. Like Ceretto's other 2001 Barolos, Prapó is beautifully balanced. It's fresh and fruity without being candied or simple; meaty and earthy without being heavy or dull. Bright red fruit mingles easily with dusty earth, finishing with powdery-feeling tannins and a refreshing hint of anise. **92** —*J.C. (3/1/2006)*

Ceretto 1999 Prapó Nebbiolo (Barolo) $80. Charry and smoky, with masses of red fruit and some citrusy overtones, this medium-weight wine features a long, chewy, cranberry-ish finish that raises it to the elite level. Drink 2008–2015. **90** *(4/2/2004)*

Ceretto 1997 Prapó Nebbiolo (Barolo) $74. Dried roses highlight the nose, followed by aromas of red berries, plums, and mushrooms. Full-bodied and rich, this delivers layers of ripe fruit that turn chocolatey on the finish, where firm tannins take hold. Should be long-lived; try this Ceretto wine in 2010 or beyond. **92** *(9/1/2001)*

Ceretto 1999 Zonchera Nebbiolo (Piedmont) $40. **89** *(4/2/2004)*

Ceretto 1998 Zonchera Nebbiolo (Piedmont) $40. Aromas of pure, sweet fruit and very ripe pomegranates. The palate is balanced, with great ripe fruit over pure acidity and lively, vibrant red flavors. This is a great fruity wine, with crisp acidity and wood flavors to finish. **93 Editors' Choice** —*R.V. (11/15/2002)*

CERRAIA

Cerraia 1996 Sangiovese (Vino Nobile di Montepulciano) $27. **83** —*M.S. (9/1/2000)*

CERRI DEL PALAGIO

Cerri del Palagio 2002 Sangiovese (Chianti Classico) $12. Light and lean, but still good. The nose is a mixture of berry fruit, leather, and herbs, while the mouth offers crisp cherry and mild earth notes. Clean, tight, and basic, with pedestrian features. **85** *(4/1/2005)*

Cerri del Palagio 2000 Riserva Sangiovese (Chianti Classico) $20. A bit over-ripe, with Port and sherry aromas, mushroom, and a whiff of anise. Black cherry and plum fruit seems plump at first but thins quickly. A touch lean and starchy, but mostly it's good to go. **84** *(4/1/2005)*

CESARI

Cesari 1999 Mara Corvina (Valpolicella Classico) $13. Fresh and racy, but not lean. The fruit is powerful and forward, as if it were getting a push from the ripasso technique. The palate is broad and full of berry flavor and bright acidity. Supple tannins and a fine structure with no rough edges enhance. **90 Best Buy** *(5/1/2003)*

Cesari 2004 Due Torri Pinot Grigio (Delle Venezie) $10. Roasted caramelized almond, banana bread, and candied fruit smells characterize a wine that is smooth, but tangy in the mouth, with good persistence. **88 Best Buy** —*M.L. (2/1/2006)*

Cesari 2005 Fiorile Pinot Grigio (Delle Venezie) $16. A bouquet dominated by banana with some spicy vanilla notes and more banana in the mouth. Has more persistence than most Grigios, with a lean, spicy finish. **87** —*M.L. (6/1/2006)*

Cesari 1998 Fiorile Pinot Grigio (Trentino) $11. **84** *(8/1/1999)*

Cesari 2000 Red Blend (Amarone della Valpolicella Classico) $40. Generous and a touch racy, with a good amount of spice, chocolate, licorice, and coffee on a traditional Amarone bouquet. Quite harmonious and satisfying in the mouth, with a bit of supple richness and forward plum, cherry, and cedar-like flavors. Fairly smooth and drinkable over the near term. **90** *(11/1/2005)*

Cesari 1998 Red Blend (Amarone della Valpolicella Classico) $40. We loved the root beer, cola, and charcoal notes to the big, voluptuous black-fruit bouquet. And then nothing on the palate diminished our opinion: pure cherry and chocolate with a hint of Cognac and vanilla. Overall, it's a modern wine with a clean, bright presence. **92 Editors' Choice** *(5/1/2003)*

Cesari 1997 Bosan Red Blend (Amarone della Valpolicella) $80. Built like a house, with seductive prune, sandalwood, and root beer aromas. Very dense, with a firm foundation. Thus the palate is heavy, but it's loaded with plum, cherry, raisin, and chocolate. It's pretty much everything you'd expect from Amarone, and the tannins are smooth but active. Should hold for another three to five years. **90** *(11/1/2005)*

Cesari 2000 Il Bosco Red Blend (Amarone della Valpolicella) $60. Ample toast and smoke announce plenty of barrique aging, but in this case it works like a charm because there's marzipan, baked fruit, and coffee playing second fiddle. Super deep in the mouth, with prune, date, and cinnamon notes. Finishes big and toasty, with succulence and supreme balance. **93** *(11/1/2005)*

Cesari 1997 Il Bosco Red Blend (Amarone della Valpolicella) $52. Intense, with aromas of kirsch, smoked meat, and oiled leather. The palate features lavish oak, but there's plenty of cherry and red plum fruit to stand up to it. And after all that force the finish is smooth and supple. **89** *(5/1/2003)*

Cesari 2000 Recioto della Valpolicella Red Blend (Valpolicella) $30. By nature, recioto (sweet) wines sometimes carry some sharp vinegar aromas, but after that it's all about sweetness. This fine example fits that model to a T. The nose is grapey and full of bitter chocolate. The palate, meanwhile, is rich and pruney, with chocolate and blackberry jam notes. The finish is long and layered. **89** *(5/1/2003)*

CEUSO

Ceuso 1998 Custera Bordeaux Blend (Sicilia) $37. Bordeaux varietals, Cabernet Sauvignon 30% and Merlot 20%, are blended with 50% Nero d'Avola for this Sicilian blend whose earthy, herbal flavors and dusty tannins are the essence of Old World style. The finish is a little one-dimensional. **86** —*C.S. (5/1/2002)*

Ceuso 2004 Scurati Nero d'Avola (Sicilia) $18. This is a non-filtered red with aromas of prune, wet earth, moist tobacco, slate, and a touch of something lactic, along the lines of milk chocolate. It's big and brawny in the mouth, with tight tannins. **87** —*M.L. (7/1/2006)*

Ceuso 2003 Scurati Nero d'Avola (Sicilia) $19. With deep, meaty red fruit, leather, and a natural, unadulterated sweetness to it, this is one likable Nero d'Avola. The palate is ripe and modern, but the flavors are traditional: spicy plum fruit, nutmeg, earth, and oak. Long and dessert-like on the finish, with vanilla and licorice notes. A prototype for the new Sicily. **91** —*M.S. (2/1/2005)*

Ceuso 2001 Ceuso Red Blend (Sicilia) $41. Here's a toasty and earthy wine that is given more dimension thanks to lush notes of vanilla, blackberry, leather, and pipe tobacco. The finish rides long over spicy notes and the tannins are tight and dusty. **90** —*M.L. (7/1/2006)*

Ceuso 2000 Custera Red Blend (Sicilia) $39. Solid stuff from Sicilia, and in many ways it sets the standard for what Southern Italy can do with native grapes. This wine offers meaty, earthy fruit, cola, oak, and leather all wrapped into a presentable whole. And it improves with airing. **89** —*M.S. (7/1/2005)*

Ceuso 2000 Fastaia Red Blend (Sicilia) $31. Big and brooding, with animal notes and a hint of smoked fish to the nose. Don't be put off by these terroir-driven aromatics; the wine is firm, solid, and well-made. Dark berry and smoke flavors lead to a finish that carries firm, full-strength tannins. **88** —*M.S. (10/1/2003)*

CEUSO DI MELIA VIGNA CUSTERA

Ceuso di Melia Vigna Custera 1996 Vino da Tavola Red Blend (Sicilia) $23. **90** —*M.S. (11/15/1999)*

CHIANTI TRAMBUSTI

Chianti Trambusti 1998 Celsus Sangiovese (Sangiovese di Toscana) $22. This wine from the Trambusti company features a nose of pepper, leather, and mint. The palate runs sharp, with berry fruit, black pepper, and some pronounced bell pepper. Ripeness is in doubt here; the back end is extremely green and peppery, and just doesn't have the fruit flavors of a well-ripened Sangiovese. But structure seems right. **84** —*M.S. (11/15/2003)*

Chianti Trambusti 1999 Il Perticato Sangiovese (Chianti Classico) $17. Citrus rind and dried fruit comprise the snappy nose, while strawberry, chocolate, and oak dominate the palate. Snappy and fresh. **86** —*M.S. (11/15/2003)*

Chianti Trambusti 2001 Val Serena Sangiovese (Chianti Rufina) $12. Pale in color and with scents of wet dog, this doesn't seem promising from the start. Warms up a little on the palate, with modest cherry fruit, but seems a bit unclean. **82** *(4/1/2005)*

CHIGI SARACINI

Chigi Saracini 2001 Poggiassai Sangiovese (Toscana) $40. Talk about a nose that announces what's to come: coffee, licorice, dark spice, and sensual black fruit aromas all indicate richness and modernity. Very much a 21st-century wine in that it pours on those ripe, extracted, lush characteristics. Soft but balanced; it's 90% Sangiovese with 10% Cabernet. **93 Editors' Choice** —*M.S. (9/1/2006)*

Chigi Saracini 2003 Villachigi Sangiovese (Chianti) $13. Deep and modern, with ripe black fruit, bacon, and cedar to the full-framed nose. The mouth is just as good, with dense plum, black cherry, prune, and vanilla. Lasting on the finish, with a spicy, warm aftertaste. A sure-fire powerhouse and a winner from Chigi Saracini. **92 Best Buy** *(4/1/2005)*

CIACCI PICCOLOMINI D'ARAGONA

Ciacci Piccolomini d'Aragona 2000 Brunello (Brunello di Montalcino) $65. Red and jammy, with a lot of sweet raspberry on the bouquet. Not much meat or darkness here; instead it's overtly bright on the palate, where cherry pie, cranberry, and apple skins reign. Simple in its singular focus on red fruit. Could be perfect for those who don't want to taste a lot of oak. **87** —*M.S. (7/1/2005)*

Ciacci Piccolomini d'Aragona 1999 Brunello (Brunello di Montalcino) $65. Pretty raspberry and cream aromas convey richness, and it is indeed an easy drinker with warmth and body to it. Core flavors of strawberry, cherry cough drop, and brown sugar are sweet and likable, but ultimately the wine doesn't have that last kick to push it to another level. **89** —*M.S. (6/1/2004)*

Ciacci Piccolomini d'Aragona 2001 Vigna di Pianrosso Brunello (Brunello di Montalcino) $65. This wine boasts a very nice balance of enticing aromas such as cola, mint tea, basil leaf, chocolate, and dried tobacco. Yet there was enough fruit and berry flavors to ensure a long cellar life. Plump and velvety in the mouth, with mouth cleansing freshness on the finish. A Marc de Grazia selection, various U.S. importers. **91** *(4/1/2006)*

CIAO BELLA

Ciao Bella 2004 Pinot Grigio (Delle Venezie) $10. Simple melon, honey, and almond aromas set up citrus, melon, and apple flavors. Quite basic and easy, with a medium mouthfeel and finishing flavors of papaya and peach. **84** *(2/1/2006)*

CIELO

Cielo 2001 Pinot Grigio (Veneto) $8. Just what consumers expect at this level of Pinot Grigio: a light, refreshing wine with pear, apple, and citrus aromas and flavors. **83** —*J.C.* *(7/1/2003)*

Cielo 1997 Red Blend (Veneto) $7. **85** *(11/15/1999)*

CIELO BLEU

Cielo Bleu 2001 Vermentino (Vermentino di Sardegna) $14. Mildly oxidized and caramelized to the nose, but fresher on the tongue. Chunky apple, melon, and spice flavors are persistent, and while the wine lacks sex appeal and polish, it's mature and has its charms. **85** —*M.S.* *(8/1/2004)*

CISPIANO

Cispiano 1998 Sangiovese (Chianti Classico) $16. Medium cherry aromas and flavors and cedary, toasty oak mark this wine. The tart fruit and bright acidity are classic Chianti, and it calls out for food. **86** *(4/1/2001)*

CITILLE DI SOPRA

Citille di Sopra 2001 Brunello (Brunello di Montalcino) $NA. This Brunello takes a little while to open, but when it does it reveals vanilla wafers, herbs, roasted coffee bean, tannery smells, sweet bread, leather, earth, and herbal notes. Engaging and complex with good structure and solid tannins. **91** *(4/1/2006)*

CITRA

Citra 2002 Montepulciano (Montepulciano d'Abruzzo) $5. The nose is green and fiery; it lacks pure fruit. The palate is sharp, with cherry pie and rhubarb flavors along with citric edges. Tangy and loaded with lean berry extract. **81** —*M.S.* *(11/15/2003)*

CLERICO

Clerico 1997 Trevigne Barbera (Barbera d'Alba) $20. **89** *(4/1/2000)*

Clerico 1999 Ciabot Mentin Ginestra Nebbiolo (Barolo) $75. Long considered a member of Barolo's New Wave vanguard, Clerico's wines are still unabashedly oaky, featuring aromas of toast and vanilla liqueur and lush masses of soft tannins underneath. Drink now–2015. **90** *(4/2/2004)*

CLETO CHIARLI

Cleto Chiarli 2005 Pruno Nero Lambrusco (Lambrusco Grasparossa di Castelvetro) $10. This is a bright, vibrant, and fruity wine that recalls vino novello or Beaujolais. Blueberry aromas come first, followed by blackberry and tart cherry on the palate, fueling a sour note on the finish. Pleasant, thin, and not particularly long lasting, the wine has enough going for it to be paired with pasta or light meat dishes. **84** —*M.L.* *(12/15/2006)*

Cleto Chiarli 2005 Vigneto Enrico Cialoini Lambrusco (Lambrusco Grasparossa di Castelvetro) $18. Good fizz, dimension, intensity, and a darker ruby color, this dry wine offers plenty of rich berry and almond skin aromas. It falls short in the mouth where its tartness is out of tune. **84** —*M.L.* *(12/15/2006)*

COCCINELLA

Coccinella 1999 Pinot Grigio (Veneto) $11. Green grassy aromas with a sharper herb or chemical note open this round, soft wine. With its melony flavors and feel, it's a simple, slightly sweet wine with a hay note on the back end. **82** —*M.M.* *(9/1/2001)*

COL D'ORCIA

Col d'Orcia 2001 Brunello (Brunello di Montalcino) $46. Blueberry, forest berry, and a delicate floral touch round off richly toasted notes that glide smoothly over a harmonious whole. It lacked some of the building blocks to see it through the years, but we saw this as a gentle, easy wine to enjoy now with roasted or grilled meats. **89** *(4/1/2006)*

Col d'Orcia 2000 Brunello (Brunello di Montalcino) $49. Lighter-bodied, with an emphasis on leather, pepper, and red fruit. Strawberry and raspberry flavors are front and center, while a bit of oak-based milk chocolate provides support. Hard to find fault here, but by the same token it's rather simple and antiseptic. Good in a clean, light way. **88** —*M.S.* *(7/1/2005)*

Col d'Orcia 1999 Brunello (Brunello di Montalcino) $50. Lean and tight, with sharp aromatics that veer in the direction of powdered fruit drink. In the mouth, it's dry and fresh, with snappy acidity defining a svelte frame. For a Brunello '99, it's light-bodied. Tasted twice. **87** —*M.S.* *(6/1/2004)*

Col d'Orcia 1999 Banditella Red Blend (Rosso di Montalcino) $18. What a pretty aromatic combination of smoky bacon and bold, natural berries. The no-holes flavor profile is all about cherries and plums, while the finish is just as it should be; clean, simple, and fresh, with nothing out of place or outlandish. An excellent wine for everyday purposes. **87** —*M.S.* *(12/31/2002)*

Col d'Orcia 2004 Spezieri Red Blend (Toscana) $13. Raw and scattered, with aromas of cherry liqueur and berry jam. More tart than expected, with lean cherry and berry building a staunch flavor profile. Finishes a bit starchy and tannic. Not poor or funky, just lacking. **83** —*M.S.* *(9/1/2006)*

Col d'Orcia 1997 Sangiovese (Rosso di Montalcino) $14. **89** *(11/15/1999)*

COL DE' SALICI

Col de' Salici NV Extra Dry Champagne Blend (Prosecco di Valdobbiadene) $15. **87** —*S.H.* *(12/31/2000)*

Col de' Salici NV Extra Dry Prosecco (Prosecco di Valdobbiadene) $15. Neutral aromas are nothing if not medicinal. Some lime and banana flavors come across the palate, and there's a bit of pop to the finish. But otherwise it's flat, dull, and mostly lamentable. **81** —*M.S.* *(12/31/2002)*

COL DI LUNA

Col di Luna NV Cuvée Brut White Blend (Italy) $12. An unusual blend of 50% Prosecco and 50% Chardonnay; it smells very much like ginger ale, while the flavors trigger citrus, apple, and mild spice. Fairly clean and persistent; neither complex nor flawed. **85** —*M.S.* *(6/1/2005)*

COL VETORAZ SPUMANTI

Col Vetoraz Spumanti NV Brut Prosecco (Prosecco di Valdobbiadene) $23. Scented candle and floral notes are well-integrated with tart citrus, pineapple, and sour grapefruit. A simple, fresh bubbly with a slightly rounder, fatter mouthfeel than most. **86** —*M.L.* *(6/1/2006)*

Col Vetoraz Spumanti NV Extra Dry Prosecco (Prosecco di Valdobbiadene) $23. A pale hay shade of gold with perky fruity tones and loads of lemon-lime crispness. A festive, balanced Prosecco with a line of crispness that cuts straight through its creamy, foamy consistency. **87** —*M.L.* *(6/1/2006)*

COLDISOLE

Coldisole 2001 Brunello (Brunello di Montalcino) $NA. A smoky, charcoal quality is rendered broader thanks to sour cherry, herbal, or menthol notes, plum and toasted wood. Gripping tannins give solid structure but ride out smooth on the finish. **91** *(4/1/2006)*

COLI

Coli 1995 Brunello (Brunello di Montalcino) $34. From a small plot within the Brunello region, Coli makes approximately 1,000 cases of this wine per year, aged traditionally for 48 months in oak. Soft and light for a Brunello, it's still a good wine, with pretty aromas of tobacco, earth, and tart cherries. **85** *(11/1/2002)*

Coli 2000 Montepulciano (Montepulciano d'Abruzzo) $7. Starts off with peach, almond, and cherry aromas and stays light and fruity in the mouth, with simple stone fruit flavors. With its light tannins, it's made to drink now. Suck it down with a quick bite at your local pizza place. **84 Best Buy** *(11/1/2002)*

Coli 1999 Primo di Montignana Red Blend (Toscana) $48. Fairly intense, with mineral notes to the deep plum and black cherry nose. Raspberry and toast flavors lead into a smooth and supple finish that's a touch tangy and tart. Lacks a great wine's depth of flavor, but it's pretty good nonetheless. A blend of Sangiovese and Merlot. **87** —*M.S.* *(11/15/2003)*

Coli 2001 Sangiovese (Orvieto) $7. This is an example of what Coli does best: A light, fruity wine that would be perfect washing down some fried calamari. The lemon and pear flavors have just enough acidity to ready your palate for the next bite, while the finish displays a moderately rich, dusty texture. **85 Best Buy** *(11/1/2002)*

Coli 2000 Sangiovese (Chianti) $10. Earth, cherry, and tobacco aromas and flavors let you know it's mostly Sangiovese, but it also contains small amounts of Canaiolo, Trebbiano, and Malvasia. Its tart cherry flavors leave a lean impression on the palate that's followed by a dose of chocolate on the finish. **83** *(11/1/2002)*

Coli 2000 Sangiovese (Chianti Classico) $13. This is a step up from Coli's straight Chianti, with bolder, more forceful aromas of earth, cherry and tobacco and an extra layer of weight on the palate. Like all of the Coli wines, it's based solely on traditional grapes; in this case, 80% Sangiovese, with lesser amounts of Canaiolo, Trebbiano, and Malvasia. **85** *(11/1/2002)*

Coli 1999 Sangiovese (Chianti) $7. Light and well-balanced, this is nice entry-level juice with a classic Chianti flavor profile of cherries, herbs, and earth. Even finishes with a little length and some spicy notes. Drink now through 2002. **85 Best Buy** *(4/1/2001)*

Coli 1998 Sangiovese (Chianti Classico) $10. Light, with some sour cherry fruit on the nose and palate that's outweighed throughout by a dry, woodiness that enters early and persists. **83** *(4/1/2001)*

Coli 1998 Montignana Riserva Sangiovese (Tuscany) $23. Violet in color, with full-bore aromas of plum, perfume, and graham cracker. This is a thick, chunky wine that tastes a lot like Dolcetto or Gamay. It's round, firm, very fruity, and a touch candied. It's also fresh and mildly oaky, with a modest hint of pepper. **84** *—M.S. (11/15/2003)*

Coli 1998 Pratale Sangiovese (Chianti Classico) $22. This wine makes an interesting contrast to the rest of the Coli line, which is otherwise very traditional in style. Pratale is a modern style, with a vibrant purple color and scents of cherries, cream, and vanilla, backed up by tobacco and tea leaves on the finish. **86** *(11/1/2002)*

Coli 1997 Pratale Sangiovese (Chianti Classico) $19. The strong start—a nose full of slightly candied cherries, plums, cloves, prunes, and cinnamon—is a great setup, but the expected richness does not materialize on the palate. Rather it's a bit lean and tart and the wood overpowers the fruit, which oddly seems to be fading already. **84** *(4/1/2001)*

Coli 1999 Riserva Sangiovese (Chianti Classico) $18. Some toasty oak starts it on its way, and in support is some dried red fruit. A sweet and puckery berry-driven palate leads you to a mildly lean but still cuddly finish, while overall it's modern and shows a fair amount of pop and zest. That said, the wine backs off a touch at the end. **87** *—M.S. (11/15/2003)*

Coli 1998 Riserva Sangiovese (Chianti) $12. This wine lacks a bit of intensity, but does boast a wonderfully smooth, supple mouthfeel. Aromas of leather give way to flavors of dried fruits and nuts on the palate. **84** *(11/1/2002)*

Coli 1997 Riserva Sangiovese (Chianti) $11. The tart cherry and earth flavors here have a green hay-like note around the edges. It's a touch light, but the fruit is decent and it's not buried under massive doses of oak. The medium-length finish has modest tannins. Drink now. **86** *(4/1/2001)*

Coli 1995 Villa Montignana Riserva Sangiovese (Chianti Classico) $23. There's a soft, almost plush mouthfeel and a creamy quality to this wine's aromas and flavors. The dark cherry fruit sports both chocolate and vanilla accents. A touch of espresso on the finish is accompanied by full but soft tannins, giving this wine the structure to age a few years. **88** *(4/1/2001)*

Coli 2003 Vernaccia (Vernaccia di San Gimignano) $10. Fairly mute, with light aromas of green melon and apple. For certain this is a simple, basic white, but its simplicity is its best attribute. Correct acidity and balance make it a worthwhile quaffer. Drink soon, and drink well chilled. **85** *—M.S. (8/1/2004)*

Coli 1999 Vernaccia (Vernaccia di San Gimignano) $8. A fine trattoria-type white, best matched to light seafood antipasto or served alone as an apéritif. Aromas of clover-blossom honey and almond paste give way to flavors of unripe honeydew melons and tart limes. **83** *—J.C. (9/1/2001)*

COLLAVINI

Collavini 2004 Villa Canlungo Pinot Grigio (Collio) $17. A bit funky at the start, but give it time to open and ripe cantaloupe and rich pear emerges. Expressive and velvety in the mouth, and a good match to chicken with garlic. **87** *—M.L. (6/1/2006)*

COLLE NERO

Colle Nero 2003 Sangiovese (Chianti) $8. A ripe Chianti with raspberry and blue flower aromas that are only slightly cooked despite the hot vintage. The wine boasts a saturated ruby color and ends with tight, dusty tannins. **85 Best Buy** *—M.L. (10/1/2006)*

COLLE S. MUSTIOLA DI FABIO CENNI

Colle S. Mustiola di Fabio Cenni 1999 Poggio Ai Chiari Sangiovese (Toscana) $48. Thick, grapey aromas accented by coffee and mocha get it going, with traditional cherry and leather flavors following thereafter. The finish is round and expansive, with distinct flavors of coffee and fudge. This is full and ripe stuff, but it stops short of being heavy. **88** *—M.S. (12/31/2002)*

COLLELCETO

Collelceto 2001 Brunello (Brunello di Montalcino) $50. This wine has a very pretty nose with a delicate embroidery of forest berry and wild flowers. Yet its structure is full and round with a deep ruby color. Thicker, denser favors come through on the palate like smoked ham and sweet cherry followed by a zesty touch of basil or green herb. **90** *(4/1/2006)*

COLLI AMERINI

Colli Amerini 1998 Carbio Red Blend (Umbria) $18. The aromas are beautiful, showing field flowers, toasted cedar, and red raspberries. Flavors are lean and finish simple but juicy. **88** *—C.S. (2/1/2003)*

COLLI DELLA MURGIA

Colli della Murgia 1998 Selvato Red Blend (Apulia) $11. **84** *(9/1/2000)*

COLLOSORBO

Collosorbo 2001 Brunello (Brunello di Montalcino) $59. A standout wine thanks to lush red apple and cinnamon, coffee, tobacco, cherry cola, spice, and peach cobbler-like aromas. Tasty, long finish with firm tannins and a flavorful, fruity tail in an ageworthy wine. A Marc de Grazia selection, various U.S. importers. **92** *(4/1/2006)*

Collosorbo 1999 Brunello (Brunello di Montalcino) $56. Truly classy, with a deep nose of earth, tar, and pure berry fruit. This wine delivers both the sweetness and ripeness that it should along with some rugged, spicy edges. The finish is big and packed with licorice, spice, and pepper. A fine wine. Hold until 2006. **92** *—M.S. (6/1/2004)*

Collosorbo 1999 Riserva Brunello (Brunello di Montalcino) $65. A bit lighter in color than most of the '99 riservas, but still a very nice wine offering easy drinkability. Toasty, foresty notes accent the nose, while the palate is sweet at the core with ripe plum and cherry. Excellent on its own; will certainly please. A Marc de Grazia Selection, various importers. **91** *—M.S. (7/1/2005)*

COLMELLO DI GROTTA

Colmello di Grotta 2004 Pinot Grigio (Collio) $9. A copper-colored wine with pinenut, almond skin, melon, and peach. Although the aromas are discernable, they seem weighed down by a touch of reductiveness. **84** *—M.L. (2/1/2006)*

Colmello di Grotta 2004 Pinot Grigio (Isonzo del Friuli) $10. This stainless-steel-fermented Pinot Grigio has hints of rhubarb and sweet-smelling cabbage. A brief hint of sulfur seems to blow off quickly but the mouthfeel is neutral. **83** *—M.L. (6/1/2006)*

COLOGNOLE

Colognole 2001 Sangiovese (Chianti Rufina) $12. This strident, youthful wine could use a year or two to settle down, but it offers solid potential, combining sappy red raspberry fruit with iron-like mineral notes. Firmly structured; try in 2006. **88 Best Buy** *(4/1/2005)*

Colognole 1997 Chianti Rufina Sangiovese (Chianti Rufina) $12. This is a big burly wine that just has too many off aromas. Heavy barnyard scents mix with tart berry and espresso elements, and although there's body here, and what seem to be basically good elements, the stable-like odors stop the show. **81** *(4/1/2001)*

COLONNARA

Colonnara 2003 Cuprese Verdicchio (Verdicchio dei Castelli di Jesi Classico) $15. An incredibly fresh example of young Verdicchio. It exudes confident aromas of pear, almond, and mineral, and then hits you with a round, pure palate stuffed with apple, pear, and a certain stoniness. Best of all, this wine makes its point without thumping your tastebuds. It arrives, pleases, then fades away quietly, leaving a dash of vanilla and cream. **91 Best Buy** —*M.S. (8/1/2004)*

Colonnara 2003 Lyricus Verdicchio (Verdicchio dei Castelli di Jesi Classico) $11. The bouquet is razor clean, lucid, and smooth, with aromas of peach blossom and a hint of citrus. Fruity and less refined than the sensational Cuprese, with grapefruit and toasted almond controlling the palate. Finishes tight and sturdy. **88 Best Buy** —*M.S. (8/1/2004)*

COLOSI

Colosi 1999 Nero d'Avola (Sicilia) $12. Six months of aging in Slavonian oak has imparted a delicate cedary sheen to the juicy black cherry flavors. Balancing acidity prevents it from being just another fruit bomb, and it develops some intriguing leather notes with air. Made of 90% Nero d'Avola, with 10% other mixed indigenous varieties, and from a small (five hectare) estate, this is just one example of why Sicily is a hotbed for bargain hunters. Modern technology and careful viticulture combined with hot sunny weather and unique grapes are yielding great wines at great prices. **87** —*J.C. (5/1/2002)*

Colosi 2002 Red Blend (Sicilia) $11. Attractive on the nose, with plum, raisin, and chocolate. However, it's ultra-sweet and candied, as if some sugar were left in it. As for the finish, it's syrupy. **83** —*M.S. (2/1/2005)*

Colosi 2001 Red Blend (Sicilia) $10. Pungent and earthy, with aromatic notes of aged cheese and chocolaty oak. This wine features a sweet streak that is reminiscent of sugared raspberries and/or cherries. **85** —*M.S. (10/1/2003)*

CÒLPETRONE

Còlpetrone 1999 Red Blend (Montefalco) $14. Gorgeous and intriguing scents of mustard, herbs, and root beer mix with lively black fruit on the nose. The palate is perfectly ripe and supple, featuring bold berry fruit and chocolate. The finish is like a warm brownie, it's that good. **91 Best Buy** —*M.S. (2/1/2003)*

Còlpetrone 2001 Sagrantino (Sagrantino di Montefalco) $65. Smoke, leather, gingerbread, and cake aromas and flavors are found in this wine from enologist Lorenzo Landi who oversees winemaking at all Saiagricola properties. Intense, drying tannins make the wine difficult to pair with most foods now, but just wait a few years. **89** —*M.L. (9/1/2005)*

COLSANTO

Colsanto 2002 Sagrantino (Sagrantino di Montefalco) $NA. Leather, tar, pencil shavings, graphite, and smoked wood from the Livon family of Friuli who recently acquired this Umbrian winery and 20 hectares of vineyard not far from Assisi. **87** —*M.L. (9/1/2005)*

COLTERENZIO

Colterenzio 2001 Lafoa Cabernet Sauvignon (Alto Adige) $65. There's a very pretty and refined quality to this 100% Cabernet Sauvignon that distinguishes it from the others. From a mountainside vineyard in alpine Alto Adige, the variety expresses itself with delicate aromas of forest berry, menthol, sweet clove, porcini mushroom, and moist tobacco. Complex, linear, intense, and very persistent in the mouth, this is a showcase wine for Northern Italy. **93** —*M.L. (9/1/2006)*

Colterenzio 2004 Pinot Grigio (Alto Adige) $12. Some wet slate smells emerge on the rear of a fruity, aromatic composition that also has a touch of yellow bell pepper. Not huge, but refreshing and satisfying. **87 Best Buy** —*M.L. (2/1/2006)*

Colterenzio 1997 Praedium Pinot Grigio (Alto Adige) $17. **82** *(8/1/1999)*

Colterenzio 2004 Puiten Pinot Grigio (Alto Adige) $18. There's a fleshier element to this wine that translated into green overtones: cut grass, kiwi,

and pear that are typical of the mountainous Alto Adige region. Makes a good show in the mouth with ample spice and power. **87** —*M.L. (6/1/2006)*

COLUTTA

Colutta 2004 Pinot Grigio (Colli Orientali del Friuli) $12. This 18-hectare vineyard at the heart of the appellation includes an ancient villa turned fermentation cellar. The Pinot Grigio makes a very good show with loads of freshly cut pear and baked banana chips. Smooth and creamy in the mouth. **87 Best Buy** —*M.L. (6/1/2006)*

Colutta 2002 Tocai Friulano Tocai (Friuli) $17. A complex white wine that combines metallic mineral, lime zest, and white pepper flavors that are highlighted by high acidity. Bone dry, it will be a classy companion for a wide spectrum of foods. **86** —*S.H. (10/1/2004)*

CONCILIO

Concilio 2001 Chardonnay (Trentino) $10. Rather simple, blending ripe pear and citrus, but offers a full-bodied mouthful of clean fruit character. **85** —*J.C. (7/1/2003)*

Concilio 2001 Riserva Merlot (Trentino) $10. Here's a single-varietal wine from Italy's northern-most Trentino region that boasts all the sensual roundness and softness of Merlot with the fresh forest berry and spicy acidity of cool climate growing conditions. Tobacco, mineral tones, dried hay, nutmeg, black pepper, and bay leaf render a wine of deep aromatic intensity that undergoes an impressive evolution in the glass. **88 Best Buy** —*M.L. (11/15/2005)*

Concilio 2004 Pinot Grigio (Delle Venezie) $11. Standard Pinot Grigio that has been fleshed out with peach, pineapple, and pear. Lean but compact in the mouth, with a refreshing, crisp finish. Try it with Indian food or Chinese take-out. **85** —*M.L. (6/1/2006)*

Concilio 1998 Pinot Grigio (Trentino) $9. *(8/1/1999)*

Concilio 2003 Contessa Manci Pinot Grigio (Trentino) $15. Smooth and round, with sweet aromas of caramel, chamomile, and pear. Fairly citrusy and sharp, with green pear and sour apple flavors. Offers good snap and pop but a tart overall flavor profile. **83** *(2/1/2006)*

Concilio 1997 Single Vineyard-Manci DOC Pinot Grigio (Trentino) $13. **85** *(8/1/1999)*

CONTADI CASTALDI

Contadi Castaldi NV Brut Champagne Blend (Terre di Franciacorta) $13. Vanilla and toast aromas are pleasant, as are the apple, pear, and sweet coconut flavors. The finish is toasty, smooth, and fairly long. Overall this spumante is a touch chunky and awkward, but it's also quite solidly structured, with good lemon-lime undertones. **86 Best Buy** —*M.S. (12/31/2002)*

Contadi Castaldi 1998 Rose Champagne Blend (Terre di Franciacorta) $27. The color is so light that it wouldn't pass for rosé in most circles. The bouquet is equally light, so much so that it's boring. The palate features a struggling mix of banana, clove, and resin flavors, and the finish seems heavy more than it is clean. Lacks pop and pizzazz. **83** —*M.S. (12/31/2002)*

Contadi Castaldi 1997 Saten Champagne Blend (Terre di Franciacorta) $27. Toasted aromas take the form of coconut and roasted hazelnuts. On the palate, the unmistakable flavor of popcorn over-rides what apple fruit might want to show its face. The finish is heavy and dry, and all in all it really doesn't offer much to win you over. **82** —*M.S. (12/31/2002)*

Contadi Castaldi NV Chardonnay (Terre di Franciacorta) $11. **84** —*J.C. (9/1/2000)*

Contadi Castaldi NV Brut Sparkling Blend (Franciacorta) $24. Peach, pear, and white mushroom appear on a well-balanced nose that is very attractive, albeit less intense than some others. This sparkler delivers fine and persistent perlage, toasted flavors, and a silky mouthfeel. **91** —*M.L. (6/1/2006)*

Contadi Castaldi NV Brut Sparkling Blend (Franciacorta) $28. Smells wonderful, like butter-sautéed mushrooms served over toast, showing nuances of fat and earth. It's medium-weight and creamy in the mouth, with flavors of apples and pears, turning fresh and citrusy on the finish without becoming sharp or angular. **90** —*J.C. (12/31/2003)*

ITALY

Contadi Castaldi 2001 Rosé Sparkling Blend (Franciacorta) $46. Redolent of cran-raspberry, peach, pink grapefruit, and yeast, or fresh baked bread and butter. The acidity is fresh and crisp with medium to long persistency on the finish. Try is with finger food appetizers. **88** —*M.L. (6/1/2006)*

Contadi Castaldi 1999 Rosé Sparkling Blend (Franciacorta) $35. This rosé isn't as strong an offering as Contadi Castaldi's other Franciacortas. It provides a mix of sour gumball and cherry flavors combined with a rich mouthfeel and a finish that is both slightly sweet and slightly alcoholic. **84** —*J.C. (12/31/2003)*

Contadi Castaldi 1999 Satèn Sparkling Blend (Franciacorta) $35. Starts with aromas of buttered toast, white chocolate, and lemon rind, then yields silky-smooth flavors of ripe apples and pears on the palate. Tart and youthful on the finish, this sparkler can be consumed now for its freshness, but should age nicely for several years. **89** —*J.C. (12/31/2003)*

Contadi Castaldi 2001 Satén Sparkling Blend (Franciacorta) $26. Dried herbs and banana, followed by crushed stone and spice, comprise a layered and striking bouquet. You'll taste intense banana fruit in the mouth with tart acidity and pizzazz on the close. **91** —*M.L. (6/1/2006)*

CONTE COLLALTO

Conte Collalto NV Prosecco (Prosecco di Conegliano e Valdobbiadene) $10. Here's a pale, straw-colored sparkler with such decisive aromatic intensity, it borders on being pungent. Notes of melon, apricot, and yellow flower are delivered in a direct, vertical manner. The wine is crisp, but very tender on the tongue. **86** —*M.L. (12/15/2006)*

Conte Collalto NV Brut Prosecco (Prosecco di Conegliano e Valdobbiadene) $15. White flowers and stone fruit come together to form a feminine and refined whole. Although the nose is intense and generous, the mouthfeel is a bit less so, with some bitterness on the close. **86** —*M.L. (6/1/2006)*

Conte Collalto NV Brut Prosecco (Prosecco di Conegliano e Valdobbiadene) $14. Clean, linear, and crisp with lemon-lime notes and stone fruit, this is a tangy, refreshing sparkler that would work wonders with finger food cocktails. It boasts a light straw color and comes off clean as a whistle. **86** —*M.L. (12/15/2006)*

Conte Collalto NV Extra Dry Prosecco (Prosecco di Conegliano e Valdobbiadene) $13. Peach, apricot, exotic fruit, apple, lemon rind, and white stone characterize this fruity and fresh bubbly. It's slightly sweet but with a refreshing vein of tartness that completes a pretty picture. **87** —*M.L. (12/15/2006)*

Conte Collalto NV Extra Dry Prosecco (Prosecco di Conegliano e Valdobbiadene) $15. The aromas are not in your face, and that's what makes them more seductive: delicate melon and stone fruit have floral notes at the edges. Plush and creamy in the mouth, with zippy freshness at the end. **87** —*M.L. (6/1/2006)*

CONTE DELLA VIPERA

Conte della Vipera 2001 Sauvignon Blanc (Umbria) $22. Interesting on the nose, where pineapple, licorice, and mint vie for attention. But in the mouth it's a low-acid flat-liner with pickled flavors and a sour aftertaste. **81** —*M.S. (10/1/2004)*

CONTE FERDINANDO GUICCIARDINI

Conte Ferdinando Guicciardini 2002 Massi Di Mandorlaia Red Blend (Morellino di Scansano) $NA. Heavily sulfuric and gaseous. Below is a meaty, plummy, fat wine with heavy edges and dark flavors. More country in style; possibly a troubled vintage. **84** —*M.S. (10/1/2004)*

Conte Ferdinando Guicciardini 2001 Massi di Mandorlaia Riserva Sangiovese (Morellino di Scansano) $40. Incredibly rich and ripe, a total departure from traditional dry Morellino. Cola, chocolate, caramel, and blackberry aromas emanate from the bouquet, while the palate is loaded with black fruit and coffee. Finishes sweet, with fudge and mocha notes. A layered, meaty wine. **91** —*M.S. (11/15/2004)*

CONTERNO FANTINO

Conterno Fantino 2003 Vignota Barbera (Barbera d'Alba) $27. The barrique regime at Conterno Fantino seems to work wonders for this Barbera, adding just the right amount of menthol, vanilla, cinnamon, and chocolate to the black cherry flavors. Long and supple on the finish, with a creamy mouthfeel. Drink now. **91 Editors' Choice** —*J.C. (3/1/2006)*

Conterno Fantino 2002 Vignota Barbera (Barbera d'Alba) $28. A bit green for Barbera, with strawberry-rhubarb aromas, and flavors that feature fresh herbs intertwined with crisp red fruit. Finishes with notes of dark chocolate. **85** —*J.C. (11/15/2004)*

Conterno Fantino 1999 Vignota Barbera (Barbera d'Alba) $22. Everything works well here, starting with the chocolate and black cherry nose with its oaky wrap and slightly earthy notes. The wine is medium-bodied with a velvety mouthfeel. Elements of the nose show again on the long finish, where a dollop of black pepper is added. Drink now. **87** —*M.N. (9/1/2001)*

Conterno Fantino 1998 Bricco Bastia Dolcetto (Dolcetto d'Alba) $19. **88** *(4/1/2000)*

Conterno Fantino 2002 Monprá Nebbiolo (Langhe) $46. Marked by 18 months in oak, this blend of Nebbiolo, Barbera, and Cabernet Sauvignon boasts scents of coffee, leather, vanilla, and hummus. Creamy-textured, with tremendously supple tannins, it's flashy, but don't be deceived—there's a deep core of cherry fruit at its center. Drink now–2010. **90** —*J.C. (3/1/2006)*

Conterno Fantino 2001 Parussi Nebbiolo (Barolo) $81. In 10 years' time, this rating may look stingy, but at this tasting the wine wasn't showing all that much. A bit lean and closed in, with leather, dusty earth, vanilla, and hints of maraschino cherries followed by a tight, firm finish. **89** —*J.C. (3/1/2006)*

Conterno Fantino 2000 Parussi Nebbiolo (Barolo) $81. Boasts knock-out aromas of flowers and herbs—a haunting perfume that adds cherry and balsamic notes as it develops. It's not a blockbuster on the palate, but relies on silkiness and finesse to make an impression, its long finish couched in supple tannins. **92** —*J.C. (11/15/2004)*

Conterno Fantino 1998 Parussi Nebbiolo (Barolo) $65. Very oceany aromas of seaweed and saltwater. The flavors are of burnt match, ash, and vanilla. Perhaps a bit too much toasted oak. There are some red cherry fruits that fight their way through. Tannins on the finish are a little gritty. Give this one some time to see if it comes around. **87** —*C.S. (11/15/2002)*

Conterno Fantino 2000 Sorì Ginestra Nebbiolo (Barolo) $99. A softer, gentler Barolo, with Nebbiolo's hard edges tamed by a combination of the vintage, short, rotary fermentation and new oak. Yet as if to thwart critics of the modern style, it retains the essence of Nebbiolo in its floral, cherry, and leather aromas—vanilla plays only a small part. Firms up considerably on the finish, suggesting greater ageability than at first glance, picking up hints of citrus peel and tea leaves. **89** —*J.C. (11/15/2004)*

Conterno Fantino 1998 Sorì Ginestra Nebbiolo (Barolo) $99. Vanilla and coconut lead the way; the aromas are dominated by oak, and the flavors follow suit, developing coffee, nougat, and vanilla notes. It's a definite oak bomb, but a soft, supple, and seductive one, with a long finish and nary a hard edge. **88** *(4/2/2004)*

Conterno Fantino 2001 Sorí Ginestra Nebbiolo (Barolo) $99. Full-bodied and richly textured, this wine nevertheless retains the essence of Nebbiolo in its delicately floral aromas and complex flavors. Cherries, plums, and prunes all mingle on the palate, picking up nuances of vanilla and spice. Long and silky on the finish. Drink 2009–2016. **93** —*J.C. (3/1/2006)*

Conterno Fantino 2001 Monprà Red Blend (Langhe) $59. Starts off nicely, with aromatic notes of cinnamon, graham cracker, and mint. There's some solid cherry fruit in the mouth, but it gets a little swamped by oaky notes of cedar and vanilla, finishing with soft tannins and tart acids. The barrique-aged blend is approximately 50% Nebbiolo, 40% Barbera, and 10% Cabernet Sauvignon. **87** —*J.C. (11/15/2004)*

CONTI COSTANTI

Conti Costanti 2001 Brunello (Brunello di Montalcino) $74. Spice bread, almond paste, cinnamon, fudge, and orange peel with dry, dusty earth notes are amplified by a lavish, velvety structure with menthol freshness on a long, firm finish. Would pair with tarragon-based sauces or herb-roasted meats. **92** *(4/1/2006)*

Conti Costanti 2000 Brunello (Brunello di Montalcino) $70. Blackberry, cherry, vanilla, cedar, and resin add a layer of complexity to a wine with a prominent cooked or roasted characteristic at its center. Smooth and silky in the mouth with a firm tannin backbone. **89** *(4/1/2006)*

Conti Costanti 1998 Brunello (Brunello di Montalcino) $62. Not showing a lot of fruit, but smooth on the palate, with rich aromas of leather, old wood, and a touch of chlorine or ink. Turns tart, dry, and tannic on the finish; try in 2008 or beyond. **88** *(11/15/2003)*

Conti Costanti 1997 Riserva Brunello (Brunello di Montalcino) $97. With bold cherry, dusty earth, and tobacco nearly blowing out of the glass, you get Brunello's aromas at their finest. Across the palate flows plum and offsetting pepper, while on the finish the wine gets tight as a drum courtesy of those patented fierce Brunello tannins. Very fruity but tight; drink 2005 or later. **92** —*M.S. (11/15/2003)*

Conti Costanti 1998 Vermiglio Red Blend (Toscana) $46. Hailing from Montalcino, this wine has a modest, reserved bouquet that offers the basics in terms of fruit as well as some charcoal and mint. The peppery palate deals a strong hand of oak atop ripe berry fruit, while the finish is spicy, woody, and firm. The only problem, if you can call it that, is that the tannins are gritty and grabbing. Time should soothe that fault. **89** —*M.S. (12/31/2002)*

CONTI FORMENTINI

Conti Formentini 2000 Torre di Tramontana Chardonnay (Collio) $25. A wood-aged 100% Chardonnay, named after the wind that blows regularly in the region. It is citric, crisp, with wood flavors showing through. Spice and vanilla balance with flavors of tropical fruits and a touch of honey. **89** —*R.V. (7/1/2003)*

Conti Formentini 1999 Torre di Tramontana Chardonnay (Collio) $25. **83** —*J.C. (7/1/2003)*

Conti Formentini 2004 Pinot Grigio (Collio) $15. This estate boasts five centuries of wine-making tradition and is one of the most-recognized ambassadors of Collio wine. The Pinot Grigio has almond and vanilla extract over fruity aromas and a crisp, filling presence. **87** —*M.L. (2/1/2006)*

Conti Formentini 2001 Pinot Grigio (Collio) $15. Slightly gingery on the nose, but marked more by fresh greens and limes. Its relatively light-weight flavors of apples and limes are joined by an herbal tang on the short but refreshing finish. **84** —*J.C. (7/1/2003)*

Conti Formentini 1999 Pinot Grigio (Collio) $14. This Pinot Grigio has a nice heft to it. The lime, lemon peel, and apple flavors are lively and full. A biscuity, bread-dough note on the nose and palate adds some dimension. A hint of bitter almond livens up the finish. **85** —*J.F. (9/1/2001)*

Conti Formentini 1996 Pinot Grigio (Collio) $13. **84** *(8/1/1999)*

Conti Formentini 2001 Rylint White Blend (Collio) $NA. This is the first vintage of this blend of Chardonnay, Pinot Grigio and Sauvignon Blanc, named after the 16th-century abbess Rylint Formentini. Peppery in character, with rich, complex fruit, it has citric flavors, along with a sense of structure and acidity. **87** —*R.V. (7/1/2003)*

CONTI ZECCA

Conti Zecca 2003 Cantalupi Negroamaro (Salento) $10. Shows mature aromas of cherry and balsam wood, with men's cologne wafting in the background. Tastes a bit sweet, yet it's lively; the strawberry and blueberry flavors stop short of syrupy. Not a refined wine but it's full, clean, and tasty. Great for casual drinking. **86 Best Buy** —*M.S. (10/1/2006)*

Conti Zecca 2003 Primitivo (Primitivo del Salento) $18. Big and meaty, with a woodsy personality that makes it more lumberjack than ballerina. The palate is extracted and full, with real-deal tannins that frame solid blackberry and plum flavors. Finishes dark and rich, with a hint of raisin. Very nice Primitivo. **88** —*M.S. (10/1/2006)*

Conti Zecca 2003 Cantalupi Primitivo (Salento) $10. Starts out reticent, with hard spice and bramble aromas over-riding the fruit. Finds its way later on, as raspberry, strawberry, and rhubarb flavors make for a zesty palate. Finishes warm and tannic, with strong front-line flavors trumping a mild note of green. **86 Best Buy** —*M.S. (10/1/2006)*

Conti Zecca 2002 Nero Red Blend (Rosso del Salento) $45. Ripe and earthy, with savory aromas of cinnamon and spice backed by rich, dark berry scents. Nicely-balanced and thorough, with bright cherry and plum flavors sweetened by vanilla. Finishes creamy and oaky, but precise. 70% Negroamaro and 30% Cabernet Sauvignon. **90** —*M.S. (10/1/2006)*

Conti Zecca 2001 Terra Riserva Red Blend (Leverano) $30. Violets, leather and some sweet cookie aromas carry the nose to a ripe, juicy palate that pumps ample amounts of black cherry, chocolate and spice. Balanced nicely and shows a completeness as well as overall harmony. It's 70% Negroamaro and the rest Aglianico. **88** —*M.S. (10/1/2006)*

CONTINI

Contini 2002 Vermentino (Vermentino di Sardegna) $15. Strong, smoky, and meaty at first, and then giving way to more expressive and subtle fruit and sea notes. The palate offers a delicious mix of ripe apple, lemon, and papaya, while the finish is very full and complex. A good match for seafood or poultry. **88** —*M.S. (8/1/2004)*

Contini 2002 Karmis Vernaccia (Vernaccia delle Valle del Tirso) $15. One of the few Vernaccia that doesn't carry the San Gimignano pedigree (it's from Sardegna). And it is indeed different; it is more full-bodied than most, with so much pepper and citrus pith that it almost seems bitter. That said, it's firm as a rock with serious backbone. **86** —*M.S. (8/1/2004)*

CONTRATTO

Contratto 1997 Panta Rei Barbera (Barbera d'Asti) $15. **86** *(4/1/2000)*

COPPO

Coppo 1997 Camp du Rouss Barbera (Barbera d'Asti) $18. **88** *(4/1/2000)*

Coppo 1997 L'Avvocata Barbera (Barbera d'Asti) $14. **85** *(4/1/2000)*

Coppo 1996 Pomorosso Barbera (Barbera d'Asti) $35. **92** *(4/1/2000)*

Coppo 1997 Monteriolo Chardonnay (Piedmont) $43. **84** *(9/1/2000)*

CORDERO DI MONTEZEMOLO

Cordero di Montezemolo 1998 Annata Barbera (Barbera d'Alba) $25. **90** *(4/1/2000)*

Cordero di Montezemolo 1998 Dolcetto (Dolcetto d'Alba) $17. **88** *(4/1/2000)*

CORINO

Corino 1999 Vecchie Vigne Nebbiolo (Barolo) $105. If you like your Barolos young and oaky, then this is the wine for you. It's filled with plush layers of milk chocolate, vanilla, and hints of cedar and maple syrup. Yet somewhere under there is a Barolo whose cherry and citrus flavors emerge the day after you open the bottle. Accented by anise and floral notes; drink now, or try in 10 years. **90** *(4/2/2004)*

Corino 1999 Vigneto Rocche Nebbiolo (Barolo) $70. Is this really Barolo? Tastes so exotic, featuring raspberry and blackberry liqueur splashed with oodles of vanilla, that Barolo origins seem questionable, yet try it the next day and more traditional Barolo flavors have emerged—cherries, tar, and tobacco. Crisp acids and firm tannins suggest cellaring until 2012. **88** *(4/2/2004)*

CORMÒNS

Cormòns 2004 Pinot Grigio (Collio) $16. Low key aromas concentrate on peach and melon with some exotic fruit. In the mouth, the wine is supple and graceful, but it's also rather neutral. Try it with falafel. **85** —*M.L. (6/1/2006)*

Cormòns 2004 Pinot Grigio (Friuli Isonzo) $14. It's a little difficult nailing down descriptors for these aromas: There's a smoky quality, pink grapefruit, and a dose of minerality. The mouth, on the other hand, is very defined, with well-balanced crispness. **86** —*M.L. (6/1/2006)*

Cormòns 2004 Rosänder Pinot Grigio (Friuli Isonzo) $14. You don't see rosé Pinot Grigio every day. Made by a 200-member cooperative in Gorizia, it has a beautiful cranberry-raspberry color and is redolent of the same fruits, plus forest berry and passion fruit. Very refreshing and almost tart in the mouth. **87** —*M.L. (6/1/2006)*

ITALY

CORTE PAVONE

Corte Pavone 2001 Brunello (Brunello di Montalcino) $45. A dark wine with purplish pigmentation, excellent concentration, and intensity. Has cherry, leather, and loads of toasted notes that do not overwhelm. Smooth, silky, and spicy in the mouth, this textbook Brunello is almost too much of a good thing. **92 Editors' Choice** (4/1/2006)

CORTE SANT' ALDA

Corte Sant' Alda 1999 Corvina (Amarone della Valpolicella) $94. Jammy and ripe, with prune and other soft fruit aromas. The palate is quite soft, with distant acids and virtually no tannic verve. But it still has sweetness, purity, and richness. It's just that it lacks the edge necessary to propel it to greater heights. **87** (11/1/2005)

CORTE VECCHIA

Corte Vecchia 1997 Red Blend (Amarone della Valpolicella Classico) $45. A rich and raisiny bouquet with nuances of orange peel, cedar, and clove kicks things off. The next act is a textbook palate of leather, mature fruit, chocolate, and fresh mushroom. This wine is snappier than some of its neighbors, and we liked that youthful feel. **90** (5/1/2003)

CORTEFORTE

Corteforte 1995 Amarone Riserva Red Blend (Amarone della Valpolicella) $33. Aromas of cured meats, graham cracker, mint, and scented candles render this wine unique. And the flavor profile is equally unusual, as it offers menthol and smoked fish atop sweet dried cherries. The feel across the palate is smooth, and while one of our panelists found this wine too abnormal to recommend, two others admired its qualities. **88** (5/1/2003)

Corteforte 1998 Ripasso Red Blend (Valpolicella Classico Superiore) $17. This wine is all about sweetness, cinnamon, and chocolate. From the nose to the finish, there's a creamy woodiness that mixes with exotic baking spices. The texture is thick, and you will have to favor oak to enjoy it to its fullest. **87** (5/1/2003)

CORVO

Corvo 2003 Bianco Inzolia (Sicilia) $10. Made from Inzolia, a local Sicilian grape, this is a round, perfectly clean example of a fish-friendly summer white. Peach and melon on the nose is backed by citrus and apple on the palate. Tangy and refreshing. **86** —M.S. (10/1/2004)

Corvo 2004 Rosso Red Blend (Sicilia) $9. Everyone recognizes the Corvo brand but few of us are familiar with the three indigenous grapes that make up this popular Sicilian blend: Nero d'Avola, Nerello Mascalese, and Pignatello. Together they offer cherry, blueberry, pomegranate and plum with a touch of minerality and soft tannins. **86 Best Buy** —M.L. (7/1/2006)

Corvo 2002 Rosso Red Blend (Sicilia) $10. This Nero d'Avola is simple, light and smooth, with aromatics of red fruits and leather. Plum and berry flavors are solid, while the finish offers integrated oak and vanilla. A correct, feel-good red for easygoing occasions. **86 Best Buy** —M.S. (11/15/2004)

Corvo 2001 Rosso Red Blend (Sicilia) $10. This was probably the first Sicilian red I tasted, and then it was full of exotic flavors and mysterious scents. Then the wine went downhill for a few years. But now this 3 million-bottle brand is back on form and full of the same herbal, spicy flavors it always had, with the plus of ripe, sweet dark cherry fruit and easy tannins. I drank it recently with a plate of grilled vegetables, and it was a great partnership. **86** —R.V. (11/15/2004)

Corvo 2000 Rosso Red Blend (Sicilia) $10. Has an herbal bouquet with cherry and tomato notes. Some sweet plum with accents of baking spices comes next. It starts better than it finishes; along the way a chewy, textured, coffee-laden character emerges. **86 Best Buy** —M.S. (10/1/2003)

Corvo 2005 Bianco White Blend (Sicilia) $9. Corvo's well-known Insolia-Grecanico white blend is rich with peach and floral notes and is totally uncomplicated. It's clean and refreshing in the mouth, easy to drink but not totally anonymous thanks to its Sicilian core. **85 Best Buy** —M.L. (7/1/2006)

Corvo 2004 Bianco White Blend (Sicilia) $10. This friendly and familiar Sicilian blend of Insolia and Grecanico grapes delivers notes of citrus fruit, honeysuckle, cut grass, or sweet peas and mineral tones. The mouthfeel is simple but genuine with enough refreshing acidity to do the trick with grilled fish or summer pastas. **86 Best Buy** —M.L. (7/1/2006)

Corvo 2002 Bianco White Blend (Sicilia) $10. A blend of local grapes, Inzolia, Catarratto, and Grecanico, this wine has clean, fresh fruit, simple crisp, apple flavors and light acidity at the end. **83** —R.V. (10/1/2003)

Costanza Malfatti 2001 Sangiovese (Morellino di Scansano) $47. Heavily oaked, with cedar, mint, and lemon-rind aromas. Becomes more integrated with airing, showing ripe red fruit and a dose of chocolate. Plenty of open-grained wood, vanilla, and cocoa on the finish. A woody Sangiovese that can handle the bulk of its oak. **89** —M.S. (11/15/2004)

Costanza Malfatti 2000 Sangiovese (Morellino di Scansano) $39. A bit dried out and oaky, but a sincere food wine. The nose hints at red berry, but there's a lot of wood grain, too. A bit sour and leafy, but also clean and crisp, with a firm, tight, real structure. **86** —M.S. (10/1/2004)

COTTANERA

Cottanera 2002 Barbazzale Inzolia (Sicilia) $18. Vaguely floral on the nose, this Inzolia is lighter-weight than many of its brethren, with crisp, refreshing pear flavors. **85** —J.C. (10/1/2003)

Cottanera 2000 Grammonte Merlot (Sicilia) $50. This wine has the pedigree and aspirations, but it falls way short of striking the right chords. It's astringent in the nose, with far too much obvious oak. The mouth is sharp, with razor-like acids that scorch. It tastes like a powdered drink mix more than a fine red wine. **81** —M.S. (10/1/2003)

Cottanera 1999 L'Ardenza Mondeuse (Sicilia) $38. Mondeuse is the varietal in this one, from a line of Cottanera wines. Great color extraction in this blue-black wine. It delivers in the nose with intense blackberry and plum fruit. A modern-styled and gorgeous fruit palate drops in the middle, but finishes juicy and full. **89** —C.S. (5/1/2002)

Cottanera 2002 Barbazzale Nerello Mascalese (Sicilia) $17. Bulky and grapey to the nose, with ample chocolate and raisin notes. Quite full and plump on the palate, with plum, prune, and tomato flavors. Finishes in one-note style, with spiked acidity. **84** —M.S. (7/1/2005)

Cottanera 2001 Fatagione Nerello Mascalese (Sicilia) $28. Forward all the way, with raspberry, cherry, and smoke aromas. The palate is round and broad, with virtually no edges. Thus it finishes heavy and meaty, without much subtlety. It's rugged, acidic, tannic, and tasty. Patience is required. **87** —M.S. (7/1/2005)

Cottanera 1999 Fatagione Nerello Mascalese (Sicilia) $25. There's plenty of complexity in the nose, with creamy cassis and cocoa plus a light dusting of oak. The flavors are welcomed with soft tannins and a chalky mouthfeel, altogether a memorable performance from this blend of indigenous Nero Mascalese and Nero d'Avola grapes. **90** —C.S. (5/1/2002)

Cottanera 2001 Barbazzale Red Blend (Sicilia) $19. Sweet and raisiny, with mineral and graham cracker aromas. Lots of red fruit—think raspberry, red plum, and apple skin. The finish goes spicy and a touch hot; ultimately it offers a clean, lithe mouthfeel. **87** —M.S. (10/1/2003)

Cottanera 1999 Grammonte Red Blend (Sicilia) $38. It's all Merlot, and it's all good. This is a wine that would make our Sexiest Wines of the Year list, if we had one. Lush and medium-full in the mouth, Grammonte has chewy tannins and a palate full of ripe blackberry, toast, chili pepper, and a dash of red berry. Good acidity keeps the tannins in line; it finishes very long with more of the same flavors, plus some black pepper. Bouquet is a tantalizing mix of blackberry and cedar, doused in brown sugar and olive oil. **91 Editors' Choice** —C.S. (5/1/2002)

Cottanera 2001 L'Ardenza Red Blend (Sicilia) $45. Weighs in on the heavy side, and that's obvious from the color as well as the tomato and beet aromas. Yet just when you think it's too stewy, a blast of black plum and licorice hits and the wine is salvaged. Not a dancer; more of a plodder with local appeal. **85** —M.S. (7/1/2005)

Cottanera 2000 Sole di Sesta Syrah (Sicilia) $50. Saturated in color and packed full of oaky aromas that turn spicy and hickory-like with airing. Flavors of half-ripe boysenberry, plum, and rhubarb carry the palate, which leads into a sour finish that's both thick and over-aggressive. A late rush of acidity leaves you with a long-lasting sour impression. **83** —M.S. (10/1/2003)

Cottanera 1999 Sole Di Sesta Syrah (Sicilia) $38. Fresh berries and sweet cream accented with black pepper are found in the nose of this Sicilian Syrah. Tar, creosote, and succulent blackberries burst on the palate. A wine with this much fruit would normally be perceived as sweet, but its complexity saves the day. **87** —C.S. (5/1/2002)

CROCE DI MEZZO

Croce di Mezzo 2001 Brunello (Brunello di Montalcino) $NA. There's a unique exotic quality to this wine that translates into red cherry, spice, dark peach, incense, and sandalwood. Medium-bodied but extremely flavorful and tangy in the mouth, with integrated tartness and supple tannins. **90** (4/1/2006)

CUSUMANO

Cusumano 2002 Nadarìa Alcamo (Alcamo) $10. Earthy and minerally on the nose, plus fresh melon and anise on the palate. Medium-weight, very clean, and fresh. A blend of Inzolia and Müller-Thurgau. **88** —J.C. (10/1/2003)

Cusumano 2004 Jal Chardonnay (Sicilia) $18. This is a more elaborate Sicilian Chardonnay and you can definitely taste the workmanship in the results: Toasted vanilla bean, honey, ripe melon, and peach are backed by some green notes that add complexity. It's luminous and golden with subtle wooden tones. **87** —M.L. (7/1/2006)

Cusumano 2001 Jalé Chardonnay (Sicilia) $28. Standard New World Chardonnay, with pineapple and pear notes and hints of vanilla and toast allied to a rich, viscous mouthfeel. Hints of plastic and anise creep in on the finish. **84** —J.C. (10/1/2003)

Cusumano 2005 Insolia (Sicilia) $10. Run by brothers Diego and Alberto, Cusumano consistently delivers some of Sicily's best-valued red and white wine year after year. This delicate white, made from the island's native Insolia variety, goes down particularly well thanks to its white flower and almond paste aromas. It is clean and refreshing in the mouth but has just enough build and intensity to remind you of its sunny, Sicilian roots. Yet the wine is not overwhelming in any way and that's what makes it such a good match to pasta or fish dishes. **86 Best Buy** — M.L. (7/1/2006)

Cusumano 2004 Insolia (Sicilia) $11. There's a pretty golden tinge to this white dominated by floral and mineral tones with exotic fruit, banana, and some vanilla. It offers a nice, full feel in the mouth with stone fruit and pineapple flavors. **86 Best Buy** —M.L. (7/1/2006)

Cusumano 2004 Cuba Insolia (Sicilia) $13. A delicately straw-colored white with a nice, compact aromatic portfolio of melon, stone fruit, almond skin, and citrus; it's pleasantly tart and crisp in the mouth, with a sleek build. **87** —M.L. (7/1/2006)

Cusumano 2004 Cubìa Insolia (Sicilia) $11. The toasted notes come through crystal clear followed by exotic fruit, citrus, and almond paste. Toasty wood dominates the mouth but makes room for more fruit on the finish. A well-built wine that would go well with most Italian pasta dishes. **88** —M.L. (9/1/2005)

Cusumano 2001 Cubìa Inzolia (Sicilia) $20. Smells flinty and minerally, suggesting leanness and austerity, but comes across as full-bodied despite a lack of fruit flavors. **84** —J.C. (10/1/2003)

Cusumano 2002 Nadarìa Inzolia (Sicilia) $10. Shows more tropical fruit than the Alcamo D.O.C. wine, but less minerality and complexity. The flavors are easier, with pear and pineapple offering a clean, refreshing drink. **87** —J.C. (10/1/2003)

Cusumano 2005 Merlot (Sicilia) $10. This is a totally friendly and youthful Sicilian Merlot that presents cherry, blackberry, coffee, and toast. It's not exceedingly deep or complex but that's what's nice about it: balanced, smooth, and soft in the mouth. **87 Best Buy** —M.L. (7/1/2006)

Cusumano 2005 Rosato Nerello Mascalese (Sicilia) $10. Why more Italian producers don't make rosé is anyone's guess. This raspberry-colored wine illustrates Sicily's potential with a varied aromatic offering of blueberry, marzipan, white chocolate, and berry pannacotta. It is a consistent and creamy wine that can stand up to usually difficult to pair fish soup. **86 Best Buy** —M.L. (6/21/2006)

Cusumano 2004 Nero d'Avola (Sicilia) $10. An intriguing wine with thickly layered aromatics that encompass cherry fruit, anise seed, mineral notes, and a touch of green bean. Medium-bodied but very supple and refined. A great friend to food. **87 Best Buy** —M.L. (7/1/2006)

Cusumano 2002 Nadarìa Nero d'Avola (Sicilia) $10. A gulpable, fresh wine with pure raspberry fruit complemented by cocoa. Despite a hint of hard candy on the nose, it achieves greater vinosity on the finish, blending herbs and bitter chocolate with soft tannins. **87** —J.C. (10/1/2003)

Cusumano 2005 Nero d'Avola (Sicilia) $10. This is a no-fuss, approachable Nero d'Avola that rides solely on the fruit's inherent qualities and never sees wood. The raspberry and strawberry notes are definitely on the ripe side but leave a young, fruity impression in the mouth. **87 Best Buy** —M.L. (7/1/2006)

Cusumano 2003 Sagana Nero d'Avola (Sicilia) $NA. A fruit-forward nose with emphasis on dried fruit, prunes, raisins, and currant berries. Ripe cherry comes through in the mouth where the wine shows good structure; shows Nero d'Avola as the elegant grape it is. **88** —M.L. (7/1/2006)

Cusumano 2004 Sàgana Nero d'Avola (Sicilia) $30. Here is a vivid and inviting rendition of Nero d'Avola that sees one year in oak casks and delivers layers of blueberry fruit, cigar box, almonds, spice, and a hot sensation reminiscent of kirsch spirit. It has feather-soft tannins, good balance, and a fruit-driven close. **87** —M.L. (7/1/2006)

Cusumano 2001 Sàgana Nero d'Avola (Sicilia) $21. Marred by a trace of acetate on the nose, this is otherwise a juicy, medium-weight wine that combines herbs, berries, and dark chocolate with modest tannins. **85** — J.C. (10/1/2003)

Cusumano 2005 Benuara Red Blend (Sicilia) $15. Just released but already mature and composed in presentation (20% sees oak), this Nero d'Avola and Syrah blend has rich aromas of milk chocolate, blackberry, earth, and moist tobacco with moderately soft tannins on the persistent finish. **88** —M.L. (7/1/2006)

Cusumano 2001 Benuara Red Blend (Sicilia) $15. A 70-30 blend, this is a lush, fruity wine. Displays mixed berry flavors, with the Syrah really showing on the finish, where the wine evokes juicy blueberries and blackberries. **88** —J.C. (10/1/2003)

Cusumano 2004 Noa Red Blend (Sicilia) $28. The most likeable aspect of this wine is how faithfully it mirrors the land it comes from. In the spring, Sicily is blanketed with wild fennel and if you pay close attention you'll smell it on the nose of this Nero d'Avola, Cabernet Sauvignon, and Merlot blend. That dill-herbal touch translates over to the mouth with pine and resin flavors; there's both the softness of the Merlot and the muscle of the Cabernet. **88** —M.L. (7/1/2006)

Cusumano 2001 Noa Red Blend (Sicilia) $30. Inky in color, you can tell just by looking at it that it's an ambitious effort. But the aromas and flavors carry traces of overripe fruit; it's a little pruny on the nose and in the mouth. And for a full-bodied wine of considerable ripeness it's surprisingly hard, with firm acids and tannins on the finish. **84** —J.C. (10/1/2003)

Cusumano 2005 Syrah (Sicilia) $10. Here is a younger, less imposing Syrah (that only sees stainless steel) with a ruby red color and notes of cherry, prune, tobacco, and something lactic. The mouthfeel is full and penetrating with soft tannins and a clean finish. **86 Best Buy** —M.L. (7/1/2006)

Cusumano 2005 Alcamo White Blend (Sicilia) $10. This white blend offers exotic fruit, almond, and some banana on the nose; the alcohol notes seem a bit pungent as it warms in the glass. The wine is lean and crisp in the mouth. **85 Best Buy** —M.L. (7/1/2006)

Cusumano 2005 Angimbé White Blend (Sicilia) $13. On informal occasions, you can't go wrong with a bottle of this 70-30% Insolia-Chardonnay blend. The nose offers generous whiffs of pineapple, stone fruit, marzipan, and bread crust. Zesty, flavorful, smooth, and consistent. **87** —M.L. (7/1/2006)

Cusumano 2002 Angimbé / Insolia-Chardonnay White Blend (Sicilia) $15. Rich, thick with plenty of nutty notes balanced against melon and peach pit. Finish brings almond flavors to the fore. **86** —J.C. (10/1/2003)

ITALY

D'ANGELO

D'Angelo 1997 Canneto Aglianico (Aglianico del Vulture) $23. Dry and lean, with a surprising paucity of fruit, there is nevertheless a lot of complexity in this Aglianico-based wine. Cedar, green herbs, and pine branches start things off, followed by sun-baked, dusty earth flavors. **84** —C.S. (5/1/2002)

D'Angelo 2001 Sacravite Aglianico (Aglianico del Vulture) $12. A spicy, sun-baked Aglianico that deals cherry, bourbon, and piles of hard spice. The flavors of dried cherries and cinnamon are subtle and enticing, while the tight, hard finish offers raisin and other baked fruits. Not complex but good in a finite way. **88 Best Buy** —M.S. (2/1/2005)

DA VINCI

Da Vinci 2001 Brunello (Brunello di Montalcino) $70. A medium-bodied, silky wine that delivers generous whiffs of coffee, vanilla, maple syrup, and sweet fruit. There's an herbal tea quality to the berry-driven flavors. Power and tannins back a vein of refreshing crispness. **89** (4/1/2006)

Da Vinci 2001 S. to Ippolito Merlot-Syrah (Toscana) $42. It's near black in color and boldly styled, but where is it headed? Right now it's a tart, disjointed mix of berries and earthy, chocolaty notes. Crisply acidic and firmly tannic on the finish. Give it some time in the cellar and hope this 50-50 blend of Merlot and Shiraz comes around better than we've predicted. **86** (12/31/2004)

Da Vinci 2003 Sangiovese (Chianti) $14. Smells really nice, with floral notes alongside black cherries, tobacco, and hint of graham cracker. Flavors are fully ripe, blending black cherry and plum, but retaining Chianti's essential leanness. Finishes a bit ungenerous and hard, or it would have scored higher. **85** (12/31/2004)

Da Vinci 2002 Sangiovese (Chianti Classico) $17. Sweet and juice-like, with a strong whiff of artificiality. Lacks the structure, depth, and guts of a major wine, and the finish is syrupy. **82** (4/1/2005)

Da Vinci 2001 Sangiovese (Chianti Classico) $17. Attains a level of intensity not matched by the other Da Vinci wines, with bold aromas of tobacco, earth, and cedar matched on the palate by flavors of cherry, plum, and dried spices. This 100% Sangiovese possesses a long finish and supple tannins; it should drink well for 4–7 years. **88** (12/31/2004)

Da Vinci 2001 Riserva Sangiovese (Chianti) $20. Slightly fuller-bodied than the 2003 Chianti, with ripe, chocolaty, slightly raisiny flavors blending with black cherry, plum, and earth. Folds in cedar and anise notes on the finish. 100% Sangiovese. **87** (12/31/2004)

Da Vinci 2000 Riserva Sangiovese (Chianti) $20. Dark to the eye, with round plum and berry aromas jazzed up by a mix of chocolate and herbs. A forward palate presses ripe cherry/berry fruit, while the finish is collected and pure. Well-made and on the money. Of note, this is a Gallo project. **88** —M.S. (10/1/2004)

DAL FORNO ROMANO

Dal Forno Romano 1999 Corvina, Rondinella, Molinara (Amarone della Valpolicella) $459. Is this a bruiser or what? Opaque in color, with monster aromatics that run from tar and espresso to maple, violets, cumin, and finely scented candle wax. Deep and intense as they come, with charcoal and menthol on top of primary blackberry and cassis. No other word besides "massive" describes it. Hugely tannic and weighing in at 17%; needs five to seven years minimum in the cellar. **95 Cellar Selection** (11/1/2005)

Dal Forno Romano 1997 Red Blend (Valpolicella Superiore) $70. This "young" powerhouse has barely got its legs under it, yet it's ready to run. It opens with smoky bacon and rubber notes. In the mouth, big cherry flavors bolstered by firm tannins and potent acids make for a full-force ride. The finish, now tannic and tight as a drum, is ripe and sweet at its center. Hold for several more years. **90** (5/1/2003)

Dal Forno Romano 1996 Red Blend (Amarone della Valpolicella) $300. At 17.5% alcohol with a color akin to ink or oil, overwhelming berry flavors and massive tannins, this drew mixed reviews from our tasting panel. Advocates loved its intensity and viscosity. The extraction is unparalleled, they noted. Detractors, however, found it sweet and unbalanced. **91** (5/1/2003)

DALFIUME

Dalfiume 1999 Rubicone Sangiovese (Emilia-Romagna) $6. 87 Best Buy —M.N. (12/31/2000)

DAMILANO

Damilano 1999 Barbera (Barbera d'Alba) $25. Pure and strapped, with plenty of oak but even more racy blackberry and pepper. The power is on here; cherry, plum skin, and currant are wrapped snugly amid tight tannins. Overall it's lean and inspired, and it would be sensational with meat-filled tortelloni. **90** —M.S. (12/15/2003)

Damilano 1999 Cannubi Nebbiolo (Barolo) $72. Like Damilano's Liste bottling, this one also has a strong vegetal streak to its aromas. Black cherry and coffee flavors are ripe and loaded with chewy tannins. If you can get past the green, you'll like this better than we did. Drink 2008–2015. **88** (4/2/2004)

Damilano 1998 Cannubi Nebbiolo (Barolo) $70. Licorice and cocoa aromas are accentuated by a touch of char. Flavors are of blackberry, cherry, and bresaola. There is good balance and depth. **91** —C.S. (11/15/2002)

Damilano 1999 Liste Nebbiolo (Barolo) $65. This wine has a persistent vegetal note to its aromas that may put some tasters off; others may not be bothered by it. Flavors are earthy and moderately rich, blending sweet notes of dried fruit with mushroom and tar. Long, tannic finish picks up hints of coffee beans. **85** (4/2/2004)

Damilano 1998 Liste Nebbiolo (Barolo) $98. An appealing bouquet of stable, earth, and underbrush lure you to believe there's not much fruit here. Once the wine is in your mouth you see that this is not true. The flavors are bursting with juicy blackberries drizzled with tar, then the wine finishes full and silky. **93 Editors' Choice** —C.S. (11/15/2002)

DANZANTE

Danzante 2001 Merlot (Sicilia) $11. Chunky and green, with caramel oak sitting on top as camouflage. Modest berry fruit leads into a lean, quick finish. Over and out. **81** —M.S. (10/1/2004)

Danzante 2000 Merlot (Sicilia) $11. This textbook entry-level Merlot combines plum, mocha, and herb shadings in a soft, almost sweet-tasting wine that's sure to be poured by the glass at innumerable restaurants nationwide. There's just enough tannin on the finish to give it the strength to pair with red meats. **84** (9/1/2002)

Danzante 1999 Merlot (Sicilia) $11. This Frescobaldi/Mondavi Merlot offers sweet raspberry aromas doused in spices (anise, ancho chili, black pepper, cinnamon). On the dry side in the mouth, ordinary blackberry fruit competes with char and toast for top billing. Ditto for the finish, which is on the acidic side. **86 Best Buy** —C.S. (5/1/2002)

Danzante 2004 Pinot Grigio (Delle Venezie) $10. Frescobaldi's Pinot Grigio proves to be a well-constructed and composed wine with green fruit like kiwi and honeydew backed by a pine resin, cut-grass quality. Silky smooth in the mouth. **87 Best Buy** —M.L. (6/1/2006)

Danzante 2003 Pinot Grigio (Delle Venezie) $10. Subtle pear and melon aromas are pleasant enough, and the mouthfeel is plump and low-acid. Easy-drinking and innocuous. **83** —J.C. (12/31/2004)

Danzante 2001 Pinot Grigio (Delle Venezie) $10. With its crisp pear, apple, and citrus flavors, this lightweight wine would work well as an apéritif. Some orange-blossom notes on the nose and a slight bitterness on the finish give it additional dimension. A small amount of Riesling boosts the aromatics further. **86** (9/1/2002)

Danzante 2002 Sangiovese (Marche) $10. Smoky and heavy, with a charred nose that masks strawberry and mineral notes. A bit shrill, but at least the cherry and raspberry fruit pops on the palate. Finishes warm and long, with a blast of fresh tomato. **84** —M.S. (6/1/2005)

Danzante 2000 Sangiovese (Marche) $11. It's tough to find good inexpensive Sangiovese, but this one fits the bill. Plum and black cherry aromas and flavors are followed by a somewhat hard, unyielding green-tobacco finish that's sure to cut through the mozzarella at your favorite pizza joint. **84** (9/1/2002)

DARDANO

Dardano 1999 Nebbiolo (Barolo) $25. Another late-arriving 1999 Barolo, Dardano's boasts a rich, expansive mouthfeel allied to flavors of prune, dried cherry, leather, and earth. It's a sturdy, chewy wine, one that could use a few years in the cellar to round into shape. Try after 2010. **89** —J.C. (11/15/2004)

Dardano 1997 Nebbiolo (Barolo) $23. Bitter cherry flavors mixed with soy are enhanced by dustiness laced with vanilla and seaweed. Not a very powerful Barolo, but an enjoyable one now. And for Barolo, it's a good value. **87** —C.S. (11/15/2002)

Dardano 2000 Primitivo (Salento) $9. Aromas and flavors of clean blackberry jam, cinnamon, and a hint of Grandma's baked cherry pie make an enjoyable, simple libation. **86 Best Buy** —C.S. (5/1/2002)

DEI

Dei 1999 Red Blend (Rosso di Montepulciano) $15. Rosso di Montepulciano is the Junior Varsity version of Brunello di Montalcino and is often a very good value for current consumption. Cherry and plum aromas and flavors abound, supported nicely by a solid but not hard acid and tannic structure. This balanced, medium-bodied wine is a fine everyday red that's ready to drink now. **87** —M.N. (9/1/2001)

Dei 2002 Sangiovese (Vino Nobile di Montepulciano) $30. Fairly fruity, without a ton of overt new oak. Aromas of plum and berry are jazzed up by spearmint, while the palate is ample, round, and chewy. Finishes modestly tannic yet sturdy, with just enough vanilla and brown-sugar flavors to keep it friendly. A Marc de Grazia Selection, various importers. **87** —M.S. (7/1/2005)

Dei 2001 Bossona Sangiovese (Vino Nobile di Montepulciano) $45. Super-tight yet smooth; this reserve-quality Sangiovese is exactly as it should be. Chocolate, raspberry, and leather aromas lead to a corpulent but structured body veiling ultrapure red fruit flavors. Neither tannic nor hard; hold for another 12 to 18 months. **91 Editors' Choice** —M.S. (7/1/2005)

DELLA STAFFA

Della Staffa 1997 Chardonnay (Alto Adige) $15. 86 (9/1/2000)

DELLATORRI

Dellatorri 2003 Pinot Grigio (Delle Venezie) $12. That extra year in the bottle seems to have dulled the wine's natural freshness leaving a musky, hummus-like element that is uncharacteristic of Pinot Grigio. **82** —M.L. (2/1/2006)

DESSILANI

Dessilani 1997 Reserve Selection Barbera (Barbera di Piemonte) $16. 86 (4/1/2000)

DEZZANI

Dezzani 2000 Gli Scaglioni Barbera (Barbera d'Asti) $17. Starts with penetrating cherry scents married to sappy or resinous nuances, then offers big, mouth-filling flavors of cherries supported by a subtle oak framework. Long and intense on the finish. **90 Editors' Choice** —J.C. (11/15/2004)

Dezzani 2004 Il Gavi Cortese (Gavi) $15. Starts off smelling pretty standard, with apple, pear, and melon scents mingling on the nose, then takes it a step further on the palate with bold, ripe tropical flavors playing against crisp, mouth-watering acids and minerals. Drink now. **88** —J.C. (3/1/2006)

Dezzani 2004 I Morelli Moscato (Moscato d'Asti) $12. The nose is ripe with floral, fruit, honey, and those trademark soapy notes with rose petal, dried grass, and citrus in the mouth. A beautiful single-vineyard wine from Terzo d'Acqui with a creamy texture and a saccharine-sweet finish. **88 Best Buy** —M.L. (12/15/2005)

DI LENARDO

Di Lenardo 2004 Pinot Grigio (Friuli Grave) $10. The candied fruit, lemon zest, orange blossom, and mineral notes make this wine stand out. It has a rounded, soft body with well-integrated crispness. **87 Best Buy** —M.L. (2/1/2006)

DI MAJO NORANTE

Di Majo Norante 2001 Contado Aglianico (Molise) $12. Deep, ripe, and syrupy on the nose, with leather, brambly red fruit, and licorice. Seemingly on the ripe side, but still juicy and fresh. The plum and berry fruit is mature, while proper aging has added a smoky edge along with carob, earth, and coffee nuances. **89 Best Buy** —M.S. (2/1/2005)

Di Majo Norante 2002 Ramitello Red Blend (Terra degli Osci) $14. I am simply delighted with the latest releases from Molise's Di Majo Norante. This luscious red blend is made from two little-known, organically grown native varieties (85 percent Prugnolo and 15 percent Aglianico) and has been deftly transformed thanks to consulting enologist Riccardo Cotarella into a thick, inky garnet wine with black cherry, tar, leather, bitter chocolate, and never-ending layers of aromatic intensity. A gorgeously concentrated and velvety body leaves zesty spice in the mouth until you're ready for the next sip. **89 Best Buy** —M.L. (11/15/2005)

Di Majo Norante 2001 Ramitello Red Blend (Terra degli Osci) $14. An Adriatic Coast wine made from Prugnolo and Aglianico; it's not terribly elegant but it does sport meaty fruit that falls into the boysenberry/blackberry category. Fairly creamy on the back end, while overall it comes across as well-made. Soft tannins make for an easy, almost lactic finish and mouthfeel. **87** —M.S. (2/1/2005)

Di Majo Norante 2003 Sangiovese (Terra degli Osci) $10. Full and purple, with a meaty bouquet that dishes bacon, berry, and cookie dough. Great feel, assuming you like yours big. As for flavor, look for plum, blackberry, and spice cake. With modest tannins, this is a drink-me-now kind of red, perfect with pizza or pasta. **86 Best Buy** —M.S. (2/1/2005)

Di Majo Norante 2002 Apianae 500ml White Blend (Molise) $19. This dessert wine ventures far beyond classic dried fruit and nuts to offer fresh peach, apricot lavender, lemon rind, dried basil, and pine nuts. It has a winning combination of herbs and sweetness that recalls tea with honey and lemon. Made from late-harvest (as late as November) and very rare Moscato Reale grapes. **93** —M.L. (10/1/2006)

Di Majo Norante 1999 Biblos White Blend (Molise) $11. Falanghina and Greco di Tufo comprise the mix in this wine. It comes from Molise, an area described by some as the appendix of the Abruzzi. The medium-gold color of this '99 makes me think that something went awry here. This is confirmed by the predominantly caramel flavors and the mouth-watering acid levels. **81** —M.N. (9/1/2001)

DI MEO

Di Meo 2004 G Greco (Greco di Tufo) $NA. Winemaker Roberto Di Meo is one of those people you instinctively like. He laughs loud and loves practical jokes and his good cheer is reflected in the long portfolio of wines he produces from grapes native to the Campania region. This single varietal Greco di Tufo has tangible almond, creamy peach, and Golden Delicious apple and is round and full with mouth-puckering tartness on the finish. Elegant packaging makes for a handsome table presentation. **88 Best Buy** —M.L. (11/15/2005)

DIEVOLE

Dievole 2001 Sangiovese (Chianti Classico) $20. Begins with scattered, funky aromas of barnyard and volatility before finding a smoother stride. Flavors of bright cherry and citrus are high-toned, while the mouth is filling, with only medium-weight tannins. **86** (4/1/2005)

Dievole 1999 Broccato Sangiovese (Toscana) $29. A little bit flat on the bouquet, with prune, graham cracker, and tobacco aromas. Flavors of plum and black cherry are fine, but there's more acid and tannin than flesh. Solid but not spectacular; there's a bit too much displaced tannin to rate at the next level up. **88** —M.S. (9/1/2006)

Dievole 2000 Novecento Riserva Sangiovese (Chianti Classico) $37. Exotic, luxurious, and lush; super-ripe and intense, but cuddly and lush, with a splendid texture. Aromas of smoked meats, cinnamon, and coffee are more savory than sweet. Tastes generous, with black fruit floating on ripe tannins. Finishes very long. **93 Editors' Choice** (4/1/2005)

ITALY

Dievole 1998 Riserva Sangiovese (Chianti Classico) $35. 92 —*R.V.* *(8/1/2002)*

DILEO

DiLeo 1996 Cabernet Sauvignon (Sicilia) $22. When's the last time you saw mature Cabernet from Sicily on your retailer's shelf? This is medium-weight, but very supple and smooth on the finish. Some berries are hanging in there, but this is more about wood, earth, and soy sauce than fruit. Drink now. **85** —*J.C.* *(10/1/2003)*

DiLeo 1998 Achilles Nero d'Avola (Sicilia) $14. This dull, earthy blend of Nero d'Avola and Sangiovese is light in color and browning at the rim. **80** *(10/1/2003)*

DiLeo 1999 Sangiovese (Sicilia) $20. Tastes prematurely old, and looks a little brown around the edges, but makes up for it with a smooth, supple mouthfeel and polished finish. **84** —*J.C.* *(10/1/2003)*

DOLMEN

Dolmen 2000 Nebbiolo (Colli del Limbara) $24. This barrique-aged Nebbiolo from Sardinia won't be mistook for Barolo. It's richer, friendlier and softer. But even with that concession it's still got some nail-like tannins. The flavors, meanwhile, are precise, and the balance is there. It's got structure and bold flavors. All in all, it's a fine discovery that's worth more than a look. **88** —*M.S.* *(12/15/2003)*

DOMENICO DE BERTIOL

Domenico de Bertiol NV Prosecco (Prosecco di Conegliano) $13. Attractive aromas of acacia blossom and lime are followed by zippy citrus and tart apple flavors. Drier and leaner than most Proseccos, finishing crisp and clean. **86** —*J.C.* *(12/31/2003)*

DOMÌNI VENETI

Domìni Veneti 2000 Corvina (Amarone della Valpolicella Classico) $39. Bacon, mocha, and coffee, all courtesy of some full-fledged oaking, are attractive in a manly, tough-guy sort of way. The palate is solid as a brick, with flavors of dates, medicinal cherry, and chocolate. Warm and spicy at the end, maybe even a touch hot. **89** *(11/1/2005)*

Domìni Veneti 1997 Vigneti di Jago Corvina (Amarone della Valpolicella Classico) $52. Starts out with crusted red fruit and chocolate before turning decidedly more oaky. Aromas of molasses, tar, and wood grain take over, setting a path toward cherry and chocolate flavors. Finishes warm and quick, with softening tannins. The time to drink it is now. **88** *(11/1/2005)*

Domìni Veneti 2002 Ca' de napa Garganega (Soave Classico) $17. Round, floral, and chunky, with creamed corn and honey aromas. The palate begins with smoky citrus and honey and then veers to melon. It's a bit soft and mealy in the middle, but it should hold one's interest. **86** —*M.S.* *(10/1/2004)*

Domìni Veneti 2002 Red Blend (Amarone della Valpolicella Classico) $39. Dark as night, with touches of aged balsamic vinegar, black olive, and fruitcake on the rich, youthful bouquet. As a brand new Amarone, it's full of rock-hard tannins and intensity. Definitely chewy and big at this point, but with plenty of fruit in reserve. It should settle down in the years to come. **91 Editors' Choice** *(11/1/2005)*

Domìni Veneti 1999 Red Blend (Amarone della Valpolicella Classico) $39. Immensely sweet, both in terms of aromatics and flavors. The bouquet oozes bacon, vanilla, blackberry, and coconut-tinged oak. The palate delivers layers of black fruit as well as pepper, bitter chocolate, and caramel. The finish is firm yet not overbearing. Give it five years and it should be a stellar wine. **93 Editors' Choice** *(5/1/2003)*

Domìni Veneti 1999 La Casetta Ripasso Red Blend (Valpolicella Classico Superiore) $20. This is an excellent ripasso, one that is loaded with plum, raisin, and earth. The flavors are a perfect combination of toast, black cherry, blueberry, and baking spices. And the finish is healthy: There's length, ripe tannins, good acids, and lots of chocolate and licorice. Full-bodied, chewy, and rewarding. **91 Editors' Choice** *(5/1/2003)*

Domìni Veneti 2000 Vigneti di Jago Red Blend (Amarone della Valpolicella Classico) $60. Rather lactic and buttery, according to two of our tasters, and slightly cooked. But it's also got some good fruit in its center and a lot of fudge, molasses, and spice. Improves with airing; needs a few years on its side. **88** *(11/1/2005)*

Domìni Veneti 1997 Vigneti di Lago Red Blend (Valpolicella Classico) $48. At first the smoky, meaty aromas seem a bit like cured meat, but with airing they morph into more typical chocolate, vanilla and prune. The palate is richer than most, featuring boysenberry and black cherry with an under-current of vanilla. The finish is creamy and long, just as it should be. **89** *(5/1/2003)*

Domìni Veneti NV Vigneti di Moron Red Blend (Recioto della Valpolicella) $23. Rich and floral, with piercing aromas of grape skins and blackberry preserves. The texture is thick, while the flavor profile is boldly sweet. But it's got moderate tannins and good acidity, so it's not cloying. A fine match for chocolate-based desserts. **90 Editors' Choice** *(5/1/2003)*

DON GATTI

Don Gatti NV Amabile Frizzante Malvasia Bianca (Colli Piacentini) $9. A sparkler made from this grape is going to be funky by nature, so don't be shocked by the unconventional aromas of smoked meat, mustard seed, and basil. The flavor profile is exceedingly sweet, but the acidity is correct so the balance seems solid. This is a strange wine, a mixed bag of flavor and funk. **82** —*M.S.* *(12/31/2002)*

DONATELLA CINELLI COLOMBINI

Donatella Cinelli Colombini 2001 Brunello (Brunello di Montalcino) $55. Enthusiastic applause across the panel for this blockbuster wine made by superstar enologist Carlo Ferrini. Modern, concentrated, and packed with plump fruit, black pepper highlights, vanilla, and chewy meatiness. One panelist likened it to Californian Syrah. Does not bode well for Brunello purists, but it is a rich, powerful wine that leaves a dry, chewy finish and a huge impression in the mouth. **95 Editors' Choice** *(4/1/2006)*

Donatella Cinelli Colombini 2000 Brunello (Brunello di Montalcino) $49. The brilliant ruby color conveys density, and the bouquet is deliciously smooth. The palate exhibits fine integration of oak, tannin, and ripe berry flavors, while the mouthfeel is nothing if not heavenly. With appropriate oak and extract, it flows in rich, creamy style. Warm, meaty, and wickedly good. **92** —*M.S.* *(7/1/2005)*

Donatella Cinelli Colombini 1999 Brunello (Brunello di Montalcino) $45. Nice and sweet to the nose, with black fruit, ample body, and modest tannins awaiting. This wine isn't hard to like; it's chewy and full, with simple, clean flavors. **88** —*M.S.* *(6/1/2004)*

Donatella Cinelli Colombini 1997 Brunello (Brunello di Montalcino) $38. When Donatella Colombini left the family estate of Fattoria dei Barbi, she set up her own production network at Fattoria del Casato. Here she has made an elegant 1997 Brunello, brimming with black tar and cherries, and balanced ripe, sweet tannins and acidity. While it is not powerful, it is smooth, ripe, and seductive. **91** —*R.V.* *(8/1/2002)*

Donatella Cinelli Colombini 2000 Prime Donne Brunello (Brunello di Montalcino) $65. A wine in which the grapes were selected by four women, hence the name. This version is more ripe and chewy than the normale, and it exhibits plum, raisin, chocolate, and licorice aromas and flavors. Very nice in its own right, but not quite as balanced and upright as the basic wine. Also, there's more barrique influence here. **90** —*M.S.* *(7/1/2005)*

Donatella Cinelli Colombini 2000 Riserva Brunello (Brunello di Montalcino) $65. A unique treat from a winery managed by women only. It offers a delicate nose with dried oregano, floral notes, cedar wood, mint candy, and dark cherries. Lively and intense in the mouth and tightly framed by a compact structure and soft wood tones. Beautiful, tingly sensation in the mouth that lasts a very long time. **94 Editors' Choice** *(4/1/2006)*

Donatella Cinelli Colombini 1999 Riserva Brunello (Brunello di Montalcino) $65. Saturated to the max, with a violet/ruby tint that shows no breaks. If it looks like an extracted bruiser, it is. The tannins are big and precise, however, they aren't aggressive or mean. In a fine-tuned cellar this will come around in about five years to show amazing black cherry and plum fruit, and lots of style. **95 Cellar Selection** —*M.S.* *(7/1/2005)*

DONNA CRISTINA

Donna Cristina 2004 Pinot Grigio (Lazio) $8. Light-weight and casual, with white flower, flinty tones, lime, and stone fruit. Crisp and refreshing, with a sour note on the finish. **85** —*M.L. (2/1/2006)*

DONNA OLGA

Donna Olga 2001 Brunello (Brunello di Montalcino) $75. This wine has a cookie dough-like quality that pairs interestingly with herb, spice, cherry and vanilla aromas. Firm, drying tannins tune down the wine's fruitiness and make it hard to see where it might be headed a few years from now. **87** *(4/1/2006)*

DONNAFUGATA

Donnafugata 2004 Vigna di Gabri Ansonica (Sicilia) $NA. This is a crisp summer wine with more dimension and personality than your standard Italian white. The toasted notes are obvious and are embroidered with delicate notes of pineapple, honeysuckle, and almond. **87** —*M.L. (7/1/2006)*

Donnafugata 2004 Sedàra Nero d'Avola (Sicilia) $15. This is a finely tuned Nero d'Avola with blueberry, wet earth muskiness, and pine resin presented in carefully measured doses. Nothing is out of place and the wine boasts a pleasant smoothness in the mouth (a small percentage of the wine matures for nine months in oak). **87** —*M.L. (7/1/2006)*

Donnafugata 2003 Sedàra Nero d'Avola (Sicilia) $15. Takes a moment to give off cherry fruit with mint, herbal notes, aged cheese rind, tobacco, and cigar box. Shows red fruit and toasted notes in the mouth with a silky feel and well-integrated parts. A perfect pasta wine. **87** —*M.L. (7/1/2006)*

Donnafugata 2003 Mille e Una Notte Red Blend (Contessa Entellina) $60. Here's a Nero d'Avola (with a small percentage of mystery grapes) that delivers the goods year after year: cinnamon, vanilla bean, pine nut, curry spice, and leather round off a deeply concentrated and layered wine that sees 16 months of new French oak. Flavors are reminiscent of Indian spice and turmeric with tight, dusty tannins. **92 Cellar Selection** —*M.L. (7/1/2006)*

Donnafugata 2002 Mille e Una Notte Red Blend (Sicilia) $69. Elsewhere in Italy, 2002 was considered too soggy for quality grapes, but not in Sicily. This wine is a true expression of the vintage with almonds and pistachio nuts, full, red berry fruit, and toasted notes over a long finish. Comprised of Nero d'Avola, with a tiny percentage of mystery grapes thrown in. **91** —*M.L. (7/1/2006)*

Donnafugata 1999 Mille e Uno Notte Red Blend (Contessa Entellina) $65. The wine has a rich, open, generous character, with a fascinating sweet and sour fusion of sweet dried fruits and acidity. The wine could certainly age, over 5–10 years. **90** —*R.V. (10/1/2003)*

Donnafugata 2002 Sedàra Red Blend (Sicilia) $12. With its soft stalky fruit and red fruit flavors, this wine is easy, chunky, and juicy. **86** —*R.V. (10/1/2003)*

Donnafugata 2003 Tancredi Red Blend (Contessa Entellina) $30. There's always been debate over which international varieties blend best with Nero d'Avola and this wine proves that Cabernet Sauvignon makes an ideal partner. Earth and toasty with plum and prune, tobacco, and dusty mineral tones, this is a spicy wine with tight tannins that drinks beautifully now. **90** —*M.L. (7/1/2006)*

Donnafugata 2002 Tancredi Red Blend (Contessa Entellina) $30. Ruby-colored and concentrated, this blend of Nero d'Avola (70%) and Cabernet Sauvignon sees 14 months of oak and is clean, refined and perfumed with berry fruit, earthy notes, smoke, vanilla, tobacco, and tight tannins. Drink now with red meat. **91 Editors' Choice** —*M.L. (7/1/2006)*

Donnafugata 2001 Tancredi Red Blend (Contessa Entellina) $25. Named for one of the characters in The Leopard, a book by Guiseppe di Lampedusa and film set at the estate. The fruit is solid, with raisins, sweetness, and chunkiness. Firmness and acidity give it great structure. **88** —*R.V. (10/1/2003)*

Donnafugata 2003 Anthilia White Blend (Sicilia) $15. This blend of local varieties Ansonica and Catarratto is open and soft, with full melon aromas preceding flavors of apple, cinnamon, and baking spices. The finish is soft, almost to the point of mushy, but not quite. An interesting wine to drink this year; don't sit on this one. **86** —*M.S. (10/1/2004)*

Donnafugata 2005 Anthilia White Blend (Sicilia) $15. This is a very friendly and approachable Ansonica-Catarratto blend fermented in stainless steel with pretty, feminine aromas of white flowers, white stone, and a light touch of peach. Lavender-like flavors appear in the mouth with a crisp close. **86** —*M.L. (7/1/2006)*

Donnafugata 2004 Anthilia White Blend (Sicilia) $15. This is a crisp white with interesting dimension thanks to solid fruit flavors and minced herb aromas. You'll find basil, wild sage, and white pepper on the nose. This Ansonica and Catarratto (two Sicilian indigenous grapes) blend is creamy but less intense in the mouth. **86** —*M.L. (7/1/2006)*

Donnafugata 2002 Anthilia White Blend (Sicilia) $12. A blend of Ansonica and Catarratto, this wine has green, crisp, fresh fruit. But is not light-weight, powering fruit, and creamy ripe flavors. **84** —*R.V. (10/1/2003)*

Donnafugata 2001 Chiarandà del Merlon Contessa Entellina White Blend (Sicilia) $35. A 50/50 blend of Chardonnay and Ansonica. Elegant yet rich, dominated by peaches and vanilla, mixed with layers of toasty wood. **89** —*R.V. (10/1/2003)*

Donnafugata 2004 Chiarandé White Blend (Contessa Entellina) $36. The color and bouquet alone denote an elaborate wine-making style with generous vanilla, pineapple, peach, and melted butter on the nose. It's fleshy and creamy in the mouth with satisfying length. This is a 50-50 Ansonica-Chardonnay blend that sees oak. **88** —*M.L. (7/1/2006)*

Donnafugata 2004 Ben Ryé Zibibbo (Passito di Pantelleria) $38. Sicilians are notorious for an insatiable sweet tooth and a talent for making dessert wines: Hands down, the best of the best is Ben Ryé. The aromatic layers are infinite: maple syrup, orange zest, almond paste, dried banana, and crème caramel. This amber-colored dessert wine is dessert on its own. **95 Editors' Choice** —*M.L. (7/1/2006)*

Donnafugata 2004 Kabir Zibibbo (Moscato di Pantelleria) $NA. A surprisingly delicious but lighter Zibibblo-based dessert wine that would pair beautifully with aged cheese. The nose is redolent of honey, apricot, lavender, and rosemary and the endnote enough acidity to cut through creamy, fatty foods. **90** —*M.L. (7/1/2006)*

DRAGANI

Dragani 1996 Selva de' Canonici Montepulciano (Montepulciano d'Abruzzo) $14. This wine has a fragrant nose of violets, chocolate, and tobacco. It's medium-bodied and succulent with soft cherry, tobacco, and mineral flavors. Not complicated, but it shows more style and refinement than many wines of this type. **87** —*J.F. (9/1/2001)*

DRIUS

Drius 2004 Pinot Grigio (Isonzo del Friuli) $NA. There are Golden Delicious apple and almond flavors that fill the mouth nicely and have some acidity at the end. **86** —*M.L. (2/1/2006)*

DRUSIAN

Drusian NV Brut Prosecco (Prosecco di Valdobbiadene) $15. A Prosecco with personality and unique strong points: There's a toasty, bread-like element to the nose with generous peach, apricot, almond, and crushed stone. Has a thicker, creamier consistency with lingering freshness on the medium finish. **88** —*M.L. (6/1/2006)*

Drusian NV Extra Dry Prosecco (Prosecco di Valdobbiadene) $15. Has robust mineral tones with lemon meringue pie, lemon grass, and almond skin. Creamy and frothy, but also light-weight in the mouth with a zesty citrus finish. **86** —*M.L. (6/1/2006)*

DUCA DI CASTELMONTE

Duca di Castelmonte 2002 Notorious Syrah (Sicilia) $16. Not sure what's notorious about this Syrah, which tastes more like a good but generic red wine than anything identifiable as Syrah. That said, the nose is jammy, with hints of bacon, soy, and teriyaki. Toasted nuances and buttery notes add a barrel influence to the palate. Finishes with a spiced-ham flavor and drying tannins. **86** —*M.S. (11/15/2004)*

ITALY

ITALY

DUCA DI SALAPARUTA

Duca di Salaparuta 2002 Bianca di Valguarnera Insolia (Sicilia) $40. This exemplifies a more evolved style with vanilla, butter, exotic fruit, almond skin, lavender, and a flatter, broader nose than most. It's three dimensional, toasted and creamy in the mouth. **88** —M.L. (7/1/2006)

Duca di Salaparuta 2004 Colomba Platino Insolia (Sicilia) $18. Here is a flatter, broader Sicilian white with nutty, pistachio, and marzipan-like notes, crushed white stone, and lighter touches of fruit intensity. Altogether, it's a delicate and likeable package that is easy to drink and refreshes the palate. **87** —M.L. (7/1/2006)

Duca di Salaparuta 2003 Colomba Platino Insolia (Sicilia) $18. Quite tropical on the nose, with floral aromas. Flavors of cantaloupe and papaya are reserved but fresh, while the finish is entirely refreshing. On the plump side, but still balanced and upright. A blend of Insolia and Grecanico. **87** —M.S. (2/1/2005)

Duca di Salaparuta 2000 Bianca di Valguarnera Inzolia (Sicilia) $35. This 100% Inzolia has toasty aromas along with citrus and green fruit flavors. Spends six months in new wood, which gives flavor but does not dominate the fruit. **88** —R.V. (10/1/2003)

Duca di Salaparuta 2001 Duca Enrico Nero d'Avola (Sicilia) $50. Nero d'Avola grapes for this flagship wine are picked from alberello-trained vines to make one of Sicily's most unique and distinctive wines. Instead of the standard ripe cherry and almond paste, here you get a deep, dark green vein with vegetal, rhubarb, herbal notes, chopped sage and fennel, and loads of forest berry. **91 Cellar Selection** —M.L. (7/1/2006)

Duca di Salaparuta 1999 Duca Enrico Nero d'Avola (Sicilia) $55. Made from 100% Nero d'Avola, this wine is a Sicilian flagship. With its firm tannins, solid chunky raisin and sweet ripe fruit and herb flavors and acidity at the end, it is a powerful red with good aging potential. **89** —R.V. (10/1/2003)

Duca di Salaparuta 2000 Terra D'Agala Red Blend (Sicilia) $18. Lots of tight oak results in aromas of resin, mint, and burnt grass. Runs a bit light and tart, given all that oak. The flavors are of raspberry and cranberry with an artificial vanilla sweetness and full tannins. **84** —M.S. (7/1/2005)

Duca di Salaparuta 2002 Terre d'Agala Red Blend (Sicilia) $14. An interesting blend of Nerello Mascalese (from 600 meters above sea level) and Merlot that sees 12 months of oak. Toasted notes are embellished with granite, resin, tobacco, and forest berry; nice, linear, and supple in the mouth. Drink now. **89 Best Buy** —M.L. (7/1/2006)

Duca di Salaparuta 1999 Terre D'Agala Red Blend (Sicilia) $16. Smoky and herbal, with attractive red licorice and tomato aromas. Raspberry and strawberry drive the light palate. Good acids make for a lean and tasty finish. Drink soon. **87** —M.S. (10/1/2003)

Duca di Salaparuta 2000 Trislelè Red Blend (Sicilia) $NA. The name of the wine comes from the three-legged mythological Greek figure that is the ancient symbol of Sicilia. The wine, though, is modern in style with ripe raisins and solid cherry flavors. **88** —R.V. (10/1/2003)

Duca di Salaparuta 2002 Colomba Platino White Blend (Sicilia) $15. This wine has smooth, creamy flavors with just a touch of toast. A floral, fruity blend of Inzolia and Catarratto grapes. **85** —R.V. (10/1/2003)

Duca di Salaparuta 2001 Colomba Platino White Blend (Sicilia) $16. Mild toast aromas add a modern touch to this plump, viscous white that's built around a core of pear and lemon flavors. Seems as if it would be a good companion to oily Mediterranean fish dishes. **86** —J.C. (10/1/2003)

DUCA LEONARDO

Duca Leonardo 2000 La Gioiosa Montepulciano (Montepulciano d'Abruzzo) $6. Aromas of cotton candy, toasted white bread, raisins, and cherry lead you to a fairly sour, almost citrusy palate. The flavor mix of blackberry and grapefruit is odd and clashing. A bit lean and scattered overall. **83** —M.S. (11/15/2003)

DUCAROSSO

Ducarosso 2001 Riserva Sangiovese (Chianti) $11. This is a light ruby Chianti that delivers nice cherry, cedar wood, raspberry roll-up, cola, and some menthol tones. It has a medium structure with a medium finish and soft tannins. **86 Best Buy** —M.L. (10/1/2006)

ECCO DOMANI

Ecco Domani 2000 Merlot (Delle Venezie) $10. Aromas of char, leather, and earth, but not much fruit, start things off. The light palate has some cherry and strawberry, but also some unwelcome weediness and the finish is candied and sweet. **83** (5/1/2003)

Ecco Domani 2005 Pinot Grigio (Delle Venezie) $11. Round and intense, with crisp grapefruit, pear, toast, and floral flavors. It has a full bouquet with kiwi and lime, but a flatter feel to the mouth. **86** —M.L. (6/1/2006)

Ecco Domani 2003 Pinot Grigio (Delle Venezie) $10. Starts better than it finishes, with promising scents of pears, honey, and lemon rind. Light in body, which is fine, but the flavors are an unbalanced blend of ripe pears and stridently sour lemons, turning a bit metallic on the finish. **82** —J.C. (12/31/2004)

Ecco Domani 2002 Pinot Grigio (Delle Venezie) $10. Fairly simple on the nose, but solid, with ripe pears leading the way. The flavors pick up some interesting graphite notes, extending through the minerally finish. Surprisingly full-bodied. **85** —J.C. (7/1/2003)

Ecco Domani 2001 Maso Canali Pinot Grigio (Trentino) $17. An odd style that may not appeal to everyone, with apple and pineapple flavors marked by butter and vanilla. It's medium bodied, and picks up a hint of lemon on the finish. **84** —J.C. (7/1/2003)

Ecco Domani 2004 Sangiovese (Chianti) $11. The lead aromas of red fruit register a bit herbal, while the palate runs a touch darker, offering berry and plum flavors. Fairly full and solid in the mouth, with a modicum of lushness. **84** —M.S. (10/1/2006)

Ecco Domani 2000 Sangiovese (Chianti) $10. Raspberry aromas, cherry, and strawberry flavors, and a strong hint of milk chocolate throughout best define this Gallo-owned wine. Some raisins and a touch of buttery oak appear late, rendering it a simple quaff. **84** (8/1/2002)

ELENA WALCH

Elena Walch 2002 Castel Ringberg Chardonnay (Alto Adige) $18. This unoaked Chardonnay has ripe, creamy fruit, along with acidity that seems typical of the 2002 vintage. Elegant and lively, with nice crispness. **86** —R.V. (7/1/2003)

Elena Walch 2001 Cashmere Gewürztraminer (Alto Adige) $25. Botrytised Gewürztraminer produces a rich, intense, luscious wine with layers of complex spice. A touch of Sauvignon Blanc introduces some clean, crisp freshness to give the wine a fine sense of balance. **91** —R.V. (7/1/2003)

Elena Walch 2002 Kastelatz Gewürztraminer (Alto Adige) $25. A hugely spicy wine, with ripe, full-bodied fruit and a touch of toast. Peaches and lychees give this wine power and richness. **89** —R.V. (7/1/2003)

Elena Walch 2002 Pinot Bianco (Alto Adige) $13. Ripe, fresh, and crisp, this wine has layers of apples and cream, a sense of structure, and full-bodied, lively fruit. This is a great apéritif wine. **86** —R.V. (7/1/2003)

Elena Walch 2002 Kastelatz Pinot Bianco (Alto Adige) $23. A soft, rounded wine with hints of oak from the one-third barrel aging. Concentrated and firm, it is already well in balance, with soft, creamy flavors. **87** —R.V. (7/1/2003)

Elena Walch 1997 Pinot Grigio (Alto Adige) $13. 87 (8/1/1999)

Elena Walch 2004 Pinot Grigio (Alto Adige) $14. Floral notes are carefully preserved: honeysuckle, lilies, and jasmine—and there's a dash of cinnamon snap on the finish. **87** —M.L. (2/1/2006)

Elena Walch 2002 Pinot Grigio (Alto Adige) $12. This is an elegant, smooth wine with fresh clean fruit aromas. It has crispness, concentration, and just a hint of spice. **85** —R.V. (7/1/2003)

Elena Walch 2004 Castel Ringberg Pinot Grigio (Alto Adige) $18. There's plenty of snap and pop on this peach and melon-infused Pinot Grigio. The snap comes from finely chiseled aromas of cinnamon and orange zest. The flavor profile is good in the mouth, too, where the wine coats evenly and shows balanced acidity. **87** —M.L. (2/1/2006)

Elena Walch 2002 Castel Ringberg Pinot Grigio (Alto Adige) $16. A light, crisp style that hints of spice but shows delicious fresh fruit. The acidity shows through, giving a vibrant character to the fruit. **86** —*R.V. (7/1/2003)*

Elena Walch 1998 Castel Ringberg Pinot Grigio (Alto Adige) $20. **87** *(8/1/1999)*

Elena Walch 2002 Castel Ringberg Sauvignon Blanc (Alto Adige) $23. Fragrant, aromatic, grassy aromas give way to fresh, crisp, green fruit and gooseberry flavors. Finishes lively and vibrant. **88** —*R.V. (7/1/2003)*

Elena Walch 2001 Beyond the Clouds White Blend (Alto Adige) $40. Elena Walch's fantasy wine is a blend of Chardonnay and four other varieties that she does not reveal. Eighteen months in oak give the wine a fine, toasty character and creamy fruit, but still leaves the hallmark Alto Adige crispness and freshness. **90** —*R.V. (7/1/2003)*

ELIO ALTARE

Elio Altare 1996 Larigi Barbera (Langhe) $70. **90** *(4/1/2000)*

Elio Altare 1998 Dolcetto (Dolcetto d'Alba) $19. **89** *(4/1/2000)*

Elio Altare 1998 Nebbiolo (Barolo) $60. Dense and chocolaty, yet also imbued with airy scents of red berries, this is a finely tuned wine worthy of attention despite not being a cru. Tar and cherries take charge on the palate, picking up nuances of tree bark, leather, and citrus, before ending with velvety tannins. Drink now–2015. **90** *(4/2/2004)*

ELIO GRASSO

Elio Grasso 1996 Vigna Martini Barbera (Barbera d'Alba) $21. **87** *(4/1/2000)*

Elio Grasso 1998 Vigna Dei Grassi Dolcetto (Dolcetto d'Alba) $14. **88** *(4/1/2000)*

Elio Grasso 1999 Ginestra Vigna Casa Maté Nebbiolo (Barolo) $53. Turns the neat trick of being big and mouth-filling yet not heavy, packing in spiced prune and date flavors wrapped in dark chocolate and tar. The finish shows this wine's true potential, ending with big fruit, big tannins, mouth-watering acids, and great length. **93 Editors' Choice** *(4/2/2004)*

ELIO PERRONE

Elio Perrone 2004 Clartè Moscato (Moscato d'Asti) $18. Less intense than the other samples, but once you dig your nose into the glass those fresh peach and soapy notes translate into a correct and genuine Moscato d'Asti. Crisp and peachy in the mouth. **85** —*M.L. (12/15/2005)*

Elio Perrone 2004 Sourgal Moscato (Moscato d'Asti) $16. I liked this vineyard-designate wine better than the producer's Clartè Moscato d'Asti (from an east-facing vineyard) thanks to its truly gorgeous and feminine nose. It is delicate and floral and the word "pretty" sums it up just right. Great for a romantic picnic in the park. **87** —*M.L. (12/15/2005)*

ELISABETTA

Elisabetta 1998 Le Marze Bordeaux Blend (Toscana) $40. From near the Tuscan coast comes this Bordeaux-style blend of Cabernet Sauvignon, Merlot, and Cab Franc. It's a little rusty in color, with aromas of molasses and plums. The balance is classic, and there's a hint of Médoc earthiness to it, maybe from the Cab Franc. With softer tannins than many, it's already drinkable. **89** —*M.S. (8/1/2002)*

Elisabetta 1999 Aulo Sangiovese (Toscana) $12. Here's a country-style, rustic blend of Sangiovese, Canaiolo, and Cabernet from the Maremma, and it fits the bill perfectly as an everyday red with some character. It's dry, full of cherry and plum fruit, and it finishes warm. Nothing too complex, but plenty to sink your teeth into. **86** —*M.S. (8/1/2002)*

ELORINA

Elorina 1999 Eloro Nero d'Avola (Sicilia) $11. The color is turning fast, while the nose shows some oxidized, stewed notes. But don't give up on it entirely; the flavor profile brings cherry, currant, and fresh tomato, while the spicy finish hits squarely with a blast of pepper. Probably past its prime, but what's here isn't bad. **83** —*M.S. (10/1/2003)*

Elorina 1998 Pachino Nero d'Avola (Sicilia) $17. **84** —*M.S. (10/1/2003)*

ELVIO COGNO

Elvio Cogno 1999 Bricco dei Merli Barbera (Barbera d'Alba) $34. This is a clean Barbera, but one with individual personality. The palate is tight and tart, with cherry and cranberry. The finish is mellow and cooling, with notes of cola, root beer, and bark. The structure is tight as a drum. This is a fine wine to accompany Italian dishes. **90** —*M.S. (11/15/2002)*

Elvio Cogno 1997 Bricco del Merli Barbera (Barbera d'Alba) $30. **87** *(4/1/2000)*

Elvio Cogno 2003 Vigna Del Mandorlo Dolcetto (Dolcetto d'Alba) $20. Nicely concentrated, with a depth of fruit and richness of texture uncommon to Dolcetto. Grapey, with black cherry and plum flavors taking the lead, but elegant at the same time, with a long, layered finish. **90 Editors' Choice** —*J.C. (3/1/2005)*

Elvio Cogno 1998 Vigna del Mandorlo Dolcetto (Dolcetto d'Alba) $16. **88** *(4/1/2000)*

Elvio Cogno 1999 Ravera Nebbiolo (Barolo) $63. In need of bottle aging, Cogno's '99 Ravera blends molasses with dates and figs to give the impression of a spiced fruitcake impregnated with tannins instead of rum. Give it until 2010, when it should begin to open up. **91** *(4/2/2004)*

ENRICO

Enrico NV Brut Prosecco (Prosecco di Valdobbiadene) $11. Crisp and natural, with some bread dough on the less than expressive nose. Distant citrus carries the flavor profile, while the finish is dry and natural. Washes the palate in fresh fashion. Made by Bellussi. **84** —*M.S. (12/15/2005)*

ENRICO SANTINI

Enrico Santini 2004 Poggio al Moro Red Blend (Bolgheri) $25. Lean and almost weedy. The ripeness is in question from the start. In the mouth, it pulses with awkward, green, plum flavors in front of a non-descript, narrow finish. Picks up some steam with time but fails to get over the hump. **82** —*M.S. (9/1/2006)*

Enrico Santini 2001 Montepergoli Sangiovese (Bolgheri) $65. Big and clumsy upon opening, as nutty, earthy aromas dominate the fruit. Airing reveals lively black cherry and snappy plum flavors, but also a distant taste of sugar beet. Brightly acidic and almost tangy; it's obviously a good wine but it has a short zestiness that brings it down a notch. **87** —*M.S. (9/1/2006)*

Enrico Santini 2004 Campo alla Casa White Blend (Bolgheri) $20. A blend of 60% Vermentino and 40% Sauvignon Blanc that runs heavy and ripe but not out of control. The flavor profile entails dry pit fruits such as peach and nectarine, while the finish is defined by soda cracker dryness and citrus rind. Balanced and zesty, if a touch lean on flavor. **86** —*M.S. (9/1/2006)*

ENZO BOGLIETTI

Enzo Boglietti 1999 Barbera (Barbera d'Alba) $17. Cherry, black pepper, and vanilla greet you and appear again in the long finish. The hollow middle, however, detracts from an otherwise fine effort. **84** —*M.N. (9/1/2001)*

Enzo Boglietti 1998 Brunate Nebbiolo (Piedmont) $60. The long, 38-month wood aging has produced a ripe, heady wine with some juicy, tarry fruit. Sweet and dry tannins combine with powerful ripe, dark fruits but the overall aftertaste is of dry wood and fruit tannins. **89** —*R.V. (11/15/2002)*

Enzo Boglietti 1998 Casa Nere Nebbiolo (Piedmont) $60. The tiny, 2.4-acre vineyard of Casa Nere in La Morra has produced a wine with dominant rustic characteristics from its high alcohol (14.6%). Under these almost heady aromas there is also sweet, open fruit with firm, dry tannins and toasty wood flavors. Dry wood comes through on the finish, along with flavors of black cherries. **88** —*R.V. (11/15/2002)*

Enzo Boglietti 1998 Fossati Nebbiolo (Piedmont) $60. This is a wine with sweet tarry aromas, and rich, sweet fruit with flavors of new wood and black figs. Powerful tannins dominate the fruit at this stage, but they will soften over the next five years or so. **90** —*R.V. (11/15/2002)*

ITALY

Enzo Boglietti 1998 Buio Red Blend (Langhe) $35. This Piedmontese blend of 80% Nebbiolo and 20% Barbera is strongly marked by new wood, which, in this instance, imparts a smoky, meaty character to the aromas of cherries and berries. The bright fruit flavors later fold in cocoa notes and finish long and tart, with an under-current of dried brush and herb that adds complexity. Hold til 2005. **91** —*J.C. (9/1/2001)*

ESPERTO

Esperto 2004 Pinot Grigio (Delle Venezie) $12. Floral aromas are more defined than the fruity ones. Still, they leave room for attractive almond skin, flint, and eucalyptus accents. Simple and lightweight in the mouth, with a sour note on the finish. **85** —*M.L. (6/1/2006)*

Esperto 2001 Pinot Grigio (Delle Venezie) $13. A rather hard, minerally wine, without the approachability of so many Pinot Grigios, but showing a more stony and focused side to this grape's personality. The flavors are clean and crisp; lime and barely ripe nectarines provide tartness and vivacity. **86** —*J.C. (7/1/2003)*

F PRINCIPIANO

F Principiano 1996 La Romualda Barbera (Barbera d'Alba) $36. 87 *(4/1/2000)*

F Principiano 2000 Sant'Anna Dolcetto (Dolcetto d'Alba) $19. Earth and coffee add a dark element to the otherwise red fruit nose. The palate runs lean and tight, with cranberry and cherry fruit. Quite tight and acidic, but with food it has the clarity of flavor and fruit to work. **85** —*M.S. (12/15/2003)*

F Principiano 1997 Sant'Anna Dolcetto (Dolcetto d'Alba) $17. 90 *(4/1/2000)*

FABIANO

Fabiano 1999 Corvina, Rondinella, Molinara (Amarone della Valpolicella) $39. A bit more racy than most, with fresh fruit on the nose, some minerality, and quite a bit of snap. Cherry and cranberry flavors vie with richer dark fruit notes, while the finish is spicy and long. More of an old-school wine, and one that should do well with meat and hearty pastas. **89** *(11/1/2005)*

Fabiano 1998 Corvina, Rondinella, Molinara (Amarone della Valpolicella Classico) $39. Charged up and a bit acidic, with aromas of smoke, under-brush and leather along with some nicely integrated wood. Solid, with requisite dark fruit and chocolate flavors. But there's no doubt that it's zesty, bordering on racy. Nice but could use more mouthfeel. **87** *(11/1/2005)*

Fabiano 1999 I Fondatori Corvina, Rondinella, Molinara (Amarone della Valpolicella Classico) $55. Basic but very solid, with leather, cedar, earth, and mild red fruit aromas. Feels nice on the tongue, with raspberry flavors, some citrus, and a bit of rubber. Nicely textured and big on the finish. Overall it's satisfying and solid. **89** *(11/1/2005)*

Fabiano 1997 I Fondatori Corvina, Rondinella, Molinara (Amarone della Valpolicella Classico) $55. Fairly round and harmonious, with spice, leather, and some sweaty rubber on the nose. Comes along snappy once it hits the palate, thus the cherry and raspberry flavors are a touch sharp. Seems to have a touch of bretty character. **86** *(11/1/2005)*

Fabiano 1998 IGT Del Veneto Pinot Grigio (Del Veneto) $7. 85 *(8/1/1999)*

Fabiano 2000 Red Blend (Amarone della Valpolicella Classico) $37. Round with some prune-based aromas. The palate runs soft and smooth, but with good balance. Flavors dominated by black cherry are enlivened by a shot of citrus, but it's not an overly acidic wine. Fairly standard fare in the final analysis, but pleasant. **87** *(11/1/2005)*

Fabiano 1998 I Fondatori Red Blend (Amarone della Valpolicella Classico) $50. Good and rich, with bacon, lavender, leather, and prune aromas. At all points this wine comes across well-balanced, with ace-level tannins and just the right amount of acidity. Finishes long and leathery, with hints of chocolate and supple tannins. Features a splendid mix of finesse and power. **91** *(11/1/2005)*

FALCHINI

Falchini 2002 Vigna a Solatio Vernaccia (Vernaccia di San Gimignano) $14. Extremely lively, to the point of being spritzy. The nose is full of cit-rus and a hint of anise, while the palate, while not particularly complex, is zesty and deals active melon and mineral flavors. A likable wine, one from a single vineyard. **86** —*M.S. (8/1/2004)*

Falchini 2001 Vinea Doni Vernaccia (Vernaccia di San Gimignano) $25. Gold in color, with unusual aromas of spiced ham and sawdust. The wine contains 10% Chardonnay, likely barrel-aged based on the strength of the wine's wood aromas and resinous aftertaste. Other flavors of maderized apple and banana are acceptable but strange for the variety. **83** —*M.S. (8/1/2004)*

FALESCO

Falesco 2003 Marciliano Cabernet Blend (Umbria) $50. Here is a knock-out wine from one of Italy's most talented enologists, Riccardo Cotarella, that delivers classic Cabernet green notes followed by bursting tones of blackberry, tobacco, toasted coconut flakes, apple pie crust, and even some distant hints of black licorice. The aromatic complexity is stellar and so is the velvety mouthfeel; a genuine crowd pleaser. **93 Editors' Choice** —*M.L. (9/1/2006)*

Falesco 2003 Vitiano Rosso Red Blend (Umbria) $10. Every year this wine proves itself as a value champ. The '03, even though it hails from a hot year, is still a balanced, full-bodied example of fine everyday wine. The nose offers smoke, game, and jammy dark fruit, and the palate is fresh and full, with big cherry and plum flavors. **88 Best Buy** —*M.S. (7/1/2005)*

Falesco 2001 Vitiano Rosso Red Blend (Umbria) $10. You could drink this wine everyday with your dinner. It's fun to drink and made that way. Aromas are of wild flowers, huckleberries, and horse tail. The coffee and raspberry flavors have a juicy, enjoyable finish. **88 Best Buy** —*C.S. (2/1/2003)*

Falesco 2003 Ferentano Roscetto (Lazio) $25. A pure expression of the little-known Roscetto grape skillfully worked by the talented Cotarella brothers. Intense peach, pineapple, toasted nuts, and a playful hint of aged Parmigiano cheese rind. Good length and depth on the body and perfectly integrated acidity. **90 Editors' Choice** —*M.L. (9/1/2005)*

FANTI

Fanti 2001 Brunello (Brunello di Montalcino) $90. Bold brushstrokes of cocoa fudge, lavish vanilla, espresso bean, plum, leather, and Indian spice create an expressive and flavorful whole. Silky tannins are framed by ripe red fruit and smoky roasted notes. A very good showing from one of Brunello's most recognized names. **93** *(4/1/2006)*

Fanti 2000 Brunello (Brunello di Montalcino) $75. Strong-willed and pure-smelling, with lush cherry, cola, and tree bark aromas mingling with berry and cherry. While it sits on the fence between racy and creamy, it delivers vanilla and chocolate flavors along with pure plum and black cherry. Features sharp tannins and bracing acidity. **91** —*M.S. (7/1/2005)*

Fanti 1999 Brunello (Brunello di Montalcino) $80. Rich, dark, and lush, with liqueur-like aromas wafting upward from a sea of purple. An obvious entry into the "modern" category of Brunello. There's jammy, mouth-coating fruit and only modest acidity. Detractors may find it heavy and bruising, but fans will adore its weight and creaminess. **92** —*M.S. (6/1/2004)*

Fanti 1997 Brunello (Brunello di Montalcino) $58. Flavio Fanti's tiny 12-acre vineyard is treated almost like his backyard, with a scrupulous attention to detail and now a dense planting that has definitely improved the quality of the wines. The 1997 shows modern, spicy wood, violet and rose aromas. The palate is rich, firm, and dry, but with attractive bitter chocolate and licorice flavors. The new wood shows through but never throws the wine off-balance. **90** —*R.V. (8/1/2002)*

Fanti 2000 Sangiovese (Sant'Antimo) $17. This is but the second vintage in the states of this rich, internationally-styled Sangiovese from this catch-all DOC near Montalcino. It's chewy, thick, and packed full of black plum and blackberry. Full yet non-aggressive tannins solidify the balance, while potent hints of bitter chocolate and coffee rise up on the finish. **88** —*M.S. (8/1/2002)*

FASSATI

Fassati 2000 Selciaia Sangiovese (Rosso di Montepulciano) $11. Seems quite a bit late for a Rosso di Montepulciano. The wine is sweet and candied, with tannin and a dull aftertaste. **81** —*M.S. (11/15/2004)*

FATTOI

Fattoi 2001 Brunello (Brunello di Montalcino) $NA. Barnyard notes first meet the nose but lessen in intensity to reveal cherry cola, dark plum, forest floor, moist tree bark, and tobacco. Offers a medium-to-full build with persistent length and a firm, spicy finish. **89** *(4/1/2006)*

FATTORIA CARPINETA FONTALPINO

Fattoria Carpineta Fontalpino 1997 Gioia Sangiovese (Chianti Colli Senesi) $13. Full, with a pruny note to the grape and chocolate aromas. The espresso and licorice flavors are mature, but there are mouth-coating tannins on the back end. Evolved in flavor, youthful in structure; only time will tell where it's headed. **86** *(4/1/2001)*

FATTORIA CORONCINO

Fattoria Coroncino 1999 Gaiospino Verdicchio (Verdicchio dei Castelli di Jesi Classico) $27. A wine like this proves that Verdicchio, if made right, has staying power. At five years of age it's showing no signs of tiring. The nose is rich and sensuous, offering a load of dried apricot and peach. The mouth is round and full, with white stone fruits, salt, nuts, and white pepper. A classy and full-bodied white from the Marche. **90** —*M.S. (8/1/2004)*

Fattoria Coroncino 2001 Il Coroncino Verdicchio (Verdicchio dei Castelli di Jesi Classico Superiore) $18. Full and fresh, with a little bit of youth. The nose is delightful as if offers almond, peach, and vanilla cream. The palate is equally nice, with its cashew, citrus, and spice notes. A lively white that's primed to run. **89** —*M.S. (8/1/2004)*

Fattoria Coroncino 1999 Gaiospino White Blend (Marche) $25. This simple wine has aromas of mustard grains and cream cheese, which lead into more cream cheese—plus lime and an arugula-like bite—in the mouth. Slightly high acidity translates into a medium-length finish with a super-citrusy tang. **84** —*D.T. (9/1/2001)*

FATTORIA DEL CERRO

Fattoria del Cerro 1999 Prugnolo Gentile (Rosso di Montepulciano) $14. Wonderful smelling, with leather, clove, and powerful black fruit. How nice to see a '99 rosso doing so well now. The flavors on this wine are dynamite, a rustic and ready combo of cherry, cassis, and blackberry. Finishes tight and firm, meaning it still has some time to go. **90 Best Buy** —*M.S. (11/15/2003)*

Fattoria del Cerro 2002 Sangiovese (Vino Nobile di Montepulciano) $28. Colorful and jammy, with a sweet nose of red licorice, cherry cough drop, and violets. Quite a simple wine, with a soft, plump body and medium tannins. Seems a touch overweight and a bit short on balance. **85** —*M.S. (7/1/2005)*

Fattoria del Cerro 1999 Sangiovese (Vino Nobile di Montepulciano) $30. Full and round, with plum, berry, and herbal aromas. The racy, mouth-filling palate features raspberry, cherry, and oak, while the finish delivers coffee and vanilla. A well-made Tuscan red. **87** —*M.S. (10/1/2004)*

Fattoria del Cerro 1996 Sangiovese (Vino Nobile di Montepulciano) $17. **82** —*J.C. (9/1/2000)*

Fattoria del Cerro 1995 Antica Chiusina Sangiovese (Vino Nobile di Montepulciano) $35. **86** —*J.C. (7/1/2000)*

Fattoria del Cerro 2001 Riserva Sangiovese (Vino Nobile di Montepulciano) $NA. The polar opposite of austere, this chunky Sangiovese yields bold aromas of berry syrup, cherry cough drop, and cola. The palate is rich, with modest tannic firmness. Not overly concentrated or tight; it's actually rather chewy and candied. Finishes meaty and easy. **87** —*M.S. (7/1/2005)*

FATTORIA DI BASCIANO

Fattoria di Basciano 2001 Riserva Sangiovese (Chianti Rufina) $22. Deceptively soft and easy, this creamy-textured wine also boasts a sense of wiry power underneath briary, blackberry-scented fruit. It's soft

enough to drink on its own, yet the inner strength will allow it to pair with assertive flavors as well. **89** *(4/1/2005)*

FATTORIA DI CINCIANO

Fattoria di Cinciano 1999 Sangiovese (Chianti Classico) $12. A youthful wine with fat, berry-packed aromas. Unremarkable but forceful berry fruit along with apple skins appear on the palate. It starts better than it finishes, and the lasting impression is drying and a touch bitter. (The tannins are fairly severe. **85** —*M.S. (12/31/2002)*

FATTORIA DI FELSINA

Fattoria di Felsina 1995 Fontalloro Sangiovese (Tuscany) $60. **93** *(11/15/1999)*

FATTORIA DI GRACCIANO SVETONI

Fattoria di Gracciano Svetoni 1999 Calvano Sangiovese (Vino Nobile di Montepulciano) $20. Aromas of red berries, licorice, and tobacco create a sweet sensation, which is followed by more common berry and cherry flavors. Finishes with tons of fruit and weight. What it lacks in polish and complexity is made up for in density and depth of flavor. **88** —*M.S. (10/1/2004)*

FATTORIA DI LUCIGNANO

Fattoria di Lucignano 2002 Sangiovese (Chianti Colli Fiorentini) $12. Questionable cleanliness, with aromas of compost and peanuts. Tangy and thin, with notes of pickle. Does not offer much. **80** *(4/1/2005)*

FATTORIA IL COLLE

Fattoria il Colle 2001 Leone Rosso Sangiovese (Toscana) $17. This red from Brunello specialist Donatella Cinelli Colombini is firm and woody, with aromas of horse stable, sawdust, rubber, and ultimately black cherry. The palate melds oak, almond, and red fruit, while the finish is spicy and plump. A wine with a casual presence; good for simple drinking. **87** —*M.S. (10/1/2004)*

FATTORIA IL PALAGIO

Fattoria il Palagio 2002 Chardonnay (Toscana) $15. This Tuscan wine has some cheesy aromas and loose fruit. It's zesty on the palate, with apple and white pepper. Finishes zingy, with overt acids. **83** —*M.S. (6/1/2005)*

Fattoria il Palagio 2003 Sangiovese (Chianti) $12. Greetings come in the way of fresh cherry, plum, and raspberry aromas topped off with some vanilla and leather. Good and round, and solid all the way home. Flavors of cherry and apple skins are supported by modest tannins along with slight herb and tobacco notes. **87 Best Buy** *(4/1/2005)*

Fattoria il Palagio 2001 Sauvignon Blanc (Toscana) $12. There is a surprising amount of fruit in this Italian Sauvignon, which more often than not tend to be overly herbal. Pungent grapefruit and jalapeño aromas are reminiscent of a New Zealand Sauvignon Blanc. Spicy orange and grapefruit flavors are vivid and have a refreshing finish. **88 Best Buy** *(12/31/2002)*

FATTORIA LA LECCIAIA

Fattoria la Lecciaia 2001 Brunello (Brunello di Montalcino) $38. Intriguing floral notes like rose tea and pressed violet blend with briar patch, anise, leather, cigar box, cherry wood, and earth. Not a modern blockbuster but delicious and refined with menthol-like freshness on the finish. **89** *(4/1/2006)*

Fattoria la Lecciaia 2001 Manapetra Brunello (Brunello di Montalcino) $45. One of the top wines of the tasting thanks to intriguing complexity and depth of character. Cassis, herbal, smoked notes, and snappy acidity are woven tight to establish texture and balance. It's hard to separate the well-amalgamated flavors. **93 Editors' Choice** *(4/1/2006)*

FATTORIA LA LECCIAIA DI PACINI MAURO

Fattoria la Lecciaia di Pacini Mauro 1999 Brunello (Brunello di Montalcino) $43. Aromas of tree bark, damp earth, and leather are not what you'd call pure and polished. The flavor profile has its issues, particularly a vegetal streak. However, there's also good berry notes and a solid feel. Not bad overall, but playing in a tough league. **85** —*M.S. (10/1/2004)*

ITALY

FATTORIA LE SORGENTI

Fattoria le Sorgenti 1998 Sangiovese (Chianti Colli Fiorentini) $12. Much more than one would expect at this price, with an inviting dark plum, menthol-toast bouquet. The positive fruit-to-acid balance, solid plum, and chocolate flavors, and fairly big tannic finish are a find at any price. Will be even better in a year. **91 Best Buy** *(4/1/2001)*

FATTORIA LICIA

Fattoria Licia 2000 Il Colle Ruzzo Red Blend (Montepulciano d'Abruzzo) $10. Violet in color, with heavy aromas of black fruit, ink, rubber, and mint. Sweet and round, with a rich, borderline unctuous mouthfeel. Toward the back end you get nuances of black licorice, spice, and grape skins. Tasty and fat, yet completely basic. **86 Best Buy** *—M.S. (1/1/2004)*

FATTORIA NITTARDI

Fattoria Nittardi 2003 Nectar Dei Sangiovese (Maremma) $90. Incredibly ripe and ready, with aromas of rubber, bacon, and deep, luscious plum. Good fruit carries the palate, and along the way you'll get cherry, strawberry, and distant coconut flavors. With vanilla and cream on the finish, all is complete. **90** *—M.S. (9/1/2006)*

FATTORIA POGGIOPIANO

Fattoria Poggiopiano 1998 Sangiovese (Chianti Classico) $21. Aromas of cherry and leather mingle with an oaky perfume. On the smooth palate, the cherry fruit wears vanilla accents, but the wine turns drier and woodier on the back end. **86** *(4/1/2001)*

FATTORIA RODANO

Fattoria Rodano 2001 Sangiovese (Chianti Classico) $18. Light and rusty at the edges, with aromas of smoke, leather, and tobacco. More savory than sweet, with mature dried fruit flavors, i.e. raspberry and cherry. Finishes dry, with serious tannins. Seems thin to the eye but has some muscle. **86** *(4/1/2005)*

Fattoria Rodano 1999 Riserva Viacoste Sangiovese (Chianti Classico) $28. Talk about the perfect mouthfeel; this baby has it. But first you get a bouquet of fine herbs, molasses, forest floor, and meaty black fruit. Back to the mouth, there's pure, developed fruit, tobacco and earth notes; overall it's exactly what you want from a middle-age wine: minerality, smoothness, and deep flavors. **92 Editors' Choice** *(4/1/2005)*

FATTORIA SAN FRANCESCO

Fattoria San Francesco 1998 Ronco Dei QuatroVenti Red Blend (Cirò Classico) $28. If you like your wine clean and fruity, steer clear of this individualistic effort, which leads off with barnyard and dirty Band-Aid aromas and folds in tar and hummus notes. There are drying tannins and crisp acids, plus solid black cherry and plum flavors to hold everything together, so the overall result is a complex, interesting wine that would pair well with full-flavored meat dishes. **85** *—C.S. (5/1/2002)*

FATTORIA SAN LORENZO

Fattoria San Lorenzo 2002 di Gino Verdicchio (Verdicchio dei Castelli di Jesi Classico) $10. Talk about a nose that reflects the ocean: Initial aromas of clam shells and sea foam are almost offputting, but once you taste the wine there's a good mix of papaya, green banana, and dried stone fruits. On the finish, cinnamon-spiced applesauce flavors mingle with hints of white pepper. Not bad, but a little shaky on the nose. **85** *—M.S. (8/1/2004)*

Fattoria San Lorenzo 2001 Vigna delle Oche Verdicchio (Verdicchio dei Castelli di Jesi Classico Superiore) $15. Lovely on the nose, with a round bouquet featuring honey and almond in addition to fresh sea air. Impeccably smooth and whole across the palate, with pure stone-fruit flavors and a subdued nuttiness. Polished, full, and complex, with subtlety. **89** *—M.S. (8/1/2004)*

FATTORIA SCOPONE

Fattoria Scopone 2001 Brunello (Brunello di Montalcino) $39. Clean, well-made, and inviting with toasted notes, vanilla, anise seed, milk chocolate, and coffee bean. A wine with bold personality, finesse, a velvety mouthfeel, and great potential at the dinner table. **91 Editors' Choice** *(4/1/2006)*

FATTORIA SONNINO

Fattoria Sonnino 2001 Chianti Montespertoli Sangiovese (Chianti Montespertoli) $12. Rich and modern, with a dark, saturated color and aromas of graham cracker and lemon rind. A juicy palate packed with plum and raspberry is carried by a creamy texture that's rather toasty in terms of flavor. The finish is round, full, and chocolaty. **87** *—M.S. (11/15/2003)*

FATTORIA SOVESTRO

Fattoria Sovestro 1998 San Domenico Vineyard Sangiovese (Chianti Colli Senesi) $13. Cherry, leather, and stewed fruits mark this medium-weight Chianti. Tangy, with nice fruit-to-acid balance, it shows sweet cherry fruit and a slightly raisiny note with earthy accents. Soft leather and slight old wood notes on the finish. Drink now. **85** *(4/1/2001)*

FATTORIE AZZOLINO

Fattorie Azzolino 2002 Chardonnay (Sicilia) $27. Gold in color, with a ton of oak. But you know what? It works. The resin and vanilla aromas over time become attractive, while the rich palate deals coconut, toffee, and baked white fruits. Yes, it's a barrique bomber from a hot climate, but it's interesting and should go well with roast fowl or foie gras. **87** *—M.S. (2/1/2005)*

Fattorie Azzolino 2002 Nero d'Avola (Sicilia) $15. Fruity and tight, with a reduced nose of raspberry and red plum. The palate is fresh, fruity, and tasty, with healthy acidity and grabby tannins. Fairly tart and red-fruit dominated, but ultra-crisp and clean. A sure thing with pizza. **87** *—M.S. (2/1/2005)*

Fattorie Azzolino 2001 Di'More Red Blend (Sicilia) $27. A touch scattered on the nose, with leather, oak, and bright berry fruit. Surprisingly tart on the palate, with plum, cherry, and berry flavors. A snappy wine with a good core of cherry, but ultimately more racy than classy. **86** *—M.S. (2/1/2005)*

Fattorie Azzolino 2003 Tranùi White Blend (Sicilia) $15. Nice and natural, with moderate spice and stone fruit aromas. A bit zippy and sharp courtesy of full-form acidity, but that just makes it all the more forward and food-friendly. Pineapple and green apple flavors are what to expect. More zesty than charming. **87** *—M.S. (2/1/2005)*

FAUNUS

Faunus 1998 Riserva Red Blend (Salice Salentino) $11. Very dark, with damp earth, cola, and meaty fruit aromas. A bit pruny, with a fudge-like flavor. But for all its darkness and rich suggestions, it's surprisingly hard and tannic, with a mouthfeel that is tight and tough. **84** *—M.S. (1/1/2004)*

FAUSTO GEMME

Fausto Gemme 1998 La Merlina Cortese (Gavi di Gavi) $16. 83 *(4/1/2000)*

FAZI BATTAGLIA

Fazi Battaglia 1998 Passo Del Lupo Riserva Red Blend (Rosso Conero) $34. Saucy and spicy on the nose, and from that point on it never really gets better. The palate is jacked up with acidic plum and cherry fruit, and the finish is overt, apparently stuck in overdrive. **82** *—M.S. (10/1/2004)*

Fazi Battaglia 2004 Verdicchio (Verdicchio dei Castelli di Jesi Classico) $10. Those nostalgic for Italy's most famous amphora-shaped bottle that was ubiquitous during the roaring Dolce Vita will be happy to know that Marche producer Fazi Battaglia continues to supply great value for your dollar. The 2004 vintage is especially delicious with crisp green apple, pear, and sharp and delineated minerality. The slight sourness in the mouth is countered by generous exotic fruit and roundness making it perfect for most fish dishes. **87 Best Buy** *—M.L. (11/15/2005)*

Fazi Battaglia 2002 Verdicchio (Verdicchio dei Castelli di Jesi Classico) $10. Light and clean, with a proper level of nuttiness, peach, and flowers to the nose. Simple on the palate, with lime, pear, and peach flavors. With its clean finish, this wine is a good example of a functional, medium-weight Verdicchio. Likely good with seafood-based appetizers. **86 Best Buy** *—M.S. (8/1/2004)*

Fazi Battaglia 2001 Arkezia Muffa di San Sisto Verdicchio (Marche) $65.
Verdicchio grapes from the San Sisto vineyard are left on the vine until they have shriveled up and show signs of botrytis, or noble rot, and are harvested in late December to produce an impressive dessert wine with thick layers of aromas and flavor. The almond paste and honey backed by herbal notes and crisp acidity are simply irresistible. **92 Editors' Choice** —*M.L. (7/1/2006)*

FAZIO

Fazio 2005 Insolia (Sicilia) $16. A sweet, floral wine with acacia, honeysuckle, peach, and loads of yellow fruit. Clean and polished with a lean mouthfeel. An informal, easy to drink white. **86** —*M.L. (7/1/2006)*

Fazio 2004 Insolia (Sicilia) $17. Clean and sharp, with citrus rind, stone fruit and almond paste flavors. Correct albeit uneventful in the mouth, with medium intensity and depth. **85** —*M.L. (7/1/2006)*

Fazio 2004 Torre dei Venti Nero d'Avola (Sicilia) $19. Vinous, fresh, and young in the mouth with nutty notes, almond skin, some chocolate fudge, and lavender soap. With young tannins and a spicy finish, it's not clear where the wine will go from here. **87** —*M.L. (7/1/2006)*

Fazio 2002 Torre dei Venti Nero d'Avola (Sicilia) $21. Simple but pleasing, with a ruby-red color and matching ruby-red fruit on the nose. There's also some forest floor, white mushroom, and dried grass flavors. Has firm tannins; a general crowd-pleaser at dinner. **86** —*M.L. (7/1/2006)*

Fazio 2004 Capo Soprano White Blend (Sicilia) $11. Here's an innovative Old World take on the Australian model. Sicily's Fazio Wines—run by brothers Girolamo and Vincenzo—has cooked up snazzy packaging for a Catarratto (an indigenous grape) and Chardonnay blend that definitely delivers the goods. Fresh-cut grass, honey, citrus, and exotic fruit with moderate acidity and good structure are perfect for everyday drinking. Thanks to its affordable price, buy this wine by the case. **86 Best Buy** —*M.L. (11/15/2005)*

FELLINE

Felline 2000 Alberello Negroamaro (Salento) $15. Earthy and slightly rustic, but still possessing plenty of tart red fruit, this 50-50 blend of Primitivo and Negroamaro is a touch too tannic for its own good; try taming the tannins with a slab of rare beef. **84** *(5/1/2002)*

Felline 2000 Primitivo (Primitivo Di Manduria) $19. You can taste the Primitivo grape's relationship to Zinfandel in wines like this one, which bursts with mixed berries and black pepper. It's a soft, easy quaff, with juicy acidity and just enough ripe tannin to give it shape in the mouth. A sure hit with pizza or pasta. **87** — *(1/1/2004)*

Felline 2000 Vigna Del Feudo Red Blend (Puglia) $28. A single-vineyard wine that's mostly Primitivo—blended with small amounts of Montepulciano, Cabernet Sauvignon, and Merlot—this is the big brother to Felline's Primitivo di Manduria. The red berry flavors are ratcheted up a notch and pick up some peach and apricot notes of sur-maturité. Some time in barrique has imparted creamy milk chocolate, vanilla flavors, and fine tannins to the finish. Try in 2–3 years. **88** —*C.S. (5/1/2002)*

FELSINA

Felsina 2002 Berardenga Sangiovese (Chianti Classico) $23. One of Chianti's stalwarts lacks depth and intensity in this troubled vintage, yet what's here satisfies. The nose offers fresh cherry and wintergreen, while the racy palate flows with red plum, raspberry, and chocolate. High-toned and linear; not rich and deep as is customary. **87** *(4/1/2005)*

Felsina 1996 Berardenga Sangiovese (Chianti Classico) $18. **90** —*M.M. (5/1/1999)*

Felsina 2000 Berardenga Rancia Reserva Sangiovese (Chianti Classico) $46. Pretty intense on first take, but a little lean and light upon further evaluation. Rancia is one of those classic Chiantis that connoisseurs are usually willing to pay for, but in '00 it seems short on substance. Yes, there's ample cherry, but the acidity is pronounced, thus creating an overriding citrusy personality. **87** *(4/1/2005)*

Felsina 2000 Berardenga Riserva Sangiovese (Chianti Classico) $32. Plenty of intensity, with a pleasant spice element that runs from the smooth berry nose onto the serious palate. Flavors of cherry and black-berry rise to the top level, while spice, chocolate, and medium tannins ensure easy drinkability. Not overly concentrated; drink now. **89** *(4/1/2005)*

Felsina 1995 Riserva Sangiovese (Chianti Classico) $25. **92** —*M.M. (5/1/1999)*

FENECH

Fenech 2004 Red Blend (Sicilia) $NA. Composed of mostly Nero d'Avola with smaller percentages of Nerello Mascalese and Corinto Nero the wine is redolent of berry fruit, wet earth, almond, exotic spice, and blackberry jam. **87** —*M.L. (7/1/2006)*

Fenech 2004 Passito White Blend (Malvasia delle Lipari) $NA. Here's a luscious, succulent passito with layers of maple syrup, honey, marzipan, toast, and white stone. It's creamy and sweet in the mouth with copperish reflections but ends on a crisp, clean note. **89** —*M.L. (7/1/2006)*

FERDINANDO GUCCIARDINI

Ferdinando Gucciardini 1999 Castello di Poppiano Riserva Sangiovese (Chianti Colli Fiorentini) $18. There's plenty of body and stuffing to this fine Chianti. Also a good deal of cherry and plum fruit, some oak and vanilla, and a touch of earth. A plush, solid wine from a good Chianti vintage. Drinkable now through 2006. **90** —*M.S. (10/1/2004)*

FERESIN DAVIDE

Feresin Davide 2004 Pinot Grigio (Isonzo del Friuli) $NA. This wine has a creamy consistency that coats the mouth with Caribbean fruit, minerals, and almond paste. It's thick, silky, and extremely food friendly. **87** — *M.L. (2/1/2006)*

FERRARI

Ferrari NV Brut Chardonnay (Trento) $25. A delightful sparkling wine that is generous with its aromas of toasted almond, nuts, and freshly-baked sourdough bread. There is the tiniest hint of lavender at the very back. It glides down with buttery charm and a long, frothy finish. **88** —*M.L. (12/15/2004)*

Ferrari NV Brut Chardonnay (Trento) $28. A tightly-packed, mineral-driven sparkler with aromas of crushed vitamins, bread, white stone, almond, pear, banana, and cracked white pepper. The mouth is rendered lively and fresh thanks to fruit and toast accents; a taut, yet expressive whole. **92** —*M.L. (6/1/2006)*

Ferrari 1996 Giulio Ferrari Riserva del Fondatore Chardonnay (Trento) $90. Many Italian wine enthusiasts consider this 100% Chardonnay their country's number one metodo classico sparkler—the wine that sets the bar for all the rest. Yet the 1996 vintage has sparked controversy because of uneven reviews. We, however, loved its complex bouquet of honey, dried lavender, tealeaf, pear, bread crust, and unexpected mint-like notes. The mouthfeel is intense, smooth, and long on the finish. **93** —*M.L. (6/1/2006)*

Ferrari 1997 Giulio Riserva del Fondatore Chardonnay (Trento) $90. One of the best vintages yet from one of Italy's best sparkling wines. The nose is a true knock-out with deep layers of intensity and perfectly seamless aromas: cookie dough, almonds, peppermint ice cream, and campfire ash. The flavors unfold delicately in the mouth and are reinforced by persistent pearls of effervescence. **93** —*M.L. (12/15/2006)*

Ferrari 2001 Perlé Chardonnay (Trento) $30. The theme here is dryness with dried apricot, pressed rose petal, banana, dried herbs, tealeaf, and pungent, toasted, and smoky tones. Together this medley of aromas is delicate and caressing on the nose, and equally tender in the mouth. **92** —*M.L. (6/1/2006)*

Ferrari 1998 Perlé Chardonnay (Trento) $30. The complexity is intriguing and the overall impact on the nose and mouth denotes a wine of defined character. Notes of butterscotch, toast, and fresh croissants create a creamy and rich feeling in the mouth. Put this bubbly aside for a special occasion. **89** —*M.L. (12/15/2004)*

Ferrari NV Rosé Metodo Classico Pinot Noir (Trento) $28. The first metodo classico rosé in Italy, this sparkler has a peachy-pink color and aromas that span from peach to yeast. The wine makes a strong impact on the palate with a velvety fruity texture and a long finish. Definitely up to accompanying an entire meal from antipasto through dessert. **87** —*M.L. (12/15/2004)*

Ferrari NV Maximum Rosé Sparkling Blend (Trento) $34. Baked fruit pie, red apple, cranberry, and raspberry characterize the nose of this pretty, pale pink sparkler. The wine performs nicely in the mouth where it delivers crisp acidity and a long, tasty finish. **89** —*M.L. (12/15/2006)*

Ferrari 1994 Riserva del Fondatore Brut Sparkling Blend (Trento) $75. An excellent sparkler by any measure, with deep, rich aromas of toast, sautéed mushrooms, and hint of citrus. Creamy and full-bodied, the flavors expand to include apple and spice notes, finishing elegantly and long. **92** *(12/15/2004)*

Ferrari NV Rosé Sparkling Blend (Trento) $30. This is a unique sparkler that probably won't appeal to everyone. Delicate notes of pink grapefruit, rose petal, honey, and cranberry greet the nose. Yet these fragrances are underscored by a yeasty tone that is almost exaggerated. **88** —*M.L. (6/1/2006)*

FERRERO

Ferrero 2001 Brunello (Brunello di Montalcino) $45. Smoke, raspberry, tart cherry, vanilla, dried basil leaf, plum, caramel, and smoked ham work well together as a whole. Juicy acidity and firm but ripe tannins are drawn over a good mouthfeel that could be more compact and complex.es. **89** *(4/1/2006)*

FEUDI DI SAN GIULIANO

Feudi di San Giuliano 2004 Cjatomé Chardonnay (Sicilia) $NA. Peach, citrus, banana nut, some mineral notes, and lemon grass sum up a clean but not terribly intense nose. The wine is refined in tonneaux and offers a spicy, bright note on the close. **87** —*M.L. (7/1/2006)*

Feudi di San Giuliano 2004 Nicasio Nero d'Avola (Sicilia) $NA. This wine is harder to read due to a metallic smell that rides parallel to pistachio nut and cherry fruit aromas. It's lean and clean in the mouth with a short, spicy finish. **85** —*M.L. (7/1/2006)*

Feudi di San Giuliano 2003 Kundisa Red Blend (Sicilia) $NA. This is a fresh and uncomplicated Nero d'Avola and Cabernet Sauvignon blend that steps forward with aromas of strawberry, blackberry, tar, resin, and some dried herbs. Fundamentally it's a very fruit-forward red that is well-constructed and tight. **87** —*M.L. (7/1/2006)*

Feudi di San Giuliano 2005 Vento di Majo White Blend (Sicilia) $NA. This is an interesting blend of Catarratto, Bianco Lucido, and Grillo that appears very floral and perfumed on the nose: like a bouquet of white flowers. The wine is moderately crisp in the mouth and satisfied the palate. **86** —*M.L. (7/1/2006)*

FEUDI DI SAN GREGORIO

Feudi di San Gregorio 1994 Aglianico (Taurasi) $25. 92 —*M.S. (11/15/1999)*

Feudi di San Gregorio 2000 Patrimo Aglianico (Irpinia) $115. Although officially classified as Aglianico, it now appears that the vines may be Merlot. It certainly tastes more like Merlot, with creamy mocha, black cherry, and tobacco-leaf aromas and flavors. The mouthfeel is impressively smooth and rich, blending in supple tannins that pick up hints of black tea on the finish. **91** *(12/1/2002)*

Feudi di San Gregorio 2000 Rabrato Aglianico (Irpinia) $17. Feudi's basic red is a supple, modern-style Aglianico that displays smoky, lactic notes layered over a core of berry and plum fruit. The creamy, richly textured mouthfeel is a treat, but a slight herbal tang that enlivens the finish may prove too green for some tasters. **87** *(12/1/2002)*

Feudi di San Gregorio 1998 Selve di Luoti Aglianico (Taurasi) $36. Close to 18 months in barriques has given this rugged Aglianico polished wisps of cedar, wood smoke, and vanilla. A massive dose of tannin follows the chocolate, coffee, and black cherry flavors, but the tannins are ripe and soft. Hold for 5–10 years. **88 Cellar Selection** *(12/1/2002)*

Feudi di San Gregorio 1997 Selve di Lvoti Aglianico (Taurasi) $38. Dusty tar, with a light floral bridge, is realized on the nose and palate along with vivid, underlying black fruits and vanilla. Chewy tannins and black pepper finish it off. **88** —*C.S. (5/1/2002)*

Feudi di San Gregorio 2000 Serpico Aglianico (Irpinia) $62. Smells enticing, with gorgeous aromas of dried spices and Mexican chocolate, plum, and black cherry fruit. But despite a rich, velvety texture, this Aglianico-based wine seems to be in a bit of a closed phase, showing little fruit on the palate and drying tannins on the finish. Give it some time. **89** *(12/1/2002)*

Feudi di San Gregorio 1999 Serpico Aglianico (Irpinia) $57. Complexity is the key in this Aglianico-Merlot blend. A hefty richness from the Aglianico combines with a velvety softness from the Merlot, which also supports the midpalate. Flavors of fresh blackberries executed in a modern style couple with dried spices and smoke. **94 Editors' Choice** —*C.S. (5/1/2002)*

Feudi di San Gregorio 1997 Serpico Aglianico (Campania) $60. The flagship of the Feudi fleet, this powerful wine is 70% Aglianico and 30% Merlot, Shiraz, and Piedirosso. The wine is complex from the start with cherry, plum, chocolate, black pepper, and toasted oak. With standing, even more nuances appear. On the palate, it is rich and robust—the tannins just need a little softening. The persistent finish replicates the initial aromatics. A true tour de force. **92 Cellar Selection** —*M.N. (9/1/2001)*

Feudi di San Gregorio 2004 Falanghina (Campania) $18. A beautiful, straw-colored wine with a little more brawn to its body reveals itself elegantly in the form of honeydew melon, pineapple, and exotic fruit. Falanghina's busy repertoire of sweet fruit smells are cleverly balanced by long-lasting crispness. **87** —*M.L. (9/1/2005)*

Feudi di San Gregorio 2001 Falanghina (Falanghina) $16. Falanghina is both the grape variety and the Italian DOC. It's another of southern Italy's indigenous varieties that is experiencing a comeback. Pear and stone fruit aromas and flavors lead the way, but there's also a strong sense of minerality and spice that's not obscured by any oak treatment and a fresh, citrusy finish. **87** *(12/1/2002)*

Feudi di San Gregorio 2004 Fiano (Fiano di Avellino) $23. A handful of producers have worked hard to turn the image of Campanian wines around, and this wine is a fine example of the extraordinary potential of the region's indigenous grapes. Ripe peach, pineapple, and pine resin blend with sea breeze-like notes that come from the volcanic soils. **89** —*M.L. (9/1/2005)*

Feudi di San Gregorio 2004 Fiano (Fiano di Avellino) $18. A strange perfume comes off this wine; it's almost like soap dish meets daisies, and while that's not bad it's not that wine-like, either. Flavors of apple cider and chunky melon are standard and soft. Not a ton of finish or flair. **84** —*M.S. (10/1/2006)*

Feudi di San Gregorio 2001 Fiano (Fiano di Avellino) $21. Explodes with orange-blossom and peach scents that evolve on the palate into rich, full flavors of peach and pineapple. Seems almost sweet because of the richness and ripeness of the fruit (the wine is dry), but it's balanced by a tart, hard-edged finish that's long and oily. **89** *(12/1/2002)*

Feudi di San Gregorio 2000 Fiano (Fiano di Avellino) $20. Pineapple, citrus, and wet stones greet you on the nose and continue into the long finish, where pineapple takes the lead. All of this is admirably supported by a medium-bodied structure, lively acids, and a round texture. Not as forthcoming as the '99, but no slouch, either. **86** —*M.N. (9/1/2001)*

Feudi di San Gregorio 1999 Privilegio Fiano (Irpinia) $55. This dessert wine, made from Fiano grapes, is bursting with honeyed apricot and lychee aromas. The flavors turn simpler, leaning toward ripe peaches and corn syrup. It's a soft, luscious wine that fades a bit on the finish but would make a killer pairing with Gorgonzola dolce. **90** *(12/1/2002)*

Feudi di San Gregorio 2004 Greco (Greco di Tufo) $23. Opens with a slight turpentine touch that quickly blows off, leaving space for rose and less pungent fruit, like pear and apple. The tickling acidity and that ever-present Campanian minerality cap the experience. **87** —*M.L. (9/1/2005)*

Feudi di San Gregorio 2001 Greco (Greco di Tufo) $21. Perhaps the least aromatic of the Feudi lineup, this wine shows restrained scents of pear and mint. It's a harder, more minerally wine than the others, with vague flavors of pears, white peaches, and herbs mixing in. The long finish blends gravel and grapefruit in a pleasant finale. **88** *(12/1/2002)*

Feudi di San Gregorio 2000 Greco (Greco di Tufo) $20. As evidenced by its solid structure, this is a good wine. The palate sensation is top-notch

ITALY

with good weight, crisp acidity, and a smooth mouthfeel. However, the fruit is missing in action. **83** —*M.N. (9/1/2001)*

Feudi di San Gregorio 2001 White Blend (Falanghina) $12. 87 Best Buy —*D.T. (11/15/2002)*

Feudi di San Gregorio 1999 White Blend (Fiano di Avellino) $20. 91 —*M.N. (12/31/2000)*

Feudi di San Gregorio 2004 Campanaro White Blend (Fiano di Avellino) $40. A golden, intense wine that offers tiers of citrus from orange blossom to lemon pie. Dig in there with your nose and uncover honey and dried apricot as well. This barrel fermented and aged Fiano and Greco blend sees less oak than it did in past vintages. The mouthfeel is dense and persistent. **90** —*M.L. (9/1/2005)*

Feudi di San Gregorio 2002 Campanaro White Blend (Fiano di Avellino) $40. Starting to show some signs of peaking, but there's still vital dried fruit aromas, particularly mango and apricot, to get jazzed about. Honey, cantaloupe, and orange flavors are ripe, and there's a hint of butterscotch on the finish. Drink real soon. **89** —*M.S. (11/17/2005)*

Feudi di San Gregorio 2001 Campanaro White Blend (Irpinia) $36. This big, rich, barrel-fermented blend of Fiano and Greco comes close to being too much of a good thing. Buttery, nutty aromas accent sweet pears and tropical fruit, while the mouthfeel is oily and dense, leaving a long, toasty finish behind. **87** *(12/1/2002)*

Feudi di San Gregorio 1998 Falanghina White Blend (Campania) $10. 88 —*M.S. (11/15/1999)*

Feudi di San Gregorio 2000 Falanghina Sannio White Blend (Campania) $15. The name of the wine and the grape is Falanghina. It was well-liked by Pliny, Horace, and Virgil—and who could argue with them? Clean and fresh, this rendition opens with pineapple, banana, citrus, and pear scents. The palate displays vibrant acidity, excellent balance, medium body and a velvety mouthfeel. The finish is long and echoes the opening notes. **89 Editors' Choice** —*M.N. (9/1/2001)*

Feudi di San Gregorio 2002 Privilegio White Blend (Campania) $56. Everything about this dessert wine—its color, consistency, and body—is smooth and seductive until your nose encounters a solid wall of wood. A tad too much toast, in my opinion, translates into blackened bread crust and peanut oil warming in an iron skillet and makes it difficult to locate the dried flowers and fruit aromas. Yet the wood does frame the wine's sweetness nicely and some may love it. **87** —*M.L. (10/1/2006)*

FEUDO ARANCIO

Feudo Arancio 2004 Cabernet Sauvignon (Sicilia) $9. Cherry, blackberry, espresso, and vanilla appear on the nose of this powerful and amicable Sicilian red. The mouthfeel is medium to compact and the tannins are soft, inviting you to drink it at dinner without a second thought. **87 Best Buy** —*M.L. (7/1/2006)*

Feudo Arancio 2005 Chardonnay (Sicilia) $8. A genuine and upfront wine with banana, citrus, peach, and attractive notes of crushed stone that are almost brackish. Simple, polished, and a good bet when you want a reliable white. **87 Best Buy** —*M.L. (7/1/2006)*

Feudo Arancio 2004 Chardonnay (Sicilia) $8. Attractive as a whole, and ready to drink at any point in the near future. This is Sicilian Chardonnay in its most mainstream, mass-market form. The nose deals pineapple and a bit of herb or pine, while the palate is pure and full of citrus and apple. No complaints and satisfying. **87 Best Buy** —*M.S. (7/1/2005)*

Feudo Arancio 2003 Chardonnay (Sicilia) $9. A low-oak Chard (15%, the rest sees only stainless), this wine boasts a plump, appealing texture and scents of pear and citrus. Brings in some peachy flavors, then turns tangy and fresh on the finish, folding in hints of orange and lemon. **85 Best Buy** *(2/1/2005)*

Feudo Arancio 2002 Chardonnay (Sicilia) $10. A plump Chardonnay with its aromas and flavors of butter, toast, and peaches. A long, citrusy finish caps it off. **87 Best Buy** —*J.C. (10/1/2003)*

Feudo Arancio 2005 Grillo (Sicilia) $8. Offers measured peach, melon, and grass aromas. In the mouth it is balanced, creamy, and rich, with apple and white stone fruit flavors. **86 Best Buy** —*M.L. (7/1/2006)*

Feudo Arancio 2004 Grillo (Sicilia) $7. Lots of peach and honey aromas create a big, heavy bouquet. Golden Delicious apple and pineapple flavors are prominent, while the finish provides a full mix of apple and citrus notes. A bit sticky on the back palate, but good for the money. **86 Best Buy** —*M.S. (7/1/2005)*

Feudo Arancio 2003 Grillo (Sicilia) $7. Winemaker Statella says that Sicily's native Grillo is easily oxidized, so he he uses "hyper-reductive" techniques. Made entirely in stainless steel, this attractive white features delicate almond and peach aromas, followed by peach and citrus flavors. Finishes with lean, grapefruity flavors. **84 Best Buy** *(2/1/2005)*

Feudo Arancio 2002 Grillo (Sicilia) $10. After a muted nose, this wine perks up on the palate, offering hints of peach and pineapple. Medium-weight, it finishes with traces of almond and pine resin. Grillo is the primary grape of Marsala. **84** —*J.C. (10/1/2003)*

Feudo Arancio 2004 Merlot (Sicilia) $8. Notes of tobacco leaf, cherry preserve, soy sauce, and toasted almond are attractive and polished but less deeply etched making this an easier, more approachable wine without the bruising of other Sicilian reds. **87 Best Buy** —*M.L. (7/1/2006)*

Feudo Arancio 2001 Merlot (Sicilia) $10. Lush and clean in the nose, with black cherry and licorice aromas. In the mouth, cherry and berry flavors pop with pizzazz. A tasty finish bursting with ripe, fresh fruit leaves you happy and wanting more. **88 Best Buy** —*M.S. (10/1/2003)*

Feudo Arancio 2001 Merlot (Sicilia) $9. Soft and easy, with plum and prune flavors that turn a bit dull on the finish. Decent but not up to the level of Arancio's other wines. **83** *(2/1/2005)*

Feudo Arancio 2001 Merlot (Sicilia) $9. 83 *(2/1/2005)*

Feudo Arancio 2004 Nero d'Avola (Sicilia) $8. Bravo to Feudo Arancio for producing a Nero d'Avola of this caliber at such an attractive price point. Its nose is rich with floral and rose-like notes backed by blueberry and vanilla. The structure is firm and the tannins give backbone. It's informal but refined at the same time. **88 Best Buy** —*M.L. (7/1/2006)*

Feudo Arancio 2003 Nero d'Avola (Sicilia) $7. This winery seems to have mastered the formula for making clean, approachable wines that have mass appeal while staying true to their roots. Here you get leather, plum, and pepper on the nose, with ripe black cherry and a touch of candied berry on the palate. Finishes with blueberry sweetness and just enough kick. Bargain hunters should buy this in quantity. **87 Best Buy** —*M.S. (7/1/2005)*

Feudo Arancio 2002 Nero d'Avola (Sicilia) $7. Shows decent varietal character in its crisp chocolate and black cherry aromas and flavors. Also boasts a slight nuttiness that winemaker Calogero Statella calls "hazelnut"—a character he attributes to Nero d'Avola grown in the southwestern portion of Sicily. **84 Best Buy** *(2/1/2005)*

Feudo Arancio 2001 Nero d'Avola (Sicilia) $10. Grapey and sweet, and much like a confection. The color is bold and purple, and the palate is lively and easygoing, with flavors of blackberry and licorice. The finish is lean, light, and clean. **87 Best Buy** —*M.S. (10/1/2003)*

Feudo Arancio 2004 Syrah (Sicilia) $8. A slightly more subdued Sicilian Syrah with notes of toasted espresso bean, berry fruit, and some white peppercorn. Nothing is overwhelming about the wine and that's what makes it nice. **87 Best Buy** —*M.L. (7/1/2006)*

Feudo Arancio 2002 Syrah (Sicilia) $7. The nose is on the herbal-peppery side, with hints of mint and ground spice, while the palate shows off more berry flavors. Medium-weight, picks up leather and spice on the dry, smooth finish. Drink now. **86 Best Buy** *(2/1/2005)*

Feudo Arancio 2001 Syrah (Sicilia) $10. The Syrah is rich, smooth, dark, and sweet; the graham cracker and mineral nose sings a pretty tune, while the palate delivers plenty of blackberry, chocolate, and coffee flavors. This is quite the full, tasty, modern wine. **88 Best Buy** —*M.S. (10/1/2003)*

Feudo Arancio 2004 Hekate Passito White Blend (Sicilia) $29. Made from a blend of air-dried grapes, this amber-colored dessert wine delivers dried apricot, orange peel, honey, and almond skin flavors over a creamy finish. Aromas are intense and rich. **89** —*M.L. (7/1/2006)*

ITALY

ITALY

FEUDO DI SANTA TERESA

Feudo di Santa Teresa 2001 Nìvuro Red Blend (Sicilia) $15. A blend of 70% Nero d'Avola and 30% Cabernet Sauvignon from the Casa Girelli estate in southeast Sicily. The fruit is hugely ripe, soft, with deceptively easy tannins which underlie good concentration and some elegance. **88** —R.V. (10/1/2003)

FEUDO MACCARI

Feudo Maccari 2003 Saia Nero d'Avola (Sicilia) $33. Here's a relatively new name in Sicilian viticulture to watch out for. Entrepreneur Antonio Moretti (owner of Tuscany's Sette Ponti) and consulting enologist Carlo Ferrini have created a blockbuster Nero d'Avola with big, round ripe cherry, smoked wood, firm tannins, and a velvety smooth finish. **91** —M.L. (9/1/2005)

Feudo Maccari 2002 Saia Nero d'Avola (Sicilia) $35. This Nero d'Avola is the inaugural Sicilian wine from Antonio Moretti, proprietor of Sette Ponti in Tuscany. It's big and stylish, with baked, spicy black fruit and a good deal of French oak. Expressive on the palate, with plum, boysenberry, and chocolate. Finishes with some typical raisin and earth. More polished and woody than your standard Southern Italian wine. **90** —M.S. (2/1/2005)

Feudo Maccari 2004 Re Noto Red Blend (Sicilia) $13. From one of Sicily's most quality-minded producers, Re Noto (85-15% Nero d'Avola and Syrah) has both a fruity component in the form of blackberry and blueberry and a toasted, nutty one. The wine is equally balanced in terms of flavors and boasts an appealing dusty or spicy quality in the mouth. **88 Best Buy** —M.L. (7/1/2006)

FEUDO MONACI

Feudo Monaci 2000 Negroamaro (Salice Salentino) $9. Burnt cedar and slightly dusty raspberries on the nose introduce the dominant, raspberry note on the palate. The finish is clean, short, and very berry. An easy-drinking beverage. **83** —C.S. (5/1/2002)

Feudo Monaci 2003 Primitivo (Puglia) $9. Fruity, plump, and inexpensive, perfect as a burger or pizza wine. Raspberry-cherry fruit features a hay-like or briary note that keeps it from being overly simple. **85 Best Buy** (8/1/2005)

Feudo Monaci 2002 Primitivo (Puglia) $9. Pretty and light, with dried fruit, herbs, belt leather, and a distant woodsy scent. An example of a lighter-bodied wine made well; it's got life, structure, and acidity, but nothing too demanding. A real pop and drop type of wine. Best Buy. **89 Best Buy** —M.S. (2/1/2005)

Feudo Monaci 2000 Primitivo (Puglia) $9. This "exceptionally bright" purple-colored Primitivo's nose offers understated cola and black pepper aromas and super-ripe blackberry flavors, dusted with a little dirt, on the palate. More of the same brightness shows through on the finish, couched in some chocolate and cocoa flavors. **87 Best Buy** —C.S. (5/1/2002)

Feudo Monaci 2003 Red Blend (Salice Salentino) $9. Complex and inviting on the nose, which features hints of clove, leather, chocolate, and dried cherries. It's medium in body and fully dry, an authentic-tasting wine at a reasonable price. **87 Best Buy** (8/1/2005)

FEUDO MONTONI

Feudo Montoni 2003 Classico Nero d'Avola (Sicilia) $16. An excellent introduction to Nero d'Avola with rich layers of dried currant, tobacco, white mushroom, clove, and toasted almond backed by delicate forest floor notes. Sweet, chewy tannins appear over a smoky finish. **90 Editors' Choice** —M.L. (7/1/2006)

Feudo Montoni 2003 Vrucara Nero d'Avola (Sicilia) $32. A wonderfully rich and concentrated Sicilian red that reflects the hard work of Fabio Sireci, who oversees 73 acres and is carefully dedicated to understanding the potential of each one. Shows intense red fruit with tobacco leaf, porcini, and soft, chewy tannins. **92 Editors' Choice** —M.L. (7/1/2006)

FEUDO PRINCIPI DI BUTERA

Feudo Principi di Butera 2004 Cabernet Sauvignon (Sicilia) $13. This Cabernet Sauvignon is redolent of blackberry, dark fruit, wet earth,

cedar, toast, and vanilla with graceful notes of dried herb or wild sage. The tannins are soft, inviting you to drink it now. **87** —M.L. (7/1/2006)

Feudo Principi di Butera 2001 Cabernet Sauvignon (Sicilia) $20. Spicy, herbal aromas with hints of pickle, leather, and coffee. The flavor profile runs sweet and plummy, with a note of pepper. The finish is a bit lean. **85** —M.S. (10/1/2003)

Feudo Principi di Butera 2001 San Rocco Cabernet Sauvignon (Sicilia) $50. Sicily has proved itself a worthy territory for Cabernet Sauvignon and this wine from the island's southeast corner is tightly packed with aromas of spice, licorice, vanilla, earth, iron, bay leaf, dried herbs, and a playful touch of crushed raspberry. It does not boast the same density as other over-extracted Cabernets because it counts on elegance, not muscle. **90** —M.L. (9/1/2006)

Feudo Principi di Butera 2000 San Rocco Cabernet Sauvignon (Sicilia) $60. Cabernet can be hit-or-miss in Sicily, but this one's a hit. The dusty cassis and field-green aromas lead to rich dark fruit flavors with plenty of tobacco, bitter chocolate, and coffee grinds. A full, plush mouthfeel with lots of oak balances the other components. This wine is approachable now but will hold well through 2010. **90** (12/31/2002)

Feudo Principi di Butera 2005 Chardonnay (Sicilia) $13. Very floral, very crisp, and very fresh, linear and simple with peach and citrus flavors; but there's also a slightly rubbery note that you may or may not pick up. Almost lean in the mouth, with spice on the finish. **86** —M.L. (7/1/2006)

Feudo Principi di Butera 2001 Chardonnay (Sicilia) $26. Lemon flavors vie with toasty, smoky wood in this wine, which has a rich, ripe California feel to it. Vanilla and honey flavors on the finish. **85** —R.V. (10/1/2003)

Feudo Principi di Butera 2005 Insolia (Sicilia) $13. Light and straw-colored, boasting exotic fruit, citrus, crushed stone, and almond paste. Fruit flavors seem more apparent in the mouth, where the wine has a plush, creamy feel. **87** —M.L. (7/1/2006)

Feudo Principi di Butera 2004 Insolia (Sicilia) $13. A crisp and luminous white of medium intensity with a pretty ensemble of stone fruit, pineapple, cut greens, and white stone. Coats the mouth, yet has enough acidity to keep it clean. **86** —M.L. (7/1/2006)

Feudo Principi di Butera 2002 Inzolia (Sicilia) $20. Nutty and round, with plump tropical fruit on the nose and palate. Apple, melon, and spice flavors work well together, while the almond-packed finish is on the mark. Drink soon to enjoy the wine's balance. It won't wait around forever. **88** —M.S. (2/1/2005)

Feudo Principi di Butera 2001 Inzolia (Sicilia) $20. Lees contact gives this wine great creamy fruit, along with a mineral character and some fresh, tropical fruit flavors. **84** —R.V. (10/1/2003)

Feudo Principi di Butera 2004 Merlot (Sicilia) $13. Definitely a hot climate Merlot with toasted almond, raspberry, and a spicy, cooked quality that rides over a sweet, soft finish. That sweet, soft nature of Merlot is magnified under the Sicilian sun. **87** —M.L. (7/1/2006)

Feudo Principi di Butera 2001 Merlot (Sicilia) $26. Ripe, jelly flavors sit alongside a touch of barnyard aromas and tannins. The wine still needs to fully blend together, but it has great tannins and fruit, and should develop well. **84** —R.V. (1/1/2004)

Feudo Principi di Butera 2000 Merlot (Sicilia) $20. Starts with fragrant cola and leather aromas before opening to reveal the scent of violets and other dark flowers. Pure plum and berry fruit makes for a harmonious whole, while the finish is pleasant, toasty, round, and full. **90** —M.S. (10/1/2003)

Feudo Principi di Butera 2000 Calat Merlot (Sicilia) $60. The bouquet offers cola, red licorice, and some mushroom before giving way to sweet, rich fruit that carries woody notes and a buttery texture. Medium-full in body, with some smoky, burnt flavors and peppery black fruit. **89** —M.S. (10/1/2003)

Feudo Principi di Butera 2004 Nero d'Avola (Sicilia) $13. Earthy and spicy, with leather, almond, tobacco, plum, and deep, concentrated flavors. The tannins are there, but are very soft. **87** —M.L. (7/1/2006)

Feudo Principi di Butera 2003 Nero d'Avola (Sicilia) $NA. Here's a Nero d'Avola with velvety roundness and a smooth mouthfeel. The nose is not very intense, offering just cherry preserves lavished over more delicate almond nut tones. An approachable, likeable red wine that calls out for pasta dishes. **86**—*M.L. (7/1/2006)*

Feudo Principi di Butera 2000 Nero d'Avola (Sicilia) $20. Sweet and spicy, with overt wood notes doctoring the aromas of currants and raspberries. That red fruit character continues onto the palate, preceding a finish of dry tannins and oaky spice. **86**—*M.S. (10/1/2003)*

Feudo Principi di Butera 2002 Deliella Nero d'Avola (Sicilia) $NA. One of the estate's top wines, this attractive Nero d'Avola delivers precise, but not overly intense, notes of cherry wood, sandalwood, forest berry, and vanilla bean. It appears more flavorful in the mouth with a firm, tannic bite that calls for succulent foods. **87**—*M.L. (7/1/2006)*

Feudo Principi di Butera 2001 Deliella Nero d'Avola (Sicilia) $30. This wine boasts a mature, dark edge with resin, cigar box, and smoked tones over ripe blackberry and cherry. But in the mouth there is a refreshing blast of menthol and almond paste backed by well-integrated acidity that leaves the palate crystal clean. **88**—*M.L. (7/1/2006)*

Feudo Principi di Butera 2000 Deliella Nero d'Avola (Sicilia) $60. **85**—*M.S. (10/1/2003)*

Feudo Principi di Butera 2004 Iperion Red Blend (Sicilia) $18. The newest addition to this estate's portfolio of wines made from international and indigenous varieties, Iperion (made from 70-20-10% Nero d'Avola, Merlot, and Cabernet Sauvignon) is a nutty and harmonious wine with blackberry, blueberry, pistachio, bread crust, and a spicy, cinnamon-like note on the close. **88**—*M.L. (7/1/2006)*

Feudo Principi di Butera 2004 Syrah (Sicilia) $13. This estate has just recently started making a 100% Syrah and their efforts bring us a cedar- and cherry-rich red that is both low key and compact. This is a steady and approachable wine with a delicate touch. **87**—*M.L. (7/1/2006)*

FIBBIANO

Fibbiano 2003 Sangiovese (Chianti) $13. Well-toasted, with blackberry and raspberry backing up the oak on the nose. Tastes ripe and full, with plum and berry supported by big, almost thunderous tannins. Not a shy wine; offers a ton of grip and feel. **85**—*M.S. (10/1/2006)*

Fibbiano 2000 Ceppatella Sangiovese (Tuscany) $18. None of the Fibbiano wines scored big, and this was the best of the lot. It's toasty and woody, bordering on burnt. That heavy wood masks the cherry fruit that battles unsuccessfully to show itself on the palate. When someone talks about an over-wooded red wine, they mean something like this. It has fruit, but also too much oak for its own good. **83**—*M.S. (12/31/2002)*

Fibbiano 2002 L'Aspetto Sangiovese (Toscana) $18. Ripe, slightly char-broiled, and pure, with compact red fruit aromas. Broader on the tongue, with tasty black cherry and blackberry. Tight and tannic, but with enough girth and glycerol to fatten it up to a balanced level. **87**—*M.S. (9/1/2006)*

Fibbiano 2000 L'Aspetto Sangiovese (Toscana) $14. Citrus peel and chemical aromas? That's not what the average Tuscan red delivers. And the palate is strange, with a seemingly injected wood-spice flavor. Feel and finish are not the big issues: They are o.k. But there's something weird here, something that's hard to put a finger on. Borderline at best. **80**—*M.S. (12/31/2002)*

Fibbiano 2004 Le Pianette Sangiovese (Rosso di Toscana) $10. Initial smoked meat and pickle aromas yield more of a deli sandwich nose than Tuscan wine, but with airing it settles to yield black cherry and plum. Those fruit flavors stay firm on the palate, which has a hard, tannic feel. Not that lush; more of a cheek blaster than anything. **83**—*M.S. (9/1/2006)*

FILIPPO GALLINO

Filippo Gallino 2001 Barbera (Barbera d'Alba) $13. Light and simple, and far from excessive or expressive. Candied red fruit carries the palate into a juicy, rather sharp finish. Meanwhile, pronounced acids exceed the fruit quality, leaving an angular, tangy feel. **83**—*M.S. (12/15/2003)*

Filippo Gallino 1998 Barbera (Barbera d'Alba Superiore) $25. Despite some lacquer-like aromas and a raw, grabby palate-feel, this wine has a few virtues. The fruit is largely ripe and forward, and all in all it isn't

timid. Pie cherry and blackberry flavors come prior to a finish that's firm and weighty. Awkward but decent. **84**—*M.S. (12/15/2003)*

Filippo Gallino 2000 Superiore Nebbiolo (Roero) $27. A bit of sweetness to the bouquet, with an underlay of oak and violets. Apple skin and sour cherry flavors come in front of a short, raw finish. Quite lean and stripped down, with tough tannins. Begs for food to soften it up. **84**—*M.S. (12/15/2003)*

FLOURISH

Flourish 2003 Pinot Grigio (Veneto) $11. Creamy banana and vanilla with distinct sawmill notes make up a simple but correct nose. The grapes afford some honeysuckle and green apple, with a bitter touch and a long crisp finish. **85**—*M.L. (2/1/2006)*

FOFFANI

Foffani 2004 Pinot Grigio (Friuli Aquileia) $14. The flatter Friuli Aquileia area has produced a wine with notes of green grass and some vegetal tones with peach and melon. But the ensemble seems slightly disjointed, and the wine is light and simple in the mouth. **84**—*M.L. (6/1/2006)*

Foffani 2000 Pinot Grigio (Friuli Aquileia) $14. Clean, crisp, and fresh, which is enough to satisfy most Pinot Grigio drinkers. This one blends Asian pear with hints of green herbs and lemon to make a refreshing summertime quaff. **86**—*J.C. (7/1/2003)*

Foffani 2000 Sauvignon Blanc (Friuli Aquileia) $19. Mildly grassy in the nose, with accents of fig, melon, and citrus rind. It's got some hay and funky earthiness to the otherwise tangy, citrus-driven palate. The acidity isn't overpowering, so the mouthfeel is a bit creamy. Overall it's a good mainstream wine unlikely to offend anyone. **88**(8/1/2002)

Foffani 1999 Superiore Sauvignon Blanc (Friuli Aquileia) $13. Pungent aromas of ammonia and cat pee feature hints of gooseberry and grape-fruit. Once past the nose, things settle down, with melon, fig, and grapefruit flavors that finish a bit rough. **83**(9/1/2001)

FOLONARI

Folonari 2003 Garganega (Soave) $8. Modest pear and herb aromas in this lean, focused Soave. It's clean and fresh, a citrusy wine that finishes tart and short. Doesn't have a lot of stuffing to stand up to food, so drink as an apéritif. **84 Best Buy**—*J.C. (12/31/2004)*

Folonari 2004 Pinot Grigio (Delle Venezie) $8. Grapes for this bargain wine are sourced from both Trentino and Veneto and consequently the nose is redolent of green grass, chamomile, melon, and fig. **85 Best Buy**—*M.L. (2/1/2006)*

Folonari 2003 Pinot Grigio (Delle Venezie) $8. Light and seems a bit lacking in concentration, with modest spice aromas and flavors but not a lot else going on. Clean and fresh on the finish. **83**—*J.C. (12/31/2004)*

Folonari NV Brio Prosecco (Prosecco del Veneto) $10. Light lemon-lime and slight mineral aromas lead to standard apple, lime, and orange zest flavors. It's refreshing, easygoing, totally as expected and not the least bit disappointing, which is really what you're looking for from $10 Prosecco. **87 Best Buy**—*M.S. (12/15/2006)*

Folonari 2004 Sangiovese (Chianti) $9. Light and leafy to begin with, while time unleashes touches of smoke, cooked meat, and even some sea foam. The palate skips to the beat of strawberry, while the slim finish is juicy and medium in length. A solid but standard everyman's red. **83**—*M.S. (10/1/2006)*

FONGOLI

Fongoli 2002 Sagrantino (Montefalco) $21. Here is a nicely compact Sagrantino with a ruby-red, purplish color and a nose that is dominated by candied cherry and ripe blackberry. On the nose it has pleasing balsam, resin, and menthol notes. The tannins are tame, making this a good match for stewed game meat. **86**—*M.L. (9/1/2005)*

FONTALEONI

Fontaleoni 2003 Sangiovese (Chianti Colli Senesi) $12. Big and round, with a rubbery note to the forceful, heavy bouquet. Comes across snappy, with cherry and plum. Definitely this is a stuffed, big red, but it runs unwaveringly along one note. And it's stern and tannic come the finish. **86** *(4/1/2005)*

ITALY

Fontaleoni 1999 Sangiovese (Chianti Colli Senesi) $11. Once a sulfury note blows off, this wine reveals dark cherry fruit with licorice, tar, and spice accents. Nice texture. Plum and black pepper notes add interest and the long, dry finish closes it nicely. Drinkable now, but better in a year. **86** *(4/1/2001)*

FONTANA

Fontana 1996 Dolcetto (Dolcetto d'Alba) $19. 84 *(4/1/2000)*

FONTANA CANDIDA

Fontana Candida 2004 Pinot Grigio (Delle Venezie) $9. This historic Lazio-based producer has segued into the competitive Pinot Grigio market and whether it can hold its own remains to be seen. The nose is ripe with fruit but there's also a stain of burnt matchstick and the body is lean. **84** —*M.L. (2/1/2006)*

Fontana Candida 2001 Pinot Grigio (Veneto) $8. Yes, it's light, but it's also clean and fresh, blending pear and lime flavors pleasantly into a decent apéritif. **83** —*J.C. (7/1/2003)*

FONTANAFREDDA

Fontanafredda 2004 Millesimato Moscato (Asti) $23. The perfect wedding cake bubbly has aromas of fresh Muscat grapes, dried grass and flowers, chalkboard, and lingering fruit. Those qualities make it pleasantly refreshing in the mouth, where it boasts a nice balance between sweetness and crispness. **87** —*M.L. (11/15/2006)*

Fontanafredda 2004 Moncucco Moscato (Moscato d'Asti) $23. You'll love the dried sage and chamomile tea aromatics with the peach cream texture of this golden hued semi-sparkler. The back offers tingling acidity that is perfect for cutting through cream-based desserts. **90** —*M.L. (12/15/2005)*

Fontanafredda 2000 Coste Rubín Nebbiolo (Barbaresco) $48. Filled with luscious red fruits and vanilla, this is a supple, medium-weight wine destined for early consumption. Strawberry and cherry flavors don't develop a lot of complexity, but this easy to drink wine is nevertheless satisfying. **86** *(4/2/2004)*

Fontanafredda 1998 La Rosa Nebbiolo (Piedmont) $68. The huge, 240-acre estate of Fontanafredda has suddenly won a new lease on life after lying almost dormant for several years. This is the second vintage produced under new management, and the style is open and accessible, but still powerful. There is pure ripe fruit on the nose, flavors of black figs, and wild strawberries and dry tannins, which still do not dominate the fruit. **90** —*R.V. (11/15/2002)*

Fontanafredda 1998 Lazzarito Nebbiolo (Piedmont) $68. There is power in this wine, with its tarry black fruit aromas. Rich and dark, with solid, dry tannins, there are still generous fruit flavors that will make it accessible over the next five years. **90** —*R.V. (11/15/2002)*

Fontanafredda 1998 Serralunga d'Alba Nebbiolo (Piedmont) $44. The standard blend of Barolo, with a production of 100,000 bottles, is very much up to the new standards of Fontanafredda. Aromas of wood and ripe fruit on the nose, with firm, dry tannins over the ripe fruit, give some sense of hidden power. **89** —*R.V. (11/15/2002)*

FONTERUTOLI

Fonterutoli 2002 Sangiovese (Chianti Classico) $26. Heavily oaked, resulting in a saucy, spicy nose. Full and tannic, with a grabby mouthfeel. But also masculine and forward, with black fruit, vanilla, and coffee. If there's a bug in the system, it's that the finish seems tangy and monotone. So while it's not the best effort from this top house, it's still laudable for an '02. **89** *(4/1/2005)*

Fonterutoli 2000 Sangiovese (Chianti Classico) $26. Very dark, rich, and chocolaty—and pretty darn oaky, too. But oh, what size and prowess. The nose is pure hickory smoke, leather, and black fruit, while the palate overflows with cassis, black plum, and pepper. The mouthfeel is silky yet aggressive, with big tannins and pulsating acids. And the coffee and cacao on the finish go on and on. **93 Editors' Choice** —*M.S. (11/15/2003)*

Fonterutoli 1999 Sangiovese (Chianti Classico) $25. Dark and dense from the get-go. Initial earth, black plum, tomato, and smoke aromas air out nicely with a bit of time, exposing a complex connoisseur's wine that is

the perfect candidate for three to five years in the cellar. Now it has such a pure, chewy palate that once the overt oak wears off, it'll be terrific. **91 Cellar Selection** —*M.S. (1/1/2004)*

Fonterutoli 1998 Sangiovese (Chianti Classico) $27. Shows overpowering cedar and heavy toast aromatics and an even feel, but the impressions are more oak than fruit-derived. Still, black plum and sweet spice flavors are in there. Finishes with cocoa notes and chalky, broad tannins. This may merit a higher score in time. **86** *(4/1/2001)*

Fonterutoli 2001 Poggio Alle Badiola Sangiovese (Toscana) $13. A bit woody and spicy, but our guess is that most folks will like that. It's 80% Sangiovese and the rest is Cabernet and Merlot. The palate provides a good dose of plum, cherry, and raspberry, while the finish is snappy and acid-driven. Fairly pure, with less oak in the mouth than on the nose. **87** —*M.S. (11/15/2003)*

FONTEVECCHIA

Fontevecchia 2001 Brunello (Brunello di Montalcino) $50. A wine with stinging freshness delivered in the form of menthol, fresh green herbs, and cracked peppercorn, with solid, underlying fruit and vanilla. Creamy and consistent in the mouth with lipsmacking acids and modest tannins. **90** *(4/1/2006)*

Fontevecchia 1998 Brunello (Brunello di Montalcino) $40. Give this wine a few minutes and it'll display a fine bouquet of black cherry, sweet almond paste, and cedar. The palate veers a bit toward the lean, red fruit spectrum of Brunello, but the more air and time it's given, the more open it becomes. Decant and drink slowly for best results. **89** —*M.S. (10/1/2004)*

Fontevecchia 2001 Sangiovese (Rosso di Montalcino) $16. Leather and cherry aromas fade fast, leading to lean strawberry flavors and some cherry skins. Not offensive, but lean and hollow. **81** —*M.S. (12/15/2003)*

Fontevecchia 2000 Sangiovese Grosso (Brunello di Montalcino) $50. This is a firm and compact wine that holds the Brunello banner high; cherry, leather, tobacco, and loads of clove spice linger on the nose and palate. The wine has a medium body with an interesting sweet and sour tug of war on the finish. **90** —*M.L. (11/15/2006)*

Fontevecchia 1997 Riserva Sangiovese Grosso (Brunello di Montalcino) $65. A rich, textured, and velvet-like wine with cherry, cedar, cigar box, spice, tobacco, leather, and ginger aromas followed by gorgeous toasted flavors in the mouth. It boasts firm tannins and a long, spice-driven finish. **92** —*M.L. (11/15/2006)*

FONTODI

Fontodi 2001 Sangiovese (Chianti Classico) $32. Begins with a blast of bright cherry fruit, backed by subtle leather and tobacco aromas, before subsiding into a creamy mouthful of cherries and vanilla. A slight herbal note adds complexity. Finish is rich and filled with supple tannins. **90** *(4/1/2005)*

Fontodi 2000 Vigna del Sorbo Riserva Sangiovese (Chianti Classico) $63. Lush and extracted, with laser beam intensity, smoke, and all the black cherry and herbs you could ask for. Gorgeous blackberry, plum, and cherry flavors announce total ripeness, while the tannins are present but integrated. Modern in style, with a barrique-based personality. **92 Editors' Choice** *(4/1/2005)*

FORACI

Foraci 2004 Galhasi Nero d'Avola (Sicilia) $12. Rich and distinctive fruit and berry notes, but it also has a touch of something lactic. There's nice exotic spice in the mouth, with a lean build and almost sweet tannins. **85** —*M.L. (10/1/2006)*

Foraci 2002 Tenute Dorrasita Nero d'Avola (Sicilia) $29. Penetrating and more concentrated, red with finely developed notes of licorice, blackberry, wet earth, and porcini mushroom over a medium build and capped by soft tannins. **88** —*M.L. (10/1/2006)*

Foraci 2004 Galhasi Nero d'Avola-Syrah Red Blend (Sicilia) $15. Ruby colored and not as concentrated, this is an easily approachable wine with inviting notes of peppermill, meat, and blackberry. The alcohol sticks out a bit and the mouthfeel is lean and tight. **86** —*M.L. (10/1/2006)*

Foraci 2005 Conte Ruggero White Blend (Alcamo) $11. The aromatic intensity is one notch higher on this wine compared to this producer's other white blend, yet the peach, almond nut, and floral aromas are similar. This wine also has a creamier quality with pretty vanilla flavors and a smooth texture. **87 Best Buy** —*M.L. (10/1/2006)*

Foraci 2005 Galhasi Inzolia-Catarratto White Blend (Sicilia) $12. You can't go wrong with this clean and light blend that delivers tight floral and fruit notes with white stone, kiwi, and peach flavors. Serve it very chilled. **86** —*M.L. (10/1/2006)*

FORADORI

Foradori 2002 Teroldego (Rotaliano) $23. Foradori's main cuvée doesn't come close to equaling its big brother, offering tobacco, herbs, and fresh cherries in a light to medium-bodied format. It's pleasant and quaffable, finishing on a herbal note. **84** —*J.C. (12/31/2004)*

Foradori 2001 Granato Teroldego (Vigneti delle Dolomiti) $60. Elisabett Foradori's top Teroldego spends 18 months in 70% new French oak barriques, and you can definitely taste their influence in its toast, cedar and vanilla flavors. But the concentrated fruit comes through as well, in the form of blueberry and cassis, blending supply harmoniously with the oak. Delicious already, but should hold for many years as well. **90** —*J.C. (12/31/2004)*

FORCHIR

Forchir 2004 Rosadis Pinot Grigio (Friuli Grave) $10. If you were to send a bottle out in a space capsule to represent the Pinot Grigio category, this might well be your choice. There's a lot going on in the nose: green apple skin and almonds or almond blossoms. It's light, refreshing, and easy to drink. **87 Best Buy** —*M.L. (6/1/2006)*

Forchir 2004 Villa del Borgo Pinot Grigio (Friuli Grave) $10. This is standard Pinot Grigio redolent of florists' shop, peach, and jasmine. It doesn't make a huge impression in the mouth, but does successfully deliver the crispness and easiness you can expect of well-made Grigio. **86 Best Buy** —*M.L. (6/1/2006)*

FORNACINA

Fornacina 2001 Brunello (Brunello di Montalcino) $60. A special, gentle wine with caressing persistence, campfire toastiness, black forest berries, and a creamy, velvety mouthfeel. Tannins flare up on the rear but leave drying elegance on the close. **92** *(4/1/2006)*

FORTETO DELLA LUJA

Forteto della Luja 2004 Piasa Sanmaurizio Moscato (Moscato d'Asti) $18. With a slightly copperish hue and plenty of persistent effervescence, this Moscato d'Asti from Loazzolo smells of Golden Delicious apple, dried flowers, and lavender honey. It has a broader and less defined mouthfeel than other wines of its kind. **85** —*M.L. (12/15/2005)*

FOSS MARAI

Foss Marai NV Prosecco (Prosecco di Valdobbiadene) $12. 88 Best Buy —*P.G. (12/15/2000)*

Foss Marai NV Dry Prosecco (Prosecco Superiore di Cartizze) $30. Perfectly fresh and open as a pasture of wild flowers in full bloom. Delicious, easy-to-take flavors of orange and pineapple are zesty and clean as a whistle. Excellent mouthfeel and tingly bubbles are the coup de grace. **90** —*M.S. (12/15/2005)*

Foss Marai NV Extra Dry Prosecco (Prosecco di Valdobbiadene) $12. Dry enough, but still just a touch sweet and candied, and doesn't that fit the model for extra dry? Full in the mouth, with citrus, a spot of mineral, and purity. It's quite simple, but still it has just enough of an elevated quality to rank with the best of the bunch. **88 Best Buy** —*M.S. (12/15/2005)*

Foss Marai NV Cuvée Vino Spumante Brut Sparkling Blend (Italy) $18. Apple and green herbs on the nose are more convincing than the flavor profile, which deals applesauce and buttered toast. Fairly weighty on the palate, but clean and correct as a whole. **85** —*M.S. (6/1/2005)*

Foss Marai NV Cuvée Brut White Blend (Italy) $18. Slightly drier than your average extra dry, with aromas of soda crackers and sugared pastry. The palate deals apple and just-ripe nectarine along with notes of white pepper and citrus pith. Almost toasty in the end, with a shot of fresh celery. **88** —*M.S. (12/15/2005)*

FOSSACOLLE

Fossacolle 2001 Brunello (Brunello di Montalcino) $64. Tight menthol, currant berry, cedar wood, and dusty mineral notes eventually waft off a wine that seems reluctant to open at first. The structure is solid without being hard, with espresso, leather, and a powerful, dry finish. **89** *(4/1/2006)*

FOURPLAY

Fourplay 2001 No 1 Red Blend (Sicilia) $12. A wine from the minds of the local Saro di Pietro winery and Tuscany's Dievole. This blend of four Sicilian grapes is dark, cherry-laden, and just oaky enough to register. Good as an everyday pizza and pasta wine, with plenty of zest and forward character. Balanced but basic. **86** —*M.S. (7/1/2005)*

FRANCESCO BOSCHIS

Francesco Boschis 1998 Vigna del Prey Dolcetto (Dolcetto di Dogliani) $19. 90 *(4/1/2000)*

FRANZ HAAS

Franz Haas 2003 Lagrein (Alto Adige) $33. Known for excellent Pinot Nero from the slopes of the Cislon mountain in Alto Adige, this family-run estate also does a fine job with late ripener Lagrein. A spectacular, inky red color, the wine opens with multiple layers of mild cherry and wild fennel that will transform into coffee and black pepper with age. There's plenty of spice already but the structure is bony. **87** —*M.L. (9/1/2005)*

Franz Haas 2004 Kris Pinot Grigio (Delle Venezie) $10. Mineral and candy-like notes create an ensemble that recalls a lime margarita. Nice mouthfeel with a tangy sour point at the back. **87 Best Buy** —*M.L. (2/1/2006)*

Franz Haas 2002 Kris Pinot Grigio (Delle Venezie) $9. This inexpensive, delicious fresh wine has good depth of concentration and long, vanilla flavors. **85** —*R.V. (7/1/2003)*

Franz Haas 2001 Manna Bianco di Mitterberg White Blend (Alto Adige) $24. This wine, which takes the family name of Franz Haas's wife, is an extraordinary blend of 50% Riesling, 20% Chardonnay, 20% Traminer, and 10% Sauvignon Blanc. And yet these disparate elements come together in a harmonious, ripe wine, with just a hint of toast from the barrel-fermented Chardonnay. It is powerful, rich, and complex. **92** —*R.V. (7/1/2003)*

FRATELLI BERLUCCHI

Fratelli Berlucchi 1999 Brut Champagne Blend (Franciacorta) $27. Fairly encouraging on the nose, what with honey and floral aromas floating above sautéed mushroom. The flavors, however, don't really sing. Mostly orange and grapefruit on the full, bulky palate, followed by a modest finish. **85** —*M.S. (12/15/2004)*

Fratelli Berlucchi 2000 Satèn Champagne Blend (Franciacorta) $NA. A blanc de blancs (Chardonnay and Pinot Bianco) that boasts a slightly greenish tint with servings of apple and peach on the nose. The most mature grape clusters are selected to go into this beautifully rich wine. **88** —*M.L. (12/15/2004)*

Fratelli Berlucchi 2000 Pas Dosé Chardonnay (Franciacorta) $NA. Another gorgeous wine from 100% Chardonnay. The nose yields more spice and nuttiness but the floral and fruit aromas keep pace. An elaborately refined product, both in the bottle and in the glass. Only 5,000 bottles produced per year. **89** —*M.L. (12/15/2004)*

Fratelli Berlucchi 2000 Brut Sparkling Blend (Franciacorta) $30. A beautiful wine with beautiful packaging to match (a truly museum-worthy bottle). Green apple, honeydew melon, and yeast reveal themselves after the creamy mousse has finished its show. Hits the palate with enough personality and precision to accompany a full meal. **90** —*M.L. (12/15/2004)*

Fratelli Berlucchi 2000 Brut Rosé Sparkling Blend (Franciacorta) $30. Blueberry, raspberry, and some crisp cranberry greet the nose on this playfully pink rosé (derived from Pinot Nero with Chardonnay and Pinot Bianco). Ideal with spicy Indian foods. **87** —*M.L. (12/15/2004)*

Fratelli Berlucchi NV Cuvée Imperiale Brut Sparkling Blend (Franciacorta) $NA. The multiple layers of this wine are like the pages of an encyclopedia of tastes: from almond to nougat to baked apple tart to flinty minerality. There are no rough edges and the wine hits the mouth with sassy smoothness. **89** —*M.L. (12/15/2004)*

Fratelli Berlucchi NV Cuvée Imperiale Max Rosé Sparkling Blend (Franciacorta) $NA. This is a wine to fall in love with. Pale rose petal pink in color, the wine greets the nose with a refreshing medley of raspberry, strawberry, and peach—but never too much of any one aroma to offset the others. Its evolution is quite remarkable and after a few sips, cinnamon, spice and Christmastime cookies come to mind. **91** —*M.L. (12/15/2004)*

FRATELLI FICI

Fratelli FICI 2000 Baglio Fici Syrah (Sicilia) $NA. No, it's not terribly recognizable as Syrah, but it tastes good, with cherries and vanilla framed by dried spices and garnished with an overlay of fresh herbs. Medium-weight and very smooth. Drink now–2006. **87** *(10/1/2003)*

FRATELLI GANCIA

Fratelli Gancia 2000 Carlo Gancia Cuvée del Fondatore Brut Champagne Blend (Asti) $20. Extremely oaky for a sparkler, with a heavy, forceful nose that's dominated by toasted wood grain. The equally woody palate is round, with hints of apple and caramel. Smoky on the finish, with a smack of banana and lemon. **83** —*M.S. (12/15/2004)*

Fratelli Gancia NV Castello Gancia Brut Champagne Blend (Piedmont) $12. **85** *(11/15/1999)*

Fratelli Gancia NV Gancia Moscato (Asti) $13. Fruity and floral, with attractive apple, mango, and melon notes. It's like a trip to carbonated Fruitopia, a place where there's plenty of pop and pizzazz but not a whole lot of substance. This wine will tame the toughest sweet tooth. **85** —*M.S. (12/15/2004)*

Fratelli Gancia NV Gancia Spumante Moscato (Piedmont) $9. Sweet, with vanilla cream, melon, and banana. Sugary on the palate, with a bit more banana. Confectionary, but tasty. **83** —*M.S. (12/15/2004)*

Fratelli Gancia 1999 Marchesi Spinola Nebbiolo (Nebbiolo d'Alba) $15. This understated wine features modest cherry and citrus fruit, alongside tea and tobacco. It's lightweight and lacks intensity on the finish, but offers recognizable Nebbiolo character at a reasonable tariff. **84** —*J.C. (11/15/2004)*

Fratelli Gancia 1998 Marchesi Spinola Nebbiolo (Barolo) $35. Shows some oak on the nose, marked by vanilla and a hint of maple syrup. Lush plum fruit, some leather, and orange zest on the palate before the tannins clamp down on the anise-tinged finish. Try after 2008. **87** *(4/2/2004)*

Fratelli Gancia 2000 Torrebianco Negroamaro (Salento) $8. Black cherry, caramel, and toffee create a sweet bouquet. Flavors of raspberry, smoke, and coffee work well together, and the mouthfeel is easy. However, it turns thin on the back palate and dilute on the back end. **85** —*M.S. (11/15/2004)*

Fratelli Gancia 2002 Della Serenissima Pinot Grigio (Friuli) $22. Herbal and under-ripe on the nose, with green notes that translate into grapefruit and herb flavors on the palate. Does pick up some riper, peachier notes on the finish. **83** —*J.C. (12/31/2004)*

Fratelli Gancia 2000 Torrebianco Primitivo (Salento) $9. Licorice, raisin, and marinade make for a spicy, saucy nose. The palate is developed and ripe, with black cherry, plum, and raspberry resulting in a standard but good flavor profile. Smooth and big on the finish, with legs. **86 Best Buy** —*M.S. (11/15/2004)*

Fratelli Gancia NV Gancia Extra Dry Prosecco (Veneto) $10. Fresh and clean, like a forest after the rain. Flavors of apple, green melon, and celery are lean and crisp, while the finish deals nothing but citrus. Rather monotone in style, but good. **86 Best Buy** —*M.S. (12/15/2004)*

Fratelli Gancia 1999 Della Serenissima Red Blend (Amarone della Valpolicella) $34. Overtly heavy and stewy on the nose, and quite citrusy

in the mouth, almost to the point of being sour. Finishes too sharp and bitter to rate higher. **83** *(11/1/2005)*

Fratelli Gancia 2002 Torrebianco Red Blend (Sicilia) $6. Light red fruit throughout, and mostly soft and clean. Some strawberry and raspberry on the palate leads into a light-weight finish. Easygoing and inoffensive. **84 Best Buy** —*M.S. (10/1/2004)*

Fratelli Gancia 2001 Torrebianco Locorotondo White Blend (Italy) $7. Nothing special, but clean and authentic. The aromas are of candied citrus, while the palate is almost entirely lime. Low-acid and flat on the tongue. **82** —*M.S. (10/1/2004)*

FRATELLI GIULIARI

Fratelli Giuliari 1998 Red Blend (Valpolicella Classico Superiore) $9. The color is brown-ish and the aromas are of earth and raisins. Citrus zest and sharp red fruit drives the palate, while the finish is tannic, especially considering how little richness is on offer. **84** *(5/1/2003)*

Fratelli Giuliari 2000 La Piccola Botte Red Blend (Amarone della Valpolicella Classico) $45. More of a stout, round wine with an emphasis on lush berry fruit and raisins. And that is what we liked about it. It doesn't deal much wood or acid; instead it shoots for a creamy, somewhat spicy personality. And it hits that target squarely. **89** *(11/1/2005)*

Fratelli Giuliari 1998 La Piccola Botte Red Blend (Recioto della Valpolicella Classico) $31. Heavy and browning, with aromas and flavors that are raisiny. The finish is like spiced tea, and the tannins are soft. If you enjoy the essence of raisins, this wine has potential. Not as fresh as the others. **85** *(5/1/2003)*

Fratelli Giuliari 1995 La Piccola Botte Red Blend (Amarone della Valpolicella Classico) $37. The barrel regimen is reflected in the charred, leathery components on the nose. In the mouth, it's heavy, with black plum, burnt sugar, and even some vinegar notes. This wine has its attributes but also some rough edges. **84** *(5/1/2003)*

FRATELLI ZENI

Fratelli Zeni 1998 Red Blend (Bardolino Classico) $12. If light makes right, this is right on. Lean in color, with mild cherry aromas and some lead pencil. The mouth is bright and acid-driven, with cherry and raspberry flavors along with a hint of cocoa. Tangy and zippy from front to back. **84** *(5/1/2003)*

Fratelli Zeni 1995 Red Blend (Amarone della Valpolicella Classico) $38. This wine seems overtly oaky, with notes of lemon and sawdust. Beyond that, there's plum and berry along with some woody vanilla character. The tannins border on firm. But there's good power and zing throughout, which keeps it highly respectable in a category that includes so many well-rated wines. **88** *(5/1/2003)*

Fratelli Zeni 1998 Vigne Alte Red Blend (Valpolicella Classico) $11. Thin, grassy aromas make for a tough, sharp nose. The flavor profile runs toward cranberry and rhubarb, but for those who like crisp, snappy reds, that may be okay. The finish is tart, and then some buttery notes take over. **83** *(5/1/2003)*

Fratelli Zeni 2000 Vigne Alte White Blend (Bianco di Custoza) $11. It's testament to this wine's balance that it remains so alive and fresh long after many other Biancos have faded. Intensely mineral aromas mix with notes of smoke and fresh apples; the flavors are earthy and hint at mineral oil. Long on the finish. Best Buy. **88 Best Buy** —*J.C. (7/1/2003)*

FRATTA PASINI

Fratta Pasini 2002 Corvina, Rondinella, Molinara (Amarone della Valpolicella) $53. Begins with sweet, floral aromas of red fruit, which one of our tasters found to be a bit too much like perfume or nail polish. The rest of our panel liked the wine's berry flavors, no-fuss style, and length on the finish. "Size with stamina," was how one taster described the body. **89** *(11/1/2005)*

FRESCOBALDI

Frescobaldi 1998 Nipozanno Riserva Red Blend (Chianti Rufina) $15. A pile of earth, smoke, leather, and dark chocolate is about all you can pull from the dense, closed nose. The palate is only a bit more open, and on the back palate the full allotment of berries and oak comes on hard. It's grapey and tannic, but it should be more friendly in due time, say two more years. **88 Best Buy** —*M.S. (12/31/2002)*

Frescobaldi 1999 Castiglioni Sangiovese (Chianti) $13. Full aromas of rich blackberry fruit with licorice and cocoa notes are followed by more of the same on the palate. The dense fruit picks up a sweet-and-sour quality and coffee tones on the lengthy finish. Not a particularly deep wine, but a very satisfying one. **89 Best Buy** *(4/1/2001)*

Frescobaldi 1995 Montesodi Sangiovese (Chianti Rufina) $49. 87 —*M.M. (5/1/1999)*

Frescobaldi 1999 Montesodi Castello Di Nipozzano Sangiovese (Chianti Rufina) $40. Racy and quick, with modest tannins and deep black fruit and berry flavors. Traditional Chianti is defined by wines like this. It has a solid and necessary tannic structure but enough richness to offset any hardness that may stem from the tannins. The finish is plush and easy, with a full batch of chocolate and coffee. Give it a year or two if possible. **90** —*M.S. (12/31/2002)*

Frescobaldi 1997 Montesodi Castello di Nipozzano Sangiovese (Chianti Rufina) $54. The black cherry, plum, and soy elements of the deep, almost profound, bouquet set you up for a serious wine. Full and powerful—but supple and even; reserved—but subtly strong, it offers up seamless black cherry, chocolate, and earth flavors. Finishes long, with firm but refined tannins and polished, dark fruit flavors. Best from 2004–2015. **92 Cellar Selection** *(4/1/2001)*

Frescobaldi 1995 Mormoreto Sangiovese (Toscana) $45. 87 —*M.M. (5/1/1999)*

Frescobaldi 1997 Nipozzano Riserva Sangiovese (Chianti Rufina) $22. The bouquet of this elegant, reserved wine is muted right now, but the berry and leather notes that show display real class. Medium-bodied, with tart cherry flavors and an appealing slate-chalk element, this wine has a distinctive palate and profile. Closes beautifully with even tannins, nice cassis, and licorice notes and a handsome perfume. **91** *(4/1/2001)*

Frescobaldi 1996 Nipozzano Riserva Sangiovese (Chianti Rufina) $20. 86 —*M.S. (7/1/2000)*

Frescobaldi 1999 Pomino Rosso Sangiovese (Pomino) $25. Here's a Tuscan red that's racy and lean, a pure shot of cherry and cranberry fruit with little else mucking it up. The nose has a hint of tree bark and cola in addition to expressive red fruit, while the palate is all zippy cherries, vanilla, and pepper. Almost certainly a winner with food due to its streamlined body, which features racy acids. **89** —*M.S. (12/31/2002)*

Frescobaldi 1996 Pomino Rosso Sangiovese (Pomino) $25. 86 —*L.W. (3/1/2000)*

Frescobaldi 2001 Remole Sangiovese (Toscana) $9. Spicy and fruity up front, but a bit shy on the nose. A mouthful of plum and pie cherry creates a tight mouthfeel. Slightly piquant and snappy, but ripe and tasty. Will be helped along by the right food. **87** —*M.S. (10/1/2004)*

Frescobaldi 1998 Remole Sangiovese (Toscana) $9. 87 *(11/15/1999)*

Frescobaldi 1997 Remole Sangiovese (Toscana) $9. 83 —*L.W. (3/1/2000)*

Frescobaldi 2001 Benefizio White Blend (Pomino) $NA. This fragrant white, with its boisterous bouquet of designer soap, perfume, and gardenia, is exotic, but it's hard to say that the palate that follows is as exciting. In fact, it's soft and bland, with banana, citrus, and nutmeg flavors that don't come in layers but all at once. A blend that's mostly Chardonnay. **86** —*M.S. (10/1/2004)*

FULIGNI

Fuligni 2001 Brunello (Brunello di Montalcino) $74. Delicate balsam, evolved cherry-berry, and smoky roundness are delicious. A good, compact structure with untamed tannins. **92** *(4/1/2006)*

Fuligni 2000 Brunello (Brunello di Montalcino) $74. This winery is always at the top of the heap, and it's 2000 shows true depth of flavor, texture, and nuance. Seemingly approachable now, with classy plum and berry aromas and flavors. Softening any astringency is vanilla and tobacco, while a distant shot of citrus adds life. The whole speaks louder than the parts; a super overall package. **93 Editors' Choice** —*M.S. (7/1/2005)*

Fuligni 1999 Brunello (Brunello di Montalcino) $82. Anyone who loves great Sangiovese should snap up this star-quality wine. Always a personal

favorite, the '99 doesn't disappoint. It's lively and electric, with structure equal to the Tuscan fort in which it was tasted. As for flavors, look for overflowing blackberry, cola, mocha, and more. A wine that can probably last for 15 years. **95** —*M.S. (6/1/2004)*

Fuligni 1998 Brunello (Brunello di Montalcino) $65. A big, rich, Port-like Brunello that found controversy with our panel. While some admired it for its ripeness, others felt it a bit raisiny. Regardless, all agreed that it possesses intense concentration, a creamy mouthfeel, and a long, softly tannic finish. **92** *(11/15/2003)*

Fuligni 1997 Riserva Brunello (Brunello di Montalcino) $100. Incredibly pure fruit defines the sturdy, entirely inviting nose. This is one juicy, rock steady wine; the tannic structure is that of a fortress. There's unadulterated fruit at every checkpoint, and it hits like a hammer as it transitions from palate to finish. To drink now would require rich, rich food. It's such a baby; drink not before 2007, if possible. **94 Editors' Choice** —*M.S. (11/15/2003)*

Fuligni 1999 S.J. Red Blend (Tuscany) $37. Even though this wine starts out weaker than it finishes, the whole package is really nice. Some earthy, stewed fruit aromas lead into a broad and spicy black-fruit palate. Well-applied wood tones add character to the finish. And the balance seems spot on. While it's firm and tight, you don't get hit with hard tannins or overt oak. In a word, it's balanced. **89** —*M.S. (12/31/2002)*

FURLAN

Furlan 2000 Castelcosa Pinot Grigio (Friuli) $12. Aging, with shellac and mineral-spirits aromas and flavors creeping in over the pear and mint. Drink up. **83** —*J.C. (7/1/2003)*

Furlan 2000 Castelcosa Sauvignon Blanc (Friuli Venezia Giulia) $12. A simple, citrusy quaff that leans heavily toward pineapple and grapefruit. Some melon flavors round out the package. **84** —*J.C. (7/1/2003)*

Furlan 2000 Cuvée Tai White Blend (Friuli) $14. Heavy and alcoholic in the mouth, with aromas of fresh corn husks and limes. Tastes simple, with hints of oranges, and finishes short. **82** —*J.C. (7/1/2003)*

G CONTRATTO

G Contratto 1995 Solus Ad Barbera D'Asti Superiore Barbera (Barbera d'Asti) $24. 89 *(4/1/2000)*

G D VAJRA

G D Vajra 1997 Barbera (Barbera d'Alba) $17. 88 *(4/1/2000)*

G D Vajra 1997 Dolcetto (Dolcetto d'Alba) $13. 86 Best Buy *(4/1/2000)*

G D Vajra 1997 Coste & Fossati Dolcetto (Dolcetto d'Alba) $18. 87 *(4/1/2000)*

G.A. ROSSI DI MEDELENA

G.A. Rossi di Medelena 2000 Lupicaia Cabernet Sauvignon-Merlot (Toscana) $120. From what was once called Castello del Terriccio comes this Tuscan blend of Cabernet and a little Merlot. It has fine-grained cinnamon oak on the nose, but not too much stuffing backing it up. Still, it's a very good red that offers black cherry, plum, and coffee notes. That said, it runs a bit heavy with tobacco and leather, especially on the nose. **89** —*M.S. (10/1/2004)*

GABBIANO

Gabbiano 2003 Pinot Grigio (Delle Venezie) $10. Delicate peach and pear fruit carries a minerally or graphite note. Crisp and clean on the finish, this is a solid, harmonious wine that delivers what you expect for the price. **85 Best Buy** —*J.C. (12/31/2004)*

Gabbiano 2003 Bonello Red Blend (Sicilia) $9. Thanks to tempting and evolving notes of black pepper, Indian spice, toast, espresso, cola, menthol, and Pastis this Merlot-Nero d'Avola blend strikes all the right chords and is a flat out bargain for $9 a bottle. It boasts a brick red color with good structure and persistency and is the ultimate consumer-friendly wine. Part of the Beringer Blass Wine Estates' project in Sicily. **87 Best Buy** —*M.L. (11/15/2005)*

Gabbiano 2001 Sangiovese (Chianti Classico) $14. Vulcanized rubber, iodine, and molasses aromas, with simple berry flavors. Carries a bit of green on the palate, but finishes solid. **82** *(4/1/2005)*

ITALY

Gabbiano 2001 Riserva Sangiovese (Chianti Classico) $17. Woody but smooth, with classic cedar, tobacco, and leather aromas along with sturdy plum and cherry fruit. Good feel, as it sits nicely on the tongue. Finishes reasonably long and straight, with solidity. Traditional and tasty, with no frills. **88** *(4/1/2005)*

GAGLIOLE

Gagliole 2001 Red Blend (Colli della Toscana Centrale) $56. Smooth and sophisticated, with cool menthol aromas and rich oak. Dynamite flavors of cherry, raspberry, and plum form a cornucopia of fruit, while toward the back chocolate and espresso rise up a take over. It's a packed wine with high-voltage power, and just enough poise. **92 Editors' Choice** — *M.S. (11/15/2003)*

Gagliole 2003 Pecchia Red Blend (Colli della Toscana Centrale) $155. Very tense and tight is the nose: It contains precise fruit, baking spice, toasted oak, and mint. Wonderfully structured on the palate, which shows bright berry flavors and grainy, grabby tannins. Finishes on the chocolaty side, with length and power. A big boy for sure. **93** *—M.S. (9/1/2006)*

Gagliole 2003 Rosso Red Blend (Colli della Toscana Centrale) $75. Lovely flower, mineral, baked cookie, and cherry aromas are lusty and inviting, and the palate is exceedingly fresh for a 2003. The fruit is snappy, legitimately healthy, and tight. Finishes with chocolate and ripe tannins. Excellent stuff, and it should be at the price. **91** *—M.S. (9/1/2006)*

Gagliole 1999 Pecchia Sangiovese (Colli della Toscana Centrale) $93. Oaky and dense, with an oily nose that loses clarity with airing. This is one of those high-flying, pricey super Tuscans that has its virtues but doesn't sing as a package. It just doesn't have much charm. And at 14.5% alcohol it's tough to swallow. **85** *—M.S. (11/15/2003)*

GAIERHOF

Gaierhof 2004 Pinot Grigio (Trentino) $17. Very appetizing, fresh, and fragrant of fruit Macedonia and lemon sorbet. Lean but pleasing in the mouth. Its fruity freshness would serve well with a lighter fish dish, such as John Dory fillets braised in butter. **86** *—M.L. (6/1/2006)*

Gaierhof 2001 Pinot Grigio (Trentino) $11. A bit rough and rustic, but packs in plenty of sweet pear-nectar flavors dusted with dried spices. **83** *—J.C. (7/1/2003)*

GAJA

Gaja 1999 Darmagi Cabernet Sauvignon (Langhe) $224. Here is a rock-solid Cabernet embellished by a delicate aromatic embroidery that gives its Piedmont origins away. Dark ruby in color, the nose is perfectly seamless with ripe fruit nuances at the core and generous notes of asphalt, resin, and blackberry. The tannins and structure are solid and the wine's enduring persistence can be counted in long, delicious minutes. **94 Cellar Selection** *—M.L. (9/1/2006)*

Gaja 2001 Nebbiolo (Barbaresco) $185. Gaja's Barbaresco is a blend of 14 different vineyard sites, aged approximately 12 months in barriques and 12 months in larger oak casks. Shows plenty of spice on the nose—clove, cinnamon, anise—but also loads of cherry and red plum fruit. Sneakily tannic; it starts off silky, then the tannins build in intensity, coating the mouth. Drink 2010–2025. **92** *(7/1/2005)*

Gaja 2001 Conteisa Red Blend (Langhe) $205. Elegantly perfumed, with touches of cinnamon, ground pepper, and dusty earth accenting notes of black cherries and chocolate. On the palate, there's powerful plum and black cherry flavors, but also a strong minerality that adds an extra dimension to this compelling wine. Soft enough to begin drinking around 2010, it should keep for a couple of decades after that. **94** *(7/1/2005)*

Gaja 2001 Costa Russi Red Blend (Langhe) $350. Darker, richer, and earthier than Gaja's Barbaresco, picking up notes of coffee, vanilla, and toast as well. Yet on the palate there's wonderfully bright cherry-raspberry fruit and masses of lush, velvety tannins that will give this wine plenty of life in the cellar. Drink 2012–2030. **95** *(7/1/2005)*

Gaja 2003 Rossj-Bass Red Blend (Langhe) $57. Mainly Chardonnay (with up to 5% Sauvignon Blanc) from several vineyards in Barbaresco and Serralunga, fermented in stainless, then matured in oak. The result is a mealy, toasty wine full of honeysuckle and pear fruit. Soft and round in the mouth, yet it firms up nicely on the finish. **89** *(7/1/2005)*

Gaja 2001 Sorì San Lorenzo Red Blend (Langhe) $350. Perhaps less nuanced than the Sorì Tildìn, but more powerful, with round, mouth-filling flavors and firm tannins. Hints of tobacco and vanilla add complexity to rich plum and black cherry notes, finishing with a lovely touch of anise. Drink 2015–2030 and beyond. **95** *(7/1/2005)*

Gaja 2001 Sorì Tildìn Red Blend (Langhe) $350. Filled with intoxicating perfume reminiscent of dried spices, fine leather, exotic woods, then delivers bold black cherry, plum, and Asian spice flavors tightly wrapped in a velvety blanket of tannin. Long and richly chewy on the finish, yet minerally as well. Drink 2015–2030. **95** *(7/1/2005)*

Gaja 2001 Sperss Refosco (Langhe) $200. Lots of spice, with black pepper and leather notes leading the way, followed by a core of plum, black cherry, and earth flavors. Structured for the long haul, it's dense and firm right now, but you can sense the enormous potential. Drink 2015–2030 and likely beyond. **94** *(7/1/2005)*

GALLI & BROCCATELLI

Galli & Broccatelli 1998 Sagrantino di Montefalco Sagrantino (Sagrantino di Montefalco) $25. Violet and dried meat aromas lead to red berry fruit flavors that are a bit weedy. The wine lacks depth and finishes tart but with some tannin structure. **85** *—C.S. (2/1/2003)*

GALTAROSSA

Galtarossa 2000 Red Blend (Amarone della Valpolicella) $54. All over the map. There's maple, acetone, and candy on the nose, and the fruit flavors morph from sweet to sugary sweet to artificial all in one sip. Saving graces come in the cinnamon and cocoa powder nuances. **84** *(11/1/2005)*

GAROFOLI

Garofoli 2000 Grosso Agontano Riserva Montepulciano (Rosso Conero) $25. This Montepulciano is seductively smoky, with bacon and spice aromas courtesy of full-fledged oak. The flavors run toward plum, blackberry, currants, and bitter chocolate. Extracted, dense, and dark; almost a star. **88** *—M.S. (6/1/2005)*

Garofoli 2001 Piancarda Montepulciano (Rosso Conero) $13. Simple red fruit from the berry and plum family defines the nose, which is a bit herbal as well. Black plum and raspberry flavors are tight, lean, and juicy due to lively acidity. Turns a little green in the midpalate as the fruit thins. Good for everyday drinking. **85** *—M.S. (6/1/2005)*

Garofoli 2001 Podium Classico Superiore Verdicchio (Verdicchio dei Castelli di Jesi Classico) $15. Rich and stately, with superior aromas of honey, almond, peach, and pear. The palate is nicely developed; it's simultaneously soft and extracted as well as defined and structured. The spicy finish blends pepper with cinnamon. A great match for fish. **88 Best Buy** *—M.S. (8/1/2004)*

Garofoli 2002 Serra del Conte Verdicchio (Verdicchio dei Castelli di Jesi Classico) $8. Simple but hefty aromas of banana and lemon precede a clean but underwhelming palate of papaya and tangerine. Fairly reserved and lean, with proper acidity and a full finish. A good entry into the variety. **85 Best Buy** *—M.S. (8/1/2004)*

GASTALDI

Gastaldi 1997 Moriolo Dolcetto (Dolcetto d'Alba) $18. **85** *(4/1/2000)*

GATTAVECCHI

Gattavecchi 1998 Sangiovese (Chianti Colli Senesi) $11. Possesses some decent black cherry aromas and flavors with leathery, earthy accents, but also a sour streak and a sulfurous note that refused to yield. The wine finishes dry, with some of the astringency shown by many 1998s. **84** *(4/1/2001)*

GATTINARA

Gattinara 1997 Estate Bottled Nebbiolo (Gattinara) $30. Leather and sweat combine with dusty, dry fruit to create a lean bouquet. Cranberry, sour cherry, and leather make for a tight, tart palate. There's not much here beyond tannin and acid. **82** *—M.S. (12/15/2003)*

GERETTO

Geretto 2001 Merlot (Delle Venezie) $10. The nose offers a lot of spice, lavender, and desert sage, but oddly little fruit, especially when contrasted to the simple grapey flavors on the palate. **83** *(5/1/2003)*

Geretto 2005 Pinot Grigio (Delle Venezie) $10. A full, almost sweet nose, with peach, melon, citrus, and crushed stone. Although the mineral presence is there, so is the fruit. Has a nice consistency with a sour note on the finish. **86 Best Buy** —*M.L. (6/1/2006)*

Geretto 2004 Pinot Grigio (Delle Venezie) $10. An intriguing nose features cola, lemon rind, tangerine, and a touch of rubber without being unattractive. But the wine does not deliver as successfully in the mouth. **86 Best Buy** —*M.L. (2/1/2006)*

Geretto 2001 Pinot Grigio (Delle Venezie) $9. Unexpectedly thick and mouth-filling, with generous peach aromas and flavors underscored by mustard greens and citrus. Clean and refreshing on the finish. **87 Best Buy** —*J.C. (7/1/2003)*

GERMANO ETTORE

Germano Ettore 2001 Pra Di Po Dolcetto (Dolcetto d'Alba) $17. Spicy, leathery aromas lead it off, and at no point is this a pure and polished prince. It's a touch wild, as there's lots of leather and drying tannins. Better at first, the fruit thins during tasting. Still, there's more good cherry and earth here than mitigating factors. **86** —*M.S. (12/15/2003)*

Germano Ettore 1998 Cerretta Nebbiolo (Barolo) $45. Modern, but not excessively so, Germano's Barolo Cerretta combines cedar and vanilla seamlesssly with supple black cherry fruit. Long on the finish, the ripe tannins provide a rich, chewy texture. Drink 2005–2015. **91** *(4/2/2004)*

GHIONE

Ghione 2005 Piccole Gioie Moscato (Moscato d'Asti) $17. The best sweet wine for informal sipping on a hot summer day is Piedmont's Moscato d'Asti, and this version embodies all the stone fruit, floral, and musky lavender aromas you should expect; foamy and creamy in the mouth, with a good level of crispness. **87** —*M.L. (11/15/2006)*

GIACOMO ASCHERI

Giacomo Ascheri 1998 Podere di Sorano Barolo Bordeaux Blend (Barolo) $40. The long wood aging in large Slavonian oak barrels has given this a dryness and austerity. The fruit is there, with red fruit flavors and ripeness, but it is the dryness and tarry black flavors that dominate. It is very young, and should develop over the next 10 years. **89** —*R.V. (11/15/2002)*

Giacomo Ascheri 1997 Poderi di Sorano Nebbiolo (Barolo) $40. A much more traditional style of wine than the 1998, with meaty, rustic aromas. The palate is ripe, with earthy, bacon, and farmyard flavors, strong acidity and dry tannins. **87** —*R.V. (11/15/2002)*

Giacomo Ascheri 1996 Poderi di Sorano Nebbiolo (Barolo) $40. Meaty, farmyard aromas characterize this wine. Ripe tannins, rustic flavors, and solid acidity follow through to a dry, almost Port-like finish. **87** —*R.V. (11/15/2002)*

Giacomo Ascheri 1999 Sorano Coste & Bricco Nebbiolo (Barolo) $55. This wine is nicely balanced, with a full, rich mouthfeel and supple tannins that admirably support the cherry and leather fruit. Traces of herbs and tobacco enhance the mouth-watering finish. Drink now–2015. **89** *(4/2/2004)*

Giacomo Ascheri 1999 Vigna dei Pola Nebbiolo (Barolo) $55. Starts off a bit subdued, with leather and cherries only emerging slowly over the half hour or so it is in the glass. But the flavors are solid, blending cherries with dried spices and some floral elements, and the mouthfeel is full and rich. Finishes on a tangy plum note. **90** *(4/2/2004)*

GIACOMO BREZZA

Giacomo Brezza 1996 Cannubi Muscatel Barbera (Barbera d'Alba) $20. 90 *(4/1/2000)*

Giacomo Brezza 1998 San Lorenzo Dolcetto (Dolcetto d'Alba) $16. 87 *(4/1/2000)*

GIACOMO BREZZA & FIGLI

Giacomo Brezza & Figli 1997 Nebbiolo (Piedmont) $45. Brezza's main blend of Barolo shone in 1997. There is pure, ripe, but concentrated fruit and ripe, sweet, and sour tannins over new wood flavors and black tarry flavors. This is a serious, condensed wine typical of the powerful nature of the vintage. **91** —*R.V. (11/15/2002)*

Giacomo Brezza & Figli 1998 Cannubi Nebbiolo (Piedmont) $55. The attractive aromas of pure, juicy fruit appear on the palate as super-ripe, almost over-ripe fruit flavors. At this stage, the wine doesn't balance, but there is some power and it should develop. **85** —*R.V. (11/15/2002)*

Giacomo Brezza & Figli 1998 Sarmassa Nebbiolo (Piedmont) $55. Brezza's Sarmassa has attractive aromas of sweet red fruits. Ripe fruits follow on the palate, with sweet tarry flavors, a hint of orange zest, and chocolate, and a finish of sweet and sour acidity. **87** —*R.V. (11/15/2002)*

GIACOMO CONTERNO

Giacomo Conterno 1998 Cascina Francia Barbera (Barbera d'Alba) $24. 90 *(4/1/2000)*

Giacomo Conterno 1998 Cascina Francia Dolcetto (Dolcetto d'Alba) $22. 88 *(4/1/2000)*

GIACOMO FENOCCHIO

Giacomo Fenocchio 1999 Bussia Nebbiolo (Barolo) $45. The best of a disappointing group of wines from Fenocchio, this has some volatile acidity and very tart cherry flavors that finish tannic and sharp. **82** *(4/2/2004)*

GIACOMO MARENGO

Giacomo Marengo 2001 Castello Di Rapale Sangiovese (Chianti) $23. Browning, with unmistakable paint and lacquer aromas. Already thinning out, with staunch acids and tannins making for a hard ride. Not much on display, and from a standout vintage. **83** *(4/1/2005)*

Giacomo Marengo 2002 Le Tornanie Sangiovese (Chianti) $19. Strange on the nose, with tobacco, green bean, and coffee. While it has the size, it lacks character and composition. And the pickled aftertaste does it no favors. **82** *(4/1/2005)*

Giacomo Marengo 1998 Tenuta del Fondatore La Commenda Riserva Sangiovese (Chianti) $33. Spiky hard and downright traditional, but still attractive in a modern way. The nose offers roasted fruit, cinnamon, and herbs, and the taste profile follows suit. Along the way come notes of mocha, coffee, and milk chocolate. If there's a pitfall, it's that it hits like a jackhammer on the palate. Begs for food. **87** *(4/1/2005)*

GIACOMO MORI

Giacomo Mori 2002 Sangiovese (Chianti) $18. Fairly jammy and muscular, but not overly tannic. The nose delivers spice, leather, tree bark, and marinade, while the round palate carries plum, berry, and vanilla. A larger-scale wine, but not monstrous or heavy. Good for drinking now. **87** *(4/1/2005)*

Giacomo Mori 1999 Sangiovese (Chianti) $15. An attractive retro label doesn't set you up for the very ripe fruit and almost Californian profile of this new-wave style Chianti. The black cherry, vanilla, and coffee flavors, soft tannins, and plenty of toasty oak comprise a satisfying package. It's a stylish, appealing wine that's drinking well right now. **87** *(4/1/2001)*

Giacomo Mori 2001 Castelrotto Sangiovese (Chianti) $30. Not exactly powerful, but subtle as it deals wintergreen, leather, and cedar in addition to black cherry. Quite oaky, but with enough blackberry, vanilla, and tannin to come across balanced. Still condensed and tight, with the majority of the wine resting in the center as opposed to on the edges. **88** *(4/1/2005)*

Giacomo Mori 1998 Castelrotto Sangiovese (Chianti) $26. As much as we like the retro package, this time the contents are just too one-dimensional. The heavily toasted oak over the narrow fruit from the '98 vintage reads as just that—toast, with vanilla and coconut shadings. Dry powdery tannins mark the taut finish. **83** *(4/1/2001)*

GIACOSA FRATELLI

Giacosa Fratelli 1997 Vigna Mandorlo Borolo Nebbiolo (Barolo) $NA. This is a dense, dark tannic wine with firm, huge tannins and wood flavors.

ITALY

Big, solid, and chunky, full of powerful, ripe, dark fruits and flavors of cocoa and licorice. It should develop well over the next 10 years, and then mature for another 10 at least. **93** —*R.V. (11/15/2002)*

GIANNI BRUNELLI

Gianni Brunelli 2001 Brunello (Brunello di Montalcino) $NA. There's something enticing but atypical to this wine that was received by our tasting panel with varying degrees of enthusiasm. Hints of barnyard or horsiness preface fruity black cherry, herbal or grassy notes, chocolate and plum. Firmly tannic with spice over a long finish. **89** *(4/1/2006)*

Gianni Brunelli 2000 Brunello (Brunello di Montalcino) $75. Plum, cranberry, and cherry—but not too much oak—make for a lovely nose, while the soft-ish palate is more round than blisteringly tannic. Midpalate and finishing flavors of espresso and chocolate seem oak-related, yet there's no woody resin flavors to detract from the purity. Meets all the standards of a fine wine without forcing it. **90** —*M.S. (7/1/2005)*

Gianni Brunelli 1999 Brunello (Brunello di Montalcino) $NA. Smooth and cool, with mellow cola and menthol aromas atop a full, rich palate. This wine pours on the berry, chocolate, and oak, and the finish is pure and ripe. It's a good one for sure, a full package with polish and pizzazz. **91** —*M.S. (6/1/2004)*

GIANNI DOGLIA

Gianni Doglia 2004 Moscato (Moscato d'Asti) $15. Bruno and Gianni Doglia oversee five hectares of vineyard with 20-year-old vines near Castagnole Lanze. This is interesting Moscato d'Asti, with unexpected hits of nutmeg, clove, gingerbread, and Indian spice backed by cream soda and lemon Fruit Loops. Thick and lathery in the mouth with layers of peach, jasmine, pear, and fig. **90 Editors' Choice** —*M.L. (12/15/2005)*

GIANNI VESCOVO

Gianni Vescovo 1997 Pinot Grigio (Isonzo del Friuli) $12. 86 *(8/1/1999)*

GIANNI VOERZIO

Gianni Voerzio 1996 Ciabot della Luna Barbera (Barbera d'Alba) $27. 88 *(4/1/2000)*

Gianni Voerzio 1998 La Serra Nebbiolo (Piedmont) $93. A powerful wine from this La Morra-based winery. There is rich fruit, with flavors of ripe acidity, dark plums, dried fruit, and tar. Underlying these fruit flavors are structured, dusty tannins. **91** —*R.V. (11/15/2002)*

GIANNINA

Giannina 2002 Vernaccia (Vernaccia di San Gimignano) $11. From Giannina di Puthod, this is Vernaccia at its near best. The laser-beam nose offers lemon-lime to the max, and that's followed by a round palate with fresh citrus and green apple flavors. It's weighty but upright, with a dry-as-a-bone crystalline finish. **89 Best Buy** —*M.S. (8/1/2004)*

Giannina 2002 Villa Laura Vernaccia (Vernaccia di San Gimignano) $15. Not great on the nose; aromas are of corn, applesauce, and cheddar cheese. However, the wine does a bit better on the palate. It's round, modestly flavorful, and features midlevel acidity. **83** —*M.S. (8/1/2004)*

GIGI ROSSO

Gigi Rosso 1997 Cascina Rocca Giovino Barbera (Barbera d'Alba) $12. 87 Best Buy *(4/1/2000)*

Gigi Rosso 1998 Moncolombetto Dolcetto (Dolcetto d'Alba) $14. 87 *(4/1/2000)*

Gigi Rosso 1999 Arione Nebbiolo (Barolo) $48. Deeply earthy on the nose, with tobacco and dried fruits mixing with saddle leather, tar, and hints of citrus. Richly tannic, this wine deserves all the time you can give it; try in 2010 or beyond. **89** *(4/2/2004)*

GILIA

Gilia 2004 Pinot Grigio (Delle Venezie) $8. A touch of anise and melon on the dry nose. Distant pear on the palate with apple juice toward the finish. A touch metallic and more empty than full. **82** *(2/1/2006)*

GINI

Gini 2000 Sorai Chardonnay (Delle Venezie) $24. A wood-aged Chardonnay from the hills above Soave, this is rich, honeyed from the malolactic fermentation, and full of tropical fruit flavors. It is rich and delicious, but also well structured. **89** —*R.V. (7/1/2003)*

Gini 1999 La Frosca Soave Classico Superiore Garganega (Soave) $18. 90 Editors' Choice —*M.N. (12/31/2000)*

Gini 1998 La Frosca Soave Classico Superiore Garganega (Soave) $18. 89 *(4/1/2000)*

Gini 2003 Villa Fortuna Sangiovese (Chianti) $9. Warm, baked, and a bit vegetal, with soft plum and berry flavors. Herbal throughout, with decent feel but dry, simple flavors. If you don't mind a touch of tomato, this wine will strike a chord. Otherwise, it may not work for you. **83** —*M.S. (10/1/2006)*

Gini 1999 Villa Fortunato Sangiovese (Chianti) $7. Tart cherry aromas and flavors are graced by herb and leather accents in this welterweight. It has good balance and the finish is dry and even. Drinks nicely in its youth and should improve short-term. **86 Best Buy** *(4/1/2001)*

Gini 2002 Classico White Blend (Soave) $10. A fresh, crisp style of Soave, brimming with green plum and light acidity. It has concentration and a light touch in equal measure. **88** —*R.V. (7/1/2003)*

Gini 2001 Contrada Salavrenza Vecchie Vigne White Blend (Soave Classico Superiore) $24. From a single vineyard's old vines, here is a full, very rich wine, packed with flavors of almonds and ripe nuts. Layers of wood give it a toasty character, but never one that dominates the quality fruit. **91** —*R.V. (7/1/2003)*

Gini 2001 La Frosca Classico White Blend (Soave) $18. From a single vineyard, this exemplary Soave has great intensity and concentration, with flavors of peppers and ripe, green fruits. The wine's long fermentation wine gives it structure and great extraction of flavor. **89** —*R.V. (7/1/2003)*

Gini 2000 Soave Classico Superiore White Blend (Soave) $12. This lively, affordable Soave has opening and closing notes of apple, pear, and wet stones. The wine is nicely poised—it has crisp acidity, yet a smooth, evenly textured mouthfeel. It finishes bright and long. This would pair well with a shrimp risotto. **88 Best Buy** —*M.N. (9/1/2001)*

GIOVELLO

Giovello 2004 Pinot Grigio (Veneto) $10. Peach, apricot, melon, and pineapple add fruity sweetness to the nose, but leave room for a defined mineral quality. There's crisp acidity in the mouth, with an almond-like finish. **86 Best Buy** —*M.L. (6/1/2006)*

GIRIBALDI

Giribaldi 1997 Barbera (Barbera d'Asti) $10. 84 *(4/1/2000)*

Giribaldi 1999 Barbera (Barbera d'Alba Superiore) $11. The nose is ripe, bordering on over-ripe. There are scents of fading flowers mixed with raisins and licorice. The chewy palate is on the big side, with loads of plum and cherry fruit. The best part of this wine is a pleasant smoothness on the palate; the edges are round and not the least bit hard. **87 Best Buy** —*M.S. (11/15/2002)*

Giribaldi NV Selezioni Rodellisa Dolce Brachetto (Piedmont) $15. The note on the label, "Nel tentative di catturare l'attenzione," ("looking to catch your eye") rightly refers to this elegantly crafted Brachetto. In store for your senses is a package of watermelon, raspberry, caramel apple, apricot, strawberry, toast, and cranberry aromas and flavors. A fine complement to an intimate evening. **88 Best Buy** —*K.F. (12/31/2002)*

Giribaldi 2000 Cortese (Gavi) $16. Light, clean, and overall quite nice. There's nothing particularly distinctive about the aromas, but they are fresh and full. Good acids and some white pepper nuance balance flavors of melon, apple, and pear. Even a bit of green herb shows up on the zesty finish. Not a complex wine, but it is tasty. **87** —*M.S. (12/15/2003)*

Giribaldi 1997 Dolcetto (Dolcetto d'Alba) $14. 85 *(4/1/2000)*

Giribaldi 2000 Vigna Cason Dolcetto (Dolcetto d'Alba) $14. A nose of carob, licorice, and earth carries a touch of green bean. The palate is grapey and sweet, especially at first. What some might call a cloying finish, others might find rich and chewy. Overall it's a dicey but hedonistic mix of sticky black fruit, prune, and tannins. **85** —*M.S. (12/15/2003)*

Giribaldi 1999 Nebbiolo (Barolo) $39. Supple and oaky, this modern-style Barolo boasts ample plum fruit that's backed by cinnamon, vanilla, and toast. A solid restaurant Barolo, not needing years to reach its peak. **86** —*J.C. (11/15/2004)*

Giribaldi 1998 Nebbiolo (Barbaresco) $28. Faint orangey-brown hints at the edges indicate this classically-styled wine is just starting to mature. It's tasty, with deep, pruney Nebbiolo fruit sporting tobacco and spice accents. The mouthfeel is lean and elegant, and the fruit-to-acid balance excellent. Finishes long, with good, even tannins. A very impressive normale (village wine). Drink this from 2004–2010. **91** —*M.M. (11/15/2002)*

Giribaldi 1997 Nebbiolo (Barolo) $30. Aromas of slow-roasted tomato and dill pickles are stimulating. Cherry and roasted corn flavors show more red fruit than dark fruit, for a wine that finishes with smooth, non-aggressive tannins. **90** —*C.S. (11/15/2002)*

Giribaldi 1998 Riserva Nebbiolo (Barolo) $37. Slightly herbal or floral notes mark the nose of this wine, layered over a core of rich milk chocolate, black cherries, and hints of roasted meat or tar. The extra aging has imparted a creamy, supple mouthfeel. One reason we liked this wine so much was its easy accessibility; not all Barolo has to have massive tannins. Drink now–2010. **92 Editors' Choice** *(4/2/2004)*

GIRLAN

Girlan 2004 Pinot Grigio (Alto Adige) $15. Make sure you serve this wine well-chilled, otherwise the high alcohol masks the more delicate aromas. Slightly copperish in color, this Pinot Grigio does boast a refreshing, long finish. **84** —*M.L. (6/1/2006)*

Girlan 2004 Filadonna Pinot Grigio (Valdadige) $14. This pinkish-colored wine boasts toasted almond, exotic spice, and eucalyptus oil. On the palate, the wine is viscous and spicy, with mustard-green flavors. **86** —*M.L. (2/1/2006)*

Girlan 2004 Filadonna Pinot Grigio (Alto Adige) $15. Better than this producer's Valdadige Pinot Grigio thanks to its delineated crispness, fruitiness, and green apple flavors. A straight shooter that's fresh and citrusy in the mouth. **87** —*M.L. (2/1/2006)*

GIROLAMO DORIGO

Girolamo Dorigo 2000 Chardonnay (Colli Orientali del Friuli) $35. A rich, aromatic, honeyed style of Chardonnay, with 100% malolactic fermentation to increase the softness and sweet wood flavors. Soft peach flavors increase the tropical intensity of the wine. **87** —*R.V. (7/1/2003)*

Girolamo Dorigo 2001 Ronc di Juri Sauvignon Blanc (Colli Piacentini) $35. A single-vineyard Sauvignon from high-density vineyards in eastern Friuli. The wine has some wood aging, which shows through the crisp, fresh fruit, green fruit, and hazelnut flavors. **85** —*R.V. (7/1/2003)*

Girolamo Dorigo 1999 Ronc di Juri Sauvignon Blanc (Friuli) $37. **82** *(1/1/2004)*

GIULIO FERRARI

Giulio Ferrari 1994 Riserva del Fondatore Chardonnay (Trento) $75. Careful selection of grapes goes into this wine—considered the grandfather of Italian sparking wine (and for very good reason). You'd be hard pressed to find another bubbly as well-balanced and refreshing in the mouth. Green apples are the preface and nutty vanilla tones pop up on the finish. **92** —*M.L. (12/15/2004)*

GIUNTI

Giunti 2001 Il Monte Riserva Sangiovese (Chianti) $25. Dark and intense, with a hint of paste or glue that eventually yields to leather, tree bark, and earth. Quite rich, with plum, baked berry, and coffee making for a manly flavor profile. Drinkable now, even with its mouth-coating tannins. **88** *(4/1/2005)*

GIUSEPPE CORTESE

Giuseppe Cortese 1998 Trifolera Dolcetto (Dolcetto d'Alba) $15. **88** *(4/1/2000)*

Giuseppe Cortese 2000 Rabajá Nebbiolo (Barbaresco) $45. Scents of warm, roasted fruit emerge from the glass, along with notes of molasses, soy sauce, and leather. Prunes and dates in the mouth, nestled in soft tannins. Drink now–2015. **89** *(4/2/2004)*

GORETTI

Goretti 2000 Le Mura Saracene Sagrantino (Sagrantino di Montefalco) $NA. Imagine being inside a gingerbread house and breath in slowly. Christmas spice, nutmeg, clove, cinnamon, and everything nice shape a divine aromatic ensemble. The structure is solid but not overwhelming. Put aside for this holiday season and drink by the fireplace. **90 Editors' Choice** —*M.L. (9/1/2005)*

GRADIS'CIUTTA

Gradis'ciutta 2000 Chardonnay (Collio) $13. Butterscotch Lifesavers with a tinny, metallic finish. **80** —*J.C. (7/1/2003)*

Gradis'ciutta 2000 del Bratinus Bianco White Blend (Collio) $13. **81** —*J.C. (7/1/2003)*

GRASSO FRATELLI

Grasso Fratelli 1999 Nebbiolo (Barbaresco) $30. Cherries and dark chocolate mingle in this tightly coiled, muscular wine that needs 5–8 years to strut its stuff. Anise notes add complexity, while the finish is long and filled with firm but ripe tannins. **89** *(4/2/2004)*

Grasso Fratelli 1999 Bricco Spessa Nebbiolo (Barbaresco) $36. Features a complex and intriguing nose, filled with aromas of graham crackers, toast, and hints of cherries and herbs, but it's a bit grapey and unformed on the palate, with a loose structure that doesn't offer the structure expected of a top-flight Barbaresco. It's good and ready to drink, just doesn't fit the classic mold. **89** *(4/2/2004)*

GRU

Gru 2003 Montepulciano (Montepulciano d'Abruzzo) $7. Lean and short on stature, with rubbery, spicy aromas jazzing up what would otherwise not register. Tastes tangy and a bit reduced, with raspberry and cherry flavors. Runs thin and a bit sour. **81** —*M.S. (10/1/2006)*

GUALDO DEL RE

Gualdo del Re 1994 Val Di Cornia Suvereto Riserva Sangiovese (Barolo) $27. **88** —*J.S. (5/1/1999)*

GUARNIERI

Guarnieri 1999 Le Masse di Greve Sangiovese (Chianti Classico) $19. Opaque in color and deep in the nose; based on this you hope for a bit more once the wine hits your palate. But it's hard as nails, with tannins that strike like a sledgehammer. The tannic structure is monstrous, and the feel of those tannins overwhelms the tasty black cherry and black olive flavors. **84** —*M.S. (12/31/2002)*

Guarnieri 1998 Le Masse di Greve Sangiovese (Chianti Classico) $19. Smooth, with a slightly barnyardy element in the midst of the creamy cherry and oak nose. The fruit on the palate is tart black cherry; the texture smooth, silky. **85** *(4/1/2001)*

GUASTI CLEMENTE

Guasti Clemente 2004 Moscato (Moscato d'Asti) $12. Larger bubbles dot a delicately colored wine bursting with crisp peach, green apple, figs, kiwi, wax, and a frothy bubble bath smell. Creamy in the mouth yet with enough acidity to fuel a zesty, long-lasting finish. **87** —*M.L. (12/15/2005)*

GUERRIERI RIZZARDI

Guerrieri Rizzardi 1998 Red Blend (Amarone della Valpolicella Classico) $70. Rustic and a bit sour, with rhubarb and pie cherry. But there's also a sweet, caramelized element as well. Overall it's just not that focused or charming. **84** *(11/1/2005)*

Guerrieri Rizzardi 1997 Red Blend (Amarone della Valpolicella Classico) $59. The nose starts out with cedar and lemon notes before it shifts to dried stone fruits and strawberry. The flavors run sweet, emphasizing

ITALY

candied red fruit, most of all cherry. The finish is drying and mildly medicinal, but not so much that it gets in the way. **87** *(5/1/2003)*

Guerrieri Rizzardi 1998 Calcarole Red Blend (Amarone della Valpolicella Classico) $95. Funky and green on the nose, with blasts of peach pit, mint, rhubarb, and spice. A fair amount of fruit graces the mouth, but still there remains some green flavors. The mouthfeel, meanwhile, is grabby. Overall it's fine but is missing some components. **86** *(11/1/2005)*

Guerrieri Rizzardi 1995 Calcarole Red Blend (Amarone della Valpolicella Classico) $82. If you enjoy a mildly barnyardy wine, say, something akin to a French Syrah, this should appeal to you. The nose is earthy for sure. The palate is dense and brooding, and a tad bit bitter. But there's also a load of leather and tannin, which give it texture and some positive rusticity. **87** *(5/1/2003)*

Guerrieri Rizzardi 2000 Estate Bottled Classico Superiore Red Blend (Bardolino) $12. A whiff of ballpark hot dogs is about all you can pull from the dull nose. This wine is watery thin, with just the minimum in terms of cherry fruit and body. The finish is tight-grained and hard. Whether food might save it remains to be seen. **81** *(5/1/2003)*

Guerrieri Rizzardi 2000 Pojega Red Blend (Valpolicella Classico Superiore) $15. Some rubber and grassy notes combine on the nose to cover up what strawberry fruit there is. The palate is rather sweet, dealing mostly candied cherry fruit. And the finish is tight and stemmy, which creates an overly tight feel across the palate. **82** *(5/1/2003)*

Guerrieri Rizzardi 2001 Tacchetto Estate Bottled Classico Red Blend (Bardolino) $15. Some pepper and cherry defines the nose. More pepper and spice are detectable on the sharp, lean palate. On the finish, dried cherries and plum skins make for astringency. Persistency is it's quality, but with that comes some persistent roughness. **82** *(5/1/2003)*

GUICCIARDINI STROZZI

Guicciardini Strozzi 2000 Millanni 994 Red Blend (Toscana) $55. A high-priced wine that seems to have never found its prime. It's heavily oaked, which is as apparent as the char, coffee and lemon on the nose. The palate is monstrously tart, with pie cherry and red raspberry. And it's tannic. Not flawed; just not very pleasant for what it costs. **84** —*M.S. (9/1/2006)*

Guicciardini Strozzi 2001 Selvascura Red Blend (Toscana) $29. A super solid super Tuscan that mostly blends Merlot and Colorino with nice results. Berry marmalade with hints of marzipan, cinnamon and vanilla work the nose, backed by tangy but serious red fruit. This is a very drinkable wine that's ready to go today. **90** —*M.S. (9/1/2006)*

Guicciardini Strozzi 2003 Titolato Sangiovese (Chianti Colli Senesi) $10. To the nose it's simultaneously soft and sweet while also smoky, leathery, and earthy. This one gives a little of this and that; the fruit is medium and bright, with full supporting tannins. But it also pours on the red fruit in doses, meaning it's snappy and sharp. **88 Best Buy** *(4/1/2005)*

GULFI

Gulfi 2000 Nero Bufaleffi Nero d'Avola (Sicilia) $33. Wild aromas of roasted meats and dried spices mingle with dark berries and plum. It's full-bodied and tannic, but the tannins are soft enough to make the wine approachable now. Bears a resemblance to Châteauneuf-du-Pape in its warm climate, untamed flavors and richness. **91** —*J.C. (10/1/2003)*

Gulfi 2000 Nero Ibleo Nero d'Avola (Sicilia) $16. Smoky and pungent, blending notes of earth, toast, and plum. It's lush, full, and soft, caressing the mouth with ripe tannins. Lacks a bit of complexity compared to Gulfi's single-vineyard wines, but is an outstanding value. **90 Editors' Choice** —*J.C. (10/1/2003)*

Gulfi 2000 Nero Maccari Nero d'Avola (Sicilia) $33. The aromas of clove, plum, and earth are rustic but attractive. On the palate, spices and earth combine in a rich, full-bodied wine that blends in just enough red berries on the long finish. Should prove to be long-lived, but the tannins are soft enough to make it drinkable now. **92** —*J.C. (10/1/2003)*

Gulfi 2002 Nerobaronj Nero d'Avola (Sicilia) $40. Gulfi strikes again with overt aromas, this time settling on bread crust, cookie dough, and pressed currant berry. The wine is broad and intense, and leaves a long-lasting impression in the mouth. **87** —*M.L. (7/1/2006)*

Gulfi 2002 Nerobufaleffj Nero d'Avola (Sicilia) $40. Cherry, charcoal, graphite, and toasted bread crust emerge on the nose. This intense and ripe wine is ready to drink now; pair with honey-smoked ham or pork dishes. **87** —*M.L. (7/1/2006)*

Gulfi 1999 Neroibleo Nero d'Avola (Sicilia) $12. Nero d'Avola at its best. Aromas of fleshy plums and ripe, juicy blackberries join toasty oak. In the mouth, bright cherry flavors swim with chocolate, coffee, and abounding oak. The finish is long and full. Made to drink now, but will last 3-5 years. **90 Best Buy** —*C.S. (5/1/2002)*

Gulfi 2003 Nerojbleo Nero d'Avola (Sicilia) $18. Ruby-colored and intense, this is one of Gulfi's many takes on Nero d'Avola; ripe blackberry and blueberry fruit, pistachio nut and earth tones sum up the nose. Concentrated and thick in the mouth with a tart note on the finish. **89** —*M.L. (7/1/2006)*

Gulfi 2002 Nerosanlorenzj Nero d'Avola (Sicilia) $40. Wine doesn't get more intense than this: Peanut butter, Nutella, cookie dough, bread crust, and dried berry sum up the biggest peaks in the bouquet. Flavors include clove and toast. Will overpower most foods. **88** —*M.L. (7/1/2006)*

Gulfi 2001 Rosso Ibleo Nero d'Avola (Sicilia) $11. Starts off slowly, with some slightly reductive, sulfury notes that clear up quickly, opening into bittersweet chocolate and raspberry notes tinged with leather and earth. Creamy, mouth-filling, and with a long finish. **88 Best Buy** —*J.C. (10/1/2003)*

Gulfi 2005 Rossojbleo Nero d'Avola (Sicilia) $15. This wine is a hair away from being too cooked and offers very ripe notes of prune and berry preserves. It's spicy and tight on the finish with mild bitterness in the tannins. **86** —*M.L. (7/1/2006)*

Gulfi 2000 Caricanti White Blend (Sicilia) $22. An interesting blend of Carricante and Albanello, with pungent, smoky aromas that also bear some resemblance to brie cheese mold. Flavors are reminiscent of apple, melon, and pear. **85** —*J.C. (10/1/2003)*

Gulfi 2004 Carjcanti White Blend (Sicilia) $20. The nose is slightly muted and mineral but does open to peach, melon, almond paste, and supple apple and peach aromas. Lively marzipan flavors appear in the mouth. **85** —*M.L. (7/1/2006)*

Gulfi 2001 Valcanziria White Blend (Sicilia) $11. This blend of Chardonnay, Carricante, and Albanello is partially barrel-fermented, imparting cinnamon and toast to go with ripe peach flavors. Finishes dry and slightly nutty. **88 Best Buy** —*J.C. (10/1/2003)*

Gulfi 2005 Valcanzjria White Blend (Sicilia) $15. This is a very likable white wine with intense notes of marzipan, walnut, passion fruit, and freshly minced garden herbs. It offers a nutty texture in the mouth accompanied by more almond-like flavors on the finish. **86** —*M.L. (7/1/2006)*

H. LUN WINERY

H. Lun Winery 2004 Pinot Grigio (Alto Adige) $16. A clean and simple wine defined by crisp grapefruit and honeysuckle notes. Some of the appeal waned in the mouth because of its lean and neutral appearance. **84** —*M.L. (6/1/2006)*

HAUNER

Hauner 1999 Agave Red Blend (Sicilia) $15. Our tasters had varying impressions of this wine's quality, but all agreed it tasted somewhat awkward at present—the cherry-berry fruit vying with horsey, leathery components. It's big, burly, and tannic, but while some reviewers felt it had the stuffing to develop positively, others felt the fruit would dry up long before the tannins softened. **86** *(5/1/2002)*

I CASALI SELECTION

I Casali Selection 2004 Pinot Grigio (Friuli Grave) $14. It's hard to imagine a wine more floral than this. Florist shop aromas include roses and lilies but leave room for peach and pear, too. Spicy and tart in the mouth. **87** —*M.L. (2/1/2006)*

I FEUDI DI ROMANS

I Feudi di Romans 2004 Pinot Grigio (Isonzo del Friuli) $14. A very linear and clean wine with a strong mineral component that would do absolute wonders accompanied by salmon croquettes, asparagus canapés or fish soup. **87** —*M.L. (6/1/2006)*

I GIUSTI E ZANZA

I Giusti e Zanza 2003 Dulcamara Cabernet Blend (Toscana) $55. Chocolate fudge, vanilla, black cherry, cassis, and blueberry essence waft from the surface of this deeply extracted, corpulent ruby-colored wine. Modern and beautifully-executed, you'll also pick up well-integrated wood tones and refreshing herbal notes. A Merlot component is blended in for softness and smoothness. **92** —*M.L. (9/1/2006)*

I Giusti e Zanza 1999 Belcore Sangiovese (Toscana) $24. This relative newcomer from near Pisa is three-fourths Sangiovese and the remainder Merlot, and the mix is delightful. Black plum aromas are hardened by the background scents of tar and leather, while soft, smooth tannins allow for a chocolaty, soft mouthfeel that steals the show. Rich, sweet, and smooth. **89** —*M.S. (8/1/2002)*

I Giusti e Zanza 1999 Dulcamara Sangiovese (Toscana) $55. A persistent ripe cheesy aroma is the only thing that mars this Cabernet-based big brother to Belcore. There's ample black fruit to the palate and a full blast of espresso on the smooth finish. It's young now, but already it's opening up. Maybe the funky aromatics will subside with additional bottle age. **88** —*M.S. (8/1/2002)*

I VIGNAIOLI DI SANTO STEFANO

I Vignaioli di Santo Stefano 2004 Moscato (Moscato d'Asti) $20. One of the best recognized Italian Moscato d'Astis in the U.S. and for good reason. Young winemaking brothers with I Vignaioli di Santo Stefano work under the guidance of Piedmont's historic Ceretto to produce a lusciously sweet semi-sparkler with vivid white flowers and stone fruits. A correct and consistent wine year after year. **88** —*M.L. (12/15/2005)*

IL CIRCO

Il Circo 2001 La Violetta Uva di Troia (Castel del Monte) $15. So Randall Grahm of Bonny Doon finally got to Southern Italy, and thus comes this berry and licorice red. It's all about color, zest, forward fruit, and tannins. Lots of backbone and boldness, and some chocolaty substance to the finish. **88** —*M.S. (10/1/2004)*

Il Circo 2000 La Violetta Uva di Troia (Castel del Monte) $15. Uva di Troia is the name of the grape, and it was grown in Puglia, in Italy's heel. It's an old grape that dependably produces a ripe, rustic wine, dry and smooth, and rich in tannins and fruit. Randall Grahm attempts to bring finesse, with some success. **86** —*S.H. (1/1/2002)*

IL CONTE

Il Conte 2002 Marinus Red Blend (Rosso Piceno) $14. Violet in color, as if it were berry syrup. And that same thick, oozing character is noticeable on the sweet, gooey nose as well as the extracted, low-acid palate. Richness and sweetness are not in question; but overall balance is. Flavorful but a hard pill to swallow. **83** —*M.S. (7/1/2005)*

Il Conte 2000 Zipolo Red Blend (Marche) $24. Menthol and eucalyptus notes to the nose indicate fairly heavy oak, which is confirmed by a latent blast of bacon fat. Blackberry, milk chocolate, and resin flavors on the palate together resemble Raisinets. Cola and chocolate notes round out the chewy finish. **85** —*M.S. (7/1/2005)*

Il Conte 2003 Donello Sangiovese (Marche) $13. Dark in color, with sappy raisin and blackberry jam aromas. While it runs a bit reduced across the tongue, there's still more than enough quality plum flavors to save the day. Not a ton of nuance and subtleties here; it's more about ripe, dark fruit and some earth. **85** —*M.S. (7/1/2005)*

Il Conte 2003 Aurato White Blend (Falerio del Colli Ascolani) $10. Shows a certain over-ripe sweetness on the nose, but also some toffee, wheat bread, and candied fruit. Lemon, apple, and almond flavors make for a full palate, which carries an equally full and creamy feel. Quite ripe and a bit sunbaked, but still a respectable white wine from central Italy. **86 Best Buy** —*M.S. (7/1/2005)*

Il Conte d'Alba NV Moscato (Moscato d'Asti) $10. I like this greenish-hued wine for its very linear and sharp mineral, graphite, green apple, and lemon rind aromas. Those defined fragrances make it a perfect pair with cream- or butter-based desserts. **87 Editors' Choice** —*M.L. (12/15/2005)*

IL FALCHETTO

Il Falchetto 2004 Ciombi (Not Imported) Moscato (Moscato d'Asti) $NA. Pretty, delicate, and foamy, this dessert wine seems sweet and fruity, yet elegant. Would pair best with desserts with higher acidity such as kiwi tart or fresh fruit salad. **87** —*M.L. (12/15/2005)*

Il Falchetto 2004 Tenuta del Fant Moscato (Moscato d'Asti) $17. Delicate and feminine with tight peach and apricot weaved into an attractive aromatic embroidery. Extremely dense lather builds up each time you swirl your glass, making this wine perfect for dried or baked desserts. **86** —*M.L. (12/15/2005)*

IL FEUDUCCIO DI S. MARIA D'ORNI

Il Feuduccio Di S. Maria D'Orni 2001 Montepulciano (Montepulciano d'Abruzzo) $29. Who knew that Montepulciano could be brought to such heights? This is a special, uncommon wine. It's ripe, from a great vintage, and it is shining brightly now but will hold for another three to five years at least. Full of black cherry, berry skins, and generous but balanced tannins. Perfect with osso buco or rack of lamb. **90 Editors' Choice** —*M.S. (10/1/2006)*

Il Feuduccio Di S. Maria D'Orni 1999 Margae Montepulciano (Montepulciano d'Abruzzo) $75. Higher up the pecking order than Il Feuduccio's others, this wine is heavily extracted and a bit raisiny. Late-harvest comes to mind, although it's far more fresh and dry than that. Still, the flavor profile is heavily slanted toward raisin and prune, while the stocky palate is soft and lush. Drink now. **90** —*M.S. (10/1/2006)*

Il Feuduccio Di S. Maria D'Orni 1999 Ursonia Montepulciano (Montepulciano d'Abruzzo) $39. Satisfying and delicious at every point. The bouquet is lovely; it delivers dense plum fruit, chili-like spice, and mounds of wet earth. The palate is pure blackberry and dark plum, and it finishes smooth as silk, with just enough coarseness to add texture and grit. Firm but not hard. A definite winner from Abruzzo. Drink by the end of 2004. **91** —*M.S. (11/15/2003)*

Il Feuduccio Di S. Maria D'Orni 1998 Ursonia Montepulciano (Montepulciano d'Abruzzo) $31. Like the '99 normale, this wine doesn't smell or taste like standard fare Montepulciano. It has more character and quality, and it's entirely rich, oaky, and stylish. Modern in every sense of the word, with plum, blackberry, and bitter chocolate flavors. The finish is smooth, solid, and complete, and the mouthfeel sizzles courtesy of fine acids and light-framed tannins. **90** —*M.S. (11/15/2003)*

Il Feuduccio Di S. Maria D'Orni 2003 White Blend (Colline Teatine) $18. Harsh and oaky at first, with astringent aromas. Ultra-lemony and singular in its focus. The blend is an odd mix of Falanghina, Greco, Sauvignon Blanc, and something called Pecorino (no, not the cheese), and all together it's sour. Barely acceptable. **80** —*M.S. (7/1/2005)*

IL GRILLESINO

Il Grillesino 1999 Sangiovese (Morellino di Scansano) $14. Lean, spicy aromas set up a smoky, plum-filled palate that's probably a bit too toasty for its own good. The body weight here is moderate, but there's lots of length to the smoke-filled, oak-driven finish. **86** —*M.S. (8/1/2002)*

Il Grillesino 1999 Ceccante Sangiovese (Toscana) $43. Super-ripe, with vivacious, youthful plum and berry fruit. This Sangiovese/ Cabernet Sauvignon blend from near Scansano is solid and sassy, with lots of spunk. The finish is long and very fruity, with lively tannins. It can be drunk now, but it could probably use a couple of years to fully come together. **90** —*M.S. (8/1/2002)*

IL MARRONETO

Il Marroneto 2001 Brunello (Brunello di Montalcino) $NA. This Brunello lacked aromatic intensity compared to the others. Dig deep down to draw out berry flavors, smoke, pipe tobacco, leather, and vanilla. A juicy finish and nice, medium structure yield more tobacco and vanilla in the mouth. **87** *(4/1/2006)*

IL NURAGHE

Il Nuraghe 1999 Chio Red Blend (Cannonau di Sardegna) $22. Very intense, with root beer, leather, and dried fruit aromas. The full allotment of cherry and plum skin makes for a flavorful yet dry palate, one that's far more precise than it is fat or chewy. With a long, lean finish that's one part pepper and another part tangy red fruit, this wine can match many foods with no problem. **88**—*M.S. (12/15/2003)*

Il Nuraghe 2000 Colle Moresco Red Blend (Monica di Sardegna) $12. Basic aromas of cherry and orange rind are reserved and proper, and at the bottom of the bouquet is a bit of tire rubber. Flavors of cherry, cranberry, and pepper are carried by lively acidity. This is fresh, quaffable and dry; it isn't a packed-to-the-brim wine, but with food it'll work nicely. **87**—*M.S. (12/15/2003)*

Il Nuraghe 1998 Nabui Red Blend (Monica di Sardegna) $21. The nose is challenging at first: There's tree bark, sarsaparilla, lots of spicy oak, and even some barnyard. Expressive cherry, plum, and blackberry flavors peer out from underneath a cover of creamy oak that carries onto the finish. It's quite svelte and racy for a ripe wine, and everything seems to be firmly in place. **89**—*M.S. (12/15/2003)*

Il Nuraghe 2000 San Bernardino Red Blend (Monica di Sardegna) $15. Very cheesy in the nose, and that scent of English cheddar just won't go away. Otherwise, the wine has some starchy tannins propping up stewy plum and blackberry flavors. The finish of bitter chocolate and molasses is heavy and lacking in purity. **83**—*M.S. (1/1/2004)*

Il Nuraghe 2001 Vignaruja Red Blend (Cannonau di Sardegna) $15. Plenty of fruit is on display. The nose is packed with earthy cherry and leather, while the palate is developed, with pure cherry and blackberry flavors. Here's a complete wine with a light frame and present but subtle tannins. It's easygoing as it makes the grade at all checkpoints. **87**—*M.S. (12/15/2003)*

IL PALAGIONE

Il Palagione 2002 Hydra Vernaccia (Vernaccia di San Gimignano) $14. One look shows a heavy tint, and an initial nosing reveals burnt, aggressive notes that seem barrel-driven. With time the nose smoothes out, and in the mouth there's banana, mango, and papaya. A bit heavy and sticky on the palate, and arguably a case of more not being more. **85**—*M.S. (8/1/2004)*

IL PALAZZINO

Il Palazzino 1998 Sangiovese (Chianti Classico) $18. The ripe, lean, smooth fruit is complemented by tobacco and cedar accents. Has a refined feel and classic tartness to the cherry flavors. Tight now, the full tannins on the finish can use a year or two to resolve, but handsome tar and licorice accents already show, and the solid components will knit themselves together well with a little time. **90 Editors' Choice** *(4/1/2001)*

Il Palazzino 1997 Grosso Sanese Riserva Sangiovese (Chianti Classico) $35. Vibrant dark cherry is handsomely balanced against toasty oak in this elegant bottling. The solid fruit wears coffee accents and a mineral note; bright acidity keeps the fruit and palate lively. Finishes long with tart cherry flavors and solid, even tannins. With the new DOCG laws, this former Super Tuscan Vino da Tavola is now a Chianti Classico Riserva. **90** *(4/1/2001)*

IL PALAZZONE

Il Palazzone 2001 Brunello (Brunello di Montalcino) $85. This wine nails that difficult spot between finesse and power. Cranberry and cherry, leather, tobacco, earth, herbs, rose petal, and mineral or graphite add texture and complexity. A silky wine with a medium structure from a winery owned by AOL Time Warner chief executive Dick Parsons. **92** *(4/1/2006)*

Il Palazzone 2000 Brunello (Brunello di Montalcino) $85. Excellent from the initial nosing through the polished palate and onto the hedonistic finish. This wine from the estate of Time Warner chairman Richard Parsons offers robust aromas of forest floor and black cherry, followed by a sleek, silky palate. Creamy and sweet on the finish, with chocolate and vanilla in spades. **92**—*M.S. (7/1/2005)*

Il Palazzone 1999 Riserva Brunello (Brunello di Montalcino) $95. A gorgeous wine with amazing texture and integration. The nose and feel are so soft and silky, and the fruit is as expressive as Sangiovese gets. Plush and royal, with perfect tannic structure, smiling acidity, and smoky shadings. A dream in the glass, with meters of depth. **96 Editors' Choice**—*M.S. (7/1/2005)*

IL PICCOLO BORGO

IL Piccolo Borgo 2002 Sangiovese (Chianti Classico) $16. Quite good for an '02, even if the nose is so heavily toasted that it smells like a hickory pit with bacon on the grill. Tastes of plum, black cherry, and vanilla, with spice and tobacco on the medium-length finish. Good mouthfeel with proper acidity is a bonus. **87**—*M.S. (10/1/2006)*

IL POGGIOLINO

Il Poggiolino 1998 Riserva Sangiovese (Chianti Classico) $25. **87**—*R.V. (8/1/2002)*

IL POGGIONE

Il Poggione 2001 Brunello (Brunello di Montalcino) $62. Vibrant ruby color with dark berry and a ripe, sweet edge followed by menthol notes. There's a sour and mildly acetic note and powerful, raw tannins that seem very sharp against the wine's medium weight. A nervous wine that could benefit from a few more years in the bottle. **89** *(4/1/2006)*

Il Poggione 2000 Brunello (Brunello di Montalcino) $60. Enticing and attractive, with no weaknesses. The nose deals all the plum, black cherry, and crafty oak that you'd expect, while the palate is snappy and attentive, not fat or creamy. Not flashy but professional; a solid and controlled Brunello. **91**—*M.S. (7/1/2005)*

Il Poggione 1999 Brunello (Brunello di Montalcino) $62. This excellent wine represents a model for straddling the line between the past and current styles of Brunello. The cherry and raspberry fruit gets a kick from oak-based notes of charcoal and vanilla. Hold for at least four years, if possible. **93**—*M.S. (6/1/2004)*

Il Poggione 1998 Brunello (Brunello di Montalcino) $63. Well-oaked and woodsy, with some earthy nuances as well as scents of campfire and rubber. This is a youngster with aggressive tannins and sharp edges. With a bit of time it'll soften, leaving a top-flight wine with cherry, citrus rind, and a hint of sweet oak. **90** *(11/15/2003)*

Il Poggione 1997 Brunello (Brunello di Montalcino) $60. A firm, classic, upstanding wine, with dry, firm fruit tannins that support generous ripe fruit. Aromas of violets and toasty wood are followed on the palate with flavors of herbs and dark chocolate. The finish is concentrated, firmly dry with a good backbone of rich fruit. Age for at least 10 years before drinking. **91**—*R.V. (8/1/2002)*

Il Poggione 1999 Riserva Brunello (Brunello di Montalcino) $80. Strong as a cement block, with aromas of charcoal, leather, and intense plum/berry. Still, in the mouth it's luscious. In addition, there's a sublime spice element playing in the background that only makes it more complete. Finishes with the essence of fruit cake and marzipan. A pleasure. **94**—*M.S. (7/1/2005)*

Il Poggione 1997 Riserva Brunello (Brunello di Montalcino) $71. Loaded with pepper, hard spice, and leather, but there's also plenty of bursting red fruit to this traditional Brunello. With every minute it's open the wine evolves: At first it's sweet and forward, but with time it turns earthy and leathery, and ultimately it gets very tight and brooding. Full acids, hammer-like tannins, and major-league structure say hold for a minimum of six more years. **92 Cellar Selection**—*M.S. (11/15/2003)*

Il Poggione 2002 Sangiovese (Rosso di Montalcino) $28. Once again, this is one of the pace-setters for Rosso. The quality and complexity are great, considering the adverse conditions of the '02 harvest. That aside, the wine shines with red fruit, medium tannins, and a graceful finish. Super with food. **90**—*M.S. (6/1/2004)*

Il Poggione 1999 Sangiovese (Rosso di Montalcino) $19. Year in and year out this estate leads the way with so-called Baby Brunello. And this version may be one of the best yet. A pure-fruit nose sets things up and the palate, redolent with fresh raspberry, leather, and spice, doesn't disappoint. It's both deep and light, medium-bodied, but still pretty full. **90** —*M.S. (8/1/2002)*

Il Poggione 1999 San Leopoldo Sangiovese (Toscana) $41. This blend of 50% Sangiovese and 50% Cabernet Sauvignon and Cab Franc is a fine example of the super Tuscan concept. It's rich, deep, and grapey, a sensationally ripe wine, loaded with tobacco, bacon, and cassis. It's lush, with only modestly full tannins, so it won't require years in the cellar before it can be drunk. The finish is smooth and delightfully layered, with ample force and clarity. **92 Editors' Choice** —*M.S. (12/31/2002)*

IL ROVERONE

Il Roverone 2000 Corvina, Rondinella, Molinara (Amarone della Valpolicella Classico) $47. This makes a great first impression in a flight of dry Amarones—lush, rich, and balanced, with a blend of dried fruit (prune, dates, figs), spice and chocolate that end in soft, plush tannins. But it's on the finish that a touch of sweetness comes through, probably limiting the food-pairing options to the cheese course. This would be delicious with pecorino or Parmigiano. **92** —*J.C. (10/1/2006)*

Il Roverone 1999 Corvina, Rondinella, Molinara (Amarone della Valpolicella Classico) $47. Doesn't quite reach the heights of the 2000 edition, but it's still darn good, featuring finely tuned scents of dried fruit and spice that dance on the nose. In the mouth, it's a bit sweet, without the richness of texture to match, finishing with some dusty tannins. Best with hard cheeses. **89** —*J.C. (10/1/2006)*

IL SOGNO DI ANNIBALE

Il Sogno di Annibale NV Extra Dry Prosecco (Prosecco di Conegliano e Valdobbiadene) $13. Textbook Prosecco, with clean citrus notes, peach, apricot, and white flowers. There's also a smooth, creamier texture to this wine that yields depth and a longer finish. **87** —*M.L. (6/1/2006)*

IL TASSO

Il Tasso 1999 Sangiovese (Chianti) $11. Herb and licorice notes complement the berry and sour cherry fruit in this bright offering. Quite youthful, a sulfur note on the nose has to blow off to reveal the essentially good fruit within. The acids here are high and the wine is a touch too racy now, but it will cut right through your pasta's tomato sauce. **86** *(4/1/2001)*

IL VESCOVADO

Il Vescovado 2001 Sangiovese (Chianti) $10. Thin and orange in color, with a cooked, lean nose and palate. In the mouth there's nothing left but acid and dry tannin. **81** *(4/1/2005)*

IL VIGNALE

Il Vignale 1997 Pinot Grigio (Veneto) $10. 86 *(8/1/1999)*

IMPERO

Impero 2001 Red Blend (Amarone della Valpolicella Classico) $48. Round, pure, and smooth, with solid, praise-worthy aromas of toast, coffee, prune, and licorice. Seems more subtle than some, and the flavors of kirsch, raspberry, and vanilla are hardened just enough by coffee and tobacco nuances. Finishes long and soft, with chocolaty sweetness and textbook tannins. **90** *(11/1/2005)*

INAMA

Inama 2001 Vulcaia Sauvignon Blanc (Delle Venezie) $21. A soft, full style of Sauvignon Blanc, with tropical fruits and rich, toasty flavors. But there is a layer of gooseberries and herbs to give the wine some freshness. **88** —*R.V. (7/1/2003)*

Inama 2001 White Blend (Soave Classico Superiore) $13. Offers soft, ripe fruit, powered with acidity and flavors of hazelnuts and ripe apples. A touch of caramel completes the wine's complexity. **89** —*R.V. (7/1/2003)*

Inama 2001 Vigneti di Foscarino White Blend (Soave Classico Superiore) $19. Full of the concentration lacking in so many Soaves, this single-vineyard wine is intense, with ripe toast and nut flavors. The fruit has a touch of honeyed botrytis, balanced with a light layer of acidity. **90** — *R.V. (7/1/2003)*

INNOCENTI

Innocenti 2001 Brunello (Brunello di Montalcino) $49. Leather and horse saddle round off bright cherry, menthol, and spicy notes. Restrained yet densely packed and tight in the mouth, the wine has good substance, a firm structure and an intense finish. **90** *(4/1/2006)*

INSTITUO ENOLOGICO ITALIANO

Instituo Enologico Italiano 2001 Duca di Camastra Nero d'Avola (Sicilia) $9. Unusual but with virtues. The nose features a toasted lid that sits snugly on top of peach and mineral aromas. The palate offers orange and lemon, while the finish dries out, sporting apricot. A touch odd and hard to place, but likable. **85 Best Buy** —*M.S. (10/1/2004)*

ISIDORO POLENCIC

Isidoro Polencic 2004 Pinot Grigio (Collio) $20. Not very expressive and weighed down by some plastic notes that weaken the clean fruit ones. Tart nectarine on the palate. **83** —*M.L. (6/1/2006)*

ISOLE E OLENA

Isole e Olena 2001 Collezione de Marchi Cabernet Sauvignon (Toscana) $60. A wine that plays the finesse card like an ace: Elegant fragrances of blackberry, clove, cinnamon, toasted nuts, and smoky oak spice are woven tightly together without ever being overstated. Dusty tannins and cherry-mint flavors kick in and fuel a long, satisfying finish. There is a small Cabernet Franc component. **92** —*M.L. (9/1/2006)*

J. HOFSTATTER

J. Hofstatter 2002 Chardonnay (Alto Adige) $NA. A soft, creamy wine, with crispness on the palate. It is ripe and clean with a touch of vanilla and appley acidity. **86** —*R.V. (7/1/2003)*

J. Hofstatter 2002 Kolbenhof Gewürztraminer (Alto Adige) $26. A spicy, creamy wine that manages to give freshness and intense varietal character at the same time. The overall effect is of lightness and elegance as well as spiciness and richness. **89** —*R.V. (7/1/2003)*

J. Hofstatter 1997 Pinot Grigio (Alto Adige) $18. 80 *(8/1/1999)*

J. Hofstatter 2002 Barthenau Vigna San Michele White Blend (Alto Adige) $16. This single-vineyard wine blends 60% Pinot Bianco with 30% Chardonnay, plus smaller amounts of Sauvignon Blanc and Riesling. Complex flavors come from this blend and from the wood aging, giving a wine that is rich and ripe with acidity at the same time. **88** —*R.V. (7/1/2003)*

JERMANN

Jermann 2002 Mjzzu Blau & Blau Blaufränkisch (Delle Venezie) $36. Give it time to open and the vegetal, beet-like tones are replaced with warm earth, clove, and raspberry tart. Has a chewy, thick consistency and a rigid tannic backbone; would pair nicely with stewed or oven-roasted meats. Made with 90% Blaufrankisch and 10% Blauburgunder (Pinot Noir). **88** —*M.L. (9/1/2005)*

Jermann 2003 Chardonnay (Venezia Giulia) $32. This is a light but flavorful expression of Italian Chardonnay. Aromas are akin to Muscat or Gewürz, yielding pear and musky spice scents, but the flavors are more Chardonnay-ish with a cavalcade of fruit-cocktail notes including peach and pear. Finishes with some peppery spice and citrus notes. **86** —*J.C. (12/31/2004)*

Jermann 2001 Chardonnay (Venezia Giulia) $27. This lightweight Chardonnay is fresh and flavorful, featuring sweet nuances of nectarine balanced by tart limes on the finish. The aromas suggest a bigger, richer wine than the palate delivers, but overall the wine is balanced and refreshing, a nice change from heavily oaked Chardonnay. **85** —*J.C. (7/1/2003)*

Jermann 2000 Were Dreams, Now it is Just Wine Chardonnay (Venezia Giulia) $55. This barrique-aged Chardonnay tastes a bit too much of barrique, with toasty, cinnamon, and vanilla flavors dominating the underlying melon and peach fruit. It's sexy wood, but it's just too prominent; tone down the makeup and let this beauty's natural good looks shine through. **85** —*J.C. (7/1/2003)*

Jermann 2001 Pignacolusse Pignolo (Venezia Giulia) $52. A stellar example of the potential of Italian indigenous grapes this is 100% Pignolo, a

ITALY

small-clustered variety that faced almost certain extinction. This robust, succulent single-vineyard wine has blackberry, prunes, cigar box, and sticky melted milk chocolate aromas and flavors. Rich in soft tannins and fruity concentration. Delightful. **94 Editors' Choice** —*M.L.* *(9/1/2005)*

Jermann 2001 Pinot Bianco (Venezia Giulia) $25. This nicely balanced Pinot Bianco is fresh and crisp, blending peach, apple, and grapefruit aromas and flavors together into a cohesive whole. Plump on the mid-palate, yet steely and food-friendly on the finish. **89** —*J.C. (7/1/2003)*

Jermann 2004 Pinot Grigio (Venezia Giulia) $34. Starts with toasty, nutty notes, then adds dried sage and a silky feel in the mouth. The wine has enough bulk and texture to be a structured Pinot Grigio—a rare feat, indeed—without compromising its perky personality. **88** —*M.L. (2/1/2006)*

Jermann 2003 Pinot Grigio (Venezia Giulia) $32. Don't be put off by this wine's slightly coppery hue—it's from a short length of skin contact. Aromas of Red Delicious apples ease into flavors of fresh apples sprinkled with dried spices like cinnamon and clove. Medium-bodied, with a finish that shows hints of appleskin and some phenolic notes. **87** —*J.C. (12/31/2004)*

Jermann 2001 Pinot Grigio (Venezia Giulia) $27. This relatively full-bodied Pinot Grigio leans toward warm, baked apple scents and flavors, blending ripe fruit with dried cinnamon and folding in hints of peach on the long finish. Has a lovely, caressing mouthfeel that underscores its comforting flavors. **90** —*J.C. (7/1/2003)*

Jermann 2003 Sauvignon (Venezia Giulia) $33. Round and waxy on the nose, with an oily note alongside minerality and apple. Quite toasty and baked on the palate, with applesauce, grapefruit, and stone fruit flavors. Very dry and long on the tail, with soda cracker flavors. Ultra textured. **87** *(7/1/2005)*

Jermann 2000 Capo Martino in Ruttaris White Blend (Venezia Giulia) $48. Toasty, buttery, and spicy, this blend's aromas and flavors are heavily influenced by barrique. So if you are oak-averse, be warned. The lavish wood is adequately supported by a wine that has good weight and density but doesn't contribute much additional flavor. **86** —*J.C. (7/1/2003)*

Jermann 2001 Vintage Tunina White Blend (Venezia Giulia) $49. Shows a rich blend of citrus and stone fruits on the nose and on the palate, easily combining grapefruit, passion fruit, and nectarines into a cohesive package. Finishes long, with tangy, lip-smacking acids that beg you to give this wine some time in the cellar. It's tasty now, but should be better in 2005. **90** —*J.C. (7/1/2003)*

Jermann 1997 Vintage Tunina White Blend (Collio) $43. **87** *(11/1/1999)*

JERZU ANTICHI PODERI

Jerzu Antichi Poderi 1998 Josto Miglior Riserva Grenache (Cannonau di Sardegna) $32. Cherry, licorice, and floral notes on the nose continue with a spicy, juicy fruit that integrates well on the palate. The finish is bone dry. **89** —*C.S. (5/1/2002)*

Jerzu Antichi Poderi 1998 Marghia Red Blend (Cannonau di Sardegna) $17. Though it has nice white pepper notes that coat maple and black berry fruit aromas, there's lots of wood here from start to finish. Charred oak envelopes mixed berry fruit in the mouth, where the wine's texture falls flat. Residual woodiness on the back end lasts a little longer than we would have liked. **82** —*C.S. (5/1/2002)*

JOSÉ MARIA DA FONSECA

José Maria da Fonseca 1999 Alambre Moscatel (Abruzzo) $19. A younger version of the 20-year-old Moscatel, this is sweeter and much less complex. But it is soft and fresh, with flavors of nuts and burnt fruits alongside sweetness and intense perfumes. Light and fresh at the same time. **88** —*R.V. (12/31/2002)*

JOSEF BRIGL

Josef Brigl 1997 Pinot Grigio (Alto Adige) $10. **84** *(8/1/1999)*

Josef Brigl 2004 Altanuta Pinot Grigio (Alto Adige) $17. Floral, with a strong shot of pineapple up front. Apple, nectarine, and pear comprise a

solid, fruity palate. On the spot in terms of feel, with a grippy finish that offers both citrus and honey. **86** *(2/1/2006)*

JOSEF NIEDERMAYR

Josef Niedermayr 2004 Pinot Grigio (Alto Adige) $NA. Wines from the Alto Adige region, where mountains lock in cool temperatures, promise rich aromatics, and crisp acidity. Thanks to malolactic fermentation, this wine also has rich layers of apple, pineapple, and silkiness. It's sweet and light in the mouth and carries a bitter note at the end. **86** —*M.L. (2/1/2006)*

JOSEF WEGER

Josef Weger 2004 Pinot Grigio (Alto Adige) $9. This wine seems hotter than it actually is at 12.5% alcohol, thanks to its aromas of candied fruit under spirit, white cherry liquor, and rum spongecake. Beyond these more recognizable elements is a smooth background of fruit. **85 Best Buy** —*M.L. (6/1/2006)*

Josef Weger 2004 Maso delle Rosé Ruländer Pinot Grigio (Alto Adige) $11. This Ruländer (another name for Pinot Grigio) has almond skin and slight pine resin on the nose and a spicy, nutmeg-like impression in the mouth. The wine has the grit to pair with pork or pheasant. **86 Best Buy** —*M.L. (6/1/2006)*

KISMET CELLARS

Kismet Cellars 2002 Montepulciano (Montepulciano d'Abruzzo) $10. Sweet cherry, red licorice, and some sugar beet comprise the nose on this grapey, full-acid red. Pie cherry, raspberry, and nutmeg flavors carry the palate, followed by a dark finish with some toasty notes. Maybe a bit sharp but largely balanced and ripe. **84** —*M.S. (11/15/2003)*

Kismet Cellars 2004 Pinot Grigio (Veneto) $9. Moderate lemon and melon aromas to start, backed by apple, pineapple, and a shock of lemon Pledge. Fresh enough, with an o.k. feel. Nothing special; good enough on its best day. **83** *(2/1/2006)*

Kismet Cellars 2002 Sangiovese (Veneto) $10. Not bad for a Veneto Sangiovese. Cherry cola and leather aromas add something to the simple, clean bouquet. A palate of cherry and rhubarb precedes the fresh, lively finish. Dry, tense, and solid, with good tannins and balance. **84** —*M.S. (12/15/2003)*

KRIS

Kris 2003 Pinot Grigio (Delle Venezie) $11. Delicate and graceful, this Franz Haas selection is redolent of almonds and acacia flowers, lightly laced with green fruits and flowers. It is everything that Pinot Grigio can be and Pinot Gris rarely is: elegant and subtle, with flowers and honey, rather than barrels, adding the grace notes. Supple and balanced, it continues along a smooth path through a lingering finish. **90 Best Buy** —*P.G. (11/15/2004)*

KRIZIA

Krizia 1996 Pinot Grigio (Colli Orientali del Friuli) $23. **82** *(8/1/1999)*

KUPELWIESER

Kupelwieser 2004 Pinot Grigio (Alto Adige) $13. I was delighted to find more evolved pastry shop smells like baked apple and cinnamon instead of the simple floral and exotic fruit aromas usually associated with Alto Adige. A great effect in the mouth: The wine is crisp and coats evenly. **87** —*M.L. (6/1/2006)*

LA BRACCESCA

La Braccesca 1996 Sangiovese (Vino Nobile di Montepulciano) $26. **86** —*J.C. (7/1/2000)*

LA CARRAIA

La Carraia 2001 Fobiano Cabernet Sauvignon-Merlot (Umbria) $40. Fully-oaked, with red fruit as well as a strong hint of canned pea or green bean. Simple cherry, plum, and raspberry flavors set up a snappy, acidic finish. Seems a touch backward as it condenses and crystallizes on the finish. **84** —*M.S. (7/1/2005)*

La Carraia 1999 Fobiano Red Blend (Umbria) $35. This Merlot, Cabernet Sauvignon blend has aromas of currants, tar, and treebark. The flavors are of juicy blackberries touched with a bit of char. There is an even balance and a smooth finish for a well-made Bordeaux blend. **89** —C.S. (2/1/2003)

La Carraia 2003 White Blend (Orvieto Classico) $9. Apple and citrus aromas are standard, while the palate of the same fruits plus some almond is decent even if it fails to stun. Finishes with clean flavors and moderate length. Watery but acceptable. **83** —M.S. (7/1/2005)

LA CASA DELL'ORCO

La Casa Dell'Orco 1996 Red Blend (Taurasi) $25. Dried cherries, bay leaves, and a whiff of smoked bacon tease the nose. The mouthfeel is hefty and tannic, but there is little fruit to support it. The finish is dusty and dry. **83** —C.S. (5/1/2002)

LA COLOMBAIA

La Colombaia 1997 Monopolio Montresor Pinot Grigio (Valdadige) $11. 88 Best Buy (8/1/1999)

La Colombaia 2000 Red Blend (Amarone della Valpolicella) $50. Coffee is a dominant element of the raw bouquet, which comes across a touch burnt. Modest red fruit carries the somewhat tannic palate. More elegant than opulent, and ready to drink soon if not now. Of note: one reviewer did not like this wine, noting charred, grassy aromas and off flavors. **89** (11/1/2005)

LA COLOMBINA

La Colombina 2001 Brunello (Brunello di Montalcino) $45. Clover, dried grass, Oriental spice, rhubarb, and intense balsam notes highlight a cherry-vanilla driven wine. Thickly concentrated with very solid tannins and mineral notes woven throughout a long finish. **91** (4/1/2006)

La Colombina 2000 Brunello (Brunello di Montalcino) $45. Starts with a lot of creamy vanilla and berry perfume aromas, which don't really tip you off to the zesty, racy fruit that's been crammed onto the palate. Medium tannins and fairly chewy on the tongue, with a juicy finish that still has plenty of sweet vanilla and chocolate characteristics. **92 Editors' Choice** —M.S. (7/1/2005)

La Colombina 1999 Brunello (Brunello di Montalcino) $NA. Dark and muscular up front, with aromas of tar, smoke, and charred beef. Below that brooding surface you'll find jammy fruit mixed with tobacco and herbs. Not a classic, but still a very good wine on the chunky side. **89** —M.S. (6/1/2004)

LA CONTEA

La Contea 1999 Ripa Sorita Nebbiolo (Barbaresco) $40. A uniquely scented and flavored Barbaresco, with touches of melon rind and stone fruits, chocolate, and a touch of white pepper. The creamy mouthfeel and ripe tannins offer early accessibility; the finish lingers, picking up hints of spice. Drink now–2010. **89** (4/2/2004)

LA CORTE

La Corte 2004 Anfora Primitivo (Puglia) $14. A textbook fruit bomb from Southern Italy that is linear and one dimentional but nevertheless delivers the goods. Candied cherries and strawberries accent a wine made with grapes from 35-year-old vines. You'll taste its youth. **86** —M.L. (9/1/2005)

La Corte 2002 Zinfandel Primitivo (Puglia) $25. An extremely quaffable wine that reflects the authentic, saturated colors and flavors of Puglia despite being marketed with the "American" moniker for Primitivo. Red fruit is backed by tangy cinnamon and spice and the attractive wood tones recall the centuries-old olive trees of the "heel" of the boot of Italy where Zinfandel is said to have its genetic roots. **87** —M.L. (9/1/2005)

La Corte 2003 Red Blend (Salento) $49. A velvety, rich Negroamaro (65%) and Primitivo (35%) blend that has horse saddle, toasted coffee beans, and cloves. Definitely dark and brooding with a smoky, beefy finish. Ready to drink this winter. **87** —M.L. (9/1/2005)

LA DIACCETA

La Diacceta 2000 Vernaccia (San Gimignano) $11. The bouquet of white peach and wet stones is fresh as can be. There's a rich texture to the palate, with flavors of cinnamon and spice accenting ripe pear. Finishes long and fairly full with some banana flavor. **87** —M.S. (8/1/2002)

LA FORTUNA

La Fortuna 2000 Brunello (Brunello di Montalcino) $48. Potent, tight, and condensed on the nose, with a blast of woody smoke. Brighter on the palate, where cherry and plum ride high and confident. This is a lively, fresh wine with an extended finish of cherry, plum, and licorice. It also shows a raw, leathery streak, good tannins, and solid aging ability. **90** —M.S. (7/1/2005)

La Fortuna 1999 Riserva Brunello (Brunello di Montalcino) $70. Smoky and dark, with potent char and tar elements to the bouquet. Look for sweet cherry and plum flavors floating on a bed of soft, smooth tannins. And in the end there's a heaping of chocolate and espresso. This is like a liquid dessert for adults. **93** —M.S. (7/1/2005)

LA FRANCESCA

La Francesca 2001 Cabernet Sauvignon (Veneto) $6. Thin and hollow, with only modest red fruit to go along with some pickled, vegetal aromas and flavors. Not flawed, but not particularly good either. A wine on the proverbial brink. **80** (5/1/2003)

La Francesca 2001 Chardonnay (Veneto) $6. Clean and correct, but very light, with lime scents that vie for prominence with aromas of green ferns. **82** —J.C. (7/1/2003)

La Francesca 2002 Merlot (Veneto) $6. Smooth and clean on the nose, with light cherry and berry fruit. A palate of red apple and strawberry is fresh, while the finish is light and clean. Pedestrian but serves its purpose. **84 Best Buy** —M.S. (12/15/2003)

La Francesca 2001 Merlot (Veneto) $6. Pungent leather and pepper aromas are what you get from the nose of this non-vintage wine. The palate features sour cherry, some fleshy plum, and a hint of earth. Overall it's simple and clean, a Beaujolais imitator from northeastern Italy. **84** (5/1/2003)

La Francesca 1998 Pinot Grigio (Veneto) $5. 86 Best Buy (8/1/1999)

La Francesca 2003 Pinot Grigio (Veneto) $7. No, this is not a concentrated intense Grigio. But it is light-boded, clean and refreshing, with ample pear and apple flavors perked up by crisp lemony notes on the finish. A wine for busy weeknights or big parties. **84 Best Buy** —J.C. (12/31/2004)

La Francesca 2001 Pinot Grigio (Veneto) $6. Musky pear aromas start things off, but the flavors are in sharper focus—a blend of pears and green herbs, finishing with a touch of anise. A bit sweet-tasting, so serve well-chilled as an apéritif. Best Buy. **84 Best Buy** —J.C. (7/1/2003)

La Francesca 2000 Pinot Grigio (Veneto) $5. Sweet lemon, mineral, and vanilla aromas lead to a very lightweight palate. Citrus and apple notes are lively but somewhat dilute, but it's refreshing nonetheless. **83** (9/1/2001)

La Francesca 2001 Red Blend (Valpolicella) $6. The nose is packed with cedar, but not much else. Some cherry and berry fruit is accentuated on the palate by chocolate and drying woody notes. The finish is clean, smooth, and of proper length. It's fine, but it lacks punch. **84** (5/1/2003)

LA GERLA

La Gerla 1993 Brunello (Brunello di Montalcino) $45. 88 —M.M. (5/1/1999)

La Gerla 2001 Brunello (Brunello di Montalcino) $45. This wine left our panel deeply divided and tested our threshold for modern Brunello. One panelist loved the chocolate fudge, black cherry, fennel seed, bacon fat, and toasted notes. To a second panelist, the wine was disjointed and over-oaked. Drink by 2015. **92 Editors' Choice** (4/1/2006)

La Gerla 2000 Brunello (Brunello di Montalcino) $60. Dark and chunky, both in sight and smell. Nevertheless, it's fairly nice on the palate, but it's soft. The black plum, cherry and licorice flavors are warm although not overly precise. Finishes with a decent kick as well as balancing flavors of fresh tomato and cherry. **88** —M.S. (7/1/2005)

La Gerla 1999 Brunello (Brunello di Montalcino) $NA. Slight tobacco and pepper notes vie with solid red fruit on the nose. It tastes full, with proper acid-tannin balance. Finishes dry and woody. What's here is nice, but it doesn't have a penthouse level, so to speak. **88** —M.S. (6/1/2004)

La Gerla 1997 Brunello (Brunello di Montalcino) $55. The land from which this wine comes was once owned by the Biondi-Santi family. It forms part of an 18-acre estate belonging to Sergio Rossi. It is a stunning wine, with a sense of fine poise combined with solid tannins and firm, ripe fruit. At the back of the palate is a lingering flavor of violets and sweet herbs. Drink from 2005; the wine should age well. **93 Editors' Choice** —R.V. (8/1/2002)

La Gerla 1999 Riserva Brunello (Brunello di Montalcino) $100. Perfect color and a round, smooth nose draw you in like a moth to a flame. The palate is classy and full of brown sugar, chocolate, and vanilla all wrapped around a core of black cherry. Very nice and incredibly easygoing, with just enough tannic firmness. **91** —M.S. (7/1/2005)

La Gerla 2001 Vigne gli Angeli Brunello (Brunello di Montalcino) $65. Dense and concentrated, this is a modern and flavorful Brunello that delivers vinous and fruity aromas such as cherry, plum, and even apricot. Lush and meaty with espresso bean, mushroom and exotic spice. Scores sky high on the power meter. **90** (4/1/2006)

LA GUARDIENSE

La Guardiense 2003 Greco (Sannio) $10. Acacia flowers, honey, kiwi, grapefruit, and honey appear on the nose and are followed by flavors of green apple and peach. The wine is medium-bodied and somewhat flat. **84** —M.L. (10/1/2006)

LA LASTRA

La Lastra 1999 Sangiovese (Chianti Colli Senesi) $12. Opens with a potent bouquet of deep cherry, earth, and mint. This is chewy on the palate, with solid fruit flavors, cola, and clove accents and more weight than many other Chiantis. The ample fruit carries the dusty tannins and chocolate well on the finish. **87 Best Buy** (4/1/2001)

LA MANNELLA

La Mannella 2001 Brunello (Brunello di Montalcino) $45. With vineyards north and southeast of Montalcino, this family-run winery is relatively new on the scene. Opens with floral and fruity intensity: ripe forest berry, blueberry, rose tea, and violet and follows with cedar, leather, tobacco, and mineral-like, iron notes. Silky, supple, and medium-bodied. **91** (4/1/2006)

La Mannella 2001 I Poggiarelli Brunello (Brunello di Montalcino) $50. Oak tonneaux aging renders a rounder, softer, and easier-to-drink Brunello. Beautiful layers of aromatic intensity include white mushroom, herbal notes, sweet cedar wood, tobacco, vanilla, and cherry. **90** (4/1/2006)

LA MARCA

La Marca 1998 Pinot Grigio (Veneto) $8. **84** (8/1/1999)

La Marca 2003 Winemaker's Collection Pinot Grigio (Piave) $11. Light and lemony, with hints of green peas and fresh apples. Finishes tart and clean. **83** —J.C. (12/31/2004)

La Marca NV Extra Dry Prosecco (Prosecco di Conegliano e Valdobbiadene) $10. Very intense and pleasing with a beautiful medley of floral, mineral, and soapy notes that add complexity and charm. Light to medium structure in the mouth, with that trademark Prosecco crispness at the end. **87 Best Buy** —M.L. (6/1/2006)

La Marca 2004 Prestige Cuvée Prosecco (Prosecco di Conegliano e Valdobbiadene) $13. A bigger, toastier style that emphasizes banana, yellow rose, and well-etched mineral tones. It has a silky mouthfeel with a bit more bulk than your standard Prosecco and a crisp, snappy close. **88 Best Buy** —M.L. (6/1/2006)

LA MASSA

La Massa 2003 Sangiovese (Toscana) $29. A well-oaked specimen, one with sandalwood, hickory, coffee, and Middle Eastern spice notes on the nose. Big and generous with its plum, berry, and thick but slick oak flavors. Simply put, this is a modern but finely made red that doesn't require cellar time; the blend is Sangiovese, Merlot, and a splash of Cabernet. **91** —M.S. (9/1/2006)

La Massa 2001 Sangiovese (Toscana) $37. Rich and ripe-smelling, with lovely plum and blackberry flavors. The feel is righteous and big, while the finish brings a blend of toast, pepper, and soft tannins. Almost jammy but it holds the line. Drink now through 2010. **93 Editors' Choice** —M.S. (9/1/2006)

La Massa 2001 Giorgio Primo Sangiovese (Chianti Classico) $75. Broadly textured and rich, with dark aromatics leaning toward coffee, blackberry, and a sniff of lemon zest. Dense plum, toast, and licorice notes control the palate, and then a clean blast of chocolate rushes through. Very sweet and unctuous for Chianti, almost like dessert in a glass. **92** (4/1/2005)

LA MONACESCA

La Monacesca 2002 Verdicchio (Verdicchio di Matelica) $19. Gold in color, with mushroom and honey on the nose. Round in the mouth, with mild flavors of orange, grapefruit and pineapple. Quite thick and substantive, with a big, grabbing finish. **85** —M.S. (8/1/2004)

LA MONTECCHIA

La Montecchia 1997 Red Blend (Colli Euganei) $13. **85** —M.S. (9/1/2000)

LA NUNSIO

La Nunsio 1997 Barbera (Barbera d'Asti) $22. **89** (4/1/2000)

LA PALAZZOLA

La Palazzola 1999 Rubino Grilli Red Blend (Umbria) $40. Floral aromas, and leathery, red berry flavors integrate well with the tannins, but could use a little more complexity and depth on the finish. **86** —C.S. (2/1/2002)

LA PESCAIA

La Pescaia 2001 Brunello (Brunello di Montalcino) $NA. Greets the nose in a nice, easy manner with cherry, currants, forest floor, rose petal, milk chocolate, and an attractive touch of musty earthiness. Silky tannins glide easily across the palate. **90** (4/1/2006)

La Pisara 2004 Primitivo (Salento) $9. Heavy, with prune, raisin and syrup on the nose. The palate holds onto that sweetness, while the finish is inky and rich. Teeters on being out of balance but holds the line. A chewy, sweet red. **83** —M.S. (10/1/2006)

La Pisara 2003 Red Blend (Salice Salentino) $8. Spice and jam get it going, but then it turns more grassy and lean. Cranberry and pie cherry are the lead flavors, and the feel is kind of raw and hard. Almost refreshing in its steeliness, but ultimately it's pretty thin. **83** —M.S. (10/1/2006)

LA PODERINA

La Poderina 2001 Brunello (Brunello di Montalcino) $75. Red berry fruit, anise seed, mint tea, and dried flowers are attractive components to a bouquet with a strong fruit compote or jammy quality. Flavors include dark plum, vanilla, and raisin and there's a nice smoothness to the tannins. **91** (4/1/2006)

La Poderina 2000 Brunello (Brunello di Montalcino) $65. Downright purple in color, so much so that it looks more like Merlot than Sangiovese. Smells incredibly rich, but not stewy. Concentrated and extracted palate, with no hard tannins or acids. Very smooth but short on the finish. Good for near-term drinking. **90** —M.S. (7/1/2005)

La Poderina 1999 Brunello (Brunello di Montalcino) $69. Open-knit and scattered on the nose; simply put, it doesn't have the density and strength of the big boys. But in the mouth, it offers lovely fruit, modest thickness, and racy acids. In many ways it's akin to a Rosso di Montalcino or Chianti. **88** —M.S. (6/1/2004)

La Poderina 2000 Poggio Banale Brunello (Brunello di Montalcino) $118. There's nothing banal about this reserve wine. Full-throttle from the start with meaty, smoked cedar wood, clove spice, cinnamon, and a hint of barnyard or wild mushroom that blows off fast. The fruity tones are not absent and slice through the mouth with a juicy, tart close. **91** (4/1/2006)

La Poderina 1999 Poggio Banale Brunello (Brunello di Montalcino) $125. Beautiful on the nose, with density and power. Very tannic on the palate, but interspersed are pockets of delicious cherry and berry flavors. With great color, tightness, and pulsing acids, this is one for the cellar. Put it away and revisit in 2007 to 2010. **91** —M.S. (6/1/2004)

LA RASINA

La Rasina 2001 Brunello (Brunello di Montalcino) $56. Toasted oak at the front with thick berry ripeness and unique layers of aromas that include plum, vanilla, resin, and even asphalt. A New World-style wine that should integrate beautifully in a few more years. **91** *(4/1/2006)*

LA ROCCA

La Rocca 1998 Pinot Grigio (Collio) $10. 81 *(8/1/1999)*

LA RONCAIA

La Roncaia 1999 Il Fusco Red Blend (Friuli Venezia Giulia) $50. The bouquet is fragrant, with notes of graham cracker, pepper, leather, and coffee. Some dry, dark fruit that's one part cassis and another part peppery (think Syrah) graces the firmly tannic palate. The finish is long, spicy, and borderline hot. Has more weight than depth. **89** *(5/1/2003)*

La Roncaia 2002 Eclisse Sauvignon-Picolit Sauvignon (Colli Orientali del Friuli) $34. One of the most fragrant, subtle Sauvignons you'll encounter. The nose spreads out like a garden in spring, with honeysuckle supported by chalky minerality. The palate delivers lemon chiffon along with light tropical fruit, while the finish is creamy, long, and flawless. Could have scored even higher, but one reviewer she said it lacked varietal character (could be the Picolit) and fell off on the back end. **90** *(7/1/2005)*

LA SCOLCA

La Scolca 1999 Cortese (Gavi di Gavi) $19. Lean, sharp, and herbal, this is a true apéritif wine that whets the appetite. A slight sour cream note on the palate is offset by a tangy citrus-laden finish that blends in some cinnamon-spiced pear flavors. **84** *(9/1/2001)*

La Scolca 2001 Bianco Secco Cortese (Gavi di Gavi) $19. Very sulfuric at first, such that it takes too much time to find its legs. Flavors of citrus and herbs are marred by an egg flavor created by the sulfur. Just not that fresh due to funky aromas, although in its favor, it improves with time. **83** —*M.S. (12/15/2003)*

La Scolca 2002 Black Label Cortese (Gavi di Gavi) $42. I have to admit: I've never "gotten" this wine, and this Gavi just doesn't do it for me. Vaguely sweaty aromas join almond and unripe peach scents on the nose, followed up by lemony, under-ripe flavors. **84** —*J.C. (11/15/2004)*

La Scolca 2002 Il Valentino Cortese (Gavi di Gavi) $14. Standard tart and refreshing stuff, with added notes that hint at anise and sour cream. Light-bodied, drink as an apéritif. **84** —*J.C. (11/15/2004)*

La Scolca 2001 il Valentino White Blend (Gavi) $13. Unexciting and borderline scouring. Citrus and pepper flavors compete with some vegetal notes. The finish is exceedingly lean and zippy. **80** —*M.S. (12/15/2003)*

La Scolca NV Soldati LaScolca Brut White Blend (Gavi) $26. Very toasty aromas, with scents of baked apples and honey. The wine seems slightly overdone, maybe a tad over-ripe. You get that from the mushroom and heavy apple flavors on the palate. And the finish is hot. However, with nothing terribly off, the wine is solid. **87** —*M.S. (12/31/2002)*

LA SELVACCIA

La Selvaccia 2001 Brunello (Brunello di Montalcino) $55. Zonin, in collaboration with Montalcino's Tenuta di Sesta, has delivered a sexy wine with dark cherry fruit, mocha, leather, earth, white mushroom, exotic spice, and an attractive menthol-like finish. The mouthfeel is tart, supple, and persistent. **91** *(4/1/2006)*

La Selvaccia 2000 Brunello (Brunello di Montalcino) $50. If you've never tried Brunello this is an excellent wine to wet your taste buds for this extraordinary Italian red. The aromatic intensity is incredible: blackberry, wet earth, cherry preserves, and leather. Its color is inky black and the wine closed with a nice, smoky finish. **90** —*M.L. (11/15/2006)*

LA SERA

La Sera 1997 Barbera (Barbera del Monferrato) $12. 87 Best Buy *(4/1/2000)*

La Sera 1997 Il Cielo Barbera (Barbera d'Alba) $17. 89 *(4/1/2000)*

LA SERENA

La Serena 2001 Brunello (Brunello di Montalcino) $NA. Generous dollops of coffee bean, cherry syrup, cedar wood, and tobacco greet the nose. Lacks nuances but does deliver creamy consistency and attractive espresso notes on the finish. **90** *(4/1/2006)*

La Serena 2000 Brunello (Brunello di Montalcino) $NA. Pure violet in color, with a nose packed full of creamy oak, sweet plum, and blackberry. This is your prototypical modern-day bruiser. The palate offers a powder keg of sweet, chewy fruit, yet the acidity is right there corralling it all. Properly applied oak cuddles rather than overwhelms the fruit, while the full tannins make it a lion heart. Fabulous for a 2000 normale. **94 Editors' Choice** —*M.S. (7/1/2005)*

La Serena 1999 Brunello (Brunello di Montalcino) $NA. Earthy and rusty in color, but liquid gold in the mouth. It's round, complete, and subtle. The dry red fruit is touched up by accents of root beer, smoke, and brown sugar. When drinking, a vise grip of tannins clamp down. That said, maturity seems in sight. Start drinking in 2005. **92** —*M.S. (6/1/2004)*

LA SPINETTA

La Spinetta 2004 Bricco Quaglia Moscato (Moscato d'Asti) $18. Pink grapefruit, peach, mint candy, rose petal, chamomile, mineral tones, and dried grass make for a surprisingly complex nose. Correct in every way, including bubble persistency, liveliness, and impact in the mouth. Watch out for this producer's excellent Moscato Passito and red wines as well. **88** —*M.L. (12/15/2005)*

La Spinetta 2000 Oro Moscato Passito Moscato (Piedmont) $NA. A very impressive and sensual late-harvest wine from Piedmont that delivers an incredible complexity of aromas including roasted honey, apricot honey, and maple syrup. But what really delighted and surprised me was its sudden burst of fresh flowers—like walking into a florists' shop. With a beautiful polished copper color and a dense and concentrated finish. **93 Editors' Choice** —*M.L. (11/15/2006)*

LA SPINONA

La Spinona 1999 Vigna Qualin Dolcetto (Dolcetto d'Alba) $15. This is an easygoing lighter-style Dolcetto. Cherry and mocha flavors predominate throughout, and the finish is long and dry. Would go well with pizza. **86** —*M.N. (9/1/2001)*

La Spinona 1998 Vigneto Qualin Dolcetto (Dolcetto d'Alba) $15. 83 *(4/1/2000)*

LA TORRE

La Torre 1999 Brunello (Brunello di Montalcino) $NA. Smoky and leathery on the nose, but not particularly rustic. When drinking, you'll encounter a forward wine with pronounced acidity. It runs a touch sharp overall, and a tiny bit tangy. Certainly nice, but shy of the star players. **88** —*M.S. (6/1/2004)*

LA VELONA

La Velona 2001 Brunello (Brunello di Montalcino) $NA. Dark, concentrated, and brooding, this Brunello is lavish with the bold vanilla, cherry, and cedar notes that are so typical of the genre. A nicely made, clean wine with cushiony, soft tannins and lemon twist on a persistent finish. **91** *(4/1/2006)*

LA VIARTE

La Viarte 2003 Sauvignon Blanc (Colli Orientali del Friuli) $20. Strange on the nose, with hints of cat box, crushed vitamins, iodine, and yeast. Quite rubbery and pithy on the palate, with papaya, green melon, and some vegetal notes. And it's spritzy across the tongue. **83** *(7/1/2005)*

LA VILLA

La Villa 2005 Pinot Grigio (Veneto) $8. Not much to the nose but a light touch of honeydew. The wine gives a better performance in the mouth, with decent consistency and zesty citrus flavors through the finish. **84 Best Buy** —*M.L. (6/1/2006)*

ITALY

LA VILLA VENETA

La Villa Veneta 2000 Merlot (Veneto) $8. Light and innocuous, with simple aromas and basic cherry and earth-tinged flavors. The acids are healthy, so the mouthfeel is snappy. **83** (5/1/2003)

La Villa Veneta 2001 Pinot Grigio (Veneto) $8. Smells strongly of lemongrass, and this character carries over onto the palate, which is flavored by lemon, pear, and herbs. Feels a bit heavy in the mouth, but finishes clean and lemony. **83** —J.C. (7/1/2003)

LA VIS

La Vis 2001 Chardonnay (Trentino) $11. Smells rich, with aromas redolent of honey and clove, peaches and pears. And in the mouth, it is medium- to full-bodied, but there's also a long, mouth-watering finish with enough acidity to keep the wine from being too heavy. **86** —J.C. (1/1/2004)

La Vis 2000 Ritratti Chardonnay (Trentino) $13. Rich, even a bit heavy, in the mouth, with canned corn, citrus, and melon aromas and flavors that offer plenty of substance but less style. **84** —J.C. (7/1/2003)

La Vis 2000 Maso Roncador Müller-Thurgau (Trentino) $14. Smells of honey and lychee fruit, but without the bold exuberance of Gewürztraminer. Pear flavors the midpalate, then turns citrusy on the finish. **86** —J.C. (7/1/2003)

La Vis 2005 Pinot Grigio (Vigneti delle Dolomiti) $11. Floral and fruity notes are direct and linear. This is an easy, well-made Grigio with perky freshness and good length. There's nothing not to like about it. **87 Best Buy** —M.L. (6/1/2006)

La Vis 2004 Ritratti Pinot Grigio (Trentino) $15. A clear-cut crowd pleaser, with dried grass and green olive notes backed by fresh white peach. Twenty percent sees two months of barrel aging and although you don't taste the wood, it does render a tighter, more compact structure in the mouth. **87** —M.L. (2/1/2006)

La Vis 2001 Rosso dei Sorni Red Blend (Trentino) $15. Creamy and milky in the nose, with chocolate, earth, and a cool, dense essence. It's plump and round, with coffee and bitter chocolate flavors. It doesn't exactly sing and dance, but for a blend of Teroldego and Lagrein, it's a solid middle-weight. **85** —M.S. (12/15/2003)

La Vis 2000 Masso Tratta Sauvignon Blanc (Trentino) $13. This Trentino Sauvignon is surprisingly rich and viscous, coating the mouth with mixed fruit flavors, including tangerine, lime, and pineapple. Despite the rich mouthfeel, the flavors linger delicately on the finish, giving an unexpected feeling of elegance. **88 Best Buy** —J.C. (7/1/2003)

La Vis 2001 Bianco dei Sorni White Blend (Trentino) $15. This blend of Chardonnay, Nosiola, and Pinot Bianco offers up apples and cream on the nose, along with flavors of peach and citrus. It's a comfortable mix of fruit that finishes lively and fresh, making it a fine apéritif. **88** —J.C. (7/1/2003)

LAGARIA

Lagaria 2003 Chardonnay (Delle Venezie) $10. A low-acid, fruit-forward Chardonnay for $10? What's not to like? Honeyed pear and dried spices upfront, a slightly viscous mouthfeel and lots of ripe pear, spicy pepper, and dried clove flavors make this a solid value. **87 Best Buy** —J.C. (12/31/2004)

Lagaria 2001 Chardonnay (Delle Venezie) $8. Inviting aromas of butter, almond, and citrus open into a rich, thickly textured wine studded with peach, almond butter, and citrus pith. The slightly bitter notes echo through the finish, providing a welcome sense of balance to round mouthfeel and fatty flavors. **87 Best Buy** —J.C. (7/1/2003)

Lagaria 2000 Merlot (Delle Venezie) $8. The nose is redeeming; there's some leather, smoke, and rubber along with cotton candy. In the mouth, dusty, earthy flavors add a leathery quality to the otherwise plum and cherry palate. **83** (5/1/2003)

Lagaria 2005 Pinot Grigio (Delle Venezie) $10. A very fruity, almost peach, juice-like wine with layers of honeydew melon and apricot. There's an interesting tug of war between sweet and sour in the mouth that promises to pair well with exotic foods. **86 Best Buy** —M.L. (6/1/2006)

Lagaria 2004 Pinot Grigio (Delle Venezie) $10. Very mild nose that releases weak bursts of flowers and honey. Not complex or structured but with just enough crispness to make your mouth pucker. The nice thing about less intense wines is they are easier to pair with a larger assortment of foods. **84** —M.L. (2/1/2006)

Lagaria 2001 Pinot Grigio (Delle Venezie) $8. While there's a decent amount of weight to this wine—enough to stand up to food—the flavors seem a bit dilute, showing only hints of almond and melon. **83** —J.C. (7/1/2003)

Lagaria 1999 Pinot Grigio (Trentino) $7. This pleasant lightweight wine opens with floral notes followed by apple and almond flavors. Adequate acidity and a medium body complete the picture. A nice apéritif. **83** —M.N. (9/1/2001)

Lagaria 1997 Pinot Grigio (Trentino) $8. **82** (8/1/1999)

LAMBARDI

Lambardi 2001 Brunello (Brunello di Montalcino) $NA. Candied cherry, toasted vanilla, and Dr. Pepper-like intensity is layered over a strongly rooted, firmly structured wine. Still young. **90** (4/1/2006)

LAMBERTI

Lamberti 2001 Santepietre Merlot (Delle Venezie) $9. A nose of molasses and popcorn, and a palate of brown sugar and very ripe grapes didn't do much for our panel. Neither did the tart, tannic finish that runs heavy with residual sugar. **81** (5/1/2003)

Lamberti 1998 Corte Rubini Red Blend (Amarone della Valpolicella) $30. Tasted in a blind flight, this wine simply didn't fare that well. It comes across thin and slightly weedy, with cherry and leather notes. **84** (5/1/2003)

Lamberti 2001 Tenuta Pule Red Blend (Amarone della Valpolicella) $31. Seems a touch sour to the nose, and maybe slightly reductive. Time allows it to improve, unveiling ripe cherry, plum, and tea flavors. Finishes with chocolate and soy flavors as well as warmth. But it's also fairly short. **86** (11/1/2005)

LAMBORGHINI

Lamborghini 2000 Campoleone Red Blend (Umbria) $75. A 50% Merlot-50% Sangiovese blend that has aromas of vanilla and new leather. The flavors of currants and cedar combine with big tannins in this powerful wine. Give this some time. Drink 2004–2010 **91** —C.S. (2/1/2003)

Lamborghini 2000 Trescone Red Blend (Umbria) $12. Earth driven aromas, and dark cherry flavors are touched with charcoal. The finish is easy and pleasant. This is a good simple red to enjoy by itself or with a pizza. **87 Best Buy** —C.S. (2/1/2003)

LAMOLE DI LAMOLE

Lamole Di Lamole 2001 Sangiovese (Chianti Classico) $18. Simple yet reserved, with jammy aromas of black cherry and raisin. There is also a sharp element to the nose, which one of our tasters pegged as vinegar. Overall, however, the palate is racy and tight, with high-toned raspberry and strawberry flavors. Finishes snappy, with a touch of sugar beet. **86** (4/1/2005)

Lamole Di Lamole 2000 Blue Label Sangiovese (Chianti Classico) $20. Simple, inoffensive, and easy, with mild leather and raisin notes. Tastes a touch sour at first before showing adequate cherry and smoke flavors. Light and dusty on the finish, with snap. **85** (4/1/2005)

Lamole Di Lamole 2000 Riserva Sangiovese (Chianti Classico) $24. Slightly roasted on the nose, with pure saddle leather and a bit of prune. Runs a bit lean and tight across the palate, but it still delivers a juicy ride due to crisp acids and power tannins. More traditional, with a brick-colored tint. **89** (4/1/2005)

Lamole Di Lamole 1999 Vigneto di Campolungo Riserva Sangiovese (Chianti Classico) $36. Just a bit of rusticity in the form of jerky, tobacco, and leather adds a manly touch to the otherwise sweet nose. Perhaps this one veers into the land of over-ripe, but still we like the raisin and plum flavors along with the smooth, supple mouthfeel. Talk about harmony and an easy feel. **89** (4/1/2005)

LANARI

Lanari 2002 Red Blend (Rosso Conero) $20. Forward and tight, with lean berry and plum flavors. Feels a touch hard, with strawberry and raspberry notes. Seems mildly burnt on the finish, and tannic. Too rustic and raw to rate higher. **83** —*M.S. (6/1/2005)*

Lanari 2001 Fibbio Red Blend (Rosso Conero) $47. Big-time Montepulciano-based wine, with monster tannins, deep color, and girth. With its bold berry, graham cracker and chocolate aromas, you could call the nose oversized. Aggressive in the mouth, with a wall of tannin and acid. But does it taste good or what? Fantastic coffee and blackberry marmalade flavors on the back end. Age until 2006, or serve with meat. **91** —*M.S. (6/1/2005)*

LANCIOLA

Lanciola 2001 Sangiovese (Chianti Colli Fiorentini) $16. Funky at first, with an amalgam of lactic, meat, and smoke aromas. Seems a touch soft on the palate, where prune and coffee flavors match wits with black cherry. Minty green on the finish, which may be construed as tobacco. **86** *(4/1/2005)*

Lanciola 1999 Sangiovese (Chianti Colli Fiorentini) $9. Intense from the start, and quite rambunctious. The fruit is healthy and powerful, with ample leather and chocolate to add complexity. This wine surely has better days ahead, but opening it now and serving it with hearty food should allow it to show its best. **87** —*M.S. (12/31/2002)*

Lanciola 1998 Sangiovese (Chianti Colli Fiorentini) $12. Rustic in a positive sense, this medium-weight, supple wine shows dark cherry fruit once a touch of sulfur blows off. Finishes long, with black cherry, licorice, and espresso flavors. It could use a year to even out and integrate its parts. **87 Best Buy** *(4/1/2001)*

Lanciola 1999 Antiche Terre De' Ricci Terricci Sangiovese (Toscana) $37. Dark and fruity on the nose, with a touch of gritty leather. Brighter on the palate, where cherry and raspberry hold court and oak plays in the background. Juicy, fresh, immensely solid, and just short of excellent.

A very good Tuscan red with a little bit of everything. Drink now through 2008. **89** —*M.S. (9/1/2006)*

Lanciola 1998 Antiche Terre de' Ricci Terricci Sangiovese (Toscana) $40. Full and penetrating aromas get it started, but beware of some horsehide and leather that some might term barnyard. Flavors of plum and berry are round and pleasing, while the mouthfeel is a touch heavy, especially when the tannins crash down on the finish unsupported by lively acidity. **87** —*M.S. (9/1/2006)*

Lanciola 2002 Le Masse Di Greve Sangiovese (Chianti Classico) $29. Cooked and beefy, with stewed fruit and molasses on the nose. Has color and size, but the flavor profile is narrow, consisting solely of candied cherry and mint. Finishes syrupy and short. **83** *(4/1/2005)*

LAZZERETTI

Lazzeretti 2001 Brunello (Brunello di Montalcino) $NA. Located at the foot of Montalcino, Marco Lazzeretti's vineyard produces concentrated Brunello highlighted by brilliant notes of almond nut, sweet red fruit, menthol, and cedar wood. The tannins are thorny and sharp, so much so that it's hard to imagine them tamed with time. **88** *(4/1/2006)*

LE BELLERIVE

Le Bellerive NV Di Cartizze Prosecco (Prosecco di Valdobbiadene Superiore) $47. Much more mature and round than your typical Prosecco, yet it doesn't necessarily hit the right chords. There's a wheaty, burnt-grass quality to the fruit, smoke, and toast, and then residual sugar. The goal here seems to be Champagne-like complexity and size, but the result is not fully convincing. **85** —*M.S. (12/15/2005)*

Le Bellerive NV Frizzante Prosecco (Prosecco di Valdobbiadene) $19. Full, round, and earthy, with gritty citrus flavors that veer toward pink grapefruit. Not the most lively wine, with toast, mineral, and admirable depth. Slightly sweet but also sort of tart. **85** —*M.S. (12/15/2005)*

LE BOCCE

Le Bocce 1998 Sangiovese (Chianti Classico) $14. The tart berry and plum fruit wears a good dose of cocoa on the nose and picks up nice herb and licorice shadings on the smooth medium weight palate. Finishes long and dry with dusty tannins, and pronounced herb and mineral notes. **87** *(4/1/2001)*

Le Bocce 1997 Riserva Sangiovese (Chianti Classico) $24. Good balance and a sense of proportion characterize this handsome, classically-styled Chianti. Displays aromas of cherry, leather, and spice and dark cherry flavors, cocoa accents, and nice acidity on the palate. The long and flavorful finish makes it very appealing for current consumption, and it should improve further over the next year or two. **89** *(4/1/2001)*

LE CALVANE

Le Calvane 1999 Trecione Riserva Sangiovese (Chianti Colli Fiorentini) $25. Jammy for starters, but with an attractive sweetness along with some chocolate. The epitome of a sugary berry ball. The palate is soft and easy, maybe borderline chunky, but there's enough tannin and acid to ensure an even flow. Drink now. **87** *(4/1/2005)*

LE CHIUSE

Le Chiuse 2001 Brunello (Brunello di Montalcino) $50. A well-received Brunello with characteristic notes of earth, blackberry, cherry, dried spice, cola, and cedar wood. We appreciated the balance, length, and dusty tannic finish. Try with stewed game meat. **90** *(4/1/2006)*

Le Chiuse 2000 Brunello (Brunello di Montalcino) $55. Gets going with hard, funky aromas resulting from either too much sulfur or heavily toasted barriques. The palate starts out leathery, although time reveals maple and additional sweetness. Flavorwise, we're talking cranberry, cherry, and plum. Peppery on the finish. **86** —*M.S. (7/1/2005)*

Le Chiuse 1999 Brunello (Brunello di Montalcino) $NA. Dense and reduced, with cola and root beer aromas. This is not the liveliest Brunello going, which is proven by the modest tannins and equally moderate acids. Nonetheless, it's not flabby or disproportionately flat. The flavors are good and the finish is long. But with a touch more zest it could be a high-flyer. **89** —*M.S. (6/1/2004)*

Le Chiuse 2000 Riserva Brunello (Brunello di Montalcino) $70. The wine is burdened by a tired, heavy quality and most probably suffers from mild oxidation. Our second bottle was fresher at the beginning, but any fruit tones start to fade fast in the glass. Initial pie crust, almond, and baked cherry are nice while they last. **84** *(4/1/2006)*

LE CINCIOLE

Le Cinciole 1998 Sangiovese (Chianti Classico) $18. A rich nose with deep cherry and spice notes opens this dense, even jammy wine. It's not often you find Sangiovese this ripe from Tuscany, but the fruit here is very good, and there's a lot of it. The finish is full and juicy, with mild tannins and good length. In weight and texture, almost like an Aussie Shiraz, but with Sangiovese flavors. **89** *(4/1/2001)*

Le Cinciole 2000 Petresco Riserva Sangiovese (Chianti Classico) $33. Sour from the start, with grapey flavors and even some chemical. Bitter chocolate on the finish. Harsh on the palate. **80** *(4/1/2005)*

Le Cinciole 1997 Petresco Riserva Sangiovese (Chianti Classico) $30. Ripe grape and cherry aromas presage the flavorful core of fruit upon which this wine is built. The mouthfeel is creamy, and dark plum and cocoa flavors prevail. The finish shows lots of spice, good length, and full but even tannins. Delicious now; will be better still in two or three years. **88** *(4/1/2001)*

LE COLTURE

Le Colture NV Cartizze Prosecco (Prosecco Superiore di Cartizze) $35. Has beautifully elongated strings of bubbles and an elegant aromatic package including dusty chalk, flowers, and white peach. The foam is silky and cushiony in the mouth. **87** —*M.L. (6/1/2006)*

Le Colture NV Cruner Dry Prosecco (Prosecco di Conegliano e Valdobbiadene) $19. Offers white flower and cracked white pepper, crushed stone, peach, fresh apricot, and grapefruit flavors. This is a polished bubbly with a light mouthfeel and a snappy, spicy close. **87** —*M.L. (6/1/2006)*

Le Colture NV Fagher Brut Prosecco (Prosecco di Conegliano e Valdobbiadene) $19. Tangerine, lemon-lime, and white peach are the main components of the nose, but there's also a touch of fresh garden

ITALY

ITALY

greens. Spicy mineral notes appear over a refreshing dose of crisp acidity. **87** —*M.L. (6/1/2006)*

Le Colture NV Pianer Extra Dry Prosecco (Prosecco di Conegliano e Valdobbiadene) $19. Very aromatic; yields generous white peach, melon, and candied lime. A blast of intense freshness in the mouth lingers and makes this a perfect prelude to a dinner with friends. **87** —*M.L. (6/1/2006)*

LE CORTE

Le Corte 2001 Anfora Zinfandel (Puglia) $11. **87** Best Buy —*R.V. (11/15/2002)*

LE CORTI

Le Corti 2000 Sangiovese (Chianti Classico) $15. Very woody, with distinct aromas of vanilla and sawdust. The tight-knit palate has hidden black fruit and lots of bitter chocolate, the latter courtesy of some heavy barrel char. If the dark elements of barrel aging; i.e., charcoal and espresso, turn you on, then give this a go. But if not, the advice here is probably to steer clear. **84** —*M.S. (12/31/2002)*

Le Corti 1999 Cortevecchia Riserva Sangiovese (Chianti Classico) $23. The bouquet is fun: Leather, violets, and a strange, lean spiciness come up and out. The palate is tight, with lots of spice and nondescript berry fruit. The finish is hard and dry, and the mouthfeel is grainy, a reflection of young, robust tannins. **86** —*M.S. (12/31/2002)*

Le Corti 2000 Don Tommaso Sangiovese (Chianti Classico) $29. The bouquet is nicely perfumed and floral, with noticeable oak and spice augmenting plum aromas. The palate offers some heft, although it's maybe a bit overoaked. But that oak does contribute mocha and coffee flavors. The finish is expressive and tannic enough to apply a firm grip. **86** —*M.S. (12/31/2002)*

Le Corti 2000 Marsiliana Sangiovese (Toscana) $15. Mineral aromas lead the muscular nose forward in powerful fashion. The palate yields some spicy mint and clove but also a lot of oak-covered fruit; it's not entirely dissimilar to chocolate-covered cherries. The finish seems a bit thick, and it's also sweet, much like the wine as a whole. **86** —*M.S. (12/31/2002)*

LE DUE TERRE

Le Due Terre 2000 Sacrisassi Bianco White Blend (Colli Orientali del Friuli) $42. Tocai Friulano and Ribolla Gialla give this wine attractive floral aromas and full flavors of tropical fruits (lychees?), while the Sauvignon Blanc in the blend provides grapefruity notes that perfectly balance the effusiveness of the other varieties. **88** —*J.C. (7/1/2003)*

LE FILIGARE

Le Filigare 1997 Sangiovese (Chianti Classico) $19. This has a supple feel, but the berry and cherry fruit has a quite tart and woody quality. There are interesting herb and dark chocolate notes, but the tannins seem more oak than fruit derived. It's still good, though perhaps the potential for better is there. **85** *(4/1/2001)*

LE FIORAIE

Le Fioraie 2000 Sangiovese (Chianti Classico) $20. Tomato and light fruit on the nose. Blanched strawberry on the palate. Turns sweet and tangy late. **81** —*M.S. (10/1/2004)*

Le Fioraie 1998 Riserva Sangiovese (Toscana) $28. Fairly dull on the nose, with light tea and cherry aromas. On the palate, full strawberry and raspberry flavors precede a chunky, full finish. A bit of an awkward heavyweight, but friendly enough. **85** —*M.S. (10/1/2004)*

LE FONTI

Le Fonti 1999 Fontissimo Sangiovese (Toscana) $46. Mildly weedy and a bit burnt on the nose, indicating a heavy barrel regimen designed to cover modest fruit. The palate yields mostly dry raspberry in front of an equally dry, traditional finish. A decent wine but underwhelming, given the price tag. **85** —*M.S. (10/1/2004)*

LE GINESTRE

Le Ginestre 1997 Pian Romaldo Barbera (Barbera d'Alba) $19. **85** *(4/1/2000)*

Le Ginestre 1998 Chardonnay (Langhe) $13. **85** *(9/1/2000)*

Le Ginestre 1999 Madonna di Como Dolcetto (Dolcetto d'Alba) $16. This on-target wine shows why Dolcetto is the everyday red of choice in Piedmont. Vibrant cherry-chocolate aromas and a velvety, balanced palate are complemented by a long black pepper finish. It's ready to drink tonight. **88** —*M.N. (9/1/2001)*

Le Ginestre 1997 Madonna Di Como Dolcetto (Dolcetto d'Alba) $16. **84** *(4/1/2000)*

Le Ginestre 1998 Nebbiolo (Barolo) $45. Already brick at the rim, this wine smells mature, yielding scents of cedar, leather, and hints of raisins and figs. Flavors are sweet and caramelized; the tannins supple. Drink now–2008. **87** *(4/2/2004)*

LE GODE

Le Gode 2001 Brunello (Brunello di Montalcino) $67. Brawny and thick in the mouth but less intense aromatically with Brunello's trademark notes of wet tobacco, cherry, anise, and forest floor. Full-force flavors fill the palate to complete a velvety, extracted wine with a dark edge. **87** *(4/1/2006)*

LE MACCHIOCHE

Le Macchioche 2000 Brunello (Brunello di Montalcino) $60. Astringent at first, but better with airing. Strawberry, raspberry, and mint aromas precede jammy red fruit flavors. Exceedingly likable if not particularly complex or stately. Amid all the high fliers, this is an approachable, solid wine with chocolate notes and an easy finish. A Marc de Grazia Selection, various importers. **89** —*M.S. (7/1/2005)*

LE MACCHIOLE

Le Macchiole 1998 Paleo Cabernet Blend (Bolgheri) $84. From Bolgheri, what's fast becoming the Tuscan Gold Coast, this Cabernet Sauvignon (with 15% Sangiovese) offers complex aromas of bacon, rose hip, and vanilla. The palate is more basic than one might expect, given the exclusive neighborhood it comes from. There's round plummy fruit and creamy oak. The chewy, weighty finish is filled with residual plum and cherry flavors. **87** —*M.S. (8/1/2002)*

LE MACIOCHE

Le Maciocche 2001 Brunello (Brunello di Montalcino) $65. This is a wine you'll love or you won't. Our panelists came up with a long list of descriptors for the nose: strawberry, rhubarb, pastry crust, smoked bacon fat, resin, rubber, and tar. In the mouth, it delivers a stone-mineral quality and tart acidity that is almost excessive. A Marc De Grazia Selection, various U.S. Importers. **89** *(4/1/2006)*

Le Maciocche 1999 Brunello (Brunello di Montalcino) $NA. With integrated leather, dried fruit, and tomato aromas, this is just what textbook Brunello is all about. It's sly, deep, and complex, albeit a wee bit tight and tangy. Time should soften it up, and then it will deliver all the goods. Drink in 2007. **92** —*M.S. (6/1/2004)*

LE MICCINE

Le Miccine 2002 Sangiovese (Chianti Classico) $20. A fragile wine that doesn't seem meant for the cellar. In the meantime enjoy the racy mouthfeel, red cherry flavors, and mild tobacco and citrus peel nuances that improve the lengthy finish **85** *(4/1/2005)*

Le Miccine 2001 Sangiovese (Chianti Classico) $20. A bit sweet on the nose, with aromas of candied fruit and root beer. Flavors of sweet raspberry and tart pie cherry form a decent palate, which finishes with tea and red fruit notes. **86** —*M.S. (10/1/2004)*

Le Miccine 2000 Sangiovese (Chianti Classico) $22. A bouquet of ink, dark fruit, and dried cheese kicks things off. Next comes a candied raspberry flavor and lots of wood spice. But with that woodiness you'll notice piercing tannins that really dry things out. It needs time to soften. **87** — *M.S. (11/15/2003)*

Le Miccine 1999 Sangiovese (Chianti Classico) $24. Aromas of berry, wet earth, creamy oak, and a touch of horsehide reveal a sweet raspberry-tinged palate that seems to want to wrestle with the oak. The finish is medium to heavy, and a bit hot. There's plenty of verve and fruit here, just not much polish or complexity. Best in a trattoria setting. **86** —*M.S. (8/1/2002)*

Le Miccine 2000 Don Alberto Riserva Sangiovese (Chianti Classico) $40. Heavily oaked; frankly too much so. It smells at first like ham hocks and tar spread over bacon-covered marmalade. Once it opens, there's only modest berry fruit to support the thick, lemony oak that's all over the palate and finish. Ultimately, it tastes resiny. **83** —*M.S. (10/1/2004)*

Le Miccine 1999 Don Alberto Riserva Sangiovese (Chianti Classico) $40. Aromas of cassis, cola, and a hint of lemon make for an attractive bouquet. The mouth is a bit tangy due to electric red fruit bolstered by powerful acids. But it's one snappy, clean package. Gets better with airing, so try to give it time before drinking. **90** —*M.S. (11/15/2003)*

Le Miccine 1997 Don Alberto Riserva Sangiovese (Chianti Classico) $40. **89** *(9/1/2000)*

Le Miccine 1998 Riserva Don Alberto Sangiovese (Chianti Classico) $40. Very ripe, with earthy aromas of black plum, berry liqueur, and bitter chocolate. The mouthfeel is meaty and muscular, but not hard. A wall of moderate tannins builds after a few sips, but the overall feel is still soft. The finish is medium in length, with adequate depth. **88** —*M.S. (8/1/2002)*

Le Miccine 2001 Riserva Don Alberto Sangiovese (Chianti Classico) $40. Very tight and woody, with aromas of charred hamburger, leather, and toast. Cherry, burnt bread crust and smoked meat on the palate lead into a fresh but oaky finish, where popcorn is identifiable. Overall it's racy and tasty. A stand-up contender. **88** *(4/1/2005)*

LE MUSE

Le Muse 1997 Pinot Grigio (Piave) $7. **81** *(8/1/1999)*

LE POTAZZINE

Le Potazzine 2001 Gorelli Brunello (Brunello di Montalcino) $55. Aromatics are not very intense but do yield leather, earth, and tobacco over cherry fruitiness with vigorous swirling. Moderately toasty, with sweet spice accents and a dry finish on this medium-bodied Brunello. There is harmony, but no poetry here. **86** *(4/1/2006)*

LE RAGOSE

Le Ragose 1999 Estate Bottled Red Blend (Valpolicella Classico Superiore) $14. Simple but attractive aromas of bacon, tree bark, and red fruit get it off to a fine start. The second act is a palate of cherry, vanilla, and chocolate. The finish is long, creamy, and ultimately satisfying. This might be standard, but it's a great take on standard. **89 Best Buy** *(5/1/2003)*

Le Ragose 1999 Estate Bottled Red Blend (Amarone della Valpolicella) $60. Snappy and zesty from the very start, something we describe as "elegant." This wine has some of the requisite richness and prune character of a good Amarone, but it leans more to red fruit, freshness, and pop than heaviness. A sure thing with food, something many can't offer. **91** *(11/1/2005)*

Le Ragose 1997 Estate Bottled Red Blend (Amarone della Valpolicella) $53. Some clove and cardamom notes add character to the toasty, barrel-driven nose. In the mouth, rich black cherry and blackberry flavors seem as though they were infused with some brandy or Port. The finish is all fruit, so much so that one reviewer called the wine a fruit ball that departs from tradition. Still it's ripe, healthy, and should age for quite some time. **89** *(5/1/2003)*

LE SALETTE

Le Salette 2000 La Marega Amarone (Amarone della Valpolicella Classico) $63. Gets off the blocks with sly baked fruit aromas, notes of berry liqueur, and just enough exotic fragrance to lock you in. Tastes great as well, with cherry, chocolate, and cinnamon, all underscored by fine acidity. Always a great Amarone and the 2000 doesn't disappoint. **91** *(11/1/2005)*

Le Salette 1999 Pergole Vece Amarone (Amarone della Valpolicella Classico) $120. Definitely smooth and woody, with plenty of toast, cedar, and coffee along with black cherry. Shows a lot of the right stuff throughout, from the broad palate that sports sweet notes of caramel, coffee, and root beer to the easy finish. Only a bit of hard tannin makes it firm; otherwise it registers as soft. **89** *(11/1/2005)*

Le Salette 2000 Ca' Camocchio Red Blend (Valpolicella Classico Superiore) $35. Pure and pungent up front, with hints of horsehide and sawdust. The ripe, round palate is pleasing and borders on being lus-

cious; the flavors veer toward berry fruit with hints of green tobacco and tomato. The finish is long and softly tannic. **88** *(5/1/2003)*

Le Salette 2000 I Progni Red Blend (Valpolicella Classico Superiore) $25. Very clean and textbook from the fresh cherry and leather nose through the smooth red fruit and vanilla palate and all the way to the creamy, well-wooded finish. While this wine may not be uniquely individual, it sings the praises of the Veneto in perfect pitch. **90** *(5/1/2003)*

Le Salette 1999 La Marega Red Blend (Amarone della Valpolicella Classico) $60. Deep and full; a thoroughbred with firm tannins and ample acidity. The nose of cherries, mint, and licorice draws you in. Next comes brandied cherry flavors touched up by hints of black pepper, herbs, and chocolate. The finish is lengthy and layered, and overall this is one complete, smooth wine. **90** *(5/1/2003)*

Le Salette 1998 Pergole Vece Red Blend (Amarone della Valpolicella Classico) $115. Here's a spicy, brooding beauty, one that could use a few years before it's at its best. Aromas of pepper, earth, mushroom, and spiced cherries are interesting and inviting. We also liked the explosive flavors of dried cherries, blackberries, chocolate, and vanilla. Some tannins add grip. **93 Cellar Selection** *(5/1/2003)*

LE TORRI

Le Torri 1998 Sangiovese (Chianti Colli Fiorentini) $10. Light berry aromas carry smoke and cedar accents. The mouthfeel is even and dry, and tart cherry and cocoa flavors carry from the palate through the moderate finish. A good quaff in a lighter style. **84** *(4/1/2001)*

LE VIGNE

Le Vigne 2003 Sangiovese (Chianti) $12. Somewhat lean, yet chunky enough. Aromas of candied berry and green tobacco lead to a plum and cherry palate with medium tannins and a mildly chewy feel. Short and dusty on the tail, but with ample acidity. **85** *(4/1/2005)*

Le Vigne 2002 Sangiovese (Chianti) $12. Fat and flat, with a deep color but not much clarity. The fruit is stewy and devoid of pop, while the finish is starchy and lemony. Little to no balance or charm to speak of. **82** *(4/1/2005)*

LEONE DE CASTRIS

Leone de Castris 1996 Donna Lisa Riserva Negroamaro (Salice Salentino) $30. Buttercream, lemon zest, vanilla—most of the panel found the bouquet on the sweet side. However, some reviewers also saw fresh garden vegetables and earth on the nose. The palate offers blackberry, herb, and chocolate flavors, though reviewers were divided as to whether the mouthfeel was cloying or well-balanced. Finishes with lots of herb and ash. One to try for yourself. **86** —*C.S. (5/1/2002)*

Leone de Castris 1999 Riserva Negroamaro (Salice Salentino) $12. **85** —*P.G. (5/1/2002)*

Leone de Castris 1998 Riserva Negroamaro (Salice Salentino) $12. **85** —*C.S. (5/1/2002)*

Leone de Castris 1999 Santera Primitivo (Primitivo Di Manduria) $15. **81** —*C.S. (5/1/2002)*

LEPORE

Lepore 1996 Montepulciano (Colonella) $13. **85** *(9/1/2000)*

LETRARI

Letrari 1995 Brut Riserva Champagne Blend (Trento) $19. **91 Best Buy** *(12/31/2000)*

LIBRANDI

Librandi 1999 Gaglioppo (Cirò Classico) $10. This wine is 100% Gaglioppo, which is the primary red grape of Calabria. The color is light to medium ruby with some brown at the edge. The structure is good, and the flavors are dry fruit and earth. Although this is a '99, the wine just seems old before its time. **84** —*M.N. (9/1/2001)*

Librandi 1997 Duca Sanfelice Riserva Gaglioppo (Calabria) $13. A riserva Gaglioppo, this wine is characterized by dry fruit, tea, and tobacco flavors. An earthy nuance brings the curtain down. Medium-bodied and well-balanced, the mouthfeel is smooth. This fully mature wine is ready

ITALY

for drinking now. With it, the Calabrese recommend a spicy sausage from Calabria…and why not? **86** —*M.N. (9/1/2001)*

Librandi 1996 Gravello Gaglioppo (Calabria) $29. The mix in this deep, ruby, purple- colored wine is 60% Gaglioppo and 40% Cabernet Sauvignon. The structure is of good weight, and is round and finely balanced. Initially reticent with its aromatics, after breathing, the wine opens with a deep cherry, dry fruit, and woody bouquet. The flavors continue into the long finish where earthy nuances then appear. This one needs some patience. **88** —*M.N. (9/1/2001)*

Librandi 2000 Rosso Classico Gaglioppo (Cirò) $10. Already browning at the rim, this wine seems prematurely old, with mature stewed fruit and leather aromas and flavors. **81** —*C.S. (5/1/2002)*

Librandi 1999 Magno Megonio Magliocco (Calabria) $35. Starts off with sweet confectionary aromas of crystallized berries and powdered sugar, then turns tarry and oaky on the finish. The drying wood tannins so apparent now should resolve relatively quickly; try in 2003 with light ragus or pizza. **85** —*C.S. (5/1/2002)*

Librandi 1998 Gravello Red Blend (Calabria) $29. This complex but modern blend of Cabernet Sauvignon and Gaglioppo features plenty of toasty oak, red berries, and vanilla with a honeyed overlay that's akin to maple syrup. The fruit turns darker in the mouth, developing blueberry and blackberry flavors. A long, tangy finish bodes well for short-term (2–4 years) aging. **89** —*C.S. (5/1/2002)*

LIS NERIS

Lis Neris 2004 Pinot Grigio (Venezia Giulia) $15. This wine favors fruit over nuttiness, with opulent melon and pear on an intense and complex nose. There's lovely depth and texture. **88** —*M.L. (2/1/2006)*

Lis Neris 2003 Pinot Grigio (Venezia Giulia) $16. A gorgeously smooth wine with toasted notes, walnut husk, and wood woven successfully into a creamy, fruity nose. Creamy and chewy with snappy spice on the finish. **88 Editors' Choice** —*M.L. (2/1/2006)*

LISINI

Lisini 2001 Brunello (Brunello di Montalcino) $60. Delicate mint and herb shadings back red berry fruit and vanilla-nutmeg spice. There's a creamy almost blueberry muffin dough quality that lends character but is not heavy in the least. Dry firm tannins and a tight, clean close. **90** *(4/1/2006)*

Lisini 2000 Brunello (Brunello di Montalcino) $69. Dark and masculine, with smoky black cherry notes carrying the sturdy bouquet. It pops with bright plum, black cherry, and chocolate flavors, and it has proper tannins that give it some edge. **90** —*M.S. (7/1/2005)*

Lisini 1999 Ugolaia Brunello (Brunello di Montalcino) $122. Intoxicatingly smoky nose, like fine wood burning slowly on a cold night. The mouth is jam-packed with vanilla, chocolate, and cream as well as black cherry and dark currants. Sweet and easy throughout, with a touch of coffee on the finish. Lovely, chewy stuff. **92** —*M.S. (7/1/2005)*

LIVIO FELLUGA

Livio Felluga 1997 Esperto Chardonnay (Friuli) $16. **86** *(9/1/2000)*

Livio Felluga 1995 Sosso Riserva Merlot (Colli Orientali del Friuli) $35. **89** —*M.S. (9/1/2000)*

Livio Felluga 2000 Vertigo Merlot-Cabernet Sauvignon (Friuli Venezia Giulia) $21. This Merlot-Cabernet blend has a broad, expressive bouquet that features hickory smoke, molasses, pepper, and olive. Black cherry with vanilla and white pepper carry the palate, which is far from heavy but not lean in the least. The finish is lengthy, juicy, and fruity. **89** *(5/1/2003)*

Livio Felluga 2000 Illivio Pinot Bianco (Colli Orientali del Friuli) $NA. A 100% Pinot Bianco wine, aged in wood. This is an exotic, complex wine, with layers of different characters. Ripe flavors and spice go with the aromas of white flowers and tropical fruits. **89** —*R.V. (1/1/2004)*

Livio Felluga 1999 Pinot Grigio (Friuli Venezia Giulia) $21. **90** —*M.S. (9/1/2000)*

Livio Felluga 1997 Pinot Grigio (Friuli Venezia Giulia) $20 **85** — *(8/1/1999)*

Livio Felluga 2004 Pinot Grigio (Collio) $25. It's rare to find Grigios that reflect the grape's natural copperish or pinkish skin tone like this one does. Its silky mouthfeel and bursting acidity are also unique. Only the nose, which is dominated by a multivitamin-like smell, didn't win me over. **87** —*M.L. (2/1/2006)*

Livio Felluga 2002 Pinot Grigio (Friuli Venezia Giulia) $23. Pinot Grigio grape berries aren't actually gray; instead they are tinged with pink or purple. Maybe it is just the power of suggestion, but this wine even seems to taste pink, showcasing ripe berries and apples that are backed by tangy acids and great length. Classy stuff. **90** —*J.C. (7/1/2003)*

Livio Felluga 2001 Pinot Grigio (Friuli Venezia Giulia) $24. There's a slight coppery tinge to this wine's color, which sets it apart from the vast majority of other Grigios on the market. And maybe it's just the suggestion of the hue, but it seems to taste "pink" as well, showcasing ripe berries and appples backed by tangy acids and great length. Classy stuff. **90 Editors' Choice** —*J.C. (7/1/2003)*

Livio Felluga 2000 Pinot Grigio (Friuli Venezia Giulia) $21. This full and tangy Pinot Grigio opens with a subdued orange, mineral, and tropical fruit nose. There's a good citrus-herb tension to the palate, and darker and spicier flavors here than usually encountered in Italian versions of the grape. Nicely balanced, the wine has a long, citrus-spice finish. **88** —*M.M. (9/1/2001)*

Livio Felluga 2002 Sauvignon Blanc (Colli Orientali del Friuli) $NA. Delicious grassy fruits and a fine mineral taste, give this wine plenty of character. It is fresh, crisp, green and herbaceous, very much in a cool climate style. **88** —*R.V. (1/1/2004)*

Livio Felluga 1998 Tocai (Colli Orientali del Friuli) $20. **86** *(9/1/2000)*

Livio Felluga 2002 Tocai (Friuli Venezia Giulia) $22. Boasts penetrating grapefruit aromas but also some warm, peachy accents. On the palate, its stony and minerally flavors play against a richly textured mouthfeel. The long, delicate finish shows hints of pepper and grapefruit. **88** —*J.C. (7/1/2003)*

Livio Felluga 2001 Tocai (Friuli Venezia Giulia) $24. **90 Editors' Choice** —*J.C. (7/1/2003)*

Livio Felluga 2000 Terre Alte Rosazzo Bianco White Blend (Colli Orientali del Friuli) $41. In general, we love Felluga's wines. So why the modest score on the winery's top white? One simple word: oak. With this wine's buttery, oaky aromas and flavors of peach, cinnamon, and brown sugar, it could pass for a decent Chardonnay. But this blend of Tocai Friulano, Pinot Bianco, and Sauvignon Blanc from a great producer should do so much more. **86** —*J.C. (7/1/2003)*

LIVIO SASSETTI

Livio Sassetti 2001 Pertimali Brunello (Brunello di Montalcino) $NA. There's a tutti-frutti glossiness to this wine that helps liven understated aromas such as light coffee, rose pedal, white cherry, cinnamon, and violet. Well-structured and constructed with tight, sour tannins on the end. **88** *(4/1/2006)*

LIVON

Livon 1997 Pinot Grigio (Collio) $15. **85** *(8/1/1999)*

Livon Erte 1997 Braide Grande Vineyard Pinot Grigio (Collio) $20. **83** *(8/1/1999)*

LOBSTER COVE

Lobster Cove 2004 Pinot Grigio (Veneto) $11. A tiny bit floral and out of the ordinary. Shows apple, pineapple, and muscat aromas, with similar flavors that offer spice and pepper. Short but clean on the finish, with a hint of tarragon and lemon. **84** *(2/1/2006)*

LODOLA NUOVA

Lodola Nuova 2002 Sangiovese (Vino Nobile di Montepulciano) $22. Fairly full on the bouquet, with a dense roundness that cups charcoal and shoe polish aromas along with berry fruit. A bit more harsh than desirable on the palate, with sweetness lacking. That said, it pours on the plum, cherry, and cranberry in fist-like fashion. **84** —*M.S. (7/1/2005)*

Lodola Nuova 2001 Riserva Sangiovese (Vino Nobile di Montepulciano) $35. As herbal as they come, with an aromatic cornucopia of oregano, basil, and rosemary alongside raspberry, tomato, and leather. A touch raw and hard for an '01 riserva, but interesting if you prefer a traditionally styled wine. **86** —*M.S. (7/1/2005)*

LODOVICO ANTINORI

Lodovico Antinori 1995 Ornellaia Bordeaux Blend (Bolgheri) $63. **96** — *M.S. (5/1/1999)*

LOHSA

Lohsa 2000 Sangiovese (Morellino di Scansano) $18. Fresh and full, with a deep berry nose, drying tannins, and ample but not overdone oak. In the mouth, it's pretty solid, and the cherry and black plum fruit is clean and tasty. It's on the stout side, with youthful acidity and a good deal of warmth to the smoky finish. From Poliziano. **88** —*M.S. (8/1/2002)*

LOREDAN GASPARINI

Loredan Gasparini 2005 Pinot Grigio (Delle Venezie) $16. A bigger, bolder style with rich toasted notes of almond, vanilla, and stone fruit. Very clear, with a lean, fresh mouthfeel yet those strong toasted notes might not appeal to everyone. **87** —*M.L. (6/1/2006)*

Loredan Gasparini 2004 Pinot Grigio (Delle Venezie) $16. Features clean, delineated mineral tones and feminine floral notes. The wine is elegant, subtle, but stylistic, crisp but not sharp. Drink now. **88** —*M.L. (2/1/2006)*

LORENZON

Lorenzon 2004 Grigio Mascalzone Pinot Grigio (Friuli Isonzo) $16. The wine's name: Grigio Mascalzone (loosely translated as "troublemaker") pays homage to some of the difficulties winemakers may encounter when making Pinot Grigio. This copper-tinged wine boasts applesauce and cinnamon aromas, a spicy elegance and a tart mouthfeel. **87** —*M.L. (6/1/2006)*

LOSI

Losi 1997 Millennium Riserva Sangiovese (Chianti Classico) $30. Funky at first, then better. The nose deals stewed fruit dressed in mocha and a blast of char. Slightly muddled on the palate, with beefy, sugary red fruit that sports some bell pepper. Finishes crunchy and gritty, with a sweet-and-sour component. **85** *(4/1/2005)*

LUCCIO

Luccio 2002 Merlot (Veneto) $7. Light in color and already showing some browning at the rim, this Merlot is cleanly made, but only shows tart, leafy flavors of tomato and dried cherries. Lean, thins out on the finish. **82** —*J.C. (12/31/2004)*

Luccio NV Moscato (Moscato d'Asti) $9. Bright, floral aromas give way to ripe stone fruit and tangerines. This is concentrated and flavorful, but not overly rich or heavy; sweet, yet balanced by orangy acids. **87 Best Buy** —*J.C. (11/15/2004)*

Luccio NV Spumante Moscato (Asti) $8. This little Moscato is floral, tight, and loaded with honey aromas. The palate is fairly smooth, with melon and dried mango flavors. An easy wine, one that's slick on the finish and sweet. A touch candied and syrupy, but a good deal. **86 Best Buy** —*M.S. (12/15/2004)*

Luccío 2002 Sangiovese (Chianti) $7. Lean and drying on the bouquet, with rhubarb, campfire, and citrus notes. Flavorwise, we're talking tart cherry and raspberry, while the finish is simple and mainstream in scope. **84 Best Buy** *(4/1/2005)*

Luccío 1998 Reserva Sangiovese (Chianti Rufina) $14. Dark, but with an aromatic hint of shoe polish along with blackberry and prune. Hardly an expressive wine, but not bad. The plum and raisin flavors are middle of the road, arguably a touch over-ripe. Meanwhile, the finish is surprisingly tangy, seemingly on the verge of volatile. **84** *(4/1/2005)*

LUCE

Luce 1998 Red Blend (Toscana) $75. This much touted blend of Sangiovese and Merlot from Robert Mondavi and the Frescobaldi winery is expensive and uninteresting. You can tell what they're striving for, a complex wine of early drinkability, but it's merely simple. and the best

French oak doesn't improve it. It's not bad, just dull, and it won't age. **84** —*S.H. (9/12/2002)*

Luce 2001 della Vite Sangiovese (Toscana) $75. Takes a while to rev up, but once it gets going it can't be stopped. Beautifully ripe and defined across the palate, with rich black fruit on level one and licorice and vanilla on level two. Finishes long, smooth, and spicy, with concentration throughout. Probably our favorite Luce to date. **92 Editors' Choice** —*M.S. (9/1/2006)*

Luce 2000 Della Vite Sangiovese (Toscana) $75. This Frescobaldi/Mondavi joint venture got it right in 2000. The wine, a blend of 60% Merlot and 40% Sangiovese, is rich, forward, and hedonistic, a cuvée made more for now than down the line. The nose is lovely, with floral aromas in front of baked berry pie. The palate is sweet and ripe, but balanced by spice and pepper notes. **92** —*M.S. (10/1/2004)*

Luce 1999 della Vite Sangiovese (Toscana) $75. This super Tuscan blends 50% Sangiovese with 50% Merlot for a wine that combines some of the wiry structure of Sangiovese with the plump flesh of Merlot. Filled with more opulent fruit than the '98, this vintage may be the best yet, bursting with plum and mocha flavors that extend through the dry, toasty finish. **90** *(9/1/2002)*

Luce 2001 Lucente Sangiovese (Toscana) $25. Luce's second wine is violet in color, with profound cola and root beer aromas, lots of oak, and a rich personality. The flavor profile goes straight to cassis, cherry, and cola, while the live-wire finish is young, fresh, and clean. Arguably a bit overoaked and syrupy, but still a fun wine. **89** —*M.S. (10/1/2004)*

LUCENTE

Lucente 1999 Sangiovese (Toscana) $28. Dusty and dry, this wine uses a higher percentage of Sangiovese than Luce and the result is a tougher, more austere wine that gets much of its character from dried spice and toast. Understated and restrained, you can almost taste the influence of co-creator Tim Mondavi. **85** *(9/1/2002)*

Lucente 1998 Sangiovese (Toscana) $28. Interesting and complex, combines sweet raspberry and black cherry flavors with earthy notes. Soft tannins make it instantly accessible, while crisp acidity provides balance. Turns simple in the middle palate, but is saved by a rich finish. A blend of 85% Sangiovese and 15% Merlot. **89** —*S.H. (8/1/2002)*

Lucente 2001 La Vite Sangiovese (Toscana) $26. Earthy and ripe, with lovely black fruit mixing with cedary wood on the nose. Plum, blackberry and chocolate flavors make for a well-known and likable flavor profile, while the toasty finish deals touches of balsamic vinegar and licorice. Unassailable as a total package. **90** —*M.S. (9/1/2006)*

LUCIANO SANDRONE

Luciano Sandrone 2003 Dolcetto (Dolcetto d'Alba) $20. The 2003 Dolcettos have enough boldly flavored fruit to hang with your best blue-cheese burgers, enough spice to stand up to jerk chicken—and enough tannin to cut through the fattiest slab of ribs. What sets Sandrone's version apart is the sense of elegance that suggests it would be just as home on a white tablecloth as a rustic wooden table. A Marc de Grazia Selection, various U.S. importers. **90** —*J.C. (8/1/2005)*

Luciano Sandrone 1998 Cannubi Boschis Nebbiolo (Barolo) $125. Expensive, but worth every penny to experience such a big, lush, juicy mouthful of Barolo. Hints of dark-roasted coffee and wisps of maple syrup wrap around flavors of strawberries and tar, but this wine is all about the seduction of texture—velvety and supple, it leaves you wanting more and more. **93 Cellar Selection** *(4/2/2004)*

LUIANICO

Luianico 2003 Rosso Sangiovese (Toscana) $8. More of a traditional, simple table wine as opposed to a high flier. The nose is lightweight and offers soft strawberry hints. Citrus, pie cherry, and apple skin make for a crisp, almost tart palate. Fortunately there's enough fruit to keep it steady. **85 Best Buy** —*M.S. (9/1/2006)*

LUIANO

Luiano 2002 Sangiovese (Chianti Classico) $16. Cherry, open-cut wood, and rubber dominate the nose, which is backed by harsh, lemony fruit. Exceedingly tart, with a lean streak to the palate. **83** *(4/1/2005)*

ITALY

ITALY

Luiano 2000 Sangiovese (Chianti Classico) $16. Open in the nose, with aromatic notes of blackberry. Although it's rather simple and straightforward, it's a good wine. The cherry and ripe plum fruit come up to the brim, while the big, tasty finish is perfectly balanced and accessible. **89** —M.S. (11/15/2003)

Luiano 1998 Estate Bottled Sangiovese (Chianti Classico) $16. This well-made wine shows good cherry fruit and a licorice or mint note on the nose. Round and fairly full on the palate, it shows complex and classic Chianti flavors—cherries, plums, cinnamon, and leather—and the modern addition of toasty oak. Shows good length and some dusty tannins on the back end. **89** (4/1/2001)

Luiano 1998 Gold Label Sangiovese (Chianti Classico) $25. Dry, dusty aromas precede more common olfactory notes such as leather and rhubarb. The palate is a bit lean, showing cherry and spice. Subdued and simple. **86** —M.S. (11/15/2003)

Luiano 1999 Gold Label Riserva Sangiovese (Chianti Classico) $24. A bit of leather and raisin get it going, followed by berry, citrus, and tannins. Comes on lean, where it resembles the whicker-basket wines of the old days. A touch too rudimentary and tart to score higher. **84** (4/1/2005)

Luiano 1996 Riserva Sangiovese (Chianti Classico) $23. Cedar, cherry, and menthol aromas open to a classic tart black cherry and cinnamon-accented palate. Full, smooth, and dry, it finishes long with some leather and black tea flavors and solid tannins. Very handsomely constructed, this superbly balanced wine is already drinking well and should continue to improve. **91** (4/1/2001)

LUIGI EINAUDI

Luigi Einaudi 1997 Vigna Tecc Dolcetto (Dolcetto di Dogliani) $20. 89 (4/1/2000)

Luigi Einaudi 2001 Costa Grimaldi Nebbiolo (Barolo) $86. This plump, full-bodied Barolo features an almost creamy texture, making it attractive in the relatively short term (5–8 years). Fatty, cedary notes on the nose are joined by super-ripe black cherries and dried spices. Finishes long, with plush tannins. **91** (3/1/2006)

Luigi Einaudi 2001 Nei Cannubi Nebbiolo (Barolo) $100. Ripe, black cherry fruit is framed by lashings of vanilla and dried spice in this lush yet tannic Barolo that ends with a mouthfeel like chewy velvet. Throughout, there's a charred-roasted caramel note that stands a bit apart from the rest of the wine. **90** (3/1/2006)

LUIGI RIGHETTI

Luigi Righetti 2000 Capital de Roari Amarone (Amarone della Valpolicella) $24. Spice on a light bouquet is the calling card of this more elegant wine. The nose offers cinnamon, cedar, and herbs in addition to red berry scents. The palate is refined and precise, although not particularly deep or dense. Slightly piquant and made more for the dinner table than for in front of the fireplace. **90 Editors' Choice** (11/1/2005)

Luigi Righetti 1995 Capitel de' Roari Corvina (Amarone della Valpolicella) $25. 87 —M.N. (12/31/2000)

Luigi Righetti 1995 Ca' del Monte Red Blend (Amarone della Valpolicella) $36. Sweet aromas of butterscotch, cherry, and caramel combine and carry through to the palate along with licorice, toast, and minerals. But there's a distinctly fiery note of alcohol that seems to dominate the palate. Firmly structured, this wine needs time to tone down and develop some nuance. **86** —J.F. (9/1/2001)

Luigi Righetti 1999 Campolieti Red Blend (Valpolicella Classico) $12. A floral nose with some leather, coffee, and bread dough does nothing to turn one away. The raspberry flavors with light oak in support are nice but simple, while the finish is dry, fruity enough, and layered. **87 Best Buy** (5/1/2003)

Luigi Righetti 2001 Capitel de Roari Red Blend (Amarone della Valpolicella Classico) $26. Burnt and harsh relative to the field, with sweaty leather and some barnyard on the nose. The palate keeps hold of that cooked quality with its charred burger and baked fruit flavors. Finishes hot and spicy, and a touch metallic. **84** (11/1/2005)

LUNA DI LUNA

Luna Di Luna 2002 White Blend (Veneto) $10. This blend is very light in color and similarly shy on the nose, where it takes coaxing to find some citrus fruits and dried spices. Tastes like mixed citrus, but folds in a dash of cherry juice as well. **83** —J.C. (7/1/2003)

Luna Di Luna NV Extra Dry White Blend (Veneto) $12. 82 —M.M. (12/31/2000)

LUNGAROTTI

Lungarotti 2001 Cabernet Sauvignon (Torgiano) $22. A Cab that amounts to a starter wine. It lacks the cassis and berry flavors and aromas of a big boy while pouring on red fruit and acidity. Fairly monotone in its approach, with big Umbrian tannins. **84** —M.S. (11/15/2004)

Lungarotti 2002 Chardonnay (Umbria) $16. Ultra floral, with fresh, clean honeysuckle aromas. In the mouth, apple and peach flavors are fresh and fun, while the finish is smooth and nutty. Soft and meant to drink now; good in its class. **87** —M.S. (6/1/2005)

Lungarotti 2002 Aurente Chardonnay (Umbria) $40. Attractive apricot, peach, and honey aromas vie with a strong dosing of oak on the bouquet. Second and third takes, however, unveil additional smoky nuances. Apple and melon flavors are true, while the finish is soft and smooth. Easygoing and textured; a positive example of high-end Umbrian Chardonnay. **89** —M.S. (6/1/2005)

Lungarotti 1998 Pinot Grigio (Umbria) $12. 83 (8/1/1999)

Lungarotti 2004 Pinot Grigio (Umbria) $17. This appealing Pinot Grigio from Central Italy conveys heavier aromas like warm honey, loads of ripe melon, and summer flowers. Soft and creamy in the mouth. **86** —M.L. (2/1/2006)

Lungarotti 2000 Giubilante Red Blend (Umbria) $18. Chunky up front, with some green tobacco to go with mocha and blackberry aromas. Plum and berry flavors are ripe and aggressive, and it's a bit chewy, with some toast and coffee. Lightweight acidity and tannins makes it somewhat short on structure. **85** —M.S. (12/15/2003)

Lungarotti 1998 Giubilante Red Blend (Umbria) $18. 85 —M.S. (2/1/2003)

Lungarotti 1998 Rubesco Red Blend (Torgiano) $15. 87 —M.S. (2/1/2003)

Lungarotti 1992 Rubesco Vigna Monticchio Red Blend (Torgiano Rosso Riserva) $43. 89 —M.S. (2/1/2003)

Lungarotti 1997 San Giorgio Red Blend (Umbria) $67. A classic, old-style blend of Sangiovese, Canaiolo, and Cab Sauvignon. It's dry, aging and lighter in frame. Which isn't to imply that it's short of structure. It has bracing acidity and a racy mouthfeel. Along the way catch pure, oak-draped berry character. **88** —M.S. (11/15/2004)

Lungarotti 1993 San Giorgio Red Blend (Umbria) $58. 90 —M.S. (2/1/2003)

Lungarotti 1990 San Giorgio Red Blend (Rosso dell'Umbria) $49. 90 —M.S. (3/1/2000)

Lungarotti 1990 Rubesco Monticchio Sangiovese (Torgiano Rosso Riserva) $35. 95 (3/1/2000)

Lungarotti 2002 Torre di Giano White Blend (Torgiano) $18. Simple, with bland citrus aromas and flavors. Finishes watery. **81** —M.S. (10/1/2004)

LUWA

Luwa 1997 Selezione Luwa Collio DOC Pinot Grigio (Collio) $14. 80 (8/1/1999)

MACHIAVELLI

Machiavelli 1998 Riserva Fontalle Sangiovese (Chianti Classico) $NA. 85 —R.V. (8/1/2002)

MACULAN

Maculan 2003 Fratta Cabernet Sauvignon (Veneto) $80. Seductive, succulent, and hedonistic. This 77% Cabernet Sauvignon and 33% Merlot blend is incredibly forthcoming and ready to drink immediately thanks to its rich toasted notes, chocolate fudge, blackberry, leather, tobacco, menthol, and herbal aromas. There's a ton of vanilla and sweet spice on the velvety finish and melted chocolate on the close. **94 Editors' Choice** —*M.L. (9/1/2006)*

Maculan 2001 Brentino Cabernet Sauvignon-Merlot (Veneto) $14. Here's a pleasant, easy-to-drink blend of Merlot and Cab Sauvignon that begins with earth, bacon, and blackberry aromas, which in turn are trailed by basic berry and plum-like flavors. The finish is mildly toasty, with notes of coffee and bramble. The tannins are soft, so the wine feels substantive and rich. **87** *(5/1/2003)*

Maculan 1999 Fratta Cabernet Sauvignon-Merlot (Veneto) $80. Clearly this 67% Cabernet Sauvignon, 33% Merlot blend is designed to appeal to the international market, meaning it's extracted, rich, supple, and at 14.5%, rather high in alcohol (for a Veneto wine). That said, it is truly luscious and delicious, with black fruit pouring out of the glass. Accents of oak, tobacco and vanilla make it all the more friendly. **91 Cellar Selection** *(5/1/2003)*

Maculan 1999 Breganze di Breganze White Blend (Veneto) $15. Breganze is a village in the hills north of Venice. The grapes, Tocai and Pinot Bianco, also come from Breganze—hence the wine's name. The bouquet is primarily pear with some petrol in the distance. Good balance and weight, together with the crisp acidity and an oily mouthfeel, complete the structure. The finish is long with some almond and petrol notes. **84** —*M.N. (9/1/2001)*

Maculan 2002 Pino & Toi White Blend (Veneto) $10. This blended white combines Tocai Friulano (60%) with Pinot Bianco (25%) and Pinot Grigio (15%) in a tasty, corpulent wine well worth its modest price. Bold flavors of oranges, pink grapefruits, and ripe cherries mingle in the mouth; the only quibble is that it finishes a little short. **87 Best Buy** — *J.C. (7/1/2003)*

Maculan 2000 Pino & Toi White Blend (Veneto) $11. Not a vaudeville act, but the second edition of a new wine. The name refers to the wine's mixture—Pino for Pinot Bianco (25%) and Pinot Grigio (15%) and Toi for Tocai (60%). That said, the wine starts with lovely grapefruit, pear, and almond scents. On the palate, there is good weight, lively acidity, and a viscous mouthfeel. The finish, however, is somewhat short with an unusual petrol-like note. **85** —*M.N. (9/1/2001)*

Maculan 2001 Pino & Toi White Blend (Veneto) $11. 88 Best Buy —*C.S. (11/15/2002)*

MADONNA ALTA

Madonna Alta 2002 Sagrantino (Montefalco) $NA. The Ferraro family bought beautiful property surrounding a 15th-centruy chapel dedicated to the Madonna in 1992 and today 14 hectares are planted to vines. Here's an example of a more traditional take on Sagrantino Montefalco aged 18 months in Slovenian oak with vegetal, pea pod tones and a tannic explosion that makes your mouth go tight. **85** —*M.L. (9/1/2005)*

MADONNA DELLE GRAZIE

Madonna delle Grazie 2001 Selezione Brunello (Brunello di Montalcino) $NA. This wine divided our panelists—two who enjoyed it very much, and one less so. The supporters described a creamy and complex wine with cherry, herbs, and just the right touch of supporting woodspice. The finish could be longer, but did carry bold berry flavors. **91** *(4/1/2006)*

MALGRA

Malgra 2001 Cortese (Gavi di Gavi) $16. A touch sweet from front to back, but a pretty good Gavi. Heady aromas of candy and banana yield after airing to subdued pear. The palate is typically full of citrus, primarily orange and grapefruit. That same citrus carries out all the way through the finish. A touch oversized, but flavorful. **85** —*M.S. (12/15/2003)*

MALIBRAN

Malibran NV Gorio Extra Dry Prosecco (Prosecco di Valdobbiadene) $NA. Lime soda and lollipop-like aromas are flanked by stone fruit and grapefruit. Crisp, clean characteristics are carried through to the mouth, where more candy flavors ride over a crisp finish. **86** —*M.L. (6/1/2006)*

Malibran 2005 Ruio Brut Prosecco (Prosecco di Valdobbiadene) $NA. This bubbly has a soda pop feel and flavors of flowers, stone fruit, and white pepper. Lean and could be livelier on the palate. **85** —*M.L. (6/1/2006)*

MANDRAROSSA

MandraRossa 2004 Cabernet Sauvignon-Shiraz (Sicilia) $9. The Mandrarossa line delivers good value for your dollar and this powerful blend of blockbuster grapes presents deep notes of cedar, cherry preserve, and dried herbs. Some elements of the nose have traces of over-ripe fruit. **86 Best Buy** —*M.L. (7/1/2006)*

MandraRossa 2005 Chardonnay (Sicilia) $9. The nice orange blossom and peach tones reflect a precise and clean winemaking approach. You'll get orange and cream in the mouth, and a crisp finish. **86 Best Buy** —*M.L. (7/1/2006)*

MandraRossa 2003 Chardonnay (Sicilia) $9. Gold in color and sweet, but still healthy enough to rate well. Honey, syrup, and peaches carry the nose, while the palate is full of pear, banana, and toasted nuts. The soft, chewy mouthfeel warns that this should be drunk soon. **86 Best Buy** — *M.S. (2/1/2005)*

MandraRossa 2005 Fiano (Sicilia) $9. Fun and cheerful with notes of banana, pineapple, vanilla, peach, and herbal tea. It is green-gold in color, with a touch of sourness on the finish. **86 Best Buy** —*M.L. (7/1/2006)*

MandraRossa 2004 Fiano (Sicilia) $9. A golden-hued wine with a thicker consistency that packs walnuts, peanut shell, and exotic fruit. The mouthfeel is buttery, fleshy, and smooth, making it an ideal match for spicy foods. **86 Best Buy** —*M.L. (9/1/2005)*

MandraRossa 2003 Fiano (Sicilia) $9. Quite gold for Fiano, with a thick apricot and peach syrup nose. Quite cushy, with ripe melon and peach flavors. Finishes short but round, with soft acids. **85 Best Buy** —*M.S. (2/1/2005)*

MandraRossa 2004 Nero d'Avola (Sicilia) $9. A casual dinner wine with spunk, blackberry, coffee bean, and a straightforward, crowd-pleasing nose. There are some faint but typically Sicilian smells that come in the form of dried brush and sea breeze. **86 Best Buy** —*M.L. (9/1/2005)*

MandraRossa 2004 Shiraz (Sicilia) $9. This is one of those hammer-over-your-head reds that takes aromatic intensity to the stratosphere. Inky black in color with cracked white pepper, exotic spice, resin, crushed stone, cedar, cherry fruit marmalade; there are no subtle nuances here, only bold statements. **87 Best Buy** —*M.L. (7/1/2006)*

MandraRossa 2005 Pinot Grigio Grecanico White Blend (Sicilia) $9. This is an interesting blend between a powerhouse white grape from the north and one from the south of Italy. It's sweet smelling with notes of aromatic flowers and exotic fruit and has an almost Moscato-like soapy fragrance. **85 Best Buy** —*M.L. (7/1/2006)*

MARCARINI

Marcarini 2003 Ciabot Camerano Barbera (Barbera d'Alba) $17. Pleasant and easy to drink, this Barbera blends sour cherry fruit with supporting notes of milk chocolate, cedar, and vanilla. Full-bodied and a bit creamy in the mouth, it ends with hints of dill. **86** —*J.C. (3/1/2006)*

Marcarini 2002 Ciabot Camerano Barbera (Barbera d'Alba) $18. Showing a premature brown edge to its hue, this is a lightweight effort marked by flavors of leather, brown sugar, and herbs and an astringent finish. There's just enough red fruit flavor to give it interest. **83** —*J.C. (11/15/2004)*

Marcarini 1998 Ciabot Camerano Barbera (Barbera d'Asti) $15. 86 *(4/1/2000)*

Marcarini 2003 Fontanazza Dolcetto (Dolcetto d'Alba) $15. Not one of Marcarini's best efforts, this Dolcetto is a bit lean and drying, with rubbery notes that intrude on the otherwise pleasant ripe plum and fudge flavors. Astringent on the finish. **83** —*J.C. (3/1/2006)*

Marcarini 1998 Fontanazza Dolcetto (Dolcetto d'Alba) $14. 85 *(4/1/2000)*

Marcarini 2003 Moscato (Moscato d'Asti) $16. This reliable Barolo producer has turned out a balanced Moscato from a ferociously hot vintage. Apricot, honey, and pink grapefruit aromas and flavors all swirl together in a harmonious whole that's not profound, simply very enjoyable. **87** —*J.C. (11/15/2004)*

Marcarini 2001 Brunate Nebbiolo (Barolo) $54. Deceptively soft and supple, this plump, full-bodied wine features ripe black cherries, a dose of chocolate liqueur, and hints of citrus zest. Firms up on the finish, which boasts mouth-watering length and substantial tannic heft. Try after 2008. **93** —*J.C. (3/1/2006)*

Marcarini 2000 Brunate Nebbiolo (Barolo) $64. Explosive Barolo, with scents of roses and cherries that just burst from the glass. There are boatloads of tannins, but they're ripe and soft, and the wine just seems to add complexity and elegance with every sip, picking up hints of licorice, red plums, leather, spice, and earth. Long and velvety on the finish. Drink 2010–2020, possibly longer. **93 Cellar Selection** —*J.C. (11/15/2004)*

Marcarini 1998 Brunate Nebbiolo (Barolo) $50. Brunate is one of the most famous vineyard sites in Barolo. There is a dirty, dusty nose that carries a whiff of hard cheese. Flavors are of caramel, cherries, and underbrush. This is a very good wine that is tight now but will evolve over time. **89** —*C.S. (11/15/2002)*

Marcarini 2001 La Serra Nebbiolo (Barolo) $54. This full-bodied, tannic Barolo is firmly astringent on the finish, but there's enough fruit behind the tannins to emerge with proper aging. The complex aromas and flavors showcase cherries and plums, but also darker, earthier notes of tobacco, hummus and spice. Try after 2010. **92 Editors' Choice** —*J.C. (3/1/2006)*

Marcarini 2000 La Serra Nebbiolo (Barolo) $65. Somewhere between traditional and modern, Marcarini's La Serra features scents of tar and rubber, flavors of ripe cherries and plums, and a full, rounded mouthfeel. There's a hint of volatility, but not enough to be worrisome. Finishes long, powerful, and tannic, but fully ripe. **90** —*J.C. (11/15/2004)*

Marcarini 1998 La Serra Nebbiolo (Barolo) $50. Wines from the vineyards of La Serra have a remarkable drinkability when young, something that can't be said for all Barolos. There are dusty aromas of wild game and red fruits. The acidity is bright and the mouthfeel shows nice complexity. A great drinking wine now and over the next 10–15 years. **92** —*C.S. (11/15/2002)*

Marcarini 2001 Donald Red Blend (Langhe) $28. The Donald—a blend of 60% Barbera, 30% Nebbiolo, and 10% Syrah—is named after Donald Rossi, who devoted his life to aiding under-privileged youth, and part of the proceeds go support the association that bears his name (www.associazionedonaldrossi.it). Even at just 10% the Syrah seems to exert a lot of influence on the finished wine, imparting pepper and blackberry aromas and flavors. Seems a bit thin and astringent at this stage of its evolution. **84** —*J.C. (11/15/2004)*

MARCHESATO DEGLI ALERAMICI

Marchesato degli Aleramici 2000 Brunello (Brunello di Montalcino) $45. Wonderful, almost flowery, perfume on the nose. There are also hints of men's cologne and lemon peel. Chewy and meaty across the palate, where black cherry and plum dominate. The finish shows ample oak, chocolate, and butter. Will be round and easy upon maturity, which should come in a couple of years. **91** —*M.S. (7/1/2005)*

Marchesato degli Aleramici 1999 Brunello (Brunello di Montalcino) $45. True yet reserved, with a full nose that deals a total package rather than parts. Dried cherry, raspberry, and leathery tannins are softened by a hint of vanillin. The finish is spicy and lengthy. Tannic, but will come together more if given five years. **90** —*M.S. (6/1/2004)*

Marchesato degli Aleramici 1999 Riserva Brunello (Brunello di Montalcino) $60. Despite starting out a bit mute, what lurks below is nothing short of stellar. Fine black licorice and ripe, meaty fruit creates a dark, manly flavor profile, while the finish deals a layer cake's worth of fudge, vanilla, and espresso. Virtually anything you would want in a Brunello is here. **93** —*M.S. (7/1/2005)*

MARCHESE ALFIERI

Marchese Alfieri 1996 Alfiera Barbera D'Asti Superiore Barbera (Barbera d'Asti) $28. **85** *(4/1/2000)*

MARCHESE ANTINORI

Marchese Antinori NV Nature Sparkling Blend (Oltrepò Pavese) $25. This wine waltzes up to the nose with the most delicate steps to offer crisp aromas of roses, golden apples, and kiwi. It offers a pleasant balance that finishes on a dry and clean note. **87** —*M.L. (12/15/2004)*

MARCHESE CARLO GUERRIERI GONZAGA

Marchese Carlo Guerrieri Gonzaga 1999 San Leonardo Bordeaux Blend (Vallagarina) $75. This Bordeaux-style blend offers plump aromas touched up by wet earth and herbaceousness. Flavors of dried cherry and jerky sport drive and intensity, but in the end notes of beets and tobacco bring overall ripeness into question. **83** —*M.S. (12/15/2003)*

Marchese Carlo Guerrieri Gonzaga 1998 Merlot di San Leonardo Estate Bottled Merlot (Trento) $18. A bit old for a current release, which is why it seems scattered and a few grades shy of whole. The nose has some strawberry, but it's funky and takes too long to unfold. The finish is dry and starchy, although it's not offensive nor does it bring with it any blatant off flavors. **83** —*M.S. (12/15/2003)*

MARCHESE DE PETRI

Marchese de Petri 1997 Il Valore Riserva Sangiovese (Chianti) $15. A solid wine, with a core of cherry and dark plum fruit. The nose is especially nice, with prune, leather, and clove accents. Turns spicier and somewhat woodier through the palate and onto the finish. Shows good acidity and even tannins. Drink now. **87** *(4/1/2001)*

MARCHESI ANTINORI

Marchesi Antinori 2003 Solaia Cabernet Blend (Toscana) $155. Despite the heat, this vintage lives up to the Solaia reputation with a slightly more ripe rendition. Toasted and oak spice aromas hit the nose first followed by strawberry and blackberry preserves. The elegance is not lost and the wine performs nicely in the mouth with chewy succulence, dusty tannins, and a long finish. **92** —*M.L. (9/1/2006)*

Marchesi Antinori 2000 Guado al Tasso Red Blend (Bolgheri Superiore) $80. This wine towers over others in terms of excellence. This blend of 60% Cabernet Sauvignon, 30% Merlot, and 10% Syrah and other varieties (that sees 14 months of barrique) is the epitome of grace and elevates wine drinking to almost spiritual heights: The nose is horizontal, wide, vast, and infinite with extraordinary tobacco, leather with fine cherry at its core, and toasted almond and herbal notes at the extremities. The palate is treated to soft tones of vanilla, silky tannins, and overall finesse that can be savored over long minutes. **95 Cellar Selection** —*M.L. (11/15/2006)*

Marchesi Antinori 2000 Tenute Marchesi Antinori Riserva Red Blend (Chianti Classico) $30. Thick, inky, and concentrated in appearance, this 90-10 Sangiovese-Cabernet Sauvignon blend presents a vast and varied aromatic portfolio that includes black cherry fruit, graphite, leather, and some barnyard for a complex and intense whole. It's a big and powerful wine that maintains its finesse and elegance. **91** —*M.L. (10/1/2006)*

Marchesi Antinori 2001 Tignanello Red Blend (Toscana) $70. One of Italy's most recognized labels, this blockbuster 85-10-5% Sangiovese-Cabernet Sauvignon-Cabernet Franc blend evolves slowly and seductively under your nose to reveal blackberry, black cherry, graphite notes, and well-integrated vanilla. The mouthfeel is lush and concentrated with silky smooth tannins and a long finish that revisits those gorgeous tobacco, berry, and dusty notes. **93** —*M.L. (11/15/2006)*

Marchesi Antinori 2002 Villa Antinori Red Blend (Toscana) $22. A surprisingly good show for a soggy vintage, this is ripe, bordering on stewy, with rich notes of prune, blueberry, mushroom, and forest floor. The tannins are hard but there's plenty of toast and spice on the finish of this 60-20-15-5 percent Sangiovese-Cabernet Sauvignon-Merlot-Syrah blend. **88** *(9/1/2006)*

Marchesi Antinori 2004 Tenuta Guado al Tasso Vermentino (Bolgheri) $20. Not that many Italian Vermentinos are imported into the U.S., and of the ones that are, this Tuscan version is among the best. This wine has an extraordinary ability to pair with foods thanks to its creamy, fruit-driven nose and overall smoothness. There are no sharp points. **90** —*M.L. (10/1/2006)*

Marchesi Antinori 2003 Cervaro della Sala White Blend (Umbria) $42. A top-notch white wine made with 80% Chardonnay and 20% Grechetto that stands above the rest thanks to its silky, soft feel. It is as smooth and supple as vanilla custard with peach pulp blended within. Yet, it leaves its mark in the mouth thanks to its supple roundness and lingering fruit flavors. **92 Editors' Choice** —*M.L. (10/1/2006)*

ITALY

MARCHESI BISCARDO

Marchesi Biscardo 2000 Red Blend (Amarone della Valpolicella) $65. Saddle leather, horsehide, and dried cherry comprise the lean, rustic nose. The flavors veer toward fresh fruits and spice, with a bit of chocolate hiding below the surface. Not that deep or complex, with a short, crisp, clean finish. **86** *(11/1/2005)*

MARCHESI CATTANEO DI BELFORTE

Marchesi Cattaneo di Belforte 2001 Etichetta Bianca Brunello (Brunello di Montalcino) $40. Starts off with a whiff of cola or tree bark, then smooths out with air into red berries and spice. Earthy on the palate, adding notes of tobacco, red cherries, and cedar, carried along by a slightly creamy texture. Turns crisp on the finish, with tart cherries framed by sturdy tannins. **90 Editors' Choice** *(4/1/2006)*

Marchesi Cattaneo di Belforte 2000 Etichetta Bianca Brunello (Brunello di Montalcino) $40. Earthy and cedary, with only modest fruit flavors peeking out from behind a wall of tobacco and coffee. Serve with herb-crusted meats to help bring out the fruit. **89** *(4/1/2006)*

Marchesi Cattaneo di Belforte 2001 Riserva Sangiovese (Chianti Classico) $23. Mildly baked on the nose, with aromas of fired clay, roast plum, and fresh tomato. It maintains a heavy, roasted personality through the palate, which is carried by plum and raspberry, all the way to the savory finish. Registers as a wide, tannic red with bulk. **87** —*M.S. (10/1/2006)*

MARCHESI DE' FRESCOBALDI

Marchesi de' Frescobaldi 2000 Castelgiocondo Brunello (Brunello di Montalcino) $55. Seductive floral aromas are jazzed up by healthy red fruit scents, and once you get to the mouth the wine becomes precise and tight. This is a defined Brunello with clear plum and black cherry flavors that are sweetened by hints of almond candy and red licorice. Sturdy, mildly tannic, and full. Should be just right in about three years. **92** —*M.S. (7/1/2005)*

Marchesi de' Frescobaldi 1999 Castelgiocondo Riserva Brunello (Brunello di Montalcino) $100. Tight as nails on the nose before it explodes on the palate in a cacophony of cherry, cassis, black plum, tobacco, and chocolate. It's like the best cigar and a great red wine rolled into one. Yes, the tannins are hammering and yes, the acidity is forward. But that only means this brilliant Brunello should age for 15 years without batting an eyelash. **97 Cellar Selection** —*M.S. (7/1/2005)*

Marchesi de' Frescobaldi 2000 Metodo Classical Brut Champagne Blend (Trento) $25. A more serious attempt at serious Champagne-style wine. Aromas of vanilla cream and toast are smooth, and the heavy palate offers lemon-lime and orange. Finishes full, maybe a bit flat. Nice overall. **87** —*M.S. (12/15/2004)*

Marchesi de' Frescobaldi 2002 Benefizio Bianco Chardonnay (Pomino) $27. Deep gold in color, with sunny aromas of peaches and flowers. In the mouth, however, it's shrill, with blasting acidity and a sour flavor profile. Disappointing because the nose seems promising. **83** —*M.S. (6/1/2005)*

Marchesi de' Frescobaldi 1999 Lamaione Merlot (Toscana) $85. This full-throttle wine needs some time to settle down, for it is not a soft, supple easy-drinking Merlot. It's a big, richly extracted wine loaded with ripe black cherries, vanilla, and toast, joined by a healthy dollop of tannins on the finish. Will be released this fall, but cellar it 5–10 years for it to reach its full potential. **92 Cellar Selection.** *(9/1/2002)*

Marchesi de' Frescobaldi 1998 Lamaione Merlot (Toscana) $64. This Merlot is super and it's destined to become a literal super Tuscan. It's dense and dark, with brooding notes of cola, damp earth, and tobacco. The texture is fine, really fine, and the manner in which the natural flavor has been extracted yet not overblown is masterful. Very luxurious and plush; when you drink this you know it's meant to be the real thing among so-called super Tuscans. **92 Cellar Selection** —*M.S. (12/31/2002)*

Marchesi de' Frescobaldi 2000 Campo ai Sasso Red Blend (Rosso di Montalcino) $NA. This is the first vintage of this wine that will be available in the United States and it makes a positive first impression. It's a delicious blend of spice, floral notes, and strawberries that finishes with soft, caressing tannins. **87** *(9/1/2002)*

Marchesi de' Frescobaldi 2000 Castiglioni Red Blend (Chianti) $13. Burly and chunky, with jammy black fruit aromas that come across fresh and attractive. The palate veers toward black cherry and blackberry, and the finish is racy and spicy. For an everyday red wine, this one has ample fruit and some subtleties, so it will likely fit the bill if expectations aren't too high. **85** —*M.S. (12/31/2002)*

Marchesi de' Frescobaldi 2002 Castiglioni Sangiovese (Chianti) $13. Chunky and obtuse, with hints of horse hide, smoke, and non-descript fruits. Medium in weight, with cherry, leather, and berry on the palate. Finishes with plum and a slight pickled flavor. **85** *(4/1/2005)*

Marchesi de' Frescobaldi 2001 Nipozzano Riserva Sangiovese (Chianti Rufina) $22. Tight and piercing at first, and then air pushes up spice, leather, and exotic dried fruits. Solid in the mouth, with zesty raspberry and plum flavors. Not a huge, modern wine; it's more traditional, with concise structure and a lot of terroir. **90** —*M.S. (10/1/2006)*

Marchesi de' Frescobaldi 2000 Nipozzano Riserva Sangiovese (Chianti Rufina) $22. One of the few ratings where unanimity was lacking. Part of the panel appreciated the wine's assertiveness, while finding a wiry blackberry foundation and character-adding herbal qualities, while the other part disapproved of the fruit quality, finding it stewed yet still too tannic. **86** *(4/1/2005)*

Marchesi de' Frescobaldi 2000 Remole Sangiovese (Toscana) $9. Mostly Sangiovese, with a touch of Cabernet Sauvignon, this "mini" Tuscan blends fruit from Chianti and Scansano in a spicy, lightweight red. Leather and chocolate accent the juicy finish. **83** *(9/1/2002)*

Marchesi de' Frescobaldi 2001 Vigneto Montesodi Castello di Nipozzano Sangiovese (Chianti Rufina) $45. Lovely aromas of black cherries and plums bust from the glass, followed by hints of vanilla and cedar. This lush, richly textured wine never seems overly ripe or heavy, delivering ample fruit and cigarbox flavors. Finishes long, with hints of anise and tobacco. Balanced to drink or age; drink now-2015. **93 Editors' Choice** *(4/1/2005)*

MARCHESI DI BAROLO

Marchesi Di Barolo 1998 Barbera (Monferrato) $10. Brisk acidity and a lean but smooth profile characterize this taut, somewhat tart wine. A very inviting bouquet with cherry, cinnamon, clove, cedar, and tobacco notes sets a pretty stage for the palate, but after the great setup the wine delivers rather uninspired and predictable tart berry and sour cherry Barbera flavors. The sour plum and earth finish is full but quite dry. **84** *(3/1/2001)*

Marchesi Di Barolo 1999 Le Lune Cortese (Gavi) $14. Clean and fresh, this Piedmontese white offers lively almond, pear, and grapefruit aromas. Light and even melon and pear flavors with herb accents grace the palate and the fairly extended finish shows an attractive, slight spiciness. **86** *(3/1/2001)*

Marchesi Di Barolo 1999 Nebbiolo (Barbaresco) $39. Displays only modest cherry and citrus notes on the nose, but in the mouth this wine is loaded. Dried black cherries, plums, and dark chocolate give an impression of richness. A big, expansive mouthfeel turns velvety on the finish. Drink 2008–2020. **89** *(4/2/2004)*

Marchesi Di Barolo 1996 Nebbiolo (Barolo) $40. Displaying a ripe, multi-faceted nose with violets, cumin, licorice, tar and chocolate elements, this wine shows class and grace with classic dry cherry flavors. Possessing lovely weight and balance, it is full without being heavy, and finishes with dusty rose and even tannins. **89** *(3/1/2001)*

Marchesi Di Barolo 1995 Nebbiolo (Barolo) $50. Great depth of fruit characterizes this wine from its beautiful bouquet of ripe sour cherries, tar, taragon, earth, and tobacco right through its solid palate where the rich dry cherry flavors open up and show some mineral accents. Long and elegant, the finish has even, ripe tannins and a fine chalky note. Deserves cellaring for two to four more years. **92 Cellar Selection** *(3/1/2001)*

Marchesi Di Barolo 1998 Cannubi Nebbiolo (Piedmont) $65. This historic producer owns a large portion of the Cannubi vineyard. The 1998 is highly perfumed, with aromas of roses and strawberries. It is powerful and chunky, with dry tannins and wood flavors, along with finishing sweetness. **90** —*R.V. (11/15/2002)*

Marchesi Di Barolo 1998 Sarmassa Nebbiolo (Piedmont) $55. As with the Cannubi, this is a solid, chunky wine, but here the fruit is drier, with dusty tannins and acidity. Flavor of dark plums and raisins are hidden underneath the tannins at this stage. **89** —*R.V. (11/15/2002)*

Marchesi Di Barolo 1998 Vigne di Proprieta Nebbiolo (Barolo) $45. Lush berry fruit and a plump, juicy mouthfeel scored big with our tasters, who also remarked on this wine's complex notes of meat, black cherries, and anise. Supple and easy on the finish, making it ready to drink now and over the next decade. **90** *(4/2/2004)*

MARCHESI DI GRESY

Marchesi di Gresy 1998 Monte Arribaldo Dolcetto (Dolcetto d'Alba) $15. **88** *(4/1/2000)*

Marchesi di Gresy 2004 La Serra Moscato (Moscato d'Asti) $13. You can't beat the activity in the glass. Persistent bubbling and frothy mousse hint at what's to come: The zesty mineral and floral notes are so intense they are almost spicy in the mouth but soon yield to creamy softness and melted honey on the finish. **89 Editors' Choice** —*M.L. (12/15/2005)*

Marchesi di Gresy 2000 Martinenga Nebbiolo (Barbaresco) $45. Seems to be a fruit-forward style on the nose, with berries and vanilla leading the way. Yet it develops more nuance and elegance on the palate, revealing delicate cherry and tobacco shadings. Finishes with a flourish of supple tannins. Drink now–2010. **87** *(4/2/2004)*

MARCO BONFANTE

Marco Bonfante 2001 Dolcetto (Dolcetto d'Alba) $17. A balanced, medium-weight Dolcetto with aromas of cherries, clove, and an intriguing note of balsam fir. Delivers sappy cherry flavors on the palate, finishing with dashes of caramel and dark chocolate. **86** —*J.C. (11/15/2004)*

Marco Bonfante 2000 Nebbiolo (Nebbiolo d'Alba) $18. A bit disjointed, this wine offers alcoholic scents of brandy-soaked cherries, then follows that with flavors of anise, dried fruit, and a hint of soy sauce. Lightweight, without much depth, and finishes with a slight astringency. **83** —*J.C. (11/15/2004)*

MARCO CECCHINI

Marco Cecchini 2004 Pinot Grigio (Venezia Giulia) $16. One of the best performers in our Pinot Grigio tasting, Cecchini has crafted just 400 cases of wine with wonderfully intense aromas of dried banana, fresh stone fruit, and peach. He relies on oxygen-free vinification to preserve fruit flavors. Drink immediately. **90 Editors' Choice** —*M.L. (6/1/2006)*

Marco Cecchini 1999 Careme Red Blend (Colli Orientali del Friuli) $23. Fairly smooth and subtle, with pure black cherry aromas along with a hint of leather. In the mouth, things turn a bit sharp as sour cherry and rhubarb take over. But if you dig a bit deeper, it has the structure and depth of fruit to stand up to dry cheeses or other foods. **86** —*M.S. (12/15/2003)*

MARCO DE BARTOLI

Marco de Bartoli 2003 Grappoli Del Grillo (Sicilia) $34. Clean and medium in weight, with apple, pineapple, and a shot of mineral to the nose. Pure citrus and sunshine in the mouth, with a finish of orange peel and pepper. Acidic and snappy, but crafty. Simple yet solid. **87** —*M.S. (7/1/2005)*

MARCO FELLUGA

Marco Felluga 2004 Pinot Grigio (Collio) $15. A successfully executed wine, redolent of pear, peach, and a dab of something green. An excellent food wine and especially well-suited for pasta and white meats. **85** —*M.L. (6/1/2006)*

Marco Felluga 2004 Russiz Superiore Pinot Grigio (Collio) $20. Keep your eye out for this producer and his elegant Russiz Superiore Pinot Grigio that delivers top marks in terms of fruitiness and freshness. Loads of fruit from melon to apple to pineapple, with solid weight in the mouth. **87** —*M.L. (6/1/2006)*

MARCO NEGRI

Marco Negri 2002 Marsillo Moscato (Moscato d'Asti) $13. Pretty in the nose, with textbook aromas of lime and gardenia. The palate offers soft,

citrusy fruit, with flavors of orange and melon. Totally sleek and correct, with a fine level of natural carbonation and a delicious balancing sweetness. **90 Best Buy** —*M.S. (12/15/2003)*

MAREA

Marea 2005 Pinot Grigio (Delle Venezie) $10. Stone fruit and white flowers characterize a delicately perfumed Grigio that is linear but refined. Lean but crisp and refreshing in the mouth with pear, apple, and banana flavors. **87 Best Buy** —*M.L. (6/1/2006)*

MAREGA

Marega 1998 Chardonnay (Collio) $15. This unwooded Chardonnay shows a good deal more character than most of the Italian wines made of the grape. Pear, peach, anise, and mineral aromas and flavors show considerable complexity and the texture on the long finish is quite full and almost buttery—surprising in a wine that sees no oak and no malolactic fermentation. **88 Best Buy** *(4/1/2001)*

Marega 1998 Malvasia Istriana (Collio) $15. If you enjoy picking apart a wine—finding all of its tiny nuances and eccentricities—you'll find plenty here. From its smoky, beeswax-like and menthol aromas to its flavors of melon and citrus, there's plenty of interest, yet the wine delivers more intellectual excitement than hedonism. **84** —*J.C. (7/1/2003)*

Marega 1997 Merlot (Collio) $14. **87** —*M.S. (5/1/1999)*

Marega 2004 Pinot Grigio (Collio) $15. After fermentation, this wine rests on the lees for two months, which explains its very nutty nose: almonds and pine nuts over pineapple and pear. Light and lean in the mouth. **85** —*M.L. (2/1/2006)*

Marega 1998 Holbar Red Blend (Friuli Venezia Giulia) $25. At 80% Merlot, 15% Cabernet, and 5% Gamay (of all things), this is clearly not your average Italian red wine. It's got some raisin, spiced cherry and oak aromas, which are followed by baked apple and cinnamon flavors. It's dry and woody, with developed but integrated tannins. Multifaceted and different, and definitely not New World in style. A bit too stretched and acidic to rank higher. **87** —*M.S. (12/15/2003)*

Marega 1994 Holbar Red Blend (Friuli Venezia Giulia) $20. Unusual and elegant, this red from northeastern Italy is mostly Merlot, blended with Cabernet Franc and a small amount of Gamay. The complex plum, ripe berry, herb, and cedar notes of the nose open to a medium-weight palate of dry cherry and earth flavors. It's quite alive and graceful at six years, and closes handsomely with even tannins on the finish. **91 Editors' Choice** *(4/1/2001)*

Marega 1993 Holbar Rosso Red Blend (Friuli) $25. **90** —*M.S. (5/1/1999)*

Marega 1995 Holbar White Blend (Friuli Venezia Giulia) $20. This Riesling-Chardonnay blend is named after and aged in Holbars, traditional acacia-wood casks. Nut, spice, lychee, honey, and black pepper elements all vie for attention in the intense bouquet. Dry, very ripe melon, orange honey, and spice flavors derive from the late-picked (but not late harvest designated) fruit, and (presumably) the acacia. This distinctive white finishes long, with peach and spice notes. **89** *(4/1/2001)*

MARENCO

Marenco 2004 Scrapona Moscato (Moscato d'Asti) $17. Start or finish your big night with something special. This is that rare Moscato that achieves greater heights. It's pure as flower blossoms, with ideal lime, lychee, and ginger flavors. Perfect as an apéritif; even better with dessert or as a nightcap. And at a meager 5.5% alcohol it might just come in handy if you're hoping to make it the whole nine yards. **90** —*M.S. (8/1/2005)*

Marenco 2003 Scrapona Moscato (Moscato d'Asti) $17. A bit richer and sweeter than it might be in more typical vintages, Marenco's Moscato lacks the touch of acidity that would have focused its flavors more effectively. The honey, peach, and pineapple flavors are rich and concentrated, they just seem a bit heavier than they should. Serve well chilled. **84** —*J.C. (11/15/2004)*

Marenco 2002 Scrapona Moscato (Moscato d'Asti) $16. Easy and mildly candied, with sweet aromas offset by lemon peel and green apple. Quite flavorful and ripe, with cinnamon apple, pineapple, and Bartlett pear flavors. Truly zesty and smooth, with top-notch bubbles and body. **89** —*M.S. (12/15/2003)*

MARETIMA

Maretima 1999 Fabula Sangiovese (Tuscany) $16. This is 100% Sangiovese made outside the Chianti DOC, but it drinks like a Brunello. There are fine leather, dried fruit, and earth aromas that create a tight bouquet. The plum, cherry, and raspberry flavors are pure and not mucked up by oak, while zippy acidity really drives the finish forward. Sturdy stuff with a subdued personality in a world of wines gone wild. **91 Editors' Choice** —*M.S. (11/15/2003)*

MARIO SCHIOPETTO

Mario Schiopetto 2001 Pinot Bianco (Collio) $35. Mario Schiopetto and his sons, Carlo and Giorgio, draw astonishingly intense flavors from the lees contact this wine has until bottling. It is powerful with rich, spicy fruit and flavors of pepper, vanilla, and apricot. **90** —*R.V. (7/1/2003)*

Mario Schiopetto 2004 Pinot Grigio (Collio) $37. There's fresh pear, nectarine, and a prominent mineral vein, rendering an elegant and snappy wine. Pair this with shellfish or creamy soufflés. **88 Editors' Choice** —*M.L. (2/1/2006)*

Mario Schiopetto 2001 Pinot Grigio (Collio) $32. A wonderful, concentrated, lightly spicy wine from the Schiopetto family, with rich flavors of honey and almonds. It has power, but also elegance. **91** —*R.V. (7/1/2003)*

Mario Schiopetto 2001 Tocai (Collio) $35. There is an amazing medley of aromas and flavors in this powerful Tocai. Aromas of perfumed spring blossom, and almonds follow through on the palate with flavors of pears, almonds, and spice, with just a touch of pepper. **93** —*R.V. (7/1/2003)*

Mario Schiopetto 2001 Blanc des Rosis White Blend (Friuli Venezia Giulia) $31. A blend of Tocai Friulano, Pinot Bianco, Sauvignon, and Malvasia, this crisp, fresh wine has elegant, refreshing acidity, flavors of white currants, and lychees and a soft, ripe aftertaste. **89** —*R.V. (7/1/2003)*

MARION

Marion 1999 Corvina, Rondinella, Molinara (Amarone della Valpolicella) $80. A touch charred and meaty, as it starts with strong coffee, smoked meat, and bark-like aromas. Opens with flavors of prune and black cherry, with shades of vanilla, leather, and brown sugar. Rather lush and soft, with guaranteed appeal for those with a sweet tooth. Of note: it's not that edgy, so drink it soon and try not to lose it in your cellar. **93** *(11/1/2005)*

MARISA CUOMO

Marisa Cuomo 1997 Furore Riserva Piedirosso (Campania) $32. Toasted oak, chocolate, and dark, jammy fruits make up the flavor profile for this Piedirosso (70%) and Aglianico (30%) blend. It is rich, yet well structured, as the bright acidity cleanses the broad tannins. Enjoy now or in 3–5 years. **91** —*C.S. (5/1/2002)*

Marisa Cuomo 1996 Ravello Riserva Piedirosso (Campania) $30. The Ravello is softer and more elegant than its big brother, Furore, due to a cooler microclimate. Spiced huckleberry jam and toasted almonds highlighted with vanilla make this a perfect match for lamb and wild mushrooms. **89** —*C.S. (5/1/2002)*

MAROTTI CAMPI

Marotti Campi 2002 Luzano Classico Verdicchio (Verdicchio dei Castelli di Jesi Classico) $11. Slightly sweet on the nose, with whiffs of Bartlett pear followed by flavors of lemon, lime, soda cracker, and mineral. The mouthfeel is good and the finish is springy, with lively acidity and straightforward flavors. **86** —*M.S. (8/1/2004)*

MARTINI & ROSSI

Martini & Rossi NV Moscato (Asti) $12. Creamy froth is short-lived but the peach and mineral notes come through clean and sharp followed by zest and soothing sweetness in the mouth. One of Italy's most recognized brands presents its most famous sweet sparkler: that's always a joy to revisit. **86 Best Buy** —*M.L. (12/15/2006)*

Martini & Rossi NV Asti Moscato (Piedmont) $13. 88 *(11/15/1999)*

Martini & Rossi NV Asti Spumante Moscato (Moscato d'Asti) $10. 87 —*S.H. (12/31/2000)*

Martini & Rossi NV Vino Frizzante Prosecco (Marca Trevigiana) $14. Heavy and out of the ordinary, with funky aromas of gardenias and mustard seeds. The palate shows tart apple and a cured meat flavor akin to bologna or salami. The finish is open but short. **83** —*M.S. (12/15/2004)*

MASCHIO DEI CAVALIERI

Maschio dei Cavalieri NV Brut Prosecco (Prosecco di Valdobbiadene) $20. There's a slightly lactic quality to the wine that muddles the flavors and aromas. Instead of peach, you get peach yogurt and instead of citrus, you get lemon cream. Feels very creamy in the mouth as well. **85** —*M.L. (6/1/2006)*

MASCIARELLI

Masciarelli 2000 Villa Gemma Montepulciano (Montepulciano d'Abruzzo) $80. This is big wine in every sense. Scratch that: it's huge and inky black in color. Evolving aromatics include leather, vanilla, tobacco, toasted wood, and red fruit. Firmly cemented tannins balanced to alcohol and acidity make this a bold and brave protagonist of the Abruzzo region. **90 Cellar Selection** —*M.L. (9/1/2005)*

Masciarelli 2004 Trebbiano (Trebbiano d'Abruzzo) $8. This wine has a pale straw color with abundant apple, citrus, and mineral aromas. There's a faint nutty, almond skin taste in the mouth and refreshing acidity. The wine underwent soft pressing, cold controlled fermentation, and refinement in stainless steel. **86 Best Buy** —*M.L. (9/1/2005)*

Masciarelli 2002 Marina Cvetic' Trebbiano (Trebbiano d'Abruzzo) $55. This wine is named after Gianni Masciarelli's wife and is usually cited as the benchmark for Trebbiano. This vintage boasts a deep golden color with toasted almonds, apples, vanilla, and lots of new oak. Indeed, the woodshop aromas are just shy of too much. **89** —*M.L. (9/1/2005)*

MASI

Masi 2000 Campolongo di Torbe Amarone (Amarone della Valpolicella Classico) $126. Just like fruitcakes themselves, fruitcake notes in wines can be really good or really bad. In this case, it's like one of the best fruitcakes you've ever had, incredibly nuanced and complex with dried fruit and spices that join easily into an integrated whole. Firm on the finish, so age, or serve with hefty main courses or cheeses. **92** —*J.C. (12/31/2006)*

Masi 1990 Campolongo di Torbe Amarone (Amarone della Valpolicella Classico) $NA. The bouquet is smoky and meaty in character, without obvious fruit, but waves of cherries and prunes emerge on the palate. This is still richly textured and tannic. Hold. **93** —*J.C. (12/31/2006)*

Masi 2001 Costasera Amarone (Amarone della Valpolicella Classico) $55. This is Masi's main Amarone bottling, and it's a beauty. Toasted almonds and ripe cherries mark the nose, while the structure of the wine is round and lush without ever seeming overly full or soft. Made in a dry, food-friendly style, with some firm tannins on the finish, this is approachable now, but looks to be capable of aging 5–10 years. **90** —*J.C. (12/31/2006)*

Masi 1990 Costasera Amarone (Amarone della Valpolicella Classico) $NA. This is a bit lighter in color than it's younger sibling, the 2000, but still shows no obvious bricking in color. This is nicely supple and softened with age, but still shows plenty of cherry fruit and leather subtleties. Drink or hold. **90** —*J.C. (12/31/2006)*

Masi 2000 Mazzano Amarone (Amarone della Valpolicella Classico) $140. Shows more leather and cedar than the Campolongo di Torbe, but even more richness and intensity. Slightly pruny, dried fruit notes are accompanied by hints of apricot, game, and dried spices. Lush and long on the finish; the best of the 2000s. It's approachable, but age-worthy. **95** —*J.C. (12/31/2006)*

Masi 1990 Mazzano Amarone (Amarone della Valpolicella Classico) $NA. This is wonderfully integrated and complex, offering a dizzying array of spices that blend seamlessly with notes of leather and cherries. Wonderfully velvety in texture and round in the mouth, but also boasting a long, spice-filled finish. A tremendous effort. Drink now–2020. **97** —*J.C. (12/31/2006)*

ITALY

ITALY

Masi 2000 Serego Alighieri Vaio Armaron Amarone (Amarone della Valpolicella Classico) $75. This is lighter and more elegant than the two crus—a practiced stylistic difference. Cherry blossoms come through here, accented by cinnamon, and showing great intensity without excess weight. Spice and delicate herbal notes mark the long finish. Drink or cellar. **92** —J.C. (12/31/2006)

Masi 1990 Serego Alighieri Vaio Armaron Amarone (Amarone della Valpolicella Classico) $NA. Delicate cherry and dried spice notes mark the nose of this wine, which is almost delicate relative to Masi's other Amarones. Elegant and complex. Drink now. **91** —J.C. (12/31/2006)

Masi 1998 Brolo di Campofiorin Corvina (Rosso del Veronese) $24. Young and still showing reductive character: rubber and tar scents dominate the nose. Yet it's lush and creamy on the palate, showing wonderfully soft tannins and at the same time, crisp acidity on the long finish. Just needs time. **89** (12/1/2004)

Masi 1997 Brolo di Campofiorin Corvina (Rosso del Veronese) $NA. Seems a bit closed and in need of more cellaring. You can sense the depth of black cherry fruit rather than smell or taste it. Finishes long and tannic. Try in 2010. **89** (12/1/2004)

Masi 1995 Brolo di Campofiorin Corvina (Rosso del Veronese) $NA. A touch richer and meatier than the '95 Campofiorin, featuring plenty of caramel and brown sugar from oak aging, plus firmer, chewier tannins. Hold another couple of years. **90** (12/1/2004)

Masi 2001 Campofiorin Corvina (Rosso del Veronese) $16. Like the '98 Brolo, this is still showing some reductive notes of rubber on the nose, but boasts plenty of lush, ripe black cherries and dried spices on the palate. It goes down deceptively easy, yet should improve for another few years at least. **90 Editors' Choice** (12/1/2004)

Masi 1999 Campofiorin Corvina (Rosso del Veronese) $15. Lush and soft on the palate, without the tannins that mark some vintages, making this one to drink young. Fresh cherries, a hint of green herbs, and a pinch of pepper ease into a long, fruit-filled finish. **89** (12/1/2004)

Masi 1997 Campofiorin Corvina (Rosso del Veronese) $NA. Nearing maturity, but still fresh, showing brown sugar, black cherry, and plum aromas and flavors. The tannins this vintage are very supple, with perhaps slightly less body. **88** (12/1/2004)

Masi 1995 Campofiorin Corvina (Rosso del Veronese) $NA. Fresh and still relatively youthful, this vintage boasts lively cherry fruit allied with leathery, cedary notes. Finishes long, with soft tannins. Seems at peak. **89** (12/1/2004)

Masi 1993 Campofiorin Corvina (Rosso del Veronese) $NA. An understated vintage that seems to be tiring, with subtle notes of molasses and soy sauce, modest cherry fruit, and a finish that fades quickly. **86** (12/1/2004)

Masi 1985 Campofiorin Corvina (Rosso del Veronese) $NA. Fully mature, but still going strong, with black cherry, tar, and cedar notes on the nose, followed by sweetly ripe fruit flavors backed by earth and dark chocolate. Long finish. Boscaini calls this "one of the most elegant vintages." **91** (12/1/2004)

Masi 1983 Campofiorin Corvina (Rosso del Veronese) $NA. Shows a lot more fruit that the '77, packing cherry and brown sugar flavors onto a rounder, softer frame. Finishes with hints of tobacco and tea. Fully mature, or maybe a little past peak. **87** (12/1/2004)

Masi 1977 Campofiorin Corvina (Rosso del Veronese) $NA. Starts with intriguing scents of molasses and almonds along with peppery, meaty notes. The fruit is fading, but there's still a lingering sensation of softness and ripe tannins. Drink up. **85** (12/1/2004)

Masi 1983 Campofiorion Corvina (Rosso del Veronese) $NA. 87 (12/1/2004)

Masi 1977 Campofiorion Corvina (Rosso del Veronese) $NA. 85 (12/1/2004)

Masi 2003 Bonacosta Corvina, Rondinella, Molinara (Valpolicella Classico) $14. Veneto's classic Corvina, Rondinella, and Molinara blend has tart fruit like cranberry skins, white cherry, and crushed red rose petal with a subtle menthol endnote. Good companion for a full meal, from appetizer to the meat course. **86** —M.L. (9/1/2005)

Masi 2002 Colbaraca Classico Garganega (Soave) $11. A Soave that has been partially barrel fermented is unusual, but it works in this wine, which has great concentration, roundness, and softness and the complexity of toast. **87** —R.V. (7/1/2003)

Masi 2000 Colbaraca Soave Classico Superiore Garganega (Soave) $12. Opens with full, nutty aromas. It's 98% Garganega Rosa, a variant of the regular grape, and receives 35% barrel fermentation. It's larger on the palate than most Soaves, with nicely defined apple and peach flavors. The dry, lingering finish shows elegant mineral-tinged notes. **89 Best Buy** (9/1/2001)

Masi 2001 Brolo di Campofiorin Red Blend (Rosso del Veronese) $25. Smoky and slightly cedary at first—it is aged in barrique—the fruit emerges with swirling to reveal plum and cherry notes and some slightly tough tannins. But the finish is long and laden with cherries, so let there be no concerns about this wine's balance—just give it 2–3 years in the cellar. **89** —J.C. (12/31/2006)

Masi 1998 Brolo di Campofiorin Red Blend (Rosso del Veronese) $24. Essentially a top selection of the company's Campofiorin that's refermented solely with Corvina grapes, Brolo has a similar nose, full of cherries and cocoa. Shows greater length and intensity on the palate and a full, velvety mouthfeel. **91 Editors' Choice** (5/1/2003)

Masi 2003 Campofiorin Red Blend (Rosso del Veronese) $15. This light-to medium-bodied red boasts bright scents of cherries with a dusting of cinnamon, backed by silky tannins and delicate minerality. It's rather Burgundian in style and feel, without any over-ripe notes. **88** —J.C. (12/31/2006)

Masi 1997 Campofiorin Red Blend (Rosso del Veronese) $16. Easy yet complex, this ripasso-method red is ultra-smooth, with rich, dark cherry and plum fruit riding the velvety palate. This supple, full-flavored red delivers plenty of pleasure. Will pair well with dinner, yet is round enough to sip. **88** (9/1/2001)

Masi 1999 Campofiorin Ripasso Red Blend (Rosso del Veronese) $15. Offers an incredible bouquet for a $15 wine—a beautiful floral bloom of cherry blossoms and cocoa that leaves your mouth watering. Rich chocolate and cherry flavors finish with baby-soft tannins. **90 Best Buy** (5/1/2003)

Masi 1999 Campolongo di Torbe Red Blend (Amarone della Valpolicella Classico) $110. Dried fruit with a lot of woody, spicy aromas make for an alluring, somewhat rustic nose. The palate, however, delivers round fruit flavors touched up by plenty of sweet mocha and vanilla notes. Finely textured, with a long, supple finish. Almost a no-brainer as goes Amarone. **91** (11/1/2005)

Masi 1997 Campolongo di Torbe Red Blend (Amarone della Valpolicella) $70. The dense, rich nose is full of spice cake, prune, and cinnamon. In the mouth, chocolate is so dominant that you'd think it's a liqueur. Raisins and dried cherries make their appearances, too. The finish is long, deep, and tannic, with a boatload of chocolate. If you like fudge, you'll love this wine young. Otherwise hold for several years. **92 Editors' Choice** (5/1/2003)

Masi 1993 Campolongo di Torbe Red Blend (Amarone della Valpolicella Classico) $62. The nose is a bit briny, with some interesting nuances of soy and leather. Flavors of sweet stewed plums, pepper, and smoked meat confirm its maturity and readiness. The finish is layered and rich, with some leftover tannins keeping it solid. **88** (5/1/2003)

Masi 2001 Costasera Red Blend (Amarone della Valpolicella) $53. A touch rowdy and sulfuric, although constant airing and swirling opens it up. Still, the nose must be characterized as burnt and funky. Underneath dwell date, prune, black cherry, and other overtly sweet, candied fruit flavors. Finishes lively, with full tannins. **86** (11/1/2005)

Masi 1999 Costasera Red Blend (Amarone della Valpolicella Classico) $40. "Costasera" means "evening slopes," referring to the west-facing hillsides that are said to yield the best Amarones. This is Masi's "basic" Amarone, and a fine effort, giving up leather and date aromatics and chewy coffee, molasses, and black cherry flavors. **91** (5/1/2003)

Masi 1997 Costasera Red Blend (Amarone della Valpolicella) $41. Immediately impressive, with an ultra-ripe nose of black currants, nuts, and blueberries. The flavors follow suit, giving the palate a dense black plum and cocoa coating. Fat and plush, with very broad, well-structured tannins, this is tempting now, and should be even better in three to five years. **91 Cellar Selection** *(9/1/2001)*

Masi 1999 Mazzano Red Blend (Amarone della Valpolicella Classico) $140. Exotic and mature, with a classic nose of prune, licorice, maple, and sweet sherry. The palate is quite round and generous, and it spreads out like a comfortable blanket on a feather bed. Finishing touches of smooth tannins and flavors of coffee and anise are ideal. **93** *(11/1/2005)*

Masi 2000 Modello Red Blend (Delle Venezie) $10. A soft, easy-drinking wine made for early consumption, Modello is a blend of Corvina and Raboso aged in large Slavonian oak. Cherry and chocolate flavors are plump and medium-weight, yet finish with a juicy, tart edge that emphasizes its role as food accompaniment, not cocktail wine. **87 Best Buy** *(5/1/2003)*

Masi 1998 Serègo Alighieri Red Blend (Valpolicella Classico Superiore) $15. For all intents and purposes, Masi makes this wine (but in conjunction with the Alighieri family). It's leathery in the nose, with chocolate and raisin aromas. Prune and milk chocolate flavors dominate prior to a fairly long, textured finish. Let it be noted that one reviewer liked this wine quite a bit more than the other panelists, even going so far as to recommend it as an accompaniment to meats and cheeses. **85** *(5/1/2003)*

Masi 1995 Serègo Alighieri Red Blend (Amarone della Valpolicella) $54. Tight and a bit hot, this single-vineyard bottling from Masi shows sour cherry, cranberry, chocolate, and mint flavors along with some chalky mineral notes. It's quite youthful and restrained, with firm, even biting, tannins. It's nicely extracted and should show more in three to four years. **87** —*J.F. (9/1/2001)*

Masi 1999 Serego Alighieri Possessioni Red Blend (Valpolicella Classico Superiore) $17. Matured in large cherrywood casks, which Boscaini claims helps to emphasize the cherry fruit of the Corvina grape. It's light, yet very flavorful, packing in lots of dried spices, leather, and cocoa, along with floral and cherry notes. Finishes long and spicy. **88** *(5/1/2003)*

Masi 1997 Serego Alighieri Vaio Red Blend (Amarone della Valpolicella) $60. Much brighter and fresher than many of its Amarone counterparts. Cherry blossoms, cedar, and a just a hint of volatility make for a knock-out bouquet, and it's followed up on the palate by lively red cherries and a kitchenful of dried spices. Long and firmly tannic, the '97 Vaio should age well for at least 10 years. **93** *(5/1/2003)*

Masi 1996 Serego Alighieri Vaio Red Blend (Amarone della Valpolicella) $55. A browning tint indicates that it's starting to mature, but it's still ripe and ready. The nose carries typical raisin and spice notes, which are backed up on the palate by flavors of plum, dried fruits, sage, and brown sugar. It's a touch hard and tannic, but unlike many Amarones, it should go well with food. **89** *(5/1/2003)*

Masi 1999 Serego Alighieri Vaio Amaron Red Blend (Amarone della Valpolicella) $75. One whiff is all it takes to draw you in, and subsequent sniffs bring you back for more. Cherry liqueur, toasted wheat bread, and leather are all convincing, attractive aromas, while the palate is snappy and racy, with no dead weight at all. This is a tight, structured wine with textbook flavors and a long, chocolate-laden finish. **91** *(11/1/2005)*

Masi 2002 Classico White Blend (Soave) $15. An easy, full-flavored wine, with crisp, clean fruit, flavors of almonds, and a touch of soft ripeness. **86** —*R.V. (7/1/2003)*

Masi 2005 Masianco White Blend (Delle Venezie) $12. There's so much Italian Pinot Grigio on the market today and so much of it tastes exactly the same. Among the exceptions is this Pinot Grigio (75 percent) and Verduzzo blend. Thanks to its thicker skins, Verduzzo undergoes extra ripening on drying racks after a late harvest for further concentration of flavors and mouth texture. The Pinot Grigio component reinforces the wine's citrus freshness and peach-like aromas. This is an easy-to-drink white wine with a charismatic and sophisticated edge. **89 Best Buy** —*M.L. (11/15/2006)*

Masi 2004 Masianco White Blend (Delle Venezie) $14. A happy marriage between two white grapes from a winery known for its deep, rich reds. Pinot Grigio adds cut grass and zest and the slightly over-ripened Verduzzo gives structure and smoothness. **89 Best Buy** —*M.L. (9/1/2005)*

Masi 2002 Masianco White Blend (Delle Venezie) $12. This wine is the white partner to Masi's familiar Campfiorin. In this case, it is the 25% of Verduzzo grapes in the blend that have gone through the drying process known as passito. The 75% of Pinot Grigio adds spice, while the Verduzzo gives great richness and ripeness. **90** —*R.V. (7/1/2003)*

Masi 2001 Serego Alighieri Possessioni White Blend (Veneto) $15. Said to be the only white wine produced in the Valpolicella region, this is a blend of 75% Garanega and 25% Sauvignon Blanc. The result is a tasty mélange of pear, peach, and passion fruit flavors, accented by peppery notes. Finishes tart and grapefruity, even slightly bitter. **87** *(5/1/2003)*

MASO CANALI

Maso Canali 2005 Pinot Grigio (Trentino) $23. Some fruit comes from the Canali family's original 17-acre Trentino vineyard that was first planted in 1893, while the rest is sourced from other vineyards in the region. The result is a wine rich in honey, vanilla, banana, acacia, and almond. **88** —*M.L. (6/1/2006)*

MASO POLI

Maso Poli 1997 Pinot Grigio (Trentino) $13. **85** *(8/1/1999)*

Maso Poli 2004 Pinot Grigio (Trentino) $21. Not intense but delicately fragrant with jasmine, lemon blossom, and peach. A very feminine wine that is fresh and crisp in the mouth and has a sour, grapefruit-like finish. Would work well with snow crab or snapper. **87** —*M.L. (6/1/2006)*

Maso Poli 2003 Estate Bottled Pinot Grigio (Trentino) $21. Not cheap, but this Pinot Grigio offers more character than most, combining dusty earth, dried spices, and powdered minerals with ripe apples. On the spicy, earthy side, yet light in body and clean on the finish. **87** —*J.C. (12/31/2004)*

MASOTTINA

Masottina 1997 Montesco Bordeaux Blend (Colli di Conegliano) $35. Earthy, herbal, and definitely oaky. The palate offers plum and cherry fruit with a defined as well as refined herbal note. Think Cabernet Franc and that's what you have here. The finish, meanwhile, is broad and textured, with dusty tannins and some tang. **87** *(5/1/2003)*

Masottina 2003 Pinot Grigio (Piave) $14. The variety's typical fruity freshness has been dulled by an extra year in the bottle, but the wine compensates royally with baked apple, spicy cinnamon, nutmeg, and peach cobbler. Good acidity renders a youthful appearance in the mouth. **87** —*M.L. (6/1/2006)*

Masottina 2003 Ai Palazzi Pinot Grigio (Piave) $21. Yellow in color and dull on the nose, with almost no fruit and a strong whiff of varnish. A big, bulky palate is devoid of flavor beyond some rudimentary citrus. Not worth the price. **81** *(2/1/2006)*

Masottina 2001 Vigneto Ai Palazzi Pinot Grigio (Piave) $15. This luscious, balanced Pinot Grigio isn't overly complex, but scores for its cactus pear and toasted almond aromas and flavors and its peppery, refreshing finish. It's medium-bodied, with just a hint of unreleased CO2 to enliven it. **87** —*J.C. (7/1/2003)*

Masottina NV Prosecco (Prosecco di Conegliano e Valdobbiadene) $14. A nosing reveals a pungent bouquet of lemon-lime and clover. The flavors of ripe apple and Bartlett pear are pure and unmistakable, while more apple comes on strong on the powerful finish. Very good and balanced, with just the right touch of sugar. **89** —*M.S. (6/1/2003)*

Masottina 2004 Cartizze Dry Prosecco (Prosecco Superiore di Cartizze) $35. A Prosecco that stands apart from the crowd thanks to its mineral and crushed vitamin notes, soapy floral tones like dried lavender and sage, and nutty aromas. Pretty perlage and loads of complex, almond-like flavors in the mouth. **90** —*M.L. (6/1/2006)*

Masottina 2004 Extra Dry Prosecco (Prosecco di Conegliano e Valdobbiadene) $15. Very nice and intense, with baskets of exotic fruit, plush peach flavors, and a creamy, full mouthfeel. Ends crisp and polished, and has enough acidity to set your palate back to zero. **88** —*M.L. (6/1/2006)*

Masottina NV Spumante Extra Dry Prosecco (Prosecco di Conegliano e Valdobbiadene) $NA. Slightly sweet to the nose, with hints of crushed vitamins and fresh-baked doughnuts. Sugary white fruits control the siz-

ITALY

able palate, while the overall character is one of simple sweetness. Veers a little toward soda pop in the final analysis. **86** —*M.S. (6/1/2005)*

Masottina 1999 Vigneto Rizzardo White Blend (Colli di Conegliano) $25. This blend of Pinot Bianco, Chardonnay, Sauvignon Blanc, and Riesling starts off with barrel-fermented notes of butter and baked apples, then folds in tropical fruit flavors. But for all its buttery ripeness, it avoids going over the top, and finishes long, with lemony acids holding its components together. **89** —*J.C. (7/1/2003)*

MASSERIA DEL FEUDO GROTTAROSSA

Masseria del Feudo Grottarossa 2003 Haermosa Chardonnay (Sicilia) $30. A deeply golden and saturated Chardonnay wine that sees both steel and barrique but seems to have lost its freshness along the way. There is toasted almond, melon, and vanilla but the mouthfeel is a bit heavy. **84** —*M.L. (7/1/2006)*

Masseria del Feudo Grottarossa 2004 Nero d'Avola (Sicilia) $14. Cherry, plum, vanilla, and toast make for a well-balanced wine of medium intensity that goes down smooth thanks to its soft tannins and silky consistency. It would pair beautifully with stewed meats or pork dishes. **87** —*M.L. (7/1/2006)*

Masseria del Feudo Grottarossa 2003 Rosso delle Rose Red Blend (Sicilia) $20. This is a truly delightful 50-50 Nero d'Avola-Syrah blend with an inky-purplish color and penetrating aromas of menthol, fennel seed, cherry or currant and cough drop. Extracted in color and flavor, it has a defined personality and a zippy, clean finish with soft tannins. **88 Editors' Choice** —*M.L. (7/1/2006)*

MASSOLINO

Massolino 1995 Vigna Margheria Nebbiolo (Barolo) $60. 82 —*M.S. (9/1/2000)*

MASTROBERARDINO

Mastroberardino 2003 Aglianico (Irpinia) $22. Earthy and leathery, with aromas and flavors of black olives and dried cherries. It's medium-bodied, with a chewy tannic structure that calls for rare beef at this stage of its development. **87** *(12/1/2005)*

Mastroberardino 2000 Radici Aglianico (Taurasi) $41. A bottle to save for a special, home-cooked dinner. The nose has black cherry, dried fruit, spice, cinnamon, and intense mineral notes typical of Campanian wines. The tannins are present but softened beautifully with age. Zesty and crisp on the finish. **91 Cellar Selection** —*M.L. (9/1/2005)*

Mastroberardino 1995 Radici Aglianico (Taurasi) $42. 89 *(3/1/2000)*

Mastroberardino 2002 Coda di Volpe (Lacryma Christi del Vesuvio) $18. Bold but balanced; this represents good Campanian white wine that most folks can appreciate. The aromas of lemon blossom, pine, and apple are refreshing, as is the palate, which offers green apple, cinnamon, and mineral. Long on the finish, and fairly stylish. **88** —*M.S. (10/1/2004)*

Mastroberardino 2004 Falanghina (Sannio) $19. A stronger hue and heavy thickness in the glass make you think of anything but a flinty Campanian white. Despite volcanic soils and the use of steel tanks, flavors of candied orange peel and honey graham cracker come through nicely. Oiliness and lower acidity make it less exciting in the mouth although the overall structure suggests a good match for shellfish. **86** —*M.L. (9/1/2005)*

Mastroberardino 2004 Radici Fiano (Fiano di Avellino) $25. A wonderful expression of one of Campania's most consistent varieties. Aged four months in oak; acacia, toasted almond, and Golden Delicious apples round off a well-balanced and crisp feel in the mouth. **90 Editors' Choice** —*M.L. (9/1/2005)*

Mastroberardino 1998 Radici Fiano (Fiano di Avellino) $26. Balanced and complex, this satisfying white from Campania is ripe and flavorful without being heavy. Beautifully poised, it has a rich nuttiness, adequate acidity, and impressive length. Will pair well with any white fish or pasta and vegetable dish, but is delicious to sip on its own as well. **89** —*M.M. (9/1/2001)*

Mastroberardino 1997 Radici Fiano (Fiano di Avellino) $26. 84 —*M.S. (4/1/2000)*

Mastroberardino 1997 Greco (Greco di Tufo) $25. 92 *(4/1/2000)*

Mastroberardino 2004 NovaSerra Greco (Greco di Tufo) $25. As its name suggests, the Greco grape is thought to have originated in ancient Greece. Peach and pineapple hit the nose and the wine goes down with crisp acidity and lingering flint or chalk dryness in the mouth. Perfect with pasta or rice salads, grilled fish or on its own as an apéritivo. **88** —*M.L. (9/1/2005)*

Mastroberardino 1998 Piedirosso (Lacryma Christi del Vesuvio) $23. 86 —*L.W. (3/1/2000)*

Mastroberardino 1997 Piedirosso (Lacryma Christi del Vesuvio) $23. 91 —*M.S. (3/1/2000)*

Mastroberardino 1997 Red Blend (Aglianico d'Irpinia) $22. 91 *(11/15/1999)*

Mastroberardino 2004 Red Blend (Lacryma Christi del Vesuvio) $22. Fresh and cheery, this cranberry-, cherry-, and spice-scented wine is relatively light in body but long on flavor, with hints of anise, mineral, and pepper that linger on the finish. It's 100% Piedirosso, aged in large barrels for six months before release. **87** *(12/1/2005)*

Mastroberardino 2000 Red Blend (Lacryma Christi del Vesuvio) $20. The nose picks up notes of black ground pepper, oregano, and marjoram. This spice-rack theme continues on the palate, where it's joined by a touch of dark cherries. A dry finish makes this a food-friendly wine. If you are a spice lover, this is for you. **86** —*C.S. (5/1/2002)*

Mastroberardino 1998 Mastro Red Blend (Campania) $17. 82 —*C.S. (5/1/2002)*

Mastroberardino 2000 Naturalis Historia Red Blend (Irpinia) $65. Mostly Aglianico, but its blended with approximately 15% Piedirosso from Vesuvio. This is Mastroberardino's luxury cuvée, so it's aged in barrique, but the influence isn't overdone. Rhubarb and mulling spices on the nose gradually deepen with air into cherry and plum, with hints of mint and olive adding complexity. Long and elegant on the finish. **90** *(12/1/2005)*

Mastroberardino 1998 Naturalis Historia Red Blend (Irpinia) $70. Piercing and powerful up front, with aromatics of black cherry and tree bark. Flavors of raspberry and cherry come next, followed by a finish that's crisp and rock solid. Toward the end the tannins rise up and become a bit fierce. The remedy to that is a meat dish or a hearty pasta. That'll take care of it. **88** —*M.S. (12/15/2003)*

Mastroberardino 1997 Naturalis Historia Red Blend (Irpinia) $70. Ideally, Aglianico shows finesse balanced with richness, and that can be difficult to achieve. But that's the case here. Big, full tannins do not overpower the plum fruits and chocolate. The finish is warm and lingering. **90** —*C.S. (5/1/2002)*

Mastroberardino 2002 Villa dei Misteri Red Blend (Pompeiano) $217. This curiosity comes from a single hectare of land planted within the ruins of Pompeii. Plum and black cherry notes mingle with mineral, finishing with firm, dusty tannins. Elegant in the Mastroberardino style. In this, the second vintage of this wine, a blend of Piedirosso (90%) with Sciascinoso (10%), only 200 cases were produced. **89** *(12/1/2005)*

Mastroberardino 1998 White Blend (Coda di Volpe d'Irpinia) $13. 88 —*L.W. (4/1/2000)*

Mastroberardino 2004 Bianco White Blend (Lacryma Christi del Vesuvio) $19. From the grape variety known as Coda di Volpe ("fox's tail"), this is a fresh, flowery white loaded with apple, pineapple, and mineral flavors. Ends with spice and mineral notes. Drink now. **88** *(12/1/2005)*

Mastroberardino 1998 Sireum White Blend (Campania) $NA. 87 —*L.W. (4/1/2000)*

MASTROJANNI

Mastrojanni 2001 Brunello (Brunello di Montalcino) $55. A zippy, snappy wine with forest berry and menthol freshness, bitter tea tannins, ripe blueberry flavors, and background aromas such as resin and wet slate. A big Brunello nose with a medium-length finish. **90 Cellar Selection** *(4/1/2006)*

Mastrojanni 2000 Brunello (Brunello di Montalcino) $50. Tight, with briar, leather, and smoke aromas, along with plum and cherry. The palate on this one seems a bit jumpy, with live-wire fruit and bright acidity. So it's interesting that the finish carries some coconut, vanilla, and sweet butter flavors. Needs a couple of years to knit together. **88**—*M.S. (7/1/2005)*

Mastrojanni 1999 Brunello (Brunello di Montalcino) $55. A touch rusty and weathered given its young age, but classic on the nose, where there's tomato, pepper, and dried red fruit. This is very drinkable now, and after a few minutes in the glass it begins to show more. Traditional, and just perfect for restaurants and early drinking. **89**—*M.S. (6/1/2004)*

Mastrojanni 1997 Brunello (Brunello di Montalcino) $60. Antonio Mastrojanni has made a classic, old-style Brunello. There is a chunky solidity to the wine, with black, tarry fruit over toasty, but not new wood, flavors. It is firm, robust and, at this stage, still very dry from fruit tannins. Like many Mastrojanni vintages, it needs time—in this case, at least 10 years. **93 Cellar Selection**—*R.V. (8/1/2002)*

MASÙT DA RIVE

Masùt da Rive 2004 Pinot Grigio (Isonzo del Friuli) $19. If you appreciate what Italians refer to as "balsam" notes in a wine —menthol and eucalyptus—this Grigio has them. Steel fermentation leads to explosive zest and crispness in the mouth. **89**—*M.L. (2/1/2006)*

Masùt Da Rive 2001 Sauvignon (Isonzo del Friuli) $22. The nose offers a bit of northern Italian funk, with aromas frighteningly close to smelling of garlic. The palate is a bit sour, with generic, mildly bitter flavors of pineapple and peach. Better weight and feel. **82** *(7/1/2005)*

MAURO BUSSI

Mauro Bussi 2000 Nebbiolo (Barbaresco) $55. Anise, black cherry, and peach aromas and flavors give this Barbaresco an exotic twist. It's lush and warm in the mouth, finishing easy, but with decent grip. Drink now–2010. **90** *(4/2/2004)*

MAURO MOLINO

Mauro Molino 1997 Vigna Gettere Barbera (Barbera d'Alba) $33. **89** *(4/1/2000)*

MAURO SEBASTE

Mauro Sebaste 1999 Brunate Nebbiolo (Barolo) $75. Scents of smoke and toast, cedar, and tobacco signal a wine with a modern touch. Yet this perfectly melds oak with spice and black cherries, yielding a lush, harmonious wine that still tastes like Barolo. Drink now—2010. **91** *(4/2/2004)*

Mauro Sebaste 1999 La Serra Nebbiolo (Barolo) $54. Coffee and tree bark aromas lead into flavors of cola and tart cherries. This is interesting from a structural standpoint, with soft, supple tannins, but it has very high, tart acids. Finish picks up hints of hickory smoke and lemon. **87** *(4/2/2004)*

Mauro Sebaste 1995 Monvigliero Nebbiolo (Barolo) $66. **86** *(7/1/2000)*

Mauro Sebaste 2001 Parigi Nebbiolo (Nebbiolo d'Alba) $32. Fairly heavily oaked, with resin and pine-needle aromas atop lean red fruit. Comes across firm and tart on the palate, with a tight, drying finish. Grippy and lean when it comes to the cherry and strawberry flavors. **84**—*M.S. (12/15/2003)*

Mauro Sebaste 1999 Prapo Nebbiolo (Barolo) $75. Wood influence dominates the aromas of this wine, imparting scents of cinnamon, bacon, and cedar. Cherry fruit shines through on the palate, joining flavors of vanilla and dried spices. Drink 2005–2015. **90** *(4/2/2004)*

MAURO VEGLIO

Mauro Veglio 1998 Castelletto Nebbiolo (Barolo) $60. Toasty, showing some obvious new wood aromas, balanced by Porty scents—the densely packed fruit is on the verge of being over-ripe, yet there are also some faint green notes. Firm tannins cut the finish short, but should enable the wine to age for at least 5–10 years. **87** *(4/2/2004)*

MAZZEI

Mazzei 2000 Badiola Sangiovese (Toscana) $13. Black in color, with foresty aromas of smoke and leaves. Unfortunately there's also some murky aromas and a hint of cheese. The palate has basic berries and oak, while the finish is overtly woody, with a note of strawberry. The wine has its good points, namely spice and heft. But it's also off the mark in a few areas, namely the confusing nose and a heavy dose of vanilla. **85**—*M.S. (12/31/2002)*

Mazzei 1999 Fonterutoli Sangiovese (Chianti Classico) $27. Dark and dense from the get-go. Initial earth, black plum, tomato, and smoke aromas air out nicely with a bit of time, exposing a complex connoisseur's wine that is the perfect candidate for three to five years in the cellar. Now it has such a pure, chewy palate that once the overt oak wears off, it'll be terrific. **91**—*M.S. (8/1/2002)*

MAZZI

Mazzi 2001 Punta di Villa Red Blend (Amarone della Valpolicella Classico) $60. Raw at first, but it comes around. Early sauvage aromas yield to dried fruit, a touch of dill and butter, and char. The palate is all about red fruit, with cherry and tar dominant. Has a bit of a lactic, creamy quality at the end. **87** *(11/1/2005)*

MAZZINO

Mazzino 1998 Barbera (Barbera d'Alba) $12. Burnt and roasted aromas come in front of tart cherry and cranberry flavors. Very monotone in its attack, and a bit hot and wiry. **82**—*M.S. (12/15/2003)*

Mazzino 1997 Nebbiolo (Barolo) $35. This wine from the Garbelletto winery is juicy and basic. It has good fruit, smoky qualities and some coffee and chocolate. Is it structured like a major-league Barolo? No. But for drinking now, it delivers some true-form character and flavor. **86**—*M.S. (12/15/2003)*

MEDICI ERMETE

Medici Ermete 2005 Concerto Lambrusco Reggiano Secco Lambrusco (Emilia-Romagna) $21. If you thought Lambrusco (a fizzy, red wine often served chilled) cannot pair with food, think again. The wine's effervescence and acidity make it perfect for cutting through cream- and cheese-based dishes. This dry version has a dark, ruby color with red berry aromas, clove, and a touch of mint tea. **86**—*M.L. (12/15/2006)*

Medici Ermete 2005 Solo Lambrusco Reggiano Secco Lambrusco (Emilia-Romagna) $15. Here's a traditional Lambrusco with a concentrated ruby color and loads of blueberry aromas. Beyond the berry notes, you'll find a nice touch of almond paste. Although the nose is simple, the wine offers good structure and body. **85**—*M.L. (12/15/2006)*

Medici Ermete 2005 Daphne Malvasia Frizzante Malvasia Bianca (Emilia-Romagna) $21. "Pear" sums up the most obvious component of this wine's aromatic offerings. You'll find pineapple, peach, and exotic fruit as well, but in much smaller doses. All in all, this is a fun and pleasant sparkler, made from aromatic Malvasia grapes, with an attractive nose and a lean mouthfeel. **85**—*M.L. (12/15/2006)*

MELINI

Melini 1997 Coltri 2 Cabernet Blend (Tuscany) $33. This wine from Melini is maturing nicely and seems to be in perfect drinking form. It's a blend of 70% Cabernet and 30% Sangiovese, and it shows patented dried fruit, leather, and caramel aromas, a peppery, cherry palate, and some light oak on the finish. A hefty tannic structure is keeping this wine from fading, but get after it sooner rather than later. **90**—*M.S. (11/15/2003)*

Melini 1999 Bonorli Merlot (Tuscany) $35. The bouquet is full of roasted red fruit and sweetness. Flavors of blackberry follow in high-voltage manner. This is no plump California Merlot; instead it's firm and juicy, courtesy of piercing yet proper tannins and lively acids. Quite a grip is applied by the tannin-acid package, but it tastes really good. **88**—*M.S. (11/15/2003)*

Melini 2002 Borghi D'Elsa Sangiovese (Chianti) $10. Sharp aromas of rhubarb, leather, and barnyard keep this one from blossoming. The palate, however, is light and fresh, with thin but pleasant strawberry and raspberry flavors preceding a peppery, mildly lemony finish. **84** *(4/1/2005)*

Melini 1998 Borghi D'Elsa Sangiovese (Chianti) $9. There's cherry and licorice on the nose of this crisp, lighter-style wine. Bright, tart fruit and cocoa accents follow on the palate, and it's bright and moderately tannic on the finish. A good pizza-pasta partner, this will even out over the next 12 months and drink well through 2004. **87 Best Buy** *(4/1/2001)*

ITALY

Melini 2000 Isassi Sangiovese (Chianti Classico) $16. Solid, with restrained red fruit, tea, fallen leaves, and leather on the nose. Old school all the way, with raspberry and black cherry flavors and little to no perceivable oak. It expands nicely on the finish, offering a glance into the lighter style of Chianti. **87** —*M.S. (11/15/2004)*

Melini 1999 Isassi Sangiovese (Chianti Classico) $15. Exotic aromas of orange peel, licorice, and leather mask some of the light red fruit that seems to want to step out. Dried cherry, raspberry, and apple skin carry the solid if standard palate, while the finish is clean, light, moderately tannic, and modest in length. **87** —*M.S. (11/15/2003)*

Melini 1997 Isassi Sangiovese (Chianti Classico) $13. The bright acid spine of this sassy wine shows off its sour cherry fruit and cinnamon-charcoal accents. Finishes dry, with some lingering toast flavors and mildly astringent tannins. **85** *(4/1/2001)*

Melini 1999 Laborel Riserva Sangiovese (Chianti Classico) $19. A bit rusty and orange in color, with light, herbal aromas of cherry and leather. Quite light on the palate, with cherry and citrus notes. The long, dry finish is a bit smoky but not that fruity. Already mature or beyond. **86** —*M.S. (11/15/2004)*

Melini 1998 Laborel Riserva Sangiovese (Chianti Classico) $19. The scents of sandalwood, pepper ,and dried cherry dominate a nose that indicates a wine that's fading more than growing. There's a bit of apple skin and cherry to the mouth, and then some spicy oak on the back end. Lean, with a tight feel and citrusy, acidic edges. **85** —*M.S. (11/15/2003)*

Melini 1995 Massovecchio dai Vigneti Terrarossa Riserva Sangiovese (Chianti Classico) $35. 91 *(11/15/1999)*

Melini 1998 Riserva La Selvanella Sangiovese (Chianti Classico) $23. Melini's Riserva, from a 98 acre vineyard in Radda in Chianti, is still firmly traditional in character. With its firm, dry bitter cherry fruit flavors and just a light touch of wood, it shows how classic Chianti winemaking still has a place, provided it is used in the right way. **87** —*R.V. (8/1/2002)*

Melini 1999 Riserva Massovecchio Sangiovese (Chianti Classico) $30. Jammy and broad, with cola and loud fruit aromas. With time it picks up focus, showing tangy cherry/berry fruit and a live-wire finish full of leather, smoke, tomato and chocolate. Fairly complex yet ripe and forward. The best of both worlds. **90** —*M.S. (10/1/2004)*

Melini 1999 Vigneti La Selvanella Riserva Sangiovese (Chianti Classico) $24. Kicks off with a bouquet of leather, burnt wood, and mint. The palate is less than eventful, but there is solid packed-down red fruit. Finishes rather sweet and sour, but without that level of balance one hopes for. **86** —*M.S. (10/1/2004)*

Melini 2002 Vernaccia (Vernaccia di San Gimignano) $12. Lucid almost to the point of looking like water, but with an easygoing palate of apple and citrus. This is an innocuous white, the quintessential apéritif. Served well-chilled, it should please. **85** —*M.S. (8/1/2004)*

Melini 2002 Le Grillaie Vernaccia (Vernaccia di San Gimignano) $20. A bit pricey for Vernaccia, especially when you consider that the wine doesn't really show more than the basics: citrus and melon notes, and some soda-cracker dryness along with white pepper. All in all, however, it's perfectly good and entirely traditional. **87** —*M.S. (8/1/2004)*

MELONI

Meloni 2001 Le Ghiaie Cannonau (Cannonau di Sardegna) $21. Kind of big up front, with creamy oak aromas along with smoky notes of molasses and barbecue. Thick and fruity on the palate, with milk chocolate draping raspberry and cherry fruit. Staunch tannins on the finish are softened by sweet fudge flavors. And through it all you get a little tomato. **88** —*M.S. (2/1/2005)*

MERK

Merk 2001 Pinot Bianco (Friuli Aquileia) $16. This is an oversized Pinot Bianco, fat and fleshy, oozing with peaches, pears, and dried spices. Yet there's a tingle of acidity holding it together, preventing the wine from busting out of its seams. **86** —*J.C. (7/1/2003)*

Merk 2004 Pinot Grigio (Friuli Aquileia) $16. A subdued note of soybean and water chestnut backed by candied pear washes through to the back of the palate with a mineral finish. You couldn't ask for a better match for Chinese take-out. **89** —*M.L. (6/1/2006)*

Merk 2001 Pinot Grigio (Friuli Aquileia) $16. Atypically gold in color, this also smells atypically ripe, of red apples and strawberries. Flavors are of baked Golden Delicious, complete with a dusting of cinnamon. Low acid makes it plump, and it finishes short. **85** —*J.C. (7/1/2003)*

Merk 2001 Tocai (Friuli Aquileia) $16. A taut, citrusy, and minerally wine from a grape variety that's often more open and fruity, this offering is nonetheless impeccably fresh and clean, picking up some minty notes on the finish. **87** —*J.C. (7/1/2003)*

MERONI

Meroni 1997 Il Velluto Red Blend (Valpolicella Classico Superiore) $24. A touch volatile, with raisiny, leathery aromas that are much like Port. Some cola and black cherry make for a classic ripasso palate, while the finish is smooth and slightly bitter. Drying, fading tannins, however, render it already past its prime; drink now if at all. **83** *(5/1/2003)*

Meroni 1997 Il Velluto Riserva Red Blend (Amarone della Valpolicella Classico) $80. Slightly gaseous on the nose and losing freshness with each passing day. Zingy acids are keeping it alive but the flavors are slipping toward cranberry and tomato. Not much else is left. **83** *(11/1/2005)*

MEZZACORONA

Mezzacorona 2004 Cabernet Sauvignon (Vigneti delle Dolomiti) $9. Grapes are harvested north of Lake Garda, where temperatures are more moderate, to produce a lighter and fresher style of Cab that boasts intense notes of forest berry and cut greens. It's clean, smooth in the mouth, and easy to drink. **87 Best Buy** —*M.L. (10/1/2006)*

Mezzacorona 2003 Cabernet Sauvignon (Vigneti delle Dolomiti) $8. Solid cassis and plum aromas and flavors lead the way, with just hints of dried herbs and leather. Supple in the mouth, yet not soft, finishing on a crisp note. **85 Best Buy** *(6/1/2005)*

Mezzacorona 2005 Chardonnay (Vigneti delle Dolomiti) $9. This is textbook cool-climate Chardonnay with banana, nut, vanilla, and exotic fruit packaged within compact and polished aromas. Lemon rind and floral flavors render crispness and freshness. **86 Best Buy** —*M.L. (10/1/2006)*

Mezzacorona 2004 Chardonnay (Vigneti delle Dolomiti) $7. This bargain-priced Chardonnay delivers the goods. Hints of butter on the nose come from 25% barrel fermentation and malolactic, while the fresh pear and ripe apple flavors come straight from the fruit. Clean on the finish. **85 Best Buy** *(6/1/2005)*

Mezzacorona 2003 Chardonnay (Vigneti delle Dolomiti) $8. The heat of 2003 seems to have brought out some exotic tropical flavors in this bargain-priced Chard. Guava and melon notes are tinged with honey, while the finish turns pineapple-y. **84 Best Buy** —*J.C. (12/31/2004)*

Mezzacorona 2002 Vigneti delle Dolomiti Chardonnay (Trentino) $8. Highly perfumed, with delicate floral and peach notes leaping out of the glass. Melon and peach flavors combine on the palate. Light-weight and finishes short, but it's a solid apéritif. **85 Best Buy** —*J.C. (7/1/2003)*

Mezzacorona 2003 Merlot (Vigneti delle Dolomiti) $10. Solid red wine at an affordable price, boasting black cherry and mocha scents and flavors, tinged with a hint of dried herbs. Medium-weight, with no tannin to speak of, finishing crisp and clean. **85 Best Buy** —*J.C. (12/31/2004)*

Mezzacorona 2001 Merlot (Trentino) $8. This is a perfectly good, garden-variety Merlot, one done in the leaner Northern Italian style. Nonetheless, it has some pop to it. Blackberry and chocolate grace the palate prior to a lengthy finish that showcases healthy, round fruit. Is it a blockbuster? No. Is it an eminently drinkable red wine? Definitely. **86 Best Buy** —*M.S. (12/15/2003)*

Mezzacorona 1998 Merlot (Trentino) $8. Fragrant floral notes with good ripe, sleek fruit behind it. An herbaceous tinge to predominantly citrus flavors. Long, clean, spicy finish. Pleasing and elegant. **86** *(1/1/2004)*

Mezzacorona 1998 Pinot Grigio (Trentino) $8. 86 Best Buy *(8/1/1999)*

Mezzacorona 2005 Pinot Grigio (Vigneti delle Dolomiti) $9. Yellow fruit aromas like melon, peach, and banana give way to a crisp and polished

Grigio, with all its elements in place. This is a friendly, playful and food-friendly wine for informal occasions. **86 Best Buy** —*M.L. (6/1/2006)*

Mezzacorona 2004 Pinot Grigio (Vigneti delle Dolomiti) $8. Peach and pear notes vie with almond skin scents in the bouquet of this mainstream Pinot Grigio. It's medium-bodied and plump in the mouth, with pear and citrus flavors that yield a fresh, clean finish. **84 Best Buy** *(6/1/2005)*

Mezzacorona 1999 Pinot Grigio (Trentino) $7. 83 —*M.N. (12/31/2000)*

Mezzacorona 2001 Millesimato Pinot Grigio (Trentino) $NA. A rich, complex style, with good concentration. There is some spice, along with citrus acidity and softness. It is immediately attractive, but also has pretensions to a more serious depth of flavor. **85** —*R.V. (7/1/2003)*

Mezzacorona 2004 Riserva Pinot Grigio (Trentino) $13. Partial barrique fermentation and barrel aging add dimension to this Pinot Grigio. Rich with flavors of toasted nuts, honey, banana bread, yellow rose, and Golden Delicious apple. It's creamy and slightly sweet in the mouth backed by a long, crisp finish. **89 Best Buy** —*M.L. (2/1/2006)*

Mezzacorona 2003 Riserva Pinot Grigio (Trentino) $13. Slightly less generous than the 2004, but with similar notes of toast and baked apple. Feels thick and creamy in the mouth with a long, nutty persistency. Cold maceration keeps floral and fruity notes intact. **88 Best Buy** —*M.L. (2/1/2006)*

Mezzacorona 2002 Riserva Pinot Grigio (Trentino) $14. An oak-aged Pinot Grigio, with notes of cinnamon and buttered toast to complement the fruit elements of poached pears. In a world of tart, tangy Grigios, this one stands out. **85** —*J.C. (12/31/2004)*

Mezzacorona 2000 Riserva Teroldego (Italy) $14. A bit herbal and weedy, but also packs in plenty of ripe cassis fruit alongside meaty notes and a hint of dark earth. Loosely-knit structurally, it still offers a rich mouthful of flavors, ending on a chocolaty note. **85** —*J.C. (12/31/2004)*

Mezzacorona 2000 Riserva Superiore Teroldego (Teroldego Rotaliano) $NA. A special bottling produced for the 100th anniversary of the cooperative, this is creamier and much more supple than the regular riserva, reviewed in our December 31, 2004 issue. Smoky, toasty, and loaded with berry fruit on the nose, dusty and smooth on the finish, this wine shows what large co-ops can achieve but rarely accomplish. **89** *(6/1/2005)*

MICHELE CHIARLO

Michele Chiarlo 1998 Barbera (Barbera d'Asti) $13. 87 **Best Buy** *(4/1/2000)*

Michele Chiarlo 1997 Barbera (Barbera d'Asti) $12. 83 *(4/1/2000)*

Michele Chiarlo 2000 La Court Barbera (Barbera d'Asti) $35. This is a full-blown barriqued version of Barbera, with powerful aromas of cedar and vanilla making a clear statement. On the palate, there's plenty of tart cherry fruit, wearing a heavy coat of new French oak. The overall result is pleasing, ending with easy suppleness. **88** —*J.C. (11/15/2004)*

Michele Chiarlo 1996 La Court Barbera (Barbera d'Asti) $46. 87 *(4/1/2000)*

Michele Chiarlo 1999 La Court Superiore Barbera (Barbera d'Asti) $NA. Cola, coffee, and cherry aromas lead off this barrique-aged wine that features lots of intensity and style. Yes, it's slathered throughout with spicy but smooth vanilla oak, but that oak works wonders with the fruit. The finish tosses up coffee and superior length. As a whole, it's racy and refined, with nuances of bacon and smoke. **91 Editors' Choice** —*M.S. (11/15/2002)*

Michele Chiarlo 2001 Le Orme Barbera (Barbera d'Asti) $11. A tart, juicy, cherry-flavored wine, couched in nuances of leather and cinnamon from a year in oak. Picks up hints of chocolate on the finish. **86 Best Buy** —*J.C. (11/15/2004)*

Michele Chiarlo 2000 Superiore Barbera (Barbera d'Asti) $10. Quite fragrant, with aromas of blueberries and graham crackers. The flavors run toward the sweet side, emphasizing boysenberry and vanilla. The finish is tight more than expansive, with grapey flavors and notes of coffee. Overall it's pretty soft, without much edge. **86 Best Buy** —*M.S. (11/15/2002)*

Michele Chiarlo 1995 Valle del Sole Barbera (Barbera d'Asti) $29. 88 *(4/1/2000)*

Michele Chiarlo 1998 Cortese (Gavi) $15. 86 *(4/1/2000)*

Michele Chiarlo 2002 Cortese (Gavi) $14. Nectarine and lemon dance all around and straight through the middle of this fruity, drink-me style of Gavi. It's not a tight, dry wine—it's more like a burst of fruit salad, one comprised of nectarine and lemon, but also melon, pineapple, and lime. Well-balanced and food friendly. **87** —*M.S. (11/15/2003)*

Michele Chiarlo 1998 Rovereto Cortese (Gavi di Gavi) $24. 86 *(4/1/2000)*

Michele Chiarlo 2004 Nivole Moscato (Moscato d'Asti) $12. Good things come in little packages and this half bottle Moscato d'Asti is hugely satisfying. It boasted the most crystalline luminosity of all the wines I tasted and among the thickest, foamiest froths. I also loved the nose with limestone and peach notes backed by characteristic muskiness. **89 Best Buy** —*M.L. (12/15/2005)*

Michele Chiarlo 1998 Nebbiolo (Piedmont) $30. This is a blend of tannic wines from the communes of Serralunga, and Castiglione Falleto, and fruitier wines from La Morra and Barolo itself. The two characters come together well in the sweet fruit and vanilla on the nose and the flavors of rich, bitter cherry, with a layer of structured dryness underneath. **90** —*R.V. (11/15/2002)*

Michele Chiarlo 1995 Nebbiolo (Barbaresco) $35. 88 —*M.M. (5/1/1999)*

Michele Chiarlo 2000 Brunate Nebbiolo (Barolo) $85. Like Chiarlo's 2000 Cerequio, this wine's aromas are dominated by burnt-match scents. Underlying are some attractive black cherry and tar flavors, nestled in a surprisingly supple, medium-weight mouthfeel. **88** —*J.C. (11/15/2004)*

Michele Chiarlo 1998 Brunate Nebbiolo (Piedmont) $81. From one of the top vineyard sites in Barolo, Michele Chiarlo produces an elegant wine. Aromas of dried raisins and figs follow through with flavors of fig jelly and tarry fruits along with great, ripe acidity. Despite the elegance, it can still pack a punch. **93 Cellar Selection** —*R.V. (11/15/2002)*

Michele Chiarlo 1999 Cannubi Nebbiolo (Barolo) $81. This full-bodied wine caresses the palate with soft, mouth-filling flavors of coffee, molasses, and dried fruit. Leather and dried spice notes add complexity, while the finish boasts a rich, chewy texture. **87** *(4/2/2004)*

Michele Chiarlo 1998 Cannubi Nebbiolo (Piedmont) $81. The parcel of the Cannubi vineyard owned by Chiarlo is so steep that it has been terraced to make it manageable. Aromas of dried figs and sweet toast are instantly attractive. Ripe black fruit is the hallmark flavor of this wine, with dry, classically tarry tannins. **92** —*R.V. (11/15/2002)*

Michele Chiarlo 2000 Cerequio Nebbiolo (Barolo) $85. Burnt-match aromas meld with burnt coffee on the nose, lending a slightly off note to this otherwise very fine wine. Black cherry and mushroom flavors are wrapped in a soft, supple package that reflects the great ripeness achieved in the 2000 vintage. **87** —*J.C. (11/15/2004)*

Michele Chiarlo 1999 Cerequio Nebbiolo (Barolo) $84. Nicely balanced and already approachable, Chiarlo's '99 Cerequio boasts textbook aromatics and flavors of anise, cherries, leather, and asphalt. It's firmly structured, but not overbearing or too tannic. Drink 2008–2015. **88** *(4/2/2004)*

Michele Chiarlo 1998 Cerequio Nebbiolo (Barolo) $45. A typical '98, softer than the '97s and much more approachable. The nose has sweet red apple and root beer notes. Flavors of tart cherries and oak are balanced nicely by an easy-to-drink finish. The tannins are silky and not too aggressive. **90** —*C.S. (11/15/2002)*

Michele Chiarlo 1995 Cerequio Nebbiolo (Barolo) $89. 88 *(7/1/2000)*

Michele Chiarlo 1998 Tortoniano Nebbiolo (Barolo) $44. Dry earthy notes dominate the nose, but the palate features plenty of plum, prune, and tar, densely packed and framed by substantial tannins. Finshes long, with a puckering tart note and firm tannins. Try after 2010. **90** *(4/2/2004)*

Michele Chiarlo 1995 Countacc Red Blend (Monferrato) $40. 91 —*M.M. (5/1/1999)*

MIONETTO

Mionetto NV Champagne Blend (Prosecco di Valdobbiadene) $24. This Prosecco has a more refined and delicate style, with flavors of peach and citrus. Lots of fruit and a creamy finish make for an easy-drinking glass of bubbles. **89** *(11/15/2002)*

ITALY

Mionetto NV Cartizze Champagne Blend (Prosecco di Valdobbiadene) $47. 88 (11/15/2002)

Mionetto NV Casada Extra Dry Spumante Champagne Blend (Prosecco di Valdobbiadene) $14. In the mouth, the bead is big and coarse (like soda carbonation), and the flavors minerally and toasty over a bed of pear and honey notes. Opens with faint apple and floral notes. 85 —M.M. (12/31/2001)

Mionetto NV Frizzante (Soft White Wine) Champagne Blend (Prosecco di Valdobbiadene) $12. Clean and lively, this is just what most people seek in a Prosecco. The initially faint citrus bouquet opens nicely, and the medium-dry lemon-lime palate is light and refreshing, but with presence and texture. The surprisingly fine bead is steady and the floral citrus finish a very pretty close. 88 Best Buy —M.M. (12/31/2001)

Mionetto NV Sergio Extra Dry Champagne Blend (Prosecco di Valdobbiadene) $18. Full and soft in the mouth, but not overly effervescent. Pleasingly sweet honey and floral notes unfold in the mouth; they are prefaced by slight citrus and yeast notes in the bouquet. Meringue, chalk powder, and lemon peel flavors sum things up. It's yummy, easy to drink, balanced, and not at all cloying. 88 Best Buy —D.T. (12/31/2001)

Mionetto NV Sergio Extra Dry Spumante Champagne Blend (Prosecco di Valdobbiadene) $16. This sparkler's aromatic nose provides floral scents and a touch of anise. The rich, creamy mouthfeel ends slightly sweet, making this an enjoyable beverage with a unique style. Has enough depth to match with oysters or lobster. 92 (11/15/2002)

Mionetto NV Spumante Champagne Blend (Prosecco di Valdobbiadene) $12. Flavors of peach and lime have a light feel and elegant balance. There is a touch of sweetness on the finish. Great by itself, or with a little prosciutto at the start of the meal. 87 (11/15/2002)

Mionetto NV Spumante Brut Champagne Blend (Prosecco di Valdobbiadene) $11. A bigger toastier style, but the floral and citrus aromas aren't masked by the toast, creating a pleasant balance that finishes dry and clean. Drink by itself or as a base for your Bellini or mimosa. 89 Best Buy (11/15/2002)

Mionetto NV Superiore di Cartizze Champagne Blend (Prosecco di Valdobbiadene) $47. This limited-appellation wine shows complexity, but is not entirely harmonious. The floral and tobacco bouquet also has an odd, wet wood-like note. Sweet, with lemon and herb accents, the palate has an even, soft feel. Closes with an odd marriage of a sugary fade and tobacco notes. 84 —M.M. (12/31/2001)

Mionetto NV Il Moscato (Moscato delle Venezie) $10. Full of ripe apples, honey and citrus, but it could use just a bit more zip and freshness to help balance the sugar. Crown-capped for easy opening; try this instead of a soda or cocktail when you want something sweet at the bar. 84 —J.C. (12/31/2003)

Mionetto NV Prosecco (Prosecco di Valdobbiadene) $13. In a bottle closed with the traditional string over the cork, this Prosecco is the lightest shade of gold with pearl-like strings of bubbles. There's pear, some citrus, white peach, and a dab of almond followed by a refreshing jolt of crispness. 85 —M.L. (12/15/2004)

Mionetto NV Prosecco (Prosecco di Valdobbiadene) $15. Starts with the aroma of gunpowder before turning warm and dusty. Quite zesty and lime-based, with a burnt, undertone to the flavor profile. Finishes with apple and mushroom. 85 —M.S. (6/1/2005)

Mionetto NV Prosecco (Prosecco di Conegliano e Valdobbiadene) $13. This Prosecco delivers heavier, fuller aromas of graham cracker, mature peach, lemon zest, kiwi, and yellow rose. It's not as crisp as others, but is an easygoing sparkler with a playful touch of sweetness. 85 —M.L. (12/15/2006)

Mionetto NV Brut Prosecco (Prosecco di Valdobbiadene) $11. The most noticeable aroma is marzipan, which also comes though beautifully in the mouth. You'll also get pine nut, peach, melon and yellow rose. This Prosecco is broader and softer than most, although its crispness remains intact. 87 —M.L. (12/15/2006)

Mionetto NV Brut Prosecco (Prosecco di Valdobbiadene) $12. A bigger style with more complex aromas that range from melon to honey to clove. An elegant product, with thick foam and golden luminosity that calls out for finger foods and antipasti. 88 Best Buy —M.L. (12/15/2004)

Mionetto NV Brut Spumante Prosecco (Prosecco di Valdobbiadene) $12. Juicy and clean, although you don't really pull much from the quiet nose. Round and citrusy on the tongue, with crisp apple flavors. Runs long and standard on the finish, with a mix of sweet and tart flavors. Easy to drink. 87 Best Buy —M.S. (6/1/2005)

Mionetto NV Cartizze Prosecco (Prosecco Superiore di Cartizze) $24. Clean, polished; the Cartizze cru yields delicate crushed stone and floral notes with background tangerine and cracker notes. A bubbly with a light, delicate touch that would pair well with finger foods. 90 Editors' Choice —M.L. (6/1/2006)

Mionetto NV Cartizze Dry Prosecco (Prosecco di Valdobbiadene) $25. Fragrantly sweet, with lush, candied aromas of lime lollipops and jelly doughnuts. The palate holds onto that sweetness as it offers ripe apple, pear, and pink grapefruit. Nice texture, maybe a bit sticky, but likable. This one is hard to knock. 89 —M.S. (6/1/2005)

Mionetto NV Extra Dry Prosecco (Prosecco di Valdobbiadene) $13. Fat, sweet aromas such as fruit salad and poached pear greet the nose, but there's also a lactic element at the back. Light and lean, with a blast of refreshing crispness on the finish. 87 —M.L. (6/1/2006)

Mionetto 2005 Extra Dry Prosecco (Prosecco di Conegliano e Valdobbiadene) $17. This is a very beautiful rendition, with ripe flavors of honeysuckle, mature melon, pear, Golden Delicious apple, and rose. It fills the mouth with creamy froth and tastes great when served very chilled. 87 —M.L. (12/15/2006)

Mionetto NV Extra Dry Linea Mó Prosecco (Prosecco di Valdobbiadene) $15. Elegant and linear with crushed stone and lively fruit notes that are toned down compared to other Proseccos, but are seductive and pleasing nonetheless. There's a very enjoyable crystalline, perky quality to this bubbly. 88 —M.L. (6/1/2006)

Mionetto NV Frizzante Prosecco (Prosecco di Valdobbiadene) $12. Basic, but 100% good. This is a perfect cocktail-party drink, one with baked-apple aromas and a round, apple-and-citrus palate. Finishes fresh, long and pure. Nothing sensational, just good, clean fun. 88 Best Buy —M.S. (6/1/2005)

Mionetto NV Il Prosecco (Prosecco di Valdobbiadene) $11. Fastened with a yellow bottle cap, this is an informal, cool Prosecco that is low in alcohol and long in charm. Easy to drink, it presents pretty floral aromas followed by flavors of straw, herbs, lime, and honey. Light and clean in the mouth, it makes an excellent cocktail wine. 86 Best Buy —M.L. (12/15/2006)

Mionetto NV IL Prosecco (Prosecco del Veneto) $10. Easygoing, with apple and citrus on both the nose and palate. Good acidity, upright in the mouth, and quaffable. Topped like a beer bottle; we can see it flowing freely over the course of the summer. 86 Best Buy —M.S. (6/1/2005)

Mionetto NV Il Prosecco Prosecco (Prosecco del Veneto) $11. Fresh and clean, with aromas of slate, citrus, and green herbs. The palate delivers lemon-lime flavors and a modest bubble bead that doesn't overwhelm. And when folks say packaging means nothing, ignore them. This one comes in a cool bowling pin-shaped bottle that's capped like a beer. The tagline on the label points out that Prosecco is the "gentle" sparkling wine. Yeah, gentle on your wallet. 86 Best Buy —M.S. (12/15/2004)

Mionetto NV Il Prosecco (Prosecco del Veneto) $10. Packaged under a convenient crown cap, this is no doubt intended for the bar crowd. It would also be perfect for picnics, featuring floral aromas of orange blossom and tangerine backed by orange and melon flavors. Light and frothy. 85 —J.C. (12/31/2003)

Mionetto NV Sergio Extra Dry Prosecco (Prosecco di Valdobbiadene) $18. There's a lot more flinty chalkiness in this wine, beyond the apple and melon, which makes it stand out from others. Prosecco, Chardonnay, Bianchetta, and Verdiso go into this wine, vinified without skin contact, which explains its pale, delicate hue. 87 —M.L. (12/15/2004)

Mionetto NV Sergio Extra Dry Prosecco (Prosecco del Veneto) $NA. Floral, perfumy, and a bit sweet-smelling, this sparkler packs notes of honey, orange blossoms, and ripe apples into a balanced, frothy whole. It is a little sweet, but finishes with good length and enough tartness to achieve a sense of balance. 89 —J.C. (12/31/2003)

Mionetto NV Sergio Extra Dry Spumante Prosecco (Prosecco di Valdobbiadene) $18. Light and garden fresh, with apple-based aromas. Not excessively expressive, but still full of chunky green apple, citrus, and honeydew melon flavors. Cleansing, with a sorbet quality. Off-dry but not sugary sweet. Shows decent style and precision. **88** —*M.S. (6/1/2005)*

Mionetto 2002 Marca Trevigiana Novello '02 Red Blend (Marca Trevigiana) $10. Like Beaujolais Nouveau, this young wine has sweet cherry and cookie aromas, followed by bubble gum flavors. It features a crisp, fresh finish and a youthful overall personality. **83** *(5/1/2003)*

Mionetto NV Extra Dry Sergio Sparkling Blend (Prosecco del Veneto) $17. Often, extra dry Prosecco offers a deceptively sweet bouquet. Part of the reason for this is that smaller percentages of Chardonnay, Verdisio, and Bianchetta have been added to the Prosecco blend. That is the case here, though this wine has a broader, fuller nose with ripe peach, honey, flowers and a chalky element. **88** —*M.L. (12/15/2006)*

MOCALI

Mocali 2001 Brunello (Brunello di Montalcino) $45. Coffee, chocolate, plum, and spicy clove add highlights to a dark, textured wine rich with sour chocolate, tar, and black cherry. The mouthfeel is creamy, supple, juicy and concentrated with menthol freshness on the finish. **91** *(4/1/2006)*

Mocali 2001 Vigna delle Raunate Brunello (Brunello di Montalcino) $23. Dark ruby with purplish highlights, this wine boasts bold cherry, forest berry, fennel, dried tobacco, tealeaf, soil, and generous cola notes. Full and richly textured in the mouth, the tannins are soft and limber with decent length. **91** *(4/1/2006)*

MOCCAGATTA

Moccagatta 2000 Cole Nebbiolo (Barbaresco) $60. The wood on this wine is either permanently out of whack or just going through the ultimate awkward phase. Features big scents of burnt popcorn and earthy, charred flavors. Yet it finishes supple and long. Hmmm. **83** *(4/2/2004)*

MOLETTO

Moletto 2000 Selecti Cabernet Sauvignon (Veneto Orientale) $62. Just by looking at its ruby color you can tell that you're in for a fantastic ride. The nose is beautifully balanced and confirms that the magic of aging is well underway: Prune, dried currant, pencil shavings, and graphite notes. On the palate, licorice, toast, vanilla, and leather with a dusty quality to the finish; very layered and rich in the mouth. **92** —*M.L. (9/1/2006)*

Moletto 1999 Merlot (Veneto) $10. Rich earth and green herbs are much more prevalent in the nose than any fruit. Some raspberry flavors do come through in the palate with additional earthiness and soft tannins. This soil-driven style will drink well now or age 2–3 years. **86 Best Buy** *(5/1/2002)*

Moletto 1998 Merlot (Piave) $20. Real varietal character shows in this wine's full, dry plum, and berry fruit. There are some slight green notes, but they're more tobacco-like than bell-peppery. With its moderate tannins and acidity, medium-weight and earthy elements, this could be mistaken for a Right Bank Bordeaux. **87** *(9/1/2001)*

Moletto 2004 Pinot Bianco (Veneto Orientale) $13. A clean and luminous appearance set the stage for what follows: aromas of citrus, white stone, wildflowers, and grass. Crisp and refreshing citrus flavors follow through to the palate and finish. **85** —*M.L. (12/15/2006)*

Moletto 2005 Pinot Grigio (Piave) $13. The nose is awkward, with wet hay or white mushroom delivered over fresh garden greens and stone fruit, but this Grigio polishes and primes the palate with almond skin flavors and a touch of bitterness. **85** —*M.L. (6/1/2006)*

Moletto 2004 Pinot Grigio (Piave) $13. The immediate rush of floral intensity is like opening the door to a cooled florist's shop on a summer day. Violets, honeysuckle, and daisy or dandelion are present, as is a soothing honey-like aroma. Lightweight and crisp in the mouth, but fun and pleasing. **87** —*M.L. (2/1/2006)*

Moletto 2003 Pinot Grigio (Veneto) $11. A great buy in Grigio. Don't be put off by a slight hint of copper in the wine's color, the aromas and flavors are fresh and filled with apples, pears, and almonds. Picks up hints of anise on the surpisingly persistent finish. **86 Best Buy** —*J.C. (12/31/2004)*

Moletto 2000 Pinot Grigio (Veneto) $10. This wine's faint rose hue shows the rarely seen but true pink color of the Pinot Grigio grape. A fragrant peach-and-herb nose, crisp but not hard texture, and decent weight mark this solid example. Fruity but dry on the palate, a chalky note adds interest, and the wine closes with decent length. **87 Best Buy** *(9/1/2001)*

Moletto 1998 Pinot Grigio (Piave) $10. **86** *(8/1/1999)*

Moletto NV Prosecco (Marca Trevigiana) $8. I love this $8 pale-gold sparkler with lively pearling, creamy mousse, and tight acidity in the mouth. It has lemon-lime, grassy, and floral notes and some bitter almond skin but it also has something that resembles the yellow center of a daisy or a dandelion, giving it distinct personality. Moletto is a dynamic, family run company in the province of Treviso. **88 Best Buy** —*M.L. (11/15/2005)*

Moletto 2000 Prosecco (Veneto) $10. Floral aromas of peach and mango. The palate has a slight creamy texture, which is cleaned by the mineral effervescence. Not just an apéritif or base for your bellini, this sparkler is a great lunch wine to be enjoyed with grilled fish. **85** *(5/1/2002)*

Moletto NV Extra Dry Prosecco (Prosecco di Valdobbiadene) $14. Tart and crisp, more austere than many Proseccos, with hints of anise providing interest. Light and refreshing. **84** —*J.C. (12/31/2003)*

Moletto NV Extra Dry Spumante Prosecco (Veneto) $13. The absolute lightest shade of gold, this lively Prosecco tickles the nose with bitter apple, honeydew melon, lychee fruit, and stone fruit, with the emphasis on white peach. A touch of sweetness in the mouth is offset by enough tartness to achieve overall harmony. **87** —*M.L. (12/15/2004)*

Moletto NV Frizzante Prosecco (Marca Trevigiana) $13. Cotton candy on the nose indicates a sweet wine, and joining that sensation is wildflower and lemon-lime. Flavors of tangerine and papaya are relaxed, and there's some light banana to the finish, which is here one minute and gone the next. **87** —*M.S. (12/15/2004)*

Moletto NV Frizzante Prosecco (Marca Trevigiana) $13. This Prosecco comes with a bottle cap closure to seal in green aromas such as garden greens, daisy flower, kiwi, and lime. The wine itself even boasts a slight green hue. Refreshing and dry, with a spicy note at the end. **87** —*M.L. (6/1/2006)*

Moletto NV Spumante Extra Dry Prosecco (Veneto) $15. A lively Prosecco that yields sweet melon, lollipop, lemon-lime, and clean mineral notes. Silky in the mouth and snappy on the finish: This a solid, satisfying, informal bubbly. **87** —*M.L. (6/1/2006)*

Moletto 1998 Colmello Rosso Red Blend (Veneto) $20. From the Colmello vineyard, this Bordeaux blend has an addictive nose of milk chocolate, clove, and pine needles. Toasty flavors amid vanilla cream and raspberries are accented by an underlying earthiness. There is a complex structure that finishes soft yet rich, with velvety tannins. **89** *(5/1/2002)*

Moletto 2005 Rosa Tocai Rosso (Veneto Orientale) $13. The year's biggest trend from Italy's Prosecco region is rosé sparkling wine. These wines embody the fresh buoyancy of traditional Prosecco with a fruitier, richer aromatic ensemble. Moletto's Rosa, made from Tocai Rosso grapes, is a perfect example: The nose is redolent of raspberry and cranberry but also has an interesting brambly edge for added dimension. The piquancy of the bubbles hits the palate first but is smoothed out by crème de cassis-like flavors and pink grapefruit. **85 Best Buy** —*M.L. (11/15/2006)*

MONASTERO DI CORIANO

Monastero di Coriano 1996 White Blend (Vin Santo del Chianti) $21. Dark golden in color, with toffee, caramel, espresso, orange liqueur, and smoky aromas and flavors. Pretty darned sweet, with a thick, viscous texture and orangey flavors. Simple, one-dimensional, a little soft. **84** —*S.H. (1/1/2002)*

Monastero di Coriano 1994 Regina White Blend (Tuscany) $24. A dark golden, glyceriney wine with burnt, charry aromas of orange honey, apricot jam and vanilla, and similar flavors. Its fairly sweet, not too much, with a nice burst of acidity. Could use more concentration and focus, because it turns watery in the middle palate, and finishes sugary. **84** —*S.H. (1/1/2002)*

ITALY

ITALY

MONCARO

Moncaro 2002 Terrazzo Verdicchio (Verdicchio dei Castelli di Jesi Classico Superiore) $13. Fat and heavy on the nose, with some initial barnyard/animal notes that raise questions about cleanliness. However, in the mouth it seems clean, with apple and spice notes preceding the potent finish. Of note, this is a well-packaged wine with a nice label. **84** —*M.S. (8/1/2004)*

MONCHIERO CARBONE

Monchiero Carbone 1996 Mon Birone Barbera (Barbera d'Alba) $20. 86 *(4/1/2000)*

MONDORO

Mondoro NV Moscato (Asti) $14. Inside the decorative green bottle is garden-scented, softly sparkling bubbly loaded with sugar. The sweet, flower-and-fruit-salad flavors are a bit cloying, unbalanced by acidity or fizz. **82** —*J.C. (12/31/2001)*

MONROSSO

Monrosso 2005 Red Blend (Chianti) $10. Stay-at-home pasta or pizza dinners call out for a simple but solid Chianti and Monrosso fits the bill beautifully. The ruby-colored wine (80 percent Sangiovese with smaller components of Canaiolo and Merlot) is fermented in steel and aged six months in oak casks for fresh, fruit-forward results. It is redolent of cherry, plum, milk chocolate, and has distant hints of spice and licorice. It's light-weight consistency and subtle tannins make it an excellent, no-brainer match for most foods. **85 Best Buy** —*M.L. (11/15/2006)*

MONTE ANTICO

Monte Antico 2000 Red Blend (Toscana) $8. This by-the-glass performer is spicy and decent, with some oak-driven maple aromas coming up late. It's more or less a simple fruit ball that delivers ample raspberry and cherry flavors. Spice on the finish provides some needed character. **84** —*M.S. (12/31/2002)*

Monte Antico 1998 Sangiovese (Toscana) $10. A value stalwart, this 100% Sangiovese blends leather, spice, and tobacco with sour cherries on a lithe frame. Finishes with cinnamon, clove, and orange-peel notes. **85** *(10/1/2001)*

Monte Antico 2003 Rosso Sangiovese (Toscana) $12. Upright, with notes of cinnamon candy on a nose dominated by bright red fruit. Quite clean and free flowing, with snappy strawberry and cherry flavors resting comfortably on a fresh, acid-driven palate. The opposite of dead weight; this is a lively wine. **86** —*M.S. (9/1/2006)*

MONTE CAMPO

Monte Campo 2005 Pinot Grigio (Delle Venezie) $10. Not intense but pleasing nonetheless, with tempered peach, apple, pear, and more body and breadth than your standard Grigio in this price range. You'll also encounter the variety's trademark sour note on the finish. **86 Best Buy** —*M.L. (6/1/2006)*

Monte Campo 2004 Pinot Grigio (Delle Venezie) $8. Produced especially for the U.S. market by Zonin, Monte Campo has lively exotic fruit, yellow rose petal, and acacia. Textbook Pinot Grigio with slight bitterness on the finish. **85 Best Buy** —*M.L. (2/1/2006)*

MONTE FAUSTINO

Monte Faustino 1998 Red Blend (Amarone della Valpolicella Classico) $75. Opens with deep cola, menthol, cinnamon, and chocolate in addition to tobacco and black fruit. Fairly sweet in the mouth, and maybe a touch too syrupy for those who prefer a drier version. Undoubtedly ripe and chocolaty, with a bit of caramel corn on the finish. **90** *(11/1/2005)*

MONTE ROSSA

Monte Rossa NV Brut Saten Champagne Blend (Franciacorta) $30. Peach and smoke aromas open this dry bubbly, but these pretty notes are marred by a soapy element. It's fairly dry, with faintly peachy flavors, intense mineral, and even slightly medicinal accents. **81** —*S.H. (6/1/2001)*

Monte Rossa NV Satén Chardonnay (Franciacorta) $38. A very attractive and seductive Satén sparkler with plush notes of toasted almond, dried apple skin, and poached pear. What really stands out is its texture in the mouth: fleshy, soft, round, and extremely creamy. The foamy mousse is divine, like whipped cream. **90** —*M.L. (6/1/2006)*

Monte Rossa 2001 Cabochon Brut Sparkling Blend (Franciacorta) $53. This sparkler has a uniquely chiseled, polished, or fine-tuned quality to it that sets it apart and gives it loads of spectacular character. The aromas are reminiscent of finely minced spice, white flowers, and crushed stone; flavors simple, yet restrained and elegant. **92** —*M.L. (6/1/2006)*

Monte Rossa NV Prima Cuvée Brut Sparkling Blend (Franciacorta) $28. A yeasty and buttery sparkler with banana, yellow rose, walnut, bread crust, and a sharp point of minerality. Fruit flavors of Golden Delicious apple roll over the palate, followed by crisp acidity. **90** —*M.L. (6/1/2006)*

MONTECARBELLO

Montecarbello 2001 Brunello (Brunello di Montalcino) $NA. Ripe strawberry, cherry, and chocolate fudge aromas make for an attractive nose. Very ripe and saturated in the mouth with tar, resin, and cooked quality. A massive presence in the mouth with soft tannins. **89** *(4/1/2006)*

MONTELVINI

Montelvini 2004 Pinot Grigio (Delle Venezie) $12. Fruit notes play second fiddle to green notes like celery leaf and dried basil. The wine is lean in the mouth with grapefruit on the finish. **85** —*M.L. (6/1/2006)*

Montelvini NV Spumante Extra Dry Prosecco (Montello e Colli Asolani) $12. Light and basic, with a bouquet of mineral, flowers, and citrus. Easy but dilute apple and melon flavors set up a soft, inconsequential finish. Pretty nice mouthfeel; slightly creamy on the palate. **85** —*M.S. (6/1/2005)*

MONTEMARO

Montemaro 2004 Pinot Grigio (Veneto) $8. Zesty lemon rind, nectarine, peach, and pear scents drift off this golden-hued Grigio. Sticky and a tad sweet in the mouth but with a spicy aftertaste and good mouthfeel. **86 Best Buy** —*M.L. (2/1/2006)*

MONTENISA

Montenisa NV Satén Chardonnay (Franciacorta) $44. A crowd-pleasing, Chard-based sparkler with freshness, a lively personality, and generous aromas of pear and kiwi fruit. The yeast-buttery notes come through clean and sharp and render a delicate, soft wine with bold aromas and flavors. **90** —*M.L. (6/1/2006)*

Montenisa NV Brut Sparkling Blend (Franciacorta) $30. Nice and smooth, with pure green apple, citrus, and rosemary aromas. Bold in the mouth, with melon, pineapple, and subtle spice flavors. Finishes seductively dry, with stylish mushroom and toast flavors, almost like a good dry Sherry. **92 Editors' Choice** —*M.S. (12/15/2005)*

Montenisa NV Brut Sparkling Blend (Franciacorta) $30. A pretty patchwork of delicate aromas such as grapefruit, white peach, and crushed stone set the tone for a sparkler that delivers similar restraint and elegance in the mouth. It's fleshy and fresh, with a citrus and toasted nut finish. **90** —*M.L. (6/1/2006)*

Montenisa 2000 Riserva Contessa Maggi Sparkling Blend (Franciacorta) $NA. A 70% Chardonnay and 30% Pinot Noir sparkling blend from Antinori's Franciacorta estate near the village of Calino. This elegant bubbly is packed tight with apple, apricot, lemon rind, and nutty-smoky notes. Deep fruit flavors are accented by a full, round mouthfeel. **92** —*M.L. (6/1/2006)*

MONTESEL RENZO

Montesel Renzo 2004 Brut Prosecco (Prosecco di Conegliano e Valdobbiadene) $20. A more exotic take on the Prosecco genre with sweet yellow fruit, peach, melon, and a mineral-vitamin vein at the core. Crisp acidity adds to the refreshing ensemble. **86** —*M.L. (6/1/2006)*

Montesel Renzo 2004 Millesimato Dry Prosecco (Prosecco di Conegliano e Valdobbiadene) $20. Boasts ample roundness and softness with some exotic fruit notes on the nose. There's a general broadness and expansiveness to this wine that sets it apart from other, younger Proseccos. **88** —*M.L. (6/1/2006)*

Montesel Renzo 2005 Vigna del Paradiso Extra Dry Prosecco (Prosecco di Conegliano e Valdobbiadene) $20. Stone fruit, lemon rind, tangerine, and mineral notes make up a pretty bouquet that suffers somewhat from a distant medicinal smell. Lightweight in the mouth with a sour note on the close. **85** —*M.L. (6/1/2006)*

MONTESOLE

Montesole 2003 Fiano (Fiano di Avellino) $18. Floral, with aromas of pollen and scented candle wax. Tight and structured, with a very nice mouthfeel. Along the way enjoy grapefruit, tangerine, and apple flavors, weighted about 60/40 in favor of the citrus. Finishes clean and fairly long. **88** —*M.S. (2/1/2005)*

MONTEVETRANO

Montevetrano 1999 Montevetrano Red Blend (Campania) $70. Bright raspberry, violets, and a Bordeaux quality on the nose makes this a wine you will want to linger over. Thankfully, the elegant character continues on the palate with toasty cherries and raspberries that are very well balanced and integrated. An exceptional wine with an exquisitely long, supple finish. **94 Cellar Selection** —*C.S. (5/1/2002)*

MONTI

Monti 2001 Barbera (Barbera d'Alba) $NA. Cedar and leather combine with dried spices on the nose, only gradually giving way to a bit of cranberry fruit on the palate. It's a big-boned wine, with plenty of size (alcohol), yet remains crisp thanks to good acidity. **86** —*J.C. (11/15/2004)*

Monti 1999 Barbera (Barbera d'Alba) $37. Barbera has an uneven record, but the best can be quite impressive, and this is a fine example. From the opening notes to the long finish, it offers loads of cherry, spice, and vanilla. Well-balanced, with medium body, soft tannins, and good acid, this handsomely crafted wine should provide great drinking over the next two to six years. **92** —*M.N. (9/1/2001)*

Monti 1997 Barbera (Barbera d'Alba) $35. **85** *(4/1/2000)*

Monti 2000 Bussia Nebbiolo (Barolo) $NA. Strong oak influence here, with toast, vanilla, and scorched wood dominating the nose at this point. But given the wine's core of cherry fruit, this should come into better balance within a couple of years. Finishes tart, with soft tannins, a short-term ager for the non-oak averse. **87** —*J.C. (11/15/2004)*

Monti 2000 L'Aura White Blend (Langhe) $28. Light in color but very flavorful, this Chardonnay-Riesling blend serves up a full nose and mouth of pineapple and spice with light herb accents. Its bright and tangy personality will take the edge off a hot evening—try it with some grilled shrimp or chicken. A touch sweet, it will also have broad appeal. **88** —*M.M. (9/1/2001)*

MONTICELLO VINEYARDS

Monticello Vineyards 2001 Riserva Sangiovese (Chianti Classico) $25. Starts out by pushing sweet cherry and tea aromas before shifting to leather and sawdust. Yes, it's oaky, but the wood falls into place on the palate, where it shares time with cherry and plum. Just shy of elaborate, with palate-friendly tannins and ample spice. Great for near-term drinking. **89** *(4/1/2005)*

Monticello Vineyards 1997 Riserva Sangiovese (Chianti Classico) $16. A complex bouquet offers black cherry, soy, game, and anise notes, and opens nicely to an expansive palate with earth and leather notes accenting the fruit. The dark finish, with its coffee and orange peel notes, shows some of the intrigue of the nose. Beautiful in its youth, it should get even better in a year or two. Beautiful price, too. **90 Best Buy** *(4/1/2001)*

MONTRESOR

Montresor 1999 CS del Veneto Campo Madonna Cabernet Sauvignon (Veneto) $17. The nose is light and floral, with tea notes, mint, pepper, and herbs. On the palate, raspberry and plum flavors carry some earthiness. The finish is short and clean, with only modest tannins grabbing at one's cheeks. **87** *(5/1/2003)*

Montresor 2001 Garganega (Bianco di Custoza) $11. A plump, juicy mouthful of citrusy fruit, worth trying with grilled or broiled seafood. The zesty lime aromas broaden out on the palate to include orange and

tangerine flavors, making it tart but not too tart. **88 Best Buy** —*J.C. (7/1/2003)*

Montresor 2004 La Colombaia Pinot Grigio (Valdadige) $13. Ripe and smooth, with a lot of melon on the nose. Easygoing yet not paunchy, with honey, melon, and banana making for a full but likable flavor mix. Dry, long, and melony on the finish, with some chalky minerality. Fills the mouth well. **87** *(2/1/2006)*

Montresor 2004 La Colombaia Pinot Grigio (Valdadige) $12. Here's a nose with prominent lemon cream pie and apple granola. There's dimension and smoothness in the mouth, and nothing seems out of place. **87** —*M.L. (2/1/2006)*

Montresor 2002 La Colombaia Pinot Grigio (Valdadige) $13. Every value Italian roundup should include at least one Pinot Grigio, and there are many contenders. La Colombaia is a well-made, mass-appeal wine, one with flowery aromas, expressive flavors, and just a hint of late-game sweetness. Some heft and zest is what pushes it past the ordinary competition that dots the Pinot Grigio landscape. **87** —*M.S. (11/15/2003)*

Montresor 1997 Capitel della Crosara Red Blend (Amarone della Valpolicella Classico) $55. Condensed black fruit aromas are accented by notes of bacon, earth, and chocolate. The flavors run sweet and forceful; cherry and blueberry stand out. The finish is tannic, with cocoa and coffee. Everything is in its proper place. **90** *(5/1/2003)*

Montresor 1998 Recioto re Tiodorico Red Blend (Amarone della Valpolicella) $33. Dark and purple, with plum, licorice, and mineral aromas. The palate is broad and bold, with sweet red apples, plum cake, and blackberry. Viscous for sure, but not thick. Try with flourless chocolate torte. **89** *(5/1/2003)*

Montresor 1999 Valpolicalla Capitel della Crosara Red Blend (Veneto) $13. The nose is dominated by horsehide and an offputting acetone-like note. The flavor profile fares better, although it's red fruit flavors are modest, in addition to pepper and other spices. The texture is decent, although it borders on gritty. **83** *(5/1/2003)*

MORELLONE

Morellone 1999 Le Caniette Red Blend (Rosso Piceno) $23. This Sangiovese-Montepulciano blend from the Marche is funky and obtuse. It's got some gassy, rubbery aromas that blow off after persistent swirling, but even then the plum and blackberry fruit is tannic and excessively broad. While it shows glimpses of quality, it struggles for an identity. **83** —*M.S. (12/15/2003)*

MORGANTE

Morgante 2004 Nero d'Avola (Sicilia) $18. A young wine that showed very well thanks to its bursting ripe fruit, crushed black pepper, and toasty nuttiness. The tannins are lusciously soft and the wine's medium body make it an excellent drink-now proposition. **87 Best Buy** —*M.L. (9/1/2005)*

Morgante 2002 Nero d'Avola (Sicilia) $15. A lively purple color, and aromas of spicy fruit and stalky tannins give this wine high marks in the easy-drinking stakes. Sweet fruit and dry tannins balance fresh cherry flavors and acidity. **84** —*R.V. (10/1/2003)*

Morgante 1999 Nero d'Avola (Sicilia) $12. Soft tannins along with vivid flavors of blackberries and spice make this a wonderful, effortless wine. **88 Best Buy** —*C.S. (5/1/2002)*

Morgante 2003 Don Antonio Nero d'Avola (Sicilia) $30. You can usually count Don Antonio as one of Sicily's very best Nero d'Avolas. But the 2003 heat seems to have left a slight jammy quality that butts awkwardly against the blackberry and crunchy toasted almond. The tannic structure is firm, which bodes well for its evolution over time. **87** —*M.L. (9/1/2005)*

Morgante 2003 Don Antonio Nero d'Avola (Sicilia) $28. Hats off to Don Antonio and this tight, ripe, and concentrated red that ages 12 months in oak. Leather, prunes, cherry, charcoal, and wet earth shape a bold, blockbuster Sicilian red; wood tones add texture and richness in the mouth where the wine caresses with its silky tannins. Drink now. **91 Editors' Choice** —*M.L. (7/1/2006)*

ITALY

Morgante 2001 Don Antonio Nero d'Avola (Sicilia) $30. Aromas of wood and dark fruits; flavors of dense chewy black fruits, spices, and fruit cake. This is a big but structured wine, with generous fruit and nice acidity on the finish. **88** —R.V. (10/1/2003)

Morgante 1999 Don Antonio Nero d'Avola (Sicilia) $30. Black raspberry and sweet cinnamon-toast aromas lure you into the glass. The alcohol is 14%, but the intense dark fruit and substantial tannins give it balance. Delicious now but will age well for a number of years. **90** —C.S. (5/1/2002)

MOSSIO

Mossio 2000 Dolcetto (Dolcetto d'Alba) $19. A red-carpet bouquet of mint, fresh-baked bread, blackberry, and tar is as welcoming as can be. This is top-flight Dolcetto: The mouth overflows with well-matched and balanced plum, berry, and earth flavors. Expectedly, the finish is spot on; it flows just right, leaving a slick, but solid, aftertaste. Drink now for top results. **90** —M.S. (12/15/2003)

MOTTA

Motta 1999 Sangiovese (Morellino di Scansano) $15. This solid Tuscan red comes from the seaside area of Tuscany, not the zone of our usual image of this historic region, but one of great recent activity. Dark cherry, earth and spice aromas open to a full and ripe mouth, with rich, dry, cherry fruit, and moderate acidity. Finishes dry with a mild chalky element. Very drinkable now; should improve over one or two years. **89 Best Buy** —M.M. (1/1/2004)

Motta 1998 Morellino Di Scansano Sangiovese (Morellino di Scansano) $14. 86 (9/1/2000)

MURI-GRIES

Muri-Gries 2004 Pinot Grigio (Alto Adige) $19. Very pretty and very floral although the 13.5% alcohol does hit the palate in a rather determined manner. The result is marzipan and candied fruit aromas. Would pair well with sweet and sour pork. **87** —M.L. (6/1/2006)

MUSELLA

Musella 1999 Corvina, Rondinella, Molinara (Amarone della Valpolicella) $32. Finely textured with exemplary aromatics. The bouquet is graced by cola, black licorice, marzipan, pipe tobacco, and other alluring smells in addition to pure, dark fruit notes. Flashy and smooth in the mouth, where the berry and prune notes are touched up by leather and spice. Just right, with more potential if given a few more years of cellar time. **93 Editors' Choice** (11/1/2005)

Musella 1997 Red Blend (Amarone della Valpolicella) $45. Starts with meaty notes to the nose along with leather, barnyard, and a certain rooty quality. Cherry and citrus work the palate, which is a bit austere. Thus the high-toned finish with rather strong acidity is almost as expected. Will do best with food. **87** (11/1/2005)

MUSSO

Musso 1999 Bricco Rio Sordo Nebbiolo (Barbaresco) $38. Rio Sordo is acknowledged as a top cru, and Walter Musso has struck gold in 1999. Toasty hints of cedar blend harmoniously with succulent cherries, picking up notes of cured meat and vanilla. Long and richly textured on the finish, this should be approachable young, yet age well. Drink 2005–2015. **92** (4/2/2004)

Musso 1999 Pora Nebbiolo (Barbaresco) $38. Dense and meaty at first; with air, purer fruit scents emerge, along with vanilla highlights. The fruit really sings on the palate, with luscious, lipsmacking black cherries captivating the tastebuds. Finishes slightly tart, like berry zinger tea. **90** (4/2/2004)

MUZIC

Muzic 2001 Moresco Pinot Grigio (Collio) $NA. Bland and beery, with a slight spritz and some burnt-matchstick aromas. **81** —J.C. (1/1/2004)

NANDO

Nando 2000 Corvina (Amarone della Valpolicella Classico) $42. Deep and eminently attractive, with huge aromas of raisin, fudge, prune, and fruit-cake. As broad and smooth goes, this is it. The feel is velvety, the depth coming in several layers. Elegant, forceful, and a bit hedonistic. **92 Editors' Choice** (11/1/2005)

Nando NV Moscato (Asti) $9. Odd aromas of candy, Windex, and lime lead into an overtly sweet and cloying palate of lime and seedless white table grapes. Some Asti sparklers are good despite their sweetness, but this one is borderline acceptable. **80** —M.S. (1/1/2004)

Nando NV Moscato (Asti) $9. Almost overly floral and sweet, with the palate showing an overdose of heavy citrus fruit. Finishes expectedly sweet, with a good mouthfeel. Attacks forcefully. **84** —M.S. (12/15/2004)

Nando 1998 Nebbiolo (Barolo) $41. Tarry and pruny, with meaty, leathery accents, this is a big-boned, firmly structured wine. Turns spicy and shows its alcohol a little on the tannic finish. Drink now–2010. **85** (4/2/2004)

Nando 2004 Pinot Grigio (Isonzo del Friuli) $11. Honeyed apple and cream on the nose, with chunky, spiced apple and pear flavors. Full bodied, with plenty of flavor but not much zest. **85** (2/1/2006)

Nando 2001 Pinot Grigio (Isonzo del Friuli) $10. A minty nose blends in some floral and citrus scents as well, giving this light-bodied wine some interest. Flavors are minty, too, verging on wintergreen, and finishing clean and fresh. **83** —J.C. (7/1/2003)

Nando 1997 Red Blend (Amarone della Valpolicella Classico) $36. The nose on this wine was difficult at first, yielding sulfur and some barnyard. The palate, however, issues chocolate and cherries, while the finish is mildly bitter and thick. Two of our panelists thought it good, but much like a liquid confection. Our third reviewer gushed over its soft, supple feel and early drinkability. **86** (5/1/2003)

Nando 2002 Sangiovese (Chianti Classico) $12. Dried cherry, leather, tomato, and spice make for a common, recognizable bouquet, while the palate offers fresh plum and raspberry with shadings of cedar and vanilla. Lighter tannins, decent acidity, and good on the tongue. All in all, it does not push the envelope. **86** (4/1/2005)

Nando 2001 Sangiovese (Chianti Classico) $11. Light, tight, and leathery, a living version of a stripped down wine. The emphasis is squarely on red fruit, and that means it's a bit sour. Nonetheless it's innocuous and goes down easy. **84** (4/1/2005)

Nando 2000 Sangiovese (Chianti Classico) $11. Powerful and serious, with condensed aromas of cassis and spice. This wine features a racy, lithe feel that's fostered by puckering acidity and lively but not over-aggressive tannins. The mouth deals a mixed bag of sweet, snappy fruit, and fortunately very little in the way of intrusive characteristics. **89 Best Buy** —M.S. (11/15/2003)

Nando 1998 Sangiovese (Chianti Classico) $11. The nose offers a full, interesting blend of Oriental spice, cherry, ginger, and soy elements. The flavors turn to tart cherry, and brisk, slightly drying tannins show on the finish. **83** (4/1/2001)

NATURA IBLEA

Natura Iblea 2004 Archimede Nero d'Avola (Sicilia) $35. Here is another hot-climate wine that stretches fruit ripeness to the very limit. The nose is redolent of blackberry jam and smoked ham, although you'll also find refined notes of crushed stone and forest floor as well. **87** —M.L. (7/1/2006)

Natura Iblea 2004 Don Pasquale Nero d'Avola (Sicilia) $23. This Nero d'Avola has small doses of berry fruit and too many sharp points (including black rubber and Band-Aid aromas) to make it totally enjoyable. It lacks finesse and has a slightly bitter note on the close. **84** —M.L. (7/1/2006)

Natura Iblea 2004 Don Paolo Red Blend (Sicilia) $25. This red blend is 70-30 Nero d'Avola and Syrah that sees four months in French oak. Offers notes of blackberry, leather, tobacco, black pepper and a hint of burnt rubber that some may find interesting and others less so. Otherwise this is a meaty, intense wine with smoked flavors and soft tannins. **87** —M.L. (7/1/2006)

Natura Iblea 2005 Impronta White Blend (Sicilia) $20. Banana, exotic fruit, citrus, and almond tones best describe this Insolia-Chardonnay blend. It's lightweight but fresh in the mouth and a perfect wine for a summer garden lunch. **86** —M.L. (7/1/2006)

NEIRANO

Neirano 2000 Barbera (Barbera d'Asti) $10. Burly, but not overly fruity. Flavors of plum and berry lead into a tight, dry finish. Juicy on the palate, with a ripe profile and good texture. Not a thriller, but competent. **85** —*M.S. (12/15/2003)*

Neirano 1998 Le Croci Superiore Barbera (Barbera d'Asti) $24. Jazzy juice like this is why savvy enthusiasts are big on Barbera. Showcases the fine fruit typical of the Piedmont's recent hot streak of vintages. It's also an example of a more confident, balanced use of oak in the best examples of this workhorse grape. Presents stylish chocolate, dark berry, and game notes, bright acidity and firm, even tannins. Will compliment almost any hearty food. Drink now–2006. **91** —*M.M. (11/15/2002)*

Neirano NV Spumante Dolce Brachetto (Brachetto d'Acqui) $12. 82 —*J.C. (1/1/2004)*

Neirano 2002 Dolcetto (Dolcetto d'Alba) $10. Minty, with cinnamon on the nose but not much fruit. Subtle flavors of raspberry and blackberry poke forward on the palate, and the finish is nice, with cherry candy and bitter chocolate flavors. Not terribly complex, but it holds the line and keeps itself together from front to back. **85** —*M.S. (12/15/2003)*

Neirano 2004 Pitulè Moscato (Moscato d'Asti) $11. Moscato often offers a musky smell, and this wine delivers just that. There's wet earth, moss, and strong, creamy aromas that smell very much like peach yogurt. Tingling acidity lingers in the mouth. **83** —*M.L. (11/15/2006)*

Neirano 1997 Nebbiolo (Barolo) $32. Flavors of cherry tomato and dried cherries with a little saltiness need pasta or grilled meat to show their best. The aroma is a meal in itself, with chestnuts, hard salami, and roasted game. A little tart on the finish, but quite enjoyable. **89** —*C.S. (11/15/2002)*

Neirano 1995 Nebbiolo (Barolo) $18. 86 *(9/1/2000)*

NICOLIS

Nicolis 2000 Red Blend (Amarone della Valpolicella Classico) $52. Highly attractive and rich, with lovely marzipan, blackberry, raisin, and toast. Seductive and stylish, with loads of black fruit and chocolate. Chewy, long, and succulent. If you like yours big, pour a glass of this and dig in. **91** *(11/1/2005)*

Nicolis 1998 Red Blend (Amarone della Valpolicella Classico) $50. Scents of onion and wet fur are at first disconcerting, but with time the wine finds prettier, fruitier aromas as well as its legs. The palate delivers a full blast of tart red berries. Some chocolate notes contribute richness. The finish is chewy, tannic, and tight, and there's a hint of lemon, which seems out of place. **87** *(5/1/2003)*

Nicolis 2000 Ambrosan Red Blend (Amarone della Valpolicella Classico) $75. Exotic and dense, with tar, tree bark, leather, and a sweet blast of cola all making for an alluring, magnetic bouquet. Racy and snappy in the mouth, but rich and relaxed enough. And the flavors of black cherry, vanilla, and spice sing in perfect harmony. Deep and on the mark. **93** *(11/1/2005)*

Nicolis 1998 Ambrosian Red Blend (Amarone della Valpolicella) $75. The nose is inky and syrupy at first, but then raisin comes to the fore. The mouth is rich and chocolaty, with mocha, cassis, and black cherry flavors. The finish is a tad bit hot, but espresso flavors keep your interest. **90** *(5/1/2003)*

Nicolis 2001 Classico Red Blend (Valpolicella Classico) $11. Some volatile acidity seems present on the plum and vanilla nose. The mouth is thick and packed with cherry, cola, and earth, but also some tartness that one reviewer called citrus and another pegged as vinegar. The finish is short and tight, with stark acidity. **80** *(5/1/2003)*

Nicolis 2000 Seccal Red Blend (Valpolicella Classico Superiore) $20. This ripasso-styled red is more sweet and grapy than stylish. It has fat, forward plum fruit that seems more sweet and roasted than maybe it should be. The finish is on the short side, but shows some tannins. **84** *(5/1/2003)*

Nicolis 2000 Testal Red Blend (Veronese) $28. Black cherry, tobacco, and grape stems comprise the nose, while the palate is mostly standard-fare cherry, plum, and toast. The finish is kind of thick, with raisin flavors along with herbal notes. Soft tannins make for medium to full mouthfeel. **86** *(5/1/2003)*

NINO FRANCO

Nino Franco NV Brut Champagne Blend (Prosecco di Valdobbiadene) $14. Faintly sweet aromas of sugar and caramel open the Nino Franco; apples, sour apple, and talcum powder round out the palate flavors. Finishes with a cottony texture, and faux-apple flavors. Tastes artificially sweetened, but that may appeal to some. **83** —*D.T. (12/31/2001)*

Nino Franco 2000 Primo Franco Champagne Blend (Prosecco di Valdobbiadene) $16. Light, fragrant aromas of flowers, hay, and herbs open this steadily bubbly, but very soft, sparkler. Decidedly sweet tropical fruit notes show in the mouth and on the medium-length finish. Still it carries its sweetness with more style than most. **84** —*M.M. (12/31/2001)*

Nino Franco 2000 Rive di San Floriano Champagne Blend (Prosecco di Valdobbiadene) $15. Soft yet big in the mouth, this Proseccco opens with light aromas of apple, toast, and talcum powder. The same apple-mineral profile, plus a little pear, shows up on the palate. On the back end, there's a tart, tangy metallic note. **83** —*D.T. (12/31/2001)*

Nino Franco NV Rustico Champagne Blend (Prosecco di Valdobbiadene) $12. One of a number of rather split-personality sparklers we encountered, this opens with ginger ale and even beer-like aromas. In the mouth, the flavors are more floral and green, with mild lime notes. It feels brisk and the mousse is frothy, even bracing. Finishes dry with herb and grass accents. **84** —*M.M. (12/31/2001)*

Nino Franco NV Rustico Champagne Blend (Prosecco di Valdobbiadene) $12. Sharp and defined aromas of white flowers and dried cheddar cheese make for an interesting nose. Tart but ripe apricot and pear flavors work well together on the tongue. The dry, simple finish is apropos for an easy drinker such as this. When asked if you'd like an apéritif, say "yes," if this one is on offer. **87** —*M.S. (12/31/2002)*

Nino Franco 2002 Primo Franco Prosecco (Prosecco di Valdobbiadene) $17. Extremely floral and perfumed, like lilacs and tangerines layered over Granny Smith apples. Quite sweet, yet appealing, with a creamy, low-acid mouthfeel. **86** —*J.C. (12/31/2003)*

Nino Franco 2001 Rive di San Floriano Brut Prosecco (Prosecco di Valdobbiadene) $17. Remember creamsicles—vanilla ice cream coated or swirled with orange sherbet? You'll swear the scent of them is in the glass, balanced by tart citrus and green apple flavors. Finishes a bit hard, with a faintly metallic note. **84** —*J.C. (12/31/2003)*

Nino Franco NV Rustico Prosecco (Prosecco di Valdobbiadene) $10. If someone says bubbly by the glass, I think Prosecco. Among the handful of very good ones is this spry offering. Bartlett pear aromas precede a smooth palate accented by soda crackers, apple cider, and lime. Fairly long on the finish, and above average in complexity. And remember: A bottle of this sassy stuff is less expensive than a glass of the cheapest Champagne at a bar or restaurant. **83** —*M.S. (11/15/2003)*

NINO NEGRI

Nino Negri 1995 Inferno Nebbiolo (Valtellina Superiore) $16. 88 —*R.V. (5/1/1999)*

Nino Negri 1996 Mazer Inferno Nebbiolo (Valtellina Superiore) $16. 88 *(7/1/2000)*

NOCIANO

Nociano 1998 Red Blend (Umbria) $9. 90 —*M.S. (2/1/2003)*

NOTTOLA

Nottola 1996 Vigna del Fattore Sangiovese (Vino Nobile di Montepulciano) $24. 84 *(7/1/2000)*

OCONE

Ocone 2000 Aglianico (Aglianico del Taburno) $12. Dark at first, with raspberry emerging. Throughout it's snappy, with red fruit dominant. Finishes clean, tight, and crisp, with solid tannins that don't go overboard. An everyday, drink-me style of Aglianico. **86** —*M.S. (11/15/2004)*

Ocone 2003 Greco (Taburno) $11. Fleshy aromas of honey and butterscotch. The plump mouthfeel cuddles melon and orange, while the

ITALY

ITALY

finish is dry, heavy, and loaded with extract. A touch clumsy, but with pop. **85** —*M.S. (11/15/2004)*

Ocone 2003 Piedirosso (Taburno) $12. The prime red fruit here jolts your palate to attention. Even so, it's sweet and ripe at its center. The mouth deals light but fresh strawberry and cherry, while the minerally finish is sound. A tad bit jumpy and acidic, but still a real wine for real people. **87 Best Buy** —*M.S. (2/1/2005)*

ODOARDI

Odoardi 1998 Garrone Red Blend (Calabria) $30. With a blend of Aglianico, Merlot, and two varieties of Cabernet you would expect this to be a little more complex than it is. The hollow midpalate is overwhelmed by the tannic and gamy mouthfeel, but fresh tar and beets show through. Tannins cross the finish line, but fruit falls short. **82** —*C.S. (5/1/2002)*

OGNISSOLE

Ognissole 2003 Primitivo (Primitivo Di Manduria) $22. Despite high expectations surrounding Feudi di San Gregorio's Puglia property, this nicely packaged Primitivo fails to deliver the goods. The nose is vegetal and stewy resembling minestrone. But the wine does improve in the mouth with spice and good length. **83** —*M.L. (9/1/2005)*

ORIEL

Oriel 2003 Palio Montepulciano (Montepulciano d'Abruzzo) $15. Hefty and aggressive, with an initial volatile blast that gives way to more traditional barnyardy notes. Shows big but hard plum and blackberry flavors on a tannic palate, while the finish is heavy, earthy, and ultimately a touch clumsy. **83** —*M.S. (10/1/2006)*

ORIGIN

Origin 2002 Collection Series Montepulciano (Montepulciano d'Abruzzo) $22. A nice wine with smoky, slightly rubbery aromas that open toward more herbal, peppery notes. Cherry and strawberry flavors on the soft, slightly buttery palate are pleasing. Finishes with chocolate and some additional creamy characteristics. **86** —*M.S. (10/1/2006)*

Origin 2003 Pinot Grigio (Delle Venezie) $9. The first impression is a good one with ripe cantaloupe melon, pineapple, and almond praline. But come back for a second whiff and the wine appears flat, bordering on oxidized, and is somewhat flabby in the mouth with a short finish. **82** —*M.L. (2/1/2006)*

Origin 2002 Pinot Grigio (Delle Venezie) $NA. An oxidized-like musky smell hits the nose, followed by burnt matchstick. Feels lean in the mouth. An example of unsuccessful Pinot Grigio bottle aging. (I tasted both bottles). **81** —*M.L. (2/1/2006)*

Origin 2002 Riserva Sangiovese (Chianti) $20. Fairly roasted and earthy, with a lot of coffee, leather, and dark berry to the bouquet. Definitely weighs in as full bodied, and flavor-wise the fruit runs dark, with licorice and toast shadings. Finishes kind of grabby and tannic, but generally speaking it's solid stuff. **86** —*M.S. (10/1/2006)*

PALADIN

Paladin 2004 Pinot Grigio (Delle Venezie) $14. This Grigio boasts fragrant summer flower tones in the foreground and fruity ones at the back. The mouthfeel is lean, making this a good candidate to enjoy with pesto-based dishes. **86** —*M.L. (2/1/2006)*

PALARI

Palari 1998 Faro Red Blend (Sicilia) $45. Complex flavors of tar, ripened blackberries, and white pepper stay surprisingly soft in this immense wine. The balance of full tannins and dark fruit, from five indigenous grapes, will make this enjoyable for a long time to come. **93 Cellar Selection** —*C.S. (5/1/2002)*

Palari 1998 Rosso Del Soprano Red Blend (Sicilia) $31. Leather, red berries, and a little rustic smokiness on the nose. The red berries repeat in the palate, then are joined by earth and a woody char. A fully-layered wine consisting of Nerello, Mascalese, and three other indigenous Sicilian grapes. Drink in 3–5 years. **91** —*C.S. (5/1/2002)*

PALAZZETTI

Palazzetti 1995 Brunello (Brunello di Montalcino) $56. Old, with a browning color and dry, raisiny aromas. There's not much left here except dried red fruits and plenty of acid. It's sharp and tastes a bit sour, and the mouthfeel seems to be thinning as we speak. **82** —*M.S. (11/15/2003)*

Palazzetti 1998 Sangiovese (Rosso di Montalcino) $23. Ripe and earthy, and teetering on over-ripe. That it's hanging around as a basic rosso after five years is a testament to the wine, which is still kicking with blackberry flavors, firm tannins, and power. Drink now. **88** —*M.S. (11/15/2003)*

PALAZZI

Palazzi 2004 Pinot Grigio (Veneto) $9. Loads of honey-related aromas jive well with a green element that resembles cloverleaf. Some soda pop and candy-like sweetness emerges, balanced by a relatively lean body. **86 Best Buy** —*M.L. (2/1/2006)*

PALAZZINA

Palazzina 1993 Le Macioche Brunello (Brunello di Montalcino) $41. **88** —*J.C. (3/1/2000)*

PALAZZO

Palazzo 2001 Brunello (Brunello di Montalcino) $74. A deep mineral vein adds gorgeous depth and complexity: polished stone, schoolroom chalkboard, and campfire coals. Bursting berry fruit and boysenberry with lemon grass highlights. Flavors are ripe and round without sacrificing complexity and the wine will stretch its legs with a few more years in the cellar. **92** *(4/1/2006)*

Palazzo 2000 Brunello (Brunello di Montalcino) $69. Fairly heavy on the nose, with a whiff of wet pooch and damp earth. Somewhat stewy on the nose, while the palate features fat plum flavors and oversized tannins. Not quite up to snuff. **84** —*M.S. (7/1/2005)*

PALAZZO ROSSO

Palazzo Rosso 1999 Brunello (Brunello di Montalcino) $36. The smoky bouquet is sleek and sly, with genuine leather and floral notes. It's very classy and already into its development. The fruit is pure and dark, and the finish is what some might call "monster," which is a good thing. A winner with all the right stuff. Hold three to four years before drinking. **95** —*M.S. (6/1/2004)*

PALLADIO

Palladio 2003 Sangiovese (Chianti) $10. Sweet, earthy, and largely clean, with some tart cherry and red plum flavors comprising the palate. Finishes largely fresh, with an acid-based crispness. **84** *(4/1/2005)*

PALMADINA

Palmadina 2004 Pinot Grigio (Friuli Isonzo) $12. Offers loads of roses, acacia, and honeysuckle fleshed out by peach and melon. Not very acidic in the mouth. **85** —*M.L. (6/1/2006)*

PANZANELLO

Panzanello 2001 Sangiovese (Chianti Classico) $27. Meaty and rich on the nose, a combination that's nothing but promising. Arguably on the over-ripe side, with aromas of Port, dates, and prunes. Yet there's enough freshness and acidic drive to keep it balanced. Yes, the tannins are extruding, but air and food will keep them in line. Finishes with coffee and earth notes. **89** *(4/1/2005)*

Panzanello 2000 Riserva Sangiovese (Chianti Classico) $35. A dark, fully-oaked, flavorful wine with aromas of blackberry, molasses, coffee, and smoke. Rich and woody on the palate, with black cherry, cedar, and vanilla. Runs a little sweet and soft, with noticeably soft tannins and modest acidity. Drink now for maximum pleasure. **90** *(4/1/2005)*

PAOLO BEA

Paolo Bea 2000 Sagrantino (Sagrantino di Montefalco) $NA. A purist, environmentalist, and activist winemaker, Paolo Bea uses native yeasts, does not filter, and believes in long macerations. Absent is the usual oak overkill and the result is a fruity, wine with firm tannins, sourness, and spicy acidity. **86** —*M.L. (9/1/2005)*

PAOLO RODARO

Paolo Rodaro 2004 Pinot Grigio (Colli Orientali del Friuli) $26. The nose has vanilla bean and caramel but also something that reminded me of rubber tire or asphalt. It shows good structure in the mouth, where is it thick and refreshing. **84** —*M.L. (6/1/2006)*

PAOLO SCAVINO

Paolo Scavino 1998 Dolcetto (Dolcetto di Diano d'Alba) $20. 91 *(4/1/2000)*

Paolo Scavino 1999 Nebbiolo (Barolo) $60. Intense from start to finish, Scavino's blended Barolo packs plenty of power into a lush, thoroughly modern frame. Toasty oak embraces the fruit without obscuring it, allowing flavors of cherry liqueur to burst across the palate. Tempting now, better in 5–7 years. **90** *(4/2/2004)*

Paolo Scavino 1999 Bric dël Fiasc Nebbiolo (Barolo) $85. Slightly herbal or minty on the nose, but the palate is all that we've come to expect from Scavino, with wonderfully pure red fruits and subtle notes of mineral and sous bois for complexity. Tar and dark chocolate wrap up the supple finish. Drink 2005–2020. **91** *(4/2/2004)*

PAOLO TOSCANO

Paolo Toscano 2000 Red Blend (Chianti) $8. This wine is light to the eye, with leather and distant dried fruit aromas. The palate is thin and starched out, with some raspberry fruit barely helping out the tomato flavor that drives the palate. Even the name on this made-for-export wine, "Paul the Tuscan," is weak. **80** —*M.S. (12/31/2002)*

PARUSSO

Parusso 1998 Piani Noce Dolcetto (Dolcetto d'Alba) $15. 90 *(4/1/2000)*

Parusso 1999 Bussia Vigna Fiurin Nebbiolo (Barolo) $70. Unabashedly modern in style, with layers of menthol and toast surrounding immense depths of dark fruit. Plum, black cherries, and tar fill the mouth with a texture that's simultaneously rich and supple, silken yet velvety. Picks up more oak-induced notes of maple syrup and coffee on the finish. **94 Editors' Choice** *(4/2/2004)*

Parusso 2001 Bricco Rovella Sauvignon Blanc (Langhe) $36. You don't come across too much Sauvignon Blanc from Piedmont, and this older example is mid-tier. The nose is smoky from oak aging, while the palate is primed with meaty, herbal flavors. An uncommon take on the grape that purists may not like. If you're experimental, it could work. **85** *(7/1/2005)*

PASQUA

Pasqua 1998 Vigneti del Sole Pinot Grigio (Pavia) $8. 82 *(8/1/1999)*

Pasqua 1999 Sagramoso Red Blend (Valpolicella Classico Superiore) $NA. Smoky and leathery, with snappy raspberry fruit and a fairly strong dose of cinnamon-tinged oak. The finish is smooth and medium in length, and for a ripasso the freshness is commendable. **86** *(5/1/2003)*

Pasqua 1998 Sagramoso Red Blend (Amarone della Valpolicella) $30. One sniff indicates that this wine saw some potent oak. The nose has distinct aromas of barrel char, sawdust, and espresso. But it still rocks on with roasted dark fruit flavors that are enhanced by hints of chocolate and vanilla. The finish is sweet and firm. **91** *(5/1/2003)*

Pasqua 2002 Vigneti Del Sole Red Blend (Montepulciano d'Abruzzo) $7. Ripe and raw, but quite clean. No doubt this is a mass-market red, but still it retains an above-average level of quality from start to finish. The nose is big and bold, with rowdy berry fruit that never shies away or breaks up. Soft tannins create a soft finish as it ends with a blast of raspberry flavor. Just right for big parties and events. **85** —*M.S. (11/15/2003)*

PATERNOSTER

Paternoster 1997 Aglianico (Aglianico del Vulture) $20. Okay, so there isn't much fruit to this wine's aromas, which instead focus on smoke, dried oregano, and leather, but don't let that deter you from trying this spicy, complex wine. Bright cherry fruit underpins pipe tobacco and cinnamon flavors on the palate, and the wine finishes with dusty tannins. **86** —*C.S. (5/1/2002)*

Paternoster 2000 Don Anselmo Aglianico (Aglianico del Vulture) $47. May well be Basilicata's best wine with flinty, graphite notes derived from volcanic soils and loads of dried prunes, cassis, intense blackberry, leather and toast. The aromas go on and on and constantly evolve in your glass. Aged in barrique and Slovenian casks, the mouthfeel is solid yet smooth, powerful yet elegant. **92 Cellar Selection** —*M.L. (9/1/2005)*

PATRIARCA DI PICCINI

Patriarca di Piccini 1998 Rosso Sangiovese (Toscana) $16. Well-utilized oak offsets deep, sweet black cherry fruit in this Sangiovese-Cabernet Sauvignon blend. The cabernet plays a supporting role as a relatively minor component (about 10%) but adds just enough weight and density to differentiate the wine from the other offerings. The wine shows bright acidity and finishes long, with substantial but even tannins. **88** *(11/15/2001)*

PATRIGLIONE

Patriglione 1994 Red Blend (Salento) $NA. Smells fortified and stewy—think Port, raisins, and dried fruit. Ripasso-styled, with dry, cedary-cooked fruit flavors in the mouth and on the finish. Full tannins, but not as integrated as we'd like. **83** —*D.T. (5/1/2002)*

PECCHENINO

Pecchenino 1996 Bricco Botti Dolcetto di Dogliani Superiore Dolcetto (Dolcetto di Dogliani) $27. 89 *(4/1/2000)*

Pecchenino 2002 San Luigi Dolcetto (Dolcetto di Dogliani) $18. Among the 2002 Dolcettos we've sampled, the ones from Dogliani have stood out for their greater depth and intensity of flavor. This one boasts a dark purple hue and dense, plummy fruit. It's a supple mouthful of flavor that goes down easily yet retains a sense of structure and balance. **90 Editors' Choice** —*J.C. (11/15/2004)*

Pecchenino 2003 Siri D'Jermu Dolcetto (Dolcetto d'Alba) $29. Some slightly smoky, herbal notes add an extra dimension to this full-bodied, richly textured wine that pumps out ripe black cherry flavors from the start all the way through the long, mouth-watering finish. **90** —*J.C. (3/1/2006)*

PERE ALESSANDRO

Pere Alessandro 1999 Barbera (Barbera d'Alba) $16. Some early spice and tobacco grace the nose, but that same bouquet turns grassy and green real quick. Chunky on the palate, with disparate raspberry and cranberry flavors. Quite grippy, and veering toward sour. **82** —*M.S. (12/15/2003)*

Pere Alessandro 2001 Barbera (Barbera d'Alba) $15. Tart and lean, with aromas that range in a narrow band from green tobacco to tomato leaf and flavors that are also tomatoey and a bit unripe. **82** —*J.C. (11/15/2004)*

Pere Alessandro 2001 Moscato (Moscato d'Asti) $16. This straggler from the fine 2001 vintage has dusty aromas and a nose similar to 7-Up. A palate of Mandarin orange, sweet melon, and sugarcomb precedes a slightly tiring finish. Tasty and fruity, but not as zesty as the best. **87** —*M.S. (12/15/2003)*

Pere Alessandro 1998 Nebbiolo (Barolo) $49. A word of warning: Decant. If you are planning to drink this within the next few years, decanting should help the sulfur aromas dissipate—then you'll be able to enjoy the chewy prune and date flavors. Brutally tannic at this juncture, but the tannins taste ripe, so just hold on until 2010 or beyond. **86** *(4/2/2004)*

Pere Alessandro 1997 Nebbiolo (Barolo) $44. This rock solid, earthy rendition comes from an Alba co-op, proving that good things come in all shapes and sizes. Lots of leather and mushroom guard the fruit on the nose, while in the mouth, prune and black cherry score points. It's a wine that's in form; a dark, delicious, coffee-laden middleweight. **90** —*M.S. (12/15/2003)*

Pere Alessandro 2000 Vigna Giaia Nebbiolo (Barbaresco) $55. Dull and earthy on the nose, with tree bark aromas and not a lot of fruit. Thankfully, it recovers on the palate, offering up intense black cherry flavors and a helping of dusty earth couched in supple tannins. Long and powerful on the finish. **89** *(4/2/2004)*

ITALY

PERLAGE

Perlage NV Canah Brut Prosecco (Prosecco di Valdobbiadene) $14. There's something beautifully unique about this Prosecco that is best described as a dusty, chalky, mineral—almost salty—element. An organic wine that begs for dishes with sweet cream or cheese. **88** —M.L. (6/1/2006)

Perlage 2005 Col di Manza Extra Dry Prosecco (Prosecco di Valdobbiadene) $12. An organic and biodynamic Prosecco with extra green tones such as cut grass, kiwi, lime, and some crushed stone. Polished and clean in the mouth, with noticeable acidity. **87** —M.L. (6/1/2006)

PERTICAIA

Perticaia 2001 Sagrantino (Sagrantino di Montefalco) $46. Guido Guardigli bought this 20-hectare property in 2000. This vintage boasts flavors of alcohol-soaked candied cherries and a very light touch of vanilla or toast. The mouthfeel is intense; finishes long. Would go well with game. **87** —M.L. (9/1/2005)

PERTINACE

Pertinace 2004 Dolcetto (Dolcetto d'Alba) $14. Starts off with modest cherry fruit and an earthy under-current, and never really develops anything else. Crisp cherry flavors turn herbal on the finish **84** —J.C. (3/1/2006)

Pertinace 2001 Nebbiolo (Barbaresco) $32. A relatively light-weight Barbaresco, Pertinace's normale features a delicately floral bouquet tinged with almonds and cherries. Dried cherries, chocolate, and earth flavors gain in intensity on the finish, adding firm tannins to the mix. Drink 2005–2015. **87** —J.C. (3/1/2006)

Pertinace 2001 Nebbiolo (Barolo) $32. On the traditional side of the spectrum, with scents of tar, prune, and herbs followed by flavors of dried fruit and marinated meat. Round in the mouth, then clamps down on the finish with some drying tannins. Try in 2010. **89** —J.C. (3/1/2006)

Pertinace 2001 Vigneto Marcarini Nebbiolo (Barbaresco) $45. This medium-bodied wine is firmly structured, with solid doses of acids and tannins to keep it focused. Dried cherries, leather, prune, and herb flavors pick up shadings of cedar and tobacco on the finish. Try in 2012. **91** —J.C. (3/1/2006)

PETER ZEMMER

Peter Zemmer 2004 Pinot Grigio (Alto Adige) $14. A nice dose of floral, chamomile, and peach notes with lemon rind and citrus zest on the finish. A food-friendly wine. **86** —M.L. (2/1/2006)

Peter Zemmer 1998 Pinot Grigio (Alto Adige) $11. 88 (8/1/1999)

Peter Zemmer 2004 La Lot Pinot Grigio (Vigneti delle Dolomiti) $11. Floral and fruity in all the right ways. Honeysuckle and pineapple round off a wine that shows strength and warmth on the palate. Some spice and good body on the medium-length finish. **87 Best Buy** —M.L. (2/1/2006)

PETRA

Petra 1999 Riserva Cabernet Sauvignon-Merlot (Toscana) $50. Robust, with meaty aromas of earth, leather, and oak. Quite sweet and expressive, with pulsating dark fruit and zippy, racy acidity. Drinking this is like savoring the essence of liquid fruitcake; it's that dense. Good now, but it should improve with a couple of years on its side. **92** —M.S. (11/15/2003)

Petra 1998 Riserva Cabernet Sauvignon-Merlot (Toscana) $50. Hailing from the town of Suvereto in the southern Maremma, this sophomore Cabernet-Merlot blend from the same owner as Bellavista and Contadi Castaldi in Franciacorta is flat-out awesome. One whiff of the bouquet says it all: earth, currant, blackberry, and coffee. The palate is equally sensational—a magic carpet ride of plum fruit, pure oak, and solid but forgiving tannins. Drink and enjoy any time through 2006. **95** —M.S. (8/1/2002)

Petra 2000 Val di Cornia Suvereto Sangiovese (Toscana) $29. From the southern coastal area of Tuscany comes this light red that offers smoky aromas, some rubber, and light red fruit. Currant and other sour berries carry the palate toward a dry, mildly tannic, and oaky finish. Has merits

but also a funky burnt quality and light, vegetal flavors. **84** —M.S. (11/15/2003)

PETROLO

Petrolo 2003 Galatrona Red Blend (Toscana) $84. A slight opening on the nose houses flowery red fruit; it's decidedly not a dark, heavy wine. But it does show some oak. The palate is hard-driving, with firm tannins supporting zesty, almost racy fruit. Nothing manipulated here; just ripe, ready rosso. **90** —M.S. (9/1/2006)

Petrolo 1999 Terre di Galatrona Sangiovese (Toscana) $16. Bold and earthy in the nose, but also maybe a tad murky. The flavor profile is forward, mostly just grapes and licorice, and while the palate is precise and on the sharper side, the finish is lighter; it just fades away without saying much. **87** —M.S. (12/31/2002)

Petrolo 2003 Torrione Sangiovese (Toscana) $36. Nice and smoky, with a solid, healthy nose that covers the bases. Good and snappy on the tongue, where zest and sweetness convene and deliver cherry, vanilla, and chocolate flavors. Medium in terms of intensity and depth. Best now–2008. **88** —M.S. (9/1/2006)

Petrolo 2001 Torrione Sangiovese (Toscana) $47. After stumbling in 2000, Petrolo is back on target with this wine. The nose immediately strikes as harmonious, with gentle earth and spice notes supporting solid berry aromas. The palate is ripe and smooth, with a fine structure that features proper acids and integrated tannins. **90** —M.S. (9/1/2006)

Petrolo 2000 Torrione Sangiovese (Toscana) $47. Weak berry aromas and candied fruit along with whacked-out acids and too much body weight. Finishes sweet and leaves a cloying tail. **80** —M.S. (10/1/2004)

PETRUSSA

Petrussa 2003 Sauvignon (Colli Orientali del Friuli) $27. Sulfuric and reductive to start, with heavy aromas of match stick, barnyard, and algae. But if you haven't tossed it aside after the first sniff or two, there's a lot below the surface. For starters, the richness and pungency of the melon and peach flavors is something. So is the briny character of the palate. But let it be noted: one of our panelists simply did not like this wine, proclaiming it "oily and dominated by salinity." **88** (7/1/2005)

PIANCORNELLO

PianCornello 2001 Brunello (Brunello di Montalcino) $50. Smokey, toasted qualities are backed by ample cherry, coffee, molasses, white peppercorn, and pine resin. Elegant and restrained without overt intensity, but well integrated and velvety in the mouth with drying tannins. **92 Editors' Choice** (4/1/2006)

PIAZZANO

Piazzano 1997 Rio Camerata Riserva Sangiovese (Chianti) $12. Very darkly fruited, this full-bodied wine offers layered bark-chocolate, cherry, and espresso aromas and flavors. The palate is smooth and suavely textured, and this sleeper has refined tannins on the long, classy finish. **89 Best Buy** (4/1/2001)

PIAZZO ARMANDO

Piazzo Armando 2005 Moscato (Moscato d'Asti) $17. The floral and fruity intensity of this wine is splendid and sets the tone for its soft impact in the mouth, which is sweet, creamy, and accented by lemon pie flavors. **85** —M.L. (12/15/2006)

Piazzo Armando 2004 Moscato (Moscato d'Asti) $15. I really enjoyed this wine with its super-thick froth, creamy peach, floral tones, intense fruit aromas, and higher than normal (for a Moscato d'Asti) alcohol. A great aperitivo or dessert drink. **89** —M.L. (12/15/2005)

PICCIAU

Picciau 1998 Vermentino (Vermentino di Sardegna) $13. This wine's banana bread, butter and yeast aromas—coupled with its deep gold, almost Muscat color—prepare you for a supersweet and creamy wine. That's not at all what it delivers. Tangy apple and grapefruit flavors on the palate give this Vermentino a bright, zippy mouthfeel and a medium-long, tangy lemon finish. **84** —D.T. (9/1/2001)

PICCINI

Piccini 2004 Sangiovese (Chianti) $8. Some situations simply demand solid, dependable Chianti that is rich in fruity notes but not too heavy in the mouth. Recognized by its eye-catching orange label, Piccini won't let you down. Red forest berries, clove, and cinnamon round off an extremely quaffable and affordable wine. Its lean consistency is accented by crispness and a fruit-driven finish that would be an ideal match with cheese-topped pizza or pasta. **87 Best Buy** —M.L. (11/15/2005)

Piccini 2003 Sangiovese (Chianti) $8. Leathery and more lean than fat, with a rustic, Rhône-like nose. Crisp and taut on the tongue, with pie cherry and plum flavors. Good length and depth for its class, with a dry cleanliness to it. **86 Best Buy** (4/1/2005)

Piccini 2002 Sangiovese (Vernaccia di San Gimignano) $10. Honey and a slight almond note at first, evolving in the glass to show more pear and citrus flavors. Medium-weight, and finishes with a slight chalkiness. **85** (7/1/2003)

Piccini 2001 Sangiovese (Chianti Superiore) $10. Simple black cherry and earth flavors in a medium-weight wine that finishes with more than a hint of citrus. **84** (7/1/2003)

Piccini 2001 Sangiovese (Chianti) $10. Light, and seems mature already, with modest cherry and tobacco flavors and tea leaves on the finish. **83** (7/1/2003)

Piccini 2000 Sangiovese (Chianti Superiore) $10. Light and pleasing with mild chalk and anise accents on the cherry fruit, the superiore is slightly more elegant than Piccini's normale. It again reflects the house preference for wines made 100% of Sangiovese with good acidity and balance as opposed to blending, extraction, and weight. Finishes with modest length and slightly peppery tannins. **86** (11/15/2001)

Piccini 2000 Sangiovese (Chianti) $8. This easy-drinking Chianti is a perfect pizza-and-pasta red with bright, dry, red cherry fruit and just a hint of chalk on the palate. Tangy but not sharp tannins and judicious use of oak make this forward, flavorful, agreeably priced wine a winner. **85 Best Buy** (11/15/2001)

Piccini 1999 Sangiovese (Chianti) $6. Though young in age, this has a light brown tinge and an orange-peel edge to its berry and herb aromas and flavors. There's a touch of soy and leather for complexity, and an even finish, but not the life or verve that makes us enthusiastic. **82** (4/1/2001)

Piccini 1998 Sangiovese (Chianti Classico) $11. The cherry fruit in this lighter-style wine shows definite herb accents. Bright acidity and a touch of mint come out on the palate, and it finishes with tart fruit flavors and slightly prickly tannins. **84** (4/1/2001)

Piccini 1999 Patriale Sangiovese (Toscana) $10. Piccini's nod to the '90s (the other wines are fairly traditional) is this internationally styled "mini Tuscan" that blends ripe plum fruit with the chocolate and vanilla flavors imparted by oak. **86 Best Buy** (7/1/2003)

Piccini 2000 Riserva Sangiovese (Chianti) $10. Although woody on the nose, there's also an attractive floral note and fresh, snappy flavors of black cherries. Finishes tart and lemony—built to accompany red sauce. **85** (7/1/2003)

Piccini 1998 Riserva Sangiovese (Chianti Classico) $16. A ripe, simple, open, fresh-fruited wine. Attractive, sweet fruit with ripe, light tannins make it immediately attractive to drink. For a Riserva, this is too lightweight. As an easy-drinking wine, it's fine. **84** —R.V. (8/1/2002)

Piccini 1997 Riserva Sangiovese (Chianti Classico) $13. The red cherry fruit bears some mushroom notes among the cedar and clove accents, and there's a sense of hollowing-out that should not be evidenced at this age. It's light, showing some nice berry and spice flavors and a sweet woodiness. But it's too developed now for a 1997 riserva. **83** (4/1/2001)

PIERO BUSSO

Piero Busso 2003 Majano Barbera (Barbera d'Alba) $30. Weirdly floral and perfumed—a potential turn-on for some tasters, while others may be turned off. It's relatively light in body for a wine carrying 14.5% alcohol, with floral grape and cherry flavors dominating. Tastes sweetly candied, balanced by bright acids. **85** —J.C. (3/1/2006)

Piero Busso 1996 Vigna Majano Barbera (Barbera d'Alba) $20. 90 (4/1/2000)

Piero Busso 1997 Vigna Majano Dolcetto (Dolcetto d'Alba) $19. 84 (4/1/2000)

Piero Busso 1999 Gallina Nebbiolo (Barbaresco) $174. Available only in magnums, Busso's '99 Gallina is a standout that should easily age past 2010. It shows some new oak in its scents of toast and vanilla, but also ample cherry fruit and strong elements of earth and tobacco. The finish is long and mouth-watering, yet still firm in its youth. **92** (4/2/2004)

Piero Busso 1999 Vigna Borgese Nebbiolo (Barbaresco) $57. The cedary, creamy, vanilla-laden nose comes across as a bit too "international." The mouthfeel is pleasantly chewy, but the flavors are limited to citrus and cedar, finishing with furry-textured wood tannins. **87** (4/2/2004)

PIEROPAN

Pieropan 2004 Garganega (Soave Classico) $18. Italy's comeback kid, Soave, has grown up. Fleshy peach and juicy grapefruit add depth to a wine that is smooth and oily in the mouth but does not lack zesty acidity. Everybody is saying it and it's true: it's a perfect match for Chinese food. **86** —M.L. (9/1/2005)

Pieropan 2003 La Rocca Garganega (Soave) $43. This elaborate interpretation of Soave is made with late-harvest Garganega grapes fermented and aged in oak barrels to yield intense depth and a bigger, bolder body. Creamy butter, toasted nuts, and vanilla play supporting roles to a predominately fruity nose. **88** —M.L. (9/1/2005)

Pieropan 1997 Soave Classico Superiore Garganega (Soave) $13. 84 (11/1/1999)

Pieropan 1997 Soave Classico Superiore Garganega (Soave) $17. 88 (11/1/1999)

Pieropan 2001 White Blend (Soave Classico Superiore) $14. Aromas of ripe pears and peaches jump out of the glass, and the flavors follow suit, bouncing across the palate in a display of stone fruits. It's relatively full bodied, but a garnish of grapefruit zest on the finish keeps it balanced and lively. **90 Best Buy** —J.C. (7/1/2003)

Pieropan 2003 Calvarino White Blend (Soave) $30. This Garganega-Trebbiano blend from the estate's original vineyard has a greenish tinge and more refreshing flowers, citrus and lime than the others in this portfolio. **87** —M.L. (9/1/2005)

Pieropan 2001 Calvarino White Blend (Soave Classico Superiore) $20. Not your grandmother's Soave, this is fully-loaded, from its charming, fresh aromas of peaches and orange blossoms to its plump, fleshy flavors of stone fruits. And it's all backed by bracing acidity that keeps the ripe flavors lively right through the long, minerally finish. **91 Editors' Choice** —J.C. (7/1/2003)

Pieropan 2000 La Rocca White Blend (Soave Classico Superiore) $30. Pieropan's La Rocca distinguishes itself from the Calvarino bottling by firmer structure and greater ageability. Tasted in spring 2003, this effort still has plenty of life left. Mimics Sauvignon a little in its gooseberry and red-currant flavors and grapefruity acidity. **89** —J.C. (7/1/2003)

Pieropan 1998 La Rocca Soave Classico Superiore White Blend (Soave) $25. The product of low yields and barrel fermentation and aging, this single-vineyard wine will change the way you think about Soave. Apples, tropical fruits, apricots, and vanilla abound, all offset by a firm mineral element. This balanced wine has zesty acidity—the long and complex finish will amaze you. To boot, the wine has a track record of aging well for six or more years. **91** —M.N. (9/1/2001)

Pieropan 1999 Soave Classico Superiore White Blend (Soave) $15. 88 —M.N. (12/31/2000)

PIERPAOLO PECORARI

Pierpaolo Pecorari 1997 Pinot Grigio (Venezia Giulia) $17. 83 (8/1/1999)

Pierpaolo Pecorari 2004 Pinot Grigio (Venezia Giulia) $10. A nutty, but not intense wine, with peach, pear, and mineral notes on what is a simple but clean nose. The mouthfeel is lean, with well-integrated acidity over a medium finish. **85 Best Buy** —M.L. (2/1/2006)

ITALY

Pierpaolo Pecorari 2004 Olivers Pinot Grigio (Venezia Giulia) $20. A copperish colored wine with opulent yellow fruit notes and a subtle toastiness render a unique nose and give the wine a distinct personality. Good consistency and finish. **87** —*M.L. (6/1/2006)*

Pierpaolo Pecorari 2000 Isonzio Sauvignon Blanc (Friuli Venezia Giulia) $15. Any baseball fan will peg the nose as being that of ballpark franks with yellow mustard. That strange meaty, pickled, spicy character carries onto the palate, where there's also some mineral character. The finish is clipped and short, which is probably a benefit after all the funky aromatics and flavors that come before. **82** *(8/1/2002)*

PIETRACOLATA

Pietracolata 2003 White Blend (Orvieto Classico) $8. Light pear and vanilla aromas get it started, followed by melon and tangerine flavors. Mostly clean, with lightweight citrus nuances to the finish. Doesn't really register on the scale, but likely good as a well-chilled quaff. **84 Best Buy** —*M.S. (11/15/2004)*

Pietracolata 2002 White Blend (Orvieto) $8. Floral and fresh, with melon and apple aromas. More melon, especially cantaloupe, on the palate. Well-balanced and flavorful; a good quaffer. **84** —*M.S. (10/1/2004)*

Pietracolata 2004 Secco White Blend (Orvieto Classico) $10. Almost neutral on the nose, with just an inkling of melon. Dry as a bone, with lean apple and green pear on the palate. Finishes as it starts: distant and short on fruit. **82** —*M.S. (10/1/2006)*

PIETRAFITTA

Pietrafitta 2000 La Sughera Rosso Red Blend (San Gimignano) $25. Exceedingly lean and tart, with crisp cherry aromas that indicate that what's to come will be stripped back and tight. And what do you know? The palate is all about tart cherry, cranberry, and red raspberry, all sitting on a bed of prickly acidity. Not what most are looking for in a full-priced Tuscan red. **83** —*M.S. (9/1/2006)*

Pietrafitta 2003 Sangiovese (Chianti Colli Senesi) $12. Earthy, with a tightly wound bouquet of black fruit, lacquer, and acetone. Once the chemical character subsides you get moderately deep plum and blackberry, while the finish spreads out in palate-coating fashion. Still, it could stand to be more concentrated. **85** *(4/1/2005)*

Pietrafitta 2001 Sangiovese (Chianti Colli Senesi) $11. The bouquet of strawberry and plum is simple and open. The palate, meanwhile, is tangy, with raspberry and cherry flavors. A bit of licorice and wood spice on the finish adds character. Still, it's a lean, juicy, acidic red. **85** —*M.S. (10/1/2004)*

Pietrafitta 2000 Sangiovese (Chianti Colli Senesi) $11. Floral aromas carry with them touches of apricot and strawberry. The palate is loaded with bright raspberry and cherry fruit, and the finish is broad and mildly oaked, but not too much so. It's a tad candied and somewhat short of substance, but it seems to have what it takes to appeal to a wide audience. **85 Best Buy** —*M.S. (12/31/2002)*

Pietrafitta 1998 Sangiovese (Chianti Colli Senesi) $10. A traditional Chianti blend is used here, including a small proportion of white grapes, and it shows how good an inexpensive wine made well in the traditional manner can be. The ripe cherry core sports tea and spice accents, and a chalk note appears on the palate. It closes with fine tannins and a dusty rose note. **88 Best Buy** *(4/1/2001)*

Pietrafitta 1999 La Sughera Sangiovese (San Gimignano) $18. The smoked meat and sugar beet nose is not that opulent, but it's generally clean and welcoming. The palate offers your basic berry fruit mix, which is followed by a tight, mildly tannic finish with a long espresso-like tail. It's a solid if pedestrian wine that shouldn't disappoint the average red-wine drinker. **86** —*M.S. (12/31/2002)*

Pietrafitta 1998 La Sughera Rosso Sangiovese (San Gimignano) $18. Built like a modern Chianti, with 90% Sangiovese supported by 10% Merlot and Cabernet, this red from the south of Tuscany is lean and dry. It has an elegant texture and feel, and black cherry and cedar aromas and flavors. Fine tannins and a leathery note mark the finish. **89** *(4/1/2001)*

Pietrafitta 2004 Vernaccia (Vernaccia di San Gimignano) $13. Nice enough on the bouquet, but not overly expressive or defined. Almond, pear, and freshly creamed butter carry the palate, followed by an airy, simple finish that's fresh but once again, not overly flavorful. Basic Vernaccia to the core. **85** —*M.S. (10/1/2006)*

Pietrafitta 2002 Vernaccia (Vernaccia di San Gimignano) $12. A bit flat and dusty at first, but then it opens to reveal aromas of peach and flowers. Flavors of pineapple and green apple are clean and solid, while the finish offers a bit of chewable vitamin flavor along with good acidity. Tang and crispness are the wine's over-riding characteristics. **86** —*M.S. (8/1/2004)*

Pietrafitta 2002 Borghetto Vernaccia (Vernaccia di San Gimignano) $16. A bit yellow in color, with licorice gumdrop, anise, and mineral aromas. It offers a tight grip across the palate and good balance. Flavors of citrus and papaya are smooth, and the finish is drying. Overall, there's just the right amount of apple, mineral, and soda cracker to warrant the thumbs up. **87** —*M.S. (8/1/2004)*

Pietrafitta 1999 Borghetto White Blend (Vernaccia di San Gimignano) $15. Aromas of grapefruit, herb, and almonds open to a mouthful of melon and peach in this medium-weight dry white. It has a bit more texture than most Vernaccias, a clean, crisp finish and an attractive back perfume with a touch of bitter almond. **88** *(4/1/2001)*

Pietrafitta 1992 Vin Santo White Blend (Colli della Toscana Centrale) $16. The Trebbiano grapes for this delicious dessert white are hung in the attic for three months in the traditional manner. Aromas of ripe grapes, citrus fruits, butterscotch, and hazelnuts yield to a nutty palate more rich than sweet. Still has plenty of acid backbone and finishes long with apricot notes. **90 Editors' Choice** *(4/1/2001)*

PIETRASERENA

Pietraserena 2003 Sangiovese (Chianti Colli Senesi) $11. Sweet, jammy, and simple, with a touch of chemical grapiness to the nose. The flavors, meanwhile, are lighter in force, emphasizing raspberry and strawberry. Decent size and length add weight to the finish, which seems a bit alcoholic when put to the test. **85** *(4/1/2005)*

PIETRATORCIA

Pietratorcia 1998 Riserva Red Blend (Ischia) $36. This wine has an attractive nose that swims with earth, dates, and figs. These jammy dried fruits continue on the palate, joined by stewed tomatoes. This is the perfect wine to pair with pasta in a pommodoro sauce. Campania is an agricultural region known for its delicious tomatoes, and wines from the region will naturally match. **87** —*C.S. (5/1/2002)*

PIETRO BARBERO

Pietro Barbero 1996 Bricco Verlenga Barbera D'Asti Superiore Barbera (Barbera d'Asti) $20. 86 *(4/1/2000)*

Pietro Barbero 1996 La Vignassa Barbera D'Asti Superiore Barbera (Barbera d'Asti) $35. 90 *(4/1/2000)*

PIETROSO

Pietroso 2001 Brunello (Brunello di Montalcino) $NA. Has textbook Brunello aromas of toasted almond, coffee, cedar bark, spice, blueberry, and herbal cough drop. A lean but well-balanced mouthfeel is accented by tart cherry and herb tea-like flavors with long, gentle tannins. **89** *(4/1/2006)*

PIEVE DI SPALTENNA

Pieve di Spaltenna 2000 Sangiovese (Chianti Classico) $15. Dull and vinegary, with a pickled quality. Strawberry and pie cherry on the palate, along with tangy, sharp apple skins. Finishes in short fashion. **83** *(4/1/2005)*

PIEVE SANTA RESTITUTA

Pieve Santa Restituta 1999 Rennina Brunello (Brunello di Montalcino) $95. Doesn't seem that concentrated at first, but builds powerfully on the finish, giving it good promise for the future. Combines ripe cherries, tobacco and leather with a silky mouthfeel in a classic Brunello style, finishing with firm tannins. Try in 2008. **92** *(7/1/2005)*

PIGHIN

Pighin 1998 Pinot Grigio (Grave del Friuli) $13. 85 *(8/1/1999)*

Pighin 1997 Pinot Grigio (Collio) $13. 82 *(8/1/1999)*

Pighin 2004 Pinot Grigio (Collio) $23. Crisp celery, pear, and a bit of resin set up ripe apple and spice flavors. Moderate length, decent depth and breadth. Not the most zesty, bouncy wine but flavorful. **85** *(2/1/2006)*

Pighin 2004 Pinot Grigio (Friuli Grave) $15. Apple cider, pear, and honey on the full, round nose. The body is fairly heavy and low in acidity, while the flavor profile pushes round apple and dried spice notes. **84** *(2/1/2006)*

PININO

Pinino 2001 Brunello (Brunello di Montalcino) $NA. Call it personality, this Brunello stands apart from the rest. Standard coffee and fudge are offset by tangy red berry, apple, candy cherry cough drop, putty, and what one panelist pinned down as roasted artichoke. A crisp close to a full, soft round wine. **89** *(4/1/2006)*

PINOCCHIO

Pinocchio 2003 Nero d'Avola (Sicilia) $9. A delicious, well-made, and spunky wine from Saro di Pietro and Dievole. Very ripe and open, with black fruit, charred wood, and mineral on the nose. High-toned but balanced red fruit hits hard on the palate but isn't shrill, while the finish is a bonus: weight, warmth, and brightness are all right there. A complete wine that handled the heat of the '03 vintage. **88 Best Buy** —*M.S.* *(7/1/2005)*

PINTAR

Pintar 1997 Single Vineyard Pinot Grigio (Collio) $20. 85 *(8/1/1999)*

PIO CESARE

Pio Cesare 1998 Arneis (Langhe) $23. 88 —*L.W. (11/15/1999)*

Pio Cesare 2001 Barbera (Barbera d'Alba) $26. Piercing, with rubber and sharp berry aromas. Very tight, with apple skin, raspberry, and a hint of oak to the flavor profile. Finishes dark, with chocolate and berries. A touch woody, but overall it's more crisp and crunchy than thick and lush. Nothing fancy, but it's good, clean Barbera. **86** —*M.S. (12/15/2003)*

Pio Cesare 2000 Fides Barbera (Barbera d'Alba) $40. Lavishly oaked, but not overdone, which is really the key. Quite sweet and spicy at first, with raisin aromas. Later come notes of fine-grained wood and toast. The body is round and lush, with cassis and blackberry flavors that give it a Merlot-like personality. Texture-wise, it's firm and solid, with healthy acids and live tannins. Can probably age for another several years. **90** —*M.S. (12/15/2003)*

Pio Cesare 1996 Fides Barbera (Barbera d'Alba) $38. 89 *(4/1/2000)*

Pio Cesare 1998 Chardonnay (Piedmont) $18. 88 —*M.S. (4/1/2000)*

Pio Cesare 1998 Chardonnay (Piedmont) $18. 84 —*L.W. (11/15/1999)*

Pio Cesare 2003 L'Altro Chardonnay (Piedmont) $24. Hints of toasted almond mark the nose, followed by peach and apple scents. It's medium-bodied, with almond and peach flavors that flow easily across the palate, ending on a citrusy note. **88** —*J.C. (3/1/2006)*

Pio Cesare 2002 L'Altro Chardonnay (Piedmont) $20. Heavily oaked and full-throttle when it comes to the banana notes. There's not much zest to this heavy, awkward Chardonnay. Yes, it offers texture, but there isn't much to latch on to. In the end, it just lays there in tired, dull fashion. **82** —*M.S. (12/15/2003)*

Pio Cesare 1999 Piemonte Chardonnay (Piedmont) $19. Light-to medium bodied, this Chardonnay is characterized by a strong floral-herb note that shows early. This almost flowershop-like quality shows more on the palate than do fruit flavors, and persists through the dry finish. **83** —*M.M. (9/1/2001)*

Pio Cesare 2003 Piodilei Chardonnay (Langhe) $49. Cesare's top Chard is a winner, balancing toasty, mealy notes from oak aging with honeyed peaches from fully ripe grapes. Hints of butter garnish this full-bodied wine, which ends with mingling nuances of citrus and toasted nuts. **90** —*J.C. (3/1/2006)*

Pio Cesare 2001 Piodilei Chardonnay (Langhe) $40. Basic melon, pear, and dough create a round, soft nose. Lemon, lime, and some tangerine define the palate. This in a monotone wine that delivers dull flavors and some body, but nothing more. **83** —*M.S. (12/15/2003)*

Pio Cesare 1997 Piodilei Chardonnay (Langhe) $39. This lavishly oaked wine with a big fruit foundation is very much in the California style, though it is made in Piedmont. The full, smooth mouthfeel is large but not fat, and the supple palate delivers apple, caramel, spice, and toast. Finishes long and toasty, with a leesy, earthy note. **90** —*M.M. (9/1/2001)*

Pio Cesare 1998 Cortese (Cortese di Gavi) $20. 86 *(4/1/2000)*

Pio Cesare 2003 Cortese (Cortese di Gavi) $23. Smells like ripe peaches with hints of anise and almond. Tastes similar, with a plump mouthfeel that carries the flavors across the palate to a short but pleasant finish. Nice as an apéritif, or with mildly flavored fish or poultry. **87** —*J.C. (11/15/2004)*

Pio Cesare 2002 Cortese (Cortese di Gavi) $20. This basic Gavi is muscular and ripe, with some creaminess to both the nose and mouthfeel. White peach and lemon flavors start to burn when put under the microscope, and the finish seems heavy. Has elements but is not complete. **83** —*M.S. (12/15/2003)*

Pio Cesare 2003 Dolcetto (Dolcetto d'Alba) $24. A youthful, exuberant wine, crammed with cherry and plum fruit. It's mouth-filling, and shows some characteristic Dolcetto tannins on the finish, which also picks up hints of chocolate and powdered charcoal. **88** —*J.C. (11/15/2004)*

Pio Cesare 2002 Dolcetto (Dolcetto d'Alba) $26. Clean, with spiced cherry and mint on the nose. A touch tart and snappy, thus it's angular and just a bit tough. Yet within the tart cherry flavor profile is an appealing tightness and fresh quality. Good if you like firm, tart reds. **86** —*M.S. (12/15/2003)*

Pio Cesare 1998 Dolcetto (Dolcetto d'Alba) $19. 85 —*L.W. (11/15/1999)*

Pio Cesare 2003 Moscato (Moscato d'Asti) $26. Seems a trifle fuller-bodied and less sweet (although it's still a dessert wine) than most Moscatos, yielding instead anise, white peach, and gumdrop aromas and flavors. **85** —*J.C. (11/15/2004)*

Pio Cesare 2001 Nebbiolo (Barbaresco) $35. Shows some wood touches, but the fruit sings loudest in this light and silky yet tannic Barbaresco. Cedar and caramel notes accent cherries, herbs, and spice. Anticipated maturity: 2010–2018. **90** —*J.C. (3/1/2006)*

Pio Cesare 2000 Nebbiolo (Nebbiolo d'Alba) $23. A hint of mint and licorice adds character to the simple, sharp nose of dried red fruit and leather. Racy and acidic, with tart flavors and fresh, drying tannins. Old-school all the way, with a clean, lean mouthfeel. **84** —*M.S. (12/15/2003)*

Pio Cesare 1999 Nebbiolo (Barolo) $79. Cherry and leather mark the nose, while the flavors are dominated by very sweet-seeming fruit—kirsch and vanilla accented by peppery spice. High acids, but tannins are very soft and supple, making the wine approachable now. Drink or hold until 2010. **89** *(4/2/2004)*

Pio Cesare 1999 Nebbiolo (Barbaresco) $71. This historic producer has developed into a reliable source for Barolo and Barbaresco, scoring uniformly well in our tastings. This offering boasts delicate aromas of cherries, leather, and tea. It's plump in the mouth, then finishes with firm tannins. Drink 2008–2016. **89** *(4/2/2004)*

Pio Cesare 1998 Nebbiolo (Barbaresco) $60. This is typical dry, leathery Barbaresco, with aromas of spice, smoked meat, and rubber. The palate is tight as a drum, with smoky flavors and the essence of dried red fruit. The finish is also dry and leathery. Drink now with meat dishes or hold for a couple of years. **89** —*M.S. (11/15/2002)*

Pio Cesare 1998 Nebbiolo (Barolo) $58. This wine is for lovers of an older style of Barolo. It has cherry and leather aromas, a touch of mint, and white chocolate. On the palate, though, there is some leaness and astringency that is certainly classic and even elegant, but might not appeal to everyone. It should age, however, and the astringency should soften. **87** —*R.V. (11/15/2002)*

Pio Cesare 1997 Nebbiolo (Nebbiolo d'Alba) $23. 88 —*L.W. (11/15/1999)*

Pio Cesare 1997 Nebbiolo (Barbaresco) $60. Creamy, with milk-chocolate and vanilla aromas and flavors alongside strawberries, cherries, and tobacco. This is a full-bodied, concentrated wine that's lush enough to

ITALY

ITALY

drink now but should develop some additional complexity with five years of cellaring. **89** *(9/1/2001)*

Pio Cesare 1999 Il Bricco Nebbiolo (Barbaresco) $137. A rich, velvety wine that falls firmly into the modern camp without losing its regional or varietal identity. The 1999 Il Bricco boasts aromas of toast and vanilla layered against a backdrop of ripe cherries and plums, adding in notes of cinnamon and clove. It's rich and velvety in the mouth, with substantial, supple tannins on the long finish. **91** —*J.C. (11/15/2004)*

Pio Cesare 1996 Il Bricco Nebbiolo (Barbaresco) $105. This Barbaresco is big and maybe a touch "international" for some purists, but it maintains a sense of place through its classic structure. Chocolate, blueberry, black cherries, smoke, and coconut macaroons all mingle on the nose, then turn dark and brooding on the palate, where the primary flavors are black cherry and dark coffee. A velvety mouthfeel and plenty of supple tannins make this wine one for the cellar. **91 Cellar Selection** *(9/1/2001)*

Pio Cesare 2001 Ornato Nebbiolo (Barolo) $146. A creamy-textured, supple Barolo with strong oak overtones, it boasts aromas of coffee and vanilla layered over black cherries. It's nicely balanced in terms of alcohol and acid, with a creamy mouthfeel and dried-spice notes on the finish. Give it a few years in the hope that the oak recedes over time. **90** —*J.C. (3/1/2006)*

Pio Cesare 1999 Ornato Nebbiolo (Barolo) $110. A plush, soft Barolo, the '99 Ornato blends rich black cherry fruit with tobacco and dark earth. Coffee, hazelnut, and caramel notes add layers of sweetness without obscuring the fruit. Deceptively approachable, its best drinking probably lies between 2010 and 2020. **91** *(4/2/2004)*

Pio Cesare 1998 Ornato Nebbiolo (Barolo) $135. A very sexy, soft, and ripe wine, with sweet prune and date flavors that caress the palate with supple tannins. Looks to be an early-maturing wine; drink now–2010. **89** *(4/2/2004)*

Pio Cesare 1997 Ornato Nebbiolo (Barolo) $110. A finely dense wine, with aromas of prunes, coffee, and dried herbs. On the palate, the texture is almost velvety, with raisins and red plums. Certainly it leaves a dry aftertaste, but that is from the concentrated tannins. This is still a young wine, from a great vintage, but it promises well for long-term aging. **90** —*R.V. (11/15/2002)*

Pio Cesare 1996 Ornato Nebbiolo (Barolo) $110. Very ripe aromas of spice cake, prunes, and candied fruit are complemented by chocolate and briary berry flavors. Acidity keeps the rich flavors in check. Tannins are caressingly soft, which make it surprisingly approachable now, though it should age well for a decade or more. **90** *(9/1/2001)*

Pio Cesare 1995 Ornato Nebbiolo (Barolo) $100. **87** *(7/1/2000)*

PLACIDO

Placido 2004 Pinot Grigio (Delle Venezie) $9. Texbook Pinot Grigio with fresh apple and pear flavors and a crisp, clean finish. This is exactly the kind of wine you'll want to drink for friendly, informal dining. **86 Best Buy** *M.L. (6/1/2006)*

Placido 1998 Pinot Grigio (Veneto) $8. 85 Best Buy *(8/1/1999)*

Placido 2003 Sangiovese (Chianti) $9. Shows full ripeness along with aromatics of leather, tobacco, and earth. Keeps a snappy but rewarding form from the cherry and red fruit palate through the full, juicy finish. More than solid, with medium weight. **87 Best Buy** *(4/1/2005)*

Placido 1998 Sangiovese (Chianti) $8. Nice cherry, anise, and cedar aromas open this affordable surprise. It follows through with good mouthfeel and balance, and black plum and chocolate flavors. Closes with ripe and even tannins, dark cherry flavors, and toast shadings. Perfect for drinking this year and the next, and worth buying by the dozen. **89 Best Buy** *(4/1/2001)*

PLANETA

Planeta 2000 Burdese Cabernet Sauvignon (Sicilia) $38. A solid, chunky wine, very New World in its rich, sweet, soft fruit and clean flavors. Black fruits and tannins give structure and power to this concentrated, dense wine. **89** —*R.V. (10/1/2003)*

Planeta 2004 Chardonnay (Sicilia) $43. From one of Sicily's flagship Chardonnay producers, here is a very attractive and luminous white with loads of butter, nut, almond, vanilla, and banana. Dig in there and you get Golden Delicious apple and pineapple, too. Creamy and textured, this is an oak-dominated wine (10 months of barrel aging) with a crisp close. **90** —*M.L. (7/1/2006)*

Planeta 2001 Chardonnay (Sicilia) $16. Exotic, tropical fruit and rich, open flavors with some Old World complexity. Acidity, toast and spice all add to the mix. **88** —*R.V. (10/1/2003)*

Planeta 2004 Cometa Fiano (Sicilia) $43. The wine's deep golden color sets the stage for the luscious notes of peach, honey, lychee, and passion fruit that follow. In the mouth, it delivers exceptional creaminess and roundness with a vein of crispness and a spice-driven finish. **90** —*M.L. (7/1/2006)*

Planeta 2003 Merlot (Sicilia) $43. The intense spiciness of this wine cannot be exaggerated: Indian spice, nutmeg, cinnamon, cigar, and toasted nuts appear full and thick on the nose and preface a dark, concentrated wine that leaves a velvety coating in the mouth. **90** —*M.L. (7/1/2006)*

Planeta 2001 Merlot (Sicilia) $38. Ripe Merlot that has intensity and concentrated black fruit flavors: this is a wine of depth as well as herbal and fruit flavors. Twelve months in French oak give a layer of vanilla, but the main effect is of the rich fruit. **90** —*R.V. (10/1/2003)*

Planeta 1999 Merlot (Sicilia) $39. Bright mixed berry aromas are revved up even more with lots of black pepper on the nose. A creamy-cheese note from the bouquet carries over onto the palate, where the black fruit is tart and coated with charred-barrel flavors. Finish is dry and long, with lots of oak. **87** —*C.S. (5/1/2002)*

Planeta 2003 Santa Cecilia Nero d'Avola (Sicilia) $43. This is a delicate, polished, and graceful wine that paints one of the most attractive portraits yet of the Nero d'Avola grape. Although some have criticized the fact its alcohol has increased over the last few years (now 14.5%), I would argue that its power is well integrated within its multifaceted and well-composed whole. **92 Cellar Selection** —*M.L. (7/1/2006)*

Planeta 2002 Santa Cecilia Nero d'Avola (Sicilia) $41. Massive amounts of extracted, sun-baked fruit is on display, which may be a hedonistic blast for some and just too syrupy and ripe for others. The bouquet is dense and sugary, with little to no spice or rusticity. That same blackberry quality controls the palate. But right when you want to dismiss it as too fat and fruity, it shows pure nuances of Nero d'Avola and Sicilian soul. **86** —*M.S. (7/1/2005)*

Planeta 2004 Red Blend (Cerasuolo di Vittoria) $26. This is a luscious, clean, and berry-driven wine that could be served slightly chilled. The nose offers bright red fruit, plum, black pepper, and tealeaf. This Nero d'Avola and Frappato-based wine has soft tannins and is refreshingly light. **87** —*M.L. (7/1/2006)*

Planeta 2003 Red Blend (Cerasuolo di Vittoria) $26. Exotic aromas of crushed lavender, violets, cherry, and molasses give hints as to what this wine is about. The palate, however, is a bit more mundane, albeit healthy in its own right. Bold plum and boysenberry is almost Zinfandel-like, while the finish is full and chewy. Drink now. **89** —*M.S. (7/1/2005)*

Planeta 2002 Red Blend (Cerasuolo di Vittoria) $12. A ripe, fresh, juicy wine with cherry flavors and sweet, soft fruit. Could well be served slightly chilled. **87** —*R.V. (10/1/2003)*

Planeta 2003 Burdese Red Blend (Sicilia) $43. Inspired by French winemaking and named after a Sicilian word for Bordeaux, this is a Cabernet Sauvignon and Cabernet Franc based wine with loads of personality. You can't miss the vegetal notes on the nose that span from sweet peas to tomato leaf and are backed by plum, spice, and those pretty almond notes present in so many Sicilian wines. **91** —*M.L. (7/1/2006)*

Planeta 2005 La Segreta Red Blend (Sicilia) $16. Blackberry, prune, pencil shavings, charcoal, and a rubber-like note sum up the aromas of this Nero d'Avola, Merlot, and Syrah blend. The wine is penetrating and intense on all levels with ripe fruit flavors and dusty tannins in the mouth. **88** —*M.L. (7/1/2006)*

Planeta 2002 La Segreta Red Blend (Sicilia) $16. Dark in color, with youthful aromas of black plum and leather. Fruity and forward the palate, with plum and chocolate flavors. Yes, it's fairly tannic and heavy, but today most folks like a big, bulky wine that has something to say. **88 Editors' Choice** —*M.S. (10/1/2003)*

Planeta 2000 La Segreta Red Blend (Sicilia) $16. Plum, grilled meat, and arugula aromas preface black fruit and animal-earthy flavors on the palate. Tannins aren't too aggressive, and the mouthfeel is round and smooth. Finishes a bit on the dry side, but with juicy fruit. A blend of 70% Merlot, 30% Nero d'Avola. **88 Best Buy** —*C.S. (5/1/2002)*

Planeta 2003 La Segreta Rosso Red Blend (Sicilia) $17. Ripe and heady, with aromas of crushed cherry and berry jam. Tons of red fruit flows on the palate, and the result is a basket of unbridled, acid-jolted flavor. Finishes full, fruity, and doused with chocolate. Very good as an every-day red. **87** —*M.S. (7/1/2005)*

Planeta 1999 Santa Cecilia Red Blend (Sicilia) $39. If you love sweet dark fruit—indeed, if the word "carnival" appeals to you when applied to wine—this is a keeper. Aromas of pine trees and cloves are echoed in the mouth with candy apple flavors, big dark fruit concentration, and cotton candy. It's a triumph of a certain style. **90** —*C.S. (5/1/2002)*

Planeta 2003 Syrah (Sicilia) $43. This red offers profound layers of sandalwood, clove, and black pepper. Those distinctive spice-box characteristics are truly unique to Planeta and shape a wine with personality that always stands out in a crowd. **90** —*M.L. (7/1/2006)*

Planeta 2001 Syrah (Sicilia) $38. This wine spends 12 months in wood, half of it new. But from the taste, all you find is the fruit. It is a fine contrast of sweet fruit and dry tannins, power, but also elegance. **88** —*R.V. (10/1/2003)*

Planeta 2005 La Segreta White Blend (Sicilia) $16. Planeta consistently delivers tasty whites and La Segreta (a Grecanico-Chardonnay-Viognier-Fiano blend) is no exception. The nose is layered with banana, pineapple, stone fruit, and a good dose of nuttiness; it's lean in the mouth with a sprinkling of spice on the close. **87** —*M.L. (7/1/2006)*

Planeta 2002 La Segreta White Blend (Sicilia) $15. A wild blend of Grecanico, Chardonnay, Viognier, Sauvignon Blanc, and Fiano, this is a crisp wine with a spicy character and rich tropical fruit. **86** —*R.V. (10/1/2003)*

Planeta 2003 La Segreta Bianco White Blend (Sicilia) $17. Yellow in color and a touch syrupy on the nose, with plowing aromas of apricot and creamed corn. More tangy and leaner than expected in the mouth, with citrus and some vanilla oak. Not really going places, so drink now. **84** —*M.S. (7/1/2005)*

Planeta 2004 Moscato di Noto White Blend (Sicilia) $46. The nice thing about Planeta's dessert wine is that it lacks the aromatic overstatement that Sicily's sweet wines are famous for. This is a more compact, clean, and linear version with notes of pine nut, yellow rose petal, Sicilian oranges, and honey. It's penetrating and textured in the mouth. **91** —*M.L. (7/1/2006)*

PLOZNER

Plozner 2003 Chardonnay (Friuli Grave) $14. Marred by a bit of sulfur on the nose, and this wine never recovers, delivering lean, clipped flavors of under-ripe pineapple and grapefruit. **82** —*J.C. (12/31/2004)*

Plozner 1997 Pinot Grigio (Friuli Grave) $12. 84 *(8/1/1999)*

Plozner 2001 Pinot Grigio (Friuli Grave) $13. Smells lemony, making you brace for a lean mouthful of tart fruit. But the flavors are riper, offering pear as well as citrus, and the finish actually ends up slightly soft. **85** —*J.C. (7/1/2003)*

Plozner 1999 Pinot Grigio (Friuli Grave) $10. This wine's earthy nose offers some hazelnut and apple nuances, and those flavors carry to the palate assertively but with a slight edge. It could use a little more acidic zing, but it would still be appealing served with mozzarella and prosciutto. **84** —*J.F. (9/1/2001)*

Plozner 2001 Tocai (Friuli Grave) $10. A pungent Tocai, full of passionfruit and grapefruit aromas reminiscent of Sauvignon Blanc. The grassy and herbal flavors are similarly evocative. **86 Best Buy** —*J.C. (7/1/2003)*

PODERE IL CAIO

Podere il Caio 2004 Grechetto (Umbria) $13. Catches your eye with its brassy hue, and also makes its mark with an overtly sweet nose of peach blossom and melon. In the mouth, however, it struggles a bit, offering cider and melon flavors on a soft, rather punchless palate. **83** —*M.S. (10/1/2006)*

PODERE IL PALAZZINO

Podere IL Palazzino 2002 Argenina Sangiovese (Chianti Classico) $20. Nicely smoked on the nose, with a leafy underbelly as well as leather and licorice. As a whole, it's a serious wine, with black cherry, vanilla and some tart cranberry comprising the palate. A touch rough around the edges, but overall it's pleasingly snappy and smooth. **88** *(4/1/2005)*

PODERE LA CAPPELLA

Podere La Cappella 1997 Querciolo Riserva Sangiovese (Chianti Classico) $22. A medium-weight contender whose fruit struggles to be acknowledged above the oak. There are some dark cherry and cocoa notes, especially on the nose, but in the end the oak rules, through the toasty, medium-length finish. **84** *(4/1/2001)*

PODERE LA VIGNA

Podere La Vigna 2001 Brunello (Brunello di Montalcino) $NA. Cherry, tobacco, earth, sandalwood, with balsam notes and a touch of horse saddle for a warmer, earthier veneer. The tannins are firm and drying but not aggressive and there's some wet slate or crushed stone on the finish. **90 Cellar Selection** *(4/1/2006)*

PODERE PROVINCIALE CANTINA LAIMBURG

Podere Provinciale Cantina Laimburg 2004 Pinot Grigio (Alto Adige) $18. The aromas of Alpine meadows, wild clover, and herbs are delicate and elegant but not intense. Regrettably they do not transfer to the mouth, which is best described as neutral. **84** —*M.L. (6/1/2006)*

PODERE RUGGERI CORSINI

Podere Ruggeri Corsini 1999 Nebbiolo (Barolo) $45. Explosive aromatics are frankly a touch over the top, bursting with cherry, leather, and touches of cedar, vanilla, coffee, and maple syrup. It's very rich, big, and bulky on the palate; gangly in its youth, it may settle down with some time in the bottle, but for now it's fruity and unformed. Try after 2009. **87** *(4/2/2004)*

Podere Ruggeri Corsini 1996 Corsini-Barolo Nebbiolo (Barolo) $45. This is a full sensory package of cinnamon, caramel, black cherry, char, apple, and procciutto aromas and flavors. What really won us over was the well-balanced, even mouthfeel. **91** *(11/15/2002)*

PODERI ALASIA

Poderi Alasia 2003 Rive Barbera (Barbera d'Asti) $26. Nice, easy-drinking Barbera, with nothing too complex or in your face. Medium-weight blackberry fruit is framed by hints of cocoa, turning crisp and citrusy on the finish. **87** —*J.C. (3/1/2006)*

Poderi Alasia 2000 Rive Barbera (Barbera d'Asti) $22. This is kicking Barbera! It's smoky, with big and ready plum and blackberry aromas. A rich, fully-oaked palate of plum and cherry fruit turns spicy and peppery on the finish, with hints of espresso. You even get some sweet marzipan in the middle of the tannins. Can age for another couple of years, but it's already sporting excellent body and feel. **91 Editors' Choice** —*M.S. (12/15/2003)*

Poderi Alasia 2000 Luca Monaca Red Blend (Monferrato) $27. Dark and dense, with tight lemony oak controlling a nose that also features some promising black fruit. Very precise across the palate, with delicious blackberry flavors. Some dark chocolate and berry pie notes carry the forward finish. With multiple layers and blaring class, this is one attractive Piedmontese red. **90** —*M.S. (12/15/2003)*

Poderi Alasia 2003 Camillona Sauvignon Blanc (Monferrato) $28. Rather smoky and round, with aromas of baked peaches, melon, and cream. Adequately fruity on the palate, with mid-level flavors of grapefruit, melon, and peach. Finishes a little bit sticky, with a bitter note akin to citrus pith. **85** *(7/1/2005)*

ITALY

PODERI ALDO CONTERNO

Poderi Aldo Conterno 2003 Printanie Chardonnay (Langhe) $35. Comprised entirely of Chardonnay, this medium-weight white blends ripe fruit aromas and flavors of peach and pear with less ripe notes of sweet peas and green beans. It's not truly vegetal, but straddles the line. **84** —*J.C. (3/1/2006)*

Poderi Aldo Conterno 1998 Nebbiolo (Barolo) $100. Dessicated fruit notes dominate the aromas, then develop more depth and complexity on the palate. Supple tannins accent dried cherry and orange notes, developing layers of additional flavor on the mouth-watering finish. **89** *(4/2/2004)*

Poderi Aldo Conterno 1999 Cicala Nebbiolo (Barolo) $126. We found some inconsistency in the lineup from Aldo Conterno, but this wine flat-out rocks. The rich, intense aromas layer vanilla, coffee, and buttercream over a framework of tart cherries, which explode in the mouth into a panopoly of red fruits. The tannins are plentiful—creating a rich texture—yet supple, showing great ripeness on the finish. **93** *(4/2/2004)*

Poderi Aldo Conterno 1998 Cicala Nebbiolo (Barolo) $112. The Conterno wines have long set the standard for more traditional Barolo. With its brown-red color and its aromas of ripe strawberries and dark plums, this wine combines powerful dried fruits with modern tannins and great concentration. It is an enormous wine that will age well over 15 years or more. **95 Editors' Choice** —*R.V. (11/15/2002)*

Poderi Aldo Conterno 1999 Colonello Nebbiolo (Barolo) $126. Dark plums, black cherries, and cola notes mingle effortlessly in this expressive offering. Tobacco, earth, and the merest hints of roasted meat add layers of complexity, while the mouthfeel is silky smooth without sacrificing any of the wine's fresh acidity. Drink 2005–2020. **91** *(4/2/2004)*

Poderi Aldo Conterno 1998 Colonnello Nebbiolo (Barolo) $116. Decidedly not a powerhouse this vintage, the '98 Colonnello is a pretty, relatively light-weight wine, displaying a range of aromas and flavors from cherries to cigarbox and dried spices. Drink now–2015. **89** *(4/2/2004)*

Poderi Aldo Conterno 1999 Monforte Bussia Nebbiolo (Barolo) $100. There's a lot to like in this wine: dried fruit and spices, leather and citrusy, floral aromatics. It's plump and relatively full-bodied, featuring cherry, cranberry, and milk chocolate flavors. Turns a bit too tart and citrusy on the finish, but it's a solid effort best consumed from 2008–2016. **87** *(4/2/2004)*

Poderi Aldo Conterno 1998 Monforte Bussia Nebbiolo (Barolo) $86. New wood aromas dominate this wine. But underneath all that expensive wood there is a fine wine waiting to emerge. It has flavors of almonds, cherries, and citrus peel, bound up in a rich, meaty stew. It is powerful and substantial, with a long vanilla and leather aftertaste. **89** —*R.V. (11/15/2002)*

PODERI BRIZIO

Poderi Brizio 1998 Brunello (Brunello di Montalcino) $70. Deep and ripe; once inside, you'll find a jumpy blend of ripe black stone fruits laid over a leathery texture. On the finish, coffee and toast offer darkness and coarseness. Firm tannins suggest a few years more aging. **91** —*M.S. (11/15/2003)*

Poderi Brizio 2000 Sangiovese (Colli della Toscana Centrale) $50. Light at first, with distant aromas of raspberry and milk chocolate. The flavor profile runs toward strawberry and red cherry, and there's zest and zip from front to back. It's full of fruit and spirit. **87** —*M.S. (11/15/2003)*

PODERI COLLA

Poderi Colla 1997 Barbera (Barbera d'Alba) $18. 88 *(4/1/2000)*

Poderi Colla 2001 Costa Bruna Barbera (Barbera d'Alba) $20. Immediately attractive, with black cherries laced with vanilla and a hint of cinnamon on the nose. Similar on the palate, but it turns a bit herbal and astringent on the finish, keeping the score relatively modest for a wine that started off so well. **86** —*J.C. (11/15/2004)*

Poderi Colla 1996 Dolcetto (Dolcetto d'Alba) $17. 83 *(4/1/2000)*

Poderi Colla 2001 Bricco del Drago Dolcetto (Langhe) $35. Lovely stuff, showing much better fruit than the 2000 did. Slightly floral on the nose (like rose petals), but complex and earthy as well, with hints of iron ore, black cherries, and tobacco. This is 85% Dolcetto, 15% Nebbiolo, and is nicely balanced, with masses of soft tannins on the finish. Drink now–2010. **92 Editors' Choice** —*J.C. (3/1/2006)*

Poderi Colla 2003 Pian Balbo Dolcetto (Dolcetto d'Alba) $17. Seems a bit muted aromatically, but still delivers pleasant black cherry and plum flavors. A bit light in body, with decent length on the finish alongside some drying tannins. **86** —*J.C. (3/1/2006)*

Poderi Colla 2002 Pian Balbo Dolcetto (Dolcetto d'Alba) $17. Has some pretty, floral aromas to go along with scents of plums, anise, and tobacco. The palate is clean and fruit-driven, picking up hints of black tea on the finish. Nicely done. **87** —*J.C. (11/15/2004)*

Poderi Colla 2002 Nebbiolo (Nebbiolo d'Alba) $24. Light in color, with some bricking at the rim, but this wine still offers plenty to like, from its intensely floral aromas to its round mouthfeel and prune-and-chocolate flavors. Clamps down with some astringent tannins on the finish, but probably better to drink near-term, before the fruit fades. **88** —*J.C. (3/1/2006)*

Poderi Colla 1999 Bussia Dardi le Rose Nebbiolo (Barolo) $60. After revealing its identity, we confess to being slightly disappointed by this wine's showing. It was good, but not as good as we would have hoped. Modest cherry, tar, and earth flavors seem less concentrated than many of the other wines in the tasting, but the finish is long and complex, with intriguing notes of sous-bois. **86** *(4/2/2004)*

Poderi Colla 1998 Bussia Dardi le Rose Nebbiolo (Barolo) $48. Aromas of grilled steak with A-1 sauce. The flavors are complex: black pepper accented with clove, cooked cherries, and a hint of tar. The wine has a nice balance of earth, fruit, and tannins, which finish long but soft. **90** —*C.S. (11/15/2002)*

Poderi Colla 2001 Dardi Le Rose Bussia Nebbiolo (Barolo) $60. Smells a bit earthy and rustic, with scents of leather and iron ore, but the fruit emerges on the palate, slowly unfolding to reveal layers of plums and black cherries. This is a wine whose true potential is seen most clearly on the finish at this early stage of its evolution, where it gains in fruit intensity and complexity, boding well for the future. Try in 10 years. **91** —*J.C. (3/1/2006)*

Poderi Colla 2000 Dardi le Rose Bussia Nebbiolo (Barolo) $64. A bit herbal on the nose, with other scents of cherries and dusty spices. It's more powerful in the mouth, where the cherries seem to expand and flow silkily across the palate. Finishes long and elegant, with a hint of chocolate. Uncommonly supple for Barolo, suggesting early drinkability. **89** —*J.C. (11/15/2002)*

Poderi Colla 2001 Roncaglie Nebbiolo (Barbaresco) $56. This is a big, mouth-filling wine, and one that suggests good things to come from the 2001 vintage in Piedmont. Starts off with clean, pure scents of cherries, plums, and vanilla, with flavors that lean toward Queen Anne cherry, black-skinned plum, earth, and cedar. Lush tannins cushion the long finish. **90** —*J.C. (11/15/2004)*

Poderi Colla 2000 Roncaglie Nebbiolo (Barbaresco) $56. Hints of tea and flowers dress up the briary, berry-scented nose of this Barbaresco. Boasts fresh acidity, which accents the berry fruit flavors and offsets the rich notes of dark chocolate and tar. Drink now–2015. **87** *(4/2/2004)*

Poderi Colla 1999 Tenuta Roncaglia Nebbiolo (Barbaresco) $46. What a gorgeous nose—it's all sweet dried cherries, root beer and leather. The flavors are ripe and pronounced. Cherries, raspberries, and cola are front and forward. Like any proper young Nebbiolo, it's tight and tannic, with a dry coffee-tinged finish. But the fruit dominates over astringency. **91** —*M.S. (11/15/2002)*

Poderi Colla 2000 Bricco del Drago Red Blend (Langhe) $35. This blend of 85% Dolcetto and 15% Nebbiolo is certainly soft and lush, but ends up tasting more like expensive oak than fruit. If vanilla, toast, and dried spices ring your chimes, go for it. **85** —*J.C. (11/15/2004)*

Poderi Colla 1996 Dardi Le Rose Bussia Red Blend (Barolo) $46. Already shows a bit of brown to its hue, but that's not terribly unusual for Nebbiolo. Aromas of leather, soy sauce, and tar are classic, followed up on the palate by tart cherry flavors that come across as a bit lean. Firmly structured, this wine needs time to resolve its tannins; give it three years or more in the cellar. **87** —*J.C. (9/1/2001)*

PODERI LUIGI EINAUDI

Poderi Luigi Einaudi 2003 Vigna Tecc Dolcetto (Dolcetto di Dogliani) $27. A top-notch Dolcetto virtually every year, Einaudi's 2003 Vigna Tecc features masses of bold dark fruit (black cherries and plums), some tarry notes, and hints of dried spices (cinnamon and clove). This big, full-bodied, tannic Dolcetto needs another year or two of cellaring, then should drink well until 2012. Impressive. **91 Editors' Choice** —*J.C. (3/1/2006)*

Poderi Luigi Einaudi 2002 Vigna Tecc Dolcetto (Dolcetto di Dogliani) $26. Deep and plummy on the nose, this fine Dolcetto delivers bass notes of earth and chocolate on the palate, with lingering notes of coffee and anise on the finish. **89** —*J.C. (11/15/2004)*

Poderi Luigi Einaudi 2000 Nebbiolo (Barolo) $73. Einaudi's 2000 Barolo is a big, mouth-filling wine, in keeping with the ripeness achieved that vintage. Boatloads of cherries and plums balance hints of vanilla and spice. Finishes with firm, yet fully ripe and supple tannins. Try after 2010. **90** —*J.C. (11/15/2004)*

Poderi Luigi Einaudi 1999 Nebbiolo (Barolo) $68. There's a nice combination of red and black fruit in this wine: dark chocolate and plums on one hand, fresh cherries on the other. Anise notes add complexity. The mouthfeel is plump and juicy; the finish long and peppery. Modest tannins suggest a drinking window between 2005 and 2015. **88** *(4/2/2004)*

Poderi Luigi Einaudi 1998 Nebbiolo (Barolo) $52. Luigi Einaudi was Italy's first president. The estate was founded in 1897, and to this day is run by his granddaughter, Paola Einaudi. The wine has a very floral nose of rose petals and lavender. Raspberry flavors and a woodiness derived from Slavonian oak are complex yet finish soft and appealing. **91** —*C.S. (11/15/2002)*

Poderi Luigi Einaudi 2000 Costa Grimaldi Nebbiolo (Barolo) $90. Measured use of barrique (20%) means this wine retains all of its essential Barolo-ness. It's taut and a little hard-edged in its youth, with aromas and flavors of sour cherry, leather, citrus, and just hints of flowers and underbrush. Should develop well in time; try in 2010 or later. **88** —*J.C. (11/15/2004)*

Poderi Luigi Einaudi 1999 Costa Grimaldi Nebbiolo (Barolo) $81. Despite this wine's ample weight, it retains a remarkable sense of elegance and complexity, blending minor amounts of toast and vanilla with dried cherries, cinnamon, citrus peel, licorice, and dates. The tannins are well rounded and supple, the finish long. Drink now–2020. **91** *(4/2/2004)*

Poderi Luigi Einaudi 2000 Nei Cannubi Nebbiolo (Barolo) $100. Elegant and supple upfront, then hits you with masses of rich, soft tannins on the finish that alleviate any initial concerns about ageability. Aromas and flavors run the gamut from earth and tobacco, to cherry and plum, to cedar and vanilla. Drink 2010–2020. **91 Cellar Selection** —*J.C. (11/15/2004)*

Poderi Luigi Einaudi 1999 Nei Cannubi Nebbiolo (Barolo) $93. Toast and vanilla aromas and flavors suggest a certain amount of new oak, but there are also ample quantities of cherry- and citrus-tinged fruit. Full-bodied, with a tannic finish. Drink 2010–2020. **90** *(4/2/2004)*

Poderi Luigi Einaudi 1998 Nei Cannubi Nebbiolo (Barolo) $50. Cannubi is the superstar of Barolo. This wine possesses cinnamon, clove, and caramel aromas. The palate brings juicy blackberries and toast. There is a rich, sweet mouthfeel that is derived from fruit concentration, and not residual sugar. The tannins are sizeable but are in balance with the fruit and acidity, and all the components fall brilliantly into place to make a great wine. **93 Cellar Selection** —*C.S. (11/15/2002)*

Poderi Luigi Einaudi 2001 Luigi Einaudi Red Blend (Langhe) $73. A proportioned blend of Nebbiolo, Barbera, Cabernet Sauvignon, and Merlot, you can taste each of the components in the finished wine: earth, cherries, tobacco and cassis, and plums, respectively. It's deceptively easy to drink, with broad, expansive tannins on the finish. You could drink it now, but it should be even better in a few years' time. **88** —*J.C. (11/15/2004)*

PODERI SALVAROLO

Poderi Salvarolo 1997 Ser Mílion Cabernet Sauvignon-Merlot (Veneto Orientale) $27. Some cola, green bean, and tobacco notes can be extracted from the nose of this Cabernet-Merlot blend. The palate is medium in weight, with berry and herb flavors. The finish runs tart, with drying tannins. One-dimensionality is this wine's pitfall; it just doesn't have much complexity. **84** *(5/1/2003)*

POGGIO AI CHIARI

Poggio Ai Chiari 2001 Sangiovese (Toscana) $43. Berry and cherry aromas get it started, followed by notes of cinnamon and alfalfa. Raspberry and sweet cherry flavors dominate, but at the same time you can taste a tiny bit of green in the middle. Overall it's a structured, healthy wine with ample wood and tannin. **89** —*M.S. (9/1/2006)*

POGGIO AL CASONE

Poggio al Casone 2004 La Cattura Red Blend (Toscana) $22. Lightly perfumed on the nose, with notes of plum, violet, and also some unwelcome pickle. The palate delivers strawberry and raspberry, while the short finish ends on a chocolaty upswing. Good overall but nothing mysterious or complex. **85** —*M.S. (9/1/2006)*

Poggio al Casone 2001 Sangiovese (Chianti Superiore) $13. Seemingly light and jammy; the strawberry and raspberry aromas are soft but fragrant. In the mouth, however, it gets tart fast, where citrus and red cherry mingles. Could use some pizza or pasta to absorb the crispness. **86** *(4/1/2005)*

Poggio al Casone 1997 Sangiovese (Chianti Superiore) $15. There's super-ripe fruit and a soft, easy feel to this very jammy wine. Although not complex, the big black cherry fruit delivers a lot of flavor and the supple texture is quite pleasurable. The finish is plush, with tart acids. Widely appealing for current consumption. **87** *(4/1/2001)*

Poggio al Casone 1999 Pog Sangiovese (Chianti Superiore) $12. This wine from the Castellani group begins with earthy, smoky aromas and some warmth. The palate unfolds as a grapey sort of fruit salad, but one without a lot of structure or tannins. The finish features a fair amount of coffee and oak. Overall it starts better than it ends, as it seems to be lacking something. **86 Best Buy** —*M.S. (12/31/2002)*

Poggio al Casone 2002 Poggio al Casone Sangiovese (Chianti Superiore) $13. Opens with light berry aromas that are similar to raspberry and strawberry. It's tangy in the mouth, with red plum and raspberry controlling the board. Shows hints of vanilla and brown sugar on the snappy finish. More racy than rich. **85** —*M.S. (10/1/2006)*

POGGIO AL MULINO

Poggio Al Mulino 1997 Pancarta Sangiovese (Toscana) $32. With an abundance of deep black cherry, molasses, and leather aromas, this is dynamite in terms of intensity and concentration. In the mouth, it's smooth and stylish, with a tight black fruit core and a suave finish. Built like a house with a very dark interior; it'll be alive and kicking through 2008. **91** —*M.S. (8/1/2002)*

POGGIO ALLE SUGHERE

Poggio alle Sughere 2001 Splendido Sangiovese (Toscana) $45. Plum and blackberry coat the plump nose, backed by ripe black fruit that registers as pure but standard. Still fairly tight and tannic, and not showing any signs of maturity as of now. Potent and tight, with lots of oak and chocolate on the finish. **88** —*M.S. (9/1/2006)*

POGGIO ANTICO

Poggio Antico 2001 Brunello (Brunello di Montalcino) $74. A dark, ruby-colored wine with generous but sharp blackberry backed by white mushroom, coffee, leather, tobacco, and earthy resin-like notes. Firm, smooth structure with black tea tannins and a berry finish. Drink from 2010–2020. **91** *(4/1/2006)*

Poggio Antico 2000 Brunello (Brunello di Montalcino) $72. Big and brawny, with a blinding violet color and a bouquet bursting with rich oak. In fact, this wine features as much new oak as any normale on the market. But with such quality fruit, the nose quickly morphs into high-grade tobacco and pure vanilla. In the mouth, things run deep and thick, and any potential corpulence is balanced by ripe tannins and fresh acids. **93** —*M.S. (7/1/2005)*

Poggio Antico 1999 Brunello (Brunello di Montalcino) $76. The color is literally purple, while the nose is layered with toasty oak and coffee atop pound cake and berry jam. The palate is powerful yet restrained, and

ITALY

with a mile-long finish propped up by jackhammer tannins, you just know it's built to last. This will drink fabulously in about six years. **94** —M.S. (6/1/2004)

Poggio Antico 1998 Brunello (Brunello di Montalcino) $58. A big cherry-vanilla style of Brunello, with bold aromas and flavors held in check by a slightly acrid, weedy note. Warming on the finish, with a dose of spice and supple tannins. **89** (11/15/2003)

Poggio Antico 1997 Brunello (Brunello di Montalcino) $60. Paola Gloder's estate can do better than this, especially in a vintage like 1997. The wine is already showing signs of aging and it has a lightweight character. The fruit is pleasant enough, with soft tannins and ripeness, but it should be more exciting. Tasted twice. **84** —R.V. (8/1/2002)

Poggio Antico 2001 Altero Brunello (Brunello di Montalcino) $82. Very toasty upfront with a lot going on inside the glass. Cherry fruit is delivered with coffee bean, leather, cigar box, vanilla, and a touch of Band-Aid. Has some rustic notes but an overall elegant mouthfeel with a long, velvety, supple finish. **91** (4/1/2006)

Poggio Antico 2000 Altero Brunello (Brunello di Montalcino) $74. Concentrated and super-ripe with blackberry, plum, cedar, clove, and coffee over a long, spicy finish. Firm, velvety tannins and toasted notes render a modern yet age-worthy wine. **90** (4/1/2006)

Poggio Antico 1998 Altero Brunello (Brunello di Montalcino) $57. This wine really grows on you. It starts off with slightly acrid, coarse elements of briar patch and weeds, but it explodes on the palate, turning rich, chocolaty, and refined. Deep layers of softly tannic, plum-flavored fruit caress the mouth, leaving a lasting aftertaste. **92** (11/15/2003)

Poggio Antico 2000 Riserva Brunello (Brunello di Montalcino) $129. Saturated and deep purple in color, this wine yields loads of toastiness, dry woodiness, soy and vanilla with a ripe undercurrent of blackberry and raspberry. Modern and built like a tank, it serves up velvety tannins and a spicy, long finish. **94 Cellar Selection** (4/1/2006)

Poggio Antico 1999 Riserva Brunello (Brunello di Montalcino) $125. Here's a huge, stately wine with a brick-based structure and mounds of lovely oak that is already so well-integrated you barely notice it. Quite tannic, and will require come cellaring. When you do drink it, expect warm flavors, liqueur-soaked berry fruit, and a mile-long finish. Hold until 2010, at least. **95 Cellar Selection** —M.S. (7/1/2005)

Poggio Antico 1995 Riserva Brunello (Brunello di Montalcino) $56. The brownish color indicates that it's fading, and the raisiny, stewed fruit on the nose confirms that initial indications are on target. In the mouth, it's soft, and the cherry fruit has a kirsch-like liqueur quality to it. Faded tannins and barely vital acids say it's going, going, and soon to be gone. **84** —M.S. (8/1/2002)

Poggio Antico 2001 Madre Cabernet Sauvignon-Sangiovese (Toscana) $64. One sniff delivers heavenly aromas of liqueur, plum, and licorice. This 50/50 blend of Sangiovese and Cabernet represents the Super Tuscan concept at its best. The fruit is dynamite, the oak front and center, and the aging potential great. Hold for about five years then unleash an avalanche of class and flavor. **94 Editors' Choice** —M.S. (10/1/2004)

POGGIO ARGENTIERA

Poggio Argentiera 2002 Finisterre Red Blend (Toscana) $62. Heady and ultra rich; it's a Syrah-Alicante marriage that's on the cusp of syrupy and overdone. Aromatically, we're talking caramel and toast, while the palate is so loaded with black plum and berry that it's straddling the breaking point. Ultimately it's just too heavy, oaky, and clumsy to make the grade in the class it's playing in. **85** —M.S. (9/1/2006)

Poggio Argentiera 2002 Bellamarsilia Sangiovese (Morellino di Scansano) $18. Dense, with bacon aromas as well as murkiness. Not terribly defined, but it does pick up confidence with time. Plum, berry, and cherry flavors precede a round finish that starts off fruity then turns warm. Tastes better than it smells. **86** —M.S. (11/15/2004)

POGGIO BERTAIO

Poggio Bertaio 2000 Cimbolo Sangiovese (Umbria) $20. 90 —M.S. (2/1/2003)

POGGIO BONELLI

Poggio Bonelli 2001 Sangiovese (Chianti Classico) $30. Raw but lively, with mega intensity. Big and leathery, with tight tannins. The flavor profile is sure, as robust dried fruit morphs into coffee and chocolate. And there's a fine minty undercurrent keeping everything in focus. Worth aging for several more years. **90 Cellar Selection** (4/1/2005)

POGGIO DEI POGGI

Poggio Dei Poggi 1997 Sangiovese Grosso (Chianti Classico) $13. Sour cherry, leather, and a ginger note mark the nose of this lighter-style wine. The tart cherry and licorice flavors and the dry, lean feel are on the mark. Closes with a chalk and anise note. **85** (4/1/2001)

Poggio Dei Poggi 1995 Riserva Sangiovese Grosso (Chianti Classico) $20. Classic elements—a nose of cherry, herbs, cedar, licorice, and a tart, dry, cherry-fruited palate—mark this wine. It has solid pieces and good length, but they're not as well-integrated as they might be. The finish turns a bit woody, but this could work well with grilled meat or vegetables. **85** (4/1/2001)

POGGIO DI SOTTO

Poggio di Sotto 2001 Brunello (Brunello di Montalcino) $NA. A racy, perky wine that appealed enthusiastically to two of three panelists. One found that it lacked intensity but the others enjoyed its herbal, high-toned cherry flavors. A hint of pastry crust or graham cracker adds complexity and depth to an otherwise lean and elegant wine. **88** (4/1/2006)

Poggio di Sotto 1999 Riserva Brunello (Brunello di Montalcino) $NA. Leather, tannery, fruit-forward but lighter in color and consistency that the other wines in its flight. There are fine-tuned notes of elegance in the form of drying minerality and rose tea sweetness. Soft and silky in the mouth with a nice, fresh finale. **91** (4/1/2006)

POGGIO IL CASTELLARE

Poggio il Castellare 2001 Brunello (Brunello di Montalcino) $NA. Toast, cedar wood, sweet berries, and mint with a smooth mouthfeel dominated by cherry-vanilla. Long and lush with chewy tannins and a nice finish, this is an easy to appreciate wine. **89** (4/1/2006)

POGGIO NARDONE

Poggio Nardone 2001 Brunello (Brunello di Montalcino) $65. Here is a vanilla- and cedar-infused wine that sparked discord among our panelists. One loved its complexity and spicy notes layered over ripe fruit, while another took issue with its stewiness. Plush tannins and fruit glide over a long finish. **92** (4/1/2006)

POGGIO SALVI

Poggio Salvi 1998 Sangiovese (Chianti Colli Senesi) $15. After an unusual, almost saline note passed, this wine presented a bouquet of dark cherry, chocolate, and toast. This opens to a mouth of mild cherry flavors with a dry even feel and a black plum and cocoa finish that displays slightly edgy tannins. **84** (4/1/2001)

POGGIO SAN POLO

Poggio San Polo 2001 Brunello (Brunello di Montalcino) $NA. Black cherry cola, forest floor, coffee, wet tobacco, and drying wood notes with a hint of wild mushroom are firmly fastened to a medium-structured wine with a eucalyptus-laden finish. **89** (4/1/2006)

POGGIO VALPAZZA

Poggio Valpazza 1997 Monteregio Sangiovese Grosso (Monteregio Rosso) $47. 88 (7/1/2000)

POGGIO VERRANO

Poggio Verrano 2004 Dròmos Red Blend (Maremma) $60. Although it is too young to drink now, the second edition of Dròmos (an intricate blend of five red varieties) already boasts beautiful development with notes of blackberry, cherry fruit, smoke, granite, clove, spice with oak balance. It's smooth, creamy, and mouth-wateringly succulent in the mouth. **92** —M.L. (11/15/2006)

Poggio Verrano 2003 Dròmos Red Blend (Maremma) $60. Francesco Bolla is a man with a mission: To make the best red blend in Maremma. This beautifully balanced assembly of Cabernet Sauvignon, Merlot, Sangiovese, Alicante, and Cabernet Franc is the estate's sole product. It has weighty plum and red cherry fruit, ground coffee bean, hay, white peppercorn, dried rose petal, and leather. It is firmly tannic and persistent in the mouth, while the nose offers hickory and berry aromas. **90** *(9/1/2006)*

POJER & SANDRI

Pojer & Sandri NV Cuvée Vino Spumante Extra Brut Champagne Blend (Trento) $30. The nose is downright flat, with just a hint of burnt vegetable. The palate is rather hollow, while the finish is tart and unexciting. The mouthfeel is fine, and overall the wine isn't overtly flawed. But it is dull as old nails and elicits no excitement whatsoever. **82** —*M.S. (12/31/2002)*

Pojer & Sandri 2001 Müller-Thurgau (Trentino) $16. It is rare to find a Müller-Thurgau with such flavor, but Pojer and Sandri have a penchant for getting more than most out of lesser grape varieties. This wine has broad fruit flavors along with a crisply aromatic aftertaste. **88** —*R.V. (7/1/2003)*

Pojer & Sandri 2001 Traminer (Trentino) $18. A rich, spicy wine, full of intense fruit, produced by Mario Pojer and Fiorentino Sandri. They conjure ripeness and balance from the Traminer, giving it power but also food-friendly subtlety. **90** —*R.V. (7/1/2003)*

POLIZIANO

Poliziano 2002 Sangiovese (Vino Nobile di Montepulciano) $25. Smoky as a campfire, with heavy barrique-driven aromas along with lemon, bitter chocolate, and cherry. Model intensity, the hallmark of Poliziano, is on display across the palate, where firm tannins clamp down like a vise. Not a great wine, but plenty dark and manly. **87** —*M.S. (7/1/2005)*

Poliziano 2001 Sangiovese (Rosso di Montepulciano) $16. Initial aromas of menthol and mushroom give way to black fruit and smoked meat, but all the while the bouquet seems a touch flat. On the palate, there's plum, black cherry, and a fair amount of acid and tannin. The finish is expansive yet mild. Juicy, fruity and forward, but not exactly loaded with style. **86** —*M.S. (11/15/2003)*

Poliziano 2000 Sangiovese (Rosso di Montepulciano) $20. This little brother to vino Nobile embodies the essence of ripe, lip-smacking country wine. But it's no piece of candy; quite the contrary, it's full, rustic and fruit-forward. If elegance isn't the game here, then the big plum flavor and meaty, berry-loaded finish is. **87** —*M.S. (8/1/2002)*

Poliziano 1999 Sangiovese (Vino Nobile di Montepulciano) $23. Raspberry, herbs, and a touch of grain on the nose. Flavors of raspberry and sweet plum take over on the palate, and finally a spicy, lively finish with solid tannins closes things out. There's good berry fruit here, a clean overall profile, and only modestly hard tannins. **87** —*M.S. (11/15/2003)*

Poliziano 1998 Sangiovese (Vino Nobile di Montepulciano) $29. Open and friendly, this is the epitome of a newly-released wine that should sell well in restaurants and fly off the shelves of wine shops. Not only will it go nicely with pasta or grilled meat, it's properly balanced and solid on its own feet. Cherry is the predominant flavor, and on the finish there's vanilla and tannins that won't quit. **87** *(8/1/2002)*

Poliziano 2001 Asinone Sangiovese (Vino Nobile di Montepulciano) $40. Huge and powerful, yet tannic and oaky. The purest example of what a barrique-aged Sangiovese (with 10% Merlot and Colorino) is all about. The bouquet exudes espresso, bitter chocolate, and lemon peel, while the dark fruit palate is beyond reproach in terms of ripeness. A great marriage of new age and old; hold until 2008. **91 Cellar Selection** —*M.S. (7/1/2005)*

Poliziano 1999 Asinone Sangiovese (Vino Nobile di Montepulciano) $43. Here's a live wire, with lemony, fine-grained oak aromas and a starchy, hard-tannin feel. Flavor-wise, it's about fleshy berry fruit and (what else?) piercing oak. Fortunately, there's enough fruit and body to support it. Quite compact, ripe, and sturdy. **87** —*M.S. (12/15/2003)*

Poliziano 1998 Asinone Sangiovese (Vino Nobile di Montepulciano) $45. This is a complex bruiser that will appeal to those willing to give it at least three years in the cellar; it's that tight and young now. Oak is a big player on the nose and in the mouth, and the acids are very alive, so as a

result some might find it aggressive (all the more reason to lay it down until 2006). There is plenty of earth and minerals throughout, and it's tight as nails on the finish. **89** *(8/1/2002)*

POWERS

Powers 1998 Merlot (Colonella) $12. The nose is jammy and ripe, forward, and vividly fruity, suggesting strawberry or rhubarb preserves. Nice flavors, light and elegant, with the fruit showing polish and a gentle hand with the oak. This winery is making great strides with their new releases. **89 Best Buy** —*P.G. (12/31/2001)*

POZZI

Pozzi 2001 Merlot (Delle Venezie) $9. The bouquet features charred elements and a certain cedar and leather quality. The palate is heavy, with acids and fat fruit doing battle. The finish is bulky, short, and sweet, with aggressive tannins. **82** *(5/1/2003)*

Pozzi 2002 Rosso Nero d'Avola (Sicilia) $10. Bulky on the nose, with malted chocolate, caramel, and soft red fruit. Broad and clumsy in the mouth, with strawberry at first and tomato toward the finish. Probably best as a bar wine, and hopefully you catch it freshly opened. **83** —*M.S. (10/1/2004)*

Pozzi 2001 Rosso Nero d'Avola (Sicilia) $10. A dark, pruny wine, with a soft, supple mouthfeel and fruit flavors that are drying out and turning to soy sauce. Made from 100% Nero d'Avola, although that's not indicated on the front label. **83** *(10/1/2003)*

Pozzi 1999 Rosso Nero d'Avola (Sicilia) $9. A sweet, jammy whiskey-barrel nose promises more than this wine can deliver. The mouthfeel is somewhat syrupy, the sweet dark fruit flavor grows cloying, and the finish is rather thin. **82** —*C.S. (5/1/2002)*

Pozzi 2001 Pinot Grigio (Delle Venezie) $10. A light, easy-drinking Pinot Grigio, with peach, lime, and fresh herb aromas and flavors. The lemony finish shows fine persistence. **84** —*J.C. (7/1/2003)*

PRADIO

Pradio 1999 Teraje Chardonnay (Friuli Grave) $10. Despite the modest price, this wine needs some time in the glass or in a decanter to open up. It starts off slowly, then builds pear and quince aromas and flavors through the long, tart, minerally finish. **87 Best Buy** —*J.C. (7/1/2003)*

PRIMA & NUOVA CANTINA

Prima & Nuova Cantina 2004 Pinot Grigio (Alto Adige) $12. Mature apple, canned pineapple, and traces of burnt matchstick hit the nose. The mouthfeel is hollow and uneventful. **83** —*M.L. (6/1/2006)*

PRIMA TERRA

Prima Terra 2004 Pinot Grigio (Lazio) $6. Shares the peach, pear, and pineapple characteristics of Grigios from northern Italy. Although the aromas are pretty, the flavors lack a bit of intensity. Still, it features lingering spice on the finish. **85 Best Buy** —*M.L. (2/1/2006)*

PRIMOSIC

Primosic 1997 Gmajne Pinot Grigio (Collio) $18. **85** *(8/1/1999)*

Primosic 2004 I Classici Pinot Grigio (Collio) $16. A fine and well-made white with a silky mouthfeel and attractive fruit aromas including mango, pineapple, and tangerine. It boasts persistent flavors and more fruit notes on the close. **87** —*M.L. (6/1/2006)*

Primosic 2004 Murno Pinot Grigio (Collio) $20. Here's a vineyard-designate Collio Grigio that shows the grape's potential. The wine is surprisingly refined and elegant with a copperish hue and full fruit aromas of melon, banana, and spice. Round and smooth in the mouth with a long, satisfying finish. **89** —*M.L. (6/1/2006)*

PRINCIPE DI CORLEONE

Principe di Corleone 2004 Inzolia (Sicilia) $18. A round, soft, and easy white with stone fruit aromatics and crisp mineral tones that add dimension to the nose. This is an easy-to-drink wine and a classic pairing partner to non-fussy dishes like grilled chicken breast or roasted vegetables. **86** —*M.L. (7/1/2006)*

Principe di Corleone 2002 Nero d'Avola (Sicilia) $18. Very youthful and fruit-forward with an emphasis on blueberries and violets. The finish is nice, not incredibly lengthy, but determined and linear. A nicely packaged Sicilian red with finesse and power. **87** —*M.L. (7/1/2006)*

Principe di Corleone 2003 Red Blend (Sicilia) $18. Nero d'Avola and Merlot are blended to produce a wine that delivers power but lacks complexity. Beyond the red fruit is some moist tobacco and very soft tannins. **86** —*M.L. (7/1/2006)*

Principe di Corleone 2005 White Blend (Alcamo) $18. This is a well-built Catarratto and Insolia blend from the Alcamo zone in Western Sicily that delivers toasted nut, stone fruit, mineral, and some soapy aromas. It has good balance and a zesty, fresh finish. **86** —*M.L. (7/1/2006)*

PRINCIPESSA GAVIA

Principessa Gavia 2004 Cortese (Gavi) $14. Light in weight, but slightly oily in texture, this Gavi packs in the basics: apple, pear, and citrus fruit and a hint of almonds. Dry and citrusy on the finish, making it a candidate for seafood or assorted hors d'oeuvres. **85** —*J.C. (3/1/2006)*

Principessa Gavia 2003 Cortese (Gavi) $12. Wonderfully user-friendly white, balanced equally well to serve on its own or with food. Almond, citrus, and white peach aromas and flavors, a plump, slightly custardy mouthfeel, and it finishes with a refreshing hint of citrus. **87 Best Buy** —*J.C. (11/15/2004)*

Principessa Gavia 2002 Cortese (Gavi) $12. Super-fresh, snappy, lip-smacking and almost sweet. Is there mass appeal written on this wine? You bet, what with sweetness interwoven into the pineapple, green apple, and lime flavor profile. Even the finish has some layers and a band of complexity to accent otherwise pleasurable flavors. **88 Best Buy** —*M.S. (12/15/2003)*

Principessa Gavia 1999 Cortese (Gavi) $18. This 100% Cortese wine has a slight fizz and an almost imperceptibly faint touch of sweetness. Hay and herb aromas open to grapy flavors accented by smoky notes. A crisp mouthfeel and classic Gavi almond, lime, and smoke notes close this pleaser. **87** *(2/1/2001)*

Principessa Gavia 1998 Cortese (Gavi) $11. **85** —*M.S. (4/1/2000)*

PRINCIPI DI SPADAFORA

Principi di Spadafora 2004 Don Pietro Red Blend (Sicilia) $24. An intense blend of Nero d'Avola, Cabernet Sauvignon, and Merlot that beautifully underlines the producer's individualistic winemaking philosophy. There are earthy, iron-like tones with blackberry, spice, and cracked white pepper. The Cabernet portion renders a tight, tannic backbone. **90** —*M.L. (7/1/2006)*

Principi di Spadafora 2004 Monreale Syrah Red Blend (Sicilia) $18. A well-executed Syrah with a small component of Nero d'Avola that exhibits deep ruby youthfulness with notes of cherry, prune, resin, chocolate fudge, and loads of blueberry and blackberry. Its mouthfeel is thick and luscious with dusty tannins, but at the end of the day this is a young, easy wine. **88** —*M.L. (7/1/2006)*

Principi di Spadafora 2002 Sole dei Padri Syrah (Sicilia) $80. If one man is to be named producer of Sicily's best Syrah, that honor must go to Francesco Spadafora. This monumental wine is a thick, inky-black bruiser that delivers a big rush of flavor: thick ripe cherry, tobacco, leather, smoked ham, cracked black pepper, charcoal, cedar wood, and the list goes on. Intense, delightful, and complex, the tannins are soft as silk and the flavors, multilayered. **93 Editors' Choice** —*M.L. (7/1/2006)*

Principi di Spadafora 2002 Syrah Schietto Syrah (Sicilia) $42. Another blockbuster Sicilian Syrah from Spadafora that appears splendidly concentrated and inky with deep and penetrating toasted notes and aromas of prune, leather, pipe tobacco, and granite. The wine sees 12 months of barrique aging, which gives it a silky, tight texture. **92** —*M.L. (7/1/2006)*

Principi di Spadafora 2005 Don Pietro Bianco White Blend (Sicilia) $17. A polished and linear white with standard aromas of peach and white stone backed by an interesting touch of green herb. Part of this Insolia-Catarratto-Grillo blend sees wood, resulting in a fresh wine with a creamy layer. **86** —*M.L. (7/1/2006)*

PRINCIPIANO FERDINANDO

Principiano Ferdinando 1999 Boscareto Nebbiolo (Barolo) $60. Creamy and lush, this wine will be derided in some quarters for being too New

Wave, but to us it strikes a fine balance between lush fruit and lavish oak without losing its identity as Barolo. Drink now–2015. **91** *(4/2/2004)*

PRODUTTORI COLTERENZIO

Produttori Colterenzio 2001 Cornell Chardonnay (Alto Adige) $33. A hugely ripe, wood-dominated Chardonnay, which had 11 months of wood aging. Vanilla and tropical fruit aromas lead to a palate with almonds, apples, and cream flavors, layers of spice, and a rich, soft aftertaste. **89** —*R.V. (7/1/2003)*

Produttori Colterenzio 1997 Pinot Grigio (Alto Adige) $12. **85** *(8/1/1999)*

Produttori Colterenzio 2001 Cornell Pinot Grigio (Alto Adige) $24. A blend of Pinot Grigio with a small percentage of Pinot Bianco that was aged in wood. The result is a full wine with aromas of white flowers, opulent and spicy on the palate, and leaving crisp acidity in the mouth. **89** —*R.V. (7/1/2003)*

Produttori Colterenzio 2001 Lafoa Sauvignon Blanc (Alto Adige) $35. This is a rare example of a successful wood-aged Sauvignon Blanc. The fruit comes from the Lafoa vineyard in Cornaiano. Half the wine has new oak barrel fermentation, the other was kept in stainless steel, cutting the wood flavors to an elegant balance with the floral and mineral flavors. **90** —*R.V. (7/1/2003)*

Produttori Colterenzio 2002 Praedium Sauvignon Blanc (Alto Adige) $19. From the Prail region of Alto Adige, this stunning, intense Sauvignon is full of grassy, herbaceous flavors. It is still young, needing time to lose its grapefruit character and ripen into a fine, aromatic wine. **89** —*R.V. (7/1/2003)*

PRODUTTORI DEL BARBARESCO

Produttori del Barbaresco 2003 Nebbiolo (Langhe) $18. Features a delicate, Burgundy-like nose of roses, herbs, and cherries, followed by a high-alcohol, round mouthfeel and flavors of Maraschino cherries and dusty earth. Ends with firm tannins and a mineral note. Drink now–2010. **87** —*J.C. (3/1/2006)*

Produttori del Barbaresco 2001 Nebbiolo (Barbaresco) $33. A solid effort from Barbaresco's local cooperative, which should augur well for its single-vineyard riservas that will be released later this year. The normale is a fairly priced, somewhat herbal and tannic wine that shows enough cherry fruit and minty complexity to anchor it in the Very Good range. Astringent on the finish, so give it some time in the cellar or drink with rare beef. **87** —*J.C. (3/1/2006)*

Produttori del Barbaresco 1999 Nebbiolo (Barbaresco) $20. The region's famous co-op continues to turn out solid, traditionally styled wines. Although the crus are the ones to seek out, the blended wine is often a good value. This vintage seems built with firmer structure than in the past, finishing hard and tannic. Aromas and flavors are pretty amalgams of cherries, tea leaves, and stone fruits, but will they outlast the tannins? **86** *(4/2/2004)*

PRODUTTORI MOSCATO D'ASTI ASSOCIATI

Produttori Moscato d'Asti Associati 2004 Moscato (Moscato d'Asti) $NA. Flinty mineral tones back up fruit ranging from dried apple skins to kiwi and grapefruit. The froth is less thick than other samples but this wine offers a refreshing and unique lemon soda crispness in the mouth. **87** —*M.L. (12/15/2005)*

PROMESSA

Promessa 2003 Negroamaro (Puglia) $9. The sister project to A-Mano is a touch awkward, with loud aromas of red fruit and Kool-Aid. Luckily it finds its stride in the mouth, where you'll find berry liqueur, chocolate, and pepper. Slightly roasted on the finish. **86 Best Buy** —*M.S. (2/1/2005)*

Promessa 2003 Rosso Salento Red Blend (Apulia) $9. A stunning package sets the bar pretty high for this southern Italian red from winemaker Mark Shannon, who is the hand behind the enormously successful A-Mano wines. Here Primitivo is just 30% of the blend, the rest being Negroamaro. The wine is big, bold, punchy, and generous. Fruit cascades through the mouth, thickly layered with clove and nutmeg and bitter chocolate, like spice on a Thanksgiving ham. Distinctive and powerful, bursting with a spicebox-full of exotic nuances, this wine will light your flavor fuse. **90 Best Buy** —*P.G. (11/15/2004)*

Promessa 2001 Rosso Salento Red Blend (Salento) $8. This perennial value favorite scores again in 2001. It's a young, fruity, sweet wine with just enough snap to ensure balance. Aromas of cured meat, lavender, and leather all signal a wine of class, and the peppy palate pours on the red fruit and candied cinnamon. A blend of Negroamaro and Primitivo that's jammy and easy to quaff. **88 Best Buy** —*M.S. (12/15/2003)*

Promessa 2000 Rosso Salento Red Blend (Puglia) $8. The aromas of red cherries and gingersnaps carry a distinctive hint of bitter almonds. Supple and plush in the mouth, the fleshy black cherry flavors fan out smoothly across the palate. A blend of Negroamaro and Primitivo. **87 Best Buy** *(5/1/2002)*

PROVOLO

Provolo 2001 Red Blend (Valpolicella) $12. There is size to the bouquet, but not too much definition. On the palate, the raspberry and cherry fruit is a bit tart and hollow, but in the same breath it's clean and fresh. Vibrant acids make it seem a bit thinner and more starching than one might wish. **84** *(5/1/2003)*

Provolo 1999 Red Blend (Amarone della Valpolicella) $54. Apple skin aromas are prominent, and the flavor profile runs to cherry. Along the way are nice toast and licorice notes, and the finish carries familiar chocolate and peppery spice characteristics. Solid if not overwhelming. **88** *(11/1/2005)*

Provolo 1997 Red Blend (Amarone della Valpolicella) $49. Interesting aromatics like sandalwood, violets, and bitter herbs make this wine a bit out of the ordinary but no less likable. The palate is fairly rich, yielding Port, kirsch, and pepper in addition to oak. The warming finish is equally rich with buttercream and milk chocolate. With good structure and tannins, there is a lot to like. **89** *(5/1/2003)*

Provolo 1998 Campotorbian Red Blend (Valpolicella Classico Superiore) $19. Deep and dark, with a unique and chameleon-like nose that at first throws off cured meat and then toasted wheat and barrel char. Despite its dark color, the fruit is tart red berries. And the finish is one-dimensional: It's dry and woody, especially for a ripasso. **85** *(5/1/2003)*

PRUNETO

Pruneto 1996 Riserva Sangiovese (Chianti Classico) $28. The juice here seems good, with dark cherry, licorice, and chocolate elements, decent structure, and fine tannins. However, you need to get past a strong sulfur component on the nose that just doesn't yield. **82** *(4/1/2001)*

PRUNOTTO

Prunotto 2003 Fiulot Barbera (Barbera d'Asti) $13. A warm, generous wine with good, meaty, intense fruit, from the Piedmont region of Italy. It shows the accessibility of Barbera, but also its potential richness and concentration. Layers of soft wood and herbs add complexity. In the local dialect, "fiulot" means "young man," and Prunotto, which is owned by Antinori, has chosen the name for the most youthful style of wine in its range. **88 Best Buy** —*R.V. (11/15/2004)*

Prunotto 1997 Pian Romualdo Barbera (Barbera d'Alba) $28. 90 *(4/1/2000)*

Prunotto 1997 Dolcetto (Dolcetto d'Alba) $15. 84 *(4/1/2000)*

Prunotto 2004 Moscato (Moscato d'Asti) $21. An upfront and genuine dessert wine with a refreshing mineral prelude that yields to lush floral and stone fruit roundness. Zippy and slightly tart in the mouth with lots of foam and overall prettiness. **88** —*M.L. (12/15/2005)*

Prunotto 1996 Nebbiolo (Barbaresco) $43. 84 *(9/1/2000)*

Prunotto 1999 Nebbiolo (Barolo) $45. Tar and dried cherry aromas and flavors. This wine boasts a supple, creamy mouthfeel and a finish graced with notes of dark chocolate. Drink now–2010. **86** *(4/2/2004)*

Prunotto 1998 Nebbiolo (Piedmont) $42. The wine has attractive aromas of musky roses and green figs. The fruit is pure, with dusty tannins and flavors of sweet plums and wood. A modern style of wine, which still retains the typical Nebbiolo dried-fruit characters. **91** —*R.V. (11/15/2002)*

Prunotto 1998 Bussia Nebbiolo (Piedmont) $70. Owned by Marchese Antinori of Tuscany, Alfredo Prunotto makes a modern style of Barolo. This is elegant, with ripe sweet fruit on the nose. A smoothly polished wine, it is rich in dark fruit and new wood flavors along with solid tannins. There is power here and the Nebbiolo dryness comes through on the finish. **93** —*R.V. (11/15/2002)*

PUIATTI

Puiatti 2004 Ruttars Pinot Grigio (Collio) $18. Delivers nicely integrated floral and fruity aromas such as acacia, peach, and exotic fruit. None of these elements are very intense and the wine appears simple and clean—although somewhat lean—in the mouth. **85** —*M.L. (6/1/2006)*

PUNSET

Punset 1996 Nebbiolo (Barbaresco) $38. 86 —*J.C. (9/1/2000)*

QUADRA

Quadra 2003 Brut Sparkling Blend (Franciacorta) $35. A nicely layered sparkling wine with fresh fruit and menthol or herb-like notes. Orange zest or tangerine crispness appears on the palate, punctuated by a sour note on the close. **87** —*M.L. (6/1/2006)*

QUADRI

Quadri 2005 Mátraalja Pinot Grigio (Trento) $8. Zippy and fresh, with floral aromas and beautifully underscored mineral notes that reinforce its overall snap and pop. More stone fruit and floral flavors in the mouth are accompanied by mouth-cleansing acidity. **87 Best Buy** —*M.L. (6/1/2006)*

QUERCETO

Querceto 1997 Sangiovese (Chianti Classico) $11. 90 Best Buy *(7/1/2000)*

Querceto 2004 Sangiovese (Chianti) $8. Lightweight but smooth, with open-knit aromas of red fruits. The palate shows more richness than you might expect, with black cherry and dark plums controlling the flavor profile. With meat on its bones and a persistent finish, this is bargain Chianti at its best. **87 Best Buy** —*M.S. (10/1/2006)*

Querceto 2003 Sangiovese (Chianti) $9. Pleasant all the way, starting from the cedar, leather, and dark fruit aromas, to the zippy cherry and raspberry palate, to the clean, spicy finish. Tart, linear, and refreshing, a Chianti in textbook proportions. **88 Best Buy** *(4/1/2005)*

Querceto 2003 Sangiovese (Chianti Classico) $13. Smoky on one hand, but also featuring a touch of burnt grass on the nose. Tart cherry and thin plum flavors with hints of leather and spice comprise the palate. Finishes lemony crisp. **83** *(4/1/2005)*

Querceto 2002 Sangiovese (Chianti Classico) $12. Fairly scattered and unfocused on the nose, with herb, gumdrop, and barrel aromas. Light on the palate, with oak and simple red fruit. Finishes zesty, but on the thin side. **84** —*M.S. (10/1/2004)*

Querceto 2001 Sangiovese (Chianti) $8. Earthy and round, with a saturated hue. In the mouth, berry and plum flavors precede a clean, moderately long finish that scores points for its cleanliness and simplicity. Nothing overtly thrilling but certainly no faults either. It's yet another easy drinking Chianti from the fine '01 vintage. **86 Best Buy** —*M.S. (11/15/2003)*

Querceto 2000 Sangiovese (Chianti Classico) $11. Clean fresh berry aromas lead into a lean, leathery palate with tart cherry fruit and tight, astringent tannins. It isn't a bad wine; but it's definitely lean as a wisp and drying. Undoubtedly it will work best with food. **83** —*M.S. (8/1/2002)*

Querceto 2000 Riserva Sangiovese (Chianti Classico) $20. Starts with heavy sulfuric aromas, which fade to unveil espresso, leather, and chunky fruit. Boysenberry and vanilla flavors are bolstered by a streak of oak-based lemon, while the finish is dry and tight, leaving coffee flavors in its wake. **87** *(4/1/2005)*

Querceto 1996 Riserva Sangiovese (Chianti Classico) $18. The elements of cherry, mint, and cedar on the nose show a touch of age, and the dry cherry fruit on the palate seems to vie with wood for prominence. Overall it's quite angular, but does show some attractive earthy notes and a chalky element on the finish. **84** *(4/1/2001)*

Querceto 1995 Riserva Sangiovese (Chianti Classico) $18. 88 *(7/1/2000)*

QUERCIAVALLE

Querciavalle 1997 Sangiovese (Chianti Classico) $18. There's sweet dark cherry and plum fruit here, but to get to it you need to give the sulfur on the nose time to blow off. When it does, the wait is worth it. A full, lush mouthfeel caresses your palate, and the finish is dry and even. Decant if drinking now, or wait a year or two. **89** *(4/1/2001)*

Querciavalle 1999 Riserva Sangiovese (Chianti Classico) $28. Pungent and peppery, but also short on the nose and throughout. The palate offers herbs and tart cherry, while the one-note finish is gritty. Rather lean and snipped, with a slight pickled quality. **84** *(4/1/2005)*

Querciavalle 1995 Riserva Sangiovese (Chianti Classico) $25. Opens with aromas of red plums, cedar, leather, and meat. Flavors of dark cherry and earth, and a light, bright mouthfeel follow. Finishes dry and even with soft tannins, dark fruit and chocolate. **86** *(4/1/2001)*

QUINTARELLI

Quintarelli 1997 Corvina, Rondinella, Molinara (Amarone della Valpolicella Classico) $300. Big in alcohol at 16% and big in reputation; we liked this wine but did not really find it up to its icon status. The nose shows a bit of volatile acidity as well as a hint of horseradish, but it also delivers fine cherry and sugared cake notes. Rather intense in the mouth, with a touch of cherry skin and grit along with cola. Finishes long and correct. **89** *(11/1/2005)*

Quintarelli 1999 Primofiore Red Blend (Veronese) $32. A clean and easy wine from a venerable producer. While not a blockbuster, Giuseppe Quintarelli has made an earthy, leafy interesting wine with cherry and vanilla characteristics and some leathery qualities. Moderate tannins and a short finish indicate that it's a drink-now type of wine. **86** *(5/1/2003)*

RAIMONDI

Raimondi 1998 Villa Monteleone Corvina, Rondinella, Molinara (Amarone della Valpolicella Classico) $49. Gets off the mark with some murk and earth, but clears up to display aromas of apple skin, horsehide, and dark fruits. Decent weight and only modest tannins create a chunky, almost syrupy personality that fosters flavors of chocolate, liqueur, and coffee. **88** *(11/1/2005)*

Raimondi 1997 Red Blend (Amarone della Valpolicella Classico) $53. A rich, hedonistic wine. The nose is Port-like, with resounding depth in addition to strong scents of prune and chocolate. The palate has an almost Bourbon-like quality to it; it's that rich and warm. And the finish is soft and plush, with bitter chocolate and espresso flavors. **91** *(5/1/2003)*

RAMPOLDI

Rampoldi 2000 Riserva Negroamaro (Copertino) $9. Somewhat spicy but also a bit stewed, so it's odd that it's racy on the palate, with cherry and raspberry flavors. Goes down acidic, so it makes a statement. Touches of root beer and cola help it along. **84** *—M.S. (10/1/2006)*

RASHI

Rashi 2003 Moscato (Moscato d'Asti) $11. Properly floral and orangey on the nose, with lightly sweet pineapple and orange juice flavors. Lacks a bit of vigor on the finish, but decent overall. **83** *—J.C. (4/1/2005)*

Rashi 2002 Moscato (Moscato d'Asti) $11. A pleasant enough wine, with pretty spice aromas. On the palate it's got a strong herbal and citrus quality. Moderate length on the finish. Kosher. **84** *—J.M. (4/3/2004)*

Rashi NV Kosher Moscato (Asti) $12. Neutral at first, and then a bit mealy and dusty. Sweet almost beyond belief, with over-ripe apricot and mango flavors. Lots of sugary sweetness at all points. A dessert wine (kosher) by default. **82** *—M.S. (6/1/2005)*

Rashi 1999 Select Nebbiolo (Barolo) $38. Quite toasty, with powdery tannins and moderate body. The wine holds back on the fruit, with a lean delivery. Herbs and hints of cherries are in evidence. Maybe cellaring will round things out. Kosher. **83** *—J.M. (4/3/2004)*

Rashi NV Pinot Brut Kosher Pinot Blanc (Italy) $12. This kosher bubbly is unusual in that it offers doughy aromas that morph into fruit blossom and honey. But it's really tart stuff once you taste it. Sour, in fact, with nothing but lemon and grapefruit on the palate and finish. **82** *—M.S. (6/1/2005)*

RE MANFREDI

Re Manfredi 2000 Aglianico (Aglianico del Vulture) $30. Starts off with a wonderfully fragrant nose, complex and bursting with floral, anise. and cherry notes. Firmly structured on the palate, where it adds elements of plum, leather, tobacco, and black pepper. Best with rare beef now, or hold three years and let the tannins mellow a bit. **90** *(8/1/2005)*

REMO FARINA

Remo Farina 2000 Red Blend (Amarone della Valpolicella Classico) $40. A touch piercing and spicy on the nose, with sweaty leather and wood notes. The flavor profile revolves around zesty red fruits like raspberry and strawberry, while the back end is mildly toasty. **86** *(11/1/2005)*

Remo Farina 1998 Red Blend (Amarone della Valpolicella Classico) $34. Menthol aromas suggest some barrique aging. And in the mouth, you get some green oak along with sweet cherry fruit. The mouthfeel is generated by firm tannins, and the finish is oaky, with some chocolate and pie cherry. At this stage, wood is a dominant feature. We think that will fade in about five years. **89** *(5/1/2003)*

Remo Farina 1998 Corte Conti Cavalli Red Blend (Rosso del Veronese) $45. Seemingly mature beyond its relative youth. There's a browning color and some earthy, chocolaty aromas to the nose. The palate is intense, with dried cherry, plum, nutmeg, and vanilla. A big and long espresso-tinged finish is the final act. Drink sooner rather than later. **88** *(5/1/2003)*

Remo Farina 2000 Montecorna Red Blend (Valpolicella) $19. With toasted aromas as well as whiffs of bacon, leather, cola, and hickory, this offers a mighty fine nose. The palate is equally impressive: It's rich and meaty, with expressive cherry fruit and lots of spice. The chocolaty, firmly tannic finish completes this rich wine. **90 Editors' Choice** *(5/1/2003)*

Remo Farina 2000 Ripasso Red Blend (Valpolicella Classico Superiore) $13. Barrel aromas are front and center, and basic sweet red fruit, with just enough oak and spice, make for a pleasurable drinking experience. The finish boasts ample acidity and some modest oak notes. **87 Best Buy** *(5/1/2003)*

Remo Farina 1997 Ripasso Red Blend (Valpolicella Classico Superiore) $12. 82 *—M.N. (12/31/2000)*

Remo Farina 1999 Soave Classico Superiore White Blend (Soave) $NA. The nose mixes aromas of Wrigley's spearmint gum and peaches. The body is on the full side, with bright white stone fruit flavors, particularly white peaches. Some grapefruit works it's way in there too. Although it's fairly non-descript, it offers all the traditional flavors of this regional white wine and vital acidity. Finsihes warm and clean. **86** *—M.S. (1/1/2004)*

RENATO RATTI

Renato Ratti 1997 Barbera (Barbera di Piemonte) $14. 86 *(4/1/2000)*

Renato Ratti 1997 Torriglione Barbera (Barbera d'Alba) $14. 88 Best Buy *(4/1/2000)*

Renato Ratti 1998 Dolcetto (Dolcetto d'Alba) $14. 87 *(4/1/2000)*

Renato Ratti 1998 Conca Marcenasco Nebbiolo (Piedmont) $62. Ratti's Conca single-vineyard wine is made only in selected vintages. Aged in small French and large Slavonian oak barrels, the wine is full of aromas of violets and old-fashioned roses. The palate is deliciously open, with ripe fruits, flavors of dark cherries, and plums. A dry, tannic layer gives it structure, the acidity gives it freshness. **95 Editors' Choice** *—R.V. (11/15/2002)*

Renato Ratti 1998 Marcenasco Nebbiolo (Piedmont) $40. This is the third wine Ratti makes from its Marcenasco vineyard at La Morra. Aromas of fine ripe fruit and a hint of truffles lead to powerful, rich fruit flavors with layers of tarry dryness. A great, ripe wine, destined for long aging. **93** *—R.V. (11/15/2002)*

Renato Ratti 1998 Rocche Marcenasco Nebbiolo (Piedmont) $60. Pietro Ratti makes wines from vineyards around the Abbey of the Annunziata, locally called the Marcenasco. This single-vineyard Rocche is deep brick red in color. With its brooding black fruit aromas and firm, dry tannins over immense fruit flavors, it is a huge wine, showing great potential. It should keep forever. **96 Cellar Selection** *—R.V. (11/15/2002)*

ITALY

RENZO MASI

Renzo Masi 2003 Sangiovese (Chianti) $8. Bulky and awkward at first, with grapey, powdery aromas. A touch green and funky at its core, but with enough surrounding black cherry and blackberry to hang in there. Finishes with firm tannins. **84 Best Buy** *(4/1/2005)*

Renzo Masi 1999 Sangiovese (Chianti Rufina) $8. A muted nose of red berries and earth opens to an even palate of cherry fruit with mineral and cocoa accents. This smoothly textured, lighter-styled wine is a good choice for antipasto, served a little cool. Still very young, it should be better in six months, too. **85 Best Buy** *(4/1/2001)*

Renzo Masi 1997 Riserva Sangiovese (Chianti) $10. Plum and anise surround the berry fruit in the bouquet of this stylish medium-weight bottling. There's a slightly chalky feel to the palate. Cherries, with more anise notes and a dry finish of powdery tannins, close this attractive value. Best now through 2002. **87 Best Buy** *(4/1/2001)*

RICCARDO ARRIGONI

Riccardo Arrigoni 2003 Ampelos Vermentino (Colli di Luni) $17. This Ligurian Vermentino is very clear and light, almost the polar opposite of the meaty, warmer styles that come from Sardegna or the Maremma. But still it pours on lime, mineral, and stony notes, and ultimately it's a healthy, crisp wine that will cut through vinaigrettes and garlic like a hot knife through butter. **86** *—M.S. (8/1/2004)*

RICCI

Ricci 2001 Brunello (Brunello di Montalcino) $52. Tart cherry, plum, strawberry, coffee, leather, and resiny-plasticy notes greet the nose. Generous red apple and spice in the mouth but also youthful red berry and lush field flowers. Crisp and structured in the mouth with a softer, rounder endnote. **92** *(4/1/2006)*

RIECINE

Riecine 1998 Sangiovese (Chianti Classico) $23. Deep berry aromas accented by chocolate and multiple spices provide an inviting opening to this sturdy wine. The mouthfeel is full, and here the wine shows a much toastier, oak-driven profile than suggested by the bouquet. Lots of charcoal, licorice and earth flavors follow on the long, evenly tannic finish. **87** *(4/1/2001)*

Riecine 1997 Riserva Sangiovese (Chianti Classico) $35. Opaque and very dark in color and flavor, toasty oak is handsomely wrapped around the black-cherry and plum fruit. Shows a slight animal note. Well textured and full, almost viscous, in the mouth, it finishes long with a nice blend of black-licorice, cherry and clove notes. **90** *(4/1/2001)*

RISECCOLI

Riseccoli 1998 Sangiovese (Chianti Classico) $18. Black cherry, cocoa, and toast mark the nose of this very dark and refined wine. The supple, appealing mouthfeel displays a similar flavor profile, and it closes with smooth tannins, tart black fruits, and an espresso note. This example of new-wave Chianti is done with style and even a sensuous note. **88** *(4/1/2001)*

Riseccoli 1997 Riserva Sangiovese (Chianti Classico) $26. Quite full and very New World in style, this is a fruit and oak-loaded wine with a creamy texture. Plum, vanilla, cocoa, and cedar work in harmony on the nose and palate to create a supple, elegant impression. Finishes long and very dark, with fine but firm tannins and black chocolate and espresso notes. Very approachable, but has the structure to last as well. **90** *(4/1/2001)*

RIVALTA

Rivalta NV Brut Convivio Rivalta Prosecco (Prosecco di Valdobbiadene) $18. Very citrusy, with freshly squeezed lemon-lime flavors that leave room for more delicate floral overtones. Perky, snappy, and fresh, with not too long a finish. **86** *—M.L. (6/1/2006)*

Rivalta NV Incontri Extra Dry Prosecco (Prosecco di Valdobbiadene) $18. Intensely floral, with toasted almond, green apple, and peach notes backed by talc powder and mineral. Smooth and refreshing on the palate, with good persistence. **87** *—M.L. (6/1/2006)*

RIVE DELLA CHIESA

Rive Della Chiesa NV Frizzante Prosecco (Colli Trevigiani) $12. Extremely apple-like on the nose—like fresh Golden Delicious, but with some floral notes mingled in as well. Lightweight and refreshing, this is a good palate primer for the holidays. **85** *—J.C. (12/15/2004)*

Rive Della Chiesa NV Frizzante Prosecco (Colli Trevigiani) $10. Light and apple-driven, and clean. The flavors are like lime lollipops and orange juice, which may sound unappealing but that's not the case. The wine tastes good, but ultimately it's rather simple and basic. But if you like a fresh bubbly with some candied sweetness and decent balance, you get that here. **85** *—M.S. (6/1/2003)*

Rive Della Chiesa NV Spumante Extra Dry Prosecco (Montello e Colli Asolani) $12. Dry and dusty, with an aromatic note of white pepper. The palate is fruity and sweet, but it's also got some complexity going for it. The flavors are well-blended and the grapefruit notes are ripe and sweet rather than tart. And the finish is pleasantly dry, with licorice notes. **87** *—M.S. (6/1/2003)*

Rive Della Chiesa NV Spumante Extra Dry Prosecco (Montello e Colli Asolani) $14. Austere and minerally on the nose, with hints of yeastiness and citrus. This is much less fruity and floral than most Proseccos, yielding instead flavors of stones and limes. The slightly chalky finish is clean and refreshing. **87** *—J.C. (12/15/2004)*

RIVETTO

Rivetto 2001 Zio Nando Barbera (Barbera d'Alba) $20. Smooth and stylish, with cedar notes and energetic fruit that falls toward raspberry and cherry. Quite delicious and full of verve; it jumps from the glass, showing acidity and pizzazz before fading gracefully. A bit of oak and licorice on the finish is good for an extra bump in character. **89** *—M.S. (12/15/2003)*

Rivetto 2002 Ercolino Dolcetto (Dolcetto d'Alba) $15. Blackberry, licorice, and mint aromas are followed by plum and other red fruit flavors. Quite fleshy on the back end, and admittedly a bit heavy. Still, there's good cherry flavor and ripe tannins. **86** *—M.S. (12/15/2003)*

Rivetto 1999 Nebbiolo (Barbaresco) $30. Chalk dust and leather aromas set this wine apart from the ordinary, and then it picks up notes of citrus fruits, chocolate, and cherries. It's supple and mouth-filling, ending with juicy acids and a soft dose of tannins. Drink now–2015. **91 Editors' Choice** *(4/2/2004)*

Rivetto 1999 Giulin Nebbiolo (Barolo) $38. A pretty, delicate, feminine style of Barolo, with minty, herbal hints layered over black cherry fruit. The mouthfeel is supple, never overpowering, finishing with soft, chewy tannins. Drink now–2010. **88** *(4/2/2004)*

Rivetto 1999 Leon Nebbiolo (Barolo) $45. Fruity and kirsch-like, this is a big, supple fruit bomb of a Barolo that should firm up and develop extra complexity in time. For now, it's a bit raw and unformed. Drink 2008–2015. **87** *(4/2/2004)*

Rivetto 2001 Lirano Nebbiolo (Nebbiolo d'Alba) $11. Sharp black cherry aromas carry notes of cocoa and leather. Typically tight and tannic, with flavors of meaty plum, earth, and cherry zest. Modest on the finish and clean. Also very drying from front to back. **85** *—M.S. (12/15/2003)*

RIZZI

Rizzi 2000 Nebbiolo (Barbaresco) $42. Herbal at first, marked by green notes that at times seem dominant. Yet the fruit is plump and mouth-filling, with sour cherry flavors that build in intensity on the mouth-watering finish. Drink 2008–2015. **89** *(4/2/2004)*

Rizzi 2000 Boito Nebbiolo (Barbaresco) $45. This plump, moderately rich wine impressed with its complex scents of leather, asphalt, and fennel that accent plum and cherry fruit. Turns chewy and tarry on the finish, suggesting decent longevity; try after 2008. **92** *(4/2/2004)*

Rizzi 2000 Fondetta Nebbiolo (Barbaresco) $45. This oddball bundle of flavors contrasts medicinal cherry-herb notes with leather and raisins. Finishes firm, with hints of tart, sour cherry fruit. Drink 2010–2020. **86** *(4/2/2004)*

ROBERTO COSIMI

Roberto Cosimi 2001 Beato Brunello (Brunello di Montalcino) $30. Made by Il Poggiolo's Rodolfo Cosimi, this wine is loaded with vanilla, floral intensity, berry fruit, cigar box, anise seed, roasted espresso, and an unexpected twist of orange peel. Firm tannins with cinnamon, clove, and a smoky finish. Ripe, full, and immediately drinkable. **91 Editors' Choice** *(4/1/2006)*

Roberto Cosimi 2001 Podere il Poggiolo Brunello (Brunello di Montalcino) $50. Young Rodolfo Cosimi carries forth the legacy of his winemaker father, Roberto, with this spectacularly expressive and elegant wine. Endless layers of aromas: cedar wood, cherry, forest berry, mint tea, black licorice, dried spices, and vanilla. Long finish, lip-smacking, firmly tannic and ageworthy. **93 Editors' Choice** *(4/1/2006)*

ROCCA

Rocca 2000 Mitico Red Blend (Salento) $22. Lots of alcohol as well as a syrupy, sweet red that is so rich and unctuous that it's tough to sip. For the prune flavor and outright size it's almost worth taking a look. But beware. **83** —*M.S. (10/1/2004)*

ROCCA DELLE MACIE

Rocca delle Macìe 1997 Ser Gioveto Cabernet Sauvignon (Toscana) $30. This wine is big and burly, yet also velvety, with cassis and dark tea and tobacco aromas and flavors. There's plenty of black fruit, licorice, and cocoa—all wrapped in toasty oak—and the fine fruit-acid-tannin balance here portends a long life. Hold for four years; will keep a long time. **92 Cellar Selection** *(8/1/2001)*

Rocca delle Macìe 2000 Roccato Cabernet Sauvignon-Sangiovese (Toscana) $46. Deeply colored, with intense crude oil, black plum, and tobacco aromas. The palate is chunky as can be, with dark plum, blackberry, and char. Where this one steers off course is on the mouthfeel, where extruding tannins create a raw, scratchy feel on the insides of one's cheeks. **85** —*M.S. (9/1/2006)*

Rocca delle Macìe 2003 Sangiovese (Chianti Classico) $16. Perfectly nice but a little heavy, with low-to-medium acidity and a stout mouthfeel. Along the way there's rubber, violet, and berry aromas as well as chewy cherry and raspberry flavors. Modest on the finish, with easy tannins. **87** —*M.S. (10/1/2006)*

Rocca delle Macìe 2002 Sangiovese (Chianti Classico) $16. The red fruit on the nose conjures memories of lollipops and/or Jell-O, and there's just enough herbal rusticity to offset the wine's candied nature. In the mouth, plum, raspberry, and black cherry flavors are textbook typical, while the finish is round and solid. **86** *(4/1/2005)*

Rocca delle Macìe 1998 Sangiovese (Chianti Classico) $13. This textbook Chianti is medium weight and shows good fruit. Classically styled, the tart cherry and chocolate elements are supported by good acidity and not overwhelmed by oak. Firm tannins on the dusty cocoa finish round out this solid 1998. **87** *(8/1/2001)*

Rocca delle Macìe 1999 Campomaccione Sangiovese (Morellino di Scansano) $14. This solid Sangiovese-based red from the southwestern area of Tuscany is lighter, but more evenly textured than Rocca delle Macìe's Rubizzo. The black cherry, slate, and leather aromas and flavors are on the mark, as are the firm tannins on the moderately long finish. **87 Best Buy** *(8/1/2001)*

Rocca delle Macìe 2000 Riserva Sangiovese (Chianti Classico) $22. More herbal and spicy than fruity, as the nose shows cumin, and molasses in spades. Seems a touch stewed, with flavors of black-cherry jam, dates and brown sugar. A heavyweight in that the palate is soft and the body creamy. **86** *(4/1/2005)*

Rocca delle Macìe 1998 Riserva Sangiovese (Chianti Classico) $18. Here is a popular winery that just keeps on producing attractive, well-priced wines. This Riserva 1998 manages to combine soft, quaffable fruit with generous, almost opulent richness. There's something brooding about the firm tannins and tarry flavors, but the fruit is just deliciously ripe. **90** —*R.V. (8/1/2002)*

Rocca delle Macìe 1997 Riserva Sangiovese (Chianti Classico) $21. The cherry aroma of this smooth and well-balanced wine is graced by tobac-co, spice, orange, and cedar accents. Black tea flavors mark the palate, and it closes dry and spicy, with firm tannins. Will improve over the next two or three years. **89** *(8/1/2001)*

Rocca delle Macìe 2000 Riserva Di Fizzano Sangiovese (Chianti Classico) $29. On the border of overdone, this is one intense ripe, pruney wine that carries just enough acid and tannin to rank as a crowd pleaser. Secondary flavors or root beer, pepper, raisin, and dried herbs are luring, while the smooth finish is graced by leather and tea. Really settles in after ten minutes of airing. **90** *(4/1/2005)*

Rocca delle Macìe 1997 Riserva di Fizzano Sangiovese (Chianti Classico) $25. Ripe black cherry aromas with cedar and clove accents open this big yet supple wine. A mouthful of licorice and plum, wrapped in toasty menthol oak, follows. Bright acidity keeps the supple texture from becoming flabby. Full tannins and tart black plum flavors on the finish promise a great life. Best held for two or three years. **90** *(8/1/2001)*

Rocca delle Macìe 1997 Roccato Sangiovese (Toscana) $25. From the cherry, violet, and tobacco nose through the full-flavored palate, this wine hits the right notes. The flavors follow the aromas, the finish is long and polished, with firm, ultra-fine tannins. Inviting now, it will really shine after 2003. **92 Editors' Choice** *(8/1/2001)*

Rocca delle Macìe 2001 Rubizzo Sangiovese (Sangiovese di Toscana) $12. Aromas of tobacco, field greens, and mint gum drops emerge, and all together they make a nice bouquet. The palate is peppy as it deals cherry candy and plenty of pulsing red fruit. Has a sweet, snappy, acid-packed finish. **86** —*M.S. (11/15/2003)*

Rocca delle Macìe 1999 Rubizzo Sangiovese (Toscana) $12. There's nice depth and a slight rusticity to the black cherry and licorice aromas and flavors. This Sangiovese Grosso-based wine has 5% Merlot in the blend, which adds a softening touch. Offers good body and length for a value red, and the warm, spicy finish shows clove and sweet-and-sour fruit notes. **87 Best Buy** *(8/1/2001)*

Rocca delle Macìe 2000 Ser Gioveto Sangiovese (Toscana) $42. Slightly rustic but still polished. The nose is toasty and full of bramble, spice, and zesty red fruit. Rich and meaty in the mouth, where exotic but clear flavors of berries, toast, and vanilla draw you in. Fairly lush in the long run, with commendable acidity and overall balance. A fine Tuscan red. **91** —*M.S. (9/1/2006)*

Rocca delle Macìe 2000 Tenuta Sant'Alfonso Sangiovese (Chianti Classico) $23. Leather, tart cherry, and green tobacco form a bouquet that's entirely familiar. Flavors of marinated meat, cherry, plum, and citrus are sizable and good, albeit not particularly developed or refined. Dry tannins and citrusy acidity finish things off. **86** *(4/1/2005)*

Rocca delle Macìe 1999 Ser Gioveto Sangiovese Grosso (Toscana) $42. Graham cracker, raisin, and citrus peel match wits with dark fruit aromas; ultimately the bouquet is quite nice. Forward and full in the mouth, with black cherry and dark plum flavors. With no holes and plenty of ripeness, this is a fine wine that will appeal to those who like their bold fruit. **90** —*M.S. (9/1/2006)*

Rocca delle Macìe 2003 Vernaccia (Vernaccia di San Gimignano) $11. Light in color, with aromas of pear and applesauce. Fairly soft and bland on the palate, with a hint of white pepper. Also shows some apple and white grapefruit. **84** —*M.S. (8/1/2004)*

Rocca delle Macìe 1999 Vernaccia (Vernaccia di San Gimignano) $12. Herb, white peach, and hay aromas and flavors show in this round, fairly soft Tuscan white. Slightly fuller than the Orvieto, it finishes with good length and a touch of bitter almond. **85** *(8/1/2001)*

Rocca delle Macìe 1999 White Blend (Orvieto Classico) $10. A straight-ahead white containing melon, herb, and peach elements. This evenly textured wine is not at all sweet, with a slight mineral note to the citrus and dry stone fruit flavors and a medium-length finish that's redolent of lemon peel. **84** *(8/1/2001)*

ROCCA DI CASTAGNOLI

Rocca di Castagnoli 1998 Sangiovese (Chianti Classico) $13. After some sulfur blows off, dark cherry aromas with leather accents come forward. This wine has a bright, slightly expansive feel in the mouth, and plum and toast notes around the cherry core. There's decent length to the dry, mildly pepper-and-licorice-tinged finish. **87** (4/1/2001)

ROCCA DI FABBRI

Rocca di Fabbri 1999 Red Blend (Sagrantino di Montefalco) $35. Chalk, and leather aromas are dry and earthy. The flavors of cherries with tar and dusty oak lead to a rich juicy finish with big, but non aggressive tannins. **88** —C.S. (2/1/2002)

Rocca di Fabbri 2000 Rosso di Montefalco Red Blend (Montefalco) $20. 90 —M.S. (2/1/2003)

Rocca di Fabbri 2001 Sagrantino (Sagrantino di Montefalco) $NA. Under this leadership of the Vitali sisters, Rocca di Fabbri has released a gorgeous ruby red Sagrantino with loads of spice, tar, dried prunes, and vanilla. This grape makes some of the most beautifully-colored wines in Italy. Twelve months in stainless steel and 18 months in wood, of which 70% in oak and 30% in barrique. **88** —M.L. (9/1/2005)

Rocca di Fabbri 2000 Satiro Sangiovese (Colli Martani) $12. 88 Best Buy —M.S. (2/1/2003)

ROCCA DI MONTEGROSSI

Rocca di Montegrossi 2001 Sangiovese (Chianti Classico) $23. The bouquet is good, with aromas of rubber, spice, leather, and plum-style fruit. Seems a little grippy and starchy on the palate, where big tannins take over and mask the rest of the show. Ultra-firm and tannic on the back end, where more grab than flavor is on display. **86** (4/1/2005)

Rocca di Montegrossi 1998 Sangiovese (Chianti Classico) $18. This full-bodied, weighty wine displays a bouquet of dark cherries, cinnamon-clove spice, and toast. Quite dry on the palate, it has dense fruit, but fairly high acidity and plenty of oak. The finish shows tart cherry flavors and big, fairly angular tannins. Cellar for three years. **88** (4/1/2001)

Rocca di Montegrossi 1999 Geremia Sangiovese (Toscana) $35. Round and minty up front, with stylish dark fruit aromas and a touch of char. An intense wine with deep cherry, toast, and coffee flavors. The finish is ripe and moderately tannic, with herb notes and a lot of bitter chocolate. Sangiovese with 7% Merlot. Should age nicely through 2010. **91** —M.S. (9/1/2006)

Rocca di Montegrossi 1998 Riserva Sangiovese (Chianti Classico) $NA. 85 —R.V. (8/1/2002)

Rocca di Montegrossi 1997 San Marcellino Sangiovese (Chianti Classico) $30. A solid package, offering cherry, coffee, and chocolate aromas, a substantial but smooth mouthfeel and cherry flavors with licorice accents. The long finish displays hearty tannins along with licorice and black plum flavors. This can use a few years to polish its rusticity. **88** (4/1/2001)

Rocca di Montegrossi 1999 Vigneto San Marcellino Sangiovese (Chianti Classico) $40. Dark and roasted on the nose, but short on the palate. The tannins are green and rock-hard, yet there's some meatiness and plum-based darkness to the flavors. In the end, however, it's a touch rough and unyielding. **84** (4/1/2005)

ROCCHE CASTAMAGNA

Rocche Castamagna 1999 Annunziata Barbera (Barbera d'Alba) $17. With its deep, tart-sweet black plum aromas and flavors wrapped in a toasty oak blanket, this is appealing, modern-style Barbera. The grape's native acidity is well-tamed, but enough remains to make it a great food match. Has good tannic structure, yet has immediate appeal. Finishes long, dark, and handsome. **88** —M.M. (9/1/2001)

Rocche Castamagna 1997 Annunziata Barbera (Barbera d'Alba) $20. 86 (4/1/2000)

Rocche Castamagna 2000 Annunziata 2000 Barbera (Barbera d'Alba) $20. Sweet and basic, with a can't-miss note of candy in the center. Decent acids and tannins ensure that it doesn't come across flabby or out of whack. However, in terms of flavor and style, it's average. **84** —M.S. (12/15/2003)

Rocche Castamagna 1996 Rocche delle Rocche Barbera (Barbera d'Alba) $27. 89 (4/1/2000)

Rocche Castamagna 1998 Dolcetto (Dolcetto d'Alba) $14. 82 (4/1/2000)

Rocche Castamagna 2001 Dolcetto (Dolcetto d'Alba) $13. Sweet and attractive, with everything in its proper place. Dusty red fruit and gum-drop aromas draw you in, where you come face to face with juicy, plump, berry fruit, a tasty, chocolaty finish and a layer or two of complexity. With zest, power, and poise, this wine hits the style head-on. **90 Best Buy** —M.S. (12/15/2003)

Rocche Castamagna 1999 Dolcetto (Dolcetto d'Alba) $13. No oak is used on this full- fruited red. Just a hint of chocolate-cocoa is evident, but what's on display are rich, dry cherry flavors and a ripe, supple mouthfeel. Though it doesn't have great length, it offers lots of flavor and feel—a great wine to share with friends. **87** —M.M. (9/1/2001)

Rocche Castamagna 1998 Bricco Francesco Nebbiolo (Barolo) $50. Seems a bit leathery and potentially dull at first, but it really opens up nicely to reveal sweetly ripe black cherries and dried figs. Picks up hints of oranges and tea leaves on the finish. Drink 2005–2015. **87** (4/2/2004)

Rocche Castamagna 1998 Rocche Dell'Annunziata Nebbiolo (Barolo) $39. Seems to be nearing maturity already, with aromas of leather, dates, and herbs leading into a round, rich palate. Plum, earth, and tobacco notes build in intensity on the supple, spicy finish. Drink now–2010. **90** (4/2/2004)

ROMOLO BUCCELLATO

Romolo Buccellato 1999 Tre Vigne Frappato (Sicilia) $11. Light in color, with mature, almost oxidized aromas to go with notes of matchstick, caramel, cranberry, and bitter greens. Tart and lean goes the palate, while it finishes equally thin and short. **82** —M.S. (12/15/2003)

Romolo Buccellato 1999 Il Cigno Nero White Blend (Cerasuolo di Vittoria) $10. Aromas of cherry, berries, and graham cracker; has red licorice and raspberry flavors, and a warm, balanced finish. This wine is well proportioned, with solid length, ample body, and pleasant fruit. **87 Best Buy** —M.S. (10/1/2003)

RONCHI DI GIANCARLO ROCCA

Ronchi di Giancarlo Rocca 1999 Nebbiolo (Barbaresco) $40. Shows sturdy dried fruit—dates and prunes—but also fresher notes of cherries and orange peel along with a large helping of rich earthy complexity. Plump on the palate, but firm on the finish, where it shows ample tannins. Try in 2010 and beyond. **92** (4/2/2004)

RONCHI DI MANZANO

Ronchi di Manzano 2004 Pinot Grigio (Colli Orientali del Friuli) $16. A somewhat clumsy and disjointed wine with sulfur, matchstick, and green notes that don't seem to blow off. It's not very exciting in the mouth either. **82** —M.L. (2/1/2006)

Ronchi di Manzano 1999 Colli Orientale del Friuli Superiore Tocai (Colli Orientali del Friuli) $NA. 91 —M.N. (12/31/2000)

RONCO BLANCHIS

Ronco Blanchis 2004 Pinot Grigio (Collio) $17. A wine with a strong personality. On the upside is its crisp finish that is lively, long, and persistent. On the downside is the wine's nose, which is reminiscent of multivitamin tablets or chalk dust and won't appeal to everyone. **85** —M.L. (2/1/2006)

RONCO DE TASSI

Ronco de Tassi 1997 Pinot Grigio (Collio) $15. 84 (8/1/1999)

RONCO DEI PINI

Ronco Dei Pini 2004 Pinot Grigio (Collio) $16. A satisfactory Pinot Grigio with lemon-lime, mineral notes, and dried field grass. A bit neutral and watery in the mouth, this wine would pair well with smoked cheese or sun-dried tomato pasta. At 13.5% alcohol, you'll feel the heat too. **84** —M.L. (2/1/2006)

RONCO DEL GELSO

Ronco del Gelso 1999 Chardonnay (Friuli) $21. This medium-weight wine flows effortlessly from start to finish, blending aromas of smoke and nuts with a citrusy core. Picks up savory nutty, cheesy notes (like a good Gruyère) on the long finish. **88** —J.C. (7/1/2003)

ITALY

Ronco del Gelso 2004 Pinot Grigio (Isonzo del Friuli) $25. Steel-tank maturation renders a fresh and crisp wine with lychee and passion fruit, kiwi, and pear. **87** —M.L. (2/1/2006)

Ronco del Gelso 2004 Sot Lis Rivis Pinot Grigio (Isonzo del Friuli) $22. Six months of oak aging have imparted a dense and creamy consistency. The only element out of place is the nose, which delivers a blast of multivitamins that might not appeal to everyone. **86** —M.L. (2/1/2006)

RONCO DEL GNEMIZ

Ronco del Gnemiz 2003 Sauvignon (Colli Orientali del Friuli) $23. Interesting on the nose because it mixes sweet, spicy elements with more standard citrus and mineral. Fairly ripe and rich across the palate, where melon, pineapple, and honey flavors run sweet. Has a bit of pop to the finish but not a ton. Hefty in terms of weight. **87** (7/1/2005)

RONCO DELLE BETULLE

Ronco delle Betulle 1997 Pinot Grigio (Colli Orientali del Friuli) $21. 85 (8/1/1999)

ROSA DEL GOLFO

Rosa Del Golfo 1997 Portulano Red Blend (Salento) $15. Distinctive gamey, cigar box and saddle leather aromas give this wine rustic appeal. It's fat and a bit tannic in the mouth with unpolished leather, tobacco, and cherry flavors. Well-structured, it's just a bit low in acidity but finishes nicely with lingering leather and tobacco flavors. **88** —J.F. (5/1/2002)

Rosa Del Golfo 1999 Scaliere Red Blend (Salento) $10. Some slightly skunky aromas give way to orange, anise, and earth. Cranberry, orange, and chocolate flavors are tartly appealing, but there's a tannic edge and a chalkiness that muffles the nuances. **83** —J.F. (5/1/2002)

ROTARI

Rotari NV Arte Italiana Champagne Blend (Trento) $11. 83 (7/1/2000)

Rotari NV Arte Italiana Brut Champagne Blend (Trento) $11. Rotari's non-vintage bubbly places the emphasis on fruit, not yeasty, toasty elements. Pear and lemon curd notes glide into a soft, easy finish. **85** (6/1/2005)

Rotari NV Arte Italiana Brut Champagne Blend (Trento) $11. This wine is 90% Chardonnay and 10% Pinot Noir. It's fresh and fragrant, just sweet enough to draw you in. The fruit, however, is on the leaner, tighter side of things, and the feel across the palate is high-toned. With a touch more richness it would be friendlier. **86 Best Buy** —M.S. (12/31/2002)

Rotari NV Blanc de Noir Brut Champagne Blend (Trentino) $11. An attractive pinkish-gold color announces the full, attractive juice of this Blanc de Noirs. Apple, hay, and toast flavors, plus an even, fairly full mouthfeel and long finish with dry, appley flavors wrap up the neat package. **87 Best Buy** —M.M. (12/31/2001)

Rotari NV Blanc de Noir Brut Champagne Blend (Trentino) $11. 87 Best Buy —M.S. (12/15/2000)

Rotari NV Blanc de Noir Brut Rose Champagne Blend (Trento) $11. Smoky and toasty, but lean. The palate is sour, with a heavy shot of lime pith. The tangy, thin finish doesn't bring it back from the edge. Lean and mean. **80** —M.S. (12/31/2002)

Rotari NV Brut Champagne Blend (Trento) $11. 86 —S.H. (12/15/2000)

Rotari 1997 Brut Riserva Champagne Blend (Trento) $15. Seductive flower and pear aromas create a pretty nose. The mouth is solid although not terribly lively, with distinct orange and apple flavors. The finish is dry and chalky, with a tight grip and mouth-coating viscosity. **87** —M.S. (12/31/2002)

Rotari 1995 Brut Riserva Champagne Blend (Trento) $15. 87 Best Buy (7/1/2000)

Rotari 1995 Brut Riserva Champagne Blend (Trentino) $15. Full apple aromas with minty accents open this vintage bottling and lead to a dry, lime-mint-chalk palate. The bead is fine, and only lack of a firmer mouthfeel keeps this from being a more serious sparkler, but the softness undoubtedly has wide appeal. A decently long, dry, green apple finish closes it nicely. **86** —M.M. (12/31/2001)

Rotari 2000 Riserva Brut Champagne Blend (Trento) $14. Pungent and aggressive. The nose offers hints of hard cider and toast, while the palate is crisp and fresh. Good mouthfeel, but lacks depth of flavor. **84** —M.S. (6/1/2005)

Rotari NV Arte Italiana Brut Chardonnay (Trento) $11. Aromas of vanilla, pear, and banana are light and sweet, almost like a glazed doughnut might smell. Apple and melon carry the palate, while the fresh finish is fruity and a little bit sharp. **85** —M.S. (12/15/2004)

Rotari NV Arte Italiana Brut Chardonnay (Trentino) $11. This pleasant, straightforward sparkler, displays a steady bead and an even, soft mousse. Mild apple, earth, and plum aromas, and crisper green apple flavors have appeal, and it never descends to sweetness or mushiness. Not complex, but on target. **84** —M.M. (12/31/2001)

Rotari 1999 Riserva Brut Chardonnay (Trento) $15. Dry and lively, with some soda and light toast to the nose. Spunky on the palate, with tangerine as the lead flavor. Finishes clean and aggressive, with some lemony tartness. **85** —M.S. (12/15/2004)

Rotari NV Blanc de Noir Pinot Noir (Trento) $11. Pink in color, with a light, fading bubble bead. Simple in terms of aromatics, showing a hint of peach and berry. Zesty stone fruit flavors are offset by some drying soda cracker notes. Finishes clean and zesty. **86 Best Buy** —M.S. (12/15/2004)

Rotari NV Arte Italiana Sparkling Blend (Trento) $11. This smells and tastes very much like a still Chardonnay, with aromas and flavors of apple and peach, smoke and toast. And why shouldn't it? It's 90% Chardonnay, with the balance Pinot Noir. It is lighter in weight than a still wine, and finishes pleasantly tart. **86 Best Buy** —J.C. (12/31/2003)

Rotari NV Arte Italiana Sparkling Blend (Trento) $11. Festive and less formal, this is a luminous sparkler with ripe melon, peach, and toasted nutty notes that hits all the right marks. Nicely tart on the close with clean flavors and tight structure. The price tag is on target, too. **88 Best Buy** —M.L. (6/1/2006)

Rotari NV Arte Italiana Brut Sparkling Blend (Trento) $11. Gold in color, with aromas of wheat bread and Golden Delicious apples. Lots of fresh peach, apple, and tangerine on the palate make for a pleasing flavor profile, while it finishes full and toasty. Nothing overwhelming, but rock solid as a whole. **87 Best Buy** —M.S. (12/15/2005)

Rotari NV Blanc de Noir Sparkling Blend (Trento) $11. Has only the barest hint of copper or brass color. Nose of apple, toast, and cherry leads to flavors of sour cherry, green apple, and citrus. The finish is positively lime-like. Crisp and clean. **85** —J.C. (12/31/2003)

Rotari 1998 Brut Riserva Sparkling Blend (Trento) $13. This blend of Chardonnay (90%) and Pinot Noir (10%) offers hints of toast and butter on the nose, then broadens to include some pear flavors on the palate. It's a bit simple, but perfectly pleasant. **86** —J.C. (12/31/2003)

Rotari NV Demi-Sec Sparkling Blend (Trento) $11. A new entry to the U.S. market, the Demi-Sec is slightly sweet, but probably not sweet enough to go with a full-blown dessert. It starts with attractive pear and anise notes, then finishes with hints of maple syrup and malt. **84** (6/1/2005)

Rotari NV Demi-Sec Sparkling Blend (Trento) $12. Definitely off-dry in character, with caramel corn, doughnut, and apples on the nose. Additional applesauce flavors blend with canned pear to create a sweet, sugary, lingering whole. Not bad but simple and candied. **84** —M.S. (12/15/2005)

Rotari 2001 Riserva Sparkling Blend (Trento) $13. Creamy and toasty in the mouth, with nice acidity to give it structure. A consistent sparkler with enough versatility to be consumed with a meal; not just for toasting. **89 Best Buy** —M.L. (6/1/2006)

Rotari 2000 Riserva Brut Sparkling Blend (Trento) $15. Toasty to the point of having a popcorn-like quality, but in between those toasted, buttery notes you'll find zesty lemon and apple. Solid if a bit of a one-note pony, but it's spunky and clean, and the overall impression is largely positive. **87** —M.S. (12/15/2005)

Rotari NV Rosé Sparkling Blend (Trento) $11. A delicately perfumed rosé that yields soft and feminine notes of forest berry and cranberry. Those fruit and rose-like aromas are carefully wrapped within yeast and baked bread flavors. Closes on a refreshing, crisp note. **87 Best Buy** —*M.L. (6/1/2006)*

RUFFINO

Ruffino 2000 Greppone Mazzi Brunello (Brunello di Montalcino) $65. There is a touch of herb and tomato on the nose, but also plenty of solid plum and cherry. A good wine but one that doesn't stray far from the beaten path. In the mouth, there's red fruit, licorice and hard tannins. Fails to wow, but it's solid. **87** —*M.S. (7/1/2005)*

Ruffino 1999 Greppone Mazzi Brunello (Brunello di Montalcino) $65. From Ruffino, this Brunello is ripe yet earthy, with a touch of forest and moss to the nose. It may be softer and riper than many, but it's definitely balanced. Meanwhile, fine black cherry and plum fruit steals the palate, which also dishes hints of chocolate and fennel. Good tannins and grip ensure its longevity. **92** —*M.S. (6/1/2004)*

Ruffino 1997 Greppone Mazzi Brunello (Brunello di Montalcino) $70. **89** —*R.V. (8/1/2002)*

Ruffino 1997 Greppone Mazzi Brunello (Brunello di Montalcino) $60. Muscle-bound with an earthy, spicy character to the nose. The body is fleshy but pure, offering black cherry flavors accented by tar and licorice. It finishes smooth, with just the right touch of vanilla oak. It's a polished Brunello, good for near-term drinking, but also a candidate for the cellar. **90** —*M.S. (8/1/2002)*

Ruffino 1996 Greppone Mazzi Brunello (Brunello di Montalcino) $60. This is medium-bodied and even—almost delicate for a Brunello, offering dried fruit, cedar, leather, and tobacco aromas and flavors. Full but not particularly deep, it feels mature and ready to drink. Finishes long and dry with a smoky note. Not a long-term keeper, drink now–2004. **87** *(3/1/2002)*

Ruffino 1999 Greppone Mazzi Riserva Brunello (Brunello di Montalcino) $95. Oaky at first, with strong hints of coconut and sawmill. Below there is nice cherry, raspberry, and plum fruit, which meets the bill even if the palate doesn't veer into the land of dark and deep. Good tannins, fine acidity, and a proper structure are all on display. **91** —*M.S. (7/1/2005)*

Ruffino 1998 La Solatìa Chardonnay (Toscana) $20. Nutty and complex, this single-vineyard barrique-aged Chardonnay shows apple and tropical fruit aromas and flavors lavishly wrapped in toasty oak. Citrus, honey, and oatmeal notes add interest to this round, supple, internationally styled white. Finishes long and tangy, with lingering oak and apple notes. Our panel was of decidedly different minds about this wine and the rating is truly an average. If you like this style, you'll rate this considerably higher—if not, you'll like it less. **86** *(3/1/2002)*

Ruffino 2000 Libaio Chardonnay (Toscana) $9. Opens light and dry with peach, green apple, and herb aromas. A tart and lemony Chardonnay, it's not at all fat or new-worldy. It displays the faintly bitter, almost quinine-like element some Italian whites show and closes crisply with an anise note. Formerly a Chardonnay-Pinot Grigio blend, Libaio is now 100% Chardonnay, while the Pinot Grigio is bottled as Lumina. **84** *(3/1/2002)*

Ruffino 2004 Lumina Pinot Grigio (Venezia Giulia) $13. This Tuscany-based estate has ventured into the Pinot Grigio race with a luminous and fresh wine, rich in the fruit aromas you should expect: melon, peach, and banana. **86** —*M.L. (6/1/2006)*

Ruffino 2002 Lumina Pinot Grigio (Venezia Giulia) $13. Aromas of pear, anise, and lemondrops lead into a bracingly citric wine. A modest amount of spice-driven complexity makes it more than just a bracing mouthful of acid. Finishes tart and clean. **85** —*J.C. (1/1/2004)*

Ruffino 2000 Lumina Pinot Grigio (Toscana) $12. Forward melon, grass, and bitter pear aromas open Lumina's debut bottling. The wine is medium-weight and even a touch syrupy in texture, particularly for a Pinot Grigio. The tasty almond-peach flavors fade effortlessly into the juicy, bright finish in this flavorful easy drinker. **84** *(3/1/2002)*

Ruffino 1997 Modus Red Blend (Toscana) $40. This super Tuscan shows fine aromatics with a ripe and dark cherry, cream, cedar, and chocolate nose. Balanced and dry, it offers a ripe, slightly viscous mouthfeel with black cherry, espresso, and toast flavors. Very appealing in the modern manner, it's satisfying, if not terrifically subtle. There's an underlying sense that more depth and intensity could come from the fruit here, even as one enjoys it for its undeniable suave appeal. **88** *(3/1/2002)*

Ruffino 2001 Romitorio di Santedame Red Blend (Toscana) $70. Big, black, and textured, but even with all of its guts, color, and polish, it isn't very unique, and that's despite the 60% Colorino and 40% Merlot it's made of. Blackberry and plum dominate the muscular palate, while the roasted finish is nice but simple. Very good on its best day. **89** —*M.S. (9/1/2006)*

Ruffino 1999 Romitorio di Santedame Red Blend (Toscana) $NA. Solid and intense, the first vintage of this wine to hit U.S. shores is an auspicious start. It's lush and juicy, with a nose- and palate-caressing black cherry, mocha cream, and chocolate profile. This Colorino-Merlot blend successfully pushes all the pleasure buttons while maintaining structure and showing substance. With a long, dry finish sporting soft ripe tannins, this is tempting now, but will be best from 2004–2010. **91 Cellar Selection** *(3/1/2002)*

Ruffino 1997 Tenuta Lodola Nuova Red Blend (Vino Nobile di Montepulciano) $17. Deep cherry, sour plum, smoke, and leather all mark this lean, handsomely textured wine. Earth and bittersweet chocolate accents compliment the fruit flavors. In a split decision, some tasters found it too lean and bitter for their taste. It finishes long, with some firm tannins to lose; best 2003–2008. **88 Editors' Choice** *(3/1/2002)*

Ruffino 1999 Aziano Sangiovese (Chianti Classico) $15. The light cherry aromas and flavors with herb accents show a slight candied quality. Decent structure, but overall the wine is a bit narrow and closes with sharp, quite tart cherry fruit. It's youthful, for sure, and perhaps will even out with six to nine months in the bottle. **84** *(4/1/2001)*

Ruffino 2000 Fonte al Sole Sangiovese (Toscana) $8. A straightforward red displaying good Sangiovese character in its tart cherry fruit accented by meat, leather, and coffee elements. Lean on the tongue and nicely balanced, this fine pizza-pasta wine closes with tangy tannins and decent length. **84 Best Buy** *(3/1/2002)*

Ruffino 2000 IL Leo Sangiovese (Chianti Superiore) $10. Smooth and structured, this Chianti delivers deep, tart black cherry flavors on a medium frame with a nice, chewy mouthfeel. Attractive licorice, earth, tobacco, and cocoa accents add interest right through the dry finish. Tasty now and should hold through 2004. A solid value, especially if found on sale. **86 Best Buy** *(3/1/2002)*

Ruffino 1999 Modus Sangiovese (Toscana) $40. Saturated purple in color; this Sangiovese-Cabernet-Merlot blend is heavily oaked, so much so that it hints at popcorn. Beyond the wood, however, are notes of root beer and smoked meat. The palate has some hard tannins and the oak is once again strong; it literally takes on a buttery flavor. The finish is the best part: It's all about thick black fruit. **88** —*M.S. (8/1/2002)*

Ruffino 2001 Riserva Ducale Sangiovese (Chianti Classico) $27. Rubber, sulfur, and mushroom are tough starting aromas, but with time it opens to offer cherry, plum, and tomato. Fairly forward and edgy, with brisk tannins. Slightly green at the center. **85** *(4/1/2005)*

Ruffino 2000 Riserva Ducale Oro Sangiovese (Chianti Classico) $39. Heavy, with some burnt aromas. Stewy on the palate, with deep plum and blackberry accented by a firm dose of cedary oak. To call it syrupy would not be an exaggeration. Not stellar for a wine with a reputation. **86** *(4/1/2005)*

Ruffino 1997 Riserva Ducale Tan Label Sangiovese (Chianti Classico) $20. This balanced and supple wine offers stylish cherry, licorice, and leather aromas and flavors. The long finish is dry, with full, well-dispersed tannins and sour cherry flavors. Not dense, but flavorful, balanced and well-built for drinking over the next few years. **89** *(4/1/2001)*

Ruffino 1995 Tenuta Lodola Nuova Sangiovese (Vino Nobile di Montepulciano) $20. **86** —*M.S. (7/1/2000)*

Ruffino 1998 Tenuta Santedame Sangiovese (Chianti Classico) $16. A dense smoke and toast cocoon envelops the dark fruit in this supple wine. Our tasters found the oak overbearing, obscuring the fruit. If it's juicy, it's in an unusual, cedary, raisiny way, with leathery accents. The wine seems at once young and closed, yet rather mature for its age. A curious offering. **85** *(3/1/2002)*

Ruffino 1997 Tenuta Santedame Sangiovese (Chianti Classico) $18. Dark berry, cherry, and herb aromas blossom into full flavors and pick up handsome tar and licorice accents on the palate. Full but smooth on the finish, it doesn't settle for superficial appeal, but has substance, good structure, and it will age nicely. **87** *(4/1/2001)*

RUGGERI & C.

Ruggeri & C. NV Gold Label Extra Dry Prosecco (Prosecco di Valdobbiadene) $18. A less intense Prosecco but attractive nonetheless. Has fragrant flowers and stone aromas, and an angular or sharp quality rendered by tasty citrus overtones. This bubbly is characterized by a lemon pie-like tug of war between sweet and sour. **86** *—M.L. (6/1/2006)*

Ruggeri & C. NV Quartese Prosecco (Prosecco di Valdobbiadene) $NA. Less fruity and dry overall, compensating with delicate tones of white flower and talc powder. A subdued wine, with a light, citrus-driven mouthfeel and a short finish. **86** *—M.L. (6/1/2006)*

Ruggeri & C. NV Santo Stefano Dry Prosecco (Prosecco di Valdobbiadene) $21. Dusty mineral tones are in line with aromatic white flowers, crisp green apple, and almond skin. A festive and seductive nose opens onto fruit candy flavors and a tart, crisp endnote. **87** *—M.L. (6/1/2006)*

RUGGERI GIULIANO

Ruggeri Giuliano NV Santo Stefano Champagne Blend (Prosecco di Valdobbiadene) $16. The nose is proper and smooth, but a touch sweet. That sweetness is confirmed on the palate, where pear flavors veer toward syrupy. The finish is simple and once again sweet, which fits the pattern. If you like yours sugary and somewhat like liquid candy, this is for you. **85** *—M.S. (6/1/2003)*

Ruggeri Giuliano 2001 Giustino B. Extra Dry Prosecco (Prosecco di Valdobbiadene) $20. Very light in color, with pleasant soda and flower-like aromas. This is the epitome of a free and easy bubbly, one that's super easy to drink. It's sweet and fruity, with the full allotment of citrus. Not complex or stately, but solid and fun. **87** *—M.S. (6/1/2003)*

Ruggeri Giuliano NV Gold Label Prosecco (Prosecco di Valdobbiadene) $15. Dry, dusty aromas of lemon-lime and aged cheese start it off. Tangerine and lemon flavors follow on both the palate and finish. The one fault here is the wine's weight: It's too light and dilute, which conveys a flatness despite good fruit flavors. **86** *—M.S. (6/1/2003)*

Ruggeri Giuliano 1999 Rosso Sagrantino (Montefalco) $15. **84** *—M.S. (2/1/2003)*

Ruggeri Giuliano 1998 Sagrantino di Montefalco Sagrantino (Sagrantino di Montefalco) $35. Chocolate and ripe red plums are prominent on the nose. Rich but balaned sweet dark fruit match with firm, well-intigrated tannins. **89** *—C.S. (2/1/2002)*

SALADINI PILASTRI

Saladini Pilastri 2003 White Blend (Falerio) $10. The Falerio DOC is in the Marches region of Italy. This white, a blend of Trebbiano, Pecorino, Passerina, and Chardonnay is rich and full-bodied, flavored with fresh almonds, peaches, and a touch of cilantro. There's very intense, ripe fruit here; the wine is perfect to serve with fish or white meat. **88 Best Buy** *—R.V. (11/15/2004)*

SALICUTTI

Salicutti 2000 Brunello (Brunello di Montalcino) $95. Tight as a drum, almost to the point that it's constricted. Airing it unlocks cinnamon, chocolate, and smoky leather aromas on top of blackberry, cherry, and vanilla. Full in the middle, and less oaky and chunky than many others. This is a wine with guts and framing, yet it goes easy on the finish. **92 Editors' Choice** *—M.S. (7/1/2005)*

Salicutti 2001 Piaggione Brunello (Brunello di Montalcino) $110. Expressive and intense with dried spices, distinct minerality, cherry cola, coffee grinds, and just enough soft vanilla toastiness to fill in the blanks. Medium build with modest tannins and a long, herbaceous finish. **90** *(4/1/2006)*

Salicutti 1999 Sangiovese (Rosso di Montalcino) $33. This is no simple red; deep black fruit and leather aromas suggest an intense, young, untamed wine. It's rugged and muscular, with an opaque color, tight tannins that starch the cheeks, and a powerful, multilayered finish. Baby Brunello? Hardly. This is a full-grown wine all its own, and it still needs several more years to open up. **90** *—M.S. (8/1/2002)*

SALUSTRI

Salustri 2002 Grotte Rosse Sangiovese (Montecucco) $40. A very good wine from a not-so-good vintage. The bouquet hits firmly with black cherry, almond paste, leather, and even a touch of refined horseradish. It's as precise and tight as the palate, which offers tannic but rewarding cherry and plum. A lively, racy, real wine that's playing at the highest level. Holding it to high standards, we find it just short of excellent. **89** *—M.S. (9/1/2006)*

Salustri 2004 Marleo Rosso Sangiovese (Montecucco) $19. Nice and ripe, with sweet plum and black cherry on the open, well-padded nose. Full in the mouth, with satisfying cherry, plum, and chocolate flavors. And it holds its form through the long, smooth finish. Just an easy wine to like and drink. Requires no serious contemplation. **87** *—M.S. (9/1/2006)*

Salustri 2003 Santa Marta Sangiovese (Montecucco) $28. The appellation isn't well known but based on the current line of Salustri reds we can say that Sangiovese from Montecucco in Tuscany has its merits. This wine is ripe with black cherry aromas and flavors. It's pure, sweet, balanced and tasty. Best from 2007 through 2011. **92** *—M.S. (9/1/2006)*

SALVANO

Salvano 1998 Dolcetto (Dolcetto di Diano d'Alba) $9. **87** *(4/1/2000)*

SALVATORE MOLETTIERI

Salvatore Molettieri 1996 Vigna Cinque Querce Aglianico (Taurasi) $32. The "vineyard of five oaks" yielded a rich, dark, earthy wine in '96, with sweet notes of molasses, brown sugar, and soy sauce. Full-bodied and low in acidity, with plenty of tannin to lose, the question is whether the tannins will ever soften enough to come into balance. **85** *—C.S. (5/1/2002)*

SALVIANO

Salviano 1999 Turlo Red Blend (Umbria) $10. **86** *—M.S. (2/1/2003)*

Salviano 2003 White Blend (Orvieto Classico Superiore) $13. Fairly spicy for an Orvieto, with aromas of pepper, wasabi, and green herbs in addition to almond and mild white fruits. Nice on the palate, with just enough acid push so that it avoids blandness. Mild apple and peach flavors lead to a round, almondy finish. **85** *—M.S. (7/1/2005)*

Salviano 2003 Superiore White Blend (Orvieto Classico) $13. Light and open, but with purity and more power than normal. Starts with lime and citrus pith and finishes with grip, an acid wave, and some white pepper. Long on the back end for Orvieto, and well-made. **87** *—M.S. (11/15/2004)*

SAN ANGELO

San Angelo 1998 Single Vineyard Pinot Grigio (Toscana) $13. **87** *(8/1/1999)*

SAN BONIFACIO

San Bonifacio 1998 Pinot Grigio (Veneto) $10. **86** *(8/1/1999)*

SAN CARLO

San Carlo 1999 Brunello (Brunello di Montalcino) $NA. The closed nose offers a slight paint or chemical aroma that hopefully will subside with aging. Very tight and dry on the palate, with cherry notes and strong hints of black pepper. Fairly lean and basic Brunello, with medium-level oak. Of note: Very little of this wine (about 20 cases) makes it to the U.S. **86** *—M.S. (6/1/2004)*

SAN FABIANO

San Fabiano 2002 Sangiovese (Chianti) $12. Sweet, with red licorice, caramel, and raisin aromas. Stewy in the mouth, with a medicinal aftertaste. Ponderous and striving for balance. **82** *(4/1/2005)*

San Fabiano 1998 Sangiovese (Chianti) $8. The nose shows dried black cherry fruit with tobacco and a Play-doh-like note. Light to medium-weight, the mouth offers more dried cherries, some chocolate, and then a hint of tarragon on the finish. **85** *(4/1/2001)*

San Fabiano 2000 Borghini Baldovinetti (Armaiolo) Sangiovese (Colli della Toscana Centrale) $43. Ripe to the point of raisiny, with milk chocolate and berry jam on the nose. The palate mixes the sweetness of liqueur with core tartness, and the final result isn't overly impressive. Leaves a shallow imprint at the finish line. **84** *—M.S. (9/1/2006)*

SAN FABIANO CALCINAIA

San Fabiano Calcinaia 2002 Sangiovese (Chianti Classico) $23. Attractive scents of tree bark, toast, and bacon announce it as a serious entry. The nose offers more toast backed by raspberry, plum, and distant citrus. Plush and full, with tannins galore. But also creamy and satisfying. Very good; just shy of excellent. **89** *(4/1/2005)*

San Fabiano Calcinaia 2001 Sangiovese (Chianti Classico) $23. Spicy and foresty up front, with aromas of hickory and pine. That heavy oak quotient creates a chocolaty nuance in the mouth, where wood meets ripe red berry fruit square on. The finish holds on to that smoky, woody quality. The tannins turn starchy and hard at the end, indicating that food should be present. **86** *—M.S. (11/15/2003)*

San Fabiano Calcinaia 2000 Sangiovese (Chianti Classico) $19. The bold, meaty nose portends a wine of strength, which is basically what you get. It's burly and fresh, with blackberry and blueberry fruit bolstered by tasty spice. It's a bit hard and tannic, and the acidity fosters a juicy sense. By no means is this a petite, elegant wine, but it's still satisfying. **86** *—M.S. (12/31/2002)*

San Fabiano Calcinaia 1998 Sangiovese (Chianti Classico) $18. Dark is the word here, with lots of deep toast, licorice, chocolate, and coffee notes throughout. The pleasurable mouthfeel has nice weight and the finish offers solid cherry and cocoa notes and good length. This wine has some tannins to lose and can be cellared for a year or two. **87** *(4/1/2001)*

San Fabiano Calcinaia 2001 Cellole Riserva Sangiovese (Chianti Classico) $38. Gorgeous stuff; the real deal in terms of meaty, modern Chianti. And from an excellent year, which explains why it's so saturated and rich. For lovers of hefty, fruity reds that have tannin and structure but can still be enjoyed now, this is your ticket. It is deep, full-bodied, and packed with tobacco, chocolate, and Tuscan sunshine. **93 Editors' Choice** *(4/1/2005)*

San Fabiano Calcinaia 2000 Cerviolo Sangiovese (Toscana) $63. As Super Tuscans go, this is a model wine, always consistent and exciting. This version is a rich, deep, balanced beauty with aromas of mocha, molasses, fudge, and plum. The palate bursts with boysenberry, plum, and chocolate, while the mildly tannic finish is toasty and full of coffee. Modern in style but lovely. **93** *—M.S. (10/1/2004)*

San Fabiano Calcinaia 1999 Cerviolo Sangiovese (Toscana) $45. This perennial knock-out is excellent again. It has maple, coffee, and other wood-driven aromatics. The mouth is like a bowl of black plums mixed with mocha, coffee, and bitter chocolate. And the finish is ultra-smooth, with light but welcome intrusions of vanilla. In a perfect world it could use at least two to three years of aging. **90** *—M.S. (12/31/2002)*

San Fabiano Calcinaia 1997 Cerviolo Sangiovese (Toscana) $45. The nose of this winning wine has coffee, vanilla, and cassis aromas. Smooth but firm, the palate leaves a slight pucker while providing rich coffee, vanilla, mint, and cherry flavors with style. Will be better with a bit of age—let it soften for a year or so. **90** *—J.F. (9/1/2001)*

San Fabiano Calcinaia 1996 Cerviolo Sangiovese (Toscana) $37. 90 *— M.S. (9/1/2000)*

San Fabiano Calcinaia 2000 Cerviolo Rosso Sangiovese (Tuscany) $65. Muscular and power-packed, with a deep-purple tint, saturated berry aromas, and a strong whack of oak. The mouth is deep, dense, and chock full of blackberry, chocolate, coffee, and cinnamon. No complaints about the richness and fruit quotient, but it's arguably too oaky. Should improve with time. **88** *—M.S. (11/15/2003)*

San Fabiano Calcinaia 1998 Riserva Cellole Sangiovese (Chianti Classico) $31. The label is from San Fabiano Calcinaia, and the wine opens with clean berry aromas and plenty of oak. The palate is overtly fruity, with bright cherry and blueberry flavors. The finish brings back some of that

powerful oak from the nose, and you taste mocha and coffee as a result. Well-balanced, so the whole sings louder than the parts. **89** *—M.S. (12/31/2002)*

San Fabiano Calcinaia 1997 Riserva Cellole Sangiovese (Chianti Classico) $28. An oak cloak envelopes this smooth, medium-weight wine, yielding a seamless black-plum and espresso profile. It's handsome, even seductive, in the modern manner, with earth, licorice, and caramel notes. **87** *(4/1/2001)*

SAN FELICE

San Felice 2001 Campogiovanni Brunello (Brunello di Montalcino) $70. A smoky, meaty core is rounded off at the edges by black cherry, maple syrup, and a green-herbal note. Sour berry, cassis, peppercorn, and wet pebble minerality ride over a long finish. **90 Cellar Selection** *(4/1/2006)*

San Felice 2002 Sangiovese (Chianti Classico) $18. Leathery and meaty on the nose, with hints of baked plum, jerky, and tobacco. Plump on the tongue, with raspberry, cherry, and herb flavors. Turns slightly sour on the finish, but to some that may represent zest and freshness. **86** *(4/1/2005)*

San Felice 2000 Sangiovese (Chianti Classico) $18. 86 *(1/1/2004)*

San Felice 2000 Il Grigio Riserva Sangiovese (Chianti Classico) $26. Soy, marinade, and sweaty leather meet on the nose, giving way to dilute plum and cherry. Just not much fruit here, at least not enough to match the heavy oak that dominates. **83** *(4/1/2005)*

San Felice 1999 Il Grigio Riserva Sangiovese (Chianti Classico) $26. 89 *(1/1/2004)*

San Felice 1999 Poggio Rosso Riserva Sangiovese (Chianti Classico) $55. 91 *(1/1/2004)*

San Felice 1999 Poggio Rosso Riserva Sangiovese (Chianti Classico) $50. Starts with attractive cherry, blackberry, and charred bacon aromas, but turns more monotone and tart than expected once you get down to drinking it. One of our panelists found "clipped, narrow" flavors and sharp "one-note" acids, while another was more positive, locking in on the wine's chewy tannins and power. **86** *(4/1/2005)*

San Felice 1999 Vigorello Sangiovese (Toscana) $43. 90 *(1/1/2004)*

SAN FILIPPO DI GIANNELLI

San Filippo di Giannelli 2001 Brunello (Brunello di Montalcino) $56. The pleasure factor is cut somewhat short by abrupt sour cranberry and apple cider that over-rides blueberry, spicy herbal, and menthol notes. Lean and exceedingly tart in the mouth. **85** *(4/1/2006)*

SAN FRANCESCO

San Francesco 1999 Rosso Gaglioppo (Cirò Classico) $12. Crisp bacon and herbal tannins are pretty much all you'll find. The finish is tannic and watery. Overall, you wonder, where's the fruit? **80** *—C.S. (5/1/2002)*

SAN GIULIO

San Giulio 2004 Pinot Grigio (Delle Venezie) $10. The nose is somewhat awkward with loads of thick honey and beeswax backed by a prominent vegetal smell that resembles stewed greens. It has a light straw color, lean consistency, and medium finish. **82** *—M.L. (2/1/2006)*

SAN GIUSEPPE

San Giuseppe 2001 Merlot (Veneto) $9. Herbal aromas with some mint and pepper comprise the nose. Some candied cherry fruit is what you get on the thick, cloying palate. Residual sugar seems to be over-abundant as the wine finishes sweet and sticky. **81** *(5/1/2003)*

San Giuseppe 2004 Pinot Grigio (Veneto) $11. Easy to like at all checkpoints. Almond, pear, and chunky apple aromas lead into lemon-lime, melon, and green apple flavors. A lightly candied finish keeps its freshness, and the overall impression is positive. **87 Best Buy** *(2/1/2006)*

San Giuseppe 2003 Pinot Grigio (Piave) $18. Minerally aromas, backed by modest pear fruit and flavors more reminiscent of earth and wet gravel. Tangy and clean on the finish. **83** *—J.C. (12/31/2004)*

San Giuseppe 2002 Pinot Grigio (Veneto) $9. Light and lean pear fruit, with subtle lime notes and a hint of sweetness appearing on the finish. **83** *—J.C. (7/1/2003)*

San Giuseppe 2001 Pinot Grigio (Veneto) $9. A bizarre blend of lime, unipe pineapple, banana, and tropical fruit marks this clumsy, disjointed wine. It's not bad, but it's all elbows, with hard edges sticking out all over. **82** —*J.C. (7/1/2003)*

San Giuseppe 2004 Pink Pinot Grigio (Veneto) $11. Copper-pink in color, with a light, floral bouquet. Yes, it's a bit sweet in a White Zin way, but it holds its form and balance courtesy of berry fruit, nectarine flavors, and firm acidity. Lasting on the finish; stands out from the crowd. **86 Best Buy** *(2/1/2006)*

San Giuseppe 2005 Brut Prosecco (Prosecco di Conegliano) $NA. A golden-hued Prosecco with less fruit intensity on the nose that is compensated with crisp mineral notes, bread crust, and background banana and peach flavors. Light and super crisp in the mouth, with a spicy finish. **85** —*M.L. (6/1/2006)*

San Giuseppe 2005 Extra Dry Prosecco (Prosecco di Conegliano) $NA. Very intense with floral notes in the center, and mineral ones at the seams. There's a slightly loose or disjointed quality to the nose, but the mouthfeel is intact with a touch of spice on the finish. **85** —*M.L. (6/1/2006)*

San Giuseppe 2002 Sangiovese (Chianti) $10. Weak in color, and dilute, but not a disaster. The nose is a bit horse-like, but otherwise the dried fruit flavors and peppery tannins are acceptable. **83** *(4/1/2005)*

SAN GIUSTO A RENTENNANO

San Giusto a Rentennano 1998 Sangiovese (Chianti Classico) $19. A lush and beautiful rendition of well-oaked, new-style Chianti. Inviting dark chocolate and cherry aromas and flavors and an even, full texture mark this affordable sophisticate. The long, densely fruited finish of this exceptional value shows lots of creamy vanillin oak and tart black cherry and espresso flavors. Perhaps hard to find, but worth the hunt. So seductive now, it will be hard to cellar for long. **92 Editors' Choice** *(4/1/2001)*

SAN JACOPO DA VICCHIOMAGGIO

San Jacopo da Vicchiomaggio 2003 Sangiovese (Chianti Classico) $18. A nice mineral edge helps out the smooth, slightly herbal nose. Solid on the palate, where cherry, berry, and plum flavors are clean and forward. The feel is commendable and cuddly, while the finish has toast, earth, and chocolate. A satisfying red wine that does the region's reputation proud. **89** —*M.S. (10/1/2006)*

SAN MICHELE EPPAN

San Michele Eppan 2002 Sanct Valentin Gewürztraminer (Alto Adige) $30. Aromas of roses, pepper, and spices make this an enticing wine. On the palate, it is ripe, soft, full-bodied, and rich, lacking acidity, but otherwise classic Gewürztraminer. **88** —*R.V. (7/1/2003)*

San Michele Eppan 2002 Sanct Valentin Pinot Bianco (Alto Adige) $30. This wood-aged Pinot Bianco offers ripe, full fruit with accompanying wood and spice flavors. It is rich and quite soft, but has a touch of crisp acidity. **88** —*R.V. (7/1/2003)*

San Michele Eppan 2002 Sanct Valentin Sauvignon Blanc (Alto Adige) $29. The top range of wines from this highly rated cooperative is called Sanet Valentin, after the patron saint of lovers. This Sauvignon is crisp, herbaceous, and very fresh, with light layers of mouth-watering acidity. **87** —*R.V. (7/1/2003)*

SAN PATRIGNANO

San Patrignano 2001 Montepirolo Cabernet Sauvignon (Colli di Rimini) $45. This Cabernet starts with mild but inoffensive coconut aromas that are backed by pungent red fruit and a hint of herbaceousness. Plum, blackberry, and chocolate flavors dominate, but there's a shock of oregano in there, too. Lasting on the finish, and saturated. Not stylish but sound. **87** —*M.S. (7/1/2005)*

San Patrignano 2002 Noi Red Blend (Colli di Rimini) $36. Full-bodied and earthy, with lots of meat on its bones. Black fruits with a bit of acidic tang control the flavor profile, while the finish is easy, full and of moderate length. Quite juicy and satisfying, with smoke, rubber and coffee nuances. **86** —*M.S. (7/1/2005)*

San Patrignano 2001 Avi Sangiovese (Sangiovese di Romagna) $45. Spicy and sweet, with a full blast of oak on the nose. Palate flavors of vanilla, boysenberry, cinnamon, and cola work well as a team, while the textured finish offers leather, pepper, and some wayward oak. A chewy, chunky red that should satisfy on most occasions. **87** —*M.S. (7/1/2005)*

SAN QUIRICO

San Quirico 2003 Sangiovese (Chianti Colli Senesi) $12. Dark and brooding, with aromas that are all over the map. There's some Port, mint, and funk preceding a leafy, slightly musty palate. Not the cleanest, most upright wine. **83** *(4/1/2005)*

San Quirico 1999 Sangiovese (Chianti Colli Senesi) $12. Aromas of black currants and anise mark the nose of this dry, medium-weight wine. It offers dark cherry and semisweet chocolate flavors on the palate, and closes nicely with a chalk-mineral element on the finish. **86** *(4/1/2001)*

San Quirico 2004 Riserva Proprietà Vecchione Vernaccia (Vernaccia di San Gimignano) $16. Thick and slightly golden, this Vernaccia offers an intense nose and a palate full of dried herbs, mint tea, ripe melon, some green vegetables, and faint rubber tire that adds to its eccentric but likeable character. **86** —*M.L. (9/1/2005)*

SAN SIMONE

San Simone 2004 Pinot Grigio (Friuli) $15. Neutral but normal, with apple and citrus aromas backed by tangy orange, apple, and melon flavors. A touch of herb flavor adds character to what is otherwise a fairly lean, acidic white wine. **84** *(2/1/2006)*

SANDRA LOTTI

Sandra Lotti 2000 Saporita Sangiovese (Toscana) $23. The nose opens with a standard offering of leather, mint, and berries. The palate is plump in terms of fruit, but the feel turns skinny and firm. Has good flavors but seems a bit jumpy and hot. **86** —*M.S. (10/1/2004)*

SANDRONE

Sandrone 2003 Barbera (Barbera d'Alba) $29. Unusually full-bodied and creamy textured for a Barbera, but also unusually good, with vibrant black cherry fruit artfully framed by hints of vanilla and cinnamon. The long, mouth-watering finish is a treat. Drink now. **90 Editors' Choice** —*J.C. (3/1/2006)*

Sandrone 2004 Dolcetto (Dolcetto d'Alba) $19. Lighter and fresher than previous vintages, with vibrant black cherry, plum—even a hint of peach—fruit flavors, backed by bright acids and some atypically hard tannins. **86** —*J.C. (3/1/2006)*

Sandrone 1998 Dolcetto (Dolcetto d'Alba) $25. **93** *(4/1/2000)*

Sandrone 2001 Cannubi Boschis Nebbiolo (Barolo) $135. Absolutely lovely. It starts off dense and tarry on the nose, with plum and chocolate fudge scents, then adds layers of bright floral and cherry notes with airing, while the palate is a whirl of mouth-coating flavors that never seem hamhanded despite the great intensity. Finishes with wonderfully plush tannins, making this approachable now, yet capable of evolving for 20 years. **97 Editors' Choice** —*J.C. (3/1/2006)*

Sandrone 2001 Le Vigne Nebbiolo (Barolo) $120. Great stuff, combining traditional Barolo flavors—dusty earth, leather, floral notes, and cherries—with modern touches, like the supple tannins and hints of hickory smoke. This is a big, powerful wine that manages to be burly without being clumsy, intellectually challenging and complex while still delivering lush fruit. Drinkable now, but better several years from now. **96** —*J.C. (3/1/2006)*

Sandrone 2003 Valmaggiore Nebbiolo (Nebbiolo d'Alba) $45. Given the heat of the vintage, it's no surprise that this wine carries some stewed, caramelized flavors along with strawberries, cocoa, and herbs. Round and soft in the mouth, with a supple finish. **87** —*J.C. (3/1/2006)*

SANGERVASIO

Sangervasio 1998 Le Stoppie Sangiovese (Chianti Colli Pisani) $9. Black cherry and creamy chocolate flavors play on the nose and in the mouth. The wine is light but harmonious, with a smooth texture and a dry cherry finish. **85 Best Buy** *(4/1/2001)*

SANSONINA

Sansonina 1998 Merlot (Veneto) $60. Very modern and rich; truly a New World Merlot from the Old World. This new wine is made by the Zenato family, and it should please fans of thick, ripe reds. The color is virtually black, the nose a mix of stewed plums, toasty oak and maple extract. There is plenty of mocha character on top of black cherry on the palate, while the finish is cuddly soft, with plenty of chocolate nuance and supple tannins. **90** *(5/1/2003)*

SANT' ELENA

Sant' Elena 1998 Pinot Grigio (Venezia Giulia) $15. **86** *(8/1/1999)*

SANT'EVASIO

Sant'Evasio 1999 Cortese (Gavi di Gavi) $13. This crisp, clean white is filled with tart green apple and lime aromas and flavors. Throw in hints of almonds and herbs and a slightly creamy texture, and this represents a patio wine supremo. **84** *(9/1/2001)*

Sant'Evasio 1995 Red Blend (Barolo) $34. Barolo isn't known for producing ready-to-drink wines, but this one is already showing signs of maturity and should be consumed soon. Aromas of earth and cherries turn complex with airing, taking on strong licorice and fruitcake scents as well. The tannins on the long finish are soft and ripe. **91** —*J.C. (9/1/2001)*

SANTA ANASTASIA

Santa Anastasia 1999 Passomaggio Red Blend (Sicilia) $14. **90 Best Buy** —*C.S. (11/15/2002)*

SANTA MARGHERITA

Santa Margherita 2003 Chardonnay (Veneto Orientale) $16. Simple and fruity, with modest aromas and flavors of pineapple and grapefruit. Finishes crisp and clean. **83** —*J.C. (12/31/2004)*

Santa Margherita 2003 Chardonnay (Alto Adige) $21. Buttery and toasty on the nose, followed by obvious flavors of vanilla, pear, and apple. This is a little bulky and lacking a sense of elegance, but is still a solid mouthful of flavorful Chardonnay. **86** —*J.C. (12/31/2004)*

Santa Margherita 2001 Versato Merlot (Veneto) $21. Aromas are dominated by scents of coffee, chocolate, and tobacco, but this wine reveals more fruit on the palate, where tart cherries kick in. It's soft and light—a pretty wine, not a blockbuster, with modest tannins on the finish. Drink now. **85** —*J.C. (12/31/2004)*

Santa Margherita 2002 Pinot Bianco (Alto Adige) $NA. This is an attractive, soft, fresh wine, with concentration and structure, as well as a light, rounded aftertaste. **84** —*R.V. (7/1/2003)*

Santa Margherita 2004 Pinot Grigio (Alto Adige) $22. This bestselling Pinot Grigio is the envy of other Grigio producers and often takes a beating back in Italy. Truth is, the wine lives up to expectations: It is informal, easy-to-drink, food-friendly, and uncomplicated. Typical of the variety, with contrasting green notes and sweet honey. **85** —*M.L. (2/1/2006)*

Santa Margherita 2003 Pinot Grigio (Alto Adige) $25. America's most recognized brand of Pinot Grigio is crisply focused this year, with almond paste and ripe apple aromas backed by fresh apple and pear flavors. Clean and citrusy on the finish. **86** —*J.C. (12/31/2004)*

Santa Margherita 2002 Pinot Grigio (Valdadige) $22. The bestselling Pinot Grigio on the market is full of forward fruit and balancing acidity. It succeeds in epitomizing why Pinot Grigio is so popular, with its slight spice and crisp, soft, clean, and fresh flavors, with just a touch of citrus and lychees. **87** —*R.V. (7/1/2003)*

Santa Margherita 1998 Pinot Grigio (Valdadige) $19. **84** *(8/1/1999)*

Santa Margherita NV Brut Prosecco (Prosecco di Valdobbiadene) $21. Here's a Prosecco with a surprisingly rich, toasted quality that translates into roasted almond, walnut, and yellow fruit flavors. The toasted notes add unexpected complexity to a dry, crisp apéritif wine. **88** —*M.L. (6/1/2006)*

Santa Margherita NV Brut Prosecco (Prosecco di Valdobbiadene) $21. Mildly toasty, with hints of bread dough in addition to crisp white fruits. The palate is lean but pleasing, with pineapple, peach, and apple.

Finishes moderately long, with some talc. Tangy and tasty overall. **87** —*M.S. (12/15/2004)*

Santa Margherita NV Brut Prosecco (Prosecco di Valdobbiadene) $21. The lemon-lime nose is true to form, and the palate is perfectly zesty, with citrus dominating a full package of Prosecco-like flavors. Slightly sweet later on, which carries the finish. Plucky and solid. **88** —*M.S. (12/15/2005)*

SANTA SOFIA

Santa Sofia 2004 Garganega (Soave Classico) $11. Pretty neutral-smelling, with just hints of Golden Delicious and melon on the nose. But it's a bit bland and light on the palate—a well-made if somewhat innocuous white that finishes clean and crisp. **83** —*J.C. (10/1/2006)*

Santa Sofia 2000 Red Blend (Valpolicella Classico) $10. Light and color and a bit dull in the nose. Dig deep for some floral notes and also some leather and orange peel. But there isn't a whole lot of ripe fruit; it's mostly lean strawberry and dried cherry. **83** *(5/1/2003)*

Santa Sofia 2000 Red Blend (Amarone della Valpolicella Classico) $55. Starts out sly and smooth and gains complexity as it opens. The bouquet is classy, with scents of black cherry, fine leather, and spice. Perfectly balanced on the palate, and sporting a classic mix of cherry, plum, and vanilla flavors. Feels great at all stops, with some chocolate to the everlasting finish. Can drink now or hold for up to 10 years. **92** *(11/1/2005)*

Santa Sofia 1997 Classico Red Blend (Amarone della Valpolicella Classico) $40. Raisins, ash, dried cherry, and baking spices create a delicious bouquet that is backed up by a smooth palate that delivers prune, coffee, and mocha. The texture is great and so is the interplay of smooth but firm tannins and lively but hidden acidity. **92** *(5/1/2003)*

Santa Sofia 1998 Gioé Red Blend (Amarone della Valpolicella Classico) $72. Intriguing and complex, with alluring aromas of campfire, citrus peel, cinnamon, and cedar. Offers fine fruit and highly commendable balance, as the palate is juiced with acidity, cherry, and raspberry flavors, and more. Smoky on the finish, with a bit of sweet caramel. **92** *(11/1/2005)*

Santa Sofia 1995 Gioé Red Blend (Amarone della Valpolicella Classico) $45. The complex nose features tobacco, raisin, rum liqueur, and apple peel. The mouthfeel is racy courtesy of healthy acids, and delivers ripe red fruit. Substantial yet fine-grained tannins give the finish a necessary edge. In addition, latent bitter chocolate and coffee flavors add to the overall character. **89** *(5/1/2003)*

Santa Sofia 1998 Monte Gradella Red Blend (Valpolicella Classico Superiore) $20. Raisins, plum skins, and root beer make for an attractive ripasso-style nose. Dried cherries and chocolate carry the palate, which is generally smooth and silky in terms of feel. The finish is fairly delicate and understated, but long. **86** *(5/1/2003)*

SANTADI

Santadi 1997 Terre Brune Carignane (Sardinia) $37. Big berries and char are predominant on the nose. Tar and dried fruit on the palate transition nicely to a lingering finish. This is a succulent wine that will mellow with age. **89** —*C.S. (5/1/2002)*

Santadi 1998 Grotta Rossa Grenache (Cannonau di Sardegna) $10. Lean red berry fruit on the palate has earth and leather accents; the wine opens with similar aromas, plus dried herb and gamy notes. Hefty tannins suggest that it'll be at its best with food. **85 Best Buy** —*C.S. (5/1/2002)*

Santadi 1998 Rocca Rubia Riserva Red Blend (Sardinia) $19. Burnt caramel and zesty red berries showed a lot of promise on the nose, but the raspberry flavors were a bit one-dimensional on the palate. It finishes with a simple but structured herbal note. **86** —*C.S. (5/1/2002)*

Santadi 1997 Shardana Red Blend (Valli di Porto Pino) $24. An inky, bright purple color lures you into the glass. Your nose will find aromas of buttercream frosting, spice, and sweet toasted oak. On the mouth, fleshy plums, candy apples, and blackberry jam make this a complex wine. Made from century-old prephylloxera Carignano vines, plus a touch of Shiraz. **90 Editors' Choice** —*C.S. (5/1/2002)*

ITALY

Santadi 1996 Shardana Red Blend (Valli di Porto Pino) $21. Dark chocolate, Kahlua, and toffee flavors mark this dense, syrupy wine. Not overly heavy, it has just enough viscosity to announce its presence in the mouth. Attribute this to the maritime winds of Sardinia, which add to the acidity of the wine. It finishes with olives, leather, and tar. **86** —*C.S. (5/1/2002)*

SANTI

Santi 1999 Merlot (Delle Venezie) $10. Tree bark, sulfur, and leather aromas interfere with the fruit. It's herbal, with dried cherry and raspberry providing what hook there is. It's lean, with firm acidity, thus it comes across fresh. But the flavors aren't pure enough to take it further. **83** *(5/1/2003)*

Santi 2005 Sortesele Pinot Grigio (Delle Venezie) $14. Toasted almond notes rise above well-integrated fruit flavors like peach, pineapple, and banana. This wine isn't so fleshy, but offers a nice palate-cleansing freshness instead. **87** —*M.L. (6/1/2006)*

Santi 2004 Sortesele Pinot Grigio (Delle Venezie) $12. An intensely fragrant and perfumy wine with fresh flowers, honey, and apple from the Sortesele vineyard along the Adige River. Sweet and endearing with prominent acidity. Drink within the next two years. **87 Best Buy** —*M.L. (2/1/2006)*

Santi 2002 Sortesele Pinot Grigio (Trentino) $13. Flavors of ripe peaches and fresh, clean fruit make for an immediately attractive wine. It is balanced with a layer of acidity and vibrant white currants. **85** —*R.V. (7/1/2003)*

Santi 2001 Sortesele Pinot Grigio (Trentino) $12. Shows the ill effects of age on this style of wine already. The vibrant, fresh fruit is fading, being replaced by some dusty spice notes. **83** —*J.C. (7/1/2003)*

Santi 2001 Red Blend (Amarone della Valpolicella) $40. Modest red fruit aromas in the cherry and rhubarb category start it toward a fresh, light, zesty palate. Don't be looking for depth and meatiness here or you'll be disappointed; it's a lot more like a simple Valpolicella table wine than classic Amarone. That said, it's clean and focused. **86** *(11/1/2005)*

Santi 1996 Proemio Red Blend (Amarone della Valpolicella) $51. Wonderful flavors of dark fruits, minerals, and licorice comprise this brawny red. There's also a nice toasty element, like roasted nuts, which is probably a result of new oak aging that brings added complexity. The alcohol is in balance. This fine wine will be best enjoyed in 2003 and beyond. **91** —*J.F. (9/1/2001)*

Santi 1999 Solane Red Blend (Valpolicella Classico) $10. A tired, browning hue is confirmed on nose and palate, where citrus rind and leather mix with fast-fading dried cherry fruit. The finish is dry and herbal. For a '99 this seems prematurely aged, yet it has some of the better qualities of an older wine: texture, tannins, and leather. **83** *(5/1/2003)*

SANTINI

Santini NV Spumante Moscato (Moscato d'Asti) $7. **84** —*P.G. (12/31/2000)*

SAPÍENS

Sapíens 2003 Chardonnay (Sicilia) $10. Heavy and ripe, with sweet apple and pear aromas. Not terribly fresh, with canned peach flavors prior to a sweet, weighty finish. Already tiring. **83** —*M.S. (7/1/2005)*

SARACCO

Saracco 2004 Moscato (Moscato d'Asti) $15. Boasts frothy mousse, good persistency, and a clearly defined mineral tenor backed by sweet green apple, honey, jasmine, and a touch of clove. Sweet peach cream in the mouth makes this parkler an ideal match for baked desserts. **90 Best Buy** —*M.L. (12/15/2005)*

SARDUS PATER

Sardus Pater 2002 Vermentino (Vermentino di Sardegna) $15. Yellow in color, with oxidized notes to the nose. This wine runs a touch sweet, heavy, and candied, with foreign but decent tasting fruit and a large, rushing finish. Turns peppery late, almost to the point of bitterness. **84** —*M.S. (8/1/2004)*

Sardus Pater 2003 Albus Vermentino (Vermentino di Sardegna) $14. Extremely oxidized, with an amber-gold color and aromas straight from a Sherry bodega. Only acceptable for its richness and nuttiness. If you expect any freshness or zip, take a pass. Tasted twice; funky both times with one sample corked. **80** —*M.S. (7/1/2006)*

SARTARELLI

Sartarelli 2003 Verdicchio (Verdicchio dei Castelli di Jesi Classico) $13. Opens with plump pear and peach aromas. Smooth in the mouth, with layered almond, pear, pepper, and ocean-influenced flavors. Quite deep and big on the finish, and as a whole it speaks well for the region and grape type. **87** —*M.S. (8/1/2004)*

Sartarelli 1999 White Blend (Verdicchio dei Castelli di Jesi Classico) $11. **83** —*M.N. (12/31/2000)*

SARTORI

Sartori 1991 Corte Brá Corvina (Amarone della Valpolicella) $40. **94** — *M.G. (5/1/1999)*

Sartori 2000 Corvina, Rondinella, Molinara (Amarone della Valpolicella Classico) $33. There's a slightly nutty-almondy edge to the black cherry and plum aromas, then lovely flavors of brandied fruitcake laden with baking spices and dried fruit. Yet at the same time, it's not over-the-top rich, and very drinkable with food. A long, supple, fruit-filled finish seals the deal. Drink now-2015. **91 Editors' Choice** —*J.C. (12/31/2004)*

Sartori 1995 Corvina, Rondinella, Molinara (Amarone della Valpolicella Classico) $31. **87** —*M.S. (9/1/2000)*

Sartori 1997 Merlot (Friuli Venezia Giulia) $9. **83** —*M.S. (9/1/2000)*

Sartori 1997 Pinot Grigio (Grave del Friuli) $9. **80** *(8/1/1999)*

Sartori 2004 Pinot Grigio (Delle Venezie) $9. Chrysanthemum, dandelion, sweet papaya, and guava compose a nose that is almost too much of a good thing. On the palate, you get what you'd expect from $9 Pinot Grigio: crispness but not a lot of complexity. **86 Best Buy** —*M.L. (6/1/2006)*

Sartori 2003 Pinot Grigio (Delle Venezie) $9. A pleasant, medium-weight cocktail white, Sartori's 2003 Pinot Grigio boasts hints of blanched almonds alongside more assertive flavors of peaches and pears. Picks up an anise note on the citrusy finish. **85 Best Buy** —*J.C. (12/31/2004)*

Sartori 2002 Pinot Grigio (Delle Venezie) $9. With flavors of unripe pineapple and a jarringly tart finish, you might not object if a friend handed you a plastic cup of this at a poolside party, but you probably wouldn't search out the label either. **81** —*J.C. (7/1/2003)*

Sartori 2001 Red Blend (Amarone della Valpolicella) $34. Medium in force, with modest tannins and a lot of crispness. Approachable and easy, with date, dried cherry, and liqueur-like flavors. An unflappable, solid wine, but not overwhelming in any way. It's juicy, structured, and pretty easy to wrap yourself around. **88** *(11/1/2005)*

Sartori 1995 Cent'Anni Red Blend (Valpolicella) $33. **84** —*M.S. (9/1/2000)*

Sartori 1998 Corte Brà Red Blend (Amarone della Valpolicella Classico) $40. Lower in alcohol than most, so consequently it's pushing bright fruit notes and a lot of cinnamon, clove, and other wood-based aromas. The palate offers a nice berry component, cherry, herbs, and cigar tobacco. Finishes with crisp acids and a spot of chocolate. **89** *(11/1/2005)*

SASSO

Sasso 1997 Covo dei Briganti Aglianico (Aglianico del Vulture) $15. Whoa—the tannins in this will parch your mouth like Death Valley. There's some question as to whether the fruit that's present will outlast them, so serve this now with hearty, rustic fare that can stand up to this wine's earth, spice, and dried fruit flavors. **85** —*C.S. (5/1/2002)*

SCAGLIOLA

Scagliola 2004 Volo di Farfalle Moscato (Moscato d'Asti) $17. A luminous, golden wine with intense mineral and chalkboard aromatics backed by less intense honey, earthy, musty, and fruity smells. Floral notes do not emerge strong on the nose, but they certainly do in the mouth, where sweet honeysuckle lingers on a foamy finish. A true specimen of the Moscato Bianco di Canelli grape from a 15-hectare, family-run vineyard near Calosso. **88** —*M.L. (12/15/2005)*

SCARLATTA

Scarlatta 1997 Merlot (Veneto) $5. 81 —*M.S. (9/1/2000)*

Scarlatta 1997 Pinot Grigio (Veneto) $5. 84 *(8/1/1999)*

SCARPA

Scarpa 1990 Tettimorra Barolo Nebbiolo (Barolo) $NA. Something of a curiosity, because Scarpa waits for the wines to be mature before their release. This is certainly mature, perhaps too mature, with high, dry tannins and mature, earthy fruit. This is a very dry, traditional style of wine. 81 —*R.V. (11/15/2002)*

SCARZELLO

Scarzello 1998 Vigna Merenda Nebbiolo (Barolo) $75. Plummy and chocolaty, with big black cherry flavors that seem a trifle hollow at the core. Tangy acids on the finish add to that impression. If this knits together and fills out over the next several years, this rating will seem conservative. 85 *(4/2/2004)*

SCIARRA

Sciarra 1998 Roccarosso Red Blend (Marche) $18. Deadpan aromas of cigar and cherry Life Saver are okay as parts but less than stellar when melded. The palate is candied and lean; not much there. Exceedingly light on the finish, which breaks up quickly. A '98 now? Kind of makes you wonder. 83 —*M.S. (10/1/2006)*

SCOPETANI

Scopetani 2004 Sangiovese (Chianti Rufina) $6. The formula for traditional Chianti sees Sangiovese blended with white grape varieties for a fruitier nose, fresher mouthfeel and an easy-to-approach drink. This Chianti follows that tradition with its blend of Sangiovese, Malvasia, and Trebbiano. The nose offers forest berry and blue flowers with background notes of marzipan, minerals, and crushed mint. And there's enough acidity in the mouth to keep it lively and food-friendly. 86 Best Buy —*M.L. (11/15/2006)*

Scopetani 2001 813 Riserva Sangiovese (Chianti Rufina) $14. By happy coincidence, the Tampa area code is 813, but the wine is named for the number of days from harvest to bottling. Cedar and dried cherry aromas are classic Chianti, picking up tobacco notes on the palate and finish. 85 *(11/15/2006)*

Scopetani 2004 Angelicus Sangiovese (Chianti) $9. Light, fresh, and clean as a whistle. Here's an easygoing Chianti that pushes red-fruit aromas toward a palate that's zesty and full of crisp cherry and raspberry flavors. Some might find it too tangy and racy; but if you like a leaner version of red wine it will do the trick. 85 Best Buy —*M.S. (10/1/2006)*

Scopetani 2003 Angelicus Sangiovese (Chianti) $8. Dark and manly from the get-go, with aromas of melted brown sugar, black cherry, and charbroiled beef. Next up you'll encounter fresh red fruit, peppy acids, and enough body to provide balance and a perceived creaminess. Very easy to like. 89 Best Buy *(4/1/2005)*

SECCO-BERTANI

Secco-Bertani 2000 Red Blend (Valpolicella Valpantena) $13. Dusty cherry and leather aromas come first, followed by chocolate and wood spice. Plum and cherry fruit make for a fine flavor profile, while the finish is touched up by just a hint of oak and some proper bitterness. Substantive yet smooth, with good balance throughout. 88 *(5/1/2003)*

SEGHESIO

Seghesio 1997 Vigneto della Chiesa Barbera (Barbera d'Alba) $30. 91 *(4/1/2000)*

SELLA & MOSCA

Sella & Mosca 1995 Marchese Di Villamarina Cabernet Sauvignon (Sardinia) $35. 84 —*M.N. (12/31/2000)*

Sella & Mosca 1996 Raím Red Blend (Isola dei Nuraghi) $12. 85 —*M.N. (12/31/2000)*

Sella & Mosca 2002 Riserva Red Blend (Cannonau di Sardegna) $16. Light in color, with a rosy tint. Aromas of burnt grass, pepper, and red fruit are distant and unconvincing, while the palate is generic and rud-

derless. Not a terrible wine, but lacking in substance. 82 —*M.S. (10/1/2006)*

Sella & Mosca 1997 Riserva Red Blend (Cannonau di Sardegna) $11. 86 —*M.N. (12/31/2000)*

Sella & Mosca 1995 Tanca Farra Red Blend (Sardinia) $16. 88 —*M.N. (12/31/2000)*

Sella & Mosca 1999 Le Arenarie Sauvignon Blanc (Sardinia) $12. 88 —*M.N. (12/31/2000)*

Sella & Mosca 2003 La Cala Vermentino (Vermentino di Sardegna) $13. At less than 12% alcohol, this is a lighter-styled Vermentino. Nevertheless, it has forward aromas of tropical fruit and flowers, and then flavors of tangy apple, papaya, and lime. It's snappy on the tongue and clean. Very easygoing and solid. 87 —*M.S. (8/1/2004)*

Sella & Mosca 1999 La Cala White Blend (Sardinia) $11. 88 Best Buy —*M.N. (12/31/2000)*

SELVO DEL MORO

Selvo del Moro 2001 Sangiovese (Chianti Classico) $22. Leathery and lean, which makes it a bit dull. Generic plum and berry fruit flavors come across mildly tart, while the finish is open but unexciting. Standard stuff that doesn't offend. 85 *(4/1/2005)*

SEMIFONTE

Semifonte 1997 Riserva Sangiovese (Chianti Classico) $31. Tart berries—almost rhubarb or cranberry—blend with dark toast. Cherry, toast, and a licorice note show on the palate; it's nicely balanced and feels food-friendly. Finishes dry, with medium to full tannins. 86 *(4/1/2001)*

SESTA DI SOPRA

Sesta di Sopra 2001 Brunello (Brunello di Montalcino) $55. Applause to Brunello tipicity in the form of balsam notes (menthol cough drop), forest berry, black licorice, tar, and background vanilla to smooth over the sharp points. The tannins are still thorny but the finish is long and limber. 91 *(4/1/2006)*

SESTI

Sesti 2001 Brunello (Brunello di Montalcino) $60. A distinct barnyard note does not distract from ripe black cherry, leather, tobacco, and cedar wood and in fact integrates well within the whole. The mouthfeel is silky and smooth, and there's a playful, clove-like sensation on the finish. 88 *(4/1/2006)*

Sesti 2000 Phenomena Riserva Brunello (Brunello di Montalcino) $45. Blueberry, fennel seed, forest berry, and rhubarb with a slightly lactic, sour note. Full and creamy in the mouth and tangy but not extremely tannic or long. Because this wine does not overwhelm your taste buds, it has great food pairing potential. 90 *(4/1/2006)*

SIGNANO

Signano 2001 Sangiovese (Chianti Colli Senesi) $14. Raisiny, with additional tar and rubber aromas. Short, flat, and medium-weight, with midland cherry flavor and not much nuance. Lacks character. 82 *(4/1/2005)*

Signano 2002 Vernaccia (Vernaccia di San Gimignano) $17. The funky nose is hard to peg; there's some cantaloupe but not much else is recognizable. Fortunately, good acidity keeps the mouthfeel fresh, while flavors of orange, lemon, and grapefruit are a bit high-toned. Decent on the finish. 84 —*M.S. (8/1/2004)*

SIMONE SANTINI

Simone Santini 2003 Tenute Le Calcinaie Sangiovese (Chianti Colli Senesi) $20. Lots of black cherry, burnt match, and talcum powder to the nose, which is followed by sweet black fruit that veers toward plum and prune. The finish is rich and full, with licorice and dry, firm tannins. Shows good size and complexity. 88 *(4/1/2005)*

SINFAROSA

Sinfarosa 1998 Zinfandel (Puglia) $24. Indian spices (particularly curry and turmeric) plus cola and black fruit notes stand out on the nose. Dry and somewhat thin in the mouth; raisiny-sweet black fruit and dry wood flavors bring you from palate to finish. 82 —*C.S. (5/1/2002)*

ITALY

SIRO PACENTI

Siro Pacenti 2001 Brunello (Brunello di Montalcino) $70. Intense black cherry, raspberry, and vanilla are amplified by maple syrup, chestnut, dried red rose petal, exotic spice, plum, earth, and mushroom. Supple, round, and soft with a young, fresh finish and coffee cacao at the end. **89** (4/1/2006)

Siro Pacenti 2000 Brunello (Brunello di Montalcino) $75. This perennial stud struts its stuff once again. Smoke, spice, and red fruit aromas are perfectly interwoven, while the wine itself flows with agile zest. Maybe it doesn't have the layering of the amazing '99, but it's gargantuan on the midpalate and the finish is exotic as it deals nutmeg, marzipan, chocolate, cassis, and mint. A proverbial kitchen-sink wine worthy of its reputation. **93 Editors' Choice** —M.S. (7/1/2005)

Siro Pacenti 1999 Brunello (Brunello di Montalcino) $NA. A stunningly complete, cool-as-can-be modern wine with great color, lush plum, and berry fruit, and very little of the earth and leather notes that some Brunello-istas may be seeking. However, if you like texture, sublime flavors of chocolate and charcoal, and perfectly integrated oak, this is for you. Consider drinking in 2005 or 2006. **95** —M.S. (6/1/2004)

Siro Pacenti 2002 Sangiovese (Rosso di Montalcino) $NA. This wine is better than many Brunellos. It offers laudable richness, excellent balance, and pure chocolate and berry flavors along with captivating spice notes. Yes, it's another modern, chewy red from Pacenti, one that will surely please the new-age palate. **91** —M.S. (6/1/2004)

SOLARIA

Solaria 2001 Brunello (Brunello di Montalcino) $45. Generous vanilla with delicate menthol, basil, and fresh herbs, eucalyptus, cherry, exotic spice, cloves, and cigar box. Wood notes are a tad dull and lackluster but the wine boasts a supple feel, solid tannins, and fruity notes on the finish. **89** (4/1/2006)

Solaria 2000 Brunello (Brunello di Montalcino) $70. Stout but intoxicating, with floral aromas along with hints of maple, leather, and pepper. For some it might come across heavy, as the ultra-ripe plum and cherry fruit almost veers toward medicinal. Fortunately, however, it holds the line. Powerful and heady, but plenty elegant. **92** —M.S. (7/1/2005)

Solaria 1998 Brunello (Brunello di Montalcino) $70. Penetrating and intense, with reserve-level qualities. The nose is full of bacon, leather, and sandalwood in addition to pulsating red fruit. It represents the purest form of ripeness; the nose, the palate, the finish—everything is so forward it seems to be dripping juice. More chewy and soft than some of its neighbors, this may be the perfect wine to drink in the near future. **92 Cellar Selection** —M.S. (11/15/2003)

Solaria 2002 Sangiovese (Rosso di Montalcino) $29. This fine producer chose not to make Brunello in 2002 due to below-average harvest conditions, so its Rosso benefited. The wine delivers sweet prune and chocolate aromas prior to a stylish, delicious palate. This one is really easy to drink and should be a no-brainer for restaurateurs. **89** —M.S. (6/1/2004)

Solaria 2001 Sangiovese (Rosso di Montalcino) $30. Very youthful, with tire rubber, burnt sugar and ripe fruit on the nose. The body is big enough to make an impression, while the red fruit conjures cherry and cassis. Things turn a touch snappy and piquant toward the end, but it's snazzy and defined enough to do the job. **87** —M.S. (11/15/2003)

SOLDIMELA

Soldimela 1999 Sangiovese Grosso (Monteregio di Massa Maritima) $8. Full, tart black cherry fruit and an appealing earthiness give character to this modestly priced red from Tuscany's western coastal region. Sangiovese Grosso (as in Brunello) fruit expressed in limestone soil make this notable value a flavor-packed mouthful. Medium-weight and dry, the wine closes moderately long with fine tannins. **87 Best Buy** —M.M. (11/15/2001)

Soldimela 2000 Vermentino (Maremma) $8. Vermentino is a grape most associated with the island of Sardinia, but it has been cultivated along the Tuscan coast for some time, and recently more examples have been reaching our shores. This rendition is crisp and dry, with an attractive dried herb and mineral profile and a lingering finish. Light, yet very flavorful. Serve this as an apéritif, or with hors d'oeuvres or salads. **87 Best Buy** —M.M. (11/15/2001)

SOLDO

Soldo 2001 Cabernet Sauvignon (Veneto) $6. The nose is slightly pickled; in addition, there's some caramel and marshmallow. Flavors of roasted coffee, tart cherry, and cranberry rule the palate, while it finishes with ample acidity but also a hint of the veggies. Mouthfeel is better than the flavor package. **83** (5/1/2003)

Soldo 2001 Merlot (Veneto) $6. Aromas akin to gravy as well as pasta smothered in red sauce and processed cheese do nothing to draw you in. The palate brings even more tomato and oregano, and the finish is thick and grabby. This wine is barely acceptable. **80** (5/1/2003)

Soldo 2001 Pinot Grigio (Veneto) $6. Light but clean, with aromas of anise, pears, and green apples and modest flavors of pear, watermelon rind, and lime. **83** —J.C. (7/1/2003)

Soldo 2000 Red Blend (Valpolicella) $6. This light rendering is quite the quaffing wine. The nose is floral, with dried red fruit. The palate delivers more of that dried fruit, particularly currants and raspberry. It feels good on the palate and goes down easy, without a fuss. **85 Best Buy** (5/1/2003)

Soldo 2000 Red Blend (Montepulciano d'Abruzzo) $6. Aromas of forest floor, wet dog, and wheat bread are awkward and far short of refined. The palate runs sweet and slightly muddled, with sugary boysenberry popping up only to veer off the mark. A chocolaty, thick finish with some baking spice flavors are okay but fail to save the day. **81** —M.S. (11/15/2003)

Soldo 2000 White Blend (Soave) $6. Some faintly floral aromas and a hint of baking soda add interest to simple lemon-lime flavors. Turns watery on the finish. **82** —J.C. (7/1/2003)

SORELLE BRONCA

Sorelle Bronca NV Extra Dry Prosecco (Prosecco di Valdobbiadene) $14. This is a remarkably fresh, floral Prosecco, with delicate apple and citrus flavors buoyed by its light, frothy texture. It's drier than most, with a tart, cleansing finish. **86** —J.C. (12/31/2003)

SPADINA

Spadina 2002 Nero d'Avola (Sicilia) $10. A touch stewy, with molasses and sherry aromas on top of earthy fruit. Flavors of pie cherry and cranberry are more austere than the bouquet might indicate, yet that tight, starchy fruit will do well washing down pizza or rigatoni alla vodka. **86 Best Buy** —M.S. (2/1/2005)

Spadina 2002 Una Rosa Signature Nero d'Avola (Sicilia) $15. Dark and intense, with lemony oak on the nose that you can't miss. In the mouth, licorice, plum, and pepper wrestle with some oakiness, but the whole is successful. Finishes with tight tannins that create a thinning sensation. More good than flawed. **88** —M.S. (2/1/2005)

SPALLETTI

Spalletti 2004 Sangiovese (Chianti) $11. Rubbery berry aromas accompany notes of smoke and leather. The palate is medium in weight but fairly robust in terms of acidity. And the cherry, plum, and berry flavors are good yet common. Middle-of-the-road red wine meant for pizza and pasta. **84** —M.S. (10/1/2006)

Spalletti 1997 Riserva Sangiovese (Chianti Rufina) $20. This round, darkly-hued, well-balanced wine has deep cherry fruit and cedar accents. Hints of licorice, mineral, and toast complement the fruit. Nice balance and mouthfeel, too, and it's lively right through the finish. Drinking well now. **90** (4/1/2001)

SPANO

Spano 1996 Annata Red Blend (Salento) $40. A deeply colored, opaque wine. Chocolate, cassis, and lanolin dominate the nose. The palate is a bit woody, almost stemmy, with kitchen herbs but very little fruit on a medium-bodied structure. **84** —C.S. (5/1/2002)

SPERI

Speri 2000 Corvina (Amarone della Valpolicella Classico) $60. Sweet and rich, with a big overlay of caramel, cola, and burnt sugar. Sweet and gooey as that may sound, it has gorgeous balance and does not taste heavy or candied. Still, it's overtly ripe, as the cherry and plum flavors sing. Lip-smacking good, and fleshy. **91** *(11/1/2005)*

Speri 2001 Corvina, Rondinella, Molinara (Amarone della Valpolicella Classico) $60. Pitch black and full of asphalt, tar, coffee, and meat aromas. The feel right now is a touch raw due to its youth, but as it sizzles and scours it shows masculine, smoky flavors and a lot of bitter chocolate. Comes on with guns blazing and full tannins. Needs several years to mellow out. **91** *(11/1/2005)*

Speri 1997 Red Blend (Amarone della Valpolicella Classico) $48. This is A-1 Amarone. It has a classy, traditional prune and chocolate nose, which comes in front of a perfectly pure palate of dried cherry, plum, and dark chocolate. The finish answers the challenge, delivering black tea and tannins, but in layer upon airy layer. **91** *(5/1/2003)*

Speri 2003 La Roverina Red Blend (Valpolicella Classico Superiore) $16. A garnet-red wine with a vegetal touch and some white mushroom backed by raspberry jam and red cherry. Sits well in the mouth with a medium build and finish but lower acidity. **86** *—M.L. (9/1/2005)*

Speri 1999 Sant'urbano Red Blend (Valpolicella Classico Superiore) $21. Dark in color and commensurately packed with aromas of black plum, blackberry, and chocolate. The texture is kind of jammy, yet full-level acids make for a juicy feel. The finish is smooth but short. **86** *(5/1/2003)*

Speri 1998 Sant'urbano Red Blend (Valpolicella Classico Superiore) $22. Some funk on the nose finally yields to reveal toasty, foresty notes. Plum, apple skin, cherry, and raspberry all share the palate prior to a chalky, dry finish. **85** *(5/1/2003)*

Speri 2000 Vigneto La Roverina Red Blend (Valpolicella Classico Superiore) $12. Some black raspberries and vanilla on the nose indicate that there is substance to come. The palate is chunky with cherry, plum, and berry fruit, while the mouthfeel is dry and full, with buttery notes. **85** *(5/1/2003)*

SPORTOLETTI

Sportoletti 2004 Grechetto (Assisi) $12. Brilliant straw-yellow color and layers of delicate aromas that span cut grass, stone fruits, and white flowers. Elegance continues in the mouth but ends on a suddenly tart note that works well in this case. Vines benefit from reddish, calcium-rich soils. Fermented in steel tanks. **87** *—M.L. (9/1/2005)*

Sportoletti 2001 Assisi Rosso Red Blend (Umbria) $15. Named after the 20 acre vineyard Assisi. The wine has dark chocolate, and black cherry flavors. A medium bodied wine that is pleasant, and easy to drink. **86** *—C.S. (2/1/2003)*

Sportoletti 2000 Villa Fidelia Rosso Red Blend (Umbria) $55. Cedar, chocolate, and black plum aromas introduce a rich, juicy mouthfeel and a long, complex finish. Made in a modern style, this delicious red is approachable now but will last for some time. **92 Editors' Choice** *—C.S. (2/1/2003)*

ST. MICHAEL EPPAN

St. Michael Eppan 1998 Pinot Grigio (Alto Adige) $10. **86** *(8/1/1999)*

St. Michael Eppan 2000 Sanct Valentin Sauvignon Blanc (Alto Adige) $28. Sharp aromas of citrus mix with the odd note of petrol. Lime and apple-skin flavors fade into an acid-driven, orange-flavored finish that's also musky and quite long. While not initially appealing, this wine opens up with airing to reveal some hidden qualities. **87** *(8/1/2002)*

St. Michael-Eppan 2004 Pinot Grigio (Alto Adige) $11. Lime, lemon blossom, and a nice mineral quality describe this wine. Light-weight, but with well-integrated acidity, it makes a safe match for seafood, vegetables, and white meat. **85** *—M.L. (2/1/2006)*

St. Michael-Eppan 2004 Anger Pinot Grigio (Alto Adige) $14. Loads of honey, peach, and melon shape a softer, rounder Pinot Grigio that is not big in the mouth but is well-made all around (partially aged in oak casks). **86** *—M.L. (2/1/2006)*

St. Michael-Eppan 2003 Sanct Valentin Pinot Grigio (Alto Adige) $22. This producer's star slugger boasts vanilla, toast, banana, and fresh sawdust. Despite being a tad monothematic and too focused on wood, the

nose is attractive. It's too bad the wine is not more structured or concentrated in the mouth. **86** *—M.L. (2/1/2006)*

STELLA

Stella 1998 Pinot Grigio (Umbria) $8. **83** *(8/1/1999)*

Stella 2000 Pinot Grigio (Umbria) $6. Umbrian Pinot Grigio may not be as well known as the crisp, elegant (and pricey) wines from veneto, but for six bucks you get a plump, round, fruity delight, with true varietal character. Its fresh, sweet pears, weightier and less steely than the versions from northern Italy, end in a clean, full finish. **87** *—P.G. (11/15/2001)*

Stella 2003 Sangiovese (Puglia) $7. Funky on the nose, with indistinct berry fruit that takes on a strange peanut character. In the mouth the fruit is tart, short, and somewhat green. **80** *—M.S. (2/1/2005)*

STIVAL

Stival 2000 Cabernet Sauvignon (Veneto) $6. Mixed berries and aromas of green vegetables start off this blend of Cabernet Sauvignon and Cabernet Franc. Lightly spiced blueberry flavors interact with creamy light tannins, and a simple finish wraps up this clean Cabernet, that for $6 won't offend anyone. **85 Best Buy** *(5/1/2002)*

Stival 2000 Chardonnay (Veneto) $6. A brilliant, pale straw-yellow color is an indication of the freshness of this wine. Tropical aromas of mangos and bananas start with flavors of citrus and a sharp but not overpowering acidity finishing. A nonmalolactic, simple yet pleasant Chardonnay. **85 Best Buy** *(5/1/2002)*

Stival 2000 Merlot (Veneto) $6. Deep earth and toasty aromas of fresh ground coffee prep you for an easy-drinking wine experience. The flavors of chocolate and wild berries make this Merlot a by-the-glass pleasure. **86 Best Buy** *(5/1/2002)*

Stival 1998 Pinot Grigio (Veneto) $6. **85 Best Buy** *(8/1/1999)*

Stival 2005 Pinot Grigio (Veneto) $7. Dried herbs, grass, and hay with some pear, apple skin, and crushed stone sums up the nose. The mouth delivers less excitement; a sour note interrupts what would otherwise be a smoother ride. **85 Best Buy** *—M.L. (6/1/2006)*

Stival 2004 Pinot Grigio (Veneto) $7. There's a copperish tinge to the color and although the nose is not intense, it does deliver clear notes of pear, pineapple, chamomile, and chopped basil or mint. The lower alcohol helps it go down easily. **85 Best Buy** *—M.L. (2/1/2006)*

Stival 2003 Pinot Grigio (Veneto) $6. Hints of almond paste and nectarine on the nose are followed by clean, fruity flavors of stone fruits, oranges, and grapefruit. A bit low in acidity, but user-friendly, with notes of almond reprising on the finish. **84 Best Buy** *—J.C. (12/31/2004)*

Stival 2000 2000 Pinot Grigio (Veneto) $6. Exactly what you want in a mainstream Pinot Grigio; light, crisp, and refreshing. The tart citrus flavors show some minerality, which adds a bit of complexity to this clean-finishing, drink-on-its-own wine. **84** *(5/1/2002)*

STRACCALI

Straccali 2003 Sangiovese (Chianti) $9. Pungent and rubbery, with aromas of leather and pie cherry. Tart red fruit is about all you get from the palate, which has a stripped-down but solid texture. Juicy and simple, with serious acidity. **84** *(4/1/2005)*

Straccali 2001 Sangiovese (Chianti Classico) $13. Roasted and herbal, with green pepper aromas mixed with prune. Very heavy, as if it were left too long on the vines. Too raisiny. **82** *(4/1/2005)*

Straccali 1999 Sangiovese (Chianti) $10. The dark cherry fruit bears some leather and earth accents that add complexity. Bright acidity marks this lean, angular wine, making it a great choice for pasta with tomato sauce. The high-toned fruit shines right to the end. **85** *(4/1/2001)*

Straccali 1998 Sangiovese (Sangiovese di Toscana) $8. The angular frame of this light red sports dry cherry aromas and flavors with leather accents. The palate shows some tobacco notes and it closes dry, with slightly prickly tannins. **84** *(8/1/2001)*

ITALY

ITALY

TALAMONTI

Talamonti 2004 Trebì Trebbiano (Trebbiano d'Abruzzo) $NA. Started in 2001, Cantine Talamonti is determined to put the spotlight on the region of Abruzzo and its native grapes. Winemaker Lucio Matricardi has produced a crisp white bursting with flowers, apples, and subtle mineral notes. **86** —M.L. (9/1/2005)

TALENTI

Talenti 2000 Brunello (Brunello di Montalcino) $60. A big-time barrique wine, with lemony, sawdust-based aromas in front of sweet, ripe fruit. Quite amped up, with lots of cherry and chocolate on the midpalate and finish. Rich and pure, although it sits firmly on one plane and doesn't show much complexity. **88** —M.S. (7/1/2005)

Talenti 1997 Brunello (Brunello di Montalcino) $NA. Riccardo Talenti, grandson of Pierluigi Talenti, the grand old man of Montalcino, currently makes one of the finest Brunellos with the help of consultant Carlo Ferrini. They are now using new wood for aging, and the extra layer of richness this brings is apparent in the comparative accessibility of this wine. Yet it is also huge, with classic tannins and intense, concentrated flavors of sweet blackberry jelly. **95 Editors' Choice** —R.V. (8/1/2002)

Talenti 2001 Pian di Conte Brunello (Brunello di Montalcino) $53. Bold, ripe, and concentrated, you can pluck out cedar, ripe berries, vanilla, cassis, spice, black pepper, and mineral notes. A big, brawny wine with a playful sour vein that delivers power, but little mystery. **92** (4/1/2006)

Talenti 1998 Reserva Brunello (Brunello di Montalcino) $NA. Rather reduced, with a touch of peanut to the tight nose. The question here is whether more time will allow this wine to open, or is it simply lacking in complexity? For now it seems condensed and punched down, good but plain as the category goes. Hold until 2006. **88** —M.S. (6/1/2004)

Talenti 1999 Riserva Brunello (Brunello di Montalcino) $85. A touch of barnyard at first gives way to deep, dark fruit that's spun tight on the palate. As it opens, bigger berry and black cherry flavors emerge. Tight and tannic on the back palate, with an uncomplicated finish. An excellent wine, but one competing in a talented field. **90** —M.S. (7/1/2005)

TASCA D'ALMERITA

Tasca d'Almerita 2003 Cabernet Sauvignon (Contea di Sclafani) $60. Each spring, Sicily is covered with bushes of wild fennel and if you pay close attention you can smell its pungent fragrance on this 100% Cabernet. You'll also get generous notes of sage, green herb, red cherry, exotic spice, smoke, vanilla, and toasted almond. This is a well-made and concentrated wine with tight tannins and an overall chewy quality. **91 Editors' Choice** —M.L. (9/1/2006)

Tasca d'Almerita 1998 Cabernet Sauvignon (Sicilia) $48. There's not much in the way of forward fruit here, but this Cab offers plenty of other appealing aspects. Charred oak and dry herbs dominate the palate and the finish; herb, oak, vanilla cream, and plum fruit show on the nose. **85** —D.T. (5/1/2002)

Tasca d'Almerita 1998 Cabernet Sauvignon (Sicilia) $48. 85 —C.S. (5/1/2002)

Tasca d'Almerita 2000 Chardonnay (Sicilia) $50. A big, full-bodied wine with spicy wood aromas and flavors. There is some peppery, spicy charcater. **87** —R.V. (10/1/2003)

Tasca d'Almerita 2004 Chardonnay Chardonnay (Contea di Sclafani) $29. This is a golden-hued Chardonnay that sees seven months of French oak with a rich, creamy quality that is not always easy to read. The aromas span from exotic fruit to Parmigiano cheese rind, but the mouthfeel is jazzy and cool. **87** —M.L. (7/1/2006)

Tasca d'Almerita 2001 Regaleali Bianco Inzolia (Sicilia) $11. A clean, simple white made from the native Inzolia grape that blends pear and peach flavors into a crisp, refreshing whole. Finishes with a hint of almond skin. **86** (6/1/2003)

Tasca d'Almerita 2005 Le Rosé Nerello Mascalese (Sicilia) $12. A beautifully luminous rosé with a peach-raspberry hue made from Nerello Mascalese (vinified white) that sees contact with Nero d'Avola skins for color. The pretty aromas include raspberry, strawberry, and stone fruit and the wine's freshness and structure is reminiscent of rosés from southern France. **86** —M.L. (6/21/2006)

Tasca d'Almerita 2004 Lamuri Nero d'Avola (Sicilia) $19. Here is a lusciously concentrated and inky red packed tight with big flavor: plum, fruit preserve, spice, clove, cinnamon, and nutmeg. It's sweet at the core with spice bread flavors in the mouth. **89** —M.L. (7/1/2006)

Tasca d'Almerita 2004 Regaleali Nero d'Avola (Sicilia) $15. This is a very ripe, hot climate wine with lavish chocolate fudge, minced clove, cinnamon, and blackberry jam on the nose. But it also has a green component, like grilled bell pepper. **87** —M.L. (7/1/2006)

Tasca d'Almerita 2003 Regaleali Nero d'Avola (Sicilia) $15. The cherry fruit, pistachio nut cream flavors, and chewy consistency make this an extremely attractive match for grated cheese-topped pasta dishes and grilled meats. **87** —M.L. (9/1/2005)

Tasca d'Almerita 2002 Regaleali Nero d'Avola (Sicilia) $14. Nice and jammy; the quintessential ripe, easy quaffer. Plenty of black fruit and licorice cover the bouquet, followed by deep plum and black-cherry fruit. The finish is fat, full, and continuous. A fine effort among its type. **88** —M.S. (2/1/2005)

Tasca d'Almerita 2003 Rosso del Conte Nero d'Avola (Contea di Sclafani) $49. Rosso del Conte is a landmark Sicilian red that boasts deep and penetrating concentration, finesse with light berry fruit, and mineral notes, and extraordinary intensity in the mouth. This is a profound wine that sees 18 months of French oak. The tannins are still tight, so drink after 2008. **92 Cellar Selection** —M.L. (7/1/2006)

Tasca d'Almerita 2001 Rosso del Conte Nero d'Avola (Contea di Sclafani) $45. Powerful and poised, with subdued but serious aromas of charred black fruit, raisin, and coffee. Ripe but linear, with intense pie cherry, rhubarb, and blackberry flavors. Ample acidity pushes it forward, while the tannins are tight, almost harsh. Will age for another five to eight years. Drink now with good food, or hold through 2005. **90** —M.S. (2/1/2005)

Tasca d'Almerita 1998 Rosso Del Conte Nero d'Avola (Sicilia) $42. A very sexy, deep wine with cedar, fresh coffee and milk chocolate aromas guiding you into spicy, black cherry warmth. It's the kind of wine that elicits a spontaneous, sensual "mmmm." A blend of Nero D'Avola (90%) and Perricone (10%). **91** —C.S. (5/1/2002)

Tasca d'Almerita 2003 Camastra Red Blend (Sicilia) $NA. A blend of Nero d'Avola and Merlot with 14 months in French oak, this ruby colored wine has loads of exotic spice— especially clove—cracked black pepper and blackberry. It's expressive, intense, and lively in the mouth with a persistent finish. **90** —M.L. (7/1/2006)

Tasca d'Almerita 2000 Camastra Red Blend (Sicilia) $24. A blend of Nero d'Avola with Merlot gives a ripe, juicy, fruity wine, with a flavor of dark chocolate and dense young tannins. This wine should age well. **87** —R.V. (10/1/2003)

Tasca d'Almerita 2003 Cygnus Red Blend (Sicilia) $30. This is a gorgeous and concentrated 60-40 Nero d'Avola-Cab Sauvignon blend with loads of exotic spice, cinnamon bread, blackberry, and dark fruit. There's a touch of sweetness in the mouth followed by tight tannins and a long, penetrating finish. Sees 14 months in French oak. **91 Editors' Choice** —M.L. (7/1/2006)

Tasca d'Almerita 1999 Cygnus Red Blend (Sicilia) $21. This winning blend of 75% Nero d'Avola and 25% Cabernet Sauvignon is firm and structured, but coddles that structure in a layer of lushness. Briary, raspberry fruit is balanced by darker notes of cassis and chocolate. Drink now-2010. **90 Editors' Choice** (6/1/2003)

Tasca d'Almerita 1997 Regaleali Red Blend (Sicilia) $12. 90 Best Buy —M.N. (12/31/2000)

Tasca d'Almerita 2001 Regaleali Rosso Red Blend (Sicilia) $16. This is a fine blend of Nero d'Avola and Syrah giving ripe, soft fruit which has a delicious layer of acidity to give balance. Flavors of raisins and dried fruits give an exotic element to the wine. **84** —R.V. (10/1/2003)

Tasca d'Almerita 2000 Regaleali Rosso Red Blend (Sicilia) $9. 86 Best Buy —R.V. (11/15/2002)

Tasca d'Almerita 2000 Rosso del Conte Red Blend (Sicilia) $37. A powerful, classic wine, full of raisin flavors, layers of wood, sweet tannins, and perfumed, ripe black fruits. A blend of Nero d'Avola and Perricone, this is a big, firm wine with aging potential over 10 years or more. **91** —*R.V.* *(10/1/2003)*

Tasca d'Almerita 1998 Rosso del Conte Red Blend (Sicilia) $40. A proprietary blend inspired by Chateauneuf-du-Pape, the Count's Red is more closed than the other offerings from Tasca, showing little on the nose beyond chocolate. In the mouth, raspberry fruit begins to emerge; the wine is obviously big, full-bodied, and tannic. It's meant to age, and we think it will do so just fine. Try in 2008, or pair it with hearty meat dishes if you can't hold out that long. **91** *(6/1/2003)*

Tasca d'Almerita 2001 Rose di Regaleali Rosé Blend (Sicilia) $11. The perfect picnic wine? Bold, floral, and berry aromas, black cherry fruit, and some light tannins will make this the most versatile wine in your hamper this summer. This blend of Nero d'Avola and Nerello Mascalese is grown specifically for rose production—it is not a saignee used to increase the concentration of the estate's reds. **90 Best Buy** *(6/1/2003)*

Tasca d'Almerita 2005 Leone d'Almerita White Blend (Sicilia) $16. This Catarratto-Chardonnay blend exhibits a luminous, straw color with aromas of white flower, stone fruit, and talc powder. It's a clean, well-balanced summertime wine with peach flavors; would pair well with salmon. **87** —*M.L.* *(7/1/2006)*

Tasca d'Almerita 2002 Leone d'Almerita White Blend (Sicilia) $18. High-altitude vineyards in central Sicily yield a finely concentrated wine, with fruit aromas and crisp, green fruit. **86** —*R.V.* *(10/1/2003)*

Tasca d'Almerita 2001 Leone d'Almerita White Blend (Sicilia) $15. This blend of Inzolia and Chardonnay displays slightly creamy, lactic aromas, along with hints of toast and an intriguing peppery note. The flavors are more delicate, featuring peaches and pears and an elegant finish. **87** *(6/1/2003)*

Tasca d'Almerita 2000 Nozze d'Oro White Blend (Sicilia) $23. A rich and full-bodied white blended from Sauvignon Blanc and Inzolia, the Nozze d'Oro begins with lightly buttery aromas of passion fruit, before developing melon and peach flavors in the mouth. Finishes long, with a refreshing note of bitter almond. **90** *(6/1/2003)*

Tasca d'Almerita 2005 Regaleali White Blend (Sicilia) $12. A pure blood Sicilian blend of the white indigenous grapes Insolia, Grecanico, and Catarratto, this wine delivers soapy, fruity tones balanced by pleasant minerality. It's lightweight but clean and crisp on the palate, making it a good pairing partner to Mediterranean or Asian foods. **86** —*M.L.* *(7/1/2006)*

Tasca d'Almerita 2004 Regaleali White Blend (Sicilia) $13. Delightful and delicately pale blend of three native Sicilian grapes: Insolia, Grecanico, and Catarratto. Hands off to the winemaker who extracted intense jasmine and citrus blossom characteristics and pink grapefruit acidity in the mouth. An extremely feminine wine. **90 Best Buy** —*M.L.* *(9/1/2005)*

Tasca d'Almerita 2002 Regaleali Bianco White Blend (Sicilia) $12. Attractively fresh, perfumed wine with a light tropical fruit flavor giving crispness, acidity, and a clean, elegant aftertaste. **84** —*R.V.* *(10/1/2003)*

Tasca d'Almerita 1998 Regaleali Bianco White Blend (Sicilia) $10. 90 *(11/15/1999)*

TASSAROLO

Tassarolo 1997 S Cortese (Gavi) $17. 86 *(11/1/1999)*

Tassarolo 1996 Vigneto Alborina Cortese (Gavi) $30. 89 *(11/1/1999)*

TAURINO

Taurino 1994 Patriglione Negroamaro (Salento) $41. 85 *(5/1/2002)*

Taurino 1998 Riserva Negroamaro (Salice Salentino) $10. The nose offers an unusual bouquet of dusty-attic-meets-fresh-asphalt aromas, plus some sweet red berry. Cedar and taut red berry carry through from palate to finish, where there's also a little char. Easy to drink and balanced, but quite typical. **85 Best Buy** —*C.S.* *(5/1/2002)*

Taurino 1997 Riserva Red Blend (Salice Salentino) $9. From Apulia, in the Italian heel, a blend of Negroamaro and Malvasia Rosso. Long a supermarket favorite, the brand has always been rustic and powerful, but

flavorful and inexpensive. Those are still its virtues. Big aromas of wild cherries and tar, with powerful berry flavors, it's dry and clean, the perfect gulp for barbecue. **85** —*S.H.* *(7/1/2001)*

Taurino 1996 Salice Salentino Riserva Red Blend (Apulia) $9. 90 *(11/15/1999)*

TEDESCHI

Tedeschi 2001 Corvina, Rondinella, Molinara (Amarone della Valpolicella) $49. It's the rare Amarone that demands cellaring these days, but this is definitely a candidate. Grilled black plum scents lead the way, followed by plum, prune, and dark chocolate flavors. Dusty, cocoa-powder-like tannins and a small amount of sweetness should mellow in four or five years, so drink from 2010. **91 Cellar Selection** —*J.C.* *(10/1/2006)*

Tedeschi 1999 Capitel Monte Olmi Red Blend (Amarone della Valpolicella Classico) $82. Earthy and meaty, with a touch of early sulfur that blows off quickly. The palate is rich and plentiful in terms of raisin, blackberry, and plum. And the finish is full and forward, with some tannic power. Candied but solid, and probably in need of more aging to soften those hard tannins. **89** *(11/1/2005)*

TENIMENTI ANGELINI

Tenimenti Angelini 2000 Brunello (Brunello di Montalcino) $64. Open knit, with raw cherry aromas. This wine has sweet and common flavors, with a fresh, fast mouthfeel. It's fairly chocolaty on the finish, with a hint of cherry cough drop. Good, but fails to stand out in a high-class field. **87** —*M.S.* *(7/1/2005)*

Tenimenti Angelini 2001 Val di Suga Brunello (Brunello di Montalcino) $53. A spice-driven wine that makes ample room for leather, cola, smoked ham, cedar, pipe tobacco, licorice, dark plum, and barnyard notes. There's an earthy, dusty quality to the mouth that amplifies the wine's smoothness. **92** *(4/1/2006)*

Tenimenti Angelini 1997 Val di Suga Brunello (Brunello di Montalcino) $80. Modern, polished fruit and new wood flavors blend well in this wine. The fruit is clean, ripe, bright with sweetness, and flavors of black cherries. The wine is generous, full, and opulent, with softer tannins than many Brunellos. Despite this nod in the direction of an

international style, the wine still has the classic Brunello power and potential for aging. **92** —*R.V.* *(8/1/2002)*

Tenimenti Angelini 1999 Vigna del Lago Riserva Brunello (Brunello di Montalcino) $134. Kicks off with a lot of maple, coffee, and espresso, and in the mouth the tannins are spiky and aggressive. Nonetheless, there's dynamite classic fruit here and structure to burn. A classic Brunello with a rugged edge. Needs five to ten years on its side. **92 Cellar Selection** —*M.S.* *(7/1/2005)*

Tenimenti Angelini 2000 Vigna Spuntali Brunello (Brunello di Montalcino) $86. More ethereal than brawny, licorice, balsam notes, forest berry, smoked cedar wood, anise seed, and menthol notes are woven carefully together. Plum and cinnamon spice come though in the mouth followed by bitter coffee and firms tannins. **93** *(4/1/2006)*

Tenimenti Angelini 2004 TuttoBene Red Blend (Toscana) $11. Maybe this producer of top-flight Brunello should stick to that; Angelini's value-priced blend of Merlot, Sangiovese, and Canaiolo has a strong green element; taken with the tomatoey fruit it doesn't add up to much. On the edges there's adequate raspberry and cherry, but it's not enough to elevate things. **83** —*M.S.* *(9/1/2006)*

Tenimenti Angelini 2002 Sangiovese (Vino Nobile di Montepulciano) $22. Smoky, with additional aromas of leather, cedar, and berries. Full, complete and flush with blackberry flavors and easygoing tannins. Due to the vintage there's not a ton of stuffing; drink now for maximum enjoyment. **87** —*M.S.* *(7/1/2005)*

Tenimenti Angelini 2001 La Villa Sangiovese (Vino Nobile di Montepulciano) $41. Weighty yet bright, with aromas of charred hamburger, leather, and plum/berry jam. Complex and interwoven on the palate, with kirsch, cassis, red plum, and chocolate flavors. Finishes smooth and stylish. Textbook stuff; hold until 2007. **90** —*M.S.* *(7/1/2005)*

ITALY

Tenimenti Angelini 2001 San Leonino Sangiovese (Chianti Classico) $17. Starts with full-bore rotten egg and dairy barn aromas, which blow off after persistent airing and swirling. If you can wade through the off-putting initial aromas you will find meaty black fruit and a rubbery, smoky finish. The mouth out-performs the nose by a factor of ten, but can you get that far before tossing it aside? Tasted twice with a consistent reading. **86** (4/1/2005)

Tenimenti Angelini 1999 San Leonino Riserva Sangiovese (Chianti Classico) $34. Plenty of wood to the nose, leaving aromas of smoke, cedar, leather, and lemon. That tangy, barrique-based lemon character lasts through the cherry-dominated palate and onto the juicy finish. With a bit less citrus and more harmony it would be right up there with the best. **87** (4/1/2005)

Tenimenti Angelini 2002 Sanleonino Sangiovese (Chianti Classico) $18. Early on it smells a touch cooked, as if there's burnt grass and leather on the nose. But airing reveals fruit and style. The palate runs toward heavy, with plum and cherry flexing collective muscle that puts it on the edge of being raisiny. Still, it holds the line and delivers good overall density and bulk. **88** —M.S. (10/1/2006)

TENIMENTI CA'BIANCA

Tenimenti Ca'Bianca 2003 Anté Barbera (Barbera d'Asti) $14. Juicy and fresh, with black cherry fruit that ends in a squirt of lemony acidity. Drink now. **84** —J.C. (3/1/2006)

Tenimenti Ca'Bianca 2004 Cortese (Gavi) $14. This medium-bodied Gavi boasts a decent bouquet that includes pear, melon, and spice scents. Lacks a bit of punch on the midpalate, but still manages to pump out enough pear, lime, and peppery flavors to earn solid marks, ending on lemon-lime and anise notes. **86** —J.C. (3/1/2006)

Tenimenti Ca'Bianca 2004 Moscato (Moscato d'Asti) $15. Gruppo Italiano Vini's take on Moscato d'Asti delivers the goods with confidence and character. White flowers, peach, and honey are beautifully integrated with a frothy mousse and acidity for that difficult-to-achieve balance between sweet and sour. **90 Best Buy** —M.L. (12/15/2005)

TENIMENTI LUIGI D'ALESSANDRO

Tenimenti Luigi D'Alessandro 2003 Il Bosco Syrah (Cortona) $49. One sniff delivers berry aromas and a blast of maple, but alongside that there's some barnyard and funk. When you accept that it's Italian Syrah some of the herbal, funky qualities become more understandable; still, you have to be able to deal with the leather, spice, tannin, and aggressiveness or it won't be your bag. **87** —M.S. (9/1/2006)

TENUTA ALZATURA

Tenuta Alzatura 2001 Uno di Quattro Sagrantino (Sagrantino di Montefalco) $45. From the Umbrian holding of Tuscany's Cecchi family, this wine opens with charred meat, leather, earth, beets, and an interesting mineral dimension. Aged 16 months in barrique, its aggressive tannins will need a few years of cellar aging to soften up. Drink after 2007. **87** —M.L. (9/1/2005)

TENUTA BELGUARDO

Tenuta Belguardo 1999 Sangiovese (Morellino di Scansano) $20. Mazzei, the family behind Fonterutoli in Chianti, is the maker of this 100% Sangiovese, which offers a strong, piercing nose of earth, leather, red fruit, and oak. If given time in the glass, the muscular palate loosens its stern grip, unveiling a nice underlay of plum, berries, and oak. Far better than pedestrian, this is a sturdy, well-made Tuscan red. **89** —M.S. (8/1/2002)

Tenuta Belguardo 2001 Poggio Bronzone Sangiovese (Morellino di Scansano) $29. Fine-tuned aromas of mint, licorice, herbs, and berries hit, while oak comes on with airing. Racy and exuberant, with forceful acidity pushing stylish dark fruit and tannin. It's hardcore Sangiovese, so it needs a couple of years to soften; to drink now consider pulling out the decanter. **90** —M.S. (10/1/2004)

Tenuta Belguardo 2001 Serrata di Belguardo Sangiovese (Maremma) $44. A rich and full wine, with raisin, licorice, and cassis on a semisweet nose. Plum and juicy berry define the palate. Finishes alive and fast, with ripe-edged fruit and some leathery tannins. Packed fairly full with Cabernet Sauvignon and Merlot, in addition to Sangiovese. Made by Marchese Mazzei. **90** —M.S. (10/1/2004)

TENUTA BELTRAME

Tenuta Beltrame 2004 Pinot Grigio (Friuli Aquileia) $19. A pretty, fruit-forward PG with plenty of Caribbean flavors backed by peach, floral, and lychee overtones. There's a trace of bitterness in the mouth but otherwise it goes down smoothly **86** —M.L. (2/1/2006)

TENUTA CA' VESCOVO

Tenuta Ca' Vescovo 2005 Pinot Grigio (Friuli Aquileia) $12. Has a brilliant golden hue and a bit more depth to the nose with baked apple and lavender. The refreshing acidity is welcome and makes for solid pairing potential with informal meals. **86** —M.L. (6/1/2006)

Tenuta Ca' Vescovo 2004 Pinot Grigio (Friuli Aquileia) $12. This Pinot Grigio has all its cards in order but lacks intensity. It offers citrus and attractive mineral notes and even a distant hint of cheese rind. Sudden sourness knocks it down a few points. **84** —M.L. (2/1/2006)

Tenuta Ca' Vescovo 2002 Sauvignon Blanc (Friuli Aquileia) $12. Lean and grassy, with lime, grapefruit, and green bell pepper all playing equal roles. Tart on the finish, which also carries a metallic or bitter note. **83** —J.C. (12/31/2004)

TENUTA CAPARZO

Tenuta Caparzo 2001 Brunello (Rosso di Montalcino) $18. Supple and forward, just the way a good rosso should be, with cherry and tobacco aromas and flavors backed up by a plump mouthfeel and a long, softly tannic finish. Good value. **88** (3/1/2005)

Tenuta Caparzo 2001 Brunello (Brunello di Montalcino) $64. Ground espresso bean, chocolate fudge, and toasted almond aromas are enticing, but distant whiffs of matchstick and muted flint stopped us short. The mouth texture demonstrated less intensity, with cherry and damp clay minerality. **88** (4/1/2006)

Tenuta Caparzo 1999 Brunello (Brunello di Montalcino) $60. Classically styled, Caparzo's regular Brunello reveals plenty of leather and cherry aromas and flavors. But it also offers additional hints of chocolate, cedar, and raspberry that put it on another level. Finishes long and softly tannic with firm acidity. **90** (3/1/2005)

Tenuta Caparzo 1997 Brunello (Brunello di Montalcino) $65. A smooth, polished performance from this 100-acre estate. The 1997 is modern in style, exhibiting huge but not too-dominant wood aromas and flavors, balancing with sweet, ripe berry fruit and black cherry jam. This is a wine that should be accessible young in four or five years, but should certainly age well over the following 10 or more. **92** —R.V. (8/1/2002)

Tenuta Caparzo 1999 La Casa Brunello (Brunello di Montalcino) $120. Fuller, richer, and creamier-textured than the normale, La Casa, from a single vineyard, starts with showy scents of smoked meat, cedar, and black cherries, then moves into vanilla, black cherry, earth, and tobacco flavors. Tannic on the finish, but also very long—promising much for the future. Try in 2010. **93 Cellar Selection** (3/1/2005)

Tenuta Caparzo 2001 Vigna La Casa Brunello (Brunello di Montalcino) $120. Menthol, toast, and modest berry offset a stern and firmly tannic wine that needs more time in the cellar. Wood notes tend to obscure the fruit and the finish is dry and somewhat astringent. **89** (4/1/2006)

Tenuta Caparzo 2002 Sangiovese (Toscana) $10. A victim of the vintage, this light-bodied wine styled for early drinking shows decent cherry, earth, and tobacco flavors but comes up lean and drying on the finish. **83** (3/1/2005)

Tenuta Caparzo 2000 Sangiovese (Rosso di Montalcino) $21. Smoky and tight, with a hint of lemony oak on the nose. The palate bursts with ripe cassis, cherry, and tannin, while later on you get a smack of cough drop as the red fruit unfolds. This is ripe as all get-out, a firm, chewy specimen for sure. **90** —M.S. (11/15/2003)

Tenuta Caparzo 2000 Sangiovese (Toscana) $14. Hail the ultimate pizza wine! It's bold and fruity, but also spicy and just a little bit more. Notes of clove and bramble mix with the juicy raspberry fruit and big but not overwhelming tannins. Finishes clean and short. **86** —M.S. (11/15/2003)

Tenuta Caparzo 1999 Borgo Scopeto Sangiovese (Chianti Classico) $20. Raspberry melds with sweet oak on the nose. On the palate, snappy cherry fruit gets clamped down by hard tannins, while late in the game chocolate and butter emerge. This isn't a heavy wine, despite its darker shadings. There are citrusy acids and the fruit is squarely out of the red berry family. **86** —*M.S. (11/15/2003)*

Tenuta Caparzo 1999 Borgo Scopeto Borgonero Sangiovese (Toscana) $35. With its sawmill aromas, lemon accents, and sharp, piercing feel, this wine seems disappointing after last year's great effort. It lacks a certain richness expected of today's super Tuscans, and it seems bitter, thin, and lacking in foundation. **83** —*M.S. (11/15/2003)*

Tenuta Caparzo 1999 Borgo Scopeto Riserva Misciano Sangiovese (Chianti Classico) $35. This single-vineyard Chianti smells a touch horsey, but if you like a heavy leather and barnyard scent, then dig in. Beyond that, there's some lavender and violet aromas, cherry and wood flavors, and a toasty, full-oak finish. The feel is ultra-tight and there's a lot of kick toward the end. Maybe it still needs more time. **87** —*M.S. (11/15/2003)*

Tenuta Caparzo 1994 Ca del Pazzo Sangiovese (Toscana) $33. **87** —*J.C. (3/1/2000)*

Tenuta Caparzo 1999 Ca' del Pazzo Sangiovese (Sant'Antimo) $40. This 50-50 blend of Sangiovese and Cabernet Sauvignon is really dominated by Cabernet at this stage of its evolution, delivering lots of cassis and tobacco flavors. This medium-weight wine is supple and creamy enough to enjoy tonight, but holding it will likely bring out more Sangiovese character. **92 Editors' Choice** *(3/1/2005)*

Tenuta Caparzo 2000 La Grance White Blend (Sant'Antimo) $21. This kitchen-sink blend of Chardonnay, Trebbiano, Sauvignon, and Traminer shows a bit of toast and lemon custard on the nose, then leesy, minerally and citrus flavors on the palate. Finishes on mealy, toasty notes alongside a beam of bright acidity. **85** *(3/1/2005)*

Tenuta Caparzo 1998 Le Crete White Blend (Toscana) $15. Signs point to this wine being prematurely old, from its medium-straw color to its slightly varnishy aromas and tired, woody palate. Look for a more recent vintage, which may show more freshness and vitality. **81** —*J.C. (9/1/2001)*

TENUTA CARRETTA

Tenuta Carretta 2002 Dolcetto (Dolcetto d'Alba) $16. Leather and animal notes mar the nose. The palate is chunky and firm, with a touch of cabbage flavor that interferes with the dark fruit. Has it mostly together, but a mild yet persistent vegetal note holds it back. **83** —*M.S. (12/15/2003)*

Tenuta Carretta 1997 Cannubi Nebbiolo (Barolo) $54. Cannubi is one of Barolo's most prestigious properties, but in this case the fruit is handled only so well. Heavy oak, which carries a hickory scent and flavor, is the mask of Zorro. You can't get much from the wine other than wood. Deep diggers will find black cherry and leather, and also some starchy tannins. **85** —*M.S. (12/15/2003)*

Tenuta Carretta 1998 Cannubi Barolo Nebbiolo (Barolo) $NA. Tenuta Carretta, under the ownership of the Miroglio family, has a small portion of the Cannubi vineyard. The 1998 is elegant and well-balanced. There are aromas of vanilla with some soft, ripe fruit. The palate is dry, especially on the finish, but the fruit underneath is soft and sweet. **89** —*R.V. (11/15/2002)*

TENUTA COCCI GRIFONI

Tenuta Cocci Grifoni NV Passerina Champagne Blend (Marche) $10. **88 Best Buy** —*S.H. (12/15/2000)*

Tenuta Cocci Grifoni 2001 Il Grifone Red Blend (Offida Rosso) $49. An excellent vintage for Il Grifone, which is a blend of 80% Montepulciano and 20% Cab Sauvignon. The nose is slightly leathery, with hints of crude oil, dark berry, and toast. It's tight in the mouth, but serious, with tannins as well as ripe, complex plum, and berry flavors. Should be great with grilled meats and the like. **91** —*M.S. (10/1/2006)*

Tenuta Cocci Grifoni 2000 Il Grifone Red Blend (Rosso Piceno Superiore) $48. Ample black fruit along with mint and herbs make for a solid if unusual bouquet. It's fairly ripe and sweet to the taste, with bold cherry and raspberry flavors. Textured on the finish, with zest. The only nega-tive is that it's rowdy and unrefined, but hey, that's rosso piceno. **88** —*M.S. (7/1/2005)*

Tenuta Cocci Grifoni 2000 Vigna Messieri Red Blend (Rosso Piceno Superiore) $12. A touch rosy and rusty in color, with a bouquet that exudes red fruit swaddled in oak and leather. Lively but simple in the mouth, with medium tannins and an under-current of charred brush. This is a true indigenous wine that won't register with a lot of people. **86** —*M.S. (7/1/2005)*

Tenuta Cocci Grifoni 1997 Sangiovese (Rosso Piceno Superiore) $10. **83** *(9/1/2000)*

Tenuta Cocci Grifoni 1997 Il Grifone Sangiovese (Rosso Piceno Superiore) $36. This intriguing blend of 70% Montepulciano, 15% Sangiovese, and 15% Cabernet Sauvignon shows deep earth and leather flavors tinged with sweet toasted almonds. It's rich, alcoholic, and full—a mouthful of distinctive flavor. **87** *(10/1/2001)*

Tenuta Cocci Grifoni 2003 Le Torri Sangiovese (Rosso Piceno Superiore) $13. Young and spunky, but very good when placed under the microscope. The nose is forward and fruity, with animal cracker and juniper as secondary aromas. The mouthfeel is full and ripe, and that's backed by tasty berry flavors. With tannin and chocolate on the finish you can safely say that's it's a full package in its price range. **88 Best Buy** —*M.S. (10/1/2006)*

Tenuta Cocci Grifoni 2001 Vigna Messieri Sangiovese (Rosso Piceno Superiore) $24. Heavily roasted, with coffee and toast riding high alongside dark fruit. It's burly in the mouth, with burnt notes darkening plum, blackberry, and black cherry flavors. Definitely rich, with creamy chocolate and peppery spice on the finish. The blend is 80% Montepulciano and 20% Sangiovese. **90** —*M.S. (10/1/2006)*

Tenuta Cocci Grifoni 2004 Podere Colle Vecchio White Blend (Offida Pecorino) $23. Another interesting wine made from an obscure indigenous grape, this white is very fragrant and rich with tones of grapefruit, yellow flowers, white powder, pear, and melon. It has strong and attractive mineral characteristics in the mouth and ends on a bitter note. **86** —*M.L. (10/1/2006)*

Tenuta Conti Attems 2004 Pinot Grigio (Collio) $19. This is a gorgeous wine that sees both steel and French barrique. Delivers candied chestnuts, banana nut bread, and lavender-infused honey. Although this pinkish Pinot Grigio is soft and creamy in the mouth, the alcohol is notable. **87** —*M.L. (2/1/2006)*

TENUTA DEL NANFRO

Tenuta del Nanfro 2001 San Mauro Nero d'Avola (Sicilia) $18. Vegetal, sharp, and sulfuric in the nose, and that just doesn't go away. Deeper down you'll find cherry flavors and a decent finish, which makes you wonder if the offputting aromas will fade at some point down the line. But that's a big leap of faith. **81** —*M.S. (10/1/2003)*

Tenuta del Nanfro 2000 Cerasuolo di Vittoria Red Blend (Sicilia) $18. Quite burnt in the nose, with dead-on aromas of brush fire, broccoli rabe, and charred beef. The palate is infused with that same burnt quality, thus it has bitter edges that carry onto the finish. There's a hint of life and fruit at the core, but the roasted surroundings never give way, making it virtually impossible to penetrate. **82** —*M.S. (12/15/2003)*

TENUTA DELL'ORNELLAIA

Tenuta dell'Ornellaia 2000 Ornellaia Bordeaux Blend (Bolgheri) $145. Deep and delicious, with an earth-driven nose that conveys quality. Chunky plum pervades the chewy, dark palate, which offers a gorgeous mouthfeel and admirable depth. Only on the finish do you get a slight hint of oak. Overall it's entirely solid and very likable, but as good as it is, it's not quite on the level of the '98 or '99, which were amazing. **94 Cellar Selection** —*M.S. (11/15/2003)*

Tenuta dell'Ornellaia 2000 Le Serre Nuove Cabernet Sauvignon-Merlot (Bolgheri) $50. The second wine of Tenuta dell'Ornellaia is smoky, leathery, and packed full of plum and leather. The jammy palate is tasty and spicy, with ample red plum and berry flavors. The finish is rich enough to make you smile, yet the winery has done right by keeping this wine a cut below its stellar premium cuvée. **90** —*M.S. (11/15/2003)*

ITALY

Tenuta dell'Ornellaia 2002 Le Serre Nuove Red Blend (Bolgheri) $50. Blame it on the vintage, but this blend from an esteemed Bolgheri estate seems a little under-ripe and volatile, even if it's mostly balanced, upright, and serious. The plum and raspberry flavors are short but good, while the finish is easy and wet, albeit dilute. Has its moments and its weaknesses. **86** —*M.S. (9/1/2006)*

Tenuta dell'Ornellaia 1996 Masseto Red Blend (Bolgheri) $138. A rich, concentrated wine, bulging with ripe, extracted tannins. This is smooth and opulent, with flavors of fruitcake and an underlying spiciness from the wood. A delcious, powerful wine, ready to drink now, but still likely to mature. **93** —*R.V. (12/31/2001)*

Tenuta dell'Ornellaia 1999 Ornellaia Red Blend (Bolgheri) $125. Spicy and full of cassis, tobacco, and coffee aromas. Texture and mouthfeel are what this wine is all about; it is plush like velvet carpet. Deep, satisfying flavors of plum, black currant, and vanilla lead into an ultrasmooth finish that is clean as a hospital emergency room. **96** —*M.S. (8/1/2002)*

Tenuta dell'Ornellaia 1995 Sangiovese (Toscana) $63. **96** —*M.S. (5/1/1999)*

Tenuta dell'Ornellaia NV Le Volte Sangiovese (Toscana) $20. **87** —*M.S. (3/1/2000)*

Tenuta dell'Ornellaia 1996 Ornellaia Sangiovese (Bolgheri) $73. **92** —*M.S. (7/1/2000)*

TENUTA DI ARCENO

Tenuta di Arceno 2002 Arcanum I Cabernet Blend (Toscana) $96. With burnt popcorn as the lead scent and an herbal streak that can't be denied, Kendall-Jackson's attempt at Tuscan Cabernet Franc (with 18% Cabernet Sauvignon and Sangiove) requires too much sacrifice. The flavors are of rhubarb and raspberry, with spice and tomato sauce along for the ride. Has size and potency, but not much charm. **83** —*M.S. (9/1/2006)*

Tenuta di Arceno 2002 Arcanum II Merlot (Toscana) $96. From Kendall-Jackson, this Merlot is warm and toasty, with aromas of popcorn, roasted plum, and leather. The palate is a bit more settled, and it's where you'll find dark cherry flavors resting on a bed of rubbery, lively tannins. Finishes with toast, vanilla, and char, along with another dose of spiky tannins. **85** —*M.S. (9/1/2006)*

Tenuta di Arceno 2003 Arcanum III Red Blend (Toscana) $100. Kendall-Jackson's super Tuscan is Cab-based and very ripe. It's black as coal, with leather, earth, and dark fruit aromas. It's more soft than steely, with blackberry and plum flavors softened by molasses and licorice. A real beast of a wine that includes 15% Merlot and Syrah. **88** —*M.S. (9/1/2006)*

Tenuta di Arceno 2003 Ataison Sangiovese (Toscana) $40. Wide on the bouquet and extremely sulfuric. No amount of swirling succeeds in dispersing the gassy aromas, but underneath there's plum, berry, and cherry flavors that are healthy and round. Nice mouthfeel and grabby tannins ensure a proper mouthfeel. **84** —*M.S. (9/1/2006)*

Tenuta di Arceno 2002 Ataison Sangiovese (Toscana) $48. So burnt and dark on the nose that it smells like old coffee, lemon rind, and charred toast. The palate is piqued and hard, with firm tannins. At times this wine shows something; at other times it seems lost. **83** —*M.S. (11/15/2004)*

Tenuta di Arceno 2003 PrimaVoce Sangiovese (Toscana) $20. A lot of sulfur at first, and that creates a cloud over the nose. Underneath, however, there's quality black plum, berry, and earth notes. Finishes dark, with a lot of espresso-like character. Has its strong points and a few faults. Fortunately the good outweighs the bad. **86** —*M.S. (9/1/2006)*

TENUTA DI ARGIANO

Tenuta di Argiano 1997 Brunello (Brunello di Montalcino) $56. The large 246-acre estate is owned by Countess Noemi Cinzano, of the vermouth family. With Giacomo Tachis as consultant, the vineyard has produced a powerful, rich wine that combines dryness, bitter fruits, and dark tannins with generous tarry, super-ripe fruit that promises to come through and dominate as the wine ages. Drink after 7–8 years. **92 Cellar Selection** —*R.V. (8/1/2002)*

TENUTA DI BLASIG

Tenuta di Blasig 2004 Pinot Grigio (Isonzo del Friuli) $NA. Exotic fruit, dried banana chips, Granny Smith apple, kiwi, and lime pie are deeply etched into a wine with medium body and finish. A correct and enjoyable Pinot Grigio. **86** —*M.L. (2/1/2006)*

TENUTA DI NOZZOLE

Tenuta di Nozzole 2001 Il Pareto Cabernet Sauvignon (Toscana) $60. Nothing is understated here. This is a huge, brawny red wine with ripe cherry preserve, prune, chocolate fudge, smoke, tobacco, black pepper, and resin-like notes that sees 16 months of oak aging. It's very ripe and concentrated, with velvety tannins and a smoky aftertaste. **90** —*M.L. (9/1/2006)*

Tenuta di Nozzole 2004 Le Bruniche Chardonnay (Chardonnay di Toscana) $14. Light and crisp, with flowery aromas that are more subtle than forced. Pear, apple, and banana flavors are smooth yet a touch dilute, while the finish is dry and tight, but short. Would make for a nice apéritif if properly chilled. **86** —*M.S. (10/1/2006)*

Tenuta di Nozzole 2002 Le Bruniche Chardonnay (Toscana) $12. Full and aromatic, yet it holds the line on sweetness and oak flavor, something many value-priced Chardonnays fail to do. This wine is all about pear, peach, and apple fruit, a modestly rich texture and a light, toasty finish. There's a solid core to this puppy, and it tastes every bit like a real white wine, not liquid candy. **86** —*M.S. (11/15/2003)*

Tenuta di Nozzole 2001 Riserva Sangiovese (Chianti Classico) $22. Minty and tight on the nose, with a hint of green pepper, plum, and earth. Weighs in heavy but not fat; the body is smooth and creamy but snappy enough to remain upright. A bit tannic, but not enough to worry about. Finishes round, with coffee and smoke notes. **89** *(4/1/2005)*

Tenuta di Nozzole 2000 Riserva Sangiovese (Tuscany) $22. Starts with plum, berry, and light wood aromas. The flavor profile is pure red fruit, mostly plum, with nice acidity keeping things propped up. A bit of excess tannin on the finish roughs it up a bit, but with food that will not be an issue. Improves with airing. **88** —*M.S. (10/1/2004)*

Tenuta di Nozzole 1997 Riserva Sangiovese (Chianti Classico) $38. A complex nose of cherry, soy, leather, and pine opens to a mouthful of red berry, pepper, and spice flavors. An elegant rather than weighty wine, with bright acidity to keep it lively. Finishes with tangy tannins and a black-tea note. **86** *(4/1/2001)*

TENUTA DI RISECCOLI

Tenuta di Riseccoli 2001 Sangiovese (Chianti Classico) $26. A touch on the soft side, as if it doesn't have the legs to run long. But for now it's a meaty brew of jammy fruit, licorice, and leather. The palate shows enough complexity in the way of chocolate, espresso, and herbs to rate highly, while the finish flows smoothly due to ripe tannins. Drink now. **89** *(4/1/2005)*

Tenuta di Riseccoli 1999 Sangiovese (Chianti Classico) $12. Attractive in the nose, with typical and traditional aromas of cherry and underbrush. Mild oak adds some vanilla to the cherry-laden palate, which also offers a fine touch of cinnamon. The finish is round and modestly tannic. All in all this one comes real close to the bull's eye. It's solid and largely complete. **89 Best Buy** —*M.S. (12/31/2002)*

Tenuta di Riseccoli 2000 Riserva Sangiovese (Chianti Classico) $43. Attractive, big, and lush, with defined leather, dried plum, and clove aromas. If there were ever a Chianti that was interbred with Port, it's this one. The palate shows spice cake, liqueur, and fudge, and the texture is downright thick. It's borderline medicinal in its richness, but for many that won't be a problem. **89** *(4/1/2006)*

Tenuta di Riseccoli 2000 Saeculum Sangiovese (Tuscany) $75. Oily and rich, yet smooth, deep, and woodsy. In a word, it has it all. The tight palate offers ripe blackberry and boysenberry flavors, while the finish is seductively secure, with chocolate and truffle notes. It still has a fair amount of wood on it, but that stretches out the finish. Will cellar well for another four or five years. **91 Cellar Selection** —*M.S. (9/1/2006)*

TENUTA DI SESTA

Tenuta di Sesta 2001 Brunello (Brunello di Montalcino) $75. Almond paste, cinnamon, bright cherry, crisp pomegranate, vanilla, and cedar waft off a very fruit-driven Brunello. There's a tart, almost sour, quality here; and one of our panel members was put off by a medicinal edge. **87** *(4/1/2006)*

Tenuta di Sesta 1997 Brunello (Brunello di Montalcino) $45. Sesta is one of the wines coming out of Montalcino that manages to combine the old-world power and tannin of Brunello with top-quality fruit flavors. It is firm and concentrated, showing dry tannins that go right through the palate. At the same time, there is delicious ripe, violet-flavored fruit and balancing acidity. Drink after 10 years. **94 Cellar Selection** *—R.V. (8/1/2002)*

TENUTA FARNETA

Tenuta Farneta 2001 Bentivoglio Sangiovese (Toscana) $18. Rusty in color, with tree bark and mulch on the nose. As for the fruit, it has mostly left the building. Thus what remains is stewy and soft. **81** *—M.S. (9/1/2006)*

Tenuta Farneta 2000 Bongoverno Sangiovese (Toscana) $38. The super Tuscan category is infested with wines that just don't justify their price. A case in point: this vegetal, tannic red with murky fruit, coffee, and heavy tannins. It's not particularly bad, just unblanced and underwhelming. **83** *—M.S. (9/1/2006)*

TENUTA FARNETA DI COLLATO

Tenuta Farneta di Collato 2002 Sangiovese (Chianti Colli Senesi) $8. More saturated than many in this class, yet while it broods and emits dark notes of charcoal and burnt toast, the fruit is modest. In the mouth, black cherry and plum make an early flavor impression then fade. A finish with hints of chocolate and coffee is of medium length. **85 Best Buy** *—M.S. (10/1/2004)*

Tenuta Farneta di Collato 2003 Tenuta Farneta Sangiovese (Chianti Colli Senesi) $8. A bit reduced, with meaty black fruit aromas accompanied by hints of grass and hay. The palate is spicy and full of plum and cherry, while the rest of the mouth and finish are carried by short acidity. Hits hard toward the back while scoring points along the way. **86 Best Buy** *(4/1/2005)*

Tenuta Farneta di Collato 2003 Vendemmia Sangiovese (Chianti Colli Senesi) $9. Quite sweet, with red licorice, bubble gum, and berry jam aromas. The wine keeps its candied persona through the palate and onto the soft, ripe finish. It's an easy drinker with a pleasant character and some modest punch. **86 Best Buy** *(4/1/2005)*

TENUTA FRIGGIALI

Tenuta Friggiali 2001 Brunello (Brunello di Montalcino) $66. Cherry-berry, vanilla, herbal notes, and forest floor are the dominant aromas. But there's also a slightly lactic quality in the form of milk chocolate. Not a hugely complex wine, but a straightforward and friendly one with a medium body and a spicy finish. **89** *(4/1/2006)*

TENUTA IL BOSCO

Tenuta Il Bosco NV Philèo Pinot Nero (Oltrepò Pavese) $15. This is an interesting wine: A charmat-method sparkler made with 100% Pinot Noir that could pass for a classic method one. For this reason, the pricing is attractive and the wine delivers sweet fruit aromas and a tart note on the finish. **86** *—M.L. (6/1/2006)*

Tenuta Il Bosco 1997 Millesimato Brut Sparkling Blend (Oltrepò Pavese) $25. A metodo classico, or bottle-fermented sparkler, with yellow fruit, rose petal, and toasted-nutty notes. The wine's color is brilliantly golden and its flavors are very much on the toasty side, even 10 years later. **88** *—M.L. (6/1/2006)*

Tenuta Il Bosco NV Philèo Brut Sparkling Blend (Oltrepò Pavese) $NA. An enjoyable sparkling wine with citrus, pears, and toasted almonds on the nose. Shows similar flavors on the palate, where it reveals a surprise splash of hazelnut. Refermented using the long charmat process, the bubble size and persistence makes you think it was done in the metodo classico. **84** *—M.L. (12/15/2004)*

TENUTA IL POGGIONE

Tenuta Il Poggione 1993 Riserva Brunello (Brunello di Montalcino) $67. **84** *—J.C. (3/1/2000)*

TENUTA IL TESORO

Tenuta Il Tesoro 2000 La Fonte Red Blend (Toscana) $15. Light in color but not in quality of flavors and balance. While the nose isn't that rich—it offers mostly pine needles and underbrush in addition to light red fruit—the feel is nice and it packs some punch given its lightweight frame. Easy to drink. **86** *—M.S. (12/31/2002)*

TENUTA LA FUGA

Tenuta La Fuga 2001 Brunello (Brunello di Montalcino) $65. Rich and plump with marzipan, cherry-berry, menthol, violet, and medicinal notes. Some sweaty, band-aid like notes add complexity. A bit austere and stern in the mouth thanks to drying tannins, but would show well over the course of a long satisfying meal. **90 Cellar Selection** *(4/1/2006)*

Tenuta La Fuga 1997 Brunello (Brunello di Montalcino) $NA. This wine comes from the branch of the Folonari family that moved out of Ruffino after a recent re-organization of the company. It is a nicely understated wine, showing great style, with new wood and dusty tannin flavors combining with smooth, modern fruit. The acidity is just too dominant at the end, but otherwise a delicate, elegant performance. **90** *—R.V. (8/1/2002)*

Tenuta La Fuga 1999 Sangiovese (Rosso di Montalcino) $NA. Raspberry aromas are a bit earthy and muddled. The palate is on the heavy side, fully laced with a strawberry lollipop flavor. A light, creamy, oaky finish seals the deal. **83** *—M.S. (8/1/2002)*

TENUTA LE QUERCE

Tenuta Le Querce 2001 Il Viola Aglianico (Aglianico del Vulture) $18. Bulky fruit, leather, and some overt wood manifesting itself as dry cheese comprise the bouquet. Plum, red currant, and cherry tomato make for a tight, snappy palate. Lots of zip, although tannic and tight. **85** *—M.S. (2/1/2005)*

Tenuta Le Querce 2000 Rosso di Costanza Aglianico (Aglianico del Vulture) $40. Stylish but bold. The nose is bruising but lively, with pepper, plum, and overall punch. In the mouth, black cherry and raspberry fruit is both snappy and rich. A wine with personality. And it's not fading. **90** *—M.S. (10/1/2006)*

Tenuta Le Querce 1999 Il Viola Red Blend (Aglianico del Vulture) $11. Smells a bit like fresh veggies—like a clean earthy or dusty character—but also of stone fruits like apricot and peach; aromas and flavors you might find in some Grenache-based wines from the southern Rhône. It's round and full in the mouth, with gritty tannins that give a hard edge to the finish. **86 Best Buy** *—C.S. (5/1/2002)*

Tenuta Le Querce 1999 Rosso Di Costanza Red Blend (Aglianico del Vulture) $26. With its powerful aromas of toast and caramel, lush but indistinct black fruit flavors and soft, ripe tannins framed by oak, this could be the poster child for the "international" style. It may not be the most individual or distinctive wine, but our panel enjoyed it for its sheer lusciousness and pure hedonism. **88** *(5/1/2002)*

TENUTA MONACI

Tenuta Monaci 1997 Simposia Negroamaro (Puglia) $12. The dusty dryness that the Negro Amaro brings to the nose is very prominent. After the leather-saddle flavors come menthol, cinnamon, and a hint of cherry. Finishes with a note of dried meat. **85** *—C.S. (5/1/2002)*

TENUTA OLIVETO

Tenuta Oliveto 2001 Brunello (Brunello di Montalcino) $48. A brawny Brunello with a modern, velvety smoothness that does not overpower finesse or ethereal mineral and fruit notes. Ripe, chewy tannins ripe over a long, leisurely finish. Appetizing and food-friendly. **92 Editors' Choice** *(4/1/2006)*

TENUTA RAPITALA

Tenuta Rapitala 2001 Bianco Chardonnay (Sicilia) $10. A rich, toasty, 100% Chardonnay full of ripe, citric fruit. The wood shows in aromas

ITALY

ITALY

and taste, but never dominates the green plum fruit flavors. **88**—*R.V. (10/1/2003)*

Tenuta Rapitala 2003 Hugonis Red Blend (Sicilia) $37. This successful marriage of Nero d'Avola and Cabernet Sauvignon boasts a vibrant ruby color and candy-like cherry fruit with cola, resin, cedar, and deeper toasted, leather-like notes. There's both pepper and spice in the mouth with smooth tannins and a smoky close. **89**—*M.L. (7/1/2006)*

Tenuta Rapitala 2002 Hugonis Red Blend (Sicilia) $37. A 50-50 blend of Nero d'Avola and Cabernet Sauvignon, this effort reveals attributes of both varieties: dense chocolate and plum fruit alongside mint and green pepper notes. It's big and fully extracted; firmly tannic on the finish. **88** *(8/1/2005)*

Tenuta Rapitala 2002 Nu har Red Blend (Sicilia) $11. A light and pleasant blend of 70% Nero d'Avola and 30% Cabernet. The bouquet features red raspberry, fresh tomato, and crushed spice. Flavors of berry jam and chocolate are easy to like, while the finish is warm and textured. With proper grip and lively, sticky tannins, this is no weakling. **87 Best Buy**— *M.S. (11/15/2004)*

Tenuta Rapitala 2002 Nu-har Red Blend (Sicilia) $13. This is Rapità's entry-level red, a blend of 70% Nero d'Avola matured in stainless and 30% Cabernet Sauvignon matured in used oak. The result is a pleasantly structured red with notes of plum and chocolate accented by hints of mint and dusty earth. **87** *(8/1/2005)*

Tenuta Rapitala 2001 Nuhar Red Blend (Sicilia) $11. Has light dill aromas and spicy berry fruit. Loads of wood-spice flavor accents plum and berry. Full and textured, and almost chewy in its richness. It's 70% Nero d'Avola and 30% Cabernet. **86**—*M.S. (10/1/2003)*

Tenuta Rapitala 2004 Nadir Syrah (Sicilia) $15. This historic Sicilian estate is another protagonist when it comes to Syrah. Nadir is a surprisingly floral interpretation of the hearty grape with notes of herbal tea, rose petal, and raspberry tea. It's leaner in the mouth with soft tannins. **89**—*M.L. (7/1/2006)*

Tenuta Rapitala 2003 Solinero Syrah (Sicilia) $41. Gorgeous, rich, and velvety, this Syrah boasts blueberry, almond, pistachio, and delicate menthol notes that are usually difficult to draw out in hot climates. A flavor-rich and commanding wine with silky tannins. **91**—*M.L. (7/1/2006)*

Tenuta Rapitala 2002 Solinero Syrah (Sicilia) $42. This dark, richly saturated in color Syrah features scents of baked plums, dusted with cinnamon and white pepper. Oak aging for 18 months has imparted a silky texture to the mouth-filling fruit and a touch of vanilla on the finish. Has enough structure to suggest holding 3–5 years, but is approachable now. **89** *(8/1/2005)*

Tenuta Rapitala 2000 Solinero Syrah (Sicilia) $NA. A huge, black fruit flavored wine, and based on 100% Syrah. It has power, tannins, concentration, solidity. There is no question this is one blockbuster of a wine. **90**—*R.V. (10/1/2003)*

Tenuta Rapitala 2004 Casalj White Blend (Sicilia) $11. Casalj is a popular Catarratto-Chardonnay blend with an intense and horizontal nose that encompasses citrus, stone fruit, almond paste, and green grass notes. The mouthfeel is creamy and consistent, and the zesty finish is longer than most. **87**—*M.L. (7/1/2006)*

Tenuta Rapitala 2003 Casalj White Blend (Sicilia) $11. Always a bit funky and unusual, this blend of 70% Catarrotto, a native Sicilian white grape, and 30% Chardonnay is mildly viscous but still quite fresh. It offers a medium-weight mouthfeel and a good amount of apple-driven flavor. Not hugely complex, but works as an apéritif or with fettuccine Alfredo, baked salmon, or grilled veggies. And as reliably out of the mainstream as it is, it's also a perennial value. Give it a shot; there's nothing not to like about it. **87 Best Buy**—*M.S. (11/15/2004)*

Tenuta Rapitala 2003 Casalj White Blend (Sicilia) $13. Don't be put off by the odd name: The J at the end is pronounced like an I. What's important is the wine itself, a blend of 70% Catarratto and 30% Chardonnay that boasts assertive aromas of orange blossom and honey. Tropical fruit notes mark the plump, mouth-filling palate, while the finish is citrusy with acidity. **88 Best Buy** *(8/1/2005)*

Tenuta Rapitala 2001 Casalj White Blend (Sicilia) $11. The letter "j" in the name is pronounced as an "i", but refers to the Arabic history of the estate. The wine is weighty and rich, but simple and neutral, with clean, fresh fruit flavors. **83**—*R.V. (10/1/2003)*

TENUTA ROVEGLIA

Tenuta Roveglia 2000 Vigne di Catullo White Blend (Lugana) $17. Light and citrusy, blending limes with green herbs, and finishes on a chalky note. Might work well with herbed, pan-roasted trout or similar dishes. **82**—*J.C. (7/1/2003)*

TENUTA SAN GIORGIO

Tenuta San Giorgio 2001 Ugolforte Brunello (Brunello di Montalcino) $50. Here's a deviation from Brunello's standard aromatic portfolio with herbal, bay leaf like aromas, pomegranate and grassy notes. Not as full and dense as others but pleasantly lush and fruity in the mouth. **88** *(4/1/2006)*

TENUTA SAN GUIDO

Tenuta San Guido 2003 Sassicaia Cabernet Sauvignon (Bolgheri) $180. It's almost criminal to taste Sassicaia before its prime. The 2003 vintage should be ready after 2010. A blend of 85% Cab Sauvignon and 15% Cab Franc that aged 24 months in barrique, notes of cassis, exotic spice, menthol, and green olive come through despite the hot vintage. It's powerful in the mouth with crispness and refined tannins. **91 Cellar Selection** —*M.L. (9/1/2006)*

Tenuta San Guido 2002 Sassicaia Cabernet Sauvignon (Bolgheri) $180. Not the best vintage for Sassicaia enthusiasts or collectors, but certainly noteworthy thanks to defined herbal aromas such as rosemary and sage backed by black plum, black berry, tobacco, cigar box, and leather. The mouthfeel is velvety and supple with unmistakable elegance delivered over a long, menthol-like finish. **90**—*M.L. (9/1/2006)*

Tenuta San Guido 2004 Guidalberto Sangiovese (Toscana) $50. Here is a more affordable wine created by the makers of Italy's legendary Sassicaia that has truly come into its own in 2004. The wine has a playful linearity to it accented by many rich mineral tones such as granite and slate roof. Take a second sniff and you'll get chocolate, leather, and toasted nut. Good acidity, succulent tannins, and persistence make it a stand out wine. **90**—*M.L. (11/15/2006)*

Tenuta San Guido 2003 Guidalberto Sangiovese (Toscana) $50. Almost catches the upper echelon, but some burnt, grassy character on the nose holds it back just a little. That said, the wine sings with round berry fruit that's accented by chocolate. Medium in weight and forcefulness. Very good but can be better. **89**—*M.S. (9/1/2006)*

Tenuta San Guido 2000 Guidalberto Sangiovese (Bolgheri) $52. Starts with a confusing nose of tobacco, smoked ham, and overt leather and animal aromas; a staid, simple wine this is not. The palate, which has a feel that's thick and chewy, is bulked up with baked black fruits. The finish, meanwhile, is dark, with berry flavors and fading spice. The blend is Cabernet, Merlot, and Sangiovese. **89**—*M.S. (10/1/2004)*

TENUTA SANT'ANTONIO

Tenuta Sant'Antonio 1999 Capitello Cabernet Sauvignon (Veneto) $45. The aromas are of red fruit, leaves, black pepper, and olives. Combined, that signals a bit of green, which is confirmed on the palate, where tasty plum fruit mixes with oak-driven caramel and a touch of the veggies. Chalky tannins dominate the finish. **86** *(5/1/2003)*

Tenuta Sant'Antonio 1998 Capitello Chardonnay (Friuli) $27. Scents of honey, pear, and cinnamon waft from the glass; the flavors are of baked pears and apples, but never turn too soft or blowsy. Warming on the finish, with lots of dried spices and toast. **89**—*J.C. (7/1/2003)*

Tenuta Sant'Antonio 1999 Campo dei Gigli Corvina, Rondinella, Molinara (Amarone della Valpolicella) $98. This wine runs a bit jammy, with a closed structure and less texture and balance than ideal. We found it a touch reductive and simple, with berry marmalade as a base flavor and a slick mouthfeel. Not quite convinced, we suggest trying it again a few years down the line. **86** *(11/1/2005)*

Tenuta Sant'Antonio 1998 Campo dei Gigli Corvina, Rondinella, Molinara (Amarone della Valpolicella) $64. Smoky notes and cured meat dominate the bouquet, which is enticing despite a moderately strong hint of green. The palate runs a bit sugary, but some cinnamon adds necessary nuance to the candied flavor profile. The mouthfeel and finish are both smooth, yet firm tannins contribute structure. **88** *(5/1/2003)*

Tenuta Sant'Antonio 2002 Selezione Antonio Castagnedi Corvina, Rondinella, Molinara (Amarone della Valpolicella) $50. It's already showing a touch of color degradation, but don't let that stop you. This is a smooth, creamy, elegant Amarone, with flavors of dried figs and cherries accented by hints of cocoa. Richly textured on the finish, where the fruit shines through. **92** *—J.C. (10/1/2006)*

Tenuta Sant'Antonio 2000 Selezione Antonio Castagnedi Corvina, Rondinella, Molinara (Amarone della Valpolicella) $50. This is one beautiful wine, something our tasting panel could agree on to a person. We loved the meaty, smoky nose along with the lush palate that oozes pure red fruit, vanilla, chocolate, and dried spices. It's everything you'd want in a young Amarone, and a little bit more. **93** *(11/1/2005)*

Tenuta Sant'Antonio 1998 La Bandina Red Blend (Valtellina Superiore) $34. The nose delivers plenty of cedary notes on top of cherry fruit, which makes perfect sense considering it was aged 30 months in oak. The palate seems fresh; the acidity is vital and the red fruit flavors are forward. The finish is more tart than rich, and a bit short. **88** *(5/1/2003)*

Tenuta Sant'Antonio 2004 White Blend (Soave) $11. This plump, medium-bodied wine starts with hints of honey, mint, and pears, then delivers well-ripened fruit flavors on the palate. Shows good concentration and length on the finish, picking up just enough spice and mineral nuances to retain interest throughout a meal. **88 Best Buy** *—J.C. (10/1/2006)*

Tenuta Sant'Antonio 2003 Monte Ceriani White Blend (Soave) $18. Perhaps this wine is showing the effects of 2003's torrid summer, but it doesn't show the fresh, vibrant fruit that characterizes the best Soaves. It's still a good, serviceable drink, but one that relies on a certain weight in the mouth and baked apple flavors bolstered by a grapefruity finish. **85** *—J.C. (10/1/2006)*

TENUTA SANTOMÉ

Tenuta Santomé NV Extra Dry Prosecco (Veneto) $13. True to what Prosecco should be, this is an informal but exceedingly fresh wine to enjoy at all occasions. Peach aromas are the most obvious but are joined by delicate tones of straw, citrus, and white stone. **84** *—M.L. (12/15/2006)*

TENUTA SETTE PONTI

Tenuta Sette Ponti 2003 Poggio al Lupo Red Blend (Toscana) $55. Here's a portly offering, and then some. Talk about a dark, soft, meaty wine. This one is so rich, ripe and loaded with black plums and berries that it's almost sleepy. But fierce tannins and lasting espresso darkness keep it going. Very good but heavier than the excellent 2001. **89** *—M.S. (9/1/2006)*

Tenuta Sette Ponti 2001 Poggio Al Lupo Red Blend (Toscana) $50. One whiff followed by a sip or two confirms that this is a different breed for the Maremma. Why? Because there's zero Sangiovese in it; instead the blend is 70% Cab with equal parts Alicante and Petit Verdot. The wine is big, broad, chocolaty, almost raisiny, and ultimately it scores for being full-force but perfectly balanced. **91** *—M.S. (9/1/2006)*

Tenuta Sette Ponti 2003 Crognolo Sangiovese (Toscana) $35. Nice and solid, but not quite up to the level of previous vintages. Maybe it was the heat of the year, but this Crognolo has more raisin and heft than its predecessors. That said, it's also a touch jumpy and grabby. As for flavors, look for raspberry and earthy strawberry. Sangiovese with 10% Merlot. **88** *—M.S. (9/1/2006)*

Tenuta Sette Ponti 2001 Crognolo Sangiovese (Toscana) $32. Huge and meaty, with round berry and plum aromas propped up by a healthy load of lumber. The palate is loaded with plum and chocolate, while the finish is ultra-rich and smooth, bordering on buttery. In the end it all comes together. Give this Sangiovese ample air and it's sure to please. **91 Editors' Choice** *—M.S. (10/1/2004)*

Tenuta Sette Ponti 2000 Crognolo Sangiovese (Toscana) $32. At 90% Sangiovese and 10% Merlot, this is a sculpted, perfumed second-vintage

red with cranberry as well as cherry fruit and well-integrated oak. What makes this a winner, especially with food, is that the crystalline, racy fruit far outshadows the oak. It's not old-school, but you'd still have to call it a traditional Tuscan wine. **92** *—M.S. (8/1/2002)*

Tenuta Sette Ponti 2003 Oreno Sangiovese (Toscana) $100. Tenuta Sette Ponti's internationally styled blend is heavy and dense, a mirror image of the hot '03 vintage. Thus it pours on the blackberry, plum, and fudge flavors with gusto. This is a seriously fat, opulent red that would weigh in as a heavyweight at any wrestling match. Still, it's delicious and quite balanced. Drink from 2007 through 2009. **90** *—M.S. (9/1/2006)*

Tenuta Sette Ponti 1999 Oreno Sangiovese (Toscana) $90. Hail the first vintage of this international-style blend of Sangiovese, Merlot, and Cabernet Sauvignon from a new quality-minded producer near Arezzo. It's deep with saturated blackberry and hints of dried citrus rind and smoked meat. The round, full-bodied, ripe fruit palate is sure to please fans of big, modern wines. **91** *—M.S. (8/1/2002)*

TENUTA SETTEN

Tenuta Setten 2001 Vigneto S. Antonio Pinot Grigio (Piave) $14. Exotic and enticing at first, with penetrating lime, muskmelon, and floral aromas. Flavors of melon and tropical fruit are simpler. A good bet for outdoor dining, thanks to its standout nose. **85** *—J.C. (7/1/2003)*

Tenuta Setten 1999 Moresco Raboso (Raboso) $24. Stemmy and minty, with a strong aromatic resemblance to a field on a hot summer day. Cherry fruit and spice on the palate gives way to rock-hard tannins and a firm, unwavering finish. Needs time, but during that time it might dry out. **84** *(5/1/2003)*

TENUTA TERACREA

Tenuta Teracrea 1999 Tocai Italiano Tocai (Lison-Pramaggiore) $13. More enthusiasts should stretch their horizons and try wines like this engaging Northeastern Italian white. Orange and mineral aromas give way to a dry, even palate in this tasty, medium-weight wine. Good acidity and a slight spiciness on the finish make this a great food wine and an unusual white. Worth the hunt. **88** *—M.M. (9/1/2001)*

TENUTA VALDIPIATTA

Tenuta Valdipiatta 2002 Sangiovese (Vino Nobile di Montepulciano) $29. Straightforward and a touch sharp, with cherry, earth, and leather aromas. Red plum, pie cherry, and vanilla flavors carry the palate toward a peppery, lean finish. Fresh enough but not very loving. **84** *—M.S. (7/1/2005)*

Tenuta Valdipiatta 2001 Vigna d'Alfiero Sangiovese (Vino Nobile di Montepulciano) $50. A bit rusty in tint, with lean, dry aromas of leather and leaves. That same earthy, slightly dried-out character is noticeable on the palate as well, where tomato, cherry, and smoke are the dominant flavors. Fades fast on the finish, with a hint of buttery oak. **85** *—M.S. (7/1/2005)*

TENUTE DEI VALLARINO

Tenute dei Vallarino 2001 Bricco Asinari Superiore Barbera (Barbera d'Asti) $36. Assertively oaky on the nose, with strong aromas of charred wood and cedar. But there's sufficient fruit to back it up, lending tart cherries and a lingering finish to the harmonious, medium-weight whole. **88** *—J.C. (11/15/2004)*

Tenute dei Vallarino 2001 La Ladra Barbera (Barbera d'Asti) $18. Smells like vanilla extract alongside liquid smoke, yet has enough fruit to get by. Flavors of tobacco and cedar are wrapped around a bright core of lemony acids. **86** *—J.C. (11/15/2004)*

Tenute dei Vallarino 2004 Castello di Canelli Moscato (Moscato d'Asti) $15. A brilliant semi-sparkler with persistent bubbles, lush grassy notes, citrus, kiwi, lavender, honey, and peach. You can really taste the Moscato grape in the glass. The wine also delivers sweet lime pie, cream, and a medium finish. Tenute dei Vallarino is part of Fratelli Gancia, one of the grandfather companies of Italian sparkling wines. **88** *—M.L. (12/15/2005)*

Tenute dei Vallarino 2001 Dialogo Red Blend (Monferrato) $41. This microproduction (275 cases) blend of 60% Cabernet Sauvignon, 25% Barbera, 10% Nebbiolo, and 5% Merlot is lean and lemony at its core,

ITALY

surrounded by a thick blanket of cedar, cinnamon, and coffee flavors. **84** —*J.C. (11/15/2004)*

TENUTE DETTORI

Tenute Dettori 2001 Badde Nigolosu Tenores Cannonau (Romangia) $91. Big and rubbery, with 17.5% alcohol and a backpalate burn that will bring you to the brink. Licorice, stewed fruit, and kirsch make for a heady nose. The palate is just as demanding, with reduced flavors of chocolate and raisins. Quite difficult to score; this burly Sardinian red needs a pungent sheep's milk cheese or something similar to show its best. **87** —*M.S. (7/1/2005)*

Tenute Dettori 2001 Badde Nigolosu Tuderi Cannonau (Romangia) $57. This Sardinian red is light in color, with dry, seductive aromas of cherry, clove, and mint. Excellent ripeness, meanwhile, is presented in a sub-dued manner; the palate is pure and sweet at the core yet framed with old-school acidity and tannins. Lean by New World standards, but unique and iconoclastic. Made from Cannonau (Grenache), and definitely worth trying. **90** —*M.S. (7/1/2005)*

Tenute Dettori 2003 Badde Nigolosu Bianco Vermentino (Romangia) $40. This Sardinian white is so much the opposite of a quaffer that it actually suffers a bit. Lofty intentions and a warm vintage have produced excess weight and sweetness; the banana and vanilla flavors overwhelm. That said, some folks will appreciate the immense flavor and intensity of this Vermentino. **86** —*M.S. (7/1/2005)*

TENUTE NICCOLAI

Tenute Niccolai 2001 Podere Bellarina Brunello (Brunello di Montalcino) $NA. Fruit plays second fiddle to dark aromas such as resin, pine nut, fennel seed, maple syrup, mint, and exotic spice. Lush cherries and ripe forest berries do come forward in the mouth. Good structure with a dusty, anise-driven finish. **91** *(4/1/2006)*

TENUTE RUBINO

Tenute Rubino 2002 Marmorelle Red Blend (Salento) $10. At 85% Negroamaro and 15% Malvasia Nera, this jammy, berry-packed Southern Italian is the type of red wine most folks can sink their teeth into. Prepare for graham cracker aromas, bold fruit, and deep espresso shadings. It attacks with juicy strawberry and raspberry, and then turns spry as the acids take over. Fades with chocolate and a hint of butter. The consulting winemaker is Riccardo Cotarella, a master of extraction and balance regardless of region and price. **88 Best Buy** —*M.S. (11/15/2004)*

TENUTE SILVIO NARDI

Tenute Silvio Nardi 2001 Brunello (Brunello di Montalcino) $50. Very ripe cherry, strawberry, forest floor, vanilla, and grape juice notes render a lush, medium-bodied wine with creamy smoothness in the mouth. Sour acidity is a slight distraction. **89** *(4/1/2006)*

Tenute Silvio Nardi 2000 Brunello (Brunello di Montalcino) $55. Exceptionally spicy on the nose, with forest floor, leather, and pepper as well as ample berry fruit. Round and likable, with plum, chocolate, vanilla, and toast flavors. What brings this wine up is that it has a few levels of complexity. The finish, for example, is at first juicy. But then it runs long and spicy. Rock-solid Brunello from a consistent producer. **91** —*M.S. (7/1/2005)*

Tenute Silvio Nardi 1999 Brunello (Brunello di Montalcino) $55. Full, classy, and exciting from the first sniff to the last essence of the finish. Along the way is a largely flawless wine that bobs and weaves; at one moment it seems forward and modern; next, classic. Overall it's a beauty with structure and style. The real deal in newer-style Brunello. **93** —*M.S. (6/1/2004)*

Tenute Silvio Nardi 1997 Brunello (Brunello di Montalcino) $60. Emilia Nardi, daughter of Silvio Nardi, is doing all the right things at this huge estate, especially with the development of clonal selection and denser planting of the vines. Her 1997 is a modern, new wood-dominated wine, but it also shows beautifully judged ripe fruits and sweet acidity. The overall effect is of great elegance, with good long-term aging potential. **92** —*R.V. (8/1/2002)*

Tenute Silvio Nardi 1998 Manachiara Brunello (Brunello di Montalcino) $65. This tannic beauty shows earth, coffee, and caramel aromas prior to big-time plum, cherry, and blackberry flavors. It's huge in the mouth, with chewy, round tannins and uplifting acids. All the way through it's integrated and smoky. Hold through 2006. **92** —*M.S. (10/1/2004)*

Tenute Silvio Nardi 2002 Sangiovese (Rosso di Montalcino) $22. Wonderful in the nose, with snappy fruit and plenty of light but fragrant wood. The palate is nothing but red fruit, while the body is not too thick but substantive enough. It finishes smooth and easy, and it improves with airing. A perfect wine for cheeses or pasta, or with lunch. **90** —*M.S. (6/1/2004)*

TENUTE SOLETTA

Tenute Soletta 1997 Soletta/Reserva Grenache (Cannonau di Sardegna) $24. This Sardinian Grenache has aromas of mulling spices, green olives, and tobacco. The taste of pepper, dried fruit, and a little salinity mix with the soft tannins. Drink soon. **85** —*C.S. (5/1/2002)*

Tenute Soletta 2002 Prestizu Vermentino (Vermentino di Sardegna) $17. Modest flower blossom and earth aromas are a bit heavy, which is typical for the variety and region. Fairly full and round on the palate, with dry apple and papaya flavors. Not an overly expressive wine, but solid. **86** —*M.S. (8/1/2004)*

TERCIC

Tercic 2004 Pinot Grigio (Collio) $22. Fairly full and beefy, with apple, banana, papaya, and other tropical flavors. More soft than firm, with golden apple and cinnamon nuances. Shows ample intensity, with the slightest hint of coconut. **86** *(2/1/2006)*

TERESA RAIZ

Teresa Raiz 2004 Pinot Grigio (Colli Orientali del Friuli) $15. Lively and expressive, with a rich, creamy feel in the mouth and flavors of yellow flowers, grated lemon zest, and Golden Delicious apple. **89 Editors' Choice** —*M.L. (2/1/2006)*

Teresa Raiz 2004 Le Marsure Pinot Grigio (Venezia Giulia) $13. Banana, pineapple, sweet melon, peach, and even a pinch of basil leaf make a tight package of pleasing aromas. The wine performs well in the mouth, where tangy crispness arrives on a medium-length finish. **87** —*M.L. (2/1/2006)*

TERLAN

Terlan 2005 Pinot Grigio (Alto Adige) $19. There's a linear character to this Grigio that is really quite attractive. Ever so slightly copper-toned in color, its edginess is accented by perky mineral tones, white peach flavors, and snappy acidity. **90 Editors' Choice** —*M.L. (6/1/2006)*

Terlan 2003 Sauvignon (Alto Adige) $30. Melon and tart apple along with a musky scent get it going. The palate is mostly linear citrus, apple, and melon, while the finish offers crisp, basic flavors. Not a whole lot of excitement or complexity to this wine, but functional and solid. **86** *(7/1/2005)*

TERRA DEI REI

Terra dei Rei 2001 Divinus Aglianico (Aglianico del Vulture) $35. Full, floral, and sophisiticated, with leather, earth, licorice, and floral aromas. Very rich, tight, and masculine, with big-time tannins pushing heavy plum, fudge, and tobacco flavors. Nothing timid here. **89** —*M.S. (10/1/2006)*

Terra dei Rei 2001 Vultur Aglianico (Aglianico del Vulture) $20. Not entirely convincing up front, where raisin and cranberry aromas are a bit less than commited. Plum, raisin, and cough syrup are the primary flavors, with even more raisin lurking on the finish. Extremely tannic; more of a traditional Aglianico. **83** —*M.S. (10/1/2006)*

TERRA ROSSA

Terra Rossa 2001 Brunello (Brunello di Montalcino) $50. Rodolfo Cosimi of Il Poggiolo started this second line of Brunello, which is named after a red-soil vineyard dear to his late father. You'll taste ripe blueberry or currant backed by drying mineral notes, earthy tones, and generous menthol. Supple and elegant with dusty tannins. **92 Cellar Selection** *(4/1/2006)*

TERRA SERENA

Terra Serena NV Extra Dry Prosecco (Prosecco di Conegliano e Valdobbiadene) $15. Starts off with yellow rose, apple cider, clove, and bread dough aromas. The atypical bouquet is a bit heavy and unpolished compared to that of most Proseccos but the wine does deliver the crisp acidity you should expect. Tasted twice. **84** —*M.L. (6/1/2006)*

TERRABIANCA

Terrabianca 2003 Ceppate Cabernet Blend (Toscana) $37. With 10% Merlot for extra smoothness, this Cabernet Sauvignon has amazing intensity with plum, blackberry, leather, spice bread, clove, chocolate, and menthol notes that leap out of the glass. It's a beautifully harmonious wine with no aromatic element out of place and black fruit and spice flavors that are nicely rounded out by the oak. Soft, yielding, and ready to drink now. **92** —*M.L. (9/1/2006)*

Terrabianca 1999 Campaccio Red Blend (Toscana) $24. A blend of 70% Sangiovese with 30% Cabernet. The nose is like a hit of pure leather bootstraps, and it just won't yield much more than that. Cherry, plum, and dark chocolate flavors carry the palate, while the finish is layered with notes of meat, licorice, and vanilla. Overall this is structured and tasty, a well-made, big-boned wine. **89** —*M.S. (12/31/2002)*

Terrabianca 2001 Campaccio Sangiovese (Toscana) $38. Interesting bouquet, with early lactic notes giving way to blueberry and then sawdust, root beer, and finally Christmas spice. A bit flat on the palate, but still pushing lively raspberry and strawberry flavors. Tight on the finish, with lively acidity and fierce tannins. **87** —*M.S. (11/15/2004)*

Terrabianca 2000 Campaccio Sangiovese (Toscana) $24. Full and bulky, with raisiny aromas. Doesn't quite impress due to some sharpness at first and then a flatness late. Balance is lacking amid the plum, cherry, and raspberry flavors. Just an average wine from a usually good producer. **85** —*M.S. (10/1/2004)*

Terrabianca 2001 Campaccio Selezione Riserva Sangiovese (Toscana) $72. Reticent for a 2001. The nose is leathery, with more smoked meat and tomato than bright fruit. Quite classical in style, blending 70% Sangiovese with 30% Cabernet. Tart cherry and cranberry control the palate, which has a nice center cut of fruit but not a lot of obvious charm. More of a connoisseur's wine than mainstream juice. **88** —*M.S. (9/1/2006)*

Terrabianca 1998 Ceppate Sangiovese (Tuscany) $22. This wine is Cabernet-based, with 25% Sangiovese. It has overly powerful wood aromas along with bacon and bramble. The palate is bright, serious, and loaded with cherry, plum, coffee, and bitter chocolate, and the finish is dark and layered. The problem, however, is the tannins, which are exceedingly hard and aggressive. **86** —*M.S. (12/31/2002)*

Terrabianca 2001 Croce Riserva Sangiovese (Chianti Classico) $31. Saddle leather and dried spices mark the nose, while the flavors run toward black cherries and cedar. It feels a little light in the mouth, finishing crisp and tart. **87** *(4/1/2005)*

Terrabianca 2000 Croce Riserva Sangiovese (Chianti Classico) $25. A bit of bramble and root beer add sweetness to the toasty, oaky nose. The palate is lush with plum, berry, and a slight hint of tomato. Finishes broad, but oak pops up, forming a soft carpet to this new-age Chianti. **90** —*M.S. (10/1/2004)*

Terrabianca 1997 Croce Riserva Sangiovese (Chianti Classico) $25. Very big and dark, the deep cherry fruit here is cloaked—some might say overshadowed—by the intensity of the oak. Still, it possesses a stylish, suave quality and a good mouthfeel, even if it loses some typicity in the robe of international-style toast. Will be better in two or three years. **87** *(4/1/2001)*

Terrabianca 2001 La Fonte Sangiovese (Toscana) $20. More dry, toasty wood than fruit creates a modest, distant nose. The palate is quite lean and acid-packed, with cherry and apple skin carrying the flavor profile. More zesty and sharp than ideal; not caustic but raw. **85** —*M.S. (10/1/2004)*

Terrabianca 2000 Piano del Cipresso Sangiovese (Toscana) $22. Quite a heavy wine, with deep aromas of rubber, blackberry, smoked meat, and prune. A load and a half of blackberry and cherry hit hard across the palate, carried by serious tannin. A finish of plum and chocolate turns a touch flat. Very oaky. **88** —*M.S. (10/1/2004)*

Terrabianca 1999 Piano Del Cipresso Sangiovese (Tuscany) $22. Leather and violet aromas kick off this 100% Sangiovese, which is more racy than burly. A potentially excellent wine with food due to its sculpted structure and modest tannins; this is a fresh and expressive version of Tuscany's prime red grape. In terms of flavor, expect cherry fruit and supporting vanilla. For feel, it's round and chunky while deftly avoiding heaviness. **90** —*M.S. (12/31/2002)*

Terrabianca 2003 Scassino Sangiovese (Chianti Classico) $24. Seems as though the heat of 2003 sapped this wine of its vitality. The nose is soft and leathery, with sausage and vanilla aromas dominating. Tomato and root vegetables control the palate, while the finish is scrambled and stewy. Not a fresh wine. **82** —*M.S. (10/1/2006)*

Terrabianca 2002 Scassino Sangiovese (Chianti Classico) $22. Closed but a little spicy, with hints of cola, damp leather, and coffee. Modest in its force, with cherry and citrus creating a fresh, zesty palate feel. Stays mostly in the middle of the road, with supple tannins and a modest finishing flavor of root beer. **86** *(4/1/2005)*

Terrabianca 2001 Scassino Sangiovese (Chianti Classico) $20. A touch brown and rusty in color, with a heavy dose of bacon/pancetta on the nose and throughout. The palate is roasted, with mild fruit and forceful oak. To some it might taste more like breakfast, what with its campfire-driven flavors of smoked meat, coffee, and toast. **85** —*M.S. (10/1/2004)*

Terrabianca 2000 Scassino Sangiovese (Chianti Classico) $20. Bramble and mixed berries comprise the nose of this youthful Chianti, which offers doses of leather, earth, cherry, and boysenberry. On the finish, it fans out in an airy sort of way, which means it should be at its best over the next year or so. **87** *(8/1/2002)*

Terrabianca 1999 Scassino Sangiovese (Chianti Classico) $14. The bouquet is round and friendly, with a full offering of cherry. The palate follows suit, delivering some earth alongside cherry and strawberry. The finish is equally friendly, and not ponderous or heavy. From start to finish it flows without flaws, even if it never quite rises to a higher status. **87** —*M.S. (12/31/2002)*

Terrabianca 1998 Scassino Sangiovese (Chianti Classico) $18. As in this producer's '97 Croce Riserva, an even palate-feel is among the best features here. The aromas and flavors are very dark and the oak quite dense. A core of sour black plum fruit wears mild vanilla accents and the balance is attractive. Pleasing and stylish. **87** *(4/1/2001)*

TERRALE

Terrale 2002 Catarratto (Sicilia) $8. A fresh, rich wine, with some good exotic fruit flavors and a clean, green aftertaste. **83** —*R.V. (10/1/2003)*

Terrale 2000 Primitivo (Puglia) $8. Not a super jammy-style Primitivo, which makes it all the more interesting because of the earthiness and spice that enhance the structure and complexity of the wine. Great with tomato- and garlic-based pastas or Bolognese. **85 Best Buy** *(5/1/2002)*

Terrale 1998 Primitivo (Puglia) $5. 83 —*M.N. (12/31/2000)*

Terrale 2000 Nero D'Avola/Syrah Red Blend (Sicilia) $8. Nero d'Avola (80%) gives this a rich, juicy berry flavor and the Syrah (20%) adds backbone and fresh-ground pepper flavors. Interesting and fruit-forward. **86 Best Buy** *(5/1/2002)*

Terrale 2000 Sangiovese (Puglia) $8. A pleasant, dusty nose redolent of brewing coffee picks up a smoky char on the palate, though it finishes a touch flat. It could use a bit more fruit and acidity, but it's a nice, simple wine nonetheless. **84** *(5/1/2002)*

Terrale 1998 Bianco White Blend (Sicilia) $5. 82 —*M.N. (12/31/2000)*

TERRALSOLE

Terralsole 2001 Brunello (Brunello di Montalcino) $NA. A perfumey and sensual wine with dried lavender, rosehip tea, violets, cranberry, and herbal notes. Very floral in the mouth as well, where it boasts a crisp, clean impact, medium-weight, firm tannins and long persistency. **89** *(4/1/2006)*

ITALY

ITALY

TERRAZZE DELLA LUNA

Terrazze Della Luna 2004 Pinot Grigio (Trentino) $12. Fragrant flowers, fresh banana, pear, and nectarine typify the nose and wash through to the mouth over a medium finish. An excellent everyday meals wine. **86** —M.L. (6/1/2006)

TERRAZZO

Terrazzo 2000 Sangiovese-Montepulciano Sangiovese (Marche) $7. Mildly horsey at first, with sharp fruit aromas and burnt edges. Strawberry mixed with oak defines the palate, while on the finish it's more tannic than the fruit can handle. Runs high on spice, particularly chili and black pepper. The blend is 60% Sangiovese, 40% Montepulciano. **83** — M.S. (11/15/2003)

TERRE DA VINO

Terre da Vino 1998 Barbera (Barbera d'Asti) $11. **88 Best Buy** (4/1/2000)

Terre da Vino 2003 La Bella Estate Moscato Passito Moscato (Piedmont) $NA. A Moscato Passito with a light amber color and abundant peanut shell, honey, dried sage, and sun-dried fruit aromas. Svelte in the mouth and not syrupy, with tight concentration and a medium finish. **87** — M.L. (11/15/2006)

Terre da Vino 2004 La Gatta Moscato (Moscato d'Asti) $12. Here is a vine-yard-designate wine bursting with floral notes: jasmine, honeysuckle, and orange blossom. Exotic fruit takes over in the mouth leaving a trail of kiwi, lime, and peach backed by thick, creamy mousse. **87 Editors' Choice** —M.L. (12/15/2005)

Terre da Vino 2004 Monti Furchi Moscato (Asti) $NA. I loved the fresh fruit and delicate floral notes that seemed to drift off the nose with amazing intensity. Peach, honeydew, and honeysuckle strike a harmonious chord and accent the sparkler's residual sugar. **89** —M.L. (11/15/2006)

TERRE DE TRINCI

Terre de Trinci 2000 Ugolino Sagrantino (Sagrantino di Montefalco) $35. This wine has a great nose: layers of spice, leather, black cherry, prunes, candied licorice, and cinnamon. Oak aging renders a smooth, round mouthfeel and good structure. **87** —M.L. (9/1/2005)

TERRE DEGLI SVEVI

Terre Degli Svevi 1999 Re Manfredi Aglianico (Aglianico del Vulture) $30. Vital and tannic after a number of years, a testament to this grape's aging ability. The bouquet deals strawberry, raspberry, mint, and sage. In the mouth, hard tannins frame plum and cherry fruit, which is backed by a racy, no-holds-barred finish. Nothing out of place; well-structured. **90** — M.S. (11/15/2004)

TERRE DEL PRINCIPE

Terre del Principe 1998 Sangiovese (Chianti) $11. There's berry and rhubarb-like aromas and dried cherry flavors that have hints of tobacco, vanilla, and leather. All of this sounds good, but the elements seemed to disappear too quickly in the glass. After only a few moments the wine seemed a pale shadow of the initial elements, and finished dry and a bit hollow. **84** (4/1/2001)

Terre del Principe 2002 Vernaccia (Vernaccia di San Gimignano) $13. Quite flowery on the nose, almost to the point of smelling like a tree grove in bloom. But beyond that there's little stuffing to this wine. It's got some lime and tangerine at its edges, but not too much at the core. A decent quaff; nothing faulty or off. **84** —M.S. (8/1/2004)

TERRE DI GENESTRA

Terre di Genestra 1999 Catarratto (Sicilia) $13. **87** (4/1/2002)

Terre di Genestra 2002 Nero d'Avola (Sicilia) $13. A powerful, complex wine showing solid tannins along with black fruits and acidity. Raisin flavors give sweetness to the aftertaste. **87** —R.V. (10/1/2003)

Terre di Genestra 1999 Nero d'Avola (Sicilia) $13. This wine has a lovely, dark, sweet nose of plums and cassis accented with toasted oak and a touch of dill. It's all there in the mouth as well. A delicious wine that will appeal to both the New World and Old World palates. **88 Best Buy** (5/1/2002)

TERRE DI GER

Terre di Ger 2004 Pinot Grigio (Friuli) $15. Not subtle, with a solid, pro-truding aroma of perfume and flowers. The palate, however, is not bad. There's spiced melon along with apple, and those flavors lead to a siz-able, persistent finish. **84** (2/1/2006)

TERRE DI GINESTRA

Terre di Ginestra 2002 Catarratto Chardonnay (Sicilia) $9. Creamy, rich wine, with layers of wood. Like Chardonnay in its openess and fullness. **87** —R.V. (10/1/2003)

TERRE DI GIURFO

Terre di Giurfo 2004 Kuntéri Nero d'Avola (Sicilia) $11. Opens with some-thing a bit funky, reminiscent of Band-Aid, but those notes blow off to reveal cherry fruit, toast, and tobacco. The tannins are soft. As a whole, it promises to be very food friendly. **87** —M.L. (7/1/2006)

Terre di Giurfo 2004 Maskarìa Red Blend (Cerasuolo di Vittoria) $10. The cherry and blackberry-driven nose of this attractively ruby-colored wine is offset by Band-Aid or animal notes that disturb an otherwise pretty picture. On the upside is the wine's crisp mouthfeel. **85** —M.L. (7/1/2006)

Terre di Giurfo 2004 Ronna Syrah (Sicilia) $10. Unmistakably a hot-climate wine, the Syrah delivers blueberry and blackberry with musty, earth tones, tight tannins, and a pleasant finish. Would pair nice-ly with grilled sausage peppered with fennel seed. **87** —M.L. (7/1/2006)

TERREDORA

Terredora 2004 Aglianico (Irpinia) $15. Aged six months in stainless steel, here is a fruity and frivolous version of this otherwise austere and brood-ing southern Italian grape. Red berry fruit meets interesting mineral notes; the wine would pair wonderfully with pasta. **87** —M.L. (10/1/2006)

Terredora 2000 Fatica Contadina Aglianico (Taurasi) $48. This is an intriguing and complex red with loads of minerality, black pepper, charred meat, earth, and charcoal. But the fruit notes are in there, too: prunes and red, ripe cherry. The tannins are a bit nervous still and the wine should be cellared a few more years. **91 Cellar Selection** —M.L. (10/1/2006)

Terredora 2002 Il Principio Aglianico (Irpinia) $NA. Aged eight months in barrique, this powerhouse Aglianico from Campania delivers a rush of fresh berry fruit, chewy ripe blackberry and raspberry, forest floor, mushroom, stone, and charcoal-like nuances. The mineral notes appear on the palate rendering a beautifully dry, almost dusty, quality. **89** — M.L. (10/1/2006)

Terredora 1998 Il Principio Aglianico (Aglianico d'Irpinia) $9. Hints of smoke and herb accent this wine's bright strawberry-rhubarb aromatics. Red berries and milk chocolate then take over and dominate the palate, which features a textured, grainy mouthfeel. Finishes long, with soft, ripe tannins. **85 Best Buy** —C.S. (5/1/2002)

Terredora 2003 Red Blend (Lacryma Christi del Vesuvio) $27. Made from one of Southern Italy's most eclectic indigenous grapes, this is a less aro-matic red that delivers small, but equal doses of blackberry, licorice, resin, and slate. The mineral component is the most noticeable: As if the vines sucked it straight up from volcanic soils. **86** —M.L. (10/1/2006)

Terredora 1999 Red Blend (Aglianico d'Irpinia) $12. **87 Best Buy** —M.N. (12/31/2000)

Terredora 1996 Fatica Contadina Red Blend (Taurasi) $38. **89** —M.N. (12/31/2000)

Terredora 1999 Terre di Dora White Blend (Fiano di Avellino) $20. **91** — M.N. (12/31/2000)

TERREDORA DI PAOLO

Terredora Di Paolo 2003 Aglianico (Irpinia) $14. A young, chunky heavy-weight is the only way to describe this black wine, which smells of fruitcake and herbs, and tastes of baked plums and chocolate. Rich and overflowing, and building to a tannic crescendo. One can see the mass appeal here. **87** —M.S. (2/1/2005)

Terredora Di Paolo 2003 Loggia Della Serra Greco (Greco di Tufo) $21. Heavily reduced citrus on the nose, with more piercing citrus and mango on the palate. Finishes racy but scouring. Some nuttiness and charm lurks below the spiked acidity, but you have to work to find it.**83** —*M.S. (2/1/2005)*

Terredora Di Paolo 1999 Fatica Contadina Red Blend (Taurasi) $49. A large, complex, forceful wine that requires time to show off. What starts out murky, heavy, and clumsy becomes more lovable once it gets some air. Along the way come plum, chocolate, and raisin characteristics, and as expected, hammer-time tannins. Very hard on the cheeks, but such is Taurasi.**89** —*M.S. (2/1/2005)*

TERUZZI & PUTHOD

Teruzzi & Puthod 2001 Peperino Sangiovese (Toscana) $15. Lean and almost citrusy on the nose, with some green notes as well. Spicy but thin, with cherry and chocolate flavors in front of a lively, high-pitched finish.**83** —*M.S. (10/1/2004)*

Teruzzi & Puthod 2004 Vernaccia (Vernaccia di San Gimignano) $13. Said to be the favorite après-sculpting drink of Michelangelo, Vernaccia is one of Italy's oldest natives grapes. This version from a 235-acre vineyard near Tuscany's famed "city of towers" is not aromatically intense but it does offer nice melon and floral tones. Tart and flinty in the mouth.**85** —*M.L. (9/1/2005)*

Teruzzi & Puthod 2003 Vernaccia (Vernaccia di San Gimignano) $13. You get the impression this was a hot year thanks to the ripe cantaloupe, pineapple fruit tart, and wood notes. But mineral tones and sour grapefruit astringency manage to break free in the mouth.**84** —*M.L. (9/1/2005)*

Teruzzi & Puthod 2002 Vernaccia (Vernaccia di San Gimignano) $12. Aromas of stone fruits, particularly apricot, are light but nice. The palate offers lightweight lemon and tangerine, while the finish is dry and simple. Nicely textured but a bit weak on flavor.**85** —*M.S. (8/1/2004)*

Teruzzi & Puthod 1997 Vernaccia (Vernaccia di San Gimignano) $11.84 *(11/1/1999)*

Teruzzi & Puthod 1997 Terre di Tufi Vernaccia (Vernaccia di San Gimignano) $21.86 *(11/1/1999)*

Teruzzi & Puthod 2004 Terre di Tufi White Blend (Toscana) $25. Colorful, bold, and sweet smelling, with hay, butterscotch, and peach on the uncommon nose. More of a big-boned wine with ripe, intriguing apple, almond, lemon, and butter flavors. Finishes smooth, with background notes of vanilla and citrus pith. Based on Vernaccia, with other grapes blended in.**88** —*M.S. (9/1/2006)*

TESEO

Teseo 2002 Chardonnay (Terre di Chieti) $15. From the Marche, this Chardonnay is creamy and thick, with aromas of buttered corn and pancakes. It's bland and heavy on the palate, with modest melon and apple flavors.**83** —*M.S. (10/1/2004)*

TIAMO

Tiamo 2004 Pinot Grigio (Delle Venezie) $10. Slightly floral and just a bit zesty, with pink grapefruit, apple, and citrus aromas and flavors. Not that deep; almost dilute; moderately peachy. Clean and fresh as a whole. **84** *(2/1/2006)*

Tiamo 2004 Pinot Grigio (Delle Venezie) $10. I absolutely love the eye-catching daisy-shaped label but was less enthused during our blind tasting by the wine's aromatic ensemble that had a strong lactic quality to it in the form of pineapple or peach yogurt. Tart and slightly bitter in the mouth.**84** —*M.L. (2/1/2006)*

TIBERINI

Tiberini 1998 Podere le Caggiole Prugnolo Gentile (Vino Nobile di Montepulciano) $20. Lighter in color, with aromas of dried fruit, leather, and smoke. The berry and cherry flavors run a touch sour, but it seems ripe and textured, with hints of chocolate working in its favor. Offers a good mix of dryness and power. Probably best with food.**86** —*M.S. (11/15/2003)*

Tiberini 2000 Virgulto Prugnolo Gentile (Rosso di Montepulciano) $30. Full, dense, and packed with fruit and oak, nothing is left to the imagination here, as sweet fruit pours forth on the palate. The basics are in form, but there isn't any nuance or character.**84** —*M.S. (11/15/2003)*

TIEFENBRUNNER

Tiefenbrunner 1999 Linticlarus Chardonnay (Alto Adige) $20. This is a rich, full-bodied Chardonnay, full of wood aromas from its 11 months aging in barriques. It has big, creamy fruit with touches of honey, and ripe, long-lasting, spicy flavors.**89** —*R.V. (7/1/2003)*

Tiefenbrunner 2003 Castel Turmhof Lagrein (Alto Adige) $18. Rounder and softer than other interpretations of Lagrein, this wine is dominated by red cherry and black fruit. Twelve months between barrique and larger barrels gives it a broader structure and makes it ready to drink now.**88** —*M.L. (9/1/2005)*

Tiefenbrunner 2002 Feldmarschall von Fenner Vino da Tavola Müller-Thurgau (Alto Adige) $27. From what is claimed to be the highest vineyard in Europe, at 3,000 feet, comes this surprisingly ripe, full-flavored Müller-Thurgau, with soft acidity and a fine, crisp, green finish. **87** —*R.V. (7/1/2003)*

Tiefenbrunner 2004 Pinot Grigio (Delle Venezie) $15. Gorgeous example of the successful integration of fruit and mineral tones. Peach and green melon seem accented by lemon zest or lime. Elegant but structured in the mouth.**87** —*M.L. (6/1/2006)*

Tiefenbrunner 2002 Kirchleiten Sauvignon Blanc (Alto Adige) $21. This wine from the Tiefenbrunner estate at Castel Turmhof is a lively, crisp, fresh style of wine, with flavors of green peppers and mint, and good acidity.**86** —*R.V. (7/1/2003)*

Tieffenbrunner 2000 Pinot Bianco (Alto Adige) $12. The wine's structure has all the requisite parts and then some. It has good weight, crisp acidity and fine balance. Unfortunately, there's little fruit for it to support, and therein lies the problem.**83** —*M.N. (9/1/2001)*

Tieffenbrunner 2000 delle Venezie Pinot Grigio (Alto Adige) $13. Tiefenbrunner is an old reliable when it comes to Pinot Grigio, and its 2000 is no exception. Pear and citrus are the flavors. The palate is well-balanced and the mouthfeel round and smooth. Vibrant acidity accentuates the long, fruity finish.**86** —*M.N. (9/1/2001)*

TIEZZI

Tiezzi 2001 Brunello (Brunello di Montalcino) $50. Crisp and astringent, this is not a wine for fans of big-barriqued wines. Instead, it promises to be a solid, food-friendly companion at the table thanks to its tart acidity and overall finesse. A lean but structured wine with baked apple pie, cranberry, and eucalyptus.**88** *(4/1/2006)*

Tiezzi 2000 Brunello (Brunello di Montalcino) $50. Red licorice, raspberry jam and a hint of cherry tomato make for a modest but open bouquet. To the contrary, the palate is hard, with fierce tannins. As for flavors, the wine locks into that familiar black cherry, medicinal tune before finishing with vanilla and milk chocolate.**87** —*M.S. (7/1/2005)*

Tiezzi 1999 Brunello (Brunello di Montalcino) $NA. Sweet and liqueur-like, with aromas of red licorice, candied cherries, and caramel. In the mouth, the flavor of brown sugar rides high over the creamy palate. Too heavy for the category, and lacking in excitement.**85** —*M.S. (6/1/2004)*

TIZIANO

Tiziano 2003 Sangiovese (Chianti) $10. Solid and chunky, with aromas of sawdust, cinnamon, and clove. Full enough, with strawberry, cherry, and spice flavors. A touch tart on the finish, but with enough length and weight to push it forward. Not profound but 100% likable.**87 Best Buy** *(4/1/2005)*

Tiziano 2001 Sangiovese (Chianti) $8. Woody and smoky, with a sweet-fruit quotient to the nose that's a lot like red licorice. Strawberry and cherry fruit works well enough on the racy palate, while a finish of strawberry, pepper, and light oak is satisfactory. Light and easy, with pronounced acidity.**85 Best Buy** —*M.S. (11/15/2003)*

Tiziano 1999 Sangiovese (Chianti) $7. Opens with a complex nose of cherry, plum, cocoa, and leather elements that promise much. On the palate, however, it turns much more tart—even sharp—with mild cherry

ITALY

fruit and a light body. Finishes with modest length and a sour cranberry-herb note. **83** *(4/1/2001)*

Tiziano 2001 Gold Sangiovese (Chianti Classico) $16. Tobacco, plum, and a sharp wine-vinegar note create a bouquet that's slightly pickled, but overall it offers more positives than negatives. The palate is bright and intense, while the gutty finish packs coffee, licorice, and dried fruits in a medicinal robe. **86** *(4/1/2005)*

Tiziano 2001 Riserva Sangiovese (Chianti) $12. Lots of leather, coffee, and campfire aromas are followed by tart plum, cherry, and hickory smoke flavors. A bit tangy, and not subtle in the least. There is also a whiff of green to the middle. **85** *(4/1/2005)*

Tiziano 1999 Riserva Sangiovese (Chianti) $10. Tight and complete, with raspberry fruit, some chocolate and a touch of buttery oak. Quite snappy on the finish, with a tannic shot that is reminiscent of cherry or plum skins. Textbook but entirely satisfactory. **86 Best Buy** —*M.S. (11/15/2003)*

TOFFOLI

Toffoli 2005 Brut Prosecco (Prosecco di Conegliano e Valdobbiadene) $12. Here's a Prosecco at a crossroads. The nose is complex and rich with exotic spice, peach, melon, and dried herbs that wins it high marks. Yet the mouthfeel lacks the crispness and sharpness you expect from this kind of wine. **85** —*M.L. (6/1/2006)*

Toffoli 2005 Extra Dry Prosecco (Prosecco di Conegliano e Valdobbiadene) $12. A wonderfully summerish bubbly with layers of exotic fruit, toasted almond, pear, and kiwi. The wine boasts a creamy, full mouthfeel and crisp acidity on the finish. **86** —*M.L. (6/1/2006)*

TOLAINI

Tolaini 2002 Tenuta S. Giovanni Duesanti Bordeaux Blend (Toscana) $40. Forward but comfortable, with dark fruit, forest, and bacon aromas. It's dominated by Cabernet, with Merlot and Cab Franc playing in the background. Ripe, tasty, and sweet, with black cherry and raspberry hitting with some force. Arguably a bit oaky and close, but still very good. **88** —*M.S. (9/1/2006)*

TOLLOY

Tolloy 1998 Pinot Bianco (Alto Adige) $11. 86 *(7/1/2000)*

Tolloy 2005 Pinot Grigio (Alto Adige) $10. Very compact and clean in its aromatic delivery with banana, Golden Delicious apple, and attractive hints of toasted almond in the background. Creamy, smooth, and supple in the mouth with a touch of zesty spice on the finish. **88 Best Buy** —*M.L. (6/1/2006)*

Tolloy 2004 Pinot Grigio (Alto Adige) $12. From the mountainous Alto Adige region, this Grigio is rich with peach, melon, honey, and apple flavors. Not huge in the mouth, but enjoyable, with just the right touch of acidity. **87** —*M.L. (2/1/2006)*

Tolloy 1999 Pinot Grigio (Alto Adige) $10. 88 Best Buy —*M.N. (12/31/2000)*

Tolloy 2003 Cantina Salorno Pinot Grigio (Alto Adige) $12. Shows decent weight and richness in the mouth, along with flavors of pear, melon, and fresh herbs. Picks up some Gewürz-like spice as well, giving it greater complexity than most inexpensive Grigios. Worth a try with unsweetened Asian dishes. **86** —*J.C. (12/31/2004)*

Tolloy 1997 Pinot Nero (Alto Adige) $11. 86 *(7/1/2000)*

TOMMASI

Tommasi 2001 Vigneto Santa Cecilia Chardonnay (Valdadige) $9. This lovely Chardonnay has just the right blend of juicy peaches and subtle herbs and flowers to make it easy to drink, yet interesting enough to hold your attention. Finishes long and mouth-watering. **88** —*J.C. (7/1/2003)*

Tommasi 2001 Rafael Corvina (Valpolicella Classico Superiore) $11. A light, easily enjoyed red, this is Valpolicella at its most basic, quaffing level. Dried spices accent leather and cherry flavors, mixing in hints of earth and citrus on the finish. A fine choice for picnics or casual lunches. **86 Best Buy** —*J.C. (12/31/2004)*

Tommasi 2001 Ripasso Corvina (Valpolicella Classico Superiore) $18. Starts off a bit horsey and leathery, but has ample depth of fruit lurking behind. Dark plum and earth flavors are tinged with meat on the palate. Shows good complexity and a long, supple finish. Drink now and over the next few years. **88** —*J.C. (12/31/2004)*

Tommasi 2001 Corvina, Rondinella, Molinara (Amarone della Valpolicella Classico) $60. A bit understated on the nose, yielding just plum and leather at first, but this really blossoms on the palate, revealing layers of black cherry and plum fruit, framed by hints of vanilla and toast. Ripe and round without being heavy, this excellent Amarone finishes with dusty tannins and another gush of fresh fruit, suggesting 10 years of aging is not out of the question. **92** —*J.C. (10/1/2006)*

Tommasi 2000 Corvina, Rondinella, Molinara (Amarone della Valpolicella Classico) $60. A full-bodied, corpulent Amarone, this doesn't have a great deal of grace just yet. Instead, its bold flavors of cinnamon and clove, cherry and plum plow ahead ruggedly, finishing long and tannic. This has all the right stuff, it just needs time to settle down; try after 2008. **90** —*J.C. (12/31/2004)*

Tommasi 1997 Corvina, Rondinella, Molinara (Amarone della Valpolicella Classico) $49. Some smoke, burnt sugar, and molasses notes on the nose; black cherry fruit, licorice, and bitter chocolate on the palate. The finish is more fruity than dark or dense, dealing clove, raspberry, and more chocolate. **88** *(5/1/2003)*

Tommasi 2001 Ca' Florian Corvina, Rondinella, Molinara (Amarone della Valpolicella Classico) $68. In contrast to Tommasi's regular Amarone, this is a darker, richer, more brooding wine, loaded with chocolaty, fudge-like flavors and roasted fruit. It's mouth-filling and supple, with a lingering finish that bodes well for cellaring, although it's certainly approachable now. **92** —*J.C. (10/1/2006)*

Tommasi 2000 Ca' Florian Corvina, Rondinella, Molinara (Amarone della Valpolicella Classico) $60. Charred to the max, as if you were poking your nose into a can of coffee. But we sort of liked that heavily burnt character, which gives way after time and should subside even more if this wine is cellared. In the meantime, be on the lookout for rich, ripe black fruit, a velvety feel, and subtle notes of licorice and syrup. **90** *(11/1/2005)*

Tommasi 1997 Ca'Florian Corvina, Rondinella, Molinara (Amarone della Valpolicella) $55. Here's an Amarone with something for everyone. The aromas of leather, smoked meat, tar, cola, and menthol combine into a delicious, complex whole. The meaty palate has powerful black cherry fruit and firm, forward acids. And the finish is long and warming, with licorice and spice. Will age well for years to come. **93 Editors' Choice** *(5/1/2003)*

Tommasi 2000 Il Sestante Vigneto Monte Masua Corvina, Rondinella, Molinara (Amarone della Valpolicella Classico) $58. Fairly tight and snappy, but weighs in more rich than lean. The palate deals cherry, plum, and earth, while the finish offers lavender, fudge, and pepper. Well balanced stuff, and pretty easy to get into; this one doesn't need a ton of time in the cellar. **89** *(11/1/2005)*

Tommasi 1997 Vigneto Il Sestante Corvina, Rondinella, Molinara (Amarone della Valpolicella) $50. Leathery aromas combine forces with wet moss, bramble, and tobacco to make for a pleasant, welcoming bouquet. The palate offers more leather and some prune and coffee flavors. The finish is tightly structured, offering modest to full tannins and plenty of bitter chocolate flavor. **87** *(5/1/2003)*

Tommasi 2003 Le Volpare Garganega (Soave Classico) $10. There's been a renaissance in Soave, and tasty, inexpensive wines like this one are the result. There's a burst of fruit opn the nose, ranging from melon and pear to white peaches and almonds, a plump, medium-weight presence on the palate, and some citrusy length to the finish. A solid choice for holiday entertaining and into the warmer months ahead. **87 Best Buy** —*J.C. (12/31/2004)*

Tommasi 2004 Le Rosse Pinot Grigio (Delle Venezie) $10. This Pinot Grigio has a note of candied fruit under white spirit, orange peel, almond, and vanilla bean. A powerful nose, but not a complex one, with spicy overtones. **85** —*M.L. (2/1/2006)*

Tommasi 2003 Le Rosse Pinot Grigio (Delle Venezie) $10. This is a weighty, corpulent wine, enlivened by a dash of citrusy acidity. Bold melon, ripe apple, and dried spice flavors make for a satisfying mouthful that could pair with fish or light chicken dishes. **86 Best Buy** —*J.C. (12/31/2004)*

Tommasi 1997 Le Rosse Pinot Grigio (Colli Orientali del Friuli) $10. 85 *(8/1/1999)*

Tommasi 1997 Campo Fiorato Red Blend (Recioto di Soave) $20. A bit brown but not necessarily in decline. The leather and soy aromas are a departure from some of its inky, rich brethren, while the palate offers dates, cinnamon, and cooked brown sugar. Very nuanced and complex. **87** *(5/1/2003)*

Tommasi 2000 Crearo della Concaa d'Oro Red Blend (Veronese) $25. Smooth and loaded with berry fruit and vanilla aromas. The palate is bright and expressive, a tasty mix of plum, cherry, earth, and dried spices. The finish is perfectly clean, with cocoa and berry flavors resting on fine yet firm tannins. Quite the pretty and precise blend of Corvina, Cab Franc, and the once-forgotten but now revived Oseleta. **89** *(5/1/2003)*

Tommasi 1998 Ripasso Red Blend (Valpolicella Classico Superiore) $30. Typical ripasso notes of Port, cola, chocolate, and dried black cherries are all over the nose. The palate is rich and smooth, with additional black cherry and chocolate flavors. The finish is layered and satisfying, with sweetness at the center and edges that are properly bitter. **87** *(5/1/2003)*

Tommasi 2004 Poggio al Tufo Vigneto Rompicollo Sangiovese (Maremma) $12. This Sangiovese-Cabernet blend yields soft strawberry aromas along with rose petals. As it opens it grows loose with its aromas, and what follows is mostly jammy, chewy berry flavors and not too much pop. Finishes a touch candied, with sugary sweetness. **85** —*M.S. (9/1/2006)*

Tommasi 2001 Vigneto Le Volpare White Blend (Soave Classico Superiore) $9. 82 —*J.C. (7/1/2003)*

Tommasi 2001 Vigneto San Martino White Blend (Lugana) $NA. Much riper, fatter, and fuller-bodied than most Luganas, this offering boasts grapefruit and passion fruit aromas nicely balanced by sweet pear and melon flavors. Finishes short. **84** —*J.C. (7/1/2003)*

TORMARESCA

Tormaresca 2002 Bocca di Lupo Aglianico (Castel del Monte) $27. Here's a wine that epitomizes the winemaking potential of Puglia, in southern Italy. This Aglianico, with a small percentage of Cabernet Sauvignon, is a vibrant ruby color and is bursting with ripe cherry, cigar box, black slate, resin, and toast. It is a complex wine with a particularly succulent quality in the mouth that finishes with dusty tannins. **91 Editors' Choice** —*M.L. (10/1/2006)*

Tormaresca 2000 Bocca di Lupo Aglianico (Castel del Monte) $28. How smooth is this luscious bruiser—a combination of 90% Aglianico and 10% Cab Sauvignon? Pull out the knife and fork and find out. The color is splendidly opaque, and the palate is packed with cherry, cassis, mint, and menthol. The finish is chewy, with mouth-coating tannins. Very pretty and wall-to-wall in terms of structure. From Antinori's Puglian operation. **93 Editors' Choice** —*M.S. (12/15/2003)*

Tormaresca 2004 Chardonnay (Puglia) $8. Bargain wine hunters can count on Tormaresca (Antinori's Tuscany estate) to deliver the goods when it comes to good value. This barrel-fermented Chardonnay is the product of fertile soils, strong sunshine, and cutting-edge technology. Aromas of apricot, yellow rose, honey, and cantaloupe melon are both intense and inviting. In the mouth, the wine is creamy and filling with penetrating stone fruit flavors and persistency. Try it with shrimp cocktail or spicy chicken. **87 Best Buy** —*M.L. (10/1/2006)*

Tormaresca 2002 Chardonnay (Puglia) $10. Distant on the nose, offering only light banana and butterscotch. Simple flavors of lemon and apple are carried on a flat palate. **82** —*M.S. (10/1/2004)*

Tormaresca 2002 Masseria Maìme Negroamaro (Salento) $28. Roasted and spicy up front, not unlike a good sauce or BBQ rub. The palate is big and chewy, with sweet plum, blackberry, and hard spice flavors. Plenty of clove and pepper carry the tannic, pumped-up finish. It's

100% Negroamaro made in a modern, well-oaked style. **90** —*M.S. (10/1/2006)*

Tormaresca 2000 Masseria Maìme Negroamaro (Salento) $28. This new Negroamaro-based wine from Piero Antinori's Southern Italian venture is quite the powerhouse. If you like digging into a meaty, tight, minerally red with loads of ripeness and complexity, then here's your ticket. It's ultra everything: black fruit, cassis, vital acidity, you name it. The finish is spectacular as it unfolds in waves. Really a super wine, drinkable now and into the near future. **92** —*M.S. (12/15/2003)*

Tormaresca 2003 Torcicoda Primitivo (Salento) $20. Antinori's Puglia estate launches a powerful rocket that rips through the mouth leaving a smoldering trail of cassis, bitter chocolate, and black cherry preserves. The mouthfeel is equally intense with rounded tannins and a lingering taste of smoked ham. **88** —*M.L. (9/1/2005)*

Tormaresca 2001 Torcicoda Primitivo (Salento) $20. Antinori has made a rich, leathery, modern rendition of this Zinfandel kin. The bouquet is forward and round, with deep black fruit, clove, and earth. Roast meat, jerky, and spice flavors dance with black plum and cherry on the palate. Dark and long on the finish; chewy and full-bodied. **89** —*M.S. (11/15/2004)*

Tormaresca 2000 Red Blend (Puglia) $11. A powerful, rich wine at a great price. This blend of Cabernet Sauvignon (55%) and Aglianico (45%) offers flavors of chocolate-covered blueberries with a light dusting of oak. The tannins here are full, but integrate well with the fruit. **86 Best Buy** —*C.S. (5/1/2002)*

TORNESI

Tornesi 2001 Brunello (Brunello di Montalcino) $44. An inky-dark wine with an assortment of pleasing aromas: tobacco, leather, plum, resin, and bacon fat. This wine evolves over time in the glass with increasing intensity of flavors. **90** *(4/1/2006)*

TORRE DI LUNA

Torre di Luna 1997 Pinot Grigio (Trentino) $8. 83 *(8/1/1999)*

Torre di Luna 2004 Pinot Grigio (Delle Venezie) $12. Truckloads of fresh banana emerge from the nose, and are backed by vanilla bean, chalky minerality, and some vitamin-like aromas. Somewhat dilute on the palate, but those banana notes put in another strong appearance. **85** —*M.L. (6/1/2006)*

Torre di Luna 2003 Pinot Grigio (Delle Venezie) $13. This wine has plenty of mouth-filling pear and melon fruit, carried along by a broad, expansive mouthfeel and low acidity. Lacks a refreshing bite on the finish, probably because of the warm vintage. **84** —*J.C. (12/31/2004)*

Torre di Luna 2001 Pinot Grigio (Delle Venezie) $12. Light. Light in color, light in body, light on flavor. What's there is pretty—featuring hints of peaches, mint, and lime—so this is best as an apéritif. It runs the risk of being overpowered by food. **84** —*J.C. (7/1/2003)*

TORRE DI MONTE

Torre di Monte 2001 Pinot Grigio (Umbria) $10. Light, with vanilla, banana and caramel aromas. Not a zesty, snappy Pinot Grigio at all, and likely at the end of its life span. What's here is tasty, albeit dilute. **82** —*M.S. (10/1/2004)*

TORRE MASCOLI

Torre Mascoli 2001 Niró Red Blend (Murgia) $10. Nail polish and other sweet, somewhat artificial aromas lead to raspberry flavors. It's a tight, lean wine with more acidity than flesh. A little bit sour but drinkable. Blends Sangiovese, Uva de Troia, Cabernet, and Merlot with modest results. **83** —*M.S. (10/1/2006)*

TORRE ROSAZZA

Torre Rosazza 1997 Pinot Grigio (Colli Orientali del Friuli) $12. 86 *(8/1/1999)*

TORRE SVEVA

Torre Sveva 1998 Castel del Monte Red Blend (Apulia) $8. 85 Best Buy —*L.W. (3/1/2000)*

ITALY

ITALY

TORRE VIGNE

Torre Vigne 1997 Aglianico (Taurasi) $20. Seems a bit late to just be making the market, but Taurasi has staying power and this wine is far from over the hill. Spice, cinnamon, and root beer mix with black fruit on the loud nose, while the palate spins mostly cherry and raspberry. Lively but raw, with outsized tannins that pound away without mercy. **86** —M.S. (2/1/2005)

TORRESELLA

Torresella 2000 Cabernet Sauvignon (Veneto) $10. An herbal wine, one that won't appeal to those put off by leafy, vegetal flavors. One of our reviewers liked the minty, herbal quality, while two others detected hints of asparagus and bell pepper. Still, the mouthfeel is good and the acidity is correct. **82** (5/1/2003)

Torresella 2002 Chardonnay (Veneto) $14. A light-bodied wine, with a faint scent of clove and modest flavors of pineapple and lemon. Finishes with a hint of anise. **83** —J.C. (12/31/2004)

Torresella 2000 Merlot (Veneto) $10. Leathery, sharp aromas get things on the march. Then lean cherry and raspberry flavors carry the tangy palate, while lively acidity keeps the finish fresh and hopping. **83** (5/1/2003)

Torresella 2003 Pinot Grigio (Veneto) $10. This light-bodied, one-dimensional wine features scents and flavors of white gumdrops, while a burst of citrus on the finish imbues it with some refreshing qualities. **82** —J.C. (12/31/2004)

Torresella 2001 Pinot Grigio (Veneto) $10. The color is very light, and so are the flavors. Although it lacks intensity, this faintly lemony wine is crisp, clean, and moderately refreshing. **83** —J.C. (7/1/2003)

Torresella 2002 Sauvignon Blanc (Veneto) $14. Shows some slightly vegetal notes of green bean and asparagus, but not so much that the crisp grapefruity flavors don't shine through. Not a blockbuster, but certainly varietally correct. **84** —J.C. (12/31/2004)

TOSCA

Tosca 2004 Pinot Grigio (Friuli Grave) $9. There's a very enticing toasted quality to this wine that translates as banana bread, walnut husk, and roasted chestnuts. Those same qualities add breadth and dimension to its texture. **86 Best Buy** —M.L. (6/1/2006)

TOSCOLO

Toscolo 2004 Sangiovese (Chianti) $11. Always a solid value contender, Toscolo really nailed it in 2004. This wine is clean and ripe, with familiar raspberry and strawberry aromas. It's not heavy at all; in fact, it's light, bright, and clear, with pure cherry and raspberry flavors that are sure to please. A pizza wine to the max. **88 Best Buy** —M.S. (10/1/2006)

Toscolo 2003 Sangiovese (Chianti) $11. Dark in color, with cherry, leather, and lemon to the nose. The palate also tastes of lemon, and there's some plum in there to soften things up. Snappy, simple, and lean; a wine that perpetuates everyday Chianti's pedestrian reputation. **84** (4/1/2005)

Toscolo 2003 Sangiovese (Chianti Classico) $20. Almost stewy but not totally over the top. The nose offers more earth and oak than brightness, while the palate is herb-infused, with berry and tomato. Fairly classic in style, but not as fresh as desirable. **84** —M.S. (10/1/2006)

Toscolo 2001 Sangiovese (Chianti Classico) $20. The bouquet blends darker notes of mocha and chocolate with red fruit aromas. The palate is fine and crisp, with no added weight whatsoever. Acidity is its calling card, so labeling it lean and precise would be accurate. For some, however, its freshness could be construed as gritty and closed. **87** (4/1/2005)

Toscolo 2001 Sangiovese (Chianti) $9. Pungent, with earthy blackberry aromas. Flavors of black cherry and cola lead into a smooth finish with ample tannins and an appropriate dry quality. This is a solid wine with a firm feel and modest oak. Good stuff for everyday trattoria fare. **86** — M.S. (11/15/2003)

Toscolo 2000 Sangiovese (Chianti) $8. This simple, light quaff combines bright cherries and milk chocolate in a squeaky clean wine that should have broad appeal. Citrusy acidity gives zip and length to the finish. **84** (10/1/2001)

Toscolo 2000 Sangiovese (Chianti Classico) $19. Saucy and spicy to the nose, with hints of chocolate, mocha, and damp earth. Plum flavors and a smooth, moderately long finish keep this wine's head above water. Nonetheless, it's not real strong in the middle. **85** —M.S. (10/1/2004)

Toscolo 1999 Sangiovese (Chianti Classico) $14. If this is an indicator of what consumers have to look forward to from the 1999 vintage, things are looking pretty sunny. Black cherries and cedar aromas and flavors carry touches of prunes and tobacco. There's some chocolate as well, and the finish blends in enough dusty tannins to give the suggestion of cocoa. **86** (10/1/2001)

Toscolo 2001 Riserva Sangiovese (Chianti Classico) $24. Smoky and savory on the nose, with saucy fruit sitting below a veil of firm oak. Runs a bit tart and racy in the mouth, where cherry and plum flavors are boosted by blazing natural acidity. Not a sour wine, but definitely crisp and racy. **87** —M.S. (10/1/2006)

Toscolo 1999 Riserva Sangiovese (Chianti Classico) $24. A bit lean and chemical, with earth, chocolate, and blackberry aromas. Plum, berry, and distant green notes define the palate. Tight and a touch bitter at the end, with coffee and cocoa. Heavily tannic. **84** —M.S. (10/1/2004)

Toscolo 1997 Riserva Sangiovese (Chianti Classico) $17. The first riserva under the Toscolo label, it boasts dark, earthy aromas capped off by a hint of citrus peel and followed by textbook Chianti flavors of sour cherries, earth, and tobacco. Smoke and cocoa notes grace the finish. Contains 10% Cabernet Sauvignon and 5% Merlot. **87** (10/1/2001)

TRABUCCHI

Trabucchi 2000 Corvina, Rondinella, Molinara (Amarone della Valpolicella) $50. A bit rooty and spicy, with aromatic notes of root beer, cinnamon, tea, and cedar. Features somewhat of a tannic, racy feel, with flavors running toward cherry. One taster found it a touch minty and leafy, but two-thirds of our panel approved of the wine's zesty, snappy characteristics. **89** (11/1/2005)

TRAMIN

Tramin 2003 Sauvignon (Alto Adige) $20. Slightly gold in color, with pungent, pure aromas of grapefruit and pine touched up by a whiff of flinty smoke. Round yet minerally in the mouth, with pink grapefruit and bright lime flavors. Long and tangy on the finish, with a crystalline aftertaste. **91 Editors' Choice** (7/1/2005)

TRANCHERO OSVALDO

Tranchero Osvaldo 2004 Casot Moscato (Moscato d'Asti) $15. This vineyard-designated Moscato d'Asti didn't quite deliver the pizzazz and spunk we expected. The bubbles are large and not very frothy, but the nose had an interesting mix of charcoal, chalk, lavender, peach, soap, and graham cracker. **84** —M.L. (12/15/2005)

TRAVAGLINI

Travaglini 1997 Nebbiolo (Gattinara) $30. Made from the Nebbiolo grape, a ruby-colored agreeable wine with opening aromas of black cherries, chocolate, and tar. In the mouth it's bone dry and delicate, with soft tannins, although the acidity is high enough to burn on the finish. **87** —S.H. (11/15/2002)

Travaglini 1995 Nebbiolo (Gattinara) $29. **92** (11/15/1999)

Travaglini 1996 Riserva Nebbiolo (Gattinara) $35. Held in oak for a year longer than the regular release, this wine is woodier and drier, and seems more acidic, too. Hints of black cherries tease the palate but it's an austere drink, with light tannins. Cries out for olive oil, butter, and marbled beef. **89** —S.H. (11/15/2002)

Travaglini 1997 Tre Vigne Nebbiolo (Gattinara) $40. A three-vineyard Nebbiolo blend (hence the name), which the winery calls "New World" because of the extra fruit and oak. But it's certainly not fruity or oaky from a New World perspective. It's earth, tomato, mushroom, and tannin, and the acids are bitter. It needs time, lots of it. **88** —S.H. (11/15/2002)

TREFIANO

Trefiano 1997 Sangiovese (Carmignano) $37. Clean and correct, with leather and sour cherry aromas and flavors that just seem to lack added dimension. Finishes hard and slightly bitter, with peppery spice and drying tannins. **84** —*J.C. (9/1/2001)*

Trefiano 1995 Sangiovese (Carmignano) $37. 88 —*M.S. (11/15/1999)*

TREVISIOL

Trevisiol NV Vino Spumante Brut Champagne Blend (Prosecco di Valdobbiadene) $14. This gets points for its unusual and quite grapey (but not sweet) quality. There's interest in the mature liqueur-like note on the nose, and a full, toasty, yet still grape-flavored palate. It's a soft sparkler, but with a fine bead and long finish that continues to showcase its individual character. **86** —*M.M. (12/31/2001)*

TRIACCA

Triacca 1998 La Palaia Red Blend (Chianti Classico) $NA. You can almost tell from the look that this is dense and heavy. It has a huge bouquet of wet earth, spice, and oak, but not much fruit. In the mouth, it is drying and on the flat side, although still-kicking tannins reach up and grab the palate. The finish is soft and losing life. Some oxidation and over-ripeness hold it back. **84** —*M.S. (8/1/2002)*

TURNING LEAF

Turning Leaf 1997 Pinot Grigio (Delle Venezie) $12. 82 *(8/1/1999)*

UCCELLIERA

Uccelliera 2001 Brunello (Brunello di Montalcino) $65. Brawny and bold with impeccable depth and balance. Dark fudge, forest berry, and coffee take center stage with menthol coolness, caramel, and marzipan from the chorus line. A deeply satisfying and plush wine with solid tannins and chewy concentration that is both mysterious and inviting. A Marc de Grazia selection, various U.S. importers. **93 Cellar Selection** *(4/1/2006)*

Uccelliera 2000 Brunello (Brunello di Montalcino) $62. One of the more unique, complex 2000s from Montalcino. Citrus peel, lavender, and basil are just some of the aromas that waft from the nose. In the mouth, there's good coverage and solid tannins. To that end, black cherry, plum, and other usual suspects make for a fine flavor profile, while the acidity is right for aging. A Marc de Grazia Selection, various importers. A Marc de Grazia Selection, various importers. **92 Editors' Choice** —*M.S. (7/1/2005)*

Uccelliera 1999 Brunello (Brunello di Montalcino) $NA. A touch rusty to the eye, but pretty to the nose. Aromas of mint, clove, and dried fruits elicit excitement, as does the lovely round palate that's loaded with flavors of smoked meat and herbal but ripe berry fruit. Quite full-bodied and sly, although its aging potential could be limited. Likely best over the next three to five years. **92** —*M.S. (6/1/2004)*

Uccelliera 1999 Riserva Brunello (Brunello di Montalcino) $90. Wonderfully toasted up front, with baked, but not cooked, fruit aromas. There's also plenty of coffee, earth, and leather to the bouquet. Initial live-wire flavors settle to reveal marzipan and dried stone fruits, while the sly finish is so complex that the wine ultimately registers as a different breed. Drinking this is like navigating a maze. A Marc de Grazia Selection, various importers. **94 Editors' Choice** —*M.S. (7/1/2005)*

UGO LEQUIO

Ugo Lequio 2000 Gallina Nebbiolo (Barbaresco) $50. Young and tight on the nose, this blossoms in the mouth, yielding a creamy, rich mix of dried cherries, leather, and chocolate. Exceptionally smooth and supple on the finish, suggesting early drinkability. **90** *(4/2/2004)*

Ugo Lequio 1999 Gallina Nebbiolo (Barbaresco) $49. This is a soft, silky, feminine Barbaresco that's already approachable. Pretty aromas of cherry preserves and spring flowers fold in vanilla notes on the palate. Drink now–2010. **88** *(4/2/2004)*

UMANI RONCHI

Umani Ronchi 2002 Jorio Montepulciano (Montepulciano d'Abruzzo) $13. There's a distinctive aromatic element to this single-vineyard wine that resembles dried sweet herb or basil followed by generous tones of sweet berry fruit, toasted nuts, and vanilla. Made from the hearty Montepulciano grape, the wine sees 11 months of wood aging (in both larger casks and smaller barrique) that help render flavors of exotic spice and cigar box. It's chewy and rich in the mouth and would pair well with grilled meats. **86 Best Buy** —*M.L. (11/15/2006)*

Umani Ronchi 2002 Casal di Serra Verdicchio (Verdicchio dei Castelli di Jesi Classico Superiore) $14. Well-positioned almond, honey, and pear aromas lead into a textured palate enlivened by melon, pear, and apple. It's a bit like Chardonnay in terms of size and mouthfeel, but with pulsing acidity it's not as blowsy. Finishes rich and round, a winner with a full, meaty character. **87** —*M.S. (8/1/2004)*

Umani Ronchi 2003 Casal di Serra Vecchie Vigne Verdicchio (Verdicchio dei Castelli di Jesi Classico Superiore) $22. Aromas of honey, spring flowers, grapefruit, and almond skin are intact and beautifully presented thanks to stainless steel fermentation. This is a late harvest wine from 30-year-old vines that earns points for its natural ability to pair with food. **87** —*M.L. (10/1/2006)*

Umani Ronchi 2002 Plenio Riserva Verdicchio (Verdicchio dei Castelli di Jesi Classico) $22. Here is a golden-tinged wine that demonstrates the aging potential of Verdicchio. A third of the blend undergoes fermentation in oak and this extra step adds pretty vanilla and toasted notes that work well with the wine's natural minerality. **87** —*M.L. (10/1/2006)*

Umani Ronchi 2004 Villa Bianchi Verdicchio (Verdicchio dei Castelli di Jesi Classico Superiore) $10. Matured only in stainless steel, this is a fresh and citrusy wine with aromas of lavender honey, cut grass, and almond paste. There's a sour note on the finish that offsets an otherwise pretty picture. **85 Best Buy** —*M.L. (10/1/2006)*

Umani Ronchi 2002 Villa Bianchi Verdicchio (Verdicchio dei Castelli di Jesi Classico Superiore) $12. Opens with full pear, tangerine, and flower aromas, which are backed by basic apple and melon flavors. It's a fairly plump, heavy wine in terms of mouthfeel, yet it finishes a touch hollow. Still, it's flavorful and true throughout. **86** —*M.S. (8/1/2004)*

Umani Ronchi 2003 Le Busche White Blend (Marche) $25. This is an oak-fermented Verdicchio and Chard blend with a wonderfully rich and creamy mouthfeel, and a layered nose offering yellow fruit, butter, vanilla bean, and spice aromas. **90** —*M.L. (10/1/2006)*

UMBERTO CESARI

Umberto Cesari 2003 Colle Del Re Albana (Albana di Romagna) $8. Nice nose, with clear aromas of bread dough, almond paste, and pear. A bit brighter on the palate, where citrus and peach flavors are nice if not exactly imposing. Finishes with a hint of cream and banana. **85 Best Buy** —*M.S. (7/1/2005)*

VAGNONI

Vagnoni 2000 Riserva Sangiovese (Chianti Colli Senesi) $24. Candied cherry and raspberry aromas give off a jammy sensation, while the plum and berry fruit that carries the palate also brings with it some severely spiked acidity. Mainstream Chianti, with a slight scouring edge. **85** *(4/1/2005)*

Vagnoni 1997 Riserva Sangiovese (Chianti Colli Senesi) $14. A slightly muted nose of dark cherry and toast offers hints of rose and tar. Similar flavors play on the palate with a touch of chocolate and a smooth mouthfeel. Long and dry, the espresso-tinged finish is elegant. The depth of fruit can be sensed and this should open up with short-term cellaring, displaying more depth and richness in a year's time. **87** *(4/1/2001)*

Vagnoni 2002 Vernaccia (Vernaccia di San Gimignano) $15. Muddled and sulfuric at first, with matchstick aromas preceding a palate of citrus and apple. That heavy, burnt note burns off with time, leaving a tangy apple and citrus palate. Nothing spectacular, but better than initial impressions indicate. **84** —*M.S. (8/1/2004)*

VAL D'OCA

Val d'Oca 2004 Pigià Pinot Grigio (Marca Trevigiana) $9. Reminiscent of a Prosecco wine with peach, apricot, citrus notes, and an overall tutti-frutti character. It's a still wine but you'll notice the slightest touch of effervescence in the glass that helps accentuate those aromas. **85 Best Buy** —*M.L. (10/1/2006)*

Val d'Oca NV Brut Prosecco (Prosecco di Valdobbiadene) $14. A bit flat, with lime and cracker aromas. Mostly dry citrus on the palate, which puckers up your lips and cheeks. Finishes tart, with celery and green-apple notes. **85** —*M.S. (12/15/2004)*

Val d'Oca 2004 Brut Prosecco (Prosecco di Valdobbiadene) $16. Light, yeasty, and dusty, with subtle fruit aromas. Equally light but fresh on the tongue, with crisp lime flavors. Precise but simple; likable and very easy to quaff. Classic mainstream Prosecco. **86** —*M.S. (12/31/2005)*

Val d'Oca 2004 Extra Dry Prosecco (Prosecco di Valdobbiadene) $16. Clean, fresh, and full of apple on both the nose and palate. Citrus and other tangy fruits work nicely on what is a rather full-bodied and chunky palate. Round on the finish, with a bit of citrus peel that offers offsetting dryness. **87** —*M.S. (12/31/2005)*

Val d'Oca 2003 Millesimato Extra Dry Prosecco (Prosecco di Valdobbiadene) $14. Dry and leafy, with aromatic notes of fresh spinach and green tobacco. As it opens it loses some of that green character and adopts a more typical stone fruit and apple personality. Finishes on the spot, with a good mouthfeel. **85** —*M.S. (12/15/2004)*

Val d'Oca NV VSAQ Extra Dry Prosecco (Italy) $11. Despite the blue bottle, this is right on the money as extra dry (i.e. sweet) Prosecco goes. The nose features gardenia, citrus, and mineral, while the melon and apple flavors are A1. A hint of green herb and scallion on the finish adds depth and complexity. **89 Best Buy** —*M.S. (12/15/2004)*

VAL DELLE ROSE

Val delle Rose 2003 Sangiovese (Morellino di Scansano) $15. Sweet, ripe, and welcoming, with aromas of cherry, cotton candy, and rubber. More cherry and raspberry come forward as you taste, while the finish is short and a bit tart. Pretty good, with snap, crackle, and pop. **84** —*M.S. (11/15/2004)*

Val delle Rose 2002 Sangiovese (Morellino di Scansano) $15. Jumpy and scattered on the nose. Shows green flavors intermixed with raspberry and cherry. Never finds its stride; previous vintages were better. **82** —*M.S. (10/1/2004)*

Val delle Rose 1999 Sangiovese (Morellino di Scansano) $14. There's plenty of pop to this bright, tight versatile red. Pretty full-fruited aromas rise up along with earth, leather, and spice. The lively palate races with blackberry, and the finish is satisfyingly long and clean as a whistle. Youth should be served here; drinking this Sangiovese now is the way to go. **88** —*M.S. (8/1/2002)*

Val delle Rose 2000 Riserva Sangiovese (Morellino di Scansano) $19. Jammy and high strung, with nice red fruit aromas and even more zesty raspberry on the palate. Finishes chunky and fleshy, but without a ton of acidity. Flavors of cola, coffee, and mocha are the end touches. **87** —*M.S. (11/15/2004)*

Val delle Rose 1998 Riserva Sangiovese (Morellino di Scansano) $19. Some cool earth, leather, and smoked meat aromas get this ripe, full-bodied Sangiovese going. The palate is fairly soft, a reminder of blackberry pie. And there's plenty of unmistakable milk chocolate, too. Look at it as a tamed, rich, enjoyable red; a wine well-suited to an autumn dinner. **88** —*M.S. (8/1/2002)*

VAL DI SUGA

Val di Suga 1999 Brunello (Brunello di Montalcino) $54. Surprisingly mature in color, with hues of rust and brown. It smells gorgeous as it offers intoxicating floral aromas mixed with rooty notes and earth. With spice and dried fruit enveloping the palate, it's all you could want. And the texture is easy enough to allow for drinking within two years. **91** —*M.S. (6/1/2004)*

Val di Suga 1993 Vigna del Lago Brunello (Brunello di Montalcino) $92. **93** —*M.S. (3/1/2000)*

Val di Suga 1998 Vigna del Lago Riserva Brunello (Brunello di Montalcino) $120. Classy and cool, and showing the true essence of complexity. Aromas of earth, coffee and vanilla lead into a healthy, acid-driven palate full of cherry and raspberry. Lots of depth, with nuances of mint and other spices. Not particularly rich, however. In fact, it's quite traditional. **91** —*M.S. (6/1/2004)*

Val di Suga 1999 Vigna Spuntali Brunello (Brunello di Montalcino) $50. A single-vineyard Brunello that's unconventional from the get-go. Not

unkind aromas of mineral, peanut, and curry suggest unusual new-barrel oaking, while the palate beats fast with racy acids and broad, heavy tannins. The finish, meanwhile, is airy and long. Hold until 2008. **91** —*M.S. (6/1/2004)*

VALCHIARÒ

Valchiarò 2000 Sauvignon Blanc (Colli Orientali del Friuli) $15. There isn't much in the way of attractive fruit on the musky, sweaty nose. Lemony, spicy flavors are also broken up by the unwelcome taste of chicken soup. As a whole it's fairly dull and chunky, and not very evolved or fancy. **83** *(8/1/2002)*

VALDICAVA

Valdicava 2001 Brunello (Brunello di Montalcino) $110. Inkjet black and super concentrated, the wine actually delivers fresh fruit and squeezed berry youthfulness. By the looks of it, you'd expect a massive, oaked, tannic beast, but instead are treated to a wine full of creamy coffee and velvety tobacco leaf flavors. **91** *(4/1/2006)*

Valdicava 2000 Brunello (Brunello di Montalcino) $89. Pitch black, like midnight on a country road. Talk about saturated: the nose yields tar, char, and more, and in the mouth it has that mid-level intensity that many of the 2000s don't have. Earthy at one moment, polished the next. It finishes with a sweet blast of molasses, black cherry, and coffee. A head-turner, one that gets better with every sip. **93** —*M.S. (7/1/2005)*

Valdicava 1999 Brunello (Brunello di Montalcino) $NA. Full-force and also full of new oak. The nose deals charcoal, cola, and root beer, while the palate offers blackberry and sweet cherry flavors. This one is extracted and rich, and while it lacks some edginess and foundation, overall it's a very nice wine. **89** —*M.S. (6/1/2004)*

Valdicava 1997 Brunello (Brunello di Montalcino) $90. This wine is surprisingly accessible for a 1997 Brunello, which is both its attraction and its failing. It lacks the power of many wines of this vintage, but has generous ripe fruit and dry tannins that balance well. A medium-term wine. Drink after seven or eight years. **88** —*R.V. (8/1/2002)*

Valdicava 1999 Madonna del Piano Riserva Brunello (Brunello di Montalcino) $130. Fresh asphalt, burning timber, bitter chocolate, and anything else that connotes "darkness" is what this heavyweight is about. And as rough as that may sound aromatically, on the palate it's polished like a gemstone, with just enough grit and guts to push it forward. The fruit, meanwhile, is sensational, a panoply of black plums and cherries infused with cocoa and vanilla. This offers a clear look into 21st-century Brunello, and the picture is breathtaking. **97 Editors' Choice** —*M.S. (7/1/2005)*

VALDIPIATTA

Valdipiatta 1998 Sangiovese (Rosso di Montepulciano) $15. **88** —*M.M. (9/1/2000)*

VALDO

Valdo NV Cartizze Cuvée Viviana Prosecco (Prosecco Superiore di Cartizze) $25. Stone fruit and crisp mineral notes, with melon, peach, pear, and distinct green notes, like cut grass or kiwi fruit. Has loads of lime flavors, medium-weight, and a burst of refreshing crispness. **87** —*M.L. (6/1/2006)*

Valdo NV Cuvée di Boj Prosecco (Prosecco di Valdobbiadene) $19. A unique nose: it has cola-like fizz, followed by sea breeze, polished stone, and rubber-like aromas. Those dry, mineral-driven flavors make this the kind of Prosecco you could easily drink with a meal. **87** —*M.L. (6/1/2006)*

Valdo NV Marca Oro Prosecco (Prosecco di Valdobbiadene) $15. A less intense extra dry Prosecco compared to others, but very floral with pleasant streaks of banana, melon, white stone, and peach. Nicely balanced, this wine imparts a fresh, perky feeling in the mouth. **87** —*M.L. (6/1/2006)*

Valdo NV Marca Oro Extra Dry Prosecco (Prosecco di Valdobbiadene) $12. Smells like lilacs in the spring, tinged with apple blossoms as well. Fresh, light, and frothy, with simple, soft flavors of apples, pears, and citrus. **87** —*J.C. (12/31/2003)*

Valdo NV Selezzione Oro Brut Prosecco (Prosecco di Valdobbiadene) $14. Begins with floral aromas, then adds in some earthier scents of damp leaves. Chalky, mineral notes underscore modest pear flavors. Finishes almost dry, but a bit short. **86** —*J.C. (12/31/2003)*

VALFIERI

Valfieri 2001 Arneis (Roero Arneis) $17. Simple and open, with a touch of vanilla to the pear-driven nose. Sweet apple defines the hefty palate, while it finishes long and lasting. If there's a fault, it's that it comes across fat, with too much papaya and banana. But mostly it's satisfying. **84** —*M.S. (12/15/2003)*

Valfieri 2001 Cortese (Gavi di Gavi) $17. A little mute on the nose, with hints of chewing gum. A mouth of peach and melon with off-setting spice is nice, but the texture runs soft. Dried citrus notes come on late, and overall it's full-flavored yet slightly rubbery. **85** —*M.S. (12/15/2003)*

Valfieri 1997 Nebbiolo (Barbaresco) $42. This vintage was hailed throughout Italy as being one of the best of the 20th century, so what went wrong here? The caramel, toffee, and raisin nose is much like Sherry. The raisiny palate indicates over-ripeness, and despite some tannins, there isn't much structure or pulse. **82** —*M.S. (11/15/2002)*

VALIANO

Valiano 2001 Sangiovese (Chianti Classico) $15. This sleek, easy-to-drink wine starts off with aromas of plum and lack cherry allied to subtle scents of sandalwood. The wood continues on the palate, but just as an accent—the emphasis is on the fruit. **87** *(7/1/2003)*

Valiano 1997 Sangiovese (Chianti Classico) $15. The modest cherry, dark berry, and black tea notes of this light wine show tell-tale orange-peel notes of decline. This feels just too thin and tired at an early age. **81** *(4/1/2001)*

Valiano 2000 Poggio Teo Sangiovese (Chianti Classico) $20. A raw, tight, ready wine with a spot of green on the nose along with leather and damp earth. Airing freshens it up, revealing berry fruit flavors with accents of soy. Crisp on the finish, with acids at work. **88** *(4/1/2005)*

Valiano 1999 Poggio Teo Sangiovese (Chianti Classico) $20. A single-vineyard Sangiovese from Piccini's top estate, Poggio Teo, offers up aromas of black tea and anise balanced by flavors of black fruit. It's smooth in the mouth, but not particularly lush, finishing with plenty of juicy acidity. **87** —*J.C. (7/1/2003)*

Valiano 2000 Riserva Sangiovese (Chianti Classico) $25. Smooth and minty, with aromas of cedar, cherry, and milk chocolate. Definitely a fresh and racy offering, as citrus and cherry mix with leather and chocolate to create a classic Chianti flavor profile. Neither modern nor old fashioned; this is what most folks are seeking. **88** *(4/1/2005)*

Valiano 1999 Riserva Sangiovese (Chianti Classico) $25. 86 *(7/1/2003)*

Valiano 1995 Riserva Sangiovese (Chianti Classico) $22. Looking brown around the edges, this wine is showing decline at an age when a good riserva should be hitting full stride. The fruit is stylishly sweet, but attenuated, and past its best in this pretty, older wine. Fading elegance, but why at just past five years of age? **83** *(4/1/2001)*

Valiano 1999 Vino in Musica Sangiovese (Toscana) $40. Piccini's top wine is this super Tuscan that puts 60% Sangiovese with Cabernet Sauvignon, Cabernet Franc, and Merlot in a successful blend of tobacco, earth, and dark fruit flavors. The '99 is firmer in structure than the '97, a reflection of the vintage. **90** *(7/1/2003)*

Valiano 1997 Vino in Musica Sangiovese (Toscana) $40. A soft, ripe wine that manages to showcase tobacco, earth, and black cherry flavors in a relatively light-weight format, finishing long and tart. **88** *(7/1/2003)*

VALLE DELL'ACATE

Valle dell'Acate 2004 Frappato (Sicilia) $20. Frappato is a lighter, fruitier red grape that could almost be described as Sicily's Pinot Noir. The aromas are of berry fruit and are delicate and feminine. Simple, lean, and spicy-crisp on the finish, this is an un-oaked alternative to Sicily's powerhouse reds. **86** —*M.L. (7/1/2006)*

Valle dell'Acate 2002 Il Frappato Frappato (Sicilia) $19. Fresh and fruity, with strawberries and vanilla, cream and dried spices. **86** —*J.C. (10/1/2003)*

Valle dell'Acate 2004 Il Moro Nero d'Avola (Sicilia) $24. A fruit-driven wine that leaves ample space for blackberry-velvet to come through. Overall, it's clean and compact in the mouth but there's also a distant hint of rubber on the nose; spicy and flavorful on the palate. **88 Editors' Choice** —*M.L. (7/1/2006)*

Valle dell'Acate 2000 Il Moro Nero d'Avola (Sicilia) $23. Shows a bit of browning at the rim and some balsamic notes on the nose, but it's still very tasty stuff, with strawberries and herbs on the nose and sweet, attenuated fruit backed by hints of soy sauce. **88** —*J.C. (10/1/2003)*

Valle dell'Acate 2004 Poggio Bidini Nero d'Avola (Sicilia) $12. Less intense than others but redolent of coffee, chocolate, and cherry, this wine is subdued in a good, approachable way. Herbal notes appear in the mouth. **87 Best Buy** —*M.L. (7/1/2006)*

Valle dell'Acate 2002 Poggio Bidini Nero d'Avola (Sicilia) $12. Seems as if it's designed to be Sicily's answer to Beaujolais, with exuberant young, grapy aromas and bright, fresh fruit flavors. **86** —*J.C. (10/1/2003)*

Valle dell'Acate 2001 Poggio Bidini Nero d'Avola (Sicilia) $9. 88 Best Buy —*C.S. (11/15/2002)*

Valle dell'Acate 2000 Poggio Bidini Nero d'Avola (Sicilia) $11. On the nose, roasted red berry, stable, and spice aromas predominate. On the palate, juicy blackberries and dusted cinnamon flavors are cleaned by bright acidity. This Nero d'Avola is an excellent by-the-glass selection. **89 Best Buy** —*C.S. (5/1/2002)*

Valle dell'Acate 2004 Red Blend (Cerasuolo di Vittoria) $24. This historic Nero d'Avola and Frappato-based wine delivers fresh cherry and menthol notes in the foreground and distant barnyard or animal notes in the background. This is a compact and solid wine with dry, dusty tannins. **86** —*M.L. (7/1/2006)*

Valle dell'Acate 1999 Cerasuolo Di Vittoria Red Blend (Sicilia) $24. 88 —*C.S. (5/1/2002)*

Valle dell'Acate 2000 Cerauolo della Vittoria Red Blend (Sicilia) $20. This blend of Nero d'Avola and Frappato combines vibrant cherry and mixed berry fruit with a briary, herbal streak in a complex, harmonious whole. It's plump and round, spicy yet smooth on the finish. **90** —*J.C. (10/1/2003)*

Valle dell'Acate 2000 Frappato Red Blend (Sicilia) $22. Frappato, a little-known grape in the States, brings a fresh, juicy character to this wine, which is like a well-structured cherry Kool-Aid with a touch of herbs. A pleasant quaffer, perfect for a picnic. **84** —*C.S. (5/1/2002)*

Valle dell'Acate 2003 Tané Red Blend (Sicilia) $60. Ripe and powerful, this is a big, bold, unfiltered Sicilian red that delivers dried figs, tobacco, and berry preserves. It's almost too much of a good thing and will appeal to those looking to make a statement. **90** —*M.L. (7/1/2006)*

Valle dell'Acate 2002 Tané Red Blend (Sicilia) $60. An impressive performance from a winery in southeastern Sicily, this 85% Nero d'Avola and 15% Syrah blend boasts smoked ham, prunes, and dried figs; tight tannins in the mouth, and a sweet blueberry note on the close. Limited availability. **91** —*M.L. (7/1/2006)*

Valle dell'Acate 2004 Bidis White Blend (Sicilia) $25. This is a very successful Insolia-Chardonnay blend that is creamy in the mouth—like a banana smoothie—and nicely layered with peach pie, exotic spice, pineapple, and tomato leaf aromas. **88** —*M.L. (7/1/2006)*

VALLE REALE

Valle Reale 2003 Montepulciano (Montepulciano d'Abruzzo) $15. Owned by the Abruzzo's Pizzolo family, Valle Reale's Montepulciano d'Abruzzo sees two years of oak aging and four months in bottle. The result is an inviting wine with smoke and black cherry. Thanks to the high tannins it becomes very tight in the mouth. **87** —*M.L. (9/1/2005)*

VALLEBELBO

Vallebelbo 2004 Moscato (Moscato d'Asti) $11. A frothy, fun, and festive wine from one of the area's biggest producers. This wine shows grassy notes, mineral tones, generous peach, and honey. **86 Best Buy** —*M.L. (12/15/2005)*

ITALY

ITALY

VALLEROSA

Vallerosa 2001 Carpaneto Vineyard Verdicchio (Verdicchio dei Castelli di Jesi Classico) $12. At first you might find this wine on the border of oxidized and mealy, but the palate is crisp and lean, and very dry. Lean, linear flavors of dried apples and apricot lead into an expansive finish. A much better wine on the back end than on the bouquet. **86** *—M.S. (8/1/2004)*

VARALDO

Varaldo 1999 Bricco Libero Nebbiolo (Barbaresco) $62. Slightly herbal, but balanced by gobs of blackberry fruit and creamy vanilla oak. Coconutty notes on the palate are backed by rich berry flavors and lush, soft tannins. Drink now–2015. **90** *(4/2/2004)*

Varaldo 1999 Sorì Loreto Nebbiolo (Barbaresco) $62. This wine is big, bouncy, and almost Zinfandel-like, with candied cherry-berry aromas and flavors that turn mouth-watering on the finish while picking up nuances of dark chocolate. Drink now–2010. **89** *(4/2/2004)*

Varaldo 1995 Vigua di Aldo-Barolo Nebbiolo (Barolo) $45. Hard cheese, leather, char, and baked apple aromas mix well with flavors of raspberry, earth, and leather. Tannins are smooth but bracing. The medium-length finish is clean and herbal. **87** *(11/15/2002)*

VARRAMISTA

Varramista 1997 Syrah (Toscana) $51. Cherries, leather, and tobacco aromas segue into plum, cedar, and earth flavors. Mouthfeel is taut—this wine certainly needs 3–5 years to unwind—and the light but long finish shows tart berry, black tea, and more tobacco. **89** *(11/1/2001)*

VASARI

Vasari 1998 Sangiovese (Chianti Colli Aretini) $11. Opens with an appealing bouquet of dark cherry and chocolate, cedar and leather accents. In the mouth simple berry flavors sporting wood and leather accents take over. Finishes with tart cherry notes and moderate length. **84** *(4/1/2001)*

VASCO SASSETTI

Vasco Sassetti 2001 Brunello (Brunello di Montalcino) $30. Earthy, tannery, spicy and berry notes form a harmonious whole but don't leave much room for complexity. Nonetheless, this is a potent and piercing wine with dried spice, firm, dusty tannins and a mouth-drying finish. **88** *(4/1/2006)*

Vasco Sassetti 2000 Brunello (Brunello di Montalcino) $NA. Tight and chemical at first, with leather and smoke aromas later. Hard on the palate and lacking the flesh typical of Brunello. Simply put, it has the right flavors but it pounds down like an anvil. Maybe time will soften it up. **86** *—M.S. (7/1/2005)*

VECCHIE TERRE DI MONTEFILI

Vecchie Terre di Montefili 1998 Sangiovese (Chianti Classico) $21. A mildly gamy, slightly sauvage note adds interest to this well-oaked wine. Cherry, cinnamon-toast, and menthol aromas open to a palate of deep cherry fruit with earthy accents. The feel is supple, and black-cherry and licorice notes show on the long, smoothly tannic finish. The toasty oak and fruit work in harmony here. **87** *(4/1/2001)*

VENEGAZZU

Venegazzu NV Venegazzu Brut Champagne Blend (Prosecco del Montello e Colli Asolani) $11. Aside from having one of the longest appellation names we've ever seen, this has mature aromas of hay, vanilla, and herbs. Tart and dry unripe pear and herb notes mark the palate, and the sweet and sour finish is long. Dry, elegant, and full with a unique, rather serious personality. **86** *—M.M. (12/31/2001)*

VENICA

Venica 2000 Bottaz Collio Refosco (Venezia Giulia) $30. This family-operated winery in Friuli is known for excellent Sauvignon. But their dedication to Italian natives is evident with this up-and-coming variety. Refosco has pizzazz that comes through as cinnamon spiciness and bitter cherry liqueur. Tannins are still a bit thorny. **86** *—M.L. (9/1/2005)*

VENICA & VENICA

Venica & Venica 2004 Jesera Pinot Grigio (Collio) $17. This Pinot Grigio sees only stainless steel but nevertheless boasts creamy, buttery qualities such as crème caramel, banana milkshake, and peach cobbler. A thick mouthfeel is amplified by well-integrated acidity and a persistent finish. **90 Editors' Choice** *—M.L. (2/1/2006)*

VENTURINI MASSIMINO

Venturini Massimino 2001 Red Blend (Valpolicella Classico) $12. Creamy vanilla aromas add character and identity to the otherwise modest nose. In the mouth, the cherry and plum fruit seems a bit sweet and thick; in fact, the mouthfeel is creamy, much like the bouquet. Some tart, lemony notes detract from the finish. **85** *(5/1/2003)*

Venturini Massimino 1998 Red Blend (Amarone della Valpolicella Classico) $42. There's a pretty nose, one that offers violets, vanilla, raisins, and cigar tobacco. The palate runs over with cherry, blackberry, plum, and chocolate, while it finishes deep and smooth, and in multiple layers. All in all, it's plush yet firm, just as it should be. **91** *(5/1/2003)*

VERBENA

Verbena 2001 Brunello (Brunello di Montalcino) $NA. Burnt coffee, black tar, cherry cola, almond paste, stewed strawberries, and a note of rubber create a dramatic, slightly over-the-top Brunello. There's a viscous fullness to the mouth that makes a good match for the wine's fruity, clean finish. **89** *(4/1/2006)*

VERETO

Vereto 1995 Red Blend (Salice Salentino) $8. 85 Best Buy *—L.W. (3/1/2000)*

VEZZANI

Vezzani 2000 Rosso Red Blend (Salice Salentino) $6. The star-bright ruby color will entice you, but there the excitement ends. Overall, it's thin and disappointing, and the finish is short. **82** *—C.S. (5/1/2002)*

Vezzani 2002 Sangiovese (Rubicone) $7. This simple red comes from the hills near Bologna, not exactly prime Italian wine country. It's lean, with a hint of spice and chocolate. It's also tart and tight on the palate. Starts better than it finishes. **83** *—M.S. (10/1/2004)*

Vezzani 2002 Bianco White Blend (Sicilia) $7. Mostly burnt aromas carry the nose. Lemon-lime and apple control the palate, with more of the same on the finish. Bland but basic in the mouth. **81** *—M.S. (10/1/2004)*

VIA FIRENZE

Via Firenze 2004 Pinot Grigio (Venezie) $9. Apples and citrus make for a common nose, while the palate is pure Granny Smith with a spot of lemon-lime. Crisp as a razor on the finish, with green herb and citrus as the lasting notes. **84** *(2/1/2006)*

VIBERTI

Viberti 1999 Bricco Airoli Barbera (Barbera d'Alba) $27. Murky in color, and unfocused on the nose. Aromas of coffee and burnt rubber lead toward a palate of sugar beets and cranberry. Just too sharp, with glaring gaps. **81** *—M.S. (12/15/2003)*

Viberti 2001 Toni 'D Giuspin Dolcetto (Dolcetto d'Alba) $21. Muscular and meaty up front, with enough barnyard, earth, and leather to qualify as rustic. Things turn more peppy and perky in the mouth, where tight red fruit takes over. A firm and tight finish is wholly expected and it arrives, confirming the wine's concrete structure. **87** *—M.S. (12/15/2003)*

Viberti 1999 Buon Padre Nebbiolo (Barolo) $42. This tannic Barolo needs another 10 years to show its stuff. Right now it's hiding its plum and cherry fruit behind a wall of mouth-drying tannins, and the nose exhibits a bit of funk that also needs time to resolve. Try in 2015. **90 Cellar Selection** *—J.C. (11/15/2004)*

Viberti 1998 Buon Padre Nebbiolo (Barolo) $42. Starts off shaky, with burnt matchstick and slightly herbal aromas. Yet it recovers nicely with air, losing the offending scents and developing lovely black cherry and hickory notes. Medium- to full-bodied, it boasts a creamy texture and dry, tea-like tannins on the finish. Drink 2010–2015. **88** *(4/2/2004)*

VICARA

Vicara 1996 Barbera (Barbera del Monferrato) $15. 87 *(4/1/2000)*

Vicara 1999 Cantico della Crosia Barbera (Monferrato) $23. Despite a leafy, damp nose that takes forever to open, this wine has plenty to offer once you start drinking it. The palate is packed with raspberry, chocolate, and buttery oak. Even more oak comes on late in the finish. Full and vital acidity keeps it vibrant, making it a fine wine for dinner. **88** *—M.S. (11/15/2002)*

Vicara 1997 Cantico della Crosia Barbera (Barbera del Monferrato) $21. 85 *(4/1/2000)*

VICCHIOMAGGIO

Vicchiomaggio 2002 La Lellera Sangiovese (Chianti Classico) $15. Stewed and reduced, with herbal/vegetal aromas of bell pepper and oregano. What saves this wine from a worse fate is the decent body and acceptable mouthfeel. Still, it's too scattered and baked to rate higher. **84** *(4/1/2005)*

Vicchiomaggio 2003 La Lellera di Vicchiomaggio Sangiovese (Chianti Classico) $15. Smooth and nice on the nose, with cola, crushed slate, and ample black fruit. In the mouth, plum, blackberry, cola, and chocolate all make an appearance, while the feel is generally balanced and friendly. A very nice wine that should please almost everyone; with another jolt of intensity it would make the next level. **88** *—M.S. (10/1/2006)*

Vicchiomaggio 2000 La Prima Riserva Sangiovese (Chianti Classico) $35. Our unanimous favorite of the tasting, La Prima comes from the oldest vines on the property, and is a blend of 90% Sangiovese, 5% Canaiolo, and 5% Colorino aged in barriques. Dark color, with black plums and hints of violets on the nose, the oak is understated, allowing the blackberry, plum, and floral notes to shine through. Finishes rich, chewy, and long. **90** *(11/15/2004)*

Vicchiomaggio 2000 Petri Riserva Sangiovese (Chianti Classico) $27. Petri spends part of its maturation in barriques and part in larger oak to help preserve its fruit. The aromas are not particularly fruity, boasting tobacco and earth alongside dried herbs and mocha, but the palate shows dark fruit flavors and a bright beam of acidity before finishing with echoes of earth and tea. **89** *(11/15/2004)*

Vicchiomaggio 2000 Ripa delle Mandorle Sangiovese (Toscana) $20. Named for the little hill's almond trees, this modestly priced super Tuscan is a blend of 80% Sangiovese and 20% barrique-aged Cabernet Sauvignon. The Sangiovese provides black cherry and tobacco flavors, while the Cab contributes toasty, buttery oak, and herbal notes. Drink now and over the next several years. **86** *(11/15/2004)*

Vicchiomaggio 2000 Ripa delle More Sangiovese (Toscana) $NA. From the "little hill of blackberries," this is Vicchiomaggio's top modern wine, a blend of 90% Sangiovese and 10% Cabernet Sauvignon that stays in barrique for 18-24 months before bottling. It's toasty as a result, but also laden with blackberries and plums, then strikes a brighter, cranberryish note on the finish. Try in 2006, when the oak should be more integrated and the tannins more supple. **89** *(11/15/2004)*

Vicchiomaggio 2001 San Jacopo da Vicchiomaggio Sangiovese (Toscana) $18. Traditional Chianti, with no small oak aging and no Cabernet or Merlot. Leathery, with dried cherry aromas and a hint of tobacco on the nose, then shows bright, focused fruit flavors on the palate. Finishes with bass notes of dark chocolate and earth. **87** *(11/15/2004)*

VIE DE ROMANS

Vie de Romans 2001 Ciampaign Vieris Chardonnay (Friuli Isonzo) $24. A delicious, ripe Chardonnay, fermented in stainless steel, and keeping all the freshness of the fruit. White currant flavors, flowers, and subtle aromas give this wine elegance and great drinking pleasure. **90** *—R.V. (7/1/2003)*

Vie de Romans 2004 Dessimis Pinot Grigio (Friuli Isonzo) $24. A beautifully executed wine, from its copper-tinged color to its opulent nose. Aromas drift off layer after layer, revealing banana bread, peach cobbler, almond paste, and sliced pear. A solid and compact wine in the mouth that could match heavier foods such as crepes and soufflés. **90 Editors' Choice** *—M.L. (6/1/2006)*

Vie de Romans 2003 Dessimis Pinot Grigio (Friuli Isonzo) $24. A carefully crafted wine that shares little in common with the Pinot Grigios we nor-

mally drink. The aromas and the mouthfeel are opulent and silky and the wine's solid structure is built for elaborate dishes. A Marc de Grazia Selection, various U.S. importers. **89** *—M.L. (6/1/2006)*

Vie de Romans 2001 Dessimis Pinot Grigio (Friuli Isonzo) $28. The name of the wine is an old word used to measure fields, and reflects the Gallo (no connection with the California winery) family's use of traditional ideas and techniques at Vie de Romans. This wine has full, ripe fruit, soft and with layers of attractive wood and vanilla flavors. **87** *—R.V. (7/1/2003)*

Vie de Romans 2001 Piere Sauvignon Blanc (Friuli Isonzo) $29. Fresh, crisp, lightly grassy flavors make this wine instantly refreshing. There are touches of apricots and green plums, and a center which is ripe and full. **86** *—R.V. (7/1/2003)*

Vie de Romans 2001 Flors di Uis White Blend (Friuli Isonzo) $27. A blend of Malvasia, Riesling, and Tocai Friulano, the name of the wine means flowers of the grapes. It is a deliciously aromatic wine, spicy, perfumed, with flavors of honey and citrus. Light acidity at the end stops it being too over the top. **88** *—R.V. (7/1/2003)*

VIETTI

Vietti 1996 La Crena Barbera (Barbera d'Asti) $30. 90 *(4/1/2000)*

Vietti 2003 Scarrone Vigna Vecchia Barbera (Barbera d'Alba) $78. A super-concentrated, ruby red, New World-style Barbera d'Alba tightly packed with red fruit, toast, Indian spice, coffee bean, chocolate, and roasted nuts. Those super-charged flavors follow through to the mouth, where solid tannins open onto a long, toasted finish. **89** *—M.L. (11/15/2006)*

Vietti 1998 Tre Vigne Barbera (Barbera d'Alba) $18. 90 *(4/1/2000)*

Vietti 1998 Lazzarito Dolcetto (Dolcetto d'Alba) $19. 90 *(4/1/2000)*

Vietti 2003 Sant'Anna Dolcetto (Dolcetto d'Alba) $20. The potential of Piedmont's lesser-known Dolcetto grape is unmasked in this wine's complex aromatic profile that encompasses toast, cherry fruit, and menthol-like notes. Concentrated with snap and spice in the mouth. It shows plenty of personality. **90** *—M.L. (11/15/2006)*

Vietti 1998 Sant'anna Dolcetto (Dolcetto d'Alba) $19. 89 *(4/1/2000)*

Vietti 1998 Tre Vigne Dolcetto (Dolcetto d'Alba) $18. 86 *(4/1/2000)*

Vietti 2002 Cascinetta Moscato (Moscato d'Asti) $12. Vietti, which makes some of Piedmont's most user-friendly wines across the full spectrum of price ranges, scores major points with this light-bodied, sweet frizzante. It smells of gardenias and fresh summer herbs, and it pulses with kiwi, nectarine, and pineapple flavor. There's nothing not to like about this low-alcohol (5.5%) liquid dessert—surely the perfect match for ice cream or fruit salad. **89** *—M.S. (11/15/2003)*

Vietti 1998 Brunate Nebbiolo (Piedmont) $84. This is a light-weight, with soft, strawberry fruit flavors and just a layer of soft, dry tannins that hint at a sense of missed power. **85** *—R.V. (11/15/2002)*

Vietti 2000 Lazzarito Nebbiolo (Barolo) $100. Sumptuous and beautiful Barolo with subtle toasted notes, forest floor, cigar box, and dried berries all vying for your attention. Powerful but elegant, with soft tannins, balanced acidity, and remarkable persistence. A truly amazing wine that yields generously each time you come back to it. **93 Editors' Choice** *—M.L. (11/15/2006)*

Vietti 1998 Lazzarito Nebbiolo (Piedmont) $84. This elegant Lazarito Barolo has attractive aromas of ripe, tarry fruit, and truffles. The palate has dry tannins, which overlay dark plums and figs. The fine, pure acidity gives it a sense of balance. **88** *—R.V. (11/15/2002)*

Vietti 2001 Masseria Nebbiolo (Barbaresco) $92. Another excellent component of the Vietti portfolio, this elegant Barbaresco is scented by wild sage, dried mint, cigar box, and rose petal. A wine capable of a long and complex evolution in the glass with clearly etched tannins over a lean body. **91** *—M.L. (11/15/2006)*

Vietti 2000 Rocche Nebbiolo (Barolo) $100. This is not an in-your-face-wine. Instead it is reserved and refined yet coquettish enough to dabble out enticing traces of candied cherry, pine resin, cigar box, forest truffles, and dried mint leaves. The tannins are round and full, with a touch of perky spice. **91** *—M.L. (11/15/2006)*

ITALY

ITALY

Vietti 1998 Rocche Nebbiolo (Piedmont) $84. The pale color and aromas of ripe strawberries and ripe fruit blend comfortably with the new wood flavors. This is a light, almost fresh style of wine. **84** —R.V. (11/15/2002)

Vietti 1996 Villero Riserva Nebbiolo (Piedmont) $145. With its sweet dried fruits on the nose, and solid, almost dusty tannins and wood flavors, it has repaid the extra wood aging. The wine is only released six years after harvest and produced in small quantities. **93** —R.V. (11/15/2002)

VIGNA PICCOLA

Vigna Piccola 1996 Sangiovese (Chianti Classico) $18. Shows modest dark cherry fruit with cedar and leather accents. A lean, even mouthfeel and moderate acidity mark the palate. The tart, dried fruit flavors turn somewhat sour on the back end. **83** (4/1/2001)

Vigna Piccola 1997 Riserva Sangiovese (Chianti Classico) $26. A complex bouquet of berries, cedar, cinnamon, and earth leads into a chewy, full palate of cherries supported by brisk acidity. Young and frisky, it closes with zingy tannins that are a little astringent now, but give it a year or two; there's good fruit here. **89** (4/1/2001)

VIGNE REGALI

Vigne Regali 2003 L'Ardi Dolcetto (Dolcetto d'Acqui) $9. A great bargain, this soft, supple Dolcetto is loaded with plum and berry fruit, backed by hints of apple blossom on the nose and tobacco on the palate. A bit drying on the finish, so drink it with rare beef or burgers to help bring that element into line. **88 Best Buy** —J.C. (3/1/2006)

VIGNETI DI UMBERTO FRANCASSI RATTI MENTONE

Vigneti di Umberto Francassi Ratti Mentone 1998 Nebbiolo (Barolo) $47. This interesting wine is going brown at the rim already, yet still packs a tannic wallop. Aromas of fig and walnut give way to surprisingly delicate flavors of cherries and orange zest. Try in 2010. **90** (4/2/2004)

VIGNOLE

Vignole 1998 Sangiovese (Chianti Classico) $13. Opens with clean and bright aromas of juicy black cherries, earth, and cedar, followed by a wine with a lean, even texture and lively tart cherry fruit accented by leather shadings. Finishes dry, with firm tannins, and has the structure to age a few years. **88** (4/1/2001)

VILLA ABA

Villa Aba 1998 Pinot Grigio (Grave del Friuli) $13. **84** (8/1/1999)

VILLA ARCENO

Villa Arceno 1999 Pozzo di San Donato Cabernet Sauvignon (Toscana) $35. From mountain vineyards, a dense, concentrated wine. Drinks very much like a big Napa Cab, with focused cassis and black currant flavors, and of course, French oak. Dry, with stylishly soft but complex tannins. But this is a wine with Italian acids. It is very tart, especially in the finish. **88** —S.H. (1/1/2002)

Villa Arceno 1999 Merlot (Toscana) $35. A wine of high aspirations. Quite extracted and ripe, stuffed with blackberry and herb flavors and richly oaked. Dry and supple and clean. It's also pretty tannic and acidic. You'll want lasagna or lamb for all that sharpness to cut through. The finish is tart and bitter. Try aging it. **86** —S.H. (1/1/2002)

Villa Arceno 1998 Merlot (Toscana) $20. **86** —S.H. (1/1/2002)

Villa Arceno 1999 Arguzzio Red Blend (Toscana) $60. High class Super-Tuscan blend of Sangiovese, Merlot, and Cabernet owned by Kendall-Jackson. Notable for intense, ripe, concentrated flavors, notably cassis and blackberry, and mouth-coating tannins that are thick and fine. Quite acidic, lending it a youthful bite that will soften with midterm aging. **91** —S.H. (1/1/2002)

Villa Arceno 1999 Riserva Red Blend (Chianti Classico) $25. Very dry, rather bitter, sharp in acids and tannins, and with austere flavors of tobacco and herbs with just a trace of black cherry. Mainly Sangiovese, and 15 percent of Merlot barely begins to soften it. Very clean and scouring on the palate, this is a food wine if ever there was one. Try with the richest meats and cheeses you can find. **87** —S.H. (1/1/2002)

Villa Arceno 1998 Arguzzio Sangiovese (Toscana) $50. Berry fruit and oak-based spice set this one in motion, but surprisingly, given the fat

nose, the palate is rather lean. It's mostly dry, with tart cherry, cranberry, and red currant. The finish is also leaner than many from this class, and although the wine is hardly devoid of fruit, it lacks style. A blend of Sangiovese, Cabernet, and Merlot. **86** —M.S. (12/31/2002)

Villa Arceno 1997 Riserva Sangiovese (Chianti Classico) $20. **91** —S.H. (1/1/2002)

Villa Arceno 1999 Syrah (Toscana) $20. This Kendall-Jackson-owned property is turning out a bevy of very good offerings. The best is their Syrah, which boasts plenty of toast and vanilla but also blackberry and dried-herb shadings. The finish is powerful and tannic, yet ripe and supple. **88** —S.H. (1/1/2002)

Villa Arceno 2000 Il Boschetto Syrah (Toscana) $35. Here's a big, thick wine, international in style with its ripe, extracted flavors of cherries, plums and other stone fruits. Tannins are pronounced and gritty, and there's plenty of powerful, spicy oak. Doesn't seem especially varietal. **87** —S.H. (1/1/2002)

VILLA BANFIO

Villa Banfio 2000 Il Torrione Sangiovese (Tuscany) $20. Aromas of fruit cake, molasses, and black plum lead off. In the second slot is ripe but simple red plum along with accents of chocolate and cinnamon. A tannic rush comes on late, but that's abated by a smooth, easy fade. Offers ripeness and clean, full flavors. **87** —M.S. (11/15/2003)

VILLA BETTA

Villa Betta 2002 Pinot Grigio (Sicilia) $9. Apparently this is what Pinot Grigio from the hot South is like. It's low-acid and flabby, with bananas and cornflakes for a flavor profile. Strange indeed. **80** —M.S. (10/1/2004)

VILLA BORGHETTI

Villa Borghetti 1998 Grigio Luna Pinot Grigio (Valdadige) $9. **81** (8/1/1999)

VILLA BRANCA

Villa Branca 2001 Alef Kosher Sangiovese (Chianti Classico) $29. Not a great Chianti, but it's certainly true to the DOCG, with lean, tart cherry fruit and nuances of cedar, leather, and dry, dusty earth. Doesn't have the depth to age further, so drink now. **85** —J.C. (4/1/2006)

VILLA CAFAGGIO

Villa Cafaggio 1997 Cortaccio Cabernet Sauvignon (Tuscany) $50. Plenty of leather, cassis, plum, and tobacco aromas show on the nose of this 100% Cabernet Sauvignon wine. The full palate has full, dark berry Cabernet flavors and pronounced tobacco-herb-earth shadings. Has depth and character, but also shows a slightly rustic feel with full tannins, espresso flavors, herb, and bell pepper notes on the finish. Best held until 2004. **90** (5/1/2001)

Villa Cafaggio 1998 Sangiovese (Chianti Classico) $17. Starts with a rich nose of dark cherry, milk chocolate, and anise. It shows the typical espresso and toast flavors of the new style, but with more nuance and better balance than many others. There's a lot of oak here, but it's a very good example of the style, and should improve through 2003. **88** (4/1/2001)

Villa Cafaggio 1997 Chianti Classico Riserva Sangiovese (Tuscany) $30. This 100% Sangiovese bottling serves up a textbook Chianti bouquet of black cherries, leather, and earth. The same range, with good fruit focus, shows on the flavorful palate, with its dense, chewy texture. Fine, well-structured tannins indicate that this should improve over the next three years and age well. **89** (5/1/2001)

Villa Cafaggio 1997 San Martino Sangiovese (Tuscany) $50. Older vines from the named vineyard provide the fruit for this 100% Sangiovese, barrique-aged Super Tuscan. The cherry, tart berry, and chocolate aromas pick up vibrant licorice accents as they blossom into full flavors on the palate. The already svelte mouthfeel should only improve, as the still substantial, firm tannins on the cocoa-tinged finish resolve. Hold for three years; drink 2004–2010. **91 Cellar Selection** (5/1/2001)

VILLA CALCINAIA

Villa Calcinaia 2000 Casarsa Rosso Merlot (Colli della Toscana Centrale) $38. This wine is starting to round into a mature stage. The bouquet pushes light leather, forest, earth, and secondary fruit aromas. Black cherry and plum work well together on the tight, mildly tannic palate, while the finish is concentrated and rewarding. Will be good with food. **88** —*M.S. (9/1/2006)*

Villa Calcinaia 2003 Sangiovese (Chianti Classico) $18. Round up front, with an earthy, leathery nose housing solid red fruit that's comfortable and familiar. Both plum and raspberry work the palate, and then comes toast, chocolate, and smooth tannins. Not overpowering but it's in equilibrium. **88** —*M.S. (10/1/2006)*

Villa Calcinaia 2001 Sangiovese (Chianti Classico) $15. Spicy and raw at first, with cinnamon, clove, and hard cheese aromas. Quickly things turn to red cherry, raspberry, and vanilla, while the lasting notes consist of mature red fruit and toast. Standard Chianti the way it should be. **88** *(4/1/2005)*

Villa Calcinaia 2001 Riserva Sangiovese (Chianti Classico) $24. Fairly oaky, with strong aromas of sawdust morphing into vanilla and butter. Fortunately there's plenty of fruit backing it up. In the mouth, it's firm, with bright cherry and plum; then even more vanilla shows up. Finishes with rubbery tannins and the flavor of black tea. **89** *(4/1/2005)*

Villa Calcinaia 2000 Riserva Sangiovese (Chianti Classico) $24. From Conti Capponi, this medium-intensity Chianti offers basic berry and plum aromas along with plump strawberry and plum flavors. Finishes clean, with a touch of vanilla and butter. A touch bulky. **85** —*M.S. (10/1/2004)*

VILLA CARRA

Villa Carra 2001 Selection Castellarin Merlot (Delle Venezie) $7. With aromas of pickles and bath soap, the nose is volatile and astringent. The mouth is sharp, with nebulous black fruit. This is a wine that is sitting precariously on the cusp of acceptability. Some size and mouthfeel is all that saves it. **80** *(5/1/2003)*

Villa Carra 2001 Pinot Grigio (Friuli Grave) $11. Not a typically fruity Grigio, this one relies more on spices and minerals to make a palate impression. Hints of almond and dried cinnamon start things off, followed by stony, mineral flavors backed by pears and allspice. **87** —*J.C. (7/1/2003)*

VILLA CERNA

Villa Cerna 2001 Riserva Sangiovese (Chianti Classico) $22. Big and brawny, with a strutting bouquet the spills earth, leather, coffee, and cedar-lined cigar box. The fruit is fine and dandy as well, with black cherry, plum, and raspberry dominating. Finishes solid, warm, and mildly tannic. Quite tasty and satisfying as a whole. **90 Editors' Choice** *(4/1/2005)*

Villa Cerna 2000 Riserva Sangiovese (Chianti Classico) $22. Mildly rusty in color, with early dust and leather aromas. It picks up the pace upon airing, showing herb and charcoal scents. In the mouth, there's snappy pie cherry and red plum, while the finish is clean and substantive. Another wine from Cecchi. **87** —*M.S. (10/1/2004)*

Villa Cerna 1997 Riserva Sangiovese (Chianti Classico) $21. Lush oak lends coconut and toast notes to the cherry fruit in this international-style wine. Fairly full, it displays a supple texture and offers dark rich flavors on the palate. Closes with espresso notes and even tannins. Has class and flavor, but it's very much of the new school . . . not for traditionalists. Drink now through 2006. **89** *(4/1/2001)*

VILLA DANTE

Villa Dante 1997 Vocato Red Blend (Toscana) $10. **86** *(9/1/2000)*

Villa Dante 1995 Sangiovese (Vino Nobile di Montepulciano) $18. **84** *(7/1/2000)*

Villa Dante 2000 Oak Aged Sangiovese (Toscana) $12. An early whiff of barnyard gives way to more standard plum and berry aromas. After that, you'll taste chunky raspberry and plum backed by healthy acidity. Finishes fairly long and strident, with cherry tomato making an appearance. **85** —*M.S. (9/1/2006)*

VILLA DEI LECCI

Villa dei Lecci 1999 Sangiovese (Chianti Colli Senesi) $9. A young wine with classic tart cherry flavors and an added chalky note that provides

some complexity. Finishes with firm tannins and some dark chocolate and licorice notes. Should be even better in a year. **85 Best Buy** *(4/1/2001)*

VILLA DI BAGNOLO

Villa di Bagnolo 1997 Marchesi Pancrazi Pinot Noir (Toscana) $43. Wipe away all Pinot pre-conceptions based on Burgundy, Oregon, or elsewhere. This is the Tuscan version, and it has its own character, which is ripe, forward, hot and spicy, and overall much closer in style to the native Sangiovese than to typical Pinot. Racy acids pump loads of cranberry fruit, backed by a forest of spice-laden vanilla oak. **86** —*M.S. (8/1/2002)*

VILLA FIORE

Villa Fiore 2004 Pinot Grigio (Delle Venezie) $7. Sweet corn dominates the nose. Tastes of under-ripe apricots and vague yellow vegetables. Turns a bit more sharp on the finish, with grapefruit taking over. Not a lot of style or flavor. **82** *(2/1/2006)*

VILLA FRATTINA

Villa Frattina 1997 Pinot Grigio (Lison-Pramaggiore) $12. **81** *(8/1/1999)*

VILLA GIADA

Villa Giada 2004 Andrea Moscato (Moscato d'Asti) $15. Classic Muscat muskiness greets the nose and is followed by grass, citrus, dried flowers, and rubber. The dried flower notes are particularly attractive and beg for hazelnut tarts, as producer Andrea Faccio suggests. **86** —*M.L. (12/15/2005)*

VILLA GIRARDI

Villa Girardi 1997 San Giuseppe Pinot Grigio (Valdadige) $11. **81** *(8/1/1999)*

VILLA GIULIA

Villa Giulia 2001 Alaura Sangiovese (Chianti) $10. Light in color and aromas. The nose is mostly dried red fruit and spice. The palate is tart yet precise; it's not sour but it's very peppy, with bright acids and plenty of red fruit in the raspberry or pie cherry vein. A light, airy finish with a modicum of creaminess closes the package. **85** —*M.S. (11/15/2003)*

Villa Giulia 2000 Alaura Sangiovese (Chianti) $9. With cherry aromas, some cedar, and a perfectly clean, unmuddled palate, this is what an affordable Chianti should be like. Simple and easy to drink, it will go fine with basic fare. **85** —*M.S. (8/1/2002)*

Villa Giulia 1998 Alaura Sangiovese (Chianti) $10. **86 Best Buy** —*M.S. (3/1/2000)*

VILLA IL MEXXINO

Villa il Mexxino 1998 Nebbiolo (Barolo) $NA. A big, bulky wine, showing slightly dried black cherries on the nose and adding in leather, dried spices and earth on the palate. The finish is long, tart and features some intriguing coffee notes. **90** *(4/2/2004)*

VILLA ILARIA

Villa Ilaria 2000 Nebbiolo (Barbaresco) $18. Seems a bit green and under-ripe, with aromas that range from tobacco to herb to green bean, but slightly more generous on the palate, where tart cherries come into play. Picks up hints of anise and citrus on the finish. **85** —*J.C. (11/15/2004)*

Villa Ilaria 1999 Nebbiolo (Barolo) $24. Already showing signs of development, this is one 1999 Barolo that you won't need to wait 10 years to sample. Coffee and leather on the nose, followed by cherry flavors carried along by silky tannins. Finishes with more coffee and charred wood. **87** —*J.C. (11/15/2004)*

VILLA LA SELVA

Villa La Selva 1997 Selvamaggio Cabernet Sauvignon (Toscana) $27. Here's a super Tuscan that's made for food, not fireside sipping. It's full of red fruit, mostly currants and plum. There's a menthol/eucalyptus element in there as well. It's already into its aging process and it'll be at its best in another couple of years. However, for a well-regarded wine that's all Cabernet, it is a tad thin in the middle. **88** —*M.S. (8/1/2002)*

Villa La Selva 2001 Merlo Rosso Cabernet Sauvignon-Sangiovese (Toscana) $54. Just reaches the cut of excellence with its attractively stewed nose that packs in plenty of blueberry and other jammy dark fruit aromas. Well-oaked but not overdone, with cherry, cassis, tobacco, and chocolate all in equal, balanced portions. Villa La Selva is a good label with true-to-form Tuscan wines; its blend of Sangiovese and Cabernet is on the money.**90** —M.S. (9/1/2006)

Villa La Selva 2001 Felciaia Sangiovese (Toscana) $28. Encouraging from the beginning, where aromas of cherry, plum, wood grain, lemon peel, and olive draw you in. Deep and pure on the palate, with ultra-ripe, defined and delicious red fruit flavors. Smooth and lasting, with mouth-filling tannins and snap.**90** —M.S. (9/1/2006)

Villa La Selva 1998 Felciaia Sangiovese (Toscana) $20. Round and power-ful, she's a brick house. This wine features a tough exterior with a piercing streak of ripe cherry running through the middle. Boxed-in cherry and raspberry flavors grace the firm palate, and there's more than enough tannins to the starching finish. Now it's probably better with food; in a couple of years it should soften up.**88** —M.S. (12/31/2002)

Villa La Selva 1999 Felciaia Sangiovese (Toscana) $23. Chunky and meaty, with broad fruit spread across a full bouquet. The palate deals a wave of cherry cola and plum before a clean, fruity finish. An upright wine with snappy acids and tasty core flavors. A good food wine for sure. **88** —M.S. (10/1/2004)

Villa La Selva 1999 Selvamaggio Sangiovese (Toscana) $28. Some tobac-co, vanilla, and toasty oak mingle with rich black fruit on the bouquet. The palate offers plum and berry fruit along with some black pepper. A fruity 100% Cabernet with a chocolate- and coffee-tinged finish.**89** — M.S. (11/15/2003)

Villa La Selva 1998 Selvamaggio Sangiovese (Toscana) $27. This 100% Tuscan Cabernet has struggled for ripeness in the past couple of vintages, and the 1998 is fairly green at the core. Beyond that it has a nice feel and racy tannins. But the murky, somewhat under-ripe flavor profile is a hurdle that it just can't clear. This type of wine makes one wonder about Cabernet's performance in central Tuscany.**86** —M.S. (12/31/2002)

VILLA LANATA

Villa Lanata 1998 Sucule Barbera (Barbera d'Alba) $18. This wine is smooth and aromatic in the nose, with a hint of tree bark. The palate is racy and full of cherry, but that cherry fruit carries a streak of sweetness that seems a bit out of place, given the usual darkness of the grape. Finish is full and round, with big tannins.**87** —M.S. (11/15/2002)

Villa Lanata 2004 Cardinale Lanata Moscato (Moscato d'Asti) $13. From one of Asti's biggest and most established producers. Good mousse and green notes on the nose, such as lemon rind, bay leaf, fresh grass, and dried mint, round off a perky dessert wine ripe with honey and peach. **87** —M.L. (12/15/2005)

VILLA MAISANO

Villa Maisano 1997 Sangiovese (Chianti Classico) $15. The berry fruit here bears an herb-floral note on the nose, and opens to a light, supple palate of cherries accented by herb and chocolate accents. The finish shows good fruit and decent length, if slightly edgy tannins.**85** (4/1/2001)

Villa Maisano 1997 Questo Sangiovese (Chianti Classico) $30. Again a good melding of fruit and oak. The nose of this single-vineyard wine dis-plays ripe cherry fruit, cinnamon, and clove spice accents and a unique mint note. Balanced and lithe on the tongue, its dried plum and spice flavors play out attractively on the finish.**90** (4/1/2001)

Villa Maisano 1997 Riserva Sangiovese (Chianti Classico) $27. A very pleasing marriage of high-quality fruit and oak. Cloves, cocoa, and licorice accent the dark plum aromas. Chocolate and hints of black tea complement the fruit, the palate is medium-full and supple, even creamy. Soft tannins and cherry fruit with coffee-chocolate accents mark the long finish. Best after 2003.**90** (4/1/2001)

VILLA MALIZIA

Villa Malizia 2004 Pinot Grigio (Venezie) $6. Rhubarb, daisy flowers, orange peel, and candy smells emerge from this slightly copper-tinged wine. Although the nose is sure to spark lively conversation, the mouth is less interesting with sharp sourness on the finish.**83** —M.L. (2/1/2006)

VILLA MASSETO

Villa Masseto 2004 La Quarta Luna Chardonnay (Toscana) $NA. An intensely floral Tuscan Chardonnay (from producer Scopetani) with some exotic fruit, mineral tones, and chopped parsley. Delicate flavors of lemongrass, soy sauce, and citrus liven a medium-structured and food-friendly wine.**86** —M.L. (10/1/2006)

VILLA MATILDE

Villa Matilde 1999 Aglianico (Falerno del Massico) $15. A modern-style effort, the entry-level bottling from Villa Matilde blends a hefty dose of toffee, toast, and coffee flavors from oak with blackberry fruit tinged with green, herbal notes. Ultimately, it's a decent, simple quaff.**84** —C.S. (5/1/2002)

Villa Matilde 1998 Camarato Aglianico (Falerno del Massico) $45. This 100% Aglianico from Campania offers layers of lavender, dark fruits, eucalyptus, mint, and clove in its intoxicating bouquet. Sweet vanilla cream adds to the richness of this skillfully balanced wine that you can drink now or hold for another 10 ten years.**92 Cellar Selection** —C.S. (5/1/2002)

Villa Matilde 2004 Falanghina (Falerno del Massico) $15. A luminous, linear, and crisp white wine that offers Campania's trademark mineral tones, white flowers, and stone fruit. Its intensity and body could be edged up a notch although the mouth-cleansing acidity is there.**86** — M.L. (9/1/2005)

Villa Matilde 2000 Falanghina (Falerno del Massico) $14. Composed of 100% Falanghina, this wine disappoints. The fruit is primarily pear with a resinous component. The palate weight is sufficient, but the acid is too high.**82** —M.N. (9/1/2001)

Villa Matilde 2003 Tenuta Rocca dei Leoni Falanghina (Falanghina del Beneventano) $14. Moderate vanilla and flower aromas are unconvinc-ing, while the palate is lemony and overdosed with pineapple. Barely in balance, with a beam of acidity in the midpalate but nothing to the edges.**82** —M.S. (7/1/2005)

Villa Matilde 2002 Red Blend (Falerno del Massico) $20. Roasty, toasty, rubbery, and smoky goes the nose, which is backed up by quality plum and boysenberry flavors. Quite condensed and firm, with a chalky, air-tight finish. Not complex, but likable. A true Campanian food wine for every day.**87** —M.S. (2/1/2005)

Villa Matilde 1999 Cecubo Red Blend (Campania) $28. Dusty black cher-ries, with cayenne and licorice aromas, give way to a mouth full of sopressata and tart cherries. The finish is dry and a bit brief, but the wine is versatile in that it can be enjoyed by itself, or with roasted meat.**87** — C.S. (5/1/2002)

Villa Matilde 1998 Rosso Red Blend (Falerno del Massico) $16. Thanks to the investigative work of Francesco Paolo Avallone of Villa Matilda, the Falerno of classic history lives again. Now, as then, the grapes are Aglianico and Piedirosso. In this offering, the bouquet is deep cherry and chocolate with barrique oak off in the distance. The medium body and fine balance lead to a smooth mouthfeel and long finish featuring cherry, oak, and earth.**88** —M.N. (9/1/2001)

VILLA PATRIZIA

Villa Patrizia 2000 Orto di Boccio Sangiovese (Montecucco) $36. Bulky but not clumsy; the nose evolves with airing to offer black licorice and clove along with chunky black plum. Firm tannins on the palate support plum and cherry flavors, while the finish is tannic but not overbearing. It's 80% Sangiovese, with Merlot and Cabernet filling it out.**88** —M.S. (11/15/2003)

VILLA PETRIOLO

Villa Petriolo 2002 Sangiovese (Chianti) $13. Earthy enough, with hints of mushroom, vanilla, and prune. The weight is there, although the power is only middle of the road. Finishes mildly tangy, with acidity pushing it. Overall it's an easy drinker.**86** (4/1/2005)

VILLA PILLO

Villa Pillo 1998 Vivaldaia Cabernet Franc (Toscana) $16. Among all the Sangiovese from Tuscany, this blend of Cabernet Franc, Cab Sauvignon, and Merlot seems a bit out of place. It has all the requisite leafy, earthy, spicy characteristics that come courtesy of Cab Franc, but it is also extremely light and airy in the body. To this reviewer it didn't sing, but fans of dry, spicy reds, like Chinon from France, might find more in it. **84** —*M.S. (12/31/2002)*

Villa Pillo 2003 Borgoforte Cabernet Sauvignon-Sangiovese (Toscana) $12. Quite full and ripe, a sure reflection of a warm year. Dark berry and prune aromas start it off, followed by ripe, oozing, black fruit flavors. Extracted but not overdone, with a touch of complexity and depth. A lot of wine for the money. **89 Best Buy** —*M.S. (9/1/2006)*

Villa Pillo 1998 Estate Bottled Merlot (Tuscany) $16. Herbal and woody aromas make up the nose, which also carries a strong hint of black olives. Basic plum and cherry fruit carries the flavor profile, and when it comes to the finish things turn decidedly lean and acidic. Decent for quaffing but not much more than that. **84** —*M.S. (12/31/2002)*

Villa Pillo 2000 Sant' Adele Merlot (Toscana) $23. There's pepper, oregano, and root beer on the nose, but no fruit to speak of. The palate is burly, bordering on hefty, with flavors of candied cherries and black-berries. It's too much like a confection. It just doesn't seem balanced and whole. **83** —*M.S. (12/31/2002)*

Villa Pillo 2004 Sant'Adele Merlot (Toscana) $13. Here's a lovely Merlot from Tuscany that boasts big, chewy cherry, leather, chocolate fudge, and vanilla spice for under $15. The wine is aged in new French oak barrels for 15 months to achieve smooth tannins and toasted nut flavors that are well-integrated without being overwhelming. Everything about the wine's mouthfeel is soft, supple, and caressing, including the finish. Try it with duck or oven-roasted tomatoes stuffed with goat cheese. **86 Best Buy** —*M.L. (11/15/2006)*

Villa Pillo 2003 Sant'Adele Merlot (Toscana) $16. Firm from the start, with centered black cherry aromas that are easy and recognizable. Very ripe and fruity, with cherry and raspberry flavors that are ordinary but nice. Flush in the mouth and on the finish, where spice and drying tannins make their mark. **87** —*M.S. (9/1/2006)*

Villa Pillo 2001 Borgoforte Sangiovese (Tuscany) $12. Snappy and full of cherry, but also a tad green. There's cherry, raspberry, and plum across the palate, and ample sweetness to the finish. It's not heavy, but the tannins are full. **88 Best Buy** —*M.S. (11/15/2003)*

Villa Pillo 2000 Borgoforte Sangiovese (Tuscany) $12. Lighter framed, and a touch on the traditional side in terms of its lean color and subdued aromas of dried fruits and herbs. In the mouth, cherry, beet, and choco-late mix nicely, while it finishes fairly large and expansive. Still firm and needing a few years of cellar time. The blend is Sangiovese, Cabernet, and Merlot. **89** —*M.S. (11/15/2003)*

Villa Pillo 2003 Syrah (Toscana) $16. Chunky, open aromas start it off, and the bouquet is likable if nothing special. Dense and grapy fruit car-ries the palate, surrounded by spiky tannins. An extracted Syrah with zero gamy, spicy character. This is a black, ripe wine with size but limits. **85** —*M.S. (9/1/2006)*

Villa Pillo 2000 Syrah (Tuscany) $15. Rich, with bacon, mineral, and a certain horsey note that interferes with the rest of the bouquet. The palate is sweet as it deals beet, caramel, and carob, but there doesn't seem to be much spice to this warm-weather Syrah. Good tannins and acids keep it fresh. **86** —*M.S. (11/15/2003)*

Villa Pillo 1998 Syrah (Tuscany) $15. Starts off with aromas of licorice, earth, and roasted red berries. The flavors are predominately tart berry, but fold in some complex smoke and game notes. Decently structured, this is one value-priced Syrah that may repay short-term cellaring. **87 Editors' Choice** *(10/1/2001)*

VILLA POGGIO SALVI

Villa Poggio Salvi 2000 Brunello (Brunello di Montalcino) $65. Offers an attractive and smoky bouquet, which might indicate that it has the full-ness and depth to run long. However, it's fairly compact and juicy on the palate, with cherry, berry, and vanilla in control. On the money, if a bit tannic. Ageworthy, too. **90** —*M.S. (7/1/2005)*

Villa Poggio Salvi 1999 Brunello (Brunello di Montalcino) $NA. A bit lean throughout but with its good points. Mild aromas of tobacco and greens suggest some under-ripeness, but there's also good raspberry and straw-

berry flavors. The proper tannic structure makes it crisp and precise on the finish. From Biondi Santi. **87** —*M.S. (6/1/2004)*

VILLA PUCCINI

Villa Puccini 2005 Pinot Grigio (Friuli Grave) $10. Intense soda pop and citrus smells are backed by toasted almond and balanced minerality. Lean, with moderately intense fruit flavors in the mouth. **85** —*M.L. (6/1/2006)*

Villa Puccini 2004 Pinot Grigio (Friuli Grave) $10. The nose is wrapped in a pretty floral bouquet with a saccharine-coated, candy-like center. Like other large case-production Pinot Grigios, this is tasty, just lacks a bit of weight. **85 Best Buy** —*M.L. (2/1/2006)*

VILLA RUSSIZ

Villa Russiz 2001 Gräfin de la Tour Chardonnay (Collio) $31. Named after the last private owner of what is now a charitable foundation, this ripe, full Chardonnay has enormous flavors. Wood, sweet caramel, and vanilla aromas are balanced on the palate with tropical fruits, peaches, apples, and creamy acidity to give it a touch of freshness. **92** —*R.V. (7/1/2003)*

Villa Russiz 2002 Pinot Bianco (Collio) $22. Offers rich, concentrated fruit with lovely apple and cream flavors, a touch of vanilla, and super-ripe fruit. The aftertaste has a touch of acidity, but richness rather than acidity is what this wine is about. **88** —*R.V. (7/1/2003)*

Villa Russiz 1999 Pinot Bianco (Collio) $19. Distinctive notes of almond butter mingle with pears and a mélange of spices in a wine that turns lemony and zesty on the lingering finish. A green sauce of garlic and pars-ley will bring out the fruit and give even more pleasure. **87** *(9/1/2001)*

Villa Russiz 2004 Pinot Grigio (Collio) $28. Soft pear and light herb aro-mas make for a common bouquet. Apple, pear, almond, and a smidgen of butter on the tongue. Lightly mineral on the finish, with adequate crispness. **84** *(2/1/2006)*

Villa Russiz 2003 Pinot Grigio (Collio) $28. Peanut shell, ripe melon, rich mineral tones, and a blast of something lactic give this wine aromatic lat-itude. Softer than other Pinot Grigios with a medium, mineral-like finish. **85** —*M.L. (2/1/2006)*

Villa Russiz 2001 Pinot Grigio (Collio) $22. Upon pouring, there's a slight haze of CO2 visible in the glass—but that's a good thing in this case, because the unreleased fermentation gasses help enliven the otherwise fat mouthfeel. With aromas of pears and fresh parsley and flavors of pears and pineapple, it's pretty standard stuff, but executed well. **86** —*J.C. (7/1/2003)*

Villa Russiz 2003 Sauvignon (Collio) $28. Abundant mineral aromas on the nose, with melon, lime, and spice notes riding shotgun. A little bit hot and aggressive on the palate, but commendable for its ripeness. Probably a touch bulkier than normal given the hot vintage, but solid nonetheless. **87** *(7/1/2005)*

Villa Russiz 2002 Sauvignon (Collio) $28. Grassy and herbal on the nose. On the palate there's peachy fruit to counter the green, herbal elements, and a strong foundation built upon grapefruit. Herbal notes reprise on the finish. **86** —*J.C. (12/31/2004)*

Villa Russiz 1997 Sauvignon Blanc (Collio) $21. 88 *(11/1/1999)*

Villa Russiz 2002 Sauvignon Blanc (Collio) $22. An intense, herbaceous wine that also manages to be light. Acidity and green fruits keep the poise and the freshness, while the flavors of green plums and gooseber-ries are balanced with some structure. **87** —*R.V. (7/1/2003)*

Villa Russiz 2002 Sauvignon de la Tour Sauvignon Blanc (Collio) $47. The 2002 vintage may not be one of the all-time greats for this top-flight Collio Sauvignon, but it still towers over its peers. Flinty, grassy aromas lead into ripe pink grapefruit flavors and a powerful, lingering finish. A unique expression of Sauvignon. **89** —*J.C. (12/31/2004)*

Villa Russiz 2001 Sauvignon de la Tour Sauvignon Blanc (Collio) $38. If you enjoy a really pungent, intensely grassy Sauvignon, then you'll love this wine, but for many consumers it will be too much. The descriptor "cat pee" may sound unkind, but it's apropos in this case, balanced by passion fruit and a long, lemony finish. **87** —*J.C. (7/1/2003)*

Villa Russiz 1998 Tocai (Collio) $21. 87 *(11/1/1999)*

ITALY

Villa Russiz 2002 Tocai (Collio) $22. This is still a closed, young wine, but the potential of the spicy, ripe, but still light and elegant fruit is going to be great. Intense concentration seems to be the hallmark of the wines made by Gianni Menotti at this great estate. **90** —R.V. (7/1/2003)

Villa Russiz 2001 Tocai (Collio) $22. Slightly musky apple and pear aromas segue into purer flavors suggestive of apples, grapefruits, and minerals. Grapefruit pith makes a brief appearance on the long finish. **87** —J.C. (7/1/2003)

VILLA SANDI

Villa Sandi 2002 Marinali Cabernet Blend (Marca Trevigiana) $20. Here is a deep ruby wine that sees 12 months of barrique and delivers distinct and pleasant notes of tomato leaf, sweet greens, and floral tones. Its slightly more vegetal than other Cabernet-based wines from further south but its toasted and vanilla notes are also beautifully put into evidence. **89** —M.L. (11/15/2006)

Villa Sandi 1998 Marinali Rosso Cabernet Blend (Veneto) $20. A blend of Cabernets Sauvignon and Franc that offers charred meat, rubber, and cedar aromas on top of some lighter-weight red fruit. The palate is on the thin side, with cherry and plum flavors mixing with a hint of leather. The finish is of moderate length, with a nice, inoffensive texture. The tannins and acids, both of which are prominent, indicate that it should be drunk with food. **86** (5/1/2003)

Villa Sandi 1999 CS Glaxa Cabernet Sauvignon (Piave) $10. A nosing says it all: This wine is over the hill. Aromas of raisins and must conjure images of sherry that's past its prime. The flavors are dry and leafy, and all that's left is acids and tannin. Think old, mediocre Rioja and that's what you have here. **81** (5/1/2003)

Villa Sandi NV Champagne Blend (Prosecco di Valdobbiadene) $10. Smells like tangerines in a flower shop, then turns watery, with hints of apple and orange on the palate. Slightly sweet and a bit dull in the mouth, thanks to a paucity of bubbles. **82** —J.C. (12/31/2001)

Villa Sandi 2000 Estate Bottled Merlot (Piave) $10. The bouquet of cinnamon, dried fruits, and tobacco is attractive. The palate is earthy and dry, but ripe fruit isn't really on display, and that point is driven home on the dry, tannic finish. Nonetheless it should accompany food quite well. **85** (5/1/2003)

Villa Sandi 2005 Pinot Grigio (Piave) $14. There's a pretty sweet side to the aromatics generated by this Grigio that resembles lemonade or lime candy, yet the mouthfeel is dry with full fruit flavors and a crisp close. **87** —M.L. (6/1/2006)

Villa Sandi 2003 Pinot Grigio (Piave) $12. Medium-bodied, with decent depth and complexity. Bold pear and apple flavors accented by intriguing dried-spice notes elevate this to a level above basic Pinot Grigio. **86** —J.C. (12/31/2004)

Villa Sandi 2001 Estate Bottled Pinot Grigio (Veneto) $10. Rather simple but cleanly made, with pear and pineapple fruit in a medium-bodied format. Not for wine-geek contemplation, rather for casual drinking with grilled fish or chicken. **84** —J.C. (7/1/2003)

Villa Sandi NV Prosecco (Prosecco di Valdobbiadene) $10. With dusty honey aromas and a sweet apple-and-pear palate, this simple little sparkler should satisfy the masses with ease. The finish is fruity, with a mild dose of sugar, and overall it is tasty and sweet. **86** —M.S. (12/31/2002)

Villa Sandi NV Prosecco (Prosecco di Valdobbiadene) $20. Light and friendly on the nose, with floral and green herb aromas. Fairly round on the palate for Prosecco, with melon, honey, and candied almond flavors. Finishes simple and clean, an unbroken continuation of the palate. **86** —M.S. (12/15/2004)

Villa Sandi NV Brut Prosecco (Prosecco di Valdobbiadene) $12. Has subdued aromas of garden greens, herbs, white fruit, pear, and wild flowers. This is a clean and crystalline sparkler with a refreshing, lime-driven finish. **87 Best Buy** —M.L. (6/1/2006)

Villa Sandi NV Dry Cuvée Prosecco (Prosecco di Conegliano e Valdobbiadene) $19. Villa Sandi consistently delivers top-notch Prosecco and this cuvée is no exception. The aromas are delicate and elegantly understated: lemon lollipop, stone fruit, and field flowers. You'll detect a candy-like flavor in the mouth and a frothy, creamy mouthfeel. **88** —M.L. (12/15/2006)

Villa Sandi NV Extra Dry Prosecco (Prosecco di Conegliano e Valdobbiadene) $15. Instead of obvious fruit aromas, this extra dry sparker delivers graham cracker, nicely chiseled mineral tones, plus kiwi and stone fruit in smaller doses. Fuller and thicker in the mouth with a touch of sweetness, it could pair well with spicy finger foods. **87** —M.L. (12/15/2006)

Villa Sandi NV Extra Dry Prosecco (Prosecco di Valdobbiadene) $12. Small and fine perlage makes this a visually attractive apéritif choice, as do the soft floral aromas. Creamy and soft in the mouth with grapefruit and mineral flavors and a fizzy, fresh close. **88 Best Buy** —M.L. (6/1/2006)

Villa Sandi NV Il Fresco Prosecco (Veneto) $12. Fresh and crisp without being thin or hollow, this Prosecco offers polished aromas of lime, kiwi, honey, white stone, lemon candy, and white flowers. Once it hits the palate, it becomes creamy and silky thanks to its playful effervescence. **86** —M.L. (12/15/2006)

Villa Sandi NV Brut Sparkling Blend (Prosecco di Valdobbiadene) $12. Lemonade-like sweetness on the nose is enhanced by notes of green herbs. Flavors of pineapple and nectarine carry the palate, while the finish is quick and clean. Adequately round and thorough. Solid and entirely functional. **87 Best Buy** —M.S. (12/15/2005)

Villa Sandi NV Cuvée Sparkling Blend (Prosecco di Valdobbiadene) $20. Sweet peach, apricot, and lemon-lime aromas are inviting, as are the flavors, which veer toward ripe apples, dried Turkish apricots and cinnamon. Quite flush, bordering on rich, with a sweetness that most folks should like. However, if you like yours very dry and tart, this might not be the one. **89** —M.S. (12/15/2005)

Villa Sandi NV Extra Dry Sparkling Blend (Prosecco di Valdobbiadene) $12. This is the quintessentially perky wine: Crisp and snappy with bursting citrus notes including lemon drop, pink grapefruit, and candied orange peel backed by delicate floral and jasmine aromas. Chalky, mineral notes round off a gorgeous nose. Designed according to Palladian principals in 1622, Villa Sandi is one of the most beautiful estates near Treviso. Owned by shoemaker Giancarlo Moretti Polegato, it has a one-kilometer long underground 17th-century gallery for red wine barrique aging. **89 Best Buy** —M.L. (11/15/2005)

Villa Sandi NV Opere Trevigiane Brut Sparkling Blend (Veneto) $23. Because this sparkler goes through secondary fermentation in the bottle (metodo tradizionale) you can count on rich, saturated tones of honey, apple pie, roasted nuts, and cookie dough. There's more weight and consistency too, making it an excellent match to lightly fried finger foods. **90** —M.L. (12/15/2006)

Villa Sandi NV Cuvée Prosecco White Blend (Prosecco di Valdobbiadene) $15. This reserve-level Prosecco strikes all the right chords. The nose is dry and, at first, chalky. With time it opens up nicely, leading to a palate full of orange, melon, and other citrus. The sweet, sassy finish is just right. Overall it's quite a well-rounded wine that plays a merry tune. **88** —M.S. (12/31/2002)

Villa Sandi 2000 Marinali Bianco White Blend (Marca Trevigiana) $20. This blend of Chardonnay and Pinot Bianco is dark-gold in color, with citrus and green apple aromas that get riper as the wine gradually warms in the glass, eventually developing peach overtones. Flavors are of buttered stone fruits. Drink up. **84** —J.C. (7/1/2003)

VILLA SELVAPIANA

Villa Selvapiana 2000 Vigneto Bucerchiale Riserva Sangiovese (Chianti Rufina) $31. 90 Villa Selvapiana 2000 Vigneto Bucerchiale Riserva (Chianti Rufina); $31. Lots of mature complexity on display here. The nose delivers classy tobacco, rubber, and smoky tar aromas as well as mature dry fruit, and the palate is lively and tight. Blackberry, cinnamon, and vanilla flavors lead into a tannic but healthy finish. Maturing as we speak; drink through 2007. **90** (4/1/2005)

VILLA SPARINA

Villa Sparina 1996 Rivalta Barbera (Barbera del Monferrato) $40. **85** (4/1/2000)

Villa Sparina 1997 Bric Maioli Dolcetto (Dolcetto d'Acqui) $7. 85 *(4/1/2000)*

Villa Sparina 1997 D Giusep Dolcetto (Dolcetto d'Acqui) $11. 88 Best Buy *(4/1/2000)*

VILLA VISTARENNI

Villa Vistarenni 2000 Codirosso Cabernet Sauvignon-Sangiovese (Toscana) $33. Appealing on the bouquet, with fresh foresty aromas off-setting cherry and berry notes. Crisp and pure in the mouth, where quality fruit pushes forward unhindered by heavy oak and extract. A solid food wine if there ever was one. **88** —*M.S. (9/1/2006)*

Villa Vistarenni 1999 Riserva Sangiovese (Chianti Classico) $25. Smooth and complete, with cherry, chocolate, fresh herbs, and burnt leather aromas. On the palate, fresh red fruit is dressed in a robe of tasty oak, which creates the flavor sensation of raspberries topped with chocolate. Medium tannins; not too heavy; well-balanced. **89** *(4/1/2005)*

VILLABELLA

Villabella 2000 Red Blend (Amarone della Valpolicella Classico) $20. Earthy for certain, with clear scents of tobacco, dry leaves, and dried cherry. Much more mature than its age might indicate, with a lean flavor profile and a lot of savory flavors. More of a drink-now kind of wine, and snappy enough to offset meats and other rich foods. **86** *(11/1/2005)*

Villabella 1999 Fracastoro Red Blend (Amarone della Valpolicella Classico) $60. Nice and sweet on the bouquet, where ripe plum, marzipan, and milky coffee hold court. Mouth-filling and ripe, if not all that powerful. It's well made and easy to like, with ample dark berry and chocolate flavors. Very much standard fare yet likable. **87** *(11/1/2005)*

VILLADORIA

Villadoria 2000 Arneis (Roero Arneis) $9. Light floral aromas fade with airing. Flavors of lemon and cabbage lead into a sharp finish. Sour and strange, and just not that good. **80** —*M.S. (12/15/2003)*

Villadoria 1999 Barbera (Barbera d'Alba Superiore) $9. The bouquet is earthy, with aromas of bacon, wood, root beer, and raisins. Conversely, the palate is fairly sharp, with a tart center of pie cherry and rhubarb. But the finish is open and airy, and as a whole this wine is solid and should work well with food. **86 Best Buy** —*M.S. (11/15/2002)*

Villadoria 1997 Barbera (Barbera d'Alba Superiore) $10. 87 *(1/1/2000)*

Villadoria 1999 Nebbiolo (Barbaresco) $21. Herbal and peppery on the nose, this is a lean, hard, tannic wine that some tasters felt would blossom in time, while others questioned its balance. If you buy it, give it a good long time in the cellar, then write us a letter and tell us who was right. **87** *(4/2/2004)*

Villadoria 1997 Nebbiolo (Barolo) $23. An array of stimulating aromas of tar, dill, and salinity. The flavors are beefy—like dried meats with a touch of steak sauce. The mouthfeel is juicy; the finish tart. Try with grilled meats. **88** —*C.S. (11/15/2002)*

Villadoria 1995 Nebbiolo (Serralunga D'Alba) $NA. 90 Best Buy *(1/1/2000)*

VILLADORO

Villadoro 2002 Montepulciano (Montepulciano d'Abruzzo) $12. The murky nose deals mushroom, soy, and earth, while the palate mixes hints of green vegetables with limited red fruit. Finishes tangy and sharp. **83** —*M.S. (10/1/2004)*

VILLANOVA

Villanova 2004 Pinot Grigio (Friuli Isonzo) $NA. Pine nuts, flint stone, baked banana, roasted nuts, and acacia are delivered on the back of a well-structured Pinot Grigio. A prominent vein of acidity slices straight down the middle, leaving a vaguely sour note on the finish. **88** *M.L. (2/1/2006)*

Villanova 1997 Pinot Grigio (Isonzo del Friuli) $12. 82 *(8/1/1999)*

Villanova 2004 Ronco Cucco Pinot Grigio (Collio) $20. Apple, pear, and licorice aromas go beyond neutral, while the palate is sweet, ripe, and veers toward apple. Honey, anisette, and heft define the weighty finish. **86** *(2/1/2006)*

VINAGRI PUGLIA

Vinagri Puglia SRL 2000 Limitone Dei Greci Primitivo (Salento) $30. With rubber, earth, and black cherry aromas, you expect a bigger wine than you get. The fruit is a bit tart and veers toward red plum, raspberry, and red currant. The mouthfeel is lean more than full, while the overall flavor impression is rather tart. If you're wondering: Primitivo is a kissing cousin of Zinfandel. **84** —*M.S. (12/15/2003)*

VINARTE

VinArte 1998 Sangiovese (Chianti) $7. The juicy berry fruit on the nose carries a green herb element. While smooth in texture, the black cherry flavors of the palate seem a touch sharp and under-ripe. A touch of leather and caramel picks up the finish. **84** *(4/1/2001)*

VITANZA

Vitanza 2001 Brunello (Brunello di Montalcino) $40. A modern Brunello with dark, inky concentration and toasted wood notes that underscore cracked black pepper, spicy cherry wood, charcoal, and chocolate-covered strawberries. As soft, cushiony, and velvety as your most comfortable couch, with a powerful tannin punch at the end. **92** *(4/1/2006)*

VITICCIO

Viticcio 1998 Sangiovese (Chianti Classico) $12. Offers aromas and flavors of cherry, cedar, licorice, and menthol. The mouthfeel is even, full and supple, and the long, dry finish displays substantial tannins as well as earth and spice accents. Can be held for three to five years. **88 Best Buy** *(4/1/2001)*

Viticcio 1997 Lucius Riserva Sangiovese (Chianti Classico) $25. Closed now, but the impressive depth and richness of fruit and texture are still evident. Opens with aromas of black and blueberries, touches of carob, and cinnamon. Chewy, yet smooth and polished, cocoa and espresso accent the subdued very dark cherry fruit. Shows dusty tannins and a leathery note on the long finish. Cellar til 2005. **90** *(4/1/2001)*

Viticcio 1998 Riserva Sangiovese (Chianti Classico) $18. Bright and intense berry aromas lead into a tart palate that runs heavy with pie cherry and leather. It's probably a tad too tight, tart, and hard to merit higher, but with food it should do the trick. Some dark black coffee notes on the finish add to the wine's drying character. **85** —*M.S. (8/1/2002)*

Viticcio 1997 Riserva Sangiovese (Chianti Classico) $20. Very dark espresso, leather, and black plum aromas and flavors. The mouthfeel is full and balanced by good acidity. The very dry, long finish shows tar, licorice, and bitter chocolate flavors, along with some tannins to shed. Time should allow the solid fruit to come from behind the lavish toast that now veils it. **87** *(4/1/2001)*

Viticcio 2000 Rosarossa Sangiovese (Toscana) $9. On the nose, creamy oak sits atop bright plum and raspberry fruit, followed by a friendly, fruity palate with just the right amount of toast, vanilla, mild tannins, and sweetness. A mild, warm finish makes this an entirely quaffable Sangiovese. **85** —*M.S. (8/1/2002)*

VOGA

Voga 2004 Pinot Grigio (Delle Venezie) $13. Wine packaging doesn't get cooler than this. Instead of a bottle, this new concept wine is presented in a very cool glass cylinder. As to the wine, it's standard Pinot Grigio with pleasant apple pie, poached pear, and wilted rose petal aromas. **85** —*M.L. (6/1/2006)*

VOLPAIA

Volpaia 1998 Sangiovese (Chianti Classico) $19. A medium-weight wine built on a core of tart cherry fruit that wears licorice and tobacco accents. Even and dry on the palate, it has a good chalky mouthfeel and dry, even tannins on the finish. Not flamboyant, but solid. **85** *(4/1/2001)*

VOLPE PASINI

Volpe Pasini 2004 Pinot Grigio (Colli Orientali del Friuli) $12. This producer's un-barriqued Pinot Grigio has standard cantaloupe, peach, and pear aromas and a lean consistency that would pair well with wok-fried chicken or pork chow mein. **86** —*M.L. (6/1/2006)*

ITALY

ITALY

Volpe Pasini 2001 Ipso Pinot Grigio (Friuli Venezia Giulia) $18. This tremendous wine is 100% Pinot Grigio, of which 50% was aged in new wood. It is rich and full-bodied, with complex layers of vanilla. It comes from low-yielding, old vines. Only 8,000 bottles were produced. **91** —R.V. (7/1/2003)

Volpe Pasini 2002 Zuc de Volpe Pinot Grigio (Colli Orientali del Friuli) $18. A well-judged, well-structured wine that balances fresh, crisp, and light fruit against flavors of peaches, almonds, and cinnamon. It will be better in two or three years' time. **88** —R.V. (7/1/2003)

Volpe Pasini 2003 Zuc di Volpe Pinot Grigio (Venezia Giulia) $23. Very toasty, with spicy wood supported by banana, nutmeg, and cinnamon. Try it with rich seafood dishes such as lobster bisque. **88** —M.L. (6/1/2006)

Volpe Pasini 2002 Zuc de Volpe Ribolla Gialla (Colli Orientali del Friuli) $18. The rare local Friulan grape Ribolla Gialla is planted only in 240 acres in the whole region. This typical example is soft, with a clean, light acidity, white currant flavors, and a racy, crisp aftertaste. **86** —R.V. (7/1/2003)

Volpe Pasini 2002 Luc de Volpe Tocai Friulano Tocai (Colli Orientali del Friuli) $18. An excellent example of this local grape variety, this is an aromatic, full-bodied wine, with ripe fruit. Aromas of lavender are followed on the palate by flavors of almonds and fresh, green fruits. **89** —R.V. (7/1/2003)

WALTER FILIPUTTI

Walter Filiputti 1997 Pinot Grigio (Venezia Giulia) $24. 83 (8/1/1999)

ZARDETTO

Zardetto NV Prosecco Brut DOC Prosecco (Veneto) $11. Light in color and lithe, with flowery aromas along with hints of orange blossom and lemon-lime. There's a good reason why this Prosecco is so popular: it's sleek and smooth, with a graceful mouthfeel and perfect acidity. At restaurants it's the prescribed palate prep, a wine to sip casually before moving on to bigger things. And the flavors of pears, apples, and lime soda are just right. **89** —M.S. (6/1/2003)

Zardetto 2004 Zeta Prosecco (Prosecco di Conegliano) $19. Sweet and floral, with lime and gardenia on the nose. Nice lemon-lime flavors are tasty and just crisp enough. Finishes a touch like Sprite, with lingering tangerine and pineapple flavors. **87** —M.S. (12/15/2005)

Zardetto 2004 Zeta Dry Prosecco (Prosecco di Conegliano) $20. Shows lemongrass, garden greens, orange blossom, and lemon-lime with sweet, mature honeydew on the nose. On the sweet side, but tasty, with a creamy, frothy finish. **87** —M.L. (6/1/2006)

ZENATO

Zenato 2000 Sergio Zenato Corvina, Rondinella, Molinara (Amarone della Valpolicella Classico) $90. Slightly heavy, but by no means has it lost its style, balance, or zip. The bouquet is packed with road tar, dark cherry, and chocolate, and all together we found it "simpatico." As for flavors, look for chocolate, cherries, and Middle Eastern spices. Loaded with size and subtleties. **92** (11/1/2005)

Zenato 2004 Pinot Grigio (Delle Venezie) $12. Apricot juice, cantaloupe, and pineapple are accented by crisp notes of kiwi and lime. Coats the mouth very well, with a silky, long-lasting finish. **87 Best Buy** —M.L. (6/1/2006)

Zenato 1998 Pinot Grigio (Delle Venezie) $10. 85 (8/1/1999)

Zenato 2000 Red Blend (Amarone della Valpolicella Classico) $65. Kicks off with a touch of wood sap before unveiling more typical aromas of fudge, raisin, and dried red fruits. Probably a bit more acidic than one might expect, which goes to explaining the racy mouthfeel and zesty cherry flavors. Fairly intense, with a late blast of heat and spice. **88** (11/1/2005)

Zenato 1998 Red Blend (Amarone della Valpolicella Classico) $50. Powerful and spicy, with aromas of black fruit, pepper, baking spices, and herbs. This is soft, modern Amarone, a wine that you could drink now. The palate is rich, with chewy fruit and plenty of nuance. Overall it's clean, easy, and perfectly textured. **91** (5/1/2003)

Zenato 1999 Ripassa Superiore Red Blend (Valpolicella) $19. Pretty aromas of smoked meat, tire rubber, and ripe plums. The flavors run toward black cherry and pepper, with a touch of creaminess making for an easy mouthfeel. Very silky and full; quite a pleasure to drink. **91 Editors' Choice** (5/1/2003)

Zenato 2001 San Benedetto Trebbiano (Lugana) $10. 87 Best Buy —R.V. (11/15/2002)

Zenato 2002 San Benedetto White Blend (Lugana) $NA. This wine from the shores of Lake Garda has fresh, attractively crisp fruit, and a touch of acidity over some broad, food-friendly fruit. **86** —R.V. (7/1/2003)

ZENNER

Zenner 1999 Nero d'Avola (Sicilia) $20. Fasten your seatbelts—this is one intense wine, packed with sweet, candied berries, near-pain-inducing vanilla oak, and screaming acidity. Tolerance for brash, loud flavors is a prerequisite for enjoyment. **86** —C.S. (5/1/2002)

ZISOLA

Zisola 2004 Nero d'Avola (Sicilia) $NA. This is an exciting new addition to the family of Sicilian reds brought to us by one of Tuscany's most prominent wine families (Mazzei of Fonterutoli); beautiful and elegant packaging too. Grapes come from the Noto area and the wine sees 10 months of oak: ripe cherry, nutty notes, plum, vanilla, and wet earth are inviting and intense. **90** —M.L. (7/1/2006)

ZONIN

Zonin 1999 Amarone (Amarone della Valpolicella) $35. Round, smoky, and solid, with all components in their proper places. We liked this wine's ripe black cherry and plum flavors and found the mouthfeel to be rock solid and the acid-tannin balance just right. Maybe it doesn't stand out, but it will fit the bill with nary a problem. **90** (11/1/2005)

Zonin NV Chardonnay (Italy) $10. Sort of sweet and candied for a blanc de blancs, with sugary apple and mango flavors. On the palate there's a touch of off-setting citrus, primarily white grapefruit and orange, but the over-riding characteristic is one of sweet, almost cloying white fruits. It's not bad but it's also not very zesty. **84** —M.S. (12/15/2005)

Zonin NV Brut Chardonnay (Italy) $10. Perfectly fine bubbly, with a pale color and fine bead, citrusy, gingery flavors, and a short, dry finish. Best as an apéritif. **85 Best Buy** —J.C. (12/15/2004)

Zonin NV Brut Blanc de Blanc Chardonnay (Piedmont) $15. Very pale straw in color, this sparkler delivers measured aromas of honeydew, pear, and crushed stone. It's a direct and genuine wine that delivers the goods at an attractive price. Tasty and clean in the mouth. **87** —M.L. (6/1/2006)

Zonin 2000 Corvina, Rondinella, Molinara (Amarone della Valpolicella) $35. The Amarones from Zonin have been consistently good the past few vintages, and this one is no exception, offering dark plum-prune and chocolate notes laced with hints of spice and tobacco. It's round and mouth-filling without being unstructured, giving the impression that it has more to give in another few years. Tastes dry, unlike some Amarones these days. **90** —J.C. (10/1/2006)

Zonin 2004 Il Giangio Garganega (Gambellara Classico) $12. Fruit for this 100% Garganega comes from the vineyards beyond Zonin's Veneto headquarters. This makes an easy summer drink with rich stone fruit, peach, and a generally attractive nose. Good acidity and moderate structure. **87** —M.L. (9/1/2005)

Zonin 2002 Podere il Giangio Garganega (Gambellara Classico) $NA. A 100% single-vineyard Garganega from the home vineyards of Zonin, this has ripe, soft almond-flavored fruit with touches of vanilla and citrus. **86** —R.V. (7/1/2003)

Zonin 2002 Podere il Giangio Recioto Garganega (Gambellara Classico) $NA. Made with indigenous Garganega grapes that are air dried on special mats, Recioto is a dessert wine that is delicately balanced between sweetness and finesse with almond skin, chestnut, peach, and honey notes. **88** —M.L. (10/1/2006)

Zonin 2002 Terre Mediterranee Insolia (Sicilia) $9. Heavy and syrupy, especially at first. Flavors of baked corn and mealy apple don't amount to much. A bit of mushroom on the finish indicates early oxidation. Nothing special. **82** —M.S. (2/1/2005)

Zonin 2000 Terre Mediterranee Insolia (Sicilia) $NA. With aromas that bring hints of mineral spirits and turpentine, you might not take a second look at this wine. But they are interesting enough to bring you back, and the slightly tart, citrusy flavors finish clean and crisp. **84**—*J.C. (10/1/2003)*

Zonin NV Lambrusco dell'Emilia Lambrusco (Emilia-Romagna) $6. This is a perky, sweet frizzante red with limited appeal among top-brass wine connoisseurs. It does, however, make a fine Sunday afternoon picnic drink with fruit candy and soda pop aromas, lower alcohol, and big berry flavors. **81**—*M.L. (12/15/2006)*

Zonin 2001 Merlot (Veneto) $7. Sweet yet bold aromas of mint, cherry, and meat. The flavor profile is straight ahead roasted cherry, and some coffee comes up on the tannic, tight finish. Very sturdy, with healthy acids. **84** *(5/1/2003)*

Zonin 2000 Montepulciano (Montepulciano d'Abruzzo) $7. Bright purple to the eye, with a syrupy, grapey nose that runs deep. The palate is snappy, lively, and loaded with blackberry, while the feel is entirely round and soft. Good acids make it a healthy drink. Overall it bears a strong resemblance to Beaujolais. **85 Best Buy**—*M.S. (11/15/2003)*

Zonin NV Moscato (Asti) $7. 80—*J.C. (1/1/2004)*

Zonin NV Dolce Moscato (Asti) $11. Aromas of peach, apricot, and Golden Delicious apple; the wine is tangy, simple, and sweet in the mouth, hence the "Dolce." Best paired with dried biscuits or shortbread. **84**—*M.L. (11/15/2006)*

Zonin NV Dolce Moscato (Italy) $10. This one is out there in terms of its sweet lemon-lime character. Alongside that you'll get dried mango and other sweet fruits. Good in terms of feel, with no residue or cloying character. But it's supersweet, hence the "dolce" designation. And even for Moscato it's like liquid sugar. **84**—*M.S. (12/15/2005)*

Zonin NV Moscato Dolce Moscato (Asti) $11. You get the peach and floral aromas you expect from the aromatic Moscato grape with an added layer of minerality that lessens some of the sweetness in the mouth. **85**—*M.L. (11/15/2006)*

Zonin NV Spumante Moscato (Asti) $10. Features floral, muscat aromas, and tropical fruit and citrus flavors. Finishes short; a pleasant quaff but lacking in concentration. **83**—*J.C. (12/15/2004)*

Zonin 2000 Terre Mediterranee Nero d'Avola (Sicilia) $9. This grape is increasing in popularity due to its fruit-forward and full-bodied style. Bright blackberry fruit with cinnamon spice finishes rich and juicy, with hints of chocolate. **85 Best Buy** *(12/31/2002)*

Zonin 2004 Pinot Grigio (Friuli Aquileia) $10. Green apple, hay, minerals, and some peach flavors with a hint of dried basil or sage make this a good value for wine. Tart, acidic, and persistent on the finish. **86 Best Buy**—*M.L. (2/1/2006)*

Zonin 2003 Pinot Grigio (Delle Venezie) $9. Has some odd pine resin notes that creep in on the nose and palate, joining predominantly simple apple flavors. Finshes clean and citrusy. **83**—*J.C. (12/31/2004)*

Zonin 2001 Pinot Grigio (Delle Venezie) $7. Just what you would expect from a $7 Pinot Grigio. Pleasant citrus and peach aromas and flavors are accented with a touch of almond. A crisp and simple wine. **84** *(12/31/2002)*

Zonin 2005 Terre Palladiane Pinot Grigio (Delle Venezie) $8. A luminous Grigio, with fruit and nut characteristics layered over melon and citrus. Lean and fresh in the mouth— albeit a little light—with a zesty finish. **85 Best Buy**—*M.L. (6/1/2006)*

Zonin 2004 Terre Palladiane Pinot Grigio (Delle Venezie) $8. Similar in taste and philosophy to Zonin's Monte Campo brand, this wine offers notes of dried lavender, lemongrass, and apple peel. Clean, simple, mainstream. **85 Best Buy**—*M.L. (2/1/2006)*

Zonin NV Brut Prosecco (Veneto) $10. An enjoyable bubbly with good creamy froth, white peach, mineral, and hard candy tones that are nicely balanced and spread throughout. It has a thick consistency and a snappy, crisp close. **87 Best Buy**—*M.L. (6/1/2006)*

Zonin NV Brut Prosecco (Italy) $10. Aggressive in a soda-like fashion, with light fruit aromas and plenty of warm, dusty qualities. Apple and peach carry the palate, while the finish is fresh in terms of feel but a touch mealy as far as flavor. **84**—*M.S. (12/15/2005)*

Zonin NV Special Cuvée Brut Prosecco (Italy) $10. Slightly floral and citrusy on the nose, with fresh, grapy flavors and a soft, creamy mouthfeel. A bit simple, but a welcome apéritif with a mouth-watering finish. **86 Best Buy**—*J.C. (12/15/2004)*

Zonin NV Special Cuvée Brut Prosecco (Italy) $10. The best bubbly in the Zonin portfolio. The nose is yeasty, with moderate richness and enough apple and citrus to register. The palate features green melon, apple, and toast, while the finish is mildly yeasty and fairly full. Satisfying as it fills the mouth. **87 Best Buy**—*M.S. (12/15/2005)*

Zonin NV Special Cuvée Extra Dry Prosecco (Prosecco di Conegliano) $13. Light-weight and a little sweet, with classy lime and lemongrass aromas backed by orange and tangerine flavors. Finishes a bit short, but crisp and clean. **86 Best Buy**—*J.C. (12/31/2003)*

Zonin 1997 Red Blend (Amarone della Valpolicella) $35. Some leather and hickory smoke dot the nose, and there's some maple and whisky notes, too. The mouth is fruity and fresh, although deep at its core there seems to be a vegetal hint. The finish is spicy and warm. **89** *(5/1/2003)*

Zonin NV Baccorosa Sparkling Blend (Asti) $10. Made from an assortment of aromatic grapes, this is a super sweet raspberry-colored sparkler with loads of berry notes and lemon zest on the close. It's soda pop-sweet in the mouth. **84**—*M.L. (11/15/2006)*

Zonin NV Baccorosa Dolce Sparkling Blend (Italy) $10. Similar in style to Bracchetto, this is a light red-dark pink, sweet sparkling wine. Candied strawberry flavors finish short. **82**—*J.C. (12/15/2004)*

Zonin 2002 Classico White Blend (Soave) $NA. An immediately attractive, quaffable wine with clean, fresh flavors. This is a light, fresh wine designed to go with summer foods. **84**—*R.V. (7/1/2003)*

ITALY

New Zealand

In recent years, the New Zealand wine industry has mushroomed in size like no other. New Zealand now boasts more than five hundred wineries in a country with a total human population of only four million. The reason behind this growth has been exports. From 1995 to 2005, United States imports of New Zealand wine went from just over NZ$1 million to more than NZ$113 million. The result is that consumers in the United States are seeing more and more New Zealand wines on store shelves and restaurant wine lists. Thankfully, quality has remained generally excellent, thanks to a rigorous export certification process, a solid technological base, and a rapidly expanding understanding of viticulture.

NEW ZEALAND WINE REGIONS

Marlborough The engine driving New Zealand's growth, Marlborough wine production is dominated by Sauvignon Blanc. With its crisp, grassy, herbal-yet-tropical style, it has become the hallmark of New Zealand. Yet Marlborough is also capable of making other fine aromatic white wines, as well as Pinot Noir and Chardonnay.

Fairhall Downs Estate produces wine in the Brancott Valley, Marlborough, New Zealand.

Hawkes Bay Known for its Bordeaux-style reds from Merlot and Cabernet Sauvignon, which can be very fine in warm vintages, but excessively herbal in others. Alternative reds, such as Malbec and Syrah, are gaining in popularity, with Syrah in particular likely to emerge as a star.

Martinborough Together with the surrounding Wairarapa, Martinborough is Pinot Noir country. The wines marry cherry fruit with an often intense, wiry-herbal character that adds character and staying power.

Central Otago The world's southernmost wine-growing region has gained a reputation for its bold, dramatically fruity Pinot Noirs, but also makes some surprisingly good Rieslings.

Other important parts of New Zealand include Waipara for Riesling and Burgundy varieties, Gisborne for Chardonnay, and Nelson for a spectrum of grape varieties similar to Marlborough's.

AKARUA

Akarua 2003 Pinot Noir (Central Otago) $40. Nicely complex on the nose, with cola, clove, and caramel accenting bright cranberry aromas. Ripe cherries pick up hints of beets and caramel on the finish. Sturdy and well-oaked. **88** —*J.C. (12/1/2005)*

Akarua 2003 The Gullies Pinot Noir (Central Otago) $33. Charred and cola-laden on the nose, then delivers crisp, tart berry, and roasted beet flavors on the palate. Solid but not terribly distinguished. **85** —*J.C. (12/1/2005)*

ALANA ESTATE

Alana Estate 2003 Pinot Noir (Martinborough) $40. Heavily toasted and smoky on the nose, followed by lots of cola flavors and modest cherry fruit. Shows decent Pinot character, but a little short on charm. **84** —*J.C. (12/1/2005)*

ALEXANDRA WINE COMPANY

Alexandra Wine Company 2002 Davishon Pinot Noir (Central Otago) $35. Herbal and minty up-front, but then some pleasant cherry flavors take over. Turns a bit hard and drying on the finish. **84** —*J.C. (12/1/2005)*

Alexandra Wine Company 2001 Davishon Alexandra Pinot Noir (Central Otago) $35. Winemaker Matt Dicey has fashioned a rich and supple Pinot, with expansive black cherry aromas and flavors that deepen with time in the glass. French oak provides a subtle framework and adds layers of spice and chocolate. **90** —*J.C. (9/1/2003)*

Alexandra Wine Company 2001 Crag an Oir Riesling (Central Otago) $20. Mt. Difficulty winemaker Matt Dicey has made another fine Otago Riesling, this from a single vineyard whose name is Gaelic for "Hill of Gold." It smells of honey and marmalade, with strong citrus overtones and a sweet attack. Zesty acids on the long, crisp finish provide balance. **88** —*J.C. (8/1/2003)*

ALEXIA

Alexia 2001 Chardonnay (Nelson) $20. Starts off very tart and citrusy, almost sour in its intensity, with unripe pineapple and plum aromas. It really smooths out on the finish, picking up weight, a creamy texture, and length. Seems to need 6-12 months to round into form. **86** —*J.C. (9/1/2003)*

Alexia 2002 Sauvignon Blanc (Nelson) $18. Tart grapefruits and gooseberries leave a high-strung impression on the palate. This is a taut, grassy wine best paired with shellfish or other briny delights. **87** —*J.C. (9/1/2003)*

ALLAN SCOTT

Allan Scott 2000 Chardonnay (Marlborough) $20. Medium-weight and structured, this Marlborough Chardonnay shows light aromas of baked apple (or applesauce?) and toast on the nose, and mealy banana and caramel flavors in the mouth. Its profile makes sense—it's aged in French oak barrels and goes through partial mallactic fermentation. Lemon, pineapple, chalk, and sage perk up the finish. **87** —*D.T. (12/15/2001)*

Allan Scott 1999 Chardonnay (Marlborough) $18. Not shy on the oak, this full-bore wine features toast, butter, and oak-imparted spice, backed up by baked pears garnished with cinnamon. Yet it manages to hold together with a finish that echoes with pineapple and citrus. **88** —*J.C. (5/1/2001)*

Allan Scott 2002 Vineyard Select Chardonnay (Marlborough) $15. I suspect there will be those who criticize this wine for being too fruity—too full of pear and nectarine aromas, too full of ripe, fruity flavors. Where's the minerality, the terroir? they'll ask. And, in fairness, that's what keeps this wine from achieving a higher rating. Still, its lush fruit, combined with a long, mouth-watering finish, make this a winning Chard at a fair price. **88** —*J.C. (7/1/2005)*

Allan Scott 2002 Pinot Noir (Marlborough) $24. A poster boy for what is wrong with New Zealand Pinot Noir, the 2002 Allan Scott takes some delicate cherry fruit and covers it with oak that tastes like caramel or toasted marshmallows. Finishes short. It's not bad, but could have been so much better. **83** —*J.C. (7/1/2005)*

Allan Scott 2001 Pinot Noir (Marlborough) $23. Boasts sturdy plum and blackberry fruit, edged by cinnamon and clove spice. It's medium-weight, supple in the mouth and finishes moderately long. **87** —*J.C. (9/1/2003)*

Allan Scott 2001 Riesling (Marlborough) $14. Medium-weight, with a touch of apparent sweetness, this tart-apple and lime-scented wine should prove versatile at the table. Pair it with anything from wursts and kraut to Thai dishes. **87** —*J.C. (8/1/2003)*

Allan Scott 2000 Riesling (Marlborough) $14. There's a small amount of residual sugar left in this wine (about 4g/L); not enough to taste, just enough to add weight to the palate. Soft peach and pear fruit is accented by musky, spicy flavors that turn lean and citrusy on the finish. **86** —*J.C. (5/1/2001)*

Allan Scott 2000 Sauvignon Blanc (Marlborough) $15. The proprietor—you guessed it, Allan Scott—doesn't like herbaceousness in Sauvignon Blanc and you can tell from the ripeness and lack of green flavors in his wine. Instead, there's mild grapefruit coupled with melon and passion fruit. **87** —*J.C. (5/1/2001)*

Allan Scott 2004 Vineyard Select Sauvignon Blanc (Marlborough) $15. Delivers really nice complexity and balance at a bargain price. The nose combines green leafy notes, a bit of asparagus and a hint of jalapeño with riper notes suggestive of honey and stone fruits. Round in the mouth, with nectarine flavors that turn citrusy and grassy on the finish. **90 Best Buy** —*J.C. (7/1/2005)*

ALPHA DOMUS

Alpha Domus 2002 The Aviator Bordeaux Blend (Hawke's Bay) $50. This is a supple, savory, and cedary Bordeaux-style blend—albeit one that indulges the current NZ fancy for Malbec (18%). Aromas are mainly black cherries and smoke, but there's an herbal under-current that seems to intensify with time in the glass. Does show good length and complexity, so it maybe worth gambling on for the future. **87** —*J.C. (7/1/2006)*

Alpha Domus 2000 The Aviator Bordeaux Blend (Hawke's Bay) $37. Smoky and toasty at first, slowly giving up hints of Provençal herbs and dark fruit. Opens on the palate to show bright, concentrated berry fruit underscored by smoky oak and a bed of dried herbs. Crisp and fresh on the palate, this Bordeaux Blend could age into something interesting, or it could lose its fruit and show more tart-edged acids. Drink now. **88** —*J.C. (4/1/2004)*

Alpha Domus 2002 The Navigator Bordeaux Blend (Hawke's Bay) $20. This blend of Merlot and Cabernet Sauvignon (with small amounts of Cabernet Franc and Malbec) reflects Bordeaux sensibilities. That is, it's on the light, lean side, and shows hints of green pepper, cedar and tobacco. Still, the tannins are supple and there's good complexity—even some slightly meaty, savory notes on the finish—making it a pleasure to drink now. **87** —*J.C. (7/1/2006)*

Alpha Domus 2001 The Navigator Bordeaux Blend (Hawke's Bay) $23. A respectable effort, the 2001 Navigator shows a little too much of the herbal side of Hawke's Bay to rate higher. Smoky and herbal, it skates dangerously close to green pepper and green bean before bursting into big, black currant flavors on the palate. Supple; drink now. **87** —*J.C. (4/1/2004)*

Alpha Domus 2004 Chardonnay (Hawke's Bay) $13. Simple, fruity, and fresh—not the stuff legends are made of, but a fine everyday Chard that should please most everyone. Tangy tropical and citrus fruit flavors carry a bit of weight, yet end crisp and tart. **86** —*J.C. (7/1/2005)*

Alpha Domus 2002 Chardonnay (Hawke's Bay) $14. Limes and tangerines at first, later opening up to reveal hints of stone fruits alongside the mixed citrus flavors. A slightly creamy mouthfeel is a plus, and the finish is very fresh and fruity. **86** —*J.C. (9/1/2003)*

Alpha Domus 2001 Chardonnay (North Island) $14. Peach, mint, and toasted hazelnut aromas lead into bright, citrusy peach and pear flavors. Finishes clean and crisp, albeit a little short. A tasty lightweight built to serve as an apéritif or with light fish and chicken preparations. **85** —*J.C. (7/1/2002)*

Alpha Domus 2005 Unoaked Chardonnay (Hawke's Bay) $14. Doesn't show the vibrant, tropical features you might expect from an unwooded New

Zealand Chardonnay, instead offering understated apple and lime fruit and a certain austerity in the finish. **84** —*J.C. (7/1/2006)*

Alpha Domus 2004 Merlot (Hawke's Bay) $14. A fresh, rather light-weight Merlot, the 2004 from Alpha Domus does have some tomato-leaf character, but also supple tannins and enough cherry fruit to balance out. There's decent length on the finish, where it turns a bit tart and peppery. **85** —*J.C. (11/1/2006)*

Alpha Domus 2002 Merlot (Hawke's Bay) $16. Bottled under screwcap, this wine starts off a bit rubbery and sulfurous before revealing fresh black cherry and vanilla flavors that finish snappy and crisp. **84** —*J.C. (12/15/2003)*

Alpha Domus 2004 Sauvignon Blanc (Hawke's Bay) $13. This plump, medium-weight Sauvignon Blanc features simple grapefruit aromas and flavors. Turns a little tart, almost metallic, on the finish. **84** —*J.C. (7/1/2005)*

AMISFIELD

Amisfield 2005 Pinot Gris (Central Otago) $24. Winemaker Jeff Sinnott had the grapes harvested in three passes through the vineyard, then fermented the early-picked fruit in steel. The resulting blend is seamlessly integrated and harmonious, offering the merest hints of toast and butter alongside ripe apples and melons. Tastes close to dry, with a clean, fresh finish. **88** —*J.C. (11/1/2006)*

Amisfield 2004 Pinot Gris (Central Otago) $20. A disappointing effort from winemaker Jeff Sinnott in light of his stellar 2004 Sauvignon Blanc, this wine is light and frankly a little bland, with modest melon flavors that never really get revved up. **83** —*J.C. (7/1/2005)*

Amisfield 2004 Pinot Noir (Central Otago) $32. Very cleanly made and modern in style, with pure cherry flavors accented by vanilla and dried spices from new oak. This is a creamy, medium-bodied wine that isn't Burgundian by any measure, but represents textbook New World Pinot Noir. **88** —*J.C. (12/1/2005)*

Amisfield 2003 Pinot Noir (Central Otago) $30. There's a bit of wood shavings and toast on the nose, but also plenty of ripe black cherries to balance out the new oak. Flavors turn redder—more toward Maraschino cherry—and a bit candied, but this is still a satisfying mouthful of New World Pinot. **88** —*J.C. (12/1/2005)*

Amisfield 2005 Sauvignon Blanc (Central Otago) $24. Relatively simple and fruity, this Sauvignon Blanc from a Pinot Noir hotbed is a good wine, just not at the same level as some of New Zealand's best. On the light side, with passion fruit and citrus flavors that finish clean and crisp. **85** —*J.C. (9/1/2006)*

Amisfield 2004 Sauvignon Blanc (Central Otago) $20. Shows all the requisite pea, pepper ,and tropical fruit in front of an intense palate that comes on like an explosion of melon, nectarine, and grapefruit. On the finish it runs calmer, and the flavors and feel are harmonious. Says a lot for New Zealand, at least their Sauvignon Blanc. **91 Editors' Choice** *(7/1/2005)*

ASHWELL

Ashwell 2003 Pinot Noir (Martinborough) $NA. Starts with slightly garlicky scents that never really blow off, then delivers tart cherry fruit flavors that turn herbal and drying on the finish. **83** —*J.C. (12/1/2005)*

ATA RANGI

Ata Rangi 2003 Pinot Noir (Martinborough) $39. Worth decanting if you open a bottle now, as this wine really blossoms with time in the glass, opening to reveal floral, rose-petal notes. Mouthfeel is big, but buffered by soft tannins and cherry, cola, and herb flavors. Finishes long, with tangy acidity and dusty tannins. Hold 3–4 years. **90 Cellar Selection** —*J.C. (12/1/2005)*

Ata Rangi 2001 Pinot Noir (Martinborough) $55. Delicate and herbal, with layers of briary and nettley complexity, this wine constantly challenges the intellect. Dried spices and cherries flesh it out without making it rich or chewy. A wine you can pleasantly linger over. **88** —*J.C. (9/1/2003)*

Ata Rangi 1999 Célèbre Red Blend (Martinborough) $36. This plump, appealing wine offers hints of smoked meat and black pepper (courtesy of the blend's 30% Syrah) along with cream and brown-sugar laced

coffee, cherries, and green herbs. The rest of the blend is Cabernet Sauvignon (60%) and Merlot (10%). **87** —*J.C. (12/15/2003)*

AUNTSFIELD

Auntsfield 2005 Long Cow Sauvignon Blanc (Marlborough) $17. A green style, but in this case those grassy, herbal aromas and flavors are amply backed by honeyed tropical fruit. Drink now. **88** —*J.C. (5/1/2006)*

BABICH

Babich 1998 Chardonnay (Gisborne) $10. 87 Best Buy —*S.H. (8/1/1999)*

Babich 1996 Irongate Chardonnay (Hawke's Bay) $22. 91 —*S.H. (8/1/1999)*

Babich 2000 Unwooded Chardonnay (Hawke's Bay) $11. Tasted blind, this would confuse many Chardonnay drinkers used to the oaked-up, caramel-flavored concoctions typically associated with the variety. The fruit comes through vibrant and pure, with lots of tart apple and pear flavors buttressed by a healthy squirt of citrus. Long and clean on the finish, perfect with shrimp cocktail. **87** —*J.C. (11/15/2003)*

Babich 1998 Sauvignon Blanc (Marlborough) $10. 87 Best Buy —*S.H. (8/1/1999)*

Babich 2005 Sauvignon Blanc (Marlborough) $13. Aromas of peach and pineapple give way to tropical fruit flavors with just a trace of passion fruit. A bit fat and soft on the palate, then picks up a slightly bitter note on the finish. **84** —*J.C. (5/1/2006)*

BALD HILLS

Bald Hills 2004 Pinot Noir (Bannockburn) $40. This relatively new Bannockburn producer has turned out a supple, creamy 2004 that boasts plenty of red fruit aromas and flavors, ranging from raspberry to cherry and strawberry. Crisp and juicy on the finish. **87** —*J.C. (9/1/2006)*

BANNOCK BRAE

Bannock Brae 2003 Barrel Selection Pinot Noir (Central Otago) $36. Starts off with a lovely, complex mix of cola, caramel, cherries, vanilla, ,and herbal notes, but seems a bit simpler on the palate, delivering cherry and vanilla flavors. Thins out on the finish, where the herbal, tea-like elements turn drying. **86** —*J.C. (12/1/2005)*

Bannock Brae 2002 Barrel Selection Pinot Noir (Central Otago) $38. Starts off with scents of toast, black cherries, and cola, while the flavors follow along, picking up hints of chocolate and plum. Supple and ready to drink. **87** —*J.C. (7/1/2005)*

BELMONTE

Belmonte 2004 Sauvignon Blanc (Marlborough) $20. Musky and aggressive, but that's what we liked about it. Aromas of grapefruit and flower blossom mix with notes of asparagus and green bean to yield that classic New Zealand bouquet. The palate is forceful and zesty, with flavors of citrus, fresh vegetables and grass. Finishes long, citrusy and focused. **89** *(7/1/2005)*

BILANCIA

Bilancia 2003 Syrah-Viognier Shiraz-Viognier (Hawke's Bay) $30. With no La Collina bottling in 2003, all the best fruit is in this single bottling—and the quality shines. Lovely pepper and berry scents pick up a touch of meaty complexity. Smooth and richly textured, with clean blackberry flavors that end in supple tannins. **89** —*J.C. (5/1/2006)*

Bilancia 2002 La Collina Syrah (Hawke's Bay) $80. This top New Zealand Syrah starts with lifted, floral peach and apricot notes, followed by a freight train of blackberries. The lush fruit persists on the palate, ending in a slow swell of ripe tannins. A triumph for winemakers-owners Warren Gibson and Lorraine Leheny. Drink now–2015. **91** —*J.C. (5/1/2006)*

BLADEN

Bladen 2000 Riesling (Marlborough) $11. This wine has a hardness to it that's only partly offset by a touch of residual sugar. The yellow plum and citrus fruit is tart and ungenerous, marked by a slight prickle on the tongue and a lingering mineral finish. **86** —*J.C. (8/1/2002)*

Bladen 2001 Sauvignon Blanc (Marlborough) $11. Softer, riper, and sweeter than most current offerings, and so the apple and citrus flavors feel a bit flabby in the mouth. It's a rich, creamy wine, and finishes spicy and ripely fruity. **85** —*S.H. (11/15/2002)*

BLIND RIVER

Blind River 2003 Sauvignon Blanc (Marlborough) $13. A recent entrant into the U.S. market, the wines here are made under the direction of John Belsham, long-time wine judge and proprietor of his own Foxes Island label. This bargain-priced offering features ripe notes of melons, nectarines, and figs, with a touch of smoke and mineral for complexity. Lingers on the finish. **89 Best Buy** —*J.C. (8/1/2004)*

BLIND TRAIL

Blind Trail 2003 Pinot Noir (Central Otago) $25. Smoky, earthy, and cola-scented, this is a soft, plushly textured wine that's not very fruity, yet features ample flesh in the form of earth, mushroom, spice and cola. Seems mature, so drink now. **87** —*J.C. (12/15/2006)*

BORTHWICK VINEYARD

Borthwick Vineyard 2005 Sauvignon Blanc (Wairarapa) $17. Distinctively smoky and grassy on the nose, marked by fumé notes and bold gooseberry aromas. This is full, ripe, and round in the mouth, bursting with melon and pink grapefruit flavors that finish long. **90 Editors' Choice** — *J.C. (12/15/2006)*

Borthwick Vineyard 2004 Sauvignon Blanc (Wairarapa) $18. Full yet steely, with melon, passion fruit, peach, and a smidgen of smoked meat. Quite the powerball, with aggressive flavors of nectarine, peach and citrus. Finishes bold, with mouthwatering acidity. **90** —*J.C. (7/1/2005)*

BOULDERVINES

Bouldervines 2005 Single Vineyard Sauvignon Blanc (Marlborough) $NA. Refreshingly combines stone fruit with grapefruit on the nose, then shows decent plumpness and weight on the palate. Turns simple, tart, and grapefruity on the finish. **86** —*J.C. (5/1/2006)*

BRANCOTT

Brancott 1997 Fairhall Estate Cabernet Sauvignon (Marlborough) $22. Rich cassis and chocolate aromas and flavors are offset by wisps of green bell pepper that comes and goes—one sniff it's there, the next it's not. Displays good richness and warm, supple tannins but may be too "green" for some consumers. **87** —*J.C. (5/1/2001)*

Brancott 2002 Chardonnay (Gisborne) $11. This light-bodied, fresh-tasting Chardonnay is driven by tart, citrusy flavors, cushioned by riper notes of nectarines and peaches. **85** —*J.C. (8/1/2004)*

Brancott 2000 Chardonnay (Gisborne) $10. The ripe yellow peaches and buttered tropical fruits feature just a hint of vanilla. Fairly rich and weighty on the palate, this is a good party wine that provides a mouthful of Chardonnay flavor at a reasonable price. **85 Best Buy** —*J.C. (5/1/2001)*

Brancott 2004 Ormond Chardonnay (Gisborne) $24. Toasty, mealy, and custardy on the nose, yet this wine has the stuffing to handle it, balancing all those aromas with apple, pear, and lemon fruit that steers clear of the overtly tropical notes often found in Gisborne Chardonnay. Slightly long and nutty on the finish. **90** —*J.C. (5/1/2006)*

Brancott 1999 Ormond Estate Chardonnay (Gisborne) $30. Ripe tropical fruit and toasty American oak are a traditional match in Gisborne, and the Ormond bottling from Brancott is a fine example. Sweet caramel, toast with honey and mixed tropical fruit aromas and flavors are rich and full but not heavy. **87** —*J.C. (8/1/2002)*

Brancott 1998 Ormond Estate Chardonnay (Gisborne) $25. Toasted oats impart a mealy texture and sophisticated complexity. The fruit core consists of oranges and nectarines, shot through with tropical fruits. Finishes clean and bright. Easy to like and easy to drink. **88** —*J.C. (5/1/2001)*

Brancott 1998 Renwick Estate Chardonnay (Marlborough) $25. The distinctive nutty oatmeal aromas and flavors found in this wine give it a rich, toasty character without an overbearing oak presence. Ripe pear fruit provides depth, while lemony acidity carries the finish. **89** —*J.C. (5/1/2001)*

Brancott 1999 Reserve Chardonnay (Gisborne) $17. Opening aromas of butter, vanilla, and cream (and a creamy mouthfeel) almost make you wistful for overoaked Claifornia Chards, but the Brancott is lighter and

more elegant. Airy marshmallow and butterscotch flavors are balanced by loads of pear. Finishes with a lean, pear skin, mineral back end. **88** — *D.T. (12/15/2001)*

Brancott 1999 Reserve Chardonnay (Gisborne) $NA. Complex, with a melange of flavors ranging from apples, peaches, and pears all the way to mangos. Upfront acidity makes the wine come alive. It seduces the palate with fresh fruitiness and creaminess, and is spectacularly food friendly. **90** —*S.H. (1/1/2002)*

Brancott 1998 Reserve Chardonnay (Gisborne) $15. A clear step down from Brancott's single-estate Chardonnay bottlings, this wine offers vanilla and spice notes, modest fruit, and a menthol-tinged finish. **84** — *J.C. (5/1/2001)*

Brancott 2004 Unoaked Chardonnay (Gisborne) $12. An obvious, unsubtle Chardonnay that flashes peaches, pineapple, and tropical fruit on a curvaceous frame, then turns tart and citrusy on the finish. **85** —*J.C. (5/1/2006)*

Brancott 2004 Patutahi Estate Gewürztraminer (Hawke's Bay) $25. Based on a number of the wines, Gisborne's climate seems well-suited to Gewürz, in this case producing a rich, deep bottling that may not be as flamboyant as some but still displays textured flavors of pear, rose petal, and spice without any bitterness. **89** —*J.C. (5/1/2006)*

Brancott 1998 Patutahi Estate Gewürztraminer (Gisborne) $25. Smells great, with rose petals and lychees leading the way, then blends in some aromas reminiscent of Earl Grey tea (bergamot). Doesn't quite live up to expectations on the palate, where it could use more weight and a plusher texture, but the flavors sure are nice. **86** —*J.C. (5/1/2001)*

Brancott 1999 Reserve Merlot (Marlborough) $17. Toast and chocolate notes vie with bright cherry-berry fruit in this middleweight. Some herb aromas creep in, but they're dried herbs, not the offensive green variety, and they add complexity to this straightforward red. **86** —*J.C. (5/1/2001)*

Brancott 2004 Pinot Noir (Marlborough) $11. This, the largest winery in New Zealand, is capable of turning out some good-value offerings, evidenced by this light yet reasonably elegant Pinot Noir. Beets and cranberries pick up some mushroom and herb complexity. Finishes crisp. **84** —*J.C. (7/1/2006)*

Brancott 2003 Pinot Noir (Marlborough) $11. Starts with some caramelly, cola-like notes, then adds cherries and a hint of green. Develops sassafras-wintergreen-root beer flavors, all carried across the palate on a soft, fruity core. Good value. **85** *(12/31/2004)*

Brancott 2002 Pinot Noir (Marlborough) $11. A plump, corpulent wine with just enough tannin to give it structure in the face of relatively low acidity. It's lush and chocolaty, adding hints of vanilla and dried spices. Drink now. **86 Best Buy** —*J.C. (8/1/2004)*

Brancott 2000 Reserve Pinot Noir (Marlborough) $20. Seems a bit lighter than previous vintages, but it's still a smooth, supple, enjoyable Pinot. Suede and red cherries, chocolate and tart berries mark the aromas and flavors. Picks up some charred oak notes on the finish. **86** —*J.C. (8/1/2002)*

Brancott 1999 Reserve Pinot Noir (Marlborough) $17. Elegant and well-integrated, with the oaky touches of caramel and toast playing off black cherries and a faint stemminess that gives added grip to the faintly tannic finish. Nice wine at a nice price for Pinot. **88 Best Buy** —*J.C. (5/1/2001)*

Brancott 2003 Terraces Estate Pinot Noir (Marlborough) $25. Brancott's top-of-line Pinot boasts a sappy, creamy texture, combining herbal notes with bright cherry fruit, then adding cola and plum bass notes. It's an approachable, drink-now style, one that ends with a food-friendly, crisp finish. **88** —*J.C. (12/1/2005)*

Brancott 2002 Terraces Estate Pinot Noir (Marlborough) $22. A big step up from Brancott's basic Pinot Noir, this offers substantially more richness and concentration, a smoother, creamier mouthfeel, and more intense and complex flavors. Smoke, cola, and earth aromas give way to black cherries and vanilla, finishing with a subtle note of dried spice and tea leaves. **88** *(12/31/2004)*

Brancott 2005 Sauvignon Blanc (Marlborough) $11. Brancott's best-ever regular SB bottling boasts grassy, sweet-pea aromas but also plenty of nectarine and floral notes. It's plump and fleshy on the palate, adding pink grapefruit and herbal notes to the mix, then finishing with hints of green pepper and honey. **88 Best Buy** —*J.C. (7/1/2006)*

Brancott 2004 Sauvignon Blanc (Marlborough) $11. Filled with bright, fresh fruit, this is an easy-drinking introduction to NZ Sauvignon Blanc. Ripe passion fruit and pineapple flavors carry a hint of sweetness, balanced by tangy acids and an herbal note on the finish. **86 Best Buy** *(12/31/2004)*

Brancott 2003 Sauvignon Blanc (Marlborough) $11. Shows some sweaty notes, but also plenty of zippy, peppery fruit backed by ripe melon flavors. It's surprisingly weighty for an entry-level bottling, its slightly oily texture offset by a tangy finish. **86** —*J.C. (8/1/2004)*

Brancott 2001 Sauvignon Blanc (Marlborough) $13. Extremely dry lime and green pepper aromas don't really roll out the welcome mat. Nor are the lean, tangy green flavors fully up to par. However, served chilled in a less than formal setting, say a picnic, it should work well enough. There's ample citrus and zest to save the day. **85** *(8/1/2002)*

Brancott 2000 Sauvignon Blanc (Marlborough) $22. Provides a good jolt of pungent and aggressively green aromas (boxwood) balanced by sweet gooseberries and passion fruit. Representative of the "New Zealand" style of Sauvignon Blanc, this is a perfect introduction to the genre for new consumers. **86 Best Buy** —*J.C. (5/1/2001)*

Brancott 1999 Sauvignon Blanc (Marlborough) $24. This Wairu Valley wine's nose is like a patch of green beans in a vast field: distinctly legumey, but open and fresh, with a tinge of chalky soil. The palate has citrus, banana,, and mineral flavors and a chalky mouthfeel. It would be better if it didn't have the lemon-acid notes that start on the palate and end when the last drop goes down your throat. Finishes with herb, hay, and tangy tropical fruit. **84** —*D.T. (12/15/2001)*

Brancott 1998 Brancott Estate Sauvignon Blanc (Marlborough) $25. Hints of mint on the nose give added nuance to this unusual, almost honeyed-tasting Sauvignon Blanc. Oranges and vanilla-cream are complemented by toast notes from aging in French oak. **87** —*J.C. (5/1/2001)*

Brancott 2000 Brancott Estate ("B") Sauvignon Blanc (Marlborough) $30. The smell of canned mushy peas pours out of the glass and just won't release its iron-handed grip. That same intense vegetal character is present at all other points as well, from the thick palate to the murky finish. It doesn't have much going for it, but at least it's consistent. **83** *(8/1/2002)*

Brancott 2004 Reserve Sauvignon Blanc (Marlborough) $18. More pungent and powerful than the regular bottling, this wine shows more grass, more asparagus, and yet more ripe stone fruit flavors. Fuller and richer on the palate, with a hint of oiliness to its texture and a slightly peppery aspect to the grapefruity finish. **89** *(12/31/2004)*

Brancott 2002 Reserve Sauvignon Blanc (Marlborough) $18. Textbook Marlborough, with tart, mouth-watering flavors of gooseberries and limes, wrapped in a high-acid wine. Packs a punch in the mouth and finishes very dry and rich. May be too strongly flavored for some, but it's very good. **88** —*S.H. (1/1/2002)*

Brancott 2001 Reserve Sauvignon Blanc (Marlborough) $18. This restaurant favorite struts its stuff in the nose, providing an ample blast of pungent grapefruit, passion fruit and mint. The palate is mildly grassy, with yet more grapefruit along with touches of flint and stone. The finish is clean and proper, with citrus flavors flowing on a stream of vital acidity. **88** *(8/1/2002)*

Brancott 2000 Reserve Sauvignon Blanc (Marlborough) $15. Young and tight, this wine needs a few months to unwind. Still, you can taste the quality, from a delicate herbal note to the green-pea flavors and long, tart, lime-and-herb-accented finish. **88** —*J.C. (5/1/2001)*

BURINGS

Burings 2004 Pinot Noir (Martinborough) $NA. Blends cola and cherry in a medium-bodied format that turns a bit lean and astringent on the finish. **84** —*J.C. (12/1/2005)*

C.J. PASK

C.J. Pask 2002 Reserve Syrah (Hawke's Bay) $NA. Impressively dark in color, but shows more wood than fruit from start to finish. Toasty and

cedary on the nose, patially balanced by white pepper and modest cherry fruit. No known U.S. importer. **84** —*J.C. (5/1/2006)*

CADWALLADERS RIVERSIDE

Cadwalladers Riverside 2004 Chardonnay (Hawke's Bay) $15. Another citrus- and tropical fruit-laden Chardonnay from New Zealand. Pear and peach notes on the nose, along with hints of nut meat add complexity, but the alcohol shows through a bit on the finish. **85** —*J.C. (7/1/2005)*

Cadwalladers Riverside 2004 Sauvignon Blanc (Hawke's Bay) $15. Less vegetable and more stone fruit suggests a slightly warmer climate, or a later harvest than a typical Marlborough Sauvignon Blanc. Nectarine and lime flavors are medium-weight and tangy on the finish—a bit simple, but appealing. **86** —*J.C. (7/1/2005)*

CAIRNBRAE

Cairnbrae 2000 Chardonnay (Marlborough) $14. Melon and tropical fruit aromas and flavors appear early and linger delicately through the clean crsip finish. Despite overtones of buttered toast and vanilla, the fruit stays on top, focused, and fresh. The oak is in check, so it should prove versatile in food pairings. **86** —*J.C. (7/1/2002)*

Cairnbrae 1999 Chardonnay (Marlborough) $15. Honey, melon, pineapple, apricot, and vanilla are all prominent players on the nose of this offering. The fruit was obviously picked very ripe; add to that a caramel-vanilla suggestion of sweetness from American oak and the overall impression is almost of a dessert wine, without the sugar. **85** —*J.C. (5/1/2001)*

Cairnbrae 2001 Pinot Noir (Marlborough) $NA. This is an interesting wine that ultimately turns out a bit muddled and unclear. Toasty oak, chocolate and caramel on the nose and dark, plummy fruit on the palate are promising, but the finish turns sappy and greenish, with hints of roasted nuts. **84** —*J.C. (4/1/2004)*

Cairnbrae 2000 Old River Riesling (Marlborough) $12. Intriguing aromas of florists' greenery (ferns), mint, green apple, and pears whet the palate. The flavors are more subtle, ranging from Anjou to Chinese pears. Tart, lime-like flavors appear on the long finish. **87 Best Buy** —*J.C. (5/1/2001)*

Cairnbrae 1998 Sauvignon Blanc (Marlborough) $12. 87 —*S.H. (8/1/1999)*

Cairnbrae 2003 The Stones Sauvignon Blanc (Marlborough) $13. Smells of pineapple and grapefruit at first, laced with plenty of herbal nuances. But the flavors are solid, citrusy at the core, and garnished by riper melon notes. Racy throughout, finishing with zippy acids. **87** —*J.C. (4/1/2004)*

Cairnbrae 2001 The Stones Sauvignon Blanc (Marlborough) $15. Lime, mineral, and grass make up the pungent, pulsating bouquet. Apricots and peaches comprise the stone-fruit-dominated palate, which is touched up by a pinch of honey. There's a nice tang and snap to the finish, which offers a little white pepper just to make things interesting. **90 Editors' Choice** *(8/1/2002)*

Cairnbrae 1999 The Stones Sauvignon Blanc (Marlborough) $13. This "Savvy" boasts textbook aromas of passion fruit, gooseberries, green peas, and even a touch of mint. Supple and almost soft on the palate, it doesn't quite have the zing you expect but still manages to satisfy. **86** —*J.C. (5/1/2001)*

CANTERBURY HOUSE

Canterbury House 2000 Chardonnay (Waipara) $17. Crisp green-apple and grass aromas open this lean wine. A softer, almost candied pear and melon note, as well as brisk acidity, shows on the palate. Closes tangy and mineral-tinged, with medium-length. **84** —*M.M. (12/15/2001)*

Canterbury House 2000 Pinot Gris (Waipara) $14. Smells white peppery and oily—like canola oil. Flavors are honey and diesel oil, but it's not sweet, just thick and full-bodied. Finishes with some alcoholic warmth and peppery spice. **82** —*J.C. (8/1/2002)*

Canterbury House 1999 Pinot Noir (Waipara) $19. Almost translucent, with a mixed-spice nose that doesn't offer much fruit. It's got some strawberry and raspberry flavors, but it's also slightly sour. Milk chocolate shows up on the finish, which is otherwise overly oaky. Lacks polish. **82** —*M.S. (12/15/2001)*

Canterbury House 1999 Riesling (Waipara) $13. A full-bodied, slightly heavy style with a thick texture. Smells like warm baked apples, complete with cinnamon and clove accents; tastes similar, picking up some oily-diesely nuances. Despite the heft, finishes a bit short. **84** —*J.C.* *(8/1/2002)*

Canterbury House 2000 Sauvignon Blanc (Waipara) $14. Cooked green vegetables, particularly mushy peas, dominate the nose and just won't let go. In the mouth, some fruit tries to fight through that vegetal character, but it's a mighty struggle. In the end, the bad outweighs the good and the wine suffers for it. **82** *(1/1/2004)*

CAROLINE BAY

Caroline Bay 2000 Cabernet Sauvignon (Hawke's Bay) $20. The nose is an interesting blend of cocoa, dill, cassis, and lemon. Flavors pretty much follow suit, sneaking in some tobacco and cedar shadings before turning lean and lemony. The finish shows off a whack of dry, cedary French oak. Hard to know where this will be in five years—might dry out, might get interestingly complex. **85** —*J.C. (8/1/2002)*

Caroline Bay 2000 Chardonnay (Hawke's Bay) $16. An oaky style, yet one that doesn't seem heavy or overdone. Buttered apple and toast aromas set off cinnamon and cashew flavors and a long, spicy-nutty finish. **86** —*J.C. (7/1/2002)*

Caroline Bay 2003 Sauvignon Blanc (Marlborough) $18. Plump, rounded and a bit soft overall, with musky, ripe melon and stone fruits. A pleasant mouthful that lacks the zip and freshness of the very best examples. **86** —*J.C. (8/1/2004)*

Caroline Bay 2002 Sauvignon Blanc (Marlborough) $16. This is a softer, rounder style of Sauvignon Blanc than many Marlborough versions, with sweet pink grapefruit flavors creamily sweeping across the palate. Yet there are enough lively, zesty character and hints of pepper to provide varietal and regional identity. **88** —*J.C. (9/1/2003)*

Caroline Bay 2001 Sauvignon Blanc (Marlborough) $16. Pink grapefruit is most pronounced on the otherwise soft, sweet bouquet. The mouth is tangy, with green apple and crisp pear and green melon. In the mouth, there's a welcome creaminess, then a long citrusy finish that offers plenty of sweetness closes things out. **90 Editors' Choice** *(8/1/2002)*

CARRICK

Carrick 2003 Pinot Noir (Central Otago) $40. Bigger and more fruit-driven than the delicately styled '02, but also less complex. Shows some slightly roasted cherry notes and hints of caramel on the finish. Drink now. **87** —*J.C. (12/1/2005)*

Carrick 2002 Pinot Noir (Central Otago) $40. Delicately herbal on the nose, with dry, dusty scents of earth that accent pretty cherry aromas. Not a blockbuster, this is a more delicate, feminine style of wine from Central Otago. Finishes with a silky flourish. **89** —*J.C. (12/1/2005)*

Carrick 2001 Bannock Burn Pinot Noir (Central Otago) $40. This slightly rough-edged wine needs 2–3 years to round into shape. Right now, it shows some rustic, tree bark aromas alongside coffee and cocoa scents, while the cherry flavors are candied and intense. These elements carry the intensity needed for aging, and should come into greater harmony in time. **87** —*J.C. (9/1/2003)*

Carrick 2001 Bannockburn Riesling (Central Otago) $20. A light-weight but intensely flavored Riesling, with stony, fern-like and lime-ridden aromas. Elegantly intertwined lime and green apple flavors dominate the palate, finishing long and minerally. Just slightly off-dry. **90 Editors' Choice** —*J.C. (8/1/2003)*

CHANCELLOR ESTATES

Chancellor Estates 2000 Mt. Cass Road Chardonnay (Waipara) $17. A heavier style, seeming almost slightly oxidized in its ripe apple and honey flavors. Picks up some interesting mineral and sage notes along the way to a long, spicy finish. **84** —*J.C. (7/1/2002)*

Chancellor Estates 2000 Mt. Cass Road Pinot Noir (Waipara) $24. The delicate cherry-berry flavors of this light-weight Pinot can't quite stand up to the oaking it received—the result is a toasty, cedary wine with a slightly hollow midpalate. **83** —*J.C. (8/1/2002)*

Chancellor Estates 2000 Mt. Cass Road Riesling (Waipara) $13. Smells of vegetable oil and farm-fresh sweet corn still in the husk, but the flavors are more like what you expect from a Riesling: green apples and under-

ripe Asian pears. The finish is a bit metallic, but otherwise features fresh lime zest. **84** —*J.C. (8/1/2002)*

Chancellor Estates 2000 Mt. Cass Road Sauvignon Blanc (Waipara) $15. This is a typically snappy New Zealand Sauvignon featuring mildly vegetal aromas along with the required touch of cat pee and grapefruit. Bold lemon and tangerine flavors comprise the citrus palate, which leads into a tangy acid-driven finish full of lemon and grapefruit. Tart, juicy, and pleasant. **88** *(8/1/2002)*

CHARLES WIFFEN

Charles Wiffen 2000 Chardonnay (Marlborough) $15. Clean and refreshing are the operative words. With only three months aging in oak and partial malolactic fermentation, this light-weight Chard toes the line of balance nicely, even coming across as crisp. Honeydew and nectarine aromas dominate. Fresh green melon drives the long, dry finish. **88 Best Buy** —*M.S. (12/15/2001)*

Charles Wiffen 2000 Riesling (Marlborough) $12. Ripe peach and apricot aromas and a touch of honey are clear signals of the white stone fruit character of the wine. A little natural vanilla and some minerals grace the finish. The fruit here is reserved, and because of that it's sturdy more than it is spectacular. **85** —*M.S. (12/15/2001)*

Charles Wiffen 2001 Sauvignon Blanc (Marlborough) $30. Powerful lemon and lime flavors are pure and bright, flattering the palate with an assault of fruity ripeness. There's certainly a lot of acidity, to judge by the tingly feeling on the tongue, but the round, sweetish, honeyed texture softens this lush, seductive wine. **89** —*S.H. (11/15/2002)*

Charles Wiffen 2000 Sauvignon Blanc (Marlborough) $14. A light floral, hay, and fresh cut grass bouquet prefaces a palate with clover honey, citrus, mineral and fresh dill flavors, balanced by plenty of yellow fruit. It's medium-weight and angular, but classy, and finishes taut with lemon-slate flavors. **89** —*D.T. (12/15/2001)*

CLEARVIEW

Clearview 2004 Old Olive Block Bordeaux Blend (Hawke's Bay) $37. A Bordeaux-inspired blend of 46% Cabernet Sauvignon, 45% Merlot, 8% Cabernet Franc, and 1% Malbec, this is a firmly structured wine that seems meant to age. Dark coffee and plum aromas are garnished with a dash of vanilla, while the flavors add tobacco to the mix. Finishes crisp and somewhat tannic, so hold 2–3 years and see what develops. **87** —*J.C. (11/1/2006)*

Clearview 2004 Reserve Chardonnay (Hawke's Bay) $46. This is a full-bodied, lush, creamy Chardonnay, but it has something extra to recommend it—a long, mouthwatering finish. The aromas are toasty, but the oak is well integrated and softly frames rich melon, peach and citrus flavors, while secondary accents of butter-toasted nuts and vanilla add layers of complexity. **91** —*J.C. (11/1/2006)*

Clearview 2002 Reserve Chardonnay (Hawke's Bay) $42. Lovely Chard that should improve with a year or two of cellaring. Scents of smoke and roasted notes ease into flavors of grilled peaches, vanilla and toasted nuts, all tied together by bright acids that elongate the finish. **89** —*J.C. (8/1/2004)*

Clearview 2001 Reserve Chardonnay (Hawke's Bay) $45. Buttery and lactic, with big aromas of caramel-laced baked apples. It's sweet-tasting and laden with vanilla and dried spices, then turns tangy and citrusy on the finish, no doubt intended to balance the sensations of sweetness and butter. **83** —*J.C. (4/1/2004)*

Clearview 2005 Unwooded Chardonnay (Hawke's Bay) $28. As always, this is a rather big wine, with plump, melony fruit. Honey and smoky-minerally notes mark the nose, while the palate adds spicy complexity. Powerful and long on the finish. **90 Editors' Choice** —*J.C. (11/1/2006)*

Clearview 2004 Unwooded Chardonnay (Hawke's Bay) $27. This is a big, round and fully ripe wine, weighing in at more than 14% alcohol, but aside from the wine's size and weight the alcohol is well concealed by the wealth of ripe melon fruit. Soft and easy on the finish. **87** —*J.C. (7/1/2006)*

NEW ZEALAND

NEW ZEALAND

CLIFFORD BAY ESTATE

Clifford Bay Estate 2004 Single Vineyard Pinot Noir (Marlborough) $NA. Tart and juicy, with understated cherry and herb aromas and flavors. Solid Marlborough Pinot that's a bit racier than typical. **85** —*J.C. (12/1/2005)*

CLOS MARGUERITE

Clos Marguerite 2005 Sauvignon Blanc (Marlborough) $19. Fairly aggressive on the nose, with pungently grassy aromas that lead into a fresh, citrusy palate. Light in body, there's a dusty chalkiness to the mouthfeel and a tart, zesty finish. **86** —*J.C. (9/1/2006)*

Clos Marguerite 2003 Sauvignon Blanc (Marlborough) $17. An interesting rendition of Marlborough Sauvignon Blanc that comes close, but doesn't quite cross the line into vegetal. Tart, almost sour, passion fruit flavors are joined by piquant citrus and pungent earth notes. **86** —*J.C. (7/1/2005)*

CLOUDY BAY

Cloudy Bay 2004 Chardonnay (Marlborough) $29. Cloudy Bay is better known for its Sauvignon Blanc, but their Chardonnay is dependably good as well. This vintage seems a little lighter than previous efforts, but it still offers flavorful notes of cashew butter atop a base of pineapple and lemon fruit. **87** —*J.C. (9/1/2006)*

Cloudy Bay 2003 Chardonnay (Marlborough) $28. Smoky on the nose, with some pineapple and citrus notes, but this is not an aroma-driven wine. It's more about the plump, custardy texture and gentle nut, white peach and pineapple flavors. Finishes on a tangy citrus note. **89** *(12/15/2005)*

Cloudy Bay 2002 Chardonnay (Marlborough) $29. This well-balanced example of cool-climate Chard features aromas of buttered cashews balanced by ample flavors of pear and melon. It's restrained and elegant, ending on lingering notes of smoke and nuts. **88** —*J.C. (8/1/2004)*

Cloudy Bay 1999 Chardonnay (Marlborough) $28. Ripe white stone fruits dominate, with just hints of oak and butter. Clean and crisp, elegant and harmonious; pears and nectarines emerge on the long finish. **89** —*J.C. (5/1/2001)*

Cloudy Bay 2004 Pinot Noir (Marlborough) $30. The result of a difficult vintage, CB's 2004 Pinot Noir is an attractive, pretty wine. Scents of mushroom, cinnamon and black cherry lead the way, followed by a supple mouthfeel and cedary flavors. It seems a bit oakier and less distinctive than either of the previous two vintages. **86** —*J.C. (9/1/2006)*

Cloudy Bay 2003 Pinot Noir (Marlborough) $29. With a core fashioned from older clonal material, this wine doesn't have quite the same vibrancy and fruit of some flashier counterparts. What it does have is some wonderful underbrushy complexity: earth, mushrooms, bracken, and spice, balanced by just enough cola and cherry fruit. Finishes wiry and a bit herbal. **88** *(12/15/2005)*

Cloudy Bay 2002 Pinot Noir (Marlborough) $29. Not a fruit bomb at all, featuring scents of cinnamon, clove, glove leather,, and herbs wrapped around a core of black cherries and cola. Amply complex, yet plump and easy to drink. Definitely user friendly. **88** —*J.C. (8/1/2004)*

Cloudy Bay 2005 Sauvignon Blanc (Marlborough) $25. This is the highest this benchmark wine has ever scored with our tasters, from what is beginning to look like an excellent year for Marlborough Sauvignon Blanc. It's still in an early estery phase right now, marked by honeyed tropical fruits, nectarines, and grapefruit, but you can sense the herbal-jalapeño flavors lurking in the background. Rich and powerful on the palate, long on the finish, with this wine, Cloudy Bay is on top of its game. **91** *(12/15/2005)*

Cloudy Bay 2004 Sauvignon Blanc (Marlborough) $26. Fine New Zealand Sauvignon, with passion fruit and a whole lot of snappy green aromas ranging from scallion and celery to green pepper and asparagus. But this isn't one of those green meanies; it has loud tropical fruit and plenty of peach and nectarine to offer. Long on the finish and a good bet with food. **89** *(7/1/2005)*

Cloudy Bay 2003 Sauvignon Blanc (Marlborough) $29. Marlborough's standard bearer is always reliable, even if it no longer stands far above the pack. The 2003 is a worthy effort, combining grassy, herbal notes with a core of grapefruit and gooseberry flavors. A safe, solid choice, with enough weight in the mouth to pair with a variety of foods. **88** —*J.C. (8/1/2004)*

Cloudy Bay 2001 Sauvignon Blanc (Marlborough) $22. Round and fruity, with aromas of ginger, pineapple, and mango. This is one of the most popular SBs in the world, and it's easy to see why. It's loaded with sweet, inoffensive citrus fruit and it comes with a soft, plush mouthfeel that's sure to win people over. **89** *(8/1/2002)*

Cloudy Bay 2000 Sauvignon Blanc (Marlborough) $24. The wine that made Marlborough famous continues to impress, vintage after vintage. Ripe gooseberries and a hint of grapefruit flow through the broad mid-palate into a long, lime-tinged finish. Rich enough to pair with sauced fish dishes, yet bright enough to go with simpler preparations as well. **90 Editors' Choice** —*J.C. (5/1/2001)*

Cloudy Bay 2002 Te Koko Sauvignon Blanc (Marlborough) $35. Championed by former winemaker James Healy, Te Koko is an attempt to take Marlborough Sauvignon in a very different stylistic direction. Barrel fermented with indigenous yeasts, it offers sweaty-musky scents intermingled with honey, melon, and quince. Rich and oily, it coats the palate with slightly nutty flavors. This is unique stuff, well worth trying. **90** *(12/15/2005)*

COOPERS CREEK

Coopers Creek 1998 Reserve Cabernet Sauvignon-Merlot (Hawke's Bay) $24. Rich cassis aromas also carry a leafy, tobacco-like note. Then some chocolate emerges on the palate, along with dried herbs. Despite this wine's Cabernet content, it's ready to drink now. **88** —*J.C. (5/1/2001)*

Coopers Creek 1998 Swamp Reserve Chardonnay (Hawke's Bay) $26. Toasty, with menthol overtones from French oak (50% new), but the new wood is well-balanced by intensely musky pear fruit. The long finish shows off complex nuances of oatmeal, lees, and hazelnuts. **91** —*J.C. (5/1/2001)*

Coopers Creek 1998 Merlot (Hawke's Bay) $14. Oregano and thyme notes that add complexity without becoming overwhelming mark the bright cherry fruit in this medium-weight wine. For current consumption. **86** —*J.C. (5/1/2001)*

Coopers Creek 1998 Riesling (Hawke's Bay) $9. 88 Best Buy —*S.H. (8/1/1999)*

Coopers Creek 2000 Riesling (Hawke's Bay) $12. Hawkes Bay's slighter warmer temperatures have given this N.Z. Riesling a softer, more approachable nature than many of its compatriots. With its barely perceptible residual sugar, it almost tastes "fuzzy" like peach or apricot skins, but with a core of pear and spice flavors. **87 Best Buy** —*J.C. (5/1/2001)*

Coopers Creek 1997 Sauvignon Blanc (Marlborough) $11. 87 —*S.H. (8/1/1999)*

Coopers Creek 2005 Sauvignon Blanc (Marlborough) $15. Lean and tart, this wine shows notes of green pepper, herb and passion fruit at the core. Finishes crisp and citrusy, marrying lime and grapefruit. **87** —*J.C. (5/1/2006)*

Coopers Creek 2000 Sauvignon Blanc (Marlborough) $10. Tart and crisp, this is a fairly "green" version, boasting plenty of gooseberry and jalapeño-pepper aromas and flavors. Residual sugar is just below the typical detection threshold of 5g/L; there's enough to add weight without making the wine seem sweet. **86** —*J.C. (5/1/2001)*

Coopers Creek 2001 Reserve Sauvignon Blanc (Marlborough) $15. A nice, all-around sipping wine. Strikes a middle path, with well-ripened apple and citrus fruit flavors and crisp acidity, and just a touch of balancing sweetness. This versatile wine is wonderful now in its expressive youth. **88** —*S.H. (11/15/2002)*

Coopers Creek 1999 Reserve Sauvignon Blanc (Marlborough) $18. Steer clear of this one if you like your Sauvignons done in stainless. This one is 100% barrel fermented, yielding some toasty, smoky aromas that blend well with the forceful tropical fruit flavors. There's guava and pineapple, smoke and menthol on the long finish. **90** —*J.C. (5/1/2001)*

CORBANS

Corbans 1998 Winemaker's Cottage Block Bordeaux Blend (Hawke's Bay) $22. Corbans' top-of-the-line red is a big wine in the warm '98 vintage, filled with rich cassis and black cherry fruit tinged with licorice and graham cracker crumbs. Firm tannins on the finish are joined by intricate dried-herb shadings. **90 Editor's Choice** —*J.C. (5/1/2001)*

Corbans 1998 Winemaker's Private Bin Bordeaux Blend (Hawke's Bay) $20. Juicy, briary blackberry fruit is spiced up by hints of mint, smoke, chocolate, and cedar. Tannins are ripe and soft, making this approachable right now. **88** —*J.C. (5/1/2001)*

Corbans 1999 Winemaker's Private Bin Chardonnay (Gisborne) $18. Extremely nutty and vanilla-filled aromas lead into a palate that reveals traces of mixed tropical fruits buried under an avalanche of toasty oak. The fruit shows even more on the juicy finish, making me think this wine will be better in another six months. **86** —*J.C. (5/1/2001)*

Corbans 1999 Winemaker's Selection Chardonnay (East Coast) $13. A soft, lush mouthful of baked apples, layered with dark toast and dried spices. Cinnamon and clove notes add to the allusion. Soft and buttery. **85** —*J.C. (5/1/2001)*

Corbans 1999 Winemaker's Selection Merlot (East Coast) $13. Black cherries, dried herbs, and a hint of toast make for a flavorful mouthful. Fleshy without being soft, thanks to vibrant acidity that will cut through rich meat dishes. No tannins to speak of, so there's no need to wait before popping the cork on this one. **87** —*J.C. (5/1/2001)*

Corbans 1999 Winemaker's Private Bin Sauvignon Blanc (Marlborough) $18. Pleasant enough, but the lime and grapefruit flavors are a bit dilute. Lacks intensity overall; well-chilled, the mild flavors would make a nice counterpoint to strongly flavored foods. **83** —*J.C. (5/1/2001)*

Corbans 1999 Winemaker's Selection Sauvignon Blanc (Marlborough) $13. The Corbans house style seems to de-emphasize the ultra-pungent elements of Sauvignon Blanc, focusing instead on grapefruit and, in this case, white nectarine. It's a delicate wine that goes down easy. **85** —*J.C. (5/1/2001)*

COTTIER

Cottier 2005 Trillo Sauvignon Blanc (Wairarapa) $20. Odd stuff, with honeyed sweet green pea aromas and flavors suggestive of older New Zealand Sauvignon, turning lemony on the finish. **81** —*J.C. (11/1/2006)*

COURTNEY'S POST

Courtney's Post 2002 Sauvignon Blanc (Marlborough) $16. Starts off with cat pee and asparagus, but also some honey-laced grapefruit. Medium-weight, with more grapefruit on the finish. A bit green, but o.k. **84** —*J.C. (4/1/2004)*

CRAGGY RANGE

Craggy Range 2004 Sophia Gimblett Gravels Bordeaux Blend (Hawke's Bay) $60. Shows all the intensity you could want from a New Zealand Merlot (there's just 7% Cab Franc and 1% Cab Sauvignon in the blend), but seems to be in a bit of an awkward stage right now. Back in June it showed great finesse and elegance to go with its power, but tasted again in September it seems chunkier, with some rough edges of wood and alcohol poking out. Try in 2009. **90** —*J.C. (12/15/2006)*

Craggy Range 2002 Sophia Gimblett Gravels Bordeaux Blend (Hawke's Bay) $55. Roughly two-thirds Merlot and one-third Cabernet Franc, this dense, plummy wine is New World all the way, with incredibly ripe fruit that approaches chocolate fudge wedded to sexy hints of coconut and vanilla. Yet the wine is balanced and structured, with lush, chewy tannins that demand a couple of years' cellaring. Tannic on the finish, but the fruit shines through. **92** —*J.C. (7/1/2005)*

Craggy Range 2002 Les Beaux Cailloux Chardonnay (Hawke's Bay) $50. A full-bodied Chard (14.9% alcohol), but one that boasts a lush softness, delivering layers of toast, cinnamon and lusciously ripe peaches. Has a mealy, leesy side to its character, and a hint of butter on the finish. Goes down easy, without a trace of heat. **89** —*J.C. (7/1/2005)*

Craggy Range 2004 Les Beaux Cailloux Gimblett Gravels Chardonnay (Hawke's Bay) $60. Craggy's Chardonnay is a big boy, with fully ripe fruit (14.5% alcohol) that's framed by ample oak. Yet it shows some restraint as well, with aromas of pencil shavings and minerals that nicely complement pear and melon fruit. With a richly textured, almost gravelly mouthfeel, the wine shows good depth and richness. The overall impression is of a wine that's a bit oaky now, but should integrate nicely in a another 12 months or so. **89** —*J.C. (12/15/2006)*

Craggy Range 2000 Seven Poplars Vineyard Chardonnay (Hawke's Bay) $NA. A moderately disappointing effort from winemaker Steve Smith, MW. It starts off with promise, with buttery, toasty, reserve-style aromas, then picks up pear and tropical fruit notes. So far, so good. But it doesn't have the depth to rate any higher. **85** —*J.C. (11/15/2002)*

Craggy Range 2003 Gimblett Gravels Vineyard Merlot (Hawke's Bay) $35. Firmly structured and dominated for the moment by its veneer of oak, this Merlot appears in need of 1-2 years of bottle age prior to consumption. There's solid black cherry fruit underneath, tinged with dried herbs and an anise note that just needs time to emerge. **86** —*J.C. (7/1/2006)*

Craggy Range 2002 Gimblett Gravels Vineyard Merlot (Hawke's Bay) $35. Starts off promising, with scents of blackberries, vanilla, and graham crackers, but does not live up to that promise on the palate. It's big, black, and softly tannic, with coffee and vanilla shadings but not that much fruit or minerality. **86** —*J.C. (8/1/2004)*

Craggy Range 1999 Seven Poplars Vineyard Merlot (Hawke's Bay) $NA. A big, mouth-filling Merlot, loaded with mocha, black cherries, and dried herbs and picking up anise and vanilla notes on the finish. The mouthfeel is special, leaving a creamy coating of tannins behind as the flavors do a slow, delicate fade. Food pairing might be problematic in its youthful baby fat—it's probably best alone or with cheese now, or age it a few years and serve with herb-crusted roasts. **90** —*J.C. (8/1/2002)*

Craggy Range 2003 Te Muna Block 1 Doug Wisor Memorial Pinot Noir (Martinborough Terrace) $60. Full-bodied, yet soft and enveloping, this silky-smooth wine seduces with its lush mouthfeel and ripe, plummy fruit, then layers on spice and savory complexities including hints of coffee, game, cola and earth. Just 42 cases imported. **93** —*J.C. (12/1/2005)*

Craggy Range 2004 Te Muna Road Vineyard Pinot Noir (Martinborough) $40. Full-bodied but supple, with plenty of black cherry and plum fruit accented by touches of cola and caramel. Soft tannins make this approachable now, while dusty floral notes add another layer of complexity. **89** —*J.C. (9/1/2006)*

Craggy Range 2003 Te Muna Road Vineyard Pinot Noir (Martinborough) $40. Intriguingly complex aromas of plum, herb, and game don't quite follow through on the palate, where the fruit becomes more dominant, delivering super ripe blackberry flavors. Mouthfeel is round and soft but not unstructured; drink now or hold 2–3 years. **88** —*J.C. (12/1/2005)*

Craggy Range 2001 Old Renwick Vineyard Sauvignon Blanc (Marlborough) $17. Citrus and gooseberry define the all-fruit nose. In the mouth, you'll encounter the full allotment of cantaloupe, citrus, and green herbs, particularly basil. The tangy finish is like grapefruit sorbet after a nice meal; it cleanses the palate, leaving no residue at all. It's refined, racy, and tips the scale at just the right weight. **90 Editors' Choice** *(8/1/2002)*

Craggy Range 2005 Te Muna Road Vineyard Sauvignon Blanc (Martinborough) $22. Shows wonderfully ripe, round character in its peach and tangerine aromas and flavors, yet also offers good complexity and length. There's a smoky, fumé note to the aromas and lingering citrus notes on the finish. **90 Editors' Choice** —*J.C. (9/1/2006)*

Craggy Range 2004 Te Muna Road Vineyard Sauvignon Blanc (Martinborough) $20. Intense stuff; hits on the nose like a bomb packed with fresh green veggies and vibrant passion fruit, mango, and stone fruits. Slides across the palate with ease courtesy of prime acidity. Tastes much like it smells, with jolting flavors of gooseberry, pineapple, and orange. **90 Editors' Choice** *(7/1/2005)*

Craggy Range 2003 Te Muna Road Vineyard Sauvignon Blanc (Martinborough) $18. This is a full, ripe style of Sauvignon Blanc, one that layers generous peach and nectarine flavors over a citrusy core. There's a hint of honeyed ripeness, and the finish is refreshingly zingy without being overly acidic. Beautifully balanced. **90 Editors' Choice** —*J.C. (4/1/2004)*

NEW ZEALAND

Craggy Range 2002 Le Sol Syrah (Hawke's Bay) $60. Major-league Syrah from New Zealand? You bet. Tips the scales at 15.4% alcohol, yet never seems hot. Instead, you get a wonderfully balanced wine loaded with cassis and blackberry fruit, but also notes of coffee and ground pepper. Chewy tannins on the finish suggest it could age, but the wine is soft enough that there's no need to wait. **92** —*J.C. (7/1/2005)*

CROSSROADS

Crossroads 2002 RGF Bordeaux Blend (Hawke's Bay) $30. Crossroads' top-of-the-line red delivers really good fruit—notably black cherries—garnished with vanilla and toast from new oak. Could use a richer mouthfeel, but offers nice flavors before turning a bit tart on the finish. **87** —*J.C. (5/1/2006)*

Crossroads 2004 Chardonnay (Hawke's Bay) $17. This is 100% barrel-fermented, which has left its mark on the wine. There's some crisp apple and citrus fruit flavors, but toast and butter notes play the starring role. It's a well-made, New World, oaky Chardonnay. **86** —*J.C. (5/1/2006)*

Crossroads 2005 Gewürztraminer (Hawke's Bay) $NA. Broad and soft in the mouth (there's nearly 3% residual sugar), this wine features plenty of pear and peach fruit, without much of the intriguing spice of the variety. **85** —*J.C. (5/1/2006)*

Crossroads 2003 Merlot-Cabernet Sauvignon (Hawke's Bay) $NA. Shows flashes of beauty on the nose, combining vanilla barrel notes with herbs and black cherries. Light and herbal on the palate, this blend of Merlot and Cabernet Sauvignon seems a bit like a Loire Cabernet Franc, without the minerality. **85** —*J.C. (5/1/2006)*

Crossroads 2005 Destination Series Sauvignon Blanc (Marlborough) $14. Simple and fruity, with grapefruit and passion fruit flavors leading the way. Picks up hints of green pepper on the finish. **85** —*J.C. (5/1/2006)*

Crossroads 2004 Destination Series Sauvignon Blanc (Marlborough) $14. This Hawke's Bay winery has turned a credible example of Marlborough Sauvignon Blanc. Medium-weight, likely fattened up by a hint of residual sugar, but the flavors are sure: celery leaf and bell pepper joined by grapefruit and red berries. Tart and tangy on the finish. **85** —*J.C. (7/1/2005)*

DANIEL SCHUSTER

Daniel Schuster 2002 Selection Chardonnay (Waipara) $29. Not your typical New Zealand Chardonnay, this wine starts off with an odd, feral note, then shows lean and minerally on the palate, with subtle apple and peach fruit and a crisp finish. Aged in large oak puncheons. **87** —*J.C. (5/1/2006)*

Daniel Schuster 2003 Pinot Noir (Waipara) $27. Restrained floral aromas (violets) mark the nose, then this wine adds lush black cherry flavors allied to wiry strength. Silky, then builds to a richer, briary finish. Nicely balanced. **89** —*J.C. (12/1/2005)*

Daniel Schuster 2002 Omihi Hills Vineyard Selection Pinot Noir (Waipara) $30. Schuster's top wine comes from a single estate vineyard planted 20 years ago—ancient by New Zealand standards. Aromas are floral, layered over earthier notes of mushroom and sous bois, then flavors add black cherries to the mix. Still firm enough to warrant cellaring. Drink 2006–2012. **90** —*J.C. (12/1/2005)*

Daniel Schuster 2004 Twin Vineyards Pinot Noir (Waipara) $18. While only light ruby in color, this wine doesn't lack for flavor, showing plenty of ripe cherry fruit. It's a bit simple, but it offers a pleasingly silky mouthful of Pinot Noir. Seems like a perfect match for salmon. **87** —*J.C. (12/1/2005)*

Daniel Schuster 2004 Riesling (Waipara) $NA. A bit heavy for Riesling, with pretty pear and peach aromas but a broad, soft mouthfeel and a touch of bitterness on the finish. Best served well-chilled to help pull it together. **85** —*J.C. (5/1/2006)*

Daniel Schuster 2004 Hull Family Vineyard Late Harvest Riesling (Waipara) $30. Rich and sweetly peachy, with rather low acidity but pleasant, succulent sweetness. Shows some slightly bitter notes on the finish, or it would have scored higher. **87** —*J.C. (5/1/2006)*

DASHWOOD

Dashwood 2005 Sauvignon Blanc (Marlborough) $15. Vavsour's entry-level brand goes by the name of Dashwood, and offers a light, crisp introduction to NZ Sauvignon Blanc. Aggressively herbal on the nose at first, it tones down to yield grassy citrusy flavors and a focused finish. **85** —*J.C. (9/1/2006)*

Dashwood 2001 Sauvignon Blanc (Marlborough) $NA. This crisp, zingy Sauvignon Blanc displays classic aromas and flavors of green apple, lime peel, and gooseberry. It's a food-friendly wine whose tart acidity will support a wide range of poultry, cheeses, and grilled veggies. The pretty finish is long and spicy. **88** —*S.H. (11/15/2002)*

DAVIS FAMILY

Davis Family 2002 Gusto Sauvignon Blanc (Marlborough) $18. For fans of extreme pungency only. There's some grapefruit, but also large amounts of asparagus and hints of cat pee. Finishes tart, but not terribly fresh—after all, it is a 2002. Why is Russian River producer Davis Family Vineyards bringing this stuff in? **83** —*J.C. (7/1/2005)*

DELTA VINEYARD

Delta Vineyard 2005 Pinot Noir (Marlborough) $19. An excellent value in Pinot Noir, this wine is made by Matt Thomson, also chief winemaker for Saint Clair. It's dark and beefy in color, with brooding black cherry fruit on the nose that freshens a bit on the palate, adding beet notes and subtle shadings of herb and spice. Nicely balanced, with a long, silky finish. **89** —*J.C. (9/1/2006)*

Delta Vineyard 2005 Hatter's Hill Pinot Noir (Marlborough) $29. This is a full-bodied, supple rendition of Marlborough Pinot Noir, boasting smoky, slightly herbal-peppery scents and bold cherry and plum fruit. There's a suggestion of sassafras or cola as well, which gives this wine an almost Californian flavor. Long and velvety on the finish. **90 Editors' Choice** —*J.C. (11/1/2006)*

DISCOVERY

Discovery 2005 Sauvignon Blanc (Marlborough) $15. A brand-new wine from importer George Galey, this debut Sauvignon blends fruit from the Awatere and Wairau valleys under the watchful eye of Vavasour winemaker Glenn Thomas to make a mouth-filling wine loaded with gooseberry and pink grapefruit flavors. Drier than many NZ Sauvignons, it picks up intriguing hints of tangerine, musk, and spice on the finish. **88** —*J.C. (9/1/2006)*

DOMAINE GEORGES MICHEL

Domaine Georges Michel 2004 Golden Mile Chardonnay (Marlborough) $23. This is a tropical fruit salad sort of Chardonnay, the kind that will go down easy ice cold on a warm summer day. Fruit ranges from banana to peach and pear, on through to bright citrus notes. **85** —*J.C. (9/1/2006)*

Domaine Georges Michel 2000 Golden Mile Chardonnay (Marlborough) $16. Toasty and rich, this is the best of this estate's recent bottlings, offering up creamy oak and ripe tropical fruits in a plump, user-friendly format. Given its late arrival in this market, drink up over the next six months or so, before the fruit begins to fade. **88** —*J.C. (9/1/2003)*

Domaine Georges Michel 2001 Golden Mile Pinot Noir (Marlborough) $25. Nice wine—if you're a beaver. Dry cedar and toast overwhelms the modest fruit. **82** —*J.C. (9/1/2003)*

Domaine Georges Michel 2005 Golden Mile Sauvignon Blanc (Marlborough) $18. This tightly wound Sauvignon needs time to unfurl. Tasted just after bottling, it offers little more than hints of peaches and lees, but you can sense the potential within. Finishes long and lean, with grapefruity overtones. Try it in summer '06, but it might even improve for a year beyond that. **89** —*J.C. (5/1/2006)*

Domaine Georges Michel 2002 Golden Mile Sauvignon Blanc (Marlborough) $15. Herbal, bordering on vegetal, yet rich and viscous in the mouth thanks to high alcohol and a dash of residual sugar. **83** —*J.C. (9/1/2003)*

NEW ZEALAND

DRY GULLY

Dry Gully 2001 Alexandra Pinot Noir (Central Otago) $35. Reasonably fruity, but lean, with tart berry flavors underscored by toasty oak. Finishes tart, with cranberry and cinnamon notes. **86** —*J.C. (9/1/2003)*

DRY RIVER

Dry River 2004 Chardonnay (Martinborough) $45. Toasty and mealy on the nose, but those characters are well-balanced by honeyed peach and citrus scents. Tasted over two days, on the first it seemed quite open and welcoming, lush and richly textured, while on the second it had closed down a bit and seemed tighter and more citrusy. Finishes long, with marked smoky notes. **92** —*J.C. (11/1/2006)*

Dry River 1999 Pinot Gris (New Zealand) $NA. A luscious wine with considerable residual sugar that manages to stay balanced because of its healthy acid levels. The rich pear and citrus flavors are thick in texture. Stylistically, this is reminiscent of Zind-Humbrecht's vieilles vignes bottling from Alsace. **90** —*J.C. (5/1/2001)*

Dry River 2004 Pinot Noir (Martinborough) $NA. This, one of New Zealand's cult wines, should retail for about $85 when it hits a select few retailers' shelves this fall. Although not perhaps the strongest vintage in Martinborough, the 2004 Dry River Pinot Noir features incredibly kaleidoscopic forward fruit that ranges from cherry to plum to mixed berries and back again. It's lush and round, yet still structured to age, with a long, silky finish. **92** —*J.C. (11/1/2006)*

Dry River 1999 Amaranth Pinot Noir (Martinborough) $NA. A mild disappointment from one of New Zealand's storied wineries, the 1999 Pinot Noir seems a touch over-ripe, with aromas and flavors of black cherries and plum pudding. A touch of alcoholic warmth shows up on the finish. **87** —*J.C. (11/1/2006)*

Dry River 2000 Arapoff Syrah (Martinborough) $NA. Boasts a flamboyant bouquet of blackberries and black pepper upon opening, then settles down into a medium-bodied wine with nice density and flavor persistence. There's no question that it's well-balanced and has a lovely nose, but this is not a great wine, merely very good. **88** —*J.C. (11/1/2006)*

DRYLANDS

Drylands 2004 Pinot Noir (Marlborough) $14. Fairly priced, this entry-level New Zealand Pinot offers herbal and black cherry aromas and flavors. It's a bit simple and fruity, but finishes clean, with crisp acids. **86** —*J.C. (12/1/2005)*

Drylands 2005 Sauvignon Blanc (Marlborough) $16. This brand's Sauvignon is from siltier, Rapaura soils, according to winemaker Alistair McIntosh. It's pungent and seaty, with hints of green bell pepper. There's a big, round mouthfeel, but the flavors are green and herbal. **87** *(3/1/2006)*

Drylands 2001 Winemakers Reserve Sauvignon Blanc (Marlborough) $19. Rich and creamy, a fat wine with considerable body. The flavors are strong and clean, of lemons, limes, peaches, and those fabled gooseberries. Feels limpid and sweet on the palate, like mountain stream water. **90** —*S.H. (11/15/2002)*

DRYSTONE

Drystone 2003 Pinot Noir (Central Otago) $30. Supple, silky, and lush on the palate, with complex aromas and flavors of cola, cherries and peppery-minty herbs, like wintergreen and sassafras. There's a dusting of cinnamon and clove as well, and a long, graceful finish. **90** —*J.C. (12/1/2005)*

DYED-IN-THE-WOOL

Dyed-In-The-Wool 2005 Ram's Reserve Pinot Noir (Marlborough) $16. Lighter than most Marlborough 2005 Pinot Noirs, but this still packs plenty of flavor. It's a snappy, fresh Pinot with slightly peppery notes that call to mind pepper-dusted cherries. Finishes crisp and clean. **84** —*J.C. (12/15/2006)*

Dyed-In-The-Wool 2003 Ram's Reserve Pinot Noir (Marlborough) $20. Herbs and pie cherries form the base flavors for this modestly priced reserve bottling. Full-bodied, with soft tannins, yet turns crisp and tangy on the finish. **85** —*J.C. (12/1/2005)*

Dyed-In-The-Wool 2002 Ram's Reserve Pinot Noir (Marlborough) $20. Solid NZ Pinot, with full, ripe fruit that's partially obscured by heavy chocolate and coffee-scented oak. There are cola and plum flavors on the modest finish. **86** —*J.C. (4/1/2004)*

Dyed-In-The-Wool 2003 Unchangeable Pinot Noir (Canterbury) $14. Light in color and already showing some disturbing bricking at the rim, this Pinot is rather light-bodied, with dusty, earthy scents and flavors of cherries, herbs, and crushed pepper. Finishes with crisp acidity. **83** —*J.C. (12/1/2005)*

Dyed-In-The-Wool 2002 Unchangeable Pinot Noir (Canterbury) $14. Said to be from the oldest commercial vines in New Zealand, this shows lovely aromatics of sour cherries, sous bois, and black pepper, but while the palate is lush and soft, it lacks the same appeal and complexity. Finishes with notes of coffee and burnt caramel. Drink now. **87 Best Buy** —*J.C. (8/1/2004)*

Dyed-In-The-Wool 2005 Sauvignon Blanc (Marlborough) $10. This consistent value performer is made specially for the U.S. importer by a winery whose "name" wine is imported by someone else. Too confusing? Try this: Winery A makes wine under the Winery A label and sells it for a premium price through Importer A. Then, since it has additional wine, it bottles more under Label B and sells that through Importer B. (No, I'm not going to spill the grapes and tell you the name of the winery in question.) A slightly musky scent imparts an exotic note to the passion fruit aromas, while the grapefruity notes on the palate are pleasantly plump before turning a bit chalky on the finish. **86 Best Buy** —*J.C. (11/1/2006)*

Dyed-In-The-Wool 2001 Estate Grown Unchangable Sauvignon Blanc (Marlborough) $12. Ripe melon and passion fruit aromas and flavors blend in hints of green pepper—just enough to give it complexity without becoming objectionable. Turns a bit narrow and grapefruity on the moderately long finish. **87 Best Buy** —*J.C. (9/1/2003)*

Dyed-In-The-Wool 2003 Unchangeable Sauvignon Blanc (Marlborough) $12. Grassy notes are nicely balanced by stone fruit and melon in this medium-weight wine that offers good length. A grapefruity tang on the finish gives it a refreshing feel. **87 Best Buy** —*J.C. (8/1/2004)*

Dyed-In-The-Wool 2002 Unchangeable Sauvignon Blanc (Marlborough) $13. Starts off with modest passion fruit and grapefruit scents that deepen on the palate into stone fruit flavors. Finishes on a tangy note, with lemons and unripe peaches vying for the lead. **85** —*J.C. (4/1/2004)*

ELSTREE

Elstree 1998 Reserve Riesling (Marlborough) $20. **90** —*S.H. (8/1/1999)*

Elstree 1998 Reserve Sauvignon Blanc (Marlborough) $19. **87** —*S.H. (8/1/1999)*

ESCARPMENT

Escarpment 2004 Pinot Gris (Martinborough) $30. Spicy, with muted apple and pineapple scents on the nose, but this wine is weighty and rich on the palate. Broad and mouth-filling, with a hint of bitter nut skin on the finish. A textural wine, more than a flavorful one, but enjoyable. **88** —*J.C. (2/1/2006)*

Escarpment 2002 Station Bush Vineyard Pinot Gris (Martinborough) $31. Viscous, mouth-coating flavors of honey and bitter almond are pleasing and food-friendly—try with salmon or other rich fish. A slight bitterness on the finish is distracting when tasted alone. **84** —*J.C. (8/1/2004)*

Escarpment 2001 Station Bush Vineyard Pinot Gris (Martinborough) $23. This wine, from a much-hyped enterprise led by winemaker Larry McKenna (formerly of Martinborough Vineyard), was somewhat disappointing. The delicate nuances of Pinot Gris are swept away by a tidal wave of oak—yummy-tasting French oak—but oak nonetheless. **85** —*J.C. (9/1/2003)*

Escarpment 2004 Pinot Noir (Martinborough) $35. Winemaker Larry McKenna's Pinots tend to be more muscular and ageworthy than this example, perhaps the result of vintage conditions rather than any stylistic change. In any event, it's a pretty, lighter-styled wine, with cherry fruit flavors enhanced by chocolate, caramel, and touches of celery seed and spice. Silky and delicate in the mouth, but the flavors fade a little too quickly on the finish. **86** —*J.C. (9/1/2006)*

NEW ZEALAND

Escarpment 2003 Pinot Noir (Martinborough) $45. Starts with a dusty, savory, spicy bouquet, then unfurls ripe black cherry flavors on the palate. Shows some slightly animale and sous-bois notes on the finish. Firmly structured, this should age well for the next five years or so. **88**—J.C. (12/1/2005)

Escarpment 2002 Pinot Noir (Martinborough) $42. This is a big, extracted wine that winemaker Larry McKenna would like to see customers lay down for a few years. Right now, it's a little rough around the edges, with tart cherry flavors edged out by earth, dried spices and some tougher-than-expected tannins. **86**—J.C. (8/1/2004)

Escarpment 2003 Kupe Pinot Noir (Martinborough) $60. Impressively big, rich, and well-extracted, with bold black cherry flavors, but also complex hints of cinnamon and other spices, floral notes, and a pleasant herbal tinge to the softly tannic finish. Approachable now, but probably better in 3–4 years. Just 500 cases produced. **93**—J.C. (12/1/2005)

ESK VALLEY

Esk Valley 2002 Chardonnay (Hawke's Bay) $15. This Hawke's Bay Chardonnay shows the warmer climate of that region in its ripe, plump flavors of stone fruits backed by hints of honey and smoke. It's a pleasingly harmonious rendition of Chardonnay from a region known more for its red wines. **88**—J.C. (9/1/2003)

Esk Valley 2000 Red Blend (Hawke's Bay) $15. This wine shows substantially less ripeness than the Reserve, with earth and tobacco aromas and flavors dominating the black cherry fruit. Finishes peppery, picking up coffee notes. **84**—J.C. (12/15/2003)

Esk Valley 2000 Reserve Red Blend (Hawke's Bay) $40. This wine is closed up tight right now, only stubbornly offering up whiffs of herbs and toast. But the flavors are more impressive, with pure cassis augmented by toast and vanilla. It's fairly rich and powerful, and the herbal element is well under control. Try in 2005. **89**—J.C. (12/15/2003)

Esk Valley 2002 Riesling (Hawke's Bay) $19. Austere and minerally, not exactly what you'd expect from a "warm" part of New Zealand. Some green apple and lime aromas lead into a refreshing palate laden with Green Gage plums. It's lean and wiry, a firmly structured wine that finishes long and minerally. **90**—J.C. (8/1/2003)

Esk Valley 2002 Sauvignon Blanc (Hawke's Bay) $19. Hawke's Bay is on the North Island of NZ, slightly warmer than Marlborough, and thus yielding wines that tend to be less pungently herbaceous. Ripe fruit and a proportion of barrel fermentation give this wine a plump, creamy texture, flavors of nectarines and passion fruit, and just a pinch of fresh herbs. **90 Editors' Choice**—J.C. (9/1/2003)

Esk Valley 2001 Sauvignon Blanc (Hawke's Bay) $19. Hawkes Bay is typically slightly warmer than Marlborough and its Sauvignons less green; this one bucks the trend, showing green bell pepper, herbs, and lime, layered with warm apricot fruit. Lacks only a little cut to elevate it into the 90s, but that same softness makes it very approachable and easy to enjoy. **89** (8/1/2002)

FAIRHALL DOWNS

Fairhall Downs 2000 Pinot Gris (Marlborough) $20. This single-vineyard wine captures plenty of varietal character in its waxy pear and melon aromas. A medium-bodied wine, with a crisp, slightly spicy-bitter finish, it should prove versatile with food or as an apéritif. **87**—J.C. (5/1/2001)

Fairhall Downs 2004 NA in US Pinot Noir (Marlborough) $NA. Darn tasty, combining cherry and cola flavors with dried spices. Plump and soft in the mouth, with a creamy, caressing mouthfeel, it's surprisingly long on the finish as well. Bravo. **90**—J.C. (12/1/2005)

Fairhall Downs 2005 Sauvignon Blanc (Marlborough) $16. This winery has raised its game in 2005, turning out a ripe, showy Sauvignon Blanc filled with gooseberry, pink grapefruit, and stone fruit aromas and flavors. Despite its fruit-forward nature, it is reasonably complex, adding mineral and passion fruit flavors on the finish. **90 Editors' Choice**—J.C. (7/1/2006)

Fairhall Downs 2001 Sauvignon Blanc (Marlborough) $18. Pretty as a picture, a very slightly sweet wine of great fruit and perfect, rich acidity. It doesn't pall after the first few sips but retains its interest through the long, refreshing finish. Defines Marlborough class. **91**—S.H. (11/15/2002)

Fairhall Downs 2000 Sauvignon Blanc (Marlborough) $18. Pungent; filled with boxwood and gooseberry aromas, this is a character-filled wine that's not for the faint-hearted. The mouthfeel is ripe and weighty, nicely balanced by a tart, bitter-grapefruit-pith finish that lingers enticingly on the tongue. **88**—J.C. (5/1/2001)

FAUNA

Fauna 2005 Sauvignon Blanc (Marlborough) $12. This medium-weight, fleshy Sauvignon offers aromas of ripe gooseberries and stone fruits, then backs that up with nectarine and citrus, just tinged with herbal character. Good length on the finish for such an inexpensive wine, a tribute to winemaking consultant Alan McCorkindale. **88 Best Buy**—J.C. (7/1/2006)

FELTON ROAD

Felton Road 2004 Barrel Fermented Chardonnay (Central Otago) $NA. Subtly toasty on the nose, adding bits of apple and peach flavors to the mix. This vintage of Felton Road's Chard isn't as rich or weighty as some years, but its quality still shines through on the bright, citrusy finish. The 2005 will be imported by Wilson Daniels Ltd. **90**—J.C. (5/1/2006)

Felton Road 2002 Barrel Fermented Chardonnay (Central Otago) $30. Nutty and toasty, but also profoundly fruity, loaded with ripe citrus fruit and peaches. The midpalate is rich and shows excellent fat, while the finish brings all the elements together in a long, tart finale laced with grapefruit and smoke. **90**—J.C. (4/1/2004)

Felton Road 2000 Barrel Fermented Chardonnay (Central Otago) $30. This is a big, ripe wine, yet it showcases cool-climate-influenced citrus fruits. Lemon-lime, ginger, and pie crust open to sweet citrus and vanilla, with just a touch of butter. A hint of grapefruit pith on the finish provides additional structure. **88**—J.C. (7/1/2002)

Felton Road 1999 Barrel Fermented Chardonnay (Central Otago) $34. Very fragrant, loaded with toasty, crème brûlée aromas and followed by oranges, vanilla, and custard. A big, ripe wine with some oatmeal character that finishes spicy and complex. **90**—J.C. (5/1/2001)

Felton Road 2004 Block 6 Chardonnay (Central Otago) $44. Having now tasted this wine on three separate occasions, I'm certain it will continue to improve in the bottle, but how stingy my current rating will ultimately seem is an open question. From tank prior to bottling, it was a rich, custardy, vibrant wine that I would have rated in the low 90s. Tasted blind after bottling, I've not yet found that same level of quality, but my ratings have climbed from low-mid 80s (back in the early part of this year) to high 80s now, as the wine seems to be regaining some of its rich, velvety texture to help balance its formidable acidity. Worth trying again in another year or two. **88**—J.C. (9/1/2006)

Felton Road 2004 Pinot Noir (Central Otago) $44. Herbal on the nose, with hints of mint and spice, yet it also boasts full-bodied black cherry and plum flavors. Supple, velvety tannins provide a great mouthfeel, with little oak in evidence. Drink now–2010. **90**—J.C. (12/1/2005)

Felton Road 2002 Pinot Noir (Central Otago) $43. This emerges from the bottle in a slightly reduced state, but the off aromas fade quickly, replaced by smoky, dense fruit scents. Black cherries and plums predominate, yielding exciting layers of fruit and finishing with extraordinary persistence. **91**—J.C. (4/1/2004)

Felton Road 2000 Pinot Noir (Central Otago) $40. The undesignated Pinot from Felton Road is normally a pretty approachable bottling, but in 2000, it's a big, brooding wine that needs time to unwind. Complex aromas of chocolate, dark plums, and smoke are complemented by a hint of root vegetables. Finishes with notes of coffee and tart cherries. **90**—J.C. (8/1/2002)

Felton Road 1999 Pinot Noir (Central Otago) $45. Felton Road's "entry-level" Pinot is better than many producers' top-end bottlings, and priced accordingly. The blend of sour and black cherries combines cola, cocoa, and thyme notes with deep earthy flavors and a silky texture. Drink now and over the next few years. **89**—J.C. (5/1/2001)

Felton Road 2004 Block 3 Pinot Noir (Central Otago) $60. Adds a meaty, bacony edge to broad, mouth-filling flavors of black cherries and herbs.

There's plenty of concentration in this wine, more than in many '04s, and some silky tannins on the finish that ideally deserve another 2–3 years of cellaring. Another winner from Felton Road. **91** —*J.C. (12/1/2005)*

Felton Road 2002 Block 3 Pinot Noir (Central Otago) $53. Dark and intense, with a rich, full, velvety mouthfeel. The fruit measures up, bringing big-time flavors of black cherries and plum, but it has a slightly herbal-vegetal side reminiscent of beet greens or cabbage that holds this otherwise impressive wine back. If this element fades or integrates, this rating could look stingy. **90** —*J.C. (4/1/2004)*

Felton Road 2000 Block 3 Pinot Noir (Central Otago) $50. In time, this may surpass the regular bottling, but for now it trails by a nose, thanks to some mushroom, bracken, and lima bean scents that dampen the cola and beet flavors. As always, it's big, rich, and full-bodied. Try in 2005. **89** —*J.C. (8/1/2002)*

Felton Road 1999 Block 3 Pinot Noir (Central Otago) $70. Despite 60% new oak, the first thing you notice about this wine is its gorgeously pure black cherry fruit. Sure, there's a hint of toast and cedar, but the size and weight comes from ripe fruit and skilled winemaking, not cooperage. Low acidity and soft tannins make this easy to drink now but it should easily last 5–7 years. **91** —*J.C. (5/1/2001)*

Felton Road 2004 Block 5 Pinot Noir (Central Otago) $62. Full-bodied yet supple, this darkly colored Pinot marries a slight leafiness with black cherry fruit. Subtle spice shadings add nuance, while the standout finish lingers, playing a citrusy tang against deeper plum bass notes. Another solid effort from a consistently excellent producer. **90** —*J.C. (9/1/2006)*

Felton Road 2003 Block 5 Pinot Noir (Central Otago) $62. Yes, it's expensive, and no, it's not showing its full potential right now; prospective purchasers should be prepared to wait 2–3 years before opening. That said, it's an excellent wine, combining dried spices, a wiry, herbal note, and vibrant red cherries. An under-current of earth and chocolate provides the bass. Firmly structured, it's built to age. **91 Cellar Selection** —*J.C. (12/1/2005)*

Felton Road 1999 Block 5 Pinot Noir (Central Otago) $80. A big, rich, structured wine, with cola and rosemary notes that give nuance to the strong black cherry aromas and flavors. With its plentiful but ripe tannins, it could use a couple years' of cellaring before being ready for prime time. **91** —*J.C. (5/1/2001)*

Felton Road 2005 Riesling (Central Otago) $26. Only 56 cases imported, but worth searching for if you like Riesling. The aromas combine floral notes with stone and mineral, then the palate offers a vivacious counterweight in the form of ripe pineapple-y fruit and bold citrus flavors. Low alcohol (9%) and a slight tickle of CO2 enliven the mouthfeel and help balance the slightly sweet flavors. **90** —*J.C. (7/1/2006)*

Felton Road 2002 Riesling (Central Otago) $23. This bold, off-dry Riesling is loaded with flavors of poached pear and baked apple, with a lavish dusting of dried spices adding complexity. Tongue-tingling acidity provides great balance and lengthens the finish. **91 Editors' Choice** —*J.C. (8/1/2003)*

Felton Road 2000 Riesling (Central Otago) $26. The very ripe flavors of pears and peaches are a little sweet, but nicely balanced by a cool edge of lime-tinged acids that provide focus to the fruit-bowl flavors. Typical New Zealand style of fairly high alcohol (for Riesling), coupled with slight residual sugar and intense acidity. **88** —*J.C. (5/1/2001)*

Felton Road 2002 Block 1 Riesling (Central Otago) $25. The sweetest and ripest of Felton Road's 2002 Rieslings, the Block 1 boasts 5-6% residual sugar balanced by a long, citrusy finish. Aromas of green ferns, limes, and powdered sandstone provide a pretty counterpoint to the powerful flavors of ripe peaches and pears. **90** —*J.C. (8/1/2003)*

Felton Road 2002 Dry Riesling (Central Otago) $23. This powerful expression of Riesling blends floral aromas with scents of lime, pineapple, and crushed stone, then finishes with great length and intensity. The strident citrus and mineral notes seem to echo on the palate, filling the mouth with their characterful flavors. **92 Editors' Choice** —*J.C. (8/1/2003)*

Felton Road 2000 Dry Riesling (Central Otago) $21. Wow. Ripe pears, peaches, and nectarines cascade over the palate. Despite the suggestion of sweet, luscious fruit, this wine is dry, with a long, lime and pineapple finish. This is world-class dry Riesling. **91 Editors' Choice** —*J.C. (5/1/2001)*

FIRSTLAND

Firstland 2000 Pinot Noir (Marlborough) $25. Light and woody, with flavors of cola and tart berries partially masked by a veneer of dry, toasty oak. **83** —*J.C. (9/1/2003)*

Firstland 2002 Sauvignon Blanc (Marlborough) $19. Bright and vibrantly fruity, with passion fruit and gooseberry aromas along with lemongrass and bell pepper. This is a crisp, clean expression of Marlborough Sauvignon Blanc, unblemished by barrel fermentation or aging. **86** —*J.C. (9/1/2003)*

Firstland 2001 Sauvignon Blanc (Marlborough) $NA. Here's an extraordinarily fragrant and flavorful wine, as lush as a late-harvest, yet dryish. It has amazing extraction, like a fruit cocktail, a mixture of grapefruit, apple, tangerine, even melon. There's a little residual sugar in it, just enough to offset high acidity. **91** —*S.H. (11/15/2002)*

FOREFATHERS

Forefathers 2005 Sauvignon Blanc (Marlborough) $16. Winemaker Nick Goldschmidt has returned to his native country to craft this prototypical Marlborough Sauvignon. Herbal, grassy scents accent pink grapefruit and melon aromas, while these same notes persist on the palate and through a moderately long finish. **89** —*J.C. (9/1/2006)*

Forefathers 2002 Sauvignon Blanc (Marlborough) $13. 90 —*J.M. (1/1/2003)*

Forefathers 2000 Sauvignon Blanc (Marlborough) $13. Fresh grapefruit and passion fruit form the center of this refreshing, zingy, full-bodied yet elegant Sauvignon Blanc. The finish is bright and lemony with just a hint of grassiness for added complexity. A knockout from Simi winemaker Nick Goldschmidt, who returned to his native country to make this wine. **91** —*J.M. (11/15/2001)*

Forefathers 1999 Sauvignon Blanc (Marlborough) $14. Initial aromas of boxwood give way to melon, cream, and grapefruit. In the mouth, this offering is mellow and a bit sweet. A soft and easy drinker for folks new to Kiwi Sauvignon Blanc. **84** —*J.C. (5/1/2001)*

FORREST ESTATE

Forrest Estate 2000 Cornerstone Cabernet Sauvignon-Merlot (Hawke's Bay) $25. Surprisingly light in body, with sweet cassis, cherry, and herb flavors that finish minty and fresh. **84** —*J.C. (12/15/2003)*

Forrest Estate 1997 Chardonnay (Marlborough) $15. 90 —*S.H. (8/1/1999)*

Forrest Estate 2004 Pinot Noir (Marlborough) $20. A credible effort in what was not an easy vintage for Marlborough Pinot Noir, Forrest Estate's 2004 is a light, silky-textured wine with scents of mushroom and earth followed up by flavors of cherry and cola. Drink now. **86** —*J.C. (11/1/2006)*

Forrest Estate 2003 Pinot Noir (Marlborough) $20. Nicely done at an affordable price, this wine starts off a bit slow, with tea and cranberry aromas leading the way. But it deepens and darkens with air, developing cherry, plum, and cola flavors and finishing with a hint of coffee. **87** —*J.C. (12/1/2005)*

Forrest Estate 2001 Pinot Noir (Marlborough) $20. Quite oaky, but classy nonetheless, with cinnamon, cedar, and a hint of hickory playing leading roles in shaping the modest cherry fruit. The mouthfeel is the star, boasting a wonderfully supple texture that's the goal of every Pinot maker. **88** —*J.C. (4/1/2004)*

Forrest Estate 2001 Riesling (Marlborough) $15. Though in the bottle for three years, this wine still shows evidence of too much sulfur: It's rubbery and tarry on the nose. Underneath, there's some rich tropical fruit, off-dry, finishing in a rush of tart pineapple flavors. **85** —*J.C. (8/1/2004)*

Forrest Estate 1997 Sauvignon Blanc (Marlborough) $15. 88 —*S.H. (8/1/1999)*

Forrest Estate 2005 Sauvignon Blanc (Marlborough) $16. A big, round Sauvignon Blanc, but it never seems too big or too bulky, instead delivering ripe melon, nectarine, and gooseberry flavors crisply balanced by citrusy acids. Long and intense on the finish. **91 Editors' Choice** —*J.C. (7/1/2006)*

Forrest Estate 2002 Sauvignon Blanc (Marlborough) $15. A big, mouthfilling Sauvignon Blanc, with smoky, toasty notes gracing ripe, full peach fruit. Finishes a touch soft, yet shows surprisingly good length. A rather late release, yet one that could go another six months before peaking. **90 Best Buy** —*J.C. (4/1/2004)*

Forrest Estate 2001 Sauvignon Blanc (Marlborough) $19. This round, lush wine has a great deal of charm. There's a fair amount of residual sugar to balance out the intense acidity, and the apple and peach flavors are profoundly rich. This is a very satisfying wine, juicy and delicious. **88** —*S.H. (11/15/2002)*

FOXES ISLAND

Foxes Island 2004 Chardonnay (Marlborough) $37. Quite toasty and mealy, with delicate hints of peach on the nose. Rich and weighty on the palate, delivering loads of baked apple, spice, and brown sugar. Yet for all this weight and power, it doesn't seem ponderous at all, finishing long and gracefully. **91 Editors' Choice** —*J.C. (12/1/2005)*

Foxes Island 2002 Chardonnay (Marlborough) $30. Intensely smoky on the nose, with powerful grilled fruit aromas that echo on the palate. These grilled peach flavors are tasty on their own, then pick up an added citrusy dimension on the tart, lemony finish. **87** —*J.C. (7/1/2005)*

Foxes Island 2001 Chardonnay (Marlborough) $32. Solid, straightforward Chard, with a toasty, buttery veneer over tropical fruit. Medium-weight, and picks up tasty notes of vanilla cream and citrus on the finish. **86** — *J.C. (8/1/2004)*

Foxes Island 2000 Chardonnay (Marlborough) $26. Toasty and creamy, this is a richly wooded style of Chardonnay that fans of oak will find grossly under-rated. A core of fading tropical fruit supports oak-derived spice, toast and vanilla, finishing with cinnamon and clove. **85** —*J.C. (9/1/2003)*

Foxes Island 1999 Chardonnay (Marlborough) $21. Toasted wheat bread is layered with fresh peaches and honey in this light-weight yet flavorful Chardonnay. Peach and vanilla flavors finish cleanly, marked by a lingering toasty edge. **86** —*J.C. (7/1/2002)*

Foxes Island 1998 Chardonnay (Marlborough) $28. Initial aromas of buttered popcorn and tropical fruit fade, then reawaken as butterscotch candy. Caramelized pears are topped with lots of oaky spice on the finish. **83** —*J.C. (5/1/2001)*

Foxes Island 2004 Pinot Noir (Marlborough) $42. A bit of a disappointment from Foxes Island. Already lightening at the rim, this has the same pretty texture that previous vintages have shown, but not the same levels of fruit. Slightly charred, meaty notes accent mushroom and herbal cherry aromas and flavors. Tart on the finish. **84** —*J.C. (11/1/2006)*

Foxes Island 2002 Pinot Noir (Marlborough) $40. Mmmmm, toasty. But it's a good toasty, with elegant nuances of smoke and dried spices, all backed up by plenty of black cherry fruit. It's medium-weight, with a supple mouthfeel and a long, spice-driven finish. **88** —*J.C. (7/1/2005)*

Foxes Island 2001 Pinot Noir (Marlborough) $38. A delicately flavored, yet impressively plush wine, with scents of woodsmoke, black cherries and mushrooms echoed on the palate with added notes of sous bois and plums. **89** —*J.C. (8/1/2004)*

Foxes Island 2000 Pinot Noir (Marlborough) $28. In contrast to this winery's soft and beguiling '99, the 2000 is a bigger, burlier offering, without as much of the previous vintage's seductive charm. Plum and spice cake aromas and flavors are solid enough—maybe this wine just needs a few months to soften. **87** —*J.C. (9/1/2003)*

Foxes Island 1999 Pinot Noir (Marlborough) $24. Its soft, beguiling aromas of brown sugar, cinnamon, pie crust, and cranberries pull you in, then bright cherry flavors take over on the palate. Mouthfeel is light, yet caressing, and the flavors fan out on the finish, picking up notes of spice and cola. A pretty wine from start to finish. **88** —*J.C. (8/1/2002)*

Foxes Island 1998 Pinot Noir (Marlborough) $30. Ripe black cherries infused with cola on the nose, but like so many N.Z. Pinots it doesn't follow through on the palate, where elements of sur-maturité war with tart, almost astringent acidity. **81** —*J.C. (5/1/2001)*

Foxes Island 2005 Sauvignon Blanc (Marlborough) $25. Rather restrained for Marlborough Sauvignon, showing more stony, minerally notes than most. With coaxing, modest passion fruit and honey notes emerge, carried along by a plump mouthfeel. A solid effort, but one that doesn't match winemaker John Belsham's more consistent touch with Chardonnay and Pinot Noir. **85** —*J.C. (11/1/2006)*

Foxes Island 2004 Sauvignon Blanc (Marlborough) $NA. Made from young vines in the Awatere Valley, this lovely Sauvignon features a bit of smoky pungency on the nose, then honeyed citrus and stone fruit flavors before turning minerally and taut on the finish. Drink now. Not imported. **91 Editors' Choice** —*J.C. (11/1/2006)*

FRAMINGHAM

Framingham 2000 Chardonnay (Marlborough) $16. Though there's lots of creamy oak on the nose, the aromas aren't as cloying as they would be in a California Chard. People used to California Chards wouldn't know what to make of the palate flavors, either: Reserved, steely mineral notes overlay banana, citrus, and a tiny bit of oak. Soft and minerally in the mouth, it closes with more stony-gravelly notes. (Their webite says that the grapes are grown in stony soil.) **87** —*D.T. (12/15/2001)*

Framingham 2004 Pinot Noir (Marlborough) $26. Light but pretty, offering up floral, cola, and cherry scents. It's a soft, easy-drinking style, with a tart, pie cherry note on the finish. **86** —*J.C. (12/1/2005)*

Framingham 2001 Classic Riesling (Marlborough) $15. With almost 2% residual sugar, you might expect this wine to taste sweet. It does—to a point. The strong lime-like finish provides a balancing counterpoint that makes this floral wine very drinkable with food. Clove and cinnamon notes add complexity to ripe pear fruit. **88** —*J.C. (8/1/2002)*

Framingham 2005 Sauvignon Blanc (Marlborough) $17. Combines dusky peach and passion fruit aromas and flavors in a wine that's a bit softer and sweeter-tasting than many Marlborough Sauvignon Blancs, yet still carries a refreshing touch of acid on the finish. **86** —*J.C. (5/1/2006)*

Framingham 2001 Sauvignon Blanc (Marlborough) $14. Young, fresh, and still a bit sulfury, it has pretty apple and citrus aromas and flavors. Polished and supple, it's a strongly flavored wine with penetrating acidity and a dry finish. This tart, crisp, flavorful wine is exciting and completely refreshing. **88** —*S.H. (11/15/2002)*

FROMM WINERY

Fromm Winery 2002 Clayvin Vineyard Pinot Noir (Marlborough) $49. With its medium body and supple texture, this is harmonious, solid stuff. Aromas and flavors of cola, cherries, and earth are true to the variety, finishing on a herbal, tea-like note. Savor the mouthfeel, which comes as close to silk as vinously possible. **88** —*J.C. (7/1/2005)*

Fromm Winery 2002 Fromm Vineyard Pinot Noir (Marlborough) $55. Much like in their Clayvin Vineyard bottling, Fromm has nailed the textural element so vital to good Pinot Noir—this light-bodied, tart wine features supremely elegant, silky tannins. Delicate cherry and spice nuances are accented by smoky, toasty barrel notes. Drink now. **87** —*J.C. (7/1/2005)*

Fromm Winery 2002 La Strada Pinot Noir (Marlborough) $36. Seems a bit too oaky, with cedar and mint aromas covering the fruit, while the flavors veer toward chocolate and plum. Finishes tart and crisp, with bright acidity. **85** —*J.C. (7/1/2005)*

Fromm Winery 2004 La Strada Riesling (Marlborough) $31. A disappointment, given this wine's reputation in New Zealand. It's a light, sweet wine, with 95 g/L of residual sugar that's not quite balanced by corresponding acidity. There's a hint of vinyl on the nose, while pear, apple, and honey notes are enlivened by a streak of lime but never truly sing. **84** —*J.C. (7/1/2006)*

GIBBSTON VALLEY

Gibbston Valley 2001 Pinot Gris (Central Otago) $22. Just as fresh and crisp as a wine can be, this vibrantly fruity wine brims with peach and citrus flavors with a nice grassy nuance. The acidity is very high and provides a needed counterpoint to the rich, slightly sweet flavors. **88** —*S.H. (1/1/2002)*

Gibbston Valley 2000 Pinot Noir (Central Otago) $30. If you're familiar with Santa Barbara Pinots, this is eerily reminiscent, with its bright raspberry and cherry flavors accented by tomato and crushed brown spices. Of course, the whole is framed in fancy oak. The big difference is acidity. This wine shines with New Zealand crispness, a tart, zingy mouthfeel you never get from California. **88** —*S.H. (1/1/2002)*

GIESEN

Giesen NV Voyage Special Cuvée Brut Champagne Blend (Canterbury) $10. An ideal party pour, with a slight mint-herb tang to the fresh, lemon-lime flavors. There's even a hint of toast or biscuits that adds complexity. Tart and light, this would best as an apéritif. **86 Best Buy** —*J.C. (5/1/2001)*

Giesen 1999 Reserve Barrel Selection Chardonnay (Marlborough) $20. Oily and buttery, the green apple fruit blends in some peach and pear notes along with plenty of mentholly French oak. Finishes long, with echoes of smoke and toast. **88** —*J.C. (5/1/2001)*

Giesen 1998 Reserve Barrel Selection Chardonnay (Canterbury) $20. The cool climate of Canterbury shows through in this wine's lemony fruit and tangy acidity. Add to that a touch of toast and a custardy, leesy mouthfeel and the wine comes out a winner. **88** —*J.C. (5/1/2001)*

Giesen 1999 Pinot Noir (Canterbury) $16. Rather light, with delicate cherry fruit that comes across as elegant and pretty. Some tart weedy notes on the nose and finish add definition and structure. **85** —*J.C. (5/1/2001)*

Giesen 2004 Riesling (East Coast) $13. Round and fleshy in texture, this blended Riesling evinces no hard edges. Petrol and mineral scents are followed by modest melon flavors. Drink now. **85** —*J.C. (7/1/2006)*

Giesen 2000 Riesling (Canterbury) $12. It's the odd Kiwi producer whose Riesling is more expensive than their Sauvignon Blanc, but it shows where the priorities are at this winery. Softly fragrant pears and limes meld with ripe golden apples on the soft, somewhat sweet (17g/L residual sugar) palate. **86** —*J.C. (5/1/2001)*

Giesen 1999 Noble School Road Late Harvest Riesling (Canterbury) $18. This blend of Riesling (usually 60–70%) and Müller-Thurgau gets musky, spicy notes from the M-T, while the bulk of the flavors and aromas are apricot and orange from the Riesling. Sweet and fairly low in alcohol (10%), this would make a nice pairing with various fruit desserts. **88** —*J.C. (5/1/2001)*

Giesen 2008 Sauvignon Blanc (Marlborough) $13. Prototypical Marlborough Sauvignon Blanc, marrying pungent red pepper and passion fruit notes with round, ripe melon flavors. It's a little soft, with a hint of honey on the finish, so serve it well-chilled to help give it more cut. **85** —*J.C. (12/15/2006)*

Giesen 2005 Sauvignon Blanc (Marlborough) $12. Prototypical Marlborough Sauvignon, from the herbal, grassy aromas to the stone fruit flavors on the midpalate and green pepper accents. Tart and chalky on the finish. **87 Best Buy** —*J.C. (5/1/2006)*

Giesen 2000 Sauvignon Blanc (Marlborough) $10. A mainstream, commercial style that blends green peppers and green peas with a sweet midpalate. Not overly aggressive or pungent, just a soft, lightly sweet sipper. **85 Best Buy** —*J.C. (5/1/2001)*

Giesen 2003 Single Vineyard Selection Sauvignon Blanc (Marlborough) $20. Lime and lemon zest along with green pepper on the nose, and then sour fruit and too much canned pea flavor on the palate. Hard to describe other than to say that it lacks fruit. **82** *(7/1/2005)*

GLADSTONE

Gladstone 2003 Auld Alliance Bordeaux Blend (Wairarapa) $20. This blend of 42% Cabernet Sauvignon, 33% Merlot, and 25% Cabernet Franc boats ample cassis fruit and is soft and supple in the mouth. So what is holding it back? It thins out a bit on the finish, and some weedy and stable-y notes mark the bouquet. If you're turned off by ultra-clean wines made with super-ripe fruit, give this one a spin. **84** —*J.C. (7/1/2006)*

Gladstone 2004 Pinot Gris (Wairarapa) $20. Lemon-lime aromas would seem a bit monochromatic, but they're enlivened by the addition of ripe apple and tropical fruit. It's off-dry, weighty, and creamy, with flavors that add spice and mineral nuances on the finish. **89** —*J.C. (2/1/2006)*

GLAZEBROOK

Glazebrook 2002 Chardonnay (Gisborne) $16. Starts off with expansive aromas of honey, ripe apples, and sweet nectarines, then seems to tighten up a bit on the palate, yielding reined-in flavors of pear, pineapple, and a hint of toast. **85** —*J.C. (8/1/2004)*

Glazebrook 2000 Chardonnay (Gisborne) $11. This is prototypical Gisborne Chardonnay, featuring a whack of spicy oak and buttered popcorn allied to tropical fruit and peach flavors, brought into focus by mild citrus (tangerine) on the finish. A very fruity and somewhat simple style, yet executed perfectly. **87** —*J.C. (7/1/2002)*

Glazebrook 2000 Merlot-Cabernet Sauvignon (Hawke's Bay) $18. Unwelcome hints of green bell pepper and fresh parsley offset positive notes of black cherries and chocolate. A smooth mouthfeel and fresh finish make the wine, on balance, a pleasant experience. **84** —*J.C. (12/15/2003)*

Glazebrook 1999 Merlot-Cabernet Sauvignon (Hawke's Bay) $19. The bright cherry flavors carry a bit of toast and herb; together with a smoked meat quality that emerges, it all makes for a complex wine. Smooth, soft tannins on the finish are complemented by juicy acids. **87** —*J.C. (5/1/2001)*

Glazebrook 2003 Sauvignon Blanc (Marlborough) $14. Smoke and mineral notes dominate the nose, picking up hints of green pepper along the way. These elements are repeated on the palate, offering solid varietal typicity. Finishes with a refreshing citric tang. **86** —*J.C. (8/1/2004)*

Glazebrook 2002 Sauvignon Blanc (Marlborough) $13. A racy style, with lime-like acidity on the finish that's complemented by aromas of less-than-fully ripe nectarines and a dash of leafy green herbs. Flavors are melon and stone fruits, along with a helping of green pepper. **88 Best Buy** —*J.C. (9/1/2003)*

Glazebrook 2000 Sauvignon Blanc (Hawke's Bay) $12. Strong grassiness is nicely offset by flavors of peaches and tropical fruits in this offering from UC Davis-trained Alwyn Corban. Finishes with juicy grapefruit, jalapeño pepper and spicy herbs, giving it a little extra kick. **88 Best Buy** —*J.C. (5/1/2001)*

GOLDWATER

Goldwater 1998 Bordeaux Blend (Waiheke Island) $60. Fairly herbaceous, with aromas and flavors of green tea, herbs, and tobacco that are complemented by cherry fruit. The soft tannins on the long, echoing finish bode well for the cellar. **89** —*J.C. (5/1/2001)*

Goldwater 1997 Cabernet Sauvignon-Merlot (Waiheke Island) $60. Quite green at first, with asparagus and green bean aromas that become mellower and more tobacco-like with time in the glass. The mouthfeel is supple and easy, the finish pleasantly chocolaty, but there's too much green for this wine to rate as highly as it's capable of in riper vintages. **84** —*J.C. (12/15/2003)*

Goldwater 2002 Roseland Chardonnay (Marlborough) $24. Displays copious amounts of tropical fruit, all underscored by delicate buttered toast notes. It's medium-weight and plump on the palate, showing pear, vanilla, and toast on the moderately long finish. **89** —*J.C. (4/1/2004)*

Goldwater 2001 Roseland Chardonnay (Marlborough) $22. Offers lush tropical fruit and a healthy dose of butter, framed by toasty oak, and kept in check by just-adequate acidity. Delicious now, so drink up—the precarious balance that has been achieved won't last for more than a year or two. **90** —*J.C. (9/1/2003)*

Goldwater 1999 Roseland Chardonnay (Central Otago) $27. A rich, toasty, buttery Chardonnay, filled with aromas and flavors of baked golden-delicious apple, which somehow manages to retain a sense of balance. The thick mouthfeel seems to last into the lingering finish. **90** —*J.C. (5/1/2001)*

Goldwater 1998 Roseland Chardonnay (Marlborough) $20. 87 —*J.C. (10/1/2000)*

Goldwater 2002 Zell Chardonnay (Waiheke Island) $40. Nicely done, with toasty, mealy notes that are balanced by ripe pear and peach fruit. Hints

NEW ZEALAND

of grilled fruit and roasted nuts complete the picture, finishing with lingering echoes of smoke. **90** —*J.C. (8/1/2004)*

Goldwater 2000 Zell Chardonnay (Waiheke Island) $40. You may mistake this light and elegant Chard for a white Burgundy; It's light on the nose, with flour-chalk and herbal notes. Apple skin and tart pear flavors take over in the mouth. Even and medium-bodied on the palate, it finishes gravelly in texture, with lime -rind and herb flavors. **89** —*D.T. (12/15/2001)*

Goldwater 2002 Esslin Merlot (Waiheke Island) $100. This particular bottling from Goldwater continues to be an enigma. Despite the wine's fame (and price), I've never been moved by it. The 2002 shows pretty, Bordeaux-like nuances of earth and tobacco on the nose, then charming cherry and vanilla flavors on the palate. Yet it never really fleshes out, and it turns a bit herbal and lean on the finish. **86** —*J.C. (7/1/2005)*

Goldwater 1999 Esslin Merlot (Waiheke Island) $98. This elegant, medium-weight Merlot shows a Bordeaux-like nose of damp earth and tobacco, but also more New World-ish cherry and vanilla flavors. Tobacco and chocolate shadings add depth and complexity. **87** —*J.C. (12/15/2003)*

Goldwater 1998 Esslin Merlot (Waiheke Island) $99. Shows obvious oak influence that seems almost like maple syrup in character; also solid black cherry fruit that has just a hint of dried herbs. Low acidity gives it an appealing lushness. **87** —*J.C. (5/1/2001)*

Goldwater 2005 Sauvignon Blanc (Marlborough) $20. As this wine's grape sourcing has changed over the years, Goldwater has struggled to maintain its quality. This year's version is lean and tart, zesty and citrusy. Lime and orange notes turn crisp and grape-fruity on the finish. A bit simple, but cleansing and refreshing. **84** —*J.C. (5/1/2006)*

Goldwater 2000 Sauvignon Blanc (Marlborough) $20. Pungent aromas of grapefruit and gooseberries lead into a wine that shows good richness in the mouth—it's almost creamy. Finishes long, with grapefruit and mint overtones. **89** —*J.C. (5/1/2001)*

Goldwater 2002 Dog Point Sauvignon Blanc (Marlborough) $20. After a disappointingly vegetal 2001, Goldwater's Dog Point Sauvignon Blanc has returned to form, offering citrus and stone fruits allied to fresh herbs and peppery spice. The creamy mouthfeel adds a touch of roundness to this lively, vivacious wine. **89** —*J.C. (9/1/2003)*

Goldwater 2001 Dog Point Sauvignon Blanc (Marlborough) $20. Passion fruit and melon vie for attention on the bouquet with grassy, vegetal, herbaceous scents. In the mouth, citrus and dry Asian pear flavors intermingle with additional grassy, asparagus tones. The acids on the back end are intense, so the tang and zip on the finish is powerful. The biggest problem here is a persistent vegetal quality that won't let up. **85** *(8/1/2002)*

Goldwater 2004 New Dog Sauvignon Blanc (Marlborough) $20. Big-time vegetal, with aromas of cooked asparagus and canned peas. In the mouth, you'll find citrus, but on the finish that vegetal character comes back with vengeance. **84** *(7/1/2005)*

Goldwater 2003 New Dog Sauvignon Blanc (Marlborough) $20. Brimming with bright passion fruit and green apple aromas, the wine shows classic New Zealand character for this variety; bright and fresh, with zippy acidity and a fine blend of melon, grapefruit, lemon, and herb flavors. **89** —*J.M. (4/1/2004)*

GRAVITAS

Gravitas 2004 Saint Arnaud's Vineyard Reserve Chardonnay (Marlborough) $20. Made in a mouth-watering, brisk style, this Chardonnay emphasizes the citrusy side of the grape, weaving in modest apple and biscuit notes. Medium-bodied, it turns crisp and lemony on the finish. **85** —*J.C. (11/1/2006)*

Gravitas 2005 Pinot Noir (Marlborough) $20. This is a big, burly, Syrah-like Pinot that delivers impressive color, alcohol levels, and tannins, just not a lot of aroma, flavor, or texture. **82** —*J.C. (12/15/2006)*

Gravitas 2005 Saint Arnaud's Vineyard Sauvignon Blanc (Marlborough) $NA. Flinty, fumé-style scents add interest to the aromas, which also include bright, citrusy elements. It's plump and custardy-leesy in the

mouth, then turns tart and racy on the finish, ending with strong lime overtones. **89** —*J.C. (5/1/2006)*

GREENHOUGH

Greenhough 2004 Chardonnay (Nelson) $20. New World Chardonnay, done well. Toasty, mealy aromas accent slightly tropical, peach-like scents on the nose, while the flavors are ripe and fruit-driven, suitably framed by butter and toast. It's a medium- to full-bodied wine, its long finish tinged with hints of butter and tropical fruit. **87** —*J.C. (12/15/2006)*

Greenhough 2004 Pinot Noir (Nelson) $25. The 2004 vintage wasn't an easy one for Nelson Pinot Noir, and this wine reflects that. The aromas are slightly earthy and herbal, marked by tomato and beet elements, while the flavors are herbal to the point of mintiness but also fresh and appealing. Ultimately, it's an attractive effort destined for short-term drinking. **85** —*J.C. (12/15/2006)*

Greenhough 2000 Riesling (Nelson) $12. Lime, white flowers and a strong hint of minerals and petrol announce that, yes, it's definitely Riesling. The palate is stony-smooth, and distinct lemon-lime flavors shoot through the wine from start to end. Acidity is moderate and there's no spritz at all. Pronounced "Grennock." **86** —*M.S. (12/15/2001)*

Greenhough 2000 Sauvignon Blanc (Nelson) $12. More indistinct than extreme, the tangy citrus and herb aromas and flavors need more weight and definition to stand up to the bracing acidity. Finishes tart and more vegetal than it reads on the nose and palate. **82** —*M.M. (12/15/2001)*

GROVE MILL

Grove Mill 2001 Chardonnay (Marlborough) $18. Restrained use of oak allows the bright citrus and tropical notes of this wine to shine. Yet despite modest oaking, extended lees contact has given the wine a fine custardy texture and a plump roundness on the palate. **87** —*J.C. (9/1/2003)*

Grove Mill 1999 Chardonnay (Marlborough) $18. Pears and pineapples turn buttery and oaky in the mouth without being overdone. A lush, easy-drinking wine that's fairly soft and designed for immediate gratification, unlike some of Grove Mill's other offerings. **86** —*J.C. (5/1/2001)*

Grove Mill 2005 Pinot Gris (Marlborough) $20. Pretty sweet and fat, with honeyed flavors that lean toward apple, melon, and pear. There's just enough citrus on the finish to pull it all together and give it some semblance of balance, but this will not be to all tastes. **88** —*J.C. (2/1/2006)*

Grove Mill 2002 Pinot Gris (Marlborough) $18. Fairly thick and viscous in the mouth, with flavors of apple and quince. There's also a subtle herbaceousness reminiscent of the region's Sauvignon Blancs. **86** —*J.C. (9/1/2003)*

Grove Mill 2000 Pinot Gris (Marlborough) $19. A unique-tasting wine that mixes minty herbs with nectarines, oranges and red apple skin. It's off-dry, and in no need of aging. 400 cases imported. **86** —*J.C. (5/1/2001)*

Grove Mill 2004 Pinot Noir (Marlborough) $25. This winery is normally pretty reliable, so one has to wonder what happened here. Brown sugar and mushroom aromas give way to earthy flavors and not much fruit. Tasted twice, with consistent results. **82** —*J.C. (12/1/2005)*

Grove Mill 2002 Pinot Noir (Marlborough) $23. A full-bodied, zaftig Pinot, with dark aromas of coffee, dark chocolate, and black cherries. Tannins are pillowy and soft, picking up anise notes on the finish. **89 Editors' Choice** —*J.C. (8/1/2004)*

Grove Mill 2001 Pinot Noir (Marlborough) $23. Grove Mill has been working hard on getting their Pinot Noir right, and the staff there have finally succeeded, crafting a lush, mouth-filling wine filled with black cherries and cocoa that linger elegantly on the long finish. **90** —*J.C. (9/1/2003)*

Grove Mill 1999 Pinot Noir (Marlborough) $27. The majority of this wine (85%) is from plantings of new-to-New Zealand Clone 5 (Pommard), which gives it some smooth black cherry flavors. But a lot of this wine's character comes from the barrels: chocolate, toast, and smoked-meat aromas and a buttered toast finish. **86** —*J.C. (5/1/2001)*

Grove Mill 2004 Wairau Valley Reserve Pinot Noir (Marlborough) $30. Not overly rich or concentrated, this is a light- to medium-bodied Pinot with a hard, woody shell. Cedar hits the senses first, followed only slowly by modest cherry fruit and more and more wood spice. Still, it shows some class and a reasonably long finish. Try in another year or two, when the oak may be more integrated, but before the fruit falls away.**86** —*J.C. (11/1/2006)*

Grove Mill 2005 Riesling (Marlborough) $17. A bit disjointed, perhaps just due to its youth, but this wine features a sweet-sour tang to the finish that's not entirely harmonious. Still, the aromas are attractive—ripe apple, pear, pineapple, and honey—balanced by stony, minerally, slightly sweet flavors and strong acids.**86** —*J.C. (7/1/2006)*

Grove Mill 2002 Riesling (Marlborough) $15. The medium-weight, off-dry Riesling boasts fresh aromas of pear and quince, enriched by a touch of honey. The flavors of baked apples and poached pears are bolstered by firm, lime-like acids that impart a refreshing quality to the finish.**89** —*J.C. (8/1/2004)*

Grove Mill 2001 Riesling (Marlborough) $15. An solid introduction to the world of New Zealand Sauvignon Blanc, it's off-dry in style, with melon and honey flavors given structure by lime-like acids. Pleasant, and even if it is a bit simple, it's easy to like.**84** —*J.C. (8/1/2003)*

Grove Mill 2000 Riesling (Marlborough) $16. I've recommended this wine in previous vintages and the 2000 is another fine example. There's a fair degree of sweetness (17g/L residual sugar) but it's balanced by a slight pétillance and zesty acidity. Ripe peaches and pears turn to oranges and limes on the finish.**88** —*J.C. (5/1/2001)*

Grove Mill 2005 Sauvignon Blanc (Marlborough) $16. Starts off zesty, with bold scents of passion fruit accented by lemon and lime, then turns softer and less racy on the finish. Worth trying with ceviche.**86** —*J.C. (5/1/2006)*

Grove Mill 2002 Sauvignon Blanc (Marlborough) $17. Pungent and grassy, yet thickly textured, this wine is a study in contradictions. The fruit is pineapple and passion fruit, but hints of asparagus creep in, giving a slight greenish cast to the flavors.**85** —*J.C. (9/1/2003)*

Grove Mill 2000 Sauvignon Blanc (Marlborough) $17, Tight on the nose, not showing much except for aggressive jalapeño and herb. Intense and structured; winemaker David Pearce believes this wine will last up to eight years.**87** —*J.C. (5/1/2001)*

Grove Mill 2005 17 Valley Reserve Sauvignon Blanc (Marlborough) $22. Grove Mill's upper-tier Sauvignon is aggressively pungent and herbaceous, with gooseberry aromas and flavors tying it all together. This medium-bodied wine is more impressive for its concentration, power, and length than for its charm or complexity, but it could work exceptionally well with the right foods—perhaps cod braised with tomatoes and onions.**87** —*J.C. (11/1/2006)*

GUNN ESTATE

Gunn Estate 1998 Skeetfield Chardonnay (Ohiti Valley) $17. Ohiti is a subregion of Hawkes Bay, one of New Zealand's warmer wine-growing areas, but this Chardonnay is tight and tart. Orange and lime, also tart pear flavors dominate. Needs time, but will the flavors ever truly unfurl? **84** —*J.C. (5/1/2001)*

Gunn Estate 1998 Woolshed Merlot-Cabernet Sauvignon (Ohiti Valley) $17. The black cherry flavors that carry this wine seems over-ripe and a bit pruny, but work well in combination with the chocolate and tea shadings that persist into the long, tart finish.**86** —*J.C. (5/1/2001)*

GYPSY DANCER

Gypsy Dancer 2004 Pinot Noir (Central Otago) $40. Mineral dust scents accent ripe cherries in this medium-bodied offering from American Gary Andrus. Smooth and well-structured on the midpalate, turning spicy and briary on the finish.**87** —*J.C. (12/1/2005)*

Gypsy Dancer 2003 Gibbston Home Estate Vineyard Pinot Noir (Central Otago) $50. From Gary Andrus's NZ venture, this is a plump, appealing Pinot that boasts scents of smoke and black cherries, followed by flavors of woodsmoke and plum. A bit astringent on the finish, with firm tannins that deserve to be cellared 2–3 years.**88** —*J.C. (7/1/2005)*

HATTON ESTATE

Hatton Estate 2003 Carsons Cabernets Cabernet Blend (Hawke's Bay) $25. Starts off with attractive scents of hickory smoke and cedar, but these wood-derived elements never fully merge or give way to the modest plum fruit. Dry and dusty on the finish.**82** —*J.C. (12/15/2006)*

Hatton Estate 2005 EC2 Gimblett Gravels Chardonnay (Hawke's Bay) $20. This is pretty solid as far as unoaked Chardonnay goes, with clean mixed fruit flavors of apple, melon, and pear providing modest complexity and weight. Finishes crisp, citrusy, and refreshing.**86** —*J.C. (12/15/2006)*

HAWKDON RISE

Hawkdon Rise 2001 Red Barnais Alexandra Pinot Noir (Central Otago) $40. A solid Pinot, with sturdy black cherries and toasty oak wrapped in a medium-weight package. Seems slightly weighted toward tannins, so drink it young while the fruit is forward and fresh.**86** —*J.C. (9/1/2003)*

HERZOG

Herzog 1999 Bordeaux Blend (Marlborough) $45. This Bordeaux-inspired blend seems a touch overdone—the fruit has a dried quality to it reminiscent of prunes and dates; the oak is chocolaty and rich. Seems supple enough on the palate, then firm tannins grab on the finish.**85** —*J.C. (4/1/2004)*

Herzog 2001 Chardonnay (Marlborough) $30. Don't confuse this for the kosher line of wines under a similar name. A nicely balanced Chardonnay, balancing ripe pear and peach fruit against lightly buttered toast to produce a really pleasing whole.**88** —*J.C. (4/1/2004)*

Herzog 2001 Montepulciano-Cabernet Fanc Montepulciano (Marlborough) $34. When you need to stump your wine-geek friends in a blind tasting, here's the perfect choice. After all, how many of them even know that Montepulciano is grown outside Italy? It's even pretty palatable, if somewhat heavy and low acid. Blackberry, blueberry, and chocolate flavors are chewy and mouth-filling.**86** —*J.C. (4/1/2004)*

Herzog 2002 Pinot Noir (Marlborough) $35. The Swiss folk at Herzog are making some interesting wines. Even this Pinot isn't without merit, although it's definitely weird. The nose is full of cola and wintergreen, with hints of cured meat, while the flavors resemble camphor and hickory smoke. Turns dry and astringent on the finish.**83** —*J.C. (7/1/2005)*

HIGHFIELD ESTATE

Highfield Estate 2001 Pinot Noir (Marlborough) $23. This pretty, relatively light-weight Pinot boasts a skinny thread of red cherry fruit wrapped in layers of root beer, dried spices, and brown sugar. Finishes with some woody notes of dark coffee and chocolate.**86** —*J.C. (8/1/2004)*

Highfield Estate 1998 Riesling (Marlborough) $12.87 —*S.H. (8/1/1999)*

Highfield Estate 2004 Sauvignon Blanc (Marlborough) $20. Always a nice wine, the '04 succeeds by pushing steely, sharp aromas of nettles, grapefruit, and citrus, and then following that up with passion fruit, grapefruit, and melon flavors. Basically, it tastes as it smells, and it finishes crystal clean if a tiny bit short.**89** *(7/1/2005)*

Highfield Estate 2002 Sauvignon Blanc (Marlborough) $18. This assertive wine adds just the right embellishments of complexity to its ripe fruit flavors: smoke on the nose and a creamy texture on the palate. Fresh herb flavors add a piquant touch to remind you that you're drinking Sauvignon Blanc.**89** —*J.C. (9/1/2003)*

Highfield Estate 2001 Sauvignon Blanc (Marlborough) $NA. Starts off with super-rich, ripe, exotic lemon-and-lime aromas and a luscious, unusual note of white chocolate. It's bone dry, but it's so fruity rich, so extracted and hedonistic, it's as decadent as a dessert wine. Amazingly long finish. **90** —*S.H. (11/15/2002)*

Highfield Estate 1998 Elstree Cuvée Brut Sparkling Blend (Marlborough) $30. This New Zealand winery excels with Sauvignon Blanc and offers some good Pinot Noir, and it's bubbly isn't bad at all. It's robust and toasty on the bouquet, and fairly full-force. The mouth is large and creamy, with typical apple and citrus flavors and also a hint of mustard. The feel across the palate is good, but also a touch aggressive.**87** —*M.S. (6/1/2003)*

NEW ZEALAND

NEW ZEALAND

HOLMES

Holmes 2003 Pinot Noir (Nelson) $25. Leathery and leafy on the nose, although the bouquet also incorporates some cherry scents. It's a lean, focused wine, one that finishes tart and zingy. **84** —*J.C. (12/1/2005)*

HOUSE OF NOBILO

House of Nobilo 1998 Fall Harvest Chardonnay (Gisborne) $12. 90 Best Buy —*S.H. (8/1/1999)*

House of Nobilo 2004 Regional Collection Chardonnay (East Coast) $12. Well-crafted and well-priced, with gentle scents of toasted nuts and grilled peaches picking up additional notes of pear and melon. Medium-weight, with a soft, easy finish. **87 Best Buy** —*J.C. (7/1/2005)*

House of Nobilo 2005 Icon Pinot Gris (Marlborough) $22. There's a copper tinge to this wine's color, the result some skin contact. The result is a richly fruity wine blessed with layers of ripe apples and berries. Zesty and a bit phenolic on the finish, helping to balance the .8% residual sugar. **88** —*J.C. (2/1/2006)*

House of Nobilo 2004 Icon Pinot Gris (Marlborough) $20. Given its pronounced copper tinge, this wine likely sees some skin contact. The result is an almost berry-like aroma, along with more typical apple and almond notes. It's also big, weighty, and slightly sweet, making a powerful flavor statement. **87** —*J.C. (7/1/2005)*

House of Nobilo 2002 Icon Pinot Noir (Marlborough) $20. Don't look for big fruit in this wine—you'll be disappointed. What you will find is plenty of earthy, spicy complexity. The flavors are slightly herbal and mushroomy, yet with a supple, rich texture. A bit tannic right now, so give it a year or two before pulling the cork. **88** —*J.C. (4/1/2004)*

House of Nobilo 2005 Icon Riesling (Marlborough) $20. A new addition to the Icon line from Nobilo and one that still needs a little work. It's good, with lifted floral and lime aromas, but seems overwhelmingly citrusy on the palate, with tangy notes that turn slightly pith-like on the finish. **84** —*J.C. (11/1/2006)*

House of Nobilo 2001 Fall Harvest Sauvignon Blanc (Marlborough) $10. Hay, grass, and intoxicating garden vegetable notes waft from the nose. It almost has the apple-citrus texture and flavor of a sparkling wine; Afterward, though, it tastes green and granite-y, like licking cilantro off a mortar and pestle. It's a little thin, and finishes long with minerals, fresh herb, and a bit too bright of a citrus-acid note. **85 Best Buy** —*D.T. (12/15/2001)*

House of Nobilo 2000 Fall Harvest Sauvignon Blanc (Marlborough) $10. Fresh and light; the grapefruit and gooseberry aromas and flavors are tinged with capsicum and green peas. The residual sugar is noticeable, at 6–7 g/L, but balanced by brisk acidity. **86 Best Buy** —*J.C. (5/1/2001)*

House of Nobilo 1998 Fall Harvest Sauvignon Blanc (Marlborough) $11. 88 Best Buy —*S.H. (8/1/1999)*

House of Nobilo 2005 Icon Sauvignon Blanc (Marlborough) $20. Produced off dry, bony sites in the Wairau, resulting in a ripe wine that retains the sweaty, passion fruit and gooseberry flavors that make Marlborough Sauvignon so unique, while adding layers of peach and pink grapefruit. Round in the mouth and easy to drink. **89** *(3/1/2006)*

House of Nobilo 2004 Icon Sauvignon Blanc (Marlborough) $20. A wine that evoked no consensus among our tasters. Is more less or is it more? The nose is rich and packed full of asparagus, canned pea, and pickled bell pepper, and the palate is thick and syrupy. One reviewer called it "good within the paradigm;" another found it mushy and lacking in balance. **85** *(7/1/2005)*

HUIA

Huia 2001 Chardonnay (Marlborough) $19. Seems almost too delicate for its own good, with toasted-oat scents gliding over melon, citrus, and pineapple aromas and flavors. The orchestra is playing a lovely melody, but you have to listen closely to hear it, so try with understated foods, such as simply prepared white fish dishes. **87** —*J.C. (4/1/2004)*

Huia 2003 Gewürztraminer (Marlborough) $19. Subtly flowery on the nose, with hints of pear and spice, Claire and Mike Allen's Gewürz is more restrained and controlled than many. Understated poached pears feature only a modicum of spice. Gewürztraminer is one grape that can

benefit from full volume, and this one is just too quiet. **85** —*J.C. (7/1/2005)*

Huia 2002 Gewürztraminer (Marlborough) $17. A bit reticent at first, but with time the aromas open up to display rich lychee and floral scents. This is a ripe, mouth-filling example of Gewürz that offers decent competition for entry-level bottlings from Alsace. **87** —*J.C. (9/1/2003)*

Huia 2004 Pinot Gris (Marlborough) $19. This off-dry rendition of Pinot Gris (the "it" grape in NZ right now) boasts a lovely, rich mouthfeel. Aromas of pear, almond, and apple, then more of the same on the palate, picking up some pineapple notes on the finish. Not complex enough to rate higher, but a very pleasing wine. **86** —*J.C. (7/1/2005)*

Huia 2003 Pinot Noir (Marlborough) $26. Leans toward a feminine style, with complex, mysterious aromas of herbs, smoke, and flowers that lead into a superbly textured midpalate—like crushed silk. Lovely floral and cherry notes linger on the finish. **90** —*J.C. (12/1/2005)*

Huia 2002 Pinot Noir (Marlborough) $27. Plump and juicy, but missing some of the velvety texture that has marked this wine in the past. Roasted cherries and fresh herbs join dark chocolate, coffee, and caramel flavors. **86** —*J.C. (8/1/2004)*

Huia 2001 Pinot Noir (Marlborough) $24. This normally reliable winery has turned out a thin, tartly acidic effort this vintage, with cranberry fruit backed by leathery spice. What happened? **83** —*J.C. (9/1/2003)*

Huia 2000 Pinot Noir (Marlborough) $24. Builds complexity through skillful layering of ripe black cherries, fresh greens (ferns or parsley stems), leather, and earth. The mouthfeel is spot-on, rich and plush without seeming heavy. Tart cherry and dusty cocoa notes on the finish and a fine sense of balance make it drinkable now or in several years. **90** —*J.C. (8/1/2002)*

Huia 2004 Riesling (Marlborough) $18. A bit disappointing from this producer, but still a good wine, the 2004 Huia Riesling seems a bit muted on the nose and lacking in intensity on the palate. On the plus side, there's some pretty pear fruit and a minerally, chalky finish. **84** —*J.C. (7/1/2005)*

Huia 2002 Riesling (Marlborough) $15. The aromas are a refined blend of peaches, pears, and citrus fruits, but don't adequately prepare the taster for the bold, striking flavors that follow. Despite being relatively light-bodied, tropical fruits, stone fruits, and citrus cascade across the palate, finishing a touch soft. If more structure becomes apparent as this wine's "baby fat" recedes, this wine's rating may prove conservative. **89** —*J.C. (8/1/2003)*

Huia 2004 Sauvignon Blanc (Marlborough) $18. A riper, gentler version of New Zealand Sauvignon Blanc, with scents of nectarine and grapefruit, nary a trace of green vegetables. Plump and amply textured on the palate, it delivers ripe peach and citrus flavors before finishing with a soft flourish of fruit. **87** —*J.C. (7/1/2005)*

Huia 2003 Sauvignon Blanc (Marlborough) $18. Concentrated, racy, and intense, packed with ever-changing notes of fruit that range from peach and melon to passion fruit, pineapple and grapefruit. The long, tangy finish reverberates across the palate long after the wine is gone. **91 Editors' Choice** —*J.C. (4/1/2004)*

Huia 2001 Sauvignon Blanc (Marlborough) $16. The bouquet here is confounding. It has some green vegetable and cat-pee qualities as well as white stone fruits, sulfur, and popcorn. In a word, it's complicated. In the mouth, grapefruit and celery flavors mingle with green grapes, while on the back end it's chalky and rather tart. The overall acidity is high, and there's one important thing missing here: balance. **86** *(8/1/2002)*

Huia 2000 Brut Sparkling Blend (Marlborough) $33. Disjointed, with ample toast, eggs and baked apple flavors but also a citrusy note that turns metallic on the finish. A disappointing effort from one of NZ's artisanal producers, or just a badly handled batch of bubbly? Tasted twice. **83** —*J.C. (6/1/2005)*

HUNTAWAY

Huntaway 1998 Reserve Limited Edition Bordeaux Blend (North Island) $15. A powerful red that relies more on non-fruit aromas and flavors for its character: smoke, cedar, cocoa, and a large helping of bitter herbs all shift and intermingle over, under, and through cassis and black cherries. **87** —*J.C. (5/1/2001)*

Huntaway 1998 Reserve Chardonnay (North Island) $15. No doubt a blend of Hawkes Bay and Gisborne fruit that's unfortunately lost its way in a lumberyard. It's full, indicating adequate sugar levels, but lacks fruit flavor, instead relying on wood for much of its character. **82** —*J.C.* *(5/1/2001)*

HUNTER'S

Hunter's 1996 Chardonnay (Marlborough) $21. 90 —*S.H. (8/1/1999)*

Hunter's 2003 Pinot Noir (Marlborough) $18. Relatively light in color, but very nicely perfumed and floral on the nose. Flavors are a bit simpler, focusing on cherries and vanilla. This soft, easy-drinking wine would make a fine accompaniment to delicate salmon dishes. **87** —*J.C. (12/1/2005)*

Hunter's 2005 Sauvignon Blanc (Marlborough) $15. Grassy and herbal on the nose, then shows more stone fruit flavors on the palate. Turns dry and stony on the finish. **86** —*J.C. (5/1/2006)*

Hunter's 2002 Sauvignon Blanc (Marlborough) $19. Smells zesty and piquant, with passion fruit and jalapeño scents wafting from the glass. Even better, the flavors back up this positive first impression, filling out this medium-weight wine with nuances of passion fruit and grapefruit. The finish is clean, tangy, and refreshing. **88** —*J.C. (9/1/2003)*

Hunter's 1999 Sauvignon Blanc (Marlborough) $12. Starts with strong, nuanced aromas of spiced green apples, citrus, melon, and fig, and turns explosively fruity in the mouth, with tiers of ripe, spicy juniper berry, and lime. Bone dry, it's fruit is highlighted by high acidity. The finish is remarkably long, rich, and spicy. **90** —*S.H. (6/1/2001)*

ISABEL ESTATE

Isabel Estate 1999 Chardonnay (Marlborough) $22. Mild toast accents the delicate white peaches and Bosc pears found in this full-bodied, spicy Chard from the Mendoza (Wente) clone. Finishes lemony and long; should age a few years at least, but it's good now as well. **89** —*J.C. (5/1/2001)*

Isabel Estate 1997 Chardonnay (Marlborough) $20. 91 —*S.H. (8/1/1999)*

Isabel Estate 2005 Pinot Gris (Marlborough) $22. A bit waxy on the nose, followed by scents of lemon and pineapple. It's medium- to full-bodied, ending dry, lemony, and long, with enough ripe apple flavor to carry the midpalate. **88** —*J.C. (2/1/2006)*

Isabel Estate 2000 Pinot Gris (Marlborough) $16. Hard to believe that first crop fruit went into this wine. Peaches, honey, and nuts on the nose; lime and white stone fruits on the palate. Good acidity and a bit of black pepper on the finish. Limited availability. **87** —*J.C. (5/1/2001)*

Isabel Estate 2004 Pinot Noir (Marlborough) $29. A disappointment from a winery and vineyard that has produced some very good Pinot in the past, this shows plenty of smoky, meaty complexity, and slightly herbal, cherry fruit. Light in weight, with a caramel edge to the finish. **82** —*J.C. (11/1/2006)*

Isabel Estate 2001 Pinot Noir (Marlborough) $30. A graceful, elegant Pinot that doesn't rely on weight or massive extraction to carry its flavors of cherries and herbs. Dried spices accent the finish. **86** —*J.C. (9/1/2003)*

Isabel Estate 1999 Pinot Noir (Marlborough) $26. From one of the older and more densely planted Pinot vineyards in the region, this is a wine of uncommon finesse and elegance. Black cherries and cola are touched with a hint of green tea and a kiss of toasty oak. Silky soft on the finish, making it great to drink now, but with this balance it should age at least a few years without a problem. **90 Editors' Choice** —*J.C. (5/1/2001)*

Isabel Estate 2000 Riesling (Marlborough) $18. A dry, steely Riesling that demands time in the cellar. Aromas of lime, with a hint of peach; assertive lime-citrus finish. Displays great depth and intensity, possibly due to the relatively low (by New Zealand standards) yields of 2.5 tons per acre. **90** —*J.C. (5/1/2001)*

Isabel Estate 1998 Sauvignon Blanc (Marlborough) $18. 89 —*S.H. (8/1/1999)*

Isabel Estate 2005 Sauvignon Blanc (Marlborough) $22. This light- to medium-bodied Savvy boasts flinty, minerally aromas, and an array of flavors that includes mixed citrus and tea leaves. Dusty, minerally notes add interest, particularly on the crisp, zesty finish. **89** —*J.C. (9/1/2006)*

Isabel Estate 2004 Sauvignon Blanc (Marlborough) $21. Hits this country's style like an arrow to the bull's eye. Fragrant as can be, with aromas of pineapple, passion fruit, tomatillo, fresh pea, and wheat grass. If that's not enough, the palate is round and spotless, with a tropical overload of sweet and tart tastes. Finishes long and precise, with radiant zest. **91 Editors' Choice** *(7/1/2005)*

Isabel Estate 2002 Sauvignon Blanc (Marlborough) $20. Tangy, grassy, and tight, this vintage of Isabel's Sauvignon Blanc seems as if it would benefit from a few more months in the bottle. It's sullen and angry now, with its honeyed, citrus flavors just waiting to unfurl. **88** —*J.C. (9/1/2003)*

Isabel Estate 2001 Sauvignon Blanc (Marlborough) $18. A remarkably complete and satisfying wine, showing exquisite balance and charm. Gooseberry, peach, and apple flavors have a sharp, minerally streak, while the crisp acids and opulent structure are near-perfect. Strikes a delicate balance between dry and honeyed. **92** —*S.H. (11/15/2002)*

Isabel Estate 2000 Sauvignon Blanc (Marlborough) $18. Shows a lot of citrusy fruit flavors—grapefruit and oranges—and passion fruit as well. Slightly creamy on the midpalate, before finishing with a faint herbal edge and strong lime-like acidity. **89** —*J.C. (5/1/2001)*

Isabel Estate 1999 Noble Sauvage Sauvignon Blanc (Marlborough) $35. All Sauvignon Blanc, and it shows in aromas of gooseberries, passion fruit, and chili peppers. This intensely sweet and honeyed wine also blends in an array of apricot-botrytis flavors. This is a wine that tastes great now and should also age gracefully. **92** —*J.C. (5/1/2001)*

JACKSON ESTATE

Jackson Estate 1999 Chardonnay (Marlborough) $15. The fruit may be tiring a little, but you can still taste its admirable citrus and peach qualities. Judicious oaking supports the fruit rather than overwhelming it, but this wine's clock is ticking. Drink up. **84** —*J.C. (9/1/2003)*

Jackson Estate 1998 Reserve Chardonnay (Marlborough) $25. Shows admirable restraint in its judicious use of French oak, resulting in menthol and pencil notes that play off pear and quince fruit. Solid, just needs more intensity overall; it's perhaps too elegant for its own good. **84** —*J.C. (5/1/2001)*

Jackson Estate 2005 Shelter Belt Chardonnay (Marlborough) $18. This reasonably complex Marlborough Chardonnay features pear and citrus fruit accented by hints of butter and spice. Add in layers of melon and anise, and the result is a very good wine that could just use a little more textured mouthfeel and longer finish. **87** —*J.C. (12/15/2006)*

Jackson Estate 2003 Unoaked Chardonnay (Marlborough) $16. Despite the rather late arrival of this wine into the market, it still shows plenty of freshness and vibrant fruit. Mango and banana scents lead into a plump wine with mixed tropical fruit flavors. It's a bit soft, but round and mouth-filling. **86** —*J.C. (7/1/2006)*

Jackson Estate 2002 Unoaked Chardonnay (Marlborough) $15. A solid example of unoaked Chardonnay, this boasts a rich, viscous mouthfeel usually reserved for more expensive wines. Flavors are tart and simple, consisting of tart pears and flourish of lime. **85** —*J.C. (9/1/2003)*

Jackson Estate 2001 Unoaked Chardonnay (Marlborough) $15. Made in a lean, high-acid style, with tart citrus aromas backed by light apple and pear fruit. **82** —*J.C. (11/15/2002)*

Jackson Estate 2000 Pinot Noir (Marlborough) $30. While it's a touch flat at first, airing brings this wine to life in no time. Cherry fruit is the calling card, and some creamy oak offers a sweet backdrop. More forward and full than it's racy or complex; Jackson's 2000 should satisfy anyone seeking a down the middle modern Pinot with structure and Burgundy-like acidity. **87** —*M.S. (12/15/2001)*

Jackson Estate 2005 Vintage Widow Pinot Noir (Marlborough) $23. This winery seems to be at the top of its game in recent vintages, and this Pinot Noir is a good value as well. Slightly dusty, floral notes add complexity to its spice and cherry aromas, while the mouthfeel is silky but not too soft. Finishes with hints of tea and rose petals. No need to wait on this one; drink now. **89** —*J.C. (12/15/2006)*

Jackson Estate 2000 Dry Riesling (Marlborough) $15. A racy, lean version of New Zealand Riesling, with crushed limestone, tart apples, and fresh limes combining on the palate. Citrusy acids on the finish bring it

NEW ZEALAND

NEW ZEALAND

sharply into focus. Worth a try with shellfish or as an apéritif. **87** —*J.C.* (8/1/2003)

Jackson Estate 1999 Dry Riesling (Marlborough) $15. Classic N.Z. Riesling aromas of pears, limes, and Granny Smith apples lead into a medium-weight version that's less austere and citrusy than many of its compatriots. Drink near-term, unless you like the petrol aromas likely to develop with age. **86** —*J.C.* (5/1/2001)

Jackson Estate 2005 Sauvignon Blanc (Marlborough) $20. This winery's Sauvignon is reassuringly back on form following a tough 2004 vintage. Peach and pink grapefruit lead the way, bolstered by wonderful ripeness and texture on the midpalate. Finishes on a crisp, grapefruity note. **90 Editors' Choice** —*J.C.* (5/1/2006)

Jackson Estate 2004 Sauvignon Blanc (Marlborough) $13. Citrusy and grassy on the nose, picking up hints of boxwood on the way to a surprisingly plump yet neutral midpalate. Tangy on the finish. **85** —*J.C.* (7/1/2005)

Jackson Estate 2003 Sauvignon Blanc (Marlborough) $17. Grassy and strikingly herbal on the nose, but it's all backed up by ample passion fruit notes. Zesty yet rounded on the palate, with more passion fruit, lime and a hint of jalapeño, finishing long, crisp, and refreshing. **90** — *J.C.* (8/1/2004)

Jackson Estate 2002 Sauvignon Blanc (Marlborough) $17. Fresh citrus and herb notes carry this zesty wine from start to finish, beginning with aromas of gooseberries, green peppers, and grapefruit and ending in a long, tangy finish laden with jalapeños and limes. **90 Editors' Choice** —*J.C.* (9/1/2003)

Jackson Estate 2000 Sauvignon Blanc (Marlborough) $15. Smells ripe, with melon and passion fruit pre-dominating, but by the finish Marlborough's trademark green pepper and grapefruit flavors come on strong—maybe too assertively for some tasters. Crisp and dry; a good palate refresher. **85** —*J.C.* (5/1/2001)

KAHURANGI

Kahurangi 2004 Mt. Arthur Chardonnay (Moutere) $22. This top-of-the-line Chard gets the full Monty—barrel fermentation, lees-stirring, malolactic fermentation—resulting in a toasty, buttery wine that's oaky from start to finish. Thankfully, there's also decent pear and apple fruit underneath and a lingering finish. **89** —*J.C.* (5/1/2006)

Kahurangi 2004 Unwooded Chardonnay (Nelson) $17. Unoaked, yet this wine still has a welcome creaminess in the midpalate that helps carry the ripe apple and tropical fruit flavors. Nicely balanced, and it should be versatile at the table, pairing with a wide array of dishes. **87** —*J.C.* (5/1/2006)

Kahurangi 2004 Moutere Gewürztraminer (Nelson) $24. Not explosively aromatic, but that may make this Gewürz easier to warm up to for some consumers. It's filled with pear and peach flavors, rounded out by a touch of residual sugar (to most tasters, it will come across as dry), and finishes with a pinch of peppery spice. **87** —*J.C.* (5/1/2006)

Kahurangi 2004 Pinot Noir (Nelson) $24. Aims at a perfumed, elegant style and partially succeeds. There's a bright, floral bouquet, but the flavors are tart, with shadings of cherry and chocolate that finish short. **84** —*J.C.* (12/1/2005)

Kahurangi 2003 Late Harvest Riesling (Moutere) $20. This lush, dessert-style Riesling is impeccably balanced. It's sweet but not overly so, with hints of dried apricot and honeyed peach on the nose and bergamot and orange marmalade flavors lingering on the finish. **92** —*J.C.* (5/1/2006)

Kahurangi 2004 Old Vines Riesling (Moutere) $20. This wine is distinctive, but not easy to cozy up to, with its dry, steely, lime, and green apple aromas and flavors. On the finish, chalky, minerally notes seem almost tannic. A bit weird, but will have its fans. **84** —*J.C.* (5/1/2006)

Kahurangi 2004 Sauvignon Blanc (Nelson) $18. Green from head to toe, with herbal, grassy notes, hints of bell pepper, and tangy passion fruit flavors barely rounded out by grapefruit. **85** —*J.C.* (5/1/2006)

KAIKOURA

Kaikoura 2002 Sauvignon Blanc (Marlborough) $14. Zesty and grapefruity, with plenty of limes, grassiness, and touches of green peppers to add

interest. A lean, racy wine to pair with shellfish or serve as an apéritif. **87** —*J.C.* (9/1/2003)

KATHY LYNSKEY

Kathy Lynskey 2004 Godfrey Reserve Chardonnay (Marlborough) $29. Subtly nutty on the nose, balanced by mixed citrus scents and hints of mint. Full-bodied and richly textured, with ample apple, pear, and tangerine flavors backed by toasty oak. Long and citrusy on the finish, with echoes of toasted nuts. Drink now. **90** —*J.C.* (7/1/2006)

Kathy Lynskey 2003 Godfrey Reserve Chardonnay (Marlborough) $29. Starts off a bit floral, then picks up hints of toast and lemon curd on the nose. In the mouth, it's a plump, medium-weight wine, with crisp citrus flavors that linger on the finish. **87** —*J.C.* (7/1/2005)

Kathy Lynskey 2004 Single Vineyard Gewürztraminer (Marlborough) $25. This is a well made Gewürz that just lacks a bit of intensity. Pear, spice, and a hint of pineapple on the nose; pineapple and pear flavors in the mouth. Finishes crisp and mouth-watering, bringing you back for another sip. **85** —*J.C.* (7/1/2005)

Kathy Lynskey 2004 15 Rows Reserve Merlot (Marlborough) $45. After years of trying, Lynskey has finally broken through with her Marlborough Merlot. This year's version features a better balance of fruit to oak than the 2001, and better ripeness than the 2002. Toasty wood and vanilla notes still lead the way, but underneath there's lush black cherry fruit tinged with olive and tobacco. Supple and creamy on the palate, with a long, layered finish. **90** —*J.C.* (11/1/2006)

Kathy Lynskey 2005 Single Vineyard Pinot Gris (Marlborough) $25. This is a plump—verging on corpulent—Pinot Gris, but one that avoids heaviness through decent acidity and a hint of tannin. Starts with fresh apples and melons, then adds a strong appleskin note, especially on the finish. **85** —*J.C.* (11/1/2006)

Kathy Lynskey 2004 Single Vineyard Pinot Gris (Marlborough) $25. Starts with a nutty, almond-like note, then delivers lots of ripe melon flavors in a plump, appealing format. Slightly off-dry, but well-balanced, without any cloying sweetness on the finish. **87** —*J.C.* (7/1/2005)

Kathy Lynskey 2004 Block 36 Reserve Pinot Noir (Marlborough) $39. This reserve effort comes across as a bit hard, combining some drying tannins with ample acidity. The bouquet features pleasant notes of cherries, milk chocolate, and powdered cinnamon, but the flavors turn toward tea, pie cherries, and cinnamon bark. **85** —*J.C.* (7/1/2006)

Kathy Lynskey 2003 Block 36 Reserve Pinot Noir (Marlborough) $39. Amply oaked, with menthol and chocolate scents that need time to integrate with cherry and anise aromas. Flavors veer toward cola, wintergreen, and red cherries, finishing on a slightly dry, woody note. **86** —*J.C.* (12/1/2005)

Kathy Lynskey 2005 Vineyard Select Sauvignon Blanc (Marlborough) $19. Peachy; quite ripe and round on the palate, filled with stone fruit, yet it's not fat and never loses its focus. This is nicely balanced Marlborough Sauv, even if in a somewhat riper style than expected. **88** —*J.C.* (5/1/2006)

Kathy Lynskey 2004 Vineyard Select Sauvignon Blanc (Marlborough) $19. A bit richer than most NZ SBs, this wine also incorporates chalky-minerally notes that elevate it above the crowd. Take complex aromas of peach, apple, grapefruit, and mineral, add nectarine flavors and a long finish, and you've got a winning recipe. Drink over the next year or so. **90 Editors' Choice** —*J.C.* (7/1/2005)

KEMBLEFIELD

Kemblefield 2002 Winemakers Signature Cabernet Sauvignon-Merlot (Hawke's Bay) $12. Modest cassis flavors are heavily burdened with green, herbaceous notes that swerve toward vegetal. Not imported to the U.S. **81** —*J.C.* (5/1/2006)

Kemblefield 2002 Distinction Chardonnay (Hawke's Bay) $16. Not overly toasty or buttery, but there's enough of each to make a statement. Honey and peach flavors end on lingering notes of lime and dried spices. **87** — *J.C.* (5/1/2006)

Kemblefield 2004 Winemakers Signature Chardonnay (Hawke's Bay) $13. Fruit-forward, with green apple and lime aromas that are rounded out on the palate by a bit of peach. Light to medium in body, this fresh, crisp Chardonnay picks up citrusy notes on the finish. **87** —*J.C. (5/1/2006)*

Kemblefield 2004 Distinction Gewürztraminer (Hawke's Bay) $14. Starts off with lovely rose petal and spice aromas, then delivers broad, mouth-filling flavors without being heavy. On the dry side for NZ Gewürz; finishes clean but a bit short. **86** —*J.C. (5/1/2006)*

Kemblefield 2002 Reserve Malbec-Merlot (Hawke's Bay) $16. Tastes exactly like you might expect a blend of these two grapes to taste, with blackberry and spice notes from the Malbec (55%) and black cherry and dried herb shadings from the Merlot (45%). Although not hugely complex or rich, it's a pretty wine that shouldn't be overlooked. **87** —*J.C. (5/1/2006)*

Kemblefield 2002 Distinction Merlot (Hawke's Bay) $14. A bright and bouncy Merlot, with charming cherry flavors accented by hints of tobacco, cinnamon and clove. A dollop of Malbec (15%) contributes acidity and spice. **86** —*J.C. (5/1/2006)*

Kemblefield 2005 Distinction Pinot Gris (Hawke's Bay) $15. Smells attractively fruity, like ripe peaches and melons. This medium-bodied Pinot Gris is broad and fat in the mouth, then turns dry and zippy on the finish. **87** —*J.C. (2/1/2006)*

Kemblefield 2005 Winemakers Signature Sauvignon Blanc (Hawke's Bay) $14. Ripe pink grapefruit aromas and flavors are almost red-berryish, really, but balanced by crisp acids. Plump in the mouth and very easy to drink, this should be a picnic staple. **88 Best Buy** —*J.C. (5/1/2006)*

Kemblefield 2004 Distinction Sémillon (Hawke's Bay) $16. Slightly nutty and leesy on the nose, followed by a medium-bodied, peach and orange-flavored midpalate. Turns very citrusy and tight on the finish, much like some Hunter Valley Sémillons. Not imported in the U.S. **86** —*J.C. (5/1/2006)*

Kemblefield 2002 Reserve Zinfandel (Hawke's Bay) $25. With its medium body and berry-tea flavors, this is more a claret-style Zin than is the current rage in California, but it nicely balances ripe berry flavors with peppery, leafy and rhubarb notes. Drink now. **90** —*J.C. (5/1/2006)*

KIM CRAWFORD

Kim Crawford 2000 Tané Bordeaux Blend (Hawke's Bay) $25. Starting with its perfumed nose of flowers, tobacco, and black cherry, this shows lovely balance in a Bordeaux-style red, layering fruit flavors with notes of herbs, dried spices, and black olive. Approximately one-third Cabernet Franc, the rest Merlot. Drink now–2012. **90** —*J.C. (5/1/2006)*

Kim Crawford 1999 Tané Cabernet Franc (Hawke's Bay) $30. With 95% Cabernet Franc and only 5% Merlot, there's plenty of floral and leafy, tobacco-like complexities and a certain austerity to the plummy, meaty flavors. Drink over the next few years with grilled or roasted meats. **89** —*J.C. (5/1/2001)*

Kim Crawford 1996 Rory Brut Champagne Blend (Marlborough) $NA. A crisp sparkler that features a nice blend of tropical fruit with green apples and limes. Some biscuity and yeasty notes provide added complexity. **87** —*J.C. (5/1/2001)*

Kim Crawford 1999 Pia Chardonnay (Hawke's Bay) $30. The blend of this proprietary wine can vary from year to year, but in 1999 it's all Chardonnay. The honeyed peach and pear fruit is oaky, but not over the top, as the wine's vibrant acidity holds everything together. **90** —*J.C. (5/1/2001)*

Kim Crawford 2000 Tietjen Chardonnay (Gisborne) $20. Don't look for subtlety here. This is a lush, lusty offering that's loaded with coconut and toast from American oak upfront, but also oozes with oranges and mangos. Drink this one young to enjoy its plump exuberance. **91 Editors' Choice** —*J.C. (5/1/2001)*

Kim Crawford 2004 Tietjen-Briant Chardonnay (Gisborne) $25. A lush marriage of tropical fruit and toast, coconut and vanilla notes, this is a big, ripe creamsicle of a wine, finishing with a flourish of oak. **89** —*J.C. (5/1/2006)*

Kim Crawford 2005 Unoaked Chardonnay (Marlborough) $17. A reliably fruit-filled offering, the 2005 version offers honeyed apple, melon, and

pear flavors carried by a well-rounded and slightly viscous wine. On the soft side, with a pithy note to the finish. **84** —*J.C. (11/1/2006)*

Kim Crawford 2002 Unoaked Chardonnay (Marlborough) $18. Undeniably well made, but I've yet to see the attraction of unoaked Chardonnay from anywhere outside of Chablis or the Maconnais. This attempt is more successful than most—it's a simple, fruit cocktail quaffer with decent mouthfeel and adequate concentration. **85** —*J.C. (4/1/2004)*

Kim Crawford 2000 Unoaked Chardonnay (Marlborough) $17. Ripe, lightly buttered pears are tinged with a light muskiness and married to tropical fruits like guava in this soft, easy-to-drink wine that tastes like Chardonnay, without the overlay of oak to which consumers are so accustomed. **88** —*J.C. (5/1/2001)*

Kim Crawford 1999 Unoaked Chardonnay (Marlborough) $15. **89** —*M.S. (10/1/2000)*

Kim Crawford 1998 Unoaked Chardonnay (Marlborough) $15. **90** *(11/15/1999)*

Kim Crawford 2002 Merlot (East Coast) $18. So young, it's like a barrel sample, with immature primary fruit accompanied by sharp acids that slice across the palate with a steely edge. The flavors suggest jammy blackberries. Badly in need of a year or so of bottle age. **84** —*S.H. (1/1/2002)*

Kim Crawford 1999 Te Awanga Merlot (Hawke's Bay) $21. Avoids the herbal elements of Merlot and instead emphasizes the smoky, meaty complexities to its robust flavors of black cherry and plum. Ready to drink now, or age up to five years. **88** —*J.C. (5/1/2001)*

Kim Crawford 2005 Pinot Gris (Marlborough) $17. Now owned by Constellation Brands, but at least for the moment Kim Crawford is still the winemaker, and continuing to turn out fresh, fruit-driven, character-filled wines. Vibrant lime and papaya scents ease into flavors of melon, tropical fruit, and a dash of citrus. Plump and easy to drink, with a touch of residual sugar. **87** —*J.C. (11/1/2006)*

Kim Crawford 2004 Pinot Gris (Marlborough) $17. Smells like pear nectar, but it's close to dry tasting, with bold pear and apple flavors accented by hints of fresh herbs. Medium in weight, with a long, refreshing finish. Should prove very versatile at the table; serve as an apéritif, with seafood or white meats. **88** —*J.C. (7/1/2005)*

Kim Crawford 2000 Boyzown Vineyard Pinot Gris (Marlborough) $18. Mild aromas of peaches and nectarines lead into a fairly full-bodied wine that ends with notes of grapefruit and lemon. **88** —*J.C. (5/1/2001)*

Kim Crawford 2005 Pinot Noir (Marlborough) $17. Frost trimmed the yields in 2005, seemingly adding an extra layer of concentration to this wine. While still not a heavyweight, it's a lush, layered wine with slightly meaty nuances to its plum and cola flavors. Good length on the finish. **89** —*J.C. (11/1/2006)*

Kim Crawford 2004 Pinot Noir (Marlborough) $17. Light in hue, featuring delicate cherry and crushed spice aromas and flavors that lean toward black pepper. It's on the light side, but still attractive, and would work well with delicate salmon preparations. **86** —*J.C. (12/1/2005)*

Kim Crawford 2002 Pinot Noir (Marlborough) $14. For the price, this is a good introduction to NZ Pinot Noir, showing a smooth mouthfeel and smoky, briary complexities layered over tangy beet and cherry fruit. **86** —*J.C. (4/1/2004)*

Kim Crawford 2000 Pinot Noir (Hawke's Bay) $NA. Simple cherry flavors are clean, pure, and easy-to-drink. At the suggested price of $15, this would be a Best Buy if it were available in the United States. Future vintages will be Marlborough-Hawkes Bay blends and be available in the U.S.; let's hope the quality stays at this level or even improves. **87** —*J.C. (5/1/2001)*

Kim Crawford 2000 Anderson Vineyard Pinot Noir (Marlborough) $35. Deep in color with a friendly back-fruit-dominant bouquet. This is all about ripe blackberries, with just the slightest touch of meatiness giving it some teeth. If you're seeking plump, New World Pinot Noir, this fits the bill. Round and cheery; the low acidity says,"drink me now." **90** —*M.S. (12/15/2001)*

Kim Crawford 2004 Dry Riesling (Marlborough) $17. Green leafy notes combine with mouth-watering ripe apple and lime scents on the nose of this crisp, stylish Riesling. It's reasonably full-bodied at 12.5% alcohol but dry, finishing fresh and minerally. **87** —*J.C. (12/1/2005)*

Kim Crawford 2000 Dry Riesling Riesling (Marlborough) $16. With only a hint of residual sugar, this wine leaves you free to focus on the intense peach, pear, and lime fruit. Great balance and racy acidity prolongs the extended finish. **90 Editors' Choice** —*J.C. (5/1/2001)*

Kim Crawford 2000 Reka Riesling (Marlborough) $NA. A slightly botrytized Riesling that's not available in the U.S., thanks to BATF regulations regarding permissible levels of volatile acidity. That said, I didn't find the VA objectionable in this or many other Kiwi dessert wines. Light apricot accents the ripe pineapple fruit. Richly viscous in the mouth, much like a good Alsatian *vendanges tardives*. **90** —*J.C. (5/1/2001)*

Kim Crawford 1998 Sauvignon Blanc (Wairau) $15. 88 —*S.H. (8/1/1999)*

Kim Crawford 2005 Sauvignon Blanc (Marlborough) $17. Shows hints of green on the nose, but the focus in this vintage is on riper, more tropical flavors. Soft and easy to drink, with an edgy shot of lime on the finish. **87** —*J.C. (5/1/2006)*

Kim Crawford 2004 Sauvignon Blanc (Marlborough) $17. Not overly aggressive, this light- to medium-weight Sauvignon Blanc features fresh leafy herbs, but also boasts plenty of melon and grapefruit to maintain its balance. A little soft on the finish, but clean, with lingering notes of pink grapefruit. **88** —*J.C. (7/1/2005)*

Kim Crawford 2002 Sauvignon Blanc (Marlborough) $18. Another dry, crisp Sauvignon from this fine producer, highlighted by gooseberry and lime flavors and intense acidity. The tartness startles the palate and carries the bright flavors all the way through the long, spicy finish. **89** —*S.H. (1/1/2002)*

Kim Crawford 2000 Sauvignon Blanc (Marlborough) $17. A soft, gentle style of Sauvignon Blanc, with gooseberry and nectarine fruit that seems almost creamy across the palate. Approximately 25% went through malolactic fermentation to smooth out the edges, and the result is a plush, creamy wine quite different from most N.Z. Sauvignon Blanc. **87** —*J.C. (5/1/2001)*

Kim Crawford 1999 Sauvignon Blanc (Marlborough) $15. 92 —*L.W. (4/1/2000)*

Kim Crawford 1998 Awatere Sauvignon Blanc (Awatere Valley) $20. 89 —*S.H. (8/1/1999)*

KINGSLEY ESTATE

Kingsley Estate 2000 Cabernet Sauvignon-Merlot (Hawke's Bay) $55. American consumers benefit from the late arrival of this wine on the market, as initial reports out of New Zealand suggested it was a tannic beast. Now, the wine is ready to drink, with dark, earthy flavors of plum and tobacco riding atop soft, enveloping tannins. Drink now or hold another 2–3 years. **88** —*J.C. (7/1/2005)*

KIWI

Kiwi 2004 White Table Wine Chardonnay (New Zealand) $14. This is a blend of tank- and barrel-fermented Chard put together at Kahurangi in Nelson for importer Russell Briggs. Green apple aromas and flavors, a slightly creamy texture and a crisp finish make this a simple yet satisfying quaff. **86** —*J.C. (5/1/2006)*

Kiwi 2004 Red Table Wine Pinot Noir (New Zealand) $15. This is Pinot Noir that in some perverse marketing twist doesn't have the variety prominently displayed in big, bold letters to snare the *Sideways* fan. Scents of celery leaf and white pepper are echoed on the light-weight palate, where cherry flavors chime in. Peppery and fresh on the finish. **83** —*J.C. (7/1/2006)*

KONO

Kono 2005 Unoaked Chardonnay (Marlborough) $17. Broad on the palate, with a slightly corpulent mouthfeel, this wine features a pleasant bouquet of spice drop, honey, and melon, followed by slightly more neutral flavors and a fast-fading finish. **86** —*J.C. (11/1/2006)*

Kono 2004 Unoaked Chardonnay (Marlborough) $15. Straightforward and fruity, with papaya and orange notes that turn crisper and more citrusy

on the palate. It's a clean, fresh, unoaked style that finishes with lemon and green apple tartness. . **86** —*J.C. (7/1/2006)*

Kono 2005 Pinot Noir (Marlborough) $17. Has a pretty appearance and bouquet, with a ruby red color and sappy scents of herbs and raspberry, but doesn't quite measure up on the palate, where it's rather light and fluid, with herbal flavors only just buffered by pretty cherry notes. Picks up slightly bitter chocolate notes on the finish. **84** —*J.C. (9/1/2006)*

Kono 2005 Sauvignon Blanc (Marlborough) $15. Perfectly serviceable Marlborough Sauvignon, with slightly sweaty-musky aromas and passion fruit scents, followed by more subdued flavors and a short, fresh finish. **84** —*J.C. (9/1/2006)*

Kono 2004 Sauvignon Blanc (Marlborough) $15. This is a full-bodied, ripe style of Marlborough Sauvignon. It starts with aromas of warm, sun-ripened stone fruits then adds hints of honey and dried herbs. Flavors of peach, melon, and fig turn a bit grapefruity on the finish, but this is a lusciously fruit-filled wine. . **88** —*J.C. (7/1/2006)*

KONRAD

Konrad 2005 Sauvignon Blanc (Marlborough) $18. Despite some obvious green notes, this Sauvignon Blanc seems rather weighty, without the crisp zest expected from this variety in Marlborough. Instead, there's more tropical fruit—even some guava notes—and an abbreviated finish. **84** —*J.C. (12/15/2006)*

KONRAD & CONRAD

Konrad & Conrad 2001 Sauvignon Blanc (Marlborough) $15. What a clean, pretty fruit-and-flowers nose this has, and the flavors don't disappoint. Melon and citrus dominate, but it's all ripe fruit and not the least bit lean. The tail end is lengthy and layered, if maybe a bit chalky. But all in all this wine delivers the goods with a smile. **90 Editors' Choice** *(8/1/2002)*

KOURA BAY

Koura Bay 2001 Whalesback Awatere Valley Sauvignon Blanc (Marlborough) $18. This wine is a bit rough around the edges, with strong citrus flavors and high acids. It's very dry and rather tart and astringent, with virtually no residual sugar. Yet it's clean and refreshing, a minerally, metallic wine that would be good with shellfish. **85** —*S.H. (11/15/2002)*

KUMEU RIVER

Kumeu River 2004 Chardonnay (Kumeu) $33. This may not be as long-lived as its Matés's Vineyard stablemate, but is it ever luscious now. Toasty, mealy aromas carry hints of roasted nuts, but this flamboyantly oaky wine features fruit to spare, adding layers of apple and citrus flavors that round out the wine without becoming soft or flabby. Drink now. **91 Editors' Choice** —*J.C. (7/1/2006)*

Kumeu River 2003 Chardonnay (Kumeu) $32. Just a bare step behind Kumeu's Mate's Vineyard, the regular Chardonnay is still a special wine. The aromas meld smoke, butter, and tropical fruit, while the palate is a bit hard-edged at this stage, yielding mostly crisp, citrusy flavors. Give it a year or two in the bottle to soften. **89** —*J.C. (7/1/2005)*

Kumeu River 2002 Chardonnay (Kumeu) $26. A Kiwi classic, Michael Brajkovich's latest release shows its trademark toasted-oat aromas combined artfully with white peaches and other undefinable stone fruits. It's full and soft, easy to drink, yet possessed of a fine core of citrusy acids. Delicious now, but likely won't peak until 2007. **90** —*J.C. (4/1/2004)*

Kumeu River 1999 Chardonnay (Kumeu) $23. Light toast notes over pears, framed by citrusy acidity. The lemon-and-lime flavors come to the fore on the elegant finish, prolonging it. Not a fruity blockbuster; rather a model of restraint and class. **90 Editors' Choice** —*J.C. (5/1/2001)*

Kumeu River 1998 Chardonnay (Kumeu) $33. 91 —*J.C. (10/1/2000)*

Kumeu River 1997 Chardonnay (Kumeu) $25. 90 —*S.H. (8/1/1999)*

Kumeu River 2004 Matés Vineyard Chardonnay (Kumeu) $43. A bit more understated than this wine has been in past vintages, but still of excellent quality, with lovely toasted-oat notes framing pear, melon, and citrus flavors. It's full-bodied and long, with some youthful oaky notes still showing on the finish. Drink 2007–2010. **90** —*J.C. (7/1/2006)*

Kumeu River 1997 Matés Vineyard Chardonnay (Kumeu) $40. 90 —*J.C. (10/1/2000)*

Kumeu River 2003 Mate's Vineyard Chardonnay (Kumeu) $37. One of New Zealand's perennial award-winners, the 2003 Mate's Chard features wonderfully complete aromas that combine scents of smoke and toasted oats with grilled fruit and nut meat. It's full-bodied, drenching the palate with grilled nut and citrus flavors, before finishing on a long, harmonious note. **91 Editors' Choice** —*J.C. (7/1/2005)*

Kumeu River 1999 Mate's Vineyard Chardonnay (Kumeu) $33. Smokier and toastier than Kumeu's regular Chardonnay, the fruit is also dialed up, with ripe pears, peaches, and even orange blossoms. The long, citrusy finish leaves you searching for another pour. Should be long-lived as well. **92** —*J.C. (5/1/2001)*

Kumeu River 2005 Village Chardonnay (Kumeu) $19. A straightforward, easy-drinking Chardonnay from one of New Zealand's best Chardonnay producers. Peach, pineapple, and citrus fruits give a round impression on the palate, finishing with a tart edge. Drink now. **85** —*J.C. (11/1/2006)*

Kumeu River 2004 Village Chardonnay (Kumeu) $19. Kumeu River's entry-level Chard is now available in the U.S., but it doesn't really compare to its upscale brethren. It's got pretty peach and citrus aromas and flavors, but not the richness, weight, or length to warrant a higher rating. **84** —*J.C. (9/1/2006)*

Kumeu River 2005 Pinot Gris (Kumeu) $19. Starts off citrusy, but those notes are rounded out by ripe apple and melon flavors. This off-dry, round-in-the-mouth Pinot Gris then picks up subtle spice and pepper notes on the finish. **87** —*J.C. (11/1/2006)*

Kumeu River 2004 Pinot Gris (Kumeu) $19. A cleanly made, straightforward Pinot Gris, with ripe apple and citrus aromas and flavors that finish crisp despite having noticeable residual sugar on the palate. Nicely balanced. **88** —*J.C. (2/1/2006)*

Kumeu River 2000 Pinot Gris (Kumeu) $15. A bit muted on the nose, but this wine scores points for its bold flavors of peach and citrus and oily texture. Flirts with sweetness, with 8g/L (0.8%) residual sugar. **85** —*J.C. (5/1/2001)*

Kumeu River 2003 Pinot Noir (Kumeu) $30. Marked by its stay in barrel, this rare Pinot Noir from near Auckland displays smoky, bacon-scented aromas, followed up on the palate by savory flavors of dried mushrooms and cured meats. Not a wine for lovers of New World fruit, it appears to be aiming for more sous bois complexity. **85** —*J.C. (11/1/2006)*

Kumeu River 2002 Pinot Noir (Kumeu) $30. A lightweight, delicate style, with slightly stinky, smoky, and cedary aromas that give way only stubbornly to cherry and herb flavors. Tart and clean on the finish. **86** —*J.C. (6/6/2005)*

Kumeu River 1999 Pinot Noir (Kumeu) $30. There's an herbaceous streak to this wine but it's more than compensated for by black cherry fruit and exciting smoked meat aromas that kept me going back for another sniff. Supple and ready to drink now and over the next few years. **90** —*J.C. (5/1/2001)*

Kumeu River 1998 Pinot Noir (Kumeu) $18. 87 —*M.S. (10/1/2000)*

Kumeu River 1998 Melba Red Blend (Kumeu) $23. In a hot vintage like 1998, Kumeu's proprietary blend of Merlot (65%), Malbec (30%), and Cabernet Franc (5%) gets ripe enough to avoid any suggestion of weediness. Strong cinnamon notes from new oak complement plush black-cherry fruit. Anise and leather nuances spice up the finish. **90** —*J.C. (5/1/2001)*

Kumeu River 2004 Sauvignon Blanc (Marlborough) $19. In a startling departure, the Brajkovich family has made their first wine from outside the winery's Kumeu region. The result is a classy Sauvignon Blanc, bursting with passion fruit and hints of nectarine, jalapeño, and mineral smoke. The only quibble is that it seems a bit tart—verging on metallic—on the finish. **87** —*J.C. (7/1/2005)*

Kumeu River 1997 Sauvignon Blanc (Kumeu) $17. 88 —*S.H. (8/1/1999)*

KUSUDA

Kusuda 2003 C Pinot Noir (Martinborough) $NA. The "C" stands for clay, the predominant soil type in the vineyard. Well-oaked, with smoke and berry aromas and flavors and a wiry, herbal thread wrapped around a core of bright boysenberry fruit. Shows some sturdy tannins on the finish, so hold 2–3 years. **89** —*J.C. (12/1/2005)*

Kusuda 2003 G Pinot Noir (Martinborough) $NA. Lush and supple, boasting ample cherry and vanilla aromas and flavors. It's easily approachable, yet still shows decent complexity in a slightly herbal-briary nuance. The "G" stands for gravel, which in this vintage produced a less powerful wine than the "C" (clay) bottling. **88** —*J.C. (12/1/2005)*

Kusuda 2002 Syrah (Martinborough) $NA. Impressive purple color, but less intense on the nose. White pepper notes add complexity to modest plum flavors, while a herbal note carries the finish. **84** —*J.C. (5/1/2006)*

LAKE CHALICE

Lake Chalice 2003 Pinot Noir (Marlborough) $20. A big-bodied, somewhat beefy Pinot, with rustic herbal tendrils giving the cherry fruit an earthy, beet-like nuance. Delivers a mouthful of flavor, but it's missing the silky mouthfeel of great Pinot. **86** —*J.C. (7/1/2005)*

Lake Chalice 2002 Pinot Noir (Marlborough) $22. An easy-to-drink and easy-to-like Pinot, Lake Chalice's 2002 melds smoky, herbal nuances with cola and black cherries in a tart, light-weight format. Try it with a simple, herb-rubbed roast chicken. **87** —*J.C. (4/1/2004)*

Lake Chalice 2004 Riesling (Marlborough) $16. Reasonably full-bodied despite only 12.5% alcohol, this off-dry Riesling features aromas and flavors of ripe peaches and vanilla, while a shot of grapefruit cleans things up nicely, adding needed delineation to the finish. **87** —*J.C. (7/1/2005)*

Lake Chalice 2002 Falcon Vineyard Botrytised Riesling (Marlborough) $20. Shows some wonderful botrytis aromas of dried apricots, but also a disturbing amount of volatile acidity. If you can tolerate notes of shoe polish and nail polish, you may find this rating woefully conservative. **84** —*J.C. (8/1/2003)*

Lake Chalice 2001 Falcon Vineyard Late Harvest Riesling (Marlborough) $17. Piny and minty, which combine to give the pineapple fruit a decidedly medicinal edge. It's lightly sweet, balanced by healthy acidity, so it might work well with herb-scented desserts, like lavender sorbet. **83** —*J.C. (8/1/2003)*

Lake Chalice 2005 Sauvignon Blanc (Marlborough) $17. Nicely ripened without being overripe, this rather soft Sauvignon marries peach and melon fruit with a dollop of grassy herbaceousness. Pretty and easy to drink; best yet from this winery. **88** —*J.C. (5/1/2006)*

Lake Chalice 2004 Sauvignon Blanc (Marlborough) $16. Seems a bit soft on the finish, but otherwise packs in plenty of pink grapefruit and passion fruit. Herbal, vegetal hints provide extra kick, but this medium-weight wine is made to go down easy, without any sharp edges. **86** —*J.C. (7/1/2005)*

Lake Chalice 2001 Sauvignon Blanc (Marlborough) $15. Odd aromas of peanuts and asparagus are a bit off-putting. And in the mouth, the vegetal character is over-riding. This wine has its qualities, but nonetheless it's just loaded with too much green veggies, primarily asparagus and green beans. And what's with the peanut butter quality? **84** *(8/1/2002)*

LAWSON'S DRY HILLS

Lawson's Dry Hills 2001 Chardonnay (Marlborough) $22. Subtle toast and peach notes are wrapped around a core of apple and pear fruit. There's a certain tension created by the interplay of weighty fruit and crisp acidity. Lingers delicately on the finish, blending hints of butter, yellow plum, and pineapple. **87** —*J.C. (4/1/2004)*

Lawson's Dry Hills 2004 Gewürztraminer (Marlborough) $16. Rather honeyed and peachy, with lychee and some extremely ripe grapefruit scents that presage broad, mouth-filling flavors of lychee, stone fruits, and citrus. Shows good weight and concentration on the palate and a long, spicy finish. Even the price is right. What's not to like? **90 Editors' Choice** —*J.C. (7/1/2005)*

Lawson's Dry Hills 2002 Gewürztraminer (Marlborough) $15. Wow. This is a steal, and a dead-ringer for a top Alsace Gewürztraminer. Effusive scents of lychees and rose petals are textbook Gewürz; the weight and viscosity on the palate provide heft and the flavors linger delicately on the finish, without any bitterness at all. **90 Best Buy** —*J.C. (8/1/2004)*

Lawson's Dry Hills 2004 Pinot Noir (Marlborough) $22. Yet another well-priced offering from Marlborough, Lawson's Pinot is a plump, fruity wine framed by ample oak. Toasty and cedary on the nose, it finishes with some dry wood tannins. Give it another year to smooth out. **87** —J.C. (12/1/2005)

Lawson's Dry Hills 2002 Pinot Noir (Marlborough) $18. Very good Pinot at a very good price. It's actually somewhat reminiscent of some Russian River Valley examples, with ample cherry and cola flavors amplified by hints of birch root and wintergreen. Caramel creeps in on the finish. **88** —J.C. (4/1/2004)

Lawson's Dry Hills 2005 Sauvignon Blanc (Marlborough) $16. Wonderfully ripe and tropical, bursting with stone fruits as well, with just a hint of capsicum to remind you it's Sauvignon Blanc. Round-bodied and concentrated, yet fresh and clean. **90 Editors' Choice** —J.C. (5/1/2006)

Lawson's Dry Hills 2004 Sauvignon Blanc (Marlborough) $16. Smells just right, with bits of passion fruit and grassy notes, and also riper hints of apricot. But it just delivers on the palate, where it seems a bit light and hollow before finishing tart and shrill. A wine of unfulfilled promise. **84** —J.C. (7/1/2005)

Lawson's Dry Hills 2003 Sauvignon Blanc (Marlborough) $16. Grassy and herbal, but with a solid under-pinning of grapefruit to tie things together. Picks up hints of cilantro and peach while remaining light and fresh. Measures a bit light on the concentration meter, but it's pretty nonetheless. **86** —J.C. (8/1/2004)

Lawson's Dry Hills 2002 Sauvignon Blanc (Marlborough) $16. Yet another fine effort from this Marlborough winery, the 2002 Sauvignon Blanc is a big, rich, mouth-filling wine. Hints of honey and smoke accent gooseberries and nectarines. Drink now. **88** —J.C. (4/1/2004)

Lawson's Dry Hills 2001 Sauvignon Blanc (Marlborough) $16. The bouquet here is not for the weak; it's intense, with cat pee, herbs, and some sulfur. Passion fruit, pineapple, and green apple flavors vie for first billing in the mouth, while the finish is long and tight. It's a funky wine, one that tastes better than it smells. **87** (8/1/2002)

LEGRYS

LeGrys 2000 Adam's Estate Pinot Noir (Marlborough) $26. Heavy oak and tart berries come together in this modest effort. Taken individually, the parts of this wine are impressive, boasting bright berries, coffee, and chocolate, but they fail to comply harmonize, leaving one wondering what might have been. **83** —J.C. (9/1/2003)

LeGrys 2001 Sauvignon Blanc (Marlborough) $17. Blends, only partly successfully, vegetal notes with sweet fruit flavors. Peas and asparagus are countered by melons and peaches. Finish seems slightly sweet, leaving open the question of residual sugar. **85** —J.C. (9/1/2003)

LINACRE LANE

Linacre Lane 2003 Pinot Noir (Martinborough) $NA. Herbal, with green aromas that come awfully close to green bean. Earthy and mushroomy on the palate, with a short finish. **83** —J.C. (12/1/2005)

LINDAUER

Lindauer NV Brut (New Zealand) $13. This bargain bubbly from New Zealand's largest winery is light and fresh, with floral notes atop apple and ginger aromas. Snappy and citrusy in the mouth, finishing with grapefruit and green apple flavors. **85** —J.C. (12/31/2004)

LINDEN ESTATE

Linden Estate 2000 Merlot (Hawke's Bay) $13. Relative to this producer's fine Sauvignon Blanc, this light-weight Merlot is a bit of a disappointment. Herbal and a bit briary, with tomato-leaf and cherry flavors. **83** —J.C. (12/15/2003)

Linden Estate 2002 Sauvignon Blanc (Hawke's Bay) $11. Surprisingly ripe and creamy for a Sauvignon Blanc in this price range, with stone fruit aromas and flavors backed by citrus and mild herbs. The warm, rich nature of this wine underscores the differences between most Hawke's Bay and Marlborough Sauvignon Blancs. **90 Best Buy** —J.C. (9/1/2003)

LOBSTER KEY

Lobster Key 2004 Pinot Noir (East Coast) $14. Brings cola and cherry on the nose, but also some slightly vegetal notes. A supple, creamy mouthfeel isn't enough to rescue this wine from its dull flavors. **82** —J.C. (7/1/2006)

LONGRIDGE

Longridge 1999 Chardonnay (Hawke's Bay) $10. This one's an odd duck. Ripe, honeyed peach and caramelized pineapple aromas and flavors turn tart and metallic on the finish, resulting in a package that's disjointed and ultimately unsatisfying. **81** —J.C. (5/1/2001)

Longridge 1998 Sauvignon Blanc (Hawke's Bay) $10. **89 Best Buy** —S.H. (8/1/1999)

LYNSKEYS WAIRAU PEAKS

Lynskeys Wairau Peaks 2002 Chardonnay (Marlborough) $25. Smoky, toasty, and mealy on the nose, but those oaky and yeasty aromas are joined by mouth-watering scents of peaches and nectarines. The flavors are of grilled peaches—smoky and slightly caramelized, yet retaining juicy acidity that elegantly prolongs the finish. **90** —J.C. (9/1/2003)

Lynskeys Wairau Peaks 1999 Chardonnay (Marlborough) $20. Pretty oaky, with buttered toast and oatmeal over modest pineapple and pear fruit. Not just another flabby oak and malo bomb, as it does have good acidity and a racy structure, but the oak does play a major role. **84** —J.C. (5/1/2001)

Lynskeys Wairau Peaks 2001 Reserve Chardonnay (Marlborough) $25. Disappointing in the context of this winery's outstanding 2002 Chardonnay, the 2001 Reserve is nonetheless a very good wine, albeit loaded with spicy oak that at times seems to overwhelm the delicate peach fruit. **87** —J.C. (9/1/2003)

Lynskeys Wairau Peaks 2002 Gewürztraminer (Marlborough) $18. Showcases Gewürztraminer's flamboyant rose petal and lychee aromas, folding in flavors of pears and dried spice on the palate. **87** —J.C. (9/1/2003)

Lynskeys Wairau Peaks 2000 Gewürztraminer (Marlborough) $17. At first sniff, this seems almost simple in its overwhelming resemblance to Bartlett pears. With swirling, however, you can dig into roses and lychees. Medium-weight on the palate, and finishes with trademark spice notes. Dry. **87** —J.C. (5/1/2001)

Lynskeys Wairau Peaks 2003 Single Vineyard Gewürztraminer (Marlborough) $25. Varietally correct, but also somewhat subdued, with muted lychee and rose petal aromas and flavors backed by pear-like fruit. Finishes a little short and without much spice. **85** —J.C. (8/1/2004)

Lynskeys Wairau Peaks 2002 15 Rows Reserve Merlot (Marlborough) $49. Marlborough Merlot is a chancy proposition—and this wine shows why. Despite the care and attention lavished on it, it still shows some herbal, grassy notes on the nose. On the palate, the fruit is big and jammy, dense and concentrated, yet there's a slightly drying note to the finish that suggests less than complete physiological ripeness. **87** —J.C. (4/1/2004)

Lynskeys Wairau Peaks 2001 Merlot (Marlborough) $45. Smooth, supple, and relatively open, this wine boasts lots of sweet, vanilla-laden oak but also copious blackberries and black cherries in support. There are no New Zealand veggies in evidence here, just ripe fruit and loads of oak. **88** —J.C. (12/15/2003)

Lynskeys Wairau Peaks 2002 Pinot Noir (Marlborough) $33. This is a sturdy, chunky NZ Pinot with plenty of black cherry fruit. It's also marked by distinctive herb and smoke shadings that give it a welcome degree of complexity. Despite the relatively short finish, it's a strong effort overall. **87** —J.C. (4/1/2004)

Lynskeys Wairau Peaks 2000 Pinot Noir (Marlborough) $33. A big style that manages to avoid tasting rustic or heavy. Starts with baked pastry shell, black cherry and plum, then adds in hints of licorice and black pepper. Could use a touch more richness in the midpalate, but closes nicely, with fresh acidity that perks up the fruit flavors. **87** —J.C. (8/1/2002)

Lynskeys Wairau Peaks 1999 Pinot Noir (Marlborough) $33. Starts with promising aromas of dark toast, vanilla, cola, and beets, but turns coarse on the palate, where rough oak flavors and alcohol dominate. **82** —*J.C. (5/1/2001)*

Lynskeys Wairau Peaks 2002 Sauvignon Blanc (Marlborough) $18. A riper style, with nectarine and other stone fruits layered over melon and shaded with just a hint of fresh herbs. Yet this vintage seems to lack a bit of concentration, ending somewhat short and with the powdery sensation of chalk dust. **86** —*J.C. (9/1/2003)*

Lynskeys Wairau Peaks 2001 Sauvignon Blanc (Marlborough) $17. The rather mute nose fights to offer up some anise, white pepper, and melon, but it's a deep dig to find it. Green apple, pineapple, and some orange rind define the flavors, while the weight of the wine seems heavy due to lower than ideal acidity. Then again, such weight might be welcomed by the Chardonnay-drinking crowd. **87** *(8/1/2002)*

Lynskeys Wairau Peaks 2000 Sauvignon Blanc (Marlborough) $17. A distinctive wine that features prominent aromas of sweet red peppers allied to round passion fruit flavors. Seems a bit heavy on the palate, and doesn't finish as crisply as you'd expect from an N.Z. Sauvignon Blanc. **84** —*J.C. (5/1/2001)*

Lynskeys Wairau Peaks 2003 Vineyard Select Sauvignon Blanc (Marlborough) $19. Seems light and a little dilute for this bottling, with pleasant aromas of passion fruit, pineapple, bell peppers and a hint of asparagus, but relatively neutral flavors, ending clean and fresh. **84** —*J.C. (8/1/2004)*

MAIN DIVIDE

Main Divide 2002 Chardonnay (Waipara) $20. Creamy and smooth in the mouth, this Chardonnay from Pegasus Bay offers scents of citrus and under-ripe pineapple along with flavors of pineapple, butter and caramel. Finishes on a slightly tinny note. This is good, but the 2003 looks to be a better bet. **84** —*J.C. (8/1/2004)*

Main Divide 2004 Pinot Noir (Canterbury) $25. From the folks at Pegasus Bay, this is a blend of purchased and estate fruit. Cherry notes blend with hints of mint, giving a bit of a medicinal edge to the flavors. Supple, but picks up a touch more green on the finish. **86** —*J.C. (12/1/2005)*

Main Divide 2002 Sauvignon Blanc (Canterbury & Marlborough) $15. A richer, lower-acid style of SB than most Americans are accustomed to, with smoke and nectarine dominating the flavor and honey and dried spices playing a role on the short finish. **86** —*J.C. (4/1/2004)*

MANA

Mana 2004 Pinot Noir (Marlborough) $15. Cranberryish on the nose, but there's also a note of sour red cabbage. Light and candied on the palate, combining candied cherry flavors with a soft, caramelly finish. **81** —*J.C. (7/1/2006)*

MARGRAIN

Margrain 2003 Pinot Noir (Martinborough) $25. Toasty and bacony on the nose, but there's also a helping of black cherries. Shows more mushroom and forest-floor character with time in the glass, and the fruit moves toward the background. **86** —*J.C. (12/1/2005)*

MARLBOROUGH WINES

Marlborough Wines 2003 Pinot Noir (Marlborough) $23. Combines slightly confectionary notes of graham cracker crumbs, vanilla, and cherries with herb and mushroom aromas. Sappy cherry flavors take on a resiny character, finishing crisp and persistent. **85** —*J.C. (12/1/2005)*

Marlborough Wines 2005 Sauvignon Blanc (Marlborough) $16. Aside from some hints of garlic on the nose, this is a clean, somewhat light Sauvignon with ripe melon and fig flavors. Picks up notes of citrus zest on the palate, turning tangy and spicy on the finish. **84** —*J.C. (7/1/2006)*

Marlborough Wines 2003 Sauvignon Blanc (Marlborough) $16. Plump and welcoming, this is an easy-to-drink introduction to New Zealand Sauvignon. Slightly grassy on the nose, but not aggressive, with a core of ripe nectarine and pink grapefruit flavors. Drink now. **88** —*J.C. (7/1/2005)*

MARTINBOROUGH VINEYARD

Martinborough Vineyard 1997 Chardonnay (Martinborough) $26. **93** —*S.H. (8/1/1999)*

Martinborough Vineyard 2003 Pinot Noir (Martinborough) $40. Favors a meaty, savory style, with ample dried spice and underbrush character. There's enough cherry fruit to support the other elements, along with an herbal edge on the finish. **85** —*J.C. (12/1/2005)*

Martinborough Vineyard 2002 Pinot Noir (Martinborough) $NA. A dry, savory Pinot, with plenty of sous bois and a riary under-current to the black cherry fruit. Drink or hold another 3-4 years. **88** —*J.C. (11/1/2006)*

Martinborough Vineyard 2001 Riesling (Martinborough) $15. Muskmelon and lime flavors start off tasting sweet, but are quickly reined in by brisk acidity, finishing chalky and tart. This is a fine Riesling, yet slightly disappointing in the context of previous vintages. **86** —*J.C. (8/1/2003)*

Martinborough Vineyard 1999 Late Harvest Riesling (Martinborough) $29. Intense dried apricot aromas and flavors indicate a high degree of botrytis, which would be overwhelming except for the trademark New Zealand acidity. Despite the heavy botrytis and sweet mango fruit, a sharp lime-citrus edge cuts through the richness, suggesting that cellaring 3–5 years is possible. **93** —*J.C. (5/1/2001)*

MATAHIWI

Matahiwi 2004 Pinot Noir (Wairarapa) $NA. Comes across as slightly light on fruit and herbal, but delivers a plump mouthfeel. In the end, there's enough cherry fruit to give it a charming personality. **86** —*J.C. (12/1/2005)*

Matahiwi 2004 Holly Pinot Noir (Wairarapa) $NA. Darker and toastier than Matahiwi's regular bottling, but not appreciably more likable, with black cherry fruit and a slightly herbal note on the finish. **86** —*J.C. (12/1/2005)*

MATARIKI

Matariki 1999 Chardonnay (Hawke's Bay) $22. A lush wine, filled with ripe pears and nectarines. Barrel-fermented in all new French oak, yet the richness of the fruit is such that the oak plays only a supporting role on the spicy, toasty finish. **89** —*J.C. (5/1/2001)*

Matariki 1997 Chardonnay (Hawke's Bay & Waipara) $23. **93** —*S.H. (8/1/1999)*

Matariki 1999 Merlot (Hawke's Bay) $25. Solidly plummy, but also tastes a little roasted or stewed, with raisiny notes. Ready to drink now. **83** —*J.C. (5/1/2001)*

Matariki 2004 Pinot Noir (Hawke's Bay) $31. This is from a part of New Zealand not known for its Pinot Noir, but don't discount it for that—it offers plenty of Pinot character, from its earth, mushroom and cola-scented bouquet to its plump, silky texture and tart, sour cherry finish. Drink now. **86** —*J.C. (12/15/2006)*

Matariki 2001 Quintology Red Blend (Hawke's Bay) $33. This medium-weight red blend is very drinkable already, with soft tannins framing juicy flavors of plums, black cherries, and vanilla. Notes of smoke, toast, and dried herbs add a layer of complexity. **89** —*J.C. (8/1/2004)*

Matariki 2000 Quintology Red Blend (Hawke's Bay) $26. As you might guess from the name, this blend contains five grape varieties: 33% Cabernet Sauvignon, with smaller amounts of Merlot, Cabernet Franc, Syrah, and Malbec. The result is a supple, charming wine that offers modest cherry fruit flavors and some notes of herbal, fresh-cut greens. **86** —*J.C. (12/15/2003)*

Matariki 2000 Late Harvest Riesling (Hawke's Bay) $30. The Matariki style of late harvest wine is to avoid overly sugary renditions in favor of balance. In this, the 2000 succeeds admirably, combining bergamot, pineapple, and apricot flavors in a lightly sweet yet tart wine. Best with fresh fruit and cheeses, as it's not rich enough to match with anything sweeter. **87** —*J.C. (8/1/2003)*

Matariki 1997 Sauvignon Blanc (Hawke's Bay) $19. **88** —*S.H. (8/1/1999)*

Matariki 2005 Sauvignon Blanc (Hawke's Bay) $18. A step down from the superbly concentrated 2004, Matariki's Sauvignon features modest grapefruit flavors allied to racy acidity this vintage. Light and zippy on the palate, it's tart and refreshing. **84** —*J.C. (11/1/2006)*

NEW ZEALAND

Matariki 2004 Sauvignon Blanc (Hawke's Bay) $18. This Sauvignon has moved toward a grassier style in recent vintages, but it's still darn good. Lime and herb notes dominate the nose, but it adds just enough chalk and grapefruit nuances on the palate to give it needed complexity. Plump yet crisply acidic at the same time, ending on racy grapefruit notes that finish without any trace of harshness. **90** —*J.C. (7/1/2005)*

Matariki 2003 Sauvignon Blanc (Hawke's Bay) $19. Matariki's 2003 Savvy displays copious scents of peaches, melons, and limes. Flavors are ripe and stone-fruity, firming up considerably on the finish, where grapefruit notes take charge. A ripe, medium-weight quaffer that would make a nice apéritif or companion to shellfish. **87** —*J.C. (8/1/2004)*

Matariki 2002 Sauvignon Blanc (Hawke's Bay) $14. Matariki's entry-level Sauvignon Blanc (they also make a Reserve) is a basic, grass-and-grapefruit version of New Zealand "Savvy." It's relatively light in body, with crisp acidity and a cleansing finish. **84** —*J.C. (9/1/2003)*

Matariki 2001 Sauvignon Blanc (Hawke's Bay) $15. Smells lush and opulent, almost like a barrel-fermented wine, and it's astonishing that the wine never saw oak. The evocative fruity flavors are extravagant and juicy, ranging from fresh lime to ripe peaches. Drinks dry, yet with a honeyed ripeness, accompanied by a great burst of mouth-watering acidity. **91** —*S.H. (11/15/2002)*

Matariki 2000 Sauvignon Blanc (Hawke's Bay) $16. Avoids the overtly herbal-vegetal aspects of Kiwi Sauvignon Blanc, instead opting for deep passion fruit and nectarine flavors. Turns just a bit green on the finish, with a welcome hint of jalapeño. **87** —*J.C. (5/1/2001)*

Matariki 1999 Reserve Sauvignon Blanc (Hawke's Bay) $25. A rich, lush blend of tropical and stone fruits, partially barrel-fermented to add a creamy texture and subtle spice notes. Seductive and supple in the mouth but with a solid backbone of acidity that keeps it from turning soft or mushy. **90** —*J.C. (5/1/2001)*

Matariki 2001 Syrah (Hawke's Bay) $30. Shows the characteristic herbal and peppery notes of Rhône-style Syrah, accenting crisp blackberry fruit. Complex on the palate, wrapping the herbs and peppers tightly around rich fruit to the point that they're really inseparable. **89** —*J.C. (4/1/2004)*

Matariki 1999 Gimblett Road Syrah (Hawke's Bay) $30. Fine cool climate Syrah, with characteristic cracked black pepper aromas and ample acidic backbone to support rich blackberry fruit. Tannins are firm, but ripe. Not a fat, jammy style at all, but based on structure and spicy nuance. **90** —*J.C. (5/1/2001)*

MATUA VALLEY

Matua Valley 1998 Bordeaux Blend (Hawke's Bay) $16. **87** —*J.C. (10/1/2000)*

Matua Valley 1996 Ararimu Bordeaux Blend (Hawke's Bay) $45. **86** —*J.C. (10/1/2000)*

Matua Valley 1998 Matheson Vineyard Bordeaux Blend (Hawke's Bay) $20. **87** —*J.C. (10/1/2000)*

Matua Valley 1999 Cabernet Sauvignon-Merlot (Hawke's Bay) $17. A soft, herbaceous wine that's destined for early drinking. The black cherry and tobacco flavors are a bit weedy, but tasty. **84** —*J.C. (5/1/2001)*

Matua Valley 2001 Ararimu Cabernet Sauvignon-Merlot (Hawke's Bay) $23. An interesting wine that blends some super ripe notes of stone fruit with under-ripe herbal elements that come dangerously close to being vegetal. Yet the mouthfeel is supple and smooth, and the peach notes on the finish are intriguing. **86** —*J.C. (12/15/2003)*

Matua Valley 1999 Matheson Vineyard Cabernet Sauvignon-Merlot (Hawke's Bay) $17. A wine that amply demonstrates the importance of site and barrel selection, as it lacks the weediness found in the non-vineyard-designated bottling. Instead it has ripe cassis and blackberry flavors marked by an intriguing hint of hickory smoke. **89** —*J.C. (5/1/2001)*

Matua Valley 2004 Chardonnay (Gisborne) $12. Starts with plenty of buttered toast or popcorn on the nose, then reveals leaner pear and citrus flavors on the palate. This medium-bodied wine finishes crisp and tart, making it suitable as an apéritif. **84** —*J.C. (12/1/2005)*

Matua Valley 2003 Chardonnay (Gisborne) $11. A fresh, vibrant style of Chardonnay, with pineapple and pear aromas and flavors laced with vanilla. Chill it well and drink it as a cocktail wine this spring and summer. **86** —*J.C. (4/1/2004)*

Matua Valley 1999 Chardonnay (Eastern Bays) $15. Luscious peaches and pears blend with sweet vanilla oak. Soft and supple, this is a drink-me-now wine that defines what many consumers mean when they ask for Chardonnay. **86** —*J.C. (5/1/2001)*

Matua Valley 1998 Ararimu Chardonnay (Gisborne) $45. Much more retrained and understated than the other Matua Valley offerings, this wine still needs a few months to blossom. Tight aromas of pear and apple and a long, powerful finish bode well for the future. **90** —*J.C. (5/1/2001)*

Matua Valley 2004 Judd Estate Chardonnay (Gisborne) $17. Gisborne made its reputation with Chardonnay, and this is a decent representative. There's a bit of matchstick scent to get past on the nose, then reined-in apple and melon fruit, a bit of sweet corn and butter, and some oaky notes that turn slightly varnishy on the finish. **86** —*J.C. (11/1/2006)*

Matua Valley 2003 Judd Estate Chardonnay (Gisborne) $17. Toasty and mealy on the nose, evidencing good integration of oak with the lush tropical fruit flavors typical of Gisborne Chardonnay. Plump on the palate without being heavy, then unleashes notes of buttered popcorn on the finish. **87** —*J.C. (5/1/2006)*

Matua Valley 2002 Judd Estate Chardonnay (Gisborne) $17. An excellent example of Gisborne Chardonnay, with lush peach and tropical fruit framed by warm vanilla oak. Finishes with flourishes of butter, honey, and caramel, along with bracing tartness. **89** —*J.C. (4/1/2004)*

Matua Valley 1999 Judd Estate Chardonnay (Gisborne) $20. Heavily oaked, with lots of toast aromas, yet the full, tropical fruit flavors handle the oak well. Buttery movie popcorn makes an appearance as well, followed by a nutty sensation on the finish. **89** —*J.C. (5/1/2001)*

Matua Valley 1998 Judd Estate Chardonnay (Gisborne) $18. **89** —*J.C. (10/1/2000)*

Matua Valley 1997 Judd Estate Hand Picked Chardonnay (Gisborne) $40. **90** —*J.C. (10/1/2000)*

Matua Valley 1998 Judd Estate Innovator Handpicked Chardonnay (Gisborne) $45. Buttered hazelnuts lead the flavor charge, followed by full, rich fruit that's creamy and marked by lees contact rather than primary fruit. The finish picks up dried spice flavors of cinnamon and clove. **90** —*J.C. (5/1/2001)*

Matua Valley 1999 Matheson Vineyard Chardonnay (Hawke's Bay) $20. Gentle toast nuances grace boatloads of peaches, pears and limes. The full fruit stands up to the oak well, while picking up dried-spice shadings on the finish. **88** —*J.C. (5/1/2001)*

Matua Valley 2002 Bullrush Merlot (Hawke's Bay) $20. Slightly jammy on the nose, blending in hints of graham cracker. This low-tannin, fruit-forward wine is a decent cocktail Merlot, laden with sweet black cherries but without a strong backbone from which to hang all of its flesh. **85** —*J.C. (4/1/2004)*

Matua Valley 2003 Bullrush Vineyard Merlot (Hawke's Bay) $20. A step up from the somewhat simple 2002 version of this wine, the 2003 Bullrush Merlot boasts ample weight on the palate and a long finish to go with its expansive black cherry flavors shot through with dried herbs. **88** —*J.C. (5/1/2006)*

Matua Valley 1998 Smith Dartmoor Estate Merlot (Hawke's Bay) $18. At first sniff, it's a plummy, toasty wine, without the herbal characteristics that in excess can mar N.Z. reds. Strongly focused, even a little austere right now, this needs some time to flesh out—if it ever does. **87** —*J.C. (5/1/2001)*

Matua Valley 1996 Smith-Dartmoor Estate Merlot (Hawke's Bay) $18. **82** —*J.C. (10/1/2000)*

Matua Valley 1998 Ararimu Merlot-Cabernet Sauvignon (Hawke's Bay) $44. Complex aromas of cedar, smoke, and cassis set the stage for what should be a long-lived wine. Structure is provided by juicy acidity and firm, yet ripe, tannins. Good now; better in four years. **90** —*J.C. (5/1/2001)*

Matua Valley 2003 Matheson Merlot-Cabernet Sauvignon (Hawke's Bay) $NA. Shows some pleasant dark toasty aromas to go with its pretty blackberry flavors, but this lacks texture and weight in the mouth. Crisp on the finish. **86** —*J.C. (5/1/2006)*

Matua Valley 2000 Late Harvest Muscat (Eastern Bays) $13. Only lightly sweet, with simple orange-blossom and lime flavors that are crisp and inviting. To drink alone, or maybe with foie gras, not with a sticky dessert. **86** —*J.C. (5/1/2001)*

Matua Valley 1996 Late Harvest Muscat (Gisborne) $12. **86** —*J.C. (10/1/2000)*

Matua Valley 2004 Pinot Gris (Marlborough) $12. Finding good Pinot Gris at this price is a challenge, but Matua Valley, part of Beringer-Blass Wine Estates, has hit a home run with its fresh herb- and citrus-laced 2004. There's just enough plumpness to make it satisfying in the mouth, while the flavors of pear and apple end on a clean, refreshing note. **87 Best Buy** —*J.C. (7/1/2005)*

Matua Valley 2004 Pinot Noir (Marlborough) $15. Light in color, but don't let that deceive you. This is a full-flavored wine, with candied cherry and caramel notes in abundance. Supple and easy to drink, although it turns slightly herbal-medicinal on the finish. **85** —*J.C. (12/1/2005)*

Matua Valley 2002 Pinot Noir (Marlborough) $11. It's supple, smooth, and the price is right, but the flavors are herbaceous and menthol-like, with sour cherry fruit and white gumdrop notes. **83** —*J.C. (8/1/2004)*

Matua Valley 2004 Estate Series Pinot Noir (Marlborough) $20. A well-extracted Pinot, with a dark color and relatively full mouthfeel, this is a step up from Matua's regular Pinot Noir offering. Plum fruit is garnished by vaguely floral notes as well as some vanilla and dried spices. It's supple and easy on the finish, so there's no point in waiting to drink this one. **87** —*J.C. (11/1/2006)*

Matua Valley 2002 Ararimu Merlot-Syrah-Cabernet Red Blend (Hawke's Bay) $25. Toast, dark fruit, and leafiness on the nose; cherries, cigarbox, and vanilla on the palate. This is a creamy, well-balanced wine with modest tannins. Roughly half Merlot, with almost equal amounts of Syrah and Cabernet making up the balance. Drink now–2010. **88** —*J.C. (8/1/2004)*

Matua Valley 2005 Sauvignon Blanc (Marlborough) $12. Bursting with ripe tropical flavors, lush and fruity. There's just a hint of green herb—enough so that you know it's Sauvignon Blanc—but the emphasis here is on forward fruit. Finishes with crisp acids and more and more fruit. **88 Best Buy** —*J.C. (12/1/2005)*

Matua Valley 2003 Sauvignon Blanc (Marlborough) $13. Since its recent acquisition by Beringer Blass, this winery's offerings have become more widely available in the States—there are 25,000 cases of this affordable gem in the U.S. market. This ripe, adequately concentrated Sauvignon Blanc is built around flavors of melon and stone fruits without forsaking the variety's characteristic notes of gooseberries and grapefruit. **88 Best Buy** —*J.C. (4/1/2004)*

Matua Valley 2002 Sauvignon Blanc (Hawke's Bay) $11. Very fruity and forward, with powerful flavors of lime, citrus, gooseberry, and oriental spices. The acidity is irresistibly refreshing. Bright and focused, it's a standup dry white wine of distinction. **88 Best Buy** —*S.H. (11/15/2002)*

Matua Valley 2000 Sauvignon Blanc (Hawke's Bay) $12. Warmer weather in Hawke's Bay means this wine shows less of the aggressively pungent grapefruit and herb aromas of Marlborough Sauvignon Blanc. This is a soft, creamy, very approachable wine that finishes with just a hint of grapefruit. **85** —*J.C. (5/1/2001)*

Matua Valley 1999 Matheson Vineyard Sauvignon Blanc (Hawke's Bay) $15. Toasty aromas mingle with vanilla and cream on the nose before giving way on the palate to melons and a strong fig component, possibly from the 15% Sémillon that's been blended in. A ripe, barrel-marked style. **88** —*J.C. (5/1/2001)*

Matua Valley 2005 Paretai Sauvignon Blanc (Marlborough) $17. Much like the 2004, this is an aggressively herbal style of Sauvignon that some consumers will love. Pungent, sweaty scents on the nose are followed by green, herbal notes and lashings of passion fruit. Slightly oily in texture, yet the wine still ends on a fresh, zesty note. **87** —*J.C. (7/1/2006)*

Matua Valley 2004 Paretai Sauvignon Blanc (Marlborough) $17. Lean and racy, Matua has chosen to go for an extremely pungent, herbal style that

may please some consumers more than me. Lime and green pea flavors are buttressed by bracing acidity in this crisp, citrusy wine. **84** —*J.C. (7/1/2005)*

Matua Valley 2003 Innovator Bullrush Syrah (Hawke's Bay) $NA. A bit jammy, with aromas and flavors of slightly cooked or overripe blackberries. Fruity and clean, but the acids stick out a little, lending a tart quality to the finish. **85** —*J.C. (5/1/2006)*

Matua Valley 2004 Matheson Syrah (Hawke's Bay) $NA. Light and a bit herbal, like a pleasant St.-Joseph. White pepper and celery-leaf notes accent tart cherries. **84** —*J.C. (5/1/2006)*

MAVEN

Maven 2005 Sauvignon Blanc (Marlborough) $17. This new label's wines come off an extremely young vineyard and are made by winemaker Mike Just, formerly of Lawson's Dry Hills. Soft honey, fig, and tropical fruit notes are pleasant and the wine seems full and lush on the palate, yet it falls off quickly on the finish. **85** —*J.C. (11/1/2006)*

MEBUS

Mebus 2000 Dakins Road Bordeaux Blend (Wairarapa) $25. Malbec is gaining popularity in New Zealand, adding color and acidity to that country's Bordeaux-style reds. This medium-weight wine boasts plenty of dark plummy flavors along with hints of chocolate and anise and cinnamon. **87** —*J.C. (12/15/2003)*

Mebus 2001 Dakins Road Cabernet-Merlot-Malbec Bordeaux Blend (Wairarapa) $21. In beneficent vintages, Wairarapa is warm enough to yield good results with Bordeaux varieties, but this wine is just too green and herbaceous, bordering on green peppery. **82** —*J.C. (5/1/2006)*

MILLS REEF

Mills Reef 1998 Elspeth Cabernet Sauvignon-Merlot (Hawke's Bay) $30. **90** —*J.C. (10/1/2000)*

Mills Reef 1999 Reserve Chardonnay (Hawke's Bay) $17. The aromas of butter and tropical fruits are bit muted at first, only strengthening with air into peach and melon. Some slightly bitter citrus notes add complexity to this understated wine. **84** —*J.C. (5/1/2001)*

Mills Reef 2000 Mere Road Elspeth Merlot (Hawke's Bay) $30. Here you have a massively constituted wine joined to well-charred oak that results in an enormously rich, satisfying and, more importantly, balanced sip. The fruit and berry flavors are hugely extracted, the tannins gentle but complex, the acidity near perfect. It all adds up to a young bruiser. If you must drink it now, have with rich foods like well-marbled beef or lamb. **93 Editors' Choice** —*S.H. (11/15/2002)*

Mills Reef 2004 Reserve Merlot-Malbec (Hawke's Bay) $20. A chunky, soft wine with a strong wood influence, very much in keeping with the winery's style. This 51% Merlot-49% Malbec blend features a smoky, cedary, vanilla-laden bouquet, dark fruit flavors, supple tannins, and a smooth finish. **85** —*J.C. (12/15/2006)*

Mills Reef 2002 Elspeth One Red Blend (Hawke's Bay) $35. Big, black, and dense—who knew that New Zealand could make wines this big and burly? It's grapy and concentrated, with hints of licorice and mouthdrying tannins. Could improve with age, hopefully picking up some grace and nuance. Drink now–2010+. **87** —*J.C. (8/1/2004)*

Mills Reef 2000 Elspeth One Red Blend (Hawke's Bay) $35. This is a rich, sumptuous red wine. It looks, smells, and tastes opulent. Ripe, forward berry flavors, wrapped in considerable oak, taste full and long, and the wine flatters with thick, velvety but fine tannins. The finish is a wonder, long and intricate. The aftertaste lasts for a full minute. It's wonderful now, but should age effortlessly for many years. A blend of Bordeaux varieties and Syrah. **94 Cellar Selection** —*S.H. (11/15/2002)*

Mills Reef 1998 Sauvignon Blanc (Hawke's Bay) $13. **87** —*S.H. (8/1/1999)*

Mills Reef 2005 Reserve Sauvignon Blanc (Hawke's Bay) $15. Almost more of a white Graves style than a traditional New Zealand Sauvignon Blanc, featuring a kiss of French oak and ample body without any overt pungency. Ripe melon and fig flavors easily accompany slightly grassy notes, accented by grapefruit on the finish. Drink now. **89** —*J.C. (12/15/2006)*

NEW ZEALAND

NEW ZEALAND

Mills Reef 2003 Reserve Sauvignon Blanc (Hawke's Bay) $14. An interesting and different take on Sauvignon Blanc, one that lacks the variety's distinctive herbaceousness, opting instead for scents of green apples, pear, and lime. It's broad and fleshy in the mouth, firming up and turning grapefruity on the finish.**88** —J.C. (8/1/2004)

Mills Reef 2002 Reserve Sauvignon Blanc (Hawke's Bay) $14. Creamy textured, the wine seems quite ripe at first, only later adding in a slightly green streak reminiscent of sweet bell peppers.**87** —J.C. (9/1/2003)

Mills Reef 2001 Reserve Sauvignon Blanc (Hawke's Bay) $15. Some oak adds butter, vanilla, and cream to the nose, and then melon, banana, and citrus come on in spades on the palate. The barrel influence provides a fine mouthfeel, and the finish is properly acidic, tangy, and eminently clean. Even with the oak, this is a sure thing with shellfish.**88** (8/1/2002)

Mills Reef 2000 Reserve Sauvignon Blanc (Hawke's Bay) $14. Almost too subtle and understated, this wine's faint melon and grapefruit aromas and flavors are tinged with honey, giving a sweet-sour impression on the palate.**83** —J.C. (5/1/2001)

Mills Reef 1999 Reserve Sauvignon Blanc (Hawke's Bay) $13.87 —J.C. (10/1/2000)

Mills Reef 1998 Reserve Sauvignon Blanc (Hawke's Bay) $13.90 Best Buy —L.W. (8/1/1999)

Mills Reef 2002 Elspeth Syrah (Hawke's Bay) $NA. This is a dark, ripe expression of Syrah, with coffee and blackberry scents that pick up molasses, cola and black pepper notes on the palate. Firm, gripping tannins on the finish suggest this has a few years to go before reaching maturity.**87** —J.C. (5/1/2006)

Mills Reef 2001 Elspeth Syrah (Hawke's Bay) $29. Mills Reef is becoming a top source for Hawke's Bay reds, particularly those sourced from its Mere Road Vineyard in the Gimblett Gravels subregion. The 2001 Elspeth Syrah is nicely peppery and filled with ripe blackberry fruit. Not terribly complex, but very satisfying.**88** —J.C. (4/1/2004)

Mills Reef 2000 Mere Road Elspeth Syrah (Hawke's Bay) $30. Strong and distinguished, this is a wine with the concentration of a winner. The dark purple and black color suggests the enormous extract, which is confirmed by the first sniff. The nose is packed with powerful black currant aromas, enhanced by fine smoky oak. In the mouth, it's full-bodied, dense, and immature. A chewy core of fruit and thick but fine tannins suggest aging through 2006.**92 Editors' Choice** —S.H. (11/15/2002)

Mills Reef 1999 Mere Road Vineyard Syrah (Hawke's Bay) $28. Dark cherry, leather, and coffee aromas lead into more of the same flavors on the palate. Medium-weight with moderate tannins, this New Zealand Syrah could almost be mistaken for a Crozes-Hermitage. It finishes with dry mineral and pepper flavors. It's lean and structured, and would benefit from 2–3 years of cellaring.**89** (11/1/2001)

MONKEY BAY

Monkey Bay 2004 Chardonnay (Gisborne) $10. Modest pear and melon scents mark the nose, while the palate delivers oodles of pears and tropical fruits. Soft and easy, nicely done at this price point.**84** (3/1/2006)

Monkey Bay 2005 Sauvignon Blanc (Marlborough) $10. A bit simple, but loaded with pungent boxwood and passion fruit notes, and backed by crisp grapefruit flavors. Relatively light in body, with a short, clean finish.**84** (3/1/2006)

Monkey Bay 2004 Sauvignon Blanc (Marlborough) $10. Ripe, not bracing, this new star in the Constellation portfolio boasts subtle aromas of stone fruit and citrus that become more apparent on the palate, emerging as nectarine and pink grapefruit. Plump and easy to drink; a real crowd-pleaser at a crowd-pleasing price.**87 Best Buy** —J.C. (7/1/2005)

MORWORTH ESTATE

Morworth Estate 2000 Chardonnay (Marlborough) $25. Plain pear and pineapple aromas and flavors in a medium-weight format. Picks up a hint of butterscotch on the tart, metallic finish.**83** —J.C. (11/15/2002)

Morworth Estate 1999 Pinot Noir (Canterbury) $NA. Camphor and cedar oak aromas partially mask flavors that center around earth and pie cherries. The fruit is a little thin and the overlay of oak only emphasizes that.**82** —J.C. (8/1/2002)

Morworth Estate 1999 Riesling (Canterbury) $NA. Not a typical New Zealand Riesling, but one worth trying for its bold, oily apricot and tangerine aromas and flavors that smell sweet but taste dry, ending in a stone-cold finish.**85** —J.C. (8/1/2002)

Morworth Estate 2001 Sauvignon Blanc (Marlborough) $11. Smells enticing, with hints of apricot and river stones embellishing a grapefruit core. But in the mouth, the wine lacks flesh and lushness to cover its impressively fashioned bones; it ends up seeming hard and lacking much generosity.**85** —J.C. (9/1/2003)

MOUNT CASS

Mount Cass 2004 Chardonnay (Waipara) $20. Not that expressive on the nose, giving up little more than some faintly nutty-leesy scents. But this is nicely weighty on the palate without being heavy, with custardy accents to its complex citrus and tropical flavors. Long on the finish, where it picks up hints of dried spices.**91 Editors' Choice** —J.C. (5/1/2006)

Mount Cass 2004 Late Harvest Chardonnay (Waipara) $20. Quite sweet, but ultimately a bit simple, this partially botrytized Chardonnay clocks in at 12% residual sugar. A fleeting whiff of volatile acidity might bother sensitive tasters, but there's also plenty of ripe pineapple and dried apricot flavors.**86** —J.C. (5/1/2006)

Mount Cass 2004 Unoaked Chardonnay (Waipara) $NA. Quite attractive, with flinty aromas backed by scents of apple and pear. More fleshy and ripely tropical in the mouth, giving an impression of richness without oak.**88** —J.C. (5/1/2006)

Mount Cass 2003 Pinot Noir (Waipara) $27. A rather delicate style, with bits of smoke, dried herbs, and spice accenting cherry fruit. Light-bodied, but with pretty aromatics and good flavor intensity. Drink now–2008.**87** —J.C. (12/1/2005)

Mount Cass 2002 Pinot Noir (Waipara) $NA. Features a delicate and pretty bouquet, offering up hints of smoke, dried herbs, and cherries, but turns a bit blocky and chunky on the palate, with powerful chocolate notes.**85** —J.C. (11/1/2006)

Mount Cass 2004 Riesling (Waipara) $16. A bit sweet, with green apple and citrus aromas and flavors that lack cut but still seem attractive, backed by a talc-like, powdery mouthfeel.**87** —J.C. (5/1/2006)

Mount Cass 2004 Waipara Gravels Reserve Riesling (Waipara) $18. A bit floral on the nose, then that gives way to pear and apple fruit aromas. It's medium-bodied, nicely balancing the 7g/L residual sugar with crisp acidity that makes it appear virtually dry. Tart and appley on the finish.**89** —J.C. (5/1/2006)

Mount Cass 2004 Sauvignon Blanc (Waipara) $17. Boasts plenty of tropical fruit on the nose, fleshed out by passion fruit and pineapple flavors on the palate. Intense and flavorful; a crisp and fruity Sauvignon for early consumption.**88** —J.C. (5/1/2006)

Mount Cass 2004 Sauvignon Blanc (Marlborough) $15. Bits of boxwood and sweet pea add layers of green to this nicely harmonious and well-balanced effort from Marlborough. Not particularly intense or concentrated, but a pretty rendition of Sauvignon Blanc.**87** —J.C. (5/1/2006)

MOUNT EDWARD

Mount Edward 2003 Pinot Noir (Central Otago) $39. Relatively light in color, but long on flavor, this is a light-bodied, silky wine that comes across as very Burgundian. Subtle herb and spice notes accent delicate cherry flavors, and there's a wiry, tensile strength to it despite the softness of the tannins.**89** —J.C. (12/1/2005)

MOUNT NELSON

Mount Nelson 2005 Sauvignon Blanc (Marlborough) $16. This Italian outpost of the Antinori clan has crafted an elegant yet mouth-filling Sauvignon that manages to inject a sense of Old World minerality into its New World fruit. Pungently grassy scents are backed by stone fruit and citrus, while a trace of minerality graces the long, pink grapefruit finish.**90 Editors' Choice** —J.C. (9/1/2006)

Mount Nelson 2004 Sauvignon Blanc (Marlborough) $16. A joint venture of brothers Piero and Lodovico Antinori, this is the first vintage to reach

U.S. shores, and it is a promising first step. Melon and peach notes on the nose are garnished with fresh herbs, and on the palate the wine hews a line between round and ripe and lean and grapefruity, striking a fine balance. **88** —*J.C. (7/1/2005)*

MOUNT RILEY

Mount Riley 2001 Chardonnay (Marlborough) $13. Dips into the current style of fat, blowsy Chards left to hang on the vine until they develop tropical fruit flavors, and then drenched in oak and spiced up with lees. In this case, stunning acidity provides welcome relief to all that flab. The resulting wine isn't for everyone, but connoisseurs will appreciate it. **91 Best Buy** —*S.H. (11/15/2002)*

Mount Riley 2005 Pinot Noir (Marlborough) $17. Sturdy black cherry and cola notes anchor this fairly priced offering from Marlborough. It's a bit chunky, without Pinot's classic silky mouthfeel, but solid and dependable, picking up some menthol notes on the finish. **87** —*J.C. (12/15/2006)*

Mount Riley 2004 Pinot Noir (South Island) $17. Light in color, but flavorful, boasting hints of cherry, mushroom, and mint. Medium-bodied, with a supple mouthfeel and a lingering finish. A blend of fruit from Brightwater (Nelson) and Wairau (Marlborough). **87** —*J.C. (12/1/2005)*

Mount Riley 2001 Pinot Noir (Marlborough) $20. A plump, soft style, with ample black plum and cherry flavors supported by clove and cinnamon. Finishes with notes of toast and caramel slightly dominating the fruit. **87** —*J.C. (9/1/2003)*

Mount Riley 2005 Sauvignon Blanc (Marlborough) $13. Starts off well, with aromas that strike a pretty balance between gooseberry and passion fruit, then layer on ripe melon and nectarine as well. In the mouth, it's big, delivering bold, fruity flavors underscored by crisp acids. It lacks a bit of elegance and length on the finish, but this wine delivers plenty of flavor and pleasure for the price. **88 Best Buy** —*J.C. (7/1/2006)*

Mount Riley 2004 Sauvignon Blanc (Marlborough) $16. Zesty, crisp, and racy, this wine begins with scents of passion fruit and crystallized lime and doesn't deviate from this course all the way through the lingering finish. A bit simple but satisfying; try with ceviche. **88** —*J.C. (7/1/2005)*

Mount Riley 2001 Sauvignon Blanc (Marlborough) $15. Right from the start this is clean, snappy, and peppery, with an added touch of butter and honey. Lemon-lime flavors get a boost from fresh green herbs and white pepper, while the finish is spot-on. At one moment it's razor-sharp and cleansing, and then it opens up to offer citrus and mineral. **90 Editors' Choice** *(8/1/2002)*

MOUNTFORD

Mountford 1999 Chardonnay (Waipara) $25. This relatively understated wine is less ebullient than the 2000s it was tasted alongside, but held its own, with green apple and lemon fruit underscored by smoky, earthy flavors. The lemony finish lingers a long time. **89** —*J.C. (7/1/2002)*

MT. DIFFICULTY

Mt. Difficulty 1999 Chardonnay (Central Otago) $17. A blend of barrel-fermented (60%) and tank-fermented (40%) juice, that displays elegant pear-citrus flavors combined with toasted marshmallows. The oak shows strongest on the finish, where it develops caramel and spice notes. **88** —*J.C. (5/1/2001)*

Mt. Difficulty 2003 Not imported Chardonnay (Central Otago) $NA. Toasty and nutty on the nose, but the 20% new oak is well-integrated, adding spice to the apple and citrus flavors and contributing a plump, mealy texture. **88** —*J.C. (5/1/2006)*

Mt. Difficulty 2004 Pinot Gris (Central Otago) $24. A bit muted on the nose, but this nicely balanced, mouth-filling wine offers juicy apple and melon flavors that coat the mouth, showing a touch of honeyed sweetness on the finish. **87** —*J.C. (5/1/2006)*

Mt. Difficulty 2000 Pinot Gris (Central Otago) $15. For a crisp, fresh white that dances with fish or shrimp, look no further. The wine saw some malolactic fermentation and even less barrel fermentation, but both are noticeable in the round body. As far as aromas and flavors, it's citrusy, emphasizing grapefruit and orange rind. In many ways it's akin to

Sauvignon Blanc; steely and lean, but hardly weak. **88 Best Buy** —*M.S. (12/15/2001)*

Mt. Difficulty 2003 Pinot Noir (Central Otago) $30. A much better value than the more complex Target Gully bottling, this Bannockburn Pinot offers up dark chocolate and cola flavors, blended with tree bark and plum. Dark, earthy notes are borne on a plump, medium-bodied mouthfeel that maintains decent structure. Drink or hold through 2010. **88** —*J.C. (12/1/2005)*

Mt. Difficulty 1999 Pinot Noir (Central Otago) $24. Deep black cherry and cola aromas pick up subtle chocolate and toast notes. In the mouth, the fruit flavors come to the fore, with sour cherries accented by cocoa-powder tannins on the finish. **88** —*J.C. (5/1/2001)*

Mt. Difficulty 2004 Roaring Meg Pinot Noir (Central Otago) $20. Mt. Difficulty's entry-level Pinot is from young vines. It features perfumed scents of cherries and a plump, juicy, fruit-laden midpalate, then thins out a bit on the finish, where it picks up some herbal notes. **86** —*J.C. (12/1/2005)*

Mt. Difficulty 2003 Target Gully Pinot Noir (Central Otago) $80. The U.S. pricing for this wine is a bit extravagant, but the wine delivers wonderful spicy and savory aromas, backed by loads of cherries, a creamy mouthfeel, and hints of vanilla briars and spice. Firm on the finish; try again in 2008. **90** —*J.C. (12/1/2005)*

Mt. Difficulty 2000 Riesling (Central Otago) $15. Lemongrass and Granny Smith apple aromas introduce chalk and floral flavors. Zingy and tangy in the mouth, it closes long, with a little pineapple-lemon sweetness and minerals. **84** —*D.T. (12/15/2001)*

Mt. Difficulty 2004 Dry Riesling (Central Otago) $NA. This apple and lime-scented wine offers wonderfully pure, delicate flavors without being unassertive. It's medium-bodied, easily carrying its 12.5% alcohol and tastes quite dry. Lingers elegantly on the finish. **90** —*J.C. (5/1/2006)*

Mt. Difficulty 2004 Long Gully Riesling (Central Otago) $NA. At 7.5% alcohol and 70g/L of residual sugar, this is more of an auslese-style Riesling, marrying petrolly, minerally notes to sweet apple, melon and peach flavors. Long and clean on the finish. **90** —*J.C. (5/1/2006)*

Mt. Difficulty 2004 Target Gully Riesling (Central Otago) $NA. At 10.5% alcohol and 25 g/L of residual sugar, this is a beautifully balanced spätlese-styled Riesling. Apple and pineapple aromas and flavors are tinged with honey. Like the 2004 Dry Riesling, this is delicate without being frail. **90** —*J.C. (5/1/2006)*

Mt. Difficulty 2004 Sauvignon Blanc (Central Otago) $19. Fresh and initially fruity, marked by bold passion fruit and tropical flavors. It's relatively light in body, making it ideal as a starter white, then finishes on a crisp, chalky note that sets it apart from Marlborough Sauvignons. **88** —*J.C. (5/1/2006)*

Mt. Difficulty 2001 Sauvignon Blanc (Central Otago) $16. Hard to believe there's no oak aging or lees contact, it's so incredibly rich and creamy. Offers ripe, fruity flavors of peaches and sweet apples, although the wine is bone-dry, with excellent acidity. Concentrated, dense, and opulent, it's a real treat to the palate. **93** —*S.H. (11/15/2002)*

Mt. Difficulty 2000 Sauvignon Blanc (Central Otago) $13. Despite the fact that Otago isn't known as Sauvignon Blanc country, winemaker Matt Dicey has bottled a lean, racy Sauvignon that's herbaceous, not vegetal. Some melon-like fruit provides the flesh, and lime-like acidity keeps it fresh and lively. **88** —*J.C. (5/1/2001)*

MUD HOUSE WINE COMPANY

Mud House Wine Company 2000 Chardonnay (Marlborough) $17. An award-winning wine back in New Zealand, time and travel seem to have taken their toll. It's still tasty, but relies heavily on oak for its character. Dried spices and butterscotch are just barely balanced out by peach and papaya notes. **86** —*J.C. (9/1/2003)*

Mud House Wine Company 1999 Black Swan Reserve Merlot (Marlborough) $25. This tart, sour cherry-flavored wine is dominated by shrill acidity. Disappointing. **82** —*J.C. (12/15/2003)*

Mud House Wine Company 2001 Pinot Noir (Marlborough) $33. Starts off with pretty aromas of truffles and earth before opening up on the palate to show plum and cherry flavors. Finishes a bit rough and rustic. **85** — J.C. (9/1/2003)

Mud House Wine Company 2002 Sauvignon Blanc (Marlborough) $16. Lean and razor-sharp, this wine is best suited for simply prepared or raw shellfish. Melon and green pepper aromas and asparagus and tart grapefruit flavors will accent the sweet brininess of fresh oysters. **83** —J.C. (9/1/2003)

MUDDY WATER

Muddy Water 2000 Chardonnay (Waipara) $20. Based on these tastings, 2000 must have been a great vintage for the eastern coast of NZ's South Island. Here's another top-notch Chard, this one loaded with buttered, toasted whole wheat bread and vanilla custard, spiked with tropical fruit and citrus. It's rich but not heavy, with a finely etched finish and ample structure. **90** —J.C. (7/1/2002)

Muddy Water 2003 Pinot Noir (Waipara) $31. Crisp and relatively high in acidity, but that's partially offset by soft, supple tannins. Tangy cherry flavors pick up meaty, leathery nuances. **84** —J.C. (12/1/2005)

Muddy Water 1999 Pinot Noir (Waipara) $25. Toasty, but backed up by solid black cherry fruit that fills the mouth with a touch of creaminess. The dark fruit flavors persist well into the finish where they are joined by a hint of mint and smoke. **87** —J.C. (5/1/2001)

MURDOCH JAMES

Murdoch James 2004 Pinot Noir (Martinborough) $20. A bit on the simple side, but lively, fresh, and ultimately satisfying. Impressively pure black cherry fruit does pick up a hint of spice on the finish. A nice introduction to NZ Pinot that should drink well from now through 2010. **87** —J.C. (12/1/2005)

Murdoch James 2003 Salesyards Syrah (Martinborough) $33. Herbal, peppery, and minty on the nose, with pleasant, bright berry and tea flavors. Firm on the finish. **85** —J.C. (5/1/2006)

MURDOCH JAMES ESTATE

Murdoch James Estate 2002 Blue Rock Pinot Noir (Martinborough) $36. Starts with notes of toasted cinnamon, cola, and root beer on the nose that give way to flavors of sour cherries, beets, and sasparilla in the mouth. Light in body, with crisp acids yet virtually no tannins. Drink now. **85** —J.C. (7/1/2005)

Murdoch James Estate 2001 Waiata Pinot Noir (Martinborough) $27. Sturdy flavors of plum and coffee and a firm tannic structure allow you to match this Pinot up against big gamy meats, such as venison. **86** — J.C. (9/1/2003)

Murdoch James Estate 2002 Sauvignon Blanc (Martinborough) $17. Has some pleasant currant aromas and stone fruit flavors, but also a strong bell pepper component, which tends to overshadow the fruit. **83** —J.C. (9/1/2003)

Murdoch James Estate 2001 Syrah (Martinborough) $27. Thin and herbal, with tart cherry fruit and loads of white pepper but no real depth or texture. **82** —J.C. (12/15/2003)

NAUTILUS

Nautilus 1998 Chardonnay (Marlborough) $17. 86 —J.C. (10/1/2000)

Nautilus 1999 Chardonnay (Marlborough) $18. A crowd-pleaser for sure. This wine is full of the stuff Americans seem to love: butter, toast, ripe pears, and pineapples. It's full and oaky. There's even some citrus-like acidity on the finish to cut through the sweet flavors. **86** —J.C. (5/1/2001)

Nautilus 2002 Pinot Gris (Marlborough) $18. What a gorgeous cocktail wine this is. In fact, it's perfect at the end of a long day. Bright and shining citrus and peach flavors are set in beautifully crisp acids, and there's just enough residual sweetness to satisfy. Positively addictive, and will be great with seared scallops in a buttery sauce. **89** —S.H. (1/1/2002)

Nautilus 2001 Pinot Gris (Marlborough) $18. Near-perfect balance, with a modest 13.5% alcohol, residual sugar of 3.5g/L, and crisp acids. Add citrus and peach flavors and a long, clean finish, and you've got a heck of a nice wine. **88** —S.H. (11/15/2002)

Nautilus 2005 Pinot Noir (Marlborough) $20. Disappointingly light in weight, this is nonetheless a pretty wine, featuring modest cherry and cola elements backed by leathery, mushroomy notes. Nothing flashy, but it should partner well with farm-raised venison or other mild game. **84** —J.C. (12/15/2006)

Nautilus 2003 Pinot Noir (Marlborough) $23. Combines hints of dried herbs and spice with super-ripe black cherry aromas. It's a soft, supple, easy-to-drink Pinot that relies heavily on ripe fruit to carry it rather than extra layers of depth or complexity. **87** —J.C. (12/1/2005)

Nautilus 2001 Pinot Noir (Marlborough) $20. A nice surprise, the Nautilus Pinot offers a silky smooth texture allied to lush flavors of black cherries and cocoa. There's even a touch of underbrush thrown in for additional complexity. While the price isn't low enough to warrant a "Best Buy" commendation, it's more fairly priced than much of its competition. **89** —J.C. (9/1/2003)

Nautilus 1999 Pinot Noir (Marlborough) $25. A light-weight but pretty wine, featuring just enough black cherry fruit to stand up to some minty overtones. Shows a hint of alcohol on the finish, along with citrusy acidity. **84** —J.C. (5/1/2001)

Nautilus 1999 Sauvignon Blanc (Marlborough) $16. 86 —M.M. (10/1/2000)

Nautilus 2005 Sauvignon Blanc (Marlborough) $17. This mainstream Sauvignon Blanc shows some herbal, grassy notes on the nose, but also ripe nectarine and stone fruit scents. It's round in the mouth, with a silky texture and a similar blend of flavors, with tropical and stone fruits accented by slight herbaceousness. Smooth and softly lingering on the finish. **88** —J.C. (12/15/2006)

Nautilus 2002 Sauvignon Blanc (Marlborough) $17. There's no oak to buffer your palate from the strong lime and gooseberry aromas and flavors. If this is your style, this is a great wine. The acidity is enormous and explosive, almost prickly, and the wine is so dry it makes your palate pucker. **87** —S.H. (1/1/2002)

Nautilus 2001 Sauvignon Blanc (Marlborough) $18. Like a fairway splitting drive in golf, this wine is just what the masses want: It's full of grapefruit, passion fruit, gooseberry, and citrus rind. The acidity, however, is pounding, so the finish might sweat your tongue a bit, thereby yielding a juicy mouthfeel. Overall, it starts well and then fades a bit. **88** (8/1/2002)

Nautilus 2000 Sauvignon Blanc (Marlborough) $16. I'll fess up—I really don't like asparagus aromas in my wine, which accounts for this wine's low score. That aside, there are some decent grapefruit and gooseberry flavors in there, and the finish is crisp and clean. **82** —J.C. (5/1/2001)

NEUDORF

Neudorf 2004 Chardonnay (Nelson) $30. Not quite as special as the Moutere bottling, but Neudorf's Nelson Chardonnay, which contains mostly Moutere fruit, is still a standout. Toasty, pineapple aromas are more obvious than those in Moutere, and the wine is slightly less textured but carries more upfront tropical and peach fruit. Ends on a spicy, oaky note. Drink now-2010. **90** —J.C. (5/1/2006)

Neudorf 2003 Moutere Chardonnay (Nelson) $NA. Neudorf's reign as one of NZ's top Chardonnay producers continues with this effort from its Moutere plantings. Rich melon aromas are bolstered by subtle toasty notes that are more nutty than overtly oaky, then powerful citrus fruit shines on the richly textured palate. Turns nutty again on the extended finish. Drink now-2010. **92** —J.C. (5/1/2006)

Neudorf 2003 Moutere Chardonnay (New Zealand) $53. Toasty, but with the fruit to back it up. Peach and caramel scents on the nose, then layers of ripe tropical and citrus fruit on the palate that keep pumping out flavor through the long finish. Another top effort for one of New Zealand's benchmark Chardonnays. **90 Editors' Choice** —J.C. (7/1/2005)

Neudorf 2001 Moutere Chardonnay (New Zealand) $49. Pricy, but this is one of NZ's top Chardonnays, and production is quite small. Subtle smoke and toast accent peaches and custard, but despite the lush aromas and plumpness, strong citrusy acids keep it all in balance. Lemon and lime last forever on the finish, rounded out by a toasty, mealy note. **91** —J.C. (9/1/2003)

Neudorf 2004 Pinot Gris (Moutere) $NA. Broad, mouthfilling, and rich, filled with aromas and flavors of melon and ripe red apples. Picks up hints of dried spice on the finish, along with a modestly tannic quality. **90** —*J.C. (2/1/2006)*

Neudorf 2004 Pinot Noir (Nelson) $30. The 2004 vintage wasn't all that kind to many Pinot Noir producers at the northern end of NZ's South Island. Neudorf's 2004 Nelson bottling shows some herbal, beet-like notes on the nose, and the tannins and acids both have a slightly green edge to them. Still, there's ample cherry fruit and some mushroomy complexity to round it out. **86** —*J.C. (11/1/2006)*

Neudorf 2003 Pinot Noir (Nelson) $46. Made from young vines, this wine nonetheless boasts a fantastically perfumed nose of flowers, cherries, and spice. On the palate, there's tea and Asian spices, followed by waves of lush cherries. Could use more length to the finish, but lovely. **89** —*J.C. (12/1/2005)*

Neudorf 2003 Pinot Noir (Moutere) $55. Shows that great wines can be made from the 10/5 clone, with lots of dried spice and leather aromas that are balanced on the palate by a rich, sturdy core of ripe cherries. Great persistence on the finish adds another dimension. **91** —*J.C. (12/1/2005)*

Neudorf 2003 Home Vineyard Pinot Noir (Moutere) $NA. Based on old (20–25-year-old) plantings of Pommard clone, this fabulous wine blends savory, spicy scents with floral elements on the nose, then delves deep into black cherries in the mouth. Rich and velvety on the palate, with powerful fruit and the structure to age. One of the best New World Pinots I've ever tasted. **94** —*J.C. (12/1/2005)*

Neudorf 2003 Riesling (Moutere) $NA. At only 10.5% alcohol and approximately 40g/L residual sugar, this is a spätlese-style Riesling from the clay soils of Moutere. Smells of sweet apples and baking spices with a hint of petrol character that adds complexity and a texture reminiscent of fine chalk dust. Enjoyable now, and should hold up to 5 years, possibly longer. **88** —*J.C. (5/1/2006)*

Neudorf 2004 Brightwater Riesling (Nelson) $22. Off alluvial gravel soils that have much in common with Marlborough, this off-dry Riesling features the bright, fruity notes common to the region, combining green apple and citrus aromas and flavors with a lean, chalky texture. Pretty, but not that concentrated. **85** —*J.C. (5/1/2006)*

Neudorf 2004 Sauvignon Blanc (Nelson) $24. Quite vegetal, even more so than what is normal. The nose reeks of canned peas and asparagus, and the mouthfeel is rather heavy. Mixed in between, however, is enough citrus to keep it afloat. **83** *(7/1/2005)*

Neudorf 2003 Sauvignon Blanc (Nelson) $23. A big, ripe style of Sauvignon Blanc, one that sacrifices herbal notes in favor of peach, melon, and fig flavors. This full-bodied wine comes across as rich and honeyed, yet dry and persistent on the finish. **89** —*J.C. (8/1/2004)*

Neudorf 2002 Sauvignon Blanc (Marlborough) $22. A small proportion of this wine was barrel-fermented, which gives it greater richness and a creamier mouthfeel than many of its counterparts. The flavors are ripe and fresh, with hints of tropical fruits, citrus, and a pinch of herbs. **88** — *J.C. (9/1/2003)*

NEVIS BLUFF

Nevis Bluff 2003 Pinot Noir (Central Otago) $24. Doesn't have the richness, mouthfeel, or intensity of the winery's 2002, but the vintage was more challenging. Crisp cherry fruit boasts hints of celery seed and a long, tart finish. **87** —*J.C. (12/1/2005)*

Nevis Bluff 2002 Pinot Noir (Central Otago) $24. The product of a great vintage in Central Otago, this wine shows why the region is so promising for Pinot. It delivers earthy, savory, meaty notes that never seem heavy thanks to its rich, velvety texture and copious ripe cherry fruit. **90 Editors' Choice** —*J.C. (12/1/2005)*

NEW Z LAND

New Z Land 2002 Merlot (Wairarapa) $17. Cool-climate Merlot can be a tricky proposition. This one features a reasonably smooth, supple texture, but boasts rather vegetal flavors of tomato, fresh herbs, and black olives, then turns lemony on the finish. **81** —*J.C. (11/1/2006)*

New Z Land 2005 Sauvignon Blanc (Marlborough) $11. Pungent and herbal, with fresh passion fruit and grassy notes that make a statement. Light and crisp on the palate, finishing with hints of pink grapefruit. **86 Best Buy** —*J.C. (7/1/2006)*

NEWTON FORREST ESTATE

Newton Forrest Estate 2002 Gimblett Gravels Cabernet-Merlot-Malbec Bordeaux Blend (Hawke's Bay) $31. A pleasant surprise in a recent sampling of Hawkes Bay blends, this wine verges on being over-ripe, yet still boasts ample structure. Black cherry and plum fruit is marked by vanilla and cinnamon, while the mouthfeel is one of contained lushness, not gloppy or syrupy. Drink now-2012. The blend is roughly one-third of each variety. **89** —*J.C. (7/1/2006)*

NGA WAKA

Nga Waka 2000 Chardonnay (Martinborough) $30. Starts off with toasted almond, pear, and citrus aromas, evolving into pear and orange in the mouth. This medium-weight Chard is a nice drink that finishes with some slightly aggressive wood and a trace of grapefruit. **86** —*J.C. (7/1/2002)*

Nga Waka 1999 Chardonnay (Martinborough) $25. Shows good intensity of pineapple, citrus, and buttered toast flavors, but still seems a bit gawky and young. Give this one another six months or a year to knit together before hitting its stride. **87** —*J.C. (5/1/2001)*

Nga Waka 2003 Pinot Noir (Martinborough) $NA. Seems to have a bit of a volatile acidity issue, with lifted aromas and a slightly pickle-y taste that distract from the cherry fruit. **81** —*J.C. (12/1/2005)*

Nga Waka 2001 Pinot Noir (Martinborough) $35. It's the same grape variety, the same vintage, and the same growing region as the identically rated Ata Rangi, but couldn't be more different, offering bold black cherry and spice in a satisfyingly rich mouthful of flavor. **88** —*J.C. (9/1/2003)*

Nga Waka 2001 Riesling (Martinborough) $20. It's the rare NZ Riesling we see in this country that's from Martinborough, but Nga Waka's 2001 makes a strong case for the continued production of Riesling in an area that's better known for Burgundian varieties. Floral on the nose, with bright citrusy fruit on the palate and almost ephemerally light, this is an ideal apéritif wine. **87** —*J.C. (8/1/2003)*

Nga Waka 2002 Sauvignon Blanc (Martinborough) $17. Taut and lean, with lemon, lime, and green apple flavors that come across as tart and ungenerous. Still, it's crisp and refreshing and would cut through a plate of oily sardines. **84** —*J.C. (8/1/2004)*

Nga Waka 2001 Sauvignon Blanc (Martinborough) $20. Hay, mint, and grass add a green touch to the nose, which also features nectarine. Citrus, but nothing really defined, dominates the flavor profile. More citrus and zippy acids run wild on the finish. It doesn't offer any one thing for you to hang your hat on. **87** *(8/1/2002)*

Nga Waka 2000 Sauvignon Blanc (Martinborough) $20. From a region better known for Burgundian varieties, this Sauvignon Blanc has turned out well. Passion fruit, peaches, and gooseberries flow across the palate, which features a bit of creaminess. A hint of capsicum (green pepper) intensifies on the finish. **88** —*J.C. (5/1/2001)*

NGATARAWA

Ngatarawa 2005 Glazebrook Sauvignon Blanc (Marlborough) $14. Grassy and herbal on the nose, this medium-weight Sauvignon epitomizes the Marlborough style, blending hints of tropical fruit with grapefruit and herbs in an easy-to-drink wine. Crisp and clean on the finish. Steam some mussels in herbed stock and let the Sauvignon flow. **86** —*J.C. (9/1/2006)*

Ngatarawa 2004 Glazebrook Sauvignon Blanc (Marlborough) $14. Grassy and herbal-smelling, but there's also lots of grapefruit and nectarines to provide a fruity counter-balance. Light in weight, with a hint of unreleased CO_2 to provide additional freshness, this is a mouth-watering summer refresher. **87** —*J.C. (7/1/2005)*

NO 1 FAMILY ESTATE

No 1 Family Estate NV Cuvée No 1 Blanc de Blancs Chardonnay (Marlborough) $25. Shows a bit more complexity than the Number Eight, but also a softer, less-focused finish. Understated aromas of toast,

NEW ZEALAND

earth, and citrus are backed by richly fruity pineapple flavors. **88** —*J.C.* *(12/15/2003)*

No 1 Family Estate NV Cuvée Number Eight Brut Sparkling Blend (Marlborough) $20. Creamy and elegant, with a fine bead and subtle aromas of toast, earth, and citrus. Picks up pineapple and chalk flavors on the palate, finishing like a crisp Granny Smith—tart and mouth-watering. **90 Editors' Choice** —*J.C. (12/15/2003)*

NOBILO

Nobilo 2002 Chardonnay (East Coast) $10. Subtle butter and toast notes frame the core of peach and pear fruit in this well-priced offering made from predominantly Gisborne-grown fruit. Finishes with spicy oak and vanilla. **86** —*J.C. (4/1/2004)*

Nobilo 2000 Fall Harvest Chardonnay (Gisborne) $10. Oaky and buttery, with loads of sweet vanilla and baking spices over modest peach and pear fruit. Turns toasty on the finish. **83** —*J.C. (5/1/2001)*

Nobilo 1999 Poverty Bay Chardonnay (Gisborne) $NA. The strong toasted-oak aromas ride heavy over melon and pear fruit, but this wine manages to keep it together, turning almost elegant on the finish, where the oak is reflected in a long menthol echo. **87** —*J.C. (5/1/2001)*

Nobilo 2004 Regional Collection Merlot (East Coast) $12. Although the majority of the fruit comes off a 300-acre Hawke's Bay vineyard planted in 2000, there is some Gisborne Merlot in this wine as well. Combines cherry fruit with bits of chocolate and caramel, with just a hint of herb. Soft and easy to drink while being light and fresh. **85** *(3/1/2006)*

Nobilo 2003 Icon Pinot Gris (Marlborough) $20. A big, ripe, slightly alcoholic wine, this is meant to make a statement. The color is coppery, suggesting some skin contact and there are even some red fruit flavors mixed in with the layers of peaches and honey. Slightly off-dry and low in acidity, this rich Pinot Gris would be lovely by itself on a lazy, late-summer day. **87** —*J.C. (8/1/2004)*

Nobilo 2005 Icon Pinot Noir (Marlborough) $22. Robust and flavorful, Nobilo's top Pinot Noir is undeniably toasty, but it also features burly cola and plum flavors to match the oak. Big-boned and firmly structured, drink 2008–09. **88** —*J.C. (12/15/2006)*

Nobilo 2003 Icon Pinot Noir (Marlborough) $20. Nobilo's top Pinot is a supple, pretty wine that's ready to drink now. It offers black cherries, plums, and dried spices, with a medium body and slightly creamy texture. Spicy and long on the finish. **88** —*J.C. (7/1/2005)*

Nobilo 2003 Sauvignon Blanc (Marlborough) $12. A fine value, Nobilo's latest SB shows a fine bouquet of musk, lime, and passion fruit paired with flavors of pink grapefruit and white currants. The slightly creamy texture glides into a zesty, clean, refreshing finish. **88 Best Buy** —*J.C. (4/1/2004)*

Nobilo 2000 Sauvignon Blanc (Marlborough) $NA. Representative Marlborough Sauvignon Blanc: melon, grapefruit, and passion fruit in abundance, followed by a finish that's marked by green herbs and bell pepper. **88** —*J.C. (5/1/2001)*

Nobilo 2000 Fall Harvest Sauvignon Blanc (Marlborough) $10. Fresh and light; the grapefruit and gooseberry aromas and flavors are tinged with capsicum and green peas. The residual sugar is noticeable, at 6-7 g/L, but balanced by brisk acidity. **86 Best Buy** —*J.C. (5/1/2001)*

Nobilo 2000 Icon Series Sauvignon Blanc (Marlborough) $19. Ultrarich and creamy, with an abundance of fruity flavors that are powerfully extracted and bold. Despite the size, you'll find lovely balance and finesse. The mealy taste of lees shows up in the rich finish. **88** —*S.H. (11/15/2002)*

Nobilo 1999 Icon Series Sauvignon Blanc (Marlborough) $NA. This is a full, rich bottling, with few of the green notes found in so many Kiwi Sauvignon Blancs. Grapefruit and passionfruit flavors coat the mouth in a creamy wave. **89** —*J.C. (5/1/2001)*

Nobilo 2005 Regional Collection Sauvignon Blanc (Marlborough) $12. With production edging up past 300,000 cases, there should be plenty of this bargain-priced Sauvignon in the market. Understated herb and green pepper scents are complemented by passion fruit and citrus. Soft and easy, this is a good introduction to Marlborough Savvy. **87 Best Buy** —*J.C. (12/1/2005)*

Nobilo 2004 Regional Collection Sauvignon Blanc (Marlborough) $12. Fits the New Zealand stereotype to a T, boasting pungent, earthy aromas, then a burst of passion fruit and citrus on the palate. Zippy and fresh, this is a wine to gulp down over the hot summer months. No food necessary, although a bowl of moules would seem appropriate. **87 Best Buy** —*J.C. (7/1/2005)*

OLSSENS

Olssens 2001 Barrel Fermented Chardonnay (Central Otago) $NA. Toasty on the nose and the palate, buffered by sour apples. Superficially likeable, but in the end you're left with soft, somewhat hollow fruit under layers of smoky, spicy oak. **85** —*J.C. (5/1/2006)*

Olssens 2004 Gewürztraminer (Central Otago) $17. Despite 14% alcohol, this Gewürz comes across as rather light in weight and deceptively easy to drink. Restrained pear and rose petal notes turn crisper and more citrusy on the finish. A good choice with Indian cuisine, so long as the heat isn't too intense. **87** —*J.C. (7/1/2005)*

Olssens 2004 Gewürztraminer (Central Otago) $17. This dry-styled Gewürz offers restrained scents of roses and lychee fruit. In the mouth, it gives an impression of broad, mouth-filling softness, but then turns a bit hard and tart on the finish. **86** —*J.C. (5/1/2006)*

Olssens 2004 Jackson Barry Pinot Noir (Central Otago) $33. Kicks off with lovely herbal, floral, and spice elements, creating an intriguing bouquet, then adds bass notes of flavor—cherries and chocolate. Finishes well, picking up hints of cola. **88** —*J.C. (12/1/2005)*

Olssens 2002 Jackson Barry Pinot Noir (Central Otago) $29. Just short of excellent, this 2002 is the best wine I've yet tasted from Olssens. Dense aromas of tree bark and dark chocolate are accented by hints of strawberries. Round and ripe, the mouth-filling cherry-berry flavors pick up hints of cola before finishing with a tart juiciness. **89** —*J.C. (7/1/2005)*

Olssens 2003 Slap Jack Creek Pinot Noir (Central Otago) $48. From its lovely dusty, dried spice aromas to its pretty cherry flavors, this is all Pinot. Medium in body, it's neither too heavy nor too light, ending with a delicate overlay of fine tannins. **89** —*J.C. (12/1/2005)*

Olssens 2004 Riesling (Central Otago) $17. Tastes just like spring, with hints of delicate pear and apple blossoms on the nose, followed by green apple flavors. It's light-bodied, low in alcohol, and low in sugar, making it tart, crisp, and dry—a refreshing apéritif. **88** —*J.C. (7/1/2005)*

Olssens 2004 Riesling (Central Otago) $17. Lightly floral on the nose, this medium-bodied Riesling (12.5% alcohol) picks up notes of fresh greens and apples on the palate alongside plenty of bright citrus flavors. Despite over 6g/L residual sugar, crisp acidity keeps the finish fresh. **88** —*J.C. (5/1/2006)*

Olssens 2003 Desert Gold Late Harvest Riesling (Central Otago) $NA. Produced from "cordon-cut" bunches, Riesling offers up intense honey, apple and pear aromas and flavors. With more than 11% residual sugar, you might expect this wine to be sticky-sweet, but thanks to crisp acids, it's not cloying. Tasty, well-balanced wine that just finishes a bit short. **86** —*J.C. (5/1/2006)*

OMAKA SPRINGS

Omaka Springs 2002 Chardonnay (Marlborough) $18. Buttery and fruity, strongly marked by the 55% of the wine that went through malolactic fermentation, as if melted butter was drizzled over ripe tropical fruit. Finishes juicy and fresh, if somewhat simple. **85** —*J.C. (9/1/2003)*

Omaka Springs 1998 Reserve Chardonnay (Marlborough) $NA. Simple and sweet-smelling, like butterscotch Lifesavers; a caramel-candy beverage. **80** —*J.C. (5/1/2001)*

Omaka Springs 2002 Winemaker's Selection Chardonnay (Marlborough) $24. Buttery on the nose, but nicely balanced, with scents of honey, peaches, and limes giving way to apple, peach, and citrus flavors. Plump in the mouth without being heavy, and it even picks up a hint of chalky minerality on the finish. **90 Editors' Choice** —*J.C. (7/1/2005)*

Omaka Springs 2001 Merlot (Marlborough) $18. Smoky and herbal, with hints of cabbage vying with over-ripe cherries and tree bark. Seems big in the mouth, then you realize it's missing flesh on the midpalate. **84** —*J.C. (12/15/2003)*

Omaka Springs 1999 Merlot (Marlborough) $15. Aromas of cherries and vanilla, with berry-zinger tea accents. The mixed red fruits are bright enough to carry this light but zippy wine. Would make a good picnic quaff. **85**—*J.C. (5/1/2001)*

Omaka Springs 2005 Pinot Gris (Marlborough) $17. This plump, medium-bodied Pinot Gris has lots of bold fruit on the nose, ranging from luscious pears and ripe melons to crisp apples. The flavors aren't quite as clean and expressive, but there's still decent fruit along with tarry, rubbery notes. Finishes dry and chalky. **88**—*J.C. (2/1/2006)*

Omaka Springs 2002 Pinot Gris (Marlborough) $15. Pinot Gris is quickly becoming the hot white grape in New Zealand, and this is a fine example. Ripe, honeyed pear and apple fruit provides plenty of weight, but there's also crisp acidity to provide balance. Going by taste alone, it may have a touch of residual sugar to help round out the mouthfeel and counter the zesty acids, but the hint of sweetness will only make it partner even better with many Asian dishes. **88**—*J.C. (11/15/2003)*

Omaka Springs 1998 Reserve Pinot Noir (Marlborough) $NA. Subtle toast and black cherry flavors anchor this solid example of Marlborough Pinot. Finishes lean and dry, with firm acidity and a touch of greenness. **85**—*J.C. (5/1/2001)*

Omaka Springs 2001 Winemaker's Selection Pinot Noir (Marlborough) $19. Earthy and a bit sour, with hints of sweaty socks alongside cola and tart cherry flavors. Shows decent complexity, but finishes short and with slightly drying tannins. **83**—*J.C. (4/1/2004)*

Omaka Springs 2004 Riesling (Marlborough) $17. Made in a lean, racy style, this Marlborough Riesling combines moderate alcohol (12.5%) with minimal residual sugar to make a crisp, refreshing wine well-suited to washing down shellfish. Scents of stones (flint) and lime pick up hints of nectarine before finishing tart and clean. **88**—*J.C. (7/1/2005)*

Omaka Springs 2003 Riesling (Marlborough) $17. Apple, pear and quince aromas segue into a pleasant mix of tree and stone fruits on the palate, wrapped up by a zippy, citrusy finish. Best Riesling yet from this producer, worth trying if you can find it. **89**—*J.C. (8/1/2004)*

Omaka Springs 2002 Riesling (Marlborough) $15. An eccentric version of Marlborough Riesling that tastes reminiscent of Marlborough Sauvignon Blanc, with a green, under-ripe quality and some goosberry aromas on the nose. There's also a hint of riper, cinnamon-scented fruit and a clean, crisp finish. **85**—*J.C. (8/1/2003)*

Omaka Springs 2001 Riesling (Marlborough) $14. A classic NZ Riesling that's all about fruit: apples, pears. and limes on the nose, with more of the same in the mouth. Medium-weight, but balanced by plenty of racy acidity that turns tart and malic on the finish. **88**—*J.C. (8/1/2002)*

Omaka Springs 1998 Riesling (Marlborough) $NA. Earl Grey tea is a classic, and its trademark flavor of bergamot shows up in this spicy Riesling. Other flavors are pear, green apple, and lime. This is a full-bodied wine that should be consumed soon. **85**—*J.C. (5/1/2001)*

Omaka Springs 2005 Sauvignon Blanc (Marlborough) $17. Less showy than many of its brethren, Omaka Springs's 2005 Sauvignon instead shows touches of smoke and minerals in its subdued aromatics. Flavors combine citrus and melon on the midpalate, then veer towards crisp lime and grapefruit on the persistent finish. **87**—*J.C. (7/1/2006)*

Omaka Springs 2004 Sauvignon Blanc (Marlborough) $17. Notes of peach and nectarine on one hand, and grassy herbs on the other, adorn a solid core of passion fruit and grapefruit. Nicely balanced, but not overly concentrated; clean on the finish, but not that long. A solid effort. **86**—*J.C. (7/1/2005)*

Omaka Springs 2003 Sauvignon Blanc (Marlborough) $17. This slightly clumsy, heavyhanded wine boasts a sweet, honeyed attack that turns tart and grapefruity somewhere midpalate, resulting in a sweet-and-sour combination that's not entirely convincing. **83**—*J.C. (4/1/2004)*

Omaka Springs 2002 Sauvignon Blanc (Marlborough) $18. Displays authentically grassy aromas, with passion fruit and gooseberry scents, then turns more tropical on the palate. At almost 0.5% residual sugar, sensitive palates might detect some sweetness that adds weight to the palate. **86**—*J.C. (9/1/2003)*

Omaka Springs 2001 Sauvignon Blanc (Marlborough) $17. Sharp, piercing aromas of pineapple and steel yield a bit prior to a tangy, citrusy palate. There's some chalk and slate on the finish, which adds an element of complexity. The only noticeable fault here is a candied sweetness at the tail end. **89**(8/1/2002)

Omaka Springs 1999 Sauvignon Blanc (Marlborough) $15. A softer, gentler Marlborough Savvy, with warm melon and passion fruit accented by only a touch of gooseberry. Pink grapefruit flavors accent the finish. **86** —*J.C. (5/1/2001)*

ORIGIN

Origin 2004 Sauvignon Blanc (Marlborough) $14. Shows some flinty-chalky notes that resemble a decent Pouilly-Fumé alongside grapefruit and bell pepper fruit. Light in body, with a long, citrusy finish. Ideal with shellfish or simple fish dishes. **88**—*J.C. (7/1/2005)*

OYSTER BAY

Oyster Bay 2005 Chardonnay (Marlborough) $13. This medium-bodied Chardonnay features plenty of tropical fruit flavors, but not much else except a distracting rubbery, tarry scent. **82**—*J.C. (12/15/2006)*

Oyster Bay 2004 Chardonnay (Marlborough) $13. Crisp without being overly racy, this mostly tank-fermented Chardonnay features bright, citrusy fruit with just hints of oak. A food-friendly style at an affordable price. **86**—*J.C. (5/1/2006)*

Oyster Bay 2002 Chardonnay (Marlborough & Hawke's Bay) $15. Smells of powerful stone fruits such as nectarines and plums. Leaves a sweet, fruit cocktail-like impression on the palate, but finishes clean and citrusy. A bit simple, but it makes for a satisfying, flavorful mouthful of wine. **86** —*J.C. (9/1/2003)*

Oyster Bay 2004 Merlot (Hawke's Bay) $13. Slightly herbal on the nose, but that's balanced by black cherry fruit and a tobacco note. Medium body and a soft finish make this Merlot easy to drink. **84**—*J.C. (5/1/2006)*

Oyster Bay 2005 Pinot Noir (Marlborough) $13. A step up in quality from the 2004, and a step down in price make this Pinot a hit any way you slice it. Black cherry and plum fruit is balanced by hints of menthol and vanilla from oak. It's on the full-bodied, muscular side and admittedly a bit chunky, but does show fine dusty tannins and decent length on the finish. **87**—*J.C. (9/1/2006)*

Oyster Bay 2004 Pinot Noir (Marlborough) $17. Starts off a bit muted on the nose, then delivers sweet cherry flavors upfront. The flavors veer toward cola and spice on the finish, where the tannins turn a bit drying. **85**—*J.C. (12/1/2005)*

Oyster Bay 2005 Sauvignon Blanc (Marlborough) $13. Solid, mainstream Marlborough Sauvignon at an attractive price, the 2005 Oyster Bay offers tropical notes on the nose, then turns more citrusy on the palate as peach and melon notes give way to lime and mineral. **87**—*J.C. (5/1/2006)*

PALLISER ESTATE

Palliser Estate 2004 Chardonnay (Martinborough) $NA. Although Palliser's wines are represented in the U.S., the Chardonnays are not, which is a shame given the evident quality. This is a medium- to full-bodied wine, marked with honey, toast, peach, and orange aromas and bold pineapple flavors, yet it finishes crisp, not sweet, buttery, or cloying. **88**—*J.C. (5/1/2006)*

Palliser Estate 1999 Chardonnay (Marlborough) $23. A soft, round wine that's filled with pineapples, oranges, and cream. A bit of alcoholic heat on the finish combines with spicy new oak to give it added kick, with a buttery aftertaste. **87**—*J.C. (5/1/2001)*

Palliser Estate 2004 Pencarrow Chardonnay (Martinborough) $NA. Palliser's second-tier Chardonnay isn't imported to the U.S., but for readers where it is available, it probably offers decent value. Subtle toast and lees add complexity to apple and citrus fruit. Crisp acidity and a chalky, slightly tannic feel make it a good with food. **87**—*J.C. (5/1/2006)*

Palliser Estate 2004 Pinot Gris (Martinborough) $19. Seems just the tiniest bit heavy, but offers ample compensation by way of bold pear and black pepper aromas, apple, and spice flavors and an orangey citrus finish. Off dry. **86** —*J.C. (7/1/2005)*

Palliser Estate 2002 Pinot Gris (Martinborough) $19. Relatively thin, but with charming apple and pear aromas and flavors. The wine is pretty, it just lacks a little palate presence. **84** —*J.C. (9/1/2003)*

Palliser Estate 2000 Pinot Gris (Martinborough) $20. Starts out soft, with warm peach and nectarine notes that turn leaner and more citric on the finish, even folding in a touch of green pepper. **85** —*J.C. (5/1/2001)*

Palliser Estate 1998 Pinot Noir (Martinborough) $24. **87** —*M.S. (10/1/2000)*

Palliser Estate 2003 Pinot Noir (Martinborough) $27. Complex and meaty on the nose, blending layers of dried spices, roasted meat, and spring flowers. Adds cola, clove, and crisp cherry flavors on the palate before finishing firm, almost tough. Give it a few years. **86** —*J.C. (12/1/2005)*

Palliser Estate 2000 Pinot Noir (Marlborough) $26. A clean wine that pushes acidity front and center to play a starring role. The flavors are international Pinot Noir, with red raspberry or cherry, beetroot, and crushed hard spice, and that silky mouthfeel that comes with light tannins. It's addictively drinkable, yet could have more depth and substance. **88** —*S.H. (11/15/2002)*

Palliser Estate 1999 Pinot Noir (Martinborough) $26. Features a sandy, earthy, beetroot character on the nose, then sweet black cherry and tea flavors on the palate. The long, moderately tannic finish suggests it will hold for a few years, but it's enjoyable even now. **88** —*J.C. (5/1/2001)*

Palliser Estate 2003 Pencarrow Pinot Noir (Martinborough) $18. Palliser's second label lacks the easy approachability expected from such an offering, instead giving up tart cherries, leather, and spice. Finishes with firm tannins, but not necessarily built for longevity. **84** —*J.C. (12/1/2005)*

Palliser Estate 2002 Pencarrow Pinot Noir (Martinborough) $18. Looks and tastes tired, with a light, rusty hue and leafy, tomatoey flavors. **81** —*J.C. (12/1/2005)*

Palliser Estate 2001 Pencarrow Pinot Noir (Martinborough) $20. Pencarrow is Palliser's second label, which helps explain this wine's lack of body; presumably the richer lots went into the Palliser Estate bottling (not yet tasted). That said, it offers pretty cherry and herb flavors and a lingering finish. **84** —*J.C. (9/1/2003)*

Palliser Estate 2000 Riesling (Martinborough) $NA. A hint of green herbs on the nose gives way to more generous flavors of grapefruit and peach. The fleshy midpalate and lime backbone bode well for aging. As an example, the '94 and '95 are drinking well now. **87** —*J.C. (5/1/2001)*

Palliser Estate 1999 Sauvignon Blanc (Martinborough) $17. **89** —*J.C. (10/1/2000)*

Palliser Estate 2005 Sauvignon Blanc (Martinborough) $19. Pungently herbal at first, accented by bold passion fruit flavors that set the original paradigm for New Zealand Sauvignon Blanc. Rather plump on the palate, but it finishes crisp and clean, with mouth-watering acidity. **87** — *J.C. (12/15/2006)*

Palliser Estate 2004 Sauvignon Blanc (Martinborough) $19. Bold peach and apricot notes on the nose, with only a trace of herbaceousness. Plump and medium-weight on the palate, with more stone fruit flavors that finish a trifle short. Drink now. **87** —*J.C. (12/1/2005)*

Palliser Estate 2002 Sauvignon Blanc (Martinborough) $17. There's too much asparagus for this reviewer in this zesty, grapefruity wine that's otherwise clean and fresh. **83** —*J.C. (9/1/2003)*

Palliser Estate 2001 Sauvignon Blanc (Marlborough) $18. Another brilliantly evocative Marlborough wine, full of the most beautiful, complex flavors. Apple, peach, and citrus fruits roll down the palate in waves, made shining bright by high acids, and finish dryish and opulent. This is simply a joy to sip. **91** —*S.H. (11/15/2002)*

Palliser Estate 2000 Sauvignon Blanc (Martinborough) $19. This perennial favorite is a hit again. There's all the ingredients you expect in Kiwi Sauvignon Blanc: intense green herbs, tropical fruit, and a long, crisp finish. **89** —*J.C. (5/1/2001)*

Palliser Estate 2004 Pencarrow Sauvignon Blanc (Martinborough) $14. Starts with notes of peach, pineapple, and jalapeño oil. Light in body,

the flavors just slip away, leaving behind hints of peaches and green peppers. **85** —*J.C. (5/1/2006)*

Palliser Estate 2002 Pencarrow Sauvignon Blanc (Martinborough) $13. **86** —*J.C. (9/1/2003)*

PEGASUS BAY

Pegasus Bay 2005 Sauvignon-Sémillon Bordeaux White Blend (Waipara Valley) $25. This is the most Sémillon (30%) I can recall in this wine, and it's also the best I can remember this wine showing, with slightly musky aromas of gooseberry, honey, and fig leading into a creamy, richly textured wine loaded with melon and fig fruit. Long on the finish, where it seems to build even higher in flavor intensity. **92 Editors' Choice** —*J.C. (11/1/2006)*

Pegasus Bay 1998 Maestro Cabernet Sauvignon-Merlot (Waipara) $52. This blend of 50% Merlot, 45% Cabernet Sauvignon, and 5% Cabernet Franc is ambitiously priced, but the quality is in the bottle. Next time you need a ringer for a right-bank Bordeaux tasting, here's a perfect candidate. Dried spices and a smooth, rich texture are the only hallmarks left from two years of barrel aging—the mocha and black cherry fruit is rich and luscious, developing tobacco nuances on the moderately tannic finish. Drink now and over the next 10 years. **92 Cellar Selection** —*J.C. (8/1/2002)*

Pegasus Bay 2005 Chardonnay (Waipara Valley) $35. One of New Zealand's most consistently good wineries, Peg Bay has turned in an excellent 2005 Chardonnay. The bouquet is packed with smoke and toasted nuts, but the fruit easily emerges on the palate, opening into peach, honey, and bright citrus flavors. Creamy in texture, with a long finish that folds in a lovely honey-nut character. **90** —*J.C. (11/1/2006)*

Pegasus Bay 2004 Chardonnay (Waipara) $35. Toasty on the nose, but not as rich or opulently fruity as some previous vintages. Instead, it's a leaner style, with tart, grapefruity flavors that finish long and intense. **88** —*J.C. (12/1/2005)*

Pegasus Bay 2001 Chardonnay (Waipara) $34. Huge aromas of butter and toast explode from the glass of this ripe, opulent Chardonnay. It's full bodied, featuring waves of peach compote flavors that pick up dried spice accents on the finish. Bold and flavorful. **89** —*J.C. (8/1/2004)*

Pegasus Bay 2000 Chardonnay (Waipara) $30. Full of butter notes, along with toasted oatmeal and Brazil nuts, this rich, oily Chard is all about New World power, yet allied to an Old World sense of balance. Honey and tropical-fruit flavors play out on the palate; toast and tangerines extend through the finish. **91** —*J.C. (7/1/2002)*

Pegasus Bay 1998 Whole Bunch Pressed Chardonnay (Waipara) $33. Amply oaked, but with sufficient fruit to back it up, this wine starts with aromas of buttered toast, roasted nuts, crème brûlée, and pineapple. Then it turns richly earthy and custardy on the palate, while still retaining a sense of balance through a beam of citrus-like acidity that adds cut to the finish. **90** —*J.C. (5/1/2001)*

Pegasus Bay 2001 Maestro Merlot-Malbec (Waipara) $NA. Peg Bay's Maestro is only bottled in the best vintages, the last being 1998, a wine that continues to age beautifully. In 2001, it's predominantly (75%) Merlot, with the remainder mainly Malbec (15%), with smaller proportions of Cabernet Franc and Cabernet Sauvignon. Combines toasty new oak with cassis and dried spices in a medium-weight wine, then adds an explosive, tobacco-laden finish. Not available in the US. **90** —*J.C. (5/1/2006)*

Pegasus Bay 2003 Pinot Noir (Waipara) $40. Seems a bit tight and sinewy, with dried spices and black cherries at the fore. Earth, sous bois, and chocolate provide the underpinnings, while crisp cranberry notes emerge on the finish. **87** —*J.C. (12/1/2005)*

Pegasus Bay 2001 Pinot Noir (Waipara) $48. A perennial favorite, this year's Pegasus Bay is no disappointment. Wisps of dried herbs add complexity to the black cherry aromas, with barrel-imparted hints of vanilla and dried spices buttressing the richly fruity flavors. Add a full, supple mouthfeel and a long, mouth-watering finish, and you've got all the ingredients for world-class Pinot Noir. **91** —*J.C. (9/1/2003)*

Pegasus Bay 1999 Pinot Noir (Waipara) $39. Intense and extracted, this wine has strong cola, chocolate, black cherry, cinnamon, and peppermint

NEW ZEALAND

aromas that border on eccentric and over-the-top, yet somehow stay in balance. Good acidity provides a foil against which the rich flavors play, and persists well through the long, softly tannic finish. Drink now and over the next few years; there's no telling how it will age. **91** —*J.C. (5/1/2001)*

Pegasus Bay 2003 Prima Donna Pinot Noir (Waipara) $74. For Peg Bay's high-end bottling, this is a bit of a disappointment. It offers dried spices and cherries on the nose, then adds sour cherry flavors on the palate. With time, darker cherry flavors emerge, showing a slight element of sur-maturité. It's medium-bodied, with some firm tannins still in evidence. Hold through 2008 and hope for improvement. **88** —*J.C. (12/1/2005)*

Pegasus Bay 2001 Prima Donna Pinot Noir (Waipara) $88. For the second consecutive release, I've rated Prima Donna lower than the regular Pinot from Peg Bay. Maybe it's just more closed at this stage, or maybe I'm looking for something different in Pinot than this wine's architects have in mind. It's nice enough, offering plenty of spice and earthy complexity, but also a dark, brooding character reminiscent of coffee and dark chocolate. Try in 2008. **88** —*J.C. (8/1/2004)*

Pegasus Bay 1999 Prima Donna Pinot Noir (Waipara) $63. Although a fine wine when taken on its own, in the context of Pegasus Bay's other wines, this is something of a let down. Either that, or it was in an awkward stage when we tasted it, showing some beet and cola notes but dominated by sweet, caramelly oak. Tasted twice, with consistent notes. **87** —*J.C. (9/1/2003)*

Pegasus Bay 2005 Riesling (Waipara Valley) $25. Plump and sweet, but reasonably balanced, with a dash of CO_2 for extra zest, this vintage of Peg Bay's Riesling seems just a touch behind their previous few releases. Baked apple, peach, cinnamon, and tangerine notes make it easily accessible now, but it may not have the same longevity as the 2004, for example. Drink now to enjoy its fresh fruit. **88** —*J.C. (11/1/2006)*

Pegasus Bay 2004 Riesling (Waipara) $24. Smells fresh enough to make your mouth water, filled with scents of lime zest and green apples. On the palate, it's nicely balanced, not as rich or sweet as a tank sample of the '05, but crisp and elegant, with superb concentration. **90** —*J.C. (12/1/2005)*

Pegasus Bay 2003 Riesling (Waipara) $25. This off-dry Riesling boasts bold scents of honey and dried apricots, then delivers baked apple and dried fruit flavors that coat the palate. It's ample-bodied, yet not heavy or fat, reminiscent of a big spätlese or auslese made in a somewhat dry style. **90 Editors' Choice** —*J.C. (7/1/2005)*

Pegasus Bay 2002 Riesling (Waipara) $24. Smells considerably riper than most Otago Rieslings, with nectarine and apricot aromas giving way to a thickly textured wine with bold stone fruit flavors and just enough citrusy acidity on the finish to keep the wine balanced. Most comparable in style to off-dry Alsatian Rieslings, possibly even vendanges tardives wines. **90 Editors' Choice** —*J.C. (8/1/2003)*

Pegasus Bay 2000 Riesling (Waipara) $20. Ripe apples and pears are accented by orange blossoms in this opulent and open-knit Riesling. Lush and viscous, it also has a subtle under-current of lime-like acidity that keeps it from being fat. Residual sugar seems to be about Spätlese level. **89** —*J.C. (5/1/2001)*

Pegasus Bay 2004 Sauvignon Blanc (Waipara) $24. There's 15% Sémillon blended into this wine, which helps add a bit of creaminess to the texture. It's reasonably rich on the palate as a result, with ripe stone fruit flavors that taper off toward grapefruit on the finish. **87** —*J.C. (12/1/2005)*

Pegasus Bay 2002 Sauvignon Blanc (Waipara) $26. The philosophy at Peg Bay, as it's sometimes called, aims for high ripeness levels. The result in the case of its Sauvignon Blanc (blended with a fair proportion of Sémillon) is an almost honeyed character to the ripe stone fruits and plenty of heft on the palate. Unusual for NZ Sauvignon Blanc, and delicious. **88** —*J.C. (8/1/2004)*

Pegasus Bay 2001 Sauvignon Blanc (Waipara) $19. A rich, mouthcoating, viscous style, with 24% Sémillon blended in and kept on the lees for nine months prior to bottling. Honeyed stone fruits (plum and peach) and its round, supple nature make it easy to drink. **88** —*J.C. (9/1/2003)*

Pegasus Bay 2000 Sauvignon Blanc (Waipara) $19. Aromas of toast, apricot, mint, honey, and field dust make for a complex bouquet. The honeyed palate yields a trace of green herbs along with lemon rind and white pepper. Obviously there's a lot going on here, and for some it may be too "out there." For others it will be a spot-on Kiwi offering with lots of individuality and character. **89** *(8/1/2002)*

Pegasus Bay 1999 Sauvignon Blanc (Waipara) $20. Weighty and extracted, this Sauvignon Blanc is atypically rich and low-acid. Grapefruit, gooseberry, and honey flavors are finished off with a hint of bitter pith. **85** —*J.C. (5/1/2001)*

PENINSULA ESTATE WINES

Peninsula Estate Wines 1998 Hauraki Bordeaux Blend (Waiheke Island) $45. Seems tired already—or possibly heat-damaged in transit. Browning at the rim. Leather, mushrooms, and molasses offer a sense of bottle sweetness, but the wine dries out on the finish, ending with starching tannins. **84** —*J.C. (8/1/2004)*

Peninsula Estate Wines 2000 Zeno Syrah (Waiheke Island) $40. A decent quaff—a bit light and herbal—but probably tasty with grilled lamb chops. Its leafy, eucalyptus aromas and light red cherry fruit are pleasant enough and would complement simply prepared grilled meats. **85** —*J.C. (8/1/2004)*

PEREGRINE

Peregrine 1999 Gewürztraminer (Central Otago) $NA. Oily and showing good varietal character in its rose-petal and lychee aromas. Tastes more pear-like, with loads of musk and spice that give it an exotic, perfumed character that persists through the long finish. **90** —*J.C. (5/1/2001)*

Peregrine 2005 Pinot Gris (Central Otago) $29. In a flight of other Kiwi Pinot Gris, this one shows more of a stony, minerally character, but also less ripeness and opulent fruit. It's medium-bodied, with a layer of lemon-lime flavors over an apple base. Finishes on a slightly bitter note. **84** —*J.C. (11/1/2006)*

Peregrine 2003 Pinot Gris (Central Otago) $26. This medium-weight wine carries its ample alcohol well, hidden in a rush of jasmine, honey, and baked apple and pear aromas and flavors. A slightly bitter or metallic note on the finish is the only thing holding it back. **85** —*J.C. (8/1/2004)*

Peregrine 2002 Pinot Gris (Central Otago) $19. So floral on the nose that you might mistake it at first for a Riesling, but the flavors of baked apples and pears and mouth-coating texture speak of Pinot Gris. **88** —*J.C. (9/1/2003)*

Peregrine 2003 Pinot Noir (Central Otago) $38. Features hints of herb and pepper on the nose, but this wine is mostly about the fruit—ripe black cherries, soft tannins, and a round, inviting mouthfeel. Picks up hints of vanilla on the silky finish. **88** —*J.C. (12/1/2005)*

Peregrine 2002 Pinot Noir (Central Otago) $34. This is a big, burly Pinot, with bold black cherry aromas marked by some herbal, beet-like notes. Broadens out with air to show deeper, darker flavors, including plums, earth, and coffee grounds. Give it 2–3 years in the cellar, then drink it over the next five. **89** —*J.C. (8/1/2004)*

Peregrine 2001 Pinot Noir (Central Otago) $34. Starts off lean and herbal, then sweetens slightly with air, developing charming cherry flavors but remaining a bit tart and narrowly constructed. **85** —*J.C. (9/1/2003)*

Peregrine 2005 Rastasburn Riesling (Central Otago) $25. This medium-bodied Riesling combines relatively high alcohol (13%) with ample residual sugar to add even greater richness and mouthfeel. But because of its excellent levels of acidity, it doesn't come across as particularly sweet or heavy. Tangerine, apple, and spice notes linger elegantly on the finish. **90 Editors' Choice** —*J.C. (11/1/2006)*

PHEASANT GROVE

Pheasant Grove 2004 Sauvignon Blanc (Marlborough) $15. Fresh and snappy, with green pea, celery, and nectarine/peach to the bouquet. This is a pleasing, smooth wine with quite a bit of natural sweetness. Finishes slightly chalky, but with enough zest to prevent any stickiness. **88** —*J.C. (7/1/2005)*

NEW ZEALAND

NEW ZEALAND

PISA RANGE

Pisa Range 2003 Black Poplar Block Pinot Noir (Central Otago) $35. From a warmer subregion of Otago, but despite 14.5% alcohol, the wine doesn't show the heat at all, instead delivering tangy cherry flavors backed by cola, vanilla and citrus. Soft and creamy in feel, with a tangy finish. **87** —*J.C. (12/1/2005)*

POND PADDOCK

Pond Paddock 2003 Hawk's Flight Pinot Noir (Martinborough) $NA. Crisply acidic, with tart cherry notes alongside mushroom and spice. Turns tea-like on the finish—a bit leafy and drying. **85** —*J.C. (12/1/2005)*

QUARTZ REEF

Quartz Reef 2004 Pinot Gris (Central Otago) $26. Smooth, plump, and elegant, this Otago Pinot Gris is easy to drink and easy to like. Apple, pear, and melon flavors offer enough fruity facets to charm without being overly complex—just chill and enjoy. **87** —*J.C. (5/1/2006)*

Quartz Reef 2002 Pinot Gris (Central Otago) $20. A delicate rendition of Pinot Gris, with charming apple, spice, and pear aromas and flavors in a relatively light-weight wine. So pretty on the nose, you'll want to smell the glass even after it's empty. **87** —*J.C. (9/1/2003)*

Quartz Reef 2004 Pinot Noir (Central Otago) $NA. Winemaker Rudi Bauer has turned in another fine Pinot, marrying floral complexity to ripe cherries in a medium-bodied wine. Subtle spice and vanilla notes add nuance, while fine tannins on the finish suggest this wine may be consumed young or held 5–8 years. **89** —*J.C. (11/1/2006)*

Quartz Reef 2003 Pinot Noir (Central Otago) $30. Starts off a bit herbal or hay-like on the nose, but gradually develops in the glass to reveal ripe cherry scents. Supple; less dense and powerful than the 2002, but still a very pretty wine. **87** —*J.C. (12/1/2005)*

Quartz Reef 2002 Pinot Noir (Central Otago) $NA. From a top vintage in the region, this is the sort of wine that has won such acclaim for Central Otago. Deep, dark color, bold aromatics, and a full, lush feel on the palate imbue this wine with the complete package. Black cherries predominate, but there's also a spicy, wild, briary note on the finish. Drink now-2010. **91 Editors' Choice** —*J.C. (11/1/2006)*

Quartz Reef 2001 Pinot Noir (Central Otago) $30. Winemaker Rudi Bauer crafted one of the finest NZ Pinots I've tasted (the Giesen 1994 Isabel Vineyard), so despite this wine's lithe structure, look for it to improve over the next couple of years, adding deeper, savory dimensions to its modest cherry fruit. **86** —*J.C. (9/1/2003)*

Quartz Reef 2004 Bendigo Estate Vineyard Pinot Noir (Central Otago) $NA. From the Bendigo subregion, which has seen enormous expansion over the past several years, this is minor step up from Quartz Reef's regular bottling, with similar floral qualities on the nose and bright cherry fruit, but also more substantial tannins. Cellar for 2–3 years. **90** —*J.C. (11/1/2006)*

Quartz Reef 2003 Bendigo Estate Vineyard Pinot Noir (Central Otago) $NA. Like the regular 2003 bottling, there's a slightly herbal or hay-like note on the nose of this wine, but also floral hints and bright cherry aromas. Lacks the depth and drama of the superb 2002, but still a nice wine. Finishes with some dry ng tannins, so hold a couple of years before opening. **88** —*J.C. (12/1/2005)*

Quartz Reef 2002 Bendigo Estate Vineyard Pinot Noir (Central Otago) $NA. Tasted from magnum, this is a simultaneously floral and rich wine, filled with cherry blossoms and cherries. Creamy and supple in the mouth, it folds in vanilla and spice on the finish, ending on a briary note. **91** —*J.C. (11/1/2006)*

Quartz Reef 2001 Chauvet Sparkling Blend (Central Otago) $28. This sparkling blend of 65% Chard and 35% Pinot spends a minimum of 42 months on the lees prior to disgorgement, giving it a toasty, autolytic bouquet that marries well with the crisp, clean, lemony flavors. Verging on austere, but in a mouth-watering way. Try as an apéritif. **90** —*J.C. (5/1/2006)*

RAIN

Rain 2008 Sauvignon Blanc (Marlborough) $14. A solid example of Marlborough Sauvignon Blanc at a reasonable price, this shows off hints of stone fruit accented by jalapeño pepper. It's plump and a bit soft, with flavors of melon, fig, and peach. Reasonably intense and very fruity. Drink now. **87** —*J.C. (12/15/2006)*

REBECCA SALMOND

Rebecca Salmond 2000 Cabernet Sauvignon-Merlot (Kumeu) $18. Smoky-smelling and closed at first, showing little more than dried herbs. It opens up on the palate to reveal creamy black cherry flavors, dried herbs, and a lip-smacking mocha finish. The blend is 80% Cabernet, 20% Merlot. **88** —*J.C. (12/15/2003)*

Rebecca Salmond 2001 Reserve Chardonnay (Gisborne) $25. Much like here in the States, "Reserve" tends to mean oaked to within an inch of its life. This wine shows little more than toasty oak and sweet vanilla flavors, with a flourish of buttered popcorn on the finish. Some peach aromas testify to the fruit's promise, if you enjoy heavily oaked Chardonnay, you may like this one more than the rating suggests. **84** —*J.C. (9/1/2003)*

Rebecca Salmond 2002 Merlot (Kumeu) $18. This producer is turning out some interesting wines. The 2002 Merlot displays slightly candied cherry flavors along with a lactic note that brings to mind cherry cheesecake. Picks up hints of lemon and mocha on the tart finish. **86** —*J.C. (12/15/2003)*

Rebecca Salmond 2001 Sauvignon Blanc (Marlborough) $15. Really tart and zippy, with lime, passion fruit, and herb flavors. Best with shellfish. **83** —*J.C. (9/1/2003)*

RED HILL

Red Hill (NZ) 2001 Riesling (Marlborough) $NA. Starts off tight, only stubbornly giving up hints of kerosene and unripe peaches—the rock-hard kind you see on sale for a price that's too good to be true. Light in body, with almost a hint of prickle in the mouth, it tastes of unripe stone fruit and lime. **84** —*J.C. (8/1/2002)*

Red Hill (NZ) 2001 Sauvignon Blanc (Marlborough) $11. Quite lean and pungent, as so many Kiwi Sauvignon Blancs are, but there's a definable tart grapefruit element amid the more pungent, feline notes. The sharp, puckery finish is right in line with the rest of the package. **83** —*M.M. (12/15/2001)*

REDCLIFFE

Redcliffe 2005 Sauvignon Blanc (Marlborough) $11. New Zealand Sauvignons near the $10 mark that aren't being churned out by a huge multi-national corporation are getting hard to find, but here's one example, and it's available in magnums too, which should be even more economical—provided you've got a big enough thirst or enough guests to down all that wine. This excellent value in NZ SB is a bit understated on the nose, but still offers herbal flourishes, stone fruit, and citrus in a medium-bodied, well-rounded package. Picks up refreshing passion fruit notes on the finish. **87 Best Buy** —*J.C. (9/1/2006)*

Redcliffe 2004 Sauvignon Blanc (Marlborough) $10. Quite pungent on the nose, with aggressive Sauvignon character: green pepper, passion fruit, even a bit of cat pee. Fans of the style will find a lot to like for the price. Flavors are softer and easier, with the focus shifting to melon and peach. **86 Best Buy** —*J.C. (7/1/2005)*

RIMU GROVE

Rimu Grove 2005 Pinot Gris (Nelson) $27. This ripe, off-dry wine comes across as rather full-bodied, balancing melon and pear flavors against zesty lemon and peppery spice notes. Picks up a chalky, flinty note on the finish. **87** —*J.C. (2/1/2006)*

Rimu Grove 2004 Pinot Gris (Nelson) $19. Reductive on the nose, with tar, rubber, and chocolate notes that make the flavors challenging to find. There are some modest citrus notes on the finish. Try vigorous decanting to help it along. **82** —*J.C. (7/1/2005)*

Rimu Grove 2003 Pinot Noir (Nelson) $30. Smoky and complex, with herb, earth, and mixed berry aromas setting the stage for a supple mouthfeel and pleasant red berry and earth flavors. Finishes a little short, but pretty good stuff overall. **87** —*J.C. (12/1/2005)*

Rimu Grove 2001 Pinot Noir (Nelson) $35. Black cherry and vanilla start strong enough, and touches of herbs and black pepper add complexity to the nose. The palate is a bit candied and simple, turning very tangy on the finish. **84** —*J.C. (4/1/2004)*

RIPPON

Rippon 2003 Pinot Noir (Central Otago) $25. Spicy, mushroomy, and earthy, full of forest floor character, what the French would call sous bois. It's nicely textured as well, supple and round, just don't expect a fruit explosion. **87** —*J.C. (12/1/2005)*

RIVER FORD

River Ford 1999 Saint Clair Estate Sauvignon Blanc (Marlborough) $16. **87** —*M.M. (10/1/2000)*

RIVERSIDE

Riverside 1998 Chardonnay (Gisborne) $13. **81** —*J.C. (10/1/2000)*

Riverside 1997 Reserve Chardonnay (Stirling) $20. **83** —*J.C. (10/1/2000)*

Riverside 1999 Sauvignon Blanc (Hawke's Bay) $12. **85** —*J.C. (10/1/2000)*

ROARING MEG

Roaring Meg 2002 Pinot Noir (Central Otago) $25. Seems a little under-ripe—surprising for a 2002 wine from Central Otago. Ashy, peppery aromas and flavors mix with sour cherries and earth. Herb-crusted meat dishes will help bring out the fruit and tame the wine's dry tannins. **84** —*J.C. (8/1/2004)*

ROCKBURN

Rockburn 2003 Chardonnay (Central Otago) $23. Kicks off with hints of banana and other tropical fruits, delivered in an easy-going, soft wash over the palate, then turns dry, stony and spicy on the finish. **86** —*J.C. (5/1/2006)*

Rockburn 2003 Pinot Noir (Central Otago) $30. Starts with bold aromas and flavors of cola, caramel, and roasted fruit. Creamy-smooth tannins combined with low acidity give this wine a lush mouthfeel, but it's less vibrant and spicy than the still-delicious and gracefully aging 2002. Drink now–2010. **87** —*J.C. (12/1/2005)*

Rockburn 2002 Pinot Noir (Central Otago) $38. A big, extracted Pinot with lots of dusty earth and dried spice components. Cola, coffee and plum flavors round it out, wrapped in firm tannins. Give it a few years to mel-low. **89** —*J.C. (8/1/2004)*

Rockburn 2003 Riesling (Central Otago) $21. Starts off rockin' with lime and mineral aromas, then turns a bit soft on the palate, offering up only non-descript citrusy flavors. Ends on a dry, chalky note. **85** —*J.C. (5/1/2006)*

ROWLAND

Rowland 2001 Jill's Vineyard Pinot Noir (Central Otago) $26. Rowland's Pinot has always had a heavy oak influence, but this year it seems toned down a bit, or maybe the fruit is ratcheted up a notch. Mixed red and black berries are framed by cinnamon and Asian spices in this silky, medium-weight offering. **87** —*J.C. (9/1/2003)*

Rowland 2000 Jill's Vineyard Pinot Noir (Central Otago) $28. Smoky, meaty, and spicy, this wine boasts plenty of oak influence. The red berry fruit is somewhat subdued, with the flavors centered on earth and spice. Though lean, the mouthfeel is admirably silky, and pretty cranberry shadings appear on the finish. **87** —*J.C. (8/1/2002)*

Rowland 1999 Jill's Vineyard Pinot Noir (Central Otago) $22. Fairly herbal on the nose, with some sour overtones. Tart cherry fruit is accented by some chocolate and smoke complexities, making for an interesting and largely intellectual wine. **84** —*J.C. (5/1/2001)*

Rowland 1998 Jill's Vineyard Pinot Noir (Central Otago) $22. **86** —*J.C. (10/1/2000)*

SACRED HILL

Sacred Hill 1997 Basket Press Cabernet Sauvignon (Hawke's Bay) $20. **87** *(9/1/2000)*

Sacred Hill 1998 Helmsman Cabernet Sauvignon (Hawke's Bay) $40. Dark cassis aromas and flavors are accented by green herbs and a touch of raisiny character. Despite the wine's dark, saturated color and adequate

structure, the combination of green and over-ripe notes suggests drink-ing over the short term. **87** —*J.C. (5/1/2001)*

Sacred Hill 1999 Barrel Fermented Chardonnay (Hawke's Bay) $20. Lush tropical fruit is joined by vanilla and spice. Starts out a bit tight and restrained but blossoms with time in the glass, displaying good richness and intensity. **88** —*J.C. (5/1/2001)*

Sacred Hill 1998 Barrel Fermented Chardonnay (Hawke's Bay) $20. **88** *(9/1/2000)*

Sacred Hill 1997 Barrel Fermented Chardonnay (Hawke's Bay) $21. **89** —*S.H. (8/1/1999)*

Sacred Hill 1999 Rifleman's Chardonnay (Hawke's Bay) $36. A structured and intense Chardonnay that should improve over the next few years, it's tight at first but opens with air. Pear and guava are set off by toast and menthol, which turn into lightly toasted hazelnuts on the extended fin-ish. **90** —*J.C. (5/1/2001)*

Sacred Hill 1997 Rifleman's Chardonnay (Hawke's Bay) $33. **92** *(9/1/2000)*

Sacred Hill 1998 Whitecliff Chardonnay (Marlborough & Hawkes Bay) $16. **89** *(9/1/2000)*

Sacred Hill 1998 Broken Stone Merlot (Hawke's Bay) $40. This 100% Merlot is packed with black cherries, lusciously ripe and silky in the mouth. Black tea notes on the finish hint at the complexities to be gained with bottle age. Try after 2003. **92** —*J.C. (5/1/2001)*

Sacred Hill 1999 Whitecliff Merlot (Hawke's Bay) $16. **87** *(9/1/2000)*

Sacred Hill 1999 Basket Press Merlot-Cabernet Sauvignon (Hawke's Bay) $20. A ready-to-drink wine that sports cherry-berry fruit and a hint of mint and tea. Soft tannins and a light finish make it a solid lunch choice. **86** —*J.C. (5/1/2001)*

Sacred Hill 2005 Sauvignon Blanc (Marlborough) $22. On the full, ripe side of Marlborough Sauvignon Blanc, but it stays true to its varietal nature, never getting sweet or sloppy. Honeyed peach and grapefruit fla-vors finish clean and fresh. Drink now. **87** —*J.C. (11/1/2006)*

Sacred Hill 1997 Barrel Fermented Sauvignon Blanc (Hawke's Bay) $20. **88** *(9/1/2000)*

Sacred Hill 1998 Sauvage Sauvignon Blanc (Hawke's Bay) $32. Steer clear of this one if you like your Sauvignons done in stainless. This one is 100% barrel fermented, yielding some toasty, smoky aromas that blend well with the forceful tropical fruit flavors. There's guava and pineapple, smoke and menthol on the long finish. **91** —*J.C. (5/1/2001)*

Sacred Hill 1999 Whitecliff Sauvignon Blanc (Hawke's Bay) $13. **88** *(9/1/2000)*

Sacred Hill 2000 Whitecliff Vineyards Sauvignon Blanc (Hawke's Bay) $20. This wine pretty much typifies what people mean when they talk about "New Zealand Sauvignon Blanc." There's a grassy, herbaceous, and green-pea edge to the lime and tropical fruit flavors. **85** —*J.C. (5/1/2001)*

SAINT CLAIR

Saint Clair 2004 Omaka Reserve Chardonnay (Marlborough) $25. Ultratoasty and vanilla-laden on the nose, but peeking out from behind the boards are ripe peaches and oranges. This is lavishly oaked, but it works, with peach and tropical fruit flavors buttressing layers of vanilla and toast. Drink over the next year or two. **90 Editors' Choice** —*J.C. (9/1/2006)*

Saint Clair 2005 Unoaked Chardonnay (Marlborough) $16. Lacks obvious fruitiness on the nose, showing instead stony-minerally notes. In the mouth, there's a slightly pulpy texture along with hints of honey. The fruit is understated, but this wine offers a refreshing New World alterna-tive to oaky Chardonnays. **85** —*J.C. (11/1/2006)*

Saint Clair 2005 Vicar's Choice Chardonnay (Marlborough) $14. Lacks a bit of intensity, both in terms of aroma and flavor, but this is a nice, easy-drinking Chardonnay that won't overwhelm whatever you choose to serve alongside. Vanilla and caramel notes support peach and melon fruit. **84** —*J.C. (11/1/2006)*

Saint Clair 2005 Pinot Noir (Marlborough) $16. Slightly herbal and pep-pery, but in a good, complexity-inducing way, not a stemmy, under-ripe way. There's plenty of cherry-berry fruit as well, plus some coffee and

NEW ZEALAND

NEW ZEALAND

caramel notes. A solid, well-made Pinot at a fair price. **85** —J.C. (9/1/2006)

Saint Clair 2004 Pinot Noir (Marlborough) $16. A nice effort at an attractive price, this Marlborough Pinot features more complexity than typical at this price range. Smoke and herbal notes verge on meaty and mushroomy, while the mouthfeel is smooth and supple. Ends with a bit of orange zest. **87** —J.C. (7/1/2006)

Saint Clair 2004 Doctor's Creek Reserve Pinot Noir (Marlborough) $26. Not that expressive on the nose, but does offer some lightly floral aromas and hints of cinnamon and mushroom. On the palate, there's more: black cherries, dried spices, and cocoa flavors carried on a velvety mouthfeel and moderate weight. Picks up some briary complexity on the firm finish. **88** —J.C. (9/1/2006)

Saint Clair 2004 Omaka Reserve Pinot Noir (Marlborough) $29. This wine isn't particularly dark in color, but it still tastes pretty good, blending cherry, beet, and cola flavors and accenting them with hints of mushroom, coffee, and cinnamon. It's medium-bodied, with a creamy mouthfeel and silky finish—ready to drink now and over the next few years. **88** —J.C. (9/1/2006)

Saint Clair 2004 Vicar's Choice Pinot Noir (Marlborough) $13. Yes, this value-priced Pinot is slightly herbal, but it's also got some pretty cherry fruit and a plump, appealing mouthfeel. With its delicate fruit and slightly drying finish, this won't last, so drink up before the end of the year. **85** —J.C. (7/1/2006)

Saint Clair 2002 Vicar's Choice Pinot Noir (Marlborough) $15. This is a big, bulky wine with a slightly syrupy mouthfeel, yet it doesn't show much in the way of fruit. Instead, it's minty and herbal, with wintergreen and cherry cough medicine flavors. **83** —J.C. (4/1/2004)

Saint Clair 2002 Riesling (New Zealand) $14. This is a very fruit-forward and flashy version of New Zealand Riesling. Aromas of tangerines, nectarines, and pears are followed by ripe stone fruit flavors that even bring a hint of red berries. Limes provide focus and delineation to the finish. **87** —J.C. (8/1/2003)

Saint Clair 2008 Sauvignon Blanc (Marlborough) $16. A good value for fans of the style, Saint Clair's 2006 Sauvignon Blanc continues this winery's leaning toward bell pepper and passion fruit aromas buoyed by bold, flashy tropical fruit flavors. Round and soft in the mouth, but shows good persistence on the finish. **88** —J.C. (12/15/2006)

Saint Clair 2005 Sauvignon Blanc (Marlborough) $16. Features classic Marlborough aromas, marrying grapefruit with grass, plus a dollop of green pepper alongside, but it's a bit soft on the palate. Some might find it more approachable for that reason, but others will find it flabby. **84** —J.C. (5/1/2006)

Saint Clair 2002 Sauvignon Blanc (Marlborough) $13. Adds a pungent, smoky-mineral note to otherwise straightforward Marlborough flavors of passion fruit and limes. Fresh and bright; best to drink young. **87** —J.C. (9/1/2003)

Saint Clair 2006 Vicar's Choice Sauvignon Blanc (Marlborough) $14. Saint Clair's entry-level Sauvignon is a flashy, fruit-driven wine with a touch of green that's keeping reams of peach and grapefruit reined in. Not quite as rich as the regular bottling, but the Vicar's Choice is a couple of bucks less expensive and still offers a characterful Sauvignon Blanc with a long, vibrant finish. **87** —J.C. (12/15/2006)

Saint Clair 2005 Wairau Reserve Sauvignon Blanc (Marlborough) $25. Powerfully herbal and dangerously close to being vegetal, but balanced by a full, oily mouthfeel and ripe melon flavors. Turns grapefruity on the finish, not green. Would be a good match for the region's green-lipped mussels cooked in white wine and aromatic herbs. **90 Editors' Choice** —J.C. (7/1/2006)

SANCTUARY

Sanctuary 1997 Sauvignon Blanc (Marlborough) $12. **87** —S.H. (8/1/1999)

SANDIHURST

Sandihurst 2004 Pinot Noir (Canterbury) $18. Spicy and floral, with a light, silky mouthfeel and flavors of cranberries, cherries, and hints of

mushroom. This is a pretty style, best paired with chicken or salmon rather than heavier meats. **87** —J.C. (12/1/2005)

Sandihurst 1998 Premier Pinot Noir (Canterbury) $18. Light in color but certainly not shy on flavor, this Pinot begins with toasty, smoky oak aromas coupled with chocolate and berries. It's fairly full on the palate, then turns spicy on the finish. **86** —J.C. (5/1/2001)

SAUVIGNON REPUBLIC

Sauvignon Republic 2005 Sauvignon Blanc (Marlborough) $18. This ambitious international effort stretches across several continents, aiming to produce hallmark Sauvignons from various regions. The Marlborough offering is pretty standard fare, featuring some grassy aromas and simple passion fruit flavors that finish a bit short. **85** —J.C. (9/1/2006)

SCHUBERT

Schubert 1999 Cabernet Sauvignon (Hawke's Bay) $40. This is likely to be a controversial wine, as some folks will no doubt love its lavish levels of sweet, vanilla-laced oak while others will despise that same feature. The color is vibrant purple, and there is substantial black cherry fruit, but it all ends up somewhat jumbled and disconnected. **85** —J.C. (12/15/2003)

Schubert 2003 Pinot Noir (Wairarapa) $50. Relatively lightweight, with modest cherry flavors, some funky forest-floor elements and some unintegrated oak. **84** —J.C. (12/1/2005)

Schubert 2002 Syrah (Wairarapa) $54. Lovely on the nose, blending peppery, meaty scents with floral notes. On the palate, there's blackberry and cherry fruit, accented by black pepper. A little short on the finish, but a noteworthy effort. **89** —J.C. (5/1/2006)

Schubert 1999 Syrah (New Zealand) $24. This impressive effort blends Hawke's Bay and Martinborough fruit to deliver enticing aromas of cracked black pepper, licorice, and blackberries. Lushly fruity on the palate, with hints of vanilla adding an elegant note. Has some tannins to lose; try from 2005–2010. **90 Editors' Choice** —J.C. (12/15/2003)

Schubert 2000 Tribianco White Blend (New Zealand) $10. Lean and lemony, this blend of Chardonnay, Pinot Gris, and Müller-Thurgau displays a sharply focused, linear personality that would make it a fit partner with raw shellfish. **83** —J.C. (9/1/2003)

SEIFRIED

Seifried 2002 Bordeaux Blend (Nelson) $16. **87** —J.C. (8/1/2004)

Seifried 2004 Malbec-Merlot-Cabernet Bordeaux Blend (Nelson) $15. It's rare to see a Bordeaux-style blend from New Zealand's South Island, but this is a notable exception that can be even better in other vintages. In 2004, it seems a little light and delicate, with slightly herbal, tomatoey aromas, and cherry and herb flavors. The tannins are well-managed, giving it an easy-drinking quality, and you might even try this with the sorts of fish dishes you'd serve with Pinot Noir. **84** —J.C. (12/15/2006)

Seifried 2002 Malbec-Merlot-Cabernet Bordeaux Blend (Nelson) $16. Half Malbec, with the balance equally split between Merlot and Cabernet. Does have an herbal streak throughout, but also more welcoming qualities: cassis and vanilla flavors, a creamy texture, and a firmly tannic finish. Drink now–2010. **87** —J.C. (8/1/2004)

Seifried 2004 Chardonnay (Nelson) $NA. A solid, mainstream NZ Chard, balancing toasty, mealy notes from oak against melon and pear fruit. A bit oaky, but well made and clean. **86** —J.C. (5/1/2006)

Seifried 2003 Unoaked Chardonnay (Nelson) $16. Packs boatloads of tropical fruit into a medium-weight package that's clean and fresh, if somewhat fruity and simple. Good party Chardonnay. **85** —J.C. (8/1/2004)

Seifried 2004 Winemakers Collection Barrique Fermented Chardonnay (Nelson) $NA. Toasty and nutty on the nose—the barrel influence is obvious, but it's backed by nicely balanced flavors of melon and spice and a lingering finish. Not a blockbuster or simple oak-bomb, this shows a fair amount of elegance. Drink now. **89** —J.C. (5/1/2006)

Seifried 2005 Gewürztraminer (Nelson) $NA. Light in weight despite nearly 2% residual sugar, this nice, easy-drinking Gewürz features varietally correct aromas and flavors of roses, lychees, and spice. **86** —J.C. (5/1/2006)

Seifried 2005 Winemakers Collection Gewürztraminer (Nelson) $NA. Intensely flavored, with bold rose and lychee notes. With only 4 g/L of residual sugar, it comes across as dry and a bit lean, but very crisp and precise, with a long finish. **88** —*J.C. (5/1/2006)*

Seifried 2005 Pinot Gris (Nelson) $17. Pinot Gris isn't often explosively aromatic, and this example is no exception, offering little more than modest melon and apple scents. Where the wine excels is in the mouth, marrying rich palate weight with density and a citrusy-chalky finish. A bit sweet, at 1.2% residual sugar. **86** —*J.C. (2/1/2006)*

Seifried 2004 Pinot Noir (Nelson) $25. Tasted shortly after bottling, this wine was showing some of the effects, displaying a slightly muted nose and closed palate. It's still a pretty wine, blending cherries and vanilla in a light-bodied format. **86** —*J.C. (12/1/2005)*

Seifried 2002 Pinot Noir (Nelson) $25. This pretty, delicately scented wine blends notes of cherries, leather, and cinnamon into a promising nose, followed by herbal, mushroomy flavors. Lithe, and a bit lean in texture, finishing with hints of coffee and charred wood. **86** —*J.C. (8/1/2004)*

Seifried 2004 Winemakers Collection Pinot Noir (Nelson) $35. Richer and more concentrated than Seifried's regular Pinot, with bold black cherry and cola flavors that linger on the finish, adding hints of vanilla and spice. **89** —*J.C. (12/1/2005)*

Seifried 2005 Riesling (Nelson) $25. Tasted just after bottling, this wine was a bit closed, but still showed enough bright lime and apple flavors to merit a recommendation. It's slightly sweet (12 g/L residual sugar), but balanced by crisp acidity. **86** —*J.C. (5/1/2006)*

Seifried 2004 Riesling (Nelson) $15. From the little-known region of Nelson, this Riesling bursts with petrol and lime scents. Quite full-bodied for a Riesling, with a touch of residual sugar and plenty of alcohol (12.5%), yet it retains a sense of grace and a finely developed minerality not often found in New World Riesling. **90 Best Buy** —*J.C. (7/1/2005)*

Seifried 2003 Riesling (Nelson) $16. Attractive nose successfully melds floral scents with hints of diesel. Rich and slightly sweet—even a bit heavy—but the flavors of pears and mineral oil stay with you on the finish. **87** —*J.C. (8/1/2004)*

Seifried 2005 Winemakers Collection Riesling (Nelson) $NA. A ripe, fruity style of Riesling off the gravels of the Brightwater region, this wine features apple and pear flavors, medium body, lovely balance and a long, mostly dry finish. **89** —*J.C. (5/1/2006)*

Seifried 2008 Sauvignon Blanc (Nelson) $17. Shows good intensity and varietal character, offering up gooseberry and passion fruit flavors with just hints of sweat and bell pepper. Seems plump at first, but firms up on the finish, finishing quite grapefruity in the end. **86** —*J.C. (11/1/2006)*

Seifried 2005 Sauvignon Blanc (Nelson) $17. Well-made, with traces of asparagus and green pepper that accent bold passion fruit flavors. Tangy and long on the finish. **86** —*J.C. (5/1/2006)*

Seifried 2004 Sauvignon Blanc (Nelson) $17. A riper style of SB, built around a core of passion fruit. Ripe fig and melon notes accent the strident tropical fruit, while the harmonious finish picks up hints of grapefruit. Medium-to-full-bodied; richer than most despite having only 12.5% alcohol. **89** —*J.C. (7/1/2005)*

Seifried 2003 Sauvignon Blanc (Nelson) $18. This zippy, fresh Savvy wakes up the palate like a citrus sorbet after a big meal. It's refreshing with bright acidity and flavors of limes, smoke, and just the barest hint of green pepper. **88** —*J.C. (8/1/2004)*

Seifried 2005 Winemakers Collection Sauvignon Blanc (Nelson) $NA. Light in body, this crisp Sauvignon captures green, grassy flavors and marries them to grapefruit and mineral notes. A summer refresher. **86** — *J.C. (5/1/2006)*

Seifried 2004 Sylvia Zweigelt (Nelson) $NA. A tribute to the family's Austrian heritage, this oddity—it's made from Zweigelt—features perfumed strawberry fruit, crisp acidity and soft tannins. Drink now. **86** —*J.C. (5/1/2006)*

SELAKS

Selaks 2000 Chardonnay (Marlborough) $15. Shows restrained oaking, with subtle toast and menthol aromas serving to accent the delicate peach and pear flavors. Well-balanced, this would be fine with many lighter fish dishes or poached chicken breasts. **88 Best Buy** —*J.C. (5/1/2001)*

Selaks 2000 Drylands Chardonnay (Marlborough) $NA. A stylish and understated wine featuring finely etched peach and guava flavors accented by subtle French oak. Here's a wine that doesn't shout for attention, but nonetheless holds you with an earnest whisper. **89** —*J.C. (5/1/2001)*

Selaks 1999 Drylands Merlot (Marlborough) $NA. A solid offering, with bright cherry fruit that's marked by herb notes. There's more oak evident on the palate, as flavors of vanilla and cream sneak up on you. Very soft tannins make this a wine to drink now, not to age. **86** —*J.C. (5/1/2001)*

Selaks 1998 Founders Estate Merlot (Hawke's Bay) $NA. Richly oaked and spicy, with a cinnamon-cocoa-espresso character. Earthy and dark; the black cherry flavors poke through on the spicy, peppery finish. This one could age or could fall apart, so why risk it? Drink now. **88** —*J.C. (5/1/2001)*

Selaks 2000 Drylands Pinot Gris (Marlborough) $NA. An impressive debut release for this bottling, which boasts juicy ripe-peach aromas. The cantaloupe-like palate is soft and smooth and the wine goes down easy, with just enough acidity on the finish to keep it fresh. **88** —*J.C. (5/1/2001)*

Selaks 2002 Founders Reserve Pinot Noir (Marlborough) $NA. Earthy and mushroomy, with lots of dried spice and cola notes layered over ripe black cherries. Reasonably full-bodied and weighty, yet balanced. Shows that big companies (Selaks is part of Constellation) can make good Pinot. **89** —*J.C. (12/1/2005)*

Selaks 1999 Riesling (Marlborough) $NA. Made in an off-dry style, the ripe pear and guava fruit seems a bit heavy and sweet; then some green acidity comes through on the finish to pull things back into balance. Drink now. **85** —*J.C. (5/1/2001)*

Selaks 2001 Sauvignon Blanc (Marlborough) $14. Very forward and ripe, offering a blast of citrus and riper notes of quince and passion fruit. The spicy lemon and cinnamon flavors are complemented by high acidity. **88** —*S.H. (11/15/2002)*

Selaks 2000 Sauvignon Blanc (Marlborough) $11. A crisp, refreshing drink that shows typical N.Z. Sauvignon character—gooseberries, grapefruit, green pepper—without tasting aggressively green or under-ripe. The tart acids on the finish would make this pair nicely with steamed mussels and the like. **88 Best Buy** —*J.C. (5/1/2001)*

Selaks 2000 Drylands Sauvignon Blanc (Marlborough) $18. This comes from older vines than Selaks' regular bottling, and it shows in the wine's greater intensity. Peach and melon flavors caress the palate, and a bright zing of jalapeño keeps the finish lively and focused. **90** —*J.C. (5/1/2001)*

Selaks 1998 Founders Reserve Sauvignon Blanc (Marlborough) $NA. A nice counterpoint to Selaks' Drylands bottling, this one is aged in oak, giving it a creamy texture and toast accents. The melony fruit carries through the lingering finish, accented by subtle herb notes. **90** —*J.C. (5/1/2001)*

SENTINEL

Sentinel 2005 Sauvignon Blanc (Marlborough) $NA. Plump and leesy, but slightly inscrutable—the aromas and flavors are understated and difficult to read. Some pleasant peach notes eventually emerge, turning herbal on the finish. **86** —*J.C. (5/1/2006)*

SERESIN

Seresin 2005 Chardonnay (Marlborough) $22. Lush on the palate, with a silky-creamy texture that's to die for, this is New World Chardonnay all the way, but it's so seductive you might forgive its lack of minerality. Honeyed peach flavors easily carry touches of smoky oak into a long, luscious finish. No point in waiting for this to open up; drink now–2007. **92 Editors' Choice** —*J.C. (11/1/2006)*

Seresin 2005 Sauvignon Blanc (Marlborough) $21. Seresin, under the capable guidance of winemaker Brian Bicknell, continues to turn out exemplary Sauvignon Blanc. The 2005 is a great success, boasting sexy

NEW ZEALAND

aromas of ripe peaches, gooseberries, and pink grapefruit, all touched with a hint of honey. Nectarine and pink grapefruit flavors seem made for each other on the plump but not soft palate, while the finish features excellent length and intensity. A benchmark Marlborough Sauvignon. **92 Editors' Choice** —*J.C. (11/1/2006)*

Seresin 2004 Sauvignon Blanc (Marlborough) $20. A bit of a letdown for Seresin, but this was a difficult vintage, and we received the samples late in the cycle, when they could have been fresher. It's still a solid Sauvignon, with classic flavors of capsicum and passion fruit, just not at the level we've come to expect from this estate. Given a choice, go for the 2005. **85** —*J.C. (11/1/2006)*

Seresin 2003 Sauvignon Blanc (Marlborough) $23. Pointed and crisp, but with complex aromas of herbs and mineral along with more typical passion fruit and citrus. Explodes in the mouth with flavors of pineapple, pink grapefruit, and more passion fruit. Citric and fresh as a whistle. What Kiwi S.B. is all about. **91 Editors' Choice** *(7/1/2005)*

Seresin 2001 Sauvignon Blanc (Marlborough) $20. Flowery in the nose, with hints of grass, green melon, and mustard seed. The tangy, crystal-clean palate is loaded with orange, tangerine, nectarine, and apricots. The long, flavorful finish features citrus pith, lime, and minerals. If you want a combination of complexity and forwardness, this is your wine. **91** *(8/1/2002)*

Seresin 2004 Márama Sauvignon Blanc (Marlborough) $32. This is an intriguing attempt at stretching the boundaries of Marlborough Sauvignon, featuring natural yeasts, barrel fermentation, and *sur lie* aging. The result is a wine with somewhat weird ginger, cashew and coffee-like scents, but also some attractive grapefruit and nectarine flavors. Full and round in the mouth, it finishes dry and minerally. **88** —*J.C. (11/1/2006)*

SEVEN TERRACES

Seven Terraces 2005 Pinot Noir (Marlborough) $20. Has a green, chlorophyllic edge to its bright cherry flavors, but this is a plump, easygoing Marlborough Pinot Noir with solid appeal. Not as soft or supple as many, it instead offers slightly drying tannins and a crisp finish. **86** —*J.C. (12/15/2006)*

Seven Terraces 2004 Pinot Noir (Marlborough) $20. Kicks off with scents of caramel, chocolate and cola, but they're all backed by some pretty cherry fruit. Lightweight and silky on the palate, easy to drink without seeming dumbed down. A good value in Marlborough Pinot Noir. **87** —*J.C. (12/1/2005)*

Seven Terraces 2005 Sauvignon Blanc (Marlborough) $15. Refreshingly austere and flinty on the nose for a Marlborough Sauvignon Blanc, this offering from winemaker John Belsham also shows some citrusy aromas. White grapefruit powers the palate, accented by passion fruit. Relatively light in weight, with a crisp, mouth-watering finish. Might be just the ticket to accompany oysters this fall. **86** —*J.C. (11/1/2006)*

Seven Terraces 2004 Sauvignon Blanc (Marlborough) $15. A bit reined in aromatically, with modest passion fruit scents. But this wine is very bold and assertive on the palate, combining bright citrus and tropical fruit with hints of bell pepper. Good value. **88** —*J.C. (12/1/2005)*

Seven Terraces 2003 Sauvignon Blanc (Marlborough) $14. A new label from Foxes Island, Seven Terraces' Sauvignon Blanc is under the same capable winemaking hands of John Belsham. It's a big, mouth-filling blend of passion fruit, melon, and citrus flavors that finishes long and tangy. Drink now. **89 Best Buy** —*J.C. (7/1/2005)*

SHAKY BRIDGE

Shaky Bridge 2003 Pinot Noir (Central Otago) $36. Shows lovely complexity on the nose, blending floral notes with spice and herbs. This is light on its feet, verging on delicate, yet delivers plenty of flavor. Silky tannins and a long finish suggest this has the balance to age, despite not being a massive blockbuster. Elegant. **90** —*J.C. (12/1/2005)*

SHEPHERDS RIDGE

Shepherds Ridge 2004 Sauvignon Blanc (Marlborough) $15. Technically sound, and some consumers will enjoy its blatantly sweaty, pungent aromas, but these same scents seem at odds with the slightly sweet flavors and chalky finish. **84** —*J.C. (7/1/2005)*

Shepherds Ridge 2002 Sauvignon Blanc (Marlborough) $15. The hint of cat pee isn't strong enough to overwhelm this wine's pleasing passion fruit and gooseberry aromas and flavors. Finishes strong, blending grapefruit with tropical fruit for a lively finale. **86** —*J.C. (9/1/2003)*

Shepherds Ridge 2001 Sauvignon Blanc (Marlborough) $15. Pink grapefruit, gooseberries, and a floral accent mark the attractive bouquet of this winner. Round melon, kiwi, and natural spice flavors do a dance on the palate, which also features red currants and more of the grapefruit present in the nose. The finish is lengthy and amply layered, so it goes out the way it comes in: with class. **90 Editors' Choice** *(8/1/2002)*

SHERWOOD ESTATE

Sherwood Estate 2000 Reserve Chardonnay (Canterbury) $20. Very fresh and vibrant, filled with zesty pear, citrus, and pineapple fruit. Just a pleasure to drink, balancing lush fruit with zippy acids. Hints of apples and butter linger in the background. **89** —*J.C. (7/1/2002)*

Sherwood Estate 2005 Pinot Noir (Marlborough) $18. This may be atypically dark and powerful, but this wine provides a rich, satisfying drink that hopefully presages more good things to come from the 2005 vintage Pinots. Despite its inky color and plum and chocolate flavors, the texture is still very Pinot—silky and round but not flabby, with crispness and lift on the finish. **88** —*J.C. (12/15/2006)*

Sherwood Estate 2005 Sauvignon Blanc (Marlborough) $15. Fresh and zippy, this is one 2005 Marlborough Sauvignon Blanc that held onto the variety's typical racy edge. If you're one of those consumers who frown on the round, ripe flavors achieved by some in 2005, this is one to seek out. Brisk passion fruit, grapefruit, and herb flavors finish crisp and clean. **88** —*J.C. (12/15/2006)*

SHINGLE PEAK

Shingle Peak 2000 Pinot Noir (Marlborough) $15. Rich, textured aromas of raspberry puree, cinnamon, warm cherry tart, smoky vanilla, leather, and mint. In the mouth, stunning fruit and spice, gorgeous balance, perfectly ripe, oak so well-integrated, racy, silky tannins, and brilliant acidity, this beauty's got it all. Dusty tannins suggest midterm aging. Super value. **92** —*S.H. (6/1/2001)*

Shingle Peak 2001 Sauvignon Blanc (Marlborough) $12. Bright, pure, well-etched fruit defines this delicious wine. Bursts of lemon and lime, peach and ripe apple are almost jammy, punctuated by high acidity, which heightens the spicy palate. A dollop of sweetness completes the package. **90** —*S.H. (11/15/2002)*

SILENI

Sileni 1998 EV Merlot-Cabernet Franc (Hawke's Bay) $80. Price aside, this is an outstanding effort in need of several years' cellaring. Smoky, meaty aromas open into cherry-berry fruit. Rich and full on the palate, it closes with a long dusty finish. Anticipated maturity: 2003-2015. **92** —*J.C. (5/1/2001)*

Sileni 2004 Cellar Selection Pinot Noir (Hawke's Bay) $16. There's isn't much Pinot Noir being grown in Hawke's Bay, but this bottling is solid, offering up slightly briary scents of plum and black cherries that carry slightly feral notes. Medium-weight on the palate, with supple tannins. **86** —*J.C. (7/1/2006)*

Sileni 2005 Cellar Selection Sauvignon Blanc (Marlborough) $14. Like several other Hawke's Bay wineries, Sileni has moved their Sauvignon Blanc sourcing to Marlborough. In this case, the results are pretty impressive. Pineapple, passion fruit, and grapefruit notes all ring harmoniously on the nose and palate, yielding a fruity, crisp wine that satisfies the craving for solid Sauvignon Blanc. **87** —*J.C. (5/1/2006)*

SILVER BIRCH

Silver Birch 2005 Sauvignon Blanc (Marlborough) $14. A bit fat for Marlborough Sauv, with ripe peach and gooseberry aromas and flavors that aren't entirely typical, but still pack in the flavor. Orange-citrus notes on the finish. **86** —*J.C. (7/1/2006)*

SOUTHBANK ESTATE

Southbank Estate 2005 Pinot Gris (Hawke's Bay) $NA. A soft, round, easy-to-drink Pinot Gris. Peach and melon flavors end on a note of ripe apples. **86** —*J.C. (2/1/2006)*

Southbank Estate 2004 Pinot Noir (Marlborough) $10. There's an herbal tinge to this wine's bright cherry and rhubarb aromas and flavors. Lean on the palate, with a modest finish. **84**—*J.C. (12/1/2005)*

Southbank Estate 2004 Sauvignon Blanc (Marlborough) $12. On the vegetal side, with fresh green bean and sweet pea notes underscored by racy citrus flavors. **84**—*J.C. (5/1/2006)*

Southbank Estate 2004 Syrah (Hawke's Bay) $NA. This lightweight, peppery Syrah offers modest cherry flavors, soft tannins, and a tart finish. **84**—*J.C. (5/1/2006)*

SPY VALLEY

Spy Valley 2004 Chardonnay (Marlborough) $25. Smoky and nutty on the nose, with ample oak layered over buttered corn and a hint of mint. It's a pleasant enough wine, but lacks the richness and flavor on the midpalate to raise it to nother level. Smoke and melon on the finish. **85**—*J.C. (7/1/2006)*

Spy Valley 2003 Chardonnay (Marlborough) $25. A plump, fleshy Chardonnay that delivers plenty of pear and peach aromas and flavors. It's pleasing, if a bit simple, with just some modest hints of smoke and popcorn on the finish to add complexity. **86**—*J.C. (7/1/2005)*

Spy Valley 2005 Gewürztraminer (Marlborough) $20. Starts with scents of roses and lychees, then adds stone fruit and super-ripe pear flavors to the mix. Plump and even a little oily on the palate, picking up a bit of spice on the finish. Contains 7g/L residual sugar, but comes across as dry. **88**—*J.C. (5/1/2006)*

Spy Valley 2004 Gewürztraminer (Marlborough) $17. A fat, fleshy Gewürz that seems to have decent lychee and pear flavors, but they're marred by an off note reminiscent of boiled egg yolks. **82**—*J.C. (7/1/2005)*

Spy Valley 2001 Gewürztraminer (Marlborough) $12. Crisp and refreshing for a Gewürz, a variety that can often get overblown. Peppery floral scents mingle with green apples, moving smoothly into pineapple, peach, and pear fruit flavors. Minty-fresh greens emerge to play a leading role on the long, clean finish. **88**—*J.C. (8/1/2002)*

Spy Valley 2001 Gewürztraminer (Marlborough) $12. Veteran winemaker Alan McCorkindale has his own label, sourced largely from the same vineyard, so he knows these grapes. The resulting wine is crisp and refreshing for a Gewürz, a variety that can often get overblown. Peppery, floral scents mingle with green apples, moving smoothly into pineapple, peach, and pear fruit flavors. Minty-fresh greens emerge to play a leading role on the long, clean finish. The winery takes its name from a nearby electronic communications interception station, locally nicknamed "Spybase." **88 Best Buy**—*J.C. (11/15/2002)*

Spy Valley 2005 Pinot Gris (Marlborough) $23. This plump, corpulent Gris is richly textured, adding another favorable element to its flavors of melon, apple, and citrus. Finishes with hints of peppery spice. **87**—*J.C. (2/1/2006)*

Spy Valley 2004 Pinot Gris (Marlborough) $20. There's a hint of rubber on the nose at first, but it quickly dissipates in favor of ripe pear aromas. Off-dry and reasonably weighty on the palate, it has flavors of spiced honey drizzled over poached pears before finishing fresh and clean. **87**—*J.C. (7/1/2005)*

Spy Valley 2005 Pinot Noir (Marlborough) $29. Another inky-dark 2005 Marlborough Pinot, Spy Valley's rendition is assertive and plummy, but perhaps lacking a little bit of perfume. Slightly creamy in texture without being particularly lush, it finishes long and clean. **88**—*J.C. (12/15/2006)*

Spy Valley 2003 Pinot Noir (Marlborough) $30. A bit floral or herbal on the nose, but there's also plenty of vibrant cherry fruit that broadens out on the midpalate, giving a nice feeling of fat. Soft tannins are accented by touches of black tea and anise on the black cherry finish. **89**—*J.C. (12/1/2005)*

Spy Valley 2005 Riesling (Marlborough) $20. Aromatic whites seem to be one of the strengths of this winery, named for its proximity to an electronic eavesdropping facility. Flinty, minerally notes add complexity to honeyed pear and citrus scents, while on the palate the citrus flavors show great precision and focus. Long and mouth-watering on the finish. **90 Editors' Choice**—*J.C. (7/1/2006)*

Spy Valley 2004 Riesling (Marlborough) $14. Wonderfully clean and pure, with aromas of peaches, limes, and wet stones. On the palate, there's soft, ripe stone fruit, but also powerful citrus notes to provide focus. Finishes dry and tart, crisp and refreshing. **90 Best Buy**—*J.C. (7/1/2005)*

Spy Valley 2005 Sauvignon Blanc (Marlborough) $18. A soft, easy-to-drink style of Sauvignon, with subtle aromatics and fleshy flavors of honey, pineapple, and tropical fruit laced with crisper, green apple notes. **87**—*J.C. (5/1/2006)*

Spy Valley 2004 Sauvignon Blanc (Marlborough) $18. Much like Spy Valley's 2004 Pinot Gris, this wine comes out of the chute with a blast of reductive, rubbery notes. Thankfully, these quickly fade in favor of ripe pink grapefruit aromas and flavors. A bit simple, but zesty, fresh, and ultimately satisfying. **87**—*J.C. (7/1/2005)*

Spy Valley 2001 Sauvignon Blanc (Marlborough) $13. No wood to interfere with the bright, citrusy flavors of this polished wine, although *sur lies* aging provides rich, creamy complexities. Dry and balanced, this is a versatile wine for the table. **88 Best Buy**—*S.H. (11/15/2002)*

Spy Valley 2000 Sauvignon Blanc (Marlborough) $12. Smells rich and creamy, with peach custard, apple turnover, and cinnamon-smoke aromas and a hint of white chocolate and tangerine peel. The flavors have an oriental complexity, explosive, with waves of exotic fruits and spices, and yet it's dry as dust. **90**—*S.H. (6/1/2001)*

STONECROFT

Stonecroft 2000 Chardonnay (Hawke's Bay) $22. Complex from start to finish, beginning with aromas of smoke, kumquats ,and grilled pears and ending cleanly, with tart pineapple notes. The texture is a compelling mix of gravel and custard, yet the wine never seems heavy. **89**—*J.C. (7/1/2002)*

Stonecroft 2003 Syrah (Hawke's Bay) $30. An interesting contrast to many of the other Hawke's Bay Syrahs, this one features red raspberries, white pepper, and hints of rhubarb. It's a brighter, fruit-driven style, but one that features a reasonably plump texture and a mouth-watering finish. **87**—*J.C. (5/1/2006)*

STONECUTTER

StoneCutter 2003 Pinot Noir (Martinborough) $35. Shows good complexity, marrying cherries, beets, and herbs on the nose with some oak and hickory smoke on the finish. In between is a medium-weight, slightly creamy-textured Pinot with cherry and herb flavors—nice. **87**—*J.C. (11/1/2006)*

STONELEIGH

Stoneleigh 1998 Chardonnay (Marlborough) $10. **87 Best Buy**—*S.H. (8/1/1999)*

Stoneleigh 2003 Chardonnay (Marlborough) $15. Nicely balanced and harmonious, with toast and yellow fruits mingling easily on the nose before giving way to pineapple and melon flavors that seem to have no sharp edges. There's a hint of caramel from oak on the finish, but it doesn't overwhelm. **88**—*J.C. (7/1/2005)*

Stoneleigh 1999 Chardonnay (Marlborough) $12. Aromas of Sieckel pears and ripe melons are joined by a hint of butter and an interesting anise note. On the palate the flavors are pear, with a strong citrus undercurrent. The lemon-lime acidity is practically searing at its crescendo on the finish. **84**—*J.C. (5/1/2001)*

Stoneleigh 2004 Pinot Noir (Marlborough) $16. The higher yields of 2004 seem to have lightened this wine compared to the same bottling in 2003, but it's still a charming wine, featuring light-weight cherry fruit coupled with briary nuances. Silky tannins grace the finish. **85**—*J.C. (12/1/2005)*

Stoneleigh 2003 Pinot Noir (Marlborough) $15. This vintage from Stoneleigh nails the Pinot mouthfeel—supple and velvety—while delivering smoky and earthy flavors. There's enough black cherry fruit to keep it lively, but this wine's just not that fruity, instead relying on cola, coffee and earth flavors for interest. **87**—*J.C. (12/1/2005)*

Stoneleigh 1999 Pinot Noir (Marlborough) $15. Another N.Z. Pinot that smells better than it tastes: attractive toast, black cherry, and cola aromas give way to lean flavors of tart berries and a persistent green tannic edge that seems unlikely to fade; drink it soon. **83**—*J.C. (5/1/2001)*

NEW ZEALAND

Stoneleigh 2003 Rapaura Series Pinot Noir (Marlborough) $19. A really pretty and elegant rendition of Pinot Noir, with supple tannins and soft dustings of herbs and spice atop ripe cherry fruit. **87** —*J.C. (12/1/2005)*

Stoneleigh 2004 Riesling (Marlborough) $16. This medium-bodied Riesling does a lovely job combining warm aromas of honey and cinnamon-baked apples with stonier, more mineral flavors and crisp acids. Persistent on the finish, ending with hints of lime. **89** —*J.C. (7/1/2006)*

Stoneleigh 2003 Riesling (Marlborough) $15. Shows some fine minerally notes on the slaty nose, while the flavors are fruitier and more accessible. Apple and citrus flavors, a slightly oily mouthfeel, and a hint of residual sugar give it a sense of ripeness. Clean and refreshing, thanks to a squirt of lemon on the finish. **87** —*J.C. (7/1/2005)*

Stoneleigh 2004 Sauvignon Blanc (Marlborough) $15. Standard stuff, with passion fruit and green pepper aromas, tropical and citrus fruit flavors, and a crisp, jalapeño-accented finish. Clean and well-made, a solid introduction to the Marlborough style. **85** —*J.C. (7/1/2005)*

STRATFORD

Stratford 2003 Pinot Noir (Martinborough) $40. Peppery and mushroomy on the nose, this wine also features earthy, leathery notes that call to mind the Rhône. It's a pleasant drink in a rustic red sort of way, distinctive for NZ Pinot. **86** —*J.C. (12/1/2005)*

SUNSHINE BAY

Sunshine Bay 2004 Pinot Noir (Marlborough) $15. Racy and fresh, with crisply acidic red berry fruit and grace notes of green herbs. Quaffable, and worth considering as a Bourgeuil stand-in. **87** —*J.C. (12/1/2005)*

SYREN

Syren 2001 Pinot Noir (Central Otago) $27. Chunky, but filled with gutsy black cherry fruit that makes up in intensity what it may lack in elegance. This is a sturdy, well-oaked wine that should hold for a number of years. **89** —*J.C. (9/1/2003)*

TE AWA

Te Awa 2002 Boundary Bordeaux Blend (Hawke's Bay) $32. Te Awa's Bordeaux-style red is a blend of 68% Merlot and 16% each Cabernet Sauvignon and Cabernet Franc. Dried herb, plum, and mocha notes give an almost St.-Emilion flavor to the wine, but the fruit is definitively New World in style. Supple and creamy enough to drink now, but should also hold a few years. **89** —*J.C. (11/1/2006)*

Te Awa 2001 Boundary Bordeaux Blend (Hawke's Bay) $25. This top-level red is more complex than the other Te Awa wines, blending tobacco and black olive aromas with savory flavors of earth and leather. There's also a core of black cherries, a creamy texture, and an elegant finish. Drink or hold 2–3 years. **89** —*J.C. (5/1/2006)*

Te Awa 2004 Chardonnay (Hawke's Bay) $21. Why can't more New World Chardonnay taste like this? Barrel fermentation has imparted a toasty, nutty richness without dominating the ripe peaches and tropical fruit. There's no malolactic fermentation and hence no buttery notes, but instead the fruit shines on the finish, offering up hints of Mandarin oranges and pineapple. **91 Editors' Choice** —*J.C. (5/1/2006)*

Te Awa 2002 Merlot (Hawke's Bay) $16. In all of the Te Awa offerings, winemaker Jenny Dobson emphasizes texture, and nowhere is this more important than in her Merlot. This is rich, ripe, round, and lush— almost fruitcake-like—without ever seeming heavy. Black cherry fruit is dusted with dried herbs and spices, then fades gently on the finish. **89** — *J.C. (5/1/2006)*

Te Awa 2005 Sauvignon Blanc (Hawke's Bay) $20. A distinctly different style of Sauvignon Blanc than that found in Marlborough, this is riper and rounder, with more potential for evolution in the bottle. Notes of citrus custard mark the bouquet, while the flavors veer toward melon and fig, with hints of peach or nectarine. It's velvety-textured, and long on the finish. **91 Editors' Choice** —*J.C. (11/1/2006)*

Te Awa 2004 Sauvignon Blanc (Hawke's Bay) $16. Aromas and flavors of white grapefruit, honeyed stone fruits, and lemon custard complement the ample mouthfeel. Finishes on a bright, citrusy note that's balanced and rounded out by a light touch of toast. **90 Editors' Choice** —*J.C. (5/1/2006)*

Te Awa 2004 Syrah (Hawke's Bay) $27. Like many Hawke's Bay producers, Te Awa is experimenting with Syrah; this bottling features bold blackberry fruit with just a hint of peppery spice. Big, round, and lush in the mouth, it's easy to drink and easy to like. Better still is the Zone 2 Syrah (aged in no new oak) that has been bottled separately—limited quantities of that wine may be available this fall. **88** —*J.C. (11/1/2006)*

Te Awa 2002 Syrah (Hawke's Bay) $20. The opening aromas feature a hint of white pepper, but the emphasis is on ripe blackberries. That ripe character carries over to the texture, which features lush, creamy fruit that retains a sense of freshness. Dusty tannins on the finish suggest some ageability; drink now–2010, or possibly even longer. **90 Editors' Choice** —*J.C. (5/1/2006)*

TE AWA FARM

Te Awa Farm 1998 Boundary Bordeaux Blend (Hawke's Bay) $23. This top-of-the-line offering from Te Awa Farm displays extraordinary richness and complexity. The aromas of dried spices (cinnamon and clove), cocoa, mocha, and black cherries slide gracefully into a multi-layered palate that caresses the mouth. Can be drunk now, but has the structure to age up to 10 years. **91 Editors' Choice** —*J.C. (5/1/2001)*

Te Awa Farm 1999 Longlands Bordeaux Blend (Hawke's Bay) $16. Chocolate, cassis, and cream are joined on the nose by hints of dried herbs. The black currant flavors turn tobaccoey on the palate, but the rich texture holds the wine together. Soft tannins make this a wine for current consumption. **87** —*J.C. (5/1/2001)*

Te Awa Farm 1998 Frontier Chardonnay (Hawke's Bay) $20. None of winemaker Jenny Dobson's wines are shy on flavor. This one is loaded with ripe peach fruit, buttressed by a healthy dose of toasty French oak, which comes across reminiscent of hazelnuts. At three years of age, this top-notch Chard is just entering its prime-drinking window and should last another few years. **89** —*J.C. (5/1/2001)*

Te Awa Farm 2000 Longlands Chardonnay (Hawke's Bay) $14. This is a weighty, lavishly oaked Chardonnay, allowing only the modest tropical and citrus notes to peek through. There's decided appeal in it's oak-derived, rich feel and long finish, but we wonder if the fruit will ever really sing. **87 Best Buy** —*M.M. (12/15/2001)*

Te Awa Farm 1999 Longlands Chardonnay (Hawke's Bay) $16. Starts off with appealing oatmeal and toast aromas that complement ripe peaches and oranges. The fruit shines on the palate up until the finish, when some rough oak edges show through. Like all of the Te Awa Farm wines, the texture really stands out: a perfect blend of weight and viscosity that's mouth-filling without being heavy. **88** —*J.C. (5/1/2001)*

Te Awa Farm 1999 Longlands Merlot (Hawke's Bay) $16. A bigger, richer wine than Te Awa Farm's Longlands Cabernet blend, this Merlot is packed with black cherry and chocolate aromas and flavors. A supple texture makes this drinkable now, but some black tea notes on the finish argue in favor of at least short-term cellaring. Try in 2003 if you can wait that long. **88** —*J.C. (5/1/2001)*

Te Awa Farm 1999 Pinotage (Hawke's Bay) $16. Thick aromas of cocoa and leather are accented by bright cherries. Rich and full-flavored without being heavy, the wine's strong coffee flavors are counter-balanced by a beam of cherry fruit that persists through the finish. Ready to drink now. **88** —*J.C. (5/1/2001)*

Te Awa Farm 2000 Frontier Sauvignon Blanc (Hawke's Bay) $20. Whether you like this wine or not will depend largely on how oak-tolerant you are—it's 100% barrel fermented and shows plenty of smoky, nutty nuances. It's also markedly creamy, with rich fruit flavors that lean toward white peach, melon, and fig. The long, layered finish has enough acidity to carry the weight and oak. **89** —*J.C. (5/1/2001)*

Te Awa Farm 2000 Longlands Sauvignon Blanc (Hawke's Bay) $12. Grapefruit and melon are the predominant aromas and flavors, with a few sprigs of minty green herbs tossed over the top. Finishes with a bitter pith note that seems a little out of place in this otherwise harmonious offering. **85** —*J.C. (5/1/2001)*

Te Awa Farm 2000 Longlands Syrah (Hawke's Bay) $21. Quite black peppery, through and through, but the pepper doesn't overpower the wine's other flavors. Smoked meat and black pepper spice up the palate's juicy red cherry and blackberry flavors. These same flavors, plus vanilla and a slight lemon tang, spill over to the finish. **Top Value. 89** *(11/1/2001)*

TE HERA

Te Hera 2004 Pinot Noir (Martinborough) $NA. This wine's bouquet, redolent of roses and ripe cherries, immediately grabs your attention. Yet it's not a heavyweight, playing off faintly herbal notes and a silky-smooth mouthfeel instead of raw power. Nicely balanced. **89** —*J.C. (12/1/2005)*

TE KAIRANGA

Te Kairanga 1999 Cabernet Sauvignon (Martinborough) $15. Shows a lot of tart vegetal flavors, including tomato and bell pepper. Why drink this when you coulda had a V-8? **80** —*J.C. (5/1/2001)*

Te Kairanga 2004 Chardonnay (Martinborough) $20. Standard Chardonnay, done well, TK's 2004 boasts scents of buttered toast, yellow plums, and ground clove, then shows a leaner, more citrusy character on the palate. Crisp on the finish. **87** *(12/15/2006)*

Te Kairanga 2002 Chardonnay (Martinborough) $18. Bold and flashy, with layers of smoke and toast wrapped around a core of mixed citrus and riper stone fruits. It's a tasty mouthful of Chard that picks up some mineral notes along the way to complement its brash flavors. **89** —*J.C. (9/1/2003)*

Te Kairanga 2005 Casarina Reserve Chardonnay (Martinborough) $30. More restrained on the nose than the regular Chardonnay, but with greater depth, richness, and texture, the 2005 Casarina Reserve Chardonnay is a selection of older vines, mainly the Mendoza clone. Subtle popcorn and cereal grain notes add elegance to the melon fruit, finishing with crisp acids that balance the wine's weight. **91** *(12/15/2006)*

Te Kairanga 1999 Reserve Chardonnay (Martinborough) $20. A whole mélange of sautéed tropical fruits jump out at you, accented by hints of vanilla oak. The finish is long and citrusy, reminiscent of carambola (star fruit). **88** —*J.C. (5/1/2001)*

Te Kairanga 2004 Pinot Noir (Martinborough) $20. A bit light compared to the 2005 offerings, but supple and round, with flavors of cherries, rhubarb, and some leafy, herbal complexity. Drink now. **88** *(12/15/2006)*

Te Kairanga 2003 Pinot Noir (Wairarapa) $20. Light and herbal on the nose, but boasts friendlier flavors of black cherry and cola. Turns a bit hard on the finish, where it could use more suppleness and length. **84** —*J.C. (12/1/2005)*

Te Kairanga 2002 Pinot Noir (Martinborough) $26. Supple and smooth in the mouth, this relatively light-hued Pinot shows elegant aromas of tea, cinnamon, vanilla and sour cherries. Finishes with tart berry and citrus flavors. **87** —*J.C. (4/1/2004)*

Te Kairanga 2000 Pinot Noir (Martinborough) $23. Hailing from the North Island, this is a confounding wine that seems to want to be better than it is. It's foxxy and funky in the nose, even a little burnt, yet the candy-like black-cherry palate is fairly pleasant. While hardly perfect, there's enough true Pinot character here to make it worthwhile. **84** —*M.S. (12/15/2001)*

Te Kairanga 2005 John Martin Reserve Pinot Noir (Martinborough) $42. TK's top Pinot is impressively dark, a result of the season's low yields. The alcohol is only 12.6%, giving it a rather Burgundian feel, while the flavors run toward dried spices, mushroom, and plum, with youthful tannins and crisp acidity. Cellar through 2008. **90** *(12/15/2006)*

Te Kairanga 2003 Reserve Pinot Noir (Martinborough) $42. Nails Pinot's texture, boasting a supple, velvety mouthfeel; also its complexity, blending savory spice and mushroom notes with bright pie cherry flavors. There's also an earthy, slightly vegetal beet nuance. **88** —*J.C. (12/1/2005)*

Te Kairanga 1999 Reserve Pinot Noir (Martinborough) $35. Needs a bit of time to integrate all of the heavy-toast oak. Strong overtones of pain grillé and caramel currently dominate the dark fruit flavors, particularly on the finish, where fine dusty tannins linger. **85** —*J.C. (5/1/2001)*

Te Kairanga 2005 Runholder Pinot Noir (Martinborough) $30. Yields in 2005 were so low that "we had to send out search parties at harvest time," jokes winemaker Peter Caldwell. This is a dark, almost inky, wine, with aromas and flavors of black cherries and plums, all wrapped in a slightly herbal edge of drying tannins. Hold and see if another year or two takes some of that edge off. **89** *(12/15/2006)*

Te Kairanga 2004 Runholder Pinot Noir (Martinborough) $30. Te Kairanga continues to refine its Pinot Noir program, now making this Runholder bottling as a mid-range offering. It's a nice wine for early consumption, combining soft tannins with floral (violet) scents and black cherry and plum flavors. Finishes with dried spice notes. **90 Editors' Choice** —*J.C. (9/1/2006)*

Te Kairanga 2008 Sauvignon Blanc (Martinborough) $18. Fresh, vibrant, and tropical, this is a plump Sauvignon Blanc that replaces the green flavors of Marlborough Sauvignon with riper notes of cassis and pink grapefruit. Long on the finish. **89** *(12/15/2006)*

Te Kairanga 2001 Sauvignon Blanc (Martinborough) $14. Unusually lush, even for this vintage, it starts with pronounced aromas of limes and lemons, fresh green apples, and juniper berries, and turns luscious in the mouth. Partial barrel fermentation and lees aging create a creamy, smoky mouthfeel, while the fruity flavors are volcanic. But it's dry and elegant. Virtually flawness Sauvignon Blanc. **93 Best Buy** —*S.H. (11/15/2002)*

Te Kairanga 2000 Sauvignon Blanc (Martinborough) $15. Martinborough isn't known for Sauvignon Blanc, but this is a solid example. A complex nose of melon, passion fruit, green pea and bitter green herbs turns crisp and bright in the mouth, with sweet pea and mint flavors. **86** —*J.C. (5/1/2001)*

TE MATA

Te Mata 2004 Woodthorpe Pinot Noir (Hawke's Bay) $25. From a region not generally known for Pinot Noir, Te Mata's version features herbal and mushroom accents balanced nicely by brighter berry flavors. Medium-bodied and supple, it picks up cocoa and cola notes on the finish. **87** —*J.C. (11/1/2006)*

Te Mata 2005 Woodthorpe Sauvignon Blanc (Hawke's Bay) $18. On the grassy, leaner side of the New Zealand Sauvignon Blanc spectrum, with grapefruit aromas accented by pungent, herbal scents. Despite the citrus and herb flavors, it's actually a bit weightier than many Marlborough Sauvignons, yet finishes clean and fresh. **86** —*J.C. (11/1/2006)*

Te Mata 2002 Woodthorpe Sauvignon Blanc (Hawke's Bay) $18. Unlike many Hawke's Bay Sauvignon Blancs, this one is not barrel fermented, so it stays crisp and tart, offering grassy, herbal aromas and grapefruity flavors. **86** —*J.C. (9/1/2003)*

TERRACE HEIGHTS ESTATE

Terrace Heights Estate 2003 Pinot Noir (Marlborough) $NA. Standard Marlborough fare, with cola and smoke adding complexity to cherry fruit. Turns earthy and tannic on the finish. **85** —*J.C. (12/1/2005)*

Terrace Heights Estate 2005 Sauvignon Blanc (Marlborough) $20. This lightweight Sauvignon is built on the grassy side, with herbal overtones only partially rounded out by modest passion fruit and peach on the midpalate. Despite some citrusy notes, it finishes soft, rather than bracing. **85** —*J.C. (7/1/2006)*

TERRACE ROAD

Terrace Road 2001 Sauvignon Blanc (Marlborough) $17. Defines the balance of Marlborough, from the upfront, juicy-fruity flavors of apples, citrus, and gooseberry, through the bright acidity and honeyed texture to the long, satisfying finish. A gorgonzola cheese with this wine is a textbook combination. **91** —*S.H. (11/15/2002)*

TERRAVIN

Terravin 2003 Pinot Noir (Omaka Valley) $36. A bit oaky on the nose, with cedar and toast notes that coast easily over hints of cola and cherry. Soft, silky, and fruit-driven on the palate, yet the wine finishes on a savory note. **87** —*J.C. (12/1/2005)*

Terravin 2003 Hillside Selection Pinot Noir (Omaka Valley) $59. Lovely Pinot aromas, with layers of flowers and herbs atop black cherry. Smooth, supple fruit, but not superficial, as there's also a deeper core of earth and chocolate. Velvety on the finish. Drink now–2010. **88** —*J.C. (12/1/2005)*

Terravin 2004 Sauvignon Blanc (Omaka Valley) $21. More subtle and understated than most NZ Sauvignon Blancs, with modest passion fruit zing. It's more on the austere and minerally side, but elegant and refined. **87** —*J.C. (5/1/2006)*

NEW ZEALAND

THE CROSSINGS

The Crossings 2005 Pinot Noir (Marlborough) $20. A strong effort from this project in Marlborough's Awatere Valley, the 2005 Crossings Pinot Noir features an elusive perfume-scented bouquet of flowers and black cherries, silky tannins, and crisp acids. Cocoa and cherry flavors linger prettily on the finish. **88**—*J.C. (12/15/2006)*

The Crossings 2004 Pinot Noir (Marlborough) $20. Shows some briary and herbal notes alongside dried spice and graham cracker scents, then the cherries blossom on the palate. Firmly structured for a Marlborough Pinot, with bright acids and firm tannins that could use a year or two to soften. **89**—*J.C. (12/1/2005)*

The Crossings 2003 Pinot Noir (Marlborough) $20. Powerful aromas of black cherries and anise make a big initial impression, followed by waves of big, soft fruit. Rich black plum and cherry flavors firm up a little on the finish, making this a wine that's more about immediately satisfying fruit than structure or complexity. **88**—*J.C. (8/1/2004)*

The Crossings 2005 Sauvignon Blanc (Marlborough) $16. Pungently herbal, but filled with grapefruit and a hint of peach at the same time, offering a wonderful balance of ripe fruit character with herbal, savory notes. Easy to drink: It's full and round in the mouth, with good persistence. **91 Editors' Choice**—*J.C. (7/1/2006)*

The Crossings 2004 Sauvignon Blanc (Marlborough) $17. Crisply aromatic, with sharply defined scents of passion fruit, pineapple, grapefruit, and hints of mineral. Bright and intense on the palate, finishing pleasantly herbal and fresh. **89**—*J.C. (12/1/2005)*

The Crossings 2003 Sauvignon Blanc (Marlborough) $16. Ripe notes of honey and peaches are balanced on the nose by celery, dill-like, herbal qualities. The palate features mouth-filling flavors of white nectarines, melons, and figs that fade gently into smoky complexity on the finish. **90 Editors' Choice**—*J.C. (8/1/2004)*

The Crossings 2002 Sauvignon Blanc (Awatere Valley) $16. From the Awatere Valley, this wine is densely packed with tightly wound fruit flavors reminiscent of passion fruit, melon, and grapefruit. A touch of smoke adds complexity. Fairly full-bodied, with good length and intensity, it picks up some extra spice notes on the finish. As good as it is now, it may even improve over the next six months. **90 Editors' Choice**—*J.C. (9/1/2003)*

The Crossings 2001 Awatere Valley Sauvignon Blanc (Marlborough) $16. From the Awatere subsection of Marlborough, this wine is all about balance and tang. The nose offers cantaloupe, white peach, and a welcome hint of green pepper. Tangerine and melon fruit mix on the palate, which is defined by its stony feel. The finish is ample and quite citrusy, and overall this wine features a bright, likable disposition. **90 Editors' Choice** *(8/1/2002)*

The Crossings 2004 Catherine's Run Sauvignon Blanc (Awatere Valley) $20. Starts off with hints of bell pepper and grapefruit, then adds stone fruit flavors on the palate. It remains focused and citrusy throughout, with a strong, minerally core. Powerful, yet lingers elegantly on the finish. **91 Editors' Choice**—*J.C. (5/1/2006)*

The Crossings 2002 Catherine's Run Reserve Sauvignon Blanc (Awatere Valley) $25. This smoky, creamy, barrel-fermented style doesn't have the same vivacious quality that makes the regular Crossings bottle such a success. It's still a fine wine, blending stone fruits with smoke and toast. **87**—*J.C. (9/1/2003)*

THE JIBE

The Jibe 2004 Pinot Noir (Marlborough) $15. Light and crisp, with plenty of cherry fruit. This is a bit simple, but tasty, and reasonably priced. **85**—*J.C. (12/1/2005)*

The Jibe 2005 Sauvignon Blanc (Marlborough) $15. Combines passion fruit and herbal notes on the nose, then offers plump white peach and melon flavors. There's a bit of a chalky note on the green, herbal finish. **86** *(3/1/2006)*

THE RED SQUARE

The Red Square 2004 For The People Pinot Noir (Hawke's Bay) $20. This wine, a partly charitable endeavor aimed at furthering the educations of top Hawke's Bay students, is rather dark and earthy. Roasted meat and coffee notes, with some modest cola accents, aren't easily accessible, and it finishes with charred tomato flavors. **84**—*J.C. (12/15/2006)*

THORNBURY

Thornbury 2004 Pinot Gris (Marlborough) $21. Pear, almond, and citrus aromas lead the way, followed by flavors of appleskin, pear, and dried spices. Pretty, but it doesn't have a great deal of richness on the palate. Finishes fresh but short. **86**—*J.C. (7/1/2005)*

Thornbury 2004 Pinot Noir (Marlborough) $24. Smells fruitier than it tastes, with scents of cherries and berries that give way to earthier, more beet-like flavors. Reasonably full-bodied and ripe, finishing with tangy acids. **86**—*J.C. (11/1/2006)*

Thornbury 2003 Pinot Noir (Marlborough) $NA. Bold and fresh, but also a bit rough and loud. Has some grassy elements on the nose, along with chocolate and carob flavors and some zesty, lemony acids on the finish. **83**—*J.C. (12/1/2005)*

Thornbury 2002 Pinot Noir (Marlborough) $25. With a published alcohol level of 14.5%, you wouldn't think ripeness would be an issue. But this wine, despite a supple mouthfeel and bright cherry flavors, shows some pungent tomato-leaf notes that hold it back. Finishes with some astringency; try again in six months or a year. **87**—*J.C. (4/1/2004)*

Thornbury 2005 Sauvignon Blanc (Marlborough) $17. Thornbury's 2005 Sauvignon is rather tropical in style, with ripe fruit flavors enlivened by healthy doses of herb and citrus notes. It's plump and medium-bodied, finishing with a touch of easy-to-drink softness. **86**—*J.C. (11/1/2006)*

Thornbury 2004 Sauvignon Blanc (Marlborough) $19. Mildly grassy and grapefruity on the low-intensity nose, this effort from winemaker Steve Bird lacks some of the vigor that has characterized his previous efforts. Modest herbal and citrus flavors pick up riper, stone fruit accents on the crisp finish. **85**—*J.C. (7/1/2005)*

Thornbury 2002 Sauvignon Blanc (Marlborough) $17. Wisps of smoke garnish melon and peach aromas and flavors in this full-bodied, ripe rendition of Kiwi Sauvignon Blanc. It's plump and juicy, laden with fruit, yet finishes with a burst of limes that give it length. **89**—*J.C. (9/1/2003)*

Thornbury 2001 Sauvignon Blanc (Marlborough) $17. The nose is grassy and full of grapefruit. In a word, it's a sharp bouquet. The mouth offers more of that grassiness and touches of green apple and lemon zest. The finish is smooth enough, and it fades off the palate nicely. A touch of spritz keeps things lively. **87** *(8/1/2002)*

THREE MINERS

Three Miners 2003 Pinot Noir (Central Otago) $38. Initial sulfur scents quickly blow off to reveal modest herb and cherry aromas. Flavors are solid—cherries and cola, turning herbal on the finish, where it picks up some citrusy notes. **85**—*J.C. (12/1/2005)*

TOHU

Tohu 2001 Chardonnay (Gisborne) $15. Golden in color, with tight-grained oak on the nose despite the fact that 20% of the wine spent just four months in barrel. Baked apple flavors carry the palate, followed by mild fruit notes and more oak on the finish. A toasty golden eagle with elegance. **88** *(9/1/2003)*

Tohu 2000 Chardonnay (Gisborne) $16. Bright and easy to drink, this Chardonnay has a super smooth mouthfeel—it's well balanced, round, and on the creamy side. Smells yellow—butter, pear skin, and white peach stand out. In the mouth, caramel and almost tropical-fruit notes dominate. It's more reserved than it sounds. **88**—*D.T. (12/15/2001)*

Tohu 2002 Reserve Chardonnay (Gisborne) $22. Well-toasted, with pleasant popcorn aromas. Apple, pear, and more toasty popcorn on the palate, with a warm finish devoid of overt buttery notes. A subdued wine with more pear and papaya than anything loud and forceful. It spent 11 months in new French oak. **88** *(9/1/2003)*

Tohu 2000 Reserve Chardonnay (Gisborne) $22. A buttery, smoky, toasty wine that echoes with oak influence: coconut, vanilla, and dill aromas and flavors ring throughout. Tasty in a one-dimensional way, it appeals to the oak-lover in all of us. **85**—*J.C. (7/1/2002)*

Tohu 2003 Unoaked Chardonnay (Gisborne) $10. One of the best unoaked Chards I've tried, with enough leesy, mealy notes to impart complexity to the waves of pear and melon fruit. Nicely balanced, with enough weight to match with food and enough freshness to serve alone. A versatile wine that's worth keeping on hand for any occasion. **88 Best Buy** —*J.C. (8/1/2004)*

Tohu 2004 Pinot Noir (Marlborough) $20. Smells lovely, with perfumed, floral notes elevating the ripe cherry scents, but doesn't quite follow through on the palate, where the flavors turn herbal and cranberryish. Tart, with crisp acidity on the finish. **85** —*J.C. (7/1/2006)*

Tohu 2002 Pinot Noir (Marlborough) $20. Notice the price decrease for this wine, which boasts young cherry, cranberry, and herbal notes. There's even some bacon in there. The palate is snappy and defined by strawberry, while orange peel and pepper notes drive the finish. This wine should hit stride in late 2003/early 2004. Right now it's a bit young and tangy. **90** *(9/1/2003)*

Tohu 2001 Pinot Noir (Marlborough) $25. Quite purple, with sweet cherry, dried herb and flower petal aromas. The palate is smoky and modestly complex, with a fine mix of cherry and chocolate. The finish grows deeper and darker, emphasizing tar and espresso. Medium in body, but packing punch. The feel is fresh yet firm. **91** *(9/1/2003)*

Tohu 2005 Sauvignon Blanc (Marlborough) $16. A solid representative of the Marlborough style, the 2005 Tohu Sauvignon fairly exudes passion fruit aromas and flavors, but also manages to sneak in hints of peaches (on the ripe side) and cooked peas (on the vegetal side). Medium in body, with some refreshing citrus on the finish. **85** —*J.C. (11/1/2006)*

Tohu 2003 Sauvignon Blanc (Marlborough) $14. Prototypical New Zealand Sauvignon Blanc, boasting pungent aromas of passion fruit and capsicum. The slightly oily texture allows the flavors—green pepper balanced by riper notes of melon and fig—to slowly unfurl across the palate, finishing clean and refreshing. **88 Best Buy** —*J.C. (8/1/2004)*

Tohu 2002 Sauvignon Blanc (Marlborough) $14. Very typical of Marlborough Sauvignon Blanc. It has piercing green pepper and snap pea aromas along with hints of jalapeño, lychee, passion fruit, and grapefruit. There are lively apple and gooseberry flavors, and then comes a tangy tangerine finish. The epitome of a pick it, crush it, and tank it white wine. **89 Best Buy** *(9/1/2003)*

Tohu 2001 Sauvignon Blanc (Marlborough) $15. Gooseberry and white pepper aromas are followed by a bold, clean palate that is so racy it's like taking a drink of cold mountain spring water. Lime and green melon shift in and out in layers. The finish is lean and long, driven by vital acidity. An idal apéritif wine. **87** —*M.S. (12/15/2001)*

Tohu 1999 Sauvignon Blanc (Marlborough) $15. 88 —*M.S. (10/1/2000)*

TOM EDDY

Tom Eddy 2004 Tenz Sauvignon Blanc (Marlborough) $17. California winemaker Tom Eddy's New Zealand adventure is off to a solid start with this bottling of Sauvignon. Light in body and lean, with modest grapefruit aromas giving way to stony, melon-flavored fruit. Crisp and clean on the finish. **87** —*J.C. (7/1/2005)*

TORLEESE

Torleese 2002 Sauvignon Blanc (Waipara) $16. Grassy, with intense passion fruit and lime aromas and flavors driving through the finish. A strident loudmouth of a wine that shouts its fruit flavors at the world. **87** —*J.C. (9/1/2003)*

Torlesse 2004 Pinot Noir (Canterbury) $23. Light in color and light in body, with pretty cherry flavors and hints of herb. A bit simple, ending on a dusty, tactile note. **85** —*J.C. (12/1/2005)*

Torlesse 2002 Pinot Noir (Canterbury) $18. A light, quaffable Pinot, with cola and caramel dominating the nose. Flavors are similar, picking up earth and herb nuances; this is not a terribly fruity wine, but delivers some interesting flavors nonetheless. **84** —*J.C. (7/1/2005)*

Torlesse 2004 Riesling (Waipara) $18. This light-bodied Riesling offers hints of fresh limes and crushed stones on the nose, followed up by bright citrus flavors of lime and grapefruit. Tart and brisk on the finish, making it a mouth-watering apéritif. **87** —*J.C. (11/1/2006)*

Torlesse 2004 Riesling (Canterbury) $13. Stony and minerally on the nose, with some lime and pear notes that hover in the background. Despite its off-dry nature, it's similarly austere in flavor, offering up only modest fruit to go with its dry, minerally notes. A bit of a 'tweener, not sweet, fruity, and luscious, but not fully dry and bracing. **87** —*J.C. (7/1/2006)*

Torlesse 2003 Riesling (Marlborough) $16. Starts off with a whiff of diesel or kerosene, but also fruitier-spicier notes of Golden Delicious apples and dried cinnamon. Medium in body, with dry, broad, apple-like flavors that turn tart and citrusy on the long finish. **89** —*J.C. (7/1/2005)*

Torlesse 2005 Sauvignon Blanc (Waipara) $19. Plump and mouth-filling, this Sauvignon Blanc offers ripe pink grapefruit and gooseberry flavors that veer toward red berries and stone fruits, yet maintain a sense of focus thanks to crisp lime and grapefruit notes on the finish. **89** —*J.C. (9/1/2006)*

Torlesse 2004 Sauvignon Blanc (Waipara) $15. Starts with promise, showing fresh scents of stone fruit, melon, passion fruit, and green pepper, but they don't quite blend properly on the palate, where there's juicy tropical fruit but also a crisp, hard layer of acidity that tastes metallic on the finish. **84** —*J.C. (7/1/2005)*

TRINITY HILL

Trinity Hill 1998 Gimblett Road Cabernet Sauvignon (Hawke's Bay) $30. The intense combination of vanilla, cassis, and black cherry aromas results in an almost syrupy sensation—before even tasting the wine. On the palate, it is rich and full, but not cloying in the least, thanks to juicy acids and a strong streak of mint. Mildly tannic; can be drunk now or aged a few years. **90** —*J.C. (5/1/2001)*

Trinity Hill 1998 Gimblett Road Chardonnay (Hawke's Bay) $30. Golden delicious apples and tropical fruits form the core of this elegant wine, accented by oak-imparted hints of toast, menthol, and coconut. Finishes impressively, with the intensity building to a loud crescendo. **90** —*J.C. (5/1/2001)*

Trinity Hill 1999 Gimblett Merlot (Hawke's Bay) $35. Starts off well, with aromas of toast, vanilla, and black cherries. The attack is rich and sweet as well, but then the wine turns a bit drying and herbal on the finish. Needs time—but will the fruit hold? **86** —*J.C. (5/1/2001)*

Trinity Hill 2003 High Country Pinot Noir (Hawke's Bay) $30. From a region of New Zealand better known for its Bordeaux varieties and gaining a growing reputation for Syrah, this Pinot delivers smoky, charred scents, meaty, plum, and black cherry flavors and a finish that's surprisingly firm given the softness of the mouthfeel. **87** —*J.C. (12/1/2005)*

Trinity Hill 2004 Riesling (Marlborough) $15. Features some slightly smoky, flinty notes on the nose, then gives up flavors of wet stones, limes and hard peaches on the dry, full-bodied palate. Crisp and tart on the finish. **88** —*J.C. (7/1/2006)*

Trinity Hill 1999 Gimblett Road Syrah (Hawke's Bay) $35. Aims at a northern Rhône style and succeeds, with modest oak levels and some smoky, meaty nuances. The boysenberry and blackberry fruit flavors are juicy and tart, leading into a dusty finish. **87** —*J.C. (5/1/2001)*

Trinity Hill 2002 Homage Syrah (Hawke's Bay) $100. Much like the Bilancia La Collina, also crafted by winemaker Warren Gibson, there's a touch of stone fruit character to this wine, along with plenty of black-and blueberry fruit. Rich, intense, and tannic, this needs time to show additional complexity. Hold 3–5 years. **90** —*J.C. (5/1/2006)*

TROUT VALLEY

Trout Valley 2001 Chardonnay (Nelson) $12. Light in body, with pineapple and mint aromas and tart, citrusy, and green flavors. Metallic on the finish. **82** —*J.C. (9/1/2003)*

Trout Valley 2001 Chardonnay (Marlborough) $14. This seems to be tiring, with lactic notes, sour fruit, and toasty oak starting to dominate its bouquet. Yet it's much better on the palate, with powdered cinnamon and cloves sprinkled over buttered toast and orange marmalade. Drink up. **84** —*J.C. (8/1/2004)*

NEW ZEALAND

TUATARA

Tuatara 2001 Chardonnay (Nelson) $16. Very fresh and appealing in its lean, citrusy flavors of orange and lime. This Chard finishes hard and tart enough to cut through fatty foods or act as a mouth-watering apéritif. **85** —*J.C. (9/1/2003)*

Tuatara 2001 Pinot Noir (Nelson) $NA. Pretty sulfury on the nose, but it begins to blow off after an hour in the glass. Underneath, the wine is big-boned but slightly hollow, with herbal accents to the cherry fruit. **84** —*J.C. (4/1/2004)*

Tuatara 2002 Sauvignon Blanc (Nelson) $12. Named after a nearly extinct species of lizard said to be dinosaur-like, this is more of what we've come to expect from New Zealand: another well-made Sauvignon Blanc with grassy, herbal aromatics and lime and grapefruit flavors. **86** —*J.C. (9/1/2003)*

TWIN ISLANDS

Twin Islands 2001 Pinot Noir (Marlborough) $13. Light in color, almost translucent, with simple aromas of earth, sweet tobacco, and cherries. Drinks tart roughly earthy, with silky tannins. Has some Pinot character but it's a very simple, direct wine. **84** —*S.H. (1/1/2002)*

Twin Islands 2002 Sauvignon Blanc (Marlborough) $12. Yikes. If you like cat pee, this wine's for you! Some call it gooseberry. Either way, it's at the extreme end of that limey, flinty flavor. It's also dry as the grave, with plenty of cool, crisp acids that make your mouth water. **85** —*S.H. (1/1/2002)*

TWO TAILS

Two Tails 2004 Sauvignon Blanc (Marlborough) $9. Screams of its place, with strident passion fruit, citrus, and capsicum all bursting from the glass yet blending harmoniously into a single whole. Medium-bodied, with a lingering finish. Bold enough to try alongside assertively spiced or slightly sweet fish dishes. **88** —*J.C. (7/1/2005)*

UNISON VINEYARD

Unison Vineyard 1999 Unison Red Blend (Hawke's Bay) $25. Seems a bit uninspired and earthy. Lacking ripe fruit, it compensates by pumping out boatloads of charred, chocolaty oak on the finish. **83** —*J.C. (12/15/2003)*

Unison Vineyard 1999 Unison Selection Red Blend (Hawke's Bay) $25. The mouthfeel is reasonably rich, but this offering lacks the vibrant fruit exhibited by the 1998, instead offering subdued aromas and flavors of smoke, tobacco, coffee grounds, and earth. **85** —*J.C. (12/15/2003)*

VAVASOUR

Vavasour 1999 Awatere Valley Chardonnay (Marlborough) $23. Excellent integration of fruit and wood means it's hard to know where the flavors of one stop and the other start. It's toasty, nutty, and peachy, rich and creamy, and ends with a flourish of crème brûlée. **90** —*J.C. (5/1/2001)*

Vavasour 1999 Pinot Noir (Marlborough) $19. Seems mature and ready to drink now, with earth and mushroom flavors layered over black cherries and finishing with a touch of anise. An easy-drinking Pinot that's not heavy or extracted yet displays complexity and balance. **86** —*J.C. (5/1/2001)*

Vavasour 1999 Awatere Valley Sauvignon Blanc (Marlborough) $19. The restrained nose shows little in the way of herbal or grassy aromas, instead offering up melon and passion fruit. Full-bodied and intense, with a long citric finish that would make a perfect partner for a bowl of moules. **89** —*J.C. (5/1/2001)*

Vavasour 1999 Single Vineyard Sauvignon Blanc (Awatere Valley) $23. Almost seems creamy, perhaps because half of the juice was fermented in neutral barrels. Grapefruits, green plums, and a pinch of black pepper lead into a long, broad finish. **90** —*J.C. (5/1/2001)*

VIDAL

Vidal 2003 Syrah (Hawke's Bay) $NA. Starts with scents of anise and blackberry, then adds hints of tea and pepper combined with a soft, creamy mouthfeel. A barrel sample of the '04 was more promising, with substantially greater intensity. **85** —*J.C. (5/1/2006)*

VILLA MARIA

Villa Maria 2001 Cellar Selection Cabernet Sauvignon-Merlot Cabernet Blend (Hawke's Bay) $20. Think cru bourgeois from a ripe vintage: smoke, dried herbs, and cassis, medium body, and a lingering finish that picks up touches of earth and vanilla. **88** —*J.C. (8/1/2004)*

Villa Maria 2002 Private Bin Cabernet Sauvignon-Merlot Cabernet Blend (Hawke's Bay) $13. Soft and supple, but some notes of green pepper sneak in to impinge on the black cherry and cassis flavors. Smoky and meaty on the finish. **86** —*J.C. (8/1/2004)*

Villa Maria 2000 Cellar Selection Cabernet Sauvignon-Merlot (Hawke's Bay) $23. Steers clear of nasty herbal or vegetal elements in favor of clean, pure fruit, and oak. Black cherries combine with toast, menthol, and vanilla to offer straightforward drinking pleasure. **86** —*J.C. (12/15/2003)*

Villa Maria 2001 Private Bin Cabernet Sauvignon-Merlot (East Coast) $13. There's a fair amount of Syrah (13%) blended into this entry-level red, but the wine is still relatively soft and easy, its modest cherry fruit underpinned by bell pepper. **83** —*J.C. (12/15/2003)*

Villa Maria 2000 Private Bin Cabernet Sauvignon-Merlot (Hawke's Bay) $19. Rounder and plummier than you might expect, thanks to only 61% Cabernet Sauvignon, with the rest being Merlot, Cabernet Franc, and Malbec. Nicely integrated cedar, mocha, and dried herb notes round out the flavors, finishing with fresh acidity. Drink now–2005. **88** —*J.C. (8/1/2002)*

Villa Maria 1999 Private Bin Cabernet Sauvignon-Merlot (Hawke's Bay) $13. Spice notes play heavily on the brambly, herbal nose. This a full-bodied, chunky mix of 53% Cabernet, 24% Merlot, 13% Pinotage, and 10% Syrah. No grape type in particular sticks out on the palate, which is heavy with oregano and basil notes in addition to red plum fruit. Best for casual drinking; anything left will help out a red sauce. **85** —*M.S. (12/15/2001)*

Villa Maria 2005 Private Bin Chardonnay (Hawke's Bay) $15. Fresh and fruity upfront, with tropical aromas and flavors that veer toward guava and banana. This is a medium-bodied wine with a fair amount of viscosity to its mouthfeel, but it seems a bit soft on the finish. Serve well-chilled to give it a little extra zip. **85** —*J.C. (7/1/2006)*

Villa Maria 2003 Private Bin Chardonnay (Marlborough) $13. Clean, fruity, and tropical, with a slightly creamy mouthfeel and hints of vanilla, mint, and flowers. This is a solid everyday Chardonnay at an everyday price. **85** —*J.C. (7/1/2005)*

Villa Maria 2002 Private Bin Chardonnay (Marlborough) $15. Middle-of-the-road stuff at a fair price, with peach and pear aromatics, clean, fresh fruit flavors, and a bright, tangy finish. With its mainstream style, easy accessibility, and modest price tag, this is a perfect choice for large gatherings. **85** —*J.C. (9/1/2003)*

Villa Maria 2001 Private Bin Chardonnay (Marlborough) $15. Very fresh pear, melon, and tropical fruit, medium body, and a clean, crisp, citrusy finish make this a wine to rely on with a wide range of foods. It should pair well with just about anything that normally works with white wine. **87** —*J.C. (7/1/2002)*

Villa Maria 2000 Private Bin Chardonnay (Marlborough) $13. Tart tropical fruit and green apple aromas and flavors mark this mid-weight, slightly syrupy wine. It's not fat, but has a round, full mouthfeel. Vanilla, hay, and a mild earthiness show on the moderate finish. **86** —*M.M. (12/15/2001)*

Villa Maria 1999 Private Bin Chardonnay (East Coast) $15. Wood and spice accents are married to a strong pineapple, peach, and papaya core. Cream and vanilla flourishes add to the impression of lushness. Finishes with a blast of toasty oak. **86** —*J.C. (5/1/2001)*

Villa Maria 2004 Private Bin Merlot-Cabernet Sauvignon (Hawke's Bay) $15. From a top-notch vintage in Hawke's Bay, Villa Maria's entry-level Bordeaux-style red is an undeniable success. It's slightly herbal, but manages to integrate that with ripe plum flavors and tobacco and cedar overtones. The silky, supple mouthfeel is a treat. Drink now. **87** —*J.C. (12/15/2006)*

Villa Maria 2003 Cellar Selection Pinot Noir (Marlborough) $28. Stays true to Villa's track record of building big fruit, softly tannic Pinots. Herb and black cherry aromas and flavors finish on a crisp note. **88** —*J.C. (12/1/2005)*

Villa Maria 2002 Cellar Selection Pinot Noir (Marlborough) $28. Not that dissimilar from Villa's reserve Pinot, just scaled back a bit, with the same black cherry cola flavor profile, just less weight, texture, and body. **87** *(8/1/2004)*

Villa Maria 2004 Private Bin Pinot Noir (Marlborough) $19. A good value in Pinot Noir, Villa's entry-level bottling offers a subdued nose, but perks up on the palate, delivering vibrant, tart cherries backed by notes of mushroomy sous bois, cola, and chocolate. Silky tannins provide plushness despite a narrow finish. **86** —*J.C. (9/1/2006)*

Villa Maria 2003 Reserve Pinot Noir (Marlborough) $37. Villa continues to refine its Pinot program, and this may be the breakthrough vintage. Complex aromas include hints of flowers, spicy stems, and dusky cherries. Round and broad in the mouth, it coats the palate with flavor before featuring firm, age-worthy tannins on the finish. **90** —*J.C. (12/1/2005)*

Villa Maria 2002 Reserve Pinot Noir (Marlborough) $35. The 2002 vintage was kind to Marlborough Pinot Noir, and this wine shows the beneficence of the weather in its plump, rounded flavors and supple tannins. Boasts ample black cherry, earth, and cola and root beer flavors. **88** —*J.C. (8/1/2004)*

Villa Maria 2001 Reserve Pinot Noir (Marlborough) $37. A big, rich, mouth-filling wine, with ample plummy fruit and oak-imparted spice and vanilla. Tipping the scales at 15% alcohol, it finishes with a burst of warmth that acts to accentuate the oak. **87** —*J.C. (9/1/2003)*

Villa Maria 2002 Botrytis Selection Reserve Noble Riesling (Marlborough) $45. Fairly full-bodied and a bit alcoholic, a testament to the immense ripeness achieved. Apricot, pineapple, and lime notes provide a fruit salad of flavors that linger on the finish. **90** *(8/1/2004)*

Villa Maria 2001 Cellar Selection Riesling (Marlborough) $22. A rich, full-bodied Riesling that's soft on the outside, but whose inner core of acids comes through on the powerful citrus-and-spice finish. Starts off with apple blossom, peach and guava aromatics that give way to ripe apple and pear flavors, layered with dried spices. Tastes good now but don't be afraid to age it—it should last easily through 2008. **91** —*J.C. (8/1/2002)*

Villa Maria 2005 Private Bin Riesling (Marlborough) $15. As always, this is an excellent value in Riesling, balancing floral, perfumy notes with lime and minerals. It's a taut, high-acid style that appears to be on the dry side, just broadening out enough on the finish to show hints of honey and ripe apples. Drink now as a mouth-watering apéritif. **88** —*J.C. (7/1/2006)*

Villa Maria 2004 Private Bin Riesling (Marlborough) $13. This Riesling packs in a lot of character at a modest price. The fern-scented bouquet of warm stones and ripe apples is enticing, the weight—not too heavy, not too light—is just right, and the flavors of apple, lime, and peach hit the pleasure buttons. Finishes fresh and clean. **89 Best Buy** —*J.C. (7/1/2005)*

Villa Maria 2003 Private Bin Riesling (Marlborough) $13. Smells lovely, with pineapple, peach, and pear notes pumped up by hints of chalk and citrus. It's clean and fresh, finishing in a rush of tart limes and a hint of sweetness. Residual sugar is a modest 0.8%. **88 Best Buy** —*J.C. (8/1/2004)*

Villa Maria 2001 Private Bin Riesling (Marlborough) $15. Lifted floral aromas include a hint of white pepper and green apples. Flavors are fresh and zesty, showing more mineral notes than fruit. This would be a nice match with chicken satay on the patio. **86** —*J.C. (8/1/2002)*

Villa Maria 2000 Private Bin Riesling (Marlborough) $14. A semi-dry bottling that's almost fat. Ripe peaches are center-stage, ushered in by a minty-herbal edge and out by gentle lime notes. Provides an easy introduction to the Kiwi style of Riesling—there's no intimidating austerity or need to age this wine; just pull the cork and pour. **85** —*J.C. (5/1/2001)*

Villa Maria 1999 Private Bin Riesling (Marlborough) $12. **87** —*M.S. (10/1/2000)*

Villa Maria 2004 Cellar Selection Sauvignon Blanc (Marlborough) $20. Bold and spunky, with passion fruit, grapefruit, and bell peppers covering the warm, exotic bouquet. Shows a touch of pickle flavor in addition to peach, citrus pith, and more green pepper. Plenty of power, in fact almost too much. But better aggressive than meek, and this is certainly a forward, acidic wine. **89** *(7/1/2005)*

Villa Maria 2003 Cellar Selection Sauvignon Blanc (Marlborough) $19. Starts off with some sweaty, passion fruit scents, then glides into passion fruit and pineapple flavors. Feels creamy and supple on the palate, finishing with some soft spice notes. **88** —*J.C. (8/1/2004)*

Villa Maria 2002 Cellar Selection Sauvignon Blanc (Marlborough) $22. This is the middle tier of Villa Maria's three Sauvignon Blancs and it seems to be caught in the middle stylistically, as well. It's full-bodied and creamy in the mouth, yet shows the sort of green, herbal flavors that seem to work better with racy, light-weight versions. The end result is good, but it lacks the sense of harmony that would elevate it to the next level. **85** —*J.C. (9/1/2003)*

Villa Maria 2001 Cellar Selection Sauvignon Blanc (Marlborough) $22. Tropical fruit aromas feature some gooseberry and grassy notes. Melon, nectarine, and passion fruit flavors also bring white pepper and a hint of bell pepper. Tangerine fruit highlights the drying finish, which is a bit chewy and full given the flavor profile and normal perceptions of New Zealand Sauvignon Blanc. **86** *(8/1/2002)*

Villa Maria 2000 Cellar Selection Sauvignon Blanc (Marlborough) $22. On-the-lees aging accounts for the added richness of this bottling. It's quite unyielding at first, then opens up slowly to reveal green peas and stone fruits accented by just a hint of chili pepper. **87** —*J.C. (5/1/2001)*

Villa Maria 2004 Clifford Bay Reserve Sauvignon Blanc (Marlborough) $32. Like so many New Zealand wines, this one blends vegetal notes of peas and beans with tropical fruit, and the whole is quite nice. Along the way there's some sweat, a bit of salt, and a touch of grass. Lengthy on the finish, with grapefruit and a certain sweetness. **88** *(7/1/2005)*

Villa Maria 2003 Clifford Bay Reserve Sauvignon Blanc (Marlborough) $30. Villa's top Sauvignon delivers the goods in 2003, offering up rich and creamy tropical fruit flavors offset by hints of green pepper. Finishes long and tangy. Only 200 six-bottle cases imported. **90** —*J.C. (8/1/2004)*

Villa Maria 2002 Clifford Bay Reserve Sauvignon Blanc (Marlborough) $30. This rich, full-bodied wine is ripe and round, offering peaches and nectarines along with notes of cream and smoke. Finishes long, with lingering notes of lemons and gooseberries. **88** —*J.C. (9/1/2003)*

Villa Maria 2000 Clifford Bay Reserve Sauvignon Blanc (Marlborough) $30. Intense gooseberry and green pea aromas and flavors are balanced by weighty stone fruits (white peaches and nectarines, green plums). Riper and less herbal than most Marlborough SBs. **89** —*J.C. (5/1/2001)*

Villa Maria 2006 Private Bin Sauvignon Blanc (Marlborough) $19. The first SB of the new vintage to cross our tasting table, and hopefully a sign of good things to come, with bold gooseberry aromas and hints of melon, peach, and sweat. Medium-bodied, with a creamy mouthfeel and a long, spicy finish. Drink now. **90** —*J.C. (9/1/2006)*

Villa Maria 2005 Private Bin Sauvignon Blanc (Marlborough) $15. After a big crop in the 2004 vintage, Marlborough suffered from poor weather during flowering, leading to lower-than-normal yields and more concetrated wines in 2005. In a recent tasting of 20-odd new releases, this offering proved to be the best value. It shows less pungency and more ripeness than most years, starting with grapefruit and adding layers of stone fruits and ripe, tropical flavors. **88** —*J.C. (5/1/2006)*

Villa Maria 2004 Private Bin Sauvignon Blanc (Marlborough) $13. This workhorse NZ Savvy delivers just what you'd expect: an initial blast of pungent herbal and passion fruit scents, followed by bright tropical fruit on the palate and a crisp, clean finish. Good value. **86** —*J.C. (7/1/2005)*

Villa Maria 2003 Private Bin Sauvignon Blanc (Marlborough) $13. Basic, straightforward NZ Sauvignon Blanc, with hints of asparagus and green pepper enlivening pink grapefruit flavors. Soft and creamy in the mouth, yet clean and crisp on the finish. **86** —*J.C. (8/1/2004)*

Villa Maria 2002 Private Bin Sauvignon Blanc (Marlborough) $13. Blends grapefruit and green pepper aromas and flavors in a rich, viscous wine that strikes a nice balance between fruity and herbal. Seems to have just a bit of sugar in it, but finishes tangy and fresh, with vivacious acids. **86** —*J.C. (9/1/2003)*

Villa Maria 2001 Private Bin Sauvignon Blanc (Marlborough) $15. Fans of New Zealand's SBs will like this wine's racy nose, which is packed with minerals, some stoniness, melon, and a hint of grassiness. Citrus is in full force in the mouth, aided by a touch of green herbs and a white pepper spice. The finish is elegant and offers hints of grapefruit. It's a youthful, fresh wine; one that will go well with salads or fish. **90 Editors' Choice** *(8/1/2002)*

Villa Maria 2000 Private Bin Sauvignon Blanc (Marlborough & Hawke's Bay) $12. Sweet peas and gooseberries put a subtle mark on this full, soft wine that's only mildly herbaceous. The residual sugar is just at the threshold of perceptibility, imparting greater weight without making the wine taste sweet. **86** —*J.C. (5/1/2001)*

Villa Maria 2001 Reserve Sauvignon Blanc (Clifford Bay) $29. Opens with a powerful explosion of lime, grass, gooseberry, and apple aromas. In the mouth, it shows the fantastic concentration and extraction of an atom bomb, yet it's balanced, complex, and harmonious. It's quite dry, with extraordinarily high acidity. **93** —*S.H. (11/15/2002)*

Villa Maria 1998 Reserve Sauvignon Blanc (Clifford Bay) $25. **89** —*S.H. (8/1/1999)*

VINOPTIMA

Vinoptima 2003 Reserve Ormond Gewürztraminer (Gisborne) $53. Musky and spicy on the nose, with hints of rose petal and pineapple. With 16 g/L residual sugar, this is noticeably off-dry but not sweet by any measure, balanced by ample acidity and modest (13.5%) alcohol. A pre-release sample of the '04 shows greater richness and length, and should be a wine to watch. **89** —*J.C. (5/1/2006)*

VOSS

Voss 2003 Pinot Noir (Martinborough) $40. Savory meat and mushroom scents lead the way, followed by a lovely silky texture that caresses the palate. Has some very positive attributes, but doesn't seem to have the same intensity of fruit character that marked this estate's great 2001. **87** —*J.C. (12/1/2005)*

Voss 2002 Pinot Noir (Martinborough) $41. A bit of a come-down after this winery's outstanding 2001, but still a very good effort, with black cherry and mushroom notes intertwined with strands of coffee and earth. Finishes long, with hints of tea and black pepper. **87** —*J.C. (8/1/2004)*

Voss 2001 Pinot Noir (Martinborough) $40. Convincingly demonstrates that a wine can be rich and well-extracted, yet retain a sense of balance and elegance. Ripe, plummy fruit is framed by dry spices and toasty oak; the wine is full-bodied but seems almost weightless. An intriguing herbal thread winds through the wine from start to finish, offering a compelling note of complexity. **92** —*J.C. (9/1/2003)*

Voss 2005 Riesling (Martinborough) $21. A change in style from the soft, round version produced in 2004, this is a light, fresh, virtually dry (7g/L residual sugar) Riesling. Strident citrus notes on the nose mingle with hints of mineral, while the palate delivers crisp green apple and citrus flavors. **86** —*J.C. (11/1/2006)*

Voss 2004 Riesling (Martinborough) $20. This round, mouth-filling Riesling is on the fullish side, but still retains a sense of focus thanks to steely-minerally notes that balance the softer honey and lime flavors. **87** —*J.C. (7/1/2006)*

VYNFIELDS

Vynfields 2003 Reserve Pinot Noir (Martinborough) $NA. Amply oaked, but it works well in the context of this wine, adding hints of bacon and wood dust to the lovely rose petal and cherry aromas. Medium-bodied, with silky tannins on the finish that add just enough structure for balance. **89** —*J.C. (12/1/2005)*

WAIHEKE VINEYARD

Waiheke Vineyard 1998 Te Motu (The Island) Cabernet Sauvignon-Merlot (Waiheke Island) $48. What went wrong here? A warm vintage should

have yielded ripe fruit but what's in the bottle shows notes of decaying vegetation along with brown sugar and vanilla. **82** —*J.C. (12/15/2003)*

WAIRAU RIVER

Wairau River 1998 Chardonnay (Marlborough) $25. Smells ripe and rich, with aromas of Golden Delicious apples mixing with butter and caramel. The flavors are much leaner and more focused, emphasizing green apples and lemons. The contrast makes for an interesting wine. **84** —*J.C. (7/1/2002)*

Wairau River 1997 Chardonnay (Marlborough) $20. A deft touch with oak leaves this wine's green apple and citrus flavors with only the barest hints of toast, wood smoke and spice. Bears a resemblance to well-made Macons. **87** —*J.C. (5/1/2001)*

Wairau River 1997 Reserve Chardonnay (Marlborough) $22. The philosophy here is to rely on bottle age to bring the acids into balance, rather than doing a lot of malolactic fermentation. The current release is this '97 when most producers are onto the '99s. Despite only 15% malo, there's a creamy richness to this wine in the mouth to go with delicate toast and bold pineapple flavors that pick up anise and black pepper notes on the finish. **89** —*J.C. (5/1/2001)*

Wairau River 2004 Home Block Pinot Noir (Marlborough) $25. Light ruby in color, this wine doesn't appear to be terribly rich or concentrated. But it's a charming, soft little Pinot, intended to caress the palate rather than stun it. Sous bois and cherries are framed by barrel-derived notes of caramel, cedar, and vanilla. Ends slightly woody, but should smooth out in another few months. **85** —*J.C. (9/1/2006)*

Wairau River 1999 Reserve Botrytised Riesling (Marlborough) $24. Simply gorgeous. This honeyed, apricot-laden, rich, plush dessert wine is balanced by zippy acidity and leaves the palate fresh, clean, and satiated. Peach, orange, and nectarine flavors add interest. Complex. **93 Editors' Choice** —*J.M. (12/1/2002)*

Wairau River 1998 Reserve Botrytised Riesling (Marlborough) $58. The proprietors spray the vines with water to encourage botrytis formation, then turn off the water and let nature take its course. The result is a fabulously rich dessert Riesling, full of dried apricots and tangerines. There's a musky, spicy character too, and a strong under-current of acidity keeps it from being cloying. **90** —*J.C. (5/1/2001)*

Wairau River 2005 Sauvignon Blanc (Marlborough) $19. A pungent, grassy wine, layered with green pepper and herbal notes. Leaner than most 2005 Marlborough Sauvignons, finishing with sharp strokes of lime and grapefruit. **86** —*J.C. (5/1/2006)*

Wairau River 2002 Sauvignon Blanc (Marlborough) $17. This is an "easy" style of Sauvignon Blanc, with stone fruit flavors that never get overly herbaceous. It's crisp enough to serve as an apéritif, yet not possessed of bracing acidity. In short, it's easy to drink and easy to like. **87** —*J.C. (9/1/2003)*

Wairau River 2001 Sauvignon Blanc (Marlborough) $17. The bouquet here is confounding. It has some green vegetable and cat pee qualities as well as white stone fruits, sulfur, and popcorn. In a word, it's complicated. In the mouth, grapefruit and celery flavors mingle with green grapes, while on the back end it's chalky and rather tart. The overall acidity is high, and there's one important thing missing here: balance. **87** *(8/1/2002)*

Wairau River 2000 Sauvignon Blanc (Marlborough) $20. Asparagus and green herb aromas run smoothly into grapefruit, passion fruit, and sweet green pea flavors. More citrus fruits emerge on the tart, cleansing finish. **86** —*J.C. (5/1/2001)*

Wairau River 2004 Home Block Sauvignon Blanc (Marlborough) $25. On the lean and mean side, with green bean aromas and sour melon flavors that veer toward pickled jalapeño on the finish. Characterful and distinctive, but not my style. **82** —*J.C. (12/15/2006)*

Wairau River 2002 Reserve Sauvignon Blanc (Marlborough) $25. Extremely green, with aromas of pole beans and asparagus along with faint whiffs of lime. In the mouth it's hard to wade through the pea and green bean flavors, but if you're intrepid you will find some grassy citrus notes. **83** *(7/1/2005)*

Wairau River 2001 Reserve Sauvignon Blanc (Marlborough) $24. A disappointing effort from this respected producer, the 2001 reserve has turned out unusually heavy and ponderous, with sweet, passion fruit-laced flavors that turn slightly metallic on the finish. **84** —*J.C. (9/1/2003)*

Wairau River 2000 Reserve Sauvignon Blanc (Marlborough) $24. Melon, citrus, and green bean aromas get a lift from some smoky oak. The thick, meaty palate is also a tad oaky, but it comes through with plenty of ripe melon, citrus, and a hint of butterscotch—presumably from the oak. The finish is full and evolves in layers, always a good sign of a wine's overall quality. **89** *(8/1/2002)*

Wairau River 1999 Reserve Sauvignon Blanc (Marlborough) $28. 86 —*(11/15/2002)*

Wairau River 1998 Reserve Sauvignon Blanc (Marlborough) $24. Asparagus and green herb aromas run smoothly into grapefruit, passion fruit and sweet green pea flavors. More citrus fruits emerge on the tart, cleansing finish. **86** —*J.C. (5/1/2001)*

WHITEHAVEN

Whitehaven 2004 Pinot Noir (Marlborough) $30. This full-bodied, round, softly textured Pinot Noir should win many friends for New Zealand, easily blending black cherries with cola and spice. It's smooth and supple on the palate, with just enough acidity to keep it from becoming too bulky. **88** —*J.C. (7/1/2006)*

Whitehaven 2003 Pinot Noir (Marlborough) $28. Boasts a Russian River Pinot-like nose of cola and cherries. Picks up flavors of vanilla and tart cherries, carried along by soft, creamy tannins, then turns crisp on the finish. **86** —*J.C. (12/1/2005)*

Whitehaven 2002 Pinot Noir (Marlborough) $29. This pretty wine artfully blends earth and fruit—cherries and beets with sous bois and leather—but the best part is its mouthfeel, silky, and caressing, lingering delicately on the finish. **89** —*J.C. (8/1/2004)*

Whitehaven 2000 Pinot Noir (Marlborough) $22. This precocious Pinot is the whole package. With its immaculately clean berry aromas and piercing red berry fruit, it's smooth, sweet, and just smoky enough, with perfect vanilla oak kissing the full, ripe finish. Whitehaven's Pinot is clearly a fine estate-grown wine made in the artisan style. **92 Editors' Choice** —*M.S. (12/15/2001)*

Whitehaven 2001 Estate Grown Pinot Noir (Marlborough) $24. A bit charred and roasted tasting, with sweet oak flavors that underscore the dark fruit notes of black cherries and plums. Plump and satisfying, if not hugely complex. **87** —*J.C. (9/1/2003)*

Whitehaven 2005 Sauvignon Blanc (Marlborough) $20. This label has grown so quickly, perhaps a slight downturn in quality was inevitable. The 2005 is still a good wine, but doesn't show quite the interest of the previous two vintages. Passion fruit and pineapple aromas and flavors are a bit simple, carried by a slightly syrupy mouthfeel (7.7 g/L residual sugar). **84** —*J.C. (9/1/2006)*

Whitehaven 2004 Sauvignon Blanc (Marlborough) $16. Winemaker Simon Waghorn has crafted a mainstream Sauvignon that's sure to please. There's a hint of asparagus, but the core of this medium-weight wine is built around passion fruit flavors that cruise on through the crisp, clean finish. **87** —*J.C. (7/1/2005)*

Whitehaven 2003 Sauvignon Blanc (Marlborough) $17. Light to medium in body, but with a suggestion of oiliness to its flavors, which boast a solid core of melon and stone fruit wrapped in layers of green. Herbs and jalapeños can be sharp, but in this wine they actually finish quite easy and soft. **87** —*J.C. (8/1/2004)*

Whitehaven 2001 Sauvignon Blanc (Marlborough) $16. Score another for this Marlborough winery. Its SB mixes healthy doses of green pepper and snap peas with requisite citrus characteristics, and then underneath the surface there are notes of peach, melon, and cream. It's a full-bodied wine, with a medium-length citrus finish and lots of texture and character. All in all it represents its homeland and the grape variety well. **90 Editors' Choice** *(8/1/2002)*

Whitehaven 2000 Sauvignon Blanc (Marlborough) $15. 80 —*M.M. (1/1/2004)*

Whitehaven 2002 Estate Grown Sauvignon Blanc (Marlborough) $15. Seems more vegetal than last year's stunner (90 points), with green peas and bell peppers running neck and neck with the underlying stone

fruits. Full-bodied and a bit chunky, which doesn't mesh as well with the herbal flavors. **86** —*J.C. (9/1/2003)*

WILD EARTH

Wild Earth 2004 Pinot Noir (Central Otago) $30. Not a stereotypical New World fruit-driven Pinot, this is a dark and stormy night—filled with earthy notes, tobacco, soy, and root vegetables, with a wiry structure and firm finish that call Burgundy to mind. Drink 2007–2010. **89** —*J.C. (12/15/2006)*

WILLOW CREEK

Willow Creek 2000 Pinot Noir (Canterbury) $16. A tartly acidic wine, with some sweet molasses aromas but also hints of decaying vegetation. **80** —*J.C. (9/1/2003)*

WITHER HILLS

Wither Hills 2002 Chardonnay (Marlborough) $20. Right now this wine is a little rough, but give it another couple months and it should knit together nicely, as all the ingredients are present: hints of toast and vanilla, ripe peaches, and pinches of cinnamon and clove. **87** —*J.C. (8/1/2004)*

Wither Hills 2004 Pinot Noir (Marlborough) $36. Just after bottling, but this seems to have recovered from that shock nicely, with lush cherry-berry fruit that picks up some darker earth and cola notes that extend through the finish. **88** —*J.C. (12/1/2005)*

Wither Hills 2003 Pinot Noir (Marlborough) $NA. Starts with attractive cola and herb shadings, then adds super-ripe flavors of black cherries and plums. Yet for all the ripe-seeming fruit, there's also a tart edge to the finish. **87** —*J.C. (11/1/2006)*

Wither Hills 2002 Pinot Noir (Marlborough) $32. A thick veneer of smoky oak, cedar, and vanilla seems to recede with airing, allowing black cherries dusted with cinnamon and clove to emerge. Tannins are creamy and supple, so there's no need to delay gratification, just decant a little in advance to allow the wine to find its balance. **87** —*J.C. (8/1/2004)*

Wither Hills 2005 Sauvignon Blanc (Marlborough) $20. Textbook Marlborough SB, from a large winery that helped establish the style. Passion fruit and kiwi aromas are marked by grassy notes, then rounded out on the midpalate by peach flavors. Crisp and refreshing, with a hint of chalky minerality on the finish. **89** —*J.C. (5/1/2006)*

Wither Hills 2004 Sauvignon Blanc (Marlborough) $23. Tons of passion fruit, melon, celery, nettles, and grass create that telltale N.Z. bouquet. In the mouth, fresh acidity pushes ripe citrus, mango, and melon flavors. Quite healthy, with a solid, satisfying mouthfeel. Razor clean and crisp. **89** *(7/1/2005)*

Wither Hills 2003 Sauvignon Blanc (Marlborough) $20. A slightly riper style of Marlborough Sauvignon Blanc, with hints of ripe stone fruits accenting passion fruit and grapefruit aromas. Light-bodied, smoky, and minerally on the palate, the wine picks up a tinge of anise on the finish. **88** —*J.C. (8/1/2004)*

WOOLLASTON

Woollaston 2004 Pinot Noir (Nelson) $30. A light, easy-drinking wine from the first crop off Woollaston's Nelson Pinot Noir vineyard. Tea, cinnamon, and clove notes accent vanilla and cherry flavors. Soft tannins build a little on the relatively short finish. **86** —*J.C. (12/1/2005)*

Woollaston 2005 Pinot Rosé Pinot Noir (Nelson) $16. Light and fresh, this is an easy-to-glug rosé that's fruity—think strawberries and cherries—simple and clean, with a reasonably persistent finish. **87** —*J.C. (12/1/2005)*

Woollaston 2005 Sauvignon Blanc (Nelson) $NA. This ambitious project, partly owned by Las Vegas-based Glenn Schaeffer, head of Fontainebleau Resorts, has succeeded admirably in its first vintage processed in its new winery. Lovely stoniness and minerality buttress ripe Sauvignon flavors of stone fruit and pink grapefruit. **89** —*J.C. (5/1/2006)*

Woollaston 2005 Morgan Leigh Sauvignon Blanc (Nelson) $NA. Tropical and stone-fruity on the nose, with follow-on flavors that are a bit soft and sweet (there's 7.8 g/L residual sugar). Well-made and clean, it's more of a mass-market wine than the regular Woollaston Sauvignon. **86** —*J.C. (5/1/2006)*

NEW ZEALAND

Woollaston 2001 Sémillon-Sauvignon Blanc (Nelson) $14. Grassy to the point of excess, this wine's lean, herbal flavors and lemony acids are tart and mouth-puckering. **82** —*J.C. (9/1/2003)*

WYCROFT

Wycroft 2003 Old River Terrace Pinot Noir (Wairarapa) $NA. Boasts an alluring bouquet of tea, jasmine, and other other floral notes, then adds ample ripe cherry flavors on the palate. Not deep or rich enough to merit an Excellent rating, but a pretty, relatively light-weight wine for early drinking. **88** —*J.C. (12/1/2005)*

ZEAL

Zeal 2005 Sauvignon Blanc (Marlborough) $13. A bit heavy and syrupy in the mouth, with white grapefruit and muted passion fruit flavors that can't be enlivened by a slight spritz. **82** —*J.C. (5/1/2006)*

ZENITH

Zenith 2001 Sauvignon Blanc (Marlborough) $11. Dull, waxy, and smelling of over-cooked vegetables, this admirably full-bodied effort is just too green to be considered good. **81** —*J.C. (9/1/2003)*

NEW ZEALAND

Portugal

Portugal has always had Port. Vintage Port and Late Bottled Vintage Port are the best sellers in the United States, but aged tawnies should command increasing interest. With the great strides in winemaking techniques and the results of great research into grape varieties and vineyard sites being put into practice, Portugal's Port is entering a golden age.

What makes Portugal so exciting at the moment is that the same can now be said of Portuguese table wines. The days of Portugal being known for only lightly sparkling Rosé are long gone, although the wines themselves are still widely available. Increasingly, wines with the quality to be poured at the top international tables are arriving in America from Portugal, and the number of these wines is increasing with each new harvest.

Terraced vineyards at Taylor's Quinta da Vargellas, high in the Dours Valley east of Prinhão, Portugal

Encouragingly, Portugal has not copied the rest of the world. As with the Italians, Portuguese winemakers have not capitulated to international grape varieties and tastes. But, unlike the Italians, who enjoy playing with Cabernet, Chardonnay, and have acres of Merlot, Portuguese vineyards are still almost entirely planted with the great native varietals.

The boiler house of new developments in Portugal is the Douro Valley. Many of the same people who also make Port are making the greatest table wines. They use Portugal's greatest red grape varieties, Touriga Nacional, Tinta Roriz, Tinta Franca, Souzão, Tinta Cão, and Tinta Barroca, generally blended, invariably wood aged (although often in large wood barrels). The tastes are powerful, intense, tannic; the wines are long-lived.

South of the Douro, the Dão region also makes reds, which can be ageworthy (see Glossary). The Dão, lacking the same wealth of winemaking talent, has lagged behind, but there are now enough producers of quality to show that the style of the reds is going to be less intense than the Douro, more mineral, more herbal.

But Portugal is not only a red wine country. One of the country's most famous wines, Vinho Verde, produced in the far north of the country, is normally seen overseas in its white version (the tart, acid red stays at home and is drunk with sardines). At its best, Vinho Verde can equal some of the whites of the Rías Baixas region of Spain.

More southerly regions of Portugal bring us back to red wine. The Alentejo, the Ribatejo, and Estremadura are three vineyards that straddle the center of the country. These are the good value areas, which can often reach fascinating heights of quality. Warmer and softer wines than the tannic giants of the Douro are produced in greater quantities, making these regions the best way of starting into the adventure of today's Portuguese wines.

ADEGA COOPERATIVA DE VILA NOVA DE TAZEM

Adega Cooperativa de Vila Nova de Tazem 2000 Alfrocheiro Red Blend (Dão) $18. Toasty, smoky oak on the nose, featuring hints of smoked meat as well. Modest cherry fruit on the satiny-smooth palate is wrapped in copious amounts of toasty oak. **86** —*J.C. (11/15/2003)*

Adega Cooperativa de Vila Nova de Tazem 2000 Touriga Nacional (Dão) $18. Sappy and intense on the nose, with cherries, blackberries, and toast. Although some tasters used to the lush midpalates of New World wines may find this a little lacking in that department, it comes across as smooth and supple, with finely etched fruit flavors elegantly framed by oak. **90 Editors' Choice** —*J.C. (11/15/2003)*

ADEGA COOPERATIVA PONTE DE LIMA

Adega Cooperativa Ponte de Lima 2005 Portuguese White (Vinho Verde) $9. A simple, rather earthy, dry style of vinho verde, a blend of Loureiro, Trajadura, and Pederna. It's somewhat reductive, which rather spoils the freshness. **83** —*R.V. (7/1/2006)*

Adega Cooperativa Ponte de Lima 2005 Adamado Portuguese White (Vinho Verde) $9. Although it is a sweeter style, this is much fresher than the dry vinho verde from this huge cooperative. There is some crispness, but the soft aftertaste gives the sugar away. **84** —*R.V. (7/1/2006)*

ADEGA DE MONSÃO

Adega de Monsão 2005 Alvarinho Deu la Deu Alvarinho (Vinho Verde) $16. This is impressive, both for Vinho Verde and for a cooperative wine. The Alvarinho grape shows its best here with richness, intensity, and flavors of plums, pineapple, and ripe pears. **90 Editors' Choice** —*R.V. (7/1/2006)*

Adega de Monsão 2005 Danaide Branco Portuguese White (Vinho Verde) $NA. A fresh, light blend of Alvarinho and Trajadura, this dry wine from the Monsão cooperative shows touches of honey, some fresh grapefruit, and pear skin flavors. Not available in the U.S. **87** —*R.V. (7/1/2006)*

Adega de Monsão 2005 Muralhas de Monsão Portuguese White (Vinho Verde) $11. One of the most familiar brands of Vinho Verde in Portugal, with a production of 2.5 million bottles, this bone-dry, supremely crisp wine has apple and sharp pear flavors, and ripe and concentrated, but very fresh fruit. **89** —*R.V. (7/1/2006)*

ALTANO

Altano 2000 Portuguese Blend (Douro) $8. The company that makes Dow's Port entered the table wine market with the release of this wine and the joint venture Chryseia. Charles Symington's experience in the Rioja vineyards shows through in this attractive, ripe, juicy wine, whose name refers to the Douro wind. This seems designed for great rustic eating. **87 Best Buy** —*R.V. (12/31/2002)*

Altano 2003 Tinta Roriz-Touriga Franca Portuguese Red (Douro) $7. Altano, a table-wine project of the Symington family, famous for their various Port houses (among them, Dow's, Graham's, and Warre's), takes a two-pronged approach to marketing. A pricier Reserva offers greater richness and texture along with hints of oak, but while the entry-level Altano lacks the rich texture and density, it offers good value. Cherries and sappy green herb notes combine in a light-weight, easy quaffer that folds in dark chocolate and black tea notes on the finish. **84 Best Buy** — *J.C. (11/1/2006)*

Altano 2001 Tinta Roriz-Touriga Franca Portuguese Red (Douro) $7. This wine from the Symington Port company is ripe, juicy, and packed with red fruits. It is designed for early drinking, with its fresh bright flavors and light acidity. **85 Best Buy** —*R.V. (11/1/2004)*

Altano 1999 Portuguese Red (Douro) $8. Thin and a bit one-dimensional, Altano opens with aromas of cracked black peppercorns and green bell peppers, more green pepper, plus loads of oak, flavor the palate and the finish. **82** —*D.T. (12/31/2001)*

Altano 2003 Reserva Portuguese Red (Douro) $18. This Symington family table wine program is going well, to judge by this excellent 2003 Reserva. It packs plenty of lush blackberry fruit into a creamy, medium-bodied wine with supple tannins. Accents of vanilla and spice add nuance to the nose and midpalate, while some peppery notes add length to the finish. Drink now–2010, possibly longer. **90 Editors' Choice** —*J.C. (11/1/2006)*

Altano 2000 Reserva Portuguese Red (Douro) $NA. A Reserva which was made because of the quality of the year. The wine has fine, juicy fruit, with some red flavors. Warmth and generosity come from the ripe fruit. It will be ready to drink over the next 2–3 years. **87** —*R.V. (11/1/2004)*

ANDREZA

Andreza 2003 Reserva Red Blend (Douro) $15. A touch deeper and richer than the regular bottling, this reserva features scents of plum, cola, and earth to start, then shows off an ample, soft texture in the mouth. Flavors are rich and loamy, with flecks of bright fruit that shine through. Round, mouth-filling, and easy to drink. **88** —*J.C. (11/1/2006)*

Andreza 2003 Vinho Tinto Red Blend (Douro) $13. A perfectly solid Douro offering, one that easily blends dusty earth and mineral notes with black cherry fruit and a touch of herbs. Medium-bodied, it ends on a tea-like note. **85** —*J.C. (11/1/2006)*

ANSELMO MENDES

Anselmo Mendes 2005 Muros Antigos Alvarinho (Vinho Verde) $16. Mendes specializes in Alvarinho in the far north of Portugal. With this powerful, intense wine he shows how good the grape can be and how good the 2005 vintage was. It's full-bodied and intense, with just a touch of mineral and spritz. **91 Editors' Choice** —*R.V. (7/1/2006)*

Anselmo Mendes 2004 Muros de Melgaço Alvarinho (Vinho Verde) $20. Here six months in wood have enhanced the fruit, rather than giving a toasty character. There are tropical, apricot flavors, while even in a lesser year like 2004, the flavors are rich and intense. **89** —*R.V. (7/1/2006)*

ANTONIO ESTEVES FERREIRA

Antonio Esteves Ferreira 2001 Soalheiro Alvarinho (Vinho Verde) $15. Forceful and intense, but very green, with tart, shrill acids and under-ripe flavors of green apple and lime. **83** —*J.C. (11/15/2003)*

AVELEDA

Aveleda 2005 Alvarinho (Vinho Verde) $11. From Monsão, this is quintessential Alvarinho, ripe and full-bodied, with the typical apple skin structure and the hint of tropical fruits. Even though it is so ripe, it remains crisp and fresh. **90 Best Buy** —*R.V. (7/1/2006)*

Aveleda 2000 Alvarinho (Vinho Verde) $11. Aromas and flavors of lightly spiced white peaches. There's a firm round mouthfeel, enlivened by a slight prickle of carbon dioxide. Turns almost powdery on the finish, the dusting of cinnamon coming to the fore. **85** —*J.C. (12/31/2001)*

Aveleda 2000 Loureiro (Vinho Verde) $8. Loureiro is a key component in most blended Vinho Verdes; here it stands alone admirably, but one can see why it's not at its best flying solo. Piercing lemon comes on top of honey and litchi aromas. Give it a try if you want something uniquely Portuguese. **84** —*M.S. (12/31/2001)*

Aveleda 2005 Grinalda Portuguese White (Vinho Verde) $9. Aveleda's more traditional Vinho Verde is still perfectly fresh, with crisp green plum and grapefruit flavors. A blend of Trajadura and Loureiro, it is fresh but full-bodied with good intensity of fruit. **88 Best Buy** —*R.V. (7/1/2006)*

Aveleda NV White Blend (Vinho Verde) $6. This Vinho Verde's lively, soft mouthfeel and low alcohol content (8.5%) make it a perfect wine to serve at large, informal gatherings where the palate diversity is wide, and the other beverages on tap are beer. A bright floral, lemon-lime, and sour apple bouquet segues into a slightly fruity-sweet palate, where apple and white peach flavors take center stage. Finishes with mineral and lime flavors. **86 Best Buy** —*D.T. (12/31/2001)*

Aveleda NV Casal Garcia White Blend (Vinho Verde) $6. Floral and pretty in the nose; this captures the spritzy Vinho Verde style to a tee. A lemony profile with vital acids makes this the right counterpart to crab, lobster, or shrimp salad. It'll cut through the mayonnaise, augmenting the flavors of the sea. **85 Best Buy** —*M.S. (12/31/2001)*

BACALHÔA WINES OF PORTUGAL

Bacalhôa Wines of Portugal 2003 Quinta da Bacalhôa Cabernet Sauvignon (Terras do Sado) $29. The renaissance estate that gives JP Vinhos its new name of Bacalhôa Wines of Portugal was the first in Portugal to have Cabernet Sauvignon in the vineyard, planted by its former American owner. It is an elegant rather than powerful wine, with a green character probably from the cool year. The tannins are very precise, poised,,, and fine, with black currant flavors rounding the wine off. **89** —*R.V. (3/1/2006)*

Bacalhôa Wines of Portugal 2003 Tinto da Anfora Red Portuguese Red (Alentejano) $10. Produced since 1978, this is one of the more familar brands from central Portugal. It is solid, chunky, and ripely fruity, without the complexity of the reserve Grande Escholha version of the same wine. But it has good plum flavors, along with some fresh acidity to give it a final lift. **87 Best Buy** —*R.V. (3/1/2006)*

Bacalhôa Wines of Portugal 2003 Tinto da Anfora Grande Escolha Red Blend (Alentejano) $29. A delicious, perfumed wine, with intense, ripe, juicy blueberry flavors. It's dark, dense, and packed with richness and opulence. Underneath, though, there are tannins, and the wine should age well over five years. "Grande Escolha" indicates a limited release and special selection. **90** —*R.V. (3/1/2006)*

Bacalhôa Wines of Portugal 2003 Só Syrah (Terras do Sado) $25. This finely crafted wine, with its perfumed, juicy, solid character, is both powerful and elegant. It is certainly dry in the approved Portuguese manner, but the fruit powers through the tannins and leaves a rich aftertaste. **91** —*R.V. (3/1/2006)*

Bacalhôa Wines of Portugal 2003 Só Touriga Nacional (Terras do Sado) $25. From vineyards on the slopes of the Arrabida mountains south of Lisbon, this Touriga Nacional is earthy, tangy, packed with black fruits and dry acidity. The aftertaste is very dry. The producer was formerly known as JP Vinhos. **87** —*R.V. (3/1/2006)*

BARÃO DE VILAR

Barão de Vilar NV 10-Year Old Tawny Port $26. From property owned by the Kopke and Van Zeller families (Fernando van Zeller is Baron de Vilar), this classically attractive 10-year style has deep gold/brown color and is ripe and almost sweet (but with just enough dryness). It also has freshness, young fruit flavors, and just a hint of an attractive, burnt character. To find a fine example of a 10-year-old, look no further. **90 Editors' Choice** —*R.V. (8/1/2006)*

Barão de Vilar NV 20-Year Old Tawny Port $42. This is an impressive wine, all power and concentration. Flavors of bitter chocolate and arabica coffee are balanced with citrusy freshness. It's relatively lively and vibrant, but there are also plenty of mature flavors. **92** —*R.V. (8/1/2006)*

Barão de Vilar 2003 Vintage Port $38. Owned by the Kopke and Van Zeller families (Fernando van Zeller is Baron de Vilar), this Port comes from vineyards in Moncorvo and San João de Pesqueira. It is a beautifully perfumed wine, with solid tannins, balancing rich fruit with a firm structure. **90** —*R.V. (11/15/2005)*

BARROS

Barros NV 10 Years Old Port $25. Barros's tawnies are worth seeking out. This young example shows the house's signature smoky, nutty aromas but adds more fruity scents of raisins and prunes. Supple in the mouth, with a long, toffee-filled finish. **90** —*J.C. (11/15/2003)*

Barros NV 10-Year Old Tawny Port $22. Barros is not well known outside Portugal, but this wine suggests it should be. Delicate and perfumed, this has a fine balance that leaves a fresh, fruity aftertaste. There is structure, sweetness, and ripeness. **88** —*R.V. (8/1/2006)*

Barros NV 20 Years Old Port $35. Portuguese-owned Port houses, such as Barros, have long made terrific tawnies. This version is smoky and minerally, with nuts and citrus peel. It's supple and not very sweet, with a freshness and vibrancy that belie its age. Peppery on the finish. **90** —*J.C. (11/15/2003)*

Barros 1977 Colheita Bottled 2002 Port $75. Effectively a 25-year-old tawny, this wine starts off slowly, with restrained aromas of nuts and dried fruit. Then it caresses the palate with silky, lush, honeyed flavors of walnuts, oranges, cinnamon, and clove, building to a crescendo on the long, anise-tinged finish. **91** —*J.C. (11/15/2003)*

Barros NV Hutcheson Porto Rocha Vintage Character Port $17. The wine is perfumed with violets and a touch of nutmeg, but that is counter-balanced by its stalkiness. To taste, it is soft, but rather green and

light-weight. It is pleasant enough, but doesn't have much character. **83** —*R.V. (3/1/2005)*

Barros 1994 LBV Bottled 2000 Traditional Unfiltered Port $24. Already showing hints of brown at the rim and the beginnings of decay on the nose, this is still eminently drinkable, especially if you prefer a little age on your Port. It's supple in the mouth, with flavors of spice and brown sugar, finishing with a hint of licorice. **88** —*J.C. (11/15/2003)*

Barros 1996 LBV Bottled 2001 Port $20. Molasses, brown sugar, and cinnamon flavors finish with a flourish of chocolate fudge. But where's the fruit? This wine, from a tough vintage, is doing a slow fade. Drink soon. **85** —*J.C. (11/15/2003)*

Barros 1997 LBV Bottled 2002 Port $19. This is for Port lovers who want a soft, fruity style. Yet, despite these obvious attractions, there is a shot of dryness that suggests the wine could age—maybe over five years. **86** —*R.V. (3/1/2003)*

Barros NV Special Reserve Port $NA. An easy drinking, ready to drink Port, with few pretensions. But it is soft and pleasant enough, with its flavors of gum arabic and soft, rich fruit. Some bitterness in the aftertaste lets the wine down. **84** —*R.V. (3/1/2005)*

BARROS ALMEIDA

Barros Almeida NV 20-Year Old Tawny Port $42. A well-balanced, simple wine, with pleasant rich fruit and refreshing acidity. This tastes younger than a 20-year-old, but is still attractive enough. **85** —*R.V. (8/1/2006)*

Barros Almeida NV 30-Year Old Tawny Port $85. An attractive, relatively simple wine with dense chocolate flavors and some good, concentrated fruit. **86** —*R.V. (8/1/2006)*

Barros Almeida NV 40-Year Old Tawny Port $130. Lovers of Italian bitters should pay attention to this wine. It's medicinal character is very intense, very herbal. Good for the stomach, maybe, but it's not Port. **82** —*R.V. (8/1/2006)*

Barros Almeida 2003 Vintage Port $40. A very fruity, rich Port, but there is also some solidity and density. Shows polished winemaking, elegance, perfume, it's very approachable already. **88** —*R.V. (11/15/2005)*

BERCO DO INFANTE

Berco Do Infante 2003 Reserva Portuguese Red (Estremadura) $6. From a sun-baked region in the south, and this wine does show some of that heat in its slightly stewed fruit aromas and flavors. But there's also decent concentration, some pleasant strawberry and black pepper notes, and a juicy, mouth-watering finish. Drink now. **85 Best Buy** —*J.C. (6/1/2006)*

BLANDY'S

Blandy's NV Alvada 5 Year Old Rich Madeira Blend (Madeira) $15. Amber-colored, with a green tinge to the rim, this is a medium-weight, not-terribly sweet Madeira imbued with flavors of walnuts and dried figs. Lots of acidity on the finish. **86** —*J.C. (3/1/2005)*

Blandy's NV 10 Years Old Rich Malmsey (Madeira) $37. Mildly syrupy in texture, this is an intensely sweet Madeira balanced by racy acidity. Rancio and brown sugar aromas lead the way, followed by flavors of caramelized nuts, molasses, and burnt citrus peel. Excellent length on the finish, where the crisp acids really shine. **91** —*J.C. (11/1/2006)*

Blandy's NV 5 Year Sercial (Madeira) $21. In a recent series of entry-level Madeiras, this was a standout, offering excellent complexity and richness at a reasonable price. Nuts, toffee, and dried fruit aromas and flavors swirl together, balancing moderate sweetness with harmonious acids. Long on the finish. **91 Editors' Choice** —*J.C. (11/1/2006)*

Blandy's NV 5 Year Verdelho (Madeira) $21. More elegant than many Madeiras in this price range, with delicate aromas and flavors of nuts, coffee, and toffee that aren't overpowering. It's sweet and very smooth in the mouth, ending with honeyed flavors that are balanced by a lemony tang. **87** —*J.C. (11/1/2006)*

BOA NOVA

Boa Nova 2002 Tinto Portuguese Red (Alentejano) $16. A disappointing effort, the 2002 Boa Nova is rather light in color and already showing slight bricking at the rim. Earthy flavors of mushroom and cola are

PORTUGAL

tinged with prune and caramel. A blend of Alicante Bouschet, Aragonês, Cabernet Sauvignon, and Castelão. **82** —*J.C. (11/1/2006)*

BORGES

Borges 2003 Vintage Port $30. Over-floral and over-perfumed aromas lead to a Port that is lean, with rather too many green flavors. The dry tannins are too much for the fruit. **81** —*R.V. (11/15/2005)*

Borges 2000 Meia Encosta Red Blend (Dão) $5. This little Portuguese red packs in a surprising amount of complexity for the price. Starts off smoky, with hints of bacon and herb layered over modest cherry fruit aromas. The fruit drops away a bit on the palate and finish, replaced by intriguing notes of herbs and spice. Serve with strongly seasoned pork, which should accentuate the wine's fruit. **85 Best Buy** —*J.C. (11/15/2003)*

Borges NV Gatão White Blend (Vinho Verde) $6. **83** —*R.V. (8/1/2004)*

BROADBENT

Broadbent 2003 Vintage Port $85. This is a vintage made specifically for San Francisco importer Broadbent Selections. It is dark, dry, and very structured. Intense blackberry flavors dominate this wine, built for long-term aging. **90** —*R.V. (11/15/2005)*

BURMEISTER

Burmeister NV Sotto Voce Port $NA. This really fits the bill for an easy-drinking, rich style of Port. Packed with aromatic fruit, herbs, chocolate, and tannins, it combines sweetness with ripeness and structure. There is a dark, dry aftertaste that adds complexity. **90** —*R.V. (3/1/2005)*

Burmester 2003 Vintage Port $NA. Apart from a slight hint of volatility, this wine has much to commend it: good fruit, dense tannins, and some elegance. Maybe the volatility will blow away as it develops. **85** —*R.V. (11/15/2005)*

Burmester 2002 Tavedo Red Blend (Douro) $8. Burmester's entry into the Douro table wine sweepstakes is a medium-bodied, somewhat leathery wine. Some glue and vinyl notes on the nose, strawberry and rhubarb notes on the palate, and a dry, dusty finish all make for a wine that's decent, nothing more. **82** —*J.C. (11/1/2006)*

C DA SILVA

C da Silva NV Presidential 20-Year Old Tawny Port $50. An easy, fresh, ripe style, with dried fruits and a perfume note that is spoiled by the rubber character and some old wood. Anybody who stays in Portugal's pousadas, the state-run hotels, will have had this brand. **84** —*R.V. (8/1/2006)*

C da Silva NV Presidential 30-Year Old Tawny Port $80. A dense, firm style of wine from this small Dutch-owned Port house. Offers good acidity, old wood, and very bitter chocolate flavors. The aftertaste, by contrast, is sweet. **87** —*R.V. (8/1/2006)*

C da Silva NV Presidential 40-Year Old Tawny Port $100. While this wine certainly tastes old, it has a delicious golden glow from the richness of the apricot jelly-flavored ripe fruit. There is just a touch of spirit, but this adds to the warmth. **89** —*R.V. (8/1/2006)*

CALÇOS DO TANHA

Calços do Tanha 1997 Reserva Portuguese Red (Douro) $19. Meaty, dense, and smoky, with a touch of mushroom up front. This was a good vintage for the Douro, and here you get some deep plum and berries along with ample oak and full tannins. Only a little sourness at the core and a slightly hot finish hold it back. **86** —*M.S. (12/31/2001)*

Calços do Tanha 1996 Tinto Portuguese Red (Douro) $14. **86** —*J.C. (12/15/2000)*

Calços do Tanha 1999 Touriga Francesa Portuguese Red (Douro) $26. Touriga Francesa is one of the grapes used in Port production, but this is a dry table wine version that comes across as a jammy fruit bomb, with blackberry preserves and a hint of cracked pepper. Medium weight, with good balance, the wine finishes dry, with firm but ripe tannins. Solid now, may be better with a couple of years' cellaring. **86** —*J.C. (12/31/2001)*

Calços do Tanha 1998 Vinho Tinto Portuguese Red (Douro) $15. Smells of baking spices like vanilla and cinnamon, but there's also a dusty, earthy note. Simple flavors of black plum finish dry, with hints of cement dust and a resinous, sappy edge. **84** —*J.C. (12/31/2001)*

CÁLEM

Cálem 1994 LBV Bottled 1998 Port (Douro) $19. Although this wine is now mature and certainly ready to drink, there is still a lively freshness from the dried fruit and sweet sultana flavors and the acidity which comes through to finish. **89** —*R.V. (3/1/2003)*

Cálem 1997 LBV Bottled 2002 Port $23. The extra year's wood aging has given this wine great depth of flavor and richness. It is concentrated, balancing sweet chocolate flavors and dry tannins to produce a finely structured wine that should age in bottle for another five years or more. **90** —*R.V. (3/1/2003)*

Cálem NV Old Friends Fine Ruby Port $14. Starts off with hints of mint, baked berries, and earth, then delivers slightly herbal, medicinal fruit and chocolate flavors. Feels lush in the mouth, with no rough edges. **85** —*J.C. (11/1/2006)*

Cálem NV Reserva Ruby Port $NA. A soft ripe wine, with caramel aromas, dense perfumed fruit, and considerable sweetness. It has good, intense flavors, but is not hugely fruity, showing maturity instead. This is in the same soft style as Càlem's tawny Ports. **86** —*R.V. (3/1/2005)*

Cálem 2003 Vintage Port $85. There are all the right elements in this rich, smooth Port: good acidity, firm tannins, power, and fine flavors of figs, sultanas, and sweet jelly. This is a very attractive wine, likely to age well over the medium term. **89** —*R.V. (11/15/2005)*

Cálem 2000 Vintage Port $80. Reasonably lush but not unstructured, Cálem's 2000 vintage Port is a solid effort. Eucalyptus, coffee, and plum scents mark the nose, while the flavors are fruit-forward plum and blackberry, with a smidgen of dark chocolate. Long and textured on the finish. Drink now-2020. **89** —*J.C. (11/1/2006)*

CALHEIROS CRUZ

Calheiros Cruz 1999 Touriga Nacional Tinta Roriz (Douro) $26. This 50-50 blend of Tinta Roriz and Touriga Nacional is aged in new oak; only 7,500 bottles are produced. Buttercream frosting, cassis, and a hint of chlorine characterize the bouquet; very sturdy blackberry, plus oak and more cream, round out the palate. Sturdy tannins and a slight metallic note close the medium-length finish. **87** —*D.T. (12/31/2001)*

Calheiros Cruz 1999 Touriga Nacional (Douro) $25. Dark fruit and a creamy, toasty nose in the international style mark this medium-weight wine. The palate is quite dry, showing black plum and berry flavors wrapped in an oaky cocoon. Smoothly textured, it's tasty despite the overly prominent oak. Two years may balance the fruit and wood. Best after 2003. **86** —*M.M. (12/31/2001)*

CAMPO ARDOSA

Campo Ardosa 2000 Quinta da Carvalhosa Red Blend (Douro) $28. The first release of a joint-venture wine made by Bernhard Breuer and Bernd Philippi from the Rheingau in Germany. This 15-acre estate has produced a wine that shows just how impressive Douro wines can be. Its dark, brooding presence is immediately apparent in the almost opaque black color. On the palate, plums and black currants combine with new wood and tannins, leaving a complex aftertaste. Power and elegance blend effortlessly. Age for another five years before opening. **94** —*R.V. (12/31/2002)*

CANTANHEDE

Cantanhede 2000 Marqués de Marialva Reserva Baga (Bairrada) $10. A layer of dry fruits comes with a rustic, earthy element. There is a touch of green acidity typical of the Baga, along with fine tannins. This is a great food wine, not a great wine. **85** —*R.V. (12/31/2002)*

Cantanhede 2001 Marqués de Marialva Reserva Seleccionada Baga (Bairrada) $17. A firm wine, with dry but well-extracted tannins and solid black fruit. Fine, ripe fruit offers good concentration. The aftertaste, though, shows some green acidity. **86** —*R.V. (12/31/2002)*

Cantanhede 1999 Marqués de Marialva Reserva Red Blend (Bairrada) $10. Soft open style of wine, with light fruit, pleasant red berry flavors, and easy tannins. A touch of acidity lies alongside the jelly softness. **83** —*R.V. (12/31/2002)*

Cantanhede 2001 Marqués de Marialva White Blend (Bairrada) $NA. **85** —*R.V. (8/1/2004)*

CARDOSO DE MENEZES

Cardoso de Menezes 1999 Quinta da Murqueira Red Blend (Dão) $NA. A balanced wine, with dusty wood and herb aromas and firm tannins but also good, juicy fruit. At the end, there are reminders of old-style Dão in its dryness and toughness. **85** —*R.V. (12/31/2002)*

Cardoso de Menezes 1998 Quinta da Murqueira Reserva Red Blend (Dão) $NA. Over-ripe fruit and sweetness yield a somewhat clumsy wine, but there are good deep flavors and tarry fruit. It would be great with hearty food, as long as you don't think about it too much. **83** —*R.V. (12/31/2002)*

Cardoso de Menezes 2000 Quinta da Murqueira Touriga Nacional (Dão) $NA. This is a huge, powerful wine, from the almost black color to the aromas of tarry fruit, and the flavors of wood and sweet blackberries. It will certainly age well—10 years or more. **91** —*R.V. (12/31/2002)*

Cardoso de Menezes 2001 Quinta da Murqueira Reserva White Blend (Dão) $5. **87** —*R.V. (8/1/2004)*

CASA CADAVAL

Casa Cadaval 1999 Muge Merlot (Ribatejano) $13. Starts off well, with red raspberries and a touch of graham cracker on the nose, but turns Sweet Tart in the mouth, with tart winning out on the finish, along with a hint of plastic. **83** —*J.C. (11/15/2003)*

CASA DA ALORNA

Casa da Alorna 2003 Colheita Seleccionada Portuguese Red (Ribatejo) $14. A terrific value, Casa da Alorna's 2003 Colheita Seleccionada is a darkly colored wine imbued with a round, lush mouthfeel and long, velvety finish. Slightly herbal (mint?) and meaty notes add complexity to black cherry and plum flavors. A blend of Castelão (Periquita), Trincadeira, and Tinta Miúda. **90 Best Buy** —*J.C. (11/1/2006)*

CASA DE SANTAR

Casa de Santar 2001 Outono de Santar Vindima Tardia Encruzado (Dão) $14. An unique dessert wine, this is a late-harvest effort made from Encruzado grapes. Its deep golden color and scents of burnt orange peel and honey lead into a wine that's not very sweet—and so best paired with foie gras or a cheese course. Traces of nuts, oranges, and honey finish a bit short. **87** —*J.C. (3/1/2005)*

Casa de Santar 1999 Castas de Santar Portuguese Red (Dão) $8. Formerly called Casa de Santar, this usually dependable red bore an off-putting, green edge that yielded a bit with time, but never fully dissipated. The juicy fruit comes forward a bit on the palate, but the wine is thin and dry nevertheless, and ends with edgy, mouth-coating tannins. **83** —*M.M. (12/31/2001)*

Casa de Santar 2000 Reserva Portuguese Red (Dão) $20. A very perfumed wine with great sweet ripe tannins, packed with rich fruit. The wood and fruit balance gives the wine complexity, directness, and the potential of aging over at least 10 years. A classic. **92** —*R.V. (11/1/2004)*

Casa de Santar 1998 Reserva Portuguese Red (Dão) $16. Take a deep whiff and you'll find black pepper and brambleberry duking it out with an odd, not entirely positive perfumed note. But the wine improves with airing, offering strawberry and raspberry fruit and a full allotment of herbs. It comes on strong in the finish, all the while maintaining an edge. **85** —*M.S. (12/31/2001)*

Casa de Santar 2001 Castas de Santar Red Blend (Dão) $8. This blend of Touriga Nacional, Tinta Roriz and Alfrochiero receives six months' aging in second-use French oak, which keeps the price moderate while imparting a subtle smoky, chocolaty note. Cherry and leather flavors pick up a slight bitter almond note on the finish. **86 Best Buy** —*J.C. (11/15/2003)*

Casa de Santar 2000 Castas de Santar Red Blend (Dão) $8. A ripe, raisiny wine which has attractive soft, earthy fruit flavors. A blend of the local red varieties from younger vines on the Santar estate: Touriga Nacional, Tinta Roriz, Alfrocheiro, and Jaen. **87 Best Buy** —*R.V. (12/31/2002)*

Casa de Santar 1999 Reserva Red Blend (Dão) $15. A big, rich, well integrated wine, showing solid tannins and huge black-fruit flavors, along with some spice from 12 months aging in new French oak. The Touriga

Nacional in the blend (50%) dominates, with its restrained power and elegance. **90** —*R.V. (12/31/2002)*

Casa de Santar 2001 Tinto Superior Red Blend (Dão) $14. A ripe, modern-style wine, with clean black cherry and chocolate aromas. Medium-bodied, it's good, solid red wine filled with black cherry flavors and finishing with a race of heat. **85** —*J.C. (11/1/2004)*

Casa de Santar 2000 Touriga Nacional (Dão) $43. A highly perfumed wine, which is packed with herbal, ripe fruit. The aromas of lavender and mint are matched by the dark, firm tannins and solid fruit. One of Casa de Santar's varietal wines, this has a good aging potential over 5 years. **88** —*R.V. (11/1/2004)*

Casa de Santar 2000 Touriga Nacional (Dão) $43. Starts off a bit floral and toasty, but the blueberry-scented fruit quickly asserts itself. Masses of soft, ripe fruit come through on the palate, along with a rich, dense mouthfeel and soft but plentiful tannins. **91** —*J.C. (11/15/2003)*

Casa de Santar 2001 Castas de Santar Touriga Nacional (Dão) $10. A finely constructed wine which shows rich herbal flavors, dry tannins, and also solid, structured fruit. With its black fruits, its dense texture, and its dark acidity, this is a wine which will age well, over 4–5 years. **88 Best Buy** —*R.V. (11/1/2004)*

Casa de Santar 2001 Reserva Touriga Nacional Blend (Dão) $19. This lean, almost delicate, wine offers decent complexity: Scents of tea, chocolate, cherries, and herbs emerge from the glass. On the palate, there's lots of tea, tobacco and herb, with just enough fruit to carry the flavors. **86** —*J.C. (11/1/2004)*

CASA DE SEZIM

Casa de Sezim 2003 Portuguese White (Vinho Verde) $NA. Light, delicate and fresh, this wine is classic bone dry Vinho Verde. It has a touch of tannin from the green grapes, the acidity is very present, but it makes a great, refreshing summer drink. **87** —*R.V. (8/1/2005)*

Casa de Sezim 2005 Grande Escolha Portuguese White (Vinho Verde) $8. This is serious Vinho Verde. It has all the fresh, crisp, acidic character but, because of the year, it is also full, ripe, with green apple skin flavors, green plums, and intense fruit. **89 Best Buy** —*R.V. (7/1/2006)*

Casa de Sezim NV Sezim Portuguese White (Vinho Verde) $7. A light, flowery style of wine, with a touch of almonds and crisp, clean, lightly sweet fruit. At 9% alcohol this is a good summer quaff. **84 Best Buy** —*R.V. (7/1/2006)*

Casa de Sezim 2001 Sociedade Agricola Pecuaria White Blend (Vinho Verde) $NA. **89** —*R.V. (8/1/2004)*

CASA DE VILA VERDE

Casa de Vila Verde 2005 Alvarinho (Vinho Verde) $12. As it should be from the year and the grape, this is a full-bodied wine, with some good green plum flavors. But its intensity of flavor is spoiled by the soft, lightly sugary aftertaste. **85** —*R.V. (7/1/2006)*

Casa de Vila Verde 2004 Alvarinho (Minho) $14. A single-vineyard wine made from the sought after Alvarinho grape. It's fuller than the average Vinho Verde, packed with ripe green fruits and flavors of pink grapefruit and white peaches. Drink now. **90 Best Buy** —*R.V. (8/1/2005)*

Casa de Vila Verde 2005 Portuguese White (Vinho Verde) $8. The estate wine from Vila Verde which is in Lousada in the southern Vinho Verde region. It is a simple wine, fresh, but just too light-weight and bland. **82** —*R.V. (7/1/2006)*

Casa de Vila Verde 2003 White Blend (Vinho Verde) $9. Very nice Vinho Verde, with fresh, green apple and lime aromas and a clean, crisp finish. Maybe a little fuller and plumper than typical, but still balanced, with no shortage of apple and citrus fruit. **86 Best Buy** —*J.C. (3/1/2005)*

Casa de Vila Verde 2004 Estate White Blend (Vinho Verde) $10. Floral and apple-y, with overtones of smoke and slate that add an intriguing mineral component. Green apple, citrus and chalk flavors finish short and clean. **84** —*J.C. (12/31/2005)*

CASA DI TONDA

Casa di Tonda 2004 Quinta dos Grilos Portuguese Red (Dão) $11. Look at the label of this Dão red wine, and there is a cricket (in Portuguese a grilo) lurking in one corner. Perfumed, deeply colored, this is a blend of Alfrocheiro and Touriga Nacional. With flavors of new wood, raisins, and dried prunes, this is a great, fruity wine that combines tannins with its powerful, ripe fruit flavors. Oenologist Carlos Moura, part of the dynamic team that runs Dão Sul and Quinta do Cabriz, shows the modern side of the region with a wine that has juicy red berries, mint, spice, and a well-integrated, polished wood character. A powerful but balanced wine. **89 Best Buy** —*R.V. (11/15/2006)*

CASA FERREIRINHA

Casa Ferreirinha 2001 Esteva Portuguese Red (Douro) $10. A plump, medium-weight wine, this is an easy-going quaff suitable for any occasion. Mixed berries on the nose and palate, joined by vanilla and cedar. Drink now and over the next few years. **85 Best Buy** —*J.C. (12/1/2004)*

Casa Ferreirinha 1991 Barca Velha Red Blend (Douro) $80. 90 *(10/1/2000)*

Casa Ferreirinha 1997 Esteva Red Blend (Douro) $10. 87 Best Buy *(10/1/2000)*

Casa Ferreirinha 1989 Reserva Red Blend (Douro) $46. 87 *(10/1/2000)*

Casa Ferreirinha 1994 Vinha Grande Red Blend (Douro) $19. 88 *(11/15/1999)*

CASA SANTA EUFEMIA

Casa Santa Eufemia NV 10-Year Old Tawny Port $39. Santa Eufemia is a new name on the U.S. market, from a vineyard in the Baixo Corgo, the western end of the Port vineyards. This is a mature 10-year-old, light in color and dry, with coffee and cocoa flavors. There is a delicious, lightly acidic, long-lasting aftertaste. **88** —*R.V. (8/1/2006)*

Casa Santa Eufemia NV 20-Year Old Tawny Port $NA. This tastes very old, and any fruit is suppressed by flavors of licorice and burnt wood. **82** —*R.V. (8/1/2006)*

Casa Santa Eufemia NV 30-Year Old Tawny Port $NA. Oreo eaters will enjoy the aromas of this wine, with its sweet, milk chocolate tastes. But apart from that it is unbalanced, too acid for real pleasure. **84** —*R.V. (8/1/2006)*

Casa Santa Eufemia NV 40-Year Old Tawny Port $NA. This is very burnt, offering concentrated old fruit flavors and tasting very mature, straight from the barrel. There's some bitterness, but the main impression is of very old wine. **85** —*R.V. (8/1/2006)*

CASA SANTOS LIMA

Casa Santos Lima 2000 Palha-Cana Vinho Tinto Red Blend (Estremadura) $9. 85 Best Buy —*D.T. (11/15/2002)*

CASAL DE VALLE PRADINHOS

Casal de Valle Pradinhos 2001 Porta Velha Red Blend (Trás-os-Montes) $10. Black cherries, vanilla, and a slightly creamy, lactic note on the nose are followed up by a wine that's filled with mocha, earth, and chocolate flavors. Finishes with firm tannins and juicy acids, folding in hints of red berries. Drink now and over the next 2–3 years. **86 Best Buy** —*J.C. (3/1/2004)*

Casal de Valle Pradinhos 2000 Valle Pradinhos Red Blend (Trás-os-Montes) $15. At first glance, this wine, with its modest cherry and cedar aromas and flavors seems too acidic and too tannic. But it seems to fill out a little as it sits in the glass, giving some hope that it will evolve in a positive direction. **85** —*J.C. (3/1/2004)*

CASAL DOS JORDÕES

Casal dos Jordões NV Finest Reserve Port $NA. This Port from the organically farmed Casal dos Jordões certainly has pure fruit flavors. But the main impression is of a green, herbal character with bitter chocolate which spoil the balance. The spirit could be better integrated, as well. **82** —*R.V. (3/1/2005)*

Casal dos Jordões 2000 Vintage Port) $NA. Slapping "wine made from organic grapes" on the label shouldn't be a license to market a subpar vintage Port in what was a great year in the Douro. Muddy aromas and flavors of charred fruit are barely acceptable, as is the thin, harsh finish. **80** —*J.C. (11/1/2006)*

Casal dos Jordões 2003 Reserva Touriga Franca (Douro) $NA. This big, fruity wine shows the liveliness and vivacity of the Touriga Franca grape. It certainly has plenty of dry tannins, but it also has great blackberry fruits, some figs, as well as tarry and violet perfumes. A delicious wine, ready to drink now, but will age over five years. **89** —*R.V. (3/1/2006)*

CASTELLO D'ALBA

Castello d'Alba 2003 Colheita Seleccionada Red Blend (Douro) $12. This is a fun, bouncy wine that actually seems a bit Syrah-like. Juicy cherry-berry flavors follow plum and black pepper scents, while the finish is mouth-watering and fresh. Perfect for casual grilling. **86** —*J.C. (11/1/2006)*

Castello d'Alba 2003 Tinto Reserva Red Blend (Douro) $12. Dark-fruited and earthy, with cedar and coffee shadings that give the wine an even darker demeanor. This medium-bodied wine boasts some dry, woody tannins that suggest another year or two of cellaring prior to primetime consumption. Sturdy rather than charming. **86** —*J.C. (11/1/2006)*

Castello d'Alba 2005 Branco Reserva White Blend (Douro) $12. The name sounds Italian, but this is made in Portugal's Douro Valley, up in the hills near the Spanish border. According to the importer, it's a blend of indigenous Códega, Viosinho, and Rabigato grapes. Whatever it is, it shows skillfully managed barrel treatment in its lush, rich, creamy texture and vanilla notes, but those elements seamlessly blend with ripe citrus (think oranges or tangerines) and gingery spice. A long finish cements this wine's impressive quality. **90 Best Buy** —*J.C. (11/1/2006)*

Castello d'Alba 2004 Vinhas Velhas Branco White Blend (Douro) $17. From a mix of old indigenous white grapes, this wine reveals a producer making a stab at something different with character. It's broad and mouth-filling, framed by plenty of toasty oak and dried spices, but it also features honey and melon flavors that help support the wood. **87** —*J.C. (11/1/2006)*

CAVES ALIANÇA

Caves Aliança 2004 Galeria Bical (Bairrada) $8. A fresh green wine that shows good, crisp acidity. The Bical grape, the standard white of Bairrada, gives a good tannic structure, as well as flavors of gooseberries and hedgerow fruits. **85 Best Buy** —*R.V. (8/1/2005)*

Caves Aliança 2001 Alabastro Portuguese Red (Alentejano) $8.5. A soft, simple, pleasurably fruit wine, which has flavors of dried berries and perfumed violets. Fresh and ripe, it is ready to drink. **84** —*R.V. (12/1/2004)*

Caves Aliança 2003 Alabastro Reserva Portuguese Red (Alentejano) $14. A delicious, easy wine, with good, spicy fruit and soft tannins. It has some toast from wood aging, but the dominant character is of ripe, red fruit flavors. **86** —*R.V. (3/1/2006)*

Caves Aliança 2001 Alabastro Reserva Portuguese Red (Alentejano) $13. A selection of grapes from the Quinta de Terrugem, including Cabernet Sauvignon. Eight months barrel aging give this wine richness and layers of toast, as well as solid tannins. Underneath ripe, generous fruit, there is a layer of dryness which indicates it will age 5 years or more. **89** —*R.V. (12/1/2004)*

Caves Aliança 2000 Aliança Particular Portuguese Red (Dão) $10. A single-vineyard wine, that has ripe, perfumed fruit and dry, firm, structured tannins. A great food wine, with its dryness and intense fruit flavors. Ripe blackberries and acidity give it a lift. **89 Best Buy** —*R.V. (11/1/2004)*

Caves Aliança 1996 Particular Portuguese Red (Dão) $11. 87 Best Buy —*M.S. (10/1/1999)*

Caves Aliança 2001 Quinta da Terrugem Portuguese Red (Alentejo) $20. A ripe, tarry-flavored wine, with great tannins and red berry fruits. With its layers of dryness, and sweet and sour acidity, this would be excellent with fatty meats. Will age well over the next five years. **88** —*R.V. (3/1/2006)*

Caves Aliança 2000 Quinta da Terrugem Portuguese Red (Alentejo) $24. An elegant blend of Aragonês and Trincadeira from the single vineyard Quinta da Terrugem. Some dense, dusty tannins soften to give juicy fruit and fine, sweet ripeness. **87** —*R.V. (12/1/2004)*

Caves Aliança 2001 Quinta das Baceladas Portuguese Red (Beiras) $25. With consultant Michel Rolland on board, it's hardly surprising that this is a supremely polished wine. It emphasizes elegance, new wood, and ripe fruit. The Merlot and Cabernet Sauvignon in the blend meld well with the local Baga grape to form a structured, generous wine. **91** —*R.V. (11/1/2004)*

Caves Aliança 2001 Quinta dos Quatro Ventos Reserva Portuguese Red (Douro) $45. This wine, with its rich, smooth fruit, shows the effects of consultancy from Michel Rolland and Pascal Chatonnet. A blend of Tinta Roriz, Touriga Nacional, and Tinta Barroca, it has elegance, juicy black fruits and some subtle wood flavors. **90** —*R.V. (11/1/2004)*

Caves Aliança 2001 T da Terrugem Portuguese Red (Alentejo) $60. Consultant Michel Rolland and Caves Aliança winemaker Francisco Atunes have produced a rich, smooth, polished blend of Aragonês and Trincadeira. Flavors of wood, chocolate, spice and deep black fruits combine richly and with intensity. This is a limited production of 21,000 bottles. **90** —*R.V. (12/1/2004)*

Caves Aliança 2002 T Quinta da Terrugem Portuguese Red (Alentejo) $57. Terrugem in the Borba region was acquired by Aliança in 1991, and now has 147 acres of vines. Bringing together the winemaking talents of Francisco Atunes and Bordelais Pascal Chatonnet, this is the top wine from the estate. It is smooth, polished, packed with dry tannins, as well as intense blackberry jelly flavors. This is a fine, deep-flavored wine, great for sophisticated cooking or just some good pork. **92** —*R.V. (3/1/2006)*

Caves Aliança 2004 Portuguese White (Dão) $7. A soft, simple wine with flavors of green fruits, and a layer of tannins. Medium-bodied and floral, it has a soft, medium-sweet aftertaste. **83** —*R.V. (8/1/2005)*

Caves Aliança 1998 Alianca Classico Reserva Red Blend (Beiras) $9. Aromas of sweet raisins and a rich concentrated palate make this an immediately attractive wine. The dusty, ripe tannins and flavors of black fruit, chocolate, and wood show its time in French and American oak. **87** —*R.V. (12/31/2002)*

Caves Aliança 1999 Alianca Floral Reserva Red Blend (Douro) $7. The initial impression of generous fruit, and flavors of wood and black raisins are spoiled by dryness and bitterness on the finish. **84** —*R.V. (12/31/2002)*

Caves Aliança 1999 Alianca Particular Red Blend (Palmela) $15. A smooth wine with racy acidity that lies alongside plums and earthy fruits. Layers of wood, a little dry tannin and a finish of dried raisins give balance to this solid, intense wine. **88** —*R.V. (12/31/2002)*

Caves Aliança 1998 Alianca Particular Red Blend (Dão) $13. The dull red color, the aromas of black, tarry fruits, and the heavily perfumed candied flavors are all part of this old-style wine. At the end, there is leanness and dryness. **83** —*R.V. (12/31/2002)*

Caves Aliança 1998 Alianca Reserva Red Blend (Dão) $7. This wine's color is already fading. Aromas of old wood are followed on the palate by juicy and jammy flavors. It is ripe, light, and easy, with a dusty layer. **82** —*R.V. (12/31/2002)*

Caves Aliança 1998 Floral Grande Escolha Red Blend (Douro) $13. An intensely perfumed wine, made from selected lots. Initially, it tastes almost artificial with flavors of violets and candies, along with dry tannins. But there is good development potential, especially when the rich dark plums and acidity begin to come to the fore, in four or five years. **88** —*R.V. (12/31/2002)*

Caves Aliança 1995 Floral Grande Escolha Red Blend (Douro) $13. 87 *(11/15/1999)*

Caves Aliança 1996 Foral Reserva Red Blend (Douro) $9. 85 *(11/15/1999)*

Caves Aliança 1997 Quinta da Terrugem Red Blend (Alentejo) $20. A deliciously ripe wine, with sweet mulberry and cranberry flavors alongside rich wood tannins. The wine, a blend of Aragonês and Trincadeira, has great tarry flavors and a solid, chunky structure. It could well age for five years or more, but is certainly ready to drink now. **90** —*R.V. (12/31/2002)*

Caves Aliança 1999 Quinta das Baceladas Single Estate Red Blend (Beiras) $26. This is one of the wines made by Caves Aliança using Bordeaux's Michel Rolland as consultant. It has all the hallmarks of a Rolland wine:

a smooth, polished purple color; soft, rich new wood flavors with dark tannins, and firm, juicy fruits. But it is an international wine, missing a regional identity. It gets high marks for craftsmanship, not so high for individuality. **89** —*R.V. (12/31/2002)*

Caves Aliança 1999 Quinta dos Quatro Ventos Red Blend (Douro) $30. This wine comes from Aliança's new estate in the Douro, whose name means four winds. Made with consultant Michel Rolland, it is purple in color, with dominant aromas of new wood. To taste, it is rich, but the wood and sawdust flavors are too prominent for the spicy black fruit. This could integrate better in the next five years. **88** —*R.V. (12/31/2002)*

Caves Aliança 1999 Galeria Tinta Roriz (Douro) $9. Here are aromas of smoky, juicy fruit along with a palate of firm tannins, prominent overtones of new wood, with ripe acidity. This is a young wine, with good modern potential, which will age well over the next 5–10 years. **90 BestBuy** —*R.V. (12/31/2002)*

CAVES DO CERCA

Caves do Cerca 2005 Famega Portuguese White (Vinho Verde) $7. A low-alcohol (9.5%), apéritif style of Vinho Verde, which certainly has some sweetness, but which also balances it with plenty of crisp, green fruit flavors. **85** —*R.V. (7/1/2006)*

CAVES DO SOLAR DE SÃO DOMINGOS

Caves do Solar de São Domingos 2000 Prestígio Red Blend (Beiras) $14. Swings for the fences . . . fouls out to the first baseman. A lean, herbal wine with a finish reminiscent of over-steeped tea and chocolate. **81** — *J.C. (11/15/2003)*

CAVES DOM TEODOSIO

Caves Dom Teodosio 2005 Lagosta Portuguese White (Vinho Verde) $7. This relatively dry style is crisp, fresh, and acidic. The name "Lagosta" means "lobster," and this would be a great seafood accompaniment. **85** —*R.V. (7/1/2006)*

Caves Dom Teodosio 1995 Quinta de S. Joao Batista Reserva Red Blend (Douro) $13. The nose has a smashed red berry theme to it, and that carries onto the palate, where it's all about red cherry, cranberry, and rhubarb. If that sounds tart, it is. But it's not a sourball. Still, the overriding theme is one of acidity and lean, dry red fruit. **82** —*M.S. (11/15/2002)*

CAVES MESSIAS

Caves Messias 2003 Vintage Port $NA. A ripe, open style of wine, generous and fruity. This is not a Port for the long-term, but for the next 5–10 years it will be a delicious, enjoyable wine. **86** —*R.V. (11/15/2005)*

CAVES SÃO JOÃO

Caves São João 1990 Quinta do Poço do Lobo Cabernet Sauvignon (Bairrada) $20. 89 *(10/1/1999)*

CHARAMBA

Charamba 1999 Portuguese Red (Douro) $6. Light and flavorful, this red has a dryly fruited nose and palate and a chalky note, adding interest. Smooth on the palate and not at all pretentious, it's a choice red at a great price to accompany hors d'oeuvres or a light supper. **84 Best Buy** — *M.M. (12/31/2001)*

CHURCHILL'S

Churchill's NV 10-Year Old Tawny Port $30. Ripe and fresh. There are touches of bitter oranges, lemon peel and ginger. The aftertaste is soft and sweet. **87** —*R.V. (8/1/2006)*

Churchill's NV 20-Year Old Tawny Port $51. A big, sweet, soft wine, with lively fruit, some bitter coffee and sweet treacle flavors. This is an elegant, attractive wine. **89** —*R.V. (8/1/2006)*

Churchill's NV Finest Vintage Character Port $17. A sweet, slightly spirity Port that lacks any real depth or complexity, yet still provides a modicum of pleasure in its sugary, cooked-fruit flavors of prunes, dates and raisins. **83** —*J.C. (12/1/2004)*

Churchill's NV Finest Vintage Character Port $17. Not an intense or concentrated wine, perhaps, but this Reserve Port from Churchill's is well balanced and finely structured. There are flavors of green figs that give it

PORTUGAL

freshness, and a dry aftertaste. A slight stalky flavor is the only off note. **86** —*R.V. (3/1/2005)*

Churchill's 1998 LBV Port $24. A strong showing for Churchill's, the 1998 LBV shows delicate aromas of walnuts and flowers, while the flavors are an ineresting blend of nuts, leather, and dried fruits. Soft and easy on the finish; clearly destined for short-term drinking. **87** —*J.C. (12/1/2004)*

Churchill's 1996 LBV Port $24. Red licorice and cherry cola announce it as a sweet, wild, young Port, but it's much more intriguing than that. The palate is intense; it literally explodes with yummy cherry and chocolate. But it's not that heavily bodied, which makes it quite drinkable. And for that you will be happy. **89** —*M.S. (11/15/2002)*

Churchill's 1997 LBV Bottled 2001 Port $21. Churchill Graham is the youngest of the Port shippers, established in 1981. The Churchill LBV is a traditional, unfiltered wine, which can age well. This wine has richness and sweetness tempered with a layer of dry tannins and concentration. **87** —*R.V. (3/1/2003)*

Churchill's 1998 Quinta Da Agua Alta Port $60. Here's a straigh ahead Port that holds nothing back. It's sweet, with defined, full-bore black fruit. It's nicely balanced, with creamy mild chocolate propped up by bright acidity. It is also easy to drink now, which is no small accomplishment for a baby vintage Port. **89** —*M.S. (11/15/2002)*

Churchill's 1999 Quinta da Gricha Port $64. Full-throttle cherry and plum fruit is in full force, backed by tons of chocolate. It's down-the-middle Port, yummy and hedonistic. Plenty of power, weight, and balance. Give it until 2010 to fully come around. **89** —*M.S. (11/15/2002)*

Churchill's 2003 Quinta da Gricha Vintage Port $85. Bought by Churchill in the 1990s, this is a single-quinta wine kept apart from the firm's true vintage. It is a rustic, earthy wine, and the fruit cannot break through that rusticity. Hints of potential, but not enough. **83** —*R.V. (11/15/2005)*

Churchill's 2001 Quinta da Gricha Vintage Port $80. As you might expect, this is very young Port, capable of aging for a couple of decades. Exuberant, youthful fruit spills forth in scents of mulberries; the mouthfeel is firm and taut, finishing with firm tannins. **88** —*J.C. (12/1/2004)*

Churchill's 2000 Quinta da Gricha Vintage Port $83. Starts off a bit floral, then develops raspberry and chocolate nuances as it sits in the glass. Seems a bit light and hard-edged, with dry, unyielding tannins. It's a pretty wine, but in an ice princess sort of way—more admirable than something you'd necessarily cozy up to. **87** —*J.C. (11/15/2003)*

Churchill's NV Tawny Ten Years Old Port $30. Boasts youthful aromas of red fruits, with just a hint of golden raisins and toffee. Strikes a fine balance between vigorous young fruit and aged notes of caramel and raisin. **88** —*J.C. (11/15/2003)*

Churchill's NV Tawny Ten Years Old Port $30. Sweet and mild aromas are highlighted by a touch of fresh prune. The mouthfeel is buttery, with plenty of toffee/coffee flavors poking through. Although it's a tad simple and straightforward, as a whole there is nothing not to like about this easy-to-drink Port. **87** —*M.S. (7/1/2002)*

Churchill's NV Ten Years Old Tawny Port $30. An earthy, spicy, mushroomy style, with lots of cinnamon and clove alongside modest amounts of plummy fruit. Develops some bittersweet chocolate notes on the finish. **85** —*J.C. (12/1/2004)*

Churchill's 2003 Vintage Port $95. An impressive, finely tannic Port with solid, ripe fruits and great black jelly and fig flavors. **92** —*R.V. (11/15/2005)*

Churchill's NV Vintage Character Port $17. Raw and wild best describe this plum-packed sweetie, which has all the elements of the real thing, i.e., vintage Port, but not much style or polish. On the plus side, the finish isn't too hot or heavy, and overall it's fairly seamless. **86** —*M.S. (11/15/2002)*

Churchill's 2000 Vintage Port $82. Perhaps the best young Churchill's I've tasted, the 2000 blends complexity with structure to create an eminently ageable Port. For fruit lovers, there's crushed berries and plums, but notes of dried spices and earth add depth. Estimated maturity: 2020–2050. **93 Cellar Selection** —*J.C. (11/15/2003)*

Churchill's 1997 Vintage Port $82. Big, bold, and grapey best describe the nose on this slightly syrupy offering. Chocolate and blackberry come in

spades on the palate, all prior to an assertive, persistent finish that's defined by a shot of raisin at the tail end. **87** —*M.S. (11/15/2002)*

Churchill's NV White Port $17. Billed on the label as a "dry apéritif," white Port on ice isn't a bad drink at all, although it probably won't fit everyone's taste. It's a bit like spiked apricot juice with the added note of brandy. Fortunately, it's neither cloying nor sweet, but it's not exactly refined or exotic. Adventurous types should try it. Conventional types might want to take a pass. **83** —*M.S. (11/15/2002)*

CISTUS

Cistus 2002 Reserva Red Blend (Douro) $14. This dark purple wine opens with a trace of animale or game, but also boasts intense aromas and flavors of roasted blackberries, accented by pinches of cinnamon and clove. Broad in the mouth, it would be a solid choice to serve with grilled or roasted meats. **88** —*J.C. (6/1/2006)*

COCKBURN'S

Cockburn's NV 10-Year Old Tawny Port $30. A hugely, almost uncomfortably sweet wine with strong aromatics. It has some attractive acidity, but the sweetness detracts from any other character. **83** —*R.V. (8/1/2006)*

Cockburn's NV 20-Year Old Tawny Port $50. Dry, rather burnt, with sweetness, but dominated by unbalanced spirit. **82** —*R.V. (8/1/2006)*

Cockburn's 1996 LBV Port $20. Successfully marries young, grapy aromas with notes of maple syrup. The flavors are slightly pruny and raisiny, but an elegant overlay of caramel smoothes things out. This is a supple, easy-to-drink LBV for current consumption. **85** —*J.C. (3/1/2004)*

Cockburn's 1998 Quinta dos Canais Port $50. Something as syrupy and rich as this—and also packed with dark bitter chocolate and espresso—is like dessert. A lot of thick, sticky plum fruit precedes an equally thick finish. A tad clumsy, but packed with flavor. Give it time. **88** —*M.S. (11/15/2002)*

Cockburn's 2003 Quinta dos Canais Vintage Port $56. A single-quinta Port from Cockburn's vineyard in the Douro Superior. It is surprisingly fresh, despite its hot vineyard provenance; it's perfumed with flavors of hedgerow fruits. There is a structure, but the main character is elegance. **87** —*R.V. (11/15/2005)*

Cockburn's 2001 Quinta dos Canais Vintage Port $NA. The blackest, inkiest wine of the tasting, it's incredibly rich and dense. Round and mouth-filling, packed with mixed berries and chocolate. The vintage's flesh is obscuring the wine's structure for the moment, but this should age magnificently. Drink 2011–2040. **93** —*J.C. (3/1/2004)*

Cockburn's 2000 Quinta dos Canais Vintage Port $60. Although 40% of the blend of Cockburn's 2000 "classic" vintage Port is from Quinta dos Canais, enough high-quality wine remained to bottle a single-quinta Port as well. Canais is slightly lighter in color and in weight, yet still boasts wondrous aromas of blueberries, licorice, and sun-warmed schist. The wine's red berries wrapped around a chocolaty core should be hitting their stride in only five years or so. **91** —*J.C. (3/1/2004)*

Cockburn's 1999 Quinta dos Canais Vintage Port $NA. Dark, close to inky in color. Intense, youthful aromas of plums and berries are firmly backed by a chocolaty core. Soft and full in the mouth, the masses of ripe fruit make this wine almost approachable. Hold a few more years, and try it in 2009. **92** —*J.C. (3/1/2004)*

Cockburn's 1995 Quinta dos Canais Vintage Port $NA. Cockburn's purchased this property in 1989. Historically, grapes from Canais accounted for approximately half of the blend in Cockburn's vintage Port, and Côrte-Real describes the '95 Canais as "very much Cockburn." The color is a dark saturated ruby, the aromas combine meat, chocolate, and plum. Côrte-Real says that the vintage was even hotter than '94 during harvest and fermentation, and some of that shows in the finished wine's hint of raisined fruit. Creamy, ripe tannins and a hint of pepper mark the finish. Hold. **89** —*J.C. (3/1/2004)*

Cockburn's NV Special Reserve Port $16. Basic Port, slightly syrupy and sweet, with dried cherry and chocolate flavors and a plump, easygoing mouthfeel. **83** —*J.C. (11/1/2006)*

Cockburn's 2003 Vintage Port $65. Fruity and floral wine with an attractive, fresh, lifted aroma. The fruit is soft, with light tannins. This is a wine that will develop quickly. **86** —*R.V. (11/15/2005)*

Cockburn's 2000 Vintage Port $90. Incredibly juicy and fruit-filled, with mixed berries leading the charge, backed by cocoa, chocolate, and dried spices. It's deceptively easy to drink now, but the structure should become more obvious in time. Côrte-Real considers it "one of the best vintages ever made." Worth cellaring some for 50 years to see how it compares with the '27 and '55. Hold. **92** —*J.C. (3/1/2004)*

Cockburn's 1994 Vintage Port $NA. This seems lighter in weight than expected, despite an impressively dark, saturated color. Lots of cherries and dried spices on the palate, along with aromas of walnuts and smoked meat. "Passing through some middle-age disturbances," as Côrte-Real said, or just very good Port, not great? Hold. **88** —*J.C. (3/1/2004)*

Cockburn's 1977 Vintage Port $NA. The 1977 vintage was not officially declared by Cockburn's—this sample was from a small stock of 1,000 bottles that was not released commercially. According to Côrte-Real, the staff at Cockburn's felt that '77 was "not as great as people thought." The company also had ample supplies of the 1975 in the market, which also may have influenced the decision not to declare. Based on the showing of this bottle, it was a big mistake. Ruby-colored, with only traces of brick and a nose of exuberant fruit joined by toffee and floral elements, you can tell immediately this is special. In the mouth, it's very supple and elegant, what Côrte-Real describes as "a little feminine. Not exactly in the house style." Drink or hold. **93** —*J.C. (3/1/2004)*

Cockburn's 1970 Vintage Port $NA. Ruby color, with just a hint of brick at the rim. Mouth-filling red berries and plums, finishing with chocolate and peppery spice. Overall, it's a bit austere, but pretty, and capable of another decade or two of further aging. Drink or hold. **91** —*J.C. (3/1/2004)*

Cockburn's 1963 Vintage Port $NA. Lighter in color than the other wines in the flight ('47 and '55) and slightly less impressive, with hints of tomato and herb sneaking in. It shows a decent amount of ripe fruit, but it's harder and more austere than either the '47 or '55, with a greater dependence on dried spices and cocoa in place of fruit. It's hard to tell whether this wine is in a closed phase or starting to slide. Drink or hold. **90** —*J.C. (3/1/2004)*

Cockburn's 1955 Vintage Port $NA. Slightly deeper and richer in color than the 1947, featuring rich cassis aromas, violets, and dried spices. It's wonderfully rich in the mouth—expansive and mouth-filling, yet not lacking at all for nuance or complexity. Tannins are resolved, but the wine is still sturdy and holding well. Drink now or, based on the strength of the '27, hold up to 20 more years. **96** —*J.C. (3/1/2004)*

Cockburn's 1947 Vintage Port $NA. "A small vintage," according to Côrte-Real, and one declared only by Cockburn's, Ferreira, Sandeman, and Warre. The color is a translucent ruby, with obvious bricking. The aromas and flavors are intoxicating: perfumed floral notes blend with red berries, chocolate and toffee, picking up some peppery, anise-tinged notes on the finish. This is a soft and approachable vintage Port, one that might be termed feminine or "sexy," in the words of Côrte-Real. Drink up. **93** —*J.C. (3/1/2004)*

Cockburn's 1935 Vintage Port $NA. Entirely amber colored, this has taken on many qualities of a fine old tawny, boasting aromas of toffee and citrus peel, flavors that include nuts and maple syrup. The fruit is tired, but the wine still shows beautiful tawny character. Drink up. **88** —*J.C. (3/1/2004)*

Cockburn's 1927 Vintage Port $NA. Served alongside the 1912 and the 1935, this was by far the darkest and reddest-colored of the flight. Rich berry aromas soar from the glass, graced by notes of toffee and coffee. The alcohol is well-integrated, almost hidden in the masses of rich, chocolaty fruit and supple, velvety mouthfeel. Shows great length on the finish, which picks up gorgeous hints of toffee and caramel. Absolutely delicious; it would be hard to say this is fading because it's so good right now. Drink or hold. **97** —*J.C. (3/1/2004)*

Cockburn's 1912 Vintage Port $NA. Côrte-Real brought six of the company's last 12 bottles to the U.S. for these tastings, making this vintage by far the scarcest of those tasted. It is translucent throughout, but still

shows some ruby color at its core, with amber at the rim. Slightly spirity on the nose, with delicate notes of dried cherries and leather. In the mouth, it's full-bodied, with pepper, nut, and toffee flavors. A bit hot on the long, mouth-coating finish, the tannins fully resolved. The fruit has almost faded away, yet the wine still seems vigorous. Drink up. **89** —*J.C. (3/1/2004)*

Cockburn's NV Fine Tawny Red Blend (Port) $12. Murky, earthy aromas make a mediocre first impression that's partly countered by raucous red berries and mellower caramel notes on the palate. **82** —*J.C. (11/15/2003)*

COMPANHIA DAS QUINTAS

Companhia das Quintas 2001 Quinta da Romeira Arinto (Bucelas) $NA. **87** —*R.V. (8/1/2004)*

Companhia das Quintas 2002 Tradição Tinto Castelão (Palmela) $10. Starts with pleasant notes of black cherries, leather, and a hint of game, but also features a slightly drying, stalky note that shortens the finish. Tasted twice, with consistent notes. **84** —*J.C. (6/1/2006)*

Companhia das Quintas 2000 Cado Portuguese Red (Douro) $14. With its well-integrated scents of cedar, plum, and tobacco, this is a medium-weight wine whose hallmark is its balance. Vanilla and dried spices meld nicely with cherry and plum fruit, finishing smooth, with modest tannins. Drink now-2008. **87** —*J.C. (3/1/2005)*

Companhia das Quintas 2004 Quinta da Romeira Prova Régia Portuguese White (Bucelas) $7. Great delicacy and intense flavors work together here. There are citrus and tropical fruits, with a touch of pineapple. Fresh and crisp. **88 Best Buy** —*R.V. (8/1/2005)*

Companhia das Quintas 2004 Quinta do Cardo Portuguese White (Beira Interior) $6. Grapefruit and other citrus dominates this cool, fresh wine. It's not delicate, but is packed with crisp, white fruits and green acidity. This is a great fish or seafood wine, in the style of a good Muscadet. **88 Best Buy** —*R.V. (8/1/2005)*

Companhia das Quintas 2004 Quinta do Cardo Síria Portuguese White (Beira Interior) $7. The Síria grape is crisp, green, and aromatic, which in this northern interior of Portugal makes a full-bodied, lightly toasty wine, with flavors of kiwis. The wine has great, refreshing acidity. **89 Best Buy** —*R.V. (8/1/2005)*

Companhia das Quintas 2000 Aristocrata Red Blend (Estremadura) $6. Earthy fruit on the nose. Barnyard flavors with some bitter, rustic fruits. A blend of Castelão and Tinta Miúda, it is traditional in style and very dry. **82** —*R.V. (12/31/2002)*

Companhia das Quintas 1999 Fronteira Red Blend (Douro) $NA. **87** —*R.V. (12/31/2002)*

Companhia das Quintas 1999 Fronteira Reserva Red Blend (Douro) $NA. **89** —*R.V. (12/31/2002)*

Companhia das Quintas 2000 Quinta do Cardo Red Blend (Beira Interior) $10. With its spicy wood aromas and sweet raisin fruit, this is a well-balanced wine. Attractive black fruit flavors, plus firm acidity, suggest this would be great with hearty stews. **85** —*R.V. (12/31/2002)*

Companhia das Quintas 2000 Tradicao Red Blend (Palmela) $6. "Tradition" is its name, and traditional is its style. This is an old-fashioned wine, with over-ripe fruit and soft tannins, plus spicy wood from aging in American oak. **85** —*R.V. (12/31/2002)*

Companhia das Quintas 2000 Tradicao Red Blend (Beira Interior) $6. **82** —*R.V. (12/31/2002)*

Companhia das Quintas 1999 Quinta do Cardo Touriga Nacional (Beira Interior) $14. This wine, from the Castelo Rodrigo subregion, is intensely rich, with aromas of sweet sultanas, dusty tannins, and layers of ripe figs and chocolate. This should age well over the next 10 years, but is ready to drink now. **88** —*R.V. (12/31/2002)*

Companhia das Quintas 1999 Quinta do Cardo Reserva Touriga Nacional Blend (Beira Interior) $11. A blend of Touriga Nacional, Touriga Francesa and Tinta Roriz, this is a solid, chunky wine, with firm, dry tannins and old wood tastes. Raisin flavors give it some sweetness, yet the wood leaves a dry aftertaste. **86** —*R.V. (12/31/2002)*

Companhia das Quintas 2001 Calhandriz White Blend (Estremadura) $NA. **82** —*R.V. (8/1/2004)*

PORTUGAL

Companhia das Quintas 2001 Quinta do Cardo White Blend (Beira Interior) $NA.81 —*R.V. (8/1/2004)*

COOPERATIVA AGRICOLA DE SANTO ISIDRO DE PEGOES

Cooperativa Agricola de Santo Isidro de Pegoes 2000 Fontanario de Pegoes Portuguese Red (Palmela) $NA. Although the spicy wood is dominant in this wine at this stage, it has great potential. Under that wood, there are fine, rich red fruits and good jelly flavors. Given three or four years, it should balance out.**88** —*R.V. (12/31/2002)*

Cooperativa Agricola de Santo Isidro de Pegoes 2000 Adega de Pegoes Colheita Seleccionada Touriga Nacional-Cabernet Sauvignon (Terras do Sado) $13. This big, ripe, dark, brooding wine has fine, concentrated fruit. Solid and chunky, the dryness is balanced with the huge fruits and powerful tannins. A blend of Touriga Nacional and Cabernet Sauvignon, with a limited production of 20,000 bottles.**90** —*R.V. (12/31/2002)*

Cooperativa Agricola de Santo Isidro de Pegoes 2001 Adega de Pegoes Colheita Seleccionada White Blend (Terras do Sado) $NA.90 —*R.V. (8/1/2004)*

Cooperativa Agricola de Santo Isidro de Pegoes 2001 Vale de Judia White Blend (Terras do Sado) $NA.89 —*R.V. (8/1/2004)*

CORTES DE CIMA

Cortes de Cima 2002 Portuguese Red (Alentejano) $18. The estate wine of Cortes de Cima is an all-encompassing blend of Aragonês, Syrah, Touriga Nacional, Trincadeira, and Cabernet Sauvignon. Somehow it all works, producing a wine that has depth of flavor and solid tannins, as well as intense juicy black flavors and fine finishing acidity. Drink after 3–5 years.**91** —*R.V. (3/1/2006)*

Cortes de Cima 2001 Portuguese Red (Alentejano) $18. A firm, tarry wine with ripe blackberry juicy fruits, layering fresh acidity and tannins. This has some wood flavors and fresh fruits. It is ready to drink now, but would repay cellaring for three to four years.**88** —*R.V. (12/1/2004)*

Cortes de Cima 2002 Chamine Portuguese Red (Alentejano) $12. Packed with ripe, juicy fruits, this is one of the fine range wines from Cortes de Cima. A blend of Aragonês and Syrah, it has fresh, black flavors and a lively tannic character. This wine would be great with barbecues.**86 Best Buy** —*R.V. (12/1/2004)*

Cortes de Cima 2004 Chaminé Portuguese Red (Alentejano) $11. A fresh, fruity, lightly earthy style of wine, which is packed with red berry flavors, soft tannins, and balancing acidity. This attractive wine is ready to drink now.**86 Best Buy** —*R.V. (3/1/2006)*

Cortes de Cima 2002 Incognito Portuguese Red (Alentejano) $NA. A smooth, rich wine, full of young berries and lively acidity. There are tannins but they are covered with the ripe, jammy fruits which are so full and delicious.**88** —*R.V. (12/1/2004)*

Cortes de Cima 2003 Incógnito Portuguese Red (Alentejano) $45. This is the young vines cuvée from Cortes de Cima, fruity and juicy, with great dark color, smooth, ripe tannins, and big, open fruit flavors. The aftertaste is hot, from the high (14.5%) alcohol and the jammy berry flavors. **87** —*R.V. (3/1/2006)*

Cortes de Cima 2001 Reserva Portuguese Red (Alentejano) $NA. This is a beautifully crafted wine, full of sweet tannins, spice flavors and dark perfumes. A blend of Syrah and Aragonês, it shows elegance and power. The wood flavors from the French and American wood aging are kept restrained and in the background to the intense fruit and herbs.**92 Editors' Choice** —*R.V. (12/1/2004)*

Cortes de Cima 2001 Red Blend (Alentejo) $21. Jammy blackberries blend with vanilla-scented oak in this rather New World-styled wine. It's supple and fully ripe, with smooth tannins and very berry fruit. Might pass for a Zin in a blind tasting. Drink now–2008.**89** —*J.C. (3/1/2004)*

Cortes de Cima 2000 Red Blend (Alentejano) $20. This is an immediately attractive wine, with a bright purple hue and juicy, raisiny fruit. There are spicy wood flavors and ripe, bright fruit. A blend of Aragonês and Syrah, it is a softly tannic but also rich wine with great forward fruit.**87** —*R.V. (12/31/2002)*

Cortes de Cima 2000 Chamine Red Blend (Alentejo) $12. This blend of Aragonês and Trincadeira boasts hints of smoke, herbs, pepper, and meat

on the nose, along with plenty of cherry-scented fruit. Although it sounds like a cacophony, the reality is harmonious and smooth, finishing with a twist of peppery spice. Drink now.**87 Best Buy** —*J.C. (1/1/2004)*

Cortes de Cima 2000 Chamine Red Blend (Alentejano) $11. The current-drinking wine from Cortes de Cima has spicy aromas and black currant and tar flavors. It's big, but has streaks of acidity and lots of elegant red berries.**86 Best Buy** —*R.V. (12/31/2002)*

Cortes de Cima 2000 Incognito Red Blend (Alentejano) $33. This is a big, rich fruity wine made from young vines, with ripe, juicy black fruit. Polished touches of wood and lovely berries along with a soft, juicy mouthfeel, make this immensely drinkable.**88** —*R.V. (12/31/2002)*

Cortes de Cima 1998 Reserva Red Blend (Alentejano) $45. This is the star wine from Cortes de Cima, owned by Dane Hans Jorgenson and his California wife Carrie. It boasts aromas of dark, mature tarry fruits on the nose and a palate of big, sweet fruit, with layers of wood and sweet black currant jelly, balanced with ripe but firm tannins that give a great sense of structure and purpose. The fruit (which includes Cabernet Sauvignon in the blend) makes it drinkable now, but it will age well.**91** —*R.V. (12/31/2002)*

Cortes de Cima 2001 Incógnito Syrah (Alentejo) $37. This cleverly packaged Syrah (check the back label) tastes more like an Aussie Shiraz than a Northern Rhône, but given Alentejo's climate, that's to be expected. Vanilla-laced oak frames big blackberry flavors that finish with a slight sensation of sweetness. It's a mouth-filling, fruity wine that doesn't lack for flavor.**88** —*J.C. (1/1/2004)*

Cortes de Cima 2003 Touriga Nacional (Alentejano) $43. Portugal's icon grape has only recently made it out of northern Portugal, but it obviously thrives in the Alentejo. This 100% Touriga Nacional has elegance, fine acidity, ripe juicy black fruits, and layers of dry, but soft tannins. With its wood flavors, this is a wine for aging over 5 years.**90** —*R.V. (3/1/2006)*

Cortes de Cima 2002 Touriga Nacional (Alentejano) $NA. A 100% Touriga Nacional from the Cortes de Cima vineyard, this wine exhibits a very spicy character, packed with berry fruits and sweetness. This is a wine that is ready to drink now, with soft tannins.**85** —*R.V. (12/1/2004)*

COSSART GORDON

Cossart Gordon NV 15 year Medium Rich Bual (Madeira) $34/500ml. Surprisingly light in body, a result of this wine's elegantly wrought balance between acid and sugar. The aromas are fresh, almost briny, while the flavors marry honey and dried apricots without intense sweetness. Long on the finish, where it folds in nutty notes.**88** —*J.C. (11/1/2006)*

Cossart Gordon 1990 Colheita Medium Rich500ml. Bual (Madeira) $32/500ml. Incredibly nutty on the nose, with hints of citrus and caramel. On the palate, lemon and orange flavors take off, although hints of honey-roasted nuts continue in the background. This is a fresh, mostly dry-seeming Madeira with a long, intense finish.**90** —*J.C. (11/1/2006)*

Cossart Gordon NV 5 year Malmsey (Madeira) $21. Don't let the medium fool you—that's how this is supposed to look. Malmsey is the sweetest of the Madeiras, and this one is intensely sweet, yet also lemony-tart at the same time, with flavors of black walnuts, molasses, and coffee.**90 Editors' Choice** —*J.C. (11/1/2006)*

Cossart Gordon NV Rainwater Medium Dry Tinta Negra Mole (Madeira) $15. This pale amber Madeira is lightly sweet, with nutty, slightly oxidized aromas that stay fresh and briny. Nuts and candied lemon flavors join coffee and caramel flavors on the finish, along with racy acidity. Worth trying with soup as a start to the evening.**85** —*J.C. (11/1/2006)*

CROFT

Croft NV 10-Year Old Tawny Port $30. Great ripe fruits dominate this young, fresh wine. There is balancing sweetness and delicate, lightly burnt acidity. Now under the same management as Taylor and Fonseca, Croft is a name that should be as well known for Port as for Sherry.**89** —*R.V. (8/1/2006)*

Croft NV 20-Year Old Tawny Port $53. Very burnt and harsh, with spirit dominating, this is a sad showing for such a famous name.**82** —*R.V. (8/1/2006)*

Croft NV Distinction Special Reserve Port $17. Now under the same ownership as Taylor and Ferreira, Croft Ports have taken on a new lease of life. This is a classic Port from a classic name, with its ripe fruit and structure. It has flavors of dried raisins, figs, and dark chocolate, along with firm, dusty tannins and a dry aftertaste. **88** —*R.V. (3/1/2005)*

Croft 1997 LBV Bottled 2002 Port $19. Aromas of wild berry fruits immediately make this wine attractive. To taste, there are raisins and dried fruits along with light-weight soft fruits. The tannins come through to finish, leaving a pleasantly dry aftertaste. **87** —*R.V. (3/1/2003)*

Croft 1983 Quinta da Roeda Port $56. This oldie isn't much of a goodie, and it goes to prove that holding wine beyond its time is a mistake. The aromas are strong and not very nice. The sweet, one-dimensional palate is still lively and relatively clean, but it lacks anything special. It may or may not have been better years ago. **82** —*M.S. (11/15/2002)*

Croft 2003 Vintage Port $72. A soft, floral style of wine, with attractive sweetness. Its tannins are subdued by the sweet fruit. **85** —*R.V. (11/15/2005)*

DÃO SUL

Dão Sul 2004 Berco do Infante Portuguese Red (Estremadura) $6. A blend of Aragonês and Castelão from the vineyards of Quinta do Gradil, and made by the star winemaking team at Dão Sul. This is a ripe, red-fruited wine, but at this early stage it is dominated by considerable acidity and dry tannins. Give this wine at least five years, and then it will all come together. **88 Best Buy** —*R.V. (3/1/2006)*

Dão Sul 2003 Monte de Cal Reserva Portuguese Red (Alentejano) $15. An extravagantly fruity wine that has delicious ripe flavors. This blend of Trincadeira, Syrah, and Alicante Bouschet comes together in a harmonious, full-flavored whole. No wood was used in maturation, and with such great black fruits, none was needed. **89** —*R.V. (3/1/2006)*

Dão Sul 2002 Quinta das Tecedeiras Reserva Portuguese Red (Douro) $20. Produced in conjunction with Dão Sul, this Douro wine is rich and finely balanced. It has all the power of a top Douro wine, with immediate accessibility. There are lovely ripe black fruits, flavors of herbs, and rich, soft tannins. Drink over the next 5 years. **89** —*R.V. (11/1/2004)*

Dão Sul 2002 Quinta de Cabriz Colheita Seleccionada Portuguese Red (Dão) $7. A delicious, very drinkable wine from a light year. The tannins are soft, the fruit is forward, fresh, and balanced with acidity. This is an immediate wine, great for fatty foods, and a pleasure to drink now. **87 Best Buy** —*R.V. (11/1/2004)*

Dão Sul 2000 Quinta de Cabriz Reserva Portuguese Red (Dão) $14. Sweet, ripe fruit with supporting acidity go with the dark, brooding tannins in this wine. It is rich, almost opulent, and packed with ripe, generous fruit. From the ripe 2000 vintage, this shows great potential. Give it at least 5 years before drinking. **91 Best Buy** —*R.V. (11/1/2004)*

Dão Sul 2001 Quinta do Encontro Portuguese Red (Bairrada) $7. Produced by Dão Sul, this wine is a blend Baga, Touriga Nacional and Tinta Roriz. With its savory berry fruits and chewy tannins, it is rich, powerful, and well-balanced. There's great black fruit there, powering through the dry tannins. Ready to drink, it will age well over 5 years. **89 Best Buy** —*R.V. (11/1/2004)*

Dao Sul 2003 Quinta do Gradil Portuguese Red (Estremadura) $6. This estate on the outskirts of Lisbon has a 17th-century castle as well as 240 acres of vines. This is a serious blend of Touriga Nacional, Syrah, and Alicante Bouschet with great, dark tannins, as well as flavors of red plums. It is still young—give it 4 or 5 years, but it will age well. **90 Best Buy** —*R.V. (3/1/2006)*

Dao Sul 2000 Quinta da Cabriz Colheita Seleccionada Red Blend (Dão) $6. The immense, amazingly heavy bottle somehow goes with this big, dense wine. Concentrated, black currant fruit and powerful tannins. Dark cherries and a hint of herbs complete the balance. **89 Best Buy** —*R.V. (12/31/2002)*

Dao Sul 1999 Quinta de Cabriz/Alfrocheiro Preto Red Blend (Dão) $16. The local Alfrocheiro grape, when ripe like this, yields broad sweeps of ripe black, tarry fruit. This wine is big, fat, and stately. It will offer a great time if you drink it now, but it will certainly age well over the next 5–10 years. **91** —*R.V. (12/31/2002)*

Dão Sul 2000 Quinta de Cabriz Touriga Nacional (Dão) $19. Dão Sul wines are produced by a star-studded team of Portuguese winemakers, including Virgilio Loureiro, professor of enology at Lisbon University. They have produced a series of classics from the granite landscape of Dão. This wine has deep purple color and aromas of black dusty fruit. There are big tannins, but also opulent, sweet fruit with black currant and cherry flavors. Spices and herbs complete the mix, along with the essential acidity. **91** —*R.V. (12/31/2002)*

DELAFORCE

Delaforce NV 20-Year Old Tawny Port $35. More in the elegant style, this Delaforce wine shows plenty of ripe flavors, but then restrains them. It is very pure, a delightful wine that is very drinkable. **89** —*R.V. (8/1/2006)*

Delaforce 1997 Curious & Ancient 20 Yrs. Old Port $46. The soft, honeyed nose is entirely inviting, hinting at the refinement this wine carries from start to finish. Though not a heavyweight, there's a goodly amount of apricot and quince mixed with toffee and crème brûlée. Scrumptious, racy, and recommended for those who like good Port. **91** —*M.S. (7/1/2002)*

Delaforce NV His Eminence's Choice 10-Year Old Tawny Port $23. Very soft, but with good concentration, this bitter orange flavored wine has ripeness, but also acidity, finishing with some bitter chocolate flavors. Attractively balanced. **88** —*R.V. (8/1/2006)*

Delaforce 1992 LBV Port $19. Most LBVs are more in-your-face than this, but so what? It's clean, reserved, and generally quite good. A little metallic tinge and a tad of heat can be caught on the otherwise nice and multifaceted finish. Definitely interesting for a 10-year-old LBV. **87** —*M.S. (11/15/2002)*

Delaforce 1996 LBV Bottled 2002 Port $17. Delaforce has produced a dry style of LBV, with a light, elegant touch and freshness. Raisins, firm tannins and berry fruits all give the wine poise. **86 Editors' Choice** —*R.V. (3/1/2003)*

Delaforce 2003 Vintage Port $58. Now under the same ownership as Taylor Fladgate and Fonseca, this is the best Delaforce vintage Port in many years. It is a big, ripe, full-flavored Port with bitter chocolate and solid black fruit flavors. The dry finish suggests good aging potential. **89** —*R.V. (11/15/2005)*

DFJ VINHOS

DFJ Vinhos 2004 Grand'Arte Alicante Bouschet (Estremadura) $15. Dark in color, with full-bodied black fruit flavors and a savory minty character, this wine is solid, with dry tannins and some spiciness. The aftertaste is dry, with considerable acidity. Give this at least a year's aging. **89** —*R.V. (3/1/2006)*

DFJ Vinhos DFJ Vinhos 2000 Grand Arte Alicante Bouschet (Estremadura) $20. In France, Alicante Bouchet is frowned upon for its poor quality. In Portugal, it is capable of making some of the country's finest wines. This is typical, with its sweet, jelly-like aromas and ripe, dense fruit. There's an evocative, herby, Mediterranean sunshine feel to it. **91** —*R.V. (12/31/2002)*

DFJ Vinhos 2000 DJF Cabernet Blend (Estremadura) $9. The local grape, Tinta Miúda, combines well with classic Cabernet Sauvignon to give a wine that has sweet black currant aromas and dense, dark fruit with elegance as well as ripe tannins. **90 Best Buy** —*R.V. (12/31/2002)*

DFJ Vinhos 2000 Grand Arte Cabernet Sauvignon (Estremadura) $20. The Cabernet on its own doesn't succeed as well as it does in the blend with Tinta Miúda. Although there are juicy black currant aromas, the fruit is slightly green, with herbs and dry tannins. At this stage, wood tannins come through and dominate. Given time, it could develop. **88** —*R.V. (12/31/2002)*

DFJ Vinhos 1999 Grand Arte Caladoc (Estremadura) $20. The Caladoc is a curious cross between Grenache and Malbec, developed in the Rhône to lessen the likelihood of uneven flowering in the Grenache. The wine has sweet, jelly-like aromas. The palate is soft, juicy with sweet acidity, soft, light tannins and an almost piercing fruitiness. **86** —*R.V. (12/31/2002)*

DFJ Vinhos 2004 Grand'Arte Caladoc (Estremadura) $15. The Caladoc grape is quite a rarity. A cross between Grenache and Malbec, it was developed for aroma and color. As a stand alone, it makes a spicy style of wine, with high tannin content, but also some juicy red fruits. It's intriguing, but in the end seems to lack a lot of depth. **86** —*R.V. (3/1/2006)*

DFJ Vinhos 2004 Grand'Arte Merlot (Estremadura) $15. A soft, gentle wine with some vanilla character along with some spiciness and blackberry jelly flavors. Dried fruits and acidity complete the finish. **85** —*R.V. (3/1/2006)*

DFJ Vinhos 2003 Consensus Portuguese Red (Ribatejo) $35. A huge, deep-colored wine, with intense, juicy fruit flavors and a layer of dry tannin. Touriga Nacional, Trincadeira, and Alicante Bouschet are blended, with the Touriga showing dominance, giving a serious, solid structure, black fruits, and dusty texture. Very ripe, this still has aging potential. **90** —*R.V. (3/1/2006)*

DFJ Vinhos 2003 Francos Portuguese Red (Alenquer) $35. This wine from the Alenquer DOC in the coastal Estremadura region is soft, smooth, and generous. With its ripe damson fruits and light acidity, balanced with some dusty tannins, it is ready to drink. A great, warm wine that is designed to go with hearty winter meals. **88** —*R.V. (3/1/2006)*

DFJ Vinhos 2000 Red Blend (Estremadura) $10. Rich tobacco and wood aromas follow through on the palate to sweet, dark berries and ripe tannins. This is a finely structured wine, with acidity balancing the firm fruit and flavors of sweet fruitcake. **91 Best Buy** —*R.V. (12/31/2002)*

DFJ Vinhos 2000 Grand Arte Touriga Franca (Estremadura) $20. Super-ripe fruit is the hallmark of this wine. The aromas are sweet, juicy, almost Porty; the palate is huge, with rich fruit flavors and great power. **88** —*R.V. (12/31/2002)*

DFJ Vinhos 2004 Grand'Arte Touriga Franca (Estremadura) $15. One of the major Douro grapes, Touriga Franca was formerly known as Touriga Francesa until the French objected. Further south in the relatively cool conditions of Estremadura it makes this very perfumed wine, with a slight green character. It leaves very firm, dry tannins in the mouth. Would benefit from a year's aging. **88** —*R.V. (3/1/2006)*

DFJ Vinhos 2000 Grand Arte Touriga Nacional (Estremadura) $30. DFJ is a combination of the initials of the two owners—Dino Ventura and Fausto Ferraz—and those of winemaker José Neiva. The Grand'Arte range consists of single-varietal wines grown in the company's 148-acre vineyard. This wine, with its aromas of pepper and herbs, and its powerful black cherry flavors and vanilla layers, is stunning. **92** —*R.V. (12/31/2002)*

DFJ Vinhos 2003 Grand'Arte Touriga Nacional (Estremadura) $15. This powerful, dry wine shows all the density and structure of the Douro's most famous grape variety. Offers solid black fruit, followed through by intense acidity, and a satisfying black currant fruit taste. This is certainly the most impressive wine in this Grand'Arte range. **90 Best Buy** —*R.V. (3/1/2006)*

DFJ Vinhos 2000 DFJ Touriga Nacional Blend (Estremadura) $23. Another fine wine from the DFJ stable, blending the two top Douro grape varieties. The aromas of sweet, juicy fruit on the nose are complemented by firm, dry tannins and rich, concentrated fruit. It's big but never clumsy. **90** —*R.V. (12/31/2002)*

DFJ Vinhos 2000 Grand Arte Trincadeira (Ribatejano) $20. The wine has firm, ripe sweet fruit with some good red fruit flavors. It is juicy, but there is also some barnyard earthiness, typical of Trincadeira on its own. **85** —*R.V. (12/31/2002)*

DFJ Vinhos 2003 Grand' Arte Trincadeira (Ribatejano) $15. Trincadeira (a k a Tinta Amarela in the Douro) produces great spicy, juicy wines in central Portugal. This is fresh, with soft tannins and easy, ripe fruit; it can put many New World wines to shame. Drink and enjoy. **87** —*R.V. (3/1/2006)*

DOMINGOS ALVES DE SOUSA

Domingos Alves de Sousa 2003 Quinta da Gaivosa Vintage Port $42. A rare vintage Port from a producer, normally known for table wines, in the Baixo Corgo region (the most westerly Port area). This is a success, a rich Port with plenty of sweet fruit, flavors of black currants, and sweet tannins. At this stage though, the spirit is still not fully integrated. **89** —*R.V. (11/15/2005)*

DONA MARIA

Dona Maria 2003 Reserva Red Blend (Alentejano) $39. This ambitious wine from the south of Portugal blends Alicante Bouschet, Aragonês, Syrah, and Cabernet Sauvignon, then covers much of the nuance with a veil of charred oak. Tarry, meaty, cedary notes on the nose; some cola, coffee, and beet flavors. Woody on the finish. Hold 2–3 years and hope the impact of the wood lessens over time. **86** —*J.C. (11/1/2006)*

DONA MARIA ANTONIA FERREIRA

Dona Maria Antonia Ferreira 2000 Vallado Red Blend (Douro) $22. From estates still owned by the Ferreira family, this wine is dark black in color. It is a huge, juicy wine, with ripe fruit and a young, almost Porty character. The sweet, jammy fruit needs time to settle. **86** —*R.V. (12/31/2002)*

DOW'S

Dow's NV 10-Year Old Tawny Port $29. A wine that is in the fresh, sweet style of 10-year-old, while balancing chocolate, cocoa, and dark fig flavors. A firm structure keeps this profusion of flavors in order. **90** —*R.V. (8/1/2006)*

Dow's NV 20-Year Old Tawny Port $50. A fresh, delicate wine. It has a fine array of orange flavors and a light touch of acidity and caramel. **89** —*R.V. (8/1/2006)*

Dow's NV 30-Year Old Tawny Port $98. A superbly dense, concentrated wine so rich in flavor that it almost has a brooding, dark quality. The hint of medicinal character just gives all this intensity a lift, and goes with flavors of roasted nuts and licorice. The aftertaste has just the right acidity. **94 Editors' Choice** —*R.V. (8/1/2006)*

Dow's NV 40-Year Old Tawny Port $148. A dark, concentrated wine, very impressive. But with all this concentration, there is also sweet fruit, flavors of apricots that have been bottled in spirits. This is a lovely wine, with just a hint of mature, medicinal character. **93** —*R.V. (8/1/2006)*

Dow's 1992 Colheita Port $30. Caramelly and sweet, without the usual complexity or elegance that are Dow's hallmarks. Smoother and silkier than run-of-the-mill tawnies, but a disappointing effort given the house's fine track record. **84** —*J.C. (12/1/2004)*

Dow's NV Crusted Porto, Bottled 1998 Port $23. This is meant to provide a touch of vintage Port character at a reasonable price, and it does—albeit in a light-weight and slightly spirity form. Cinnamon and prune flavors finish in a burst of heat. **84** —*J.C. (11/15/2003)*

Dow's 2000 LBV Port $20. With its gorgeous scents of spice cake and dates, this is a seductive LBV from the very start. It's ripe and round in the mouth, soft and lush on the finish, with a cavalcade of fig, date, chocolate and dried spice flavors. Drink now. **89** —*J.C. (6/1/2006)*

Dow's 1998 LBV Port $19. Shows good complexity for an LBV, with aromas of smoke, herb, and black cherries. Tobacco, dark chocolate, and tea notes emerge on the palate, which is drier than most LBVs and in keeping with the house style. **85** —*J.C. (12/1/2004)*

Dow's 1996 LBV Bottled 2002 Port $20. While this is typical of the Dow's style, with its dryness and structure, it also has great elegance. That dryness is balanced with the fine, ripe dark berry fruit flavors and by the fresh acidity that tops it off. **90** —*R.V. (3/1/2003)*

Dow's 1997 LBV Port $18. You get a glimpse of the fine qualities of the 1997 vintage in this bottling, which displays lush black cherry and plum aromas and flavors against a backdrop of supple tannins and a velvety texture. The elements are well-integrated, and the finish is long and fruity. **89 Editors' Choice** —*J.C. (11/15/2003)*

Dow's 1986 Quinta Do Bomfim Vintage Port $36. While some houses now release their single-quinta wines just two years after the harvest, others hold them until they are deemed mature. This recent release from Dow's is a boon to vintage Port lovers who lack adequate cellaring facilities, or to restaurateurs who don't want to hit the auction circuit. Prunes and plums combine with tea and spice notes in this fully mature wine, with subtle hints of maple sugar and anise coming up on the finish. **88** —*J.C. (12/1/2004)*

PORTUGAL

Dow's 2001 Senhora da Ribeira Vintage Port $50. This dense wine is packed with fruit. The blackberry and anise aromas give an impression of the wine's impressive size that is confirmed on the palate. This seems sweeter than most vintages of Dow's flagship wine, but the extra sugar is balanced by big tannins. This is one single-quinta Port that doesn't seem destined for early drinking. Try in 2015. **92** —*J.C. (11/15/2003)*

Dow's NV Trademark Finest Reserve Port $17. A disappointing wine from such a distinguished name, spoiled by greenness, and lacking richness or depth. It certainly tastes young, so it could develop but in weight it feels almost like a table wine, not a Port. **83** —*R.V. (3/1/2005)*

Dow's 2003 Vintage Port $80. A dark, dense wine, packed with dry fruits and firm tannins. There are coffee and bitter cherry flavors. All these elements come together to produce a dry but fruity style of wine, which, like all Dow wines, is sure to age well. **93** —*R.V. (11/15/2005)*

Dow's 2004 Vale do Bomfim Reserva Portuguese Red (Douro) $12. This is a bold, exuberantly fruity blend of 40% Touriga Franca, 40% Tinta Roriz, and 20% Tinta Barroca. Mulberry and boysenberry flavors pick up hints of baked pie crust. A bit drying on the finish, but it also shows good depth of fruit. A new wine, with no track record for aging, so drink now and over the next few years. **88 Best Buy** —*J.C. (6/1/2006)*

DUAS QUINTAS

Duas Quintas 1996 Vinho Tinto Portuguese Red (Douro) $11. 85 *(11/15/1999)*

ENCOSTAS DO DOURO

Encostas do Douro 2001 Vinha Palestra Portuguese Red (Douro) $NA. A light, fresh, perfumed wine that has good, dry tannins along with bright red fruits. This is ripe, easy drinking and ready to go now. **84** —*R.V. (11/1/2004)*

ERMELINDA FREITAS

Ermelinda Freitas 2003 Dona Ermelinda Red Blend (Palmela) $7. Slightly stewed or baked, but there's enough plum and herb complexity to keep it interesting. Soft and low in acid; supple and easy to drink over the next few months. **84 Best Buy** —*J.C. (6/1/2006)*

Ermelinda Freitas 2000 Dona Ermelinda Red Blend (Palmela) $7. A lean, focused wine, with delicate aromas and flavors of strawberries and cream. Vanilla and chocolate notes add interest to the short finish. **84** —*J.C. (11/15/2003)*

EVEL

Evel 2002 Red Portuguese Red (Douro) $9. The understated fruit in this light, lean wine has a character reminiscent of tart berries and sour cherries, framed by balsa wood. Turns lemony and dry on the finish. The crisp acids make it best with fatty meat dishes. **83** —*J.C. (6/1/2006)*

Evel 2004 White Portuguese White (Douro) $9. Smells of honey, nectarine, and apricot. Medium- to full-bodied, with ripe melon flavors and a finish that's seemingly off-dry, spicy, and long. With its apparent sweetness, it might work well with Asian dishes. **86 Best Buy** —*J.C. (12/31/2005)*

Evel 2001 Vinho Tinto Red Blend (Douro) $10. This fruity, easy-to-drink wine seems made for burgers on the grill. The juicy red berry core is dressed up with notes of bitter chocolate, yet stays fresh and quaffable. **86 Best Buy** —*J.C. (3/1/2004)*

Evel 2002 Vinho Branco White Blend (Douro) $NA. A blend of four indigenous Douro grape varieties, this wine blends pineapple and lychee aromas and flavors in medium-weight package. Picks up hints of wet stones as well, adding a welcome layer of minerality, but finishes slightly bitter, with a note of citrus pith. **85** —*J.C. (1/1/2004)*

FALDAS DA SERRA

Faldas da Serra 2000 Quinta das Maias Red Blend (Dão) $13. The palate of this wine is fresh and fruity, with juicy flavors and generous, forward fruit. It is an easy style of wine that would be great with barbecued meat. **85** —*R.V. (12/31/2002)*

Faldas da Serra 2000 Quinta das Maias Jaen Red Blend (Dão) $22. The 73-acre Quinta das Maias, under the same ownership as Quinta dos Roques, is located on the slopes of Portugal's highest mountain range, the Serra da Estrela. The Jaen vines planted there have produced a densely fruity wine, dark purple in color, with rich, black, juicy fruit. Flavors of cranberries and dry tannins come along with firm wood, but dominating it all is richness. **91** —*R.V. (12/31/2002)*

Faldas da Serra 2001 Quinta das Maias Verdelho (Dão) $14. 88 —*R.V. (8/1/2004)*

Faldas da Serra 2001 Quinta das Maias Malvasia Fina (Dão) $14. 88 —*R.V. (8/1/2004)*

FALUA

Falua 1999 Duas Castas Portuguese Red (Ribatejo) $9. Light in weight and evenly textured, this dry, flavorful red is a fine choice for everyday drinking. The cherry, herb, and tree bark bouquet opens to a dry, just slightly puckery mouth of spice-accented light berry flavors. Finishes clean and dry, with moderate length. **85** *(12/31/2001)*

FEIST

Feist NV 10 Years Old Port $19. 89 Best Buy *(3/1/2000)*

Feist NV 10-Year Old Tawny Port $23. This has a burnt, dry style, with high acidity. It tastes more mature than a 10-year-old. **82** —*R.V. (8/1/2006)*

Feist NV 20-Year Old Tawny Port $49. The burnt character is too dominant in this wine, and it smothers any fruit there is. Just a touch dry as well. **81** —*R.V. (8/1/2006)*

Feist NV 30-Year Old Tawny Port $98. An impressively concentrated wine from this firm owned by Barros. There's a dark toffee flavor that runs parallel to fine acidity throughout. The aftertaste is fresh, but still full of concentration. **90** —*R.V. (8/1/2006)*

Feist NV 40-Year Old Tawny Port $150. Dry, with some burnt character, this 40-year old from one of the companies owned by Barros also has great sweet fruit, lime marmalade and layers of acidity. It's well in balance, leaving acidity to finish. **89** —*R.V. (8/1/2006)*

Feist 1997 LBV Bottled 2002 Port $18. Feist is now a brand owned by Barros Almeida, but it has a history dating back to 1836. This LBV is immediately attractive, with perfumed aromas, and flavors of raisins and sweet fruits. It is not a wine for aging, with few tannins, but it makes a very pleasant drink. **85** —*R.V. (3/1/2003)*

Feist 2003 Vintage Port $NA. Part of the large Barros Almeida group, Feist is one of those names that has an illustrious history in Port. This 2003 is a fine, ripe wine with plenty of rich, dark fruit flavors. There is a pronounced dry character as well, which promises well for the future. **90** —*R.V. (11/15/2005)*

Feist NV Vintage Character Port $NA. This is a dry style of wine, with a touch of cistus aroma and lean acidity. There are good tannins, some fresh black fruits, but it needs more intensity to really show up the herbal flavors. One of the many brand names of the Barros group, Feist has a history dating back to the 1830s. **84** —*R.V. (3/1/2005)*

FERREIRA

Ferreira NV 10-Year Old Tawny Port $NA. A sadly unbalanced wine from a company that has a name for tawny Ports. With its sweetness, marred by a touch of reduction (too long in old barrels?), it has a curious sweet/sour aftertaste. **84** —*R.V. (8/1/2006)*

Ferreira NV Dona Antonia Personal Reserve Port $22. The color is a cross between violet and brick red. The nose is muddled, bordering on dull. The palate feel is on the heavy side. It seems a bit clumsy and chunky. The nutty, warm finish helps, but overall it lacks sophistication and its parts aren't in full unity. **83** —*M.S. (7/1/2002)*

Ferreira NV Duque de Bragança 20-Year Old Tawny Port $70. Always one of the best 20-year-olds, and this is no exception. The secret is in the velvet-like smoothness, which combines with a balanced mix of fig and caramel flavors, just a touch of burnt vanilla, and the sort of acidity that makes you want another glass. Delicious. **94 Editors' Choice** —*R.V. (8/1/2006)*

Ferreira 1997 LBV Bottled 2001 Port (Douro) $34. A very soft, sweet, easy style of wine, with raisins and forward, mature fruit flavors. Produced by a firm whose Port reputation lies in its aged tawny Ports, this is almost like a young, fruity tawny in style. **86** —*R.V. (3/1/2003)*

Ferreira NV Tawny Port $14. Bright, intense, and attractive, with quite a bit of red color to it. It's overtly sweet, yet entirely pleasant, with lively fruit and solid edges. For an everyday classic tawny that's neither complex nor simple and dull, this is it. Lots of toffee-like nuttiness graces the tail end. **86** —*M.S. (7/1/2002)*

Ferreira 1994 Traditional LBV Port $20. When a wine is as dense, plummy, and pretty as this, you're in business. It's somewhat round and fat, but it's rightly balanced by driving cherry fruit and bitter chocolate. An LBV rich enough to top off vanilla ice cream yet vital enough to be drunk by the glass is a good thing to have in the house. **89** —*M.S. (11/15/2002)*

Ferreira 2003 Vintage Port $78. Caramel aromas give a strange, unbalanced nature to this wine. It is soft, with ripe, but unfocused fruit. **82** —*R.V. (11/15/2005)*

FONSECA

Fonseca NV 10-Year Old Tawny Port $30. A hugely rich, sweet wine, full of concentration and very ripe fruit flavors. This is the classic Fonseca style, all richness and depth of flavor. There's power here, but it is all clothed in acidity and great fruits. **90** —*R.V. (8/1/2006)*

Fonseca NV 20-Year Old Tawny Port $50. This is a sweet, dense wine, balancing lively dried fruit flavors against intense coffee and treacle. It has great style, a powerful wine that manages to present a softer side. **91** —*R.V. (8/1/2006)*

Fonseca NV 40-Year Old Tawny Port $157. A very sweet rich wine, in the Fonseca house style. But it lacks the intensity, going more for sweet almonds, along with some bitter marmalade, and a young taste. **88** —*R.V. (8/1/2006)*

Fonseca NV Bin 27 Port $20. One of the big brands in Reserve Ports, Bin 27 is long and well-established. So it's good to report that it is great wine, with sweetness and balancing acidity and fruit. Soft and juicy, it is ready to drink, but there are structure and flavors of dried raisins to give it some aging potential. **88** —*R.V. (3/1/2005)*

Fonseca 1984 Guimaraens Port $44. Still muscular and just now beginning to turn older, this is a tasty, stylish aged wine with a dominant cherry cough drop flavor that flows seamlessly onto a long, smooth, classy finish. Not fully mature, but entirely drinkable. **90** —*M.S. (11/15/2002)*

Fonseca 2000 LBV Port $25. Plummy on the nose, with the ripe aromas accented by hints of dried flowers. In the mouth, the texture is rich—almost syrupy—and the flavors head toward prune and chocolate fudge, finishing on drier, more complex notes of cocoa powder and spice. **90 Editors' Choice** —*J.C. (6/1/2006)*

Fonseca 1996 Port $21. A rich, sweet wine, this is typical of the wonderfully powerful Fonseca style. The fruit is enormous and black, with sweet chocolate and ripe tannins. Drink it now, but it could age over five years or more. **91 Editors' Choice** —*R.V. (3/1/2003)*

Fonseca 2001 Quinta Do Panascal Vintage Port $50. A strong candidate for Port of the vintage, Fonseca's 2001 Quinta do Panascal boasts a nose filled with rich, dense, brooding fruit. Blackberries and plums rush the palate; it's lush and fruity, yet given shape by some dusty tannins. Turns chocolaty on the finish. Likely to be an early-maturing vintage; drink 2010–2020, possibly beyond. **91 Cellar Selection** —*J.C. (12/1/2004)*

Fonseca 2003 Vintage Port $92. Fonseca vintage Ports are always among the most attractive and long-lived. This 2003 conforms magnificently to that model. It is structured, rich, powerful, and opulent. There are cassis and black fig flavors, as well as sweet tannins. It is delicious already, and will remain delicious throughout its long life. **97** —*R.V. (11/15/2005)*

FRANCISCO NUNES GARCIA

Francisco Nunes Garcia 1999 Colheita Seleccionada Aragonês (Alentejo) $45. Clearly made with lofty aims, this wine displays great intensity. The aromas of fresh-sawn wood and vanilla are nearly overpowering, while the fruit is concentrated and plummy, with a large dose of tannins that

dry out the finish. Give it a few years to settle down and it will be more approachable and hopefully more complex as well. **87** —*J.C. (3/1/2004)*

FUNDAÇÃO EUGENIO ALMEIDA

Fundação Eugenio Almeida 1994 Pera-Manca Portuguese Red (Alentejo) $60. 91 *(10/1/1999)*

GLORIA

Gloria 2002 Tinto Portuguese Red (Douro) $16. This medium-bodied blend of Tinta Roriz, Touriga Nacional, and Touriga Franca boasts plenty of plump, juicy fruit backed by hints of cocoa and spice. The ripe cherry flavors are easy to enjoy, finishing on a fresh, mouth-watering note. Would be a great choice with grilled meats. **88** —*J.C. (6/1/2006)*

GOULD CAMPBELL

Gould Campbell NV 10-Year Old Tawny Port $24. An attractively dry style of wine, with a concentrated inner core of firm acid and lightly burnt flavors. It has intensity, along with good fruitiness. This lesser brand of the Symington group is worth seeking out, both for its quality and for its good value. **90 Editors' Choice** —*R.V. (8/1/2006)*

Gould Campbell 1996 LBV Bottled 2002 Port $20. Gould Campbell, one of the smaller Port houses owned by the Symington family, is often underrated. But it shouldn't be, as this LBV shows. With its big, sweet, ripe fruit character, flavors of dried sultanas, and dark chocolate and its structured tannins, it has all the right ingredients for a classic Port. **91** —*R.V. (3/1/2003)*

Gould Campbell 2003 Vintage Port $50. This may be one of the "lesser" Symington brands, but this Port shows very well. It is a beautifully perfumed wine, fragrant with ripe fruit. Balanced, with dusty tannins, there is a touch of chocolate to give richness, and at the end, the tannins turn dry and firm. **91** —*R.V. (11/15/2005)*

GRANTOM

Grantom 2001 Reserva Portuguese Red (Trás-os-Montes) $40. This was once one of Portugal's famous wine brands, which disappeared 15 years ago. Now revived by Real Companhia Velha, it is a blend of Cabernet Sauvignon, Touriga Nacional, and Touriga Franca. With 18 months in Portuguese oak, this is a powerful wine with dark fruits, vanilla, and chocolate flavors. **89** —*R.V. (11/1/2004)*

HERDADE DA CALADA

Herdade da Calada 2000 Baron de B Reserva Red Blend (Alentejo) $25. This attempt at a modern, heavily extracted red packs in plenty of bulky blackberry and oak flavors but not much finesse. It's simply a satisfying mouthful of fruit and wood. **85** —*J.C. (11/15/2003)*

Herdade da Calada 2000 Vale da Calada Red Blend (Alentejano) $11. A ripe wine, with soft tannins. It is juicy and uncomplex, with fresh redfruit flavors. **83** —*R.V. (12/31/2002)*

HERDADE DA MADEIRA

Herdade da Madeira 1999 Roquevale Red Blend (Alentejo) $16. This has rustic flavors with soft tannins and some attractive red berry fruits, but finishes green. **82** —*R.V. (12/31/2002)*

Herdade da Madeira 2000 Roquevale Chao de Xisto Red Blend (Alentejano) $6. The wine has a pleasant color, but rustic, barnyard aromas, and is rather lean. The aftertaste is more pleasant, with some soft tannins and easy ripeness. **81** —*R.V. (12/31/2002)*

HERDADE DA MALHADINA NOVA

Herdade da Malhadina Nova 2004 Aragonês de Peceguina Aragonês (Alentejo) $NA. Great red berry fruits mark this wine made from Portugal's Tempranillo. But it also has typical firm Portuguese dry tannins and a solid structure, which are underlined by the 6 months' wood aging. A powerful, dense wine that will age over the next 5 years. **90** —*R.V. (3/1/2006)*

Herdade da Malhadina Nova 2004 Malhadina Portuguese Red (Alentejo) $NA. A beautifully crafted wine, layering dusty fruits and tannins with new wood flavors. This is a warm, rich wine, which also manages to have a great structure balanced with acidity and juicy fruit. This is a great start to a new project in the southern Alentejo. **92** —*R.V. (3/1/2006)*

Herdade da Malhadina Nova 2004 Monte da Peceguina Portuguese Red (Alentejano) $NA. This is the first vintage from the Malhadina Nova vineyard in the southern Alentejo. This wine, a blend of Syrah, Touriga Nacional, Aragonês, and Alicante Bouschet, is one of an impressive range. With its deep, black fruits, smooth tannins, and touch of vanilla, it is ready to drink, but should age over the next 2-3 years. **89**—*R.V. (3/1/2006)*

HERDADE DE ESPORÃO

Herdade de Esporão 2003 Alicante Bouschet (Alentejano) $19. A typical production from this fruity grape, this is an easy-drinking, juicy style of wine, full of red berry flavors, just a touch of wood, and gentle but dry tannins. **86**—*R.V. (3/1/2006)*

Herdade de Esporão 2003 Aragonês (Alentejano) $18. The Portuguese version of Spanish Tempranillo, this Aragonês has a smooth, velvety character that shows bright black fruits, but also lively acidity, and a toasty flavor. This is a sophisticated wine, with dusty tannins giving extra structure. **89**—*R.V. (3/1/2006)*

Herdade de Esporão 2002 Aragonês (Alentejano) $20. The Aragonês is the Alentejo's name for the Spanish Tempranillo. This 100% version, with its huge, solid tannins, and layers of spicy wood, is definitely a hot climate wine. It has richness and ripe, almost new world flavors, while still preserving some element of tannin and dryness which would support some aging. **89 Best Buy**—*R.V. (12/1/2004)*

Herdade de Esporão 2000 Aragonês (Alentejano) $14. This toasty, tannic, firmly structured wine still manages to show that the rich, silky fruit underneath will blossom when the spicy wood flavors have blended in. Give it two to three years. **88**—*R.V. (12/31/2002)*

Herdade de Esporão 2002 Esporão Reserva Portuguese Red (Alentejo) $16. The estate wine of Esporão is a big, powerful blend of Trincadeira, Aragonês, and Cabernet Sauvignon, with great structure and fruit. It is dense, with dark, firm tannins and powerful, ripe black fruits. Acidity and dryness give this wine the possibility of good aging. **91**—*R.V. (3/1/2006)*

Herdade de Esporão 2001 Esporão Reserva Portuguese Red (Alentejo) $17. Of the many wines from Esporão, this is the most traditionally Portuguese in its dark black tannins, acidity, and leather and spice aromas. It is powerful, at 14.5% alcohol, and a touch hot but it is a great wine with richly flavored dishes. **88**—*R.V. (12/1/2004)*

Herdade de Esporão 2000 Garrafeira Portuguese Red (Alentejo) $38. Intense rich licorice and chocolate flavors typify this rich, structured wine. Fresh acidity gives the wine a delicious lift to finish. Garrafeira means special selection or wine for cellaring, and this blend of juicy Alicante Bouchet and tannic Aragonês is definitely worth keeping for at least five years. **91 Cellar Selection**—*R.V. (12/1/2004)*

Herdade de Esporão 2001 Garrafeira Private Selection Portuguese Red (Alentejo) $38. "Garrafeira" means "special selection," and this wine is definitely at the top of the Esporão range. Eighteen months in French oak gives it sophistication and elegance, while its powerful fruit and red berry flavors combine with vanilla and toast to show off its richness. This is an impressive wine, packed with dense tannins as well as fruit, and is certainly suitable for aging. **93**—*R.V. (3/1/2006)*

Herdade de Esporão 2003 Monte Velho Portuguese Red (Alentejano) $8. A powerful, tannic wine which shows big spice and ripe berry flavors. From the 1500 acre Esporão vineyard, this wine has layers of dark fruits and richness. There is a juicy element which gives freshness, but this is a wine which needs another 3-4 years before drinking. **85**—*R.V. (12/1/2004)*

Herdade de Esporão 2002 Quatro Castas Reserva Portuguese Red (Alentejano) $20. A blend of Trincadeira, Aragonês, Syrah, and Touriga Nacional, this is a refreshing, easy wine, with bright red fruit aromas and fresh flavors. There are red plum and spice flavors. Six months' wood aging leaves a touch of toast, and brings out the soft tannins. **88**—*R.V. (3/1/2006)*

Herdade de Esporão 2003 Vinha da Defesa Portuguese Red (Alentejano) $11. A heady, spicy blend of Aragonês and Castelão Frances, this is packed with mint and raspberry red fruit flavors. It is firm, tannic to finish, but shows great soft fruits as well. **85**—*R.V. (12/1/2004)*

Herdade de Esporão 2004 Monte Velho Portuguese White (Alentejano) $8. A smooth, creamy ripe wine from the 1,500-acre Esporão estate, this blended wine has richness, and almond and green plum flavors. It is intense, dense, and polished, with good acidity. **90 Best Buy**—*R.V. (11/15/2005)*

Herdade de Esporão 2003 Reserva Portuguese White (Alentejo) $12. An intensely spicy, herbal wine, with just a touch of wood from the American oak. This top white from Esporão is rich, modern in style, and powerful, but never loses sight of its origins. **91 Best Buy**—*R.V. (11/15/2005)*

Herdade de Esporão 2004 Vinha da Defesa Portuguese White (Alentejo) $11. A blend of Antão Vaz, Arinto, and Roupeiro, this full-bodied white is ripe and modern, with delicious tropical fruit and lime flavors. It makes a great accompaniment to fish or chicken. **87 Best Buy**—*R.V. (8/1/2005)*

Herdade de Esporão 2000 Esporao Reserva Red Blend (Alentejo) $15. The estate wine of Esporão is this huge property's best wine (apart from the limited-release Garrafeira). Its Aragonês, Trincadeira, and Cabernet Sauvignon are aged in American oak. With its hugely concentrated black fruit flavors and smooth, ripe tannins, it should age well. **91**—*R.V. (12/31/2002)*

Herdade de Esporão 2001 Monte Velho Tinto Red Blend (Alentejano) $6. The inexpensive brand from Esporão is a forward, fruity combination of spicy, peppery fruit with light tannins and pleasant acidity. **84**—*R.V. (12/31/2002)*

Herdade de Esporão 2000 Quatro Castas Reserva Red Blend (Alentejano) $21. Herbal and briary, featuring ample red berry fruit and some pleasant spice notes. Open and accessible, this is a solid offering that would go well with char-broiled steak. **86**—*J.C. (11/15/2003)*

Herdade de Esporão 2000 Vinha da Defesa Red Blend (Alentejano) $14. Attractive, soft, raspberry flavors, laced with spice and wood, make for a smooth, easily quaffable wine. The 2000 is a little young still, but a year will bring it all into balance. **85**—*R.V. (12/31/2002)*

Herdade de Esporão 2003 Syrah (Alentejano) $19. For Esporão's winemaker, Australian David Baverstock, this Syrah must seem like a wine from home. He makes a rich, meaty wine, but it has more structure than a New World version, balancing acidity and firm, dry tannins against the sweetness of the fruit. Great to drink, but could age. **89**—*R.V. (3/1/2006)*

Herdade de Esporão 2000 Syrah (Alentejano) $11. The aromas are of spicy American oak, but the palate has great fruit, with flavors of chocolate, vibrant, black fruit and sweetness. To finish, there is a suggestion of herbal tea. **89**—*R.V. (12/31/2002)*

Herdade de Esporão 2003 Touriga Nacional (Alentejano) $19. A powerful, elegant wine, pulsating with big black fruit flavors, and firmly dominated by tannins from the wine and the wood aging. This is a serious, concentrated wine, which shows the breeding of Portugal's finest grape variety. **90**—*R.V. (3/1/2006)*

Herdade de Esporão 2002 Touriga Nacional (Alentejano) $22. Aged in half and half French and American oak, this intense wine has aromas of violets, spice, and flavors of black fruits. It has more power than elegance, but it still has class from the balancing tannins, acidity, and dry fruit flavors. Age for 5 years. **88**—*R.V. (12/1/2004)*

Herdade de Esporão 2000 Touriga Nacional (Alentejano) $15. The 1,000-acre vineyards of Esporão are the largest in Portugal. Under the tutelage of Australian winemaker David Baverstock, this aristocrat of Portuguese grapes wins again in the Esporão's range of single-varietal wines. It is rich, it is vibrant, it has complexity. It is certainly ripe, but also elegant, along with lingering plum flavors. **90**—*R.V. (12/31/2002)*

Herdade de Esporão 2003 Trincadeira (Alentejano) $19. A big, beefy wine from this southern version of Tinta Amarela, this is rich, solid, and full of fine black currants. There is some wood, but it underlines the fruit and leaves a rich, satisfying, fresh wine but with structure. **88**—*R.V. (3/1/2006)*

Herdade de Esporão 2000 Trincadeira (Alentejano) $14. Plums, herbs and pepper come together. It is soft and ripe, streaked with American oak spice, which gives it a fine lift on the finish. **86**—*R.V. (12/31/2002)*

Herdade de Esporão 2004 Verdelho (Alentejano) $11. This grape variety produces a delicate, flowery wine, with mango and citrus flavors and good structure. **86 Best Buy** —*R.V. (8/1/2005)*

Herdade de Esporão 2001 Reserva White Blend (Alentejo) $14. Although this wine is a blend of the indigenous Roupeiro, Arinto, and Antão Vaz grapes, you might mistake it for any barrel-fermented white. Pear, peach, and buttered toast aromas and flavors aren't much different from a well-made, warm-climate Chardonnay. **86** —*J.C. (11/15/2003)*

HERDADE DE SANTA MARTA

Herdade de Santa Marta 1999 Red Blend (Alentejano) $10. This offering from J.P. Vinhos starts off with high-toned cherry fruit graced with vanilla and herbs, and stays on a steady course through the lean, focused finish. A bit lacking in concentration, but supple and easy to drink. **84** —*J.C. (3/1/2004)*

HERDADE DOS COELHEIROS

Herdade dos Coelheiros 2001 Tapada de Coelheiros Chardonnay (Alentejano) $NA. 81 —*R.V. (8/1/2004)*

Herdade dos Coelheiros 1999 Tapada de Coelheiros Red Blend (Alentejano) $32. A dark, tarry, tannic wine with old-style fruit, with rich black fruit flavors underneath it all. The huge, dry tannins make this a wine that will need at least 5 years of cellaring. **87** —*R.V. (12/31/2002)*

Herdade dos Coelheiros 1999 Tapada de Coelheiros Garrafeira Red Blend (Alentejano) $42. Garrafeira means a wine designed for cellaring. From this small 50-acre vineyard in Arraiolos in the the Alentejo, this powerful concentrated wine is a blend of Caberenet Sauvignon and Aragonês. Almost black in color, this is a hugely rich, almost impenetrable wine, with dark, tarry fruit and big solid tannins. With its dryness it is quite old fashioned, but the richness that comes from the fruit more than balances. **90** —*R.V. (12/31/2002)*

Herdade dos Coelheiros 2000 Vinha da Tapada Red Blend (Alentejano) $15. A dry wine, with a touch of greeness to it. The dryness is softened a little by some black fruit. **81** —*R.V. (12/31/2002)*

Herdade dos Coelheiros 2001 Tapada de Coelheiros White Blend (Alentejano) $NA. 83 —*R.V. (8/1/2004)*

HERDADE GRANDE

Herdade Grande 2003 Portuguese Red (Alentejano) $11. Shows some definite sous bois elements—including damp moss, mushroom, and cola notes—then adds tart berries and an easy, facile mouthfeel. Crisp and fresh on the finish. A pleasant light-weight red for everyday drinking. **86 Best Buy** —*J.C. (11/1/2006)*

Herdade Grande 2003 Condado das Vinhas Portuguese Red (Alentejano) $8. Reasonably complex for a modestly priced table wine, with intriguing notes of wintergreen, birchbeer, mushrooms, and beet root. For some tastes, it could use a stronger fruit component, but despite that it's supple enough on the palate to charm. Finishes crisp, with some tart berry flavors. A blend of Trincadeira, Aragonês, and Alfrocheiro. **86 Best Buy** —*J.C. (11/1/2006)*

Herdade Grande 2005 Colheita Seleccionada White Blend (Alentejano) $11. A blend of indigenous varieties from the south of Portugal, this wine smoothly blends green apple and citrus flavors with a slightly creamy texture, yet finishes zesty and fresh, with a hint of anise. **86 Best Buy** —*J.C. (11/1/2006)*

Herdade Grande 2004 Condado das Vinhas White Blend (Alentejano) $8. Starts off with a bit of matchstick on the nose, then opens to reveal a fairly bland, innocuous white with a plump mouthfeel. **82** —*J.C. (11/1/2006)*

HOOPERS

Hoopers 2003 Vintage Port $NA. From one of the brand names of the Royal Oporto group, this is impressive. It is perfumed, firm, solid with dense tannins. The balance and structure are already there in a Port that shows sweetness as well as concentration. **90** —*R.V. (11/15/2005)*

HUTCHESON FEUERHEERD

Hutcheson Feuerheerd 2003 Vintage Port $NA. This is one of the brands owned by Barros Almeida. This vintage Port has hints of volatile acidity,

which leaves dirty flavors. Has tannins and some fine blackberry flavors, but overall, it's not an impressive wine. **83** —*R.V. (11/15/2005)*

J. H. ANDERSEN

J. H. Andersen NV Special Reserve Port $15. A big, chocolaty wine, packed with intense, almost over-powering ripe fruit. Dark cocoa flavors and big black, jammy fruit leave very little to the imagination, and make it one-dimensional. But for those who like power, here it is. **86** —*R.V. (3/1/2005)*

J. H. Andresen 2003 Vintage Port $32. Founded in 1845 by a Danish sea captain, Andersen remains a tiny, independent shipper, run by the Santos family. It certainly knows how to make some good vintage Port, with its fragrant flavors, big, dark fruits and rich raisins. There is a fine mélange of fruit flavors, balanced with a touch of acidity. **90** —*R.V. (11/15/2005)*

J. PORTUGAL RAMOS

J. Portugal Ramos 2004 Aragonês (Alentejano) $15. A fresh, light, fruity wine that has some soft tannic structure. Has flavors of red cherries, plums, and a touch of spice from the aging in American oak. Great acidity rounds it off attractively. **86** —*R.V. (3/1/2006)*

J. Portugal Ramos 2002 Conde de Vimioso Portuguese Red (Ribatejano) $8. A blend in which Portuguese varieties meld with Cabernet Sauvignon, here is a wine that gives depth of flavor and tannins as well as good, fresh red fruits. It is spicy, with a touch of wood and ripe flavors. **87 Best Buy** —*R.V. (11/1/2004)*

J. Portugal Ramos 2001 Conde de Vimioso Reserva Portuguese Red (Ribatejano) $20. This maturing version of the Conde de Vimioso reveals old-fashioned, tarry, licorice flavors that are well-balanced and enjoyable. A blend of Trincadeira, Aragonês, Touriga Nacional, and Cabernet Sauvignon, it seems to be dominated by the first two, warm southern grapes, which give a generous, ripe character, and a rich aftertaste. **90** —R.V. (3/1/2006)

J. Portugal Ramos 2001 Conde de Vimioso Reserva Portuguese Red (Ribatejano) $20. An impressive wine, packed with serious, dark, intense and concentrated fruits, and dusty tannins. Spices, dried fruits, vanilla, and herbs are all there, giving a complex blend that would benefit from 5 years' bottle aging. Beautifully crafted. **91 Editors' Choice** —*R.V. (11/1/2004)*

J. Portugal Ramos 2004 Marquês de Borba Portuguese Red (Alentejo) $10. This popular Portuguese brand is all about dry, tannic, rich, food-friendly wines. There are also black fruit flavors, and a dry, spicy aftertaste with layers of acidity. **86 Best Buy** —*R.V. (3/1/2006)*

J. Portugal Ramos 2003 Marquês de Borba Portuguese Red (Alentejo) $12. A fruity quaff, with aromas of mixed berries and cotton candy, flavors that are similarly simple. The mixed berries turn tart and piquant on the finish. A blend of Aragonês (Tempranillo) and Trincadeira. **83** —*J.C. (12/1/2004)*

J. Portugal Ramos 2001 Marquês de Borba Portuguese Red (Alentejo) $10. A blend of Aragonês, Trincadeira, and Periquita, this wine shows a strong note of charred wood and roasted or caramelized fruit. In a way, it's cherries jubilee in a glass—alcohol, caramelized cherries, and a dusting of cinnamon for good measure. **85** —*J.C. (11/15/2003)*

J. Portugal Ramos 1999 Marquês de Borba Portuguese Red (Alentejo) $11. After a youthful stink blows off, sweet scents of black cherries emerge, gently swathed in folds of toasty oak. Despite the attractive aromas, the palate is a bit thin, albeit silky smooth. A sappy edge suggests a portion of Portuguese oak was used in the upbringing of this Aragones, Trincadeira, and Periquita blend. **86** —*J.C. (12/31/2001)*

J. Portugal Ramos 2000 Marquês de Borba Reserva Portuguese Red (Alentejo) $50. A classic Alentejo brand, the Marquês de Borba exists and has lent his name to a range of wine hugely popular in Portugal. This is big, packed with raisins and generous fruit, and solid, dry tannins. A great wine with powerful fruit and the potential for aging. It's traditional, but like this, tradition is good. **90** —*R.V. (12/1/2004)*

J. Portugal Ramos 2000 Marquês de Borba Reserva Portuguese Red (Alentejo) $48. Marqués de Borba is one of Portugal's bestselling brands. This Reserva version, aged in wood, and in bottle, is richer and more intense in flavor than the normal version, but it still has the same attractively old-fashioned, ripe, tarry fruit flavors and layers of acidity. Drink now. **90** —*R.V. (3/1/2006)*

J. Portugal Ramos 2000 Marquês de Borba Reserva Portuguese Red (Alentejo) $45. The Marquês de Borba is João Portugal Ramos's uncle, so the name and the fame has stayed in the family. This is one of the cult wines of Portugal, but the style is definitely old-fashioned, an interesting contrast to the other wines from this entirely new winery. Its smooth fruit and tarry, dry layers give it great strength and power, yielding a great partner for rich foods. **89** —*R.V. (12/31/2002)*

J. Portugal Ramos 1999 Marquês de Borba Reserva Portuguese Red (Alentejo) $45. This tasty, well-made red features a sweet, smoky oak-heavy nose and then a dense, rich palate of sweet cherries and ripe plums floating in vanilla. Smooth and stylish at all key points, it's easy to drink and easy to like. A calling card for Portugal. **88** —*M.S. (12/31/2001)*

J. Portugal Ramos 1999 Sinfonia Portuguese Red (Alentejo) $9. This blended red would make a perfect match with a lunch quiche or picnic. It's gutsy enough without being heavy, refined without being overly polished. Blackberry and black cherry aromas and flavors are joined by chocolate and a dusting of cinnamon. **86 Best Buy** —*J.C. (12/31/2001)*

J. Portugal Ramos 2004 Vila Santa Portuguese Red (Alentejano) $16. A dark, black-fruited wine that shows freshness as well. Dusty tannins give the wine a layer of dryness; the aftertaste is filled with lively sweet-and-sour acidity. **87** —*R.V. (3/1/2006)*

J. Portugal Ramos 2003 Vila Santa Portuguese Red (Alentejano) $18. This is an exotic blend of Aragonês, Trincadeira, Alicante Bouschet, and Cabernet Sauvignon. With sophisticated tannins and layers of wood, this is a powerful, full-bodied wine, with just a touch of earthiness. Spice and herbs give extra complexity. **90 Editors' Choice** —*R.V. (12/1/2004)*

J. Portugal Ramos 2004 Antão Vaz Portuguese White (Alentejano) $10. Delicious, fresh, fruity, and clean; great acidity, creamy flavors, and aromas of summer hedgerow flowers. **87 Best Buy** —*R.V. (8/1/2005)*

J. Portugal Ramos 2005 Marquês de Borba Portuguese White (Alentejo) $13. Deliciously spicy and citrusy, this blend of Arinto, Rabo de Ovelha, and Roupiero is quickly becoming one of Portugal's go-to whites. Pepper and ginger notes lead the way, backed by fresh pineapple fruit. A slightly oily mouthfeel gives it some heft, but the finish is spice-driven and refreshing, not heavy. Drink now. **89 Best Buy** —*J.C. (11/1/2006)*

J. Portugal Ramos 2004 Marquês de Borba Portuguese White (Alentejo) $14. For a wine from such a hot region as Alentejo, this is a deliciously delicate, fresh wine. Packed with acidity and flavors of almonds and green fruits, it is ripe but always crisp and clean. **88** —*R.V. (8/1/2005)*

J. Portugal Ramos 2003 Marquês de Borba Portuguese White (Alentejo) $11. A blend of four native Portuguese white grape varieties, this is a light-weight wine ideal for simply prepared fish or shellfish. Fresh green apple aromas and flavors, accented by hints of peach and citrus, finishing clean and refreshing. **85** —*J.C. (11/1/2004)*

J. Portugal Ramos 2001 Aragones Red Blend (Alentejano) $18. A big, spicy wine that layers smooth vanilla, dry tannins, and rich, ripe, powerful red fruit. The American oak used to age the Aragonês, the local name for Tinta Roriz or Tempranillo, gives the fruit just the lift it needs. **88** —*R.V. (12/31/2002)*

J. Portugal Ramos 2000 Falua Duas Castas Red Blend (Ribatejo) $9. This wine boasts a lovely, supple, and smooth mouthfeel, but also some off-beat aromas and flavors. It's herbal and leafy, yet also has some meaty notes similar to beef gravy. **86 Best Buy** —*J.C. (11/15/2003)*

J. Portugal Ramos 2001 Tinta Caiada Red Blend (Alentejano) $18. The Tinta Caiada is the local name for Bastardo, which some believe to be identical to the Trousseau of eastern France. Putting the name aside, the wine is sweet but elegant, with flavors of new wood underlining the black fruit rather than dominating it. **89** —*R.V. (12/31/2002)*

J. Portugal Ramos 2002 Vila Santa Red Blend (Alentejano) $15. João Portugal Ramos remains one of Portugal's most respected winemakers, but even he had a tough time with the 2002 vintage. His Vila Santa, which scored 90 points in both the 2001 and 2003 vintages, manages just 85 this time out, with stewed rhubarb notes and hints of prune

backed by black cherries. Soft and easy to drink, with a tangy finish. **85** —*J.C. (12/31/2005)*

J. Portugal Ramos 2001 Vila Santa Red Blend (Alentejano) $20. A good example of what a real blend can do. With Aragonês, Trincadeira, Alicante Bouschet, and Cabernet Sauvignon all mixed together, the result works out magnificently. The oak may dominate at the moment, but the power and the gloriously opulent fruit will certainly come right through in a year or two. **90** —*R.V. (12/31/2002)*

J. Portugal Ramos 2004 Syrah (Alentejano) $16. Portugal Ramos believes that Syrah has great potential in the Alentejo, and this wine, with its ripe fruits, perfumed aromas, and ripe, earthy character shows why. There is richness as well as elegance, but power is the main aspect of this deeply flavored wine. **90** —*R.V. (3/1/2006)*

J. Portugal Ramos 2003 Syrah (Alentejano) $19. Syrah is a grape with a great future in the Alentejo, according to João Portugal Ramos. This wine shows that potential. Soft and rich with fine perfumes and some mineral character, it is full, powerful, and immediately appealing. There is some wood, but it just underlines the rich fruit. **89** —*R.V. (12/1/2004)*

J. Portugal Ramos 2001 Syrah (Alentejano) $18. João Portugal Ramos has surrounded the fortress city of Estremoz with his vineyards. The Syrah just loves it in this hot, dry climate, giving a wine with aromas of violets and leather, huge tannins, rich jammy flavors, and a sense of restrained power. Yet Portugal Ramos has also managed to get some elegance in this otherwise bruising wine. **90** —*R.V. (12/31/2002)*

J. Portugal Ramos 2004 Tinta Caiada (Alentejano) $16. Thought to be related to the Douro grape, Bastardo, and the Savoy (French) grape, Trousseau, the Tinta Caiada is something of a curiosity. It makes a tannic, smoky wine with flavors of figs and a bitter character from the intense dryness of the aftertaste. **87** —*R.V. (3/1/2006)*

J. Portugal Ramos 2003 Quinta da Viçosa Touriga Merlot Touriga Nacional Blend (Alentejano) $26. An unusual but successful blend, the Touriga Nacional giving structure, the Merlot giving softness. There is good concentration, layers of acidity, and a deep color from the partial foot treading in open lagares. Towards the end, spicy wood comes through from the barrel aging. **88** —*R.V. (3/1/2006)*

J. Portugal Ramos 2004 Trincadeira (Alentejano) $15. A big, dark wine that is full of black plums, figs, and spice. Firm, dry tannins support the intense fruit flavors. Aging in French oak gives the wine a richness, a touch of vanilla and smooths the edges. **89** —*R.V. (3/1/2006)*

J. Portugal Ramos 2003 Trincadeira (Alentejano) $17. Earthy, meaty aromas are a prominent character of this single varietal wine. They are balanced by very ripe, raspberry flavors, with a layer of dry tannin. This is an open, fresh wine that would be great with barbecues. **87** —*R.V. (12/1/2004)*

J.M. DA FONSECA AND VAN ZELLER

J.M. da Fonseca and Van Zeller 2003 Vintage Port $NA. A joint venture between J.M. da Fonseca, one of the largest Portuguese wine producers, and Cristiano van Zeller. This is a curious wine, which is spoiled by caramel flavors and some toast. Not a success overall, although there is certainly some good black fruit there. **83** —*R.V. (11/15/2005)*

J.P. VINHOS

J.P. Vinhos 2000 Quinta da Bacalhôa Cabernet Blend (Terras do Sado) $27. The beautiful vineyard of Quinta da Bacalhôa was established along with the palace in the 15th century. It was replanted with Cabernet Sauvignon and Merlot by American owners in the 1970s. This 2000 vintage is as good as ever, rich and tannic, with dark fruits and intensity along with wood flavors. A great wine for short-term aging, it is very drinkable already. **89** —*R.V. (11/1/2004)*

J.P. Vinhos NV J.P. Branco Moscatel (Terras do Sado) $NA. **83** —*R.V. (8/1/2004)*

J.P. Vinhos 1999 Herdade de Santa Marta Portuguese Red (Alentejano) $10. A big, round, juicy wine which is a perfect barbecue wine. Packed with berry and herbal flavors, it is soft, ripe, with a light layer of tannins. From a blend of local grapes, this is ready to drink now. **84** —*R.V. (12/1/2004)*

J.P. Vinhos NV J.P. Tinto Portuguese Red (Terras do Sado) $7. From the vast vineyard area that lies south of Lisbon, this simple, fresh red is made of 100% Castelão. Ripe, soft tannins and fresh juicy fruit make this easy to drink. **83** —*R.V. (11/1/2004)*

J.P. Vinhos 2003 Santa Fé de Arraiolos Portuguese Red (Alentejano) $9. Smells slightly roasted or caramelized, then picks up dried cherries, citrus fruit, and herbs in the mouth. A smooth, rounded mouthfeel adds interest. Chocolate and raisin notes on the finish suggest pairing with hard cheeses at the end of a meal. **85 Best Buy** —*J.C. (12/31/2005)*

J.P. Vinhos 2003 Serras de Azeitão Portuguese Red (Terras do Sado) $8. Castelão, Aragonez, Syrah, and Merlot come together in this young, fresh wine that is drinkable already. Flavors of dark berries and soft tannins support a ripeness and full flavor from the warm 2003 vintage. **86 Best Buy** —*R.V. (11/1/2004)*

J.P. Vinhos 1994 Tinto da Anfora Portuguese Red (Alenteo) $11. 87 Best Buy *(10/1/1999)*

J.P. Vinhos 2001 Tinto da Anfora Grande Escolha Portuguese Red (Alentejano) $29. Long wood aging for 14 months has enhanced the delicious black fruits and spices of this broad, complex wine. The tannins are dense with dryness over the rich fruit. There's power, but good balance. Drink in 3/4 years. **90** —*R.V. (12/1/2004)*

J.P. Vinhos 2004 Catarina Portuguese White (Terras do Sado) $9. Musky on the nose, picking up hints of honey and peaches with air. Smells as if it might taste sweet, but it's dry on the palate, with floral, spicy, and melon flavors that finish short and clean. **86 Best Buy** —*J.C. (12/31/2005)*

J.P. Vinhos 2003 Catarina Portuguese White (Terras do Sado) $10. It is the Chardonnay that gives this wine its character, its creaminess, and flavor of green plums. There is just a touch of more aromatic flavors and a light hint of wood. **88 Best Buy** —*R.V. (8/1/2005)*

J.P. Vinhos 2003 J.P. Branco Portuguese White (Terras do Sado) $7. A soft, gentle, honey-and-spice wine that gives immediate pleasure as an apéritif. There is just a touch of acidity to keep it all in balance. **83** —*R.V. (8/1/2005)*

J.P. Vinhos 2004 Serras de Azeitão Portuguese White (Terras do Sado) $9. A fascinating blend of Fernão Pires, Moscatel, and Chardonnay. It's the Moscatel, with its honeyed fragrance that is the most obvious, but the roundness comes from the other two grapes. The grapes are grown on the Setúbal peninsula, just south of Lisbon. **89 Best Buy** —*R.V. (8/1/2005)*

J.P. Vinhos 2003 Serras de Azeitão Portuguese White (Terras do Sado) $8. This white wine is a blend of Fernão Pires and Moscatel, giving an aromatic style which has attractive apples and cream flavors. It is fresh, rich, and soft, with a touch of tropical fruits to round it off. **85 Best Buy** —*R.V. (11/1/2004)*

J.P. Vinhos 1999 Herdade de Santa Marta Red Blend (Alentejano) $8. A light, perfumed wine, with fresh red fruits and soft tannins. It is attractive and ripe, but light-weight. **84** —*R.V. (12/31/2002)*

J.P. Vinhos 1995 J.P. Garrafeira Red Blend (Palmela) $10. A fine old-style wine, with solid dusty tannins balancing big, black, concentrated fruit. Dry tannins and dried fruits give a sense of richness and dark power. This powerful wine has been aged six years before release, but it could benefit from another four or five in the cellar. **91 Best Buy** —*R.V. (12/31/2002)*

J.P. Vinhos 2000 Monte das Anforas Red Blend (Alentejano) $9. This heady, perfumed wine is produced in the Alentejo. Soft, lingering, and fruity, it has soft black fruits. It's an easy, ready-to-drink wine in the New World style. **85** —*R.V. (12/31/2002)*

J.P. Vinhos 2001 Monte das Anforas Vinho Tinto Red Blend (Alentejano) $8. This starts off with pure cherry aromas, but they quickly turn more herbal as the wine sits in the glass. In the mouth, the candied, brandied cherries compete with a broad swathe of herbal flavors, finally finishing a tart, sour cherry finale. Shows good concentration, a smooth mouthfeel, and unique flavors. **84** —*J.C. (3/1/2004)*

J.P. Vinhos 2000 Quinta da Bacalhoa Red Blend (Terras do Sado) $20. The beautiful quinta, now part of the J.P. Vinhos winery, was until recently owned by the family of American Elizabeth Scoville, who filled it with antiques. The family also planted the first Cabernet Sauvignon in Portugal. The wine today remains elegant, with solid but restrained tannins, but there is an awkward edge of green pepper. **86** —*R.V. (12/31/2002)*

J.P. Vinhos 2001 Tinto da Anfora Red Blend (Alentejano) $12. Sure, purists may quibble that it's international, but so what? It tastes good. Vanilla and chocolate notes from the oak caress blueberry and blackberry flavors in a smooth, creamy embrace that goes down easily. The finish echoes with vanilla, spice, and fruit. No point in aging this puppy—drink it now. **90 Best Buy** —*J.C. (3/1/2004)*

J.P. Vinhos 1999 Tinto da Anfora Red Blend (Alentejano) $13. This is a Portuguese classic, made for at least 20 years. A blend of Trincadeira, Aragonês, Castelão, and a whole basketful of other local grapes, it's a big, generous wine with bags of ripe, soft fruits. A long streak of tannin gives structure but the overall effect is open and fruity. **87** —*R.V. (12/31/2002)*

J.P. Vinhos 1999 Tinto da Anfora Grande Escohla Red Blend (Alentejano) $30. 90 —*R.V. (12/31/2002)*

J.P. Vinhos 2000 Só Syrah (Terras do Sado) $18. Starts off with briary, herb-accented fruit that acquires a strawberry-rhubarb edge to the flavors. It's medium-weight and slightly creamy in the mouth, yet finishes with coffee-laced, cranberryish fruit. **85** —*J.C. (3/1/2004)*

J.P. Vinhos 2002 Catarina White Blend (Terras do Sado) $8. A light-weight wine with aromas of apple, anise, and a hint of fresh greens. The delicate flavors evoke rainwater seasoned with touches of green apples and lime, finishing tart and clean. A blend of Fernão Pires, Tamarez, Rabo de Ovelha, and—finally a grape variety we all know—Chardonnay. **85** —*J.C. (3/1/2004)*

J.P. Vinhos 2001 Monte das Ânforas White Blend (Alentejano) $NA. 87 —*R.V. (8/1/2004)*

JOÃO PIRES

João Pires 1997 Muscat (Terras do Sado) $11. 85 *(10/1/1999)*

João Pires 2004 Muscat (Terras do Sado) $14. Very perfumed and floral on the nose, with spicy, lychee notes that almost suggest Gewürztraminer, but don't have the same weight or unctuous feel on the palate. It's a light-bodied dry Muscat, rather unique and interesting, and makes, nice counterpoint to various tapas. **86** —*J.C. (11/1/2006)*

João Pires 2003 Muscat (Terras do Sado) $13. Immediately striking, with bold musk and floral aromas that burst from the glass. Ripe, expansive melon and spice notes on the palate. Full-bodied and soft; not as refreshing as some vintages, but still a nice way to start a meal. Drink now. **85** —*J.C. (3/1/2005)*

João Pires 1999 Muscat (Terras do Sado) $9. Get after this one soon, for it seems to be fading. It's already quite gold in color, indicating maturity. What it lacks in vivacity, however, is made up for in the bright lemon, pineapple, and melon flavors. It's a mixed bag of fruit, yet nothing really stands out. **84** —*M.S. (12/31/2001)*

João Pires 1998 Muscat (Terras do Sado) $7. 87 Best Buy —*J.C. (12/15/2000)*

João Pires 2002 Dry Muscat (Terras do Sado) $11. This is a perennial favorite and, outside of Vinho Verde, probably the best-known white of Portugal. Floral aromas bring to mind scents of lemongrass, lime, and orange blossom, while the flavors brim with tangerines and tropical fruit, yet finish crisp and clean. It's dry, light and mouth-watering, making it an ideal apéritif. **88 Best Buy** —*J.C. (11/15/2003)*

João Pires 2001 Muscat of Alexandria Muscat (Terras do Sado) $10. With its flamboyant aromas of oranges, tangerines, and apricots, this screams "Muscat" at the top of its lungs. The plump flavors of tropical and citrus fruits make it easy to like and easy to drink. Great as an apéritif. **87** —*J.C. (7/1/2003)*

JOSÉ MARIA DA FONSECA

José Maria da Fonseca 2001 Periquita Castelão (Palmela) $7. This is J.M. da Fonseca's big brand, the name meaning "little parrot," from the plot of vines that went into the original blend back in the 19th century.

Made from the Castelão grape, it is soft, juicy, and impressively easy to drink. **85 Best Buy** —*R.V. (11/1/2004)*

José Maria da Fonseca NV Alambre 20 Anos Moscatel (Setubal) $45. If Portugal's third fortified wine (after Port and Madeira) can taste like this, it should be better known. Dark gold color, the wine has burnt, Maderized aromas. This is a wonderful old wine, with the youngest wine in the blend being 18 years old. Tastes of burnt old wood and old gold fruits complete a sensous experience. Sensibly, the wine also comes in half bottles. **93** —*R.V. (12/31/2002)*

José Maria da Fonseca NV Alambre 20 years Moscatel (Moscatel de Setúbal) $62. A classic fortified wine from just south of Lisbon, this Moscatel de Setúbal is a beautifully smooth, nutty wine, with acidity and freshness along with sweetness. Surprisingly light, despite its 18% alcohol, its closest parallel is Madeira rather than Port. **92** —*R.V. (11/15/2005)*

José Maria da Fonseca 2001 Domingos Soares Franco Colecção Privado Moscatel (Moscatel de Setúbal) $NA. After a trial of different brandies to fortify the wine made from the Moscatel grapes in Setúbal, winemaker Domingos Soares Franco found that adding Armagnac resulted in a more supple, fresh, and complex Moscatel de Setúbal. This is certainly complex and rich, but also with a distinct dry element, a great grapey character, and a delicious poise. This is still fresh, and will continue to age in bottle. **92** —*R.V. (11/15/2005)*

José Maria da Fonseca NV Moscatel Roxo 20 years Moscatel (Moscatel de Setúbal) $NA. Called Moscatel Roxo because of the slight red tinge to the old gold color of the wine, this is a stunning, mature wine, whose youngest component is 20 years old. It is deep, with a tannic element, and a dry, acidic streak over the intense sweetness. This is a beautiful wine, one of the world's classics. **94** —*R.V. (11/15/2005)*

José Maria da Fonseca 2003 Domingos Soares Franco Colecção Privado Portuguese Red (Terras do Sado) $NA. Domingos Soares Franco, the winemaking director of J.M. da Fonseca, has sought to make a wine using old techniques such as open lagares with foot treading for fermentation. Made entirely from Touriga Nacional, this is a rich and juicy fruited wine, with wood flavors and elegant, soft tannins. **93 Editors' Choice** —*R.V. (11/15/2005)*

José Maria da Fonseca 2001 Domini Portuguese Red (Douro) $14. A joint venture between J.M. da Fonseca chief winemaker Domingos Soares Franco and Cristiano van Zeller, this wine packs ripe, toasty fruit and flavors of dark plums, herbs, and bitter cherries. It is rich, ripe, but juicy, and so elegant. **89** —*R.V. (11/1/2004)*

José Maria da Fonseca 2001 Domini Plus Portuguese Red (Douro) $26. A finely crafted wine, offering ripe dark cherries and plums along with sophisticated acidity and tannins. This top wine from the joint venture between J.M. da Fonseca and Cristiano van Zeller has elegance as well as a fine tarry aftertaste. **92** —*R.V. (11/1/2004)*

José Maria da Fonseca 2001 DPT Garrafeira Portuguese Red (Palmela) $NA. J.M. da Fonseca is renowned for its Garrafeira wines, every one different, every one with its own three-letter code. This wine lives up to the reputation, full of dark, tarry fruit, dusty tannins, and intense flavors. This is great, a link with the positive past of Portuguese wines. **92** —*R.V. (11/1/2004)*

José Maria da Fonseca 2001 FSF Fernando Soares Franco Portuguese Red (Terras do Sado) $NA. A wine made in homage to the father of the present directors of J.M. da Fonseca. This is a fascinating blend of Syrah, Trincadeira, and Tannat. It is beautifully perfumed, with huge tannins and powerful intense fruit. This is a wine to cellar, but already its great, ripe fruit is delicious. This is a great wine, showing how good serious winemaking can be in the south of Portugal. **94 Editors' Choice** —*R.V. (11/15/2005)*

José Maria da Fonseca 1999 Garrafeira CO Portuguese Red (Palmela) $20. A Garrafeira (special selection) from the Castelão grape, aged in wood and tank for four years. It has dense tannins and shows a completely different view of a grape equally at home in fresh, juicy wines. Big and powerful, it should age well over 5–7 years, maybe more. **89** —*R.V. (11/1/2004)*

José Maria da Fonseca 2000 Hexagon Portuguese Red (Terras do Sado) $50. A blend of six grape varieties (hence the name of the wine) also celebrates the six generations of the family at the helm of J.M. da Fonseca. It is a rich wine, full of sweet tannins and powerful acidity in balance. Flavors of herbs combine with black fruit. It should age well over 8 years at least. Tasted in magnum. **92** —*R.V. (11/1/2004)*

José Maria da Fonseca 2003 Jose de Sousa Portuguese Red (Alentejano) $NA. A wine from the Jose de Sousa estate in Alentejo, now owned by J.M. da Fonseca. Fermented partly in traditional clay pots, and then aged in wood, it is a generous, fruity wine with just a touch of tobacco and firm but soft tannins. **88** —*R.V. (11/15/2005)*

José Maria da Fonseca 2001 José de Sousa Mayor Portuguese Red (Alentejano) $NA. A traditionally fermented wine, using foot-treading for a part and clay pots for the rest, this is the top wine from the J.M. da Fonseca-owned José de Sousa estate. It is big and toasty with dry wood and juicy fruit flavors, which set comfortably together. Very dry to finish. **91** —*R.V. (11/15/2005)*

José Maria da Fonseca 2001 Periquita Portuguese Red (Terras do Sado) $10. One of the classic Portuguese red wine brands, with a production of around 4.5 million bottles, this has flavors of ripe red berries, spice, and soft balanced acidity. This is a wine that does not need any aging, but is great for everyday drinking. **87 Best Buy** —*R.V. (11/15/2005)*

José Maria da Fonseca 2001 Periquita Classico Portuguese Red (Terras do Sado) $19. This limited production version of the multimillion-bottle Periquita brand was aged for 24 months in American oak. Made from the Castelão grape, it is rich and velvety with flavors of dark figs. This is a wine that can certainly age—keep it for 5 years or more. 1,000 cases produced. **90** —*R.V. (11/15/2005)*

José Maria da Fonseca 1996 Primum Portuguese Red (Terras do Sado) $11. 89 *(11/15/1999)*

José Maria da Fonseca 2003 Septimus Portuguese Red (Terras do Sado) $12. A fat and juicy wine, with soft tannins that promises great herbal pleasure. This blend of Touriga Nacional and Touriga Franca is ripe, with fresh red fruits and some hint of wood. The name celebrates the arrival of a new, seventh generation in this family winery. **87** —*R.V. (11/1/2004)*

José Maria da Fonseca 2000 Domini Red Blend (Douro) $15. A younger, less complex brother to the Domini Plus, this is still a finely balanced wine in its own right. The aromas are of bright purple fruits. To taste, there is vibrant fruit and finely judged acidity to balance the sweet fruit. **89** —*R.V. (12/31/2002)*

José Maria da Fonseca 2000 Domini Plus Red Blend (Douro) $25. This is one of two wines (and a Port) which are the product of a joint venture between Setúbal-based Domingos Soares Franco of J.M. da Fonseca and Cristiano van Zeller, a leading Port producer. It is a powerful, black-fruited wine with balanced new wood and tarry fruit flavors. Still young, its exudes potential with its layers of richness. The relatively high alcohol (14.5%) is held in check by the power of the fruit. **93** —*R.V. (12/31/2002)*

José Maria da Fonseca 1999 Periquita Red Blend (Azeitao) $8. 85 Best Buy —*D.T. (11/15/2002)*

José Maria da Fonseca 1995 Periquita Classico Red Blend (Terras do Sado) $19. A selection of Castelão grapes gives a wine of greater power than the normal Periquita. The wood flavors marry well with the crisp red fruits, and tarry flavors give complexity to the aftertaste. **87** —*R.V. (12/31/2002)*

José Maria da Fonseca 2000 Primum Touriga Nacional Blend (Terras do Sado) $13. From the Palmela vineyards of José Maria da Fonseca, comes this ripe, red-fruited wine. Flavors of herbs, red peppers and dark plums move effortlessly to a dry finish. **88** —*R.V. (12/31/2002)*

José Maria da Fonseca 2001 Primum White Blend (Terras do Sado) $15. 90 —*R.V. (8/1/2004)*

José Maria da Fonseca 2002 Primum Sauvignon-Arinto White Blend (Terras do Sado) $15. This clean, refreshing white features a floral, citrusy nose that never lets up. Orange blossom, tangerine, and pineapple flavors fill out the midpalate, while the finish is crisp and tart. **87** —*J.C. (11/15/2003)*

PORTUGAL

PORTUGAL

KOPKE

Kopke NV 10-Year Old Tawny Port $28. A firm style of wine, from the oldest Port producer. With tannins and bitter almond and chocolate flavors, this is certainly on the drier side. **88** —R.V. (8/1/2006)

Kopke NV 20-Year Old Tawny Port $56. Although part of Barros, Kopke still operates relatively independently, and obviously can draw on good stocks of aged tawnys. This wine certainly tastes all of 20 years, with its richness and dryness finely in balance, and with lemon jelly and intense ripe fruits shining through. **92** —R.V. (8/1/2006)

Kopke NV 30-Year Old Tawny Port $122. A fine, sweet, fresh wine, which tastes younger than 30 years. The flavors are ripe, layering milk chocolate with acidity in good balance. **87** —R.V. (8/1/2006)

Kopke NV 40-Year Old Tawny Port $180. A very old, too concentrated, medicinal, Italian bitters-flavored wine that tastes too herbal to give much pleasure. **83** —R.V. (8/1/2006)

Kopke NV Barão de Massarelos Ruby Reserve Port $NA. A very light style, with raisins, currants, and mature fruit flavors. There are sweetness, softness and a touch of acidity, leaving a clean, light aftertaste. **83** —R.V. (3/1/2005)

Kopke 2003 Vintage Port $NA. An attractive, fresh wine from one of the oldest Port companies, founded in 1638. The fruit is ripe and forward; this is a Port that will develop quickly. There are good tannins to round off an attractive wine. **86** —R.V. (11/15/2005)

Kopke NV Vintage Character Port $NA. This is one of the sweetest Reserve Ports on the market. As such, it is an acquired taste for those used to the more classic, drier styles. But it holds together well, with its ripe fruit, tastes of raisins, and richness. **87** —R.V. (3/1/2005)

LAVRADORES DE FEITORIA

Lavradores de Feitoria 2001 Portuguese Red (Douro) $9. Lavradores is an innovative project that brings together 15 growers (lavradores) and estate owners in the Douro to make and market their own wine. This first vintage, an amazing bargain at the price, justifies the innovation. It has a fine, earthy character, with rich, dark tannic fruit and big blackberry fruit flavors. A powerful and impressive wine which talks of schist rocks and mountain vineyards. **90 Best Buy** —R.V. (11/15/2005)

LEACOCK'S

Leacock's NV 10 Year Medium Rich Bual (Madeira) $36. Less nutty than other Madeiras despite being 10 years of age, this Bual has a striking bouquet that includes notes of fresh orange rinds. Flavors add dark honey notes to orange marmalade. Silky and smooth in the mouth, with a long, tangy finish. **88** —J.C. (11/1/2006)

Leacock's NV Rainwater Tinta Negra Mole (Madeira) $13. On the lighter, fresher side of Madeira, with candied citrus flavors edging out honey and nut notes. Ends with a smoky, citrusy tang. **86** —J.C. (11/1/2006)

LUIS MARGARIDE

Luis Margaride 1996 Dom Hermano Reserva Portuguese Red (Ribatejo) $9. Deep red-brown, like a mature Cab, this Ribatejo has tangy citrus and peanutty aromas, and distinct dried herb and tree bark flavors. Thin in the mouth, it closes with more green wood and herb flavors. Tastes like it's a little under-ripe. **83** —D.T. (12/31/2001)

LUIS PATO

Luis Pato 2003 Casta Baga (Beiras) $9. Pato is the master of the broody grape that is Baga, the grape of the central coastal region of Bairrada and Beiras in Portugal. He tames the tannins, smooths the rough edges, and makes a great, soft, generous wine. With flavors of yellow plums and thyme with good acidity, this ripe wine has a fine, razor-sharp streak of tannin holding it all together. **87 Best Buy** —R.V. (11/15/2006)

Luis Pato 2001 Casta Baga (Beiras) $14. Not even the magician of Baga, Luis Pato can make a lush, fruity Baga wine at this price point. Shows some horsey, leathery notes as well as black cherry and plum fruit. But it's also lean and hard. Drink now with rare beef, or hold and hope for the best. **85** —J.C. (11/15/2003)

Luis Pato 2001 Casta Baga (Beiras) $8. A fresh, juicy varietal wine (from the Baga grape), a lighter cousin to Pato's Vinha Pan, this wine will

mature over the next 2–3 years. It has some cool tannins, layers of acidity, and vibrant red fruits. **86** —R.V. (11/1/2004)

Luis Pato 2001 Quinta do Moinho Baga (Beiras) $60. Luis Pato's Bairradas used to be the standouts of the D.O. In a sense they still are, although he has chosen to label them with the regional denomination of Beiras in protest over restrictive practices. In this example, Pato has harnessed the rough tannins and brash acidity of Baga into a rich creamy wine filled with blackberries and anise. It's still tannic and crisp, but it just needs another 10 years in the cellar to become fully appreciable. **91** —J.C. (11/15/2003)

Luis Pato 2003 Vinha Formal Bical (Beiras) $19. A full-flavored, wooded wine that shows flavors of ripe grapefruit, white currants, and a generous richness. Made from the local Bical grape, this is Luis Pato's top white. **90** —R.V. (8/1/2005)

Luis Pato 2004 Maria Gomes (Beiras) $8. Green fruits dominate this wine, with their tannins and lime and citric flavors. It's fresh, crisp, and acidic, with just a touch of toast. **86 Best Buy** —R.V. (8/1/2005)

Luis Pato 2002 Maria Gomes (Bairrada) $13. A tart, malic white, with a slightly creamy texture and flavors of under-ripe pineapple, green apples, and pears. Dried spice notes add a modicum of complexity. **85** —J.C. (11/15/2003)

Luis Pato 2001 Quinta do Ribeirinho Primeira Escolha Portuguese Red (Beiras) $20. This is a single-vineyard blend of Baga and Touriga Nacional, making an intensely dense and rich wine, packed with sweet tannins and great ripe fruit. There is a juicy element that suggests it will age relatively quickly, but those dark, dry tannins should give it a long life. This is a fine wine, to be drunk after 5 years. **89** —R.V. (11/1/2004)

Luis Pato 2001 Vinha Barrosa Portuguese Red (Beiras) $NA. The 65-year-old Barrio vineyard, planted with Baga, has produced a ripe, relatively soft wine, with earthy, juicy flavors and fine concentration. The tannins are only dry to finish, but still the leathery aromas and acidity dominate. **88** —R.V. (11/1/2004)

Luis Pato 2001 Vinha Pan Portuguese Red (Beiras) $50. Named after the village of Panasqueira, where the vineyard is situated, this wine is made from the local Baga grape. Packed with rich black fruits, ripe but firm tannins, and layers of wood, this is an intense wine that would repay cellaring. Pato believes the Baga softens and becomes more like Pinot Noir as it ages—give it 10 years. **91** —R.V. (11/1/2004)

Luis Pato 2001 Vinhas Velhas Portuguese Red (Beiras) $19. From 45-year-old vines, this impressive 100% Baga wine is aged for 12 months in a mix of new and old wood. It is smooth, rich, with tarry dusty tannins and some acidity. This is concentrated, dense, and certainly a great wine, and will age well over 10 years. **91 Editors' Choice** —R.V. (11/1/2004)

Luis Pato 2001 Vinha Formal Portuguese White (Beiras) $NA. This wood-aged wine, made from the local Bical grape, is reminiscent of an Australian Sémillon, packed with oily, citrus fruit, with toast and rich flavors. Who says Portugal can't produce white wines which are age-worthy? **88** —R.V. (11/1/2004)

Luis Pato 2000 Red Blend (Beiras) $13. This soft, supple wine has a layer of tannins but fresh, light red fruits and flavors of herbs dominate the palate. **86** —R.V. (12/31/2002)

Luis Pato 1999 Quinta do Moinho Red Blend (Beiras) $45. Ripe fruit and aromas of bitter coffee, with some firm, dry tannins but also juicy black fruits, make this single-vineyard 100% Baga firm but generous. Age it for another 4–10 years. **88** —R.V. (12/31/2002)

Luis Pato 2000 Quinta do Ribeirinho Red Blend (Beiras) $30. Because the Quinta do Ribeirinho is planted on sandy soil, phylloxera cannot attack the vine roots, so they can be ungrafted. Pato aims to make this wine in a prephylloxera style. It is certainly different, with flavors of bitter coffee and dry, intense curiously juicy sweet and sour acidity. **85** —R.V. (12/31/2002)

Luis Pato 2000 Quinta do Ribeirinho Primeira Escolha Red Blend (Beiras) $29. Pato is a Pinot Noir lover, and you can see his affection for Burgundy in this wine. Deep, rustic aromas lead to fresh fruit, with fine blackberry flavors and lovely, juicy acidity. This softly tannic wine is a blend of Baga and Touriga Nacional, with power but also elegance. **90** —R.V. (12/31/2002)

Luis Pato 2000 Vinha Barrio Red Blend (Beiras) $29. A dense, darkly tannic wine, with impenetrable dryness and concentrated "black" flavors. Under those tannins, some juicy acidity is struggling to get escape. It may actually do so in four or five years. 87 —R.V. (12/31/2002)

Luis Pato 2000 Vinha Barrosa Vina Velha Red Blend (Beiras) $29. Luis Pato, whose name means "duck" in Portuguese, is the man who has tamed the local Baga grape by keeping its acidity and tannins in check. Made from 70-year-old vines, this is a stunningly concentrated wine, with sweet chocolate flavors and silky, tarry tannins. The juicy black currant fruit makes it very drinkable. 92 —R.V. (12/31/2002)

Luis Pato 2000 Vinha Pan Red Blend (Beiras) $13. Dusty, tarry fruit aromas come from this deep, nearly black-colored wine. It is smooth, almost velvety, with strong, dry tannins under the fruit. Intensely concentrated, it is certainly age-worthy, probably maturing well over the next five years. Vinha Pan is short for Vinha Panasqueria, the name of the vineyard. 90 —R.V. (12/31/2002)

Luis Pato 2000 Vinhas Velhas Red Blend (Beiras) $13. Made from Baga grapes, this is a deep purple wine with aromas of ripe figs and licorice. Ripe spices and dense tannins are tinged with a touch of bitterness, finishing with noticeable acidity. 88 —R.V. (12/31/2002)

Luis Pato 1997 Vinhas Velhas Red Blend (Bairrada) $20. 90 (11/15/1999)

Luis Pato 2000 Vinha Formal White Blend (Beiras) $NA. 87 —R.V. (11/1/2004)

Luis Pato 2001 Vinhas Velhas White Blend (Beiras) $15. 90 —R.V. (11/1/2004)

MARGARIDA CABACO

Margarida Cabaco 2001 Monte dos Cabacos Portuguese Red (Alentejano) $19. Like many of the Alentejano wines, this one is a blend of several grape varieties. In this case, it's Syrah, Cabernet Sauvignon, Touriga Nacional, and Alicante Bouschet. The result is a broad, mouth-filling wine but one that lacks depth or richness. Black cherry and leather flavors are pleasant enough for washing down weeknight burgers. 84 —J.C. (12/31/2005)

MARQUÉS DE BORBA

Marqués de Borba 2000 Portuguese White (Alentejo) $11. Fans of austere Sauvignon Blancs need only apply here: You'll like this blend of Arinto, Rabo de Ovelha, and Roupeiro grapes, and its tangy cotton-lemon-mineral flavors. Its bouquet smells clean and fresh, with lemon, lime, and slight vanilla aromas; it finishes with mineral and citrus flavors. Drink well chilled—some might find it overly tangy otherwise. 85 — D.T. (12/31/2001)

MARTINEZ GASSIOT

Martinez Gassiot 1995 Quinta da Chousa Port $40. 86 —J.C. (3/1/2000)

Martinez Gassiot 1995 Quinta da Eira Velha Port $43. 89 —J.C. (3/1/2000)

MESSIAS

Messias NV 10-Year Old Tawny Port) $20. Rather brown in color, this wine is sweet, soft, and chocolaty, spoiled by volatility and unbalanced acidity. 82 —R.V. (8/1/2006)

Messias NV 20-Year Old Tawny Port) $40. Tart, hard, and burnt, this wine is completely spoiled by the harsh spirits which dominate. 81 —R.V. (8/1/2006)

Messias NV 30-Year Old Tawny Port $60. This is more like an Italian bitters than a Port, with its roasted coffee aromas, and bitter flavors. Almost medicinal. 84 —R.V. (8/1/2006)

MONTEZ CHAMPALIMAUD

Montez Champalimaud 1999 Quinta do Cotto Red Blend (Douro) $20. A disappointment from one of the Douro pioneers of table wines. Light, with red fruit and meaty aromas, it is rather lean and displays tart acids and bitterness. Offers high acid and low richness. 80 —R.V. (12/31/2002)

Montez Champalimaud 10-Year Old Tawny Port $44. As so often, Niepoort comes through with a fabulous wine. It is dry and structured, with mature flavors that suggest there are wines in the blend that are older than 10 years. There is a bitter chocolate character, intense bitter

almonds, and finishing freshness and acidity. The whole comes in a concentrated, intense package. 93 Editors' Choice —R.V. (8/1/2006)

NIEPOORT

Niepoort NV 20-Year Old Tawny Port $40. At first sip, this seems gentle and soft. But behind this smooth, glossy exterior, there are delicious flavors waiting to emerge. With caramel, oranges, acidity and a twist of treacle, this becomes a fine, balanced wine. 92 —R.V. (8/1/2006)

Niepoort NV 30-Year Old Tawny Port $174. This impressively concentrated wine has classic burnt caramel aromas, with dense fig and bitter chocolate flavors. It is rich, delicious, and tastes somewhat older than its 30-year label. 92 —R.V. (8/1/2006)

Niepoort 1997 LBV Bottled 2001 Port $22. Balance, dryness, and elegance are the hallmarks of this wine. It is fruity, with a sense of structure and delicious acidity to give it freshness. The wine was bottled unfiltered, meaning it should age well in bottle. 90 —R.V. (3/1/2003)

Niepoort 1998 LBV Bottled 2002 Port $22. A Port that is close to a classic vintage Port in quality, because Niepoort makes a traditional style of LBV, which can age in the bottle. This wine is big and tannic, with acidity and flavors of dried fruits. Its dry style and tannins mean it will show well beyond its LBV pedigree, and age well over 10 years. 90 —R.V. (3/1/2003)

Niepoort 2003 Secundum Vintage Port $58. This may be called "Secundum," or "second wine," but this is as fine a vintage Port as many so-called first wines. The tannins are huge, dense, dry, designed for the long haul. The Port is packed with ripe fruit, cassis flavors, and an herbal layer. The style is big and opulent, backed up with tannins. 93 —R.V. (11/15/2005)

Niepoort 2003 Vintage Port $84. A great wine from master winemaker Dirk van Niepoort. It is big, solid, chunky and packed with ripe fruit flavors. It also has fine acidity and a layer of dry, woodsy tannins. To finish, there are good bitter chocolate flavors. 95 —R.V. (11/15/2005)

Niepoort NV Vintage Character Port $18. A well-balanced Port from master winemaker Dirk Niepoort. It is soft, with delicate flavors of black cherries, and young, fresh fruit. In keeping with what a Reserve Port should be, this is easy to drink, just hinting at a tannic structure. 88 — R.V. (3/1/2005)

Niepoort 2000 Vintage Port $80. A prodigious effort from a small house that's becoming one of the Douro's best. The fruit is massive; huge and inky and filled with blackberries and chocolate. Yet for all its size, it finishes with finesse-filled layers of flavor that fold in mint and black pepper notes. 97 Cellar Selection (11/15/2003)

Niepoort 2001 Batuta Portuguese Red (Douro) $71. A great wine, which has the richness and the intense concentration of the Douro with a world-class style. This blend of Douro grapes is full of black fruits, of new wood flavors, of solid, dry tannins. But it also has tastes of prunes, of brooding dark fruits, and balancing acidity. This is undoubtedly one of the greatest wines from the Douro. 94 —R.V. (11/1/2004)

Niepoort 2001 Redoma Portuguese Red (Douro) $43. A powerful wine, full of hot country aromas and dark tannins. This has old leather richness along with great ripe fruit. Acidity and young black fruit flavors suggest a good aging potential. Don't come to this wine expecting elegance, but enjoy it for its power and sheer exuberance. 90 —R.V. (11/1/2004)

Niepoort 2001 Vertente Portuguese Red (Douro) $26. A rich, smooth, concentrated wine that shows great juicy fruit along with soft, cigar box tannins. It has vibrant fruit along with dark black flavors. This wine, from the hands of Douro master winemaker Dirk van Niepoort, could well be drunk now, but would certainly benefit from 5 years' cellaring. 89 —R.V. (11/1/2004)

Niepoort 1999 Batuta Red Blend (Douro) $60. Master Portmaker Dirk Niepoort seems also to excel at table wines. Dark and purple in color, it is filled with great black fruits, with blackberries and huge dark wood tastes. Smoky flavors combine with dark raisins and big fruits. Well-balanced, despite the high alcohol (14.5%), it is a stunning wine. 92 —R.V. (12/31/2002)

Niepoort 1999 Redoma Red Blend (Douro) $41. A more leathery, hot-country wine than Batuta, but this is still mighty impressive. Huge, dark, and black, it has dark, rich fruit flavors with great power and concentration. Acidity shows through at the end to just give it a lift. **92** —*R.V. (12/31/2002)*

Niepoort 2000 Redoma Reserva White Blend (Douro) $41. 91 Editors' Choice —*R.V. (11/1/2004)*

NOVAL

Noval NV LB Finest Reserve Port $18. Freshness and fruitiness are the hallmarks of this wine, from French-owned Noval. It is easy and simple, but some herbal flavors add an edge of interest and there is structure as well. The bitter aftertaste spoils the rest of the wine. **85** —*R.V. (3/1/2005)*

OFFLEY

Offley NV 10-Year Old Tawny Port $26. A very sweet style, with flavors of Hershey bars, figs, vanilla and caramel. Rather out of balance. **86** —*R.V. (8/1/2006)*

Offley NV 20-Year Old Tawny Port $48. A smooth, ripe, caramel- and toffee-flavored wine, with sweet fruit. Tastes young for a 20-year old, this still has good structure and is well integrated. **89** —*R.V. (8/1/2006)*

Offley NV 30-Year Old Tawny Port $45. This is a finely balanced, rich but elegant wine, from a company owned by Sogrape, Portugal's largest wine producer. There is some good burnt caramel flavor, as well as ripe fruit, and a delicious, just lightly fresh aftertaste. **90** —*R.V. (8/1/2006)*

Offley NV Baron de Forrester Reserva Port $NA. Aromas of raisins lead to sweet fruit and intense ripe flavors. The wine has richness but the main impression is of smoothness and softness, along with sweetness. Now owned by Portugal's largest wine company (also owner of Ferreira, Sandeman, and Mateus Rose Offley Ports bear the name of Baron Forrester, the Englishman who created the modern style of Port in the 19th century.) **87** —*R.V. (3/1/2005)*

Offley 1997 Boa Vista Port $19. There's hardly any tawny color to speak of here; it's actually deep red, much like a dry table wine. On the palate, candied flavors mingle with powerful berries. The finish is heavy and exceedingly long, offering flavors of coffee and burnt toast. This tawny is youthful and warm, emphasizing fruit over typical toffee and caramel characteristics. **84** —*M.S. (7/1/2002)*

Offley 2003 Boa Vista Vintage Port $50. A fine, structured wine from one of the Port houses now owned by Sogrape (Portugal's largest wine producer). It is in a relatively fast maturing style, but the Port has great, ripe blackberry jelly flavors, some dry tannins, and a full, fleshy feel. **90** —*R.V. (11/15/2005)*

Offley 1997 LBV Bottled 2001 Port) $23. Offley's Ports have improved considerably in quality. This LBV is the first fruits of new owners Sogrape, Portugal's largest wine company (who also own Ferreira and Sandeman Ports). It is ripe, elegant, and immediately fruity, with an attractive aroma of tea roses. But with its tannins and balance between sweetness and dryness, there is a more serious side to the wine, which suggests an aging potential. **89** —*R.V. (3/1/2003)*

OSBORNE

Osborne NV 10 Years Old Tawny Port $25. Light in body, which contributes to this wine's sense of being easy to drink. Coffee and caramel flavors mix creamily on the supple palate, finishing with elegant flourishes of nuts. **88** —*J.C. (3/1/2005)*

Osborne 1997 LBC Port $16. Shows floral aromas alongside fresh black cherries, leather, and anise. It's a pretty Port, much like Osborne's 2000 vintage wine, without bone-crushing concentration or extract yet possessed of an easy harmony. **86** —*J.C. (3/1/2004)*

Osborne 1999 LBV Port $14. Cherry and chocolate flavors abound in this rather simple LBV. It's clean and well-made, just doesn't show much depth or complexity, finishing on a tart note. **84** —*J.C. (3/1/2005)*

Osborne NV Special Reserve Master of Port $16. Very light, actually nearly translucent. Aromatics of caramel and butter lead into a super-sweet palate with plenty of vanilla and caramel flavors. The texture is creamy and there's ample woody character along with toasted nuts on the finish. It's quite sweet, yet structured. **87** —*M.S. (7/1/2002)*

Osborne 2003 Vintage Port $50. A disappointing Port from a firm that is better known for its Sherries and brandies. The fruit is highly perfumed,

with aromas of geraniums, but is not at all structured. Instead, it is much more in a light, fresh style. **84** —*R.V. (11/15/2005)*

Osborne 2000 Vintage Port $45. A solid, medium-weight offering that boasts supple tannins and pretty floral notes. Not a blockbuster, but a fruity vintage Port that should mature relatively quickly and provide ample enjoyment while you wait for the big boys to shed their massive tannins. **87** —*J.C. (3/1/2004)*

Osborne 1995 Vintage Port $40. This house was one of only a few that declared '95 a vintage year, but the proof is in the bottle: the decision was a good one. There's tons of stuffing and structure here, and it's just starting to come around to show defined plum, licorice, and coffee flavors. It's a tad hot on the finish, but that should fade if given another 10 years in the cellar. **88** —*M.S. (11/15/2002)*

PALACIO DE BREJOEIRA

Palacio de Brejoeira 2004 Alvarinho (Vinho Verde) $24. This is one of the flagship estates of Vinho Verde, based in the northern Monsão region: its VVs are based on Alvarinho. Has Riesling-like perfumes, but the intensity, green fruit and citrus flavors are all Vinho Verde. **90** —*R.V. (7/1/2006)*

PENINSULA

Peninsula 2003 Red Blend (Estremadura) $9. A fresh, fruit-driven style, marked by a touch of nail polish on the nose. It's medium-bodied, with tart cherry flavors on the palate. **84** —*J.C. (11/1/2006)*

PINHAL DA TORRE

Pinhal da Torre 2003 Two Worlds Portuguese Red (Ribatejano) $16. A blend of Cabernet Sauvignon and Touriga Nacional, so called because producer Paulo Cunha and US importer Robert Kacher felt the Cabernet was new world in its contribution, while the Touriga was firmly in the old world. Very ripe and juicy, this wine is full of black fresh fruits, just underlined by a touch of dry tannin. There is an openness as well as a dry aftertaste. **89** —*R.V. (7/1/2006)*

Pinhal da Torre 2003 Quinta do Alqueve Touriga Nacional (Ribatejano) $29. A powerful, impressive wine, which brings together very ripe fruit and fine juicy acidity and solid tannins. The fruit is concentrated, with black plums and a herbal layer. The aftertaste has acidity, but also ripeness. **92 Editors' Choice** —*R.V. (7/1/2006)*

Pinhal da Torre 2003 Quinta do Alqueve Touriga Nacional-Syrah (Ribatejano) $32. As a contrast to the great fruity straight Touriga Nacional from the same producer, this is a much drier, firmer wine. The tannins are very dry, packed with wood flavors as well as berry fruits and layers of acidity. A wine for aging, this needs a good 5 years. **92 Cellar Selection** —*R.V. (7/1/2006)*

PINTAS

Pintas 2002 Portuguese Red (Douro) $NA. Tasted as a cask sample, this wine was packed with new wood and red fruit flavors. It will not be as powerful, or as long-lasting as the 2001, but it has the potential for great drinkability within 5 years. **88** —*R.V. (11/1/2004)*

Pintas 2001 Portuguese Red (Douro) $60. Sweet ripe fruit, packed with flavors of blackberry juice, and balanced by new wood. This is a serious wine, showing pepper, herbs, firm, dry tannins, and great aging potential. It is certainly a world-class wine, but it also keeps its roots firmly in the Douro, with its solid structure, opulent ripe fruit, and food-friendly character. **91** —*R.V. (11/1/2004)*

PONTUAL

Pontual 2004 Reserva Portuguese Red (Alentejano) $38. It's mainly (80%) Alicante Bouschet with 10% each Syrah and Touriga Nacional, but this wine bears something of a resemblance to Port. Dark chocolate and blueberry notes show up on the nose, although there are also bright raspberry and vanilla flourishes. Long and a bit peppery on the finish, this is a winter-weight red to have alongside braised meats. **90** —*J.C. (11/1/2006)*

Pontual 2004 Touriga Nacional-Trincadeira Portuguese Red (Alentejano) $23. Weirdly floral on the nose, reminiscent of strawberry- or cherry-scented candles and somewhat akin to air freshener. Very red-fruity on the medium-weight palate, with a Sweet Tart quality. Tasted three times, with consistent notes. **84** —*J.C. (11/1/2006)*

Pontual 2004 Syrah (Alentejano) $23. Dark and meaty, this Syrah shows its hot weather climate without losing all of its nuance. Hints of anise, meat, and dried spices add a layer of flavor atop the chocolate and black cherry base, while the supple tannins and soft texture end gracefully. **89** —J.C. (11/1/2006)

PORCA DE MURCA

Porca de Murca 2000 Reserve Red Blend (Douro) $16. Leathery, with slightly raisiny fruit flavors reminiscent of prune or dried cherries. The tough tannins are mouth-drying and may not have the fruit behind them to support extended aging. Drink now with hearty foods that need an austere counterpoint. **83**—J.C. (3/1/2004)

Porca de Murca 2001 Tinto Red Blend (Douro) $10. Soft and supple on the finish, this leathery, medium-weight wine could substitute for a decent Côtes-du-Rhône. Chocolate and cherries fill out the midpalate. **85**—J.C. (3/1/2004)

Porca de Murca 2002 Branco Reserva White Blend (Douro) $10. This unique blend of 50% Sémillon, 25% Gouveio, and 25% Cerceal (Sercial) is plump and aromatic enough (pears, tropical fruit) but the flavors are less pronounced. Finishes on a tart, grapefruity note. **84**—J.C. (3/1/2004)

PORTAL

Portal NV Cellar Reserve Port $NA. This comes from Quinta do Portal, well known for its Douro table wines. It is a fine, concentrated Port which shows tannins, fresh fruit and flavors of cherries. It is spoiled by the stalky aromas, but the taste is good compensation. **86**—R.V. (3/1/2005)

PORTAL DO FIDALGO

Portal do Fidalgo 2004 Alvarinho (Vinho Verde) $15. From the sub region of Monção, this is a richly fruity Alvarinho, featuring pineapple and pears. It's ultimately a little simple, but satisfying and cleanly made. **84** —J.C. (12/31/2005)

Portal do Fidalgo 2002 Alvarinho (Vinho Verde) $15. Pricey for a Vinho Verde, but one of the best we've tasted on this side of the Atlantic. It's lean and minerally, with hints of green apple, lime, and fresh fennel. Finishes long and crisp, with a mineral note that lingers gracefully. **87 Editors' Choice**—J.C. (3/1/2004)

PORTO POÇAS

Porto Poças NV 10-Year Old Tawny Port $20. This independent company has a reputation for its aged tawnies. This 10-Year Old is in the sweet style, but it has a fine freshness, as well as flavors of figs and firm, structured fruit at its core. **86**—R.V. (8/1/2006)

Porto Poças NV 20-Year Old Tawny Port $50. A generally balanced sweet wine, with layers of candied fruits, and sweet marmalade flavors. The ripeness and the sweetness are spoiled by the volatility that shows in the finishing acidity. **87**—R.V. (8/1/2006)

Porto Poças NV 30-Year Old Tawny Port $60. This is dry, with burnt aromas. The palate is very concentrated, packed with bitter fruits and hints of lemon. A sipping Port, just ready for contemplation. **89**—R.V. (8/1/2006)

Poças NV 40-Year Old Tawny Port $130. This is a very old 40-year old, with some harsh, burnt, and rubber flavors. There's high acidity and caramel toffee, masking the mature fruit. **84**—R.V. (8/1/2006)

Poças 2003 Director's Choice Vintage Port $19. A big, perfumed, delicious wine that seduces with its opulence and generosity. It also offers some dry tannins which beautifully frame the ripe, red fruits. **91**—R.V. (11/15/2005)

Poças 2003 Vintage Port $46. This house is still a relative newcomer to vintage Port, having declared its first vintage in 1960. The style of this Port is very rich and concentrated, with a full, sweet character. To judge by the sweet tannins, it is a Port for medium-term aging. **91**—R.V. (11/15/2005)

Porto Poças NV Director's Choice Tawny Port $20. Starts with aromas of dried cherries, a slight nuttiness, and hints of smoke. Elegant and smooth in the mouth, its lovely nutty flavors are buffered by dried cher-

ries and honey. Finishes long, just a touch on the tart side. **89**—J.C. (3/1/2005)

Porto Poças 1998 LBV Port $23. This is a dense, chocolatey, and plummy wine, on the full-bodied side, with modest tannins to provide balance. A bit chunky, but satisfying, with bold, fleshy flavors and hints of caramel. **88**—J.C. (3/1/2005)

Porto Poças NV Quinta Vale de Cavalos Special Reserve Ruby Port $19. A single quinta Reserva, which is young and seems to have the potential to age in bottle. The aromas are fresh and lightly stalky. It is well-made and fruity with layers of tannins along with firm fruit flavors. It would be worth buying this now and keeping it until the end of the year. **88**—R.V. (3/1/2005)

Porto Poças NV Ruby Port $14. Starts with dusty earth scents alongside black plums, then develops flavors of chocolate and earth as well. Supple and fleshy, with little in the way of tannin, just a slightly tart edge to the finish to keep things in balance. **85**—J.C. (3/1/2005)

Porto Poças NV Tawny Port $14. Earthy and a bit simple, with modest dried fruit flavors and hints of candied orange peel. Lacks concentration, making it seem a little warm on the finish, but it's a solid performer in its class. **84**—J.C. (3/1/2005)

Porto Poças 2001 Vintage Port $70. Floral and spicy on the nose, leading into ripe blackberry and blueberry flavors. Not the richest mouthfeel or deepest flavors, but a pretty Port that finishes with crisp acidity and firm tannins. Drink 2010–2020. **89**—J.C. (6/1/2006)

PORTO SOLENE

Porto Solene NV Ruby Special Reserve Port $40/500 ml. Even for a ruby, this is dark purple in color and attractively saturated in the glass. It's somewhat grapey, but avoids simplicity by blending in hints of mulberries, chocolate, and spice. Full-bodied and slightly tannic, it shows good grip for a basic ruby, although a touch of heat does show through on the finish. Not available in the U.S. **88**—J.C. (11/1/2006)

PRATS & SYMINGTON LDA

Prats & Symington LDA 2003 Chryseia Portuguese Red (Douro) $66. As you might expect—but see all too rarely—this Douro table wine comes close in character to Port, with bold, blackberry fruit-filled aromas that verge on being over-ripe. It's got ample alcohol but not to excess, with a firm structure of acid and tannins to hold things in place. Long on the finish; give this 3–5 years to round out and develop some more nuances. **92**—J.C. (11/1/2006)

Prats & Symington LDA 2000 Chryseia (Douro) $45. A joint venture between the Symington family and Bruno Prats, formerly of Château Cos d'Estournel in Bordeaux, has produced Chryseia. The name is Greek for "gold," a play on the River Douro's name (which means "gold" in Portuguese). It is a fully extracted wine, with purple colors and rich tannins, but it is also finely balanced and very elegant. Still young, with a dry finish, it should develop in a classic Bordeaux way over the next 5–10 years. **92**—R.V. (12/31/2002)

Prats & Symington LDA 2004 Post Scriptum de Chryseia Portuguese Red (Douro) $24. It's a second label, but the quality is still very good, with blackberry and black cherry fruit amped up by the addition of wood spice and vanilla. Tannins are supple, yet firm enough to give the bold fruit focus and structure on the finish. Drink now–2010. **89**—J.C. (11/1/2006)

Prats & Symington LDA 2001 Chryseia Portuguese Red (Douro) $25. The joint venture between Bruno Prats, formerly of Cos d'Estournel in Bordeaux, and the Symington family has already produced some great wines. This latest release of Chryseia, a blend of classic Douro varieties, is packed with intense cigar box aromas, with elegant tannins and with flavors of ripe, almost juicy red fruits. A herbal character is also in the blend to give a warm feel to what is a sophisticated wine. **91 Editors' Choice**—R.V. (11/1/2004)

Prats & Symington LDA 2002 Post Scriptum de Chryseia Portuguese Red (Douro) $NA. The poor-quality 2002 vintage encouraged partners Bruno Prats and the Symington family not to make Chryseia, but to make a second wine instead. This is a wine that will age fast, and already has soft

PORTUGAL

tannins and attractive dark fruit flavors. The acidity still needs to soften before it is completely ready to drink. **88** —*R.V. (11/1/2004)*

PRESIDENTIAL

Presidential 2000 LBV Port $20. Less lush and welcoming than the other LBVs reviewed for this issue, C. da Silva's Presidential brand instead shows more acidity and tannin. The result is a crisp, pepper-, and plum-flavored Port with a slight rancio quality. **87** —*J.C. (6/1/2006)*

Presidential 2003 Vintage Port $55. Sold mainly to the Pousadas, the state-owned hotel chain of Portugal, Presidential is nevertheless a brand worth looking out for, especially for tawnies. This vintage is well structured, firm, and ripe. **88** —*R.V. (11/15/2005)*

PROVAM

Provam 2005 Alvarinho Portal do Fidalgo Alvarinho (Vinho Verde) $15. Provam is a grouping of 10 growers in the Monsão area. Citrus and green fruit flavors dominate this Alvarinho-based wine. Intensely flavored wine, dry, and great for food. **90 Best Buy** —*R.V. (7/1/2006)*

Provam 2005 Varanda do Conde Portuguese White (Vinho Verde) $10. This blend of Alvarinho and Trajadura comes from the former vineyard of a local nobleman. It is a great, ripe wine, packed with tropical fruits, only very slightly off-dry because of its richness. **89** —*R.V. (7/1/2006)*

QUARLES HARRIS

Quarles Harris NV 10-Year Old Tawny Port $NA. A dry, fruity wine, burnt with acidity and somewhat unbalanced spirit. It's firm, dry, but rather dull. **85** —*R.V. (8/1/2006)*

Quarles Harris 2003 Vintage Port $NA. A dry, power-packed Port from one of the Symington-owned brands. The wine is dense, structured, and full of big, firm fruit flavors. A touch of stalkiness is a discordant note. **88** —*R.V. (11/15/2005)*

QUINTA D'AGUIEIRA

Quinta d'Aguieira 2000 Alvarinho Chardonnay (Beiras) $10. An unusual Chardonnay, in which green, fresh wood flavors (Portuguese oak?) meld with sweet, juicy tropical fruit. It's light to medium weight, with a slightly slick mouthfeel and decent length, but the green note persists and doesn't meld harmoniously with the fruit's pear-guava-nectar sweetness. **84** —*M.M. (12/31/2001)*

Quinta d'Aguieira 2001 Touriga Nacional-Cabernet Sauvignon (Beiras) $13. This blend is 60% Cabernet Sauvignon, and it really dominates the wine, imparting black olive and bell pepper aromas that merge with cherry fruit and sweet oak on the palate. Supple and chewy, finishing with dry oak and firm tannins. **84** *(1/1/2004)*

Quinta d'Aguieira 1999 Touriga Nacional-Cabernet Sauvignon (Bairrada) $13. This uncommon marriage of big-boned red grapes seems over-ripe and bloated. Flavors of rum-drenched fruitcake and black plums mingle with dark chocolate and meat in the middle, but it's around the edges where it suffers. It has no noticeable acidity or balance. Hot, heavy, raisiny, and seemingly stewed. **80** —*M.S. (12/31/2001)*

Quinta d'Aguieira 2002 White Blend (Beiras) $8. The Maria Gomes variety is said to provide this wine's floral aromas, the Bical, its structure. Starts off with scents of flowershop greens and peaches, showing some apple flavors on the palate. Finishes tart, lemony, and chalky; a fine palate refresher that has enough weight to accompany food. **86 Best Buy** *(12/15/2003)*

Quinta d'Aguieira 2000 White Blend (Beiras) $8. Bical and Maria Gomes are the grapes. The aromas are floral, verging on Muscat- or Riesling-like. Flavors are green apple, pears, tropical fruit, and tangerine, finishing spicy, with a hint of orange rind. **85 Best Buy** —*J.C. (12/31/2001)*

QUINTA DA AVELEDA

Quinta da Aveleda 2000 Alvarinho Alvarinho (Vinho Verde) $12. **88** —*R.V. (8/1/2004)*

Quinta da Aveleda 2001 Loureiro (Vinho Verde) $7. Green apple notes give way to grapefruit and melon, but tart lime and green apple flavors power this wine. **84** —*J.C. (7/1/2003)*

Quinta da Aveleda 2005 Portuguese White (Vinho Verde) $8. One of the markers for Vinho Verde, this brand gets better and better. The 2005 is a new blend, with 10% of Alvarinho from the Aveleda estate. It is ripe and rich, with great solid full fruits in the mouth, tropical but with some citrus character. It's bone dry, with fine finishing acidity. **89 Best Buy** —*R.V. (7/1/2006)*

Quinta da Aveleda 2000 Aveleda Red Blend (Estremadura) $6. With its purple color, aromas of bitter chocolate and coffee flavors, along with acidity and raspberry fruits, this is an easy but appealing wine. Finishes dry. **86 Best Buy** —*R.V. (12/31/2002)*

Quinta da Aveleda 2000 Charamba Red Blend (Douro) $7. Rather light weight, but with its charming aromas of black cherries, smoke, and herbs and flavors of cherry and earth, this is a pretty wine. With more weight and intensity, this would be a stunning value. **85 Best Buy** *(1/1/2004)*

Quinta da Aveleda 1999 Charamba Red Blend (Douro) $7. A simple but lightweight wine, with freshness and fruitiness, good acidity, and some sweet jelly flavors. In the end, though, the fruit is too lean. **83** —*R.V. (12/31/2002)*

Quinta da Aveleda 2000 Quinta da Aguieira Touriga Nacional (Beiras) $26. The wine comes from Aveleda's latest purchase, a vineyard in Bairrada region. Made under the supervision of Bordeaux winemaker Denis Dubourdieu, it strives to combine the wild dark acidity, black fruit, and wood flavors of Portugal with the more restrained elegance of Bordeaux. At this stage, the combination needs time to work—maybe three or four years would help. **85** —*R.V. (12/31/2002)*

Quinta da Aveleda 2000 Quinta d'Aguiera Touriga Nacional-Cabernet Sauvignon (Beiras) $16. Dusty black currant aromas with some wood are accompanied on the palate by lean, slightly green fruit, with dusty tannins and flavors of bell peppers. **84** —*R.V. (12/31/2002)*

Quinta da Aveleda 2001 Trajadura (Vinho Verde) $7. A whiff of peach or apricot gives this Vinho Verde a little extra interest beyond its green apple and citrus flavors. Crisp and refreshing, with a tart, chalky finish. **86** —*J.C. (7/1/2003)*

Quinta da Aveleda 2002 Aveleda Trajadura (Vinho Verde) $8. One of several single-variety Vinho Verdes made by Aveleda, the Trajadura is plump, offering more tropical fruit aromas and flavors than the typical Vinho Verde blends. Finishes soft and easy, not at all bracingly tart. **84** *(12/15/2003)*

Quinta da Aveleda 2000 White Blend (Vinho Verde) $9. Clean, with a light spritzy feel on the palate, this offers nice hay, melon, and even tangerine notes on the nose. The mouth shows more of the same, with green apple and herb flavors as well. Completely correct Vinho Verde, this finishes dry, with a mineral citrus tang that fairly begs for seafood. **85** —*M.M. (12/31/2001)*

Quinta da Aveleda 2002 Alvarinho White Blend (Vinho Verde) $12. Slightly floral nose boasts hints of apple and pear alongside more prominent notes of mint and fresh greens. Plump apple and pear flavors on the palate, finishing clean and herbal. **86** *(12/15/2003)*

Quinta da Aveleda NV Aveleda White Blend (Vinho Verde) $6. With 1.5% residual sugar, this doesn't show the same crispness or clarity of flavor as the 2002 vintage wine, blending dusty apple and earth notes with prickly acidity. **83** *(12/15/2003)*

Quinta da Aveleda NV Aveleda White Blend (Vinho Verde) $6. **84** —*R.V. (8/1/2004)*

Quinta da Aveleda NV Casal Garcia White Blend (Vinho Verde) $6. A light spritz gives this wine some of the character of club soda and lime, with a slight brininess to add interest. **82** —*J.C. (7/1/2003)*

Quinta da Aveleda NV Casal Garcia White Blend (Vinho Verde) $6. This simple Vinho Verde's spice, melon, and lime flavors and prickly, aggressive mouthfeel are somewhat reminiscent of a gin and tonic. Serve it the same way—well chilled as an apéritif. **84** *(12/15/2003)*

Quinta da Aveleda 2001 Grinalda White Blend (Vinho Verde) $8. **87** —*R.V. (8/1/2004)*

Quinta da Aveleda 2000 Grinalda White Blend (Vinho Verde) $9. Pineapple and pear aromas lead into a ripe (for Vinho Verde) wine that at first seems a bit soft. Give it some time though, and a steely edge of lime-like acidity emerges, giving it just the requisite bite to cut through a plate of grilled sardines. A blend of Loureiro and Trajdura. **84** —*J.C. (12/31/2001)*

Quinta da Aveleda 2002 Quinta da Aveleda White Blend (Vinho Verde) $7. The basic blend shows typical green lime and grassy-herbal aromas, lean, citrusy flavors and a clean, refreshing finish. Perfect for washing down a plate of grilled or fried sardines. **84** *(12/15/2003)*

Quinta da Aveleda 2001 Quinta de Aveleda White Blend (Vinho Verde) $7. **88** —*R.V. (8/1/2004)*

QUINTA DA CARVALHOSA

Quinta da Carvalhosa 2002 Ardosino Portuguese Red (Douro) $18. This is the second wine from Carvalhosa. It manages to bring great black currant fruit and firm tannins to the lightweight 2002 vintage. There are flavors of tar, and of acidity balanced with fine wood. Drink after 4–5 years. **88** —*R.V. (11/1/2004)*

Quinta da Carvalhosa 2001 Campo Ardosa Portuguese Red (Douro) $30. Matured in new oak, this shows how the Douro is capable of great elegance. Flavors of dark fruits balance dry tannins and spice. This wine will age, for 10 years or more. **94 Editors' Choice** —*R.V. (11/1/2004)*

Quinta da Carvalhosa 2001 Ardosino Red Blend (Douro) $22. Richly fruity, with aromas of raspberries and cherries, joined by leathery complexities and a hint of vanilla. This is a fresh, easy-drinking wine with enough crispness and tannic structure to stand up to roast pork. Picks up intriguing smoky, meaty notes on the finish. **87** —*J.C. (3/1/2004)*

QUINTA DA CORTEZIA

Quinta da Cortezia 2005 Vinho Branco Arinto (Estremadura) $12. For a white wine from hot Estremadura, this shows admirable freshness, with apple, pear, and nectarine flavors touched with hints of mint and graphite. It's medium- to full-bodied, but finishes dry and steely without being hard. **86** —*J.C. (11/1/2006)*

Quinta da Cortezia 2004 Reserve Red Blend (Estremadura) $16. For a wine from warm Estremadura, this is a rather bright wine, marked by red cherries and sandalwood. Touches of dry oak and cocoa emerge on the finish. **86** —*J.C. (11/1/2006)*

Quinta da Cortezia 2004 Vinha Conchas Red Blend (Estremadura) $8. A great value in everyday table wine, Quinta da Cortezia's second label offers bright cherry fruit accented by just enough mineral and spice elements to keep you coming back for another sip. A slightly creamy texture is balanced by crisp acids on the finish. Drink now. **87 Best Buy** —*J.C. (11/1/2006)*

Quinta da Cortezia 2004 Vinha Conchas Special Selection Red Blend (Estremadura) $11. This is a subsidiary label of Quinta da Cortezia that comes in two levels: Special Selection and regular. It's a modern-styled, fruit-focused wine, with blackberries leading the way, but buttressed by hints of mineral, peppery spice, and chocolate. Long and mouth-watering on the finish. Drink now–2010. **88 Best Buy** —*J.C. (11/1/2006)*

Quinta da Cortezia 1997 Touriga Nacional (Estremadura) $33. **91** *(10/1/1999)*

Quinta da Cortezia 1999 Reserva Touriga Nacional Blend (Estremadura) $32. Voluptuous, sweet tannins and intense dark wood are balanced by ripe, sweet acidity. A blend of Touriga Nacional, Tinta Roriz, and Merlot, it brings together style and complexity with immediate appeal. **90** —*R.V. (12/31/2002)*

QUINTA DA ESTEVEIRA

Quinta da Esteveira 2003 Colheita Seleccionada Portuguese Red (Douro) $NA. A classic Douro blend of Touriga Franca, Tinta Roriz, and 5% Touriga Nacional, this wine comes from vines in São João de Pesqueira. It is very classy and elegant, with very ripe tannins, powerful black fruits, and intense, perfumed flavors. This wine could certainly age for 5–10 years. **92** —*R.V. (3/1/2006)*

QUINTA DA FOZ

Quinta da Foz 1996 Vintage Port $50. This 1996 is finely poised, elegant, and has a sweetness and richness that makes it immediately appealing. But its fruit is shot through with tannins that suggest 10 years' aging potential. **90** —*R.V. (3/1/2004)*

Quinta da Foz 1992 Vintage Port $NA. Foz, a classic vintage for some shippers, was bottled as a single quinta by Cálem. It is solid, mature, but still

with a good tannic mouthfeel. It's not a heavyweight, but the fruit has the potential to last another 5 to 10 years. **89** —*R.V. (3/1/2004)*

QUINTA DA MANUELA

Quinta da Manuela 2000 Portuguese Red (Douro) $61. Starts off with lovely mixed berry scents, including hints of raspberry, blackberry, and mulberry, accented by hints of toast and cedar. Darker fruit flavors emerge on the palate, adding earth, anise, and chocolate notes. For a full-bodied wine, it shows remarkable poise, balanced by modest tannins and decent acidity. Drink now-2010, possibly longer. **90** —*J.C. (3/1/2005)*

QUINTA DA MIMOSA

Quinta da Mimosa 2001 Periquita (Palmela) $16. Sure, it's oak-laden, but it's tasty oak, with vanilla and coconut flavors framing red raspberry fruit. The mouthfeel is creamy and smooth, the finish tart and tangy. **88** —*J.C. (11/15/2003)*

Quinta da Mimosa 2000 Tinto Red Blend (Palmela) $15. The toast and blackberry aromas seem to lighten with air, giving way to raspberry and strawberry scents. Flavors of sweet red berries and cream and a long, oaky finish. **88** —*J.C. (7/1/2003)*

QUINTA DA MURTA

Quinta da Murta 2005 Vinho Branco Seco Arinto (Bucelas) $10. Primarily Arinto, this distinctive, interesting white comes across as a citrus-flavored spice drop, blending tangerine and lime with pepper and anise. It's not particularly fleshy, turning crisp on the finish. Probably best with simple seafood dishes. **86 Best Buy** —*J.C. (11/1/2006)*

QUINTA DA PACHECA

Quinta da Pacheca 2003 Vintage Port $NA. The Serpa Pimentel family's estate is located on the south side of the Douro, in the hills leading to Lamego. This Port is a triumph for an estate better known for table wines. It is very pure, and flavored with dark red fruits, blackberry jelly, and a touch of bitter chocolate. A solid, enjoyable wine. **91** —*R.V. (11/15/2005)*

QUINTA DA PEDRA

Quinta da Pedra 2005 Alvarinho (Vinho Verde) $13. A 100% Alvarinho from this small, 34-acre estate near Monsão. This is a delicious, fresh wine, with great piercing acidity and bright pink grapefruit flavors. **89 Best Buy** —*R.V. (7/1/2006)*

QUINTA DA ROMEIRA

Quinta da Romeira 2003 Arinto (Bucelas) $9. Lime and chalk dust aromas ease into flavors of green apples and minerals. Finishes with mild citrus flavors that seem a bit softer than usual for this wine, giving it an atypically plump mouthfeel. **85 Best Buy** —*J.C. (3/1/2005)*

Quinta da Romeira 2002 Arinto (Bucelas) $8. Starts off with notes of honey and green apple, later showing more citrus and fresh pineapple flavors. It finishes crisp and clean, with a slightly creamy mouthfeel that keeps it from being too lean and citrusy. **85** —*J.C. (11/15/2003)*

Quinta da Romeira 2001 Estate Bottled Arinto (Bucelas) $7. Light and simple, with green apple and citrus aromas and flavors. Use it to wash down steamed shellfish at the beach. **83** —*J.C. (7/1/2003)*

Quinta da Romeira 2001 Morgado de Santa Catherina Arinto (Bucelas) $14. **90** —*R.V. (8/1/2004)*

Quinta da Romeira 1999 Morgado de Sta. Catherina Arinto (Bucelas) $13. On its own, you might fault this wine for seeming a bit dull and woody. But with the right food pairing, preferably something fruity seasoned with cumin and cinnamon, this wine can sing. Butter and nut aromas take hold, while dry notes of clove, mace, and cinnamon echo the food spices and a lemony tang comes through on the finish. **83** —*J.C. (12/31/2001)*

Quinta da Romeira 2004 Arinto Portuguese White (Bucelas) $NA. Delicious citric flavors and aromas dominate this fresh, green wine from the coast near Lisbon. It is crisp, with some layers of tannin and grapefruit. Drink within two years. **86** —*R.V. (8/1/2005)*

Quinta da Romeira 2003 Morgado de Santa Catherina Portuguese White (Bucelas) $NA. A finely poised wine from this appellation close to Lisbon. Made from the Arinto grape, it is delicate, but still has a creaminess almost like Chardonnay, from the wood aging and the lees stirring during and after fermentation. **88**—*R.V. (8/1/2005)*

Quinta da Romeira 2000 Calhandriz Red Blend (Estremadura) $7. A sweetly perfumed wine, light and fresh, with curious flavors of candies. **82**—*R.V. (12/31/2002)*

Quinta da Romeira 1999 Tradicão Red Blend (Palmela) $7. 87 Best Buy— *J.C. (12/15/2000)*

Quinta da Romeira 1999 Prova Regia Touriga Nacional (Estremadura) $13. A supple, oaky red, infused with aromas of sandalwood and flowers and flavors of roasted cherries and dried spices. Finishes smooth and creamy, with hints of vanilla. **88**—*J.C. (7/1/2003)*

QUINTA DAS BALDIAS

Quinta das Baldias 2003 Vintage Port $NA. José and Manuel Vizeu have been grape growers for three generations, and have been bottling their own wine since the 1980s. This is a dense, deep powerful Port, with firm tannins. It is sweet, structured, and impressive. **93**—*R.V. (11/15/2005)*

QUINTA DAS HEREDIAS

Quinta das Heredias NV 10-Year Old Tawny Port $28. With French winemaker Jean-Hugues Gros (who used to work in Burgundy with Jacques Prieur) in charge, Heredias is producing both table wines and Ports. This 10-Year Old is sweet, fresh, with caramel flavors, leavened with fresh acidity in the aftertaste. **86**—*R.V. (8/1/2006)*

Quinta das Heredias NV 20-Year Old Tawny Port $50. There are many failings here: reductive, volatile, unbalanced acidity. But just somewhere there is a small streak of orange marmalade. **80**—*R.V. (8/1/2006)*

Quinta das Heredias NV 40-Year Old Tawny Port $130. This wine certainly doesn't taste its age. It has more to do with sweet almond cookies and unbalanced spirit than mature flavors. **83**—*R.V. (8/1/2006)*

QUINTA DAS MAIAS

Quinta das Maias 2003 Malvasia Fina (Dão) $15. The exotic honey and spice character of the Malvasia shines through. It is full and light on the acidity, but that's compensated for by the power of the lychees, Asian fruits, and the touch of wood. **87**—*R.V. (8/1/2005)*

Quinta das Maias 2001 Portuguese Red (Dão) $18. This wine offers great power, despite the relatively low (12.5%) alcohol. That gives it balance, and drinkability, which makes it a pleasure. Rich, earthy fruit flavors are balanced by some dry tannins and soft acidity. Definitely food friendly. **89**—*R.V. (11/1/2004)*

Quinta das Maias 2000 Jaen Portuguese Red (Dão) $29. Under the same ownership as Quinta dos Roques, this estate, in the eastern Dão, has more granitic soil, producing softer, hotter wines. This 100% Jaen (the grape is also known as Tinta Mecilla in northeast Spain), is rich, fat, spicy, and generous. **89**—*R.V. (11/1/2004)*

Quinta das Maias 2000 Reserva Portuguese Red (Dão) $29. From 70-year-old vines, this is a ripe wine, packed with fruit and soft, dusty tannins. Aged 12 months in wood; a blend of Tinta Amarela, Tinta Roriz, and Touriga Nacional, this has lovely, generous, opulent flavors, and yet remains restrained in its alcohol (13%). **90**—*R.V. (11/1/2004)*

Quinta das Maias 2003 Portuguese White (Dão) $10. A generous ripe wine, with flavors of green fruits, grapefruit, and spice. A touch of wood gives complexity. A great food wine. **86 Best Buy**—*R.V. (8/1/2005)*

QUINTA DAS TECEDEIRAS

Quinta das Tecedeiras 2003 Vintage Port $35. Owned by Dão Sul, well-known as table wine producers, this is a fragrant, floral wine with soft, easy, raisiny flavors. There are some good dusty tannins, but this is a wine for early, enjoyable drinking. **88**—*R.V. (11/15/2005)*

Quinta das Tecedeiras 2001 Reserva Red Blend (Douro) $NA. This plump offering shows oak influence on the nose in its aromas of vanilla and toast, but considerably less on the palate, where flavors of road tar and blackberries kick in. Some slightly gritty tannins on the finish provide grip to this low-acid wine. **86**—*J.C. (11/15/2003)*

QUINTA DE CABRIZ

Quinta de Cabriz 2003 Colheita Seleccionada Portuguese Red (Dão) $7. This blend of Alfrochiero, Tinta Roriz, and Touriga Nacional is a steal at the $7 price. The meaty, peppery, blackberry nose and bouncy, medium-weight palate makes this wine a ringer for a good Côtes-du-Rhône, at a fraction of the price. Even shows good length on the peppery finish. Drink now–2008. **89 Best Buy**—*J.C. (6/1/2006)*

Quinta de Cabriz 2000 Colheita Seleccionada Red Blend (Dão) $20. A pleasant, simple quaffer, with baked red fruit flavors of strawberry and cherry. It's relatively light in body, with a short, chocolatey finish. **85**— *J.C. (11/15/2003)*

QUINTA DE CHOCAPALHA

Quinta de Chocapalha 2001 Portuguese Red (Estremadura) $NA. This is a dense, intense wine, a blend of Touriga Nacional, Tinta Roriz and Alicante Bouchet. It is firmly tannic, but there is plenty of powerful fruit as well. Dark fruit flavors give depth and concentration. This is a fine wine, which will repay several years aging. **91 Editors' Choice**—*R.V. (11/1/2004)*

QUINTA DE COVELA

Quinta de Covela 2001 Colheita Seleccionada Portuguese Red (Portugal) $NA. This oak-aged wine, a blend of Touriga Nacional, Cabernet Sauvignon, and Merlot, is a successful balancing act between ripe acidity and cool-climate fruit. It has red fruits, lively flavors, and just a touch of wood, which certainly doesn't detract from the fruit. **87**—*R.V. (11/1/2004)*

Quinta de Covela 2002 Tinto Escolha Portuguese Red (Portugal) $NA. A fresh, fruity red wine, which is light and vibrant. A blend of Touriga Nacional, Merlot, Syrah, and Cabernet Franc, it is lively, full of red currants, and would be great with oily foods. Produced in the Minho region of northern Portugal, this cool climate wine has strong affinities with red Vinho Verde. **84**—*R.V. (11/1/2004)*

Quinta de Covela 2003 Branco Escolha Portuguese White (Portugal) $NA. This unoaked wine follows the same blend of Avesso and Chardonnay as Covela's oaked Colheita Seleccionada. Lighter in style and fresh, it is an equal success with its ripe apple flavors and full richness, a reflection of the warm 2003 vintage. **88**—*R.V. (11/1/2004)*

Quinta de Covela 2002 Colheita Seleccionada Portuguese White (Portugal) $NA. A great white wine, a blend of Avesso and Chardonnay, aged for 6 months in new French wood. It has richness, fine acidity, a creamy character, and flavors of ripe pears. It shows how northern Portugal, with its tradition of crisp Vinho Verde, is also able to produce top white wines. **90**—*R.V. (11/1/2004)*

Quinta de Covela 2004 Covela Portuguese White (Minho) $21. This floral wine is a successful blend of Gewürztraminer, Chardonnay, and the local Avesso. It is perfumed, but also full-bodied with a great layer of acidity. Drink by 2006. **86**—*R.V. (8/1/2005)*

Quinta de Covela 2003 Covela Colheita Seleccionada Portuguese White (Minho) $NA. A great creamy wine, with a lift of acidity. This blend of Chardonnay and Avesso, aged in French wood, has tropical fruits, vanilla and richness. Smooth and ripe. **89 Best Buy**—*R.V. (8/1/2005)*

Quinta de Covela 2003 Covela Fantástico Portuguese White (Minho) $NA. A hugely toasty, woody wine at this stage, but there is also ripe fruit with flavors of ripe quince, lychees, and spice. Made from a selection of wines, this is the Reserve wine from Quinta de Covela. **90**—*R.V. (8/1/2005)*

Quinta de Covela 1999 Vinho Branco White Blend (Portugal) $13. This is more or less a Douro Valley white made of Avessa and Chardonnay. It features some tangy fruit and a pleasant sweet almond core, but it seems to be losing its edge. At one moment it's fairly harmonious, but in the next moment it seems tired. **83**—*M.S. (12/31/2001)*

QUINTA DE LA ROSA

Quinta de la Rosa NV 10-year old Tawny Port $37. This deliciously nutty tawny has old wood and concentrated flavors. They balance against fresh, sweet fruit and coffee flavors, along with some acidity and elegance. **88**—*R.V. (3/1/2004)*

Quinta de la Rosa NV Finest Reserve Port $28. This is a structured style of Port, which hangs together well, with its ripe fruit and flavors of tar, rosewater, and black figs. The tannins and the structure blend combine with sweetness to give an attractive balanced wine. The quinta of la Rosa, owned by the Bergqvist family, is perched dramatically on the north bank of the Douro close to Pinhão. **88** —*R.V. (3/1/2005)*

Quinta de la Rosa 1997 LBV Bottled 2002 Port $26. The quinta of la Rosa is perched dramatically on the north bank of the Douro close to Pinhão. The house itself has great views of the river. This LBV is attractively fruity, with sweetness, generosity, and soft tannins. Flavor of sweet chocolate and dried fruits make it very appealing. **87** —*R.V. (3/1/2003)*

Quinta de la Rosa 1999 Vale do Inferno Vintage Port $52. From a small, low-yielding parcel of old vines, this Port comes with huge intensity and concentrated flavors. It is dark, powerful, and almost brooding. The potential in this wine, with its dry tannins over the juicy fruit, is impressive—15–20 years at least. **92 Cellar Selection** —*R.V. (3/1/2004)*

Quinta de la Rosa 2003 Vintage Port $NA. Owned by the Bergqvist family, this stunning quinta, on the banks of the Douro near Pinhão, produces both Port and table wines. This 2003 vintage is a fine, firmly tannic wine, which also manages to push through with sweet fruit. The structure and the aging potential are both excellent. **94** —*R.V. (11/15/2005)*

Quinta de la Rosa 2000 Vintage Port $NA. The Bergqvist family has made a sweet ripe 2000, flavored with red and dried fruits. The tannins are well-structured and concentrated, powering through the fruit and the sweetness. The wine has a medium-term aging potential of 8-12 years. **89** —*R.V. (3/1/2004)*

Quinta de la Rosa 2001 Portuguese Red (Douro) $NA. Rich, juicy fruit with great acidity and firm, but not overpowering, tannins. It has tarry and juicy black fruits which give concentration. The finishing acidity and the wood flavors give it complexity. **89** —*R.V. (11/1/2004)*

Quinta de la Rosa 2001 Vale de Clara Portuguese Red (Douro) $NA. This blend of Tinta Roriz, Tinta Barroca, and Touriga Franca grapes is the second label of the Quinta de la Rosa estate, and is made from young vines. It is fresh and packed with vibrant red fruit flavors. Great to drink over the next several years. **86** —*R.V. (11/1/2004)*

Quinta de la Rosa 2001 Quinta la Rosa Red Blend (Douro) $18. The attractive Quinta de la Rosa, at Pinhão, under the ownership of the Bergqvist family, is aquiring a good name for its table wines as well as its Ports. This vintage has delicious, ripe, sweet fruit on the nose and fine forward fruit and sweetness. The ripeness and almost-jelly juiciness give a real sense of the wine being made from serious Port fruit. **90** —*R.V. (12/31/2002)*

Quinta de Pancas 1996 Cabernet Sauvignon (Estremadura) $13. 83 — *(10/1/1999)*

Quinta de Pancas 2003 Cabernet Sauvignon (Estremadura) $15. Seems relatively mature already, showing herbal, tobacco-like scents and some earthy, loamy flavors. Leather and spice notes add complexity to the dry, dusty finish. **84** —*J.C. (11/1/2006)*

Quinta de Pancas 2003 Special Selection Cabernet Sauvignon (Estremadura) $35. Ripe, full-bodied, and powerful, this is a delicious, velvety wine. The tannins are tamed by richness and wood flavors, and balanced with licorice flavors and opulent, jammy fruits. **89** —*R.V. (3/1/2006)*

Quinta de Pancas 2003 Premium Red Portuguese Red (Estremadura) $80. A limited release (4,000 bottles) of wine from the best casks of 2003, selected after 18 months of wood aging. It certainly is a stunning wine: big, rich, tarry, very polished, and ripe. There is great depth of flavor here, solid figs, and dried fruits along with ripe black plums. There's a layer of dry tannin that will soften as the wine ages. Give it another five years. **94** —*R.V. (3/1/2006)*

Quinta de Pancas 2003 Reserva Especial Red Portuguese Red (Estremadura) $38. Bordeaux meets Douro in this wine, a blend of Cabernet Sauvignon, Petit Verdot, and Touriga Nacional. They seem to like each other in this powerful, explosive wine. It is dense, perfumed,

with very ripe tannins and a great balance between dryness and big, black fruits. This could age well over 5–10 years. **93** —*R.V. (3/1/2006)*

Quinta de Parrotes 2002 Red Wine Portuguese Red (Alenquer) $9. Despite containing only a small percentage of Cabernet Sauvignon, the herbal—almost vegetal—scent of unripe Cabernet dominates this wine. It's plump and round in the mouth, yet has a distinctly unripe character to it. If you can, track down the 2001 instead—it's much better. **82** —*J.C. (6/1/2006)*

Quinta de Parrotes 2001 Red Blend (Alenquer) $9. Tastes more than a little like a decent cru bourgeois, with scents of leather and cedar and flavors of tea, tobacco, and cassis. Medium-weight and surprisingly elegant. A blend of Castelão and Cabernet Sauvignon. **86 Best Buy** —*J.C. (11/1/2004)*

Quinta de Roriz 1999 Vintage Port $50. Top wine from this smaller estate. It's incredibly stylish, even as young as it is now. A lighter body featuring more liquid and less plum pudding should mean that it will be an easy drinker come maturity. With pure fruit, spice, and lots of coffee already poking through, it has a fine future. Drink after 2010. **91** —*M.S. (11/15/2002)*

Quinta de Roriz 2003 Vintage Port $57. Jointly owned by the Symington family and João van Zeller, this Port is charming, with balanced, attractive, open fruit. If there is a touch of greenness in the wine from the tannins, it is still going to be a delicious Port. **87** —*R.V. (11/15/2005)*

Quinta de Roriz 2002 Vintage Port $52. Very fruity, elegant, and supple for a vintage Port, with waves of raspberry and mulberry fruit that cascade across the palate. Some dusty tannins and tart acidity show on the finish, so this does have some structure, but it's likely destined for early drinking, not old bones. **90** —*J.C. (12/1/2004)*

Quinta de Roriz 2001 Vintage Port $48. Richly textured, verging on opulent, this should be a relatively early-maturing Port. Complex and intriguing on the nose, where smoky, minerally aromas evoke memories of sun-baked Douro schist, backed by plush blackberry fruit and a dash of maple syrup. Best from 2010. **92 Editors' Choice** —*J.C. (11/15/2003)*

Quinta de Roriz 2004 Prazo de Roriz Portuguese Red (Douro) $14. The Symington family continues to make strides in their table wine production. This is a full-bodied, smooth-textured bistro-styled red that's more of a dark purple in hue, bringing blackberry, blueberry, and spice and mineral notes to the table. Enjoy it over the next year or two for its exuberant fruit. **89 Best Buy** —*J.C. (6/1/2006)*

Quinta de Roriz 2003 Prazo de Roriz Portuguese Red (Douro) $13. Shows excellent complexity and minerality for a wine of this price, with smoke and stone dust notes layered elegantly over cherry-berry fruit. It's medium-bodied, with creamy tannins that make it immediately approachable. Drink now. **87** —*J.C. (12/31/2005)*

Quinta de Roriz 2002 Prazo de Roriz Portuguese Red (Douro) $13. The second label of Quinta de Roriz, from the lighter 2002 vintage, is a wine for early drinking. It has fresh red fruits, soft tannins, and good balancing acidity. The word "prazo," meaning "lease," was the name given to the quinta in the 18th century. **85** —*R.V. (11/1/2004)*

Quinta de Roriz 2002 Reserva Portuguese Red (Douro) $26. This medium-bodied blend of Touriga Nacional (45%), Touriga Franca (35%), and Tinta Roriz (20%) lacks a bit of flesh, but you wouldn't call it lean, either. Instead, it's sinewy in texture and feel, with masses of blackberry and mulberry fruit upfront and dusty, slightly drying notes on the finish. **87** —*J.C. (11/1/2006)*

Quinta de Roriz 2001 Reserva Portuguese Red (Douro) $23. A joint venture between the quinta's owner João van Zeller and the Symington family, this wine was aged in new oak for 12 months. The result is rich, with sweet but firm tannins, with flavors of red currant fruits and sweet figs. It could well age for 10 years or more, with its dark, intense aftertaste. **90 Editors' Choice** —*R.V. (11/1/2004)*

Quinta de Roriz 2001 Reserva Portuguese Red (Douro) $24. Smoky and charred, with scents of coffee and game that dominate the pleasant dark-skinned plum fruit underneath. Smooth and creamy in the mouth, with a long, softly tannic finish. **86** —*J.C. (12/31/2005)*

Quinta de Roriz 2000 Reserva Portuguese Red (Douro) $23. A powerful, oak-aged wine with fine, ripe red fruits and black tannins. This Reserva wine has 12 months French oak aging, which gives it complexity, but the richness of the fruit gives a great firm balance to the wood. It is still young; age for at least 5 years. **91 Editors' Choice** —*R.V. (11/1/2004)*

Quinta de Roriz 2001 Prazo de Roriz Red Blend (Douro) $13. This wine is made from new plantings at Roriz, which is controlled by a partnership of the Symington family and João van Zeller. A blend of Tinta Roriz, Tinta Franca, Touriga Nacional, and Tinta Barroca, it was matured in French oak. It's a big, generous, fruity wine and plenty of dusty tannins and bright fruit give a big, structured feel. **88** —*R.V. (12/31/2002)*

Quinta de Roriz 2000 Quinta de Roriz Reserva Red Blend (Douro) $29. The dark purple color, the huge, solid tannins, and new wood flavors make this a powerful but still elegant wine, produced by the Symington family in partnership with João van Zeller. A layer of dryness gives structure to the powerful, concentrated young fruit. **91** —*R.V. (12/31/2002)*

QUINTA DE SAES

Quinta de Saes 1996 Vinho Tinto Red Blend (Dão) $25. 87 *(10/1/1999)*

QUINTA DE VENTOZELO

Quinta de Ventozelo 2000 LBV Port $19. A very ripe style, with baked plum and prune aromas and flavors supported by hints of pastry crust and dried spices. Medium-to-full in body, with soft tannins and a long, spicy finish. **89** —*J.C. (6/1/2006)*

Quinta de Ventozelo NV Reserva Port $15. A pleasant, straightforward aromatic wine which is given a dark side by herbs and a slight touch of bitterness. Eucalyptus and stalkiness don't quite come together. **83** —*R.V. (3/1/2005)*

Quinta de Ventozelo 2003 Vintage Port $60. Still in the flush of youth, this creamy-textured vintage Port strikes all the right notes, from complex aromas to powerful flavors. Blackberry, plum, and earth notes finish long, buttressed by supple tannins. Based on the rapid maturation of the 2001 and 2002, drink this one from 2010-2020. **92** —*J.C. (6/1/2006)*

Quinta de Ventozelo 2002 Vintage Port $50. Already throwing considerable sediment and possessed of a creamy, supple mouthfeel, this is a vintage Port that should probably be consumed young. Enjoy its lush blueberry fruit, chocolate, and spice complexity over the next 10 years. **92** —*J.C. (6/1/2006)*

Quinta de Ventozelo 2001 Vintage Port $50. Doesn't show the richness or complexity of its younger counterparts, but this effort from Ventozelo is still pretty good. Modest floral and chocolate notes and youthful grapey flavors hint at further aging potential, but the tannins are already soft. Better to err on the young side and drink it over the next several years. **88** —*J.C. (6/1/2006)*

Quinta de Ventozelo 2000 Vintage Port $50. A lovely single-quinta wine that can be drunk now and over the next 10–15 years, Ventozelo's 2000 is a supple, creamy-textured Port that features slightly briary herbal-floral accents to its dark berry flavors. Picks up some intriguing spice notes on the finish, so it's not just a fruit bomb. **89** —*J.C. (11/1/2006)*

Quinta de Ventozelo 2000 Portuguese Red (Douro) $12. Not for the oak-averse, this is layered in cedar and vanilla, yet remains lean and focused, with roasted plum flavors supporting the oak. Finishes on a tart note, couched in soft, woody tannins. **86** —*J.C. (12/31/2004)*

Quinta de Ventozelo 2003 Amostra de Casco Portuguese Red (Douro) $15. Not up to the level of the single-variety bottlings, but still a decent drink, this offering from Quinta de Ventezelo offers coffee and roasted marshmallows layered over some rather herbal cherry fruit. Green and astringent on the finish. **84** —*J.C. (12/31/2005)*

Quinta de Ventozelo 2001 Cister da Ribeira Portuguese Red (Douro) $9. Presents admirably pure black cherry fruit in a medium-bodied format. What it lacks in weight and texture it makes up for in flavor, delivering fruit, mineral, and spice in a harmonious package that builds in intensity on the finish. **87 Best Buy** —*J.C. (12/31/2005)*

Quinta de Ventozelo 2000 Cistera da Ribeira Tinto Portuguese Red (Douro) $9. This wine starts off with distinctive and promising aromas of smoked and cured meats and tea leaves, but it falls off a bit on the palate, turning lean and cranberryish. **84** —*J.C. (12/11/2004)*

Quinta de Ventozelo 2001 Reserva Portuguese Red (Douro) $22. Another winner from Quinta de Ventozelo, the 2001 Reserva features complex, Rhône-like scents of leather, game, and spice alongside bold cherry flavors. Smooth and supple, with a long, piquant finish endowed with crisp acids and soft tannins. **89** —*J.C. (12/31/2005)*

Quinta de Ventozelo 2002 Tinto Portuguese Red (Douro) $15. This Douro red speaks clearly of its origins, blending anise and mineral notes with ripe fruit. Resin and spice notes add interest to the black cherry flavors, backed by just a hint of toasty oak. Structured and firm, this wine could use a bit more lushness and flesh, but nicely conveys its sense of place. **87** —*J.C. (6/1/2006)*

Quinta de Ventozelo 2000 Tinto Reserva Portuguese Red (Douro) $45. This oaky blend of Touriga Nacional, Touriga Franca, and Tinta Roriz is a pleasant wine, but one that ultimately lacks distinction, its fruit and terroir buried under an avalanche of admittedly tasty wood. Cedar and vanilla aromas and flavors dominate, coating the palate with soft tannins. **85** —*J.C. (12/1/2004)*

Quinta de Ventozelo 2003 Tinta Roriz (Douro) $16. A bit of a disappointment from this winery, but the flavors here seem a touch over-ripe, with pruny notes intruding into the blackberries. Obvious American oak marks the nose with herbal, dill-like notes and the finish with dry, woody tannins and caramel flavors. **85** —*J.C. (6/1/2006)*

Quinta de Ventozelo 2003 Touriga Franca (Douro) $16. Smoky, toasty, and vanilla-laden on the nose, but turns juicy and filled with cherry-berry fruit in the mouth. Medium-bodied, with more vanilla and some dry, woody notes on the finish. Good, if somewhat oaky. **86** —*J.C. (12/31/2005)*

Quinta de Ventozelo 2003 Tinto Touriga Nacional (Douro) $16. Lovely aromas of blackberries and coffee are laced with hints of cinnamon and vanilla. Bursts with fresh fruit—blueberries and blackberries—on the palate, but the flavors aren't simple, they're backed by layers of minerality and stone dust. Supple enough to drink now, but should hold up to five years, maybe longer. **90 Editors' Choice** —*J.C. (12/31/2005)*

QUINTA DO AMEAL

Quinta do Ameal 2004 Loureiro (Vinho Verde) $13. This top estate in the Ponte de Lima area produces beautiful, hand-crafted wines. This 100% Loureiro is almost Riesling-like in its perfumes, while its green fruit shows hints of an almond character, as well as piercingly clean ripeness and acidity. **91 Best Buy** —*R.V. (7/1/2006)*

Quinta do Ameal 2003 Escolha Loureiro (Vinho Verde) $25. Wood and Vinho Verde don't mix, say the pundits. They can, if the wood is handled as sensitively as it is here. The toast is there, but its job is to enhance and enlarge the dense, intense green fruit flavors. A fine white wine that's creamy and delicious. **92 Editors' Choice** —*R.V. (7/1/2006)*

QUINTA DO CARMO

Quinta do Carmo 2002 Portuguese Red (Alentejano) $23. Combines tobacco and baked fruit scents on the nose, then delivers flavors reminiscent of charred leather and cooked plums. Medium-bodied, with a supple, earth-and-tobacco finish. **82** —*J.C. (11/1/2006)*

Quinta do Carmo 2001 Portuguese Red (Alentejano) $30. This Lafite-owned venture in the south of Portugal has turned out a round, softly fruity wine dominated by chocolate and plum aromas and flavors. A blend of Aragonês, Alicante Bouschet, Trincadeira, Castelão, Cabernet Sauvignon, and Syrah. **86** —*J.C. (12/31/2005)*

Quinta do Carmo 2000 Portuguese Red (Alentejano) $25. A fine, elegant blend which shows restrained leather and herbal aromas and flavors of wood. This estate wine from the Rothschild-owned property is soft, with a layer of dark black cherries and prominent acidity. It should age over 4-5 years. **87** —*R.V. (12/1/2004)*

Quinta do Carmo 2003 Dom Martinho Portuguese Red (Alentejano) $13. This could use a little more intensity, but it's a decent quaff, offering bright scents of sour plum and cherry alongside a duller, charred note.

Chocolate and cherries on the palate, which is smooth and slightly creamy. Supple on the finish, this is ready to drink now. **84** —*J.C. (11/1/2006)*

Quinta do Carmo 2001 Dom Martinho Portuguese Red (Alentejano) $11. This is the second wine of the Rothschild-owned Quinta do Carmo. It is soft and supple with dry tannins and fresh, juicy fruit flavors. The tannins suggest it could age, but it is not a complex wine and is good to drink now. **84** —*R.V. (12/1/2004)*

Quinta do Carmo 2003 Reserva Portuguese Red (Alentejano) $55. Looking for a Portuguese Bordeaux? This offering from the Lafite branch of the Rothschild family fits the bill, despite its inclusion of indigenous Portuguese grape varieties. A veneer of cedary oak coats an earthy core of mulberry flavors in this medium-bodied red wine. Supple and earthy on the finish. Drink now–2015. **87** —*J.C. (11/1/2006)*

Quinta do Carmo 2001 Reserva Portuguese Red (Alentejano) $40. Spicy, smoky aromas give a French gloss to this first vintage of a reserve wine from the Rothschild owned estate. It is by far the most satisfying wine from Quinta do Carmo, showing good balance to go with the red fruits and sweet tannins. It should age well over the next 4-5 years. **89** —*R.V. (12/1/2004)*

Quinta do Carmo 2000 Red Blend (Alentejano) $25. Well-balanced, with alcohol levels under control and acids providing a tangy finish, despite coming from a hot growing region. The heat shows up in the wine's flavors, which lean toward dried or roasted cherries. Hints of caramel and oak intensify on the finish. **86** —*J.C. (12/10/2003)*

Quinta do Carmo 1999 Red Blend (Alentejano) $24. This property, close to Estremoz, is run by the Rothschilds of Château Lafite in Bordeaux. They have gone for Bordeaux elegance, with dark purple fruits mingled with some stalky dry tannins. But some of the richness and softness of the Alentejo has been lost. **85** —*R.V. (12/31/2002)*

Quinta do Carmo 1998 Red Blend (Alentejo) $30. This blend of four red grapes, none of which is Cabernet or Merlot, strives for a Bordeaux-like style, but only half achieves that goal. It has the right weight and body, but it lacks clarity of flavor and punch. The nose is smoky, with burnt-rubber notes. There's moderate cherry fruit at the core. The finish is long and amply smooth. **85** —*M.S. (11/15/2002)*

Quinta do Carmo 2002 Dom Martinho Red Blend (Alentejano) $12. An interesting wine—one that combines a certain sour, resinous quality with hints of sur-maturité. Add leather, clove, and cinnamon and the result is a reasonably complex wine for a reasonable price. **85** —*J.C. (6/1/2006)*

Quinta do Carmo 2000 Dom Martinho Red Blend (Alentejano) $10. Aromas of dried cherries and baking spices presage an earthy, leathery wine that seems a bit heavy without being particularly rich. The finish picks things up a notch, layering dark chocolate over dried fruit. **84** —*J.C. (3/1/2004)*

Quinta do Carmo 1999 Dom Martinho Red Blend (Alentejano) $10. The second wine of Quinta do Carmo is dominated by earthy, meaty aromas. While the fruit has some richness and solid fruit, it is also dry, with awkward, earthy tannins. **82** —*R.V. (12/31/2002)*

Quinta do Carmo 1998 Dom Martinho Red Blend (Alentejo) $15. The baby brother to the richer, more robust Carmo red is light and fruity enough, with an emphasis on red raspberries and some buttery oak.
Unfortunately, it doesn't really have the stuffing to hold up to food. And it isn't a sipping wine, either. So it sort of falls neither here nor there. **84** —*M.S. (11/15/2002)*

Quinta do Carmo 2002 Reserva Red Blend (Alentejano) $40. Strongly scented of oak, with toasty, mentholated scents alongside vanilla, cinnamon, and clove. The texture is creamy, with vanilla and tobacco flavors backed by soft black cherries. Should integrate better in another year or two but there's no need to hide this away. Drink now–2010. **87** —*J.C. (12/31/2005)*

Quinta do Carmo 2001 Reserva Red Blend (Alentejano) $40. This is a big, burly wine that needs some time to come into its own. Right now, the nose is way ahead of the palate, boasting smoky, herbal complexity layered over toast and blackberries, while the flavors are harder to read, being dominated by wood. A few years of cellaring should see the oak flavors integrating more with the underlying berries. Try in 2007. **88** —*J.C. (3/1/2004)*

Quinta do Carmo 2000 Reserva Red Blend (Alentejano) $NA. A toasty, cedary wine that features lots of vanilla-tinged oak slathered over black cherries. The mouthfeel is creamy, and the rough wood tannins apparent now on the finish should smooth out in a couple of years. **87** —*J.C. (7/1/2003)*

QUINTA DO CASAL BRANCO

Quinta do Casal Branco 1999 Capucho Cabernet Sauvignon (Ribatejo) $20. This is Cabernet Sauvignon fermented in lagares. The result has great depth, from the purple color to the ripe but dry fruit and firm tannins alongside modern wood and black fruit. Overall, it is a solid, chunky wine. **88** —*R.V. (12/31/2002)*

Quinta do Casal Branco 2002 Falcoaria Fernão Pires (Ribatejo) $9. This is the estate wine from the huge property of the Vasconcellos family. It is rich, creamy, and toasty, with good acidity. The name comes from a dovecote on the estate. **87 Best Buy** —*R.V. (8/1/2005)*

Quinta do Casal Branco 2002 Capucho Merlot Merlot (Ribatejano) $NA. With its grassy, herbaceous aromas and bell pepper flavors, this wine accurately reflects the cool 2002 vintage. But as a cool climate wine produced in a normally hot climate, it somehow works, giving fresh, fruity drinking, and a dry, tannic aftertaste that is ready now. **83** —*R.V. (11/1/2004)*

Quinta do Casal Branco 1999 Falcoaria Portuguese Red (Ribatejo) $15. A blend of Trincadeira and Castelão, named after a dovecote on the estate, this wine is soft, with smoky tannins and some mature fruit. This is certainly ready to drink, and, with its light, drinkable acidity, goes well with pasta or oily foods. **85** —*R.V. (11/1/2004)*

Quinta do Casal Branco 2001 Falcoaria Reserva Portuguese Red (Ribatejo) $NA. A fine, wood-aged wine which shows good, dense, but dusty tannins and sweet, ripe fruit. Flavors of dark plums and cherries come through the wood. This is a wine that should age well over 5 years. **89** —*R.V. (11/1/2004)*

Quinta do Casal Branco 2000 Globus Portuguese Red (Ribatejano) $NA. A soft, mature wine, with some ripe black fruits, this has layers of wood to give some complexity. From the good 2000 vintage, it has richness in its blend of Castelão and Trincadeira. The tannins are dry and firm. **86** —*R.V. (11/1/2004)*

Quinta do Casal Branco 2002 Terra de Lobos Portuguese Red (Ribatejano) $7. A soft, juicy wine, shot through with new wood flavors and fresh red fruit. This blend of Cabernet Sauvignon and Castelão is soft, forward, and ready to drink. **84 Best Buy** —*R.V. (11/1/2004)*

Quinta do Casal Branco 2003 Portuguese White (Ribatejano) $6. This is a serious, complex wine, from the Casal Branco estate. It has aromas of wood, spice, toast, and white fruits. The palate is packed with intense, dense fruit, shot through with fresh acidity and wood. Ageworthy, it should mature for 5 years or more. **91 Best Buy** —*R.V. (11/15/2005)*

Quinta do Casal Branco 2002 Falcoaria Branco Portuguese White (Ribatejo) $10. This white version of Casal Branco's Falcoaria brand is a blend of Fernão Pires and Trincadeira das Pratas. Partly fermented in oak, it has a fine, creamy, almost Chardonnay-like richness, tempered with crisp, appley acidity. The combination is immensely drinkable. **88 Best Buy** —*R.V. (11/1/2004)*

Quinta do Casal Branco 1999 Falcoaria Red Blend (Ribatejo) $15. Blending Castelão and Trincadeira, this wine comes from the large 283-acre vineyard of Quinta do Casal Branco. Fermented in open lagares, it is powerful and big, with plenty of dusty tannins and dry fruits. Certainly the wine is still young and needs time, but it will emerge as a great bruiser of a wine with fine style. **90** —*R.V. (12/31/2002)*

Quinta do Casal Branco 2001 Falcoaria White Blend (Ribatejo) $NA. 91 —*R.V. (8/1/2004)*

QUINTA DO CÔA

Quinta do Côa 2004 Red Blend (Douro) $16. Seems a touch less than fully ripe, dominated by grassy-herbal notes and strawberry fruit. Some drying tannins on the finish contribute to that same impression, but it might be just the thing with rare burgers. **83** —*J.C. (11/1/2006)*

QUINTA DO CÔTTO

Quinta do Côtto 2002 Paço de Texeiró Avesso (Minho) $26. From the local Minho grape Avesso, this is a full-bodied white, with some crisp acidity. Flavors of green plums, white currants, and a touch of grassiness make this a great wine to drink with white fish. **87** —*R.V. (11/1/2004)*

Quinta do Côtto 2001 Paço de Texeiró Avesso (Minho) $18. A powerful white wine, with green fruits, some tannins, and flavors of quince. It has fresh fruit, rather than ripe, and looks set for some bottle aging (2–3 years) before it's drinkable. **88** —*R.V. (11/1/2004)*

Quinta do Côtto 2002 Portuguese Red (Douro) $19. Soft, warm, spicy aromas give this wine immediate attraction. Produced from one of the original Douro top table wine quintas, this 2002 shows the lighter side of the vintage, but still manages to have great flavors of sweet fruits and dry tannins. Drink over 5 years. **87** —*R.V. (11/1/2004)*

QUINTA DO CRASTO

Quinta do Crasto 1998 Late Bottled Vintage Port $14. Traditional unfiltered LBV, which has richness and concentration. Flavors of raisins and ripe, fresh fruit suggest this will evolve in the bottle over the next four or five years. **88 Best Buy** —*R.V. (3/1/2004)*

Quinta do Crasto 1997 LBV Bottled 2001 Port $20. The beautiful Quinta do Crasto, with its tiny chapel perched on a mountain top overlooking the Douro, is a leading producer of Douro table wines as well as Ports. This LBV is in a lighter style, with enticing perfumes and fresh, balanced, elegant fruit. **89** —*R.V. (3/1/2003)*

Quinta do Crasto 1996 LBV Bottled 2000 Port $20. In the British wine trade, when a wine is called "pretty," it means it is attractive, seductive, and just plain delicious. This wine is pretty. The black fruits and suppressed tannins give structure, and the balance of sweetness and acidity suggest aging potential as well. **90** —*R.V. (3/1/2003)*

Quinta do Crasto 2003 Vintage Port $94. This beautiful quinta, high above the Douro, has produced a generous, raisin, and black fig-flavored Port. It is ripe, plummy, and sweet in style, although the tannins at the end show good structure. **88** —*R.V. (11/15/2005)*

Quinta do Crasto 1995 Vintage Port $33. An immensely satisfying Port from one of the top single quinta vineyards. Crasto also makes table wines, and this shows in its finely structured Ports with firm tannins. Flavors of enticing nuts and spices give complexity to a wine which should last over the next 10-15 years. **90** —*R.V. (3/1/2004)*

Quinta do Crasto 2001 Vintage Port) $63. It is still very young, but this wine has enormous potential, with its black fruit, flavors of crushed blackberries, and wild cherries and layers of dense tannins. Give it at least 15 years. **90** —*R.V. (3/1/2004)*

Quinta do Crasto 1999 Vintage Port $NA. This is lighter than the 1995 Crasto, perfumed and fresh. The elegant black fruits are highlighted by acidity and sweet tannins. Some sweetness shows through initially, but it is balanced by a dry aftertaste. **89** —*R.V. (3/1/2004)*

Quinta do Crasto 2002 Portuguese Red (Douro) $15. A fine, fresh wine, from the light 2002 vintage, which has fresh red fruit flavors and a touch of wood. It is not powerful, but it will be very drinkable over the next 4–5 years. **86** —*R.V. (11/1/2004)*

Quinta do Crasto 1996 Reserva Portuguese Red (Douro) $18. **90** *(11/15/1999)*

Quinta do Crasto 2001 Reserva Old Vines Portuguese Red (Douro) $33. A smooth, spicy, juicy wine that is packed with ripe, fresh, black fruit flavors. It has dry tannins but these are balanced by the acidity and forward fruit. Quinta do Crasto was one of the first estates on the Douro to make top-class table wines, and it still sets a benchmark. **90** —*R.V. (11/1/2004)*

Quinta do Crasto 2001 Vinha Maria Teresa Portuguese Red (Douro) $125. This dark, inky wine is produced from the Quinta's oldest vines. Packed with dense blackberry fruit, it also blends hints of cedar and vanilla. For all its weight and full-bodied flavor, it also boasts surprisingly crisp acidity,

which compresses the finish. Try around 2010 for a more harmonious drinking experience. **91 Cellar Selection** —*J.C. (3/1/2005)*

Quinta do Crasto 1997 Reserva Red Blend (Douro) $22. **89** —*J.C. (10/1/2000)*

Quinta do Crasto 1999 Vinho Tinto Red Blend (Douro) $14. The aromas show great complexity, blending hints of forest underbrush and game with spicy cranberry and chocolate. A supple mouthfeel and moderate tannins make this accessible now, while a squirt of acidity on the finish means it should work well with food. **87** —*J.C. (12/31/2001)*

Quinta do Crasto 1998 Vinho Tinto Red Blend (Douro) $14. **86** —*J.C. (10/1/2000)*

Quinta do Crasto 2001 Touriga Nacional (Douro) $100. This pure varietal has great perfumed fruit, and smoky aromas. Smoky wood flavors and black currant fruit, balanced with ripeness, create a gallery of intense black fruit characters. This manages to balance power with elegance, a great achievement. **92** —*R.V. (11/1/2004)*

QUINTA DO ESTANHO

Quinta do Estanho 1996 Vintage Port $28. Situated in the heart of the Pinhão Valley, Estanho began to produce good vintage Port in the 1990s. This 1996 shows the style well. Big and ripe, quite dry with acidity and solid tannins, it is built for long aging. **88** —*R.V. (3/1/2004)*

QUINTA DO FOJO

Quinta do Fojo 2000 Fojo Portuguese Red (Douro) $84. One of Portugal's priciest table wines, this vintage boasts cherry and plum aromas that just don't seem all that intense, followed by bright cherry flavors accented by modest cedar. The long finish is evidence of its quality, but it turns astringent and one wonders whether the fruit will outlast the tannins. **87** —*J.C. (3/1/2005)*

Quinta do Fojo 1999 Vinha do Fojo Portuguese Red (Douro) $51. Smells a bit under-ripe, with weedy, green notes that ride atop sour cherries. Tart and sour-tasting, yet it does pick up an intriguing licorice note on the finish. Not bad, but not worthy of its reputation. **84** —*J.C. (3/1/2005)*

QUINTA DO GRIFO

Quinta do Grifo 2004 Reserva Portuguese Red (Douro Superior) $16. Starts with simple aromas of roasted berries, but soon reveals a more complex side, marrying slightly herbal-grassy notes with ripe fruit and picking up hints of cocoa and dark chocolate on the finish. **85** —*J.C. (11/1/2006)*

QUINTA DO INFANTADO

Quinta do Infantado NV 10-year old Tawny Port $35. This fruity style of aged tawny, with its gold color and dark raisin and dried fruit flavors, makes a great food partner, leaving a dry, nutty flavor. **86** —*R.V. (3/1/2004)*

Quinta do Infantado LBV Port 1998 $23. An opulent, fruity LBV, full of black fruits and layers of tannins over the sweetness. It is young and will develop some good bottle age, giving elegance as well as richness. **87** —*R.V. (3/1/2004)*

Quinta do Infantado 2003 Vintage Port $52. This traditional quinta, close to Pinhão, still uses lagares for vintage Port. There certainly is a rustic character to the wine, but at this stage it is still very restrained, only giving hints of red berry fruits. **86** —*R.V. (11/15/2005)*

Quinta do Infantado 2000 Vintage Port $50. One of the pioneers of single-quinta Ports under the ownership of the Roseira family, Infantado's wines can be impressively powerful. This wine from the great 2000 vintage has power, but it also has great structured tannins, piled with firm, ripe fruit. It's packed with potential to age over the next 10–15 years. **91** —*R.V. (3/1/2004)*

Quinta do Infantado 1997 Vintage Port $NA. A medium-weight perfumed wine, with soft fruit and mature tannins. The lavender and wild flower perfumes are followed by flavors of sweet fruit, finished by a shot of dryness. **86** —*R.V. (3/1/2004)*

Quinta do Infantado 1995 Vintage Port $NA. Infantado has produced a 1995 full of ripe tannins, powerful black fruits, and sweetness. There is a layer of dryness but the ripeness and sweetness means the wine is ready to drink now. **89** —*R.V. (3/1/2004)*

QUINTA DO JUDEU

Quinta do Judeu 2003 Portuguese Red (Douro) $15. Surprisingly light in weight for a Douro wine, with taut mulberryish fruit that seems a bit reined in and tight at this stage of its evolution, but does show an attractive cocoa tinge to its finish. Try in six months.**85** —*J.C. (12/31/2005)*

QUINTA DO NOVAL

Quinta do Noval NV 10-Year Old Tawny Port $28. The legendary Noval has produced a deliciously attractive, light, and poised wine, with fresh fruit and acidity. It is dry in style, with some tannins, and a layer of spirit that is well in balance. The aftertaste floats with acidity and fruit.**91 Editors' Choice** —*R.V. (8/1/2006)*

Quinta do Noval NV 20-Year Old Tawny Port $60. There is plenty going on in Noval's 20-year-old. It is a dry style, but the generous fruit combines marmalade and fresh citrus flavors, along with powerful ripeness. Acidity is there too, giving a lift at the end.**89** —*R.V. (8/1/2006)*

Quinta do Noval NV 40-Year Old Tawny Port $125. This is a sweet but deliciously mature wine that exudes the richness of its burnt orange flavors, layers of sweet toffee, and clean, hugely rich aftertaste. A great wine.**94** —*R.V. (8/1/2006)*

Quinta do Noval 1971 Colheita Port $40.85 —*M.S. (3/1/2000)*

Quinta do Noval 1997 LBV Bottled 2001 Port $23. Bottled unfiltered, Noval's LBV is dry in style, with concentrated fruit. With the fruit quality, it should be great, but it is spoiled by the brandy, which is too prominent, and by a layer of lean tannins.**85** —*R.V. (3/1/2003)*

Quinta do Noval 2003 Silval Vintage Port $45. The second label of Quinta do Noval is a more open Port than its big brother. Its stalky character, dark fruits, and considerable acidity come together well, leaving a dry but fresh aftertaste.**88** —*R.V. (11/15/2005)*

Quinta do Noval 2000 Silval Vintage Port $37. A reasonably good buy in vintage Port, Silval is something of a second label for Quinta do Noval. It's less concentrated and suppler in the mouth than its sister wine, but still boasts compelling floral aromas allied to prune, berry, and chocolate flavors. Worth trying a bottle before 2010.**90** —*J.C. (11/15/2003)*

Quinta do Noval 2003 Vintage Port $95. A pure fruited wine, with an unusual touch of toast and new wood. The fruit is well-structured with flavors of thyme and rosemary. This is a smooth, polished Port, which is definitely in a modern style of winemaking.**90** —*R.V. (11/15/2005)*

Quinta do Noval 2000 Vintage Port $65. One of the vintage's standouts, the 2000 Quinta do Noval is incredibly rich and intense, with a density that made me think I should reach for a spoon. Chocolate and coffee, prune and date aromas; plum cake flavors. Despite the richness, there is a superb backbone of acidity and ripe tannins that suggests peak maturity is probably two decades or more away.**95 Cellar Selection** —*J.C. (11/15/2003)*

QUINTA DO PASSADOURO

Quinta do Passadouro 2000 Vintage Port $70. A lighter (though not to say light), more floral style of vintage Port, with ethereal aromatics buttressed by blackberries and caramel. Finishes with bright acids and supple tannins that make it almost drinkable already. Try in 2008 and beyond.**91** *(11/15/2003)*

QUINTA DO PORTAL

Quinta do Portal NV 10-Year Old Tawny Port $22. A very soft, easy wine, with some good concentration that just lacks a central core.**85** —*R.V. (8/1/2006)*

Quinta do Portal NV 20-Year Old Tawny Port $52. Another Port success from the Branco family of Quinta do Portal, following their success with the 2003 vintage. This is a lovely, lively wine, with fresh acidity alongside good, mature fruit. It is ripe but very elegant, with a sweet, dried fruit aftertaste.**92** —*R.V. (8/1/2006)*

Quinta do Portal NV Cellar Reserve Port $16. Muddy, indistinct fruit aromas offer hints of almond paste and cherries before giving way to flavors of prune, dried cherries, and chocolate on the palate. A bit heavy and lacking cut and clarity, but you could do worse.**83** —*J.C. (3/1/2004)*

Quinta do Portal 1994 Colheita Port $28. A rare category, Colheita Ports are vintage wines aged in barrel (this was aged for eight years before bottling in 2002). This gives a wine with huge concentration, and dense flavors of sweet plums. The wood aging has softened the tannins, meaning that it is ready to drink.**90** —*R.V. (3/1/2004)*

Quinta do Portal 1996 LBV Port $15. It's light and relatively dry, with aromas and flavors of prune and Mexican chocolate. Turns spicy and peppery on the finish.**87** —*J.C. (11/15/2003)*

Quinta do Portal 2000 Portal Vintage Port $33. This is a densely concentrated wine, powering through with tannins and dry concentration over the young black fruits. It's young, showing sweetness and acidity still coming into balance, but over the next 10 years it will develop well.**89** —*R.V. (3/1/2004)*

Quinta do Portal NV Tawny Reserve Port $14. A soft, easy tawny that represents a solid value, Portal's Reserve displays earthy, spicy characteristics and a warming finish. Cinnamon and white pepper notes add complexity.**87** —*J.C. (11/15/2003)*

Quinta do Portal NV Ten Year Old Aged Tawny Port $24. At 10 years of age, Portal's tawny is still showing some rough edges of youth; it's big and brawny, with plump cherry-berry fruit joined by citrus and caramel. A fine café au lait note comes through on the finish.**89** —*J.C. (11/15/2003)*

Quinta do Portal NV Twenty Year Old Aged Tawny Port $49. Smooth and supple, with caramel scents backed by hints of berries and citrus. Marries still-vigorous fruit with warm, honeyed notes.**87** —*J.C. (11/15/2003)*

Quinta do Portal 2003 Vintage Port $60. Potentially one of the best wines of the vintage, this is an extraordinary performance from a producer not previously noted for making such high-quality Vintage Ports. The wine—a special selection that at this stage, has no name—has great ripe fruit and huge tannins combined to make a dense, intense wine. It is dark, brooding, and rich. There are also layers of dryness which shows the aging potential of this great wine.**95** —*R.V. (11/15/2005)*

Quinta do Portal 2003 Vintage Port $57. Better known for its table wines, this Port is a great success for Portal. It is dark, dry, and very firmly tannic. There is a powerhouse of fruit, but at this stage—and for several years—that fruit will be buried under a layer of strength and structure. A great wine for maturing.**94** —*R.V. (11/15/2005)*

Quinta do Portal 1999 Vintage Port $33. Promising aromas of black cherries and mulberries carry hints of dust and mineral. Fairly lightweight, with simpler flavors that finish clean and crisp.**87** —*J.C. (11/15/2003)*

Quinta do Portal 1997 Vintage Port $54. This young vintage Port is quite big, with plenty of lush fruit and some herb and spice notes. It's also on the dry side for vintage Port, and it lacks the hulking tannins you might expect. Surprisingly ready to drink, even at this age.**90** —*J.C. (11/15/2003)*

Quinta do Portal 1995 Vintage Port $33. Plums, dusty earth, and dried spice mingle on the nose of this older release that actually seems more ageworthy than Portal's 1997 and 1999. It's supple, medium-weight wine, with plum, prune, and spice flavors that finish with modest tannins and pleasing berry and spice notes.**89** —*J.C. (11/15/2003)*

Quinta do Portal 2001 Auru Portuguese Red (Douro) $75. Dense, dusty tannins and powerful black fruits give this wine a huge sense of concentration and richness along with dryness. Pure plum flavor, ripe acidity, and new wood complete an impressive wine.**91** —*R.V. (11/1/2004)*

Quinta do Portal 2000 Grande Reserva Portuguese Red (Douro) $35. The top wine from Quinta do Portal, only made in the best years, this has great ripe flavors and delicious richness. It is packed with sweet tannins and red fruits, along with flavors of wood and tastes of rich currants. It is still young, and will benefit from at least 7–8 years bottle age.**90** —*R.V. (11/1/2004)*

Quinta do Portal 2000 Portal Portuguese Red (Douro) $13. This is a big, powerful, extracted wine, packed with solid fruit and ripe tannins. New wood flavors are well in balance. There's good acidity and some great black fruit tastes. It is not a wine for long aging, drink over 5–7 years.**87** —*R.V. (11/1/2004)*

Quinta do Portal 2000 Reserva Portuguese Red (Douro) $17. With the 2000 vintage, Portal was able to make a Grande Reserva as well as this

Reserva. It has fine, ripe fruit, but is a wine for early drinking. The tannins and the wood flavors are there, but it is the fruit, rich, red, and generous, that makes this wine so attractive. **88** —*R.V. (11/1/2004)*

Quinta do Portal 1999 Red Blend (Douro) $NA. A leaner version of this wine than the 2000 vintage. It is firm with ripe, meaty flavors and solid, very dry tannins. The high acids give this wine obvious staying power, but seem to dominate the fruit at this stage. **86** —*R.V. (12/31/2002)*

Quinta do Portal 2000 Grande Reserva Red Blend (Douro) $NA. Bordeaux winemaker Pascal Chatonnet, whose family owns property in Lalande-de-Pomerol, is consultant at Quinta do Portal. His expertise shows in the blend of Bordeaux classicism and powerful, sweet fruit. New wood and deep purple fruits yield a modern wine that combine power and balance. **91** —*R.V. (12/31/2002)*

Quinta do Portal 1996 Grande Reserva Red Blend (Douro) $29. Smoky and earthy, with intertwining notes of anise, hung game, and plum. The mouthfeel is creamy and soft, the flavors oaky, especially on the finish, but amply backed by lush fruit. Drink now. **88** —*J.C. (11/15/2003)*

Quinta do Portal 1996 Mural Red Blend (Douro) $7. Cedary, with a sappy, resinous quality to the cherry and strawberry fruit flavors. It's lean on the palate, and finishes short. **84** —*J.C. (11/15/2003)*

Quinta do Portal 1999 Muros de Vinha Red Blend (Douro) $8. Leathery, with a lean core of tart red cherries, this wine is relatively high in acid, made to cut through a haunch of roasted pig or other fatty foods. **85** —*J.C. (11/15/2003)*

Quinta do Portal 1999 Quinta do Portal Reserva Red Blend (Douro) $NA. Smoky, meaty aromas lead into perfumed fruit flavors. The tannins are soft but dry; the fruit is very aromatic with a touch of violets and some rich, dark tannins underneath. The wine will age well—probably 5–10 years. **90** —*R.V. (12/31/2002)*

Quinta do Portal 2001 Tinta Roriz (Douro) $35. A powerful, but soft wine, with tannins that are so ripe that they are hardly noticeable. Flavors of very ripe black cherries blend with more concentrated herbal and spice tastes. This is rich and hot, with a peppery character from the alcohol. **88** —*R.V. (11/1/2004)*

Quinta do Portal 2001 Touriga Franca (Douro) $35. The first varietal release of Touriga Franca from Quinta do Portal is packed with cedar and coffee aromas, and flavors ripe figs and red plums. This is rich, but balanced with some wood flavors balancing the ripe fruit. Good tannins suggest aging potential. **89** —*R.V. (11/1/2004)*

Quinta do Portal 2001 Touriga Nacional (Douro) $35. Rich fruit with flavors of blackberries, notes of spice, and deep, brooding tannins give all the right intensity of flavor to this wine from Portugal's top varietal. Aged in new French oak, flavors of dark plums and cassis give a great juicy character. **88** —*R.V. (11/1/2004)*

QUINTA DO REGUENGO DE MELGACO

Quinta do Reguengo de Melgaco 2005 Alvarinho (Vinho Verde) $15. This small estate bottling is an attractive, full-bodied wine, ripe, with a touch of tropical fruit flavors. Fine, clean and fresh. **88** —*R.V. (7/1/2006)*

QUINTA DO TEDO

Quinta do Tedo NV Finest Reserve Port $NA. This wine from the single quinta Quinta do Tedo, owned by Napa-based Vincent Bouchard, is sweet and soft, but has good flavors of raisins and a solid structure. The black fruit tastes are fresh, juicy, and lively. A classic, easy drinking Reserve style. **85** —*R.V. (3/1/2005)*

Quinta do Tedo 1997 Late Bottled Vintage Port $22. A well-balanced LBV, showing dry raisins, dark plums and some firm tannins, along with a layer of sweetness and balancing acidity. **86** —*R.V. (3/1/2004)*

Quinta do Tedo 2000 Savedra Vintage Port $55. From a small parcel of old vines, this wine is dense, very firm, and closed. It is in a dry style, layering richness rather than sweetness, with solid black fruit. Give this wine at least 10 years. **88** —*R.V. (3/1/2004)*

Quinta do Tedo 1999 Traditional Single Quinta Port $NA. Vincent Bouchard, owner of Tedo, divides his time between the Douro and Napa Valley. This small property is located where the River Tedo joins the Douro, downriver from Pinhão. This wine is still young, dominated by

fresh black fruits, firm tannins, and layers of dryness. It is certainly destined for a 15 year aging. **89** —*R.V. (3/1/2004)*

Quinta do Tedo 2000 Vintage Port $45. Rich, soft, and seductive, this Port has aromas of caramel, and ripe, sweet tannins. It's very attractive, but likely to age fast. **85** —*R.V. (3/1/2004)*

QUINTA DO VALE MEÃO

Quinta do Vale Meão 2003 Vintage Port $30. Shows a lifted fruit character on the nose—maybe even a little hint of nail polish—but also some earth and berry scents. Bright raspberry flavors on the palate are backed by mineral notes, finishing crisp. Lacks the weight and structure of the best vintage Ports. **87** —*J.C. (6/1/2006)*

Quinta do Vale Meão 2001 Vintage Port $35. This great quinta is owned by the Ferreira family and was the former home of the legendary table wine, Barca Velha. This 2001 is a great example of the power of the wines from this sun-baked vineyard. Young black fruits are balanced with perfumes and tarry flavors. It's dark, intense, and likely to be long lasting. **88** —*R.V. (3/1/2004)*

Quinta do Vale Meão 2000 Vintage Port $45. This lushly fruity Port folds in enough intriguing floral aromas to be more than a simple fruit bomb. Briary notes add another element to the creamy boysenberry flavors that are incredibly rich but not cloying or syrupy. Likely to mature early but hold well, thanks to masses of supple tannins. Great quality for the price. **92 Editors' Choice** —*J.C. (11/15/2003)*

Quinta do Vale Meão 2003 Portuguese Red (Douro) $55. A star among dry Douro wines, the 2003 Quinta do Vale Meão boasts a deep, intense bouquet of ripe grapes, spring flowers, and anise-like spice. Plum, spice, and vanilla flavors flow seamlessly across the palate, weighty yet never heavy, with a creamy texture. Long, lush, and vibrant on the finish, with a hint of French roast coffee. Drink now–2015. **94 Editors' Choice** —*J.C. (12/31/2005)*

Quinta do Vale Meão 2002 Portuguese Red (Douro) $50. A bit crisper and lighter in weight than top vintages of this wine, but pleasing nevertheless, with cedar, herb, and cherry flavors that merge harmoniously on the finish. **88** —*J.C. (12/31/2005)*

Quinta do Vale Meão 2001 Portuguese Red (Douro) $49. The great estate of Vale de Meão, established in the 19th century by Dona Antonia Ferreira, is still in the family hands. It has produced this intense, fruit powered wine which packs herbs, dark tannins, and sweet wood flavors. It oozes concentration from low yields and great ageability. **93 Cellar Selection** —*R.V. (11/1/2004)*

Quinta do Vale Meão 2000 Portuguese Red (Douro) $65. Made from grapes that used to go into Barca Velha, Portugal's most-storied table red, this wine represents the New Wave of Douro wines. It's inky and intense, with whiffs of smoke and toast from new oak barrels, but also incredible fruit concentration. Blackberries, coffee, and dried spices on the palate; it finishes long and firm, with hints of licorice. **93 Editors' Choice** —*J.C. (11/15/2003)*

Quinta do Vale Meão 2003 Meandro Portuguese Red (Douro) $20. Rich and thickly textured on the palate, this is a big, ripe, jammy wine filled with blackberries and dried spices. Long, tannic, and layered on the finish. Hard to believe this is a second label. **91 Editors' Choice** —*J.C. (12/31/2005)*

Quinta do Vale Meão 2002 Meandro Portuguese Red (Douro) $20. Shows a bit of tar or treebark on the nose, then reveals crisp, mulberry-flavored fruit on the palate before picking up hints of chocolate on the tart, tangy finish. **87** —*J.C. (12/31/2005)*

Quinta do Vale Meão 2001 Meandro Portuguese Red (Douro) $19. The second wine of Quinta do Vale Meão is inevitably much less powerful than the estate wine. It has ripe, earthy fruit, with flavors of spices and warm, southern herbs. The tannins are there, but only serve to balance the wine's immediate drinkability. **87** —*R.V. (11/1/2004)*

Quinta do Vale Meão 2000 Meandro Portuguese Red (Douro) $19. A selection of lots not deemed worthy of inclusion in this estate's flagship red, Meandro is nevertheless a fine wine and an even better value. Smoke and herbs add complexity to the blueberries and blackberries found on the

PORTUGAL

nose, while the flavors combine lush fruit with intense notes of spice and anise. Drink now–2008. **90 Editors' Choice** —*J.C. (11/15/2003)*

QUINTA DO VALLADO

Quinta do Vallado NV 10-Year Old Tawny Port $NA. A very soft style from a vineyard run by the Olazabal family. There is sweetness, allied with cocoa flavors and a touch of burnt coffee. There's a very attractive sweet black fig character to finish. **87** —*R.V. (8/1/2006)*

Quinta do Vallado NV 20-Year Old Tawny Port $NA. A full-bodied, dense, and very concentrated wine that just misses being intensely rich because of a touch of burnt rubber. It is certainly powerful, and the dried prune flavors are ripe and sweet. **88** —*R.V. (8/1/2006)*

Quinta do Vallado 2002 Vallado Portuguese Red (Douro) $NA. Produced at the Ferreira family-owned estate near Regua, this wine is fresh, fruity, and for early drinking. It has great, easy fruit and flavors of plums, fresh green figs, and light acidity. **85** —*R.V. (11/1/2004)*

Quinta do Vallado 2003 Portuguese White (Douro) $18. A highly perfumed wine, with spice and melon flavors. There is just a hint of spicy wood. The wine comes from a top Douro estate, close to Regua. **89** —*R.V. (8/1/2005)*

Quinta do Vallado 2002 Vallado Branco Portuguese White (Douro) $NA. A heady blend of Malvasia, Moscatel, Rabigato, Verdelho, and almost unknown Viosinho provides an aromatic, creamy wine, with great fat fruit and flavors of almonds. Low acidity means it is ready to drink now. **87** —*R.V. (11/1/2004)*

QUINTA DO VENTOZELO

Quinta do Ventozelo NV 10-Year Old Tawny Port $30. This is a very easy, light and fresh style, with sweet caramel flavors balanced by sweet figs and milk chocolate. It finishes clean, with just a touch of acidity. **87** —*R.V. (8/1/2006)*

Quinta do Ventozelo NV 20-Year Old Tawny Port $40. Layers of dried fruits and prunes give a fruity character to this gently sweet wine. It's very elegant and delicate, but certainly very drinkable. **88** —*R.V. (8/1/2006)*

QUINTA DO VESUVIO

Quinta do Vesuvio 2003 Vintage Port $78. The Symingtons' showpiece vineyard in the upper Douro continues to make great vintage Port. This 2003 shows the estate's potential for big, luscious wines that are both powerful and tannic. It is opulent and generous, with the potential for good aging. **93** —*R.V. (11/15/2005)*

Quinta do Vesuvio 2000 Vintage Port $NA. Quinta do Vesuvio is owned by the Symington family but managed separately from the family's shipping brands (Dow, Graham, Warre). Vesuvio's immense terraces and vast open lagares for fermentation have produced a suitably dense, dark, brooding 2000, perfumed with violets and bursting with solid tannins. This is a great vintage wine. **93** —*R.V. (3/1/2004)*

Quinta do Vesuvio 2001 Vintage Port $56. A brooding nose of sullen blackberries and earth presages a wine that shows wonderful balance between fruit, alcohol, acidity, and tannin. It's not a huge, extracted Port, but one that carries itself with grace, finishing with good length and soft tannins. Drink 2010–2030. **91** —*J.C. (11/15/2003)*

Quinta do Vesuvio 1998 Vintage Port $50. This wine has the dark fruit typical of this quinta, but this year shows more elegance than usual, with dusty tannins and concentrated, sweet fruit. **90** —*R.V. (2/1/2001)*

QUINTA DOS ACIPRESTES

Quinta dos Aciprestes 2003 Portuguese Red (Douro) $12. A bit understated on the nose, but what's there is nice, offering modest cherry fruit alongside dried spices and cocoa. A bit creamy in the mouth, with smooth, supple tannins, and cherry and blackberry flavors that pick up pretty spice notes on the finish. **87 Best Buy** —*J.C. (6/1/2006)*

Quinta dos Aciprestes 2001 Portuguese Red (Douro) $12. A wine from old vines grown across the river from Tua in the upper Douro, owned by the Royal Oporto company. With its ripe, juicy fruits, flavors of firm, solid tannins, and attractive herbal flavors, this is a wine that could be drunk soon, but will age well over 5 years. **87 Best Buy** —*R.V. (11/1/2004)*

QUINTA DOS ROQUES

Quinta dos Roques 2000 Alfrocheiro (Dão) $29. The Alfrocheiro grape, also known as Alfrocheiro Preto, gives color to the wines of the Dão. In its pure form, it makes a soft wine, with intense forward fruit and fine, ripe acidity. It would be great with oily foods, even with that Portuguese favorite, sardines. **88** —*R.V. (11/1/2004)*

Quinta dos Roques 2000 Garrafeira Portuguese Red (Dão) $39. The idea of a Garrafeira is a special selection, and this wine from Quinta dos Roques, with its smooth, rich tannins and intense fruit flavors, is certainly special. Aged in wood for 13 months, it is packed with ripe black fruits, leaving sweet acidity and a dry aftertaste. Has good aging potential. **91** —*R.V. (11/1/2004)*

Quinta dos Roques 2000 Reserva Portuguese Red (Dão) $29. This is a powerful, serious, wood-aged wine that blends rich, tarry black fruit flavors and dark, brooding tannins. A mouthful of fruit from the great 2000 vintage, it powers through with a burst of richness to the finish. **90** —*R.V. (11/1/2004)*

Quinta dos Roques 2003 Encruzado Portuguese White (Dão) $18. A hearty, ripe wine, packed with flavors of green plums, layers of wood, spice, and a complex herbal character. This is rich, intense, and full-bodied, great with food. **90** —*R.V. (8/1/2005)*

Quinta dos Roques 2000 Red Blend (Dão) $13. After the success of the varietal wines from this producer, this is something of a disappointment. Despite the attractive dried-fruit aromas, the palate is over-ripe and jammy, with acidity and sweetness in conflict. It is pleasant enough but lacks structure. **84** —*R.V. (12/31/2002)*

Quinta dos Roques 2000 Alfrocheiro Preto Red Blend (Dão) $22. At this stage, wood dominates this wine, although there are dark, brooding blackberry aromas and spices underneath. There are ripe flavors and sweet fruit but the new wood spices and wood tannins are prominent. It should develop, and needs 6–8 years at least. **88** —*R.V. (12/31/2002)*

Quinta dos Roques 2000 Tinta Roriz (Dão) $29. An earthy, soft, ripe wine which has good flavors of herbs and soft crushed fruits. This is an early drinking wine, ready in 2-3 years. Great for barbecues. **86** —*R.V. (11/1/2004)*

Quinta dos Roques 2000 Tinta Roriz (Dão) $22. A great sweet, Porty wine, soft and immediately fruity. There's big, ripe, generous fruit with great acidity and lovely, ripe red berry flavors. Wood tannins at the heart give structure to the juicy fruit; it should age well over the next five years. **90** —*R.V. (12/31/2002)*

Quinta dos Roques 2000 Touriga Nacional (Dão) $22. Like the Tinta Roriz from the same producer, this wine is only produced in years that are good to the Dão. The grapes are selected before fermentation and aging for 11 months in French oak. The result is spicy and dusty, with big, juicy black fruit and layers of dryness and pepper. The spicy wood element gives complexity but does not dominate. **89** —*R.V. (12/31/2002)*

Quinta dos Roques 2000 Touriga Nacional (Dão) $29. This 100% varietal wine shows the Touriga Nacional well. With its bright red fruits, herbal flavors, the taste of dark plums, and brooding tannins, here is a wine from a world-class grape variety. In the Dão, it exhibits more fruit, lower alcohol, and less tannin than in the Douro, but there is still enough power there. **89** —*R.V. (11/1/2004)*

Quinta dos Roques 2001 White Blend (Dão) $9. **90** —*R.V. (12/31/2002)*

QUINTA SANTA EUFEMIA

Quinta Santa Eufemia NV 10-Year Old Tawny Port $23. A delicate style, balancing freshness and dryness. There is good acidity and lightness, finishing with almost bashful sweetness. **88** —*R.V. (8/1/2006)*

Quinta Santa Eufemia NV 20-Year Old Tawny Port $40. A very sweet style, but with some good fruit flavors: orange peel, dried berries, and fig jelly. The sweet and sour aftertaste is attractive. **88** —*R.V. (8/1/2006)*

Quinta Santa Eufemia NV 30-Year Old Tawny Port $43. Somewhat medicinal in character, this wine still holds together because of its underlying sweet, very ripe fruit. The pale color suggests that there are younger wines in the blend. **87** —*R.V. (8/1/2006)*

PORTUGAL

QUINTA SEARA D'ORDENS

Quinta Seara d'Ordens 2003 Vintage Port $NA. A quinta on the western edge of the Port region, owned by the Moreira family, who also produce a Douro table wine. New wood aromas are unusual for a vintage Port, and the wood dominates the black fruit flavors. This is an unusual, modern style of Port, one that doesn't quite come off. **83** —R.V. (11/15/2005)

QUINTA VALE D. MARIA

Quinta Vale D. Maria NV Reserve Port $NA. The small Vale Dona Maria quinta in the Rio Torto valley is making a name for its vintage Ports. This Reserve follows in a serious, vintage style, with ripe, attractive perfumed fruit, and rich, complete flavors of sweet figs and chocolate. The aftertaste is dry, just slightly bitter. **89** —R.V. (3/1/2005)

Quinta Vale D. Maria 2003 Vintage Port $NA. A dry, ripe wine with some firm tannins. Flavors of raisins and dry figs lead to a dry finish. At this stage in its development, the spirits element dominates. **85** —R.V. (11/15/2005)

Quinta Vale D. Maria 2001 Vintage Port $55. This small jewel of an estate in the Torto Valley is owned by Cristiano van Zeller, who has transformed the vineyard. The 2001 is a rich, luxurious vintage Port, solid but shot through with ripe, concentrated fruit, flavors of dark plums, and a dry aftertaste. **92** —R.V. (3/1/2004)

Quinta Vale D. Maria 2001 Portuguese Red (Douro) $NA. A spicy, elegant wine that has all the hallmarks of great style as well as power. From the hot valley of the Torto, a tributary of the Douro, the wine still manages to retain dry tannins along with plums and sultana fruit flavors. It is designed for aging, but drinkable in 4–5 years. **90** —R.V. (11/1/2004)

QUINTAS DE MELGACO

Quintas de Melgaco 1998 Couto de Frades Alvarinho (Vinho Verde) $10. **85** —J.C. (12/15/2000)

Quintas de Melgaco 1998 QM Alvarinho (Vinho Verde) $11. **82** —J.C. (12/15/2000)

Quintas de Melgaco 1998 Torre de Menagem White Blend (Vinho Verde) $8. **83** —J.C. (12/15/2000)

RAMOS-PINTO

Ramos-Pinto NV 30 Year Tawny Port (Douro) $90. Like so many of the Portuguese houses, Ramos-Pinto takes special pride in its tawnies, with the 30-year being the crowning glory. It's a delicate wine, one that has gained many times in complexity what it has lost in weight. Almeida likens it to "an aged person who has a lot of things to tell you." Hazelnuts and walnuts, dried apricots, and citrus fruits, honey, the list of descriptors goes on and on. **92** (10/1/2004)

Ramos-Pinto NV Collector Reserva Port $19. This basic Port is well-balanced for its type, not syrupy or hot, but blessed with grapey prune and chocolate flavors and a smooth, not-too-sweet finish. **86** —J.C. (3/1/2004)

Ramos-Pinto NV Collector Reserva Port $19. **85** (11/1/2004)

Ramos-Pinto 1997 LBV Port $21. Fairly big and chunky, a solid mouthful of Port that packs in leather, chocolate, prune, and blackberry flavors. Fruit-forward, but with enough complexity to keep it from becoming tiring. **88** (10/1/2004)

Ramos-Pinto 1996 LBV Port $19. Grapey and full up front, with a palate of candied red and black fruits and loads of smooth dark chocolate. Sure, it's a little overt and it wouldn't hurt from a booster shot of complexity, but it's neither thick nor cloying, and it is almost certain to go down easily. **89** —M.S. (11/15/2002)

Ramos-Pinto 1995 LBV Bottled 1999 Port $15. This is an almost black colored wine, soft, ripe, and very sweet. There are some soft, mature tannins, but the richness of the fruit and the sweetness dominate. **88** —R.V. (3/1/2003)

Ramos-Pinto 1998 LBV Bottled 2002 Port (Douro) $18. Roederer Champagne-owned Ramos Pinto has gone for a young style of LBV, exhibiting ripe fresh fruit. Flavors of dark plums and blackberries give it exuberance. Age for five years, but it is drinkable now. **86** —R.V. (3/1/2003)

Ramos-Pinto NV Quinta Bom Retiro 20-Year Old Tawny Port $75. From its vineyard in the hot Torto Valley, Ramos-Pinto has produced a rich, densely sweet, lightly burnt wine. It's deliciously attractive, very smooth, and flavored with perfumed dried apricots. **91** —R.V. (8/1/2006)

Ramos-Pinto NV Quinta da Ervamoira Port $34. **90** (3/1/2000)

Ramos-Pinto 1994 Quinta da Ervamoira Port $45. The earthy nose is a little mute, but the maturing palate is rich and full of softening black fruit. The wine is now coming into its own, and while it lacks the complexity and punch of a great Port, it has plenty going on in its favor, including layers of spice and sweetness on the finish. Will be at its best in 3–4 years. **88** —M.S. (11/15/2002)

Ramos-Pinto NV Quinta Ervamoira 10-Year Old Tawny Port $41. This wine comes from a wildly remote vineyard high in the Upper Douro. It is a fine, balanced wine, packed with acidity to balance the sweetness. It's relatively soft and gentle, with good, fresh flavors of figs. **89** —R.V. (8/1/2006)

Ramos-Pinto NV Reserva Collector Port $19. Roederer-Champagne owned Ramos Pinto has produced a soft, easy, and ripe Reserve. Aromas of cistus flowers are off-putting, but the flavors of sweet milk chocolate are attractive. It just lacks structure. **84** —R.V. (3/1/2005)

Ramos-Pinto NV Urtiga Vintage Character Port $16. This spunky Port offers just what it advertises: vintage character. It's a robust confection, for sure. Candied black cherry fruit dominates, with a moderate amount of chocolate and coffee on the broad, bold finish. There's heat and acidity along the way, making for a potent, powerful drink. **88** —M.S. (11/15/2002)

Ramos-Pinto 2003 Vintage Port $65. The wine is big, full, opulent, and super-ripe. But the tannins are also there, giving a dark, brooding edge, which comes through powerfully on the finish. This is the best vintage yet from this Roederer-owned house. **94** —R.V. (11/15/2005)

Ramos-Pinto 2000 Vintage Port $63. Showing slightly better than it did a year ago when last reviewed, the 2000 boasts sweet plum fruit, ample earthiness, and refined spice flavors. As vintage Ports go, it's not the biggest or most concentrated, but shows a fine sense of harmony and balance. **91** (10/1/2004)

Ramos-Pinto 1997 Vintage Port $50. Light in body and showing some alcohol, I suspect this is in a bit of awkward phase. Black cherry, plum, and berry fruit is joined by a slightly under-ripe weedy note. The wine finishes short, with modest tannins. **86** —J.C. (11/15/2003)

Ramos-Pinto 1994 Vintage Port $NA. Beginning to show some development, the 1994 starts with hints of mint and maple syrup, blended with sturdier notes of tar, molasses, and prunes. Supple and powerful on the finish; drink now or hold another 10-plus years. **91** (10/1/2004)

Ramos-Pinto 1983 Vintage Port $NA. Almeida refers to this vintage as playing Mozart compared to the 1994's Beethoven and 2000's Bach. At 20 years of age, it seems pretty much mature, with hints of coffee and maple syrup adding complexity to plum and cherry fruit. Drink now–2015. **91** (10/1/2004)

Ramos-Pinto 2003 Adriano Estate Bottled Red Wine Portuguese Red (Douro) $15. A bit herbal and resiny, but those elements are mostly balanced by cherry fruit, giving it a slightly medicinal aspect. Supple in texture and medium-bodied, it finishes crisply, with hints of cocoa and citrus. **86** —J.C. (12/31/2005)

Ramos-Pinto 2000 Duas Quintas Red Blend (Douro) $12. **86** Best Buy — R.V. (11/15/2002)

Ramos-Pinto 1999 Duas Quintas Red Blend (Douro) $12. The fresh, popping all-fruit style of this light-bodied red makes it the cru Beaujolais of the Douro Valley. A distinct cherry flavor with some flowery accents renders it pleasant to quaff with grilled meats, or grilled vegetables, if that's your preference. It's a pop-the-cork-and-enjoy wine. **85** —M.S. (11/15/2002)

Ramos-Pinto 2000 Duas Quintas Reserva Red Blend (Douro) $34. The senior partner of the popular Duas Quintas brand, this wine from the Ramos-Pinto stable has a dark, intense color. It is a big and black wine, with serious tannins and powerful fruit. Still young, this should develop into a solid, chunky wine. **92** —R.V. (12/31/2002)

PORTUGAL

Ramos-Pinto 1999 Duas Quintas Reserva Red Blend (Douro) $34. The Quinta da Ervamoira, high up in the Alto Douro, supplies the fruit for this wine. The quinta is now also famous for its prehistoric wall paintings. It has the hot climate to produce a hugely concentrated, rich wine like this. Smooth and ripe, it has soft wood flavors, dry tannins, and a touch of raisins. **91** —R.V. (12/31/2002)

Ramos-Pinto 1999 Duas Quintas Reserva Especial Red Blend (Douro) $11. Boasts flavors of prune and plum, with hints of alcohol, clove, and cinnamon, almost like a rum-soaked spice cake. A bit heavy and low-acid; could use more freshness. **85** —J.C. (11/15/2003)

Ramos-Pinto 1997 Duas Quintas Reserva Touriga Nacional (Douro) $34. This is in transition. When young, it was impressive for its rich fruit and texture, but now it's showing hints of green bean on the nose and a leaner, more compact profile. Give it another few years to see if it turns around. **85** —J.C. (7/1/2003)

Ramos-Pinto 2001 Duas Quintas Touriga Nacional Blend (Douro) $NA. This blend of Tinta Roriz, Touriga Francesa, and Touriga Nacional is appreciably lighter than the Touriga Nacional-dominated Reserva, but similar in flavor, with dark fruit and baking spices enlivened by a beam of bright acidity on the finish. **86** (10/1/2004)

Ramos-Pinto 2000 Duas Quintas Reserva Touriga Nacional Blend (Douro) $37. Shows plenty of dark fruit aromas and flavors, with notes reminiscent of blueberry pie and black cherries, picking up subtle shadings of black pepper, cinnamon, and clove. Chewy yet supple, its long finish is filled with soft tannins. **90** (10/1/2004)

Ramos-Pinto NV Fine White Port (Douro) $14. We don't see much white Port in this country, but in Portugal it's often served as an apéritif. This is a fine example, a little sweet but also possessing bracing acidity for balance. Mouth-watering aromas and flavors run toward nuts and stone fruits, with a hint of honey. **88 Editors' Choice** —J.C. (3/1/2004)

REAL COMPANHIA VELHA

Real Companhia Velha 2003 Quinta de Cidrô Reserva Chardonnay (Trás-os-Montes) $12. This 100% Chardonnay wine is a smooth, modern style of wine, with tropical fruit flavors, and touches of toast and vanilla. There are green fruits and spice to give the wine complexity. **87** —R.V. (8/1/2005)

Real Companhia Velha 2002 Quinta do Cidrô Chardonnay (Trás-os-Montes) $12. The cooler climate of the far north-east of Portugal allows this creamy Chardonnay to also have good fresh acidity balancing its layers of wood. It is not complex, but is a fine, well-made, lively wine. **87 Best Buy** —R.V. (12/1/2004)

Real Companhia Velha 2001 Evel Grande Escholha Portuguese Red (Douro) $22. A fat, juicy wine with some tannins to give structure. There are aromas of figs and flavors of new wood and dried herbs. This is solidly made, powerful, old fashioned in its bone-dry tannins, and ready to drink. **86** —R.V. (11/1/2004)

Real Companhia Velha 2001 Porca de Murça Portuguese Red (Douro) $8. The curious name of this wine celebrates a prehistoric cave painting of a pig at Murça. Thankfully, the wine bears no relationship to its name. It is ripe, sweet, and juicy with good fresh, clean fruit flavors. There are some good dry tannins which suggest 5-year aging potential. **88 Best Buy** —R.V. (11/1/2004)

Real Companhia Velha 2004 Quinta de Cidrô Sauvignon Blanc (Trás-os-Montes) $10. High up above the Douro Valley, Quinta de Cidró is a large estate on the plateau. This Sauvignon Blanc, taking advantage of the high altitude, is green, ripe, and clean. Finishes crisp and light. **85 Best Buy** —R.V. (8/1/2005)

Real Companhia Velha 2003 Porca de Murça White Blend (Douro) $12. A dense wine, packed with wood, complex green and white fruit flavors, and a definite touch of pepper and spice. Made from the Codega, Cerceal, and Gouveio grapes. **88 Best Buy** —R.V. (8/1/2005)

REAL VINICOLA

Real Vinicola 1998 Porca de Murça Reserva Red Blend (Douro) $17. 89 (10/1/1999)

Real Vinicola 1997 Porca de Murça Reserva Red Blend (Douro) $17. 87 (10/1/1999)

ROBEREDO MADEIRA

Roberedo Madeira 2000 Carm Classico Red Blend (Douro) $18. With its aromas of smoke, mineral, blackberries, and blueberries, this Douro blend tastes like a dry Port—without the alcohol, tannins, or sugar that relegate Port to the end of the meal. Drink now–2010. **87** —J.C. (11/15/2003)

Roberedo Madeira 1999 Carm Praemium Touriga Nacional (Douro) $27. A big, burly wine with a firmly tannic finish, the 1999 Praemium needs a few years to shed its youthfulness. The subtle toast and vanilla notes are in proportion with the intense blackberry fruit, and it picks up some coffee notes on the finish. **89** —J.C. (11/15/2003)

Roberedo Madeira 2000 Carm Reserva Touriga Nacional (Douro) $23. Toast and vanilla notes from oak barrels are layered over aromas of cured meat and blackberries. On the palate, it's lush but not overly weighty or rich, just nicely balanced. There's plenty of spicy oak, especially on the finish, but also the fruit to support it. **90 Editors' Choice** —J.C. (11/15/2003)

ROMARIZ

Romariz 2003 Vintage Port $NA. One of the smaller brands produced by the Fladgate Partnership, also producer of Taylor Fladgate and Fonseca. This is a light, fresh floral Port with sweet, soft fruit, which is going to age relatively quickly. **84** —R.V. (11/15/2005)

ROQUEVALE

Roquevale 1999 Redondo Portuguese Red (Alentejo) $6. Dark cherry aromas with faint meaty accents open this light red. Juicy, but not jammy, the red fruit really takes over on the palate. Straightforward flavors and a clean even finish make this a commendable quaff. **83** —M.M. (12/31/2001)

ROYAL OPORTO

Royal Oporto NV 10-Year Old Tawny Port $29. While it is quite dark in color, this wine still has plenty of good, 10-Year Old fresh fruit flavors. Perfumed and delicate, it has light sweetness and a good layer of fruit and wood acidity, leaving a dry aftertaste. Its quality is an indication of the impressive improvements that have occurred at Royal Oporto in recent years. **90** —R.V. (8/1/2006)

Royal Oporto NV 20-Year Old Tawny Port $48. A delicious, easy wine that floats by with orange marmalade and fresh acidity. Marred on the finish by some volatility. **87** —R.V. (8/1/2006)

Royal Oporto NV 40-Year Old Tawny Port $128. An intensely sweet wine, with mature fruit that shows some richness and orange marmalade flavors. It is spoiled by a hint of volatility, which leaves a sharp aftertaste. **88** —R.V. (8/1/2006)

Royal Oporto 2003 Vintage Port $44. Once a byword for indifferent Ports, Royal Oporto has totally revamped its winemaking, and this 2003 vintage is the result. It is dark and dry, with layers of firm fruit. Flavors of black figs give a lift to the Port. **88** —R.V. (11/15/2005)

ROZES

Rozes NV 10-Year Old Tawny Port $27. Rozes has always supplied the French market with inexpensive Port. But it is also able to produce some more serious aged tawnies, such as this fresh, ripe, fig-flavored wine. **86** —R.V. (8/1/2006)

Rozes NV 20-Year Old Tawny Port $50. If it wasn't for the unbalanced spirity element to this wine, it would rate higher. The concentration and the dried fruit and lemon jelly flavors are attractive. But that spirit comes through at the finish. **87** —R.V. (8/1/2006)

Rozes NV 40-Year Old Tawny Port $120. A very old wine which smells medicinal and tastes like sweet cough syrup. It's so concentrated as to be almost undrinkable. **83** —R.V. (8/1/2006)

Rozes 1994 Reserve Edition LBV Port $19. 86 —M.S. (3/1/2000)

Rozes NV Reserve Port $NA. An attractive, fruity Port, which has perfumed aromas, young, fresh fruit, and flavors of raisins. It is sweet,

PORTUGAL

flavored with black cherries and figs. This is an easy drinking style, which fits the profile of Reserve Ports perfectly. **88** —*R.V. (3/1/2005)*

Rozes 2000 Vintage Port $90. A round, lushly fruited vintage Port, the 2000 Rozès boasts scents of toffee, chocolate, and prune, then follows up with flavors of chocolate fudge and dark plum. Has enough structure to age another 10 years, just lacks a little length on the finish. **88** —*J.C. (11/1/2006)*

Rozes 1997 Vintage Port $60. Very dense in the nose, with nuances of rubber and ripe black plum. The palate thrusts with cherry, raspberry, and raisin. Now, it's all fruit, showing only a smidgen of chocolate and a hint of espresso. But with time—8 to 10 years—it will reveal the full allotment of refinement and class. **92 Cellar Selection** —*M.S. (11/15/2002)*

SANDEMAN

Sandeman NV 20-Year Old Tawny Port $50. It is the harshness, with unbalanced spirit, that mars what is otherwise a mature, dry style with good burned caramel flavors. **85** —*R.V. (8/1/2006)*

Sandeman NV 40-Year Old Tawny Port $135. At first taste, this appears amazingly fresh for a 40-year-old, but then the older flavors kick in. There is concentration, ripeness, and huge intensity of flavor. It's a beautiful wine, with dried apricots giving freshness. **93 Editors' Choice** —*R.V. (8/1/2006)*

Sandeman NV Founder's Reserve Port $17. One of the most familiar of Reserve Port brands, this is a fruity, soft wine, which seems to have aging potential as well as present drinking pleasure. The flavors are open, generous, easy, with just a touch of tannin to give it structure. A definite success. **86** —*R.V. (3/1/2005)*

Sandeman 1997 LBV Bottled 2001 Port (Douro) $19. Sandeman has produced a dark-colored, fruity wine, with aromas of chocolate, which is soft, easy-to-drink and certainly not for aging. With its sweetness and richness, it is almost like a New World table wine in style—enjoyable but maybe not Port. **84** —*R.V. (3/1/2003)*

Sandeman 1997 Quinta do Vau Port $38. **93** *(12/15/1999)*

Sandeman NV Ruby Port $12. A solid value in ruby Port, Sandeman's bottling pairs dried fruits with leathery notes to offer more than simple, grapey fruit. Finishes with fresh, spicy notes. **86** —*J.C. (11/1/2006)*

Sandeman NV Tawny Port $12. Slightly hot, this chunky, full-bodied tawny reveals flavors of earth and prune. Hints of caramel and maple syrup on the finish, but also a slightly bitter note of scorched earth. **83** —*J.C. (12/1/2004)*

Sandeman 2000 Vau Vintage Port $45. Intentionally made in a friendly, fruit-forward style, Vau doesn't disappoint in 2000. It delivers what we've come to expect from this relatively recent creation, lush blackberry and plum flavors backed by clove and spice. If you like your Ports young and fruity, try this one soon; its longevity is untested. **90** —*J.C. (11/15/2003)*

Sandeman 1999 Vau Vintage Port $30. A decent value in vintage Port, Sandeman's 1999 Vau doesn't offer long-term ageability, but should provide peak enjoyment from 2005–2015. Dusty prune aromas and flavors are framed by modest tannins, while a pleasant earthiness lingers on the finish. **88 Editors' Choice** —*J.C. (12/1/2004)*

Sandeman 2003 Vintage Port $60. A wine which, to smell, has a rustic, earthy character. The taste is cleaner, fresher, more solid, and with attractive raspberry and wild strawberry flavors vying with acidity. **87** —*R.V. (11/15/2005)*

Sandeman 2000 Vintage Port $60. Clove, dried spices, and plum-scented fruit on the nose; straightforward blackberry and plum flavors. It's reasonably rich and supple in the mouth, but doesn't seem to have a great deal of depth to support aging. **86** —*J.C. (11/15/2003)*

SANTA VITORIA

Santa Vitoria 2004 Red Blend (Alentejano) $13. In complete contrast to the same winery's Versátil, this wine's blend of cherries, dried spices, and vanilla is terrifically appealing, with a firm structure that helps carry the weight of the fruit. Drink now or hold 3–4 years. **88 Best Buy** —*J.C. (11/1/2006)*

Santa Vitoria 2004 Reserva Red Blend (Alentejano) $25. A blend of Syrah, Touriga Nacional, and Alfrocheiro, this wine is loaded with bold blackberry fruit and lashings of vanilla. Definitely not for the shy, it's intense but adds enough spice and tobacco flavors to avoid any claims of simplicity or jamminess. Drink now or hold 4–5 years. **90** —*J.C. (11/1/2006)*

Santa Vitoria 2004 Versátil Red Blend (Alentejano) $13. The Alentejo is a warm region, and this wine, in this vintage, seems to have gotten a bit too warm. The cherry fruit is a bit dulled and baked, but then there's enough acidity to bring it into some semblance of balance. Dusty and soft on the finish. **82** —*J.C. (11/1/2006)*

SAO PEDRO

Sao Pedro 1995 das Águias LBV Port $NA. Supple and lightweight, with raisiny fruit and flavors of molasses, maple syrup, and a trace of honey. Seems to be fading, so drink up. **84** —*J.C. (11/15/2003)*

SENHORA DO CONVENTO

Senhora do Convento NV Quinta das Heredias Ruby Special Reserve Port $NA. Sweet, soft, and light, this is an enjoyable, but discreet wine, hiding its charms under fresh perfumes and juicy, young fruit. After the first taste, it opened up in its glass, and showed good black fruit aromas and direct, ripe fruit flavors. **85** —*R.V. (3/1/2005)*

Senhora do Convento 2003 Vintage Port $NA. A rich wine with a touch of new wood. The fruit is huge but restrained, giving ripeness and black jelly sweetness. This is a fine wine that will age well. **89** —*R.V. (11/15/2005)*

SENTUS

Sentus 1997 Portuguese Red (Douro) $18. Toasty on the nose, with hints of animale and a pinch of pepper. Smooths out a bit on the palate, with flavors of black cherries, plums, and tree bark. But then it finishes green and sappy—almost resinous. Pair with spicy, hearty foods to tame the rough edges. **84** —*J.C. (12/31/2001)*

SMITH WOODHOUSE

Smith Woodhouse NV 10-Year Old Tawny Port $28. Another Symington family brand that often shows well, Smith Woodhouse's 10-Year Old is big and firm, quite tannic even, and very rich and dry. This is a good, solid, powerful wine, with great finishing acidity. **90** —*R.V. (8/1/2006)*

Smith Woodhouse 1986 Colheita Port $41. On the nose, nuts and caramel dominate, but in the mouth enough stone fruits emerge to bring to mind peaches and cherries drizzled with the liquid nuts from the ice cream parlor. It's elegant—almost delicate—bringing complexity and flavor without heaviness, and it ends on a lingering smoky, coffee-like note. **90 Editors' Choice** —*J.C. (12/1/2004)*

Smith Woodhouse 1976 Colheita Single Year Tawny Port $43. Nutty and earthy, with maple sugar flavors and just a hint of red-skinned fruit. Sweet and a bit simple, but satisfying nonetheless. **87** —*J.C. (11/15/2003)*

Smith Woodhouse 1994 LBV Port $25. Bottled in 1998, this is a delicious, immediately approachable LBV. The intensity of sweet, soft fruit is balanced by a dark, dry element that gives it structure. **87** —*R.V. (3/1/2004)*

Smith Woodhouse 1992 LBV Port $25. Bottled in 1996, but just being released to the U.S. market, this is a relatively mature LBV, with aromatic notes of caramel and dried cherries. Flavors are a bit simple and sweet, revolving around dates, figs, and cherries, while the mouthfeel is soft and jammy right up until the finish, which picks up a scour of acidity. **85** —*J.C. (12/1/2004)*

Smith Woodhouse 1990 LBV Bottled 1994 Port $27. A traditional crusted LBV that has had plenty of time to mature in the bottle. Perhaps a little too much time, since the brandy is beginning to show through as the wine dries out. But it is still a delicious, mature Port, worth enjoying now. **88** —*R.V. (3/1/2003)*

Smith Woodhouse NV Lodge Reserve Port $16. This fresh, fruity wine comes from one of the Symington Group's second labels, one which often impresses by its quality. This Port is herbal, with chocolate flavors, black fruits, and a good, clean, dry aftertaste. **85** —*R.V. (3/1/2005)*

Smith Woodhouse 1999 Quinta de Madelena Vintage Port $32. Saturation is the key here, in the nose and especially on the palate. It's thick and very candied, probably a result of how hot it gets at the Madalena site. Still, there's plenty of delicious black fruit and chocolatey stuffing. In the end, though, its full weight indicates it may not age forever. **87**—*M.S. (11/15/2002)*

Smith Woodhouse 2003 Vintage Port $60. A fine, foursquare wine from one of the Symington-owned Port houses. It shows good tannins, delicious perfumed fruit, and great ripeness. Along with this attractive fruit, there is an impressive streak of dry tannins which promise good aging. **90**—*R.V. (11/15/2005)*

SOGRAPE

Sogrape 2004 Morgadio da Torre Alvarinho (Vinho Verde) $12. This is a 100% Alvarinho, perfumed with hints of honey and melon. It is a ripe, intense wine, dry but rich, showing a lemon tea character, a touch of spritz, and fresh, dry finish. **89 Best Buy**—*R.V. (7/1/2006)*

Sogrape 1998 Morgadio da Torre Alvarinho (Vinho Verde) $13. 87 Best Buy—*M.S. (10/1/1999)*

Sogrape 2003 Callabriga Portuguese Red (Douro) $NA. This and a partner wine from the southern Alentejo region of Portugal are a new pair from Portugal's largest producer, Sogrape. Named after an ancient settlement in northeast Portugal, close to the Douro, this Tinta Roriz-based wine revels in the harsh landscape of the Douro with its strong tannins, and dryness layered over dense fruit. It is certainly age-worthy, keep for the next 5–10 years. **90**—*R.V. (11/15/2005)*

Sogrape 2003 Callabriga Portuguese Red (Alentejo) $NA. Named after the old Roman name for a fortified settlement in northeast Portugal, there are two wines in this new range from Portugal's largest producer, Sogrape. Both are based on the Tinta Roriz grape. This wine from the southern Alentejo shows the rich, ripe, open character of many southern Italian wines. Great fruit, great value. **89**—*R.V. (11/15/2005)*

Sogrape 1997 Duque de Viseu White Table Win Portuguese Red (Dão) $10. 84—*M.S. (10/1/1999)*

Sogrape NV Duque du Viseu Portuguese Red (Dão) $11. 87 Best Buy—*M.S. (10/1/1999)*

Sogrape 1997 Grão Vasco Portuguese Red (Dão) $6. 86 Best Buy—*M.S. (10/1/1999)*

Sogrape 2003 Herdade do Peso Vinha do Monte Portuguese Red (Alentejano) $9. A smooth, elegant wine, with soft fruits which are overlain with dusty tannins. This is packed with ripe fruit, but also has structure, solid dry fruits, and a layer of wood. A wine that impresses with its balance. **89 Best Buy**—*R.V. (3/1/2006)*

Sogrape 2002 Reserva Portuguese Red (Alentejo) $15. A special selection from Portugal's largest wine company, showing huge, concentrated flavors of dark black fruits and powerful tannins. The wine is opulent, intense, but also elegant. It's a wine of style, which would certainly repay aging, but which also is delicious to drink now. **92 Best Buy**—*R.V. (3/1/2006)*

Sogrape 1996 Reserva Portuguese Red (Douro) $13. 87—*M.S. (10/1/1999)*

Sogrape 1999 Vinha do Monte Portuguese Red (Alentejo) $9. 84 *(12/31/2001)*

Sogrape 1997 Vinha do Monte Portuguese Red (Alentejo) $10. 85—*M.S. (10/1/1999)*

Sogrape NV Gazela Portuguese White (Vinho Verde) $6. A fresh, uncomplicated wine, made and sold in large quantities. There is sweetness, along with clean, easy lemon fruits and a touch of acidity. Don't think, drink. **84 Best Buy**—*R.V. (7/1/2006)*

Sogrape 1999 Casa do Douro Reserva Red Blend (Douro) $13. Soft, sweet flavors dominate this wine. Red fruit and vanilla give it softness and richness with a touch of spice. This is an attractive wine, ready to drink now, but with a touch of dryness for the future. **87**—*R.V. (12/31/2002)*

Sogrape 1999 Duque de Viseu Red Blend (Dão) $11. This has long been the best-known wine from the Dão. Good, simple ripe fruit and spicy, toasty wood flavors make it an easy wine. Finishes with soft tannins and plenty of attractive red berry fruit. **85**—*R.V. (12/31/2002)*

Sogrape 1999 Reserva Red Blend (Alentejo) $9. A superb wine from the company that also brings you Mateus Rosé. It is mainly made from the local Aragonês, with vibrant perfumed aromas and dry tannins alongside rich, juicy fruit. Wood flavors lend complexity to a wine that should age well for 5 years or more. **90**—*R.V. (12/31/2002)*

Sogrape 2000 Vinha do Monte Red Blend (Alentejano) $11. A blend of Castelão, Aragonês, Trincadeira, and Alfrocheiro grapes. Ripe red fruit on the nose; dense tannins, firm acidity, and big fruit in the mouth. **87 Best Buy**—*R.V. (12/31/2002)*

Sogrape 1996 Quinta dos Carvalhais Touriga Nacional (Dão) $39. 89—*M.S. (10/1/1999)*

Sogrape 2001 Duque de Viseu White Blend (Vinho Verde) $11. 85—*R.V. (8/1/2004)*

TAYLOR FLADGATE

Taylor Fladgate NV 10-Year Old Tawny Port $30. This is a great, fresh, young style of wine, with figs and bitter marmalade flavors. There's a touch of orange peel, a hint of vanilla, and very ripe, delicious fruit. **91**—*R.V. (8/1/2006)*

Taylor Fladgate NV 20-Year Old Tawny Port $53. Although this famous name has produced quite a light 20-year-old, that lightness is more than made up for by the beautiful, smooth flavors, the taste of lemon jelly, dried apricots, and peaches, and fine, fresh acidity. **90**—*R.V. (8/1/2006)*

Taylor Fladgate NV 30-Year Old Tawny Port $115. Apart from the fact that this tastes too fresh to be a 30-year-old, this is a delicious wine, with ripe, sweet fruits, caramel, and just the right layer of dryness. **88**—*R.V. (8/1/2006)*

Taylor Fladgate NV 40-Year Old Tawny Port) $154. A superb wine, elegance and weight combined magisterially. It has all the right mature flavors, ripe fruit, intense marmalade and concentration. This is a wine with a great reputation, and the taste doesn't let that reputation down. **95 Editors' Choice**—*R.V. (8/1/2006)*

Taylor Fladgate NV First Estate Reserve Port $18. With its dried raisin aromas and fresh, sweet, fruity character, this is a great example of Reserve Ports. It has a touch of tannin to go with the soft fruits, and flavors of ripe black figs and dark plums. First Estate is produced at Taylor Fladgate's original vineyard at Regua, which was bought in 1744. **87**—*R.V. (3/1/2005)*

Taylor Fladgate 2000 LBV Port $25. With its charming aromas of spice drop, ripe cherries, and schistous minerality, this Taylor looks set to zoom. And it is tasty, but also a bit soft and lacking structure—something unexpected from a Port under the Taylor label. Turns chocolaty on the finish. Drink now. **88**—*J.C. (6/1/2006)*

Taylor Fladgate 1997 LBV Bottled 2002 Port $21. The best-selling LBV keeps up its quality impressively. With its flavors of rich fruit cake and ripe tannins, it is soft and supple, and ready to drink without aging. But it has a touch of elegance and style that pushes it well up in quality. **89**—*R.V. (3/1/2003)*

Taylor Fladgate 2001 Quinta De Vargellas Port $50. Seems tight at first on the nose, but after a few minutes the wine opens up and becomes surprisingly approachable. It's sweet and a bit raisiny, and doesn't have that classic Taylor structure and firmness. Drink 2010–2020. **89**—*J.C. (12/1/2004)*

Taylor Fladgate 1998 Quinta de Vargellas Port $42. A powerful, solid wine, packed with luscious fruit. The perfumes and the ripeness of the fruit are currently covered with a firm tannin layer, but this should develop well as a medium-term wine. **90**—*R.V. (2/1/2001)*

Taylor Fladgate 1995 Quinta de Vargellas Vinha Velha Port $NA. At almost 10 years of age, this mammoth effort is just starting to budge along the path to maturity. The nose is rich with scents of baking spices; the palate shows plenty of plum and blackberry fruit, but is more about earth, spice, and raw power. This tremendously deep, powerful, and structured wine should be even better by 2010, with a plateau of maturity that should extend out to 2040 or beyond. **97 Cellar Selection**—*J.C. (12/1/2004)*

Taylor Fladgate 1997 Vargellas Vinha Velha Port $NA. The most forward of the trio of Vargellas Vinha Velhas, the 1997 may be approachable by

PORTUGAL

2010, but should last until 2030 or beyond. It's lush, yet powerfuly structured, filled with a complex array of flavors that includes earth, tobacco, tea, and gobs of briary, berry-scented fruit. **94 Cellar Selection** —*J.C. (12/1/2004)*

Taylor Fladgate 2000 Vargellas Vinha Velha Vintage Port $NA. The youngest of Taylor Fladgate's Vargellas old vines bottling offers considerable aging potential. It's richly tannic and chewy in the mouth; firm on the finish. The noble structure amply supports dried spices, chocolate, and plum flavors. Try after 2015. **95 Cellar Selection** —*J.C. (12/1/2004)*

Taylor Fladgate 2003 Vintage Port $92. Hugely ripe fruit dominates this wine. But, as so often with a Taylor Fladgate Port, this fruit is balanced out with beautiful perfumes, elegant tannins, and complex layers of dryness, sweetness, and acidity. This is a great wine, maybe not as long-lived as some Taylor Fladgate vintages of the past, but certainly destined for many years of aging. **95** —*R.V. (11/15/2005)*

TERRACOTA

Terracota 2003 Fernão Pires (Ribatejo) $9. With its caramel and green fruit aromas, and flavors of toast, white fruits, honey, and sweet caramel, this is an immediately attractive wine. Acidity complements the generosity of the palate. **86 Best Buy** —*R.V. (8/1/2005)*

Terracota 2001 Portuguese Red (Ribatejo) $NA. An impressive blend of Cabernet Sauvignon and Castelão, this is richly wood-aged. With its juicy, jelly tastes (from the Castelão) and the tannins from the Cabernet, this has power as well as immediate drinkability. **86** —*R.V. (11/1/2004)*

Terracota 2003 Branco Portuguese White (Ribatejo) $9. A lively, perfumed wine, fresh and crisp, which also has a hint of new wood from six months barrel aging. The best things about the wine are its lightness and poise which make it delicious and fragrant. **87** —*R.V. (12/1/2004)*

TERRAS DE PAUL

Terras de Paul 2004 Portuguese Red (Ribatejano) $17. This medium-bodied red features decent balance between tannins, alcohol, and acids, but the flavors are just a little different. There are some cherry flavors, maybe even black cherry, but also herbal, chlorophyllic notes that start on the nose and persist through the finish. **84** —*J.C. (6/1/2006)*

TERRAS DO GRIFO

Terras do Grifo 2005 Selected Harvest Malvasia Fina (Douro) $16. This medium-bodied white is a bit prickly and tough to like, with citrus pith aromas and largely neutral flavors that turn chalky and peppery on the finish. **82** —*J.C. (11/1/2006)*

THE RARE WINE CO.

The Rare Wine Co. NV Historic Series Boston Bual Special Reserve (Madeira) $40. Slightly richer than the Charleston Sercial, the Boston Bual boasts knockout aromas of toasted nut oil, orange peel, and hints of dark honey or maple syrup. Despite the extra weight and sweetness, it's not cloying at all—the finish is mouth-watering and long. **93 Editors' Choice** —*J.C. (11/1/2006)*

The Rare Wine Co. NV Historic Series Charleston Sercial Special Reserve (Madeira) $40. The Historic Series are simply great Madeiras at reasonable prices. The Charleston Sercial is the driest of the collection, offering nutty aromas tinged with honey, caramel, and maple syrup. Dried figs, honey, and candied citrus flavors mark the palate, which is wonderfully smooth. The long finish features racy yet balanced acidity. **93 Editors' Choice** —*J.C. (11/1/2006)*

The Rare Wine Co. NV Historic Series New York Malmsey Special Reserve (Madeira) $40. The sweetest and richest in the Historic series, the New York Malmsey unfolds slowly in the glass, gradually revealing layers of depth and flavor. Coffee, toffee, and date notes emerge, followed by earthy, almost truffley flavors. Powerful and assertive on the long finish. **93 Editors' Choice** —*J.C. (11/1/2006)*

VALLEGRE

Vallegre 2003 Valle Longo Vintage Port $NA. Shows a somewhat earthy character, which leaves it unfocused and dominated by rustic perfumes. **82** —*R.V. (11/15/2005)*

VARANDA DO CONDE

Varanda do Conde 2004 Alvarinho (Vinho Verde) $10. Not a typical Vinho Verde with a slender body and floral scents, but instead one that features petrol and ripe apple scents and a distinctive mineral note on the palate. Medium-bodied, with a long, citrusy finish. **85 Best Buy** —*J.C. (12/31/2005)*

VEIGA TEIXEIRA

Veiga Teixeira 2001 Horta da Nazaré Castelão Red Blend (Ribatejo) $13. A powerful, tannic wine that deserves to be cellared 2–3 years, or served alongside some rare lamb or beef to help tame the tannins. There's a blast of black cherries, graham crackers, and vanilla right out of the glass, and plenty of weight to support the hearty flavors. **88 Best Buy** —*J.C. (11/1/2004)*

Veiga Teixeira 2002 Quinta de Santo André Red Blend (Ribatejo) $9. Nicely crafted, blending chocolate and cinnamon notes artfully with bold cherries. Medium-weight. Picks up soft, tea-like tannins and subtle toast shadings on the finish. **87 Best Buy** —*J.C. (11/1/2004)*

Veiga Teixeira 2003 Quinta de Santo André White Blend (Ribatejo) $8. A bit similar to a white Rhône in style, with delicate floral aromas combined with nutty scents, then chunky, slightly neutral flavors on the palate of melon and spice. Full enough to handle delicate cream sauces. **84 Best Buy** —*J.C. (11/1/2004)*

VINHOS BORGES

Vinhos Borges 2005 Alvarinho (Vinho Verde) $15. A finely balanced wine, creamy and smooth, with good dense flavors. Green plums, apple skins, and ripe acidity blend well in this fresh wine. **89** —*R.V. (7/1/2006)*

Vinhos Borges NV Gatão Portuguese White (Vinho Verde) $6. The standard style of inexpensive Vinho Verde, this is a simple wine, clean, but with layers of sugar to coat and mask the fresh, crisp acidity. **82** —*R.V. (7/1/2006)*

Vinhos Borges 2000 Meia Encosta Red Blend (Dão) $8. This popular brand in Portugal is easy, light and fresh, with a touch of sweetness. It has red berries and easy flavors, but also an uncomfortable streak of rusticity. **83** —*R.V. (12/31/2002)*

VINHOS JUSTINO HENRIQUES, FILHOS

Vinhos Justino Henriques, Filhos 1996 Colheita Sweet Madeira Blend (Madeira) $25. Plump and sweet, this single-vintage Madeira boasts slightly nutty aromas allied to scents of dried figs and dates. The sweet dried fruit and Christmas spice flavors come on strong on the palate, balanced by tangy acids on the long finish. **88** —*J.C. (3/1/2005)*

VINHOS MESSIAS

Vinhos Messias 2000 Quinta do Cachao Tinta Roriz (Douro) $20. This is a light, fresh wine with some pleasant, soft tannins, but it is somewhat dilute. Pleasant red fruits give this wine a fresh aftertaste. **83** —*R.V. (12/31/2002)*

Vinhos Messias 1999 Quinta do Cachão Touriga Nacional (Douro) $5. A bulky, fruity wine that makes up in size and flavor what it lacks in finesse. Bold blackberry and grape flavors finish with ash and charcoal notes. Grilled burgers would be the perfect food pairing. **85 Best Buy** —*J.C. (12/31/2001)*

Vinhos Messias 2000 Quinta do Cachão/Colheita Touriga Nacional (Douro) $20. The Quinta de Cachão is also used to produce Messias Port. This could almost be a Port, with its soft, juicy fruit, sweetly perfumed blackcurrant flavors and soft tannins. **87** —*R.V. (12/31/2002)*

Vinhos Messias 2001 Quinta do Valdoeiro Touriga Nacional (Beiras) $20. The 172-acre Quinta do Valdoeiro is just outside Mealhada in the Bairrada region. This wine is made from the Douro grape, Touriga Nacional, rather than the local Baga. It has a dark purple color and yeasty, toasty aromas. The palate is dark and withdrawn, with powerful toast flavors and black fruits. **87** —*R.V. (12/31/2002)*

Vinhos Messias NV Santola White Blend (Vinho Verde) $11. This low-alcohol (9%) Vinho Verde carries some obvious residual sugar, which in this case works well. Some lively upfront spritz is replaced by a respectable smoothness on the finish. And the acid structure is just right, as it keeps

PORTUGAL

things tangy and lively. With a seafood salad at lunch, this would work perfectly. **85** —*M.S. (12/31/2001)*

VISTA ALEGRE

Vista Alegre 1995 LBV Bottled 2000 Port $NA. This is dry, dense, and raisiny, with dry tannins, and acidity. Towards the aftertaste, the solidity of the wine is spoiled by a touch of green tannin. The name of the wine comes from the principal quinta owned by Barros Agricola near Pinhão. **86** —*R.V. (11/1/2004)*

Vista Alegre 1996 LBV Bottled 2002 Port $NA. Plums, black fruits, and ripe raisins all blend to give this wine a fine, fruit-driven character. The downside to all this fruit is that there is little sense of structure, and this is a wine which needs to be drunk now. **86** —*R.V. (11/1/2004)*

Vista Alegre 2003 Single Estate Vintage Port $NA. From the Vista Alegre vineyard in the Pinhão valley, this Port is powerfully perfumed, with great black cherry flavors and acidity. It has good structure, but is generally relatively simple and easy to appreciate. **88** —*R.V. (11/15/2005)*

Vista Alegre NV Vintage Character Port $NA. A jammy, herbal flavored wine, which is well enough balanced but seems to lack much intensity. The fruit is soft, sweet, with black jam flavors and a light touch of acidity. With just an extra touch of concentration, this would be a classic wine. The name of the wine comes from the principal quinta owned by Barros near Pinhão. **85** —*R.V. (3/1/2005)*

W. & J. GRAHAM'S

W. & J. Graham's NV 10-Year Old Tawny Port $31. Powered with acidity and its firm structure, this is an intensely dry, concentrated, powerful wine. It certainly has wines in the blend that are older than 10 years, yet it is definitely a 10-Year Old in style, as the fresh fruit to finish confirms. **92 Editors' Choice** —*R.V. (8/1/2006)*

W. & J. Graham's NV 20-Year Old Tawny Port $52. This is a hugely dry, burnt style, very concentrated. The licorice and bitter coffee flavors are dense, layered, and well-balanced with the acidity. A serious wine that demands attention. **90** —*R.V. (8/1/2006)*

W. & J. Graham's NV 40-Year Old Tawny Port $152. An old, mature wine, but one that has kept its ripeness and richness. The concentration is so intense that one glass is almost enough (except it tastes so good). There are walnuts, bitter chocolate, and a delicious clean aftertaste. **94** —*R.V. (8/1/2006)*

W. & J. Graham's NV Aged 20 Years Finest Cask Matured Tawny Port $45. This 20-year-old shows some surprisingly youthful notes of red fruits along with layers of caramel, honey, maple syrup, and walnuts. Nicely balanced, and it comes in half-bottles too—the perfect size for smaller gatherings. **90** —*J.C. (11/15/2003)*

W. & J. Graham's NV Crusted Port Bottled 1999 Port $NA. Crusted Port is an intermediate category between LBV and vintage. It is bottled with a crust or sediment, allowing it to age in the bottle like a vintage Port, but is not released until three years after bottling. Graham's Crusted is still young, showing bright, peppery fruit, ripeness, and dryness along with sweet black flavors and vibrant acidity to finish. **89** —*R.V. (11/1/2004)*

W. & J. Graham's 1995 LBV Bottled 2000 Port $20. An attractive, soft, mature wine, which has rich sweetness. The obvious richness, though, is balanced by flavors of ripe plums and by the acidity that gives a sense of freshness in the aftertaste. It's ready to drink now. **88** —*R.V. (3/1/2003)*

W. & J. Graham's 1996 Malvedos Vintage Port $42. 86 —*J.C. (11/15/2003)*

W. & J. Graham's NV Six Grapes Reserve Port $21. W & J Graham makes one of the best-known Reserve Port brands. And a great wine it is, too. It is soft, but there are tannins. It is fruity, but there is good concentration. And with its flavors of ripe black figs and dark chocolate, it is an immediately appealing wine. **89** —*R.V. (3/1/2005)*

W. & J. Graham's 2003 Vintage Port $100. This is a great Port, from a great brand. It is packed with solid, structured, rich, and intense black fruit flavors. Its tannins show considerable aging potential. It is a big, ripe wine, balanced by a long, lingering dark aftertaste. **96** —*R.V. (11/15/2005)*

WARRE'S

Warre's NV King's Tawny Port $13. 85 *(3/1/2000)*

Warre's 1992 LBV Bottled 1996 Port $23. Warre's LBV is a crusted, traditional style, which has been bottled unfiltered and which matures in the bottle. That's why this wine is so fine and rich and only now reaching maturity. It is dry, with layers of tannins and dried fruit flavors. Tasted blind, it would certainly be mistaken for a vintage Port. **92** —*R.V. (3/1/2003)*

Warre's NV Otima 10-Year Old Tawny Port $25. This recent launch from Warre's is delicious. It's a fruity tawny, with delicious acidity and touches of bitter orange and chocolate. Classically balanced and fresh. **91** —*R.V. (8/1/2006)*

Warre's NV Otima 20-Year Old Tawny Port $42. Warre's seems to have found just the right formula for its tawnys. The 10-Year Old Otima is a fine wine, and so is this Otima 20. It has aromas of almonds, layers of acidity and sweetness, the flavor of bitter oranges, and a round, ripe aftertaste. **90** —*R.V. (8/1/2006)*

Warre's NV Plus 20-Year Old Tawny Port $46. This is a huge, concentrated, dry wine, which is left very unbalanced by the burnt character and the dominance of the spirit. The acidity, at least, leaves freshness. **85** —*R.V. (8/1/2006)*

Warre's 1986 Quinta Da Cavadinha Port $42. 87 —*J.C. (3/1/2000)*

Warre's 1987 Reserve Tawny Port $28. A knockout of a 12-year-old tawny, with heavy, inviting caramel aromas and flavors. The color is still slightly rosy, showing that this wine has retained its fruity roots. Structured and weighty in the mouth, with notes of cloves and ginger throughout. **93** *(1/1/2004)*

Warre's 1961 Reserve Tawny Port $111. 89 *(3/1/2000)*

Warre's NV Sir William 10-Year Old Tawny Port $26. Caramel, white chocolate aromas, and unbalanced sweet and sour flavors just do not show well together in this disappointing wine. **83** —*R.V. (8/1/2006)*

Warre's 2003 Vintage Port $82. A fine, perfumed wine with great fruit. It's ripe, with lovely rich flavors and a backbone of firm tannins. This is a good, solid, classic wine. **90** —*R.V. (11/15/2005)*

Warre's NV Warrior Special Reserve Port $16. Smells attractive enough, offering up chocolate, blackberry, and spice aromas, but seems a bit thin and lacking in texture on the palate, finishing with some unintegrated alcohol. **82** —*J.C. (11/1/2006)*

WIESE & KROHN

Wiese & Krohn NV 10-Year Old Tawny Port $25. A clean, very poised style, with attractive acidity and good balance. It's just as deliciously fresh as a 10-Year Old should be. **88** —*R.V. (8/1/2006)*

Wiese & Krohn NV 20-Year Old Tawny Port $50. A dense, concentrated, but deliciously clean wine, with balanced fruit, marmalade flavor and a touch of spirit to finish. This is a wine that shows considerable character and style. **90** —*R.V. (8/1/2006)*

Wiese & Krohn 2003 Vintage Port $NA. Normally known for relatively soft vintages, Wiese & Krohn have changed style with this 2003. This Port is firm, solid with intense fruits, black figs and fine tannins. It should have a good, medium-term future. **89** —*R.V. (11/15/2005)*

WINE & SOUL

Wine & Soul 2003 Pintas Vintage Port $55. For Sandra Tavares da Silva and her husband, Jorge Serodio Borges, already well-known for great Douro table wine, this is a first vintage Port. For such a modern couple, the Port has a comfortingly old-fashioned feel. The tannins are dusty and solid, but generous. The style is dry, while the fruit has fine dried fruit flavors. An impressive start. **90** —*R.V. (11/15/2005)*

ZIMBRO

Zimbro 2004 Tinto Red Blend (Douro) $16. A bit confected, with aromas and flavors of jumbleberry pie drizzled with chocolate syrup. That's not to say it tastes sweet—it's dry—but the flavors boast a candied quality that limits their otherwise considerable appeal. **84** —*J.C. (11/1/2006)*

PORTUGAL

South Africa

After a slow start, South Africa's wines have reached international heights. The wines are sold at an impressively good value, and the country offers styles and tastes that are special and—importantly—enjoyable.

South Africa has been producing wine since the first vineyards were planted by the French in the seventeenth century, brought to the country by the Dutch governors of Cape Colony. At one time, the sweet wine of Constantia was the most prized in the world. For decades, South Africa, as part of the British Empire, sent shiploads of fortified wines to London.

This luxurious past can still be seen in the stunningly beautiful Cape vineyards, and the elegant, gabled Dutch Cape houses that form the centerpieces of many wine estates. But the future has also made its mark in South Africa's vineyards, where local winemakers (joined by an increasing number of European and American winemakers and investors) are creating a new generation of wines.

Boschendal Estate, Groot Drakenstein Valley, Franschhoek, Cape Province, South Africa.

The style, the character of the wines, is somewhere between California or Australia and Europe. Food friendly and equally elegant and powerful, there are many wines here for drinkers tired of alcoholic blockbusters.

All South Africa's vineyards are within an hour or three of Cape Town, in the southwest corner of the country. South Africa has its own appellation system, Wine of Origin, which is indicated on the label and on a government-issued neck sticker.

The most important quality wine areas are around the two cities of Stellenbosch and Paarl. All wine styles are made here: the country's greatest reds are from Stellenbosch, but Paarl's sub-district of Franschhoek runs a close second. Increasingly, other areas are being developed: the west coast, which makes great cooler-climate Sauvignon Blanc and red wines under the Darling and Swartland Wine of Origin, and the south coast at Walker Bay and Elgin, from which the country's best Pinot Noir comes.

The other famed quality area (although tiny in volume) is Constantia, almost in the suburbs of Cape Town. The original Cape vineyards now make impressive reds and whites in the country's most historic wine estates.

Larger-volume areas are further north and east than these classic heartland areas: Robertson, known for its Chardonnay, Worcester, for inexpensive volume wines, and Oliphants River, better known for reds and fortified wines.

South Africa's wine styles are evolving. Chenin Blanc, the local white workhorse grape, is also capable of making some impressive dry and sweet wines. Sauvignon Blanc has the potential to be more exciting than Chardonnay.

For reds, Pinotage, South Africa's own red grape (a cross between Pinot Noir and Cinsaut) still leaves wine critics divided, but can make great things, especially if found in Cape Blend wines (Pinotage blended with other red grapes). Shiraz is seen as the new hope for red wine, but Cabernet Sauvignon, Merlot, and Bordeaux blend wines are still the country's top reds.

ABRAHAM PEROLD

Abraham Perold 1996 Op Die Berg Shiraz (Paarl) $145. Ultra-toasty, but in a sweet, appealing way, featuring enveloping flavors of caramelized sugar and vanilla, marinated pork, and cherries. The texture is full and verging on custardy in this smooth, luxurious wine from South Africa. **90** *(1/1/2004)*

ALEXANDERFONTEIN

Alexanderfontein 2003 Chenin Blanc (Coastal Region) $10. A classy Chenin Blanc that offers an intriguing profile with smoke and mineral notes over a dry green apple and citrus foundation. It's restrained, but shows good fruit intensity. Tasty and long, it will pair beautifully with lobster or a fleshy, white fish like sea bass, and is delicious on its own. **88 Editors' Choice** *—M.M. (7/1/2005)*

ALLESVERLOREN

Allesverloren 1999 Estate Cabernet Sauvignon (Swartland) $22. Aromas of cocoa, applesauce, red plum, and mild toast travel to the palate. The acidity gives the wine an overall feel of cleanliness and juiciness. **86 —K.F. (8/1/2003)**

AMBELOUI

Ambeloui 2000 Valley Road Hout Bay Christo Champagne Blend (Constantia) $20. This Pinot Noir-Chardonnay brut from South Africa smells yeasty and doughy, with a hint of citrus and smoke. Drinks dry and citrusy, and there's a real bite of acidity, but it's rough on the palate, and finishes with peppery sharpness. **84 —S.H. (12/1/2002)**

ANURA

Anura 2004 Private Cellar Chenin Blanc (Paarl) $18. Not known for whites, Anura has crafted a very nice Chenin. This golden-hued wine exudes aromas of cooked peanuts, soy dumplings, and Asian spices, all wrapped in toasty oak. Nutty and toasty in the mouth, with flavors of olive oil and spice coating moderate white stone fruit. The full, creamy mouthfeel borders on bulky. **88 —M.D. (7/1/2006)**

Anura 2004 Private Cellar Syrah-Mourvèdre Red Blend (Paarl) $30. A huge wine, clocking in at 15% alcohol, this liqueur-like offering has aromas of plum, mint, cinnamon, and hints of lemon. Warm, with sweet blackberry flavors to match the moderate tannins, it borders on raisiny, with plenty of oak-driven spice, and more heat on the finish. **87 —M.D. (7/1/2006)**

ARNISTON BAY

Arniston Bay 2003 Chenin Blanc-Chardonnay (Western Cape) $10. A well-made easy drinker with clean apple-pear fruit and some mineral-chalk accents. Not really sweet, but the fruit is strong enough to make it seem slightly so. A refreshing wine that could satisfy a wide range of palates. It's uncomplicated, but satisfying rather than dull or cloying. **85 Best Buy** *—M.M. (7/1/2005)*

Arniston Bay 2003 Merlot-Shiraz (Western Cape) $11. Not your usual red blend, this light wine has a red berry and rhubarb profile. The feel is easy, but with slightly high-strung fruit and acidity, and some peppery tannins on the close. **82 —M.M. (7/1/2005)**

Arniston Bay 2004 Rosé Pinotage (Western Cape) $10. A straightforward rosé with bright color and flavors. Not at all sweet, and will go well with many light foods. Shows hints of funkiness, but they add some complexity to this decent patio or light-dining wine. Closes with a dry, spice-tinged finish. **84 —M.M. (7/1/2005)**

ASHANTI

Ashanti 2001 Chiwara Red Blend (Paarl) $24. Aromas of toasted marshmallow and new glove leather meet sweet raspberry and blueberry notes on the palate. The marshmallow streaks through the whole wine to the lengthy finish flavored with dried herbs and pepper. **87 —K.F. (9/1/2003)**

Ashanti 2001 Joseph's Hat Red Blend (Paarl) $10. The simple flavors of sweet red plum are pleasantly hailed by aromas of dry fruit, baking spices, dried herbs, tobacco, and glove leather. Fruit displaying more complexity would contribute to a higher rating. **86 —K.F. (9/1/2003)**

Ashanti 2001 Nicole's Hat White Blend (Paarl) $10. Zesty aromas reminiscent of orange blossom and lime carry well to the citrusy palate tinged with shale. Although light on the nose, the citrus flavors are worth investigating. **85 —K.F. (9/1/2003)**

AVONDALE

Avondale 2004 Chenin Blanc (Coastal Region) $NA. A fascinating, serious, full-bodied style of wine from this Paarl winery, which was founded in 1997. The wine is packed with nutmeg and almond flavors, which join concentrated vibrant fruits. **89 —R.V. (11/15/2005)**

BACKSBERG

Backsberg 2002 Cabernet Sauvignon (Paarl) $12. Medium-weight with good flavor and varietal character after a slightly muddy opening. The wine expands, improving in the glass where the dark berry fruit and tobacco, earth, and toasty oak accents gain focus. Solid, basic Cabernet with a decently long finish. **86 —M.M. (11/15/2004)**

Backsberg 1997 Cabernet Sauvignon (Paarl) $14. Dark cherry and toast shows on the nose of this straightforward Cabernet. The wine offers more of the same and some earthy shadings on the dry and even palate. Finishes with medium length, and displays a hint of chocolate on the back end. **85 —M.M. (3/1/2001)**

Backsberg 2002 Klein Babylons Toren Cabernet Sauvignon-Merlot (Paarl) $15. Opaque and hard to read, with deep, toasty, menthol-tinged oak over dark and dense fruit. Built for the cellar. Taut structure and firm tannins here demand keeping both the wine until 2006–7. **87 —M.M. (11/15/2004)**

Backsberg 2003 Chardonnay (Paarl) $10. This is a good wine for this price. Tropical notes of mango and guava are accented with some vanilla. Menthol and smoke notes add some complexity, and the full body has enough balancing acidity. **86 Best Buy** *—M.D. (3/1/2006)*

Backsberg 2002 Chardonnay (Paarl) $10. Straightforward mainstream Chardonnay with lavish oak over apple fruit. Has a decent medium-weight mouthfeel and a fairly long, if woody, close. If you like 'em oaky you'll like this more than me. I'd prefer to see this fruit done in an unwooded style. **84 —M.M. (7/4/2004)**

Backsberg 2001 Chardonnay (Paarl) $13. A world away from any traditional Kosher wine concept, this South African white is crisp and light with citrus-hay aromas. It nearly takes on a Sauvignon Blanc profile with its tart lemony flavors and bright feel, closing crisply with modest length. Looks just like the regular Chardonnay bottling, but with a background blue Star of David on the label, indicating its Kosher (and Kosher for Passover) status. **84 —M.M. (4/1/2002)**

Backsberg 2000 Chardonnay (Paarl) $13. This medium-weight Chardonnay has its own style somewhere between Old and New World in manner. It's dry, with a bouquet of hay and faint orange, tangy and slightly grainy—in flavor and texture—on the tongue, showing more citrus hints. Turns nutty on the finish. Drink now–2003. **85 —M.M. (4/1/2002)**

Backsberg 1999 Chardonnay (Paarl) $14. A light and basic Chardonnay that lacks the fruit to match the oak utilized. There's structure and it finishes long, but the wine is dominated by toasted oak. **82 —M.N. (3/1/2001)**

Backsberg 2002 Babylons Toren Chardonnay (Paarl) $25. Backsberg's top offerings, its Babylons Toren range, are impressive, showing a focus, quality, and style not seen before. This is suave, with vibrant pineapple, mango and apple aromas and flavors, and ample French oak. The texture is very good—a positive tension between rich and zingy notes. **91 Editors' Choice** *—M.M. (11/15/2004)*

Backsberg 2005 Chenin Blanc (Western Cape) $12. Strange, dry aromas of peanut shell are off-putting, but the wine comes back with flavors of cashews and white fruit. Dry, with good acidity, it finishes with hints of spice. **85 —M.D. (7/1/2006)**

Backsberg 2003 Chenin Blanc (Paarl) $10. An interesting wine that's dry, yet shows some distinctly sweet notes. The apple-grape front end is fruity, somewhat Riesling-like. The appealing, tart green apple close turns crisper and drier. Light-weight with good acidity, a good choice for moderately spicy foods, and pretty tasty on its own. **86 —M.M. (7/4/2004)**

Backsberg 1998 Merlot (Paarl) $14. A medium to deep ruby color opens things up. The wine is well-balanced and the tannins soft. Unfortunately, however, this structure is fleshed out with only light coffee notes, and therein lies the problem.**82** —*M.N. (3/1/2001)*

Backsberg 1998 Klein Babylonstoren Merlot-Cabernet Sauvignon (Paarl) $18. Stylistically, this blend is much like a Bordeaux. At first, bright cherry and raspberry fruit ride atop a racy, dry palate. With deeper inspection comes the integration of earthy aromatics with oak, plum, and kirsch notes. A little more richness wouldn't hurt.**87** —*M.S. (4/1/2002)*

Backsberg 2004 Kosher Pinotage (Paarl) $14. This young wine is reminiscent of Beaujolais, with fresh aromas of crushed grapes and berries. Light-bodied, it's vibrant, fruity, and fun with bright fruit on the palate. **84** —*M.D. (4/1/2006)*

Backsberg 2002 Babylons Toren Red Blend (Paarl) $30. At once overtly woody, yet lithe and elegant. Black fruits, tobacco and even shoe polish hints show on the nose. Toast and espresso flavors abound—the tart, dark side of the force rules here. Many will love it just as it is, and it's an undeniably handsome acute oakster. But only time will tell if the fruit evers comes out from behind the veil.**87** —*M.M. (7/1/2005)*

Backsberg 2005 Sauvignon Blanc (Western Cape) $12. Green bean and dill lead off the nose, but white fruits emerge on the palate to counter the vegetal notes. Good intensity of flavor, with acidity that borders on tart.**86** —*M.D. (3/1/2006)*

Backsberg 2003 Sauvignon Blanc (Western Cape) $10. Round with perfectly accurate, varietally correct aromas and flavors. Bright without being sharp, showing sweet-sour fruit and pepper hints on the close. Quite drinkable and quite mainstream.**85 Best Buy** —*M.M. (11/15/2004)*

Backsberg 2003 John Martin Sauvignon Blanc (Paarl) $15. Achieves a fine balance of tangy and rich elements. Grapefruit, fig, and vanilla aromas and flavors abound, with a lovely tension. The texture is great, and tart citrus notes linger on the long finish. Not the zingiest, nor the weightiest, but an excellent all-around Sauvignon Blanc.**90 Best Buy** —*M.M. (11/15/2004)*

Backsberg 1998 Shiraz (Paarl) $14. Has what seems like grain-like aromas to go with grapey, blackberry-plum fruit. Turns tart and somewhat green on the palate, offering little more than tart berry and leafy flavors that turn lemony on the finish.**82** *(10/1/2001)*

Backsberg 2003 Pumphouse Shiraz (Paarl) $20. Although this wine boasts 15% alcohol, it's very well-balanced. It's dark and spicy, with flavors of black olive and cooked berry, picking up hints of lemon custard that continue to the long, coffeE and olive finish. A big wine that packs plenty of punch and just enough tannin to make it work.**88** —*M.D. (5/1/2006)*

Backsberg 2002 Pumphouse Shiraz (Paarl) $18. Tasty, very international-style Shiraz that will have broad appeal. This delivers ample ripe berry, stewed fruit, and leather aromas. On the tongue, it's firm and dry, with coffee-chocolate accents on the tangy fruit. Closes with even tannins, and is very drinkable now.**87** —*M.M. (11/15/2004)*

Backsberg 2004 Babylons Toren Viognier (Paarl) $30. Heavily oaked, with toasty vanilla aromas, this full wine still manages a high acidic core along with a round exterior. Peach pit and melon flavors stand up to buttery oak, while the finish is long. The alcohol (15.5%) does show on the finish, leaving the throat warm.**89** —*M.D. (9/1/2006)*

Backsberg 2003 Babylons Toren Viognier (South Africa) $25. This tasty Viognier hits all the right notes, presenting very appealing honeysuckle-spice aromas and flavors. It's not heavy or sappy, and good acidity supports the fruit. Finishes long and with a very nice blend of spice and mineral notes.**88** —*M.S. (11/15/2004)*

BAOBAB

Baobab 2002 Chardonnay (Western Cape) $8. Solidly middle of the road, New World Chard, a little sweet, a little oaky, and very ripe. Peaches, apples, and pears all mingle together in the flavors. Simple and a little thin, but an easy sipper.**84** —*S.H. (1/1/2002)*

Baobab 2001 Chenin Blanc (Western Cape) $7.85 —*S.H. (4/1/2002)*

Baobab 2004 Merlot (Western Cape) $10. If more inexpensive Merlots were as good as this, maybe the category could regain some of its lost cachet. Plum, black currant, and chocolate flavors pack enough punch to stand up to such boldly flavored foods as cheeseburgers, spare ribs, and barbecued chicken.**85 Best Buy** —*J.C. (11/15/2005)*

Baobab 2002 Merlot (Western Cape) $8. Nicely opposed berry, earth, and smoke elements riff in this tasty over-achiever. Bordeaux-like, with solid dry fruit, earth and herb accents. Shows good length and even a touch of elegance. Outperforms most value Merlots, regardless of origin.**87 Best Buy** —*M.M. (11/15/2004)*

Baobab 1998 Merlot (Western Cape) $10. Packs plenty of flavor for the price, with great heaps of berries and stone fruits, earth, mushroom, and sweet vanillins and spice. You can taste the sunny ripeness through the rich finish, but the wine is dry and balanced. This is a very good value. **87** —*S.H. (1/1/2002)*

Baobab 2004 Pinotage (Western Cape) $10. Massive cherry aromas erupt from the glass, and they swamp the palate, too, quite deliciously. The texture is less pleasing, and is rough and sharp.**84** —*M.D. (3/1/2006)*

Baobab 2001 Pinotage (Western Cape) $10. Grilled meat, black plum, peppercorns, and caramel aromas carry through to the palate. Fine tannins and peppery black fruit deliver pleasure.**88 Best Buy** —*K.F. (4/1/2003)*

Baobab 2001 Sauvignon Blanc (Western Cape) $8.84 —*S.H. (4/1/2002)*

BEAU JOUBERT

Beau Joubert 2002 Cabernet Sauvignon (Stellenbosch) $17. A wonderful wine for the price, with aromas of berry and plum wrapped in tobacco leaf and coffee. Smooth and full in the mouth, this dry wine's flavors of dark berry, coffee, and graphite are touched with balsam, showing character and complexity. A hint of lemon creeps through on the finish.**89** —*M.D. (7/1/2006)*

Beau Joubert 2005 Chardonnay (Stellenbosch) $14. Pretty uncharacteristic Chardonnay; offers scents of lemon verbena and scented oils. The floral theme continues in the mouth with flavors of honeysuckle and melon. Has an oily, round feel, although acidity is also a player. Different, but good.**86** —*M.D. (7/1/2006)*

Beau Joubert 2005 Oak Lane Chenin Blanc-Sauvignon Blanc (Stellenbosch) $8. Tart apple is the main player in the mouth. Zesty and ripe, the 85% Chenin Blanc is beginning to show nutty flavors, too. A good bargain from Beau Joubert's second label.**85 Best Buy** —*M.D. (7/1/2006)*

Beau Joubert 2004 Oak Lane Merlot-Cabernet Sauvignon (Stellenbosch) $8. This inexpensive Stellenbosch wine has lots to offer. Cassis aromas mix with hints of forest floor and mint. Plum and cassis star in the mouth, with graphite notes adding complexity. Finishes firm.**86 Best Buy** —*M.D. (5/1/2006)*

Beau Joubert 2005 Sauvignon Blanc (Stellenbosch) $13. A ripe nose of tropical fruit, honey, and baked apple leads to more of the same in the mouth, plus some spicy fruit and citrus pith. Full-bodied for a Sauvignon Blanc; pair it with grilled shrimp.**87** —*M.D. (7/1/2006)*

Beau Joubert 2005 Oak Lane Shiraz (Stellenbosch) $8. This wine has lots going on, but no focus. A grapey nose is marred by grassy aromas, while band-aid flavors play as much a role as the plum and vanilla. Despite heavy tannins the wine remains hollow. Finishes spicy.**83** —*M.D. (7/1/2006)*

BEAUMONT

Beaumont 2001 Ariane Bordeaux Blend (Walker Bay) $20. The dry nose of thyme and oregano lets the fresh flavors of red plum and currant carry the punch, with a leathery dried-herb finish providing follow through. Balancing the fruit are forward tannins and soft acids.**87** —*K.F. (8/1/2003)*

Beaumont 2004 Chenin Blanc (Walker Bay) $15. A wine that spent two months in wood, giving it a ripe, fruity character, with spice, cinnamon, acidity, and tropical fruits. This cool-climate Walker Bay winery is now highly rated under the hands of winemaker Sebastian Beaumont.**88** —*R.V. (11/15/2005)*

Beaumont 2004 Hope Marguerite Chenin Blanc (Walker Bay) $21. Named after winemaker Sebastian Beaumont's grandmother, this is a fine, barrel-fermented Chenin that balances elegant citrus fruit with spice and fresh toast. A delicious, dry food style of Chenin. **91** —*R.V. (11/15/2005)*

Beaumont 2000 Shiraz (South Africa) $18. This inky glassful is a little tight now, with firm acidity and coating, sandy tannins. A bit of aging will gently loosen the copious black plum, pepper, char, grilled meat, and violet aromas and flavors for extended enjoyment. **88** —*K.F. (8/1/2003)*

BELLINGHAM

Bellingham 2003 Our Founder's Cabernet Sauvignon (Coastal Region) $12. Stewed fruit is joined by cigar box on the nose, while the palate delivers dark berry, menthol, and a hint of raspberry to jazz things up. A bit soft from start to finish. **84** —*M.D. (3/1/2006)*

Bellingham 2004 Our Founder's Chardonnay (Coastal Region) $11. This wine has vanilla scents. The mouth pleases with white fruit, hints of oak, and a crisp finish. **84** —*M.D. (3/1/2006)*

Bellingham 2003 Our Founder's Pinotage (Coastal Region) $12. Heavy aromas of roasted berry lead to caramel, meat, and berry flavors. Despite the dark flavors this wine is simple, although with good balance. **84** —*M.D. (5/1/2006)*

Bellingham 2004 Our Founder's Sauvignon Blanc (Coastal Region) $11. Peach aromas waft from the glass, mixed with vanilla spice. The palate is light, with flavors of white peach and orange peel, and good acidity. Finishes with a dash of oak. **85** —*M.D. (3/1/2006)*

Bellingham 2003 Shiraz (Coastal Region) $12. Earthy aromas lead to a palate that lacks fruit but shows cedar and spice notes, along with some olive. The acidity of this wine really kicks in on the finish, which is otherwise oily, creating a strange dichotomy. **83** —*M.D. (5/1/2006)*

BERGSIG

Bergsig 2003 Pinotage (Breede River Valley) $13. This wine has plenty of flavor, from mulberry to cherry cola to spice, as well as high acidity and hints of minerality. The nose offers red berry and rhubarb. All in all it's good, but it would be better if it were more integrated. **84** —*M.D. (12/31/2006)*

Bergsig 2001 Pinotage (South Africa) $12. A whiff of pepper blows off, revealing red cherry and grilled meat notes. Ripe, sweet red-plum flavors have a similar meatiness with toasty caramel accents. A bit green toward the finish, but with a heat not unlike pepper chaff. **87** —*K.F. (4/1/2003)*

Bergsig 2004 Sauvignon Blanc (Breede River Valley) $9. Oak asserts itself on the nose with aromas of caramel and walnut. The age is also apparent, as this wine lacks the zippy feel of similarly priced 2005s. But it's a good wine, nicely balanced with acidity, a rounded body, and oaked flavors of caramel, nut, and spice. You just wish there were a little more fruit. **84** —*M.D. (12/31/2006)*

Bergsig 2002 Sauvignon Blanc (Breede River Valley) $10. Light and gently tangy, the hay, herb, and melon notes predominating here make this a softly straightforward wine. Decidedly not in the extreme style, this has easy drinking appeal, closing with gentle spice and grapefruit tones. **84** —*M.M. (3/1/2004)*

BEYERSKLOOF

Beyerskloof 2001 Cabernet Sauvignon-Merlot (Stellenbosch) $35. Beyers Truter, legendary winemaker of Kanonkop (which he left in 2004) also produces wines from his own estate, Beyerskloof. This Cab-Merlot blend is a smooth, ripe wine, with full-on juicy fruit backed up by sweet, ripe tannins. But it is not excessive, as the brakes of restraint are put on just at the right moment. **93 Editors' Choice** —*R.V. (11/1/2006)*

Beyerskloof 2005 Pinotage (Stellenbosch) $12. Starts off beautifully with aromas of mulberry, smoke, eraser, and a hint of lemon leading to dark berry fruit flavors. Then notes of leather crop up, and later gain strength. Yet this wine is smooth with a medium-full body and plenty of fruit to keep pace over the next year. **86** —*M.D. (12/31/2006)*

Beyerskloof 2000 Pinotage (Stellenbosch) $10. A strong rendition of this distinctive South African variety that shows bouncy, exuberant fruit. Sweet plum aromas and flavors, a ripe mouthfeel, and an almost jammy blackberry finish make it a winner. Possesses Shiraz-like qualities, but its own unique flavor profile. **89 Best Buy** *(9/1/2001)*

Beyerskloof 2003 Cape Blend Red Blend (Stellenbosch) $20. Pinotage aromas of woodsmoke and sour cherry segue into Bordeaux scents of dried tobacco and cassis. This blend of 45% Pinotage with the rest Cabernet Sauvignon and Merlot juxtaposes the former's vibrant fruit with structured tannin and brown leaf flavors. Smooth, incorporating high acidity, the oak still needs time to fully integrate. **88** —*M.D. (9/1/2006)*

BILTON

Bilton 1999 Merlot (Stellenbosch) $18. A nose of flavorful, plummy fruit with clove accents pulls you right in to this winning medium-weight wine. The fruit reads rich and bright on the balanced, not-at-all-weighty palate, with its very smooth feel. Finishes with a long dance of ripe plum and sweet oak, a statement of fine fruit handsomely rendered that will drink well through 2005. **89** —*M.M. (4/1/2002)*

Bilton 2002 Shiraz (Stellenbosch) $25. Shows a hint of volatility in its high-toned, mixed-berry and pie crust aromas, then settles down a bit on the palate, where the predominant flavors are of tart cherries and cranberries. Finishes with flourishes of toast and vanilla. **85** —*J.C. (11/15/2005)*

BLAAUWKLIPPEN

Blaauwklippen 2000 Barrel Selection Zinfandel (Stellenbosch) $19. That's right, a Zinfandel from South Africa. The acid-tannin backbone holds up the notes of cocoa powder and ripe, spiced plum, but none of the parts puts a damper on the growing herbal component. **85** —*K.F. (9/1/2003)*

BLACK PEARL

Black Pearl 2003 Shiraz (Paarl) $33. An exciting and explosive wine, this packs a punch with syrupy flavors of cassis, plum, and a touch of coffee. Full-bodied, with sweet tannins and smokey notes to the cassis-laden nose, this highly pleasurable wine can be drunk over the next five years. **92 Editors' Choice** —*M.D. (12/31/2006)*

BLACK ROCK

Black Rock 2004 White Blend (Swartland) $24. A blend of 75% Chenin Blanc with some Chardonnay and Viognier, the fruit for this wine comes from cool, dry-farmed vineyards in Swartland. It has a great, pure fruit character, and it's ripe, generous, balancing wood and acidity along with white fruit flavors, peaches, and green plums. A touch of minerality completes the picture. **91** —*R.V. (11/15/2005)*

BOEKENHOUTSKLOOF

Boekenhoutskloof 2004 Cabernet Sauvignon (Franschhoek) $47. Young, vibrant fruit dominates this dense, ripe wine. Not as powerful as the 2003, this shows elegance and some restraint, but there is still a punch of rich black currant, dark plum, and coffee flavors. Expect to cellar this wine for at least six years. **92** —*R.V. (11/1/2006)*

Boekenhoutskloof 2003 Cabernet Sauvignon (Franschhoek) $46. Very ripe and powerful, this Cabernet is built for aging. Dry, firm tannins overlay cassis and herbal flavors, while cedar and toast aromas come from new French wood aging. Sourced from a top Franschhoek Valley vineyard, this is impressive. **94** —*R.V. (11/1/2006)*

BOSCHENDAL

Boschendal 2001 Cabernet Sauvignon (Coastal Region) $16. This medium weight red is not unpleasant, yet fails to achieve a graceful balance. One has to wonder why all the wood? The oak over-indulgence renders the wine decidedly drier and more one-dimensional than it need be, as the fruit struggles to present itself. **85** —*M.M. (7/1/2005)*

Boschendal 2000 Reserve Cabernet Sauvignon (Coastal Region) $20. The oak is dark and heavy here, but the fruit core is strong and not entirely obscured. This medium-to-full-bodied red shows nice weight and good tannic structure, plus a long close. Tasty now in a woody way, it will be better after 2006 and hold well to 2010+. **88** —*M.M. (7/1/2005)*

Boschendal NV Le Grand Pavillon Blanc de Blancs Champagne Blend (Coastal Region) $15. A commendable bubbly from the "other

Down-Under," this South African is dryly fruited, with good bead and decent complexity. Toast, cracker, and earth aromas open to an even, herb tinged palate that offers a full, soft mouthfeel. It closes with citrus, chalk and a faint hint of bitters. **87** *(12/1/2001)*

Boschendal NV Le Grand Pavillon Brut Champagne Blend (Coastal Region) $13. 87 *—M.M. (3/1/2004)*

Boschendal 2004 Chardonnay (Western Cape) $16. Lightly oaked, with a moderate nose of yellow fruit and spice. The palate is round, with a dusty feel and flavors of peach and vanilla. Finishes warm, with acidity. **85** *—M.D. (9/1/2006)*

Boschendal 2003 Chardonnay (Coastal Region) $14. Nicely balanced, with apple-pear fruit offset by mineral and oak accents. Dry and tasty, if not terribly deep, with a long, even finish. A solid, dry white from a venerable estate with 300+ years of Cape winemaking experience. **86** *—M.M. (4/1/2005)*

Boschendal 2000 Chardonnay (Coastal Region) $NA. A wine for those who like their Chardonnays big and fat. With its honey and caramel aromas, its spice and toast flavors, and ripe, tropical fruit, it may lack acidity, but it makes up for this in opulence and openness. **85** *—R.V. (7/1/2002)*

Boschendal 2003 Reserve Chardonnay (Coastal Region) $18. Mint, toast, and spice are dominant on the nose, while the palate is laden with toasty, nearly over-ripe fruit. Retains some tropical fruit character, namely mango, and the oak is flavorful, if heavy handed. **86** *—M.D. (11/1/2006)*

Boschendal 2001 Reserve Chardonnay (Coastal Region) $16. A light note of banana accompanies aromas of pineapple and white peach that sway to the sweet, semi-viscous palate. Finishes with creamy vanilla and plenty of heat. **87** *—K.F. (4/1/2003)*

Boschendal 2005 Le Pavillon Chardonnay-Semillon (Western Cape) $9. Like biting into a peach, this bargain-buster has intense peach and yellow fruit flavors with a dry, pithy edge. Touches of butter and spice suggest oak, while grassy notes and acid give it backbone. Beyond an apéritif, this wine has the stuffing to stand up to many a chicken dish. **87 Best Buy** *—M.D. (11/1/2006)*

Boschendal 2001 Reserve Merlot (Coastal Region) $20. A tart berry profile prevails in this firm red. It's structured and Bordeaux-inspired, with some earth and mineral accents. Hard and very dry. Try with grilled meats. **84** *—M.M. (7/1/2005)*

Boschendal 2001 Lanoy Red Blend (Coastal Region) $15. This firm, balanced a red is solidly built, if slightly hard. Dark berry-currant fruit wears spice and earth accents. Closes with good length and taut tannins. It's a bit closed now but well-constructed with good fruit at the center. Best 2008 and after. Will reward cellaring. **88** *—M.M. (7/1/2005)*

Boschendal 2004 Sauvignon Blanc (Coastal Region) $12. Quite pale, but shows its substance quickly with a lively green apple, grass, and mild tropical fruit bouquet. Seems like it might be sweet, but turns considerably more citrusy and spritzy on the tongue. A surprise that closes clean, refreshingly tart-sweet, and tangy. **86** *—M.M. (4/1/2005)*

Boschendal 2002 Sauvignon Blanc (Coastal Region) $12. Sweet aromas of mango, dried oregano, vanilla, and saltwater taffy are matched on the palate by honeysuckle and more mango. This wine is very flavorful and fresh with brisk, engaging acidity, and like the Grand Cuvée, it is sweet yet dry. **88 Best Buy** *—K.F. (4/1/2003)*

Boschendal 2003 Grand Cuvée Sauvignon Blanc (Franschhoek) $14. Everything's in place as the complex grapefruit, pineapple, and tangy-spice nose opens to a full, similarly flavored palate. The feel is ripe and full yet alive with vibrant acidity, the finish long and clean with zesty pepper notes. **90 Editors' Choice** *—M.M. (4/1/2005)*

Boschendal 2004 Grande Cuvée Sauvignon Blanc (Franschhoek) $14. This appealing wine's super-clean grapefruit-pineapple-herbgrass aromas and flavors really sing. It's 'well-tuned,' to quote a J. S. Bach title, finely balancing its rich/smooth and tangy/angular elements—something as appealing as Bach. Displays lovely feel and flavor right through the long, herb-tinged finish. Cries out for sea bass, sole, or shell fish. **90 Best Buy** *—M.M. (4/1/2005)*

Boschendal 2005 Grande Cuvée Sauvignon Blanc (Coastal Region) $17. Dark yellow, the color speaks to this wine's richness. Pithy peach and vanilla waft from the glass, but this wine has plenty of body to stand up to oak, also delivering rich tropical fruit with citrus undertones. Despite the rich flavors, acidity offers a careful balance. **89 Editors' Choice** *—M.D. (12/31/2006)*

Boschendal 2002 Grande Cuvée Sauvignon Blanc (Coastal Region) $14. Dusty hay, citrus, and butter icing stretch from the nose to the palate in lovely layers. The flavors are full and sweet, like cantaloupe rind, but are never cloying, thanks to the spritzy acidity. Finishes dry and faintly chalky with herbs. This is a lightweight and warm style with fine depth. **89** *—K.F. (1/1/2004)*

Boschendal 1999 Grande Cuvée Sauvignon Blanc (Coastal Region) $12. Another strong showing by Boschendahl, the 1999 Sauvignon Blanc offers grapefruit, smoke, and melon aromas. The supple palate has a good acid spine, plus apple-vanilla accents—perhaps from the 15% Chardonnay in the blend. Finishes long, with a slight peppery note. **88 Best Buy** *(9/1/2001)*

Boschendal 2005 Reserve Sauvignon Blanc (Coastal Region) $12. Vanilla, lime, and a hint of salinity make for an interesting bouquet, while vanilla and toast dominate in the mouth. With time key lime and citrus notes emerge. Smooth on the palate with enough acid to keep it lively. **87 Best Buy** *—M.D. (3/1/2006)*

Boschendal 2004 Le Pavillon Semillon-Chardonnay (Western Cape) $9. The vanilla and pear nose shows this white's ripe easy style up front. Just unexpectedly turns too sweet and soft on the tongue. Good fruit, but simple, and to this palate cloying, though it could have broad appeal in our sweet-tooth nation. The clean close shows some spice. Try with spicy chicken dishes. **83** *—M.M. (4/1/2005)*

Boschendal 2003 Shiraz (Coastal Region) $19. Lively acidity keeps the mouthfeel tight in this wine, which has stony cherry and chocolate aromas. Cherry-esque fruit and dark berries dance on the tongue, matched and mineral. Finishes with tar and pain grille. **88** *—M.D. (9/1/2006)*

Boschendal 2002 Shiraz (Coastal Region) $16. A tasty, reserved Shiraz with compact, briary dark fruit and spicy accents. Very solid and well-structured at this price, this shows much more restraint than usually seen in this price range. Not at all jammy, it's attractively understated, an elegant affordable red. **87** *—M.M. (7/1/2005)*

Boschendal 2001 Grand Pavillon Sparkling Blend (Franschhoek) $15. An aggressive bead leads to a frothy mouthfeel which is cleaned up by bright acids. Dry toast, intense hay, and grassiness characterize the nose and palate. **86** *—K.F. (12/1/2003)*

BOSCHKLOOF

Boschkloof 1999 Cabernet Sauvignon-Merlot (Vlootenburg) $15. The light, one-dimensional body of red plum, toast, and brown sugar is finished off with dried herbs and another wisp of brown sugar. The delicate touch that this wine has would be better suited to more complex fruit, thus attaining elegance over transparency. **84** *—K.F. (4/1/2003)*

Boschkloof 1998 Reserve Cabernet Sauvignon-Merlot (Vlootenburg) $20. Racy acidity and herbiness combine in a slightly awkward manner. The aromas of red pepper, espresso bean, dark cocoa, and meat are joined by currant and red plum on the palate. **85** *—K.F. (4/1/2003)*

Boschkloof 2000 Syrah (Vlootenburg) $18. Oaken layers make themselves known from nose to finish, with notes of cream, vanilla, and cinnamon. The fruit thins out midpalate, revealing bright acidity and insistent tannins. A good pour for an everyday dinner. **85** *—K.F. (8/1/2003)*

BOUCHARD FINLAYSON

Bouchard Finlayson 2000 Crocodile's Lair/Kaaimansgat Chardonnay (Overberg) $20. Delicate aromas of dried herbs, dusty basement, cedar, and lemon peel herald complementary flavors of hay and caraway. Dried herbs repeat on the palate, while the finish is a peppery blend of sausage and bread. Classy and full flavored to the end. **88** *—K.F. (4/1/2003)*

Bouchard Finlayson 2001 Sans Barrique Chardonnay (Overberg) $18. The caramel and sugared lemon aromas and flavors of this wine are sweet, and although clean, the mouthfeel is somewhat viscous. **86** *—K.F. (4/1/2003)*

Bouchard Finlayson 2001 Blanc de Mer Meritage (Hemel en Aarde) $12. A straightforward nose of sweet peas and honeysuckle lead to citrus and faint melon on the palate; finishes with a bit of grassiness. Although a bit simple, this is rather nice, with a light body and lively acidity. **87** —*K.F. (4/1/2003)*

Bouchard Finlayson 2001 Galpin Peak Pinot Noir (Walker Bay) $40. Tannins gently support the fresh acidity and light, easy raspberry and plum fruit with notes of white chocolate and earth adding weight. **86** —*K.F. (9/1/2003)*

Bouchard Finlayson 2001 Hannibal Cuvée Red Blend (Walker Bay) $30. This well-balanced red has light brown sugar, vanilla, and cinnamon aromas that belie the oak layering on the palate of ripe cherry, dried basil, and meat juices. This wine will pair well with mild meats, but is just as tasty alone. **87** —*K.F. (9/1/2003)*

BOUWLAND

Bouwland 2003 Chenin Blanc (Stellenbosch) $NA. One of the new generation of wineries run by South African blacks, under an empowerment program, this winery's 2003 Chenin is full and rich, with great aromas of mangoes and flavors of tropical fruits. For lovers of a ripe, full style of Chenin, this is an essential. **88** —*R.V. (11/15/2005)*

BOWE JOUBERT VINEYARD & WINERY

Bowe Joubert Vineyard & Winery 2001 Cabernet Sauvignon (Stellenbosch) $18. Ripe red to black plum blankets the senses. Aromatic accents of currants and lettuce become molasses and fennel on the palate. The ever-present element of toast turns to a slightly sweet and herby char on the finish. **88** —*K.F. (4/1/2003)*

Bowe Joubert Vineyard & Winery 2002 Cuvée Emmerentia Chardonnay (Stellenbosch) $13. Golden in color, with a smooth mouthfeel and decent balance, this dishes up an interesting, mature mix of apple, hay spice, and wood notes. It's flavorful and shows surprising elegance. **87** —*M.M. (3/1/2004)*

Bowe Joubert Vineyard & Winery 2001 Cuvée Emmerentia Chardonnay (Stellenbosch) $15. Clarified butter and toasty fruit aromas and flavors follow through to the palate, where there's thin lemon fruit. The finish is layered in butter and lemon zest. **85** —*K.F. (4/1/2003)*

Bowe Joubert Vineyard & Winery 2001 Oaked Chenin Blanc (Stellenbosch) $10. Lovely aromas of starfruit, honey, herbs, and oak transfer to the palate with a bit of heat. This is slightly viscous throughout, but the acidity keeps it from feeling too thick. **86** —*K.F. (4/1/2003)*

Bowe Joubert Vineyard & Winery 2001 Merlot (Stellenbosch) $18. Dusty cocoa, cherry, and faint menthol aromas agree with the simple palate of caramel and continued cherry. Strikes a fine balance between soft tannins and juicy acidity. **87** —*K.F. (4/1/2003)*

Bowe Joubert Vineyard & Winery 2001 Sauvignon Blanc (Stellenbosch) $11. Citrus, melon rind, and a faintly smoky salinity appear on the nose and palate. The hints of toast, herbs, and cinnamon extend to the medium-length finish. **87** —*K.F. (4/1/2003)*

Bowe Joubert Vineyard & Winery 2003 JB Sauvignon Blanc (Stellenbosch) $12. Tasty Sauvignon, with grass, grapefruit, and slate elements in nice balance. It's crisp without being sharp, as too many are, and just slightly tangy on the tongue. An attractive wine with a spicy satisfying finish. **88 Best Buy** —*M.M. (3/1/2004)*

Bowe Joubert Vineyard & Winery 2001 Mosaïc White Blend (Stellenbosch) $8. Opens with light toast, citrus juice, and peel. Thin lemon flavors and a hint of grass play on the finish. A bit of depth would go a long way with this simple, everyday pour. **84** —*K.F. (4/1/2003)*

BRADGATE

Bradgate 2002 White Blend (Stellenbosch) $9. This everyday wine's aromas satisfy, with sesame seed, thin citrus, and a hint of thyme. Clean on the palate, with soft citrus, fresh herbs and toasty accents, this is a natural choice for a light luncheon. **85** —*K.F. (4/1/2003)*

Bradgate 2005 Chenin Blanc/Sauvignon Blanc White Blend (Stellenbosch) $9. A full style of wine, named after the home of the Jordan family, who produce this wine. It is packed with great acidity balancing nutty fruit flavors. A touch of vanilla comes through, leaving a wine that is generous and full, but still leaves a fresh, crisp aftertaste. **89 Best Buy** —*R.V. (11/15/2005)*

BRAHMS

Brahms 2004 Chenin Blanc (Paarl) $17. Two Cape Town lawyers hung up their robes and bought vineyards in Paarl in 1989. Their winery produces a well-made Chenin from a single vineyard on Paarl mountain, which gives a nutty aroma, flavors of salted peanuts, as well as a touch of apple fruits. This wine needs to age for another year. **87** —*R.V. (11/15/2005)*

BRAMPTON

Brampton 2004 Cabernet Sauvignon (Stellenbosch) $14. This is Rustenberg's second label, and the wine is packed with a screw cap top. But the wine itself still has considerable weight, fine dry tannins, and balanced stalky fruit. Drink now, but it could certainly age a couple of years. **87** —*R.V. (11/1/2006)*

Brampton 1996 Cabernet Sauvignon-Merlot (Stellenbosch) $14. 86 *(9/1/1999)*

Brampton 2005 Unoaked Chardonnay (Coastal Region) $10. All the Brampton wines have a focus on fruit that makes them instantly appealing. This Chardonnay, unoaked to retain the fruit flavors, shows ample apple and tropical pineapple on the nose and palate. Good acidity give it a light feel, and the finish is clean. **87 Best Buy** —*M.D. (12/31/2006)*

Brampton 2001 Red Blend (Stellenbosch) $15. This is a one-way sensory package of cherry candy and vanillin oak that shows a bit of aggressivity in the tannins. In fact, the tannins carry far past the finish. Beyond its simplicity, there is nothing really out of order. **84** —*K.F. (4/1/2003)*

Brampton 1997 Sauvignon Blanc (Stellenbosch) $14. 86 —*M.S. (9/1/1999)*

Brampton 2004 Shiraz (Coastal Region) $12. Rustenberg's second label, Brampton, enclosed in screwcap, shines because of its focus on fruit. This Shiraz glows with aromas of cola, sour cherry, lemon, and spice. Underneath the veneer are layers of red berry and blueberry flavors, tempered with coffee, lemon, and just the right amount of oak. Full but silky, with sweet tannins, this is enjoyable now and can stand up to rich dishes like braised ribs or filet mignon. **89 Best Buy** —*M.D. (9/1/2006)*

Brampton 2005 Viognier (Coastal Region) $14. A great value in Viognier, thanks to moderate use of oak, which also brightens the fruit in this wine. It has vibrant citrus in the mouth, with cantaloupe and a hint of vanilla from older oak. The aromas are similar, with some honeysuckle, while the body is full and creamy, despite racy acids. The alcohol (15.5%) shows through a bit on the finish, but overall a harmonious wine. **88** —*M.D. (9/1/2006)*

BUITENVERWACHTING

Buitenverwachting 2001 Chardonnay (Constantia) $15. The pleasant nose of meatiness and mild yellow mustard ushers in flavors of tropical fruit and notes of toast that strengthen by the minute. Although the finish is herbal and short, the heat holds out long after it is gone. **85** —*K.F. (9/1/2003)*

Buitenverwachting 2005 Rhine Riesling (Constantia) $12. You may find a bit of CO2 remaining in this wine, not enough to bubble but enough to add zest and liveliness. Citrusy white fruits on the nose lead to ripe white stone fruits with a hint of straw and spice in the mouth. A fine quaffer that should be drunk in the next year. **85** —*M.D. (12/31/2006)*

Buitenverwachting 2005 Sauvignon Blanc (Constantia) $12. From a region renowned for its dessert wine comes this easy-to-love white. Despite a lightness to the medium body, this wine has plenty of guts, evident in the liquid gooseberry mouth mixed with lime and dusted with chalk. The flavor of the wine carries through to the long finish, while aromas of pure gooseberry dance in the glass. Drink now, and enjoy. **88 Best Buy** —*M.D. (9/1/2006)*

Buitenverwachting 2002 Sauvignon Blanc (Constantia) $13. This wine is likeable for its warm, round aromas of canned peas, banana peel, and a hint of toast. The grapefruit and herbs on the palate lack complexity. **83** —*K.F. (9/1/2003)*

SOUTH AFRICA

CAMBERLEY

Camberley 2000 Cabernet Sauvignon-Merlot (Stellenbosch) $18. Aromatic, ashy oak wafts around a slip of sweet red fruit. This thin, plummy fruit is sustained on the palate, where the acidity keeps it from being too sweet. The finish is chock-full of eucalyptus and dried mint. **85** —*K.F. (8/1/2003)*

CAPE HAVEN

Cape Haven 2004 Chenin Blanc (Swartland) $12. This rich style of Chenin has aromas of ripe currants; full-bodied fruit, with accents of almonds, spices and herbs, marks the palate. **88 Best Buy** —*R.V. (11/15/2005)*

CAPE INDABA

Cape Indaba 1998 Chardonnay (Western Cape) $10. 82 *(9/1/1999)*

Cape Indaba 1998 Pinotage (Coastal Region) $10. 86 —*J.C. (11/15/1999)*

Cape Indaba 1998 Sauvignon Blanc (Robertson) $8. 82 *(9/1/1999)*

CAPE VIEW

Cape View 1999 Merlot (Stellenbosch) $23. Earthy aromas are accompanied by driftwood and endive. These repeat on the palate, accompanied by cinnamon, dried meat, and dried herbs. The finish has eucalyptus up front and a sweet, fruity bloom at the back end. Lovely wine, but without appropriate heft. **86** —*K.F. (4/1/2003)*

Cape View 1999 Pinotage (Stellenbosch) $28. Although a bit vegetal, there are worthwhile notes of plum, cherry, and caramel. The palate is lightweight, with salad greens, tomato and basil flavors. Finishes peppery. **84** —*K.F. (4/1/2003)*

CEDERBERG

Cederberg 2003 Cabernet Sauvignon (Cederberg) $28. There's a touch of austerity to this wine, a firm set of tannins, and some herbal character, all coming from the high-altitude (3,000-foot) vineyards of Cederberg. These suggest aging potential, because the fruit is there as well as a range of berry flavors to go with the dryness. **89** —*R.V. (11/1/2006)*

Cederberg 2002 Cabernet Sauvignon (South Africa) $25. Elegant wine with an attractive bouquet of dark fruit, Oriental spice, cinnamon, and cocoa. Quite dry, with a similar palate profile. This has Tuscan manners—it's solid, tasty, and firm—and demands food. Possible big league potential with greater depth of fruit and a bit more back-end length. Keep your eye on this producer. **88** —*M.M. (12/15/2004)*

Cederberg 2003 Five Generations Cabernet Sauvignon (Cederberg) $49. The Nieuwould family has farmed at Cederberg for five generations—hence the name. This top Cabernet from the estate vineyards comes from old vines, giving huge concentration and elegance. Aged for 18 months in wood, this intense, berry-dominated wine also shows big, dry fruit tannins, and should age for a good 10 years. **93 Cellar Selection** — *R.V. (11/1/2006)*

Cederberg 2005 Chenin Blanc (Cederberg) $17. High mountain vineyards in the spectacular Cederberg wilderness produce a great, crisp wine, full of citrus character and fresh, green fruit. This is a delicious, dry wine made from old vines, just pure fruit. **89** —*R.V. (11/15/2005)*

Cederberg 2004 Chenin Blanc (South Africa) $15. This rich, almost Viognier-like Chenin Blanc offers lots of melon, apricot, tropical fruit, and citrus on the nose and palate. The nose is slightly over-sweet, but the wine turns more tangy and spicy on the tongue. Try this flavorful, persistent white with grilled pork chops. **86** —*M.M. (7/1/2005)*

Cederberg 2003 Dry Chenin Blanc (South Africa) $15. Tangy and dry, with subdued pear-citrus-tropical fruit flavors and plenty of chalk-mineral-herb notes. This classy wine can hold its own with good Loire Chenin Blancs. It will sing with broiled or grilled seafood and most Asian cuisine. **90 Editors' Choice** —*M.M. (12/15/2004)*

Cederberg 2003 Five Generations Chenin Blanc (Cederberg) $35. Five generations of the Nieuwoud family have run the Cederberg farm, and this wine, along with a Cabernet Sauvignon, are here to commemorate. This is a great full-bodied white, showing a successful marriage of wood and peachy, aromatic fruit, layered with acidity. A delicious wine with aging potential. **93** —*R.V. (11/15/2005)*

Cederberg 2003 Cederberger Red Blend (Cederberg) $20. Half Merlot, 15% Pinotage, and the remainder Ruby Cabernet (a cross between Cab Sauvignon and Carignan), this wine has nice structure backed by refined tannins. A creamy nose of vanilla and cassis touched with mint leads to a full mouth of dark berry, coffee, balsam, and barnyard. Has enough body to pair well with assorted cheeses. **87** —*M.D. (7/1/2006)*

Cederberg 2005 Sauvignon Blanc (Cederberg) $19. A wine that comes together with all the right parts: freshly crushed gooseberry aromas, tropical fruit, gooseberry and mineral flavors, and an elegant yet powerful feel that is finely balanced. Simple and effective. **87** —*M.D. (12/31/2006)*

Cederberg 2004 Shiraz (Cederberg) $29. This Shiraz has a vibrant purple hue and aromas of cassis, dark berries, leather, and grilled meats. Nicely balanced, with acidity playing counterpoint to sweet tannins, the wine offers cassis and black fruit flavors with hints of lemon and leather. Picks up coffee notes on the impressively long finish. **90** —*M.D. (12/31/2006)*

Cederberg 2003 Shiraz (South Africa) $30. Starts off promising, with scents of mixed berries and lashings of vanilla and dried spices that continue onto and through the palate. A nicely balanced wine, one that may be a bit on the tart side, with metallic hints on the finish that may prove troublesome with age. Drink now. **86** —*J.C. (11/15/2005)*

Cederberg 2002 Shiraz (South Africa) $25. Deep and fairly tightly wound, with ripe berry, leather, and tobacco aromas and flavors. Stylish herb and mildly metallic notes yield a very Rhônish character once it breathes some. Starts dry—almost hard—then opens, developing nicely in the glass. Firm now, structured, and handsome, and can age for three to six years. **88** —*M.M. (12/15/2004)*

CHAMONIX

Chamonix 2000 Troika Bordeaux Blend (Franschhoek) $25. This balanced wine has a nose of vanilla, cardamom that lingers on to the mouthful of simple, oaky red fruit. There is an herby note of radicchio that clings from the nose to the cinnamon toast finish. **86** —*K.F. (8/1/2003)*

Chamonix 1998 Chardonnay (Franschhoek) $16. A whiff of provolone cheese and cured meat bears out this wine's age. After that, it is a delicate assembly of slightly bitter herbs, lemon, and firm toast. This may sound odd to some, but the combination works, with cleansing acids on the finish. **85** —*K.F. (9/1/2003)*

Chamonix 1998 Reserve Chardonnay (Franschhoek) $25. An enticing nose of apricot, maple syrup, and sweet, reduced vinegar plays well with the toasty mango flavors ribboned with smokiness. Finishes juicy, with a lingering toasty, herbal character. The acidity is a little soft, but that shouldn't prevent you from drinking it now. **87** —*K.F. (9/1/2003)*

Chamonix 2000 Pinot Noir (Franschhoek) $25. The sandy tannins and upfront, almost tart, acidity keep the cocoa, cherry, strawberry, and raspberry flavors from being too sweet. The finish has an interesting note of white pepper. **85** —*K.F. (9/1/2003)*

Chamonix 2001 Pinotage (Franschhoek) $17. This full-bodied wine seems mature but still has time for enjoyment. It is meaty and smoky on the nose, with a charry hint of pencil shavings. The flavors of leather and tobacco sprinkled with dried herbs are tasty accessories to the ripe red plum fruit. Drink until 2006. **88** —*K.F. (9/1/2003)*

CLOS MALVERNE

Clos Malverne 1998 Cabernet-Pinotage Cabernet Blend (Stellenbosch) $17. The aromas of red plum, anise, leather, brown sugar, and sawdust repeat on the palate with an herby edge. Endive and white pepper carry on the finish. The moderate balance makes for an easy-drinking experience anytime. **85** —*K.F. (4/1/2003)*

Clos Malverne 2000 Basket Pressed Cabernet Sauvignon (Stellenbosch) $16. Opens with black cherry, toast, and dark chocolate aromas. Followed by green herbs and grass that chase the tight, well-oaked fruit on the palate. Comes off as eucalyptus on the cherry-chocolate finish. **83** —*K.F. (9/1/2003)*

Clos Malverne 2004 Cabernet Sauvignon-Merlot (Stellenbosch) $NA. Named by a previous owner after the Malvern Hills in England, and Frenchified by the current owner, Seymour Pritchard. Clos Malverne benefits from the cool-climate of the Devon Valley to produce structured

SOUTH AFRICA

wines, like this still-young 2004. With juicy, blackberry flavors, and layers of toast and herbs, this is a finely balanced wine. **92**—*R.V. (11/1/2006)*

Clos Malverne 2001 Limited Release Cabernet Sauvignon-Merlot (Stellenbosch) $67. If any proof were needed that South African wines are stylistically as close to Europe as they can be to California, it would be in this wine. With its tight structure, mineral fruit character, and enclosed layer of cassis fruits, this is as Bordeaux as it gets outside southwest France. **90**—*R.V. (11/1/2006)*

Clos Malverne 2002 Cabernet Sauvignon-Shiraz (Stellenbosch) $16. Suave and dark, with blackberry-licorice aromas and flavors, a full mouthfeel, and substantial tannins. If this comes off as slightly facile due to the very pronounced oak, it still has great appeal. Finishes long and smooth, with black coffee and espresso notes, and the structure to age for a few years. **88**—*M.M. (4/1/2005)*

Clos Malverne 1999 Basket Pressed Cabernet Sauvignon-Shiraz (Stellenbosch) $16. Sweet and sour fruit, not unlike stewed rhubarb, colors the nose and palate. Although it is a little watery, peppery tannins pick up the slack. Closes with eucalyptus, char, and bitter herbs. **83**—*K.F. (9/1/2003)*

Clos Malverne 2001 Pinotage (Stellenbosch) $16. Sharp, with tart red fruit, green tobacco, and a deep elefunkiness that doesn't let go. The modest fruit is overwhelmed by the earthiness and harder, more bitter metallic elements that ascend on the finish. **82**—*M.M. (4/1/2005)*

Clos Malverne 2002 Reserve Pinotage (Stellenbosch) $17. This wine has an appealing, roasted quality to the dark berry flavors. A roasted game note mixes with berry in the nose, and comes through again in the mouth. Medium-bodied, with good tannin and a sweet and tangy oak finish. **86**—*M.D. (5/1/2006)*

Clos Malverne 2001 Reserve Pinotage (Stellenbosch) $17. Stewed plums meld with brown sugar and toast on the pleasantly soft palate, accented by slightly bitter notes of plum skin. From start to finish, toasty oak spice abounds. **86**—*K.F. (9/1/2003)*

Clos Malverne 2000 Reserve Pinotage (Stellenbosch) $17. Plum skin and mesclun greens sharpen the palate, but the oak holds sway with warm, toasty char and molasses notes. An oak lover's cocktail pour. **84**—*K.F. (9/1/2003)*

Clos Malverne 2001 Auret Red Blend (Stellenbosch) $17. Cherry, plum, and toast elements mingle in this stylish but rather dry, lean red. Nevertheless, the oak bears heavy on the fruit. Shows substantial structure and should hold well though the decade. But a more refined fruit-to-wood balance could elevate this red to the heights it clearly aspires to. **85**—*M.M. (4/1/2005)*

Clos Malverne 1999 Auret Red Blend (Stellenbosch) $17. A pleasant, full nose of earth, hickory, apple, and a note reminiscent of rum-raisin does not extend to the toasty, brown sugar palate. The eucalyptus-laden finish is sharp and minty. **84**—*K.F. (1/1/2004)*

Clos Malverne 2001 Sauvignon Blanc (Stellenbosch) $15. A flourish of floral perfume lingers until the last moments of tasting. Lime and candied lemon carry from the nose to the palate, with an accent of honey. The bright acidity and a food-friendly herbal tang on the finish lend stability to the sweet expression of fruit. **88**—*K.F. (4/1/2003)*

Clos Malverne 1999 Shiraz (Stellenbosch) $13. Like many South African Shirazes, this one emphasizes the earthy, leathery side of the grape's flavor spectrum, with only hints of dark plum fruit. Still, the damp earth and hummus notes are pleasant, and the right food match (perhaps a grilled steak topped with chimichurri sauce) would help accentuate the fruit. **83** *(10/1/2001)*

CULRAITHIN

Culraithin 2002 Syrah (Paarl) $34. A dark and robust wine, inky to the eye, with voluptuous aromas of chocolate, coffee, black fruits, and a hint of lemon. The tannins are big but harnessed, showing ample ripeness, as do the full-on flavors of cassis, black plum, coffee, and leather that will only develop more with age. Finishes with a touch of lemon. Enjoyable now, but can last for over ten years. 380 cases produced. **91 Cellar Selection**—*M.D. (12/31/2006)*

DANIE DE WET

Danie de Wet 2000 Bateleur Chardonnay (Robertson) $31. This is rather hot on the nose, but past that are aromas of banana, pineapple, and melon. These lovely fruits carry to the refreshing palate, finishing with hay, light cream, and toast. **88**—*K.F. (4/1/2003)*

DARLING CELLARS

Darling Cellars 1999 DC Cabernet Sauvignon (Coastal Region) $13. The brick rim is tinted with orange, and the feel is a little loose—odd for such a young vintage. A hint of animal aroma is followed by sausage and caraway. Leather, dry tobacco, and cedar flavors complete the package that has distinct roasted red peppers throughout. **87**—*K.F. (4/1/2003)*

Darling Cellars 1999 Onyx Cabernet Sauvignon (Groenekloof) $20. The perks of this wine are the cherry fruit aroma, the tannins, and the caramel at the backend of the finish. The aromas of asparagus and radicchio are awkward company to the tomato and toast flavors. **82**—*K.F. (4/1/2003)*

Darling Cellars 2000 DC Chardonnay (Swartland-GroeneKloof) $13. This is deceptively soft at the start but quickly gains heat when the acidity creeps in. Simple aromas and flavors of sweet hay, light cream, and a pat of butter finish with white-hot pepper. **84**—*K.F. (4/1/2003)*

Darling Cellars 1999 Onyx Chardonnay (Groenekloof) $15. The thin mouthfeel is rather smooth, with clean acidity and light flavors of citrus, toast, and herbs, finishing with a lemony tang. The nose is where all the action is, with honey, lush tropical fruit, apricots, figs, herbed butter, and so much more. **85**—*K.F. (9/1/2003)*

Darling Cellars 1999 DC Merlot (Swartland-GroeneKloof) $13. Offers loam, driftwood, toast, cinnamon, caramel, and red plum aromas. The fruit is good, the acidity tingly, but the bitter greens hinted at on the palate and on the finish are a bit too much. **84**—*K.F. (4/1/2003)*

Darling Cellars 1999 DC Pinotage (Coastal Region) $22. Aromas and flavors of red plum, caramel, and toast, with accents of cherry. Dried herbs and cinnamon fill out the finish. The acids are a bit spritzy, then settle down. **85**—*K.F. (4/1/2003)*

Darling Cellars 1999 Onyx Pinotage (Swartland-GroeneKloof) $22. Throughout the nose and palate, a suggestion of gamy meat is accompanied by tart red plum, toasty caramel, and cherry. The finish is marred by bitter green herbs. **83**—*K.F. (4/1/2003)*

Darling Cellars 2001 Onyx Kroon Red Blend (Groenekloof) $25. The body of this wine is appealing and food friendly, with slightly mouth-watering acids and peppery, particulate tannins. The oak influence shows light brown sugar and vanilla cream over slightly tart red plum with fresh herbs. **85**—*K.F. (9/1/2003)*

Darling Cellars 2001 DC Sauvignon Blanc (Swartland-GroeneKloof) $13. Aromas of fresh-mown hay and sweet peas are accompanied by simple yellow fruit. The hay and peas repeat on the finish. This is unadorned, with soft acids. **84**—*K.F. (4/1/2003)*

DASHBOSCH

Dashbosch 2005 Chenin Blanc (Worcester) $NA. A floral, fresh wine, very aromatic, with flavors of pears. From the Dashbosch winery in Worcester, this is an attractive, ripe and soft wine, fruity and easy. **85**—*R.V. (11/15/2005)*

Dashbosch 2005 Cape Concert Seaside White Chenin Blanc (Worcester) $NA. This ripe, very soft wine has attractive currant flavors, layers of sweetness and an easy fruit character. Crisp and fresh but slightly sulfured to finish. **84**—*R.V. (11/15/2005)*

DAVID FROST

David Frost 2000 Chardonnay (Western Cape) $NA. A bright, Northern California-style wine, brimming with ripe, expressive flavors of peaches, tangerines, tropical fruits, and oaky-spicy notes. It's technically dry, but filled with the honeyed richness of oak and fruit, supported by good acids. Calls to mind many a Sonoma County bottling. **87**—*S.H. (1/1/2002)*

David Frost 2001 Sauvignon Blanc (Western Cape) $NA. Comes down firmly on Sauvignon's aggressively grassy, herbal side. Smells like

SOUTH AFRICA

three-day old mown hay, at the point it's going from green to dry. In the mouth, it's citrusy and grassy, but with softer notes of figs and wood. A perfectly pleasant wine, very clean and flavorful, that will go with a huge range of foods. **87** —S.H. (1/1/2002)

DC

DC 1999 Shiraz (Coastal Region) $23. As the wine airs, the faint note of sawdust gains strength. This is backed by rawhide, and a whiff of figs that carry to the palate. Pleasant, fresh blackberry fruit is accented on the finish with a minty note. **88** —K.F. (4/1/2003)

DE MEYE

De Meye 1999 Cabernet Sauvignon (Stellenbosch) $16. This is pleasant, but the fruit lacks depth. Aromas and flavors of cherry, leather, cedar, and menthol sweeten the deal. Finishes with herbed meat and a hint of melon rind. **85** —K.F. (4/1/2003)

De Meye 2000 Shiraz (South Africa) $16. Radicchio, toast, and mushroom aromas meld with delicate black fruit flavors and green herbs that carry to the finish. This wine seems simple, almost stark; wants more complexity. **86** —K.F. (4/1/2003)

DE TRAFFORD

de Trafford 1999 Reserve Bordeaux Blend (Helderberg) $35. This red blend shows its 51% Cabernet roots with strong red cherry and ripe plum fruit. Throughout, the notes of vanilla, cinnamon toast, and cream vie for attention over the likeable fruit. The snug, particulate tannins and alcohol heat make for a mouth-filling experience. **87** —K.F. (8/1/2003)

de Trafford 2004 Chenin Blanc (Stellenbosch) $25. A wood-aged style that works, and works well. Balanced with its touch of spice and some vanilla flavors from the American wood, there is fresh fruit, delicious acidity, and flavors of apples. De Trafford is a top quality, small-scale producer, high up in the mountains above Stellenbosch. **91** —R.V. (11/15/2005)

de Trafford 2002 Chenin Blanc (Helderberg) $17. Aromas of dusty citrus, pear, cilantro and spice meet similar flavors on the palate, plus a bit of green apple. Finishes with herbs, pepper and citrus. This is well-balanced and very fresh. **86** —K.F. (4/1/2003)

de Trafford 2001 Straw Wine Chenin Blanc (Helderberg) $25. This wine is a seamless mélange of apricot nectar, honey, dried pineapple, golden raisin, and orange zest. It is a sweet, fruity, not-too-viscous wine made, per the label, "from naturally dried grapes." Well-balanced throughout, and not too deep. **88** —K.F. (12/1/2003)

de Trafford 2001 Pinot Noir (Helderberg) $40. The edgy, attention-getting note of funky earth holds on through shades of cherry, cocoa, and white pepper. The well-balanced acids and tannins make the fruit attractive. **86** —K.F. (9/1/2003)

de Trafford 2000 Shiraz (Helderberg) $40. This is a very lovely choice for an evening in with its sweet plum, pepper, and blackberry flavors couched in smooth, powdery tannins. A thin vein of eucalyptus and a bit of acidity complements the peppercorn finish. This is sure to please each time it is uncorked. **88** —K.F. (8/1/2003)

DE WETSHOF

De Wetshof 2000 Bateleur Chardonnay (Robertson) $20. This is the midrange wine in Danie de Wet's clutch of Chardonnays, proof that the hot climate of Robertson is no bar to making fine white wines. With its steely character, this is the most French wine, almost Chablis in style, from this producer. Spices, green plums, and kiwi fruit are all there, as is fresh, crisp acidity. **90** —R.V. (7/1/2002)

De Wetshof 2002 Bon Vallon Chardonnay (Robertson) $14. Mango, papaya and banana aromas are wrapped in a gauze of hay. The spritzy, refreshing acidity is a fine, dry compliment to the light hay and tropical flavors that finish with good length. **87** —K.F. (4/1/2003)

De Wetshof 2001 Bon Vallon Chardonnay (Robertson) $12. A ripe but lively wine, from this master of Chardonnay. Danie de Wet's entry point wine is full, fat, and toasty but also has fresh, green fruit flavors and a layer of cinammon and tropical fruits. It is great Chardonnay, delicious and tasty. **90 Best Buy** —R.V. (7/1/2002)

De Wetshof 2000 Bon Vallon Chardonnay (Robertson) $10. A crisp, unwooded wine, at once tangy and full. Citrus, melon, and herb aromas lead into a palate that pops with sweet and sour orange-pineapple fruit and clove accents. Despite the lean profile, it even has a buttery note. Refreshingly clean Chardonnay. **89 Best Buy** (9/1/2001)

De Wetshof 2002 D'Honneur Chardonnay (Robertson) $24. Danie De Wets has steadily demonstrated both what he and the Robertson region—for many still an unknown—can deliver. He does it again in this convincing white, built (of course) on a solid Chardonnay fruit core. Rich but not sappy, it offers abundant flavor, a solid mouthfeel, elegant style, and a spicy, long finish. An impressive white with balance and finesse well beyond its price and rustic origins. **91 Editors' Choice** —M.M. (4/1/2005)

De Wetshof 2002 Lesca Chardonnay (Robertson) $16. Buttered toast and cream aromas lead the way to toast, lemon, and a hint of hay on the palate. The finish is lemony, with crisp acids and a sweet herbal streak at the back end. **86** —K.F. (4/1/2003)

De Wetshof 2001 Lesca Chardonnay (Robertson) $14. Named after Danie de Wet's wife, this elegant Chardonnay balances smooth fruit with crisp acidity and a spice-and-toast finish. There have been better, more concentrated, vintages of this wine—notably the 1998 and 1993—but it will develop well over the next four or five years. **87** —R.V. (7/1/2002)

De Wetshof 2000 Edeloes Noble Late Harvest Riesling (Robertson) $65. The deep golden color of this wine stands out. The nose offers light wafts of loft-dried hay, sweet toast, lychee, and apricot. An herbal note surfaces, but is hard to distinguish, reminding this taster of dessert-style Sauvignon Blanc. **88** —K.F. (12/1/2003)

De Wetshof 2002 Rhine Riesling (Robertson) $12. This straightforward wine shows lime flower, chalk, and confectioner's sugar on the nose. The flavors of lime zest and white grapefruit carry to the finish. This wine is fresh and simple with a spine of good acidity. **85** —K.F. (8/1/2003)

DEWAAL/VITERWYK ESTATE

DeWaal/Viterwyk Estate 2001 Pinotage (Stellenbosch) $17. An interesting note of bran flakes leads to blackberry, molasses, toast, and sweet fresh herb aromas and flavors. This is clearly a wine that is all about the rich black fruit, which is accented by layers of oak, talcy tannins, and a char-washed finish. **88** —K.F. (4/1/2003)

DeWaal/Viterwyk Estate 2001 Top of the Hill Pinotage (Stellenbosch) $45. Like the regular Pinotage, this leads with an aroma of bran flakes. Black plum, blackberry jam, and caramel are soon to follow, with a cool, eucalyptus-like char on the finish. Seems to have more finesse, but less weight than its compatriot. **88** —K.F. (4/1/2003)

DIEU DONNE

Dieu Donne 2000 Merlot (Franschhoek) $18. Foresty earth notes wrap spiced plum, vanilla, and toast flavors. The light-weight and refreshing acids lead to the clean, toasty finish. More depth would contribute to a higher score. **86** —K.F. (8/1/2003)

Dieu Donne 1999 Merlot (Franschhoek) $17. Blackberry jam, portobello mushroom, forest floor, and dry leather aromas; the palate adds peppery spice. Smooth but powerful tannins balance the sweet, ripe fruit in a decidedly New World style. **88** —K.F. (4/1/2003)

Dieu Donne 1999 Pinotage (Franschhoek) $17. Smoke and beef stock meet red apple, molasses, and toast on the nose. The apple and molasses appear again on the palate, joined with grilled meat and distinct cherry accents. Well-developed fruit, refreshing acidity, and fine tannins make this a very good wine. **88** —K.F. (4/1/2003)

Dieu Donne 2001 Sauvignon Blanc (Franschhoek) $15. The initial aromatics are of grapefruit, a grassy field, a nip of lilac, and some pine. The flavors that follow are mostly in the pear, apple, and lemon categories, while a little vanilla manages to work itself onto the short, clean finish. The mouthfeel is perfectly adequate, while overall it provides good character. **87** (8/1/2002)

DOUGLAS GREEN

Douglas Green 2004 Sauvignon Blanc (Western Cape) $10. This wine has an enticing nose of toast and vanilla spice that can't quite hide tropical fruit aromas. The palate backs that up with good body and great acidity,

SOUTH AFRICA

more tropical fruit, and plenty of vanilla spice. Ends with a nice citrusy tang. **87 Best Buy** —*M.D. (3/1/2006)*

Douglas Green 2003 Shiraz (Western Cape) $10. This wine starts off with nice aromas of cedar and spice, but the palate entry is dull, and spiking acidity plays an off note. Flavors of dark red berry just can't seem to bring it together. **81** —*M.D. (5/1/2006)*

DU PREEZ ESTATE

Du Preez Estate 2000 Merlot (Goudini) $11. Blackened meat, brown sugar, and wet, dark earth aromas are countered by black cherry and plum, which extend to the palate along with notes of radicchio and eucalyptus. Toasty layers of oak are present at all stages, similar to cinnamon breakfast cereal. **88 Best Buy** —*K.F. (4/1/2003)*

Du Preez Estate 2001 Sauvignon Blanc (Goudini) $9. This is a very good example of the varietal's telltale aromas of sweet peas and boxwood. Comparative aromas of fresh herbs and toasty tropical fruit carry vividly to the palate. The finish offers toast and herbs. **88 Best Buy** —*K.F. (4/1/2003)*

Du Preez Estate 2000 Shiraz (Goudini) $11. Scents of greens and baked acorn squash are tinged with gaminess, while the palate offers unsweetened tea, red plums, and an odd note of MSG. This finishes with a not unpleasant vegetal ray. **86** —*K.F. (4/1/2003)*

Du Preez Estate 1999 Hanepoot Estate Wine White Blend (South Africa) $10. This family winery's fortified wine is made every year, but only 200 cases make it to the U.S. What is a hanepoot? This "honey pot" of a wine is made from Muscat d'Alexandria, or Muscatel to some. In the bottle, it is full of complex flavors. Notes of luscious honey, candied lemon peel, dried pineapple, papaya, and mango all vie for center stage. Extremely viscous and rich, this might benefit from a touch more acidity. **86** —*K.F. (11/15/2003)*

DURBANVILLE HILLS

Durbanville Hills 2005 Sauvignon Blanc (Durbanville) $12. Burnt match and other sulfuric smells dominate, although the wine has nice melon and white stone fruit flavors. A bit tart throughout, with a finish that borders on harsh. **83** —*M.D. (3/1/2006)*

Durbanville Hills 2003 Sauvignon Blanc (Durbanville) $12. Lean, grassy, with ample tangy herb and lime elements from start to even finish. The slight note of CP (that's cat pee) in the bouquet is right in line with the angular, crisp neo-New Zealand style. **87 Best Buy** —*M.M. (11/15/2004)*

Durbanville Hills 2002 Durbanville Hills Sauvignon Blanc (Durbanville) $12. Enticing aromas of tropical fruit, toast, and canned peas herald fresh pineapple, lime, and herb flavors. Good acids and a little heat spice up the herby finish. Not a deep wine, but still a good value. **86** —*K.F. (4/1/2003)*

Durbanville Hills 2001 Rhinofields Sauvignon Blanc (Durbanville) $17. Warm aromas of melon rind and canned peas are balanced by citrus and fresh-cut grass, and ride out to the long finish. A great example of Sauvignon Blanc with spine in a well-integrated presentation. **88** —*K.F. (4/1/2003)*

Durbanville Hills 2003 Shiraz (Durbanville) $14. Though this Shiraz has round mouthfeel, good tannin, and flavors of charred meat and grapes. It also shows some mousiness on the nose and a medicinal edge that detracts, especially on the tart finish. **84** —*M.D. (5/1/2006)*

Durbanville Hills 2001 Durbanville Hills Shiraz (South Africa) $15. Toasty aromas and flavors of thick, sweet blackberries match the interesting sensation of viscosity to the mouthfeel. Dried herbs and peppered meat round out the palate. **87** —*K.F. (4/1/2003)*

EIKENDAL

Eikendal 2000 Classique Bordeaux Blend (Stellenbosch) $30. Inky-dark with toasty oak over blackberry and dark chocolate aromas and flavors. Displays some nice forest floor notes plus a winning, smooth feel from midpalate through the finish. This taut, structured, darkly appealing 57% Cab Sauv, 35%Merlot, 8% Cab Franc blend should improve further for another year. **87** —*M.M. (11/15/2004)*

Eikendal 2003 Chardonnay (Stellenbosch) $22. Ample toasty oak here, but it doesn't entirely bury the sweet apple-pear-and tropical fruit. Styled like many New World Chardonnays, and fits comfortably in that league. If woody, it's tasty and well-made. Shows potential to be a serious player, with some fine tuning and restraint on the wood. **87** —*M.M. (12/15/2004)*

ENGELBRECHT ELS VINEYARDS

Engelbrecht Els Vineyards 2003 Red Blend (Western Cape) $45. A collaboration between Rust en Vrede's Jean Engelbrecht and golf star Ernie Els, this blend shows off Shiraz's spicy, peppery nose and Bordeaux's classic dry, earthy feel. Oak plays an integral part, offering woody flavors and big tannins. Warm throughout, this wine could use cellar time to integrate, but don't wait too long. **89** —*M.D. (7/1/2006)*

ERNIE ELS

Ernie Els 2003 Limited Release Bordeaux Blend (Stellenbosch) $93. All the Bordeaux grapes are here, making this one of the most complete Bordeaux blends from South Africa. They go with the golfing legend of owner Ernie Els and the winemaking skills of Louis Strydom of Rust en Vrede to produce a very impressively elegant wine, which has delicious mint and smooth black fruit flavors over layers of dark tannins. Great aging potential for this world-class wine. **95 Editors' Choice** —*R.V. (11/1/2006)*

EVENTIDE CELLAR

Eventide Cellar 2002 Wellington Shiraz (South Africa) $15. Richly scented, with aromas that resemble a cross between graham crackers and Nilla Wafers, plus a few tablespoons of blackberry preserves. It's still young and rambunctious, with assertive oak warring a bit with the jammy fruit, but should settle down in another year or two, while still retaining a bit of an untamed, rustic edge. **87** —*J.C. (11/15/2005)*

EXCELSIOR

Excelsior 2002 Estate Chardonnay (Robertson) $8. Throughout this wine is an herbiness typical to South African wines. In this case, the herbal notes are offset by toast, cream, peach, and lemon. This has very good body, finishing with intense fruit. **85** —*K.F. (9/1/2003)*

Excelsior 2004 Paddock Shiraz (Robertson) $10. Many good bargains like this interesting Shiraz can be found from the Robertson region. Vanilla and leather play large roles, with Provençal herb aromas and flavors of purple fruit. Firm tannins and a hint of sweetness keep high acidity in check. **85 Best Buy** —*M.D. (9/1/2006)*

FAIRVALLEY

Fairvalley 2004 Cabernet Sauvignon (Western Cape) $9. Medium-bodied with dry tannins yet a smooth, approachable feel, this wine has sweet black current and plum flavors wrapped in a light layer of leather that picks up intensity towards the finish. **85 Best Buy** —*M.D. (12/31/2006)*

Fairvalley 2004 Pinotage (Coastal Region) $9. The Fairvalley Workers Association was founded in 1997 by workers from the Fairview Wine & Cheese Estate with funds from Fairview's owner Charles Back and the South African government. This young Pinotage (the first was in 2001) is a standout. Plush and inviting, modern and sexy, it has deep aromas of berry, plum, and barnyard nuanced with lemon and spice. There are pure fruit flavors of plum and berry, and hints of leather and spice to add character. This wine shows what Pinotage can be. **88 Best Buy** — *M.D. (11/15/2006)*

FAIRVIEW

Fairview 2002 Pegleg Carignane (Paarl) $23. A dark fruit-oak-spice profile and supple feel offer lots to like in this mid-weight red. Shows solid fruit and surprising underlying structure. **88** —*M.M. (12/15/2004)*

Fairview 2001 Pegleg Carignane (Paarl) $25. This wine would soothe most ills with its comforting, deep aromas of wheat bread, black plums, and blueberry jam. Ditto for the palate, which also offers some toasty char. Finishes with an herbal twinge. **89** —*K.F. (4/1/2003)*

Fairview 2004 Mourvèdre (Coastal Region) $17. A ripe and lush wine with plummy, brambly aromas. Heavy tannins take a backseat to sweet berry fruit, and a nice, chocolaty feel. The alcohol (14%) shows through on the finish, tinged with lemon. **86** —*M.D. (7/1/2006)*

SOUTH AFRICA

Fairview 2003 Pinotage (Coastal Region) $14. This wine has aromas of green olive and wood branch in addition to tart cherry. The palate is full and smooth, with mild tannins and flavors of dark berry, vanilla and a touch of spice. **85** —*M.D. (3/1/2006)*

Fairview 2002 Pinotage (Coastal Region) $12. Handsome red currant fruit and oak work well together, yielding a tasty Pinotage from this dependable producer. Some typical Cape funkiness shows, but it's well under control, and it closes dry. A good example with which to get to know this grape, or revisit it, if you've been previously disappointed. **86** —*M.M. (12/15/2004)*

Fairview 2001 Pinotage (Coastal Region) $13. This is a simple but enjoyable wine with fine, chalky tannins. Cinnamon, caramel, sweet cherries, and toast, with sweet herbs on the close. **87** —*K.F. (4/1/2003)*

Fairview 2001 Primo Pinotage (Paarl) $8. This wine is meaty, with chalky tannins. Bacon, caramel, red plum, cherry blossom and herbs are well integrated, making for a balanced and interesting wine. The finish is full of pepper, bacon fat, and herbs. **86** —*K.F. (4/1/2003)*

Fairview 2001 SMV Red Blend (Coastal Region) $17. Handsome, almost too suave, with a complex, supple, tawny fruit wearing spice, coffee, and oak accents. The flavors are darker, the feel a bit lighter than expected. Totally appealing, if a bit facile. Deeper, better defined fruit could propel this into the upper echelon. But it's delicious as it is now. **88** —*M.M. (12/15/2004)*

Fairview 2005 Sauvignon Blanc (Coastal Region) $12. With enticing melon and creamy vanilla aromas, this wine starts off on the right foot. In the mouth tropical fruit is on offer, then picks up notes of honeydew and a bit of celery. There is a touch of sweetness to this light wine, but it doesn't detract from the tart acids. **84** —*M.D. (3/1/2006)*

Fairview 2002 Sauvignon Blanc (Coastal Region) $10. On the nose, the fresh herbs so typical of Fairview's other recent efforts appear in the form of hay and fresh peas. The palate offers citrus rind and toast; the finish is grassy. This displays good weight and soft acids. **85** —*K.F. (4/1/2003)*

Fairview 2001 Oom Pagel Sémillon (Paarl) $25. Alluring orange pith and blossom aromas are dusted in cinnamon and paired with cardamom and clover honey. All of this corresponds on the palate, with a hint of sweet golden apple. The herbed butter finish and clean acidity keep the supple viscosity from becoming thick or sticky. **89** —*K.F. (4/1/2003)*

Fairview 2001 Shiraz (Paarl) $13. Solid, medium-weight Shiraz with some structure. Displays briary, dark fruit with pepper and toasty oak accents. Very drinkable, with good fruit, not at all overly sweet or jammy, and mildly tangy tannins on the close. **86** —*M.M. (11/15/2004)*

Fairview 1999 Shiraz (Paarl) $15. Dominated by sweet sexy oak, this soft, creamy wine boasts aromas and flavors of caramel, nuts, and chocolate— a sort of liquid Snickers bar that sneaks in a bit of dried plum flavor just to remind you that it's made from grapes. **84** *(10/1/2001)*

Fairview 2002 Beacon Shiraz (Paarl) $28. Opaque and very dense on the nose with deep, focused, black plum, and berry fruit. Toasty oak is nicely melded with the strong fruit, adding smoke and tobacco notes. A chewy mouthfeel and long dark finish complete the package. Should improve through 2006, and hold well beyond that. **90 Cellar Selection** —*M.M. (11/15/2004)*

Fairview 2001 Beacon Shiraz (Paarl) $30. Aromas of baking spices, dried herbs, and toast lead to endive and tart blackberry on the lean palate. After the green note on the finish, a bloom of blueberry toast lasts all too briefly. **87** —*K.F. (4/1/2003)*

Fairview 2001 Cyril Back Shiraz (Paarl) $26. Even and smooth yet somewhat thin, this is light in feel but with dark aromas and flavors. The tart blackberry-currant fruit wears dense, oak-derived espresso-black coffee accents. Still this vintage doesn't deliver the weight or depth I had hoped for. **85** —*M.M. (11/15/2004)*

Fairview 1999 Cyril Back Shiraz (South Africa) $24. Some reviewers liked it much more than this final score indicates, and some liked it much less (this 88-point average really is just that—the average of vastly differing scores). To some, the nose was mute; others found roasted blackberries, vanilla, and graham cracker aromas that they liked quite a bit. Though all reviewers recognized the wine's blackberry, white-peppercorn, and anise flavors, they differed on whether the palate also showed milk chocolate, coffee or cream cheese highlights. Finishes long and firm, with tannins and a slight metallic bite. One to evaluate with friends. **88** *(11/1/2001)*

Fairview 2000 Cyril Back Shiraz Shiraz (Paarl) $20. A toasty, earthy nose also carries a note of rice cereal. This is countered on the palate with thin fruit and bites of menthol and char. Although tannins are strong, the fruit and midpalate lacks weight and depth. **85** —*K.F. (4/1/2003)*

Fairview 2003 Jakkalsfontein Shiraz (Swartland) $35. This atypical wine has aromas of licorice, hickory, dark red fruit, paprika, and other dried spices. The tannins are firm, the mouthfeel is smooth and balanced, and the luscious fruit is laden with spice, harmonious oak, and crushed rock flavors. An individual wine of unquestionable quality. Drink now–2014. **91** —*M.D. (7/1/2006)*

Fairview 2002 Jakkalsfontein Shiraz (Swartland) $28. Classic Shiraz. Tart, sweet berry flavors and ample oak are in full play. It's already flavorful and well-balanced, with even, smooth tannins. Should be even better in six to twelve months. **88** —*M.M. (11/15/2004)*

Fairview 2002 Solitude Shiraz (Paarl) $34. A bit of horse funk opens up the nose, but it never overpowers. Some fresh herb notes add nuance to black pepper, dark berry, and menthol flavors. Finishes warm and spicy. Despite 15% alcohol, this wine is nicely balanced, with dusty tannins. **89** —*M.D. (5/1/2006)*

Fairview 2001 Solitude Shiraz (Paarl) $20. Opens with a bouquet of molasses, dry earth, wheat bread, anise, and raspberry aromas. On the palate, lush black plum flavors are layered in peppery, blackened oak that is a bit intense for young consumption. **87** —*K.F. (4/1/2003)*

Fairview 2004 Viognier (Coastal Region) $19. Burnished gold, even the nose is creamy, offering heavily oaked aromas of caramel, toast, and vanilla that neatly encase citrus and peach pit. Oak leads the way in the mouth as well, although there are plenty of citrusy fruits along with peach mineral. Despite the creamy feel, there is plenty of acidity, and this great value will drink well over the next 3-4 years. **88** —*M.D. (9/1/2006)*

Fairview 2003 Viognier (South Africa) $18. Ripe, fairly soft, and tasty with a nice spice butter and honeysuckle nose. The orange-tangerine-almond palate is drier than expected. Solid Viognier, closing with decent length. **85** —*M.M. (12/15/2004)*

Fairview 2002 Viognier (Paarl) $18. Meat juices, banana peel, and smoky toast aromas lead to citrusy, yellow fruit on the palate. The back palate displays a streak of bitter herbaceousness. **83** —*K.F. (9/1/2003)*

FALSE BAY

False Bay 2002 Chardonnay (South Africa) $NA. Presents good appley fruit accented by oak and mineral notes. Think of it as a New World striver with modest Burgundian influences. Would go well with hors d'oeuvres or salads. Drink now. **85** —*M.M. (7/4/2004)*

False Bay 2000 Chenin Blanc (Coastal Region) $9. Inoffensive, simple aromas set the stage for basic pear and apple flavors. There's some pear early in the finish, but then a sour lemon characteristic comes on heavy. Simple but steady white wine is what you get here—but nothing more than that. **84** —*M.S. (4/1/2002)*

False Bay 2002 Merlot (South Africa) $NA. Plum and herb aromas and flavors vie with more extreme herb and metallic notes here. Finishes tart and stern, almost like a hard Tuscan wine. Could work with grilled meats and veggies, but it's definitely not a sipper. **84** —*M.M. (7/4/2004)*

False Bay 2002 Pinotage (South Africa) $NA. Flavorful, uncomplicated Pinotage showing good depth of fruit with solid berry and tart cherry flavors. Leather and metallic notes creep in towards the finish, but don't predominate. A good basic version of this South African Pinot Noir-Cinsault hybrid. **85** —*M.M. (7/4/2004)*

False Bay 2000 Pinotage (Coastal Region) $9. This light- to medium-weight red is an interesting marriage of grapes. The palate feel is soft and the fruit sweet, yet dry, with the Pinotage's (78%) earthy rusticity offsetting the neo-Australian jamminess of the Shiraz (22%). The finish of this fairly unique easy drinker turns more brisk, with more of the dry fruit and earth, plus some pepper notes and mildly tangy tannins. **85** —*M.S. (4/1/2002)*

SOUTH AFRICA

False Bay 2000 Rhône Red Blend (Coastal Region) $9. 85 —*M.M. (4/1/2002)*

False Bay 2002 Sauvignon Blanc (South Africa) $NA. Tart but not extreme, with sour grapefruit, lime, and slate notes. Medium bodied, it's fuller than many Sauvignon Blancs with a round, slightly slick feel. Melon-like flavors show on the back end. A decent everyday drinker. **84** —*M.M. (7/4/2004)*

FISH HOEK

Fish Hoek 2005 Sauvignon Blanc (Western Cape) $11. Almost creamy, despite its lively acidity, this SB offers tropical fruit flavors and white pepper, finishing with pear and more spice. Simple but enjoyable; would go well with summer salads. **85** —*M.D. (7/1/2006)*

FISH HOOK

Fish Hook 2005 Merlot (Western Cape) $11. Dark purple fruit aromas are paired with vanilla, lemon, and spice from oak. Retains its grapey feel in the mouth, although high acid gives it a tart blueberry taste. The oak is lemony, adding a straw-like character. **83** —*M.D. (11/1/2006)*

FLAGSTONE

Flagstone 2003 The Music Room Cabernet Sauvignon (South Africa) $40. Earthy red berry aromas lead to nice flavors of dark berry, leather, and barnyard. Full and ripe in the mouth, with plenty of acidity and chalky tannins. Finishes hot, with a metallic feel. **87** —*M.D. (9/1/2006)*

Flagstone 2004 Dark Horse Shiraz (Western Cape) $40. Don't let the screwcap fool you: this wine has quality written all over it. Twelve months in mostly American oak yields graham cracker and lemon aromas, with young blackberry and herbs supporting. Oak again shows in the mouth, supporting dark fruit flavors. It will be interesting to see how the big tannins age under screwcap, as this wine has years to go. **89** —*M.D. (7/1/2006)*

FLAMINGO BAY

Flamingo Bay 2001 Red Blend (Coastal Region) $7. Ripe raspberry, sweet red plum, and a hint of eucalyptus on the nose prepare you for the bitter herb and acid lying in wait on the finish. Serve with food. **84** —*K.F. (4/1/2003)*

Flamingo Bay 2001 White Blend (Coastal Region) $7. Aromas of yellow nectarine, lemon peel, and toast are simply delicious. In the mouth, this falls a bit flat with transparent, anonymous yellow fruit slightly lifted by an herby tang on the finish. Strangely, the acidity actually nosedives in intensity by midpalate. **84** —*K.F. (4/1/2003)*

FLAT ROOF MANOR

Flat Roof Manor 2004 Pinot Grigio (Stellenbosch) $NA. Modest pear and pineapple aromas are alluring and fresh. The palate is crisp, defined by lime and orange. It's just jumpy and jagged enough to rise above the masses; fruity and medium-bodied. **87** *(2/1/2006)*

FLEUR DU CAP

Fleur du Cap 1992 Cabernet Sauvignon (Coastal Region) $12. 84 *(9/1/1999)*

Fleur du Cap 2001 Cabernet Sauvignon (Coastal Region) $14. A bit earthy and leathery on the nose, with undertones of dark berry, this wine is still dark after five years, with charred meat, leather, and blueberry flavors. A sweet palate entry dries out with good tannins, and overall it's a smooth, easy-drinking wine. **86** —*M.D. (12/31/2006)*

Fleur du Cap 2000 Cabernet Sauvignon (Coastal Region) $13. Steamed vegetables, cinnamon, and baked apple aromas join red plum, black pepper, and grilled meat flavors. Tannins are dry, and the finish is lean and peppery, with a nice plum note at the end. **85** —*K.F. (4/1/2003)*

Fleur du Cap 1998 Cabernet Sauvignon (Stellenbosch) $10. Red and black fruit and spicy oak aromas segue into a palate that offers green herb, black fruit, and lots of oak. Ditto for the finish, with its dry earth and plum skin flavors. Not the fullest-bodied wine out there, either. 45,000 cases made. **84** *(11/15/2002)*

Fleur du Cap 2000 Unfiltered Cabernet Sauvignon (Stellenbosch) $15. This Cab's mouthfeel is chalky and clay-like, but juicy, with loads of black plum and blackberries, and a nice earthy component. Bouquet has green herb and tree bark notes accenting the soft black fruit. Only 1,100 cases made. **87** *(11/15/2002)*

Fleur du Cap 1998 Unfiltered Cabernet Sauvignon (Coastal Region) $23. A little browning at the rim combined with stewy and baked aromas confirm age. Oaking shines through with notes of char, cedar, and smoke over meaty-tasting, but thin fruit and dried herbs. **84** —*K.F. (8/1/2003)*

Fleur du Cap 1998 Chardonnay (Coastal Region) $9. 85 —*M.S. (9/1/1999)*

Fleur du Cap 2001 Chardonnay (Stellenbosch) $9. This Chard is 100% barrel fermented, with battonage once a week; 70% of the barrels were new. Snyman admits that it saw "maybe a touch too much new wood," a statement with which the panel was inclined to agree. Yellow fruit and toasty wood stand out on the palate; the nose offers nice nut and floral notes, and gets toastier with aeration. 15,000 cases produced. **85** *(11/15/2002)*

Fleur du Cap 2000 Chardonnay (South Africa) $9. Pleasant, slightly sweet apple and spice aromas open this straightforward, mainstream crowd-pleaser. It's medium-weight, with a slightly sappy feel and a round apple-oak flavor profile that carries nicely through the close. Uncomplicated and certainly ready to drink now. **85** —*M.M. (4/1/2002)*

Fleur du Cap 2000 Unfiltered Chardonnay (Coastal Region) $15. Gentle acidity is a good foil to the bright pineapple, nectarine, and lemon flavors. The fruit rings on the finish, followed by a streak of herbs and wispy toast before falling off. **86** —*K.F. (9/1/2003)*

Fleur du Cap 2001 Unfilterted Chardonnay (Stellenbosch) $15. Like Fleur du Cap's entry-level Chard, this one sees 100% barrel fermentation, but these barrels are all French. Woody peach pit and white pepper notes envelope the yellow fruit flavors; it's creamy and medium-weight, and closes with nut and toast. **86** *(11/15/2002)*

Fleur du Cap 2003 Chenin Blanc (Stellenbosch) $10. A heavily wooded, spicy wine that has little connection with Chenin Blanc. **83** —*R.V. (11/15/2005)*

Fleur du Cap 2004 Merlot (Stellenbosch) $12. A bright yet full-bodied red, this wine has nice raspberry, tobacco, and plum aromas. It is an early drinking wine, jumping from the glass with cassis and red fruit flavors with root nuances, and it's high acidity makes it ideal with food. **87 Best Buy** —*M.D. (12/31/2006)*

Fleur du Cap 2001 Merlot (Coastal Region) $15. Dusty tannins with a fair amount of grip are a good match to the plum, white chocolate, and intense, dusty earth. A note of oaky vanilla carries through to the slightly herby finish. **86** —*K.F. (8/1/2003)*

Fleur du Cap 2000 Merlot (Stellenbosch) $10. With 40,000 cases produced, FDC's entry-level Merlot is the biggest Merlot brand in South Africa—and this wine tastes it. It's a big-production, safe Merlot with anise-tinged oak and indistinct berry fruit flavors. A bit one-dimensional in the mouth, it closes with dried herb, and a tarry, minerally finish. **84** *(11/15/2002)*

Fleur du Cap 1996 Merlot (South Africa) $12. 82 *(9/1/1999)*

Fleur du Cap 2001 Unfiltered Merlot (Coastal Region) $23. Many South African Merlots show some bell pepper components, like this one. It can sometimes be overwhelming, but in this case it adds nuance to nice flavors of blueberry, coffee, and pekoe tea. It's more powerful on the nose, where it's joined by chocolate, coffee, blueberry, and mesquite aromas, but doesn't affect the lively, full-bodied mouthfeel or long, juicy, and smokey finish. **88** —*M.D. (12/31/2006)*

Fleur du Cap 2000 Unfiltered Merlot (Stellenbosch) $15. "Unfiltered," we believe—this Merlot's wild and rustic in the mouth, with earthy, foresty flavors, dark black fruit, and gritty tannins. Finishes with clove and char flavors. **86** *(11/15/2002)*

Fleur du Cap 1998 Unfiltered Merlot (Coastal Region) $15. The browning rim, light tannins, and fair acidity make this a wine for drinking now. The notes of earth, spiced plum, toast, and sweet, stewed rhubarb are complimented throughout with vanilla and cinnamon. **85** —*K.F. (8/1/2003)*

Fleur du Cap 1993 Pinotage (Coastal Region) $12. 83 *(9/1/1999)*

Fleur du Cap 2004 Pinotage (Stellenbosch) $14. Inky purple, this has a beautiful nose of crunchy blueberry, plum, and oak. The plum continues in the mouth, with hints of eraser, while the palate is dry but meaty. A racy finish complements the total package. **85** —M.D. (12/31/2006)

Fleur du Cap 2000 Pinotage (Coastal Region) $13. Strong aromas of black cherry, brown sugar, and toast continue on through to the palate and the finish, which is tinged with meat. Overall, this is simple yet satisfying. **86** —K.F. (4/1/2003)

Fleur du Cap 2004 Sauvignon Blanc (Coastal Region) $11. Clean and well-defined with abundant green apple, herbgrass, and mineral notes. It's subtle, with a fine, high strung balance, becoming more impressive with time in the glass. A brisk finish closes this tasty, affordable example of the elevated confidence and performance so many Cape wineries now demonstrate with Sauvignon Blanc. **87 Best Buy** —M.M. (4/1/2005)

Fleur du Cap 2003 Sauvignon Blanc (Coastal Region) $10. Tasty straight-ahead Sauvignon Blanc with dry lemon-lime fruit offset by mild grass and tropical fruit accents. A tangy feel and crisp finish complete this fine everyday drinker. **86 Best Buy** —M.M. (11/15/2004)

Fleur du Cap 2002 Sauvignon Blanc (Stellenbosch) $9. A tangy, palate-cleansing Sauvignon Blanc if ever there was one, this wine has a grapefruit, green herb, and mineral core. It's as fresh and lively as if it were bottled yesterday. 15,000 cases produced. **86 Best Buy** — (11/15/2002)

Fleur du Cap 2000 Sauvignon Blanc (Coastal Region) $13. Here's a big, burly-full style SB (14% alcohol) that offers plenty of citrus rind, apple, and lemon character as well as some starching dryness on the palate. Unfortunately, it never delivers much sweetness; it's more about dried fruits (apricots and apples). **85** —M.S. (4/1/2002)

Fleur du Cap 2002 Unfiltered Sauvignon Blanc (Stellenbosch) $15. This wine has plenty of racy citrus flavors, but doesn't have the bracing tanginess of Fleur du Cap's regular Sauvignon Blanc. The bouquet's herb and grapefruit notes wear a soft, cream-and-talc cloak. Ginger, citrus pith, and bell pepper flavors characterize the palate. 2,000 cases produced. **87** (11/15/2002)

Fleur du Cap 2001 Unfiltered Sémillon (Stellenbosch) $15. It's 100% Sémillon, 100% barrel fermented—and it's 100% obvious that the two preceding statements are true. Snyman describes this white as a science experiment of sorts—"everything we could play with, we played with"—including 14 different yeasts and 10 barrel types. Mallowy cream and caramel aromas elbow out white peach flavors on the nose. Nutty peach pit, toast, and tropical fruit flavors come to a dried herb-and-mineral point on the back end. 750 cases produced. **87** (11/15/2002)

Fleur du Cap 2000 Shiraz (Coastal Region) $15. The nose on this is built of delicate cherry and red plum fruit with accents of light brown sugar and breadiness. The palate of the same cherry fruit is wrapped in endive, toast and dry herbs. **85** —K.F. (4/1/2003)

Fleur du Cap 1996 Noble Late Harvest White Blend (Coastal Region) $8. **87 Best Buy** (9/1/1999)

FORRESTER'S

Forrester's 2002 Petit Chenin Chenin Blanc (Stellenbosch) $9. Core aromas and flavors of tropical fruit and honeysuckle are accented with fresh green beans and a dash of coconut. The finish is slightly herbal, but full of fruit. **87 Best Buy** —K.F. (4/1/2003)

FORT SIMON

Fort Simon 2004 Chenin Blanc (Stellenbosch) $NA. While the aromas of this wine showed a slight reductive character, on the palate it is much better—dry, full but also crisp with excellent acidity. The finish is soft and creamy. **85** —R.V. (11/15/2005)

GENERAL BILIMORIA

General Bilimoria 2002 Pinotage (Stellenbosch) $11. Creamy oak mingles here with tart dry berry fruit and the usual earth-iron-iodine element. Straightahead Pinotage, and you'll like it or not, depending upon how you react to the earth-metal component. The tart berry finish has tangy tannins. **84** —M.M. (7/4/2004)

General Bilimoria 2003 Olifants River Red Blend (Olifants River) $8. Dry and fairly thin, with a tart edge. The Pinotage fruit must be potent since it seems to outweigh the predominant (76%) Shiraz here. Sour on the finish. **80** —M.M. (7/4/2004)

General Bilimoria 2003 Olifants River White Blend (Olifants River) $8. This Colombard-Chardonnay blend has a chewing gum-like quality. Might work with South Asian cuisine or as a quaff for casual circumstances. But the cheap-perfume notes are hard to get past. **82** —M.M. (7/4/2004)

GENESIS

Genesis 1999 Shiraz (Stellenbosch) $25. Opens with a full, handsome nose displaying a vibrant spectrum of ripe berry cream, coffee, smoke, bacon, and spice aromas. Evenly textured and not at all heavy, the palate offers similar flavors framed by judiciously used oak. Finishes with modest tannins and more smoky oak notes. It's delicious if not terrifically deep. Drink now through 2004. **89** —M.M. (4/1/2002)

GILGA

Gilga 2000 Shiraz (Stellenbosch) $45. An aroma evocative of a dry wood-pile mingles with dried pipe tobacco and charred meat. This readies the palate for the cool, smooth, red plum fruit that is carefully layered in oak. This is no blockbuster, but a pleasant quaff that comes in under the radar. **87** —K.F. (8/1/2003)

GLEN CARLOU

Glen Carlou 2004 Chardonnay (Paarl) $16. Plantain and banana bread seem pleasant enough in the nose, but the wine turns a bit sour in the mouth, with over-ripe melon and a soft mouthfeel. **81** —M.D. (3/1/2006)

Glen Carlou 2001 Chardonnay (Paarl) $14. Translucent stone fruit aromas and flavors are lightly peppered with oak. Overall, this is incredibly light-weight, bordering on hollow, but it never strays into unpleasantness. **83** —K.F. (4/1/2003)

Glen Carlou 2000 Chardonnay (Paarl) $14. The regular cuvée from Glen Carlou is a weighty wine, spicy, with toffee and cream flavors and some attractive green fruit to give it a fresh aftertaste. While this is not as serious as the Reserve Chardonnay, it makes a delicious apèritif wine, that will pair well with light fish dishes. **86** —R.V. (7/1/2002)

Glen Carlou 1999 Chardonnay (Coastal Region) $14. The Finlaysons, father and son, have made some impressive Chardonnays in the dozen years since they took over this Paarl estate. This is not as fine as some (1995 was exceptional), but it has many of the same characteristics: ripe, tropical, fat fruit, with an element of complexity provided by the lees. Yet, the high toast flavors tend to spoil and dominate the fruit. **87** —R.V. (7/1/2002)

Glen Carlou 2002 Grand Classique Meritage (Paarl) $18. Dark red in color, this Bordeaux blend offers sexy aromas of chocolate and cigar box, and has earthy flavors of forest floor, and tobacco with a nice spice. Aside from a bulky feel in the mouth, it's got the whole package, including firm acidity and dry tannins. **87** —M.D. (5/1/2006)

GOATS DO ROAM WINE CO.

Goats do Roam Wine Co. 2004 Bored Doe Bordeaux Blend (Coastal Region) $14. Young and purple, with dark plummy fruit aromas tempered by smoke, this is another cleverly named wine from The Goats do Roam line of Charles Back. It's smooth, simple, and easy to drink, with straightforward grape and plum flavors. **84** —M.D. (9/1/2006)

Goats do Roam Wine Co. 2005 Goat Door Chardonnay (Coastal Region) $14. Banana and popcorn vie on the nose before continuing in the mouth, where oak offers dusty vanilla flavors along with white citrus. Medium-bodied, this wine has plenty of acidity, giving it a tart finish with more popcorn flavors. **85** —M.D. (9/1/2006)

Goats do Roam Wine Co. 2001 Goat-Roti Red Blend (Western Cape) $17. The leading component of acidity only serves to enhance the fruit, making for a refreshing wine. Red plum, dusty baking spices, and leather are accented by radicchio and herbs. which carry to the finish of good length. This is a blend of Shiraz, Mouvèdre, and Viognier. **86** —K.F. (9/1/2003)

Goats do Roam Wine Co. 2003 Goats do Roam Red Blend (Western Cape) $10. Red currant flavors, earth, and toast prevail in this medium weight Cape Rhone blend. Undeniably tasty, if a bit woody and slightly one-dimensional, though it improves in the glass. Decent everyday wine, if less dynamic and impressive than some other Goats du Roam offerings. **85 Best Buy** —M.M. (4/1/2005)

Goats do Roam Wine Co. 2002 Goats do Roam Red Blend (Paarl) $10. A bit of airing will reduce the palate-numbing, fiery qualities. The cocoa and graham cracker nose leads to flavors of red plum and raspberry. The finish is slightly peppery, with fresh herbs. **84** —K.F. (1/1/2004)

Goats do Roam Wine Co. 2003 Goat-Roti Rhône Red Blend (Western Cape) $18. From Charles Back comes another play on a Rhône wine, although this has Grenache and Carignan in addition to the Shiraz and Viognier. A tight nose of ripe, red fruit leads to a jammy, plum-filled palate layered with chocolate, oak spice, and vanilla. Rich and dark, with a round mouthfeel, it finishes with spice and a little warmth. **88** —M.D. (7/1/2006)

Goats do Roam Wine Co. 2004 Goats do Roam in Villages Rhône Red Blend (Coastal Region) $13. This inky purple wine offers aromas of carob and smoke. Chunky, with a hint of sweetness and solid tannins, this wine nevertheless has spiky acids that show through and call for food. Flavors of plum, carob, and vanilla are rich, finishing with over-ripe prune. **87** —M.D. (7/1/2006)

Goats do Roam Wine Co. 2003 Goats do Roam Rosé Blend (South Africa) $10. Full bodied, darker in hue than many rosés, this is tasty and substantial, with full dry cherry and mineral aromas and flavors. There's more positive things going on here than in many light reds. Very good job, showing again why this Fairview brand has been the biggest South African success to date in the U.S. **87 Best Buy** —M.M. (12/15/2004)

Goats do Roam Wine Co. 2002 Goats do Roam White Blend (Western Cape) $10. This blend of Crouchen, Clairette, and Grenache Blancs contains a small dose of Muscat de Frontignan. The herby lemon aromas are filled out on the palate with grapefruit, a hint of pineapple, and orange peel. **86** —K.F. (1/1/2004)

Goats do Roam Wine Co. 2003 Goats do Roam in Villages White Blend (Western Cape) $14. This attractive white's dry mineral-herb nose, round, full feel, and tasty pear spice flavors add up to a winner. Yet another very credible psuedo-Rhône Capester from Charles Back and the Fairview crew. French authorities should lighten up on their (serious) case against his harmless, tongue-in-cheek name, while Rhône winemakers ought to note it as an homage and laud Back's good work with their native grapes. **87** —M.M. (4/1/2005)

GÔIYA

Gôiya 2004 Cabernet Sauvignon (Western Cape) $8. Cherry and dark berry signify this wine, both in the nose and in the mouth. A good quaffer, with just enough tannin and wood spice to brighten it up. **86 Best Buy** —M.D. (3/1/2006)

Gôiya 2004 Chardonnay (Western Cape) $7. Has some tasty elements, ranging from grilled peaches to roasted nuts, but they fail to come together with a true sense of harmony, leaving rough edges behind on the slightly bitter finish. **82** —J.C. (11/15/2005)

Gôiya 2004 Chardonnay-Sauvignon (Olifants River) $7. This 50-50 blend is dominated by the Sauvignon Blanc, but tamed by the Chardonnay. Smoky and flinty on the nose, with mineral and fresh herb flavors, and a citrusy finish. It's light in weight, without a lot of intensity, but what did you expect for $7? **84 Best Buy** —J.C. (11/15/2005)

Gôiya 2004 Merlot (Western Cape) $8. This is what easy-drinking Merlot is all about. Chocolate, cassis, and eraser form a nice bouquet, while vanilla and tobacco meld with red fruit and cassis in the mouth. Stock up, then drink up. **85 Best Buy** —M.D. (3/1/2006)

Gôiya 2003 Merlot (Western Cape) $7. Light red fruits with herb accents mark this value red. Not sweet or jammy, it's rather more like a petit-château Bordeaux. Has some tang and tannins, and it's a refreshing change from other soft, often cloying, inexpensive Merlots. **84 Best Buy** —M.M. (7/1/2005)

Gôiya 2004 Shiraz (Western Cape) $7. Starts with some rather baked fruit aromas, but quickly settles down to deliver balanced plum and cherry fruit on a medium-bodied frame. Dry and slightly peppery on the finish. **85 Best Buy** —J.C. (11/15/2005)

GOLDEN KAAN

Golden Kaan 2004 Cabernet Sauvignon (Western Cape) $10. This wine leads off with dark berry and a touch of herbs. A dusty and dry wine, it has some tart raspberry notes that lead to darker fruit, finally picking up some tobacco leaf. A good, everyday quaff. **85 Best Buy** —M.D. (3/1/2006)

Golden Kaan 2003 Cabernet Sauvignon (Western Cape) $10. Modest cherry scents combine with dried herbs on the nose, followed by earthy flavors and black cherry fruit. Medium-bodied, ending on dusty, earthy notes that will complement rare burgers nicely. **84** —J.C. (11/15/2005)

Golden Kaan 2003 Reserve Selection Cabernet Sauvignon (Western Cape) $14. Golden Kaan's best wine to date, this competes with some of South Africa's much pricier wines. There are cola, balsam, coffee, and mixed berry aromas, while the mouthfeel is creamy, with dry tannins. On the palate, the wine picks up some earthy flavors in addition to mixed berry, and has good length on the finish. **88** —M.D. (7/1/2006)

Golden Kaan 2005 Chardonnay (Western Cape) $10. Heavily wooded for a bargain wine, this has decent tropical fruit aromas and a sweet, chunky palate with pineapple and wood flavors. A bit flat on the palate, but certainly quaffable. **84** —M.D. (12/31/2006)

Golden Kaan 2004 Chardonnay (Western Cape) $10. This medium-bodied Chardonnay opens with understated scents of apples and honey, then follows with earthy, minerally flavors that fold in hints of apple, citrus, and pear. **84** —J.C. (11/15/2005)

Golden Kaan 2005 Chenin Blanc (Western Cape) $10. This newly created South African brand, a joint venture between the German firm Racke and the South African KWV, is producing some well-made, immediately attractive wines, such as this Chenin Blanc. It has good, Golden Delicious apple flavors, richness, and just a touch of toast. The aftertaste is dry, but leaves some softness as well. **85 Best Buy** —R.V. (11/15/2005)

Golden Kaan 2004 Merlot (Western Cape) $10. Cabernet-like on the nose with aromas of cassis, plum, tobacco, and lemon peel. The mouth is all Merlot, however, with soft red fruit and a touch of sweetness. A little disjointed, but good. **84** —M.D. (3/1/2006)

Golden Kaan 2003 Merlot (Western Cape) $10. Herbal, with aromas reminiscent of dried grass alongside modest cherry flavors. A lightweight. **82** —J.C. (11/15/2005)

Golden Kaan 2004 Pinotage (Western Cape) $10. Vibrant and racy, this wine offers an oaky nose of vanilla and dill, but carries enough dark berry and mineral on the palate to compensate. This wine would pair well with mild cheeses and crackers. **85 Best Buy** —M.D. (3/1/2006)

Golden Kaan 2003 Pinotage (Western Cape) $10. Tart but tasty, with lots of rhubarb, cranberry, and red currant fruit. Bright acidity yields a lively light palate, with sour plum and even some citrus notes. This decent everyday red closes clean and tangy. **84** —M.M. (12/15/2004)

Golden Kaan 2005 Sauvignon Blanc (Western Cape) $9. With a stated mission of making consumer-friendly wines for today's marketplace, Golden Kaan, a joint venture between South Africa's KWV and European-based wine company Racke GmbH, pumps out exactly that. This Sauvignon, light in color and aroma, has a nice perfume with vanilla, citrus, and spritzy tropical fruit. The mouth is fairly round, but with supporting acids, and displays solid flavors of citrus and tropical fruit with a slatey edge. Crisp on the finish, this is meant to be enjoyed young. **85 Best Buy** —M.D. (11/15/2006)

Golden Kaan 2004 Sauvignon Blanc (Western Cape) $10. This crisp Sauvignon doesn't wow with intensity, weight, or complexity. But it is a clean, well-crafted wine at an excellent price. Snappy grapefruit flavors are buttressed by hints of honeyed peach and a refreshing finish. **84** —J.C. (11/15/2005)

Golden Kaan 2003 Sauvignon Blanc (Western Cape) $10. On the round and easy-drinking end of the Sauvignon Blanc spectrum, with melon, hay, and peach aromas and flavors. An even feel and slightly drier close

SOUTH AFRICA

with spice notes give this everyday appeal, in a decidedly softer style. **84** —*M.M. (12/15/2004)*

Golden Kaan 2005 Reserve Selection Sauvignon Blanc (Western Cape) $14. Creamy in the nose, with banana and oak aromas, and yellow fruits and straw in the mouth. Creamy and soft in the mouth, this is a simple yet enjoyable wine. **84** —*M.D. (5/1/2006)*

Golden Kaan 2004 Shiraz (Western Cape) $10. Fresh grapey aromas are mixed with cinnamon and vanilla, which carries over to the palate. Dark berry flavors are also present in the mouth, although they don't mesh well with the oak notes, but seem to be dancing their own tune. **83** —*M.D. (3/1/2006)*

Golden Kaan 2003 Shiraz (Western Cape) $10. Attractive everyday wine with a red berry-spice profile, and a nice mouthfeel—neither too soft or hard. Shows good if slightly candied fruit with leather-herb accents. Uncomplicated, enjoyable. This relatively unknown brand delivers dependable quality in this price range. **85 Best Buy** —*M.M. (12/15/2004)*

Golden Kaan 2003 Reserve Selection Shiraz (Western Cape) $14. Golden Kaan is known for their bargain-priced bottlings, and this wine shows the extra effort. Ruby-purple in color and medium in body, this wine has typical South African funk on the nose mixed with stewed fruit and a hint of tar. The mouth delivers stewed plummy fruit with pepper, and a nice, spicy finish. **85** —*M.D. (5/1/2006)*

GRAHAM BECK

Graham Beck 2000 Chardonnay (Robertson) $10. Along with De Wetshof, the Graham Beck winery shows that it is possible to produce fine Chardonnay in the hot, dry Robertson climate. This wine is fruit-driven, dominated by green and fresh citrus and lime flavors, and only lightly touched by wood. **85** —*R.V. (9/10/2002)*

GRANGEHURST

Grangehurst 1997 Cabernet Sauvignon-Merlot (Stellenbosch) $30. The chunky, heavy tar and smoked meat aromas are a bit over the top, and the plump and juicy cherry fruit doesn't quite flow off of the bouquet. All in all, though, it's pleasant even if it's overwhelmingly fruity and lacking nuance. **84** —*M.S. (4/1/2002)*

Grangehurst 2000 Pinotage (Stellenbosch) $20. Pinotage is known to be long lived, and this 6-year-old still seems young. Smoky aromas of roasted salsa, dark berry, and brown leaf are forceful, while the cherry/berry flavors are plenty fruity, mixed with tobacco, mineral, and smoke. Good tannin and acidity are tinged with sweetness, but the finish is smoky and dry. **87** —*M.D. (9/1/2006)*

Grangehurst 2000 Nikela Red Blend (Stellenbosch) $30. This blend of 51% Cabernet Sauvignon, 38% Pinotage, and the remainder Merlot has nice aromas of balsam, red fruit, and spice. But the palate is heavy and chunky, with the 14% alcohol showing through. Sour cherry and dark berry flavors dominate, but are marred by band-aid flavors. **84** —*M.D. (7/1/2006)*

GREAT WHITE WINES

Great White Wines 2004 Chardonnay (Western Cape) $9. Another wine from the label with the smiling shark I've come to call Jovial Jaws. Simple, generic Chardonnay, with a bit-too-sweet-perfumy profile, though the palate is actually drier than the nose or close. This can pass muster at a large party or gallery opening. **83** —*M.M. (12/15/2004)*

Great White Wines 2004 Chenin Blanc (Western Cape) $9. This dry, refreshing white might surprise many tasters, as it did this reviewer. Expecting another undistinguished (to be generous) animal-label wine, found really unexpected flavorful, lively Chenin Blanc fruit and a crisp, cleansing palate feel. 10% of proceeds go to preserve this top-of-the-food-chain predator. **86 Best Buy** —*M.M. (12/15/2004)*

Great White Wines 2004 Sauvignon Blanc (Western Cape) $9. A clean, simple wine that's very pale in color and on the rounder, pear-melon end of the grape's profile. Mild spice notes show on the back end. Basic and mild, but correct, with reasonable typicity. **84** —*M.M. (12/15/2004)*

GROENLAND

Groenland 2000 Cabernet Sauvignon (Stellenbosch) $13. This simple, somewhat hollow wine has apple peel, pipe tobacco, earth, and

eucalyptus wrapped around a tart red fruit core. The balance is snug and the finish has a hint of lemon to it. A great start, but not enough stuffing or complexity to follow through. **84** —*K.F. (9/1/2003)*

Groenland 2001 Shiraz (Stellenbosch) $13. This wine's modest fruit is submerged under a suffocating oak veneer. If you love intensely oaky wines, you'll find this palatable. If not, this woody won't provide pleasure. **82** —*M.M. (3/1/2004)*

GROOT CONSTANTIA

Groot Constantia 2003 Gouverneurs Reserve Bordeaux Blend (Constantia) $32. A subtle, elegant nose displays cassis, soy, vanilla, and green bean aromas. Many of Groot Constantia's wines, including this one, have a silky mouthfeel, with just the right amount of oak balancing the soft tannins and acidity. Mixed berry, bell pepper, and tobacco flavors continue through a decently long finish. **89** —*M.D. (9/1/2006)*

Groot Constantia 2001 Cabernet Sauvignon (Constantia) $14. This historic property's 2001 Cabernet is lean and tart, with aromas and flavors more mineral, iodine, and even animal, than of fruit or tobacco. A little barn-yardiness can add complexity, but the forward elements here will overtly challenge most palates. **81** —*M.M. (3/1/2004)*

Groot Constantia 2001 Gouverneur's Reserve Cabernet Sauvignon-Merlot (Constantia) $19. The nose shows variety and nuance, with light tart berry, menthol, cream, and smoke aromas. The berries are always there, but an intense, toasty oakiness comes up and keeps coming on. The wine is relatively light on the tongue, still the woody tannins get intense and the wine closes rather puckery. **85** —*M.M. (3/1/2004)*

Groot Constantia 2001 Merlot (Constantia) $17. Faint hints of underlying [and under-ripe] fruit here are swamped by a dominant earth-metal profile and hard tannins. Yes, this shows some interesting smoke and saddle-leather notes, but overall it's tough, closing with fairly bitter metallic notes. **82** —*M.M. (7/1/2005)*

Groot Constantia 2002 Pinotage (Constantia) $21. Although it comes from despite a cooler climate than Stellenbosch, this wine achieved 14.5% alcohol. But you wouldn't know it, as it has elegant flavors of ripe cherry, plum, and chocolate in a beautifully balanced framework. Groot Constantia's reds all have a silky texture, and this one is no different. The nose favors brown sugar and chocolate over muted red berry, but this wine will drink well over the next five years, and possibly beyond. **89** —*M.D. (9/1/2006)*

Groot Constantia 2001 Pinotage (Constantia) $16. Nicely balanced, with medium weight, good acidity, and tart black cherry flavors sporting dark chocolate accents. Yes, the funky earth, game, and menthol oak bouquet will challenge some, but there's a good, tasty wine here. Closes dry with smooth, even tannins. **86** —*M.M. (3/1/2004)*

Groot Constantia 2004 Sauvignon Blanc (Constantia) $16. More New Zealand than South African on the nose, with green bean and cat pee aromas. Tangy and high in acid, the wine nevertheless has enough body to round it out. Try pairing with grilled fish. **86** —*M.D. (3/1/2006)*

Groot Constantia 2003 Sauvignon Blanc (Constantia) $16. Lean and green, showing the same tang seen in many New Zealand Sauvignon Blancs. Lime and bright green pepper notes abound and bracing acidity wakes up the taste buds. Quite tart, but decently made, and will appeal to fans of the style. **86** —*M.M. (3/1/2004)*

Groot Constantia 2000 Sauvignon Blanc (Constantia) $11. This wine pushes the envelope with its high acidity and strong green pepper and lime elements. A touch of the extreme "cat pee" notes some Sauvignon Blancs exhibit will appeal to some consumers, but many will find it lean and green. **83** *(1/1/2004)*

Groot Constantia 1997 Shiraz (Constantia) $12. **82** —*M.S. (5/1/2000)*

Groot Constantia 2001 Shiraz (Constantia) $17. An overwhelmingly inky and toasty wine, with a semi-sweet chocolate / black coffee profile. Hints of black cherry fruit do peek through the round mouthfeel and smooth texture. An opaque yet supple cup of vinous espresso, that will have grand appeal to fans of lavishly oaked wines. **86** —*M.M. (4/1/2005)*

Groot Constantia 1999 Shiraz (Constantia) $13. There's a slight acrid tinge to the primarily woody nose and the fruit on the palate is tart and thin. Pleasant leathery and dried spice notes partially redeem it. **82** *(10/1/2001)*

Groot Constantia 2001 Gouverneurs Shiraz (Constantia) $36. Has dominant stably, earthy aromas and flavors. While not a fruity wine, it still has a beautiful mouthfeel, creamy, yet with good acidity. Finishes spicy and long. 89—M.D. (7/1/2006)

GROOTE POST

Groote Post 2005 Chenin Blanc (Coastal Region) $12. Tropical fruit aromas pick up candy and sugarcane accents, but the palate is dry to austerity, with a citrus pith flavor and feel. Despite its dryness, the wine does have a nice rounded feel, and finishes with hints of nut and lanolin. 86—M.D. (11/1/2006)

Groote Post 2004 Chenin Blanc (Coastal Region) $11. From vineyards in the cool Darling region, this ripe but dry wine has mineral austerity to balance its lively acidity. There are some caramel flavors, and a touch of grapefruit, leaving a fresh, crisp taste in the mouth. 88 Best Buy—R.V. (11/15/2005)

Groote Post 2002 Darling Hills Road Chenin Blanc (Coastal Region) $13. This simple wine's anchor is its solid acidity. The stone fruit, spice, and dried herb aromas and flavors are pleasant, down to the herb-tinged finish. 86—K.F. (4/1/2003)

Groote Post 2004 Darling Hills Road Sauvignon Blanc (Coastal Region) $13. Ripe, full, and decidedly different from the lean, rather sharp style currently in vogue. The mild, tropical fruit and grapefruit flavors show good intensity. It's an interesting change of pace, low-acid though satisfying, in a softer style. 86—M.M. (7/1/2005)

Groote Post 2005 The Old Man's Blend White Blend (Coastal Region) $15. The bouquet may take a while to come around, but when it does you'll know what you're in for. Strong tropical fruit aromas have a citrusy side, leading to a very tropical mouthfeel with a smooth, oaked feel and solid acidity. Its 60% Sauvignon Blanc offers grippy grass and grapefruit flavors, while 40% Chenin Blanc adds mango and nutty notes. Finishes with warm, spicy oak. 90 Best Buy—M.D. (11/1/2006)

GUARDIAN

Guardian 2002 Chardonnay (Western Cape) $7. This simple cocktail white shows cilantro and thyme on the nose and finish. In between, toast and wispy licorice veil fresh white grapefruit flavors. 85—K.F. (9/1/2003)

GUARDIAN PEAK

Guardian Peak 2004 Lapa Cabernet Sauvignon (Stellenbosch) $33. Owned by the same team that makes the Ernie Els wines, the Guardian Peak winery concentrates mainly on Rhône grapes. But it also produces this Cabernet Sauvignon, which is a ripely smooth wine, packed with dusty tannins and a ripe, jammy, densely fruity character that is very Australian in style. 89—R.V. (11/1/2006)

Guardian Peak 2001 Cabernet Sauvignon-Syrah (Stellenbosch) $10. This has a lovely nose of cocoa, endive, and black plum, and upon palate entry, the acidity is almost spritzy. The flavors are where the gratification is, with blackberries, allspice, black plums, baking chocolate, raisins, and dried herbs, all with measure of rich sweetness. Charry herbs and black fruit combine on the finish. 89 Best Buy—K.F. (4/1/2003)

Guardian Peak 2002 Frontier Red Blend (Western Cape) $13. Though light-weight and smooth with dry, even tannins, the modest tart red fruit of this blend is overpowered by unrelenting, intense funky earth, game and metallic notes, rendering it out of balance. 82—M.M. (4/1/2005)

Guardian Peak 2004 Shiraz (Western Cape) $12. Scents of herb mix with freshly crushed grapes, while the palate delivers a sweet mix of plums and purple berries. Finishes a bit harsh. 83—M.D. (3/1/2006)

Guardian Peak 2001 Shiraz (Western Cape) $9. Start to finish, this is a pleasure: char, endive, anise, and buttered toast aromas couple with ripe black plums, blueberries, and blackberries. Finishes with some beef bouillon and greens. An interesting blend of Old World simplicity and fruit-forward New Worldliness. 88 Best Buy—K.F. (4/1/2003)

HAMILTON RUSSELL

Hamilton Russell 2005 Chardonnay (Walker Bay) $27. A perennial powerhouse Chardonnay from the Cape, this vintage starts off with strong aromas of popcorn and butter before smoothing out and offering flowery orange and white stone fruit notes. Full-bodied, with beautiful balance, the flavors of papaya, mango, spice, and vanilla are perfectly integrated. The finish is long; the only thing this winner really needs is a little more heft in the midpalate. 90—M.D. (7/1/2006)

Hamilton Russell 2003 Chardonnay (Walker Bay) $25. A taut and fine-tuned, yet large-scale, lavishly oaked white that projects suave appeal and will wow fans of the WTNFO (well-toasted new French oak) style. Lives up to its bold Burgundian pretensions with a lean, angular stance and long, stylish finish. The persistent intense wood leads one to ponder which shines more brightly—the fruit or the classy oak suit it wears. But tasty? Oh, yes indeed. 88—M.M. (4/1/2005)

Hamilton Russell 2000 Chardonnay (Walker Bay) $22. Produced from the cool vineyards at the southern tip of Africa, Hamilton Russell's Chardonnays are world-class wines, fine examples of French winemaking in a South African context. This 2000 is one of the estate's finest to date, a melange of lemon and nuts, mingled with smoky wood flavors, with a layer of acidity and structure that give it great aging ability. 92—R.V. (7/1/2002)

HAVANA HILLS

Havana Hills 2000 Merlot (Western Cape) $33. Salad greens, like chicory and endive, carry through this wine from start to finish in a strangely pleasant fashion. The fresh red plum, toast, earth, and dusty cocoa fill out the palate. 85—K.F. (1/1/2004)

Havana Hills 2000 Du Plessis Reserve Merlot (Western Cape) $33. Typical South African earthiness with a large dose of green—at first minty, then turning more vegetal—charcterize this curious red. The flavors are indistinct, with the dark berry in there under some serious wood and the herb-pepper cascade. Closes very dry and woody. 83—M.M. (3/1/2004)

Havana Hills 2000 Sauvignon Blanc (Western Cape) $15. The somewhat muted nose displays fresh peas, honeydew melon, and freshly snipped herbs, while the palate shows herbs and grapefruit pith. It lacks weight and is watery at times. 84—K.F. (9/1/2003)

Havana Hills 2000 Shiraz (Western Cape) $33. A tight, green note of eucalyptus persists throughout the cherry, plum, and oaken layers. The tannins are powdery and strong while the acidity is clean and refreshing. 85—K.F. (8/1/2003)

Havana Hills 1999 Shiraz (Western Cape) $33. Approachable, fresh flavors of red plum, toast, tobacco, and apple peels finish with a cedary zing. The body of this wine is light-weight, with good acids and particulate tannins with a fair grip. 86—K.F. (8/1/2003)

Havana Hills 2000 Du Plessis Reserve Shiraz (Western Cape) $33. The sheer layers of oak wrap up round plum, light cherry, dried tobacco, and herbs. The acidity is a refreshing counter-weight to the tannins and the style is elegantly simple. 87—K.F. (8/1/2003)

HELDERBERG

Helderberg 2003 Chardonnay (Western Cape) $9. Buttery aromas fold in apple and plantain, while in the mouth, tropical fruit, dusty oak, and baked apple take over. Goes down smooth, but finishes warm. 87 Best Buy—M.D. (3/1/2006)

Helderberg 2000 Chardonnay (Stellenbosch) $8. Simple fruit, with green aromas and soft, creamy, honeyed wood. The flavors are light, somewhat dilute, but make pleasant, easy drinking as an apèritif wine. 81—R.V. (1/1/2003)

Helderberg 2001 Chenin Blanc (Stellenbosch) $6. Clean, bright peach-like aromas precede a tight, acidic, well-defined palate that opens significantly with just five minutes of airing. This will work wonders with Asian appetizers because it's round, weighty, and citrusy. If South Africa is to have a signature white, it may as well be this tasty style of Chenin Blanc. 87 Best Buy—M.S. (1/1/2003)

Helderberg 1999 Shiraz (Stellenbosch) $9. This commendable offering from South Africa confirms the grape's potential there. The nose is complex, with animal, earth, and herb notes on tart berry fruit. Modest dark fruit, coffee accents, and an even, balanced texture show in the mouth. Turns woodier on the back end, with sour cherry notes and light tannins. 86 Best Buy (1/1/2003)

SOUTH AFRICA

HELGERSON

Helgerson 2002 Reserve Cabernet Sauvignon (Franschhoek) $9. A tasty, bottle-aged Cab for under $20? Believe it. This medium-bodied Cabernet is oaky but dry, with plums, black currants, and mint on the nose, wrapped in gentle coffee and chocolate notes and framed by soft tannins. Spend the extra cash on a good beef roast and serve this alongside. **86 Best Buy** —*J.C. (11/15/2005)*

HERDING CATS

Herding Cats 2005 Chenin Blanc-Chardonnay (Western Cape) $9. Banana, citrus and scents of nut start this wine off, then lead to flavors of banana and papaya in the mouth. Full-bodied and creamy, the wine lacks good acidity, while alcoholic heat creeps in. **83** —*M.D. (7/1/2006)*

Herding Cats 2004 Merlot/Pinotage Red Blend (Western Cape) $9. Tomato leaf and red fruit aromas lift from this 80/20 blend. Despite the young age, it's starting to rust at the rim. The wine is on the soft side, creamy and smooth, with with flavors of red berry, vanilla, and green leaf. **83** —*M.D. (7/1/2006)*

HIDDEN VALLEY

Hidden Valley 2000 Limited Release Cabernet Sauvignon (Stellenbosch) $25. More herbal than other Stellenbosch offerings, but this wine has plenty of Cabernet character, including tobacco and dark berry aromas. Chewy in the mouth, the palate delivers charred wood, berry fruit, tobacco, spice, and eucalyptus flavors. Complex, despite subtle green bean notes. This is a wine to enjoy now. **89** —*M.D. (7/1/2006)*

Hidden Valley 2001 Limited Release Pinotage (Stellenbosch) $20. Though the wine has aromas of roasted meat, dark berry, and clove, it lacks weight on the palate. Oak flavors overpower the fading berry fruit flavors. Drink up. **83** —*M.D. (5/1/2006)*

Hidden Valley 2003 Hidden Agenda Red Blend (Stellenbosch) $15. Smooth and simple, this wine comes on strong with dark red berry flavors then fades quickly. Solid tannins and a bit of sweetness add to the mouthfeel, but aromas of red berry and clay are marred by the smell of band-aid. **84** —*M.D. (7/1/2006)*

HOOPENBURG

Hoopenburg 1998 Winemaker's Selection Cabernet Sauvignon (Stellenbosch) $18. Cedar, leather, black plum, and meat juice aromas are contradicted on the palate by tart red fruit and stemminess. A bit of air brings leather and medium char, but the greenery on the finish is a tad bitter. It's Cabernet all right, but lacks some of the richness associated with the varietal. **86** —*K.F. (4/1/2003)*

Hoopenburg 1999 Merlot (Stellenbosch) $18. Aromas of baby spinach and stewy rhubarb meet with cherry tomatoes that carries to the palate of tart red plum. Overall this is a bit tart, finishing with bitter greens. **83** —*K.F. (4/1/2003)*

INDABA

Indaba 2005 Chardonnay (Western Cape) $9. A clean gold color and varietal Chardonnay aromas will seduce you, leaving you vulnerable to its sweet and succulent tropical fruit flavors. Sweet oak wraps the fruit, but it is wholly dry, with high acid to lift it and give it zip. This is a Chardonnay that can pair with a variety of foods, and will not overpower them. **86 Best Buy** —*M.D. (11/15/2006)*

Indaba 2002 Chardonnay (Western Cape) $9. Typical aromas of toast, buttered popcorn, and creaminess extend to the thinly fruited palate, finishing with a toasty bite. This is very light-weight in body and fruit, but the softer acids are a good match. **84** —*K.F. (9/1/2003)*

Indaba 2002 Chenin Blanc (Western Cape) $7. The nose is a pretty arrangement of fresh white grapefruit, new grass, and jícama. This carries, but becomes dilute, on the palate, finishing with some grassiness. **83** —*K.F. (9/1/2003)*

Indaba 2005 Merlot (Western Cape) $9. This wine has flavors from ripe and unripe grapes, dark fruit vying with green bean. Additional aromas of balsam, grape, and spice are pleasant, if unfocused, but the Band-Aid finish is not. **81** —*M.D. (11/1/2006)*

Indaba 2005 Sauvignon Blanc (Western Cape) $9. The nose has a dry almond note and a touch of green in addition to the expected citrus. The green fades in the mouth in favor of melon and citrus with a touch of mineral. A wine with good intensity, nice body, and backing acidity. Nothing stands out, making this a well-balanced quaff. **86 Best Buy** —*M.D. (12/31/2006)*

Indaba 2002 Sauvignon Blanc (Western Cape) $8. Aromas and flavors of grass clippings, green peas, and white grapefruit are tinged with marshmallow. This acidity-driven wine finishes short and herbal. **83** —*K.F. (9/1/2003)*

Indaba 2004 Shiraz (Western Cape) $10. Earth and chocolate aromas soon give way to less appealing Band-Aid, but the flavors maintain their integrity, showing plenty of plummy dark fruit, leather, and sweet oak. Smooth tannins and high acidity leave your mouth clean after each sip. **83** —*M.D. (9/1/2006)*

JABULANI

Jabulani 2004 Chardonnay (Western Cape) $10. Jabulani seems aimed at bargain buyers who like fruity wines. This one is right on track: it's easy to drink, with caramel and tropical fruit flavors. Simple and forward, with some toast notes bringing up the rear. **84** —*M.D. (5/1/2006)*

Jabulani 2004 Merlot (Western Cape) $10. This wine has a sexy nose displaying cassis, cigar box, vanilla, chocolate, and even some herbal notes. The full-throttle nose leads to cherry and cassis tempered with tobacco leaf in the mouth that has a short but sweet finish. And at this price, it's worth buying by the case. **85 Best Buy** —*M.D. (3/1/2006)*

Jabulani 2003 Merlot-Cabernet Sauvignon (Western Cape) $10. An excellent bargain, this wine has attractive fruit with complexity to match. Aromas of woodspice and eraser dance with plum, while the palate adds some graphite to the mix before finishing with tobacco. Full in the mouth, with smooth tannins, this is a wine that will go down easily. **87 Best Buy** —*M.D. (5/1/2006)*

Jabulani 2004 Shiraz (Western Cape) $10. This wine is young and harsh. Burnt-match marred the oaky plum aromas, while the palate's harsh tannins overpowered the simple grape flavors. **82** —*M.D. (3/1/2006)*

JACOBSDAL

Jacobsdal 1998 Pinotage (Stellenbosch) $17. This is a smooth, light-weight wine, but still waters run deep: The talcy tannins provide structure to the dry palate of leather, bitter cocoa, apple skin. The toasty, leathery finish has a hint of fresh mint leaf. **87** —*K.F. (9/1/2003)*

Jacobsdal 1996 Pinotage (Stellenbosch) $15. This wine emphasizes some of the tougher elements of the Pinotage aroma/flavor profile, with lots of barnyard, earth, and leather. The light cherry fruit struggles to balance with the rustic notes. **83** *(3/1/2001)*

JARDIN

Jardin 2003 Cobblers Hill Bordeaux Blend (Stellenbosch) $38. A classic Bordeaux blend, featuring 55% Cabernet Sauvignon, 30% Merlot, and 15% Cabernet Franc. It is packed with great cassis flavors that mesh well with the coffee and mocha flavors, dry tannins, and hints of spice from 24 months in new wood. The hill in the name recognizes hillside vineyards, Cobblers recognizes that ancestors of the owning Jordan family were in the shoe business. **91** —*R.V. (11/1/2006)*

Jardin 2004 Cabernet Sauvignon (Stellenbosch) $20. This is a seriously impressive wine. Its black currant fruit, rich smoky flavors, and soft tannins come straight out of the glass. But it is very young, needing three years for aging to show its prune, black plum, and herbal character blending well with the great layers of y showing some wood. **93 Best Buy** —*R.V. (11/1/2006)*

Jardin 1998 Chardonnay (Stellenbosch) $17. Exuding style and power, this Chardonnay shows complexity with great depth—and breadth—of aromas and flavors. Tropical fruit, citrus, butterscotch, toasted oak, and spice are beautifully melded together to achieve a harmonious whole. Near-perfect fruit/acid balance, a supple mouthfeel, and a superlong finish displaying orange and toast notes wrap it up. **92 Editors' Choice** *(3/1/2001)*

SOUTH AFRICA

Jardin 1999 Fumé Blanc (Stellenbosch) $13. Barrel fermented in French oak, this wine is made in a full style with plenty of nut, herb, and fig aromas and flavors. Big, even fat on the palate, it offers considerable weight and texture. The lengthy finish with herb and mineral accents is particularly appealing. **88** —*M.M. (3/1/2001)*

Jardin 1998 Merlot (Stellenbosch) $17. Displaying style and character, this mid-weight Merlot's complex nose shows classic berry, plum, mocha, and earth flavors, with interesting cinnamon and olive accents. The round palate shows solid flavors of plum, cocoa, and coffee as well as good texture and fruit to acid balance. Finishes with moderate tannins, offering good near-to mid-term aging potential. **90 Editors' Choice** *(3/1/2001)*

Jardin 2005 Sauvignon Blanc (Stellenbosch) $15. Slatey mineral aromas have touches of green bean, while the palate deals smokey flint with asparagus and green flavors. Very enjoyable for its core of acidity and minerally feel and clean finish. **85** —*M.D. (12/31/2006)*

Jardin 2002 Sauvignon Blanc (Stellenbosch) $12. The zippy, acidity provides spine for the full tropical fruit, shelled peas, and citrus-rind flavors. This light-bodied wine finishes with a bit of white pepper and herbs. **85** —*K.F. (9/1/2003)*

Jardin 1999 Chameleon White Blend (Stellenbosch) $16. The attractive opening notes of orange blossom and mild spice are quickly overwhelmed by an off-putting asparagus and sulfur note that just doesn't yield. Light on the palate, the wine finishes lean with a pronounced vegetal element. This producer has impressed us with other offerings, but this one misses the mark. **83** —*M.M. (3/1/2001)*

JEAN TAILLEFERT

Jean Taillefert 2002 Shiraz (Paarl) $68. Soundly built, this wine has heavenly aromas of dark berry, forest floor, and an overlay of oak that keeps evolving in the glass. Full-bodied but lithe, the wine dances on the tongue with cinnamon, smoke, leather, and a dark core of fruit which balances the smooth tannin and firm acidity. Exiting the stage with lasting traces of smoke, leather, and coffee, this wine is drinking beautifully now, and will last through 2012. **91** —*M.D. (5/1/2006)*

Jean Taillefert 2001 Shiraz (Paarl) $66. Well-built, with deep tart-sweet fruit and hefty American oak. Perhaps Aussie-inspired, but the subtle hints of typical Cape earthiness are a plus here, adding unique character. Closes long and very smooth with polished cocoa, smoke and dark cherry-plum notes. **90** —*M.M. (11/15/2004)*

JOHN B.

John B. 2003 Bouquet Rouge Cabernet Blend (Robertson) $9. This simple but tasty blend of Cabernet Sauvignon and the Portuguese Tinta Barocca grape. Offers ample rich fruit flavor and a chewy feel, with easy tannins on a lighter-weight frame. This is what good everyday wine is about, and increasingly, some producers in South Africa grasp it. **86 Best Buy** — *M.M. (12/15/2004)*

KAAPZICHT

Kaapzicht 2001 Estate Cabernet Sauvignon (Stellenbosch) $NA. At first smell this seems to be maturing fast, with cedar and pencil shaving aromas. But in fact the tannins are still firm and dry, the ripe black fruit is all there, and it will certainly improve for a few years yet. But it is ready to drink now. A restrained, elegant wine overall. **90** —*R.V. (11/1/2006)*

KANONKOP

Kanonkop 2002 Paul Sauer Bordeaux Blend (Simonsberg-Stellenbosch) $39. Dry, with high acidity streaking through a medium-full body, this wine has powerful onion aromas that take over. Brown stemmy notes poke through the dark berry fruit flavors, while tannins coat the mouth on the finish. **86** —*M.D. (9/1/2006)*

Kanonkop 2002 Cabernet Sauvignon (Stellenbosch) $33. This indigo-colored wine has a cacophony of aromas ranging from barnyard and leather to eucalyptus and dark berry. The flavor profile is nearly identical, the eucalyptus taking on more of a balsam note and additional dashes of forest floor and spice. The gritty tannins may soften, but the acidity will always be high. This wine has a lot going on, but after four years it still doesn't mesh. **85** —*M.D. (9/1/2006)*

Kanonkop 2000 Cabernet Sauvignon (Stellenbosch) $30. This claret-like Cabernet with Cape accents shows tea, plum, berry, and tobacco on the nose, which opens to a solid fruit core accented by spice, dark chocolate, and earth-mineral tones. Crisp acidity recommends it as a food wine, while the ripe fruit and good tannic structure suggest it will improve with age. Best after 2005. **89** —*M.M. (3/1/2004)*

Kanonkop 2003 Pinotage (Simonsberg-Stellenbosch) $33. The nose is a bit muddled, with earth and brown sugar, but the finish is long and fruity. You don't have to think about the fruit in this wine: it embraces with open arms from the first sip. Plum and cassis flavors abound, wrapped in big tannins and a full body. **87** —*M.D. (9/1/2006)*

Kanonkop 2001 Pinotage (Stellenbosch) $28. All the potentially challenging notes Pinotage can present are well tamed in this carefully crafted wine. The nose of dark red fruit and smoke opens to a solid fruit core— and that's what it's all about, isn't it? This handsome blend of physical and intellectual winemaking closes long and even, with firm, even tannins. Drink now through 2010. **88** —*M.M. (3/1/2004)*

Kanonkop 2000 Pinotage (Stellenbosch) $27. Jerked meat aromas herald toasty red plum that follows through to the palate. This has a lean, herbal finish, but the fine tannins and firm acids make it rather agreeable. **86** —*K.F. (1/1/2004)*

Kanonkop 2001 Kadette Red Blend (Stellenbosch) $12. Offers lots of dark berry fruit with a healthy dose of typical South African earthiness. The wine is dry, of medium weight, with a slightly chewy texture. Moderate tannins show on the mineral-tinged finish. **86** —*M.M. (3/1/2004)*

Kanonkop 2000 Paul Sauer Red Blend (Stellenbosch) $35. A brooding and serious wine, showing very good depth and intense dark cherry and cassis fruit on a nicely structured frame. There's tobacco and cocoa hints throughout, as well as oak. Finishes long, with firm tannins. Best cellared three or four years, and could easily hold for 10–15. **90 Cellar Selection** —*M.M. (3/1/2004)*

KANU

Kanu 2004 Chardonnay (Stellenbosch) $17. Medium-bodied and nice in the mouth, displaying flavors of pineapple, apricot, and sweet oak. The oak offers a toasty nose coating Macintosh apple, as well as a spicy, vanilla-laden and lengthy finish. **87** —*M.D. (9/1/2006)*

Kanu 2004 Chenin Blanc (Stellenbosch) $10. A beautifully crisp, unoaked Chenin that jumps from the glass with its vibrant spicy, floral fruit aromas. Just off dry, this wine's crisp acidity is nicely balanced with just a hint of sweeter Chenin used as part of the blend. **90 Best Buy** —*R.V. (11/15/2005)*

Kanu 2004 Limited Release Wooded Chenin Blanc (Stellenbosch) $18. This is Kanu's signature wine, with its soft toast and wooded character layering with perfumed, crisp gooseberry and tropical fruit flavors. New winemaker Richard Kershaw dropped the 2003 vintage while he settled in, but now the wine is back, and very much on form. **91** —*R.V. (11/15/2005)*

Kanu 2005 Sauvignon Blanc (Stellenbosch) $12. There's a subtle hint of green to this wine's light yellow color, but there's nothing subtle about green bean aromas that blast from the glass. The wine also has an intense mouthfeel with zippy acidity, which pairs well with the vegetal flavors that also include citrus and a hint of smoke. A bit too green but certainly intense, with a tart finish. **84** —*M.D. (12/31/2006)*

KEN FORRESTER

Ken Forrester 2005 Chenin Blanc (Stellenbosch) $15. A wine that shows that, with care, it is possible to make a successful wooded Chenin Blanc. This is currently a little closed up, but the wine shows great potential, with its spice, toast, dried fruits, and touch of spicy pepper. This would work as a partner to Thai food. **90 Best Buy** —*R.V. (11/15/2005)*

Ken Forrester 2003 Forrester Meinert Chenin Chenin Blanc (Stellenbosch) $65. A rich, nutty style of wine, which has 12 months of barrel aging. Added complexity comes from the addition of some noble late harvest (botrytis) fruit to the blend. Apple and cream flavors make the wine very attractive. **88** —*R.V. (11/15/2005)*

Ken Forrester 2002 Helderberg Chenin Blanc (Stellenbosch) $14. This is full-flavored with a light-bodied, accessible style. The mellow apricot and

SOUTH AFRICA

tropical fruit aromas repeat on the palate, with fresh herb flavors that extend to the long finish. **87**—*K.F. (4/1/2003)*

Ken Forrester 2004 Petit Chenin Chenin Blanc (Stellenbosch) $9. "Petit" in the case of this wine refers to the fact that this is the good-value Chenin from Forrester Vineyards. With its flowery aroma, ripeness, mature fruit, layers of nuts and just a hint of a soft aftertaste, this is a great value wine. **90 Best Buy**—*R.V. (11/15/2005)*

Ken Forrester 2001 Helderberg Grenache-Syrah (Stellenbosch) $20. Coffee bean, cocoa, and brown sugar aromas are enticing, while the palate offers only thin red fruit. The tannins are chalky but strapping, leading to a peppery, mouth-puckering finish. **84**—*K.F. (4/1/2003)*

Ken Forrester 2000 Helderberg Grenache-Syrah (Stellenbosch) $20. Throughout this wine is a sensation of fortification, but without the sweetness or viscosity. On the nose, it reads as rum, with flavors of currant, golden raisin, and candied citrus rinds. The drying tannins pull no punches and serve to draw everything together. **86**—*K.F. (4/1/2003)*

Ken Forrester 2001 Merlot (Stellenbosch) $20. The acidity is in the forefront, with little structure or fruit to fill it out. The fruit displays notes of milk chocolate, red plum, and fresh herbs. The toast and oakspice ride nicely on the clean finish. **85**—*K.F. (8/1/2003)*

Ken Forrester 2002 Sauvignon Blanc (Stellenbosch) $14. The aromas of papaya, honeydew melon, tarragon, and coriander seed are quite lovely. The simple melon and citrus flavors finish clean, with a hint of dried herbs. **86**—*K.F. (4/1/2003)*

KLEIN CONSTANTIA

Klein Constantia 1999 Estate Cabernet Sauvignon (Constantia) $22. The thin aromas of leather, old book paper, and horsiness carry to the palate with notes of meat juices and stewy red fruit. This wine is a hint watery, finishes with some eucalyptus, and there is enough structure to drink now. **85**—*K.F. (8/1/2003)*

Klein Constantia 2005 Marlbrook Cabernet Sauvignon (Constantia) $NA. From one of the Cape's coolest wine regions, this Marlbrook, grown in Constantia, has great structure and dry tannins that reveal cassis fruit underneath. It is very dry at present, a sign of aging potential, but also means it will be a great accompaniment to rich meat dishes. **90**—*R.V. (11/1/2006)*

Klein Constantia 2005 Riesling (Constantia) $15. A bit of a disappointment from this famed producer of Vin de Constance. Lanolin and spice aromas have a touch of peanut butter, while the palate offers lemony citrus and more lanolin. A dry Austrian-styled Riesling that lacks the mineral, acidity, and intensity of flavor of finer wines. **83**—*M.D. (12/31/2006)*

Klein Constantia 2004 Marlbrook White Blend (Constantia) $20. From the historic Constantia Valley comes this beautiful blend of Sémillon, Chardonnay, Sauvignon Blanc, and Muscat. Broad aromas of peachy tropical fruit are brushed with grass and toast notes that add complexity, leading to a round, medium-bodied wine that is sculpted with a dry, grassy feel. Tropical fruit and green bean flavors play cat and mouse, finishing with grapefuit. **89**—*M.D. (11/1/2006)*

KLEINE ZALZE

Kleine Zalze 2004 Bush Vines Chenin Blanc (Stellenbosch) $NA. A fascinating wine from this new Stellenbosch estate. It has ripeness, almost sweetness, certainly weight, which comes through as a creamy character, and just a touch of botrytis to give a honey edge to the wine. **89**—*R.V. (11/15/2005)*

KUMALA

Kumala 2004 Cabernet Sauvignon (Western Cape) $9. A bit on the candied side, but easy enough to drink, with black cherry and graham cracker notes that seem sweet and simple on the midpalate, then turn dry on the finish. **83**—*J.C. (11/15/2005)*

Kumala 2004 Chardonnay (Western Cape) $9. South Africa has emerged as a top source for bargain-priced wines, but remains a bit of a minefield, as many of the less expensive wines continue to exhibit various winemaking faults. Not so this wine, part of the Vincor portfolio. This plump, easy-to-drink Chardonnay boasts oodles of tropical and citrus fruit flavors

that finish clean and fresh. It's in the uncomplicated fruit cocktail style popularized by mass market Australian brands, but remarkably well done. **85 Best Buy**—*J.C. (11/15/2005)*

Kumala 2004 Merlot (Western Cape) $9. Not completely clean, with some sulfury notes that linger annoyingly throughout. Aside from that, there's some decent plum and black cherry fruit and a soft, easy finish. **81**—*J.C. (11/15/2005)*

Kumala 2005 Sauvignon Blanc (Western Cape) $9. This wine is simple but pleasant, with flavors and aromas of ripe white fruit with a touch of vanilla. Plump, despite being light-medium bodied, this is good for keeping cool in the summer. **83**—*M.D. (7/1/2006)*

Kumala 2004 Shiraz (Western Cape) $9. Earthy and dry, with flavors reminiscent black cherries covered in fine, wind-borne dust. **83**—*J.C. (11/15/2005)*

KUMKANI

Kumkani 2000 Cabernet Sauvignon-Shiraz (Stellenbosch) $13. Kumkani means "king" in Xhosa, and this has a rather royal bearing, displaying good depth of fruit and the unique earthiness particular to certain South African reds. The fruit positively shines on the dry, supple palate, picking up earth, game, and herb notes. A structured wine, it's built to last, with solid tannins on the lengthy close. Drink from 2004 to 2006 and beyond. **90 Best Buy**—*M.M. (4/1/2002)*

Kumkani 2004 Pinotage (Stellenbosch) $14. Despite 14.5% alcohol, this wine won't overwhelm you. There are hints of alcohol to the nose, but not enough to overpower plum, spice, and sawdust, while the cassis, mixed berry, earth, and vanilla flavors are rounded and intense, finishing with a hint of leather. **86**—*M.D. (12/31/2006)*

Kumkani 2004 Sauvignon Blanc (Stellenbosch) $12. Clean and taut, with a citrus-floral-herb nose opening to a very dry, minerally mouthfeel. It's bright, bracing, and palate-cleansing, though some might find it sharp-edged. Will shine with shellfish or a salad. **86**—*M.M. (7/1/2005)*

Kumkani 2001 Sauvignon Blanc (Stellenbosch) $11. Light and lucid in the glass, with vegetal overtones on the nose and in the mouth. What little dry apple fruit there is isn't allowed to show itself. The cucumber quality isn't helpful. **80**—*M.S. (1/1/2003)*

Kumkani 2005 Single Vineyard Lanner Hill Sauvignon Blanc (Groenekloof) $22. The flavors and aromas of this wine are green, showing asparagus, green bean, and smoke, but they have a nice intensity and a full, serious feel that can withstand the high acidity. Not a wine for everyone, but certainly enjoyable to some for its power and grace. **88**—*M.D. (12/31/2006)*

Kumkani 2002 Shiraz (Stellenbosch) $15. This medium-weight, supple wine stood apart from the other South African Shirazes in its flight for its dark, meaty aromas and flavors. Roast beef-like flavors add coffee and plum notes, then finish crisp. **85**—*J.C. (11/15/2005)*

Kumkani 2000 Shiraz (Stellenbosch) $15. A well-structured wine with fine fruit-acid balance, this has a quite dry dark berry core accented on the nose by smoky oak, anise, and tarragon notes. Licorice and leather add palate interest, and firm, drying tannins show on the finish. Dark and handsome, it's drinkable now, but will be at its best from mid-2003 through 2006. **88**—*M.M. (4/1/2002)*

Kumkani 2002 Shiraz-Cabernet Sauvignon (Stellenbosch) $13. An outgoing wine well-poised to make friends for South African wine in general. It's tasty, even, and stylish, if not that deep. Yes, it could lacks much Cape 'typicity,' if you accept that sort of stuff—and I do. But at at this price, just enjoy the tasty dark fruit, smoke-earth accents, and supple feel. **87 Best Buy**—*M.M. (7/1/2005)*

KWV

KWV 2003 Cathedral Cellar Triptych Bordeaux Blend (Coastal Region) $NA. A ripe plum and black cherry-flavored wine that shows wood tannins from aging in small French oak barrels. This blend of Cabernet Sauvignon, Merlot, and Shiraz (hence the name Triptych) is full-blooded, dense, and very rich. **89**—*R.V. (11/1/2006)*

SOUTH AFRICA

KWV 2003 Cabernet Sauvignon (Western Cape) $9. Weedy, with modest black cherry fruit that loses its way in a bog of dried leaves, coffee, and green herbs. **81** —*J.C. (11/15/2005)*

KWV 2002 Cabernet Sauvignon (Western Cape) $10. Medium berry flavors, a slight juiciness, and easy palate feel make this a very likeable wine. Oak is used gently on this pleasant, entry-level South African. Though not complex, the wine has good balance and a dry finish with even tannins. **85** —*M.M. (3/1/2004)*

KWV 2001 Cabernet Sauvignon (Western Cape) $10. The accessible, global style of this wine shows why KWV is a smart bet for everyday dining and casual entertaining. This vintage is no exception, displaying a lovely nose of toast, cinnamon, and vanilla with intriguing notes of cardamom, black olives, and baking chocolate. The deep currant flavors mix with pepper notes and firm tannins. This will suit a range of foods, from hamburgers and pizza to pepper steak and phutu. **89 Best Buy** —*K.F. (11/15/2003)*

KWV 2000 Cabernet Sauvignon (Western Cape) $10. The nose of buttered toast, golden raisins, dried herbs, oiled leather, black olives, and radicchio extends to the palate. A slightly herby tang to the finish imparts cleanness on the palate. A delicious expression of fruit that is subtle but well structured, not to mention inexpensive. **90 Best Buy** —*K.F. (4/1/2003)*

KWV 2002 Cathedral Cellar Cabernet Sauvignon (Coastal Region) $18. KWV, the huge combine that once dominated the South African wine industry, has turned into a quality producer, and it shows in this fine wine. It has elegance and sophistication in the way it balances big flavors of spice and black plums with considerable restraint, and in the way the fruit is layered with dry Cabernet tannins. This needs some aging—three to four years would be good. **90 Editors' Choice** —*R.V. (11/1/2006)*

KWV 2001 Cathedral Cellar Cabernet Sauvignon (Paarl) $17. Beautiful aromas of eucalyptus and Chinese spices accent red berry fruit, while the palate is a bit darker, showing forest floor, mulberry, and spice all coated with still-young tannins. Finishes a bit chewy, with balsam notes. **87** —*M.D. (11/1/2006)*

KWV 2000 Cathedral Cellar Cabernet Sauvignon (Coastal Region) $15. Modest, dry dark fruit flavors struggle for presence in this opaque, toasty-oak-veiled red. Medium-full in weight, it's even in texture and has some length. But the overoaking is intense and it's doubtful the fruit will ever have a major role in this play. **83** —*M.M. (7/1/2005)*

KWV 1999 Cathedral Cellar Cabernet Sauvignon (Coastal Region) $15. Wheat toast, caramel, and golden raisin aromas open up to brown sugar, cedar, leafy green herbs, and roasted red pepper on the palate. Throughout there is dark fruit that also coats the moderate length finish. Nothing is awry or out of place, rather, this seems very 'safe.' **88** —*K.F. (4/1/2003)*

KWV 1997 Cathedral Cellar Cabernet Sauvignon (Stellenbosch) $15. This very drinkable red shows impressive depth of fruit marked by solid cassis aromas and flavors bearing smoke, toast, and mint accents. It's full and round, but not flabby, and displays very good body and structure. Finishes dry and even, with good length and powdery tannins. **90 Editors' Choice** *(9/1/2001)*

KWV 2003 Reserve Cabernet Sauvignon (Stellenbosch) $NA. A very intense, perfumed wine, with great blackberry and spice flavors. Ripe and juicy, it has soft tannins and a firm, dry layer from wood aging. Big and concentrated, this wine is ready to drink now. **88** —*R.V. (11/1/2006)*

KWV 2005 Chardonnay (Western Cape) $9. KWV has been on a streak, making quality wines that would make any cooperative jealous. This Chardonnay is simple and straightforward, but in a delightfully delicious way. Sweet yellow fruits entice the nose, while the medium-bodied palate is balanced with good acidity, ripe tropical fruit flavors, and just the right amount of oak treatment. Not a wine to dwell on; just pop the cork and enjoy. **86 Best Buy** —*M.D. (11/15/2006)*

KWV 2004 Chardonnay (Western Cape) $10. On the heavy side, with baked apple and spiced orange flavors that finish soft. **83** —*J.C. (11/15/2005)*

KWV 2003 Chardonnay (Western Cape) $10. A simple, easy-drinker offering mild citrus and tropical fruit on a light frame. The soft palate shows

a melony quality, in both flavor and texture. On the sweet side, this should have mainstream appeal. **83** —*M.M. (3/1/2004)*

KWV 2004 Cathedral Cellar Chardonnay (Coastal Region) $14. The oak in this wine is heavy-handed, with charred wood and toast flavors and aromas, but it still can't hide the wine's harsh acidity. Finishes with baked banana flavors. **82** —*M.D. (3/1/2006)*

KWV 2003 Cathedral Cellar Chardonnay (Coastal Region) $17. Solid mainstream Chardonnay whose ripe nose shows apple-pear fruit and oak-butterscotch accents. Medium-full in feel, with maybe just a touch of alcoholic heat, its broad, friendly profile will enjoy wide appeal. Direct rather than complex, and rich and flavorful, closing with good length. **87** —*M.M. (4/1/2005)*

KWV 2002 Cathedral Cellar Chardonnay (Coastal Region) $16. An unusual perfume like chestnut—or is it acacia—suffuses this intriguing medium-weight white. It envelops classic apple, hay, and mild citrus Chardonnay qualities. The spicy finish wraps it up nicely. This atypical wine has a unique appeal. **87** —*M.M. (3/1/2004)*

KWV 2001 Cathedral Cellar Chardonnay (Western Cape) $12. The name of the top brand from the massive KWV winery refers to the cathedral-like roof of its main winery. This is a rich, generous wine, with spice, ripe fruit, and a good layer of toasty wood flavors. There is complexity also, introduced by the crisp acidity that complements the opulent fruit. **90 Best Buy** —*R.V. (7/1/2002)*

KWV 2000 Cathedral Cellar Chardonnay (Western Cape) $12. The unexpectedly complex nose of this Chardonnay value shows tangerine and white peach, toast, and nut accents. Pineapple, cinnnamon-clove, and roasted cashew flavors show on the full, ripe, and oaky palate. Finishes with good length and toasted-oatmeal flavors. **89 Editors' Choice** *(9/1/2001)*

KWV 2002 KWV Chardonnay (Western Cape) $10. From the nose to the palate, this wine is easily described by lemon buttercreme icing with citrus zest. If that sounds too cloying, no worries thanks to the dried herbs and lightbodied style. **86** —*K.F. (4/1/2003)*

KWV 2004 Steen Chenin Blanc (Western Cape) $8. Ripe fruit and bubblegum hints open this clean, angular white. Quickly turns much less sweet than expected, its ample melon and tropical fruit supported by brisk acidity. A refreshing value Chenin Blanc (Steen in South Africa) that closes very clean, surprisingly long. **85 Best Buy** —*M.M. (4/1/2005)*

KWV 2003 Steen Chenin Blanc (Western Cape) $8. Steen is the common name for Chenin Blanc in the Cape, and how KWV has labeled this bottling. It's round, with a pronounced melon-grapefruit profile and a mouth-filling quality. The tangy finish offers some lychee notes. **84** —*M.M. (3/1/2004)*

KWV 2002 Steen Chenin Blanc (Western Cape) $8. This is a simple, easy-going wine with hallmark aromas and flavors of citrus and fresh herbs. The notes of durum and meat juices are especially interesting. **85** —*K.F. (4/1/2003)*

KWV 2003 Merlot (Western Cape) $9. This wine starts off light, with acidity pushing it towards tartness. Cranberry flavors match the light feel, accompanied by cedary spice. The nose is unrevealing, but at this price just sip, swallow and enjoy. **84** —*M.D. (9/1/2006)*

KWV 2002 Merlot (Western Cape) $10. Very cherry is a good way to describe this tasty, firm value red. Bright acidity supports the ample fruit, while toasty oak and restrained earthy notes add flavor interest. Quite structured, with tangy, almost edgy back end tannins—good for grilled meats. **85 Best Buy** —*M.M. (4/1/2005)*

KWV 2001 Merlot (Western Cape) $10. A watery rim color of light brick heralds the faint aromas of baking spices, cherry, caramel, and meat juices. The palate is not as muted, with cinnamon spice and a hint of melon providing interesting flavor counterparts to the ripe cherry fruit. Light-bodied, but well layered, almost slick toward the finish. **88 Best Buy** —*K.F. (4/1/2003)*

KWV 2002 Cathedral Cellar Merlot (Coastal Region) $17. Pleasant whiffs of mint mix with blueberry and eraser, leading to a palate full of holiday spice, dark berries, cedar, and mint. Medium-bodied with moderate tannins and a dash of acidity, this wine is light enough to be drunk in warm weather but sturdy enough to pair with roast fowl. **86** —*M.D. (9/1/2006)*

KWV 1996 Cathedral Cellar Merlot (Coastal Region) $15. With its dried fruit, leather, and mint scents, this lean wine could easily be mistaken for a modest Bordeaux. The tart cherry flavors on the lithe palate bear tobacco accents. Closes tart and dry, with a cocoa note. **86** *(9/1/2001)*

KWV 2003 Pinotage (Western Cape) $9. This wine smells like flowers and sour cherries. It's light and soft in the mouth, with enjoyable flavors of sweet-and-sour cherries lightly dusted with vanilla and cedar. **85 Best Buy** —*M.D. (3/1/2006)*

KWV 2002 Pinotage (Western Cape) $10. An attractive, accessible Pinotage with berry, mint, and tar aromas. The nose opens to a brisk, dry, but not heavy palate of red fruit and pepper flavors. This perfect introduction to South Africa's synthetic-indigenous red (a hybrid of Pinot Noir and Cinsault) finishes with decent length and a pleasant aftertaste. **85** —*M.M. (3/1/2004)*

KWV 2001 Pinotage (Western Cape) $10. This wine will please many with its round, currant-like fruit tinged in herbs, green pepper, and meat juices. Even the soft mouthfeel aims to please, making the wine friendly enough for a meal or by itself. **85** —*K.F. (9/1/2003)*

KWV 2000 Pinotage (Western Cape) $11. Baked apple aromas are met by toast and red plums on the palate. The finish is herbal, but with a last minute bloom of sweet plum and cinnamon. **86** —*K.F. (4/1/2003)*

KWV 1999 Pinotage (Western Cape) $9. Smoke, game, and leather accent the sweet berry fruit. The medium-weight berry-cherry palate shows the characteristic earthy—some say horsey—quality of the Pinotage grape, a Pinot Noir/Cinsault hybrid. Opens with airing to reveal a licorice note. Finishes tart and smoky. **86** *(9/1/2001)*

KWV 1999 Cathedral Cellar Pinotage (Western Cape) $17. An odd but not unbecoming note of book paper starts off the nose of cooked meat and red fruit peels. The tart red fruit and char is basic and balanced on the palate, finishing with a wisp of bitter chocolate. **84** —*K.F. (9/1/2003)*

KWV NV Full Ruby Port (Western Cape) $9. Bottled in 2003, the exuberant notes of leather, toast, licorice root, and schnapps-like blackberry fruit are tasty for sipping now. The firm, peppery tannins, bright acidity, and 19.5% alcohol indicate that this package will take some aging. **87** —*K.F. (12/1/2003)*

KWV NV Full Tawny Port (Western Cape) $9. Like the Full Ruby Port, this was bottled in 2003. Simple notes of tobacco, leather, citrus oil, and apricot do well to overpower the hint of bitterness at the backpalate. A coating of caramel completes the package. **87** —*K.F. (12/1/2003)*

KWV 1993 Late Bottled Vintage Port (Western Cape) $15. Beginning to brown a little at the rim and show off a little maturity by way of the structured, leathery body. Notes of mulling spice, exotic woods, and toast offset those of taut, simple fruit, a thin whiff of varnish, and a hint of bitterness. A great ending for a holiday meal. **88** —*K.F. (12/1/2003)*

KWV 2005 Sauvignon Blanc (Western Cape) $9. Nice, soft aromas of gooseberry and peach lift from the glass, and this wine has a polished feel. Citrus and white fruit flavors carry a hint of nut, giving this an almost Chenin taste. Nice and correct, but lacking excitement. **84** —*M.D. (12/31/2006)*

KWV 2001 Cathedral Cellar Sauvignon Blanc (Western Cape) $15. The sweet tropical fruit on the nose turns flinty and almost citrusy on the palate. The aromas and flavors of fresh peas, sweet fresh herbs, and grass clippings also appear on the palate, slightly diluted, with good length. The acidity is a bit spritzy at the start. **87** —*K.F. (4/1/2003)*

KWV 2002 Shiraz (Western Cape) $10. Simple dark juice, though not sappy and sweet like so much value Shiraz. Undefined dark fruit is accented by toast and leather notes in this tangy, lean light-weight. **84** —*M.M. (4/1/2005)*

KWV 2000 Shiraz (Western Cape) $10. Cedar, leather, white pepper, and grilled meat smell fantastic, but only the leather lasts to the palate. The currant-flavored fruit is marked by a slight tartness, toast, and eucalyptus that carries to the very end. Among all of this is a strange, spicy, green bell pepper note not usually associated with the variety. **84** —*K.F. (9/1/2003)*

KWV 1999 Shiraz (Western Cape) $9. An earthy, rustic wine, with mushroom and earth aromas that lead into leathery, sour berry flavors on the palate. Coffee and cocoa notes add life to the finish. Complex, but not for fans of fruity wines. **84** *(10/1/2001)*

KWV 1999 Cathedral Cellar Shiraz (Western Cape) $15. **81** —*D.T. (1/1/2002)*

KWV 1999 Cathedral Cellar Shiraz (Coastal Region) $17. Creamy, yet slightly tangy on the tongue, this juicy yet not sweet Shiraz has decent light fruit. Yet again, this would be better served by more judicious use of wood. It displays sour cherry and berry fruits with mild leather and pepper accents, a good straightforward wine deserving a lighter oak regime that would let the fruit show more. **83** —*M.M. (3/1/2004)*

KWV 1998 Cathedral Cellar Shiraz (Coastal Region) $15. Scents of sawdust, kiln-dried wood, and scorched oak bring the lumberyard to life. There's some coffee and licorice at this wine's core, plus a beam of lemony acidity that helps keep it balanced. This is definitely a wine for oakophiles. **83** *(10/1/2001)*

KWV 2005 Steen (Western Cape) $7. Outside the U.S., this wine is normally found as Chenin Blanc, and it seems sad that the U.S. importer wanted to revert to the old South African name for the varietal. It is particularly a shame because this is a good value wine, with ripeness, softness, and plenty of acidity to go with the pear fruit flavors. **86 Best Buy** —*R.V. (11/15/2005)*

L'AVENIR

L'Avenir 2005 Chenin Blanc (Stellenbosch) $NA. This estate is widely reputed for its Chenin Blanc. And no wonder, with this very dry, ripe character wine spiced with cinnamon and citrus. This is a full, creamy style, which matures well, and will certainly be even more impressive in 8–9 years. **91** —*R.V. (11/15/2005)*

L'Avenir 2004 Pinotage (Stellenbosch) $20. A deliciously juicy version of Pinotage, which starts with open aromas of plums and beetroot and follows with soft, ripe, sweet flavors. It flows generously over the earthy edge of Pinotage, and would be great with spicy food. **87** —*R.V. (11/1/2006)*

L'Avenir 2004 Grand Vin Pinotage (Stellenbosch) $NA. Rich and silky, this wine is full of very soft, sweet fruit. It has the texture of treacle, dense but without any sense of tannins. The dusty, superripe fruit (14.5% alcohol) makes it very enticing, but the structure and the acidity seem to have disappeared. **89** —*R.V. (11/1/2006)*

L'Avenir 2005 Sauvignon Blanc (Stellenbosch) $NA. With its softness, its layers of wood, this wine has delicious apple and cream flavors, giving a tropical style of Sauvignon Blanc. But there is also great acidity and a hint of a mineral character to give it structure. **87** —*R.V. (11/1/2006)*

LA MOTTE

La Motte 1999 Estate Cabernet Sauvignon (Franschhoek) $20. Although relatively balanced, this wine has simple sensory findings of cherry, plum and cocoa. A note reminiscent of mint tea transforms to eucalyptus on the palate. **84** —*K.F. (8/1/2003)*

LABORIE

Laborie 2001 Estate Cabernet Sauvignon (Paarl) $12. Focused, lush aromas and flavors of ripe black plum, apple peel, star anise, and woodsmoke are well-balanced and unwavering. Finishes with a cozy hint of fresh bread. Satisfies the senses and the budget. **89 Best Buy** —*K.F. (1/1/2004)*

Laborie 1998 Blanc de Noir Champagne Blend (Paarl) $18. Pink in color, with modest fruit redolent of peach and apple. Hints of spice and a nutty note dress up the finish of this South African bubbly. **83** —*J.M. (12/1/2002)*

Laborie 1995 Cap Classique Brut Champagne Blend (Paarl) $18. This mild-mannered bubbly comes from South Africa. It's easy to drink, with soft apple, pear, and citrus notes. **85** —*J.M. (12/1/2002)*

Laborie 2003 Chardonnay (Paarl) $11. Very pale in color with a clean mild citrus nose. Simple and clean, the only issue being there's not enough 'there' there. It's subdued to the point of being almost indistinct. There are no off-putting elements here, just show us more fruit. **83** —*M.M. (3/1/2004)*

Laborie 2001 Chardonnay (Paarl) $11. The KWV-owned estate in Paarl has produced an old-style Burgundian wine with animal aromas. These may wear off with age, but currently it still has charm, and certainly character, with its layers of spice and yeasty fruits. **84** —*R. V. (7/1/2002)*

Laborie 1998 Cap Classique Chardonnay (Paarl) $18. This accessible, acidity-driven pour showcases a light body and vanillin toast flavors. Straightforward throughout, with some grassiness on the finish. **86** —*K.F. (12/1/2003)*

Laborie 2001 Estate Wine Merlot-Cabernet Sauvignon (Paarl) $12. Sweet Tart, candied cherry, and plum is wrapped in sweet, toasty oak. Notes of dried herbs, eucalyptus, and coffee grounds are found throughout. The peppery tannins provide grip and firm support to the palate. **85** —*K.F. (9/1/2003)*

Laborie 1998 Pineau de Laborie Pinotage (Paarl) $16. The label declares this a "Pinotage dessert wine . . . fortified with Pinotage spirit." The firm, plummy fruit has just a bit of eucalyptus running along the edges, and is completed with notes of cigar smoke and toast, wrapped in white pepper tannins. Though the varietal character is spot-on, the sweetness does not seem fully integrated. **87** —*K.F. (12/1/2003)*

Laborie 2003 Sauvignon Blanc (Paarl) $11. The opening bouquet has an almost quinine-like perfume. On the tongue it's a bit thin, with green pepper and citrus notes that fail to mesh in a complimentary manner. A Cape Sauvignon Blanc that aims high, for a point somewhere between Sancerre and Marlborough, but veers off course. **84** —*M.M. (3/1/2004)*

Laborie 2002 Sauvignon Blanc (Paarl) $11. KWV purchased Laborie in 1972, and the estate and its restaurant have since become well-known Cape wine country destinations because of their proximity to Paarl Mountain. The plantings are primarily red varieties, but this Sauvignon Blanc is a light and easy offering, showcasing bright yellow stone fruit and clean lemon flavors tempered with grassiness. Zippy acidity makes this a natural with fresh oysters. **87** —*K.F. (11/15/2003)*

Laborie 1999 Blanc de Noir Sparkling Blend (Paarl) $13. A short note of bitters is overcome by the cedar, toast, pithy strawberry, and light cherry notes on the palate. The slight presence of vanilla and cinnamon throughout is uplifting, and the strawberry notes carry through to the end. Without a doubt, a delicious starter sparkling rosé. **87 Best Buy** —*K.F. (12/1/2003)*

LAMMERSHOEK

Lammershoek 2001 Barrique Chenin Blanc (Coastal Region) $10. Austrians Paul and Anna Kretzel co-own this winery with the Stephan family from Germany. The best fruit from their 600-ton production launches a fleet of proprietary wines. This flagship white is barrel-fermented in French oak, which produces a strong whiff of buttered wheat toast at the start. The flavors of dried pineapple, sweet basil, and white pepper are supported by good acidity. Try this with a summery fruit salad. **87** —*K.F. (1/1/2004)*

Lammershoek 2001 Red Blend (Coastal Region) $13. This 60% Shiraz/40% Carignan blend shows a decidedly Rhônish profile with a (challenging?) mix of sweet lavender and vanilla with some very gamy notes accenting the dry red fruits. Medium weight, with decent acidity, this is no juiceball or fruitbomb, but shows a reserved slight tartness throughout, with even a traditional bitter herb touch at the close. **84** —*M.M. (3/1/2004)*

Lammershoek 2002 Roulette Red Blend (Coastal Region) $28. An interesting, medium-weight red and a sort of Cape-o-neuf de Pape—comprised of four Rhône grapes. It's ripe and juicy, with dark berry fruit accented by menthol and mint notes. The close of this nicely fruited blend shows classy drier, slightly metallic Grenache notes. **86** —*M.M. (7/1/2005)*

Lammershoek 2005 Aprilskloof Sauvignon Blanc (Coastal Region) $10. This wine has pleasant aromas of apple, pear, and dusty vanilla, which carry through to the mouth. A bit soft, this wine nevertheless finishes with a citric tang. **84** —*M.D. (3/1/2006)*

LANDSKROON

Landskroon 2002 Cabernet Sauvignon (Paarl) $16. A leathery wine, linear and lean in the mouth with dry tannin and acid that lends a mineral feel.

Mint and modest red fruit aromas are secondary to leather, which also frames tangy dark berry in the mouth, then grabs hold on the spicy finish. **85** —*M.D. (9/1/2006)*

Landskroon 2001 Cabernet Sauvignon (Paarl) $15. Light but quite tasty with red berry, black plum, herb, and licorice aromas and flavors. An even mouthfeel and mild, smooth tannins complete the profile in this very drinkable, claret-like wine. **85** —*M.M. (11/15/2004)*

Landskroon 2000 Cabernet Sauvignon (Paarl) $16. A satisfying nose of red plum, anise, melon rind, and red licorice whet the palate, where the full plum and anise flavors are accompanied by dry toast. A shot of bitter herbs are sensed at the backpalate and on the medium length finish. **87** —*K.F. (4/1/2003)*

Landskroon 2000 Merlot (Paarl) $16. Nose offers loam, button mushroom, dry leather, and rhubarb aromas. The palate is slimmer, with light fruit and leather that carries over to the lightly toasted finish. Simple and straightforward, but good. **86** —*K.F. (4/1/2003)*

Landskroon 2003 Jerepico Morio Muskat (Paarl) $15. Bright, focused, classic orange-apricot Muscat aromas and flavors shine in this fortified wine from Paarl. Though light in feel, it shows a little heat—no surprise with its 18% alcohol. Refreshing very cold from the nose right through the tangy citrus-spice close. **87** —*M.M. (11/15/2004)*

Landskroon 1999 Pinotage (Paarl) $15. A simple nose of sweet red plum and toasty caramel; the plum repeats on the palate, accompanied by green pepper and vegetal notes. The finish is rather green and bitter. **83** —*K.F. (4/1/2003)*

Landskroon 1999 Cape Vintage Port (Paarl) $20. This squat-bottled offering shows a rich and dense stewed fruit, dried plum, and raisin platform. The fruit's up front, with attractive nut and smoke accents showing as this opens up in the glass. Even in feel, not overly dense or heavy, and accessible now. **88** —*M.M. (11/15/2004)*

Landskroon 2002 Shiraz (Paarl) $16. Even and medium weight, with sweet berry-plum fruit, plus nice oak. The wine is not terrifically complex, but is handsomely balanced. All components are in harmony—including a modest dose of South African earthiness, closing with smooth, dry tannins. **86** —*M.M. (11/15/2004)*

Landskroon 2000 Shiraz (Paarl) $18. An uncharacteristic note of cucumber blows off, leaving simple aromas of light toast and red fruit. These continue on the hollow palate, with an odd note of spinach blooming through tart fruit on the finish. **84** —*K.F. (4/1/2003)*

LANZERAC

Lanzerac 1998 Cabernet Sauvignon (Stellenbosch) $27. The slight brown edge reads age, which this has. Plus handsome dried raspberry, cedar, leather, and cigar box aromas and flavors. Elegantly constructed, this shows many admirable qualities of mature Bordeaux, but also a large dose of greenness. **86** —*M.M. (11/15/2004)*

Lanzerac 2003 Chardonnay (Stellenbosch) $20. Opens handsomely with green apple, smoke, and herb aromas. The oak shows in the palate's toast and butterscotch sheen. Slightly viscous on the tongue, with a long minerally finish, this is elegant, taut Chardonnay. Rewarding now, and will improve further. **89** —*M.M. (11/15/2004)*

Lanzerac 1999 Chardonnay (Stellenbosch) $22. Lovely popcorn and toast aromas whet the appetite for the thin, cool lemon flavors accented by spice. The finish shows the popcorn, plus an herbal tang. **85** —*K.F. (4/1/2003)*

Lanzerac 2000 Pinotage (Stellenbosch) $26. The black cherry-dark berry fruit here is simply overwhelmed by massive oak. Overwooded and edgy, fundamentally out of balance, offering little but sharp acidity, bracing tannins, and a hard, dry, gum-numbing finish. It's supposed to be about the grapes. **80** —*M.M. (12/15/2004)*

Lanzerac 2004 Sauvignon Blanc (Stellenbosch) $21. A goodly amount of stoniness and mineral offset any candied fruit element, and the whole is largely on the money. Flavors of ripe melon, grapefruit, and other citrus fruits are sweet but pleasant, while the finish is concentrated and forward, with ample pith and zesty dryness. **87** *(7/1/2005)*

LE BONHEUR

Le Bonheur 2000 Cabernet Sauvignon (Simonsberg-Stellenbosch) $25. You can smell and taste the good red and blackberry fruit here, but the menthol-toast oak weighs on it heavily. The mouthfeel is supple and filling, yet the package doesn't cohere quite as expected. Yes it is good, but the whole seems less-than-what-was-aimed-for, or the sum of its parts. **85** — *M.M. (4/1/2005)*

Le Bonheur 1997 Cabernet Sauvignon (Stellenbosch) $18. Intense aromatics of field greens and rhubarb seem indicative of unripe fruit. That impression is echoed by the palate, where there's cherry cola and root-like qualities. As a package, it's unbalanced, with a berry-syrup quality dominating the core. **82** —*M.S. (1/1/2004)*

Le Bonheur 1996 Cabernet Sauvignon (Stellenbosch) $9. Cassis well-integrated with the oak used here dominate from the nose to the long finish. The medium body weight fits well with the harmonious palate. A fine companion for tonight's steak frites. **89 Best Buy** —*M.N. (1/1/2004)*

Le Bonheur 2003 Chardonnay (Simonsberg-Stellenbosch) $13. Pale gold, with pear-tangerine fruit and a sweet, almost juicy-fruit-gum note that persists all the way through. This round, easy-drinking mid-weight Chardonnay's candied edge is more like a value white than what an estate wine could deliver. **84** —*M.M. (4/1/2005)*

Le Bonheur 1999 Chardonnay (Stellenbosch) $11. This wine suffers from the excessive use of oak. A little Chardonnay character is discernible, but toast, caramel, and a resinous element predominate. **81** —*M.N. (1/1/2004)*

Le Bonheur 2001 Landgoed Chardonnay (Stellenbosch) $12. The aromas of lemon-infused honey and creamy toffee are tied in with a waft of alcohol. The palate is almost unflavored, with thin lemon and toast that trail off on the finish. This lacks depth of flavor, weight, and acidity, but the aromas are nice. **83** —*K.F. (9/1/2004)*

Le Bonheur 2001 Prima Merlot-Cabernet Sauvignon (Stellenbosch) $16. A bit stewy at first sniff, heavy plum aromas having a cooked quality, but the flavors aren't overboard, maintaining some chocolate, cola, and plum, while the mouthfeel is pleasant, medium-full bodied with soft tannins. A blend of Merlot and Cabernet Sauvignon. **86** —*M.D. (12/31/2006)*

Le Bonheur 2000 Prima Merlot-Cabernet Sauvignon (Simonsberg-Stellenbosch) $15. A tasty 75% Merlot- 25% Cabernet blend with a dark berry, earth, and toast profile. Just slightly tart, this will stand up well to full-flavored and spicy foods. Shows good fruit-acid balance plus hints of sous-bois (under the trees) woodsiness . . . not just oaky woodiness. A firm structured middle-weight with solid appeal. **88** —*M.M. (4/1/2005)*

Le Bonheur 1999 Prima Merlot-Cabernet Sauvignon (Stellenbosch) $15. Though a Merlot-Cabernet blend, this wine's pronounced tart cherry and spice elements call to mind a Chianti. Then again, it's named Prima, so maybe the Italian profile was intended. It's flavorful and fairly light-bodied, with licorice and earth accents. Finishes with even tannins and a mineral note. **87** —*M.M. (3/1/2004)*

Le Bonheur 1998 Prima Red Blend (Stellenbosch) $15. This delicate wine features an interesting nose of leather, dried herbs and arugala. Ripe red plum flavors lead to an herbal finish with a hint of faint leather and vanilla curling up at the very end. The tannins provide gentle support to the soft acids and light-weight body. **86** —*K.F. (1/1/2004)*

Le Bonheur 2005 Sauvignon Blanc (Stellenbosch) $12. A good wine with flavors of citrus and yellow fruits, but it lacks the intensity and lively acids of previous vintages. Has aromas of white stone fruits and orange peel. **83** —*M.D. (12/31/2006)*

Le Bonheur 2003 Sauvignon Blanc (Stellenbosch) $11. Light and even with mild citrus herb and grass elements throughout. A slightly too-green note showed early on the nose, but was not on the palate. A good, straightforward example that's lean but not sharp, and finishes clean. **84** —*M.M. (11/15/2004)*

Le Bonheur 2000 Sauvignon Blanc (Stellenbosch) $13. **85** —*M.S. (1/1/2004)*

Le Bonheur 2004 Landgoed Sauvignon Blanc (Simonsberg-Stellenbosch) $13. Tasty juice with ample tangy citrus-herb tones over ripe melon and tropical fruit aromas and flavors. Has pizzazz, but no sharp edges, and finishes long with nice spicy notes. Easy to like and easy to drink, with good balance and some complexity. **87** —*M.M. (4/1/2005)*

Le Bonheur 2002 Landgoed Sauvignon Blanc (Stellenbosch) $11. The aromas of melon, white pepper, and fresh thyme meet with citrus and dry herbs on the palate. A lovely Sauvignon Blanc in a light style, with very clean acidity. **87** —*K.F. (1/1/2004)*

LE RICHE

Le Riche 1999 Reserve Cabernet Sauvignon (Stellenbosch) $30. Nicely balanced from nose to finish, this medium-weight Cabernet is more French than New World in style, with tart berry and tobacco elements prevailing. Very smooth on the palate, it finishes with fine tannins and a lingering tobacco note. **86** —*M.M. (3/1/2001)*

LEIDERSBURG

Leidersburg 2005 Vintner's Reserve Sauvignon Blanc (Coastal Region) $18. Offers mild aromas of mint and tropical fruit. It's a flavorful wine, with tropical and white stone fruit flavors, but it lacks some zest. **84** — *M.D. (3/1/2006)*

Leidersburg 2004 Vintner's Reserve Sauvignon Blanc (Coastal Region) $23. Super-clean and fresh, with pineapple, pink grapefruit, and ample minerality. Quite snappy and tasty, with mostly tropical fruit flavors and grassy notes. Graceful, with a light to medium palate feel. **87** *(7/1/2005)*

Leidersburg 2003 Vintner's Reserve Sur Lie Sauvignon Blanc (Coastal Region) $19. This even, elegant white is medium-weight and balanced, with a gentle citrus-hay bouquet. Shows poise, if less depth than the *sur lie* designation might suggest. A tasty and attractively tangy wine, with lemon-lime flavors and a dry, minerally close. **85** —*M.M. (7/1/2005)*

LONG NECK

Long Neck 2003 Cabernet Sauvignon (Western Cape) $8. A solid medium-weight with good fruit and mouthfeel. Perfect for burgers—better yet, blue or cheddar cheeseburgers. Yeah, the label sports a giraffe. But, in the end it's about the juice, and tasty and inexpensive always wins. **85 Best Buy** —*M.M. (12/15/2004)*

Long Neck 2003 Chardonnay (Western Cape) $8. Vaguely sweet and perfumy on the nose, but also shows nice mild tropical fruit and avoids cloying sweetness on the tongue. A modest but enjoyable simple Chardonnay, with a smooth feel and clean finish. An off-the-beaten-track choice for an inexpensive by-the-glass pour. **84 Best Buy** —*M.M. (12/15/2004)*

Long Neck 2003 Merlot (Western Cape) $8. Light red berry Merlot fruit wears a strong green bell pepper element from the nose on, and it stays out front all the way. The fruit is simply under-ripe. **80** —*M.M. (12/15/2004)*

Long Neck 2003 Shiraz (Western Cape) $8. Nose mostly mute; light in feel, it lacks fruit presence and flavor. Very mild red berry, cocoa, and toasty oak shadings show, mostly on the finish. Yes, it's a simple value wine, but where's the fruit? **82** —*M.M. (12/15/2004)*

LONGRIDGE

Longridge 1998 Merlot (Stellenbosch) $20. The right elements are here and show on the nose-berry/plum, a touch of earth and leather. On the palate, though, the wine displays sharp acidity, an angular profile, and tart plum flavors. Finishes lean, and could use more flesh, less bite. **84** — *M.M. (3/1/2001)*

Longridge 1999 Bay View Merlot (Stellenbosch) $10. This well-balanced Merlot displays a deep ruby/purple color and plenty of plum flavors. Coffee and herb notes add a touch of complexity and the texture is smooth and even. The finish has good length for a modestly priced red. **87 Best Buy** *(3/1/2001)*

Longridge 1998 Pinotage (Stellenbosch) $20. Dark cherry, toasted oak, and licorice notes mark the nose of this fairly full wine. Sweet and sour flavors, a smoky note, and an even finish with tarry elements all have significant appeal. The toasted-oak notes seem a bit heavy handed, but tasty. **87** *(3/1/2001)*

SOUTH AFRICA

Longridge 1999 Bayview Pinotage (South Africa) $10. This medium weight example shows Pinotage fruit in a forward, correct manner. Tart plum and berry, cherry, and leather aromas abound. Earth and dried plum flavors on the palate are kept lively by decent acidity; touches of tart red berry, rhubarb, and anise show on the moderately long finish. **86** *(3/1/2001)*

Longridge 1999 Bayview Syrah (Stellenbosch) $10. Tart, tart, tart. Did we mention tart? There's just not much here other than acidity. **80** *(10/1/2001)*

Longridge (S.Af) 1999 Chardonnay (Stellenbosch) $19. This well-oaked Chardonnay has a full apple and caramel bouquet, flavors that follow in suit, and a pleasing, round mouthfeel. There are no surprises here, but no let-downs either. A middle-of-the-road pleaser with nice toast and butterscotch notes on the back end. **87** *—M.M. (3/1/2001)*

LONGRIDGE BAY VIEW

Longridge Bay View 1999 Merlot (Stellenbosch) $10. This well-balanced Merlot displays a deep ruby/purple color and plenty of plum flavors. Coffee and herb notes add a touch of complexity, and the texture is smooth and even. The finish has good length for a modestly priced red. **87 Best Buy** *(3/1/2001)*

LOST HORIZONS

Lost Horizons 2001 Cabernet Sauvignon-Merlot (Western Cape) $8. This offers little complexity, but enough pleasure and tannins for a red meat pairing. Thin cherry, bread, and floral aromas carry to the palate, where the sweet, almost dried fruit shows some herbal bite at the back end. **85** *—K.F. (4/1/2003)*

LOUISVALE

Louisvale 2000 Chardonnay (Stellenbosch) $NA. A crisp style of wine, with green plums, lime, and kiwi fruit flavors. There's a fresh, poised balance between the light taste of wood and lively acidity, and just a touch of nutmeg and almonds to give it extra interest. **87** *—R.V. (9/10/2002)*

MALAN

Malan 2000 Family Vinter's Chardonnay (Stellenbosch) $8. This wine is produced by the Malan family of Simonsig Estate from purchased grapes. Light, fresh, with crisp, green fruit, it is an easy, pleasant wine to drink, well-made and delicious. There's a lovely, creamy, toffee aftertaste. **86 Best Buy** *—R.V. (7/1/2002)*

Malan 1999 Pinotage (Stellenbosch) $9. Berry, rhubarb, and cocoa show on this flavorful red's deep nose. It's even and lithe in feel, with substantial tart berry flavors offset by more cocoa notes and earthy accents. As in their Sauvignon Blanc, Malan displays a deft winemaking touch, allowing the handsome depth of fruit to shine, showing good extraction and balance. Drink now through 2004. **88 Best Buy** *—M.M. (4/1/2002)*

Malan 2001 Family Vinters Sauvignon Blanc (Stellenbosch) $8. Fragrant and very well-balanced, this opens with a grapefruit, grass, and mild tropical fruit nose. It's even and full on the tongue, with a ripe melon-spice palate. The long, smooth finish has a melony feel and tangerine hints. Shows fine Sauvignon Blanc character and avoids edgy, exaggerated herbaceousness. **89 Best Buy** *—M.M. (4/1/2002)*

MAN VINTNERS

MAN Vintners 2005 Cabernet Sauvignon (Coastal Region) $10. The MAN in the name is the initial letters of the wives (Marie, Anette, and Nicky) of the three partners in this 75,000-case joint venture between Charles Back of Fairview, José Condé of Stark-Condé, and Tyrrel Myburgh of Joosetenberg. This is a ripe, juicy fruity wine that bounces with energy and fresh vitality if not much subtlety. **85 Best Buy** *—R.V. (11/1/2006)*

MAN Vintners 2004 Cabernet Sauvignon (Western Cape) $10. Nice redberry dominate the nose and palate, with aromas of menthol mixing in, and flavors of tobacco emerging with time. Smooth and simple, this wine finishes a bit warm. **85 Best Buy** *—M.D. (3/1/2006)*

MAN Vintners 2005 Chardonnay (Coastal Region) $10. This wine doesn't seem to know where it's going. Nice tropical fruit and stone aromas lead to more generic white fruit in the mouth, but then picks up some butterscotch notes that don't match with the lean feel and tart finish. Nice

in parts, but doesn't add up to an integrated whole. **83** *—M.D. (5/1/2006)*

MAN Vintners 2005 Chenin Blanc (Coastal Region) $9. A joint venture with the Myburgh brothers of Joostenberg and Jose Conde of Stark-Conde has produced an attractive, aromatic Chenin—it's very floral. It has good acidity, a fresh, soft easy style and lifted acidity to the finish. **86 Best Buy** *—R.V. (11/15/2005)*

MAN Vintners 2004 Pinotage (Western Cape) $10. This wine packs the usual from a young Pinotage: cherry and cassis, with some dill and lemon peel one the nose. But the mouthfeel is harsh, with acids overpowering the feel of the wine. **81** *—M.D. (5/1/2006)*

MAN Vintners 2005 Sauvignon Blanc (Western Cape) $10. The aromas of this wine are all over the place: Grassy and green; chalk and sawdust; and grilled plantains. In the mouth the grassy element dominates, with some sweet corn and mild fruitiness. Simple in the mouth, with a cleansing finish. **83** *—M.D. (5/1/2006)*

MAN Vintners 2004 Shiraz (Western Cape) $10. This purple wine has a brambly quality to the sweet vanilla-and-plum nose. Oak is apparent in the mouth, with dusty vanilla flavors. Simple, with a bit of a weedy quality to the finish. **83** *—M.D. (3/1/2006)*

MAS NICOLAS

Mas Nicolas 2000 Cape Shiraz-Cabernet Sauvignon (Stellenbosch) $34. This wine has a thin streak of eucalyptus throughout. As a foil to that green note, there is red licorice, cassis, sweet cherry, and black plum to entice. Pleasant notes of molasses, oiled leather, and white pepper round out the palate. **86** *—K.F. (8/1/2003)*

MATUBA

Matuba 2003 Premium Select Cabernet Sauvignon (Coastal Region) $12. Dry, chalky tannins frame this woody wine with modest aromas of berry, earth, and leather. The finish shows a hint of lemon and more leather, but the wood overpowers the dark berry fruit in the mouth. **85** *—M.D. (9/1/2006)*

Matuba 2004 Premium Select Chardonnay (Coastal Region) $12. Rounded in the mouth, with decent balance, this has nice fruit and spice, even if the impression is not lasting. Citrus pith, oak spice, and a touch of petrol surround tropical fruit flavors. Finish is brief. **84** *—M.D. (11/1/2006)*

Matuba 2004 Vineyards Specific Chardonnay (Coastal Region) $15. Has sweet white fruit aromas, like peaches that have been sitting in the sun too long. Citrusy in the mouth, with a medium body but a flat feel. Finishes with a hint of spice. **84** *—M.D. (9/1/2006)*

Matuba 2004 Premium Select Chenin Blanc (Western Cape) $12. Light gold, this has a touch of oak to the nose, adding sweetness to aromas of tropical fruit. Rounder and fuller than unoaked Chenins, with a touch of sweetness from the oak, this nevertheless has good acidity propping up yellow fruit flavors touched with spice. **85** *—M.D. (11/1/2006)*

MEERLUST

Meerlust 2001 Rubicon Bordeaux Blend (Stellenbosch) $30. Over a quarter of a century ago, this was one of the first South African Bordeaux blends. It is still one of the best, a ripely tannic, firm wine that owes a lot to the structure given by ripe grapes from mature vines. Great acidity, great black currant fruits, and great style. **94 Editors' Choice** *—R.V. (11/1/2006)*

Meerlust 2003 Chardonnay (Stellenbosch) $19. Heavy notes of vanilla and caramel, char, and menthol herald the oak in this wine. But on the palate the oak is well-integrated with white stone fruit and crème brûlée flavors. Seemingly soft at first, this wine has a strong, fruity core that carries it right through the buttery finish. **88** *—M.D. (3/1/2006)*

Meerlust 1998 Chardonnay (Stellenbosch) $20. Light notes of firm cheese, brown mustard, and toast confirm this wine's age. Following on the palate are watery fruit and herb flavors accented by soft acids and finishing with a toasty, herbal streak. **83** *—K.F. (9/1/2003)*

Meerlust 2000 Merlot (Stellenbosch) $25. Chocolaty and ripe on the nose, with cassis, plum, cola, and eucalyptus aromas. As complex in the mouth, with blueberry and oak in addition to plum and cola. The wine has a racy mouthfeel yet is full-bodied, with nice tannins and a solid finish. **90** —*M.D. (12/31/2006)*

Meerlust 2000 Rubicon Red Blend (Stellenbosch) $30. This Cab-dominant Bordeaux blend opens slowly, eventually showing blueberry, pastry, and cedar aromas. Tobacco and earth take the stage in the mouth, along with more blueberry and pie crust. The smooth, evolved tannins offer a seamless mouthfeel; will continue to evolve over the next five years. **90** —*M.D. (7/1/2006)*

Meerlust 1997 Rubicon Red Blend (Stellenbosch) $28. Rich red plum and currant notes contrast with leafy herbs and leather on the palate. All of this carries to the well-balanced finish. This wine is hearty enough for a solid red meat pairing. Drink 2003–2008. **87** —*K.F. (9/1/2003)*

MEINERT

Meinert 2000 Cabernet Sauvignon (Devon Valley) $25. The red plum and cassis aromas are meaty and oak-laden and carry to the smoky palate. This simple wine shows firm tannins and good acids, finishing with a toasty herbal note. **84** —*K.F. (8/1/2003)*

Meinert 2000 Merlot (Devon Valley) $20. The clean, juicy acidity provides a consistent backdrop to the thinned flavors of dark earth, plum, and dark chocolate. Throughout, and especially on the finish, is an oaky overlay with a hint of herbs. **84** —*K.F. (8/1/2003)*

Meinert 2000 Synchronicity Red Blend (Devon Valley) $35. This wine is the unequivocal standout of the Meinert portfolio. From nose to palate, just-crushed dried herbs, sprinkles of light brown sugar, and thick, lush plum, blueberry, and blackberry fruit serenade the senses. The oaking is interlaced at every step with the fresh fruit. Trust your heart and take it home to meet the parents. **90** —*K.F. (9/1/2003)*

MIDDELVLEI

Middelvlei 1995 Cabernet Sauvignon (Stellenbosch) $17. This medium-weight Cabernet displays plum, slightly candied cherry, and a little smoke on the nose and palate. Well-balanced with good persistence, this is an easy, pleasing glass of red that's ready to drink now. **87** —*M.N. (3/1/2001)*

Middelvlei 1996 Pinotage (Stellenbosch) $17. This light offering shows berry-cherry fruit and an herb note on the nose. The palate is even and dry with bing cherry flavors, but an evident greenness keeps the wine from blossoming fully. Finishes dry, with a mildly astringent and slightly woody note. **84** *(3/1/2001)*

Middelvlei 1998 Red Blend (Stellenbosch) $16. A jammy and meaty nose with dark currant, plum, and leather accents opens this straight-ahead, pleasing wine. Dark berry flavors fill the mouth and the tart-sweet fruit works well with the modest wood. Displays judicious use of the differing attributes of the blended grapes and oak. **86** *(3/1/2001)*

Middelvlei 1996 Syrah (Stellenbosch) $17. Brine, pine, and camphor on the nose obscures what black fruit lies beneath. Odd chestnut, acorn, and shoe polish notes on the thin palate lead into a salty, corned beef-meets-menthol finish. **81** *(10/1/2001)*

MILES MOSSOP

Miles Mossop 2004 Saskia White Blend (Coastal Region) $35. Tokara's winemaker has crafted this full-bodied wine under his own label. It has plenty of flesh and orange and apricot flavors from Viognier, despite the other two-thirds being Chenin Blanc. But the real dominant force here is the oak, which the wine wears tightly wrapped, hiding the fruit character. Vanilla and spice hit the palate and continue through the finish, where alcohol warms things up. **87** —*M.D. (11/1/2006)*

MISCHA

Mischa 2004 Shiraz (Wellington) $27. There's a bit of a bubble gum quality to the full fruit flavors, but aside from that this wine shows lots of promise. Graham cracker spices up a fruity nose of cassis and crushed grapes, while the flavors are as purple as the color. A bit tart in acid with tannins on the chalky side. **87** —*M.D. (12/31/2006)*

MISSIONVALE

Missionvale 2000 Walker Bay Chardonnay (South Africa) $NA. The team of Peter Finlayson (brother of Walter from Glen Carlou) and Burgundian

Paul Bouchard make great Pinot Noir and Chardonnay in the cool climate of Hermanus, just a ridge away from the ocean. The palate is concentrated, spicy, and smoky, with smooth ripe fruit, flavors of butter, and hot toast. It is all topped off with a delicious, fresh layer of acidity. **91** —*R.V. (9/10/2002)*

MONTEROSSO

Monterosso 2005 Bush Vine Chenin Blanc (Stellenbosch) $NA. Very soft, without a huge lift or character, but the wine does have freshness and cleanness and a low price. Some currant flavors in the aftertaste give a lift. **84** —*R.V. (11/15/2005)*

MONTESTELL

Montestell 2002 Reserve Cabernet Sauvignon (Paarl) $18. Aromas of menthol and stewed berry translate to the mouth, with some additional green pepper flavor. This wine's structure is hollow and flabby, with a sharp, tangy finish. **82** —*M.D. (3/1/2006)*

Montestell 2000 Reserve Cabernet Sauvignon (Paarl) $20. Oiled leather, cocoa, and red delicious apple aromas work well with the palate of sweet blackberries and cedar. Ripe red plum and anise serve as ample support through to the pepper and blackberry layered finish. This is uncomplicated and fruit-forward. **88** —*K.F. (4/1/2003)*

Montestell 2001 Reserve Pinotage (Paarl) $14. The tart berry flavors here wear some cinnamon, chocolate, and earth accents. Still, they can't rise above stronger bitter notes and sharp tannins. **82** —*M.M. (11/15/2004)*

Montestell 2000 Reserve Pinotage (Paarl) $16. Red plum, caramel and dried meat aromas and flavors. The toasty finish has herbal and vegetal qualities. **84** —*K.F. (4/1/2003)*

Montestell 2002 Reserve Shiraz (Paarl) $18. Flavorful, with plenty of dark fruit accented by ample toasty oak and good mouthfeel. Has classic tart-sweet Shiraz flavors plus a subtle, complimentary undertone of Cape earthiness. Closes smoothly and smokily. **86** —*M.M. (11/15/2004)*

MOOIUITZICHT

Mooiuitzicht NV Old Tawny Port (Western Cape) $16. Light tawny in color, with dried fruits and caramel on the nose and palate. Not heavy in feel, but a touch hot with some tangy tannins. **85** —*M.M. (11/15/2004)*

MÔRESON

Môreson 2003 Magia Bordeaux Blend (Coastal Region) $27. A Bordeaux blend, with 60% Cabernet Sauvignon, 16% Cabernet Franc, and 24% Merlot, supposedly named because a passing Bulgarian described the wine as Magia (magical). In fact, it is in an elegant style, not hugely intense, but with good berry flavors, some herbal character, and a sweet, juicy finish. **87** —*R.V. (11/1/2006)*

Môreson 2004 Cabernet Sauvignon (Coastal Region) $27. A fruit-packed wine that shows varietal character with its dusty tannins and black currant flavors. Layers of chocolate and toast go with the finishing intense, young acidity. Give this 2–3 years. **89** —*R.V. (11/1/2006)*

Môreson 1998 Cabernet Sauvignon (Coastal Region) $20. Woody notes mix with leather and light brown sugar that carry to the palate with cedar, tobacco, and meaty red plum. The oaking is well-integrated, the meatiness is attractive, and the wine is a great example of South Africa's Old World bent. **87** —*K.F. (8/1/2003)*

Môreson 1997 Cabernet Sauvignon (Franschhoek) $25. The aromas and flavors of tobacco, anise, and apple peels are fleshed out with vivid fruit, in the form of blackberries and plums. A bit of air develops the consuming sensation of pepper into an herby char on the finish, and chalky, coating tannins on the body. **88** —*K.F. (4/1/2003)*

Môreson 2004 Premium Chardonnay (Franschhoek) $19. Nice Chard fruit has just enough oak on the nose, leading to a smooth, creamy mouth with tropical and white stone fruits whetted with mint and oak. Despite the fruitiness, this is dry, with plenty of spicy oak on the finish. **87** —*M.D. (11/1/2006)*

Môreson 2004 Chenin Blanc (Franschhoek) $14. From mature bush vines, this wine is fresh, balanced, and with just a fine touch of spice and some honey. The Môreson vineyard is on the flat valley floor of the

Franschhoek valley, giving some ripe, full-bodied fruit. 85 —R.V. (11/15/2005)

Môreson 2001 Chenin Blanc (Franschhoek) $13. The acidity of this wine is simply refreshing. Distinct honey and lemon peel aromas follow through the palate to the long, herbed finish. 86 —K.F. (4/1/2003)

Môreson 1999 Merlot (Franschhoek) $23. This delicate wine is well balanced, with fine tannins and an elegant sensory package. Lightly grilled meat, potting soil, cinnamon, vanilla, and cherry aromas meet with toast, leather, cherry, and dried herb flavors. 88 —K.F. (4/1/2003)

Môreson 2004 Pinotage (Coastal Region) $20. Nice berry flavors are nuanced with chocolate and oak, leading to a lighter style of Pinotage with lifting acidity and sweet purple fruit. Lemony oak and Rainier cherry flavors follow through to the quick finish. 86 —M.D. (11/1/2006)

Môreson 1999 Magia Red Blend (Coastal Region) $25. A medicinal note goes hand in hand with those of cedar, char, and dried mint on the nose. The palate is full of sweet, ripe currants with pepper, cinnamon, and more char and mint. Sandy tannins are well-matched with refreshing acidity and a good-length finish. 87 —K.F. (9/1/2003)

Môreson 2001 Sauvignon Blanc (Franschhoek) $16. This is a grassy, lean bottling with a bit too much asparagus and vegetal notes on both the nose and palate. The flavor profile features some grapefruit and green apple, but the fruit is rather dilute and distant. Beyond that, the finish is dry, almost like drinking club soda. 85 (8/1/2002)

Môreson NV Blanc de Blanc Brut Sparkling Blend (Franschhoek) $19. Yeasty to start, with moderate yellow fruit aromas that transfer to a soft and creamy mouthfeel. A bit too soft, though, with low acidity letting the wine get flabby. 90% Chardonnay, 10% Chenin Blanc. 83 —M.D. (12/31/2006)

MORGENHOF

Morgenhof 2001 Premiere Selection Bordeaux Blend (Stellenbosch) $35. A classic Bordeaux blend, dominated by 60% Cabernet Sauvignon, Premiere Selection is a ripe wine, layered with sweet fruit dominating firm tannins. Despite those tannins, the big fruit flavors mean the wine is ready to drink now. 91 —R.V. (11/1/2006)

Morgenhof 1997 Premiere Selection Cabernet Blend (Stellenbosch) $20. The dry, tart berry, earth, and tobacco profile is appealingly elegant, as is the lean but solid feel and good acidity. Closes long with tobacco and spice notes, and could pass for a Bordeaux cru bourgeois, or even a lesser classified growth. It's drinking well now, but should improve further through 2004. 90 Editors' Choice —M.M. (4/1/2002)

Morgenhof 2001 Reserve Cabernet Sauvignon (Stellenbosch) $45. Matured in 100% new French oak, and it shows on the palate with tight wood tannins. This concentrated wine shows a dense, dark, brooding power from the estate's oldest block of Cabernet vines. The tannins at the end are dry, and the wine deserves another four or five years to mature. 89 —R.V. (11/1/2006)

Morgenhof 1999 Estate Chardonnay (Stellenbosch) $12. This French-run estate (the family is involved with Gosset Champagne and Cointreau liqueurs) has produced a stunning Chardonnay. Big on creamy fruit and nutty, buttery flavors, this wine pairs toast, acidity, and ripe fruit in a fine, complex balance. 90 Best Buy —R.V. (7/1/2002)

Morgenhof 1998 Merlot (Stellenbosch) $16. Very international in style, with a dark berry and sweet oak bouquet. It's smooth on the tongue, with licorice accents and a similar profile to that of the nose. Picks up a nice cocoa note on the long, even finish. This can be criticized for being a bit anonymous with its ultra-smooth feel and dark toast patina, but it sure is tasty, and will have wide appeal. Drink now–2004. 88 —M.M. (4/1/2002)

Morgenhof 2001 Sauvignon Blanc (Stellenbosch) $9. That the aromas are sweet and perfumed is unconventional, given that South African SBs tend to be on the sharper side. In the mouth, lime and peach flavors are solid until the finish. Detracting from the overall package, however, is a somewhat flat-feeling palate. 85 —M.S. (4/1/2002)

MOUNTAIN GATE

Mountain Gate 2000 Cabernet Sauvignon (Stellenbosch) $15. Accessible, medium-weight, and in the international style. The typical South African earth and iodine notes are nicely tamed here. They compliment rather than obscure the dry, dark berry fruit, offering just enough character keep this from being generic. Finishes with cocoa hints. 86 —M.M. (3/1/2004)

Mountain Gate 2001 Sauvignon Blanc (Stellenbosch) $9. Opens with enticing aromas of hay, fresh peaches, and boxwood. The distinct flavors of white peach, nectarine, and sweet pear juice are fresh and rich. The weighty fruit sings through to the finish, where it closes with an herbal tang. 87 —K.F. (9/1/2003)

MULDERBOSCH

Mulderbosch 2003 Chardonnay (Stellenbosch) $24. Although not barrel fermented, there is still plenty of oak to this wine. A toasty nose of vanilla and caramel caresses green fruit, and in the mouth steely acidity undergirds intense flavors of tropical fruit, citrus, and sweet oak. The harmonious balance suggests this wine will maintain its character throughout this decade. 88 —M.D. (9/1/2006)

Mulderbosch 2002 Barrel Fermented Chardonnay (Stellenbosch) $38. A touch buttery on the nose at first, this wine quickly shows mango, vanilla and toast aromas. Big in the mouth, but with a firm line of acidity to hold it in check, the warm flavors of tropical fruits are backed by plenty of toasty, spicy oak. An intense finish is magnified by a dash of lasting acidity. 89 —M.D. (9/1/2006)

Mulderbosch 1999 Barrel Fermented Chardonnay (Stellenbosch) $23. Mike Dobrovic, winemaker at Mulderbosch, coaxes a blend of open rich fruit with a spine of steel from his fruit. The wine is definitely New World in style with its creamy wood flavors, yet it also has the ability to age, which is more Burgundian in character. 91 —R.V. (7/1/2002)

Mulderbosch 2004 Chenin Blanc (Stellenbosch) $14. From bush vines on slopes just north of Stellenbosch, this wine has crisp apple and toast flavors, balanced with lively acidity. There is some gooseberry character, plus just a hint of honey from the noble rot grapes that were used in the blend to leave just a touch of sweetness. 87 —R.V. (11/15/2005)

Mulderbosch 2002 Shiraz (Western Cape) $69. A very smooth, dry wine with tight acidity and a hint of alcohol to the palate. Aromas of dark fruits are a bit roasted, while plum and blueberry flavors are tinged with leather bordering on Band-Aid. Finishes warm, with vanilla accents. 87 —M.D. (9/1/2006)

NATURAL STATE

Natural State 1999 Cape Soleil Shiraz (Coastal Region) $12. This lightweight, juicy, organically farmed South African wine has a coffee edge to its tart berry fruit. Even on the palate, it turns harder on the finish with edgy, metallic tannins—too much for the weight and density of fruit. 82 (10/1/2001)

NEDERBURG

Nederburg 2002 Cabernet Sauvignon (Western Cape) $10. An attractive claret-style red whose dark fruit wears tea, earth, and forest-note accents. With its positive mouthfilling feel, good balance, and dark fruit/coffee close, this is good, lighter-styled Cabernet at a light price. 85 Best Buy —M.M. (4/1/2005)

Nederburg 2001 Cabernet Sauvignon (Western Cape) $11. A light Cabernet Sauvignon, with tart cherry and cranberry aromas and flavors. Not unlike the estate's Private Bin wine, but with less weight, texture, and length . . . and price. Closes with wood-mineral accents over dry fruit. 82 —M.M. (3/1/2004)

Nederburg 2001 Private Bin Cabernet Sauvignon (South Africa) $18. A mid-weight with a pleasing, smooth palate feel and tart, dried cherry and cranberry qualities. But it's also rather woody, and the oak starts to dominate as it opens. Still, many people enjoy lots of oak, here used interestingly against atypical-for-Cabernet light berry fruit. Closes long with dry, even tannins. 84 —M.M. (3/1/2004)

Nederburg 2002 Edelrood Cabernet Sauvignon-Merlot (Western Cape) $11. This simple Bordeaux blend opens with an attractive red berry-rhubarb

SOUTH AFRICA

and toast nose, but not much follows. It's light-weight and not amply fruited, closing tart with quite drying tannins. **83** —*M.M. (4/1/2005)*

Nederburg 2001 Chardonnay (Western Cape) $10. The nose is a delicate blend of toasting bread, tropical fruit, and hayloft aromas. The tropical fruit extends to the palate of caramel and toast, with a twang of drying bitterness at the back. The acidity is almost spritzy. **86** —*K.F. (4/1/2003)*

Nederburg 2003 Pinotage (Western Cape) $11. This ruby-red wine has a lot to offer. It offers vanilla, spice, Maraschino cherry, and cola in the nose, while the palate is packed with more cherry, vanilla, a mild minerality and some lemon notes. It finishes smooth, with coffee and spice. **88 Best Buy** —*M.D. (3/1/2006)*

Nederburg 2003 Paarl Riesling (Western Cape) $10. Light and taut, with bright acidity underlying grass and mineral aromas and flavors, plus kerosene hints. The light lemon and grape flavors are appealing. An attractive, inexpensive white for sipping or light dining. **85 Best Buy** —*M.M. (7/1/2005)*

Nederburg 2005 Sauvignon Blanc (Western Cape) $11. This wine has a vegetal character, but tropical fruit flavors are just as dominant. Intense flavors and aromas, lively acidity, and a warm finish make this an ideal match for oily foods. **87 Best Buy** —*M.D. (3/1/2006)*

Nederburg 2003 Sauvignon Blanc (Western Cape) $9. This opens to display classic herb-grass-grapefruit aromas. A lively zing and bright citrus-grass notes show on the tongue. Shines most, with some class, on the longer-than-expected, lime, and mineral-tinged finish. **87 Best Buy** —*M.M. (3/1/2004)*

Nederburg 2003 Private Bin Sauvignon Blanc (South Africa) $15. Shows an angular profile, with amped-up grassy-gooseberry-cat pee elements, though warmer spice notes appear on the close. Different and more intense, but not necessarily better than the winery's regular bottling—it's more a matter of style. **87** —*M.M. (3/1/2004)*

Nederburg 2002 Shiraz (Western Cape) $11. On the nose, plum and juicy berry are joined by cocoa powder and vanilla. With air, grilled meat aromas emerge. The palate starts out a bit sweet with vanilla, but quickly picks up fruit, spice, and charred meat notes. All this in a package that is soft without being simple. **88 Best Buy** —*M.D. (5/1/2006)*

Nederburg 2001 Shiraz (Paarl) $11. This wine is on the fringe from the funky opening notes of gamy Syrah fruit with their almost fishy tinge. The mouthfeel is soft, but the flavors sour. A wine that simply doesn't cohere or recommend itself. **80** —*M.M. (3/1/2004)*

Nederburg 2001 Private Bin Shiraz (South Africa) $18. Why does the perception that more oak makes a better wine persist? This basic, solid wine, like too many others, suffers from an excess of oak. The sound black plum fruit, with its nice earthy accents, struggles to assert itself. When it peeks through, it's lovely. Black pepper notes show on the even finish. **85** —*M.M. (3/1/2004)*

Nederburg 2005 Lyric White Blend (Western Cape) $11. Pungent, grassy aromas herald Sauvignon Blanc, which makes up 60% of this blend. There's also good intensity in the mouth, with Chenin adding flavors of almond, as well as high acidity and a grassy bite, and the 19% Chardonnay possibly responsible for tropical fruit notes. Finishes clean, with a hint of oak. **87 Best Buy** —*M.D. (11/1/2006)*

Nederburg 2004 Lyric White Blend (Western Cape) $10. This floral white will win lots of fans if you bring it to a family dinner. Nothing wrong here, just a sweet and soft puffball. Perfect for relatives who can't comprehend how or why we love and drink some of the denser, drier, or more offbeat, challenging wines we do. **83** —*M.M. (4/1/2005)*

Nederburg 2003 Special Late Harvest White Blend (Western Cape) $10. A tasty, vaguely spritzy and ethereal dessert wine that opens with faint white peach and apricot-lemon aromas. Lacks body, but has tasty sweet apricot, baked apple, and honey flavors. It's not very complex but also avoids being cloying. Finishes with a drier mineral undertone. **85 Best Buy** —*M.M. (4/1/2005)*

Nederburg 2005 Stein White Blend (Western Cape) $11. A blend of four white grapes, this semisweet white has pineapple and citrus aromas mixed with menthol. In the mouth it's creamy, with flavors of white fruits, nuts, menthol, and flowers. Enjoy with mild curry dishes. **87 Best Buy** —*M.D. (7/1/2006)*

NEIL ELLIS

Neil Ellis 2003 Cabernet Sauvignon (Stellenbosch) $23. This excellent Cab has a Bordeaux-like nose, with forest floor meeting meaty red fruit and oak. Big tannins offer great structure without over-powering, and the wine has enough acid to feel alive. Barnyard flavors show on the palate, accompanied by complex coffee and red berry. A juxtaposition of Old World structure and New World fruit—this is why South African wine can excel. **90** —*M.D. (7/1/2006)*

Neil Ellis 1999 Cabernet Sauvignon (Stellenbosch) $17. Sweet and smoky berry fruit greets you. Black cherries with ample vanilla oak warm the core. The acids are racy, and drive the wine through the lengthy, round finish. Give it another year or two, if possible. **87** —*M.S. (4/1/2002)*

Neil Ellis 2003 Vineyard Selection Cabernet Sauvignon (Jonkershoek Valley) $43. Nearly black, this big wine smells like dark berries dipped in vanilla cream, with a hint of barnyard. The barnyard carries to the palate, where it's joined by leather and blackberry. Tannins start off smooth, but develop plenty of grip with time. Warm throughout, this is one that should be decanted a few hours before serving. **88** —*M.D. (9/1/2006)*

Neil Ellis 2003 Cabernet Sauvignon-Merlot (Stellenbosch) $20. Old World aromas of earth, tobacco, and pencil shavings blend nicely with cassis. The combination continues through the dry, chalky palate. Some vegetal flavors mar the palate, as does a tart feel, but give this wine some time to develop and it should reward you. **87** —*M.D. (7/1/2006)*

Neil Ellis 2002 Cabernet Sauvignon-Merlot (Stellenbosch) $15. A 61% Cabernet Sauvignon and 39% Merlot black beauty with some intriguing tart berry, Indian spices, popcorn, and licorice whiffs on the nose. It's quite dark, adding espresso and smoke notes on the palate and a very dry, briskly tannic finish. **86** —*M.M. (11/15/2004)*

Neil Ellis 2004 Chardonnay (Stellenbosch) $20. Compared to Neil Ellis's Elgin Chard, this one, from the warmer Stellenbosch region, has more banana and other white fruit components but less acidity. Plenty of oak character shows through, even some popcorn on the nose; finishes with a dash of spicy white fruit. **87** —*M.D. (7/1/2006)*

Neil Ellis 2004 Chardonnay (Elgin) $23. Subdued yet elegant, with a heavily oaked, toasty vanilla nose. Big and plump in the mouth, this wine retains a creamy feel, its tropical fruit flavors taking some time to emerge. The long, lingering finish attests to the wine's depth of character. **90 Editors' Choice** —*M.D. (7/1/2006)*

Neil Ellis 2003 Chardonnay (Stellenbosch) $17. Classy, dry Chardonnay with an angular flint-smoke-lime bouquet. There's ample oak here, and the fruit is present but quite reigned-in, with a crisp palate feel similar to Chablis. Tasty, long, and drinkable now, this will benefit from a year in the bottle. **89 Editors' Choice** —*M.M. (11/15/2004)*

Neil Ellis 2000 Chardonnay (Elgin) $20. While Neil Ellis's winery is in Stellenbosch, he gets his Chardonnay for this wine from the cooler region of Elgin. It has sweet, almost tropical fruit aromas, followed through with spicy, creamy, wood flavors and ripe, generous acidity. Despite its richness, it also has delicacy, as much in the finely judged use of wood as in the clean, elegant fruit. **91** —*R.V. (7/1/2002)*

Neil Ellis 2005 Sauvignon Blanc (Stellenbosch) $18. Moderate white stone fruit aromas lead to greener flavors of asparagus, edamame and gooseberry. This is a wine with a lot of kick, but finishes on the tangy side. **85** —*M.D. (7/1/2006)*

Neil Ellis 2004 Sauvignon Blanc (Groenekloof) $14. Light on its feet yet with surprising substance, another tasty, winning white from Neil Ellis. Early-on his wines helped introduce South Africa as a serious producing region to unacquainted American enthusiasts. Herb, grass, papaya, and mineral notes are juxtaposed handsomely here. The feel is taut and angular, the finish long, and a screwtop cap again puts him in the forward guard. **89 Best Buy** —*M.M. (4/1/2005)*

Neil Ellis 2003 Sauvignon Blanc (Groenekloof) $14. Starts with soft ripe melon, pear, and tropical fruit notes. Turns crisper and more typically Sauvignon Blanc on the tongue, where satisfying grapefruit flavors show classic herb and pepper accents and a fairly full yet crisp feel. **88** —*M.M. (11/15/2004)*

SOUTH AFRICA

Neil Ellis 2001 Sauvignon Blanc (Groenekloof) $15. Powerful and steely best describe the nose, and the palate is equally racy and intense. But sheer zest doesn't make up for the fact the fruit is lean and distant. No matter how hard you dig, there's only some lean green apple prior to a short, clean, tight finish. **85** —*M.S. (4/1/2002)*

Neil Ellis 2000 Sauvignon Blanc (Groenekloof) $15. Fat-bodied but tangy, with grapefruit and lime aromas and flavors. A touch of figginess and a tangerine note on the palate balance the flavor profile. There's lovely texture—quite full for Sauvignon Blanc—and a long ripe finish. **90** —*M.M. (3/1/2001)*

Neil Ellis 2005 Sincerely Sauvignon Blanc (Western Cape) $15. Banana and pear with green notes grace the nose and palate in a simple, soft wine with only moderate acidity. Best for summer afternoon quaffing. **84** —*M.D. (7/1/2006)*

Neil Ellis 2003 Shiraz (Stellenbosch) $23. Starts off with wonderful, very fragrant aromas of pepper, smoke, vanilla, tobacco, mint, and ripe black currant. It's smooth in the mouth, with mouthcoating flavors of sweet purple fruit and oak spice caressing the tongue. The only flaw is that the oak is a bit overpowering, with vanilla shadowing the fruit. **88** —*M.D. (7/1/2006)*

Neil Ellis 1999 Shiraz (Stellenbosch) $19. Coffee, earth, and sour herb aromas (some described the bouquet as also having cola and sausage-y notes) show up again on the palate—the coffee and herb flavors are particularly prevalent, and seem to envelope the blueberry and blackberry palate flavors. Mouthfeel is even, though on the lean side; finishes with smoked meat and pepper flavors. **86** *(10/1/2001)*

Neil Ellis 2004 Sincerely Shiraz (Western Cape) $15. Vibrant purple in color, with fresh aromas of grapes, violets, and vanilla, this wine has smooth tannins, nice body, and pleasing dark berry fruit. Some Band-Aid character shows through, but this wine is good overall. Would go well with braised ribs. **86** —*M.D. (7/1/2006)*

Neil Ellis 2003 Vineyard Selection Syrah (Jonkershoek Valley) $43. The Jonkershoek Valley receives more rain than almost anywhere else in South Africa, but that hasn't negatively affected this wine. Big, chewy, and warm, at 15% alcohol, this Shiraz has solid tannins and flavors of blueberry, coffee, earth, and a touch of vanilla. The nose offers much of the same, with semisweet chocolate adding to the complexity. Finishes with good length and plenty of spicy fruit. **89** —*M.D. (7/1/2006)*

NEW WORLD

New World 2002 Sémillon-Chardonnay (Western Cape) $9. The tasty tropical fruits of papaya and dried pineapple are wrapped in hay, toast, and oak. This starts off a bit soft, but gets racier, with the acidity cleaning up the fruit on the creamy finish. **85** —*K.F. (4/1/2003)*

New World 2002 Syrah (Western Cape) $10. This wine seems to reach out to the mainstream: flavors and aromas of sweet vanilla, cinnamon toast, and brown sugar are met with lightweight red fruit, a soft balance, and just a touch of white pepper. Inoffensive on all counts, but lacks the depth needed to set it apart. **86** —*K.F. (8/1/2003)*

NIEL JOUBERT

Niel Joubert 2001 African Tradition Collection Leopard Cabernet Sauvignon (Paarl) $12. A heavy note of baking spices is found throughout those of fleshy red plum, brown sugar, and sweet red licorice, finishing with mild dried herbs. The bracing acidity makes this a natural for the cheese course. Try with blue cheese. **86** —*K.F. (8/1/2003)*

Niel Joubert 2002 African Tradition Collection Buffalo Chardonnay (Paarl) $12. This wine offers lots of toast, cream, and brown sugar, with notes of pineapple and white nectarine. Some herbaceous notes make it taste less than fully ripe, yet it's soft and quite viscous on the palate. A good quaffer at a fair price. **86** —*K.F. (9/1/2003)*

Niel Joubert 2000 African Tradition Collection Lion Merlot (Paarl) $12. This wine is a delightful nod to Old World styling. The nose of dry leather, humidor, and earth carries to the palate with additional notes of dried herbs, plum, and apple skins. The light weight balance should give this wide appeal. **87** —*K.F. (8/1/2003)*

Niel Joubert 2001 African Tradition Collection Rhinoceros Red Blend (Paarl) $12. Dry earth, leather, and a spiciness reminiscent of cayenne pepper fill the nose and spread out across the palate, accented by plummy fruit. This youthful wine is a little spritzy, but should mellow within a few months, or just decant prior to serving. Try with pork tenderloin or lamb. **87** —*K.F. (9/1/2003)*

Niel Joubert 2000 African Tradition Collection Elephant Shiraz (Paarl) $12. The balance of this wine has slightly spritzy acidity in the lead, wrapped with sheer tannins. Rich aromas of earth, leather, and toast are contrasted by the bright fruit which is a sweet candylike strawberry-cherry at the forepalate. **86** —*K.F. (8/1/2003)*

NITÍDA

Nitída 2003 Calligraphy Bordeaux Blend (Durbanville) $25. A blend of almost equal parts Merlot, Cab Franc, and Cab Sauvignon, this wine has nice cassis and tobacco notes on the nose that translate to the mouth, adding some spicy earth and tart berry. Big on the palate, with solid tannins to back it up, it picks up some lemony notes on the finish. **87** —*M.D. (5/1/2006)*

Nitída 2002 Pinotage (Durbanville) $15. There's a ripe core of fruit under this wine's massive veneer of animal funkiness, but it's hard to find. Complex tart red berry, vanilla, and licorice notes on the nose are quickly buried. A funky metallic-earthiness—too much for most noses and palates—takes over, and that's the whole story here. **81** —*M.M. (12/15/2004)*

Nitída 2005 Sauvignon Blanc (Durbanville) $15. A strong nose of cat pee and green bean leads to pleasing flavors of gooseberries. The high acidity in this wine calls for food, so try it with oysters. **85** —*M.D. (5/1/2006)*

Nitída 2003 Sauvignon Blanc (Durbanville) $15. Clean and fresh, with lime-herb aromas and flavors. Taut mineral and sour grass elements here are on a par with solid Loire or New Zealand Sauvignon Blanc. A firm acid backbone sits over lurking ripe tropical fruit notes. This begs for grilled seafood or pork in a lime marinade. **88** —*M.M. (12/15/2004)*

Nitída 2003 Sémillon (Durbanville) $13. A dry white with a smooth mouthfeel and some typical Sémillon waxiness to boot. Still, a strong, unyielding bell pepper quality detracts throughout. Closes clean with a slight grainy feel, but it's just too green and lean. **82** —*M.M. (12/15/2004)*

OMNIA

Omnia 2005 Arniston Bay Bush Vines Chenin Blanc (Coastal Region) $NA. One of South Africa's successful brands, especially in the British market, this wine goes for the gooseberry spectrum of Chenin Blanc, emphasizing green flavors along with its sweetness. It is well-made, but does lack some character. **84** —*R.V. (11/15/2005)*

ONE STROKE ONE

One Stroke One 2003 Cabernet Sauvignon (Stellenbosch) $28. Tasted in a flight with other 2003 Stellenbosch Cabs, this wine stood out due to its higher acidity which lifted the flavors of cassis and blackberry. Unfined and unfiltered. **87** —*M.D. (11/1/2006)*

ONYX

Onyx 2000 Shiraz (Groenekloof) $20. This wine, produced by Darling Cellars, features a meaty nose of black cherry and cinnamon toast that leads to red plum and white pepper on the palate. Tannins are there, but the acidity isn't. The cinnamon finish is accompanied by bitter herbs. **85** —*K.F. (4/1/2003)*

ORACLE

Oracle 2002 Cabernet Sauvignon (Western Cape) $8. Curious, with some dark sweet fruit and spice accents, but also a less enjoyable, sharp tart note that really takes over. Shows decent mouthfeel and even tannins, but the bitter element predominates, leaving a strong sour aftertaste. **81** —*M.M. (11/15/2004)*

Oracle 2002 Pinotage (Western Cape) $8. Rich, juicy Pinotage from Aussie Linley Schultz, über-winemaker at Distell. The grape's harder-to-handle elements are neatly restrained, becoming interesting accents here. Displays a ripe feel, dark fruit with Bordeaux-like tobacco shadings, and a smooth finish. More renditions like this will expand the grape's possibilites and make it more friends. **87 Best Buy** —*M.M. (7/4/2004)*

SOUTH AFRICA

Oracle 2003 Sauvignon Blanc (Western Cape) $8. Impressive, with good tang and surprising persistence. Tends towards the crisper Sauvignon Blanc style in aromas and flavors, but a fairly round, smooth mouthfeel provides a nice counterpoint, and subtle figgy notes keep the sharper elements in check. Focused and tasty. **88** —*M.M. (7/4/2004)*

Oracle 2002 Shiraz (Western Cape) $8. Solid, tart-sweet fruit shines in this flavorful Western Cape Shiraz. Winemaker Linley Schultz's confident hand shows in the judicious use of oak, balanced mouthfeel, and tasty, lingering close. Shows some complexity and the structure to evolve. Enjoy through 2007, maybe longer. **87** —*M.M. (7/4/2004)*

ORIGIN

Origin 2005 Sauvignon Blanc (Western Cape) $10. Ripe fruit aromas of papaya and grapefruit virtually disappear in the mouth, where a hint of white fruit remains. Soft and flabby, without an acidic kick to bolster the mouthfeel. **82** —*M.D. (7/1/2006)*

Origin 2004 Syrah (Western Cape) $10. Sweet aromas of raspberry and grape soda set the stage, while sweet plum, grape, and vanilla flavors play their parts. Fairly full-bodied, but residual sweetness makes this wine eminently drinkable. **83** —*M.D. (9/1/2006)*

OUT OF AFRICA

Out of Africa 2002 Cabernet Sauvignon (Western Cape) $9. Light, with typical berry and herb elements, but with an overwhelming greenish, seemingly under-ripe edge. Smooth and even-textured, but lacking concentration or depth of fruit to overcome the green. **82** —*M.M. (11/15/2004)*

Out of Africa 2003 Chardonnay (Western Cape) $9. Work-a-day Chardonnnay with apple-and-melon profile and a moderately slick feel. Not cloying or sweet. Okay for the patio and with light foods. **84** —*M.M. (7/4/2004)*

Out of Africa 2002 Pinotage (Western Cape) $9. Tasty wine similar to a basic Bordeaux. The very dry tart berry fruit wears a dose of earthiness, but it comes off less overtly South African as the iron-iodine element is suppressed here. As such, it's less typical of its origins. Putting whether that's a plus or minus aside, it should afford the wine wider mainstream appeal. **85** —*M.M. (7/4/2004)*

Out of Africa 2003 Sauvignon Blanc (Western Cape) $9. Tangy grass and gooseberry aromas and flavors sit on a light- to medium-weight frame. Mellows a bit towards the back end. Has appeal as an everyday alternative to fans of Sancerre and New Zealand Sauvignon Blanc. **85** —*M.M. (7/4/2004)*

Out of Africa 2003 Shiraz (Western Cape) $9. Solid and inky, with an earthy, slightly metallic South African typicity on the dark berry-licorice Shiraz fruit. Has good flavors and medium-weight feel. Closes with some dry tannins, making it a good companion to grilled meat. **86** —*M.M. (7/4/2004)*

PAUL CLUVER

Paul Cluver 2005 Gewürztraminer (Elgin) $13. A bright and festive wine with a powerful nose of tropical fruit, lychee, and rose and a touch of mineral. Lively in the mouth, with zippy acidity playing against a good dose of sweetness, the flavors pour on rose petal, lychee, and spice, everything you could want from a Gewürz. **88 Best Buy** —*M.D. (12/31/2006)*

Paul Cluver 2005 Riesling (Elgin) $13. From Elgin, a cooler coastal area, comes this citrusy, slatey wine that speaks with the authority of this majestic grape. Whiffs of citrus and lanolin add to the nose, while flavors of nectarine and orange complement the minerally mouthfeel. **87** —*M.D. (12/31/2006)*

PEACOCK RIDGE

Peacock Ridge 2005 Chardonnay (Stellenbosch) $19. Sweet yellow fruit flavor is plentiful if simple; oak, as usual, adds a touch of flavor and spice through the finish. This is a fine wine for buttery lobster, as its fresh fruit nose and big, sweet body can stand up to butter, and its low acid won't interfere. **84** —*M.D. (11/1/2006)*

Peacock Ridge 2005 Merlot (Stellenbosch) $19. A meaty, spicy nose offers plum and cassis along with prune and brown raisin, leading to a palate ripe with more of the same flavors. Lean and dry, with dusty tannins.

Leathery notes develop, then follow through to the finish. **83** —*M.D. (11/1/2006)*

Peacock Ridge 2005 Sauvignon Blanc (Stellenbosch) $19. Nail polish aromas blow off to reveal white fruit, but in the mouth there is no missing the depth of gooseberry and pineapple flavors that abound. Mild acids are a sign of the ripeness of this wine, as is the alcohol (14.5%). Finishes with crisp minerality and a touch of heat. **87** —*M.D. (9/1/2006)*

PEARLY BAY

Pearly Bay NV Celebration Champagne Blend (South Africa) $7. Very fruity and sweet, like an inexpensive Moscato, this has a bubble gum, candied quality and a very soft feel. In truth, it makes no pretense, bearing the name vin doux, or sweet wine. Simple, with sweet-tooth appeal and very low apparent acidity. **82** —*M.M. (12/1/2001)*

Pearly Bay NV Celebration Champagne Blend (South Africa) $7. Quite sweet, with tangy spice, menthol, and tangerine notes backed by peach and apricot flavors. A bit like Asti Spumante. **84** —*J.M. (12/1/2002)*

PECAN STREAM

Pecan Stream 2005 Chenin Blanc (Stellenbosch) $14. One of South Africa's star winemakers, Kevin Arnold, has produced an impressive, dry wine, with intense apple and grapefruit flavors. It is crisp, with a delicious lift at the end, and a dry, green aftertaste. **90 Best Buy** —*R.V. (11/15/2005)*

PINE CREST

Pine Crest 2004 Cabernet Sauvignon (Coastal Region) $15. A big, dry style of Cabernet, more going towards dusty tannins and black currants. It is serious, likely to age well, with a firm hold on the structure of Cabernet. **87** —*R.V. (11/1/2006)*

Pine Crest 2003 Cabernet Sauvignon (Coastal Region) $15. Meaty, with dark fruit flavors, this wine has dry, hefty tannins that power through to the finish, picking up notes of leather and Band-Aid along the way. **84** —*M.D. (11/1/2006)*

Pine Crest 2001 Chardonnay (Coastal Region) $13. This wine has a full, rich nose of whipping cream, yellow stone fruit, slate, and parsley. The palate offers watery flavors of grapefruit and toast; it finishes with dried herbs. Wants more substance. **84** —*K.F. (9/1/2003)*

Pine Crest 2000 Chardonnay (Franschhoek) $13. A varietally correct combination of vanilla, toast, and light butterscotch aromas play into lemon and citrus-rind flavors. The cleansing acidity starts off almost spritzy and the finish is toasty and hot with an herby tang. **88** —*K.F. (4/1/2003)*

Pine Crest 2001 Chenin Blanc (Franschhoek) $10. Buttered toast, radicchio, and durum flour on the nose are complimented by honey and grapefruit flavors on the palate. Through to the toasty finish, the acids ride just under the radar; oak adds some spice. **85** —*K.F. (4/1/2003)*

Pine Crest 2004 Pinotage (Coastal Region) $14. Bright purple, with aromas of clove, plum, cherry, and leather. Plump in the mouth, with mild, dusty tannins, good acidity, and a hint of fruity sweetness. Cassis coats the tongue while spice entices the taste buds. Finishes on the leathery side. **85** —*M.D. (11/1/2006)*

PLAISIR DE MERLE

Plaisir De Merle 1998 Merlot (Paarl) $22. Mature fruit is veneered with oak and kissed with dusty cocoa and dry earth. Although this is losing freshness, it comes off as elegant and the tannins suggest that it may age for just a year or two longer. **86** —*K.F. (8/1/2003)*

Plaisir De Merle 2005 Sauvignon Blanc (Coastal Region) $22. A sweet palate entry and rich, ripe tropical fruit flavors say "sweet," but this wine is dry and balanced. Notes of ginger and petrol grace the otherwise fruity nose, and there's lime on the palate, but it stays shy of tart through the long, rich, lime-laden finish. **90** —*M.D. (12/31/2006)*

PORCUPINE RIDGE

Porcupine Ridge 2005 Cabernet Sauvignon (Coastal Region) $12. A hefty nose offers plum, black fruits, and spice, a nice combo, but the flavors are more stalky, with red fruit flavors. On the zesty side, with light tannins and a dry, stalky, and spicy finish. **83** —*M.D. (12/31/2006)*

SOUTH AFRICA

Porcupine Ridge 2004 Cabernet Sauvignon (Coastal Region) $12. There's 11% Malbec in this wine which gives it a purplish hue, but the flavors are all Cab. Cassis, raspberry, and chocolate meld in the mouth, with dill and tobacco influencing the mixed-berry nose. A supple mouthfeel and solid tannins back it up, although the finish is a bit short. **86** —*M.D. (3/1/2006)*

Porcupine Ridge 2001 Cabernet Sauvignon (Coastal Region) $13. Very dry tannins and near-mouth-watering acidity are worth noting. The nose of bread, sawdust, and dry basement hides anonymous red fruit. On the palate, the fruit is wrapped in herby endive. Throughout, a note of peppery gaminess. **84** —*K.F. (4/1/2003)*

Porcupine Ridge 2004 Merlot (Coastal Region) $12. This wine doesn't quite come across as full-bodied, with a lean streak through the mid-palate. But it does have plenty of character, along with cassis, tobacco, and herbal flavors backed by solid tannins, and a chocolate-laden finish. **86** —*M.D. (3/1/2006)*

Porcupine Ridge 2003 Merlot (Coastal Region) $11. An opening display of solid berry and plum fruit is over-taken by wood. The wine turns astringent rather quickly, with drying tannins and difficult earth and vitamin-tablet notes predominating. **83** —*M.M. (11/15/2004)*

Porcupine Ridge 2001 Merlot (Coastal Region) $13. Light, with fine tannins and plenty of fruit. Red Delicious apple peels, cinnamon and delicate cranberry-raspberry fruit are layered in oak. **88** —*K.F. (4/1/2003)*

Porcupine Ridge 2005 Sauvignon Blanc (Western Cape) $10. This Sauvignon Blanc smells and tastes of lime peel. With a tart entry that rounds out to a creamy feel and green apple flavors, it's quite enjoyable, although the finish is a bit warm. **85 Best Buy** —*M.D. (3/1/2006)*

Porcupine Ridge 2003 Sauvignon Blanc (Western Cape) $9. With a light, even feel, this is rather unique for its mix of typical high-strung citrus with dense floral notes. Tangy and round at once, with good fruit, this finishes bright, tasty and refreshing, with a lot of appeal. **86 Best Buy** —*M.M. (11/15/2004)*

Porcupine Ridge 2002 Sauvignon Blanc (Western Cape) $10. This is very clean, lightweight and tasty. The nose has a lovely note of lychee, along with citrus peel, fresh-cut grass, and a hint of basil that extend to the palate, finishing with toast and grass. **87 Best Buy** —*K.F. (4/1/2003)*

Porcupine Ridge 2004 Syrah (Coastal Region) $12. Hit or miss the past couple of years, Porcupine Ridge has a winner this year with its Syrah. Intense aromas of plum, cassis, graham cracker, coffee, and lemon mingle with floral notes in the nose. Creamy in the mouth, it has dark coffee and blueberry flavors with hints of vanilla and herbs. A pleasant wine hitting on all cylinders. **88 Best Buy** —*M.D. (7/1/2006)*

Porcupine Ridge 2003 Syrah (Coastal Region) $11. A tart cranberry-rhubarb and stewed tomato bouquet opens this lean wine. As it opens, a predominant green quality ascends on the palate and takes over. This simply seems under-ripe. **82** —*M.M. (11/15/2004)*

Porcupine Ridge 2000 Syrah (Coastal Region) $13. The opening aromas of dark berries and earth are marred by an odd briny note reminiscent of a wet bathing suit or raw clams. But once past that, there are sturdy flavors of espresso, dark toast, and a pleasant sweet-and-sour quality. Finishes tannic and toasty. **84** *(10/1/2001)*

POSITIVELY ZINFUL

Positively Zinful 2001 Zinfandel (Coastal Region) $10. Not your father's Porto, this ruby-style, fortified wine is made of 100% Zinfandel at Lammershoek Winery. The low-yielding bush vines produce just enough to make this hedonistic delight. Strong Zin hallmarks of loamy earth, dried figs, and pepper all support the shameless cinnamon candy flavors. Although this is primarily a sweet tooth's delight, the acidity prevents it from becoming too cloying. Only 200 cases imported to the U.S. **87** —*K.F. (11/15/2003)*

POST HOUSE CELLAR

Post House Cellar 2002 Chenin Blanc (Stellenbosch) $NA. A wood-aged wine that has achieved some good balance. It is big and rich, almost like Chardonnay in weight, but it seems to have little of Chenin's varietal character. **87** —*R.V. (11/15/2005)*

PROSPECT

Prospect 1870 1998 Cabernet Sauvignon (Robertson) $30. The palate is drenched in sweet oak and sugarplums. This is not to say that it is a syrupy quaff: there is also cocoa, toast, dried herbs, and a note of eucalyptus that pinches at the finish. **85** —*K.F. (8/1/2003)*

RAATS FAMILY

Raats Family 2004 Chenin Blanc (Stellenbosch) $23. This lightly wooded interpretation from Bruwer Raats is a superb wine. Its acidity and delicious pure fruit character are in no way lessened by the touch of vanilla from the wood. In fact they are heightened, bringing out their density and concentration. A great Chenin Blanc. **93** —*R.V. (11/15/2005)*

Raats Family 2005 Original Chenin Blanc (South Africa) $13. One of South Africa's best with Chenin, Bruwer Raats has hit another home run with this unwooded wine. It kicks off with perfumed citrus aromas, then lets fly with lively almond-tinged flavors of orange and peach. Vibrant in the mouth with beautifully matching acidity, this is a wine that calls for food, but can certainly be enjoyed alone. **89 Best Buy** —*M.D. (11/1/2006)*

Raats Family 2004 Original Chenin Blanc (Stellenbosch) $13. Bruwer Raats is a Loire wine lover, and he expresses this love in two distinct styles of Chenin Blanc. The unwooded Original is packed with apples, almonds, and nuts, as well as flinty mineral character. It is almost bone dry, and is crisp and fresh. **89 Best Buy** —*R.V. (11/15/2005)*

RADFORD DALE

Radford Dale 2004 Shiraz (Stellenbosch) $20. This wine has an amazing mouthfeel, finely balanced and silky smooth, with just enough tannins to stand up to the medium-full body. Coffee aromas lead to a sweet entry of dark plum and cassis flavors. The only caution: There are notes of barnyard, which may develop more with time. **88** —*M.D. (12/31/2006)*

RAKA

Raka 2002 Biography Shiraz (Western Cape) $23. This dark wine hints at Cabernet with aromas of cassis, tobacco, menthol, and coffee. The palate entry offers up vanilla and coffee, backed by red berry. Smooth and firm in the mouth, this wine is beautifully proportioned, ending long with dark berry and coffee notes. **91 Editors' Choice** —*M.D. (5/1/2006)*

RAWSON'S

Rawson's 2002 Chardonnay (Worcester) $9. This is rather appealing for such a simple, soundly balanced package. Dried tarragon, poppy seed, lemon, and toast please the senses. Easy to drink, and even easier to buy. **87 Best Buy** —*K.F. (4/1/2003)*

Rawson's 2001 Pinotage (Breede River Valley) $10. This medium-weight wine is well-balanced and accessible. A whiff of rhubarb and gum rubber blows away to make way for flavorful red plum, grilled meat dashed with pepper, and a hint of herbs. **85** —*K.F. (9/1/2003)*

Rawson's 2002 Shiraz (Breede River Valley) $10. A light barnyard note is accompanied by grilled meat, red plum, and tobacco that carries to the palate. The acidity is somewhat spritzy and the tannins are sheer, so this is very juicy and suited to everyday fare. **86** —*K.F. (8/1/2003)*

Rawson's 2001 Revelry White Blend (Worcester) $8. Honeysuckle and vanilla toast open into citrus aromas that repeat on the slightly gamy palate. The medium-length finish is tinged with herbs. **86** —*K.F. (4/1/2003)*

REMHOOGTE

Remhoogte 2003 Bonne Nouvelle Cabernet Blend (Stellenbosch) $45. The second vintage from this joint venture between Remhoogte owner Murray Boustred and new partner Michel Rolland. This blend includes Merlot, Cabernet Sauvignon, and Pinotage. It is an impressively perfumed wine that gets away from the juicy Pinotage flavors and goes for a densely packed, woody taste, with great black plum flavors. **92** —*R.V. (11/1/2006)*

Remhoogte 2002 Bonne Nouvelle Cabernet Blend (Stellenbosch) $40. This is the first vintage of the joint venture between Remhoogte owner Murray Boustred and consultant Michel Rolland. And it certainly

SOUTH AFRICA

started with a bang, exploding in the mouth with intense packed fruit flavors, big spicy wood, and juicy, ripe tannins. **89** —*R.V. (11/1/2006)*

Remhoogte 2003 Estate Wine Cabernet Blend (Simonsberg-Stellenbosch) $28. The estate wine from Remhoogte in which Michel Rolland is both consultant and partner. This Bordeaux Blend is serious stuff with dry tannins that promise good aging. There is some Pinotage in the blend, but it is hardly noticeable; the main flavors come from the textured cassis of Merlot and Cabernet Sauvignon. **92 Editors' Choice** —*R.V. (11/1/2006)*

Remhoogte 2000 Cabernet Sauvignon (Stellenbosch) $22. This estate-bottled Cabernet's dark fruit tries to project but is dominated, as in too many South African reds, by untamed notes of earth, animal, and iodine. Whether from soil, vines, or wine-making practices, these elements lack appeal and render the wine out-of-balance when present to this extent. Closes long and very dry, with a bitter note. **81** —*M.M. (3/1/2004)*

RIETVALLEI ESTATE WINE

Rietvallei Estate Wine 2002 Cabernet Sauvignon (Robertson) $13. A lightweight red with good fruit-acid balance and some even, dusty tannins. Displays a rather neo-Tuscan profile—the fruit is sour cherry, with dry leather tones. Not typical Cabernet, but with individual character. **86** —*M.M. (11/15/2004)*

Rietvallei Estate Wine 2003 Chardonnay (Robertson) $11. Rather puckery throughout, with strong tart citrus notes over modest hay and tropical fruit aromas and flavors. Lean in manner, this finishes quite dry with some spice accents. **84** —*M.M. (11/15/2004)*

Rietvallei Estate Wine 2003 Gewürztraminer (Robertson) $10. Mild spice and some faint tangy fruit on the nose introduce this as Gewürztraminer, but straightaway a cloying sweetness takes over. It's just too soft and sweet, a cross between tropical fruit juice and drugstore perfume. Needs both more spine and concentration. **82** —*M.M. (12/15/2004)*

Rietvallei Estate Wine 2002 Muscadel (Robertson) $11. A distinctive sweet wine that's labeled red but is more rosé in color. Deep floral aromas open to a rich but not cloying palate of strawberry, caramel, and chocolate flavors. Very ripe, and smoothly textured with a long finish, this can work either as an apéritif or a dessert drink. **88 Editors' Choice** —*M.M. (11/15/2004)*

Rietvallei Estate Wine 2002 Shiraz (Robertson) $15. Some handsome, dense fruit shows through this wine's overall rather inky, toasty facade. Oaky? Yes, but a black beauty with a still healthy, positive Shiraz fruit presence, right through the long, even finish. **87** —*M.M. (11/15/2004)*

Rietvallei Estate Wine 2003 John B. Bouquet Blanc White Blend (Robertson) $9. A dry, four-grape white blend (Chenin Blanc, Colombard, Sauvignon Blanc and Chardonnay) with citrus-mineral-hay aromas. The palate is similar, and reminiscent of some Italian Pinot Biancos. Finishes clean, with some lemony notes. A decent quaff, with a somewhat unique composition. **84** —*M.M. (12/15/2004)*

RIJK'S PRIVATE CELLAR

Rijk's Private Cellar 2004 Chenin Blanc (Tulbagh) $NA. This barrel-fermented wine shows great wood flavors, but very little fruit. Caramel and vanilla elements dominate, along with spice and pepper. The aftertaste is creamy and soft. **85** —*R.V. (11/15/2005)*

Rijk's Private Cellar 2003 Chenin Blanc (Tulbagh) $35. Wood and Chenin Blanc can go together, if handled judiciously, as this fabulous wine shows. Nuts and almonds make classic mature Chenin Blanc aromas, while the dense ripe fruit flavors with a complex interplay between wood and fruit give this wine great depth. **93** —*R.V. (11/15/2005)*

ROBERT'S ROCK

Robert's Rock 2004 Cabernet Sauvignon-Merlot (Western Cape) $8. This self-proclaimed "lifestyle brand" from giant South African wine company KWV boasts the usual trappings: brightly colored label, flanged top. What's unusual is that the wine in the bottle is pretty good. Cherry, leather, and chocolate notes provide a modicum of complexity, while the finish is soft and clean. A solid choice to accompany burgers on the patio. **84 Best Buy** —*J.C. (11/15/2005)*

Robert's Rock 2003 Cabernet Sauvignon-Merlot (Western Cape) $9. This basic Bordeaux blend's solid, dry cherry fruit and herb-chalk accents are focused and attractive, if not very deep. The dry, slightly tart profile will compliment many foods and make for good sipping, as well. A good value red. **84** —*M.M. (4/1/2005)*

Robert's Rock 2002 Cabernet Sauvignon-Merlot (Western Cape) $8. The insubstantial nose of this wine is spotted with dried herbs, baking spices, and a whiff of pickle jar. The palate is thin, the tannins are sheer, but the flavors are of sweet, fresh red plum and cinnamon. **84** —*K.F. (8/1/2003)*

Robert's Rock 2005 Chenin Blanc-Chardonnay (Western Cape) $8. Chenin, South Africa's most widely planted grape, plays its role once again, this time in the lead with 48% Chardonnay supporting. Citrus on the nose, with strong vanilla accents, is followed by racy tropical fruits in the mouth giving life to the smooth, demure feel. Finishes with a bang, leaving grapefruit, papaya, vanilla, spice, and a craving for another sip. **86 Best Buy** —*M.D. (11/1/2006)*

Robert's Rock 2004 Chenin Blanc-Chardonnay (Western Cape) $8. A good basic white blend offering apple hay and mild tropical fruit aromas and flavors. The feel is smooth and easy, the palate a touch sweet, but the wine closes neatly—crisper and drier than expected, nice to find in this price range. **84 Best Buy** —*M.M. (4/1/2005)*

Robert's Rock 2003 Chenin Blanc-Chardonnay (Western Cape) $8. Pleasingly plump, this soft white grape blend shows pear and melon aromas and flavors. Definitely low-acid, but this vaguely Viognier-like wine finishes drier and longer than expected. **85 Best Buy** —*M.M. (3/1/2004)*

Robert's Rock 2000 Chenin Blanc-Chardonnay (Western Cape) $6. Chenin Blanc, aka Steen, has for years been South Africa's work-a-day white. Paired here with Chardonnay, it shows a nice green apple, and floral bouquet, similar brisk flavors and finishes with a lemony tang. It's a good white wine quaff that's not overly soft or sweet. **84** *(9/1/2001)*

Robert's Rock 2003 Shiraz-Cabernet Sauvignon (Western Cape) $9. A light, simple red with less substance than expected considering the grapes and the brand's usual good hand with value wines. Some grapey and tart red berry flavors here wear smoke and toast accents. Lean, with a short, earthy dry finish. **83** —*M.M. (4/1/2005)*

Robert's Rock 2003 Shiraz-Malbec (Western Cape) $9. Simple, yet with plenty of straightforward appeal, this attractive wine is a credible light red (read Beaujolais-style) alternative. Ample strawberry-raspberry aromas and flavors prevail, while a smooth feel and clean finish complete this modest yet attractive offering. **85 Best Buy** —*M.M. (4/1/2005)*

Robert's Rock 2001 Shiraz-Malbec (Western Cape) $9. This intriguing blend shows plenty of individuality: leathery, slightly horsey aromas and dark berry and earth flavors. Hints of sour herbs and lemon on the finish give it enough bite to serve alongside burgers and the like. No need for additional age; drink it now. **85 Best Buy** —*J.C. (7/1/2004)*

ROBERTSON WINERY

Robertson Winery 2004 Cabernet Sauvignon (Robertson) $10. A lovely nose of cassis and herbal notes, with hints of eucalyptus and chocolate, leads into a dark palate with plenty of tannin, cassis, and tobacco leaf. Should be drunk now, but has enough grace to last for the next few years. A bargain at this price. **88 Best Buy** —*M.D. (3/1/2006)*

Robertson Winery 2003 Cabernet Sauvignon (Robertson) $10. Light, with an under-ripe quality, showing tart berry flavors and green tobacco accents. Also has a substantial dose of the iodine-earth-vitamin character of some South African wines, off-putting when too prominent. **80** —*M.M. (11/15/2004)*

Robertson Winery 2002 Cabernet Sauvignon (Robertson) $10. Notes of cedar, paper, and leather carry to the cassis laden palate, with meat juices and a hint of plum. Light in weight, with talcy tannins, this wine is straightforward and an easy drinking entertainer. **87** —*K.F. (8/1/2003)*

Robertson Winery 2003 Prospect Hill Cabernet Sauvignon (Robertson) $20. Smooth and even, this is grapey and pretty soft. Chocolate and caramel notes accent the ripe berry fruit. It's a refined take on the low-acid easy drinker—think of it as an upscale quaff. Finishes gently with good length. **86** —*M.M. (7/1/2005)*

Robertson Winery 2005 Chardonnay (Robertson) $10. Despite this wine's golden hue, it has many green characteristics. Herbal notes come through in the nose and mouth, mixing with mineral and banana. The mouthfeel, simple and dusty at first, picks up more acidity, giving a raw feeling that climaxes with a medicinal finish. **82** —M.D. (5/1/2006)

Robertson Winery 2003 Chardonnay (Robertson) $10. On the sweet side, with a floral nose followed by apple and tropical fruit flavors. Too candied for my taste, but will have its fans. **82** —M.M. (7/4/2004)

Robertson Winery 2002 Chardonnay (Robertson) $9. This wine's toast, thyme, and amber maple syrup notes are a little mute to start, but gain on the palate with a little yellow fruit peeking through. Light and clean throughout, this is a natural for cocktail hour. **84** —K.F. (9/1/2003)

Robertson Winery 2003 Kings River Chardonnay (Robertson) $19. Solid Chardonnay with tasty citrus-apple-pear fruit that's nicely wrapped in oak. Subdued toffee-butterscotch notes add appeal. Shows a nice chewiness, with an almost grain-like, oaty flavor and feel on the finish. **87** —M.M. (7/4/2004)

Robertson Winery 2005 Chenin Blanc (Robertson) $10. From the Robertson cooperative, this is a sweet style of Chenin, but one that is balanced by vibrant fruit; fresh acidity gives a crisp, poised aftertaste. **87 Best Buy** —R.V. (11/15/2005)

Robertson Winery 2004 Chenin Blanc (Robertson) $10. Ripe, fruity, slightly sweet Chenin Blanc—think Vouvray—with a bright feel. Ample chalk-mineral notes on the fruit keep it refreshing. Solid as an apéritif or with light foods. **84** —M.M. (12/15/2004)

Robertson Winery 2003 Chenin Blanc (Robertson) $9. Simple and cloying. Has a heavy perfumey quality on the nose and on the palate. **80** —M.M. (7/4/2004)

Robertson Winery 2004 Special Late Harvest Gewürztraminer (Robertson) $10. Quite similar to the tasty 2003, if a little less concentrated. Light on the tongue with an attractive lychee-citrus-pineapple profile. Closes drier than expected. Again, an interesting, affordable surprise and a perfectly sufficient dessert wine for many situations. **85 Best Buy** —M.M. (12/15/2004)

Robertson Winery 2003 Special Late Harvest Gewürztraminer (Robertson) $10. This interesting dessert-styled wine is not too heavy or sweet. An odd earthy note on the nose is a bit strange at first, but the mild lychee-pineapple-candied pear aromas and flavors have definite appeal, and linger nicely on the close. An interesting offering from one of South Africa's more outlying regions. **86 Best Buy** —M.M. (12/15/2004)

Robertson Winery 2003 Merlot (Robertson) $10. Bricking already at this young age, with herbal notes and dried-out fruit. Light and inoffensive, but surprisingly past its prime. **80** —J.C. (11/15/2005)

Robertson Winery 2002 Merlot (Robertson) $10. Tasty in a lighter style, with red raspberry and cranberry flavors on a lithe frame. This appealing easy drinker improves in the glass, shedding some early astringency as the fruit builds and comes forward. Closes with light tannins. **85 Best Buy** —M.M. (11/15/2004)

Robertson Winery 2001 Merlot (Robertson) $10. This acidity-driven wine has a sheer veneer of tannins over thinned red fruit, earth, and cocoa powder. With such a light, simple touch, this wine is a good choice for those who usually order white wine. **84** —K.F. (8/1/2003)

Robertson Winery 2003 Pinotage (Robertson) $10. Tart-sweet cherry-berry fruit shines through the earthy notes here. The typical metallic quality is present but restrained. This light to medium-weight wine is tasty, focused basic Pinotage. A nice casual choice for grilled meats. **85** —M.M. (7/4/2004)

Robertson Winery 2002 Pinotage (Robertson) $10. This wine is moving in a couple of directions at once: it is light-bodied, acidity-driven, and the tannins are on the soft side. From there, the red plum fruit on the palate is tinged with slightly bitter bell pepper. **84** —K.F. (9/1/2003)

Robertson Winery 2004 Phanto Ridge Pinotage (Robertson) $20. This soft wine has pleasant aromas of red berry and menthol, and the palate has loads of baked red fruits plus oaky vanilla and a hint of tart lemon. Drink now. **85** —M.D. (3/1/2006)

Robertson Winery 2003 Almond Grove Noble Late Harvest Riesling (Robertson) $18. A very smooth Riesling, a handsome dessert wine with an aromatic and flavorful citrus-apricot profile. Fine, ripe fruit yields appealing richness without being overly sweet, supported by good acidity all the way. Needs only greater length to kick it up into the top echelon. Worth seeking out. **88 Editors' Choice** —M.M. (12/15/2004)

Robertson Winery 2005 Sauvignon Blanc (Robertson) $10. The ripeness of the grapes used for this wine is apparent in the tropical fruit aromas it offers. Creamy and full, the wine offers flavors of melon, mango, and pink grapefruit that carry through the finish. **87 Best Buy** —M.D. (3/1/2006)

Robertson Winery 2004 Sauvignon Blanc (Robertson) $10. A soft wine with faint, sweet perfume notes on the nose. Tastes more like a Chardonnay or white blend. Simple, and could have some mainstream appeal with its slightly over-ripe hints and short, clean finish. **83** —M.M. (12/15/2004)

Robertson Winery 2003 Sauvignon Blanc (Robertson) $10. Muted but accurate Sauvignon Blanc. Straightforward, with clean herb and mild citrus aromas and flavors. It's neither clumsy or flawed, and has the right stuff—it just could use a little more of it. **84** —M.M. (7/4/2004)

Robertson Winery 2002 Sauvignon Blanc (Robertson) $9. This wine has simple aromas of fresh herbs and banana pith. The acidity is a likeable counterpart to one-dimensional tropical fruit flavors. Finishes with another dose of fresh herbs. **84** —K.F. (9/1/2003)

Robertson Winery 2004 Retreat Sauvignon Blanc (Robertson) $20. Classy, vibrant lime-herb bouquet. A finely tuned fruit/acid balance yields positive flavor intensity without sharpness. Finishes long with nice back end pepper notes. Commendable for its handsome play of crisp and full elements. Best wine yet from this producer. **90 Editors' Choice** —M.M. (12/15/2004)

Robertson Winery 2004 Shiraz (Robertson) $10. Robertson Winery has made a name for itself with affordable wines, and this one is no different. While the nose carries graham cracker and menthol, this wine doesn't lack fruit, with plenty of sweet red berry in the mouth. Although soft, this wine has a meaty quality to it that would make it a good bet for barbecue. **84** —M.D. (3/1/2006)

Robertson Winery 2003 Shiraz (Robertson) $10. Shows plenty of character, but it's not always entirely pleasant, combining leather, horse sweat, and Band-Aid aromas with a smooth, medium-weight mouthfeel. **82** —J.C. (11/15/2005)

Robertson Winery 2002 Shiraz (Robertson) $10. The sweet, easy-drinking flavors of cherry and plum are countered by pipe tobacco, with gentle layers of oak throughout and some eucalyptus on the finish. The acids lend a pleasant bite and are well offset by the tannins which have some grip. **87** —K.F. (8/1/2003)

Robertson Winery 2003 Wolfkloof Shiraz (Robertson) $20. Presents tasty dark berry fruit accented by mocha and dense oak. The hints of earthiness are modest and controlled, adding positively to the sensory mix. Closes with full coffee-chocolate notes and some spicy, tangy tannins. Good wine, if a bit on the oaky side. **86** —M.M. (12/15/2004)

ROCKFIELDS

Rockfields 2005 Chenin Blanc (Worcester) $NA. Rather thin and dilute, this wine succeeds because of its easy style and total lack of complexity. Pleasant and clean. **81** —R.V. (11/15/2005)

ROODEBERG

Roodeberg 2002 Red Blend (Western Cape) $13. A sprightly red blend—light, tangy, and flavorful. Sour cherry fruit abounds, accented by leather, toast, cocoa and earth. Quite dry and slightly tart on the close. **87** —M.M. (3/1/2004)

Roodeberg 2001 Red Blend (Western Cape) $13. This wine is a straightforward package of mulch, sweet dried herbs, anise, leather, cedar, and blackberry. The consistency and style of the fruit are very likeable, as is the ever-so-light herby char on the finish. Has good tannins, but doesn't delve too deep. **88** —K.F. (1/1/2004)

SOUTH AFRICA

Roodeberg 1998 Red Blend (Western Cape) $11. The bouquet of this Cabernet-Shiraz-Merlot-Ruby Cabernet blend shows intriguing berry, mint, anise, earth, and tobacco-herb aromas. Bright acidity keeps the berry fruit lively, and the finish is long and earthy. Good now, and should improve over the next two-plus years. **88** *(9/1/2001)*

Roodeberg 1997 Red Blend (Western Cape) $12. This blend of five red grapes has been the hallmark wine for KWV for 50 years. This rendition has foresty aromas mixed with earthy, peppery scents. Round and soft, with tannins that are smooth. Given time, this will open up into something special. Luscious and rewarding, and all for a song. **91 Best Buy** —*M.S. (1/1/2004)*

RUDERA

Rudera 2004 Cabernet Sauvignon (Stellenbosch) $44. A perfumed, jammy wine, full of flavor. There is also a more serious element to this wine from the Hall's first vintage in their own winery. The tannin dryness, ripe wood flavors, and cassis flavors suggest good aging, as well as good food pairing. **89** —*R.V. (11/1/2006)*

Rudera 2003 Cabernet Sauvignon (Stellenbosch) $46. Heavy aromas of well-oiled leather and pepper obscure fruit, while the plum and dark fruit flavors are over-powered by leather with a hint of Band-Aid. Nice tannins and moderate acidity give the wine a smooth feel. **85** —*M.D. (9/1/2006)*

Rudera 2004 Chenin Blanc (Stellenbosch) $20. This could be an impressive wine, but the overwhelming wood element makes it hard to taste the fruit. There are just hints of ripe spice and creamy apples, and the aftertaste is just off dry. **89** —*R.V. (11/15/2005)*

Rudera 2002 Robusto Chenin Blanc (Stellenbosch) $NA. Rated the top Chenin in South Africa in 2005, this is a serious but delicious wine. It has a toasty character from wood fermentation and aging, but a character which does not dominate the sweet fruit. Spice and honey come from the tropical flavors, but the final taste is of crispness and acidity. **92** — *R.V. (11/15/2005)*

Rudera 2003 Syrah (Stellenbosch) $27. A mild nose of dark berries and violets uncovers grilled meat, mineral, and finely oaked berry fruits. The structure is tightly wound, acidity wrapping tannins in a silky feel. Lacks the power of some other Syrahs, but a fine wine nevertheless. **87** —*M.D. (9/1/2006)*

RUPERT & ROTHSCHILD

Rupert & Rothschild 1999 Baron Edmund Bordeaux Blend (Coastal Region) $45. This Cabernet-based blend opens with deep cassis and herb aromas. A svelte, evenly textured palate follows, with dark berry and plum flavors sporting tobacco accents. Finely balanced, it finishes long, with full, even tannins. **88** —*M.M. (12/15/2004)*

Rupert & Rothschild 2001 Classique Bordeaux Blend (Coastal Region) $19. This, the less-expensive red from Rupert & Rothschild, has been a consistent performer since its introduction. It's smooth and elegant, with dark fruit, tasty oak, and tobacco-espresso accents. Classique is like an attractive potential partner in a singles bar—perhaps not terribly deep, but undeniably seductive, with plenty of up-front appeal. **87** —*M.M. (12/15/2004)*

Rupert & Rothschild 2000 Classique Bordeaux Blend (Coastal Region) $20. Cassis, leather, spice, and faint creamy notes open this nicely balanced claret-like red. The dry cherry, licorice, and earth palate, very even tannins, and lingering finish offer plenty of appeal, and it's built to be consumed within the next few years. **88** —*M.M. (3/1/2004)*

Rupert & Rothschild 1998 Classique Bordeaux Blend (Coastal Region) $20. Berry, bark, herb, and green tobacco aromas open this Bordeaux blend. Earth and herb accents show strongly on the palate. Ready to drink, it's elegant if not particularly weighty. Closes slightly short, with more earth and herb elements. **87** *(2/1/2002)*

Rupert & Rothschild 2001 Baron Edmond Cabernet Sauvignon-Merlot (Coastal Region) $45. **88** —*J.C. (7/1/2005)*

Rupert & Rothschild 2003 Baroness Nadine Chardonnay (Western Cape) $25. Full-bodied, and full of flavor. Displaying aromas of tropical fruits, butterscotch, and menthol, this wine has a ripe feel about it, but is still balanced by lively acidity. Some notes of corn show through, as does some heat on the finish, but it's still very good. **87** —*M.D. (3/1/2006)*

Rupert & Rothschild 2000 Baroness Nadine Chardonnay (Coastal Region) $26. Rather lean and tart, a crisp wine that feels tight in the mouth right now. May open up with a year or so of age to reveal underlying flavors of peaches and apples. Finishes with a bitter bite of lees. **85** —*S.H. (1/1/2002)*

Rupert & Rothschild 1999 Baroness Nadine Chardonnay (Coastal Region) $26. Full, supple, and tasty, this Chardonnay named for Benjamin's mother strikes a nice balance between crisp and creamy elements. The nose and palate show apple, lemon, caramel, oak, and spice. Medium-bodied and richly textured, this wine closes with good length, lees notes, butterscotch, and toast. Drink now through 2004. **89** *(2/1/2002)*

Rupert & Rothschild 1999 Classique Red Blend (Coastal Region) $20. A simple aroma and flavor package of endive, eucalyptus, fresh herbs, ripe red plum, sweet raspberries, coffee, and light toast. A simple, well balanced blend for anytime. **86** —*K.F. (4/1/2003)*

RUST EN VREDE

Rust en Vrede 1998 Estate Wine Bordeaux Blend (Stellenbosch) $33. Earthy, meaty, and full of smashed berries. Red currant and plum flavors dominate, with a touch of green pepper in there as well. It's a brawny wine that's more rustic than refined. The balance and acid structure, however, is right on. The blend is Cabernet Sauvignon, Shiraz, and Merlot, in descending order. **87** —*M.S. (1/1/2004)*

Rust en Vrede 2002 Cabernet Sauvignon (Stellenbosch) $29. This is one of South Africa's great Cabernets, a particular success in a difficult vintage. It has all the richness and power, but it combines that with elegance and structure. The tannins are dry, promising good aging, while the acidity comes from ripe black currant and black plum fruits. Age for another five years at least. **93 Editors' Choice** —*R.V. (11/1/2006)*

Rust en Vrede 1999 Cabernet Sauvignon (Stellenbosch) $20. Odd aromas and indistinct, sour fruit are loosely knit together in this wine. A spine of dry herbs and sour cherry are accented by paraffin, cedar, and vaccum powder on the nose and palate. **83** —*K.F. (4/1/2003)*

Rust en Vrede 1998 Cabernet Sauvignon (Stellenbosch) $23. Earthy, deep, and brooding are words that best describe the robust nose, which is followed by cherry, plum, and apple-skin flavors. Overall it's sweet and juicy, with fine acidity and a touch of tomato and earth that make it similar to a Bordeaux red. **88** —*M.M. (4/1/2002)*

Rust en Vrede 2004 Merlot (Stellenbosch) $21. Firm tannins and good acidity suggest you can enjoy this wine over the next 10 years, but with beefy flavors of cassis, blackberry, and tobacco you may not want to wait. Meaty on the nose, with ample oak spice and a touch of pepper adding to powerful fruit aromas, and a long, spicy finish. **91 Editors' Choice** — *M.D. (12/31/2006)*

Rust en Vrede 2003 Merlot (Stellenbosch) $23. Packed with character, from aromas of red berries wrapped in wet tobacco, anise, hazelnut, and vanilla; to flavors of pistachio, blueberry, and tobacco leaf. Despite 14.5% alcohol it comes across less than full-bodied, with fine tannins and high acidity that gives it a minerally feel. Warms up on the long blueberry finish. **88** —*M.D. (9/1/2006)*

Rust en Vrede 2001 Merlot (Stellenbosch) $14. Fragrant notes of spiced plum, cherry, and milk chocolate are met with toast and herbs on the palate. The acidity is a façade to smooth, sheer tannins and the finish is layered in oak and cocoa. **85** —*K.F. (8/1/2003)*

Rust en Vrede 2002 Estate Wine Red Blend (Stellenbosch) $46. From a famed Stellenbosch estate comes another fantastic vintage of the Estate red. A blend of Cabernet (53%) and Shiraz (33%), with Merlot picking up the slack, this awesome wine shows all that the Stellenbosch region can be. Nearly black in color, the nose is awash with clove, cinnamon, and coffee notes that don't overpower the dark, plummy fruit. Its rich mouthfeel is loaded with dark plum and cassis flavors and sprinkled coffee grounds, ending in a long, earthy finish. Drink now and over the next 8 years. **92 Editors' Choice** —*M.D. (7/1/2006)*

Rust en Vrede 1999 Shiraz (Stellenbosch) $35. Aromas run the gamut from red plum, cranberry, and sourdough to wood stain and meat marinade. On the palate, red plum, leather, and beef stock are accented with bay leaf. Juicy acidity merits pairing with food. **87** —*K.F. (4/1/2003)*

Rust en Vrede 1998 Shiraz (Stellenbosch) $22. The earthy, stably aromas that are so characteristic of South African Shiraz also leave their marks on this one. The bouquet is mostly leather and "tree-leafy;" tobacco and tree bark overlay tart red berries in the mouth. A medium-length finish offers sour leather and black tea notes. Unusual and not for everyone, but worth exploring. **87** *(11/1/2001)*

RUSTENBERG

Rustenberg 2004 John X Merriman Bordeaux Blend (Stellenbosch) $30. John X. Merriman purchased part of the Rustenberg farm in 1892 (it was subsequently bought by the current owners, the Barlow family, in 1940) and this Cabernet-dominated blend is named after him. As with all Rustenberg wines, this is a fine, structured bottling that's more than New World. Offers smoky fruit, a mineral character, and dry tannins. This has potential to age for at least five years. **93** —*R.V. (11/1/2006)*

Rustenberg 2002 John X Merriman Bordeaux Blend (Stellenbosch) $30. A heavy-weight, this Cabernet-Merlot blend tips the scales with full-on pruned berry flavors that are almost candied. Jammy, the big tannins are coated with a touch of sweetness. Acidity is low, giving the wine a lush, portly feel, with a warm, sweet finish. **87** —*M.D. (9/1/2006)*

Rustenberg 2003 Peter Barlow Cabernet Sauvignon (Stellenbosch) $48. Vibrant red, with a spicy nose of pepper, graham cracker, mint, plum, and a hint of bramble. Full-bodied and big, with chalky tannins and high alcohol (15.5%), the loaded dark fruit flavors lean towards prune, with coffee and chocolate riding shotgun. The long finish is smooth, but the heat in this wine makes it near impossible to pair with food. **87** — *M.D. (9/1/2006)*

Rustenberg 2003 Five Soldiers Chardonnay (Stellenbosch) $38. Rustenberg has been one of South Africa's top estates in recent years, and this wine is one of the reasons. Big, modern, and heavily oaked, the 2003 vintage has plenty of ripe tropical fruit and firm acidity to match the brawny power and toasty flavor. The finish is amazing, leaving a warm fuzzy sensation that travels beyond the mouth. Elite and awesome. **90** —*M.D. (9/1/2006)*

Rustenberg 1999 Five Soldiers Chardonnay (Stellenbosch) $33. One of South Africa's oldest wine estates, established in 1692, has revolutionized its wine cellar and its wine in the past five years. This Chardonnay is typical of the estate's wines, oozing rich fruit and modern wood flavors, yet retaining a style and elegance that is as much French as South African. **91** —*R.V. (7/1/2002)*

SANCTUM

Sanctum 2003 Shiraz (Western Cape) $48. With time to open in the glass, this wine shows what it's made of. Dark berry and Melba sauce aromas have a creamy quality, while the mouth is loaded with dark chocolate, plum, and smoke. The tannins are already smooth, along with easy acids that lead to a long, smoky finish. **90** —*M.D. (9/1/2006)*

SAUVIGNON REPUBLIC

Sauvignon Republic 2005 Sauvignon Blanc (Stellenbosch) $18. The first South African wine from this Sauvignon Blanc specialist. Has some grassy aromas that open up to show plenty of tropical fruit. In the mouth it's clean, with good balance, and shows both ripe flavors of mango, peach, and pear as well as a hint of asparagus. Complex, with a citrusy finish. **88** —*M.D. (7/1/2006)*

SAXENBURG ESTATE

Saxenburg Estate 2003 Private Collection Cabernet Sauvignon (Stellenbosch) $NA. A very herbal wine, with sage and thyme flavors. There are solid, dry tannins that mask the black fruits and red berry tastes. This is a wine that obviously needs time to develop, promising a serious, tannin-layered style. **89** —*R.V. (11/1/2006)*

Saxenburg Estate 2000 Private Collection Chardonnay (Stellenbosch) $15. A heavyweight, dominated by candy and toffee aromas. Its lack of acidity is redeemed by the concentration of the fruit and by the intensity of the wood and spice, which make a firm background. **84** —*J.M. (7/1/2002)*

Saxenburg Estate 1998 Merlot (Coastal Region) $15. More than a touch of green tobacco leafiness shows here. The berry fruit is light, the wine somewhat astringent. There's a touch of earthy complexity, but not much depth or length. **82** —*M.M. (3/1/2001)*

Saxenburg Estate 1998 Private Selection Merlot (Stellenbosch) $20. This opens with a complex bouquet of dark berry, earth, soy, pine, and herbs. It's balanced, lean, and darkly fruited on the palate, but though nicely flavored, it's a little hollow, and doesn't show the depth hoped for from the dimensions of the nose. Finishes dry, with even tannins. Drink through 2005. **86** —*M.M. (4/1/2002)*

Saxenburg Estate 1999 Private Collection Sauvignon Blanc (Stellenbosch) $14. Hits the fat and the lean of Sauvignon Blanc with both fig and grassy flavors. A well-balanced wine, it shows a smooth mouthfeel and a long finish. This is one to have with grilled fish. **85** —*M.N. (3/1/2001)*

Saxenburg Estate 1998 Private Collection Shiraz (Stellenbosch) $30. Intense earth, meat, and game aromas accent the blackberry and blueberry fruit in this somewhat controversial, medium-weight wine. The peppery finish offers dried plum and fig, a tart smoky note, and metallic elements. The earthiness, even dung-iness, while complex and challenging, is not for everyone. **86** *(11/1/2001)*

SCALI

Scali 1999 Pinotage (Paarl) $25. Appealing aromas of currants, dates, and nutmeg accent those of red plum, currant, and toast, which carry to the palate. The fruit is pleasant, if simple, with a greenish tinge to the finish. **86** —*K.F. (4/1/2003)*

SEIDELBERG

Seidelberg 2000 Roland's Reserve Estate Wine Cabernet Sauvignon (Paarl) $32. The nose of sweet tobacco, black plum, blackberry, dry earth, and cedar is a pleasant invitation to the licorice, molasses, and black plum on the palate. Finishes with herby char. Juicy acidity and light tannins make this a fine mealtime selection. **87** —*K.F. (4/1/2003)*

Seidelberg 2001 Chardonnay (Paarl) $15. Toast, salinity, and meatlean, the mouthfeel is somewhat viscous. **87** —*K.F. (4/1/2003)*

Seidelberg 2005 Estate Chenin Blanc (Paarl) $12. There is some peanut shell to the nose, but also banana and citrus. Medium-full in the mouth, the wine is smooth, with citrus flavors tempered by spice and nut. Picks up some lime on the sweet finish. **86** —*M.D. (7/1/2006)*

Seidelberg 2000 Roland's Reserve Estate Wine Merlot (Paarl) $32. Veiled by aromas of dry peat, cigarbox, and caramel you'll find black cherry fruit on the palate. A sip reveals the same, with the addition of green herbs that come off a touch bitter. **87** —*K.F. (4/1/2003)*

Seidelberg 2003 Pinotage (Paarl) $13. Tart sour cherry and lemon aromas have a smoky quality, but the palate delivers a very solid core of chunky plum, leather, charcoal, and spice. Its 15% alcohol is evident—the wine is pretty big on the palate, but it's balanced. With such tight tannins, this could use another year to open up, although it probably won't pull together any better than it is now. **87** —*M.D. (7/1/2006)*

Seidelberg 2003 Roland's Reserve Pinotage (Paarl) $22. Oak is a key player in this wine, caressing purple fruit aromas with vanilla and spice. Full-bodied and vibrant in the mouth, with moderate acid and tannins, the oak lends a hint of spice to young plum and sour cherry flavors. A warm, smoky finish of lemon-rubbed leather lingers on the palate. Will improve over two years. **88** —*M.D. (7/1/2006)*

Seidelberg 2001 Roland's Reserve Estate Wine Pinotage (Paarl) $32. Blackberry, black cherry, and molasses coat the nose and palate. The finish of toast and rich caramel is a sweet treat. The tannins are fine, but have plenty of grip to compete with the gooey black fruit. **89** —*K.F. (4/1/2003)*

Seidelberg 2002 Un Deux Trois Red Blend (Paarl) $22. Starting to show some age with a rusty color at the rim. Black olive and earth dominate the mouth, although aromas of red berry and some woody notes of spice and pastry shine through. With smooth tannins and a nice mouthfeel, this is a solid wine. **88** —*M.D. (5/1/2006)*

Seidelberg 2005 Sauvignon Blanc (Paarl) $14. This is a straightforward wine, filled with gooseberries in every aspect. Ripe and round in the mouth, with a bit of sweetness balanced against moderate acidity, it has flinty aromas and good length on the finish.**85** —*M.D. (9/1/2006)*

Seidelberg 2004 Sauvignon Blanc (Paarl) $12. With a golden hue and a fuller body than many other Sauvignon Blancs tasted from South Africa, this wine oozes mango and apple on the nose. It carries through with more apple and tropical fruit in the mouth and finish, and balancing acidity.**88 Best Buy** —*M.D. (3/1/2006)*

Seidelberg 2002 Estate Wine Sauvignon Blanc (Paarl) $13. The miniscule bubbles rising from the bottom of the glass, paired with cleansing acidity, make for a slightly spritzy wine. Classic citrus flavors and aromas are accented by the scent of a freshly mown field.**86** —*K.F. (4/1/2003)*

Seidelberg 2003 Roland's Reserve Syrah (Paarl) $24. This wine shows good extraction with dark color and flavors of charred meat and black fruit, but also has aromas of raspberry and a tinge of green to the plum. The juxtaposition works, although the wine could use a little more oomph midpalate.**86** —*M.D. (5/1/2006)*

Seidelberg 2001 Roland's Reserve Estate Wine Syrah (Paarl) $32. Red-plum aromas mix with brown sugar and sweet leather; plum, caramel, and cedar show on the palate. Rich fruit, chalky tannins and bright acidity make for a delicious, well-balanced wine.**88** —*K.F. (4/1/2003)*

SERENGETI

Serengeti 2003 Pinotage (Coastal Region) $13. This simple wine has straightforward Beaujolais-like aromas, with grapy flavors and sour lemon flavors on the finish.**83** —*M.D. (3/1/2006)*

Serengeti 2004 Sauvignon Blanc (Coastal Region) $13. Veers a bit too far into the vegetal lane for this reviewer, although others may find it simply herbal. Passion fruit and citrus elements lose out to green pepper and asparagus notes. Short finish.**82** —*J.C. (11/15/2005)*

Serengeti 2003 Shiraz (Coastal Region) $13. A trifle soft, but otherwise very drinkable, this medium-bodied Shiraz boasts ample red raspberry and vanilla flavors sure to please most drinkers. Shows more elegance and better integration of components than many of its brethren, ending on a supple, harmonious note.**87** —*J.C. (11/15/2005)*

SHARK TRUST

Shark Trust 2005 Great White Unwooded Chardonnay (Western Cape) $10. A value-oriented brand that makes donations to shark research and preservation, this Chardonnay has front-running pineapple and other tropical fruit flavors that are a touch candied, but not short on intensity. Rounded in the mouth, with a smoky aftertaste.**85 Best Buy** —*M.D. (12/31/2006)*

Shark Trust 2005 Whale Shark Chenin Blanc (Western Cape) $10. Like biting into a peach that isn't fully ripe, this wine has crunch and accessibility in one. Almond also plays a part, and it smells like a semi-sweet Vouvray, with lanolin taking center stage. Try with scallops wrapped in bacon: The acidity will cut right through the dish.**87 Best Buy** —*M.D. (11/1/2006)*

SIGNAL HILL

Signal Hill 2003 Tete Blanche Chenin Blanc (Stellenbosch) $15. Though it gets its Chenin Blanc from vineyards on the Simonsberg mountain slopes, this winery is actually within Cape Town city limits. The wine is rich and wooded, with vanilla and caramel flavors, currants and spice. This is a well-made wine, lacking much varietal character, but with plenty of attractive flavors.**88** —*R.V. (11/15/2005)*

Signal Hill 2000 Gamay Noir (Stellenbosch) $10. Aromas of sweet plum, cocoa, and brown sugar are contrasted by a whiff of dried sausage. This note of dry, cured meat carries to the palate where the plum and cocoa dominate. The body weighs more on acidity, making the fruit a bit lemony on the finish.**87** —*K.F. (9/1/2003)*

Signal Hill 2000 Petite Verdot (Western Cape) $25. The ripe, sweet, red and black fruit is somewhat lush, with a bit of meatiness and molasses-flavored oaken layers throughout. The acidity and tannins are a delightful match to the weight of the fruit.**87** —*K.F. (9/1/2003)*

SIMONSIG

Simonsig 2000 Tiara Bordeaux Blend (Stellenbosch) $30. This mature wine is the top Bordeaux blend from the Malan family estate. With rich, red plum, and black jammy fruits, this wine does not hold its big, bold tastes back. But with great, spicy flavors and a layer of dry tannins that appears at the end, it will stand up to rich foods.**90** —*R.V. (11/1/2006)*

Simonsig 1996 Tiara Bordeaux Blend (Stellenbosch) $25.86 —*M.S. (5/1/2000)*

Simonsig 1996 Cabernet Sauvignon (Stellenbosch) $14.82 —*M.S. (5/1/2000)*

Simonsig 1998 Cabernet Sauvignon (Stellenbosch) $15. This big boy greets us with his deep ruby/black cloak. Loaded with cassis from start to finish, there is tremendous fruit depth here and a full, supple mouthfeel. Reminiscent of one of the successful large-scale '97 California Cabernets. Has tannins to resolve, best held for a year or two.**93 Editors' Choice** —*M.N. (3/1/2001)*

Simonsig 2002 Cabernet Sauvignon Cabernet Sauvignon (Stellenbosch) $18. A spicy, forward, and fruity wine that maintains ample balance. It shows red fruits, spice and dry tannins. This is fresh, elegant, and ready to drink now.**88** —*R.V. (11/1/2006)*

Simonsig 2000 Chardonnay (Stellenbosch) $14. The Malan family makes a ripe, balanced Chardonnay, 100% wood-fermented in French oak. The style is rich and creamy, and there are attractive hints of honey from the partial use of malolactic fermentation. The downside of that is a lack of acidity, but for those who want rich, fat Chardonnay, this is it.**88** —*R.V. (7/1/2002)*

Simonsig 1998 Chenin Blanc (Stellenbosch) $8.87 —*M.S. (11/15/1999)*

Simonsig 2005 Chenin Blanc (Stellenbosch) $10. An intense, extracted, and flowery wine that is full but balanced. Flavors of white currants and gooseberries give some freshness as well as crisp fruitiness. A little sweet on the soft finish.**87 Best Buy** —*R.V. (11/15/2005)*

Simonsig 2004 Chenin Blanc (Stellenbosch) $10. Attractive in an over-ripe way with a core of tangerine and papaya fruit and lime-herb accents. It's rich, with botrytis-like notes, yet shows a faint petillance. Turns drier on the finish, where lemony notes ascend. This is a fine match for spicy foods.**86 Best Buy** —*M.M. (7/1/2005)*

Simonsig 2003 Chenin Blanc (Stellenbosch) $8. When measuring straight-forward quality against price, you won't do any better than with this South African white, which has the weight and mouthfeel of a fine Chardonnay. Seductive aromas of pear, apple, and peach lead to a mus-cular mouthful of Bartlett pear and just-ripe banana. No gimmicks here, just pure, unadulterated fruit balanced by just-right acids. Bar none, this is one of the best values in white wine. Must be that Chenin is still grossly under-appreciated.**88 Best Buy** —*M.S. (11/15/2004)*

Simonsig 2001 Estate Wine Chenin Blanc (Stellenbosch) $7. Sweet, ripe, and fruity in the nose, with a heavier palate than the rest of the wine's components can support. The mouth is all about ripe peach and citrus. It finishes fairly smooth and dry, with some nice nutty qualities.**85** —*M.S. (4/1/2002)*

Simonsig 2002 Pinotage (Stellenbosch) $14. With big tannins and high acidity, this wine is explosive and fruity. Red cherry and mulberry flavors are barely kept in check with a dash of minerality and ripe fruit is layered on a structured frame. This wine could easily please at the next barbecue, washing down a mouth-watering rack of baby back ribs.**88** —*M.D. (9/1/2006)*

Simonsig 2003 Redhill Pinotage (Stellenbosch) $30. Despite straightfor-ward flavors of purple berry fruit and vanilla, this wine's nose speaks volumes, with rich dark fruit and chocolate in addition to the plum and vanilla. Smooth and full in the mouth, with good balancing acidity, this wine will drink well over the next 5 years.**89** —*M.D. (7/1/2006)*

Simonsig 2005 Sauvignon Blanc (Stellenbosch) $13. Fresh and fruity, this wine offers ripe flavors of mango and grapefruit, along with a whiff of cat pee. A great wine for sipping before dinner or when the weather warms up.**85** —*M.D. (3/1/2006)*

Simonsig 2000 Sauvignon Blanc (Stellenbosch) $13. Just what Sauvignon Blanc should be. Fresh and clean with grassy and melon notes present

SOUTH AFRICA

throughout. Vibrant acidity, a smooth mouthfeel and a long finish complete this very lively wine. Would make a great aperitif. **90 Best Buy** —*M.N. (3/1/2001)*

Simonsig 2001 Estate Wine Sauvignon Blanc (Stellenbosch) $11. Tropical fruit makes up the nose, with hints of mint and honey poking through. The body is more full than lean, with light lemon flavors mixing into the richer fig element. Apple dominates the finish. **84** —*M.S. (4/1/2002)*

Simonsig 1998 Shiraz (Stellenbosch) $15. Dangerously stinky, with aromas of unclean stable and sweaty horses. Worse, it doesn't redeem itself in the mouth. **80** *(10/1/2001)*

Simonsig 1998 Merindol Shiraz (Stellenbosch) $45. A funky (but decidedly characteristic South African) earth-meets-barbecue, "horsey" bouquet intrigued some reviewers, but puzzled others. The palate was similarly outdoorsy—earth, oak, and herb enveloped the wine's sour red-fruit flavors. Finishes with tangy, dry wood. **86** *(11/1/2001)*

SIMONSVLEI

Simonsvlei 2005 Lifestyle Chenin Blanc (Western Cape) $NA. An apple- and cream-flavored wine; soft and easy with some crisp apple flavors. It's a great apéritif style. **85** —*R.V. (11/15/2005)*

Simonsvlei 2005 Premier Chenin Blanc (Western Cape) $NA. From fruit mainly grown on the eastern slopes of the Pederberg mountain in Swartland, this is a toasty-edged wine, with fat spicy fruit and light acidity. Because of its dry style, this is a wine which should age, for a couple of years at least. **86** —*R.V. (11/15/2005)*

SINNYA

Sinnya 1998 Bordeaux Blend (Robertson) $11. **85** *(9/1/1999)*

Sinnya 1998 Chardonnay (Robertson) $11. **82** *(9/1/1999)*

Sinnya 2002 Chardonnay (Robertson) $10. At the start, the nose of honey, papaya, brown sugar, and ripe fruit begins to fade. The palate comes off a bit watery, with lemon and herb flavors carrying to the finish. **83** —*K.F. (9/1/2003)*

Sinnya 2001 Merlot-Cabernet Sauvignon (Robertson) $10. The thin, tart palate displays cranberry-plum fruit and the nose is of newsprint, driftwood, and currants. This sensory combo is not as odd as it sounds, but the wine could use more depth. **84** —*K.F. (8/1/2003)*

Sinnya 2002 Pinotage (Robertson) $10. Toast, meat juices, plum and raspberry come off a bit hollow on the midpalate. The flavors carry to the finish, which blooms with a thin layer of eucalyptus. **85** —*K.F. (9/1/2003)*

SIYABONGA

Siyabonga 2001 Cabernet Sauvignon-Merlot (Western Cape) $28. Toast, breadiness, and simple cherry read a bit thin on the nose and palate. This is lightweight, with gripping tannins and a eucalyptus trail to the finish. **84** —*K.F. (1/1/2004)*

Siyabonga 2001 Severney White Blend (Western Cape) $16. French vanilla and marshmallow aromas are accented by a lemony, fresh-herb veneer. Offers ultra-light fruit and a medium-length, herbed finish. A fresh alternative, best served on a hot patio. **84** —*K.F. (1/1/2004)*

SLALEY

Slaley 1999 Hunting Family Shiraz (Stellenbosch) $28. Its leather and dark cherry bouquet is infused with outdoorsy scents (some described it as "animal" and some called it "tree bark"), but that's just fine by us. South African "intensely gamy and earthy" flavors, plus more leather and dry red berry, round out the palate. Long coffee-meets-smoke and gunpowder finish. **89** *(11/1/2001)*

SLANGHOEK

Slanghoek 2001 Private Reserve Pinotage (South Africa) $13. A good example of the modern Pinotage style, in which the grape's sometimes challenging game and metallic qualities are well-tamed. The attractive nose offers tart berry jam, smoke and tar, while the drily fruited palate shows good, brisk acidity. A touch puckery on the close, but tasty overall. **84** —*M.M. (3/1/2004)*

Slanghoek 2002 Private Reserve Sauvignon Blanc (South Africa) $11. Its recent plantings of Touriga Nacional, Malbec, Petit Verdot, and Barbera give every indication that this winery's new offerings will be worth watching. In the meantime, this wine is a fine everyday white with firm, yellow stone fruit and crisp citrus flavors rounded out by hints of vanillin, toast, and hay. There is a certain leanness to the herbal notes and just-right acidity. Drink young, with goat cheeses and chicken dishes. **86** —*K.F. (11/15/2003)*

Slanghoek 2000 Private Reserve Shiraz (South Africa) $14. Decent Shiraz fruit here is regrettably obscured by a heavy toasty oak overlay. With less wood, this might really shine. Typical dark berry, sour herb, and leather flavors play on a mid-weight frame. The feel is tangy, while the finish shows spice, cocoa, and Rhônish metallic hints. **84** —*M.M. (3/1/2004)*

Slanghoek NV Vin Doux Sparkling Blend (South Africa) $14. This wine boasts elements of pale hay, distinct lychee, and candied grapefruit, with a grassy edge. There is a slight flinty, metallic note towards the finish. Although well made, the dosage stands out against the low acidity, and the mouthfeel is on the fierce side. **86** —*K.F. (12/1/2003)*

SOUTHERN RIGHT

Southern Right 2004 Pinotage (Walker Bay) $20. A fully purple wine unleashes dark aromas of leather and black olive, while in the mouth those two flavors dominate. The palate is nice enough—full-bodied with sweet tannins and moderate acidity—but wants more fruit. **84** —*M.D. (11/1/2006)*

Southern Right 2002 Pinotage (Western Cape) $15. Solid, straight ahead, and amply oaked, this Pinotage keeps the tart berry fruit focused and the funky earth note under control. There's plenty of espresso and even some intriguing mint notes here. Finishes fairly long with tangy tannins, great for grilled meats. **86** —*M.M. (11/15/2004)*

Southern Right 2003 Sauvignon Blanc (Western Cape) $10. Grass, lime, even asparagus notes show in this decidedly Kiwi-inspired Sauvignon Blanc. Lean and tangy to the max. **87 Best Buy** —*M.M. (11/15/2004)*

SPICE ROUTE

Spice Route 2004 Chenin Blanc (Coastal Region) $17. The brand is well-known, but this wine does not live up to the hype. It is fat, full, oaky, and toasty, while the fruit seems too soft for the layers of wood, and throws the whole wine out of balance. **82** —*R.V. (11/15/2005)*

Spice Route 2000 Flagship Merlot (Swartland) $35. Deep aromas of smoke, loam, grilled meat, and salinity provide a wrap for red fruit that carries hints of leather, toast and cedar. The salinity and smoke pair with char on the finish, while dusty tannins add structure. **88** —*K.F. (4/1/2003)*

Spice Route 2004 Mourvèdre (Swartland) $18. More Rhône varietals are making it to the U.S. from South Africa, and for good reason. This Mourvèdre showcases plenty of ripe, plummy fruit in the nose and mouth, with additional aromas of mineral and lemon. Plenty of tannins back the full, lush mouthfeel. A bit of warmth shows on the chocolaty finish. **89** —*M.D. (7/1/2006)*

Spice Route 2004 Pinotage (Swartland) $23. Deep purple in color, this wine smells of eraser, dill, and cherries. Vanilla and graham cracker hide a deep core of dark berry fruit, and a bit of spice adds to the mix. The mouthfeel is supple, but has solid tannins to support it. **88** —*M.D. (3/1/2006)*

Spice Route 2000 Flagship Pinotage (Swartland) $23. The oaking provides notes of toast, brown sugar, and dried, sweet herbs while the fruit is translated as plum skin and cherry with accents of cocoa. This is snug, with good acidity, but more depth of fruit would be a boon. **86** —*K.F. (9/1/2003)*

Spice Route 2005 Sauvignon Blanc (Coastal Region) $15. This straw-colored wine has grassy aromas of cat pee and asparagus, a precursor to the zesty, lively mouthfeel. Peach and green apple show in the mouth, but overall, it seems more green than tropical. **85** —*M.D. (7/1/2006)*

Spice Route 1999 Shiraz (Swartland) $20. Reviewers debated whether this bouquet was more redolent of cardboard, green beans, or fresh fish. In any case, the vegetal-tanginess that the aromas promise shows up again on the palate. Finishes sharp, with tobacco notes. **80** *(10/1/2001)*

Spice Route 2001 Flagship Syrah (Swartland) $34. Aromas are of earth, meat, and Indian spice, plus a dash of vanilla. This Syrah picks up some barbecue flavors in the mouth, along with spice and red berry. Soft on the palate, it finishes quickly with menthol and dark berry. **87** *—M.D. (5/1/2006)*

Spice Route 2000 Flagship Syrah (Swartland) $34. Very tart berry Syrah fruit with espresso, tar, and clove accents struggles against overbearing earthiness. The funky element sometimes called South African terroir, which variously appears as iodine, vitamin, metal, or dung, can work in modest doses, just as barnyardiness can in Burgundy. But not to this degree. **83** *—M.M. (11/15/2004)*

Spice Route 1999 Flagship Syrah (Swartland) $35. A complex, individual wine from South Africa that boasts earthy, horsey aromas mixed with briary scents of blackberries and eucalyptus. The earth flavors persist right through to the peppery finish, joined by hints of black olive and hickory smoke. **88** *(11/1/2001)*

Spice Route 2005 Viognier (Swartland) $23. Full-bodied, but with plenty of acidity, this wine has moderate banana and yellow fruit aromas with a hint of nail polish. Dark oak shows through on the palate, along with bruised peach and a streak of stony minerality. A wine with potential, but it doesn't reach it. **85** *—M.D. (9/1/2006)*

SPIER

Spier 2005 Classic Chenin Blanc (Western Cape) $9. Juicy, with ripe, open fruit and a touch of toast from a small amount of barrel fermentation. Pears and citrus fruit have interesting spice notes that add to the complexity. **87 Best Buy** *—R.V. (11/15/2005)*

Spier 2005 Discover Steen (Western Cape) $7. A tropical fruit style of Chenin, marketed as Steen, the old South African name for the grape. This version has too much weight. With green plum flavors and only a touch of crispness, it ends up being rather too full and fat. **83** *—R.V. (11/15/2005)*

SPRINGFIELD ESTATE

Springfield Estate 2001 The Work of Time Bordeaux Blend (Robertson) $30. The is the first vintage of this Bordeaux blend, after 10 years of planning and waiting. But the wine is excellent—there's plenty of juicy fruit, dry wood, and tannin, along with chocolate and plenty of firm berry flavors. **90** *—R.V. (11/1/2006)*

Springfield Estate 1999 Cabernet Sauvignon Methode Ancienne Cabernet Sauvignon (Robertson) $52. From its wax seal, its older vintage (this is the current release) and its name, expect interesting things. You won't be disappointed. The wines come from a small parcel of land on the estate that was long considered too poor to plant. Native yeasts, whole berry fermentation, and no filtering—that's the *methode ancienne* part. There are just 20 barrels of poised, elegant wine with huge depth of flavor, black cherries, and dense tannins blending well together. **92** *—R.V. (11/1/2006)*

Springfield Estate 2004 Whole Berry Cabernet Sauvignon Cabernet Sauvignon (Robertson) $22. Whole-berry fermentation in open-top fermenters allows fermentation to take place slowly and gently. That's the basis behind this open, generous wine, which has great black fruit flavor, good intensity, and soft, ripe tannins. **89** *—R.V. (11/1/2006)*

STARK-CONDÉ

Stark-Condé 2004 Condé Cabernet Sauvignon (Stellenbosch) $42. A single-vineyard wine from land high in the dramatic Jonkershoek valley, this is an intriguingly perfumed wine that still shows a fine sense of structure. The fruit is certainly ripe—it is 14.5% alcohol—but that is lost in the balance with acidity and fine black currant flavors. **89** *—R.V. (11/1/2006)*

Stark-Condé 2003 Condé Cabernet Sauvignon (Stellenbosch) $42. The more expensive of Stark-Condé's Cabs, this one was picked very ripe, evident in the 15% alcohol and stewed fruit aromas. Full but dry in the mouth, it has dark flavors of plum, coffee, and graphite, with similar aromas. The acidity seems high, particularly on the plummy finish. **87** *—M.D. (7/1/2006)*

Stark-Condé 2004 Stark Cabernet Sauvignon (Stellenbosch) $27. A very pure line of blackberry and dark cherry flavors distinguish this wine. It is certainly structured—underneath the fruit there are plenty of fruit and wood tannins—but the ripe fruit flavors dominate. Based on fruit from the Jonkershoek valley, this shows a fine minerally side, compliments of the granite subsoil. **90** *—R.V. (11/1/2006)*

Stark-Condé 2003 Stark Cabernet Sauvignon (Stellenbosch) $27. Though Syrah has been touted as South Africa's best variety, Cabernet has been making quite a name for itself. Bordeaux-like aromas of pencil shavings, brown leaf, and loads of plummy fruit are only slightly marred by a tomato-y note. Lush but dry, with mineral undertones, this dark, fruit-laden wine has a bit of a stewy quality on the finish. Very enjoyable now, and will drink well over the next five years. **89** *—M.D. (7/1/2006)*

Stark-Condé 2003 Condé Syrah (Stellenbosch) $35. Chocolate, cigar leaf, and plum fruit aromas lead to a big, full-bodied wine with great balance and plenty of ripe tannins. Kirsch, black currant, and spice flavors are plenty deep; tobacco shines through on the long, smooth finish. **90** *—M.D. (7/1/2006)*

Stark-Condé 2003 Stark Syrah (Stellenbosch) $26. Not as complex as the Condé, this wine still has rich, plummy fruit matched with sexy oak. The oak shows as chocolate and vanilla on the nose. Full, with a barely noticeable 15% alcohol, the palate offers dry tannins and just enough acidity. The dark fruit flavors have hints of spice, and pick up herbal notes on the finish. **89** *—M.D. (7/1/2006)*

STELLAR ORGANICS

Stellar Organics 2003 Cabernet Sauvignon (Western Cape) $9. Smells raisiny and over-ripe, with a heavy mouthfeel and baked fruit flavors. **80** *—J.C. (11/15/2005)*

STELLEKAYA

Stellekaya 2002 Cabernet Sauvignon (Stellenbosch) $29. A big, beefy red that spent 22 months in oak. The oak imparts a slight sweetness that softens the tannins without impairing the dark, meaty fruit. Chocolate-espresso notes play in the nose and on the tongue, while the wine picks up flavors of leather and balsam. Finishes as big as it lives, with coffee grounds and dark fruit. **88** *—M.D. (11/1/2006)*

STELLENRYCK

Stellenryck 1996 Cabernet Sauvignon (Coastal Region) $16. Restrained and refined, this lighter-weight Cab satisfies with dark cherry/berry aromas and flavors offset by earth and tobacco elements. Possessed of flavor and texture that should pair very well with a wide range of foods, think of this as an attractive South African claret. Drink now through 2004. **87** *—M.M. (3/1/2001)*

STELLENZICHT

Stellenzicht 2002 Golden Triangle Chardonnay (Stellenbosch) $15. Muted, and rather elegant. Shows some finesse, with lots of mineral notes. The taut apple and citrus fruit wears plenty of stony accents, presenting a fairly Burgundian profile. Toasty oak shows more on the close, but doesn't overwhelm. Laudable, a solid, non-fruit-driven offering. **88 Editors' Choice** *—M.M. (7/4/2004)*

Stellenzicht 2001 Golden Triangle Pinotage (Stellenbosch) $18. Elegant Pinotage, smooth but not heavy, classily oaked and rather Pinot Noir-like—of course, that's 50% of its lineage. This is an appealingly tasty, if overtly woody, example. There's very good fruit here; in time I think the elements will resolve positively. Impressive structure too, with back end tannins to lose. Time will surely tell. Enticing now, best 2006–2010. **88** *—M.M. (7/4/2004)*

Stellenzicht 2003 Golden Triangle Sauvignon Blanc (Stellenbosch) $13. Flavorful wine with good focus and fruit-acid balance. Prominent grapefruit, grass, and fig elements recall a Bordeaux Blanc. A good one. This has style and length, fairly begs for fish or shellfish, and is worth looking for. **87** *—M.M. (7/4/2004)*

Stellenzicht 2002 Reserve Sémillon (Stellenbosch) $25. Delicious and full-bodied with fine depth of flavor and excellent texture. Ample oak compliments dry pear, herb-tinged fruit aromas and flavors. Most

Chardonnays don't offer this elegance, structure, or food-friendliness. Will cellar well for 4–8 years. **90 Editors' Choice** —*M.M. (11/15/2004)*

Stellenzicht 2001 Golden Triangle Shiraz (Stellenbosch) $18. Plush, very internationally styled Shiraz showing handsome deep fruit and lavish, toasty oak. Yes, it's a bit generic—meaning maybe you can't tell where it's from—but it's undeniably delicious. The coffee-smoky oak nose, tart-sweet plum fruit, and briary accents leave no doubt about the quality or pleasure quotient here. Seductive now, even better 2005-2008. **89** —*M.M. (7/4/2004)*

Stellenzicht 2000 Syrah (Stellenbosch) $60. The tart-sweet fruit says Syrah, and the potent earthiness is distinctively South African. But the game-earth notes are overpowering here. Neither the fruit nor the texture offer enough positive counterbalance in this shot at a serious Syrah gone awry. **83** —*M.M. (11/15/2004)*

SWARTLAND

Swartland 1997 Cabernet Sauvignon (Swartland) $12. 85 *(9/1/1999)*

Swartland 2004 Indalo Cabernet Sauvignon (Swartland) $14. An oaky, spicy Swartland version of this popular variety, the wine has nice dark fruit flavors with touches of chocolate and a medium-full body that is just shy of showing alcoholic heat in the mouth. Finishes with a hint of leather. **87** —*M.D. (12/31/2006)*

Swartland 1997 Chardonnay (Swartland) $10. 81 *(9/1/1999)*

Swartland 2005 Chenin Blanc (Swartland) $NA. An overly soft wine that is good because of its pleasant, refreshing acidity, leaving a taste of crisp freshness. **83** —*R.V. (11/15/2005)*

Swartland 2005 Indalo Chenin Blanc (Swartland) $14. From the highly rated Swartland cooperative, this wine has fresh fruit, a touch of softness, and ripe, clean apple flavors. It balances richness and freshness very easily. **86** —*R.V. (11/15/2005)*

Swartland 1997 Merlot (Swartland) $12. 82 *(9/1/1999)*

Swartland 2003 Indalo Pinotage (Swartland) $14. From an area formerly known for wheat and tobacco comes this co-op produced premium wine. This Pinotage is inky-purple in color with fresh, grapey whiffs of dark berry and spice, with lemony overtones. Full-bodied and creamy in the mouth, it has flavors of spice, purple fruit, and straw with a lemony-citrus finish. **86** —*M.D. (7/1/2006)*

Swartland 1997 Shiraz (Swartland) $10. 86 *(9/1/1999)*

TALL HORSE

Tall Horse 2003 Cabernet Sauvignon (South Africa) $8. This wine has plenty of oak to the nose, with vanilla and butterscotch dominating, but it fails to excite in the mouth. A soft wine, the palate first delivers sweet mixed berries but is quickly overpowered by oak. **82** —*M.D. (3/1/2006)*

Tall Horse 2004 Chardonnay (Western Cape) $8. White fruit aromas waft from the glass like perfume. This wine has a dusty, creamy feel and melon flavors. Quite a bargain at this price. **84 Best Buy** —*M.D. (3/1/2006)*

Tall Horse 2003 Merlot (Western Cape) $8. Dark red at the rim with cigarbox aromas, this wine packs plenty of fruit for the buck. Cassis, plum, and raspberry all vie for attention in the mouth; while it's a bit sweet, the wine has plenty of tannin and acidity to back it up. Finishes with chocolate notes. **84 Best Buy** —*M.D. (3/1/2006)*

Tall Horse 2003 Shiraz (South Africa) $8. Aromas of smoke, menthol, and cedar don't prepare you for the wealth of spicy berry fruit and vanilla flavors this wine contains. With a lively mouthfeel, this wine is a winner at this price. **84 Best Buy** —*M.D. (5/1/2006)*

TEDDY HALL

Teddy Hall 2005 Chenin Blanc (Stellenbosch) $12. From 20-year-old bush vines, this is a balanced, full-bodied wine, packed with ripeness, but also good acidity. A soft but not sweet wine, named after the owner of the Rudera Winery. **88 Best Buy** —*R.V. (11/15/2005)*

THANDI

Thandi 2001 Cabernet Sauvignon (Coastal Region) $14. Nice accents show here, including some associated with expensive red wines—leather,

tobacco, cedar, shoe polish. But the modest red fruit is overpowered by the amount of oak used, making this overly drying. Some good parts, but the whole is less than the sum. **83** —*M.M. (12/15/2004)*

Thandi 2002 Chardonnay (Western Cape) $13. Good mid-weight Chardonnay with nice apple fruit, notable but not overwhelming oak, nice texture, and a dry finish. As so often, it seems that 15% less oak would yield an improved, better balanced wine. Still, this is even and tasty. **85** —*M.M. (12/15/2004)*

Thandi 2002 Pinot Noir (Elgin) $15. A tangy cherry and smoke bouquet opens this light, attractively balanced wine. Shows interesting chalk hints, but also too much of a green element for it to really sing. Still, they've gotten the feel just right, hard enough with Pinot Noir. Deeper, more focused fruit could make this an impressive contender. I hope the Thandi team stays with it in upcoming vintages. **84** —*M.M. (12/15/2004)*

THE BERRIO

The Berrio 2003 Cabernet Sauvignon (South Africa) $20. A fairly big wine, with big tannins and high acidity, that lets its flavors do the talking. Lush purple fruit and coffee is streaked with lemon and mineral. A bit tart on the finish, but with food this is enjoyable for its swagger. **87** —*M.D. (9/1/2006)*

The Berrio 2005 Sauvignon Blanc (Elim) $20. From this still-young maritime ward comes a zesty, pungent wine. Aromas of asparagus and gooseberry lead to flavors of citrus and mineral with a touch of fresh green herb. Medium-bodied, with zesty acidity throughout. **85** —*M.D. (7/1/2006)*

THE BIG FIVE COLLECTION

The Big Five Collection 2003 Lion Cabernet Sauvignon (Western Cape) $10. Rich, almost sweet cherry fruit has pine/menthol accents and a caramel-like note on the nose. The dry palate shows firmer-than-expected tannins but ample cherry-chocolate flavor, as well. Decent in a lighter style for this grape, though it starts stronger than it closes. **84** —*M.M. (4/1/2005)*

The Big Five Collection 2004 Leopard Chardonnay (Western Cape) $10. This attractive white opens with a handsome peach and herb nose. The even palate's good fruit/acid balance supports solid fruit in the style of the bouquet. Closes clean with drier mineral notes. Flavorful, with some unique character, and commendably off the predictable track. **87 Best Buy** —*M.M. (4/1/2005)*

The Big Five Collection 2003 Elephant Pinotage (Western Cape) $10. Lean and dry with very dark red fruit, tobacco, menthol, and plenty of that specific South African earthiness. It's even, but thin and closes dry, the fruit squelched by the strong green and even funkier notes. **83** —*M.M. (4/1/2005)*

The Big Five Collection 2004 Rhino Sauvignon Blanc (Western Cape) $10. Opens with a soft mineral-herb bouquet. The rounder style continues on the palate, but ample citrus and white pepper notes keep it from being flaccid or mushy. Closes fairly long with a nice reprise of the early mineral notes. An appealing, well-done mainstream white. **85 Best Buy** —*M.M. (4/1/2005)*

The Big Five Collection 2003 Buffalo Shiraz (Western Cape) $10. Attractive lighter-style Shiraz with a complex nose offering berry fruits, herbs, incense, and shoe polish notes. Lithe and racy, with bright red fruit flavors and tangy acidity, it's appealing and not entirely typical—this one shows a little character. **85 Best Buy** —*M.M. (4/1/2005)*

THE FOUNDRY

The Foundry 2003 Cape of Good Hope Syrah (Coastal Region) $41. A full, chewy mouthfeel and dry tannins keep deep, pure plum flavors in check. A straightforward wine at first, time reveals aromas of bramble and a minty finish. With its strong fruit core and young tannins, this may turn into a beautiful wine as secondary flavors develop over the next 5 years. **89** —*M.D. (9/1/2006)*

The Foundry 2005 Cape of Good Hope Viognier (Coastal Region) $20. Toasty vanilla meets peach, apricot, and honeysuckle in a classic Viognier nose. Round in the mouth, with moderate acidity, the melon

SOUTH AFRICA

and peach flavors are brushed aside by toasty, buttery oak. Give the oak another six months to a year, then try with potato gnocchi slathered in a rich alfredo sauce. **87** —*M.D. (9/1/2006)*

THE WOLFTRAP

The Wolftrap 2003 Red Blend (Western Cape) $10. There's ample cherry fruit in this simple, juicy, tasty red from Boekenhoutskloof. The soft, ripe feel will be a crowd pleaser, and slight hints of funkiness are positive here, preventing this from being just another bland blend. Closes drier, showing its Rhônish roots with slight herb-metal notes and modest tannins. **85 Best Buy** —*M.M. (12/15/2004)*

THELEMA

Thelema 1995 Cabernet Sauvignon (Stellenbosch) $30. 85 *(9/1/1999)*

Thelema 2003 Cabernet Sauvignon (Stellenbosch) $41. This wine brings fine Bordeaux to mind, with aromas of eucalyptus and mint, black currant flavor, and firm tannin, and a finish of forest floor. But it's also its own wine, with leather accents, a big, silky body, tart berry and cola, and a warm finish. **88** —*M.D. (9/1/2006)*

Thelema 2004 Chardonnay (Stellenbosch) $25. Although this wine deals some mealy corn aromas, it is still solid. Nicely balanced, with moderate acid pairing a bit of sweetness, the mouth is flush with peach, papaya, and vanilla, tempered with spicy oak. All the cards fall into place with a long, harmonious finish. Drink over the next three years. **88** —*M.D. (9/1/2006)*

Thelema 2002 Chardonnay (Stellenbosch) $25. Usually a good wine, but this vintage the wine seemed to lose steam quickly. Mild, sweet aromas of caramel and butter lead to more of the same in the mouth. Nicely structured, with firm acidity backing medium weight, but the flavors don't quite match up, finishing with a note of corn. **83** —*M.D. (9/1/2006)*

Thelema 2000 Chardonnay (Stellenbosch) $25. Gyles Webb, whose spectacular vineyards drench the slopes of the Simonsberg mountain, was once better known for his great-value Sauvignon Blanc and for his reds. But his Chardonnay is as good as the rest of the range, full of tangy marmalade flavors and a well-judged use of oak, which supports rather than dominates the delicious citrus character of the wine. **90** —*R.V. (7/1/2002)*

Thelema 2003 Merlot (Stellenbosch) $29. Rich and dark, with full, smooth tannins, this big wine explodes with flavors of tar, cassis, plum, and integrated oak. The warm graham cracker finish is as deep as the nose, which displays aromas of cigar box, ripe dark fruits, and cedar; eucalyptus emerging with time. A stellar wine from the premier red wine area in South Africa. **89** —*M.D. (9/1/2006)*

Thelema 1999 Merlot (Stellenbosch) $22. Damp, foresty earth aromas meet those of cherry and dusty cocoa, which carry to the palate of lightweight red fruit. The balance of smooth tannins and gentle acidity is pleasant, but there is room for more heft and complexity overall in this wine. **86** —*K.F. (8/1/2003)*

Thelema 2004 Rhine Riesling (Stellenbosch) $17. This wine has freshly picked apple aromas and nice flavors of peach and mango with some varietal petrol thrown in. There's even a bit of slate, although not as concentrated as some better versions. It also has enough sugar to give it a bit of sweetness and body, but not enough acidity to balance it out. All in all good. **84** —*M.D. (12/31/2006)*

Thelema 2005 Sauvignon Blanc (Stellenbosch) $19. Stellenbosch, like Napa Valley, can produce ripely flavored whites like this. Packed with character, from citrus, peach, and lime flavors to the energizing acidity and fresh fruity nose. Finishes with solid length and intensity. **89** —*M.D. (12/31/2006)*

THORNTREE

Thorntree 2004 Chardonnay (Western Cape) $9. Melon and grassy aromas waft from the glass. The palate delivers plenty of green melon and crème brûlée flavors. The feel is a little oily. Despite its texture, there is still enough acidity to match this with plenty of foods. **85 Best Buy** —*M.D. (5/1/2006)*

Thorntree 2003 Merlot (Western Cape) $9. Merlot has had its ups and downs, but it has always been accessible. This version is medium-to-full bodied, with oozing black fruits and mint notes on the nose and palate. The mouth offers additional spice from a light touch of oak, with a hint of vanilla sweetness. Offers the flavor intensity of a wine three times the cost. **85 Best Buy** —*M.D. (9/1/2006)*

Thorntree 2004 Sauvignon Blanc (Western Cape) $9. This wine has a nice nose of melon, smoke, and mineral, all overlaid with vanilla. Fleshy in the mouth, but with good acidity, it picks up flavors of peaches before toasty oak takes over. **84** —*M.D. (5/1/2006)*

Thorntree 2003 Shiraz (Western Cape) $9. Floral notes mix with heady aromas of red berry and clay. This wine is soft and dry in the mouth but seems a bit hollow, despite delivering some nice chalky berry flavors that turn to plum on the finish. **83** —*M.D. (5/1/2006)*

TOKARA

Tokara 2004 Chardonnay (Stellenbosch) $36. Big in the mouth, with moderate acid, this Chardonnay got plenty ripe in the hot Stellenbosch sun. Yellow fruit flavors have a nice oaky touch, adding plenty of vanilla spice character. The nose is airy, with a straw-like character. Overall a nice wine, with some complexity for a wine of this price. **86** —*M.D. (11/1/2006)*

Tokara 2003 Zondernaam Chardonnay (Stellenbosch) $20. Flavors of white stone fruits, peach pit, and spicy oak are a surprise after a modest nose of melon. The finish carries more of the oak-spice flavors and alcoholic warmth, while the acidity seems high for this medium-bodied wine. **86** —*M.D. (9/1/2006)*

Tokara 2005 Zondernaam Sauvignon Blanc (Western Cape) $17. A nice combination of gooseberry and mineral on the nose, while the palate entry is round, wrapping gooseberry flavors into a seamless wine. Soft acidity and hints of green bean keep it lively, and green peppercorn adds to the finish. **86** —*M.D. (12/31/2006)*

Tokara 2003 Zondernaam Shiraz (Stellenbosch) $20. Not your average Shiraz, this has touches of tobacco, eraser, and mineral to the raspberry and dark berry fruit aromas. More plummy in the mouth, with spicy pepper and layered oak and acidity to match the still young tannins. Leave it on its side for a couple years, or give it at least an hour in a decanter. **88** —*M.D. (9/1/2006)*

TRIBAL

Tribal 2003 Chardonnay (Western Cape) $7. Simple Chardonnay with a pleasant, smooth feel that avoids being cloying. Shows a little heat on the nose at first but evens out on the palate. Ends with mild apple and cream notes. **83** —*M.M. (7/4/2004)*

Tribal 2003 Merlot (Western Cape) $7. The fruit here is enveloped and subdued by much stronger earth-iodine notes that dominate. Closes tart and hard. **80** —*M.M. (7/4/2004)*

Tribal 2003 Pinot Noir (Western Cape) $7. Shows sour cherry fruit, some oak, and a dose of that metallic earthiness Cape wines often show. A little lighter in weight, but not far from a Pinotage in manner—then again, it is a parent grape (with the Rhône's Cinsault) to that South African hybrid. **83** —*M.M. (7/4/2004)*

Tribal 2002 Pinotage (Western Cape) $7. Tasty, solid Pinotage fruit here is nicely wrapped in oak. The tart berry flavors will pair well with lamb or game. Shows surprising substance and good back end grip, with some tannins to lose. Would be interesting to try in two years, too. **85** —*M.M. (7/4/2004)*

TUKULU

Tukulu 2003 Chenin Blanc (Groenekloof) $12. Dry and very refreshing, a fine example of the potential of Cape Chenin Blanc. Slate and mineral notes over fine dry white peach and citrus fruit make for a tasty, refreshing wine. **87 Best Buy** —*M.M. (11/15/2004)*

Tukulu 2005 Papkuilsfontein Chenin Blanc (Darling) $13. From a black empowerment-managed vineyard, jointly owned with giant winery Distell, this wine comes from the Papkuilsfontein vineyard on the west coast. It is a ripe wine, but its chief attraction is the white fruit and crisp, herbaceous flavors. It already has good balance, but its very dry character promises some good development. **90 Best Buy** —*R.V. (11/15/2005)*

TUMARA

Tumara 2002 Titan Bordeaux Blend (Stellenbosch) $16. With powerful aromas of tobacco and menthol this earthy wine definitely pleases, although a medicinal note detracts a bit. In the mouth, red berry is muted by forest floor, tobacco, and mint, and the wine coats the palate with some gritty tannins. Finishes smooth, ending with mixed berry. **88** —M.D. (5/1/2006)

Tumara 2002 Malbec (Stellenbosch) $13. Good fruit meets intense elefunkiness (my term for that Cape earthy element) in this even, mid-weight red. Black raspberry, licorice, toast, and asphalt notes play on the palate. But on the back end, full, spiky tannins and fierce funk prevail. Still, it's interesting, atypical, and feels like it may show improved focus and balance with a little age. **85**—M.M. (4/1/2005)

Tumara 2004 Bellevue Estate Pinotage (Stellenbosch) $16. Fans of oldstyle Tuscan wines, take note. This easy-to-like wine has plummy-cherry fruit flavors wrapped in a leathery skin. Some barnyard and cola are apparent on the nose, while sweet tannins coat the palate. **86**—M.D. (11/1/2006)

Tumara 2003 Bellevue Estate Pinotage (Stellenbosch) $12. This wine shows a healthy dose of oak with scents of vanilla and dill, but also a good amount of sour cherry. Full and smooth, with flavors of dark berry and cola, the only thing this wine is lacking is the structure it needs to age over the long term. Enjoy it now. **87 Best Buy**—M.D. (3/1/2006)

Tumara 2002 Bellevue Estate Pinotage (Stellenbosch) $13. A reasonably tasty if very dark wine in which oak dominates the black cherry fruit. It's medium weight, with stylish toast-espresso flavors. Has appeal, but the attraction here isn't robust fruit. Still, legions of fans of the 'quercus maximus' style have plenty to savor here. **85**—M.M. (4/1/2005)

Tumara 2001 Bellevue Estate Pinotage (Stellenbosch) $13. Plenty of flavor shows in this zingy Pinotage from the first estate to ever plant the grape commercially. Dry, sour cherry fruit is offset by toast and herb accents. **85**—M.M. (3/1/2004)

TWEE JONGE GEZELLEN

Twee Jonge Gezellen NV The Rosé Brut Sparkling Blend (Tulbagh) $17. There's a bit of copper to the color of this wine, and aromas of cola. Fairly intense flavors follow the nose, sassafras, and cherry cola leading the way, and the wine has a nice creaminess to it. Could use a bit more acidity to liven it up. **85**—M.D. (12/31/2006)

TWO OCEANS

Two Oceans 2004 Cabernet Sauvignon-Merlot (Western Cape) $8. This lively wine has a deep nose of cassis, pencil eraser, and tobacco. A Bordeaux blend, it tastes like a fine wine of that region, with a core of dark berry fruit accented by some tobacco. Wrapped in moderate tannins with a dry, dusty feel and finishing with cassis, this is a value-priced wine to stock up on. Drink over the next two years. **87 Best Buy**—M.D. (5/1/2006)

Two Oceans 2004 Chardonnay (Western Cape) $8. Better than many more expensive wines, this wine delivers a solid package without trying to do too much. Toast and vanilla accompany white stone fruit aromas and flavors, while the palate is round, with just the right amount of acidity. **87 Best Buy**—M.D. (5/1/2006)

Two Oceans 2003 Chardonnay (Western Cape) $8. This basic Chardonnay opens with floral aromas. Mildly sweet pear fruit is accented by straw and vanilla. Finishes clean with apple and citrus notes. **83**—M.M. (7/4/2004)

Two Oceans 2002 Chardonnay (Western Cape) $7. Creamy oak and tropical fruit aromas are tinted with grapefruit peel. The palate displays white peach and starfruit aromas that finish with herbs and heat. **87 Best Buy** —K.F. (4/1/2003)

Two Oceans 2005 Sauvignon Blanc (Western Cape) $8. This wine is clumsy in the mouth for a Sauvignon Blanc, with little acidity. It's sweet, with aromas and flavors of yellow fruit and straw, and a bit of sulphur note on the nose. **82**—M.D. (5/1/2006)

Two Oceans 2004 Shiraz (Western Cape) $8. This wine is easy to drink, relatively complex, and a great value. Meaty, barnyardy scents open to reveal toast and dark berry, and flavors of ripe plum and meat. Full-bodied and warm, despite only 13.5% alcohol, this wine has good acid and tannin, and a dry mouthfeel. Finishes ashy and warm. **87 Best Buy**— M.D. (7/1/2006)

Two Oceans 2002 Shiraz (Western Cape) $8. Good everyday Shiraz with an even, light to mid-weight mouthfeel. Not at all sweet or candied; stewy, dark berry fruit, earth, and mineral accents make this tasty red an attractive value-priced choice. **85**—M.M. (7/4/2004)

Two Oceans 2001 Shiraz (Western Cape) $7. A mouth-filling wine with fine tannins; tart blackberry, endive, and pastry aromas add to the flavors of fresh figs, apple peel, and leather. Black pepper and meat flavors show on the finish. **88 Best Buy**—K.F. (4/1/2003)

UITKYK

Uitkyk 1998 Cabernet Sauvignon (Stellenbosch) $17. Cherry and apple peel aromas are veiled in caramel and light brown sugar. The cherry and apple transform on the palate, coming across as tawny-red fruit with toasty caramel. The finish is vegetal. **84**—K.F. (4/1/2003)

Uitkyk 1999 Estate Cabernet Sauvignon (Stellenbosch) $18. Oak runs rampant here, swamping the dark red berry fruit with asphalt, licorice, and toast, toast, toast. The modest fruit is hard to find. Quite dry and not well-balanced, with overtly woody tannins. **83**—M.M. (4/1/2005)

Uitkyk 2003 Chardonnay (Stellenbosch) $18. A handsome, mid-weight white with tasty apple-oak flavors supported by ample acidity. There's a ripe, even feel, while spice accents and tropical fruit notes keep it lively and engaging. Closes with more tangy spice, subtle mineral hints. The name reads 'ooyt-kick' to Anglo eyes, but from the Afrikaans, it's pronounced more like 'ate-cake.' **89**—M.M. (4/1/2005)

Uitkyk 2001 Chardonnay (Stellenbosch) $17. Slightly sweet aromas of toast and lemon cake are accompanied by a bloom of alcohol. The lightweight palate offers herbs, lemon, and white pepper, and bright acidity. **85**— K.F. (4/1/2003)

Uitkyk 2004 Sauvignon Blanc (Stellenbosch) $18. Peach, mild apple, and tropical fruit notes prevail in this light, lean white. No problems here, just doesn't emphatically grab the senses. Maybe an understated manner causes it to recede in a rather vibrant crowd. Still, it's a good match for salads, closing clean, with mild white pepper notes. **84**—M.M. (4/1/2005)

Uitkyk 2002 Sauvignon Blanc (Stellenbosch) $11. The colorless appearance of this wine extends to its very delicate and dilute style. Marshmallow, mango, coconut water, and orange blossom carry to the palate, with a hint of licorice and grassiness on the finish. **84**—K.F. (9/1/2003)

Uitkyk 2001 Sauvignon Blanc (Stellenbosch) $11. Fresh hay, light tropical fruit, and dried herb sachet aromas repeat on the palate with less depth. The finish is herby, clean, and maybe the most outstanding element when compared to the undistinguished fruit. **84**—K.F. (4/1/2003)

UMKHULU

Umkhulu 2004 Dry White White Blend (Stellenbosch) $NA. A wine with a fine, nutty complexity over ripe fruit, with a touch of toast and a full, buttery flavor. This is developing well, but could age another 18 months. **89**—R.V. (11/15/2005)

URBANE

Urbane 2005 Chenin Blanc (Walker Bay) $NA. A crisp, easy style, with sweet apple flavors and some good crisp acidity. The wine finishes soft and lightly sweet. **84**—R.V. (11/15/2005)

Urbane 2002 Sauvignon Blanc (Stellenbosch) $10. The aromas and flavors here are green, in the Kiwi (that's New Zealand) style, but the mouthfeel is much softer than most wines of this profile. It's clean from start to finish, and for drinking near term. And soon after opening—it softened up too much, too quickly. **83**—M.M. (3/1/2004)

Urbane 2002 Shiraz (Stellenbosch) $10. Correct Syrah elements here in an unusually soft package. The very plush—nearly mushy—mouthfeel provides barely adequate support for the sound berry, herb, and earth notes. Some commendable leather and game accents even show. Could sing if it had more spine to hold it together. **84**—M.M. (3/1/2004)

VAN LOVEREN

Van Loveren 2003 Reserve Chardonnay (Robertson) $15. A nose of hay and sweet perfume opens to over-ripe and slightly oxidized flavors. Just too soft and too sweet. **80** —*M.M. (11/15/2004)*

Van Loveren 2002 Reserve Chardonnay (Robertson) $16. The thin fruit here is utterly overwhelmed by oak from stem to stern. **80** —*M.M. (7/4/2004)*

Van Loveren 2001 Reserve Chardonnay (Robertson) $16. Citrus, toast, and cream aromas are followed up by watery citrus on the palate. There's enough acidity to hold interest through the herbal, toasted finish. **84** —*K.F. (4/1/2003)*

Van Loveren 2002 Riesling (Robertson) $13. Aromas of golden apples and raisins are lifted by pretty blossom aromas and a zing of lime juice. The clean acidity paired with flavors of lime and grapefruit, make this very pleasant and fresh. **87** —*K.F. (4/1/2003)*

Van Loveren 2003 Sauvignon Blanc (Robertson) $10. Sauvignon Blanc with unusual acacia wood-like aromatics and a slightly over-ripe fruit quality. The feel is easy, almost plush, and on the sweet and soft side for a grape known more for zesty acidity and tangy flavors. Could have everyday appeal as a Chardonnay alternative. **83** —*M.M. (12/15/2004)*

VEENWOUDEN

Veenwouden 1998 Classic Bordeaux Blend (Paarl) $37. There's very little to take issue with here. It's an intense, extracted mouth-filling beauty with leather, black plum, and licorice aromas. The palate is plush, creamy, and packed full of vanilla and kirsch. What a ripe and ready red you'll find in this Bordeaux-style blend; drink sooner rather than later. **91** —*M.S. (4/1/2002)*

Veenwouden 1998 Merlot (Paarl) $37. The color is opaque and the nose is tight, meaty, and earthy. The mouth offers layers of bittersweet chocolate and powerful blackberries. It's a tad hedonistic and heavy, with all sorts of overflowing fruit, but isn't that what most people want in a modern red wine? **90** —*M.S. (4/1/2002)*

VERGELEGEN

Vergelegen 2001 Red Cabernet Blend (Stellenbosch) $59. Much better than a bottle previously reviewed, this wine shows ample tobacco, earth, and slate to combine with its admittedly green flavors. It's structured like a tightrope, linear and strong, with more acidity than many Cabernets of its caliber. It will pair beautifully with a pot roast, and develop more complexity with age. **88** —*M.D. (5/1/2006)*

Vergelegen 2001 Red Cabernet Blend (Stellenbosch) $59. Shows good ripeness by some measures—smooth tannins, relatively high alcohol—but not by others, as it also exhibits plenty of roasted green pepper aromas. Chocolate and cassis give it some redeeming flavors, and they pick up hints of black pepper on the finish. Might get better with age. **82** —*J.C. (11/15/2005)*

Vergelegen 2001 V Cabernet Blend (Stellenbosch) $145. 91% Cabernet Sauvignon, plus Merlot and Cabernet Franc, Vergelegen's ultra-premium cuvée is tightly structured, harmoniously balanced, and built to age, although it has a greener flavor profile than many modern wines—bell pepper and bramble aromas and green bean flavors—there is still plenty of underlying cassis, tobacco, and chocolate to make this a keeper. Polished tannins lead to a long, powerful finish. **92** —*M.D. (9/1/2006)*

Vergelegen 2003 Cabernet Sauvignon (Stellenbosch) $34. Cassis, herbs, char, and a touch of green pepper create an interesting bouquet, while the palate is supple, creamy, and delivers nice cassis and forest-floor flavors. A finely made wine in a classic Bordeaux style. **88** —*M.D. (3/1/2006)*

Vergelegen 2003 Reserve Chardonnay (Stellenbosch) $31. This wine shows plenty of char, butter, and eucalyptus aromas layered over banana and mango. On the palate the feel is round with full flavors of tropical fruit and baked banana bread. Finishes dry and crisp. **88** —*M.D. (3/1/2006)*

Vergelegen 2003 Mill Race Merlot-Cabernet Sauvignon (Stellenbosch) $22. A delicious wine, loaded with cassis and kirsch liqueur. The complex nose offers tobacco and menthol in addition to the deep fruit,

similar to the spice and tobacco on the fruity finish. A wine to drink over the near term. **89** —*M.D. (5/1/2006)*

Vergelegen 2005 Sauvignon Blanc (Western Cape) $22. Like many of Vergelegen's wines, this Sauvignon Blanc has aromas touched with green bean; in this case the aromas are of chalk, flint, and lime. Flavors of key lime border on unripe, while tropical fruits add a pleasant dimension, making this an ideal summer quaff. Finishes with a chalky, tart intensity. **86** —*M.D. (9/1/2006)*

Vergelegen 2004 Sauvignon Blanc (Western Cape) $22. Citrus, flint, and stone scents join riper peach and melon aromas to create a full, solid bouquet. The palate is plump, a bit pithy, and overall the wine is a straightforward, well-made easy drinker. Nothing weird or wild, just a pure wine with mass appeal. **87** *(7/1/2005)*

VERGENOEGD

Vergenoegd 2001 Estate Wine Bordeaux Blend (Stellenbosch) $35. This Cabernet Sauvignon-Merlot-Cabernet Franc blend is full-bodied and rich, with sweet fruit overflowing an impressive structure that seems effortless. It is near maturity, possibly benefiting from a few more years in the cellar, but those generous, full-power flavors could well be enjoyed now. Until this 2001 vintage, this wine was labeled as Reserve. **92** —*R.V. (11/1/2006)*

Vergenoegd 2001 Cabernet Sauvignon (Stellenbosch) $28. An opulently rich wine from very ripe fruit giving soft tannins, a delicious layer of red berries, and mature Cab flavors. There is structure there, buried under all the ripeness, but this is a wine to sink into, ready for immediate drinking. **91** —*R.V. (11/1/2006)*

Vergenoegd 2000 Estate Cabernet Sauvignon (Stellenbosch) $32. Seems dominated by brett, with sweaty leather, cedar, and hickory smoke aromas and flavors, like a horse that's been ridden hard and put away wet. Metallic on the finish, coupled with drying tannins. **82** —*J.C. (11/15/2005)*

Vergenoegd 2000 Estate Merlot (Stellenbosch) $31. Red berry fruit fights to show through a heavy cloak of toasty-oak. The smooth mouthfeel and even finish are appealing, but the overall profile is too indistinct. Lovers of dark, lavishly oaky wines will find lots to like and my score stingy, but I prefer the fruit more forward. **84** —*M.M. (11/15/2004)*

Vergenoegd 1998 Old Cape Colony Port (Stellenbosch) $30. Tasty but very dark, even black, with a dense oak veneer over its solid fruit core. The ripe crushed blackberry and blueberry fruit and nutty accents work hard to come forward. Structured and tannic now, but should improve and open a bit more through 2006. This might really sing with less overbearing dark, toasty oak. **86** —*M.M. (11/15/2004)*

Vergenoegd 2000 Estate Shiraz (Stellenbosch) $40. Nice parts try to surface here, showing hints at a serious Shiraz: Very dark, tart, sweet fruit, herb and tar accents, and a mouthfilling, if dryly woody feel. The problem? Massive, overbearing oak that envelops and submerges all else, even after an hour of breathing. **82** —*M.M. (12/15/2004)*

VILAFONTÉ

Vilafonté 2004 Series C Bordeaux Blend (Paarl) $70. Series C is the Cabernet-dominated version of a wine that brings together the winemaking talents of California winemaker Zelma Long and her viticulturist husband Phil Freese, along with Warwick Estate's Mike Ratcliffe and San Francisco-based importer Bartholemew Broadbent. Coffee, chocolate, and dark berry fruits dominate this brooding wine that shows intensity and power. Yet it never becomes heavy or over-ripe—here there is a good sense of balance that lifts the wine, especially in the aftertaste. **94** —*R.V. (11/1/2006)*

Vilafonté 2003 Series C Bordeaux Blend (Paarl) $70. A fairly big (14.5% alcohol), chewy wine, but one that delivers waves of lush fruit. Plum and cassis notes are framed by hints of smoke and cedar; the merest hint of green herbs adds complexity without detracting. Long and supple on the finish. Drink now–2015. **92** *(11/15/2005)*

Vilafonté 2004 Series M Bordeaux Blend (Paarl) $50. Series M is based on Merlot and Malbec, with the two Cabernets also in the blend. Very modern in style, it has polished elegance, packs a punch of black fruits, dense mulberry flavors, and long, smooth oak tastes. **93** —*R.V. (11/1/2006)*

Vilafonté 2003 Series M Bordeaux Blend (Paarl) $50. Rounder and softer in the mouth than the Series C, with plump plum and chocolate flavors that pick up hints of caramel, toast, and dried herbs on the finish. Soft but not unstructured, this is immediately likeable. Drink now–2010. It might last longer, but why chance it? **91** *(11/15/2005)*

VILLIERA

Villiera NV Tradition Brut Champagne Blend (Paarl) $16. Deeper in color than many, with caramel and toffee aromas as well as some hints of cheese and popcorn. The palate is developed and mature, with baked apple and melon flavors. But then comes a sharp note akin to lemon, which does create a lean and tart impression. But overall it has good character. **86** —*M.S. (6/1/2003)*

Villiera 2005 Chenin Blanc (Stellenbosch) $12. One of the top wineries of Stellenbosch, the Villiera winery has a fine reputation for strongly ter-roir-based wines. This Chenin, with its mineral character, shows good structure to go with the tropical fruit flavors, the almonds and some cit-rus. **89** —*R.V. (11/15/2005)*

Villiera 2004 Cellar Door Chenin Blanc (Stellenbosch) $24. There's just too much wood with this wine. It dominates the ripe fruit, leaving high toast flavors and spice. This is a wine for lovers of heavily oaked wines, but not for lovers of Chenin Blanc. **85** —*R.V. (11/15/2005)*

VINAY

Vinay NV Rosé Blend (South Africa) $12. A very cherry bouquet opens this surprisingly flavorful rosé. The tangy mouthfeel, spicy cherry flavors, and meaty accents have appeal. Though a touch metallic on the close, it's far ahead of most white zins as a tasty, inexpensive quaff. Non vintage and in a 1-liter bottle, to boot. **84** —*M.M. (3/1/2004)*

VINUM AFRICA

Vinum Africa 2004 Cabernet Sauvignon (Stellenbosch) $14. Dark red in the glass, this wine slowly reveals itself as a wolf in sheep's clothing. Hints of leather and barnyard lift to show dark berry aromas, while the entry is smooth and silky, a chocolate under-current leading towards more substantial cassis and mixed berry with cola and leather notes. Firm in the mouth, it has graceful tannins that will evolve over the next few years. A wine true to Stellenbosch at an affordable price. **89 Best Buy** —*M.D. (11/15/2006)*

Vinum Africa 2004 Chenin Blanc (Stellenbosch) $12. Just a hint of wood from a small percentage of barrel aging gives this wine an open, buttery character. From vines on the slopes of the Helderberg mountain outside Stellenbosch, the wine lacks pure Chenin varietal character, but there are great, ripe flavors. **89 Best Buy** —*R.V. (11/15/2005)*

Vinum Africa 2002 Chenin Blanc (Stellenbosch) $12. Grassy aromas meet those of papaya and banana, while the palate displays similar tropical notes with citrus and grassiness. Light and thin throughout, this finishes with bitter herbs. **84** —*K.F. (9/1/2003)*

VREDE EN LUST

Vrede en Lust 2003 Classic Bordeaux Blend (Simonsberg-Paarl) $20. "Classic" means Bordeaux in this case, with four of the varieties included (65% Cabernet, 26% Merlot, and the rest Malbec and Petit Verdot). Shows a lot of leather on the nose, with dark plummy fruit underneath, while the palate is extracted, showing a full body, good acid, and plenty of fine tannins. Dark berry flavors, almost charred, cover cherry flavors. **87** —*M.D. (12/31/2006)*

WARWICK

Warwick 2002 Reserve Bordeaux Blend (Stellenbosch) $32. A firm, dry, and elegant red whose earth and mineral notes accent a solid, dark cherry-berry fruit core. A modest amount of typical South African funkiness shows. But well-handled here, rather than detracting, it adds complexity, Closes long, with good tannic structure. Should improve through this decade. **90** —*M.M. (7/1/2005)*

Warwick 2003 Tilogy (Estate Reserve) Bordeaux Blend (Stellenbosch) $30. Smooth and sexy, this trilogy of Cabernet Sauvignon, Cabernet Franc, and Merlot offers a wood-driven nose with eucalyptus, brown sugar,

vanilla, and chocolate, all tinged with spice. The flavors of dark berry, eucalyptus, and earth, while more subdued, still manage to convey strength, and lead to smooth tannins and chocolate on the finish. **90** —*M.D. (5/1/2006)*

Warwick 2001 Tilogy (Estate Reserve) Bordeaux Blend (Simonsberg-Stellenbosch) $30. Offers interesting Oriental spice, leather, popcorn, and earth notes over deep cassis fruit. Full and smooth, with excellent balance and an espresso-dark finish. Perhaps oak-heavy, but delicious in weight and style not unlike some very good modern-style Graves. **88** —*M.M. (11/15/2004)*

Warwick 1998 Tilogy (Estate Reserve) Bordeaux Blend (Stellenbosch) $22. The dark, dry cherry, tobacco, and earth aromas and flavors in this mid-weight red are attractive, but without tremendous depth. It offers cocoa and anise notes, but also fairly high acidity, and on the back end, some prickly tannins. A good dining wine—food will lessen its edge. Drink this year and next. **86** —*M.M. (4/1/2002)*

Warwick 2004 Trilogy (Estate Reserve) Bordeaux Blend (Stellenbosch) $32. This was the first Bordeaux blend from the Cape, and remains one of the very best. This 2004 is stylish, very Bordeaux in its structure, yet shows a richness of fruit that Bordeaux can only envy. Black currants, dry tannins, and a sense of great ageability—they are all there. **95 Editors' Choice** —*R.V. (11/1/2006)*

Warwick 2004 Chardonnay (Stellenbosch) $25. Aromas are of white stone fruits, which continue on the palate, where there's also freshly peeled bananas. Creamy through and through, but not all that complex. **85** —*M.D. (3/1/2006)*

Warwick 1999 Chardonnay (Stellenbosch) $18. Stan and Norma Ratcliffe made their names as producers in the first wave of South Africa's wine Renaissance. Their consistency of style keeps them there. This Chardonnay, aged for four months in French oak, is rich, with creamy, mature fruit, just spiced with wood, and an enticing lemongrass per-fume. **89** —*R.V. (9/10/2002)*

Warwick 1998 Merlot (Stellenbosch) $19. Black fruit and plenty of oak create a dark flavor profile for this Merlot. The animal and earth ele-ments noted in more than a few South African reds adds an unexpected complexity, but like Burgundian barnyard, some tasters will have trouble with it. The long finish of tart plum, chocolate and oak wraps it up nicely. Best drunk now through 2004. **87** —*M.M. (4/1/2002)*

Warwick 1997 Merlot (Stellenbosch) $18. Plum, chocolate, and herba-ceous notes make for an attractive flavor package. A smooth mouthfeel, medium body, and a long finish add further positive notes. You won't go wrong with this one. **87** —*M.N. (3/1/2001)*

Warwick 2004 Old Bush Vines Pinotage (Stellenbosch) $17. "Old Bush Vines" must mean an extra dose of fruit, because this wine has it in waves. Offers crushed berries on the nose and sweet mixed berries in the mouth, mixed with just enough vanilla to keep it interesting. **86** —*M.D. (3/1/2006)*

Warwick 2003 Old Bush Vines Pinotage (Stellenbosch) $21. Opens with a lovely raspberry, chocolate, and spice nose. Strong and solid, with deep fruit, a nicely balanced mouthfeel, and well-employed oak, this closes long and dry with mildly tangy tannins. **88** —*M.M. (11/15/2004)*

Warwick 1999 Old Bush Vines Pinotage (Stellenbosch) $17. Made of fruit from 27-year-old vines, this is built on a solid core of deep dark berry fruit nicely framed in toasty oak. The full, smooth palate is nuanced, showing plenty of character in its barnyard notes and accents of leather and bitter chocolate. Impressive Pinotage that closes with good length. Drink now through 2005. **89** —*M.M. (4/1/2002)*

Warwick 1998 Old Bush Vines Pinotage (Stellenbosch) $18. Earth and wood aromas open to a tart berry palate. The wine has a mildly creamy texture, but the fruit seems clipped with a slight green note. High acidity gives the wine an edgy feel and it closes a bit short, with more tart berry fruit. **84** —*M.M. (3/1/2001)*

Warwick 2001 Three Cape Ladies Red Blend (Simonsberg-Stellenbosch) $21. The three Cape ladies are the Cabernet Sauvignon, Merlot, and Pinotage in this tasty, accessible blend. Shows attractive dry berry fruit, tobacco and forest floor accents, and very good fruit/acid balance. Drink through 2007–8. **86** —*M.M. (11/15/2004)*

SOUTH AFRICA

Warwick 2003 Three Cape Ladies Cape Blend Red Blend (Stellenbosch) $25. A fun wine, with plenty of plum and berry flavors cloaked in oak, with a hint of earth to add interest. Quaffable for its smooth mouthfeel and moderate tannins, the nose has a hint of sour cherry. A Pinotage, Cabernet, and Merlot blend. **85** —*M.D. (7/1/2006)*

Warwick 2002 Three Cape Ladies Cape Blend Red Blend (Stellenbosch) $29. Sexy, forward wine with ample fruit and easy tannins. Plush— almost soft, yet not entirely simple. This vinous menage-a-trois has some depth and may easily seduce you. Nothing wrong with that . . . just don't seek a long term relationship. It's not for cellaring, drink thru 2007. **88** —*M.M. (7/1/2005)*

Warwick 2004 Winemaker Guild Blend Red Blend (Stellenbosch) $60. The Winemakers Guild is a grouping of South African winemakers and members who can submit wines for approval and release under the Guild name. This impressive 2004 Cabernet is still very young, firmly under the control of fine tannins, but showing ripe but structured dark plums and herbs underneath. **92** —*R.V. (11/1/2006)*

Warwick 2005 Professor Black Sauvignon Blanc (Stellenbosch) $17. Warwick makes good wines in a variety of categories, and Professor Black is a standout in South African Sauvignon Blanc every year. The white fruit aromas have a crunchy, crisp feel that speaks of freshness and flavor, with a dollop of creamy vanilla. Tasty peach along with refreshing citrus and lime offer waves of flavor, and it maintains a crisp feel without losing body. Great balance between flavor and feel. **88** —*M.D. (12/31/2006)*

Warwick 2004 Professor Black Sauvignon Blanc (Simonsberg-Stellenbosch) $18. Initially rather simple and sweet, offering ripe tropical-citrus fruit plus a round, soft feel, behind that veneer lurked an impressive wine. With time emerged Sauvignon Blanc's brighter citrus and grass tanginess, and much higher apparent acidity. It's full yet crisp, closing long with rich fruit and mild pepper notes. Grab now, but wait until 2005 to drink. **90 Editors' Choice** —*M.M. (11/15/2004)*

Warwick 2001 Estate Shiraz (Simonsberg-Stellenbosch) $20. Elegant, but overly woody, with smoke and cedar aromas dominating the nose. The palate offers indistinct black fruit wrapped in dark toast that's a bit astringent. There's simply too much oak and not enough fruit. **84** — *M.M. (11/15/2004)*

Waterford 2004 Cabernet Sauvignon (Stellenbosch) $29. From this beautiful Helderberg estate, this Cabernet Sauvignon is in a leaner style than some vintages, reflecting the cooler conditions of 2004. There are flavors of dark chocolate, juicy black cherries, and damsons, while the wine is suffused with layers with acidity. Has great aging potential. Available in the U.S. next summer. **92** —*R.V. (11/1/2006)*

Waterford 2003 Cabernet Sauvignon (Stellenbosch) $27. A big, fat, juicy wine that nonetheless preserves elegance and freshness. There's a touch of eucalyptus and mint, plus an herbal character. The acidity holds the whole thing in balance. From master red winemaker Kevin Arnold, this is a wine that needs aging. Give it three to four years before opening. **93 Cellar Selection** —*R.V. (11/1/2006)*

Waterford 2001 Cabernet Sauvignon (Stellenbosch) $27. This is more herbal than other recent vintages from Waterford, a stalky Cabernet style. The tannins are firm, dry, and solid, the fruit leaning towards hedgerow black fruit flavors. It is ready to drink now, and delicious. **89** —*R.V. (11/1/2006)*

Waterford 2000 Cabernet Sauvignon (Stellenbosch) $22. A good aromatic setup of anise, faint eucalyptus, cigar box, and enticing ripe fruit. The ripe red to black fruit in a veil of cedar on the palate is pleasurable, but relatively one-dimensional. The firm structure will chase away any lengthy consideration of the fruit. **87** —*K.F. (4/1/2003)*

Waterford 1999 Chardonnay (Stellenbosch) $15. Everything about this elegant Chardonnay says balance and proportion. The tropical fruit shadings are carried by a solid acid backbone and accented smartly by mineral notes. A subtle yet rich perfume provides unexpected pleasure, and this wine has structure, reserve, and depth. Can last two to five years. **90 Best Buy** —*M.M. (3/1/2001)*

Waterford 2000 Sauvignon Blanc (Stellenbosch) $13. Lively, with brisk lime and herb aromas opening into a mouthful of tart grapefruit flavors. Shows a nice mouthfeel and a long finish with a crisp citrus tang and a slight mineral note. This zinger is right up there with the best in this style from New Zealand. **90 Best Buy** —*M.M. (3/1/2001)*

Waterford 1999 Kevin Arnold Shiraz (Stellenbosch) $30. The earth, smoke, saddle-leather aromas and flavors are powerful and distinctive but probably not to all tastes. The lavish high-toast oak is nearly over-the-top, but a creamy mouthfeel and long finish tip the scales to the pleasure side. Complex and challenging . . . but not for those averse to the elements mentioned. **88** —*M.M. (3/1/2001)*

Waterford 2001 Nadine Shiraz (Stellenbosch) $34. An animal note quickly blows off, leaving lovely menthol-eucalyptus, blackberry, and molasses aromas. The animal note returns on the palate, pleasantly integrating with rich blackberry, black plum, coffee, pepper, cinnamon, and clove flavors. Mentholated char and fresh herbs carry out the long finish. **89** —*K.F. (4/1/2003)*

Waterkloof 2005 Sauvignon Blanc (Stellenbosch) $45. Passionfruit and mineral leap from the glass, while the flavors of honeydew, peach and a spritz of lime have good intensity. Ripe in the mouth, but with good matching acidity, the alcohol (14.5%) shows a bit warm on the finish, giving the key lime notes a feel of austerity. **87** —*M.D. (9/1/2006)*

Webersburg 1999 Cabernet Sauvignon (Stellenbosch) $35. This plump, medium-bodied wine boasts plenty of briary, blackberry flavors laced with notes of beefy meatiness and vanilla. Despite its age, it's still relatively youthful, with dry tannins on the finish that may never fully integrate. Drink now. **84** —*J.C. (11/15/2005)*

Wild Rush 2003 Cape Red Cabernet Blend (Robertson) $9. A dry and balanced blend of Cabernet Sauvignon and Tinta Barroca. Opens with a creamy dark nose of berry, cinnamon, and leather elements that prevail through the palate and out onto the smoothly tannic finish. Solid and slightly offbeat. **85** —*M.M. (11/15/2004)*

Wild Rush 2003 Cape White White Blend (Robertson) $8. A blend of Chenin Blanc, Colombard, Sauvignon Blanc, and Chardonnay, this easy-drinking white recalls many everyday Pinot Grigios. It's a little sweet, with a mild citrus, grass, and herb profile. This uncomplicated refresher is best served well-chilled. **83** —*M.M. (11/15/2004)*

Wildekrans 2005 Chenin Blanc (Walker Bay) $15. A totally dry Chenin, and as a consequence great with food, this wine comes from the cool-climate Elgin region close to the ocean. The acidity is great, and the only thing that spoils this wine initially is a touch of sulfur, but it blows away after some time in the glass. **86** —*R.V. (11/15/2005)*

Wildekrans 2001 Reserve Estate Wine Chenin Blanc (Walker Bay) $9. Yellow nectarine and toffee aromas are accented by hints of banana and fresh green beans. The palate is similar, less the beans. Overall, it's crisp and fresh; finishes with nectarine, herbs, and a hint of menthol. **85** —*K.F. (4/1/2003)*

Wildekrans 2001 Barrel Selection Estate Wine Pinotage (Walker Bay) $25. The smoky meat and cherry flavors are relatively fresh, while the feel is a bit bracing. This is nicely done, probably best paired with rustic or grilled fare. A little more time in the bottle should shine this up even more. **87** —*K.F. (9/1/2003)*

Wildekrans 2001 Estate Wine Pinotage (Walker Bay) $15. This well-balanced wine tastes deliciously Old World. Aromas of herbs, pastry dough and cocoa powder are unique to the nose. Reserved plum skin and cherry flavors blend nicely with those of meat juices, leather, and dried tobacco. **87** —*K.F. (9/1/2003)*

Wildekrans 2001 Estate Wine - Cabernet Franc/Merlot Red Blend (Walker Bay) $13. With 91% Cabernet Franc, this wine displays strong, vegetal, reedy aromas and flavors. There is red plum and cedar laid out over supportive acidity and tannins, but the finish is of bitter eucalyptus. **83** —*K.F. (9/1/2003)*

Wildekrans 2000 Warrant Estate Wine Red Blend (Walker Bay) $25. A faint herbal note ribbons around creamy vanilla, currant, and plum skin flavors. The tannins are snug and mouthcoating, carrying out to the herbal finish. **84** —*K.F. (9/1/2003)*

Wildekrans 2002 Estate Wine Sauvignon Blanc (Walker Bay) $8. Aromas of stone fruit, lemon candy, fresh-mown hay, and toffee meet on a light-weight palate that is rife with flinty citrus. The finish has quite an herbal streak that borders on spearmint. **85** —*K.F. (4/1/2003)*

Wildekrans 2001 Estate Wine Sémillon (Walker Bay) $15. Very yellow coloring paves the way to aromas of dusty newsprint and meat juices. Dig deep to find light citrus fruit that carries to the palate with a dose of eucalyptus. Its odd notes are slightly more acceptable than the lack of body and focus. **84** —*K.F. (4/1/2003)*

WINERY OF GOOD HOPE

Winery of Good Hope 2005 Chenin Blanc (Stellenbosch) $9. A delicious example of dry Chenin Blanc. With currant aromas, and a full, fruity palate, this is big, rich and concentrated, with flavors of pears, white currants, and a touch of mint to give it a lift. From the same winery as the Black Rock range, this is a fine wine. **91 Best Buy** —*R.V. (11/15/2005)*

ZELPHI WINES

Zelphi Wines 2001 Simunye Sauvignon Blanc (Coastal Region) $17. Produced by South Africa's Michael Back, flying winemaker Zelma Long and her winegrower husband Phillip Freese under the Simunye label, this wine displays simple aromas of warmed peas, cardamom, and sweet cream. The palate and finish are couched in herbs and delicate citrus, with accents of sweet grass. **85** —*K.F. (4/1/2003)*

ZEVENWACHT

Zevenwacht 2005 Chenin Blanc (Stellenbosch) $NA. A well-made, big, fat wine, which brings in some toasty elements, along with dense white fruits, honey, nuts, and dried apricots. While the previous vintage clocked an overwhelming 14.5% alcohol, this wine at 13.5% is much better balanced. **88** —*R.V. (11/15/2005)*

ZONNEBLOEM

Zonnebloem 2003 Chardonnay (Western Cape) $10. Tasty apple-pear aromas and flavors, fine balance, and good fruit-acid balance are a winning combination (as always) in this appealing mid-weight white. Tasty and surprisingly stylish at the price, with (again, as always) good fruit at the core. Worth seeking out, the equal of many more costly Chardonnays of diverse origin. **87 Best Buy** —*M.M. (4/1/2005)*

Zonnebloem 2000 Chardonnay (Stellenbosch) $10. A quick hint of herby char on the nose is followed by buttered toast that extends to the delicate flavors of stonefruit and citrus peel. This comes off semi-viscous but clean, with a short, lemony finish. **86** —*K.F. (4/1/2003)*

Zonnebloem 2004 Merlot (Stellenbosch) $11. Plum, blueberry, leather and spice waft from the glass, followed by a lean, dry, almost metallic note. Light in the mouth, with tart plum peeking through, this would be a tough match for food. **80** —*M.D. (11/1/2006)*

Zonnebloem 2004 Pinotage (Stellenbosch) $10. Young and lush, this wine has strong purple fruit flavors, aromas of creamy vanilla, lemony oak and leather, with moderate tannins and spice to support. Pinotage can age, but this comes across as forward and fruity, so the best bet is to enjoy it now. **87 Best Buy** —*M.D. (11/1/2006)*

Zonnebloem 2005 Sauvignon Blanc (Western Cape) $11. Zonnebloem is one of South Africa's biggest-selling brands, able to produce wines at affordable prices. This medium-bodied wine offers something not many can at this price: ripe fruit flavors, intensity and depth. A nose of pithy white fruit leads to a crisp framework with peach, kiwi, and lime dancing on the tongue. No frills necessary, a fine accompaniment to lunch and light conversation. **87 Best Buy** —*M.D. (11/15/2006)*

Zonnebloem 2002 Shiraz (Stellenbosch) $10. Juicy, ripe Shiraz fruit is accented by ample toasty oak and a lively citrus note in this tasty, even welterweight. There's more tangy acidity and tannins here than is usually found in a value red. Closes dry with espresso and black fruit notes. **85 Best Buy** —*M.M. (4/1/2005)*

SOUTH AFRICA

Spain

Among European countries with long wine-making histories, no country has come further in recent years than Spain. As the nation with more acreage under vine than any of its continental mates, Spain is no longer simply a producer of overcropped, basic wines destined for domestic consumption. Just the opposite: in less than two decades, Spain has evolved into one of Europe's most exciting and progressive wine producers.

Today, Spanish winemakers are making sought-after wines at almost every price point and quality level, and in most of the country's sixty-plus denominated regions. From everyday reds made from grapes including Tempranillo, Monastrell, and Garnacha, to crisp whites like Albariño and Verdejo, to frothy Cava and some of the world's finest and richest red and dessert wines, Spain is offering the consumer variety and value at almost every turn.

Harvesting Xarel-lo grapes in a vineyard at Cavas Chandon, the Spanish branch of Moët et Chandon.

Talk about a 180-degree turnabout; twenty years ago, nobody thought much of Spain's wines. In those early post-Franco years, the country featured one collectable red—the idiosyncratic and esoteric Vega Sicilia (still one of the world's great red wines). Meanwhile, Rioja boasted a few highly traditional wines (read: not that fruity, with a lot of American oak flavor) in López de Heredia's Viña Tondonia, Marqués de Riscal, and CUNE, among others. Beyond that, there wasn't much to talk about besides Torres' Sangre de Toro and the dry and sweet fortified wines coming from Jerez in the south.

By the middle of the 1990s and into the twenty-first century, however, the world's thirst for better, more distinctive wines gave Spain the necessary spur in the side that it needed to push the envelope. Younger winemakers, many trained outside the country, started to replace their more traditional predecessors. Older regions that had fallen out of style were invigorated with new plantings and the construction of modern wineries. And almost before you could say Olé, quality wines were emerging from all four corners of the country and quite a few places in between.

SPAIN'S WINES AND REGIONS

There are currently more than sixty regulated wine regions in Spain. The most prominent denominaciones de origen, as the regions are called, have been around for decades if not longer; places like Rioja, Ribera Del Duero, Jerez, Rías Baixas, Priorat, Penedès, Navarra, La Mancha, and Valdepeñas. Others have risen to prominence during the aforementioned growth boom: Rueda, Bierzo, Toro, Cigales, Somontano, Yecla, Jumilla, and Montsant, while not all young, fit the mold of up and coming. And there are still a few DOs that seem stuck in time; outposts like Extremadura, located along the border with Portugal, and Utiel-Requena (inland from Valencia) that may have their day down the line.

Among red-wine regions, the spotlight is shining brightest on Rioja, Ribera Del Duero, Priorat, and, to a lesser degree, Toro and Bierzo. Rioja is one of Spain's larger DOs, and the focus here is on Tempranillo. Rioja came to prominence in the 1800s when French

SPAIN

winemakers fled their country's phylloxera (see Glossary) epidemic, and over time three main styles of red wine have evolved: crianzas, which are wood-aged wines generally of lighter stature; reservas, which spend extended time in barrel; and gran reserva, theoretically the ripest and most ageworthy of wines. Look for modern, extracted, flavorful wines from the likes of Allende, LAN, Muga, Remelluri, Remírez de Ganuza, Roda, and a host of other newcomers. Marqués de Murrieta, Marqués de Cáceres, Montecillo, and the previously mentioned CUNE and Riscal comprise the respected old guard.

Ribera Del Duero, Toro, Cigales, and other sections of Castilla y León province are also prime Tempranillo areas. Modern wineries like Alion, Pingus, Viña Sastre, and others in Ribera, as well as Numanthia-Termes in Toro are the new-wave leaders, while Vega Sicilia, Pesquera, Protos, and Pérez Pascuas have been plying their trade in Ribera for longer, with commendable results.

Just to the southwest of Barcelona lies Penedès, the heart of Spain's sparkling wine industry. Here wineries harvest the white grapes Macabeo, Parellada, and Xarello before blending them into what's known as Cava. This sparkling wine is made similarly to Champagne but is lighter and far less complex than France's prized bubbly. Penedès is also home to Miguel Torres S.A., one of Spain's preeminent wineries, a survivor of the Spanish Civil War, and for many years when Spain was overlooked, a major exporter to the United States.

A little further southwest of Penedès are Priorat and Montsant, regions that can trace their winemaking roots back to the Romans and later Carthusian monks. Here Garnacha and old Cariñena vines yield powerful wines, and the current crop of winemakers is, almost to a person, young, ambitious, and iconoclastic. Today Priorat is producing some of the world's finest red wines, ones that compare with the best of France, Italy, and California.

Lastly, Sherry is the fortified sipper of Andalusia. From crisp fino and manzanilla up to richer, nuttier amontillado and oloroso, Sherry is a unique wine for either before a meal or after. Sherry predates Spain's vinous renaissance by centuries, but never has it gone out of style.

SPAIN

1+1=3

1+1=3 NV Brut Sparkling Blend (Cava) $13. The nose kicks up ginger ale and a touch of lime, and that's followed by apple and mild citrus flavors. The mouthfeel is good and the finish crisp, clean and full of vibrant acidity. A perfectly fine and pleasant cava, but nothing out of the ordinary. **86** —*M.S. (12/15/2006)*

7 LUNAS

7 Lunas 2003 Campo Góticos Tempranillo (Ribera del Duero) $55. Big and charred, but under the veil of new oak there's violet, blackberry, and savory spice notes. Full throttle on the palate, with quality plum and cherry flavors. Tight and tannic late, but not overly rough. Should be at its best in 2007–08. **90** —*M.S. (11/1/2006)*

AALTO

Aalto 2001 PS Tinto del Pais (Ribera del Duero) $105. Aalto is one of several smaller projects being led by former Vega Sicilia head winemaker Mariano García, and we think this 2001 Pagos Seliccionados (PS) is his best effort to date. The wine is dark, with charcoal, lemon, and pure black-fruit aromas. It features a brilliant luster and deep, rich, syrupy flavors of maple, boysenberry, and black cherry. Shows a beautiful finish and amazing depth. Hold until 2006–07. **95 Editors' Choice** —*M.S. (6/1/2005)*

ABADIA RETUERTA

Abadia Retuerta 1996 Pago Valdebellon Cabernet Sauvignon (Vino de Mesa de Castilla y León) $100. Rich and earthy, with dark cassis fruit accented by chocolate, coffee, and licorice. This 100% Cabernet Sauvignon packs immense flavor into a dense package that doesn't seem heavy, thanks to its creamy, velvety texture in the mouth. **92** —*J.C. (11/1/2001)*

Abadia Retuerta 1998 Red Blend (Sardon de Duero) $10. 86 —*M.M. (8/1/2000)*

Abadia Retuerta 1997 Red Blend (Sardon de Duero) $26. 89 —*M.M. (8/1/2000)*

Abadia Retuerta 2000 Primicia Red Blend (Vino de la Tierra de Castilla y León) $10. A young, fruity wine that's meant to be consumed in its first year or two, it's a blend of 60 percent Tempranillo, 20 percent Cabernet, Sauvignon, and 20 percent Merlot. Winemaking tricks like partial carbonic maceration and varying fermentation temperatures for separate parts of the blend accentuate bright berry and cherry fruit. No oak means the fruit speaks loud and clear. **87 Best Buy** —*J.C. (11/1/2001)*

Abadia Retuerta 1998 Rívola Red Blend (Sardon de Duero) $12. 90 *(11/15/1999)*

Abadia Retuerta 1998 Selección Especial Red Blend (Vino de Mesa de Castilla y León) $24. Despite the name, this is the winery's standard bottling (sold without a designation in previous vintages). The blend this year is 75% Tempranillo, 20% Cabernet Sauvignon, and 5% Merlot, aged in a mix of French and American oak. It's weedy, with some rhubarb notes amid the cherries and cassis, and seems a bit tart and hard, with toasty oak showing on the finish. **87** —*J.C. (11/1/2001)*

Abadia Retuerta 1999 Selección Especial Unfiltered Red Blend (Sardon de Duero) $27. Masculine but not brooding, with an encouraging, lightly perfumed nose that really draws you in. Pulsating red fruit carries the earthy palate into a soft but dynamic finish that fills all corners of your mouth. With a good feel and subtleties, this wine is drinking well right now. **89** —*M.S. (3/1/2004)*

Abadia Retuerta 1997 Cuvée El Campanario Tempranillo (Sardon de Duero) $50. 95 —*M.M. (8/1/2000)*

Abadia Retuerta 1998 Cuvée El Campanario Tempranillo (Vino de Mesa de Castilla y León) $50. The rich black-cherry fruit in this 100% Tempranillo is blessed with enormous depth and solid structure. Dark earthy flavors mingle with brighter notes of cherries and berries on the palate. The slightly drying tannins on the finish suggest this wine is best saved for a special occasion in 2005. **91 Cellar Selection** —*J.C. (11/1/2001)*

Abadia Retuerta 1997 Cuvée El Palomar Tempranillo (Sardon de Duero) $48. 89 —*M.M. (8/1/2000)*

Abadia Retuerta 1997 Lapsus Tempranillo (Sardon de Duero) $130. 90 —*M.M. (8/1/2000)*

Abadia Retuerta 1996 Pago Negralada Tempranillo (Sardon de Duero) $140. 90 *(8/1/2000)*

Abadia Retuerta 1999 Rívola Tempranillo (Sardon de Duero) $12. 88 —*M.M. (8/1/2000)*

Abadia Retuerta 1998 Cuvée El Palomar Tempranillo-Cabernet Sauvignon (Vino de Mesa de Castilla y León) $45. A blend of 50% Cabernet Sauvignon and 50% Tempranillo from separate parcels of the estate. The Tempranillo, from a lime hillside, brings exotic floral aromas and red cherries; the Cabernet, from vines butting up against the Duero, provides structure and black currants. Hints of rhubarb and herbs accent the long finish. **89** —*J.C. (11/1/2001)*

Abadia Retuerta 2000 Cuvée Palomar Tempranillo-Cabernet Sauvignon (Vino de la Tierra de Castilla y León) $48. Patience is a must to make it through this burly, earthy, almost murky blend of Tempranillo and Cabernet Sauvignon. Early aromas of mulch and coffee morph into black fruit and leather, while initially reduced black cherry and currant flavors take on more character and depth with time. Never does it really shine, but it is a serious wine that has its merits. **88** —*M.S. (12/15/2006)*

Abadia Retuerta 2001 Rívola Tempranillo-Cabernet Sauvignon (Vino de la Tierra de Castilla y León) $14. Earthy and dark, with forward fruit and plenty of overt wood. With lots of berry fruit, a smooth feel, and fine overall integration, this is a quintessential, well-priced Spanish wine for 2004. There's no flab or fat, but it's not hard, either. A drying, coffee-filled finish with bitter chocolate is the final act. **88** —*M.S. (3/1/2004)*

Abadia Retuerta 1999 Rívola Tempranillo-Cabernet Sauvignon (Vino de Mesa de Castilla y León) $11. A rich, earthy wine that blends black cherries and chocolate with hints of mixed green herbs—even dill. Shows enough structure and balance to last a few years, and picks up an anise note on the finish. A blend of 60% Tempranillo, 40% Cabernet Sauvignon that spends a year in a mix of French and American oak. **89 Editors' Choice** —*J.C. (11/1/2001)*

ABANDO

Abando 2001 Crianza Tempranillo (Rioja) $NA. Red licorice and cherry candy aromas blend with mint and grass to form a simple, candied, somewhat green bouquet. The palate delivers standard cherry and raspberry, while the finish is easygoing as it displays mild chocolate and vanilla touches. **86** —*M.S. (8/1/2005)*

ABRAZO

Abrazo 2003 Garnacha (Cariñena) $7. Sharp and edgy, with burnt leather on the piquant nose. Some red fruit and also a lot of spicy, green notes. Finishes swift and peppery. **81** —*M.S. (12/31/2004)*

Abrazo 2001 Garnacha (Cariñena) $5. Full and minty, and quite the bargain at five bucks. This bargain buster features some cherry liqueur and sucking-candy flavors, while the finish is not devoid of some class, as it offers coffee and chocolate notes. Yes, it's a bit like cherry soda without the bubbles, but what's not to like at this price, especially if the menu calls for burgers or London broil? If Two Buck Chuck is so popular, try giving this wine "hug," the English translation for abrazo. **84 Best Buy** —*M.S. (8/1/2003)*

Abrazo 1999 Crianza Garnacha-Tempranillo Red Blend (Cariñena) $8. Sharp and rubbery on the nose, with a racy, spirited red-cherry character. Trouble is, the acidity is piercing and the fruit, if there ever was any, is quickly exiting stage left. **81** —*M.S. (6/1/2005)*

Abrazo 1996 Gran Reserva Red Blend (Cariñena) $13. Sulfuric, with quite a bit of green character mixed into the fruit. Tastes lean, with herbal notes of raspberry and apple skins. Long and persistent on the finish, but bland in its length. **82** —*M.S. (6/1/2005)*

Abrazo 1996 Gran Reserva Red Blend (Cariñena) $11. Lots to like in this dry, earthy wine, with its flavors of black cherries, tobacco, and sage. The tannins are practically non-existent, but it's crisp and tart enough to stand up to chorizo and similar fare. **86** —*S.H. (1/1/2002)*

Abrazo 1997 Reserva Garnacha-Tempranillo Red Blend (Cariñena) $10. An old wine that now carries only tart cherry and acidity. Yes, it's clean, just not friendly. Barely acceptable at this stage. **80** —*M.S. (6/1/2005)*

ADEGA MARTÍNEZ SERANTES

Adega Martínez Serantes 2005 Alba Rosa Albariño (Rías Baixas) $15. A lower selection of grapes than the winery's superior Dona Rosa results in a fresh wine full of apple, nectarine, and minerality. Not particularly complex but goes down nicely. Classic everyday Albariño. **87** —*M.S. (9/1/2006)*

Adega Martínez Serantes 2005 Dona Rosa Albariño (Rías Baixas) $17. A powerful wine with forceful minerality. Still, it's loaded with expressive fruit that falls squarely into the pineapple/mango category. Finishes crisp but precise, with notes of wet stone and lingering nips of green apple and peach. **91 Editors' Choice** —*M.S. (9/1/2006)*

ADEGAS GALEGAS

Adegas Galegas 2003 O Deus Dionisos Albariño (Rías Baixas) $22. Light and easy, with simple aromas of lemon and wildflowers. Fairly forward and pronounced in terms of fruit; the lemon, pineapple, and peach are all right there and lively. Finishes smooth and easy, if maybe a touch watery. **86** —*M.S. (9/1/2004)*

ADEGAS GRAN VINUM

Adegas Gran Vinum 2005 Mar De Viñas Albariño (Rías Baixas) $22. Brass colored, with aromas of apple cider and mineral. Heavy in the mouth with jumpy, tangy fruit and overt acidity. Okay if a bit mealy. **82** —*M.S. (9/1/2006)*

ADEGAS VALMIÑOR

Adegas Valmiñor 2005 Davila White Blend (Rías Baixas) $15. Valmiñor's signature wine since 2001 is 75% Albariño, with 20% Loureira and 5% Treixadura. Which means it is ultra floral and a touch sweeter than a varietal Albariño. A pleasure to quaff, with citrus and mango flavors. **88** —*M.S. (9/1/2006)*

AGRAMONT

Agramont 2000 Chardonnay (Navarra) $9. The bright golden color and mounds of buttery oak don't do this varietally incorrect Chard much service. Then giant oaky flavors dominate what little pear fruit exists, while the finish is grainy and resinous. Overall it lacks focus and style. **81** —*M.S. (11/1/2002)*

AGREST DE GUITARD

Agrest de Guitard 2003 Cabernet Sauvignon-Merlot (Penedès) $10. Quite raw and rubbery, with loud aromas that offer more power than harmony. In the mouth, strawberry fruit precedes a tight, hard finish. **82** —*M.S. (3/1/2005)*

AGRICOLA CASTELLANA

Agricola Castellana 2005 Veliterra Joven White Blend (Rueda) $9. Short and slightly chemical on the nose, with hard-to-define melon, citrus, and apple flavors. A tart wine without too much going on. **81** —*M.S. (12/15/2006)*

AGRICOLA FALSET-MARCA

Agricola Falset-Marca 2001 Etim Garnacha (Montsant) $14. Sweet red-fruit and red-licorice aromas are attractive and round. The palate of peppy cranberry and plum is moderately tart, although it opens up and gets much friendlier if given time. While many wines from this section of Catalonia are big and modern, this one is more restrained and will perform well with food. **88** —*M.S. (3/1/2004)*

AGRO DE BAZÁN

Agro de Bazán 2005 Contrapunto Albariño (Rías Baixas) $13. Soft aromatically, with notes of pear, vanilla, and banana. Surprisingly, the palate is short and tart, with sharp citrus and pineapple flavors. Entirely basic and lacking punch. Already seems to be in decline and it's brand new. **82** —*M.S. (12/15/2006)*

Agro de Bazán 1999 Granbazán Albariño (Rías Baixas) $19. **83** —*M.S. (1/1/2004)*

Agro de Bazán 1999 Granbazán Albariño (Rías Baixas) $13. Nearly the color of Sherry, this is pure burnished gold, which announces oxidation and/or some heavy oaking. Aromas of butterscotch and baked apples are momentarily intriguing, but in the mouth the wine is lean and acidic, with a fiery quality. Safe to say this is not the Albarino most of us are seeking. **83** —*M.S. (3/1/2004)*

AGUSTÍ TORELLÓ

Agustí Torelló 1999 Barrica Reserva Extra Brut Macabeo (Penedès) $25. This is an austere, uncommon wine made entirely from Macabeo. The nose offers baked apple and bread dough, which is followed by green apple and melon flavors and a touch of smoky dryness. It's an agile wine with a dry, snappy finish that offers some lime and talc. **89** —*M.S. (12/31/2002)*

Agustí Torelló 1999 Kripta Gran Reserva Brut Nature Sparkling Blend (Cava) $52. I love the funky amphora-shaped bottle as much as the forward nature of the wine. Starts with a full blast of toast, which is backed by a richer butterscotch aroma. This is a cava that provides a big mouthful; the palate is dry and wheaty, while the backing flavors of cinnamon and apple are live-wire. **90** —*M.S. (6/1/2005)*

Agustí Torelló 1999 Brut Riserva White Blend (Penedès) $12. This is a bit spunkier and sweeter than its more refined big brothers. It has a fresh eggy nose, a dry apple-dominated palate, and a fresh, zippy, cleansing finish. It is a perfect apéritif or party bubbly, one with a smooth, defined character and lots of punch, but not a ton of complexity. **88 Best Buy** — *M.S. (12/31/2002)*

Agustí Torelló 1998 Gran Reserva Extra Brut White Blend (Penedès) $16. The soft, attractive mildly yeasty nose leads into a pear-and-apple palate with shades of vanilla. The grapes for this wine come from vines that are at least 30 years old, and because of that there's richness and depth not offered by most other cavas. On the finish, sublime notes of melon and papaya are present. This could be Torelló's most elegant cava. **89** —*M.S. (12/31/2002)*

Agustí Torelló 1997 Kripta Extra Brut White Blend (Penedès) $45. If this isn't one of the best bubblies in Spain, then what is? It gets no dosage, so what you taste is just the natural flavor of top-shelf Macabeo, Xarello, and Parellada—aged four plus years on its yeast. The flavors are pure light citrus and tropical fruit along with some toast and cream. The finish is persistent, the mouthfeel ethereal. **91 Editors' Choice** —*M.S. (12/31/2002)*

ALABANZA

Alabanza 2001 Crianza Tempranillo (Rioja) $15. Even keeled, with doughy, sweet aromas of pound cake, cherry, and plum. Mildly leathery on the tongue, with round, warm blackberry and plum flavors. Not the deepest or densest offering, but warm and pleasing, with vanilla and smoke on the finish. **87** —*M.S. (8/1/2005)*

Alabanza 1999 Reserva Tempranillo (Rioja) $24. Herbal on the nose, with tobacco, mushroom, and tomato aromas. Quite juicy, sharp and tannic, yielding apple-skin and red plum flavors. Gets better with airing, as tobacco, almond and plum flavors emerge. Struggles for the right mouthfeel and texture, but has its moments and virtues. **86** —*M.S. (8/1/2005)*

Alabanza 2001 Selección Tempranillo (Rioja) $42. Sort of heavy and herbal, with plenty of mint, beet, and sweet plum flavors. Seems on the verge of overripe; the oak takes it to chocolate and coffee before a meaty finish. **85** —*M.S. (8/1/2005)*

Alabanza 2002 Selección Tempranillo Blend (Rioja) $40. Ripe and round, with blackberry and bacon aromas. Quite modern and full for a 2002, one of Rioja's most challenging vintages in a while. Shows full berry flavors with ample oak and a touch of tannin. Finishes with mocha and spice. **89** —*M.S. (11/1/2006)*

ALBADA

Albada 2001 Garnacha (Calatayud) $12. Easy and open, with ample berry fruit on the casual nose. Cherry and red plum flavors run a touch sour, but at least it isn't overly sweet and manufactured. A warm, spicy finish is a touch rough, but overall the wine is solid. **85** —*M.S. (12/31/2004)*

Albada 2000 Garnacha (Calatayud) $8. Big and fruity, with sugary cherry fruit and a big, aggressive finish. The acidity here is abrasive as it sears your tongue. In the end, you almost feel a shock as you drink this over-done wine that tastes more like a powdered fruit drink than fine wine. **81** —*M.S. (10/1/2003)*

ALBET I NOYA

Albet I Noya 2000 Lignum Negre Red Blend (Penedès) $11. The trio of Garnacha, Carignan, and Cabernet Sauvignon yield raspberry aromas that carry nuances of earth and pepper. If you're looking for something from the Old World, a wine that has lighter fruit, bolder acidity and a subdued, open-knit palate, then try this. It's well made, with ample pop. **87 Best Buy** —*M.S. (3/1/2004)*

Albet I Noya 1999 Cava Brut Reserva Sparkling Blend (Cava) $14. Fresh and snappy, boasting hints of fresh garden produce alongside limes and racy flavors of green apples. Lean and tart, with greater cut than many Cavas. **84** —*J.C. (12/31/2003)*

ALCEÑO

Alceño 2003 Selección Crianza Red Blend (Jumilla) $18. Very nice from head to toe. The nose breathes leather, tobacco, berry fruit and spice, while the palate offers evolved, top-tier plum and cherry flavors. Exotic and concentrated, with hints of licorice. Pretty big and rich, but also quite well made. **90 Editors' Choice** —*M.S. (12/15/2006)*

Alceño 2003 Selección Roble Red Blend (Jumilla) $13. This is the type of wine that's giving resurgent Jumilla a positive reputation. The nose is smoky but still loaded with solid fruit, while the palate bubbles over with pure blackberry and plum. It's a Monastrell-dominated blend, but it tastes a lot like Tempranillo, which is only 15% of the blend. Very nice overall. **89 Best Buy** —*M.S. (12/15/2006)*

Alceño 2005 Tinto Red Blend (Jumilla) $10. Bulky and a bit stewy, but still balanced enough to earn its positive points. The palate is ripe and sweet, as it oozes with black fruit. Some might call it a touch chunky, but for the most part this blend of Monastrell, Tempranillo, and Syrah registers as a highly pleasurable red. **87 Best Buy** —*M.S. (12/15/2006)*

Alceño 2005 Rosado Rosé Blend (Jumilla) $10. This Monastrell-based rosado is indicative of the Jumilla region, meaning it's sweet, a bit heavy, and fairly candied in its aromas. Flavors of fleshy raspberry and strawberry are full, while the round finish is neutral. Low in acid; drink right away. **84** —*M.S. (12/15/2006)*

Alceño 2004 Syrah (Jumilla) $15. Very colorful and properly ripe, with lush berry aromas backed by coffee notes. The palate is lush and bal-anced, with deep blueberry, black cherry, and cola notes. A truly committed wine with a smooth, unctuous finish as the final chapter. **90 Best Buy** —*M.S. (12/15/2006)*

ALCONDE

Alconde 2001 Reserva Tempranillo Blend (Navarra) $34. This attempt at a prestige-level wine comes up a touch short. The aromas start out incredi-bly green, with can't-miss blasts of green tobacco, pole beans, and olive. There's more green in the mouth, which is backed by earthy fruit and burnt caramel. Finishes almost salty, with a streak of outsized acidity. **84** —*M.S. (11/15/2005)*

ALDOR

Aldor 2003 Verdejo (Rueda) $11. Moderate cinnamon spice notes to the nose, with thick, soft apple flavors on the palate. Not the most forward wine, with a leaden mouthfeel. Fails to improve in the glass. **83** —*M.S. (8/1/2005)*

ALENZA

Alenza 1999 Gran Reserva Tinto del Pais (Ribera del Duero) $87. A bit stewy and heavy, as if some of the zesty fruit had hit the road a while ago. What's left is coffee and some earthy dampness. But if you like a darker, meatier wine with prune-style fruit, blackberry, and oak, this is

it. Bulky and chewy throughout, with medium tannins. **87** —*M.S. (10/1/2005)*

ALIDIS

Alidis 2000 Crianza Tempranillo (Ribera del Duero) $22. Funky and gassy at first, but with time leather and wild berries emerge on the nose. The mouth offers red plum and blackberry, while the lean, starchy finish is tight, tannic and oaky. Very zippy and alive, with raisin and chocolate nuances. **86** —*M.S. (3/1/2004)*

Alidis 1999 Crianza Tempranillo (Ribera del Duero) $20. Grapy, bold and pure, with plenty of black fruit and healthy acids and tannins. Size and drive are what this wine is about; it never steps off the gas, all the while delivering tannic power, some bitter coffee and chocolate notes, and all the blackberry extract you could ask for. **88** —*M.S. (3/1/2004)*

Alidis 2001 Tinto Roble Tempranillo (Ribera del Duero) $15. A bit horsey and scattered at first, but it improves with time. Flavors of blackberry and raspberry are attractive in the glass, as is the smooth finish that comes with some bitter coffee. Very young and aggressive. Bright wine, although some might view it as slightly thin and sour. **85** —*M.S. (3/1/2004)*

ALION

Alion 1999 Tempranillo (Ribera del Duero) $50. Bacon, sawdust and earth along with cassis and raspberry kick start this lively, acid-driven red. The palate offers tart plum and raspberry, all steered to a point by piercing, laser-beam acidity. Oak plays a prominent role throughout, especially on the finish. The gritty tannins, firm feel and strong acids call for a few years of cellaring. **88** —*M.S. (3/1/2004)*

Alion 1996 Crianza Tempranillo (Ribera del Duero) $45. 95 *(8/1/2000)*

Alion 2000 Tinto del Pais (Ribera del Duero) $65. Leathery, earthy, and entirely attractive; this is a wine that doesn't seem to have come off an assembly line. The fruit is power-packed, dealing blackberry and plum along with chocolate and spice. In tasting this it's hard to find any faults. Only the hard tannins stand out, calling for several years of cellar time. From Vega Sicilia. Drink in 2008. **91** —*M.S. (6/1/2005)*

ALLENDE

Allende 1997 Aurus Red Blend (Rioja) $155. This is a dark, supple wine with toasty oak, sweet blueberry, and roasted fruit aromas. Textured on the tongue, but vintage-true, it doesn't show the depth of the stunning 1996. Still, the blackberry and prune fruit, earth and leather accents, tangy acidity and dry, peppery finish show class most wines only aspire to. Closes firm and dry. Drink 2003–2007. **91** —*M.M. (11/1/2002)*

Allende 1999 Calvario Red Blend (Rioja) $45. Plush, seamless Rioja from a single vineyard planted in 1945, this shows what old-vine fruit is about. It's at once chewy and firm, yet ripe and supple, with real depth. Classic tarragon, pine, and leather notes expand as the wine opens. The plush oak works—the solid, deep fruit keeps this from becoming a smooth, generic modern wine. Closes long, with supple tannins. Drink in 2008. **93 Editors' Choice** —*M.M. (11/1/2002)*

Allende 1999 Tempranillo (Rioja) $20. High-toned and forward, with lilac and nutmeg adding to the gorgeous bouquet. The palate is huge and ripe, with ample plum, blackberry, and coffee flavors. Finishes round with enveloping yet soft tannins. If you like your reds big and polished, then proceed happily and without caution. **91 Editors' Choice** —*M.S. (3/1/2004)*

Allende 1997 Tempranillo (Rioja) $18. 91 —*M.M. (8/1/2000)*

Allende 2000 Calvario Tempranillo (Rioja) $50. Inky and saturated, which makes sense given that it's from vines planted more than 50 years ago. Condensed blackberry aromas are a hint that big fruit is to come. And it does, in the form of a berry cornucopia accented by lavender and clove. Some might find it a touch syrupy and jacked up. But if you like big-shouldered modern wines, you'll be all over this. **91** —*M.S. (3/1/2004)*

Allende 2002 Estate White Blend (Rioja) $25. Significantly toasted and dry, the opposite of a fruitball. Heavy oak and not much fruit is the theme throughout, from the buttery, woody palate all the way through the blanched, spicy finish. Those desperate for fruit will find some banana, pear and apple notes beneath the barrel-based veneer. **87** —*M.S. (8/1/2005)*

Allende 2000 Special Reserve Dealu Mare-Ploiesti White Blend (Rioja) $18. Golden in color, with a waxy nose that's on the rich, creamy side. The mouth deals some lemon and apple, a hint of green herb, and butter. The finish is moderate and enveloping, with a soft feel. Good but fading; maybe it's best to wait for the 2001. **86** —*M.S. (3/1/2004)*

ALQUÉZAR

Alquézar 2004 Moristel (Somontano) $12. Jammy and candied to start with. Black cherry, boysenberry, and plum flavors are friendly but basic, while the texture and finish are nothing to take issue with. Perfectly fruity and easy, but runs short on complexity. **84** —*M.S. (9/1/2006)*

ALTANZA

Altanza 1998 Lealtanza Gran Reserva Tempranillo (Rioja) $33. More red than brown. Aromas of wood spice, cinnamon, and black cherry are lively, while the palate offers mostly tart cherry and raspberry. Hard and lean on the finish, with sharp acidity. **84** —*M.S. (12/31/2004)*

Altanza 1999 Lealtanza Reserva Tempranillo (Rioja) $25. Subtlety is not in the calling here. The nose is chunky, with leather and scattered fruit. Sweet plum and berry fruit is bolstered by forward acidity. Condensed and short, but undoubtedly lively. **85** —*M.S. (3/1/2005)*

Altanza 1999 Reserva Tempranillo (Rioja) $68. Saucy, with overt oak aromas that manifest themselves as espresso and charred beef. Fairly acidic and thin across the palate, where pie cherry is the dominant flavor and sourness mars the finish. **82** —*M.S. (11/1/2006)*

Altanza 1998 Reserva Tempranillo (Rioja) $47. Meaty on the nose, with chunky leather aromas along with mature fruit. In the mouth, it's a touch racy and acidic, which serves to bolster its raspberry and pie-cherry personality. Pretty good overall, with a sizable allotment of zest. **86** —*M.S. (6/1/2005)*

ALTICO

Altico 2003 Red Blend (Jumilla) $19. Starts completely jumbled, with sweaty, funky aromas that ultimately morph into bubble gum and berries. A jammy heavyweight with tangy plum and berry fruit but never any true nuance or complexity. A blimp of a wine with a soft finish. **82** —*M.S. (10/1/2005)*

ALTOS DE TAMARON

Altos de Tamaron 2003 Tinto del Pais (Ribera del Duero) $10. Toasty and rough at first, but it settles. Flavors of root beer and jammy fruit are carried on a creamy palate. Solid and round if given time, with some syrupy sweetness courtesy of the hot vintage. **85 Best Buy** —*M.S. (11/15/2005)*

Altos de Tamaron 2002 Crianza Tinto del Pais (Ribera del Duero) $14. A little bit of sweet talcum powder adds softness to the more leathery, rustic character on the nose, while the palate deals enough plump berry and pepper to impress. Warm and correct throughout, with a chewy, solid profile. Commendable for an '02. **87** —*M.S. (11/15/2005)*

ALVAREZ Y DIEZ

Alvarez y Diez 2002 Nava Real Verdejo (Rueda) $11. The nose offers some applesauce and a touch of pickle. The palate is also a bit off; popcorn and burnt toast seem to dominate. Heavy and clumsy, but not necessarily bad. **83** —*M.S. (9/1/2004)*

ALVARO PALACIOS

Alvaro Palacios 2003 Finca Dofí Red Blend (Priorat) $70. Round and lush, with immense fruit from the nose to the palate. Beautifully balanced, with sweet plum and berry flavors, a lash of smoke, and a touch of pepper and thyme. There's nothing raw or earthy about this wine; it's opulent and pure, a testament to vineyard management and great winemaking in a tough year. Doesn't even need much cellar time; drink from 2006–09. **94 Editors' Choice** —*M.S. (10/1/2005)*

Alvaro Palacios 2003 L'Ermita Red Blend (Priorat) $440. Super pricey but this is a knock-your-socks-off wine with a gorgeous bouquet that shows not even a hint of syrup or jam. The palate is like a nova; it bursts with plum, blackberry, and cinnamon. No harshness, not too tannic, and splendid on the finish, where toast and chocolate appear

and stick around for a long time. It's 80% old-vines Garnacha and 20% Cabernet, and there just aren't enough superlatives to describe it. Only 300 cases made. **98** —*M.S. (10/1/2005)*

Alvaro Palacios 2003 Les Terrasses Red Blend (Priorat) $32. Intense and colorful; one of the most flavorful and sizable versions of Terrasses on record. Flavors of boysenberry, blackberry, and plum sizzle, while the layered palate spreads out nicely upon airing. Everything about this Cariñena-dominated wine is solid and precise. A really nice taste of Priorat at a fairly affordable price. **91** —*M.S. (10/1/2005)*

ALVEAR NV SOLERA

Alvear NV Solera 1830 Pedro Ximenez (Montilla-Moriles) $NA. A bit more easygoing than the PX wines of Jerez, as it delivers white raisin, milk chocolate, and brown-sugar aromas and flavors. The palate is far from aggressive; in fact, it's a little low in acidity, which results in a soft mouthfeel and a short finish. Excellent stuff; just not a classic. **90** —*M.S. (6/1/2005)*

ALZANIA

Alzania 2002 Crianza Red Blend (Navarra) $30. Initially it's like a pungent strip of fresh-cut oak laid on a bed of leather, but airing reveals black cherry and blueberry flavors and a couple layers of warmth and style. Very nice weight and balance. A little oaky on the nose, but overall it's more than commendable. **89** —*M.S. (10/1/2005)*

Alzania 2002 Selección Privada Red Blend (Navarra) $70. Potent to start, with heavy oak notes that conjure memories of pickle barrel and malt vinegar. Airing opens it up, and below there's black cherry, cassis, and a lot of sticky, hard tannins. Patience and hearty food are needed, but it has its qualities. Suavity, however, is not among them. **88** —*M.S. (10/1/2005)*

ANIMA NEGRA

Anima Negra 1999 Red Blend (Vi de Taula de Balears) $30. From the party zone of the Balearic Islands (think Mallorca and Ibiza) comes this hedonistic wine. The dry, roasted fruit flavors and powerful cedary quality have sensuous appeal. A pronounced dusty cocoa note adds flavor and textural interest. Medium in weight and length, it closes with licorice notes and some woody tannins. Drink now through 2003. **86** —*M.N. (4/1/2002)*

ANTAÑO

Antaño 1997 Crianza Red Blend (Rioja) $10. What slight dark cherry fruit there is in this light '97 is submerged under the oak. It's a bit brown at the edges and overwooded. **80** —*M.M. (9/1/2002)*

Antaño 2000 Tempranillo (Rioja) $7. Straightforward Tempranillo aromas and flavors mark this light red. The dry berry-cherry fruit is offset by smoke, leather, and rosemary notes. It's slightly and typically on the astringent side, but turns a bit raspy on the modest finish. **83** —*M.M. (9/1/2002)*

ARADON

Aradon 2004 Rosado Tempranillo Blend (Rioja) $10. Some measurable weight to the nose, but mostly it's light and clean. Aromas of powdered drink mix and wet stones are solid, as is the raspberry, cherry, and peach flavors. Spicy and juicy, with enough body to tip the scales as a middleweight. Nice Riojano rosé. **86 Best Buy** —*M.S. (8/1/2005)*

Aradon 2003 Joven Blanco Viura (Rioja) $10. A touch chalky, but for the most part it's clean and dry. A bit of roasted corn and baked apple along with lower acidity make it a soft, drink-now kind of wine. Plump and peppery, with some pith and bitterness late. **84** —*M.S. (8/1/2005)*

ARBANTA

Arbanta 2002 Tempranillo (Rioja) $10. Leather and tar up front, followed by sweet fruit with adequate depth and plenty of plum and berry. A bit soft, touching on overripe, but pretty good despite some burnt, rubbery notes to the finish. **85** —*M.S. (9/1/2004)*

ARCO DE GUÍA

Arco de Guía 2003 Jóven Tinta de Toro (Toro) $10. Big and ripe, with marshmallow, butter, and cedar on the nose. Lots of weight but not much depth, so the black-fruit flavors attack then leave as quickly as they came. A tiny bit weedy and peppery on the finish. **84** —*M.S. (10/1/2005)*

ARCS

Arcs 2004 Carinyena (Terra Alta) $11. Violet in color, with burnt rubber, cherry and plum on the lively nose. Things go south from there, however, as the palate is too snappy and austere to support the flavors. It's 90% Carignan and much like a tart Italian Dolcetto. **81** —*M.S. (9/1/2006)*

ARES

Ares 2001 Crianza Tempranillo (Rioja) $16. Tobacco, plum, berry, and earth work the nose, followed by black plum, cherry and chocolate flavors. This is an open, medium-bodied wine that straddles the old and new styles of Riojano winemaking. A little tannic in the mouth, so prepare some cheese, ham or meat to go with it. **87** —*M.S. (4/1/2006)*

ARRIBEÑO

Arribeño 2003 Roble Tempranillo (Ribera del Duero) $9. Murky aromas of milk chocolate and cherry don't forecast the tart, snappy boysenberry flavors that follow. Very jumpy and acidic, with a shrill mouthfeel. **81** —*M.S. (11/15/2005)*

Arribeño 2004 Tinto del Pais (Ribera del Duero) $7. Gaseous, with a heavy, grapey profile and too much tannin. Comes down hard on the palate, and by any measure its faults trump its virtues. Not a polished wine by any stretch. **81** —*M.S. (4/1/2006)*

ARROYO

Arroyo 1998 Crianza Red Blend (Ribera del Duero) $32. Smoky, toasty oak dominates the aromas and flavors of this wine and it doesn't appear to have the stuffing to ever absorb all of the wood elements. That said, it is tasty oak. **84** —*J.C. (11/1/2001)*

Arroyo 1995 Reserva Red Blend (Ribera del Duero) $18. The smoky, floral aromas are pretty, but the wine shows a bit of age on the palate, where the cherry fruit seems a bit faded and light. Mature; drink now. **85** —*J.C. (11/1/2001)*

Arroyo 2000 Jóven Tempranillo (Ribera del Duero) $11. This jóven sees only stainless steel prior to bottling, so you can taste all the juicy Tempranillo fruit without any of the cluttering oak. Complex, briary spice notes on the finish accent the bright cherry and red berry flavors. It's full without being jammy or heavy, so you can pair it with burgers or sip it on its own. **88 Best Buy** —*J.C. (11/1/2001)*

ARTADI

Artadi 2002 Pagos Viejos Tempranillo (Rioja) $70. A poster child for modern Rioja. Seriously extracted, with saturated blackberry, cola, and chocolate aromas. Features excellent texture and a fine, tannic finish. If it could offer anything else, it would be additional complexity and variety. It locks onto that fruit-and-chocolate combination and doesn't let go. **91** —*M.S. (6/1/2005)*

Artadi 2002 Viña El Pisón Tempranillo (Rioja) $145. Mildly burnt smelling, with whiffs of charred toast and forest fire. Plenty of black cherry, plum, and brown sugar comprise the palate, which is also laden with licorice and spice. Numerous merits secure its place in the box seats, but could be too oaky for some folks. **90** —*M.S. (6/1/2005)*

ARTEAGA

Arteaga 2000 Crianza Red Blend (Navarra) $19. Young and jumpy is this blend of Cabernet, Tempranillo, and Merlot. The nose is dense and woody, with charcoal darkness. Tart blackberry flavors control the oily palate. Seems to be all over the place but goes down fairly well. **85** —*M.S. (9/1/2006)*

ARX

Arx 2003 Tempranillo-Cabernet Sauvignon (Navarra) $12. Smells like sweaty leather, with a certain salty, grassy quality. The mouth offers tart cherry and raspberry, quickened by mild tannins and starchy acidity. **82** —*M.S. (10/1/2005)*

ARZUAGA

Arzuaga 1996 Crianza Tempranillo (Ribera del Duero) $27. 88 *(8/1/2000)*

Arzuaga 1995 Crianza Tempranillo (Ribera del Duero) $23. 92 —*S.H. (11/15/1999)*

Arzuaga 2002 La Planta Tempranillo (Ribera del Duero) $15. A good wine, albeit a bit sharp on the tongue. On the nose, however, there's a good mix of leather, rubber, cherry, and mint. Lengthy and powerful on the back end, with bitter chocolate in support of red fruit. Very spunky; it gets your salivary glands going. **87** —*M.S. (9/1/2004)*

Arzuaga 1995 Reserva Tempranillo (Ribera del Duero) $60. 89 —*S.H. (11/15/1999)*

Arzuaga 2000 Tinto Crianza Tempranillo (Ribera del Duero) $28. Forceful and rustic, with aromas of barnyard, tree bark, and black plum. Raspberry and sour cherry flavors create a sharp-edged palate, while the finish is peppery and a touch bitter. Leaves you wanting more. **86** —*M.S. (9/1/2004)*

AS LAXAS

As Laxas 2005 Bágoa do Miño Albariño (Rías Baixas) $NA. A single-vineyard wine made from tear must that was extracted during a light pressing. It's smooth and concentrated, with apple, melon, peach, and a touch of white-pepper. Shows good acidity and style. **88** —*M.S. (9/1/2006)*

As Laxas 2005 Laxas Albariño (Rías Baixas) $NA. Zesty as all get out, with a touch of spritz. Full melon, nectarine and green-herb aromas set the stage for apricot, peach and citrus flavors. Hails from Condado do Tea and seems racier than most. **89** —*M.S. (9/1/2006)*

As Laxas 2005 Val do Sosego Albariño (Rías Baixas) $NA. Clean and expressive up front, with floral aromas shaped by doses of grass, apple, and pear. Tastes very good, with condensed fruit creating a nice mouthfeel. Very long on the back end. **89** —*M.S. (9/1/2006)*

AURA

Aura 2004 Verdejo (Rueda) $18. A touch awkward to begin with, as the bouquet exhibits corn and hay along with ripe apple. The palate offers plenty of sweet, round flavors, particularly spiced apple and quince. Finishes soft, almost lazy. Good and ripe; not too acidic. **85** —*M.S. (9/1/2006)*

AURUS

Aurus 1996 Aurus Tempranillo (Rioja) $130. 96 —*M.M. (8/1/2000)*

AVINYÓ

Avinyó 2001 Cabernet Sauvignon (Penedès) $NA. Nearly black in color, with a nose that pulses forth with tire rubber and later some lighter, more distant aromas of green vegetables. While there is a chocolaty sweetness to the cherry and cassis fruit, that same fruit has an alter ego, which is bell pepper. You taste the green mostly at the front of the palate and very late. In between is some richness and lots of extract. **86** —*M.S. (3/1/2003)*

Avinyó NV Brut Reserva Sparkling Blend (Cava) $16. Avinyo does not make cookie-cutter cavas, and thus this wine is out of the ordinary and not always the better for it. The nose is lean and spritzy, with aromas equal to lemon-lime. The palate is drawn in for a brut, with tart flavors. Slim in profile, but not a bad or indifferent wine. **85** —*M.S. (6/1/2006)*

Avinyó NV Rosado Brut Reserva Sparkling Blend (Cava) $20. Different from the crowd. The nose concedes light raspberry and cranberry aromas, while the palate is a pink passion play that's not that easy to figure out. It's tangy, with citrus and berry mixing in an unconventional manner. Interesting in the mouth; a quality wine. Not run of the mill. **87** —*M.S. (6/1/2006)*

BACASIS

Bacasis 2002 Crianza Cabernet Sauvignon-Merlot (Pla de Bages) $14. Slightly vegetal and green, with spicy, herbal aromas mixed with oak and earth. The palate is kind of light and leafy for a Cab-Merlot blend, but there's enough body and mouthfeel to keep it moving in the right direction. Decent but weighed down by the veggies. **84** —*M.S. (9/1/2006)*

BALBAS

Balbas 2003 Tradición Tempranillo (Ribera del Duero) $17. Features a nice mix of mint, herbs, spice, and black fruit. It's a touch sharp and hard, but overall the cherry and strawberry flavors work. Tannic and clean on the finish, with balance. Nothing complex or regal, but easily fits the bill. **86** —*M.S. (11/15/2005)*

Balbas 2004 Roble Tinto del Pais (Ribera del Duero) $19. Makes a great early impression via ripe blackberry and toast aromas. Overall there's not much negative to say about this meaty, fruity youngster; it has a lovely color, dark cherry and blackberry flavors, and warm vanilla and chocolate notes on the finish. Becomes more tannic and chunky as it opens; but as an easy drinker it's very good. **88** —*M.S. (11/1/2006)*

BARBADILLO

Barbadillo NV Solear Manzanilla Sherry (Jerez) $9. A classic manzanilla with aromas of honey, apple, blanched almonds, and salt air. Fresh and exuding clarity not found in every fino or manzanilla. Quite apple-driven on the palate, with hints of mushroom and buttered toast. Flavorful, lithe, and on the money. **89** —*M.S. (6/1/2005)*

BARON DE LEY

Baron De Ley 2000 Finca Monasterio Red Blend (Rioja) $42. Dark and rich, with bacon, hickory smoke, mushroom, and black-fruit aromas. A creamy mix of blackberry, dill, and woody flavors carries into a round and layered finish. Shy on complexity. **86** —*M.S. (10/1/2003)*

Baron De Ley 1996 Gran Reserva Tempranillo (Rioja) $34. A bit rough and tumble, with pepper, thick cherry, and some herbal essence to the bouquet. Black cherry is the dominant flavor, while the mouthfeel is hardened by protruding tannins and forward acids. **86** —*M.S. (4/1/2006)*

Baron De Ley 1995 Gran Reserva Tempranillo (Rioja) $32. Lacking in shine, this wine isn't showing a whole lot. Tree bark and tea aromas give way to a pruny flavor profile that doesn't match the tangy acidity that dominates the core. Ponderous and muscled up, but missing balance and vitality. **81** —*M.S. (10/1/2003)*

Baron De Ley 2000 Reserva Tempranillo (Rioja) $20. Tight-grained oak on top of slightly herbal fruit gives this wine an Old World bouquet. Juicy cherry, raspberry, and olive flavors work the palate, followed by an acidic, drying finish that lasts for quite a while. Lean and zesty; this has definite merits. **86** —*M.S. (12/15/2006)*

Baron De Ley 1998 Reserva Tempranillo (Rioja) $19. Grassy aromas with horse stable notes take descriptors like rusticity and traditional to the extreme. The palate is heavy, with deep plum and berry flavors surrounded by mounds of earth. Very big in the mouth and rather tired already. **82** —*M.S. (10/1/2003)*

Baron De Ley 2002 Finca Monasterio Tempranillo-Cabernet Sauvignon (Rioja) $44. Oaky and charred, with maple and mocha on the nose. And from there it slips. The palate is spiky and acidic, and the finish is sharp and saucy. For whatever reason this Tempranillo-Cabernet Sauvignon blend weighs in on the cusp of sour. Pricey for what you get. **83** —*M.S. (4/1/2006)*

Baron De Ley 2001 Finca Monasterio Tempranillo-Cabernet Sauvignon (Rioja) $45. Begins with cola and root beer aromas before going decidedly stewy. Ultra lemony on the palate, a combination of thin but cooked fruit along with overaggressive oak. Finishes reedy, with tomato notes. A wine with greater intentions that doesn't click. **83** —*M.S. (8/1/2005)*

BARÓN DE OÑA

Barón de Oña 1997 Reserva Tempranillo (Rioja) $24. Rusty in color, with hickory, leather, and dried currants on the traditional Rioja nose. More dried fruit creates a spicy palate, one with cinnamon, pepper, and clove. It's fading and still fairly oaky, with fruit secondary to the wood and acids. But isn't that old-school Rioja? **87** —*M.S. (3/1/2004)*

BARZAGOSO

Barzagoso 2001 Crianza Tempranillo Blend (Rioja) $14. Rose-colored, with subdued aromas of cherry tomato, dried red fruits, mint, and leather. By modern standards, it's light and starchy, but the cherry and raspberry flavors are solid and easy to like. Better than inoffensive even if it's ultimately a simple, clean wine and nothing more. **87** —*M.S. (10/1/2005)*

Barzagoso 2000 Reserva Tempranillo Blend (Rioja) $25. Light red berry aromas with touches of cinnamon and vanilla. Lean and scouring on the palate in a traditional way, with tangy cherry and berry flavors. Finishes with some caramel and leather. Old-style and probably not for the modern palate. **87** —*M.S. (11/15/2005)*

BENJAMIN ROMEO

Benjamin Romeo 2001 La Viña de Andrés Romeo Tempranillo (Rioja) $140. Here's another full-force Tempranillo made in the modern style. The fruit is from older vines, and the oak regimen lasted 20 months. The nose features a mix of tree fruits along with earth and wood, and the palate is round and tannic, with a fairly thin midsection and a sweet finish of marzipan, coffee and plum. **90** —*M.S. (9/1/2004)*

BERBERANA

Berberana 1997 Viña Alarde Reserva Red Blend (Rioja) $18. With red fruit—plum, cherry, raspberry—judicious oak, soil, and a textured, medium body, this Tempranillo, Garnacha, and Mazuelo blend is a winner. Nose has red fruit accented by peanuts and walnuts; finishes with chalky tannins. Drink 2004–2007. **89** —*D.T. (4/1/2003)*

Berberana 2002 Dragon Tempranillo (Rioja) $10. Hits the ground running with berry and spice notes courtesy of ample oak. The mouth is equally spicy, with mid-level plum and berry fruit. Finishes fairly long, and again with a shot of oakiness that is not fully integrated. **85** —*M.S. (5/1/2004)*

Berberana 2001 Dragón Tempranillo (Vino de la Tierra de Castilla y León) $8. Plump and fruity is this Tempranillo, but it's also a grapey, simple wine with blueberry flavors and some sweet wood. On the finish, a touch of pepper and coffee stem from the oak. **84** —*M.S. (3/1/2004)*

Berberana 2000 Dragón Tempranillo (Rioja) $8. On the nose, it offers briary, forest flavors and sweet plum fruit; the front of the palate has more plum, oak, plus a healthy dose of red berries. Had potential to be better than it was—this would have been a great bargain if it hadn't fallen flat on the back end. **85** —*D.T. (4/1/2003)*

Berberana 2002 Viña Alarde Tempranillo (Rioja) $13. Light in color, with leathery aromas mucked up by wet earth and caramel. The palate is tart, almost raw, with rhubarb and pie cherry flavors. Seems washed out. **80** —*M.S. (6/1/2005)*

Berberana 2001 Vina Alarde Reserva Tempranillo (Rioja) $18. Light in color, with Old-World aromas of leaves, dried cherries and leather. It's a clean, easy wine with cherry and cranberry flavors coming in front of a dry, spicy finish. With proper acids and balance, its traditional qualities are admirable. **85** —*M.S. (3/1/2004)*

Berberana 1999 Vina Alarde Reserva Tempranillo Blend (Rioja) $20. Thin and light to the eye, with a traditional light-framed nose of earth, leather, and spice. The palate offers dried cherry and orange peel, while the finish deals hints of caramel and milk chocolate. Fades away smooth and easy. **86** —*M.S. (5/1/2004)*

BLASÓN DE SAN JUAN

Blasón de San Juan 2000 Crianza Tinto del Pais (Ribera del Duero) $19. Plump and fruity, with aromatics of tobacco, leather, and dark fruits. Features sweet, sturdy black cherry and plum flavors before a finish of warm earth, plum, and vanilla. Very straightforward in its approach, but solid on all accounts. **87** —*M.S. (6/1/2005)*

Blasón de San Juan 2000 Jóven Tinto del Pais (Ribera del Duero) $10. The color is rosy, as if it's starting to fall apart. The nose stays tight courtesy of gaseous sulfur notes. Eventually some tobacco and smoke emerge. Tangy in the mouth, with thin, average red fruit. **83** —*M.S. (10/1/2005)*

Blasón de San Juan 1999 Reserva Tinto del Pais (Ribera del Duero) $27. If it seems dirty at first, time will reveal tobacco and leather aromas along with black plum and coffee. Seems more sour than you might expect, with pie cherry and rhubarb flavors. Really high-toned on the finish, where it teeters on the brink of sour. Not bad but not endearing. **84** — *M.S. (6/1/2005)*

Blasón de San Juan 2000 Roble Tinto del Pais (Ribera del Duero) $13. Shows hickory-style wood aromas along with jerky, briar patch and

SPAIN

cherry. Fairly fresh and forward, with a tangy palate dealing standard berry-cherry fare. Tight on the finish, with chocolate, pepper, and coffee notes. A cut above the mass-market products; quite acceptable for the price **86** —*M.S. (6/1/2005)*

BLECUA

Blecua 2001 Vino Tinto Red Blend (Somontano) $NA. An eye-opening, intriguing wine from Somontano, at the foot of the Pyrenees. The bouquet is quite interesting, as it offers herbs, ripeness, and intensity. Super dense in the mouth, with pure blackberry and chocolate flavors floating atop dynamite tannins. Tons of flavor; from the Viñas del Vero group. **91** —*M.S. (6/1/2005)*

BODEGA JARIO

Bodega Jario 1998 Reserva Red Blend (Rioja) $14. Leathery and maturing, as the fruit seems to be on the fade. Dry cherry and raspberry notes carry the aging palate, which is bolstered by ample vanilla. Finishes warm, with licorice and pepper notes. Likable and more traditional, but drink soon. **87** —*M.S. (6/1/2005)*

BODEGAS ABEL DE MENDOZA

Bodegas Abel de Mendoza 1999 Jarrarte Tempranillo (Rioja) $26. Pretty berry and chocolate aromas lead you to a palate that's round and pure. Right away this wine impresses; it's got all the requisite fruit as well as some peppery kick. The finish is massive, with a bitter espresso edge. Wholly modern in style, with a chewy, delicious feel/flavor combination. **91** —*M.S. (3/1/2004)*

BODEGAS AGAPITO RICO

Bodegas Agapito Rico 2004 Monastrell (Jumilla) $9. This has become a popular by-the-glass wine, and deservedly so. The color is pure, the nose a nice mix of leather, earth, and dark but healthy plum and blackberry. Hails from a hot climate, but shows balance via bright acidity and firm tannins. Finishes with a fat, spicy finish. A country wine but a good one. **87 Best Buy** —*M.S. (10/1/2005)*

Bodegas Agapito Rico 2000 Monastrell (Jumilla) $9. Dryly fruited, this light and flavorful Monastrell (aka Mourvèdre) blend is a winning, easy drinker. Clean and direct, with dry cherry licorice and mineral shadings, it's a simple and satisfying mouthful, great for patio dining with lighter grilled foods. **85** —*M.M. (9/1/2002)*

Bodegas Agapito Rico 2002 Carchelo Red Blend (Jumilla) $9. Young and candied, with more zip and zest than sophistication. It's a five-grape blend dominated by Monastrell, and it pours forth with raspberry, blackberry, and also some plump, buttery oak that may or may not be pleasing, depending on one's taste. It's fairly simple and the finish fades fast. **84** —*M.S. (3/1/2004)*

Bodegas Agapito Rico 2000 Carchelo Red Blend (Jumilla) $8. 85 Best Buy —*M.M. (9/1/2002)*

Bodegas Agapito Rico 1999 Carchelo Red Blend (Jumilla) $9. 86 —*M.S. (8/1/2000)*

Bodegas Agapito Rico 1999 Carchelo Syrah (Jumilla) $13. 84 —*M.S. (8/1/2000)*

BODEGAS ANGEL LORENZO CACHAZO

Bodegas Angel Lorenzo Cachazo 2002 Martivilli Superior Verdejo (Rueda) $10. Fine pear and apple aromas come up in force, and citrus is there, too. Very bright and forward, with pure apple and citrus flavors. A good dose of natural spice adds the perfect finishing touch. Like Las Brisas, it's from Angel Lorenzo Cachazo. **90 Best Buy** —*M.S. (3/1/2004)*

Bodegas Angel Lorenzo Cachazo 2002 Las Brisas White Blend (Rueda) $9. Angel Lorenzo Cachazo is behind this open, piquant, vibrant white that really pours on the Sauvignon character. The aromas are more to peach and pear, yet the high-voltage palate is all grapefruit and other citrus. Very refreshing, with some pepper on the finish. **89 Best Buy** —*M.S. (3/1/2004)*

BODEGAS ANTANO

Bodegas Antano 2005 Viña Mocen White Blend (Rueda) $10. A 50/50 blend of Verdejo and Viura that focuses on aromas of green herbs, citrus, and nettles. The palate offers nice grapefruit and green papaya flavors,

and they are backed by a smooth, medium-length finish. **85 Best Buy** —*M.S. (9/1/2006)*

BODEGAS ARAGONESAS

Bodegas Aragonesas 2001 Don Ramon Tinto Barrica Garnacha (Campo de Borja) $8. A bit rubbery and hot is this Garnacha/Tempranillo blend. But while it's mostly just bland and plump, some probing will uncover plum and berry notes and some good structure. But still too simple and heavy to merit higher. **84** —*M.S. (9/1/2004)*

Bodegas Aragonesas 2002 La Riada Old Vines Garnacha (Campo de Borja) $11. Aromas of red licorice are unrefined and sweet. Plum and berry flavors are intense and forward, too much so. Finishes raw and sugary. **82** —*M.S. (9/1/2004)*

Bodegas Aragonesas 2000 Don Ramon Red Blend (Campo de Borja) $6. Chunky and clumsy on the nose, with unrefined flavors of apple skins, red plum, and cranberry. Shows hints of licorice and spice late in the game, but overall it's lean and short. And what's with the Sherry bottle? Seems strange for a red table wine. **83** —*M.S. (5/1/2004)*

BODEGAS ARTESANAS

Bodegas Artesanas 2000 Campo Viejo Crianza Red Blend (Rioja) $9. Some raspberry jam on the nose, but also dried leaves, pickle barrel, and tea. Flavors of cherry and buttery oak carry the palate into a broad, bland finish. Simple and plump, and ultimately a decent baby Rioja. **84** —*M.S. (3/1/2004)*

Bodegas Artesanas 1998 Campo Viejo Crianza Red Blend (Rioja) $9. Cream, nutmeg, and vanilla aromas waft from the nose, and continue on to the palate, where they are joined by sturdy, unyielding red fruits. Light- to medium-bodied, with some woodsy tannins, it feels rustic in the mouth. A good party quaff in theory, but it isn't the fruit-forward, jammy wine that your guests might be expecting. May be at its best with cheese. **85** —*D.T. (4/1/2003)*

Bodegas Artesanas 1997 Campo Viejo Reserva Red Blend (Rioja) $15. On the weak side, in terms of body and concentration. The overall flavor impression is one of wood and generic red fruit; woodsy tannins finish things off. **83** —*D.T. (4/1/2003)*

BODEGAS B.G.

Bodegas B.G. 2001 Gueta-Lupia Red Blend (Priorat) $66. Starts promising, with its dark color and interesting aromas of violets, black cherry, and cinnamon. But it's rather heavy and tannic on the tongue, where overbaked black fruit controls the flavor profile. All in all it's fully stuffed and chewy before turning bitter on the finish. **83** —*M.S. (3/1/2005)*

BODEGAS BALCONA

Bodegas Balcona 1999 Partal Crianza Red Blend (Bullas) $23. Chances are you don't know this tasty little Crianza from near Murcia, which is close to Alicante. The wine has plum and earth aromas along with some wood smoke and citrus peel. A palate loaded with cherry, raspberry, and other red fruits is smooth, open and lively. Nice and racy throughout, with the right mouthfeel, one that's neither too much nor too little. **88** —*M.S. (3/1/2004)*

BODEGAS BERCEO

Bodegas Berceo 2000 Los Dominios de Berceo Reserva 36 Tempranillo (Rioja) $67. Floral and candied, with rosy, fresh, acid-based fruit. Very precise and tight, with size and zest. Opens a bit on the palate to show a softer, chocolaty edge. But overall it's a fruity, concentrated ride of raspberry and cherry. **88** —*M.S. (8/1/2005)*

BODEGAS BERNABE NAVARRO

Bodegas Bernabe Navarro 2003 Beryna Red Blend (Alicante) $17. One of the best red wines we've tried from Alicante. It's based on Monastrell, with other grapes thrown in. The result is a complex winner that smells like dark cherries and tastes like a swirl of raspberry, plum, and chocolate. Very well balanced considering how warm 2003 was. **90** —*M.S. (11/1/2006)*

BODEGAS BILBAINAS

Bodegas Bilbainas 1994 Viña Pomal Reserva Red Blend (Rioja) $15. 86 *(8/1/2000)*

Bodegas Bilbainas 1994 La Vicalanda Gran Reserva Tempranillo (Rioja) $46. Smooth tannins, lively cherry, and plum fruit and subtle though judicious oak—a recipe for success, in my book. Finishes medium-long with more red fruit, plus some floral notes; nose offers smoldering, musky-earth aromas. Drink 2004+. **89** —D.T. (4/1/2003)

Bodegas Bilbainas 1999 La Vicalanda Reserva Tempranillo (Rioja) $20. Super old school, featuring aromas of mint, rubber, dried red fruits and wood smoke. Turns more reduced and hard on the palate, where cherry and raspberry shift toward medicinal: think cough drops. Finishes solid, with light oak notes. **86** —M.S. (8/1/2005)

Bodegas Bilbainas 1996 La Vicalanda Reserva Tempranillo (Rioja) $20. Stewy red fruit, earth, and oak flavors are couched in woodsy tannins, which might give you the impression that this is a rustic, unfinished wine. Not true. Rather, it's a tightly wound wine that needs time in the cellar, or a big hunk of grilled meat, to show its best. **88** —D.T. (4/1/2003)

Bodegas Bilbainas 1995 La Vicalanda Reserva Tempranillo (Rioja) $20. **88** —J.C. (8/1/2000)

Bodegas Bilbainas 2000 Viña Pomal Crianza Tempranillo (Rioja) $10. Pretty heady, with baked berry fruit, wood grain and caramel on the nose. More oak frames red berry and vanilla flavors, while the light finish starts airy but loses steam quickly. Overall it's lean and lithe, like a ballet dancer. **84** —M.S. (3/1/2005)

Bodegas Bilbainas 1998 Viña Pomal Reserva Tempranillo (Rioja) $16. Starts with a blast of coconut backed by dill and crystallized red fruit. Cherry, berry, and spice on the palate, with back notes of cherry tomato and green herbs. Oaky but tight, with a lot of acidity. **86** —M.S. (8/1/2005)

Bodegas Bilbainas 1996 La Vicalanda Gran Reserva Tempranillo Blend (Rioja) $30. Charred and smoky on the nose, with solid, dry fruit notes. Very middle-of-the-road in terms of flavors and feel. There's light plum, cherry and apple skins, with acidity on the back end. Fades with a bit of oak. **87** —M.S. (9/1/2004)

Bodegas Bilbainas 1999 La Vicalanda Reserva Tempranillo Blend (Rioja) $22. Dark in color, with aromas of black plum, raisin, and spice. Fairly plump and easy, with modest richness, medium tannins and a fair amount of sweet, chocolaty oak on the finish. **87** —M.S. (9/1/2004)

Bodegas Bilbainas 2003 Vicuana Tempranillo Blend (Rioja) $24. Violet in color, with dark, rubbery aromas that scream "new" and "modern." This new-age heavyweight spent 15 months in French oak, and the nose is lemony as a result. The palate, meanwhile, is rich and full, but still rather oaky and blunt. Finishing notes of espresso, chocolate, and lemon peel preserve interest. **87** —M.S. (10/1/2005)

Bodegas Bilbainas 1997 Viña Pomal Reserva Tempranillo Blend (Rioja) $10. This wine only spends a year in oak, so it's no newbie. It's rather distinguished, with cherry and plum on the nose and clean fruit that tastes right and ripe, not covered with wood it can't handle. Refined and light, not dissimilar to a good Burgundy. Old school but good. **88 Best Buy** —M.S. (9/1/2004)

BODEGAS BLEDA

Bodegas Bleda 2002 Divus Monastrell (Jumilla) $28. Damp mushroom and pine-forest aromas are more green and woodsy than fruity. On the palate, it's tannic and drying, although there is some cherry and chocolate mixed in. Dry as a barrel in summer, with too little fruit to offset the hard oak character. **82** —M.S. (10/1/2005)

BODEGAS BRETON

Bodegas Breton 1998 Loriñon Reserva Red Blend (Rioja) $14. Dense, earthy and full of stable and tree bark aromas. Grapy, plum-skin flavors evolve with airing, leading toward a mildly tannic finish. With a hollow middle and pronounced acids, this is not perfect, but it has character. **85** —M.S. (10/1/2003)

Bodegas Breton 2001 Alba de Breton Reserva Tempranillo (Rioja) $54. For a full-priced Rioja, it's rather scattered and scouring. The nose is mildly green, while the palate and finish are both fast and raw, bolstered by a pushy streak of core acidity. From the start it strikes an acidic,

razor-sharp note, and the finish is mostly defined by oak. **83** —M.S. (11/15/2005)

Bodegas Breton 1998 Alba de Breton Tempranillo (Rioja) $50. Much more classic than nouveau, with leather, red fruit and some tomato/rhubarb on the nose. The palate has plum, berry and earth, and while acidic, it more than holds its own. A bit of a throwback wine that's prime for the dinner table. Finishes solid. **90** —M.S. (9/1/2004)

Bodegas Breton 1996 Alba de Breton Tempranillo (Rioja) $55. This Rioja with a light- to medium-weight profile elicited quite varying responses. Undeniably elegant, some found it a bit thin, the sour-cherry tartness turning a bit puckery at the end. Others found it quite complex, well-integrated, smooth and supple, very Pinot Noir-like with a long, juicy dusty-tannin finish. Drink now through 2006. **90** — (9/1/2002)

BODEGAS CAMPANTE

Bodegas Campante 2003 Gran Reboreda White Blend (Ribeiro) $16. Ultra sweet and candied up front, with bulky apple and melon flavors. Finishes thick, grapey, and innocuous. Lots of holes and flaws where they shouldn't be. **83** —M.S. (9/1/2004)

Bodegas Campante 2003 Viña Reboreda White Blend (Ribeiro) $9. Fairly youthful, light and airy, with simple nectarine and melon flavors. Finishes smooth and medium length, with adequate but reserved force. Some finishing notes of creamy pear and sugared citrus zest work well. **85** —M.S. (9/1/2004)

BODEGAS CARMELO RODERO

Bodegas Carmelo Rodero 2000 Tempranillo (Ribera del Duero) $13. Blackberry and raspberry aromas suggest that the fruit to follow will be pleasing; mouthfeel is round and juicy, almost big. But there's a heavy dose of char here that buries the palate's plum fruit. The same juicy fruit peeks out from under the char on the finish. **86** —D.T. (4/1/2003)

Bodegas Carmelo Rodero 1998 Crianza Tempranillo (Ribera del Duero) $20. Between this Tempranillo's dry tannins and herbaceous flavors, your tongue just may go numb. Still, there are nice, dark flavors underneath it all—black fruit, mocha, maybe even some chocolate. Finishes with oak and herb accents. **85** —D.T. (4/1/2003)

BODEGAS CASTEJÓN

Bodegas Castejón 2002 NOBUL red Tempranillo (Madrid) $7. Flat up front, with a gassy nose. The flavor profile offers modest red fruit and a touch of green. Lots of wood grain rears up on the finish. Covers the easy bases but goes no further. **83** —M.S. (9/1/2004)

Bodegas Castejón 2001 Viña Rey Tempranillo (Madrid) $6. A simple, drink-me-now, light- to medium-weight Tempranillo, the Viña Rey is just this side of tired. Red plum fruit wears a barky-chalky coat; plum and cherry round out the finish. **83** —D.T. (4/1/2003)

Bodegas Castejón 2002 Viña Rey 70 Barricas Tempranillo (Madrid) $9. The bouquet offers some pleasant chocolate and root beer notes, but the fruit is distant and murkiness rises with each passing minute. That said, the berry and plum fruit is pretty good, while the finish is decent. Not a lot of depth or substance, but still steady. **84** —M.S. (9/1/2004)

BODEGAS CERROSOL

Bodegas Cerrosol 2002 Verdejo (Rueda) $11. Snappy, with citrus and a certain aromatic pungency. As for flavors, it's mostly orange, green melon, white pepper, and herbs, while the feel is dry and medium-full, with adequate freshness. **86** —M.S. (3/1/2004)

Bodegas Cerrosol 2001 Verdejo (Rueda) $9. There are a number of sensational Verdejo-based whites from this region, but this isn't one of them. The nose is heavy and creamy, while the palate is overdone yet bland. The dry, acidic palate is fresh enough, but where's the flavor? Not terrible, but not very good. **80** —M.S. (3/1/2004)

Bodegas Cerrosal 2000 Verdejo (Rueda) $9. The orange, apple, and hay notes here taste slightly mature, but have character and appeal. Medium weight, with a faintly viscous feel, the wine finishes dry and smooth. Verdejo generally shows better younger and brisker, but this is still good current drinking. **84** —M.M. (9/1/2002)

SPAIN

BODEGAS CONCAVINS

Bodegas Concavins 2000 Proyecto 4 Red Blend (Conca de Barberà) $10. Sometimes concept exceeds the wine itself, and this may be a case in point. The blend is odd, and the fact that each grape comes from a different part of Spain is potentially more odd. As for the wine, it has a nice perfume to it, courtesy of the Rhône varieties in the mix. And while the cherry/berry fruit is forward, it's maybe too sweet and basic in terms of length, structure and mouthfeel. Still, it's worth a try for the experimental tasters out there. **85** —M.S. (8/1/2003)

BODEGAS CONDE

Bodegas Conde 2001 Neo Punta Esencia Tinto del Pais (Ribera del Duero) $96. Inky dark, with coconut, baking spice, and leather on the otherwise fruity nose. There's a lumber yard's worth of oak here, but overall it works. The spice element is undeniable, while the quality of the fruit supercedes any raw wood quality. A bit simple and forward, but nothing to take issue with. **91** —M.S. (6/1/2005)

BODEGAS DIOS BACO S.L.

Bodegas Dios Baco S.L. NV Pedro Ximenez (Jerez) $18. Raisiny and extremely ripe, with licorice on the nose. Prune, chocolate, and fig flavors dominate, while the palate runs as viscous as possible without it turning solid. Probably a bit too syrupy, but loaded with flavor. **88** —M.S. (10/1/2005)

Bodegas Dios Baco S.L. NV 1970 Oxford Pedro Ximenez (Jerez) $40. Not as fresh forward as it could be, with mushroom and leather along with the requisite raisin and toffee aromas and flavors. Also it runs hot on the palate. Has some good points but in such a sweet category it isn't lovable. **85** —M.S. (12/31/2004)

Bodegas Dios Baco S.L. NV 20 Yr. Imperial Amontillado Sherry (Jerez) $75. Dark in color and extremely nutty. Along the way there are notes of seawater and white plum. The palate is a bit tangy and sharp, with orange peel, almond, and butter. Oily and complex on the finish, with a buttery tail and plenty of palate presence. **90** —M.S. (10/1/2005)

Bodegas Dios Baco S.L. NV 30 Yr. Imperial Oloroso Sherry (Jerez) $90. Piercing and pungent, with a bit of alcohol on the nose as well as campfire smoke and citrus zest. Smoky and round on the palate, with big-time nuttiness and plenty of mushroom. A condensed, explosive Sherry that hits hard. **89** —M.S. (10/1/2005)

Bodegas Dios Baco S.L. NV Amontillado Sherry (Jerez) $20. Pristine aromas of caramel, orange peel, and leather are both powerful and pure. Flavors of toffee, cinnamon, cheddar cheese and raisin are first-rate, while the sum of the parts is brightened and heightened by perfect acidity. A fine Amontillado that should please anyone with a fondness for good Sherry. **91** —M.S. (10/1/2005)

Bodegas Dios Baco S.L. NV Cream Sherry (Jerez) $20. Sweet and a bit unusual, with aromatic notes of cheddar cheese and barnyard along with more typical toffee and caramel. The palate is confectionary and sturdy, with vanilla, maple and mushroom flavors. Plump and rich on the finish. **90** —M.S. (10/1/2005)

Bodegas Dios Baco S.L. NV Fino Sherry Sherry (Jerez) $18. Yellow in tint, with slightly pasty aromas that quickly morph into nuttiness. The palate is full of nuts and butter, while the finish throws off mushroom. Not oxidized, but on the round side. **87** —M.S. (4/1/2006)

Bodegas Dios Baco S.L. NV Manzanilla Sherry (Jerez) $9. Top-notch manzanilla, plain and simple. What's not plain and simple is the fact that this is so pure and smooth that it dances across your palate. From the vanilla and almond on the nose to the pastry and mushroom on the palate to the creamed butter on the finish, this is as good as it gets in this class. **91 Editors' Choice** —M.S. (4/1/2006)

Bodegas Dios Baco S.L. NV Oloroso Sherry (Jerez) $20. Dark in color, with round, malty aromas that run deep. The palate is a bit sweet as well as a bit sharp; think citrus mixed with caramel. And along with that there's pumpkin pie and allspice. Flavorful and nicely balanced. **89** — M.S. (10/1/2005)

BODEGAS EL MOLAR

Bodegas El Molar 2001 Araviñas Semi-Crianza Tempranillo (Ribera del Duero) $14. Light and flowery in the nose, with delicate notes of lavender and smoke. The palate, however, is compact and intense. The cherry fruit is so acid-driven and reduced that it tastes a bit like a powdered drink mix. Probably best with burgers or steak. **86** —M.S. (3/1/2004)

BODEGAS FONTANA

Bodegas Fontana 1999 Fontal Crianza Tempranillo (La Mancha) $11. The nose offers some full fruit, but also a few gaps and a touch of cheesiness. Cherry and pepper define the tight, lean palate, which shows flashes but also recedes into that bland, tart underworld of the average wine. **84** — M.S. (5/1/2004)

Bodegas Fontana 2001 Fontal Roble Tempranillo (La Mancha) $9. Full and convincing at first, but with airing some of the wine's holes become apparent. Nevertheless, this oak-aged Tempranillo delivers good plum and raspberry fruit and a smoky, woody finish. Solid and flavorful, but with a thin midsection. **86** —M.S. (5/1/2004)

Bodegas Fontana 2002 Mesta Tempranillo (Vino de la Tierra de Castilla) $6. Shows tree bark and exotic spice aromas, while the palate runs fast and basic, with berry fruit and plenty of oak. Notes of licorice, cardamom and other spices push it forward and above the fray. **87 Best Buy** —M.S. (5/1/2004)

BODEGAS FUENTESPINA

Bodegas Fuentespina 1998 Crianza Red Blend (Ribera del Duero) $17. Unlike many crianzas, this one's oak is understated on the nose— instead, you get lots of delicate cherry aromas. That all changes in the mouth, with a healthy whack of vanilla. Spicy, creamy-oak finish. **85** — J.C. (11/1/2001)

Bodegas Fuentespina 1998 Reserva Red Blend (Ribera del Duero) $25. Don't underestimate this wine—though it seems approachable at first, it seems to bulk up the longer that it sits in the glass. Add woodsy tannins to a dark profile of black soil, black plum, and charred oak, and you've got a wine that could use at least another year (but more like two or three) in the bottle. **88** —D.T. (4/1/2003)

Bodegas Fuentespina 1996 Reserva Especial Red Blend (Ribera del Duero) $65. Wispy tendrils of smoky, toasty, vanilla oak are wrapped firmly around delicate cherries and strawberries and never let go, becoming slightly tougher on the finish. Drink now. **87** —J.C. (11/1/2001)

Bodegas Fuentespina 2002 Tempranillo (Ribera del Duero) $12. Pretty and lush, with a succulent nose. The palate is young, bright and fruity, with lots of raspberry flavor. The tail end is solid, balanced and expansive. With some lavender and crushed rose-petal notes, it has just enough ancillary accents to rise above the masses. **87 Best Buy** —M.S. (3/1/2004)

Bodegas Fuentespina 2001 Tempranillo (Ribera del Duero) $12. Jammy and sweet up front, and almost like a fruit roll-up as far as aromatics go. The palate is chewy and sweet, with boysenberry and plum flavors. Pretty nice in terms of mouthfeel, and for the most part it's right there. This is ultimately a basic Tempranillo, just the right wine for everyday drinking. **87** —M.S. (3/1/2004)

Bodegas Fuentespina 2000 Tempranillo (Ribera del Duero) $12. Medium-bodied, juicy and this side of bouncy, this Tempranillo packs what feels like two pounds of plums into every glass. Meaty, peppery notes add interest on the nose and finish. Drink now. **86** —D.T. (4/1/2003)

Bodegas Fuentespina 1999 Crianza Tempranillo (Ribera del Duero) $22. Cool and collected, with a deeply fruity nose. The palate pours forth with red fruit, particularly cherry and raspberry, with some vanilla shadings to prop it all up. Fairly lush and chocolaty, with a fine transition from palate to finish. **90** —M.S. (3/1/2004)

Bodegas Fuentespina 1997 Reserva Tempranillo (Ribera del Duero) $NA. Looking for a mature reserva at a reasonable price? This one boasts aromas of damp soil, cedar, clove, and wood, followed by rich flavors of sweet cherries and sauna cedar. Thins out on the finish, so drink now. **88** —J.C. (11/1/2001)

Bodegas Fuentespina 1998 Reserva Especial Tempranillo (Ribera del Duero) $72. Rich and attractive to the nose, with hints of smoked meat, tobacco, and black fruit. The palate is both developed and enveloping; it blends meat, berries, earth, and spice into a whole that's beyond the ordinary. The finish drives on for minutes with mocha, coffee, and charred meat. This has all the right components in all the right places. **92** —*M.S. (3/1/2004)*

Bodegas Fuentespina 1999 Cosecha Tempranillo Blend (Ribera del Duero) $12. Starts well, with mouthwatering aromas of smoke, cedar, cured meat, tobacco, and bright cherries. Simpler on the palate and a bit hollow, with cherry and cedar dominating, before perking up again on the finish, with notes of cigar tobacco and smoke. **85** —*J.C. (11/1/2001)*

BODEGAS GODEVAL

Bodegas Godeval 2001 Viña Godeval Godello (Valdeorras) $14. One of Rueda's top producers strikes gold here. Brilliant peach and pear aromas carry a hint of fresh cream, and the palate of pure apple and white pepper is dynamite. Some lemon and hard spice create a firm, biting and lasting finish. Drink this one up while it lasts. **90 Best Buy** —*M.S. (3/1/2004)*

BODEGAS GUELBENZU

Bodegas Guelbenzu 2002 EVO Cabernet Blend (Ribera del Queiles) $22. Dark and clearly shooting for the stars. Problem is, there's a fair level of green at the core. You get cassis, rubber, and earth aromas, but also some celery and green bean. In the mouth, it's mostly ditto: blackberry, milk chocolate, and a strong wave of bell pepper. Texture-wise, it's nearly perfect. Those unopposed to herbal influences will like it most. **87** —*M.S. (9/1/2004)*

Bodegas Guelbenzu 1999 Guelbenzu EVO Cabernet Blend (Navarra) $22. An opaque wine with a bright purple color brings red raspberries and fresh vegetables that integrate well with toasty cedar. Tannins are firm but not aggressive in this Cabernet Sauvignon (70%), Tempranillo (20%), and Merlot (10%) blend. **89** —*C.S. (4/1/2002)*

Bodegas Guelbenzu 2002 Azul Tempranillo Blend (Ribera del Queiles) $14. Pretty and floral, with sleek cherry fruit but also a slight hint of green that keeps it from achieving greater heights. The finish is simple and solid, with notes of burnt wood and pepper, both black and green. Will work best with food. **86** —*M.S. (9/1/2004)*

Bodegas Guelbenzu 1999 Guelbenzu Azul Tempranillo Blend (Navarra) $13. Starts off a little slow, taking a few minutes to open from dull, forest-floor aromas into a mix of dried spices and vanilla. Where it starts to sing is on the palate, with berry and black cherry flavors that mingle enticingly with notes of pepper, smoke, and herb. Finishes with tobacco flavors and enough ripe tannins to carry it through 2004. **88 Best Buy** *(1/1/2004)*

BODEGAS GUTIÉRREZ DE LA VEGA

Bodegas Gutiérrez de la Vega 2000 Casta Diva Reserva Real Moscatel (Alicante) $NA. Moscatel from the hot plains of Alicante doesn't get much better than this. Yes, it's a bit oxidized and overloaded with caramel, but otherwise it's stellar. Lovely brown sugar, cinnamon, and vanilla aromas lead the way for the sun-drenched fruit to do its thing. The result is an over-the-top sweetie that excites. **90** —*M.S. (6/1/2005)*

Bodegas Gutiérrez de la Vega 2003 Casta Diva Cosecha Miel Muscat (Alicante) $25. Funky to say the least, with aromas of canned pear and pumpkin pie. Big and sweet on the palate; like candy in a cup. Clunky and chunky, but pretty good if you're taking one nicely chilled glass with a fruit dessert. **85** —*M.S. (8/1/2005)*

BODEGAS HEREDEROS RIBAS

Bodegas Herederos Ribas 1998 Ribas de Cabrera Red Blend (Vi de Taula de Balears) $53. The Balearic Islands seem to have what it takes when it comes to fine reds, especially when importer supreme Jorge Ordonez is the one ferreting them out. This three-grape blend is fascinating and flavorful; it has a floral nose, gorgeous plum, berry, vanilla, and cinnamon flavors, and a smooth, chocolaty finish. The wine is round, complete, and unusual; it's a real find. **92** —*M.S. (3/1/2004)*

BODEGAS HIDALGO

Bodegas Hidalgo NV La Gitana Manzanilla Sherry (Jerez) $10. The benchmark among fino-style Sherries is La Gitana. Simply put, it's a classic.

Pour yourself a copita of this beauty and sip it while munching some olives, peanuts, or pistachios. Shazzam! You're transported to a white-washed village in Andalusia. Aromas of mushroom and yeast are just as they should be. And deep within are subtle flavors of marzipan and citrus. The long, salty, bone-dry finish cleanses the palate and primes your appetite for better things to come. **89 Best Buy** —*M.S. (11/15/2004)*

BODEGAS INVIOSA

Bodegas Inviosa 1999 Lar de Barros Crianza Tempranillo (Ribera del Guadiana) $10. An altogether unusual wine, with a melange of fruits at its core—really, it's reminiscent of a fruit-juice punch you drank as a kid. Nose shows anise, meat, and blood orange notes over a foundation of red berries; finishes with a tangy, spritzy texture. **83** —*D.T. (4/1/2003)*

Bodegas Inviosa 1998 Lar de Barros Crianza White Blend (Ribera del Guadiana) $10. The nose offers interesting spice and tarragon notes. Bitter chocolate and a berry festival dominate the palate, which was surprising because the nose did not show much fruit. Great acid, fruit, tannin balance that left you thirsty for more. **87 Best Buy** —*C.S. (4/1/2002)*

BODEGAS IRANZO

Bodegas Iranzo 2004 Mi Niña Tempranillo (Utiel-Requena) $11. Black raspberry and raisin control the bouquet on this carbonically macerated wine from inland Valencia. Lively plum and black cherry work the rubbery, mildly tannic palate, while the finish is leisurely enough. A touch narrow in flavor but broad in feel. **84** —*M.S. (12/15/2006)*

Bodegas Iranzo 2002 Vertus Reserva Tempranillo-Cabernet Sauvignon (Utiel-Requena) $35. Almost volatile with its cooked rhubarb and berry aromas. Screechy black cherry and raspberry flavors don't really help it along. Simply a hard, closed-down wine that isn't up to its price tag. **80** —*M.S. (12/15/2006)*

BODEGAS JULIÁN CHIVITE

Bodegas Julián Chivite 2003 Colección 125 Chardonnay (Navarra) $NA. A modern, ripe, full-bodied Chardonnay that sports an Australian personality and a bright gold luster. It's richly buttered, with lemon, pineapple, green apple, and cinnamon flavors. Creamy on the finish yet it holds onto its minerality. An atypical Navarran white due to its richness. **89** —*M.S. (10/1/2004)*

Bodegas Julián Chivite 2000 Colección 125 Chardonnay (Navarra) $50. Offers mealy, white-peach and melon notes from beginning to end. Mouthfeel is full and rich, even custardy, and turns powdery on the long finish. Comprised of three different Chardonnay clones. Hold 1–2 years. **90** *(4/1/2003)*

Bodegas Julián Chivite 1999 Colección 125 Chardonnay (Navarra) $49. This Chard has viscous, resiny mouthfeel, with pear, yellow fruit, and almond butter flavors. It's aged on lees in second-year, French oak barrels, which explains the nuttiness on the nose and the lingering finish. **89** *(4/1/2003)*

Bodegas Julián Chivite 2005 Gran Feudo Rosé Garnacha (Navarra) $12. For years this wine was a big-time bargain from Navarra. Now it's not so inexpensive yet the quality is the same. There's common nectarine and raspberry aromas before snappy peach and berry flavors. It's juicy and modest, with crispness and a drying finish. **85** —*M.S. (12/15/2006)*

Bodegas Julián Chivite 2002 Colección 125 Vendimia Tardía Moscatel (Navarra) $40. The epitome of freshness and complexity is on offer in this delicious late-harvest Moscatel from Navarra's most innovative bodega. Lemon peel, wild flowers, and piercing apricot and peach aromas carry the ultra pure nose. There's nothing funky or odd about this barrel-fermented wine; it will appeal to almost everyone who likes a well-made sweet white. **92** —*M.S. (6/1/2005)*

Bodegas Julián Chivite 2000 Colección 125 Vendimia Tardía Muscat (Navarra) $35. Made, according to Fernando Chivite, "in the Barsac way of winemaking," this Muscat is at once seductive and restrained. It's viscous, but is the farthest thing from syrupy; its honeysuckle, jasmine, beeswax, and sugarcane flavors are as close as you'll get to ambrosia for a long time to come. **91** *(4/1/2003)*

Bodegas Julián Chivite 2001 Colección 125 Reserva Tempranillo Blend (Navarra) $NA. A masterful mixture of Tempranillo, Merlot, and

SPAIN

Cabernet Sauvignon. Aromas of wood smoke, blackberry, and plum. An open wine for near-term drinking. Sweet and rich at the core, while pure cacao darkens the tail end. **92** —*M.S. (10/1/2004)*

Bodegas Julián Chivite 2000 Colección 125 Reserva Tempranillo Blend (Navarra) $NA. On par with Chivite's other Reservas, but this infant just isn't talking much quite yet. Nuances of black pepper, plum, and oak play on the nose. Rich mouthfeel; juicy red berry and earth flavors peeking from the palate. Wake this one up 2005–2015. **90** *(4/1/2003)*

Bodegas Julián Chivite 1999 Colección 125 Reserva Tempranillo Blend (Navarra) $46. A juicy, plump wine, but still two-plus years away from its peak, the 1999's palate and nose are brimming with fleshy, juicy plum and blackberry flavors—even a little red fruit. Nose beguiles with fat fruit and a little spice. Drink 2005–2015. **90** *(4/1/2003)*

Bodegas Julián Chivite 1998 Colección 125 Reserva Tempranillo Blend (Navarra) $42. Unique flavors, especially considering that this is Tempranillo, not a Bordeaux blend. Cherry fruit and lead pencil predominate, with a hint of weediness; mint and green-wood flavors stick out on the long finish. Drink from 2008. **88** *(4/1/2003)*

Bodegas Julián Chivite 2002 Gran Feudo Crianza Tempranillo Blend (Navarra) $11. Red fruit, hints of spice, and a touch of herbal essence kick it off. The palate is leafy and drying, with medium-ripe cherry and berry flavors. Quite your basic red table wine, and if that's what you're looking for it's not disappointing. **85** —*M.S. (12/15/2006)*

Bodegas Julián Chivite 2001 Gran Feudo Reserva Tempranillo Blend (Navarra) $15. Red fruit is the focus of this zesty, rugged Tempranillo-based wine. The palate is lively and acidic, as plum and berry flavors get lots of boost. The finish is firm and medium in depth, with a stout amount of tannin. Drink now, preferably with food. **87** —*M.S. (12/15/2006)*

Bodegas Julián Chivite 2000 Señorío de Arinzano Tempranillo Blend (Navarra) $NA. Rich, big and burly, this blend of Tempranillo, Cabernet Sauvignon and Merlot is juicy, with full-on black cherry, plum, soil, ink, and oak flavors. The nose is somewhat closed, but with aeration reveals black pepper and vanilla nuances. Finishes with black tea, char, and dry, chalky tannins. Still a baby, but so promising. Give it 5+ years. **93 Cellar Selection** *(4/1/2003)*

BODEGAS LA CERCA

Bodegas La Cerca 2001 Don Cecilio Red Blend (Mentrida) $10. This 70% Tempranillo and 30% Garnacha Vieja is a dark, straightforward quaffer with an earth and black fruit core. Brewed, malty notes on the nose and finish, however, make more sense in beer than wine. **85** —*D.T. (4/1/2003)*

Bodegas La Cerca 2000 Milino Viejo Crianza Red Blend (Mentrida) $18. This wine from the La Cerca winery hails from near Toledo. It's dark and ripe, with plum, currant, and oak on the nose. Syrupy cassis notes carry the palate toward and extracted, tannic finish. Quite deep and rich, but arguably a touch grapy. Worth a look. **87** —*M.S. (3/1/2004)*

Bodegas La Cerca 1999 Molino Viejo Crianza Red Blend (Mentrida) $20. This Tempranillo-Garnacha blend is full in the mouth, with a palate brimming with juicy black plums and oak. With this kind of extraction (and the caramelly, creamy oak that goes along with it), you might mistake it for a Cabernet. Finishes medium-long, though a little dry, with oak and nut flavors. **88** —*D.T. (4/1/2003)*

BODEGAS LAN

Bodegas LAN 2003 Crianza Red Blend (Rioja) $11. Hits with force as well as notes of raisin and Sherry. No doubt this comes from a hot vintage, evidenced by the prune, brandied cherry, and chocolate flavors. Still there's some tannin to keep it moving ahead. Overall, however, it's pretty heavy and condensed. **84** —*M.S. (12/15/2006)*

Bodegas LAN 1998 Gran Reserva Red Blend (Rioja) $25. Quite rooty and earthy, with brandied cherry aromas. Not too pure and fruity, as green bean and carob creep onto the palate. Finishes a touch dry and tannic. Seems caught in Neverland. **83** —*M.S. (11/1/2006)*

Bodegas LAN 1999 Reserva Red Blend (Rioja) $17. Traditional in the way it displays molasses, tobacco, and cherry cola among its aromatics. Satisfying in the mouth, with lightweight cherry supported by oak-driven vanilla. Crisp acids are keeping it healthy. Drink now for a taste of Old World Rioja. **86** —*M.S. (11/1/2006)*

Bodegas LAN 1999 Crianza Tempranillo (Rioja) $11. Sweet on the nose, with aromas of molasses, burnt sugar, and fresh-cut wood. The palate runs tart, with spiky red-berry flavors. Firm on the finish, with genuine tannins. Still, it seems diluted. **83** —*M.S. (6/1/2005)*

Bodegas LAN 1996 Gran Reserva Tempranillo (Rioja) $25. Heavy and high-voltage, with a strong whiff of green bean to the nose. Flavors of raisin, raspberry, and green pepper combine to create a palate that has its high moments as well as its faults. Tight on the finish, with lots of tobacco and bell pepper. **84** —*M.S. (6/1/2005)*

Bodegas LAN 1999 Viña Lanciano Reserva Red Blend (Rioja) $25. Dark in color, with brawny aromas of oak, clove and leather. In the mouth, there's a mix of black plum and cherry but also a streak of bell pepper. Finishes round, spicy, properly tannic and dark, with coffee and a light hint of green. **87** —*M.S. (12/15/2006)*

Bodegas LAN 2000 Crianza Tempranillo (Rioja) $10. A little heavier than ideal, with a touch of raisin along with candied black cherry on the bouquet. Better in the mouth, where it comes to life on the wings of good acids, modest tannins, and simple but proper berry fruit flavors. **84** —*M.S. (6/1/2005)*

Bodegas LAN 1994 Culmen de LAN Tempranillo (Rioja) $162. Tasters praised the solid, dark cherry fruit core of this well-poised, medium-weight offering. They diverged beyond that, some enjoying the wine's cedar, meat, and earth elements, others finding, along with tasty coffee and licorice notes, a slightly edgy astringency. Drinkable now, it's still evolving. Best from 2004–2010+. **89** —*M.M. (9/1/2002)*

Bodegas LAN 2003 Edición Limitada Tempranillo (Rioja) $45. LAN's modern interpretation of Rioja is ripe, fragrant, and beefy, with mineral, charcoal, pine, and black cherry coating the unctuous nose. Runs a touch soft and plump on the palate, probably a reflection of the hot '03 vintage. But along the way there's black plum, licorice, molasses, and maple flavors. A big, new-wave wine that has a lot going for it. **89** —*M.S. (11/1/2006)*

Bodegas LAN 2002 Edición Limitada Tempranillo (Rioja) $38. Ultra sweet and intriguing; you'd have to say, given the vintage, that LAN has done a great job with this prestige wine. It's loaded with sandalwood, plum, and cassis aromas. Best of all, it's fresh and lively, not a dull heavyweight that trips over itself. As for flavors, look for dark plum, coffee, and black currant. **91** —*M.S. (3/1/2005)*

Bodegas LAN 2001 Edición Limitada Tempranillo (Rioja) $38. This is everything a modern-day super red is supposed to be. It's bold, smoky, and masculine beyond reproach. The body is sturdy as a brick, yet it's cuddly and smooth. Flavorwise, you won't believe the cascade of cassis, black cherry, vanilla, and licorice that flows from the palate. And the finish lasts an eternity. Hold until 2006-07, and then let it rip. **95 Editors' Choice** —*M.S. (3/1/2005)*

Bodegas LAN 1996 Viña Lanciano Reserva Tempranillo (Rioja) $30. Sly and expressive, with traditional aromas of wood, earth, and leather along with telltale dried fruit. The palate is racy and reduced, a combination of apple skins, cherry and red plum. Finishes tight and concentrated before giving way to mature chocolaty notes. Drink or continue to hold. **89** —*M.S. (3/1/2005)*

Bodegas LAN 2001 Culmen Tempranillo Blend (Rioja) $75. With color akin to crude oil with a violet tint, this is one tank of a wine. The nose is massively roasted, with espresso, bacon fat, and blackberry melding in monster fashion. In the mouth, there's more licorice, pepper, and syrup than bounce, which makes it somewhat of a one-trick pony. Heady for sure, but lacking that extra nuance or two that the great ones have. **90** —*M.S. (3/1/2005)*

Bodegas LAN 1996 Edición Limitada Reserva Tempranillo Blend (Rioja) $39. Some Russian oak was used on this wine, which is 80% Tempranillo, and it has a nose of bell pepper and dill that could stem from that. The body, however, is good as is the acidity, but the flavor profile comes up midland. From the older school and Bodegas LAN, and in essence lost in space. **86** —*M.S. (9/1/2004)*

Bodegas LAN 1998 Reserva Tempranillo Blend (Rioja) $17. Solid as can be, with powerful black cherry, earth, and leather on the nose. Attractive berry and plum fruit carries the sturdy palate toward a spicy, chocolaty finish that deals firm tannins, leather, and mushroom. Round, satisfying, and complete. **89** —*M.S. (6/1/2005)*

Bodegas LAN 1999 Viña Lanciano Tempranillo Blend (Rioja) $30. Dark and saturated, like a New World wine should be. The nose is lush and smoky, with deep prune, violet, and rubber aromas. Rich and lusty on the palate, with bacon, mustard green, clove, and cinnamon. Finishes with brown sugar, licorice, and coffee. Very easy to drink; a likely crowd favorite. **90** —*M.S. (6/1/2005)*

Bodegas LAN 1998 Viña Lanciano Reserva Tempranillo Blend (Rioja) $30. Dark and deep, with maturity as well as kept-up youth. Odds are you will love this alta expression Rioja for its violet and blackberry aromas, its stately overall bouquet, and its sweet, smooth plum, black cherry, and smoke flavor profile. With coffee and chocolate coming in layers, the finish is excellent. From Bodegas Lan; and while it claims to be a limited-edition wine, production exceeds 2,000 cases. **92 Editors' Choice** —*M.S. (3/1/2005)*

BODEGAS LEDA

Bodegas Leda 2002 Viñas Viejas Tempranillo (Viño de la Tierra de Castilla y León) $60. Round up front, although not terribly fragrant. The nose shows only subtle berry and game aromas, with a hint of bacon. Very tannic, with a foundation of bitter chocolate and earth. Tastes good, as it should, but still not the best Leda in terms of depth and mouthfeel. **89** —*M.S. (6/1/2005)*

Bodegas Leda 2000 Viñas Viejas Tempranillo (Viño de la Tierra de Castilla y León) $50. Made by Mariano Garcia, the same winemaker as Mauro, this is the third vintage of the Leda old-vine Tempranillo, and it scores big for its soy, hickory and exotic spice notes. Richness is the wine's calling card. The palate is a real berry ball, one with blackberry, raspberry, and cassis. The smooth finish carries some chalky tannins, but the whole is in fine balance. **92 Editors' Choice** —*M.S. (3/1/2004)*

BODEGAS LUZON

Bodegas Luzon 2004 Verde Monastrell (Jumilla) $8. Smells like fruit bubble gum and even though it settles down with time in the glass, it really doesn't offer much besides jumpy fruit. Devoid of complexity despite being clean and juicy. **82** —*M.S. (11/15/2005)*

BODEGAS MARTINEZ LACUESTA

Bodegas Martinez Lacuesta 1996 Campeador Reserva Tempranillo (Rioja) $18. 84 *(8/1/2000)*

BODEGAS MARTINEZ PAYVA

Bodegas Martinez Payva 2003 Payva Tempranillo (Ribera del Guadiana) $8. This hot-climate chunkster hails from Extremadura, and you can tell it's warm there by the wine's heavy color and nose. It's fairly soft on the palate, however, with flavors of cough syrup, wood, and brandied fruit. Some pepper and spice on the finish add a rustic touch. **84** —*M.S. (9/1/2004)*

BODEGAS MAURO

Bodegas Mauro 1999 Red Blend (Viño de la Tierra de Castilla y León) $37. Tasted just days after bottling, this wine was nevertheless showing well. Rich chocolate and earth aromas complement the red berry and black cherry fruit. Mauro is not huge or overly weighty, but displays notable intensity and persistence of flavor. The finish lingers delicately, folding hints of vanilla, licorice, and cinnamon. **90 Editors' Choice** —*J.C. (11/1/2001)*

Bodegas Mauro 1998 Vendimmia Seleccionada Red Blend (Viño de la Tierra de Castilla y León) $90. This wine has already been bottled, but likely won't reach U.S. shores until 2002. It needs the additional time, because aromatically it's closed right now, tight as a drum. Still, you can taste the potential in its earthy, dark fruit, and coffee flavors. With this kind of depth and intensity and a long, supple but tannic finish, 91 points may seem conservative in five years' time. **91 Cellar Selection** —*J.C. (11/1/2001)*

BODEGAS MAURODOS

Bodegas Maurodos 2000 San Roman, Unfiltered Tinta de Toro (Toro) $38. Dark and pungent, with heavy but integrated oak. Notes of peanut and coconut are detectable, but they aren't out of place. In the mouth, black plum flavors get a lift from cola, coffee, and nutmeg accents. The finish is lively and moderately tannic, but overall this wine hits the bull's eye. **92 Editors' Choice** —*M.S. (3/1/2004)*

BODEGAS MURIEL

Bodegas Muriel 1995 Reserva Tempranillo (Rioja) $13. 86 *(8/1/2000)*

BODEGAS MURVIEDRO

Bodegas Murviedro 2003 Tinto Bobal (Valencia) $6. The nose of this Bobal-based red displays soft, candied fruit aromas and something akin to citrus. Light plum and peach flavors carry the short, simple palate. Tastes pretty good but lacks depth and stuffing. **84 Best Buy** —*M.S. (8/1/2005)*

Bodegas Murviedro 2000 Los Monteros Crianza Monastrell (Valencia) $11. This Valencian Monastrell, with its juicy, mixed black and red fruit, had potential to be something better than it is. On the front end, it offers cream, caramel, and blackberry aromas. The wine is mouthfilling though rather simple; its appreciable fruit falls off on the back end. At the very least shows that Valencia's a region to watch in future vintages. **85** —*D.T. (4/1/2003)*

Bodegas Murviedro 1996 Reserva Red Blend (Valencia) $15. With red plum skin flavors, and an undercurrents of eucalpyptus and herb, the overall impression here is a tart, almost lean, one. Tart red fruit lingers on the finish; the nose offers earth, eucalyptus and red berry aromas. 2,000 cases produced. **84** —*D.T. (4/1/2003)*

Bodegas Murviedro 1999 Tinto Crianza Red Blend (Valencia) $10. The nose shows sweet pastry dough and oak notes; however, this Tempranillo, Monastrell, and Bobal blend has drying tannins and oak to spare, with black fruit underneath that can't quite overcome the wood. Might drink better if paired with chorizo, or other grilled meats. **83** —*D.T. (4/1/2003)*

Bodegas Murviedro 2003 Agarena Tempranillo-Cabernet Sauvignon (Utiel-Requena) $7. Overall it's a sweet, solid wine. Aromas of smoke, berry, and marinade precede an avalanche of blackberry in the mouth. That same power pushes onto the finish, where warm pepper notes take over. A good warm-climate red from central Spain. **87 Best Buy** —*M.S. (8/1/2005)*

Bodegas Murviedro 2001 Agarena Tempranillo-Cabernet Sauvignon (Utiel-Requena) $8. Medium-weight and approachable now, this Cab-Tempranillo from southern Spain offers juicy (though a little sour) red cherry and plum fruit, with smoke and char accents. Piquant red fruit and earth aromas waft from the nose. Try this at your next barbecue—at this price, how can you go wrong? 60,000 cases produced. **87 Best Buy** —*D.T. (4/1/2003)*

Bodegas Murviedro 2003 Blanco White Blend (Valencia) $6. Enormously fragrant, with sunny aromas of honeysuckle, gardenia, and lemon juice. Softer flavors of melon, papaya, and lime are solid and supported by fresh acidity. Mild vanilla and honey sweeten the finish. Surprisingly satisfying, with few to no faults. **88 Best Buy** —*M.S. (8/1/2005)*

BODEGAS NAIA

Bodegas Naia 2004 Las Brisas White Blend (Rueda) $10. Amazingly expressive stuff from Spain. A mix of Verdejo, Sauvignon Blanc, and Viura that delivers a cornucopia of citrus. Grapefruit, passion fruit, and lime aromas and flavors abound, and the finish is so fresh and scouring that it can't help but quench your thirst. A superb summer sipper from the constantly improving Rueda region. **89 Best Buy** —*M.S. (8/1/2005)*

BODEGAS NAVAJAS

Bodegas Navajas 2002 Vega del Rio Crianza Red Blend (Rioja) $14. Heavy and green, with nutty, leathery aromas. Rather candied and less than fresh in the mouth, with a weedy underbelly on the palate. Finishes herbal, minty, and burnt, but with a lot of size and power. **82** —*M.S. (11/1/2006)*

Bodegas Navajas 2003 Vega del Rio-Jóven Tempranillo Blend (Rioja) $10. Not much color, but a lot of aromatics in the form of milk chocolate, sawdust, and coconut. Broad and woody on the palate, with light fruit flavors. A bunch more wood and butter comes forth on the finish. Leaves a somewhat leafy, wanting impression. **82** —M.S. (2/1/2006)

Bodegas Navajas 2003 Vega del Rio Crianza Viura (Rioja) $14. Wheat and corn aromas announce the soft, oaky personality that this wine brings to the table. Grainy and heavily oaked, it sits on toast, vanilla, and creamy, buttery flavors without offering any serious fruit or style. **80** —M.S. (11/1/2006)

BODEGAS NEKEAS

Bodegas Nekeas 2003 Vega Sindoa Cabernet Sauvignon-Tempranillo (Navarra) $10. "Oaky" is the first word that comes to mind, as the bouquet is full of cinnamon and cedar shavings. The mouth deals clove and vanilla notes along with meaty, somewhat dense fruit that doesn't really rise above first impressions. **85 Best Buy** —M.S. (11/15/2005)

Bodegas Nekeas 2001 Vega Sindoa Cabernet Sauvignon-Tempranillo (Navarra) $11. This wine from Bodegas Nekeas is overtly green. It smells and tastes of bell peppers and green beans, and despite a perfectly good mouthfeel and tannic structure, the underripe aromas and flavors drag it down. **82** —M.S. (3/1/2004)

Bodegas Nekeas 2001 Vega Sindoa Chardonnay (Navarra) $10. Even if the nose is slightly bland, the wine perks up on the palate, where it delivers apple and papaya in nice, round bursts. The finish is full and long, with a likable woody undertone. Sweet, easy, and ripe, with adequate acidity at its base. **85** —M.S. (3/1/2004)

Bodegas Nekeas 2001 Vega Sindoa El Chaparral, Old Vines Garnacha (Navarra) $11. Racy and rambunctious, with a potent yet pretty nose featuring tons of red licorice and cassis. This is old-vines Garnacha, and it has some tannins that could use a few years to settle in. Nonetheless the chocolate and coffee flavors are fine, and there's a sweetness that grows on you. Drink beginning in late 2004. **89 Best Buy** —M.S. (3/1/2004)

Bodegas Nekeas 2000 Vega Sindoa Merlot (Navarra) $12. Strong bell pepper and red pepper aromas lead into a similar palate, one dominated by peppery, vegetal fruit. It's not the Merlot most of us are used to; fortunately the farm-influenced flavors aren't offensive, just overwhelming. **81** —M.S. (3/1/2004)

Bodegas Nekeas 2002 Vega Sindoa Rosé Blend (Navarra) $7. Such a pretty pink is this little Garnacha/Cabernet mix; and it tastes and smells great, too. Fruity raspberry aromas blend into the flowery bouquet, while the palate is streamlined by watermelon notes that prime the peach flavors that dominate. A mild dose of pepper on the finish is nice. **88 Best Buy** —M.S. (3/1/2004)

Bodegas Nekeas 2002 Vega Sindoa White Blend (Navarra) $7. At 75% Viura, this is a hollow wine with dull aromas and midland apple and pear flavors. The finish is oaky and plump, but not very exciting. **82** — M.S. (3/1/2004)

BODEGAS ONTANON

Bodegas Ontanon 1998 Crianza Tempranillo (Rioja) $NA. 86 —M.M. (9/1/2002)

Bodegas Ontanon 1994 Gran Reserva Tempranillo (Rioja) $NA. This mature red's complex, enticing nose offers wood, spices, brown leaves, and hint of funky mushroom-earth. It's not weighty, but very aromatic and flavorful. The elements above continue to play out over a solid dried fruit core on the palate. Finishes beautifully with very good length and subtle spice notes. **91** —M.M. (9/1/2002)

BODEGAS ORVALAIZ

Bodegas Orvalaiz 1998 Cabernet Sauvignon (Navarra) $8. Funky aromas of red cabbage, green herbs, and sweet cherries lead into a lean, herbaceous wine that finishes on a metallic note. Tasters' views were more consistent on this wine than on this winery's Merlot. **82** (1/1/2004)

Bodegas Orvalaiz 1999 Merlot (Navarra) $8. Downrated by some tasters for its "metallic, abrupt finish," and praised by others for its "black cherry, milk chocolate, coffee, and dried herb" flavors, which gave it away as Merlot despite being tasted blind. "Out of whack" or "varietally correct"? —that is the question. **82** (1/1/2004)

Bodegas Orvalaiz 1999 Tempranillo (Navarra) $8. Red plums and candied fruit, with a touch of old wood flavor make this a pleasant wine. The nose brings chocolate and mint with focused deep red berry fruit. Drink soon and enjoy. **85** —C.S. (4/1/2002)

Bodegas Orvalaiz 1999 Viña Orvalaiz Tempranillo Blend (Navarra) $9. A simple wine with aromas of blackberry jam and Bing cherries. Slightly nutty flavors, accompanied by a touch of dustiness, make this an enjoyable quaffing wine. **84** —C.S. (4/1/2002)

BODEGAS OTTO BESTUE

Bodegas Otto Bestue 2002 Finca Rableros Tempranillo-Cabernet Sauvignon (Somontano) $13. The country-style nose deals beets and crystallized fruit at first, and then comes sweaty leather and earth notes. In the mouth, raspberry, strawberry, and spice come in layers, while the finish is plump and shows some muscle. Bold and satisfying, yet somewhat rustic. **87** —M.S. (5/1/2004)

BODEGAS PALACIO

Bodegas Palacio 2004 Tempranillo (Rioja) $9. Starts with lightly roasted aromas of herbal fruit and pepper, while the palate is deeper and more pure, with raspberry, cherry, and cranberry flavors. Finishes medium in terms of power and length, but short on complexity. Good in a basic sense, with proper balance. **84** —M.S. (11/1/2006)

Bodegas Palacio 2002 Crianza Tempranillo (Rioja) $10. Easy and fruity, with light cherry aromas. Juicy on the palate, with raspberry, apple skin, and plum flavors. Zesty as they go, with good natural acidity and ample freshness. **85 Best Buy** —M.S. (11/1/2006)

Bodegas Palacio 1998 Gran Reserva Tempranillo (Rioja) $28. Needs ample air to shake its early stewy, earthy character, and even then it recedes into a place best described as traditional. That means the nose is rustic, leathery, and oaky, and the fruit is reserved, teetering toward drying and fading. A throwback with merits and demerits. **86** —M.S. (11/1/2006)

Bodegas Palacio Especial 2000 Reserva Tempranillo (Rioja) $33. Red berry aromas are backed by crisp, almost sour flavors of cherry skins and red plum. Quite acidic and lean by modern standards, with some toast and earth on the finish. **84** —M.S. (11/15/2005)

BODEGAS PIRINEOS

Bodegas Pirineos 2002 Montesierra Macabeo (Somontano) $7. Macabeo, a grape usually used in the cava blend, stands alone here. And it struggles. The palate on this wine is of lime and underripe peach, while the compact finish is dry and edgy. Sparse in terms of flavor, but not bad when it comes to freshness and feel. **82** —M.S. (3/1/2004)

Bodegas Pirineos 2001 Moristel (Somontano) $13. Scattered and woody, with grainy notes to the red-fruit nose. This is Mourvèdre, or if you prefer, Monastrell, but any way you cut it the fruit is big and ripe yet somewhat sour, with a lot of dry oak in support. Promising at first but it doesn't hit with much force. **84** —M.S. (3/1/2004)

Bodegas Pirineos 1999 Moristel (Somontano) $10. A slight whiff of animale and spiced pie crust melds seamlessly into a brightly fruited, light-weight wine that's loaded with cherry and blackberry fruit. The tannins are negligible, but the acidity is pure and clean, giving a juicy, palate-cleansing effect that finishes with a hint of green herbs. A perfect picnic red to go with sandwiches or quiche. **87 Best Buy** —J.C. (4/1/2002)

Bodegas Pirineos 1999 Marbore Red Blend (Somontano) $28. Offers Syrahlike, rich blackberry fruit and a slight caramel-oak twinge. It's mouthfilling and brimming with promise, but it wants the power and richness that could have catapulted it over the "excellent" mark. Nose offers liqueurish, black-peppery aromas. **86** —D.T. (4/1/2003)

Bodegas Pirineos 2001 Marboré Red Blend (Somontano) $34. A bit of brett and barnyard on the nose, with minty raspberry coming on to take over. A little leafy on the midpalate, but not what you'd call green. Bitter chocolate carries the finish. A blend of five red grapes, a couple of which are local and virtually unknown. **87** —M.S. (6/1/2005)

Bodegas Pirineos 2000 Marboré Red Blend (Somontano) $28. Very woody, with overt menthol and lemony aromas that cover up what black cherry fruit there is. The palate is fairly lean and sour, and with that funky lemon-tinged oak, it tastes almost of citrus. A five-grape blend with hard tannins and bite. **82** —M.S. (3/1/2004)

Bodegas Pirineos 1999 Montesierra Tinto Red Blend (Somontano) $7. 81 —M.M. (9/1/2002)

Bodegas Pirineos 2002 Montesierra Rosado Rosé Blend (Somontano) $10. Heavy, forceful aromas make it tough and rough to get into, but with time it opens to display tea, raspberry and nutty flavors. The finish is clean and the weight throughout is good. But when you get down to it it's fairly innocuous. **83** —M.S. (3/1/2004)

BODEGAS REAL

Bodegas Real 2000 Vega Ibor Crianza Tempranillo (Valdepeñas) $10. Bland at first, with light berry aromas. It opens to offer a bit more, such as dry berry fruit and a starchy, firm finish. It's a zesty somewhat sharp red, but as a whole it's good. Just don't be expecting a thriller. **85** —M.S. (5/1/2004)

BODEGAS REMIREZ DE GANUZA

Bodegas Remirez de Ganuza 1998 Reserva Tempranillo Blend (Rioja) $65. Dark in color, with dynamite bacon, boysenberry, and lavender aromas. Quite a saturated wine, with smoke and earth surrounding cola and dried fruit. This is killer Rioja, one with all the trimmings. There's racy spice, pencil lead and push. Sensationally snazzy and stylish. **92 Cellar Selection** —M.S. (3/1/2004)

BODEGAS RIOJANAS

Bodegas Riojanas 2001 Gran Albina Tempranillo Blend (Rioja) $35. The nose deals dill, coconut, vanilla, and a lot of plum and berry. Soft but not really, with a lively but plush palate that starts with cranberry and raspberry and then deepens to show chocolate and spice. More of a middleweight, but one packing punch; would be nice with roast lamb, etc. **89** —M.S. (10/1/2005)

Bodegas Riojanas 2000 Puerta Vieja Crianza Tempranillo Blend (Rioja) $13. Shows some funk at the start, with red berry, earth, and spice playing second fiddle. Raspberry and cherry skins are a force on the palate, with tangy acidity and mild tannins working the oaky finish. A simple, traditional Rioja. **85** —M.S. (2/1/2006)

Bodegas Riojanas 1999 Reserva Viña Albina Tempranillo Blend (Rioja) $20. An old-school offering with earth, light wood, stewed fruit, and tomato on the bouquet. Like a throwback to the days of yore, this wine emphasizes dried cherry, plum tomatoes, and leather, all framed by tight tannins and lots of acidity. Not a lot of flesh on the bones, but will stand the test of time. **87** —M.S. (2/1/2006)

BODEGAS RODA

Bodegas Roda 2001 Cirsion Tempranillo (Rioja) $200. Dark as night, pure as silk, and rich as a sultan. This one wine defines the best of the new wave; a great high-end product from a perfect vintage. It's intense, spicy, racy, and still soft enough to wrap yourself around. Licorice, crushed peppercorn, chocolate, espresso, and blackberry are just some of what you can pull from this baby. Cellar a few years then explore. **97 Editors' Choice** —M.S. (9/1/2004)

Bodegas Roda 1998 Cirsion Tempranillo (Rioja) $215. 94 (8/1/2000)

Bodegas Roda 2000 Roda I Tempranillo Blend (Rioja) $60. It's hard to imagine the subsequent vintage surpassing this purring monster, but it could and probably will. That said, the current 2000 is magnificent in its dark masculinity and layered complexity. The fruit aromas are perfect, the spice notes exotic, and overall it's just a blast to drink. Lots of sweet oak is still front and center, so give it until 2006 for it to show even better. **95 Cellar Selection** —M.S. (9/1/2004)

BODEGAS SILVANO GARCIA

Bodegas Silvano Garcia 2003 Dulce Monastrell (Jumilla) $24. Licorice, pepper and raisin join forces on a can't-miss bouquet that's all Monastrell and all southern Spain. Dark and candied, with tons of cooked brown sugar. This is what you'd call big and tannic, with a hard, grabby mouthfeel. One glass we can recommend; two or more might be tough to handle. **86** —M.S. (6/1/2006)

Bodegas Silvano Garcia 2004 Viña Honda Red Blend (Jumilla) $12. Thick on the nose, with prickly, mildly pickled aromas. Typical of Jumilla, the wine is big and candied, with soft tannins and spiky, out-of-place acidity. Finishes tart and crisp with virtually no second level to speak of. **81** — M.S. (9/1/2006)

BODEGAS TINTORALBA

Bodegas Tintoralba 2000 Crianza Red Blend (Almansa) $19. Starts out showing aromas of turned earth, cedar, and embedded plum and raisin. Upright and solid on the palate, where cherry and raspberry flavors are ripe, smooth and moderately complex. Layered on the finish, with fruit, herbs, and acidity. Hails from the Alicante/ Valencia region. **87** —M.S. (9/1/2006)

Bodegas Tintoralba 2003 Higueruela Red Blend (Almansa) $10. Dry leather, leaves, burnt spice, and pepper lead it off, followed by tart flavors of plum and berry. Never seems to find a higher level of quality as it falls off on the palate, finishing with rhubarb and cranberry. **83** —M.S. (9/1/2006)

BODEGAS TORREDUERO

Bodegas Torreduero 2002 Peñamonte Tinta de Toro (Toro) $10. Fairly classic in style, with hard spice, leather and dark fruit on the nose. A bit tough and chewy. The palate features raspberry and cola flavors, and the finish is long, if a bit racy and tannic. **86** —M.S. (2/1/2006)

BODEGAS VALDEÁGUILA

Bodegas Valdeáguila 2003 Viña Salamanca Rufete (Sierra de Salamanca) $8. This rosé is made from the obscure Rufete grape, and it's nearly red in color, with rose petal and cinnamon aromas. It starts off impressive enough, with cherry and raspberry flavors. The finish, however, is monotone and fades quickly, despite bold acidity. **83** —M.S. (9/1/2004)

Bodegas Valdeáguila 2003 Viña Salamanca Verdejo (Sierra de Salamanca) $8. Candle wax, vanilla, and a foxy, wet-animal aroma define the nose. Starts off spicy and racy but doesn't hold the pace. Finishes creamy and modestly thick. **82** —M.S. (9/1/2004)

BODEGAS VALDEMAR

Bodegas Valdemar 2004 Esencia Valdemar Rosé Garnacha (Rioja) $7. Heavy aromas with soft, dense flavors of apple skin and black plum. Slightly reduced on the finish, but surprisingly sharp and scouring on the tongue. There's a lot of zest and acid for a wine with a meatier flavor profile. **83** —M.S. (2/1/2006)

Bodegas Valdemar 2001 Inspiración Valdemar Graciano (Rioja) $95. Most of the credit here goes to the fact that is a varietal Graciano, something you just don't see much of. But in tasting it we learn why this grape is usually blended into Tempranillo to provide acidic structure. As a varietal there's flesh and berry flavors, but the feel is kind of racy and sharp. More applause for the approach than the end result. **86** —M.S. (4/1/2006)

Bodegas Valdemar 2001 Inspiración Valdemar V.O.4 Tempranillo Blend (Rioja) $45. Soft and sweet, with raisin and red-licorice aromas. This wine seems caught between the new style of Rioja and the traditional. The result is that it vacillates between lean and dry, rich and sweet, without settling on either. **85** —M.S. (10/1/2005)

BODEGAS VALDERROA

Bodegas Valderroa 2005 Montenovo Godello (Valdeorras) $10. Crisply made, with a strong emphasis on green apples. This is a zesty, flinty white made for warm-weather drinking. Despite being 100% Godello, it has a lot in common with Sauvignon Blanc. **87 Best Buy** — M.S. (9/1/2006)

Bodegas Valderroa 2004 Pedrouzos 1.5L Godello (Valdeorras) $80. From extremely old Godello vines, this barrel-fermented wine comes only in magnums. It's currently showing a lot of oak, but it's also extremely well structured. It has an acid backbone that nobody could crack. Very serious, with intense apple, pear, and minerality. Much like a fine Burgundy. **92** —M.S. (9/1/2006)

Bodegas Valderroa 2004 Val de Sil Godello (Valdeorras) $18. This wine shows the potential and power of Valdeorras Godello, but at a fair price. It has a lot of minerality and acidity, but also a boatload of kiwi, green apple, papaya, and white pepper. Unconventional for Spanish white wines and very much worth a look. **90 Editors' Choice** —*M.S. (9/1/2006)*

Bodegas Valderroa 2004 Pezas da Portela White Blend (Valdeorras) $35. Pezas is the Meursault of Valdeorras. It starts with a smoky, slate-driven nose and then opens to reveal pear, green apple, and vanilla flavors. Shows excellent backbone courtesy of refined but powerful acidity. One of Galicia's few ageworthy whites; good through at least 2008. **92** —*M.S. (9/1/2006)*

BODEGAS VIDAL SOBLECHERO

Bodegas Vidal Soblechero 2001 Viña Clavidor Tempranillo (Rueda) $11. Dark like crude oil, with a rich, raisiny nose that conveys thickness. This is pure Tempranillo, made ripe and sweet. Flavors of prunes and blackberry are full and forward. The tannins are soft. Not overly complex, but chewy and of a certain style. **88 Best Buy** —*M.S. (5/1/2004)*

Bodegas Vidal Soblechero 2002 Viña Clavidor Verdejo (Rueda) $11. Round and waxy, with very little verve. The flavors are of banana, bitter almonds, and vanilla, yet there's no pulse or excitement here. Finishes dilute. **82** —*M.S. (5/1/2004)*

BODEGAS Y VINEDOS DE JALÓN

Bodegas y Vinedos de Jalón 2002 Viña Alarba Old Vines Grenache Grenache (Catalonia) $6. Sweet and grapey, but pleasurable and well made. The candied palate of sugar beets, raspberry, and mocha is juicy, and there's decent grip to the mouthfeel. The tail end then fans out and showcases nice acidity, integrated tannins, and a juicy personality. Drink now and throughout the year. **87** —*M.S. (3/1/2004)*

BODEGAS Y VINEDOS DE RIBERA DEL DURATON

Bodegas y Vinedos de Ribera del Duraton 2000 Duraton Red Blend (Vino de la Tierra de Castilla y León) $18. Interesting and meaty on the nose, with plenty of pepper and herbs. This is not a garden-variety red that fits into some preconceived box; actually, it's an unusual wine, one with a dark, ripe character and a masculine personality. It offers plenty of cooked, roasted notes and monstrous tannins. Hold until 2008. **89** —*M.S. (3/1/2004)*

BODEGAS Y VIÑEDOS DEL JARO

Bodegas y Viñedos del Jaro 2001 Sed de Caná Tinto del Pais (Ribera del Duero) $NA. My first look at this fledgling project from the folks at Osborne left me impressed. Sed de Caná is a well toasted, masculine Tempranillo with raw, smoky aromas and a broad-shouldered palate. It toes the line between spunky and tannic, but there's so much forward fruit thrown in that you can't help but like it. Needs several years to settle; best by 2008. 145 cases made. **92** —*M.S. (6/1/2005)*

BOHIGAS

Bohigas 1999 Brut Champagne Blend (Cava) $11. The sweet, smooth nose is very basic—some might say nondescript. Some lemony flavors are touched up by ample spice, while the finish is dry and the mouthfeel, like the Brut Nature, is flat as a Midwestern highway. Decent flavors but nothing much beyond that. **84** —*M.S. (12/31/2002)*

Bohigas 2000 Chardonnay (Catalonia) $12. The apple, hay and earth aromas and flavors of this Chardonnay from northeastern Spain are in the right range, but lack the liveliness and definition I sought. Medium-weight, it finishes a bit short, a bit dull and uninspired. **80** —*M.M. (9/1/2002)*

Bohigas 1999 Brut Nature-Reserva Limitada Chardonnay (Cava) $12. The soda-like nose is simpler than it is captivating. The palate provides some citrus and tropical fruit, but it's borderline tart, too. The finish is dry and crisp, but the mouthfeel seems flatter than it should be. **84** —*M.S. (12/31/2002)*

Bohigas NV Gran Reserva Brut Nature Sparkling Blend (Cava) $18. Apple and peach define the bouquet, but where's the pop? This cava seems a touch quiet and reticent. It's drying, with flavors of apple, white corn, and soda cracker. But the bead is weak and the overall personality is shy.

Has 15% Chardonnay in addition to the traditional cava three-pack of Macabeo, Parellada, and Xarello. **84** —*M.S. (12/15/2006)*

Bohigas NV Rosado Sparkling Blend (Cava) $14. Light and modest in aromas, although scents of citrus blossom and nectarine manage to work their way to the top of the bouquet. The palate is smooth and creamy, with flavors of red plum, melon, and chocolate. A good wine that won't make you go crazy looking for complexities and depth. **85** —*M.S. (12/15/2006)*

Bohigas 1999 Tempranillo Blend (Catalonia) $10. This stylistic wine shows red cabbage and borscht, plus a slight dill character, on the nose. The palate follows suit, with Bing cherries and cedar that integrate with the full, nonassertive tannins. **88 Best Buy** —*C.S. (4/1/2002)*

BORSAO

Borsao 2000 Tres Picos Garnacha (Campo de Borja) $13. Every now and then a knockout wine comes along that doesn't cost a fortune, like this star. Full, ripe fruit and deftly used oak team up to provide an inviting nose and compelling palate. The strength and depth of the fruit is impressive—it just continues to open and shine, as opposed to being embalmed in oak. Keeps you wanting more, right through the satisfying finish. Buy this model of affordable excellence by the case. You could hold this through 2005—but I bet you won't. **91 Editors' Choice** —*M.M. (4/1/2002)*

Borsao 2002 Red Blend (Campo de Borja) $6. The essence of mint and orange peel add character to the youthful red fruit that defines the bouquet of this 100% Garnacha. Cherry, plum skin, and red licorice flavors come in front of a zesty, sharp, lean finish. There's not much fat or waste to this wine; it's precise and racy, and eminently tasty. It's a fine starter Garnacha. **87 Best Buy** —*M.S. (3/1/2004)*

BOUZA DO REI

Bouza do Rei 2005 Albariño (Rías Baixas) $15. Plenty of white flowers and tropical-fruit aromas signal that this is special. The palate is full to the brim with pure flavors of melon, nectarine, and green herbs, while the finish is exact. Drinking this baby is like taking a trip to the heart of Salnés. **91 Best Buy** —*M.S. (9/1/2006)*

BOUZA GRANDE

Bouza Grande 2003 Condado de Tea Albariño (Rías Baixas) $22. An Albariño-dominated middleweight with pure and pleasant aromas of pineapple, citrus, and slate. Rich, round, and defined, with orange, banana, and melon flavors. Very much on the money, with curvy acids as opposed to spiky ones. **89** —*M.S. (3/1/2005)*

BUIL & GINÉ

Buil & Giné 2002 17-XI Red Blend (Montsant) $23. Quite sweet and borderline raisiny on the nose, yet red and tart in the mouth, with pie cherry and red raspberry flavors. Quite basic and straightforward, with a touch of green spiciness to the racy finish. **84** —*M.S. (10/1/2005)*

Buil & Giné 2000 Pleret Red Blend (Priorat) $45. Rich and syrupy, so much so that you get Port-like aromas and flavors. The palate is dark and grapy, with sugar beet and chocolate. The sweet finish is a bit clunky and out of whack, but overall it's an easy drinker despite its size. **86** —*M.S. (3/1/2004)*

Buil & Giné 2004 Nosis Verdejo (Rueda) $19. Pungent and grassy, with a scrappy sharpness that softens with time. Flavors of passion fruit and orange create a juice-like palate, while sweet and tart flavors carry the finish. Nice Verdejo but not quite up there with the region's best. **86** —*M.S. (10/1/2005)*

BURGÁNS

Burgáns 2005 Albariño (Rías Baixas) $12. To date, this year's best value among Spanish white wines is this simple but lovely fruit bomb of an Albariño from the quality-driven Martín Códax cooperative. It literally overflows with peach blossom aromas and melon flavors. Brightly labeled with orange print, it's hard to miss. And you wouldn't want to. **90 Best Buy** —*M.S. (9/1/2006)*

Burgáns 2000 Albariño (Rías Baixas) $16. This is a tasty, fairly round rendition of Albariño. Dry, with mineral and grass elements, it also displays an intriguing faint orange-tangerine element throughout. The wine maintains a clean crispness without being sharp. This will seem soft to some Albariño purists—and it is—but it's flavorful and will make converts for the grape among consumers previously unacquainted with this Galician prize. **86** —*M.M. (4/1/2002)*

CALDERONA

Calderona 1999 Crianza Red Blend (Cigales) $12. Chewy and medium-bodied, this is an easy, interesting choice for a weeknight dinner, or a friend's BYO party. Mixed red and black fruit have oak and mocha nuances; tree bark and herb aromas add interest to red plum and raspberry on the nose. **86** —*D.T. (4/1/2003)*

Calderona 1996 Reserva Red Blend (Cigales) $17. From the Frutos Villar bodega comes this friendly if a bit lean reserva with cherry, leather, and rubber aromas and a snappy, clean palate of cherry and raspberry fruit. The finish is lightweight and pure, and slightly warming, while overall it comes across fresh and solid, with just enough oak to give it heft and substance. **87** —*M.S. (8/1/2003)*

CALIU

Caliu 2001 1+1=3 U més U fan tres Tempranillo-Cabernet Sauvignon (Penedès) $13. Starts by emitting baked plum and leather aromas, and the bouquet is backed by solid but lean black cherry, plum, and raspberry flavors. Light to medium in build, with a moderately strong but bland finish that's only slightly toasted. Short on substance but good as far as what's here. **84** —*M.S. (9/1/2006)*

CALLEJO

Callejo 2002 Crianza Tempranillo (Ribera del Duero) $26. Rooty and rich, and it hits stride with some airing. Fairly woody stuff, with maple and toast accenting beefy, sweet fruit flavors in the black cherry and plum category. Long and lasting late, with coffee and some lemon peel. **88** —*M.S. (2/1/2006)*

Callejo 2001 Reserva Tempranillo (Ribera del Duero) $42. Quite dense and ripe, a trademark of 2001. The bouquet is bold and packed deep and full; you'll find stewed plum, molasses, root beer, and black cherry in quantity. The ripe, tannic palate is chewy and broad, with vanilla, brown sugar, and spice. **89** —*M.S. (2/1/2006)*

Callejo 2002 Reserve Tempranillo (Ribera del Duero) $44. Shows good fruit aromas, moderate depth and a touch of sandalwood on the nose. The palate features ripe blackberry and chocolate, while the feel is cushioned and chewy. Modern in style; just a cut below the 2001. **88** —*M.S. (12/15/2006)*

CAMPILLO

Campillo 1994 Gran Reserva Tempranillo (Rioja) $32. This shows some advanced aromatics of decayed fruit, coffee, and tobacco, but at the same time it tastes robust and youthful, with plum and dark chocolate dominating the flavor profile. Finishes long and earthy, picking up notes of tar and vanilla. **88** *(5/1/2004)*

Campillo 1998 Pago Cuesta Clara Raro Reserva Tempranillo (Rioja) $NA. A special bottling from a vineyard planted in 1969 to the Tempranillo Peludo clone. The resulting wine is exceptionally ripe and extracted, with masses of soft tannins. Subtle coffee, toast, and vanilla notes frame black cherry and plum fruit. Should age well and is bottled in mags and double-mags to help it keep. A statement wine for sure. **92** *(5/1/2004)*

Campillo 1996 Reserva Tempranillo (Rioja) $24. Across the board, the Campillo wines are bigger and more robust than their Faustino stable-mates. This reserva shows plenty of coffee and caramel aromas, allied to black cherry, plum, and tobacco flavors. Smooth in the mouth, with a long, tart finish. **88** *(5/1/2004)*

Campillo 1991 Rioja Gran Reserva Tempranillo (Rioja) $75. The bouquet of dried cherries, plums, prunes, and tobacco opens to a palate of dense fruit that's dry and structured. This wine is big, but even textured and not heavy. Shows finely focused fruit and good grip. The dark fruit flavors add spice accents on the long finish. **92 Cellar Selection** *(5/1/2001)*

Campillo 1995 Rioja Reserva Tempranillo (Rioja) $24. Nose of ripe spicy fruit with tobacco and earth accents. Similar full, chewy flavors ride the plush mouthfeel. The long finish is dense and dark. **90** *(5/1/2001)*

Campillo 1995 Reserva Especial Tempranillo Blend (Rioja) $50. This big, full-bodied, muscular Rioja is surprisingly supple, blending prune and plum fruit with notes of coffee and tobacco. The blend is 70% Tempranillo, 15% Cabernet Sauvignon, and 15% Graciano. **90** *(5/1/2004)*

CAMPO ELISEO

Campo Eliseo 2002 Tinta de Toro (Toro) $50. Big and ripe, with tobacco, blackberry and fresh-cut lumber on the nose. This big boy weighs in at 15%, so the chocolate, cassis, and rich blackberry flavors on the palate should not come as a surprise. Toasty and plush; a model New World red from Jacques and François Lurton and partner Michel Rolland. **91** —*M.S. (10/1/2005)*

CAMPO VIEJO

Campo Viejo 1995 Gran Reserva Red Blend (Rioja) $25. Aromatherapy in a bottle. Soothing cedar, sweet caramel, molasses, and toasted coconut are comforting. Chocolate and tobacco flavors integrate well with soft tannins. **90** —*C.S. (11/1/2002)*

Campo Viejo 1994 Gran Reserva Red Blend (Rioja) $25. This tasty Rioja has an almost chewy feel. Tart dried fruits, leather, licorice, and menthol oak aromas and flavors come together well in this—especially at this age—fairly full-bodied wine. Dark and handsome, it still has some tannins to shed, and finishes long and dry. Drink now–2007. **88** —*M.M. (9/1/2002)*

Campo Viejo 1996 Reserva Red Blend (Rioja) $13. The color was transparent, as were the flavors. It's a bit of a thin wine, with some strawberry fruit and accents of wood and char on the finish. **83** —*C.S. (11/1/2002)*

Campo Viejo 2002 Crianza Tempranillo (Rioja) $10. Mildly leafy, with root beer and red fruit comprising the nose. Basic but fresh in the mouth, with cherry and berry flavors, medium tannins and a laudable mouthfeel. Middle-of-the-road in terms of power, with finishing notes of tobacco and smoke. **85 Best Buy** —*M.S. (11/1/2006)*

Campo Viejo 2000 Reserva Tempranillo (Rioja) $13. A touch timid in how it doles out slight raspberry and light oak aromas. And that's in front of a mellow, quiet palate that offers basic berry flavors and not much more. Far from the most cushioned, lush wine going; it hits firmly and evenly, like a welterweight from a past era. **85** —*M.S. (11/1/2006)*

Campo Viejo 1998 Gran Reserva Tempranillo Blend (Rioja) $20. Alluring cherry and berry aromas show a touch of candied sweetness, yet overall the bouquet is magnetically attractive. And the palate is deep and spicy, with tons of red fruit accented by toast and chocolate. And as far as complexity notes go, there's rose petal, lavender, and leather. Eminently drinkable; excellent quality to price ratio. **90** —*M.S. (4/1/2006)*

CAMPOS REALES

Campos Reales 2004 Tempranillo (La Mancha) $6. Pretty darn good red wine for what it costs. Smells like pure raspberries and black cherries, with nothing mucking it up. Has balance and acid, a solid mouthfeel, and no abnormal funk or green. In its price category it's as good as you could ask for. **84 Best Buy** —*M.S. (11/15/2005)*

CANTOFINO

Cantofino 2003 Joven Garnacha (Vino de la Tierra de Castilla) $9. Gassy at first, with clumsy, bulky aromas of sun-baked fruit, cinnamon and sulfur. That heavily baked character carries onto the palate, which is defined by mildly burnt, peppery flavors. Obtuse; not much in the way of mouthfeel. **82** —*M.S. (10/1/2005)*

CAPÇANES

Capçanes 2001 Cabrida Garnacha (Priorat) $60. Pure Garnacha, which is anathema in the region. Savory on the nose, with roasted meat and spice notes as much as fruit. Once it hits the palate, however, the plum and berry flavors explode. Turns elegant as it opens, while retaining intensity. Flashy stuff. **91** —*M.S. (10/1/2005)*

Capçanes 2001 Costers del Gravet Red Blend (Montsant) $20. At 45% Cabernet Sauvignon, 40% Garnacha, and 15% Tempranillo, this is a bit like a Catalan super Tuscan. Unusual for the region because you can really pick up on the Cabernet component. Overall it's spicy, with hints of tomato, herb, and pepper along with textured dark fruit. Good for the money; drink now. **88** —*M.S. (10/1/2005)*

Capçanes 2003 Mas Donís Barrica Red Blend (Montsant) $12. This wine is a custom cuvée made by Montsant's trend-setting co-operative for American importer Eric Solomon. It's a bit like a Côtes du Rhône, but with more color, dark fruit, and body. And it displays some of the region's patented terroir, meaning it has that graphite-schist quality along with peppery notes. **86** —*M.S. (10/1/2005)*

CAPITOSO

Capitoso 2002 Tempranillo (Rioja) $12. Heavily oaked, with aromas of coconut, rubber, and fruitcake. Bold tannins warm the palate, which dishes out cherry, currant, and plum flavors. A bit too stewy on the whole, but with merits between the cracks. **84** —*M.S. (8/1/2005)*

CARE

Care 2001 Tinto Red Blend (Cariñena) $20. Tons of color but the nose is a bit soupy, with aromas of heavy oak, black fruit, tomato, and herbs. A blend of 60% Garnacha and 40% Cabernet Sauvignon that's solid but shrill. Hits with extract and tannins, but the integration and flavors don't quite achieve the next level. **84** —*M.S. (6/1/2005)*

CARMELO RODERO

Carmelo Rodero 2001 Crianza Tempranillo (Ribera del Duero) $25. Toasty and solid, with cherry, kirsch, and herbal aromas. The palate is expressive and clean, with tangy, healthy fruit that shows touches of citrus along with oak and chocolate. Seems a bit buttery on the finish, but the bet here is that it will fade with time. Nicely structured and properly tannic. Drink now through 2007. **87** —*M.S. (10/1/2005)*

Carmelo Rodero 2000 Crianza Tempranillo (Ribera del Duero) $24. Strong and oaky, without much finesse to the fast-paced nose and palate. Basic red fruit and sharp-cutting acidity defines the mouth. Rounds out some late in the game, but still it only goes so far. **84** —*M.S. (9/1/2004)*

Carmelo Rodero 2000 Reserva Tempranillo (Ribera del Duero) $43. A lot of bacon, open-cut wood and charcoal on the nose, all of which adds up to blast of heavy overt oak, clearly American. The palate is slightly choppy, with cherry and plum resting below a veneer of lively oak. Finishes a touch buttery and fat, with spunky, scouring tannins. Still, this is a true Ribera red, just not at that higher echelon. **87** —*M.S. (10/1/2005)*

Carmelo Rodero 1999 Reserva Tempranillo (Ribera del Duero) $45. Sweet and solid, with true-form tree bark, root vegetable and black fruit aromas. Ripe strawberry and raspberry carry the healthy palate toward a smooth, juicy, satisfying finish. Very well balanced and correct at all major checkpoints. **90** —*M.S. (9/1/2004)*

Carmelo Rodero 2003 Roble Tempranillo (Ribera del Duero) $15. Good and clean, and seemingly more ripe than overripe. Aromas of black grapes and plums are dark and fruity, while the palate runs syrupy and rich, with creamy notes of vanilla intermixed with blackberry and the like. Finishes like a sundae, with vanilla, carob, and coconut. **87** —*M.S. (10/1/2005)*

Carmelo Rodero 2002 Roble Tempranillo (Ribera del Duero) $17. An oak-aged vino joven with a nose of cherry, rubber, and raspberry. At first taste, it seems overtly buttery, as if the young oak were sitting atop the wine. As you get into it, that oak seems less obvious and more integrated. Still, it's a touch bland, yet competent. **85** —*M.S. (9/1/2004)*

CARREDUEÑAS

Carredueñas 2003 Tinto Roble Tempranillo (Cigales) $14. Jammy and big-boned, with ripe but reduced aromas and flavors. The palate is dark and deep, featuring prune and black cherry. Everything here is pushed to the center by jumpy acidity and firm tannins; good but shows hardly any softness or silk. **86** —*M.S. (8/1/2005)*

CASA DE LA REINA

Casa de la Reina 2003 Tempranillo Blend (Rioja) $8. See-through in color, with leafy, earthy aromas that turn more oaky with time. Almost citric in flavor, with tart, lean raspberry and strawberry flavors. Clean but missing potency; juicy nearly to the point of sour. **83** —*M.S. (11/1/2006)*

Casa de la Reina 2001 Crianza Tempranillo Blend (Rioja) $12. Light and leathery, with dried fruit notes and not much else on the lithe bouquet. Quite traditional in style, with dilute but clean cherry and cranberry flavors. A dose of wood spice pops up on the lightweight finish. Drink now. **85** —*M.S. (4/1/2006)*

Casa de la Reina 1996 Gran Reserva Tempranillo Blend (Rioja) $21. Almost orange in color but fairly lively on the nose, where cherry, vanilla, leather, and licorice come together. Firm and acidic at its center, with surrounding tobacco, cherry, and citrus flavors. Shows some toast and root beer on the finish. Very solid stuff from a good vintage. **89** —*M.S. (4/1/2006)*

Casa de la Reina 1998 Reserva Tempranillo Blend (Rioja) $18. Coffee and grilled beef provide a masculine, dark side to the bouquet. Behind it, there's nice berry and plum fruit lifted by ripe, firm tannins. Then it finishes fairly soft, with strawberry, chocolate, and vanilla notes. Very nice overall. **88** —*M.S. (4/1/2006)*

Casa de la Reina 2004 Viura (Rioja) $8. Gold in color with nondescript aromas of wheat and apple. Turns to tart on the palate, with lemon and green-apple flavors. Adequate at best. **82** —*M.S. (11/1/2006)*

CASA SOLAR

Casa Solar 2000 Plata Red Blend (Rioja) $6. Some dried fruits accent what is otherwise a dull nose. Flavors of raspberry and rhubarb are lean and tangy, while the finish is rather tight and tannic for such a basic wine. Overall, it's not sour. But to call it rich, satisfying and sweet would be out of the question. Made by the Martinez-Bujanda group. **83** —*M.S. (10/1/2003)*

Casa Solar 1999 Plata - Vino de la Tierra del bajo Aragon Red Blend (Bajo Aragon) $6. Although the nose yields slightly oxidized aromas, the spicy cherry palate is lively and clean. For a young red table wine, it provides ample pop and length along with bright strawberry flavors. The balance in the mouth and finish is entirely correct. **86** —*M.S. (11/1/2002)*

Casa Solar 1997 Tempranillo (Bajo Aragon) $4. **84** *(3/1/2000)*

Casa Solar 2003 3 Months in Oak Tempranillo (Vino de la Tierra de Castilla) $6. Lean and peppery, with more citrus than berry on the nose. The mouth is a bit grabby, with a starchy feel and far-reaching tannins. Clearly not a great wine but it holds itself together. **81 Best Buy** —*M.S. (12/15/2006)*

Casa Solar 1994 Oro Tempranillo (Sacedon-Mondejar) $6. **87 Best Buy** *(3/1/2000)*

Casa Solar 1994 Plata Tempranillo (Sacedon-Mondejar) $5. **86** *(3/1/2000)*

Casa Solar 2004 Viura (Vino de la Tierra de Castilla) $5. Light stone-fruit and vanilla aromas lead to a fresh, somewhat dilute palate that offers apple and peach flavors. Wet and juicy, with clean, medium-force acids. Easy to quaff. **84 Best Buy** —*M.S. (10/1/2005)*

CASAL CAEIRO

Casal Caeiro 2003 Albariño (Rías Baixas) $16. Yellow in color, with a round, yeasty, corn-tinged nose. That roundness is maintained on the palate, where flavors of orange, lemon, and peach lead to a mild, buttery finish. Good but a bit chunky. **85** —*M.S. (8/1/2005)*

CASAR DE BURBIA

Casar de Burbia 2003 Hombros Mencia (Bierzo) $26. For a winery in only its second year of production, this is a solid effort, matching smoky, meaty qualities with intense cherry, plum, and tea notes. Firm on the finish; try with lamb or beef. **86** *(11/15/2006)*

Casar de Burbia 2002 Hombros Mencia (Bierzo) $22. More heavy and ripe than expected, with a creamy, almost lactic nose. Round on the palate, with plum and black-cherry fruit. Good acidity and overall balance keep it afloat. Finishes with coffee, chocolate, and spice. Not a world beater but good. **85** —*M.S. (6/1/2005)*

CASTAÑO

Castaño 2000 Monastrell (Yecla) $9. Monastrell, or Mourvèdre as it is more commonly known in French- and English-speaking parts of the globe, has a reputation for producing dry, tannic wines that occasionally reek of horse manure. Not so in sunny Spain, where a growing number of clean, berry-fruited offerings are turning up at bargain prices. This medium-weight Monastrell combines forward berry fruit with chocolate notes and just a hint of tree bark on the finish. **87 Best Buy** —*J.C. (11/15/2002)*

Castaño 2001 Hécula Monastrell (Yecla) $12. A modern-style offering from the up-and-coming region of Yecla, near Alicante. The grape used is Monastrell, aka Mourvèdre. It's bold and packed with blackberry, pepper, and other spices. It's the perfect wine to enjoy with barbecue, stews and roasts. This wine busted onto the scene just a couple of years ago, earning accolades for its full flavors and overall character. For the price, it's a big-time bargain. **90** —*M.S. (11/15/2003)*

CASTEL DE BOUZA

Castel de Bouza 2005 Albariño (Rías Baixas) $17. Clean and pure to the nose, with lemon and other sheer citrus fruit aromas. Gets plump in the mouth, but not fat, with melon and orange-driven flavors. Good, full, mouthfilling, and solid. Shows nothing out of the ordinary. **87** —*M.S. (9/1/2006)*

CASTELL DE FALSET

Castell de Falset 1998 Tempranillo Blend (Tarragona) $19. Dark and a bit pruny, this blend of old-vine Grenache, Cabernet Sauvignon, and Tempranillo is quite dry, densely wooded, and firmly structured. Toasty oak, dried rose petals, and meat adorn the dark cherry and blackberry fruit. But the wine is lean, rather tart—and overly woody, at least for now. Does it have the stuff to unfold over the next few years? **86** —*M.M. (4/1/2002)*

CASTELL ROIG

Castell Roig NV Brut Nature Sparkling Blend (Cava) $20. Creamy and yeasty, with mild apple and bread-based aromas. Nice in the mouth, with citrus leading the way. Shows ample kick and acidity, with length and balance on the finish. Perfectly good overall, if not overly exciting. **87** —*M.S. (6/1/2006)*

CASTELLBLANCH

Castellblanch NV Brut Zero Reserva Sparkling Blend (Cava) $10. This producer is doing a very good job with its superaffordable, no-dosage cava. The nose is lightly floral, with the accent on apple blossom. The palate is solid and crisp, with appropriate white-fruit flavors. Crisp on the finish, with a lively feel. A pleasurable sipper for sure. **89 Best Buy** —*M.S. (12/15/2006)*

Castellblanch NV Extra Brut Sparkling Blend (Cava) $8. As under-$10 sparklers go, you'd be hard-pressed to find better than this medium-bodied and toasty version from Catalonia's White Castle. The nose is mildly yeasty but basic, while the palate deals juicy apple and white-grape flavors propelled by fresh acidity. Virtuous yet basic. But who's complaining? **87 Best Buy** —*M.S. (12/15/2006)*

Castellblanch NV Rosado Seco Sparkling Blend (Cava) $10. Yeasty and round, with aromas of citrus and spent campfire. The palate runs toward peach and cantaloupe with a brown sugar coating. A bit sweet and candied late, yet mouthfilling and pleasant. **86 Best Buy** —*M.S. (12/15/2006)*

Castellblanch NV Semi-Seco Sparkling Blend (Cava) $10. Hay, corn, and buttered toast are the initial aromas, and soon after the wine settles into a pretty good groove. The palate is pure and sweet, with sticky, ripe fruit flavors that veer toward fruit cocktail and mango but never turn cloying. This wine handles its sugar like a pro. **87 Best Buy** —*M.S. (12/15/2006)*

Castellblanch NV Brut Zero Brut Reserva White Blend (Cava) $9. An enticing nose of vanilla-cream, toast, red delicious apple, mown hay, and wet, dark earth. The frothy, mouthwatering body holds a bit of tart apple and toast. Finishes long with an enjoyable touch of toast, if you can get past the acidity that will cut through any dish. **85** —*K.F. (12/31/2002)*

CASTELLFLORIT

Castellflorit 1999 Tinto Garnacha (Priorat) $17. Sweet is the best way to describe the nose, which pushes heavy doses of maple and molasses. The palate's black cherry flavors are clean and forward, but all in all this wine suffers from too much driving acidity. The acids literally sweat the tongue. **84** —*M.S. (11/1/2002)*

CASTILLO CATADAU

Castillo Catadau 1996 Reserva Tempranillo Blend (Valencia) $9. Tasty in a tart way, with licorice hints, this well-balanced, medium-weight red shows plenty of herb-tinged, sour cherry flavor. Good acidity and moderate tannins make this a good match for grilled veal. Think Claret, but from southern Spain. Drink now–2004. **85 Best Buy** —*M.M. (9/1/2002)*

CASTILLO DE ALMANSA

Castillo de Almansa 1994 Reserva Cencibel (Almansa) $10. 87 —*J.C. (8/1/2000)*

Castillo de Almansa 2005 Tintorera Garnacha (Almansa) $9. This is a perfectly good, fairly dark Garnacha that oozes bacon smoke and blueberry syrup aromas. The palate is mildly zesty due to adequate acidity, while the blackberry flavors carry a certain savory quality along with firm tannins. **86 Best Buy** —*M.S. (12/15/2006)*

Castillo de Almansa 2002 Reserva Red Blend (Almansa) $11. This Cencibel/Monastrell blend is loaded with black fruit from the bouquet onto the palate. Round flavors of plum and raspberry are balanced and forward, while the finish is full and mouthfilling. A correct, tasty wine that would be hard not to like. **88 Best Buy** —*M.S. (9/1/2006)*

Castillo de Almansa 1995 Reserva Red Blend (Almansa) $10. Tart cherry aromas and flavors with tarragon accents are wrapped in oak in this medium-weight, mature red. The wine is evenly textured, but the oak sits well to the fore, really predominating on the very dry, tangy-in-a-woody-way finish. **84** —*M.M. (9/1/2002)*

Castillo de Almansa 1993 Reserva Tempranillo (Almansa) $10. 87 Best Buy —*J.C. (11/15/1999)*

CASTILLO DE FUENDEJALON

Castillo de Fuendejalon 2000 Crianza Garnacha (Campo de Borja) $8. This is a nice blend of three-fourths Garnacha and one-fourth Tempranillo. It smells sweet and ripe, while the palate features bright cherry and candied fruit. Finishes light and easy, with an added shot of zip and freshness. **86** —*M.S. (9/1/2004)*

Castillo de Fuendejalon 2000 Crianza Red Blend (Campo de Borja) $7. The odd yellow paper wrapping might draw attention to this modest red, which features wood spice and cinnamon atop a soft, lean core of red fruit. Flavors of cherry extract and artificial drink mix lack integrity but could please fans of sweet, simple wines. **84** —*M.S. (5/1/2004)*

CASTILLO DE JUMILLA

Castillo de Jumilla 1999 Reserva Red Blend (Jumilla) $17. Seems overripe and stewy at first; airing brings it into better form, but there's still a lot of overt oak sitting on the bouquet. Flavors of raisins, cherries, and plums are dark and chewy, while the finish offers vanilla and lively acids. Not dull but clumsy and heavy. **84** —*M.S. (10/1/2005)*

CASTILLO DE MONJARDIN

Castillo de Monjardin 1999 Reserva Barrel Fermented Chardonnay (Navarra) $20. Yellow in color and well oaked, with creamy, waxy aromas that convey richness. Flavors of honey, apple, and lemon curd, and then an average, clean finish come later. Plenty of size and power are on display; if only the wine were more complex and subtle. **87** —*M.S. (5/1/2004)*

Castillo de Monjardin 2002 Unoaked Chardonnay (Navarra) $11. Unoaked and forward, with a shot of butterscotch and fresh herbs to the nose. Banana, mango, and cucumber flavors lead toward a thin, citrusy finish. The acidity is lively but constrained. **86** —*M.S. (5/1/2004)*

Castillo de Monjardin 2002 Deyo Merlot (Navarra) $18. After a couple of vintages of really raving about this Merlot, the '02, from a cool, wet vintage, just isn't that great. The nose is dominated by rhubarb and sharpness, while the palate offers peppery flavors and a rough feel. Plenty of olive on the finish brings ripeness into question. **82** —*M.S. (12/15/2006)*

Castillo de Monjardin 2001 Deyo Merlot (Navarra) $18. Earthy at first, with foresty spice aromas that go from moss to sandalwood. Heavy and hard now, with big black fruit emboldened by full-grained tannins. Exotic on the finish, with chocolate-dipped raisin and some Bordeaux

SPAIN

fines herbes. Will hold through 2008 and probably beyond. **90** —*M.S.* *(12/31/2004)*

Castillo de Monjardin 2000 Deyo Merlot (Navarra) $15. Delightfully round and pleasant, with aromas of plum, earth, pencil lead, and redwood shavings. The palate is deep and developed, with a full allotment of berry fruits and sweet strawberry working the layer below. Finishes leathery and dry, but not drying. A centered, classy Merlot from Navarra. **91 Best Buy** —*M.S. (5/1/2004)*

Castillo de Monjardin 2000 Crianza Red Blend (Navarra) $11. Ripe and meaty, with a dark color and full, earthy aromatics. Airing and swirling break down the traditional leathery, stewy character to free black cherry and plum fruit showcased on a muscular, sturdy frame. Some chewy yet mild tannins seal the show. **88 Best Buy** —*M.S. (5/1/2004)*

CASTILLO DE MONSÉRAN

Castillo de Monséran 2005 Garnacha (Cariñena) $6. This full-bodied, cherry-dominated Garnacha is pretty good considering the price. The nose is a bit raisiny and ripe, while the palate is sweet but balanced. A standard red wine with clarity and no surprises. **84 Best Buy** —*M.S. (12/15/2006)*

Castillo de Monséran 2002 Garnacha (Cariñena) $7. Ruby in color and sweet on the nose. Yes, it's a candied Grenache from central Spain, and while it doesn't overwhelm, it's steady as she goes. Plenty of raspberry and cherry on the palate is backed by a clear, focused finish. A tasty, upright, semisweet red. **85 Best Buy** —*M.S. (9/1/2004)*

CASTILLO DE OLITE

Castillo de Olite 1998 Crianza Red Blend (Navarra) $8. This is a lighter-styled wine that is introduced by liqueur, tree bark, and charcoal aromas. The bright raspberry palate features vital acids and only in the finish does some vanilla oak raise its head. This light, somewhat tart and open wine is worth a try with food. **85** —*M.S. (11/1/2002)*

CASTILLO DE PERELADA

Castillo de Perelada NV Cresta Rosa Rosé Blend (Emporadà-Costa Brava) $18. This oddball from near Girona is a sparkling dry wine with hardly any flavor other than dried fruit and burnt toast. It isn't particularly good or bad, and finding its target market seems impossible. But what the heck, here it is, a bone-dry Rosado sparkler. Go figure. **81** —*M.S. (9/1/2004)*

CASTILLO DE URA

Castillo de Ura 1998 Tinto Tempranillo (Ribera del Arlanza) $16. This 100% Tempranillo tinto spends a year in American oak, and it tastes it. It's rustic, as though it'd be at its best with a heavy beefy stew. Distinctly bacony, smoky notes on the nose lead to more meatiness and smoke, plus red berries and oak, on the palate. Given its smokehouse flavors, it's surprisingly light in the mouth. Closes with more woody flavors. **85** —*D.T. (4/1/2002)*

CASTILLO DE URTAU

Castillo de Urtau 2001 Crianza Tempranillo (Ribera del Duero) $34. Initial aromas of tree bark, root beer, and leather give way to stronger, obvious oak notes. Very snappy on the palate; in fact, it's downright sharp and acidic in the midpalate. Has its positives but is too racy and shrill in the middle. **84** —*M.S. (8/1/2005)*

CASTILLO LABASTIDA

Castillo Labastida 1999 Reserva Tempranillo (Rioja) $18. Brick colored, with a baked, spicy nose that is true Rioja in that it also pushes Sherry, raisin, and cinnamon notes. Fairly dry, acidic, and zesty in the mouth, with cherry and cola flavors. Forceful acidity keeps it moving along. Needs food to absorb that acid. **87** —*M.S. (12/15/2006)*

CASTRO BREY

Castro Brey 2004 Albariño (Rías Baixas) $14. Green melon and white peach aromas start this monocline wine on its way. The palate offers more peach as well as underripe honeydew. Citrusy late, with clean simplicity. **83** —*M.S. (11/15/2005)*

CATALINO

Catalino 2003 Tempranillo-Cabernet Sauvignon (Catalunya) $10. Smoke and rubber aromas along with soy carry the nose. Raspberry and spice, mainly clove, kick in on the palate. Finishes sharp and juicy, with a lot of acidity. Also plenty of drawn out, unflinching wood. **84** —*M.S. (8/1/2005)*

CAVAS HILL

Cavas Hill 2000 Chardonnay (Penedès) $NA. The soft yellow fruit and nutmeg-vanilla notes are nice, though light, but this Chard-Parellada is on the flabby side. Nose offers more yellow fruit, dusted with bubble-gum powder and chalk. Wants structure and more concentration. **83** —*D.T. (4/1/2003)*

Cavas Hill 2001 Gran Civet Hill Crianza Red Blend (Penedès) $10. Smoky and dry, with strong aromas of cherry and forest floor. Flavors of raspberry and cherry blend with greener tomato and basil notes, while the finish is tight and tannic. Very standard; like something you've tasted many times before. **85 Best Buy** —*M.S. (8/1/2005)*

Cavas Hill 2000 Gran Civet Hill Crianza Red Blend (Penedès) $11. Clean and full, with nuances of tree bark, bramble, and dried cherry. This wine sports a good level of balance; there's some ripe cherry and berry fruit, and also some coffee that creates a dark side. The finish is slightly dry and bitter, but that's a welcome foil to any leftover sweetness. **86** —*M.S. (3/1/2004)*

Cavas Hill 1999 Gran Civet Hill Crianza Red Blend (Penedès) $8. For a not-so-old wine, it shows many signs of being old. A rusty color and drying cherry fruit are the most pronounced. The nose, meanwhile, has some cherry and leather aromas, but even they are weak. It's not bad, but it seems tired, and that's the most you can say **83** —*M.S. (11/1/2002)*

Cavas Hill 1998 Gran Reserva Hill Red Blend (Penedès) $25. Foresty and mature, with wood-spice aromas along with a certain leafy, herbal quality. In the mouth, it's dark and fairly intense, with black plum and cassis. And the finish is tannic, firm and enveloping. A blend of Cabernet, Tempranillo, and Syrah. **87** —*M.S. (3/1/2004)*

Cavas Hill 1997 Gran Toc Hill Reserva Red Blend (Penedès) $13. Shockingly, this wine is but three years old; it's color and faded aromas make it seem older. What's left in the wine is dried cherries and some raisin flavor. It's a mix of Tempranillo, Cabernet, and Merlot. Drink immediately to rescue what life is left. **83** —*M.S. (11/1/2002)*

Cavas Hill 2001 Sauvignon Blanc Hill Sauvignon Blanc (Penedès) $13. Aromas of sweet corn and hay create a creamy sensation, while the palate offers modest lemon and green apple. The finish is tangy, but here some celery and bell pepper appear. It's a wine seemingly on the down side; best to wait for a subsequent and hopefully fresher vintage. **83** —*M.S. (3/1/2004)*

CELLAR MARTI FABRA CARRERAS

Cellar Marti Fabra Carreras 1999 Masia Carreras Red Blend (Emporadà-Costa Brava) $29. Anyone who favors sweet, extracted, rich bruisers should snap this up. It's thick and chewy, with caramel and chocolate jazzing up deep plum and boysenberry fruit. You might think that this baby was spiked; it has kirsch and brandied fruit at its core. Fans of more traditional styles, however, should probably steer clear. **87** —*M.S. (3/1/2004)*

CELLER CECILIO

Celler Cecilio 2001 L'Espill Red Blend (Priorat) $40. A touch of early aromatic raisin gives way to spice, tobacco, tomato, and cherry, while the palate is ripe and rich, with flavors of raspberry syrup and prune. Very deep and smooth, with just enough toasty oak to keep things well framed. **90** —*M.S. (4/1/2006)*

Celler Cecilio 2003 Negre Red Blend (Priorat) $17. Spicy and saucy on the nose, with some leather and cherry mixed in. Shows attractive cherry and tobacco flavors, and they are supported by ripe, pure tannins. This is a tight, ripe wine that is drinkable now and should hold for another couple of years at the very least. **88** —*M.S. (4/1/2006)*

CELLERS BARONIA DEL MONTSANT

Cellers Baronia del Montsant 2001 Clos D'Englora Red Blend (Montsant) $40. It has been a few years since 2001 was a current vintage, and while Montsant wines can age, this one doesn't seem to be going anywhere in particular. The nose is overdone with heavy mint, menthol, and cinnamon-driven oak, while the palate is jumpy and tannic. Not a cheap wine, but also not that great. 83 —*M.S. (12/15/2006)*

CELLERS UNIO

Cellers Unio 2001 Roureda llicorella Red Blend (Priorat) $27. A co-op wine with a meaty, spicy nose that features pepper and olive-like edges. The palate runs lean but ripe, with some plum fruit coming in front of a finish that's lively and anchored by a pinch of chili pepper. 85 —*M.S. (3/1/2004)*

Cellers Unio 1999 Tendral Red Blend (Priorat) $22. Very sweet and round in the nose—a true whiff of Spanish Garnacha if there ever was one. The palate feels chewy as it delivers earthy, sweet flavors that don't really fit any one particular flavor profile. In its favor, the wine has size and guts. But it also seems a tad overripe and raisiny. 84 —*M.S. (3/1/2004)*

CERMEÑO

Cermeño 2004 Tinto Jóven Tinta de Toro (Toro) $11. Jammy and full of raisin, stewed berries, and leather. Calling it ultraripe might be an understatement because it's nearly over the top in its heft, extract, and tannin level. A high-production bruiser that has tons of power but very little precision. 84 —*M.S. (12/15/2006)*

CIMS DE PORRERA

Cims de Porrera 2001 Classic Red Blend (Priorat) $98. A beauty that represents Priorat in its most complete form. Meaty and savage at first, Cims is a terroir wine of the first order. Still, it's polished, with a soft, smooth texture and impressive cherry, cola, spice, and vanilla flavors. Coffee and mocha on the finish seal the deal. Made by Sara Pérez of Mas Martinet. 94 Editors' Choice —*M.S. (10/1/2005)*

CLOS CYPRES

Clos Cypres 2002 Tinto Red Blend (Priorat) $48. Lively and loaded with smoky aromas of beef jerky, sandalwood, and leather. Distant blackberry along with vanilla and tobacco carry the palate, while the finish is wide and smooth. Very drinkable if not a classic. 86 —*M.S. (10/1/2005)*

CLOS DE L'OBAC

Clos de L'Obac 2000 Costers del Siurana Red Blend (Priorat) $55. The pure, hedonistic bouquet is a gorgeous meld of mint and rubber, sweetness and spice, and just a touch of maple. The palate is deep and saturated, with suave plum, berry, and chocolate flavors. The finish is huge but balanced, with licorice and bitter herbs. 93 —*M.S. (3/1/2004)*

Clos de L'Obac 2000 Dolç de L'Obac Red Blend (Priorat) $100. Clos de L'Obac's dessert wine is the perfect Spanish take on recioto d'Italia. Aromas of licorice, dried cheese, balsamic vinegar, and tight-grained oak create a complex bouquet, and the palate doesn't disappoint. Cinnamon and clove notes dress up the raisiny fruit, and later on there's anisette and leather. Best with an aged cheese after dinner. 91 —*M.N. (3/1/2003)*

CLOS DELS CODULS

Clos Dels Coduls 2001 Red Blend (Montsant) $19. Seems a touch green and stripped at first, but airing brings it around. Still, there's a lot of fresh wood and resin, which somewhat masks the plum and berry fruit that's eager to emerge. Spicy on the finish, with a decent feel. 86 —*M.S. (6/1/2005)*

CLOS ERASMUS

Clos Erasmus 2002 Tinto Grenache (Priorat) $125. From Daphne Glorian, among the region's original new wavers, Clos Erasmus is simply one of the best, most typical Priorat wines out there. And while the '02 may not rank as a classic, it's still superb. Aromas of graphite, mineral, and licorice dominate, backed by layered cherry, plum, and earth notes. From four small vineyards around the town of Gratallops. About 450 cases made. 93 —*M.S. (10/1/2005)*

Clos Erasmus 1996 Grenache (Priorat) $50. 94 *(11/15/1999)*

CLOS FIGUERAS

Clos Figueras 2002 Font de la Figuera Red Blend (Priorat) $30. A lot of leather and rubber join jammy red-fruit scents on the bouquet. The palate is loaded with zesty, fairly lean raspberry and plum flavors, while the finish sports vanilla, spice, and tannin. A bit harsh and acid-driven, but still a good wine from a less-than-ideal year. 86 —*M.S. (10/1/2005)*

CLOS MOGADOR

Clos Mogador 2002 Manyetes Red Blend (Priorat) $NA. Fat and dark, with tons of rubber, smoke, licorice, and tobacco on the nose. Young and rowdy now, with a texture that's tight as a drum. Still, it exhibits fine cherry, blackberry, and flowery characteristics. Comes from a hot zone within Priorat, so it's ripe even in a cool vintage. 89 —*M.S. (10/1/2005)*

Clos Mogador 2001 Manyetes Red Blend (Priorat) $70. This monster is intensely mineral, with aromas of crushed stones mixed with leather, lavender, pepper, and cherry. In the mouth, it's heady with maple, leather, asphalt, and cola. Comes at you in layers, the last of which is a finishing flow of espresso. Aged 20 months in new 500-liter barrels, not barriques. 91 —*M.S. (10/1/2005)*

Clos Mogador 2001 Tinto Red Blend (Priorat) $75. The 2002 is the current vintage (reviewed in June), but this wine is superior and is just now entering its prime; call it red nectar with a cement foundation. Mogador offers the purest Priorat fruit going, and the '01 is ethereal, with chewy blackberry, chocolate, and vanilla flavors along with horsehide, black pepper and tobacco on the finish. 95 Editors' Choice —*M.S. (10/1/2005)*

Clos Mogador 2002 Vino Tinto Red Blend (Priorat) $75. René Barbier, the pioneer of Priorat, pulled together a beautiful wine in what was, at best, a mediocre vintage. Admittedly, it starts out coarse and grainy, but airing shows juicy red fruit and a level of complexity that's up there. More the total package than a collection of spare parts; as a result, it'll drink wonderfully around 2006-07. A mix of Cabernet, Cariñena, Garnacha, and Syrah. 93 —*M.S. (6/1/2005)*

CLOS VILÓ

Clos Viló 2002 Costers del Priorat Red Blend (Priorat) $40. Charred on the nose, as if it were burnt steak. Crusty and sharp on the palate, and seemingly dirty at first, with weird flavors of peanut skins and mushroom. Not corked but far off the mainstream. 81 —*M.S. (10/1/2005)*

CODICE

Codice 1999 Red Blend (Vino de la Tierra de Manchuela) $9. This is an easy drinker—not an intellectual, "serious" wine—but it displays more tasty ripe fruit than many more pretentious offerings. The nose is a blender-mix of ripe berry, cocoa, banana hints, and smoky, toasty oak. The palate is flavorful, with ripe but dry strawberry and raspberry fruit. It's fairly light in weight and closes with a nice berry-spice fade—a quaff with class. 87 —*M.M. (4/1/2002)*

Codice 2003 Tempranillo (Vino de la Tierra de Castilla) $9. Sweet and syrupy, but also murky, with aromas of wet dog and moist leaves. Rich on the palate, with thick, stewy flavors of prune and carob. Warm and chocolaty on the finish, but still sort of ponderous and clumsy. 84 —*M.S. (8/1/2005)*

CODORNÍU

Codorníu NV Brut Pinot Noir (Cava) $14. Pinot Noir-based cavas are touchy; sometimes they take on a rough, peppery personality that some might find offputting. This wine does that, but only to an extent. The nose pushes peach pit and campfire aromas, while the palate features dry fruits like papaya and melon, but with cinnamon and pepper shadings. Good mouthfeel and well made, but the flavors and aromas require some getting used to. 87 —*M.S. (12/15/2006)*

Codorníu NV Jaume de Codorniú Brut Sparkling Blend (Cava) $NA. More mature and minerally than most, with some earthy notes as well as a sharp smokiness. Apple, citrus, and grapefruit flavors dominate the developed, smooth-textured palate. Nice overall, with good body. A stand-up cava. 89 —*M.S. (6/1/2005)*

Codorníu NV Original Brut Sparkling Blend (Cava) $9. With some toast and popcorn to fatten up the standard apple aromas, this is a fairly rich cava, especially given the price. Apple, pear and cinnamon flavors grace the palate, while the finish is persistent beyond expectations. Not overly bubbly but still lively. Strides better than your average quaffer.**87 Best Buy** —*M.S. (12/15/2006)*

Codorníu NV Reserva Raventós Brut Sparkling Blend (Cava) $14. Crisp and clean, thus it qualifies as a perfect apéritif wine. Secure in its apple and slate aromas and flavors, with a firm but persistent bead that fosters a fine mouthfeel. Best with nuts, olives, chips, and especially seafood.**88** —*M.S. (6/1/2006)*

CONDADO DE HAZA

Condado de Haza 2003 Tempranillo (Ribera del Duero) $25. Full and toasty, with roasted fruit, meat, and leather on the ripe, robust bouquet. Blackberry and plum flavors are good, and the mouthfeel is manly if a bit tannic. Undoubtedly a warm-vintage wine with size but not a ton of depth. Drink now.**87** —*M.S. (11/1/2006)*

Condado de Haza 2002 Tempranillo (Ribera del Duero) $23. Big and round, with color and a bouquet of rubber, leather, chocolate, and berries. Plump and smoky on the palate, but kind of hard and tannic. And with time those tannins become even more monstrous in their collective intensity. Still, as a whole there's solid flavor and plenty of clout. **87** —*M.S. (10/1/2005)*

Condado de Haza 1999 Estate Bottled Tempranillo (Ribera del Duero) $20. Cassis, plum skin, and cedar accent aromas of stone dust. The flavors are meaty, with blackberry and earth dominating. Rich and full of dark fruits but lacking in real depth, this is a very approachable wine that ought to be enjoyed now.**88** —*C.S. (11/1/2002)*

CONDE ANSUREZ

Conde Ansurez 1996 Tinto Crianza Red Blend (Cigales) $13. One might think that a seven-year-old crianza would be fading, but this one isn't. Sure, it's ready to drink now, and cellaring is unnecessary, but the fruit is pure and exciting. The cherry and raspberry character is exact and lively, while the feel is lean and easy. On the finish, which isn't huge, you get a nice reflection of the wine amid some healthy tannins and acids. Almost certainly good with food.**89** —*M.S. (8/1/2003)*

CONDE DE LA SALCEDA

Conde de la Salceda 2000 Reserva Tempranillo (Rioja) $40. Spice, herbs, smoked meat, and a dark core work in harmony on the bouquet. The palate on this well-made Reserva packs black cherry, cassis, and plum, and that's followed by a stylish, smooth finish that comes on buttery at first and then settles in. Doesn't overwhelm but complements food nicely. Tasted twice.**90** —*M.S. (12/15/2006)*

Conde de la Salceda 1998 Reserva Tempranillo Blend (Navarra) $49. Mocha and Mexican cinnamon notes compete with a twinge of acetone on the nose. An upfront, easy drinker, it offers red plum from start to finish, and plenty of toasty oak (courtesy of new-wood barrels). Tempranillo-based, with about 15% total Cabernet and Merlot added. **86** *(4/1/2003)*

CONDE DE OLZINELLAS

Conde de Olzinellas 2001 Crianza Cabernet Sauvignon-Merlot (Penedès) $18. A ton of bell pepper and tomato sits front and center on the nose, which almost ensures that the flavors will be herbal and leafy. They are, yet the feel in the mouth is decent and the tannin-acid balance adequate. A blend of 50% each Cabernet and Merlot.**82** —*M.S. (9/1/2006)*

CONDE DE SIRUELA

Conde de Siruela 1996 Crianza Red Blend (Ribera del Duero) $23. Yeast, creosote, mercaptans and baked apple aromas are odd companions to flavors of blackberry and mulling spice. Although the tannins and acidity have a bit of grip, the midpalate seems a bit thin and watery.**84** —*K.F. (11/1/2002)*

CONDE DE VALDEMAR

Conde de Valdemar 2002 Crianza Tempranillo (Rioja) $12. Brambly red fruit, leather, and a strong whiff of dill pickle create a less than welcoming nose, which is backed by tart red fruit that carries a roasted overtone. Oaky and tomatoey throughout, with a lean mouthfeel.**81** —*M.S. (12/15/2006)*

Conde de Valdemar 2001 Crianza Tempranillo Blend (Rioja) $12. Clean but rugged, with meaty, solid aromas. Cherry, berry, and cola create a sturdy, fruity attack, while the finish is round and medium in size. A pedestrian, good red for everyday drinking.**86** —*M.S. (9/1/2004)*

Conde de Valdemar 1996 Gran Reserva Tempranillo Blend (Rioja) $21. A lovable throwback, with stewed fruit supporting leather, pepper, and smoke aromas. Solid as a brick, with mature berry flavors that happily carry perky citrus accents. Not a wine that's fading; the fruit is vertical, with bright, healthy acidity.**89** —*M.S. (12/31/2004)*

Conde de Valdemar 1999 Reserva Tempranillo Blend (Rioja) $18. Earthy and solid, with bacon, coffee, and leafiness to the dried-fruit nose. Chocolate and berries mix with stewed plums on the palate, and the finish is chunky. Medium in terms of tannic bite, with soft acidity. Drink now.**88** —*M.S. (2/1/2006)*

Conde de Valdemar 1998 Reserva Tempranillo Blend (Rioja) $15. Big and broad, with aromas of burnt sugar, leather, tomato, and mocha. The palate delivers ample raspberry and plum flavors amid meaty tannins and healthy acidity. Finishes lively and tannic.**87** —*M.S. (9/1/2004)*

Conde de Valdemar 2002 Viura (Rioja) $15. Barrel fermented and strange, with some likable characteristics and others you could do without. The nose features butterscotch, corn, and mustard, while the palate is flat in one sense but also shows a powerful beam of acidity. Finishes waxy yet sour. Hard to grasp.**83** —*M.S. (11/15/2005)*

Conde de Valdemar 2005 Blanco Viura (Rioja) $15. Heavy, with a lot of oak, which is reflected in both the amber color and the aromas. Flavors of vanilla, lemon drop, banana, and wood resin take a moment or two to get used to, but they grow on you. Not a lot of complexity or breadth, but interesting for what it is.**85** —*M.S. (12/15/2006)*

CONDES DE ALBAREI

Condes de Albarei 1999 Albariño (Rías Baixas) $13.86 *(8/1/2000)*

Condes de Albarei 2005 Albariño (Rías Baixas) $16. More than 80,000 cases of this wine were made, making it "mass" by local standards. But that doesn't mean it's not a quality white. In fact, everything about it is really good, from the crystalline nose to the ripe palate to the clean, exact finish.**88** —*M.S. (9/1/2006)*

Condes de Albarei 2004 Albariño (Rías Baixas) $15. Aromas of soap, flowers, and ripe white fruits are nice, while the citrusy palate veers toward lemon and tangerine. Good mouthfeel if a bit short and stout; the finish is rather condensed. But the lasting notes of riper stone fruits help it along. Nice yet basic Galician white.**87** —*M.S. (10/1/2005)*

Condes de Albarei 2003 Albariño (Rías Baixas) $12. Attractive enough, with buttercup, cashew, citrus, and canned pineapple aromas. Fairly focused and controlled on the palate, with basic apple and peach flavors. Finishes a bit chunky, with a sweet pineapple-driven roundness.**86** — *M.S. (12/31/2004)*

Condes de Albarei 2000 Albariño (Rías Baixas) $13. This lively white shows a spritz on the tongue. It's crisp without being sharp, and the citrus notes here tend to orange and they complement tasty stone fruit and floral elements. Finishes clean and light, a great choice for any seafood, any warm evening.**87** —*M.M. (9/1/2002)*

Condes de Albarei 2005 Salneval Albariño (Rías Baixas) $10. This good value features peach, apricot, and some grapefruit on the nose, and in the rear is a full blast of citrus flavors. Juicy, a bit plump and full on the finish.**86 Best Buy** —*M.S. (9/1/2006)*

CONDESA DE LEGANZA

Condesa de Leganza 2001 Crianza Tempranillo (La Mancha) $10. Typical and likable, with aromas of dark fruit, rubber, leather, and spice. Fairly broad and easy on the palate, where simple raspberry and cherry flavors lead to a light, airy finish. Solid and juicy stuff.**86** —*M.S. (8/1/2005)*

Condesa de Leganza 1998 Crianza Tempranillo (La Mancha) $9. Made from the Tempranillo grape, this wine can serve as a graduate seminar in how a wine doesn't have to be fruity to be interesting and even complex. Aromas and flavors of earth, leather, and herbs are austere, while high acidity and dusty tannins give it structure and depth. Very dry, it's a superb wine for paella.**88 Best Buy** —*S.H. (11/1/2002)*

Condesa de Leganza 1999 Crianza Estate Bottled Finca los Trenzones Tempranillo (La Mancha) $9. The vast region of La Mancha is on the prowl in the 21st century, and wines like this won't hurt the region's improving reputation. The nose here is fresh and loaded with berry sweetness and accents of cinnamon and forest floor. The palate is round and chewy, with plum and berry flavors. It's richer than many so-called alta expresión wines, and the structure goes way beyond that of most under-$10 reds. With some airing and good food, it's a certain winner. **88 Best Buy** —*M.S. (8/1/2003)*

Condesa de Leganza 1998 Los Trezones Tempranillo (La Mancha) $9. An attempt at a more "serious" style, this wine goes overboard on the oak, burying the plum, prune, and dried berry fruit. Medium- to full-bodied and even, it closes with mouth-puckering woody tannins. Those more oak-tolerant will find much more to like here. **84** —*M.M. (9/1/2002)*

CONRERIA D'SCALA DEI

Conreria d'Scala Dei 2004 Les Brugueres Garnacha (Priorat) $25. Immediately this white Garnacha registers as something totally different, but more importantly, it's really good. A mere 108 vines yield this lovely anomaly, almost all of which is imported into the U.S. Look for melon and apricot aromas and flavors, along with accents ranging from almond to peach pit to bee's wax. Spectacular texture. 375 cases made. **90** —*M.S. (10/1/2005)*

CONTINO

Contino 2001 Single Vineyard Graciano (Rioja) $95. Although this wine has been favorably reviewed in the past, this vintage seems jammy and ponderous. The color is blinding and the bouquet reduced and jammy. The palate pours on monotonous boysenberry and blackberry, while the finish is granular. A specialty wine (only 250 cases made) that proves why Graciano is rarely made by itself. **84** —*M.S. (11/1/2006)*

Contino 2000 Single Vineyard Graciano (Rioja) $95. Perfumed and polished, with tar and black-cherry aromas. Not often do you see varietal Graciano; usually it's a component supporting Tempranillo. But here it offers boysenberry flavors and a linear structure. Sturdy, a bit tangy, and different. **89** —*M.S. (8/1/2005)*

Contino 1996 Gran Reserva Tempranillo (Rioja) $50. Very healthy and lively, and positively a traditional in style Rioja. Leather, caramel, and chocolate aromas precede a dry, acid-packed palate of cherries and raspberries. The finish is tart at first, then opens into vanilla and spice. With its exciting flavor accents, this is like taking a trip back to a bygone winemaking era. **90** —*M.S. (3/1/2004)*

Contino 1996 Gran Reserva Tempranillo (Rioja) $65. Heavy and rustic, with smoked game, rubber, and bacon on a condensed nose. Woodsy and leafy, with flavors of dried cherry, vanilla, pepper, and coffee. Acidic and tannic, with structure to push it on for another 20 years. But where would be the fruit and fun? Already it needs food. **88** —*M.S. (8/1/2005)*

Contino 1999 Reserva Tempranillo (Rioja) $42. Open and downright fruity for an old-school wine. The bouquet is sweet and rubbery, while the palate delivers plum and blackberry along with chocolate and vanilla. Big tannins are firm but friendly, and the body is sturdy. Not sharp but modestly aggressive. **89** —*M.S. (8/1/2005)*

Contino 2000 Reserva Tempranillo Blend (Rioja) $42. Lots of cherry, fresh-cut wood, charcoal, and green herbs on the lively entry. A second act of snappy cherry fruit and citrus rind is zesty and might be a bit too much for some. But with food, Contino will be a fine, table-worthy companion. **89** —*M.S. (2/1/2006)*

Contino 1997 Single Vineyard Crianza Tempranillo Blend (Rioja) $20. More approachable now, perhaps, than other '97 crianzas, this Tempranillo, Mazuela, and Graciano blend has a relatively soft, medium-bodied mouthfeel, with red plums front and center. Nose carries a stemmy-ashy note over the red fruit; finishes with a disappointing lactic-oak note. **84** —*D.T. (4/1/2003)*

Contino 2001 Viña del Olivo Tempranillo Blend (Rioja) $120. With density and purity, this is yet another fine Rioja from 2001. Contino is CUNE's so-called "modern" label, and the wine delivers ripe plum and cherry, with oak-driven cinnamon, nutmeg, and chocolate playing supporting

roles. A textbook 21st-century wine, with all the right parts in all the right places **90** —*M.S. (6/1/2005)*

CONVENTO SAN FRANCISCO

Convento San Francisco 2002 Crianza Tempranillo (Ribera del Duero) $38. Exemplary Ribera del Duero, given that '02 was not a great year. This wine, however, pours on the richness fans of this region are looking for. The palate is lush and ripe, with deep plum and blackberry flavors supported by mocha and earth shadings. Offers a little bit of everything. **90** —*M.S. (12/15/2006)*

COOPERATIVO SAN ISIDRO

Cooperativo San Isidro 2002 Campo de Camarena Garnacha (Mentrida) $9. Full acidity and racy, with raspberry and strawberry flavors. The core, however, is less than ripe, while the finish is tart. **82** —*M.S. (3/1/2004)*

Cooperativo San Isidro 2001 Campo de Camarena Garnacha (Mentrida) $9. Bouncy plum fruit is tempered by oak and earth; a medium body, and an easy-on-the-wallet price tag make this Garnacha Vieja a good choice for your next BYOB gathering. Finishes with more oak and tart cherry flavors. 33,000 cases produced. **85** —*D.T. (4/1/2003)*

Cooperativo San Isidro 2001 Bastión de Camarena Red Blend (Mentrida) $11. Medium and well-balanced, this 50-50 Tempranillo-Grenache's mouthfeel is its best feature. Offers vague red fruit and oak flavors, and creamy-meaty aromas. Would have fared even better had there been more intensity on the palate. **84** —*D.T. (4/1/2003)*

CORONA DE ARAGÓN

Corona de Aragón 2004 Syrah (Cariñena) $12. Bold in color, with a stewy nose that oozes raisin and licorice. The palate is heavy, with bacon and reduced berry flavors. Flat and a touch burnt late, and in general it's in dire need of an infusion of acidity. **82** —*M.S. (12/15/2006)*

CORONILLA

Coronilla 2002 Crianza Bobal (Utiel-Requena) $12. The bouquet kicks up aromas of black fruit, bacon, and rubber. The grape type is Bobal, and the wine is grabby and rubbery, with piercing tannins supporting black cherry and pepper flavors. Tangy but not shrill on the finish. **85** —*M.S. (8/1/2005)*

Coronilla 2000 Reserva Bobal (Utiel-Requena) $23. Rubbery and tight, with an overt oakiness to the nose. But alongside that wood are serious dark-fruit aromas and a blast of floral freshness. This is Bobal, a lesser known red grape, at its best. There's attractive strawberry flavors and firm, grabbing tannins. Healthy and flavorful; no complaints. **88** —*M.S. (8/1/2005)*

Coronilla 2000 Crianza Red Blend (Utiel-Requena) $15. This Bobal-based wine shows Utiel-Requeña's potential, though it is further evidence that the region has a way to go before it's on par with Priorat or Rioja. Blackcurrant, chocolaty flavors are nice and smoldering, but drop off quickly on the finish. The mouthfeel leaves us with a similar "where's the rest?" feeling—admirable flavors, but not enough stuffing. Keep an eye out for this southeastern Spain D.O. **85** —*D.T. (4/1/2003)*

CORTE REAL

Corte Real 2000 Platinum Cabernet Sauvignon-Merlot (Extremadura) $34. Interesting, with spicy BBQ notes along with dried fruits and pine. Turns kind of woody as it spreads out, with cinnamon, pepper, and plum flavors. Gets even woodier and more raw as it finishes and by that time the fruit has left the building. **84** —*M.S. (2/1/2006)*

Corte Real 2000 Tempranillo-Cabernet Sauvignon (Extremadura) $16. Lean and spicy, with little to no fruit. Very dry and grabby, with far more tannins and acid than flesh. A genuine country wine with a few years of age on it; and what's left is kind of sour and thin. **80** —*M.S. (10/1/2005)*

COSME PALACIO Y HERMANOS

Cosme Palacio y Hermanos 2004 Tempranillo (Rioja) $13. Brawny plum and blackberry aromas feature notes of bacon, rubber, and leather, all of which lead you to expect big, ripe flavors. But the news is, those flavors aren't anywhere to be found. The profile is tangy and lean, with sharp berry notes. Quick and simple on the finish, with aggressive acidity and tannins. **83** —*M.S. (12/15/2006)*

Cosme Palacio y Hermanos 2001 Tempranillo (Rioja) $12. Heavy and sweaty at first, with a fat texture and forward fruit. It takes this wine a couple of minutes to show its black core and some spicy heat. Finishes with obvious flavors of oak and coffee. **85** —*M.S. (9/1/2004)*

Cosme Palacio y Hermanos 2001 Reserva Privada Tempranillo (Rioja) $25. Leather, berry, and slight green aromas carry the nose toward a tart, domineering palate. Quite acidic at first glance, and then buttery on the finish. **83** —*M.S. (11/15/2005)*

Cosme Palacio y Hermanos 2003 Viura (Rioja) $12. Flat and gassy. Bland apple flavors carry the palate, followed by a short, low-acid finish. **81** — *M.S. (11/15/2005)*

Cosme Palacio y Hermanos 2002 Viura (Rioja) $12. Sulfuric, with hints of wet dog and matchstick. The palate is adequate, with green bean and white pepper mixed in with some apple. Some spice and mint on the finish stirs interest in what's otherwise a bland wine. **83** —*M.S. (9/1/2004)*

COSTERS DEL PRIORAT

Costers del Priorat 2004 Abadia Mediterrània Red Blend (Priorat) $30. Far more lean, raw, and rough than ideal, with a touch of burnt field on the nose. The palate keeps that raw, reedy taste, which is smoothed out by softening oak notes. Better on the finish than up front. **83** —*M.S. (12/15/2006)*

COSTERS DEL SIURANA

Costers del Siurana 2001 Clos de L'Obac Red Blend (Priorat) $67. Plenty of smoked meat, hard spice, and pulsating fruit to the nose, which evolves greatly if given time. If there's anything to take issue with, it's that the wine is almost too much of a straight-shooter: It's a touch racy and acidic, with a single beam of bright flavors off of which it doesn't vary. **90** —*M.S. (10/1/2005)*

Costers del Siurana 2001 Dolç de L'Obac Red Blend (Priorat) $98. Sassy and forward, with ripe aromas and exotic flavors. This wine registers at 16% but it's not fortified, so it comes across more like a sweet but dry wine than, say, Port. Expressive and rich, with cherry cough drop, dark chocolate, and raisin flavors. At one moment it's table wine, the next an elixir. And the finish won't quit. Perfect with cheese. **92** —*M.S. (10/1/2005)*

Costers del Siurana 2001 Miserere Red Blend (Priorat) $60. Sleek and fruity, with round, mature aromas and flavors of strawberry and raspberry. Pleasant more than complex, with some acidic verve and a core of healthy fruit. Easy to like, with a lot of flavor. Drink now through 2006. **88** —*M.S. (10/1/2005)*

COTO DE HAYAS

Coto de Hayas 2002 Centenaria Garnacha (Campo de Borja) $14. This old-vines Garnacha has all the earmarks of a young wine. It's ripe and sweet at all checkpoints. The bouquet indicates power to come, while the palate throbs with sweet, candied fruit. Even the finish is like a dessert. Very jammy and forward. **86** —*M.S. (5/1/2004)*

Coto de Hayas 2001 Centenaria Garnacha (Tarragona) $10. Very youthful, yet from 100-year-old vines, this 100% Garnacha has a vibrant purple color and a chocolate-accented nose. Smooth and tart-sweet on the tongue, it delivers flavor and texture galore. It's a real mouthful with a fairly big, persistent finish. Delicious, yet makes you want a more serious rendering of such old, solid fruit. **86** —*M.M. (9/1/2002)*

Coto de Hayas 2003 Fagus Garnacha (Campo de Borja) $37. Smells fairly solid, with plum, prune, and leather. But the palate is ultrasweet and milky, with a strong candied essence that doesn't impress unless your thing is chocolate-covered cherries and vanilla. Way too expensive for what's in the bottle. **82** —*M.S. (11/1/2006)*

Coto de Hayas 2001 Fagus Garnacha (Campo de Borja) $30. This huge, ultrasweet Garnacha knows no boundaries. It's full of candied cherry, milk chocolate, and out-of-whack tannins. A fast ride with no guard rails. Beware! **83** —*M.S. (9/1/2004)*

Coto de Hayas 2001 Reserva Garnacha (Campo de Borja) $18. Sappy and sweet, with a ton of chocolate both on the nose and especially on the palate. This Garnacha is so chocolaty it's like digging into a Hershey bar.

Trouble is, there isn't much fruit or acid to offset the creamy, cloying vanilla and fudge flavors. Not flawed or underripe; but too chocolaty and monotone to score better. **84** —*M.S. (2/1/2006)*

Coto de Hayas 1998 Reserva Garnacha (Campo de Borja) $13. Lots of sweet mocha and milk chocolate coats the nose of this basic, chunky red. The palate offers adequate strawberry and raspberry, while the finish turns high-wire and tart. A bit syrupy in terms of mouthfeel. **84** —*M.S. (9/1/2004)*

Coto de Hayas 2003 Rosado Garnacha (Campo de Borja) $6. Flat and heavy, with pasty aromas. The palate deals bulky plum flavors, which are followed by black cherry and kirsch. Almost a red wine in its color and weight. **83 Best Buy** —*M.S. (8/1/2005)*

Coto de Hayas 2004 Rosado Grenache (Campo de Borja) $7. Oddly aromatized, with strong hints of hickory and sweets. The whole wine is a strange mix of clove and distant fruit. Finishes with weird notes of spiced tea and rubber. Made from 95% Garnacha. **81** —*M.S. (11/1/2006)*

Coto de Hayas 2000 Crianza Red Blend (Campo de Borja) $8. Roasted and creamy on the nose, with only modest fruit notes. Very sweet and thick across the tongue, with a sugary berry profile. With chocolate and carob coming on late, this wine plays up the oak element. **85** —*M.S. (5/1/2004)*

Coto de Hayas 1998 Crianza Red Blend (Campo de Borja) $7. The nose is leathery and earthy, but not very fruity. Some red plum and raspberry appears on the lean, tangy palate, while the finish is tight and hard-edged. The wine has nice fruit and a clean taste profile, but it's also a bit sharp. **85 Best Buy** —*M.S. (11/1/2002)*

Coto de Hayas 2004 Tinto Red Blend (Campo de Borja) $7. The candied red fruit on the nose is distinct and frankly quite likable. Forget about complexity, depth, and edge with this wine and go straight for the sweet, sugary fruit that's pleasant as an ice cream sundae and about as difficult to consume. **85 Best Buy** —*M.S. (2/1/2006)*

Coto de Hayas 2002 Tinto Jóven Red Blend (Campo de Borja) $6. Racy and juicy, with forward strawberry, raspberry, and leather aromas followed by a zesty, bold mouthful of plum fruit and black pepper. Long and deep for a youngster, with warmth and spice. **87 Best Buy** —*M.S. (5/1/2004)*

Coto de Hayas 2002 Tempranillo-Cabernet Sauvignon (Campo de Borja) $9. At 85% Tempranillo, it could be labeled as such. Regardless, look for a bouquet of fat black fruit and touches of earth and smoke. Flavors of plum and blackberry are warm and full, while both the back end and overall impression are positive and lusty. **87 Best Buy** —*M.S. (5/1/2004)*

Coto de Hayas 2003 Tempranillo-Cabernet Sauvignon (Campo de Borja) $10. A touch rubbery up front, with plum and cherry aromas forming a standard, quite acceptable bouquet. Sweet cherry, plum, and grape flavors are bright and zesty, and there's a hint of chocolate on the finish. Lacks nuance but is commendable in a straight-ahead kind of way. **84** — *M.S. (2/1/2006)*

Coto de Hayas 2002 Blanco White Blend (Campo de Borja) $6. Flowery on the nose, but very gentle in terms of flavors. There's some apple and citrus, but not all that much. And the mouthfeel is flat, almost flabby. Could stand a boost in acidity to liven things up. **84 Best Buy** —*M.S. (5/1/2004)*

COTO DE IMAZ

Coto de Imaz 1996 Selección Pedro Guasch Reserva Red Blend (Rioja) $45. Densely oaked, but over good fruit, this delivers fine flavor and feel. A solid, dark cherry core, very good fruit-to-acid balance and solid tannins create a handsome package. In the classic Rioja sense, it has substance, but is not fat or weighty. Tasty now, even better in two years, this will keep until 2010+. **90 Cellar Selection** —*M.M. (9/1/2002)*

Coto de Imaz 1994 Gran Reserva Tempranillo (Rioja) $29. This lighter-styled, mature Rioja shows just a hint of brown at the edges. An initial light sweaty note blows off quickly, revealing appealing dried cherry, spice, and wood aromas and flavors, and an elegant, balanced mouthfeel. Tannins are mostly resolved, drink now–2005. **87** —*M.M. (9/1/2002)*

CRATER

Crater 1998 Barrica Red Blend (Tacoronte-Acentejo) $38. Canary Islands wine? Yes indeed, with appealing black cherry fruit, dark chocolate, and tar aromas and flavors wrapped in firm, toasty oak. This 65% Listan Negro and 35% Negramoll blend rides a lean frame, similar in weight and texture to a mainstream Rioja or Tuscan red. Finishes long and smooth with even, well-dispersed tannins. Tasty now, and should hold or improve through 2004. **90** —*M.M. (4/1/2002)*

CRISTALINO

Cristalino NV Brut Sparkling Blend (Cava) $9. Light aromas of petrol and lemon-lime are entirely correct for cava, and the palate pushes fresh fruit in the tangerine and grapefruit realm. Has a bit of heft and zap, with a dry, largely clean finish. Fine on its own; maybe better in a Spanish-style mimosa. **85 Best Buy** —*M.S. (12/15/2005)*

Cristalino 2001 Brut Nature Sparkling Blend (Cava) $15. Yellow in color and heavy on the nose. Toast is the lead aroma, and with that there's some caramel and peanut butter. Dry and lean in the mouth, with lemon and grapefruit notes. Still, it has class and style to it; not a dullard. Fairly unique. **87** —*M.S. (6/1/2006)*

Cristalino 1998 Brut Nature Sparkling Blend (Cava) $12. Lean and slightly toasty, this wine doesn't show a lot of fruit yet pleases with an array of gentle earth and mineral flavors. Finishes fully dry, yet avoids any sensation of sharpness, falling away gracefully. **85** —*J.C. (12/31/2003)*

Cristalino NV Extra Dry Sparkling Blend (Cava) $9. Neutral for the most part, with a touch of toasty wheat and baked apple on the nose. Typical cava petrol invades the palate, but it's overrun by tastier, fresher apple and banana flavors. Exhibits some light toastiness on the finish. **86 Best Buy** —*M.S. (12/15/2005)*

Cristalino NV Rosé Brut Sparkling Blend (Cava) $9. A bit gaseous and funky, with simple dried-cherry and slightly mealy citrus flavors. Gets better with time but never really impresses. Not musty but definitely less than fresh. **81** —*M.S. (12/15/2005)*

CRUCILLON

Crucillon 2003 Garnacha (Campo de Borja) $6. Exhibits dry red fruits and mushroom on the nose, with accents of forest and spice. Somewhat minty and forward on the palate, and arguably a touch gritty and sweet. Raw as it might be, no one can say this wine doesn't have guts. **85 Best Buy** —*M.S. (6/1/2005)*

Crucillon 2004 Tinto Garnacha (Campo de Borja) $6. Cherry skins, red licorice and a spot of earthiness carry the sweet nose. The mouth offers additional ripe red fruits, decent tannins and perky acidity. It's a balanced, easy, no-brainer red for those not too picky about what they're drinking. Call it good, sweet fun. **85 Best Buy** —*M.S. (2/1/2006)*

Crucillon 2002 Tinto Garnacha (Campo de Borja) $5. This Garnacha has a strong berry nose with hints of leather, but it doesn't hold up to airing. Within the basics, look for loud, juicy fruit that tastes like plum, strawberry and cherry mixed together. Seems most complete on the finish. **85 Best Buy** —*M.S. (5/1/2004)*

CRUZ DE PIEDRA

Cruz de Piedra 2002 Garnacha (Calatayud) $7. Plump and grapey, with sharp raspberry and pepper controlling the palate. Fairly tart and condensed, but mostly clean. Spice on the finish, but never all that much texture. **84** —*M.S. (12/31/2004)*

Cruz de Piedra 2003 Macabeo (Calatayud) $7. Easy to dismiss at first because it's a bit acrid and raspy on the nose. But patience will be rewarded; the palate provides burnt apple and toast flavors, while the finish is alive with herb, pepper, and smoke notes. Not a familiar style, so it's hard to grasp. Interesting for Macabeo. **86 Best Buy** —*M.S. (8/1/2005)*

CUATRO PASOS

Cuatro Pasos 2004 Mencia (Bierzo) $12. Bierzo is being called the new frontier for stimulating Spanish red wines, but many are expensive. Cuatro Pasos, a new wine sourced from old hillside vineyards, is not. Still, it delivers power, freshness and flavor, all of which are attributes of the indigenous Mencía grape. With no overt oak character, good acidity and mild tannins, it's perfect for drinking now. **88 Best Buy** —*M.S. (11/15/2006)*

CUETO

Cueto 2004 Tempranillo (Rioja) $10. Jammy and sweet on the nose, like a jar of strawberry preserves. The palate, however, is light and tart, with burnt berry flavors. Finishes peppery and short, with little to latch onto. **80** —*M.S. (12/15/2006)*

CVNE

CVNE 2001 Rosado Grenache (Rioja) $11. This Grenache-based rosé's a little flat, with hard cheese and strawberry flavors and aromas. Simple; thankfully doesn't taste confected. **82** —*D.T. (4/1/2003)*

CVNE 2005 Rosado Rosé Blend (Rioja) $9. Light salmon in color, with fruity, relaxed raspberry aromas. Melon and peach flavors are pleasant but dilute, while the wine weighs in a bit watery and devoid of stuffing, even for a rosado. Finishes dry but flat. **84** —*M.S. (11/1/2006)*

CVNE 2003 Crianza Tempranillo (Rioja) $16. A sniff delivers aromas of dried fruits along with a smack of toast and char. Runs light to medium across the palate, with cranberry and raspberry rising as the primary flavors. Definitely a flyweight made in the traditional style. A new release that seems more mature than it is. Drink right away, preferably with food. **85** —*M.S. (11/1/2006)*

CVNE 1995 Imperial Gran Reserva Tempranillo (Rioja) $43. Chunky and mouthfilling, but it still has lovable characteristics of briary fruit, full-bore acids and a leathery feel. The nose is slightly grainy and animal at first, but it finds its stride. Plum and berry flavors are ripe enough, and the finish offers some chocolate. **88** —*M.S. (3/1/2004)*

CVNE 1996 Imperial Reserva Tempranillo (Rioja) $31. Juicy red berries, earth, and tea flavors are at the heart of this reserva; fresh wood-pulp notes come through on the nose and on the finish. Medium-bodied, with smooth tannins, this Spanish wine—while far from entry-level—may just be the one that wins your friends over to Rioja. **87** —*D.T. (4/1/2003)*

CVNE 1998 Imperial Reserva 125 Anniversary Tempranillo (Rioja) $45. Foresty and herbal, with Old World aromas of coconut, dill, and dried cherry. Quite acidic and sharp, but if you let it unfold you'll find cherry and cranberry along with buttery oak and vanilla. Not for everyone. **87** —*M.S. (8/1/2005)*

CVNE 2001 Pagos de Viña Real Tempranillo (Rioja) $119. Perfect color; built like a house. The bouquet is telling, as one whiff delivers cherry, cola, tobacco, and almond paste. Much to ponder on the palate, as red berry and cassis flavors are puffed up by woody waves of coconut and cream. And then there are those tight, driving tannins. You can't miss them. Hold for several years, if you can. **91 Cellar Selection** —*M.S. (8/1/2005)*

CVNE 2003 Viña Real Crianza Tempranillo (Rioja) $18. Forward and a touch racy, with moderate sweetness on the bouquet. Runs juicy and tight, with fresh, almost tart raspberry and cherry flavors. Offers the basics and not much more, but it's a balanced wine made in the traditional style, meaning it's dry, acidic, and medium-bodied. **86** —*M.S. (11/1/2006)*

CVNE 1996 Viña Real Gran Reserva Tempranillo (Rioja) $48. Intriguing earthy, leafy aromas as well as a lot of roasted meat and berry fruit to the nose. Any high expectations, however, are lost on the palate, where it's sour and scouring. Yes, there's red cherry and rhubarb for the tart-fruit lovers, but the bet here is that most will find it starched out and not that pleasant to drink. **83** —*M.S. (8/1/2005)*

CVNE 2000 Viña Real Oro Reserva Tempranillo (Rioja) $33. Starts out rather simple, with cherry, tomato, and dill notes. Picks up complexity and style as it airs, revealing plum and raspberry flavors along with herbs and leather. Toasty, with flavors of coconut to the finish. Acidic still, so serve with food. **87** —*M.S. (8/1/2005)*

CVNE 2002 Viña Real Plata Crianza Tempranillo (Rioja) $19. Dry berry aromas and a rubbery, saucy quality lead to gritty cherry and raspberry flavors. Very thin and starching, with potent tannins and astringent acids. **82** —*M.S. (8/1/2005)*

CVNE 1996 Vina Real Reserva Tempranillo (Rioja) $29. Start and finish, this reserva has some serious barnyardy, earthy elements—and that's a good thing. The palate's generic red fruit and herb flavors, though, didn't make as much of an impression on me. The wine is mouthfilling, but the flavors don't quite flesh out the frame. **86** —D.T. (4/1/2003)

CVNE 2000 Imperial Reserva Tempranillo Blend (Rioja) $45. An old-school wine done really well. It starts with cherry, tobacco, and light coconut aromas before moving on to juicy boysenberry and citrus flavors that are boosted by CUNE's trademark acids. Muscular, wiry and structured, but with restraints. Think Barry Bonds before Balco. **91** —M.S. (11/1/2006)

CVNE 1998 Imperial Reserva Tempranillo Blend (Rioja) $38. Clear and lucid, with cherry on the nose along with leather and dried fruits. Mature but not old, with a spicy palate with piquant edges. Lively but smooth enough on the finish, with peppery notes all the way out. **89** —M.S. (9/1/2004)

CVNE 2000 Real de Asúa Reserva Tempranillo Blend (Rioja) $120. Concentrated but not too heavy, at least not compared to some new-age Riojanos. Asúa shows smoky, toasty aromas and some bright cherry fruit. In the mouth, she's fresh and upright, with just a hint of Bordeaux-style leafiness but zero under ripeness. Toward the finish cola and red licorice flavors come up. Lovely and more subtle than the competition. **92** —M.S. (6/1/2005)

CVNE 2005 Monopole White Blend (Rioja) $15. Basic, fresh, and fruity, with floral aromas that capture the essence of clean, tank-made Viura. Flavors of melon, banana, and papaya are easy to like but not that serious, while the finish is soft and creamy, but not very intense. **85** —M.S. (11/1/2006)

D. PEDRO DE SOUTOMAIOR

D. Pedro de SoutoMaior 2003 Albariño (Rías Baixas) $19. Loaded with tropical fruit, with ample size to the nose and palate. Tastes more of live-wire citrus than anything else, and the zesty finish definitely hums along at a quick pace. Lasting notes of grapefruit and mineral are typical and welcome. **87** —M.S. (3/1/2005)

DAMALISCO

Damalisco 1999 Reserva Tempranillo Blend (Toro) $26. Fairly soft and fruity on first inspection, with some dusty notes to the nose along with a hint of wood. The palate shows cherry, plum, and tangy acids. It finishes dry and a bit oaky. Not a complex red, but solid enough. **86** —M.S. (9/1/2004)

DARIEN

Darien 2004 Tempranillo (Rioja) $10. The bouquet mixes bramble and berry notes, which turn rougher and more vegetal as time passes. The palate is peppery and light, with just adequate cherry and berry flavors. A light, distant wine with some similarities to Beaujolais Nouveau. **82** —M.S. (12/15/2006)

Darien 2002 Tempranillo (Rioja) $9. Smells a touch sour and leathery, with thin cherry fruit. Seems roasted and heavy on the finish, and a bit lacking in structure. The mouthfeel is starching as well. **83** —M.S. (9/1/2004)

Darien 2000 Crianza Tempranillo Blend (Rioja) $14. Slightly buttery and unstable on the nose, with popcorn and light raspberry aromas. More lightweight berry fruit comes forth on the palate, which is dominated by a dry tea-like quality. Clean but underwhelming. **84** —M.S. (5/1/2004)

Darien 2000 Reserva Tempranillo Blend (Rioja) $28. Starts shy, but then reveals a smoky nose of dried cherries and freshly fallen leaves. Still fairly youthful on the palate, where plum and cherry flavors are braced by a ripping note of hickory smoke. Barrel notes take over on the finish, but overall it has a lot of what you want from a 21st-century Rioja. **88** —M.S. (6/1/2005)

Darien 2001 Reserve Tempranillo Blend (Rioja) $28. Light raspberry along with charred wood carries the modest nose. Additional raspberry flavors blend with sweeter strawberry tastes to create a mildly creamy, easygoing palate. Finishes fairly buttery, with toast and popcorn notes. An attempt at a major-league wine that is semi-successful. **87** —M.S. (11/1/2006)

Darien 2000 Selección Tempranillo Blend (Rioja) $32. Open and simple, with fresh red-fruit flavors prior to a soft but tart finish. There's just

enough stuffing here to keep things afloat, yet it's best initially and thins as it opens up. **86** —M.S. (5/1/2004)

Darien 2001 Selección Tempranillo Blend (Rioja) $36. A mix of four grapes, headed by Tempranillo and Garnacha, this is a good, hefty blend. Plenty of red fruit and toast on the nose, with lots of color and zest. Meaty and full of new oak, with plum and berry fruit backing things up. Smooth on finish. Quite nice. **89** —M.S. (9/1/2004)

DE LOZAR

De Lozar 2004 Tinto del Pais (Ribera del Duero) $13. Nice from the get-go. Blueberry and cassis carry the nose, which offers a slight blast of pencil lead and mineral. Complete and largely harmonious on the palate, with soft oak and chunky, ripe fruit. On the mark now and it should shape up even more with additional bottle age. **88 Best Buy** —M.S. (4/1/2006)

DE MULLER

De Muller 1998 Legitim Red Blend (Priorat) $15. Tangy oak, over-the-hill, stewy fruit and earth on the palate leave a lot to be desired here. Finishes flat, with more oaky tang. **80** —D.T. (4/1/2003)

DEHESA LA GRANJA

Dehesa la Granja 2000 Selección Tempranillo (Zamora) $35. Spicy and woodsy, with a smoky lemony quality to the nose along with bold fruit and cola. Zesty and tannic, with plum and berry flavors and lots of chocolate. Seems a bit hard-edged, with plenty of pepper and spice. **86** —M.S. (10/1/2005)

DELIUS

Delius 2001 Reserva Tempranillo Blend (Rioja) $60. This Tempranillo-dominated red (it includes 25% Graciano) is oaky and drying, with cinnamon and basic red-fruit aromas on the bouquet. The palate is tannic and solid, with raspberry, plum, and spice. Turns increasingly oaky toward the end, with a rush of butter. Round and generally well balanced, yet nothing out of the ordinary. **87** —M.S. (11/1/2006)

DESCENDIENTES DE J. PALACIOS

Descendientes de J. Palacios 2001 Corullón Villa Mencia (Bierzo) $40. This rather unique wine (made from Mencía) is at the vanguard of the Bierzo revival. It's earthy and leafy, with aromas of red plums and natural spice. The mouthfeel is perfect, as it's just lush and firm enough. Nearly explodes in the mouth, with fine French oak softening the blow. **92** —M.S. (6/1/2005)

DÍA NACIENTE

Día Naciente 2004 Shiraz (Castilla La Mancha) $10. Round and sweet up front, with aromas of candied berries. More alert and red-fruit dominated on the palate, with snappy acidity keeping it well propped up. Finishes with bright acidity and modest tannins. Straight-ahead red wine with crispness. **84** —M.S. (12/15/2006)

Día Naciente 2004 Shiraz-Tempranillo (Castilla La Mancha) $10. This is a good table wine with sweet, woodsy aromas of sandalwood, clove, cinnamon, and earth. The palate turns a bit to the tangy, sharp side. But in a world with so many overripe heavyweights, this edgy, almost racy blend has the right stuff. **85 Best Buy** —M.S. (12/15/2006)

Día Naciente 2004 Tempranillo (Castilla La Mancha) $10. Light raspberry and strawberry aromas lead into snappy berry flavors. The feel is almost astringent; call it tangy and tight. Juicy but also rubbery. Shows both positives and negatives. **83** —M.S. (12/15/2006)

Día Naciente 2000 Tempranillo (La Mancha) $10. Murky and stewy, and already old for a La Mancha red. Plum and earth flavors are baked, while there is but a modicum of spice and nuance. **80** —M.S. (6/1/2005)

DIEGO DE ALMAGRO

Diego de Almagro 1991 Gran Reserva Tempranillo (Valdepeñas) $19. **87** —J.C. (8/1/2000)

DIEZ LLORENTE

Diez Llorente 2001 Crianza Tinto del Pais (Ribera del Duero) $25. Gets going in heavy, stewy fashion, with aromas of rubber, asphalt, and leather. Picks up speed and precision on the palate, where there's a good mix of strident fruit, vanilla, and smooth tannins. A lot is on offer here if you give it time to open up and show its true colors. **88**—*M.S. (10/1/2005)*

Diez Llorente 2001 Reserva Tinto del Pais (Ribera del Duero) $29. Murkier than ideal. The nose is heavy and earthy, and it's full of barnyard initially. The wine rests heavily on the tongue, with soft, mildly funky flavors of dark berry and stewed tomato. Seems a touch overripe and flaccid for an '01 reserva. **84**—*M.S. (11/1/2006)*

DINASTÍA VIVANCO

Dinastía Vivanco 1998 Reserva Tempranillo Blend (Rioja) $20. This new, showy winery in the heart of Rioja was founded by bulk brokers, and this wine still tastes as if were from the old stock. Some spice and leather aromas and then tart pie cherry and raspberry in the mouth. Not a sour, bad wine, but dull. **84**—*M.S. (9/1/2004)*

DO FERREIRO

Do Ferreiro 2001 Albariño (Rías Baixas) $20. The nose is flat, offering nothing offensive but also nothing terribly attractive. Lemon and green apple flavors define the tart palate, while the finish is zippy and acidic, but not piercingly so. **85**—*M.S. (11/1/2002)*

Do Ferreiro 2003 Cepas Vellas Albariño (Rías Baixas) $33. From the outset, this beauty oozes character. The whole exceeds the parts by a sum of three, as the wine delivers full flavors, complexity and a near Burgundian minerality. This is what great Albariño is about, even if it's from a hot vintage. Spicy yet thumping with guava, banana, and citrus. Simply delicious. **92 Editors' Choice**—*M.S. (6/1/2005)*

DOMAINE PEDRO DE SOUTOMAIOR

Domaine Pedro De Soutomaior 2000 Albariño (Rías Baixas) $15. A knockout Albariño, this one has a unique, less-typical orange cast. Very flavorful, with orange and peach-apricot hints, it's smooth and even, and closes with good length. This is an attractive, medium-weight white with real character. Worth seeking out. **89**—*M.M. (9/1/2002)*

DOMECQ

Domecq NV La Ina Fino Sherry (Jerez) $14. Clean, nutty and smooth, if a touch neutral on the nose. The palate pushes more nuts and distant white fruits, followed by a finish of fleur de sel and cashew butter. Slightly heavy but that's the style; like its sister manzanilla, this wine is very consistent year to year. **88**—*M.S. (4/1/2006)*

Domecq NV Light, Very Dry Manzanilla Sherry (Jerez) $14. Perfectly good and fresh, and consistent with years past. This manzanilla earns points for its dryness, its good mouthfeel, and its nutty finish. Is it the most complex wine from Sanlucar? Maybe not; but it's tasty and made right. **87**—*M.S. (4/1/2006)*

DOMINIO DE ATAUTA

Dominio de Atauta 2002 Tinto del Pais (Ribera del Duero) $40. With redfruit, leather, and just enough funky aromas to stir the pot, this wine deserves a whirl. The body and style is somewhat tight and narrow, maybe a reflection of less-than-stellar vintage conditions. Nevertheless, it's got all that you'd want in a young Ribera red. **89**—*M.S. (6/1/2005)*

Dominio de Atauta 2000 Tempranillo (Ribera del Duero) $30. Dense and meaty, with cured ham and earthy mineral notes. The rustic, untamed nose draws you in, but once you get inside things calm down. Yes, the palate's saturated, but it stops short of bowling you over. On the finish, cherry and chocolate flavors bring it home. From a Spanish owner/French winemaker duo. **89**—*M.S. (3/1/2004)*

DOMINIO DE EGUREN

Dominio de Eguren 1999 Protocolo Rosado Rosé Blend (Tierra Manchuela) $6. 87 Best Buy—*M.M. (8/1/2000)*

Dominio de Eguren 2001 Codice Tempranillo (Tierra Manchuela) $9. Overly sweet and syrupy you might say, but maple, caramel, and chocolate are often the types of flavors folks are seeking. The tannins are gritty, so much so that they almost run roughshod over some of the sublime characteristics hidden within. **85**—*M.S. (3/1/2004)*

Dominio de Eguren 1998 Codice Tinto Tempranillo (Tierra Manchuela) $8. 87—*M.M. (8/1/2000)*

Dominio de Eguren 2001 Protocolo Tempranillo (Tierra Manchuela) $6. Subdued and earthy, with cool, compact red-fruit aromas. The palate offers brandied cherry, plum, and apple skin flavors. The finish is long, with coffee and chocolate along with some fatty oak. Has a lot going for it, but could use more focus. **86 Best Buy**—*M.S. (3/1/2004)*

Dominio de Eguren 1998 Protocolo Tinto Tempranillo (Tierra Manchuela) $6. 85 Best Buy—*M.M. (8/1/2000)*

Dominio de Eguren 1999 Protocolo Blanca White Blend (Tierra Manchuela) $6. 86—*M.M. (8/1/2000)*

Dominio de Eguren 2002 Protocolo Blanco White Blend (Vino de la Tierra de Castilla) $6. With its succulent floral aromas, you almost have to be drawn in. Flavors of melon, apple, and banana are lengthy and delicious. The only stumbling block is a flat mouthfeel, which some might call plump. Shockingly, this wine is made mostly from the pedestrian Airen grape. **87 Best Buy**—*M.S. (3/1/2004)*

DOMINIO DE PINGUS

Dominio de Pingus 2001 Flor de Pingus Tinto del Pais (Ribera del Duero) $50. Barely a step down from the more rare and pricey Pingus, the '01 Flor should fly off store shelves and restaurant wine lists. It's that good, starting with the intoxicating nose and moving through the pure palate and onto the marvelous finish. A wine that goes all the way, with spice, leather, and mounds of rich, ripe fruit. **93 Editors' Choice**—*M.S. (6/1/2005)*

Dominio de Pingus 2001 Pingus Tinto del Pais (Ribera del Duero) $320. Huge and on the border of overwhelming. But if you like yours concentrated and forward (although arguably not that complex) then Pingus is a dream come true. Start with the bouquet of coffee, earth, black truffle, and smoked meat before digging into the wine's saturated black-fruit palate. Big tannins on the finish say lay it down for several years. **94**—*M.S. (6/1/2005)*

DOMINIO DE TARES

Dominio de Tares 2003 Mencia (Bierzo) $16. A real-deal, modern wine. Among the many imposters coming out of Spain, this beefy, ripe, muscled red tosses up cinnamon and earth before a free flow of plum, black cherry, and berry fruit. Thick, chewy, and balanced, with mounds of coffee and fudge waiting on the finish. Not subtle but a lot of fun to drink, especially given the price. **90 Editors' Choice**—*M.S. (6/1/2005)*

Dominio de Tares 2003 Albares Mencia (Bierzo) $11. Sweet and grapy on first look, but shows more complexity once you get into it. Rich plum and other black fruits carry the bulky, sizable palate. The finish offers oak in the form of chocolate and mocha. Devoid of serious nuance and depth, but charming in an easy, fruit-forward way. **88 Best Buy**—*M.S. (6/1/2005)*

Dominio de Tares 2004 Baltos Mencia (Bierzo) $16. Violets, boysenberry, and coffee make for an open, plump bouquet that functions as a red carpet for anyone willing to take the plunge. The palate is equally seductive and round, with deep, dark-fruit flavors topped with toast and chocolate. Stylish but forward; it's a wine most anyone should like. **90**—*M.S. (9/1/2006)*

Dominio de Tares 2002 Bembibre Mencia (Bierzo) $45. Lush on the nose, with wild game, smoke, and blackberry filling every void. Almost Syrah-like in its weight, more so than the other Mencía wines that are making a statement. Which only means that it's chewy, chocolaty, and creamy. Finishes slightly short, with bitter fudge and vanilla shadings. **91**—*M.S. (6/1/2005)*

Dominio de Tares 2001 Cepas Viejas Mencia (Bierzo) $26. Talk about precious aromatics; this one sports mint, licorice, dark cocoa, and spicy oak. The color is deep, the body full, and the leather, meat, and cinnamon-based woodspice flavors sublime. Made from the Mencía grape, so it's a bit shy on the midpalate. Otherwise, it's flawless. **91**—*M.S. (12/31/2004)*

Dominio de Tares 2003 Exaltos Mencia (Bierzo) $28. Ripe, robust, and not the least bit rustic. This is a polished, warm red with seductive red-fruit, vanilla, and coconut aromas along with leather and earth. Extrapolated and extended on the palate, with toasty, deep, ripe flavors. New-wave Bierzo with pizzazz. **90**—*M.S. (9/1/2006)*

SPAIN

DON OLEGARIO

Don Olegario 2004 Albariño (Rías Baixas) $21. Albariño is not known for its aging potential, and this wine already seems to be on the way out. The nose veers toward apricot and cider, as does the palate. Finishes with a final kick of acidity. Drink soon, or wait for the 2005. **84** —*M.S. (12/15/2006)*

DON PEDRO DE SOUTOMAIOR

Don Pedro de Soutomaior 2002 Albariño (Rías Baixas) $19. The dainty nose offers pound cake, citrus, and a laudable freshness, while the palate is forward and blasting with citrus and melon. Finishes with more melon. Possibly a touch flabby at the end, but still a good example of the type. **87** —*M.S. (9/1/2004)*

DON RAMÓN

Don Ramón 2002 Tinto Red Blend (Campo de Borja) $7. From Bodegas Aragonesas, this bulky, ultra sweet red sports virtually no acids and as a result tastes like candy in liquid form. Tons of raspberries and sugar before a medicinal finish. Too clumsy and strange for our taste. **83** —*M.S. (6/1/2005)*

Don Ramón 2003 Tinto Barrica Red Blend (Campo de Borja) $7. Mildly green and brambly, with touches of tomato and raspberry on the full, sun-baked bouquet. Yet in the mouth it's tart, pushing red cherry flavors onto a palate that's lactic and creamy. Settles late to show some fruit and subtleties. **83** —*M.S. (11/1/2006)*

Don Ramón 2002 Tempranillo (Rioja) $15. This co-op wine is almost a good deal, but ultimately it does not show enough depth or elegance to reach the next level. The nose is a touch stewy and lifeless, while the palate offers chewy raisin, plum, and berry. Flat on the finish, with a syrupy feel. **83** —*M.S. (6/1/2005)*

DOS VICTORÍAS

Dos Victorías 2004 José Pariente Verdejo (Rueda) $17. Round, fruity, and quite exceptional in its class. This Verdejo sets the standard for Rueda; it's loaded with green melon and pineapple up front and backed by bright apple, pear, and green herb flavors. Perfectly balanced and fresh. Stands out from the crowd. **91 Editors' Choice** —*M.S. (9/1/2006)*

Dos Victorías 2003 José Pariente Verdejo (Rueda) $16. Balanced Spanish whites were rare in the hot '03 vintage, but this one is. Two female wine-makers, hence the Two Victorías name, flat-out nailed this Verdejo, which pours on round peach, gooseberry, almond, and mineral aromas and flavors. Clean as a whistle, with a finish that hits with power. **91 Editors' Choice** —*M.S. (6/1/2005)*

DUQUE DE SEVILLA

Duque de Sevilla 1998 Reserva Garnacha (Campo de Borja) $11. A Garnacha-Tempranillo mix that's sweet and syrupy, with stewed fruit and a fair amount of wood. Aromas of cola and root beer lead into a thick palate that's sugary in the middle and tangy on the edges. **83** —*M.S. (9/1/2004)*

EL COPERO

El Copero 2004 Tinto Bobal (Valencia) $6. Simple and fruity, with red-cherry and candied aromas. The palate offers pie cherry and raspberry with a streak of acidity running through the center. Finishes light and zesty. Not much to it, but not bad. **83** —*M.S. (8/1/2005)*

El Copero 2001 Vino Rosado Rosé Blend (Valencia) $7. It's the coppery color of a French rosé, but tastes nothing like it. This Bobal-Monastrell blend is just this side of cloying, with leathery aromas and flavors reining the sweet peach fruit in before it crosses the line into Candyland. A simple quaff; a good bridge to wine, perhaps, for wine cooler drinkers. 30,000 cases produced. **82** —*D.T. (4/1/2003)*

El Copero 2001 White Blend (Valencia) $7. Yellow fruit and mineral flavors in the mouth; more of the same, plus some mustard and petrol notes on the nose. Are the flavors light and delicate, or is there just not much here? **82** —*D.T. (4/1/2003)*

El Copero 2004 Blanco White Blend (Valencia) $6. Crisp and tight, with a slate-based nose that offers citrus and melon. Quite zesty and clean on the palate, with citrus-driven flavors of tangerine and pineapple.

Compelling and precise; full, lengthy, and tasty. **88 Best Buy** —*M.S. (8/1/2005)*

EL COTO

El Coto 2004 Rosé Blend (Rioja) $12. Typical Garnacha-Tempranillo rosado, with fresh berry aromas and bright peach, nectarine, and apple flavors. More lean and streamlined than bulky, so you won't find much in the way of red-fruit character. Clean, persistent, and fresh. **87 Best Buy** —*M.S. (11/1/2006)*

El Coto 2001 Rosado Rosé Blend (Rioja) $9. A very light, almost orange-colored blend of Garnacha and Tempranillo. The palate is dry, mildly peachy, and short. A clean finish that's fresh but simple closes the show. Possibly this was more tasty a year ago. **82** —*M.S. (10/1/2003)*

El Coto 1995 Coto de Imaz Gran Reserva Tempranillo (Rioja) $38. Seductive and classy aromas of sandalwood, cola, spice, licorice, and leather amount to pretty much everything you could ask for. Ripe and complex in terms of its earth and tree-fruit flavors. Finishes svelte and sturdy, but with ample vanilla, toffee, and tobacco nuances. Classic gran reserva. **91** —*M.S. (4/1/2006)*

El Coto 1994 Coto de Imaz Gran Reserva Tempranillo (Rioja) $30. Though stewed fruit and herb aromas on the nose are rather expressive, the palate flavors are much harder to read. Vague bits of cherry and smoke pop up in the midpalate, with some hard cheese on the finish. It would have fared better had its pleasing components sung a little more loudly. **85** —*D.T. (4/1/2003)*

El Coto 2000 Coto de Imaz Reserva Tempranillo (Rioja) $21. This wine kind of misses the mark. The nose is a bit stewy and less than pure, while the palate seems tight, grabby, and herbal. At times it seems like it's almost where it should be, but then you find weaknesses. **84** —*M.S. (11/1/2006)*

El Coto 1999 Coto de Imaz Reserva Tempranillo (Rioja) $21. Brick colored, with an earthy, gritty nose that deals leather, rhubarb, and burnt fruit. The flavor package is reserved and citrusy, what some might call dilute. But it's classic old-school Rioja. Finishes light, with tea and toast. **88** —*M.S. (11/1/2006)*

El Coto 1997 Coto de Imaz Reserva Tempranillo (Rioja) $18. Aged in American oak, this Tempranillo has a round, medium body that isn't weighed down by overpowering oak or tannins. Red fruit and earth flavors dominate, with flavors concentrated in the midpalate. Fruit stays on through the long, juicy finish. Approachable now, but probably best after a few years in the cellar. **88** —*D.T. (4/1/2003)*

El Coto 1997 Coto Real Reserva Tempranillo (Rioja) $45. Bright, expressive, fleshy—all words that came up again and again describing this wine's fruit, from nose to finish. The core is mostly blackberry, with mixed plums and a dash of oak; it's medium-full, mouthfilling but not huge. Finishes with some chewy tannins, and an almost beefy flavor. Perhaps too big to fully appreciate now; best drunk from 2005. **90** —*D.T. (4/1/2003)*

El Coto 2000 Crianza Tempranillo (Rioja) $12. An easy and simple display of Rioja in fresh form. The nose is all berry fruit, quite lucid, and easygoing. On the palate, there's a smooth interplay of red fruit and light oak, and that brightness carries onto the lean, clean finish. **87 Best Buy** —*M.S. (10/1/2003)*

El Coto 1999 Crianza Tempranillo (Rioja) $12. This 100% Tempranillo has good structure and a medium body, but its slightly sour red-fruit core isn't anything to get excited about. Thanks to American oak, seeped tea, woodsy tannins, and peanut shell notes play key roles here. **85** —*D.T. (4/1/2003)*

El Coto 1998 Crianza Tempranillo (Rioja) $12. Smoky oak and dark cherry fruit with herb accents complement each other well in this medium-weight, even red. Leathery hints add complexity, and this tasty, straightforward Rioja never get harsh or astringent. Drink now–2004. **85** —*M.M. (9/1/2002)*

El Coto 2000 Coto Real Reserva Tempranillo Blend (Rioja) $48. There's no shortage of barrel-driven hickory, coffee, and chocolate on this modern-style Rioja, but there's also a spike of green on the nose and at the core of the flavor profile. Surrounding that is bright blackberry, amplified

SPAIN

tannins and bursting acidity. Needs air upon opening—that, or more time in the cellar. **89** —*M.S. (11/1/2006)*

El Coto 1998 Coto Real Reserva Tempranillo Blend (Rioja) $42. Leathery and smoky, with woodsy aromas as well as the essence of dried red fruits. Like many classic Riojas, it's a touch racy and acidic, but that zest pushes the cherry, cranberry, and raspberry fruit toward an even finish. As a whole it's snappy, with a solid core. **88** —*M.S. (6/1/2005)*

El Coto 2005 Rosado Tempranillo Blend (Rioja) $12. Salmon in color, with creamsicle aromas leading to cantaloupe and peach flavors. Runs juicy on the palate, with lean fruit, perky acids and a bitter-almond finish. Slight of frame and less than generous, but stable. A blend of Garnacha and Tempranillo. **84** —*M.S. (11/1/2006)*

El Coto 2005 Blanco Viura (Rioja) $11. Mild butterscotch aromas blend with sweeter fruit-cocktail notes, while the flavors run tangy and short, with an emphasis on lemon and green apple. Dry and lean late, with ample snap and freshness. Simple. **83** —*M.S. (11/1/2006)*

El Coto 2004 Blanco Viura (Rioja) $12. Heavy and waxy, and not all that likable. Weighs in as a dull, acidic white with a boring, sour disposition. **80** —*M.S. (11/1/2006)*

El Coto 2001 Blanco Viura (Rioja) $9. Eggy and chunky at first, with soda-like grapefruit and green pepper flavors. With time, it shows clear citrus flavors and a good mouthfeel. **84** —*M.S. (10/1/2003)*

EL PUNTIDO

El Puntido 2001 Tempranillo (Rioja) $51. Textbook alta expresión wine, with great color and a meaty, extracted ultra rich nose that oozes sandalwood, bacon, and a rush of black fruit. In a word, it's chewy. Saturated and fleshy, with all the chocolate, caramel, and prime plum and black cherry flavors possible. Almost syrupy but not; like a strong-armed buddy. **94 Editors' Choice** —*M.S. (8/1/2005)*

EL VINCULO

El Vinculo 1999 Red Blend (La Mancha) $21. The nose is unusual, offering soil, eucalyptus, and barbecue marinade aromas. Ripe red fruit is front-loaded on the palate, with the midpalate and finish showing more oak accents than fruit. Chalky tannins add texture to the otherwise light-weight mouthfeel. **85** —*D.T. (4/1/2003)*

El Vinculo 2002 Tempranillo (La Mancha) $25. Fairly deep and saturated, at least to the eye. It's a dark, soft wine with leather, earth, and blueberry aromas. The palate is alive and balanced, with black cherry and plum flavors. Not overpowering at any point, with coffee and chocolate on the finish. **87** —*M.S. (8/1/2005)*

El Vinculo 2000 Crianza Tempranillo (La Mancha) $27. Aromas of charred beef, pepper, and raspberry start it off before giving way to a questionable grassiness. Flavors of blackberry, plum, and cassis carry the forward palate, which is nothing if not power-packed and forward. Ripe tannins are highly evident but they don't pound away. **87** —*M.S. (3/1/2004)*

El Vinculo 2001 Reserva Tempranillo (La Mancha) $40. Solid and spicy, with full cherry and berry aromas that get woodier with time. Snappy red fruit carries the medium-weight palate, while it finishes tight, structured and with noticeable vanilla and chocolate. A free-flowing wine that is at its best right now. **88** —*M.S. (8/1/2005)*

El Vinculo 1999 Reserva Tempranillo (La Mancha) $19. This is a new wine made by Alejandro Fernandez of Pesquera in Ribera del Duero. It's clear, defined, and ripe, with earthy, spicy undercurrents supporting potent blackberry fruit. The chewy, deep palate is solid and saturated, leading into a coffee-tinged finish that carries echoes of chocolate. The tannins get larger with each passing minute; drink this with food. **88** —*M.S. (3/1/2004)*

ELIAS MORA

Elias Mora 2003 Tinta de Toro (Toro) $22. Big and bulky, with balsmic aromas mixed in with notes of blueberry and boysenberry. Quite extracted and meaty, which is in the Toro mode. Black plum and cassis flavors are decent, while the finish is stocky and short, with chocolate. Not refined but definitely bold. **84** —*M.S. (2/1/2006)*

Elias Mora 2001 Crianza Tinta de Toro (Toro) $30. From the talented Dos Victorías team, this is a bold Toro. Dark cherry is the fruit on the

woodsy nose, while the palate is juicing with cherry, raspberry, and plum. Lots of oak throughout; a palate coater that's still pretty tannic. Can hold for several years. **90** —*M.S. (2/1/2006)*

EMILIO MORO

Emilio Moro 1998 Crianza Tempranillo (Ribera del Duero) $24. Extremely supple and creamy, with waves of black-cherry and vanilla flavors that gently caress the palate. Earthy dark chocolate and ample cedar shadings complete the package. A great effort given the challenging vintage; should drink well now and for the next half-dozen years. **91 Editors' Choice** —*J.C. (11/1/2001)*

Emilio Moro 1997 Crianza Tempranillo (Ribera del Duero) $25. **89** —*M.M. (8/1/2000)*

Emilio Moro 1998 Malleolus Tempranillo (Ribera del Duero) $40. Starts off very cedary, showing lots of toast and vanilla—also a hint of grilled meats. Explodes on the palate with bright red cherries, powering through chocolate notes onto the sweetly tannic finish. This is the first vintage for Moro's luxury cuvée aged in French oak; barrel samples of the 1999 and 2000 vintages were even more impressive. **91** —*J.C. (11/1/2001)*

Emilio Moro 2000 Crianza Tinto del Pais (Ribera del Duero) $28. Chunky and ripe, with natural leather and barnyard notes along with a bit of surface-sitting oak. The palate is jacked up and exciting, with deep black fruit, firm tannins, and plenty of length. The finish is long and wide, with a burnt flavor note. Big-time verve and kick should maintain its following. **89** —*M.S. (3/1/2004)*

Emilio Moro 1999 Malleolus Tinto del Pais (Ribera del Duero) $40. Polished, with aromas of sweet leather and pure red fruit. The palate features bright berry and cherry, while the large finish is oaky but not overdone or tannic. It's smooth as silk with just a hint of lemony French oak. Very modern in style. Drink now. **91** —*M.S. (3/1/2004)*

Emilio Moro 2002 Malleolus de Valderramiro Tinto del Pais (Ribera del Duero) $166. Undoubtedly powerful, but lovable. The nose is wholesome and complete, a blend of earth, coffee, and heavy black cherry and plum aromas. Broad on the palate, with deep levels of dark fruit mixed with copious French oak. A big-time success in '02, and proof that good wines can come from marginal vintages. **92** —*M.S. (6/1/2005)*

EMILIO ROJO

Emilio Rojo 2001 White Blend (Ribeiro) $35. This wine from Galicia blends together four different grapes, and the mix isn't exactly a bona fide hit. The aromas come across as being slightly artificial. Applesauce flavors come next, followed by a finish that's acidic but still like flat seltzer. This wine lacks freshness despite its youth. **82** —*M.S. (11/1/2002)*

Emilio Rojo 2005 Blanco White Blend (Ribeiro) $40. This five-grape blend is based on Treixadura but also includes Albariño, Loureira, Lado, and Torrontès. The grapes were picked well into October, so the richness and alcohol are up there. Still, the flowery aromas are alluring and the flavors of mango, pear, and apple are clean despite some oak aging. Only 50 cases imported into the States. **92** —*M.S. (9/1/2006)*

Emilio Rojo 2003 Blanco White Blend (Ribeiro) $35. A blend of four white grapes, including Albariño; this is an unconventional wine made in small quantities. Starts with cinnamon and anise aromas that morph toward curry. Plenty of full-bodied spiced pear and banana flavors in the center. Unlike most everything else; could even be better in a cooler vintage like the upcoming 2004. **89** —*M.S. (6/1/2005)*

EMINA

Emina 2003 12 Meses en Barrica Tinto del Pais (Ribera del Duero) $17. The chunky fruit aromas are like chewing gum, while the palate is punchy and drying, with tannic black cherry and cranberry flavors. Sheer on the finish and slightly astringent, but serious for a big-production wine. **84** —*M.S. (11/1/2006)*

Emina 2003 Atio Tinto del Pais (Ribera del Duero) $44. Full and raring to go. This is one lively, big-boned red. It spreads out on the bouquet in peppery, boisterous fashion before unveiling lively raspberry and other red fruits on a bulky, tannic palate. Fairly big and untamed; a year or two more time might soften it up. **87** —*M.S. (11/1/2006)*

Emina 2003 Prestigio Tinto del Pais (Ribera del Duero) $26. Plum, berry, and other ripe fruits make for a solid, pure, attractive bouquet. The wine is fairly deep and plummy, with red raspberry raising the red-fruit quotient. Full and balanced, with modest complexity. Seems solid for a front-line '03. **88** —M.S. (11/1/2006)

ENATE

Enate 2000 Reserva Cabernet Sauvignon-Merlot (Somontano) $NA. Sweet and candied on the nose, which draws you in. Runs ,a touch chunky, with plum and licorice flavors. Good acidity creates a racy mouthfeel, even teetering on fiery. Tight on the finish, but crisp and fresh. The blend is 80% Cabernet and the rest Merlot. **88** —M.S. (6/1/2005)

Enate 2002 Fermentado en Barrica de Roble Chardonnay (Somontano) $NA. Rich and creamy, but lacks zest and drive. The nose and palate offer sweet banana and oak, while the feel is almost too pillowy. Tastes more like a dessert than a dry white should. Still, it's neither bad nor poorly made. **85** —M.S. (6/1/2005)

ENRIQUE MENDOZA

Enrique Mendoza 2003 Moscatel de la Marina Moscatel (Alicante) $NA. A nosing reveals just about everything but the kitchen sink. There's peanut butter, honey, mango, and banana, and then later more elaborate sweet fruits rise up on the palate. Maybe too simple to be great, but very good and likable. **89** —M.S. (6/1/2005)

Enrique Mendoza 2000 Reserva Santa Rosa Red Blend (Alicante) $35. Dark and intense is this Cabernet-Merlot-Syrah blend. The nose offers smoky leather and hot earth, but also a sweet perfume dominated by violets. Quite drinkable now, with soft tannins and easygoing black fruit. Best to get this one over the next year or two, before the fruit fades. **90** —M.S. (6/1/2005)

EOLO

Eolo 2000 Crianza Tempranillo Blend (Navarra) $13. Sometimes you come across an unfamiliar label and it strikes a chord. This wine blends several grapes with finesse and reserve. There's some cedar and toast aromas that lead to raspberry, cherry, and coffee flavors. Shows classic acidity, dryness, and balance. **89 Best Buy** —M.S. (9/1/2006)

ERMITA VERACRUZ

Ermita Veracruz 2004 Verdejo (Rueda) $16. Shows ample apple, pineapple, and apricot on the nose, and follows with sweet melon, lime, and other tropical fruit flavors. Pretty good in the mouth, as it's just sharp and balanced enough to make the grade. Fairly ripe and zesty as a whole. **85** —M.S. (9/1/2006)

ESPERANZA

Esperanza 2003 Sauvignon Blanc (Rueda) $10. The word esperanza means "hope" in Spanish, but there's almost no hope for this sharp-nosed S.B. that has little besides oversized banana and pickle flavors to offer. Barely acceptable. **80** —M.S. (3/1/2005)

Esperanza 2003 Verdejo (Rueda) $10. A bit fuller than the Verdejo-Viura blend but every bit as functional and satisfying. Melon, pineapple, and passion fruit aromas are full rather than crisp, while the grapefruit and orange flavors sizzle. More than decent length, structure and finish. **87** —M.S. (12/31/2004)

Esperanza 2003 Verdejo-Viura White Blend (Rueda) $9. Intriguing and nice, with pungent yet typical aromas of citrus, nettles, and wildflower. Citrus, chalk, and mineral character on the palate is exactly as expected, while the finish is quite long and stays the course. An enjoyable white wine. **87** —M.S. (12/31/2004)

ESSENCIA VENDIMIA

Essencia Vendima 2005 Albariño (Rías Baixas) $16. Fairly agile, floral, and friendly, with precise peach, nectarine, and citrus flavors. With its easy personality and good mouthfeel, this is what you're looking for in a solid, everyday white wine. **88** —M.S. (12/15/2006)

ESTOLA

Estola 1991 Gran Reserva Red Blend (La Mancha) $16. Like any aged gran reserva worth its weight, this wine has tomato and vanilla aromas and some oxidization. But it remains largely fresh despite its maturity. Lean strawberry flavors grace the silky palate, which is trailed by a smooth and airy finish. The intensity has faded, but given the fact that it's 10+ years old, that should be expected. **86** —M.S. (11/1/2002)

Estola 1997 Reserva 1997 Tempranillo (La Mancha) $8. With lean, leathery aromas, this wine seems like it has been stretched to its maximum. The generic raspberry fruit is clean, but fails to offer any excitement. The finish is dull and dry, but ultimately it's also clean and smooth. There is nothing really off in this wine, but by the same token there's nothing to hang your hat on, either. **83** —M.S. (11/1/2002)

FAUSTINO

Faustino 1994 Faustino de Autor Reserva Tempranillo (Rioja) $50. A lean, structured wine of great elegance and finesse. Begins with aromas of leather and vanilla, folding hints of plum, coffee, earth, and pepper. Tarter and redder on the finish, with cranberry and herb notes lingering delicately. Substantially better than a bottle reviewed in the March issue. **91** (5/1/2004)

Faustino 2000 Faustino de Crianza Tempranillo (Rioja) $13. Starts with smoky campfire aromas that soon give way to dried cherry and berry accented by coffee. Mature and ready to go, with simple acid-driven raspberry and cherry. Come the finish, the core is solid while the edges are light. **87** —M.S. (10/1/2005)

Faustino 1999 Faustino de Crianza Tempranillo (Rioja) $12. There's much to dig into here; poised berry fruit dominates the palate, with some plum and raspberry flavors present. Vanilla and chocolate notes grace the finish, which is lasting and sturdy. **86** —M.S. (3/1/2004)

Faustino 1998 Faustino de Crianza Tempranillo (Rioja) $10. Shows a fair amount of American oak on the nose, with charred aromas as well as scents of dill, caramel, and vanilla. Fruit is lean and red—reminiscent of sour cherries and cranberries. Light and supple, with a tart finish. **85** (5/1/2004)

Faustino 1999 Faustino V Reserva Tempranillo (Rioja) $19. Rusting in color, but showing some of the positive signs of maturing Rioja. For instance, the bouquet provides spiced raisin, dried plum, and cinnamon, and together the nose is as old-fashioned as it comes. Dried cherry and apricot flavors mix with pepper and tobacco on the palate, while the finish is warm and accented by vanilla. **87** —M.S. (10/1/2005)

Faustino 1995 Gran Reserva Tempranillo (Rioja) $36. Medium-weight and plump in the mouth, with mature aromas and flavors of tobacco, coffee, vanilla, and cherry. Picks up hints of anise on the long finish. Drink now. **89** (5/1/2004)

Faustino 2003 Faustino VII Tempranillo Blend (Rioja) $11. A bit leafy and smoky, with snappy red fruit and basic spice notes. Very simple and traditional, with firm acidity. Will cut through most foods like a hot knife through butter, and it's fresh. **84** —M.S. (10/1/2005)

Faustino 1997 Crianza Tempranillo Blend (Rioja) $15. Toasty oak and tobacco shadings are wrapped around the dark-cherry fruit core of this 100% Tempranillo wine. The full and supple palate shows good depth of fruit, leather, and spice accents. This handsome modern-style Rioja finishes long and tangy, with moderate tannins. **88** (5/1/2001)

Faustino 1995 Faustino de Autor Reserva Especial Tempranillo (Rioja) $50. Mature but not even close to expiring, with cola, root beer, tree bark, and leather on the bouquet. Fairly acidic, which is why it has so much verve at 10+ years. Flavors of dried cherry, raspberry and citrus peel are classic in their attack. Very good in an Old World way. **88** —M.S. (4/1/2006)

Faustino1994 Faustino I Rioja Gran Reserva Tempranillo (Rioja) $26. Deep, sweet dark-cherry fruit forms a solid foundation for this impressive wine. There's a touch of menthol oak on the nose; plenty of leather and earth accents in the mouth, coupled with good acidity, keep the palate complex and lively. Finishes long, with full—but not harsh—tannins. Editors' Choice. **92 Editors' Choice** (5/1/2001)

Faustino 1982 Faustino I Rioja Gran Reserva Tempranillo (Rioja) $72. Sweet cherry and dried-rose notes on the nose are offset by some noticeable barnyardy scents. Elegant, but less generous on the palate and decidedly drier than the much older 1970, this finishes with dry tannins. **89** (5/1/2001)

SPAIN

Faustino 1970 Faustino I Rioja Gran Reserva Tempranillo (Rioja) $125. Beautifully balanced, this shows all the positive attributes of mature Rioja. Though 30 years old, it is still very alive, with deep sweet fruit that wears tobacco and meat accents. Anise accents the ultrasmooth palate. Full of complex flavors, with a lingering finish. **92** *(5/1/2001)*

Faustino 1964 Faustino I Rioja Gran Reserva Tempranillo (Rioja) $185. With its dried-cherry and rose-petal aromas and flavors, this beautiful, mature red is every bit the equivalent of a fine, older Bordeaux or Burgundy. Cumin and cinnamon show on the palate and the refined finish is lovely, with anise and white pepper accents. **94** *(5/1/2001)*

Faustino 1999 Faustino V Rosado Rosé Blend (Rioja) $12. This Rioja rosé displays a full bouquet of rose petal, spice, and the slightly meaty element that Tempranillo so often shows. No White Zinfandel, this is a fairly lean and dry wine with spicy notes, a decent match for hors d'oeuvres or light meals. **84** *(5/1/2001)*

Faustino 1998 Faustino V Reserva Tempranillo (Rioja) $18. Straightforward vanilla and cherry flavors are joined by hints of tobacco and earth. The simple flavors thin out a little on the tart, lingering finish. **86** *(5/1/2004)*

Faustino 1995 Faustino V Rioja Riserva Tempranillo (Rioja) $17. This is classic Rioja Reserva, with textbook cherry, earth, leather, and meaty Tempranillo flavors supported by a good acid spine and moderate tannins. The elegant finish is dry and spicy. **89** *(5/1/2001)*

Faustino 2002 Faustino V Rosé Tempranillo (Rioja) $9. Very red in color, and leafy. The palate is hefty but devoid of specific flavors. You get some red berry notes, but that's it. The finish is heavy and fades away bitter. Could use more pep and elegance. **83** *—M.S. (3/1/2004)*

Faustino 2003 Faustino V Blanco Seco Viura (Rioja) $10. Dry and clean, with apple and tarragon on the nose. The palate deals crisp green apple and nectarine, with a hint of butterscotch and corn. Finishes crisp and generally fresh, with touches of butter and citrus rind. **85 Best Buy** *—M.S. (11/15/2005)*

Faustino 2002 Faustino V Blanco Seco White Blend (Rioja) $8. Pear aromas come in front of melon and peach flavors. The feel is a bit hot and racy, but the taste profile is fruity. Lots of raw zest here, but not as refined as one might want. **85** *—M.S. (3/1/2004)*

Faustino 2000 Faustino VII Tempranillo (Rioja) $10. Spicy and lean, with light pickled notes. In the mouth, however, it's got pure fruit and adequate spice. It's on the basic side, but the mouthfeel is good and it tastes fresh and lively. **86** *—M.S. (3/1/2004)*

Faustino 1998 Faustino VII Tempranillo (Rioja) $12. Dried cherry and spice aromas and flavors accented by peppery, meaty notes mark this jóven (young wine). A blend of 80% Tempranillo and 20% Mazuela, it has a light, even mouthfeel. The acids are tangy, and a little prickly now, and the bright finish shows spicy elements. **86** *(5/1/2001)*

FELIX CALLEJO

Felix Callejo 2002 Selección de Vinedos de la Familia Tempranillo (Ribera del Duero) $108. The bouquet starts out with promising whiffs of molasses, bacon, and black fruit but it loses form quickly, resulting in aromas of menthol and funky beet. In the mouth, it's ultrasweet and candied, and the tannins are jackhammer hard. **84** *—M.S. (11/15/2005)*

FELIX SOLIS

Felix Solis 2001 Los Molinos Airen (Valdepeñas) $6. Though medium-bodied, this wine is a serious lightweight in terms of flavor. If you're looking for an essence of melon water with a lemon garnish to keep you cool, look no further. If it's a complex wine you want, probably best to keep looking. **81** *—D.T. (4/1/2003)*

Felix Solis 2001 Los Molinos Tempranillo (Valdepeñas) $7. The nose is chunky and meaty, but also kind of confusing; it doesn't really lead you anywhere. The palate is intense, even if it's mildly sweet and a tad sugary. This wine is definitely one dimensional, but it has proper weight to it and a rich mouthfeel. **85 Best Buy** *—M.S. (11/1/2002)*

Felix Solis 1995 Vina Albali Gran Reserva Tempranillo (Valdepeñas) $14. The nose has earth and chocolate aromas, but mostly it's about oak—big, driving oak. That same heavy woodiness lays across the palate,

effectively masking any fruit that might lie below. And the finish is pure butter, vanilla, and menthol. Simply put: too much oak for the fruit. **84** *—M.S. (11/1/2002)*

Felix Solis 1998 Vina Albali Los Molinos Crianza Tempranillo (Valdepeñas) $9. The nose is light and airy, offering a simple set of aromas with just a modicum of red fruit. Cherry and red raspberry flavors lead into a tangy, low-voltage finish. There isn't much to gripe about here, but in the same breath there isn't much to compliment, either. **82** *—M.S. (11/1/2002)*

FIGUERO

Figuero 2001 Vendimia Seleccionada Tempranillo (Ribera del Duero) $60. Warm and rich, with rooty aromas of sarsaparilla and charred beef. The bouquet works as a welcome mat, bringing you into the deep, sassy palate, which features bold black fruit and enough smoky leather to do the trick. Smooth and fine; just a tad short of excellent. **89** *—M.S. (8/1/2005)*

FILLABOA

Fillaboa 2002 Finca Monte Alto Albariño (Rías Baixas) $27. Floral and mildly leesy, with pungent aromas of green apple, citrus, and honey. For anyone looking for steely, pure Albariño, the single-vineyard Fillaboa Monte Alto is the ticket. The fruit is crisp and zesty, the acidity just right. And the finish runs a mile long. **91 Editors' Choice** *—M.S. (6/1/2005)*

FINCA ALLENDE

Finca Allende 2001 Tempranillo (Rioja) $24. Full, rich, robust, and probably the best regular Rioja bottling yet from this vanguard producer. The '01 vintage could prove to be a benchmark year for the region, so grab up moderately priced, easy-drinking bottles like this. The berry fruit is lush yet short of syrupy, while the oak is big and forward, yet still largely integrated and appropriate. Tons of mocha and coffee on the finish is a treat. **91** *—M.S. (9/1/2004)*

Finca Allende 2001 Aurus Tempranillo (Rioja) $184. Miguel Angel de Gregorio makes wines that match his exuberant personality, and Aurus, with 85% old-vine Tempranillo and 15% Graciano, is his premier offering. The 2001's exotic nose pumps licorice, clove, nutmeg, and vanilla on top of the ripest black-fruit aromas going. With pillowy tannins, unmatched breadth, and huge flavors of blackberry, plum, and chocolate, there's no denying this wine's quality and stature. **96 Editors' Choice** *—M.S. (6/1/2005)*

Finca Allende 2000 Aurus Tempranillo Blend (Rioja) $25. A precursor to the unbelievable 2001 that's to come, this is still a beauty of a wine. Aromas of raisin, mint, and meaty black fruit create a bouquet that's nearly over the top. Not flabby; vibrant acids keep it poised and upright. A true vineyard wine in that it tastes natural despite having been vishly oaked for two full years in new French barrels. **92** *—M.S. (9/1/2004)*

Finca Allende 2001 Calvario Tempranillo Blend (Rioja) $88. Yet another portly, gorgeous wine from Allende, one that well serves the single-vineyard train of thought. Entirely international in style, with pure plum, blackberry, and vanilla aromas and flavors. Super concentrated and unctuous, with soft tannins and an all-out finish. And the acidity is as integrated and proper as possible. **94 Editors' Choice** *—M.S. (6/1/2005)*

FINCA ANTIGUA

Finca Antigua 2004 Merlot (La Mancha) $10. Fairly big and muscular, with black fruit, cinnamon, and olive notes on the nose. The palate is beefy and deep, with plum and blackberry flavors. With big tannins and a full-bodied personality, this is not a lightweight. **85 Best Buy** *—M.S. (12/15/2006)*

Finca Antigua 2003 Crianza Red Blend (La Mancha) $12. Warm and earthy, with a round, ripe nose. The palate is a touch on the sweet, cooked side, but it avoids being stewy or soupy and instead shows ripe black fruit, licorice, and smoked meat. Quite soft and low in acid. Drink right away. **85** *—M.S. (12/15/2006)*

Finca Antigua 2001 Crianza Red Blend (La Mancha) $10. Not too refined, but still pretty tasty. The palate offers chewy cherry and raspberry fruit, while the finish is spicy and zesty to the point that it creates a tingle.

Somewhat sugary, but definitely an easy one to drink. **84** —M.S. (6/1/2005)

Finca Antigua 2002 Reserva Red Blend (La Mancha) $15. For the most part this is a full-bodied, full-fruited wine that has what it takes to win people over. The nose is full of cherry, plum, licorice, and coconut, while the palate is bright and ripe. It's a bit clumsy and not all that complex, but you can't knock the power and extract. **85** —M.S. (12/15/2006)

Finca Antigua 2001 Reserva Red Blend (La Mancha) $15. Quite international in style, a direct reflection of the Merlot, Cabernet Sauvignon, and Syrah components that comprise the wine. That said, this is probably the best wine Martinez Bujanda has made at its La Mancha winery; it's plump and ripe, with nice cherry and plum flavors. It's medium in weight and length, and juicy. Likable as can be. **88** —M.S. (4/1/2006)

Finca Antigua 2003 Syrah (La Mancha) $10. Earthy and raw, with plum, berry and raisin aromas. Brighter on the palate, where black cherry is darkened up by coffee and chocolate accents. Modern in size, with a one-note personality. **83** —M.S. (11/15/2005)

Finca Antigua 2003 Tempranillo (La Mancha) $10. Good size but struggles a bit. The nose is a touch green and murky, but below the surface there's solid raspberry and plum fruit. Shows some oak and barnyard throughout, and runs fairly smooth through the finish. **83** —M.S. (11/15/2005)

Finca Antigua 2002 Tempranillo (La Mancha) $10. Not a bad little quaffer. From Martinez-Bujanda, this colorful, ripe red is solid and chunky, with sweet aromas of berries and black plum. It is what you would call straightforward, with little to no complexity but lots of girth. Finishes full, almost creamy. **85 Best Buy** —M.S. (6/1/2005)

Finca Antigua 2002 Clavis Tempranillo Blend (La Mancha) $95. It's never fun to come down heavily on a high-priced wine, but the Clavis is just too weedy and disjointed to rate any higher. It's wild, uncontrolled, and not that well balanced given the price tag. The mouthfeel is hard as a rock and it lacks harmony. Case closed! **82** —M.S. (4/1/2006)

Finca Antigua 2005 Viura (La Mancha) $10. Open on the bouquet, with a pleasant spiciness. The flavors veer toward tangy nectarine and apricot, while the snappy finish is long and slightly bitter. Shows good citrus character and plenty of pop. Quite good for a white from central Spain. **86 Best Buy** —M.S. (12/15/2006)

FINCA EL ENCINAL

Finca El Encinal 1999 Reserva Tempranillo (Ribera del Duero) $32. Light in color; almost transparent. The nose is largely as the color suggests: light and leathery, with old-school character. Leafy red fruit dominates the palate, which is dry and controlled by crisp acidity, tannin, and spice. **84** —M.S. (11/1/2006)

Finca El Encinal 2003 Roble Tempranillo (Ribera del Duero) $10. Rubbery yet light-bodied, with distant berry and burnt-wood aromas. Seems dilute and more acidic than ideal, with crisp fruit flavors that run tart and zippy. More of a wake-you-up wine than something rich and plump. **83** —M.S. (11/1/2006)

FINCA LA ESTACADA

Finca La Estacada 2002 Oak Aged 12 Months Tempranillo (Vino de la Tierra de Castilla) $16. Piercing wood intersects with cherry aromas in front of a lean, scrappy palate that features short raspberry and cherry flavors. Quite tangy, zesty stuff with no off flavors but nothing to write home about, either. **82** —M.S. (11/1/2006)

Finca La Estacada 2004 Oak Aged 6 Months Tempranillo (Vino de la Tierra de Castilla) $13. Tomato and rhubarb are present on the earthy nose, which isn't very fruity but does set the stage for solid raspberry and cherry flavors. Medium to light in weight, with a slight barnyardy, herbal quality to the finish. **83** —M.S. (11/1/2006)

Finca La Estacada 2003 Oak Aged 6 Months Tempranillo (Vino de la Tierra de Castilla) $13. Smells like cherries and fruit punch. The palate is snappy and simple, with red fruit front and center. Shows a tiny bit of wood on the finish, but overall it's a tart, lean wine that grabs at the palate. **83** —M.S. (12/15/2006)

FINCA LUZÓN

Finca Luzón 2002 Merlot (Jumilla) $8. For several years we've been impressed with this under-$10 Merlot, and this year the quality and purity are once again exemplary. Aromas of smoke, mineral, and sweet leather set the stage for amplified cherry, raspberry, plum, and chocolate flavors. A medium-bodied but healthy and spicy finish secures the final favorable votes. **88 Best Buy** —M.S. (3/1/2004)

Finca Luzón 2001 Merlot (Jumilla) $8. This blows away the majority of California Merlots retailing for two or three times as much. Dried herbs accent creamy mocha and black cherries in a supple, harmonious whole that's as true to the variety as can be. The 2001 vintage is shaping up as a great one for Spain, and here's a chance to get in on the ground floor. **87 Best Buy** —J.C. (11/15/2002)

Finca Luzón 2000 Merlot (Jumilla) $10. This Merlot is quite dark, with plentiful black plum, anise, and toasty oak aromas and flavors. Medium-weight and nicely balanced, it's smooth and jammy, yet avoids the sweet or candied quality of so many warm-climate wines. Displays a touch of class for an easy drinker, finishing with decent length and a faint earth-mineral note. Best now through 2004. **86** —M.M. (4/1/2002)

Finca Luzón 2001 Red Blend (Jumilla) $14. For several years we've been impressed with this under-$10 Merlot, and in this go around the quality and purity are shockingly good. Aromas of smoke, mineral, and sweet perfume set the stage for amplified cherry, raspberry, plum, and chocolate flavors. A medium-bodied but healthy and spicy finish secures the final favorable votes. **90 Best Buy** —M.S. (3/1/2004)

Finca Luzón 2002 Altos de Luzon Red Blend (Jumilla) $10. This wine comes in two waves. The first is youthful and aggressive; it carries maple and sawdust aromas, and tons of powerful plum, cassis and smoky oak. The next wave is textured and chocolaty, and a little bit dark. Overall, it might not ooze elegance, but it's certainly lively and big. The blend is Monastrell, Cabernet and Tempranillo. **89 Best Buy** —M.S. (3/1/2004)

FINCA MINATEDA

Finca Minateda 2000 Selección Pedro Sarrion Garnacha (Vino de la Tierra de Castilla) $18. Smoky and mildly leafy to start, with some dry, dusty aromas that lose punch with airing. Red fruit, spice, and leather appear on the palate, followed by a starchy finish with light tomato and cranberry notes. **85** —M.S. (10/1/2005)

Finca Minateda 2001 Tinto Roble Garnacha (Vino de la Tierra de Castilla) $13. Sweet and marinated at first, with a certain stewy richness. The palate is round and plump, with good berry and plum characteristics. Open-grained wood and vanilla notes dominate the finish. **85** —M.S. (10/1/2005)

FINCA SANDOVAL

Finca Sandoval 2002 Syrah (Tierra Manchuela) $39. Local wine critic Victor de la Serna is the man behind this Syrah from central Spain, and you have to admire its bright purple color and sweet plum and black-cherry flavor profile. Leaner in the middle than the downright gooey 2001, which means it's less jammy and more racy. With 7% Monastrell. **90** —M.S. (6/1/2005)

Finca Sandoval 2001 Syrah (Tierra Manchuela) $29. Violet in color, with a richness that's as visible as it is detectable in the mouth. Smoky, rubbery aromas dance around the boysenberry fruit that defines this warm-weather wine, which has 7% Mourvèdre in the blend. Flavors of berry syrup, chocolate cake, and Port are bolstered by ample acids and tannins. **90** —M.S. (3/1/2004)

FINCA ZUBASTÍA

Finca Zubastía 2003 ADA Cabernet Sauvignon-Merlot (Navarra) $10. Sweet, sour, and stewy is this Cabernet-Merlot-Garnacha-Tempranillo blend. On the nose is caramel and some light weediness. Raspberry and red plum carry the palate to a firm, tannic finish that tastes of coffee. **84** —M.S. (12/31/2004)

Finca Zubastía 2003 ADA Tempranillo Blend (Navarra) $10. Extracted and raw, but with enough rustic country charm to make it worth a go. Four major grapes were thrown together, yielding cherry, beet, and tomato aromas. The palate is ripe and edgy, with red plum and herb flavors.

A tight, basic wine with ample tannin and acid. **86 Best Buy** —*M.S. (6/1/2005)*

FLEUR DE NUIT

Fleur de Nuit NV Brut Sparkling Blend (Cava) $7. Pedestrian yet entirely solid, with nice citrus and apple flavors. A very easy wine to understand, with seltzer and grapefruit on the finish along with a slight twinge of mushroom. Good cava that will go down easy. **85 Best Buy** —*M.S. (12/15/2005)*

FLOURISH

Flourish 2002 Tempranillo (Rioja) $11. Leafy and lean, and muddy. The palate is fiery and generic, with sour flavors of red plum and cherry. Table wine on its best day. **81** —*M.S. (8/1/2005)*

FORTIUS

Fortius 1999 Tierra de Estella Merlot (Navarra) $12. Dried herbs, lots of spice, and some black raspberry carry the bouquet. Fruit is front and center; the palate is all cherry and black pepper, and the finish brings more red fruit and firm tannins. It's mostly a one-song act, meaning it's clean, spicy, and adequately fruity. **85** —*M.S. (8/1/2003)*

Fortius 1998 Tierra de Estella Tempranillo (Navarra) $12. From the Valcarlos winery, this Tempranillo has some berry aromas, earth, and a bit of grain on the nose. The flavor profile deals plum, cassis, and some green olive, while the finish is lean and toasty. The texture is nice, and, while it's not terribly packed with bold flavors or extract, it gets the job done and delivers a solid expression of the grape type and region. **86** —*M.S. (8/1/2003)*

FRA GUERAU

Fra Guerau 2002 Red Blend (Montsant) $12. This well-priced red from Tarragona shows a glimpse of what the Montsant region can produce. The nose is all red fruit, with a splinter of oak. The palate is chunky and easy as it deals blackberry and raspberry in spades. Chocolate and mocha on the thick finish should please the sugar mavens. **87 Best Buy** —*M.S. (6/1/2005)*

FRANCESC SANCHEZ BAS

Francesc Sanchez Bas 2002 Montgarnatx Garnacha (Priorat) $45. A bit transparent in color, but only by Priorat standards. The nose, however, offers all the crusty, earthy red fruit you'd expect; it leads nicely into a palate of sweet cherry, plum and vanilla. Big enough on the finish, with mouthfeel galore. The full package from the town of La Vilella Alta, and not too tannic. **88** —*M.S. (10/1/2005)*

Francesc Sanchez Bas 2001 Montgarnatx Garnacha (Priorat) $38. Open, round, and clean, with a lovely bouquet and an even better palate that offers strawberry, plum, and a full blast of creamy oak. Turns soft and friendly upon airing, and overall it provides complexity along with straightforward likeability. **91** —*M.S. (5/1/2004)*

Francesc Sanchez Bas 2001 Montsalvat Red Blend (Priorat) $72. Ethereal and sort of reminiscent of a fine Port, or maybe Banyuls. Pure and ripe on the nose, with licorice, violet, and wild blackberry aromas. This is a smooth-drinking wine that's showing some maturity; meaning the tannins are smooth and the acids not too pointed. A real mouthful, with a measure or two of depth. Finishes big. **91** —*M.S. (10/1/2005)*

Francesc Sanchez Bas 2000 Montsalvat Red Blend (Priorat) $60. A typically masculine Priorat red, one with beef jerky, leather, and reduced blackberry on the nose, and then a fully jazzed palate with lively berry fruit, chocolate, and mocha. It's not soft, but it remains round and lush, and the finish is warm and spunky. **92** —*M.S. (5/1/2004)*

Francesc Sanchez Bas 2002 Blanc de Montsalvat White Blend (Priorat) $32. A waxy, thick wine with extract but too much flatness to carry its own weight. The nose is jumbled, with mustard seed and dried fruit aromas. The palate is rich, almost creamy, with some peach and vanilla. Still, it falls short prior to the finish line. **84** —*M.S. (5/1/2004)*

FREIXENET

Freixenet NV Cordon Negro Brut Sparkling Blend (Cava) $10. Keeps the Cordon Negro reputation healthy by delivering easygoing lemon-lime aromas and round citrus and apple flavors. As correct as one can ask for, this large-production cava features pure-fruit character and a perfectly good mouthfeel. For the money, we give it the proverbial high-five. **88 Best Buy** —*M.S. (12/15/2006)*

Freixenet NV Brut de Noirs Sparkling Blend (Cava) $10. The color is an odd orange, which should come as an indicator that not all is right with this wine. The bouquet starts with dust on a warming radiator, and there's some vanilla as well. Soft citrus and nectarine flavors work the palate, followed by a round but somewhat mushy finish. **83** —*M.S. (12/15/2006)*

Freixenet 2000 Brut Nature Sparkling Blend (Cava) $14. Easygoing and balanced, with cream soda and vanilla aromas setting up orange, tangerine, and green apple flavors. Crisp and right on the palate, with flowing acidity. Solid, with a touch of green herbs. **88** —*M.S. (6/1/2006)*

Freixenet 1999 Brut Nature Sparkling Blend (Cava) $NA. Tart and sour, with unripe apple flavors joined by earth and saddle leather. **81** —*J.C. (1/1/2004)*

Freixenet NV Carta Nevada Brut Sparkling Blend (Cava) $9. Consistency at a good price is what this textbook cava is all about. The bouquet offers your basic fruit-cocktail aromas, while the palate is sort of plump as it pours on the nectarine and ripe peach flavors. Easygoing, with some weight and roundness. **87 Best Buy** —*M.S. (12/15/2006)*

Freixenet NV Carta Nevada Semi Dry Sparkling Blend (Cava) $9. Some early pickle and sauerkraut aromas were worrisome until they completely disappeared. Left in their wake are flavors of apple juice and peaches, while the mouthfeel registers as solid and full. A little funky and definitely not for everyone, given the wine's overt sweetness and oddities. **85 Best Buy** —*M.S. (12/15/2006)*

Freixenet NV Cordon Negro Extra Dry Sparkling Blend (Cava) $10. One of my personal favorites among the giant collection of Freixenet cavas is the extra dry, which isn't dry in the least. Just the opposite, it's loaded with sweet apple and apricot aromas along with peach, melon, and candied citrus flavors. Best of all, it maintains its poise while never falling toward cloying or sappy. **88 Best Buy** —*M.S. (12/15/2006)*

Freixenet 1999 Cuvée D.S. Brut Nature Sparkling Blend (Cava) $NA. Lots of yeast and lees at first, but still tight, with apple, peach, and melon flavors. Turns more toasty and yeasty as it opens, with a hint of dried herbs. A controlled buttery note makes for a fine final impression. One of Freixenet's best. **90** —*M.S. (6/1/2005)*

Freixenet NV Spumante Sparkling Blend (Cava) $10. Very round and candied, with a ton of vanilla on the nose. It's made in the supersweet style, as if it's supposed to go with wedding cake or caramel bon bons. Yet there's enough balance to keep it on an even keel, which should make it perfect for those raised on candy-sweet wines and their kin. Certainly not to everyone's liking but not a poorly made wine by any means. **86** —*M.S. (12/15/2006)*

Freixenet NV XXI Brut Sparkling Blend (Cava) $25. Not a complete swing and a miss, but nothing special despite the miniscule production and higher-than-normal price. The color is pale and the nose has some gaps. In the mouth, you get dry soda crackers and white-peach flavors. Finishes with lime and apple. No glaring faults but hollow. **85** —*M.S. (12/15/2006)*

FUENTE DEL CONDE

Fuente del Conde 2002 Rosado Rosé Blend (Cigales) $9. Minty-fresh, with aromatic hints of herbs, peach, and bread dough. With a round palate propped up by citrus, berry flavors, and modest acidity, this wine delivers the goods—but only for the short term. Drink this Tempranillo-based rosé now. **86 Best Buy** —*M.S. (3/1/2004)*

Fuente del Conde 2004 Rosado Tempranillo (Cigales) $10. Murky, with barnyard aromas. Bland but sour flavors. Not awful but not that appealing. **80** —*M.S. (8/1/2005)*

FUENTES

Fuentes 2000 Gran Clos de J.M. Fuentes Red Blend (Priorat) $50. A massive wine with lovely black fruit wrapped is a veneer of classy charred oak. A bomber but a precision one. The plum and blackberry fruit is vital and forceful, while the finish is big, aggressive, supremely built, and long lasting. The epitome of brickyard Priorat, so give it a year or two before opening. **93 Editors' Choice** —*M.S. (3/1/2004)*

GAGO

Gago 1999 Red Blend (Toro) $20. Solidly built, with the rugged, earthy manner of Toro, this dense, structured red from Telmo Rodriguez wears a heavy, toasty oak cloak over a dark fruit core. Opening aromas of black cherry, dried flowers, earth, and meat give way to a full, smooth palate of similar profile, with black chocolate and earth shadings. More black chocolate and espresso show on the long, firmly tannic finish. Give this at least two to three years; best from 2005 to 2010. **90** —*M.M. (4/1/2002)*

Gago 2000 Dehesa Gago Tinta de Toro (Toro) $12. This, the "second wine" from Gago, has less depth than its big brother, but greater overt appeal in many ways—a scaled-down version of similar elements. Decidedly more accessible, it's lighter, shows more fruit and wears less oak. On the nose, the dark fruit displays a creaminess and a faint lavender note that offsets the classic Tinta de Toro meat and earth. Round in the mouth, its dark chocolate and coffee elements play out on the long, solidly tannic finish. Drink now through 2005. **88** —*M.M. (4/1/2002)*

GANDIA

Gandia 2003 Fusta Nova Moscatel (Valencia) $12. Starts out rather unrefined, with aromas of petrol and turpentine. But in the mouth it's all about ripe Moscatel, and there's no chemical influence to speak of. Flavors of banana, caramel, and mango are sweet and sticky. An unctuous ride; pull out the knife and fork. **86** —*M.S. (8/1/2005)*

Gandia 2002 Hoya De Cadenas Reserva Tempranillo (Utiel-Requena) $9. This Tempranillo is spicy and solid enough. The wine comes across ripe and clean, with forward cherry and raspberry flavors. It's rather crisp and basic, but it seems highly food-friendly and ultimately it's easy to drink. **85 Best Buy** —*M.S. (9/1/2006)*

GLORIOSO

Glorioso 2003 Crianza Tempranillo (Rioja) $11. Round and balanced, with a nice mix of cherry, spice, and leather on the bouquet. The palate comes across as totally fresh and zesty, with ample red fruit pumped up by acidity that creates a slight citric character. Racy and crisp wine; nice with chorizo or other basic foods. **86 Best Buy** —*M.S. (12/15/2006)*

Glorioso 2001 Crianza Tempranillo (Rioja) $11. Big and dusty on the bouquet, with a lot of berry fruit. The middle is medium weight, shows good balance and sports tasty cherry, plum, and cassis. Not too hard on the finish, and fruit-forward all the way. Drink now. **85** —*M.S. (12/31/2004)*

Glorioso 2001 Reserva Tempranillo (Rioja) $15. No complaints—just praise for this clean, easy red from a great vintage. The nose is crisp and fruity, with welcome citrus and wood notes. Blackberry mixed with vanilla and chocolate create a pleasant palate, while the finish is round and tinged by mocha. **90 Best Buy** —*M.S. (11/1/2006)*

Glorioso 2000 Reserva Tempranillo (Rioja) $15. A wine that very much fits the bill. The aromas are rubbery and smoky, with plenty of dark, ripe fruit filling in the voids. In the mouth, cherry and plum runneth over, while the finish is potent. Fruit is front and center, all supported by spicy oak. Very good in a mainstream, approachable way. **88 Best Buy** —*M.S. (12/31/2004)*

Glorioso 2003 Roble Tempranillo (Rioja) $9. Citrus peel and dried tree fruits define the nose. Raspberry and strawberry flavors are light-framed, while the palate feel is coarse due to hard tannins. Decent on a good day, with some grittiness to the finish. **82** —*M.S. (2/1/2006)*

GONDOMAR DEL REINO

Gondomar Del Reino 1996 Gran Reserva Tempranillo (Ribera del Duero) $43. Hard to penetrate, with some funk. Airing reveals unchained fruit with some green flavors at the core. Stays hard and medicinal, with cherry, spice, and burnt grass. Not in line with the best of the region. **83** —*M.S. (10/1/2005)*

Gondomar Del Reino 2002 Roble Tempranillo (Ribera del Duero) $19. Stewy, with aromas of baked beans and cooked fruit. A bit more secure and balanced in the mouth, where plum, cherry, and earth notes are

heavy but inoffensive. Strives for better balance without really finding it. **83** —*M.S. (8/1/2005)*

GONZALEZ BYASS

Gonzalez Byass NV Noe Muy Viejo Pedro Ximenez (Jerez) $NA. The crude oil of PX Sherries, Noe won't appeal to everyone. For starters, it's thick as molasses, with heavy caramel and toffee aromas and flavors. And while there's nothing not to like about caramel and toffee, this wine is fat and chewy, arguably too viscous to drink with ease. **88** —*M.S. (6/1/2005)*

Gonzalez Byass NV Tio Pepe Fino Sherry (Jerez) $NA. Round and nutty, with mild floral and honey hints up front. The formula for Tio Pepe calls for a salty, crisp flavor profile with just enough complexity to thrust it into the upper echelon of finos. Slight mushroom and iodine notes appear on the finish. **88** —*M.S. (6/1/2005)*

GOSALBEZ ORTI

Gosalbez Orti 2001 Qubel Barrica Tempranillo Blend (Vinos de Madrid) $47. Pure blueberry and blackberry pour forth from this dark-as-night Tempranillo, one of tiny production made in organic fashion. Wonderful texture, excellent fruit, and a smoky, rubbery finish announce it as a major leaguer. Not overly expansive on the finish, but lovely and serious throughout. **92 Editors' Choice** —*M.S. (9/1/2004)*

GRAMONA

Gramona NV Brut Rosado Pinot Noir (Cava) $NA. Neutral on the nose, with a rough bubble bead. Tastes candied and strange, with cough-drop flavors. Seems fresh, but finishes coarse. **83** —*M.S. (6/1/2005)*

Gramona 2003 Gran Cuvée Sparkling Blend (Cava) $18. Loud and basic, with ripe fruit aromas and flavors but also a detectable heaviness. The palate pushes ripe apple and pear, while the finish is big but quiet. Deep and dense but dull along the edges. **86** —*M.S. (6/1/2006)*

Gramona 2003 Grand Cuvée Rosé Sparkling Blend (Cava) $35. Cherry and dusty cinnamon aromas blend with a touch of cough drop on the nose, while the full-bodied palate pits spicy berry and plum against rather soft acidity. Finishes sweet for a burst, then dry and peppery. Alluring rosado. **87** —*M.S. (6/1/2006)*

Gramona 1998 III Lustros Gran Reserva Sparkling Blend (Cava) $NA. It is said that at five years a good cava starts to change for the better, and this seems to be an example of that. Classic aromas of petrol, baked apple, and spiced ham precede a sly palate that's both soft and deep. Mild citrus flavors are topped by vanilla and white pepper. Mature. **91** —*M.S. (6/1/2005)*

Gramona 2001 Imperial Gran Reserva Sparkling Blend (Cava) $48. Perfectly approachable and wholesome. Aromas of bread dough, pear, and lemon-lime are alert and attractive. The palate provides a lush bowl of kiwi, apple and pear, while some citrus coats the finish. **90** —*M.S. (6/1/2006)*

GRAN CERMEÑO

Gran Cermeño 1997 Crianza Tinta de Toro (Toro) $14. From Toro, the DO that's just west of Rueda (and the last DO through which the Duero flows before it hits Portugal), comes this 100% Tinta de Toro, which is the local name for Tempranillo. Most of what you get on the nose is burned butterscotch—it's hard to tell what lies beneath. Dark berry and charred oak open the front palate; at midpalate, a little espresso joins in. Dry tannins and char flavors make for a strong, bowl-you-over finish. **84** —*D.T. (4/1/2002)*

Gran Cermeño 1996 Reserva Tinta de Toro (Toro) $19. Impressively dense, this darkly fruited, well-oaked red delivers large-scale flavor and texture. Yes, there's plenty of oak, but there's something so often lacking, too—a wealth of deep, brawny fruit. This dark berry, espresso, and licorice-tinged tour de force closes with solid tannins and will reward cellaring. Drinkable now, but best from 2004–2000. **91 Editors' Choice** —*M.M. (9/1/2002)*

GRAN GESTA

Gran Gesta NV Brut Sparkling Blend (Cava) $14. This is a pleasant surprise. From the first sniff you know it's fresh and well made. Butterscotch, apple, and yeast aromas create a swell bouquet, which is followed by round apple, pineapple, and white-raisin flavors. It's big, smooth, and stands out from the crowd in a positive way. **90 Best Buy** —*M.S. (6/1/2005)*

GRAN METS

Gran Mets 2001 Red Blend (Montsant) $15. A fine blend of Cabernet Sauvignon, Merlot, and Tempranillo. Aromas of cherry, licorice, and nutmeg are inviting, as is the palate of tobacco, cherry, and blackberry. The finish is tight and fundamentally sound, with a hint of creaminess. **88** —*M.S. (5/1/2004)*

GRAN ORISTAN

Gran Oristan 1992 Gran Reserva Cencibel (La Mancha) $13. **84** —*J.C. (8/1/2000)*

Gran Oristan 1995 Gran Reserva Red Blend (La Mancha) $14. Pleasant red fruit and oak from start to finish characterizes this light-to-medium-bodied wine. It's easy to drink, if not overly complicated. Finish offers some anise and herb. **85** —*D.T. (4/1/2002)*

GRAN VEIGADARES

Gran Veigadares 2001 Blanco Albariño (Rías Baixas) $110. With its gold luster and strong aromas of fresh-cut wood, you know it's fully oaked. To that end, an overriding resiny scent melds with hints of flowers, melon, and butterscotch. The palate kicks up applesauce and spice, while the finish is defined by dry oak and white pepper. Full-bodied and deserving of serious food. **88** —*M.S. (3/1/2005)*

GRAN VEREMA

Gran Verema 2000 Old Vines Reserva Tempranillo (Utiel-Requena) $9. Light and dry, with mild aromas of mint and red fruit. Forward and tart, with lively berry and cherry flavors. Not thrilling, but solid and balanced. From the Gandia family. **84** —*M.S. (10/1/2005)*

GRANBAZÁN

Granbazán 2005 Ambar Albariño (Rías Baixas) $19. Our favorite among this winery's 2005s, Ambar offers tight, dry, precise aromas backed by driving flavors of melon, peach, and orange-blossom honey. Very much on the spot; an Albariño that you can't go wrong with. **90** —*M.S. (9/1/2006)*

Granbazán 2005 Don Alvaro de Bazán Albariño (Rías Baixas) $24. Highly mineral, with citrus, apple, and peach aromas. A touch mute in its flavor profile but still shows enough forward fruit and restrained sweetness to please. Snappy throughout. **87** —*M.S. (9/1/2006)*

Granbazán 2005 Verde Albariño (Rías Baixas) $15. Displays pretty aromas of flowers and green apples, with bright, round flavors of peach and apple making for a pleasant palate. Offers a touch of sweetness and honey at its core. Very typical of the 2005 vintage. **88** —*M.S. (9/1/2006)*

GRANJA NTRA, SRA. DE REMELLURI

Granja Ntra, Sra. de Remelluri 2000 Tempranillo Blend (Rioja) $28. Aromas of tobacco, earth, and plenty of fresh-cut oak make for a big, boisterous nose. The mouth is opulent and fairly well loaded with cassis and cherry. The finish is wall-to-wall as far as tannins go, while overall it's a stacked wine with class and power. Best for fans of well-oaked, sweet reds. **90** —*M.S. (3/1/2004)*

Granja Ntra, Sra. de Remelluri 2001 Remelluri Blanco White Blend (Rioja) $40. Flowery, with a nice mix of sweetness, dried apricots, and vanilla. Flavors of banana, papaya, and apple dominate a textured, modestly rich palate. Remelluri blends about a half-dozen grapes together for its white Rioja, and the result is smooth, albeit not overly powerful. **88** —*M.S. (3/1/2004)*

GUELBENZU

Guelbenzu 2003 EVO Cabernet Blend (Ribera del Queiles) $25. Not easy at first, because initial and secondary sniffs deliver blasts of wet dog and cranberry. Patience will be rewarded with peppy red-fruit flavors and a lot of terroir-driven mineral and raspberry notes. This is not a cookie-cutter wine, and some folks may not find it to their liking. **86** —*M.S. (8/1/2005)*

Guelbenzu 2001 Azul Red Blend (Navarra) $13. Clean and bouncy, with fresh berry aromas. This is a pretty, lighter-framed red with expressive cherry, plum, and oak all in a row. It finishes chewy and rich enough, but it's still in balance and not overpowering. All in all, it's a good blend with proper feel and a full taste. **87** —*M.S. (3/1/2004)*

Guelbenzu 2000 Azul Red Blend (Ribera del Arlanza) $13. Pretty aromas of cherry, leather, and baking spices lead into a sturdy, structured palate featuring dark plum and bitter chocolate flavors. The finish is hard and a bit tannic, but in a way that indicates there's a good foundation for aging. Cherry and cola are the lasting flavor impressions. Drink now or hold for a year or two. **88 Best Buy** —*M.S. (11/1/2002)*

Guelbenzu 2001 EVO Red Blend (Navarra) $20. Broad-shouldered and bold, but like all Guelbenzu wines, it applies the brakes where necessary. Herbal, terroir-driven characteristics pop up in between the red berry, plum, and oak flavors, giving it some boost and nuance. And it gets better with airing, as it delivers coffee and buttery oak at the end. **88** —*M.S. (3/1/2004)*

Guelbenzu 1999 Lautus Red Blend (Navarra) $45. This mixed bag of Tempranillo, Merlot, Cabernet, and Garnacha sings a sweet tune. The nose is powerful; there's an early punch of oak then dill, earth, and red fruit. Clearly this wine benefited from some healthy sunshine in '99. It's eminently ripe and full of cassis and black-plum flavors. With some marzipan and bitter chocolate on the finish, it racks up plenty of positives. **90** —*M.S. (3/1/2004)*

Guelbenzu 1998 Tempranillo Blend (Navarra) $13. Toasty and smoky, this is a big, bulky wine loaded with burnt sugar and oak. The black cherry flavors blend in vanilla, cinnamon, and allspice, along with earth and herbs on the finish. It has nice components; they just aren't all going the same direction. **84** (1/1/2004)

Guelbenzu 2003 Azul Tempranillo Blend (Ribera del Queiles) $15. Lots of bell pepper at first, so the first take is that it's green and underripe. But swirling brings it around, revealing dried plum, smoked meat and tomato. Thickens up as it goes along; early on it seems thin and vegetal. **85** —*M.S. (8/1/2005)*

Guelbenzu 1998 EVO Tempranillo Blend (Navarra) $22. **89** —*C.S. (4/1/2002)*

Guelbenzu 1996 Lautus Tempranillo Blend (Navarra) $58. A smoky, cedar nose starts this wine off, followed by plum and black-olive flavors. Finishes with great depth and richness. A well-structured wine that is a blend of Tempranillo (50%), Merlot (30%), Garnacha (10%), and Cabernet Sauvignon (10%), Lautus is the Latin word for "magnificent," and is made only in years the winery considers exceptional. **90** —*C.S. (4/1/2002)*

GUITIÁN

Guitián 2002 Sobre Lias Godello (Valdeorras) $NA. An example of a richer-styled Godello, a grape you'll only find in this small region. The nose and body are both full, and despite no oak aging, there are licorice and vanilla shadings to the ripe apple and banana flavors. Something to chew on. Unique. **90** —*M.S. (6/1/2005)*

GUNDIAN

Gundian 2004 Albariño (Rías Baixas) $15. Melon, peach and other ripe fruits on the full-styled bouquet. Riper than some, with apple and a touch of banana carrying the flavor profile. Zesty enough, with a solid, moderately lengthy finish. **87** —*M.S. (11/15/2005)*

GUZMÁN ALDAZABAL

Guzmán Aldazabal 2000 Tempranillo Blend (Rioja) $27. Deep, earthy aromas show some stewed fruit and rubber, but the palate offers a solid blast of ripe berry mixed with chocolate and leather, and the finish is thick, smooth, a bit buttery and a touch starchy. **90** —*M.S. (2/1/2006)*

HACIENDA LA CONCORDIA

Hacienda la Concordia 1999 Reserva Tempranillo (Rioja) $25. Soft and simple, with a dry, spicy nose that's ultimately light. Adequate raspberry, cherry, and plum-skin flavors turn astringent and sour as the acidity rears up toward the finish. **83** —*M.S. (5/1/2004)*

HACIENDA MONASTERIO

Hacienda Monasterio 1997 Crianza Red Blend (Ribera del Duero) $30. Even the winemaking wizardry of Peter Sisseck couldn't save this vintage. Aromas of red earth and tobacco give way to overripe, stewed, and raisiny fruit flavors that show the alcohol. Finishes a bit sour, with cooked-fruit flavors. **83** —*J.C. (11/1/2001)*

Hacienda Monasterio 1995 Crianza Tempranillo (Ribera del Duero) $30. 92 *(11/15/1999)*

HACIENDAS DURIUS

Haciendas Durius 2002 Durius Tempranillo (Ribera del Duero) $10. Surprisingly round and earthy, with licorice and cherry aromas. The palate is sassy yet mostly sweet, and the finish is full of berries and cream. Not fat or overly modern, yet it still brings ripeness and chocolate to offset its leathery qualities. **89 Best Buy** —*M.S. (5/1/2004)*

Haciendas Durius 2003 Alto Duero Viura-Sauvignon Blanc (Vino de la Tierra de Castilla y León) $13. Quite light in color and mute on the nose, with faint apple and honeydew flavors on the smooth but soft palate. Lacks the drive normally associated with these grapes. Despite that, it tastes o.k. **84** —*M.S. (3/1/2005)*

Haciendas Durius 2002 White Blend (Ribera del Duero) $10. Smooth and stylish from the opening gun. The nose has mint, pineapple, and a piquant sharpness that work in unison. In the mouth you'll find apple, pear, grapefruit, and passion fruit. It's a real winner, with admirable balance and plenty of flavor. **88 Best Buy** —*M.S. (5/1/2004)*

HEREDEROS DE MARTÍNEZ FUENTE

Herederos de Martínez Fuente 2002 Pucho Mencia (Bierzo) $13. Made from the Mencía grape, this purple-power jóven is fresh, fruit-packed, and interesting. Aromas of rose hips and blackberry lead into a palate that's largely sweet and rich. You get candied raspberry and cherry, but it's not artificial in any way. Finishes clean and nice, with a hint of vanilla. **86** —*M.S. (3/1/2004)*

HERENCIA ANTICA

Herencia Antica 2000 Reserva Tempranillo (Utiel-Requena) $8. Brambly and pickled, with monotone flavors. Juicy on the palate, but unrefined. Overall there's a lot of acid and not much clarity or depth. **81** —*M.S. (10/1/2005)*

Herencia Antica 1998 Reserva Tempranillo (Utiel-Requena) $8. Simple and cheerful, with red-fruit and tobacco aromas. For some it could seem a bit tight and candied, yet despite it having a rubbery, tannic grip, something typical for the region, it has a good flavor profile and it's easy to drink. **85 Best Buy** —*M.S. (3/1/2004)*

HERMANOS LURTON

Hermanos Lurton 2004 Rosado Tempranillo Blend (Vino de la Tierra de Castilla y León) $11. The fresh berry, red licorice, and cherry Lifesaver aromas will make you think you've placed your nose in a bushel of summer fruit, and while this rosé from the warm plains of central Spain looks more red than pink, it shows a bit of stoniness and a ton of clean, attractive flavors. It's a blend of Garnacha and Tempranillo from vineyards around Valladolid, and it will appeal to those who prefer a bit of meat on the bones of their dry pink wines. **88 Best Buy** —*M.S. (11/15/2005)*

Hermanos Lurton 2004 White Blend (Rueda) $13. Hard and funky at first, with a nose that shows leather, scallion, and bitter herbs. Seems to find its way a bit better in the mouth, where apple and papaya flavors are in the lead. Still, it remains unfocused and clumsy throughout. **83** —*M.S. (9/1/2006)*

HERMANOS SASTRE

Hermanos Sastre 1999 Crianza Tempranillo (Ribera del Duero) $25. 89 —*C.S. (11/1/2002)*

Hermanos Sastre 2000 Roble Tempranillo (Ribera del Duero) $14. 88 Best Buy —*C.S. (11/1/2002)*

HIDALGO

Hidalgo NV Oloroso Viejo Sherry (Jerez) $116. A serious and intense wine, with coffee and mocha on the nose, and a sharp dried-apricot and toasted-nut character on the palate. Power is this wine's calling card, as it hits like a bomb. The flavors are huge, the mouthfeel big but balanced. This is aged Oloroso in top form. **93 Editors' Choice** —*M.S. (6/1/2005)*

HUGUET DE CAN FEIXES

Huguet de Can Feixes 2001 Gran Reserva Brut Nature Sparkling Blend (Cava) $25. Classic and austere, with light toast and vanilla aromas in front of stark green apple and lime flavors. A natural dosage on a cava will result in tartness and sleekness, and here that's definitely what you get. **87** —*M.S. (6/1/2006)*

Huguet de Can Feixes 1999 Brut Nature Sparkling Blend (Cava) $18. Only a slight note of cheese gets in the way of the otherwise clean nose. In the mouth, lime and lemon flavors are drying, while the finish is simple, like tonic water or something similar. Like many cavas, this one seems to have the goods to work well at cocktail parties and receptions. **85** —*M.S. (12/31/2002)*

Huguet de Can Feixes 2000 Brut Nature Reserva Champagne Blend (Cava) $23. Light and lucid, with fine pear, almond, and cream aromas. The palate splashes apple and nectarine fruit, while the acids and zest on the finish function as the perfect cleanser. Crisp, tasty, and on the dot. **89 Editors' Choice** —*M.S. (12/15/2004)*

Huguet de Can Feixes 2000 Negre Selecció Red Blend (Penedès) $22. Compact and pungent, and borderline ungenerous at first. Once it opens up, there's ripe cherry and berry fruit pumped forward by zippy acidity. Toward the back it grows darker and more masculine, and at the very end the tannins get tough. **86** —*M.S. (3/1/2004)*

Huguet de Can Feixes 2000 Can Feixes Blanc Selecció White Blend (Catalonia) $10. This structured, medium-weight wine's nose offers dried apple and nutty aromas. Crisp lime and stony notes come up strongly on the palate. The mouth shows good tension and decent acidity, the flavors are persistent on the solid finish of this tasty white. Drink now–2004. **87 Best Buy** —*M.M. (9/1/2002)*

IBERNOBLE

Ibernoble 1995 Reserva Tempranillo (Ribera del Duero) $42. Ribera Tropic? Sure seems like it, with coconut, tropical fruit, orange peel, and citrus all playing roles in this wine's makeup. There's also vanilla and red plum, and fine wood tannins on the finish. **87** —*J.C. (11/1/2001)*

Ibernoble 1999 Cosecha Tempranillo Blend (Ribera del Duero) $17. Beet and bitter chocolate aromas and flavors accent black cherries and cedar in this medium-weight red. Slightly rough acidity fails to enliven the finish. **83** —*J.C. (11/1/2001)*

IGLESIA VIEJA

Iglesia Vieja 1997 La Purisima Red Blend (Yecla) $13. Lively on the palate, this cooperative-produced wine comes from Yecla, which is just northeast of Murcia in southern Spain. Soft cocoa, licorice, and red berry aromas lead to the same flavors on the palate, plus some dusty black fruit. Only a slight hollowness on the finish brings it down; otherwise, go give this tiny DO some of your business. **87** —*D.T. (4/1/2002)*

INFINITUS

Infinitus 2004 Cabernet Sauvignon (Vino de la Tierra de Castilla) $7. Saturated and completely unidentifiable as Cabernet. It's a monster in terms of color and size, and the flavors and aromas go all over the map but settle nowhere you'd recognize. On the border of acceptable. **80** —*M.S. (11/15/2005)*

Infinitus 2005 Merlot (Vino de la Tierra de Castilla) $7. Functional and fruity, with big aromas of plum and berry on the slightly foxy nose. Fully tannic across the palate, so it feels kind of hard. The big berry flavors are loud and basic. **83** —*M.S. (12/15/2006)*

Infinitus 2004 Syrah (Vino de la Tierra de Castilla) $7. Purple in color, but clumsy from start to finish. The nose is oily and loaded with balsamic notes along with berry jam. Prune and chocolate flavors are awkward and aggressive. Extract over balance is the formula. **81** —*M.S. (11/15/2005)*

Infinitus 2005 Tempranillo (Vino de la Tierra de Castilla) $7. Full and fruity as well as dense and structured. Not bad for an inexpensive Spanish red. The palate is fairly smooth but also a tad bit juicy. Chocolate, coffee, and a dryness work the palate. Even shows some finesse along the way. **86 Best Buy** —*M.S. (12/15/2006)*

Infinitus 2004 Tempranillo-Cabernet Sauvignon (Vino de la Tierra de Castilla) $7. Sweet cherry and berry aromas are blended with cookie dough scents to create a simple, easy bouquet. The palate is a bit lean, with tight red-fruit flavors and a blast of citrus essence. Shows some kick and tannins at its core. **84 Best Buy** —*M.S. (12/15/2006)*

Infinitus 2005 Chardonnay-Viura White Blend (Vino de la Tierra de Castilla) $7. Slightly amber in color, with pastry, peach, and pear aromas. The palate is tangy, with flavors of green apple along with some bitterness. Finishes light and dry, with zest and freshness. Simple yet solid. **84 Best Buy** —*M.S. (12/15/2006)*

Infinitus 2004 Viura and Chardonnay White Blend (Vino de la Tierra de Castilla) $7. Sweet and simple, with light aromas of vanilla, pear, and melon. Very sugary and striving for balance. The feel is plump and soft, yet the flavors are unfocused and distant. **82** —*M.S. (10/1/2005)*

INSPIRACIÓN PAMPANO

Inspiración Pampano 2004 White Blend (Rueda) $10. Mildly floral and tropical at first, but then it seems to go heavy and flat on the bouquet the longer it sits. Look for decent grapefruit and tangerine flavors on a healthy but rudimentary cassis. **83** —*M.S. (12/15/2006)*

INURRIETA

Inurrieta 2002 Norte Cabernet Sauvignon-Merlot (Navarra) $13. This wine is making its American debut this fall. It's a blend of Merlot and Cabernet, with ripe plum and blackberry aromas along with balsamic notes. Flavor-packed and round; a wine to keep in mind when "value" is what you're after. **88** —*M.S. (10/1/2004)*

J. & F. LURTON

J. & F. Lurton 2001 El Albar Barricas Tempranillo (Toro) $20. Monstrously ripe, bordering on syrupy. Seems like it wants to be one part nuevo and one part Port. While soft and lush, it still has some tannic middle ground. Finishes with huge, creamy chocolate notes. Seemingly not a food wine, unless you're talking chocolate. **88** —*M.S. (12/31/2004)*

J. & F. Lurton 2001 El Albar Excelencia Tempranillo (Toro) $43. Made in the modern, ripe, soft, extracted style. The nose exudes maple, cinnamon, and chocolate but not as much fruit as you might hope for. Big plum and chocolate flavors along with a thick, smoky palate make for an easygoing, 21st-century wine. Not flawless, but real nice. **89** —*M.S. (8/1/2005)*

J. & F. Lurton 2000 El Albar Excelencia Tempranillo (Toro) $43. Sweet and stewy, with overt oak that comes across as toasted marshmallow topped with melted chocolate. Very ripe, with a rubbery mouthfeel. Finishes with strong coffee and burnt notes along with sweeter jam and fudge nuances. **86** —*M.S. (3/1/2005)*

J. & F. Lurton 2001 Campo Eliseo Tinta de Toro (Toro) $50. A new wine from François and Jacques Lurton and partners Michel and Dany Rolland. It's expectedly dark, with exotic spice aromas, stewed stone fruits, and a certain sauciness to the nose. Very dense and textured, with plum, blackberry, and fudge flavors. Finishes thick but short, with some bitterness at the end. **88** —*M.S. (9/1/2004)*

J. & F. Lurton 2003 El Albar Tinta de Toro (Toro) $20. A touch heavy, but not nearly as weighty and syrupy as this winery's '03 Excelencia. At 14%, it's a bit raisiny and blustery, but the dark plum and coffee flavors do manage to please. And the finish is full of chocolate and fudge-like residue. Big but fun; ready to be drunk now. **88** —*M.S. (12/15/2006)*

J. & F. Lurton 2002 El Albar Barricas Tinta de Toro (Toro) $20. Broad, with slightly leafy, sweet aromas that are solid but not quite convincing. Lactic and full in the mouth, with toffee, vanilla, and chocolate mixing with tannins and firm fruit. Maple and mocha carry the sweet finish. **87** —*M.S. (2/1/2006)*

J. & F. Lurton 2003 El Albar Excelencia Tinta de Toro (Toro) $40. Seems like the brutal heat of 2003 got to this wine in a negative way. The result is a thick, unctuous, syrupy wine with a ton of sweetness but not much balance. The alcohol is listed at 15.5%, and it seems bigger. Very much a heavyweight, and with no agility. **84** —*M.S. (12/15/2006)*

J. & F. Lurton 2002 El Albar Excellencia Tinta de Toro (Toro) $40. Creamy, minty and full of cedar, with sweet, ripe dark fruits backing things up. This is one rich, beefy red; it deals plenty of vanilla and butter on the palate, with clove and mint on the finish. A lot of protruding oak and tannin now; should settle and soften by 2007. **90 Cellar Selection** —*M.S. (2/1/2006)*

J. & F. Lurton 2003 Hermanos Lurton White Blend (Rueda) $12. Brothers Jacques and François seem ubiquitous, and this round, soft, melon-driven wine represents their efforts in Rueda. A bit sweet and syrupy, but not overdone or cloying. It's a weighty blend of Sauvignon Blanc, Verdejo and Viura, and it offers loads of tropical fruit but not much backbone. **85** —*M.S. (12/31/2004)*

JANÉ VENTURA

Jané Ventura 2000 Finca Els Camps Macabeo (Penedès) $21. This wine is made entirely from Macabeo, one of the three grapes that comprise cava. The wine is heavy and fairly dull in the nose; there isn't much fruit and only a distant scent of nut oil. The flavors are sharp and lemony, and the finish is equally tangy. Cheerful is not this wine's middle name. **82** —*M.S. (11/1/2002)*

Jané Ventura 1998 Gran Reserva Brut Nature Sparkling Blend (Cava) $21. Loads of white fruits and lees, resulting in a nose of pure toast and vanilla. Shows the perfect size and integration, with a creamy feel. Flavors of grapefruit, lime, and mineral are at the fore. Classy and refined, with a proper petrol characteristic. **91** —*M.S. (6/1/2005)*

JARRARTE

Jarrarte 1998 Red Blend (Rioja) $24. This is a slick, seductive pleasure-fest of sweet oak and ripe Tempranillo fruit. Pine and cocoa aromas and flavors, handsome leather accents, a mid-weight frame, and smooth mouthfeel mark this modern Rioja. It's not tremendously deep, but it's delicious, with a sense of elegance and balance. Drink now–2006. **89** —*M.M. (11/1/2002)*

Jarrarte 2001 Tempranillo (Rioja) $29. Bright in color, with a modern nose of bacon and black fruit that goes darker and smokier with time. Almost expected blackberry and plum flavors control the palate, with hammering tannins in support. Good flavor profile. **87** —*M.S. (8/1/2005)*

JARRERO

Jarrero 2001 Red Blend (Rioja) $16. Smells like slow-roasted fruit mixed with a dusting of savory spice. Not the freshest kid on the block, but it offers cherry and apple-skin flavors that are decent and smooth. Not a thriller but not bad. **84** —*M.S. (11/1/2006)*

JAUME LLOPART ALEMANY

Jaume Llopart Alemany NV Artesanal Brut Nature Sparkling Blend (Cava) $14. Though the nose nose offers a somewhat alluring bouquet of toast, caramel, herb, and earth, the rest of the wine is somewhat disappointing. It's crisp and light in the mouth—so light that it is almost too effervescent—and fairly mute on the palate. A little lemon on the palate; finishes with chalky mineral notes. **83** *(12/31/2001)*

Jaume Llopart Alemany NV Artesanal Brut Reserva Sparkling Blend (Penedès) $12. Opens with an unusual and quite green flower shop and celery-like aroma. Has slight hints of tarragon, but is very light, with just faint lemon notes. Light is all right, but lack of effervescence isn't, and this just didn't fizz. **82** *(12/31/2001)*

JAUME SERRA

Jaume Serra NV Seco Reserva Sparkling Blend (Penedès) $9. 82 *(12/15/2000)*

Jaume Serra NV Semi Seco Reserva Sparkling Blend (Penedès) $9. Shows yeasty, earthy, dusty aromas, with just a slight trace of fruit. There are also mild fruity flavors. It's slightly sweet as a semi-seco should be, but has adequate acidity and decent length finishing with some richness. **86** —*S.H. (6/1/2001)*

SPAIN

Jaume Serra 2000 Estate Bottled Chardonnay (Penedès) $9. The nose could use more freshness, while the palate features dilute apple flavors and sharp acidity, despite the fact that it was fermented in barrels. Some dryness and buttered toast define the finish. **82** —*M.S. (11/1/2002)*

JEAN LEÓN

Jean León 2000 Zemis Bordeaux Blend (Penedès) $126. A high-water mark for Jean León, which usually sticks to varietal wines. Zemis, on the other hand, is a blend of Cabernet, Merlot, and Cab Franc that makes its point. After a tight, bruising, sulfuric beginning, the wine finds its groove, showing black cherry, plum, and earth flavors. Thorough and rewarding; a fine red from Penedès. **91** —*M.S. (6/1/2005)*

Jean León 1998 Cabernet Sauvignon (Penedès) $26. Attractive to the nose, as it offers a smooth, integrated blend of dry fruit, vanilla, and spice. Equally dry on the palate, with cherry and plum and whole lot of hammering tannins. Fairly interesting and rustic, and firm. While not old or fading it's probably not improving either. **87** —*M.S. (12/31/2004)*

Jean León 1994 Gran Reserva Cabernet Sauvignon (Penedès) $33. The jewel of Jean León's current lineup. This is a pure, leafy, smoky Old World beauty with just enough modernity to keep it up to date. The flavors are big and broad, offering notes of bacon, spice, plum, and tomato. Cinnamon and other sweet nuances appear toward the end. **92** *(2/1/2003)*

Jean León 1996 Reserva Cabernet Sauvignon (Penedès) $23. More earthy and herbal than the '95, with chocolate and licorice notes. Maybe the leafy quality is from the 15% Cab Franc. Ample cherry, cassis, and licorice flavors, but it finishes tannic and hard, which shortens the finish. **88** *(2/1/2003)*

Jean León 1995 Reserva Cabernet Sauvignon (Penedès) $23. This is showing signs of early maturity. Its earthy, dusty quality suits the traditional cherry and cassis fruit. Some coffee, root beer, and herbs give the finish a touch of the unusual. Yet it all works. **90** *(2/1/2003)*

Jean León 2002 Chardonnay (Penedès) $26. Gold in color, with a cheese-filled nose that offers only a modicum of pear and butter. Tastes lemony and bland, with citrus on the palate and finish. **81** —*M.S. (12/31/2004)*

Jean León 2000 Chardonnay (Penedès) $21. A fresh Chardonnay with fresh pineapple, pear, and mild buttery aromas. The palate is solid, with good structure, while the flavors are pear, sweet golden apple, and vanilla. The wine was barrel fermented and aged on the lees, so it has a round mouthfeel. **88** *(2/1/2003)*

Jean León 2002 Terrasola Chardonnay (Catalonia) $14. Funky and strange is this blend of 85% Chardonnay and 15% Garnacha Blanca. On the tongue it's lean and citrusy, without much composition. **80** —*M.S. (12/31/2004)*

Jean León 2002 Vinya Gigi Chardonnay (Penedès) $29. Fat and melony on the nose, with tons of pear, cantaloupe, almond, and vanilla on the palate. Heavily oaked, especially on the finish, where wood resin is mostly what you get. **86** —*M.S. (6/1/2005)*

Jean León 2001 Merlot (Penedès) $26. Big and round, with heavy aromas of smoke and tar. Lively, with wild cherry and berry flavors, full tannins and ample zest. Chocolaty on the finish, and oaky throughout. **86** —*M.S. (12/31/2004)*

Jean León 1999 Merlot (Penedès) $20. Piercing aromas of bramble and herbs give it a slightly rustic bouquet. The mouth is forward and packs punch, with cherry and raspberry fruit. The finish is tight and dry, but it doesn't turn hard. Aging in used Chardonnay barrels keeps the oak element in check. **87** *(2/1/2003)*

Jean León 2002 Terrasola Syrah (Catalunya) $16. More savory and spicy than fruity, with bramble and leather aromas dominating any sweetness that might want to escape. A touch aggressive in the mouth, with lively but hard raspberry and other red-fruit flavors. Finishes dry and salty, with heat. Includes 17% Carignan. **83** —*M.S. (9/1/2006)*

JM ORTEA

JM Ortea 2000 Crianza Tempranillo (Ribera del Guadiana) $23. Cola, mushroom, and some cheesy oak make for a scattered nose. Better in the mouth, where plum and berry flavors are full if a bit heavy. Sort of

roasted and reduced, but with air it softens and ultimately rounds into form. **83** —*M.S. (10/1/2005)*

JOAN D'ANGUERA

Joan D'Anguera 2002 El Bugader Red Blend (Montsant) $60. One of the best of the region, with supreme concentration and style. It's mostly Syrah, and the color is piercing purple. On the nose, it's a touch granular and nutty at first, but eventually dark, meaty black fruit emerges. Tons of black cherry and heft on the palate, with a lasting, smoky finish. Reaches that higher level, although not quite as surely as the fabulous 2001. **89** —*M.S. (10/1/2005)*

Joan D'Anguera 2002 Finca L'Argata Red Blend (Montsant) $25. Dark as night, with smooth, deep aromas of earth, leather, and black fruit. It's a blend of four fairly common red grapes, and together they yield pleasant plum, blackberry, and other dark-fruit flavors. Sizable and tannic, but impressive for its clarity and simplicity. **88** —*M.S. (10/1/2005)*

Joan D'Anguera 1999 Finca L'Argata Red Blend (Tarragona) $21. This deep purple opaque, wine possesses dried sage and milk chocolate with an underlying dustiness on the nose. The tannins are full but will integrate with time. An enjoyable, rich chewy wine to be consumed in 1–3 years. **90** —*C.S. (4/1/2002)*

Joan D'Anguera 2000 Finca L'Argatà Red Blend (Montsant) $21. Full-force blackberry, cherry, and licorice create a lovely bouquet, which is followed nicely by cherry, plum, and additional berry flavors. The finish is broad, meaty and firm, with fine tannins. **90 Editors' Choice** —*M.S. (3/1/2004)*

Joan D'Anguera 2003 La Planella Red Blend (Montsant) $18. Dark purple in color, with heavy aromas of molasses, road tar, and baked plum. Not particularly vivid, but solid and ripe. There's ample black fruit throughout, but it lacks the edge it might have in a more balanced vintage. Remember: 2003 was a broiler, thus the grapes suffered. **84** —*M.S. (10/1/2005)*

Joan D'Anguera 2002 La Planella Red Blend (Montsant) $19. Saturated and dense, but youthful as well as a few shades shy of refined. There's herbal essence to the flavor profile, but there's also bold and tasty cassis and black plum. The finish is chewy and a bit spicy, and overall you'd have to label it rich and full. **87** —*M.S. (3/1/2004)*

Joan D'Anguera 2000 La Planella Red Blend (Tarragona) $19. La Planella is blended exclusively for the U.S. market. Extended maceration adds to the bright purple color and complexity of this wine, which has rich blackberry fruit and soft tannins. **88** —*C.S. (4/1/2002)*

Joan D'Anguera 1998 Vi Dolç Red Blend (Tarragona) $70. A Banyuls-style dessert wine made from Garnacha. Molasses and dried fruits start the nose off, jumping into flavors of caramel and toffee. The wine is sweet but not cloying, meaning it has grit for a dessert wine. Perfect at the end of a meal. Can be drunk now or will age for a number of years. **88** —*C.S. (4/1/2002)*

Joan D'Anguera 1999 El Bugader Shiraz (Tarragona) $50. "Mr. Shiraz" is what the late father Josep D'Anguerra was called. This Shiraz blend justifies that name. Josep started planting the grape back in 1977 and it is doing very well in Tarragona, giving us a wine that is bluish-black in color with a jammy blackberry nose and wisps of frying bacon. Rich tannins beautifully balance the intense fruit and tangy acids. Drink in 2–10 years. **93 Cellar Selection** —*C.S. (4/1/2002)*

Joan D'Anguera 2000 El Bugader Syrah (Montsant) $50. Here's an excellent wine from a high-flying subsection of Tarragona. It's rich, inky, and thick, but impeccably balanced. Pulsating dark-berry fruit carries the nose and palate, while chocolate comes on late. Polished and intense, with all elements squarely in place. **92** —*M.S. (3/1/2004)*

JOAN SARDÀ

Joan Sardà 2001 Criança Cabernet Sauvignon (Penedès) $13. Leather, raspberry, and earth get it going. The fruit is on the sharp side, and the wine has a raw, snappy feel to it. Shows a bit of sweat and green. Not a Cabernet for the new American palate. **82** —*M.S. (2/1/2006)*

JOAN SIMÓ

Joan Simó 2002 Les Eres Vinyas Velles Red Blend (Priorat) $66. The definition of old-vines Priorato can be found within this bottle. The

Garnacha is very old, the Cariñena even older, and some mature Cabernet Sauvignon adds spine. On the nose, there's a lot of barrique. The palate is snappy, almost acidic, and thus the flavors run toward pie cherry and raspberry. Classic in style; an Old World throwback. **91** — *M.S. (10/1/2005)*

Joan Simó 2000 Les Eres Vinyes Velles Red Blend (Priorat) $59. This blend is 55% old-vines Garnacha, 30% ancient Carignan, and the rest Cabernet. It's sweet and rich, with aromas of red fruit and a hint of coconut. The palate is classic old-vines stuff: cassis, red plum, beet, and plenty of persistence. Yet despite it's old-vines status, it still tastes young and snappy. **89** —*M.S. (3/1/2004)*

Joan Simó 2002 Les Sentius Red Blend (Priorat) $34. Brand new on the market is this blend of Garnacha, Cariñena, Cabernet, and Syrah, all planted only in 1999. And you know what? It's pretty solid, with a bright garnet color and toasty aromas. Where it shows its pedigree, or lack thereof, is in the middle, where it's lean and zesty as opposed to meaty and deep. Falls off after extended time in the glass. **85** —*M.S. (10/1/2005)*

JULIA ROCH E HIJOS

Julia Roch e Hijos 2000 Las Gravas Red Blend (Jumilla) $19. Deep and exotic, with fine black fruit and perfume on the nose. Flavors of black cherry and blackberry sing a pretty song, while the finish is racy and firm, and arguably a bit lean. Among all the big bruisers out there, it's nice to see a juicier, fruitier wine that doesn't hit like a battering ram. That said, this is no lightweight. **89** —*M.S. (3/1/2004)*

JULIO IGLESIAS

Julio Iglesias NV Julio Brut Sparkling Blend (Cava) $15. The bouquet shows some combination of (and we quote—we couldn't make this up) "wet slate," "dusty soil" and "honey mustard Chicken McNuggets sauce." Flavors are somewhat muted, with whispers of lemon, orange blossom, and herb. Soft and creamy in the mouth, it finishes with a little caramel. **83** *(12/31/2001)*

JUVÉ Y CAMPS

Juvé y Camps NV Brut Rosé Pinot Noir (Cava) $16. Much more spicy and nuanced than most cavas, whether we're talking rosado or not. This one begins with aromas of black gumdrops and orange drink. The palate echoes the nose as it displays star anise and Sambuca flavors along with distant citrus. A different breed that's both odd and intriguing. **86** — *M.S. (12/15/2006)*

Juvé y Camps 2001 Reserva de la Familia Brut Nature Sparkling Blend (Cava) $20. Quite hard on the nose, with classic petrol aromas that almost smell of rubber cement. Tough and tight on the palate; it takes some effort to penetrate. Once inside there's crisp apple and lime zest. A true "nature" in every sense. **87** —*M.S. (6/1/2005)*

Juvé y Camps 2002 Brut Nature Reserva de la Familia White Blend (Cava) $22. Light and lemony, with a hint of green astringency. Tangerine with hints of mushroom on the palate run toward a solid but lean finish. Has zest but little roundness. Fresh and crisp, but not the most friendly bubbly. **86** —*M.S. (6/1/2006)*

Juvé y Camps 2000 Gran Brut White Blend (Cava) $42. Fairly big and yeasty, with earth and mushroom notes that offer complexity to the apple and pear aromas that dominate. Fruity enough, with hints of nutmeg and white pepper. Richly textured with a ton of body. Roundness is its calling card. **89** —*M.S. (6/1/2006)*

LA LEGUA

La Legua 1999 Crianza Tempranillo (Cigales) $10. The aromas are a bit too prickly and pickled to call the nose clean, and thus the wine never really achieves solid footing. The raspberry and strawberry fruit is there, but it's marred by sharp, pickled accents, which ultimately don't work in its favor. The feel is nice, as the acidity and tannins are proper. But with too much funk to the nose and palate, it misses the upper echelon. **84** — *M.S. (8/1/2003)*

La Legua 1998 Reserva Tempranillo (Cigales) $19. From a region on the rise, this is nice Tempranillo, made in a lighter, food-friendly style. Which doesn't mean it's weak. On the contrary, the wine has good

concentration and purity to go with fresh acids and an approachable texture. The flavors are of plum, cherry, and licorice, while the finish is tight and comes in a couple of layers. Well made and easy to drink. **89** — *M.S. (8/1/2003)*

LA RIADA

La Riada 2004 Old Vines Garnacha (Campo de Borja) $10. Light reddish in color, with dry cranberry aromas and a strong hint of spearmint. Surprisingly heavy in the mouth, with slightly cooked flavors and a wave of burnt brown sugar on the finish. A wine with some issues. **81** —*M.S. (12/15/2006)*

LA RIOJA ALTA

La Rioja Alta 1987 Gran Reserva 890 Tempranillo (Rioja) $120. It's old, it's brown, and it's good. Not much red fruit is left in this classic, but the peach and apricot flavors are intriguing, and the lasting acidity is keeping it surprisingly fresh. **90** —*M.S. (10/1/2003)*

La Rioja Alta 1994 Gran Reserva 904 Tempranillo (Rioja) $53. Leaner than ideal on the nose, with hot aromas of leather, earth, and peach pit. A bit sharp in flavor, showing more pie cherry and apricot than anything else. Still a classic, however, but best be prepared for tea and juice notes more than beef and brawn. **88** —*M.S. (9/1/2004)*

La Rioja Alta 1989 Gran Reserva 904 Tempranillo (Rioja) $48. **92** *(11/15/1999)*

La Rioja Alta 1998 Vina Alberdi Reserva Tempranillo (Rioja) $23. Rather thin and transparent to the eye, but that lightness doesn't translate into it being a thin, nothing wine. Just the opposite: It's loaded with leather, cranberry, and tea aromas and brisk cherry and cranberry flavors. Some chocolate on the finish adds heft to this old-school wine that really seems to have been made to go with food. **88** —*M.S. (3/1/2004)*

La Rioja Alta 1996 Vina Ardanza Reserva Tempranillo (Rioja) $28. A classic old-school Rioja in that it has strong dill aromas on a bouquet of dried fruit, leaves, and flower petals. The color is fading, but the mouth is alive with raisin, plum, cinnamon, and tomato flavors. The acidity is huge; will be best with food. **88** —*M.S. (10/1/2003)*

La Rioja Alta 1990 Vina Ardanza Reserva Tempranillo (Rioja) $27. **86** — *J.C. (11/15/1999)*

LA VAL

La Val 2005 Albariño (Rías Baixas) $NA. Good but a bit less concentrated and pure than most. There's a whiff of sulfur on the nose, and in the mouth the fruit is solid but basic. Apple and melon are the key flavors, while the finish is clean but unspectacular. At 40,000 cases this is a large-production wine by Rías Baixas standards. **85** —*M.S. (9/1/2006)*

La Val 2005 Finca de Arantei Albariño (Rías Baixas) $NA. La Val is an O Rosal winery but its wines are 100% Albariño. This estate-grown white offers a yellowish tint with pretty aromas of buttercup and apple blossoms. It's fairly light-bodied and exhilarating, with pure flavors of apples, honeydew, and citrus. Shows good acidity. **89** —*M.S. (9/1/2006)*

La Val 2005 Orballo Albariño (Rías Baixas) $19. Pale yellow in color, with elegant aromas and flavors. To call it light would not be wrong: The wine shows grassy citrus notes but it peters out a bit on the back palate and finish. More subtle and fresh than powerful. **87** —*M.S. (9/1/2006)*

LACATUS

Lacatus 2003 Tempranillo (Penedès) $8. Straightforward, with jammy red-fruit aromas. Tastes like fresh cherries and plums, with medium depth, power, and length on the finish. Offers a little spice, a little fruit and a little heat. Overall it's solid. **85 Best Buy** —*M.S. (8/1/2005)*

Lacatus 2001 Tempranillo (Penedès) $7. The nose kicks up some acetone, and beyond that it's all about piercing raspberry aromas. The palate is simple and drying, mostly due to hard tannins that overwhelm the fruit. The finish, thus, is just as hard and tough to fight through. **81** —*M.S. (3/1/2004)*

Lacatus NV Gold Brut Nature White Blend (Cava) $13. Dry as a bone, with petrol and green-apple aromas. The palate delivers expected apple and lemon flavors, while the finish is crisp, tangy and a touch tart.

SPAIN

Simultaneously acidic and elegant. Classic no-sugar brut nature. **86** —M.S. (12/15/2005)

Lacatus NV Semi Seco White Blend (Cava) $12. Clean but quiet aromas lead to sweet flavors, predominantly candied peach, cantaloupe, and dried apricot. Fairly lively in the mouth, almost to the point of being too bubbly. Overall it tastes good even if it's jumpy. **85** —M.S. (12/15/2005)

LAGAR DE CERVERA

Lagar de Cervera 2002 Albariño (Rías Baixas) $21. Big as Albariños go, with lots of melon, apple and pineapple in the bouquet. The flavors lean toward papaya and grapefruit, with a hint of baking spice providing support. The finish is complete and integrated, with licorice and anise subtleties creating interest. **87** —M.S. (3/1/2004)

LAGAR DE COSTA

Lagar de Costa 2005 Albariño (Rías Baixas) $13. Round in style, with soft white-fruit and apple blossom aromas. Tastes a touch reduced, as if the lemon, lime, and melon flavors had been condensed and amplified. The finish is lively, with citrus and some pithiness. Good but limited. **85** —M.S. (12/15/2006)

LAGUNA DE LA NAVA

Laguna de la Nava 2000 Reserva Tempranillo (Valdepeñas) $11. Sweet and floral, like light berries with crushed flower petals. The palate is not as comforting; it's acidic and bouncy, which fosters good flavors but a jagged, jumpy mouthfeel. You want to like this wine but the feel doesn't make it easy. **84** —M.S. (12/15/2006)

LAS GRAVAS

Las Gravas 1999 Red Blend (Jumilla) $18. This easy drinker has a round feel, but enough acidity to support the sweet dark-cherry flavors and appealing clove-cocoa accents. It's smooth, goes down easy, and closes with good length, displaying a slight mineral, almost quinine-like note on the finish. Not complex, but offers a lot of flavorful character. **85** —M.M. (4/1/2002)

LAURONA

Laurona 2000 Red Blend (Montsant) $20. A powerful, pretty wine with much of the qualities of a high-end Priorat, (Which makes sense because Montsant is right next door to Priorat.) it offers a bottomless nose of deep red fruit and flowers. That's matched by the palate, which is ripe and everlasting as it transitions to the spicy, complex finish. **91 Editors' Choice** —M.S. (3/1/2004)

Laurona 2000 6 Vinyes de Laurona Red Blend (Montsant) $45. A millennium wine that's now in fine form. It's a typical Garnacha-Cariñena blend that runs heavy on Garnacha. The bouquet is strong and evolved, with leather and mineral along with aromas of crushed flower petals, asphalt, and earth. Excellent fruit quality in the mouth; vivid with raspberry and black pepper. 800 cases made. **90** —M.S. (10/1/2005)

Laurona 2001 Tinto Red Blend (Montsant) $28. Bingo! An excellent wine from a great vintage, simple as that. Exotic and complex aromas that highlight Middle Eastern spices, a silky palate and integrated tannins, what more could you want? How about a delicious mix of five grapes, incredibly harmonious and food friendly? No surprise it's this good: It's made by the team at Clos Mogador. **90** —M.S. (10/1/2005)

LEALTANZA

Lealtanza 2001 Crianza Tempranillo (Rioja) $20. Roasted and leathery but not that bright. The palate is zesty and chock full of nondescript red fruit. The finish is similar, while overall that tannins are firm if a bit spiky. **84** —M.S. (11/15/2005)

Lealtanza 2000 Crianza Tempranillo (Rioja) $16. Chunky and ripe, with more power and potency than precision or finesse. Which still means it's pleasant, warm, and tasty. The palate offers ample raisin and toffee, while the finish is aptly spicy. Good heft and texture, but short in the midsection. **87** —M.S. (6/1/2005)

Lealtanza 2000 Gran Reserva Tempranillo (Rioja) $44. Medium-strength plum and cherry aromas mix with earth and leather on a bouquet that's not all that fruity but still shows fruit. In the mouth, there's raspberry and red plum flavors floating on juicy, snappy acidity. Mouthfilling but

hardly ponderous. Stylish in a somewhat classic mode. **87** —M.S. (11/1/2006)

Lealtanza 1999 Gran Reserva Tempranillo (Rioja) $45. Initial and secondary nosings reveal some green notes and barnyard, which dissolve a bit if given time but never quite leave the scene. The mouth offers loud plum and berry flavors, with a somewhat tannic finish. Nonetheless, it features good Rioja attributes; in the final analysis it's a fairly good wine. **85** —M.S. (4/1/2006)

Lealtanza 2000 Reserva Tempranillo (Rioja) $29. Hard leather and smoke aromas are the opening salvo, and there's plenty of warm earth and cedar below deck. The palate is herbal and peppery, with a touch of burnt grass and green pepper sparring with plum and berry. Finishes a bit hot but ultimately it's a solid, old-school Rioja. **85** —M.S. (11/1/2006)

Lealtanza 2001 Reserva Selección Tempranillo (Rioja) $135. Grapy and granular smelling, with heavy, raw aromas that lack finesse and agility but offer plenty of thump. Surprisingly, the palate on this dark, more modern-styled wine is kind of tart, with racy cherry and blackberry fruit. Not an easy wine to evaluate; you want more from it but it isn't that generous. **84** —M.S. (11/1/2006)

Lealtanza 2005 Rosé Tempranillo (Rioja) $14. Dark in color. Cherry, raspberry and a touch of innertube rubber carry the nose toward a ripe palate featuring red apple and raspberry flavors. Finishes crisp and zesty, with nice acidity and commendable purity **86** —M.S. (11/1/2006)

LEGADO MUNOZ

Legado Munoz 2004 Garnacha (Vino de la Tierra de Castilla) $10. A raisiny wine of the first order. The nose is stewed, while the pruny palate is soft and chocolaty, mostly because there's no detectable acidity. Only late in the game do you catch some tannin and zest. **81** —M.S. (11/1/2006)

Legado Munoz 2004 Merlot (Vino de la Tierra de Castilla) $10. Attractive on the nose, with violet, cherry, and a bit of candy. Round and satisfying in the mouth, with full berry flavors and mouthcoating tannins. Not all that nuanced or complex, but good in a dense, hit-me sort of way. **85 Best Buy** —M.S. (12/15/2006)

Legado Munoz 2005 Tempranillo (Vino de la Tierra de Castilla) $10. Smoky, grapey, and spicy on the nose. The palate is full and aggressive in a bring-it-on sort of way. It's a touch heavy and tannic, but it's also pretty long and toasty on the finish. **84** —M.S. (12/15/2006)

LEGARIS

Legaris 2000 Crianza Tempranillo (Ribera del Duero) $15. Sweet and ripe, and a touch aggressive. That said, the spicy pepper and blackberry palate is satisfying. The finish offers vanilla, black pepper, and wood resin. Very plump and fruity, with chocolaty edges. Definitely a good Ribera red, even if it comes in below the cream of the region. **87** —M.S. (3/1/2004)

Legaris 1999 Reserva Tempranillo (Ribera del Duero) $28. Understatedly stunning, with wintergreen and licorice gumdrop notes poking through a fruit-infested bouquet. The palate is genuine and pure, with cassis and plum, spice, and loads of leather. The finish is firm, with a warm earthiness that leaves you believing that this wine is right on form. **93 Editors' Choice** —M.S. (3/1/2004)

Legaris 2002 Crianza Tinto del Pais (Ribera del Duero) $17. Jammy aromas with a lot of bramble make for a jumbled nose. The palate is thin and racy, with nondescript flavors that veer toward cherry. Finishes overtly buttery and cheesy, a result of too much oak being applied to a wine that couldn't handle it. **83** —M.S. (10/1/2005)

Legaris 2000 Reserva Tinto del Pais (Ribera del Duero) $25. Tight and grainy aromas, with strong hints of fresh-cut wood. Turns tangy on the palate, with basic plum and raspberry flavors. Rather firm and unforgiving in terms of tannins. Even veers toward lacquer at certain points. **85** —M.S. (10/1/2005)

LLOPART

Llopart 1994 Brut Leopardi Sparkling Blend (Cava) $26. Light aromas of lemon, cotton and chalk preface similar flavors, backed by pear notes, on the palate. In the mouth, it's clean, even and soft, with a little bead. Finishes with more clean lemon-mineral flavors. **85** (12/31/2001)

Llopart 2000 Leopardi Brut Nature Sparkling Blend (Cava) $18. Light and lean, with lively fruit aromas and flavors. Freshness is what this wine pushes, because there's not much weight or overt sweetness to it. Light apple, a touch of pear, and some lemon-lime is the most that you're going to get. Still, it works as a palate freshener. 87 —M.S. (6/1/2006)

Llopart 2002 Rosé Brut Reserva Sparkling Blend (Cava) $25. Alluring bubbly, regardless of origin or composition. The bouquet is dry, clean, and spicy, with crushed raspberry. Full in the mouth, with a perfect texture; the peach and nectarine flavors are delicious. Finishes a bit racy and citrusy, with pink grapefruit and passion fruit. Outstanding rosado cava. 91 Editors' Choice —M.S. (6/1/2006)

LÓPEZ HERMANOS

López Hermanos NV Don Juan Trasañejo Pedro Ximenez (Málaga) $NA. Super rich and syrupy, which is just the way you want it. But what makes it great is that there's also a giant streak of balancing acidity that runs right up the gut. Reeking of prune, coffee, and mocha is the nose, while the palate is pure bliss, a mix of spice, chocolate, and raisin. A shining star from little-known Málaga. 94 Editors' Choice —M.S. (6/1/2005)

LORIÑON

Loriñon 1997 Gran Reserva Tempranillo (Rioja) $34. Lean yet still fresh, with punchy herbal aromas of tree bark, dried fruits, and burnt grass. A bit stripped of its power by now, but still tossing up strawberry and cherry flavors in front of snappy finishing notes of nectarine and pie cherry. An old-style wine with more acidity than flesh. 86 —M.S. (10/1/2005)

Loriñon 2000 Reserva Tempranillo (Rioja) $20. Fairly sweet and medicinal on the nose, almost like a vapor rub for sore muscles. Chunky and borderline syrupy on the palate, with run-of-the-mill plum and berry flavors. Finishes with texture and lemony tinges. Good but standard. 86 —M.S. (8/1/2005)

Loriñon 2002 Crianza Tempranillo Blend (Rioja) $13. Typically dry and leathery, with only modest red-fruit aromas. It's light to medium in weight, with punchy acidity pushing clean but thin cherry and plum fruit. Not too big or spacious on the finish, but good in a mainstream, traditional sort of way. 84 —M.S. (11/1/2006)

Loriñon 2001 Crianza Tempranillo Blend (Rioja) $13. From Bodegas Bretón, this medium-weight red is a touch stewy, with peanut and black-olive aromas along with red licorice and Tootsie Roll. The palate offers strawberry and red cherry, while the finish is surprisingly tangy, with a shock of overt acidity. 85 —M.S. (6/1/2005)

Loriñon 2004 Viura (Rioja) $12. A barrel-fermented wine with soft, lactic aromas that conjure memories of a bowl of cornflakes. The palate is dry but rather tasteless except for some distant melon and citrus. Finishes bland. 82 —M.S. (11/1/2006)

LOS MONTEROS

Los Monteros 2004 Tinto Red Blend (Valencia) $10. Sharp and green at first, with cranberry and herbal aromas. Ultrafirm and smoky on the palate, with a hard-cooked flavor profile. Decent tannins and structure, but short on friendliness and depth. Typical base-level Bobal. 83 —M.S. (8/1/2005)

Los Monteros 2004 Blanco White Blend (Valencia) $10. Offers big floral aromas along with scents of honeysuckle and lemon zest. Mango, pineapple, and lime flavors are crisp and clean, while the palate is a bit acidic and sharp, but entirely refreshing. 86 Best Buy —M.S. (8/1/2005)

LUNA BEBERIDE

Luna Beberide 2004 Mencia (Bierzo) $13. You won't find a better, more affordable Bierzo than this. It carries true terroir, heft, and solidity but it's not that complicated or racy. Lush black fruit is what defines the palate, while the finish is textured and creamy. Really smacks of natural character and joy. 88 Best Buy —M.S. (9/1/2006)

Luna Beberide 2000 Tinto Red Blend (Vino de la Tierra de Castilla y León) $46. Massive yet proportional, with olive, rubber, and ripe black fruit on the manly bouquet. The palate is ponderous but tasty, with a huge dose of syrupy berry and black-plum flavors. Ripe as all get out, with firm

tannins. To call it a powerhouse would be taking things lightly. 90 — M.S. (4/1/2006)

LUSCO

Lusco 2004 Albariño (Rías Baixas) $23. Some wax on the nose along with a touch of pollen; less than fruity. The wine remains on the sharp, tangy side in the mouth, where lemon, lime, and grapefruit flavors are predominant. Crisp on the finish, what some might call short and tart. 85 —M.S. (11/15/2005)

Lusco 2003 Pazo Piñeiro Albariño (Rías Baixas) $35. Impeccably clean, with light tropical fruit gracing the bouquet. A wine that's better than the sum of its parts; the palate is lemony fresh and satisfying, while the overall impression is that of elegance and simplicity. Perfectly good but not overly flavorful. 88 —M.S. (6/1/2005)

Lusco 2002 Albariño (Rías Baixas) $20. Fairly grassy, with aromas of applesauce and wildflowers. A palate of lemon-lime, apple and grapefruit shows medium-weight intensity, while the finish is fairly sizable, with a lasting note of buttered toast (despite no oak). 85 —M.S. (3/1/2004)

Lusco 2000 Albariño (Rías Baixas) $20. The crisp lime and straw aromas of this Galician white are right on target. Tangy citrus and green apple flavors tickle the tongue atop a refreshing, even bracing mouthfeel. Finishing long with stony notes, this is a perfect shellfish wine. If you haven't yet tried an Albariño, what are you waiting for? 89 —M.M. (9/1/2002)

MAD DOGS & ENGLISHMEN

Mad Dogs & Englishmen 2004 Red Blend (Jumilla) $10. Candied and thick right from the begininning. This is a heavy, chunky southern Spanish red comprised of 60% Monastrell and 20% each of Cabernet and Syrah. The final result is rustic, stewy, and fat, with gooey chocolate and stewed plum flavors. Big and ripe but devoid of finesse. 83 —M.S. (9/1/2006)

Mad Dogs & Englishmen 2003 Shiraz Cabernet Monastrell Red Blend (Jumilla) $10. Jumilla, a hotbed of luscious new wines from Spain, had the hottest summer on record in 2003. The result is this sweet and fleshy red blend, half Monastrell, 30% Cabernet, and 20% Shiraz. Fruit flavors of plum, berry, and cherry fill a fleshy midpalate, and despite the hot weather the alcohol remains at a comfortable 13.5%. There are no pruney, raisiny notes, just fresh, sweet, supple ripe fruit and a hint of white pepper. 88 Best Buy —P.G. (11/15/2004)

MAJAZUL

Majazul 1999 Crianza Tempranillo (Mentrida) $13. Dry, and hard to love, this crianza's nose has a penetrating petrol-menthol note that all but obscures what plum fruit lies beneath. The same goes for the palate: Dry herbs and fresh-cut wood swathe the red-plum core. Finishes with charred wood. Tasted twice. 82 —D.T. (4/1/2003)

MANO A MANO

Mano A Mano 2004 Tempranillo (La Mancha) $10. Here's a good Tempranillo from a prime growing zone within the sprawling La Mancha region. The wine displays serious fruit quality as the black cherry and dark plum flavors kick it out. On the palate, the balance is right where you want it. For a joven that sees only six months in oak, it has the right amount of chocolaty framing. Not an overcropped mass-market wine; only 4,000 cases were made. 86 Best Buy —M.S. (11/15/2005)

MANYANA

Manyana 2003 Tempranillo (Cariñena) $7. Weedy and leafy, with penetrating aromas of rhubarb and burning hayfield. Never finds much fruit or style, as it finishes with a bland, raspy burn. 80 —M.S. (8/1/2005)

MAR DE CASTILLA

Mar de Castilla 2005 Tempranillo Blend (Vino de la Tierra de Castilla y León) $9. Medicinal and chalky on the nose; tart and lively, with acidic cherry and plum flavors. Short on the finish. 80 —M.S. (12/15/2006)

Mar de Castilla 2005 Verdejo (Vino de la Tierra de Castilla y León) $9. Gets off the mark a bit chunky and soft, with heavier than usual peach and melon aromas. Melon, papaya, and green banana carry the plump, full-bodied palate to a soft, easy, almost shy finish. Weighty for Verdejo. **84** —M.S. (11/1/2006)

MAR DE FRADES

Mar de Frades 2005 Albariño (Rías Baixas) $15. Sweet and fresh smelling, with aromas of lime, pear, and peach. The palate is all about citrus, with some spice and mineral thrown in for good measure. Balanced and zesty, like Albariño should be. **87** —M.S. (12/15/2006)

Mar de Frades 2004 Albariño (Rías Baixas) $15. Hard and waxy on the nose, with little to no appealing fruit aromas. The palate is loaded with sharp lemon and green apple flavors. Lacks friendliness; healthy in terms of feel but borders on sour. **82** —M.S. (9/1/2006)

Mar de Frades 2002 Albariño (Rías Baixas) $16. Made in a lush style, with melon, pear and pineapple aromas. Notes of cinnamon grace the fresh palate, which is coated from side to side with apple. Finishes in a spicy, layered crescendo. More plump than lean, but it seems to be weighted properly. **87** —M.S. (3/1/2004)

MAR DE LEÓN

Mar de León 2004 Joven Tempranillo (Vino de la Tierra de Castilla y León) $7. Stewy, with red cabbage and field funk on the nose. Limited in scope, with tart plum flavors along with a persistent infusion of green. Acceptable mouthfeel and balance are what save it from a worse fate. **81** —M.S. (11/1/2006)

MARQUÉS DE ALELLA

Marqués de Alella 1999 White Blend (Alella) $10. 87 Best Buy (8/1/2000)

Marqués de Alella 2000 Classico White Blend (Alella) $10. Appealing bright citrus and slate flavors ride a round yet faintly spritzy mouthfeel in this lively white from Spain's northeast. The flavors and textures show some depth and positive tension. Best for current drinking, it closes bright and dry, with good length. **87 Best Buy** —M.M. (9/1/2002)

MARQUÉS DE ARIENZO

Marqués de Arienzo 2001 Crianza Tempranillo (Rioja) $23. Nicely done, a touch soft, but strong as a whole. The nose shows some typical Arienzo earth and stewiness, while the balanced palate is meaty but fresh enough, with good berry fruit resting on a bed of firm tannins and proper acids. Not a complicated wine; it's classic Rioja. **87** —M.S. (11/1/2006)

Marqués de Arienzo 1999 Crianza Tempranillo (Rioja) $10. The bouquet is mostly sweet and fresh, with just the slightest hint of field greens. Adequate strawberry and raspberry fruit carries the palate toward a rubbery, spicy finish that brings pepper at the end. Easy and lean, with a good enough mouthfeel. **85** —M.S. (3/1/2004)

Marqués de Arienzo 1998 Crianza Tempranillo (Rioja) $10. This wine offers tumbleweed and leather saddle aromas, and flavors of strawberry jam. The fruit-to-acid balance is good; overall, a soft, interesting, and enjoyable wine. **88 Best Buy** —C.S. (11/1/2002)

Marqués de Arienzo 1996 Gran Reserva Tempranillo (Rioja) $15. Rusty in color, which is to be expected. The nose shows dried cherry, belt leather, and cigar box, and at this point all seems dandy. The palate, however, is short and stewy, with too little fruit to stand up to the prickly acids and herbal notes. Already past its prime. **84** —M.S. (11/1/2006)

Marqués de Arienzo 1994 Gran Reserva Tempranillo (Rioja) $25. There's lots to like in this fully mature Rioja. Substantial ripe sweet fruit, caramel, and tobacco aromas and flavors abound. The mouthfeel is light to medium weight, the acidity moderate and the tannins well resolved on the long, positive finish. Very tasty, and at its best now through 2005. **90 Editors' Choice** —M.M. (9/1/2002)

Marqués de Arienzo 1999 Reserva Tempranillo (Rioja) $13. Losing color and steam; the nose already is showing sherry, root beer, and other oxidized notes of tobacco and caramel. Tastes of rooty fruit, earth, and some citrus peel. Has seen better days. **83** —M.S. (11/1/2006)

Marqués de Arienzo 1998 Reserva Tempranillo (Rioja) $15. Rusty in color, with aromas of caramel, marshmallow, and earth. The palate is fading, with dried cherry, almond, and oregano. Finishes thin, but with moderate complexity. In terms of mouthfeel, it's tight and leathery, and a bit starchy. **84** —M.S. (3/1/2004)

Marqués de Arienzo 1996 Reserva Tempranillo (Rioja) $16. A touch of brown at the edge and a plummy, woody nose open this middleweight contender. Nicely balanced, the mouthfeel is even, but the wood is overbearing on the palate and finish. The texture is right on, but the fruit fights for presence against the oak. **84** —M.M. (9/1/2002)

Marqués de Arienzo 1997 Reserva Tempranillo Blend (Rioja) $15. Soft and flavorful, an easy drinking wine with cherry, tobacco and herb flavors. Acids are quite soft and so are the tannins. It's a very dry wine with little oak influence. **86** —S.H. (1/1/2002)

MARQUÉS DE CÁCERES

Marqués de Cáceres 2000 Crianza Red Blend (Rioja) $13. Dried red fruit, pepper, and mint on the nose, and clove, vanilla, and raspberry on the palate. It tails away in tight, dry form, yet it's largely an open, steady, and satisfying wine. Even if it doesn't pump up and thump its chest, it still scores points for its friendliness. **87** —M.S. (3/1/2004)

Marqués de Cáceres 2000 Gaudium Gran Vino Red Blend (Rioja) $50. This winery's flagship red is Tempranillo-based and it delivers round, blackberry, herb, tobacco, and earth-based aromas. It's fairly creamy in the mouth, with generous flavors that hit the berry and plum chords and the descent into a deep finish of vanilla, oak, and herbs. Not a cookie-cutter red; doesn't taste run-of-the-mill. Good through 2011. **90** —M.S. (11/1/2006)

Marqués de Cáceres 1994 Gran Reserva Red Blend (Rioja) $26. Mediumweight, with stewed fruit, smoke, and black pepper on the nose, this gran reserva (a blend of Tempranillo, Mazuelo, and Graciano) is more subtle seductress than mouthfilling bruiser. It offers lovely plum fruit, and semisweet chocolate and oak accents. Finish fades a little more quickly than you want it to, which is why it stops shy of the elusive "excellent" mark. **89** —D.T. (4/1/2003)

Marqués de Cáceres 1998 Reserva Red Blend (Rioja) $22. Gets off the mark with savory aromas akin to bean and bacon soup, wood smoke, and dried herbs. Next comes raspberry and plum fruit supported by ample oak-based vanilla. Finishes creamy, round, and solid. Just a sip or two and you know you're drinking true Rioja. **88** —M.S. (11/1/2006)

Marqués de Cáceres 1994 Reserva Red Blend (Rioja) $21. 89 (8/1/2000)

Marqués de Cáceres 2005 Dry Rosé Blend (Rioja) $8. Simple and clean, with a pretty rose tint and basic but nice berry and leather aromas. Quite natural, with fresh cherry and raspberry flavors. Full and grabby on the finish as it hits the spot. Drink this year. **87 Best Buy** —M.S. (6/21/2006)

Marqués de Cáceres 2004 Dry Rosé Rosé Blend (Rioja) $8. Chill it down and let it flow. That's the one and only secret to enjoying this textbook, inexpensive rosado from Spain. Aromas of red licorice, dried cherries, and strawberries are fresh and lucid, as is the crystal-clean palate. Spicy and wispy on the finish; will work with almost any salad or sandwich in your picnic basket. **88 Best Buy** —M.S. (8/1/2005)

Marqués de Cáceres 2003 Dry Rosé Rosé Blend (Rioja) $7. Round and fleshy, with bold aromatic notes of strawberry and watermelon candies. Finishes short. **84** (10/1/2004)

Marqués de Cáceres 2002 Rosé Blend (Rioja) $7. Leafy aromas offer some melon and earth. Flavors of strawberry and citrus seem chunkier than in previous years. Look for a smack of milk chocolate on the finish. A good quaff, but a touch meaty. **85** —M.S. (3/1/2004)

Marqués de Cáceres 1999 Rosé Blend (Rioja) $7. 84 —M.M. (8/1/2000)

Marqués de Cáceres 2004 MC Tempranillo (Rioja) $38. This wine is Cáceres' attempt at a modern (yet for the masses) Rioja, and frankly it's not working. The bouquet is nothing but an avalanche of coconut and butter, which stems from the barrel regimen the wine goes through. And the palate is loud, chunky, and clumsy. Yes, there's big fruit and bulk; but it's grabby, oversized, and overoaked. **83** —M.S. (12/15/2006)

Marqués de Cáceres 2002 MC Tempranillo (Rioja) $37. Another of the "modern" wines, MC is 100% Tempranillo that stays in French oak for 9 months and then is released quickly onto the market. It's a creamy, supple wine that packs a lot of fruit and oak into a pleasant package. **89** (10/1/2004)

Marqués de Cáceres 1995 Rioja Crianza Tempranillo (Rioja) $12. 82 —J.C. (11/15/1999)

Marqués de Cáceres 1992 Rioja Reserva Tempranillo (Rioja) $18. 88 — *J.C. (11/15/1999)*

Marqués de Cáceres 2002 Crianza Tempranillo Blend (Rioja) $14. Light and moderately oaky, with dry, herbal accents to the red-fruit aromas that are dominant. Light cherry and strawberry are the key flavors, and they're backed by notes of toast, chocolate, and leather. Classic and solid, especially for a down year. **86** —*M.S. (11/1/2006)*

Marqués de Cáceres 2001 Crianza Tempranillo Blend (Rioja) $13. A bit simple but satisfying, with ripe blackberries and vanilla on a smooth, supple frame. Picks up subtle hints of cinnamon and clove on the tart, clean finish. **86** *(10/1/2004)*

Marqués de Cáceres 1998 Gaudium Gran Vino Tempranillo Blend (Rioja) $50. This wine requires some patience and willingness, or it just might not register. The bouquet offers cooked fruits, smoky vanilla, cured meat, and earth. Blackberry, cherry and cola carry the palate, while the finish is mildly buttery, with dark chocolate. Still lively and acidic after numerous years of bottle age. Not an easy wine, but interesting. **88** — *M.S. (8/1/2005)*

Marqués de Cáceres 1996 Gaudium Gran Vino Tempranillo Blend (Rioja) $60. Cáceres's alta expressión wine gets the Full Monty: old vines (averaging 70 years of age), malolactic fermentation in new French oak, microxygenation. The result is a creamy, supple, thoroughly modern wine that blends black cherries with hints of tobacco and vanilla. **90** *(10/1/2004)*

Marqués de Cáceres 1995 Gran Reserva Tempranillo Blend (Rioja) $28. Big and bulky, with jammy, bacon-fat aromas that register as clumsy and rubbery. Seems to be on the fade; ten years into its existence the fruit has gone heavy and chewy. The plum and chocolate are still present and accounted for, but there isn't much balance or structure. Was probably better five years ago. **84** —*M.S. (10/1/2005)*

Marqués de Cáceres 1994 Gran Reserva Tempranillo Blend (Rioja) $25. One of the big differences between Cáceres and its competitors is a reliance on French rather than American oak. This gran reserva spent more than two years in barrel, and it shows wonderful leather, vanilla, and tobacco shadings layered over red plum fruit. A fully mature Rioja that offers good value. **90 Editors' Choice** *(10/1/2004)*

Marqués de Cáceres 1995 Reserva Tempranillo Blend (Rioja) $21. Back into traditional mode, this wine stayed in barrel for 2 years, then in bottle for 6 years before being released. The result is an earthy, tobacco-scented wine that still retains underpinnings of fresh blackberries. Finishes with elegant flourishes of smoke and vanilla. **89** *(10/1/2004)*

Marqués de Cáceres 1996 Reserve Tempranillo Blend (Rioja) $22. Full and still quite bright, with brandied cherry, leather, and Tootsie Roll on the nose. Quite full-force on the palate, with forward raspberry fruit. Tannic and grabby, but not raw. Solid in the classic sense, with cola, plum, and cherry Lifesaver nuances. **88** —*M.S. (10/1/2005)*

Marqués de Cáceres 2005 Viura (Rioja) $7. Once again this Viura ranks as one of the better values in white Rioja. It deals a punchbowl bouquet of round melon and pineapple, while the dry but fresh palate pushes green melon and white pepper. Limited in what it can offer but good for what it costs. **85 Best Buy** —*M.S. (11/1/2006)*

Marqués de Cáceres 2004 Viura (Rioja) $7. Always a solid Rioja white; the 2004 is ripe and refreshing, with aromas of melon and canned fruit. Fresher on the palate, with notes of green herbs, dry melon, apple and white pepper. Zesty and clean, with even more dryness and pepper to the finish. **86 Best Buy** —*M.S. (8/1/2005)*

Marqués de Cáceres 2003 Viura (Rioja) $7. Made from 100% Viura, fermented in stainless steel, this is a plump, quaffable wine laced with melon and fig flavors. **84** *(10/1/2004)*

Marqués de Cáceres 2002 Viura (Rioja) $7. Search the world over and you'll be hard-pressed to find a more pleasing low-cost white than this 100% Viura. It doesn't take an expert to appreciate the unoaked freshness of this lightweight. The seamless bouquet snaps with melon, while the palate shimmies with citrus and apple. There are no frills to this wine, just consistency and simplicity. And the cooler you serve it, the crisper it'll come across. **85** —*M.S. (11/15/2003)*

Marqués de Cáceres 2000 Viura (Rioja) $7. Round and even, this dry white from the well-known Rioja producer offers sweet hay, apple, and vanilla aromas and flavors. Nicely composed, this has decent balance and a smooth, if modest finish. Best to drink now, and a good bar or party pour. **85 Best Buy** —*M.M. (9/1/2002)*

Marqués de Cáceres 1999 Viura (Rioja) $7. 84 —*M.S. (8/1/2000)*

Marqués de Cáceres 2003 Antea White Blend (Rioja) $10. A heavy, awkward, rather tasteless blend of Viura and Malvasia. And it's barrel fermented from a hot year. So just imagine the weight. The opposite of a refreshing Spanish white, this is an oily wine with distant notes of dried apricot and vanilla. **81** —*M.S. (8/1/2005)*

Marqués de Cáceres 2002 Antea White Blend (Rioja) $9. This blend of 80% Viura and 20% Malvasia is barrel-fermented in French oak, giving the understated peach and melon flavors a heavy blanket of toast and grilled nuts. **84** *(10/1/2004)*

Marqués de Cáceres 2001 Antea White Blend (Rioja) $9. Made from Viura and Malvasia, this plump barrel-fermented white begins with refreshing, clean aromas of pear and apple. Similar flavors follow, and despite the barrel influence the oak flavor is nominal. The lengthy finish is lively but smooth. Its size, grip, and balance are all just right. **87** —*M.S. (11/1/2002)*

Marqués de Cáceres 1998 Antea White Blend (Rioja) $10. 84 *(8/1/2000)*

Marqués de Cáceres 2003 Satinela White Blend (Rioja) $7. Labeled "medium sweet," this is sweet but not cloying, with almond, citrus, and peach providing a solid base of fruit flavor. **83** *(10/1/2004)*

Marqués de Cáceres 2001 Satinela White Blend (Rioja) $9. If the question is, "what should a proper lady drink in hundred-degree weather?", Satinela is the answer. It's feminine, sweet, and zippy—even a little spritzy—in the mouth, with honeysuckle and yellow fruit flavors, and perfumed, garden-vegetable, and lemon aromas. With 3% residual sugar, it will be too sweet for many, and just right for others. **84** —*D.T. (4/1/2003)*

Marqués de Cáceres 2000 Satinela Medium Sweet White Blend (Rioja) $7. Clearly labeled as a medium-sweet wine, this wine's rather dry bouquet gives no hint of the soft, cloying palate to follow. This sweetness is more than medium to this taster, but it could be just the thing for guests who find normally dry wines puckery. **81** —*M.M. (9/1/2002)*

Marqués de Cáceres 2004 Satinela Medium Sweet White Blend (Rioja) $8. This medium-sweet wine has a lot of issues. First off, it smells like cooked bananas. Next, the palate is like mango cotton candy. Third, the juice itself will take a coat of enamel off your teeth. Need more? **80** — *M.S. (8/1/2005)*

MARQUÉS DE GELIDA

Marqués de Gelida 1997 Brut Sparkling Blend (Cava) $10. "Elegant for what it is," this Cava is soft yet zippy in the mouth, with rich apple, honey, and pear flavors. More honey and pear flavors. More honey, plus hay and mocha notes unfold on the bouquet. Finishes with grassy, creamy notes. A straightforward, affordable Cava. **86 Best Buy** —*M.M. (12/31/2001)*

Marqués de Gelida 2001 Brut Exclusive Reserva Sparkling Blend (Cava) $12. More open than many, with lemon-lime aromas that work as a nice entry. Full in the mouth, where mixed fruits mesh together. The back palate offers drier citrus on top of a smooth, creamy body. Finishing notes of green herbs and lettuce are welcome. **89 Best Buy** —*M.S. (6/1/2006)*

MARQUÉS DE GRIÑON

Marqués de Griñon 2002 Cabernet Sauvignon (Dominio de Valdepusa) $40. Toasty and solid, with wintergreen on the nose. Blackberry, cherry, and other typical Cab flavors work well together on the framed, tannic palate. Finishes ripe, with additional tannins, coffee and chocolate. Hard as a rock in terms of feel. **88** —*M.S. (2/1/2006)*

Marqués de Griñon 2001 Dominio de Valdepusa Cabernet Sauvignon (Toledo) $35. Tar, rubber, and a light chemical note turn the nose down, while rhubarb and cranberry mix with cola on the palate. Finishes sweet, with stewed fruit and carob. It's also a touch green. **83** —*M.S.* (*12/31/2004*)

Marqués de Griñon 2000 Dominio de Valdepusa Cabernet Sauvignon (Toledo) $35. Deep, chunky, and round, with a dark complexion and a rich, saturated palate. Cassis, black plum, and milk chocolate create a thick yet nonsyrupy flavor profile, while on the tail end you get ripeness and natural sugar. It could use more finesse to be great, but it still has a lot of what people are seeking. **89** —*M.S.* (*5/1/2004*)

Marqués de Griñon 1999 Dominio de Valdepusa Cabernet Sauvignon (Vino da Mesa de Toledo) $28. This bears some similarities to its Petit Verdot sibling reviewed here, but is not as well-realized. The red berry fruit wears a hint of sourness, showing a green, under ripe quality that detracts. It's slightly weightier than its stable-mate, but lags behind it in flavor and finesse. **84** —*M.M.* (*9/1/2002*)

Marqués de Griñon 2002 Petite Verdot (Dominio de Valdepusa) $40. Saturated and dark, with black pepper, leather, and boysenberry making for a fully pleasing bouquet. Juicy and serious, with berry and cherry fruit flowing on a wave of dense tannins. Finishes long and chocolaty, with a touch of prune. Layered and likable. **92** —*M.S.* (*2/1/2006*)

Marqués de Griñon 1999 Dominio de Valdepusa Petite Verdot (Vino da Mesa de Toledo) $30. A lively, flavorful, and well-balanced red made of a Bordeaux grape generally reserved for blending. Its bright berry aromas and flavors are offset by attractive black pepper and green tobacco accents. Good fruit, positive acidity, and a firm, even tannic structure mean this stylish, elegant wine has a future. Drink now through 2007, best after 2004. **88** —*M.M.* (*9/1/2002*)

Marqués de Griñon 2000 Emeritus Red Blend (Vino da Mesa de Toledo) $60. As you might expect from a wine from Spain's central plains, this is dark, stewy, ,and heavy. But it's also loaded with exotic gumdrop, spice, and plum syrup aromas, saturated deep-fruit flavors, and ultimately an ending flow of coffee and fudge. It's like drinking a confection, but one crafted for adults. **90** —*M.S.* (*3/1/2005*)

Marqués de Griñon 1998 Emeritus Red Blend (Toledo) $50. This Cabernet, Syrah, Petit Verdot blend has ripe, juicy blackberry and black cherry fruit that is muted by a heavy dose of dry, woodsy tannins. Cream, vanilla, and nut accents from start to finish underscore its seemingly liberal exposure to oak. **87** —*D.T.* (*4/1/2003*)

Marqués de Griñon 1999 Enartis Red Blend (Rioja) $30. This Tempranillo, Cabernet Sauvignon, Syrah, and Merlot blend has a nice mouthfeel and decent heft, but its flavors aren't as compelling as its body. Red plum and cherry fruit wasn't ripe or lush; dough, dry wood and meat notes round out the profile. Tasted twice. **85** —*D.T.* (*4/1/2003*)

Marqués de Griñon 2002 Syrah (Dominio de Valdepusa) $40. Dark and ethereal, with raisin and vanilla on the pitch-black, manly bouquet. One of Spain's best Syrahs, with dense cherry, raspberry, and mocha flavors. It's lavishly oaked, smooth yet big, and it's packed to the brim with full tannins and lushness. Drink now or hold. **92** —*M.S.* (*2/1/2006*)

Marqués de Griñon 2000 Dominio de Valdepusa Syrah (Vino da Mesa de Toledo) $34. Overly dense and rich. Flavors of raisins and liqueur meld into a burnt, charred center. This wine doesn't have enough balance to offset its full ripeness. To this taster there's too much marshmallow and syrup. That noted, it's quite possible that it will have its followers. **86** —*M.S.* (*3/1/2005*)

Marqués de Griñon 1999 Dominio de Valdepusa Syrah (Vino da Mesa de Toledo) $34. There's just something our tasters found hard to handle in this Syrah, made under Michel Rolland's direction, in central Spain. An odd note described variously as fishy, algae-like, or varnishy covered the dark-berry fruit. An ashy element on the palate and a thin, oily finish with light cherry fruit peeking through closes it. Tasted twice. **83** (*11/1/2001*)

Marqués de Griñon 2000 Durius Tempranillo (Douro) $9. This Tempranillo shows a burst of sweet, dark blackberries on the palate, which are thereafter overtaken by char and toast flavors. Dry, woody tannins are dominant here, and may be difficult to overcome if you don't drink this with a slab of grilled meat. Butterscotch, toast, and liqueur notes start things off. **84** —*D.T.* (*4/1/2003*)

Marqués de Griñon 2001 Durius White Blend (Douro) $9. Nose offers piquant mix of citrus, mustard seed, and yellow stone fruit. The palate is a muted extension of the same flavor profile—zippy white pepper notes over generic yellow fruit. Falls off quickly on the finish. **83** —*D.T.* (*4/1/2003*)

Marqués de Griñon 2000 Tempranillo (Rioja) $12. Fry up the chorizo—here's an easy, rustic, Tuesday-night drinker that's perfect with Spanish sausage or even paella. This Tempranillo offers a host of red fruit (raspberry, plum, cherry) on the palate, plus a hefty dose of oak. Oak-derived vanilla, cream, and caramel notes start things off. **86** —*D.T.* (*4/1/2003*)

Marqués de Griñon 1997 Colección Personal Reserva Tempranillo (Rioja) $26. Ripe, red plum is at the core of this Rioja, but "svelte" and "sophisticated" are the last words I'd use to describe it. With chewy, woodsy tannins and a healthy helping of earth and tree-bark flavors, this wine is rustic but honest—like good barbecue, which, while we're on the subject, would do this wine just right. Aged 24 months in French and American oak. **88** —*D.T.* (*4/1/2003*)

MARQUÉS DE LA CONCORDIA

Marqués de la Concordia 2000 Crianza Tempranillo (Rioja) $15. Lean and dilute from start to finish. The fruit is in the sour cherry category and the acidity is high. Finishes almost lemony. **80** —*M.S.* (*5/1/2004*)

Marqués de la Concordia 2001 Hacienda de Susar Tempranillo (Rioja) $15. Offers an attractive mix of herb, oak, and ripe fruit aromas. The palate is sunny, and thus bright fruit in the form of raspberry and cherry shines. Full and lengthy on the finish, with chocolate as the lasting flavor. **87** —*M.S.* (*6/1/2005*)

MARQUÉS DE MONISTROL

Marqués de Monistrol 1999 Masia Monistrol Single Vineyard Reserva Especial Cabernet Sauvignon-Merlot (Penedès) $20. Juicy blackberry and plum flavors have just enough of a charred-oak overlay to keep the fruit from being too jammy. A sleek and sophisticated Cab-Merlot blend, it's mouthfilling and smooth, with brambly, lush blackberry aromas wafting from the nose. Aged in new French oak for 18 months; 29,900 bottles made. **90 Editors' Choice** —*D.T.* (*4/1/2003*)

Marqués de Monistrol 2000 Cabernet Sauvignon-Tempranillo (Penedès) $7. Surely one of the better bargains this year, and with 60,000 cases produced, it can't be that hard to find. This Cab-Tempranillo is full and balanced in the mouth, with red fruit and a healthy dose of oak. Its tannins are most perceptible on the finish; letting it rest a year or two may coax more than mocha and light, jammy fruit out of the nose. **88 Best Buy** —*D.T.* (*4/1/2003*)

Marqués de Monistrol NV Brut Reserva Sparkling Blend (Cava) $9. Take a whiff and it comes across plump and traditional. The palate is less complex and toasty; grapefruit and other citrus flavors are what you get. The finish is smooth and unassuming. It's a lively type of wine, one that's neither brooding nor subdued. **88 Best Buy** —*M.S.* (*12/31/2002*)

Marqués de Monistrol NV Masia Monistrol Sparkling Blend (Cava) $7. Scents of bread dough, corn, and some sweat comprise the rustic nose. Apple and tarragon flavors come forth on the tongue, followed by a racy, lemony finish. Overall it's sort of wild and awkward, but it has its good points, too. **86 Best Buy** —*M.S.* (*12/31/2002*)

Marqués de Monistrol 1998 Reserva Privada Red Blend (Penedès) $10. Red plum and cherry fruit isn't overblown or jammy, by any means. On the contrary, there's an element of plum-skin tautness that keeps the wine a little austere, in terms of flavor. Medium-bodied and somewhat chewy, it closes with woodsy tannins and more plum fruit. A steal, for the price. 32,000 cases produced. **88 Best Buy** *D.T.* (*4/1/2003*)

Marqués de Monistrol 1999 Brut Reserva Privada Sparkling Blend (Cava) $15. This smooth, stylish wine is on the way up, as evidenced by the two-point bump it's receiving from its last review, in December 2004. Today it's round and full, with aromas of hay and popcorn that draw you in. Layered through the middle, with expressive white fruit, dryness and sweetness all in one. **90 Best Buy** —*M.S.* (*6/1/2006*)

MARQUÉS DE MURRIETA

Marqués de Murrieta 1994 Castillo Ygay Reserva Especial Red Blend (Rioja) $24. **87** (*2/1/2000*)

Marqués de Murrieta 1989 Castillo Ygay Gran Reserva Esp Red Blend (Rioja) $35. 89 *(2/1/2000)*

Marqués de Murrieta 1998 Colección 2100 Tinto Red Blend (Rioja) $11. 86 *(2/1/2000)*

Marqués de Murrieta 1997 Colección 2100 Tinto Red Blend (Rioja) $10. 83 *(2/1/2000)*

Marqués de Murrieta 1995 Dalmau Reserva Red Blend (Rioja) $75. 89 *(2/1/2000)*

Marqués de Murrieta 1995 Prado Lagar Reserva Especial Red Blend (Rioja) $27. 89 *(2/1/2000)*

Marqués de Murrieta 1995 Reserva Red Blend (Rioja) $20. 89 *(2/1/2000)*

Marqués de Murrieta 1995 Castillo Ygay Gran Reserva Tempranillo (Rioja) $45. This is a single-vineyard wine with pedigree. The tint is toward orange, with a brick center. The nose deals intoxicating vanilla, marzipan, and sweet leather, while the palate picks up the pace with fruit, density, and subtlety. Wonderful texture; drink over next five years. 91 —M.S. *(9/1/2004)*

Marqués de Murrieta 1999 Dalmau Tempranillo Blend (Rioja) $80. This old-vines blend of mostly Tempranillo, Graciano, and Cabernet Sauvignon is full of berry and cherry fruit. It comes on a lighter frame than some, with more raspberry and cherry on the palate than jam. For a new-age wine, it's textbook in that it isn't overdone. Chocolate, cherry and coffee carry the long finish. 91 —M.S. *(9/1/2004)*

Marqués de Murrieta 2000 Dalmau Reserva Tempranillo Blend (Rioja) $NA. This wine shows that old dogs can be taught new tricks. Murrieta is about as traditional as they come in Rioja yet Dalmau is ultra modern. The nose is a smooth mix of plum, raspberry, and tobacco, while the sizable palate pushes oak-backed berry fruit. Runs racy but not particularly aggressive. Long and satisfying on the finish. 92 —M.S. *(6/1/2005)*

MARQUÉS DE REALA

Marqués de Reala 2004 Grenache (Campo de Borja) $9. Young and open, with light red-fruit aromas on the candied bouquet. Nothing complicated here; just snappy raspberry and candy flavors followed by a gritty, sugary finish. Standardfare Garnacha from a warm climate. 84 —M.S. *(2/1/2006)*

Marqués de Reala 2003 Rosado Grenache (Campo de Borja) $7. Heavier than ideal, with earthy berry aromas and accents of cinnamon. Overly ripe, with a lot of meat, pepper, and baked berry flavors. Has its merits and faults. 84 Best Buy —M.S. *(3/1/2005)*

Marqués de Reala 2005 Rosé Joven Grenache (Campo de Borja) $9. Overly soft and deep in color, with heavy caramel and red licorice aromas. With no edges and little acidity, the wine seems flat. In addition, it finishes with bitterness as well as sugary sweetness. 81 —M.S. *(11/1/2006)*

Marqués de Reala 2003 Tinto Grenache (Campo de Borja) $7. Very sweet, with cherry cola and licorice nibs comprising the nose. It's nothing more than simple Garnacha, which means it's all about red fruit and sunshine. Not a fine wine, but good for those with a sweet tooth. 84 Best Buy —M.S. *(6/1/2005)*

MARQUÉS DE RISCAL

Marqués de Riscal 2004 Sauvignon (Rueda) $8. Moderately forward, with smooth, floral, comfortable aromas. The palate is loaded with citrus, mostly lime but also some grapefruit. Rock solid on the finish, with acidic snap and mineral notes. A perfect apéritif white. 87 —M.S. *(10/1/2005)*

Marqués de Riscal 2004 Riscal 1860 Tempranillo (Vino de la Tierra de Castilla y León) $8. This fruit-forward wine based on grapes mostly from the Toro region represents a relatively new project from a venerable Rioja producer. With a few years behind the wines, the '04 is highly expressive and packed with bold character. The palate is lush, saturated, and meaty, while the finish is smoky and big. This is a lot of wine for the money. 88 Best Buy —M.S. *(11/15/2006)*

Marqués de Riscal 2001 Riscal 1860 Tempranillo (Vino de la Tierra de Castilla y León) $9. Tobacco and berries join with brown sugar, cinnamon, and spice—all of the things that make oak nice. Smooth and supple, with modest plum and berry fruit layered with vanilla. 86 Best Buy *(12/31/2004)*

Marqués de Riscal 2000 Riscal 1860 Tempranillo (Vino de la Tierra de Castilla y León) $8. Bulky and clumsy, with powerful early barnyard aromas that ultimately give way to more refined plum and cherry. While this wine has its virtues, it lacks elegance. And while we admit that it's a country wine that's probably meant to be a sizable, rustic quaff, it seems a bit too basic and borderline to garner a better review. 84 —M.S. *(8/1/2003)*

Marqués de Riscal 2001 Baron de Chirel Reserva Tempranillo Blend (Rioja) $50. Dark violet in color, with plenty of wood smoke and earth to the nose, which also offers tobacco and mushroom. Dynamic on the palate, with ripe cherry and blackberry flavors. Sort of airy on the finish, with mocha and chocolate. Hefty throughout, with nice tannins. From Marqués de Riscal. 91 —M.S. *(10/1/2005)*

Marqués de Riscal 1999 Baron de Chirel Reserva Tempranillo Blend (Rioja) $60. Firmly structured and ageworthy, with loads of vanillin oak but also masses of dark fruit, earth, molasses and tobacco flavors that linger on the finish. In contrast to the rest of Riscal's offerings, this one needs time in the cellar. Try in 2008 or so. 90 *(12/31/2004)*

Marqués de Riscal 1996 Baron de Chirel Reserva Tempranillo Blend (Rioja) $60. Slick and very much in the modern international style, this smooth operator has the dark, toasty oak and vanilla over black fruit profile seen often, and from many places. But it's undeniably tasty, and its bright tart-sweet fruit, coffee, and chocolate accents and substantial feel is pleasing. Finishes long and tasty with espresso and vanilla accents, full but supple tannins. Drink now–2008. 90 —M.M. *(9/1/2002)*

Marqués de Riscal 1998 Gran Reserva Tempranillo Blend (Rioja) $36. All it takes is a quick sniff and it's clear that this is the real thing. Aromas of sweet black cherry, marzipan, and dried earth create a classic bouquet. Additional pure cherry on the palate with chocolate; together they strike the right chord. Harmonious and still worthy of some more aging. 90 —M.S. *(10/1/2005)*

Marqués de Riscal 1996 Gran Reserva Tempranillo Blend (Rioja) $35. Although this bottle didn't show quite as well as the one rated last year (92 points, 10/03), it's still a fine wine. Tobacco, earth, vanilla and coffee aromas, backed by black cherry and cassis. It's bigger than the 2000 Reserva, but just as supple and ready to drink. 90 *(11/1/2004)*

Marqués de Riscal 1996 Gran Reserva Tempranillo Blend (Rioja) $36. The nose is full of cherry, yeasty bread, and earth, while the palate is healthy and alive with plum fruit and chocolate fudge. Some oak lives on the finish, which is otherwise chocolaty and creamy. 92 —M.S. *(10/1/2003)*

Marqués de Riscal 1995 Gran Reserva Tempranillo Blend (Rioja) $36. A trip to the county fair with aromas of horse stall and prize cows. Flavors are rich: dark cherry shows through more than earth, and they lingers with firm tannins indicating that it will last till 2010. 88 —C.S. *(11/1/2002)*

Marqués de Riscal 2000 Reserva Tempranillo Blend (Rioja) $17. Starts off a little shaky, but just needs a little time in a decanter to right itself and blow off some dusty aromas. Underneath that is some toasty oak, along with cherry, vanilla, and tobacco flavors. It's relatively light, supple, and ready to drink tonight with roast lamb. 87 *(12/31/2004)*

Marqués de Riscal 1998 Reserva Tempranillo Blend (Rioja) $15. Tar, raspberry, and old wood aromas are the best part of this wine. The acidity is a little awkward, but the finish is smooth and very earthy. 86 —C.S. *(11/1/2002)*

Marqués de Riscal 2003 Verdejo (Rueda) $8. Light- to medium-bodied, and crisp, this pineappley, wine also suggests pear, citrus, and quince. Finishes long, tart, and mouthwatering—a worthy apéritif. 87 Best Buy *(12/31/2004)*

Marqués de Riscal 2000 White Blend (Rueda) $9. Even and medium-weight, this Rueda white shows hay and a slight sour-apple quality. Smoothly textured, it glides across the palate easily and into a broad, dry finish with faint white pepper notes. Appealing, if perhaps a little mature. 85 —M.M. *(9/1/2002)*

SPAIN

MARQUÉS DE TOMARES

Marqués de Tomares 2001 Crianza Tempranillo Blend (Rioja) $19. An example of a well-made, lightweight red that puts clarity and freshness ahead of bulk and oak. The palate is racy and slick, with some peppery spice and milk chocolate along with pure cherry and raspberry. Finishes warm, tight, and spicy. **88** —M.S. (6/1/2005)

Marqués de Tomares 1999 Crianza Tempranillo Blend (Rioja) $19. Smoky and saucy on the nose, with a hint of oak-based caramel. The palate features tart raspberry and light oak, while the thin, tight finish carries with it a bit of milk chocolate. Not dense or layered; mildly leafy. **84** —M.S. (12/31/2004)

Marqués de Tomares 1996 Gran Reserva Tempranillo Blend (Rioja) $50. A touch leafy, with telltale root beer and cola aromas mixing with spice and raisins. The palate is firm, with tart but precise fruit that veers toward red currants and cranberry; which isn't to say it's sour. Nuances of forest floor and tree bark are expected. **88** —M.S. (12/31/2004)

Marqués de Tomares 1995 Gran Reserva Tempranillo Blend (Rioja) $50. Root beer, cola nut, red pepper, and saddle leather together form a classic aged Rioja bouquet. Bright cherry and red currant on the palate is followed by a finish graced by vanilla and cherry tomato. Some minty, herbal nuances make it extra interesting. **89** —M.S. (12/31/2004)

MARQUÉS DE ULIA

Marqués de Ulia 1998 Reserva Tempranillo (Rioja) $15. Begins with tight sulfuric aromas that transform into rubber and red fruit. Flavors of cherry, plum, and dried herbs are tart and precise, while the finish offers some tomato. Overall it's a solid, tight wine that gets better with airing. **87** —M.S. (6/1/2005)

MARQUÉS DE VARGAS

Marqués de Vargas 1998 Reserva Tempranillo Blend (Rioja) $70. Full-bodied and earthy, with red plum, cola, and tomato aromas. The palate mixes leafy, herbal flavors with candied cherry, and the combination proves to have issues. Finishes gritty, with hard tannins. More traditional than modern in style. **86** —M.S. (3/1/2005)

MARQUÉS DE VILLALBA

Marqués de Villalba 2000 Crianza Tempranillo (Ribera del Guadiana) $15. Sharp and snappy on the nose, with green tobacco and earth notes. Turns toward red fruit on the palate, with raspberry and cherry prominent. Fairly lean and tight in terms of mouthfeel, with snappy acids and moderate tannins. **85** —M.S. (12/31/2004)

MARQUÉS DE VILLAMAGNA

Marqués de Villamagna 1997 Gran Reserva Tempranillo (Rioja) $NA. Fairly dark, with black raspberry and pepper aromas. Shows decent length and depth, with standard old-Rioja smoke and leather. Cut from the classic mold, made simply and clean by Juan Alcorta Bodegas, part of the Allied Domecq group. **87** —M.S. (9/1/2004)

MARQUÉS DE VIZHOJA

Marqués de Vizhoja 2005 Torre La Moreira Albariño (Rías Baixas) $19. A single-estate Albariño with clean minerality accenting flowery, grassy aromas. In the mouth, it's forward and finely chiseled, with pure apple, papaya, and saline flavors. Not run of the mill, and for that we like it a lot. **90** —M.S. (9/1/2006)

Marqués de Vizhoja 2005 Señor da Folla Verde White Blend (Rías Baixas) $21. With 30% Loureira and Treixadura added to 70% Albariño, this wine offers sweet pineapple aromas in front of round melon, peach and spice flavors. Rather plump and driving, with a prolonged finish and some distant minerality. **88** —M.S. (9/1/2006)

MARQUÉS DEL PUERTO

Marqués del Puerto 1997 Crianza Red Blend (Rioja) $12. 81 —M.S. (8/1/2000)

Marqués del Puerto 1991 Gran Reserva Red Blend (Rioja) $21. 84 (8/1/2000)

Marqués del Puerto 1996 Reserva Red Blend (Rioja) $13. Tasty and tart, with interesting aromas of vanilla and lemon meringue pie. Strawberry flavors were zesty and accented with a little cedar. Drink and enjoy now. **85** —C.S. (11/1/2002)

Marqués del Puerto 1995 Reserva Red Blend (Rioja) $17. 85 (8/1/2000)

Marqués del Puerto 1985 Roman Paladino Gran Reserva Red Blend (Rioja) $130. 87 (8/1/2000)

Marqués del Puerto 1996 Selección Especial MM-Reserva Red Blend (Rioja) $40. A rich but dusty wine, with aromas of grilled meat and steak sauce. Lush plum and currant fruit features a hint of salinity in the mouth. The tannins are well integrated, yielding a wine that is drinkable now but will last to 2010. **90** (11/1/2002)

Marqués del Puerto 1994 Selección Especial MM Reserva Red Blend (Rioja) $NA. 87 (8/1/2000)

Marqués del Puerto 2002 Rosado Rosé Blend (Rioja) $9. Almost red in color, with nectarine and cherry aromas. Fairly big and lively in the mouth, but the fruit is soft and simple: It's like underripe strawberry and stone fruits. The finish broadens out somewhat, but it never gets past the snappy, tart stage. **83** —M.S. (10/1/2003)

Marqués del Puerto 2000 Crianza Tempranillo (Rioja) $14. Some mint, licorice, and cinnamon makes the sweet nose fairly open, and there's plenty of snap and pop to the cherry-raspberry palate. This is a simple wine, but it's tasty and has all its ducks in a row. **84** —M.S. (10/1/2003)

Marqués del Puerto 1999 Crianza Tempranillo (Rioja) $12. This Tempranillo combines red raspberries with chalky minerals and a touch of white pepper. Flavors of grilled meat go along with raspberry fruit, then the wine finishes smooth, soft, and even. **89** —C.S. (11/1/2002)

Marqués del Puerto 1995 Gran Reserva Tempranillo (Rioja) $25. Light smoke, cedar, and raisin aromas are followed by dried cherry and currant-like flavors. At eight years of age, it's starting to cross the bridge from mature to fading. The acidity is mostly what's left, so there's a beam of tartness at the center and on the finish. **83** —M.S. (10/1/2003)

Marqués del Puerto 1999 Rosado Tempranillo (Rioja) $10. 85 (8/1/2000)

Marqués del Puerto 2003 Rosado Tempranillo Blend (Rioja) $10. Big and colorful, with strawberry and rubber aromas. A good amount of citrus and raspberry creates a lengthy palate that forces its game on you. Not a strong finish, but nice along the way. **86 Best Buy** —M.S. (9/1/2004)

Marqués del Puerto 2003 Blanco Viura (Rioja) $9. This 100% Viura is fresh and forward but not overly expressive in terms of aromas or flavors. Simple white fruits like grapes and peach carry the palate, while the finish is heavy with the aftertaste of citrus pith. **83** —M.S. (12/31/2004)

Marqués del Puerto 2002 Blanco Viura (Rioja) $9. Clean and clear, with pear and mineral aromas. There are lime, apple, and peach flavors and a crisp, fresh finish. With loads of citrus and a streamlined mouthfeel, it's quite tasty when served chilled. **86 Best Buy** —M.S. (10/1/2003)

Marqués del Puerto 2000 Cosecha 2000 White Blend (Rioja) $17. The FB stands for fermented in barrel, but everything about it is strange. The aromas are of wheat and creamed corn, while the flavors are at once citrusy and then, in the next moment, akin to pepper or chilies. The finish is slightly pickled and flat. This wine seems to have lost its verve, assuming it once had verve. **81** —M.S. (11/1/2002)

MARQUÉS DEL REAL TESORO

Marqués del Real Tesoro NV Del Principe Amontillado Muy Viejo Sherry (Jerez) $22. This Real Tesoro brand is a bit forceful and awkward, but it delivers decent toffee and apricot extract on the nose followed by butterscotch and cashew brittle on the palate. **84** —M.S. (12/31/2004)

Marqués del Real Tesoro NV Pedro Ximenez Viejo Sherry (Jerez) $16. A bit separated and orange at the edges, but full of raisin, hard spice, and power. Flavors of dried fruit, cinnamon, and brown sugar are sweet as daylights, but there's enough piercing acidity and savory qualities on keep it on line. **88** —M.S. (12/31/2004)

Marqués del Real Tesoro NV Tio Mateo Fino Seco y Suave Sherry (Jerez) $15. From Real Tesoro, this fino is dry and chalky, with spiky blanched-almond flavors and a heavy, astringent aftertaste of sautéed mushrooms. **82** —M.S. (12/31/2004)

MARTÍN CÓDAX

Martín Códax 2005 Albariño (Rías Baixas) $16. Floral, with buttercup and acacia on the nose. The mouth, however, is a bit more austere and sharp-edged. It delivers steely, bracing acids and narrow flavors of green apple, lemon, and tangerine. A tightly knit Albariño made for shellfish. **88** —*M.S. (9/1/2006)*

Martín Códax 1999 Albariño (Rías Baixas) $13. 88 Best Buy —*M.M. (8/1/2000)*

Martín Códax 1999 Burgans Albariño (Rías Baixas) $12. 85 —*M.M. (8/1/2000)*

Martín Códax 1998 Organistrum Albariño (Rías Baixas) $17. 87 —*M.M. (8/1/2000)*

MARTINEZ BUJANDA

Martinez Bujanda 2001 Finca Antigua Cabernet Sauvignon (La Mancha) $8. Decent Cabernet for the price, with minty, herbal notes joining black currants on the nose. Slightly weedy and earthy on the palate, and it finishes tart. **85** *(11/1/2003)*

Martinez Bujanda 1997 Conde de Valdemar Garnacha Reserva Garnacha (Rioja) $26. Flat and fading, with raisiny aromas and notes of caramel. The palate, at its best, has dried cherry fruit and spice, but really all that's on display here is acidity and the skeleton of what was, several years ago, a pretty tasty wine several. Tasted twice with consistent results. **82** —*M.S. (10/1/2003)*

Martinez Bujanda 1999 Conde de Valdemar Reserva Garnacha (Rioja) $25. There's a hint of peanutiness to the aromas, along with black cherry, clove, and allspice. Chocolate and black pepper sneak in on the palate, where the wine is big-boned without being overly rich or lush. In short, it's well balanced. **90 Editors' Choice** *(11/1/2003)*

Martinez Bujanda 2002 Valdemar Vino Rosado Garnacha (Rioja) $8. This rosado of Garnacha features light aromas and flavors of strawberries and watermelon, finishing tart and fresh. A super summer quaffer. **85 Best Buy** *(11/1/2003)*

Martinez Bujanda 2000 Conde de Valdemar Crianza Red Blend (Rioja) $10. Aromas of strawberry jam and green herbs greet you. Next in line is a palate of moderately rich berry fruit and some peppery accents. It finishes light, with some length. Offers good zing and some meatiness, but not too much. **85** —*M.S. (3/1/2004)*

Martinez Bujanda 1998 Finca Valpiedra Reserva Red Blend (Rioja) $32. This single-vineyard wine is beefy and bold, with a thick mouthfeel and lots of extract. Blackberry and pepper control the palate, while the finish is heavy and smoky. If there's a fault, it's that the wine is lacking in edginess. It's a tiny bit grapy and soft. Otherwise, everything else is a go. **87** —*M.S. (3/1/2004)*

Martinez Bujanda 1998 Conde de Valdemar Crianza Tempranillo (Rioja) $9. Tasty and smooth, this Rioja shows sweet black cherry fruit and licorice aromas and flavors. There's plenty of oak here, too, plus some tannins to lose on the even, dry menthol and leather-tinged close. Will benefit from a year or two in bottle, and may shine quite nicely if the fruit comes forward a bit more. Drink now–2007. **86** —*M.M. (9/1/2002)*

Martinez Bujanda 1994 Conde de Valdemar Gran Reserva Tempranillo (Rioja) $21. A flavorful, mature wine from a respected vintage, in the classic Conde de Valdemar manner, a refined, perhaps more Pinot Noir-like style of Tempranillo. Handsome dried berry fruit and a cedary sweetness mark the wine throughout. It's lithe and elegant, with an almost delicate sense of balance. Has the elements of a much more expensive aged red Burgundy. Best now through 2005. **89** —*M.M. (9/1/2002)*

Martinez Bujanda 1998 Conde de Valdemar Reserva Tempranillo (Rioja) $15. The fruit in this wine is a little thin, but you can't help but be seduced by the pretty oak shadings of sweet vanilla, clove and cinnamon. Just enough berry fruit comes through to carry the flavors on the finish. **87** *(11/1/2003)*

Martinez Bujanda 2001 Finca Antigua Tempranillo (La Mancha) $9. Varietally true, with hints of meat and tobacco layered over blackberry fruit. Some oak shows up as well, bringing notes of roasted coffee. It's clean and tart, a young Tempranillo that offers juicy, fresh fruit at a good price. **87 Best Buy** *(11/1/2003)*

Martinez Bujanda 2000 Finca Antigua Crianza Tempranillo (La Mancha) $10. Finca Anigua's crianza is a blend of mostly Tempranillo with smaller amounts of Cabernet Sauvignon and Merlot. After 14 months in oak, it's toasty and filled with aromas of dried spices and cocoa that slightly dominate the tart, cranberry fruit. **86** *(11/1/2003)*

Martinez Bujanda 1997 Finca Valpiedra Reserva Tempranillo (Rioja) $30. Fully mature and in need of current consumption, this wine reflects the difficulty of the vintage in its slightly green aromas and flavors. Finishes tart and cranberryish, with notes of coffee and earth. **87** *(11/1/2003)*

Martinez Bujanda 1997 Conde de Valdemar Gran Reserva Tempranillo Blend (Rioja) $25. Sharp and fruity, but not what you'd label as lush. Tobacco, plum, and cherry flavors are best at first; after a while a more raisiny quality arises. Midland at best; from a poor vintage. **83** —*M.S. (10/1/2005)*

Martinez Bujanda 1999 Finca Valpiedra Reserva Tempranillo Blend (Rioja) $32. A stand-alone project from Martínez-Bujanda that is spicy, leafy, and not unlike good Bordeaux. The wine is a Tempranillo-dominated blend that includes some Cabernet. It has herbal, leafy aromas along with cherry and vanilla, and then zest, acidity, and tannin on the palate. Well made and ready for the dinner table. **90** —*M.S. (9/1/2004)*

Martinez Bujanda 1996 Gran Reserva Tempranillo Blend (Rioja) $22. A reasonably priced gran reserva from a good vintage, this '96 is plump, supple, and ready to drink. Thirty months in American oak has imparted plenty of charred and smoky aromas to the meat- and berry-infused flavors. Finishes long, with some lemony acid that would work well with pork roasts. **89** *(11/1/2003)*

MARTINEZ LAORDEN

Martinez Laorden 2004 El Talud Tempranillo (Rioja) $13. Sweet and grapey, with hints of olive and balsamic vinegar. Snappy cherry and raspberry flavors are raw and flow forward on a wave of sharp, saliva-inducing acids. Finishes with chocolate and baked fruit flavors. **81** —*M.S. (2/1/2006)*

MARTINSANCHO

Martinsancho 2004 Verdejo (Rueda) $15. Crisp and green on the nose, with aromas of celery, green pepper, and passion fruit. Tight and juicy across the palate, with peach and lime flavors. Dry as a soda cracker on the finish, yet firm and food friendly. **86** —*M.S. (8/1/2005)*

Martinsancho 2003 Verdejo (Rueda) $14. Heavily aromatic, with strong scents of nettles, citrus, and mineral. This is a big-boned white, the product of a hot summer. It oozes pear and peach flavors prior to a smooth apple-coated finish. All in all, there's a nice medley of activity, with good acids to push everything forward. **89** —*M.S. (9/1/2004)*

Martinsancho 2002 Verdejo (Rueda) $12. Sharp and siren-like in the nose, with snappy green pepper and passion fruit aromas. Based on the bouquet, you'd think it Sauvignon Blanc. And the peppery, grapefruit palate wouldn't steer you away from that perception. It's not spritzy, but almost so. A real live-wire act. **85** —*M.S. (3/1/2004)*

Martinsancho 2000 Rueda Superior Verdejo (Rueda) $13. Smoothly textured with a hint of viscosity, this shows typical apple and hay flavors. Consistent from nose to close, there's nothing wrong here, but it lacks the liveliness a vibrant young Verdejo can show. Drink now. **84** —*M.M. (9/1/2002)*

MARTIVILLI

Martivilli 2000 Verdejo (Rueda) $10. Appearances can be deceiving: pale in color but angular and flavorful, this white sports attractive lime and hay aromas with fragrant honeysuckle hints. A subtle pepperiness creeps in on the light, crisp palate. Closes smoothly, with lime and white pepper notes. This shows more flavor and texture than most light whites at this price—try this instead of a Pinot Grigio. **87 Best Buy** —*M.M. (4/1/2002)*

MAS DELS FRARES

Mas Dels Frares 2004 Red Blend (Priorat) $17. A bit lighter on the nose than many, with notes of raspberry and strawberry. That same character works its way onto the palate, where raspberry and plum flavors are front and center. Fruity and balanced, with a ripe, easy-to-like personality. **88** —*M.S. (12/15/2006)*

Mas Dels Frares 2002 Crianza Red Blend (Priorat) $70. Simple plum and red-berry aromas carry the bouquet, which leads to acid-based cherry and berry flavors. Comes across hard and spotty, and the mouthfeel is reduced and too demanding. **84** —*M.S. (10/1/2005)*

MAS DOIX

Mas Doix 2002 Doix Costers de Vinyes Velles Red Blend (Priorat) $85. Like a freight train, this wine from the village of Poboleda hits with force. From Joan Doix and his winemaking nephew, Ramón Llagostera, it deftly delivers both red and black fruit notes, all on a lightly tannic frame. To call it lip-smacking and juicy would be correct. The blend is 51% old-vines Garnacha, 46% Cariñena, and 3% Merlot. 500 cases made. **91** —*M.S. (10/1/2005)*

MAS FRANCH

Mas Franch 2003 Red Blend (Montsant) $35. Black fruit, licorice, and earth are all aromas of classic Montsant, and together they are easy to enjoy and understand. Ripe black cherry, pepper, and an undercurrent of licorice and coffee work the palate, while the finish sports tight acids and smooth tannins. Good now through 2009. **89** —*M.S. (12/15/2006)*

MAS IGNEUS

Mas Igneus 2001 Mas Igneus-Garnacha Blanca Old Vines Garnacha (Priorat) $18. Made mostly from Garnacha Blanca, this wine is odd. It has sugary hay-like aromas and bland yet sweet pear flavors. It grabs a little at the edges, and it never reaches stride or makes an impact. **83** —*M.S. (3/1/2004)*

Mas Igneus 2001 Barranc Dels Closos Red Blend (Priorat) $15. Word has it that 2001 is a benchmark year for Priorat, and this early bird seems like a positive indicator. It has some earth and mushroom on the nose, but also plenty of sweet fruit and cinnamon. The palate is chunky and unbridled, with all the plum, berry, and apple skin one could ask for. A chewy finish with a creamy chocolate base seals the deal in a winning way. **91 Editors' Choice** —*M.S. (3/1/2004)*

Mas Igneus 2000 FA 112 Red Blend (Priorat) $32. Deep and wild up front, with a streak of mint and clove running through the pretty black plum that carries the nose. Cherry, raspberry, and apple skin flavors are jazzed up by pepper and nutmeg hints, while the finish is lovely. Overall it's soft, with notes of butter and baked apples. Intense and angular, age it for at least two years. **92** —*M.S. (3/1/2004)*

Mas Igneus 1999 FA 104 Blanco White Blend (Priorat) $19. A lovely and unusual Bergamot-like citrus-blossom note runs through this attractive wine. The full nose displays hay and creamy nougat, and the mouth is a melange of orange, almond, and herb flavors. This solid white has unique character and closes long, with citrus and nut flavors and a fine spicy back-bouquet. Worth seeking out, this is reminiscent of some Rhône whites. **88** —*M.M. (4/1/2002)*

MAS MARÇAL

Mas Marçal 2003 Tinto Red Blend (Catalonia) $9. Bulky and ripe, with raspberry and punch-like aromas. If you like sweet notes like kirsch, sugar beets, and coulis, this has it. Clearly the wine reflects the hot vintage, so it's soft, chewy and bent on sweetness. Good, but not an ager. **86 Best Buy** —*M.S. (6/1/2005)*

MAS MARTINET

Mas Martinet 2002 Clos Martinet Red Blend (Priorat) $58. Elevated from the first nosing through the multilevel palate and then out the door. Fragrant like an aromatic magnet, with red licorice, wild flower, and jammy fruit. A potent brew, with some medicinal cherry to the toasty finish. Super healthy, with an aggressive personality. Could use a year or two to settle because now it's rather tannic. **92** —*M.S. (10/1/2005)*

MAS VILÓ

Mas Viló 2003 Red Blend (Priorat) $26. Dry, leathery, and pungent, with plenty of pepper and earth to the nose. The blend is 60% Garnacha and the rest Cariñena, and it pushes surprisingly fresh raspberry flavors along

with a fine undercurrent of oak. Racy and cleansing, with hints of cola. A good '03 for early drinking; no need to cellar. **87** —*M.S. (10/1/2005)*

MASET DEL LLEÓ

Maset del Lleó NV Semi-Dulce Rosé Blend (Penedès) $11. Out of the ordinary, so it's hard to gauge. To enjoy this you have to appreciate the off-dry style that features residual sugar and overt sweetness. In that sense, it's a lot like White Zin. Assuming that's not your bag, it won't score big. **83** —*M.S. (8/1/2005)*

Maset del Lleó NV Brut Sparkling Blend (Cava) $13. A touch bland. Flavors of lime, apple, and almond are drying, while the finish is light, bordering on watery. Lacks zest and character, but still tastes pretty good. **83** —*M.S. (12/15/2004)*

Maset del Lleó NV Brut Nature Sparkling Blend (Cava) $14. The bouquet is flowery, with a full note of lime. The mouthfeel is a touch heavy and sticky, but the citrus (primarily orange) flavors are good. A light and easy cava. **84** —*M.S. (12/15/2004)*

Maset del Lleó NV Brut Nature Reserva Sparkling Blend (Cava) $16. Quite open, with a candied nose that's slightly aggressive. Nice on the palate, with melon, peach, and nectarine flavors. Finishes in fresh, playful fashion. Zesty and good, and ultra clean. **86** —*M.S. (12/15/2004)*

Maset del Lleó NV Brut Reserva Sparkling Blend (Cava) $15. A bit fizzy, with a nose reminiscent of lemon-lime soda. Yet while it tickles, it manages to please. The palate offers nice honeydew and nectarine flavors, which are backed by a frothy, creamy finish. Fresh and balanced. **87** —*M.S. (12/15/2004)*

Maset del Lleó NV Semi Seco Sparkling Blend (Cava) $12. Well balanced from start to finish, with rubbery, attractive aromas that also offer some smoke and cream nuances. The palate is crisp and packed densely with ripe fruit, primarily sweet apple. Its mouthfeel is a strong point. **88 Best Buy** —*M.S. (12/15/2004)*

Maset del Lleó NV Semi Seco Reserva Sparkling Blend (Cava) $14. Dosed heavily to be sweet, but still very nice. Look for ripe melon and sugared citrus on the palate, followed by a thick finish that toes the line on cloying but manages to avoid stepping on it. Not quite as clean as the bodega's normal semisweet cava. **87** —*M.S. (12/15/2004)*

Maset del Lleó NV Semi-Sweet White Blend (Penedès) $11. Light and generally unexpressive, with peach and melon aromas. Basic honeydew and nectarine flavors lead to a waxy, grippy palate that carries some pineapple and banana flavors. Sweet but not overly. **84** —*M.S. (8/1/2005)*

MASIA BACH

Masia Bach 1997 Bach Cabernet Sauvignon (Catalonia) $12. **86** —*R.V. (11/1/1999)*

Masia Bach 1997 Merlot (Catalonia) $NA. **88** —*R.V. (11/1/1999)*

Masia Bach 1996 Bach Tempranillo (Catalonia) $8. **89 Best Buy** —*R.V. (11/1/1999)*

MASIES D'AVINYO

Masies d'Avinyo 2002 Abadal Crianza Cabernet Sauvignon-Merlot (Pla de Bages) $14. Open and lighter framed, with berry aromas and a strong scent of black olive. Somewhat salty and herbal, but also fairly fruity and spunky. Shows plenty of acidity and tannin. **85** —*M.S. (2/1/2006)*

Masies d'Avinyo 2001 Abadal Merlot (Pla de Bages) $16. All the wines in the Abadal line seem commited to serious aromas and flavors supported by honest structure. This Merlot from an obscure Catalonian wine region offers blackberry, cigar box, and raisin aromas in front of additional blackberry flavor. There's also chocolate folded into the finishing layers. Integrated and properlly welded by firm tannins. **89** —*M.S. (9/1/2006)*

Masies D'Avinyo 2003 Red Blend (Pla de Bages) $12. A real surprise! Who in their right mind could expect so much quality from a Cab Franc-Tempranillo blend from Penedès? But try it and we guarantee you're going to like it. The nose is meaty, ripe, and round, while the palate features pure core fruit backed by chocolaty warmth. With kick as well as subtlety, this is a bargain hunter's dream. **91 Best Buy** —*M.S. (4/1/2006)*

SPAIN

MATARROMERA

Matarromera 2003 Crianza Tinto del Pais (Ribera del Duero) $28. Dark, with a heavy warmth to the nose and lots of earth and toast. Comes on more racy in the mouth, with snappy red-cherry and roasted plum flavors. Gets harder and harder as it opens, displaying heat and tannin. Needs better balance and cushion. **83** —*M.S. (11/1/2006)*

Matarromera 1999 Crianza Tinto del Pais (Ribera del Duero) $30. If you want a forward, intense wine with unbridled power and dynamite fruit, this is it. At first it might seem wild, almost out of whack. But once it unfolds there are cherry, coffee, and herbal subtleties. The finish is a mile long and the potency and young acids make it almost citric. This is Crianza, oaked but not overdone, that bursts with vibrancy. **91 Editors' Choice** —*M.S. (3/1/2004)*

Matarromera 1999 Grand Reserva Tinto del Pais (Ribera del Duero) $105. Smoky like BBQ, with dried fruits, leather, and heat. Maybe a bit too exuberant in how it hits the palate; the fruit is a touch tangy and clipped, while the tannins are persistent if anything. A touchy, prickly wine that will do well with grilled meats. **87** —*M.S. (11/1/2006)*

Matarromera 1999 Prestigio Tinto del Pais (Ribera del Duero) $60. A zealous wine with sweaty leather, prune, and leftover oak on the nose. The mouth is charged up and lively as the tannins and acids meet to boost cherry and raspberry fruit. Comes across too eager and hard; needs more mouthfeel and subtlety to make the next level. **85** —*M.S. (11/1/2006)*

Matarromera 2001 Prestigio Pago de las Solanas Tinto del Pais (Ribera del Duero) $300. Open-cut oak, blackberry, and chocolate are the opening shots in this plump, ripe, full-bodied red that is slightly tannic and chewy but impressive due to solid plum, cherry, and vanilla flavors. Delivers commendable RdD quality, but $300 is shockingly expensive. **89** —*M.S. (11/1/2006)*

Matarromera 2002 Reserva Tinto del Pais (Ribera del Duero) $40. Hard spices, smoke, and tar darken up the berry nose, while the palate is round and solid, with nice berry and plum fruit. The finish delivers a wave of blackened toast, while licorice plays from the second chair. Nicely made and familiar as RDD goes. **88** —*M.S. (12/15/2006)*

Matarromera 1998 Reserva Tinto del Pais (Ribera del Duero) $49. Sweet aromas hint of grassy meadows and cherry cola. The palate is open and ripe, but there's also a firm, tannic foundation to support all the ripe flavors. Time in the cellar should permit this powerhouse to shed some of its tannins. Hold for another year or so. **90** —*M.S. (3/1/2004)*

MAURO

Mauro 2000 Tempranillo (Vino de la Tierra de Castilla y León) $32. Sweet and rich, with aromatic notes of barbecued meats, blackberry, and wild flowers. Quite bold and chewy, but with an acidic middle that preserves balance like an angel. For the maximum in terms of plum, blackberry, and licorice, this one delivers the goods. It's mouthfilling and delicious, with tannic structure and a chocolaty smoothness. **92 Editors' Choice** —*M.S. (3/1/2004)*

MAYORAL

Mayoral 2000 Cosecha Tempranillo Blend (Jumilla) $7. This medium-to full-bodied red from Spain's southeast sports a potent, inviting nose. Black plum, soy, leather, and oak merge in an appealing, inky opening. The black cherry flavors are quite dry, but also rich and palate-coating. Finishes with substantial tannins. The wine should drink even better in one or two years, but should pair well with hearty fare even now. **87 Best Buy** —*M.M. (9/1/2002)*

MEDERAÑO

Mederaño 2003 Linea d'Oro Cabernet Sauvignon-Tempranillo (Catalunya) $10. Spicy and herbal, but with ample fruit backing that up it comes across as a nice everyday red wine. The palate is a bit earthy and rustic, with a touch of green. But for the most part it's a healthy, mildly tannic red that will wash down just about any food put in its path. The blend is Cabernet Sauvignon and Tempranillo. **85 Best Buy** —*M.S. (4/1/2006)*

Mederaño 2000 Tinto Red Blend (Tierra de Castilla) $7. This tinto is good, but doesn't leave much of a lasting impression. Offers vague black fruit, oak, and earth aromas and flavors, from beginning to end. Suitable for casual circumstances. **83** —*D.T. (4/1/2003)*

Mederaño 2001 White Blend (Tierra de Castilla) $7. Light mineral aroma; tastes like mineral water with an undercurrent of citrus. It's spritzy in the mouth—the vinous cousin to lemon Perrier. **80** —*D.T. (4/1/2003)*

Mederaño 2004 Linea d'Oro Chardonnay & Xarel-Lo White Blend (Catalunya) $10. Mildly sulfuric, with vitamin, bitter greens, and funk on the nose. Melon and banana flavors are of the soft, dilute type. Seems burnt and herbal. Not fresh enough. **82** —*M.S. (9/1/2006)*

MERUM

Merum 2005 Old Vines Grenache-Syrah (Spain) $16. Plump and full of plum and licorice aromas. Weighs in big and a touch sweet, with black cherry and ripe plum flavors. Very soft in the feel department, with a soft finish that's like a cushioned fall. Healthy as a whole, with lively tannins. **85** —*M.S. (12/15/2006)*

Merum 2003 Monastrell (Jumilla) $9. Bulky and fruity, with a medicinal note to the ripe nose. From a hot vintage, so it is jammy and sweet, with strawberry and chocolate flavors. Finishes creamy and thick, with heavy doses of vanilla. Also shows a mild cooked character. **83** —*M.S. (6/1/2005)*

Merum 2002 Unico Monastrell (Jumilla) $27. A Monastrell with 10% Cabernet, and it is heavily minty and woody, with leaner than expected fruit and a whole lot of resin and vanilla setting things off. Decent structure and mouthfeel, and with plenty of oak. Not bad but nothing too exciting. **84** —*M.S. (6/1/2005)*

Merum 2005 Tempranillo (Madrid) $10. A touch minty and rustic, but with enough black cherry, marmalade, and tannin to make the grade. Jammy, medium in density, and solid. A stout, friendly red made for early drinking. **85 Best Buy** —*M.S. (12/15/2006)*

Merum 2002 Tempranillo (Madrid) $7. With earth, leather, and a touch of cheese to the bouquet, this unheralded wine is rustic yet solid, quite the surprise and satisfying overall. The palate has dark plum, chocolate, and balsamic flavors, while it finishes with straight-ahead espresso and cocoa. **87 Best Buy** —*M.S. (9/1/2004)*

Merum 1999 Crianza Tempranillo (Madrid) $10. Aromas of coffee, balsamic vinegar, and cedar, but not much fruit, send this wine on its way. Flavors of plum and cherry are standard but clean, while the finish is fruity and offers hints of licorice. A touch sharp but likable. **86 Best Buy** —*M.S. (9/1/2004)*

MM MASIA L'HEREU

MM Masia L'Hereu 2000 Reserva Privada Cabernet Blend (Penedès) $10. Sweet and perfumed. The early palate is tight and tannic, with dynamic cherry and raspberry flavors. The back palate seems linear and defined at first, but what is initially snappy and crisp unfolds to display several layers of complexity and style. **90 Best Buy** —*M.S. (5/1/2004)*

MM Masia L'Hereu 1999 1882 Reserva Privada Red Blend (Penedès) $10. Dense and fruity, but not as defined or enriched as the 2000. The bouquet delivers red fruit, foresty aromas, and chocolate. Next in line is a palate of brandied berries, earth, and a touch too much acidity. No complaints as a whole, but it shows some leanness in the middle. **88 Best Buy** —*M.S. (5/1/2004)*

MONOPOLE

Monopole 2001 Blanco Seco Viura (Rioja) $20. Plump yellow fruit comprises the backbone of this Viura; sweet, musky-floral aromas and flavors add interest. Medium-bodied; yellow fruit, mineral, and resin bat cleanup. **86** —*D.T. (4/1/2003)*

MONT MARÇAL

Mont Marçal NV Brut Sparkling Blend (Cava) $11. 89 *(11/15/1999)*

Mont Marçal 2003 Reserva Brut Sparkling Blend (Cava) $12. Nice and fresh, with defined, attractive apple and pear aromas. Dry and fruity in the mouth, with a tad of sweetness to the firm papaya, lime, and apple flavors. Ripe and round enough, with balance. The total package in cava. **88 Best Buy** —*M.S. (6/1/2006)*

SPAIN

Mont Marçal 2001 Brut Reserva Sparkling Blend (Cava) $12. This is top-notch value cava, perfectly round, solid, and fruity. Pear, apple, and pastry aromas carry the nose while orange, lemon, green herb, and white pepper flavors are defined and attractive. Rarely does a sparkler at this price register so high on the quality meter, but the structure and totality of this Macabeo-Parellada-Xarello blend is nothing if not commendable. Mont Marçal ranks as a perennial value leader. **89 Best Buy** —*M.S.* *(11/15/2005)*

Mont Marçal 1999 Brut Reserva Sparkling Blend (Cava) $9. Although lacking a bit of complexity, this is an affable pour with its toast, cream, white peach, and butter aromas. Toast and lemon flavors lead to a buttercream finish. **86** —*K.F.* *(12/31/2002)*

Mont Marçal 1998 Brut Reserva Sparkling Blend (Cava) $9. Soft in the mouth and smoky on the close, expect a buttercream-vanilla-tobacco bouquet and lemon, cream, and pear flavors in the mouth. Not as much bead as we'd like, but has more complexity than you'd expect. **86 Best Buy** *(12/31/2001)*

Mont Marçal NV Brut Reserva Rosé Sparkling Blend (Cava) $15. Colorful stuff, like the flesh of a wild King salmon. The nose offers dried cherry, nectarine, and some carbon dioxide. Fresh and tangy in the mouth, with pink grapefruit as the primary flavor despite its Pinot Noir DNA. Good enough to sip on a summer day, but not what you'd call elevated. **86** —*M.S.* *(12/15/2005)*

Mont Marçal NV Extremarium Brut Sparkling Blend (Cava) $18. Open and floral, with acacia and orange blossom on the nose. The palate is full-bore citrus, dealing orange and pink grapefruit. Lots of acidity and still full-bodied, with a solid finish that's zesty and lasting. Nice brut cava; offers more than average. **88** —*M.S.* *(6/1/2006)*

MONTALVO WILMONT

Montalvo Wilmont 2003 Tempranillo-Cabernet Sauvignon (La Mancha) $11. Adequately smoky and raw, with rubber, cassis, and black cherry. A bit unfocused and clumsy, but good in a natural, no-frills kind of way. Finishes easy, with oak and some earthy mushroom. **84** —*M.S.* *(8/1/2005)*

Montalvo Wilmot 2003 Gran Baco de Oro Cabernet Sauvignon (La Mancha) $12. Questionable clarity on the nose, where stewy black cherry aromas mix with field scents. The palate isn't far from pressed beets and brandied cherries, while the finish is pruney. Cabernet from La Mancha in the hottest summer in 150 years? Hard to expect more. **82** —*M.S.* *(10/1/2005)*

MONTE DON LUCIO

Monte Don Lucio 2000 Reserva Tempranillo-Cabernet Sauvignon (La Mancha) $8. A bit brown in color, with dry, baked aromas of balsamic vinegar and raspberry. The palate is kind of tart and tangy, while the finish is tight and acid-based. Not a lot of density or sweetness but still pretty good in a Old World sort of way. **84 Best Buy** —*M.S.* *(4/1/2006)*

MONTE PINADILLO

Monte Pinadillo 1997 Crianza Tempranillo (Ribera del Duero) $20. Another '97 that shouldn't have been made—or should have already been consumed. Earthy and mushroomy, with dried leaves and dirt highlighted by piercing acidity. **82** —*J.C.* *(11/1/2001)*

MONTEBACO

Montebaco 2001 Crianza Red Blend (Ribera del Duero) $20. Fairly stylish and true to the region; the nose is both meaty and leathery, with rustic but composed notes of roast plum, earth, and oak. Blackberry and plum flavors are convincing, while the finish offers the right amount of spice and vanilla. **88** —*M.S.* *(11/1/2006)*

Montebaco 2001 Selección Especial Red Blend (Ribera del Duero) $40. A slight step up from the Crianza, mostly because it's a level or two more intense. The nose is powerful, albeit full of earthy funk and leather. The palate is snappy and full, with black cherry dominant. Finishes warm and spicy, with cola and chocolate. **89** —*M.S.* *(11/1/2006)*

Montebaco 2003 Selección Especial Tempranillo Blend (Ribera del Duero) $40. Lush and full-bodied, this Tempranillo from vines more than 65 years of age handles its size gracefully, with precise flavors of blackberries

and peppery spice rounded out by hints of vanilla and tobacco. **89** *(11/15/2006)*

Montebaco 2003 Semele Tempranillo Blend (Ribera del Duero) $16. From younger vines, this is suppler and more modest in intent than the Selección Especial, but still tasty, marrying meaty, leathery notes with plummy, earthy nuances. **86** *(11/15/2006)*

MONTECASTRO

Montecastro 2003 Tinto del Pais (Ribera del Duero) $36. A wine searching for an identity. The nose deals menthol, licorice, grilled meat, and molasses but little-to-no bright fruit. That heaviness transfers to the mouth, where marinated, baked flavors mix with green tomato. Fails to impress. **83** —*M.S.* *(12/15/2006)*

MONTECILLO

Montecillo 1994 130 Edicion Limitada Gran Reserva Tempranillo (Rioja) $50. Aromas of warm cedar planks, tobacco and mushroom turn more murky and leafy with air. Quite acidic, which is why the wine is still kicking and screaming. The fruit is slick and racy, while the finish is hot, fiery and bitter like espresso. **83** —*M.S.* *(8/1/2005)*

Montecillo 2001 Crianza Tempranillo (Rioja) $10. Starts with appropriate earth, cherry, and vanilla notes, which are followed by spicy cherry, cranberry and raspberry flavors. Shows red fruit in a more traditional style, while the finish is warm, a bit oaky, and ultimately quite fresh. **85 Best Buy** —*M.S.* *(6/1/2005)*

Montecillo 1998 Crianza Tempranillo (Rioja) $10. Angular and tasty, Montecillo's regular offering is an appealing, uncomplicated ready-to-drink red. Dried fruit, herb and oak flavors meld nicely in this light-medium weight wine best for drinking now through 2004. **85** —*M.M.* *(9/1/2002)*

Montecillo 1998 Gran Reserva Tempranillo (Rioja) $26. The bouquet delivers touches of graphite and rubber in front of traditional dried cherry and raspberry. Nice in the mouth, with softly fading fruit riding a wave of persistent acids and tannins. Snappy, old-school, and succulent. Drink now through 2010. **89** —*M.S.* *(11/1/2006)*

Montecillo 1996 Gran Reserva Tempranillo (Rioja) $23. Thinning, but with catchy aromas of leather, citrus peel, forest floor, and cola. The palate offers sweeping dried fruits, mostly cassis and cherry. Meanwhile, the finish is tight and guarded by mature tannins and vital acidity. Interestingly, root beer and turnip show up at the very end. **87** —*M.S.* *(6/1/2005)*

Montecillo 1994 Gran Reserva Tempranillo (Rioja) $23. This mature wine shows a touch of brown at the edge and a handsome cedar, tobacco, and herb nose. The finely tuned palate has good fruit-to-acid balance, and the tasty dried cherry and plum flavors are complemented by more cedar and tobacco. Lean and elegant, best drunk now through 2006. **89** —*M.M.* *(9/1/2002)*

Montecillo 2000 Reserva Tempranillo (Rioja) $16. Cherry cough drop, leather, and moss aromas open it up, followed by red raspberry and some natural bitterness. Finishes with some gritty tannin and a slightly cooked, raisiny aftertaste. More of a throwback in style. **86** —*M.S.* *(11/1/2006)*

Montecillo 1997 Reserva Tempranillo (Rioja) $17. Even and light on its feet, this tasty wine presents a cedar, meat, and cocoa-tinged nose. Soft for a Rioja, it reflects perhaps the light 1997 vintage, but neatly avoids the underripe green notes evident in so many of the year's wines. One gripe: this lacks what I consider appropriate weight or substance for a wine designated Reserva. Forgiving that, it's truly drinkable, with black plum and tar notes on the palate, and a modest but flavorful finish. **86** —*M.M.* *(11/1/2002)*

Montecillo 1996 Reserva Tempranillo (Rioja) $17. Tasty tart fruit, leather and tobacco flavors in this taut, medium-weight wine are supported by quite racy acidity, rendering it somewhat astringent. The oak here, too, seems to bear heavily on rather light fruit. With tannins to lose, this may improve with age, filling out some, but will always be lean. Drink now–2006. **86** —*M.M.* *(9/1/2002)*

Montecillo 1991 Selección Especial Gran Reserva Tempranillo (Rioja) $65. More red still than orange, with classic aromas of leather, molasses, and tobacco. Rich and developed in the mouth, with black cherry and caramel leading to a finish of chocolaty complexity. Has it now and will age for another 10 to 20 years if properly stored. **92 Cellar Selection** — *M.S. (12/31/2004)*

Montecillo 1985 Selección Especial Gran Reserva Tempranillo (Rioja) $65. Rusty, with a confounding but interesting set of aromas that include peanut, soy, and mushroom along with dried apricot. In fact, the fruit profile is all dried stone fruits, more white than red. The finish is sheer, dotted with additional mushroom, and highly reminiscent of amontillado sherry. **89** —*M.S. (12/31/2004)*

Montecillo 1982 Selección Especial Gran Reserva Tempranillo (Rioja) $75. Orange in color, with dark, burnt aromas that turn from sweet and saucy to tobacco and leaves in no time. Quite forward and zesty, with apricot, dried cherry, and tobacco flavors. Finishes a bit dry and salty, but with an undercurrent of toffee to save it. **90** —*M.S. (12/31/2004)*

Montecillo 1981 Selección Especial Gran Reserva Tempranillo (Rioja) $75. Well aged but not retired, this classic old-school Rioja smells of well-oiled leather, dried fruits, and herbs, and a smack of root beer. Sly plum flavors are sweetened by the essence of brown sugar, while the finish offers heat and mild acids. A winner among commercially available aged wines. **91** —*M.S. (12/31/2004)*

Montecillo 2004 Viura (Rioja) $8. Waxy and sweet on the nose, with aromas of corn and cotton candy. Flavors best described as apple and lemon are weak, and the finishing notes are sour. **80** —*M.S. (7/1/2005)*

Montecillo 2003 Viura (Rioja) $8. Bland apple and tart citrus with very little body. Not much here. **80** —*M.S. (12/31/2004)*

Montecillo 2002 Viura (Rioja) $10. This basic Viura has a waxy nose with hints of mineral and banana. The palate deals tart apple and lemon juice, while the finish is tight and sharp. Needs salty, basics to pump it up, something like green olives. **84** —*M.S. (9/1/2004)*

MONTEGAREDO

Montegaredo 2000 Piramide Red Blend (Ribera del Duero) $20. A very grapey wine that's reminiscent of Concord grape juice on the nose. Cranberry and strawberry flavors come through on the palate, but it's essentially tart and lemony on the finish. **83** —*C.S. (11/1/2002)*

Montegaredo 1999 Crianza Tempranillo (Ribera del Duero) $19. Bay leaf, dried spices, and violet aromas lead to juicy blackberry and unsweetened cocoa flavors. Despite the bright tannins and mellow acidity, this wine lacks a bit of weight at midpalate. **88** —*K.F. (11/1/2002)*

Montegaredo 1999 Tinto Tempranillo (Ribera del Duero) $13. Char, dried earth, potpourri, and stewy fruit aromas are followed by flavors of blueberry, strawberry, and a faint whiff of pastry. Displays good balance of acid, fruit, and tannins, but lacks richness. **88 Best Buy** —*K.F. (11/1/2002)*

MONTESIERRA

Montesierra 1999 Tinta de Toro (Somontano) $7. This medium-weight red's berry fruit and saddle leather accents can't rise above a tart, even sour, herb-vegetal note that appears early and remains throughout. Shows modest tannins and a little length on the back end, but the odd note prevails. **81** —*M.M. (9/1/2002)*

MONTSARRA

Montsarra NV Brut Sparkling Blend (Cava) $15. Nice in terms of texture, but a bit strange and hard to identify as far as aromas and flavors go. The nose tosses up Sherry and syrup notes, while the flavors run toward Granny Smith apples and lime. Shockingly, the finish is sweet. Confounding and hard to appreciate, but not a bad cava. **84** —*M.S. (6/1/2005)*

MORGADIO

Morgadio 2004 Albariño (Rías Baixas) $20. Fresh and pure, with a solid citrus quality. The nose features pineapple and peaches, with a shot of mineral. Orange is the predominant flavor, mixed with some drying soda cracker. Well balanced and properly acidic, with proper dryness on the finish. **88** —*M.S. (11/15/2005)*

Morgadio 2003 Albariño (Rías Baixas) $19. A touch prickly and odd at first, with cactus and canned peaches on the nose. More canned, sweet fruit appears on the palate, which is soft and modest from front to finish. Ends with the flavor of pineapple Lifesavers. **86** —*M.S. (9/1/2004)*

Morgadio 2002 Albariño (Rías Baixas) $18. Pineapple and flowers create a candied nose, while the flavor profile is about melon, papaya, pear, and spice. A rich and persistent finish scores this wine some points, as does the full, chewy mouthfeel. Nice and balanced. **87** —*M.S. (3/1/2004)*

Morgadio 2000 Albariño (Rías Baixas) $19. Intensely perfumed, with green herbs, floral, even lychee hints on the nose. The palate shows herb and wet-stone flavors, but also a faint musty note. Very poised in feel, this is commendable for its excellent texture and balance. Drink now. **85** —*M.M. (9/1/2002)*

Morgadio 1999 Albariño (Rías Baixas) $20. 89 —*M.M. (8/1/2000)*

MORLANDA

Morlanda 2001 Criança Red Blend (Priorat) $48. Light in color, with some cloudiness. On the nose it's fairly lean and herbal, more similar to French Cabernet Franc or Pinot Noir than your typical muscular Priorat. Flavorwise, expect raisin and raspberry notes before a short, spicy finish. **84** —*M.S. (3/1/2005)*

Morlanda 1998 Crianza Red Blend (Priorat) $46. Overtly, overwhelmingly oaky, a shot at the international style, this red from the hot region of Priorat just doesn't go anywhere beyond the wood. From stem to stern, the coconut-toasty oak renders all other elements subservient to an extent that grape and location are rendered irrelevant. **84** —*M.M. (9/1/2002)*

Morlanda 2002 Vi de Guarda Red Blend (Priorat) $48. Hard and rubbery at first; the nose requires a lot of patience. Those who have it will be rewarded with candied red fruit and a buttery, oaky finish. Somewhat of a unique, odd style for Priorat, with a broader, less mineral character. **85** —*M.S. (10/1/2005)*

Morlanda 2000 Vi de Guarda Red Blend (Priorat) $48. A touch creamy and lactic at first, but it picks up leathery, more rustic notes with airing. Flavors of plum, blackberry, and broad-grained oak lead into a spicy finish with both cinnamon and tree-bark notes. Maybe it's a bit basic, but it's juicy, well made and tasty. **88** —*M.S. (3/1/2004)*

MUGA

Muga 1996 Reserva Tempranillo Blend (Rioja) $17. 89 —*M.M. (8/1/2000)*

Muga 2002 Rosé Blend (Rioja) $9. Simple elegance defines this rosado. The color is perfect, the nose is bright, the fruit is forward . . . everything is in place. Isaac Muga and his sons know how to make rosé. They emphasize flashy fruit and a pure finish, while eschewing oak and weight. Every restaurant in America should serve this beauty by the glass, and every wine drinker should try it at least once. Impeccable with salads. **89 Best Buy** —*M.S. (11/15/2003)*

Muga 1999 Rosada Rosé Blend (Rioja) $10. 87 —*M.M. (8/1/2000)*

Muga 1991 Prado Enea Gran Reserva Tempranillo (Rioja) $41. 92 —*M.M. (8/1/2000)*

Muga 1994 Reserva Seleccion Especial Tempranillo (Rioja) $29. 91 —*M.M. (8/1/2000)*

Muga 1996 Torre Muga Tempranillo (Rioja) $60. 92 —*M.M. (8/1/2000)*

Muga 2001 Aro Tempranillo Blend (Rioja) $179. A compact red with aromatic hints of tobacco, violets, and dark berries. Fueled in high-octane fashion, meaning it's tight, tannic, and forward. While it needs five years to loosen up, now you get refined black cherry and chocolate. A stern drink for those who favor big reds. Tempranillo with 30% Graciano. **90** —*M.S. (6/1/2005)*

Muga 1995 Prado Enea Gran Reserva Tempranillo Blend (Rioja) $41. One of Rioja's unique old-school reds is lean, tangy, and herbal, with dry plum and prune aromas as well as some dill and rubber. Piquant cherry and tobacco carry the peppy palate, while the finish is warm and lengthy. Quite a throwback, but with an appealing taste and class. **90** —*M.S. (3/1/2004)*

Muga 1999 Reserva Tempranillo Blend (Rioja) $19. Sweet, ripe, and full, which is pretty much the Muga style. One whiff tells you a lot: there's nice plum and cherry, with depth. The finish lingers for a while, delivering vanilla and ample wood. This is so easy to like, and equally easy to drink. **89** —*M.S. (3/1/2004)*

Muga 1996 Reserva Selección Especial Tempranillo Blend (Rioja) $31. At first the wine seems to tip in favor of oak over substance; the nose is slightly lemony and caramelized. But as it airs out and opens up you get some juiciness but even more bruising roasted fruit. Tight and aggressive on the finish, with more than enough wood spice. Still youthful despite its 1996 birthdate. **90** —*M.S. (3/1/2004)*

Muga 1998 Torre Muga Tempranillo Blend (Rioja) $45. Deep and earthy, and packing more than a punch. This is big-time modern Rioja in brash form. The nose is gorgeous, dealing milk chocolate and fresh soil. The palate is a tight blend of tannins, acids, and zesty flavors. Big and hedonistic for sure, but you'll love the plum, pepper and espresso flavors. Still feverishly tannic; hold at least until 2005. **93 Editors' Choice** —*M.S. (3/1/2004)*

Muga 1999 Barrel Fermented White Blend (Rioja) $11. 88 Best Buy —*M.M. (8/1/2000)*

Muga 2002 Blanco White Blend (Rioja) $11. Elegant and fragrant on the nose, with wild flower, honey, and apple/pear aromas. Flavors of green apple and lemon are surprisingly tart given the barrel-fermented status of the wine. Solid and tasty for the style. **87** —*M.S. (3/1/2004)*

MURUVE

Muruve 1998 Crianza Tinta de Toro (Toro) $12. Liberally wooded, to say the least, the plum fruit at the core of this Toro wine doesn't much see the light of day. Has a nice raspberry, eucalyptus, and white-pepper nose. **82** —*D.T. (4/1/2003)*

Muruve 1996 Crianza Tinta de Toro (Toro) $13. 91 Best Buy —*M.S. (8/1/2000)*

MUSEUM

Museum 2000 Crianza Tempranillo (Cigales) $14. Heavily resiny on the nose, with strong scents of fresh-cut wood and pungent herbs. Shows moderate cherry, raspberry fruit with powerful acidity. Medium-bodied at best; it's actually fairly lean. **84** —*M.S. (9/1/2004)*

Museum 2002 Real Reserva Tempranillo (Cigales) $25. Round up front, with solid fruit aromas mixed with oak and vanilla. In the mouth, it features bold cherry and raspberry flavors supported by zesty acidity and bold tannins. Finishes full, with a lot of oak-driven butter. More than competent. **86** —*M.S. (12/15/2006)*

Museum 2001 Real Reserva Tempranillo (Cigales) $24. Gets off the blocks with Middle Eastern spice notes of cumin and curry, but later on open-cut wood and vanilla take over. Bold cherry, blackberry, and black olive flavors are solid, while the mouthfeel is tannic and rowdy. Possibly too grabby for some, but if you like Tempranillo taken to the extreme this might be your ticket. **88** —*M.S. (4/1/2006)*

Museum 2000 Real Reserva Tempranillo (Cigales) $23. Decent aromas of sun-baked fruit, leather, and oak is a known trio that spells out Spanish Tempranillo. The palate offers tangy cherry and red plum, while the finish is buttery. Piercing acidity sort of sneaks up on you as you get into it. Pretty good but lacking in mouthfeel. **86** —*M.S. (8/1/2005)*

Museum 2001 Crianza Tinto del Pais (Cigales) $14. Round and ripe, with a touch of rich prune and warm earth on the spice-cabinet nose. Fairly oaky, with coconut and raspberry flavors. That coconutty character sticks with it through the finish, which is slightly tannic. **86** —*M.S. (11/1/2006)*

MUTUO

Mutuo 2001 Crianza Organic Tempranillo Blend (Rioja) $17. An organic wine with brushy aromas of tobacco, bramble, and berry. Fairly true and full in the mouth, with a note of raisin to the black cherry and plum flavors. Gets better with time but always seems a bit grassy. **85** —*M.S. (11/1/2006)*

NAIA

Naia 2004 Verdejo (Rueda) $13. Sauvignon Blanc fans take note: this no-oak Verdejo tastes a lot like S.B., with ultrafresh tropical and citrus fruit characteristics that include aromas and flavors of pineapple, grapefruit, passion fruit, and nectarine. Extremely lively and appealing, with a good mix of acidity and body. A very good food wine. **88 Best Buy** —*M.S. (11/15/2005)*

Naia 2003 Verdejo (Rueda) $13. An aggressive example of Verdejo, one that wants to be grapefruit juice and comes very close to tasting like it. Along with the pulsating pink grapefruit aromas and flavors there's some passion fruit and pith. But you'll be hard pressed to go beyond these dominating characteristics. A proverbial one-noter, but a good one. **86** —*M.S. (8/1/2005)*

NOBUL RED

Nobul Red 2003 Tempranillo (Vinos de Madrid) $7. Colorful but candied, with a sweet, gritty nose that smells of cotton candy and reduced red fruit. High-toned cherry and raspberry flavors control the palate, followed by a sugary, forward finish. **82** —*M.S. (6/1/2005)*

NORA

Nora 2004 Albariño (Rías Baixas) $16. From the same owners of Naia in Rueda, this racy Albariño is made by Alistair Gardner, from New Zealand, and it comes across fairly crisp and tight. Lemon and green apple notes carry the nose and palate, each of which is fresh but somewhat linear and mute. A sharp, albeit clean, wine. **85** —*M.S. (11/15/2005)*

Nora 2003 Albariño (Rías Baixas) $16. Shows all the typical outward signs of the variety, including melon, peach, and citrus aromas followed by pear, orange, and biscuit-like flavors. There's just enough slate and mineral on the palate to offer some complexity, while the finish is clean and light. A satisfying Spanish white. **88** —*M.S. (8/1/2005)*

Nora 2002 Albariño (Rías Baixas) $13. This Galician white is clean and properly acidic; it'll take the coating off your palate like liquid sorbet. In the nose, aromas of lemon-lime dominate, while in the mouth, lemon, green apple, and white pepper take over. While it's a touch thin, it's fresh and likable. **86** —*M.S. (3/1/2004)*

NUMANTHIA-TERMES, S.L.

Numanthia-Termes, S.L. 2000 Numanthia Tinta de Toro (Toro) $45. Tight as nails, with earth and mint aromas leading you toward plum, black cherry, and leather-like flavors. This is fiercely tannic right now, with a hint of bitterness. But it's also a high-voltage, new-age wine with copious oak, cola, and earth characteristics. Shows good aging potential. Hold until 2005 or 2006. **89** —*M.S. (3/1/2004)*

Numanthia-Termes, S.L. 2001 Termanthia Tinta de Toro (Toro) $175. With this wine the Egurens of Rioja fame have hit the mother lode in Toro. The '01 version of Termanthia is outrageously powerful and deep, like a shot to the jaw from Lennox Lewis in his prime. It's maxed out in terms of leather, smoky oak, and depth of fruit. Almost hard to describe, it's so big and mauling. Hold until at least 2008. 330 cases made. **95 Cellar Selection** —*M.S. (6/1/2005)*

Numanthia-Termes, S.L. 2000 Termes Tinta de Toro (Toro) $21. Soft, deep and pure, and a significant step up from the fine-in-its-own-right '99. The bouquet of blackberry, bacon, and herbs is open and welcoming, while the smoky cherry and bacon palate is wonderful. Finishes sweet and easy, with warmth, size, and fine tannins. So supple and rich, yet packed with stuffing. A New World masterpiece that's made for drinking over the next several years. **93 Editors' Choice** —*M.S. (3/1/2004)*

Numanthia-Termes, S.L. 1999 Termes Tinta de Toro (Toro) $21. Less concentrated and oaky than its big brother, Numanthia, but definitely more approachable, and arguably more likable. Some earth and leather deepen and darken the nose, while in the mouth, chunky black fruit kicks up notes of cola and chocolate. Very smooth and sweet, with firm tannins but not the jack-hammer type. **90** —*M.S. (3/1/2004)*

OCHOA

Ochoa 2003 Rosado Rosé Blend (Navarra) $10. Based on Garnacha and Cabernet Sauvignon, this is a full-bodied, meal-friendly rosé with raspberry and watermelon aromas and a hint of nuttiness. Shows power, with a meaty edge. Snap, grit, and grip make this a significant wine. **88 Best Buy** —*M.S. (10/1/2004)*

Ochoa 2003 Viura-Chardonnay White Blend (Navarra) $10. Expressive, with a fresh, flowery, Moscato-like nose. Bursts with apple and grapefruit, and then a wave of pineapple. It has spine, zest, and style. A good everyday white that's balanced. **87 Best Buy** —*M.S. (10/1/2004)*

OLIVER CONTI

Oliver Conti 1999 Bordeaux Blend (Emporadà-Costa Brava) $43. Round and interesting, with a nose of sweaty leather and a hint of barnyard. The palate deals red licorice, plum, and chocolate cake, while the finish is sweet and a bit chewy. It improves with airing and tastes riper and more accessible than the greener 1998. **89** —*M.S. (3/1/2004)*

Oliver Conti 1998 Bordeaux Blend (Emporadà-Costa Brava) $39. This Bordeaux blend from extreme northeastern Spain is balanced and even, flavorful and silky. From the earth, leather and mint nose through tart berry and faintly anise-tinged flavors, it's surprisingly elegant. Finishes dry, with gentle tannins and hints of licorice, earth, and mushrooms. There's much to like in this smooth operator's impressive, supple feel and round, balanced flavors. Drink now through 2005. **89** —*M.M. (4/1/2002)*

ONIX

Onix 1999 Red Blend (Priorat) $12. Catalonia, in Spain's northeast, is a home to many grapes also grown in France's Rhône Valley. Which home is the home is a dispute to avoid here, but don't avoid this tasty, affordable 50-50 Garnacha-Cariñena (or en Français, Grenache-Carignane) blend. The complex aromas of dark fruit, rosemary, lavender, smoke, and leather are impressive. The Sweet Tart fruit, offset by game, licorice, and oak accents, rides a tangy mouthfeel, and the dry finish displays a hint of gunpowder. It's juicy, but not simple; in fact, the wine's gamy notes may be too much for some. Still, this offers real character in a price range where far too many wines lack any identity. Drink now–2006+. **88 Best Buy** —*M.M. (4/1/2002)*

ORBALLO

Orballo 2003 Albariño (Rías Baixas) $17. A bit sweet and ripe, with aromas of pineapple, canned pear, and sugared doughnuts. Round pineapple, nectarine, and apple flavors lead toward a satisfying, smooth finish. Reserved but still carries some kick. **87** —*M.S. (8/1/2005)*

ORIEL

Oriel 2004 Barona Albariño (Rías Baixas) $20. Starts with fruit cocktail aromas, which are backed by semisweet orange and lemon flavors. Zesty and clean, with pretty good mouthfeel but not much depth of flavor, complexity, or nuance. A good wine on its best day. **84** —*M.S. (9/1/2006)*

Oriel 2001 Alma de Llicorella Red Blend (Priorat) $35. Gets out of the blocks with black cherry, cinnamon, and forest-like aromas. Structured on the palate, with large tannins protecting cherry and spice flavors. Finishes with a lot of wood spice, chocolate, and warmth. Is it too tannic and oaky? Time will tell. **87** —*M.S. (10/1/2005)*

Oriel 2003 Setena Red Blend (Terra Alta) $18. This five-grape blend hails from outside Barcelona. It's mute on the nose, with hints of horseradish and vinaigrette. Seems pickled on the palate, with rubbery tannins and flavor notes of salsa and wasabi. **81** —*M.S. (10/1/2005)*

ORIGIN

Origin 2003 Tempranillo (Tierra de Castilla) $11. Green, grassy aromas precede sour plum and apple-skin flavors. Thin and weak. Not a lot going in its favor. **80** —*M.S. (8/1/2005)*

Origin 1998 Reserva Tempranillo Blend (Rioja) $24. A bit sweet on the nose, with notes of caramel, blackberry, and earth. Better at first, where it comes on ripe. But then it turns a little sluggish and heavy as it opens. Still, it's largely a good Rioja, maybe more in the "modern" style than old-school. **85** —*M.S. (6/1/2005)*

ORISTAN

Oristan 1993 Reserva Cabernet Sauvignon-Tempranillo (La Mancha) $10. **86** —*J.C. (11/15/1999)*

Oristan 1995 Reserva Cencibel (La Mancha) $10. **83** *(8/1/2000)*

OSBORNE

Osborne 2001 Dominio de Malpica Cabernet Sauvignon (Tierra de Castilla) $13. This Osborne-owned wine is like fruitcake: it's dense, a bit heavy and alcoholic, and it weighs in like a fort. The mouth is like a mound of berry fruit mixed with tomato and leaves. Meanwhile, the mouthfeel is warming and full. Green bean on the finish, however, is a detractor. **84** —*M.S. (12/31/2004)*

Osborne 2000 Solaz Cabernet Sauvignon-Tempranillo (Tierra de Castilla) $7. A tasty quaff from the well-known Sherry and Port house with good color, plummy aromas, and a soft yet full mouthfeel. The ripe cherry and cocoa flavors have instant appeal, as does the velvety texture. Though not deep, this is enjoyable. Closes easy, with cocoa and mild spice notes. Drink now–2004. **85 Best Buy** —*M.M. (11/1/2002)*

Osborne NV Fino Quinta Palomino (Jerez) $14. The differences between a good fino and a great fino are usually slight, but this one has pretty much all one could ask for. The nose is crisp, with hints of sea breeze, peanut, and tart apple showing through. In the mouth, there's snap, saline, and mineral-laden white fruits. Nothing is out of bounds. **90 Best Buy** —*M.S. (6/1/2005)*

Osborne NV Rare Sherry Pedro Ximénez Viejo (Jerez) $120. Fairly typical of a quality PX, with prune, fudge, and leather on the nose. Runs a touch syrupy, but the flavors are excellent: the chocolate, raisin, and coffee tastes are all precise and stellar. Shows some raw power at times, but also remains subdued. **91** —*M.S. (6/1/2005)*

Osborne NV 10RF Oloroso Medium Sherry (Jerez) $14. Sweet and plump in the nose, with a hint of caramel corn, burnt sugar, and char. Flavors of walnuts, dried apricots, and citrus peel carry the palate, while the lasting and tasty finish delivers the works in terms of toffee, mocha, and raisins. More fruity than many, with a touch of mushroom. **90 Best Buy** —*M.S. (8/1/2003)*

Osborne NV Bailen Dry Oloroso Sherry (Jerez) $14. Offers all the requisite almond and dried stone fruits one could ask for. The spicy palate is racy as can be, with flavors of mushroom, almond, sea salt, and white pepper. The finish is long and powerful, and overall it is a serious Sherry with no cracks or flaws. **90 Best Buy** —*M.S. (10/1/2005)*

Osborne NV Cream Sherry (Jerez) $10. Flat on the nose, with simple, toasted aromas and flavors. This is a sweet sherry for amateurs; it lacks complexity and style but comes to the plate with plenty of pop and sweetness. Finishing notes of brown sugar, coffee, and mocha is about it for nuance. **86 Best Buy** —*M.S. (10/1/2005)*

Osborne NV Manzanilla Sherry (Jerez) $14. Petrol and crisp sea air control the nose, while the palate has saline, lemon, and bitter almond flavors. Chalky and tight on the finish, with some mushroom and vanilla nuance. **87** —*M.S. (8/1/2005)*

Osborne NV Medium Amontillado Sherry (Jerez) $10. Seductive caramel, toffee, and hazelnut aromas lead to an equally nutty palate that features maple and more toffee. Not the most complex Sherry going; it's more forward and easy to grasp, so novices should enjoy the sweet and salty mix and the marathon-length finish. **88 Best Buy** —*M.S. (8/1/2005)*

Osborne NV Pale Dry Fino Sherry (Jerez) $10. Heavier in color, with a bit of yellow to the tint. Salted nut, popcorn, and light fruit flavors are solid, as is the mouthfeel. Finishes crisp and solid, but without much elegance. Sizable and weighty for a fino. **87 Best Buy** —*M.S. (8/1/2005)*

Osborne NV Pedro Ximénez 1827 Sweet Sherry (Jerez) $14. A spectacularly sweet and rich bruiser, and one that delivers the essence of raisins, toffee, and chocolate. This wine hasn't taken one turn south, and it's beckoning to be consumed. The finish is impeccably smooth and rich, and while its luscious to say the least, the amazing thing is its length, which runs a couple of minutes, no joke. A guarantee for anyone who loves the hedonistic combination of sweet fruit, brown sugar, and chocolate. **94 Best Buy** —*M.S. (8/1/2003)*

Osborne NV Solera AOS Rare Amontillado Sherry (Jerez) $60. Dark and mature, with iodine and roasted nuts on the nose. Very salty and aggressive on the palate, almost too much so. Finishes with popcorn, clarified butter, and peanuts. Better aromatics than flavors; comes off the nose and hits the wall before slumping. **87** —*M.S. (8/1/2005)*

SPAIN

SPAIN

Osborne NV Solera Primera Rare Amontillado Sherry (Jerez) $90. Almost shocking at first, due to strong, unyielding peanut and iodine aromas. Remains intense on the palate, where salt, butter, and almonds mix nicely. Sharp and racy on the finish, with good flow. A word of warning: there's nothing cuddly or sweet about this. It's old-style, traditional Sherry made for the connoisseur.**90** —M.S. (8/1/2005)

Osborne 2004 Solaz Shiraz-Tempranillo (Vino de la Tierra de Castilla) $8. Aromas of olive, tobacco, and dark plum are satisfactory and convincing. It tastes of black cherry and other berries wrapped into a short, stout package. Finishes simple.**84 Best Buy** —M.S. (11/1/2006)

Osborne 1999 Solaz Tempranillo Blend (Tierra de Castilla) $7. Striving for complexity with plenty of cedary, toasty wood over cherry fruit, this Castilian Tempranillo–Cabernet blend aims high. It falls short of its aspirations, turning lean and somewhat astringent as green tobacco, herb, and puckery, tart red fruit flavors take over. Finishes short and slightly raspy.**82** —M.M. (9/1/2002)

Osborne 2001 Tempranillo-Cabernet Sauvignon (Tierra de Castilla) $8. Known first for its Sherry, and second for its Port, Osborne is now making its mark with attractive still wines such as this excellent 80/20 Tempranillo/Cabernet blend. It cleverly bridges New and Old World styles, sending up seductive scents of dried fruits, meat, nutmeg, and Spanish leather (wait, I hear a Dylan song in here somewhere!). But there's good fruit in the core, and soft—not dusty—tannins to round out the finish. Drink now or wait five years.**88** —P.G. (11/15/2004)

Osborne 2004 Solaz Tempranillo-Cabernet Sauvignon (Viño de la Tierra de Castilla) $8. Olive, roast plum, and heavy berry aromas lead toward modest boysenberry flavors that show some weediness. The finish is tannic and hard, with a touch of red fruit as well as a burnt characteristic.**83** —M.S. (11/1/2006)

Osborne 2003 Solaz Tempranillo-Cabernet Sauvignon (Tierra de Castilla) $8. With some leather, bramble and smoky dark fruit, this Cabernet-Tempranillo blend scores as an everyday steady. But to take it farther brings caveat emptor into play. Flavorwise, it's got nice cherry and raspberry, and the finish deals vanilla and chocolate. Pleasant in every way.**86 Best Buy** —M.S. (10/1/2005)

Osborne 2001 Solaz Tempranillo-Cabernet Sauvignon (Viño de la Tierra de Castilla) $8. After tasting this wine over the past several years, it's safe to say that this is the best version yet. It's an 80/20 blend of Tempranillo and Cabernet, which shows good fruit and tree bark aromas, followed by a smooth palate that deals ample cherry and other dark fruits. Finishes rich and chewy despite having a modest pedigree and price tag.**87 Best Buy** —M.S. (9/1/2004)

Osborne 2005 Solaz Blanco Viura (Viño de la Tierra de Castilla) $8. Here's an uncomplicated but positive white wine that relies on the modest Viura grape. In its favor you'll find pear and vanilla aromas along with exact lemon, orange, and mineral flavors. Exceedingly fresh and easy, with a clean style. And at this price it can double as the perfect base wine for white sangria.**87 Best Buy** —M.S. (11/15/2006)

Osborne 2004 Solaz Blanco Viura (Viño de la Tierra de Castilla) $8. Hard apple and lemony aromas lead to a stiff palate defined by tart green apple, underripe pineapple, and green herbs. More acidic than desirable, with a clean finish.**83** —M.S. (11/1/2006)

Osborne Selección 2002 Dominio de Malpica Cabernet Sauvignon (Viño de la Tierra de Castilla) $15. A lightweight specimen with tomato, earth, leaves, and leather on the nose. Cherry and cola flavors are distant but solid, while the acidity is out there, bordering on scouring. Modest in scope, with some appeal.**84** —M.S. (11/15/2005)

Osborne Selección 2000 Señorio del Cid Crianza Tempranillo (Ribera del Duero) $20. Early mint, leather, and earth aromas quickly give way to woody notes such as cinnamon and vanilla. In between is blackberry and chocolate, the latter also oak-based. A bit rigid and hard on the palate.**85** —M.S. (12/31/2004)

OSTATU

Ostatu 2000 Crianza Tempranillo (Rioja) $16. Aromas of strawberry and plum lead into a fruity, lightly sugared palate that pours on the friendly red fruit. Well made and perfectly drinkable. What a simple, modern Rioja can and should be.**87** —M.S. (3/1/2004)

OTANON

Otanon 1998 Crianza 1998 Red Blend (Rioja) $14. This slightly brooding red has a sweet and sour, tart cherry, and toasty wood profile. As this shows some depth and has tannins to lose, it may benefit from aging another year. The tart fruit and good acidity make it a good choice to pair with lamb or other fatty meats. Drink now–2005+.**86** —M.M. (9/1/2002)

OTAZU

Otazu 2000 Chardonnay (Navarra) $11. Pale straw in color, this is a crisp, clean wine with bright aromas of grapefruit and quince, accented by chalky notes. Juicy and mouthwatering on the palate, this simple yet pleasant wine should be consumed over the next six months.**86** —C.S. (4/1/2002)

Otazu 1999 Barriqua Chardonnay (Navarra) $14. Aromas of toasted coconut, marshmallow, and caramel corn. On the palate, this wine exhibits bright acidity with flavors of creamy banana and lemon-peel with a slight minerality. Well-balanced with a clean tangy finish. Drink now til 2005.**89 Best Buy** —C.S. (4/1/2002)

Otazu 2002 Palacio de Otazu Chardonnay (Navarra) $14. Not a great quality-to-price ratio, but still a fresh Chardonnay with citrus, green apple, and tropical-fruit. Tight and lean because it's unoaked, with white pepper on the finish. Good in a scaled-back manner.**86** —M.S. (10/1/2004)

Otazu 1997 Palacio de Erite-Crianza Red Blend (Navarra) $12. Aromas of cherry, toast, straw, and fresh vegetables. On the palate the wine exhibits straightforward flavors of cherry and vanilla with soft tannins. A nice choice for an everyday wine.**86** —C.S. (4/1/2002)

Otazu 1997 Palacio de Otazu-Crianza Red Blend (Navarra) $16. Herbal aromas include everything from dill and tobacco to lima beans and earth. Leathery mouthfeel, with coffee and juicy cherries. Drink soon.**86** —C.S. (11/1/2002)

Otazu 1997 Reserva Red Blend (Navarra) $19. Deep ruby in color, with dark berry, cinnamon, wild flowers, and toasty mineral notes on the nose. This velvety wine has flavors of raspberries and bittersweet chocolate with soft chewy tannins and cedar undertones. Has potential to evolve into an even greater wine with time.**90 Cellar Selection** —C.S. (4/1/2002)

PAGO DE LA JARABA

Pago de la Jaraba 2003 Crianza Tempranillo Blend (La Mancha) $10. Woodsy and smoky up front, which sort of hides the fact that there's very little fruit on the bones of this wine. On the palate, it's peppery and firm, with spiky tannins.**82** —M.S. (12/15/2006)

PAGO DE LOS CAPELLANES

Pago de los Capellanes 1996 Crianza Red Blend (Ribera del Duero) $25. Displays smoky, grilled-meat aromas, along with vanilla and cedar. More meatiness shows up on the palate, joined by black cherries. Finishes soft and delicate; ready to drink now.**88** —J.C. (11/1/2001)

Pago de los Capellanes 2001 Jóven Roble Tempranillo (Ribera del Duero) $28.90 Best Buy —R.V. (11/15/2002)

Pago de los Capellanes 1998 Reserva Tempranillo (Ribera del Duero) $22. The dark purple color combined with deep, smoky bacon and plum aromas make this enticing from the start. The palate follows the lead laid out by the nose, as it offers mostly rich plum fruit and toasty supporting oak. This is friendly, chewy, and big—but not so big as to require extensive aging.**90 Editors' Choice** —M.S. (11/1/2002)

Pago de los Capellanes 1996 Reserva Tinto del Pais (Ribera del Duero) $37. This full-bodied wine carries a heavy load of new lumber: warm caramel, sweet vanilla, and toasted coconut aromas lead the way. Yet the underlying fruit—marked by black cherry and tobacco, with hints of apricot skin and orange peel—embodies a fragility that suggests it is best consumed now.**89** —J.C. (11/1/2001)

Pago de los Capellanes 1999 Tinto Jóven Tinto del Pais (Ribera del Duero) $13. Seems almost Port-like at first; it's slightly hot on the nose. Clove and cinnamon elements combine with toast and vanilla to carry the flavors into a cedary finish. Not a stainless-steel jóven.**84** —J.C. (11/1/2001)

Pago del Vostal 2002 Crianza Tinto del Pais (Ribera del Duero) $14. Dull and rusty in color, with tree bark and other resiny aromas. Cherry and citrus tang carry the palate, which is tannic and wide. Finishes kind of tart and starchy. The overall impression is authentic but one of sharpness. **83** —*M.S. (2/1/2006)*

Pago del Vostal 2004 Tinto Jóven Tinto del Pais (Ribera del Duero) $10. Brandied and beet-driven on the nose, with density but not much clarity or poise. It's a touch rowdy in the mouth, where the acidity creates tang and the fruit is only so-so in quality. Persistent and forward more than anything. **84** —*M.S. (4/1/2006)*

Pagos de Valde Orca 2000 Tempranillo (Rioja) $45. Light and a bit cheesy, with leafy raspberry aromas. The mouth runs a little hard, with firm but not caustic raspberry and strawberry flavors. More crisp and lean than chubby, with plenty of decent qualities but nothing outstanding. **84** — *M.S. (4/1/2006)*

Palacio de Bornos 2004 Verdejo (Rueda) $14. Clean, lucid, and attractive, with spindly tropical fruit aromas that veer toward mango, pineapple, and passion fruit. A complete Verdejo with all the hallmarks Rueda is known for: apricot and peach flavors, nice acidity, and a crisp finish. **88** —*M.S. (9/1/2006)*

Palacio de Bornos 2003 Verdejo (Rueda) $10. A total fruitball from front to finish. The nose yields pineapple, peach, and grapefruit, while the palate pumps out plenty of apple, lemon, and other citrus fruits. Finishes snappy, with zest galore. **86 Best Buy** —*M.S. (9/1/2004)*

Palacio de Fefiñanes 2005 Albariño (Rías Baixas) $20. Lemony gold in color, with mineral-infused apple as the lead aroma. Maybe a bit bigger than average, with some roundness and chunkiness to the palate. Still it's a very good wine, one with additional mineral and citrus on the finish. **87** —*M.S. (9/1/2006)*

Palacio de La Vega 2000 Conde de La Vega Selección Privada Cabernet Blend (Navarra) $20. Aromas of plum, cherry, and licorice are good, although some obvious bell pepper gets in there as well. Raspberry and cherry carry the palate, but again there's an infusion of green, which one frequently sees in the wines of Navarra. Carob and earth soften the electric, high-wire finish. **86** —*M.S. (12/31/2004)*

Palacio de La Vega 2000 Reserva Cabernet Sauvignon (Navarra) $13. Full of plum and berry, with plenty of dill pickle as well. That said, it's not vegetal. Cola, cranberry, and cherry come on strong across the palate. In total it's an aggressive wine with an obvious tannic side to it. **85** —*M.S. (12/31/2004)*

Palacio de La Vega 2000 Crianza Cabernet Sauvignon-Tempranillo (Navarra) $9. Rusty and flat, with aromas of lettuce, celery, and other dry greens. Some cherry and plum carry the palate, while the finish is dry and simple. Starchy in terms of feel. **82** —*M.S. (12/31/2004)*

Palacio de La Vega 1999 Reserva Tempranillo (Navarra) $13. Too much funk and animal on the nose, which is followed by a heavy palate of red fruit pumped forward by clamp-down tannins. Patient swirling helps it open up, but how much time should you have to give it? **81** —*M.S. (3/1/2005)*

Palacio de Villachica 2003 3T Tinta de Toro (Toro) $12. Lots of color and aggressiveness, but no polish or poise. The nose is gassy and harsh, while the palate is surprisingly boring, with little to no flavor. Finishes short and clipped, with tannins that drill your cheeks. **82** —*M.S. (10/1/2005)*

Palacio de Villachica 2001 4T Tinta de Toro (Toro) $14. Seems like the winery's 5T bottling gets the riper grapes and this one gets the thin, sour stuff. Some oak helps cover up the lean fruit, but the palate remains tart and sharp, with flavors of pie cherry and cranberry. **81** —*M.S. (10/1/2005)*

Palacio de Villachica 2001 5T Tinta de Toro (Toro) $19. Aromas of dill, char, and vanilla mix with red fruit to create a recognizable, inviting bouquet. Black cherry and plum flavors are firm and spicy, however the back palate is a bit short, verging on hollow. With gritty tannins and forward acidity, this is no slouch. **87** —*M.S. (10/1/2005)*

PALACIOS REMONDO

Palacios Remondo 2001 Propiedad Herencia Remondo Red Blend (Rioja) $28. Alvaro Palacios is indeed a great winemaker, as is evidenced by this blend of Garnacha, Tempranillo, Graciano, and Mazuelo. Aromas of bright cherry signify power and structure, yet it's easy as sin to drink. Shows model integration, bursting berry flavors and ripe tannins. Tasted several times during the past year but not rated until now; this wine just keeps getting better. **92** —*M.S. (6/1/2005)*

Palacios Remondo 2001 Propiedad Herencia Remondo Tempranillo Blend (Rioja) $25. The peak of the Palacios family's Rioja production, it's gorgeous and aromatic. It has red fruit, flowers, and handsome oak on the nose. The palate is smooth and chewy, with expressive plum, berry, and apple skin flavors. Power-packed but balanced, offering a proper jolt and immediate drinkability. **92** —*M.S. (9/1/2004)*

PAÑUELO

Pañuelo 2002 Merlot-Cabernet Sauvignon (Navarra) $11. Heavy and a bit closed, with smoky bacon notes, olive, and green pepper on the nose. The plum and cherry flavors are big but awkward, while the finish steers you to the tannic side. Still, it's a decent wine from a marginal vintage. **84** —*M.S. (10/1/2005)*

Pañuelo 2002 Garnacha-Tempranillo Tempranillo Blend (Navarra) $11. The oak on the nose seems green, which puts across minty aromas. The palate is buttery and a touch raw, but there's nice black plum and blackberry flavors. Sort of bland and woody on the finish. **84** —*M.S. (10/1/2005)*

PÁRAMO DE GUZMÁN

Páramo de Guzmán 2000 Crianza Tempranillo (Ribera del Duero) $31. Looks good in the glass, and smells pretty nice despite a hint of barnyard. In addition, there's cola, vanilla, and plum to consider. Fairly meaty in terms of feel, but not overly expressive and not quite reaching the upper echelon. Finishes with some gritty, hard-fighting tannins. **87** —*M.S. (6/1/2005)*

Páramo de Guzmán 2003 Roble Tempranillo (Ribera del Duero) $19. Jammy and sweet, with a dominant raisiny quality that comes with the midpalate and stays until the end. Along the way there's some leather and smoke, but mostly it deals raisin flavors, firm tannins and heft. **85** —*M.S. (8/1/2005)*

PARTAL

Partal 1998 Crianza Monastrell (Bullas) $25. It's all about fruit, and the depth of fruit sings in this Monastrell (a. k. a. Mourvèdre, Mataro) that's made from 50-year-old vines in the Bullas DO in Spain's southeast. Ripe and smooth, it has a rich berry and vanilla nose, and an even, spice-accented palate. Finishes dry, with cocoa and mild sweet- spice notes. **88** —*M.M. (4/1/2002)*

PARXET

Parxet 2004 Marqués de Alella Clasico Pansa Blanca (Alella) $10. A sweet-styled wine with waxy, inoffensive aromas and flavors of cinnamon-tinged applesauce. Flat and candied; made from Pansa Blanca, a.k.a. Xarello. **82** —*M.S. (2/1/2006)*

Parxet NV Brut Pinot Noir (Cava) $12. Round and fruity, with sweet, attractive aromas. The palate is a bit dark for cava, with plum and bitter chocolate flavors. The feel is soft and foamy, with a dry, roasted note on the finish. Clear as can be; easy to tell that it's Pinot Noir **88 Best Buy** —*M.S. (6/1/2005)*

Parxet NV Cuvée Dessert Dulce Pinot Noir (Cava) $20. Not every wine is easy to read: this one is a case in point. The nose offers sweet toffee and apricot, while the palate starts out toasty and dry before unveiling ripe peach and brown sugar. The dosage on this wine is unusual. A funky bubbly that's worth a try. **86** —*M.S. (6/1/2006)*

Parxet NV Aniversario PA 84 Brut Nature Sparkling Blend (Cava) $70. Lean on the bouquet; there's almost zero yeast or lees character. But there is an interesting smoked-meat aroma that conjures memories of sausage or ballpark franks. Aggressive in the mouth, with green herbs and paprika. An unusual cava with confusing characteristics. **86** —*M.S. (6/1/2005)*

Parxet NV Cuvée 21 Brut Sparkling Blend (Cava) $10. Clean and attractive, with freshness and some mineral and spice. The palate is accented by white pepper, basil, and tarragon, while the fruit leans toward pear. The finish is smooth, as is the mouthfeel. **85** —*M.S. (12/31/2003)*

SPAIN

Parxet 1999 Tionio Crianza Tinto del Pais (Ribera del Duero) $20. From a bodega better known for their cavas comes this rustic 100% Tinto del Pais(Tempranillo). It's well-structured, with a foundation of taut red fruit and sturdy oak—but the tannins are on the gritty side, which, in this case, seems to work fairly well. **87** —D.T. (4/1/2003)

Parxet 2002 Marqués de Alella Clasico White Blend (Alella) $10. Floral and fresh, with a supercharged personality and plenty of sugary sweetness. On the plus side, it's racy and lithe, and that's despite being as candied as it is. But ask yourself, what's not to like about lemon-lime and apple? And when there's smoothness and palate feel thrown in, you wind up with a warm-weather winner. **88** —M.S. (8/1/2003)

PASANAU GERMANS

Pasanau Germans 2002 Finca la Planeta Cabernet Sauvignon (Priorat) $46. From the village of La Morera, this is a jumpy, spiky wine with lively acidity and a racy personality. Aromas of lemon peel, black olive, and rock quarry precede a chiseled palate that's quite tannic. Pent-up power for sure, with a blast of toasty vanilla on the finish. Possibly a touch green at its core. **88** —M.S. (10/1/2005)

Pasanau Germans 2001 Finca la Planeta Cabernet Sauvignon (Priorat) $46. Aromas of dark fruits are distinct and defined, while hints of perfume soften the bullish, rather earthy nose. Classy berry fruit rests comfortably on the palate, while the feel is juicy and tight. Finishes strong, maybe a little sharp, but with full flavors. 100% Cabernet. **88** — M.S. (3/1/2005)

Pasanau Germans 1998 Pasanau La Planeta Cabernet Blend (Priorat) $40. Dark but alluring cola, burnt coffee, and leathery notes open onto an equally smoldering blackberry, coffee, and oak-laden palate. Richly textured in the mouth, it finishes with dry tarry flavors and intense tannins. **88** —C.S. (4/1/2002)

Pasanau Germans 2003 Ceps Nous Red Blend (Priorat) $20. Aromatically satisfying, with heat, spice, and brandied plum notes. Fairly narrow on the palate, with dark-cherry flavors softened by a light wave of vanilla and caramel. Short on the back end, with a quick finish. **85** —M.S. (10/1/2005)

Pasanau Germans 2000 Finca la Planeta Red Blend (Priorat) $34. Giant and muscled, with potent aromas of smoke, tar, maple, and prune. At 14% alcohol, not much is held back; the palate is at first sweet and rich, with the full allotment of plum, raisin, and black cherry. On the finish comes mammoth tannins and some of the toastiest, burnt coffee notes you'll find. A real bruiser with a full tank of fuel behind it. **92 Editors' Choice** —M.S. (3/1/2004)

Pasanau Germans 1999 Finca La Planeta Red Blend (Priorat) $34. Green olive and vegetal aromas are offset by Mexican spices. Flavors of coffee and brown sugar are more earthy than fruit driven, thanks to the 2,400-foot elevation of the vineyard. **87** —C.S. (11/1/2002)

Pasanau Germans 2001 La Morera de Montsant Red Blend (Priorat) $34. This wine will stick to your ribs, and it'll grab your palate on the way down, leaving quite an impression. Red fruit, leather, and toast create a rock-solid, ideal nose. Moderately syrupy and full-bodied, with smooth berry flavors and plenty of vanilla. Finishes long and classy. **90** —M.S. (10/1/2005)

Pasanau Germans 2000 La Morera de Montsant Red Blend (Priorat) $29. Young and wild, with funky nut and mineral aromas that take some time to get used to. Once you dig in, the palate is immensely ripe and dense, with black currant and blackberry fruit. Toward the back things turn even darker and tighter, with notes of burnt sugar, leather and espresso. Huge in the mouth, with expansive tannins. **90** —M.S. (3/1/2004)

PAUL CHENEAU

Paul Cheneau NV Brut Sparkling Blend (Cava) $11. Full and heavy, with mango and orange juice flavors. Creamy in the mouth, with a full, foamy feel. Good citrus and apple characteristics keep it moving forward, while the weight is definitely there. Good in cava cocktails or as a Spanish mimosa. **85** —M.S. (6/1/2006)

PAZO DE BARRANTES

Pazo de Barrantes 2005 Albariño (Rías Baixas) $14. Ripe yet a bit chunky, probably a reflection of this estate's somewhat inland location. Shows sweet grapefruit and almond flavors, with a touch of pithy bitterness on the finish. This winery is owned by Marqués de Murrieta of Rioja fame. **87** —M.S. (9/1/2006)

Pazo de Barrantes 2003 Albariño (Rías Baixas) $NA. Ripe like many of the 2003s, but still a perfectly fine Albariño. The nose is clean and peachy, while light citrus, nectarine, and apple control the palate. Nothing out of the ordinary: fine body and fresh lime on the finish. good as a first-course white. **89** —M.S. (6/1/2005)

PAZO DE EIRAS

Pazo de Eiras 2004 Albariño (Rías Baixas) $27. Pineapple, melon, and mineral on the nose are welcoming aromas. The mouth is nice, with citrus and melon flavors. Plenty of feel and body, and pleasantly wet, meaning it's fresh, properly acidic and refreshing. **87** —M.S. (9/1/2006)

Pazo de Eiras 2003 Albariño (Rías Baixas) $25. Floral and super clean, with pretty overall aromas of mineral and lemon. Round and zesty, with a modest hint of almond oil softening up vibrant orange and lemon flavors. Refreshing but hefty, with a warm finish and lots of citrus peel. **89** —M.S. (8/1/2005)

PAZO DE SEÑORANS

Pazo de Señorans 2005 Albariño (Rías Baixas) $22. A small portion of the wine went through malolactic fermentation, so it offers a lovely roundness. Features floral aromas backed by pure tangerine and nectarine flavors. Registers more fruity and smooth than mineral, with a perfect finish. **91 Editors' Choice** —M.S. (9/1/2006)

PAZO DE VILLAREI

Pazo De Villarei 2000 Albariño (Rías Baixas) $15. The bright golden color indicates age as well as oak—and that oak is confirmed on the nose, where there's a lot of corn and a strong smell of pungent wood. The palate offers mostly overripe apple and, yes, wood. The feel is flat, proving that Albariño doesn't take well to heavy oaking. **82** —M.S. (11/1/2002)

PAZO PONDAL

Pazo Pondal 2004 Albariño (Rías Baixas) $22. This Albariño exhibits good signs on the nose, where buttercup, white flowers, and apple dance together. Stays solid in the mouth, with round apple, pineapple, and light spice notes working seamlessly. Long and full late, with style and grace. **89** —M.S. (9/1/2006)

PAZO SAN MAURO

Pazo San Mauro 2005 Albariño (Rías Baixas) $19. Perfectly crisp and fresh, with touches of tangerine and lemon making it slightly sharp but not the least bit sour. More of a zesty version, with correct acidity, ripeness and balance. Yet another fine match for seafood. **89** —M.S. (9/1/2006)

Pazo San Mauro 2003 Albariño (Rías Baixas) $17. Clean and sweet, with an aromatic touch of cookies and cream. In the mouth, it's more of the standard lemon, apple, and mineral that you expect from this Galician white. Finishes easy and nice, but not too crisp. **87** —M.S. (3/1/2005)

Pazo San Mauro 2002 Albariño (Rías Baixas) $18. Open and pretty, with approachable aromas of pear, banana, and ocean air. The palate is packed full of mango, peach, and banana, while the finish is long and holds form. A hefty, forward real-deal of a white. Excellent with appetizers. **88** —M.S. (9/1/2004)

Pazo San Mauro 2001 Albariño (Rías Baixas) $17. At once lively and round, this is a not-too-racy, not-too-mushy Albariño from northern Spain. Yellow stone fruit and citrus (especially lemon pith) vie for top billing on the palate. Good with white fish, or as an apèritif. **86** —D.T. (4/1/2003)

PAZO VILADOMAR

Pazo Viladomar 2004 Albariño (Rías Baixas) $15. A bit gaseous and chunky on the nose, with a lot of heavy melon character. The palate is fatter than ideal, with dull fruit flavors. Base level, without much going on. **82** —P.P. (11/15/2005)

PECIÑA

Peciña 1997 Reserve Tempranillo (Rioja) $60. Berry fruit and underbrush on the nose, with some buttery oak standing out. Seems a bit sweet and pruny on the palate, with a ripe, medicinal finish. Not bad but also not in the top echelon of Rioja reservas. And 1997 was not a particularly good year. **85** —M.S. (4/1/2006)

PEDRO ESCUDERO

Pedro Escudero 2003 Fuente Elvira Verdejo (Rueda) $22. The gold color and heavy oak aromas indicate barrel fermentation, which for this reviewer is not the ideal way to produce Verdejo. That said, this wine is made well, with plump melon and apple flavors cuddled in vanilla and wood resin. Very thick and woody; like being lost in the forest. **86** — M.S. (9/1/2006)

PEDROSA

Pedrosa 1995 Gran Reserva Red Blend (Ribera del Duero) $79. Still very youthful-tasting and structured, this wine—which incorporates 10% Cabernet Sauvignon in the blend—also boasts admirable quantities of black cherry and blackberry fruit. Hints of smoke and grilled meat add a dose of complexity. Drink now with hearty foods or age up to 10 years. **90 Cellar Selection** —J.C. (11/1/2001)

Pedrosa 1997 Reserva Red Blend (Ribera del Duero) $45. The sweet toast and firm structure can't hide fruit that seems a little less than fully ripe. Does have attractive smoke and spice elements, but also green tannins. **87** —J.C. (11/1/2001)

Pedrosa 1998 Crianza Tempranillo (Ribera del Duero) $28. In a vintage that favored structure over opulence, Pedrosa's crianza spent 18 months in barrel, softening some of the roughness. It ends up smelling quite oaky, with toast, vanilla, and sweet cinnamon-sugar elements over black-cherry and blackberry fruit. The tannins are plentiful and the acids firm, making this another '98 that could use more aging. **88** —J.C. (11/1/2001)

PENASCAL

Penascal 2005 Sauvignon Blanc (Viño de la Tierra de Castilla y León) $7. Chunky but also lively, with pungent, aggressive Sauvignon aromas of prickly fruit, grapefruit, and greens. The palate is heavy and all about pink grapefruit, while the texture is thick. Has its good points; and it's varietally correct. **84 Best Buy** —M.S. (11/1/2006)

Penascal 2004 Sauvignon Blanc (Viño de la Tierra de Castilla y León) $6. Pungent and prickly at first, but then it loses some of that zest as it opens. Chalky on the palate, with celery and citrus flavors. Lengthy enough on the finish, with hints of peaches and mineral. **84 Best Buy** — M.S. (10/1/2005)

Penascal 2002 Sauvignon Blanc (Viño de la Tierra de Castilla y León) $7. Who knew that crisp, varietally correct Sauvignon Blanc was being made on the plains of central Spain? The nose deals pine and bell pepper, while the palate is zippy and zesty, but filled with apple and banana flavors. A tangy, precise finish with tangerine notes is the final act. **88 Best Buy** — M.S. (3/1/2004)

Penascal 2004 Shiraz (Viño de la Tierra de Castilla y León) $7. Fairly deep and dark, with ripe plum and blackberry aromas. Transitions to meaty black cherry and plum flavors, which are followed by a round finish accented by chocolate and mocha. Medium to full-bodied; good value in basic red wine. **85 Best Buy** —M.S. (11/1/2006)

Penascal 2003 Shiraz (Viño de la Tierra de Castilla y León) $6. Pretty nice for young Syrah grown on the hot plains of Spain. The nose provides more than adequate plum, blackberry, and bacon, and the palate is definitely lively, with black cherry and raspberry flavors. A ripe wine with chocolate and balance. **86 Best Buy** —M.S. (11/15/2005)

Penascal 2004 Tempranillo (Viño de la Tierra de Castilla y León) $7. Penascal has emerged as one of those value brands that delivers. This installment of Tempranillo is full of berry, prune, and leather aromas, while the palate is creamy and rather full, with smooth berry notes and more than adequate richness. **86 Best Buy** —M.S. (11/1/2006)

Penascal 2000 Tempranillo (Viño de la Tierra de Castilla y León) $7. A little funky and "country style" in the nose, with some cherry lurking in the background. Raspberry and pepper are the predominant flavors, while the finish is broad, with more than a touch of wood. Fairly modest in strength, but more than adequate. **85 Best Buy** —M.S. (3/1/2004)

Penascal 2005 Rosé Tempranillo (Viño de la Tierra de Castilla y León) $7. Perfectly nice and fresh, with fruity springtime aromas that offers slight touches of nettle and citrus. Tropical flavors emerge from the spritzy palate, while the finish is both sweet and spicy. Shows some residual sugar but not too much. **85 Best Buy** —M.S. (11/1/2006)

PERELADA

Perelada 1996 Gran Claustro Extra Brut Champagne Blend (Cava) $14. Tasty in a mature way, with some complexity to the earthy apple, hay, and mineral aromas and flavors. However, it just didn't fizz, a problem for a sparkling wine, which brought its rating down, despite the nice flavor package. Closes dry and lemony with moderate length. **83** (12/31/2001)

PESQUERA

Pesquera 1999 Crianza Tempranillo (Ribera del Duero) $23. Tight, dusty, dark, and baked on the nose. Tart cherry, caramel, leather, and tobacco follow up on the palate. Finishes a bit awkwardly, with gritty, overpowering tannins. **85** —K.F. (11/1/2002)

Pesquera 2000 Crianza Tempranillo (Ribera del Duero) $25. Grapy and youthful, with a pronounced wet-earth streak to the nose. Basic cherry and plum flavors carry the palate, which is sweet and modestly tannic. **85** —M.S. (3/1/2004)

Pesquera 1999 Tinto Reserva Tempranillo (Ribera del Duero) $40. Deep and packed with aromas of cola, earth, and violets. It's open from the gun, with a round, plummy texture, bright fruit and nuances of chocolate and coffee. Very full and balanced, with a good attack, middle, and finish. Drink now or hold for several years. **90** —M.S. (3/1/2004)

Pesquera 1998 Crianza Tempranillo (Ribera del Duero) $25. Cedar and vanilla aromas beautifully complement the blackberry fruit. Add in spicy complexities of clove and sandalwood, along with a rich smoked-meat nuance, and this medium-weight wine is another winning vintage from Alejandro Fernandez. **89** —J.C. (11/1/2001)

Pesquera 1995 Gran Reserva Tempranillo (Ribera del Duero) $99. Cedary from its long stay in American oak, it's also tightly wound and in need of six months to a year of cellaring to allow it to fill out. Despite its reticence, there's great intensity of raspberry and cherry fruit that lingers on the finish. Lucia, Alejandro's eldest daughter, says this wine should be consumed over the next 3–5 years; I suspect it will drink well for several years beyond that. **91 Cellar Selection** —J.C. (11/1/2001)

Pesquera 1996 Millennium Reserva Tempranillo (Ribera del Duero) $799. **92** (8/1/2000)

Pesquera 1997 Reserva Tempranillo (Ribera del Duero) $40. Featuring supple cherries marked by plenty of vanilla and toast, this is an easy-drinking wine made for current consumption. A good effort from a miserable vintage, this should be drunk over the next 2–3 years. **89** — J.C. (11/1/2001)

Pesquera 1996 Reserva Tempranillo (Ribera del Duero) $49. **91** (8/1/2000)

Pesquera 2001 Reserva Tempranillo Blend (Ribera del Duero) $44. Full, tight and entering its prime, this classic Spanish red offers big aromas of leather, blackberry, violets, and dried brush. Dense on the palate, with flavors of black olive, tobacco, and racy black fruit. Chewy and chocolaty on the finish, with a wash of real-deal tannins. Will age well for at least another five years. **91** —M.S. (10/1/2005)

Pesquera 2002 Crianza Tempranillo (Ribera del Duero) $27. Gritty and tight, with black cherry, kirsch, and wood on the nose. The palate features cranberry on top with deeper fruit notes below. Last but not least, toffee, coffee, and vanilla carry the finish. More than adequate, but a bit underdeveloped. **86** —M.S. (10/1/2005)

Pesquera 2001 Crianza Tempranillo (Ribera del Duero) $25. Smooth, clean and dark, with charcoal, earth, and dried-fruit aromas. For this winery's basic red, you get quite a lot: herbal cherry, plum, and berry flavors and a warm, spicy finish that has plenty of acid-based verve. Bright and lively; best with food. **88** —M.S. (9/1/2004)

SPAIN

PINTIA

Pintia 2002 Vino Tinto Tinta de Toro (Toro) $50. The newest project from Vega Sicilia comes from Toro, where the serious wines are often gargantuan. This has a blinding violet tint and equally forward aromas. In the mouth, it's rock hard, a bruiser of the first order. To drink now would be inviting a tannic overload. Best to hold a couple of years and then serve with a juicy steak. **90** —*M.S. (6/1/2005)*

PIRAMIDE

Piramide 1999 Piramide Crianza Red Blend (Ribera del Duero) $20. This wine certainly has a full package of plum skin, caramel apple, steak, cassis and pleasing warm vegetal-herbal notes. Although short on depth, the finish shows well, with juicy plum flavors and integrated tannins. **86** — *K.F. (11/1/2002)*

PISSARRES

Pissarres 2003 Red Blend (Priorat) $25. Raw and rugged at first. The mouth offers a bit more, although even here the raspberry and plum flavors are spread thin. Has its merits but also some faults, primarily a finish that's not far enough removed from cough syrup. **83** —*M.S. (10/1/2005)*

PONTALIE

Pontalie 1998 Crianza Red Blend (Mentrida) $17. A promising nose of chocolate-covered cherries and sweet cream segues to earth, char—even soap?—flavors on the palate. Finishes with herbs and resin. A strange wine, overall. **82** —*D.T. (4/1/2003)*

Pontalie 1998 Crianza Syrah-Cabernet (Mentrida) $18. Green beans and seeped tea coat the palate's tired plum fruit. Feels thin in the mouth, and overall past its prime. **81** —*D.T. (4/1/2003)*

PRADO REY

Prado Rey 1999 Real Sitio Tempranilo (Ribera del Duero) $NA. Imagine the scent of blackberry pie laced with vanilla, cinnamon, and clove. This 100% Tempranillo shows good depth and lush, silky tannins married to juicy acidity and elegant cedar notes. It's very smooth and polished—maybe too much so for some tasters. **91** —*J.C. (11/1/2001)*

Prado Rey 1998 Reserva (Ribera del Duero) $NA. For now, the U.S. importer of Prado Rey is concentrating on the roble and crianza offerings from this bodega. Which is a shame, because more consumers should have access to this rising star's top cuvées. The reserva boasts sexy aromas of black cherries and brambly spice along with subtle cinnamon and vanilla notes. Finishes smooth and creamy, with fine tannins. **90** **Cellar Selection** —*J.C. (11/1/2001)*

Prado Rey 1999 Roble (Ribera del Duero) $11. Features dark, earthy fruit topped by high-toned pie cherries. Soft and easy to drink, closing with a dusting of dried spices—the greatest evidence of its three months in oak. **86** —*J.C. (11/1/2001)*

Prado Rey 2001 Crianza Tempranillo (Ribera del Duero) $19. Riper and deeper than some in this class, but arguably overoaked and roasted, such that the finish tastes like burnt coffee and the bouquet smells of peeled tire rubber. In between look for plum, blackberry, cumin, and black pepper. **86** —*M.S. (6/1/2005)*

Prado Rey 1997 Crianza Tempranillo (Ribera del Duero) $17. **88** —*M.M. (8/1/2000)*

Prado Rey 1999 Elite Tempranillo (Ribera del Duero) $55. Quite aggressive and murky at first, with a gassy, heavy bouquet of leather, earth, and cooked plums. A lot of dryness comes out on the palate, courtesy of starchy tannins and medium-weight red fruit. Finishes with grip, size, and a heavy hand. For best results, give it as much time as you can. **86** — *M.S. (6/1/2005)*

Prado Rey 1999 Reserva Tempranillo (Ribera del Duero) $35. Earth and leather control the nose along with some barnyard. All in all, it's an old-school wine, one with plum fruit, dryness, and plenty of acidity. In the long run it's not that exciting. **83** —*M.S. (6/1/2005)*

Prado Rey 2002 Roble Tempranillo (Ribera del Duero) $14. Gaseous and murky, although time reveals cleaner plum and berry aromas and flavors.

Nothing special; just a modest, mildly woody wine with some sulfur and saline holding it back. Finishes on the bitter side. **83** —*M.S. (6/1/2005)*

Prado Rey 1998 Roble Tempranillo (Ribera del Duero) $11. **85** —*M.M. (8/1/2000)*

Prado Rey 1998 Crianza Tempranillo (Ribera del Duero) $18. The delicate strawberry, vanilla, and toast aromas open with additional air to show more black cherry and tobacco. A medium-weight blend of 95% Tempranillo and 5% Cabernet Sauvignon. **87** —*J.C. (11/1/2001)*

Prado Rey 1999 Crianza Tempranillo (Ribera del Duero) $18. Grainy, unfocused aromas start it off, and the wine just never gets back on track after that. The palate is bulky and overdone with plum and prune flavors, while the finish seems sweet and raisiny, and without a lot of harmony. As a whole it's chewy yet neither here nor there. **83** —*M.S. (8/1/2003)*

Prado Rey 2000 Roble Tinto del Pais (Ribera del Duero) $13. Meaty in the nose, with leathery aromas. The fruit flavors are in the plum class, and there seems to be a poached-fruit element there as well. The finish feels hefty and disparate; it has no real direction. Which basically describes this wine. It's full and tannic, yet it doesn't seem to have a goal, much less a path to travel upon. **84** —*M.S. (8/1/2003)*

PRINCIPE DE VIANA

Principe de Viana 1996 Tempranillo (Navarra) $11. **85** —*J.C. (11/15/1999)*

PROTOS

Protos 1994 Gran Reserva Red Blend (Ribera del Duero) $75. As you might expect, this wine's prolonged stay in oak has given it cedar and vanilla aromas and flavors, but they're well integrated with dark earth, leaf mold, and candied orange peel. Fully mature. **87** —*J.C. (11/1/2001)*

Protos 2000 Jóven Roble Tempranillo (Ribera del Duero) $11. Aromas of raw steak, black cherries, and dark chocolate set this jóven apart from the bulk of the carbonic crowd. Instead, it's a big, juicy wine that might be accused of being an overly forward fruit bomb but for its fine structure and rich finish, which folds in hints of smoked meat. **87 Best Buy** —*J.C. (11/1/2001)*

PUERTA DE GRANADA

Puerta de Granada 1997 Monastrell Crianza 1997 Monastrell (Jumilla) $15. This is a nice example of the Mourvèdre that's coming out of Jumilla in southeast Spain. It's fleshy and full, with a welcome earthiness. Flavors of black plum and cherry cover the palate prior to a drying, tannic finish. This wine manages to pick up the pace after airing, always a sign of quality. From Bodegas Huertas. **86** —*M.S. (11/1/2002)*

Puerta de Granada 1996 Puerta de Granada-Reserva Monastrell (Jumilla) $20. Medium-bodied with gritty, oaky tannins; some tart plum fruit lurks under the oak, but it's hard to find. Nose is fairly closed, but for some tarry notes. **82** —*D.T. (4/1/2003)*

Puerta de Granada 2000 Vino Tinto Tempranillo (Jumilla) $9. The nose is open and musky. Dark and deep flavors of cherry and plum seem a bit unrefined and robust. The finish is dry and tannic, so much so that it coats your mouth. It's a fruit ball with power, but one without much balance or structure. **83** —*M.S. (11/1/2002)*

PUERTA DEL SOL

Puerta Del Sol 2002 Blanco Fermentado en Roble Malvar (Madrid) $16. From Vinos Jeromín, this heavily oaked white smells of wood char and popcorn, while it tastes of coconut, more popcorn and some hard-to-peg white fruit. Weighs a ton; hard to identify and embrace. **81** —*M.S. (12/31/2004)*

PUERTA PALMA

Puerta Palma 2001 Estate Bottled Red Blend (Ribera del Guadiana) $15. From Extremadura in west-central Spain, this dark, virtually opaque red shows oak, herbs, and leather on the dense nose. The flavors to this Tempranillo-based heavyweight are of blackberry, and they're fine. But jackhammer tannins that blow away your cheek linings make it almost impossible to swallow. Bottom line: it's a high-plains tannic drifter. **83** — *M.S. (3/1/2004)*

Puerta Palma 2000 Vino Tinto Tempranillo (Ribera del Guadiana) $NA. Despite spending just six months in oak, this Tempranillo-dominated red serves up ample barrel char along with some sweet, attractive wood-driven spice. The black cherry fruit is lifted up by a pleasant vanilla flavor, which is followed by wall-to-wall tannins and a severe but welcome smokiness. **87**—*M.S. (11/1/2002)*

Puerta Palma 2003 Estate Tempranillo Blend (Ribera del Guadiana) $13. Heavy and stewy, with sweet molasses aromas but little to no freshness. Flavors of raisins and plums are dark and meaty, but lifeless. **80**—*M.S. (8/1/2005)*

Puerta Palma 2000 Finca El Campillo Reserva de la Familia Tempranillo Blend (Ribera del Guadiana) $12. Seemingly fading, with murky cedar and mint aromas and not too much fruit. Fairly gritty and tight on the back palate. A country wine that might do best with beef or lamb. **82**—*M.S. (12/31/2004)*

PUJANZA

Pujanza 2001 Tempranillo (Rioja) $30. Big and toasty, with graphite, rubber, and leather accenting pure black-fruit aromas. This is one ripe, tannic Rioja, but it's pure and the berry flavors sing a nice song. Solid on the finish, with length and feel. Shows the right stuff without blowing you away. **88**—*M.S. (4/1/2006)*

R. LOPEZ DE HEREDIA

R. Lopez de Heredia 1996 Viña Tondonia Reserva Red Blend (Rioja) $36. Not old by Tondonia standards, in fact it's a new release. Yet it's already orange and rusty in color, with aromas of citrus peel, crushed spice, and subdued berry. The palate is lean, with sharp acidity (the key to this wine's longevity). Lots of pulse and zip on the finish. Spent five years in barrel. **89**—*M.S. (9/1/2004)*

R. Lopez de Heredia 1996 Viña Bosconia Reserva Tempranillo (Rioja) $21. López de Heredia is known for classic, lightweight Riojas, and this wine fits that bill. The color is rusty, the nose raisiny and sherried. Plenty of leather and puckery acidity keep it lively, but there isn't much fruit beyond pie cherry and rhubarb. Very stylistic and not for everyone, but if you like the Old-World mode, here it is, front and center. **86**—*M.S. (3/1/2004)*

R. Lopez de Heredia 1996 Viña Bosconia Reserva Tempranillo Blend (Rioja) $32. The poster-boy wine for old Rioja is indeed tasting and acting old, even more so than its eight years. It's orange in color, with nothing but acidity on the palate. The best part is the intriguing nose, which offers vanilla, citrus peel, and saddle leather. Unfortunately, there's nothing left of this wine's body. It's emaciated. **84**—*M.S. (9/1/2004)*

R. Lopez de Heredia 2000 Viña Cubillo Crianza Tempranillo Blend (Rioja) $25. Typically brick-colored and oxidized, which leads to the idea that it's 25 years old already. Unique in every way: The nose is like deconstructed citrus, sherry, and leather, while the palate will seem sour if compared to most other reds and zesty if you're coming off a white wine. Hard to describe; a wine for some to admire and others to say, "What the hell?" **88**—*M.S. (11/1/2006)*

R. Lopez de Heredia 1997 Viña Tondonia Reserva Tempranillo Blend (Rioja) $39. Typically amber in color, with aromas of dried cherries merging into apricots. Tangy and sharp on the palate, as is standard. Neither fruity nor deep, even according to Tondonia's track record. Newcomers may not be impressed. **86**—*M.S. (6/1/2005)*

RAFAEL PALACIOS

Rafael Palacios 2005 As Sortes Godello (Valdeorras) $35. Palacios started his Valdeorras winery in 2004, and in short order he has established himself as a quality leader. His As Sortes is 100% Godello, from dry-farmed vines with age. This wine is rich, with ample oak, fresh and dry fruit flavors, and a walnut-infused finish. Quite Burgundian in style. **92**—*M.S. (9/1/2006)*

RAIMAT

Raimat 1998 Cabernet Sauvignon (Costers del Segre) $13. From Costers del Segre, in northeastern Spain, this Cab spends 24 months in American oak. Once you sample it, that fact won't at all surprise you.

Plum fruit on the nose and on the palate takes a back seat to the wood; oak is all you get on the finish. **82**—*D.T. (4/1/2003)*

Raimat 1994 El Moli Cabernet Sauvignon (Costers del Segre) $29. **93**—*R.V. (11/1/1999)*

Raimat 1994 Mas Castell Cabernet Sauvignon (Costers del Segre) $29. **90**—*R.V. (11/1/1999)*

Raimat 1995 Mas Castell Reserva Cabernet Sauvignon (Costers del Segre) $20. Grapey fruit on the nose smells confected—and that's the good news. Stemminess pervades the palate flavors, with some black fruit underneath. More stemminess and oak on the nose and the finish. **81**—*D.T. (4/1/2003)*

Raimat 1994 Vallorba Cabernet Sauvignon (Costers del Segre) $12. **94 Best Buy**—*R.V. (11/1/1999)*

Raimat 2003 Chardonnay (Costers del Segre) $9. Rather dull and oily, with lemon and apple flavors. Feels good on the palate, but lacks style and clarity. Limited in its merits. **82**—*M.S. (12/31/2004)*

Raimat 2002 Chardonnay (Costers del Segre) $8. Ripe and creamy pear aromas precede a nutty palate with basic nectarine and banana flavors. Some spice and licorice on the finish, and then more banana. The feel is thick. **84**—*M.S. (3/1/2004)*

Raimat 1996 Merlot (Costers del Segre) $12. **88**—*R.V. (11/1/1999)*

Raimat 1996 Tempranillo (Costers del Segre) $14. **89**—*R.V. (11/1/1999)*

Raimat 2000 Tempranillo (Costers del Segre) $14. The nose tosses up hints of tobacco, tree bark, and root beer. Flavors of cherry and strawberry carry a sugary beam, and the finish turns rather candied. Not the easiest wine to wrap yourself around; it has some Old-World style but also some clumsy sweetness. **85**—*M.S. (3/1/2004)*

Raimat 1999 Tempranillo (Costers del Segre) $13. Dried spices, tomato, and earthy aromas give you a hint of what's to come: This Tempranillo's red-cherry core is hidden by seeped tea and barnyardy-earthy flavors. Finishes with oak and dusty tannins. **83**—*D.T. (4/1/2003)*

Raimat 1999 Abadia Tempranillo-Cabernet Sauvignon (Costers del Segre) $10. This Cab-Tempranillo blend was aged for 12 months in American oak. Red plum fruit is taut, and dotted with wood and eucalyptus accents. Though the wine's medium bodied, the almost-tart fruit and wood make it feel leaner. Would probably be at its best with a platter of Spanish cheese and some membrillo. **85**—*D.T. (4/1/2003)*

RAIZ DE GUZMAN

Raiz de Guzman 2000 Tempranillo (Ribera del Duero) $61. Neither flabby nor fat, with aromas of leather, hard cheese, berries, and oak. Cherry, red licorice, and more oak carry the palate, while the finish is short but stout, with yet more wood-driven reinforcement. Arguably too woody for what it is, but solid nonetheless. **86**—*M.S. (10/1/2005)*

RAMIREZ DE LA PISCINA

Ramirez de la Piscina 1999 Crianza Tempranillo (Rioja) $12. Call it rustic, barnyardy or pickled, but no matter how you slice it, it comes out rather green. At first the fruit seems too dilute to matter, but with airing it develops some personality. A good mouthfeel is the high point, while too much in the way of pickle and cabbage notes is the main detractor. **83**—*M.S. (3/1/2004)*

Ramirez de la Piscina 1997 Crianza Tempranillo (Rioja) $15. **87**—*M.M. (8/1/2000)*

Ramirez de la Piscina 1995 Reserva Tempranillo (Rioja) $21. **90**—*M.M. (8/1/2000)*

RAMÓN BILBAO

Ramón Bilbao 2000 Tempranillo (Rioja) $11. Mildly warm and baked, with red fruit and coffee aromas. Fairly firm in the mouth, with rather hard tannins. A sweet finish deals chocolate chip cookies and some wood spice. Flavorful for sure, yet a bit raw and clumsy. **85**—*M.S. (3/1/2004)*

Ramón Bilbao 1999 Tempranillo (Rioja) $10. Bears a strong resemblance to Bibao's Limited Edition crianza. Though it's a few bucks cheaper, this Tempranillo has the same cocoa-and-red fruit aromas on the nose, plus a piquant hint of eucalyptus. On the palate, red plums and cherries are swathed in oak and woodsy tannins, which makes for a somewhat unapproachable bottle for tonight's dinner. Best to start drinking after 2004. **88 Best Buy** —D.T. (4/1/2003)

Ramón Bilbao 1996 Gran Reserva Tempranillo (Rioja) $20. The bouquet is lean and intriguing, with aromas of clove and violets. But the fruit is light; there's some sour cherry and rhubarb, yet even that's a little on the tight and tough side. Good spice notes add character to this wine, which hits squarely but simple. **86** —M.S. (3/1/2004)

Ramón Bilbao 1995 Gran Reserva Tempranillo (Rioja) $20. Sour cherry and red plum flavors (and a wee too much acid) are the key players on the palate. Simpler and lighter weight than you'd expect of a gran reserva. Finishes with cranberry and oak flavors. **84** —D.T. (4/1/2003)

Ramón Bilbao 1999 Limited Edition Crianza Tempranillo (Rioja) $13. Though it's a little hard-edged now, with some tannins to lose, this crianza has good structure and sturdy red fruit going for it. The nose, with some aeration, shows raspberry and cocoa powder nuances. Drink 2004 and beyond. **88** —D.T. (4/1/2003)

Ramón Bilbao 1998 Reserva Tempranillo (Rioja) $15. Ripe and rosy on the nose, with notes of milk chocolate and plum. Very zesty across the palate; the raspberry and cherry fruit almost elicits a pucker. The finish is snappy and fresh, while medium tannins fail to absorb the sharp acidity. Nonetheless it's balanced and easy to drink. **86** —M.S. (3/1/2004)

Ramón Bilbao 1996 Reserva Tempranillo (Rioja) $15. Medium and quite unyielding, this 90% Tempranillo (Mazuelo, Garnacha, and Graciano make up the rest) has tangy wood and red plum-skin flavors. Offers understated foresty aromas, plus some stewy red fruit, on the nose. Hard cheese may bring out its best. **84** —D.T. (4/1/2003)

Ramón Bilbao 2001 Limited Edition Crianza Tempranillo Blend (Rioja) $13. Clean and fruity, with yeasty, flowery scents and some snappy berry notes. It remains pure and lively in the mouth, with a smooth, late flow of chocolaty oak. Likable and noteworthy from a winery without a great track record for quality. **88** —M.S. (9/1/2004)

Ramón Bilbao 2001 Mirto Tempranillo (Rioja) $37. Clean and polished, but not as expressive as the company it's running with. The nose is spicy, forward, and full of plum and berry. A bit acidic and racy, with good flavors of cherry, mint, and oak. Finishes swift but snappy. Very good but playing in a tough division. **89** —M.S. (9/1/2004)

Ramón Bilbao 1999 Mirto Tempranillo Blend (Rioja) $37. Lush and masculine, and every bit made to emphasize extract and oak. It's dark, with heavy berry fruit, density, and ripeness. On the finish it turns even darker, with bitter chocolate and wood smoke. Arguably better at first; airing seems to close it up rather than expanding it. Drink now or cellar for up to five years. **88** —M.S. (3/1/2004)

RAMÓN CARDOVA

Ramón Cardova 2002 Tempranillo (Rioja) $12. The burnt matchstick aromas are tough to get past, but once they blow off, this joven delivers simple blackberry and citrus flavors on a lightweight frame. **83** —J.C. (4/1/2005)

Ramón Cardova 2001 Tempranillo (Rioja) $10. Sweet blueberry aromas make it attractive in a basic way. And in the mouth there's ample cherry and raspberry fruit. Where this wine turns south, however, is at the finish line; here an unwelcome and odd chicken-fat flavor not only arises but hangs around for the rest of the show. A kosher offering. **82** —M.S. (10/1/2003)

Ramón Cardova 2001 Crianza Tempranillo (Rioja) $18. This lean, oaky wine offers kosher wine drinkers an authentic expression of one style of Rioja, delivering cherry-berry fruit and a mountain of vanilla and toast. Finishes dry and woody. **83** —J.C. (4/1/2005)

RAVENTÓS I BLANC

Raventós I Blanc 1998 Gran Reserva Personal Brut Nature Sparkling Blend (Cava) $NA. Harmonious and a bit creamy to the nose, with apple, citrus, and lees. More citrus and apple on the palate, with an almondy kick. Shows fine depth on the finish, where orange notes take over. An excellent, mature cava that still has some grit. **90** —M.S. (6/1/2005)

REINO DE LOS MALLOS

Reino de los Mallos 2003 Red Blend (Vino de la Tierra Ribera del Gállego-Cinco Villas) $20. A blend of Cabernet, Merlot, and Grenache that can only be described as strange. The nose is stewy, the palate full of root beer, baked berries and syrup. It's even cloying on the finish. Yet through all that there's still a little something redeeming about it. **81** —M.S. (12/15/2006)

REJADORADA

Rejadorada 2001 Crianza Tinta de Toro (Toro) $27. Spicy and exotic, with tight fruit and plenty of tannin in the mouth. There's a lot of juicy blackberry flavors along with full-force acids and verve. Tight as a drum, with some rough edges that should mellow over the next year or so. A wine to watch from a region that's showing its stuff **89** —M.S. (4/1/2006)

Rejadorada 2001 Sango Tinta de Toro (Toro) $55. Raisin and liqueur carry the oaked nose, yet the palate is quite hard and tannic. Reduced a bit across the tongue, with prune, milk chocolate, and beet nots. Has power and a high price tag, but it fails to stir the beast. **85** —M.S. (9/1/2006)

Rejadorada 2003 Tinto Roble Tinta de Toro (Toro) $20. Starts with roasted, leathery aromas that feature hints of burnt beef and berry compote. The palate is layered and nicely balanced, with berry flavors hitting first and chocolate coming next. Espresso is the final act, as it ties the mouth to the finish in impressive fashion. A big load but one that's still manageable. **90** —M.S. (12/15/2006)

REMÍREZ DE GANUZA

Remírez de Ganuza 2001 Reserva Tempranillo Blend (Rioja) $74. Since coming into existence in 1988, this winery has made rich, modern reds that represent the best of what new-age Rioja is about. And the 2001 could be the best yet, as it offers aromas of rose petals, fresh lemon, cola, soy, coffee, leather, and more. Definitely a powerhouse, with huge fruit from front to back. Lively in terms of tannins, with the expected monster oak. Employs 10% Graciano in addition to Tempranillo. **94 Editors' Choice** —M.S. (6/1/2005)

RENÉ BARBIER

René Barbier 2002 Cabernet Sauvignon (Penedès) $7. Initial off aromas never really find their way, leaving lasting notes of red cabbage and pickle barrel. The mouth is sharp and grapey, and there isn't much charm or Cabernet-related richness. Very pedestrian. **82** —M.S. (3/1/2004)

René Barbier 1996 Selección Crianza Cabernet Sauvignon (Penedès) $14. Green olive and white pepper—then a hint of caraway—lead the nose. Flavors of blackberry and a chalky finish end this wine. A bit awkward but interesting if you like a green wine. **83** —C.S. (4/1/2002)

René Barbier 2002 Chardonnay (Penedès) $7. A zesty, lean wine, one that's not really identifiable as mainstream Chardonnay but which will go well with seafood due to its racy mouthfeel. The nose, meanwhile, is thin and prickly, while the palate offers lean apple and melon. **84** —M.S. (3/1/2004)

René Barbier 2001 Chardonnay (Penedès) $10. Some cream and stone fruits grace the nose, but beyond that you'd be hard pressed to identify anything else. The palate is fruity, with cantaloupe and banana flavors emerging. And the finish is clean, sizable, and lasting. An okay wine for the price, but don't expect miracles from this base-level Chardonnay. **83** —M.S. (3/1/2004)

René Barbier 1999 Selección Chardonnay (Penedès) $14. Loads of oak over golden apple fruit and mild tropical notes make this a New World wannabe. It's medium weight but overblown, and the flavors are fundamentally out of balance. Still, there are some folks who just want a little fruit with their oak. **83** —M.M. (9/1/2002)

René Barbier NV Mediterranean Red Red Blend (Penedès) $6. Cherry, fleshy red fruit flavors and a light, dilute mouthfeel are prefaced by earthy, resiny notes on the nose. Juicy cranberry and plum flavors, plus some wood, round out the short finish. Tasted twice. **81** —D.T. (4/1/2002)

René Barbier 2003 Tempranillo (Penedès) $7. This perennial bargain-basement red offers solid fruit with herbal overtones, while the flavor profile veers toward cherries and licorice. Gets raisiny and more ponderous the more time you spend analyzing it. **83** —*M.S. (9/1/2006)*

René Barbier 2002 Tempranillo (Penedès) $7. Bulky and simple on the bouquet, with some plum and blackberry. Flavors of cherry, plum and berry are standard fare and clean, while the mouthfeel is a touch racy as it toes the line of sharpness. A bit of chocolaty oak adds sweetness to the zesty, acid-strong finish. **84** —*M.S. (3/1/2004)*

René Barbier NV Mediterranean Rosé Tempranillo Blend (Catalunya) $6. Citrus rind on the nose, which is backed by light nectarine and table grape flavors. Sort of dilute and watery on the finish, with low acidity. Comes across sweet. **82** —*M.S. (2/1/2006)*

René Barbier NV Mediterranean White White Blend (Catalunya) $6. This simple summer sipper is clean, fresh, and grassy, with aromas of apple and green melon. Surprisingly mouthfilling for something so easygoing, but still packed with melon and citrus flavors. Fresh and zesty, and just right for patio parties. **85 Best Buy** —*M.S. (10/1/2005)*

RENTO

Rento 2003 Tinto del Pais (Ribera del Duero) $60. There's a lot of raw power on this jumbled red that starts with rubber and spice before settling on maple. The mouth is a cacophony of loud flavors, while the finish is stark. Needs finesse to match the aggressiveness. **82** —*M.S. (11/1/2006)*

RIBERAL

Riberal 2003 4 Meses Barrica Tinto del Pais (Ribera del Duero) $13. Damp and foresty, and seeming old before its time. Raisiny fruit with clove and anise accents are acceptable but heavy. Tannic and bulky. **81** —*M.S. (11/1/2006)*

RIMARTS

Rimarts 2001 Cabernet Sauvignon-Merlot (Penedès) $14. With 25% Merlot blended in, this basic Cab will serve most purposes. It's light, with raspberry aromas and plum, berry, and mild caramel flavors. Finishes fruity and on the money, with good flavors and precision. **86** —*M.S. (5/1/2004)*

Rimarts 2002 Merlot Rosé Blend (Penedès) $11. Powerful and beefy on the nose, but lacking in refinement. And overall the bouquet seems slightly pickled and prickly, while there's little identifiable fruit to the palate. Mostly it's thin and just mildly peachy. **82** —*M.S. (5/1/2004)*

Rimarts 1998 Brut Nature Sparkling Blend (Cava) $15. Fresh and slightly green, marked by aromas and flavors of herbs, green apples, and limes. It's light and lean, fairly brisk and acidic. Note that there's no vintage indicated on the bottle; this is the regular red label. **85** —*J.C. (12/31/2003)*

Rimarts 1996 Brut Nature Gran Reserva Sparkling Blend (Cava) $21. Savory, with a hint of anise and not much fruit remaining, this aged Cava finishes on a slightly sweet-and-sour note. This is the red label Gran Reserva; no vintage is indicated on the bottle, but the 1996 is the current release. **83** —*J.C. (1/1/2004)*

Rimarts 1994 Reserva Especial Brut Nature Sparkling Blend (Cava) $30. This wine is so filled with floral and herbal aromas as to be positively overbearing—like the first few breaths upon entering a flower shop. Light and frothy, it may hold more appeal for other tasters. No vintage is indicated on the bottle, but this is the current vintage of the green label Reserva Especial. **80** —*J.C. (1/1/2004)*

RIOJA VEGA

Rioja Vega 2000 Red Blend (Rioja) $8. Forward, expressive plum and raspberry fruit would leap from the glass were it not reigned in by a healthy dose of oak. Brambly, tomatoey—even Bourbonlike—accents waft from the nose. Medium-bodied, this Tempranillo, Garnacha, and Mazuelo blend is a natural match for tapas, paella, or gambas al ajillo. **87 Best Buy** —*D.T. (4/1/2003)*

Rioja Vega 2004 Tempranillo (Rioja) $8. Hard and jumbled up front, with slightly harsh peppery notes interlocking with light raspberry fruit. A light, airy, almost innocuous wine with mild bitterness on the finish. Doesn't impress. **81** —*M.S. (12/15/2006)*

RONDEL

Rondel NV Extreme Brut Sparkling Blend (Cava) $6. Early burnt-match aromas lead to more grassy, herbal scents. Fairly bulky on the palate, and oily. A persistent, hard-hitting wine, and that alone doesn't serve it well. **81** —*M.S. (12/15/2004)*

ROQUERO

Roquero 1995 Reserva Monastrell (Jumilla) $12. This wine's smooth, even mouthfeel can't compensate for an odd, cheesy note on the nose and the fact that the dark cherry and bitter chocolate flavors are deeply under wood. Shows some back-end bite, seeming past its best, as if it would have shown better earlier. **83** —*M.M. (9/1/2002)*

Roquero 1994 Reserva Monastrell (Jumilla) $12. **86** —*J.C. (8/1/2000)*

Roquero 1998 Tinto Monastrell (Jumilla) $9. **87** —*J.C. (8/1/2000)*

ROTLLAN TORRA

Rotllan Torra 2002 Amadis Red Blend (Priorat) $55. Dark in color, while one sniff indicates ripeness at the edge of stewy. There's unctuous berry jam and raisin to the bouquet, likely a result of late picking. Chunky on the palate, with plum and blackberry. Grabby yet soft, with wide-spread tannins. Finishes with coconut, vanilla, and prune. **86** —*M.S. (10/1/2005)*

Rotllan Torra 1998 Amadis Red Blend (Priorat) $45. Aromas of raisins, meat, and forest floor match the full, fleshy flavors of currant, sweet tobacco, and new leather well. Finishes with juicy acidity that holds up to the tannins. This is a big, lush, well-balanced wine that should drink well until at least 2010. **93 Editors' Choice** —*K.F. (11/1/2002)*

Rotllan Torra 1998 Balandra Red Blend (Priorat) $32. A touch gamy at first, this wine offers a complex package of curry, sweet spices, black fruit, pepper, and golden raisins. In the mouth, it is smooth, svelte and closes with an elegant yet big finish. Drink now–2008. **91** —*K.F. (11/1/2002)*

Rotllan Torra 1997 Reserva Red Blend (Priorat) $15. **89 Best Buy** —*C.S. (11/15/2002)*

Rotllan Torra 2000 Sellecció Red Blend (Priorat) $15. Unfocused, with sharp fruit that comes across borderline astringent. In terms of flavors, it's all cherry and citrus, and that's because the acidity is scorching. A hollow man of a wine; there's just not that much to like. **83** —*M.S. (3/1/2004)*

Rotllan Torra 2002 Tirant Red Blend (Priorat) $75. Ripe and rich; it pushes the limit toward raisiny but doesn't cross the boundary. As a result, the sweet bouquet oozes kirsch, licorice, and spice. Stays thick on the palate, but not particularly heavy. Flavors of baked black fruit, mocha, and espresso impress, with accents of cinnamon and herbs popping through. Complex and out of the ordinary **91** —*M.S. (10/1/2005)*

Rotllan Torra 1998 Tirant Red Blend (Priorat) $70. A huge, intense wine that still delivers complexity, it's made from 100-year-old Garnacha and Cariñena vines, finished off with small amounts of Cabernet Sauvignon, Merlot, and Syrah. The evolving aromas of licorice, black cherry, toast, and lavender lead into big, dark fruit flavors with tannins and acids to match. Drink now–2015. **94 Cellar Selection** (11/1/2002)

RUBIEJO

Rubiejo 2002 Crianza Tempranillo (Ribera del Duero) $22. **88** —*M.S. (9/9/1999)*

Rubiejo 2004 Oak Aged Tempranillo (Ribera del Duero) $17. Wines like this are good indicators that 2004 is indeed an exceptional vintage in RdD. For a Tempranillo that spent only five months in oak it's fairly settled. The nose is a touch syrupy but you can only love the concentrated berry aromas. The mouth is bulky but satisfying, with huge dark-fruit flavors and balancing tannins and acidity. Jumpy but very likable. **89** —*M.S. (11/1/2006)*

Rubiejo 2003 Oak Aged Tempranillo (Ribera del Duero) $17. This young RdD was aged only five months in barrel, yet it has weight, softness, and vanilla shadings as well as pure, unadulterated dark fruit. In a word, it's delicious; the round blackberry and cherry flavors are great and the chocolate and smoke that sneak up on the finish seal the deal. A bit too expensive to be a Best Buy, but still a very good deal. **89** —*M.S. (11/15/2005)*

Rubiejo 2004 Young Tempranillo (Ribera del Duero) $12. Talk about a colorful, bold, jammy red! It's heavily extracted and, as the label notes, young as can be. The fruit is heavy, dark to the point of teeth-staining, and tannic. Not sophisticated or meant for fine dining, but full of fruit and life. Tastes good but is unequivocally rambunctious. **85** —*M.S. (11/1/2006)*

Rubiejo 2002 Crianza Tinto del Pais (Ribera del Duero) $29. What starts as smoke and bacon quickly veers to heavy wood, rubber, vanilla, and coconut. Flavors of raspberry and strawberry are secure, while the texture is grabby and sharp. Shows good intensity. **84** —*M.S. (10/1/2005)*

Rubiejo 2003 Jóven Tinto del Pais (Ribera del Duero) $13. Seductively rich, with blackberry and vanilla aromas. Ripe and chewy, with plum, vanilla, and subtle spice in the background. Nice doses of licorice and bitter chocolate solidify the finish. Quite meaty and modern, if a bit pricy for a youngster from a hot year. **88 Best Buy** —*M.S. (10/1/2005)*

RUBINES

Rubines 2003 Albariño (Rías Baixas) $21. Big-boned and citrusy, with aromas of oranges and melon. More citrus on the palate mixes with the essence of pear and apple, while the finish is tight and rather long. A bit lacking in depth, but ripe and forward. Satisfyingly simple. **86** —*M.S. (3/1/2005)*

S'FORNO

S'forno 2003 Estate Godello (Valdeorras) $15. Reeks of burnt matchstick on the nose, and the sensation permeates the wine, turning the modest apple and mineral flavors acrid on the finish. Might be acceptable with long decanting. **80** —*J.C. (4/1/2005)*

S'forno 2002 Estate Mourvedre Monastrell (Yecla) $10. Herbal and tomatoey on the nose, this crisp, lean wine offers little beyond flavors of cherry tomatoes and citrus. Finishes tart, with drying tannins. **82** —*J.C. (4/1/2005)*

S. ARROYO

S. Arroyo 2001 Tinto Jóven Tempranillo (Ribera del Duero) $9. A monster with a forceful nose that reeks of earth, coffee grounds, and leather. Underneath is a bruiser that pumps high-octane licorice and blackberry. Along the way the tannins are young and fierce. This is not a smooth, cuddly wine. Best for fans of tannic, lusty reds. **86 Best Buy** —*M.S. (3/1/2004)*

SALNEVAL

Salneval 2004 Albariño (Rías Baixas) $10. From Condes de Albarei, this wine is solid and round, with aromas of petrol and scented oil. Peach, orange, and herb flavors are good and go the distance. Fresh and acidic, with correct feel and weight. **86 Best Buy** —*M.S. (10/1/2005)*

SAN PEDRO

San Pedro 1999 Vallobera Crianza Tempranillo (Rioja) $15. Deep but reticent on the nose, with somewhat muted cherry and blackberry aromas. Plum and black-fruit flavors come prior to a dark, mouth-filling finish that's properly tannic and entirely substantive. For a mid-price Rioja there's depth, and beyond that the flavors and feel are clean and attractive. **87** —*M.S. (8/1/2003)*

SAN ROMAN

San Roman 1998 Tempranillo (Toro) $40. 92 *(8/1/2000)*

SAN VICENTE

San Vicente 2002 Tempranillo (Rioja) $49. Lots of bacon, leather, and earth coat the nose of this vanguard-style Rioja, but unlike the spectacular 2001, the '02 is not nearly as deep and ethereal. Blame the cool, wet vintage and take solace in the fact that it's still a rich, almost syrupy red with integrated tannins and lushness. What's missing is the wine's patented layering and complexity. **89** —*M.S. (4/1/2006)*

San Vicente 2001 Tempranillo (Rioja) $51. Smoky and rich, with hints of raisin, black cherry, and chocolate scurrying about the nose. Meaty plum, cherry and blackberry flavors form a seamless palate that slides easily onto the coffee-filled finish. Everything evolves beautifully here, and it will satisfy anyone with an unbridled craving for chocolaty hedonism **94 Editors' Choice** —*M.S. (8/1/2005)*

San Vicente 2000 Tempranillo Blend (Rioja) $49. A touch of green pepper and herb character to the nose leads one to question ripeness, especially considering how rich the wine's neighbors are. But this wine is fine, with spice, balance, and character. It's the type of Rioja that can dance from a tasting to the dinner table—no small feat these days. With perfect mouthfeel and length, it's a winner. **91** —*M.S. (9/1/2004)*

SANCHEZ ROMATE

Sanchez Romate NV Cardenal Cisneros Reservas Pedro Ximénez (Jerez) $15. This reserve-level P.X. sets the gold standard for excellence in sweet sherry. The lovely bouquet straddles the line between unadulterated sweetness and impeccable slyness. The flavors of fig, chocolate, caramel, browned butter, and cinnamon are amazing. So chewy and thick, but balanced by firm acids. Brilliant. **94 Best Buy** —*M.S. (10/1/2005)*

Sanchez Romate NV Don José Oloroso Sherry (Jerez) $17. Nutty and intense, like peanut brittle reduced to liquid form—but with less than half the corn syrup. It delivers beautiful texture and intensity; it's almost fruity, but then mushroom, almond, and macadamia nut take over. With perfect weight and a finish that doesn't quit, this is a great dry Sherry. **93** —*M.S. (10/1/2005)*

Sanchez Romate NV Fino Marismeno Reservas Sherry (Jerez) $15. Quite yellow, with toffee, peanuts, and light fruit aromas. Big and round in the mouth, with dried apple, almond, and white pepper flavors. Full and long late, with tons of texture and a strong mushroom accent. Powerful, so you'd better be a fino fan if you're going to tackle this one. **90 Editors' Choice** —*M.S. (4/1/2006)*

Sanchez Romate NV Iberia Cream Sherry (Jerez) $15. It's rare that a sweet sherry reaches such heights, but here's a case in point. Iberia has impeccable prune and raisin aromas along with intoxicating scents of toffee and cane sugar. All in all, the bouquet is excellent. The palate, meanwhile, is seamless as it deals raisin, vanilla, and mocha. Spot on for a dessert elixir, with a ceaseless finish. **93 Editors' Choice** —*M.S. (10/1/2005)*

Sanchez Romate NV Imported Cream Sherry (Jerez) $7. Lively prune and raisin aromas are nice, even if a bit of alcohol mars the nose. Flavors of caramel and vanilla satisfy, while the sugary finish is borderline cloying but manages to hold the line. Very nice and just right for sweet-toothed sherry novices. **88 Best Buy** —*M.S. (10/1/2005)*

Sanchez Romate NV NPU Amontillado Sherry (Jerez) $17. Pure and nutty, with aromas of dried apricot and sea air. In the mouth you get lots of almond and butter, while the A-rate finish is buttery but also quite complex. A classic, refined wine that dances across your tongue like a ballerina. **92** —*M.S. (10/1/2005)*

Sanchez Romate NV Romate Medium Dry Amontillado Sherry (Jerez) $7. Perfectly drinkable but not that exciting. This is everyday Sherry, the type of wine you'd get in a bar in Jerez. It's mildly sweet, with adequate nuttiness. Not much flash or sizzle, however. **84 Best Buy** —*M.S. (10/1/2005)*

SANDEMAN

Sandeman NV Royal Ambrosante Aged 20 Years Old Solera Pedro Ximénez (Jerez) $24. Sandeman excels with its reserve-level sherries, as is exemplified by this stand-out PX. Figs and raisins are front and center throughout, but it never sits heavily on your palate. Just the opposite, there's plow-through acidity that creates a brilliant mouthfeel and the sensation of freshness. Fabulous by itself or on top of vanilla ice cream. **93 Editors' Choice** —*M.S. (6/1/2005)*

Sandeman NV Royal Corregidor Rich Old Oloroso Sherry (Jerez) $25. Rich and unctuous; a big, muscular, semi-sweet beauty with a meaty frame and gorgeous maple and toffee aromas. Broad-shouldered across the palate, with apricot and quince flavors accented by cinnamon and nutmeg. In terms of mouthfeel, it's like a fine liqueur, and on the finish everything you've previously smelled and/or tasted comes back into perfect focus. **94** —*M.S. (8/1/2003)*

Sandeman NV Royal Esmeralda Fine Dry Amontillado Sherry (Jerez) $25. Quite the classic, with rich toffee and nut-like aromas that come through with piercing power. The briny palate is all about dried citrus and nuts, while the earthy, long finish has an unmistakable and very nice mushroom quality. This is a precise, somewhat reserved and dainty amontillado, but it's structured and quite real as far as style and impact. **91** —M.S. (8/1/2003)

SANGENÍS I VAQUÉ

Sangenís I Vaqué 2000 Clos Monlleó Red Blend (Priorat) $60. Rock solid, with spice, leather, and piercing oak on the nose. Snappy and upright on the palate, with tons of berry fruit and nice smoky shadings. Balanced and nuanced, with vanilla, licorice, toast, and spice on the finish. A winner. **90** —M.S. (4/1/2006)

Sangenís I Vaqué 2000 Coranya Red Blend (Priorat) $45. Quite ripe, with a touch of stewiness that settles with time and morphs into a pool of ripe cherries, berries, and raisins. More soft than hard, with easygoing tannins and a meaty, chunky finish laced with licorice and cured meat. Dense and chewy. **89** —M.S. (4/1/2006)

Sangenís I Vaqué 2002 Crianza Dara Red Blend (Priorat) $14. For an affordable Priorat this wine isn't disappointing. The nose is a bit funky and gamy, but you'll also dig out mineral, leather, and bacon notes that are pleasing. Peppery and spicy more than lush and fruity, with pushy game and herbal notes on the finish. **85** —M.S. (11/1/2006)

Sangenís I Vaqué 2001 Vall Por Red Blend (Priorat) $13. Cherry, earth, and leather are nice opening notes, while some charred oak adds masculinity and depth. Almost syrupy in the mouth, with plenty of black cherry and chocolate to satisfy those with a sweet tooth. Exhibits nice core qualities. **88 Best Buy** —M.S. (4/1/2006)

Sangenís I Vaqué 2000 Vall Por Red Blend (Priorat) $34. Tight and natural, with rustic, terroir-based aromas and plenty of leather to the nose and feel. Full and ripe on the tongue, mixing chocolate and licorice into a fine swirl. A clear mocha note makes for a sweet and satisfying finish. Drinkable now and over the next few years. **90** —M.S. (3/1/2004)

SANTANA

Santana 1998 Tempranillo (Rioja) $7. A straightforward basic red, with dried cherry, oak, and slightly meaty scents. The palate shows dark fruit and spice flavors, medium weight and an even texture. Finishes with decent length and tangy, spicy notes. **84** (5/1/2001)

Santana 1999 Viura (Tierra Manchuela) $7. This pleasant wine shows clean apple, hay, and mildly floral aromas. Even and round on the tongue, it has a slightly waxy feel and decent acidity. Green apple, citrus, and slightly nutty flavors play on the finish, with a crisp, dry grapefruity aftertaste that lingers. **86 Best Buy** (5/1/2001)

SANTIAGO RUIZ

Santiago Ruiz 2005 O Rosal White Blend (Rías Baixas) $18. This winery, with its sketched labels, is classic O Rosal. The wine is 90% Albariño and Loureira, with some Caino Blanca thrown in. The color is pale but convincing, while the palate offers bright apple, apricot, and nectarine flavors meshed with cutting acidity. **89** —M.S. (9/1/2006)

SANTONEGRO

Santonegro 2005 Monastrell (Jumilla) $9. A little bit sweet and doughy, but hardly offputting. Deep flavors of cherry, raspberry, and strawberry control the palate, while the finish is chocolaty and long. This is one easy-to-like red; it's not complex but it scores plenty of simple pleasure points. **87 Best Buy** —M.S. (12/15/2006)

Santonegro 2002 Crianza Red Blend (Jumilla) $12. Warm and the slightest bit raisiny, but overall it's a bright, fruity blend of Monastrell and Tempranillo that's tasty and worth every dollar. Flavors of black cherry and vanilla are cuddly, while the finish is long and of medium potency. A treat for those who enjoy fruity, somewhat softer reds. **87 Best Buy** — M.S. (12/15/2006)

SCALA DEI

Scala Dei 2002 Negre Garnacha (Priorat) $13. Catchy aromas such as violet and exotic candle wax are encouraging, maybe a bit more so than the tangy palate, which runs toward red-apple skins and cherry. Light in the middle but tannic on the edges. Fresh and spry, but lean. **85** —M.S. (12/31/2004)

Scala Dei 2000 Prior Criança Garnacha (Priorat) $20. Ripe, earthy, and spicy, with noticeable oak. The palate is lively, packed with cherry and plum, and quite tannic. Thus the finish seems gritty and racy, bordering on raw. Give it air and food for maximum results. It's 88% Garnacha. **86** —M.S. (12/31/2004)

Scala Dei 2003 Negre Grenache (Priorat) $15. Sweet and raisiny, with a heavy profile as well as some unexpected aromatic sharpness. The fruit is more brambly and baked than usual, and there's some murkiness. Not the best example of this wine, which was not oaked; it was better in previous vintages. **83** —M.S. (10/1/2005)

Scala Dei 2001 Prior Criança Grenache (Priorat) $22. Smooth and open, with pretty cherry, fudge, and maple aromas. Rather zingy and stand-up on the palate, where big, rubbery tannins carry full-sized cherry and plum flavors. Finishes with grab and at least two waves of flavor and power. Drink through 2007. **89** —M.S. (10/1/2005)

Scala Dei 2001 Cartoixa Red Blend (Priorat) $30. Pure and cerebral, but with enough natural liveliness that you can't help but love it. Aromas of schist, lavender, and plum mix with oak-driven bacon and chocolate to create a welcoming whole. Sizable cherry and plum flavors are round but also precise and firm. Looming tannins suggest some cellaring may be warranted. The blend is Garnacha followed by Syrah and Cabernet Sauvignon. **91** —M.S. (10/1/2005)

Scala Dei 2000 Cartoixa Reserva Red Blend (Priorat) $26. Full and earthy, and very oaky. But also quite solid and forceful, with delicious cola, cherry, and plum flavors following in the wake of sweet berry and barrel-based aromas. Rich enough on the palate, with typical Priorat ruggedness. A commendable effort that offers plenty. The blend is Cabernet Sauvignon, Garnacha, and Syrah. **90** —M.S. (12/31/2004)

Scala Dei 1998 Cartoixa Reserva Red Blend (Priorat) $22. Smells like Christmas, with holly and candied plum wafting from the nose. Medium-bodied, it has a plum and cherry core, with flavors just this side of tangy. Rustic tannins and barbecue-char notes round out the finish. Try with chorizo. **86** —D.T. (4/1/2003)

SEGURA VIUDAS

Segura Viudas NV Aria Brut Rosé Pinot Noir (Cava) $12. Deep in color, falling somewhere between copper and red. The nose is forward as could be, with raspberry and a strong hint of orange blossom. Solid across the palate, with dry berry flavors and a powerful edge of pepper. Based on Pinot Noir; you can taste the essence of that variety at its core. **87** —M.S. (12/15/2006)

Segura Viudas NV Aria Estate Brut Sparkling Blend (Cava) $12. A classic cava from top to bottom. The nose offers familiar baked apple, mineral, and saline aromas, while the palate is exceedingly fresh in its delivery of pineapple, apple, and nectarine flavors. A fruity yet crisp number that foams up nicely on the palate but doesn't lose its focus or form. **89 Best Buy** —M.S. (12/15/2006)

Segura Viudas NV Aria Extra Dry Sparkling Blend (Cava) $12. This rendition of Segura Viudas's off-dry bubbly is nice and yeasty, with plenty of baked apple pie and buttered toast on the nose. The palate is spunky but round, with semi-sweet flavors of apples and ripe nectarines. Shows some complexity and depth on the finish as well as a richness that makes it to all corners of your mouth. **88 Best Buy** —M.S. (12/15/2006)

Segura Viudas NV Brut Reserva Sparkling Blend (Cava) $14. Slightly sweet on the nose, the aromas of baked fruit, cream soda, and vanilla are welcoming. Interestingly, the wine is a bit more tart and refined on the palate, where zesty but full apple and pear flavors run the show. Not lean but definitely streamlined and acidic. More of a food wine than a stand-alone sipper. **88** —M.S. (12/15/2006)

Segura Viudas NV Brut Heredad Reserva Sparkling Blend (Cava) $20. Regal in presentation, with its faux-metal label and broad-based bottle. And in every edition it's one of Spain's more elegant, serious cavas. Look for slightly toasted, charcoal-based aromas backed by ripe apple and sweet citrus flavors. Very good feel and length. One of Spain's truly consistent high-end bubblies. **89** —M.S. (6/1/2006)

SPAIN

Segura Viudas NV Brut Rosé Sparkling Blend (Cava) $10. With its citrusy nose and well-balanced palate, this is what Best Buy sparklers are all about. Tangerine and orange peel grace the bouquet, while crisp flavors of berries and stone fruits win you over. A bit of strawberry and snap close the deal. Nice stuff. **87 Best Buy** —*M.S. (12/15/2006)*

Segura Viudas NV Extra Dry Sparkling Blend (Cava) $10. A gem in the semisweet category, with touches of melon and banana on the nose. The palate pours on the sweet apple cider and warm citrus, while the finish is on the mark. This is a generous, no-brainer of a bubbly: Just uncork, pour, sip and smile. **89 Best Buy** —*M.S. (12/15/2006)*

Segura Viudas 2000 Torre Galimany Brut Nature Sparkling Blend (Cava) $NA. Begins with mature aromas of toast, sugared pastry and yeast. Ultra dry in the mouth but flavorful, with almost sterile apple and spice flavors. Crisp but forgiving on the finish; a good match for poultry. **88** —*M.S. (6/1/2005)*

Segura Viudas 2001 Mas D'Aranyó Reserva Tempranillo (Penedès) $15. Dusty and dry, with a fair amount of barnyard to the nose. Tannic and raw, with nondescript berry flavors. Acidic yet not fully scouring, with some lasting chocolate and spice. From Segura Viudas. **82** —*M.S. (10/1/2005)*

Segura Viudas 1998 Mas D'Aranyo Reserva Tempranillo (Penedès) $12. Big, bold and thoroughly modern, with pungent burnt-wood aromas and rich chocolaty flavors. The black cherry fruit is ripe and rewarding prior to a dry tannic finish. This wine is structured and woody, very typical of today's Spanish reds. **87 Best Buy** —*M.S. (11/1/2002)*

Segura Viudas 1997 Mas D'Aranyó Riserva Tempranillo (Penedès) $15. Shows some nice red berry fruit with tobacco and white pepper accents, but a negative note between green pepper and sour cream distracts and detracts considerably. A tasty wine with nice feel and decent length upon opening, it disappointingly goes downhill as the off-putting element ascends. **83** —*M.M. (9/1/2002)*

Segura Viudas 2004 Creu de Lavit Xarel-lo (Penedès) $15. This one takes some getting used to. The nose begins in crystallized, granular fashion, much like a powdered drink mix. The palate offers citrus, apple and some oak, because it was barrel fermented. Medium in depth, with tang across the tongue. Good for Penedès white table wine. **86** —*M.S. (10/1/2005)*

Segura Viudas 2003 Creu de Lavit Xarel-lo (Penedès) $15. Another table wine made from Xarel-lo, the prime white grape for sparkling cava. This one is barrel-aged, so there's a full whiff of resiny wood prior to flavors of spiced cider and smoked ham. Some cinnamon and raisin notes add character to the light, almost sleepy finish. **84** —*M.S. (12/31/2004)*

Segura Viudas 2002 Creu de Lavit Xarel-lo (Penedès) $15. Waxy on the nose, with barrel hints as well as buttered toast and vanilla. Fairly limited in scope, but nicely textured. Flavors of apple, banana, and custard lead into a lemon and pineapple finish. **84** —*M.S. (9/1/2004)*

Segura Viudas 2000 Creu de Lavit Xarel-lo (Penedès) $15. Apple, hay, and lots of toasty oak yield a very butterscotchy wine. But the oak keeps coming on, burying all else and rendering the wine ponderous. Xarello, a lighter white usually used in Cava blends, could perhaps yield an interesting still wine with mainstream appeal using less wood. **84** —*M.M. (9/1/2002)*

Segura Viudas 2001 Creu de Lavit Xarel-lo (Penedès) $15. Round and medium-bodied in the mouth, this Xarel-lo had so much ripe yellow and tropical fruit on the nose that I feared that it would be too sweet in the mouth. This wasn't at all the case. The palate's yellow fruit wore meaty, mushroomy accents that extended into the finish. A very good wine— the kind of white that sommeliers should look to as a food-friendly alternative to Chardonnay. **87** —*D.T. (4/1/2003)*

SEÑORIO DE AYLÉS

Señorío de Aylés 2004 Garnacha (Cariñena) $10. Foxy, animal aromas don't distinguish it, while robust but mulchy berry and plum flavors fail to take it very far. Barely acceptable. **80** —*M.S. (9/1/2006)*

Señorío de Aylés 2004 Tinto Jóven Red Blend (Cariñena) $11. Balsamic vinegar, burnt coffee, and pepper aromas create a bouquet that's more like salad dressing than fine wine. The flavors are peppery and herbal, yet the body is full and the mouthfeel not bad. A blend of four grapes, led by Garnacha and Tempranillo. **80** —*M.S. (9/1/2006)*

Señorío de Aylés 2003 Tempranillo-Merlot (Cariñena) $15. There's nice color to this Merlot-Tempranillo blend, and that's backed by density on the nose along with notes of balsamic vinegar and dark plums. Full and slightly herbal in the mouth, with core acids and tannins that ensure that it stays propped up. Not a factory-style wine; it's unique and well worth a go at this price. **87** —*M.S. (4/1/2006)*

SEÑORÍO DE CRUCES

Señorío de Cruces 2002 Albariño (Rías Baixas) $17. Fairly lively and forward, with apple aromas and a touch of fresh cabbage. Apricot, nectarine, and citrus dominate the zesty palate, which precedes a solid, razor-crisp finish. Nice and fresh. **87** —*M.S. (12/31/2004)*

SEÑORÍO DE CUZCURRITA

Señorío de Cuzcurrita 2001 Tempranillo (Rioja) $39. Bright in color and aromas, with pure cherry, leather, and yeast on the nose. Medium-bodied, not thick, but pretty full in terms of flavors, tannins and feel. Being young, it's rambunctious, hot, and spicy, but all bets are that it will settle down well over the next year or two. **90** —*M.S. (9/1/2004)*

Señorío de Cuzcurrita 2000 Tempranillo (Rioja) $35. Begins tight and smoky, with a chunky, earthy nose. The palate offers tart berry fruit with more than enough spicy oak. A finish that's at first peppery and later of vanilla and toast re-emphasizes the barrel influence. Nonetheless the fruit is healthy and thorough, as is the overall balance. **87** —*M.S. (5/1/2004)*

SEÑORÍO DE P. PECIÑA

Señorío de P. Peciña 2003 Tempranillo (Rioja) $15. Rusty to the eye, with grassy, burnt aromas. Dilute berry flavors and a touch of weediness don't really help things along. Finishes fairly tart and green. **81** —*M.S. (2/1/2006)*

SEÑORÍO DE SAN VINCENTE

Señorío de San Vincente 1997 San Vincente Tempranillo (Rioja) $36. **89** —*M.M. (8/1/2000)*

SEÑORÍO DE SARRIA

Señorío de Sarria 1996 Cabernet Sauvignon (Navarra) $12. Easy-drinking and smooth, this standard-issue Cab offers black plum and earth flavors from palate through to finish. Earth, oak, and nutty aromas start things off. A good (and economical) introduction to northern Spain's Cabernets. **86** —*D.T. (4/1/2003)*

Señorío de Sarria 2001 Chardonnay (Navarra) $12. Round and resinous in the mouth, there's nothing not to like about this innocuous, easy-drinking Chardonnay. With soft yellow fruit and a creamy-custardy overlay, this is the appropriate "white wine" selection for large parties. **86** —*D.T. (4/1/2003)*

Señorío de Sarria 2001 Vinedo No 7 Graciano (Navarra) $15. Chalky, oaky tannins give this wine some body, but I don't know where the fruit is hiding. A hint of tangy plum skin pops up on the back end; other than that, there's not much here. **81** —*D.T. (4/1/2003)*

Señorío de Sarria 2001 Vinedo No 4 Merlot (Navarra) $15. Black plum fruit is flattened by smooth woodsy tannins on the palate; oak and white pepper notes bookend the plum fruit core. Medium-bodied and simple. **83** —*D.T. (4/1/2003)*

Señorío de Sarria 1998 Reserva Merlot-Cabernet Sauvignon (Navarra) $18. Roasted and hard from the initial take, with earthy, leathery aromas that don't illicit a smile. Tart, dilute and fading, with apple and cherry skin on the palate. Quite sour and thin at this point of its evolution and surely not getting better. **81** —*M.S. (9/1/2006)*

Señorío de Sarria 1997 Reserva Red Blend (Navarra) $18. A black beauty, medium-weight, balanced, and chewy. This wine's all about ripe blackberry and black plum flavors, without much in the way of wood to distract you from the fruit. Deep ink, spice, and plum aromas play on the nose. **88 Best Buy** —*D.T. (4/1/2003)*

Señorío de Sarria 2001 Vinedo No 5 Rosé Blend (Navarra) $15. This rosé is a gorgeous, dark-rose hue, with strawberry, raspberry and vanilla aromas and flavors. Finishes with numbing, gravelly tannins. It's an on-the-porch-in-summertime, straightforward quaff, with earthy notes that keep the fruit on the right side of sweet. **85** —*D. T. (4/1/2003)*

Señorío de Sarria 2001 Reserva Especial Tempranillo Blend (Navarra) $65. Here's a classic Navarran blend, complete with herbal, leafy, some might say vegetal aromas and flavors. But in between the tomato and herbs are sweet plum and cherry notes, good depth and texture, and solid, serious tannins. If green notes are not a total turn-off, then add a couple of points. If that stuff bothers you, this will not be your bag. **87** —*M.S. (4/1/2006)*

SEÑORIO DEL AGUILA

Señorio del Aguila 1994 Reserva Tempranillo Blend (Cariñena) $12. The inviting nose of this mature red blends berry, vanillin oak, sweet cream, wood, and tobacco. But the wine never fully delivers on the front-end promise, as oak sits heavily on the berry-plum fruit, giving it a smooth but rather leaden feel. More woody tannins show on the modest finish. Probably would have shown more positively three years ago. **84** —*M.M. (9/1/2002)*

SEÑORIO DEL VAL

Señorio del Val 2000 Tempranillo (Valdepeñas) $7. 85 —*M.S. (11/1/2002)*

SERRA DA ESTRELA

Serra da Estrela 2004 Albariño (Rías Baixas) $15. Mildly sweet but not very exact or dilineated on the nose. Flavors of lime, papaya, and apple run toward green, but with good snap and zest the wine makes the grade. Finishes dry and snappy, with medium depth. **86** —*M.S. (9/1/2006)*

Serra da Estrela 2003 Albariño (Rías Baixas) $15. Fairly thick and creamy for the style, probably due to the hot vintage. The bouquet is sweet, with buttered corn and wildflower aromas. More citrusy on the palate, with flavors of orange, tangerine, and nectarine. Well made and textured; just a little more ripe than usual. **88** —*M.S. (12/31/2004)*

Serra da Estrela 2002 Albariño (Rías Baixas) $17. Starts off with heavy melon and citrus aromas, which are followed by tangy apple and pineapple flavors. Very zesty, with a certain sharpness that dumbs down any complexity that might be hiding. **85** —*M.S. (9/1/2004)*

SESTERO

Sestero 2003 Tempranillo-Cabernet Sauvignon (Navarra) $7. Smells like powdered cherry drink mix, and tastes like candied cherries, tomato and spice. Very familiar in its style; there's sweet fruit, jumpy acidity and lots of drying oak. Not polished. **83** —*M.S. (10/1/2005)*

SIDESHOW

Sideshow 2003 The Barker Garnacha (Calatayud) $9. The label says the Barker is big, loud, and Spanish, and it's right. This wine is a racy, ripe, lively Garnacha with weight, flavor and balance. Tastes good, with cherry, plum, coffee, and chocolate all stepping up and taking a bow. Ripe and ready at 14.5%, but on the money. **87 Best Buy** —*M.S. (9/1/2006)*

Sideshow 2004 La Rosa Rosé Blend (Campo de Borja) $9. Despite the silly packaging and strange orange tint, this is a solid if unusual rosado that registers sweet but likable. It's chunky, with berry flavors and a shot of leather and animal. By no means is it elevated or for the long haul. Drink now or hold your peace. **84** —*M.S. (11/1/2006)*

SIERRA CANTABRIA

Sierra Cantabria 2003 Tempranillo (Rioja) $10. Quite jammy with a lot of milk chocolate character courtesy of oak aging. The nose offers some depth and spice in addition to raspberry marmalade, while the palate is chunky and broad. Shows certain characteristics of a more elevated wine, but weighs in as a bit candied. **84** —*M.S. (11/15/2005)*

Sierra Cantabria 2002 Tempranillo (Rioja) $9. Ask for a glass of simple, modern Rioja and hopefully you'll get something like this. Red fruit and rubber on the nose, flavors of cherry, plum, and cotton candy, and finally some chocolate, coffee, and vanilla on the finish. Healthy, with big tannins and full acids. **87 Best Buy** —*M.S. (9/1/2004)*

Sierra Cantabria 2001 Tempranillo (Rioja) $9. The bouquet offers raspberry and strawberry fruit, which is followed by a meaty mouthful of plum, coffee, and bitter chocolate. The finish is defined by mocha, and the feel is derived from firm tannins. This wine feels warm, arguably borderline hot. But that's probably more a result of youth than anything else. **88 Best Buy** —*M.S. (3/1/2004)*

Sierra Cantabria 2001 Amancio Tempranillo (Rioja) $138. The color tells you everything you need to know; saturation overload is what this is about, with aromas of licorice, leather, pepper, and dark, masculine fruit. It comes from Sierra Cantabria, a winery known for modern-style reds. And this one fits the bill with its firm tannins, vanilla shadings, and insurmountable wall of spice on the finish. **93** —*M.S. (8/1/2005)*

Sierra Cantabria 2000 Colección Privada, Unfiltered Tempranillo (Rioja) $38. Ruby-red and colorful, with aromas of polished, fine-grained oak. Bright and fruity, but limited when it comes to complexity. It's loaded with chocolate, licorice, and espresso, while the palate feel is one of juiciness along with tight tannins. It's aggressive and muscular, not subtle. **88** —*M.S. (3/1/2004)*

Sierra Cantabria 1998 Crianza Tempranillo (Rioja) $13. Smooth and fresh, with bright berry on the nose and also some well-applied oak. In the mouth, raspberry and cherry flavors are spiced up with a note of black pepper. Lean, clean, and moderately tangy; a basic but good Rioja in the truest sense. **86** —*M.S. (3/1/2004)*

Sierra Cantabria 1999 Cuvée Especial, Unfiltered Tempranillo (Rioja) $19. Tobacco and mild green aromas take some of the ripeness off the nose, but all in all it's an electric wine with sweet plum, cherry, and boysenberry flavors. Typical oak-based notes of coffee, chocolate, and malt make an appearance on the finish. **90 Editors' Choice** —*M.S. (3/1/2004)*

Sierra Cantabria 2002 El Bosque Tempranillo (Rioja) $138. Hard and tannic to start with, so it really needs time. Aromas of beef bullion, jerky, and soy convey a certain smokiness, which is more geared to the nose than the palate. As for taste, it's laced with black cherry, cinnamon, vanilla, and chocolate. Very tight and firm, so hold for another three years. **91** —*M.S. (6/1/2005)*

Sierra Cantabria 2001 Finca El Bosque Tempranillo (Rioja) $140. Arguably the pinnacle of the Sierra Cantabria portfolio is this spicy, tasty wine that's 100% Tempranillo, and aged 16 months in French and Central European oak. The nose kicks off coffee, fudge, and bacon aromas, which are followed by flavors of black plum, berry jam, and more chocolate. A big boy still playing on the field adjacent to the super wines of the region. **92** —*M.S. (9/1/2004)*

Sierra Cantabria 1996 Reserva Tempranillo (Rioja) $19. The bouquet of this aging Rioja features a good mix of berry fruit, tree bark, and earth. Across the palate flows a stream of strawberry, cherry, and coffee. Firm tannins create a masculine mouthfeel, while the finish is dry with a tad of buttery oak. Gets better with airing and patient swirling. **88** —*M.S. (3/1/2004)*

Sierra Cantabria 2003 Organza White Blend (Rioja) $23. A blend of Viura and Malvasia that's been heavily fortified with oak. In between the folds of wood you'll find butter, cream, and resin, but not a ton of expression. Balanced and creamy, but devoid of the pop and excitement one might hope for. **87** —*M.S. (8/1/2005)*

Sierra Cantabria 2001 Organza White Blend (Rioja) $17. A bit awkward, with mild corn and wheat aromas in addition to melon and banana. The overall feel is flat, yet there's just enough acid to keep it lively. Finishes toasty, with a leesy, vanilla character. **85** —*M.S. (3/1/2004)*

SIGLO

Siglo 1998 Crianza Red Blend (Rioja) $9. This wine is thin and a bit metallic, with tart cherry flavors. The aromas are of peat moss and earth, with a touch of salinity **82** —*C.S. (11/1/2002)*

SIGLO SACO

Siglo Saco 2001 Crianza Tempranillo (Rioja) $NA. This basic red from Bodegas y Bebidas is fresh and offers ample pop across the palate. With some wood and acidity, it's a well-made everyday red with tasty fruit and mildly sharp edges. **84** —*M.S. (9/1/2004)*

SOLABAL

Solabal 1999 Crianza Tempranillo (Rioja) $13. Light and perfumed, with aromatics of lavender and flower petals. Standard-fare but healthy red berry and pepper dominate the palate, followed by a simple finish with some spice and bitterness. Lean and defined, and every bit the opposite of complicated. **86** —*M.S. (3/1/2004)*

Solabal 1997 Reserva Tempranillo (Rioja) $20. 89 —*M.M. (8/1/2000)*

SOLANES

Solanes 2000 Red Blend (Priorat) $24. With intense mineral, orange peel, and graham cracker aromas that give way to raisin, this is a beauty. There's a ton of plum fruit racing across a spicy, acid-and-tannin-packed palate. Not for the weak; this is power ready to be unleashed. **92 Editors' Choice** —*M.S. (3/1/2004)*

SOLAR DE LA VEGA

Solar de la Vega 2004 Verdejo (Rueda) $8. Aggressive on the nose, with white grapefruit and scallion aromas. There's some lemon-lime and lychee to the flavor profile, but it finishes mildly bitter, with a heavy whack of citrus peel. **83** —*M.S. (10/1/2005)*

Solar de la Vega 2004 Verdejo (Rueda) $10. Light melon and vanilla aromas are simple yet muddled, while the green melon and lemon flavors are not overly generous but acceptable. A narrow wine with a lean figure and protruding acidity. **82** —*M.S. (12/15/2006)*

SOLAR DE RANDEZ

Solar de Randez 2001 Crianza Tempranillo (Rioja) $18. Quite brambly, with a persistent burnt character that sticks with it from start to finish. Along the way there's cooked cherry and raspberry flavors supported by strong oak notes. Fails to improve in the glass; in fact it's just the opposite, as it falls apart. **83** —*M.S. (11/1/2006)*

SOLEIRA

Soleira 2004 Albariño (Rías Baixas) $20. Mealy on the nose, with corn and pear syrup making for a less than fresh bouquet. Bland apple and orange flavors are okay but not that stimulating, while the overall take is that it tastes too much like citrus juice and not enough like balanced wine. **81** —*M.S. (9/1/2006)*

SOLO

Solo 2003 Tempranillo Blend (Utiel-Requena) $20. A black-colored, deeply extracted wine with charcoal, mint, and burnt berry aromas. The palate is certainly ripe, as plum, and berry flavors hit hard. But it's also limited in scope and complexity. A big wine with average personality. The blend is Tempranillo-Bobal-Syrah. **85** —*M.S. (9/1/2006)*

TANDEM

Tandem 2004 Ars Nova Red Blend (Navarra) $25. Sweet black fruit starts up the engine, and beyond that it mostly tastes like raspberry and plum. Quite big and fruity, with a peppery streak to the finish. Registers full but a bit tough, with some tannic bite. **86** —*M.S. (12/15/2006)*

TARSUS

Tarsus 1999 Red Blend (Ribera del Duero) $25. Encouraging aromas of earth, leather, plum, and berry lead to a rather sheer, zesty palate of blackberry, cherry, and acid. It's tight in the mouth, with cheeky tannins and friction. Quite extracted and oaky; requires food or will seem astringent. **85** —*M.S. (11/1/2006)*

TELMO RODRÍGUEZ

Telmo Rodríguez 1999 Alma Garnacha (Navarra) $10. 86 —*M.M. (8/1/2000)*

Telmo Rodríguez 2002 Molino Real Mountain Wine Moscatel (Málaga) $50. More concentrated than the MR, but not necessarily better. Candle and body oil on the nose, with notes of pineapple and spice. Quite big and ripe, with intense flavors of honey, candied yams, and dripping mango. Long on the finish and persistent in its emphasis on vanilla. **90** —*M.S. (8/1/2005)*

Telmo Rodríguez 2001 Molino Real Mountain Wine Moscatel (Málaga) $48. There's not a region or grape type that Telmo Rodríguez won't tackle, and here he's on to Moscatel in the deep south. This wine exhibits lilac aromas with hints of smoked ham and hard cheese. It's not a perfect bouquet, but it is intriguing. In addition, look for a bulky but rewarding

palate featuring chewy sweet fruit and moderate acidity. **88** —*M.S. (6/1/2005)*

Telmo Rodríguez 2003 MR Mountain Wine Moscatel (Málaga) $19. Even if this Moscatel begins with waxy aromas and whiffs of hard cheese, it is one excellent elixir. The palate will please with its honey, sweet melon and guava flavors, while the additional notes of white pepper and green melon add foundation. Excellent for the price, and it won't require a Master's degree in wine to enjoy. **90** —*M.S. (8/1/2005)*

Telmo Rodríguez 2001 Matallana Red Blend (Ribera del Duero) $93. Smooth, smoky, and leathery is how this winner gets going, and backing that up is a palate of laser-beam intensity. This offers nothing less than an explosion of plum and cherry flavors, but the style is clean and fresh, not heavy or overoaked. Already it shows nice evolution, as it comes across drinkable. Ethereal in how the finish just slips away. Only 375 cases produced. **93 Editors' Choice** —*M.S. (6/1/2005)*

Telmo Rodríguez 1998 Altos Lanzaga Tempranillo (Rioja) $20. 91 —*M.M. (8/1/2000)*

Telmo Rodríguez 1999 Dehesa Gago Tempranillo (Toro) $12. 87 —*M.M. (8/1/2000)*

Telmo Rodríguez 2000 Lanzaga Tempranillo (Rioja) $20. Simply lovely in the nose, with lavender, violets, berries and cedary wood. This is quite the heavyweight, with a candied, oaky palate that offers plenty of vanilla. The mouthfeel is a touch creamy, but once you dig in, the wine shows its nuances and stuffing. Smoothness is definitely what you get here, plus major-league richness and extract. **90** —*M.S. (3/1/2004)*

Telmo Rodríguez 1998 Valderiz Tempranillo Blend (Ribera del Duero) $25. 92 —*M.M. (8/1/2000)*

Telmo Rodríguez 2002 G Dehesa Gago Tinta de Toro (Toro) $13. The initial aromas are of barnyard and medicine. But with time raspberry and blackberry emerge, and across the palate a wide blanket of tannins spreads out. Espresso, earth, and char make for a masculine, tantalizing finish. **86** —*M.S. (3/1/2004)*

Telmo Rodríguez 2002 Basa White Blend (Rueda) $9. One of the tastiest, best-made value whites in the world remains Basa, a blend of Verdejo, Viura, and Sauvignon Blanc. Since bursting onto the wine scene in the late '90s, Basa, which means "base" or "foundation" in Spanish, has never failed to excel. In the 2002 version, winemaker Telmo Rodríguez, who began his career at his father's Remelluri estate in Rioja, has managed to capture the purest grapefruit, passion fruit, and citrus flavors, all the while creating a wine with body, bracing acids and simple joy. A surefire apéritif, and also a fine bet for salads or fish. **88 Best Buy** —*M.S. (11/15/2003)*

Telmo Rodríguez 1999 Basa White Blend (Rueda) $8. 88 Best Buy —*M.M. (8/1/2000)*

TEOFILO REYES

Teofilo Reyes 1999 Crianza Red Blend (Ribera del Duero) $26. Despite this wine's heavy overlay of oak (a blend of American and French), the vintage's bright fruit shines through with stunning clarity and purity. Cinnamon and toast accent the anise-tinged cherries—some black, some red. Finishes with black tea and vanilla notes. Don't miss this wine if you are oak tolerant. **92 Editors' Choice** —*J.C. (11/1/2001)*

Teofilo Reyes 1998 Tempranillo (Ribera del Duero) $36. 89 —*M.M. (8/1/2000)*

Teofilo Reyes 1996 Reserva Tempranillo (Ribera del Duero) $150. 94 —*M.M. (8/1/2000)*

TERRAS GAUDA

Terras Gauda 2005 Abadía de San Campio Albariño (Rías Baixas) $16. Lucid in appearance, with mineral aromas adding complexity to the otherwise clean, floral nose. Very dry in style, with apple and pineapple flavors. So crisp and precise that "honest" is the best way to sum it up. **89** —*M.S. (9/1/2006)*

Terras Gauda 2004 Abadía de San Campio Albariño (Rías Baixas) $18. Peach and vanilla aromas dominate, with a touch of orange peel thrown in. The palate is surprisingly acidic, with sharp flavors of lemon, grapefruit, and green apple. Almost shocking at first; it goes out easier than it comes in. **84** —*M.S. (2/1/2006)*

Terras Gauda 2004 O Rosal Albariño (Rías Baixas) $20. Gold in color, with a chunky, oversized nose weighted down by apple and orange aromas. A lot of bulky citrus flavors carry the palate, but there isn't much balance or zest. Tastes o.k. but feels a bit mealy. **83** —*M.S. (12/31/2005)*

Terras Gauda 2005 O Rosal White Blend (Rías Baixas) $19. Starts out flowery and tropical, which is likely a reflection of the 20% Loureira in the wine. The flavor profile is dominated by peach and apple, while the finish runs long due to an infusion of Caino Blanca. A nice wine for those who like tropical fruit flavors. **88** —*M.S. (9/1/2006)*

TIBERIO

Tiberio 2003 Tinto Tinto del Pais (Ribera del Duero) $10. Fruit mixes with earth and leather to create a decent bouquet. Medicinal fruit and chocolate make for a basic palate. Has good feel and balance, but finishes sweet and a touch weedy. **82** —*M.S. (11/15/2005)*

TINAR

Tinar 2000 Crianza Tempranillo (Ribera del Duero) $32. Solid but unspectacular. The nose deals earth, leather, and blackberry in front of an austere palate defined by apple skin and cherry. Finishes with some buttery oak, soy and chocolate. Entirely drinkable but where's the bang for the buck? **85** —*M.S. (8/1/2005)*

TIONIO

Tionio 2000 Crianza Red Blend (Ribera del Duero) $20. This label is owned by Parxet, a cava producer, and it delivers a solid, youthful taste of Ribera. There's pepper and earth, and a little oak on the nose. Flavorwise, it's loaded with snappy black cherry and plum. At first take it's simple and forward, but always tasty and ripe. And with airing a bit of complexity comes on. **86** —*M.S. (8/1/2003)*

Tionio 1998 Crianza Tempranillo (Ribera del Duero) $17. Creamy vanilla and dill aromas bump up against bright cherries on the nose. In the mouth, the creaminess is noticeable, with tart cherries and weedy tobacco notes chiming in. The firm tannins on the finish need a year or two to settle down. **86** —*J.C. (11/1/2001)*

TORNASOL

Tornasol 2002 Tempranillo (Rioja) $25. This wine proves that "organic" doesn't automatically translate into great. The nose is leathery and sweet, with red licorice and peanut aromas. Sweet and sugary on the palate, with flavors of beets and fruit roll-up. Hard and reduced on the finish. **81** —*M.S. (8/1/2005)*

TORRE ORIA

Torre Oria NV Brut Nature Sparkling Blend (Cava) $20. The Nature tag indicates no dosage, and this Cava is appropriately very crisp and dry. The nose is closed, but tart green apple flavors and chalk accents enliven the palate. Light in weight, it has a soft mousse, and slightly floral close. **85** —*M.M. (12/31/2001)*

Torre Oria NV Brut Sparkling Blend (Cava) $11. Toast, butterscotch, and oxidized apple aromas precede a heavy, nearly overripe palate loaded down with sticky apple, nectarine, and banana. Where it does well is in texture, which is correct and pleasant. Finishes long and heavy. A different breed. **85** —*M.S. (6/1/2005)*

Torre Oria NV Brut Reserve Tannat (Cava) $15. From central Spain, this cava is funky for sure. Mustard seed, field greens, and a harsh astringency define the bouquet, while the palate offers a unique but odd blend of mealy apple and clove-spiked ham. Probably unrecognizable to most. **81** —*M.S. (6/1/2005)*

Torre Oria 1996 Reserva Tempranillo (Utiel-Requena) $15. Smells old and dirty, with peanut and barnyard grass on the nose. Dry and fading is the palate, and it's also rather murky. Acidity and some flesh in the middle is all that's keeping this one afloat. **80** —*M.S. (9/1/2004)*

Torre Oria 1998 Reserve Tempranillo (Utiel-Requena) $15. Mild cherry and violet aromas are the best part. The palate is tannic and bland, with flavors akin to green tobacco and cranberry. Loses clarity with airing; it turns to burnt and chemical tasting. **81** —*M.S. (10/1/2005)*

Torre Oria 2003 Superior Tempranillo (Utiel-Requena) $9. Mulchy and earthy from start to finish, with distant flavors that barely register. Not overly bad but a true cipher of a wine. **80** —*M.S. (9/1/2006)*

TORRES

Torres 2000 Reserva Real Bordeaux Blend (Penedès) $150. This Bordeaux-style blend features enticing aromas of molasses, licorice, leather, and plum, and while the palate satisfies, it doesn't quite live up to the hype built by the bouquet. The feel is soft, as if the edges had slipped away. Still, it offers good mouthfeel and decent depth. **88** —*M.S. (3/1/2005)*

Torres 1998 Gran Coronas Cabernet Sauvignon (Penedès) $19. The rustic, leathery bouquet takes a while to open, and when it does it reveals an unfortunate whiff of green pepper. Despite that, the mouthfeel is wonderful, and there's some nice cassis in there, too. But the flavors that come across loudest and clearest are green tobacco and bell pepper. **86** —*M.S. (11/1/2002)*

Torres 1999 Gran Coronas Reserva Cabernet Sauvignon (Penedès) $20. The nose is nice; there's cherry, blackberry, and mint. Loads of ripe berry fruit draw raves, and the finish is warm, with notes of cream-filled coffee. Tight and firm in terms of feel. **88** —*M.S. (3/1/2004)*

Torres 1997 Gran Coronas Reserva Cabernet Sauvignon (Penedès) $19. This Cabernet from one of Spain's best-known producers is mature and structured. An attractive, complex nose offers berry, tobacco, and leather aromas, while the wine is darkly fruited and a touch brown at the edge. Finishes long and dry, with some drying tannins. Drink now through 2006. Despite the tannins, sooner is preferable, as the fruit seems fully mature. **87** —*M.M. (9/1/2002)*

Torres 2001 Mas La Plana Cabernet Sauvignon (Penedès) $50. This icon Spanish Cabernet hails from a 72-acre plot in Penedès. It's 100% Cabernet, aged in new French oak for 18 months. It has a roasted charcoal and lemon-peel nose, followed by herbs, cherry, and cassis flavors. It has mouthfeel and structure, with fine coffee and chocolate finishing notes. Best around 2009–2112. **91 Cellar Selection** *(11/15/2005)*

Torres 2000 Mas La Plana Cabernet Sauvignon (Penedès) $49. The nose seems tight, almost reduced. In the mouth, plum and grapy fruit announce that this is pure Cabernet. It's dark and coffee-like on the finish. What the future holds for it is up for debate. Now it's sort of closed, yet still rather tasty. **88** —*M.S. (3/1/2004)*

Torres 1998 Mas La Plana Cabernet Sauvignon (Penedès) $49. The nose is generally sweet and likable, yet there's some medicinal character in there too. Very ripe and dynamic, with mint and chocolate flavors along with fast-moving currant and cherry. A bit racy and unbridled for Cabernet. **87** —*M.S. (3/1/2004)*

Torres 1997 Mas La Plana Cabernet Sauvignon (Penedès) $25. Ripe blackberry and cherry fruit and classy oak team up to deliver the goods in this palate-pleasing Cabernet Sauvignon. There's plenty of tobacco and earth, and in style and weight it's somewhere between Bordeaux and California, with a heavier nod to the former. Already delicious, this will hold well through the decade, maybe longer. It is an apt demonstration of why weight and density are less important than flavor, texture and balance. Take that, extraction junkies. Drink now through 2008 and beyond. **92 Cellar Selection** —*M.M. (4/1/2002)*

Torres 1995 Gran Coronas Cabernet Sauvignon-Tempranillo (Penedès) $18. **87** —*J.C. (8/1/2000)*

Torres 2003 Gran Viña Sol Chardonnay (Penedès) $15. Round and mostly on the money, with medium-depth fruit. The bouquet pitches melon and some richness, while the full palate deals melon, papaya, and banana. Not designed for the long haul, so drink soon for best results. **86** —*M.S. (12/31/2004)*

Torres 2002 Gran Viña Sol Chardonnay (Penedès) $14. Oak is a key feature. The nose carries some sawdust and vanilla, while the plate is creamy, with banana and pear flavors. Vanilla is also present on the oaky, airy finish. Thick and woody, but healthy and honest. **86** —*M.S. (3/1/2004)*

Torres 2001 Gran Viña Sol Chardonnay (Penedès) $14. Mallowy, toasty aromas start things off and show up again on the back end, but the palate offers only generic yellow fruit. Medium-bodied and quite resinous in the mouth, it's suitable for casual gatherings. **83** —*D.T. (4/1/2003)*

Torres 2002 Milmanda Chardonnay (Conca de Barberà) $47. Soft and buttery on the nose, with a touch of pear. Shy pear and apple flavors drive toward a modest finish that's dry and almondy. Smooth on the palate, but not dynamic. This is intended to be a prestige Chardonnay, yet while it has mouthfeel there's not a whole lot of zest or character. **86** —*M.S. (12/31/2004)*

Torres 2001 Milmanda Chardonnay (Conca de Barberà) $50. This barrel-fermented, pricey Chardonnay is heavy and doesn't have much life in it. The nose is flat and mildly oaky, while the palate is immensely woody, with low-level acidity and buttery, baked-apple flavors. To say it doesn't hit hard is an understatement. But to say it's outright bad would be overly harsh. **84** —*M.S. (3/1/2004)*

Torres 2000 Milmanda Chardonnay (Conca de Barberà) $50. Milmanda is 100% Chardonnay from Catalonia, but this vintage is a touch flatter than previous years. The nose is nice, offering spring flowers, vanilla, and nutmeg. The flavors lean toward tropical fruit, especially banana. The warm finish is where you first catch some spicy oak. Too bad it isn't more lively. **86** —*M.S. (11/1/2002)*

Torres 1999 Milmanda Chardonnay (Conca de Barberà) $48. Though handsomely balanced, this medium-weight Chardonnay shows only modest complexity, with apple, tropical fruit, and mild toasty notes on the nose and palate. A slight caramel note gives a vaguely sweet cast to the basically dry fruit flavors. Has appeal and some length, but it's not the statement one would expect at the price. **85** —*M.M. (9/1/2002)*

Torres 2005 Malena Garnacha (Catalunya) $10. Purple in color, with a sweet, fragrant bouquet featuring mostly plum and strawberry but also a touch of rusticity. Bold and full of cherry-cola flavors, while the feel is downright plush and proper. A very nice (and new to the market) wine from Torres; and there's no knocking its value qualifications. **89 Best Buy** —*M.S. (12/15/2006)*

Torres 2003 Atrium Merlot (Penedès) $16. Aggressive and candied, with boiled beet, red plum, and carob flavors. Bulky and grapey. **82** —*M.S. (12/31/2004)*

Torres 2001 Atrium Merlot (Penedès) $15. "Like lo-fi Syrah," was my first impression of this Merlot's juicy blackberry core. It's drinkable now, medium-bodied, petite, easy and bouncy. Nutty, oaky notes punctuate the finish. **86** —*D.T. (4/1/2003)*

Torres 1999 Atrium Merlot (Penedès) $14. The bouquet smells young, what with all the creamy oak and rubber that pumps forth. The mouth is drier than expected; it offers far more herbal black fruit than round red fruit. The finish is firm and tannic, even a touch hot. And there's some herb and tomato character as well. **86** —*M.S. (11/1/2002)*

Torres 2004 Viña Sol Parallada (Penedès) $8. Slightly mineral on the nose, with likable aromas of apple and white stone fruits. Downright tangy on the palate, bordering on sour, with lime, green apple, and chalk-like flavors. Finishes shy but sharp, without much in the midsection. **84 Best Buy** —*M.S. (10/1/2005)*

Torres 2003 Viña Sol Parallada (Catalonia) $9. Light and floral, with an attractive overall nose that conveys freshness. Light citrus and melon notes on the palate are pushed by good acidity, while the lemony finish is tight and right. **85 Best Buy** —*M.S. (12/31/2004)*

Torres 2000 Viña Sol Parallada (Penedès) $11. Very pale in color, this widely available Spanish white opens with a melon-lime and slightly floral bouquet. Citrus accents appear on the light- to medium-weight palate, but the floral note turns faintly candied, too. Finishes a bit short, with a little bite. Drink now. **83** —*M.M. (9/1/2002)*

Torres 2002 Mas Borràs Pinot Noir (Penedès) $30. Hazy in color, with funky aromas of cranberry, leather, and pickle. The fruit is bland, and the feel is sticky and forced. Spain has never offered much in the way of Pinot Noir, and here you see why. **82** —*M.S. (6/1/2005)*

Torres 2001 Mas Borràs Pinot Noir (Penedès) $32. A burly bomber, with a heavily barrel-influenced nose. The palate is broad and chunky, and while undeniably ripe, it's a stretch finding true Pinot Noir characteris-

tics, say something a Burgundian would recognize. Nonetheless, it's got a rich feel and it's definitely not unripe. **85** —*M.S. (3/1/2004)*

Torres 1994 Mas Borràs Pinot Noir (Penedès) $30. 90 —*R.V. (11/1/1999)*

Torres 2003 Celeste Red Blend (Ribera del Duero) $22. Torres' first-ever Spanish wine from outside Catalonia was made from purchased fruit at a newly acquired winery outside of Valladolid. The wine shows good color and nice plum and cherry character. It's a bit tart and fresh for a 2003 (hot year), yet it carries some more rugged beef and smoke notes. **86** *(11/15/2005)*

Torres 2001 Gran Sangre de Toro Red Blend (Catalunya) $15. A blend of Garnacha, Cariñena, and Syrah that starts with leather, plum, and cherry aromas. Runs a bit racy and snappy on the palate and then settles into a fairly nice groove. Still, it's kind of a spunky wine that will do better with food than as a solo sipper. **86** —*M.S. (11/15/2005)*

Torres 2000 Gran Sangre de Toro Red Blend (Catalunya) $14. This three-grape blend is led by Garnacha, and it's fun and easy, albeit kind of light. It's also a touch "country" in style, meaning it has some barnyard and leather. The flavors lean toward raspberry and cherry, and the finish snaps and pops. Very forward and drinkable. **86** —*M.S. (3/1/2004)*

Torres 1998 Gran Sangre de Toro Red Blend (Catalunya) $13. This Torres is 60% Garnacha, 25% Cariñena, and 15% Syrah, and goes down easy. Thick black fruit—think cassis meets Port—plus earth, cedar, and chocolate aromas; bright blueberries and a tree-bark-cinnamon note carry through on the palate. Finishes long, with dusty blackberry flavors. **87 Best Buy** —*D.T. (4/1/2002)*

Torres 1996 Gran Sangre de Toro Reserva Red Blend (Penedès) $11. 89 —*M.S. (8/1/2000)*

Torres 1995 Gran Sangre de Toro Reserva Red Blend (Penedès) $11. 90 —*R.V. (11/1/1999)*

Torres 2000 Grans Muralles Red Blend (Conca de Barberà) $100. Still young and jumpy, but the ripeness and pedigree of this Penedès bruiser is beyond reproach. It's big, bold, and deep as a mountain lake, with black plum, bullion, and a pile of blackberry on the palate. Tons of extract and tannins make this inky, saturated heavyweight a wine to ponder. For fans of forward, beefy reds. **91** —*M.S. (4/1/2006)*

Torres 1999 Grans Muralles Red Blend (Conca de Barberà) $98. Modern in terms of its forward oak, extraction, and deep color. The nose is packed with charcoal, tobacco, and pepper, while the fresh, forward palate pushes cherry cola and baked fruit. Firm tannins, however, close it down, leaving a clipped finish and the perception of only moderate depth. Decant to get best results. **88** —*M.S. (3/1/2005)*

Torres 1998 Grans Muralles Red Blend (Conca de Barberà) $106. The wine sounds pretty impressive: It's comprised of local Catalan grape varities Monastrell, Garnacha Tinta, Garró, Samsó and Cariñena, which are all grown at Grans Muralles, a single vineyard that dates back to the Middle Ages. And very good it is, though it doesn't taste as singular as its heritage suggests. Black plum and cherry notes are couched in brambly, oak flavors. The wine has woodsy, rustic tannins in the mouth, and even more on the finish. **87** —*D.T. (4/1/2003)*

Torres 1997 Grans Muralles Red Blend (Rioja) $103. Torres' top-end offering is quite dark, with a plum, tobacco, earth, and leather nose. Smooth and balanced, it shows good acidity and even tannins, while handsome cocoa notes adorn the almost juicy cherry fruit. Tasty now, it will improve if aged one to three years, and drink well through 2010. **90** —*M.M. (9/1/2002)*

Torres 2003 Nerola Xarello-Garnacha Red Blend (Catalunya) $18. Half of the wine here was fermented in barrel, and that yields buttercup and vanilla aromas along with lighter peach and melon notes. The flavor profile, however, is more lemony crisp. With a Gaudí-inspired label, this is a wine aimed at younger wine consumers. **85** *(11/15/2005)*

Torres 2002 Nerola Red Blend (Catalonia) $20. As we noted in an earlier article, this wine represents Torres' attempt at the so-called "modern Mediterranean" style. It features 80% Syrah and 20% Monastrell, and it comes across as successfully New World. The color is violet, the nose sweet and young, with a hint of toffee and marshmallow. The plump palate and chocolaty finish should please those who crave size and ripeness from their red wine. **88** —*M.S. (12/31/2004)*

Torres 2001 Nerola Red Blend (Catalonia) $20. Starts somewhat cooked and stewy before finding a better, fresher, fruitier groove. Weighty and full, with bright colors and aggressive flavors. Plum, berry, and cherry notes dominate. Persistent airing unveils additional ripeness and soft tannins. **84** —*M.S. (6/1/2005)*

Torres 1998 Reserva Real Red Blend (Penedès) $150. Miguel Torres is aiming high with this heavyweight single-vineyard Cabernet that was bottled back in 2000. The bouquet is classy and deep, with sweet rubber, licorice, and berry notes. Cassis, blackberry, and chocolate compete on the palate, while the finish is much like flourless chocolate cake and a cup of espresso rolled into one. Clearly the class of the Torres Cabernets. **92** —*M.S. (3/1/2004)*

Torres 2003 50th Aniversario Sangre de Toro Red Blend (Catalonia) $10. Earthy and ripe, with jammy, borderline stewy fruit that carries a meaty edge. Fairly one-line in terms of complexity, but it stands on its feet and tastes pretty solid. With some rustic character, it'll do the job. **85 Best Buy** —*M.S. (6/1/2005)*

Torres 2002 Sangre de Toro Red Blend (Catalonia) $10. Open and a bit hot, with raspberry, cherry, and bold acidity. The body is full, bordering on chunky and big. There's little in the way of nuance in this bistro-style red, but it taste nice and will wash down munchies like chorizo or pizza with no problem. **84** —*M.S. (3/1/2004)*

Torres 2001 Sangre de Toro Red Blend (Catalonia) $10. If your local wine shop carries a single Spanish wine, this one's probably it—and it's no wonder why. This Garnacha-Cariñena blend is an easy quaffer, Beaujolais-weight, and probably best appreciated by wine newbies who like a little sweetness in their glass. It offers raspberry, plum, and strawberry flavors, kept in check by a dose of oak. Drink now. **84** —*D.T. (4/1/2003)*

Torres 2000 Sangre do Toro Red Blend (Catalonia) $11. Earth, mushroom, and raspberry aromas open the show for this popular blend of Garnacha and Cariñena. Red raspberry flavors are most prominent on the palate, while the chunky finish is big but not terribly classy. This seems too awkward to rate higher, but it does have its merits. **84** —*M.S. (11/1/2002)*

Torres 1999 Sangre de Toro Red Blend (Catalonia) $11. Barnyardy-earthy aromas dominate this wine's nose; the palate offers mostly blackberry and sweet cream flavors, plus a smooth mouthfeel. Finishes tart, with herb, lemon and cheese flavors. 65% Garnacha, 35% Cariñena. **83** —*D.T. (4/1/2002)*

Torres 1998 Waltroud Riesling (Penedès) $13. 88 —*L.W. (11/15/1999)*

Torres 2004 De Casta Rosé Blend (Catalunya) $8. Full and snappy, with a touch of natural smoke and plenty of berry defining the bouquet. Strawberry, apple skin, and citrus flavors make for a spunky, clean palate, and the overall zest is admirable. **86 Best Buy** —*M.S. (2/1/2006)*

Torres 2003 Fransola Sauvignon Blanc (Penedès) $26. Grassy on the nose, with a touch of green apple to help it along. Melon, canned peach, and banana flavors indicate that it was too hot in 2003 for Sauvignon Blanc. Lacks the piquant, zesty quality the wine is known for. **83** —*M.S. (3/1/2005)*

Torres 2002 Fransola Sauvignon Blanc (Penedès) $25. Having tasted this wine year after year, I can say that the '02 version is textbook, but a bit light. The nose features bell pepper and lime, while the palate is loaded with green apple, papaya, and snap pea. Finishes round and smooth, with good acidity. A good match for vinaigrettes and shellfish. **86** —*M.S. (3/1/2004)*

Torres 2001 Fransola Sauvignon Blanc (Penedès) $25. This 90% Sauvignon Blanc, 10% Parellada is resinous in the mouth, with zingy white pepper, stone fruit, and banana flavors on the palate and the finish; ts aromas veer more toward bright citrus. The possibilities of food pairings with this wine are endless—start with Thai noodles. **87** —*D.T. (4/1/2003)*

Torres 2000 Fransola Sauvignon Blanc (Penedès) $22. This is quite meaty, oaky, and powerful, with a buttery texture supporting soft citrus, melon, and green apple flavors. A smoky, toasty finish screams of the oak treatment it went through, and while it's soft and luscious throughout, it's a tad flat as well. **88** *(8/1/2002)*

Torres 1998 Fransola Sauvignon Blanc (Penedès) $22. 84 *(8/1/2000)*

Torres 2003 Coronas Tempranillo (Catalunya) $10. Chunky and brambly, with sweet black cherry, beet, and peppery flavors. Not very complex, but solid, with licorice and berry syrup on the palate. Seems riper than in the past, a sign that it's from 2003. **85 Best Buy** —*M.S. (10/1/2005)*

Torres 2002 Coronas Tempranillo (Catalonia) $10. Initially it is harsh and on the verge of caustic, although time settles it down. Nevertheless, this basic Tempranillo has medicinal flavors along with chunky black cherry and raspberry notes. Gets better with time but fails to make its mark. **83** —*M.S. (6/1/2005)*

Torres 2001 Coronas Tempranillo (Catalonia) $10. Clean and big, with attractive baking spice and cola aromas. Bright, deep and full of cherry and blackberry flavors, and also fairly sizable and layered. This is the type of friendly, competent wine that should please everyone, from novices up to wine snobs. **88 Best Buy** —*M.S. (3/1/2004)*

Torres 2000 Coronas-Tempranillo (Penedès) $10. The bouquet starts out brawny, with foresty aromas and a touch of iodine. Big black fruit flavors run across the buttery, creamy palate, while a fine trio of fresh fruit, oak flavors, and tannins meld on the finish. This is a solid wine, a nice example of monovarietal Tempranillo from Catalonia. **87 Best Buy** —*M.S. (11/1/2002)*

Torres 1999 Coronas Tempranillo (Catalonia) $11. Earthy, gamy aromas envelop sweet plum fruit on the nose; the same black fruit-earth profile holds up on the palate, topped off with a bit of espresso and dust. Velvety in the mouth, though it may lack a little depth, this is a great tapas-bar pour. Finishes with some char and oak, and not overbearing tannins. **85** —*D.T. (4/1/2002)*

Torres 1997 Coronas Tempranillo (Penedès) $9. 84 —*R.V. (11/1/1999)*

Torres 2002 Nerola White Blend (Catalonia) $15. A mix of Xarello and white Garnacha that smells nice as well as different, with aromas of cake frosting, litchi fruit, and applesauce. Ripe and sweet, with a round, medium-weight palate. A bit fat and lacking in structure, but that's the nature of Xarello. **85** —*M.S. (12/31/2004)*

Torres 2002 Viña Esmeralda White Blend (Penedès) $13. As usual, this Moscatel-Gewürztraminer blend is light, sweet and fun. Aromas of gardenia, lemon-lime and tarragon lead toward a friendly palate of pear, ripe papaya and sugar. It's a simple, quasi-dessert wine, but it hits the spot. **87** —*M.S. (3/1/2004)*

Torres 2001 Viña Esmeralda White Blend (Penedès) $13. Here's a sweeter-style wine done well. It's 85% Moscatel; the remainder is Gewürztraminer. The aromas are hugely floral, with warm honey nuances. Given the price, the fruit quality is exemplary, with clean flavors of citrus and lychee. The finish is surprisingly powerful and entirely fresh. **87 Best Buy** —*M.S. (11/1/2002)*

Torres 2002 Viña Sol White Blend (Penedès) $10. Pine needle, lilac, and some musk on the nose. Citrus is the driving force from then on. There's tangerine and some melon for flavor, and plenty or orange and passion fruit on the finish. A drink-now citrus ball that's full and flavorful. **86** —*M.S. (8/1/2003)*

Torres 2001 Vina Sol White Blend (Penedès) $10. Light and simple, with indistinct aromas that carry a touch of honey. The wine is made from the Parellada grape, one of the components of Spanish cava. It features melon, apple, and underripe banana flavors before a dry, smooth finish. It represents the epitome of a mellow and mild, but good white wine. **85** —*M.S. (11/1/2002)*

TORRES DE ANGUIX

Torres de Anguix 2004 A Tinto del Pais (Ribera del Duero) $10. Jumpy and young, with a touch of pickle on the nose. In the mouth, it's all about high-toned red fruit, particularly cherry and raspberry. Very bright and a bit acidic, but with that comes a certain freshness that keeps the wine alert. Should get better with some bottle age. **85 Best Buy** —*M.S. (4/1/2006)*

Torres de Anguix 2000 A Tinto del Pais (Ribera del Duero) $20. Reduced, sweet aromas lead into a chunky red-fruit palate that lacks structure but remains wet and juicy. Finishes mildly hot and spicy, but without much stuffing. **83** —*M.S. (6/1/2005)*

SPAIN

Torres de Anguix 2002 Crianza Tinto del Pais (Ribera del Duero) $14. Lean and woody, with mint, herbs, and sawdust on the nose. The palate is surprisingly saturated and healthy, with pepper and vanilla running side by side with dry cherry and raspberry. A bit scouring and tannic. **85** —*M.S. (6/1/2005)*

Torres de Anguix 2003 Tinto Tinto del Pais (Ribera del Duero) $10. Black in color and saturated with plum, fruit cake, and vanilla aromas. Big in the mouth but clumsy, with dense, thumping black cherry and blackberry flavors. In fact, everything about the wine is black, including the burnt, licorice-tinged finish. Ponderous in the long run. **84** —*M.S. (6/1/2005)*

TORROXAL

Torroxal 2004 Albariño (Rías Baixas) $25. Gold in color, with musky aromas that feature hints of butterscotch, ham, and spice. Runs more racy in the mouth, with big lemon, orange, and passion fruit flavors. Seems a touch unfocused and hefty, but for a bigger-styled wine it has its virtues. **85** —*M.S. (9/1/2006)*

TR3

TR3 2002 Tinta de Toro (Toro) $30. Hard but sweet swmelling, with both barnyard and perfume. Fairly high-toned and tart on the palate, where pie cherry and red plum are firmly in control. Acidic and unyielding; too raw and forceful to rate better. **83** —*M.S. (2/1/2006)*

TRASLANZAS

Traslanzas 2000 Tinto del Pais Tempranillo (Cigales) $35. Rich and inviting, but also sly, with complexity. Aromas of cherry, cola, coffee, and hard cheese set a proper stage for roasted cherry, meat, tobacco, and toasted vanilla flavors. This is one long, dry, traditional wine, one with fine balance and character. **90** —*M.S. (5/1/2004)*

TRAVITANA

Travitana 2003 Old Vines Monastrell (Alicante) $10. Jumpy raspberry and strawberry aromas greet you, followed by plump, buttery red-fruit flavors of cherry and plum. Turns a bit hard and gritty, with woody tannins. Fortunately there are also some chocolate and juicy, sweet flavors to keep it on an even keel. **85 Best Buy** —*M.S. (8/1/2005)*

TRES LUNAS

Tres Lunas 2003 Tempranillo (Toro) $17. Generally speaking, this wine is nicely balanced and a bit less over the top than most 2003s. The nose shows mint, fresh herbs, graphite, and berry aromas. The palate is juicy, not dull or heavy, with black cherry and dark plum flavors. Finishes almost crisp, with a shot of balancing acidity. **87** —*M.S. (12/15/2006)*

TRESANTOS

Tresantos 2000 Roble Red Blend (Tierra del Viños de Zamora) $13. Deep and dark, with lots of heavy toast on the tart black and blueberry flavors, this tastes a bit like a lightweight mountain Cabernet. It's fairly full, with brisk acidity, licorice, and herb accents. Appealingly rugged, this closes solid, dry, and earthy. **85** —*M.M. (4/1/2002)*

TXOMÍN ETXANÍZ

Txomín Etxaníz 1999 Txakoli (Getariako Txakolina) $17. **87** —*M.M. (8/1/2000)*

Txomín Etxaníz 2002 White Blend (Getariako Txakolina) $14. From the heart of the Basque region, San Sebastian, comes this oddball of a wine. In and of itself Txakoli is unusual, but this one is particularly weird. It's pickled and tough to like. The feel is spritzy and the flavors biting. **81** —*M.S. (3/1/2004)*

Txomín Etxaníz 2000 White Blend (Getariako Txakolina) $16. Bright and light, this Basque-country white, literally from seaside vineyards on Spain's north coast, is full of lime and wet stone aromas and flavors and has a faint yet unmistakable saline nuance. The slight spritz on the tongue adds to the lively feel. As might be expected from a wine cultivated on hills facing the Bay of Biscay, this begs for shellfish, octopus, or other seafood. Drink it cold and young. **85** —*M.M. (4/1/2002)*

URBINA

Urbina 2001 Selección Especial Tempranillo (Rioja) $35. A lot of dill and coconut on the nose, and that dill character remains on the palate and finish. Aside from that, the red-fruit character is zesty and true, while the spice element works well. **84** —*M.S. (8/1/2005)*

VAL DE LOS FRAILES

Val de Los Frailes 2003 Jóven Tempranillo (Cigales) $8. Sharp, with harsh, reduced aromas of tar, rhubarb, and molasses. A lot of heavy plum and berry flavors raise hopes, but in the end it's just not that thrilling. Authentic, however. **83** —*M.S. (8/1/2005)*

Val de Los Frailes 2001 Pago de las Costanas Tempranillo (Cigales) $35. Dark fruit, tobacco, and leathery spice make for a nice bouquet. Tight and forceful in the mouth, with ripe black fruit and firm tannins. Chocolate and espresso come on toward the finish of this thorough, flavorful wine. Satisfying but not a spectacle. **87** —*M.S. (11/1/2006)*

Val de Los Frailes 2001 Prestigio Tempranillo (Cigales) $25. Full and smoky, with a broad bouquet of bacon, earth, and black fruit. The palate is nicely balanced between aggressive acidity and lush blackberry and cherry fruit. Exceedingly long and fresh on the finish; shows its quality from the first sip and holds it all the way through. **90** —*M.S. (8/1/2005)*

Val de Los Frailes 2001 Vendimia Seleccionada Tempranillo (Cigales) $15. Piercing and reduced, with cherry and red currant flavors. Quite tannic and acidic, with a tough personality. But the overall take remains positive and the wine seems healthy and live-wire. For best results pour with chorizo or jamón Serrano. The salt will soften it up. **86** —*M.S. (8/1/2005)*

Val de Los Frailes 2002 Prestigio Tinta Fina (Cigales) $23. Funky, with earthy, heavy aromas. Seems a bit rubbery and peppery, with cola, plum, and olive flavors. Tannic, too. Not nearly as fruity, clean, ripe and pleasing as the 2001. **84** —*M.S. (11/1/2006)*

VAL SOTILLO

Val Sotillo 1998 Crianza Temparillo (Ribera del Duero) $28. Firmly structured, this wine needs another two years to round into form. Right now, it still shows a youthful stink that quickly blows off to reveal a blend of red and black cherries allied to sturdy iron and earth elements. Firm tannins on the finish accentuate the need for aging. **88 Cellar Selection** —*J.C. (11/1/2001)*

Val Sotillo 1997 Tempranillo (Ribera del Duero) $29. **88** —*M.M. (8/1/2000)*

Val Sotillo 1996 Reserva Tempranillo (Ribera del Duero) $55. **93** —*M.M. (8/1/2000)*

Val Sotillo 1995 Gran Reserva Red Blend (Ribera del Duero) $75. The dark purple color suggests a younger wine, but one sniff and you know it spent a lot of time in oak. Toast and cedar aromas predominate, but underneath them lies black-cherry fruit and a firm iron-mineral tang. Long, dry finish. Give it 3–5 years for the oak to integrate before drinking it over the next 10. **89** —*J.C. (11/1/2001)*

Val Sotillo 1994 Gran Reserva Red Blend (Ribera del Duero) $80. **96** —*M.M. (8/1/2000)*

VALCANTARA

Valcantara 2004 Old Vine Garnacha (Cariñena) $8. Slightly prickly and green, but overall it's a decent, mildly herbal Garnacha that will do the trick. Basic red-fruit flavors carry a note of tomato and leather, while the finish is generally tight and crisp. **84 Best Buy** —*M.S. (9/1/2006)*

VALCORTES

Valcortes 2001 Crianza Tempranillo (Rioja) $15. Plump and a bit stewy, but the flavors manage to take over in a fairly positive way. Upon sipping you take in blackberry and prune, but also some murkiness. Not much in the midpalate, but decent around the edges. **84** —*M.S. (6/1/2005)*

VALDAMOR

Valdamor 2005 Albariño (Rías Baixas) $20. Fairly mineral on the nose, with tropical fruit aromas rounding out the bouquet. Quite fresh and crisp, yet a bit hollow in the midpalate and on the finish. Overall this is a perfectly good Albariño, totally competent for quaffing or drinking with fish. **86** —*M.S. (9/1/2006)*

VALDEAURUM

Valdeaurum 2000 Crianza Tempranillo (Ribera del Guadiana) $15. Despite heavy oak, this wine is lean and jagged, with sharp cherry and plum flavors offset by some spice. Quite woody throughout, with a warm, solid finish. Hard tannins create a tight mouthfeel. Flavorful and real, but unforgiving. **85** —*M.S. (3/1/2005)*

VALDEGRACIA

Valdegracia 1998 Tinto Crianza Tempranillo (Ribera del Guadiana) $14. Even and light, but with copious tart cherry aromas and flavors, this tasty red comes from rugged Extremadura, in southwestern Spain, near Portugal. Saddle leather accents add interest, and the tangy finish closes with balanced tannins that'll cut through food well. Drink now–2005. **87** —*M.M. (9/1/2002)*

VALDELANA

Valdelana 2001 Red Blend (Rioja) $8. The bright purple color and aromas of bubble gum and grape skins shout out "carbonic maceration," a technique often used to pump up young wines. The flavors are of candied black plum, licorice, and sugar. The finish, though, is only thin and tangy. It's the equivalent of Spanish Beaujolais Nouveau. **83** —*M.S. (11/1/2002)*

Valdelana 1999 Crianza Red Blend (Rioja) $11. A straightforward, simple and light wine with dusty old cedar and beet aromas. Strawberry and rhubarb flavors take it to the finish short and simple. **84** *(11/1/2002)*

Valdelana 2003 Agnus Crianza Tempranillo (Rioja) $25. Sweet and spicy stuff, with plenty of oak-based coconut and butter on the nose. In the mouth, it's quite saturated and flush, with overt plum, blackberry, and wood resin notes. A big, modern wine that's a bit oafish but also rather easy to drink. **87** —*M.S. (12/15/2006)*

VALDELAPINTA

Valdelapinta 2004 Verdejo (Rueda) $12. Gets off on the wrong foot, with aromas of corn and overripe apples. It steadies itself on the palate, where it's still sort of candied, with mango and cantaloupe stepping up. Has its qualities and registers entirely inoffensive. Good wine but not exciting. **85** —*M.S. (9/1/2006)*

VALDEMAR

Valdemar 2003 Rosado Garnacha (Rioja) $9. Aromas of overripe strawberries and caramel create a heavy bouquet. The palate offers raspberry, cranberry, and pepper. Full bodied but with adequate acidity. Not stellar but functional. **83** —*M.S. (3/1/2005)*

VALDEMORAL

Valdemoral 1998 Tinto del Pais (Ribera del Duero) $17. 85 *(8/1/2000)*

VALDETAN

Valdetan 2000 Roble Tinto Red Blend (Cigales) $10. The roble in the name indicates oak aging, but maybe this wine could have done without that oak, because the aromas and flavors are pickled and funky. Beyond that, there's candied cherry fruit and some beet flavor, while the feel, tannins and texture all seem to be in place. Simply stated, the oak on this wine hinders rather than helps. **83** —*M.S. (3/1/2004)*

Valdetan 2001 Tinto Red Blend (Cigales) $NA. Young and boisterous, but nice and tasty. The color is violet, while the aromas are unchained and saturated. Flavors of black plum, ripe grapes, and rubber make for uncommon richness, while the finish is sizable and real. Full tannins and some acidic punch ensure that it won't be taken lightly. Made by the people at La Legua. **87** —*M.S. (8/1/2003)*

VALDRINAL

Valdrinal 2002 Crianza Tinto del Pais (Ribera del Duero) $17. Robust and dark, with plum and berry aromas that also carry hints of citrus and mineral. Overall this is a balanced specimen; the palate is round and full of bright plum and berry while the feel is moderately deep, somewhat tannic, and medium in acidity. Drink now. **88** —*M.S. (12/15/2006)*

VALDUBÓN

Valdubón 2003 Tempranillo (Ribera del Duero) $14. This basic RdD delivers a smooth, ripe nose with doses of forest, bacon, road tar, and violets, and there's some plum and blackberry at the foundation. Juicy and raw on the tongue, with racy, slick blackberry fruit. Finishes broad and medicinal, likely a sign of the hot vintage. **86** —*M.S. (6/1/2005)*

Valdubón 1999 Tempranillo (Ribera del Duero) $14. There's a distinctively earthy cast to the black-cherry aromas and flavors and welcome hints of meat and smoke as well. Somehow manages to be full-bodied, full of roasted fruit flavors while lacking a bit of depth. Finishes with tobacco, espresso, and bitter chocolate notes. Drink now with grilled meats. **85** —*J.C. (11/1/2001)*

Valdubón 2004 Cosecha Tempranillo (Ribera del Duero) $17. Not a stellar effort from this winery. The nose is more pickled than ideal and no matter how much air you give it there's a strong hint of wet animal. The palate is simple, bold and grapey, while the finish is muddled and tannic. Previous wines, albeit reserve-level bottlings, have been better. **83** —*M.S. (4/1/2006)*

Valdubón 2002 Cosecha Tempranillo (Ribera del Duero) $14. Meaty and earthy, with hints of cured Serrano ham spicing up the bold black fruit. The flavor profile veers toward red fruit, with raspberry and strawberry showing most prominently. In the mouth, grippy tannins support a big finish that's wide and open. Some vanilla punctuates the finish. **87** —*M.S. (3/1/2004)*

Valdubón 2002 Crianza Tempranillo (Ribera del Duero) $18. Smooth and round, with chunky red-fruit aromas touched up by cinnamon. Tangy on the tongue, with plum and cherry balanced by firm tannins and lively acidity. Not flashy but plenty good enough to enjoy on an everyday basis. **87** —*M.S. (11/15/2004)*

Valdubón 2001 Crianza Tempranillo (Ribera del Duero) $18. Here's a crianza with kick, a wine to match up to a good steak or rack of lamb. The bouquet is leathery and ripe, with clear notes of cumin and Indian spice. Ample berry and chocolate across the palate and finish make it a very good example of mainstream Ribera del Duero. **89** —*M.S. (12/31/2004)*

Valdubón 1999 Crianza Tempranillo (Ribera del Duero) $18. An easy drinker, creamy and medium-bodied in the mouth, this crianza offers red plums and oak on the palate, and sweet caramel candy aromas on the nose. Finishes with prickly tannins and some char and herb flavors. **86** —*D.T. (4/1/2003)*

Valdubón 1998 Crianza Tempranillo (Ribera del Duero) $18. The rustic, expressive aromas of raw meat and sun-warmed black cherries are a treat—then they're followed up by dark, powerful flavors of earth and tobacco. Like many wines from this vintage, it needs a few years of aging to round out the currently rough finish. **88** —*J.C. (11/1/2001)*

Valdubón 2000 Reserva Tempranillo (Ribera del Duero) $24. Kicks off with a bouquet akin to chocolate-covered cherries before moving on to cured meat and bacon. Strawberry and cherry flavors are touched up by buttery oak, while the finish is so broad that it seems like pulled dough. Shows much of what's good about this appellation. **87** —*M.S. (6/1/2005)*

Valdubón 1999 Reserva Tempranillo (Ribera del Duero) $24. A touch creamy, but generally it's a nice, healthy, well-made wine. Flavors of bold red fruit are touched up by earth notes and overt wood. The finish is lush enough, with sweet, ripe fruit and modest tannins. Even if this wine lacks the pop of the very best, it's got plenty going for it, and its lines are clean and well fitted. **90** —*M.S. (3/1/2004)*

VALENCISO

Valenciso 2001 Reserva Tempranillo (Rioja) $35. Leans toward the modern style, with plenty of oak, bacon, and plum on the bouquet. Quite upright and balanced throughout, with cherry, raspberry, cola, and brown sugar for flavors. A thorough, heartily oaked Tempranillo with purity and style. Almost at the top echelon. **89** —*M.S. (11/1/2006)*

Valenciso 2000 Reserva Tempranillo (Rioja) $34. Broad and rubbery, with ripe black fruit and citrus peel on the nose. Good on the tongue, with a solid mouthfeel. And the finish is attractively marinated, offering hints of soy sauce, molasses, and sea salt. Fresh enough, and definitely forward in thrust. **87** —*M.S. (6/1/2005)*

VALL LLACH

Vall Llach 2000 Celler Red Blend (Priorat) $88. This one is up there with the very best of the region. It's downright purple, with a powerful, classy, dense nose that exudes pine, lemon peel, and loads of blackberry and plum. The flavor profile is a splendid mix of boysenberry, cherry, fennel, and black pepper. And the finish is driving and spicy, a wonderful blend of cola, chocolate, and berries. A dazzling wine. **95 Cellar Selection** —M.S. (3/1/2004)

Vall Llach 2002 Embruix Red Blend (Priorat) $33. More of an approachable Priorat, with plump fruit and modest tannins. It's a blend of five grapes, mostly from vineyards planted in the 1990s, and the aging takes place in one-year-old French oak. Ripe and rich enough to go with hearty foods, but it's not a full-force bruiser. Look for boysenberry and blackberry flavors, hints of cocoa, and a smooth finish. **88** —M.S. (10/1/2005)

Vall Llach 2000 Embruix Red Blend (Priorat) $28. Inky-dark and dense, with exemplary cherry and berry fruit along with tons of earth, spice and terroir. At 15% it's big, and you get more than ample blackberry and cherry fruit to chew on. The finish, meanwhile, is dark with espresso and leftover fruit. Big and boisterous, but right on the money. **94 Editors' Choice** —M.S. (3/1/2004)

Vall Llach 1998 Embruix Red Blend (Priorat) $80. The black plum and toasty oak nose of this suave button-pusher will help you make friends quickly. Very international in style, it displays black cherry, semisweet chocolate, and licorice accents on a medium frame with good acidity. It's tasty, but a bit indistinct—this oak-heavy wine could be from many places. Still, it's well rendered in a style that has broad appeal. Closes dark and toasty, with some dry tannins to lose. Good now, best from 2003 to 2005. **87** —M.M. (4/1/2002)

Vall Llach 2002 Idus Red Blend (Priorat) $62. Five grapes comprise this luscious, intense, well-rounded wine that offers jolting aromas of black cherry, violets and mineral. Fairly plump and succulent relative to the field, with moderate tannins amplifying flavors of black plum, berries, chocolate and wood. Already easy to drink and will hit its prime in 2006. **90** —M.S. (10/1/2005)

Vall Llach 2002 Vino Tinto Red Blend (Priorat) $94. More jammy than previous vintages, with blackberry aromas and notes of bitter dark chocolate. Like any young Priorat stud, it hits firmly with jackhammer tannins, but there's also a likable, soft underside to it. Starts to sing with air and swirling, indicating a bright future. Hold a few years, if possible. **91** —M.S. (6/1/2005)

VALLFORMOSA

Vallformosa 2000 Clos Maset Selección Especial Cabernet Sauvignon (Penedès) $30. A bit foresty and damp at first and then more open, fruity and lush later. The palate offers mostly snappy black cherry and cassis, while the finish is short but sturdy, with mild oak notes and decent tannins. Improves upon airing and will go with most foods. **85** —M.S. (9/1/2006)

Vallformosa 1999 Masia Freyes Collección Especial Merlot (Penedès) $30. Rusty in color, with nutty, leathery aromas that feature little to no fruit. Quite sour in the mouth, and drying on the finish. Just not that pleasant; it's definitely not what you'd expect from Merlot. **81** —M.S. (9/1/2006)

Vallformosa 1992 Gran Reserva Red Blend (Penedès) $18. Sadly, I tasted this only recently, so late in its life. It's fading—but so beautifully in this case, that it deserves mention. Rather than dry and puckery, this wine is ending its days with an almost profound elegance. **86** —M.M. (9/1/2002)

Vallformosa 2000 Mas La Roca Selección Especial Syrah (Penedès) $30. Dark and smoky, almost like a burnt wooden match on top of plum purée. Runs a bit tart in the mouth for Syrah, with red raspberry and cherry flavors. Firm and lean in the mouth. **83** —M.S. (9/1/2006)

Vallformosa 2001 Primum Vitae Crianza Tempranillo (Rioja) $19. Light red to brick in color. Starts out spicy and leathery with more rhubarb and bramble than, say, black fruit. Tastes largely of raspberry and strawberry before finishing with caramel and a touch of toast. Simple. **83** —M.S. (11/1/2006)

Vallformosa 2001 Primum Vitae Reserva Tempranillo (Rioja) $20. Here's a wine that rides heavy with smoked meat and cured ham aromas. The nose is full of bacon, rubber, spice, and peppery fruit and then it turns to a palate of basic strawberry and raspberry. Short on the finish, with a touch of vanilla. **86** —M.S. (11/1/2006)

Vallformosa NV Chantal Brut Rosé White Blend (Cava) $20. Dusty cherry aromas start out full and turn more green and grassy with time. Sweet grapefruit and tang carry the palate, and the finish is a rush of acidity. Good but odd. **85** —M.S. (6/1/2006)

Vallformosa NV Eric Brut Nature White Blend (Cava) $22. Apple to start with, with some sweet doughiness to ease things along. Rather crisp and dry, which is all very classic. Flavors of white grapefruit and lemon are laser-like, while the finish is tight, almost sharp. Good quality; a little short. Made with Chardonnay and Parellada. **87** —M.S. (6/1/2006)

VALLOBERA

Vallobera 1998 Reserva Tempranillo (Rioja) $20. Starts with a big, dusty nose of cherry, blackberry, and forest notes. Fresh and proper on the palate, with plum and boysenberry. Finishes with vanilla and toffee, while the feel is warm and round. Very functional and moderately complex. **88** —M.S. (6/1/2005)

Vallobera 2001 Crianza Tempranillo Blend (Rioja) $15. Full and fresh, with pungent leather, tobacco, and red-fruit aromas. On the mark in terms of feel, with laudable plum, cherry, and earth-like flavors. Entirely holes-free, with ripeness that matches the wine's smooth texture. **88** —M.S. (6/1/2005)

Vallobera 2002 Pago Malarina Tempranillo Blend (Rioja) $10. Murky and leathery at first, with spice, stewed meat, and herbal aromas. Chunky but mostly in balance. The thick palate offers baked plum and black raspberry, while the finish is full and earthy. Best with tapas, ideally chorizo. **85 Best Buy** —M.S. (10/1/2005)

Vallobera 1999 Tinto Crianza Tempranillo Blend (Rioja) $15. Soft in acids and tannins and limpid in the mouth, but could use a bit more fruity flavor on top of the tobacco and sage notes. Would be nice with a big paella. **84** —S.H. (1/1/2002)

VALMIÑOR

Valmiñor 2005 Albariño (Rías Baixas) $15. A bit zesty to start, with a touch of mineral on the nose. Flavorwise, we're talking apple, peach, and nectarine. A solid wine with good balance and nothing out or the ordinary. **87** —M.S. (9/1/2006)

VALPICULATA

Valpiculata 2003 Tinta de Toro (Toro) $45. Smells a touch green and pasty, and while the wine is deep and dark, there isn't a whole lot of definition or specificity to it. Sweet and heavy in the mouth, with chocolate notes. Creamy on the finish, with minimal flavor. Not bad but doesn't have an identifiable personality. **85** —M.S. (12/15/2006)

VALSACRO

Valsacro 2001 Dioro Tempranillo Blend (Rioja) $36. This is a very new wine, but one worth getting if you like the modern style Spanish red. Made from 70-year old Tempranillo as well as some Mazuelo, Graciano, and Garnacha, you'll be digging into a massively roasted, well-oaked bruiser. Caramel, mocha, and chocolate mix with full berry fruit to yield a wine of concentration and body. Thick and manly; mature and ready by 2008. **93** —M.S. (9/1/2004)

VEGA DE CASTILLA

Vega de Castilla 2000 Tempranillo (Ribera del Duero) $11. Rough-and-ready, with gravelly tannins, there's lots of red plum fruit in this Tempranillo. Meaty, toasty aromas and flavors add a rustic aspect; this baby is just begging to be paired with stew. **86** —D.T. (4/1/2003)

VEGA GITANIA

Vega Gitania 2003 Premium Rosé Tempranillo Blend (Mentrida) $15. Dark in color, with heavy, awkward aromas. Quite plump in the mouth but wanting for flavor. There just isn't much to hang your hat on. Finishes with some pepper and bitterness. **81** —M.S. (2/1/2006)

VEGA PRIVANZA

Vega Privanza 1999 Tinto Jóven Tempranillo (Ribera del Duero) $11. Starts weak, offering little more than watery vanilla, cherry, and tobacco aromas, but gradually builds through the palate until it finishes with juicy cherry fruit tinged with chocolate. **83** —*J.C. (11/1/2001)*

VEGA RIAZA

Vega Riaza 2002 Tempranillo (Ribera del Duero) $12. Nice mint notes accent berry aromas. Flavors of coffee, burnt cherry, and toast seem sturdy and legit, while the finish is lean, clean, and only modestly tannic. Nicely balanced and solid; a wine that doesn't bite off more than it can chew. **87** —*M.S. (5/1/2004)*

Vega Riaza 2002 Roble Tempranillo (Ribera del Duero) $15. Spicy and rubbery on the nose, with a touch of heavy fruit providing the base. Shows ample cherry and berry flavors, but that fruit is a bit high-toned, meaning the back palate is mildly acidic and slightly sour. Needs food, with which it should fit the bill. **85** —*M.S. (5/1/2004)*

VEGA SAUCO

Vega Sauco 2002 Roble Tinta de Toro (Toro) $10. Starts with dusty cherry, plum and green herb aromas before turning more smoky and saucy. Warm and solid, with flavors of plum, vanilla, and spice. Well constructed and balanced, if not overly exciting. **86 Best Buy** —*M.S. (10/1/2005)*

Vega Sauco 1998 Adoremus Reserva Tinta de Toro (Toro) $22. A bit tart and leathery at first, but airing reveals plum, raspberry, and chocolate. It's a well-oaked, fairly mature wine, probably at its best right now. The finish is lean, acid-packed and spicy. **87** —*M.S. (9/1/2004)*

Vega Sauco 2000 Crianza Tinta de Toro (Toro) $15. Lots of early mint and wood, but then it loses clarity with airing. Flavors of cherry, beet, and black pepper steal the palate, which is backed up by red fruit and modest tannins on the finish. Not a lot of nuance here but it's still good. **85** —*M.S. (9/1/2004)*

Vega Sauco 2001 Roble Tinta de Toro (Toro) $10. A touch heavy and sulfuric at first, but better with airing. Aromas of licorice and black plum come right off the bat, followed by flavors of raspberry, spice, and pepper. Finishes smooth and in a couple of layers, with a coffee-like bitterness at the very end. Limited but a gritty contender. **86 Best Buy** — *M.S. (9/1/2004)*

Vega Sauco 1999 Wences Reserva Tinta de Toro (Toro) $60. From the start to the end, this heavyweight from Toro never really gets it right. The burnt rubber notes on the nose fight with a more pleasant blueberry fruit component. In the mouth, there's cherry and plum, but it's kind of medicinal in character. And the palate feel is over the edge, a bit fast and gritty. **84** —*M.S. (3/1/2005)*

VEGA SICILI

Vega Sicilia 1987 Unico Red Blend (Ribera del Duero) $200. One of the mysteries of Vega is how a wine released so late can be so fresh and vibrant. The '87 is no exception, featuring red raspberries and cherries counterbalanced by cedary oak. Focused, lean, and dry, this vintage of Unico may turn out to be too elegant for its own good, but the delicately fruity, intricately wrought finish seems to go on and on. **90** —*J.C. (11/1/2001)*

Vega Sicilia 1997 Valbuena Tempranillo (Ribera del Duero) $90. A wine of exceptional elegance that starts off with delicate floral aromas of violets or lilacs, then folds in black cherries, red raspberries, and dried spices. Bright fruit flavors sing on the long finish. No Unico was made in this difficult vintage, so much of the juice that normally goes into Unico was used for this wine, while the wine that is normally Valbuena was sold off for distillation. **92 Cellar Selection** —*J.C. (11/1/2001)*

Vega Sicilia 1994 Unico Gran Reserva Tempranillo Blend (Ribera del Duero) $325. Who else but Vega holds wines for more than 10 years before their release? This gorgeous Unico spent 104 months in large casks and smaller barrels, yet there's virtually no overt wood. The nose is foresty and complex, with hints of tomato, leather, and licorice. Flavors of plum, cherry, and vanilla are otherworldly, and there's enough tobacco to conjure memories of a fine cigar. A Tempranillo-Cabernet-Merlot blend worthy of its reputation. **95 Editors' Choice** —*M.S. (6/1/2005)*

VEGA SINDOA

Vega Sindoa 2003 Rosé Cabernet Blend (Navarra) $8. Bodegas Nekeas, the owner, calls this wine rosé, not rosado. It has light strawberry and cherry aromas and flavors, sweetness, a firm body, and some pepper, anise and licorice on the finish. The color is just right. A 50/50 blend of Garnacha and Cabernet. **87 Best Buy** —*M.S. (10/1/2004)*

Vega Sindoa 1998 Cabernet Sauvignon-Tempranillo (Navarra) $7. **84** — *M.M. (8/1/2000)*

Vega Sindoa 2000 Barrel Fermented Chardonnay (Navarra) $11. There's a wealth of oak over the apple and pear fruit in this affordable white. The rich, full mouthfeel suggests a higher price point, but this year's version seems heavier on the wood than previous vintages, and to my fruit-seeking palate, pushes the edge of balance. Call it a sucker-punch—it still tastes real good. **87** —*M.M. (4/1/2002)*

Vega Sindoa 1999 Barrel Fermented Chardonnay (Navarra) $10. **86** — *M.M. (8/1/2000)*

Vega Sindoa 1998 Cuvée Allier Chardonnay (Navarra) $12. **89 Best Buy** — *M.M. (8/1/2000)*

Vega Sindoa 2002 Merlot (Navarra) $8. A good, affordable Merlot. Leather, plum, and cherry notes mix with a touch of green pepper to yield a friendly, mostly sweet red with a nice mouthfeel. Mocha, vanilla, and fudge on the finish make for a tasty end. **87 Best Buy** —*M.S. (10/1/2004)*

Vega Sindoa 1998 Merlot (Navarra) $12. **90 Best Buy** —*M.M. (8/1/2000)*

Vega Sindoa 1996 Reserva Red Blend (Navarra) $16. **86** —*M.M. (8/1/2000)*

Vega Sindoa 2001 Rosé Blend (Navarra) $7. **86 Best Buy** —*D.T. (11/15/2002)*

Vega Sindoa 2000 Rosé Blend (Navarra) $7. Even a wine geek can like this tasty, inexpensive pink-colored wine, and it's a great way to get novice enthusiasts into something other than white Zinfandel. From its rose-floral nose with subtle earth and meaty hints, through the full, dry, herb-shaded berry flavors, this wine is packed with appeal. The Garnacha-Cabernet blend provides surprising body, and it's smoother and fuller than most inexpensive rosés. The dry, light finish makes this a perfect spring choice for anything from sipping to light dining. **87 Best Buy** —*M.M. (4/1/2002)*

Vega Sindoa 1999 Rosé Blend (Navarra) $7. **86** —*M.M. (8/1/2000)*

Vega Sindoa 2002 Tempranillo-Merlot (Navarra) $7. Bodegas Nekeas should be proud of this wine. It's one of the best value reds going. Powerful berry aromas lead toward chewy plum and burnt-caramel flavors. A chocolaty essence enriches the finish. Try not to stretch the wine's virtues by taking it out of its element: It's made for Wednesday evenings at home and barbecues. The blend is 70-30 in favor of Tempranillo. **86 Best Buy** —*M.S. (11/15/2003)*

Vega Sindoa 1999 Tempranillo-Merlot (Navarra) $7. **88 Best Buy** —*M.M. (8/1/2000)*

Vega Sindoa 2000 White Blend (Navarra) $7. Smooth and round, this ripe blend offers hay, nut, and stone-fruit notes on the nose. In the mouth, the peach-apricot edge turns almost Gewürztraminer-like, picking up tangerine and lychee elements. A seductive finish completes this attractive offering. **86 Best Buy** —*M.M. (4/1/2002)*

Vega Sindoa 1999 Viura Chardonnay White Blend (Navarra) $7. **87 Best Buy** —*M.M. (8/1/2000)*

VEGAVAL PLATA

Vegaval Plata 1996 Crianza Cencibel (Valdepeñas) $10. **86** —*J.C. (8/1/2000)*

Vegaval Plata 1993 Gran Reserva Cencibel (Valdepeñas) $17. Smoky, meaty notes dominate the nose of this medium-bodied wine. Red berries plus some dark caramel notes stand out on the palate. Medium-bodied but not too complicated, it closes with a dry, toasty-oak finish and a slight acidic tang that softens at the very end. **85** —*D.T. (4/1/2002)*

Vegaval Plata 1993 Reserva Tempranillo (Valdepeñas) $12. **82** —*J.C. (11/15/1999)*

Vegaval Plata 1989 Reserva Tempranillo (Valdepeñas) $12. 83 —*J.C.* (11/15/1999)

VEIGADARES

Veigadares 2002 Albariño (Rías Baixas) $18. More action on the nose than the palate, as the bouquet pushes toasted wood along with pear. Meanwhile, the mouth is dilute, with modest apple and pineapple flavors. Finishes on the thin side, but with heavy barrel notes. An oak-aged blend of Albariño, Treixadura, and Loureiro. 84 —*M.S.* (12/31/2004)

VENTA MAZZARON

Venta Mazzaron 2000 Tinta de Toro (Toro) $10. A complex bouquet of inky fruit, meat, dry-rub spices and pronounced clove and cinnamon elements segues into deep black fruit and coffee on the smooth, mid-weight palate. The often-rustic Toro character is beautifully handled, showing elegance without losing typicity or power. This structured wine closes full and dry, with a reprise of the spice notes and mouth-coating but even tannins. Drink 2004–2010+, or now, with hearty food. 90 — *M.M.* (4/1/2002)

VICENTE GANDIA

Vicente Gandia 2004 Fusta Nova Moscatel (Valencia) $11. Honey, pear, and sugar cane are the dominating flavors in thi sticky, rich, unctuous sweet wine. There isn't a whole lot else to say about it: you have to have an aggressive penchant for candy to get into this style of wine. 84 —*M.S.* (9/1/2006)

Vicente Gandia 2001 Generacion 1 Red Blend (Utiel-Requena) $19. Composed of 50% Bobal, a rubbery, hard-tannin grape, and Cabernet Sauvignon; to call this wine shrill would be an understatement. The color is purple, the nose dense but quiet. Black cherry flavors with unforgiving acidity and tannins create a grabby, squelching palate feel. 83 —*M.S.* (6/1/2005)

Vicente Gandia 2002 Tempranillo (Utiel-Requena) $7. Some heft and rich-ness propel this bargain wine to a higher level. There are even some bacon, beef, and leather aromas in addition to the plump fruit scents. Chewy and chunky, with flavors of black cherry and raspberry. Yet still tangy and refreshing enough to avoid being clumsy. 84 Best Buy —*M.S.* (6/1/2005)

Vicente Gandia 2002 Ceremonia Reserva De Autor Tempranillo (Utiel-Requena) $15. Bacon and leather meld with modest black-fruit aromas on the nose of this Tempranillo-Cabernet Sauvignon-Bobal blend. It's fairly plump, with blackberry and vanilla flavors. Ripe and tasty enough, but neither elevated nor complex. 85 —*M.S.* (9/1/2006)

Vicente Gandia 2004 El Miracle 120 Tempranillo Blend (Valencia) $10. Deep and secure on the nose, with richness and a strong whiff of fresh leather. The palate is serious as it deals black fruit and spice. Chocolate and rugged tannins carry the hard, almost grabby finish. A powerful but approachable blend. 86 Best Buy —*M.S.* (12/15/2006)

Vicente Gandia 2000 Hoya De Cadenas Reserva Prevada Tempranillo-Cabernet Sauvignon (Utiel-Requena) $11. More minty oak than fruit on the nose, with simple but clean candied fruit flavors. A bit short on depth and complexity, but totally drinkable, especially after some airing. Decent texture to the finish, with leftover spice and wood-based flavors. 85 —*M.S.* (6/1/2005)

VILLACAMPA DEL MARQUÉS

Villacampa del Marqués 2002 Roble Tempranillo Blend (Ribera del Duero) $14. Overtly sweet and syrupy, with artificial aromas of bacon grease and air freshener. Cloying for a while, although patience does uncover some likable plum and maple notes. Overall, it's too sweet and sticky. 82 — *M.S.* (6/1/2005)

VILLACEZAN

Villacezan 2003 Doce Meses Prieto Picudo (Viño Tierra de León) $15. A masculine, rubbery nose covered with oak and dark-fruit aromas is stage one. Next up comes a spicy, solid palate that has some tannin and com-plexity to go with dry berry flavors. Not uncommon or unusual. It's got the goods, so to speak. 87 —*M.S.* (9/1/2006)

Villacezan 2003 Molendores Prieto Picudo (Viño Tierra de León) $12. Dark in color, with questionable cleanliness. In the mouth, it's meaty, big and

unbalanced. Finishes with slight mushroom and sherry notes. The grape used is Prieto Picudo. 80 —*M.S.* (3/1/2005)

Villacezan 2005 Molendores Rosado Prieto Picudo (Viño Tierra de León) $11. Candied and round, with tangy melon and citrus flavors. Does best early on before losing focus and finishing flat. There is okay feel and bal-ance to it but little in the way of backing depth. 83 —*M.S.* (9/1/2006)

Villacezan 2004 VCZ Molendores Prieto Picudo (Viño Tierra de León) $15. Prieto Picudo is the grape, and the wine yields robust aromas of radish and red fruits. Very tangy, almost citrusy on the palate. Finishes quite lean and tart. A screechy wine without a lot of happiness. 83 —*M.S.* (9/1/2006)

Villacezan 2003 Dehesa de Villacezan Red Blend (Viño Tierra de León) $11. Sweet yet snappy, with youthful aromas of candied fruit. Slightly tangy on the tongue, with raspberry and plum flavors. Tastes clean, with a soft mouthfeel. Very standard, simple, and easygoing. 84 —*M.S.* (6/1/2005)

Villacezan 2001 Doce Meses Red Blend (Viño Tierra de León) $17. Muddled to start, with chocolate and earth aromas along with heavy, seemingly chewable berry fruit. Big on the palate, with slightly overripe plum backed by overt vanilla and brown sugar. A three-grape mix of Prieto Pecudo, Mencía, and Tempranillo. 84 —*M.S.* (6/1/2005)

Villacezan 2002 Seis Meses Red Blend (Viño Tierra de León) $14. Sweet on the nose, and full of cherry, oak, and spice. The mouth features bright but unrefined red fruit, and pepper on the finish. Not outstand-ing, but also nothing too serious in the way of flaws. 83 —*M.S.* (6/1/2005)

Villacezan 2005 Elverite Verdejo (Viño Tierra de León) $11. Light and sweet to the nose, with aromas of honey, which isn't normal for the usu-ally zesty, citrusy Verdejo. Pear and apple are the dominant flavors on a palate that's more smooth and lush than racy and snappy. Strange in how it's almost creamy. 84 —*M.S.* (9/1/2006)

Villacezan 2003 Elverite Verdejo (Viño de la Tierra de Castilla y León) $11. Lightweight and flaccid, with distant melon and citrus rind flavors. Short and simple, but not at all offensive. 82 —*M.S.* (12/31/2004)

VILLAREI

Villarei 2003 Albariño (Rías Baixas) $20. Tilts the scale on the heavy side. The nose is bolstered by weighty applesauce and petrol yet the palate is surprisingly lean and lemony in terms of flavors. Rather oily, and not endowed with much brightness. 83 —*M.S.* (9/1/2006)

VILLARROYA DE LA SIERRA

Villarroya de la Sierra 2004 la Garnacha (Calatayud) $9. Sweet plum and raisin on the nose go heavy and dull after time exposed to air. The palate offers some raspberry flavor, but with tang and finishing bitterness. Thick but raw. 83 —*M.S.* (9/1/2006)

VIÑA ALARBA

Viña Alarba 2001 Old Vines Grenache (Catalonia) $6. The Best Buy of the year? The price is unbelievable for what you get: bright, crunchy Grenache fruit that overflows the glass with ripe cherries, capped off by a hint of white pepper on the finish. It's fresh, it's bouncy and it's a bit rambunctious in its exuberant youth—perfect with assertively seasoned hamburgers or meatloaf. 88 Best Buy —*J.C.* (11/15/2002)

VIÑA ALBALI

Viña Albali 1998 Gran Reserva Tempranillo (Valdepeñas) $11. Light and dry, with a touch of raisin, mint, and butter on the nose. Tomato and red cherry are the prime flavors, and the finish is fresh and lean. 83 — *M.S.* (10/1/2005)

Viña Albali 2000 Reserva Tempranillo (Valdepeñas) $8. Simple and a bit jammy, with green aromas mixed with berry and bacon. Shows raspberry and strawberry flavors with a gritty, buttery streak. Thin and acidic at the end. 82 —*M.S.* (10/1/2005)

VIÑA ARNÁIZ

Viña Arnáiz 2001 Crianza Tinto del Pais (Ribera del Duero) $28. A bit jumpy and sharp. The nose is woody and lively while the palate is accu-rate in terms of the region but rather forceful with its plum, black cherry, and vanilla flavors. Flush and acidic on the finish, with a snappy impression. Unsettled. **85** —*M.S. (2/1/2006)*

Viña Arnáiz 2000 Reserva Tinto del Pais (Ribera del Duero) $30. Traditionally leathery, with earth and bramble on the bouquet. The cherry, raspberry, and cola flavors on the palate are aggressive courtesy of sharp acidity, while some wayward oak-based butter and vanilla rises up late on the finish. Like many in its class, this wine needs food. **84** —*M.S. (11/1/2006)*

Viña Arnáiz 1999 Crianza Tinto del Pais (Ribera del Duero) $19. Wonderful vanilla and creamy aromas accented with coffee and leather. Unfortunately, the flavors of blackberry and earth did not deliver what the nose promised. The finish was long and tangy—almost a bit tart. **87** —*C.S. (11/1/2002)*

Viña Arnáiz 1998 Reserva Tinto del Pais (Ribera del Duero) $30. Dark in color, with a bouquet that is chunky and oaky, with notes of tobacco and hard cheese. Blackberry and cherry carry the palate toward a finish that's a bit hard and grippy. A touch simple when compared to the very best, but still very solid. **89** —*M.S. (3/1/2004)*

VIÑA BORGIA

Viña Borgia 2000 Garnacha (Campo de Borja) $6. Violet and herb, leather and meat accents adorn the tart plum and cherry nose, which shows plenty of Garnacha character. It's followed by a tangy, cracked-peppery mouthful of fruit that carries through the brisk, dry finish. Very few wines at this price offer this level of flavor and feel, and smart shoppers will find it on sale for even less. **86 Best Buy** —*M.M. (4/1/2002)*

VIÑA CANCHAL

Viña Canchal 2003 Tempranillo (Ribera del Guadiana) $6. Rosy in color, with simple jammy aromas. Basic strawberry and black cherry flavors are backed by rubbery tannins. Seems cleanly made; just not all that exciting. **83** —*M.S. (8/1/2005)*

Viña Canchal 2002 Crianza Tempranillo (Ribera del Guadiana) $12. Raw and barky on the bouquet, with bits of green and leather mixed in. Tastes of cherry and plum, with serious tannins making for a grabby mouthfeel. Finishes with ample vanilla and toast. **85** —*M.S. (2/1/2006)*

Viña Canchal 2001 Crianza Tempranillo (Ribera del Guadiana) $9. A commonplace yet good Tempranillo, with red-fruit aromas and some leather. Cherry and strawberry grace the racy palate, which is carried by hard tannins and raw acids. Tastes good but the mouthfeel is rough. A true country wine in every sense of the word. **86 Best Buy** —*M.S. (3/1/2005)*

VIÑA CAROSSA

Viña Carossa NV Tinto Red Blend (Spain) $6. The ultimate Spanish table wine in that it has no vintage and is likely a blend of bulk wines from various regions. Yet it's not bad; raspberry and cherry aromas and flavors are decent, while the finish is crisp, dry and fairly clean. **83** —*M.S. (5/1/2004)*

Viña Carossa NV Brut Sparkling Blend (Spain) $8. Movie popcorn, peanuts and sugared breakfast cereal dominate the heavy, overbearing nose. In the mouth, it's plump and sticky, with apple and pear fruit. Adequate, but lacks elegance and precision. **82** —*M.S. (5/1/2004)*

VIÑA COLLADO

Viña Collado 1999 Tinto Tempranillo Blend (Campo de Borja) $8. A clean, light wine with cherry and cinnamon notes on the nose and in the mouth. This isn't heavy or deep, but tasty, and evenly textured. Elegant herb and mineral shadings show on the close of this attractive easy drinker. Would do well with a very light chill. **85** —*M.M. (9/1/2002)*

VIÑA CONCEJO

Viña Concejo 2001 Crianza Tempranillo (Cigales) $19. Savory and spicy, with a lot of tree bark, licorice, and dry red fruit. Quite hard and rocky on the tongue, with jagged tannins and raw acidity. **83** —*M.S. (11/1/2006)*

Viña Concejo 1999 Crianza Tempranillo (Cigales) $20. This crianza has some stuffing and it's definitely still kicking. The nose is meaty, robust and full of spice, leather, and black fruit. The plate pours forth with blackberry and some powerful wood notes, while the finish remains

woody but flows cleanly. Solid, warm and ready to drink. **87** —*M.S. (12/31/2004)*

VIÑA FUENTENARRO

Viña Fuentenarro 2003 Cuatro Meses Barrica Tempranillo (Ribera del Duero) $14. Pickled aromas are obvious on the chunky, warm bouquet, and never does the wine shed its green personality. The palate offers brown sugar and baked fruit, while the finish leaves an impression of carob and green bean. **82** —*M.S. (11/1/2006)*

VIÑA GODEVAL

Viña Godeval 2005 Godello (Valdeorras) $15. More available than most Valdeorras wines—and very good in 2005—Godeval offers a no-nonsense version of the Godello grape. There's typical slate on the nose but even more apple, pear, nectarine, and banana. Friendly, with medium acidity. **89** —*M.S. (9/1/2006)*

Viña Godeval 2003 Godello (Valdeorras) $15. Smooth and round, with meaty melon and pear aromas as it is. Which is quite out of the ordinary for this wine, one that usually pushes crisp white fruits and minerality. But because 2003 was so hot, this vintage is a bit sugary and heavy, but still very pleasant. Drink well chilled. **87** —*M.S. (10/1/2005)*

Viña Godeval 2000 Godello (Valdeorras) $16. A graceful white made of an old Galician grape that was nearly extinct before a handful of pioneer-preservationists rescued it from oblivion. Dry and flavorful, with a lovely thyme-sage bouquet and nutty flavors, this smoothly textured wine is worth seeking out. The long finish displays a fine perfume with a similar herb-nut character. This unique white will pair well with a seafood and lighter meats. **89** —*M.M. (4/1/2002)*

VIÑA HERMOSA

Viña Hermosa 2001 Crianza Tempranillo (Rioja) $14. Pure as old-school Rioja Crianzas go. The nose is light and leathery, while the palate deals spicy cherry, cranberry, and pepper. A little bit of fading oak makes an appearance on the finish, while lasting notes of vanilla and dried fruits are pleasant. **85** —*M.S. (4/1/2006)*

Viña Hermosa 1997 Gran Reserva Tempranillo (Rioja) $30. This is a racy little wine with slightly charred aromas; it's bright and lithe, with cherry, raspberry, and distant chocolate flavors. Juicy from front to rear, with freshness and complexity playing off each other. Will go nicely with a range of foods. **88** —*M.S. (4/1/2006)*

Viña Hermosa 1998 Reserva Tempranillo (Rioja) $20. Full and ripe, with tobacco and a certain earthy nuttiness to the nose. Raspberry and plum are the leading flavors, while the mouthfeel is both textured as well as juicy. Full in the middle, with a likable personality. **88** —*M.S. (4/1/2006)*

VIÑA IJALBA

Viña Ijalba 2000 Múrice Crianza Tempranillo (Rioja) $13. The bouquet begins with uncanny aromas of Italian bitters before turning fat and sweet. The palate is thin and stretched out, with flavors of strawberry and citrus zest. Sort of spicy but more stripped down and dull than exciting. **83** —*M.S. (8/1/2005)*

Viña Ijalba 1998 Reserva Tempranillo Blend (Rioja) $20. The nose contains beet, fir, and air freshener aromas, while the acidic palate pumps red plum and raspberry without any restraint. Tannic, racy, and hard. **82** —*M.S. (10/1/2005)*

VIÑA IZADI

Viña Izadi 2000 Crianza Tempranillo (Rioja) $14. Leather and wood spice add character to the full, brooding nose. In the mouth, plum and blackberry come across tight and balanced. **86** —*M.S. (10/1/2003)*

Viña Izadi 1998 Expresión Tempranillo (Rioja) $60. Cool earth and dry leather aromas open into fleshy dark plums. On the palate, cedar, blackberry and lightly blackened meat fade gently over a long finish. Even though this is a full, rich wine, it has an elegant structure. **91** —*K.F. (11/1/2002)*

Viña Izadi 1998 Reserva Tempranillo (Rioja) $20. Aromas are of tree bark, haystack, and dried berries. The palate is fairly light and bold, courtesy of zippy acidity and forward cherry and raspberry flavors. A touch of oaky butter comes up on the dry finish. **85** —*M.S. (10/1/2003)*

Viña Izadi 1997 Selección Tempranillo (Rioja) $45. Though not as rich as Viña Izadi's 1997 Expresión, this wine still has a lot to like: aromas of toasted bagel, dried apple, and orange peel that are followed by flavors of cranberry, raspberry, clove, and fennel **89** —M.M. (9/1/2002)

Viña Izadi 2000 Blanco Viura (Rioja) $13. No cookie-cutter white, this 80% Viura and 20% Malvasia barrel-aged Rioja has vibrant aromas and flavors. The Malvasia's decidedly orange cast plays off the nuttier Viura and wood notes. Closes dry and toasty, decently long, with a faint bitter almond note. Unique, and tasty for drinking now. **86** —M.M. (9/1/2002)

Viña Izadi 2001 White Blend (Rioja) $14. A nosing delivers pure oak extract and lemon custard, all of which is confirmed by the "barrel fermented" notation on the label. Why so much wood as been thrown at this wine is a question worth asking. Heavy toast flavors dominate the palate and wood resin seems to be all that's left at the end. Obtuse and oaky, yet still fresh and round in the mouth. **83** —M.S. (10/1/2003)

VIÑA JARABA

Viña Jaraba 2002 Crianza Tempranillo Blend (La Mancha) $13. Earthy fruit aromas, blackberry and cola flavors, and a soft, saturated finish all add up to a flush wine typical of La Mancha, where elegance is fleeting. And while this fruit-filled middleweight isn't off, it's not that alluring either. **83** —M.S. (12/15/2006)

VIÑA LUCIA

Viña Lucia 1998 Cabernet Sauvignon-Tempranillo (Cadiz) $10. 88 —C.S. (4/1/2002)

VIÑA MAGAÑA

Viña Magaña 2001 Baron de Magana Merlot (Navarra) $22. Full and heavy, with a smack of berry, oak, and bouillon on the nose. Big blackberry and espresso notes on the palate seem warm and raw, while the tannins force the finish toward the bitter side. **83** —M.S. (12/31/2004)

Viña Magaña 2000 Calchetas Crianza Red Blend (Navarra) $40. Brambly and a bit green, with aromas of plum, basil, and forest floor. This is one of the more tannic wines you'll encounter; the feel is like a jackhammer pounding away. But within that tannic vise there's adequate raisin, plum, and beet-like flavors. **84** —M.S. (3/1/2005)

Viña Magaña 1998 Dignus Red Blend (Navarra) $12. Not very pleasant as the nose offers sour, burnt aromas. Then comes a palate that's weedy and tart. Some cherry and cola flavors are present, but it's still fiery and awkward. **82** —M.S. (9/1/2004)

VIÑA MAYOR

Viña Mayor 1994 Gran Reserva Red Blend (Ribera del Duero) $32. Has all the typical ingredients of an aged Ribera: toast, vanilla, earth, and tobacco and still retains a measure of plummy fruit. Seems to be drying out just a little, but it goes down gently and gracefully. **86** —J.C. (11/1/2001)

Viña Mayor 1996 Reserva Red Blend (Ribera del Duero) $16. Tiring, thinning fruit with leather and cedar accents on the nose. Flavors of red earth and molasses, finishing toasty and lean. For fans of mature wines. **84** —J.C. (11/1/2001)

Viña Mayor 1999 Secreto Reserva Red Blend (Ribera del Duero) $18. Spicy, with clean red fruit, earth, and leather aromas. Also some overt wood. Flavors of cherry, raspberry, and mocha are appealing, and then a hint of butter comes on late. Overall it's tangy, fresh, and a pretty good rendition of Ribera del Duero. Best with food. **87** —M.S. (9/1/2004)

Viña Mayor 2002 Crianza Tempranillo (Ribera del Duero) $15. 87 —M.S. (9/9/1999)

Viña Mayor 2002 Crianza Tempranillo (Ribera del Duero) $14. Lemon peel and zesty raspberry aromas greet you, and next in line comes a mouthful of sharp red-fruit flavors that are tangy and juicy. This represents the fresh, almost austere side of Tempranillo. It's also similar to most 2002s, which are more lean and tart than average. **86** —M.S. (12/15/2006)

Viña Mayor 2000 Crianza Tempranillo (Ribera del Duero) $13. Dry and lean, with apple-skin aromas. Light and fruity on the palate, with some fading raspberry and strawberry flavors. Pretty much a one-note tune. **83** —M.S. (12/31/2004)

Viña Mayor 1998 Crianza Tempranillo (Ribera del Duero) $13. This safe middle-of-the-road Ribera makes a good introduction to the region. The cedar and black cherry aromas and flavors are well integrated, blending in vanilla and toast on the finish. There are enough tannins to provide some structure, but there's no reason not to drink this wine tonight. **87 Best Buy** —J.C. (11/1/2001)

Viña Mayor 1996 Gran Reserva Tempranillo (Ribera del Duero) $30. Saucy and mildly seductive, with aromas of herbs, leather, and exotic spices. In the mouth, however, things seem a touch rustic and burnt. The palate carries some serious zing and spice, but to call it smooth would be a stretch. **86** —M.S. (6/1/2005)

Viña Mayor 1999 Reserva Tempranillo (Ribera del Duero) $19. This Ribera workhorse from before the time RDD was a hot region hangs in there. The rooty nose springs with cola and spice along with dried fruits. Red raspberry and cherry tomato make for a recognizable, traditional palate. An easy food wine; mature now but with some life still in it. **86** —M.S. (3/1/2005)

VIÑA MEIN

Viña Mein 2001 White Blend (Ribeiro) $16. Touches of nectarine, apricot, and wildflower grace the nose. The plate is equally floral and nice, and the finish is soft and mildly nutty. Where it takes a hit, however, is in the mouthfeel: it seems flat, like an older Alsatian wine or something similar. **86** —M.S. (3/1/2004)

Viña Mein 2004 Barrica White Blend (Ribeiro) $21. In the past we've found this wine to be a bit flat and overwooded, but the '04 is balanced, fresh and downright lovely. Light vanilla and toast shadings accent bright peach and melon flavors, and the texture is something to behold. Excluding Valdeorras, this is Galician white wine in its most refined state. **91** —M.S. (9/1/2006)

Viña Mein 2005 Blanco White Blend (Ribeiro) $18. Treixadura-based, with Godello, Loureira, and tiny portions of Albariño, Torrontés, Caino Blanca, and Albilla. The whole, however, is all that counts, and this is simply an excellent white that's aromatic, dry as a bone, and fresh as spring. **91 Editors' Choice** —M.S. (9/1/2006)

Viña Mein 2003 Blanco White Blend (Ribeiro) $19. Stylish and classy; about as good as you'll find for a 2003 white from Spain. Lovely fresh fruit and lemon custard aromas start it in the right direction, and the palate of melon, green apple, and citrus takes it to the finish line. Gentle, with zest and clarity. It's 80% Treixadura, with some Malvasia and other things thrown in. **90 Editors' Choice** —M.S. (8/1/2005)

Viña Mein 2000 Blanco White Blend (Ribeiro) $16. This dry, aromatic white comes from a region in northwestern Spain, north of Portugal and inland from Galicia. Hay and nut aromas open to similar flavors, adorned by bright mineral-lime notes. This blend of 75% Treixadura, 15% Godello, with the remainder a mixture of Albariño, Loureira, and Torrontes is balanced and fresh, a bright spring white that will shine with seafood and other lighter dishes, or make a fine apéritif. **86** —M.M. (4/1/2002)

VIÑA MOCEN

Viña Mocen 2005 Verdejo (Rueda) $12. A sweet, almost punch-bowl nose greets you, followed by mellow apple and tropical fruit flavors. Medium-bodied and generally balanced, with shy but layered flavors and dryness that offers a bit of complexity. **85** —M.S. (12/15/2006)

VIÑA PRÓDIGUS

Viña Pródigus 1998 Reserva Tinta de Toro (Toro) $38. Good and fruity, with smoky oak and a ton of natural and barrel-aided spice. Solid black cherry and raspberry flavors sit at the core of this fast-maturing Tempranillo, while racy acidity keeps it fresh and healthy. Notes of cedar and cinnamon are pleasant. Drink or hold through 2008. **88** —M.S. (10/1/2005)

Viña Pródigus 2001 Roble Tinta de Toro (Toro) $18. Starts with strong scents of cured meat and marinade, before turning toward hard-smoked rubber. A bit tart in the mouth, with red raspberry and green pepper notes. Not terribly ruity, with a raw feel. But overall it has more positives than negatives, and it should go well with grilled meats. **85** —M.S. (10/1/2005)

VIÑA RUFINA

Viña Rufina 2000 Alta Gama Reserva Tempranillo (Cigales) $28. Cherry and baked fruit carries the nose, followed by more cherry and some oaky vanilla. Plump but flat in terms of feel, with stewy finishing notes. Never finds much of a groove. **83** —*M.S. (11/1/2006)*

VIÑA SALAMANCA

Viña Salamanca 2004 Viura/Verdejo White Blend (Viño de la Tierra de Castilla y León) $10. Granular on the nose, with mineral-based aromas of vitamins, iron, and citrus peel. Thin and metallic on the palate, with dry citrus and not much else. Some tangerine on the tail gives it a boost, but still it is short on continuity and character. **84** —*M.S. (10/1/2005)*

VIÑA SALCEDA

Viña Salceda 2002 Crianza Tempranillo Blend (Rioja) $16. A wave of pleasant but light cherry, blackberry, and sage offers a powerful but not overpowering opening. The palate is juicy and fresh, with controlled cherry and a touch of buttered toast. Round and medium in size on the finish, with solid but correct tannins. **87** —*M.S. (12/15/2006)*

VIÑA SARDASOL

Viña Sardasol 2005 Rosado de Lagrima Garnacha (Navarra) $9. Fairly sweet and fruity, with notes of raspberry jam and cotton candy on the bouquet. Feels nice across the palate, with tangy strawberry and red-cherry flavors leading to a fresh, wet, bright finish. A good but pedestrian wine at a reasonable price. **85 Best Buy** —*M.S. (12/15/2006)*

Viña Sardasol 2004 Rosado de Lagrima Garnacha (Navarra) $9. Nice mineral and cherry aromas precede a snappy, cleansing palate that runs heavy on the berry, orange, and nectarine flavors. This wine shows why Navarra is one of Spain's best regions for rosados; it's ripe and bouncy, with balance and tang. Will work nicely with an array of foods. **87 Best Buy** —*M.S. (2/1/2006)*

Viña Sardasol 2004 Tempranillo (Navarra) $7. Foresty and smoky, with berry and earthy plum flavors. Soft in the mouth, with only mild tannins. Overall it's plump and generous, although the complexity and depth are moderate at best. **84 Best Buy** —*M.S. (11/15/2005)*

Viña Sardasol 2002 Crianza Tempranillo Blend (Navarra) $10. This Navarran winery usually does well, but its '02 Crianza isn't up to snuff. The nose is clumsy and jammy, while the fruit is underdeveloped and dull. Acceptable on its best day. **81** —*M.S. (12/15/2006)*

Viña Sardasol 2001 Crianza Tempranillo Blend (Navarra) $10. Shows real solidity and ripeness, with commendable red fruit, leather, and pepper on the nose. Fairly fresh and tight flavors of plum and black cherry ride nicely on a balanced, medium-depth palate. Neither lush nor stripped down; it's perfect for everyday drinking. **87 Best Buy** —*M.S. (11/15/2005)*

Viña Sardasol 2001 Reserva Tempranillo Blend (Navarra) $11. A Tempranillo-based blend that's not only a clear cut above most Spanish reds in this price range, it's the type of wine favored by opponents of the New World, bigger-is-better school of thought. It opens with subtle cherry and spice aromas, while the flavors are similar, with tea and a hint of leather added in. The fuel for it all is laser-like acidity, which gives the wine a ready-to-go personality. **89 Best Buy** —*M.S. (11/15/2006)*

Viña Sardasol 2000 Reserva Tempranillo Blend (Navarra) $11. A bit rubbery at first, but then it picks up steam and clarity. Raspberry, cherry, and earth flavors are good, as is the light finish that shows touches of citrus and vanilla. Nothing special but absolutely nothing to take issue with. **85** —*M.S. (11/15/2005)*

Viña Sardasol 2004 Tempranillo-Merlot (Navarra) $9. Jammy but structured red-fruit aromas mix with a little tree bark to create an attractive, wholesome bouquet. Hits with flavors of black plum and berry, and the Merlot adds some sweetness to the Tempranillo. Clean and fresh, with agility. **86 Best Buy** —*M.S. (11/15/2005)*

VIÑA SASTRE

Viña Sastre 1999 Regina Vides Tempranillo (Ribera del Duero) $175. Wow. Made from a small parcel of 80-plus-year-old Tempranillo vines, the resulting wine is packed with dense, smoky aromas wrapped around a core of brandied fruitcake. Huge, mouthfilling flavors of blackberries and roasted meat develop in the glass, all framed by wonderfully supple tannins. **95 Cellar Selection** *(4/1/2003)*

Viña Sastre 1999 Regina Vides 1998 Tempranillo (Ribera del Duero) $175. A bit toastier and more floral than the bruising 1999, but still a rich, silky wine. Roasted meats, blackberry, and tobacco give true Tempranillo flavor, finishing with hints of licorice. Like the other wines from Sastre, the tannins are plentiful but wonderfully ripe and supple. **93** *(4/1/2003)*

Viña Sastre 1999 Pago de Santa Cruz Tempranillo (Ribera del Duero) $85. A single-vineyard wine made from the fruit of 65-year-old Tempranillo vines, it spends 18 months in new French oak, yet because of the fruit concentration the wood doesn't seem overdone. Starts off with hints of clove and coffee, then develops blackberry and black cherry fruit wrapped in a cocoon of dried spices. **92** *(4/1/2003)*

Viña Sastre 1998 Pago de Santa Cruz Tempranillo (Ribera del Duero) $85. Not quite as rich or lush as the great 1999 version—a product of the weaker vintage—this is still stunning stuff. Dried spices and blackberries start and finish strong, couched in the plush tannins that are the winery's hallmark. **91** *(4/1/2003)*

Viña Sastre 1996 Pago de Santa Cruz Gran Reserva Tempranillo (Ribera del Duero) $175. Features higher-toned, redder fruit than the other vintages tasted, but the cranberry and raspberry flavors provide a bright counterpoint to dark coffee and earth on the finish. Still young and vibrant; drink 2005-2010. **90** *(4/1/2003)*

Viña Sastre 1995 Pago de Santa Cruz Gran Reserva Tempranillo (Ribera del Duero) $150. The vintage, 1995, was a good one in Ribera del Duero, and this is a solid effort, but it pales in comparison to recent vintages at Viña Sastre. Lean, with a firm backbone that supports simple blackberry fruit, it finishes with a squirt of lemony acidity and some peppery spice. **87** *(4/1/2003)*

Viña Sastre 1999 Pesus Tempranillo Blend (Ribera del Duero) $375. Old-vine Tempranillo is cut by about 15% younger-vine Cabernet and Merlot in this rich, chewy red. It's smokier and more herbal than its all-Tempranillo stablemate, the Regina Vides, yet still boasts enormous blackberry and black cherry fruit cushioned by plush tannins. **94 Cellar Selection** *(4/1/2003)*

Viña Sastre 2001 Pesus Tinto del Pais (Ribera del Duero) $395. Talk about a wine that's tight as a bank vault. You almost need a pick and axe to get into this bruiser. The bouquet is drawn in, with toast, lemon peel, and pure belt leather adding a manly element to the earthy fruit that lurks below. What a pedigree on this single-vineyard alta expressión red, and the coffee-flooded finish goes on and on. Hold until 2009. 125 cases made. **95** —*M.S. (6/1/2005)*

VIÑA SILA

Viña Sila 2003 Naia Des Verdejo (Rueda) $28. A barrel-fermented Verdejo, which will work for some and seem wrong to others. The nose is wood-heavy, with smoke, butterscotch, and licorice. In the mouth, it's ripe and full of spiced pear and vanilla flavors. A one-trick pony in that it's dominated by oak. Still, the quality of the fruit and oak is solid. **88** —*M.S. (6/1/2005)*

VIÑA SOLEDAD

Viña Soledad 2001 Crianza Tempranillo Blend (Rioja) $18. Tea and strawberry on the nose, with smoky, leathery accents to the lightweight yet somewhat grabby palate. Not too much fruit is left here, but what survives is clean and fresh, if a touch bland. Blends 20% Garnacha with Tempranillo. **84** —*M.S. (4/1/2006)*

VIÑA SOLORCA

Viña Solorca 1998 Crianza Tempranillo (Ribera del Duero) $19. Tasty coconut, vanilla, and a hint of dill would lead you to believe American oak was used to fashion this wine. Juicy plum and cassis flavors are enjoyable, but a bit hollow in the midpalate, finishing with firm, drying tannins. **87** —*C.S. (11/1/2002)*

Viña Solorca 1999 Roble Tempranillo (Ribera del Duero) $12. Aromas of celery and root beer mix with flavors of dried spice and chocolate. Not for the fruit lover, this wine needs to settle so the tannins and awkward acidity even out. **85** —*C.S. (11/1/2002)*

VIÑA SOMOZA

Viña Somoza 2004 Godello (Valdeorras) $18. Grassy apple aromas carry a note of pickle, while the palate is chunky, full and delivers melon, pear, and almond flavors. Chalk, mineral and green herbs are the secondary characteristics. Dry and long in the mouth. **85** —*M.S. (9/1/2006)*

VIÑA VERMETA

Viña Vermeta 1996 Reserva Roble Nuevo Monastrell (Alicante) $10. Dried fruits and a slight canned aroma, followed by earthy tannins with a little burnt coffee. The wine seems a little tired. **82** —*C.S. (4/1/2002)*

VIÑA VILANO

Viña Vilano 2005 Rosado Tempranillo (Ribera del Duero) $10. Reddish in color and plump on the nose. The palate, however, deals only light cherry and dilute berry flavors. Inconsequential on the finish, with little character overall. **81** —*M.S. (12/15/2006)*

VIÑALCASTA

Viñalcasta 2000 Crianza Tempranillo (Toro) $14. Thick and saucy, with a nose akin to BBQ. Along the way are chocolate, stewed prune, and bacon. The mouth sports rich, ripe cherry and berry fruit while the easygoing finish yields more of that oaky bacon found on the nose. On the heavier but not too much so. **86** —*M.S. (12/31/2004)*

Viñalcasta 1999 Reserva Tempranillo (Toro) $18. For a long while in the glass this wine seemed acrid and sulfuric. Time and air finally forced out dark plum fruit aromas, a meaty mouthfeel, and a lot of fudge and coffee on the finish. **84** —*M.S. (12/31/2004)*

Viñalcasta 2001 Reserva Tinta de Toro (Toro) $20. Jumbled, jammy, and disjointed, with a heavy load of extracted, overdone fruit. Deep and hard, with funky aromas and a disconcerting mouthfeel. A wine with issues. **81** —*M.S. (9/1/2006)*

VIÑAS DEL CENIT

Viñas del Cenit 2003 Venta Mazzaron Tempranillo (Viño de la Tierra de Manchuela) $15. This modern-style wine could be designated as Toro, but it comes from a village that predates the Toro D.O. so it keeps the "Viño de la Tierra" moniker. That said, it's a first-ever Tempranillo made by the New Zealand enologist Amy Hopkinson, and like many new-wave Spanish bruisers five times pricier, it pours on the smoky aromas in front of a textured, extracted palate. In terms of sheer flavor per dollar, you'll be hard pressed to do better **90 Best Buy** —*M.S. (11/15/2005)*

VIÑAS DEL MONTSAN

Viñas del Montsant 2001 Fra Gueralu Red Blend (Montsant) $NA. This co-op wine is a touch minty and herbal, but it has enough class and red fruit to earn props. Cherry and raspberry dominate the flavor profile, while the finish is dry and a little bit starchy. Zesty and full of pop, but lean in the middle. **85** —*M.S. (3/1/2004)*

VIÑAS DEL VERO

Viñas del Vero 2003 Clarion White Blend (Somontano) $NA. Hailing from a more obscure mountainous region, this Chardonnay-based white blend is a potent brew. The nose offers pointed lime, citrus, and cream aromas, which are followed by vanilla-tinged pear and spice flavors. Big boned yet clean, with a piquant finish. **88** —*M.S. (6/1/2005)*

VINÍCOLA HIDALGO

Vinícola Hidalgo NV Pastrana Manzanilla Pasada Sherry (Jerez) $18. The people at Hidalgo in Sanlúcar have taken dry Manzanilla and have let it age until it has turned golden and mature. The bouquet is full of exotic oils, nuts, and some horsehide. In the mouth, it's a touch salty and astringent, but there are buttery, sweet undertones and great focus. And on the back end the pure flavor of mushroom and almonds is uncanny. Sleek, acidic, and likely perfect with lobster or shrimp bisque. **92 Editors' Choice** —*M.S. (8/1/2003)*

VIÑOS JEROMIN

Viños Jeromin 1999 Cosecha de Familia Félix Martinez Reserva Red Blend (Vinos de Madrid) $45. On one hand it shows black cherry, plum, and licorice. On the other there are green, lettuce-like aromas, and flavors.

Along the way is some tang on the palate, length to the herbal finish, and an adequate mouthfeel. **84** —*M.S. (6/1/2005)*

Viños Jeromin 2000 Manu Crianza Red Blend (Madrid) $60. This crianza is saucy on the nose, with prune, berry jam, and cherry aromas. Zippy and hard, with forward black-cherry flavors. All in all it's a complete red, with nuances of chocolate and spice. Could stand for some food to tame the hard tannic structure. **85** —*M.S. (3/1/2005)*

VIÑOS SANZ

Viños Sanz 2004 Finca La Colina Sauvignon Blanc (Rueda) $NA. In Rueda, sometimes the Sauvignon Blanc and Verdejo taste similar. But in this case there's no mistaking things. This S.B. is sharp, with teeth to the nose and palate. Classic sweaty gooseberry aromas lead to pure citrus, slate, and grass on the tongue. As good as you're going to find in Spanish Sauvignon. **90** —*M.S. (6/1/2005)*

VINYA L'HEREU

Vinya L'Hereu 2002 Flor de Grealo Red Blend (Costers del Segre) $33. Dark and attractive in terms of color, with barrique-driven aromas of bacon, toast, and roasted plum and berry. This is a ripe, meaty offering with blackberry, chocolate, and warm brown sugar flavors supported by full tannins. Shows some licorice and burnt toast on the fairly long finish. **89** —*M.S. (11/1/2006)*

Vinya L'Hereu 2002 Petit Grealo Red Blend (Costers del Segre) $16. Quite a bit different than the bodega's Flor de Grealo prestige bottling; this wine is a touch stewy, with molasses and braised-beef aromas. The palate leans toward unctuous and syrupy, while the finish is flatter than ideal. A blend of Syrah, Merlot, and Cabernet Sauvignon. **83** —*M.S. (11/1/2006)*

VIONTA

Vionta 2005 Albariño (Rías Baixas) $18. Full and robust in its approach. The bouquet is fragrant and expansive, with melon and honey aromas pouring forth with gusto. The flavors are quite delicious, a near-perfect blend of apple, melon and citrus. The word on the street is that 2005 Albariños offer great fruit-to-acid balance. This wine is an example of just that. **90** —*M.S. (9/1/2006)*

Vionta 2004 Albariño (Rías Baixas) $18. Light and a bit dusty, with simple, inoffensive aromas. A bit shrill and tart, with bold acidity that overruns the fruit. Not bad but superficial; and with too much snap. **84** —*M.S. (10/1/2005)*

Vionta 2000 Albariño (Rías Baixas) $12. Positive, bright citrus elements in this Albariño are marred by uncomplimentary mushroom and sour hay notes. Though the mouthfeel is even, and one can detect the crispness behind, the odd qualities depress the flavor profile. **81** —*M.M. (9/1/2002)*

Vionta 2003 Single Vineyard Albariño (Rías Baixas) $18. Yellow in color, with a heavy disposition. The nose yields sweet and ripe mango, melon, and Lemon Pledge aromas. Additional lemon and tangerine carries the monoline palate. Best as a simple shellfish wine. **84** —*M.S. (12/31/2004)*

Vionta 2002 Estate Botted Single Vineyard Limited Release Albariño (Rías Baixas) $15. Creamy and smooth on the nose, yet a little weak. The palate is lemony, with notes of green apple poking through the citrusy veil. Finishes moderately sharp, but with verve and potency. **86** —*M.S. (3/1/2004)*

Vionta 2001 Estate Bottled-Single Vineyard-Limited Edition White Blend (Rías Baixas) $16. This single-vineyard Albariño is medium-full in body, but it's still crisp, which makes it a great alternative-to-Chard candidate for dinner. Its core is pear and apple; mustard seed, chalk and white pepper dress up the nose. **87** —*D.T. (4/1/2003)*

VITICULTORES BERCIANOS

Viticultores Bercianos 2001 Gran Riocua Mencia (Bierzo) $65. A strange brew. Starts off with charred espresso aromas, not really the way elegant Bierzo wines usually go. Lots of oak throughout, with a stewy personality. Bold but bumbling. **80** —*M.S. (6/1/2005)*

VITICULTORES DEL PRIORAT

Viticultores del Priorat 1998 Prior Terrae Red Blend (Priorat) $200. Mature, with tomato and dill aromas prior to severe cherry tomato, rhubarb, and vanilla flavors. At all points the wine places zest before richness, acid before body. And while it has its aged, old-world virtues, it fails to share much love along the way. **84** —*M.S. (3/1/2005)*

VIVIR, VIVIR

Vivir, Vivir 2004 Tempranillo (Ribera del Duero) $10. **86** —*M.S. (9/9/1999)*

VIZCONDE DE AYALA

Vizconde de Ayala 1999 Crianza Tempranillo (Rioja) $12. Thin, with flavors of cherry skins and lemon juice. Not nearly enough flesh to support the acidity. **81** —*M.S. (8/1/2005)*

Vizconde de Ayala 1994 Gran Reserva Tempranillo (Rioja) $50. Typically dry and earthy, with aromas of wet leaves, rubber, and cherry drink mix. The palate features tart red fruit floating on a wave of aggressive acids. Some spice on the finish is a decent second act. **84** —*M.S. (8/1/2005)*

YLLERA

Yllera 1986 Black Label Red Blend (Viño da Mesa de Toledo) $28. Aromas of dried spices and vanilla dominate, but the cherry fruit still tastes fresh and alive thanks to firm acidity. Turns tart on the finish, where its age becomes more obvious in the thinning flavors. **86** —*J.C. (11/1/2001)*

Yllera 1995 Red Label Red Blend (Viño de Mesa de Castilla y León) $23. Tastes fresh for a six-year-old wine, with crisp red-raspberry and cherry flavors accented by vanilla. On the light side, but streamlined and elegant; probably better with food. **86** —*J.C. (11/1/2001)*

Yllera 1999 Oak Selection Tempranillo (Viño de Mesa de Castilla y León) $9. Here's a solid—if somewhat generic—red with a touch of vanilla oak. Red raspberries, earth, and black tea shadings make for a satisfying drink. Don't be scared away by the "oak selection" moniker; this blend of 90% Tempranilllo and 10% Cabernet Sauvignon spends only four months in wood. **87 Best Buy** —*J.C. (11/1/2001)*

YSIOS

Ysios 1999 Reserva Red Blend (Rioja) $30. For years Ysios has been one of Spain's most architecturally astounding wineries, but its wines have lagged. This is not a new wine, so it falls into that simple, basic category. It's aging decently, showing citrus, root beer, and tobacco. Good but midland. **85** —*M.S. (11/1/2006)*

ZITUA

Zitua 2000 Crianza Tempranillo (Rioja) $16. Light as if it were even older than it is, but nicely perfumed and mild in scope. The nose is mature and woodsy, while the palate is light, acidic, and still dancing with plum and cherry. Best if you don't expect too much from it. **85** —*M.S. (6/1/2005)*

ZUMAYA

Zumaya 1999 Crianza Tempranillo (Ribera del Duero) $17. Light cherry, earth, and smoke notes are more encouraging than the tart, pointed palate, which features sour cherry and berry fruit. On the finish, you get lemony oak and some grabby tannins. **83** —*M.S. (12/31/2004)*

Zumaya 1999 Reserva Tempranillo (Ribera del Duero) $25. Pretty heavy on the nose, with mushroom, bacon and rubber. The palate runs extremely fast, with condensed cherry flavors that hit hard courtesy of spiky tannins. Very forward and in-your-face. **84** —*M.S. (12/31/2004)*

Zumaya 1998 Reserva Tempranillo (Ribera del Duero) $25. Raw and woody, with thin cherry fruit and hints of tangy, almost sour strawberry. Lightweight yet gritty. **80** —*M.S. (1/1/2005)*

Other International

BULGARIA AND ROMANIA

These two countries have been upgrading their vineyards and wineries for several years. Bulgaria has some 200,000 acres of vinifera vines in production, Romania has about the same. Look for good-value Chardonnays, Merlots, and Cabernets from Bulgaria in particular. Merlot and Cabernet show promise in Romania, along with indigenous reds such as Feteasca Neagra.

CANADA

The Canadian wine industry divides neatly in half. In eastern Canada, the Niagara Peninsula north of Lake Ontario produces the vast majority of the region's wines. The government-funded switch to vinifera vines in the early 1990s revolutionized the region, which produces roughly four-fifths of Canada's wine grapes. Though a wide range of varietal white and red wines are made, it is the region's ice wines, marketed in super-tall, slim, 375 ml bottles, that have brought it global acclaim. Meanwhile, British Columbia has been quietly building a substantial wine industry of its own, especially on the bluffs surrounding Lake Okanagan, where a compelling blend of wine and recreational tourism draws visitors year-round. Everything from Germanic Rieslings to Burgundian Pinots to Bordeaux-style red wines and even Syrah can be ripened here. More than one hundred wineries call British Columbia home, with more opening every month.

CROATIA

Original homeland to Zinfandel—known on the Dalmatian coast as Crljenik Kasteljanski. Plavac Mali is a similar grape, making sometimes tough, tannic wines.

GREECE

Greece's best, most distinctive wines are indigenous grape varieties that are unknown elsewhere. Moschofilero is Greece's answer to Pinot Grigio—a light, attractively fruity white that can be charming when cleanly made. Reds tend to be more rustic, whether made from Agiorgitiko or Xinomavro.

HUNGARY

Although home to the storied wines of Tokaji and Egri Bikaver (Bull's Blood), quality was stunted by the chaos that supplanted Communism. Western investment and heroic individual efforts are just beginning to bear fruit.

ISRAEL

High-tech farming is a hallmark of Israeli agriculture, and grape growing is no different, with carefully metered irrigation of international grape varieties the rule rather than the exception. A new generation of carefully sculpted reds is raising the bar.

LEBANON

For years, Lebanese wine was synonymous with Château Musar, but now other names have joined the Hochar family in making wine amidst the ruins. Reds show the most promise.

SLOVENIA

Bordering Italy's Collio region, Slovenia produces many of the same grape varieties, including pungent Sauvignon and classy Tocai, as well as blended whites.

URUGUAY

Uruguay is South America's fourth-largest wine producer (behind Chile, Argentina, and Brazil), and, in global wine terms, is best described as an emerging market.

With a couple hundred years of grape-growing history to its name, and 135 years of commercial winemaking history, Uruguay has never quite caught on the way Argentina and Chile have. Nonetheless, many vinifera grapes, most imported from France, are grown in Uruguay, including Cabernet Sauvignon, Merlot, Pinot Noir, Riesling, and Gewürztraminer. That said, the calling-card grape for the country is Tannat, a rustic variety hailing from Madiran, in southwest France. Somewhat of a chameleon, Uruguayan Tannat can be made in a racier, fruity style or in a more international, barrel-aged style.

OTHER INTERNATIONAL

BRAZIL

CORDELIER

Cordelier NV White Sparkling Wine Muscat (Brazil) $11. Made from 100% Muscat, the nose offers the usual gardenia and lily-like aromas. Melon and sweet apple flavors are clean and real, and for the most part the wine succeeds. The one place it has issues is its carbonation. It bubbles like crazy, creating foam central on the palate. **82** —*M.S. (12/31/2005)*

Cordelier NV Brut Sparkling Blend (Brazil) $13. Pretty nice for a Brazilian sparkler, with a sweet, frosted-cake nose that's a bit gassy. Plump and candied on the palate, with apple and melon flavors. Loud and full, but clumsy. Shows good base qualities; needs refinement. **84** —*M.S. (6/1/2006)*

SALTON

Salton NV Demi-Sec Sparkling Blend (Brazil) $7. Sweet. This blend of Chardonnay and Riesling from southern Brazil is sweet and a touch green. The feel is respectable and the flavors are more or less candy in a glass: look for sugary lime and melon. **84 Best Buy** —*M.S. (12/31/2005)*

BULGARIA

BALKAN HILLS

Balkan Hills 2003 Muscat (Targovishte) $8. Very floral and obvious on the nose, but also very light and fresh on the palate, without any overpowering weight or sugar. Clean and dry on the finish, with lingering notes of flowershop greens and a hint of white pepper. **85 Best Buy** —*J.C. (6/1/2005)*

DAMIANITZA

Damianitza 2002 Reserva Melnik (Melnik) $10. Light in body and lacking flesh to cover its dry, scratchy tannins. Modest cherry flavors can't compete with dull cedar and leather notes. **81** —*J.C. (6/1/2005)*

DOMAINE BOYAR

Domaine Boyar 2000 Reserve Cabernet Sauvignon (Sliven) $8. Another Bulgarian surprise, with pleasant cigar box and earth flavors wrapped in supple tannins and topped with cassis. Nicely balanced for near-term drinking. **85 Best Buy** —*J.C. (6/1/2005)*

KANOV VINEYARD

Kanov Vineyard 2003 Reserve Unfiltered Cabernet Sauvignon (Danube Hills Valley) $15. A very drinkable wine that could pass for a well-made cru bourgeois, this Cabernet was a nice surprise. Scents of smoke, cedar, and leather; crisp cherries accented by meaty, earthy notes on the palate. Claret-weight, with soft tannins. Drink now. **86** —*J.C. (6/1/2005)*

SUN VALLEY

Sun Valley 2003 Cabernet Sauvignon (Bulgaria) $10. Light and fruity, with modest black cherry flavors and helpings of herbs and earth. Short and clean on the finish. **83** —*J.C. (6/1/2005)*

Sun Valley 2003 Merlot (Bulgaria) $10. Fresh and bouncy, with grapy, fruit-juicy flavors that lack true depth or richness. Still, it's cleanly made, young and has some appeal. **83** —*J.C. (6/1/2005)*

Sun Valley 2003 Sauvignon Blanc (Bulgaria) $10. Tart, lean, and citrusy, this extremely dry, earthy white needs a suitably bracing accompaniment, like fresh oysters. **82** —*J.C. (6/1/2005)*

VINI

Vini 2004 Cabernet Sauvignon (Thracian Valley) $8. Oak plays a large role in this wine, with plenty of vanilla flavor and aroma intermixed with hung meat and pepper spice. This wine has a dark feel, with big tannins, but it still manages to be round in the mouth, with a peppery, tannic finish. **84 Best Buy** —*M.D. (6/1/2006)*

Vini 2002 Cabernet Sauvignon (Sliven) $7. Lacks intensity, giving up modest earth and tart cherry flavors. **82** —*J.C. (6/1/2005)*

Vini 2002 Meritage (Sliven) $7. Although this may not come across like a Merlot, it still offers great value. Plenty of vanilla mixes with deep berry and spice aromas, while the dark, extracted mouth offers a lush feel with good tannin matched with black berry and white pepper. **86 Best Buy** —*M.D. (6/1/2006)*

Vini 2004 Merlot (Thracian Valley) $8. Dark and extracted, with oaky aromas of cola and vanilla. While this wine has some firm tannins and acidity, the mouth offers only tar and a dark extracted, ashy taste. **80** —*M.D. (6/1/2006)*

CANADA

CAVE SPRING

Cave Spring 1997 Estate Chardonnay (Niagara Peninsula) $12. 84 —*J.C. (8/1/1999)*

Cave Spring 1997 Gamay (Niagara Peninsula) $9. 84 —*J.C. (8/1/1999)*

Cave Spring 1997 Dry Reserve Riesling (Niagara Peninsula) $12. 87 — *J.C. (8/1/1999)*

Cave Spring 1999 Ice Wine Riesling (Niagara Peninsula) $50. Wow, is this sweet—tooth-achingly sweet. The aromas and flavors are relatively pure and free of botrytis; instead you get boatloads of ripe pear and melon flavors, huge thickness and weight, and decent acidity. Almost too rich and sweet for its own good. **88** —*J.C. (3/1/2001)*

Cave Spring 1997 Ice Wine Riesling (Niagara Peninsula) $48. 86 —*J.C. (8/1/1999)*

Cave Spring 1997 Indian Summer Riesling (Niagara Peninsula) $18. 92 —*J.C. (8/1/1999)*

Cave Spring 2003 Reserve Riesling (Niagara Peninsula) $13. Dry enough to please folks who think they don't like sweet wine, yet with enough residual sugar to please those who like a touch of sweetness, this wonderfully balanced Riesling from north of the border is a perfect summer sipper. Ripe peach and green apple flavors freshen up on the citrusy finish. **87** —*J.C. (8/1/2005)*

COLIO

Colio 1998 Icewine Riesling (Lake Erie) $NA. Shows pronounced oily, earthy, almost tobacco-like elements to its bouquet; also honey and clementines. Not overly rich, but flavorful and complete, with excellent balance. Like the other Colio Estate wines, this emphasizes subtle earth shadings over slap-you-in-the-face-fruit. **90** —*J.C. (3/1/2001)*

Colio 1998 Select Late Harvest Riesling (Lake Erie) $18. Smells oily, with a diesel-fuel note that some may find offputting. Rich and earthy on the palate, this bottling emphasizes spice, mineral, and loam flavors, not the bright fruit of so many other Ontario products. **86** —*J.C. (3/1/2001)*

HENRY OF PELHAM

Henry of Pelham 1998 Botrytis Affected Riesling (Niagara Peninsula) $30. Shows ample evidence of botrytis on the apricot-scented nose, with less-dominant aromas of ultraripe pears and peaches blending in. It's very juicy and fruity, with some lime-like acidity that keeps it fresh. Best with fresh fruits, or try with a foie gras appetizer. **88** —*J.C. (3/1/2001)*

Henry of Pelham 1999 Icewine Riesling (Niagara Peninsula) $50. A bit closed at first, then swirling, characteristic Riesling aromas of pears, golden delicious apples, and superripe peaches appear. Thick and intense, it's almost overwhelming in its honeyed richness. Sweet enough to pair with many desserts, but try it with blue-veined cheeses for a special treat. **91** —*J.C. (3/1/2001)*

Henry of Pelham 1998 Select Late Harvest Riesling (Niagara Peninsula) $23. Peaches and pears, lemons and grapefruits come together in this harmonious late harvest wine that shows little evidence of botrytis. The high acidity gives it balance and makes it a great foil for fruit-garnished foie gras. **87** —*J.C. (3/1/2001)*

Henry of Pelham 1999 Special Select Late Harvest Vidal Blanc (Niagara Peninsula) $25. Vidal has a peculiar bouquet that I have a hard time describing. This one boasts muskmelon, litchi, and kumquat aromas, backed by a honeyed sweetness and grapefruit-like acids. Intense—verging on overblown—this is a fine example of what this French-American hybrid is capable of producing. **87** —*J.C. (3/1/2001)*

INNISKILLIN

Inniskillin 2004 Icewine Cabernet Franc (Niagara Peninsula) $100. Cab Franc icewines have some reddish color, this one looking a brownish-red. Cran-apple on the nose, the flavors are not traditional for an icewine, with cranberry and apple hinting at bubblegum sweetness. But the structure is, with acidity wrapping the medium-full body. **86** —*M.D. (8/1/2006)*

Inniskillin 2003 Icewine Riesling (Niagara Peninsula) $80. Lovely icewine, balancing orange-marmalade sweetness against zesty acidity. Not overly heavy, yet completely mouthfilling, with hints of apple and orange blossoms on the nose. **92** —*J.C. (9/1/2005)*

Inniskillin 2003 Icewine Vidal Blanc (Niagara Peninsula) $59. Brilliant stuff that shows not all hybrids deserve to be scoffed at. Flamboyant aromas of dried pineapple combine with fresh apricots and honey in this rich, unctuous wine that's incredibly sweet yet not cloying, thanks to vibrant acidity. **94** —*J.C. (9/1/2005)*

Inniskillin 1997 Oak Aged Ice Wine Vidal Blanc (Niagara Peninsula) $80. Inniskillin continues to push the boundaries of icewine, as evidenced by this wood-aged Vidal. The vanilla and spice of oak barrels partially masks some of the stranger Vidal aromas, allowing the apricot and peach scents to come to the fore. There are some creamy lactic notes on the finish that detract slightly, but this is a very good effort at an entirely different genre. **89** —*J.C. (3/1/2001)*

Inniskillin 2003 Oak Aged Icewine Vidal Blanc (Niagara Peninsula) $80. If you like your wines over-the-top sweet, this one's for you. Sticky and sweet, with powerful flavors of orange marmalade. Impressive, but lacking the precise, focused nature of the very best. **91** —*J.C. (9/1/2005)*

Inniskillin 2002 Sparkling Icewine Vidal Blanc (Niagara Peninsula) $90. Perfumey aromas of corn, melon, and ginger set the stage for one of the more unique wines on the market. It's a true dessert-level ice wine, but one with a creamy mouthfeel, thanks to the multitude of tiny bubbles that seem to aid in balancing the sweetness. Strange at first, but tasty. **91** —*J.C. (9/1/2005)*

Inniskillin 1998 Sparkling Icewine Vidal Blanc (Niagara Peninsula) $83. A real oddball that's musky, melony, sweet, and—yes–bubbly. Vidal is a French-American hybrid with some strange petrolly aromatics that take some getting used to, and they're well-displayed in this example that gets its bubbles from fermentation in sealed tanks, trapping the naturally occurring carbon dioxide. **84** —*J.C. (3/1/2001)*

JACKSON-TRIGGS

Jackson-Triggs 2002 Proprietor's Reserve Cabernet Sauvignon (Okanagan Valley) $15. This round, supple Cabernet boasts easy-to-drink flavors of black cherries, earth, and tobacco. Notes of vanilla add interest, while the soft tannins on the finish give it just enough structure. **85** —*J.C. (9/1/2005)*

Jackson-Triggs 2002 Proprietor's Grand Reserve Okanagan Estate Meritage (Okanagan Valley) $25. From its inviting aromas of vanilla, dried herbs, and black cherries to its lushly tannic finish, this wine strikes all the right notes. Supple and fleshy in the mouth, it lacks only the complexity and intensity to push it to the next level. Drink now–2010, although it might age even longer. **88** —*J.C. (9/1/2005)*

Jackson-Triggs 1998 Proprietor's Grand Reserve Ice Wine Riesling (Okanagan Valley) $60. Absolutely luscious, rich, viscous and full-on, with apricot, peach, caramel crème brûlée flavors at the center. Good acidity leaves a freshness on the finish, with lengthy hints of honey and vanilla. **92** —*J.M. (12/1/2002)*

Jackson-Triggs 2003 Proprietor's Grande Reserve Sauvignon Blanc (Okanagan Valley) $20. Definitely has a personality all its own. Our panel all found aromas of baby food and applesauce, but nobody called it offputting. Quite sweet throughout, with flavors of honeydew, pear, and ultraripe peach. A slick wine with no bite. **87** *(7/1/2005)*

Jackson-Triggs 2003 Proprietors' Reserve Icewine (187mL) Vidal Blanc (Niagara Peninsula) $20. The smaller bottle size makes this perfect for more intimate gatherings. Peach and creamed corn aromas give way to mouthfilling honey flavors. Fat, but not that complex or long. **87** —*J.C. (9/1/2005)*

MALIVOIRE

Malivoire 2004 Estate Bottled Pinot Gris (Niagara Peninsula) $16. Just too lean and lemony to be really pleasurable, but it's a cleanly made, tart dry wine with hints of pear. **82** —*J.C. (2/1/2006)*

MISSION HILL

Mission Hill 1999 Merlot (Okanagan Valley) $9. From a well-regarded winery in British Columbia, this rather oaky effort shows why Bordeaux varietals are a tough go that far north. Light cherry flavors and plenty of acid sum up this lightweight, simple wine. **82** —*P.G. (12/31/2001)*

Mission Hill 1999 Bin 99 Pinot Noir (Okanagan Valley) $8. From British Columbia comes this light, well-made Pinot. Miles away from the jammy, beefy Oregon style, it shows delicate flavors of beet, cola, and cracker. The tart berry fruit is delicate; light spice, stem, and leaf take over the finish. **85** —*P.G. (12/31/2001)*

Mission Hill 2004 Five Vineyards Icewine 187ML Riesling (Okanagan Valley) $20. Rich and syrupy, this wine has plenty of acidity to balance, leaving mouthwatering flavors of baked apple and golden raisin. The wine has a long finish with pineapple flavors that coat the mouth. Musky on the nose, showing vanilla bean. **91** —*M.D. (8/1/2006)*

Mission Hill 2004 Reserve Icewine Riesling (Okanagan Valley) $60. The nose explodes with oily aromas of dried apricot, golden raisin, lemon, and musk. Full, rich, and oily, with similar flavors to Mission Hill's other icewines, predominantly pineapple. Acidity tickles the tongue, leaving the mouth asking for more on the finish. **90** —*M.D. (8/1/2006)*

Mission Hill 2004 S.L.C. Icewine Riesling (Okanagan Valley) $85. This wine looks like liquid sunshine and smells like a mixture of tropical fruit nectar, vanilla, and pastry dough. Rich flavors of tropical fruits and apple custard coat the mouth, while backing acidity keeps it from being cloying. The finish is mouthwatering and long, with pineapple dominating. **92 Cellar Selection** —*M.D. (8/1/2006)*

Mission Hill 1999 Estate Syrah (Okanagan Valley) $16. Syrah's future is already secure in Washington, so why not the Okanagan Valley, British Columbia's premier region? Berry, chocolate, pepper, and spice notes in this mid-weight, even wine make a plausible case for the grape in Canada's Pacific province. Tart-sweet fruit is checked by a bit too much wood, but it's solid, closing with modest tannins. **85** *(10/1/2001)*

OSOYOOS LAROSE

Osoyoos Larose 2002 Le Grand Vin Bordeaux Blend (Okanagan Valley) $35. The second vintage of this heralded joint venture between Vincor (owner of Jackson-Triggs) and Groupe Taillan of Bordeaux is an intriguing wine that starts with vibrant red berries, dried herbs, and cracked-pepper notes but thins out a bit on the finish. Credit the creamy midpalate to consulting enologist Michel Rolland. **87** —*J.C. (9/1/2005)*

PENINSULA RIDGE

Peninsula Ridge 2003 Sauvignon Blanc (Niagara Peninsula) $25. This Canadian entry is a dead knock-off for a pungent, prickly New Zealand wine, and two of our panelists went gaga over the grassy, pickled aromas. They also enjoyed the sharp passion fruit and grapefruit aromas and had no major difficulties with the canned vegetable notes that turned off our third rater. All said, look for good weight, balance, and a forwardness not often replicated. **90** *(7/1/2005)*

CHINA

CHINA SILK

China Silk NV Marco Polo White Wine White Blend (China) $7. This Chardonnay-Riesling blend has faint hints of banana and white fruits leading to more of the same in the mouth. Dry, with an almost tannic feel and a short finish of peach. **82** —*M.D. (8/1/2006)*

CROATIA

CARA

Cara 2001 Posip (Croatia) $16. Smells rich as a dessert, with white chocolate, buttery vanilla, and lemon meringue pie aromas. But is surprisingly dry, with a rich array of lemon custard flavor and big, bright acidity. Attractive and clean, and something different for a change. **87** —*S.H. (10/1/2004)*

FERA VINO

Fera Vino NV Grasevina (Slavonija) Welschriesling (Croatia) $9. From the grape also known as Welschriesling, an aromatic, fragrant wine brimming with peach, mineral, wildflower, and citrus. Bone dry and tart with high acidity, this refreshing sipper is like a cross between Sauvignon Blanc and Riesling. **86** —*S.H. (10/1/2004)*

KATUNAR

Katunar 2002 Zlahtina (Croatia) $15. A highly fragrant white with a family resemblance to Riesling. Honeysuckle, gardenia, citrus, peach aromas lead to intense citrus flavors, with a dry streak of mineral. High acid and bone dry, this will be a great cocktail wine, or try with oysters. **87** —*S.H. (10/1/2004)*

CYPRUS

DOMAINE NICOLAIDES

Domaine Nicolaides NV Xinisteri (Lemesos) $10. A unique wine, this has sweet aromas of honeysuckle, mint, and oak. Low in acidity with a medium body, it gives the impression of oiliness, and has strange muscat-like flavors with oak and sawdust hints. **80** —*M.D. (12/15/2006)*

K&K VASILIKON

K&K Vasilikon 2003 Agios Onoufrios Red Blend (Kathikas) $10. This blend of the Cyprian Ofthalmo, Mourvèdre, and Cabernet Sauvignon has strange aromas of prune, wet grass, and beet. But rhubarb flavors and a sweetness hide the tannins and gives it a smooth feel. **81** —*M.D. (12/15/2006)*

TSIAKKAS

Tsiakkas 2003 Oak Aged Cabernet Sauvignon (Pitsilia Mountains) $22. A surprise from this region of Cyprus, this is a fully modern, smooth effort. The nose is a bit rambunctious, and the wine needs time to knit together, but it has good tannic structure and nicely integrated oak that offers cola flavors and aromas of vanilla, tobacco, and spice to accompany the sweet blackberry and cherry flavors. The finish is long and mouthwatering. **88** —*M.D. (12/15/2006)*

GEORGIA

TELAVI

Telavi 2002 Saperavi (Napareuli) $13. This late-ripening Russian grape delivers plenty of fruit and enjoyable drinking in this deep red wine. Sweet holiday spice, vanilla, and plum make for an enjoyable nose, while the fruity, round palate is backed by tobacco and more spice. The rich fruit should pair well with hamburgers. **85** —*M.D. (6/1/2006)*

Telavi 2000 Saperavi (Georgia) $13. This wine still has a purple color after six years, and fresh aromas of purple fruit, vanilla, and some bramble. Oak is displayed in the mouth with a dusty but smooth feel, counterbalancing the good acid, while the purple fruit is strong, although showing some green stemmy notes. **84** —*M.D. (6/1/2006)*

Telavi 2002 Tsinandali White Blend (Georgia) $9. Vanilla and banana herald the nose on this blend of Rkatsiteli and Mtsvane, indigenous grapes of Georgia. The wine is big and round in the mouth, but dull, with flavors of banana and vanilla dust. **81** —*M.D. (6/1/2006)*

GREECE

A. BABATZIM

A. Babatzim 2002 Domaine Anestis Babatzimopoulos Malvasia Bianca (Vin de Pays de Macedoine) $22. If you know Italian Malvasia, you know what to expect from this version—bland melon and pear flavors. What you might not expect is for the wine to be slightly off-dry and to finish with a perky tang, making it a candidate to pair with Asian dishes. **84** —*J.C. (9/2/2004)*

A. PARPAROUSSIS

A. Parparoussis 1999 Muscat de Rio Patras Muscat (Muscat of Patras) $26. Lightly sundried for 10 days and then lightly fortified to stop the fermentation, this sweet Muscat is crammed with flavors of dried apricots, pears, and oranges. Despite relatively low acidity, it doesn't seem all that sweet—probably best sipped on its own, with fresh fruit or with cheese. **87** —*J.C. (9/2/2004)*

ACHAIA CLAUSS

Achaia Clauss 2000 Agiorgitiko (Corinth) $10. 83 —*J.C. (9/2/2004)*

Achaia Clauss NV Danielis Agiorgitiko (Greece) $10. This wine has a simple mouthfeel, but plump cherry flavors make up for it. Herbal notes and aromas of cola and green bean keep it from being too straightforward. **85 Best Buy** —*M.D. (10/1/2006)*

Achaia Clauss NV Demestica Red Agiorgitiko (Greece) $9. Rosy color hints at the lightness of this wine, while sweet red fruit and spice flavors pair with gym bag aromas. **81** —*M.D. (10/1/2006)*

Achaia Clauss NV Demestica Rosé Agiorgitiko (Greece) $9. The color is in the rust-salmon family. Aromas are of cherry and rose, while the fairly lively palate has more rustic flavors of cola and cherry fruit. **82** —*M.D. (12/15/2006)*

Achaia Clauss 1998 Château Clauss Cabernet Blend (Peloponnese) $12. 82 —*J.C. (9/2/2004)*

Achaia Clauss 1996 Mavrodaphne of Patras Reserve Mavrodaphne (Peloponnese) $20. Made much like tawny Port, this russet-brown wine features aromas of coffee, toffee, and walnuts. It's sweet but not overly so, with hints of maple syrup that add a sense of refinement to the straightforward flavors. **86** —*J.C. (9/2/2004)*

Achaia Clauss NV Muscat (Muscat of Patras) $9. Aromas of orange marmalade and superripe pears fold in touches of honey and caramel in the mouth, where the wine is sweet and plump. Finishes with medium length and a slight burnt-sugar note. **84** —*J.C. (9/2/2004)*

Achaia Clauss NV Muscat de Patras Muscat (Patras) $9. 84 —*J.C. (9/1/2004)*

AGROS

Agros 2003 Agiorgitiko (Peloponnese) $10. 84 —*J.C. (9/2/2004)*

Agros 2003 Assyrtico (Santorini) $14. Peach, anise, and citrus aromas set the stage for this light, tart wine whose flavors turn lemony and crisp. Really zingy on the finish. **85** —*J.C. (9/2/2004)*

Agros 2002 Muscat de Rio Patras Muscat (Patras) $7. A heavy, rich Muscat, not as sweet as you might expect, but slightly more alcoholic. Delicate almond paste, orange zest, and melon notes are a bit over-powered by the warmth on the finish. **84** —*J.C. (9/2/2004)*

ALEXANDROS MEGAPANOS

Alexandros Megapanos 2002 Savatiano (Spata) $8. Light in body and fla-vor intensity, but boasts a helping of stone-dust minerality to go along with its clean pineapple, pear, and apple flavors. **85 Best Buy** —*J.C. (9/2/2004)*

Alexandros Megapanos 2003 Xinomavro (Amindeo) $10. 81 —*J.C. (9/2/2004)*

ALPHA ESTATE

Alpha Estate 2004 Estate Red Blend (Macedonia) $35. Syrah makes up nearly a third of Alpha Estate's vineyards and 60% of this flagship blend, with Xinomavro and Merlot splitting the difference. One of the effects of vineyards above 2,000 feet is high acidity. Although a bit tart, the wine has plenty of plum and menthol in addition to bit-ter cherry flavors and a meaty character. The acidity makes this a great match for food, and time may soften this wine. **87** —*M.D. (10/1/2006)*

Alpha Estate 2003 One Red Blend (Greece) $65. An unusual blend of 60% Tannat and 40% Montepulciano, the first from Greece (or any-where), this has a beautiful nose of cured meat, fresh crushed berries, and vibrant vanilla. Tannat's heavy tannins are present, as is plentiful acidity. Dark purple fruit and vanilla flavors are pure and modern, but this wine would be better if it wasn't so tart. **86** —*M.D. (10/1/2006)*

Alpha Estate 2005 Sauvignon Blanc (Florina) $28. Full-on aromas of fresh-ly squeezed nectarine rev up this dry white, followed by wet stone and lime. Firm in the mouth, white fruit flavors are slow to emerge, hiding behind steely mineral and a hint of crushed peanut. Lime and citrus notes finally come round, turning towards nectarine on the long, acidic finish. **89** —*M.D. (10/1/2006)*

ANTONOPOULOS

Antonopoulos 2001 Cabernet-Nea Dris Cabernet Blend (Greece) $23. This blend of Cabernet Sauvignon and Cabernet Franc has an interesting nose of cherry, menthol, tobacco, and plenty of oaky vanilla. It's full-bodied and spicy, with good tannins, and plenty of oaky shadings to the cherry fruit and chalky mouthfeel. **87** —*M.D. (10/5/2006)*

Antonopoulos 2002 Cabernet-Nea Dris Cabernet Sauvignon-Cabernet Franc (Greece) $26. Made in an Old World style, this dry, earthy wine has aromas of vanilla and Asian spice, eucalyptus, and earth that picks up secondary aromas with time. The tannins are developed, the wine having spent plenty of time in wood, while the palate has a medium weight and good acidity. Earth and eucalyptus dominate the mouth, supported by lesser flavors of red berry and cola, which linger on the long finish. This is a wine that needs a decanter or time in the glass to open up, and can be drunk over the next five years. **88** —*M.D. (12/15/2006)*

Antonopoulos 2002 Chardonnay in New Oak Chardonnay (Greece) $25. 83 —*J.C. (9/2/2004)*

Antonopoulos 2002 Moschofilero (Mantinia) $10. 84 —*J.C. (9/2/2004)*

Antonopoulos 2003 Collection White Dry Table Wine White Blend (Greece) $15. Shows some toasty, caramel-popcorn scents, but also pleasant enough peach, pineapple, and lemon flavors. Finishes intense-ly citrusy, with mouthpuckering acids that scream for food. **86** —*J.C. (9/2/2004)*

ARGYROS

Argyros 2003 Canava Assyrtico (Santorini) $19. Tastes like unripe straw-berries doused in lemon juice—but in a good way. Slightly chalky mouthfeel, with a tart, acid-dominated finish that leaves the mouth per-fectly fresh and clean, ready for the next bite of fresh sardines. **86** —*J.C. (9/2/2004)*

Argyros 2004 Estate Assyrtico (Santorini) $26. Looks like liquid sunshine, and has a creamy texture to match. Fills the mouth with warm flavors of banana and citrus, while an undercurrent of acidity keeps this struc-tured. Finishes with a nice mineral note. **87** —*M.D. (10/1/2006)*

Argyros 2004 Estate Barrel Assyrtico (Santorini) $33. Strong summertime winds helped the grapes maintain high acidity in this big wine. Toasty on the nose, buttery and smooth in the mouth. Although quite dry, it shows solid white fruit with flavors of papaya and peach. Finishes long, with a popcorn note. **88** —*M.D. (10/1/2006)*

Argyros NV Atlantis Mandilaria (Santorini) $17. Starts off a bit rough, with leather, scorched wood, and roasted fruit aromas, but airs out gracefully, delivering big, jammy plum and cherry fruit, shadings of anise and soft tannins on the finish. The grape variety is Mandilaria. **88** —*J.C. (9/2/2004)*

Argyros NV Atlantis White Blend (Santorini) $15. Starts out plump-seem-ing, then finishes with powerful acidity. In between you get flavors of apples, pears, and citrus fruits, also hints of fresh herbs. **85** —*J.C. (9/2/2004)*

Argyros 2004 Atlantis White Blend (Santorini) $16. Not a standout wine, but solid, with flavors of baked apple and holiday spice. Dry, with cit-rusy acids, and a crisp finish, this wine is suitable for oily fish served in the Greek way: grilled with olive oil and lemon. **85** —*M.D. (10/1/2006)*

AVANTIS

Avantis 2005 Roditis (Beotia) $17. Lemon skin and citrus scents are pleas-ant but mild. The wine has an almost creamy feel to it, plus lemony citrus flavors. Finishes tart and crisp. **81** —*M.D. (10/1/2006)*

Avantis 2005 Fumé Sauvignon Blanc (Beotia) $18. A crowd pleaser, this easy-to-like Sauvignon has plenty of tropical fruit wrapped in a creamy body and dashed with a hint of oak. A steely mineral core shows it's seri-ous, while the grape's aromatics are displayed in the peach fuzz and melon nose. **87** —*M.D. (10/1/2006)*

Avantis 2002 Syrah (Beotia) $25. A serious attempt, this wine has plenty of dark fruit and spice flavors, with a note of mashed raisins. A hint of sweetness softens plenty of firm, chalky tannins, while the nose offers prune and dehydrated blueberry aromas. **85** —*M.D. (10/1/2006)*

BOUTARI

Boutari 2000 Agiorgitiko (Corinth) $20. Aromas of huckleberries, dried spices, and leather lead gracefully into a soft, lush wine that avoids any sense of hardness. Very easy to drink. **87** —*J.C. (9/2/2004)*

Boutari 2004 Agiorgitiko Agiorgitiko (Nemea) $20. A simple, Beaujolais-like nose of purple fruit, grass, and earth leads to an equally simple palate with a nice, smooth feel. Cinnamon and brown spice emerge from grapey flavors while a mineral streak runs through the middle. **84** —*M.D. (12/15/2006)*

Boutari 2004 Nemea Agiorgitiko (Nemea) $14. Cherry and cinnamon emerge from darker flavors of purple fruit and a hint of barnyard, while the hard tannins outweigh this wine's medium body. **83** —*M.D. (12/15/2006)*

Boutari 2003 Assyrtico (Santorini) $15. Not only is this 100% Assyrtiko, it's fermented and aged entirely in stainless steel, which completely pre-serves its biting acidity. It has some waxy, citrusy aromas and flavors, but they are secondary to the wine's dominating acids, which leave the mouth clean and tingling after each taste. **85** —*J.C. (9/2/2004)*

Boutari 2001 Assyrtico (Cyclades) $15. This barrel-fermented Assyrtiko shows hints of toasty oak, minerality, and honeysuckle on the nose, and flavors of preserved lemons. Mouthwatering acidity with a touch of salinity. Great structure, with baked sourdough notes. A wonderful mar-riage of fruit and oak, to drink with full flavored fish dishes. **88** — *(11/15/2002)*

Boutari 2004 Kallisti Assyrtico (Santorini) $24. The shy nose hints at plantain, caramel, peach pith, and a touch of diesel. The palate follows through with tropical fruit and citrus pith, again with diesel. A very nice wine, only missing some midpalate heft to fully complete the picture.**85** —M.D. (10/1/2006)

Boutari 2002 Kallisti Assyrtico (Santorini) $19. This is 100% Assyrtiko from Santorini, barrel-fermented in French oak. As a result, it shows some nutty, toasty elements on the nose, some softer peach fruit on the palate, and then shows trademark Assyrtiko acids on the finish, finishing a bit hard and tart.**87** —J.C. (9/2/2004)

Boutari 2000 Ode Cabernet Sauvignon-Agiorgitiko Cabernet Blend (Corinth) $25. This wine ably marries the sturdy dark cassis fruit of its 50% Cabernet Sauvignon with brighter, cherry notes from its 50% Agiorgitiko. It's all supported by a framework of toast and vanilla from a year in oak barrels.**88** —J.C. (9/2/2004)

Boutari 2005 Moschofilero (Mantinia) $17. Boutari seems to make lip-smacking wine with ease, like this dry, minerally white. Aromas of citrus, peach, and even spice presage intense citrus flavors with tropical fruit accents. Simply delicious.**87** —M.D. (12/15/2006)

Boutari 2003 Moschofilero (Mantinia) $15. Moschofilero is a grape that the Boutari company has high hopes for, as sales of the wine have sky-rocketed in the U.S. Pleasant floral aromas lead into a wine with peach, strawberry, and herb flavors. The mouthfeel is plump, the finish virtually dry. A pleasant cocktail-hour white when you're looking for something a little different.**86** —J.C. (9/2/2004)

Boutari 2001 Moschofilero (Mantinia) $12. Wildflowers, roses, apricots, and peaches leap out of the glass. Lively acidity, with fruit dominating the palate. A little yeasty, with lingering floral notes.**88** (11/15/2002)

Boutari NV Muscat (Samos) $14. With only one winery on the island of Samos, the quality of this bottling depends on the Boutari company's selection of lots. This orangey, honeyed bottling was one of the best basic Muscats of Samos we tried, balancing sugar, acid, and alcohol very well.**87** —J.C. (9/2/2004)

Boutari 2002 Skalani Red Blend (Crete) $25. Aged in new oak, this impressively concentrated, dark wine has soaked up much of the oak flavor, showing only traces of vanilla and coffee. The fruit is what shows on the surface, powerful plum and licorice flavors. this blend of 70% Kotsifali and 30% Mandilari is approachable now.**89** —J.C. (9/2/2004)

Boutari 1999 Xinomavro Merlot Red Blend (Imathia) $18. An interesting blend in which the Merlot softens the tannins of the Xynomavro. Slightly toasted, with tobacco and blueberries. Medium tannins but lacking personality.**86** — (11/15/2002)

Boutari 2003 Domaine Matsa Savatiano (Attica) $20. A little bit of this and a little bit of that—this wine has it all, from peaches, to grapefruit to nuts. Lightweight, with a long, harmonious finish.**86** —J.C. (9/2/2004)

Boutari 2005 Kretikos Vilana (Crete) $10. This wine has mild aromas of macadamia, pineapple, and musky flower. On the palate, these same flavors are nice but bland. 100% Vilana.**81** —M.D. (12/15/2006)

Boutari 2003 Fantaxometocho White Blend (Paros) $20. This intriguing blend of 70% barrel-fermented Chardonnay and 30% stainless steel-fermented Vilana comes from the island of Crete. The Chardonnay component provides toasty, nutty, and peachy nuances, while the Vilana gives fine acidity and bright green apple flavors. Give it a few months in the bottle to come together.**88** —J.C. (9/2/2004)

Boutari 2004 Xinomavro (Naoussa) $15. One of Greece's biggest wine exporters, Boutari has the formula for smooth, accessible wines. A soft red color leads to a big but polished Xinomavro with chocolaty flavors of mixed berry, spice, and a spritz of lemon. A great match for roast rack of lamb.**88** —M.D. (12/15/2006)

Boutari 1999 Grande Reserve Xinomavro (Naoussa) $17. Lots of toast and dried spices, but also lovely strawberries and cream; bright red fruit with underpinnings of earth and leather. This spent two years in French oak, then two years in bottle prior to being released, so it's ready to drink now.**88** —J.C. (9/2/2004)

CALLIGA

Calliga NV Rubis Agiorgitiko (Greece) $10. Red berry and cinnamon aromas start off this wine, and it has racy red fruit in the mouth. A bit rustic, but nice.**83** —M.D. (10/1/2006)

CHÂTEAU JULIA

Château Julia 2000 Merlot (Adriani) $23. There is a lot of salinity in the bouquet of this wine, which makes it reminiscent of the seashore. But the red berry fruit comes through on the palate with char and earth. Smooth on the finish, as the acids balance the tannins.**87** —C.S. (11/15/2002)

CHÂTEAU NICO LAZARIDI

Château Nico Lazaridi 2003 White Dry Wine White Blend (Drama) $22. Gold in color, with heavy aromas of corn oil, buttered root vegetables, and chemical. A very strange bird that seems a touch oxidized. The edges are duller than a butter knife.**80** (7/1/2005)

DOMAINE CONSTANTIN LAZARIDI

Domaine Constantin Lazaridi 1998 Amethystos Cabernet Sauvignon (Drama) $30. This Cabernet Sauvignon from the Drama region might sell better in the United States if they would display that varietal on the front label. It is a nice Cab, with aromas of dried meats, black pepper, and soft cheese. The palate brings juicy cherries and a chalky minerality, with nice fruit-tannin balance and a supple finish.**89** —C.S. (11/15/2002)

Domaine Costa Lazaridi 2002 Amethystos Cabernet Blend (Vin de Pays de Macedoine) $19. With its delicate red-fruit flavors that seem to morph between cherry, raspberry, and strawberry, this blend of Cabernet Sauvignon, Merlot, and Limnio actually seems Pinot-esque. Vanilla and dried spices show on the nose, and firm tannins surface on the finish.**85** —J.C. (9/2/2004)

Domaine Costa Lazaridi 2003 Amethystos Red Cabernet Blend (Macedonia) $18. A blend of Cabernet, Merlot, and Limnio, this is a young wine with nice fruit but it's lacking in complexity. Grapey on the nose, with grass, spice and hints of coffee emerging, the palate is soft with dusty tannins. A mineral, chalky feel coats the mouth, and the grapey flavors backed by blueberry pie don't diminish it.**85** —M.D. (12/15/2006)

Domaine Costa Lazaridi 2002 Oenodea Cabernet Blend (Vin de Pays de Macedoine) $10.84 —J.C. (9/2/2004)

Domaine Costa Lazaridi 2005 Amethystos Rosé Cabernet Sauvignon (Drama) $14. Fresh, clean, and simple, this wine's raspberry-cherry flavors and crisp, dry feel make it a fine match for chicken Caesar salad.**83** —M.D. (12/15/2006)

Domaine Costa Lazaridi 2001 Cava Amethystos Cabernet Sauvignon (Drama) $30. Although the oak in this wine has settled, it still coats the mouth with a smooth film. Grape, clay, and barnyard aromas lead the way, with more barnyard and berry fruit flavors following. Drink up.**85** —M.D. (10/1/2006)

Domaine Costa Lazaridi 2002 Château Julia Chardonnay (Drama) $14.83 —J.C. (9/2/2004)

Domaine Costa Lazaridi 2005 Château Julia Chardonnay (Drama) $15. A straightforward Chardonnay, with citrus and white stone fruit flavors placed in a round, low-acid wine. Won't offend, nor will it excite.**83** — M.D. (10/1/2006)

Domaine Costa Lazaridi 2004 Amethystos Fumé Sauvignon Blanc (Drama) $16. Oak leads off the nose, then does most of the talking for this wine, with vanilla and toast notes throughout. Borders on too much oak, but some ripe white fruit shows through the toasty veneer, while time in the bottle has lent the wine an appealing creaminess.**88** —M.D. (10/1/2006)

Domaine Costa Lazaridi 2003 Amethystos White White Blend (Vin de Pays de Macedoine) $14. This open and welcoming blend of Sauvignon Blanc, Sémillon, and Assyrtiko starts off with pear and apple scents that glide easily into plump stone-fruit flavors. A bit of white-peppery spice kicks it up a notch on the finish.**86** —J.C. (9/2/2004)

Domaine Costa Lazaridi 2005 Amethystos White White Blend (Drama) $14. Sauvignon Blanc adds steel, Sémillon adds cream, and Assyrtico, body to this solid white. Flavors of peach, lime, and peanut follow a similar bouquet, and the wine has a steely finish of peach pit. A great accompaniment to grilled fish. **87** —*M.D. (10/1/2006)*

Domaine Costa Lazaridi 2002 Oenodea White Blend (Vin de Pays de Macedoine) $10. Starts off straightforward enough, with scents of green apple, pear, and citrus. Flavors are harder to describe, echoing the aromas but adding a note of vegetable oil. Medium-weight, and finishes with tart, lemon-lime flavors. **85** —*J.C. (9/2/2004)*

DOMAINE EVHARIS

Domaine Evharis 2004 Assyrtiko (Gerania) $22. Butterscotch, baked apple, and holiday spice aromas hint at the presence of oak, while the palate confirms it. Vanilla and toast flavors hide an undercurrent of pleasant musk in this medium-bodied wine. Finishes with good acidity. **84** —*M.D. (10/1/2006)*

Domaine Evharis 2003 Red Blend (Gerania) $28. A ripe, modern wine made for immediate enjoyment. A fanfare of plum and black cherry flavors usher in notes of chocolate powder and mineral. The fruit matches the full body, while smooth tannins and a hint of sweetness caress the mouth. Even the nose is burly, offering meaty aromas of kirsch liqueur, prune, caramel and coffee. **88** —*M.D. (10/1/2006)*

Domaine Evharis 2005 White Blend (Gerania) $22. Greenish-yellow, Chardonnay adds nice citrus notes to this Assyrtico-dominant wine. Crisp orange and peach flavors match well to a light-medium body and firm acidity. A great summer wine for keeping cool, or with Asian chicken salad. **85** —*M.D. (10/1/2006)*

DOMAINE GEROVASSILIOU

Domaine Gerovassiliou 2004 Chardonnay (Epanomi) $32. Evangelos Gerovassiliou has done a lot of work with French varieties in Greece, and this version has paid off. The oak is obvious but not dominant, offering aromas of butterscotch and toast and a smooth feel. The fruit stands on its own, with guava and peach flavors and aromas. Mint makes an appearance before the long, citrus-and-spice finish. **89** —*M.D. (10/1/2006)*

Domaine Gerovassiliou 2003 Malagauzia (Greece) $22. Not profoundly complex, but juicy and satisfying, this single-varietal Malagousia's aromas and flavors bring to mind nectarines and clementines harmoniously bound together with great balance and length. **88** — *J.C. (9/2/2004)*

Domaine Gerovassiliou 2002 Syrah (Epanomi) $24. A powerful wine with a fruity core, showing flavors of blueberry, cherry, and plum all wrapped in sweet tannin. Barnyard aromas add character to the ripe nose, while oak rounds out the wine, adding some dusty spice notes. **90 Editors' Choice** —*M.D. (10/1/2006)*

Domaine Gerovassiliou 2001 Syrah (Greece) $24. This is a nice facsimile of a northern Rhône, featuring a fine balance between the complementary herbs, berries and white pepper. Finishes long and crisp, with firm tannins. Drink now–2010+. **88** —*J.C. (9/2/2004)*

DOMAINE KARYDAS

Domaine Karydas 2003 Xinomavro (Naoussa) $25. A solid producer of Naoussa, Karydas has crafted a good Xinomavro with this vintage. Aromas come on strong with lush purple fruit, violets, pepper, and menthol, then pick up lemon, charred burger, and distinctive earthy elements. Flavors of pomegranate, menthol and plum all have a meaty feel, while hard tannins are matched by firm acidity. More of a curiosity wine than one to consume over light conversation. **85** —*M.D. (12/15/2006)*

Domaine Karydas 2001 Xinomavro (Naoussa) $20. At first glance, this Xinomavro seems overly tannic, but come back to it later, and the tannins have started to smooth out. Tough, leathery fruit backs sturdy, roasted plum flavors. Finishes with hints of tea and coffee. Decant in advance, or age 3–5 years. **88** —*J.C. (9/2/2004)*

DOMAINE MERCOURI

Domaine Mercouri 1999 Refosco Red Blend (Ilias) $15. Very earthy, with barnyard and bacon aromas. Fresh bright berries and cocoa on the palate. A note of toast throughout. Soft, yet structured, the tannins are velvety. Seductive and rounded. **89** — *(11/15/2002)*

DOUGOS

Dougos 2003 Methistanes Red Blend (Greece) $29. Starts off with green, herbal aromas that include spicy pepper, which is echoed on the palate in the form of green peppercorn. The mouthfeel is fine, but the lack of fruit in a wine this young doesn't bode well for the future. **82** —*M.D. (10/1/2006)*

ESTATE BIBLIA CHORA

Estate Biblia Chora 2002 Areti Red Agiorgitiko (Greece) $18. Young and grapy, with aromas of peanut and sawdust. This wine is decently structured, with young, chalky tannins supporting a medium body. Blackberry flavors add a hint of sweetness, and there are hints of holiday spice and nettles. May improve in a year. **85** —*M.D. (10/1/2006)*

Estate Biblia Chora 2004 Areti White Assyrtico (Pangeon) $18. Made from 100% Assyrtico, this starts off with a nice nose of peach, citrus, and a hint of smoke. The mouth is more muted, though flavors of yellow fruit and citrus do show through. Finishes dry, with tart strawberry flavor. **82** —*M.D. (10/1/2006)*

Estate Biblia Chora 2005 Ovilos White Blend (Pangeon) $40. A curiosity, this Assyrtico-Sémillon blend has a smooth, creamy feel that fills the mouth, and a pleasant nose of grapefruit and baked apple. Muted at first, flavors of citrus, baked apple, and vanilla toast are nicely integrated, picking up steam towards a firm, zesty finish. **87** —*M.D. (10/1/2006)*

Estate Biblia Chora 2005 Sauvignon Blanc-Assyrtico White Blend (Pangeon) $16. Cream and grapefruit aromas lead to flavors of more grapefruit, citrus, and spice. Light and creamy in the mouth, with a touch of oak, this wine is finely crafted, finishing lively. **87** —*M.D. (10/1/2006)*

GAIA ESTATE

Gaia Estate 2002 Agiorgitiko (Corinth) $30. Slightly horsey and leathery, but backed by black cherries and herbs. Despite its somewhat rustic aromas, it's smooth and plump in the mouth, with modern coffee and vanilla notes adding to the mix. Firmly tannic; might improve with 2–4 years of cellaring. **87** —*J.C. (9/2/2004)*

Gaia Estate 2003 14-18h Agiorgitiko (Peloponnese) $10. 83 —*J.C. (9/2/2004)*

Gaia Estate 2001 14-18h Koutsi Nemea Agiorgitiko (Corinth) $9. Crammed with strawberries, cranberries, and ripe cherries. Crisp acidity and soft tannins leave the palate fresh but dry. All of these qualities are enriched with 14–18 hours of skin contact (hence the wine's name). A wine for red wine drinkers when the weather is too hot. **87 Best Buy** *(11/15/2002)*

Gaia Estate 2002 Notios Agiorgitiko (Peloponnese) $11. Among several rustic and unfriendly Greek reds tasted for this report, this offering from Nemea stood out for its clean winemaking and vibrant fruit. Aromas are slightly floral, but also feature hints of strawberries and a bass note of leather; the fruit is lively and berry-flavored. It's very easy to drink and would make a fine Beaujolais alternative. Try it with lamb burgers for an interesting match. **86** —*M.S. (11/15/2003)*

Gaia Estate 2000 Superior Agiorgitiko (Corinth) $20. Licorice, blackberries, cherries, and vanilla toast. A well-balanced, ripe, fruit-forward New World-style wine with well-integrated tannins and acidity. **90** *(11/15/2002)*

GENTILINI

Gentilini 2003 Robola (Cephalonia) $15. Tart, lemony, and refreshing, with scents of green apples and lime alongside hints of peach and almond. It's a harmonious, lightweight blend of stone fruits and citrus with not an off note to be found. **87** —*J.C. (9/2/2004)*

Gentilini 2003 Classico White Blend (Cephalonia) $15. Slight copper tinge. Fresh apple and pear aromas are joined by hints of cherries and

OTHER INTERNATIONAL

anise before this lightweight wine finishes clean and a bit tangy. **85** —J.C. (9/2/2004)

GLINAVOS

Glinavos 1999 Red Velvet Red Blend (Greece) $17. 82 —J.C. (9/2/2004)

Glinavos 2001 Primus White Blend (Zitsa) $17. Made from the local Debina grape, this wine illustrates why the indigenous varieties of Greece are such a potential treasure trove: Aromas and flavors are strongly mineral, speaking of wet riverstones tinged with lime and anise. Light, clean, crisp, and well balanced. **87** —J.C. (9/2/2004)

HAGGIPAVLU

Haggipavlu 2000 Agiorgitiko (Corinth) $14. 84 —J.C. (9/2/2004)

Haggipavlu 2002 Moschofilero (Mantinia) $12. Not as plump or floral as most Moschofileros, but more minerally and intense. Mineral, lime, and ginger ale aromas are followed by lime, green apple, and mineral flavors. It's light in body, yet long on the finish. A top-notch seafood white. **87 Best Buy** —J.C. (9/2/2004)

HARLAFTIS

Harlaftis 2001 Argilos Agiorgitiko (Corinth) $12. 81 —J.C. (9/2/2004)

HATZI MICHALIS

Hatzi Michalis 2001 Kapnias Cabernet Blend (Opuntia Locris) $30. Seems rather mature for such a young wine, but that doesn't diminish its pleasure. It's a complex Cabernet Sauvignon that shows a vast array of scents and flavors, ranging from leather and damp earth to dates, plums, strawberries, and herbs. Classic tobacco flavors chime in on the finish. Drink now. **87** —J.C. (9/2/2004)

Hatzi Michalis 2002 Chardonnay (Atalanti Valley) $15. 83 —J.C. (9/2/2004)

Hatzi Michalis 2003 Laas White Blend (Opuntia Locris) $25. Smells fresh and clean, with hints of peaches and almonds followed by a citrusy finish. Brisk and refreshing. **85** —J.C. (9/2/2004)

HELIOPOULOS

Heliopoulos 2003 White Blend (Santorini) $16. Perhaps it's a trick of this wine's slightly coppery hue, but it seems to have some peach and strawberry scents along with intense pink grapefruit flavors. Its medium weight gives the impression of ripe fruit balanced by racy acids, finishing clean and crisp. **87** —J.C. (9/2/2004)

KARIPIDIS

Karipidis 2003 Cabernet Sauvignon (Thessalikos) $22. You could easily get lost in this wine's bouquet: plenty of new, spicy oak, scents of plum and blackberry pie, later picking up anise and coffee. On the palate, a streak of acidity is followed by soft, dry tannins, making way for more blackberry and anise. This wine has a lot of depth, and the firm tannins and solid acidity imply this could last for at least a decade, but it's very enjoyable now. **89** —M.D. (12/15/2006)

KATOGI & STROFILIA

Katogi & Strofilia 2000 Averoff Estate Bordeaux Blend (Metsovo) $23. International grape varieties (a blend of Cabernet Sauvignon, Merlot, and Cabernet Franc), but this is a unique wine nonetheless, with a rich texture and mouth-gripping tannins that frame ripe cassis and black cherry flavors. Drink 2007–2015. **91 Cellar Selection** —J.C. (9/2/2004)

Katogi & Strofilia 2001 Purple Earth Red Blend (Nemea) $22. Funky and rustic, this wine just makes the grade with metal-tinged flavors of pomegranate and dark fruit sitting atop dry, hard tannins. A blend of Agiorgitiko and Xinomavro. **80** —M.D. (12/15/2006)

KEO

Keo NV Domaine D'Ahera Mavro Red Blend (Cyprus) $11. A true country wine displaying aromas of black cherries, blueberries, hints of vanilla, and a whiff of Port. A little dusty with baked fruit and solid tannins but lacking acidity. **84** — (11/15/2002)

KIR-YIANNI

Kir-Yianni 2004 Paranga Red Blend (Vin de Pays de Macedoine) $13. Young flavors of grape, clay, and mineral have a touch of spice, while thyme is apparent on the nose. A food wine that calls for creamy pasta dishes to match the high acidity. **84** —M.D. (10/1/2006)

Kir-Yianni 2001 Paranga Red Blend (Vin de Pays de Macedoine) $15. 82 —J.C. (9/2/2004)

Kir-Yianni 2003 Yianakohori Red Blend (Vin de Pays d'Imithia) $25. Green bean and tobacco aromas lead to more of the same in the mouth, although grapy fruit shows through. This wine seems underripe, an oddity in 2003, with chalky tannins and spiky acidity. **82** —M.D. (10/1/2006)

Kir-Yianni 2003 Syrah (Vin de Pays d'Imithia) $40. Dark and ripe, this inky purple wine has coffee, roast plum, cherry, and leather aromas that lead to more of the same with vanilla and a touch of barnyard in the mouth. Smooth and cultivated on the palate, with a big feel cut by solid tannins, the finish turns dry with coffee grind flavors. **89** —M.D. (10/1/2006)

Kir-Yianni 2005 Samaropetra White Blend (Florina) $14. Very pale, with a green tinge and aromas of vanilla, nectarine, and lychee, this blend, (70% Roditis with Sauvignon Blanc and a touch of Gewürztraminer) is an enjoyable quaffing wine. You'll find citrus, orange, and spice flavors accented by vanilla in this fine, balanced offering. **87** —M.D. (12/15/2006)

Kir-Yianni 2003 Samaropetra White Blend (Florina) $13. This light, refreshing blend of Sauvignon Blanc, Gewürztraminer, and Roditis features peach and pear aromas accented by a permeating anise-pepper component. Flavors are less spicy, marked more by melon, white peach, and citrus. **87** —J.C. (9/2/2004)

Kir-Yianni 2005 Akakies Xinomavro (Amyndeon) $11. Hints of pickle quickly blow off to reveal juicy red berry aromas, while the smooth, almost oaky feel has good cherry, vanilla, and wafer flavors. Simply pleasurable, rather than intense. **85** —M.D. (12/15/2006)

Kir-Yianni 2003 Akakies Xinomavro (Amyntaion) $11. Boldly flavored and assertive, with distinctive aromas and flavors of strawberries, cherry tomatoes, and herbs like oregano and basil. This highly individual rosé would be a good match to various summery main-course salads. **87** —J.C. (9/2/2004)

Kir-Yianni 2001 Ramnista Xinomavro (Naoussa) $22. Xinomavro, meaning acid-black, is one of Greece's better indigenous reds and the only variety in Naoussa. It can make wines with firm acidity and jackhammer tannins, as in this example, which also shows a spicy nose of black pepper, coffee, and red fruit. Flavors are a bit darker and sweeter, to match the heavy tannins, with black spicy fruit, coffee, and a touch of chocolate. Will soften a bit with time. **89** —M.D. (12/15/2006)

KOUROS

Kouros 2000 Agiorgitiko (Corinth) $9. 80 —J.C. (9/2/2004)

Kouros 2003 Red Agiorgitiko (Nemea) $9. Cinnamon, spice, and red berry aromas are touched with coffee. Light flavors of root beer and red berry meet hints of spice. Structured for easy drinking with a smooth cola finish, this is a wine you could chill a bit and have with smoked meats. **85 Best Buy** —M.D. (10/1/2006)

Kouros 1999 Red Blend (Corinth) $9. Great aromas of marinated grilled meat and steak sauce. The flavors are also meaty and blend in mulberry and spice. Medium-weight, ending simple and soft. Have with grilled lamb or by itself. **85 Best Buy** —C.S. (11/15/2002)

Kouros 2002 Roditis (Patras) $9. Not really, but it shows some similarities in its lemon-lime and ginger aromas and lightbodied, stony, minerally flavors. Made from Roditis grapes, a main component of Retsina. **84** —J.C. (9/2/2004)

Kouros 2004 White Roditis (Patras) $9. The nose opens with a hint of oak that leads to flowery musk. Straightforward in the mouth, with evergreen and hints of white fruit. **80** —M.D. (10/1/2006)

KOURTAKI

Kourtaki NV Muscat (Samos) $9. The bouquet is filled with the aromas of honey and overripe oranges and pears. The wine is very orangey on the palate, without a lot of nuance, but it finishes long, buoyed by mouth-watering acidity. **86 Best Buy** —*J.C. (9/2/2004)*

Kourtaki 2003 Vin de Crete Red Red Blend (Crete) $8. Starts off simple and stays that way, with dark berry flavor and a strange grassy note. **80** —*M.D. (10/1/2006)*

KTIMA VOYATZI

Ktima Voyatzi 2001 Red Blend (Greece) $24. First, this wine has fruit—big fruit. Black cherries, even some grapiness. Second, the wine also has tannins—big tannins. Mouthstarching tannins. Will age bring this wine balance and harmony? Frankly, the score is a hedge—this is uncharted territory for us. **85** —*J.C. (9/2/2004)*

Ktima Voyatzi 2003 Red Red Blend (Vin de Pays de Velvendo) $28. Green herbs add some complexity to this dark wine, giving life to red fruit flavors and berry aromas. Full and dusty in the mouth, with dry tannins and a nice finish, this is a new age Greek blend, incorporating indigenous Xinomavro and Maschomavro with Cab and Merlot. **85** —*M.D. (10/1/2006)*

KYR-YIANNI

Kyr-Yianni 1997 Ramnista Xinomavro (Naoussa) $15. Big, bold nose of black olives, tobacco, leather and cinnamon. Big, aggressive tannins with taming blackberry and plum flavors. Bone-dry with a long, solid finish. Strictly a food wine, try with hearty tomato stews. **87** — *(11/15/2002)*

LAFAZANIS

Lafazanis 2005 Roditis (Peloponnese) $10. Greek producers have a wealth of indigenous grapes that have adapted to the hot Mediterranean climate. Roditis, grown in the Peloponnese for centuries, retains acidity throughout the hot summer to make a refreshing wine that is great with food. This example, from a quality-minded Greek importer with temperature-controlled shipping, marries aromas of juicy peach with flavors of lemon, mineral, white stone fruits and a dash of mint, all in an acidic framework that makes this perfect for food. Finishes crisply, with a touch of oak spice. **86 Best Buy** —*M.D. (11/15/2006)*

LAFAZANIS

Lafazanis 2005 St. George (Peloponnese) $10. Sometimes translated as "St. George" for the U.S. market, the Agiorgitiko grape can be very grapy when young, as this wine shows. Fine tannins and a mineral streak offer attractive elements, but sweaty notes mar the otherwise fine mixed berry and cola flavors. **83** —*M.D. (10/1/2006)*

Lathazanni 2003 Roditis (Corinth) $10. Lacks a bit of concentration, but showcases cleanly made pear and peach fruit on a lightweight frame. Refreshing. **85** —*J.C. (9/2/2004)*

MANOLESAKI ESTATE

Manolesaki Estate 2001 Cabernet Blend (Drama) $22. A bit rustic and tannic, but also shows some solid, ripe berry and cherry fruit. Hay, horse and spice notes add nuance without burying the fruit. Lighter-bodied, with crisp acids. **86** —*J.C. (9/2/2004)*

Manolesaki Estate 2001 Cabernet Sauvignon (Drama) $23. Strawberry isn't a typical Cabernet descriptor, but it applies to this wine, which also boasts more classic notes of dried herbs, leather and cedar. Supple tannins make this Cab instantly approachable. **87** —*J.C. (9/2/2004)*

Manolesaki Estate 2001 Merlot (Drama) $23. Firm yet fleshy, this Merlot boasts chunky black-cherry fruit swaddled in layers of toast and dark chocolate. It's medium-weight, graceful enough to drink with food, but it's still chewy enough to drink on its own. **88** —*J.C. (9/2/2004)*

Manolesaki Estate 2002 Sauvignon Blanc-Chardonnay White Blend (Drama) $22. This interesting blend boasts aromas of preserved lemons and fresh herbs, then turns a bit plumper in the mouth, with nectarine flavors joining in. Tart and high-acid on the finish, making it a natural with oily seafood dishes like fresh sardines. **85** —*J.C. (9/2/2004)*

Manolesaki Estate 2002 Sauvignon Blanc-Roditis White Blend (Drama) $18. This 60-40 blend combines ripe stone-fruit elements of nectarine and peach with firm mineral notes and a hint of anise on the lingering finish. Slightly herbal, but speaks more of ripe fruit, making for a pleasant, medium-weight sipper. **87** —*J.C. (9/2/2004)*

MANOUSAKIS

Manousakis 2002 Nostos Rhône Red Blend (Crete) $19. You can lose yourself in this wine's nose, as ripe fruit aromas of blackberry, cassis and kirsch are tempered with leather, lead and spice. Flavors of equally ripe fruit are intense and backed with a metallic edge, while the feel is smooth and dry. A blend of Syrah, Grenache, Mourvèdre and Roussanne. **89** —*M.D. (10/1/2006)*

MERCOURI ESTATE

Mercouri Estate 2005 Folói Roditis (Pisatis) $15. Made from the Roditis grape, a pink-skinned variety grown in the Peloponnese, this wine is zesty and dry, but with a pithy feel that gives body. Flavors are of citrus, orange, peach and lemon verbena, all with fine intensity. Also has a pleasant nose of citrus and peach and a fairly long, crisp finish. **88** —*M.D. (12/15/2006)*

MINOS

Minos 2002 Vilana Vilana (Crete) $16. Smells buttery and caramelly, then shows clean apple, pear and citrus fruit on the palate. Medium-weight, with a finish that turns more tropical, developing hints of pineapple, melon and citrus. Vilana is the grape variety. **85** —*J.C. (9/2/2004)*

NASIAKOS

Nasiakos 2005 Mantinia Moschofilero (Mantinia) $17. Mantinia is the appellation for Moschofilero, a versatile grape that makes fine, crisp whites. This is a good example, a light, dry, crisply acidic wine that pours on the lemon-lime from start to long finish. Perfect to pair with oysters or grilled swordfish. **87** —*M.D. (12/15/2006)*

Nasiakos 2003 Mantinia Moschofilero (Mantinia) $16. 84 —*J.C. (9/2/2004)*

Nasiakos 2005 Moschofilero White Label Moschofilero (Mantinia) $14. A nicely balanced wine that matches a mineral feel with zesty acidity and sweet citrus fruits. Crisp enough to withstand various seafood dishes or salads, but with enough flavor to stand on its own as an apéritif. **85** —*M.D. (12/15/2006)*

Nasiakos 2003 Moschofilero White Label Moschofilero (Mantinia) $13. Nicely floral, with notes of honeysuckle that seem almost Muscat- or Gewürz-like. A slightly viscous mouthfeel adds weight to apple and pear flavors that linger on the finish, picking up spice notes. **87** —*J.C. (9/2/2004)*

NICO LAZARIDI

Nico Lazaridi 2001 Château Nico Lazaridi Bordeaux Blend (Peloponnese) $17. This Bordeaux blend could use a little more ripeness—it does show hints of green beans—but overall it's a solid Cabernet-based wine accented by notes of coffee and chocolate. **83** —*J.C. (9/2/2004)*

Nico Lazaridi 1999 Magic Mountain Red Bordeaux Blend (Drama) $50. An ambitious effort, with plenty of tasty oak influence in the form of coffee and vanilla aromas and flavors. Fruit is ripe and soft; tannins are supple and harmonious, giving the impression of immediate drinkability. **86** —*J.C. (9/2/2004)*

Nico Lazaridi 2004 Lion d'Or Cabernet Sauvignon (Greece) $15. The nose starts a bit funky and earthy, but clears to reveal scents of blueberry pie and grape jelly. Full in the mouth, it has a soft, smooth feel with acidity to give it a lift. The blueberry compote flavors are a bit hidden by heavy tannins, but drink this with a steak or rack of lamb and watch the tannins melt away. **86** —*M.D. (12/15/2006)*

Nico Lazaridi 2001 Merlot (Drama) $17. 81 —*J.C. (9/2/2004)*

Nico Lazaridi 2001 Moushk Muscat d'Alexandrie (Drama) $23. Strongly floral, but also marked by a hint of nail polish. Once past that, it's sweet but well-balanced by tart acids and dominated by its powerful floral quality—clover blossoms? **85** —*J.C. (9/2/2004)*

Nico Lazaridi 2003 Magic Mountain Sauvignon Blanc (Drama) $30. Nice Greek Sauvignon showing melon, apple, and peach aromas more than piquant citrus. Offers fine balance, with the acidity propping up apple, honeydew, and peach flavors. Fairly chewy and round, with a finish that's slightly warm but satisfying. Could be nice with a salad of tomatoes and feta followed by grilled whole fish. **88** *(7/1/2005)*

Nico Lazaridi 2002 Magic Mountain White Sauvignon Blanc (Drama) $33. A valiant effort at making a full-bodied, barrel-fermented Sauvignon Blanc that falls just short. The toast and butter noes dominate the pear and peach fruit. **84** *—J.C. (9/2/2004)*

OENOFOROS

Oenoforos 2003 Cabernet Sauvignon (Aigialias Slopes) $12. Dark purple fruit and fennel open on the nose, while this wine has a lively mouthfeel with nice acidity, big tannins, and a minerally feel. Berry fruit, clay, and fennel play their role in the mouth, finishing with dark herbs. **86** — *M.D. (10/1/2006)*

Oenoforos 2001 Chardonnay (Egilias Slopes) $12. An aged style, any flavors of fruit have gone from this butter-colored wine. Butterscotch and oxidized nutty notes have replaced it, giving the impression of a full-bodied, low-alcohol Sherry. **82** *—M.D. (10/1/2006)*

Oenoforos 2005 Asprolithi Roditis (Patras) $10. Light and crisp, this 100% Roditis has moderate flavors of citrusy fruits and a short, clean finish. **82** *—M.D. (10/1/2006)*

Orphanos 2005 Assyrtico Assyrtico (Santorini) $17. Mineral and citrus flavors zip through the mouth, picking up some peach along the way. The acidity in this wine takes some time to show, but does make its presence felt, leaving a short, grippy finish. **84** *—M.D. (10/1/2006)*

PALIVOU

Palivou 2003 Agiorgitiko (Nemea) $25. So smooth and creamy. Solid oaking leads to polished tannins and flavors of cola and vanilla. The nose is Pinot-esque, while berry and plum flavors hold their own. A good rendition of the Agiorgitiko grape. **87** *—M.D. (10/1/2006)*

Palivou 2005 Agiorgitiko (St. George) Agiorgitiko (Peloponnese) $14. If you could coat purple grapes in peanut dust, you would know what this wine smells like. A strong minerally-clay element runs through the wine, joined by purple fruit flavor and hickory smoke. Solid tannins and a smooth feel round it out. **85** *—M.D. (10/1/2006)*

Palivou 2005 Agiorgitiko (St. George) Rosé Agiorgitiko (Corinth) $14. Freshly crushed raspberry and darker red fruit aromas waft from this deeply colored rosé. The wine has light tannins but lacks the acidity to lift the dark pomegranate flavors. **81** *—M.D. (12/15/2006)*

Palivou 2003 Ammos Agiorgitiko (Nemea) $35. A single vineyard wine with plenty of oak nuances, this shows darker flavors than other Agiorgitikos: Blueberry mixes with the telltale cherry, while vanilla caresses the whole. Strong tannins envelop a medium-bodied wine with good acidity, while the nose offers supple blackberry and blueberry fruit, vanilla and some meaty notes. **88** *—M.D. (12/15/2006)*

Palivou 2001 Nemea Agiorgitiko (Nemea) $20. Artfully oaked, this Agiorgitiko-based wine boasts hints of cinnamon, clove, and even a dash of coconut. Cherries and pears give a unique quality to the fruit, while the tannins are soft and impart a creamy texture to this admittedly international-style wine. **88** *—J.C. (9/2/2004)*

Palivou 2001 St. George Agiorgitiko (Corinth) $13. With its firm acids and modest tannins, tart cherries and worn leather, this is a natural burger wine—something assertive enough to pair with strong, simple flavors without being overwhelmed, yet not so complex as to demand finer fare. **85** *—J.C. (9/2/2004)*

Palivou 2002 St. George (Rose) Agiorgitiko (Corinth) $13. **81** *—J.C. (9/2/2004)*

Palivou 2001 Chardonnay (Corinth) $16. This well-oaked Chardonnay is plump and custardy in the mouth, with standard pear, cinnamon, and butter flavors all enveloped in a large helping of vanilla. **85** *—J.C. (9/2/2004)*

Palivou 2005 White Fox Roditis (Corinth) $14. Toast aromas surround baked apple, transforming to baking spice in the mouth. The oak is forward, but underneath, the fruit doesn't match up. **82** *—M.D. (10/1/2006)*

Palivou 2003 White Fox White Blend (Corinth) $13. Surprisingly low-acid compared to most Greek whites, with exotic tropical fruit aromas and flavors, maybe even some bananas. Hints of almonds, pears, and vanilla round out the flavors on the finish. **85** *—J.C. (9/2/2004)*

PAPAGIANNAKOS

Papagiannakos 2000 St. George Agiorgitiko (Attica) $18. **84** *—J.C. (9/2/2004)*

Papagiannakos 2005 Savatiano (Attica) $14. Savatiano is often used in retsina, a traditional Greek wine made with pine resin, but can also make fine table wine, such as this. A pithy, peachy nose leads to a dry, oily, medium-bodied wine with good acidity and flavors of peach, mineral, and flowers. **86** *—M.D. (12/15/2006)*

Papagiannakos 2003 Savatiano (Attica) $13. Savatiano is one of the most cultivated white grape varieties of Greece, often serving as the base for retsina. But this effort shows how good it can be, melding slightly nutty scents with peachy, melony fruit. It's plump and medium weight, finishing fresh and clean with a squirt of grapefruit. **88 Best Buy** *—J.C. (9/2/2004)*

PAVLIDIS

Pavlidis 2001 Cabernet Blend (Drama) $18. This blend of 70% Cabernet Sauvignon, 20% Merlot, and 10% Limnio offers a rush of cherries and sweet vanilla upfront, but not a lot of richness to back it up. Dry and astringent on the finish; try in a couple of years. **85** — *J.C. (9/2/2004)*

Pavlidis 2002 White Blend (Drama) $15. This blend of Sauvignon Blanc and Assyrtiko is definitely assertive, delivering pungent aromas of boxwood and grapefruit. An extreme style that may have its proponents. **82** *—J.C. (9/2/2004)*

PORTO CARRAS

Porto Carras 2003 Melisanthi Assyrtico (Côtes de Meliton) $15. **83** *—J.C. (9/2/2004)*

Porto Carras 2001 Château Porto Carras Cabernet Blend (Côtes de Meliton) $30. Black and brooding, with toast and vanilla showing on the nose, followed by earth and tobacco on the palate. It's medium-weight, slightly creamy and dense, yet with a touch of acidity on the finish to give it cut. Drink this blend of Cabernet Sauvignon, Cabernet Franc, and Limnio now–2010. **90** *—J.C. (9/2/2004)*

Porto Carras 2001 Lidia (Côtes de Meliton) $15. **84** *—J.C. (9/2/2004)*

Porto Carras 2003 Regional Wine of Sithonia Malagousia (Halkidiki) $20. A subtle and understated white from the Malagousia grape, with clean, fresh notes of grapefruit and a hint of green herbs. Light and tart; a good summertime quaff. **84** *—J.C. (9/2/2004)*

Porto Carras 1999 Syrah (Halkidiki) $80. This is a brawny, ripe wine, with fruit flavors that veer toward prune and molasses while folding in dark earthy notes. Big and bulky, with full tannins that need 3–5 years to resolve. **86** *—J.C. (9/2/2004)*

Porto Carras 2003 Blanc de Blancs White Blend (Côtes de Meliton) $10. A light, crisp seafood white, with lemons and minerals accented by notes of paraffin. Finishes long and tart; palate-cleansing. **85** *—J.C. (9/2/2004)*

PROVENZA

Provenza 2001 White Blend (Naoussa) $12. A pleasant, lemon-and-lime white, best with light fish dishes. Unlike most of its brethren, which are ready to go from the moment they're opened, this one has some burnt-matchstick aromas that need time and aeration to dissipate. Try decanting. **84** *—J.C. (7/1/2003)*

ROBOLA

Robola 2003 Robola (Cephalonia) $10. Faint scents of rainwater and rock dust mark the nose, while the palate is assertively tart and lemony. This is a lean, acidic wine best suited for washing down oily or fried foods. **83** *—J.C. (9/2/2004)*

SAMOS

Samos 2000 Grand Cru Vin Doux Naturel White Blend (Samos) $10. A seductive nose of nectarine, quince, and apricots. The mouthfeel is balanced, with high acidity and dried figs and plums. **88**— *(11/15/2002)*

SKOURAS

Skouras 2004 Grande Cuvée Agiorgitiko (Nemea) $25. The nose first offers suede and leather before showing some plummy aromas. Smooth tannins give it a refined feel, although the acids keep it on the racy side. Has nice, deep cassis flavor with a touch of cola and spice from oak. **87**—*M.D. (10/1/2006)*

Skouras 2003 Saint George Agiorgitiko (Nemea) $13. Fuller-bodied than many Agiorgitikos, this has tart, mixed berry flavors with cinnamon and spice on the nose. A bit rustic, but nobody will mind the strawberry-flavored finish. **84**—*M.D. (10/1/2006)*

Skouras 2004 Saint George-Cabernet Sauvignon Agiorgitiko (Peloponnese) $8. A Beaujolais-like nose of raspberry and clay leads to a fruity wine with blueberry and raspberry and a streak of minerality. Only 5% Cabernet, it has a medium-full body supported by good tannins, finishing with tart red fruit. **85 Best Buy**—*M.D. (10/1/2006)*

Skouras 2004 Cuvée Prestige Cabernet Sauvignon (Peloponnese) $16. The nose starts nicely, with plenty of plum and dark berry fruit, a hint of green adding character. Upon entry the wine picks up some barnyard flavors which vie with blueberry and anise. If not for this wine's dry and chalky tannins, it would have scored higher. **85**—*M.D. (10/1/2006)*

Skouras 2004 Chardonnay (Peloponnese) $14. Fermented in new oak, this wine has a nice perfume of citrus, orange marmalade and vanilla. The vanilla comes on stronger in the mouth, followed by tropical white fruit, citrus, and a hint of musk. Soft acids and a smooth oak feel finish with a citrusy burst. **85**—*M.D. (10/1/2006)*

Skouras 2005 Moschofilero (Peloponnese) $14. Lighter and lacking the acidity of Mantinia Moschofilero, this starts with aromas of springtime flowers, cola, and a lemon spritz, followed by moderate lemony citrus, orange pith and cola flavors. More of a sipping wine than one to have with food. **84**—*M.D. (12/15/2006)*

Skouras 2005 Zoë! Rosé Blend (Peloponnese) $10. This dry, vibrant wine has loads of cherry and strawberry flavors that nearly crunch in the mouth. A blend of Agiorgitiko and Moschofilero, two of Greece's most versatile grapes, this is best drunk young to retain its freshness. It should be a superb match for grilled fish and feta salad. **87 Best Buy**—*M.D. (12/15/2006)*

Skouras 2005 White Blend (Peloponnese) $8. A blend of Roditis and Moschofilero, this wine has nice aromas of grapefruit, pineapple, and honeysuckle. Crisp and dry in the mouth, the honeysuckle continues with added citrus. An enjoyable summer quaff. **84 Best Buy**—*M.D. (10/1/2006)*

SPIROPOULOS

Spiropoulos 2000 Red Stag Agiorgitiko (Peloponnese) $15. **80**—*J.C. (9/2/2004)*

SPYROS HATZIYIANNIS

Spyros Hatziyiannis 2002 White Blend (Cyclades) $10. Anise, pear, and mineral aromas and flavors imbue this wine with a fine degree of complexity. It's also richer than most of the whites from Santorini, yet it still retains a refreshing bite on its tart, minerally finish. **88 Best Buy**—*J.C. (9/2/2004)*

TECHNI ALIPIAS 2

Techni Alipias 2002 Regional Wine Sauvignon Blanc (Drama) $19. **83**—*J.C. (9/2/2004)*

TSANTALI

Tsantali 2002 Athiri (Vin de Pays de Macedoine) $10. Another light-bodied, seafood white, Athiri is most often blended with Assyrtiko. In this stand-alone version, you get hints of pear and citrus on the nose, then lime zest dusted with minerals on the finish. **84**—*J.C. (9/2/2004)*

Tsantali 1998 Cava Tsantalis Cabernet Blend (Halkidiki) $15. Kava is a Greek classification that may be applied to red wines that have aged at least one year in barrel and two additional years prior to release—that's the derivation of this wine's name. As you might expect, this is a mature wine, with leather, tobacco, and earth nuances wrapped around a core of dried fruit and molasses. A blend of Cabernet Sauvignon and Xinomavro. Drink up. **89 Best Buy**—*J.C. (9/2/2004)*

Tsantali 2001 Metoxi Cabernet Blend (Mount Athos) $20. Dark earth, graham cracker, and plush purple fruit aromas introduce a wealth of blueberry and black plum flavors wrapped in oaky spice. The wine is smooth from eight months in new French oak, though the oak could not fully tame such ripe, heavy tannins. Can be drunk over the next decade. A blend of 60% Cabernet Sauvignon and 40% Limnio. **89**—*M.D. (12/15/2006)*

Tsantali 1999 Metoxi Cabernet Blend (Mount Athos) $NA. This blend of Cabernet Sauvignon and the indigenous Limnio shows the great improvement in Greek winemaking over recent years. While the '96 version is thinning out a bit, yet stubbornly tannic, this '99 is round and supple, packed with plum, black cherry, and vanilla flavors and finishes long. **89**—*J.C. (9/1/2004)*

Tsantali 1996 Metoxi Reserve Cabernet Blend (Mount Athos) $44. Earth and tobacco, backed by modest cassis flavors that are already starting to thin out. Dry tannins mark the finish. The '99 (non-Reserve) is a better bet. **85**—*J.C. (9/2/2004)*

Tsantali 2001 Organics Cabernet Sauvignon (Halkidiki) $22. As with the previous year's bottling, this wine is shut down with tannins and toasty oak. Dark and polished, with flavors of black fruits, coffee, and spice trying to emerge, the wine's nose gives it away as an ager, offering damp earth, later transforming to coffee, spice, and rich, dark fruit. Throw a case in your cellar until 2008, then try a bottle a year after that. **91 Editors' Choice**—*M.D. (12/15/2006)*

Tsantali 2000 Organics Cabernet Sauvignon (Halkidiki) $24. Right now this vibrant, dark purple wine is closed up and dominated by toasty new oak—vanilla and cedar notes take the lead. But the wine appears to have the structure to support this ambitious oak treatment, the fruit just needs some time to re-emerge. Try in 2008. **88**—*J.C. (9/2/2004)*

Tsantali NV Cellar Reserve Mavrodaphne (Patras) $13. **84**—*J.C. (9/2/2004)*

Tsantali 2000 Halkidiki Vineyards Merlot (Halkidiki) $12. This simple, supple, modern Merlot blends black cherries and vanilla. It's well made, straightforward and easy to drink. **86**—*J.C. (9/2/2004)*

Tsantali 2003 Muscat (Lemnos) $7. **81**—*J.C. (9/2/2004)*

Tsantali 1998 Epilegmenos Reserve Red Blend (Rapsani) $18. This light-to medium-weight wine exhibits fine complexity, blending earth, tobacco, mint, and red berries on the nose, then adding in hints of vanilla and orange peel on the long, layered finish. Drink now–2010. **88**—*J.C. (9/2/2004)*

Tsantali 1997 Epilegmenos Reserve Red Blend (Naoussa) $14. Unabashedly modern, with supple tannins that impart a creamy mouthfeel to the cherry fruit, all wrapped in an oaky cocoon of toast, chocolate, and vanilla. **89 Best Buy**—*J.C. (9/2/2004)*

Tsantali 1997 Epilegmenos Reserve Red Blend (Rapsani) $13. Vibrant cherry and blueberry aromas are wrapped in understated tobacco, toasted coconut, macerated fruit, and caramel. Solid tannins lend structure to the rounded and rich flavors. **88**— *(11/15/2002)*

Tsantali 1995 Epilegmenos Reserve Red Blend (Rapsani) $35. This forceful, tannic wine appears to be still on the upswing. Meaty scents and flavors akin to beef stew, and dark fruit notes of plum and cassis all suggest it's best served as a companion to hearty dishes. Earth, leather, coffee, and bitter chocolate notes round out the medium-length finish. **87**—*J.C. (9/2/2004)*

Tsantali 1992 Rapsani Grand Reserve Red Blend (Rapsani) $43. **83**—*J.C. (9/2/2004)*

Tsantali 2002 Agiroritikos Rosé Blend (Greece) $15. **81**—*J.C. (9/2/2004)*

Tsantali 1999 Syrah (Greece) $17. Herbal, peppery overtones mark this Syrah, but the slightly creamy core of this wine is built around bright, bouncy cherry and vanilla flavors. Turns a bit green and peppery again on the finish. **85** —*J.C. (9/2/2004)*

Tsantali 2002 Agioritikos White Blend (Greece) $15. 84 —*J.C. (9/2/2004)*

Tsantali 2003 Ambelonas White Blend (Halkidiki) $23. This blend of Sauvignon Blanc and the local Assyrtiko has medium intensity and some unusual aromas of acrylic dust, lemon grass, and honey. The palate has a meaty, cured-ham quality along with flavors of grapefruit and nectarine. Lengthy enough on the finish, but a bit bland. From Greece. **86** *(7/1/2005)*

Tsantali 2002 Ambelonas White Blend (Halkidiki) $15. This attempt at a Greek white made in a fatter, riper style is partially successful, yielding rich, honeyed aromas of beeswax and hints of peach and lemon that don't deliver quite as much length on the palate. **85** —*J.C. (9/2/2004)*

Tsantali 2002 Chromitsa White Blend (Mount Athos) $16. 84 —*J.C. (9/2/2004)*

Tsantali 2003 Xinomavro (Naoussa) $13. A meaty nose muddled by aromas of leather, sweat, and coffee introduces a wine with dark, solid tannins and black fruit flavors. But the fruit is sweet and the palate smooth. **87** —*M.D. (12/15/2006)*

Tsantali 1992 Nauosa Reserve Xinomavro (Naoussa) $33. 84 —*J.C. (9/2/2004)*

Tsantali 2002 Xinomavro (Macedonia) $14. From a broader region than Naoussa, this wine has aromas of cherry, tobacco, and copper leading to some rustic flavors of mulberry, mint, and nice cherry fruit. Medium-bodied and on the soft side, with relatively mild tannins for this variety, the finish is dry with hints of tobacco. **86** —*M.D. (12/15/2006)*

TSELEPOS

Tselepos 2000 Agiorgitiko (Corinth) $15. Bursting with raspberries, cassis, tobacco, leather, and coffee beans. Truly capturing the older style and incorporating the new. Solid tannins, surprisingly good acidity and a long, soft finish. **90** — *(11/15/2002)*

Tselepos 2001 Moschofilero (Mantinia) $12. A bouquet of flowers, rose petals, and lavender with apricots and peaches. Slight effervescence on the palate with nut and orange-skin flavors. A light-bodied, clean wine that is excellent as an apéritif. **87** — *(11/15/2002)*

UNION DE COOPERATIVES VINICOLES DE SAMOS

Union de Cooperatives Vinicoles de Samos 1999 Nectar Vin de Paille Muscat (Samos) $20. Brown sugar, honey, caramelized nuts—what comforting, warming scents waft from the glass. It's plump but not overly sweet, more nutty and honeyed, with citrusy notes that give it a sense of structure. Made from sun-dried Muscat grapes, then aged in oak for three years. **90 Editors' Choice** —*J.C. (9/2/2004)*

Union de Cooperatives Vinicoles de Samos NV Samena Golden White Blend (Samos) $9. Pale straw color. This is the dry version of Muscat produced on the island of Samos. It smells sweetly fruity, with hints of pineapple, pear, and lychee, but tastes dry and a bit hard on the palate. Finishes clean and fresh. **86** —*J.C. (9/2/2004)*

VATISTAS

Vatistas 2002 Assyrtico (Peloponnese) $20. 84 —*J.C. (9/2/2004)*

Vatistas 2002 Athiri (Peloponnese) $20. Delicate peach and nut scents develop into modest peach and pear flavors. It's plump in the mouth, providing a fine alternative to Chardonnay. **85** —*J.C. (9/2/2004)*

Vatistas 2001 Cabernet-Aghiorgitiko Cabernet Blend (Peloponnese) $15. 83 —*J.C. (9/2/2004)*

Vatistas 2002 Petroulianos (Peloponnese) $20. Petroulianos is the grape variety, yielding in this case a tart, zingy white graced with hints of ginger and citrus. A simple, lemony quaffer made to refresh on hot summer days or perk up the palate alongside oily fish. **86** —*J.C. (9/2/2004)*

Vatistas 2000 Regional Wine Red Blend (Peloponnese) $14. 82 —*J.C. (9/2/2004)*

Vatistas 2002 White Blend (Peloponnese) $14. This four-variety blend starts off a little sulfury and nutty, but blossoms with time in the glass

into a light, citrusy mouthful of wine filled with hints of white nectarines and minerals. Finishes long, clean, and refreshing. **87** —*J.C. (9/2/2004)*

ZENATO

Zenato 2001 Vigneto Massoni White Blend (Naoussa) $NA. A fresh, tangy, vibrant wine that has ripe green plum and apple flavors alongside a layer of full, forward fruit. **88** —*R.V. (7/1/2003)*

HUNGARY

CRAFTSMAN

Craftsman 2003 Cabernet Franc (Szekszárd) $9. This Cab Franc offers a young, fresh side of the variety, low in tannin but high in vibrant berry flavors. Colored a rich purple, a hint of barbecue adds some character to this pleasant wine. **85 Best Buy** —*M.D. (6/1/2006)*

Craftsman 2004 Cserszegi Fuszeres (Neszmély) $9. This native variety (pronounced Chair-say-ghy Foo-seh-fresh) produces a wine loaded with lemon, from the lemon Pine-Sol nose to the lemon custard mouth and tart lemon finish. Despite the lemon, it's round in the mouth, with some spice notes. **83** —*M.D. (6/1/2006)*

Craftsman 2004 Gewürztraminer (Neszmély) $9. This wine shows the peppery side of Gewürz, pairing it with papaya and lychee in the mouth. Its medium-full body along with its spicy pepper undertones would make this the perfect pair to the traditional Hungarian dish: chicken in paprika sauce. **84** —*M.D. (6/1/2006)*

Craftsman 2004 Királyleányka (Neszmély) $9. With Muscat-like aromas of honeysuckle, lemon, and white fruit, this indigenous Hungarian white (pronounced Kee-rye-lay-ohn-kha) offers airy flavors of lemon candy and honeysuckle. Just right for sipping on a summer afternoon. **84** — *M.D. (6/1/2006)*

Craftsman 2004 Pinot Grigio (Neszmély) $9. Tropical in style, with mango and pineapple on the nose and tangy citrus and a slight mineral note on the palate. Almost Riesling-like, with a melony aftertaste. **86 Best Buy** *(2/1/2006)*

Craftsman 2003 Falconers Cuvée Red Blend (Neszmély) $9. A blend of Merlot, Cab, Pinot Noir, and Kékfrankos (aka Blaufränkisch), this wine offers lemon, vanilla, and oak on the nose, plus some herbal notes. In the mouth it's on the lean side, with flavors of green bean and vanilla, and a strong peppery spice that lasts through the finish. **83** —*M.D. (6/1/2006)*

Craftsman 2004 Sauvignon Blanc (Neszmély) $9. Pungent aromas of grapefruit, gooseberry, and straw lead to an intense mouthful of more grapefruit and spice. Although this wine has high acidity, there is a touch of sweetness to balance it. Persistent on the finish. **86 Best Buy** —*M.D. (6/1/2006)*

DISZNÓKÖ

Disznókö 1999 Aszú 5 Puttonyos Tokaji (Tokaji) $33. At 5 Puttonyos this wine is very sweet and medium to full bodied, with enough acidity it to give it mouthwatering appeal. Young citrus notes play off flavors of apricot and milk chocolate, with additional aromas of toffee and herbs. Finishes long. **91** *(6/1/2006)*

Disznókö 1999 Aszú 6 Puttonyos Tokaji (Tokaji) $43. A sweeter and rarer version of the '99 from Disznóko, this also has mouthwatering acidity that balances the wine. Honey, spice, and apricot aromas lead to more of the same in the mouth, although it develops musk scents with air time. Flavors of pineapple, citrus, and golden raisins add to the mouthfeel, and it finishes long, with tangy tropical fruit. **90** *(6/1/2006)*

DOBOGÓ

Dobogó 2004 Furmint (Tokaj) $32. One of the grapes used in the famous dessert wine, this dry-style from the village of Tokaj has a mixture of fresh, vibrant fruit with a supple, round body. Aromas of tropical fruits, mixed with straw and chalk, continue in the mouth, with some dried apricot thrown in, then it's brought home by zesty acidity and citrus pith. This could herald a bright future for Hungarian dry whites. **88** —*M.D. (6/1/2006)*

Dobogó 2003 Mylitta Furmint (Tokaji) $36. A golden-hued, late harvest style, lacking the botrytis character of an Aszú wine, but still offering plenty of sweetness. Ripe tropical fruits and spicy floral scents pervade the nose, while the medium-full palate has good acidity and flavors of citrus, guava, and allspice. Finishes a bit soft, with pineapple flavors. **87** *(6/1/2006)*

Dobogó 2000 Aszú 6 Puttonyos Tokaji (Tokaji) $87. Rich and unctuous, with flavors of apricot marmalade and honey, this wine has a dry, pithy feel, although it's also very sweet. The juxtaposition is pleasant, as is the complex nose of orange tea, cinnamon, and honeyed fig. Acidity finally emerges on the long, spicy finish. **90** *(6/1/2006)*

Dobogó 1999 Aszú 6 Puttonyos Tokaji (Tokaji) $87. Darker-colored than the 2000, this wine has more orange character on the nose, along with toffee and nutmeg. The wine offers a medium-full body and complex flavors of honey, melon, and citrus all delicately spiced, with a hint of almond. The finish is long and spicy, with tropical fruits. **89** *(6/1/2006)*

DUNAVAR

Dunavar 2004 Connoisseur Collection Pinot Gris (Felso-Magyarország) $7. Shows some tell-tale pear in the nose, with generic white fruits and a dash of oak on the palate. A little plump in the mouth, but with matching acidity and a bit of spice, this Pinot could be from anywhere. **84 Best Buy** —*M.D. (6/1/2006)*

Dunavar 2003 Egri Bikaver Red Blend (Eger) $8. Fresh and fruity, with a young, vibrant quality, this wine offers plenty of mixed berry and purple fruit flavors with just the lightest touch of oak. Perfect for a picnic. **84 Best Buy** —*M.D. (6/1/2006)*

HILLTOP NESZMÉLY

Hilltop Neszmély 1993 Aszú 5 Puttonyos Tokaji (Tokaji) $45. An older style with amber-brown color, this wine has an oxidized nose of brown sugar and aged cheese. It's medium-bodied with decent acidity and flavors of orange marmalade, tea leaves, tobacco, and a hint of chocolate. **87** *(6/1/2006)*

OREMUS

Oremus 2000 Furmint (Tokaji) $10. 89 Best Buy —*R.V. (11/15/2002)*

Oremus 2003 Mandolás Furmint (Tokaji) $17. Full, round, and spicy in the mouth, this wine offers muted aromas of beeswax and honeysuckle before showing its overpowering oak and vanilla side. Seems to have suffered from the hot vintage, with too much oak hiding the white fruit. **82** —*M.D. (6/1/2006)*

Oremus 1999 Aszú 5 Puttonyos Tokaji (Tokaji) $60. Fruity aromas of pineapple and apricot join notes of vanilla and dried spice, while in the mouth this wine is plump and round. Flavors of pineapple, citrus, and apricot coat the palate, then leave slowly, finishing with honey. **88** *(6/1/2006)*

Oremus 2002 Late Harvest Tokaji (Tokaji) $24. Buttery-gold and viscous, this wine offers earthy scents of vanilla and honeyed white fruits, developing more tropical fruit, honey, and caramel on the palate. A medium-length finish with citrusy acidity rounds out the wine. **89** *(6/1/2006)*

ROYAL TOKAJI

Royal Tokaji 2000 Aszú 5 Puttonyos 500 ml Tokaji (Tokaji) $32. An amazing wine that is a benchmark for its class. Pure scents of dried apricot, citrus, jasmine, and melon are coated with Asian spices, while the mouth is honeyed but nuanced, with flavors of dried spices, apricot marmalade, and citrus fruits. What sets this wine apart is its mouthwatering acidity. A blend of grapes from multiple vineyards, this 26,000-case production wine is a steal at this price. **94 Editors' Choice** *(6/1/2006)*

Royal Tokaji 1995 Aszú Essencia Tokaji (Tokaji) $167. The sweetest Aszú wine, with 217 grams per liter of sugar (only pure Essencia is sweeter). Honeyed nuts, brown sugar, orange blossom, and chocolate aromas waft from the glass. Full and viscous in the mouth, this balanced wine, with a

modest 8.5% alcohol, has beautiful flavors of toffee, caramel, and orange tea. Finishes long and complex. **92** *(6/1/2006)*

Royal Tokaji 1999 Betsek Aszú 6 Puttonyos Tokaji (Tokaji) $67. Made with 50% Furmint, 45% Háslevelu, and 5% Muscat, this vintage weathered two hailstorms during the summer. The surviving grapes benefited from greater concentration, leading to a more intense wine. Already developing toffee and coffee notes, this wine still shows plenty of citrus, honey, dried apricot, and fig, with a hint of nuttiness on the nose. Syrupy and round, the citrusy acids maintain a beautiful harmony. **93** *(6/1/2006)*

Royal Tokaji 1999 Birsalmás Aszú 5 Puttonyos Tokaji (Tokaji) $52. With 70% Hárslevelū, this single-vineyard bottling changes the usual formula for Tokaji, normally Furmint heavy. Amber-colored and showing some oxidation, it offers floral aromas and dried apricot, some earthy notes and a bit of volatility. Full in the mouth, with drying acidity that is just shy of tart, the wine has flavors of sweet citrus, cinnamon, and orange marmalade. **88** *(6/1/2006)*

Royal Tokaji 1995 Mézes Mály Aszú 6 Puttonyos Tokaji (Tokaji) $115. Meaning "honey pot," Mézes Mály is an esteemed south-facing, first-growth vineyard. This wine has an oxidized character resulting in nutty aromas and cheese-rind flavors. Still, this wine also showed flavors of dried apricot and raisin, although none of the namesake honey. Finishes long, but the oxidative note was still a strike against this wine. **88** *(6/1/2006)*

Royal Tokaji 1995 Nyulászó Aszú 6 Puttonyos Tokaji (Tokaji) $85. This first-growth vineyard, classified in 1700 (165 years before Bordeaux) is known for its highly perfumed wines. This example shows a complex array of clove, brown sugar, and oxidized nutty notes. Flavors of citrus are the first signs of fruit, with caramel and nuts playing secondary roles, all wrapped up in racy acids. Despite this wine's age it is fresh and shows potential to keep on going. **91** *(6/1/2006)*

Royal Tokaji 1995 Szt. Tamás Aszú 6 Puttonyos Tokaji (Tokaji) $77. From a southwest slope facing the village of Mád, this sweet Tokaji is earthier then the Nyulászó, but also has scents of brown sugar, clove, and dried figs. Medium-bodied and complex in the mouth, with citrus, earth, and honey flavors, the acidity gives good backing and a citric finish. **91** *(6/1/2006)*

TIBOR GAL

Tibor Gal 2002 Chardonnay (Eger) $12. Heady in the nose, with melon and orange rind, this wine disappoints in the mouth. An oily texture with virtually no acidity accompanies vanilla and banana flavors, then ends hot. Fails to impress. **80** —*M.D. (6/1/2006)*

Tibor Gal 2001 Chardonnay (Eger) $12. Nutty and mealy on the nose, the oak treatment blending nicely with ripe fruit notes. Flavors of buttered nuts, pears, and citrus finish on a toasty note. Solid Chardonnay at a solid price. **86** —*J.C. (6/1/2005)*

Tibor Gal 2002 Egri Bikaver Red Blend (Eger) $11. Toasty oak is displayed in the nose and mouth, mixing with flavors of modest red berry. This wine has good balance and moderate tannin, but at this age the tannin outweighs the fruit. Finishes with some spice notes. **83** —*M.D. (6/1/2006)*

ISRAEL

BARKAN

Barkan 2000 Reserve Cabernet Sauvignon (Galil) $20. With its tobacco and earth notes, this Israeli Cab could almost pass for Bordeaux, except that it also oozes cassis fruit and has the ripe, supple mouthfeel that says warm climate. Finishes with gentle tannins, hints of coffee and vanilla and a bit of lemony tartness. Drink now. **88** —*J.C. (4/1/2005)*

Barkan 1996 Reserve Cabernet Sauvignon (Galil) $19. The nose offers earthy, medicinal notes on the light black-cherry fruit. Thin on the palate, it has a cough syrup-like taste. The tannins are soft, the acids low. Finishes short. **80** *(4/1/2001)*

Barkan 2000 Superieur Cabernet Sauvignon (Galilee) $75. Full-bodied and firm textured, with ripe, smooth tannins. The wine serves up a fine blend of blackberry, cassis, coffee, toast, and herb flavors. On the finish, it's long, with a tangy citrus edge. Kosher **89** —*J.M. (4/3/2004)*

Barkan 2000 Reserve Chardonnay (Barkan) $15. Lean and tart, with initial aromas of burnt match giving way to green apple and lime flavors. Very citrusy and crisp on the finish. **84** —*J.C. (4/1/2005)*

Barkan 1998 Reserve Chardonnay (Galil) $8. A light but flavorful wine with citrus and green-apple aromas and flavors. A mild chalkiness shows on the palate and oak adds some smoke and spice to the picture. Finishes with an herb note. **84** *(4/1/2001)*

Barkan 2000 Superieur Merlot (Galil) $75. This ambitiously priced effort boasts scents of roasted fruit and charred barrels allied to flavors of caramelized cherries and dried cinnamon. Best features are the lush, velvety texture and long, tart finish. Ready to drink. **86** —*J.C. (4/1/2005)*

Barkan 2002 Reserve Kosher Pinotage (Judea) $20. Smells a bit like baked berries in pastry crust, then adds a note of carob on the palate. Medium-bodied, with zesty finishing touches of tea and orangey citrus. **84** —*J.C. (4/1/2006)*

BINYAMINA

Binyamina 2002 Special Reserve Chardonnay (Galilee) $15. Bland on the palate, with burnt, acrid notes on the nose and a lemony finish. **81** —*J.C. (4/1/2005)*

Binyamina 1999 Special Reserve Merlot (Galilee) $25. Bright and somewhat fruity, but with tannic structure to tone down any effusiveness, the wine shows a smoky, toasty core backed by cherry, raspberry, cola, and herb flavors. Kosher **85** —*J.M. (4/3/2004)*

CARMEL

Carmel 2002 Ben Zimra Single Vineyard Cabernet Sauvignon (Upper Galilee) $25. The biggest and most muscular of Carmel's single-vineyard Cabs, this wine blends hints of green bean and smoke with ripe cassis and blackberry. Extracted and tannic, and just a little rough on the finish. Try in 2007. **87** —*J.C. (4/1/2005)*

Carmel 1999 Private Collection Cabernet Sauvignon (Judean Hills) $26. Somewhat herbal, with hints of licorice, tar, smoke, blackberry, and spice. The wine is medium bodied, with reasonably round tannins that leave the palate clean on the finish. Kosher **83** —*J.M. (4/3/2004)*

Carmel 1998 Private Collection Cabernet Sauvignon (Galil) $12. **81** —*M.S. (4/1/2002)*

Carmel 2003 Private Collection Kosher Cabernet Sauvignon (Galilee) $19. Light and dry, with modest cassis fruit and some pleasant tobacco and cigarbox aromas and flavors. **83** —*J.C. (4/1/2006)*

Carmel 2002 Ramat Arad Single Vineyard Cabernet Sauvignon (Negev Hills) $28. This darkly colored wine smells not unlike some Paso Robles Cabs, combining cassis fruit with hints of herb that come dangerously close to bell pepper. The flavors follow suit with a soft mouthfeel that carries plum and pepper notes before turning dense and chocolaty on the finish. **86** —*J.C. (4/1/2005)*

Carmel 2002 Zarit Single Vineyard Cabernet Sauvignon (Upper Galilee) $25. Herbal and earthy, but this Carmel effort also features soft, slightly chewy tannins and nice cherry fruit. **85** —*J.C. (4/1/2005)*

Carmel 2003 Private Collection Cabernet Sauvignon-Merlot (Galilee) $15. Shows some potential in its youthful aromas of cassis and chocolate, but seems a little thin on the midpalate. Fresh and a bit tannic on the finish, but also tastes a little sugary. **84** —*J.C. (4/1/2005)*

Carmel 2002 Private Collection Cabernet Sauvignon-Shiraz (Galilee) $16. Shows more structure than expected, with firm, drying tannins and tart acids on the finish, but they're needed to balance the slightly baked, candied flavor of cherry Newtons. Try with rare beef. **85** —*J.C. (4/1/2006)*

Carmel 2002 Kerem Single Vineyard Merlot (Shomron) $25. Richly textured and dense, but the flavors are a touch herbal, leaning toward cherry tomatoes rather than cherries or plums. Chewy, even a bit meaty, on the finish. **87** —*J.C. (4/1/2005)*

Carmel 1998 Private Collection Merlot (Judean Hills) $12. Aromas of sweet red berries, dried fruits, and herbs open this light, accessible wine from Israel. The tone of the fruit seems to shift between a tart rhubarb and a slightly candied quality. Cherry notes show on the lean and dry back end. **84** *(4/1/2001)*

Carmel 1999 Valley Wines Petite Sirah (Shomron) $9. Opens with solid grape and red-currant fruit accented by tobacco, but on the palate the wine is light for a Petite Sirah, usually a hefty wine. As the fruit is from very young vines, it's not a terrible surprise, and it's a positive sign that Israeli winemakers are stretching their horizons. Finishes tart-sweet, with red berry fruit and a hint of licorice. **83** *(4/1/2001)*

Carmel 2003 Ramat Arad Vineyard Sauvignon Blanc (Negev Hills) $15. Eccentric stuff, with a slight coppery tinge to the hue and scents of caramel, honey, and dried spices. Seems a bit tired, finishing on an anise note. **82** —*J.C. (4/1/2005)*

Carmel 1998 Vineyards Selected Shiraz (Shomron) $12. Shows lean red berry and herb aromas. Mild tea and currant flavors play on the tongue, but the desired weight and texture of Shiraz aren't there. Finishes short, with a tea note. **82** *(4/1/2001)*

CASTEL

Castel 1999 Petite Castel Cabernet Sauvignon (Haut-Judeé) $21. Toasty, with cassis, tobacco, and smoked meat aromas. Spicy on the palate with sweet roasted tomatoes. Lacking a little depth, but generally a well-balanced, medium-bodied wine. **87** — *(11/15/2002)*

Castel 1996 Grand Vin Cabernet Sauvignon-Merlot (Haut-Judeé) $41. Big, bold, and meaty. Chocolate, coffee, and cassis aromas blend well with flavors of raspberries, tobacco, and wild mushrooms. This is a big, extracted Bordeaux-like wine that is well-supported by solid tannins. A natural pairing to lamb on an outdoor spit. **91** — *(11/15/2002)*

CHILLAG

Chillag 2003 Orna Riserva Kosher Cabernet Sauvignon (Galilee) $20. Not mevushal. If that's not a concern, this is a fine wine, lavishly oaked but nicely textured, with some bright cherry notes and supple tannins peering out from under layers of smoke, vanilla, and toast. **87** —*J.C. (4/1/2006)*

DALTON

Dalton 1999 Reserve Cabernet Sauvignon (Galilee) $37. A bit earthy and weedy, but nonetheless, it harbors some pleasing plum and black cherry notes. Tannins are ripe and the finish is moderate in length. **83** —*J.M. (4/3/2004)*

Dalton 2002 Reserve Chardonnay (Galilee) $21. Smooth and viscous, with some pretty high-toned toast upfront. Vanilla, peach, apple, pear, and Mandarin orange are at the core, finishing with a bright punch. Kosher. **87** —*J.M. (4/3/2004)*

Dalton 2000 Merlot (Galilee) $24. Kicks off with a distinct vegetal aroma, this is classic "cold-climate" wine. Herbal notes with stewed fruits take center stage. Reminds me a bit of some Chinons. Interesting, though not for everyone. Kosher. **82** —*J.M. (4/3/2004)*

Dalton 2000 Reserve Merlot (Galilee) $37. A bright wine with a cherry core framed by firm tannins. Herbal overtones, licorice, coffee, and tea notes add interest. On the finish, it remains fairly bright. Kosher **86** —*J.M. (4/3/2004)*

Dalton NV Admon Portah Port (Galilee) $16. Made in the style of Port, this sweet red wine serves up spicy rich, raspberry, chocolate, coffee, plum, vanilla, tea, and herb flavors, all couched in firm tannins. Toast and caramel frame the finish. Kosher **87** —*J.M. (4/3/2004)*

Dalton 2002 Reserve Sauvignon Blanc (Galilee) $18. A full-bodied wine that serves up zippy acidity. The flavors are bright, with hints of pineapple, lemon, and grapefruit. A touch of sourness mars the finish. Kosher. **81** —*J.M. (4/3/2004)*

DOMAINE DU CASTEL

Domaine du Castel 2003 Blanc du Castel Kosher Chardonnay (Judean Hills) $40. This ambitious attempt falls just short of the mark. The expensive

French oak is obvious in the wine's toasty, nutty aromas of dried spices, but where's the fruit? Modest apple flavors fail to round out the mid-palate, leaving this wine with a hole in the middle. Woody notes surge on the finish. Not mevushal. 82 —J.C. (4/1/2006)

GALIL MOUNTAIN

Galil Mountain 2003 Cabernet Sauvignon (Galilee) $17. Ultrayoung and ultraloud, with grapy, herbal flavors that come across as bold, assertive and unsubtle. A bit tart on the finish, cushioned by supple tannins. 86 —J.C. (4/1/2005)

Galil Mountain 2001 Yiron Cabernet Sauvignon-Merlot (Galilee) $26. A blend of 78% Cabernet Sauvignon and 22% Merlot, this wine displays decent aromas of cherries, earth, and herbs, but fails to develop a sense of verve or energy on the palate, ending on dull notes of coffee and dark chocolate. 84 —J.C. (4/1/2005)

Galil Mountain 2003 Merlot (Galilee) $16. Fruit-forward, with ripe berry aromas that fairly burst out of the glass, along with hints of vanilla, chocolate, and coffee. Tannins are soft, while the black cherry and plum flavors pick up a tart, hard edge on the finish. 85 —J.C. (4/1/2006)

GAMLA

Gamla 1996 Cabernet Sauvignon (Galilee) $12. 87 Best Buy (4/1/2000)

Gamla 2000 Cabernet Sauvignon (Galilee) $16. Plum, blackberry, and graham-cracker notes start this wine off on the right foot, but it's tart and racy on the palate, with only modest black-cherry flavors. 83 —J.C. (4/1/2005)

Gamla 1997 Cabernet Sauvignon (Galilee) $14. This international-style Cabernet from Israel boasts solid, full-flavored blackcurrant fruit wrapped in plenty of smoky oak. Not at all weighty, it's carried more by flavor than density or texture. The tannins are even and the finish clean and long. 88 (4/1/2001)

Gamla 1998 Chardonnay (Galilee) $12. Round and fairly full, this is mainstream juice in the international style, with ripe apple-citrus fruit and lots of smoky, vanilla-tinged oak. It's a straightforward crowd-pleaser that could say Coastal, but it's from the Galilee, in northern Israel. 84 (4/1/2001)

GOLAN HEIGHTS

Golan Heights 2002 Golan Cabernet Sauvignon (Galilee) $16. Herbal and briary, with some eucalyptus as well, this plump, juicy Cabernet shows some slightly stewed and medicinal notes, yet still comes across as harmonious overall. 86 —J.C. (4/1/2005)

Golan Heights 2003 Golan Chardonnay (Galilee) $15. This unwooded Chardonnay delivers a mouthful of low-acid, low-intensity fruit, ranging from pears and lemons to tropical and citrus fruits. Soft finish. 84 —J.C. (4/1/2005)

Golan Heights 2003 Golan Sion Creek Red Red Blend (Galilee) $10. This kitchen-sink blend of Sangiovese, Syrah, Pinot Noir, Gamay, and Napa Gamay delivers Beaujolais-like flavors of ripe pears and cherries. Light in body and tart on the finish. 84 —J.C. (4/1/2005)

Golan Heights 2003 Golan Emerald Riesling (Galilee) $11. Smells nice, with fresh apple and citrus scents, but the flavors seem cooked and slightly sweet, finishing on a dull note without the requisite balancing acidity. 81 —J.C. (4/1/2005)

Golan Heights 2003 Sion Creek White White Blend (Galilee) $10. Light in weight and intensity, but pretty, with floral, musky notes accenting ripe melons, spice, and citrus. Slightly chalky on the finish. 85 Best Buy —J.C. (4/1/2005)

GUSH ETZION

Gush Etzion 2000 Cabernet Sauvignon-Merlot (Judean Hills) $27. This 70-30 blend boasts attractive aromas of cherries, menthol, and vanilla, then delivers cassis and vanilla flavors tinged with hints of green bell pepper. Supple and easy on the palate. 86 —J.C. (4/1/2005)

HEVRON HEIGHTS WINERY

Hevron Heights Winery 2001 Isaac's Ram Kosher Cabernet Sauvignon (Judean Hills) $25. Easy to drink, if somewhat herbal and light in body. Cedar and vanilla notes accent cherry-rhubarb aromas and flavors,

picking up additional complexity in the form of cinnamon and mint. Tart and juicy on the finish. 85 —J.C. (4/1/2006)

Hevron Heights Winery 2002 Jerusalem Heights Barrel Selection Kosher Cabernet Sauvignon-Merlot (Judean Hills) $14. Color is already fading toward the rim, and the wine smells of roasted yet unripe fruit, blending rhubarb and cut grass with molasses and prunes. Soft and lacking structure in the mouth. 80 —J.C. (4/1/2006)

Hevron Heights Winery 2001 Makhpelah Judean Vineyards Kosher Cabernet Sauvignon-Merlot (Judean Hills) $54. To my palate, the luxury cuvées from this winery aren't quite as successful as some of the other wines, bearing a prematurely aged character of slight oxidation and dried fruit. This one folds in earth and leather flavors before thinning out a bit on the finish. 83 —J.C. (4/1/2006)

Hevron Heights Winery 2001 Pardess Kosher Merlot (Judean Hills) $25. Has some hints of green bean, but also decent cassis and chocolate flavors. There's a hint of tomato leaf as well. Velvety in the mouth, with a long, layered finish. 86 —J.C. (4/1/2006)

Hevron Heights Winery 2002 Megiddo Kosher Red Blend (Judean Hills) $84. Pricey, but one of the better efforts to come out of Israel, successfully marrying plum fruit with vanilla and toasted coconut and some fine pipe tobacco notes. Medium-bodied, turning a bit chewy on the finish, but the fruit wins out in the end. Best over the next few years. 89 —J.C. (4/1/2006)

Hevron Heights Winery 2001 Special Reserve Lasportas Brother's Selection Kosher Red Blend (Judean Hills) $69. Has some almost slightly oxidized character to it, with hints of almonds on the nose alongside superripe, chocolaty fruit. Picks up pruny notes on the palate, then dried cherries and some drying tannins on the finish. 84 —J.C. (4/1/2006)

NOAH

Noah 2002 Kosher Cabernet Sauvignon (Judean Hills) $15. Tastes a bit grapy and almost sweet, with jammy flavors accented by hints of vanilla. A chunky, straightforward wine best suited for uncritical quaffing. 83 —J.C. (4/1/2006)

Noah 2002 Kosher Merlot (Judean Hills) $15. Jammy and a bit sweet-tasting, with aromas of stewed berries and rhubarb. Medium-bodied; finishes with a raisiny tinge to the flavors. 81 —J.C. (4/1/2006)

RECANATI

Recanati 2004 Kosher Cabernet Sauvignon (Galilee) $15. Light and crisp, with herbal and red berry aromas laced with hints of carob and rhubarb. Turns drying and peppery on the finish. 84 —J.C. (4/1/2006)

Recanati 2002 Reserve Kosher Cabernet Sauvignon (Galilee) $25. Has a slightly leathery streak to the aromas, but there's also decent berry fruit underneath. This medium-bodied Cabernet offers blackberry, plum, and herb flavors that finish soft. An easy-to-drink wine that will please most palates. 85 —J.C. (4/1/2006)

Recanati 2001 Special Reserve Kosher Cabernet Sauvignon (Galilee) $35. Recanati's most ambitious effort is also its best, with ample plum, blackberry, and coffee aromas admirably echoed on the palate. Nicely balanced, with supple tannins, and spice notes that linger on the finish. 89 —J.C. (4/1/2006)

Recanati 2004 Kosher Chardonnay (Galilee) $14. Starts off with nutty, buttery notes accented by cinnamon and clove, but has just enough stuffing to carry the oak. Apple and citrus flavors help round out the plump midpalate, but this wine is ultimately dominated by oak. Finishes on a lemony note. 84 —J.C. (4/1/2006)

Recanati 2004 Kosher Merlot (Galilee) $15. A bit confected, but nice nonetheless, with berry and vanilla notes mingling with soft tannins. Shows a bit of a metallic edge on the finish. 84 —J.C. (4/1/2006)

Recanati 2002 Reserve Kosher Merlot (Galilee) $25. Toasty and very cedary, with cherry and vanilla showing through a solid wood veneer. In the mouth, it's a bit thin despite some chewy tannins, and it turns drying and lemony on the finish. 83 —J.C. (4/1/2006)

Recanati 2003 Kosher Shiraz (Galilee) $15. This medium-bodied Shiraz features an unusual celery-seed note to its aromas alongside bold cherry fruit. An herbal flavor imparts a slightly medicinal tone, but the finish is silky smooth. **85** —*J.C. (4/1/2006)*

SEGAL'S

Segal's 2000 Special Reserve Cabernet Sauvignon (Galilee) $15. Unabashedly modern in style, this Cab boasts a lush, supple mouthfeel and hits all the right flavor notes: cedar, leather, and vanilla from oak but also black cherry and cassis from ripe fruit. The long, velvety finish is its crowning glory. **90 Best Buy** —*J.C. (4/1/2005)*

Segal's 2002 Unfiltered Cabernet Sauvignon (Galil) $60. Fans of oak should lap up this wine, but this reviewer found it overly wooded, with dominant dill and vanilla notes that taste good, yet obscure the underlying fruit. An ambitious effort. **84** —*J.C. (4/1/2005)*

Segal's 2002 Special Reserve Chardonnay (Galilee) $13. Medium- bodied and well crafted, with light toast and vanilla notes preceding the melon, baked apple, and citrus flavors to follow. Moderate in length, with a clean finish. Kosher **87** —*J.M. (4/3/2004)*

Segal's 2000 Special Reserve Merlot (Galilee) $15. Segal's hit it out of the park in 2000, delivering a Best Buy Special Reserve Cab, and this Merlot, which isn't far behind. Cedar, black cherry, and herb aromas lead into a supple, richly textured palate loaded with balanced coffee and black cherry flavors. Long and harmonious on the finish. **89 Editors' Choice** —*J.C. (4/1/2005)*

TISHBI ESTATE

Tishbi Estate 2000 Chardonnay (Golan Heights) $16. A rich golden color, with tropical fruit, pineapple, and lemon aromas. A rich mouthfeel with crisp, citrusy acidity and hints of oak that do not overwhelm the fruit. **87** — *(11/15/2002)*

Tishbi Estate 2000 Baron Chenin Blanc (Galilee) $9. Ripe quince, honey, and pears with a hint of sea salt on the nose. Even on the palate with apricots and plums. A mineral-tinged wine with a short finish. **82** — *(11/15/2002)*

YARDEN

Yarden 1996 Cabernet Sauvignon (Galilee) $20. 90 *(4/1/2000)*

Yarden 1998 Cabernet Sauvignon (Galilee) $26. Fruity right from the start, with just the slightest hint of stems on the bouquet. The palate is round and bold, and entirely pleasing, with plum and cherry flavors. The clean, chunky, round finish is smooth and darn near silky. A rich and likable wine, with chocolate and oak notes in the rear. **87** — *(11/15/2002)*

Yarden NV Champagne Blend (Galilee) $22. 88 *(4/1/2000)*

Yarden NV Brut Champagne Blend (Galilee) $20. 86 *(4/1/2000)*

Yarden NV Brut NV Champagne Blend (Galilee) $24. This sparkling wine from Israel's hilly north has complex yeasty aromas and a bready, toasty palate with citrus accents. The mouthfeel is full, and the long dry finish features mild grapefruit and spice notes. **88** *(4/1/2001)*

Yarden 2000 Chardonnay (Galilee) $17. Flowery in the nose, with notes of honey, banana, and butter. Without doubt it screams "Chardonnay," and the tropical fruit and coconut flavors announce that it received plenty of oak during the making process. The finish is also full of wood, so you had better like well-oaked Chards if this is going to appeal to you. In its favor, the texture is creamy and easygoing. **85** — *(11/15/2002)*

Yarden 1998 Chardonnay (Galilee) $15. A creamy vanilla and caramel-apple nose opens to a palate of ripe peach and apple flavors bolstered by a healthy dose of oak and good acidity. Full-bodied and round, this very international wine finishes with an orange and oak tang and modest tannins. **85** *(4/1/2001)*

Yarden 1998 Blanc de Blancs Chardonnay (Galilee) $20. Light, lean, and crisp, this is a surprisingly racy bubbly from Israel. The toast and lime aromas and flavors are clean and refreshing. And yes, it's kosher, if that's important to you. **86** —*J.C. (12/31/2004)*

Yarden 2002 Katzrin Chardonnay (Galilee) $30. Yarden's top Chardonnay is top-heavy with buttered popcorn flavors, buttressed by layers of peach

and vanilla. Full-bodied, and seems a bit warm on the finish. **86** —*J.C. (4/1/2005)*

Yarden 2002 Odem Organic Vineyard Chardonnay (Galilee) $19. Smells toasty and smoky, with a plump, medium-weight mouthfeel and smoky, leesy flavors. Finishes long, and—you guessed it—smoky. An oak-lover's wine; well made and tasty. **88** —*J.C. (4/1/2005)*

Yarden 1996 Merlot (Galilee) $20. 88 *(4/1/2000)*

Yarden 1999 Yarden Merlot (Galilee) $23. The violet color and rich, supple aromas draw you in. Plum and other Merlot-like fruit shines on the racy, acid-rich palate. This is no softy, but it is still plush and deep enough to satisfy and maintain balance. Not a bad Levant red at all. **86** —*M.S. (11/15/2002)*

Yarden 2003 Mount Hermon Red Blend (Galilee) $11. This blend of 42% Cab Sauvignon, 48% Merlot, and 10% Cab Franc comes across as unevolved, showing lots of bouncy fresh black cherry flavors but not much nuance. A charred wood-coffee grounds note does come through on the finish. **84** —*J.C. (4/1/2005)*

Yarden 1998 Mt. Hermon Red Blend (Galilee) $11. 87 Best Buy *(4/1/2000)*

Yarden 2001 Syrah (Galilee) $23. Delivers a blast of jammy black cherry aromas that quickly subside into hints of raisin, dried spices, and herbs. Flavors are dull and a bit earthy, while the wine finishes on a note of alcoholic warmth. **83** —*J.C. (4/1/2005)*

YATIR

Yatir 2002 Yatir Forest Kosher Cabernet Sauvignon (Judean Hills) $50. Smooth and velvety in the mouth, with some chewy wood tannins on the finish. Aromas and flavors hint at tobacco and vanilla, with just enough earthy fruit flavors in support. Drink now–2010. **86** —*J.C. (4/1/2006)*

Yatir 2001 Cabernet Sauvignon-Merlot (Judean Hills) $30. Earthy and dull, a flat, boring wine that features modest fruit and a medicinal note. **81** —*J.C. (4/1/2005)*

Yatir 2001 Forest Cabernet Sauvignon-Merlot (Judean Hills) $49. Starts off herbal, then adds flavors of black cherries and coffee. This medium-bodied wine is smooth and supple in the mouth, finishing with soft tannins and a tea-like note. **87** —*J.C. (4/1/2005)*

LEBANON

CHÂTEAU KEFRAYA

Château Kefraya 1997 Cabernet Blend (Bekaa Valley) $23. Very earthy, with notes of cinnamon and cassis. Ripe blackberries, spice, and white pepper play out on the palate. Tannins are big and crushing but the fruit holds up in this well-balanced wine. **91** — *(11/15/2002)*

CHÂTEAU KEFRAYA

Château Kefraya 2000 La Dame Blanche Chardonnay (Bekaa Valley) $13. A slightly oxidized oloroso-like nose with yeasty, ripe banana notes. Sun-dried apricots and roasted nuts on the palate. A light-bodied wine lacking a little acidity with a very short finish. A blend of Clairette, Ugni Blanc, and Boiurboulenc. **82** — *(11/15/2002)*

CHÂTEAU MUSAR

Château Musar 1997 Red Blend (Bekaa Valley) $49. 88 —*J.C. (4/1/2005)*

Château Musar 2000 Hochar Red Blend (Bekaa Valley) $25. 89 —*J.C. (4/1/2005)*

Château Musar 1998 White Blend (Bekaa Valley) $28. Sherried-smelling, picking up nuances of anise, lacquer, and stone dust, and finishing on a lemony note. An acquired taste. **82** —*J.C. (4/1/2005)*

TISHBI ESTATE

Tishbi Estate 2000 Baron Cabernet Sauvignon (Bekaa Valley) $12. Opens with toasted vanilla, plum, spice, and tobacco aromas. Fresh, ripe, jammy berry flavors. Although a little short on the finish, this is a charming, well-rounded wine with soft tannins. **88 Best Buy** — *(11/15/2002)*

Tishbi Estate 2000 Tishbi Vineyards Cabernet Sauvignon (Bekaa Valley) $16. Wild mushrooms, herbal, earthy aromas lead to green olives on the palate with black pepper, spice, and tobacco, and ripe berries on the long finish. **90** — *(11/15/2002)*

Tishbi Estate 1999 Jonathan Tishbi Merlot (Bekaa Valley) $46. Fragrant notes of cloves, wild herbs, plums, and an earthy thread throughout. A full-bodied, rich wine with great extraction of inky blackberries, strong spices, tobacco, and supportive oak character. Tasters were pleasantly surprised by this wine due to it's unusual power. **92 Cellar Selection** — *(11/15/2002)*

MACEDONIA

BOVIN

Bovin 2000 Alexandar Red Blend (Tikves) $12. A blend of Vranec and Cabernet Sauvignon, Alexandar displays a smooth mouthfeel with soft tannins and good acidity. Spice dominates the mouth, with hints of black berries, and the wine is rounded out with holiday spice, red berry and silky chocolate in the nose. **84** —*M.D. (6/1/2006)*

Bovin 2000 Venus Red Blend (Tikves) $12. This blend of the Macedonian Vranec varietal with Merlot starts off well enough, with chocolate and red berry aromas, but falls off in the mouth. Some oak, cinnamon, and tobacco flavors emerge but fade just as quickly, leaving a round, low tannin and low acid wine with very little flavor. **81** —*M.D. (6/1/2006)*

Bovin 2000 Vranec (Tikves) $12. This grape, called Vranac in former Yuogslavia, is known for its amicable nature with oak. This wine has that, with vanilla aromas and notes of oak and mint on the tongue, but little else. Red color and a nice mouthfeel speak of youth, but the lack of fruit does not. **83** —*M.D. (6/1/2006)*

Bovin 2000 Dissan Vranec (Tikves) $25. Full, dry, round, and balanced in the mouth, this wine attempts greatness. But aside from oak-based flavors, it doesn't deliver. Toast and graham cracker waft from the glass, while flavors of tobacco, spice, and mint nearly overpower the red berry. **85** —*M.D. (6/1/2006)*

MEXICO

L.A. CETTO

L.A. Cetto 1996 Private Reserve Cabernet Sauvignon (Valle de Guadalupe) $18. Aromas of mature Cabernet: cassis, tobacco leaf, and a touch of caramel. Not overly rich or heavy, this is a pretty, lightweight Cab best enjoyed now. **87** *(7/1/2003)*

L.A. Cetto 2001 Chardonnay (Valle de Guadalupe) $10. Smells crisp and pineapple-y and tastes of tart pineapple and pear, but the mouthfeel is thick and syrupy. Finishes relatively clean and tangy. **84** *(7/1/2003)*

L.A. Cetto 2000 Private Reserve Chardonnay (Valle de Guadalupe) $14. Simple pear flavors, joined by a hint of butter. A bit thick and heavy, but it makes for a mouthfilling white. **84** *(7/1/2003)*

L.A. Cetto 1996 Private Reserve Nebbiolo (Valle de Guadalupe) $18. The color is appropriately light, the aromas appropriately floral and rose-like. Fleshy cherry flavors are balanced by a helping of greens and flowers. Light and elegant. Who would've thought Nebbiolo like this could come from Mexico? **88** *(7/1/2003)*

L.A. Cetto 1999 Petite Sirah (Valle de Guadalupe) $8. Dark and earthy, slightly pruny and alcoholic, finishing on notes of tar and molasses. **83** *(7/1/2003)*

L.A. Cetto 2001 Zinfandel (Valle de Guadalupe) $8. A surprisingly light, crisp Zinfandel, with tomato and herb aromas and flavors only partially offset by berries. But it finishes with Zin's trademark pepperiness. **83** *(7/1/2003)*

MOLDOVA

CRICOVA

Cricova 2002 Cabernet Sauvignon (Moldova) $8. At first this wine smells of stem, berry fruit, and oak, then picks up candied apple and clay notes. Fairly big and bulky, despite being dry and stemmy, the wine offers spice and chocolate in addition to red fruit flavor. **83** —*M.D. (12/15/2006)*

Cricova 1993 Collection Cabernet Cabernet Sauvignon (Moldova) $23. This is the best of Cricova's Collection series, which consists of wines that age in the winery for years. It has an evolved nose of aged cheese, earth, stem, and tobacco, with some fruit to spare. Fairly light for a Cabernet, it maintains healthy, yet dusty, tannins supporting barnyard, leather, brown spice, and chewing tobacco flavors. The fruit has gone, but what remains is an interesting, complex wine with good intensity. **86** —*M.D. (12/15/2006)*

Cricova 2001 Prestige Cabernet Sauvignon (Moldova) $16. Stemmy throughout, but in between there's aromas and flavors of spiced red plum, blueberry, and raspberry, a touch of mineral and dry, chalky tannins. Lively acidity brings this to a tart and spicy finish. **84** —*M.D. (12/15/2006)*

Cricova 2000 Codru Cabernet Sauvignon-Merlot (Moldova) $8. Heavy on the nose, this wine's prune-like aromas lead to a medium-bodied quaff with good, smooth tannins and heavy prune flavors. Finishes solid, although on the tangy side. **84 Best Buy** —*M.D. (12/15/2006)*

Cricova 1990 Collection Codru Cabernet Sauvignon-Merlot (Moldova) $22. With 75% Cabernet and 25% Merlot, this older Codru blend has a nice, smooth mouthfeel from soft, aged tannins. Light bodied, with brown tobacco and stem flavors following a nose of brown spice and smoke. Drink up, as the fruit has long since gone, but it's worth trying just for the feel. **85** —*M.D. (12/15/2006)*

Cricova 2001 Prestige Codru Cabernet Sauvignon-Merlot (Moldova) $16. Aromas offer hints of red berry under mint, spice, and heavy stem. The stemminess continues in the mouth, where this wine is gritty and dry, with mild red berry flavor. **82** —*M.D. (12/15/2006)*

Cricova 1992 Collection Dionis Red Blend (Moldova) $22. An unusual blend of 80% Pinot Noir with 20% Cabernet that has fine, dusty tannins and a lean but smooth feel. Light red fruit, tobacco, and citrus emerge on the nose, followed by flavors of tobacco, spice, and cola, with a touch of fruit. Good now, but edging toward retirement. **84** —*M.D. (12/15/2006)*

Cricova 2000 Dionis Red Blend (Moldova) $10. This wine starts off with robust aromas of purple, candied fruit and stem, but in the mouth it's too sweet, the berry and sour cherry flavors having a candied edge. **81** — *M.D. (12/15/2006)*

CRICOVA ACOREX

Cricova Acorex 1999 Riesling (Moldova) $6. **82** *(9/1/2004)*
Cricova Acorex 1999 Sauvignon Blanc (Moldova) $6. **83** *(9/1/2004)*

GRAYSTONE

Graystone 2004 Select Cabernet Sauvignon (Cahul) $13. Simple and Beaujolais-like, with purple, grapey berry fruit as well as hints of char and leather. Smooth, simple and dry, with berry aromas. **83** —*M.D. (12/15/2006)*

Graystone 2005 Select Chardonnay (Cahul) $13. A run-of-the-mill Chardonnay nose with hints of oak lead to a light, sharp white wine with bright, lively tropical fruit flavors and a touch of mineral. Finishes with oak flavor and high acidity. **83** —*M.D. (12/15/2006)*

OTHER INTERNATIONAL

Graystone 2004 Select Merlot (Cahul) $13. Purple, grapey fruit flavors are simple but good, with hints of clay. Tannins are light, offering little structure. Aromas are a bit muddled, red berry one minute then mint and leather the next, with wafts of weediness. **83** —*M.D. (12/15/2006)*

Graystone 2005 Select Pinot Gris (Cahul) $13. Hints at peanut butter on the nose, with just a hint of fruit, but in the mouth it opens a little, adding fruity flavors to the nutty ones. Smooth, but with enough acidity to finish crisply. **83** —*M.D. (12/15/2006)*

Graystone 2004 Select Pinot Noir (Cahul) $13. Rosy colored, but with heavy, chunky aromas. Stalky red fruit flavors lack excitement. A touch of cola is nice, but not enough to stand out and sing. **81** —*M.D. (12/15/2006)*

VINA LAVINA

Vina LaVina 2000 Chardonnay (Chisinau County) $9. Despite it's age, it shows pale yellow in the glass, with a greenish tinge. Some pineapple and petrol aromas lead to tart citrus fruit and more petrol in the mouth, with a round, oily feel and a lemony finish. **81** —*M.D. (6/1/2006)*

VINO VISTA COLLECTION

Vino Vista Collection 2005 Mirodia Semidry Red Blend (Codru Region) $9. Pomegranate and red berry flavors are fairly sweet, as indicated by the label, and the wine offers aromas of cinnamon, violet, candied dark fruit and honey. **82** —*M.D. (12/15/2006)*

MOROCCO

HICKORY RIDGE

Hickory Ridge 1999 Special Cuvée Shiraz (Beni M'Tir) $6. A slight saline quality marks the dark cherry fruit in one of our most exotic offerings, from Morocco. The sweet and sour stewed fruit doesn't show depth or enough definition. Turns hard, with a metallic note on the back end. **82** *(10/1/2001)*

ROMANIA

BLACK C

Black C 2001 Feteasca Neagra (Romania) $9. Cassis and fresh berry start off the nose, and are quickly enveloped by menthol aromas. In the mouth there is a hint of sweetness, but otherwise menthol and tannins prevail. **80** —*M.D. (6/1/2006)*

Black C 2000 Pinot Gris (Romania) $9. If this were game, it would be considered well hung, but since it's wine, it's just barely holding on. The aromas are an interesting blend of pear and quince with honey and tangerine, but it lacks midpalate weight, ending on a chalky, citrusy note. **83** —*J.C. (2/1/2006)*

BYZANTIUM

Byzantium 2000 Cabernet Sauvignon (Dealu Mare) $15. Chunky and on the verge of plump, this wine has turned from its fruit at this stage and shows plenty of brown leaf and earth. Probably not going anywhere, so drink up now. **83** —*M.D. (6/1/2006)*

Byzantium 2004 Chardonnay (Murfatlar Cernavoda) $15. Some sweetness in the mouth doesn't quite balance the tart feel, while candy banana flavors and peppermint aromas don't speak of this wine's varietal characters. All in all, just not put together well. **80** —*M.D. (6/1/2006)*

Byzantium 2002 Rosso di Valachia Red Blend (Dealu Mare) $15. Nice fruit aromas of blueberry and plum mingle with tobacco, with graphite adding to the mix in the mouth. Dry and light-bodied, this wine is linear in its fruit, but rewarding. **84** —*M.D. (6/1/2006)*

Byzantium 2004 Blanc de Transylvanie White Blend (Transylvanian Plateau) $15. A blend of Pinot Gris, Gewürztraminer, and the indigenous Feteasca, this wine offers perfumey scents of lychee fruit and orange blossom with some animal musk. Flavors of peppermint, lychee, and white pepper follow, and a touch of sweetness keeps it all in harmony. **84** —*M.D. (6/1/2006)*

CHERRY TREE HILL

Cherry Tree Hill 2003 Merlot (Dealu Mare) $20. A dark, meaty nose has hints of vanilla and dust, and this wine fills the mouth with a full body and dry but fine tannin. Despite being barrique aged the oak is not obvious, showing more graphite and tobacco leaf. There seems to be very little fruit at this stage, however, and an ashy finish adds an off note. **84** —*M.D. (6/1/2006)*

CRAMELE HALEWOOD

Cramele Halewood 2000 Prahova Valley Special Reserve Cabernet Sauvignon (Dealu Mare) $14. Dry tannin still characterizes this wine, which also displays sweet red berry and herb flavors. Medium-bodied, with a rustic feel and aromas of cola, tobacco, and wood. **83** —*M.D. (6/1/2006)*

Cramele Halewood 2001 Prahova Valley Special Reserve Feteasca Neagra (Dealu Mare) $14. Light aromas of red berry, cola, and brown sugar are pleasant on the nose, but the fruit gets lost in the mouth. Light and dry, with high acidity, the mineralty of this wine has very little red fruit to balance it. **83** —*M.D. (6/1/2006)*

LA BELLE AMIE

La Belle Amie 2002 Special Reserve Cabernet Sauvignon (Dealu Mare) $15. The Dealu Mare region is Romania's wine basket, with international and local varieties grown. This Cab is expressive, showing aromas of purple berry, cinnamon, and char. Flavors are similar, with meat and leather adding to the somewhat candied, mixed berry taste. Smooth and fairly light for Cabernet. **86** —*M.D. (12/15/2006)*

La Belle Amie 2001 Special Reserve Pinot Noir (Dealu Mare) $18. A light-bodied and slightly underripe wine, judging by the stalky notes, but overall it passes with peppery, red fruit aromas and flavors. **83** —*M.D. (12/15/2006)*

TERRA ROMANA

Terra Romana 2003 Muscat Ottonel Muskat Ottonel (Tarnave) $10. This Muscat is best served with mildly spicy Asian dishes, where its floral, off-dry flavors will offset some chili heat, while the refreshing acids on the finish will clean the palate. Lychee, melon, and tangerine flavors add exotic notes. **84** —*J.C. (6/1/2005)*

Terra Romana 2002 Cuvée Charlotte Red Blend (Dealu Mare) $20. Ambitiously structured, with robust tannins and stern acids, but the fruit doesn't quite measure up, yielding modest berry and earth flavors. Drink soon with hearty meat dishes, before the fruit fades. **83** —*J.C. (6/1/2005)*

Terra Romana 2000 Reserve Red Blend (Dealu Mare) $9. Fading and already brick in color, this dull, earthy wine finishes tart and watery. **80** —*J.C. (6/1/2005)*

Terra Romana 2002 Sauvignon Blanc-Feteasca White Blend (Romania) $10. Without much fruit, this is an earthy, dull, medium-bodied wine with a short finish. **80** —*J.C. (6/1/2005)*

VAL DUNÁ

Val Duná 2004 Sauvignon Blanc/Feteasca Regala White Blend (Plaiurile Drancei) $7. This wine, made with half of the Feteasca Regala, or "Royal Girl" grape, offers nice grapefruit on the nose with a hint of animal musk. Light flavors of peach and citrus, with that hint of musk, marry the medium body and fresh acidity nicely. **84 Best Buy** —*M.D. (6/1/2006)*

VOX POPULI

Vox Populi 2004 Chardonnay (Dealu Mare) $10. A thin, high-acid wine with okay flavors of citrusy white fruits. **81** —*M.D. (12/15/2006)*

Vox Populi 2003 Pinot Noir (Dealu Mare) $10. On the nose there is vanilla with decent berry-cola aromas and a hint of nail polish. The wine is medium-bodied and dry, with earthy red berry and barnyard flavors. A touch of spice picks up the finish. **84** —*M.D. (12/15/2006)*

SLOVENIA

MOVIA

Movia 2002 Sauvignon (Brda) $24. This Slovenian white shows exotic, unconventional aromas that land squarely in the realm of tropical fruit and flowers. Soft and creamy on the palate, with melon, honeycomb, and just a spritz of lemon. Subtle and sleek on the finish as it gently drifts away. Quite interesting and satisfying. **89** *(7/1/2005)*

TUNISIA

DOMAINE NEFERIS

Domaine Neferis 2005 Selian Rosé Mystère Rosé Blend (Tunisia) $NA. An irresistible rosé from Tunisia (made by Sicily's Calatrasi) that boasts a deep, penetrating raspberry color, lush berry fruit, lush peach aromas, and plenty of rose-like notes. This is a wine with promising pairing potential with couscous or grilled meat. **87** —*M.L. (7/1/2006)*

Domaine Neferis 2005 Selian White Blend (Tunisia) $NA. Sicily's Calatrasi is also present in Tunisia—a marriage between North Africa and Italian winemaking styles—to produce unique wines, like this white, redolent of white flowers, stone fruit, and a touch of something plastic or gummy in the background. This is otherwise a balanced wine with spice on the close. **85** —*M.L. (7/1/2006)*

TERRALE

Terrale 2000 Syrah/Carignan Red Blend (Tunisia) $8. **85** *(5/1/2002)*

URUGUAY

ARIANO

Ariano 2002 Cabernet Sauvignon (Canelones) $7. Peanut and leather aromas, with a candied sweetness to the palate. Sweet and sugary, maybe a likable trait for some. **80** —*M.S. (11/15/2004)*

Ariano 2003 Merlot (Canelones) $7. Innocuous; nothing forceful or impacting. Shows hints of raspberry and cinnamon, with spice and wintergreen on the rough finish. **82** —*M.S. (11/15/2004)*

Ariano 2003 Selección Red Blend (Canelones) $10. Among the Ariano line, this Tannat, Cab Franc, and Syrah blend is the best. Yet it's still light, with caramel aromas along with hints of berry fruit. Mild strawberry and plum on the palate before a finish with kick. **83** —*M.S. (11/15/2004)*

Ariano 2002 Tannat (Canelones) $9. Soy sauce and sweet fruit create a muddled, odd nose. The palate offers tart raspberry, with hints of pepper and oak. Finishes leathery and tight, with loud, drying tannins. **82** —*M.S. (10/1/2004)*

BODEGA CARLOS PIZZORNO

Bodega Carlos Pizzorno 2004 Don Próspero Tannat (Uruguay) $12. This wine captures the enigma that is Uruguayan Tannat. The nose is ripe, the color bold and purple. From that, you'd expect a lot. But the palate is wanting; the fruit is snappy and borderline tart. It just doesn't seem fully ripe. And the wine turns horsey and tannic as it airs. **82** —*M.S. (11/1/2006)*

BODEGAS CARRAU

Bodegas Carrau 2002 De Reserva Tannat (Uruguay) $13. This basic Tannat is more acceptable than the winery's higher-priced reserve wine simply because it's fruity, short, and precise. Of course, it's tannic and rough, but that's the nature of the grape and country of origin. **82** —*M.S. (11/1/2006)*

BODEGONES DEL SUR

Bodegones Del Sur 1999 Selección de Barricas Red Blend (Juanico) $22. If it were only true that the stock black cherry and earth aromas guaranteed a better wine, because this is tight, aggressive, harsh, and tannic. Plushness is absent amid the spicy, hammering pool of dark fruit and tannin. Seems professionally made but where's the pleasure? **81** —*M.S. (11/1/2006)*

Bodegones Del Sur 2003 Sauvignon Blanc (Juanico) $9. Mild citrus aromas are clouded by the scent of green pepper and peas. Flavors of apple, pineapple, and citrus are ultimately sour, as is the finish. Not much nuance is on display, and in the wide world of Sauvignon Blanc, you can surely do better. **82** —*M.S. (9/1/2004)*

Bodegones Del Sur 2000 Oak Aged Tannat (Juanico) $15. The bouquet is difficult to get into; there's peanut, popcorn, sawdust, and chili powder. So go figure. On the palate, some raspberry and cherry gets tied up in the oak, which isn't particularly flavorful. As for mouthfeel, it is tight and hard, like virtually every Uruguayan wine we've tasted. **83** —*M.S. (9/1/2004)*

Bodegones Del Sur 2000 Reserve Tannat (Juanico) $12. Like all the wines from Uruguay, this one has rock-hard tannins that clamp down on the palate. But the nose of cool earth, leather, and black fruit is nice, and the flavor profile is nothing to take issue with. The cherry and raspberry flavors are full and healthy, and the wine's acidity forms a nice base for the fruit. Drink with food due to the firm tannins. **86** —*M.S. (9/1/2004)*

BOUZA

Bouza 2004 Tannat-Merlot Red Blend (Canelones) $24. Bouza is one of the few Uruguayan wineries that's ready to compete on the world stage. This Tannat-Merlot blend is deep and dark, with saturated blackberry and dark plum flavors. It's a bit heavy and clumsy, with some chocolate on the finish. But overall it's a well-made New World red that will accompany steak and other grilled meats. **86** —*M.S. (11/1/2006)*

Bouza 2004 Special Barrel Tannat (Uruguay) $50. They call it Special Barrel, and one sniff tells you that this is a Tannat raised in pricey French oak barrels. And that's not a criticism; the wine is toasty, with alluring charcoal and smoke aromas. The palate is up to it as well, as it exhibits bright, elevated dark-fruit flavors. Nicely balanced for the most part, with plenty of cassis, berry, and plum character. **89 Editors' Choice** —*M.S. (11/1/2006)*

CASTILLO VIEJO

Castillo Viejo 2002 Catamayor Red Blend (San Jose) $13. Fairly mature and less rough than most Tannat-based wines. This one features cola, rubber, and cedar aromas followed by tangy red-berry fruit. Somewhat oily and rubbery on the palate but it tastes alright. Includes 40% Cab Franc. **83** —*M.S. (11/1/2006)*

Castillo Viejo 2004 Catamayor Sauvignon Blanc (San Jose) $10. Citrusy all the way through, with light pear and peach aromas that struggle to hold form. Grapefruit and orange flavors are reasonable; shallow on the finish. **83** —*M.S. (4/1/2006)*

DANTE IRURTIA

Dante Irurtia 2000 Reserva del Virrey Tannat (Uruguay) $18. The rubber and tree bark are common for Uruguayan Tannat. Flavors of dark cherry, cola, and coffee are the best part of yet another tough, rugged power pack that's neither plush nor all that pleasant to drink. Hard as heck in the mouth; rough stuff on the whole. **80** —*M.S. (11/1/2006)*

Dante Irurtia 2004 Posada del Virrey Reserva Viognier (Uruguay) $14. Light on the nose, offering touches of pear, vanilla and spice. Veers toward crisp lime and orange in the mouth, with even more citrus on the finish. Runs juicy and lean, but mostly it's clean. **83** —*M.S. (11/1/2006)*

OTHER INTERNATIONAL

DELUCCA

DeLucca 2001 Red Blend (El Colorado) $10. Beefy and stocky, with a dark tint, big tannins, and a very masculine personality. The palate yields blackberry fruit in ripe form, and the finish is expectedly tight and tannic, with a drying sensation that builds quickly. Still, with roast or barbecued meats, it will work. **85** —*M.S. (1/1/2004)*

DeLucca 2000 Tannat (El Colorado) $10. Round and tight, like Tannat is known to be, with burly black-fruit aromas and flavors. There's detectable cassis and raisin notes prior to a spicy, tannic finish that deals licorice and coffee. Pretty heavy, full-bodied stuff for sure, but a decent rendition of Tannat. Very much worth a go. **85** —*M.S. (1/1/2004)*

DON ADELIO ARIANO

Don Adelio Ariano 2002 Reserve Oak Barrel Tannat (Uruguay) $12. Jumbled and earthy on the nose, with a strong blast of leather. Not as tannic as the majority of Tannats, so it manages to sit on your palate without boring a hole through your cheek. But still it's rather leafy and bland. **83** —*M.S. (11/1/2006)*

LOS CERROS DE SAN JUAN

Los Cerros de San Juan 2002 S Torrens Oak Reserve Tannat (Uruguay) $18. Dark and purple, with a hard nose that's difficult to get into. Hard and dark on the palate as well, with wicked acids and rock-like tannins. It's yet another sassy, rough Tannat. **81** —*M.S. (11/1/2006)*

MOIZO HERMANOS

Moizo Hermanos 2000 Roble Reserva Tannat (Juanico) $15. The distinct smell of buttered movie popcorn smothers the nose and manages to pick up strength with time. And that doesn't bode well for the friendliness of this wine, which has some cherry and cassis flavors but also a tannic-driven, rock-hard mouthfeel that makes it seem like you're drinking gravel. **81** —*M.S. (1/1/2004)*

STAGNARI

Stagnari 2000 Salto Premier Tannat (Uruguay) $12. Almost over the top, but not quite. The nose seems a bit burnt and meaty, but the palate is all plum and blackberry fruit. There's good balance here and the tannins are not too wicked. But the finish is short and the early impression left by the wine exceeds the final impression by a healthy distance. **84** —*M.S. (1/1/2004)*

TOSCANINI

Toscanini 2002 Cabernet Sauvignon (Canelones) $9. Dark in color, with black plum along with damp earth aromas. But in the mouth it's sharp, with searing acidity. A confusing, atypical Cabernet. **80** —*M.S. (11/15/2004)*

Toscanini 2003 Sauvignon Blanc (Canelones) $8. Not great, but shows some banana and pear flavors and aromas. Weak and watery; inoffensive. **80** —*M.S. (10/1/2004)*

Toscanini 2002 Tannat (Canelones) $9. Spicy, with somewhat attractive yet hollow aromas. The palate is grapy, with oak and berry flavors. The mouthfeel is textured but comes with a bit of a burnt, cooked fruit. Still, it stirs interest for the grape and origin. **84** —*M.S. (10/1/2004)*

Toscanini 2002 Reserva Tannat (Uruguay) $30. Mildly saucy and stewy, with damp aromas. The palate is a touch green, with olive, bell pepper, and tomato notes feeding into primary plum flavors. Hard as can be on the tongue, with cheek-scratching tannins. **81** —*M.S. (11/1/2006)*

Toscanini 1999 Reserve Tannat (Canelones) $13. If this five-year-old wine is an indication, then Tannat doesn't age that well. This example is rusty and orange at the rim, with dried fruit, caramel, and earth on the nose. Over the hill. **80** —*M.S. (10/1/2004)*

Toscanini 2003 Trebbiano 70% Sémillon 30% White Blend (Canelones) $8. Odd but okay. The nose is unrecognizable as a whole, but in there is pear, apple, and butter—not your normal Sauvignon aromas. Citrus on the palate and a long, herbaceous finish. **83** —*M.S. (10/1/2004)*

VIÑA PROGRESO

Viña Progreso 2003 Reserve Chardonnay (Uruguay) $19. Butterscotch in color and aromas, with apple as the core flavor. Full and interesting, with a long, warm finish. A good deal of zest and attitude. Millions of miles away from Burgundy, but not bad. **85** —*M.S. (10/1/2004)*

Viña Progreso 2003 Reserve Tannat (Uruguay) $19. This joint venture between the Pisano and Boisset families is making an extracted, heavily oaked Tannat, and it's a good effort. The wine is dark, almost opaque. Coffee and mocha vie with ripe black plum on the nose, while flavors of bitter chocolate and pepper darken the fruity palate. The finish is both juicy and thick. An interesting Uruguayan red. **86** —*M.S. (10/1/2004)*

VIÑEDO DE LOS VIENTOS

Viñedo de los Vientos 2000 Eolo Gran Reserva Red Blend (Atlantida) $15. The bouquet has a strong lemony scent, one that seems to come from the wood treatment it went through. But there's also saturated black fruit, boysenberry flavors and, of course, huge, drying tannins. This is not an ordinary wine, or an ordinary Tannat. It certainly brings some zing to the table. **84** —*M.S. (1/1/2004)*

Viñedo de los Vientos 2002 Tannat (Atlantida) $18. Approachable on the nose, but like so many other Tannats it's like nails on the palate. And here the fruit is snappy and tangy, not dark and sweet. You could call it juicy or just as easily call it sour. **81** —*M.S. (11/1/2006)*

VINSON RICHARDS

Vinson Richards 2000 Estate Bottled Cabernet Sauvignon (Juanico) $9. At first the aromas seem reduced and inky, but with time some spice and raisin comes up. As per usual, given its origin, the wine is tannic, with a hard mouthfeel. But the flavors are solid and true, and there's just enough spicy red fruit, leather, and earth throughout. **84** —*M.S. (9/1/2004)*

Vinson Richards 2000 Merlot (Juanico) $9. The bouquet of cherry, vanilla, and leather is fairly complete and nice. Flavors of dried fruits, brandy, and chocolate pave the way to a quiet, simple, and clean finish. With a fair amount of Piedmontese character, this one has a bit in common with Nebbiolo. It's definitely leathery and tight, but the flavors are good. **85** —*M.S. (9/1/2004)*

Vinson Richards 2000 Shiraz (Juanico) $9. With its leather and peanut aromas, you wonder about the fruit. But it doesn't taste bad, although the tannins wrapped around the cherry and raisin fruit are hard as cement. It finishes dry and hard, with too much tannin and not enough pulp. **82** —*M.S. (9/1/2004)*

Vinson Richards 2000 Reserve Tannat (Juanico) $17. Inky and saturated in the nose, with aromas of chocolate, coffee, and red berries. The palate kicks up cherry, plum, and chocolate, and the finish is typically dry and tannic. But it's also tasty and comes in a couple of layers. This wine shows more style than most from Uruguay and would be worth a go with grilled steak. **86** —*M.S. (9/1/2004)*

The United States

CALIFORNIA

Vineyard on the western slopes of the Napa Valley, Oakville, Napa County, California.

California wines account for a sixty-four percent share of the United States wine market, according to the Wine Institute, the venerable trade and lobbying group whose membership includes 840 wineries. However, *Wine Business Monthly*, a trade magazine, estimates that there are 2,445 wineries doing business in California.

Whatever the number, in 2004, California wineries produced wine grown on 440,296 acres of vineyards, with about sixty percent of them planted with red or black grapes. The most widely planted major varietals, not surprisingly, are Chardonnay and Cabernet Sauvignon, although the latter has seen a slight percentage drop in recent years, as more Syrah and Pinot Noir have been planted.

The Central Valley of California contains the majority of plantings, but grapes from this hot inland region are seldom if ever included in premium bottlings. California's reputation for world-class wine rests almost entirely on coastal bottlings, "coastal" being defined as anywhere a true maritime influence penetrates the land, through gaps in the Coast Ranges that run from Oregon down to below Los Angeles. The Pacific Ocean is a chilly body of water, even in high summer. Without the gaps, California's coastal valleys would be almost as hot as the Central Valley, and incapable of producing fine, dry table wine. With the gaps, however, come the cooling winds and fogs that make for premium grape growing.

PREDOMINANT VARIETIES

Cabernet Sauvignon The great grape of the Médoc, in France's Bordeaux region, which has been the model—and point of departure—for California claret-style wines for more than a century. Napa County dominates statewide acreage of Cabernet, as well as quality. The great estates of Napa Valley have been joined by scores of small, ambitious boutique wineries on the cutting edge of viticultural and enological—and pricing—practices. California Cabernet is rich, full-bodied, opulent, fruity, and hedonistic, matching supreme power with a velvety elegance. The best will easily age for a decade or two.

Pinot Noir Undoubtedly the great varietal success story of the late twentieth century in California wine, red or white, Pinot Noir continues to make the most astounding advances. It favors the coolest climates available, although if growing conditions are too chilly, the grapes fail to ripen. Pinot Noir is far more demanding to grow than almost any other wine grape, but when conditions are right, the wines can be majestic: lush, silky, complex, and (to use an overworked but useful word) seductive.

Chardonnay For at least fifty years, Chardonnay has been California's greatest dry white wine. Although in the

1990s the media touted an "A.B.C." phenomenon—anything but Chardonnay—the wine remains a triumph. Like Pinot Noir, Chardonnay is best grown in cool coastal conditions, although it is more forgiving, and the odd bottling from anywhere can gain praise. Full-throttle Burgundian winemaking is the norm, but lately, Australian-style unoaked Chardonnay has been enjoying favor.

Zinfandel Historians still quibble about when exactly this varietal came to California. It has been here for at least one hundred and fifty years, and always has had its admirers. Zinfandel comes into and goes out of fashion, and has been made in styles ranging from sweet and Porty to dry and tannic to "white." The current thinking leans toward balance, in the model of a good Cabernet. The best Zinfandels come from cool coastal regions, especially old vines, most usually in Sonoma and Napa, but the Sierra Foothills have many old vineyards that produce great bottlings. Paso Robles occasionally comes up with a masterpiece.

Sauvignon Blanc This great grape of Sancerre and Pouilly-Fumé, in the Loire Valley, similarly produces a dry, crisp, pleasantly clean wine in California. It can be tank fermented and entirely unoaked, or just slightly oaked, in order to preserve the variety's fresh, citrusy flavors. Some producers look to Bordeaux to craft richer, barrel-fermented wines, often mixed with Sémillon, or even Viognier. "Fumé" Blanc is a synonym. If overcropped or unripe, the wines can have unpleasant aromas.

Merlot This other great grape of Bordeaux was greeted with fanfare by critics in the 1980s and 1990s, but Merlot never really reached Cabernet's superstardom. Merlot was said to be the "soft" Cabernet, but with modern tannin management, it's no softer than Cabernet, and, in fact can be quite hard. The wines, though, can be exceptional, especially in Napa Valley, Carneros, and parts of Sonoma County and Santa Barbara.

Syrah and Rhône Varieties Plantings of Syrah have increased, as consumers and critics alike welcome these deeply fruity, richly balanced wines. Syrah grapes are remarkably adaptable, and grow well almost everywhere. The wines tend to be organized into cool-climate and warm-climate bottlings, the former drier and more tannic, the latter often soft and jammy. The other red Rhône varieties, especially Mourvèdre and Grenache, are still exotic specimens, tinkered with lovingly by a coterie of Rhône Rangers.

Other Dry Whites Viognier, the darling of the Northern Rhône, grew in popularity in the 1990s. The wine achieved fame for its exotic, full-throttle fruit, floral, and spice flavors, but proved surprisingly elusive when it came to balance. An emerging handful display true Alsatian richness and complexity. The best are from cool coastal valleys, but if the climate is too cold, the wines turn acidic and green.

MAJOR CALIFORNIA WINE REGIONS

American grape-growing regions are authorized by the federal government, upon petitioning from individuals, and are called "American Viticultural Areas" (AVAs), or "appellations." Currently, there are ninety-five AVAs in California, with more petitions filed everyday.

Napa Valley The state's oldest AVA is its most famous. Napa Valley (established in 1981), at 225,000 acres, is so large that over the years, it has developed fourteen appellations within the larger one. Napa always has been home to California's, and America's, greatest Cabernet Sauvignons and blends, an achievement not likely to be upset anytime soon. In all other varieties, it strives, usually successfully, to compete.

Sonoma County Sonoma is California's most heterogeneous wine county. So diverse is its climate, from hot and sunny inland to cool, foggy coastal, that every grape varietal in the state is grown somewhere within its borders, often as not to good effect. In warm Alexander Valley and Dry Creek Valley, Zinfandel finds few peers. Out on the coast, and the adjacent Russian River Valley, Pinot Noir first proved that California could compete with Burgundy, and Pinot's huge improvements continue to startle. Chardonnay excels everywhere; Syrah is dependable. Old-vine field blends, comprised often of obscure French varieties, have their admirers. Meanwhile, Alexander Valley Cabernet, especially from the steep, rugged west-facing slopes of the Mayacamas Mountains, is showing continuing improvement.

Monterey County This large, cool growing area originally was planted with huge vineyards, making inexpensive wine in industrial-sized quantities. Serious, boutique-oriented adventurers sought out nooks and crannies where they could produce world-class wine, and the Santa Lucia Highlands AVA (1992) has been the most noteworthy result. Its slopes and benches are home to ripe, full-bodied, high-acid Pinot Noir, Chardonnay, and, increasingly, Syrah.

USA

San Luis Obispo County Sandwiched between Monterey to the north and Santa Barbara to the south, this coastal county often is overlooked. But its twin AVAs, Edna Valley and Arroyo Grande Valley, arguably produce some of California's most distinguished Pinots and Chardonnays. A few vintners have made enormous strides with cool-climate Syrah and other Rhône varieties.

Santa Barbara County If any county deserves the honor for greatest achievements in winemaking over the last twenty years, it is this South-Central Coast region. The action began in the inland Santa Ynez Valley, a warmish-to-hot AVA. Years of experiments have shown the valley's aptitude for lush, complex red Rhône wines and Sauvignon Blanc. Merlot has been an unexpected star; Cabernet Sauvignon has not yet shown greatness. Closer to the ocean, the newest AVA, Santa Rita Hills (2001), was on critics' radar for Pinot Noir for showing lush fruit with an acidity found in few other regions. Chardonnay follows the same pattern. As in most cool-climate growing areas, determined winemakers tinker with Syrah, often excitingly.

Mendocino County Inland Mendocino is hot and mountainous. Beyond an individual winery here and there, it has yet to make a name for itself. The county's cool AVA is Anderson Valley, which has shown great promise in Pinot Noir.

The Sierra Foothills This enormous, multi-county region sprawls along the foothills of the Sierra Nevada Mountains. At their best, Foothills wines can be varietally pure, with Zinfandel taking the lead, although Cabernet Franc has been an unexpected star. Too many Foothills vintners, unfortunately, produce wines whose rusticity and high alcohol outweigh their charm.

WASHINGTON

Mount Rainier viewed over vineyards near Zillah, Washington.

In barely three decades, the Washington wine industry has risen from a half-dozen wineries trying their hand at a bit of Riesling, Gewürztraminer, and experimental plots of Pinot Noir and Cabernet, to become a global player. The state now boasts more than 375 wineries, 30,000 vineyard acres, and a track record for producing crisply etched, vibrantly fruity Rieslings; sleek and polished Chardonnays; ripe and flavorful Sémillons; bold, luscious Merlots; well-defined, muscular Cabernets; and vivid, smoky, saturated Syrahs.

Though a distant second to California in terms of total production, Washington wines get more medals and higher scores and sell for lower average prices on a percentage basis. There are seven appellations, all but one (the Puget Sound AVA) lying east of the Cascade Mountains. The largest AVA by far is the Columbia Valley, a vast area of scrubby desert, punctuated by irrigated stretches of farmland with row crops, hops, orchards, and vineyards. The Cascade Mountains protect this inland desert from the cool, wet maritime climate of western Washington. Eastern Washington summers are hot and dry, and during the growing season, the vines average two extra hours of sunlight per day.

Inside the Columbia Valley AVA are the smaller appellations of Yakima Valley, Walla Walla Valley, Red Mountain, and Horse Heaven Hills. A sixth, the Columbia Gorge AVA, lies just to the west along the Columbia River.

Several factors account for Washington's unique wine-growing profile. Its vines are planted on their own roots,

USA

as phylloxera (see Glossary) has not been a problem in the state. Most vineyards are irrigated, and the scientifically timed application of precise amounts of water has become an important aspect of grape-growing and ripening. The lengthy fall harvest season, which can run from late August into early November, is marked by warm days and very cool nights. The 40 to 50 degree Fahrenheit daily temperature swings keep acids up as sugars rise, which means that in many vintages, no acidification is necessary. Alcohol levels for finished wines have risen, but are still below the numbers for California.

The exploration of Washington terroir is well underway, and the state actually has plantings of Cabernet as old or older than any in California, where vines have been ravaged by disease. Red Mountain in particular has proven itself as a spectacular region for Merlot and Cabernet, and the Red Mountain vineyards of Klipsun and Ciel du Cheval provide grapes to dozens of Washington's best boutique wineries.

Walla Walla has become an important tourist destination, with more than eighty wineries, 1,200 acres of vineyard, year-round recreational activities, and an active and fun-loving wine community. Pioneered in the early 1980s by Leonetti Cellar, L'Ecole No 41, and Woodward Canyon, the valley is now home to dozens of wineries producing small lots of rich, oaky red wines and ripe, succulent whites. Syrah does particularly well.

Eastern Washington has periodically suffered from arctic blasts that can devastate vineyards. The most recent, early in 2004, all but eliminated that year's harvest in Walla Walla. But much is being learned about Washington viticulture, and new plantings are better sited to survive the occasional frigid winters. Additionally, established vineyards are maturing, and older vines with deeper roots are far less likely to be killed by even severe cold.

Most of Washington's wineries produce fewer than two thousand cases of wine annually, and awareness of the state's best wines has been hampered by this lack of production. Additionally, there have been very few wineries large enough to produce soundly-made, inexpensive "supermarket" wines, the kind that help establish a national presence. The wines of Columbia Crest, Covey Run, and Precept brands are beginning to change that, challenging the huge California conglomerates with budget bottles that don't skimp on either character or quality.

OREGON

Vineyards of Domaine Serene, Dayton, Oregon.

Unlike Washington, where vineyards are scattered throughout the east, most Oregon vineyards lie in the state's western half. They are somewhat protected from ocean fogs and cloud cover by the coastal mountain range. The farther south you go, the hotter it gets. In the Rogue Valley appellation, centered around the town of Ashland, Syrah and Cabernet can be ripened, though with rather tough, chewy tannins. But it is the Pinot Noirs of the northern Willamette valley that have brought Oregon to the attention of the world.

Oregon became known as the Pinot Noir state at a time when decent Pinot was hard to come by outside of Burgundy. Pioneered by David Lett, David Adelsheim, Dick Ponzi, and Dick Erath, Oregon Pinot in the early years was indeed Burgundian, elegant and light, with modest color and relatively low alcohol levels.

Over the years, as viticulture improved and winemakers learned new techniques, Oregon Pinot became thicker, darker, more jammy, and hot in the ripe years; and more tannic and earthy in the cool ones. Recently, as Pinot Noirs from California, New Zealand, and elsewhere have risen in quality, Oregon vintners have begun turning their attention to other varietals. The Willamette Valley's two hundred-plus wineries still predominantly produce Pinot, but some of the state's most interesting wines are coming from other grapes grown outside the region.

The big challenges for Oregon Pinot are two-fold. First, vintage variation is a fact of life, and wines can range from thin, harsh, and weedy to hot, ripe, and impenetrable. Unlike California and Washington, where vintages are far more consistent, Oregon vintners can expect something different every year. Hail, rain, extreme heat, humidity, drought, and vast temperature swings during harvest are the norm, not the exception.

To some degree, this is a good thing, because it suggests that Oregon, like a handful of other winemaking regions scattered across the globe, has the ability to put its own distinct stamp on its wines. The plus side of vintage variation is that each harvest is unique, and imparts specific, unique qualities to the wines of that vintage. The minus side is that not every vintage is all that good, especially where Pinot Noir is concerned.

The second challenge is that there is no longer a generally identifiable Oregon Pinot "style." Some vintners make elegant, light, tannic Pinots that require years to open up, while others make wines so dark and jammy, they are dead ringers for Syrah. And finally, while there are plenty of pricey, single-vineyard Pinots being produced, it is still difficult for consumers to find drinkable, good value, every day bottles.

Oregon's Rieslings and Gewürztraminers remain well-kept secrets. These are lively, juicy, floral, and fragrant wines that are always good value. The state's signature white is Pinot Gris, and it's made in a lush, fruity style that tastes of fresh-cut pears and goes easy on the new oak. The Chardonnays, once clumsy and fat, have dramatically improved with the introduction of Dijon clones.

Some producers have demonstrated remarkable success with grapes not generally associated with Oregon. Syrah is grown in the south, and makes a big, tannic, rough-hewn red wine. At Abacela in central Oregon, Tempranillo has proved surprisingly good, and the old-vine Zinfandels of Sineann, from an eastern Oregon vineyard, are superb. Oregon has added several new AVAs in the past couple of years, but what is most exciting are these new wines from different grapes that promise to open up Oregon to its full potential in the decades ahead.

USA

USA

2820 WINE CO.

2820 Wine Co. 2002 The Ghost Bordeaux Blend (Napa Valley) $42. With Merlot and Cabernet Franc dominating the blend, this is a soft, gentle wine, with silky, light tannins and ripe flavors of cherries and oak. Drink now. **86** —*S.H. (12/15/2005)*

2820 Wine Co. 1998 Cabernet Sauvignon (Napa Valley) $32. Redolent of cassis, blackberry, herbs, anise, smoke, and toasty oak aromas, the wine fans out gracefully on the palate to reveal more layers of equally well-defined fruit. Tannins are soft and round, finishing moderately with a clean freshness. **91** —*J.M. (12/1/2001)*

2820 Wine Co. 2002 Merlot (Napa Valley) $22. Soft, easy, and flavorful, this Merlot has fruity tastes of cherries, black raspberries, and latte dusted with cocoa and cinnamon. Drink now. **85** —*S.H. (12/15/2005)*

2820 Wine Co. 1999 Tain't Hermitage Syrah (Napa Valley) $36. Some reviewers say this Syrah is "ripe" and "plush"; others call it "a fruit bomb." Whatever panelists' varying views about its balance, we all agree that it's pleasing and easy to drink. Juicy blueberry and blackberry flavors wear only a light dusting of black pepper and minerals; pie dough-meets-oak aromas dominate the bouquet. Finishes with even tannins, red-berry fruit and anise. Drink now through 2003. **88** *(11/1/2001)*

2820 Wine Co. 2003 Zinfandel (Napa Valley) $18. Very ripe, almost raisiny, with a cooked fruit flavor, although the wine is fully dry. The tannins are on the harsh side, and the stewed character seems to accentuate the acidity. Drink now. **82** —*S.H. (6/1/2006)*

2820 Wine Co. 2002 Zinfandel (Napa Valley) $18. This is one of those soft, deliciously ripe Zins that's so easy to drink. It's filled with chocolate and blackberry flavors, with a touch of raisins, and has enough tannins to lend backbone. **87** —*S.H. (8/1/2005)*

29 SONGS

29 Songs 2004 Soscol Ridge Vineyard Back Porch Block Syrah (Napa Valley) $55. From a cool vineyard in the southeast part of the valley, this wine opens with a refined scent of blackberry pie sprinkled with pepper and cocoa. It's a beautiful scent, like a pastry. In the mouth, it turns soft and slightly sweet, somewhat of a letdown. **85** —*S.H. (11/15/2006)*

4 BEARS

4 Bears 2002 Cabernet Sauvignon (Napa Valley) $15. Tastes a bit lean, with currant, herb, and coffee flavors that are wrapped in fairly hefty, dry tannins. **84** —*S.H. (12/1/2006)*

6TH SENSE

6th Sense 2003 Syrah (Lodi) $17. Downgraded by one reviewer for being sweet, this Lodi wine did have enough positives to merit a good rating, starting with hints of wintergreen on the nose and flowing into baked berry flavors. **83** *(9/1/2005)*

7 HEAVENLY CHARDS

7 Heavenly Chards 2005 Chardonnay (Lodi) $17. This is a ripely fruity wine with a dollop of French oak that's a textbook example of Lodi. Soft in acids, with powerful tropical fruit, nectarine, peach, pear, and apple flavors, it offers clean, easy drinking. **86** —*S.H. (12/15/2006)*

A DONKEY AND GOAT

A Donkey and Goat 2004 Brosseau Vineyard Chardonnay (Chalone) $40. From up in the Chalone highlands comes this very dry, acidic and rather earthy Chard. It has peach and apricot flavors, with a touch of green tea and tannins. Seems like it has the structure to age, although that has got to be considered a gamble. **86** —*S.H. (5/1/2006)*

A Donkey and Goat 2004 Carson Ridge Vineyard Syrah (El Dorado) $32. Fruity and simple, with blackberry and cherry pie flavors, this wine has a rustic texture in the attack of tannins and acids with a certain twiggy component. **84** —*S.H. (5/1/2006)*

A Donkey and Goat 2004 Vidmar Vineyard Syrah (Yorkville Highlands) $32. This is a powerfully fruity wine, packed with very ripe blackberry, black cherry, coffee, and sweet leather flavors, in a fairly tannic package. It fin-

ishes a bit sweet, but shows good control throughout. **86** —*S.H. (5/1/2006)*

A Donkey and Goat 2004 Vieilles Vignes Syrah (McDowell Valley) $34. This Mendocino region has some very old Syrah vines, and they have produced a dark, soft, lush Syrah, with an earthy component to the blackberry and mocha flavors. It's pretty tannic, but that softness makes it instantly drinkable, and it's not likely to improve with age. **87** —*S.H. (5/1/2006)*

A. RAFANELLI

A. Rafanelli 2001 Zinfandel (Sonoma County) $26. Kicks off with spicy, rich, plum, black cherry, herb, toast, anise, and cola flavors. This long-time top producer doesn't disappoint with this classy, complex array, couched in ripe, supple tannins. It finishes long and fresh, with a toasty, raspberry edge. **91 Editors' Choice** *(11/1/2003)*

A.S. KIKEN

A.S. Kiken 2001 Estate Cabernet Blend (Diamond Mountain) $30. Kind of pricy for a not-so-ripe Cab with green peppercorn and cherry flavors. There's a ton of oak, and the wine is dry, with chunky tannins. From Reverie. **84** —*S.H. (10/1/2005)*

A.S. Kiken 2000 Red Blend (Diamond Mountain) $75. From Reverie. Kind of pricey for a not-so-ripe Cab with green peppercorn and cherry flavors. There's a ton of oak, and the wine is dry, with chunky tannins. **84** —*S.H. (11/1/2005)*

ABACELA

Abacela 2005 Albariño (Southern Oregon) $23. With this bracing, bone-dry, crisply mineral white wine, Abacela continues to prove that southern Oregon is really the westernmost province of Spain. If this isn't the perfect oyster wine, I don't know what is. Like a great Muscadet, it's clean, acidic, and bracing but never thin or sour. Wonderful winemaking. **89** —*P.G. (12/1/2006)*

Abacela 2002 Cabernet Franc (Oregon) $24. I'm a big fan of Abacela's wines, and appreciate the effort to do a varietal Cab Franc, but this wine could benefit from a bit of blending. Tart, spicy, and slightly sweaty, it has the expected blueberry fruit and leathery tannins of Cab Franc, but the tannins are so dry and dominant that they undercut the middle of the wine and skew the finish. Interesting but not entirely complete. **86** —*P.G. (2/1/2005)*

Abacela 2001 Cabernet Franc (Umpqua Valley) $24. Meaty, leathery, and substantial, this wine explodes out of the glass with aggressive aromas. The fruit following is less muscular; it is lightly tart, simple, and overcome with leathery saddle notes. **86** —*P.G. (5/1/2004)*

Abacela 2000 Cabernet Franc (Oregon) $20. Rustic and funky, with a curious nose sending up scents of fruit, musk, soy, pepper and espresso. Flavors are vivid and grapey, and there is a penetrating spicy note running throughout. The finish is tannic and rough. **86** —*P.G. (8/1/2003)*

Abacela 1999 Cabernet Franc (Umpqua Valley) $22. Lovely aromas show sweet fruit, cherry candy flavors, along with some green tannins in a tart, tight finish. **86** —*P.G. (8/1/2002)*

Abacela 2004 Dolcetto (Southern Oregon) $18. Beautiful and evocative, this sensuous Dolcetto sends up beguiling aromas of dried cherry, tobacco, plum, fig, and balsamic, with flavors to follow. Tart and mouthfilling, it shows real varietal character and strength, with a persistent and stylish finish. **88** —*P.G. (9/1/2006)*

Abacela 2003 Dolcetto (Oregon) $18. There is not a great deal of Dolcetto grown in the Northwest, but this is the best version I've yet seen. Its vivid, spicy fruit core expresses the soil, the plant, and the grape in equal proportion. Sappy flavors of spiced plum and wild berry hold the fort; it's built like a race car, sleek and stylish, with a powerful, tannic frame. **88** —*P.G. (2/1/2005)*

Abacela 2002 Dolcetto (Oregon) $18. As its vineyards age, Abacela's unique lineup of varietal grapes seem to gain in intensity and concentration. This deeply fruity, spicy, sensuous wine is made with whole-berry fermentation and neutral oak. Blueberry fruit, spice, and a whiff of sage add complexity and interest. **89** —*P.G. (5/1/2004)*

Abacela 2000 Dolcetto (Umpqua Valley) $18. Intense, fruity, soft, and sensuous, this sweet and pretty wine features whole cluster fermentation. It is lively and balanced, fruity and smooth. Terrific for summer sipping. **88** —P.G. (8/1/2002)

Abacela 2004 Grenache (Southern Oregon) $22. Birds got most of the 2004 Grenache, but the 82 cases that were left are impressive. Along with biting red fruits that seem to snap and sizzle in the mouth, there is a nice, spicy edge that gives the wine dimension and scale. The tannins are austere and taste of graphite and bark. **88** —P.G. (9/1/2006)

Abacela 2003 Grenache (Umpqua Valley) $22. Abacela remains the single most iconoclastic winery in the entire Northwest, pioneering unusual estate grown varietals in Oregon's oft-neglected mid-section, the Umpqua valley. And doing it well, in all respects. The Grenache is a bruiser, extracted, sappy, and tannic, well made for its size, though lacking the super sweet extract of the Australian versions. Still it's a tasty wine, chewy and blocky, but perfect for pizza. **87** —P.G. (2/1/2005)

Abacela 2003 Malbec (Southern Oregon) $23. Black and inky, this aromatic potpourri sends up scents of wet earth, truffle, spice, wild berries, and even a bit of Provençal garrigue. Concentrated and tannic, it adds elements of raw meat, leaf, and forest floor as it rolls across the tongue. Just a bit hot in the finish. **89** —P.G. (11/15/2005)

Abacela 2002 Malbec (Oregon) $20. Don't cry for me, Argentina! This is a beautiful, pungent, two-fisted effort, which comes on like a petite sirah. At first inky, grapey and tannic, it gains complexity in the mouth, adding elements of raw meat, leaf and forest floor. At the center is a striking core of tart blueberry/boysenberry compote. This one can go awhile. **90** —P.G. (2/1/2005)

Abacela 2001 Malbec (Umpqua Valley) $20. The 2000 was a stunningly good Malbec; this is just a notch lighter. Mountain-grown fruit flavors dominate: plum, berry, and spice on the palate, with plenty of lip-smacking acids in the back end. What's missing is the weight of deep, dense fruit, but 2001 was a lighter vintage. **90** —P.G. (5/1/2004)

Abacela 2000 Malbec (Umpqua Valley) $18. This rising superstar Oregon winery, best known for its landmark Tempranillo, here showcases a stunningly good Malbec. Dense, inky purple and blue colors set up an edgy and intense wine, full of mountain-grown fruit flavors. Plum, berry, baked apple, and allspice light up the palate, arrayed over a powerful base of mineral, acid and earth. **91** —P.G. (12/31/2002)

Abacela 1999 Malbec (Umpqua Valley) $15. This unusual Oregon Malbec carries intense, rustic aromas mixing plum, grape, spice, and saddle leather. Despite its very tight tannins, the wine tastes open and grapey, reminiscent of a Washington Lemberger, though not quite as soft. **85** —P.G. (8/1/2002)

Abacela 2003 Meritage (Southern Oregon) $35. This is a detailed Bordeaux blend of 61% Cabernet Sauvignon, 14% Merlot, 12% Cab Franc, 8% Malbec, and 5% Petite Verdot, made to emulate a European style. Muscular and trim, it has compact layers of just-ripe fruit, the winery's characteristic streaks of mineral and earth, hints of tobacco leaf, and a bit of pepper. Long, tannic, slightly earthy, and smooth through the finish, it's a superb effort, beautifully blended and complete. **91** —P.G. (11/15/2005)

Abacela 2002 Merlot (Oregon) $18. Oregon Merlot can be extremely hard, green, and tannic, but this complex bottle shows that it need not be. Fruits and spices mingle perfectly, with scents of sandalwood, toffee, smoke, and leather providing depth. Plenty of serious heft to this wine, but the tannins are smoothed out and balanced. **89** —P.G. (8/1/2005)

Abacela 2001 Merlot (Oregon) $18. Abacela has made great strides with its Merlots, and here the fruit has ripened past the "green" stage while retaining plenty of tannic, earthy mineral flavors. Dense and minerally, this has a core of sweet fruit and a pretty finish. **89** —P.G. (5/1/2004)

Abacela 2000 Merlot (Umpqua Valley) $18. Actually a Bordeaux blend, this mainly Merlot wine from the Umpqua valley in central Oregon outdoes its peers with dark, plummy, even jammy fruit laced with toast, tar,

and espresso. Sweet fruit meets stiff tannins, all in the name of structure. **88** —P.G. (8/1/2003)

Abacela 1999 Merlot (Umpqua Valley) $18. Very tart, with a deep, tannic, earthy mineral streak. There's an iron/earth streak running through all Abacela wines; here it comes across as iron and slightly bitter licorice. This is still very young and green; the score might well improve with more time in the bottle. **86** —P.G. (8/1/2002)

Abacela NV Vintner's Blend #7 Red Blend (Southern Oregon) $15. Number Six had 13 varieties from seven different vineyards, but this time around it's down to just six and six. Nonetheless, no one else is doing Merlot, Tempranillo, Syrah, Cab Franc, Malbec, and Graciano. Once again, the wizards at Abacela have crafted a fragrant, spicy mutt red, with hints of leather and bark. **87** —P.G. (12/1/2006)

Abacela NV Vintner's Blend #6 Red Blend (Oregon) $15. When Abacela does a kitchen sink blend, they don't hold anything back. Thirteen varieties from seven vineyards go into this gem, but rather than creating an unfocused mélange, the result is a lush, fragrant, fruit salad of a red, with some nice new oak and a solid core of berries and plums. **88 Best Buy** —P.G. (8/1/2005)

Abacela 1999 Vintners Blend Red Table Wine Red Blend (Umpqua Valley) $11. The winery grows 17 different varietals, many in minute quantities. This is a blend of 8–12 different varietals, including such oddballs as Refosco and Freisa, along with Zin, Carignan, Tempranillo, some Cabs—in other words, it's a kitchen sink wine. Spicy and peppery, with firm acids under a forward mélange of red fruit flavors. **86** —P.G. (8/1/2002)

Abacela 2003 Syrah (Southern Oregon) $25. A blend of Umpqua and Applegate valley fruit that's scented with new oak and hints of licorice, cassis, and black olives. The ability of Abacela to evoke Spanish nuances in their many wines extends even to this Syrah. It does not taste like Syrah from elsewhere in Oregon, nor does it resemble anything from the West Coast. It is ripe, tough, spicy and tart, and it's packed with delicious fruit and well-defined acids. **89** —P.G. (12/1/2006)

Abacela 2002 Syrah (Oregon) $29. A blend of Umpqua and Applegate valley fruit, this spicy, tannic wine sports a bit of citrus peel, anise, earth, and vanilla for added interest. Tannins are characteristically hard and tight, and it is quite angular at this time, showing some green tea in the tannins. Air it out. **90** —P.G. (8/1/2005)

Abacela 2001 Syrah (Oregon) $29. Spicy and beautifully balanced, this delicious wine rings out with flavor. Pretty fruit, vivid acids, hints of mineral, and perfectly defined tannins make for a very sexy wine, with a long, concentrated finish that adds a bit of sweet, roasted, toasted nuttiness. Wow! **92** —P.G. (5/1/2004)

Abacela 2000 Syrah (Umpqua Valley) $25. Abacela does best with its Tempranillo, Dolcetto, and Syrah. This is distinctive, spicy, and loaded with powerful flavors. Licorice, blackberry, pepper, and coffee tumble together, the sweet powerful fruit held within a tight focus. Ripe, forward, appealing, and yet built for aging. **90** —P.G. (9/1/2003)

Abacela 1999 Syrah (Umpqua Valley) $27. Intense, spicy, and richly fruity nose. Already meaty, bloody, and gamey; this really hits the mark for this variety. Good acids, weight, and balance. It's a very sexy wine, with a long, concentrated finish that shows extracted berry fruit and layers of mineral and earth, with just the barest hint of roasted barrel. **90** —P.G. (8/1/2002)

Abacela 2003 Tempranillo (Umpqua Valley) $20. Abacela was founded on the premise that this unique site in central Oregon was perfectly suited to Tempranillo, and they have done an excellent job of proving themselves right. The complex aromas suggest cedar and mint, raspberries and blue fruits. The wine is tart and the tannins tight; it seems quite youthful and hard. Surely a wine to cellar for up to a decade. **88** —P.G. (9/1/2006)

Abacela 2002 Tempranillo (Umpqua Valley) $20. The winery has staked its reputation on Tempranillo of all things, and consistently over a half dozen vintages it has surprised and delighted me with the results. Good color for this pale grape, and decent varietal character, though the estate bottling is clearly superior. **87** —P.G. (8/1/2005)

Abacela 2001 Tempranillo (Umpqua Valley) $29. Abacela is pioneering this grape in the Pacific Northwest, and making a strong case for it. This is a complex wine, showing a mix of leather, herb, mineral, and dark fruits. It's balanced and tough, with a meaty concentration that suggests ageworthiness. **89** —*P.G. (5/1/2004)*

Abacela 1999 Tempranillo (Umpqua Valley) $29. Three different clones are used, all estate grown. There's a lovely wild clover scent to it, and very tart, dark fruit. Though it needs more time to smooth out, it shows streaks of iron and mineral, adding excellent flavor and depth. Structured to age. **89** —*P.G. (8/1/2002)*

Abacela 2003 Estate Tempranillo (Southern Oregon) $30. The signature wine of this pioneering central Oregon winery is their Tempranillo. Here it is nicely ripened and complex, layering boysenberries, mineral, wet earth, fennel, leaf, cedar, and whiffs of smoke. Quite tart and tannic, but clearly varietal; this excellent 2003 seems just a bit less concentrated than in the very best vintages. **89** —*P.G. (11/15/2005)*

Abacela 2002 Estate Grown Tempranillo (Umpqua Valley) $30. This is from Abacela's own grapes, which were planted in Oregon's Umpqua Valley because the winery's founders believed it was the best place in America to grow Tempranillo. So far, no one has proved them wrong. Concentrated, almost black, bursting with smoke, leather, tar, blackberry, black cherry, graphite, and more. Big, chewy and firm. **91** —*P.G. (8/1/2005)*

Abacela 2005 Rosado Tempranillo (Southern Oregon) $12. A rosé that's the color of the lipstick on the girl you lusted after in high school. It tastes of strawberry and raspberry, simple and not too sweet, and it rings just about every possible bell for a late-summer sip. **87** —*P.G. (12/1/2006)*

Abacela 2005 Viognier (Southern Oregon) $19. Whoa! Welcome to Hawaii! This is like a mouthful of the tropics, with everything from coconut oil to banana waffles. Pineapple and peach, mango, and hints of honeysuckle are all in the mix, and this aromatic, evocative wine is nicely balanced at 14.1% alcohol. It finishes bone dry, like a twist of lemon. **89** —*P.G. (12/1/2006)*

Abacela 2004 Viognier (Oregon) $19. This new vintage brings down the alcohol (from 15% to just under 14%) and the price of this pleasant, well-made Viognier. Citrus and apricot fill out the fruity midpalate, and it's a round, peachy wine without any of the bitterness or heat that can plague overripe Viognier. The aromatics are clean and simple; though it does not have the extra dimensions that the best Washington Viogniers can sometimes express, it does not suffer from the flaws that Washington Viogniers can sometimes express. **87** —*P.G. (11/15/2005)*

Abacela 2003 Viognier (Oregon) $25. A high test version at 15% alcohol, this successfully skirts the problems that can plague such wines. The high-toned, complex aromas of rose petals, spice, and citrus avoid going volatile; the tropical fruit core never descends into bubble gum, and the bitter citrus rind finish manages to hold onto a sense of appropriate balance. Whew! **88** —*P.G. (2/1/2005)*

ABANDON

Abandon 2004 Chardonnay (Carneros) $18. Simple, with earthy flavors and thinned-down peaches and apples. There's a little oak. Finishes dry and crisp. **83** —*S.H. (12/1/2006)*

ABBEY PAGE

Abbey Page 2004 Pinot Gris (Oregon) $11. This is solidly made, with a crisp entry that tastes of lemon peel. It moves into a broader midpalate, opening up with notes of pear, orange peel, and apple, then finishes dry, with a lick of licorice. **87 Best Buy** —*P.G. (2/1/2006)*

ABEJA

Abeja 2003 Cabernet Sauvignon (Columbia Valley (WA)) $35. Abeja's John Abbott belongs on anyone's short list of Washington's most talented winemakers. This supple, dense Cabernet is restrained for the vintage, but lacks nothing in terms of power, muscle or complexity. Tar, smoke, and gravel run right down its spine; tannins are substantial. But everything about the wine says class, and its compact confidence rewards patient tasters with layers of ripe, varietal flavor, perfectly matched to the oak. **94** —*P.G. (6/1/2006)*

Abeja 2004 Chardonnay (Columbia Valley (WA)) $28. Chardonnay rarely rises above the mundane, but when it does, you wonder why doesn't everyone make it like this? Big and voluptuous, this gorgeous

bottling retains enough acid and balance to deliver the big-time goods with finesse. Silky, ripe, lush yet sculpted, it plays out deliciously through an extremely long and richly fruity palate. **93** —*P.G. (6/1/2006)*

Abeja 2004 Merlot (Columbia Valley (WA)) $35. Those who miss the John Abbott Merlots from his years at Canoe Ridge can take heart. This first-time Abbott Merlot from his new winery, Abeja, is a gem. Fragrant, beautifully rendered aromas of primary red fruits, cocoa, and licorice set up firm streaks of black tea, smoke, and concentrated black cherry. There is just enough new oak to support, but not dominate, the beautiful, polished fruit. **91** —*P.G. (12/31/2006)*

Abeja 2003 Syrah (Walla Walla (WA)) $30. Firm, meaty, and substantial; this is sharply defined, tart and racy; the fruit is polished and aromatic. There is a clear, clean through-line to the wine, with a citric edge and a hint of iodine; it's persistent and clean, but at first just a bit simple in the finish. On the second day it firms up and fleshes out nicely. **90** —*P.G. (12/31/2006)*

Abeja 2005 Viognier (Walla Walla (WA)) $26. A thoroughly delicious, glorious mix of melon, lime, pineapple, and apple; the fruits—which were whole cluster pressed—just blend beautifully, with no trace of heat or bitterness. The finish wraps into a light butterscotch and lemon candy flavor; wonderfully satisfying. **92** —*P.G. (12/31/2006)*

ABIOUNESS

Abiouness 2001 Stanly Ranch Pinot Noir (Carneros) $35. A fine-tuned, complex wine that offers a beautiful blend of cherry, spice, earth, herb, leather, and coffee notes all framed in smooth, supple tannins. It's elegant and refined, long on the finish and somewhat lush. A terrific wine from a relative newcomer, Nicole Abiouness. **92** —*J.M. (6/1/2004)*

Abiouness 2000 Stanly Ranch Pinot Noir (Carneros) $40. From a Lebanese winemaker, a jammy Pinot tasting of cherries, blueberries, black raspberries and dusty oriental spices, especially clove. It is dry, with lively acids and silky tannins. **87** —*S.H. (2/1/2004)*

ABUNDANCE VINEYARDS

Abundance Vineyards 2000 Clos D'Abundance Chardonnay (Clarksburg) $13. Quite creamy on the palate, with an upfront melon and apple core. Peaches, herbs, citrus, and toast are also in evidence, finishing with moderate length. **88 Best Buy** —*J.M. (12/15/2002)*

Abundance Vineyards 2000 Talmage Block Viognier (Mendocino County) $18. Tangy and zippy, with a ginger-like quality that leads to peach, spice, apricot, and herbs on the palate. The finish is long and bright, with a lemony edge. **88** —*J.M. (12/15/2002)*

Abundance Vineyards 1999 Mencarini Vineyards Old Vine Zinfandel (Lodi) $15. A smooth, elegant wine, with subtle blackberry, licorice, and chocolate notes. It serves up an almost creamy finish. Sure, it's big and ripe, but it is also refined. Herb notes add complexity, reminding us that Central Valley grapes can make gosh-darned food wine. **90** —*J.M. (9/1/2003)*

ACACIA

Acacia 1993 Brut Champagne Blend (Carneros) $35. This is a very dry, elegant bubbly that drinks "French" because the dominant notes are earthy, minerally, and toasty, rather than fruity. At seven years of age, it's lost whatever fruit it had and is turning dusty and rich, a wine of structural austerity. Yet it's very fine. **91** —*S.H. (6/1/2001)*

Acacia 2004 Chardonnay (Carneros) $23. This lovely, delicately powerful Chardonnay has a great balance of all its parts. The ripe fruit flavors are set off by crisp acids, while toasty oak and lees add complexity. The honeyed finish is rich. **87** —*S.H. (3/1/2006)*

Acacia 2003 Chardonnay (Carneros) $20. Here's a nicely balanced Chard that combines rich fruit with impeccable style and finesse. It's ripely forward in pineapple, mango, butterscotch, buttered toast, and vanilla, and has vivacious acidity and a clean, harmonious finish. **90** —*S.H. (8/1/2005)*

Acacia 2002 Chardonnay (Carneros) $20. A flamboyant style that emphasizes well-ripened fruit flavors, including tangerine and pineapple, and quite a bit of smoky oak. Bold, rich, and opulent, with a creamy, honeyed texture. **90** —*S.H. (6/1/2004)*

Acacia 2000 Chardonnay (Carneros) $22. A pleasing and delicate wine, with hints of pear, apple, and citrus flavors. The ensemble is framed by light toast and herbs. Moderate on the finish. **87** —*J.M. (5/1/2002)*

Acacia 1998 Chardonnay (Carneros) $21. 87 *(6/1/2000)*

Acacia 1997 Chardonnay (Carneros) $20. 86 —*M.S. (10/1/1999)*

Acacia 2002 Sangiacomo Vineyard Chardonnay (Carneros) $30. Here's a deliciously drinkable Chard, sweet with pineapple and mango flavors and well-oaked, and with the excellent acidity to make it clean and bright. Lasts for a long time on the finish, turning spicy and reprising the mango theme. **90** —*S.H. (10/1/2004)*

Acacia 2001 Sangiacomo Vineyard Chardonnay (Carneros) $30. This big, bold Chard screams with flavors of tangerines, orange sorbet, vanilla, and toast. It is well oaked, and has upfront acids that make for a crisp and bright mouthfeel. Finishes with tangy spices. **91** —*S.H. (12/15/2003)*

Acacia 2003 Pinot Noir (Carneros) $20. Pretty full-bodied and rich for a Pinot, and dark, too. The flavors veer toward black cherries, coffee, and spice, and are very dry. Fortunately it's a silky wine, with zesty acids. Drink now with rich fare, like pork tenderloin. **87** —*S.H. (10/1/2005)*

Acacia 2002 Pinot Noir (Carneros) $20. Indistinct wine, with plummy, spicy flavors and gritty tannins. Has a citrus-acid tartness. Average throughout. **84** *(11/1/2004)*

Acacia 2000 Pinot Noir (Carneros) $27. Deep, tangy fruit is substantial enough to wear its toasted oak mantle gracefully. Ripe cherry-plum flavors are offset by spice, earth, meat and saddle leather—and ample charred wood—but remain sweet. It's fairly light in feel for the oak and dark fruit, closing dark and briary. **89 Drink now–2005. Editor's Choice.** *(10/1/2002)*

Acacia 1999 Pinot Noir (Napa Valley) $25. One of the first '99 Pinots to come out, this puppy from the Napa side of the American Viticultural Area is young and promising. It shows classic notes of plum, sautéed mushroom, vanilla, and smoke, and something earthy, midway between chocolate and leather. The aroma is deep; you can inhale it and feel it in your head. Also heady are the flavors, which are sumptuous, rich and complex, with plenty of fruit and spice, very dry and velvety. This workhorse release is quite good, and a fabulous omen of future '99 North Coast Pinots to come. **91** —*S.H. (2/1/2001)*

Acacia 1998 Pinot Noir (Napa Valley) $25. 90 —*S.H. (5/1/2000)*

Acacia 2000 Beckstoffer-Las Amigas Vineyard Pinot Noir (Napa Valley) $62. Woody, bordering on charred; but the ripe, full-force red fruit supports the heavy barrel influence. In the mouth, there's plenty of sweet cherry, softer strawberry and a supporting cinnamon-like undercurrent. Full tannins provide a foundation that will allow this one to age for years to come. **89** *(10/1/2002)*

Acacia 1999 Beckstoffer-Las Amigas Vineyard Pinot Noir (Carneros) $60. Dense and highly aromatic, with notes of cherry, cedar, plum cake, and brown sugar. The fruit on the palate is candied yet racy, the latter a result of intense acidity. This has a lot in common with Acacia's other single-vineyard wines: It's sweet yet acidic. **86** *(10/1/2002)*

Acacia 2004 Beckstoffer Las Amigas Vineyard Pinot Noir (Carneros) $60. From the Napa side of the appellation comes this dry, young Pinot Noir. The acids, tannins, and new oak show now, and also the intensely ripe cherry fruit, with all the parts jockeying for position. Needs time to knit together. Best after 2007, and through 2011 before it loses fruit. **90 Cellar Selection** —*S.H. (12/15/2006)*

Acacia 2001 Beckstoffer Las Amigas Vineyard Pinot Noir (Carneros) $60. This is a big, dark, jammy wine, with glycerine stains that suggest its weight. The flavors are equally balanced between earthy ones, such as tobacco, coffee, and sweet oregano, and dark fruits. It is very dry, with fine, dusty tannins. **89** —*S.H. (2/1/2004)*

Acacia 1996 Beckstoffer Vineyard Reserve Pinot Noir (Carneros) $42. 90 —*M.S. (6/1/1999)*

Acacia 2002 Beckstoffer-Las Amigas Vineyard Pinot Noir (Carneros) $60. Disappointingly simple and awkward, with candied, almost medicinal, cherry, cola, and sweet tea flavors. **83** *(11/1/2004)*

Acacia 2000 DeSoto Vineyard Pinot Noir (Napa Valley) $52. Even though it smells like burnt steak, we also caught softer aromas of grilled fruit, tea, and clove. If a huge, barrel-influenced wine is not your style, steer clear. But if you like a brawny, tannic heavyweight that can age for the better part of a decade, this is your wine. It has a massive underlay of ripe plum fruit, terrific zip and a mile-long finish. **91 Cellar Selection** *(10/1/2002)*

Acacia 1999 Desoto Vineyard Pinot Noir (Carneros) $50. Compared to other Acacia Pinots, this is the richest and densest, but it carries a common thread: ultra sweet fruit. It's all about black cherry, barrel char, and then coffee and warmth on the finish. Similar to the berry syrup you put on pancakes or vanilla ice cream. **86** *(10/1/2002)*

Acacia 2002 Field Blend Estate Vineyard Pinot Noir (Carneros) $50. Solid scores from tasters for this easy, fresh Pinot. Shows straightforward flavors of coffee, cola, cherries, and anise in a dry, supple wine with a spicy finish. **86** *(11/1/2004)*

Acacia 2001 Lee Vineyard Pinot Noir (Carneros) $50. The most complex and rewarding of Acacia's vineyard offerings, it opens with a mélange of aromas that start but do not end with white pepper. From there you go on to black cherries with a tannic edge of bitterness from skins, and the sweetening effects of good oak. It will be fine now with roast lamb but will develop for several years. **90** —*S.H. (3/1/2004)*

Acacia 1999 Lee Vineyard Pinot Noir (Carneros) $50. What some might call terroir, Burgundian or earthiness, others less enamored of funky aromas might call barnyardy. Flavors of cola, sweet cherries, and blackberries ensure that it won't be mistaken for Burgundy. There's some bitter chocolate and coffee on the back end, but also something reminiscent of iced tea. **87** *(10/1/2002)*

Acacia 1997 Lee Vineyard Pinot Noir (Napa Valley) $50. 94 —*S.H. (12/15/2000)*

Acacia 2004 Lone Tree Vineyard Pinot Noir (Carneros) $50. Very ripe and lush in blackberry, cherry, cola, and rhubarb flavors, this Pinot also shows plenty of sweet new oak. Fortunately, it has the crisp acids and dusty tannins to balance. Defines Carneros balance and elegance. **91** —*S.H. (12/15/2006)*

Acacia 1996 Reserve Pinot Noir (Carneros) $32. 89 *(11/15/1999)*

Acacia 2002 St. Clair Vineyard Pinot Noir (Carneros) $50. Opens with cooked, stewed prune aromas, but is actually balanced and charming in the mouth, with cherry and plum fruit. Fairly tough and gritty in tannins. Drink now through 2005. **86** *(11/1/2004)*

Acacia 2001 St. Clair Vineyard Pinot Noir (Carneros) $50. Rather tannic and earthy, and hard to discern much beyond the tobacco, herb, coffee, and bitter chocolate flavors. Those tannins are tough and gritty. May soften and sweeten in a year or two. **86** —*S.H. (3/1/2004)*

Acacia 2000 St. Clair Vineyard Pinot Noir (Carneros) $50. This one has extreme funky, deep aromas of tree bark and barnyard. But those smells yield to friendly layers of black cherry, plum, coffee, and kirsch. We don't think this wine is for everyone (one of our panelists flat out did not care for it), but the depth and chewiness on the palate cannot be short-changed. **90** *(8/1/2003)*

Acacia 1999 St. Clair Vineyard Pinot Noir (Carneros) $50. Full and bold, with a touch of smoked meat. The palate is really sweet, like candied cherries. The finish is smooth and clean, more or less a continuation of the palate characteristics. There's plenty of power, too, but a bit more structure would provide a helping hand. **86** *(10/1/2002)*

Acacia 1997 St. Clair Vineyard Pinot Noir (Napa Valley) $50. 93 —*S.H. (12/15/2000)*

ACKERLY POND

Ackerly Pond 2003 Cabernet Franc (North Fork of Long Island) $20. Nice aromas of pie crust, red fruit, and some barnyard lead to a tart, simple wine with watered-down flavors of red berry. **81** —*M.D. (8/1/2006)*

USA

Ackerly Pond 2004 Merlot (North Fork of Long Island) $25. Despite some pickled, stalky aromas and flavors, this wine has everything you want in an easy-drinking Merlot. Strong flavors of blueberry, cherry pie, and graham cracker are a touch sweet, and the wine has a nice fat quality to its medium body. Aromas need time to open and develop, showing cherry and spice. Oak is prominent on the finish, and this wine should drink well over the next five years. **86** —*M.D. (12/1/2006)*

Ackerly Pond 2003 Merlot (North Fork of Long Island) $18. Doesn't quite reach the potential of Merlot on Long Island, but still has aromas of vanilla, mint, and red fruit. In the mouth the fruit is tart cherry, with eucalyptus and horse starting to show. Has fine weight and tannins, but gets greener on the finish. **83** —*M.D. (8/1/2006)*

ACORN

Acorn 2003 Alegria Vineyards Cabernet Franc (Russian River Valley) $28. Acorn, which does such interesting things with Rhône varieties, shows it's no slouch with Bordeaux varieties, to judge from this fresh, succulent young red wine. It's medium-bodied and dry, with polished flavors of cherries, blueberries, leather, and herbs and a long, spicy finish. **88** —*S.H. (5/1/2006)*

Acorn 2003 Alegria Vineyards Dolcetto (Russian River Valley) $26. Acorn persists with this Italian variety despite the challenges. It's dry and medium-bodied, with a silky texture and some hot acids. The flavors are of cherries and tobacco. Overall, it's a clean country wine. **84** —*S.H. (6/1/2006)*

Acorn 2002 Alegria Vineyards Dolcetto (Russian River Valley) $22. Bone-dry, earthy, and gritty yet not really tannic, this is one of those wines that goes with almost anything calling for a dry red. There's a cherry tone and peppery finish that suggest tender beef. **84** —*S.H. (8/1/2005)*

Acorn 2001 Alegria Vineyards Dolcetto (Russian River Valley) $22. This young wine is earthy, with a core of blackberry and Chinese plum sauce sweetness, although it's really dry. It has a nice acid-tannin balance and is easy to drink. **84** —*S.H. (10/1/2004)*

Acorn 1999 Alegria Vineyards Dolcetto (Russian River Valley) $20. Made from Dolcetto, an Italian variety rare in California, this wine tries to struggle beyond an earthiness that's unnaturally sweet. The result: The berry flavors are ripe, the acidity and tannins fine, but it can't quite shake its rough, countrified edge. **82** —*S.H. (11/15/2001)*

Acorn 2003 Alegria Vineyards Medley Red Blend (Russian River Valley) $24. Dry and balanced, this multi-varietal blend of about 10 grapes, dominated by Cabernet Franc, Zinfandel, and Syrah, shows real sophistication. It's quite forward in berry-cherry fruit, but has restraint in the tannin-acid-oak-alcohol balance, and could improve over the next year. **87** —*S.H. (4/1/2006)*

Acorn 2002 Alegria Vineyards Medley Red Blend (Russian River Valley) $22. I stopped counting the number of varieties in this wine when I reached 10. It's dry, balanced, and fruity, with a good cherry-acid tension and a little bit of oak. A nice, all-purpose red wine with some flair. **85** —*S.H. (8/1/2005)*

Acorn 2001 Alegria Vineyards Medley Rhône Red Blend (Russian River Valley) $22. There are too many varietals to name, but it's sort of a Rhône blend. Drinks dry, rich and earthy, with a tobaccoey, peppery edge to the cherries and herbs. The tannins are chewy but soft. This is a nice modern-day version of an old field blend. **87** —*S.H. (10/1/2004)*

Acorn 1999 Alegria Vineyards-Axiom Rhône Cuvée Rhône Red Blend (Russian River Valley) $16. American oak seems overly aggressive on the nose, with dominating aromas of clove and vanilla-tinged wood sap. Once you get past the bouquet, the wine is limpid, silky smooth, and utterly dry, with berry flavors. **82** —*S.H. (11/15/2001)*

Acorn 2003 Alegria Vineyards Sangiovese (Russian River Valley) $22. This is a pretty good Sangiovese and Acorn has worked hard on the variety for years. It's dry and elegant, with silky, Pinot-like tannins and crisp acids. It's also very ripe in cherry and cocoa flavors. **87** —*S.H. (3/1/2006)*

Acorn 2002 Alegria Vineyards Sangiovese (Russian River Valley) $22. Rather sweetish in ripe, extracted jammy cherry, with a chocolaty finish, yet basically dry, with good acidity and silky tannins. Easy to drink with anything from pizza to vanilla ice cream. **84** —*S.H. (8/1/2005)*

Acorn 2000 Alegria Vineyards Sangiovese (Russian River Valley) $16. A single-vineyard Sangiovese made Chianti-style, meaning it's dry as dust with pronounced acidity. Pretty rich in flavor, though, with a ripe streak of cherries and sweet chocolate. Dry, dusty tannins kick in in the finish. **87** —*S.H. (7/1/2003)*

Acorn 2001 Alegria Vineyards Sangiovese (Russian River Valley) $20. This is a medium-bodied, with soft tannins and cherryish fruit. Has good acidity and a cinnamony finish. Easy to drink and easy to like. **87** —*S.H. (10/1/2004)*

Acorn 1999 Alegria Vineyards Sangiovese (Russian River Valley) $16. American oak seems overly aggressive on the nose, with dominating aromas of clove and vanilla-tinged wood sap. Once you get past the bouquet, the wine is limpid, silky smooth, and utterly dry, with berry flavors. **85** —*S.H. (11/15/2001)*

Acorn 2003 Alegria Vineyards Axiom Syrah (Russian River Valley) $30. Superripe and high in alcohol, but dry, this Syrah is rich and lush in blackberry, coffee, and chocolate flavors. It has a smooth mouthfeel and soft acids. If you like these big, luscious, New World wines, it's for you. **85** —*S.H. (4/1/2006)*

Acorn 2002 Alegria Vineyards Axiom Syrah (Russian River Valley) $28. Does a good job at the Syrah thing, namely, a full-bodied red wine, dry and rich in fruit, and soft in tannins and acids. Rises into complexity with the mélange of coffee, cocoa, and spice flavors. **86** —*S.H. (8/1/2005)*

Acorn 2001 Alegria Vineyards Axiom Syrah (Russian River Valley) $24. A good, rich Syrah, with that Northern Rhône peppery-meaty structural edge to the vibrant cherry fruit. The tannins are substantial, but that's no problem with the right foods. Has that extra dimension that marks a distinctive wine. **91** —*S.H. (10/1/2004)*

Acorn 2000 Alegria Vineyards Axiom Syrah Cuvée Syrah (Russian River Valley) $20. An interesting wine by virtue of its terroir-driven features. Low in cherry fruit, high in earthy tobacco, dry as a bone, and tart with acidity. But it has an elegantly sweet edge that cries out for richly sauced pasta and beef. **90 Editors' Choice** —*S.H. (12/15/2003)*

Acorn 1999 Alegria Vineyards-Axiom Syrah (Russian River Valley) $16. Black cherry and anise flavors are wrapped in a cedary veil in this medium-weight, balanced wine. It shows a bit of structure for its weight and style, finishing with modest, even tannins and a peppery note. **86** *(10/1/2001)*

Acorn 1998 Alegria Vineyards Heritage Vin Zinfandel (Russian River Valley) $25. **86** —*S.H. (12/1/2000)*

Acorn 2001 Alegria Vineyards, Heritage Vines Zinfandel (Russian River Valley) $28. A bright, eucalyptus edge runs through the top here, followed by creamy black cherry, blackberry, plum, chocolate, licorice, coffee, and sage notes. Smooth textured and ripe, the wine is pleasing to the end. **88** *(11/1/2003)*

Acorn 2000 Heritage Vines Alegria Vineyards Zinfandel (Russian River Valley) $28. Actually a blend of Zin plus 10 other minor varietals in an old field blend, this complex wine fascinates with its intricately interlocked flavors. There's a sensation a second. Bottom line: This wine is delicious, ripely sweet although technically dry, and ageworthy. **91** —*S.H. (7/1/2003)*

Acorn 1999 Heritage Vines Alegria Vineyards Zinfandel (Russian River Valley) $28. Starts off with wild berry, brambly aromas of earth, sun-warmes wood, coffee, and spice. In the mouth, the berry flavors are wrapped in solid tannins, The kind that make your palate numb. It's very dry with a tar, tough finish. **83** —*S.H. (12/15/2001)*

ADASTRA

Adastra 2003 Chardonnay (Carneros) $30. This toothpicky wine tastes overly oaked by far, and you have to wonder why they plastered it on, since the underlying fruit seems fine, even with the acid. Makes you appreciate the "unoaked" Chardonnay phenomenon. **83** —*S.H. (12/31/2005)*

Adastra 2002 Chardonnay (Carneros) $30. Fruity and oaky, with char and caramel dominating the apple and peach flavors. This tasty wine finishes a little sweet in fruit and wood sap. **86** —*S.H. (4/1/2005)*

USA

Adastra 2000 Chardonnay (Carneros) $28. Lean and angular, with citrus fruit flavors and tart acidity that lavish oak does little to alleviate. Many of the 2000 North Coast Chards show this lemony profile. It's very dry, with a rasp on the palate that cries out for food, and it's also heady and high in alcohol. **86** —*S.H. (5/1/2002)*

Adastra 2001 Merlot (Carneros) $30. This is a very ripe wine that floods the mouth with black cherry, chocolate, and smoky oak flavors. The tannins are soft and complex. Drinks a bit too sweet and simple, especially at this price. **86** —*S.H. (4/1/2005)*

ADEA

Adea 2000 Chardonnay (Willamette Valley) $20. A mix of clones, with some of the new Dijon included. This barrel-fermented Chardonnay has a good, fleshy, chewy mouthfeel, buttressed with plenty of oaky tannins. Simple, but tasty enough. **85** —*P.G. (9/1/2003)*

Adea 1999 Chardonnay (Willamette Valley) $24. Intriguing, forward, palate-tickling layers of spicy melon, kiwi, apple, and mango get things off to a great start. Ripe and fleshy, this is mouthfilling juice with a tasty, toasty, caramel and light butter finish, yet enough crisp acid to keep things very lively. **90** —*P.G. (2/1/2002)*

Adea 1999 Pinot Gris (Willamette Valley) $15. All from a single vineyard, this very tart wine shows green apple fruit, hints of coconut, and a bit of toast on the finish. Just 205 cases were produced. **85** —*P.G. (2/1/2002)*

Adea 2002 Pinot Noir (Willamette Valley) $25. Pungent and smoky with meat, leathery and woodsy scents, this promises big things but falls apart on the palate. Sour cherry fruit disappears after a big entry, and the finish is all oak. **85** *(11/1/2004)*

Adea 2000 Pinot Noir (Willamette Valley) $35. A middle-of-the-road Oregon Pinot, with pleasant, quite light fruit. Strawberry and light cherry flavors, followed by an ashy, grainy, earthy finish. **85** —*P.G. (4/1/2003)*

Adea 1999 Pinot Noir (Willamette Valley) $35. Light cherry flavors are swathed in smoky oak and vanilla wafer notes, with just a hint of spice. At this point, there's too much wood for the fruit, and it all leads to a quick, dry, tannic finish. Just 340 cases made. **85** —*P.G. (12/31/2001)*

Adea 2002 Coleman Vineyard Pinot Noir (Willamette Valley) $35. Fragrant with diverse, interesting, unusual floral and chocolate scents. The chocolaty oak, though appealing, runs over the light, citrus and cherry fruit, which can't stand up to it. **87** *(11/1/2004)*

Adea 2002 Dean-O's Pinot Noir (Willamette Valley) $30. This wine has plenty of color, and good, dark extract, which struck one reviewer as sappy and full-bodied, but others as blocky and disjointed. Definitely big, but lacking elegance and balance. **85** *(11/1/2004)*

Adea 2000 Reserve Pinot Noir (Willamette Valley) $42. The winery's reserve Pinot is not much different from the regular bottling. Strawberry and cherry lifesaver flavors make this a forward, fruity, quaffable wine. The simple flavors and the plastic cork suggest a $10 bottle; $42 seems like quite a stretch. **85** —*P.G. (4/1/2003)*

Adea 2002 Yamhill Valley Vineyards Pinot Noir (Willamette Valley) $35. Very oaky, with powerful vanilla scents, and grapy, candied fruit. The depth and texture of perfectly ripe, supple fruit are not there, but there's plenty of tannin and all that oak. **84** *(11/1/2004)*

ADELAIDA

Adelaida 2002 Estate Reserve Cabernet Sauvignon (Paso Robles) $45. Rustic and a little on the sweet side, with blackberry tea and cola flavors. The finish is both tannic and sugary. **82** —*S.H. (11/1/2006)*

Adelaida 2001 Viking Port Cabernet Sauvignon (Paso Robles) $30. Sweet, heavy and full-bodied, with rich chocolate and blackberry flavors. Turns a little cloying on the soft finish. **84** —*S.H. (8/1/2005)*

Adelaida 2002 Chamisal Vineyard Chardonnay (Edna Valley) $24. These Edna Valley Chards always seem to be tart in acids and fairly lean in apple and white peach fruit, with a strong minerality. Chablisian, if you will. This one fits the mold perfectly. Dry and crisp, it can easily accompany mussels or oysters. **87** —*S.H. (7/1/2005)*

Adelaida 2004 HMR Estate Chardonnay (Santa Lucia Highlands) $30. The estate is in the southern end of the appellation, toward Paso Robles, and this full-bodied Chard smacks of apricot preserves, with a spicy, peppery edge. It's adequately acidic and oaked, with a rich, creamy texture. **87** —*S.H. (11/1/2006)*

Adelaida 2002 HMR Estate Chardonnay (Paso Robles) $30. Not showing much to savor now, a flat, simple wine with earthy, vegetal flavors. **83** —*S.H. (7/1/2005)*

Adelaida 2002 Pavanne Chenin Blanc (Paso Robles) $20. One of the more serious attempts at Chenin in the state, but you can only push this varietal so far. This is a bone dry wine, with high acidity, sort of like a Sauvignon Blanc, with fruity citrus flavors and a whistle-clean finish. **85** —*S.H. (7/1/2005)*

Adelaida 2003 HMR Estate Pinot Noir (Paso Robles) $55. The vineyard is out on the cooler west side of the appellation, and it shows in the balance and acidity of this fine Pinot. At the same time, that Paso heat has brought the grapes to cherry pie ripeness. The result is a deliciously drinkable wine. **88** —*S.H. (11/1/2006)*

Adelaida 2002 HMR Estate Pinot Noir (Paso Robles) $25. From the cooler western hills of the appellation, a full-bodied Pinot that's smooth, dry, and fruity. The pretty flavors of cherries and oak have an edge of tannins that will play well off goat cheese, steak or salmon. **88** —*S.H. (4/1/2005)*

Adelaida 2002 SLO Pinot Noir (San Luis Obispo County) $15. Has the rough texture you often find in inexpensive California Pinots, but otherwise is a fine wine. The cherry and coffee flavors finish with a silky quality and a spicy taste. **85** —*S.H. (4/1/2005)*

Adelaida 2003 Vin Gris de Pinot Noir Pinot Noir (Paso Robles) $15. Dry and fruity, with peach, wild blackberry, and spice flavors, this is a crisp blush wine that has subtlety and complexity. It's fairly full-bodied, with a nice, curranty finish. Try with bouillabaisse. **85** —*S.H. (7/1/2005)*

Adelaida 2003 Glenrose Vineyard Rhône Style Red Wine Rhône Red Blend (Paso Robles) $26. With five Rhône varieties, this Châteauneuf-style wine is soft, simple, and a bit cooked. It has cherry pie filling flavors and finishes rustic, with a trace of stewed fruit. **82** —*S.H. (11/15/2006)*

Adelaida 2004 Glenrose Vineyard Roussanne-Grenache Blanc Rhône White Blend (Paso Robles) $25. Creamy in texture, with extracted, jammy flavors of tropical fruits, white raisins, caramel, and honeysuckle, this wine is dry and crisp with acids. It was barrel fermented and aged *sur lie*, giving it the weight of a Chardonnay. **85** —*S.H. (11/1/2006)*

Adelaida 2002 The Glenrose Vineyard Rhône White Blend (Paso Robles) $25. An exciting Rhône white, oaky and rich in flamboyant tropical fruit, wildflower, and spicy flavors. This big, flashy, opulent wine is a blend of Roussanne and Grenache Blanc. **90 Editors' Choice** —*S.H. (10/1/2005)*

Adelaida 1996 Syrah (Paso Robles) $24. 88 —*S.H. (10/1/1999)*

Adelaida 2003 Syrah (Paso Robles) $26. Ripe to the point of jammy, with blackberry and cherry flavors that taste like they were baked in a pie. But the wine wisely avoids any hints of overripeness. It's dry and a little soft. **86** —*S.H. (11/15/2006)*

Adelaida 2003 Glenrose Vineyard Reserve Syrah (Paso Robles) $55. Superripe and soft, with baked cherry and fudge-crust flavors and nutmeg on the finish. Not a bad wine, but certainly shows its hot terroir. **84** —*S.H. (11/15/2006)*

Adelaida 2003 Viking Estate Reserve Syrah (Paso Robles) $55. Lots of tasty cherry pie, cocoa, leather, and spice flavors here, and the wine is nicely dry, but it's too soft and there's a hot, peppery mouthfeel. **83** —*S.H. (11/15/2006)*

Adelaida 1998 Viking Estate Vineyard Syrah (Paso Robles) $40. An intense, complex cassis, toast, curry, and espresso bouquet open this dense, balanced wine. A smooth feel, creamy vanilla, tart berry, and tobacco flavors, and a long, tangy fruit finish with supple tannins complete the package. A heavily oaked wine that some tasters found sexy; others thought it overwooded—your take will depend on your appetite for oak. **87** *(11/1/2001)*

USA

Adelaida 2004 Glenrose Vineyard Viognier (Paso Robles) $30. Here's a big, full-bodied, gutsy Viognier with robust acidity and mouth-filling flavors of baked peach pie. Thoroughly dry, it also has an herbal, mineral side that anchors it. Very nice. **88** —*S.H. (11/15/2006)*

Adelaida 1997 Zinfandel (Paso Robles) $20. 83 —*S.H. (5/1/2000)*

Adelaida 2001 Zinfandel (Paso Robles) $21. A pleasant, bright-edged blend of tangy cherry, blackberry, toast, vanilla, and spice flavors with a moderately long finish. **86** *(11/1/2003)*

Adelaida 2001 Reserve Zinfandel (Paso Robles) $35. A bright-edged wine that sports chocolate, tea, black plum, spice, and cedary flavors. A bit hot on the finish, though pleasant enough, and zippy to the end. **86** *(11/1/2003)*

Adelaida 2001 Schoolhouse Zinfandel (Paso Robles) $19. Pretty plum and cherry flavors make this a pleasing quaff. The tannins are mild and the finish is moderate in length, tapering off with toasty oak and spice. **86** *(11/1/2003)*

ADELSHEIM

Adelsheim 2000 Chardonnay (Oregon) $14. There are pretty scents of tropical fruit, and just a hint of oak, but once in the mouth the flavors are still unmingled, giving the wine a somewhat disjointed structure. It mixes sweet, candied fruit with cinnamon spice and some pretty sour acids. **85** —*P.G. (4/1/2002)*

Adelsheim 2005 CH Chardonnay (Willamette Valley) $22. Adelsheim pioneered Dijon clone Chardonnay in Oregon, correctly guessing that the Burgundian grape would ripen better than the California (Wente) clones that were ubiquitous. CH is made with no oak, no malolactic fermentation, no residual sugar, and no skin contact. In a way it's the anti-Chardonnay, but at the same time it is the purest style of Chardonnay. Bracing, fresh, and zesty in the Euro mold, it's got flavors of melon, green apple, and gooseberry. **89** *(12/1/2006)*

Adelsheim 2000 Stoller Vineyard Chardonnay (Yamhill County) $30. In '99 Adelsheim bottled two separate clonal selections; this year they have elected to combine the two. This lovely, young wine, with very ripe, tight fruit, is already showing a bit more peach, apricot, and tropical scents than the previous vintage. This is a concentrated, complex, and powerful style, which harnesses the oak rather than being driven by it. Delicious and exceptionally long. **92** —*P.G. (8/1/2002)*

Adelsheim 1996 Stoller Vineyard Chardonnay (Yamhill County) $30. The winery planted several different Dijon clones a few years back, and decided to bottle them separately in 1999, hence the unwieldy name. This is a young, hard, assertive, and distinctly Burgundian effort, ripe and well structured. There is firm, tart, lemony fruit nicely layered with French oak, and nuanced with hazelnuts through the long finish. **90** —*P.G. (4/1/2002)*

Adelsheim 1999 Stoller Vineyard Clone 76 Chardonnay (Yamhill County) $30. This bottling is softer and more forward than the Clone 96, and a good case could be made for blending the two, though the winery explains that they tried it and didn't like the results. Here are tropical fruit flavors of pineapple and banana, fronting a rich, lush wine that is ready right now. **88** —*P.G. (4/1/2002)*

Adelsheim 2005 Pinot Blanc (Willamette Valley) $19. Melon, lime and apple define this wine designed for acid lovers. I am one, but this is borderline sour. It turns salty on the finish, wrapping things up with more tart acidity. **86** —*P.G. (12/1/2006)*

Adelsheim 2000 Pinot Blanc (Oregon) $12. At its best, Oregon Pinot Blanc is the most exciting white wine made in the state, and this definitely is the grape at its best. Soft scents of melon and banana lead into a panoply of lively mixed green fruits flavors. Elegant, supple, fresh, and refreshing, this is an excellent, layered, nimble food wine. **91 Best Buy** —*P.G. (4/1/2002)*

Adelsheim 1998 Pinot Blanc (Oregon) $13. 88 —*L.W. (12/31/1999)*

Adelsheim 2005 Pinot Gris (Willamette Valley) $18. Adelsheim makes 9,000 cases of this full-flavored Pinot Gris, one of the best in Oregon. A rich texture and fleshy fruit highlighted by

cinnamon-dusted pears is enhanced by hints of mint and marzipan. **89** —*P.G. (12/1/2006)*

Adelsheim 2004 Pinot Gris (Oregon) $17. A little bit of spritz livens the mouthfeel. This is very light, with herb and grass and tart green apple flavors. A good quaffing wine, not big, but clean and refreshing. **87** —*P.G. (2/1/2006)*

Adelsheim 2000 Pinot Gris (Oregon) $13. The nose lifts off with unusual scents of pears, brown sugar, and graham crackers. The wine is crisp and full-bodied, and the ripe, tropical fruits carry a slight impression of canned syrup, making it all taste a bit like fruit salad. **85** —*P.G. (4/1/2002)*

Adelsheim 2004 Pinot Noir (Willamette Valley) $29. Young and bursting with scents of crisp toast, ripe cherries, coffee grounds, and cedar, this forward, fruity Pinot unfolds with bright raspberry flavors. The tangy fruit holds down the fort, circled by marauding bands of toast and ground coffee. Expressive and flavorful. **88** —*P.G. (5/1/2006)*

Adelsheim 2000 Pinot Noir (Oregon) $22. This is the least expensive of Adelsheim's Pinots, and the first release of the new vintage. Nonetheless it shows some muscle, with a sweet, smoky nose over grapey fruit. Forward and appealing, with a tannic and quick finish. **87** —*P.G. (4/1/2002)*

Adelsheim 1997 Pinot Noir (Oregon) $20. 85 *(11/15/1999)*

Adelsheim 1998 AVS Pinot Noir (Willamette Valley) $40. 91 —*M.M. (12/1/2000)*

Adelsheim 1999 Bryan Creek Vineyard Pinot Noir (Willamette Valley) $36. The nose mixes interesting notes of beet, cola, and crème caramel, and the wine is still quite young, unresolved, and slightly prickly in the mouth. But there is good concentration and all the components for a fine Pinot, given a bit more time in bottle. **88** —*P.G. (4/1/2002)*

Adelsheim 1998 Bryan Creek Vineyard Pinot Noir (Willamette Valley) $40. 88 —*M.S. (12/1/2000)*

Adelsheim 2002 Elizabeth's Reserve Pinot Noir (Yamhill County) $40. A bit of a disappointment, this shows the horsey, barnyard notes that are consistent across the lineup from Adelsheim. Light fruit flavors of strawberry and melon make for a lean finish. **84** *(11/1/2004)*

Adelsheim 1999 Elizabeth's Reserve Pinot Noir (Oregon) $36. This has long been Adelsheim's top Pinot, sourced entirely from the winery's oldest estate vineyard, which was planted in 1974. It's a lovely effort, with a deep, seductive bouquet that mingles rose petals, vanilla, and sweet beet. Soft and layered, it shows flavors of fruit, root, spice, herb and even hints of mineral. Interesting, complex and subtle. **91 Editors' Choice** —*P.G. (4/1/2002)*

Adelsheim 1998 Elizabeth's Reserve Pinot Noir (Yamhill County) $45. 90 —*M.S. (12/1/2000)*

Adelsheim 1999 Goldschmidt Vineyard Pinot Noir (Yamhill County) $36. The vineyard is owned by the former governor of Oregon, and the wine greets you with a firm handshake and a smile. A ripe, round nose shows ripe, forward fruit, generous and spicy. In the mouth it is textured and sleek, with a sculpted, elegant mouthfeel. It is ageworthy, and not overblown. **90** —*P.G. (4/1/2002)*

Adelsheim 1998 Penta Reserve Pinot Noir (Yamhill County) $32. An interesting, soft, and sensual wine, the first blended reserve Pinot from the Adelsheim vineyard. The extra year of bottle age has rounded out the flavors, and it is a round, pleasing wine dominated by sassafras and spice. Delicious and ready to drink, it lacks only sufficient depth to merit a higher score. **87** —*P.G. (4/1/2002)*

Adelsheim 2002 Ribbon Springs Vineyard Pinot Noir (Yamhill County) $45. Earthy, lightly horsey aromas lend accents of leather, bacon, and coffee. There is some sweet, young, grapy fruit, but overall it seems one-dimensional. **84** *(11/1/2004)*

Adelsheim 1998 Seven Springs Vineyard Pinot Noir (Polk County) $30. 90 —*M.M. (12/1/2000)*

Adelsheim 2004 TF Tocai Friulano (Willamette Valley) $20. TF stands for Tocai Friulano, a perfectly legitimate grape name that has been outlawed in Oregon and will soon be illegal in its own home of Friuli. It's a fresh, herbal grape, which mixes light grassy flavors, citrus, pineapple, and honeydew, with a pleasing mineral undercurrent. **88**—P.G. (5/1/2006)

Adelsheim 2005 Auxerrois White Blend (Willamette Valley) $20. Here is Auxerrois at its very best, fragrant with orange, quince, and honey, and lively with lemon-lime and pink grapefruit on the palate. The final impression—of stone and spice—leaves you craving that next sip. **88**—P.G. (12/1/2006)

ADLER FELS

Adler Fels 1997 Chardonnay (Sonoma County) $15. **89**—S.H. (11/1/1999)

Adler Fels 2001 Gewürztraminer (Russian River Valley) $10. **87 Best Buy**—S.H. (11/15/2002)

Adler Fels 1997 Sauvignon Blanc (Sonoma County) $12. **86**—S.H. (11/1/1999)

Adler Fels 1998 Sauvignon Blanc (Russian River Valley) $11. **86**—S.H. (11/15/2000)

ADOBE CREEK

Adobe Creek 2000 Merlot (Sonoma County) $14. There's some good varietal character here, with the aromas and flavors of plums, violets, cassis, and cherry-chocolate. Feels smooth in the mouth, with dry tannins. Finishes a bit rustic, but overall, not bad. **85**—S.H. (12/31/2003)

Adobe Creek 2001 Pinot Gris (Sonoma County) $14. Simple, with the taste and feel of alcohol-laced lemonade. The citrusy, spearminty flavors are a little sweet, and the wine finishes with a thud. **83**—S.H. (12/1/2003)

Adobe Creek 2002 Sauvignon Blanc (Contra Costa County) $12. This indifferent wine has simple, watered down flavors of citrus fruits. About the only thing the palate experiences is acidity and alcohol. Yet it is technically without flaws. **82**—S.H. (10/1/2003)

ADOBE ROAD

Adobe Road 2000 Cabernet Sauvignon (Alexander Valley) $39. Raw, unripe, and unlikeable, with a bitter finish. Whatever were they thinking when they set the price? **81**—S.H. (8/1/2005)

Adobe Road 2002 Herrerias Vineyard Pinot Noir (Sonoma Coast) $30. Rather heavy and lifeless, but rescued by the pretty black cherry, cola, and spice flavors, and a silky mouthfeel. Finishes dry and oaky. **84**—S.H. (8/1/2005)

Adobe Road 2001 Zinfandel (Alexander Valley) $32. Opens with the veggies, like canned aspraragus, and drinks a little richer, with black cherries flavors and firm tannins. Okay Zin, but kind of pricey. **83**—S.H. (8/1/2005)

AGRARIA

Agraria 1999 Big Barn Red Bordeaux Blend (Dry Creek Valley) $52. A Cabernet Franc-based Bordeaux blend and quite a good one. Soft and luxurious, with forward cherry flavors backed by firm tannins. The mouthfeel is blue velvet, seductive in its own fashion. **88**—S.H. (12/1/2004)

Agraria 1999 Big Barn Red Cabernet Sauvignon (Dry Creek Valley) $52. This wine has a weird aroma of cough drops and varnish, and is sharp in acids, with a medicinal cherry taste that finishes a little sweet. Tasted twice, with consistent results. **82**—S.H. (10/1/2004)

AHLGREN

Ahlgren 1997 Bates' Ranch Cabernet Sauvignon (Santa Cruz Mountains) $35. **90** (11/1/2000)

Ahlgren 1997 Harvest Moon Vineyards Cabernet Sauvignon (Santa Cruz Mountains) $33. **82** (11/1/2000)

Ahlgren 1999 Ventana Vineyards Syrah (Monterey) $24. This even, balanced wine opens with a smooth, tart, black cherry-rhubarb, pepper, and smoke bouquet. It's medium in weight and has tangy acidity that supports the fruit well. Complex flavors with smoked meat, bitter herb, and espresso on the cherry core are appealing. Tangy tannins and coffee notes close it nicely. **87** (11/1/2001)

AIRLIE

Airlie 2002 Chardonnay (Willamette Valley) $10. Bitter oak, a sugary mouthfeel, and an earthy, chunky, pineapple candy-flavored palate. **83**—P.G. (5/1/2006)

Airlie 2004 Gewürztraminer (Willamette Valley) $9. Quite light and citric, this doesn't show much of the floral side of the grape. Mere hints of rose petal and a little bit of soapiness in the mouth, with thin, hard lemony fruit. **84**—P.G. (5/1/2006)

Airlie 2002 Gewürztraminer (Willamette Valley) $10. Bone dry style, which puts the emphasis on dusty, dried spices rather than flowers. There are concentrated fruit flavors of cantaloupe, citrus, pear, and honey, lending the impression of sweetness. Unusual and rich. **87 Best Buy**—P.G. (2/1/2005)

Airlie 2003 Maréchal Foch (Willamette Valley) $14. This winery does a fine job with this unusual, rustic red grape. Heavy, juicy black cherry fruit anchors an earthy, tannic wine, giving it a ripe, solid core to hang the tannins on. **89 Best Buy**—P.G. (5/1/2006)

Airlie 2004 Müller-Thurgau (Willamette Valley) $10. Big, round, and fruity, this is a simple, fairly sweet wine with plenty of smooth fruit enjoyment. There's just a touch of spice and an earthy finish. **85 Best Buy**—P.G. (5/1/2006)

Airlie 2003 Pinot Gris (Willamette Valley) $12. Crisp, leesy, textural varietal fruit flavors of fresh cut pear coat the palate. There is a bit of earthy follow-through, slightly musty old barrel flavors that carry into the finish. **84**—P.G. (2/1/2006)

Airlie 2002 Pinot Gris (Willamette Valley) $12. The straw brown color suggests a wine that is already slightly oxidized, and the palate confirms that the fruit is dropping out, leaving a creamy, yeasty, still flavorful wine that is ready to go. This would be particularly good with a creamy pasta dish. **87**—P.G. (2/1/2005)

Airlie 2003 Pinot Noir (Willamette Valley) $14. Scents of violets and unfermented grapes suggest a prettier wine than is actually here. It's tart and thin, with cranberry-ish fruit and an artificial, chalky, slightly candied finish. **83**—P.G. (5/1/2006)

Airlie 2002 Two Vineyard-Old Vines Pinot Noir (Willamette Valley) $20. Young, full and forward, this delivers a big burst of nice, ripe fruit right off the top. It's cherries and chocolate, all good, but it loses some points for a gritty, tannic finish. **88**—P.G. (2/1/2005)

Airlie 2004 Riesling (Willamette Valley) $10. Light and pretty, with citrus blossom scents and a gentle but pleasing palate, like a simple German kabinett from a cooler vintage. **86 Best Buy**—P.G. (5/1/2006)

AIX MONTEREY

Aix Monterey 1999 Chardonnay (Monterey) $15. Firm and smooth textured, with a toasty edge plus apple, pear, and modest citrus flavors. **86**—J.M. (12/15/2002)

AJB VINEYARDS

AJB Vineyards 1997 Syrah (Paso Robles) $21. Bold, powerful aromas of white pepper and blackberry explode, with a more mature bouquet of dried rose petal and sweet cigar box. Soft, lush tannins frame pure, supple berry fruit. Perfect now. **90**—S.H. (7/1/2002)

ALAPAY

Alapay 2000 Chardonnay (Central Coast) $17. Pretty darned nice Chard, and not too oaky or sweet, for a change. This one has fresh apple and peach flavors in a round, creamy texture, with quite a dollop of lees, which adds to the complex palate and finish. The structure is especially good. **90**—S.H. (9/1/2002)

Alapay 2004 Edna Ranch Chardonnay (Edna Valley) $22. Here's a fine, distinctive Chardonnay. It possesses classic Edna acidity and forward citrus and mineral flavors, with a luscious interweaving of honeysuckle. The wine is thoroughly dry and quite delicious. **89**—S.H. (11/1/2006)

Alapay 2004 Edna Ranch Pinot Noir (Edna Valley) $25. Delicately silky and dry, this is an elegant Pinot that's dynamic in fruity flavor. Ripe red cherry pie filling, cola, root beer, and pomegranates flood the mouth, leading to a clean, Asian spice finish. Should hold well for five years. **88** —*S.H. (10/1/2006)*

Alapay 2000 Viognier (Santa Barbara County) $19. Typically bright and floral-fruity, this offers up a big mouthful of lemonade, peach juice, and honeyed, wildlfower flavors. It's creamy and rich, and really a lot of fun, a wine to enjoy, not ponder over. **88** —*S.H. (9/1/2002)*

Alapay 1999 Zinfandel (Paso Robles) $18. Here's an absolutely classic Paso Zin. It brims with the juiciest wild berry and jam flavors, big and bold, wrapped in ultrasoft tannins and set off by low acids. It's also nicely dry, without those hot country Port notes. This all makes it a grand drink in its precocious youth. **90** —*S.H. (9/1/2003)*

ALBA

Alba 1998 East Coast Chardonnay (New Jersey) $10. **83** —*J.C. (1/1/2004)*

Alba 2003 Heritage Red Blend (New Jersey) $25. Foch, a hybrid known in France as Marécahl Foch, makes up the bulk of this wine, with Cab Sauv (30%) and Petit Verdot (5%) supporting. Smooth, with high acid, soft tannins, and a hint of sweetness. Tart plummy fruit characterizes the wine; there is also aromas of pastry and lemon meringue. The finish is mouthwatering, with good fruit, vanilla, and crisp acids. **86** —*M.D. (8/1/2006)*

Alba 2004 Riesling (New Jersey) $11. Pleasant aromas of mango, peach, and spice lead to a sweet wine that lacks acidity. The aromas don't translate to the flavor, where Bazooka Joe bubble gum dominates. Not bad, but too sweet for my taste. **81** —*M.D. (8/1/2006)*

Alba NV Delaware Dolce White Blend (America) $20. There is plenty of sweet fruit, honey, golden raisin, and spearmint in this wine, but bubble gum cheapens it a trifle. Acidity keeps the feel lively, while on a whole the experience is positive and the flavors quite good. **85** —*M.D. (8/1/2006)*

ALBAN

Alban 1996 Estate Grenache (Edna Valley) $NA. Developing bottle bouquet. Chalky-cherry nose, grilled meat, potpourri, cinnamon, nutmeg, vanilla, pipe tobacco, roses, and violets. Drinks lush, smooth, sweet in raspberries and cherries. Good acidity. Still fresh, firm, dry. Could reintensify. **90** —*S.H. (6/1/2005)*

Alban 1993 Estate Grenache (Edna Valley) $NA. The bouquet of this wine made me very happy. Pure, intense raspberry-cherry, with spicy clove, cinnamon, vanilla. Fine and alluring. Tons of raspberry fruit in the mouth, with a roast coffee earthiness. Dry, clean, supple, elegant. A chef's dream. Delicate, powerful, uplifted. **94** —*S.H. (6/1/2005)*

Alban 1997 Roussanne (Edna Valley) $32. **89** —*S.H. (10/1/1999)*

Alban 2000 Roussanne (Central Coast) $25. A startingly interesting wine that opens with powerful aromas of peaches and all sort of meaty, beefy, truffly, and mushroomy complexities. Marked by crisp, vibrant acids that boost the stone fruit flavors and make them punchy. Dry, complex, and compelling. **90** —*S.H. (6/1/2003)*

Alban 2000 Estate Vineyard Roussanne (Edna Valley) $32. Clearly a winner, a wine that shows its terroir in the mineral, slate, vanilla, and cotton candy aromas. The flavor is hard to describe, sort of a mix of tapioca, rasberry purée and gunflint. Very acidic and crisp, with a long, firm, and steely finish that cries out for rich, complex foods. **91** —*S.H. (6/1/2003)*

Alban 1998 Lorraine Syrah (Edna Valley) $45. Loaded with blackberry from beginning to end, the Alban is big, black, and velvety in the mouth. Reviewers lauded earthy-vegetal aromas, plus a little spice and pepper, in the bouquet; organic-earthy notes coat the blackberry flavor on both the palate and the slightly bitter finish. **89** *(11/1/2001)*

Alban 1996 Reva Syrah (Edna Valley) $NA. Big roasted coffeebean aroma, also mulch, wet earth, forest floor, truffles, chocolate, bark, wild red forest berries. Sweet, smooth, supple, dry, chocolatey on the palate, with a potent core of anisette-soaked cherries. Velvety mouthfeel, very nice. **91** —*S.H. (6/1/2005)*

Alban 1992 Reva Syrah (Edna Valley) $NA. Still a good color. Pepper, earth, blackberry, roasted coffee aromas. Still some sturdy tannins to shed. Tight now, with blackberry and cherry flavors, but closed, austere.

Could re-emerge from its cocoon. Drink now-2010. **90** —*S.H. (6/1/2005)*

Alban 2003 Seymour's Syrah (Edna Valley) $NA. Tremendous depth and complexity, with red and black stone fruits, berries, spices, and herbs. Layers of anise, chocolate, oak. Tannins are rich, thick, soft, and negotiable now. Huge wine. **95** —*S.H. (7/1/2006)*

Alban 1998 Viognier (Edna Valley) $28. **91** —*S.H. (10/1/1999)*

Alban 2000 Costello T.B.A. Viognier (Edna Valley) $65. Glugs out of the bottle as thick as mineral oil, a hint to the viscous texture. Don't chill this too much, because it will stun the intensely rich botrytis and apricot preserves aromas, with their edge of wild honey and cinnamon. The ultimate impression is in the mouth, where the apricot and pear tart flavors drink like a nectary syrup, but are relieved with vibrant acids. Not supersweet, and fairly low in alcohol, this is a beautiful, delicious dessert wine. **95** —*S.H. (6/1/2003)*

Alban 2001 Estate Viognier (Edna Valley) $29. Ripe, rich, forward, and exotic. From an American pioneer of Rhône varietals, the wine offers an intriguing and exciting blend of spice, apricot, peach, melon, and herb components. **91** Editors' Choice —*J.M. (12/15/2002)*

ALBEMARLE

Albemarle 2002 Simply Red Bordeaux Blend (America) $22. This blend of 51% Merlot, 30% Cabernet Sauvignon, and 19% Cabernet Franc carries a label designation as American Red Wine, which means the grapes could be from anywhere, but they were made into wine in Virginia. Pleasant spice, tobacco, and red berry flavors thin out on the finish. **83** —*J.C. (9/1/2005)*

ALDER RIDGE

Alder Ridge 2002 Cabernet Sauvignon (Columbia Valley (WA)) $30. A very fine effort. The wine is full flavored without being punishing. There's plenty of cassis and plum, and nothing syrupy about it. Great balance across the entire palate, with a Bordeaux-like elegance. Notes of iron filings, chalk, and light herb complete the picture. 150 cases produced. **92** —*P.G. (6/1/2006)*

ALDERBROOK

Alderbrook 2004 Carignane (Dry Creek Valley) $19. Here's something good and different. This wine shows exuberant wild berry and cassis flavors, like fruit plucked from thorny bushes at the height of juicy ripeness. The fresh acidity and dusty tannins call out for olive oil, butter, cheese, meats, or poultry. **87** —*S.H. (12/31/2006)*

Alderbrook 1998 Chardonnay (Dry Creek Valley) $15. **89** *(6/1/2000)*

Alderbrook 2004 Chardonnay (Russian River Valley) $18. Alderbrook's winemaker could have made a big, fruity wine in this warm vintage, but seems to have decided to make a more delicate, higher-acid Chard instead. This food-friendly sipper has nice peach, apple, and pineapple flavors, and is balanced, dry and elegant. **87** —*S.H. (11/1/2006)*

Alderbrook 2003 Chardonnay (Russian River Valley) $18. There's plenty of ripe fruit here, but the wine has too much oak, and has a weird salty flavor. The varietal identity is proper. **83** —*S.H. (11/1/2005)*

Alderbrook 2002 Chardonnay (Dry Creek Valley) $18. Charming, with a good balance of ripe tree fruits, oak, and earthy, herbal notes. Satisfies your Chardonnay tooth, but it's understated enough not to swamp food **87** —*S.H. (3/1/2005)*

Alderbrook 2000 Chardonnay (Dry Creek Valley) $NA. Combines some pretty apple flavors with earthier notes, and drinks a bit heavy in the mouth. Herbal tastes show up on the finish. Dry, with good acids and dusty tannins, and clean. **85** *(6/1/2003)*

Alderbrook 1999 Chardonnay (Dry Creek Valley) $18. Begins with classic, bright aromas of green apples, ripe peaches, and sweet oak, including buttery-vanilla overtones. The upfront, fruity flavors are wrapped in a creamy, supple texture. The dry finish suggests peaches and cream, dusted with crushed spices. **88** —*S.H. (11/15/2001)*

Alderbrook 1997 Dorothy's Vineyard Chardonnay (Dry Creek Valley) $22. **88** *(6/1/2000)*

Alderbrook 2004 Pinot Noir (Russian River Valley) $25. This isn't a cheap wine, but it's a good value compared to more costly Russian River Pinots. It's classy, showing Pinot's silky elegance with delicious cherry, cola, and tea flavors. Hard to imagine a more versatile Pinot; will go with everything from salmon to steak. **90 Editors' Choice** —S.H. (11/1/2006)

Alderbrook 2003 Pinot Noir (Russian River Valley) $24. Alderbrook's Pinots are usually clean, well made, and typically varietal, with crisp acids and ripe, pleasant flavors of cola, cherries, rhubarb pie, vanilla, and spice. Drink this light, easy wine now and over the next year. **86** —S.H. (12/15/2005)

Alderbrook 2002 Pinot Noir (Russian River Valley) $24. Earthy, simple and light, with modest cherry and herb flavors. Finishes dry, with a silky mouth feel. **84** —S.H. (3/1/2005)

Alderbrook 2000 Pinot Noir (Russian River Valley) $29. Made in a light, accessible style, it retains Pinot's character without aggressive tannins or oak. The flavors of black cherry, tea, and cinnamon are subtly spiced with toast. The dry finish is long-lasting and elegant. **89** —S.H. (2/1/2003)

Alderbrook 1999 Pinot Noir (Russian River Valley) $22. Sweet berry fruit and caramel aromas lead into a creamy black-fruit palate with touches of vanilla and coffee. The oak on the back palate and finish is powerful. **85** (10/1/2002)

Alderbrook 2003 Sauvignon Blanc (Dry Creek Valley) $14. Slightly sweet but crisp in acids, this pleasant wine features citrus, fig, tobacco, and vanilla flavors. **84** —S.H. (2/1/2005)

Alderbrook 2000 Sauvignon Blanc (Dry Creek Valley) $NA. From the cooler, southeast section of the appellation, a wine that steers clear of Sauvignon's grassy personality in favor of richer melon and fig notes. The fruity flavors are nicely balanced by crisp acidity and a dry, spicy mouthfeel that persists into the finish. **87** —S.H. (9/1/2003)

Alderbrook 1999 Sauvignon Blanc (Dry Creek Valley) $14. Delicate aromas of smoke, oak, white peach, and a hint of citrus waft from the glass. Tastes spicy, pert, and delicate, with light citrus flavors and some heat from alcohol. The final impression is of a rich, scoury, lemony burnish on the palate. **86** —S.H. (11/15/2001)

Alderbrook 2002 Syrah (Dry Creek Valley) $24. Polished and soft in texture, with decent cherry, earth, and cocoa flavors. Could use more intensity. **84** —S.H. (3/1/2005)

Alderbrook 2004 Old Vine Zinfandel (Dry Creek Valley) $20. Alderbrook just keeps on doing a good job at moderately priced wines that offer plenty of richness and varietal character. This Zin pleases for its dry, gentle flavors of berries, cherries, and spices, with a suggestion of thyme and nettles. **86** —S.H. (12/31/2006)

Alderbrook 2003 Old Vine Zinfandel (Dry Creek Valley) $21. This is one of Alderbrook's more successful wines. It's classic Dry Creek, ripe and zesty, with a pleasing balance of peppery fruit, alcohol, and tannins. Achieves real claret-like structure, while never losing Zin's wild and woolly side. **89** —S.H. (12/15/2005)

Alderbrook 2002 Old Vine Zinfandel (Dry Creek Valley) $19. This is great Zin, filled with personality. Showcases the briary, brambly wild blackberry and blueberry flavors, spices, and dusty tannins this appellation is famous for. Finishes dry and smooth. Beautiful and compelling now. **91** —S.H. (3/1/2005)

Alderbrook 2001 OVOC Zinfandel (Dry Creek Valley) $18. Spicy bright on the nose, with hints of raspberry and plums. The flavors continue on the palate, framed by toasty oak. Look for coffee, tar, black cherry, and herbs as well. The finish is firm and moderate in length. **88** (11/1/2003)

Alderbrook 2000 OVOC Zinfandel (Dry Creek Valley) $25. A ripe cherry ball, with almost a candy-like quality. Pretty herb and citrus notes follow on a somewhat moderate body. Ultrafruity is the theme here. May not be for everyone. **85** —J.M. (3/1/2002)

Alderbrook 1998 OVOC Zinfandel (Sonoma County) $18. Delicious berries and cream nose, which follows through with crisp, spicy flavors and good structure. OVOC stands for "old vines old clones" and the fruit, from head-pruned, hillside vineyards, lives up to its billing. Great all-purpose Zin. **90** —P.G. (3/1/2001)

Alderbrook 1997 OVOC Zinfandel (Sonoma County) $16. 90 —L.W. (9/1/1999)

Alderbrook 2003 Reserve Zinfandel (Dry Creek Valley) $34. Zinfandels are always worth a look. Their '03 Old Vine was very good. This is better, with greater depth and complexity. It showcases classic Dry Creek terroir in the dryness, richly tannic structure, and explosively peppery, wild berry and cherry fruit flavors. **91** —S.H. (6/1/2006)

Alderbrook 2002 Reserve Zinfandel (Dry Creek Valley) $34. Compared to Alderbrook's Old Vine Zin, this is more tannic and closed, almost brooding. It doesn't offer the immediate blast of pleasure, but is a very fine wine, with complex berry, spice, herb, smoke, and cocoa flavors. Good now, and should gain complexity over the next 5 years. **92** —S.H. (3/1/2005)

Alderbrook 2001 Reserve Zinfandel (Russian River Valley) $39. Dense and well structured, the wine serves up an elegant array of ripe plum, black cherry and blackberry flavors. Ripe, plush tannins frame the ensemble, which also features coffee, toast, cocoa, sage and spice notes. Full bodied and smooth; long on the finish. **90** (11/1/2003)

Alderbrook 2001 Reserve Zinfandel (Dry Creek Valley) $39. Smooth tannins frame the core of moderate fruit here, with cherry, berry, plum, and coffee notes in evidence. The texture beats the flavors, which are still pleasing. Moderate length on the finish. **87** (11/1/2003)

Alderbrook 2000 Reserve Zinfandel (Dry Creek Valley) $39. This is young and quite tart, still a bit closed in, but it shows pure, sweet, berry fruit that has the concentration of jammy preserves yet retain their lively acidity. Not much oak in evidence, just lovely Zinfandel fruit that speaks to the terroir of Dry Creek. **89** —P.G. (3/1/2002)

Alderbrook 2000 Reserve Zinfandel (Russian River Valley) $39. This is one of two new reserves from winemaker T.J. Evans, who set himself the goal to produce quintessential Zinfandels from both the Dry Creek Valley and Russian River Valley appellations. From 50 year old vines, the wine is fragrant with wild strawberries and enhanced with chocolatey oak. Sweet, vivid, and food friendly, it's a wonderful debut. **91** —P.G. (3/1/2002)

Alderbrook 2004 Wind Machine Zinfandel (Dry Creek Valley) $34. With the silky mouthfeel of a nice Pinot Noir, and fine varietal character, this is a French-style Zin. It's dry and balanced, with pleasant cherry cola and spice flavors that are fairly complex, though light. **85** —S.H. (12/31/2006)

ALEX SOTELO CELLARS

Alex Sotelo Cellars 2002 Dalraddy Vineyard Zinfandel (Napa Valley) $28. The front label says it's unfiltered, which may explain the spoiled, vegetal aroma. **81** —S.H. (6/1/2005)

ALEXANDER

Alexander 2000 Chestnut Hill Vineyard Chardonnay (Santa Cruz Mountains) $20. The underlying flavor of the varietal wine is good and pure, with peaches, pears, and tropical fruits, but the winemaking is heavy. Too much oak and lees results in imbalance. **84** —S.H. (6/1/2003)

Alexander 1998 Petite Sirah (Monterey) $23. It's tough enough to get big reds to ripen in Monterey, and this rainy vintage didn't help. Not a bad wine, but the green, herbal tannins are tough to get through. It's helped by a savory, rich finish. **84** —S.H. (12/31/2003)

ALEXANDER VALLEY VINEYARDS

Alexander Valley Vineyards 2002 Cyrus Cabernet Blend (Alexander Valley) $50. Named after the pioneer who settled Alexander Valley, this wine, based on Cabernet Sauvignon, is very dry and pretty tannic right now. It has a wealth of black cherry, blackberry jam, and sugared espresso flavors. Needs time, but it's a classy wine, and should be best by 2008. **89** —S.H. (9/1/2006)

Alexander Valley Vineyards 2001 Cyrus Cabernet Blend (Alexander Valley) $50. Here's a deliciously drinkable Cab, bursting with flavors of sun-ripened cassis and black currant fruit flavors, and a generous coating of well-toasted oak. It's dry, with a polished, velvety mouthfeel, and the tannins, while sturdy, are sweet enough to permit instant consumption. **92** —S.H. (10/1/2005)

Alexander Valley Vineyards 2000 Cyrus Cabernet Blend (Alexander Valley) $50. Light and oaky but delicious, like a sweet confection. Intricately laced flavors of blackberry scone, vanilla, crème de cassis, and toast are encased in an airy texture. The tannins are gentle but rich, lending a silken quality to this delicate wine. **89** —*S.H. (6/1/2004)*

Alexander Valley Vineyards 2001 Wetzel Family Estate Cabernet Franc (Alexander Valley) $20. An easy, soft wine, with well-ripened black currant, tobacco, and sweet cured olive flavors. Feels gentle in the mouth. Yet it's not flabby. The tannins and acids are ripe, and provide good balance to the rich flavors. **86** —*S.H. (11/15/2003)*

Alexander Valley Vineyards 2003 Cabernet Sauvignon (Alexander Valley) $20. A classic regional Cab. It's soft, with melted tannins, but the important thing is the complexity of flavor. Cherries, black currants, cocoa, anise, and dried herbs, as well as toasty oak, mingle on a rich finish. This fine wine should develop well over the next 10 years. **90** —*S.H. (3/1/2006)*

Alexander Valley Vineyards 2000 Estate Bottled Cabernet Sauvignon (Alexander Valley) $20. Made solidly in the house style of soft, lushly fruity Cabs that flatter the palate. The fully ripened berry flavors are rich and tasty, with only a hint of acids and tannins. The chocolatey finish is almost sweet. **86** *(11/15/2002)*

Alexander Valley Vineyards 2002 Wetzel Family Estate Cabernet Sauvignon (Alexander Valley) $20. Very nice, a ripe Cab with real elegance. Shows currant and oak flavors wrapped in firm but negotiable tannins, and is fully dry. Finishes with a scour of espresso acidity that cleans the palate. **87** —*S.H. (4/1/2005)*

Alexander Valley Vineyards 2004 Chardonnay (Alexander Valley) $15. Simple and dry, like a Petit Chablis, this wine is crisp in mouthfeel and streamlined in fruit. You'll find citrus and mineral flavors that finish clean and tart. **84** —*S.H. (2/1/2006)*

Alexander Valley Vineyards 1998 Estate Bottled Chardonnay (Sonoma County) $15. **85** *(6/1/2000)*

Alexander Valley Vineyards 2003 Wetzel Family Estate Chardonnay (Alexander Valley) $15. Lots of green apples in this crisp, clean Chard. It's lightly oaked, with a creamy texture and spicy aftertaste. Very food-friendly. **86** —*S.H. (3/1/2005)*

Alexander Valley Vineyards 2001 Wetzel Family Estate-Estate Bottled Chardonnay (Alexander Valley) $15. Easy to drink, a lemony, peachy wine with a pleasant overlay of oak and lees. It's far from a blockbuster, but pleasant enough, with good varietal character. **85** —*S.H. (12/15/2002)*

Alexander Valley Vineyards 2000 Wetzel Family Estate Reserve Chardonnay (Alexander Valley) $25. Sweet stuff, with flavors of butterscotch, vanilla, and custard. The basic fruit flavors are peaches and pears. No problem getting the grapes superripe in this warm California region. Nice on its own as a sipper, or good with barbecued scallops in a rich butter sauce. **87** —*S.H. (12/15/2002)*

Alexander Valley Vineyards 1997 Wetzel Family Reserve Chardonnay (Sonoma County) $24. **87** *(6/1/2000)*

Alexander Valley Vineyards 2000 Dry Chenin Blanc (Alexander Valley) $9. A lively blend of citrus and baked-apple flavors that are clean and spicy on the finish. Simple and fresh. **85** —*J.M. (12/15/2001)*

Alexander Valley Vineyards 2000 Gewürztraminer (Alexander Valley) $9. A spicy blend of melon, lemon, litchi, and herb flavors made in a fairly dry style with good, tangy acidity at the end. **87 Best Buy** —*J.M. (12/15/2001)*

Alexander Valley Vineyards 2003 New Gewurz Gewürztraminer (North Coast) $9. A weak white wine from Alexander Valley Vineyards. It's spicy enough, but the fruit is thin and watery. **82** —*S.H. (5/1/2004)*

Alexander Valley Vineyards 2002 New Gewurz Gewürztraminer (North Coast) $9. Pretty watered down, although the exotic flavors of stone fruits and Oriental spices are nice. So is the acid, which makes things crisp and clean in the mouth. Just off-dry, but it's dry enough for Chinese food. **84** —*S.H. (12/31/2003)*

Alexander Valley Vineyards 2001 New Gewurz Gewürztraminer (North Coast) $9. Rich and spicy, with a fine-tuned mineral element for added balance. The fruity flavors are redolent of plum, litchee, pear, and

melon. They linger nicely on a tangy, citrus-like finish. **88** —*J.M. (6/1/2002)*

Alexander Valley Vineyards 2003 Merlot (Alexander Valley) $20. Very soft in tannins and acids, this gentle Merlot has blackberry and cherry flavors with an herbaceous streak, as well as a good deal of oak. It's totally dry, and might gain a few notes of complexity with a couple years in the cellar. **85** —*S.H. (3/1/2006)*

Alexander Valley Vineyards 1997 Estate Bottled Merlot (Sonoma County) $18. **86** —*L.W. (12/31/1999)*

Alexander Valley Vineyards 2002 Wetzel Family Estate Merlot (Alexander Valley) $20. Rich and juicy in cherry and blackberry fruit flavors, with a streak of herbs and earth that makes it more food-friendly. Fully dry, this pretty wine has soft, easy tannins, although it's complex and nuanced. **87** —*S.H. (4/1/2005)*

Alexander Valley Vineyards 2000 Wetzel Family Estate-Estate Bottled Merlot (Alexander Valley) $20. There's nice, plush fruit here, plums and blackberries, framed in fairly aggressive tannins that are young and fresh. The wine is dry and round enough to drink with rich red meats, but really would benefit with a year two in the cellar. **85** —*S.H. (11/15/2002)*

Alexander Valley Vineyards 2002 Two Barrel Merlot-Syrah (Alexander Valley) $19. Here's a rustic wine that's a bit raw in green fruit, but it has a good grip and is fully dry. Syrah and Merlot. **83** —*S.H. (4/1/2005)*

Alexander Valley Vineyards 2002 Wetzel Family Estate Pinot Noir (Alexander Valley) $20. A pretty wine with nice flavors of raspberry cola, cherries, vanilla, and sweet oak. It's soft and silky in the mouth, yet has firm acidity. Lots of elegance and style. **88** —*S.H. (3/1/2005)*

Alexander Valley Vineyards 2001 Wetzel Family Estate Sangiovese (Alexander Valley) $20. A delicate wine in body and color, like a light Pinot Noir. Tannins are soft and silky, and it's easy on the palate. Flavors are decent, suggesting cherries and raspberries, in this everyday sort of wine. **85** —*S.H. (9/1/2003)*

Alexander Valley Vineyards 1999 Syrah (Sonoma County) $18. This Syrah is toast and cedar through and through, but these earthy notes were read by three different reviewers as burning leaves, roasted nuts, and eucalyptus-meets-peat. The leather, cherry, and cocoa palate finishes with a little toasty heat—but what else would you expect? Unusual, yes, but there's not a lot of fruit here. **87** *(10/1/2001)*

Alexander Valley Vineyards 2002 Wetzel Family Estate Syrah (Alexander Valley) $20. Gentle in the mouth, this easy wine has some nice complexities. It's dry, with coffee and blackberry flavors and a touch of oak. Has a good balance that adds elegance. **86** —*S.H. (4/1/2005)*

Alexander Valley Vineyards 2000 Wetzel Family Estate Syrah (Alexander Valley) $18. Warm-country red wine with very low acids framing plum and cherry flavors. They put only 2% Viognier in, but it shows up as a hint of lemons in the finish. This soft, supple sipper is clean, dry, and supple, with a touch of oak. **85** —*S.H. (12/1/2004)*

Alexander Valley Vineyards 2002 Redemption Zinfandel (Dry Creek Valley) $25. May not get you into heaven, but you'll sing its praises when you pair it with barbecued ribs or chicken. Ripe in jammy fruit and berry flavors, dry but oh so sweet in fruity essence, and perky in tannins. Classic Sonoma Zin. **89** —*S.H. (12/15/2004)*

Alexander Valley Vineyards 2001 Redemption Zin Zinfandel (Dry Creek Valley) $30. Quite toasty up front. Smooth tannins frame this bright, spicy wine that serves up rich cherry, plum, spice, menthol, herb, and pepper flavors. Full and fat, with a hint of a resiny edge at the end. A big bruiser . . . and lots of fun. **88** *(11/1/2003)*

Alexander Valley Vineyards 2002 Sin Zin Zinfandel (Alexander Valley) $20. Textbook Sonoma Zin, with its blast of spicy, brambly fruit. Floods the mouth with wild blackberries and raspberries, cola, root beer, and pepper, wrapped in big but smooth tannins. Finishes a little hot. **88** —*S.H. (6/1/2004)*

Alexander Valley Vineyards 2001 Sin Zin Zinfandel (Alexander Valley) $20. Heavily oaked, there is still a healthy core of cherry and strawberry fruit in this full-bodied wine. It's spicy and rich on the finish, though with a touch of bitterness at the end. **86** *(11/1/2003)*

Alexander Valley Vineyards 1999 Sin Zin Zinfandel (Sonoma County) $18. Simple and fruity and forward, though still unbalanced from extreme youth. It's more like a Beaujolais nouveau, with an odd, disjointed, watery finish. The price seems way out of line for what's in the bottle. **82** —*P.G. (3/1/2001)*

ALEXANDRIA NICOLE

Alexandria Nicole 2001 Lemberger (Columbia Valley (WA)) $21. A clean, bright Lem, pushing up loads of raspberry and sweet blackberry aromas, and framing the fruit with crisp natural acid. It might be mistaken for Grenache, meaty but less rustic than most Lembergers. Laying off the new oak helps; this got just four months in neutral barrels. 55 cases made. **88** —*P.G. (12/15/2005)*

Alexandria Nicole 2002 Destiny Ridge Vineyards Merlot (Columbia Valley (WA)) $24. There is a slight sweetness to the initial aroma, but it quickly blows off and reveals a wine packed with plummy, black cherry fruit, encased in appealing new oak. Good grapes, solid winemaking, and substantial tannins, leavened by the flavors of toasted coconut. **90** —*P.G. (12/15/2004)*

Alexandria Nicole 2004 Destiny Ridge Vineyard Shepard's Mark White Rhône White Blend (Columbia Valley (WA)) $18. Barrel fermented in neutral oak, this Roussanne/Viognier/Marsanne blend is full and pungent with apricot, peach, and cooked pear flavors. The fruit is nicely set off against cinnamon spice; it's a bit like drinking a baked apple tart, without the sugar. There is some kick to the finish. **88** —*P.G. (12/15/2005)*

Alexandria Nicole 2004 Sauvignon Blanc (Columbia Valley (WA)) $20. A light style, with nuances of cilantro, fresh greens, citrus, lime, and pineapple. Clean and persistent, with good acid and light but true-to-varietal grassiness. **87** —*P.G. (12/15/2005)*

Alexandria Nicole 2002 Destiny Ridge Vineyards Syrah (Columbia Valley (WA)) $27. After some initial burnt matchstick aromas blow off, this wine reveals pretty scents of raspberries, blackberries, and minerals. Juicy and medium-bodied, it picks up cedary nuances on the finish. **86** *(9/1/2005)*

Alexandria Nicole 2005 Viognier (Columbia Valley (WA)) $18. Another nicely made Viognier for this up-and-coming winery, the third in a row. Vivid acids define lemon drop fruit flavors. It's a clean, juicy style, with lip-smacking tartness and excellent focus in the midpalate. The finish is long and concentrated, with immaculately pure tasting fruit, and no alcoholic heat or excessive bitterness. **90** —*P.G. (8/1/2006)*

Alexandria Nicole 2004 Viognier (Columbia Valley (WA)) $16. Very nicely made, as was the initial vintage (2003). Sweet, lingering fruit salad flavors, emphasizing candied lemon and candied lime. **89** —*P.G. (12/15/2005)*

Alexandria Nicole 2003 Destiny Ridge Vineyards Viognier (Columbia Valley (WA)) $16. This is a producer to watch closely, as the plans include a destination winery and inn in the heart of eastern Washington wine country, and the Destiny Ridge vineyard is already showing signs of greatness, despite its youth. Plump, thick, viscous, unctuous even, this wine is packed with ripe pear, citrus, and tropical fruit, and finishes with some sweetness, but no rough edges or heat. **90** —*P.G. (12/15/2004)*

Alexandria Nicole 2004 Reserve Viognier (Columbia Valley (WA)) $21. Clean and leesy, but seems to be a lightweight, with flavors of light citrus and a slightly bitter, citrus rind finish. The regular version is much nicer. **86** —*P.G. (12/15/2005)*

Alexandria Nicole 2005 Destiny Ridge Vineyard Shepard's Mark White Blend (Columbia Valley (WA)) $18. This blend of 72% Rousanne, 16% Viognier, and 12% Marsanne is creamy and lush, powered with flavors of pears and pineapple, light spice, light floral, and citrus. A creamy, vanilla bean character is emerging as the wine gets some extra bottle time, and there is just the right touch of citrus rind on the finish. **88** — *P.G. (8/1/2006)*

ALIENTO DEL SOL

Aliento Del Sol 2003 Bien Nacido Vineyard Chardonnay (Santa Maria Valley) $24. Very dry, with apricot, hard mineral, and citrus flavors, this Chard gets better as it breathes and warms up in the glass. It's a bit quirky, but has terroir-inspired complexity and interest. **89** —*S.H. (11/1/2006)*

Aliento Del Sol 1998 Bien Nacido Vineyard Chardonnay (Santa Maria Valley) $25. **85** *(6/1/2000)*

Aliento Del Sol 1998 La Colline Vineyard Pinot Noir (Arroyo Grande Valley) $30. **84** —*M.S. (5/1/2000)*

Aliento Del Sol 1999 Loma Vista Pinot Noir (California) $25. This Monterey Pinot is quite briary, with charcoal, hickory, and toasted nut aromas. In the mouth, sour cherry and leather make it quite Burgundian in style. The acid level throughout is high, which makes the whole package a little tight and tart. **88** *(10/1/2002)*

Aliento Del Sol 2003 Sarmento Vineyard Pinot Noir (Santa Lucia Highlands) $28. Delicato is going upscale with new brands, and this is one of them. From a proven source for Pinot, this single-vineyard wine is dry, elegant, and a fine exemplar of what the Highlands can do. Hitting all the right notes, all this wine needs is greater concentration or intensity. **87** —*S.H. (12/31/2005)*

Aliento Del Sol 2002 Sarmento Vineyard Pinot Noir (Santa Lucia Highlands) $28. Well-made and tasty, a good example of cool-climate Pinot, with its fresh, citrusy acidity and layers of cherry, cola, toasty oak, and spice flavors. Juicy and nice. **86** *(11/1/2004)*

ALLORA

Allora 1999 Tresca Cabernet Sauvignon (Napa Valley) $60. Here's a good example of what's so disturbing about the rash of expensive Cabernets and blends that has possessed the minds of consumers. This is an awkward, cumbersome wine. Sure, the fruit is as ripe as anything on earth, but what good is extract if it doesn't have balance? The wine is excessively soft. It's cloying, and to add insult to injury, it's tannic. There are wines that cost one-fifth the price that are far better. **86** —*S.H. (8/1/2003)*

Allora 1999 Cielo Red Blend (Napa Valley) $45. This Super-Tuscan blend of Howell Mountain Sangiovese and Stag's Leap Cabernet Sauvignon and Cab Franc is one dark wine. It smells big, too, like an egg cream, which New Yorkers will understand. This chocolatey wine has hints of malt, while the flavors are vast, suggesting ripe blackberries. It's a huge wine in extract and mouthfeel. This creates awkward food-pairing challenges. Barbecued ribs come to mind—but at $45? **86** —*S.H. (8/19/2003)*

ALMA ROSA

Alma Rosa 2004 Pinot Noir (Santa Rita Hills) $32. Here's a heavy, dense, slightly sweet Pinot that may not be at its best now. It's young and jammy, in the way of a wine that hasn't had time to settle down. But the fruit is huge, and the tannins and acids are all there. Cellar until at least 2007. **87** —*S.H. (11/1/2006)*

Alma Rosa 2004 La Encantada Vineyard Pinot Noir (Santa Rita Hills) $48. This is the first launch of Richard Sanford's new brand. The pioneering Santa Barbara vintner is no longer connected with Sanford Winery. It's an impressive start. Power defines the wine, which detonates with explosive cherry-berry and cocoa fruit and oak, wrapped into a silky, velvety texture. It's drinkable now, but it's likely to age well for the next eight years. **92 Cellar Selection** —*S.H. (11/1/2006)*

ALTAMURA

Altamura 1995 Cabernet Sauvignon (Napa Valley) $40. **91** —*L.W. (6/1/1999)*

Altamura 2001 Cabernet Sauvignon (Napa Valley) $60. Showcases the positive qualities of '01 Napa Cabs in the well-ripened tannins and ripe cherry and cocoa flavors. Could use more depth and seriousness, but it's a lovely wine to drink now. **88** —*S.H. (10/1/2005)*

Altamura 2000 Cabernet Sauvignon (Napa Valley) $60. One of the more seductive Cabs of the vintage, a soft, lithe, fleshy wine oozing opulent flavors. Black currants and cassis, with hints of minty chocolate, are absolutely delicious, while the tannins are as finely grained as they come. It's the kind of wine you want to drink in the finest crystal you have. **93** —*S.H. (8/1/2004)*

USA

Altamura 1999 Cabernet Sauvignon (Napa Valley) $60. "Sweet" is the operative word with this wine. In the nose, a certain baked berry pie note mixes with bacon and chocolate. The palate is full of bitter chocolate and sweet black cherry, and the finish is like a shot of vintage Port or Banyuls. **89** —*M.S. (5/1/2003)*

Altamura 1996 Sangiovese (California) $26. **86** —*S.H. (12/15/1999)*

Altamura 2001 Sangiovese (Napa Valley) $30. Quite a nice wine, dry and soft, with a lush, generous mouthfeel that conveys rich cherry, chocolate, and oak flavors. There's a touch of overripe raisins, and the finish is a bit hot. **88** —*S.H. (6/1/2005)*

Altamura 1999 Sangiovese (Napa Valley) $30. Among the best bottlings of the vintage for this difficult and challenging varietal. Here, the winemaker has captured a rich streak of sweet cherry, coffee, and tobacco flavors. The texture and mouthful are a delight, packing weight but pure and supple. Long, long finish. This is a beautiful table wine. **91** —*S.H. (9/1/2003)*

ALTERRA

Alterra 1998 Syrah (Russian River Valley) $18. Buckle up your chaps, enthusiasts, because this Syrah's got truckloads of leather on the nose. Tart blackberries and blueberries, plus herbs and cedar battle moderate acidity on the palate. Finishes Rhône-ish, with herbs, metal, and unripe peach flavors. **84** *(10/1/2001)*

AMADOR FOOTHILL WINERY

Amador Foothill Winery 2002 Fumé Blanc (Shenandoah Valley (CA)) $11. One-quarter of Sémillon adds a nutty, floral accent to the otherwise grassy, citrusy Sauvignon Blanc flavors, but there's still a pleasant tartness all the way through. The finish turns a little Lifesaver candy sweet. **85** —*S.H. (2/1/2004)*

Amador Foothill Winery 2001 Fumé Blanc (Shenandoah Valley (CA)) $10. What a nice wine at this value price! It's lean and citrusy, and bone dry, a tart wine whose scouring acidity washes over the palate and cleans it. Perfect with shellfish and goat cheese. **86** —*S.H. (9/1/2003)*

Amador Foothill Winery 2000 Fumé Blanc (Shenandoah Valley (CA)) $9. Containing 25% Sémillon, this richly fragrant wine is a big drink. The citrus, melon, and spice flavors pack a whallop, while the dry acidity will complement a variety of foods. The finish makes your taste buds sing. **87 Best Buy** —*S.H. (11/15/2001)*

Amador Foothill Winery 1999 Fumé Blanc (Shenandoah Valley (CA)) $10. Citrus, buttercream, spice, and smoke mark this fruity, layered wine. The citrus and spice flavors explode in the mouth, where it turns dry, soft, round, and supple. **85** —*S.H. (8/1/2001)*

Amador Foothill Winery 2004 Katie's Cote Rhône Red Blend (Shenandoah Valley (CA)) $18. This Syrah-Grenache blend is from one of the Sierra Foothills' better appellations. It's a rustic, simple wine, jammy on the finish, with cherry pie flavors and a rich mouthfeel. **84** —*S.H. (10/1/2006)*

Amador Foothill Winery 2003 Katie's Cote Rhône Red Blend (Shenandoah Valley (CA)) $18. I like this blend of Syrah and Grenache despite its rustic nature. It's tannic, dry, and acidic, as far as you can get from today's decadently soft red wines, but it's hard to imagine anything better to set against grated cheese and olive oil. Bruschetta with an olive tapenade will be a sensation. **90** —*S.H. (12/31/2005)*

Amador Foothill Winery 2000 Sangiovese (Shenandoah Valley (CA)) $20. Few California wineries have striven more to perfect Sangiovese than Amador Foothill. This is a work in progress. The score isn't high, but it's a winery to watch. You don't perfect this varietal overnight. Dry, with black cherry flavors and pretty tannic. The challenge is to tame the tannins and create depth. **86** —*S.H. (12/1/2002)*

Amador Foothill Winery 2001 Barrel Select Sangiovese (Shenandoah Valley (CA)) $18. From a winery that's worked hard to get this tough variety, a dry, cherry-infused wine that, despite the light body, has some hefty tannins. Calls for cheeses, olive oil, and rich meats. **86** —*S.H. (11/15/2004)*

Amador Foothill Winery 2002 Estate Sangiovese (Shenandoah Valley (CA)) $18. Dry, soft, and thickly textured, with slightly sweet Lifesaver cherry flavors and robust tannins, this rustic wine calls for rich cheeses and meats. **83** —*S.H. (6/1/2006)*

Amador Foothill Winery 2001 Grand Reserve Sangiovese (Shenandoah Valley (CA)) $28. From a winery that takes Sangiovese seriously comes this dry, tannic, bitter, Chianti-like interpretation. It has California-ripe cherry flavors, but the acidity is high and cutting enough to easily handle olive oil, butter, or beef. **88** —*S.H. (12/31/2005)*

Amador Foothill Winery 2000 Grand Reserve Sangiovese (Shenandoah Valley (CA)) $30. Always an interesting wine from this winery, this is a concentrated, intense wine, darkly hued, with big flavors. Smells like cured tobacco and blackberries, with a smoky, meaty note. Drinks bone dry, with dark berry flavors and thick, dusty tannins. A bit soft, but fascinating. **89** —*S.H. (9/1/2003)*

Amador Foothill Winery 2005 Rosato of Sangiovese (Amador County) $11. Amador Foothill does a good job with Sangiovese, and this dry rosé is made from that variety. It's a cheerful wine, brisk in acidity and with delicate but complex cherry, rose petal, and lavender flavors. The winemaker recommends bouillabaisse, which is a pretty good suggestion. **86 Best Buy** —*S.H. (10/1/2006)*

Amador Foothill Winery 2004 Rosato of Sangiovese (Amador County) $10. I wish I liked this wine more. It's bone dry, with herbal, peppery notes, and a little bit of strawberry. Turns watery thin and acidic on the finish. **83** —*S.H. (10/1/2005)*

Amador Foothill Winery 2003 Rosato of Sangiovese (Amador County) $10. Relatively dry, with an edge of honey, this copper-colored wine has strawberry and pepper flavors and crisp acidity. It's a simple, easy blush wine to enjoy with fried chicken or fruit salad. **83** —*S.H. (11/15/2004)*

Amador Foothill Winery 2002 Rosato of Sangiovese (Amador County) $10. A rose of Sangiovese, and a superfine wine. Absolutely dry and crisp, with beautiful flavors of strawberries and cinnamony spice. Has enough depth to stand up to roasts, but lovely on its own, the perfect apéritif wine. A very great value. **88 Best Buy** —*S.H. (9/1/2003)*

Amador Foothill Winery 2001 Rosato of Sangiovese (Amador County) $9. A very rich and full-bodied blush wine. The flavors of strawberries and raspberries are ripe and almost sweet, although the wine is basically dry, with tart acids. My bottle was pretty sulfury, but it blew off. **84** —*S.H. (9/1/2003)*

Amador Foothill Winery 2004 Sauvignon Blanc (Shenandoah Valley (CA)) $11. This winery often turns up real jewels. Fans of dry Sauvignon Blancs need to stock up on this one by the case. It has New Zealand-like gooseberries and citrus flavors and a long, rich, spicy finish. **88 Best Buy** —*S.H. (12/31/2005)*

Amador Foothill Winery 2000 Sémillon (Shenandoah Valley (CA)) $10. Very dry and tart, an unusually minerally wine that brings to mind sun-warmed slate tiles. Other flavors veer toward honeysuckle and acidic citrus fruits, especially lemons. Has a nice, creamy texture from barrel fermentation and lees aging. This is a distinctive wine and a nice expression of a Sierra vineyard. **87** —*S.H. (9/1/2003)*

Amador Foothill Winery 2002 Barrel Select Syrah (Sierra Foothills) $15. Dry, tannic, and acidic to the point of mouth-puckering numbness, this is a difficult wine. It finishes in a swirl of raisins. **80** —*S.H. (10/1/2006)*

Amador Foothill Winery 2000 Hollander Vineyard Syrah (Sierra Foothills) $20. Captures Syrah's wild and woolly side, with jammy, wild berry flavors that taste fresh from the fermenter. The acidity is sharp, almost green, and there are stemmy, chlorophyll notes. From 3-year-old vines. Shows promise, but the vines need age, and the wine needs tweaking. **84** —*S.H. (9/1/2002)*

Amador Foothill Winery 2004 Clockspring Vineyard Zinfandel (Shenandoah Valley (CA)) $16. Dry to the point of rasping, and hot in alcohol, this is not a successful Zin. It's peppery on the finish, and the tannins are tough and astringent. **82** —*S.H. (10/1/2006)*

Amador Foothill Winery 2003 Clockspring Vineyard Zinfandel (Shenandoah Valley (CA)) $14. Defines the rustic, appealing side of Foothills Zin with its ripe wild berry, cocoa, and spice flavors and smooth, sturdy tannins. Built for standing up to BBQ and garlicky tomato sauces, and a good value. **87** —*S.H. (10/1/2005)*

Amador Foothill Winery 2001 Clockspring Vineyard Zinfandel (Shenandoah Valley (CA)) $13. Smooth and silky on the palate, the wine serves up a refined blend of black cherry, blackberry, coffee, tea, spice, and herb flavors. The tannins are soft yet firm. **88** *(11/1/2003)*

Amador Foothill Winery 2000 Clockspring Vineyard Zinfandel (Shenandoah Valley (CA)) $13. Big, hot, and peppery, a bruiser of a wine that smacks of its wild mountain origins. Flavors are big and ripe, with some dessicated notes of raisins and prunes. Absolutely dry, with gentle tannins. **86** —*S.H. (5/1/2003)*

Amador Foothill Winery 1999 Clockspring Vineyard Zinfandel (Amador County) $13. Sierra Foothills Zins can be high-alcohol and a bit clumsy. This starts out with jammy, tomato, meaty aromas, and turns unpleasantly hot in the mouth. The ripe, briary flavors are there, and it's very dry. Turns bitter and harsh in the finish. **84** —*S.H. (11/15/2001)*

Amador Foothill Winery 1997 Clockspring Vineyard Zinfandel (Amador County) $12. 84 —*P.G. (11/15/1999)*

Amador Foothill Winery 2002 Esola Vineyard Zinfandel (Shenandoah Valley (CA)) $15. I've been a critic of overripeness in red wines, but here, the raisiny flavors complement rather than hinder the fresh wild berries, lending a black currant complexity. It's high in alcohol, but totally dry, and besides, what else would you expect from a high-country Zin? **88** —*S.H. (8/1/2005)*

Amador Foothill Winery 2001 Esola Vineyard Zinfandel (Shenandoah Valley (CA)) $18. Bright and racy, with zippy-edged raspberry, strawberry, coffee, chocolate, spice, and licorice flavors. The tannins are ripe, though the finish is a bit rustic, with some spice at the end. **87** *(11/1/2003)*

Amador Foothill Winery 1999 Ferraro Vineyard Zinfandel (Shenandoah Valley (CA)) $15. You always look to the Foothills for Zin, especially inexpensive Zin, and Amador seldom disappoints. This fine vintage fully ripened the grapes, producing brambly, spicy flavors that are fully dry without excessive alcohol. It's a bit edgy and lacks finesse, but has that wild, pioneer quality associated with this mountainous region. **87 Best Buy** —*S.H. (11/1/2002)*

Amador Foothill Winery 2001 Ferrero Vineyard Zinfandel (Shenandoah Valley (CA)) $15. Extracted and jammy in black cherries and black raspberries, with hints of cocoa, this wine is fully dry and balanced. It's tasty through the smooth finish. **87** —*S.H. (3/1/2005)*

Amador Foothill Winery 1997 Ferrero Vineyard Zinfandel (Shenandoah Valley (CA)) $12. 88 Best Buy —*S.H. (5/1/2000)*

AMAVI CELLARS

Amavi Cellars 2003 Cabernet Sauvignon (Walla Walla (WA)) $22. For a Cabernet, this is almost soft, with seductive, coffee-infused flavors of plum and pie cherry. The sweet spices carry into the finish, with just a hint of herb and fresh mint to cleanse the palate. **90** —*P.G. (4/1/2006)*

Amavi Cellars 2004 Sémillon (Columbia Valley (WA)) $20. A fine effort, 100% varietal, that showcases why this grape loves Washington soil. Pear and pineapple mix with citrus zest; there is a lively, refreshing acidity, and the barrels softened up rather than flavored the wine. Flavors are crystal clear, leesy, and long-lasting. **92** —*P.G. (4/1/2006)*

Amavi Cellars 2003 Syrah (Walla Walla (WA)) $25. Smooth and smoky, with blueberry and black cherry fruit, smoked ham, light layers of coffee, and buttered toast. Deceptive; it's not a jammy or dense wine, but it's got staying power and a silky, voluptuous mouthfeel. **92** —*P.G. (4/1/2006)*

Amavi Cellars 2003 Syrah (Walla Walla (WA)) $25. Lays on a thick layer of caramel and toast, then moves into tart red berry fruit. Raspberries and vanilla on the palate, finishing with crisp acidity and a sense of elegance. **84** *(9/1/2005)*

Amavi Cellars 2002 Syrah (Walla Walla (WA)) $25. A thrilling wine, firm and supple with a core of plush, dark fruit. Generous new oak adds layers of smoke and char, while the grapes provide extra nuances of smoked meats, licorice, and mineral. **91 Editors' Choice** —*P.G. (11/15/2004)*

AMBERHILL

Amberhill 2000 Cabernet Sauvignon (California) $9. Another great value from the folks at Raymond. Blackberry and cassis, smooth, velvety tannins, dry and rich, good balance, and a long, fruity finish. **86 Best Buy** —*S.H. (10/1/2003)*

Amberhill 1997 Chardonnay (California) $8. 84 Best Buy —*S.H. (10/1/1999)*

Amberhill 2001 Chardonnay (California) $7. Pretty dismal, from the opening smells of canned asparagus and tapioca to the watery flavors, with their faint note of peach. Even at this price, there are better buys. **81** —*S.H. (10/1/2003)*

Amberhill 2000 Chardonnay (California) $8. It's a bit eccentric, with melon and butterscotch aromas and flavors that stretch the varietal boundaries, but it's not a bad everyday sipper. Clean, round and soft, an easy-drinking quaffer at a fair price. **83** —*S.H. (5/1/2002)*

AMETHYST

Amethyst 2001 Cabernet Sauvignon (Napa Valley) $36. This good, rich Cabernet brims with fancy, ripe black currant and cassis flavors, well-oaked, that are framed in suave tannins. Feels lush and creamy in the mouth, and for all the fruitiness, it's completely dry. **90** —*S.H. (2/1/2004)*

Amethyst 2001 Floralia Malvasia Bianca (Monterey County) $20. This intense wine surprises. It smells sweet, with aromas of honeysuckle, orange blossom, and apricot, but it's bone dry. The citrus and apricot flavors are accompanied by very high acidity. **90 Editors' Choice** —*S.H. (2/1/2004)*

Amethyst 2004 Pinot Grigio (Los Carneros) $18. As oaky a PG as you're likely to come across. The nose is pure buttered popcorn and mill dust with a barely detectable backing of vanilla-coated pear. Smooth in the mouth, with heft and tons of resiny flavor. The finish is, as might be expected, a wood-driven ride. Anyone adverse to barrel influences should steer clear; oak lovers could find it to their liking. **84** *(2/1/2006)*

Amethyst 1998 Vinalia Sangiovese (Napa Valley) $17. A wine strong in aromas and flavors, suggesting ripe plums, blackberries, tobacco, leather, and herbs. It's dry as they come, with the kind of sturdy tannins and acids that will stand up to a great big cheesy lasagna. A Nebbiolo-Sangiovese blend. **88** —*S.H. (3/1/2004)*

AMICI

Amici 2002 Cabernet Sauvignon (Napa Valley) $42. Showing rather heavy and closed now, this Cab may wake up one of these days. It's a dry, soft wine, with cherry-berry, coffee, and herb flavors. Gamblers will hold it until 2007. **84** —*S.H. (12/1/2005)*

Amici 2001 Cabernet Sauvignon (Napa Valley) $38. Smooth and elegant, with ripe cherry and plum flavors and soft, gentle tannins. Generously oaked, this pretty wine is drinking beautifully now. **90** —*S.H. (10/3/2004)*

Amici 2004 Chardonnay (Napa Valley) $30. Many Napa Chards taste earthy, and so does this one. The earthiness is about green herbs, tobacco, and soy-flavored tofu, but there's also plenty of pineapple fruit. On top of that, considerable new oak gives a blast of vanilla and spice. This interesting, complex Chard should challenge chefs to rise to the occasion. **90** —*S.H. (12/1/2004)*

Amici 2002 Chardonnay (Napa Valley) $25. Ripe and forward in peach, applesauce, butterscotch, vanilla, and toasty flavors, this creamy Chard is fun to drink. It explodes on the palate, and has a long, rich finish. **86** —*S.H. (4/1/2005)*

Amici 2000 Meritage (Napa Valley) $45. Here's a muscular, intense Bordeaux blend, whose proportion of hillside fruit lends it firm, dusty tannins. The explosive cherry-berry fruit and lush, sweet oak give it a savor that's drinkable now, but the balance and harmony suggest the ability to age for a long time. **92** —*S.H. (11/15/2004)*

Amici 2003 Pinot Noir (Mendocino) $42. Mixed reviews for this wine. It's light and silky in the mouth, with a delicate structure and subtle flavors of cherries, toast, herbs, and coffee. But those flavors are a bit simple and snap to a quick finish. **85** —*S.H. (12/1/2005)*

Amici 2002 Pinot Noir (Mendocino) $35. Simple, dry, and robust for a Pinot, with a heavy mouthfeel. You'll find some tannins underlying the plum and coffee flavors. **84** —*S.H. (4/1/2005)*

USA

AMICUS

Amicus 2002 Special Blend Bordeaux Blend (Napa Valley) $38. This is a pretty nice Bordeaux blend, dry and stylish, with rich, sweet tannins, rich oak, and well-ripened flavors of cassis, cherries, and mocha. It has Cabernet Sauvignon, Merlot, and Petit Verdot. **88** —*S.H. (12/31/2005)*

Amicus 2002 Cabernet Sauvignon (Napa Valley) $49. This is a big, sweetly ripe 100% Cab, a blend of Yountville and Spring Mountain fruit. It's considerably more acidic and tannic than your usual Napa Cab, but the black currant flavors are as huge as anywhere. Despite the tannins, it's best now and for a couple more years. **89** —*S.H. (12/31/2005)*

Amicus 2001 Special Blend Cabernet Sauvignon (Napa Valley) $49. Shows the superripe qualities of this vintage in the fruit that runs from sun-warmed blackberries through cherry pie, kirsch, and cassis, and also the soft, gentle tannins. Lots of oak, too. Seems best now and for a few years, due to the softness. **90** —*S.H. (10/1/2005)*

AMITY

Amity 1999 Gewürztraminer (Oregon) $12. Oregon used to produce a lot of delicious, dry, inexpensive Gewürztraminer, but there are only a handful left, and this is always one of the best. Bone dry and intense with spicy, not floral, scents and flavors. It has fine tannin structure, substantial (13.5%) alcohol, and a good balance of fruit and acid. **88** —*P.G. (11/15/2001)*

Amity 2002 Dry Gewürztraminer (Oregon) $12. Amity has made a dry gewürz since 1977, and it is frequently a standout, but seems to have slipped a bit in this vintage. It's soft and creamy, with ripe fruit flavors, but missing the snap and precision that makes the grape memorable. **86** —*P.G. (2/1/2005)*

Amity 2000 Dry Gewürztraminer (Oregon) $12. A knockout wine, with beautiful scents of flowers and herbs, smooth flavors that are perfectly balanced between fruit and acid, and a long, glissando finish that demands another sip. 656 cases made. **91 Best Buy** —*P.G. (12/1/2003)*

Amity 1998 Pinot Blanc (Willamette Valley) $12. 88 —*L.W. (12/31/1999)*

Amity 2003 Pinot Blanc (Willamette Valley) $14. The winemaking is stainless steel all the way, and the wine delivers crisp aromatics that mix rose petals, citrus, peach, and honeysuckle. It's all very appealing, with a hint of spritz to add life and lift to the finish. **88** —*P.G. (2/1/2005)*

Amity 2001 Pinot Blanc (Oregon) $12. Amity made a vociferous switch a few years back, pulling all its Chardonnay and planting Pinot Blanc in its wake. Looks like a good call, with consistently fine wines such as this new release the result. It's dry and tastes of ripe, just-sliced pears, with plenty of weight and a long, strong finish. **88** —*P.G. (12/31/2002)*

Amity 1999 Pinot Blanc (Willamette Valley) $12. After a few minutes in the glass, the wine's citrusy-pineapple aromas take on a grassy dimension. Green-apple and banana flavors brighten an even, creamy mouthfeel. Finishes a little chewy, with mango flavor and a slight metallic tanginess on the very end. An easy quaff. **85** —*D.T. (11/1/2001)*

Amity 2002 Pinot Noir (Oregon) $14. Thin, herbal, green. **83** *(11/1/2004)*

Amity 1999 Pinot Noir (Willamette Valley) $20. This Pinot's juicy and dark, gamy, and briary. It's not complex, but the deep, black cherry fruit and pepper accents are satisfying. A good choice for grilled foods, it turns tangy on the modest close. Drink now–2005. **87** *(10/1/2002)*

Amity 1998 Pinot Noir (Willamette Valley) $20. 85 —*M.S. (12/1/2000)*

Amity 1997 Pinot Noir (Willamette Valley) $16. 83 *(11/15/1999)*

Amity 1999 Eco Wine Cattrall Brothers Pinot Noir (Oregon) $14. 80 —*M.S. (12/1/2000)*

Amity 2001 Eco-Wine Pinot Noir (Oregon) $14. Amity makes this sulfite-free wine from organically farmed grapes, so it's about as politically correct as a wine can be. Fruity cranberry and strawberry flavors run into some earthy, ashy tannins. **85** —*P.G. (12/31/2002)*

Amity 2000 Eco-Wine Pinot Noir (Oregon) $15. Fruity, like a Beaujolais, with light berry and cranberry flavors, followed by some earthy, ashy tannins. The sulfite-free, organically farmed grapes come from Cattrall Brothers vineyards. **85** —*P.G. (4/1/2003)*

Amity 2002 Estate Pinot Noir (Willamette Valley) $30. Delicate, herbal, ultra light. Clean, correct, but dilute. **83** *(11/1/2004)*

Amity 1999 Estate Pinot Noir (Willamette Valley) $30. This is the last of Amity's '99s to be released; no '99 reserve was made because the juice went into three single-vineyard releases. With the extra time the wine has smoothed out a bit, but it is still tight and reticent upon first being opened. Good structure, some spicy highlights, and a concentrated, tarry finish. **90** —*P.G. (12/1/2003)*

Amity 2003 Schouten Vineyard Pinot Noir (Willamette Valley) $35. With a new focus on single-vineyard Pinot, Amity's Myron Redford has selected his favorite sites and given them a snazzy new label while improving what's in the bottle. This is still sharp, edgy, and showing some green tea flavors, but the cherry tobacco aromas add a Chianti-like elegance, and the wine shows good definition and length. **88** —*P.G. (12/1/2006)*

Amity 2002 Schouten Vineyard Pinot Noir (Willamette Valley) $30. Odd, herbal, and dry, with a bit of nuance. **84** *(11/1/2004)*

Amity 2000 Schouten Vineyard Pinot Noir (Willamette Valley) $15. Forward, clean, bright cherry fruit leads into a wine with firmness and length. Still young and compact, it hints in the finish at some interesting nuances of soil and leaf. This is the second vintage that Amity has bottled a single-vineyard Schouten, and it is their best single-vineyard effort. **89** —*P.G. (4/1/2003)*

Amity 2000 Schouter Pinot Noir (Willamette Valley) $30. The nose is kind of awkward, featuring strawberry, bubble gum, and a little cream cheese. Buttery strawberry fruit opens the palate, and there's some milk chocolate underneath that. A drying oakiness is the main feature of the finish. All in all the wine is good, but it lacks definition and pizzazz, and seems overoaked. **85** *(10/1/2002)*

Amity 2002 Sunnyside Pinot Noir (Willamette Valley) $30. Plum, cola, cocoa. Weak coffee and cherry flavors. Tart, tannic finish. **85** *(11/1/2004)*

Amity 1999 Sunnyside Pinot Noir (Willamette Valley) $30. Opening aromas of strawberries, dried grass, and brown sugar turn tangy and sour on the palate. It's mid-weight and even, with smoky notes and a slightly grainy feel. Sadly, the whole lacks dimension, seeming less than the sum of its parts. **84** *(10/1/2002)*

Amity 2003 Sunnyside Vineyard Pinot Noir (Willamette Valley) $35. Amity's Sunnyside Pinot is stylistically joined at the hip to the Schouten bottling, but with more tart, cranberry-flavored power. This shows a strong, pure resonance; a single note well struck. The fruit flavors just keep echoing down through the throat. **89** —*P.G. (12/1/2006)*

Amity 1998 Winemaker's Reserve Pinot Noir (Willamette Valley) $40. On first take, the nose is slightly grassy, murky, and lactic, but time serves it well; with airing the wine opens to reveal ripe plum and cherry fruit prior to a full and tannic finish. The heart of this maturing Pinot is solid, although the edges and polish seem a bit lacking. For best results, give it as much time as possible. **85** —*M.S. (9/1/2003)*

Amity 2001 Dry Riesling (Oregon) $12. An off-dry, delicious style, with plenty of good acid and just 10.5% alcohol. There's an abundance of rich flavor, spice, and texture to this wine, which wraps the taste buds in citrus zest, stone and hints of lemon candy. 958 cases made. **89 Best Buy** —*P.G. (12/1/2003)*

Amity 2002 Select Cluster Riesling (Oregon) $40. Peaches and honey mix it up at trockenbeerenauslese levels, all botrytis-affected. Very rich and butter soft, with 24% residual sugar and just 7.4% alcohol. There's a lot of room for further development in this very young wine. **90** —*P.G. (12/1/2003)*

Amity 2002 Wedding Dance Riesling (Willamette Valley) $14. Although this wine sports 5% residual sugar, it still has enough acid to keep it from tasting sugary. Clean and lightly effervescent, it sings of orange blossoms and light citrus, and refreshes the palate like a Moscato, with just 9.5% alcohol. **88** —*P.G. (12/1/2003)*

Amity 2002 Crown Jewel Reserve White Blend (Willamette Valley) $16. A serendipitous blending error turned into this delightful white wine, named for the Crown Jewel iris. It's 45% Pinot Blanc, 31% Riesling, and 24% Chardonnay, a wonderfully fragrant blend that seems to take the best that each grape has to offer. 100 cases made. **88** —*P.G. (12/1/2003)*

AMIZETTA

Amizetta 2002 Estate Cabernet Sauvignon (Napa Valley) $45. Really a lovely Cab, this gentle wine captivates for its soft, lush mouthfeel and sheer complexity. It's rich in black currant and cherry fruit, and generously oaked, but possesses an inherent balance and structural integrity that make it impeccable. **91** —S.H. (10/1/2005)

Amizetta 1999 Estate Bottled Vigneto del Tacchino Selvatico Cabernet Sauvignon (Napa Valley) $75. 91 (8/1/2003)

Amizetta 2002 Vigneto del Tacchino Selvatico Estate Reserve Cabernet Sauvignon (Napa Valley) $85. This is a big, young, rather tough Cab, tannic and thick. The blackberry flavors have to swim up to the surface from murky depths. But it's dry and balanced, and has the stuffing for the cellar. Best after 2008. **88** —S.H. (10/1/2005)

Amizetta 2002 Complexity Meritage (Napa Valley) $38. A little rough and ready to drink now. Sturdy and dry, with good acidity framing berry flavors; has a nice finish. **86** —S.H. (10/1/2005)

AMPHORA

Amphora 2002 Jacob's Ridge Mounts Vineyard Cabernet Sauvignon (Dry Creek Valley) $45. So ripe, it explodes, filling the mouth with intense black currant flavors. The fruit is sweet, but the wine is technically dry, and pretty tannic, too. A bit awkward now. Try holding for a few years. **85** —S.H. (10/1/2005)

Amphora 2003 Mounts Vineyard Merlot (Dry Creek Valley) $35. Easy does it with this Merlot, with its flavors of blackberries and chocolate. But it's too sweet on the finish, smacking of sugar. **83** —S.H. (10/1/2005)

Amphora 2003 Mounts Vineyard Petite Sirah (Dry Creek Valley) $30. Textbook "Pet" wine. Midnight black, dry, high in alcohol, tannic, and rich in blackberry, plum, coffee, and spice flavors. Will probably age forever. **86** —S.H. (10/1/2005)

Amphora 2001 Mounts Vineyard Petite Sirah (Dry Creek Valley) $30. Hard to find much to praise about this simple, earthy wine. The panel criticized it for excessive sweetness and harsh, astringent tannins and acids. A few tasters detected overt winemaking flaws. **82** (4/1/2003)

Amphora 2003 Mounts Vineyard Syrah (Dry Creek Valley) $30. Minty and floral at first, developing tart berry-cherry flavors with time in the glass. It's bright and tangy, making it food friendly, with just enough tannin to cut through burgers and the like. **84** (9/1/2005)

Amphora 2002 Mounts Vineyard Syrah (Dry Creek Valley) $30. Rich and spicy, with an exuberant peacock's tail of wild berry, cherry, mocha, and sweet roasted coconut spreading across the palate. The lush fruit is wrapped in easy tannins. **86** —S.H. (12/1/2004)

Amphora 2003 Mounts Vineyard Zinfandel (Dry Creek Valley) $24. A big-boned, exuberant Zin, ripe and tannic, with flavors that bring to mind wild berries growing in briar patches. Very dry and a bit hot. **85** —S.H. (10/1/2005)

AMUSANT

Amusant 2002 Cabernet Sauvignon (Napa Valley) $30. Textbook Napa Cabernet, with its rich, sweet, soft but complicated tannic structure, dry finish, and exuberantly ripe mélange of flavors. They include classic black currants and cassis, roasted coffeebean, bitter dark chocolate, and sweet, toasty oak. **91** —S.H. (8/1/2005)

Amusant 2001 Cabernet Sauvignon (Napa Valley) $30. This screwtopped wine is thin and featureless, although there are some modest flavors of blackberries and herbs. That leaves the hefty tannins, acids, and alcohol to take front and center. **84** —S.H. (11/15/2003)

Amusant 2002 Chardonnay (Napa Valley) $16. This is an earthy Chardonnay, with restrained peach and spice flavors and a kiss of oak. It's also very dry. Has some real complexity in the structure and the finish. **84** —S.H. (8/1/2005)

Amusant 2003 Sauvignon Blanc (Napa Valley) $15. This is really a nice, easy-drinking wine that avoids the overly-sweet tendency of many Sauvignon Blancs. Its fig, spearmint, and peach flavors are dry, and accompanied by fresh, clean acidity. **86** —S.H. (8/1/2005)

AMUSE BOUCHE

Amuse Bouche 2002 Merlot-Cabernet Franc (Napa Valley) $200. Winemaker-owner Heidi Peterson Barrett (Screaming Eagle, La Sirena, others) chose only Merlot and Cab Franc for this first release, obviously meant to make a statement with its fancy graphics, rock-heavy bottle, and price. The wine is delicious, but so ethereal, you wonder if it wouldn't benefit from a little Cabernet. **90** —S.H. (10/1/2004)

Amuse Bouche 2003 Red Wine Red Blend (Napa Valley) $200. Last year's bottling was elegant and refined. This year, the Merlot-Cabernet Franc blend remains an extremely elegant wine, yet is even richer in chocolate-cherry flavor, drizzled with vanilla and cinnamon, and wickedly soft on the palate. Somehow, all this richness manages to stay dry. **94 Editors' Choice** —S.H. (8/1/2006)

ANAKOTA

Anakota 2002 Helena Dakota Vineyard Cabernet Sauvignon (Knights Valley) $80. It's sometimes overlooked that Jess Jackson produces very small quantities of competitive wines such as this. This 100% Cabernet is a mountain wine, dense in tannins and very dry, yet intense in classically Cabernet black currant fruit. The all new French oak feels natural. As good as it is, more refinement is necessary, but Anakota is a label worth watching. **92** —S.H. (9/1/2006)

Anakota 2002 Helena Montana Vineyard Cabernet Sauvignon (Knights Valley) $80. Mountain grapes have yielded an intense, concentrated young Cabernet, grown on the Sonoma side of Mount St. Helena. The wine is brash, dry and astringently tannic now. But it possesses a classic elegance and refinement and a remarkable core of cassis fruit. How could it not develop, given the balance and harmony? Best 2008–2015. **92 Cellar Selection** —S.H. (9/1/2006)

ANAPAMU

Anapamu 2004 Chardonnay (Monterey County) $16. Lots of rich, ripe tropical fruit flavors in this creamy, brisk wine. Vanilla, buttered toast, and woodspice from oak add to the impact. There's nothing subtle about this bold Chardonnay. **85** —S.H. (3/1/2006)

Anapamu 2003 Chardonnay (Monterey County) $16. Earthy and tart, a meager wine without much flavor except raw citrus juice, and a lot of oak. **82** —S.H. (10/1/2005)

Anapamu 2001 Chardonnay (Monterey County) $16. From Gallo's Central Coast brand, a lean, tart, and minerally Chardonnay marked by flavors of flint and lime just veering into tart green apple. Extremely well made, and not without interest, but if big, blowsy Chards are your thing, look elsewhere. **87** —S.H. (8/1/2003)

Anapamu 2000 Chardonnay (Monterey) $16. Smells oaky and sweet, tastes oaky and sweet. Other features include apple and peach flavors, a gingery spiciness, and a rich, creamy mouthfeel. It's also round and mellow in the mouth. **86** —S.H. (5/1/2002)

Anapamu 2003 Pinot Noir (Monterey County) $16. Kind of thin, especially considering the price, but it's basically okay. The wine is totally dry and fairly acidic, with cherry flavors and a smooth, silky mouthfeel. **83** — S.H. (12/15/2005)

Anapamu 2002 Pinot Noir (Monterey County) $16. Raw and simple, with cherry flavors that feel hot through the finish. But it's clean and dry. **83** —S.H. (10/1/2005)

Anapamu 2001 Pinot Noir (Monterey County) $16. At 21,000 cases, this might be the biggest production Pinot Noir in the county. This good, introductory-level Pinot has a silky mouthfeel and crisp, refined flavors of raspberry, cherry, and beet. Don't look for complexity. Just enjoy. **86** —S.H. (7/1/2003)

Anapamu 2000 Pinot Noir (Monterey County) $16. While one reviewer called it "nice, simple stuff," another found it to have "a slight funk, like rotting hay." All agreed it's basic Pinot—tart berries and dried spices—at a fair price. **84** (10/1/2002)

Anapamu 2001 Riesling (Monterey County) $16. Showing moderate body and made in a drier style, the wine offers a hint of earthiness that's followed by pretty melon, peach, herb, and citrus flavors. Crisp and clean on the finish, with a toasty, fruity hint at the end. More complex than many of the local Rieslings. **87** —*J.M. (8/1/2003)*

Anapamu 2001 Syrah (Paso Robles) $20. A softly tannic wine with well-developed, jammy flavors of raspberries, cherries, and blackberries. Made like an Aussie Shiraz, the wine is silky in the mouth. **85** —*S.H. (12/1/2004)*

Anapamu 2001 Syrah (Paso Robles) $22. Jammy and fruity, a big, young, juicy wine with big flavors of cherries, cola, blackberries, and sweetly spiced plums. Drinks rather thick and gluey, with overt sweetness. **84** —*S.H. (12/15/2003)*

Anapamu 2000 Syrah (Paso Robles) $20. A Gallo label, and a fine wine. Shows its warm origins in easily ripened fruit, big and rich in plums and blackberries, with soft tannins and acids. Yet it's not a simple wine. It has depth and complexity, although a taste of raisins in the finish is bothersome. **86** —*S.H. (12/1/2002)*

Anapamu 1999 Syrah (Central Coast) $16. The plush, ripe mouthfeel delivers plenty of pleasure. Ripe, if darkly indistinct, fruit has coffee, smoke, and gamey notes that add depth and complexity. Finishes long and dark, with attractive pepper shadings. Pushes all the right buttons, and delivers with style. **88 Editors' Choice** *(10/1/2001)*

ANCIEN

Ancien 2000 Pinot Noir (Russian River Valley) $36. This wine possesses good elements, though not necessarily all in harmony. Caramel-toffee, cinnamon, and mint accents adorn tart black cherry fruit, but somehow this didn't come together as well as we'd hoped for, and felt quite light to some panelists. **84** *(10/1/2002)*

Ancien 2000 Pinot Noir (Carneros) $32. This juicy wine has a creamy streak through it. Cinnamon, meat, cola, and herb hints adorn mildly tart plum, cherry, and tomato fruit. The feel is medium weight and a little plush. Some tasters found the finish short on this nicely balanced wine, while others found it smoky and even, sporting soft, dry tannins. Drink now–2005. **87** *(10/1/2002)*

Ancien 1999 Steiner Vineyard Pinot Noir (Sonoma Mountain) $42. Pinot on Sonoma Mountain? Yes, if it's on the Pacific-facing side. Shares much in common with Sonoma Coast Pinots in a ripe vintage. Cherry, spice, and peppery-tobacco flavors are framed by soft tannins and crisp acidity. Complex and compelling, this wine changes every second on the palate. **93** —*S.H. (2/1/2003)*

ANDRE

Andre NV Extra Dry Champagne Blend (California) $4. 80 —*S.H. (12/15/1999)*

Andre NV Spumante Champagne Blend (California) $4. 83 —*S.H. (12/15/1999)*

ANDRETTI

Andretti 2004 Cabernet Sauvignon (Napa Valley) $38. Flashy and showy, with ripe Cabernet flavors of cassis and plenty of new toasty oak. The tannins are ripe and sweet, yet there's a jagged mouthfeel, a minty sharpness, that detracts. Probably won't age out; drink now. **85** —*S.H. (12/31/2006)*

Andretti 2002 Cabernet Sauvignon (Napa Valley) $30. There's something about this lush Cab that keeps you reaching for more. It's soft and velvety, with just enough tannins to keep things perky, but best of all are the flavors. Blackberries and cherries, dusted with cocoa, sprinkled with a dash of cinnamon, and drizzled with crème de cassis. Yummy. **90** —*S.H. (12/1/2005)*

Andretti 2002 Cabernet Sauvignon (Napa Valley) $28. Lush, delicious, and hedonistic, an instantly appealing Cab due to its long, deep flavors of black currants, rich overlay of toasty oak, and smooth texture. The tannins are strong, but they're ripe and sweet and provide a nice angular structure to this impressive wine. **92** —*S.H. (4/1/2004)*

Andretti 2000 Cabernet Sauvignon (Napa Valley) $28. A charming, delicious Cab, with pretty flavors of black currants and spiced plums, and rich, complex tannins. Feels solid and complete in the mouth, and the long, spicy finish is dry. Shows a lot of class and elegance. **89** —*S.H. (11/15/2003)*

Andretti 1999 Cabernet Sauvignon (Napa Valley) $30. Here's a wine that needs time to show its stuff, but it's very good in its youth. Dark and thick, with strong dusty tannins, but a core of blackberry fruit. Cellar it until 2005 and try again. **91** —*S.H. (11/15/2002)*

Andretti 2001 Selection Series Cabernet Sauvignon (North Coast) $12. You'll be surprised at what you get here. It's a rich, dry wine with black currant, cherry, and herb flavors that are ripe and forward, wrapped in sweet tannins. Perfectly acceptable for steaks, prime rib, and such, and at an everyday price. Good value. **85** —*S.H. (11/15/2003)*

Andretti 2001 Selections Cabernet Sauvignon (North Coast) $15. This Cab's a little too extracted, too sweet, too oaky and too soft for my tastes, but it's fundamentally clean, and will have its fans. **83** —*S.H. (12/1/2005)*

Andretti 2005 Chardonnay (Napa Valley) $24. Consider it a food wine. It's on the lean side compared to today's superripe Chards, but it sure is elegant. The peach and pineapple fruit is controlled, the oak is moderate, the alcohol is low, and acidity is crisp and clean. **85** —*S.H. (12/31/2006)*

Andretti 2004 Chardonnay (Napa Valley) $19. Here's a full-flavored Chardonnay in which toasty oak plays side by side with big, lush tropical fruit flavors to give plenty of mouth satisfaction. There's a vanilla custard and tapioca spice flavor on the finish that's especially rich. **87** —*S.H. (12/1/2005)*

Andretti 2002 Chardonnay (Napa Valley) $16. A nice, smooth Chard, solidly in the pop style with its pretty flavors of peaches, apples, sweet cream, vanilla, and oak. It's smooth in the mouth, with a spicy aftertaste. **87** —*S.H. (12/31/2003)*

Andretti 2001 Chardonnay (Napa Valley) $16. Broad flavors of apples and peaches are framed in spicy oak, with hints of vanilla and char. The wine is dry but very rich, with enough acidity to make the fruit sparkle. The finish is long. **90 Editors' Choice** —*S.H. (12/15/2002)*

Andretti 2002 Selection Series Chardonnay (Sonoma County) $10. Watery, with slight citrus flavors and a bite of heat from alcohol. Turns astringent and dry on the finish. **83** —*S.H. (4/1/2004)*

Andretti 2004 Selections Chardonnay (Central Coast) $12. This simple and dry Chard has watered down peach and apple flavors and a touch of oak. Acidity is fine. **83** —*S.H. (12/1/2005)*

Andretti 1997 Merlot (Napa Valley) $23. 89 *(7/1/2000)*

Andretti 2004 Merlot (Napa Valley) $26. Seems a bit pricey for what you get, which is a dry, clean red table wine with sturdy tannins and good cherry, herb, cocoa, and oak flavors. At its best now, this Merlot will complement beef and lamb dishes **85** —*S.H. (7/1/2006)*

Andretti 2001 Merlot (Napa Valley) $24. This beautifully crafted Merlot shows a near-perfect balance of ripe plum, cherry, and cassis-accented fruit with deeper notes of herbs, coffee, and dark unsweetened chocolate. It glides across the palate with a velvety texture and finishes long. Could use a tad more concentration, but it's a lovely wine. **90** —*S.H. (4/1/2004)*

Andretti 2000 Merlot (Napa Valley) $23. Smells great, with rich aromas of plum, blackberry, violets, and smoke. In the mouth, this wine is gentle, with easy tannins framing blackberry fruit. Fairly acidic through the finish now. Try aging until 2005. **87** —*S.H. (12/15/2003)*

Andretti 1999 Merlot (Napa Valley) $20. This is the kind of full-bodied, dry red wine that you can set on your table with complete confidence because it's world-class good. Rich, ripe fruit is nicely balanced with earthy, tobacco flavors, the whole framed in soft but complex tannins and plush oak. It's fairly high in acidity, which may have been added later, but works to offset the ripe sweetness with tart crispness. **91** —*S.H. (6/1/2002)*

Andretti 2001 Selection Series Merlot (North Coast) $11. A good little country-style wine, with its blackberry, coffee, and earth flavors and soft tannins. Turns a bit rough along the way, but carries the ripe fruit nicely through the spicy finish. **85** —*S.H. (2/1/2004)*

Andretti 2005 Pinot Grigio (Napa Valley) $18. This wine is clean enough, and has zesty, mouth-watering acidity. But there's no there there. It's watery and thin, with just a trace of citrus juice. **82** —*S.H. (7/1/2006)*

Andretti 2005 Pinot Noir (Napa Valley) $30. Flavors of raspberry and cherry Lifesavers, this silky, easy Pinot has overtones of vanilla, cinnamon,

USA

and toast. It's soft and gentle and, well, just plain likeable. **86** —*S.H.* *(12/31/2006)*

Andretti 2004 Pinot Noir (Napa Valley) $20. For a winery known for Cabernet, Merlot, and Chardonnay, this Pinot is surprisingly good. It's rich in cherry, coffee, unsweetened chocolate and spice flavors, wrapped in a silky but full-bodied texture. Try with rosemary-grilled lamb chops. **88** —*S.H. (12/1/2005)*

Andretti 2004 Zinfandel-Primitivo Red Blend (Napa Valley) $33. A 50-50 blend of the two varieties. Sweet and soft, it's like a cheap Chianti of old times. **80** —*S.H. (12/31/2006)*

Andretti 2003 Sangiovese (Napa Valley) $20. Andretti has been working on Sangiovese for years. They've succeeded in getting the fruit ripe in berries, cherries, espresso, and spices, and in a full-bodied mouthfeel with real oomph. Yet to come are layers of complexity and distinction. **85** —*S.H. (12/1/2005)*

Andretti 2001 Sangiovese (Napa Valley) $18. Explores a nice side of this emerging varietal, with soft acids and brisk tannins that frame cherry, espresso, and herb flavors. This wine strikes the palate as dry and austere, but locked in its core is a potential sweetness that needs only cheese or fatty proteins to make it companionable at the table. **88** —*S.H. (4/1/2004)*

Andretti 2000 Sangiovese (Napa Valley) $19. This is a full-bodied wine with very strong fruit, including some dark berry notes more akin to a big red like, say, Merlot—of which it contains a dash. At the same time, the tannins are light, which makes it kind of schizoid. It's also superacidic and tart. Made by respected Napa vintner Bob Pepi, it's a work in progress. **85** —*S.H. (9/1/2002)*

Andretti 2005 Sauvignon Blanc (Napa Valley) $18. Dry and grassy, even herbaceous, with a streak of cat pee, this simple wine has crisp acidity that makes the tastebuds whistle. **83** —*S.H. (7/1/2006)*

Andretti 2004 Sauvignon Blanc (Napa Valley) $16. The green grass, newly mown hay, lemon and lime, and melon aromas and flavors jump right out of the glass. Crisp acidity, a round, creamy texture and a dryish finish. **86** —*S.H. (12/1/2005)*

Andretti 2002 Sauvignon Blanc (Napa Valley) $14. Even though it strikes a familiar style, of citrus, fig, melon, and spice flavors that finish slightly sweet, this wine is unusually delicious. It has a length and richness you don't always find in a California Sauvignon Blanc. **88** —*S.H. (12/15/2003)*

Andretti 2001 Sauvignon Blanc (Napa Valley) $14. Shows unusual depth and finesse for a Sauvignon Blanc, with scads of palate impressions ranging from lemondrop candy, zesty wintergreen, apricot nectar, and white pepper. Yet it's dry and smooth, with crisp acids. **89** —*S.H. (7/1/2003)*

Andretti 2000 Sauvignon Blanc (Napa Valley) $14. Here's a complex wine with bold flavors of lemongrass and peaches that are rich and honeyed, and yet it's tart and crisp enough to be your dry white wine of the evening. Combines the best of both worlds: round, sweet fruit and dry acidity that makes your mouth water, even as it's savoring the flavor. **87** —*S.H. (9/1/2002)*

Andretti 2004 Selections Zinfandel (California) $15. Try this rustic wine with rich meats and cheeses, as it's rather sharp in acids, with a racy, raw mouthfeel. The flavors are ripe and strong in berries, chocolate, and tangy spices. **84** —*S.H. (12/1/2005)*

ANDREW GEOFFREY

Andrew Geoffrey 2002 Cabernet Sauvignon (Diamond Mountain) $75. Lacking perhaps the sheer opulence of the '01, this estate Cab compensates with ageworthiness. It's bone dry and stiff in tannins, with a new-oak veneer sheathing black currant and cherry flavors. It's so rich and balanced that it should have no trouble developing for a decade. **91 Cellar Selection** —*S.H. (2/1/2006)*

Andrew Geoffrey 2001 Cabernet Sauvignon (Diamond Mountain) $75. Diamond Mountain District Cabs always are very tannic, and so is this one, but it should reward cellaring. It's well-oaked, with balancing acids and a tremendous core of blackberry and currant fruit that penetrates

the palate and lasts through the finish. Combines power and finesse. Drink now–2015. **92 Cellar Selection** —*S.H. (6/1/2005)*

Andrew Geoffrey 2000 Cabernet Sauvignon (Diamond Mountain) $85. From this mountain district in Napa Valley, a well-tailored wine that opens with ripe aromas of blackberry, cassis, and oak. Drinks rich, layered and quite tannic, and then turns dry on the finish. Needs a few years to soften and open up. **88** —*S.H. (11/15/2003)*

ANDREW MURRAY

Andrew Murray 1997 Espérance Red Blend (Santa Barbara County) $18. **93** —*S.H. (6/1/1999)*

Andrew Murray 2001 Espérance Rhône Red Blend (Santa Ynez Valley) $22. A happy wine, easy to slurp, but with some real character. Complexly fruity, with plum, blackberry, tangerine rind, and floral notes. Beautifully lush on the palate, with soft tannins and yet a crisp mouthfeel leading to a spicy finish. A blend of Grenache, Syrah, and Mourvèdre. **88** —*S.H. (3/1/2004)*

Andrew Murray 2004 Espérance Rhône Red Blend (Central Coast) $22. So Côtes-du-Rhône-y, but so California! The kind of wine Andrew Murray produces so well. Ripe and expressive, soft and gentle, yet with a good set of tannins. Finishes with a ripe, fruity richness. **88** —*S.H. (11/15/2006)*

Andrew Murray 2004 Enchanté Rhône White Blend (Santa Ynez Valley) $22. Here's an amusing white blend of Roussanne and Marsanne that's explosive in tropical fruit, vanilla, and spice flavors. Good acidity keeps it crisp and clean. **87** —*S.H. (11/15/2006)*

Andrew Murray 1998 Roussanne (Santa Barbara County) $25. **90** —*S.H. (6/1/1999)*

Andrew Murray 1997 "Roasted Slope" Syrah (Santa Barbara County) $18. **88** —*S.H. (6/1/1999)*

Andrew Murray 2003 Estate Grown Syrah (Santa Ynez Valley) $25. Another Syrah that caused great dissent on the panel: One reviewer admired the wine's herbal, peppery accents and round, supple feel, while another thought that it smelled and tasted like a for-the-masses wine. **85** *(9/1/2005)*

Andrew Murray 2001 Estate Grown Syrah (Santa Ynez Valley) $20. The first estate-labelled Syrah off this fine property is eccentric. It has a Porty aroma with underlying currents of sweet cured tobacco, and while it is bone dry, it has a hot mouthfeel that's thin in fruit, leaving the alcohol and tannins front and center. A big disappointment. **84** —*S.H. (3/1/2004)*

Andrew Murray 2000 Hillside Reserve Syrah (Santa Ynez Valley) $45. Expensive, but this is a very rare wine and a very good one. It is young and intense, with uplifted dark stone fruit and berry aromas and flavors with a rich, peppery note. The tannins are ripe and thick. Drinkable now, but has the structure and balance to cellar. **92** —*S.H. (12/1/2003)*

Andrew Murray 1996 Hillside Reserve Syrah (Santa Barbara County) $25. **92** —*S.H. (6/1/1999)*

Andrew Murray 2000 Les Coteaux Syrah (Santa Ynez Valley) $25. Marred by an excessively Port-like character. Seems overly alcoholic, overly sweet, and overly extracted in every sense, with overripe berries that lend a raisiny flavor. **84** —*S.H. (2/1/2003)*

Andrew Murray 1999 Les Coteaux Syrah (Santa Ynez Valley) $25. From hillside vineyards, here's a concentrated, intense wine with some tongue-sticking tannins. Blackberry, espresso, and white-pepper aromas lead to a round, full-bodied and very dry wine that will benefit from a year or so of cellaring. **90** —*S.H. (7/1/2002)*

Andrew Murray 1997 Les Coteaux Syrah (Santa Barbara County) $20. **93** —*S.H. (10/1/1999)*

Andrew Murray 2003 Roasted Slope Syrah (Santa Ynez Valley) $25. Co-fermented with Viognier grapes which were so ripe they were almost late harvest. The Viognier dominates the Syrah, giving the wine a lemondrop sweetness that's weird. Too bad, because the Syrah seems fine. **84** —*S.H. (11/15/2006)*

USA

USA

Andrew Murray 2001 Roasted Slope Syrah (Santa Ynez Valley) $32. For all its obvious power, this wine is elegant and stylish. The sweet cherry fruit is wrapped in a layer of lavender, thyme, and sweet oak. The flavors coat the mouth and last for a long time. The underlying strength and staying power of this wine shows in the tannic finish. Best after 2007. **93 Editors' Choice** —*S.H. (12/1/2004)*

Andrew Murray 2000 Roasted Slope Vineyard Syrah (Santa Ynez Valley) $30. A big bold Syrah, ripe and fruity. Stuns the palate with blackberry, cassis and pepper flavors, and also a strong raisiny note. Fruity and clean in the mouth, but the tannins are considerable. Cellar this baby through 2006, then try again. **91** —*S.H. (2/1/2003)*

Andrew Murray 1999 Roasted Slope Vineyard Syrah (Santa Ynez Valley) $30. Smoky, slightly herbaceous notes over raspberry and cherry fruit give this California wine a decidedly Rhônish cast. The mouthfeel is lean and structured, the tart flavors are strawberry and rhubarb. Finishes with drying tannins. A hard, angular wine that needs time to come around. **85** *(11/1/2001)*

Andrew Murray 1999 Tous Les Jours Syrah (California) $16. Briary, sour plummy aromas on the nose are shrouded by a touch of greenness that some described as sulfur, and others called cilantro. Though the mouthfeel is soft and smooth, the wine's flavors aren't more complicated than strong blackberry and tart, toasted oak. Lengthy finish has bitter menthol-pepper flavors. **85** *(10/1/2001)*

Andrew Murray 2003 Westerly Vineyard Syrah (Santa Ynez Valley) $36. A crisp, structured wine at first blush, one that exhibits high-toned red-berry and herb aromas and flavors. With air it takes on overripe aromas, and accents of chocolate on the palate. Lipsmacking finish. **86** *(9/1/2005)*

Andrew Murray 1998 Viognier (Santa Barbara County) $25. 91 —*S.H. (10/1/1999)*

Andrew Murray 1997 Viognier (Santa Barbara County) $25. 90 —*S.H. (6/1/1999)*

Andrew Murray 2005 Viognier (Central Coast) $25. A little heavy, soft and sweet for a white wine, but appeals for its exotically rich tropical fruit, floral spice, and butterscotch flavors. **85** —*S.H. (11/15/2006)*

Andrew Murray 2001 Viognier (Santa Ynez Valley) $25. A distinctive Viognier, and easily one of the state's best. Has the usual array of stone and tropical fruit flavors, with a minerality that's refreshing. Crisp and authoritative, sleek and refined, and perfectly oaked. Stunning, with the richness of a fine Chardonnay. **92** —*S.H. (3/1/2003)*

Andrew Murray 2000 Viognier (Santa Ynez Valley) $25. Fruits, flowers, and spices mark this highly aromatic, flavorful wine. Upfront fruits include peaches, apricots, and pineapple, but it's pretty dry, with pretty acidity that creates freshness on the palate. The smooth, creamy texture is notable. **87** —*S.H. (12/1/2001)*

Andrew Murray 2002 Estate Viognier (Santa Ynez Valley) $25. Brings a level of refinement and finesse to this variety, which can be over the top in lesser hands. Has exotic notes of tropical fruits, honeysuckle, citrus, peach and honey that are rich and palate-coating, but never loses sight of its structure, with its fine mineral and acid backbone. **90** —*S.H. (10/1/2003)*

Andrew Murray 2001 Enchanté White Blend (Santa Ynez Valley) $22. A blend of Roussanne and Marsanne; complex flavors range from tangerine and peach to grapefruit and apricot. There's a lot of oak and lees here, both of which soften and fatten the mouthfeel. Finishes with a honeyed richness. **90** —*S.H. (12/1/2003)*

Andrew Murray 2000 Enchanté White Blend (Santa Ynez Valley) $22. A Rhone blend of Viognier, Marsanne, and Rousanne, it offers a myriad of fruity, flowery aromas and complex flavors ranging from banana to chocolate cream to melon. The smooth, velvety texture carries sweetly ripe fruit in waves across the palate. **89** —*S.H. (12/1/2001)*

ANDREW RICH

Andrew Rich 2004 Cabernet Franc (Columbia Valley (WA)) $20. The Alder Ridge vineyard supplied the fruit, and the blend includes 10% Malbec—"just for fun," says the winemaker. This is sure to be a crowd pleaser, showing off the smooth and sappy side of Cab Franc. Delicious from the get-go, it manages its tannins perfectly and puts the fruit in the driver's seat. **90** —*P.G. (12/31/2006)*

Andrew Rich 1998 Les Vigneaux Corral Creek Vineyard Pinot Noir (Willamette Valley) $25. 88 —*M.S. (12/1/2000)*

Andrew Rich 2004 Red Blend (Columbia Valley (WA)) $16. This Rhône-style blend, from an Oregon producer who makes half his wines from Washington fruit, is 50% Syrah, 20% Grenache, the rest evenly split between Counoise and Mourvèdre. It shows clean, spicy red fruits and a streak of ash in the tannins. **87** —*P.G. (12/31/2006)*

Andrew Rich 2004 Roussanne (Columbia Valley (WA)) $20. This is a lovely Roussanne, a white Rhône grape that is only beginning to be planted in Washington vineyards. This fruit comes from Alder Ridge and Ciel du Cheval, and the wine delivers creamy, rich flavors without becoming syrupy or overripe. Fresh, leesy, palate-cleaning acids keep it lively and lifted through the extended finish. **90** —*P.G. (12/31/2006)*

Andrew Rich 2003 Syrah (Columbia Valley (WA)) $23. This thick and quite tannic Syrah showcases the dark and earthy side of the grape. Streaks of tar and smoke add length and flavor interest; the wine does not seem overoaked. I suspect the earthy components come from the earth rather than the barrel. **90** —*P.G. (12/31/2006)*

ANDREW WILL

Andrew Will 2003 Champoux Vineyard Bordeaux Blend (Columbia Valley (WA)) $45. This wine uses the same Merlot and Cabernet Franc as the superpremium Sorella (due out in the spring), but here the Cab is a younger Champoux block, planted in 1990. Though a blend of 55% Cabernet Sauvignon, 21% Cabernet Franc, 15% Merlot and the rest Petit Verdot, the wine expresses itself with a captivating purity. The fruit almost seems to shine with glistening flavors of berries. It's a perfectly balanced and beautifully integrated mix of spicy herb, primary fruits, natural acids, and compelling density. **94** —*P.G. (4/1/2006)*

Andrew Will 2001 Champoux Vineyard Bordeaux Blend (Columbia Valley (WA)) $48. Another single-vineyard gem, solid, substantial, and sophisticated, though still quite young and tight. Fruit flavors hint at raspberry and pomegranate, along with graphite and dry, lightly chalky tannins. The mix is roughly two-thirds Cabernet Sauvignon, 18% Cab Franc, 10% Merlot and a splash of Petit Verdot. The PV is a catalyst; it puts things in play and makes the wine jump. **91** —*P.G. (7/1/2004)*

Andrew Will 2002 Champoux Vineyard Red Wine Bordeaux Blend (Columbia Valley (WA)) $55. Springs from the glass with a ripe, juicy nose of berry liqueur, hints of mocha, and a whiff of fresh cut hay. There are some whiskey barrel esters as well, and the alcohol registers a bit hot, almost like a whiff of scotch. But the tight, concentrated fruit just needs breathing time and/or decanting, and then it more than holds up to the heat. The blend is 62% Cabernet Sauvignon, 21% Merlot, 11% Petit Verdot, and 4% Cab Franc. **91** —*P.G. (12/15/2004)*

Andrew Will 2004 Ciel du Cheval Vineyard Bordeaux Blend (Red Mountain) $56. Ciel is usually the most concentrated, mineral-streaked and ageworthy of the Andrew Will lineup, but in this frost-affected vintage it's a much lighter, more forward wine, with less concentration. The fruits are bright and balanced, with a trace of herb. The blend is 15% Cabernet Sauvignon, 48% Merlot, 30% Cab Franc, and 7% Petit Verdot. **89** —*P.G. (12/31/2006)*

Andrew Will 2001 Ciel du Cheval Vineyard Bordeaux Blend (Red Mountain) $48. A big wine, but perfectly blended and balanced, with nuanced flavors that mix fruit and stone. Sweet cherry fruit stands out, with some blueberry and roasted coffee beneath. This is a complex, striated, and tight wine that needs considerable airing and will certainly cellar well over the next 6–8 years. A blend of 60% Merlot, 21% Cab Franc, 12% Cab Sauvignon, and 7% Petit Verdot. **93** —*P.G. (7/1/2004)*

Andrew Will 2002 Ciel du Cheval Vineyard Red Wine Bordeaux Blend (Red Mountain) $55. Gloriously structured, this extraordinary effort blends 44% Merlot, 28% Cab Franc, 18% Cab Sauvignon, and 10% Petit Verdot into a wine that reveals itself in sculpted layer upon layer of scent and flavor. Citrus peel, plum, wild berry, red currant, and spice are set upon a base of rich mineral and rock, with precisely cut tannins. Hold 8–10 years. **95 Cellar Selection** —*P.G. (12/15/2004)*

Andrew Will 2004 Sheridan Vineyard Bordeaux Blend (Yakima Valley) $46. The winemaker, Chris Camarda, abandoned varietal wines in favor of vineyard-designate red blends a couple of vintages ago. The Sheridan vineyard, a relatively new site in the upper elevations of the Yakima valley, is a bit tricky in a cooler vintage like this one. There are some streaks of herb evident here, along with quite tart red fruits. The blend is 43% Cab Sauvignon, 30% Merlot, 25% Cab Franc, and a splash of Petit Verdot. **87** —*P.G. (12/31/2006)*

Andrew Will 2003 Sheridan Vineyard Bordeaux Blend (Yakima Valley) $40. Here the blend is 63% Cabernet Sauvignon, 29% Merlot, and the rest Cab Franc. Winemaker Chris Camarda captures pretty fragrances of strawberries, light cocoa, and hints of ham. It's a wine that offers a lot of small pleasures; nothing on a grand scale, but stylish and balanced. **90** —*P.G. (4/1/2006)*

Andrew Will 2003 Sorella Bordeaux Blend (Columbia Valley (WA)) $65. From older Champoux Vineyard vines, Andrew Will's Tête de Cuvée is half Cabernet Sauvignon, one quarter Merlot, and the rest Franc and Petit Verdot. Tasted shortly before its official release, it was fairly reductive, extremely tight, and difficult to penetrate. Certainly a substantial and worthy Sorella, the score could go higher as it evolves. **93** —*P.G. (6/1/2006)*

Andrew Will 2001 Sorella Red Wine Bordeaux Blend (Columbia Valley (WA)) $56. The winery's premier wine showcases "Block One" Champoux vineyard fruit: about two thirds Cabernet Sauvignon, 15% Cab Franc, and the rest Petit Verdot. A big, fleshy wine, it shows rich, plummy fruit and swirling streaks of licorice, mineral, and preserves. Young and somewhat blocky, it's dominated by cassis and a broad swath of dusty tannin. Has slightly sweeter fruit and a more roasted character than the Champoux designate. **92** —*P.G. (7/1/2004)*

Andrew Will 2002 Klipsun Vineyard Cabernet Sauvignon (Red Mountain) $45. An unusual nose sends up floral and citrus scents along with the expected wild berry and black currant. There is plenty of very ripe fruit here, but Klipsun Cab also has some of the darkest, chewiest tannins in the state, and here they are still slightly out of proportion with the fruit, which needs a lot of breathing time to catch up. The finish is a bit tough; chalk it up to youth and put this one away for a few years. **92** —*P.G. (12/15/2004)*

Andrew Will 1999 Ciel du Cheval Merlot (Washington) $40. This is flat-out classy, polished, and elegant Merlot, made with fruit from a premier vineyard on Red Mountain. There's a lush mix of cherries, plums, and berries to start, a nice toasty, cocoa frame, fine balance, and a firm, confident finish. Despite its youth it's focused and appealing, but a little time will really open it up. **92 Cellar Selection** —*P.G. (6/1/2001)*

Andrew Will 2000 Ciel du Cheval Vineyard Merlot (Washington) $40. This vineyard, virtually adjacent to Klipsun, delivers equally good fruit but with a more restrained, feminine profile. Mineral, cassis, and cherry flavors are structured on an elegant, firmly sculpted framework of acid and restrained tannins. The oak treatment is just right, and lets the fruit take center stage. **93** —*P.G. (9/1/2002)*

Andrew Will 1998 Ciel du Cheval Vineyard Merlot (Washington) $45. 93 — *P.G. (9/1/2000)*

Andrew Will 2002 Cuvée Lucia Merlot (Washington) $30. The Cuvée Lucia lineup takes advantage of barrels not included in the winery's new single vineyard program. But what great juice! This is a taut, muscular, tannic wine with somewhat rough, grainy tannins. Delicious, tart, berry-flavored fruit is at the core. **89** —*P.G. (7/1/2004)*

Andrew Will 2003 Cuvée Lucia Merlot (Washington) $28. A glorious, tart and tangy Merlot, with vivid fruit that snaps the palate to attention. The acids are right upfront; if you like your fruit a bit on the sour side, as I do, this will ring your bell. **90** —*P.G. (4/1/2006)*

Andrew Will 1999 Klipsun Merlot (Washington) $40. An intense blue-purple wine, young, grapey, and striking. The classic Klipsun core of iron/mineral is there, along with tight, spicy fruit, and plenty of acid for long-term aging. The complex layers of flavor are a good way from being fully integrated, but the track record of the winery and the vineyard

suggest that they will come together beautifully over time. **90** —*P.G. (6/1/2001)*

Andrew Will 2002 Klipsun Vineyard Merlot (Red Mountain) $45. Is this the finest single-vineyard Merlot in the country? It certainly can stake a claim to that distinction, with its bright, dense, vibrant scents of berry and cherry, its muscular tannins, and deeply concentrated fruit flavors enhanced with the dark notes of earth and iron from Klipsun soil and the relentless wind that toughens the grape skins. Decant this one early. **94** —*P.G. (12/15/2004)*

Andrew Will 2000 Klipsun Vineyard Merlot (Washington) $40. A powerful, dense, blue-purple Klipsun vineyard release tops the incredible lineup from Andrew Will in the 2000 vintage. This wine features pungent black cherry and blackberry fruit, streaked with the vineyard's defining terroir flavor of iron ore. All the Andrew Will Merlots are released quite young, but are undeniably delicious, balanced, and hard to resist. **93** —*P.G. (9/1/2002)*

Andrew Will 1998 Klipsun Vineyard Merlot (Washington) $45. 92 —*P.G. (9/1/2000)*

Andrew Will 1999 Pepper Bridge Merlot (Washington) $36. High-toned blueberry, blackberry, and cherry fruit is accented with nuances of herbs and chocolate. This is still tannic, young, grapey and tight; the winery is always one of the first to release their red wines. The Pepper Bridge vineyard is in Walla Walla, though the bottle's label says Washington State. This wine clearly needs more time in the bottle to reveal its deeper mysteries **88** —*P.G. (6/1/2001)*

Andrew Will 2000 Pepper Bridge Vineyard Merlot (Washington) $36. Walla Walla's Pepper Bridge Vineyard seems to have made richer, riper wines in 2000, and there are deep and delicious flavors of strawberry, cherry, and cassis, along with a bit of licorice. Nice concentration here, more than usual, and even a hint of mineral in the finish. **91** —*P.G. (9/1/2002)*

Andrew Will 1998 Pepper Bridge Vineyard Merlot (Washington) $45. 86 — *P.G. (9/1/2000)*

Andrew Will 1999 Seven Hills Merlot (Washington) $36. Here is a surprisingly light effort, with soft plum-flavored fruit, and gentle accents of lively, peppery spice. There's a hint of asparagus flavor here too, and the finish drops off very quickly. This is an excellent vineyard, and one wonders if the wine is just at a rather unfortunate, awkward phase of its development. **87** —*P.G. (6/1/2001)*

Andrew Will 2000 Seven Hills Vineyard Merlot (Walla Walla (WA)) $36. Much improved over the previous vintage, this is a fragrant wine perfumed with cherry/berry scents and light spice. The core of sweet cherry fruit is more open and generous, more approachable than the Red Mountain vineyard wines, which are more cellarworthy. **92** —*P.G. (9/1/2002)*

Andrew Will 1998 Seven Hills Vineyard Merlot (Walla Walla (WA)) $45. 89 —*P.G. (9/1/2000)*

Andrew Will 2000 Sheridan Vineyard Merlot (Washington) $36. This is the first year Andrew Will has done a Sheridan Vineyard designation. The bouquet is like a fresh-baked blackberry pie, and the sweet, ripe, and tangy flavor of blackberries hits the palate too. It's a forward, fruit-driven wine with plenty of immediate appeal. **90** —*P.G. (9/1/2002)*

Andrew Will 2002 Seven Hills Vineyard Red Wine Merlot-Cabernet Sauvignon (Walla Walla (WA)) $55. This 62% Merlot, 38% Cabernet blend is the softest and most approachable of the new lineup from Andrew Will, showing tart cherry/berry fruit, notes of wild berry, cocoa, pepper, and coffee grounds. Nice entry into the midpalate, and then a gentle fade, rather than a drop off, as the flavors echo like distant music. **90** —*P.G. (12/15/2004)*

Andrew Will 2004 Champoux Vineyard Red Wine Red Blend (Columbia Valley (WA)) $56. Champoux comes out tops in the '04 vintage for Andrew Will. This wine has the stuffing missing from the rest, with tight, chewy young fruit that has good weight and extract. There's a hint of dried wild herb and the stiff tannins that often mark this vineyard's wines. **90** —*P.G. (12/31/2006)*

Andrew Will 2003 Ciel du Cheval Vineyard Red Blend (Red Mountain) $45. Spectacular, with opening young wine characteristics displaying naturally tart, spicy mixed red fruits. New barrel flavors of chocolate, smoke, and toast are out in front, but right behind is glorious fruit—fully ripe, sweet, and succulent, concentrated, and rich. It finishes gracefully with nuances of iron filings and fresh herb. **95 Editors' Choice** —*P.G.* *(4/1/2006)*

Andrew Will 2003 Klipsun Vineyard Red Blend (Red Mountain) $45. This will be the last Klipsun wine from Andrew Will. It's 60% Merlot and 40% Cabernet Sauvignon, and as usual with Klipsun fruit it's a big, chewy wine, though a bit monolithic. Ripe, tight, and hard, it's packed with black fruits and flavors of black tea, smoke and chalk. **91** —*P.G.* *(4/1/2006)*

Andrew Will 2002 Sheridan Vineyard Red Wine Red Blend (Yakima Valley) $55. Immediately gratifying, this loose-knit, broadly flavorful blend is like sticking your nose in a jar of fresh strawberry preserves. Layers of jam, leaf, bark, earth, and toast mingle around the ripe fruit, creating textures and flavors that extend for much longer than you would expect from the initial palate impression. Beautifully crafted. **91** —*P.G.* *(12/15/2004)*

Andrew Will 2003 Two Blondes Red Blend (Yakima Valley) $40. This is the first release from the winery's new estate vineyard. It's Cabernet all the way—two-thirds Sauv, one-third Franc. Fragrant and charming, scented with sweet strawberry, smoked ham, light cracker, and fresh herb. It's a graceful wine that shows how much elegance Yakima Valley fruit can express when carefully grown and vinified. **91** —*P.G.* *(4/1/2006)*

Andrew Will 1999 Ciel du Cheval Sangiovese (Yakima Valley) $23. 90 — *P.G. (11/15/2000)*

Andrew Will 2004 Cuvée Lucia Ciel du Cheval Vineyard Sangiovese (Red Mountain) $28. The Cuvée Lucia line from Andrew Will is moderately priced, usually limited edition and often devoted to varietal wines that don't fit the mainstream lineup. This Red Mountain Sangiovese is a light wine, with pretty strawberry/cherry fruit, plenty of acid, and just a twinge of tobacco hinting at true varietal character. **86** —*P.G.* *(12/31/2006)*

Andrew Will 2002 Cuvée Lucia du Cheval Sangiovese (Red Mountain) $28. Technically a second label, but flavorwise it's top shelf. A lovely effort from a top vineyard; this elegant, ripe, and textured wine offers true varietal flavors. Tart plum, berry, and cherry are wrapped into a tannic young wine with room to develop. A pleasing minerality underlies the fruit. **90** —*P.G. (7/1/2004)*

Andrew Will 1999 Pepper Bridge Sangiovese (Walla Walla (WA)) $23. 91 —*P.G. (11/15/2000)*

Andrew Will 2002 Annie Camarda Syrah (Red Mountain) $58. An extraordinary Syrah, from Ciel du Cheval grapes. It's supple and silky, yet retains classic fresh raspberry, cherry, and boysenberry fruit that's bright and crisply defined by natural acids. The panoply of flavors is seamlessly woven into chocolaty tannins, with a final kick of gravelly minerality. **95** —*P.G. (11/15/2006)*

Andrew Will 2002 Cuvée Lucia Seven Hills Vineyard Syrah (Walla Walla (WA)) $28. Fairly light, with cranberry/pomegranate flavors and hints of stem and earth. Plenty of acid keeps it firmed up, and there is a modest hint of milk chocolate in the broad finish. **87** —*P.G. (7/1/2004)*

ANDRUS

Andrus 1997 Reserve Bordeaux Blend (Napa Valley) $125. 94 *(11/1/2000)*

ANGELINE

Angeline 2002 Zinfandel (Russian River Valley) $10. Martin Ray's second label is proving to be a good value. This Zin is exuberantly ripe in black cherry fruit, with a rich earthiness. It's a bit sharp, but that will actually help to stand up to olive oil, cheese, butter, and meats. **85 Best Buy** — *S.H. (11/1/2005)*

ANGELO'S

Angelo's 2001 Cabernet Sauvignon (Columbia Valley (WA)) $21. Tough and chewy, with tart berry fruit leading into very thick, heavy tannins. Could be just fine with a grilled steak. **84** —*P.G. (1/1/2004)*

Angelo's 2002 Chardonnay (Columbia Valley (WA)) $18. The second label of a new Washington winery called Cave B; it's quite soft with light fruit

and hints of honey and spice. Very pleasant quaffing wine; just 270 cases produced. **86** —*P.G. (1/1/2004)*

Angelo's 2001 Merlot (Columbia Valley (WA)) $21. Strong scents of bark and dill, with a powerfully earthy flavor. The wine is quite light bodied, with chalky, unripe tannins. **83** —*P.G. (1/1/2004)*

ANNE AMIE

Anne Amie 2002 Pinot Noir (Willamette Valley) $22. Tomato and herb, with a dash of rhubarb and tart, wild berries suggesting fruit just approaching ripeness. The wine has a mix of interesting herb, leaf, and earthy flavors, but it's definitely in the earthy, herbal camp. **85** *(11/1/2004)*

Anne Amie 2002 Deux Vert Vineyard Pinot Noir (Willamette Valley) $35. Plum, cola, dried spices. Briary, burnt, harsh finish. **85** *(11/1/2004)*

Anne Amie 2002 Doe Ridge Vineyard Pinot Noir (Willamette Valley) $35. Minty, oaky vanilla. Breathes open to show black cherry and root beer, with fresh salad greens. Medium weight, supple but firm, with a spicy hint of pepper. A bit hollow in the middle. **86** *(11/1/2004)*

Anne Amie 2001 Doe Ridge Vineyard Pinot Noir (Willamette Valley) $40. Good grip, concentration, and a nice, earthy presence in the mouth. A young wine that shows some ripe, rich cherry fruit, along with textured layers of earth and stone. **89** —*P.G. (12/1/2003)*

Anne Amie 2002 Hawks View Vineyard Pinot Noir (Willamette Valley) $35. Forward, engaging, and nicely fruited wine, with a tart, dry body and pretty, dried spices. Elegant. **87** *(11/1/2004)*

Anne Amie 2001 Hawks View Vineyard Pinot Noir (Willamette Valley) $40. Fragrant and racy, with bright berry scents and flavors. Very smooth, with pretty cherry/berry fruit and a touch of spice in the finish. **88** — *P.G. (12/1/2003)*

Anne Amie 2002 La Colina Vineyard Pinot Noir (Willamette Valley) $35. Matchstick aromas, cut with vanilla and plum. Grapey, syrupy, average. **86** *(11/1/2004)*

Anne Amie 2001 Laurel Vineyard Pinot Noir (Willamette Valley) $40. Red fruits and flavors of beet, tomato, and earth mingle in this interesting and flavorful wine. Forward and tart, with a long, consistent finish. **88** —*P.G. (12/1/2003)*

Anne Amie 2002 Yamhill Springs Vineyard Pinot Noir (Willamette Valley) $35. Varietally correct but indistinct, oaky. Medium weight, with cherry and vanilla flavors. Not complex, but satisfying. **84** *(11/1/2004)*

Anne Amie 2001 Yamhill Springs Vineyard Pinot Noir (Willamette Valley) $40. Light, spicy cranberry and red fruits. It's a forward, pleasant wine that falls off in the finish. **86** —*P.G. (12/1/2003)*

ANTHONY ROAD

Anthony Road 2001 Cabernet Franc (Finger Lakes) $14. Very sweet in the nose, with vanilla and barrel char. The palate is heavy and grapey, while the finish is simple at best and unimpressive at worst. The overall take is not so much of wine but of fruit juice. Not terrible but flawed. **82** — *M.S. (3/1/2003)*

Anthony Road 2002 Semi-Dry Spring Riesling Riesling (Finger Lakes) $12. 82 —*J.C. (8/1/2003)*

Anthony Road 2002 Semi-Sweet Riesling (Finger Lakes) $11. 81 —*J.C. (8/1/2003)*

ANTICA TERRA

Antica Terra 2002 Pinot Noir (Willamette Valley) $35. A horsey nose that suggests leather and barnyard more than fruit. This may appeal to some more than others, but it renders the wine quite harsh and tannic, and kills the fruit. **83** *(11/1/2004)*

APEX

Apex 2000 Cabernet Sauvignon (Yakima Valley) $30. Tannic and dark, this Yakima Valley Cab shows good ripeness, with black currant and cherry flavors. It's hard, still tight, and nicely balanced for near-term aging. **88** —*P.G. (9/1/2004)*

Apex 1998 Cabernet Sauvignon (Columbia Valley (WA)) $30. Still firm and tight, and packed with plenty of toasty oak, this Cabernet has enough fruit and stuffing to show mixed flavors of cherry, herb, leaf, and leather. Very dry and Bordeaux-like in style. **87** —*P.G. (6/1/2002)*

Apex 2004 Chardonnay (Yakima Valley) $17. Lemon yellow, scented with Bourbon barrel, ripe apples, light honey, and tea. It's soft and round, with forward, plush flavors of very ripe apples, banana, cantaloupe, and lots of buttery oak. **88** —*P.G. (10/1/2006)*

Apex 2000 Chardonnay (Columbia Valley (WA)) $20. Crisply fruity, with apples and citrus backed by light toast and vanilla. There's a nice balance of acids, not too much, but enough to give the wine proper structure and balance. **87** —*P.G. (7/1/2002)*

Apex 2001 Outlook Vineyard Chardonnay (Yakima Valley) $25. A big, open, plush style, with the butterscotch fruit married to toasty oak. Nothing complicated, but quite tasty. **88** —*P.G. (9/1/2004)*

Apex 1998 Merlot (Columbia Valley (WA)) $30. The black cherry flavors characteristic of Washington Merlot are here, but almost buried in massive amounts of oak. The oak imparts flavors of dark, bitter chocolate, cedar, and coffee, and dries out the tannic finish, while all but obliterating the fruit. Enough already! **86** —*P.G. (6/1/2002)*

Apex 1998 Kestrel Vineyard Merlot (Yakima Valley) $60. This tangy wine is laced with plenty of toasty new oak, giving it scents and flavors of cocoa and spice. Some excellent fruit is there, tasting of tart black cherries, but it seems a bit overwhelmed. **88** —*P.G. (9/1/2002)*

Apex 2000 Dry Riesling (Yakima Valley) $15. It is helpful when wineries denote their rieslings as "dry" (if appropriate), and this one begins with pleasant scents of stone fruits—pears and white peaches. Dry it definitely is, but it also appears to be heading for the edge of the cliff, with flavors already gravitating from dry toward oxidized. **85** —*P.G. (6/1/2002)*

APEX II

Apex II 2001 Cabernet Sauvignon (Yakima Valley) $16. Yakima Valley Cab can often have a distinct herbal edge. This wine skates on that border, but never strays too far over it. Medium weight and relatively soft, it has light cranberry fruit and hints of mushroom and woodsy flavors. **87** — *P.G. (4/1/2005)*

Apex II 2003 Chardonnay (Yakima Valley) $11. A ripe, round, and deliciously fruity Chardonnay, 50% barrel fermented, with a lip-smacking mix of tropical fruit and sweet crème brulée. Pineapples, peaches, melons, and more. **90 Best Buy** —*P.G. (4/1/2005)*

Apex II 2002 Merlot (Yakima Valley) $16. Fragrant and expressive, this soft, very approachable wine offers sweet blackberry fruit stylishly arrayed against a 50/50 blend of French and American oak. Smooth, silky, and ripe, it is a can't-miss crowd pleaser. **88** —*P.G. (4/1/2005)*

Apex II 2005 Sauvignon Blanc (Yakima Valley) $12. Bright mix of pineapple, citrus, green berries, etc. with a yeasty, pleasing grassiness. A good follow up to the 2003, with precision and power. **88 Editors' Choice** —*P.G. (10/1/2006)*

Apex II 2003 Sauvignon Blanc (Yakima Valley) $11. This new, value brand from winemaker Brian Carter hits the mark with this creamy, smooth, seamless rendition of sauvignon blanc. An oxidative "*sur lie*" technique keeps it citrus fresh but cuts the herbaceousness. **90 Best Buy** —*P.G. (4/1/2005)*

Apex II 2002 Syrah (Yakima Valley) $16. Nice enough right out of the bottle, with pretty scents of raspberry and blueberry. It's clean and pleasant, but a bit insubstantial, without real definition or depth. Still, at this modest price, it's a very nice bottle. **86** —*P.G. (4/1/2005)*

AQUINAS

Aquinas 2004 Cabernet Sauvignon (Napa Valley) $12. Tastes young and jammy, with bright, acid-lifted berry-cherry flavors. Dusty tannins and a silky texture make for an instantly likeable wine. **84** —*S.H. (12/1/2006)*

Aquinas 2003 Cabernet Sauvignon (Napa Valley) $13. Don Sebastiani & Sons score big with this textured Cabernet. It's dry and velvety, with lush black currant and cocoa flavors and a coating of smoky oak. Except for the short finish, it's a very nice wine. **86** —*S.H. (12/1/2005)*

Aquinas 2002 Cabernet Sauvignon (Napa Valley) $10. Shows a hint of surmaturité in its plum and prune flavors, but also pleasant earthiness and a

soft, medium-bodied mouthfeel. Finishes with a slight rusticity of tannins that give it added character. **85 Best Buy** *(12/1/2004)*

Aquinas 2001 Cabernet Sauvignon (Napa Valley) $10. A Napa Cabernet at this price? It's pretty good, too, rich with juicy blackberry and oak flavors, with fancy, smooth tannins, and very dry. A value for its balance and harmony. **87 Best Buy** —*S.H. (10/1/2004)*

Aquinas 2003 Chardonnay (Napa Valley) $13. Packs as much flavor as you can fit in a glass. Ultraripe pineapples and peaches, caramelized oak, toasty meringue, vanilla, the works. Plus, it's creamy, smooth, and crisp. **90 Best Buy** —*S.H. (6/1/2005)*

Aquinas 2002 Chardonnay (Napa Valley) $10. A plump, low-acid Chardonnay that boasts modest fruit levels (some peach and pear) alongside nutty, custardy flavors and a toasty finish. **84** *(12/1/2004)*

Aquinas 2002 Merlot (Napa Valley) $10. Not a fruity wine, but one with various nuances of tobacco, coffee, and earth wrapped in a soft, supple mouthfeel. This easy-going red is very drinkable on its own. **84** *(12/1/2004)*

Aquinas 2005 Late Harvest Sauvignon Blanc (Napa Valley) $15. This is a great price for a dessert wine of this deliciousness. It's all apricot jam, honeysuckle and vanilla spice, and tastes botrytisy too, with a richly honeyed mouthfeel. Brings to mind sipping in a summer flower garden. **90 Best Buy** —*S.H. (12/15/2006)*

ARAUJO

Araujo 2002 Eisele Vineyard Cabernet Sauvignon (Napa Valley) $185. Stunning. Explodes with the most intricately detailed aromas: a perfume of fine smoky oak and ripe black currants. Exudes sheer power, with great weight yet no heaviness. Lush and delicious, but just tannic enough. If you can wait, cellar until 2008, it should hold and improve for many years. **96 Cellar Selection** —*S.H. (9/1/2006)*

ARBIOS

Arbios 2002 Cabernet Sauvignon (Alexander Valley) $27. So soft and melted, it has almost no backbone at all, but there's a nice, grippy dusting of tannins, and the flavors work, so it's okay. Shows berry-cherry fruit with an earthy, dried herb quality. **85** —*S.H. (12/15/2006)*

Arbios 2001 Cabernet Sauvignon (Alexander Valley) $30. Soft, flavorful and a little hot, with berry-cherry flavors and a chocolaty, mocha finish. Easy and dry. **86** —*S.H. (6/1/2005)*

Arbios 2000 Cabernet Sauvignon (Alexander Valley) $30. You'll like this wine for its easy drinkability. The texture is soft and luscious, with rich, fine tannins. Flavors of black currants, mocha, and sweet spices entice the palate. Shows complexity and finesse throughout. **90** —*S.H. (11/15/2004)*

Arbios 1999 Cabernet Sauvignon (Alexander Valley) $30. Bill Arbios was one of the pioneers in setting the standards for meritage wines while at Lyeth in 1981. He started Arbios Cellars in 1993, and since then he has been producing high-quality, reasonably priced Cabernet. His '99 Cab starts with aromas of black cherries and green olives. The fruit-to-earth balance is enjoyable through the lingering, rich finish. **91 Editors' Choice** —*C.S. (11/15/2002)*

Arbios 1997 Cabernet Sauvignon (Sonoma County) $35. **88** *(11/1/2000)*

ARBOR CREST

Arbor Crest 2002 Cabernet Franc (Columbia Valley (WA)) $16. Firm and varietal, this smooth and chocolaty wine is built upon supple cassis and plum fruit; thick but soft tannins, a powerful streak of roasted coffee and appropriate notes of leaf and stem. Nicely done. **89** —*P.G. (4/1/2006)*

Arbor Crest 1999 Conner Lee Vineyard Cabernet Franc (Columbia Valley (WA)) $25. Plum and blueberry fruit, augmented with spicy juniper berry and herb. This is a tart, minty wine, with some tough tannins and a mix of dry herbs and toasted coconut in the finish. **85** —*P.G. (12/31/2001)*

Arbor Crest 2001 Cabernet Sauvignon (Columbia Valley (WA)) $28. Pungent aromas mix blackberries with cracker and a bit of band-aid. The wine enters the palate quite hot; it actually burns, then shows a brief burst of cherry fruit before the alcohol and tannins take over and the flavors fade. **86** —*P.G. (12/1/2004)*

USA

Arbor Crest 2000 Cabernet Sauvignon (Columbia Valley (WA)) $24. Winemaker Kristina Mielke has brought welcome new energy to this winery. In this warm vintage she has made a dark, earthy, tannic Cab with excellent, textured tannins and some pleasing spice. Give it some cellar time and it will open up into something special. **89** —*P.G.* (9/1/2003)

Arbor Crest 1999 Cabernet Sauvignon (Columbia Valley (WA)) $25. This wine seems to be going through a bit of a bad patch right now. What initially came across as lightly oaked, cassis and plum-flavored fruit has acquired a reduced, odd character, and an artificial mix of herbal and sweet flavors. Perhaps it will turn around. **84** —*P.G.* (12/31/2001)

Arbor Crest 2000 Chardonnay (Columbia Valley (WA)) $14. The style is rich and ripe fruit, with the fruit pushing through into tropical. Nice handling of the oak adds just enough butter and light spice. A hint of bitterness mars the finish. **87** —*P.G.* (9/1/2002)

Arbor Crest 1999 Chardonnay (Columbia Valley (WA)) $10. Here again is fine, rich, ripe fruit, mostly pears and peaches and bananas, layered and textured. The flavors build through a full, delicious middle, with some nice creaminess from barrel fermentation. What's missing is the pleasing toast of new oak, which would etch the fruit into a bit more focus. A hint of residual sweetness rounds out the finish. **88 Best Buy** —*P.G.* (6/1/2001)

Arbor Crest 2002 Conner Lee Chardonnay (Columbia Valley (WA)) $18. Strong scents of ripe fruit and high-toned acetic acid—nail polish and rubbing alcohol. In the mouth the wine is broadly fruity, tropical and a bit heavy, with alcohol and ripe banana flavors showing the strongest. **84** —*P.G.* (4/1/2005)

Arbor Crest 1999 Conner Lee Vineyard Chardonnay (Columbia Valley (WA)) $18. This is a hot, ripe, extracted style that will be quite appealing to many consumers. However, the volatile high-toned scents and the hot edge from the excess alcohol make it a tough match for food. **85** —*P.G.* (7/1/2002)

Arbor Crest 2000 Connor Lee Vineyard Chardonnay (Columbia Valley (WA)) $18. This wine saw plenty of new French oak—it is steeped in scents of wood and butter—and the flavors inevitably conjure up Bourbon rather than wine. Tropical fruit is in there, but can't begin to take on all the wood and alcohol. **84** —*P.G.* (12/31/2002)

Arbor Crest 2000 Dionysus Meritage (Columbia Valley (WA)) $48. Concentrated scents of raspberry liqueur, with just a hint of fresh mushroom, stand out in this Bordeaux blend. The winery has held it back a bit longer than most, and consequently it is nicely softened, with maturing fruit, though the tannins are quite dry and chalky. **87** —*P.G.* (12/1/2004)

Arbor Crest 1999 Dionysus Meritage (Columbia Valley (WA)) $45. This is a 65% Cabernet Sauvignon, 25% Merlot, 10% Cab Franc blend. Big, heavy, and thick, it carries a lot of smoky oak flavors and some rough tannins right now. Time may smooth it out. **87** —*P.G.* (12/31/2003)

Arbor Crest 2001 Dionysus Red Meritage (Columbia Valley (WA)) $40. This meritage blend (65% Cabernet Sauvignon, 22% Merlot, 13% Cab Franc) is true to the house style—ripe, high-toned, tannic, and chocolaty. **87** —*P.G.* (4/1/2006)

Arbor Crest 2003 Merlot (Columbia Valley (WA)) $15. This rich, ripe wine, sourced from top vineyards such as Klipsun, Stillwater Creek, and Conner Lee, really knocks your socks off. The substantial blackberry and black cherry fruit carries unusual weight, and the tannins and barrel time give the wine layers of toast and smoke. **90 Best Buy** —*P.G.* (12/31/2006)

Arbor Crest 2002 Merlot (Columbia Valley (WA)) $15. Chocolaty and rich, with ripe blackberry and currant fruit. There's a streak of chalky mint in here also; this is a very dry, tannic wine but remains very soft and accessible. It's a big style of Merlot, even for Washington, which would be a fine match for juicy red meats. **87** —*P.G.* (4/1/2006)

Arbor Crest 2001 Merlot (Columbia Valley (WA)) $20. This is quite stiff, tannic, hard, and herbal; definitely a bigger style of Merlot with chewy tannins and dark chocolate over hard cassis and black cherry fruit. Give it plenty of breathing time. **86** —*P.G.* (4/1/2005)

Arbor Crest 2003 Sangiovese (Columbia Valley (WA)) $13. Full, almost jammy flavors of strawberry preserves and sweet cherries jump out, with light milk chocolate highlights. Though I don't find it to be particularly varietal (in terms of Tuscan sangio), it is still a very tasty wine with plenty of plump, sweet fruit appeal. **88 Best Buy** —*P.G.* (4/1/2006)

Arbor Crest 2000 Sangiovese (Columbia Valley (WA)) $18. More and more Washington wineries are making Sangio, though not always with distinction. This shows slightly unripe black fruits, hints of beet, and bean, neutral oak and soft, chalky tannins. 717 cases made. **85** —*P.G.* (12/31/2002)

Arbor Crest 2005 Sauvignon Blanc (Columbia Valley (WA)) $8. This rich and full-bodied Sauvignon Blanc is made in a soft, open, fruity, and fairly sweet style. It's bound to have plenty of consumer appeal, especially at this price. It delivers a lot of body and sweet fruit flavor, with none of the vegetal or grassy flavors found in high acid versions of this grape. **87** —*P.G.* (12/31/2006)

Arbor Crest 2003 Sauvignon Blanc (Columbia Valley (WA)) $8. Definitely the winery's shining star; this is a firm, succulent style of Sauv Blanc, lightly toasty, with good fruit flavors that seem to fall right on the cusp between citrus and stone fruits. Polished and flavorful. **88 Best Buy** —*P.G.* (4/1/2006)

Arbor Crest 2002 Sauvignon Blanc (Columbia Valley (WA)) $12. Arbor Crest has long been known for its Sauvignon Blancs, but this new release is a bit of a let-down. The fruit is ripe to the point of losing its focus, replacing crisp flavors with soft peach and tropical. But there is also a very noticeable nail polish scent, and it can also be tasted through the fruit. That's just too much volatility for some tasters. **85** —*P.G.* (12/1/2004)

Arbor Crest 2001 Sauvignon Blanc (Columbia Valley (WA)) $10. This winery excels with Sauv Blanc, which has come from the same Sagemoor Vineyard grapes for 21 years. Fermented in stainless steel, kept on the lees, and finished in a rich, thick, tropical-fruit style, it's layered and intense. Apricots and peaches dominate. **88 Best Buy** —*P.G.* (12/31/2003)

Arbor Crest 2000 Sauvignon Blanc (Columbia Valley (WA)) $10. Sauvignon Blanc has long been the winery's calling card, but this vintage isn't quite up to past standards. Some high-toned scents add edginess to the tropical fruit, and some bitter skin flavors are borderline too much. Good, but they can do better. **86** —*P.G.* (9/1/2002)

Arbor Crest 1999 Sauvignon Blanc (Columbia Valley (WA)) $8. This attractively priced Sauvignon Blanc begins with lovely scents of fig, melon, and green berry. There are some high tones too, and the sharpness of alcohol in this ultra-ripe vintage. New winemaker Kristina van Loben Sels extracts ripe, tropical fruit flavors without sacrificing complexity. The wine really delivers a lot of luscious flavor for the price. **88 Best Buy** —*P.G.* (6/1/2001)

Arbor Crest 2003 Syrah (Columbia Valley (WA)) $17. Soft and sweet, this concentrated, unblended Syrah mixes Stillwater Creek and Sundance Vineyard fruit. There is plenty of oak evident in both the nose and the mouth, and the sweetness of the fruit, dark and liquorous, gives it a Californian spin. **88** —*P.G.* (12/31/2006)

Arbor Crest 2001 Syrah (Columbia Valley (WA)) $28. Sappy, ripe fruit, packed with juicy berry flavors, gets this wine going. Clearly the right things were happening in the vineyard. But more than subtle notes of vinegar and nail polish get in the way of the fruit, and keep this wine from being all it could be. **87** —*P.G.* (12/1/2004)

Arbor Crest 1999 Syrah (Columbia Valley (WA)) $26. This big, tangy, too-oaky palate is not much consolation for the bizarre bouquet of Macadamia nut, cream cheese, and volatile acid (know what a nail salon smells like?). Finishes long, with tart toast and cocoa flavors. One reviewer noted that those who aren't sensetive to volatile acidity will like this better—but many people won't be able to get past the nose. **83** (11/1/2001)

ARCADIAN

Arcadian 2000 Bien Nacido Vineyard Chardonnay (Santa Maria Valley) $25. Seems a bit tired, with the fruit flavors turning to herbs, dried leaves, and mushroom. Finishes dry and clean, with some green-apple notes. **84** —*S.H.* (5/1/2005)

Arcadian 1998 Bien Nacido Vineyard Chardonnay (Santa Maria Valley) $30. A full and creamy bouquet announces a palate laden with ripe golden delicious apple, vanilla, and melon flavors, with chalk, mineral, and earth elements. The dry finish carries some length and builds in intensity. A straightforward wine that's ready to drink right now. **87** *(7/1/2001)*

Arcadian 2001 Sleepy Hollow Vineyard Chardonnay (Monterey) $30. One of the more distinctive Chards I've had this year, notable especially for its very high acidity and mineral and lime complex. The lime tastes like a cool custard, flavored with vanilla, while the minerals bring to mind liquid steel. One hundred percent new French oak slathers it all with buttered toast. **90** *—S.H. (6/1/2005)*

Arcadian 2001 Fiddlestix Vineyard Pinot Noir (Santa Rita Hills) $50. Curiously inert for coming from such a good vineyard. Hits you with tannins, dryness, and earthy, coffee flavors. Finishes raw and harsh in acids. **83** *—S.H. (5/1/2005)*

Arcadian 2001 Francesca Pinot Noir (Central Coast) $75. Dark, dry, heavy and rough in tannins, with plummy, herbal flavors. Isn't offering much now. Tasted twice. **84** *—S.H. (5/1/2005)*

Arcadian 2001 Gary's Vineyard Pinot Noir (Monterey) $50. Well-oaked, this wine stars char, vanilla, and woody flavors framing underlying cola and cherry flavors that, while dry, are rich enough to feel sweet on the palate. There's good acidity, and the texture is silky and smooth. Nice for immediate drinking. **87** *—S.H. (5/1/2005)*

Arcadian 1999 Pisoni Pinot Noir (Monterey County) $80. Rich and fragrant, with an abundance of earth and dense fruit to the bouquet. Roasted plums and black cherry dominate the palate, which despite being thick is amazingly balanced. This has all the components of a classy wine: ripe fruit, earth notes, and persistence. It can age for five or more years. **91 Cellar Selection** *(10/1/2002)*

Arcadian 2001 Pisoni Vineyard Pinot Noir (Monterey) $75. Heavy and soft, like a red velvet curtain. It's forward in black cherry and oak flavors, with a dusting of cocoa. It's not really showing delicacy or finesse now, but has plenty of power. Try holding until 2007. **87** *—S.H. (6/1/2005)*

Arcadian 2002 Sleepy Hollow Vineyard Pinot Noir (Santa Lucia Highlands) $45. I actually prefer this to Arcadian's 2001 Pinots, with which it was released, for its clean, pure framework of acidity and fruit. It's certainly a lively, brisk wine, with cool-climate flavors of cola, cherries, rhubarb, and oak. Showcases the delicacy yet sexiness of a fine Pinot Noir. **90** *—S.H. (6/1/2005)*

Arcadian 2001 Sleepy Hollow Vineyard Pinot Noir (Santa Lucia Highlands) $45. Here's a Pinot that's pretty big-boned but manages to hold on to elegance. It's a balancing act, but the full body is lightened by silky tannins and crisp blackberry flavors. Still, it's heavy. **86** *—S.H. (5/1/2005)*

Arcadian 1999 Gary's Vineyard Syrah (Monterey) $50. The bouquet of this "big and chewy" Syrah is a complex tiramisu, black cherry and smoke melange. More than one reviewer described this Syrah's palate as "very black," and noted distinctive charcoal, black-pepper, plum, and chocolate flavors. Finishes pretty black, too, with black pepper, toast, and even tannins. **90** *(11/1/2001)*

Arcadian 2001 Gary's Vineyard Syrah (Santa Lucia Highlands) $45. Opens with vegetal aromas that turn harsh and dry in the mouth, with a finish of sweet cherry cough medicine. **82** *—S.H. (5/1/2005)*

ARCHERY SUMMIT

Archery Summit 2000 Vireton Pinot Gris (Oregon) $26. Okay class, all together now, a vireton is "the feather on an arrow that causes it to spin in flight." A Pinot Gris-dominated, blended white that also includes some Chardonnay (12%) and Pinot Blanc (8%). Rich and lush with peachy/apricot flavors, this is a ripe, tropical wine, well-made with a complexity more characteristic of Chardonnay. **89** *—P.G. (2/1/2002)*

Archery Summit 1999 Archery Summit Estate Pinot Noir (Oregon) $115. Deep and true in the nose, featuring cherry, pine, molasses, earth and chocolate. It's perfectly balanced, with a combination of sweet cherry and snappy raspberry mixed with just the right touch of spicy, creamy

oak. Proper acidity and firm tannins close this winner. Drink now–2005. **90 Cellar Selection** *(10/1/2002)*

Archery Summit 2003 Arcus Estate Pinot Noir (Willamette Valley) $75. A disappointing vintage for the estate vineyard. It's earthy and bitter, showing far too much of the tomato-leaf herbaceousness that can plague Oregon Pinot. Leafy and chalky through the finish, it is a charmless, herbal wine. **86** *—P.G. (12/1/2006)*

Archery Summit 2000 Arcus Estate Pinot Noir (Oregon) $53. This estate's top bottling is well made in this vintage, with a nice medley of ripe berries, cassis, coffee, and earth. Quite young and firm, its tart acids are still in control, with some chalky, unresolved tannins on the finish. Time could well improve the score. **87** *—P.G. (4/1/2003)*

Archery Summit 1999 Arcus Estate Pinot Noir (Oregon) $75. I don't know why this is labeled "Oregon" rather than Yamhill county, where the vineyard sits. It is a very young, very tight wine, with flavors that run the gamut of red and black fruits, and a good bit of tannin. There's not much oak in evidence at this point; it's mostly fruit and tannin, and tough to pry loose at that. Re-tasted several days after being opened, it had not only held up but actually improved, suggesting that its layers of flavor, hidden today, will blossom in due time. **90** *—P.G. (11/1/2001)*

Archery Summit 2003 Estate Pinot Noir (Willamette Valley) $150. The best of the Archery Summit '03s, this light and tannic wine shows nicely ripened red fruits as well as hints of stone, bark, leaf, and root. Good length and balance compensate for the lack of weight or richness. **89** — *P.G. (12/1/2006)*

Archery Summit 2000 Premier Cuvée Pinot Noir (Oregon) $45. An odd bottle, with a curious set of disjointed flavors. Berries, coconut, vanilla, and a funky, microbial odor reminiscent of soy or seaweed are all mixed together. The fruit is light and sweet, like a candy Lifesaver, and the finish is flat, dull, and lifeless. **85** *—P.G. (4/1/2003)*

Archery Summit 1999 Premier Cuvée Pinot Noir (Willamette Valley) $45. This winery's "starter" Pinot is velvety smooth on the nose and in the mouth. A bouquet full of smoked meat, chocolate, caramel, and black fruit is quite welcoming. Plum, kirsch, and black currant flavors are powerful yet properly restrained. Soft tannins ensure a plush finish. **89** *(10/1/2002)*

Archery Summit 2003 Premier Cuvée Pinot Noir (Willamette Valley) $37. Light and clean, this moves beyond simple and fruity with sharp detail and a mix of strawberry, red currant, raspberry, and cherry fruit. There are characteristic streaks of root and cola, earth, and even a hint of pepper. Lots going on in a lighter style. **87** *—P.G. (12/1/2006)*

Archery Summit 2003 Red Hills Estate Pinot Noir (Willamette Valley) $75. This wine has some funky scents of soy and silage, with simple, thin fruit. It falls off quickly; there's no weight to it and the oak flavors have nothing to lean against. **86** *—P.G. (12/1/2006)*

Archery Summit 2000 Red Hills Estate Pinot Noir (Oregon) $70. Smooth on the bouquet, with a good mix of ripe red fruit and wood-driven spice. The palate deals a hand of pure but light cherry and raspberry, while the finishing act is one of oak and coffee, and a fair amount of length. This is a racy and acid-heavy wine that comes across fresh and snappy. But all told it's not packed enough to go the extra mile. **88** — *M.S. (9/1/2003)*

Archery Summit 1999 Red Hills Estate Pinot Noir (Willamette Valley) $75. Medium- weight and tasty, this shows greater extraction than most Oregon Pinot Noirs. The soft fruit displays mocha and plum aromas. Some tasters praised complex meat and mushroom accents; others found it forward and pleasing, if less finely nuanced. The wine's supple, almost creamy feel was widely praised. Drink now–2005. **86** *(10/1/2002)*

Archery Summit 2003 Renegade Ridge Estate Pinot Noir (Willamette Valley) $60. Firm and tannic, this carries a penetrating, distinct, and sharply defined cranberry and red currant core. Beyond that it heads straight for a tannic, chalky finish. **88** *—P.G. (12/1/2006)*

Archery Summit 2002 Renegade Ridge Estate Pinot Noir (Oregon) $60. There's a definite barnyard aroma of sweaty leather here, and the fruit comes across as a bit sour and green. The oak barrel flavors show a roasted, slightly burnt edge, and the tannins are toasty and astringent. **84** (11/1/2004)

Archery Summit 2000 Renegade Ridge Estate Pinot Noir (Oregon) $60. Dense, with a hint of bacon on the nose as well as black cherry. This is a youngster that takes time to open up, but once it does there's a nice package of raspberry and ripe cherry wrapped up in some chocolaty sweetness. In the end, a firm and oaky finish gives added life to a wine that hits the finish line with gas left in the tank. **90** —*M.S.* (9/1/2003)

ARCHIPEL

Archipel 2002 Bordeaux Blend (Sonoma-Napa) $40. This is one of Jess Jackson's small-production wines. The vineyards are way up in the Mayacamas range separating Alexander Valley and Napa Valley, which explains the multi-county appellation. Mostly Cabernet Sauvignon and Merlot, the wine is very dry and very tannic—too young to drink now. It should soften, but lacks the stuffing for the long haul. **87** —*S.H.* (12/31/2006)

ARCIERO

Arciero 1999 Chardonnay (California) $10. Ripe, oaky, but inexpensive Chardonnay often smells like lemon-lime soda pop, with a waft of spice and vanilla and a hint of smoke. This version tastes fruity and more than a little sweet, but it's not flat, thanks to vibrant acidity. It's geared to the American palate, at an affordable price. **83** —*S.H.* (5/1/2001)

Arciero 1998 Merlot (Central Coast) $12. Light, rustic, and brimming with black cherry fruit, with a cut of mushroom and earth. Very dry, and although the color is a bit light, it's surprisingly acidic. Finishes earthy and rough. **82** —*S.H.* (5/1/2001)

Arciero 1998 Petite Sirah (Paso Robles) $14. Some deep stone fruit flavors, like black cherry, but this wine really comes down on the earthy side, with notes of chocolate and mint. The tannins are fine but substantial; you can feel them on the finish, which leaves the palate a little numb. It's not likely to age, though, so drink it with rich foods. **84** — *S.H.* (5/1/2001)

Arciero 1998 Estate Bottled Pinot Grigio (Paso Robles) $12. 86 Best Buy (8/1/1999)

Arciero 1998 Arpeggio Red Blend (Paso Robles) $15. This blend of Nebbiolo, Sangiovese, and Zinfandel starts with aromas of black raspberries, mint, and oregano. While it's supple, it has a green harshness to it that dominates whatever ripe, fruity flavors it has. The result is a sharp, thin wine that leaves the palate stinging. **81** —*S.H.* (5/1/2001)

ARDENTE

Ardente 2000 Estate Cabernet Sauvignon (Atlas Peak) $45. A tense, tight, tannic mountain wine that's pretty closed and rough at this time. Shows herbal and blackberry flavors and is very dry. Could develop a bit with short-term aging. **85** —*S.H.* (11/15/2004)

ARGER-MARTUCCI

Arger-Martucci 2002 Cabernet Sauvignon (Napa Valley) $60. Here's an old-style Cab. Tastes like it was picked earlier than most these days, giving a dry, rich earthiness along with acidity and firm, dry tannins. Opulent it's not, but balanced and ageworthy it is, and will probably last for 20 years. **88 Cellar Selection** —*S.H.* (9/1/2006)

Arger-Martucci 2001 Cabernet Sauvignon (Napa Valley) $50. Very dry, with some tannins to shed, this full-bodied wine offers up cherry, blackberry, and herb flavors, and a generous dollop of oak. It's a very good wine, but streamlined compared to many of its '01 colleagues. **87** —*S.H.* (10/1/2004)

Arger-Martucci 2000 Cabernet Sauvignon (Napa Valley) $50. From 1,500 feet up near Atlas Peak, another mountain wine that's closed and muted now with dense, hard tannins, and cherry flavors and herbal notes. **85** — *S.H.* (11/15/2004)

Arger-Martucci 1999 Cabernet Sauvignon (Napa Valley) $50. This opening salvo is O.K., but this wine has a ways to go before it elbows its way into the top league. Dark, with earth, sage, and blackberry aromas and flavors. It's soft, with overripe, raisiny notes in the finish. **85** —*S.H.* (11/15/2002)

Arger-Martucci 2002 Chardonnay (Carneros) $22. Crisp, silky, and elegant, a wine of bright acidity that cleans the palate. Then there are the flavors, which are rich and explosive. They range from citrus fruits through apples and peaches to mango, and are well-oaked. **91** —*S.H.* (12/15/2004)

Arger-Martucci 2000 Chardonnay (Carneros) $30. This is an intense, oaky Chardonnay, massive in every way. Big, ripe fruity flavors of tropical fruits, peaches, and pears are framed in well-charred oak. The tannins and acids are well within normal limits. It finishes with a flourish of lees and pepper. **89** —*S.H.* (12/15/2002)

Arger-Martucci 2002 Pinot Noir (Carneros) $30. Feels hot and rough on the palate, although the silk is there and so are the cherry and cola flavors typical of the variety. Not going anywhere, so drink now. **83** —*S.H.* (10/1/2006)

Arger-Martucci 2000 Pinot Noir (Carneros) $40. Simple, one-dimensional and awkward, it opens with notes of tea, beets, and beefsteak tomato. There are some berry flavors but the wine is lean and herbal. The tannins and acids are fine. **85** —*S.H.* (4/1/2003)

Arger-Martucci 2004 Syrah (Napa Valley) $30. Tannic and unyielding now, this Syrah is full-bodied and soft, with cola, blackberry tea, bitter chocolate, and leather flavors. It's a young, fresh, very dry wine, with a complex, chewy mouthfeel. The tannins suggest upscale red meats and fine cheeses. **89** —*S.H.* (10/1/2006)

Arger-Martucci 2003 Syrah (Napa Valley) $25. Standard Syrah flavors—blackberries, herbs, and pepper—done very well. Soft tannins give a succulent mouthfeel, while the finish is soft and persistent, picking up hints of citrus and pepper. **88** (9/1/2005)

Arger-Martucci 2004 Viognier (Russian River Valley) $25. This is a clean, dry earthy, acidic wine, but it's a little thin in fruit, and lovers of Viognier's opulence will be disappointed, despite the elegance. The flavors veer toward lemon zest and minerals. **84** —*S.H.* (10/1/2006)

ARGYLE

Argyle 1999 Brut Champagne Blend (Willamette Valley) $21. Argyle vintage dates its Brut, a mark of extra care and quality. This is still green apple young; at first sip it could almost be hard cider. Tart, bracing, and concentrated, it tastes of fresh cut apples, pears, and yeast. **88** —*P.G.* (12/31/2004)

Argyle 1997 Brut Champagne Blend (Willamette Valley) $21. Argyle's mainstream Brut strikes a good balance all around, with bone-dry, lightly spicy flavors of fresh green apples and Bartlett pears. Crisp and slightly beery, it is well integrated through a gently toasty finish. **87** —*P.G.* (12/1/2001)

Argyle 1996 Brut Champagne Blend (Willamette Valley) $22. 87 —*S.H.* (12/1/2000)

Argyle 1999 Brut Rosé Champagne Blend (Willamette Valley) $21. This is as boldly fruity as rosé can be; it is packed with young pinot flavors of cherry candy. Youthful, big, and fruity, it is immediately engaging, quite quaffable, but ultimately much less complex and interesting than the rest of the Argyle lineup. **87** —*P.G.* (12/31/2004)

Argyle 1991 Extended Tirage-Disgorged on Demand Champagne Blend (Willamette Valley) $22. With 10 years on the yeast in the bottle, it is no surprise to find sweet cream, unsalted butter, cardamom, white bread, and lemon-candy aromas and flavors. The soft acidity and medium-length, talc-y finish leave no questions as to why this was "disgorged on demand." Drink now, only 405 cases were made of this 80% Pinot, 20% Chard blend. **88** —*K.F.* (12/1/2002)

Argyle 1989 Extended Tirage Brut Champagne Blend (Willamette Valley) $30. 86 —*M.M.* (12/1/2000)

Argyle 1989 Extended Tirage Brut Champagne Blend (Willamette Valley) $30. This is certainly one of the oldest domestic sparkling wines still in current release. As expected, it is very dry and somewhat oxidized with woody, Sherry- cask scents, and flavors. The fruit, though subdued, has some pleasant baked apple and vanilla cracker components, and it finishes with a pleasant persistence. There were 1,011 six-bottle cases produced. **87** —*P.G.* (12/1/2001)

Argyle 1997 Knudsen Vineyard Blanc de Blancs "Julia Lee's Block" Champagne Blend (Willamette Valley) $30. Perfectly aged, creamy, and round, this lovely blanc de blancs shows ripe fruits that include a touch of mango, along with fennel and other herbal notes, vanilla custard, and a smooth, pleasing finish. **90** —*P.G. (12/31/2004)*

Argyle 1997 Knudsen Vineyard Brut Champagne Blend (Willamette Valley) $30. This is 100% barrel fermented, an 80% Pinot/20% Chardonnay blend, and at this age it is already showing lovely sherry notes and lightly oxidized fruit. Yet it retains enough youthful juice to be quite refreshing, with a finish that suggests toast and slightly oily nuts, layer upon layer. **90** —*P.G. (12/31/2004)*

Argyle 1996 Knudsen Vineyard Brut Champagne Blend (Willamette Valley) $35. 89 —*P.G. (12/31/2000)*

Argyle 1996 Knudsen Vineyard Julia Lee's Block Blanc de Blancs Champagne Blend (Willamette Valley) $30. 87 —*P.G. (12/1/2000)*

Argyle 1995 Knudsen's Vineyard Julis Lee's Champagne Blend (Willamette Valley) $30. 88 *(12/15/1999)*

Argyle 1996 Knutsen Vineyard Blanc de Blancs Champagne Blend (Willamette Valley) $30. Made from 100% Dijon-clone Chardonnay, this carries delicious scents of rich, toasty oak above ripe, fleshy fruit. There is a suggestion of tropical pineapple and papaya along with the usual green apple flavors and a bigger, more fruit-forward style than is usually found in Blanc de Blancs. **88** —*P.G. (12/1/2001)*

Argyle 1996 Knutsen Vineyard Brut Champagne Blend (Willamette Valley) $35. This is the most complex and elegant sparkling wine from Argyle, who pioneered Oregon bubbly. It's a barrel-fermented, 70/30 blend of Pinot Noir and Chardonnay. In the mouth, it has a seamless, delicate presence, it's overall elegance expressed in the tiny, streaming bubbles and the crisp precision of flavors. Hints of cinnamon and licorice highlight a light, toasty finish. **89** —*P.G. (12/1/2001)*

Argyle 1999 Nuthouse Chardonnay (Willamette Valley) $28. This is soft, forward and fruity, with a somewhat flat mouthfeel. Soft, buttery oak rounds out into a smooth, silky finsh. Very seductive and caramel flavored, long, satiny finish. A drink-now bottle, not for aging. **89** —*P.G. (8/1/2002)*

Argyle 1997 Nuthouse Chardonnay (Willamette Valley) $28. 90 —*M.S. (4/1/2000)*

Argyle 1999 Reserve Chardonnay (Willamette Valley) $20. Argyle's Reserve shows less oak than the Nuthouse and Spirithouse bottlings, with more compact and vivid fruit. Nice flavors of stone fruits, grapes, and citrus, well integrated and full through the mid-palate. It rounds into a very pretty finish, fruit forward, balanced, and true. **90** —*P.G. (7/1/2002)*

Argyle 1997 Reserve Chardonnay (Willamette Valley) $21. 84 —*M.S. (4/1/2000)*

Argyle 2004 Pinot Noir (Willamette Valley) $20. An early release is often good for Oregon Pinot, bringing out the young varietal flavors with bracing freshness. Here an extended maceration, both before and after fermentation, gives it a nice mix of cherry/grapy fruit with a good tannic structure. Comes on like a cru Beaujolais, with surprising weight and length for such a young wine. **88** —*P.G. (11/15/2005)*

Argyle 2002 Pinot Noir (Willamette Valley) $18. Good varietal character, with smoky cherry, orange peel, cherry, and vanilla. Supple, creamy, and sweet with vanilla and spice. Pleasant, with nice complexity. **87** *(11/1/2004)*

Argyle 1998 Pinot Noir (Willamette Valley) $16. 87 Best Buy —*P.G. (9/1/2000)*

Argyle 2002 Nuthouse Pinot Noir (Willamette Valley) $40. Argyle has done an excellent job with this late-released '02; it's firm and toasty, cedar-scented under tart, cherry/berry fruit. Layered with earth and wood streaks, and some lightly chocolaty tannins to finish up strong. **92 Editors' Choice** —*P.G. (8/1/2005)*

Argyle 2000 Nuthouse Pinot Noir (Willamette Valley) $40. Tobacco and leather provide a rustic side to the sweet black cherry aromas. The mouth is loaded with earthy cherry and plum fruit, sweet milk chocolate, and just a snippet of green. The finish is soft, aided by velvety

tannins. The mouthfeel is on the money, with a harmonious mix of tannins and oak. **88** *(10/1/2002)*

Argyle 1998 Nuthouse Pinot Noir (Willamette Valley) $40. 92 *(12/1/2000)*

Argyle 1997 Nuthouse Pinot Noir (Willamette Valley) $35. 91 *(10/1/1999)*

Argyle 2003 Reserve Pinot Noir (Willamette Valley) $30. Silky and fresh, with berries and strawberries, natural tartness and early hints of toasted grain, cracker, and sandalwood. Certainly a wine to cellar for a few years. **89** —*P.G. (11/15/2005)*

Argyle 2002 Reserve Pinot Noir (Willamette Valley) $30. Good concentration and noticeable density, with intriguing, briary flavors that mix candied fruit with dusty herbs, cinnamon, and cocoa. **87** *(11/1/2004)*

Argyle 1998 Reserve Pinot Noir (Willamette Valley) $30. 91 —*M.M. (12/1/2000)*

Argyle 2000 Spirit House Pinot Noir (Willamette Valley) $50. There is no shortage of aromatics in this wine: leather, vanilla, popcorn, sweet cream, black cherry, brown sugar—they're all there. The mouth is all about chunky plum fruit and buttery oak, while soft tannins and a plush, airy finish guarantee that it will go down easy. **89** *(10/1/2002)*

Argyle 1998 Spirit House Pinot Noir (Willamette Valley) $50. 88 —*J.C. (12/1/2000)*

Argyle 2004 Riesling (Willamette Valley) $25. Screwcapped, pleasant-tasting effort with mixed orange, apple, and grapefruit. Tastes just a bit flat; perhaps an off-bottle? **86** —*P.G. (11/15/2005)*

Argyle 2000 Brut Sparkling Blend (Willamette Valley) $21. Argyle vintage dates its Brut, a mark of extra care and quality. As with the '99 when it was first released, this is still tight and showing crisp green apple flavors, but it opens gently into a smooth, yeasty wine with hints of toast. The blend is 55% Chardonnay and 45% Pinot Noir. **90** —*P.G. (11/15/2005)*

Argyle 2003 Brut Rosé Sparkling Blend (Willamette Valley) $25. Soft (for bubbly), light, young, and showing pretty flavors of cherry candy. It's 100% Pinot Noir, a bit foamy in the glass, but smooth and lingering, though light as a summer breeze. **88** —*P.G. (12/31/2005)*

Argyle 1994 Extended Tirage Sparkling Blend (Willamette Valley) $34. A thrilling success, with beautifully developed aromas of vanilla and buttered toast. Gorgeous mousse, and persistent, nutty, complex flavors that show hints of candied tropical fruits and sweet butterscotch. Maybe the best Argyle ever. **91 Editors' Choice** —*P.G. (12/31/2004)*

Argyle 1995 Extended Tirage Brut Sparkling Blend (Willamette Valley) $35. A lovely follow-up to the outstanding '94, this well-integrated, perfectly aged Brut is still crisp and showing hints of fresh apple, along with beeswax, citrus, and gooseberry. It shows off with a gorgeous mousse, and persistent fresh flavors that linger without cracking up. **91** —*P.G. (12/31/2005)*

Argyle 1998 Knudsen Vineyard Brut Sparkling Blend (Willamette Valley) $30. Amylic, showing rather awkward tropical fruit/bubble gum character, with banana-like softness. Blowsier than the rest of the lineup, this is perfectly drinkable but less elegant (and more expensive) than Argyle's fine vintage Brut. **86** —*P.G. (12/31/2005)*

ARISTA

Arista 2004 Pinot Noir (Russian River Valley) $28. Arista's basic Pinot, which contains some Anderson Valley fruit, is textbook cool-climate Pinot, very dry and quite acidic. It's a little diluted, but enjoyable for its cherry, cola, and toast flavors that finish in a great burst of peppery spice. **87** —*S.H. (10/1/2006)*

Arista 2003 Ferrington Vineyard Pinot Noir (Anderson Valley) $50. A tight, young Pinot, currently dominated by toasty oak aromas. It's dry and complex, with a mélange of cranberry, cherry, cola, blackberry, and oaky, wood-spice flavors that are deep and satisfying. In its structure and balance, it's the most classic of Arista's four Pinots. Drink now through 2007. **94** —*S.H. (2/1/2006)*

Arista 2004 Harper's Rest Pinot Noir (Russian River Valley) $38. This wine is very similar to Arista's regular Pinot, but considerably more concentrated. It's bone dry, silky in texture, fairly alcoholic, full-bodied, and complex in cherry, cola, rhubarb, and peppery spice flavors, with a

USA

tannin-acid backbone that suggests aging through 2011. **91** —*S.H. (10/1/2006)*

Arista 2003 Harper's Rest Pinot Noir (Russian River Valley) $35. This Pinot is a junior version of Arista's Toboni bottling, sharing many of the same characteristics, without quite the complexity or depth. It's dry and rich, and notable for its cherry, cranberry, and vanilla flavors and silky mouthfeel. **90** —*S.H. (2/1/2006)*

Arista 2004 Longbow Pinot Noir (Russian River Valley) $38. This is the driest, most austere of Arista's current Pinots. It's not a hedonistic wine. It offers a mouthful of acidity and earthy, truffly tastes, with a hint of cherries and cranberries. It doesn't slap you with fruit, but it's a wine you'll return to for a third glass when the fruit bombs have palled. Best now, but will hold for five years. **93 Editors' Choice** —*S.H. (10/1/2006)*

Arista 2003 Mononi Vineyard Pinot Noir (Russian River Valley) $50. Compared to the winery's Toboni bottling, this wine is slightly more tannic, with more body, but the two wines are similar. It's dominated by cherry and cranberry flavors, and feels soft and creamy. Seems likely to improve with a few years in the bottle. **93** —*S.H. (2/1/2006)*

Arista 2003 Toboni Vineyard Pinot Noir (Russian River Valley) $50. This bottling is the richest, most complex, and most accessible of this new winery's four single-vineyard bottlings, a textbook example of luscious Russian River Pinot. With its cherry, cola, coffee, and spice flavors, and rich but delicate tannins, it's delicious. Will hold several years, but best now in its sexy youth. **94** —*S.H. (2/1/2006)*

ARMAGH

Armagh 2003 Syrah (Sonoma Coast) $25. This vineyard established its reputation with Pinot Noir, but now comes this Syrah, from a cool area with a southern exposure. Black and peppery with an inviting aroma. In the mouth, it dominates with blackberry flavors. Dry, tannic, and complex, this is a wine to follow. **90** —*S.H. (12/31/2005)*

ARMIDA

Armida 1997 Chardonnay (Russian River Valley) $12. 87 —*J.C. (10/1/1999)*

Armida 2004 Keefer Ranch Chardonnay (Russian River Valley) $28. The vineyard is in the Green Valley, and the acidity is very high, giving a bright purity to the kiwi, Key lime pie, pineapple custard, and crème brûlée flavors. Lots of toasty new French oak and lees bring super creaminess to the mouthfeel. White Burgundy is the model, expressed California-style. **92** —*S.H. (12/15/2006)*

Armida 1997 Merlot (Russian River Valley) $22. 83 —*J.C. (7/1/2000)*

Armida 2004 Castelli-Knight Ranch Vineyard Pinot Noir (Russian River Valley) $36. Nice and ripe in black cherry pie filling, black raspberry, cola, root beer, and smoky oak flavors, this Pinot has some firm tannins that will stand up to a rich steak. It should hold through 2010. **91** —*S.H. (12/15/2006)*

Armida 2004 Sauvignon Blanc (Russian River Valley) $20. Herbal and bulky, with sweet apple, pear, and pineapple flavors. Quite heavy on the tongue, with soft acids. Seems a bit gummy and candied, and just not that precise, despite delivering some rich flavors. **84** *(7/1/2005)*

Armida 1996 Zinfandel (Russian River Valley) $20. 84 —*J.C. (9/1/1999)*

Armida 2001 Maple Vineyard Zinfandel (Dry Creek Valley) $30. Tea and herb qualities mark this wine, which also features blackberry and cassis notes that are couched in moderate tannins. Fairly smooth yet bright. **87** *(11/1/2003)*

Armida 1998 Maple Vineyard Zinfandel (Dry Creek Valley) $22. 87 —*M.S. (5/1/2000)*

Armida 2004 PoiZin Zinfandel (Sonoma County) $25. Superripe, a Zin with a soft, thick texture and almost desserty flavors of chocolate soufflé infused with crème de cassis and cherry jam. It's probably technically dry, but leaves behind a sweet aftertaste. **86** —*S.H. (12/15/2006)*

Armida 2004 Tre Torrente Vineyard Zinfandel (Dry Creek Valley) $34. Beautiful Zin, lush and decadent and heady. Hits you with the most wonderfully ripe chocolate, blackberry, and cherry marmalade, licorice, and spice flavors that are so rich, they would be gooey without the

balancing acids and tannins. Drink this wine with the richest possible fare, like short ribs of beef. **90** —*S.H. (12/15/2006)*

ARNOLD PALMER

Arnold Palmer 2004 Chardonnay (California) $15. The golf legend lends his name to this everyday, simple Chard. It has fruity flavors and a creamy texture, with smoky notes, and is dry and balanced. **84** —*S.H. (5/1/2006)*

ARNS

Arns 2000 Cabernet Sauvignon (Napa Valley) $60. Incredibly aromatic and redolent of black cherry, black currant, plum, chocolate, coffee, spice, vanilla, toast, herb, and anise. Rich, lush, long, and elegant on the palate with corresponding flavors that don't disappoint. A full-bodied expression of great Cabernet. **92** —*J.M. (11/15/2003)*

Arns 1998 Cabernet Sauvignon (Napa Valley) $50. Earthy, with sautéed mushroom aromas, although in the mouth it turns fruity with blackberry, cassis and plummy spices. Turns tannic on the finish. Could improve, but it's a gamble. **85** —*S.H. (11/15/2003)*

ARROW CREEK

Arrow Creek 2004 Pinot Grigio (California) $10. Refreshingly fruity and crisp in acids, this vibrant PG is really easy to savor. It's filled with apple, citrus, peach, fig, and honeydew flavors that finish long and spicy, with a slightly honeyed sweetness. **85 Best Buy** —*S.H. (4/1/2006)*

ARROWOOD

Arrowood 2001 Cabernet Sauvignon (Sonoma County) $45. Master vintner Dick Arrowood has crafted a sensational wine from a sensational vintage. A blend from throughout the county, it shows his discernment in the overall balance, harmony, and charm. Black currants, chocolate, green olives, sweet sage, and vanilla-scented oak flavors come together in a lush, smooth, intricately structured wine that will probably hold for 10 years, but is best in its flamboyant, exuberant youth. **93 Editors' Choice** —*S.H. (12/1/2005)*

Arrowood 2000 Cabernet Sauvignon (Sonoma County) $45. Rich in blackberry, mocha, and oak flavors, soft and lush in approachable tannins, and with a delicious overlay of smoky oak, this is a very good wine, one to drink now and for the next few years. You wish it had a little more concentration, but it's still a beauty. **90** —*S.H. (12/31/2004)*

Arrowood 2001 Grand Archer Cabernet Sauvignon (Sonoma County) $22. Plays it safe with a good varietal profile. Very dry, with a harmony of fruit, oak, tannins and acidity, a regional Cabernet with some fanciness. Might improve with a few years in bottle. **86** —*S.H. (10/1/2004)*

Arrowood 2000 Grand Archer Cabernet Sauvignon (Sonoma County) $20. Tough, lean, and tannic, but it has a core of berry fruit. It's acidic and bitter right now, and there's a flavor of unsweetened coffee on the finish. Cellar it, or if you must try it now, drink it with the richest red meats you can find. **85** —*S.H. (2/1/2003)*

Arrowood 1999 Grand Archer Cabernet Sauvignon (Sonoma County) $22. From master winemaker Dick Arrowood, and pretty good for a regional-based wine. A politically correct Cabernet with cassis flavors, good oak, very dry, stylish tannins and low acidity. There's not a lot going on below the surface but it gets the job done. **87** —*S.H. (7/1/2002)*

Arrowood 1999 Reserve Speciale Cabernet Sauvignon (Sonoma County) $85. From a legendary winemaker, a wine designed for the cellar. Dick Arrowood shunned the easy approach, instead crafting a fairly tannic wine with a solid core of blackberry, cherry, and herb flavors. Although the tannins are soft in the modern way, it's best after 2005. **92** —*S.H. (11/15/2003)*

Arrowood 2002 Chardonnay (Sonoma County) $29. Here's a powerful Chard that never loses its sense of balance. It is rich in pear, pineapple, and mango flavors accompanied by notes of smoky oak and creamy lees. Feels fat and plush in the mouth. **90** —*S.H. (9/1/2004)*

Arrowood 2001 Chardonnay (Sonoma County) $29. A well-made, attractive Chardonnay from a veteran Chard guy, this wine is fully ripened, with delicious peach and pear flavors. It's a bit soft, but sturdy oak helps to contribute structure to this polished, eminently drinkable wine. **87** —*S.H. (6/1/2003)*

Arrowood 1998 Chardonnay (South Coast) $25. Tight flavors of citrus and peach are molded by high acids and dusty tannins, while sumptuous oak treatment adds sweet vanilla nuances and a creamy, buttery mouthfeel. Drinks very complex and polished, with great weight and structure and a long, creamy, spicy finsish. **91** —*S.H. (12/1/2001)*

Arrowood 2002 Grand Archer Chardonnay (Sonoma County) $16. There's an elegant balance to this wine, a mellowness that's partly due to its age, and partly to the winemaking talents of Dick Arrowood. Belies its price with real richness of fruit, oak, cream, acids, and lees that impress. **88** —*S.H. (12/1/2005)*

Arrowood 2001 Grand Archer Chardonnay (Sonoma County) $18. A very fruity, exceptionally ripe wine, filled with sun-pure flavors of green apple, white peach, pear, and nutmeg. Oak plays a supporting role throughout. Finishes with a honey and pepper richness. **87** —*S.H. (8/1/2003)*

Arrowood 2000 Grand Archer Chardonnay (Sonoma County) $18. Nice and easy-drinking, with peach and apple flavors spiced up with the sweet vanillins and smoke of oak. Drinks a bit soft and slightly sweet, with rich extract that lasts through the finish. **85** —*S.H. (5/1/2002)*

Arrowood 1998 Reserve Speciale Cuvée Michel Berthoud Chardonnay (Sonoma County) $38. It's said that Dick Arrowood personally checks every bottle that goes out—his attention to detail shows here. A complex and refined bouquet of toasted oat, coconut, orange, and peach opens to a full palate of apple, yellow plum, and caramel flavors. Rich and creamily textured, it is also high on spice and smoky oak. The complex finish is very long, leesy and elegantly nuanced. **91** *(7/1/2001)*

Arrowood 2002 Reserve Speciale, Cuvée Michel Berthoud Chardonnay (Russian River Valley) $35. In an era where size is everything, a wine like this makes you appreciate true balance. It has all the rich fruit, spice, cream, and oak you could want in a Chard, but maintains elegance. So easy to drink, and yet so refined. **92** —*S.H. (12/1/2005)*

Arrowood 2002 Saralee's Vineyard Gewürztraminer (Russian River Valley) $20. A lovely and delicate wine, absolutely refreshing, and a versatile companion at the table. Quite dry and racy, with tingly acids and an array of flavors ranging from citrus fruits to apricots and all kinds of dusty brown Oriental spices. Perfect with everything from roasted chicken to a pear and blue cheese salad. **86** —*S.H. (7/1/2003)*

Arrowood 2001 Merlot (Sonoma County) $42. Fairly concentrated and elevated, with cherry, plum, tobacco, and light wood-based aromas. Sweet plum, brown sugar, and tobacco coat the palate, which is ripe and on the spot but not what you'd call complex. Finishes with vanilla, nutmeg and a breeze of herbs. Very nice and easy to like. **88** —*M.S. (12/31/2006)*

Arrowood 1998 Merlot (Sonoma County) $42. The nose is kind of light and shy, although airing reveals plum, bark, and rhubarb. Sweet oak dominates the palate, with underlying suggestions of blackberry and cassis. Dry, elegant, and harmonious, yet light, the wine is a success for the vintage. **89** —*P.G. (12/1/2001)*

Arrowood 2001 Grand Archer Merlot (Sonoma County) $16. This Merlot straddles that interesting line between easy, everyday drinking and real complexity. It's dry and richly tannic, and is the sort of wine that won't win a blind tasting, but leaves you reaching for a third glass with that steak. **87** —*S.H. (12/1/2005)*

Arrowood 2000 Grand Archer Merlot (Sonoma County) $18. There's lots of class in this dry, fairly tannic wine, with blackberry and plum flavors. Feels rich in the mouth, with depth and good structure. The gritty tannins are tough, though, and require aging or rich fare, like lamb, to tame them. **86** —*S.H. (2/1/2003)*

Arrowood 1999 Grand Archer Merlot (Sonoma County) $20. Nice drinking here, with modulated berry fruit and sizable tannins, which you don't see that much anymore. Dick Arrowood produced a complex, dry beverage that will complement a wide variety of foods. **90** —*S.H. (9/1/2002)*

Arrowood 2000 Unfined & Unfiltered Merlot (Sonoma County) $42. Put together from every corner of the county, this is a very good wine. It just shows that tasteful blending can be a good thing. Strikes a fine balance between the dried herb and green olive flavors and plusher ones of

cherries. There is a hollow spot in the middle that is due to the vintage, but the overall impression is upscale. **89** —*S.H. (12/31/2003)*

Arrowood 2001 Select Late Harvest White Riesling Riesling (Alexander Valley) $25. Starts with apricot, orange, honeysuckle, and vanilla aromas. Curiously, the concentration and intensity the aroma suggests isn't there. Finishes weak. **84** —*S.H. (12/1/2003)*

Arrowood 2001 Special Select Late Harvest White Riesling Hoot Owl Creek Vineyards Riesling (Alexander Valley) $40. The real deal, an unctuously sweet wine that tastes like it has some botrytis as well. The color of old gold, and oozing aromas of ripe apricots, nectarines, orange, tapioca, and vanilla custard. Turns thick and glyceriney in the mouth, with fantastic density of flavor. It's sweet but never cloying, thanks to the refreshing acids. **93** —*S.H. (12/1/2003)*

Arrowood 1999 Syrah (Sonoma Valley) $55. Quite bright, with briary, tangy, herbal, olive, and blackberry flavors. Tannins are a bit rustic and angular. Moderately long on the finish. **85** —*J.M. (12/1/2002)*

Arrowood 2001 Grand Archer Syrah (Sonoma County) $16. Plenty of ripe, juicy fruit in this wine, and it offers a pleasant experience with its smooth tannins and kiss of oak. The cherry, blackberry jam, and cocoa flavors would be a good match for charbroiled beef. **85** —*S.H. (12/1/2005)*

Arrowood 2001 Le Beau Melange Syrah (Sonoma Valley) $35. Arrowood's blended Syrah is a clean, well-made wine that won't disappoint many Syrah lovers. Aromas of vanilla, herb, and spice add mixed berries and pepper flavors on the palate. A bit less lush than the Saralee's Vineyard bottling, but still creamy and elegant. **88** *(9/1/2005)*

Arrowood 2001 Saralee's Vineyard Syrah (Russian River Valley) $39. Starts with scents of jammy blackberries and peppery spice, then adds shadings of vanilla and plum on the lush, creamy-textured palate. Finishes long, with echoes of black pepper that gracefully linger, mingling with fruity notes. **91 Cellar Selection** *(9/1/2005)*

Arrowood 1999 Saralee's Vineyard Syrah (Russian River Valley) $62. An herbal-edged wine that also sports an interesting blend of blackberry, cherry, olive, licorice, earth, and toasty oak flavors. Somewhat bright on the finish, with firm, powdery tannins. **88** —*J.M. (12/1/2002)*

Arrowood 1998 Saralee's Vineyard Syrah (Russian River Valley) $60. This wine takes some time to get going—but once it does, look out. The toast and pepper aromas broaden with air, developing blackberry and caramel notes that continue through the flavors. Full-bodied, the flavors continue to evolve in the glass, slowly giving up saddle leather, coffee, and chocolate before finishing with touches of mint and anise. **89** *(11/1/2001)*

Arrowood 2000 Saralee's Vineyard-Unfined & Unfiltered Syrah (Russian River Valley) $35. Here's a rich, flamboyant Syrah oozing with cherry liqueur and spicy flavors, with tannins as soft and melted as warm butter. It is very tasty, but a bit lacking in structure. **86** —*S.H. (12/1/2003)*

Arrowood 2000 Unfined & Unfiltered Syrah (Sonoma Valley) $40. A soft, gentle wine, flavored with red cherry, kirsch, pomegranat and raspberry, folded into easy tannins. Turns a bit hollow in the finish. **86** —*S.H. (12/1/2003)*

Arrowood 1997 Viognier (Russian River Valley) $30. 91 —*S.H. (6/1/1999)*

Arrowood 2003 Saralee's Vineyard Viognier (Russian River Valley) $30. Dick Arrowood's Saralee's Viognier is consistently one of the best in California. Dependably ripe in juicy tropical fruit, wildflower, honey, and vanilla flavors, it's balanced with acidity and minerals. **91** —*S.H. (2/1/2005)*

Arrowood 2001 Saralee's Vineyard Viognier (Russian River Valley) $30. Quite rich and creamy, with a leesy texture so thick, it's almost custardy. Flavors are exuberant, showing ripe white peach, smoky honey, apricot, and nectarine. Technically dry, but so ripe and syrupy, it's almost a dessert in itself. **88** —*S.H. (6/1/2003)*

Arrowood 2002 Saralee's Vineyard Viognier (Russian River Valley) $30. Captured at its youthful best, this wine is all about fresh apples, peaches, mangos and apricots. Master winemaker Arrowood has lavished just enough oak to provide nuances of vanilla and smoke, but the theme always returns to fruit. The finish is amazingly long, rich, and sweet. **91** —*S.H. (6/1/2004)*

ARTESA

Artesa 2001 Elements Bordeaux Blend (Sonoma-Napa) $20. Thus is a rather rustic blend. It has lots of fruit and berry flavors, ripe and round, with firm acids and soft tannins. Easy to drink, and versatile with a wide range of food. **85** —*S.H. (5/1/2005)*

Artesa 2003 Cabernet Sauvignon (Napa-Sonoma) $25. Sits on the border of ordinary and fancy, and the right food could make the difference. Dry, rich, and fruity in berry-cherry and Asian spice flavors and smoky oak, this two-county Cab has a rough edge to the softness. Cries out for a salty, peppery grilled steak. **86** —*S.H. (12/31/2006)*

Artesa 2002 Cabernet Sauvignon (Napa-Sonoma) $25. Very ripe in fruit, brimming with cherries and currants, this wine is almost medicinal-sweet on the finish. It's also a little too soft. **83** —*S.H. (12/15/2005)*

Artesa 2002 Cabernet Sauvignon (Alexander Valley) $40. Marked by those soft Alexander Valley tannins that are so much gentler than Napa's, this Cab is a regional classic. It's a little tight now, but deliciously forward in cherry and cassis fruit, with overt oak influences. Good now with beef. **91** —*S.H. (7/1/2006)*

Artesa 1998 Cabernet Sauvignon (Napa Valley) $30. What a plush red wine this is. Soft tannins and acids support blackberry fruit that's laced with olives, green herbs, and tobacco. It's very dry, and the balance and harmony are exquisite. Lacks the stuffing for aging, but this is an elegant, white-tablecloth wine to enjoy in its youth. **92** —*S.H. (11/15/2002)*

Artesa 1997 Cabernet Sauvignon (Napa Valley) $33. Cassis and black currant aromas burst forth, almost swamped in oak, with it's toasty, cedary, smoky, clove-scented elements. Oak dominates the palate, too, and fairly aggressive tannins mask underlying blackberry fruit flavors. This is a cellar candidate, unless you really like young tannic wines. **89** —*S.H. (12/1/2001)*

Artesa 2003 Reserve Cabernet Sauvignon (Napa Valley) $40. Smells great, right up there with great Napa Cab, all toast and rich blackberry chocolate, but turns a little too sweet on the finish for balance. Too bad, because it's a real beauty, except for that sugary finale. **85** —*S.H. (12/31/2006)*

Artesa 1997 Reserve Cabernet Sauvignon (Napa Valley) $70. There are few wines on earth that smell better than this one. The finest smoky oak, the best blackberry and cassis fruit are irresistible. Beautiful flavors of berries, herbs, and spices impress with their depth, while the tannin structure is the best money can buy. The fault lies in the acids. The wine is as soft as a melting Dali watch. **90** —*S.H. (6/1/2002)*

Artesa 2002 Chardonnay (Napa Valley) $16. Nowhere near as rich or compelling as the reserve, but at less than half the price, a good deal. Plenty of rich fruit and spicy oak, in a creamy texture. **86** —*S.H. (8/1/2005)*

Artesa 2000 Chardonnay (Carneros) $23. Tight and lean, an austere wine marked by citrus and tobacco and a blast of tart acidity. Feels crisp and clean, almost like a Sauvignon Blanc, although oak and lees add rich, creamy notes. Still, this is a hard-edged Chard. **86** —*S.H. (2/1/2003)*

Artesa 1999 Chardonnay (Napa Valley) $23. Explosive leesy notes dominate the aromas and flavors, with plenty of charred oak, too. Under these winemaker bells and whistles is some ripe peach and apple fruit, and the finish is long, sweet, and spicy. Emphasizes sheer size over finesse. **87** —*S.H. (12/1/2001)*

Artesa 1999 Chardonnay (Carneros) $23. Classic Carneros Chard. Aromas of apples and peaches veering into tropical fruitlead to bright, well-etched fruity flavors in the mouth. Spices, too, and smoky vanilla from oak. Malolactic fermentation and lees aging create a round, creamy feel, and the finish is spicy and smooth. **89** —*S.H. (12/1/2001)*

Artesa 2004 Estate Chardonnay (Carneros) $30. This is a good, oaky Chardonnay for those who like their Chards bright in acidity and fruit. The flavors veer toward ripe pears, buttered toast, and sweet herbs, but have an earthy undercurrent. **86** —*S.H. (6/1/2006)*

Artesa 2002 Reserve Chardonnay (Carneros) $40. If you like plenty of delicious flavor in your Chards, try this beauty. It's big and fat with butterscotch and vanilla drizzled over baked pineapple pie, in a rich, creamy texture. The spicy finish makes you want another pour. **90** —*S.H. (8/1/2005)*

Artesa 1999 Reserve Chardonnay (Carneros) $30. There is a lot of new oak on this smooth wine, with smoky, vanilla, and clove elements. Lees aging also adds creamy, milky bells and whistles. Under all of that is some nice peach-flavored fruit. It drinks dry, with refreshing acidity. Overall, there's a lot of class and elegance here. **90** —*S.H. (12/1/2001)*

Artesa 1997 Reserve Chardonnay (Carneros) $30. **88** *(6/1/2000)*

Artesa 1999 Select Late Harvest Gewürztraminer (Russian River Valley) $28. Not quite as rich and viscous as one would expect from a dessert wine. It nonetheless serves up a fine blend of melon, peach, spice, ginger, and citrus notes. **87** —*J.M. (12/1/2002)*

Artesa 1998 Merlot (Napa Valley) $22. If you've made up your mind about the '98 vintage, you'll be surprised by this ripe, complex wine, which offers enormously beautiful palate impressions. It just proves how some wineries can succeed even when the vintage is questionable. Ripe blackberries stand alongside earthy mushroom flavors, and the dry, plush tannins are a treat. **91** —*S.H. (11/15/2002)*

Artesa 1997 Merlot (Napa Valley) $24. A few years of bottle age have mellowed this wine to silky smoothness. Has the prettiest bouquet of red cherries and smoke, with hints of bacon, thyme, mint, and white chocolate. Equally complex on the palate, with the most generous texture. Pure velvet. **91 Editors' Choice** —*S.H. (12/1/2001)*

Artesa 1997 Merlot (Sonoma Valley) $24. This bottling has a very different profile from the winery's Napa version. It's earthier with coffee and rhubarb flavors along with cassis and oak, and rougher around the edges. There's a lot of power here, with elongated tannins, and a somewhat edgy feel. **88** —*S.H. (12/1/2001)*

Artesa 1999 Reserve Merlot (Sonoma Valley) $60. Slightly herbal on the nose, with caramel and vanilla scents accenting cherries and tomatoes. On the palate, alcohol is evident, matched by strident oak. Finishes lean and tart. A good wine, but something of a disappointment. **86** *(5/1/2004)*

Artesa 1997 Reserve Merlot (Sonoma Valley) $60. This is the kind of wine only severe lot selection can achieve. The flavors are deep and impressive, ranging from cassis to chocolate. Oak provides smoke and spice. It has that brilliant, velvety texture you expect from wines of this caliber, but, like so many such bottlings, it lacks the acidity to provide backbone. **91** —*S.H. (7/1/2002)*

Artesa 2002 Pinot Noir (Carneros) $22. An immensely enjoyable Pinot for its smoky, vanilla-infused aromas and flavors of red cherries, mint, and mocha, and the delicate, silky mouthfeel. The finish is long and tart in cherry fruit. **88** *(11/1/2004)*

Artesa 2000 Pinot Noir (Santa Barbara County) $24. **82** *(10/1/2002)*

Artesa 2000 Pinot Noir (Russian River Valley) $24. High-toned sour cherry and cranberry fruit combine with earthy, woodsy, leathery accents in this juicy wine. It's complex and not at all heavy, showing bright fruit and smoky notes supported by tangy acidity. Ends long with dusty, powdery tannins and hints of orange. Drink now–2006. **89 Editor's Choice.** *(10/1/2002)*

Artesa 2000 Pinot Noir (Carneros) $24. Sometimes a smoky, charry wine is all about the oak, but in this case there's plenty of barrel, but also balance, acidity, and style. Unanimously, we enjoyed the toastiness of the wine as well as the leathery palate that's balanced by cherry, plum and sweet tobacco. **91 Editors' Choice** *(10/1/2002)*

Artesa 1999 Pinot Noir (Santa Barbara County) $24. Herb, earth, and spice aromas and flavors dominate, with suggestions of rhubarb, tomato, and tea, plus pepper and smoky, oaky notes. Fills the mouth with powerful berry and fruit flavors, but it's very dry, with enough tannic structure to provide size and weight. **89** —*S.H. (12/15/2001)*

Artesa 1999 Pinot Noir (Russian River Valley) $24. Jammy and fruity-sweet, it bursts with aromas of rasberries, cherries, strawberries, and a cool waft of refreshing mint. The flavors are also berry fresh and wrapped in soft, elegant tannins. Crisp acidity provides balance. This is a nice, all-purpose wine that will go with a wide range of foods. **88** —*S.H. (12/15/2001)*

Artesa 1999 Pinot Noir (Carneros) $24. An earthy style, with rich tannins and notes of mushroom, beet, and tea riding over black raspberry and

USA

stone-fruit flavors. This full-bodied wine packs a solid punch and ends on a tannic note. Cellar-worthy for mid-term aging. **87** —*S.H.* *(12/15/2001)*

Artesa 2004 Estate Pinot Noir (Carneros) $40. Kind of full-bodied and heavy for a Pinot, with flavors of baked cherry pie, rum-soaked currants, and French roast coffee. The tannins are fairly forward and stiff too. This is a young wine, and it may throw a little sediment and lighten up with a year or so in the bottle. **85** —*S.H. (6/1/2006)*

Artesa 2004 Reserve Pinot Noir (Carneros) $50. This Pinot defines a fruit-forward, direct style, but elevates it above the obvious into sheer decadence. Offers masses of cherry pie, cola, leather, licorice, and cinnamon spice flavors, wrapped into a creamy, smoky texture that feels powerful and silky at the same time. Delicious, but drink now. So much better than the regular '05. **91** —*S.H. (12/31/2006)*

Artesa 2002 Reserve Pinot Noir (Carneros) $40. Starts with simple, pleasant cola, cherry, and vanilla aromas, and turns richly spicy, with fruity flavors in a crisp, supple package. Very drinkable and tart in acids. **86** *(11/1/2004)*

Artesa 2000 Reserve Pinot Noir (Carneros) $38. Earth, smoked meat, cherry-berry fruit, and a hint of green comprise the nose, with cherry, leather and toasty oak carrying the palate. The finish brings plummy fruit, some black pepper, and a touch of caramel sweetness. **88** *(10/1/2002)*

Artesa 1999 Reserve Pinot Noir (Carneros) $40. There's some really lovely fruit under lots of new oak, with its charry, woodsy notes. The fruit tends toward black raspberries and red cherries, with spicy, tobacco notes, but it's not jammy. It's complex, layered. Dry, with dusty, silky tannins, it's delicious and elegant. **92** —*S.H. (12/15/2001)*

Artesa 2002 Reserve Sauvignon Blanc (Napa Valley) $20. Quite weighty, with a gold tint, enormous oak-based aromas, and heavy flavors that veer toward creamed corn, cantaloupe, and guava. Finishes with yet another monstrous blast of oak, and thus lingering notes of vanilla and buttered toast. Not a poor wine by any stretch, but too oaky for us to rate higher. **86** *(7/1/2005)*

Artesa 1999 Reserve Sauvignon Blanc (Napa Valley) $19. This is a wonderfully complex wine that marches to the beat of a different drum. It's got unusual but fragrant aromas of hyacinth and guava in addition to the standard citrus notes, and is rich and creamy in the mouth. The flavors are citrusy, nutty, and bone-dry. It's pretty much as fancy as Sauvignon Blanc gets in California. **90** —*S.H. (11/15/2001)*

Artesa 2001 Syrah (Sonoma Valley) $16. Features a generous overlay of caramel and vanilla atop tart berry flavors. Plenty of herb and spice nuances, ending on a cranberry note. Seems a tad underripe by California standards. **84** *(9/1/2005)*

Artesa 1999 Syrah (Sonoma Valley) $28. The deep fruit and leather aromas of this silky wine are offset by stylish herb, earth, and mineral notes. Smooth as it is, it has body and a chewy feel on the palate, as well as a long licorice and roasted fruit finish. Admirably, it manages to be at once straightforward yet intense and complex. **90** *(11/1/2001)*

Artesa 2003 Tempranillo (Alexander Valley) $24. Midway between Cabernet and Zinfandel in flavor, this dry, soft, spicy-peppery wine has blackberry and pomegranate flavors and firm tannins. It should improve for a few years, then begin a long, slow decline. **87** —*S.H. (4/1/2006)*

ARTEVINO

Artevino 2001 Zinfandel (North Coast) $22. A sweet style, with spicy plum, black cherry, spice, and herb flavors. Tangy cinnamon and cedar notes are prominent on the finish. **84** *(11/1/2003)*

ARTEZIN

Artezin 2004 Zinfandel (Mendocino-Sonoma-Amador) $15. Nice everyday Zin, a little simple, but likeable for its wealth of blueberry, cherry, mocha, and Asian spice flavors. Finishes basically dry, with honeyed cherry pie filling. **84** —*S.H. (12/15/2006)*

Artezin 2003 Zinfandel (Mendocino-Amador-Napa) $15. This is a new brand from Hess, and a very good wine. The winemaker calls it a field blend, meaning it may or may not be Zinfandel. It doesn't taste entirely like Zin. There are blueberries and cherries in there along with the brambly, peppery stuff. The wine is claret-style, meaning it's balanced and harmonious despite 15.5% alcohol. **90 Best Buy** —*S.H. (12/15/2005)*

ASH HOLLOW

Ash Hollow 2002 Estate Blend Bordeaux Blend (Walla Walla (WA)) $30. The vineyard was wiped clean in the freeze of '04, but this fragrant, chocolatey wine suggests that it holds real potential if it can be adequately protected. Crisp cranberry and strawberry fruits are underscored with smooth, chocolatey oak flavors. The style is Walla Walla all the way; broadly accessible, smooth, and seamless. **88** —*P.G. (4/1/2005)*

Ash Hollow 2003 Cabernet Sauvignon (Walla Walla (WA)) $28. Light fruit showing simple cherry, strawberry, and watermelon flavors. The young fruit carries a hint of fresh herb. Balanced and well made. **86** —*P.G. (4/1/2006)*

Ash Hollow 2003 Merlot (Walla Walla (WA)) $24. Light and herbal, with suggestions of black cherry and a hint of gunmetal or iron ore. It falls away quickly into rather pale fruit flavors. **86** —*P.G. (4/1/2006)*

Ash Hollow 2003 Terassa Red Blend (Walla Walla (WA)) $36. The new release is a blend of one-third each Cab, Merlot, and Malbec. It carries lots of vanilla syrup and some sweet, candied cherry fruit, along with barrel flavors of espresso, caramel, and maple syrup. **87** —*P.G. (4/1/2006)*

Ash Hollow 2003 Somanna White Blend (Columbia Valley (WA)) $20. From a new Walla Walla winery comes this ripe, peachy blend of Sauvignon Blanc and Pinot Gris. The young vines delivered full, lush, forward fruit flavors, and there is some toasted cracker in the back end. A good sipping wine for easy, near term enjoyment. **87** —*P.G. (4/1/2005)*

ASHLAND VINEYARDS

Ashland Vineyards 1999 Chardonnay (Rogue Valley) $8. Barrel fermented. Scents of new wood dominate; the juice is very tart, the oak not yet well-integrated. **83** —*P.G. (8/1/2002)*

Ashland Vineyards 1999 Pinot Gris (Rogue Valley) $10. It is too bad that the winery seems to have overloaded this wine with sulfites; it's pleasant enough otherwise, and sells for less than most Oregon Pinot Gris. But the scent and taste of burnt match gives a bitter edge to the fruit, and buries the nose. **83** —*P.G. (2/1/2002)*

ASTRALE E TERRA

Astrale e Terra 2001 Arcturus Cabernet Blend (Napa Valley) $39. What a nice '01 this is. It exemplifies the ripe style, rich in black currants and cassis, and the smooth, sweet tannins of this great Napa vintage. Finishes with an edge of cocoa, anise, and oak. Drink now or over the next several years. **91** —*S.H. (10/1/2005)*

ATALON

Atalon 2002 Beckstoffer Tokalon Vineyard Cabernet Blend (Oakville) $NA. Young, dark, and smells hard and unyielding. Oak, black stone fruits and berries. Very extracted, jammy, and acidic. Sweet in fruit and oak. Somewhat astringent. Needs time, or extensive decanting. **91** —*S.H. (6/1/2005)*

Atalon 1998 Beckstoffer Vineyard Cabernet Blend (Oakville) $NA. Not half the wine of the remarkable '97. Smells oaky and of black cherries. Taste of dried herbs, cherries, coffee. Dry, with a chunky, chewy mouthfeel and unresolved, awkward tannins. Shows some elegance and finesse. Probably best now-2008. **87** —*S.H. (6/1/2005)*

Atalon 1997 Beckstoffer Vineyard Cabernet Blend (Oakville) $NA. Lovely cherry and herb aromas, a faint perfume of prunes and raisins, but not out of balance. Drinks very sweet in cherry and mocha fruit. Perfect now, soft, gentle, supple, complex. Lovely cassis finish, dry, pure. **92** —*S.H. (6/1/2005)*

Atalon 2000 Cabernet Sauvignon (Napa Valley) $35. Here's a rich wine that just drips with ripe Cabernet flavors. Black currants, cherries, dried herbs, and unsweetened chocolate are enriched with spicy, smoky notes from oak. This wine is fully dry and very balanced, and the rather rough tannins suggest a well-marbled steak. From Jess Jackson. **90** —*S.H. (12/31/2003)*

USA

Atalon 1999 Beckstoffer Cabernet Sauvignon (Oakville) $90. 91 (8/1/2003)

Atalon 1999 Beckstoffer Tokalon Vineyard Cabernet Sauvignon (Napa Valley) $NA. Rich, dusty cocoa, black currant, cherry aromas. Very rich, ripe, pure. Fabulously soft and smooth in the mouth, complex. Rich, sweet tannins. Dry and rich, with a very long, satisfying finish. Now-2020. **94 Cellar Selection** —S.H. (6/1/2005)

Atalon 1997 Mountain Estates Merlot (Napa Valley) $60. Firm, ripe tannic structure provides a nice framework for this classy wine. Blackberry, cassis, herb, tobacco, and chocolate are also at the fore. From mountainside vineyards, its angular yet powdery tannins should soften within a year or two. **92** —J.M. (11/15/2001)

ATELIER

Atelier 2003 Syrah (Alexander Valley) $28. There are lovely aromas in this wine. The scents of ripe blackberries, freshly ground French roast, cocoa dustings, and white pepper are so inviting. But the wine is way too soft. It has nice flavors, but is flat in the mouth. **83** —S.H. (12/1/2005)

ATLAS PEAK

Atlas Peak 2003 Claret Cabernet Blend (Atlas Peak) $86. Atlas Peak, now under the ownership of Beam Wine Estates, is reinventing itself. This new wine, by veteran winemaker Darren Procsal, shows promise. It's a big, dry Cab, not as astringent as in the past but still tannic enough to demand cellaring. Should be better between 2009 and 2015, but it's a gamble. **87** —S.H. (12/15/2006)

Atlas Peak 2003 Cabernet Sauvignon (Howell Mountain) $86. Immensely ripe, just explosive in young Cabernet flavors, and wrapped in those Howell tannins that require extensive cellaring. The wine, nearly 100% Cab, is totally dry and very oaky, from 100% new, small French barrels. But it's easily big enough in black currant, cherry, and cocoa flavors to handle all that wood. Drinkable now, after decanting, with rich, fatty meats, and through 2020. **92 Cellar Selection** —S.H. (12/15/2006)

Atlas Peak 2003 Cabernet Sauvignon (Mount Veeder) $86. There aren't lots of Cabs coming off this mountain but it's a pretty good guarantee of quality. This is a tannic young wine, rather dry and astringent now, but it has a huge core of molten cherry and blackberry fruit, with enough balance for the long haul. Hold until 2009, then drink for the next six years or so. **90 Cellar Selection** —S.H. (12/15/2006)

Atlas Peak 2003 Cabernet Sauvignon (Napa Valley) $42. Atlas Peak Cabernets have always seemed overly tannic, and so is this wine. But it's fruitier and riper than in the past, and may develop. It's tough and astringent, but packs a whallop with black currant flavors. Try after 2008. **86** —S.H. (11/15/2006)

Atlas Peak 2003 Cabernet Sauvignon (Spring Mountain) $86. Here's a tough, young, tannic wine, not drinkable now, but it shows promise. Those pesky tannins lock down the blackberry flavors, making the wine taste even drier than it is. Try after 2009. **87** —S.H. (12/15/2006)

Atlas Peak 2002 Cabernet Sauvignon (Napa Valley) $38. Atlas Peak is in an intense period of transition, and this is easily their best Cabernet ever. It shows its mountain origins in the tight structure and firm tannins, but they've learned how to push the fruit out, and it's a powerhouse of black currants and cherries. This is a wine to watch carefully. **91** —S.H. (5/1/2006)

Atlas Peak 1997 Consenso Cabernet Sauvignon (Atlas Peak) $30. This wine must be one of the last '97s to be released. It opens with herbal aromas verging on vegetal, and drinks simple and tannic, with cranberry, dill and coffee flavors. A very great disappointment. **84** —S.H. (6/1/2003)

Atlas Peak 1996 Consenso Vineyard Cabernet Sauvignon (Napa Valley) $30. 84 —S.H. (2/1/2000)

Atlas Peak 1998 Chardonnay (Atlas Peak) $16. 88 (6/1/2000)

Atlas Peak 2001 Chardonnay (Atlas Peak) $16. An interesting wine with tight acids and tannins and compressed fruit, the result of austere mountain growing conditions. Flavors range from lemons to green apples, but the overlay of oak is strong, with a powerful toasty note. **87** —S.H. (6/1/2003)

Atlas Peak 1999 Chardonnay (Atlas Peak) $16. Here's another good Chard from a vintage that produced a lot of them. It's ripe and aromatic, with a depth of peach-apple fruit, spices, and smoky oak. A hint of lees and a creamy texture add complexity. **87** —S.H. (5/1/2001)

Atlas Peak 2000 Atlas Peak Chardonnay (Atlas Peak) $16. From high above Napa Valley, a curiously lean wine. Except for a massive dose of oak that contributes sweet vanilla and smoke, it's tight to the point of austerity. What flavors there are veer toward lemon and apples. A leesy flavor shows up in the tart, dry finish. **86** —S.H. (12/31/2001)

Atlas Peak 2001 Sangiovese (Atlas Peak) $16. Here's a very dry red wine that will strike fruit lovers as lean and herbal, although there are some cherry flavors, as well as brisk tannins. Pretty ordinary stuff. **84** —S.H. (10/1/2005)

Atlas Peak 2000 Sangiovese (Atlas Peak) $16. This winery's workhorse red is bone-dry and tart, with puckery acids and sticky tannins that demand olive oil, butter or cheese. The flavors are lean and herbal. **86** —S.H. (2/1/2003)

Atlas Peak 1999 Sangiovese (Atlas Peak) $16. This winery continues to make major strides. Of course, in such a ripe year, the fruit is lovely, bringing forth all sorts of berries, coffee, earth, and spice. Supporting all of those sweet flavors are a soft voluptuous texture and near-perfect tannins. This is the best regular Sangiovese ever from Atlas Peak. **90** —S.H. (12/15/2001)

Atlas Peak 1999 Sangiovese (Napa Valley) $16. Starts with the prettiest black cherry and smoke aromas, mingled with vanilla and spice notes, like a warm fruit tart. Long, sweetly fruity flavors of black cherries and spices are wrapped in soft tannins and adequate acidity. Not complex, but delicious, nevertheless. **87** —S.H. (11/15/2001)

Atlas Peak 1997 Sangiovese (Atlas Peak) $16. A juicy, delicious wine; the best Atlas Peak Sangiovese so far. It's got pronounced berry-fruit flavors, with a peppery, spicy component and a rich earthiness. Soft and round, it's easy to drink, and while not especially complex, offers plenty of pleasure. Finishes with just a slight hit of tannins. **87** —S.H. (5/1/2001)

Atlas Peak 2000 Reserve Sangiovese (Atlas Peak) $30. Nobody in California has worked harder than Atlas Peak to get Sangiovese right. This vintage doesn't make it any easier. Aromas of tobacco, mushrooms, cardboard, and a hint of berry jam. In the mouth the wine is soft and gentle, with a tannic bite in the finish. **87** —S.H. (9/1/2003)

Atlas Peak 1997 Reserve Sangiovese (Napa Valley) $24. 92 (11/15/1999)

AU BON CLIMAT

Au Bon Climat 1997 Alban Vineyard Chardonnay (Edna Valley) $35. 92 —S.H. (10/1/1999)

Au Bon Climat 1997 Bien Nacido Les Nuits Blanches Chardonnay (Santa Maria Valley) $40. 92 —S.H. (10/1/1999)

Au Bon Climat 1997 Le Bouge D'a Côte Chardonnay (Santa Maria Valley) $25. 90 —S.H. (10/1/1999)

Au Bon Climat 1999 Mt. Carmel Vineyard Chardonnay (Santa Ynez Valley) $40. Some panelists praised this Chardonnay's balance and zingy citrus flavors; others were put off by its potent, even overwhelming, oak, and green woody aspects. It's full-bodied, and there are pleasant pear, lime, and butterscotch notes fighting for space on the palate. Give it a year or two and judge for yourself. **86** (7/1/2001)

Au Bon Climat 1999 Sanford & Benedict Chardonnay (Santa Ynez Valley) $35. Respected vineyard source and established record of the winemaker notwithstanding, the dense gunpowder/matchstick quality here isn't easy to take—or even read. It is stylized, and big (we can sense suppressed tropical fruit and earthy, mineral notes below the veneer). Hidden treasure...or just rough stuff? **86** (7/1/2001)

Au Bon Climat 1997 Sanford & Benedict Reserve Chardonnay (Santa Ynez Valley) $35. 91 —S.H. (10/1/1999)

Au Bon Climat 1995 Sanford & Benedict Vineyard Reserve Chardonnay (Santa Ynez Valley) $NA. Lovely, fresh, clean, with pure apricot, honey, sweet-sour pineapple, caramel, smoke, vanilla aromas. Fresh and creamy, fruity, oaky. Notable for bright acidity. Finishes complex and spicy. **91** — *S.H. (6/1/2005)*

Au Bon Climat 1997 Talley Reserve Chardonnay (Arroyo Grande Valley) $25. 90 —*S.H. (10/1/1999)*

Au Bon Climat 1998 Talley Vineyard "Rincon" Chardonnay (Arroyo Grande Valley) $25. 89 *(6/1/2000)*

Au Bon Climat 1988 (Benedict Vineyard) Pinot Noir (Santa Ynez Valley) $NA. Old Pinot aroma, a little stale, with raspberry candy and smoky, vanilla oak. In the mouth, rather too old, dry and brittle, with the fruit fading and a hint of vinegar. Praiseworthy but past its prime. **86** —*S.H. (6/1/2005)*

Au Bon Climat 1999 Knox Alexander Pinot Noir (Santa Maria Valley) $45. A gorgeously plush Pinot, redolent of bright cherry, strawberry, plum, cinnamon, and herbs. Explosively fragrant, it's rich and lively on the palate, where it finishes long and lush. A real winner from this Central Coast specialist in Pinot Noir. **93** —*J.M. (7/1/2002)*

Au Bon Climat 1998 Knox Alexander Pinot Noir (Santa Maria Valley) $45. With the extra heavy bottle and the wax seal, this is an ABC signature wine, and worthy of it. It's reminiscent of a fine Vosne-Romanée in its extreme youth. Light in color and even in body, its nevertheless got the stuffing of legend. Black cherries come to mind; plum, tobacco, chocolate, and spice, too. At the core, there's solid extract. The finish is long and spicy. This wonderfully expressive wine is for the cellar. **94** *(12/31/2001)*

Au Bon Climat 1997 Rosemary's-Talley Vineyard Pinot Noir (Arroyo Grande Valley) $50. 93 *(10/1/1999)*

Au Bon Climat 2002 Sanford & Benedict Vineyard Pinot Noir (Santa Ynez Valley) $35. Still rather young and aggressive in tannins and acids, with pronounced cherry, pomegranate, coffee, and spice flavors, as well as an overlay of toasty oak. Very dry, with good structure. Not a blockbuster, but elegant and charming. Best 2005–2008. **89** —*S.H. (6/1/2005)*

Au Bon Climat 2001 Sanford & Benedict Vineyard Pinot Noir (Santa Ynez Valley) $NA. A bunker buster of a wine. Massive cherry fruit, flavored with cinnamon, rich cola, cocoa, and toasty oak. Explodes on the palate. Yet gaining age: softly expressive, gently complex, a wine of opposites. Delicate and authoritative. Sensual. At its peak now and for the next 3 years. **95 Editors' Choice** —*S.H. (6/1/2005)*

Au Bon Climat 2000 Sanford & Benedict Vineyard Pinot Noir (Santa Ynez Valley) $NA. Alcohol: 13.5%. Fairly pale. Smells young, fresh, clean, piquant in Pinot aroma. Cherries, sweet beet, toast, sweet oriental spice, gingerbread. Acids, tannins, and oak upfront now, or is the fruit thin? Delicately structured, silky. **89** —*S.H. (6/1/2005)*

Au Bon Climat 1997 Sanford & Benedict Vineyard Pinot Noir (Santa Ynez Valley) $35. 90 —*S.H. (10/1/1999)*

Au Bon Climat 1996 Sanford & Benedict Vineyard Pinot Noir (Santa Ynez Valley) $NA. Alcohol only 13.0%. Pale, ruby-orange color. Succulent in sweet char, vanilla, cherry-raspberry meringue, nutmeggy spice, smoke. Filled with life and zest due to crisp acidity and fresh flavors. Cherries, pomegranates, sweet herbal tea. Dry, balanced, elegant. A bit sharp in the finish, though. **89** —*S.H. (6/1/2005)*

Au Bon Climat 1994 Sanford & Benedict Vineyard Pinot Noir (Santa Ynez Valley) $NA. Turning pale. Exquisitely expressive bouquet: rose petal and orange blossom potpourri, raspberry nougat, vanilla. Soft, gentle, old pinot wine, with tangerine tea, raspberry tea, oak flavors, sweet and refined. Very dry. Going down, though, so drink up. **93** —*S.H. (6/1/2005)*

AUDELSSA

Audelssa 2001 Mountain Terraces Cabernet Sauvignon (Sonoma Valley) $33. Made by the legendary Richard Arrowood, a very fine Cab. Rich and complex in black currants and oak, it shows sturdy tannins that are perfectly drinkable now, but will enable this wine to age well through the decade. **92** —*S.H. (3/1/2005)*

AUDELSSA SONOMA

Audelssa Sonoma 2000 Mountain Terraces Cabernet Sauvignon (Sonoma Valley) $27. Very tough and austere, a young wine buried under layers of oak and powerful tannins. Doesn't provide a great deal of pleasure now, but there is a powerful core of black cherry fruit that hits midpalate and kicks in on the finish. Seems to be an ager. **89** —*S.H. (11/15/2004)*

Audelssa Sonoma 2002 Mountain Terraces Syrah (Sonoma Valley) $32. What happened? This winery, which has impressed with its first few releases, seems to have stumbled here. Despite a decent alcohol number (14.5%), the wine tastes underripe and thin, dominated by green, leafy and bell pepper flavors. **80** *(9/1/2005)*

Audelssa Sonoma 2001 Mountain Terraces Syrah (Sonoma Valley) $32. Here's an interesting and unique Syrah. There's something roasted about it, in the scent and slightly bitter flavor of French roast coffee and in the charry taste of a grilled steak, although the anchor taste is of blackberries. It's totally dry, sturdy in tannins and possesses an ineffable quality of class. **91** —*S.H. (12/1/2004)*

AUDUBON CELLARS

Audubon Cellars 1997 Graeser Vineyards Cabernet Sauvignon (Napa Valley) $18. 88 —*S.H. (9/1/2000)*

Audubon Cellars 1998 Sangiacomo Vineyard Chardonnay (Carneros) $13. The underlying grape flavors are a little thin, suggesting peaches, but there's a ton of winemaker bells and whistles. French oak yields smoky, spicy, vanilla notes, while lees aging gives a creamy flavor and mouthfeel. **84** —*S.H. (11/15/2001)*

Audubon Cellars 1997 Sangiacomo Vineyard Chardonnay (Sonoma) $15. 84 *(6/1/2000)*

Audubon Cellars 1999 Juliana Vineyard Sauvignon Blanc (Napa Valley) $12. 86 —*S.H. (11/15/2000)*

Audubon Cellars 2000 Juliana Vineyards Sauvignon Blanc (Napa Valley) $12. From the warmer Pope Valley, a ripe, limpid wine brimming with melon, and citrus-peach flavors. It's soft, while a bit of lees aging provides tartness and creaminess. **83** —*S.H. (11/15/2001)*

Audubon Cellars 1997 Juliana Vineyards Sauvignon Blanc (Napa Valley) $9. 83 —*S.H. (9/1/1999)*

Audubon Cellars 1997 Picnic Hill Vineyard Late Harvest Zinfandel (Amador County) $14. 82 —*S.H. (12/31/2000)*

AUGUST BRIGGS

August Briggs 1997 Cabernet Sauvignon (Sonoma Mountain) $50. 89 *(11/1/2000)*

August Briggs 1997 Cabernet Sauvignon (Napa Valley) $50. 91 *(11/1/2000)*

August Briggs 2001 Petite Sirah (Lake County) $32. Quite dark in color, with a dark-edged flavor profile as well. Charry, smoky qualities frame black plum and cherry notes that give way to herb and spice flavors. Bright on the finish, with an herbal, slighty astringent edge at the end. **87** —*J.M. (9/1/2004)*

August Briggs 2002 Pinot Noir (Russian River Valley) $32. Shows textbook Russian River notes of cherries and sweet cola, with a silky texture and good acids. Feels a little rough around the edges, with a candied finish. Toasty oak completes the picture. **85** —*S.H. (8/1/2005)*

August Briggs 2000 Pinot Noir (Russian River Valley) $32. Supple and plump, this Pinot announces itself with a nuanced red berry, cinnamon-clove spice, soy, and tree-bark bouquet. The palate's velvety feel, subtle acidity and caramel-tinged sweet fruit have great appeal. Closes stylishly with a ripe and spicy, almost sappy-feeling, softly tannic finish. Drink now through 2006. **90** *(10/1/2002)*

August Briggs 1997 Pinot Noir (Russian River Valley) $28. 90 *(10/1/1999)*

August Briggs 2002 Dijon Clones Pinot Noir (Napa Valley) $35. What a great wine. Dry, smooth, and complex, with a silky texture and nice, firm acids, as well as an opulent layer of what tastes like fine French oak. The flavors are fully ripe, suggesting black and red cherries with a dusting of sweet cocoa. **91** —*S.H. (8/1/2005)*

August Briggs 2000 Dijon Clones Pinot Noir (Napa Valley) $35. Mature, earthy meat, leather, tobacco, mocha, and stewed fruit aromas open this controversial wine. All tasters found the cherry and sour herb flavors tasty, but some found the sharp high-acid mouthfeel unpleasant, while others thought it smooth, soft and velvety. Go figure. Drink now–2005. **87** (10/1/2002)

August Briggs 2002 Zinfandel (Napa Valley) $32. Does a great job of offering ripe, forward blackberry, black cherry, briary wild berry and peppery spice flavors upfront, with firm tannins, in a wine that's totally dry and not over the top in alcohol. You'll find Zin's muscular wild personality dressed in the Armani of Napa. **90** —S.H. (8/1/2005)

August Briggs 2001 Zinfandel (Napa Valley) $32. A fairly complex blend of toasty oak-framed black cherry, blackberry, bing cherry, spice, herb, and vanilla flavors framed in firm, supple tannins. The finish is moderate in length. **89** (11/1/2003)

AUGUST WEST

August West 2003 Rosella's Vineyard Pinot Noir (Santa Lucia Highlands) $42. What a fabulous wine. So rich and forward in black cherry, cocoa, leather, and spice flavors, yet subtle and complex. Despite a powerful start it reveals itself slowly, spreading layers of fruit, spice, and oak across the palate. The texture is wonderfully silky, backed up with lively acids. Wonderful now, but with the stuffing to develop additional complexities through the decade. **93 Cellar Selection** —S.H. (8/1/2005)

AURIGA

Auriga 2003 Max Vineyard Syrah (El Dorado County) $18. Shows firm tannins underlying a rustic structure, with lush, forward cherry, blackberry, blueberry, and cocoa fruit flavors. The finish is dry and balanced in this easy-to-like Syrah. **85** —S.H. (4/1/2006)

Auriga 2004 Zinfandel (El Dorado) $17. Rough and ready Zin, with chocolate, cherry, and blueberry flavors that are extracted and jammy. The wine is soft and dry, and so super-rich in ripe fruit it's almost sweet. **84** —S.H. (4/1/2006)

AUSTIN HOPE

Austin Hope 2003 Mer Soleil Vineyard Roussanne (Santa Lucia Highlands) $37. Terrific wine, rich as sin, oozing honey, apricot, lemondrop, and exotic quince and pineapple flavors. Yet great cleansing acidity gives it backbone. Finishes with a caramelized richness. **92** —S.H. (11/15/2006)

Austin Hope 2003 Hope Family Vineyard Syrah (Paso Robles) $42. The challenges during this hot vintage were obvious. The wine is virtually sweet in dessert pastry flavors, raspberry, fig newton, black cherry pie, and smoky, charry new oak and vanilla. It has good acidity and grip, but you find yourself wishing it were a touch drier. **86** —S.H. (11/15/2006)

AUSTIN ROBAIRE

Austin Robaire 2000 Cabernet Sauvignon (Columbia Valley (WA)) $55. A dark, firm, rich wine, with plenty of fat, meaty, oaky power. This has decent, medium-bodied fruit, and plenty of well-managed oak. But it is a bit one dimensional, without extra depth. **88** —P.G. (9/1/2003)

Austin Robaire 2001 Elerding Vineyard Reserve Cabernet Sauvignon (Columbia Valley (WA)) $115. Smells rich and jammy—loaded with cassis and vanilla. In the mouth, there's more of the same, plus added notes of coffee and blackberry allied to a creamy, supple texture. Would rate even higher if not for the relatively short, tart finish. **90** —J.C. (6/6/2005)

Austin Robaire 2002 Klipsun Vineyard Cabernet Sauvignon (Red Mountain) $55. Though Klipsun is widely regarded as an iconic vineyard for Washington, this wine smells more of raisins and prunes than of fresh, ripe grapes. The flavors are broad, baked, and pruny; yet the tannins remain a bit green and chalky. The wine doesn't knit together and seems unlikely to do so in the future. **85** —P.G. (6/1/2005)

Austin Robaire 2002 Le Petit Garçon Cabernet Sauvignon (Columbia Valley (WA)) $18. Pleasant black cherry flavors on entry, then the wine turns a bit light and tart, the fruit overshadowed by the rough tannins. **86** —P.G. (6/1/2005)

Austin Robaire 2001 Ward Family Vineyard Pinot Noir (Washington) $26. Quite light but sweetly pretty, showing some candy cherry fruit. The tannins are soft and the wine is simple and pleasant, but insubstantial. **84** —P.G. (9/1/2003)

Austin Robaire 2001 Elerding Vineyard Reserve Syrah (Columbia Valley (WA)) $85. Rather oaky, with scents of cedar and vanilla dominating the fruit. Don't get us wrong—it's good oak—it's just unintegrated and unclear if it will age into complete harmony. There is some dense blackberry fruit underneath, so maybe this will improve with further aging. **86** (9/1/2005)

Austin Robaire 2002 La Petite Fille Syrah (Columbia Valley (WA)) $18. Sweet cracker and strawberry jam are the main notes struck here, with a whiff of leather. The leather and barnyard flavors seem to gather strength, along with smoke and licorice. Some tasters will find this wine too rustic; others will love it. **85** —P.G. (6/1/2005)

Austin Robaire 2001 Charmaine Angela White Blend (Columbia Valley (WA)) $26. Already a deep gold, with hints of brown and oxidative scents of hay and honey. The mix is 55% Roussanne, 10% Viognier and 35% Chardonnay. **85** —P.G. (9/1/2003)

AUTUMN HILL

Autumn Hill 1997 Cabernet Sauvignon (Monticello) $16. **85** —J.C. (8/1/1999)

AVALON

Avalon 2003 Cabernet Sauvignon (Napa Valley) $13. A pretty good value. It's rich, ripe, dry, and balanced, with blackberry, cherry, and mocha flavors that finish with a spicy, oaky taste. **85** —S.H. (12/31/2005)

AVENUE

Avenue 2003 Cabernet Sauvignon (California) $11. Rough-and-ready Cab, with earthy, coffee-berry flavors that turn fruity and tannic on the finish. **83** —S.H. (5/1/2005)

Avenue 2003 Chardonnay (California) $11. Watery and heavy in super-oaked flavors. **82** —S.H. (5/1/2005)

Avenue 2003 Merlot (California) $11. Fruity and rustic, dry and balanced, with chocolate-cherry flavors and a good finish. **84** —S.H. (5/1/2005)

Avenue 2002 Zinfandel (California) $11. Raw and leathery, with raisin and coffee flavors, and dry. Should wake up with olive oil, cheese, and rich meats. **83** —S.H. (5/1/2005)

AVERY LANE

Avery Lane 2001 Cabernet Sauvignon (Columbia Valley (WA)) $8. Nicely styled, light, and crisply tannic. This has clean currant/plum fruit, firm tannins and good definition. **87 Best Buy** —P.G. (12/31/2003)

Avery Lane 2002 Chardonnay (Washington) $8. Simple and soft, with broad, artificial flavors suggesting microwave popcorn. **82** —P.G. (7/1/2004)

Avery Lane 2001 Chardonnay (Columbia Valley (WA)) $8. Simple, soft Chardonnay, hinting at peaches and apples, with just a touch of toast and sweetness on the finish. **85 Best Buy** —P.G. (12/31/2003)

Avery Lane 2003 Gewürztraminer (Washington) $7. Soft and oily, it's sweetly laced with scents of soap and talcum powder. It hits the palate like bubble bath hits a hot tub and tastes just as it smells. **85** —P.G. (7/1/2004)

Avery Lane 2002 Gewürztraminer (Columbia Valley (WA)) $7. A very nice, spicy, fruity style of Gewürz, with the emphasis on sweet lychee and floral spice. Sugars and acids in good balance. Serve well chilled. **87 Best Buy** —P.G. (12/31/2003)

Avery Lane 2002 Johannisberg Riesling (Columbia Valley (WA)) $7. A sweet, pretty style of Washington Riesling, this is succulent with ripe apples and honeysuckle. The sugar is offset with good, crisp acid. **88 Best Buy** —P.G. (12/31/2003)

Avery Lane 2001 Merlot (Columbia Valley (WA)) $8. A bit more substance than one expects in Merlot in this price range, counterbalanced with some hard, rubbery, reduced flavors. Try giving it some extra air time—it works well as a burger wine. **85 Best Buy** —P.G. (12/31/2003)

Avery Lane NV Red Blend (Columbia Valley (WA)) $8. The blend here is 60% Merlot, 25% Cabernet, 10% Syrah, and 5% Cab Franc. Bigger, more vivid fruit flavors than either the Cab or the Merlot, this négociant blend offers solid, clean, berry-driven fruit flavors backed with firm tannins and characteristic Washington acids. **87 Best Buy** —*P.G. (12/31/2003)*

Avery Lane 2002 Sauvignon Blanc (Washington) $7. Pungent with pine resin and pineapple scents. Sharp, aggressive, and herbal, with a bit of vitamin-pill flavor on the finish. **85** —*P.G. (7/1/2004)*

Avery Lane 2001 Sauvignon Blanc (Columbia Valley (WA)) $7. This is a light, pleasant, melony style, with a bit of citrus and lemon zest adding a hint of spice. A good all-purpose seafood white. **85 Best Buy** —*P.G. (12/31/2003)*

Avery Lane 2001 Syrah (Washington) $8. There is a bitter start to this light, innocuous, generic red wine. Some hints of graham cracker in the midpalate, and a finish that is both tarry and tannic. **82** —*P.G. (7/1/2004)*

AVILA

Avila 2004 Cabernet Sauvignon (Santa Barbara County) $13. The grapes just barely ripened, with the result that this Cab has green, minty flavors along with the berries. It's dry and acidic. **82** —*S.H. (3/1/2006)*

Avila 2003 Cabernet Sauvignon (Santa Barbara County) $14. Lots of ripe blackberry and dark chocolate flavors, in a dry wine with sharp acids and an edgy texture. Decent everyday fare. **83** —*S.H. (10/1/2005)*

Avila 2002 Cabernet Sauvignon (Santa Barbara County) $11. On the overly sweet side, and soft to the point of flaccid. The fruit's ripe in cherries and black raspberries. **83** —*S.H. (2/1/2005)*

Avila 2001 Cabernet Sauvignon (Santa Barbara County) $13. Dark and dry, a full-bodied wine with currant and oak flavors and a soft, creamy smooth texture. Not especially concentrated, but has a certain fanciness. **85** —*S.H. (2/1/2004)*

Avila 2000 Cabernet Sauvignon (Santa Barbara County) $12. This ripe Cabernet is a textbook example of the varietal in California. It oozes rich flavors of blackberries and cassis and sweet green olives, and is framed in oak. It's soft and velvety in the mouth. **88 Best Buy** —*S.H. (11/15/2002)*

Avila 2004 Chardonnay (Santa Barbara County) $13. This is a country-style Chard, a bit rough around the edges, with very ripe tropical fruit and apricot flavors, good acidity, and an overtly oaky taste. **83** —*S.H. (3/1/2006)*

Avila 2003 Chardonnay (San Luis Obispo County) $11. Lots to like in this affordable Chard, with its bright flavors of tropical fruits and apricots and brisk acidity. Finishes smooth and a little sweet. **84** —*S.H. (2/1/2005)*

Avila 2000 Chardonnay (San Luis Obispo County) $12. Avila is a new line from Laetitia and Barnwood wineries, and one that fills the important niche of affordable varietal wines. This lean Chard brims with bright flavors of lemons and grapefruits, but an overlay of oak adds richness. Intense acidity makes the wine's finish clean and zesty. **85** —*S.H. (12/15/2002)*

Avila 2002 Merlot (Santa Barbara County) $11. A bit too sweet, with cough medicincy cherry flavors. Smooth and soft in the mouth. **82** — *S.H. (2/1/2005)*

Avila 2001 Merlot (Santa Barbara County) $13. Tough, herbal, and weedy, a dryly tannic wine with modest flavors of cherries that offers little pleasure now. **83** —*S.H. (4/1/2004)*

Avila 2000 Merlot (Santa Barbara County) $12. An interesting wine that belies its price. Rich blackberry flavors ride side-by-side with earthy, herbal notes of dark coffee and tobacco. A good percentage of new French oak shows up, especially in the vanilla and toast accents of the aroma. This full-bodied, bone-dry wine has a lot of richness. **89** —*S.H. (11/15/2002)*

Avila 2003 Pinot Noir (San Luis Obispo County) $11. Starts off a little rough and raw, with some dry, chewy tannins, but when the ripe cherry and roasted coffee flavors hit mid-palate, it turns pretty. The fruit really kicks in on the finish. **85** —*S.H. (12/15/2004)*

Avila 2002 Pinot Noir (San Luis Obispo County) $13. A real charmer, this easy-drinking Pinot has lots to like. The cherry, tobacco and pepper flavors are very dry, and wrapped in silky tannins. Turns a bit harsh on the finish. **86** —*S.H. (4/1/2004)*

Avila 2001 Pinot Noir (San Luis Obispo County) $10. A second label from the folks at Laetitia Winery, which grows about 200 acres of Chardonnay and Pinot Noir grapes in the Central Coast. It's graceful, light in body, and serves up a pleasing blend of cherry, smoke, toast, blackberry, spice, and herb flavors. **86** —*J.M. (11/15/2003)*

Avila 2000 Pinot Noir (San Luis Obispo County) $12. There's a heavy overlay of toasty oak on this mid-weight wine's modest fruit. Still, its black plum-cedar aromas and flavors have real appeal, as does the round, supple mouthfeel. Finishes in similar style, quite dark, with some lemony notes. **85 Best Buy** *(10/1/2002)*

Avila 2001 Cote d'Avila Rhône Red Blend (Santa Barbara County) $13. This blend of Syrah, Grenache, and Mourvèdre suffers from the dreaded South Coast veggies. The grapes simply did not get ripe. Aromas and flavors veer toward canned asparagus and earth. Will do in a pinch, and the price isn't bad. **82** —*S.H. (5/1/2003)*

Avila 2002 Cote d'Avila Rhône Red Blend (Santa Barbara County) $11. A Rhône blend with juicy berry and cocoa flavors. Very soft and gentle through the finish. Easy with burgers and such. **84** —*S.H. (2/1/2005)*

Avila 2003 Syrah (Santa Barbara County) $13. Here's a rough, somewhat rustic Syrah, with penetrating blackberry pie aromas but flavors that seem a bit herbal. Crisp on the finish, picking up spice and tea-like notes. **84** *(9/1/2005)*

AZALEA SPRINGS

Azalea Springs 1997 Estate Grown Merlot (Napa Valley) $35. Aromas of black cherries and Stanley plums combine with dark-chocolate and tea scents to create a rich bouquet. Shows good depth on the palate, before some serious tannins clamp down on the finish. Fortunately the tannins are soft and ripe; this is one of the rare California Merlots that require cellaring. Try in 2003. **89** —*J.C. (6/1/2001)*

B.R. COHN

B.R. Cohn 1996 Olive Hill Cabernet Sauvignon (Sonoma Valley) $35. 92 *(12/31/1999)*

B.R. Cohn 2001 Olive Hill Estate Cabernet Sauvignon (Sonoma County) $50. This is a shameless palate-flatterer. It's flamboyant in sweet cassis, dark chocolate, spiced rum, and oaky flavors, with easy tannins. A little too soft for the long run, but decadently delicious now. **91** —*S.H. (10/1/2004)*

B.R. Cohn 1999 Olive Hill Estate Vineyards-Special Selection Cabernet Sauvignon (Sonoma Valley) $100. 86 *(8/1/2003)*

B.R. Cohn 1996 Olive Hill Estate Vineyards Sp Cabernet Sauvignon (Sonoma Valley) $80. 92 —*J.C. (12/31/1999)*

B.R. Cohn 1997 Olive Hill Estate Vineyards Cabernet Sauvignon (Sonoma Valley) $38. 91 *(12/31/1999)*

B.R. Cohn 1997 Olive Hill Estate Vineyards Special Cabernet Sauvignon (Sonoma Valley) $100. 88 *(11/1/2000)*

B.R. Cohn 2002 Oliver Hill Estate Vineyards Cabernet Sauvignon (Sonoma Valley) $65. This wine typically starts life out as a young, tannic puppy, and although it has ripe flavors and a suppleness that can handle rich meats and cheeses, it's best to cellar it. This vintage is quite undeveloped, wrapped in tannic astringency, but with a hopeful core of fruit that should age well from 2008 on. **90 Cellar Selection** —*S.H. (5/1/2006)*

B.R. Cohn 2003 Silver Label Cabernet Sauvignon (North Coast) $20. As good as North Coast-appellation Cabs get, this one is very dry, tannic and fleshy, with good varietal character and a rich, full-bodied mouthful of blackberries, cherries, plums, and coffee. Drink now. **85** —*S.H. (5/1/2006)*

B.R. Cohn 2001 Silver Label Cabernet Sauvignon (Central Coast) $20. Rough and unbalanced, with overripe raisiny flavors right next to underripe weedy ones. Overpriced for what you get. A mix of San Luis Obispo and Sonoma county grapes. **83** —*S.H. (10/1/2004)*

B.R. Cohn 1998 Chardonnay (Carneros) $16. 88 *(6/1/2000)*

B.R. Cohn 2001 Chardonnay (Carneros) $35. Firm and bright, with a clean, clear focus that features mineral, lemon, green apple, and grapefruit. Fresh on the finish. **87** —*J.M. (2/1/2004)*

USA

USA

B.R. Cohn 1998 Reserve Joseph Herman Vineyard Chardonnay (Carneros) $28. 87 (6/1/2000)

B.R. Cohn 1997 Reserve Joseph Herman Vineyard. Chardonnay (Carneros) $24. 93 —M.S. (2/1/2000)

B.R. Cohn 2001 Merlot (Sonoma Valley) $28. There's a gentleness here that shows up in the soft texture and pliant tannins. But the flavors are no pushover. They're very ripe in cherries and spiced blackberries, with a mocha-choca richness that seems sweet, although the wine is technically dry. 88 —S.H. (12/15/2004)

B.R. Cohn 2000 Merlot (Sonoma Valley) $28. Fairly bright, with zippy cherry notes at the center. Tannins are soft and the body is moderate in weight. There's a weedy, herbal core that permeates, so this might not be for everyone. But interesting, nonetheless. 87 —J.M. (2/1/2004)

B.R. Cohn 2003 Syrcab Red Blend (Sonoma Valley) $32. Tough, dry, and tannic, with an unrelieved quality, this is a wine that needs serious time in the cellar or major decanting to let it soften. There's a heart of blackberry and pomegranate fruit that should withstand these tests. Even 12 hours of decanting would not be too much. 87 —S.H. (5/1/2006)

BABCOCK

Babcock 2000 Fathom Bordeaux Blend (Santa Barbara County) $40. When Brian Babcock calls this "the best [Bordeaux blend] I have made" you have to take him seriously. It is indeed excellent and seductive in its rich, ripe fruit and velvety tannins. Softer and plumper than Napa, but delicious and complex. Needs tinkering to develop greater finesse, but worth watching. 90 —S.H. (11/15/2002)

Babcock 1999 Fathom Bordeaux Blend (Santa Barbara County) $35. Mainly Cabernet Franc and Merlot with a little Cabernet Sauvignon, this wine advances the case for South Coast claret. It's one of the best ever from Santa Barbara. Juicy, ripe, balanced, rich, elegant, fairly soft, and covered with lush oak, it's sheer pleasure now. 93 Editors' Choice —S.H. (12/1/2001)

Babcock 1998 Fathom Bordeaux Blend (Santa Barbara County) $30. Made largely of Cabernet Franc, this wine has all the elements of first-rate Meritage: ripe blackberry and blueberry fruit, accompanied by a blast of smoky oak. It tastes good, too, with pure, sweet, supple berry flavors; yet, it's very dry, with ample acidity. It lacks the focus of North Coast claret-style wines, but is certainly among the best of the genre from the South Coast. 89 —S.H. (2/1/2001)

Babcock 2002 Cabernet Sauvignon (Central Coast) $19. Has sharp acids and a tart flavor of sour cherries, but the smooth tannins and pretty oak soften and sweeten. 85 —S.H. (10/1/2004)

Babcock 2004 Back Roads Cuvée Cabernet Sauvignon (Central Coast) $20. If you're used to the aroma of Napa and Sonoma Cab, the first whiff of minty white pepper tells you we're in a cool climate. About half of the grapes are from Santa Ynez Valley, with a good chunk from Monterey. The wine itself is firmly structured and fairly acidic, with cherry jam flavors and some flashy new oak. 86 —S.H. (12/1/2006)

Babcock 2001 La Moda Toscana Cabernet Sauvignon-Sangiovese (Santa Ynez Valley) $28. This wine is a blend of Sangiovese and Cabernet Sauvignon. It's dark, high in acids, and very dry. Flavors are of of blackberries, black cherries, herbs, and tobacco. The acids and tannins take over on the astringent finish. 89 —S.H. (3/1/2004)

Babcock 1997 Chardonnay (Santa Ynez Valley) $25. 92 —S.H. (10/1/1999)

Babcock 2002 Chardonnay (Santa Barbara County) $19. A clean, focused Chard, with tightly wound flavors of citrus fruits, apples, and peaches. Oak adds notes of vanilla, buttered toast, and smoke. Particularly nice for its crisp acids and firm balance. 87 —S.H. (2/1/2004)

Babcock 2001 Chardonnay (Santa Barbara County) $17. Bright, forward acids and lean fruit characterize this flinty white wine. The flavors are of citrus and minerals, with riper suggestions of peaches, and are enriched with smoky oak. This Chablis-style Chardonnay is complex, and one of the year's greatest values. Enjoy it with shellfish. 93 Editors' Choice —S.H. (12/15/2002)

Babcock 2000 Chardonnay (Santa Barbara County) $17. Concentrated and intense, it's marked by stylish tropical fruit flavors and quite a dose of smoky oak. There's a mineral streak right down the middle that gives it a steely spine, and refreshing acidity adds to the structural integrity. 87 —S.H. (11/15/2001)

Babcock 2000 Chardonnay (Santa Ynez Valley) $25. If you like lees, minerals and intense acidity in your Chardonnay; if you like a spine of steel and an austere profile softened only slightly by citrus fruits, then you will love this wine. It's far sharper than most California Chards. Also more food-friendly. You might find yourself reaching for a second glass. 90 —S.H. (9/1/2002)

Babcock 1999 Chardonnay (Santa Barbara County) $18. This is the workhorse release from an always dependable producer, and it's excellent. Not enormously complex or layered, but very ripe; it offers up-front peach flavors veering into tropical fruit, with a solid dose of smoky oak that adds nuance. Vibrant and alive, with high acidity that endows it with marvelous structure. 88 —S.H. (2/1/2001)

Babcock 1998 Chardonnay (Santa Barbara County) $18. 85 (6/1/2000)

Babcock 2005 Grand Cuvée Chardonnay (Santa Barbara County) $30. Co-released with Babcock's Sta. Rita Hills Chard, somehow this wine is flatter and simpler, even though it costs ten dollars more. Go figure. It's an okay wine, dry, fruity and creamy, but lacks complexity. 84 —S.H. (11/15/2006)

Babcock 2003 Grand Cuvée Chardonnay (Santa Rita Hills) $30. This Chard is oakier and leesier than Babcock's Rita's Earth Cuvée. Consequently, it's a fuller-bodied, heavier wine. Softer and fatter, too. It has opulently ripe New World flavors of pineapple custard and vanilla cream pie. 90 —S.H. (12/31/2005)

Babcock 2002 Grand Cuvée Chardonnay (Santa Ynez Valley) $30. Crisp in acids, and not showing a lot of flavor now, except for oak. Reveals modest tree fruits in dry package. Elegant rather than opulent. 84 —S.H. (12/31/2004)

Babcock 2000 Grand Cuvée Chardonnay (Santa Ynez Valley) $25. Firm and bright, this wine serves up a tangy blend of lemon, herb, pear, and melon flavors. Toast and mineral notes add interest. Clean on the finish. 89 —S.H. (12/15/2002)

Babcock 1999 Grand Cuvée Chardonnay (Santa Barbara County) $25. A dark golden color, a big wine that starts with ultraripe tropical fruit aromas veering into banana. Aromatic complexities come from lees and oak. Drinks strong and creamy, with extracted fruit, spice and lees. A blast of sweet vanilla and dusty spices last into the finish. 89 —S.H. (12/1/2001)

Babcock 1998 Grand Cuvée Chardonnay (Santa Barbara County) $30. This is hefty, dry and structured Chardonnay. Offers a complex musky, creamy nose that ushers in a range of tart citrus, coconut, toasted nut, and mineral flavors. The smoky finish also shows a crisp, almost hard-edged metallic note. Stylized and appealing, but still tight—should be better in a year or two. 89 (7/1/2001)

Babcock 1996 Grand Cuvée Chardonnay (Santa Ynez Valley) $30. 91 —S.H. (7/1/1999)

Babcock 1997 Grand Cuvée Estate Chardonnay (Santa Ynez Valley) $30. 92 (8/1/2003)

Babcock 1998 Mt. Carmel Vineyard Chardonnay (Santa Ynez Valley) $35. The nutty, smoky notes on the nose are overshadowed by taut, high-octane alcohol-mineral scents. The stony, mineral-laden palate also shows earthy, apple-oatmeal flavors. The mouthfeel is full, yet tight (we could say ripe, but it's not fruit-driven wine). This unusual offering fades long but closed, with hints of spice and coffee. Previous tastings of Mt. Carmel have proved it a tough read when young. Hold and taste in three years. 86 (7/1/2001)

Babcock 1997 Mt. Carmel Vineyard Chardonnay (Santa Ynez Valley) $30. 92 (11/15/1999)

Babcock 2005 Rita's Earth Cuvée Chardonnay (Sta. Rita Hills) $20. Very ripe and zingy in fresh kiwi, Key lime pie, and vanilla flavors, with great acidity, this Chard could be mistaken for an Edna Valley. But it's a blend of six Santa Barbara vineyards. A bit of barrel fermentation makes it creamy and pie-crust buttery. 88 —S.H. (11/15/2006)

Babcock 2004 Rita's Earth Cuvée Chardonnay (Santa Rita Hills) $20. The first bottling of this particular cuvée, this Chardonnay is a great expression of Santa Barbara terroir, fresh, young, and racy. The flavors are explosive and complex, suggesting wildly ripe tropical fruits and Key Lime pie, with refreshingly bright acidity and rich oak and lees nuances. It's a big, assertive New World Chard, and a great value. **91 Editors' Choice** —*S.H. (12/31/2005)*

Babcock 2001 Cuvée Sublime Gewürztraminer (Santa Barbara County) $20. There is something "sublime" in the intensely apricoty, orange blossom and honeyed aromas and rich, decadent flavors. Make no mistake, this is a very sweet wine, but beautifully balanced by crisp acids. A noble dessert wine, and fairly priced for this quality. **93 Editors' Choice** —*S.H. (12/1/2002)*

Babcock 2005 Pinot Grigio (Santa Rita Hills) $15. This almost wins the white food wine of the year award. It's very dry, very crisp, and refreshingly clean, with balanced citrus zest, green melon, stony mineral, and spicy pepper flavors. The acids really come into play on the finish. Let's eat! **91 Best Buy** —*S.H. (11/15/2006)*

Babcock 2001 Pinot Grigio (Santa Barbara County) $14. A combination of grapes from around the county has produced a complex, nuanced wine. It has that dry-sweet thing going on, with no measurable sugar but layers of fruity, flowery flavors, and quite bright acids. It feels fat and oily in the mouth, and even has a touch of spicy oak. **88 Best Buy** —*S.H. (9/1/2002)*

Babcock 1998 Pinot Gris (Santa Barbara County) $14. 88 *(10/1/1999)*

Babcock 2005 Naughty Little Hillsides Pinot Gris (Sta. Rita Hills) $25. This is a white wine for red wine lovers. Full-bodied, almost heavy, the wine is enormously rich in fruit flavors that taste oven-baked. One hundred percent barrel fermentation, partially in new oak, makes it even bigger. It's an unusual, even eccentric, PG. Still, Babcock's regular '05 PG, at almost half the price, is fresher and more appealing. 89 —*S.H. (11/15/2006)*

Babcock 2001 Pinot Noir (Santa Barbara County) $23. 91 Editors' Choice —*S.H. (2/1/2003)*

Babcock 2000 Pinot Noir (Santa Barbara County) $22. A young, fresh Pinot that's very full bodied. Almost purple in color, the flavors are of black cherry marmalade, clove, allspice, and smoke, with a hint of oaky sweetness. It's very pure, with feather-soft tannins. Lip-smackingly delicious through the finish. 89 —*S.H. (12/15/2001)*

Babcock 2002 Cargasacchi Pinot Noir (Santa Ynez Valley) $40. Pleasant and clean rather than complex, with pretty black and red cherry flavors and a bit of coffee and herb. Light- to medium-bodied, this wine is good, but wants a little more concentration. 86 *(11/1/2004)*

Babcock 2004 Grand Cuvée Pinot Noir (Santa Rita Hills) $32. There's nothing "grand" about this cuvée. It's a rather ordinary Pinot Noir, tart in acids, with gentle tannins and tasty cherry, cola, and oak flavors. Drink now. 84 —*S.H. (2/1/2006)*

Babcock 2002 Grand Cuvée Pinot Noir (Santa Rita Hills) $35. All the elements of great Pinot are here except concentration. You'll find modest flavors of cherries, cola, smoke, and vanilla, in an easy, gentle wine. Good stuff, but seems overpriced for what you get. 85 —*S.H. (2/1/2005)*

Babcock 2001 Grand Cuvée Pinot Noir (Santa Ynez Valley) $35. A simple, unbalanced wine. It opens with aromas of cola, cherries, and earth that are pretty good, and the flavors of cherries are ripe and tasty. But there is a sweetness that is out of place, and the wine has little depth. 84 —*S.H. (2/1/2004)*

Babcock 2000 Grand Cuvée Pinot Noir (Santa Ynez Valley) $35. Undeniably solid yet slightly bitter and impenetrable, this left tasters confused, yielding a split panel. Still, a rich mouthfeel and submerged but strong cherry fruit accented by toffee-coffee notes hint at real substance. So tight that in three-plus years it may well be in the upper echelon. 87 *(10/1/2002)*

Babcock 2001 Grand Cuvée Pinot Noir Pinot Noir (Santa Ynez Valley) $30. This is a big, dark, rich, interesting Pinot Noir. Flavorwise, it shows black cherries, blueberries, pomegranates, and sweet rhubarb, and an edge of coffee, with an earthy, slightly bitter acidity. In the mouth it is soft and lush yet firm and assertive. 92 —*S.H. (4/1/2004)*

Babcock 1997 Grande Cuvée-Estate Pinot Noir (Santa Ynez Valley) $40. 93 **Best Buy** *(10/1/1999)*

Babcock 1997 Mt. Carmel Vineyard Pinot Noir (Santa Ynez Valley) $35. 91 *(10/1/1999)*

Babcock 2002 Fathom Red Blend (Santa Ynez Valley) $32. Babcock has wisely chosen to let Merlot dominate this blend, since it clearly performs better in the valley than Cabernet. The wine shows the herbaceousness that always accompanies Santa Barbara clarets, but achieves a new level for that county of ripe, satisfying fruity complexity. The flavor of cassis even shows up on the finish. A wine to watch. 91 —*S.H. (2/1/2006)*

Babcock 2001 Fathom Red Blend (Santa Ynez Valley) $32. No problem getting the fruit ripe, to go by the delicious black currant, cassis, cherry, and blueberry flavors that veer into chocolate. Compared to Napa tannins, this one's edgier, sharper. It doesn't have that luscious creaminess. But that may be unfair. It's a really good wine. 90 —*S.H. (2/1/2005)*

Babcock 1997 Fathom Red Table Wine Red Blend (Santa Barbara County) $30. 90 —*J.C. (11/15/1999)*

Babcock 1999 Eleven Oaks Sangiovese (Santa Barbara County) $40. This interesting Sangiovese from the Santa Ynez Valley is a big wine, with a burst of rich, ripe berry fruit in the mouth and detailed tannins. The mouthfeel is sappy, almost viscous, but saved by good acidity and a dusty dryness. 91 —*S.H. (12/1/2001)*

Babcock 1997 Eleven Oaks Sangiovese (Santa Ynez Valley) $30. 90 *(10/1/1999)*

Babcock 2002 Eleven Oaks Sauvignon Blanc (Santa Barbara County) $20. Another fine version of this wine, with its intensely flavorful notes of tart green apples, citrus fruits, and figs. Acids are bright and crisp and the wine is fully dry, with an appealingly bitter finish that cries out for food. 88 —*S.H. (2/1/2004)*

Babcock 2001 Eleven Oaks Sauvignon Blanc (Santa Barbara County) $23. Tasted twice, with divergent results; the 86 rating reflects the average of both bottles. One bottle seemed overly heavy, with an odd mix of jalapeño peppers and honey. The better (and hopefully more representative) bottle showed richness without excessive weight, hints of cream and toast and penetrating citrus flavors, and would have rated 89 points on its own. 86 *(8/1/2002)*

Babcock 2000 Eleven Oaks Sauvignon Blanc (Santa Barbara County) $23. Always loaded with character, once again this wine doesn't disappoint. The aromas are racy, stylish, and clean, filled with lime and hay, green grass and honey, fig, and melon. And what great flavors, big, ripe, and juicy. It seems a little bit sweet, but the acidity is high, creating a crisp, rich wine that's full-bodied and flavorful. **90 Editors' Choice** *(8/1/2001)*

Babcock 2003 Eleven Oaks Cuvée Sauvignon Blanc (Santa Ynez Valley) $25. Always complex and interesting, and this year shows plenty of upfront spearmint, fig, and melon flavors wrapped in a rich, creamy texture. There are oak and lees shadings that show up on the finish. 90 —*S.H. (12/31/2004)*

Babcock 2005 Estate Grown Sauvignon Blanc (Sta. Rita Hills) $21. Those who loved Babcock's old Eleven Oaks bottling, don't worry. This is similar to it, but better. To counter Santa Rita's cool climate, Bryan Babcock put in some Los Alamos fruit, partially barrel fermented the wine, and added a dollop of Chardonnay to tame the beast. The wine is rich, zesty, and balanced, and heads straight to the front of the pack. **92 Editors' Choice** —*S.H. (11/15/2006)*

Babcock 2004 Estate Grown Sauvignon Blanc (Santa Rita Hills) $23. I wish this wine were drier, because it has some excellent qualities. It has the kiwi, lime, and lemongrass flavors of a great Sauvignon Blanc, and fine South Coast acidity, but that sweetness in the finish is so unnecessary. 84 —*S.H. (12/31/2005)*

Babcock 2005 Big Fat Pink Shiraz Shiraz (Santa Barbara County) $15. California is producing the best rosés in its history, and this one, which has a dash of Cabernet Franc, is an example. It's a flavorful wine, dry and crisp in acidity, with a rich array of cherry, spice, and vanilla flavors as well as a splash of crème de cassis. The winemaker recommends cioppino. I wouldn't turn it down. 88 —*S.H. (12/1/2006)*

Babcock 2000 Syrah (Santa Barbara County) $23. This dark, young wine is brooding. It's hiding itself in a purple velvet cloak, revealing only hints of spicy blackberry fruit and smoked meat. The tannins are chewy, but yielding, like gum. It's a very beautiful wine that will improve for a couple years in the cellar. **90** —*S.H. (7/1/2002)*

Babcock 2002 Black Label Cuvée Syrah (Central Coast) $30. Pinot Noir specialist Babcock spreads his varietal wings with this rustic, simple Syrah. It's rich in blackberry, coffee, and cocoa flavors, but too sugary sweet for balance. **84** —*S.H. (3/1/2006)*

Babcock 2001 Black Label Cuvée Syrah (Santa Barbara County) $30. Jammy and thick, and in the prime of its youth showing ripe, bold flavors of black cherries, chocolate, and oaky vanilla, offset by creamy tannins. It's soft and almost sweet. Try with anything from braised ribs to vanilla ice cream. **87** —*S.H. (2/1/2005)*

Babcock 2000 Black Label Cuvée Syrah (Santa Barbara County) $40. With wines like this, Santa Barbara argues that it's the greatest home for Syrah in California. Incredibly dark and dense, the wine offers up deep flavors of plums and blackberries. It's pretty tannic now, but fat and dense, the kind of wine that will easily age. Possesses that elusive quality of elegance. **93 Editors' Choice** —*S.H. (12/1/2002)*

Babcock 1999 Black Label Cuvée Syrah (Santa Barbara County) $50. There's lots of deep blueberry and sour red-berry fruit on the Babcock's nose, which is offset by saddle-leather and wet wool notes. In the mouth, earth and tobacco flavors vie with oak; plenty of tannins give it nice structure and an almost chewy mouthfeel. Finishes with tangy acid, and black pepper and mineral flavors. **88** *(11/1/2001)*

Babcock 1997 Black Label Cuvée Syrah (Santa Barbara County) $40. 91 *(10/1/1999)*

Babcock 2003 Frying Pan Syrah (Santa Barbara County) $50. Obviously youthful, with some reductive notes that need time to dissipate. Once it comes around, you get straight-ahead plum and blackberry fruit, vanilla and coffee notes and the merest hint of bacon fat (we love that!). Really nice wine that seems to fall off a bit on the finish. **87** *(9/1/2005)*

Babcock 2003 Nook & Cranny Syrah (Santa Rita Hills) $50. Herbal and peppery on the nose, but also shows plenty of fruit, which really expands on the palate to deliver a mouthful of creamy-textured cherries and vanilla. Yet the flavors remain complex, incorporating pepper and herb notes. Ends in a long, spice-driven finish. **90** *(9/1/2005)*

Babcock 2003 Radical Syrah (Paso Robles) $50. What's radical about this wine is the amount of fruit crammed into it: jammy, superripe blackberries framed in caramel-drizzled toast. Some tough tannins on the finish need time to resolve. It's practically embryonic at this stage; hold 3–5 years. **85** *(9/1/2005)*

BACCHARIS

Baccharis 2003 Cabernet Sauvignon (Alexander Valley) $28. This is a classic old-style Alexander Valley Cabernet. By that I mean it's dry, soft and slightly herbal, with a dill and tobacco edge to the cherry fruit. It's an elegant, complex, tannic wine that should age well. **90 Cellar Selection** —*S.H. (2/1/2006)*

Baccharis 2002 Petite Sirah (Dry Creek Valley) $23. This is an old-fashioned Petite Sirah, the kind that will live for decades. It's dark and very dry, with bigtime tannins, full-bodied alcohol, and lots of dark stone fruit, leather, and cured tobacco flavors. Drink now through 2020. **87** —*S.H. (2/1/2006)*

Baccharis 2002 Floodgate Vineyard Pinot Noir (Anderson Valley) $28. This wine is like a good Zinfandel with the texture and body of a Pinot. By that, I mean it has a feral quality, with a peppery, leathery edge to the wild berry fruit, but it also has Pinot's silky texture. **87** —*S.H. (2/1/2006)*

Baccharis 2004 Sauvignon Blanc (Russian River Valley) $15. Combines basic Sauvignon savage character of wild green grasses, hay, and melon with richer fig and tropical fruit flavors, in a creamy texture. The result is a fine, somewhat complex wine, with high acidity. **86** —*S.H. (2/1/2006)*

Baccharis 2002 Zinfandel (Sonoma County) $16. Classic Sonoma Zin, ripe, dry, and luscious in blackberry, cherry, cocoa, coffee and peppery spice flavors, with rich, complex tannins and a finish of sweet fruit and oak. Has the depth and intensity of a true old vine wine. **89 Editors' Choice** —*S.H. (2/1/2006)*

BACIO DIVINO

Bacio Divino 1999 Red Blend (Napa Valley) $75. At first this is very woody, bordering on sappy. But with time the wood softens, leaving ripe and bright cassis, plum, and black cherry. The finish is toasty and creamy. And while it feels full and hearty, the wine isn't hard or tannic. An interesting blend of Cabernet, Sangiovese, and Petite Sirah. **91** —*M.S. (11/15/2003)*

Bacio Divino 2000 Pazzo Red Blend (Napa Valley) $24. A simple blend but a likeable one, due to its pretty cherry, black raspberry, and coffee flavors. Underneath the fruit, the wine is soft in tannins and acids. Mainly Sangiovese, with Cabernet Sauvignon and Zinfandel. **85** —*S.H. (12/31/2003)*

Bacio Divino 2000 Red Wine Red Blend (Napa Valley) $80. Pretty good, although it is without much depth. The tart black cherry, tobacco, and herb flavors are folded into thick tannins, and the finish is very dry and astringent. Might soften a bit with a few years of age. **85** —*S.H. (12/31/2003)*

Bacio Divino 1997 Sangiovese (Napa Valley) $75. 90 *(11/1/2000)*

BADGER MOUNTAIN

Badger Mountain 1998 Cabernet Franc (Columbia Valley (WA)) $12. Badger Mountain grows its grapes organically, but its red wines, even in a near-perfect Washington vintage like 1998, seem underripe, thin, and hard. This too is simple and tannic. **82** —*P.G. (6/1/2002)*

Badger Mountain 1998 Cabernet Sauvignon (Columbia Valley (WA)) $14. Roasted, toasty scents dominate the nose, with layers of vanilla, chocolate and coffee. The fruit is raisined and soft, already fading, and the finish is hot and slightly bitter. **83** —*P.G. (12/31/2001)*

Badger Mountain 1999 N.S.A. Cabernet Sauvignon (Columbia Valley (WA)) $14. The initials mean no sulfites added; the wine comes from organically grown grapes, but it smells of stem and root, rather than good, ripe fruit. Earthy and spare. **84** —*P.G. (6/1/2002)*

Badger Mountain 1999 Vintner's Estate Cabernet Sauvignon (Columbia Valley (WA)) $12. This is generic Cabernet, despite its organic pedigree. It's clean and balanced, and if organic is important to you, it's a very good choice. But it does not show the depth and complexity that is possible in Columbia Valley wines. **86** —*P.G. (12/31/2003)*

Badger Mountain 2000 N.S.A. Chardonnay (Columbia Valley (WA)) $10. This organically grown, no-sulfites-added Chardonnay is forward and fruity, with a nice scent of green apples and just a hint of butterscotch. Lively and made for immediate drinking. **86** —*P.G. (7/1/2002)*

Badger Mountain 1999 Vintner's Estate Meritage (Columbia Valley (WA)) $12. This is already tasting of raisins and prunes, indicators that the wine is already rapidly aging. Hints of bell pepper, mint, and stem; better drink this one right now. **85** —*P.G. (12/31/2003)*

Badger Mountain 1999 Merlot (Columbia Valley (WA)) $14. Organically cultivated and vinified, this forward, overripe wine starts off with sweet, jammy fruit then seems to fall apart in the glass. It smells and tastes baked; the finish, sour and tannic, feels manipulated. **82** —*P.G. (12/31/2001)*

Badger Mountain 1998 Merlot (Columbia Valley (WA)) $12. A hint of brick is already showing in the color, and the nose is leafy, with toasted tomato instead of ripe fruit. **83** —*P.G. (6/1/2002)*

Badger Mountain 2000 N.S.A Merlot (Columbia Valley (WA)) $14. Forward and scented with bell pepper and licorice, this organic, no sulfites added Merlot seems just a bit underripe, with some earthy tannins. Nonetheless, a solid effort, with good color, grip, and balance. **86** —*P.G. (6/1/2002)*

Badger Mountain 1998 Red Blend (Columbia Valley (WA)) $12. A 60/40 blend makes for a light, tart, fairly tough and tannic red wine. The fruit is lean and hard, the finish green and stemmy. **83** —*P.G. (6/1/2002)*

Badger Mountain 2001 N.S.A. Riesling (Columbia Valley (WA)) $8. The initials mean "no sulfites added" and that, plus the unusual blue bottle, make this a one of a kind riesling. From organically grown grapes, this is fresh, sweetly fruity, with a clean, citrusy pop. **86 Best Buy** —*P.G.* *(6/1/2002)*

Badger Mountain 2001 Vintner's Estate Syrah (Columbia Valley (WA)) $18. A sweet, sappy nose, highlighted with minty spice, leads into a chewy young wine with pleasant, innocuous fruit and a soft, smooth finish. **86** —*P.G. (12/31/2003)*

Badger Mountain 2000 Seve White Blend (Columbia Valley (WA)) $8. A neutral white wine blend, from organically grown grapes. Simple and bland. **84** —*P.G. (6/1/2002)*

BAER

Baer 2003 Ursa Red Bordeaux Blend (Columbia Valley (WA)) $29. Soft, smooth, rich, and supple, this delicious blend of Merlot and Cabernet Franc also includes a dash of Cabernet Sauvignon and Malbec. There's loads of black cherry and blackberry fruit flavor, but beyond that the wine shows real stuffing. It gently evolves in the mouth, opening up to reveal layers of tobacco, cherry, tar, and light smoke. **92** —*P.G. (10/1/2006)*

BAILEYANA

Baileyana 1998 Chardonnay (Monterey County) $17. 85 *(6/1/2000)*

Baileyana 1997 Chardonnay (Edna Valley) $22. 86 *(6/1/2000)*

Baileyana 2001 Chardonnay (San Luis Obispo) $18. No mistaking the chilly climate this tart, slightly bitter Chard hails from. Its flavors start with grapefruits and limes and manage to break through to green apples, although oak certainly adds softer, sweeter notes. It's a good, crisp wine that will be excellent with crab. **87** —*S.H. (12/31/2003)*

Baileyana 2002 55% San Luis Obispo County/45% Monterey County Chardonnay (California) $18. Way too much oak on this rustic wine, and rather insipid, too, with its too-soft mouthfeel and slightly sweet, Lifesaver flavors. **83** —*S.H. (8/1/2005)*

Baileyana 2003 Estate Chardonnay (Edna Valley) $18. Characterized by bright acidity that makes the lime custard and peach flavors dance on the palate, this Central Coast Chard is fun to drink. It finishes in a swirl of toasty oak. **86** —*S.H. (4/1/2006)*

Baileyana 2001 Firepeak Vineyard Chardonnay (Edna Valley) $30. This is a winemaker's wine. The underlying fruit flavors are tight, suggesting tart green apples and barely ripened peaches; smoky oak has added buttery, creamy notes. A very good candidate at the dinner table. **90** —*S.H. (12/15/2003)*

Baileyana 1999 Firepeak Vineyard Chardonnay (Edna Valley) $30. The bouquet offers dazzling aromas, including pineapple, banana, cinnamon, nutmeg, roasted nuts, and butter. On the palate, the wine becomes more focused: taut pear, citrus, and golden apple flavors closely wrapped in a tasty butterscotch and toast cocoon. Finishes long and even; could still use six months to a year to unwind. **88** *(7/1/2001)*

Baileyana 2004 Firepeak Vineyard El Gordo Chardonnay (Edna Valley) $30. Takes the firm, flinty steeliness, and tangy acidity of Edna Valley fruit to new heights, with powerful yet nuanced Key lime, kiwi, and tart green apple flavors and a rich, creamy, not-too-oaky mouthfeel. **93** —*S.H. (7/1/2006)*

Baileyana 2002 Grand Firepeak Cuvée Chardonnay (Edna Valley) $30. On the sharp, acidic side despite well-ripened pineapple fruit, oak, and lees. Try with boldly flavored foods that call for a big Chard. **86** —*S.H. (10/1/2005)*

Baileyana 2003 Grand Firepeak Cuvée Chardonnay (Edna Valley) $30. The acidity and asperity of this Chard are a bit beyond my comfort zone, but that's Edna Valley for you. It's certainly a distinctive wine, a best-blocks selection rich in lemon, lime, and mineral flavors, to which the winemaker has added a filigree of toasted oak. **86** —*S.H. (12/15/2005)*

Baileyana 2004 Grand Firepeak Vineyard Chardonnay (Edna Valley) $30. Baileyana's Pinot Noirs from the cool Edna Valley are right up there with the best, and so is their Chardonnay. It shows off the region's typically bright acidity and pure, clean flavors of limes, kiwis, and Asian pears, undergirded with a vibrant minerality. **92 Editors' Choice** —*S.H. (7/1/2006)*

Baileyana 2001 Pinot Noir (Edna Valley) $23. A nice coastal Pinot whose crisp acids firm up black raspberry and cherry flavors and earthier ones of white pepper and tobacco. Softly elegant and silky in the mouth. This is a classic, easy food wine that will complement, not overwhelm, everything from roast chicken to a garlicky lamb. **86** —*S.H. (4/1/2004)*

Baileyana 2000 Pinot Noir (Edna Valley) $23. This toasty, earthy wine elicited divergent responses from tasters. The dark cherry-plum fruit, charred oak and tobacco shadings were harmonious to most, but found murky and a bit hollow by others. It was described as supple and ripe, yet also as tart and lemony. The one thing agreed upon was the long dark, tangy finish. **88** *(10/1/2002)*

Baileyana 1999 Pinot Noir (Edna Valley) $23. A sour cherry and dusty saddle leather nose opens to an even palate where cocoa and anise notes nicely offset the pie cherry fruit. It's smooth and tasty in a lean, focused manner. It finishes with good length and scant tannins. **87** *(10/1/2002)*

Baileyana 2002 El Pico Firepeak Vineyard Clone 115 Pinot Noir (Edna Valley) $30. Very dry and a little disjointed now, but has great potential. The dry flavors suggest coffee, rhubarb pie, red cherries, and mushrooms. The earthiness is relieved by smoky oak that turns sweet in the finish. Give it a year or two to come together. **90 Editors' Choice** —*S.H. (11/1/2004)*

Baileyana 2003 Firepeak Vineyard Pinot Noir (Edna Valley) $23. Shows a nicely crisp, silky texture and ripe cherry flavors, but there's something about the tannic structure that's a little rustic. And despite low alcohol, there's a stewed taste in the finish. Drink now. **84** —*S.H. (8/1/2006)*

Baileyana 2002 Firepeak Vineyard Pinot Noir (Edna Valley) $23. Truly varietally correct, in the silky mouthfeel, crisp acids, delicate mouthfeel and cherry flavors, but goes the extra mile in achieving real complexity. Addictively drinkable, one of those wines whose pleasure is accentuated by a slight resistance, due to a sprinkling of dusty tannins. **92** —*S.H. (10/1/2005)*

Baileyana 2001 Firepeak Vineyard Pinot Noir (Edna Valley) $38. A single-vineyard Pinot that shows signs of those green tomato Central Coast flavors complexed with riper black cherry notes and a rich, espresso finish. It's very dry and soft in tannins, although the tart acidity stimulates the taste buds. May soften and sweeten in a few years, but is best consumed now. **87** —*S.H. (4/1/2004)*

Baileyana 1999 Firepeak Vineyard Pinot Noir (Edna Valley) $38. Rich, ripe and velvety textured, the wine offers loads of complex black cherry, herb, chocolate, spice, cedar, and anise flavors. Full bodied and plush for a Pinot, it remains long and lush on the finish. **92 Editors' Choice** —*J.M. (12/15/2001)*

Baileyana 2000 Firepeak Vineyard-Estate Bottled Pinot Noir (Edna Valley) $38. The nose is a bit charred, with popcorn that then yields to smoke and herbs. The flavors run toward strawberry and red plum, with a hint of citrus peel in the background. It finishes lean, with drying tannins. **87** *(10/1/2002)*

Baileyana 2002 Grand Firepeak Cuvée Pinot Noir (Edna Valley) $38. Over the top, with its heavy plaster of oak, and a flatness that no amount of fruit, which this wine has in spades, can overcome. **85** —*S.H. (10/1/2005)*

Baileyana 2004 Grand Firepeak Cuvée Pinot Noir (Edna Valley) $38. Showing fine varietal character in the racy, silky mouthfeel, high acidity and wonderful dryness, this Pinot brims with cool-climate cola, tart red cherry and cranberry flavors that are so ripe, they finish almost chocolate like. It's a complex, layered wine that was made for food. Great with roast duck, pork, or a nice steak. **91** —*S.H. (11/1/2006)*

Baileyana 2003 Grand Firepeak Cuvée Firepeak Vineyard Pinot Noir (Edna Valley) $38. From a very cool climate comes this high acid, brightly etched Pinot. It's not an opulent charmer, or a superripe bruiser, but shows those qualities of elegance and delicacy that mark great Pinot Noir. **90** —*S.H. (3/1/2006)*

Baileyana 2002 Halcon Rojo Firepeak Vineyard Pommard Clone Pinot Noir (Edna Valley) $30. Dry, earthy, and not fully ripe, with beetroot, tomato, and rhubarb flavors. Feels rich and earthy in the mouth, a chunky wine with crisp acids. Probably at its best now. **87** —*S.H. (11/1/2004)*

Baileyana 1997 La Colline Vineyard Pinot Noir (Arroyo Grande Valley) $30. **89** *(12/15/1999)*

Baileyana 2002 La Entrada Firepeak Vineyard Clone 777 Pinot Noir (Edna Valley) $30. Riper by a hair than its Pommard Clone neighbor, showing tart red cherry flavors. Dry and crisp in acids, with a silky, velvety texture, this medium-bodied wine has good balance. Drink now with rich meats. **89** —*S.H.* *(11/1/2004)*

Baileyana 2004 Paragon Vineyard Sauvignon Blanc (Edna Valley) $13. Edna Valley's cool maritime climate has led to a sharply acidic wine, intense and pure in Meyer lemon, ripe fig, Key lime pie, and peppery guava flavors. The wine is dry and intensely fruity. A beautiful cocktail wine. **89 Best Buy** —*S.H.* *(8/1/2006)*

Baileyana 2003 Paragon Vineyard Sauvignon Blanc (Edna Valley) $13. Consumers should not overlook the Sauvignon Blancs of the Central/South coasts, and this fine example shows why. Bone-dry, with excellently crisp acidity and telltale lemon, lime, and grass flavors enriched with riper notes of sweet fig. Finishes with a lively, spicy aftertaste. **88 Best Buy** —*S.H.* *(8/1/2005)*

Baileyana 2002 Paragon Vineyard Sauvignon Blanc (Edna Valley) $13. From a cool coastal appellation, an herbal, green wine with grassy, citrusy flavors. It's very dry and backed up with firm acids, but there's a slight vegetal note that detracts from the enjoyment. **84** —*S.H.* *(4/1/2004)*

Baileyana 2001 Syrah (Edna Valley) $18. Starts with mouthwatering (at least for carnivores) aromas of smoke, grilled meat, and pepper, then moves easily into blackberry and cherry fruit on the midpalate. Bright acids and firm tannins on the finish, giving a decent sense of structure. **88** *(9/1/2005)*

Baileyana 1999 Syrah (Paso Robles) $18. Stewed dark fruit, earth, and a smidgen of cotton-candy sweetness characterize Baileyana's nose; clove, "very grapey," and black cherry flavors show up on the mouth. Medium-weight and somewhat angular, it closes with powdery tannins and sweet cherry flavors. **87** *(10/1/2001)*

Baileyana 2003 Firepeak Vineyard Syrah (Edna Valley) $30. Shows some unripe notes in its peppery, herbal, leafy-green aromas and dry, unyielding tannins, but they're mostly balanced by bright raspberry and cherry fruit. Could mature nicely over the next several years. **86** *(9/1/2005)*

Baileyana 1999 Firepeak Vineyard Syrah (Edna Valley) $38. Cassis, fig, smoke, and toast are among the descriptors used by our panelists for this tasty South Central Coaster. It might be called a strong generalist—it has good feel and structure, espresso, and licorice accents, and a long, tart-sweet, dryly tannic finish. **89** *(11/1/2001)*

Baileyana 2003 Grand Firepeak Cuvée Syrah (Edna Valley) $38. Our panel tasted Baileyana's regular Firepeak 2003 Syrah earlier this year and found it a little green, but still a good wine. This best block selection is richer, but still fairly green and peppery, with sharp acids. **87** —*S.H.* *(12/31/2005)*

Baileyana 1998 Zinfandel (Paso Robles) $18. A Zin with nice flavors and textures, though most of them are oak-derived. Sweet cream, spice, black tea, and mixed berry; oak and pepper dominate the palate, though there is some tart black fruit underneath. Finishes woody. **86** —*D.T.* *(3/1/2002)*

BAILY

Baily 1999 Merlot (Temecula) $16. The dark, almost black color hints at the deep ripeness. Aromas of blackberry and black cherry jam, espresso, and chocolate leap from the glass, with smoke, toast, and vanilla nuances from oak aging. Very dry, with good depth of flavor and hefty tannins. Will benefit from a few years in the cellar. **88** —*S.H.* *(4/1/2002)*

BAITING HOLLOW FARM VINEYARD

Baiting Hollow Farm Vineyard 2004 Merlot (North Fork of Long Island) $NA. A lighter wine with tart acidity and moderate tannin. Brambly, fresh aromas of cranberry have green notes, leading to flavors much the same. Better with light cheese than steak. **83** —*M.D.* *(12/1/2006)*

BALBOA

Balboa 2003 Cabernet Sauvignon (Walla Walla (WA)) $16. Smooth, roasted flavors suggest a richer wine than might be expected at the price. The light cherry fruit is wrapped in smoked meat, tar, and tannin. A very tasty effort, from the winemaker for Beresan. **88** —*P.G.* *(6/1/2006)*

Balboa 2004 Sauvignon Blanc (Columbia Valley (WA)) $16. Some residual sugar and fresh flavors of peach and pineapple lift this pleasant bottle out of the realm of the ordinary. It's soft, fruity, and has not a hint of grassiness; in other words, it's very Californian. **88** —*P.G.* *(6/1/2006)*

BALCOM & MOE

Balcom & Moe 1997 Cabernet Sauvignon (Washington) $20. There's a bit of high-toned volatility in the nose, a hint of nail polish, and a light, strawberry quality to the fruit. The tannins are dense enough, but overall it's an unbalanced, slightly sweet wine which lacks focus. **83** —*P.G.* *(10/1/2001)*

Balcom & Moe 1998 Merlot (Washington) $20. Maury Balcom planted his first vineyard 30 years ago, and has supplied fruit to dozens of wineries over the years, yet the home team seems to struggle to find its own identity. This is simple, uncomplicated red wine, fine for quaffing, but indistinguishable from dozens just like it. **84** —*P.G.* *(10/1/2001)*

BALDACCI

Baldacci 2003 Cabernet Sauvignon (Stags Leap District) $49. Size isn't everything, but in this magnificent 100% Cab, it's an impressive part of the total package. The black currant and cherry flavors are massive, the oak is impressively strong and spicy, the acidity is balancing, and the tannins are a wonder, softly ripe and firm at the same time. On the finish, the flavors turn even richer, suggesting crème de cassis and chocolate. Best now–2010. **93 Editors' Choice** *(9/1/2006)*

Baldacci 2002 Cabernet Sauvignon (Stags Leap District) $44. This is a classic young Napa Cabernet. It's very forward in ripe black currant and mocha flavors, with thoroughly sweet tannins and a soft, luxurious mouthfeel. The fruit flatters the palate from entry to long finish. Drink now and for the next two years. **90** —*S.H.* *(12/15/2005)*

Baldacci 2001 Cabernet Sauvignon (Stags Leap District) $44. Pretty tannic and tight right now, with a dusty finish, although the cassis, cherry, and bitter chocolate flavors are so fruit forward, you could enjoy it tonight. Will improve through this decade. The balance and finesse are impeccable. **91** —*S.H.* *(7/1/2005)*

Baldacci 2003 Brenda's Vineyard Cabernet Sauvignon (Stags Leap District) $70. Tasted with Baldacci's regular Cab, this is a slightly tougher, less immediately opulent wine. The fruit is there, but the tannic structure makes it less accessible. Lush plum and prune flavors coat the palate, dusted with oaky notes of chocolate and smoke. Winemaker Rolando Herrera worked at Stag's Leap Wine Cellars as well as with Paul Hobbs, and he clearly knows his stuff. If you can cellar this 100% Cab though 2010, good for you, because it's just so rewarding now. **95 Editors' Choice** *(9/1/2006)*

Baldacci 2002 Brenda's Vineyard Cabernet Sauvignon (Stags Leap District) $70. Tasted alongside Baldacci's regular '02 Cab, this one's more tannic, and also more deeply flavored. There's an explosion of black currant, cherry, and mocha fruit, backed up with a firm dustiness that provides structure and balance. The wine will probably benefit from short-term aging. Drink 2006 and 2007. **92 Cellar Selection** —*S.H.* *(12/15/2005)*

Baldacci 2001 Brenda's Vineyard Cabernet Sauvignon (Stags Leap District) $70. This single-vineyard release has far more tannins than the winery's regular Cabernet. They effectively shut down the finish in a cloud of sandpapery astringency. Will it evolve in the cellar? There's a good core of cherry fruit in there, but it's a gamble. **88** —*S.H.* *(7/1/2005)*

BALISTRERI

Balistreri 2003 Cabernet Franc (Grand Valley) $26. This wine has rhubarb and cranberry aromas marred by pickle juice. In the mouth it's better, with dark, extracted flavors of cranberry and oak spice. Finishes hot and tannic. **80** —*M.D. (8/1/2006)*

Balistreri 2004 Cabernet Sauvignon (Grand Valley) $28. Dark purple, with mixed aromas of juicy plum, sawdust, and clove that pick up hints of beet. A heavy hitter, the 15% alcohol is not apparent except in the big feel, matched by dry, rough tannins and a hint of sweetness. Dark berry fruit and beet flavors coat the mouth, and the wine finishes with a medicinal feel. **83** —*M.D. (8/1/2006)*

BALLATORE

Ballatore NV Gran Spumante Champagne Blend (California) $7. **82** — *S.H. (12/15/1999)*

Ballatore NV Gran Spumante Champagne Blend (California) $7. If you like your bubbly sweet, this is an excellent choice. The cleanliness and sleek, refreshing quality is impressive. So are the flavors of peaches and raspberries. Finishes with a honeyed scour of acidity. **86 Best Buy** —*S.H. (12/1/2002)*

Ballatore NV Rosso Champagne Blend (California) $8. This is old-style pink Champagne, like they sipped from flat glasses in the 1930s. It smells like raspberry soda and cotton candy, and tastes sweet and fruity. Refreshing acidity provides the balance it needs. **85** —*S.H. (12/1/2002)*

Ballatore NV Gran Spumante Sparkling Blend (California) $6. A bit fierce in aggressive bubbles, but this sparkler is fine for everyday purposes, with its sweetened peach and vanilla flavors and brisk, clean acids. **84 Best Buy** —*S.H. (12/31/2005)*

Ballatore NV Gran Spumante Sparkling Blend (California) $9. Frankly sweet, and zesty in acidity, this is a nice, clean bubbly for those who like a bit of sugar in the finish. It has pleasant flavors of tangerine and vanilla, with a light, delicate mouthfeel. **85 Best Buy** —*S.H. (6/1/2006)*

Ballatore NV Rosso Red Spumante Sparkling Blend (California) $9. Colored a pretty salmon-pink, with inviting aromas, this bubbly is sweet and clean. It has delicious raspberry and strawberry parfait flavors drizzled with vanilla and cinnamon. Sure is easy to like at this price. **84 Best Buy** —*S.H. (6/1/2006)*

Ballatore NV Rosso Red Spumante Sparkling Blend (California) $6. Red in color, sugary sweet, this sparkler will have its fans, but it's really kind of cloying. **82** —*S.H. (12/31/2005)*

BALLENTINE

Ballentine 2003 Pocai Vineyard Cabernet Franc (Napa Valley) $24. Compared to Cabernet Sauvignon, this 100% Cab Franc, from the north part of St. Helena, is softer, much lighter in body, and marked by red, not black, fruits, especially cherries. Like a good Cab, it's dry and balanced, with rich tannins and oak. **86** —*S.H. (12/31/2005)*

Ballentine 2002 Pocai Vineyard Cabernet Franc (Napa Valley) $24. Soft and juicy in berry flavors with a streak of herbaceousness. Finishes dry, with notes of oak. **84** —*S.H. (12/31/2004)*

Ballentine 2004 Pocai Vineyard Old Vine Chenin Blanc (Napa Valley) $14. If more Chenins had this wine's balance and attractiveness, maybe consumers would drink more of it. Dry and crisp in acids, with intense, flowery peach and melon flavors. Has some real complexity. **87** —*S.H. (7/1/2005)*

Ballentine 2005 Pocai Vineyard Old Vines Chenin Blanc (Napa Valley) $14. The vines date to the early 1970s, and the vineyard is on the valley floor near Calistoga. Winemaker Bruce Devlin worked at Boschendal, South Africa's first winery to barrel ferment Chenin Blanc. Dry and crisp, this wine shows wildflower and citrus flavors, and a sweet, green-pea note with an edge of toasted wood. Not only is this an elegant table white, it should evolve over the next five to seven years. **92 Best Buy** —*S.H. (7/1/2006)*

Ballentine 2001 Merlot (Napa Valley) $22. Ripe and fruity in upfront blackberries, currants, and oak, with a hint of cocoa, this wine also shows raw tannins. It's young, and finishes with that raw quality of a juvenile Cab. Fine now with rich fare, but should mellow for a few years. Now through 2008. **88** —*S.H. (6/1/2005)*

Ballentine 1999 Merlot (Napa Valley) $25. A nice, soft, lush red wine, what Merlot is supposed to be. Has plenty of ripe berry flavors and a rich texture that coats the palate in soft, mink-coat luxury. It isn't especially deep or complex, but has a lot of surface opulence. **87** —*S.H. (11/15/2002)*

Ballentine 1997 Estate Grown Merlot (Napa Valley) $20. **87** —*J.C. (7/1/2000)*

Ballentine 2002 Pocai Vineyard Merlot (Napa Valley) $22. Too superripe with a raisiny, Porty taste. Although the wine is dry, it just can't overcome that baked-fruit quality. **82** —*S.H. (11/15/2006)*

Ballentine 2000 Integrity Merlot-Cabernet Franc (Napa Valley) $28. This unusual blend of Merlot and Cabernet Franc shows leathery, blackberry, mint, and oaky aromas and flavors, and is pretty tannic. It numbs the mouth, but there's a rich core of fruit that may age out. **86** —*S.H. (11/15/2004)*

Ballentine 2004 Petite Verdot (Napa Valley) $38. Often added to Cabernet for color and aromatics, this PV shows a saturated black color and is powerful in violet and blackberry tea flavors that are almost leathery. It's a very dry, very tannic wine, but finely structured. Treat it like an Argentine Malbec and have with steak. **88** —*S.H. (12/1/2006)*

Ballentine 2003 Zinfandel Port (Napa Valley) $40. Smooth in texture and very sweet, with flavors of cherry and black raspberry marmalade, chocolate pie, and spices. For immediate drinking. **85** —*S.H. (12/15/2005)*

Ballentine 1999 Bg Reserve Red Blend (Napa Valley) $40. This is a 50-50 mixture of Merlot and Cabernet Franc, and so you won't find any of those big Cabernet Sauvignon flavors and tannins. The wine has soft, melted tannins, and the black cherry and tobacco flavors have a rich earthiness to them. It will probably age well, but try it now with leg of lamb. **91** —*S.H. (11/15/2002)*

Ballentine 1999 Syrah (Napa Valley) $28. Very smooth and velvety texture. The tongue feels good as the dark stone fruit and peppery flavors spread over the palate like a soft blanket. The robust flavors are balanced by fine, dusty, dry tannins, further enhancing the mouthfeel. This is a very nice red wine of elegance and style. **91** —*S.H. (12/1/2002)*

Ballentine 1998 Syrah (Napa Valley) $25. Though reviewers detected a slight funkiness (plastic or game?) on the nose, we appreciated the dry leather and tart berry fruit flavors in the mouth. Finishes with a similar dryness—cedar, mostly. **86** *(11/1/2001)*

Ballentine 2003 Betty's Vineyard Syrah (Napa Valley) $22. Unanimously admired by our panel, Ballentine's Syrah boasts a big mouthful of cocoa, plum, and black cherry flavors, backed by firm acids and tannins. Has some faint rubbery notes, but they should fade with time or a brisk decanting. **88** *(9/1/2005)*

Ballentine 1999 Zinfandel (Napa Valley) $20. There's a gorgeous smell to this wine, a mixture of blueberries and smoke that's as fragrant as a warm berry tart. The flavor is pretty, too. Richly textured and smooth, dry and supple, this is first-class, elegant Zin. **90 Editors' Choice** —*S.H. (12/1/2002)*

Ballentine 1999 Bg Reserve Zinfandel (Napa Valley) $28. This is a weightier, more tannic wine than Ballentine's regular Zin, and not quite so appealing or flavorful in its youth. There's a deep core of yummy fruit buried down deep that needs the right foods to release its sweetness. **90** —*S.H. (12/1/2002)*

Ballentine 2001 Bg Zinfandel Block 9 Reserve Zinfandel (Napa Valley) $27. Smooth and pretty, with coffee, cola, dark plum, toast, smoke, and spice flavors that leave a bright, fresh finish on the palate. Lively throughout the long finish. **88** *(11/1/2003)*

Ballentine 2004 Block 11 Old Vines Zinfandel (Napa Valley) $25. Luscious, smooth, complex, complete, round, voluptuous, the adjectives go on and on with this incredibly ripe Zin. It's fully dry, with amazing blackberry tea, cherry pie, mocha, root beer, and spice flavors, but be forewarned: the alcohol is a whopping 16.7%. **90** —*S.H. (7/1/2006)*

USA

Ballentine 2000 Block 9 Zinfandel (Napa Valley) $27. This wine shows all the class and elegance of a fine Napa Cab, except it's indisputably Zin, with its brambly fruit flavors and spicy, peppery edge. The oak is rich and charred, the tannins sweet and ripe, the texture as smooth as velvet. Pretty much the best that Napa can do with Zinfandel. **92** —*S.H. (9/1/2004)*

Ballentine 2002 Block 9 Reserve Zinfandel (Napa Valley) $27. Shows the classic structure and balance of top-notch Napa Zin. From a vineyard near Calistoga, the wine is mouth-fillingly big, with black cherry, leather, spicy plum, and coffee flavors wrapped in significant tannins. Best to decant before serving. **91** —*S.H. (12/1/2006)*

Ballentine 1997 Estate Grown Zinfandel (Napa Valley) $16. **82** —*P.G. (11/15/1999)*

Ballentine 2002 Old Vines Zinfandel (Napa Valley) $18. Opens with a Provençal herb blast of thyme and lavender, then the blackberry tea and mocha aromas take over. It's a promising start to a wine that doesn't disappoint. Shows powerful fruit and spice flavors, with sweetly ripe tannins leading to a dry finish. This is a comparative bargain for a fine Napa Zin. **89** —*S.H. (11/15/2006)*

Ballentine 2001 Old Vines Zinfandel (Napa Valley) $18. Fairly elegant, with pretty toast, plum, blackberry, spice, vanilla, and licorice flavors. The tannins are ripe, firm and focused, with hints of smoke and more toast on the finish. **88** *(11/1/2003)*

Ballentine 2003 Old Vines Block 11 Zinfandel (Napa Valley) $25. Here's a Zin with the potential to develop into something very special. It should have been held back a year longer, to let the elements meld. Deliciously ripe raspberry-cherry fruit, lush, complex tannins, a subtle overlay of oak and fine acidity need until 2006 to knit, and when they do, look out. **92** —*S.H. (5/1/2005)*

BALLETTO

Balletto 2004 Pinot Grigio (Sonoma Coast) $12. Beautiful acidity, a slight dusting of tannins, perfect dryness, modest alcohol, and penetrating, ripe citrus and fig flavors add up to a lovely sipper, at a terrific price. **87 Best Buy** —*S.H. (2/1/2006)*

Balletto 2004 Estate Bottled Pinot Noir (Russian River Valley) $24. Here's a delicately structured, elegant Pinot that modulates the fruit and ups the acidity. It shows polished cherry, cola, and toast flavors, with a mushroomy, herbal earthiness and a light, silky texture. Finishes dry and spicy. **86** —*S.H. (12/1/2006)*

BANDIERA

Bandiera 2000 Vineyard Reserve Cabernet Sauvignon (California) $10. A solid, clean red wine, dry and rustic. That sounds like a backhanded compliment but it's the truth. Doesn't pretend to be anything more than a competent Cabernet at an affordable price. **84** —*S.H. (11/15/2002)*

Bandiera 1999 Vineyard Reserve Cabernet Sauvignon (California) $10. If you're a fan of Chilean Cabs, you'll like this one. It's got some real finesse and depth, with black currant and oak notes throughout. It's actually plush and opulent, although in a low-key way. Yes, it's light, but the long, rich finish points to good grape sourcing, plus, of course, a fantastic vintage. This is a great value. **87 Best Buy** —*S.H. (5/1/2001)*

Bandiera 1999 Vineyard Reserve Chardonnay (California) $10. Aromas of white peach and apple wood, with a dab of oak and butter. In the mouth it's very fruity and a bit sweet. The acidity is high and cutting. It's one-dimensional and finishes rough and earthy. **83** —*S.H. (5/1/2001)*

Bandiera 1999 Vineyard Reserve Merlot (California) $10. Starts out with aromas that are pretty typical of inexpensive California Merlots: earth, plums, and blackberries, with no noticeable oak. The aromas are dull; they don't shine. The flavors are good, though. Sharply etched fruit forces itself on the palate, ripe, sweet, and brimming with sunshine. This is simple, everyday stuff, but it's clean as a whistle and has a good amount of charm. Definitely a value in Merlot. **85 Best Buy** —*S.H. (5/1/2001)*

Bandiera 1998 Vineyard Reserve Merlot (California) $10. This wine offers some blackberry aromas and flavors. On the downside are herbaceous green notes, especially on the rather sharp finish. It's a thin wine. **82** —*S.H. (8/1/2001)*

BANDON

Bandon 2004 Pinot Gris (Oregon) $14. Soft, light flavors of fresh pear and green apple. Some nice skin flavors add a bit of punch to the finish. **86** —*P.G. (2/1/2006)*

BANNISTER

Bannister 2002 Chardonnay (Russian River Valley) $20. Kind of thin and earthy, this very dry wine has slight flavors of citrus fruits and apples. Finishes with a scoury, grapefruit and apricot fruitiness. **84** —*S.H. (10/1/2005)*

Bannister 1999 Porter-Bass Chardonnay (Russian River Valley) $38. This is a tight, taut Chard, grown very close to the Pacific Ocean. Acidity is the chief palate impression, high and tart, and the flavors veer toward minerals, stone, herbs, and citrus fruits. But this austerity is rich, complex and interesting. Seems likely to develop, but these coastal Chards are still experiments. **87** —*S.H. (12/15/2002)*

Bannister 2002 Porter-Bass Vineyard Chardonnay (Russian River Valley) $28. Quite an interesting wine, chewy and dense in apple, melon, and peach fruits and oak, with a chalky, minerally taste that adds texture. Turns tart with acids on the finish. **90 Editors' Choice** —*S.H. (10/1/2005)*

Bannister 2002 Rochioli & Allen Vineyards Chardonnay (Russian River Valley) $28. This Chard, from two famous vineyards, is a little too tart now for enjoyment. It has a roughness that detracts from the underlying fruit, while the oak sticks out. My hunch is that three or four years will reward your patience. **88** —*S.H. (10/1/2005)*

Bannister 1999 Rochioli and Allen Vineyards Chardonnay (Russian River Valley) $28. Green apples, so typical of Chards grown in these parts, dominate the aromas and flavors. The wine has a real bite of tartness and almost seems to crunch on the palate. Softer, lusher notes are provided by oak and lees, but it remains a lean, Chablisian wine. That makes it a fantastic partner for food. **90** —*S.H. (12/15/2002)*

Bannister 1999 Floodgate Vineyard Pinot Noir (Anderson Valley) $30. Starts with aromas of espresso, cola, beefsteak tomato, and black cherry, all spiced up with black pepper. Turns tart and acidic in the mouth; it's a fresh, young wine that calls for mid-term cellaring. Underlying flavors of cranberry and black cherry suggest it will soften and develop by 2004. **87** —*S.H. (2/1/2003)*

Bannister 2002 Salzgeber Vineyard Pinot Noir (Russian River Valley) $34. Hard to tell if this wine is just young and closed now and will age, or if it's a tough, earthy Pinot with no future. It's very dry, with a gritty mouthfeel and a bitter cherry finish. My guess is to drink up now. **85** —*S.H. (10/1/2005)*

BARBOURSVILLE

Barboursville 1998 Chardonnay (Virginia) $12. **83** —*J.C. (8/1/1999)*

Barboursville 1998 Merlot (Monticello) $16. **85** —*J.C. (8/1/1999)*

Barboursville 1998 Pinot Grigio (Monticello) $13. **86** *(8/1/1999)*

Barboursville 1998 Riesling (Monticello) $10. **82** —*J.C. (8/1/1999)*

BAREFOOT BUBBLY

Barefoot Bubbly NV Brut Cuvée Chardonnay Champagne Sparkling Blend (California) $9. Nice and dry, with crisp acidity and a good stream of bubbles, this sparkler has pleasantly yeasty flavors of peaches and cream. The finish is clean and satisfying. **85 Best Buy** —*S.H. (6/1/2006)*

Barefoot Bubbly NV Premium Extra Dry Chardonnay Champagne Sparkling Blend (California) $7. Frankly sweet, with sugared peach pie flavors, including the toasted crust, this sparkling wine is clean and smooth in texture. It's a good value. **84 Best Buy** —*S.H. (12/31/2005)*

BAREFOOT CELLARS

Barefoot Cellars 1999 Cabernet Sauvignon (Sonoma County) $17. An uninteresting wine, from the awkward, stemmy aromas to the rough

USA

mouthfeel. True, there's some ripe berry fruit, but the wine is soft and featureless, and has herbal flavors of bay leaf and oregano. **83** —*S.H.* *(3/1/2003)*

Barefoot Cellars 2003 Reserve Cabernet Sauvignon (Dry Creek Valley) $15. This release is soft and simple. It has thinned-down berry flavors and is dry, with some dusty tannins. **83** —*S.H. (11/15/2006)*

Barefoot Cellars 2001 Reserve Cabernet Sauvignon (Dry Creek Valley) $17. This nice, fruity wine offers pleasure and complexity in a full-bodied red, with its plum, raspberry, blackberry and tobacco flavors. The youthful tannins are sweet and chewy. Best now through 2006. **86** —*S.H. (5/1/2004)*

Barefoot Cellars 2000 Reserve Cabernet Sauvignon (Sonoma County) $17. An easy-drinking Cab with pleasant berry and earth flavors framed in supple tannins. **85** —*S.H. (10/1/2003)*

Barefoot Cellars NV Barefoot Bubbly Champagne Blend (California) $7. 81 —*S.H. (12/1/2000)*

Barefoot Cellars NV Bubbly Champagne Blend (California) $10. 80 *(12/15/1999)*

Barefoot Cellars NV Bubbly Brut Cuvée Champagne Blend (California) $7. Well, it's dry, bubbly, and clean. This blend of Chenin Blanc and Chardonnay is also inexpensive, but you'd never mistake it for Champagne. **81** —*S.H. (12/1/2002)*

Barefoot Cellars NV Bubbly Premium Champagne Blend (California) $7. Bizarre, with candied yam, pepper, and citrus smells, and a dry, rough feeling that leaves the palate exhausted. **80** —*S.H. (12/1/2002)*

Barefoot Cellars NV Cuvée Brut Champagne Blend (California) $8. Plesant and sweet spice aromas mark the nose of this easy drinker. Soft on the palatem with a frothy mousse, it has lemon candy flavors that will have broad sweet-tooth appeal. Finishes sugary, with moderate length. **82** *(12/1/2001)*

Barefoot Cellars NV Chardonnay (California) $6. A good price for a fruity dry wine with some real Chard character. Apple flavors in a creamy finish lead to a spicy finish. **83 Best Buy** —*S.H. (10/1/2005)*

Barefoot Cellars NV Chardonnay (California) $6. This is a modest Chard, yet it's clean and vibrant, with proper varietal character in the peach and apple flavors, with a dollop of oak and cream. **83 Best Buy** —*S.H. (4/1/2006)*

Barefoot Cellars NV Brut Cuvée Chardonnay (California) $7. A perfectly acceptable sparkler for parties, with its flavors of peaches and cream, and smoky notes. Finishes very dry, with a scour of acidity. **84** —*S.H. (12/1/2003)*

Barefoot Cellars NV Brut Cuvée Chardonnay (California) $7. Sometimes you need a good bubbly but can't spend a lot: weddings, bar mitzvahs, block parties, that sort of thing. This 100% Chardonnay is terrific, with apple, peach, and brioche flavors, fine mousse, and an elegant finish. **86 Best Buy** —*S.H. (11/15/2003)*

Barefoot Cellars 2004 Reserve Chardonnay (Russian River Valley) $15. There's tons of ripe peach custard and pineapple tart flavor in this wine, and also some good, crisp acidity, but it's so sweet tasting that it's really almost off-dry. That reduces its score. **83** —*S.H. (3/1/2006)*

Barefoot Cellars 2003 Reserve Chardonnay (Russian River Valley) $15. Similar to Barefoot's non-vintage Chard bottling, with apple flavors and dry, crisp acids. There's a little more oak, and a fuller body. **84** —*S.H. (10/1/2005)*

Barefoot Cellars 1997 Reserve Chardonnay (Sonoma) $NA. A very drinkable Chardonnay from this well-known producer of bargain priced wines. Clean and not overly manipulated with pleasing pear and spice aromas and flavors. The oak is nicely integrated (a pleasant surprise) and ends with a mildly spicy finish of moderate length. **87** —*M.M. (6/1/2003)*

Barefoot Cellars 2000 Reserve Impression Meritage (Alexander Valley) $18. There's some very pretty fruit in this Sonoma County Cabernet Franc-based blend. It tastes of black cherries and currants, with a tasty edge of dried herbs and oak. Be warned that the tannins are very strong and aggressive, and are not likely to age out. **86** —*S.H. (11/15/2003)*

Barefoot Cellars 2003 Reserve Merlot (Alexander Valley) $15. This round and supple Merlot is ripe in juicy blackberry and coffee flavors, framed in chewy, soft tannins. It's totally dry, and shows lots of class for the price. **85** —*S.H. (11/15/2005)*

Barefoot Cellars 2000 Reserve Merlot (Russian River Valley) $17. A young wine, from the dark, blue-black color to the immature aromas of blackberry jam and oak. In the mouth, the tannins strike hard and fast, followed up by acidity. But there's a solid core of blackberry fruit. This wine demands cellaring. Try after 2004. **86** —*S.H. (2/1/2003)*

Barefoot Cellars 1999 Reserve Merlot (Sonoma County) $17. 86 —*S.H. (9/1/2002)*

Barefoot Cellars 2001 Pinot Noir (Russian River Valley) $15. Simple and fruity, with cherry, tea, and cola flavors and soft tannins. It's an easy drinking wine, dry and clean, with Pinotesque silkiness. **85** —*S.H. (2/1/2003)*

Barefoot Cellars 1999 Pinot Noir (Sonoma County) $15. Light and delicate, it attracts more for its stylish finesse than for any power or ageability. Berry and earth flavors are framed in modest tannins and soft acids, and there's some bitterness from the middle palate through the finish. **84** —*S.H. (7/1/2002)*

Barefoot Cellars 2003 Reserve Pinot Noir (Russian River Valley) $15. You get a lot of Pinot character in this cool-climate wine, with its brisk acids, light, silky texture and pleasant flavors of cherries, raspberries, cola, and spices. Those fruity flavors sink down deep and last a long time. **87** —*S.H. (11/15/2005)*

Barefoot Cellars 2002 Reserve Pinot Noir (Russian River Valley) $16. This pale, weak wine doesn't reveal much fruit, beyond a touch of candied cherry. It's light in body, with a fast finish. **83** *(11/1/2004)*

Barefoot Cellars 2000 Reserve Pinot Noir (Sonoma County) $NA. 87 *(5/1/2002)*

Barefoot Cellars 1998 Reserve Pinot Noir (Sonoma County) $15. 86 —*J.C. (12/15/2000)*

Barefoot Cellars NV Barefoot on the Beach Red Blend (California) $5. With upfront blackberry, cherry, and raisin flavors, this dryish wine is soft, with grapeskin tannins that feel puckery. It's a simple wine that will wash down simple fare. **83 Best Buy** —*S.H. (7/1/2006)*

Barefoot Cellars 2001 Sauvignon Blanc (California) $6. A brisk, tart white wine that scours the palate with lemony flavors and leaves the throat feeling fresh and clean. The vibrancy of its lines, and the sleek, acidic structure are softened by a very slight residual sugar in the finish. **87 Best Buy** —*S.H. (1/1/2004)*

Barefoot Cellars 2004 Reserve Sauvignon Blanc (Alexander Valley) $13. So good, so refreshing, you can taste the sunshine in every savory sip of this delightful wine. It's packed with sweet citrus fruits, tangy gooseberry, ripe fig, and white pepper flavors, set up against crisp, bright acids. Finishes tart and puckery, preparing the palate for food. **87** —*S.H. (11/15/2005)*

Barefoot Cellars 2002 Reserve Sauvignon Blanc (Alexander Valley) $15. Spare and lean, a watery glassful of alcohol and acidity. Has slight peach and citrus flavors and is overpriced for what you get. **83** —*S.H. (12/31/2003)*

Barefoot Cellars 2001 Reserve Sauvignon Blanc (Dry Creek Valley) $13. Fruity, slightly sweet, and simple, with ripe flavors of citrus, fig, melon, and spices. Drinks crisp and clean, with a spicy, fruity finish. Try with fruity salsa toppings. **85** —*S.H. (3/1/2003)*

Barefoot Cellars NV Extra Dry Sparkling Blend (California) $7. A very nice sparkling wine, and a good value at this price. Makes the right moves with its delicate peach, strawberry, baked bread, and vanilla aromas, and rich, fruity flavor. A fierce burst of bubbles makes the wine crisp and bubbly in the mouth. **86 Best Buy** —*S.H. (12/1/2003)*

Barefoot Cellars NV Syrah (California) $6. You won't confuse this for Cote Rotie, but it's a nice, honest country wine. It has rich flavors of blackberries, coffee, and herbs, and is totally dry. A great value for an everyday red. **84 Best Buy** —*S.H. (11/15/2005)*

USA

Barefoot Cellars NV Syrah (California) $6. Stinky and funky, with watery berry flavors and astringent tannins. **80** —*S.H. (3/1/2004)*

Barefoot Cellars NV Barefoot on the Beach White Blend (California) $4. It's slightly sweet and quite rustic, but serviceable. **82** —*S.H. (11/15/2005)*

Barefoot Cellars NV Barefoot on the Beach White Wine White Blend (California) $5. Sugary sweet, with apricot flavors. Finishes clean and fruity, with a flourish of brisk acids. Serve well chilled. **83 Best Buy** — *S.H. (7/1/2006)*

Barefoot Cellars NV Zinfandel (California) $6. Nonvintage juice at an amazing price. It's not going to knock your favorite Zin off the shelf, but as a house pour for spaghetti and meatballs-style cooking, it would do just fine. It has some sweet, tomato-juice flavors and a fair bit of concentration in the finish. **83** —*P.G. (3/1/2001)*

Barefoot Cellars NV Zinfandel (California) $6. Weddings and block parties come to mind with this wine. At this price, it's perfect for satisfying large numbers of folks when all they need is a dry, clean, full-bodied, fruity red to wash down everything from fried chicken to BBQ. **84 Best Buy** — *S.H. (10/1/2006)*

Barefoot Cellars NV Barefoot on the Beach White Zinfandel (California) $5. Off-dry, almost semi-sweet, this wine has the twin virtues of crisp acidity and ripe, juicy fruit. Just as the name says, it suggests pleasant days on the beach, with an ample picnic hamper. **83 Best Buy** —*S.H. (7/1/2006)*

Barefoot Cellars 2001 Reserve Zinfandel (Dry Creek Valley) $10. Toasty oak leads the way here, with hints of cherry, blackberry, spice and herbs on the finish. Moderate in length. **84** *(11/1/2003)*

Barefoot Cellars 1998 Reserve Zinfandel (Sonoma County) $17. So young, fresh and frisky, it's a puppy of a wine, filled with exuberant wild-berry flavors, especially red ones, like red rasberry and strawberry. The acidity is high enough to tingle the palate, and yet it's weirdly soft, It's as if all the tannins had been strained out. **85** —*S.H. (12/15/2001)*

BARGETTO

Bargetto 2002 Chardonnay (Central Coast) $12. Mixes a rich earthiness with a ripe peach finish and lots of toasty, spicy oak. Easy to drink, and not a bad price for an everyday Chard. **84** —*S.H. (12/1/2004)*

Bargetto 2000 Chardonnay (Central Coast) $NA. Good value for the money in this easy-drinking wine, with ripe peach and apple flavors and hints of honey, smoke, and spices. It's round and supple and flavorful, and the finish is polished and ripe. **84** —*S.H. (9/12/2002)*

Bargetto 2000 Regan Vineyard Chardonnay (Santa Cruz Mountains) $20. Lush, ripe, and oaky, with oodles of juicy peach and tropical fruit flavors accented with the smoke, vanilla and spices of oak. The finish adds a burst of cleansing acidity. **89** —*S.H. (2/1/2003)*

Bargetto 2001 Regan Vineyards Chardonnay (Santa Cruz Mountains) $18. Ripe grapes went into this juicy, extracted wine, with its big, bold flavors of peaches and spice. Oak adds smoky nuances and a round, creamy texture through the long finish. **86** —*S.H. (6/1/2003)*

Bargetto 2000 Gewürztraminer (Monterey) $10. Spicy and floral, just oozing with ginger, cinnamon, Graham cracker, fig, buttercup, and honeysuckle aromas and flavors. There's a taste of fresh, ripe, spicy peaches in the finish. Slightly off-dry. Those nice Salinas Valley acids make it refreshing. **85** —*S.H. (9/1/2003)*

Bargetto 2000 Dry Gewürztraminer (Santa Cruz Mountains) $12. This single-vineyard wine smells unbelievably good, with gingerbread, honey, citrus, vanilla custard, and tropical fruit notes bursting from the glass. The flavors are as good, filled with ripe fruits and spices. It's not all that dry, but pretty much so. One of the best Gewürzes of the vintage, and an incredible value. **90** —*S.H. (9/12/2002)*

Bargetto 2001 Merlot (Santa Cruz Mountains) $20. There are many admirable qualities to this wine. Its mountain origins lend it a tight, taut structure, rich in tannins and acids, yet the berry, cherry fruit is accessible and ripe. And what a deliciously long, sweet finish it has. **90** —*S.H. (12/15/2004)*

Bargetto 2000 Merlot (California) $12. Has good acidity and lovely tannins, which are soft and plush in the mouth, with good acidity. Feels great, but loses a few points because of green, unripe flavors that ride

side by side with riper blackberry ones. That sharpness really kicks in on the finish. **84** —*S.H. (4/1/2003)*

Bargetto 1999 Merlot (Santa Cruz Mountains) $20. The problem with this wine is an excess of less-than-ripe grapes. There's some green stemminess in the aroma and this is confirmed in the mouth, where the wine turns thin. It's not a bad wine, just simple, and too expensive for this quality. **83** —*S.H. (4/1/2003)*

Bargetto 1998 Reserve Merlot (Santa Cruz Mountains) $30. A disagreeable wine. There's a medicinal quality in the aroma that suggests plastic bandages, and the flavors are thin, sharp, and acidic. It's impossible to separate your impression of the wine from the price. It's a rip off. **81** — *S.H. (9/12/2002)*

Bargetto 2003 Pinot Grigio (California) $15. A simple and likeable wine, with juicy flavors of spearmint, figs, and sweet apples. Good acidity, and a little bit of sweetness. **84** —*S.H. (11/15/2004)*

Bargetto 2001 Pinot Grigio (California) $16. Fruity, with apricot, citrus, and peach flavors that drink slightly sweet or just off-dry. Very fresh acidity helps boost the flavor profile and keep the structure keen and lively. **84** —*S.H. (9/1/2003)*

Bargetto 2000 Pinot Grigio (California) $16. Smells fresh and lemony, with accents of smoke and butter. You also get sweetish lemon flavors, with a real attack of acidity. The wine is a little spritzy, which isn't all that bad, although it may be better as an aperitif than a food wine. **84** —*S.H. (9/1/2002)*

Bargetto 2004 Pinot Gris (California) $14. This is a simple, soft, fruity wine that's also a little sweet on the finish. It has flavors of canned apricots and peaches. **83** —*S.H. (2/1/2006)*

Bargetto 2001 Regan Vineyards Pinot Noir (Santa Cruz Mountains) $20. Shows lots of finesse in addition to the pretty cherry, raspberry, and herb flavors that are wrapped in a delicately fine structure. Silky tannins and crisp acids provide the balance and strength to make this a versatile food wine. **87** —*S.H. (12/15/2004)*

Bargetto 2000 Regan Vineyards Pinot Noir (Santa Cruz County) $30. An awkward wine, it begins with plummy, black cherry aromas and earth. It's overtly fruity, almost candied, with bright, sweet cherry and other red stone fruit and sugary cola flavors. Nice texture, but too sweet, and needs more stuffing and depth. **83** —*S.H. (5/1/2002)*

Bargetto 1999 Regan Vineyards Pinot Noir (Santa Cruz Mountains) $30. 84 *(10/1/2002)*

Bargetto 2000 Regan Vineyards Reserve Pinot Noir (Santa Cruz Mountains) $40. A bit earthy, but there's a nice streak of cassis and black cherry, and the silky texture is sheer pleasure. The spicy finish is rich. **87** —*S.H. (7/1/2003)*

Bargetto 1999 La Vita Regan Vineyards Red Blend (Santa Cruz Mountains) $50. Raspingly dry and tannic, with earthy, herbal flavors and a hint of dark berry fruit, this blend of Dolcetto, Refosco, Nebbiolo, and Merlot may develop complexity with age. From Bargetto. **84** —*S.H. (12/15/2004)*

Bargetto 2002 Syrah (Monterey County) $16. Comes across as a bit Port-like, with scents of raisins and a hint of alcohol, but also a big, extracted mouthfeel. The tannins are soft and inviting and the flavors not unpleasant, just different. **83** *(9/1/2005)*

Bargetto 2002 Zinfandel (Lodi) $14. Big in berry-cherry fruit, dry, spicy and life-affirming, it has that wild and woolly edge of an authentic country wine. **86** —*S.H. (11/15/2004)*

Bargetto 2001 Rauser Vineyard Zinfandel (Lodi) $12. A tarry, licorice-like blend that shows hints of smoke and blackberry as well. The finish has a resiny edge. **83** —*J.M. (11/1/2003)*

BARLOW

Barlow 2001 Red Table Wine Cabernet Blend (Napa Valley) $30. One for the cellar. It opens with a swift kick of dusty tannins that numb the palate to the sweet black currant and cherry fruit buried far below. On the finish, tannins and oak dominate. But such is the overall balance, and the core of fruit, that putting it away for 10 years is no

USA

gamble at all. Cabernet Sauvignon (80%) and Merlot. **90** —*S.H.* *(6/1/2004)*

Barlow 2002 Cabernet Sauvignon (Napa Valley) $40. Released a year later than the '02 Merlot, this Cab is drinkable, although the tannins remain fairly astringent. The fruit is ripe, suggesting black currants and cassis. A distraction is a bitter note on the finish that is unlikely to age out. **86** —*S.H. (12/15/2005)*

Barlow 2001 Cabernet Sauvignon (Napa Valley) $39. Ripe in black currant fruit and nicely balanced in rich tannins and good acids. Just oozes flavor and character. Almost a food group of its own. Keep the food pairing simple, like a grilled steak or rib roast. **92 Editors' Choice** —*S.H. (10/1/2004)*

Barlow 2000 Cabernet Sauvignon (Napa Valley) $36. Made in a classic Napa style, with pronounced aromas of cassis and black currant and a considerably layering of well-charred, toasty oak. Doesn't disappoint on the entry, and then it spreads currant and herb flavors all over the palate, wrapped in rich, fine, ripe tannins. Very good, but lacks that extra bit of intensity. **90** —*S.H. (11/15/2003)*

Barlow 2002 Merlot (Napa Valley) $32. Takes the usual formula of cherries, blackberries, cocoa, and oak and kicks it up a notch. It has all that, but the extra layers of dusty oriental spices and a wonderful integration of oak with ripe tannins add interest. The bottom line is elegance. **91** —*S.H. (4/1/2005)*

Barlow 2001 Merlot (Napa Valley) $NA. This big, fat, sexy wine is just what Merlot is supposed to be. It's softly accessible, yet complex with rich, sweet tannins and a delicious array of cassis, plum, cherry, and herb flavors. As good as it is, it possesses a feminine complexity that suggests pairing it with food. **91** —*S.H. (6/1/2004)*

Barlow 2000 Merlot (Napa Valley) $28. Textbook Napa Merlot. Flavors of green olives, blackberries, white chocolate, and herbs, with a slight meatiness, are wrapped in delicate, fine tannins. The wine is very dry and feels great in the mouth. Has the stuffing to improve in the cellar for a few years. **91** —*S.H. (8/1/2003)*

Barlow 2002 Barrouge Red Blend (Napa Valley) $38. Very smooth and ripe, with a rich complex of black currant, cassis, cocoa, green olive, smoke, and oak flavors. It's a soft wine, but far from simple. Finishes with a peacock's tail of oriental spices. **91** —*S.H. (4/1/2005)*

Barlow 2001 Zinfandel (Napa Valley) $19. A bit dry on the tongue, with light cherry, raspberry, herb, toast, and plum notes coming through. There is a nice floral edge on the finish for added interest, though. Perhaps it will round out a bit in the bottle with time. Give it another year or so. **87** *(11/1/2003)*

BARNARD GRIFFIN

Barnard Griffin 2000 Cabernet Franc (Columbia Valley (WA)) $30. Carefully controlled yield has resulted in a splendid Cabernet Franc with classic aromas of blueberries and coffee. Austere yet complete, it shows a firm structure, well-managed tannins, good grip, and tight, muscular black fruit. Just 230 cases were produced. **90** —*P.G. (6/1/2002)*

Barnard Griffin 2003 Cabernet Sauvignon (Columbia Valley (WA)) $14. Middle of the road, simple and clean, with light herbs and a food-friendly lightness and balance at 13.8% alcohol. **87** —*P.G. (12/15/2005)*

Barnard Griffin 2001 Cabernet Sauvignon (Columbia Valley (WA)) $15. A good one, with flavors of grape and plum up front, good acid and restrained (13.1% alcohol). Well-constructed, though not deep or complex; it's ready right now. **87** —*P.G. (9/1/2004)*

Barnard Griffin 1999 Cabernet Sauvignon (Columbia Valley (WA)) $18. A budget-priced Cabernet with a sweet nose that includes a distinctive mix of talcum powder, toast, and cinnamon spice. The wine is simple, tart, and spicy, and the finish rather chalky and tannic. **85** —*P.G. (12/31/2001)*

Barnard Griffin 2000 Chardonnay (Columbia Valley (WA)) $14. This winery imprints a distinct style on virtually everything it releases; here it is a Chardonnay that smells strongly of new-mown hay, with an earthy, dusty undercurrent that carries over to the palate. Some alcoholic heat is there as well, along with the taste of grassy herbs. **86** —*P.G. (2/1/2002)*

Barnard Griffin 2000 Reserve Chardonnay (Columbia Valley (WA)) $19. Here is a well-priced Chardonnay that delivers a bit extra. Plump, soft fruit with a hint of honey and plenty of butterscotch. There's even a hint of licorice. All in all, a well-rounded, forward, fruity effort with front-loaded flavors. **88** —*P.G. (7/1/2002)*

Barnard Griffin 2000 Wahluke Slope Vineyard Chardonnay (Columbia Valley (WA)) $19. Rich and satisfying in all respects. It offers full, fat fruit flavor, a generous complement of new oak, and a juicy, oily, mouthcoating grip. Finishes with a pleasing burst of roasted nuts. **90** —*P.G. (9/1/2002)*

Barnard Griffin 2004 Fumé Blanc (Columbia Valley (WA)) $9. This dry Sauvignon Blanc, all stainless fermented, represents a change in style for B-G that puts it more in line with the lime/citrus flavors of New Zealand. Gone are the herbaceous notes; here the flavor is all about citrus zest, providing sharp relief around the good, juicy fruit. Barnard Griffin is one of the largest family-owned wineries in Washington, and winemaker Rob Griffin has been making wine in the state since 1976. "We're too available to be cultish," he modestly explains. But if there were $9 cult wines, this would qualify. **88 Best Buy** —*P.G. (11/15/2005)*

Barnard Griffin 2003 Fumé Blanc (Columbia Valley (WA)) $8. Rich, creamy, and loaded with luscious fig and melon flavors, this consistent crowd-pleaser from Rob Griffin is loaded with irresistible flavors. Round and full-bodied, it's a fruit salad of melons, figs, and grapefruit, riper than usual thanks to the extremely hot, dry vintage. There's also a toasty complexity to the finish, due to the inclusion of 16% barrel-fermented Sémillon in the blend. **88 Best Buy** —*P.G. (12/1/2004)*

Barnard Griffin 2002 Fumé Blanc (Columbia Valley (WA)) $8. A rich, creamy, textured wine; with luscious fig and melon flavors. The blend includes about 18% Sémillon, which gives it breadth. The modest, 12.6% alcohol makes it a better balanced wine as well. **89 Best Buy** —*P.G. (5/1/2004)*

Barnard Griffin 2000 Fumé Blanc (Columbia Valley (WA)) $11. This is a lovely bottle, with clean, crisp fruit providing the backbone. Complex flavors of melon, fig, and sweetpea, just the right hint of grassiness, and some good, toasty vanilla make for a full-flavored, satisfying bottle. **88 Best Buy** —*P.G. (12/31/2001)*

Barnard Griffin 2001 Merlot (Columbia Valley (WA)) $15. Straight-ahead, no frills Merlot, with plenty of up-front strawberry/cherry Lifesaver fruit flavors. There are some stiff, slightly weedy tannins as well, and the finish is quite astringent. This Pomerol wannabe would taste best with a nice cut of beef. **87** —*P.G. (9/1/2004)*

Barnard Griffin 2000 Merlot (Columbia Valley (WA)) $15. Despite its early release, this is a fragrant, approachable wine with pretty scents of cassis and vanilla. There is none of the weediness that can plague inexpensive Columbia Valley Merlot; rather it is nicely balanced and strung tight, with firm, not opulent fruit and a smooth finish. **89 Best Buy** —*P.G. (6/1/2002)*

Barnard Griffin 1998 Merlot (Columbia Valley (WA)) $17. **90** —*P.G. (6/1/2000)*

Barnard Griffin 2003 Ciel du Cheval Merlot (Red Mountain) $30. Just 175 cases were made of this 100% Merlot. Great juice, it shows concentrated cherry and blackberry aromas and flavors. Ripe and rich and voluptuous, there's a jammy sweetness to the fruit. **89** —*P.G. (12/15/2005)*

Barnard Griffin 2002 Caroway Vineyard Sémillon (Columbia Valley (WA)) $NA. Round and full, voluptuous even, this lip-smacking Sémillon blends in notes of honey and hay to expand upon its ripe peach and papaya flavors. Citrus rind completes the tangy finish. **90** —*P.G. (9/1/2004)*

Barnard Griffin 2001 Caroway Vineyard Sémillon (Columbia Valley (WA)) $13. Sémillon, a highly undervalued, food-friendly white wine, does well in Washington when handled with care. Winemaker Rob Griffin makes one of the best; fermented and aged in French oak, it has a pretty nose of sweet pea, spice, and toast. The fruit is ripe without being tropical, and it has the acid to do well with a variety of food choices. **88 Best Buy** —*P.G. (6/1/2002)*

Barnard Griffin 2002 Syrah (Columbia Valley (WA)) $14. A young, grapey, deliciously spicy Syrah with plenty of bright, juicy berry flavors. It clocks in at 14.2% alcohol, easily supported by the dense, deep fruit. Great now, or cellar it as you would a great Zinfandel.**91 Best Buy** —*P.G. (5/1/2004)*

Barnard Griffin 2000 Syrah (Columbia Valley (WA)) $30. A first for Barnard Griffin, this young Syrah is still going through a lot of changes, and needs some time to show its strength. The early impression was of a sweet, grapey, forward wine with berry-flavored fruit and hints of white pepper. A straightforward, fruit-oriented, New World style.**86** —*P.G. (6/1/2002)*

Barnard Griffin 1999 Syrah (Columbia Valley (WA)) $30. Minty-menthol, cedar and mixed-berry flavors preface a palate where bright berries and heavy oak flavors compete for top billing. Medium-weight and tannic in the mouth, this Syrah finishes with lots of dry tannins, and bitter-coffe and steeped-tea flavors.**85** *(11/1/2001)*

Barnard Griffin 2003 Zinfandel (Columbia Valley (WA)) $22. Very citrusy and lifted, forward, scented with orange and lemon peel, cranberry, and orange flesh. Unique and persistent, the orange peel character continues all the way through.**88** —*P.G. (12/15/2005)*

BARNETT

Barnett 2003 Cabernet Sauvignon (Spring Mountain) $65. This is a very fine Cabernet, a bit too young for complete enjoyment now due to tough mountain tannins, but there's a fleshy opulence to the fruit. Totally dry, the wine feels rich and balanced, and is Bordeaux-like in its feminine elegance, suggesting a fine St.-Julien. Hold until 2008.**92 Cellar Selection** —*S.H. (8/1/2006)*

Barnett 2002 Cabernet Sauvignon (Spring Mountain) $60. Here's a text-book Napa Cab. It's concentrated in black currant flavors, with the best tannic structure money can buy. Soft and elegant in the mouth, with a long, elegant finish. Could use some individuality, though, as it's firmly in the international style.**91** —*S.H. (10/1/2005)*

Barnett 2003 Rattlesnake Hill Cabernet Sauvignon (Spring Mountain) $110. The fruity intensity of this young Cabernet is impressive, an explosion of cassis and cocoa flavor that dominates the palate. Beyond that is the overall balance. The tannins are sturdy, with good, clean acidity, and the finish is exceptionally long and rich. This classic mountain Napa Cabernet is tough now, and should slowly soften over the next 15 years. **94 Cellar Selection** —*S.H. (8/1/2006)*

Barnett 1998 Chardonnay (Napa Valley) $25.88 *(6/1/2000)*

Barnett 2000 Chardonnay (Napa Valley) $25. Quite bright and lemony, with a tangy mineral core that's backed by green apple, pear, melon, and herb notes. Toasty oak frames the ensemble, which is zippy on the finish. **88** —*J.M. (5/1/2002)*

Barnett 2004 Sangiacomo Vineyard Chardonnay (Carneros) $29. This is a very nice, stylish Chardonnay that's good in varietal character, yet balanced and elegant enough not to blow away any food it accompanies. Dry and crisp in acids, it shows citrus, peach, and apple flavors that finish clean and zesty.**87** —*S.H. (8/1/2006)*

Barnett 2004 Savoy Vineyard Chardonnay (Anderson Valley) $35. This Chard has a lot of lees and oak influences. It feels overworked, especially given the high acidity and lean, citrusy fruit. Bone dry, this single-vineyard wine should work well with raw shellfish.**85** —*S.H. (8/1/2006)*

Barnett 2003 Merlot (Spring Mountain) $45. Polished and ripe, this wine has a gentle, soft mouthfeel that sports red and black cherry, mocha, and blackberry flavors. Despite the gentleness, there are firm tannins that cry out for a broiled steak. Best now through 2007.**87** —*S.H. (8/1/2006)*

Barnett 1997 Pinot Noir (Santa Lucia Highlands) $25.87 *(12/15/1999)*

Barnett 2004 Pinot Noir (Santa Barbara County) $37. Here's a nice, easy, delicate Pinot, light on the palate and drily silky, yet with ripe fruity insistence. There's plenty of elegance, with cherry, cola, and spice flavors that finish with complexity. Best now.**88** —*S.H. (9/1/2006)*

Barnett 2004 Pinot Noir (Russian River Valley) $37. Classic Russian River Pinot from a warm year. The wine is dry and crispy-soft, if that's not a

contradiction, and the cherry and cola fruit is nearly raisined, but stops just short. The texture is all silk and satin. This wine is best consumed early. Drink now.**89** —*S.H. (9/1/2006)*

Barnett 2004 Savoy Vineyard Pinot Noir (Anderson Valley) $45. This classy Pinot Noir doesn't require age, but a few years won't hurt. It's young and dry, with an elegantly silky mouthfeel framing ripe red and black cherry and mocha fruit and lots of Asian spice, especially on the finish. Yet it's also somewhat tannic. Best to decant for a few hours if you open it now. **93** —*S.H. (9/1/2006)*

Barnett 2000 Sleepy Hollow Vineyard Pinot Noir (Santa Lucia Highlands) $40. An interesting and complex wine sure to provoke discussion, the 2000 Barnett offers some starchy vegetable aromas and flavors but also pretty black cherry and plum notes that wind up on top. It's tart and tannic but well fruited, and should last for several years.**90** *(10/1/2002)*

BARNWOOD

Barnwood 1997 Trio Bordeaux Blend (Santa Barbara County) $29.88 —*L.W. (12/31/1999)*

Barnwood 2002 Cabernet Sauvignon (Santa Barbara County) $22. Ripe in juicy blackberry and cherry flavors, with an edge of sweet dried herbs and some oak, this polished Cab is soft and gentle. Has enough acidity to keep it brisk.**85** —*S.H. (2/1/2005)*

Barnwood 2001 Cabernet Sauvignon (Santa Barbara County) $22. Smells ripe and fruity, then provides a letdown once it hits the mouth. The promise of currant and cherry turns herbal, with a hint of blackberry. This dry wine finishes with astringent tannins.**83** —*S.H. (11/15/2003)*

Barnwood 2000 Cabernet Sauvignon (Santa Barbara County) $22. Sort of like a photocopy of a good Napa Cabernet. Loses a bit of detail, but still has enough fruity-berry flavors to be a good wine. The rich texture and pleasing notes added by oak are especially nice.**86** —*S.H. (6/1/2003)*

Barnwood 2004 3200 Cabernet Sauvignon (Santa Barbara County) $20. Rustic, with earth and berry flavors that finish soft and simply.**82** —*S.H. (11/15/2006)*

Barnwood 1997 Reserve Merlot (Santa Barbara County) $27.88 —*L.W. (12/31/1999)*

Barnwood 2004 Long Shadow Petite Sirah (Santa Barbara County) $20. Weedy, with menthol flavors and a touch of blackberry. The lack of fruity richness emphasizes the acidity and tannins.**82** —*S.H. (11/15/2006)*

Barnwood 2003 Long Shadow Petite Sirah (Santa Barbara County) $20. This is a very good Pet, dark, full-bodied, and dry. There's an edge of leather and coffee to the blackberry flavors, and the tannins are rich, thick, and ageworthy. It has a Cabernet-like balance that makes it very drinkable.**87** —*S.H. (3/1/2006)*

Barnwood 2002 Trio Red Blend (Santa Barbara County) $35. An interesting blend that combines ripe, juicy fruit with fairly firm tannins to make for balance. The blackberry, cherry, and coffee flavors will complement a nice steak. Cabernet, Merlot, Syrah.**85** —*S.H. (2/1/2005)*

Barnwood 2000 Trio Red Blend (Santa Barbara County) $35. Smells almost like a dessert wine, with aromas of baked cherry pie, caramel, and chocolate fudge. Yet it's not sweet at all, and has nice flavors of cherries. A bit eccentric, but pretty good. Merlot, Cabernet Sauvignon, and Syrah.**86** —*S.H. (6/1/2004)*

Barnwood 2004 Sauvignon Blanc (Santa Barbara County) $14. Clean and brisk in acidity, and dry, this pleasant wine features citrus, fig, green apple, and lemongrass flavors. It finishes long and fruity.**84** —*S.H. (3/1/2006)*

Barnwood 2003 Sauvignon Blanc (Santa Barbara County) $14. Bright in acids and refreshing, this wine features straightforward flavors of ripe citrus fruits, figs, melons, and a hint of papaya on the finish. Try with fish or pork with a fruity salsa.**86** —*S.H. (2/1/2005)*

Barnwood 2002 Sauvignon Blanc (Santa Barbara County) $14. Lots of character in this ripe, fruity white wine, with its lemon and lime, peach, grass, and herb flavors. Has a nice spine of firm acidity that boosts the fruit, and while it's dry, there's a honeyed finish.**85** —*S.H. (12/31/2003)*

Barnwood 2000 Sauvignon Blanc (Santa Barbara County) $14. From the highest vineyard in the county, more than 3,000 feet in altitude, comes this tight, lemony wine with lots of structural integrity. High acidity accentuates the ripe citrus flavors. The finish is a little sweet and spicy. **87** —S.H. (11/15/2001)

Barnwood 2005 The Border Sauvignon Blanc (Santa Barbara County) $14. Here's a wonderfully versatile Sauvignon Blanc, one that'll wash down everything from Mexican food to potstickers and friend chicken. Very crisp in acidity, it shows polished pink grapefruit, fig, honeydew, and peach flavors, and peppery spices. **86** —S.H. (11/15/2006)

Barnwood 1999 Syrah (Central Coast) $20. Plenty of interesting elements including soy, Indian spices, and cocoa accent the black-plum fruit of this solid offering. Juicy and lively on the tongue, it's a balanced and nicely textured example of what the Central Coast can do. The spice and soy notes reprise on the long finish, which turns just a bit woody. **87** (10/1/2001)

Barnwood 2004 Untamed Tempranillo (San Luis Obispo County) $20. Dark, very dry, soft, and simple. A hot wine with earthy tobacco and sour cherry flavors. Finishes dry and astringent. **83** —S.H. (11/15/2006)

Barnwood 2003 Untamed Tempranillo (San Luis Obispo County) $22. Dry and acidic, with dusty, sandpapery tannins, this is a distinctive wine. There's interest in the ripe red cherry and pomegranate flavors and the length of the finish. This is one of the best California Tempranillos on the market. **89** —S.H. (6/1/2006)

BARON HERZOG

Baron Herzog 1997 Cabernet Sauvignon (California) $13. **85** —S.H. (7/1/1999)

Baron Herzog 2002 Cabernet Sauvignon (California) $13. Here's an easy Cabernet. It's dry and medium-bodied, with black currant and cherry flavors and soft tannins. Finishes with the rich taste of cocoa. **84** —S.H. (8/1/2005)

Baron Herzog 1999 Cabernet Sauvignon (California) $13. Sawdust is the dominant aroma, a sure sign of heavy "introduced" oak. Some candied cherry fruit in the mouth offers balance, but overall it's still too heavily oaked. The flavor is almost like butter. This is a wine that needs more edge and balance. **82** —M.S. (4/1/2002)

Baron Herzog 1996 Special Reserve Cabernet Sauvignon (Napa Valley) $30. **86** —S.H. (9/1/1999)

Baron Herzog 1998 Chardonnay (California) $13. **85** —S.H. (10/1/2000)

Baron Herzog 1997 Chardonnay (California) $13. **80** —S.H. (7/1/1999).

Baron Herzog 1999 Chardonnay (California) $13. If you want to know what artificial oak smells and tastes like, it's on full display here. Sawdust aromas come before a creamy, oaky palate. It's not cloying or overly heavy, and the acidity is strong enough to keep things lively, but it still lacks a clean fruit character, and the forced oak flavor is not appealing. **80** —M.S. (4/1/2002)

Baron Herzog 1999 Chenin Blanc (Clarksburg) $6. **81** (9/1/2000)

Baron Herzog 2003 Chenin Blanc (Clarksburg) $7. Fans of slightly sweet white wines will enjoy the apple sauce and lemon custard flavors of this wine, which fortunately has excellent acidity. Finishes clean. **84 Best Buy** —S.H. (7/1/2005)

BARON HERZOG

Baron Herzog 2002 Chenin Blanc (Clarksburg) $7. This wine, from a leading kosher winery, is rich in apricot, peach, lime, kiwi, and nectarine fruit, and is without the wax-bean quality that can plague wines made from this variety. This version is not quite dry yet not quite sweet, and pairs perfectly with a salad of mixed greens, blue cheese, and ripe pears. **87 Best Buy** —S.H. (11/15/2003)

Baron Herzog 2000 Chenin Blanc (Clarksburg) $7. Slightly sweet, this easy-drinking sipper will go best with fusion foods or fresh fruit. Wildflower, honey, and smoky vanilla aromas lead to intensely fruity flavors, with soft acids. **83** —S.H. (11/15/2001)

Baron Herzog 1999 Merlot (Paso Robles) $13. Pretty cherry and herb flavors course through this medium-bodied Merlot. Tannins are a trifle coarse, but the ensemble makes a pleasing quaff. **85** —J.M. (11/15/2001)

Baron Herzog 1999 Sauvignon Blanc (California) $13. There's a touch of field greens on the nose, but beyond that there is little else to latch on to in this insipid white. Some citrus rind and a touch of sugar give the palate what personality it has. This will be at its most refreshing if served well chilled, because it's quite heavy on the finish. **80** —M.S. (4/1/2002)

Baron Herzog 2003 Syrah (California) $13. Direct and fruity, this is a bit simple but ultimately satisfying wine that would be at home with burgers or other uncomplicated fare. Black cherry and blackberry flavors pick up just a hint of pepper on the finish. Kosher. **86** (9/1/2005)

Baron Herzog 1997 Zinfandel (California) $13. **83** —S.H. (9/1/1999)

Baron Herzog 2001 Zinfandel (Lodi) $7. Smoky, charry notes kick off here, backed by hints of black cherry, plum, raspberry and herbs. The wine is relatively smooth on the palate, with a toasty licorice note at the end. **86** (11/1/2003)

Baron Herzog 2001 Old Vine Zinfandel (Lodi) $13. Fruity and intense in blackberries, black cherries, leather, sweet cocoa, and peppery spices, and totally dry, this is a mouth-filling Zin. It's soft and gentle, with a finish that's just slightly sweet. **86** —S.H. (8/1/2005)

Baron Herzog 1998 Old Vine Zinfandel (California) $13. **83** —S.H. (12/1/2000)

BARRA

Barra 2001 Cabernet Sauvignon (Mendocino) $22. Juicy and sweet. You can taste the sunny ripeness with every sip of the blackberry, cherry, and blueberry fruit. Oak plays a supporting role. This dry wine, with its sweet, gentle tannins is delicious. **87** —S.H. (4/1/2004)

Barra 1999 Muscat Canelli (Mendocino County) $12. From a longtime Redwood Valley grower, a white dessert wine, brimming with peach and apricot flavors that are well-defined and bright. It's pretty sweet. Congratulations on the acidity, which is penetrating, and does a good job of balancing the sugars. **87** —S.H. (5/1/2002)

Barra 1999 Petite Sirah (Mendocino) $27. From Mendocino, a big bruiser of a wine that tasted like Zinfandel to some tasters, with its brambly, wild berry flavors and touches of leather and tar. Everyone liked the balanced feeling, aided by rich tannins and firm acidity. **84** (4/1/2003)

Barra 1998 Petite Sirah (Mendocino County) $21. From Redwood Valley, a dark wine the color of ink, with deep, brooding and fun aromas. Try chocolate, charcoal, blackberries, cassis, and something smoky-sweet from oak. Drinks extracted and jammy, with flavors of blackberries and black cherries. Has sturdy tannins, although it's a bit soft. **90** —S.H. (5/1/2002)

Barra 1999 Pinot Blanc (Mendocino) $14. You might mistake this for Chardonnay, with the apple and peach flavors, vanilla, and oak flavorings, and complexities from what seems like lees aging. It flatters the palate with semi-sweet fruit and rich, almost candied creaminess, but has a refreshing acidity that prevents it from being cloying. **87** —S.H. (5/1/2002)

Barra 1999 Pinot Noir (Mendocino) $15. Controversial. Grown in the Redwood Valley, a hot part of inland Mendocino, the argument is that the downright cold nights preserve acidity. But it's overly soft in the mouth, with berry, peppery flavors that are almost Rhône-like. The tannins are silky enough, but the wine lacks that essential Pinot delicacy. **84** —S.H. (5/1/2002)

BARRA OF MENDOCINO

Barra of Mendocino 2002 Pinot Noir (Mendocino) $16. Not a whole lot going on in this simple wine. It's pale and light-bodied, with flavors of tea and watermelon. Turns watery on the finish. **83** (11/1/2004)

BARREL 27

Barrel 27 2004 Syrah (Paso Robles) $18. Very nice. Soft and gentle, with real class and polish. Shows refined cherry and mocha flavors with rich char and vanilla from new oak. Easy to drink, with some complexity. **87** —S.H. (11/15/2006)

Barrel 27 2002 Syrah (Paso Robles) $13. From the well-known Fralich and French Camp vineyards, a good value in a dry, full-bodied Syrah. Lots of nuance in the plumy, chocolaty, Chinese spice flavors and firm tannins. **87** —S.H. (12/1/2004)

BARRELSTONE

Barrelstone 2003 Syrah (Columbia Valley (WA)) $10. An easy quaffer, not that dissimilar from a light-bodied Australian Shiraz. Candied berry and vanilla fruit, smooth mouthfeel, and a hint of herbs make this a nice summer-weight Syrah that you could even serve slightly chilled, à la Beaujolais. **85 Best Buy** *(9/1/2005)*

Barrelstone 2001 Syrah (Columbia Valley (WA)) $14. Despite the buzz over Syrah in Washington, with more than 40 wineries making at least a few hundred cases, there is little to choose from under $20. This is very light and pleasant, with superficial cherry flavors and a whiff of toasty oak at the end. **86** *—P.G. (12/31/2003)*

BARRISTER

Barrister 2003 Cabernet Franc (Columbia Valley (WA)) $24. Substantial and concentrated, this jams the palate with layers of boysenberry, blackberry, and black cherry fruit. The oak is just right, and overall it is a very well made wine, big and a bit raw-boned but nicely defined. The finish is just a bit one-dimensional. **89** *—P.G. (4/1/2006)*

Barrister 2002 Cabernet Franc (Columbia Valley (WA)) $24. This new producer grabbed a "Best Limited Production Wine" award at the La County Fair for this herbal and flavorful effort. Once you rip past the bell pepper scents and dig into the wine, it's got dark Cab Franc fruit flavors, accented with ground coffee and plenty of smoky oak. The mid-palate is fleshy and concentrated, loaded with sweet fruit, while the finish lingers like smoke from a barbecue. **89** *—P.G. (12/1/2004)*

Barrister 2001 Cabernet Franc (Columbia Valley (WA)) $24. This is the first release from this tiny boutique winery. Good fruit is sourced from Walla Walla and Yakima Valley vineyards, and there is some spicy, well-handled oak. Just 145 cases were made. **87** *—P.G. (12/31/2003)*

Barrister 2002 Cabernet Sauvignon (Columbia Valley (WA)) $29. The winery's first Cab, this is made from a blend of Pepper Bridge and Bacchus fruit, with a smattering of Red Mountain Merlot. Tarry, smoky, dark ,and dense, it shows supple fruits and superb concentration. Black cherry, ripe berry, and espresso are wrapped together, with whiffs of fresh-cut tobacco. **92** *—P.G. (4/1/2006)*

Barrister 2003 Bacchus Vineyard Cabernet Sauvignon (Columbia Valley (WA)) $29. The winery's first vineyard-designated Cab will be released officially in February 2006. Stylish, lighter and more elegant than the 2002 Cab, this weaves leaf and herbal accents throughout. 185 cases made. **90** *—P.G. (4/1/2006)*

Barrister 2003 Merlot (Red Mountain) $28. A thick, chewy, fleshy and chocolaty wine, this is classic Washington Merlot. Nothing wimpy about it, the concentrated boysenberry, blueberry, cherry, and chocolate flavors are enhanced with cedary aromas and some streaks of cinnamon. Way better than the '02. **91** *—P.G. (4/1/2006)*

Barrister 2003 Syrah (Walla Walla (WA)) $26. The fruit, from Walla Walla's great Morrison Lane Vineyard, is flat out sensational. Co-fermented with a generous 6% Viognier, it's a gorgeously aromatic Syrah. Whiff after whiff mixes mineral, bacon fat, wild berry, and citrus rind; once in the mouth the flavors rainbow out harmoniously, elegant, and constantly shifting. **93 Editors' Choice** *—P.G. (4/1/2006)*

BARTHOLOMEW PARK

Bartholomew Park 1997 Alta Vista Vineyards Cabernet Sauvignon (Sonoma Valley) $36. **89** *(11/1/2000)*

Bartholomew Park 1997 Batto Vineyard Cabernet Sauvignon (Sonoma Valley) $36. **93** *(11/1/2000)*

Bartholomew Park 1997 Kasper Vineyard Cabernet Sauvignon (Sonoma Valley) $41. **88** *(11/1/2000)*

Bartholomew Park 1997 Parks Vineyard Cabernet Sauvignon (Napa Valley) $37. **90** *(11/1/2000)*

Bartholomew Park 1996 Weiler Vineyard Chardonnay (Sonoma Valley) $21. **86** *—S.H. (11/1/1999)*

BASEL CELLARS

Basel Cellars 2003 Claret Bordeaux Blend (Walla Walla (WA)) $24. A very dark and sappy blend of Cab, Merlot, and Syrah; it shows all three grapes' influence. The Syrah gives it color and spice; the Cab provides tannin and a hint of herb; the Merlot broadens out the mid-palate a bit. An interesting, flavorful blend; right now the fruit is young, fresh, and right out front, with a finishing lick of citrus. **87** *—P.G. (4/1/2006)*

Basel Cellars 2001 Merriment Bordeaux Blend (Walla Walla (WA)) $48. Basel Cellars' inaugural vintage displays lovely buttercream, nut, and mint aromas on the nose. The palate swells with juicy, ripe red plum fruit dressed in a caramel-and-nut cloak, with more of the mint, or eucalyptus, drawn out on the finish. It's a more supple, softer-bodied wine than its components would have you believe. Drink now, and over the next five years. A blend of 50% Cabernet Sauvignon, 40% Merlot, and 10% Cabernet Franc. **91** *(5/1/2004)*

Basel Cellars 2002 Merriment Red Wine Bordeaux Blend (Walla Walla (WA)) $48. A Bordeaux blend of 50% Cabernet Sauvignon, 40% Merlot and the rest Cab Franc; all free run juice given the full tilt new oak treatment. Big and fruity, it's immediately delicious, though acidification sticks out a bit and tangles up the finish. **88** *—P.G. (4/1/2005)*

Basel Cellars 2003 Cabernet Sauvignon (Columbia Valley (WA)) $32. A blend of Cabernet and 16% Syrah. It's quite dense and black in the style of the winery, and powerfully scented with black cherry, loganberry, and cedar. It tastes like a berry pie with cedary/leafy highlights. The finish shows interesting tobacco and cigar notes. **89** *—P.G. (4/1/2006)*

Basel Cellars 2002 Cabernet Sauvignon (Columbia Valley (WA)) $32. Winemaker Trey Busch gets more confident and assured with each new vintage, and this is his best Cab yet. It's 100% Cabernet Sauvignon, from the Lewis, Seven Hills and Spoffard Station vineyards. Light scents suggest cherry tobacco, and cherries are the main theme here, ripened to 14.7% alcohol, but balanced, firm, and packed with fruit. The blend was done right after fermentation, which gives it a head start at this young age, and the tannins and oak are beautifully managed. **90** *—P.G. (4/1/2005)*

Basel Cellars 2003 Red Blend (Walla Walla (WA)) $36. Tannic with green tea and tobacco notes prevalent. The fruit is dark and wrapped in the thick, smoky tannins; flavors show blackberry, black cherry, and roasted coffee. The Cab Franc dominates here; this is muscular and brawny; almost 15% alcohol. **87** *—P.G. (4/1/2006)*

Basel Cellars 2004 Syrah (Columbia Valley (WA)) $42. Pure Syrah from a great lineup of vineyards. In this freeze year the Walla Walla vineyard produced no fruit, so winemaker Trey Busch sourced his grapes from an all-star lineup including Lewis, Minick, Portteus, and Columbia Crest. Densely packed with mixed purple fruits, it also sports a mix of wet leaf, earth, and herb flavors that add texture and beaucoup aroma. This leans towards the funky side, in a style more reminiscent of France than Australia, but what amazing flavors. **93** *—P.G. (11/15/2006)*

Basel Cellars 2003 Syrah (Walla Walla (WA)) $42. Sharp and tart, with the biting attack of a lemon. The slightly bitter acids overcome the fruit, which is light and lightly peppery. Some smoky, roasted coffee flavors fill out the finish. **87** *—P.G. (4/1/2006)*

Basel Cellars 2002 Syrah (Columbia Valley (WA)) $48. An excellent example of spicy, peppery Washington Syrah, this has a lifted bouquet of herb, pepper, and toast, tart cherry/cranberry fruit, and fine grained tannins. Scents and flavors of coffee and toast are beginning to integrate into the body of the wine, which may well merit a higher score with another few months of bottle age. **88** *—P.G. (4/1/2005)*

Basel Cellars 2004 Lewis Vineyard Reserve Syrah (Columbia Valley (WA)) $60. Not as balanced as the winery's regular Syrah, this monster (15.9% alcohol) is thick, smoky, beefy, ripe, and extremely rich. Expect a palate-bruising, massive mix of smoke, meat, and heat. If that's your favorite style, this nails it. **89** *—P.G. (11/15/2006)*

BASIGNANI

Basignani 1999 Chardonnay (Maryland) $13. An unusual blend of fruity, peachy flavors and bright lemony tanginess. Tastes a bit sweet, like it can't decide whether it's Riesling or Chardonnay. Some might love it, but it's definitely not for everyone. **80** —*J.M. (7/1/2002)*

BASK

Bask 2005 Chardonnay (North Coast) $20. A nice Chard, grown in the up-and-coming Suisun Valley east of San Francisco in the Delta. Shows nicely ripened tropical fruit, with some oak influence and a long, spicy-fruity finish. **85** —*S.H. (12/31/2006)*

Bask 2005 Viognier (North Coast) $24. Tons of fruit in this simple, one-dimensional wine, just bursting with everything imaginable. Peaches, pineapples, mangoes, papayas, guavas, nectarines, kiwi, lime, honeysuckle, tangerine, the list goes on. It's dryish and balanced. **84** —*S.H. (12/31/2006)*

BATES CREEK

Bates Creek 1999 Cabernet Sauvignon (Napa Valley) $25. This isn't one of your over-the-top Napa Cabs. It's balanced and harmonious and doesn't let the fruit push it around. Has proper notes of black currants, olives, and herbs, a deft dose of oak and lovely tannins. **92 Editors' Choice** —*S.H. (11/15/2002)*

BATTLE CREEK

Battle Creek 2002 Pinot Noir (Willamette Valley) $50. Good color, dark and plummy, and there are strong spicy/herbal components to the nose. The wine has a tough streak of vegetal/earthy flavors, that border on canned green beans. Underneath some sweeter purple fruits can be discerned, a cross between blackberry and beet, but the rough, earthy tannins need a lot more time to soften up. **86** —*P.G. (2/1/2005)*

BAYSTONE

Baystone 2000 Saralee's Vineyard Chardonnay (Russian River Valley) $20. A full-bodied, strongly flavored wine, with green apples and citrus fruits powerfully dosed with smoky oak and lees. Very dry and well-structured. The finish is spicy and tobaccoey, and turns yeasty-sour. **87** —*S.H. (6/1/2003)*

Baystone 1998 Saralee's Vineyard Chardonnay (Russian River Valley) $20. 90 *(6/1/2000)*

Baystone 1999 Shiraz (Dry Creek Valley) $24. Medium-weight and brisk, this Sonoma wine has a blackberry, herb, and cocoa profile, accented by ginger-snap and cedar notes. Bitter chocolate and black coffee play on the slightly short, tart, and tangy, mildly tannic finish. Has appeal, even a bit of depth, but not a great deal of nuance. **86** *(11/1/2001)*

BAYWOOD

Baywood 1997 Merlot (Monterey) $18. The deep, dark red color and richly ripe fruit and berry aromas tell you just how fine the grapes got in this wonderful vintage. The essence of plums and blackberries jumps out of the glass. Full and rich; those who think Monterey can't ripen a Bordeaux varietal just might be surprised. Yes, it's a little soft, and don't look for rich, complex tannins like you find in the North Coast. But this is a deeply satisfying, serious red wine. **90 Editors' Choice** —*S.H. (5/1/2001)*

Baywood 1999 Grand Reserve Syrah (Monterey) $35. A tart-sweet fruit, smoke and dried spice bouquet opens this French-inspired Californian. Herb and bramble notes accent roasted red-berry flavors, as does an appealing, Rhônish smoked meatiness. An espresso-and- spice-rub finish with slight herb-metallic notes reinforces this Monterey offering's Gallic profile. Very drinkable, it should be even better in two years. **88** *(11/1/2001)*

Baywood 1999 Late Harvest Symphony White Blend (California) $35. A bouquet as inviting as a fancy dessert suggests fresh apricots topped with caramel sauce and dusted with confectioner's sugar. It's extremely sweet and fruity, with luscious flavors and a thick texture. Delicious, but a bit more acidity would add even more character and appeal. **89** *(8/1/2001)*

Baywood 1999 Symphony White Blend (California) $12. A fresh, fruity wine. A little soft but full of juicy flavors of lemon, lime, peach, and pear, with flowery, honeyed notes. It's pleasant rather than complex, an everyday picnic-sort-of-wine. **83** —*S.H. (5/1/2001)*

BEAR CREEK

Bear Creek 2000 Petite Sirah (Lodi) $18. Okay in flavor and style, although there are some overly sweet notes that bothered tasters. Cherries, black tea, plum, mint, and licorice are just a few of the flavors that are wrapped in soft, gentle tannins. One taster loved the rich mouthfeel. **84** *(4/1/2003)*

Bear Creek 1998 Pinot Noir (Rogue Valley) $30. 89 —*M.S. (12/1/2000)*

Bear Creek 2000 Zinfandel (Lodi) $18. Rich in wild berry fruit, with brambly, pepper flavors suggesting black raspberry jam. Abounds in spices, coffee, and tobacco. The tannins are on the aggressive side, and the wine feels jagged and edgy in the mouth. **84** —*S.H. (2/1/2003)*

Bear Creek 2001 Old Vine Zinfandel (Lodi) $16. Rich and plush in the nose, with hints of ripe fruit and toast. On the palate, it's a bit leaner than the nose would indicate. Still, it's fairly complex and silky, with good blackberry, cherry, herb, and spice notes. Tannins are firm and the finish is moderate. **89** *(11/1/2003)*

BEARBOAT

Bearboat 2002 Chardonnay (Russian River Valley) $15. Heavily oaked with well-charred wood, so you get lots of upfront toast. Below is a nice Chard with pleasant peach and apple flavors. Finishes dry and spicy. **84** —*S.H. (8/1/2005)*

Bearboat 2000 Chardonnay (Russian River Valley) $15. Rough and earthy, with some apple and peach flavors and a touch of oak, but also vegetal and mushroom elements. Very dry, with crisp acidity. **84** —*S.H. (6/1/2003)*

Bearboat 2002 Pinot Noir (Russian River Valley) $19. Nice and delicately structured in the mouth, an elegant wine with fine acidity and a silky finish. The classic Russian River flavors suggest cherries, cola, mocha, and cinnamon spice. **86** —*S.H. (8/1/2005)*

Bearboat 2000 Pinot Noir (Russian River Valley) $19. Ample cedary shadings adorn sweet fruit. Creamy mocha notes layered over pie-cherry and strawberry flavors give the palate an almost milkshake quality. Then the wine switches gears and the cedary element takes over. It closes abruptly, tart and woody. **84** *(10/1/2002)*

BEAUCANON

Beaucanon 2000 Trifecta Cabernet Blend (Napa Valley) $27. Tastes old, tired, with flattening acids and still some sticky tannins. The flavors are of blackberries and oak, with a medicinal taste in the finish. **82** —*S.H. (10/1/2005)*

Beaucanon 1998 La Crosse Cabernet Franc (Napa Valley) $12. A Loire-like red wine, pleasantly light and fruity, it has black cherry and cola flavors and a real streak of earthiness. Dry, supple tannins provide structure, but it's pretty soft. From Beaucanon. **86** —*S.H. (7/1/2002)*

Beaucanon 1998 Jacques de Connick Cabernet Sauvignon (Napa Valley) $65. The best Napa Cabs are soft, concentrated, and supple. This pretty wine is all that. It combines the power of sun-ripened fruit with a reluctance on the winemaker's part to overwhelm. This dry wine impresses through restraint, not a knock to the head. The right foods will make it sing. **92** —*S.H. (6/1/2002)*

Beaucanon 2001 Longwood Cabernet Sauvignon (Napa Valley) $26. The grapes got way too ripe for balance in this wine. It's strong in Porty raisins, with a hot, spirity mouthfeel and a dry, cassis-fueled finish. **82** —*S.H. (10/1/2005)*

Beaucanon 1999 Reserve Cabernet Sauvignon (Napa Valley) $20. Oddly thin for a Napa Cabernet from this vintage. The expected black currant, cassis, olive, sage, and tobacco fruit is there, as is fine oak, and the wine has those lovely valley tannins and acidity. The entry is great, but then you slosh and chew and look for a core of fruit and it's not there. **84** —*S.H. (6/1/2002)*

Beaucanon 1998 Reserve Cabernet Sauvignon (Napa Valley) $18. From a winery in the heart of Napa that has long been overshadowed by flashier competitors. Maybe this wine shows why. It has that Napa pedigree of fruit, but there are disturbing notes of imbalance. Some of the flavors are ripe and juicy; others are overripe and pruny, while still others are immature and green or stalky. The result is disappointing. **84** —S.H. (5/1/2001)

Beaucanon 2002 Chardonnay (Napa Valley) $15. A little earthy, with creamy apple sauce flavors dusted with cinnamon and nutmeg, but dry. There's a rough texture through the finish. **84** —S.H. (10/1/2005)

Beaucanon 1999 Chardonnay (Napa Valley) $25. A rich blend that features toasty oak, vanilla, and butterscotch on the nose. On the palate, it serves up a pleasing lineup of melon, apple, honey, spice, and toast flavors. Creamy rich on the finish, fleshy and seductive. **90** —J.M. (6/1/2003)

Beaucanon 1997 Jacques de Coninck Chardonnay (Napa Valley) $30. **85** (6/1/2000)

Beaucanon 1998 Reserve Chardonnay (Napa Valley) $15. **87** (6/1/2000)

Beaucanon 2001 Selection Reserve Jacques de Coninck Chardonnay (Napa Valley) $27. Rather earthy for a Chardonnay, but it's extremely rich earth, with suggestions of apples, clover honey, butterscotch, and toast. Something about this wine makes you reach for a second glass. **87** —S.H. (10/1/2005)

Beaucanon 2001 Merlot (Napa Valley) $25. This bizarre failure is sharp in acids, Porty in raisins, and hot. What were they thinking? **80** —S.H. (10/1/2005)

Beaucanon 1998 Jacques de Connick Merlot (Napa Valley) $75. Some wines taste fancy. They have that exquisite fruit, those sculpted tannins, that plush overlay of oak that speaks of money. This wine is fancy. Napa terroir has given lovely fruit and acids. It's not a blockbuster. It's subtle, but there are signs of quality throughout. **91** —S.H. (6/1/2002)

Beaucanon 1999 Reserve Merlot (Napa Valley) $18. Smells and tastes great. Plums, blackberry, mushroom, earth, and tobacco, with the requisite oaky notes in the aroma, and blackberry and black cherry flavors framed in smoky oak. Tannins are notable, but negotiable. The big problem is that the wine is thin. If it had more weight and density, it would be excellent. Instead, it's just very good. **87** —S.H. (6/1/2002)

Beaucanon 1999 Selection Reserve Jacques de Coninck Merlot (Napa Valley) $47. Fairly rich and ripe, with pretty balck cherry, blackberry, spice, herb, leather, and earth notes. The tannins are smooth, though the finish packs some forward brightness. A new style from a veteran winery. **88** —J.M. (8/1/2003)

BEAULIEU VINEYARD

Beaulieu Vineyard 2001 Tapestry Reserve Bordeaux Blend (Napa Valley) $40. A lovely wine, one that winemaker Joel Aiken says is more accessible than Private Reserve, but the tannins suggest ageability. Rich and full-bodied, with black currant, chocolate, coffee, and herb flavors. With a steak, it's fine now, but will develop easily for many years. A blend of four Bordeaux varieties. **92** —S.H. (10/1/2004)

Beaulieu Vineyard 1997 Tapestry Reserve Red Table Win Bordeaux Blend (Napa Valley) $50. **92** (11/1/2000)

Beaulieu Vineyard 2002 Tapestry Reserve Cabernet Blend (Napa Valley) $50. Where Beaulieu's Private Reserve is 100% Cabernet Sauvignon, this is a blend of Bordeaux grapes. It's softer and smoother than the PR, with a cherry and chocolate undertow to the currant flavor. It's a very dry, fairly tannic wine that doesn't seem to have a long life ahead, so drink up now. **90** —S.H. (12/1/2005)

Beaulieu Vineyard 2003 Cabernet Sauvignon (Napa Valley) $18. Beaulieu's basic Napa Cab is dry and balanced wine, with the accent on balance. This is a wine that stays in the background, letting food star, but that doesn't mean it's not complex. It is thoroughly rewarding, an ideal restaurant wine. Should develop well for 10 years. **89 Editors' Choice** — S.H. (9/1/2006)

Beaulieu Vineyard 2003 Cabernet Sauvignon (Rutherford) $25. What a nice job Beaulieu does every year with this wine, from their home territory. It's dry and polished, with loads of black currant, licorice, and chocolate flavors. The dusty tannins balance out the ripe fruit. Best now through 2012. **87** —S.H. (9/1/2006)

Beaulieu Vineyard 2002 Cabernet Sauvignon (Napa Valley) $17. This ripe, fruity blended Cab is bursting with cassis, mocha, and smoky oak flavors. The tannins are very smooth and ripe. A minor quibble is the alcoholic heat throughout. **85** —S.H. (12/1/2005)

Beaulieu Vineyard 2002 Cabernet Sauvignon (Rutherford) $25. Beaulieu is most known for its Private Reserve Cab, but in a way, the Rutherford Cab shows what the winery can do on an everyday basis. It's always balanced and controlled, elegant and dry. This vintage shows all those qualities, with ripe black currant fruit. Drink now through 2008. **90** — S.H. (12/1/2005)

Beaulieu Vineyard 2001 Cabernet Sauvignon (Rutherford) $25. Classic BV Rutherford, with its thick, dusty tannins, black currant flavors, dryness, and overall balance. Those tannins really hit in the finish, suggesting midterm aging. Good now, but should improve by the end of the decade. **87** —S.H. (5/1/2005)

Beaulieu Vineyard 2001 Cabernet Sauvignon (Napa Valley) $17. Gentle and uncomplicated, but with class and finesse, this dry wine shows blackberry flavors with overtones of green olives and coffee. It has a good grip and finish. **86** —S.H. (5/1/2005)

Beaulieu Vineyard 2000 Cabernet Sauvignon (Napa Valley) $17. BV does it again with this solid effort. It's as good as many Napa Cabs costing far more, with its currant, plum, and herb and lush, sweet tannins. Lots of finesse and complexity. Drink now. **88** —S.H. (6/1/2004)

Beaulieu Vineyard 2000 Cabernet Sauvignon (Rutherford) $25. Starts with black currant, olive, tobacco, and bell pepper aromas. Feels soft and smooth on the palate, and yields flavors of currants and blackberries. The tannins are dusty and easy; the wine is delicately balanced and trips off the palate to a polished finish. **87** —S.H. (12/31/2003)

Beaulieu Vineyard 1999 Cabernet Sauvignon (Rutherford) $25. For 100 years, Beaulieu's Rutherford Cabernets have been supple wines of balance and charm rather than overwhelming power. They still stubbornly are. This is classic midvalley Cabernet, with currant flavors, dusty tannins, moderate alcohol, and modest oak. It will age for many years. **90** —S.H. (11/15/2002)

Beaulieu Vineyard 1998 Cabernet Sauvignon (Rutherford) $22. The latest from this famous label begins with delicate aromas of blackberries and oak with earthy overtones. In the mouth, it's rich and supple, with velvety tannins and adequate acidity. The fruit is a little light, and it's dry as dust—Rutherford dust. **87** —S.H. (8/1/2001)

Beaulieu Vineyard 1998 Cabernet Sauvignon (Napa Valley) $17. This is a good, well-made Cab that satisfies without being particularly exciting. It's average in the blackberry and earthy aromas, and in its very dry, blackberry flavors. Then, it snaps to a quick finish. **84** —S.H. (8/1/2001)

Beaulieu Vineyard 1996 Cabernet Sauvignon (Rutherford) $12. **90** (11/15/1999)

Beaulieu Vineyard 2001 Clone 4 Cabernet Sauvignon (Rutherford) $130. Soft and lush in texture, with cedar- and vanilla-scented oak, vibrant cassis fruit, and hints of dried spices. A delicious wine, but one that needs more depth, structure, and complexity to push it into Cabernet's upper echelons. **89** (12/1/2005)

Beaulieu Vineyard 1997 Clone 4 Cabernet Sauvignon (Napa Valley) $130. **93** (11/1/2000)

Beaulieu Vineyard 1995 Clone 4 Cabernet Sauvignon (Rutherford) $100. **97 Cellar Selection** (6/1/1999)

Beaulieu Vineyard 2001 Clone 6 Cabernet Sauvignon (Rutherford) $130. Shows an awful lot of wood, with vanilla and coconut notes dominating the blackberry fruit. The chewy tannins are omnipresent, but they're soft and lasting on the finish, giving us hope that this will evolve in a positive direction. **87** (12/1/2005)

Beaulieu Vineyard 1997 Clone 6 Cabernet Sauvignon (Napa Valley) $130. **92** (11/1/2000)

Beaulieu Vineyard 2003 Coastal Estates Cabernet Sauvignon (California) $11. Baked and hot, with earth and cough medicine flavors and gritty tannins. **82** —S.H. (12/1/2005)

Beaulieu Vineyard 2003 Georges de Latour Private Reserve Cabernet Sauvignon (Napa Valley) $95. Just classic Georges, balanced, elegant, and refined, hiding its power under a blanket of controlled finesse. There's great depth of flavor, with oodles of blackberry, cherry, and raspberry, mocha, Chinese plum sauce, soy, and spicy oak, wrapped in firm, dry tannins. Just wonderful now, but with the certainty of a long life ahead. Drink–2020. **95 Cellar Selection**—*S.H. (12/31/2006)*

Beaulieu Vineyard 2002 Georges de Latour Private Reserve Cabernet Sauvignon (Napa Valley) $95. It's young, dry, tight, and tannic, although there's obviously a core of ripe black currant and cherry fruit. To evaluate this wine properly, you have to know its history as one of Napa's most ageable Cabernets. Still, it's not a great Georges. Hold until 2008 through 2010, but it could surprise. **92 Cellar Selection**—*S.H. (12/1/2005)*

Beaulieu Vineyard 2001 Georges de Latour Private Reserve Cabernet Sauvignon (Rutherford) $85. Classic Georges, balanced and ageworthy, yet riper and lusher than any Private Reserve in memory. Magnificently ripe fruit, rich in currants and cocoa, well-oaked, with ripe, supple tannins. Doesn't try to out-wow the competition in power, but the equilibrium is its strong point. Drink now–2015. **93 Cellar Selection**—*S.H. (10/1/2004)*

Beaulieu Vineyard 2000 Georges de Latour Private Reserve Cabernet Sauvignon (Napa Valley) $85. Beaulieu's flagship wine does not have the volume of the best vintages, but it is still a beautiful wine, oozing black currant and cigar-box flavors. The dusty tannins create a lush, velvety texture that displays great balance and charm. **92** *(2/1/2004)*

Beaulieu Vineyard 1999 Georges de Latour Private Reserve Cabernet Sauvignon (Napa Valley) $100. This age-old classic begins with sawdust aromas and hints of mint and green bean. Broad plum, berry, and vanilla flavors spread across the wide-open palate, followed by a finish of mocha and coffee. The wine is on the sweet side, with fairly aggressive oak, yet it manages to shine and strut its stuff. Still, more definition and delicacy would elevate it further. **90**—*M.S. (3/1/2003)*

Beaulieu Vineyard 1998 Georges de Latour Private Reserve Cabernet Sauvignon (Napa Valley) $100. Still young and jammy, with dark purple color and great heaps of cherry, blackberry, and cassis fruit, overlaid with plush, vanilla-tinged oak. There's an enormous depth of flavor in the mouth, rich and jammy, with fruity, chocolate notes. The tannins are evident now in this very dry wine. It is a cellar candidate; a very good wine, but not a great vintage. **91 Cellar Selection**—*S.H. (12/31/2001)*

Beaulieu Vineyard 1997 Georges de Latour Private Reserve Cabernet Sauvignon (Napa Valley) $100. 94 *(11/1/2000)*

Beaulieu Vineyard 1998 Reserve Tapestry Cabernet Sauvignon (Napa Valley) $40. Dark and dramtically scented, with a perfume of superbly ripe cassis and plush, smoky oak, it's a pleasure to inhale. In the mouth, it drinks round and supple, with real flair. The tannins are exquisite, the acidity soft but supportive. The one problem is a certain thinness in the middle palate, probably a fault of the vintage. Drink now, or soon. **87**—*S.H. (12/31/2001)*

Beaulieu Vineyard 2001 Dulcet Reserve Cabernet Sauvignon-Syrah (Napa Valley) $35. First produced in the 2000 vintage, this Cabernet-Syrah blend is dramatically ripe and oaky. It shows huge aromas of black currants, violets, chocolate, and smoke, and is almost sweet, but it's technically dry. Balanced with rich tannins and good acidity, it will develop complexity through the years. **92 Editors' Choice**—*S.H. (10/1/2004)*

Beaulieu Vineyard 2000 Dulcet Reserve Cabernet Sauvignon-Syrah (Napa Valley) $35. Soft, juicy, and luscious, a velvety wine that feels soft and complex in the mouth. Has herbal, cherry-berry flavors and subtle oak, and is very dry. Best now through 2005. **89**—*S.H. (2/1/2004)*

Beaulieu Vineyard 2004 Chardonnay (Napa Valley) $18. Dry, earthy, and a little simple, this Chard has flavors of herbs, pears, and oak, and is soft in acidity. For another two dollars, you're better off buying Beaulieu's beautiful Carneros Chardonnay. **84**—*S.H. (6/1/2006)*

Beaulieu Vineyard 2004 Chardonnay (Carneros) $20. I love this Chard for its bright, brisk acidity that fires up the palate, only to reward it with ripe, delicious flavors of Key lime pie, kiwi, and pineapple. Oak adds

notes of buttered toast and vanilla. The result is rich, refined, and complex, a Chardonnay to linger over. Easy to find, with 17,000 cases produced. **91**—*S.H. (6/1/2006)*

Beaulieu Vineyard 2003 Chardonnay (Carneros) $18. Joins very ripe, tropical fruits (like guavas and papayas) to vanilla-tinged, smoky oak to produce a likeable, flavorful Chard. Has a rich, almost thick, creamy texture that finishes with a swirl of spices. **86**—*S.H. (6/1/2005)*

Beaulieu Vineyard 2001 Chardonnay (Carneros) $18. A well-crafted Chard, rich and balanced. The mango and pineapple flavors are elaborated with smoky, spicy, buttery notes from oak and lees, and the creamy mouthfeel is a delight. Brims with a youthful acidity. **90**—*S.H. (12/15/2003)*

Beaulieu Vineyard 2000 Chardonnay (Carneros) $18. Captures all the notes that makes Chard the world's number one white wine: Spiced apple, ripe peach, smoky vanilla, toasty oak, and bright, crisp acidity. Add in that BV balance and harmony, and you've got a winner. **91 Editors' Choice**—*S.H. (12/15/2002)*

Beaulieu Vineyard 1999 Chardonnay (Carneros) $18. Subtle citrus and peach aromas mark this pretty wine, with light oak shadings. It's round and supple, with some nicely extracted citrus fruit and crisp acidity. It's light and elegant, but no blockbuster. **86**—*S.H. (8/1/2001)*

Beaulieu Vineyard 2000 Coastal Chardonnay (California) $11. Lemony-spicy flavors, bold and bright, in a nice, easy-drinking wine with lots of class. The crisp acids make the cinnamony fruit sing, and it finishes with a little sweetness. **85**—*S.H. (12/31/2001)*

Beaulieu Vineyard 1999 Coastal Chardonnay (California) $10. This lemony wine boasts modest citrus aromas and flavors coupled with sharp acidity. It has some pretty oak and spice notes. **83**—*S.H. (8/1/2001)*

Beaulieu Vineyard 2003 Coastal Estates Chardonnay (California) $11. There's a lot of Chard character here, in the flavors of peaches, pears, Asian spices, buttery toast, and cream. A large proportion of the grapes came from Monterey, which also helps explain the crispness. **85**—*S.H. (12/1/2005)*

Beaulieu Vineyard 2003 Reserve Chardonnay (Carneros) $28. Everything's controlled in this balanced, harmonious Chard. The tropical fruit is ripe, oak is judiciously applied, creamy lees are just right. It's a very elegant, pure wine that gets better and better with every sip. **90**—*S.H. (12/15/2005)*

Beaulieu Vineyard 1999 Reserve Chardonnay (Carneros) $30. Pear, pineapple and herb aromas intrigued some tasters, but others found an odd note in this wine's nose. Vanilla, pear, apple, and sweet spices mark the medium-weight and round palate. The back end of this wine has tangy wood and a slight chalkiness. **87** *(7/1/2001)*

Beaulieu Vineyard 1997 Reserve Chardonnay (Carneros) $24. 87 *(6/1/2000)*

Beaulieu Vineyard 1996 Merlot (Napa Valley) $16. 86—*J.C. (7/1/2000)*

Beaulieu Vineyard 2003 Merlot (Napa Valley) $18. Smooth and polished, this Merlot combines its plush texture with wonderfully ripe, rewarding cherry, blackberry, and woodspice flavors that finish with a chocolate fudginess. Yet the wine is dry. This is a good buy for a Napa wine of this complexity. **87**—*S.H. (7/1/2006)*

Beaulieu Vineyard 2002 Merlot (Napa Valley) $18. I like this wine for its voluptuousness, its creamy mouthfeel, and the long, pure flavors of cherries, chocolate, and coffee. It's dry, elegant, and completely balanced, the kind of Merlot people have in mind when they talk about "the soft Cabernet." **87**—*S.H. (12/1/2005)*

Beaulieu Vineyard 2001 Merlot (Napa Valley) $17. This wonderfully supple and rewarding Merlot offers satisfaction throughout. It's richly colored, with a velvety texture that carries waves of currant, olive, chocolate, and sweet oak flavors wrapped in soft tannins. **90**—*S.H. (5/1/2005)*

Beaulieu Vineyard 2000 Merlot (Napa-Carneros) $17. Cola, root beer, black cherry, sweet oak, and smoky vanilla highlight the flavors of this rich wine. It has a velvety texture, with soft tannins. Turns a bit cloying and syrupy on the finish. **85**—*S.H. (6/1/2004)*

Beaulieu Vineyard 1999 Merlot (Napa Valley) $18. This wine is both good and a good value. It's ripe but not cloying, teasing with plum and cherry flavors but then turning herbal and earthy. It's not an ager because it's too soft, but it was created to be consumed with food. **90** — *(11/15/2002)*

Beaulieu Vineyard 1998 Merlot (Napa Valley) $17. Soft, round, and velvety in the mouth, the texture is delightful. On the other hand, the tannins are fairly sturdy and the fruit is light, making the wine austere. The right foods will bring out the inherent sweetness, but on its own, it's a hard wine. **85** —*S.H. (8/1/2001)*

Beaulieu Vineyard 1999 Coastal Merlot (California) $12. This is the kind of wine that allows everday consumers to experience the joys of a beautifully made dry, red wine. It's not a blockbuster, but with deep berry and stone fruit flavors, pretty tannins and rich, dry texture, it's among the best of its class. Kudos to this winery for keeping the price so low. Amazing value. **88 Best Buy** —*S.H. (12/31/2001)*

Beaulieu Vineyard 1998 Coastal Merlot (California) $12. This is one of those "generic" red wines that smells and tastes of berries, with an earthy streak and a kiss of oak. It's a little soft, yet dry enough to satisfy most red wine drinkers and not bad for the price. **83** —*S.H. (8/1/2001)*

Beaulieu Vineyard 2004 Maestro Collection Pinot Gris (Carneros) $17. This elegant wine invites with aromas of lemons, limes, apricots, and milk-cream, and even an exotic green banana scent. In the mouth, it turns dry and delicate, with fruity flavors and bright acidity. **86** —*S.H. (2/1/2006)*

Beaulieu Vineyard 2003 Pinot Noir (Carneros) $18. A solid effort in a cool-climate Pinot, showing mixed berry, coffee, and cola flavors and a spicy overlay of oak. Full-bodied and dry, with a cherry-fruit finish. **87** —*S.H. (6/1/2005)*

Beaulieu Vineyard 2002 Pinot Noir (Carneros) $18. Simple and refreshing, a light-bodied wine with some black cherry, cranberry, and vanilla aromas and flavors. Tight in acidity, with a silky texture and a hint of orange peel on the finish. **85** *(11/1/2004)*

Beaulieu Vineyard 2000 Pinot Noir (Carneros) $18. **83** *(10/1/2002)*

Beaulieu Vineyard 1999 Pinot Noir (Carneros) $18. Earth, blackberry, and fudge aromas should please those with a sweet tooth. The palate is redolent with candied fruit and brown sugar; however, the finish doesn't display a whole lot of length or complexity. **86** *(10/1/2002)*

Beaulieu Vineyard 1997 Carneros Pinot Noir (Carneros) $16. **87** *(11/15/1999)*

Beaulieu Vineyard 2001 Coastal Pinot Noir (California) $11. Here's a Pinot with some varietal character, namely silky tannins, soft acids, and flavors of cherries and cola. Goes the extra mile with some additional depth of flavor and pretty oak, but it's awfully hard to get a good Pinot at this price. **85** —*S.H. (7/1/2003)*

Beaulieu Vineyard 2000 Coastal Pinot Noir (California) $11. Here's a lovely wine exhibiting true varietal character at a giveaway price. The aromas are all about beet root, racy red raspberry, tobacco, pungent spices, and smoke. The flavors are deep and impressive, and wrapped in silky but assertive tannins. This bone dry wine isn't complex, but it accomplishes its mission. **86 Best Buy** —*S.H. (12/15/2001)*

Beaulieu Vineyard 2004 Coastal Estates Pinot Noir (California) $11. Hot and rubbery, with dried-out tannins and herbal, peppery flavors. **81** — *S.H. (12/1/2005)*

Beaulieu Vineyard 2000 Maestro-Signet Collection Pinot Noir (Carneros) $100. Available only in magnum, this full-blown Pinot—a tribute to André Tchelistcheff—is inky and ripe, with prune, plum, cherry, caramel, and spice aromas and flavors. The full mouthfeel is soft and plush, but the wine shows a liqueur-like quality and some heat, as well as spice cake and chocolate flavors. The low acids and soft-tannins make this best for near-term drinking. **87** *(10/1/2002)*

Beaulieu Vineyard 2003 Reserve Pinot Noir (Carneros) $39. A little light in flavor and length, this Pinot comes down more on the elegant side than the powerful. It's silky and dry, with pleasant raspberry-cherry, mocha, vanilla, and Asian spice flavors. **87** —*S.H. (12/15/2005)*

Beaulieu Vineyard 2002 Reserve Pinot Noir (Carneros) $35. Attractive, with herb, cherry, brown sugar, and smoky oak aromas. Feels plump and juicy, flooding the palate with plum, black cherry, and herb flavors leading to a quick finish. **86** *(11/1/2004)*

Beaulieu Vineyard 2000 Reserve Pinot Noir (Carneros) $32. Multiple members of our panel detected blue cheese in the nose as well as kirsch, coffee, and sugar beets. There is full-scale cherry fruit on the palate, but also some sweet beets and prunes. The body is full, the weight quite large. But it's not as deep in the middle as it should be, especially given its full girth and heft. **87** *(10/1/2002)*

Beaulieu Vineyard 1999 Reserve Pinot Noir (Carneros) $35. Here's a wine to mull over as you sniff the complex earthy, mushroomy, black raspberry, and smoky oak aromas, infused with all kinds of spices and herbs. Take a sip, swirl. It turns even more complex. Racy, juicy fruit is framed in delicate oak. Tannins and acids are just right. Plus it has that elusive quality, elegance. It's California sweet, and needs the right foods. **92** — *S.H. (12/15/2001)*

Beaulieu Vineyard 1997 Reserve Carneros Pinot Noir (Carneros) $30. **90** *(10/1/1999)*

Beaulieu Vineyard 2002 Reserve Dulcet Red Blend (Napa Valley) $40. With three-quarters Cabernet Sauvignon and the balance Syrah, this Cali-Rhône blend sure is a good wine. It's very dry, with rich, dusty tannins, and while there's good cherry and blackberry fruit, there's also a balance of herbs and sweet leather for complexity. **89** —*S.H. (12/1/2005)*

Beaulieu Vineyard 1999 Reserve Tapestry Red Blend (Napa Valley) $50. This Bordeaux style blend smells and tastes like anything but Bordeaux, proving that similar blends do not produce similar wines if the terroir is different. The barrel influence is strong, as is the herbal quality. Richness on the palate comes to the rescue. There's nice cassis and plum flavors. And the finish is smooth and classy. Only a hint of green at the core holds it back. **89** —*M.S. (3/1/2003)*

Beaulieu Vineyard 2000 Tapestry Reserve Red Blend (Napa Valley) $40. This Cabernet-based blend seduces the palate with opulence. Cedar, toast, dark chocolate, cassis, and maple syrup flavors are couched in soft tannins. Develops even more complexity on the finish, revealing berries, coffee, and dried herbs. Drink now. **91** *(2/1/2004)*

Beaulieu Vineyard 1997 Signet Collection Beauzeaux Rhône Red Blend (California) $20. **88** —*J.C. (11/1/1999)*

Beaulieu Vineyard 2000 Signet Collection Ensemble Rhône Red Blend (California) $25. A nice, full-bodied wine with a quality of elegance. Has aromas and flavors of various berries and stone fruits, and is very dry, with soft, complex tannins. Could use more concentration. A blend of Syrah, Grenache, Mourvèdre, Carignane, and Viognier. **86** —*S.H. (6/1/2003)*

Beaulieu Vineyard 1996 Signet Collection Ensemble Rhône Red Blend (California) $25. **86** —*J.C. (11/1/1999)*

Beaulieu Vineyard 1997 Signet Collection Sangiovese (Napa Valley) $20. **87** —*S.H. (12/15/1999)*

Beaulieu Vineyard 1996 Signet Collection Sangiovese (Napa Valley) $16. **86** *(10/1/1999)*

Beaulieu Vineyard 1997 Coastal Estates Sauvignon Blanc (California) $9. **83** *(3/1/2000)*

Beaulieu Vineyard 2004 Coastal Estates Sauvignon Blanc (California) $11. Here's a bone-dry Sauvignon Blanc that's perfect as an everyday cocktail sipper, and versatile with food. It has citrus flavors and bright acidity. **84** —*S.H. (12/1/2005)*

Beaulieu Vineyard 2002 Coastal Estates Private Cellars Shiraz (California) $11. Combines mint and sour cherries in a light-bodied, simple wine. An adequate by-the-glass pour at your local family-style restaurant. **82** *(9/1/2005)*

Beaulieu Vineyard 2003 Syrah (Napa Valley) $15. A ripe, easy-drinking Syrah from a big brand, this has all the earmarks of commercial success. Jammy raspberries mingle with deft touches of vanilla, while the finish features just enough acid and tannin to remind you that you're drinking a red wine. Drink now. **85** *(9/1/2005)*

Beaulieu Vineyard 2000 Syrah (California) $15. There's some good Syrah character here, with plummy, peppery aromas and a nice mouthfeel. But the flavors are on the thin side, suggesting that the vines were over-cropped. You find yourself wishing there were more concentration. **85** —*S.H. (6/1/2003)*

Beaulieu Vineyard 1999 Syrah (California) $15. Young and jammy, it has exuberant aromas of crushed berries, smoked meat, and vanilla. It's very extracted and fresh, almost like a barrel sample with pungent, juicy fruit. But it is dry, and covered in dusty tannins. Might improve with short-term aging, or best to have with big, rich foods, like barbecued ribs. **85** —*S.H. (10/1/2001)*

Beaulieu Vineyard 1999 Signet Syrah (Napa County) $25. What aromas we can discern from this Syrah's tight nose run the gamut from vanilla and plum to plastic and resin. It's balanced in the mouth, but has a strangely gravelly mouthfeel. More minerals on the palate and on the finish obscure slight blackberry flavor. **83** *(11/1/2001)*

Beaulieu Vineyard 1996 Signet Collection Syrah (North Coast) $25. **87** — *J.C. (11/1/1999)*

Beaulieu Vineyard 1998 Winemaker's Collection Syrah (North Coast) $25. This firmly structured wine has a core of plum and black cherry fruit enveloped in toasty oak. It's decidedly dry, and the full tannins may make it seem austere—it's rather Rhône-like for a California Syrah. Solid, if slightly reserved, this wine pairs well with grilled meat and other hearty foods now, but should reward cellaring for 3–4 years. **91 Editors' Choice** *(8/1/2001)*

Beaulieu Vineyard 1997 Signet Collection Tocai (Monterey County) $15. **80** —*J.C. (11/1/1999)*

Beaulieu Vineyard 1997 Viognier (Napa Valley) $17. **88** —*S.H. (6/1/1999)*

Beaulieu Vineyard 2001 Signet Collection Viognier (Carneros) $17. Big and blowsy aromas of litchi and candied citrus are typical of California Viognier, yet more individual are the flavors of apple, spiced lemon rind, and pepper. With no one characteristic dominating, this is a wine that spreads itself all over the map. The finish is hefty, almost fat, while healthy acidity and a citrusy core keep it lively. **87** —*M.S. (3/1/2003)*

Beaulieu Vineyard 1997 Signet Collection Viognier (Napa Valley) $16. **84** —*J.C. (11/1/1999)*

Beaulieu Vineyard 1996 Zinfandel (Napa Valley) $16. **87** —*S.H. (5/1/2000)*

Beaulieu Vineyard 2003 Zinfandel (Napa Valley) $14. Many Napa Zins have a Cabernet-like quality, but this one stays true to Zin's wild and woolly character. It's briary, a little green and peppery alongside the riper berry flavors, and very dry, with mouthwatering acidity and brisk tannins. **86** —*S.H. (12/1/2005)*

Beaulieu Vineyard 2002 Zinfandel (Napa Valley) $14. Nice wine for this price. It's dry and full-bodied, and rich in plum, coffee, and herb flavors. Very balanced. The sturdy tannins call for rich fare. **86** —*S.H. (5/1/2005)*

Beaulieu Vineyard 2001 Zinfandel (Napa Valley) $14. A pretty Zin, showing good structure, fruit, and elegance. Black cherry, coffee, chocolate, and herbs are at the forefront, backed by firm, silky tannins and a finish redolent of spiced plums. **88** *(11/1/2003)*

Beaulieu Vineyard 2000 Zinfandel (Napa Valley) $15. Classic Napa Zin. Wild berry and dark stone fruit flavors drink richly ripe, with a spicy, peppery edge and a long finish. The wine is beautifully dry and balanced, with dusty tannins. It has that briary, rustic nature that makes California Zin Cabernet's country cousin. **90 Best Buy** —*S.H. (11/1/2002)*

Beaulieu Vineyard 1999 Zinfandel (Napa Valley) $14. A ripe, jammy Zinfandel that opens with a burst of peppery wild-berry aromas, and turns fruity and supple on the palate. Probably not an ager, just a nice everyday Zin to sip with pasta and tomato sauce. Finishes very dry, with moderately intense tannins. **85** —*S.H. (8/1/2001)*

Beaulieu Vineyard 1997 Zinfandel (Napa Valley) $16. Lovely attack, plummy and evolved, with no rough edges. The fruit is soft and sweet, layered and full, and the overall palate impression is of elegance and balance. This is a terrific drink-me-now bottle with nicely aged flavors. **88** —*P.G. (3/1/2001)*

Beaulieu Vineyard 1998 Coastal Zinfandel (California) $NA. **82** —*D.T. (3/1/2002)*

Beaulieu Vineyard 1997 Coastal Zinfandel (California) $10. **88 Best Buy** —*P.G. (11/15/1999)*

Beaulieu Vineyard 2003 Coastal Estates Zinfandel (California) $11. There's a lot of briary, brambly Zin character in this pleasantly dry wine. It's a full-bodied, assertive wine whose cherry, berry, and spice flavors will match up against anything from steak to pizza to a nice roasted chicken. **84** —*S.H. (12/1/2005)*

Beaulieu Vineyard 1999 Signet Collection Zinfandel (Napa Valley) $28. Black as night. If you drink this Zin with food, that food better be a charbroiled steak. Oak, blackberry, and black plum aromas lead to similar flavors in the mouth that are lightened a tad by a tart grape-blackberry-gumball note. Chewy and heavy on the tannins, it signs off with a dry, tannic, black plum-skin finish. **85** —*D.T. (3/1/2002)*

BEAUREGARD

Beauregard 2002 Bald Mountain Vineyard Chardonnay (Santa Cruz Mountains) $20. Long on fruity extract, rich in oak, this complex wine is packed with mango, papaya, apricot, peach, tapioca, vanilla, and smoky aromas and flavors. The creamy texture is smooth. **88** —*S.H. (2/1/2005)*

Beauregard 2002 Beauregard Ranch Vineyard Chardonnay (Santa Cruz Mountains) $25. Rich and ripe in pineapple, mango, vanilla, spice, and buttered toast, a smooth, succulent wine that finishes long and spicy. A tad soft and simple, but polished. **87** —*S.H. (2/1/2005)*

Beauregard 2002 Hirsch Vineyard Pinot Noir (Sonoma Coast) $35. Rather thick and extracted, almost syrupy in blackberry, spiced plum, and coffee flavors. There are some dusty tannins, and the wine turns a little cloying on the finish. **86** —*S.H. (2/1/2005)*

Beauregard 2002 Beauregard Ranch Vineayrd Zinfandel (Santa Cruz Mountains) $25. Very ripe, verging on raisins, and strong in brambly fruit, this Zin is very dry and medium-bodied. Along with the raisins you get an array of late-summer wild berries and tannins. **85** —*S.H. (2/1/2005)*

BEAUX FRERES

Beaux Freres 1997 Pinot Noir (Yamhill County) $50. **88** *(11/15/1999)*

Beaux Freres 2000 Pinot Noir (Willamette Valley) $75. Gorgeous aromas of bacon and cherry mix with toast before a palate that's full of black cherry, plum, and vanilla cream. The texture is marvelous, as is its pulse; this is a racy wine filled with rich fruit and firm acids. **92 Cellar Selection** *(10/1/2002)*

Beaux Freres 1999 Belles-Soeurs Shea Vineyard Pinot Noir (Yamhill County) $50. Winemaker Mike Etzel set out to design a more elegant, feminine companion Pinot to his much-acclaimed Beaux Frères bottling, and this wine really hits the mark. The bright fruit mixes tart raspberry/strawberry flavors that seem to gain weight and complexity in the glass. Over the course of an evening the wine draws you back to it again and again, as the fruit seems to put on flesh and nuances of spice and oak, extending into a deliciously long, sensuous finish. **93 Cellar Selection** —*P.G. (11/1/2001)*

BECKMEN

Beckmen 1997 Atelier Bordeaux Blend (Santa Barbara County) $20. **91** *(3/1/2000)*

Beckmen 1996 Cabernet Sauvignon (Santa Barbara County) $20. **92** — *M.S. (7/1/2000)*

Beckmen 1999 Cabernet Sauvignon (Santa Barbara County) $24. Made from some of the best Cabernet vineyards in the county, the wine struggles to overcome its fierce tannins and dry, herbal flavors. New French oak supplies smoky notes, but this can't cover up the lean fruit. Won't benefit from age, so drink now with rich meats and cheeses. **85** —*S.H. (11/15/2002)*

Beckmen 1998 Chardonnay (Santa Barbara County) $16. **91** *(6/1/2000)*

Beckmen 2001 Purisima Mountain Vineyard Grenache (Santa Ynez Valley) $14. It seems like there's fewer and fewer California roses every year, but here's one that could breathe life back into the genre. It's fruity and dry

USA

and crisp, with dusty tannins and plenty of charm. Fresh as the morning dew, with a subtle undercurrent of smoke from oak. **86** —*S.H. (9/1/2003)*

Beckmen 2000 Purisima Mountain Vineyard Grenache (Santa Ynez Valley) $24. Made from vines that yielded less than 2 tons per acre, the wine achieves a density unusual for Grenache. The berry and chocolate flavors are thickly textured, with velvety tannins and a long, fruity finish. The oak is neutral, but the wine might actually benefit from a bit of smoky wood. **88** —*S.H. (12/1/2002)*

Beckmen 2002 Purisima Mountain Vineyard Marsanne (Santa Ynez Valley) $16. A bit flabby and thick in the mouth despite the peach, apricot, melon, and wildflower flavors. Sits on the palate with a heavy bodiedness, and then turns slightly bitter on the short finish. **85** —*S.H. (3/1/2004)*

Beckmen 2001 Purisima Mountain Vineyard Marsanne (Santa Ynez Valley) $16. If you're not sure what a California Marsanne is supposed to taste like, don't worry. Nobody else is, either. This one is full of peach and white chocolate flavors, and has a little bit of sugar. Fortunately, good acidity creates balance. The finish is clean and candied. **85** —*S.H. (12/15/2002)*

Beckmen 1998 Purisima Mountain Vineyard Marsanne (Santa Ynez Valley) $14. 90 —*S.H. (10/1/1999)*

Beckmen 1999 Atelier Red Blend (Santa Ynez Valley) $22. Simple and straightforward, with some berry flavors but basically an earthy, herbal wine. The tannins are fairly hefty, with decent acids. This blend of Cabernet Franc and Merlot is too thin to merit a higher score. **84** —*S.H. (11/15/2002)*

Beckmen 2000 Cuvée Le Bec Red Blend (Santa Barbara County) $14. Ample berry fruit marks this full-bodied red wine, which is dry, with good tannins and soft acids. It's a Châteauneuf wannabe, a blend of Grenache, Syrah, Mourvèdre, and Counoise. Simple and direct, it will complement grilled meats. **84** —*S.H. (12/1/2002)*

Beckmen 2001 Cuvée Le Bec Rhône Red Blend (Santa Ynez Valley) $14. Everything came together to make this Grenache-based Rhône blend rich and delicious. It possesses mouthwatering jammy flavors of cherries, chocolate, and herbs, and is dry and balanced. The smooth texture makes it feel as swanky as wines costing far more. This is a great price for what you get. **90 Best Buy** —*S.H. (12/1/2003)*

Beckmen 2002 Purisima Mountain Vineyard Roussanne (Santa Ynez Valley) $16. An effusively fruity wine, with upfront flavors of peaches and cream, figs, nectarines, and even some tropical pineapple notes. It has a nice acidity that uplifts the flavors and makes the wine bright. At the same time, it's basically a simple, fruit cocktaily sipper. **85** —*S.H. (3/1/2004)*

Beckmen 2001 Estate Sauvignon Blanc (Santa Ynez Valley) $12. There's no oak evident at all in this clean, lemony wine, although it avoids overly sour flavors by veering into riper peach notes. Lees aging adds a creamy texture and bitterness. This pretty wine is a straightforward drink at a super-value price. **87** —*S.H. (9/1/2003)*

Beckmen 2001 Purisima Mountain Vineyard Sauvignon Blanc (Santa Ynez Valley) $20. The pretty lime, peach, fig, and melon flavors are well-integrated and backed up with lively acidity. It's not only delicious, it refreshes and stimulates the palate. **87** —*S.H. (12/15/2003)*

Beckmen 1999 Purisima Mountain Vineyard Sauvignon Blanc (Santa Ynez Valley) $20. This seems to be losing its freshness and appears to be on the down side; the nose is a mixed bag of burnt toast, sulfur, and dried straw. The palate offers more likable characteristics, such as green apple and citrus. But the finish is heavily wooded, and there's an element of cheese here. **86** *(8/1/2002)*

Beckmen 2000 Syrah (Santa Ynez Valley) $24. This little valley continues to press the case for California Syrah. This wine is lush and dense but not heavy. The berry and plum flavors are spiced up with pepper, and dry tannins coat the mouth. Nice now, but will improve in the next 2 or 3 years. **88** —*S.H. (12/1/2002)*

Beckmen 1999 Syrah (Santa Barbara County) $24. The near-black color warns you to expect enormous concentration—and this wine delivers just that. Aromas of leather, cracked peppercorns, blackberries, and a sweet smokiness (BBQ sauce?) give way to a mouthful of espresso and

toasty oak that's marked by deep earthiness. The rich texture and long finish are a treat; give this wine 2–3 years. **88** *(11/1/2001)*

Beckmen 1997 Syrah (Santa Barbara County) $20. 92 *(3/1/2000)*

Beckmen 2003 Estate Syrah (Santa Ynez Valley) $22. Big and brash—a little rough around the edges—but compensates with tasty blackberry, coffee, and earth flavors. Plentiful acids and tannins give this wine a leg up with leg of lamb. **85** *(9/1/2005)*

Beckmen 2001 Estate Syrah (Santa Ynez Valley) $22. An impressive estate wine that shows why Syrah is coming on like gangbusters. The flavors are richly ripe and fill the mouth with cherry, blueberry, and blackberry notes that are sweetly lush. These flavors are balanced by near-perfect tannins, soft and luxurious, and nice, crisp acids. A touch of smoky oak adds spice and vanilla accents. **91 Editors' Choice** —*S.H. (12/1/2003)*

Beckmen 2003 Purisima Mountain Vineyard Syrah (Santa Ynez Valley) $38. Quite different from Beckmen's Block Six, with cola, meat, and coffee notes in place of the Block Six's vibrant berry. There's still plenty of fruit, it's just darker and earthier, backed by a softer structure and a slightly shorter finish. **88** *(9/1/2005)*

Beckmen 2001 Purisima Mountain Vineyard Syrah (Santa Ynez Valley) $38. A tremendous wine, delicious and complex and easily drinkable on release due to the soft, velvety tannins. It has blackberry jam, raspberry, plum, and chocolate flavors, and a distinctive cool-climate note of pepper. New French oak adds fancy notes of vanilla, smoke and cream. Although this wine is dry, it drinks as rich as a fruity custard. **94** —*S.H. (12/1/2003)*

Beckmen 1999 Purisima Mountain Vineyard Syrah (Santa Ynez Valley) $35. The near-black color warns you to expect enormous concentration—and this wine delivers just that. Aromas of leather, cracked peppercorns, blackberries, and a sweet smokiness (BBQ sauce?) give way to a mouthful of espresso and toasty oak that's marked by deep earthiness. The rich texture and long finish are a treat; give this wine 2–3 years. **90** *(11/1/2001)*

Beckmen 2003 Purisima Mountain Vineyard Block Six Syrah (Santa Ynez Valley) $42. With Beckmen's Syrah seemingly back on form after a disappointing 2002 vintage, this flagship wine shows penetrating raspberry scents alongside hints of dark chocolate, blueberries, and blackberries. It's a big-body, big-fruit wine, with hints of oak and spice to add nuance. The long, firmly tannic finish suggests cellaring 2–3 years. **89** *(9/1/2005)*

Beckmen 2002 Purisima Mountain Vineyard Clone #1 Syrah (Santa Ynez Valley) $40. Feels melted and soft, with low acidity and light tannins. Would score higher if it had more fruit. The dry cocoa, bitter coffee, and tart plum flavors have a green streak throughout. **85** —*S.H. (5/1/2005)*

Beckmen 2001 Purisima Mountain Vineyard Clone #1 Syrah (Santa Ynez Valley) $40. The best Syrah of the vintage, a magnificent wine that blows you away through the force of its beauty and sheer voluptuousness. Pours dark and thick, and announces itself with muted but distinguished aromas of cassis, cherry pie, truffle, vanilla, and smoke. Only in the mouth can you begin to appreciate the fantastic wealth of flavors. All this richness is reined in by dusty, structured but easy tannins and the oak regimen. For all its size, the wine maintains delicacy and femininity. With only 125 cases produced, it's hard to find, but worth the search. **95 Editors' Choice** —*S.H. (12/1/2003)*

BEDELL

Bedell 2001 Cupola Bordeaux Blend (North Fork of Long Island) $NA. 87 —*J.C. (10/2/2004)*

Bedell 1997 Cabernet Sauvignon (North Fork of Long Island) $25. Toasty and smoky, with tea and tobacco notes accenting the powerful cassis fruit. Good acidity keeps the wine from being heavy, adding a pleasant juiciness to the finish. **87** —*J.C. (4/1/2001)*

Bedell 1997 Reserve Chardonnay (North Fork of Long Island) $15. Toast and butter aromas are joined by Granny Smith apples, Bartlett pears, and limes. This is a taut, minerally wine that shows a lot of pencilly French oak. **86** —*J.C. (4/1/2001)*

Bedell 1998 Gewürztraminer (North Fork of Long Island) $13. Boasts slightly oily rose and lychee scents that leave no doubt as to what grape variety

USA

you are smelling. This is a big-boned wine with a healthy alcohol level, but one wishes for more persistence on the finish. **83** —*J.C. (4/1/2001)*

Bedell 2002 Merlot (North Fork of Long Island) $18. Hearty aromas of mixed berries, chocolate, earth, barnyard, and spice lead to a smooth, dry, medium-bodied wine packed with flavor. Blueberry, strawberry, chocolate, earth, and spice all play an integral part in the overall package. A highly drinkable wine that will also pair well with a various assortment of foods. **88 Editors' Choice** —*M.D. (12/1/2006)*

Bedell 2000 Merlot (North Fork of Long Island) $21. **84** —*J.C. (10/2/2004)*

Bedell 1997 Merlot (North Fork of Long Island) $18. An intricate nose of floral scents, dried herbs, and cherry-berry fruit is an excellent opener. In the mouth the wine seems attractively light and lively, with some toasty oak notes emerging on the finish. **86** —*J.C. (4/1/2001)*

Bedell 2000 C-Block South Merlot (North Fork of Long Island) $39. **82** — *J.C. (10/2/2004)*

Bedell 2002 Reserve Merlot (North Fork of Long Island) $30. A finely crafted wine, but one that has some unripe elements. Sweet and supple in the mouth, this gets an A-plus for mouthfeel. But rhubarb and unripe red-fruit aromas and flavors mar the healthy chocolate, spice, vanilla, tobacco, and blueberry. Finishes with plenty of oak flavor. **86** —*M.D. (12/1/2006)*

Bedell NV Main Road Red Merlot-Cabernet Sauvignon (North Fork of Long Island) $14. **80** —*J.C. (10/2/2004)*

Bedell 1998 Cupola Red Blend (North Fork of Long Island) $30. This blend of 50% Cabernet Sauvignon and 40% Cabernet Franc, with 5% each Malbec and Petit Verdot is very primary, showing lots of bright cherry fruit and a judicious dose of vanilla oak. A juicy, fun wine that would make for good drinking this summer and on into fall. Bottled 9/00, release date undetermined. **87** —*J.C. (4/1/2001)*

Bedell 2001 Late Harvest Riesling Riesling (North Fork of Long Island) $35. It's picked late, when the grapes are superripe, then winemaker Kip Bedell puts them in a freezer prior to crush to further concentrate the resulting must. The result is a thick, gooey, unctuous dessert wine with flavors of tangerines and honey. Yum. **88** —*J.C. (8/1/2003)*

Bedell 1999 Viognier (North Fork of Long Island) $18. Not as intensely aromatic as either the sold-out 1998 or the 2000 tasted from barrel, this is nonetheless a solid example. Peach and bitter-almond flavors are carried across the palate by a wine that's rich and full but not fat. Some nice black-pepper notes punctuate the finish. **85** —*J.C. (4/1/2001)*

BEDFORD THOMPSON

Bedford Thompson 2000 Thompson Vineyard Cabernet Franc (Santa Barbara County) $20. Nice and polished, an elegant wine with flavors of cherries and oak. It's medium in body, with smooth tannins and a silky finish, and quite dry. **85** —*S.H. (12/15/2004)*

Bedford Thompson 1998 Chardonnay (Santa Barbara County) $18. **84** *(6/1/2000)*

Bedford Thompson 2002 Thompson Vineyard Chardonnay (Santa Barbara County) $20. A bit raw and green, with peach, apple, and oak flavors. Feels rough through the finish. **84** —*S.H. (12/15/2004)*

Bedford Thompson 1997 Gewürztraminer (Santa Barbara County) $12. **90** —*S.H. (9/1/1999)*

Bedford Thompson 2000 Thompson Vineyard Grenache (Santa Barbara County) $20. Light in body and flavor, a simple little wine with herbal, mushroomy flavors and puckery tannins. Feels dry and astringent because there's not enough ripe fruit to soften. **83** —*S.H. (3/1/2004)*

Bedford Thompson 2000 Thompson Vineyard Mourvèdre (Santa Barbara County) $20. Mourvèdre is almost never a great wine in California, but a good one in the right hands, as is this dry, rich, stylish version. An interesting mélange of grapey, cherry-berry flavors infused with spices, herbs, chocolate, and earth, wrapped in soft, gentle tannins. **87** —*S.H. (12/1/2003)*

Bedford Thompson 2001 Thompson Vineyard Petite Sirah (Santa Barbara County) $45. Very dry and thick in tannins, with powerful plum, coffee, and chocolate fruit and crisp acids. Those tannins really kick in

and numb the palate, leading to a dry, astringent finish. **84** —*S.H. (12/15/2004)*

Bedford Thompson 1998 Syrah (Santa Barbara County) $20. A wine of contrasting parts that just don't seem to cohere—hot, sweet, and salty, weedy and tangy, smoky and metallic. The tart fruit is a bit indistinct and the wood and fruit aren't well integrated. Disappointingly narrow and sourly fruited. **81** *(10/1/2001)*

Bedford Thompson 2000 Thompson Vineyard Syrah (Santa Barbara County) $22. This concentrated, well-wooded young wine pours black and streaky, and opens with complex scents of cassis, smoked meat, anise, smoky oak, and vanilla. It tastes rich and candied now, with red fruit flavors and an earthy, truffly streak. The tannins are a bit rough around the edges. Try aging for a year or so. **88** —*S.H. (12/1/2003)*

BEHRENS & HITCHCOCK

Behrens & Hitchcock 2002 Beckstoffer Tokalon Vineyard Cabernet Sauvignon (Oakville) $75. A difficult wine to evaluate, as it's young and unresolved. Has tobacco and mint aromas, with some cherries. Closed and on the palate shows some cassis and lots of oak. Tannins are big and astringent. Seems to lack fruit. **84** —*S.H. (6/1/2005)*

Behrens & Hitchcock 2001 Beckstoffer Tokalon Vineyard Cabernet Sauvignon (Napa Valley) $65. Black in color with well-charred oak, caramel and toast flavors. Raisins, currants and blackstrap molasses flavors. Big, Port-like in size, but dry. Finishes hot. **85** —*S.H. (6/1/2005)*

Behrens & Hitchcock 1999 Beckstoffer Vineyards Cabernet Sauvignon (Oakville) $NA. Porty. Candied raisins, caramel, stewed prunes. Raisiny, overripe, hot. **83** —*S.H. (6/1/2005)*

Bel Arbor 1999 Cabernet Sauvignon (California) $6. **86 Best Buy** —*S.H. (12/15/2000)*

BEL ARBOR

Bel Arbor 1998 Chardonnay (California) $6. **82** —*S.H. (7/1/1999)*

Bel Arbor 2000 Chardonnay (Mendocino County) $6. Has some noticeable oak, with the expected vanilla, smoke, and spicy notes floating above tangerine fruit flavors. The texture is creamy and full, although low acidity makes it flabby and robs it of life. It's a common wine but, at this price, it's pretty enough for your next block party. **84** —*S.H. (5/1/2002)*

Bel Arbor 1999 Chardonnay (California) $6. **82** —*S.H. (11/15/2000)*

Bel Arbor 2000 Merlot (Mendocino County) $6. Gets the job done with a burst of jammy Lifesaver aromas and flavors. Lightly structured. There are some less ripe, green, stalky flavors that lead to a tart finish in this dry wine. **83** —*S.H. (7/1/2002)*

Bel Arbor 1999 Merlot (California) $6. **86 Best Buy** —*S.H. (11/15/2000)*

BEL GLOS

Bel Glos 2000 Pinot Noir (Santa Maria Valley) $30. A light-textured wine, creamy smooth on the palate, with a pretty blend of raspberry, blueberry, cherry, and herb flavors that turn silky on the finish. A new release from Chuck Wagner of Caymus. **88** —*J.M. (2/1/2003)*

BELFORD SPRINGS

Belford Springs 2000 Chardonnay (California) $8. There is a lot to like in this modest but flavorful Chard, with its apple and pear flavors and fig undercurrents. A dose of oak adds creamy, smoky notes and a taste of vanilla. **86** —*S.H. (12/15/2002)*

Belford Springs 2000 Pinot Noir (California) $8. It has recognizably Pinot qualities of silky tannins and a round, easy mouthfeel. The fruit is thin, and there's some bitterness on the short finish. **84** —*S.H. (4/1/2003)*

Belford Springs 2001 Sauvignon Blanc (California) $8. What a pleasure it is to drink this wine on a warm day. It's filled with lip-smackingly good fruity flavors, apples and peaches and pears, and is clean and zesty. A sheer delight all the way from start to finish. **86** —*S.H. (9/1/2003)*

Belford Springs 2001 Zinfandel (California) $6. Smoke, toast, vanilla, and cherries are at the center of this pleasant quaffer. It's relatively smooth textured and finishes with a mildly toasty edge. **85 Best Buy** *(11/1/2003)*

Belford Springs 1999 Zinfandel (California) $8. Here's a thin, peppery wine that's very dry and tart, with pronounced tannins. There's not much fruit to be found, but it's a sprightly, clean drink that will work with rich, gooey foods like pizza. **83** —*S.H. (12/1/2002)*

BELL

Bell 2003 Claret Bordeaux Blend (Napa Valley) $30. Nice, ripe Cabernet-based wine, with a touch of Syrah. Shows Bordeaux structure and intensity, with black currants, rich tannins, and oak, while Syrah seems to bring softer, violet-infused cherries. Lots of flair and sophistication. **88** —*S.H. (12/1/2006)*

Bell 2003 Cabernet Sauvignon (Napa Valley) $40. Lots to like, lots to not like; a difficult wine. On the plus side are lush, smooth tannins and that softly luxurious mouthfeel that Napa Cabs give. On the minus side is a stewed, raisiny overripeness. New oak can't quite erase that dried-out berry taste. **84** —*S.H. (12/1/2006)*

Bell 2000 Cabernet Sauvignon (Napa Valley) $35. An awkward wine that has some pretty blackberry flavors and nice, soft tannins, but also earthy, uncured tobacco notes that verge on vegetal, and an astringency that rubs the palate all the way down. **85** —*S.H. (11/15/2003)*

Bell 1999 Cabernet Sauvignon (Napa Valley) $35. A good wine, but lean and herbal for such a ripe vintage. The dominant flavors are of sage, tobacco and coffee, accompanied by some tough tannins. The inish turns tannic and gritty. Try aging, but it's a gamble. **85** —*S.H. (5/1/2003)*

Bell 1999 Baritelle Vineyard Cabernet Sauvignon (Rutherford) $60. Opulent as heck, this is thick enough to paint with, with massive flavors of black currants, blackberries, plums, tobacco, sage, and white chocolate. An elaborate overlay of oak adds vanilla and smoke. The tannins are rich and fabulous. **92 Editors' Choice** —*S.H. (12/31/2002)*

Bell 2000 Baritelle Vineyard-Jackson Clone Cabernet Sauvignon (Rutherford) $65. An elegant Cabernet that shows off its upscale address. Has pretty aromas and flavors of black currants and blackberries and and a rich veneer of smoky oak. On the other hand, there is a thin spot in the middle palate where the wine trails off to alcohol and tannins. Drink now. **87** —*S.H. (6/1/2004)*

Bell 1998 Baritelle Vineyard-Jackson Clone Cabernet Sauvignon (Rutherford) $55. Inky dark, this wine brims with important aromas of cassis, mint, and fine, smoky oak. Fully ripe Cabernet blackberry flavors are wrapped in elegant tannins, dry and dusty. The structure is impeccable, the finish long. It's complex but approachable enough for immediate drinking. **93** —*S.H. (6/1/2002)*

Bell 1996 Baritelle Vineyard Jackson Clo Cabernet Sauvignon (Rutherford) $50. **89** —*M.S. (9/1/2000)*

Bell 1997 Baritelle Vineyard Cabernet Sauvignon (Rutherford) $60. **90** *(11/1/2000)*

Bell 2002 Clone Six Cabernet Sauvignon (Rutherford) $65. This fresh, young wine, which expresses vibrant fruit flavors of cherries and blackberries, has a slightly rustic edge. It finishes with a swirl of dried herbs and dusty tannins. **87** —*S.H. (12/15/2005)*

Bell 1999 Talianna Cabernet Sauvignon (Rutherford) $35. This interesting blend includes 20% Syrah from the Sierra Foothills. The Cabernet provides structure and varietal character. Syrah adds a fat, meaty note. New oak gives it a spicy sweetness. The result is delicious, a dry, complex wine to drink now or soon. **92** —*S.H. (6/1/2002)*

Bell 1999 Talianna Cabernet Sauvignon-Syrah (Rutherford) $35. **92** —*S.H. (6/1/2002)*

Bell 2005 Chardonnay (Napa Valley) $25. Shows richness in the ripe peach, pear, and apple flavors, although the wine, from Yountville and Oak Knoll, is a little soft and earthy compared to cool-climate Chards. Dry and clean. **85** —*S.H. (12/1/2006)*

Bell 1998 Aleta's Vineyard Chardonnay (Yountville) $24. **82** *(6/1/2000)*

Bell 2003 Merlot (Napa Valley) $30. Shows overripeness in the raisin flavors that accompany cherries and cassis. A fairly unbalanced wine that's probably at its best now. **83** —*S.H. (12/1/2006)*

Bell 2000 Merlot (Yountville) $30. Lean and earthy, marked by tobacco, dill, and less than ripe cherry flavors. Tannins are tough and gritty. The wine finishes very dry and rasping, showing little fruit. The winemaker seems to have understood the problem here, and added five percent Syrah. **85** —*S.H. (8/1/2003)*

Bell 1999 Aleta's Vineyard Merlot (Yountville) $35. This 100% Merlot starts with minty, cedary aromas tinged with smoke and vanilla and a solid cut of black raspberry. It's not a big wine, although there are some youthfully jammy berry flavors. Seems a little simple for the price, but there's no denying its elegance and charm. **88** —*S.H. (6/1/2002)*

Bell 1996 Aleta's Vineyard Merlot (Napa Valley) $28. **85** —*J.C. (7/1/2000)*

Bell 2004 Canterbury Vineyard Syrah (Sierra Foothills) $25. Nice and rich. It's one of those wines whose fruit is so powerful, it lays claim to the palate. Blackberry jam, cherry pie, pomegranate, and sweet rhubarb flavors are wrapped into finely meshed tannins. **87** —*S.H. (12/1/2006)*

Bell 2003 Canterbury Vineyard Syrah (Sierra Foothills) $24. Slightly herbal and spicy, but this wine is mostly about the fruit, which one taster described as ripe while another called it stewed. There's a backbone of chocolate and prune that's undeniably rich and gives it strength. **87** *(9/1/2005)*

Bell 2000 Canterbury Vineyard Syrah (Sierra Foothills) $28. From 2,200 feet, a single vineyard wine that's rough around the edges and pretty tannic. Flavors veer between blackberries and earthier tobacco and sage. Very dry, rather austere right now, with a bitter finish. Aging for a couple years may soften. **84** —*S.H. (6/1/2003)*

Bell 1999 Canterbury Vineyard Syrah (Sierra Foothills) $28. This wine is creamy and concentrated. Milk chocolate, briary berries and vanilla flavors join leather, stable, and citrus notes on the palate. Finishes lush and creamy, with extremely supple tannins. Drink now. **88** *(11/1/2001)*

Bell 1997 Canterbury Vineyard Syrah (Sierra Foothills) $28. **88** *(5/1/2000)*

Bell 2000 T&A Vineyard Viognier (Santa Cruz County) $28. Hints of almonds, butterscotch and peaches are at the core of this full-bodied white wine. The finish is fruity and fun. **88** —*J.M. (12/15/2002)*

BELLA

Bella 2002 Big River Ranch Syrah (Alexander Valley) $38. Made Northern Rhône style, this sturdy Syrah opens with white pepper and cherry aromas. It's a young wine, currently tight in acids and sweet in layers of toasty oak. Give it a year to come together. **89** —*S.H. (11/1/2005)*

Bella 2002 Lily Hill Estate Syrah (Dry Creek Valley) $34. This soft Syrah is forward in ripe cherries, raspberries, pomegranates, coffee, and wood spice flavors. It has an apparent sweetness that comes from the interplay of ripeness, alcohol, and oak. Feels limpid, soft, and voluptuous on the palate. **88** —*S.H. (11/1/2005)*

Bella 2001 Zinfandel (Dry Creek Valley) $24. Toasty rich and smooth, with bright-edged cherry, berry, vanilla, sage, and spice flavors. Tannins are a little tough, but the ensemble is fairly elegant. Finishes with moderate length. **88** *(11/1/2003)*

Bella 2002 Belle Canyon Estate Zinfandel (Dry Creek Valley) $30. This fine example of a Dry Creek Zin is very forward in ripe cherries and raspberries, but possesses great structure from rich tannins. Deeply satisfying, it has a fine, claret-like balance and elegance. **90** —*S.H. (11/1/2005)*

Bella 2001 Belle Canyon Estate Zinfandel (Dry Creek Valley) $28. Smooth and silky, with an elegant mix of coffee, chocolate, plum, black cherry, and spice flavors. The tannins are ripe, with moderate body and a good finish. **89** *(11/1/2003)*

Bella 2003 Big River Ranch Zinfandel (Alexander Valley) $34. This is a big, rich, forward, chocolaty Zin that flirts with overripeness. It's not as complex or balanced as Bella's superb Lily Hill bottling. It also goes a little raisiny and hot towards the finish. But it sure is a nice barbecue wine. **87** —*S.H. (7/1/2006)*

Bella 2002 Big River Ranch Zinfandel (Alexander Valley) $34. Almost Port-like in the black-purple color. Aromas are of caramel, baked brown sugar and blueberries. This is a dry wine, but an enormously fruity one,

USA

with rich, thick, soft, elaborate tannins. The blackberries reprise on the finish, ripe with sunny sweetness. **88** —*S.H. (10/1/2005)*

Bella 2001 Big River Ranch Zinfandel (Alexander Valley) $32. Smooth, silky tannins give the wine a certain elegance. The flavors are not quite as noteworthy, but they're still enjoyable, ranging from black cherry, to plum, vanilla, toast, licorice, spice, and herbs. A touch astringent on the end. **89** *(11/1/2003)*

Bella 2002 Estate Zinfandel (Dry Creek Valley) $24. With more than 15% alcohol and new oak, this Zin adds sweetness to the cherry and black raspberry flavors, but there's a good grip of acids and tannins to balance. Try with the best beef you can get. **87** —*S.H. (11/1/2005)*

Bella 2002 Lily Hill Estate Zinfandel (Dry Creek Valley) $30. Opens with an exuberant burst of briars and brambly, wild berries, and turns explosively fruity in the mouth, with firm, dusty tannins. Has an edge of ripe sweetness. **85** —*S.H. (10/1/2005)*

Bella 2001 Lily Hill Estate Zinfandel (Dry Creek Valley) $28. This one has a slight stewed-fruit quality. Prunes and berries are at the fore, with herb and spice on the follow-up. Tannins are supple and the wine sits squarely on the palate with a good finish. **86** *(11/1/2003)*

Bella 2003 Lily Hill Vineyard Zinfandel (Dry Creek Valley) $30. I discovered Bella a few years ago and was glad to find a Zin specialist with a real commitment to vineyard terroir. Bella's estate has produced a wonderfully dry Zin, as rich and balanced as a classic Cab, with Zin's briary, brambly fruit. This is really one of the best Zins out there right now. **92 Editors' Choice** —*S.H. (7/1/2006)*

BELLA VIGNA

Bella Vigna 1998 Costa Vineyard Zinfandel (Lodi) $16. Smells like a shootout in a tomato factory. It's a strong whiff of tomatoes on the vine, followed by tannin and a little sweet, grapy fruit. **82** —*P.G. (3/1/2001)*

BELLE GLOS

Belle Glos 2001 Pinot Noir (Santa Maria Valley) $30. A cool coastal Pinot with powerful aromatics and silky tannins. Flavors veer toward sweet ripe cherries, with earthy complexities of tobacco and espresso. Dry and stylish, a youthful wine that's not built for the cellar, but is delicious now. A new label from Caymus. **90** —*S.H. (7/1/2003)*

Belle Glos 2004 Clark & Telephone Vineyard Pinot Noir (Santa Maria Valley) $38. Too raw and acidic for me, with jammy blackberry and cherry flavors, this Pinot unsuccessfully tries to make up in power what it lacks in finesse. It's a good wine, but a disappointment given the lineage, which stems directly from Caymus. **84** —*S.H. (10/1/2006)*

Belle Glos 2003 Clark & Telephone Vineyard Pinot Noir (Santa Maria Valley) $38. Following on the heels of the last vintage, this Pinot is right up there in complexity and deliciousness. It's a big, young wine, dark and full-bodied, with complex fruit, herb, spice, and oak flavors that are impressive for their length and depth. It's also very dry. Fine now despite its youth, it should gain in power and subtlety through 2008. **94 Cellar Selection** —*S.H. (12/1/2005)*

Belle Glos 2002 Clark & Telephone Vineyard Pinot Noir (Santa Maria Valley) $38. This spectacular Pinot, which defines its South Coast terroir, is a great wine. The extracted fruit is massive, flooding the palate with cherries and raspberries, and the wine is well-oaked. Yet it combines its power with regal grace, which is what Pinot is supposed to do. Finishes with a silky, velvety harmony. Really an eye-opening wine, superb in every respect. **95** —*S.H. (5/1/2005)*

Belle Glos 2004 Las Alturas Vineyard Pinot Noir (Santa Lucia Highlands) $48. In true Lucia fashion, this is a dark, big, rich, ripe young Pinot, bursting with fruit, and while it's not exactly elegant, it certainly is powerful. Gobs of cherry, pomegranate, chocolate, and coffee flavors flood the palate, leading to a dry finish. Don't drink it now unless you're immune to the acidity and tannins of immature wines. Best 2008-2010. **88** —*S.H. (10/1/2006)*

Belle Glos 2004 Taylor Lane Vineyard Pinot Noir (Sonoma Coast) $50. Smells fresh and invigorating, but in the mouth it has raisiny flavors. This is a young Pinot, rich in acids and tannins, but that overripe quality

limits ageability and makes the wine a bit one-dimensional. Drink now. **85** —*S.H. (10/1/2006)*

Belle Glos 2003 Taylor Lane Vineyard Pinot Noir (Sonoma Coast) $50. Here's a dark, big, rich, dry, oaky Pinot Noir. It's huge in black cherry, cocoa, cola, vanilla, and spice flavors that dramatically swamp the palate. It's a complex, elegant, silky wine now, delicious on its own, and likely to intensify for four or five years. From Caymus. **91 Editors' Choice** —*S.H. (12/1/2005)*

Belle Glos 2002 Taylor Lane Vineyard Pinot Noir (Sonoma Coast) $50. This is a good wine, but it's really tannic and heavy for Pinot Noir. With the black color and peppery aroma, you might mistake it for Syrah. Perhaps it will age. Meanwhile, it defines a current trend in Sonoma for weighty Pinots, so be forewarned. **87** —*S.H. (4/1/2005)*

BELLE VALLÉE

Belle Vallée 2004 Pinot Gris (Willamette Valley) $13. Very crisp, clean, and leesy. This is made in a style that seems to emphasize the flavors of the yeast, giving a mouth-cleaning freshness to the flavors. **88** —*P.G. (2/1/2006)*

Belle Vallée 2004 Pinot Noir (Willamette Valley) $20. Pungent, minty and quite tannic, this young wine needs more time to pull its flavors together. There's a nice whiff of vanilla cream wrapped into the finish. **86** —*P.G. (5/1/2006)*

Belle Vallée 2002 Pinot Noir (Oregon) $20. Straightforward, with cherries and cream consistency. Despite a rather watery finish, the wine delivers some nice fruity pleasure, along with plenty of milk chocolaty oak. **86** *(11/1/2004)*

Belle Vallée 2004 Grand Cuvée Pinot Noir (Willamette Valley) $49. This opens with tart, tight leaf and beetroot flavors, which overlay quite soft, round and riper fruit. The integration of earthy tannins with the fruit is a little disjointed; what shows most clearly are the leafy, herbal plant flavors. There's plenty of stuffing here; perhaps this is one of those wines that will warrant a higher score with additional bottle age. **87** —*P.G. (5/1/2006)*

Belle Vallée 2004 Reserve Pinot Noir (Willamette Valley) $30. Herbal flavors descend into stemminess, with the aggressive tannins swamping the fruit. The finish is hard, earthy, and tasting of green tea. **86** —*P.G. (5/1/2006)*

Belle Vallée 2002 Reserve Pinot Noir (Oregon) $30. Cranberries and tart cherry fruit is awash in new oak, tannic and awkward at the moment. If the tannins smooth out, this could merit a significantly higher score. **86** *(11/1/2004)*

Belle Vallée 2004 Whole Cluster Pinot Noir (Willamette Valley) $15. This is a fun wine, with flavors like cherry candy and milk chocolate. Light and insubstantial, but it will be quite nice chilled as an apéritif. **84** —*P.G. (5/1/2006)*

Belle Vallée 2002 Whole Cluster Pinot Noir (Willamette Valley) $15. Here's an unusual mix of opening notes. Melon, meat, fig, and peanut; this is not standard stuff. But it's plenty juicy, with cranberry and pomegranate flavors, a big, cuddly Pinot. **86** *(11/1/2004)*

BELO

Belo 1999 Muscat Gris Muscat (California) $16. A Beaumes-de-Venise-style wine, sweet but not too sweet, with pleasant peach, nougat, and apricot flavors and a Sherry-like quality that adds interest. The honeyed flavors are balanced by crisp acids, finishing clean. **89** —*S.H. (9/1/2003)*

Belo 1999 Sousao Port Port (California) $15. Fairly sweet, with dark chocolate, black cherry, and sweetened espresso flavors, set off by adequate acidity. Lacks the layers and complexity of the best Portuguese stuff, but at this price, it's a nice wine to sip with chocolate desserts. **86** —*S.H. (12/1/2002)*

Belo 1999 Touriga Nacional Vintage Reserve Port (Napa Valley) $40. Very sweet and viscous in the mouth, a wine that blankets the palate with velvet and fine dusty tannins. The flavors are of sweetened espresso, blackberry, and blueberry liqueur and cassis, dark milk chocolate and rich cocoa, and a beautiful peppery note that braces against the overt sweetness. One of the best California Ports in recent memory. **96 Cellar Selection** —*S.H. (12/1/2002)*

Belo 1999 Dessert Wine Sauvignon Blanc (Napa Valley) $25. Frankly sweet, with a dollop of Sémillon, this white Bordeaux-style wine has powerful, pronounced flavors of smoky honey, peaches, and especially pears, with a finish that tastes distinctly of white chocolate. These flavors are very strong and pure, and call for similar foods. **87** —*S.H. (9/1/2003)*

BELVEDERE

Belvedere 2000 Healdsburg Ranches Cabernet Sauvignon (Sonoma County) $26. At five years-plus, this Cab is beginning to shed its aggressive tannins, allowing rich cassis, currant, and oaky flavors to emerge. It's still pretty tannic, though, and very dry, but it's balanced enough to enjoy with a good steak. **86** —*S.H. (7/1/2006)*

Belvedere 1998 Chardonnay (Russian River Valley) $18. 89 *(6/1/2000)*

Belvedere 1998 Chardonnay (Sonoma County) $18. 89 *(6/1/2000)*

Belvedere 2004 Chardonnay (Russian River Valley) $20. Clean, dry, and tart in acids, this is a minerally Chard with citrus and kiwi flavors. It has some oak that adds richness, but it's not really a rich wine. It's more of a streamlined, sleek sipper. **85** —*S.H. (12/1/2006)*

Belvedere 2002 Chardonnay (Russian River Valley) $20. More manipulated than Belvedere's Healdsburg Ranches bottling, showing the impact of *sur lie* aging in the slightly sour note that lends complexity to the oak and fruit. Dry and well-acidified, this needs something like cracked Dungeness crab to make it sing. **88** —*S.H. (8/1/2005)*

Belvedere 2000 Chardonnay (Russian River Valley) $20. Rich and ripe, with fine-tuned layers of pear, melon, citrus, apple, herb, and pretty toast notes. Well balanced and refined, the wine finishes long, with a tangy, fresh edge to the vibrant flavors. **90** —*J.M. (12/15/2002)*

Belvedere 2004 Healdsburg Ranches Chardonnay (Sonoma County) $14. Okay everyday Chard, with toned-down peach, pear, and oak flavors and a creaminess to the texture. Finishes dry, crisp, and short. **84** —*S.H. (12/1/2006)*

Belvedere 2003 Healdsburg Ranches Chardonnay (Sonoma County) $14. Well-oaked, brimming with vanilla, buttered toast, and sweet wood flavors, but the fruit below is big enough to take it. Spicy mango, guava, pineapple, and honey, in a creamy, full-bodied texture. Not a bad price for a wine of this quality. **88** —*S.H. (8/1/2005)*

Belvedere 2000 Healdsburg Ranches Chardonnay (Sonoma County) $14. Smooth and sleek, with a fine balance of acidity and body. Flavors recall lemon, melon, pear, herb, and toast, finishing fresh and full. **88 Best Buy** —*J.M. (12/15/2002)*

Belvedere 2002 Healdsburg Ranches Merlot (Sonoma County) $19. Here's a Merlot that's a little everyday, a little fancy. It has a velvety texture and currant, plum, and oaky flavors. The downside is astringent tannins—the puckery kind that make the tongue stick to the roof of the mouth. **85** —*S.H. (12/1/2006)*

Belvedere 2004 Pinot Noir (Russian River Valley) $28. Lovely and complicated; a Pinot Noir for Cabernet lovers. It has Pinot's silky texture and soft tannins, but also a full-bodied, oak-infused weight that carries wonderfully ripe cherry pie, anise, cola, and raspberry flavors that change from sip to sip. **90** —*S.H. (12/1/2006)*

Belvedere 2001 Pinot Noir (Russian River Valley) $28. At more than four years of age, this Pinot still tastes fresh and lively. It has a juicy acidity that frames classic Russian River Pinot flavors of cherries, cola, and rhubarb, and is dry and silky. There's still an edge of dusty tannins. Try this well-crafted wine with lamb or rib roast. **91 Editors' Choice** —*S.H. (7/1/2006)*

Belvedere 2000 Pinot Noir (Russian River Valley) $30. Rises to the expectations of the appellation, with classic aromas of beetroot, black raspberry, chocolate, mint, smoke, and vanilla, and a dry, voluptious mouthfeel. The berry flavors are powerful and jammy, but the wine is balanced and harmonious. This is what the California sun does for Pinot Noir. **91** —*S.H. (5/1/2002)*

Belvedere 1997 Floodgate Vineyard Pinot Noir (Anderson Valley) $20. 89 —*M.S. (10/1/2000)*

Belvedere 2005 Sauvignon Blanc (Dry Creek Valley) $18. Here's a bone-dry, high-acid, minerally Sauvignon with grapefruit, fig, and white pepper flavors. It's a racy, savory wine that will pair well with an enormous range of foods, or else serve as a warmer-upper before dinner. **86** —*S.H. (11/15/2006)*

Belvedere 1998 Syrah (Dry Creek Valley) $22. Blackberry, maple, and well-worn-baseball-glove aromas open this smooth, medium-weight wine. Plum, earth, and leather flavors dominate the palate and the medium-short finish. **87** *(11/1/2001)*

Belvedere 1999 Healdsburg Ranches Syrah (Sonoma County) $26. This is one reason why Syrah is becoming so popular. It has all the fruit you expect from a ripe vintage, but it doesn't overwhelm. It's just part of the package that includes ripe, soft tannins and acids and a subtle interplay of oak. Balanced, rich, and harmonious, it's an elaborately detailed wine meant to accompany strongly flavored foods. **92 Editors' Choice** —*S.H. (9/1/2002)*

Belvedere 1999 Zinfandel (Dry Creek Valley) $NA. This Zin has sturdy tannins and a medium-full mouthfeel, but not the black, brooding quality that you'd expect from such bigness. Cola plus bright, jammy red and black berries pave the way for cocoa and lots of ripe, mixed black fruit on the finish. Goes down really easy. **89** —*D.T. (3/1/2002)*

Belvedere 2001 Healdsburg Ranches Zinfandel (Sonoma County) $24. Quite plush, packed with elegant, sweet oak framing full-blown, ripe black cherry, plum, blackberry, chocolate, coffee, and herb flavors. The tannins are firm and ripe and the finish long and bright. **90** *(11/1/2003)*

BENESSERE

Benessere 2005 Pinot Grigio (Carneros) $24. Cool Carneros is turning out to be one of the best homes for serious PGs in the state, as evidenced by this and other examples. Benessere's '05 is rich in apple, fig, peach, and spicy punch flavors, with a refreshing spine of crisp acidity and an impressively long finish. **88** —*S.H. (12/15/2006)*

Benessere 2003 Pinot Grigio (Carneros) $22. Smooth-textured and firm, yet with just the right touch of acidity. The wine shows complexity, with layered notes of melon, lemon, herbs, and a touch of peach. Medium-bodied with a finish that's moderate in length. **88** —*J.M. (10/1/2004)*

Benessere 2002 Pinot Grigio (Napa-Carneros) $22. A steely, mineral-like wine that neatly balances firm acidity with fairly rich body. The wine is clean and crisp but also shows off pretty hints of melon, grapefruit, and lemon. Long, clean, and fresh at the end. A serious effort for this varietal. **90** —*J.M. (2/1/2004)*

Benessere 2000 Pinot Grigio (Napa Valley) $20. Pretty grapefruit, melon, mineral, pear, and herb notes form the core of this luscious yet refreshing white wine. Clean and bright on the finish. Perfect for summer. **88** —*J.M. (11/15/2001)*

Benessere 2002 Phenomenon Red Blend (Napa Valley) $60. A blend of Sangiovese, Syrah, Cab, and Merlot, this fruity wine has a forward, primary flavor of red cherries, with a nice coating of smoky oak. It's voluptuous and velvety, but too sweet on the finish. **85** —*S.H. (3/1/2006)*

Benessere 1997 Sangiovese (Napa Valley) $26. 88 —*S.H. (9/1/2000)*

Benessere 1996 Sangiovese (Napa Valley) $25. 87 —*M.S. (6/1/1999)*

Benessere 2002 Sangiovese (Napa Valley) $28. Benessere has worked hard to master this fussy variety. This version is silky and clean, with ripe cherry flavors veering into chocolate. It has a supple texture and good acids, but is a little too sweet for my taste. **86** —*S.H. (3/1/2006)*

Benessere 2001 Sangiovese (Napa Valley) $28. While others have given up on this finicky varietal, Benessere perseveres, with good results. This wine is soft and creamy in texture, with lovely flavors of fully ripe cherries, cocoa, and sweet, smoky oak. It has a crispness and delicacy that make it pleasurable. **88** —*S.H. (3/1/2005)*

Benessere 2000 Sangiovese (Napa Valley) $25. A smoky, charry edge frames the black cherry, cassis, blackberry, licorice, and spice flavors here. The wine is smooth textured, though it ends with a touch of bitterness. **87** —*J.M. (4/1/2004)*

Benessere 1999 Sangiovese (Napa Valley) $29. Incredibly velvety, with lush, cherry, floral, raspberry, herb, chocolate, and spice flavors. Smooth and sleek. A fine example of this varietal in America. **91 Editors' Choice** —*J.M. (12/1/2002)*

Benessere 1998 Sangiovese (Napa Valley) $28. Silky smooth, with velvety tannins that support a fine blend of plum, cherry, spice, herb, and anise flavors. The wine is complex and seductive; Securely one of the best Sangiovese wines to come out of California yet. **92 Editors' Choice** —*J.M. (12/1/2001)*

Benessere 2003 Syrah (Napa Valley) $40. Limited production (under 200 cases), but worth seeking out. Features bold blackberries accented by hints of savory dried herbs, pepper, and dried spices, all buoyed by a creamy, supple, mouthfeel. The long, berry-filled finish boasts hints of coffee and vanilla. Nicely done. **89** *(9/1/2005)*

Benessere 1999 Estate Syrah (Napa Valley) $38. Rich and ripe, with lush black cherry and plum flavors, hints of sage, chocolate, and smoke, all couched in toasty sweet oak highlighted by herbs and spice. A powerhouse that's long on the finish. **92** —*J.M. (12/1/2002)*

Benessere 1999 Benessere Estate Black Glass Vineyard Zinfandel (Napa Valley) $35. Rich plum and cedar notes lead the way here, backed by velvety tannins and lush black cherry, vanilla, anise, and herb notes. Beautifully balanced and brimming with character. **92 Editors' Choice** —*J.M. (12/15/2001)*

Benessere 2001 BK Collins, Old Vines Zinfandel (Napa Valley) $28. Fairly plush and smooth, but with a racy core of spice, plum, black cherry, licorice, toast, and herb flavors. The finish is moderate in length with full-on body. Quite nice. **89** —*J.M. (11/1/2003)*

Benessere 2001 Black Glass Vineyard Zinfandel (Napa Valley) $35. Sleek and plush, this elegant blend of black cherry, cola, coffee, tea, plum, spice, cedar, chocolate, blackberry, and anise flavors is set in ripe, supple tannins that carry it with muscle and finesse. Silky smooth on the finish, it lingers nicely to the end. **91** *(11/1/2003)*

Benessere 1999 Black Glass Vineyard Zinfandel (Napa Valley) $35. Rich plum and cedar notes lead the way here, backed by velvety tannins and lush black cherry, vanilla, anise, and herb notes. Beautifully balanced and brimming with character. **92 Editors' Choice** —*J.M. (12/15/2001)*

BENMARL

Benmarl 2004 Pinot Grigio (Oregon) $18. Made in New York from Oregon grapes, this is one strange cat. The nose is full of almond butter and juice-like aromas, while the palate offers a weird mix of apple and spice. Not normal; too funky to score better. Strange stuff indeed. **81** *(2/1/2006)*

BENNETT LANE

Bennett Lane 2002 Maximus Cabernet Blend (Napa Valley) $28. A Bordeaux blend with a good chunk of Syrah added, this wine is soft and luscious. Although it's a little sweet and not an ager, the blackberry, coffee, and cocoa flavors make you want another glass. **87** —*S.H. (10/1/2005)*

Bennett Lane 2002 Cabernet Sauvignon (Napa Valley) $45. This is an exuberantly ripe wine, rich in currant, blackberry, and cherry flavors. What's especially attractive is the texture, comprised of soft, intricate tannins and good acidity. At its best now. **88** —*S.H. (10/1/2005)*

BENSON FERRY

Benson Ferry 2001 Select Chardonnay (North Coast) $9. Solid middle of the road Chard, all peaches and cream and opulent spices. Dry and rich, with a creamy texture, the wine turns peppery on the finish. **86 Best Buy** —*S.H. (6/1/2003)*

Benson Ferry 2001 Syrah (Lodi) $NA. Smells and tastes harsh and hot, with pruny, raisiny aromas and a gritty, earthy flavor. Very dry, with soft tannins and acids. Try with pizza and burgers. **83** —*S.H. (9/1/2003)*

Benson Ferry 2001 Old Vines Zinfandel (Lodi) $13. A firm but supple wine that shows off rich chocolate, coffee, plum, spice, and herb flavors. The tannins frame the flavors effectively, and offer good structure to the blend. Moderate length on the finish. **88** *(11/1/2003)*

BENT CREEK

Bent Creek 2000 Cabernet Sauvignon (Livermore Valley) $20. A very ordinary wine that starts off with wobbly Cabernet aromas that veer into Port and raisins, and then turn too sweet in the mouth. **82** —*S.H. (11/15/2003)*

BENTON-LANE

Benton-Lane 2004 Pinot Gris (Oregon) $15. Fresh, round, and balanced, with simple peach and citrus flavors. Crisp and lean, with lasting notes of peach and nectarine. Wet and easy, made for simple quaffing. **85** *(2/1/2006)*

Benton-Lane 2002 Pinot Noir (Willamette Valley) $21. Quite similar to the winery's "First Class" bottling, this too offers very tart, sour red fruits, and a thin, watery texture. The herbal flavors carry into some forest floor, mushroomy notes. **84** *(11/1/2004)*

Benton-Lane 2000 Pinot Noir (Oregon) $18. The cranberry and cherry nose carries some pickle and tomato notes. The thin palate is much like cherry-flavored tea, while the finish is dry and lean, with fine tannins. This wine is sharp and probably best served at a picnic. **83** *(10/1/2002)*

Benton-Lane 1998 Pinot Noir (Willamette Valley) $17. 82 —*M.S. (12/1/2000)*

Benton-Lane 2002 First Class Pinot Noir (Willamette Valley) $35. High acid, stemmy and tasting of bark and leaf, this is a difficult, tannic wine at this stage. Tart, abrupt, and vegetal. **84** *(11/1/2004)*

Benton-Lane 1999 Reserve Pinot Noir (Oregon) $30. Right out of the bottle this is a smooth, tightly constructed Pinot, layered with beetroot, tomato, sassafras, and leaf scents, tasting spicy and firm. The fruit is dark and laced with coffee, and it seems certain to improve further with 3–5 years of bottle age. **89** —*P.G. (12/31/2001)*

Benton-Lane 1998 Reserve Pinot Noir (Willamette Valley) $30. 84 —*M.S. (12/1/2000)*

Benton-Lane 1999 Sunnymount Cuvée Pinot Noir (Willamette Valley) $65. Good texture and more flesh than the B-L reserve from the same excellent vintage. This is a beautifully crafted and balanced wine that could pass for a good Gevrey-Chambertin. Flavors of beetroot, herb, leaf, cherry and spicy oak; will certainly improve with further cellar time. Just 100 cases were produced. **91 Cellar Selection** —*P.G. (2/1/2004)*

Benton-Lane 1998 Sunnymount Cuvée Pinot Noir (Willamette Valley) $50. 85 —*J.C. (12/1/2000)*

Benton-Lane 1998 Sunnymount Cuvée Pinot Noir (Oregon) $50. In the mode of other '98s this is a forward, fruity, approachable and quite likeable wine. It shows fruity, soft scents and round, forward, fairly simple flavors. Tobacco and leaf highlight a flavorful finish. **88** —*P.G. (12/31/2001)*

BENZIGER

Benziger 2002 Tribute Cabernet Blend (Sonoma Mountain) $65. Benziger pulls out all the stops on this estate, Cabernet-based Bordeaux blend, from their hilly vineyard above Glen Ellen. It's a beautiful effort. The flavors are very close to Napa Cab, namely deliciously sweet cassis, roasted coffee, and cocoa, but there's a tannin and acid structure that in some respects outclasses even Napa's most prestigious châteaus. This is a great red wine. **94 Editors' Choice** —*S.H. (12/1/2005)*

Benziger 2001 Cabernet Sauvignon (Sonoma County) $19. Balance and user-friendliness are what this wine is all about. The blackberry and herb flavors aren't overdone. The tannins are thick and dusty, but negotiable. There's a dab of smoky oak, but just enough to season. The result is a very good dinner wine, from fast food to cookbook special. **89** —*S.H. (6/1/2004)*

Benziger 2000 Cabernet Sauvignon (Sonoma County) $19. Soft and very dry, with completely melted tannins. Flavors are classic Cabernet, showing black currant, cassis, dried herbs, and green olives. **89** —*S.H. (10/1/2003)*

Benziger 1999 Cabernet Sauvignon (Sonoma County) $19. Textbook Sonoma Cab, with good flavors of black currants and cassis, green olive,

USA

and sage. Feels a bit rough due to notable tannins, but a leg of lamb or similar fare will make for a perfect marriage with this dry, balanced wine. **86** —*S.H. (12/15/2003)*

Benziger 1999 Cabernet Sauvignon (Sonoma County) $19. Here's a soft, juicy wine with melted tannins in the modern style and some nice blackberry flavors. It's young now, a saucy wine that hasn't yet fully come together. But all the pieces are there. Drink it at three or four years of age. **90** —*S.H. (7/1/2002)*

Benziger 1997 Blue Rock Vineyards Cabernet Sauvignon (Alexander Valley) $50. Still dark and incredibly aromatic, with classic cassis, sage, and mint scents, framed in well-integrated, toasty oak. Dry, with soft, plush acids and vigorous but intricate tannins, it's approachable now. A fine example of its appellation. **90** —*S.H. (12/31/2001)*

Benziger 1996 Blue Rock Vineyard Cabernet Sauvignon (Sonoma) $30. 91 —*M.S. (7/1/1999)*

Benziger 1998 Estate Cabernet Sauvignon (Sonoma Mountain) $60. A really young wine, almost black in color, and sharply aromatic with cedar, cassis, and minty -clove note. Below woody influences are herbal-fruity aromas, including sage, oregano, and blackberry. Very dry and somewhat tannic, it's well-made and elegant, despite the vintage's shortcomings. **88** —*S.H. (12/31/2001)*

Benziger 1996 Rancho Salinas Vineyard Cabernet Sauvignon (Sonoma) $30. 87 —*J.C. (7/1/1999)*

Benziger 2001 Reserve Cabernet Sauvignon (Sonoma County) $42. This is a big, flamboyant Cab that floods the mouth with ripe, juicy flavors, but it's balanced despite the size. Blackberries, cherries, sweet red plums, cocoa, and spices, with soft, sweet tannins and a long, fruity finish. **89** —*S.H. (3/1/2005)*

Benziger 2000 Reserve Cabernet Sauvignon (Sonoma County) $42. Similar to Benziger's regular '01 release, with a shade more richness and oak. The blackberry and herb flavors are enhanced by smoky vanilla, and the dusty tannins on the finish turn dry and puckery. It's an elegant wine, not an opulent one, and should be good with steak. **90** —*S.H. (6/1/2004)*

Benziger 1998 Reserve Cabernet Sauvignon (Sonoma County) $45. The aromas are very ripe and full, packed with sweet oak, blackberry jam, cassis, smoke, and pepper. Not as concentrated as the enormous 1997, but round and harmonious and dry, with a spicy, long, peacock's tail of a finish. **91** —*S.H. (12/1/2001)*

Benziger 1997 Reserve Cabernet Sauvignon (Sonoma County) $45. 90 *(11/1/2000)*

Benziger 2001 Stone Farm Vineyard Cabernet Sauvignon (Sonoma Valley) $27. Drinks beautifully now for its rich, smooth tannins, dry balance, and complex mélange of black currant, oak, coffee, and spice flavors. Easy to toss back, but has extra layers of complexity and nuance. **91** —*S.H. (3/1/2005)*

Benziger 2003 Chardonnay (Carneros) $16. Plenty of honeyed, caramelly toast on this fruity wine. The flavors are very ripe and pineappley, with lots of spices on the finish. **85** —*S.H. (8/1/2005)*

Benziger 2002 Chardonnay (Carneros) $16. A pretty wine, spicy, and rich, with an array of vibrantly fruity flavors ranging from sweet citrus through apples and peaches to exotic mango. Winemaker bells and whistles such as barrel fermentation and lees add creamy, vanilla, buttered toast notes. **87** —*S.H. (11/15/2004)*

Benziger 2001 Chardonnay (Carneros) $16. A delicious, easy-drinking Chard with plenty of complexity to boot. The apple and pear flavors are accented with toasty oak and a dash of creamy lees. It's a dryish wine, with an harmonious flourish of ripe green apple on the finish. **88** —*S.H. (12/15/2003)*

Benziger 2000 Chardonnay (Carneros) $16. This is a bit drier and crisper than many Chards out there today. It has bracing acidity and even some scouring tannins, and what fruit there is veers toward apples and citrus rather than riper peaches. That makes it a food wine, and a very nice one, too. **86** —*S.H. (5/1/2002)*

Benziger 1999 Chardonnay (Carneros) $16. The vanilla, clove, and smoky aromas of well-charred oak dominate this pretty wine. The peach and apple fruit handles all that oak well, as does the refreshingly crisp acidity.

Ultraclean, round, and vibrant, this dry wine is built to please. **88** —*S.H. (11/15/2001)*

Benziger 2002 Reserve Chardonnay (Carneros) $27. This is an oaky Chard, brimming with vanilla, honey and smoky char, with underlying flavors of peaches and tropical fruits. There's also an earthy edge suggesting sweet dried herbs that suggests careful food pairing. A butter-sauteed filet of sole will be fine. **87** —*S.H. (3/1/2005)*

Benziger 1998 Reserve Chardonnay (Carneros) $25. 85 *(6/1/2000)*

Benziger 2002 Ricci Vineyard Chardonnay (Carneros) $25. Oaky and sweet in honey, mango, papaya, and pear flavors, swirled with vanilla. Fortunately there's a good grip of acidity to balance the sweetness. **86** —*S.H. (3/1/2005)*

Benziger 1998 Sangiacomo Vineyards Chardonnay (Carneros) $25. Beginning to show its age, with the floral, tropical fruit notes just starting to take on more intricate shades of coconut, hazlenut, and crème bruée, with a very telltale fino-Sherry finish. It's dry and a bit eccentric, calling for careful food pairing. **88** —*S.H. (5/1/2002)*

Benziger 2001 Sangiacomo Vineyards Reserve Chardonnay (Carneros) $27. This tremendously opulent wine opens with a mouthburst of well-ripened tropical fruits such as pineapples and mangoes. It is strongly oaked, but the flavors are so powerful, all that vanilla and buttered toast is balanced and harmonious. Feels lush and creamy-smooth all the way through the long, sweetish finish. **92** —*S.H. (12/15/2003)*

Benziger 1998 Yamakawa Vineyards Chardonnay (Carneros) $25. 86 *(6/1/2000)*

Benziger 2003 Fumé Blanc (North Coast) $13. Fruity and a little sweet, with apple and fig flavors and good acidity. Finishes clean and zesty. **84** —*S.H. (3/1/2005)*

Benziger 2002 Fumé Blanc (North Coast) $13. Citrus, melon, and fig flavors are backed up with firm acidity, and the finish is a little sweet. Enjoy this refresher on its own, or with figs and chevre. **84** —*S.H. (2/1/2004)*

Benziger 2001 Merlot (Sonoma County) $19. Benziger keeps the good wines coming. This one straddles the line between ripe cherry and berry fruit flavors and earthier notes of mushrooms and dried herbs. Oak provides the bass. It's dry and tannic, and cries out for fine, rich meats and cheeses. **88** —*S.H. (6/1/2004)*

Benziger 2000 Merlot (Sonoma County) $19. Plum and blackberry flavors, with edges of tobacco, meat, and herb, are wrapped in fairly rugged tannins. This is a young, fresh regional wine and a bit tough, but it could soften and sweeten in a year or two. **85** —*S.H. (12/1/2003)*

Benziger 1999 Merlot (Sonoma County) $19. Fans of ripe, forward fruit will like this wine. Opens with a burst of jammy plum and cassis and then explodes into fruit and berry sensations on the palate, but it's classically dry. Soft tannins and acids support all these luscious flavors. The finish is really long and spicy. **91** —*S.H. (7/1/2002)*

Benziger 1999 Merlot (Sonoma County) $19. Pretty tannic now, with underlying fruity flavors of plum, blackberry, herbs and earth. Drinks very dry and a bit austere, and there's tartness in the dusty finish. May gain with an additional year or two of age. **85** —*S.H. (8/1/2003)*

Benziger 2000 Blue Rock Vineyard Merlot (Alexander Valley) $30. A fat, strong, rich Merlot with potent flavors and lavish oak. When you sniff it, you get equal parts smoky, spicy vanillins from barrels and the underlying black currant of the grape. Drinks dense and refined, with creamy sweet tannins and a lavish mouthfeel. **91** —*S.H. (4/1/2004)*

Benziger 1998 McNab Ranch Merlot (Mendocino County) $35. Clear, pure aromas combine floral, black stone-fruit, and earthy notes, leading to a rich, well-structured wine with good acidity and lush tannins, framed in sumptuous oak. There's pretty blackberry fruit in the finish of this dry, appealing wine. **90** —*S.H. (12/31/2001)*

Benziger 2000 Reserve Merlot (Sonoma County) $42. Lovely and soft in the modern red style, a full-bodied wine that glides like velvet over the palate. The flavors satisfy with plums, blackberries, cocoa, and oak. **90** —*S.H. (8/1/2005)*

Benziger 1998 Reserve Merlot (Sonoma County) $42. Dark and aromatic, it displays clean, fresh plum, blackberry, and cassis aromas, with a rich

streak of earthiness. Drinks dry and nicely layered, with complex but negotiable tannins and a dense core of berry fruit. Lovely. **90** —*S.H. (12/31/2001)*

Benziger 1997 Reserve Merlot (Sonoma County) $41. Dried-herb shadings add an extra touch of complexity to this dense wine that combines rich plum, mocha, and earth elements. A big, bold Merlot that avoids being overblown by virtue of its strong undercurrent of acidity. **91** *(6/1/2001)*

Benziger 2000 McNab Ranch Petite Sirah (Mendocino) $27. You never quite know what you're getting in a "Pet," but in this case the wine rises to the height of what the variety can do. It's very dark, and absolutely dry, with substantial tannins although it's soft in acidity. The flavors are ripe and rich. They range from black cherries through blackberries, coffee, and chocolate, with a sprinkling of white pepper. **90** —*S.H. (11/15/2004)*

Benziger 1999 McNab Ranch Petite Sirah (Mendocino County) $21. A big disappointment. There's some good, ripe fruit, but the tannins are dry and rasping, and the flavors turn thin on the slightly hot finish. Seems more like a decent vin ordinaire than a serious red table wine. **83** *(4/1/2003)*

Benziger 2000 Pinot Gris (Oregon) $20. Strikes a middle-of-the-road pose, combining a nice apple and watermelon fruitiness with a little softness, a little sweetness and enough acidity to make it balanced. It's an easy wine to like and to pair with casual foods. **85** —*S.H. (8/1/2002)*

Benziger 1997 Pinot Noir (California) $15. 87 *(11/15/1999)*

Benziger 2001 Pinot Noir (Sonoma County) $22. Super-spicy, with a burst of pepper, cinnamon, nutmeg, and other Oriental spices that frame red cherry and vanilla flavors. The texture is supple and silky. This is a versatile restaurant wine. **86** —*S.H. (12/15/2004)*

Benziger 2000 Pinot Noir (Sonoma County) $21. A likeable, easy Pinot that straddles the line between simplicity and complexity. Darkly colored, with earthy, berry aromatics; in the mouth it has the soft, silky texture and crisp acids you want in a good Pinot. Flavors are of cherries and spices. Fruit-driven and a good accompaniment to a wide range of food. **86** —*S.H. (7/1/2003)*

Benziger 1999 Pinot Noir (Sonoma County) $21. Plenty of black fruit mingles with some earthy, funky complexity on the full-blown bouquet. Some minty, herbal notes sneak onto the palate at the expense of fruit clarity. The finish is dominated by coffee and smoky char. **85** *(10/1/2002)*

Benziger 1999 Bien Nacido Pinot Noir (Santa Maria Valley) $33. Cola, bramble and hot, dry wood make up the powerful bouquet, with strawberry and herbal green flavors following. Steeped tea and tangy red fruit carries the finish of this balanced Pinot that offers both nice balance and a full mouthfeel. **86** *(10/1/2002)*

Benziger 2001 Bien Nacido Vineyard Pinot Noir (Santa Maria Valley) $33. Likeable for its polished cherry, raspberry, vanilla, mocha, and smoky flavors, crisp, clean acids and bright mouthfeel. This feminine wine offers lots of enjoyment, and is elegant and complex enough for your best dinners. **87** —*S.H. (12/1/2004)*

Benziger 2000 Bien Nacido Vineyard Pinot Noir (Santa Maria Valley) $33. Plenty of flavor, with tastes of black raspberry jam, cherry, tobacco, and pepper. Has a nice texture, satiny and velvety, with good acidity. Straddles the border between simple and complex, but it's certainly tasty with a good, long finish. **87** —*S.H. (7/1/2003)*

Benziger 1999 Reserve Pinot Noir (Sonoma County) $43. Tart-sweet, with an interesting peach-apricot-mango overlay on the deep cherry fruit core. Smoke and vanilla accents and an even, dense texture give this wine the mouthfeel equivalent of a luxury car ride. Tart, dry fruit shines on the long finish. Drinkable now, it's structured enough to develop over the next two years. **88** *(10/1/2002)*

Benziger 1997 Reserve Pinot Noir (California) $40. Dark, dramatic, and showy, with smoke, blackberry, roasted coffee-bean, spice, tomato, and sweet oak aromas. Rich, full-bodied and dry, with great depth of flavor. It has finesse, harmony, and elegance. **90** —*S.H. (12/15/2001)*

Benziger 2000 Reserve Santa Barbara-Sonoma Pinot Noir (California) $42. Decently dry and silky, with earthy cherry flavors, but simple. **83** —*S.H. (8/1/2005)*

Benziger 2001 Tribute Red Blend (Sonoma Mountain) $65. Made from bio-dynamically grown estate grapes, this Cabernet-based wine is as massive as any I've tasted from this great vintage. It's like drinking liquid steel, with deep, ripe flavors of black currants, chocolate, and cherries, and plenty of new oak. Despite the size, the texture is gentle and velvety, but it's an ager if you want. Now through 2015. **94 Cellar Selection** *(4/1/2005)*

Benziger 2005 Sauvignon Blanc (North Coast) $13. The winery's basic Sauvignon is very dry, crisp, and clean, showing long, deep citrus, apricot, and melon flavors. It's a good example of the fine art of blending grapes from disparate regions. **86** —*S.H. (11/15/2006)*

Benziger 2000 Estate Sauvignon Blanc (Sonoma Mountain) $22. White stone fruits, some smoke and toast, and ample spice makes the entrance to this wine really inviting. There's plenty of richness to the mouth, which is jammed with lemon, lime, and a balancing dryness not unlike chalk. The fade is pure and dry, offering long nuances of spicy oak and white pepper. It's a wine that's integrated and satisfying. **90** *(8/1/2002)*

Benziger 2005 Paradiso de Maria Sauvignon Blanc (Sonoma Mountain) $29. Brilliantly sharp, penetrating Sauvignon. Opens with intense aromas of gooseberry, grapefruit juice, lime, apricot, tart green apple, and white pepper, leading to a rich, very dry, high-acid wine of great depth, charm and complexity. From the cool, long vintage of 2005, it is simply great Sauvignon Blanc. **92** —*S.H. (9/1/2006)*

Benziger 2004 Paradiso de Maria Sauvignon Blanc (Sonoma Mountain) $27. This is a very fine Sauvignon Blanc that has great elegance and finesse as well as power. To begin with, it's delicately structured, with a steely minerality and fine acidity, and is fully dry. The flavors are a mélange of lime, alfalfa, honeydew melon, fig, and white pepper. **91 Editors' Choice** —*S.H. (12/1/2005)*

Benziger 2004 Shone Farm Sauvignon Blanc (Russian River Valley) $27. No oak in this wine, but it's amazingly rich anyway. The wine is very dry, with Meyer lemon flavors boosted by a firm minerality and rich acidity. Absolutely defines the unoaked style of Sauvignon Blanc. **94 Editors' Choice** —*S.H. (8/1/2006)*

Benziger 1996 Syrah (Central Coast) $18. 90 —*S.H. (6/1/1999)*

Benziger 2000 Syrah (California) $22. Dark in color, with light but pleasant aromas of blackberries and espresso. Drinks soft and fruity, with easy tannins. **85** —*S.H. (10/1/2003)*

Benziger 2000 Bien Nacido Vineyard Syrah (Santa Maria Valley) $35. Dense and concentrated, a wine of considerable complexity and interest. Has a mélange of aromas including blackberries, anise, mint, and grilled meat. It's a supple, rich wine that oozes blackberry and cassis flavors on the finish. **91** —*S.H. (10/1/2003)*

Benziger 1998 Bien Nacido Vineyard Syrah (Santa Maria Valley) $24. Opens with a burst of blackberry, mint, game, and smoky oak, and turns rich and flavorful in the mouth, with enormous concentration and depth of flavor. Bone dry, the fancy berry flavors float in a silky texture framed by toasty oak. **90** —*S.H. (7/1/2002)*

Benziger 2002 Bien Nacido Vineyards Syrah (Santa Maria Valley) $35. Savory and meaty, with scents of molasses and very ripe fruit that give it an almost Australian Shiraz character. Creamy textured thanks to fully ripe tannins, with flavors of roasted meat, blackberries, and crushed pepper, yet its detractors found it overly tannic and gamy. The result is a middle-of-the-road rating that doesn't tell the full story of this love-it-or-hate-it wine. **85** *(9/1/2005)*

Benziger 1997 Viognier (Sonoma County) $18. 89 —*S.H. (6/1/1999)*

Benziger 2000 Carreras Vineyard Zinfandel (Dry Creek Valley) $35. A very good and interesting Zin that seems a bit pricy for what you get. It's luxuriously fruity, stuffed with berry, cherry, milk chocolate, and vanilla flavors that are wrapped in smooth, melted tannins. Simply delicious on its own, but with the complexity and class to accompany a great steak. **90** —*S.H. (3/1/2004)*

BERAN

Beran 2002 Pinot Noir (Willamette Valley) $30. Some stemmy, vegetal notes start things off roughly, but then the wine opens up with pleasing citrus, rosewater, and watermelon flavors. Very light, elegant, and polished through the finish. **86** *(11/1/2004)*

Beran 1998 Pinot Noir (Willamette Valley) $28. **83** —*M.S. (12/1/2000)*

BERESAN

Beresan 2003 Cabernet Sauvignon (Walla Walla (WA)) $25. This is 93% Cab from Waliser and Yellow Jacket (estate) vineyards; and 7% Pepper Bridge Malbec. Fragrant with scents of berries, red currant and spicy plum, it's a substantial and thickly tannic wine. Initially the Cab sports strong barrel flavors of chocolate and smoke, but just a little breathing time and they unwrap into appealing layers of spice, coffee, and toffee through the finish. Decant this. **92** —*P.G. (4/1/2006)*

Beresan 2002 Cabernet Sauvignon (Walla Walla (WA)) $25. Extremely likeable and accessible, this Cab includes 15% Syrah and 5% Cab Franc. It's loaded with butterscotch and mocha, but the ripe, not over-ripe fruit gives it a clear, clean focus right down the middle. **90** —*P.G. (4/1/2005)*

Beresan 2003 Merlot (Walla Walla (WA)) $25. This is pure varietal, all from the estate vineyard, and already showing the warm, round supple strength of great Washington Merlot. Rich and sweetly ripe with spicy berries, wild red fruits, and sweet chocolate. **91** —*P.G. (4/1/2006)*

Beresan 2002 Merlot (Walla Walla (WA)) $25. Like the winery's Syrah, this young wine shows a lot of spicy new oak at the moment, although the specs say only 30% of the barrels were new. There's a full, flavorful mid-palate of cherry and plum, nicely framed against toast, smoke, and char. Plenty of power and punch for a pure Merlot. **91 Editors' Choice** —*P.G. (4/1/2005)*

Beresan 2003 Stone River Red Red Blend (Walla Walla (WA)) $35. A sophisticated blend of 35% Cabernet Sauvignon, 30% Syrah, 20% Merlot, and 15% Cab Franc; the winery's top wine and very close to the quality of the phenomenal 2002. The secret sauce here is the river rock on which the vines struggle to produce fruit. The results are evident; along with a few spots on Red Mountain, these rock-strewn Walla Walla vineyards have genuine terroir. This is densely layered with tart red fruits, framed in vivid acids and already showing its signature minerality. **94** —*P.G. (4/1/2006)*

Beresan 2002 Stone River Red Wine Red Blend (Walla Walla (WA)) $28. Sophisticated winemaking meets gorgeous fruit in this unusual blend: 30% Cabernet Sauvignon, 30% Syrah, 20% Merlot, and 20% Cab Franc. The Syrah's fresh citrus flavors are perfect in the context of the sappy Merlot and harder Cabs, making a wonderful blend that is immediately accessible with sweet, round fruit; then lingers into a long, textured, lively finish. **95 Editors' Choice** —*P.G. (11/15/2004)*

Beresan 2003 Syrah (Walla Walla (WA)) $25. This is 100% Pepper Bridge fruit, from relatively older vines (13–14 years). It's bursting with berries to which are added fine-grained tannins and a sappy, tangy grip. Give it some breathing time and watch this modest wine flesh out; it seems to add spice and volume with each passing minute. **90** —*P.G. (4/1/2006)*

Beresan 2002 Syrah (Walla Walla (WA)) $30. Beresan owner Tom Waliser manages several Walla Walla vineyards, including Pepper Bridge, from which this fruit was sourced. The wine is showing a lot of fat, toasty new oak at present, but it is a delicious, plump, cherry-flavored fat boy, and needs just a bit more bottle age to knit itself together. **90** —*P.G. (4/1/2005)*

BERGEVIN LANE

Bergevin Lane 2003 Intuition Reserve Bordeaux Blend (Columbia Valley (WA)) $45. A Bordeaux blend with a textured, spicy, exotic nose that mixes its red and black fruits with pepper, ground coffee, cinnamon, and saffron. The spice box opens into a lovely, supple wine that continues to display nicely nuanced notes of mineral, leaf, and leather. **92** —*P.G. (4/1/2006)*

Bergevin Lane 2004 Cabernet Franc (Columbia Valley (WA)) $30. The winery's first-ever Cab Franc includes a generous (19%) hit of Merlot: "It cuts through the vegetative, tannic aspect," explains the winemaker. Perfectly drinkable despite its youth, it is showing some nice aromatics, with the classic green coffee notes. It finishes a bit severe,

austere; the tannins are dry and the fruit is a bit tight. **86** —*P.G. (12/31/2006)*

Bergevin Lane 2003 Cabernet Sauvignon (Columbia Valley (WA)) $25. The Cab is matched against Merlot, Cab Franc, and Petit Verdot in a slightly less intense version of the becoming quite fashionable in Washington State. The best percentage seems to be about 60% Cab to 40% Syrah, roughly the blend here, which contrasts the Cab's firm, tannic, lightly herbal character with the tart blueberry and winery's exceptional Intuition reserve. Similar flavors are here, complex and lingering, just slightly less concentration. **90** —*P.G. (4/1/2006)*

Bergevin Lane 2002 Cabernet Sauvignon (Columbia Valley (WA)) $25. Spicy and tart, with sharp, stiff, tight cranberry/currant-flavored fruit. The wine feels attenuated; it hits a wall and stops, and after 24 hours of breathing time opens only slightly more. **86** —*P.G. (4/1/2005)*

Bergevin Lane 2004 Merlot (Columbia Valley (WA)) $25. This is pure Merlot which, in Washington, does not equate to lifeless, wimpy wine. Au contraire, this reveals supple, lovely flavors of mixed red apples, plums, and cranberry. There are firm acids anchoring it, and I like the snap of the fruit as it hits the back of the palate. It is a very accessible, approachable wine that finishes with a nicely applied layer of milk chocolaty oak. **88** —*P.G. (12/31/2006)*

Bergevin Lane 2002 Merlot (Walla Walla (WA)) $30. This 100% varietal Merlot is strongly aromatic, with lovely and imposing scents of plum and licorice, citrus peel, and herb. Nuanced and lingering, it has a very French sensibility. **91** —*P.G. (4/1/2005)*

Bergevin Lane 2004 Calico Red Red Blend (Columbia Valley (WA)) $18. A mongrel blend of Cabernet, Merlot, Syrah, Zin, and Cab Franc. It's a fun, fruity blend with accents of coffee and toast; nothing serious, but good stuff. **87** —*P.G. (4/1/2006)*

Bergevin Lane 2003 Calico Red Red Blend (Columbia Valley (WA)) $16. A "kitchen sink" blend of Cabernet Sauvignon, Cab Franc, Merlot, Syrah and Zinfandel, it somehow knits itself together and avoids the broad, generic red syndrome of most cheap blends. This has sappy, sweet fruit built upon juicy berries, and that concentrated core carries right through the clean, spicy finish. **90** —*P.G. (6/1/2005)*

Bergevin Lane 2003 Sémillon (Columbia Valley (WA)) $19. This young Walla Walla winery is gaining confidence with each new release. This blend of Sémillon and Viognier (17%) is oaky and warm, with broadly fruity citrus and stone fruits. Lots of spice, vanilla, and a hint of hazelnut. **89** —*P.G. (6/1/2005)*

Bergevin Lane 2003 Syrah (Columbia Valley (WA)) $25. Among a bevy of Columbia Valley bottlings, Bergevin Lane's stood out for its complex nose of black cherry, cracked pepper, dried spices, and herbs and for its smooth, silky mouthfeel. Drink now. **88** *(9/1/2005)*

Bergevin Lane 2002 Syrah (Walla Walla (WA)) $30. Walla Walla Syrah is notable for its broad, meaty flavors, often nuanced with pretty floral and citrus notes. This is a gem, lightly herbal, persistent, and balanced throughout. **88** —*P.G. (4/1/2005)*

Bergevin Lane 2003 Jaden's Reserve Syrah (Columbia Valley (WA)) $55. This extremely limited (47 cases) Syrah is dedicated to the owners' daughter Jaden, who is pictured on the label. Very classy Wahluke Slope fruit sends up citrus, spice, pineapple, and lime aromas over bright, sappy raspberry and cherry fruit. **93** —*P.G. (8/1/2006)*

Bergevin Lane 2004 Viognier (Columbia Valley (WA)) $25. Thick and peachy, with the weight of Roussanne (19%) married to the elegance of the Viognier (81%), this barrel-fermented, oak-aged wine displays intense fruit flavors of apricot, white peach, and citrus. Round and fleshy, it retains sufficient acid to prevent a flabby impression. A nice kiss of vanilla sends it on its way. **90** —*P.G. (12/15/2005)*

Bergevin Lane 2003 Viognier (Columbia Valley (WA)) $25. Fresh, crisp, and flavorful, with a pleasing elegance. The nose mixes citrus blossom and stone, and those elements follow through on the palate. The blend includes 11% Roussanne. Just 188 cases were produced. **89** —*P.G. (9/1/2004)*

Bergevin Lane 2003 375ml Zinfandel (Horse Heaven Hills) $19. Very limited, this dry, un-oaky Zin is showing its age quickly, with flavors of strawberry preserves, bitter chocolate, and a hint of dried herb. Drink up! **87** —*P.G. (12/31/2006)*

BERGSTRÖM

Bergström 2001 Chardonnay (Willamette Valley) $28. Distinguished, with finely etched flavors of peaches and pears and subtle shadings of oak. Acidity is high and the wine has a crisp, steely backbone. Young and tight now, and will improve through 2004. **90** —*S.H. (9/1/2003)*

Bergström 2000 Chardonnay (Willamette Valley) $28. Lean and crisp despite bells and whistles of barrel fermentation and lees aging. Sure, that adds richness and depth, but the wine stays true to its roots with high acidity and the flavor profile of apples, not pineapples. It's a distinguished wine. That's not a technical term, but it gets the point across. **88** —*S.H. (8/1/2002)*

Bergström 2000 Pinot Gris (Willamette Valley) $16. If you're not sure what Pinot Gris/Grigio is like and want a good starter version, try this one. It's sweet like applesauce but dry like lemons, a seemingly impossible feat until you taste it. Plus, it's creamy from barrel fermentation, so it feels lush. **87** —*S.H. (8/1/2002)*

Bergström 2001 Pinot Noir (Willamette Valley) $18. A fascinating Pinot, utterly different from those from California, with a distinct kiss of terroir in the spicy white-pepper aromas that dust underlying black cherry-kirsch flavors. Dry and crisp, with a chunky, meaty mouthfeel. A touch of spritz quickly dies down. **90 Editors' Choice** —*S.H. (12/1/2003)*

Bergström 2000 Pinot Noir (Willamette Valley) $35. Can a wine be light and serious too? This one is both. By light, I mean it's not real concentrated, fruit-wise. It's an earth-driven wine, with tomato and beet flavors, and it's pretty tannic. It's also light in the way it floats on the tongue. It's very silky. But it's a serious wine because it makes you stop and think about it, which is half the fun. It may also be ageable. **91** —*S.H. (12/31/2002)*

Bergström 2000 Arcus Pinot Noir (Willamette Valley) $50. This sweet, extracted, creamy wine oozes lushness, ripeness, and richness. The power is intense, the flavors dark plum, blackberry, and cola. The tannins are big and plush, making for a huge, round finish. But be warned, one reviewer found it overly dry. **95 Editors' Choice** *(10/1/2002)*

Bergström 2001 Arcus Vineyard Pinot Noir (Willamette Valley) $50. From a renowned vineyard, an amazingly rich and complete wine that satisfies on every level. Has the forward flavors of raspberries and cherries that satisfy the palate, yet also possesses layers of subtle complexity in the mingling of acids, tannins, and smoky oak. As delicious as it is in youth, it's an ager through the decade. **93 Cellar Selection** —*S.H. (12/1/2003)*

Bergström 2001 Cumberland Reserve Pinot Noir (Willamette Valley) $30. Takes the regular bottling to new heights, as if everything were on steroids. Massive in the fruity, berry flavors that explode in the mouth, and yet the wine easily maintains dignity and balance. A bit of spritz suggests a secondary fermentation that is not unpleasant. **91** —*S.H. (12/1/2003)*

BERINGER

Beringer 2000 Alluvium Bordeaux Blend (Knights Valley) $30. Sonoma's most inland appellation, where days get hot, is home to this Merlot-based, five-varietal Bordeaux blend. It's ripe in blackberries and plums, with herb and coffee complexities. Completely dry, with soft, smooth tannins, it's a heck of a good food wine. **90** —*S.H. (12/1/2004)*

Beringer 1996 Alluvium Bordeaux Blend (Knights Valley) $30. 87 *(3/1/2000)*

Beringer 2002 Alluvium Red Table Wine Bordeaux Blend (Knights Valley) $30. Over the years my scores for Alluvium have been all over the board. This wine, a Bordeaux blend based on Merlot but with all five classic varieties, is a bit edgy in tannic structure, with a rustic bite. But it's ripe in blackberry, cherry, coffee, and rum flavors, and could easily soften by 2010. **87** —*S.H. (12/15/2006)*

Beringer 2001 Alluvium Red Table Wine Bordeaux Blend (Knights Valley) $30. Tastes a little raw, with still-youthful acids, although there's a softness that frames the cherry and blackberry flavors. But this isn't an ager.

It's a pleasant, clean Cabernet blend that's drinkable now and through 2006. **86** —*S.H. (12/15/2005)*

Beringer 1996 Cabernet Sauvignon (Knights Valley) $25. 87 —*L.W. (12/31/1999)*

Beringer 2002 Cabernet Sauvignon (Knights Valley) $27. The wine is ripe enough in blackberries and cherries with a leathery edge, and a pretty coating of sweet, spicy oak. Yet it feels a bit chunky and rustic. Might improve with a few years cellaring. **86** —*S.H. (12/15/2006)*

Beringer 2001 Cabernet Sauvignon (Napa Valley) $35. Shows off the best of Napa Cab with aromas of cassis and toasty oak. Turns rich and dry in the mouth, classically structured, with firm tannins and a finish of pure black currants and sweet oak. **90** —*S.H. (3/1/2005)*

Beringer 2000 Cabernet Sauvignon (Knights Valley) $26. This is a light, delicate Cab, with flavors of black currants and herbs. It is soft in acids, with a dusting of firm tannins that shows up on the finish. **85** —*S.H. (11/15/2003)*

Beringer 1999 Cabernet Sauvignon (Knights Valley) $26. Polished, with lots of flair, this well-crafted wine shows good varietal character. Cassis, olive, and herb flavors are joined by smoky oak and dry, fine tannins, with lively acids. Try cellaring for a year or two. **87** —*S.H. (2/1/2003)*

Beringer 1998 Cabernet Sauvignon (Knights Valley) $25. A very nice wine, with good, ripe black currant fruit; dry and balanced with aromas and flavors of sweet, smoky oak. The flash is on the surface and it's a little sharp, so it's not an ager. But it's a tasty wine. **87** —*S.H. (7/1/2002)*

Beringer 1999 Appellation Collection Reserve Cabernet Sauvignon (Knights Valley) $50. Overly soft and simple. The black currant and cassis flavors are pretty enough, but the wine lacks zest and life on the palate. This is a structural issue. Firmer acids and tannins would go a long way to help. **84** —*S.H. (12/15/2003)*

Beringer 2001 Bancroft Ranch Cabernet Sauvignon (Howell Mountain) $90. Like all of Beringer's 2001 gold letter single-vineyard Cabs, this one is a cellar laydown. It's hard in tannins now, a dry wine that leaves the palate rasping because it's so astringent. Yet the fruit is gigantically ripe, flooding the mouth with blackberries and cherries that are the essence of those fruits. With all that ripeness, the acidity is crisp and fine. Drink 2008–2020. **93 Cellar Selection** —*S.H. (9/1/2006)*

Beringer 1998 Bancroft Ranch Cabernet Sauvignon (Howell Mountain) $80. Extraordinarily tough, tannic, and dense, a wine that simply cannot be consumed without proper aging. The tannins are outsized by present day standards, and finish dry and rasping. Yet the wine is saved by an underlying integrity. It's a gamble for the long haul. **89** —*S.H. (11/15/2003)*

Beringer 2001 Chabot Vineyard Cabernet Sauvignon (St. Helena) $90. I have always found Beringer's limited-production, single-vineyard Cabs to be exceedingly tannic wines, and this one still is, even though it's more than four years old. Granted, there's tremendous blackberry and cherry fruit, and the wine is balanced, so it should be an ager. But unless you can deal with tannins, it will be a long time. Hold until 2008 and try again. **89** —*S.H. (8/1/2006)*

Beringer 1998 Chabot Vineyard Cabernet Sauvignon (St. Helena) $80. An extremely tannic and tough wine that numbs the palate despite polished plum, blackberry, and dry chocolate flavors. Oak adds vanilla, smoke and a richly creamy texture. Will it age? The compact berry-cherry flavors suggest yes. Try again in 10 years. **91** —*S.H. (11/15/2003)*

Beringer 2003 Founders' Estate Cabernet Sauvignon (California) $11. Owning vast vineyard acreage has paid off with this polished, supple, soft Cab. It's really nice, especially at this price. Shows real poise in the lush, smooth texture and ripe blackberry and cherry flavors that finish with a swirl of toasty oak. **86 Best Buy** —*S.H. (4/1/2006)*

Beringer 2001 Founders' Estate Cabernet Sauvignon (California) $12. Another good drink from this line, this Cab displays ripe, juicy flavors of black currants and cherries that are accented with smoky vanilla and toast. It's smooth and supple in the mouth. A good value in this price range. **86** —*S.H. (10/1/2004)*

Beringer 2000 Founders' Estate Cabernet Sauvignon (California) $12. A good wine, dry and full-bodied, made in the Beringer style, namely, instantly drinkable and likeable. Has pleasant blackberry and cassis flavors. Pulled down a notch by some rough, tart notes and a hot, peppery finish. **85** —*S.H. (3/1/2003)*

Beringer 1999 Founders' Estate Cabernet Sauvignon (California) $12. Riper blackberry flavors are side by side with less ripe, greener notes in this dry, good wine of average character. It has pretty tannins, soft acidity, and velvety mouthfeel of a great wine, minus the concentration. The difference is vine yield, but this is a good wine for the price. **84** —*S.H. (12/31/2001)*

Beringer 1997 Founders' Estate Cabernet Sauvignon (California) $11. **87** *(11/15/1999)*

Beringer 2001 Marston Vineyard Cabernet Sauvignon (Spring Mountain) $90. Enormously tannic and effectively shut down now, this nonetheless is a big, potent, dry wine that's explosive in ripe, plush Cabernet fruit flavor, and generously oaked. The finish is so sweet, so delicious. The idea clearly is an ageable mountain Cab and Beringer seems to have succeeded. Hold until 2008, at the earliest. **92 Cellar Selection** —*S.H. (9/1/2006)*

Beringer 1998 Marston Vineyard Cabernet Sauvignon (Spring Mountain) $80. One of seven limited-production, single-vineyard Cabs this vintage by Beringer, a dense, concentrated mountain wine of considerable strength. The cassis, plum, and herb flavors are just beginning to emerge from a tannic sleep, although the wine remains young and quite ageworthy. **91** —*S.H. (11/15/2003)*

Beringer 2002 Private Reserve Cabernet Sauvignon (Napa Valley) $116. Huge wine, young and tannic, almost bitter now and not offering much relief. But of course you don't buy Beringer PR tonight. There is indeed enormous Cabernet flavor deep down inside, offering oodles of blackberries and cherries and charry new oak, but there's also a warning note of prune. Best after 2008. **90** —*S.H. (9/1/2006)*

Beringer 2000 Private Reserve Cabernet Sauvignon (Napa Valley) $100. Not the greatest Beringer PR of late, this wine showcases the weakness of the vintage. It's earthy and tannic, with only a suggestion of cherries and blackberries. It's a wine to drink now and over the next few years. **86** —*S.H. (5/1/2005)*

Beringer 1999 Private Reserve Cabernet Sauvignon (Napa Valley) $75. **91** *(8/1/2003)*

Beringer 1997 Private Reserve Cabernet Sauvignon (Napa Valley) $100. Creamy blackberry, cassis, toasty oak, and vanilla aromas lead off. This elegant wine is loaded with additional flavors redolent of licorice, tobacco, spice, and dense berries. It's all couched in supple, velvety tannins. Long and lush at the end. **93** —*S.H. (12/31/2001)*

Beringer 1996 Private Reserve Cabernet Sauvignon (Napa Valley) $100. This wine is still young and precocious, but don't judge it too quickly. Let it air in your glass, and watch how it changes. One minute it's all cherries and smoke; the next it heaves up a great draught of currants, cocoa, and cedar. It's a big wine but deceptive; the tannins are airy and lilting, there's charm and underneath, enormous complexity. It's best left alone for a few more years, but it's really very lovely now. **95** —*S.H. (2/1/2001)*

Beringer 1995 Private Reserve Cabernet Sauvignon (Napa Valley) $75. **95** —*S.H. (7/1/2000)*

Beringer 2001 Quarry Vineyard Cabernet Sauvignon (Rutherford) $90. No one else in Rutherford is making Cabs this tannic, and while the wine isn't really representative of its appellation, it's a dramatic, young cellar candidate. The fruity heart is ripe in blackberry, black cherry, and unsweetened dark chocolate, with a compellingly long finish. Like its sister Cabs, it should begin to be drinkable by 2008, and hold for many years after. **92 Cellar Selection** —*S.H. (9/1/2006)*

Beringer 1998 Quarry Vineyard Cabernet Sauvignon (Rutherford) $80. Pretty tannic, a wine that makes the tongue stick to the palate, although it will soften and sweeten up with big, rich roasts. Underlying flavors are of blackberries, currants, and tobacco, and the finish is very dry. Seems to have the density and concentration to cellar for the long haul. **91** —*S.H. (11/15/2003)*

Beringer 2001 Rancho del Oso Vineyard Cabernet Sauvignon (Howell Mountain) $90. Another tight, tough single-vineyard Cab from Beringer, one likely to age well. The balance is fine, the fruit is ripe and properly varietal, and the wine has a distinguished feeling in the mouth. It's just that those tannins are so hard. Better after 2007, and should drink well for at least another 10 years after that. **92 Cellar Selection** —*S.H. (9/1/2006)*

Beringer 2001 St. Helena Home Vineyard Cabernet Sauvignon (St. Helena) $90. Dry, rich, and enormously tannic, this Cabernet, grown right around the famous winery in the capital town of Napa Valley, has been crafted for longterm aging. It's ripe in black currant, cherry, and mocha flavors, but those tannins are really tough and astringent. Hold until at least 2008. **92 Cellar Selection** —*S.H. (9/1/2006)*

Beringer 1998 St. Helena Home Vineyard Cabernet Sauvignon (St. Helena) $80. Almost indistinguishable from Beringer's Chabot bottling, perhaps a bit more aromatic and softer in tannins. Flavors range from cassis and black cherry through dark chocolate and dill. Drinkable now with rich foods, but will gain in sweetness and complexity with a few years of cellaring. **92** —*S.H. (11/15/2003)*

Beringer 1998 State Lane Cabernet Sauvignon (Napa Valley) $80. Pretty tannic, and extremely well-oaked. Char, vanilla, and smoke dominate the opening aroma, only gradually revealing underlying cassis flavors. In the mouth, the wine is tannic and young, but the solid core of cherry-berry suggests aging until 2008. **91** —*S.H. (11/15/2003)*

Beringer 2001 Steinhauer Ranch Cabernet Sauvignon (Howell Mountain) $90. These single-vineyard Beringer Cabs continue to be among the most tannic in California. They are largely undrinkable even at four-plus years, but this has got to be by design. The fruit here is enormous, gargantuan, and the balance is impeccable. There's no reason the wine shouldn't blossom by 2008, and hold for another 10 years. **92 Cellar Selection** —*S.H. (9/1/2006)*

Beringer 1998 Tre Colline Cabernet Sauvignon (Howell Mountain) $80. Quite as tannic as Beringer's other limited-release single-vineyard Cabs, although a streak of buttery softness makes it drinkable now. Richly marbled with cassis, dark chocolate, and cherry flavors, and very dry. Seems to have the depth and structure for the long haul. Try after 2006. **91** —*S.H. (11/15/2003)*

Beringer 1999 Alluvium Cabernet Sauvignon-Merlot (Knights Valley) $30. This is a true Bordeaux blend, with all five classic varieties. It opens with a blast of smoky oak and black currants, with an underlying herbal note of roasted bell pepper. Fruity, but big in tannins and acids. This young, aggressive wine might rehabilitate itself in your cellar. **87** —*S.H. (3/1/2004)*

Beringer 1998 Chardonnay (Napa Valley) $16. **86** *(6/1/2000)*

Beringer 2004 Chardonnay (Napa Valley) $16. Made in a superripe style, this Chard is jammy in apricot preserves, peaches and cream, and pineapple juice flavors, brightened with a nice cut of acidity. It's nice and dry with a brisk, spicy finish. **84** —*S.H. (8/1/2006)*

Beringer 2003 Chardonnay (Napa Valley) $16. This is an earthy, dry wine, with a little bit of oak. It shows modest fruit flavors that finish quick. Fulfills Chard's basic obligations without going much further. **84** —*S.H. (10/1/2005)*

Beringer 2002 Chardonnay (Napa Valley) $16. Bright in acidity, with nice apple, peach, and sweet oak flavors. Finishes with butter, spice, and vanilla. **86** —*S.H. (3/1/2005)*

Beringer 2001 Chardonnay (Napa Valley) $16. A junior version of the Private Reserve with many of the same qualities of opulently ripe tropical fruit, lavish oak and toast, and a rich, creamy texture. Of course, it's not as massive as the PR, but is nonetheless a good wine. Loses one point due to astringency on the finish. **86** —*S.H. (12/15/2003)*

Beringer 2000 Appellation Collection Chardonnay (Napa Valley) $16. Does Ed Sbragia know how to make good Chard, or what? This wine is as opulent as they come. It just oozes over the palate with gooey tropical-fruit flavors, wrapped in a creamy-custardy texture. Lavish oak adds vanilla, toast, and a rich, caramelized sweetness. The finish sprinkles oriental spices all down the hatch. **92** —*S.H. (12/15/2002)*

Beringer 2005 Founders' Estate Chardonnay (California) $11. Your basic inexpensive California Chard: fruity, creamy, and light, with pleasant peach, pineapple, and apricot flavors finished with a touch of spicy oak. 83 —*S.H. (12/31/2006)*

Beringer 2002 Founders' Estate Chardonnay (California) $12. Nice and fruity, with plenty of ripe flavors and pleasantly oaky shadings. Peaches, pineapples, and cream, buttered toast, cinnamonny spices, and vanilla mingle together, leading to a sweet, honeyed finish. 87 —*S.H. (8/1/2004)*

Beringer 2001 Founders' Estate Chardonnay (California) $12. Another fine varietal wine from this dependable brand. Lots of ripe, lush flavors of peaches and tropical fruit, a kiss of smoky oak, and a buttercream texture make for easy drinking at an affordable price. 85 —*S.H. (6/1/2003)*

Beringer 2000 Founders' Estate Chardonnay (California) $12. User-friendly Chard, all toasty-spicy apples, and peaches and cream. There's almond-skin bitterness in the aftertaste that sort of sets your teeth on edge, but food will take care of that. 85 —*S.H. (9/1/2002)*

Beringer 2004 Private Reserve Chardonnay (Napa Valley) $35. Drinks tighter and steelier than PR Chards of the past, and there's a lot of acidity, and even a dusting of tannins in this big, young wine. Bone dry, the minerality is enriched with white peach, honeydew, and oak flavors. Few California Chardonnays benefit from aging, but this one will. Best from 2007 through 2009. 90 —*S.H. (8/1/2006)*

Beringer 2002 Private Reserve Chardonnay (Napa Valley) $35. Another great PR from Beringer. Stays the course with lushly ripe fruit and lavish oak. Big and bold, but elegant and balanced, with mouthwatering acidity and a sense of harmony. 91 —*S.H. (12/15/2004)*

Beringer 2001 Private Reserve Chardonnay (Napa Valley) $35. Rich and concentrated, packed with flavors ranging from Golden Delicious apples through peaches, pears, and ripe mangoes. The generous dose of oak provides a blast of vanilla and sweet tannins that are balanced with the fruit. This young wine also has acidic verve that will carry it through five years or more of aging. 93 **Editors' Choice** —*S.H. (2/1/2004)*

Beringer 2000 Private Reserve Chardonnay (Napa Valley) $35. A complex Chard, brimming with bright, pure flavors of ripe green apples, spicy Bosc pears, and more exotic notes of mango. Oak brings vanilla, spice, and a rich, creamy texture. Despite its size, this delicious wine is balanced and harmonious. 91 —*S.H. (5/1/2003)*

Beringer 1999 Private Reserve Chardonnay (Napa Valley) $35. Big and oaky, as Private Reserves always are, the '99 is a textbook toasty Chardonnay. Apple, peach, and plum aromas and flavors are wrapped in a smooth, smoky cocoon. The rich and supple palate feel is a winner, the long finish still tight. Enjoyable already, but should be held for a few years. 90 *(7/1/2001)*

Beringer 1998 Private Reserve Chardonnay (Napa Valley) $36. 89 *(10/1/2000)*

Beringer 2000 Sbragia-Limited Release Chardonnay (Napa Valley) $40. An interesting juxtaposition of tangy citrus, steely mineral, melon, grapefruit, fig, herb, and toast flavors, all couched in a refreshing yet lushly textured wine. Clean and bright on the finish, which is quite long. 92 —*J.M. (12/15/2002)*

Beringer 2001 Sbragia Limited Release Chardonnay (Napa Valley) $40. If size is your thing, here's a Godzilla of a Chard, as you'd expect from Ed Sbragia. The deep gold color suggests the oak level, which is massive in vanilla and buttered toast. But the flamboyant tropical fruit easily handles it. Oily, rich, and unctuous through the spicy finish. 92 —*S.H. (12/1/2003)*

Beringer 1997 Sbragia Limited Release Chardonnay (Napa Valley) $40. 94 —*M.M. (11/15/1999)*

Beringer 1999 Sbragia-Limited Release Chardonnay (Napa Valley) $40. The third vintage of the Beringer senior winemaker's namesake bottling is robust, yet approachable. This wine is lavishly—to some, overly oaked, but it's one of the best of this style. Apple, cinnamon bun, and smoke aromas give way to caramel, vanilla, and spice flavors. Add a rich, round mouthfeel, and you've got a very seductive package. This wine is more about vigorous style, flavor, and texture than subtlety. Only die-hard anti-oaksters will be able to resist its appeal. 91 *(7/1/2001)*

Beringer 2003 Chenin Blanc (California) $6. A broadly fruity, soft wine with peach and apple flavors that are just a little off-dry. Will work just fine for a day at the beach. 83 —*S.H. (10/1/2004)*

Beringer 2002 Chenin Blanc (California) $6. Pale in color, delicate in scent, with wax bean and peach aromas. Drinks soft, semi-sweet and fruity, with a clean finish. 83 —*S.H. (12/15/2003)*

Beringer 2003 Gewürztraminer (California) $8. Smells nice and flowery-spicy, but turns disappointingly watery in the mouth. It's okay for the price, though, with some peach and candied ginger flavors. 83 —*S.H. (10/1/2004)*

Beringer 2002 Gewürztraminer (California) $6. What a pretty smell, like a freshly baked carrot cake drizzled with a sweet vanilla sauce and a sprinkle of cinnamon. The flavors are similar in this light, delicate, and off-dry wine. 84 —*S.H. (12/31/2003)*

Beringer 2003 Johannisberg Riesling (California) $8. A simple, slightly sweet wine, with some flavors of wildflowers and peaches. 83 —*S.H. (10/1/2004)*

Beringer 2002 Johannisberg Riesling (California) $6. Delicate, fragrant and charming, a light-bodied, crisp wine with fruity flavors of peaches, apricots, apples, pears, and nectarines. Off-dry, with a rich, honeyed finish. Great value in an afternoon sipper. 85 **Best Buy** —*S.H. (12/31/2003)*

Beringer 1998 Special Late Harvest Johannisberg Riesling (California) $20. At nearly six years of age, this sweetie has picked up an old gold color, and has developed true bottle bouquet: ripe apricot nectar, pear liqueur, caramel, coffee, and honey, gingersnap, vanilla custard, among other aromas and flavors. Enormously sweet, and the alcohol is only 8 percent. High acidity creates a whistle-clean finish. 94 —*S.H. (9/1/2004)*

Beringer 2001 Merlot (Napa Valley) $19. It's surprising to see a four-year-old wine released at such an inexpensive price. Maybe Beringer was hoping it would come around. Instead, it's just tired. Already losing fruit, it's dry and brittle. 83 —*S.H. (11/15/2005)*

Beringer 2000 Appellation Collection Merlot (Napa Valley) $19. Tries its hardest to be lush and balanced but can't overcome its lean, herbal core. Has the oak, firm tannins and fresh young acids you want in a young, full-bodied red wine, but the tease of cherry-berry fruit disappears instantly, replaced by a rigid dryness. 85 —*S.H. (2/1/2004)*

Beringer 1997 Bancroft Ranch Merlot (Howell Mountain) $75. Smoke and vanilla highlight pure berry aromas that seem more red-berryish than previous vintages, with some herbal notes as well. Creamy-textured, it fills the mouth with berry and cocoa flavors and finishes with firm mountain tannins. 89 *(6/1/2001)*

Beringer 1996 Bancroft Ranch Merlot (Howell Mountain) $75. 92 *(3/1/2000)*

Beringer 2003 Founders' Estate Merlot (California) $11. Fine for this price, a fruity, somewhat tannic wine that's dry and balanced and pretty rich. A little bit of Petite Syrah and Zinfandel add darker plum, roasted coffee, and chocolate layers to Merlot's cherries and blackberries. Smooth enough to drink with fine meats and cheeses. 85 —*S.H. (12/31/2006)*

Beringer 2002 Founders' Estate Merlot (California) $11. This wine has earth, blackberry, herb, and spice flavors that finish dry, with a cleansing, slightly bitter scour of acidity like the aftertaste on espresso. 83 —*S.H. (11/15/2005)*

Beringer 2001 Founders' Estate Merlot (California) $12. Lots of plump, sweet plum, blackberry, and cherry flavors mark this nice, easy wine. It's medium-bodied and dry, with a bit of smoky oak, and feels smooth through the finish. 85 —*S.H. (9/1/2004)*

Beringer 2000 Founders' Estate Merlot (California) $12. Has a lush perfume of plummy berry, oak, mushroom, and coffee. It's not a magnificent blockbuster. Still, it's a great inexpensive wine, filled with flavor, harmony and balance. 87 **Best Buy** —*S.H. (10/1/2003)*

Beringer 1999 Founders' Estate Merlot (California) $12. Nice for the price. There's some juicy fruit along with greener, thinner notes, but it's well-structured, with the velvety tannins of far more expensive wines. Dry, but a bit soft. A good everyday wine. 85 **Best Buy** —*S.H. (12/31/2001)*

USA

Beringer 2000 Private Reserve Howell Mountain Merlot (Napa Valley) $50. Hits with harsh, stinging tannins and a tantalizing hint of cherries, and quickly numbs the palate. Hard to tell where it's going. **86** —*S.H. (5/1/2005)*

Beringer 1998 Hayne Vineyard Petite Sirah (St. Helena) $35. A major disappointment from this fine producer and famous vineyard. Aims for Cabernet-style wine, with ripely extracted blackberry flavors, but struck tasters as too big and clumsy for balance. The oak is also overpowering, with huge charry wood tannins. **82** *(4/1/2003)*

Beringer 2003 Pinot Grigio (California) $7. Bone dry and very tart in acids and grapefruit flavors. This clean wine gets the job done when you need a serviceable white. **83** —*S.H. (10/1/2004)*

Beringer 2005 Founders' Estate Pinot Grigio (California) $11. This is the kind of PG Americans will buy in droves. It's soft, slightly sweet, and enormously fruity, flooding the mouth with pineapples, peaches, honeydew melons, honeysuckle flowers, green apples, and just about every other fruit in the store. **84** —*S.H. (12/31/2006)*

Beringer 2004 Founders' Estate Pinot Grigio (California) $11. Popping the cork on this wine is like walking into a fruit-packing plant. It's all about grapefruits, peaches, apples, and mangoes, with a few wildflowers thrown in for good measure. Dry, with excellent acidity. **86 Best Buy** —*S.H. (11/15/2005)*

Beringer 2004 Premier Vineyard Selection Pinot Grigio (California) $6. There's plenty of richness in this wine. It's filled with apricots, figs, melons, and nectarines, and is dry, with palate-stimulating acids. **84 Best Buy** —*S.H. (2/1/2006)*

Beringer 2003 Stone Cellars Pinot Grigio (California) $8. Easy drinking, with apple, fig, and citrus flavors. Crisp acids and a dry finish make it clean and vibrant. **84** —*S.H. (2/1/2006)*

Beringer 2004 Pinot Noir (Napa Valley) $16. Pleasant and uncomplicated, this is an easy Pinot to understand. Plays it straight down the middle, a gently silky wine with cola, cherry, vanilla, cocoa, and spice flavors. **84** —*S.H. (11/15/2005)*

Beringer 2003 Pinot Noir (Napa Valley) $16. A bit rugged and hot in the mouth. Offers a good array of plummy cherry flavor, with bright, zingy acidity and a touch of smoky oak. **84** —*S.H. (6/1/2005)*

Beringer 2002 Pinot Noir (Carneros) $16. Textbook example of a charming, young, cool-climate Pinot that's fresh and flavorful. Packs the cherry, white pepper, sweet tobacco, vanilla, and smoky tastes into soft, creamy tannins backed by a burst of clean acidity. **87** *(11/1/2004)*

Beringer 2000 Pinot Noir (Carneros) $16. Light and brisk, this opens with angular cedar, beef gravy, sandalwood, and burnt leaf aromas. Flavors of tomatoes and sour plums, follow, marked by a taut high-acid feel. Lean and lemony, the finish offers toasty oak and bitter chocolate. **84** *(10/1/2002)*

Beringer 1999 Pinot Noir (North Coast) $16. There's an accessible sweetness to this medium-weight wine's cherry, plum, and spice elements. On the tongue, it displays a slick, almost cough-drop feel. Finishes with some mild tannins, tangy acids, and cherry and pepper notes; some tasters found an odd aftertaste. **83** *(10/1/2002)*

Beringer 2005 Founders' Estate Pinot Noir (California) $12. You know how a Beaujolais Nouveau hits you with a blast of young acid and freshly picked fruit? That's this Pinot Noir. It's a simple, savory, easy wine, with cherries, strawberries, pomegranates, and rhubarbs that seem like they were picked five minutes ago. **85** —*S.H. (12/31/2006)*

Beringer 2002 Founders' Estate Pinot Noir (California) $12. While it's a light wine, this pretty Pinot has plenty of varietal appeal. It's silky and crisp, with pleasant cherry and raspberry flavors finished with vanilla and smoke. A good value in Pinot Noir. **85** —*S.H. (11/1/2004)*

Beringer 2001 Founders' Estate Pinot Noir (California) $12. Quite good for an inexpensive Pinot, especially one from a statewide appellation. Has pleasant berry-cherry, herb, and tobacco flavors wrapped in soft, silky tannins, but enough acidity to cleanse the palate. Pinot 101. **86 Best Buy** —*S.H. (12/1/2003)*

Beringer 2000 Founders' Estate Pinot Noir (California) $12. Lots of wood covers the dark cherry fruit of this full wine. With earth, leather, and

chocolate as well as an appealing woodsy character, it's tasty and straightforward, even if it's not tremendously Pinot-like. **84 Best Buy** *(10/1/2002)*

Beringer 2002 Stanly Ranch Pinot Noir (Carneros) $30. Dramatically delicious, a complex wine of great depth and interest. It takes the minty, tutti-fruity flavors of simpler Carneros Pinots and elevates them, adding swirls of cherry liqueur, kid leather, veal and, on the finish, intense cassis. Maintains essential silkiness, dryness, delicacy, and crispness. **92 Editors' Choice** —*S.H. (11/1/2004)*

Beringer 2000 Stanly Ranch Pinot Noir (Carneros) $30. Lots to like in this impressively lush Pinot Noir. The garnet color leads to aromas of raspberries, plums, smoke, and vanilla. Turns rich and delicious in the mouth, with berry and herb flavors wrapped in silky tannins and a finish of Oriental spices. Goes beyond a simple fruity wine to achieve real depth and interest. **91** —*S.H. (12/1/2003)*

Beringer 1999 Stanly Ranch Pinot Noir (Napa Valley) $30. A delicious, balanced Pinot. Will it last forever? Probably not, given that it's so rich and velvety, with modest tannins. But for now it impresses with its mocha and cedar aromas, toasty plum and black currant flavors, and easygoing, coffee-laden finish. **92 Editors' Choice** *(10/1/2002)*

Beringer 1999 Port of Cabernet Sauvignon Port (Napa Valley) $20. A good vintage Port-style dessert wine that's best consumed now. It has black currant and chocolate flavors and sturdy tannins, and is semi-sweet. Finishes a bit swift. Nice with anything chocolate. **86** —*S.H. (7/1/2005)*

Beringer 1998 Alluvium Red Blend (Knights Valley) $30. This is a good wine that just misses the big leagues. It makes all the right moves, with posh, cherry-infused Merlot flavors nicely balanced by Cabernet's stronger, more structured blackberry profile. The tannins are fine, and there's some fancy oak framing them. But bitterness in the finish and a midpalate thinness bring it down a notch. **88** —*J.M. (11/15/2002)*

Beringer 2001 Nouveau Red Blend (California) $8. This first wine of the vintage, a blend of Pinot Noir, Grenache, and Valdigue, is largely the result of carbonic maceration, a winemaking technique that creates the freshest, sharpest, zingiest aromas and flavors imaginable. It's vibrant and juicy, like Beaujolais. The gorgeous ripeness of the fruit bodes well for the 2001 vintage. Great value. **86** —*S.H. (9/1/2002)*

Beringer 2002 Riesling (Napa Valley) $16. Aromatic and pretty, a light, delicate wine that offers up plenty of flavor. White peach, honeysuckle, smoky vanilla, gingerbread, flowers, and spices mingle in complex waves. Dry, but finishes with honeyed richness **87** —*S.H. (9/1/2004)*

Beringer 1997 Johannisberg Riesling (Napa Valley) $8. 85 —*M.S. (6/1/1999)*

Beringer 1998 Rose de Saignee Rosé Blend (California) $16. 86 —*J.C. (8/1/2000)*

Beringer 1998 Sauvignon Blanc (Napa Valley) $12. 87 —*S.H. (5/1/2000)*

Beringer 2004 Sauvignon Blanc (Napa Valley) $12. Made in a bone dry style with green pepper, feline spray, and gooseberry flavors, this will appeal to those who like this type. It has a soft, creamy texture. **83** —*S.H. (11/15/2005)*

Beringer 2003 Sauvignon Blanc (Napa Valley) $12. Grassy and citrusy but enriched with sweet oak, this polished wine will be very good as a cocktail, or with a wide variety of food. It's clean and tart with acids. **85** —*S.H. (12/15/2004)*

Beringer 2002 Sauvignon Blanc (Napa Valley) $12. Smells and tastes a little sweet, with the aroma of wild honey mingled with citrus fruits and peaches. Similar flavors, with that same citrusy edge and finish of spicy, peppery honey. **85** —*S.H. (12/31/2003)*

Beringer 2004 Founders' Estate Sauvignon Blanc (California) $11. Appeals right up the middle with its range of grassy, citrusy flavors that are dry and tart, and softer peaches and cream notes. The peppery, spicy midpalate and finish make this wine especially food-friendly. **85** —*S.H. (11/15/2005)*

Beringer 2002 Founders' Estate Sauvignon Blanc (California) $11. Beringer's FE line does a good job of producing clean, varietally correct wines at fair prices. This white wine is sprightly and ripe with juicy citrus, fig, melon, and vanilla flavors. It's a bit sweet, but has good acidity for balance. **85** —*S.H. (8/1/2004)*

Beringer 2001 Founders' Estate Sauvignon Blanc (California) $11. Just what the doctor ordered in an affordable, fruity white wine. Opens with pleasant flavors of peaches and citrus fruits, and is just a little bit sweet, with a rich, honeyed finish. **86** —*S.H. (3/1/2003)*

Beringer 2000 Founders' Estate Sauvignon Blanc (California) $11. Just what you want in a clean, pleasant, everyday wine that won't break the bank. It's citrusy and fruity, with a nice cut of green-grass aromas and flavors. Drinks dry and clean. **84** —*S.H. (12/15/2001)*

Beringer 2003 Alluvium Blanc Sauvignon Blanc-Sémillon (Knights Valley) $16. Seems a bit overwrought, with too much oak framing too little fruit. But it's a pleasant, dry wine, with citrus and buttercream flavors and enough acidity for balance. **85** —*S.H. (11/15/2005)*

Beringer 2001 Alluvium Blanc Sémillon-Sauvignon Blanc (Knights Valley) $16. A Sauvignon Blanc and Sémillon blend with crisp acidity, a smooth, clean finish and citrus and fig flavors. **84** —*S.H. (7/1/2003)*

Beringer 2001 Nightingale Sémillon-Sauvignon Blanc (Napa Valley) $30. Very good as usual for this pioneering botrytized wine. It has lush and jammy apricot and vanilla flavors wrapped in a gooey texture. It's so sweet and tasty, you almost find yourself wishing it were a little more concentrated, in which case it would be a knockout. **89** —*S.H. (4/1/2004)*

Beringer 2000 Nightingale Sémillon-Sauvignon Blanc (Napa Valley) $35. This heavily botrytised Sémillon–Sauvignon Blanc blend has the smoky vanillins and apricots that you expect in such a wine. It's not as concentrated as in previous vintages, however, and there's a hollow place in the middle. **86** —*S.H. (12/1/2003)*

Beringer 1998 Nightingale Sémillon-Sauvignon Blanc (Napa Valley) $30. Made since the 1970s, and always at the top rung of California dessert wines. The cool vintage actually aided the wine, since it prodded the development of botrytis. Elaborate and unctuous, the apricot and peach flavors are very sweet, but crisp acidity provides balance. The texture is pure velvet, right through the long, sweet finish. **94 Cellar Selection** —*S.H. (12/1/2002)*

Beringer 2002 Nightingale Private Reserve Sémillon-Sauvignon Blanc (Napa Valley) $30. Quite sweet and forward in apricot nectar and crème brûlée flavors, this dessert wine is an immediate palate pleaser. It has nice citrusy acidity for clean balance. One sip leads to another, but beware. It's fairly hefty in alcohol. **90** —*S.H. (5/1/2006)*

Beringer 2003 Founders' Estate Shiraz (California) $11. An easy-drinking, pleasing Shiraz. Very ripe plum, cinnamon, and vanilla aromas are echoed on the palate, where the wine also shows hints of chocolate. Medium-bodied; falls flat on the finish. **85** *(9/1/2005)*

Beringer 1999 Founders' Estate Shiraz (California) $11. Blackberry, cinnamon, and sweet cream aromas give Beringer's bouquet a fresh-out-of-the-oven pie smell. This soft, supple Shiraz has juicy berry fruit, black chocolate, and vanilla flavors and a clean, tart berry fruit and mineral finish. An easy-to-drink crowd-pleaser. **86** *(10/1/2001)*

Beringer 2001 Marston Vineyard Syrah (Spring Mountain) $35. Really ripe-smelling, with elements of pruny fruit intertwined with hickory smoke and graham cracker on the nose. The fruit freshens up on the palate, turning plummy and velvety. Sturdy, this wine shows its mountain origins without being overly tough. **89** *(9/1/2005)*

Beringer 1997 Viognier (Napa Valley) $20. **91** —*S.H. (10/1/1999)*

Beringer 2004 Viognier (Napa Valley) $16. Soft, simple, and clean, this is a big-fruit wine that appeals for its superripe peach, mango, pineapple, honeysuckle, and citrus flavors and creamy texture. It has just enough acidity to have a balanced mouthfeel. **84** —*S.H. (11/15/2005)*

Beringer 2003 Viognier (Napa Valley) $16. Made in the exotic style, with loads of ripe tropical fruit and spice flavors, but the crisp acidity and well-defined structure lend it elegance and style. Notable for the creamy texture. **88** —*S.H. (12/15/2004)*

Beringer 2002 Viognier (Napa Valley) $16. Drinks dry and tart, not the fruitiest Viognier ever, but a nice, calm one. Reins in the peach, citrus, and apple flavors with firm acidity and a steely clean finish. **85** —*S.H. (9/1/2004)*

Beringer 2004 Alluvium Blanc White Blend (Knights Valley) $16. The hot vintage worked to the wine's benefit, making it richer and riper than the '03. All sorts of forward peaches and cream, custardy citrus, and smoky, creamy oak notes, with good acidity, make this Sauvignon Blanc-Sémillon blend a nice upscale white. **88** —*S.H. (12/15/2006)*

Beringer 2002 Alluvium Blanc White Blend (Knights Valley) $16. Almost the perfect white wine for food. It's rich in citrus, fig, spice, and sweet herb flavors, with subtle oak flavorings, but this is a dry, balanced wine. Its acids and dusting of tannins will complement almost anything, even beef. **89** —*S.H. (12/15/2004)*

Beringer 2000 Alluvium Blanc White Blend (Knights Valley) $16. Fairly rich and lush—really quite viscous—with pretty apricot, peach, honey, nut, and spice flavors. Fleshy on the finish. A blend of Sauvignon Blanc and Sémillon. **87** —*J.M. (12/15/2002)*

Beringer 1999 Alluvium Blanc White Blend (Knights Valley) $16. This is a very fruity wine, one dominated by apple and peach and citrus flavors. Good acids make it bright, and it's impeccably clean and focused. Could use some more depth and layers. **85** —*S.H. (9/1/2002)*

Beringer 1998 Alluvium Blanc White Blend (Knights Valley) $16. One of a growing family of California whites that marry unrelated varietals, this is a rich, complex, and delightful example, with a menagerie of flavors. The blending of Sémillon, Sauvignon Blanc, Chardonnay, and Viognier yields everything from apples, peaches, and grapefruit to flowers and honey. Slightly sweet, though protected by a racy acidity. The result is a lot of fun. But because the flavors are strong, it's best matched with the right foods. Smoked fish comes to mind; also fruity salsa toppings. **89** —*S.H. (5/1/2001)*

Beringer 1997 Alluvium Blanc White Blend (Knights Valley) $16. **89** —*M.S. (8/1/2000)*

Beringer 1996 Nightingale White Blend (North Coast) $30. **93** —*S.H. (12/31/2000)*

Beringer 1996 Zinfandel (North Coast) $13. **88 Best Buy** —*M.S. (9/1/1999)*

Beringer 2001 Zinfandel (California) $12. Mild-mannered, with toasty oak and mild cherry, blackberry, spice, and herb flavors. Tangy acidity lifts the finish. **82** *(11/1/2003)*

Beringer 1998 Zinfandel (Clear Lake) $14. When Beringer couldn't find Zin in Napa Valley at a decent price, they turned to this little-known appellation to the east. It's not bad. The grapes got ripe enough to produce Zin's briary, peppery flavors, but the wine has a roughness it can't overcome. These are mountain vineyards, at 2,300 feet, and the soils are volcanic, courtesy of the dormant volcano nearest to San Francisco. **86** —*S.H. (11/1/2002)*

Beringer 1999 Appelation Collection Zinfandel (Clear Lake) $14. A difficult Zin to like. Opens with funky aromas of socks and that offputting smell doesn't blow off. In the mouth, it's jammy and unnaturally sweet. **81** —*S.H. (3/1/2004)*

Beringer 1999 Founders' Estate Zinfandel (California) $12. Ripe, plump, and juicy, with flavors of wild berries, white pepper, tobacco, and herbs. This is a good, young Zin, with some sharp, aggressive acids and youthful tannins. Needs ribs and similar fare to show its best. **86** —*S.H. (2/1/2003)*

Beringer 2004 Founders' Estate Old Vine Zinfandel (California) $11. Here's a good, everyday Zin, a little peppery and briary, with ripe cherry and berry flavors. It finishes dry, with the kind of smooth, meaty tannins that cry out for olive oil, cheese, beef. **84** —*S.H. (12/31/2006)*

Beringer 2003 Founders' Estate Old Vine Zinfandel (California) $11. There's a ton of juicy Zin character in this pleasant wine. It has bigtime cherry, black raspberry, and blackberry flavors with a rich chocolate streak, and a raw, acidic edginess that cries out for food. **85** —*S.H. (11/15/2005)*

BERNARDUS

Bernardus 2000 Marinus Bordeaux Blend (Carmel Valley) $46. A Bordeaux blend with lots of richness and panache, this wine is rather tannic and acidic in its youth. It's not a blockbuster, but has a deep enough core of black cherry fruit to warrant cellaring. Best after 2006. **87** —*S.H. (10/1/2004)*

USA

Bernardus 2002 Marinus Cabernet Blend (Carmel Valley) $44. Very similar to the '01, maybe a bit more tannic, this polished blend of all five Bordeaux varieties is firm in acids and tannins. The flavors are ripe and forward, of cassis, dark chocolate, and tobacco. Might develop with four or five years of bottle age. **90** —*S.H. (9/1/2006)*

Bernardus 2001 Marinus Cabernet Sauvignon (Carmel Valley) $46. From this sheltered valley in Monterey, a lovely Cab that features ripe cassis and black currant flavors. The tannins invite a comparison to Napa Valley. They're firmer, but the wine is drinkable now. Finishes with a chocolaty taste. Mainly Cabernet Sauvignon. **90** —*S.H. (4/1/2005)*

Bernardus 1997 Chardonnay (Monterey County) $18. 90 *(11/15/1999)*

Bernardus 2004 Chardonnay (Monterey County) $20. Crisp, bright acidity marks this dry, clean Chardonnay. It's bone dry, but rewardingly fruity, showing ripe peach, pear, and pineapple flavors, with a richer streak of crème brûlée. Easy to find, with 23,544 cases made. **87** —*S.H. (10/1/2006)*

Bernardus 2003 Chardonnay (Monterey) $20. Here's one of the more complex Chards at this price. It has much in common with what California does best, namely, well-ripened fruit, with fresh, keen acidity. The winemaker bells and whistles have been tastefully applied. **91 Editors' Choice** —*S.H. (11/1/2005)*

Bernardus 2002 Chardonnay (Monterey County) $20. There's a roasted hazelnut taste to the peach, tropical fruit and oak flavors that make this fine wine distinctive. But what really makes it shine is the acidity. Clean, vibrant, and pure, with an enormous finish. **92** —*S.H. (12/15/2004)*

Bernardus 2001 Chardonnay (Monterey County) $20. Almost always distinctive, and this year has unusual flair and finesse. Shows a Chablisian style of mineral, warm stone, and citrus, but with far richer streaks, like gold embedded in flint. Oak and lees are elegantly applied. More foodworthy than most California Chards. **90 Editors' Choice** —*S.H. (8/1/2003)*

Bernardus 2000 Chardonnay (Monterey County) $20. Has well-developed tangerine, peach, and pear flavors veering into tropical fruits, and an elaborate overlay of toasty oak. Lees add a slightly sour, creamy note. Finishes soft. **88** —*S.H. (2/1/2003)*

Bernardus 1996 Bien Nacido Reserve Chardonnay (Santa Barbara County) $32. Asian pear, but also dairy-like notes of cheese, sour cream, and show on the nose. The mouthfeel is a bit heavy. Apple and woody flavors show on the palate; dry wood and spice mark the back end. A good wine, but now reading ponderously—perhaps past its prime. **84** *(7/1/2001)*

Bernardus 2002 Cypress Vineyard Chardonnay (Monterey County) $50. The vineyard is in the northeastern Salinas Valley, in the Gavilan foothills, which makes it a cool climate. The wine has adequate acidity and oak, with flavors of peaches and cream and a rich, honeyed finish. Could have more depth and complexity, though, especially at this price. **87** —*S.H. (6/1/2006)*

Bernardus 2001 Griva Vineyard Chardonnay (Monterey County) $38. A very expressive and full-bodied wine. It jolts the palate with the purest extract of ripe limes, green apples, and minerals. Wonderfully sharp acids push the flavors up and out, and cleanse the palate. Rather lean, compared to some of the fatties out there, a wine of structure and firmness. **91** —*S.H. (8/1/2003)*

Bernardus 2002 Rosella's Vineyard Chardonnay (Santa Lucia Highlands) $40. The source of dependably rich Chards, Rosella's has given Bernardus the opportunity to craft a wonderfully complex wine. It's ripe in flavors ranging from lime tart and kiwi to papaya, nectarine, and Anjou pear. Delicious, although it would benefit from higher acidity. **90** —*S.H. (6/1/2006)*

Bernardus 1996 Sangiacomo Vineyards Reserve Chardonnay (Sonoma County) $30. This Chard displays a slightly unusual but appealing sweet and sour streak. The bouquet shows tart green apples, grapefruit, stewed fruit, and sweet herbs, plus tangy green oak shadings. The palate delivers more of the same, with zingy citrus and crisp apple flavors, but also dry, leesy notes. There's both cream and pepper on the back end of this likeable, split-personality wine. **87** *(7/1/2001)*

Bernardus 1999 Marinus Estate Grown & Estate Bottled Meritage (Carmel Valley) $50. Opens with aromas of oak, mint, and herbs, with a hint of black currant. Drinks fairly tannic at the moment, and sharp in acids. There is some berry fruit buried down deep, but not offering a plush, hedonistic experience. The finish is very dry and tannic. **85** —*S.H. (8/1/2003)*

Bernardus 1996 Merlot (Carmel Valley) $30. 89 —*J.C. (7/1/2000)*

Bernardus 2000 Pinot Noir (Santa Barbara County) $28. A generic, regional South-Central Coast Pinot showing berry, cola, herb, and sautéed mushroom flavors encased in soft, silky tannins and crisp acids. Has little complexity and best consumed now. **85** —*S.H. (8/1/2003)*

Bernardus 2004 Bien Nacido Vineyard Pinot Noir (Santa Maria Valley) $34. Surprisingly weedy and thin for this vineyard, but Bernardus has struggled with this bottling over the years. Dry and mint-sharp, with cherry Lifesaver flavors and plenty of oak. **84** —*S.H. (12/31/2006)*

Bernardus 2002 Bien Nacido Vineyard Pinot Noir (Santa Maria Valley) $34. Feels heavy in the mouth, and too soft, too, which weighs the dark stone fruit flavors down. This dark, big, Rhône-style wine isn't at all like a real Pinot Noir. Maybe it will do something in four or five years. **82** —*S.H. (3/1/2006)*

Bernardus 2000 Bien Nacido Vineyard Pinot Noir (Santa Barbara County) $48. Earthier and drier than the 1999, and not as flamboyantly fruity. Shows aromas of beet, sun-dried tomato, cherry, and crushed hard spices, and drinks very dry, with silky tannins and firm acids. Quite supple and complex in its way. **87** —*S.H. (12/1/2003)*

Bernardus 2003 Rosella's Vineyard Pinot Noir (Santa Lucia Highlands) $50. I love the silky texture of this Pinot, with its crisp acids and fine, smooth tannins. The fruit is enormous, bursting with cherry and mocha flavors. It seems rather sweet now, but that may be its youth. Give it until mid-2006 to come together. **87** —*S.H. (3/1/2006)*

Bernardus 1998 Sauvignon Blanc (Monterey County) $14. 87 —*S.H. (11/1/1999)*

Bernardus 2005 Sauvignon Blanc (Monterey County) $15. Cat pee, a drop of grapefruit juice, and a clean, spicy finish. That's pretty much it. **83** —*S.H. (12/1/2006)*

Bernardus 2004 Sauvignon Blanc (Monterey County) $15. An intensely flavored white wine, totally dry and tart in zesty citrus rind and gooseberry, with shadings of fig, melon, and vanilla. It's a really good wine, fun to drink, and versatile across a range of food. **88** —*S.H. (11/1/2005)*

Bernardus 2003 Sauvignon Blanc (Monterey County) $15. Fresh and fruity in ripe peaches and figs, this wine turns creamy in the mouth, and finishes with clean acidity. **85** —*S.H. (5/1/2005)*

Bernardus 2001 Sauvignon Blanc (Monterey County) $15. What a great wine this is. It combines Chardonnay's rich, creamy texture with Sauvignon Blanc's dry, tart, lemony flavors to yield a complex wine that's a joy to drink. The acidic, peppery finish begs for food to accompany it. A very great value. **89** —*S.H. (7/1/2003)*

Bernardus 2000 Sauvignon Blanc (Monterey) $15. Passion fruit, citrus, and other nice aromatics make for a pretty nose, which is followed by genuinely good and correct flavors such as grapefruit, lemon, and citrus rind. The finish is also quite nice, with a certain roundness and acidity that makes it tantalizing and tasty. **89 Best Buy** *(8/1/2002)*

Bernardus 2005 Griva Vineyard Sauvignon Blanc (Arroyo Seco) $20. Tons of cat-pee aromas pour forth from this dry, acidic Sauvignon Blanc, so if that's not your thing, don't buy it. For you others, there are richer notes of pineapple, fig, and honeydew. **84** —*S.H. (12/1/2006)*

Bernardus 2004 Griva Vineyard Sauvignon Blanc (Arroyo Seco) $20. Three cheers for this Sauvignon Blanc. It triangulates perfectly between the variety's grassy, green apple character, richer, riper fig, and peach flavors, and an oaky veneer. But it never loses sight of its crisp, cleansing, and vital acidity. **90** —*S.H. (11/1/2005)*

Bernardus 2003 Griva Vineyard Sauvignon Blanc (Arroyo Seco) $20. Shows a touch of the Monterey veggies on the nose, where asparagus notes go head to head with melon and citrus. Softer than some on the palate, which supports the flavors of melon and peach. Goes pithy and a touch thin toward the end, with a spot of bitterness. **86** *(7/1/2005)*

Bernardus 2001 Griva Vineyard Sauvignon Blanc (Arroyo Seco) $20. Just what a cool climate Sauvignon Blanc wants to be, a bone dry, high acid wine filled with pure, bright flavors of gooseberry and lime. This is made from the Musque clone, and is appealing for its streamlined profile and clean finish. **89** —*S.H. (10/1/2003)*

BETHEL HEIGHTS

Bethel Heights 2001 Chardonnay (Willamette Valley) $15. Barrel fermented and aged on the lees, this estate-grown wine is comprised mostly of fruit from 25-year-old vines, planted on their own rootstock. The fruit is spicy, tangy and a bit tannic, still needing some time to smooth out, but the flavors, which run from citrus through tart tropical fruits, are all there. Plenty of acid keeps it food friendly. **88** —*P.G. (12/1/2003)*

Bethel Heights 1999 Estate Grown Chardonnay (Willamette Valley) $15. This taut, steely Chardonnay, muscular and firm, tastes of stone, mineral, herb, and citrus. It's a complex, appealing mix, supported by vivid acids. Fine length and precise, elegant flavors with a light touch on the oak. This is high-wire Chardonnay. **89 Best Buy** —*P.G. (4/1/2002)*

Bethel Heights 1998 Pinot Blanc (Willamette Valley) $12. 88 —*L.W. (12/31/1999)*

Bethel Heights 2002 Pinot Blanc (Willamette Valley) $12. The classic "Alsatian style" Oregon Pinot, but it's Blanc rather than Gris, giving it more acid, more steely structure, and nice mineral and stone flavors. Stylish and subtle, with citrus, melon, and herbs. **88 Best Buy** —*P.G. (12/1/2003)*

Bethel Heights 2000 Reserve Pinot Blanc (Willamette Valley) $12. Stylish and decidedly dry, this medium-weight wine shows a gentle pear-vanilla-chamomile nose. Mineral notes and a spicy tang accent the mild pear fruit. Evenly textured, but not at all bland, the mineral and spice elements carry through the clean finish. **87** —*M.M. (11/1/2001)*

Bethel Heights 2004 Pinot Gris (Oregon) $15. Full and spicy, this marries ripe, pear, and mango-flavored fruit with spicy cinnamon and green tea. It's got the harmonious integration and lingering fruitiness that makes you want second and third glasses. **90 Best Buy** —*P.G. (2/1/2006)*

Bethel Heights 2000 Pinot Gris (Willamette Valley) $12. There is good, solid fruit here, as can be expected from this quality producer, but the problem seems to be an excess of sulfur, and it spoils the nose. It also bleeds into the palate, with harsh burnt match flavors overriding the fleshy fruit and citrus components. Swirl it, decant it, anything to let it breathe, and you'll be rewarded. **86** —*P.G. (4/1/2002)*

Bethel Heights 1998 Pinot Gris (Willamette Valley) $12. 87 *(8/1/1999)*

Bethel Heights 1997 Pinot Noir (Willamette Valley) $15. 84 *(11/15/1999)*

Bethel Heights 2002 Pinot Noir (Willamette Valley) $15. Despite its soft, pretty opening scents, this wine simply lacks fruit. The middle drops out completely, resolving in some dry tannins. Bottle shock? **84** *(11/1/2004)*

Bethel Heights 2001 Pinot Noir (Willamette Valley) $25. Organically grown grapes are used here, making a lean, tart, cranberry and pomegranate-flavored Pinot. Right now it is very tight and earthy, so plenty of breathing time will be in order. **87** —*P.G. (12/1/2003)*

Bethel Heights 2000 Pinot Noir (Willamette Valley) $25. Straightfoward and tasty, this offers a core of dry cherry fruit swathed in smoke and mild leather accents. The palate has a smooth and silky texture; the finish is even and tea-flavored. For a basic Pinot, this shows hints of style and nuance. **86** *(10/1/2002)*

Bethel Heights 2002 Casteel Reserve Pinot Noir (Willamette Valley) $40. Good, varietal flavors, hints of bark and cocoa, and a solid midpalate showing plums and purple fruits, laced with vanilla. Chocolate plum cake, said one taster; but the green, tannic finish suggests a stemmy future. **86** *(11/1/2004)*

Bethel Heights 1999 Estate Grown Pinot Noir (Willamette Valley) $25. Again, this is a tight wine still wrapped up in youthful tannins. The nose hints of earth and ash, its dark fruit emerging slowly to reveal flavors of bark, root, and soil. Still quite tannic and closed up, but promising. **88** —*P.G. (4/1/2002)*

Bethel Heights 2002 Flat Block Reserve Pinot Noir (Willamette Valley) $38. Perhaps just young and closed up, but this reserve did not seem to show the extra dimensions that a reserve generally should. A mix of berry/cherry fruits, snappy acids, and a hint of new oak. Good, standard fare. **85** *(11/1/2004)*

Bethel Heights 2001 Flat Block Reserve Pinot Noir (Willamette Valley) $38. This is softer, smoother, and more forward than the West Block; it has some sweet cherry fruit and firm, earthy tannins. Give it some air and the finish opens up into some pretty, sweet black cherry and smoke. **88** —*P.G. (12/1/2003)*

Bethel Heights 2000 Flat Block Reserve Pinot Noir (Willamette Valley) $35. A medium-bodied wine with tight aromas of bacon, red raspberry, and spice. That same smoked-meat quality found in the nose carries onto the palate, where you'll also find clean cherry and raspberry flavors. An easy drinking wine. **87** *(10/1/2002)*

Bethel Heights 1999 Flat Block Reserve Pinot Noir (Willamette Valley) $35. This has long been a top Oregon Pinot, and it shows its breeding in this tricky vintage. The nose is redolent of sweet, grapey cherries, aromatic and quite pretty. In the mouth extra dimensions emerge: fruit, mineral, and earth. Balanced and tight, some additional cellaring will flesh it out and let it unwrap. **91 Editors' Choice** —*P.G. (4/1/2002)*

Bethel Heights 2002 Freedom Hill Vineyard Pinot Noir (Willamette Valley) $30. Hard and stemmy, oaky and tannic. A lot of tough, chewy flavors here, augmented with herbs and tobacco. Time may take some of the bitterness away, but it's tough sledding right now. **86** *(11/1/2004)*

Bethel Heights 2001 Freedom Hill Vineyard Pinot Noir (Willamette Valley) $30. This is quite distinctive, with spicy highlights that cut through the fruit. There is a scent and sensation of something resinous, mineral; this is clearly structured to age. Good, tart cranberry fruit, highlights of cherry, and light oak. **89** —*P.G. (12/1/2003)*

Bethel Heights 1998 Freedom Hill Vineyard Pinot Noir (Willamette Valley) $30. 89 —*M.M. (12/1/2000)*

Bethel Heights 1998 Lewman Vineyard Pinot Noir (Willamette Valley) $25. 85 —*M.S. (12/1/2000)*

Bethel Heights 2002 Nysa Vineyard Pinot Noir (Willamette Valley) $30. Very dark, purple, and extracted looking, with big, dense, plummy blue fruits beginning to show. Right now this is in a dumbed-down phase, and the reduced flavors, along with some volatile acidity, bring down the score. Has the potential to improve significantly. **86** *(11/1/2004)*

Bethel Heights 2001 Nysa Vineyard Pinot Noir (Willamette Valley) $30. This is a tight, young wine, with sleek, firm, very tart fruit. Flavors show light cherry and sour berry, with nice chocolaty toast from the barrels. **88** —*P.G. (12/1/2003)*

Bethel Heights 2000 Nysa Vineyard Pinot Noir (Willamette Valley) $30. The bouquet is like cherry and strawberry candy, but it has woody backbone, too. Plum, vanilla, and chocolate flavors are followed by a light and graceful finish that's clean and warm. This wine offers plenty of balance and drinkability. **87** *(10/1/2002)*

Bethel Heights 1999 Nysa Vineyard Pinot Noir (Willamette Valley) $30. Made from purchased grapes, this clear, bright wine offers sweet fruit packaged in a clean, elegant style. The spotlight is on the fruit, sweet and pure, accented with light spice and finishing with a hint of mocha. **89** —*P.G. (4/1/2002)*

Bethel Heights 1998 Nysa Vineyard Pinot Noir (Willamette Valley) $25. 87 —*M.S. (12/1/2000)*

Bethel Heights 2002 SE Block Reserve Pinot Noir (Willamette Valley) $38. Meaty, animal scents, along with some earthy funk, start things off; then the wine plumps out with ripe red fruits and cola. Very tannic through the finish. **86** *(11/1/2004)*

Bethel Heights 2002 Seven Springs Vineyard Pinot Noir (Willamette Valley) $38. A full, meaty style, mixing exotic fruits, tree bark, and smoky mocha. Tart, herbal, and sharp-edged, but characterful with a lively mix of layered flavors. **87** *(11/1/2004)*

Bethel Heights 2001 Southeast Block Reserve Pinot Noir (Willamette Valley) $38. The three different "Block" reserves may seem significantly distinctive to the winery, but it might serve them just as well to do a reserve and let it go at that. It's hard to distinguish between them; all show tight, herb, and earth-driven flavors. This has a softer, tutti-fruity core that might meld well with the other two. **88** —*P.G. (12/1/2003)*

Bethel Heights 2000 Southeast Block Reserve Pinot Noir (Willamette Valley) $40. Two members of our tasting panel detected some iodine and mineral aromas normally associated with chewable vitamins, but the wine also has some nice black cherry aromas. The palate is heavy with plum and dried spices, and a fair dose of buttery oak. Compact and unforgiving, time in the bottle might be the answer. **87** *(10/1/2002)*

Bethel Heights 1999 Southeast Block Reserve Pinot Noir (Willamette Valley) $40. Pretty and richly scented, this wine is stuffed with black cherry fruit, lightly accented with toast and coffee. Still so tightly wound that its richer dimensions remain a bit veiled. Needs more bottle time to really strut its stuff. **89** —*P.G. (4/1/2002)*

Bethel Heights 1998 Southeast Block Reserve Pinot Noir (Willamette Valley) $35. 90 —*M.S. (12/1/2000)*

Bethel Heights 1998 Wadenswil Block Reserve Pinot Noir (Willamette Valley) $35. 89 —*M.S. (12/1/2000)*

Bethel Heights 1999 Wädenswil Block Reserve Pinot Noir (Willamette Valley) $35. Classy and tight, with a tart cherry, herb, and tomato profile and racy acidity that is very '99. Light and smooth, with an even chalk-dust feel, it stays lean and clean through the long, sour cherry finish. This will even out a bit with time in the bottle, but not flesh out much. It will always be angular in manner, with great appeal to those who enjoy high-strung Pinot. **89** —*M.M. (11/1/2001)*

Bethel Heights 2001 West Block Reserve Pinot Noir (Willamette Valley) $38. Nice herbal and leafy accents, rather than big, jammy fruit flavors. The effect is to give the Pinot texture and depth. The oak is not intrusive. Feels just a little thin in the finish. **88** —*P.G. (12/1/2003)*

Bethel Heights 2000 West Block Reserve Pinot Noir (Willamette Valley) $35. The smoky, bacon-filled nose also offers black cherry, vanilla, and a chalky dustiness. The powerful raspberry character in the mouth is driven by healthy acidity. The finish has a lot of charred wood, and black coffee. If there's a fault, it's that this wine is hard. Time could be the answer to that. **88** *(10/1/2002)*

BETZ FAMILY WINERY

Betz Family Winery 2002 Clos de Betz Bordeaux Blend (Columbia Valley (WA)) $29. Master of Wine Bob Betz has refined his winemaking to a style that is breaking new ground for the region. The Merlot-centric Clos de Betz (57% Merlot, 33% Cabernet Sauvignon, 10% Cab Franc) is incredibly dense, concentrated and inky, yet retains amazing elegance. Its silky mouthfeel, brightness, and finesse support supple, ripe, immaculate fruit. It's all wrapped in pillowy tannins. **93 Editors' Choice** —*P.G. (6/1/2005)*

Betz Family Winery 2003 Père de Famille Cabernet Sauvignon (Columbia Valley (WA)) $45. Firm, chewy, young, tight, and yet quite supple and fulfilling, this stunning Cabernet is packed with a rainbow of fruit flavors—blueberry, black currant, and black cherry—that open into a seamless, beautifully proportioned wine. The scents and flavors run the gamut from citrus peel to clove to soy to chocolate, espresso, and beyond. **95 Editors' Choice** —*P.G. (6/1/2006)*

Betz Family Winery 2002 Père de Famille Cabernet Sauvignon (Columbia Valley (WA)) $45. The mouthfeel on this stunning Cabernet is utterly distinctive. Full, lush, packed with smoky black fruits, it seamlessly extends through the midpalate with no hint of chalk, stem, earth, or roughness. Voluptuous, smooth, and coated with chocolate, espresso, and dried orange peel. **93** —*P.G. (6/1/2005)*

Betz Family Winery 2003 Bésolei Grenache (Columbia Valley (WA)) $35. Béso is kiss, soleil is sun; the name is made up to signify "sun-kissed." The grapes are from Alder Ridge, with 14% Syrah from Red Mountain blended in. Just 82 cases were made. It's a juicy, delicious tangle of red fruits and berries, with a spicy highlight. As it unfolds you notice the fruit is lined with citrus, orange peel, and clove, then finished with sweet oak. **91** —*P.G. (12/15/2005)*

Betz Family Winery 2003 Clos de Betz Red Blend (Columbia Valley (WA)) $32. Though it gets the same care as the winery's Cab, the Clos de Betz features considerably more Merlot in the blend (59% compared with 13%). This is intensely fragrant, beautifully integrated, toasty, and lush. The mouthfeel is incredible, offering layers of caramel, butterscotch, and creamy oak around black cherry and plum. There is even a hint of camphor and five spice for still more sensory overload. **93** —*P.G. (6/1/2006)*

Betz Family Winery 2003 La Cote Rousse Syrah (Red Mountain) $44. A mix of Kiona and Ciel du Cheval Syrah is crafted into a dark, dense, tannic wine, tightly wound and vertically structured. Dark roasted scents suggest espresso and moist earth, along with classic Red Mountain minerality. Clean, silky, fully ripe but sleekly styled cherry and plum fruit finishes with dense, chocolaty tannins. Definitely a wine to tuck away for a few years. **93** —*P.G. (12/15/2005)*

Betz Family Winery 2002 La Cote Rousse Syrah (Red Mountain) $41. The second Syrah from Betz Family relies on Red Mountain fruit, and makes a fascinating contrast to the much more open and sappy La Serenne. This wine is tight, vertically structured, with far less immediate breadth. The nose grudgingly reveals cassis and sweet, toasted cracker, along with classic Red Mountain flavors of mineral and earth. Tight as a drum, the wine finishes with a hard shell of tannin, that will certainly require some years to smooth out. But the compact, dark, mysterious fruit core promises that it will be worth the wait. **92** —*P.G. (12/15/2004)*

Betz Family Winery 2003 La Serenne Syrah (Columbia Valley (WA)) $44. An elegant and tart, cool-climate style of Syrah. Betz wines are always carefully structured and beautifully proportioned, and the winery has not over-reached in this somewhat difficult vintage. Extra hang time ripened the fruit while retaining good acids and flavors of boysenberry, sour cherry, and raspberry. Hints of coffee and gravel add complexity. Best for relatively near-term enjoyment. **91** —*P.G. (12/15/2005)*

Betz Family Winery 2002 La Serenne Syrah (Columbia Valley (WA)) $41. Dense and plush with exotic scents of roasted coffee, smoke, toast, cedar, and blackberry jam, this is very young, showing mostly primary fruits and lots of new wood. But the ripe, sappy fruit, from an exceptional block in the Boushey vineyard, stands out, seamless and pure. Like a racehorse, this wine is sleek, powerful, and perfectly proportioned. It offers immense enjoyment as soon as the cork is popped, but will go for a good 10 years in the cellar. **94** —*P.G. (12/15/2004)*

BIANCHI

Bianchi 2004 Jack Ranch Signature Selection Chardonnay (Edna Valley) $20. Only Edna Valley could produce this remarkably bold, bright acidity and rich Key Lime pie and sautéed banana flavors. Oak is the perfect partner, adding smoky vanillins and buttercream. **90** —*S.H. (12/31/2005)*

Bianchi 2004 Signature Selection Pinot Grigio (Arroyo Grande Valley) $25. PG's are rare from this appellation. This one's well-acidified, leaving a bright and crisp mouthfeel to the citrus, melon, and fig flavors. But be forewarned, the wine's too sweet, almost off-dry. **83** —*S.H. (2/1/2006)*

Bianchi 2004 Signature Selection Pinot Noir (Paso Robles) $25. Pinot from Paso doesn't really work, and although this is on the cooler, western end, near the York Mountain appellation, it's unbalanced. While it's dry, it has a medicinal taste, and a burning hot mouthfeel from high alcohol. **82** —*S.H. (12/15/2006)*

Bianchi 2004 Signature Selection Sauvignon Blanc (Central Coast) $16. Grassiness and cat pee mark this wine, with clean grapefruit juice and lemon zest on the finish. It's absolutely dry, with crisp, cool-climate acidity. **84** —*S.H. (12/31/2005)*

Bianchi 2001 Zen Ranch Zinfandel (Paso Robles) $18. Toasty, smoky oak frames the spicy cherry, blackberry, coffee, and tea flavors that are most apparent here. The wine offers firm, ripe tannins and a finish of moderate length. **86** (11/1/2003)

BIG BASIN

Big Basin 2004 Mandala Syrah (Santa Cruz County) $42. Intensely jammy, with all kinds of marmalade, cherry, black raspberry, and a dusting of cocoa and white pepper and an unusually high proportion of Mourvèdre (40%). From the start the Mourvèdre is apparent, imparting hints of cola, tree bark, and dark-fruit flavors—even a hint of espresso. Yet there's also peppery spice from the Grenache, and the wine avoids any sense of heaviness or rusticity. The tannins are supple and velvety, the finish long. Drink now–2014. **89** —S.H. (11/15/2006)

Big Basin 2004 Rattlesnake Rock Syrah (Santa Cruz Mountains) $55. Maybe it's the snake venom, but this is seriously good Syrah. Blackberry and cherry pie aromas and flavors, with caramelized oak, mocha, chocolate macaroon, and vanilla extravagances that turn richer and richer with every sip. Defines Syrah's power and elegance with immediate, voluptuous pleasure. **94 Editors' Choice** —S.H. (11/15/2006)

BIG FIRE

Big Fire 2004 Pinot Gris (Oregon) $18. Rob Stuart's take on PG is very sensual, creamy, leesy, and fresh. It's got a mix of tropical fruit and crisp citrus peel, hints of wet stone, and a lingering, textured finish. **89** —P.G. (2/1/2006)

Big Fire 2001 Pinot Gris (Oregon) $14. Rob Stuart, formerly with Erath vineyards, is the winemaker. The first release for this new brand recalls his Erath days with its fleshy, ripe pear flavors. Some cinnamon spice adds interest. The wine is open and rich; solidly made. **88** —P.G. (12/31/2002)

BIG YELLOW

Big Yellow 2003 Cabernet Sauvignon (North Coast) $11. The latest in a tidal wave of mid-priced varieties under new labels, this Cab is dry and rustic, with cherry, berry, and coffee flavors that finish in a scour of tannins. **84** —S.H. (12/15/2005)

BIGHORN

Bighorn 2001 Cabernet Sauvignon (Napa Valley) $29. Starts off with a musty aroma that decanting should take care of. In the mouth, this Cab tastes good. It's sweetish-dry and very smooth, with rich cherry and blackberry flavors that veer into chocolate. **86** —S.H. (11/1/2005)

Bighorn 2002 Broken Rock Vineyard Cabernet Sauvignon (Napa Valley) $36. Ripe, smooth, and delicious, this Cab offers tiers of blackberry jam, plum sauce, chocolate, licorice, and oaky spice flavors. It's so soft, so beguiling, and despite the fruity power it's elegantly structured. A wine to savor as it warms in the glass. It wears its high alcohol well. **92** —S.H. (12/1/2006)

Bighorn 2001 Coombsville Cabernet Sauvignon (Napa Valley) $39. Marked by excessive alcohol, this is a hot, clumsy Cabernet. It's deficient in lively acidity, with worn-down cherry and mocha flavors. **83** —S.H. (11/1/2005)

Bighorn 1998 Coombsville Cabernet Sauvignon (Napa Valley) $39. From southern Napa, just beyond the Carneros border, this is a cool climate Cabernet. Well-etched cassis flavors are set off by fine acids and rich tannins. This wine is remarkable for its depth and complexity but also for its balance and restraint. It wisely avoids the modern tendency toward excessive size. **93** —S.H. (11/15/2002)

Bighorn 2002 Coombsville Vineyard Cabernet Sauvignon (Napa Valley) $36. This Cab has been variable over the years, but '02 is a wine to like for its lush flavors and overall balance. It's a superripe wine, chockablock with chocolate, crème de cassis, and oaky flavors. Drink now. **87** —S.H. (12/1/2006)

Bighorn 2000 Coombsville Vineyard Cabernet Sauvignon (Napa Valley) $30. Bigtime tannins mark this well-intentioned wine. You'll find flavors of black currants and herbs way down underneath, and a thick plastering of fine oak, but then those pesky tannins kick in and numb things down. The cassis theme picks up on the finish, suggesting cellaring until 2006. **88** —S.H. (6/1/2004)

Bighorn 2001 Grand Reserve Cabernet Sauvignon (Napa Valley) $36. The winery has a mixed record with Cabernet and this release doesn't advance the cause. It's sharp in acids, with stalky, green notes, and the thinness of flavor accentuates the tannins, making them astringent. **82** —S.H. (5/1/2006)

Bighorn 2000 Grand Reserve Cabernet Sauvignon (Napa Valley) $49. Nearly five years of aging has not helped this wine. It's hot and awkward, with low acids and an herbal edge to the blackberry fruit. **83** —S.H. (11/1/2005)

Bighorn 1998 Soda Canyon Cabernet Sauvignon (Napa Valley) $19. Earthy, with plum, sage, and raisin aromas. Very soft, pretty texture, with delicate tannins. The fruit is thin and herbal and lets the acidity dominate the palate. Still, it's saved by the pedigree of terroir. **85** —S.H. (11/15/2002)

Bighorn 2002 Chardonnay (Napa Valley) $16. Comes down on the earthy, herbal side. Apple flavors hit on entry, then turn into fresh dill and sage, with the usual oaky notes. **84** —S.H. (6/1/2004)

Bighorn 2002 Chardonnay (Carneros) $18. Surprisingly thin and watery for such a nice appellation, with a weak aroma and equally unimpressive citrus flavors. Seems like the vines were overcropped. **83** —S.H. (6/1/2004)

Bighorn 2001 Chardonnay (Carneros) $17. From the Napa side, a bells and whistles wine bursting with notes of spent lees and toasty oak. The underlying fruit veers toward ripe peaches and green apples. Clean, complex, and nuanced. **89** —S.H. (12/15/2004)

Bighorn 1999 Camelback Chardonnay (Carneros) $16. Very complex fruit, forward and brilliant, ranging from apples and peaches through pears to unctuous tropical fruits, and it's set off against a lavish display of oak and lees. It's lively in the mouth thanks to refreshing acidity. **91** —S.H. (12/15/2002)

Bighorn 2004 Camelback Vineyard Chardonnay (Carneros) $22. This is one of those Chards that's more Burgundian than Californian. There's a rich earthiness followed by a minerally date nut, dried pineapple, and spiced apple character. In the end, there's enough acidity to suggest mid-term aging. **91** —S.H. (12/1/2006)

Bighorn 2001 Coombsville Vineyard Chardonnay (Napa Valley) $15. For all its heft, and this is a heavyweight Chardonnay, it never loses its balance and harmony. Bigtime tropical fruit and spicy fig flavors are wrapped in succulently sweet, smoky oak. The creamy texture and long, rich finish make this a great wine. **93 Best Buy** —S.H. (12/15/2004)

Bighorn 1999 Grand Reserve Chardonnay (Napa Valley) $24. Considerably plumper and richer than this winery's Camelback bottling, and the burst of tropical fruit flavors fills the mouth. It's nicely accompanied by good acids, and the oak is enormous. Finishes with a buttery, creamy, oaky feel. **92** —S.H. (12/15/2002)

Bighorn 2003 Broken Rock Vineyard Merlot (Napa Valley) $30. There's lots to like in this ripe, juicy wine. The flavors are forward and ripe in black cherries and cocoa, and the tannic structure is sturdy, dry, and clean, with a long, fruity-spicy finish. It's an easy wine with some real elegance. **87** —S.H. (12/15/2005)

Bighorn 2003 Sugerloaf Mountain Vineyard Syrah (Napa Valley) $30. This rich, full-bodied Syrah aspires to a Northern Rhône style, with its dry, peppery flavors and smooth, rich tannins, although the sunny cherry and blackberry fruit is indisputably Napa. It's a sumptuous, soft wine for early drinking, from veteran William Hill. **90** —S.H. (12/15/2005)

BINK

Bink 2002 Hawks Butte Vineyard Syrah (Mendocino) $40. Focused, lean, and light in body, with strong herbal overtones of basil and oregano that aren't unattractive. Shows enough cherry fruit on the midpalate to appeal, with a long, intense finish. With only 13% alcohol, crisp acids, and herbal notes, this is in many ways a non-Californian Syrah. **87** (9/1/2005)

BIONDI

Biondi 2003 Cabernet Sauvignon (North Coast) $14. The aroma on this wine is fresh enough, with good varietal character, but in the mouth it

USA

turns soft and rustic, and there's a vegetal taste in the finish despite decent berry flavors. 83 —S.H. (4/1/2006)

Biondi 2004 Chardonnay (North Coast) $13. Earthy, simple, and slightly sweet, with candied apricot and herb flavors. Finishes soft and sugary. 82 —S.H. (4/1/2006)

Biondi NV Red Table Wine Red Blend (California) $11. Here's an old style red blend, the kind the Italian-American settlers drank. A blend of Zin, Syrah, Petite Sirah, and Carignane, it's dry, clean, full-bodied, and fruity. Cries out for pasta, tomato sauce, grated cheese, and beef. 85 —S.H. (4/1/2006)

Biondi 2004 Sauvignon Blanc (Mendocino County) $11. My gripe with this wine is that it tastes overly sweet. Too bad, because it has polished fig, melon, and citrus flavors and nice acidity. If it were drier, it would be great. But plenty of people with a sweet tooth will enjoy it. 83 —S.H. (4/1/2006)

Biondi 2004 Viognier (Mendocino) $13. This is a simple, fruity wine, tart in acidity and very dry. It's not as opulent as some Vogniers, instead showing lime and citrus flavors with a slight peachiness. 84 —S.H. (4/1/2006)

BISHOP CREEK

Bishop Creek 2002 Barrel Selection Pinot Noir (Yamhill County) $25. An odd bouquet, possibly mint, though somewhat fishy, leads into a tight, hard, slightly stemmy wine. 85 (11/1/2004)

BISHOP'S PEAK

Bishop's Peak 2002 Cabernet Sauvignon (Paso Robles) $16. Juicy enough in cassis and oak, but with a stubborn green streak, and a rather aggressive texture. 83 —S.H. (10/1/2005)

Bishop's Peak 2001 Cabernet Sauvignon (Paso Robles) $15. A bit heavy and thick, but there's a whole lot of interesting jammy blackberry and currant flavor, intertwined with coffee, chocolate, and herbs. Finishes with a prickly, peppery hotness. 84 —S.H. (6/1/2004)

Bishop's Peak 2004 Chardonnay (Edna Valley) $14. Shows all the qualities of a fine Edna Valley Chard, from the juicy acids to the laser pure lime and nectarine flavors. It's thinned down from the better stuff, but still, not bad. 85 —S.H. (11/1/2006)

Bishop's Peak 2003 Chardonnay (Edna Valley) $14. Brings the Talley touch to a high-acid Chard that has bright flavors of passionfruit and lime. The structure is great, but the finish is a little thin. 84 —S.H. (10/1/2005)

Bishop's Peak 2001 Chardonnay (Central Coast) $13. A bit old for an inexpensive Chard, but the wine is still fresh and fruity, displaying apple and pear flavors that have a thick overlay of oak. Flavor, not finesse, is what you get at this fair price. 85 —S.H. (6/1/2004)

Bishop's Peak 2000 Chardonnay (Central Coast) $13. Very acidic now, actually with a bit of spritz underscoring apple flavors. Very dry, with a bit of oak influence. The finish is tart and bitter, with the taste of pepper and apple. 85 —S.H. (2/1/2003)

Bishop's Peak 2002 Pinot Noir (Central Coast) $16. Talley, one of the best Pinot producers in the state, has come out with a pretty good wine in this second label. It's dry, with rich acids framing cherry and spice flavors, and is delicately structured. 86 —S.H. (10/1/2005)

Bishop's Peak 2001 Pinot Noir (Central Coast) $16. A nice country-style Pinot, a bit rough and earthy, but okay as a substitute for more expensive versions. Dry, with silky tannins and cherry flavors. Second label from Talley. 84 —S.H. (6/1/2004)

Bishop's Peak 2004 Rock Solid Red Red Blend (Paso Robles) $12. Delicious, with enough complexity to make it interesting. A blend of Cabernet Sauvignon and Syrah, the wine has dry, lush berry-cherry, mocha and spice flavors wrapped in ripe, gentle tannins and a balancing bite of acidity. From Talley. 86 —S.H. (9/1/2006)

Bishop's Peak 2003 Syrah (Edna Valley) $16. This second label from Talley is proving to be a good source of less expensive wines from the region. This Syrah is dry and fruity, with firm acids and weighty, but finely grained, tannins. It's a little light on the finish, but pleasant. 85 —S.H. (11/1/2006)

Bishop's Peak 2002 Syrah (Edna Valley) $16. An offshoot of the Talley winery, Bishop's Peak wines typically represent fine value, and this Syrah is no exception. Charred meat, marinade, and coffee mark the nose, while the flavors are on the meaty, savory side but feature just enough lush blackberry fruit to carry them. Ready to drink now. 89 Editors' Choice (9/1/2005)

Bishop's Peak 2001 Syrah (Edna Valley) $15. This is a seriously good wine and how the parent company, Talley, sells it at this price is a miracle. Smells grandly Rhôniste, with a burst of white pepper, blackberry, and leather. It doesn't have the density of a supreme wine, but this great value showcases Central Coast Syrah. 89 —S.H. (12/1/2004)

Bishop's Peak 2000 Syrah (Central Coast) $15. A young, fresh, juicy wine, filled with the tart, sharp acids of youth. Jammy flavors of black raspberries and cherries drink pure and strong in this simple, one-dimensional Syrah. 85 —S.H. (2/1/2003)

Bishop's Peak 2001 Zinfandel (Paso Robles) $14. A decent Zin with some good points and some not so good ones. There's plenty of fresh, succulent cherry berry fruit and spice, but also some residual sweetness that makes it taste a little like cough medicine. 84 —S.H. (6/1/2004)

BLACK BOX

Black Box 2003 Cabernet Sauvignon (Paso Robles) $18. Vintner Ryan Sproule discovered the popularity of boxed wine in Europe and came to California. The result was Black Box. This wine, the equivalent of 4 regular bottles at $4.50 each, is juicy in blackberry, blueberry, and cherry jam flavors, dry and smooth. It's easy to pour, and should stay fresh for weeks due to the vacuum packing. 86 —S.H. (11/15/2004)

Black Box 2004 Cabernet Sauvignon (Paso Robles) $18. The price is unbelievable. This is as good as many Paso Robles Cabs in a full bottle, with forward blackberry jam, coffee, and dry chocolate flavors, and it finishes in a dry, rich swirl of tannins and acids. They kept the alcohol nice and moderate. 85 Best Buy —S.H. (9/1/2006)

Black Box 2002 Cabernet Sauvignon (Paso Robles) $20. Four bottles in one box, but what you get is pretty harsh and lean. Not much going on except acidity, tannins, and a harsh mouthfeel. 82 —S.H. (8/1/2004)

Black Box 2002 Chardonnay (Napa Valley) $22. This is a nice, serviceable little Chard that fulfills the basic requirements of ripe fruit, a bit of oak, and a dry, creamy mouthfeel. It's fine for everyday occasions. 84 —S.H. (12/31/2004)

Black Box 2004 Chardonnay (Monterey County) $22. Here's a good example of a country-style Chard that offers some nice qualities, at a fair price. The equivalent of four regular bottles, it's fruity and off-dry, with peaches and cream flavors that finish clean. 83 Best Buy —S.H. (7/1/2006)

Black Box 2004 Chardonnay (Napa Valley) $24. There's lots to like in this everyday Chard in a box. It's not just the price, because the wine is dry, crisp and fruity, with plenty of creamy Chardonnay character and a refreshingly clean finish. 84 Best Buy —S.H. (9/1/2006)

Black Box 2003 Chardonnay (Monterey County) $20. From a box that holds the equivalent of four regular bottles, a nice, rich Chard. It's all about ripe tropical fruits, peaches and cream, and Asian spices. Finishes long and flavorful. 86 Best Buy —S.H. (8/1/2004)

Black Box 2001 Merlot (Sonoma County) $24. A winning wine, with plenty of personality and flair. The fruity flavors are nice and rich, suggesting black cherries. At approximately six bucks a bottle, this is a great value, and it will hold in the box for days if not weeks. 86 —S.H. (12/31/2004)

Black Box 2003 Merlot (California) $22. Dry and balanced, with a soft Merlot texture that frames cherry, herb, and coffee flavors. Perfect for parties, picnics, and other informal events. 84 Best Buy —S.H. (7/1/2006)

Black Box NV 3L Merlot (Sonoma County) $24. It's not a vintage wine, and there's a slightly green, peppery note, but that just adds a piquant touch to the cherry-cocoa fruit in this easy-to-savor Merlot. It's dry and balanced, and, and, and at the equivalent of a buck-fifty a bottle, it's a super buy. 84 Best Buy —S.H. (9/1/2006)

USA

BLACK COYOTE

Black Coyote 2002 Bates Creek Vineyard Cabernet Sauvignon (Napa Valley) $30. There's a good Cab in here, but it's surrounded by overripe raisined fruit that makes the wine drink hot. There's no quibbling with the deliciousness factor, though. **85** —*S.H. (11/1/2005)*

Black Coyote 2000 Bates Creek Vineyard Cabernet Sauvignon (Napa Valley) $25. Modest aromas of blackberries and oak lead to a thinly-flavored wine. There are some berry notes, but the oak and tannins are really the stars. Drink now. **84** —*S.H. (4/1/2004)*

BLACK CREEK

Black Creek 2000 Bates Creek Vineyard Cabernet Sauvignon (Napa Valley) $25. Modest aromas of blackberries and oak lead to a thinly-flavored wine. There are some berry notes, but the oak and tannins are really the stars. Drink now. **84** —*S.H. (2/1/2004)*

BLACK SHEEP

Black Sheep 2001 Cinsault (Calaveras County) $18. Light in color and in body, a silky wine, but with good acids. Has enjoyable flavors of cherries, rose petal, tea, and dried autumn leaves, and is very dry. **86** —*S.H. (3/1/2005)*

Black Sheep 2002 Sémillon (Calaveras County) $13. Starts with a barnyardy smell, then turns rich and creamy in the mouth, vibrant in vanilla, butterscotch, peach, and floral flavors. **84** —*S.H. (3/1/2005)*

Black Sheep 2001 Shiraz (Calaveras County) $16. Dry, robust, and full-bodied, with dusty tannins framing earth, berry, and cherry flavors. Picks up some sweet cocoa on the finish. **85** —*S.H. (3/1/2005)*

Black Sheep 1997 Zinfandel (Amador County) $14. **87 Best Buy** —*S.H. (5/1/2000)*

Black Sheep 2001 Clockspring Vineyard Zinfandel (Amador County) $16. An oak-dominated style that covers up otherwise pretty cherry, blackberry and spice flavors. Tannic and a bit harsh on the finish. **81** *(11/1/2003)*

BLACKBIRD VINEYARDS

Blackbird Vineyards 2003 Merlot (Oak Knoll) $70. Wonderful Merlot, rich and complex, with the classy mouthfeel that Napa provides so effortlessly. You might mistake it for a valley floor Cabernet for the new oak-infused blackberry, cherry, and cocoa flavors and soft, immediate appeal. The tannins are there, but they're melted, sweet, and gentle. Drink now. **90** —*S.H. (12/15/2006)*

BLACKJACK

Blackjack 1997 Harmonie Bordeaux Blend (Santa Barbara County) $32. **91** *(11/1/2000)*

Blackjack 1998 Laetitia Vineyard Pinot Noir (San Luis Obispo County) $32. **84** —*M.S. (10/1/2000)*

BLACKRIDGE CANYON

Blackridge Canyon 2001 Pinot Noir (Napa Valley) $20. A polished Pinot with good varietal character, it's showing cherry liqueur, mocha, and spicy flavors, in a delicately oaked, lightly elegant texture. **87** —*S.H. (8/1/2005)*

BLACKSTONE

Blackstone 2003 Cabernet Sauvignon (Napa Valley) $12. Here's a nice, polished Cabernet that offers easy drinking right away, yet has some extra complexity that elevates it. It's softly fruity, with finely ground tannins and a long, spicy finish. **87** —*S.H. (12/31/2006)*

Blackstone 2003 Cabernet Sauvignon (California) $12. Tastes raw and sharp in acidity, accentuating the tannins and making the wine brittle. It's very dry, with modest cherry-berry flavors. Tasted twice, with consistent results. **82** —*S.H. (4/1/2006)*

Blackstone 2002 Cabernet Sauvignon (Sonoma County) $15. Despite some nice blackberry and cassis fruit, this wine has a green stalky flavor that makes it sharp, and puts it solidly into the everyday category. **83** —*S.H. (10/1/2005)*

Blackstone 2002 Cabernet Sauvignon (California) $12. Smells of toast, vanilla, and cream. On the palate, tobacco is the dominant flavor, and earth and black currants take a backseat. Finishes lean and herbal. **83** *(6/1/2004)*

Blackstone 1998 Cabernet Sauvignon (California) $10. Country-style, with berry and dust aromas and rough, fruity flavors. It's a bit scoury around the edge, but clean, with a sweet finish. A nice everyday wine at a fair price. **84** —*S.H. (11/15/2001)*

Blackstone 2002 Reserve Cabernet Sauvignon (Dry Creek Valley) $28. The pretty aroma mingles well-toasted, caramelly oak with ripe black currant fruit. In the mouth, turns rather bitter and astringent in rugged tannins. A year or two of aging could soften it up. **85** —*S.H. (10/1/2005)*

Blackstone 1997 Chardonnay (California) $10. **84** —*L.W. (7/1/1999)*

Blackstone 2005 Chardonnay (Monterey County) $12. Rich and vibrant in acid-accented lime, peach, pink grapefruit, and tangerine flavors, this creamy, smooth Chard is partly barrel fermented, which gives it a toasty, buttery edge. **85** —*S.H. (10/1/2006)*

Blackstone 2004 Chardonnay (Monterey County) $11. This isn't a bad price for a nice, everyday Chardonnay with some pleasant peach, lemon rind, pineapple, and vanilla-oaky flavors that finish clean and dry. **84** —*S.H. (12/31/2005)*

Blackstone 2004 Chardonnay (Sonoma County) $16. Chard doesn't get any riper, unless it's late harvest. Floods the mouth with peach custard, pineapple, guava, nectarine and apple flavors, with a rich, creamy, oaky finish. It's a bit one-dimensional, but what a tasty dimension. **86** —*S.H. (12/15/2006)*

Blackstone 2003 Chardonnay (Monterey County) $10. There's a firmness in the mouth with this Chard. The fruit is ripe and spicy, the oak is just right, and the acidity is high, leading to a tart, dry finish. **85 Best Buy** —*S.H. (10/1/2005)*

Blackstone 2003 Chardonnay (Sonoma County) $16. There's some richness in this well-made wine, which is showing peach and tropical fruit flavors, with vanilla and toast accents. Finishes a bit astringent, calling for rich shellfish. **85** —*S.H. (7/1/2005)*

Blackstone 2002 Chardonnay (Sonoma County) $16. A tremendously woody wine, with butter, cream, and white pepper aromas, and toasty oak on the palate. Finishes rough, with tangy lemon flavors. **84** *(6/1/2004)*

Blackstone 2000 Chardonnay (Monterey County) $10. There are pretty aromas of tropical fruits and spices, but it turns a little hot and rough in the mouth. The fruity flavors are sugary, although the acidity is fine. Think of it as a country style wine, with all the wrappings of Chard, at an everyday price. **83** —*S.H. (12/31/2001)*

Blackstone 1999 Chardonnay (Monterey County) $10. Pleasant enough and Chard-like, with aromas of tangerine, peach, and a kiss of honeyed oak. It's got enough residual sugar to almost fall into the off-dry category. Well made and certainly affordable. **82** —*S.H. (5/1/2001)*

Blackstone 2002 Reserve Chardonnay (Santa Lucia Highlands) $26. Medium weight and well balanced, there's melon, pear, and oak on the palate, and aromas of green pea, citrus, and toast. Finishes on the short side, with smoke and toast. **86** *(6/1/2004)*

Blackstone 2005 Gewürztraminer (Monterey County) $12. This will be popular among the crowd that likes an affordable fruity wine that's just a tiny bit sweet. Packs loads of apricot, white peach, honeysuckle, pineapple, vanilla, gardenia, and Asian spice flavors, and those zesty Monterey acids make it clean and lively. **84** —*S.H. (12/31/2006)*

Blackstone 2004 Gewürztraminer (Monterey County) $11. Floral, spicy, and dry, this Gewürz shows forward flavors of pink grapefruit, with a peppery finish. It has good acidity and a clean finish. **84** —*S.H. (10/1/2005)*

Blackstone 1997 Merlot (Napa Valley) $13. **86** *(11/15/1999)*

Blackstone 2003 Merlot (Napa Valley) $18. The winery's Napa Merlot is firmer and better structured than the Sonoma Merlot, with a richer tannin structure and greater acidity. It's a dry, stylish wine, with blackberry and herb flavors enhanced with a dash of oak. **86** —*S.H. (4/1/2006)*

Blackstone 2003 Merlot (Sonoma County) $16. A nice, simple Merlot, with pleasant blackberry and cherry flavors. It's fully dry, with good tannic support, and finishes with rich, ripe fruit. **85** —*S.H. (7/1/2005)*

Blackstone 2003 Merlot (California) $12. For those everyday purposes when you need a dry, balanced, and full-bodied red, this is a good choice. It has pleasant flavors of plums, blackberries, and spice, with a chocolaty finish. **84** —*S.H. (12/15/2005)*

Blackstone 2002 Merlot (Monterey County) $17. A bit on the herbal side, showing green, woody notes. Turns tannic in the mouth, with blackberry and coffee flavors, and finishes dry. **84** —*S.H. (12/31/2004)*

Blackstone 2002 Merlot (Sonoma County) $16. Soft and juicy, this dry wine is infused with pure cherry and red plum flavors. It's tannic, but smooth and complex. Shows real finesse through the spicy finish. **87** —*S.H. (10/1/2005)*

Blackstone 2002 Merlot (Napa Valley) $17. Simple and fruity in blackberries and coffee, this wine is dry and sharp, with some stalky notes. **83** —*S.H. (5/1/2005)*

Blackstone 2002 Merlot (California) $12. The "goal is consistency" for this 950,000-case production, which is also the number-one selling red wine in the States. It's soft on the palate, with simple blackberry and raspberry fruit flavors, with briary-acorny accents. Sours up on the finish, which shows herbal, seeped-tea flavors. **84** *(6/1/2004)*

Blackstone 2001 Merlot (Sonoma County) $16. Has mocha and vanilla flavors, but also an edge of sourness. It's plump in the mouth, with soft tannins; oak is heavy on the finish. **86** *(6/1/2004)*

Blackstone 1999 Merlot (Napa Valley) $16. This Merlot shows sautéed mushroom and rich, earthy notes along with the expected blackberry aromas, and the sharp mintiness of wood. Drinks deeply fruity, with soft, velvety tannins and slightly soft acids. The finish turns sweet. **86** —*S.H. (11/15/2001)*

Blackstone 1999 Merlot (California) $10. Packed with berry and spice aromas, this rustic wine has jagged tannins. It's your basic table red, with good acidity, alcohol, a deep color, and ripe flavors. Best of all, the price tag is just right. **84** —*S.H. (11/15/2001)*

Blackstone 1998 Merlot (Napa Valley) $18. Good color and quite a bit of charm. Some impressive aromas of blackberry, mocha, violets, and smoky oak, and similar rich, deep flavors. The tannins are soft and inviting. It misses excellence by a hair, but it's a very good wine. **89** —*S.H. (5/1/2001)*

Blackstone 2001 Reserve Merlot (Napa Valley) $28. Nice and ripe, with sweet cocoa, cherry, and cola flavors, and lush, smooth tannins. Finishes with sharp acidity, and might benefit from a year or two in the bottle. **86** —*S.H. (2/1/2005)*

Blackstone 2000 Reserve Merlot (Napa Valley) $28. Nose has an herbal edge and stewy fruit aromas. Dry, woody tannins show on the palate, where the flavors are of taut plum fruit, tree bark, and a hint of stem. Finishes dry and rough. **85** *(6/1/2004)*

Blackstone 2005 Pinot Grigio (Monterey County) $12. Dry, high in acidity and fiercely clean all the way through the finish, this PG is fruitier than you might expect. Small amounts of Riesling and Tocai Friulano lend flowery citrus notes. The alcohol is a refreshingly low 12.5%. **85** —*S.H. (10/1/2006)*

Blackstone 2004 Pinot Noir (Monterey County) $12. Sideways converts looking for a relatively inexpensive Pinot will find this one a refreshing alternative to a big, heavy, tannic red wine. It's light and silky, with cherry, cola, and herb flavors, and that bright Monterey acidity. **84** —*S.H. (12/15/2005)*

Blackstone 2003 Pinot Noir (Monterey County) $12. Good value in a dry Pinot with real Salinas quality. Delicately structured and elegantly crisp, with silky tannins and cherry, cola, and herb flavors. **85** —*S.H. (5/1/2005)*

Blackstone 2002 Pinot Noir (Monterey County) $12. Proper varietal character here, a decent, regional wine with some ripe fruit and a long, tart finish. Cherries, coffee, and strawberries, with good acids. **85** *(11/1/2004)*

Blackstone 2001 Pinot Noir (Monterey County) $12. Varietally correct in the soft, silky tannins, crisp acids, and notes of berries. This simple wine also has a baked edge and finishes hot. **83** —*S.H. (9/1/2004)*

Blackstone 2002 Reserve Pinot Noir (Santa Lucia Highlands) $28. A nice Pinot with the firm backbone of acidity associated with this cool appellation. The flavors range from cherries and cola through tobacco and earthy mushrooms. Finishes a little watery and harsh. **85** —*S.H. (11/1/2004)*

Blackstone 2002 Reserve Pinot Noir (Santa Lucia Highlands) $28. On the nose, cherry aromas are accented by tea and root beer notes. It's a bit light in weight on the palate, with flavors of cherry, tree bark and beet. Tart and moderately long on the finish. 900 cases made. **86** *(6/1/2004)*

Blackstone 2005 Riesling (Monterey County) $12. Delicate and light in the mouth, with low alcohol, this clean Riesling has bright Monterey acids. The flavors are a little watery, suggesting peaches, apples, and flowers, and the finish is off-dry. **83** —*S.H. (10/1/2006)*

Blackstone 2004 Riesling (Monterey County) $11. A little bitter, especially in the finish, but offers pleasantly ripe peach and floral flavors. Thoroughly dry. **84** —*S.H. (10/1/2005)*

Blackstone 2004 Sauvignon Blanc (Monterey County) $10. This is a crisply tart, dry wine, light in body, with pleasant flavors of green apples and peaches. There's a lingering finish of tangerine that adds nuance. **85 Best Buy** —*S.H. (10/1/2005)*

Blackstone 2003 Sauvignon Blanc (Monterey County) $10. Grassy aromas are balanced out by yellow fruit and cream; citrus and more yellow stone fruit shows on the palate, which is soft and a little flabby. Finishes tart, with grapefruit flavors. **84** *(6/1/2004)*

Blackstone 2002 Syrah (Sonoma County) $16. Big-bodied yet silky-smooth, this Syrah has a slight rusticity, yet also shows some elegance and finesse, courtesy of vanilla and toast accents. With its fruit and herb flavors, it should be fine with rich fare like roast lamb with olive tapenade. **86** *(9/1/2005)*

Blackstone 2002 Syrah (California) $16. This dry, stylish Syrah shows real flair in the rich berry, herb, spice and oak flavors, and the harmonious balance of acids and tannins. Soft and velvety, it has some complexity in the finish. **86** —*S.H. (7/1/2005)*

Blackstone 2001 Syrah (California) $12. Pretty unforgiving, with pruny fruit and fireplace aromas, and sour, earthy flavors. Medium bodied, simple. **83** *(6/1/2004)*

Blackstone 2002 Hamilton Vineyards Reserve Syrah (Dry Creek Valley) $28. Earthy and sharp, with coffee and berry flavors that finish dry and harsh. **82** —*S.H. (12/31/2005)*

Blackstone 2002 Reserve Syrah (Dry Creek Valley) $28. Wine lovers who are more tolerant of lavish oak than our tasters will find a lot to like in this lush, velvety Syrah. Toasty and smoky from start to finish, but there is some superconcentrated blackberry fruit to back it up. A bit chewy on the finish, with unsubtle notes of vanilla. **86** *(9/1/2005)*

Blackstone 2003 Zinfandel (Sonoma County) $16. Textbook Zin 101 here, a dry, full-bodied wine with flavors of wild berries, cherries, raisins, and tobacco, and rich, edgy tannins. Take advantage of the acids and try this with rich cheeses and sauces. **86** —*S.H. (12/15/2005)*

Blackstone 2003 Zinfandel (California) $12. Rustic and sharp-edged in the mouth, with jagged tannins and acids, this Zin has a mixture of raisiny, just right, peppery, green fruit flavors. It finishes dry and astringent. **82** —*S.H. (10/1/2006)*

Blackstone 2002 Zinfandel (Sonoma County) $16. The wine is round and soft in the mouth, with juicy plum fruit jazzed up with a little herb. Finishes with rustic black-pepper and tree-bark flavors. **87** *(6/1/2004)*

Blackstone 2002 Zinfandel (California) $12. Hard to like for its thin, vegetal flavors and bitterness. Probably a gooey pizza will soften it up. **82** —*S.H. (8/1/2005)*

Blackstone 2002 Reserve Zinfandel (Dry Creek Valley) $28. Here's a wine that deserves its reserve status. It's pure in varietal character, from the briary, white pepper, wild berry, and coffee flavors to the sturdy tannins, and that feral edge of friendly aggression that marks a good Zin. But it's a bone dry, balanced wine, with a distinctive individuality. **90 Editors' Choice** —*S.H. (12/15/2005)*

BLISS

Bliss 2002 Heritage Series Cabernet Sauvignon (Mendocino) $11. Raw, harsh, and medicinal in berry flavors, this Cabernet is just barely acceptable. **80** —*S.H. (12/15/2005)*

Bliss 2005 Heritage Series Chardonnay (Mendocino) $12. Opens with peach and apricot aromas, then turns fruity and simple, with a dryish, creamy mouthfeel. **83** —*S.H. (12/15/2006)*

Bliss 2004 Heritage Series Chardonnay (Mendocino) $11. Clumsy and simple, with a tart, tobaccoey taste that's vaguely reminiscent of canned peaches. **81** —*S.H. (12/15/2005)*

Bliss 2004 Heritage Series Merlot (Mendocino) $12. Ripe, juicy, and simple, with blackberry-infused espresso flavors that finish with some sweetness. **82** —*S.H. (12/15/2006)*

Bliss 2002 Heritage Series Merlot (Mendocino) $25. Juicy-ripe, with tasty cherry, black raspberry, and blackberry flavors wrapped in angular tannins, and with a sharpness throughout. A pleasant, country-style wine. **83** —*S.H. (12/15/2005)*

Bliss 2002 Pinot Noir (Mendocino) $11. Smells funky and cheesy, two aromas that don't blow off in this rustic, dry wine. Too bad, because the Pinot flavors and body are nice. **82** —*S.H. (12/15/2005)*

BLOCKHEADIA RINGNOSII

Blockheadia Ringnosii 2001 Zinfandel (Mendocino) $24. A very pretty, fruit-driven wine, loaded with bright, spicy, cherry, raspberry, plum, toast, licorice, and herb flavors. Tannins are firm yet ripe, while the finish is fairly long, though quite oaky. Lingers nicely at the end with the fruit forward. **90** *(11/1/2003)*

Blockheadia Ringnosii 2001 Zinfandel (Napa Valley) $24. Smoke and tar lead the way on the nose, but rich, ripe fruit follows up on the palate. This is a firm, ripe wine, with layers of black cherry, plum, cassis, chocolate, tar, toast, coffee, spice, citrus, and herbs, all couched in supple, silky tannins. **91 Editors' Choice** *(11/1/2003)*

BLUE MOON

Blue Moon 2004 Pinot Gris (Oregon) $11. Widely available, this distinctively packaged wine has little going on in the way of flavor. Lightly herbal, citric, and thin, it could be almost any generic white grape. **83** —*P.G. (2/1/2006)*

BLUE ROCK

Blue Rock 2003 Cabernet Sauvignon (Alexander Valley) $45. Lots of upscale features in this polished Cab. It shows modern characteristics of expressively ripe, lush blackberry, blueberry, cassis, and chocolate flavors that are wrapped in a soft, velvety texture. The softness may limit ageability. **89** —*S.H. (12/15/2006)*

Blue Rock 2003 Best Barrel Malbec (Alexander Valley) $75. Owner Kenny Kahn reserves the "Best Barrel" designation for his best wine. This year it's a Malbec. Pours inky black, and explodes with blackberry pie filling, chocolate, plum sauce, licorice, and cedar aromas. Drinks as powerfully rich as it smells, offering immense flavors and luxuriously smooth, velvety tannins. Very soft. Drink now through 2009 before the fruit fades. **92** —*S.H. (12/15/2006)*

Blue Rock 2003 Syrah (Alexander Valley) $36. As softly gooey as a sauce you'd pour over sponge cake or ice cream, with blackberry, blueberry, and peppery rum and plum flavors. Dry and delicious, but really needs more acidity, structure, tannins, or all of the above. **85** —*S.H. (12/15/2006)*

BOCAGE

Bocage 2001 Chardonnay (Monterey) $11. An unoaked Chard, and it's fascinating to see what Santa Lucia Highlands fruit tastes like. It's vibrantly fruity, a wine whose citrus, apple and peach flavors are highlighted by the crisp acids characteristic of the appellation. **86** —*S.H. (12/15/2002)*

Bocage 2005 Unoaked Chardonnay (Monterey) $13. You want pure Monterey Chardonnay? Go here. It's all about peaches, apricots, pineapples, limes, and kiwis, not to mention fresh crisp acidity. Where all that

cream came from is a mystery, given that the wine is unoaked. Good wine, good price. **86** —*S.H. (12/1/2006)*

Bocage 2004 Unoaked Chardonnay (Monterey) $11. With no oak on this wine, you can taste how beautifully Monterey terroir develops Chardonnay. The wine is all crisp acids and ripe flavors of guava, pineapple, mango, and peach. Vanilla, too, which must come from the grapes, not barrels. What a delightfully drinkable wine this is. **87 Best Buy** —*S.H. (12/15/2005)*

Bocage 2003 Unoaked Chardonnay (Monterey) $11. With no oak, what you get in the aroma are the prettiest, cleanest scents of ripe apples, peaches, pears, and spices. Would earn a higher score if it weren't soft and syrupy-sweet. **85** —*S.H. (3/1/2005)*

Bocage 2004 Merlot (Monterey) $13. Rustic and simple, this Merlot smells a little vegetal, and then turns fairly sweet in fruit jam flavors. This is a second label from San Saba. **82** —*S.H. (12/15/2006)*

Bocage 2003 Merlot (Monterey) $11. This Merlot won't challenge Napa, but it's a nicely ripe, dry wine. It has powerful blackberry jam and cherry flavors and firm tannins, and finishes long in fruity taste, with a chocolaty sweetness. **84** —*S.H. (9/1/2006)*

Bocage 2002 Merlot (Monterey) $11. Soft as melted butter, and oaky with vanilla and smoke, this wine offers ripe flavors of red and black cherries and cocoa, with just enough crispness to balance. **85** —*S.H. (3/1/2005)*

BOCCE

Bocce 2004 Pinot Grigio (California) $10. Let the sulfur blow off and you've got a decently dry, crisp sipper. It's a tart wine, with mineral and citrus flavors that finish swift and clean. **84** —*S.H. (2/1/2006)*

Bocce 2001 Rosso Red Blend (California) $6. As the name implies, an old-style Italian-American type wine, full-bodied and robust but gentle in tannins. Fully dry, with earthy-berry flavors. Mix of 7 common varietals. **84 Best Buy** —*S.H. (3/1/2005)*

BOEGER

Boeger 2001 Barbera (El Dorado) $15. Big and merciless, a mountain man of a wine that has enough tannins to fell a Sierra sequoia. There are probably some berry flavors buried deep down beneath, but you won't find them for a decade or so. It's very dry, the sort of wine to gulp with hamburgers in the backyard without giving much thought to finesse. **84** —*S.H. (12/1/2003)*

Boeger 1998 Barbera (El Dorado) $14. Lots of black cherry fruit, with notes of dry, dusty earth and truffle, and a strong cola element. It's very dry and supple, a wine of character. The fruity flavors are rich, and the tannins are soft and rounded. **89** —*S.H. (8/1/2001)*

Boeger 1996 Bordeaux Blend (El Dorado County) $18. 88 —*L.W. (12/31/1999)*

Boeger 1999 Reserve Petite Sirah (El Dorado) $25. There's lots to like in this easy drinking wine, although it's a bit pricy for the quality. Tasters found the fruity flavors light but tasty, while the tannins are not a problem. It's also an oaky wine, but the smooth, gentle texture is pleasant. **85** *(4/1/2003)*

Boeger 1997 Pinot Noir (El Dorado) $20. 88 —*L.W. (5/1/2000)*

Boeger 1999 Reserve Pinot Noir (El Dorado) $25. If anyone can succeed with Pinot in the warmish Sierra Foothills, it's pioneering Boeger. This effort is a good start. It's correctly light and silky, with red cherry, espresso, cherry tomato and crushed hard spice aromas and flavors. All they need to do is put some depth and complexity in, and they'll have a winner. **85** —*S.H. (2/1/2003)*

Boeger 1998 Sauvignon Blanc (El Dorado County) $13. 87 —*L.W. (3/1/2000)*

Boeger 1998 Reserve Tempranillo (El Dorado) $25. The great grape of Spain's Rioja produces a very soft and fruity wine, with smoky strawberry flavors, and very dry. It has dusty tannins and acidity. Your tongue sticks to the roof of your mouth, suggesting that this wine needs food. There's also a hint of smoked meat in there somewhere. **86** —*S.H. (5/1/2002)*

Boeger 2001 Zinfandel (El Dorado) $15. Marked by green-edged cola notes, the wine doesn't show the hallmarks of ripe Zinfandel. Toasty oak and bright acidity are most apparent, with a touch of cherry and spice. Unusual. **84** *(11/1/2003)*

Boeger 1997 Estate Zinfandel (El Dorado) $15. Tar and cherries in the nose, and the follow-through shows thick, ripe, sweet cherry fruit with some dark, tarry underpinnings. Good concentration and a long finish. There is 11% Petite Sirah, which adds color and depth. **87** *—P.G. (3/1/2001)*

Boeger 2001 Walker Vineyard Zinfandel (El Dorado) $18. Cola and coffee notes are the watchwords here. But we're missing some primary fruit flavors. It shows interest nonetheless. Tannins are mild and the finish is moderate in length. **84** *(11/1/2003)*

Boeger 1998 Walker Vineyard Zinfandel (El Dorado County) $18. 86 *—S.H. (5/1/2000)*

Boeger 1997 Walker Vineyard Zinfandel (El Dorado) $18. Thick, chewy, cherry fruit, with lots of wood behind it. Simple, forward, and quite pleasant, without pretension. **85** *—P.G. (3/1/2001)*

BOGLE

Bogle 2003 Cabernet Sauvignon (California) $11. Made from Delta and Sonoma grapes, this is a fine Cab if you're looking for something relatively plush at an everyday price. It's soft, with melted chocolate and intense blackberry pie flavors, with a nice edge of spice. **85** *—S.H. (11/1/2006)*

Bogle 2002 Cabernet Sauvignon (California) $12. A little rustic and pruny, but not a bad little wine. The flavors are of blackberries and chocolate, and the finish is dry. **83** *—S.H. (10/1/2005)*

Bogle 1998 Chardonnay (California) $9. 86 Best Buy *—L.W. (12/31/1999)*

Bogle 2005 Chardonnay (California) $9. Soft and simple, with candied peach and pear flavors and some oaky, leesy influence that makes it a little fancier. **83** *—S.H. (12/1/2006)*

Bogle 2004 Chardonnay (California) $9. This inexpensive Chard tastes herbal, with dill and thyme flavors that turn mildly peachy and appley on the finish. **83** *—S.H. (11/1/2005)*

Bogle 2000 Chardonnay (Clarksburg) $9. Toasty oak and bright citrus flavors form the core of this snappy wine. Clean and fresh on the finish. **85** *—J.M. (11/15/2001)*

Bogle 1998 Colby Ranch Reserve Chardonnay (Clarksburg) $18. 86 *(6/1/2000)*

Bogle 2005 Chenin Blanc (California) $9. This one's off-dry to semi-sweet, which may explain the low acidity. It has forward flavors of apples, pineapples, and peaches. **84** *—S.H. (12/1/2006)*

Bogle 2004 Chenin Blanc (Clarksburg) $7. Sometimes you just want a quaffer with a trace of sweetness, lots of fruit, and acidity to make those tastebuds tingle. Clarksburg has long been known as a congenial home for Chenin Blanc, and in this wine Bogle has produced the perfect drench for watermelon, fresh fruit, cheeseburgers, and fried chicken. Just don't get sand in your glass. **84** *—S.H. (8/1/2005)*

Bogle 2003 Chenin Blanc (Clarksburg) $7. Easily earns its Best Buy status with its rich, fruity flavors and high acidity. Seems to have a little residual sugar, but those acids really balance. Try as an alternative to Sauvignon Blanc, Viognier. **86 Best Buy** *—S.H. (7/1/2005)*

Bogle 2004 Merlot (California) $11. Acceptable, but with harsh acidity and semi-sweet berry flavors. **80** *—S.H. (12/1/2006)*

Bogle 2003 Merlot (California) $9. A good price for the juicy black cherry, blueberry, and cocoa flavors, with an edge of oak, and the dry, balanced finish. Yes, it's rustic. But it will wash that steak down just fine. **84 Best Buy** *—S.H. (10/1/2005)*

Bogle 1998 Petite Sirah (California) $10. 87 *—J.C. (11/15/1999)*

Bogle 2003 Petite Sirah (California) $10. Pizza? Lasagna? This is the perfect inexpensive wine. It's full-bodied and brawny, and totally dry, with big tannins and fresh, deep flavors of blackberries, coffee, cocoa, and dried leather. Shows real character, and will develop for a few years. **87 Best Buy** *—S.H. (11/1/2005)*

Bogle 2001 Petite Sirah (California) $10. This was a panel favorite for an affordable, value wine. It's simple and richly flavored with

blackberry, cherry, and chocolate notes, and has firm, dry tannins. The pretty fruit flavors and oriental spices last through the finish. **84** *(4/1/2003)*

Bogle 2000 Petite Sirah (California) $10. Another good value from this Sierra Foothills producer, with all tasters rating it between 83 and 85 points. We liked it for its simple but tasty cherry syrup flavors and round, full mouthfeel. Don't look for added complexities, just a nice drinking quaffer. **84** *(4/1/2003)*

Bogle 2003 Phantom Red Blend (California) $16. A little soft and hot, but redeemed by rich flavors of chocolate, blackberries, coffee, and even pecan pie. There's a rusticity here, but something about the blend of Petite Sirah, Zinfandel, and Mourvèdre is appealing. **87** *—S.H. (12/1/2006)*

Bogle 1998 Sauvignon Blanc (California) $7. 85 Best Buy *—L.W. (3/1/2000)*

Bogle 2005 Sauvignon Blanc (California) $9. This fruit-forward Sauvignon is a creative blend of Monterey and Amador, combining ripe Sierra Foothills fruit with coastal acidity. Figs, citrus fruits, melons, peaches, green apples, the fruit goes on and on. **85 Best Buy** *—S.H. (11/15/2006)*

Bogle 2004 Sauvignon Blanc (California) $8. It's not unusual for a young white wine to bristle with SO2 after you pop the cork, but it's never a pleasant experience. This one was slow to blow off, marring what otherwise is a pleasantly crisp and fruity wine. **83** *—S.H. (11/1/2005)*

Bogle 2003 Old Vine Zinfandel (California) $11. Ripe enough in berry fruit and totally soft, this wine is a little too sweet for me, suggesting as it does a dessert confection, although it's probably technically dry. **83** *—S.H. (10/1/2005)*

Bogle 2001 Old Vine Zinfandel (California) $11. Smooth and supple-textured, with a modest but classy blend of cocoa, coffee, black cherry, plum, vanilla, and spice flavors, finishing with good length. **89 Best Buy** *(11/1/2003)*

Bogle 1997 Old Vine Cuvée Zinfandel (California) $10. 90 Best Buy *—P.G. (11/15/1999)*

BOITANO

Boitano 2002 Barbera (Shenandoah Valley (CA)) $18. Nice spaghetti and meatballs wine, with berry, earth, and sweet tobacco flavors and sturdy tannins. Finishes dry and robust. **85** *—S.H. (3/1/2005)*

Boitano 2002 Port (Sierra Foothills) $14. Mute aroma, but turns sweet and chocolatey-cherry in the mouth, with good acidity, and very clean. A pleasant dessert quaffer. **86** *—S.H. (2/1/2005)*

Boitano 2002 Sapore di Cielo Red Blend (Sierra Foothills) $25. Rustic, sharp in acids, with cola and rhubarb flavors. **83** *—S.H. (2/1/2005)*

Boitano 2002 Mokelumne Hill Sangiovese (Calaveras County) $24. Here's a Chianti-style wine, silky and acidic, with cherry-earthy flavors that drink very dry. It's pretty oaky, too. **84** *—S.H. (3/1/2005)*

BOKISCH

Bokisch 2004 Albariño (Lodi) $16. Like a good, unoaked Sauvignon Blanc, this wine is very dry and high in acids, with citrus, apricot, and mineral flavors that make you think of oysters. It's a very good wine, and showcases the enormous possibilities of this variety in California. **89** *—S.H. (12/31/2005)*

Bokisch 2002 Albariño (Lodi) $16. This Spanish variety, rare in California, is distinctive. It's full-bodied, with a thick texture and dense weight that carry rich, almost syrupy, flavors of peaches and apricots. But brilliant acidity keeps it all lively, and it's fully dry. **88** *—S.H. (2/1/2004)*

Bokisch 2004 Garnacha (Lodi) $18. Soft and melted in tannins and acids, this dry red wine, which is the same as Grenache, has intense flavors of perfectly ripened cherries, with a rich coat of oak. There's a peppery tingly feeling that suggests a nice barbecued steak. **85** *—S.H. (12/31/2005)*

Bokisch 2003 Graciano (Lodi) $26. Simple and soft, this rustic wine has ripe red cherry flavors. It's very dry, with all kinds of oaky, peppery spices. It's not an insult to say it's the perfect upscale cheeseburger red. **84** *—S.H. (12/31/2005)*

USA

Bokisch 2001 Graciano (Lodi) $19. Very dark, densely layered, and dramatically full-bodied, with its lush, thick tannins and gobs of rich black cherry fruit. Tastes and feels like melted jam, flooding the palate with oozy flavors. But it's bone dry. The trace of astringency in the finish may go away in a few years. **88** —S.H. (4/1/2004)

Bokisch 2003 Tempranillo (Lodi) $21. Tempranillo continues to struggle to find a California identity. This warm-climate version strikes one path, in the direction of a soft, dry and fruity wine, with cherry flavors and an earthy, dried herb edge. The next step is for depth and complexity. **84** —S.H. (12/31/2005)

Bokisch 2001 Tempranillo (Lodi) $19. A nicely fruity wine that showcases this Spanish variety's pretty cherry, rose petal, and dry chocolate aromas and flavors, and lets Lodi's heat contribute ripe, soft tannins. It's an easy wine, very dry, with a bite of acidity on the finish. **86** —S.H. (4/1/2004)

BONACCORSI

Bonaccorsi 2003 Sanford & Benedict Vineyard Pinot Noir (Santa Rita Hills) $42. Jammy and fat. All primary fruit (cherries) and loads of toast. Itï¿?s rich and ripe, with loads of cherry fruit flavor, scads of sweet oak. Juicy acidity. Best 2006–2012. **92** —S.H. (6/1/2005)

Bonaccorsi 2001 Syrah (Central Coast) $32. From Spago's former sommelier and new winery owner, Michael Bonaccorsi, a big, rich, gutsy Syrah with plenty of ripe fruit and gritty tannins. There are some nice flavors of blackberries and cassis. **89** —S.H. (12/1/2003)

Bonaccorsi 2003 Bien Nacido Vineyard Syrah (Santa Maria Valley) $50. Awesome wine, big, brooding, and tannic, yet amazingly rich in fruit, this is one for the cellar. Massive blackberry, coffee, and chocolate fruit flavors are well-integrated with smoky oak, and the finish is huge, long, and fruity-spicy. A real beauty now, but so immature, it would be a shame not to give it four or five more years to develop additional bottle complexities. **93 Cellar Selection** —S.H. (8/1/2006)

BONAIR

Bonair 2003 Cabernet Sauvignon (Yakima Valley) $16. Here is a ripe, full-flavored Cabernet that clocks in at a moderate 12.5% alcohol. The blend includes 10% Merlot and 15% Cabernet Franc. Surely a great strength of cool-climate, Yakima Valley Cabernet is its ability to obtain ripe, naturally tart, mixed fruit flavors, and avoid joining the syrupy, jammy, hedonistic crowd. What's here are pure varietal flavors of blackberry and cassis, just lightly kissed with oak. **88** —P.G. (6/1/2006)

Bonair 2002 Morrison Vineyard Cabernet Sauvignon (Yakima Valley) $21. Here is a full-blown 15% bruiser. Chewy, tannic, and rugged, from vines almost 40 years old. Thick and chalky, the fruit has plenty of blackberry and black cherry flavor, with a smoky streak and a hint of black tea in the slightly bitter tannins. All that stuffing needs some additional bottle time to loosen it up and soften the rough edges. **88** —P.G. (6/1/2006)

Bonair 2004 Chardonnay (Yakima Valley) $13. As with the reserve, the house style is to make a soft, lightly buttery, very approachable wine. Nice light tropical fruit flavors are a blend of mango, pineapple, and banana. There is nothing heavy-handed about the oak, it's nicely layered into the background. **87** —P.G. (6/1/2006)

Bonair 2003 Château Puryear Vineyard Reserve Chardonnay (Yakima Valley) $21. Bigger, rounder, toastier yet stylistically of a piece with the winery's regular Chardonnay, this appealing bottling is extra soft and extra rich. The flavors are nicely balanced and creamy, finishing with a sweet Bordeaux blend comes on with well-ripened fruit, pretty cherry flavors accented with barrel notes of kahlùa, espresso, and smoke. Concentrated and smooth throughout, it is the star of this new winery's first lineup of wines. **88** —P.G. (6/1/2006)

Bonair 2004 Port Gewürztraminer (Yakima Valley) $21. Yes it is 100% Gewürztraminer, and yes the winery calls it Port, listing the alcohol content at 19.5%. Unusual it certainly may be, but it is really quite well made, with varietal character showcasing very tasty candied citrus and sugared rose petals. The brandy is neither hot nor intrusive. All in all it's an intriguing, versatile, and unique dessert wine. **90** —P.G. (6/1/2006)

Bonair 1998 Merlot (Yakima Valley) $18. Bonair has made a big, earthy bruiser of a Merlot in this vintage, with complex aromas mixing ripe fruit, leather, earth, and a whiff of barnyard. The fruit is topnotch, showing cassis and black cherry, along with firm, dark chocolate in the tannic finish. **89** —P.G. (9/1/2002)

Bonair 2001 Riesling (Yakima Valley) $10. A pretty, forward, fruity nose with fruit and blossom scents mixed together; a lovely anise note rides over the top. This wine also has plenty of fruit power, and the fruit has some texture and flesh, extending into a smooth, spicy, lively finish. **90** —P.G. (9/1/2002)

BOND

Bond 2000 Vecina Bordeaux Blend (Napa Valley) $150. Softly textured, gentle and feminine, although rather light in body, with smooth-drinking cherry, tobacco, and dill flavors. The fruit is sweet and refined, and the wine finishes with some tannins. **89** —S.H. (12/1/2004)

Bond 2002 Melbury Cabernet Blend (Napa Valley) $225. Enormously rich, like biting into a warm chocolate truffle with a cherry-blackberry core. Ultrasmooth, a bit soft, and melted, but oh, so supple and velvety, with fine, firm tannins. Completely dry and balanced, this is a wine of harmonious complexity. **95** —S.H. (9/1/2006)

Bond 2001 Melbury Cabernet Blend (Napa Valley) $210. Has stunning fruit, for starters. Sheer, pure, concentrated nose of cassis and cherry. Subtle oak in the background, lending vanilla, toast, and caramel nuances. Fabulous texture and weight, fine as velvet. Magnificently lush, full-bodied. Fantastic finish. Drink now through 2015. **95** —S.H. (6/1/2005)

Bond 2002 St. Eden Cabernet Blend (Napa Valley) $225. More structured than the Melbury, with deeper, firmer tannins: but it's certainly not a tannic, hard wine. It's the quality of the tannins, fine, ripely sweet, intricate. The flavors are enormously rich in blue and black berries, as well as chocolate. Magnificent wine, fleshy, fat, opulent. As delicious as it is now, should age well through 2020. **96** —S.H. (9/1/2006)

Bond 2001 St. Eden Cabernet Blend (Napa Valley) $210. From Oakville, a wine quite different from Bond's Melbury. Not as immediately lush and flamboyant, it's a trace more reserved. Darker, too, more tannic and closed. Starts with an earthiness. Airing brings out cherries and cassis. There is great balance and integrity here, even though it is in desperate need of cellaring. Drink in 2009. **95** —S.H. (6/1/2005)

Bond 2002 Vecina Cabernet Blend (Napa Valley) $225. Based on Oakville fruit, Vecina is not quite as fruit-driven as the other two Bond wines. It's a bit backward, with an earthy, mushroomy, soy, and balsamic taste alongside the briary berry flavors. Has an almost feral quality that is quite interesting and different. With its big backsplash of tannins, it might age best of the current trio. Drink now–2020. **95 Cellar Selection** —S.H. (9/1/2006)

Bond 2001 Vecina Cabernet Blend (Napa Valley) $210. Very fine wine. Denser, richer, more powerful than the other Bond '01s. In the mouth, it has a molten quality, like liquid lead or mercury; strong flavors of plums, bitter chocolate, cassis, and good, rich oak. Pretty astringent now in tannins, it's firm and hard, but complex and layered. Drink now, but best beyond 2010. **96 Cellar Selection** —S.H. (6/1/2005)

Bond 2000 Melbury Red Blend (Napa Valley) $150. This wine opens with gorgeous aromatics, a waft of smoky vanilla and spicy, cherry compote that's irresistible. It's also tasty and sweetly plump, with savory cherry and blackberry flavors. On the light side, but polished and refined. **89** —S.H. (11/15/2004)

Bond 1999 Melbury Red Blend (Napa Valley) $150. Rich plum, earth, and spice aromas are followed by lush black cherry, blackberry, cassis, herb, coffee, chocolate, and raspberry flavors. An intriguing floral edge runs through the core for added interest, all supported by firm, ripe tannins and fine body. The finish is long and smooth, with just a hint of brightness on the end. Made from 100 percent Cabernet Sauvignon. A first release from the folks who also make Harlan. **94** —J.M. (7/1/2003)

Bond 1999 Vecina Red Blend (Napa Valley) $150. A smooth, round-textured wine that serves up multiple layers of complexity and flavor. Black cherry, blackberry and olive notes are at the fore. Spice, cedar, raspberry, toast and vanilla flavors are also firmly in evidence. Attractive herb notes blend seamlessly into the ensemble. Tannins are powdery smooth and the finish is long. A new label made by the folks at Harlan.**93** —*J.M. (7/1/2003)*

BONNEAU

Bonneau 2003 Private Reserve Chardonnay (Carneros) $22. This is a deeply flavored Chardonnay. Its full body embraces powerful flavors of ripe green apples, pineapples, butterscotch and spices. The wine is kept lively by good acidity.**89** —*S.H. (11/1/2005)*

BONNY DOON

Bonny Doon 2001 Freisa (Monterey County) $18. Tastes like a workhorse wine, a dry, rustic red with earth, berry and herb flavors and rugged tannins. Finishes with a bite of acidity.**84** —*S.H. (11/15/2004)*

Bonny Doon 2004 Clos de Gilroy Grenache (California) $12. This is a California-style Beaujolais Nouveau. It's fresh, jammy, racy and dry, with raspberry flavors and a crisp mouthfeel.**84** —*S.H. (6/1/2005)*

Bonny Doon 2003 Clos de Gilroy Grenache (California) $12. As light in body and texture as a Pinot Noir, almost rosé, a Provençal-style wine with the rich earthiness of herbs and leaves. Finishes dry, with sour cherry and tannins. Value in a dry blush wine.**86** —*S.H. (10/1/2004)*

Bonny Doon 2002 Old Telegram Mourvèdre (California) $32. Nice and easy marks this dry wine. It's modest but honest, with earth, herb and coffee-cherry flavors. Fairly stiff in tannins, but won't compete with rich fare. **86** —*S.H. (10/1/2005)*

Bonny Doon 2001 Vin de Glacière Muscat (California) $17. It's a blast of apricot chutney sweetened with smoky honey and a sprinkle of vanilla. The texture is glyceriney and creamy. It's very sweet, but has orange-zesty acidity that keeps it from being cloying.**92** —*S.H. (6/1/2004)*

Bonny Doon NV Angelica Red Blend (California) $18. This dessert variety, which has a long history in California, is made the old-fashioned way, with very sweet, intense flavors of cherries, apricots and white chocolate baked into a Sweet Tart, with a vanilla and butter crust. It has good enough acidity to balance, and a richly smooth, creamy texture.**90 Editors' Choice** —*S.H. (12/31/2005)*

Bonny Doon 2003 Barbera Arneis Red Blend (Monterey County) $18. With 87 percent Barbera, you get a full-bodied, dry and pretty tannic red wine, with earthy, coffee and berry flavors. The Arneis, a white grape, seems to bring much-needed acidity, as well as a floral note. Still, it's a fringe wine, a better concept than reality.**84** —*S.H. (11/1/2005)*

Bonny Doon 2004 Big House Red Red Blend (California) $10. It would take an entire review to list all the varieties in this wine, but it's mainly Carignane, Petite Sirah and Sangiovese. It's really good, and proves that Randall Grahm continues to march to his own beat. Not for him lush, ripe fruit, but leanness, acidity, elegance, structure and what you might call style. How Bonny Doon sells at this price is a mystery.**90 Best Buy** —*S.H. (10/1/2006)*

Bonny Doon NV Framboise Red Blend (California) $11. The ultimate chocolate liqueur. Winemaker Randall Grahm calls this "an infusion" that's been boosted with brandied fruit that brings it to 17% alcohol. It's gooey in raspberry essence finished with a chocolate dust, but a brilliant squeeze of lime adds life and zest.**92** —*S.H. (8/1/2004)*

Bonny Doon NV Framboise Red Blend (California) $12. Dark red in color, this sweet wine smells and tastes like a raspberry Slurpee. The fruit flavors are direct and agreeable, backed up with crisp acidity. It's a syrupy wine that could be poured over vanilla ice cream or pound cake.**86** —*S.H. (12/1/2002)*

Bonny Doon 2001 Le Cigare Volant Red Blend (California) $32. After the leanness of previous vintages, Randall Grahm is back to fruit. Namely, cherries, which ooze through this Grenache, Syrah and Mourvedre-based blend. There are also aromas and flavors of rosemary, thyme and other field herbs. This bone-dry wine is complex and interesting.**91** —*S.H. (4/1/2004)*

Bonny Doon 2000 Le Cigare Volant Red Blend (California) $32. Randall Grahm continues to make this wine harder and earthier with every vintage. The wine this year suggests sage and tobacco and black cherries,

and is fairly tannic. It's a sophisticated wine; complex, layered, and interesting. Far from flamboyant, it's understated and intense, with a dry finish.**91** —*S.H. (12/1/2002)*

Bonny Doon 1996 Le Cigare Volant Red Blend (California) $25.88 *(11/1/1999)*

Bonny Doon 1995 Le Cigare Volant Red Blend (California) $20.90 —*M.S. (6/1/1999)*

Bonny Doon NV Le Cigare Volant Riserva Triperfecto Red Blend (California) $32. Drier than usual, and earthier too, this Rhône-style blend mingles dried herb, leather, spice, and berry flavors with tannins that grip through the finish. After a while, it breathes forth a great waft of pure cherry fruit. This wine is actually very complex. Decant it for a few hours.**89** —*S.H. (11/15/2004)*

Bonny Doon 2002 Le Cigare Volant Rhône Red Blend (California) $32. A shade off prior vintages. Very dry, somewhat herbal, with modest cherry and tobacco flavors. Finishes clean and tannic, and will bounce well off a steak.**86** —*S.H. (8/1/2005)*

Bonny Doon 1999 Le Cigare Volant Rhône Red Blend (California) $30. Randall Grahm pioneered how to produce flavorful, glamorous Rhône blends, and this mixture of Grenache, Syrah, and Mourvèdre continues the tradition. It's a bit harder-edged this year, which is fine. It makes this deliciously dry, fruity wine a better companion with food.**91** —*S.H. (9/1/2002)*

Bonny Doon 1998 Dry Pacific Rim Riesling (California-Washington) $10. 90 Best Buy —*M.S. (11/15/1999)*

Bonny Doon 1997 Dry Pacific Rim Riesling (California-Washington) $9. 90 Best Buy —*M.S. (9/1/1999)*

Bonny Doon 2002 Pacific Rim Riesling (America) $10. Zippy, zingy, zesty sipping with this delightfully crisp, slightly sweet white wine. It has pretty flavors of apples, peaches, and honeysuckle, with a minerally tang.**86** —*S.H. (2/1/2004)*

Bonny Doon 1999 Pacific Rim Dry Riesling (California-Washington) $10. Riesling, when well made, is one of the great white wines, and this one is well made. There are floral, honeyed, and citrus-fruit flavors here, but what makes it notable is the steely, minerally backbone. An intensely fruity, spicy finish adds a flourish. A very good wine and an unbelievable value.**89 Best Buy** —*S.H. (5/1/2001)*

Bonny Doon 2003 The Heart Has Its Rieslings Riesling (Washington) $15. Has an off-dry sweetness that's a little cloying. It would be nice to have richer, brighter acidity. Beyond that, you'll find the flavors of apricots and ripe peaches.**84** —*S.H. (11/15/2004)*

Bonny Doon 2002 The Heart Has Its Rieslings Riesling (California) $15. Randall Grahm has made his Riesling sweet this year, and very low in alcohol, barely scraping 8 percent. The result is a light-bodied wine, with the prettiness of a summer flower. In fact the flavors suggest garden flowers, apricots, and oranges. This pleasant wine seems designed for the beach.**86** —*S.H. (12/31/2003)*

Bonny Doon 2005 Vin Gris de Cigare Rosé Blend (California) $12. Seems lighter and thinner than in previous vintages, a bone-dry, high-acid wine that just barely suggests fruit. All the pieces are there for a nice rosé, except for that watery finish.**83** —*S.H. (10/1/2006)*

Bonny Doon 2004 Vin Gris de Cigare Rosé Blend (California) $11. Randall Grahm is at the top of his game, producing Rhône wines that are inexpensive, yet incredibly complex and rewarding. This year's Cigare is bone dry, and the richest yet. With its zesty burst of acidity, the subtle flavors are of cherries, raspberries, rose petals, dried Provençal herbs, and pepper. This complex wine is a blend of Grenache, Mourvèdre, Roussanne, Cinsault, Syrah, and Marsanne.**90 Best Buy** —*S.H. (11/15/2005)*

Bonny Doon 2003 Vin Gris de Cigare Rosé Blend (California) $11. A six-variety Southern Rhône blend with bone-dry flavors of strawberries drizzled with vanilla. Served very cold, it teases the palate with the red-white line it straddles. Good value.**85** —*S.H. (10/1/2004)*

Bonny Doon 2002 Vin Gris de Cigare Rosé Blend (California) $10. The latest in a series of noteworthy blush wines from Randall Grahm, this rosé is remarkable for its insistent but delicate flavors, which include strawberries and cream, white peach, white pepper, and vanilla. It all meshes into a delicate, sleek wine with quite a bit of complexity. A blend of Grenache, Syrah, Mourvèdre, and Marsanne. **89 Best Buy** —*S.H.* *(11/15/2003)*

Bonny Doon 2000 Vin Gris de Cigare Rosé Blend (California) $9. Randall Grahm strikes again with this brilliant wine, beautiful from the pinkish-rose color to the marvelous palate sensations. A Rhône-style blend of at least eight grape varieties. it's packed with wild berry fruit, with the most delicate, supple texture. It's as dry as dust, with brittle acidity, making it the perfect accompaniment to all sorts of table fare. If you drink one rosé this year, make it this one. **90** —*S.H. (11/15/2001)*

Bonny Doon 2001 Syrah (California) $18. Made the way Randall Grahm likes Syrah, which is a dry, peppery wine with rich outbursts of sweet cherry fruit. It must be in the blending, but this wine seems to possess both warm- and cool-climate aspects, which is often what works best in a California Syrah. It's rich but dry, fruity but elegant, a Euro-wine of instant, and international, appeal. **91 Editors' Choice** —*S.H. (6/1/2004)*

Bonny Doon 2003 Le Pousseur Syrah (Central Coast) $16. An improvement from Bonny Doon's 2002 version, revealing more weight and intensity to go with its mixed berry flavors. Notes of pepper and herbs add complexity, while the finish features riper tannins than last vintage. **85** *(9/1/2005)*

Bonny Doon 2002 Le Pousseur Syrah (California) $15. Leans toward the red-fruit side of the Syrah fruit continuum, with raspberry and strawberry flavors strongly marked by herbal, peppery, menthol notes. Well made, but a bit too green for our tastes, with some hard tannins on the finish. **83** *(9/1/2005)*

Bonny Doon 2003 Doux Viognier (Paso Robles) $18. Amply displays how well Viognier takes to dessert-wine status. This frankly sweet wine has delicious flavors of apricot nectar drizzled with vanilla and white chocolate powder, with enough acidity for balance. **89** —*S.H. (10/1/2004)*

Bonny Doon 2002 Viognier Doux Viognier (Paso Robles) $18. This interesting wine has the tropical fruits and exotic wildflower aromatics you associate with Viognier. But it's sweet as honey, with a white chocolate truffle, meringue flavor on the finish. Fortunately, there's good, clean acidity. **89** —*S.H. (6/1/2004)*

Bonny Doon 2004 Big House White White Blend (California) $10. The Big House is a state prison in the Salinas Valley where Randall Grahm sources grapes. This wine, comprised of at least nine varieties, is absolutely dry and intense in acidity, with subtle earth, tobacco, herb and citrus flavors. It's quite complex and completely distinctive and, at this price, a great value. **90 Best Buy** —*S.H. (10/1/2006)*

Bonny Doon 2001 Big House White White Blend (California) $10. From iconoclast Randall Grahm, a blend of six varietals, and a very good one at that. You'll find all sorts of fruits in it, from lemons to mangoes, and refreshing acidity. It's a little on the sweet side. **86 Best Buy** —*S.H. (12/15/2002)*

Bonny Doon 2003 Le Cigare Blanc White Blend (California) $20. Rhônemeister Randall Grahm's companion to his celebrated red Rhône wine, this is mainly Roussanne with a drop of Grenache Blanc. It's a very fine and interesting wine that combines white and yellow tree-fruit flavors with melons, flowers, and a refreshing minerality. **91** —*S.H. (8/1/2005)*

Bonny Doon 2003 Cardinal Zin Zinfandel (California) $20. Smells sharp and raw, and tastes young and fresh, a juvenile wine with hard acids and primary, grapy flavors. Finishes dry and tart. Should be better with a year or two of aging. **85** —*S.H. (10/1/2005)*

Bonny Doon 2000 Cardinal Zin Zinfandel (California) $20. From warm Contra Costa County, this old vine Zin is eccentric and individualistic. It's wild, opening with a savage burst of briary fruit. The ripe fruity flavors persist in the mouth, where it's dry, kind of soft, and seems more alcoholic than the official reading of 13.5%. Finishes on a dry, bitter note. **86** —*S.H. (12/15/2001)*

Bonny Doon 2002 Cardinal Zin Beastly Old Vines Zinfandel (California) $20. Mostly from Contra Costa grapes, a plummy wine with those raisiny notes Zin can get from hot areas. Yet the alcohol is moderate, the body smooth, and the wine is fully dry. It will appeal to fans of this style. **86** —*S.H. (4/1/2004)*

Bonny Doon 2001 Cardinal Zin/Beastly Old Vines Zinfandel (California) $20. Bright, fresh, and fruity on the palate, with plenty of pretty plum, cherry, raspberry, vanilla, spice, and herb flavors. Tannins are a little rustic, but the wine is quite enjoyable and easy to drink. **87** —*J.M. (11/1/2003)*

BONTERRA

Bonterra 2003 Cabernet Sauvignon (Mendocino County) $15. The '02 was quite a good Cabernet and so is this one, from a winery whose organic grapes produce dependable wines across all varieties. This bottling is nicely dry and balanced, with a classic Cabernet profile. Drink now. **87** —*S.H. (7/1/2006)*

Bonterra 2002 Cabernet Sauvignon (North Coast) $15. Bonterra wines invariably show a great purity of flavor, and so it is with this lovely Cab. It has classic varietal flavorsof ripe black currants, with a spicy edge enriched with toasty oak. The tannins are ripe and supportive. **89** —*S.H. (12/15/2005)*

Bonterra 1999 Chardonnay (Mendocino County) $12. 87 Best Buy —*P.G. (10/1/2000)*

Bonterra 1998 Chardonnay (Mendocino) $12. 90 Best Buy —*S.H. (3/1/2000)*

Bonterra 1997 Chardonnay (Mendocino County) $11. 89 Best Buy —*S.H. (10/1/1999)*

Bonterra 2005 Chardonnay (Mendocino County) $13. There's some new oak on this Chard, but the fruit really stars. It's so pure and clean and bright, suggesting pineapples, nectarines, guavas, and Meyer lemons. It's a tiny bit sweet, but the acidity is high enough to make the finish feel dry. **85** —*S.H. (12/31/2006)*

Bonterra 2004 Chardonnay (Mendocino County) $13. They say the purity of fruit is because of the organically grown grapes. The flavors do have a laserlike cleanness, of apricots, peaches, and the sweetest green apples. And then, of course, there's that creamy, buttery aspect. **89 Best Buy** — *S.H. (12/31/2005)*

Bonterra 2000 Chardonnay (Mendocino County) $15. From Fetzer's organic offshoot winery, a terrific Chard despite a lean austerity. You won't get much more than citrus, maybe green apple, in the fruit department, but the wine is so well structured and clean, it creates interest. Oak and lees are prominent but not overwhelming. **88** —*S.H. (5/1/2002)*

Bonterra 1999 Lakeview Vineyards Marsanne (Mendocino County) $19. This pleasant wine has aromas and flavors suggesting peaches in a heavy sugar syrup, but there are also denser notes of earth and mulch. Little oak interferes with the bright, forward flavors, which are rich without being heavy. **85** —*S.H. (8/1/2001)*

Bonterra 2004 Merlot (Mendocino County) $15. Here's an extremely ripe wine brimming with cherry and black raspberry jam flavors and an edge of coffee and cocoa. The bigness is balanced by rich, finely-ground tannins and firm acidity, which makes it all bright and clean. At its best now, it's a versatile food wine. **87** —*S.H. (12/31/2006)*

Bonterra 2003 Merlot (Mendocino County) $15. Last year's release was the best Bonterra Merlot ever. This one's right up there. It's rich and dry and exceedingly fruity, with long, deep cherry, blackberry, and cocoa flavors complexed with coffee and herb nuances. The mouthfeel is vibrant and interesting. **90 Best Buy** —*S.H. (5/1/2006)*

Bonterra 2002 Merlot (Mendocino County) $15. Rich and deep are the words that come to mind for this intensely flavorful Merlot. It's as full-bodied as a Cab, with the prettiest cherry and chocolate flavors and a smooth finish that turns blueberry. **90 Best Buy** —*S.H. (12/15/2005)*

Bonterra 2000 Merlot (Paso Robles) $15. A darkly colored wine that is not as rich as it appears. The flavors are pretty earthy, suggesting tobacco, sage, and oregano, only partially relieved with a hint of blackberries. Cleanly made, but could use a lot more substance. **84** —*S.H. (12/15/2003)*

Bonterra 1998 Merlot (Mendocino County) $16. A tale of two cities: plush blackberry and plum flavors co-exist with herbal ones, and the wine is less than fully ripe in the mouth. The grapes struggled to achieve ripeness, and there's a sharp streak of tart acidity. That said, it's the best wine that could have been made from this fine vineyard. **85** —*S.H. (5/1/2002)*

Bonterra 1997 Merlot (Mendocino County) $19. A woody wine that features a shell of toasty, cedary oak over a core of black cherry fruit. The supple mouthful turns a little drying on the finish, just enough to cut through the fat of a well-marbled steak or roast. **86** *(6/1/2001)*

Bonterra 2005 Bartolucci Vineyard Muscat (Lake County) $16. Clean and vibrant, with apricot, fig, and vanilla flavors, this single-vineyard dessert wine has refreshing acidity. It's sweet, but not too sweet, and look at that nice, low alcohol, only 9%. **86** —*S.H. (11/1/2006)*

Bonterra 2004 Bartolucci Vineyard Muscat (Lake County) $16. This organically grown wine is certainly sweet, although not supersweet, and fruity, with apricot and vanilla flavors. What it's missing is acidity. It's soft and delicious, but needs that racy clean quality to lift it up. **84** —*S.H. (4/1/2006)*

Bonterra 1997 Roussanne (Mendocino) $17. 91 —*L.W. (10/1/1999)*

Bonterra 2004 Roussanne (Mendocino County) $18. You never know what you're going to get in a California Roussanne. This one's dry, very crisp in acidity and complex, with citrus, honeysuckle, white apricot, and spice flavors. Try as a substitute for an oaky Sauvignon Blanc. **88** —*S.H. (12/15/2005)*

Bonterra 1999 Lakeview Vineyards Roussanne (Mendocino County) $19. An effusively flowery, honeyed wine, brimming with bright aromas of butterscotch and smoke, apricots, vanilla, and cinnamon. It's exotically fruity and rich, with complex flavors ranging from apricot preserves to ginger. Tasty on its own. **87** —*S.H. (8/1/2001)*

Bonterra 2003 Syrah (Mendocino County) $15. From a pioneer of organic growing and biodynamic winemaking comes this clean, jammy Syrah. It has the juicy high acidity of a baby coastal wine, with dark blue and black fruit wrapped in firm tannins. Finishes dry and spicy. Drink now. **87** —*S.H. (11/1/2006)*

Bonterra 2002 Syrah (Mendocino County) $15. There's a purity to the fruit in this full-bodied wine, which brims with ripe blackberries and cherries, with an edge of sweet leather. The tannins are smooth and soft, but a sweet, sugary finish detracts. **83** —*S.H. (3/1/2006)*

Bonterra 2001 Syrah (Mendocino County) $17. Big and clunky according to one taster, but creamy-smooth and satisfying according to another. Vanilla and black cherry notes aren't hugely complex, but deliver mouth-filling flavor. Chewy and tannic on the finish. **85** *(9/1/2005)*

Bonterra 1998 Syrah (Mendocino) $19. This complex and elegant wine is certified organic. The bouquet has dimension, with cherry, leather, chalk, meat, and cigar-box notes. Lightweight on the palate, it is nicely textured and delivers lots of fruit flavor. Firm acids support the fruit and a cocoa-spice finish wraps it up neatly. **89 Editors' Choice** *(10/1/2001)*

Bonterra 1997 Viognier (North Coast) $17. 91 —*S.H. (10/1/1999)*

Bonterra 2005 Viognier (Mendocino County) $18. Bonterra has always done a good job with Viognier, and here's another one. Maybe it's the biodynamic grapes, but the fruit is so clean and pure. Apricots, peaches, papayas, and spicy flavors all come together in a honeyed texture, but the wine is dry and quite perky in acidity. **88** —*S.H. (11/1/2006)*

Bonterra 2004 Viognier (Mendocino County) $18. Organically grown, this wine is clean and vibrant, with bright acidity and a dry, crisp mouthfeel. It doesn't show Viognier's usual flamboyant, exotic flavors, but instead shows a lean, citrus, and floral elegance. **85** —*S.H. (12/15/2005)*

Bonterra 2000 Viognier (Mendocino County) $18. From well-groomed vineyards along the western foothills in Hopland, an expressive Viognier that titillates with exotic notes, but doesn't veer into eccentricity. You'll like the fresh, clean apple, citrus, peach, spice, and tropical fruit notes, and the acids are brilliant. They etch their way into the palate, underscoring the fruity flavors. **88** —*S.H. (5/1/2002)*

Bonterra 1999 Viognier (Mendocino County) $19. Showcases Viognier's exotic, flowery side, with strong aromas of honeysuckle and jasmine accented with citrus fruits and peaches, coconut, and smoke and vanilla. There's lots of extract, and it veers to stone fruits, especially peaches. It's very light and elegant, and slightly sweet. This wine would be perfect with grilled trout. **88 Editors' Choice** *(8/1/2001)*

BOOKWALTER

Bookwalter 2000 Cabernet Sauvignon (Columbia Valley (WA)) $28. A dense, dark, mysterious wine that could easily pass for a Spring Mountain Cab costing three times as much. This sensational value wine is packed with powerful, dark fruit, muscled around modest oak and buttressed with spicy acid. A knockout! **93 Cellar Selection** —*P.G. (1/1/2004)*

Bookwalter 1998 Cabernet Sauvignon (Columbia Valley (WA)) $35. Bookwalter has done an exciting turnaround as a new generation takes the reins. This is a vivid, forward, toasty and inviting Cabernet. It shows nice, round fruit and plenty of toasty oak. There are dry tannins as well, and it's all balanced out for near term enjoyment. Not a big wine, but delicious and well made. **87** —*P.G. (6/1/2001)*

Bookwalter 1999 Chardonnay (Columbia Valley (WA)) $18. 87 —*P.G. (11/15/2000)*

Bookwalter 1997 Vintner's Select Chardonnay (Washington) $20. 88 —*P.G. (11/15/2000)*

Bookwalter 2002 Johannisberg Riesling (Columbia Valley (WA)) $8. 89 —*P.G. (8/1/2003)*

Bookwalter 2001 Merlot (Columbia Valley (WA)) $NA. Powerful, pungent, ripe black cherry fruit assaults the nostrils, leading into a taut, slightly gamey, muscular and dense with layers of fruit, tar, smoke, and earth. Give it 6 to 8 years to unwrap and it will be sensational. **91 Cellar Selection** —*P.G. (1/1/2004)*

Bookwalter NV Lot 14 Red Wine Red Blend (Columbia Valley (WA)) $NA. A pleasant blend of two Cabs, Merlot, and a pinch of Syrah. Unpretentious and affordable, it's a delight, with firm, muscular fruit, compact and lightly spicy, taking the forefront. If there is oak it is invisible, and unnecessary. The wine shows the simple pleasures of well-ripened Columbia valley grapes. **88 Best Buy** —*P.G. (1/1/2004)*

BOUCHAINE

Bouchaine 1998 Chardonnay (Carneros) $20. 89 *(6/1/2000)*

Bouchaine 2004 Chardonnay (Carneros) $28. There's lots of oak on this ripe wine, which has forward tropical fruit and spice flavors and a richly creamy texture from barrel fermentation. It's a bit simple, though. **85** —*S.H. (7/1/2006)*

Bouchaine 2003 Chardonnay (Carneros) $25. Pretty tart in acids, with citrusy flavors and a fair amount of oak, this Chard pleases for its easy drinkability. Not terribly complex, just a good, dry, fruity-flinty wine. **87** —*S.H. (10/1/2005)*

Bouchaine 2001 Chardonnay (Carneros) $18. A good Chard that balances ripe, forward flavors with a degree of delicacy and balance. The flavors veer toward sweet citrus fruits, peaches, and pears, spiced up with a touch of smoky oak. Crisp acids and peppery spices hit on the long finish. **88** —*S.H. (6/1/2003)*

Bouchaine 1999 Chardonnay (Carneros) $25. Always rich and toasty, Bouchaine's '99 drinks bright and ripe. There are white peach and tropical fruit flavors dusted with crushed oriental spices, and the whole is framed in well-charred oak. This is a fat, lush, creamy Chardonnay, polished and satisfying. **90** —*S.H. (5/1/2002)*

Bouchaine 1999 B Chardonnay (Napa Valley) $13. Pretty standard stuff here, with thin, watery aromas that carry only faint traces of wood and apples, and watery flavors. It's clean, but hot from alcohol, with high acidity. **82** —*S.H. (9/1/2002)*

Bouchaine 2002 Buchli Station Chardonnay (California) $12. There's lots of rich fruit in this smooth, affordable wine. It represents a good value in a big, gooey Chard that's brimming with tropical fruit, buttered toast, and smoky spices. **85** —*S.H. (6/1/2004)*

Bouchaine 2004 Pinot Noir (Carneros) $28. Fruity and simple, with diluted cherry and oaky-vanilla flavors that finish dry and crisp. There's some green, minty stuff going on. **83** —*S.H. (12/1/2006)*

Bouchaine 2003 Pinot Noir (Carneros) $25. Seems a bit thin for this price. You get modest cherry and cola flavors in a very dry wine that actually has some tannins. Finishes dry and tart. **85** —*S.H. (10/1/2005)*

Bouchaine 2002 Pinot Noir (Carneros) $23. A pleasant, light wine, with lots of rich and refined notes of cherries, coffee, and dried herbs. Silky and delicate, showing zesty acidity, this classy wine is easy to drink. **89** *(11/1/2004)*

Bouchaine 2000 Pinot Noir (Carneros) $18. Recognizably Pinot with its raspberry, cherry, and spice flavors, silky tannins, and crisp acidity, and gets the job done. But there's an awkward sweetness of residual sugar and a thick, gluey texture that lacks zest and crispness. **84** —*S.H. (7/1/2003)*

Bouchaine 1999 Pinot Noir (Carneros) $34. Our opinions about this smooth, midweight wine varied. The nose features cherry cordial aromas complemented by cedar and herb tones. On the palate, though, some found the wine dull—a bit fat and plumy. Others lauded the fine balance and herb-tinged fruit. Drink now–2004. **86** *(10/1/2002)*

Bouchaine 1999 20th Anniversary Gee Vineyard Pinot Noir (Carneros) $50. Cherries and vanilla are all over the nose, so much so that it seems a little bit like Port. The plum and blackberry fruit is potent yet jammy, although ample acidity keeps it lively. Additional notes of tree bark, earth and dark chocolate add complexity. **86** *(10/1/2002)*

Bouchaine 2000 B Pinot Noir (California) $15. 82 *(10/1/2002)*

Bouchaine 2002 Buchli Station Pinot Noir (California) $11. Earthy, with coffee, cola, and berry-cherry flavors, and rugged tannins. Yet there's a sweet aftertaste of currants soaked in rum, and the texture is silky. **84** —*S.H. (6/1/2004)*

Bouchaine 2003 Estate Vineyard Pinot Noir (Carneros) $35. A bit richer and fruitier than Bouchaine's regular '03, this dry wine shows cherry, earth, and coffee flavors. It won't astonish you, but it's a well-made, somewhat complex Pinot. **87** —*S.H. (10/1/2005)*

Bouchaine 2002 Gee Vineyard Pinot Noir (Carneros) $40. Rather short in fruit, although there are hints of candied cherry and tea. Very delicate and feminine in the mouth, with tart, crisp acidity and an elegant, clean finish. A bit light, but this is a nice food wine. **85** *(11/1/2004)*

BOUDREAUX CELLARS

Boudreaux Cellars 2003 Cabernet Sauvignon (Washington) $40. Boudreaux has set a consistent house style in place, and it is best described as extremely smooth, chocolaty, and soft. The Cabernet has more concentrated plum, black currant, and cherry flavors than the Merlot, and here the oak lends some distinct Bourbon barrel scents rather than pure milk chocolate. Medium-bodied and easy-drinking, it's made for near-term enjoyment. **88** —*P.G. (6/1/2006)*

Boudreaux Cellars 2002 Cabernet Sauvignon (Walla Walla (WA)) $40. Seven Hills (Walla Walla) fruit, with an edgy, slightly herbal, tannic structure. The fruit is a mix of red berries, and there is lots of mixed clove and cinnamon spice from the barrels. It's nicely blended, and layered, though probably not for the long haul. Just 80 cases were made. **89** —*P.G. (4/1/2005)*

Boudreaux Cellars 2001 Seven Hills Vineyard Cabernet Sauvignon (Walla Walla (WA)) $30. This very ripe, slightly stewed wine runs right at you with full-out fruit flavors, soft and open. Soft at first, it turns tannic in the back end and finishes with somewhat cooked flavors and plenty of toasty new oak. **87** —*P.G. (11/15/2004)*

Boudreaux Cellars 2004 Chardonnay (Columbia Valley (WA)) $26. Colored a deep green/gold, this thick and viscous Chardonnay is packed with flavors of peach, apricot, and tropical stone fruits. It seems Australian in its weight and fruit power, though the acids typical of Washington grapes give it some additional lift. There's just enough oak to provide a nice dusting of spice. Definitely a wine to drink young. **89** —*P.G. (6/1/2006)*

Boudreaux Cellars 2002 Chardonnay (Washington) $20. This new winery, with excellent grape sources, jumps in with a soft, plush, buttery Chardonnay. Substantial flavors of ripe tropical fruits—bananas, peaches, and melon—are melded to buttered nuts and toast. **88** —*P.G. (11/15/2004)*

Boudreaux Cellars 2003 Merlot (Washington) $40. Very smooth, very soft, very chocolaty, with a light layer of green herb. The soft, chocolaty mouthfeel carries through a warm, slightly dilute finish. **88** —*P.G. (6/1/2006)*

Boudreaux Cellars 2001 Pepper Bridge Vineyard Merlot (Walla Walla (WA)) $25. In attempting to reach for just a bit of extra flavor the wine has gone slightly over the top, but offers many near-term pleasures. A plush mix of stewed fruits, sweet plum, and mince pie smoothes into a seductive, lush middle before hitting a wall of tannin on the way out. **87** —*P.G. (11/15/2004)*

Boudreaux Cellars 2002 Syrah (Walla Walla (WA)) $32. From the Pepper Bridge and Seven Hills vineyards, this compelling Syrah offers more than just crisp red fruits. I love the citrus rind, the floral lift, the hints of cinnamon and spice. It's a testament to sensitive winemaking, and grapes that were not pushed too far. **91** —*P.G. (4/1/2005)*

Boudreaux Cellars 2003 Pepper Bridge Vineyard Syrah (Walla Walla (WA)) $40. From an important Washington vineyard, this Syrah packs lots of slightly syrupy red fruit flavors into a supple, medium-bodied format. Hints of mint and other herbs along with dried spices and vanilla impart nuance. **87** *(9/1/2005)*

BOURASSA VINEYARDS

Bourassa Vineyards 2002 Harmony 3 Bordeaux Blend (Napa Valley) $52. Quite clean, vibrant, and forward in cassis and cherry aromas, this generously oaked wine has smooth tannins and is fairly high in acidity. It might soften and improve with several years of aging. **86** —*S.H. (5/1/2005)*

Bourassa Vineyards 2001 Block 42 Cabernet Franc (Napa Valley) $29. This is a light-bodied wine with pretty cherry and herb flavors. It's totally dry, but has some rugged tannins. Best with a juicy steak or lamb. **84** —*S.H. (5/1/2005)*

Bourassa Vineyards NV Solera3 Port (Napa Valley) $60. Very sweet but a bit thin on fruity flavor despite some chocolate and raspberry. This Port-style wine is a blend of Primitivo, Zinfandel, and Syrah. **84** —*S.H. (12/1/2006)*

Bourassa Vineyards 2003 Sauvignon Blanc (Napa Valley) $16. Aggressive in green grass, wheatberry, and gooseberry aromas and flavors, but has a creamy edge of fig and melon to soften. Appealing for its crisp acidity and balance and lingering finish. **87** —*S.H. (12/31/2004)*

Bourassa Vineyards 2004 Rhapsody 3 Syrah (Napa Valley) $30. A nice Syrah, dry and fairly tannic, with cherry-berry flavors and an earthy coffee and pepper edge. Lots of new oak brings toast, char, and vanilla. **86** —*S.H. (12/1/2006)*

Bourassa Vineyards 2003 Rhapsody 3 Syrah (Napa Valley) $32. Rich and packed with superripe fruit: blackberries, raspberries, and plums all make appearances. Add on layers of coffee, caramel, and toast notes from new oak and the result is a flashy, hedonistic wine that just lacks the complexity and structure to take it to the next level. **86** *(9/1/2005)*

Bourassa Vineyards 2003 Viognier (Napa Valley) $24. Fruity and simple, with a buttercream thick texture and flavors of peaches and oak. A bit soft in acidity, and with a long, fruity finish. **85** —*S.H. (12/31/2004)*

Bourassa Vineyards 2003 Odyssey 3 Zinfandel (Napa Valley) $32. Why did they rush this out? It badly needs more time to settle down. Smells and tastes like it's still fermenting. Shame, especially at this price. **80** —*S.H. (6/1/2005)*

BOYER

Boyer 2004 Riesling (Monterey) $14. What a delightful wine. It's low in alcohol but completely dry, with acidity that thoroughly cleanses the palate. The complex flavors suggest lime zest, pineapple, flowers, and tangy metals, and last for a long time on the finish. **89 Best Buy** —*S.H. (12/1/2005)*

BRADFORD MOUNTAIN

Bradford Mountain 1998 Block One Zinfandel (Dry Creek Valley) $36. 85 —*D.T. (3/1/2002)*

USA

Bradford Mountain 1999 Grist Vineyard Zinfandel (Dry Creek Valley) $30. Spice, leather, and cherry mix with a slightly alcoholic, floral nose in this single-vineyard Zin. The spice joins forces with a little toast and smoke on the palate, which enhance the cherry aromas and flavors, but which also cause the wine to finish with a bite of tannin. This is one that could benefit from another year or two in the rack. **89** —*T.H. (3/1/2002)*

Bradford Mountain 1998 Grist Vineyard Zinfandel (Dry Creek Valley) $24. **87** —*D.T. (3/1/2002)*

BRANDBORG

Brandborg 2005 Gewürztraminer (Umpqua Valley) $17. Good varietal scents and flavors show crushed rose petals, orange candy, and peach. Sweet as a lemon drop, it's an interesting wine with enough acidity to hold up to unusual foods. **88** —*P.G. (12/1/2006)*

Brandborg 2004 Gewürztraminer (Umpqua Valley) $14. Sweet and sugary, with orange candy flavors, almost muscat-like. It hits you with fruit and sugar, then holds through the mid-palate before fading, without much change as it goes. **82** —*P.G. (5/1/2006)*

Brandborg 2004 Pinot Gris (Umpqua Valley) $17. Quite tart and citrusy, this is a pleasant wine that offers clean and refreshing flavors of melon, grapefruit, and gin. It's not an insubstantial wine, but it does not have the fleshy fruit that Willamette Valley Gris usually shows; this is a leaner style that's well suited to shellfish. **86** —*P.G. (12/1/2006)*

Brandborg 2003 Pinot Gris (Umpqua Valley) $14. A different style, that shows a strong streak of lime flavored fruit. Tart, clean, and refreshing, but marching to its own drummer, it's like a wine version of a gin and tonic. **86** —*P.G. (2/1/2006)*

Brandborg 2001 Pinot Noir (Anderson Valley) $23. Offers some good varietal pleasure, with its silky texture and flavors of cherries, coffee, and herbs. It's a bone-dry wine and a bit acidic, and turns dustily tannic on the tart finish. Drink now. **85** —*S.H. (4/1/2004)*

Brandborg 2004 Benchlands Pinot Noir (Umpqua Valley) $21. This wine still seems to have some bottle shock. There is clean, spicy fruit and the flavors of plum and currant show through. And there's a nice streak of sassafras and cola, with just a whisper of new oak. It should open up nicely with additional bottle age. **87** —*P.G. (12/1/2006)*

Brandborg 2002 Benchlands Pinot Noir (Umpqua Valley) $18. Spice, mint, menthol, and a whiff of hickory smoke mingle in the nose. The fruit offers a bit of hard black cherry, again with a distinctive wintergreen character. It finishes tannic and slightly hot. **87** *(11/1/2004)*

Brandborg 2003 Northern Reach Pinot Noir (Umpqua Valley) $27. A pale, pretty wine that's elegantly styled. It's a pleasure to encounter Pinot from Oregon that hasn't been placed on steroids, that isn't super sweet or the color of Zinfandel. In short, Pinot that looks and smells and tastes more like Burgundy. This is a very nice effort in that lighter style. **87** —*P.G. (12/1/2006)*

Brandborg 2002 Northern Reach Pinot Noir (Umpqua Valley) $23. Blue fruits and mixed, peppery spices set the stage for this taut, supple wine. There's a fruit-salad quality to the grapes, but the winemaking is polished and appealing. **87** *(11/1/2004)*

Brandborg 2005 Riesling (Umpqua Valley) $19. A strong scent of quinine permeates this young Riesling—the tasting notes tell us that "the Elkton terrior [sic] of diesel is already beginning to show through"—one can almost hear it yapping! It's a tight, slightly bitter, spicy, and sharp wine, with fruit nuances of green apple and lime. **85** —*P.G. (12/1/2006)*

Brandborg 2004 Riesling (Umpqua Valley) $14. The nose suggests a mix of herb, citrus, and cotton candy; in the mouth you find the same odd confluence of flavors. Maybe all this will come together at some point in time, but right now it's disjointed and off-putting. **80** —*P.G. (5/1/2006)*

Brandborg 2001 Sangiovese (Russian River Valley) $18. One of the riper, fruitier Sangioveses on the market, with pronounced flavors of cherries and raspberries. It's fully dry, with a pretty layer of smoky oak. Easy drinking, with its soft tannins and smooth mouthfeel. **86** —*S.H. (4/1/2004)*

Brandborg 2004 Syrah (Umpqua Valley) $29. A tannic, slightly roasted style, with peppery tannins overtaking the tart berry-flavored fruit. Stiff,

hard, and dark, it's all about acid and tannin at this point in time, so give it a good decanting. **86** —*P.G. (12/1/2006)*

Brandborg 2003 Syrah (Umpqua Valley) $25. A bit volatile and Port-y, yet it seems to lack richness and depth at the same time. The black cherry flavors are solid and the charred oak adds a welcome touch of complexity, so it's not without some good points. **84** *(9/1/2005)*

BRANDER

Brander 2004 Bouchet Bordeaux Blend (Santa Ynez Valley) $32. Better than last year's bottling, this is a very dry, stylish wine of complexity. A blend of Cabernet Sauvignon and Cabernet Franc, it's leaner than many North Coast clarets, with an herbal edge to the cherry flavors. That restraint makes it a comfortable companion to a wide range of food. **90** —*S.H. (7/1/2006)*

Brander 2002 Bouchet (Santa Ynez Valley) $30. Mimics Cabernet with ripe flavors of black currants and cherries and the veneer of well-toasted oak. The tannins are Cab-like, too, ripe and dense. There's a swirl of sweet chocolate truffle that's distinctive and attractive. **88** —*S.H. (9/1/2004)*

Brander 2001 Bouchet (Santa Ynez Valley) $30. Ultrasoft and rather flabby, and desperately in need of some lively acidity and tannins. The plum, blueberry cream and chocolate flavors earn extra points, but they're floating around without any structure. **86** —*S.H. (12/31/2003)*

Brander 2003 Bouchet Cabernet Blend (Santa Ynez Valley) $30. A Santa Ynez Cabernet character has slowly been emerging, and this wine showcases it. This is a soft, dry wine, with an edge of green herbs and sweet peas framing red cherry and cassis flavors. **88** —*S.H. (12/1/2005)*

Brander 2005 Cabernet Sauvignon (Santa Ynez Valley) $25. Fresh and jammy, with sharp acidity and berry flavors that taste right out of the fermenter. Seems like it was released awfully young, but might calm down in a few months. **83** —*S.H. (12/1/2006)*

Brander 2004 Cabernet Sauvignon (Santa Ynez Valley) $20. This is Brander's best Cabernet yet. That's mainly due to ripeness. They achieved delicious blackberry, black currant, and mocha flavors that echo the best of the North Coast. Next on the agenda is to get those tannins to be softer and smoother and more authoritative. **87** —*S.H. (5/1/2006)*

Brander 2003 Cabernet Sauvignon (Santa Ynez Valley) $20. An awkward wine. It's very dry, with some decent blackberry flavors, but doesn't seem altogether ripe. There's some tough acidity and a peppery, bitter coffee finish. **83** —*S.H. (12/1/2005)*

Brander 2002 Cabernet Sauvignon (Santa Ynez Valley) $18. A nice effort, and not a bad wine, but it just doesn't have the well-ripened fruit and sumptuous tannins of Napa and Sonoma. Tastes a bit green. **84** —*S.H. (5/1/2005)*

Brander 2004 Reserve Cabernet Sauvignon (Santa Ynez Valley) $50. Brander keeps trying to get Cabernet ripe down in Santa Ynez, and while they sometimes come close, it's like horseshoes: close doesn't count at this price. Even in this hot vintage, the wine has a tough astringency, and less than generous flavors. Oddly, I liked the regular '04 Cab better. **83** —*S.H. (12/31/2006)*

Brander 2002 Reserve Cabernet Sauvignon (Santa Ynez Valley) $45. If I'd never tasted a Napa Cab I would think this was a nice California wine. But comparisons are inevitable. There's certainly a lot of ripe fruit here, but also a sharpness and rustic tannic structure that's disturbing, especially at this price. **84** —*S.H. (12/1/2005)*

Brander 2000 Reserve Cabernet Sauvignon (Santa Ynez Valley) $45. Ripe flavors of blackberries and cherries sink into the taste buds and last for a long, sweet time. The tannins are jagged with an edge of greenness, which makes for an unbalanced mouthfeel. **87** —*S.H. (11/15/2003)*

Brander 2003 Vogelzang Vineyard Cabernet Sauvignon (Santa Ynez Valley) $30. This single-vineyard bottling is riper and more intense than Brander's regular '04 Cab, but it's not necessarily a better wine. The angular tannins are more pronounced, giving it a jagged, sharp mouthfeel that will not age away. **87** —*S.H. (5/1/2006)*

Brander 2004 Merlot (Santa Ynez Valley) $20. Brander has struggled with Merlot. This year's bottling achieve plenty of cherry-berry and mocha fruit. The challenge continues to be the tannic structure, but improvement is notable. **87**—*S.H. (5/1/2006)*

Brander 2003 Merlot (Santa Ynez Valley) $20. This is a very dry, tannic wine, with a simple structure. But it has well-developed black cherry and mocha flavors, and is soft in acids, making it pleasant now with something rich, like short ribs of beef. **86**—*S.H. (10/1/2005)*

Brander 2002 Merlot (Santa Ynez Valley) $20. Compared to Napa and Sonoma bottlings this wine is hard and lean in fruit. The tannins stick out, and the flavors are of earthy herbs, with a hint of cherry. Bordeaux varieties can be tough to ripen in this appellation. **84**—*S.H. (12/15/2004)*

Brander 1999 Merlot (Santa Ynez Valley) $18. Even in the best of vintages it's hard to get Merlot to ripen in Santa Barbara unless it's grown well inland. This one does its best, with modest aromas of black cherry fruit accentuated by oak, but there's a green weediness throughout that age will not soften. That said, it's dry and well made, and complex enough to be a nice by-the-glass wine if the price is kept down. 1,450 cases produced. **85**—*S.H. (5/1/2001)*

Brander 2005 Château Neuf du Pink Rosé Blend (Santa Ynez Valley) $13. Easy and dry, this blend of too many varieties to name has raspberry, rosehip tea, floral, and wild herb flavors. The addition of Sauvignon Blanc seems to bring a refreshing citrus element. **86**—*S.H. (12/1/2006)*

Brander 2005 Sauvignon Blanc (Santa Ynez Valley) $13. Similar to Brander's early release Sauvignon, this is a refreshingly dry, crisp wine, rich in citrus, fig, and melon flavors, and clean as a whistle. What a great job the winery is doing with this varietal, at every price tier. **87**—*S.H. (7/1/2006)*

Brander 2004 Sauvignon Blanc (Santa Ynez Valley) $12. Fruity, floral, slightly sweet, a little spritzy, crisp in acidity, and clean. That about says it all for this easy wine. Try it with fresh fruit, or by itself as an apéritif. **85**—*S.H. (10/1/2005)*

Brander 2003 Sauvignon Blanc (Santa Ynez Valley) $12. Redolent of citrus, melon, herb, and grass, the wine is clean and fresh, with a finish that is moderate in length. Good wine at a good price. **87**—*J.M. (8/1/2004)*

Brander 1999 Sauvignon Blanc (Santa Ynez Valley) $12. Fred Brander puts out at least four different Sauvignon Blancs; this is his workhorse release and it's quite distinctive. A strong, grassy quaff with lean citrus flavors and that curious note they call essence of cat. It's clean as a whistle; bright acidity scours the palate and prepares it to receive food. Herbed goat cheese comes to mind. **86**—*S.H. (5/1/2001)*

Brander 2005 Au Naturel Sauvignon Blanc (Santa Ynez Valley) $30. Brander's stainless steel fermented Sauvignon is an exciting wine, simply brilliant in pure fruit and mouthwatering acidity. It's as fresh as a harvest morning, with intense flavors of lemongrass, gooseberry, tangerine zest, green grass, and vanilla. Certainly at the top of its class. **93 Editors' Choice**—*S.H. (11/15/2006)*

Brander 2004 Au Naturel Sauvignon Blanc (Santa Ynez Valley) $30. California's top Sauvignon Blanc specialist continues on a roll with this wonderfully pure, clean wine. It's crisp and bone dry in gooseberry, lemon and lime, and fig flavors, with an intense cassis or black currant flavor that's unusual and thrilling in a dry Sauvignon Blanc. You'll savor every sip of this exceptional wine. **92 Editors' Choice**—*S.H. (5/1/2006)*

Brander 2003 Au Naturel Sauvignon Blanc (Santa Ynez Valley) $30. Sharp and minerally at first, with aromas of cat pee, nectarine, melon, and cucumber. Rather big and meaty on the tongue, with enough tangy gooseberry and citrus to balance out the larger peach and pear flavors. Thorough and healthy as a whole, with adequate acidity and girth. **89** *(7/1/2005)*

Brander 2002 Au Naturel Sauvignon Blanc (Santa Ynez Valley) $30. Firm and crips, with a fine-tuned array of grapefruit, spice, melon, lemon, herb, grass, and mineral flavors. It's sleek, clean, and fresh, with a long, bright finish. **91**—*J.M. (8/1/2004)*

Brander 2004 Cuvée Natalie Sauvignon Blanc (Santa Ynez Valley) $16. Opens with a clean, citrus and grass aroma, with just a hint of vanilla and toast, promising a dry wine. But it turns unexpectedly sweet,

although acids are balancing. The 13 percent of Riesling in this Sauvignon Blanc-dominated wine really shows. **84**—*S.H. (10/1/2005)*

Brander 1999 Cuvée Natalie Sauvignon Blanc (Santa Ynez Valley) $15. They call this their Alsatian-style wine, and indeed, it contains smaller amounts of Gewürztraminer, Riesling, and Sylvaner. This explains the pretty flavors, which range from citrus and straw through flowers and lusher spices and fruits. Yet it's very dry and crisp and finishes tart and racy. **90 Editors' Choice**—*S.H. (5/1/2001)*

Brander 2005 Cuvée Nicolas Sauvignon Blanc (Santa Ynez Valley) $25. One hundred percent barrel fermented and aged *sur lies*, this polished wine brings the same lemon and lime and grassy flavors as Brander's unoaked Au Naturel. But for me, the oak robs the wine of some of its crispness and brightness, although it's still a high-class Sauvignon Blanc. **90**—*S.H. (11/15/2006)*

Brander 2004 Cuvée Nicolas Sauvignon Blanc (Santa Ynez Valley) $26. Shows a return to form after the '03, with brilliantly ripe guava, nectarine, and herb-infused citrus flavors and clean, crisp acids. Totally dry, the wine has a good chunk of new French oak, which assists with a creamy texture, but doesn't take over. This is great California SB. **92 Editors' Choice**—*S.H. (12/1/2005)*

Brander 2002 Cuvée Nicolas Sauvignon Blanc (Santa Ynez Valley) $25. Lemony bright upfront with melon, pear, herb, and hints of grass. It's got a slightly honeyed note on the finish. Classy Sauvignon Blanc. **89**—*J.M. (8/1/2004)*

Brander 2005 Early Release Sauvignon Blanc (Santa Ynez Valley) $12. One of the first wines of the new vintage, this nouveau-style wine is ultrafresh and fruity. It has peppy, zesty acidity, and intense flavors of limes, kiwi, figs, and vanilla. Utterly refreshing and dry, this is a wine to stock up on. **87 Best Buy**—*S.H. (5/1/2006)*

Brander 2004 Early Release Sauvignon Blanc (Santa Ynez Valley) $12. The first wine I've had from the new vintage is clean, crisp, and totally enjoyable. It has a raw, juicy quality, like biting into a fresh lime, and is dry, with a long, citrus-and-vanilla aftertaste. **87 Best Buy**—*S.H. (5/1/2005)*

Brander 2005 Purisima Mountain Sauvignon Blanc (Santa Ynez Valley) $25. From one of California's greatest Sauvignon Blanc producers comes this very interesting wine from a well-regarded part of the appellation. It's a big wine, packed with concentrated citrus, fig, melon, and peppery spice flavors. With fresh acidity, it's right up there with the best. **92 Editors' Choice**—*S.H. (12/1/2005)*

Brander 2004 Purisima Mountain Vineyard Sauvignon Blanc (Santa Ynez Valley) $22. Very clean, pure and elegant, this wine hails from one of the best vineyards in the appellation. It's savory in citrus, melon, fig and spicy vanilla flavors, with a long, rich after-taste. **87**—*S.H. (12/1/2005)*

Brander 2001 Sauvignon au Naturel Sauvignon Blanc (Santa Ynez Valley) $30. An amazingly good Sauvignon Blanc, and as close as California gets to a true Marlborough version. The flavors of passion fruit, lime, peach, and vanilla are undercut by a huge burst of acidity that cleanses the palate and carries the flavors deep into the tastebuds. It's not all on the surface. This wine has a deep undertow of black currant that shows up on the finish. **91**—*S.H. (10/1/2003)*

Brander 2003 Cuvée Nicolas Sauvignon Blanc-Sémillon (Santa Ynez Valley) $25. Big and waxy, with aromatic notes of nuts, bread dough, and toast. Contains 25% Sémillon, so it's richer and less acidic than some. The flavor profile centers around baked peach and apple, while the finish is soft yet drying, probably a result of the oak it sat in. **86** *(7/1/2005)*

Brander 2005 Cuvée Natalie White Blend (Santa Ynez Valley) $18. A blend of Sauvignon Blanc, Riesling, Pinot Blanc and Pinot Gris, this is a nice, flavorful wine with some flair and sophistication. It's not a complicated wine, but satisfies with fruity flavors that are dry and crisp through the finish. **85**—*S.H. (11/15/2006)*

Brander 2003 Cuvée Natalie White Blend (Santa Ynez Valley) $16. Here's a fun and refreshing wine that's a mélange of Sauvignon Blanc, Riesling, Pinot Gris, and Pinot Blanc. In this warm appellation the melon, fig, and citrus flavors are ripe and slightly sweet, but crisp acidity balances. **86**—*S.H. (12/1/2004)*

USA

Brander 2005 Uno Mas White Blend (Santa Ynez Valley) $25. Brander is one of the best white wine specialists in California, especially when it comes to Sauvignon Blanc, which comprises half the blend here, with Grenache Blanc. This is a marvelous wine, racy, dry, spicy, and brilliantly structured, with piquant acidity and rewarding citrus, mango, and strawberry flavors. **91 Editors' Choice** —S.H. (12/31/2006)

BRAREN PAULI

Braren Pauli 1999 Frost Reserve Cabernet Sauvignon (Mendocino) $16. Hate to say it, but this is the kind of wine Mendocino is struggling to leave behind. It's rough and earthy, and seems simultaneously underripe and overripe. Dry, with good tannins, it's not going anywhere. **83** —S.H. (5/1/2002)

Braren Pauli 1999 Busch Creek Vineyard Chardonnay (Mendocino County) $12. Opens with apple and peach aromas and a funky, off-note that bothers. The flavors are spare and common. This rather tart wine is dry, with high acidity. Finishes with an earthiness. **83** —S.H. (5/1/2002)

Braren Pauli 1998 Merlot (Redwood Valley) $14. Struggles to drum up some interest, but it's hard to get excited. The wine has hot, cardboardy aromas of stewed prunes and mushrooms, and diluted berry flavors dominated by the heat of alcohol. It's pretty common stuff, but acceptable. **82** —S.H. (5/1/2002)

Braren Pauli 1999 Roar Vineyard Pinot Noir (Mendocino) $14. Begins with cooked aromas of berries steeped in coffee and rum, with stewed tomato notes, and drinks heavy and thick, although the flavors are ripe and sweet. Good acids set off the semi-sweet fruit. Flavorful, but can be faulted for lacking the delicacy Pinot Noir should have. **85** —S.H. (5/1/2002)

BRASSFIELD

Brassfield 2003 Monte Sereno Vineyard Cabernet Sauvignon (High Valley) $40. The wine has fine tannins and a certain rustic mouthfeel. The deep Cabernet flavor is there, plus the dryness and balance. What's needed is finesse, and some great oak would help. A wine to watch. **85** —S.H. (12/31/2006)

Brassfield 2003 High Serenity Ranch Merlot (High Valley) $19. This is quite an interesting Merlot, not least because it actually lives up to Merlot's reputation as the soft Cabernet. It's ripe and juicy in cherry flavor, with a rich, olive-y earthiness enhanced and framed by oak. At the same time, it's dry. The softness is balanced by wonderfully thick, fine tannins, with a grip that cries out for steak. **91 Editors' Choice** —S.H. (12/31/2006)

Brassfield 2004 Pinot Grigio (Clear Lake) $15. Gulpable, delicious, easy, fruity, delightful; these are a few words that come to mind with this wine. The apple, peach, fig, orange zest, and vanilla flavors are framed in zesty acidity, with an ultraclean, dry but ripe finish. **86** —S.H. (12/15/2005)

Brassfield 2003 Pinot Grigio (Clear Lake) $16. Fruity and crisp, with fresh apple, lime, and fig flavors that are balanced with brisk acids. An easy sipper that finishes slightly sweet. **85** —S.H. (3/1/2005)

Brassfield 2005 High Serenity Ranch Pinot Grigio (High Valley) $15. From a Lake County high-elevation region, this is a very crisp, almost tart dry white wine, with subtle, complex citrus flavors of lime, grapefruit, and guava, a minerally midpalate and a finish of stimulating white pepperiness. So versatile, it's a sommelier's dream. **88 Editors' Choice** —S.H. (12/31/2006)

Brassfield 2005 Susan's Passion Late Harvest Riesling (High Valley) $25. A very good dessert Riesling, nice and ripe in sweet apricot, honeysuckle, and tangerine flavors, with a buttercream vanilla topping and what tastes like rich botrytis honey. Fortunately, it has crisp acidity. **90** —S.H. (12/31/2006)

Brassfield 2004 Sauvignon Blanc (Clear Lake) $15. Feline, anyone? From the pungent first whiff through the dry, acidic, citrusy finish, this is that kind of Sauvignon Blanc. You either like it or you hate it. It wouldn't be my first choice. **83** —S.H. (12/15/2005)

Brassfield 2003 Sauvignon Blanc (Clear Lake) $15. A juicy Sauvignon Blanc, rich in ripe fig, lemon, and lime and spicy melon flavors, and well acidified. Finishes with a clean, fruity note. **84** —S.H. (8/1/2005)

Brassfield 2005 High Serenity Ranch Sauvignon Blanc (High Valley) $15. This is America's answer to Marlborough, showing true Lake County terroir, with high acidity that gives a minerally, gunmetal lift to the ripe grapefruit, passion fruit, kiwi, and lime flavors. Wonderfully good, and the low alcohol makes it easy to drink. **91 Best Buy** —S.H. (12/31/2006)

Brassfield 2002 Syrah (Clear Lake) $24. A nice, clean, everyday sort of red wine, dry and smooth. Shows cherry-berry, herb and slight oaky flavors and a velvety texture. **86** —S.H. (3/1/2005)

Brassfield 2003 Monte Sereno Vineyard Syrah (High Valley) $30. Very tannic, a challenge the winemaker will have to deal with, but there's enormous promise in this new, unexplored appellation of Lake County. Complex, this wine is marked by peppery blackberry fruit and licorice, with a rich vein of sweet new leather. Has that undefinable take-a-second-sip quality. Drink now, but decant for a few hours. **91** —S.H. (12/31/2006)

Brassfield 2003 Round Mountain Vineyard Syrah (Clear Lake) $23. An interesting Syrah: a bit rustic, but intricate. Cherry pie, blackberry jam, espresso, cola, blackstrap molasses, white pepper, and tannic Chinese tea flavors lead to a dry finish. The vineyard is on an extinct volcano at a high elevation east of Clear Lake. **85** —S.H. (12/31/2006)

Brassfield 2005 High Serenity Ranch Serenity White Table Wine White Blend (High Valley) $15. This is one of those catch-all blends that seems made up of all the wines left over after the varietals have been bottled. It's Sauvignon Blanc, Pinot Grigio and Gewürz, something of a mongrel. At a low price, it would be okay, since it's acidic and dry, but this is too much. **83** —S.H. (12/31/2006)

Brassfield 2004 Serenity White Blend (Clear Lake) $15. This blend of Sauvignon Blanc, Pinot Grigio, and Gewürztraminer is simple and easy, a dry, fruity wine that finishes slightly sweet. It's picnic-style wine. **83** —S.H. (12/15/2005)

Brassfield 2001 High Valley Zinfandel (Lake County) $19. Starts off with some earth tones, then gets set in its viscous, velvety-textured tannins. It's a little on the bright side, but the flavors are ultra-ripe: prune, dried apricot, plum, and spice. Intense, if not balanced. **86** (11/1/2003)

Brassfield 2003 Round Mountain Vineyard Zinfandel (Clear Lake) $19. Sure is ripe, flooding the mouth with dry pie filling flavors of blackberries, cherries, and raspberries, with the chocolate fudge edge that so many modernly ripe red wines get. All it needs now is more classic structure and mouthfeel. **86** —S.H. (12/31/2006)

BRAVANTE

Bravante 2003 Cabernet Sauvignon (Howell Mountain) $45. This Cab is young, dry, and very tannic, a juicy wine with concentrated currant and blackberry flavors. A noble wine, but don't open now. Try after 2009. **87** —S.H. (12/31/2006)

Bravante 2001 Merlot (Howell Mountain) $35. This is a sturdy, closed young wine. It's bone dry, with powerful tannins and subtle berry, cassis, and earth flavors. It has enough fruit in the finish to warrant another glass, but won't age for a long time. Best now through 2006. **85** —S.H. (8/1/2005)

BRAY

Bray 2002 Zinfandel (Shenandoah Valley (CA)) $16. Sweet, overripe, and rough. **81** —S.H. (3/1/2005)

BREWER-CLIFTON

Brewer-Clifton 2004 Ashleys Chardonnay (Santa Rita Hills) $60. With over 16% alcohol, this wine is soft, round, lush, and utterly delicious. The citrus and tropical fruit, oak, cream, and mineral flavors don't taste at all hot, but are luscious. **93** —S.H. (3/1/2006)

Brewer-Clifton 2004 Clos Pepe Chardonnay (Santa Rita Hills) $40. This Chard showcases the Hills' wonderful mélange of ripe tropical and citrus fruit and crisp acidity. Add to that the complex toast and vanillins of the barrel, and the result is eminently drinkable. Enjoy this unctuous Chardonnay early before that babyfat melts away. **92** —S.H. (8/1/2006)

Brewer-Clifton 2004 Melville Chardonnay (Santa Rita Hills) $46. It's odd that while the alcohol here is lower than on the winery's Rancho Santa

Rosa bottling, the wine tastes hotter, with a pepper spice note that actually complements the ripe, exotic tropical fruit, pear, and buttercream flavors. This is a very big, complex wine, long-lasting in the finish and impressive for the way its mass is balanced and contained. **93** —*S.H. (8/1/2006)*

Brewer-Clifton 2004 Mount Carmel Chardonnay (Santa Rita Hills) $52. Brilliant aromatics characterize this powerful wine. It has lots of charry, fine oak and huge fruit, like apricots, peaches, pineapples, and mangoes. In the mouth, a firm minerality kicks in, based on high, clean acidity. This is a beautifully complex, dazzling Chard, intense and pure, but balanced and elegant. **95 Editors' Choice** —*S.H. (3/1/2006)*

Brewer-Clifton 2004 Rancho Santa Rosa Chardonnay (Santa Rita Hills) $46. At nearly 16% alcohol, this is one of the biggest Chards I've ever had. It's totally dry and explosive in all sorts of late-picked, effusively ripe pineapple custard, lemon drop, and apricot, caramelized brown sugar and cinnamon. A wine like this is an achievement anywhere, and while there are those who will object to its size, it is certainly delicious. **93** —*S.H. (8/1/2006)*

Brewer-Clifton 2004 Ashley's Pinot Noir (Santa Rita Hills) $50. Powerful aromatics launch this wine, which is bursting with pure cherry, raspberry, cola, rhubarb pie, beetroot, and oak notes. Totally dry, and tart in acids, it's big and young, a little brawny now. Should mellow and knit together with a year or so in the cellar. **91** —*S.H. (3/1/2006)*

Brewer-Clifton 2004 Cargasacchi Pinot Noir (Santa Rita Hills) $64. Very refined and supple, with fabulous texture, all silk and satin on the palate. Perfectly showcases Pinot's sensual, seductive side, with cherry and cola flavors and a smooth elaboration of oak. Finishes complex, spicy, and long, a brilliant wine that combines power with elegance. **93** —*S.H. (3/1/2006)*

Brewer-Clifton 2004 Melville Pinot Noir (Santa Rita Hills) $64. This tastes riper and hotter than the winery's other Pinots I tasted, almost to the point of raisins and stewed prunes. The vintage was very difficult, with stupendous heat waves that challenged both growers and vintners. The wine does its best, but can't quite overcome the ill effects of the heat. **86** —*S.H. (8/1/2006)*

Brewer-Clifton 2004 Mount Carmel Pinot Noir (Santa Rita Hills) $72. What a young, powerful wine this is. From the first sniff, an assault of dried cherry, licorice, and Asian spice, to the lasting impression of tannins, all this wine wants to do is open up. Decanting, even overnight, will help to soften and round it out. It's a superb wine, rich, and elaborate, but a little hot in alcohol, which may limit the ageworthiness. Drink now through 2008. **92** —*S.H. (8/1/2006)*

Brewer-Clifton 2004 Rancho Santa Rosa Pinot Noir (Santa Rita Hills) $56. The vineyard is owned by Foley, which produces great Pinot, and what they all have in common is rich acidity, an uncommonly complete structure, and a clean purity of Pinot Noir fruit. This bottle is dry and fuller-bodied than Brewer-Clifton's other Pinots, although it retains those lovely red stone fruits that are so elegant. It's a tight, young wine that needs to be decanted, and should drink well through its sixth birthday. **93** —*S.H. (8/1/2006)*

BRIAN CARTER CELLARS

Brian Carter Cellars 2002 L'Etalon Bordeaux Blend (Yakima Valley) $30. This is the winery's core Bordeaux blend ("étalon" means "stallion" in French), and it delivers firm, full, even fleshy flavors. All five Bordeaux varieties are included in the blend. A ripe though not quite voluptuous style, it shows the fruit well with a solid presence and nice, firm structure. Polished but still youthful, it takes the new oak in stride and should continue to evolve nicely over the next decade. **90** —*P.G. (6/1/2006)*

Brian Carter Cellars 2002 Byzance Grenache-Shiraz (Yakima Valley) $30. The blend is 60-40 Grenache-Syrah, and the name comes from French slang for something that is luxurious, really chic. Sappy, grapy, nicely lifted, and vivacious, this is a beautiful mix of fruits in a spectrum from watermelon to strawberry to red plum to raspberry and pie cherry. There's plenty of acid and just a whiff of pepper from the Syrah. **89** —*P.G. (6/1/2006)*

Brian Carter Cellars 2003 Abracadabra Red Red Blend (Columbia Valley (WA)) $16. The second label for this new winery is made from grapes and barrels left out of the other blends. The result is a "mutt" wine that's red, ripe, and slightly volatile. Though it lacks the focus and precision of the other blends, it's full of ripe, polished fruit flavors and makes a good barbecue or by-the-glass red wine. It's soft, smooth, with some citrus and tart berry flavors. **87** —*P.G. (6/1/2006)*

Brian Carter Cellars 2002 Tuttorosso Sangiovese (Yakima Valley) $30. The tart acidity of Sangiovese, along with its spicy cranberry, red currant, and lean red berry flavors are buttressed with the addition of 27% Cabernet Sauvignon and 15% Syrah. It tastes very young despite its extended bottle age. Definitely a wine for acid lovers, it rounds out in the mouth with light flavors of hazelnut and mocha. **88** —*P.G. (6/1/2006)*

Brian Carter Cellars 2004 Oriana White Blend White Blend (Yakima Valley) $24. Aromatic, rich, and dry, this wine was fermented in used Chardonnay barrels and given extended lees contact. This is a creamy, leesy, rich wine, a very stylish blend that captures the citrusy Viognier, the floral Riesling and the rich, ripe, peachy Roussanne. **90** —*P.G. (6/1/2006)*

BRICE STATION

Brice Station 2003 Gold Rush Cabernet Franc (Calaveras County) $18. A nice everyday sort of red, medium-bodied, with gentle, soft tannins and blackberry flavors. Finishes dry and clean. **86** —*S.H. (3/1/2005)*

Brice Station 2002 Gold Rush Cabernet Sauvignon (Calaveras County) $16. Rustic, simple, and sharp, with earthy-berry flavors. **83** —*S.H. (3/1/2005)*

Brice Station 2003 Chardonnay (California) $17. Rustic and sharp, and very fruit. Finishes with a blast of oak and spices. **83** —*S.H. (2/1/2005)*

BRICELAND

Briceland 2000 Elk Prairie Vineyard Pinot Noir (Humboldt County) $24. Here is a wine from a county almost unknown for Pinot Noir. It expresses some varietal character in the raspberry and cherry flavors, and its dry, silky tannins. There are also less-ripe tomato and beet notes. The next step is to develop finesse. **84** —*S.H. (4/1/2003)*

Briceland 2000 Phelps Vineyard Pinot Noir (Humboldt County) $22. Good color, with earthy, black cherry, and tobacco aromas. Drinks earthy, with cherry and sage flavors. The tannins are silky but the wine needs more delicacy and elegance if it wants to compete with coastal Pinots. **83** —*S.H. (2/1/2003)*

BRICK HOUSE

Brick House 2002 Pinot Noir (Willamette Valley) $26. It starts out dark and bold, a deep purple color reminiscent of spicy Syrah. Despite the imposing entry, the wine tastes of light strawberry fruit, clean and simple, but surprisingly thin. **84** *(11/1/2004)*

Brick House 2002 Clos Ladybug Pinot Noir (Willamette Valley) $20. Pungent and minty, with tart flavors of not-quite-ripe berries. Not a big wine, but lively with crisp, cutting acids. **86** *(11/1/2004)*

Brick House 1997 Cuvée du Tonnelier Pinot Noir (Willamette Valley) $36. **87** *(10/1/1999)*

Brick House 2002 Evelyn's Pinot Noir (Willamette Valley) $40. Organically grown and made, this is a crisp, appealing bottle with fresh, round flavors of strawberry jam, vanilla, and a touch of herb. Shows some nice complexity and texture. **87** *(11/1/2004)*

Brick House 2002 Les Dijonnais Pinot Noir (Willamette Valley) $40. One of the real success stories of the vintage, this is a big, fruity, ripe, and intensely perfumed wine that carries its plump, posh fruit flavors smoothly across the full palate. Young but seamlessly integrated, it has a juicy, substantial mouthfeel and good grip. **90** *(11/1/2004)*

BRIDGEVIEW

Bridgeview 2003 Cabernet Sauvignon-Merlot (Southern Oregon) $10. Thin, tart, tannic, and earthy. It's reminiscent of the least expensive Australian Cab-Merlot blends, with the same herbal, tannic presence. **83** —*P.G. (9/1/2006)*

Bridgeview 2001 Cabernet Sauvignon-Merlot (Oregon) $10. The nose is forward and somewhat disjointed, a broad mix of fruit, herb, and wood.

USA

Flavors of stem and dill are there, along with soft, grapey fruit. **84** —*P.G.* (8/1/2002)

Bridgeview 2000 Chardonnay (Oregon) $7. About 15,000 cases were made of this simple, stainless-fermented, very clean and fruity wine. Nice cinnamon spice and light hazelnut flavors light up the finish. A lot of flavor and style for this price. **88 Best Buy** —*P.G.* (8/1/2002)

Bridgeview 1999 Chardonnay (Oregon) $7. Bridgeview is in southern Oregon, near the California border, and its hot climate vineyards are closer in style to Washington than to the Willamette Valley wineries to the north. This is a well-made budget Chardonnay, that delivers crisp fruit, a fresh, clean palate impression, and a bit of a mineral flavor in the finish. It's a useful style that foregoes the richer pleasures of barrel fermentation and oak aging in favor of a food-friendly wine at an affordable price. **85 Best Buy** —*P.G.* (11/1/2001)

Bridgeview 2003 Blue Moon Chardonnay (Oregon) $10. Dilute and thin, with only the vaguest hint of green apple for fruit flavor. There may be some attempt to add buttered popcorn-style oak flavoring, but it doesn't really add much. **82** —*P.G.* (9/1/2006)

Bridgeview 2000 Blue Moon Chardonnay (Oregon) $10. About 40% is barrel aged and put through malolactic. This is a heavier, more substantial effort than their regular Chardonnay, with more butterscotch flavors showing. With good fruit, some weight and texture, it's well made and a good value. **88 Best Buy** —*P.G.* (8/1/2002)

Bridgeview 1999 Blue Moon Chardonnay (Oregon) $10. The success of the "Blue Moon" Riesling spawned a Chardonnay sister, packaged in an even darker blue bottle, with gold stars bespeckling the label and neck. If it's all a bit over the top, you have to admire the chutzpah. Without all the foofarol, it would be just another soft, buttery Chardonnay. This way, it's the star of the show. **86** —*P.G.* (11/1/2001)

Bridgeview 2000 Gewürztraminer (Oregon) $10. This is a soft, open wine, as might be expected from this producer located near the California border, in one of Oregon's hottest growing regions. Flavors of ripe pears and sweet spices fill the palate, making a plush, accessible wine for immediate consumption. **86** —*P.G.* (4/1/2002)

Bridgeview 2003 Merlot (Southern Oregon) $10. There's a hint of cherry in the mid-palate, and the wine delivers simple pleasures. Nothing fancy, but nothing wrong. **84** —*P.G.* (9/1/2006)

Bridgeview 2000 Merlot (Oregon) $10. The grapes come from the Applegate valley and the blend is 100% Merlot. The flavors are not particularly varietal; they are broader and more rustic, reminiscent of Carmenère. The palate impression is of soft, sweet, light blueberry fruit, for immediate drinking. **85** —*P.G.* (8/1/2002)

Bridgeview 1999 Black Beauty Merlot (Oregon) $15. This is definitely a subpar effort from this usually reliable budget producer. Dark and muddy in appearance, it tastes of burnt sugar, tired fruit, and stemmy earth. The finish is dry and chalky, with ashy tannins. **80** —*P.G.* (4/1/2002)

Bridgeview 1997 Black Beauty Merlot (Oregon) $15. A definite impression of fresh-baked bread highlights the nose, underscored with dill and charcoal. Though a fair amount of Merlot is grown in southern Oregon, it has yet to establish a clear-cut persona, and so it comes across as either light or thin or green or tannic, at least in comparison to Washington and California, where the grape shines. This is soundly made and perfectly drinkable, but it finishes with an earthy, herbal, sour note that is not attractive. I'm not sure this is the right grape in the right place. **83** —*P.G.* (11/1/2001)

Bridgeview 2000 Pinot Gris (Oregon) $11. Light and refreshing, this no-frills version offers crisp, neutral flavors of green apples and melon. Despite the fact that Bridgeview is in hot-climate southern Oregon, their style of Pinot Gris is considerably leaner than those from up north. **84** —*P.G.* (2/1/2002)

Bridgeview 2000 Reserve Pinot Gris (Oregon) $16. This is the first reserve for Bridgeview. It's a block selection, treated the same as their regular bottling; i.e., all stainless, no malolactic. That said, it has an extra dimension, good texture, more elegance, and lovely fruit. **89 Editors' Choice** —*P.G.* (8/1/2002)

Bridgeview 2004 Pinot Noir (Southern Oregon) $13. A tart, leafy Pinot, with brambly berry, tomato leaf, and light cola flavors. Light and tannic, with some earthy weight to the midpalate. **84** —*P.G.* (9/1/2006)

Bridgeview 2000 Pinot Noir (Oregon) $12. Black raspberry, mushroom, and leather comprise the attractive, seductive nose. Plum and raspberry fruit meet on the palate, which has some starching dry woodiness to it. The feel is a bit chewy, but overall it's light and airy. **87 Best Buy** (10/1/2002)

Bridgeview 1999 Pinot Noir (Oregon) $12. This Pinot has a forward, spicy scent with some very pretty cranberry/black cherry fruit. It's front loaded for flavor, and falls off in the mid-palate. The finish is tannic and quite tough, suggesting the wine was left on the skins a bit too long. **84** —*P.G.* (11/1/2001)

Bridgeview 2004 Blue Moon Pinot Noir (Oregon) $18. The Blue Moon Pinot is indistinguishable from the regular Pinot bottling; tart, herbal, tannic, leafy, and earthy. **84** —*P.G.* (9/1/2006)

Bridgeview 2002 Blue Moon Pinot Noir (Oregon) $15. This popular package has a light, floral charm. Simple, forward fruit suggests cotton candy; there's a hole in the middle and overall it is charming but nondescript. **85** (11/1/2004)

Bridgeview 2000 Blue Moon Pinot Noir (Oregon) $15. Rubber, chocolate, vanilla, and an unwelcome note of cheddar cheese open up this perennial value winner, which just isn't as good a vintage as it has been in prior years. Flavors of cherry and plum come up on the palate before a dark finish that seems low in acidity and softer than normal. **84** (10/1/2002)

Bridgeview 1998 Blue Moon Pinot Noir (Oregon) $15. **90 Best Buy** —*M.S.* (12/1/2000)

Bridgeview 1998 Oregon Pinot Noir (Oregon) $11. **88 Best Buy** (11/15/1999)

Bridgeview 1998 Red Cedar Pinot Noir (Rogue Valley) $30. This is a late-release wine from a forward vintage; it's an odd duck, with very hard, chewy, stemmy tannins taking over from the very start. The fruit is in the background, and there are some interesting herbal highlights, but oh, that tannin is too much. **84** —*P.G.* (12/1/2003)

Bridgeview 2000 Reserve Pinot Noir (Southern Oregon) $20. Strong accents of mint, tomato leaf, and clove; tannic and earthy. There's a core of leafy, earthy spice, but the fruit doesn't show much ripeness. **85** —*P.G.* (9/1/2006)

Bridgeview 1999 Reserve Pinot Noir (Rogue Valley) $18. This shows excellent focus and spice in the nose, with scents of cardamom and clove reminiscent of a good Mendocino Pinot. Plenty of flavor up front, but the wine loses it in the middle palate. It finishes with a soft, spicy, slightly banana flavor, a bit out of balance. **87** —*P.G.* (8/1/2002)

Bridgeview 1998 Reserve Pinot Noir (Rogue Valley) $20. **87** —*J.C.* (12/1/2000)

Bridgeview 2005 Blue Moon Riesling (Oregon) $10. A popular, easily-spotted wine in a distinctive blue bottle. The wine is simple, tart, and lemony. Don't look for nuance here; it's a straight-ahead, off-dry, pleasant quaffer. **84** —*P.G.* (9/1/2006)

Bridgeview 2002 Blue Moon Riesling (Oregon) $8. **87** —*P.G.* (8/1/2003)

Bridgeview 2001 Blue Moon Riesling (Oregon) $7. **82** —*J.C.* (8/1/2003)

Bridgeview 2000 Blue Moon Riesling (Oregon) $7. This pleasant, off-dry Riesling, in its blue bottle (with a cork to match), has been a runaway success for Bridgeview. It's something of a marketing triumph, as the wine is indistinguishable (in price and flavor) from dozens upon dozens of competitors. But it is reliable and fruity, with ripe apples and orange scents and flavors, and a good, clean finish. **86 Best Buy** —*P.G.* (11/1/2001)

BRIDGEWAY

Bridgeway 2003 Syrah (Central Coast) $16. Simple and fruity, a light, cheery quaff destined to accompany burgers and the like. Raspberry and strawberry fruit, laced with a dash of vanilla. **84** (9/1/2005)

BRIDGMAN

Bridgman 2002 Chardonnay (Columbia Valley (WA)) $10. Here there is plenty of oak, laid on a bit thick, and a hot, tannic, and buttery finish. **87** —*P.G. (9/1/2004)*

Bridgman 2000 Chardonnay (Columbia Valley (WA)) $11. Soundly made, straightforward Washington Chardonnay, with chunky, forward, green-apple fruit married to some butterscotchy oak. Full malolactic fermentation brings the fruit forward and keeps the acids low. **86** —*P.G. (7/1/2002)*

Bridgman 1999 Merlot (Columbia Valley (WA)) $17. A big, aggressively oaky aroma, smelling like a stroll through a sawmill, leads into a wine whose simple fruit is simply overmatched by the wood. Tough, dry, and tannic through the finish. **84** —*P.G. (6/1/2002)*

Bridgman 2002 Roussanne (Yakima Valley) $13. Soapy, lemony, and spicy; this is a pleasant drinking white wine, but shows no clear varietal character. **86** —*P.G. (9/1/2004)*

Bridgman 2000 Sauvignon Blanc (Yakima Valley) $11. Some barrel fermentation (30%) has added a lightly toasty element to this bone dry wine. It shows simple flavors of melon and citrus, along with residual yeastiness. **85** —*P.G. (6/1/2002)*

Bridgman 1998 Syrah (Columbia Valley (WA)) $18. 81 —*S.H. (9/1/2000)*

Bridgman 2001 Syrah (Yakima Valley) $13. Front-loaded flavors show clean berry fruit, but the wine stops short in the middle and quickly cuts off, finishing with somewhat green, herbal tannins. **86** —*P.G. (9/1/2004)*

Bridgman 2000 Syrah (Yakima Valley) $17. There is some nice black fruit forward in the palate, and a bit of toasty tannin in the back, but where's the middle? There's a big hole where the heart of this wine should reside, and it makes the rest seem lean and unyielding. **83** —*P.G. (12/31/2002)*

Bridgman 1999 Syrah (Yakima Valley) $18. Its complex nose—inviting, with leather green tobacco and forest floor shadings on the dark berry fruit—is followed by a narrower, greener palate. There's good texture, with creamy oak and lemony note on the palate, which give way to a taut finish with tobacco and licorice shadings. **85** *(10/1/2001)*

Bridgman 2000 Viognier (Yakima Valley) $17. 84 —*P.G. (6/1/2002)*

BRIDLEWOOD

Bridlewood 1997 Cabernet Franc (Central Coast) $28. 88 —*S.H. (7/1/2000)*

Bridlewood 1997 Chardonnay (Central Coast) $18. 86 *(6/1/2000)*

Bridlewood 2000 Chardonnay (Edna Valley) $16. Vegetal and herbal, with disageeable aromas of canned white asparagus. Tastes a little better than it smells, but hardly like a Chardonnay. Flavors are citrusy, and the wine is lean and tart. 81 —*S.H. (9/1/2003)*

Bridlewood 1999 Chardonnay (Santa Barbara County) $18. Lots of bright peach, pear, and tropical fruit here, with a lush overlay of smoky, vanilla-tinged oak. In the mouth, it turns a bit flabby. The fruity flavors are pretty, and so is the oaky spice, but the texture could use some more sparkle and life. 84 —*S.H. (12/31/2001)*

Bridlewood 1998 Chenin Blanc (Santa Barbara County) $10. An unusual white, with aromas and flavors of green and yellow plums, melons, fresh clover, wax, and honey (without the sweetness). It's quite full for a Chenin, and dry, with a stony finish. 86 —*J.C. (10/14/2003)*

Bridlewood 1997 Merlot (Santa Barbara County) $22. 88 *(7/1/2000)*

Bridlewood 1999 Merlot (Central Coast) $22. Not a complete success due to notable vegetal notes suggesting those notorious South Coast aspara-gus. The acids and tannins are fine and so is the color. Most of the grapes came from Monterey, where the trick with Bordeaux varietals always is getting them ripe. 84 —*S.H. (8/1/2003)*

Bridlewood 1998 Arabesque Red Blend (California) $14. 86 —*S.H. (11/15/2000)*

Bridlewood 1999 Arabesque Rhône Red Blend (California) $14. Smells raw and stemmy, with green wood aromas. In the mouth, it's dry, as you'd expect. Not much flavor, for those accustomed to ripe fruit. It' a struc-tural wine, meant to go with food, and could be nice with, say, a lamb curry, which would bring out the hidden sweetness. If you're careful about pairing, it's a nice wine. A Rhône blend of Carignane, Grenache, Mourvèdre and Syrah. 85 —*S.H. (12/15/2001)*

Bridlewood 1998 Ranger Red Rhône Red Blend (California) $12. 85 —*S.H. (2/1/2000)*

Bridlewood 1998 Saddlesore Rosé Rhône Red Blend (California) $12. 85 —*M.S. (8/1/2000)*

Bridlewood 1998 Sauvignon Blanc (Santa Barbara County) $14. 87 —*S.H. (2/1/2000)*

Bridlewood 2000 Sauvignon Blanc (Santa Ynez Valley) $12. A lovely wine, made even more attractive by the value price. It has flavors and lemons and limes and a ripe, sweet edge of honey, although it's technically dry. The acidity is clean and refreshing. 87 —*S.H. (7/1/2003)*

Bridlewood 1999 Sauvignon Blanc (Santa Barbara County) $12. Easy-drinking wine here, with lemon-custard flavors and textures. Nothing complicated, and it finishes with a nice, spicy aftertaste. At this price, it's a pretty good value. 84 —*S.H. (12/15/2001)*

Bridlewood 2003 Syrah (Central Coast) $8. Nice and dry, and although it's a little sharp and tart in green mint, this inexpensive wine offers plenty of black cherry and cocoa flavors wrapped into smooth tannins. **84 Best Buy** —*S.H. (12/31/2006)*

Bridlewood 2001 Syrah (Central Coast) $20. This Syrah is grapy and raw, although there's no denying the wine's size and fruit-forward nature. It could use more complexity, finesse, and length. 83 *(9/1/2005)*

Bridlewood 2000 Syrah (Central Coast) $19. An interesting wine, not without problems. Pours intensely dark, and opens with aromas ranging from blackberries to earth and white pepper. In the mouth, straddles the ripeness line, with deliciously fruity flavors kept in check by an herbal edge. A blend of Paso Robles, Edna Valley, and Santa Ynez Valley. **90 Editors' Choice** —*S.H. (6/1/2003)*

Bridlewood 1999 Syrah (Central Coast) $20. The excellent fruit-to-acid balance and dark, ripe berry fruit supports subtle flavors. The result is a sweetly smoky, complete wine with attractive aromas, flavors, and a fairly dense mouthfeel. Moderate tannins, blackberry, herb, and toast notes mark the close. 89 *(10/1/2001)*

Bridlewood 1998 Syrah (Paso Robles) $18. 89 —*S.H. (11/15/2000)*

Bridlewood 2002 Estate Syrah (Santa Ynez Valley) $40. Like the winery's reserve 2003 Syrah, this is a raspingly dry, tannic wine that offers little pleasure now. It has greater balance, though, and a stronger fruit core. Might soften and sweeten over the next five years. 85 —*S.H. (10/1/2006)*

Bridlewood 2003 Reserve Syrah (Central Coast) $24. Totally dry, with harsh tannins that lock down the palate and last through an astringent finish, this is an unsatisfying wine that makes you wonder if it will age. It may do interesting things over the next five years, but it's a big roll of the dice. 84 —*S.H. (10/1/2006)*

Bridlewood 1998 Winners Circle Syrah (Central Coast) $25. 90 —*S.H. (11/15/2000)*

Bridlewood 1999 Winners Circle Selection Syrah (San Luis Obispo County) $24. Plum, black cherry, cured-meat, and "smoke-machine smoke" aro-mas comprise the subtle yet complex nose; raspberry, red-apple, toasted-nuts, and cola flavors dominate on the palate. Mouthfeel is smooth and full; long finish shows "soft but plentiful" tannins and min-eral flavors. 89 *(11/1/2001)*

Bridlewood 2004 Viognier (Central Coast) $24. Loaded with tons of ripely opulent fruit and floral flavors that just don't quit. Peach, quince, pineapple, honeysuckle, vanilla, buttered toast, and spice all mingle through the long finish. Plus, it has a wonderfully lush and creamy tex-ture. 90 —*S.H. (9/1/2006)*

Bridlewood 2005 Reserve Viognier (Central Coast) $20. If you like your Viogniers with flamboyant, in-your-face flavors, try this one. Honeysuckle, smoky peach pie, apricot, and vanilla cream, pineapple custard, it goes on and on. There's some sweetness to the finish, with for-tunate acidity to balance and cleanse. 86 —*S.H. (12/15/2006)*

Bridlewood 2001 Estate Reserve Zinfandel (Santa Ynez Valley) $24. An intriguing blend of tea, cherry, blackberry, spice, smoke, toast, coffee, chocolate, and herb flavors, all set in smooth, velvety tannins. Toasty,

USA

charry, and exotic on the finish, with a menthol twist. **90 Editors' Choice** *(11/1/2003)*

Bridlewood 1998 French Camp Zinfandel (Paso Robles) $16. **83** —*S.H.* *(5/1/2000)*

BROADFIELDS

Broadfields 2001 Merlot (North Fork of Long Island) $NA. **86** —*J.C.* *(10/2/2004)*

BROADLEY

Broadley 1997 Reserve Pinot Noir (Willamette Valley) $23. **82** *(11/15/1999)*

BROCHELLE VINEYARDS

Brochelle Vineyards 2001 Zinfandel (Paso Robles) $30. Kicks off with ultra-ripe aromas of prune, black cherry, and spice. This is a sweet style- not quite Port- but still very fruity, with bright cherry and more spice on the palate. Not for everyone. **83** *(11/1/2003)*

BROLL MOUNTAIN VINEYARDS

Broll Mountain Vineyards 2002 Merlot (Calaveras County) $32. There's a nice peppermint patty note to the cherries, cocoa, and smoky vanilla. Drinks a bit soft, but dry, with pleasant earthy-berry flavors. **85** —*S.H.* *(2/1/2005)*

Broll Mountain Vineyards 2003 Syrah (Calaveras County) $32. This winery has shown consistency over the years in producing a sound, balanced Syrah with lots of ripe red and black stone fruit, berry flavors, and a good grip of tannins. The next step is to aim for depth and complexity. **86** —*S.H. (12/31/2005)*

Broll Mountain Vineyards 2002 Syrah (Calaveras County) $31. A wonder- fully drinkable Syrah, dry and balanced, with tart plum, blackberry, and coffee flavors and a deeper undertow of rich earth. The tannins are siz- able, but smooth. Has lots of class. **89** —*S.H. (7/1/2005)*

Broll Mountain Vineyards 2001 Syrah (Calaveras County) $31. Fruity, with black cherry, black raspberry, rose petal, blueberry, and oaky-smoky vanilla, with a hint of cocoa on the finish. In the mouth, drinks dry and elegant, with soft, smooth tannins. **88** —*S.H. (2/1/2005)*

BROMAN

Broman 1999 Cabernet Sauvignon (Napa Valley) $54. There's a weedy, cig- arette ash scent here. The fruity flavors aren't bad, but there's a rough, tannic edge all the way through the finish. Tasted twice, with consistent results. **83** —*S.H. (10/1/2004)*

Broman 2002 Sauvignon Blanc (Napa Valley) $16. Bright edged and min- erally. The wine has a strong lemon and herb component as well. Very zippy on the finish. **85** —*J.M. (9/1/2004)*

BROOKDALE VINEYARDS

Brookdale Vineyards 2002 Cabernet Sauvignon (Napa Valley) $52. With its dark purple color, dramatic aroma of ripe black currants and oak, and appealing mouthfeel, this fine Cabernet expresses very good Napa character. The black currant flavors are framed in rich, sweet, smooth tannins. Probably best now and through 2006. **90** —*S.H. (12/15/2005)*

Brookdale Vineyards 2001 Cabernet Sauvignon (Napa Valley) $52. This is a muscular wine, framed in firm, ripe tannins and blessed with a com- plex array of coffee, cassis, blackberry, blueberry, licorice, and herb flavors. The finish is smoky, rich, and long. Should age quite well in the cellar. **91** —*J.M. (6/1/2004)*

Brookdale Vineyards 2000 Cabernet Sauvignon (Napa Valley) $48. Quite spicy in the nose, with hints of pretty cedar, anise, and herb flavors up front. Zippy acidity blends well with creamy smooth tannins, all framing a complex web of chocolate, raspberry, cassis, blackberry, licorice, and earth flavors. A slight citrus edge gives lift at the end. Long on the finish; a fine first effort from this new winery. **91** —*J.M. (6/1/2003)*

BROOKS

Brooks 2002 Pinot Noir (Oregon) $20. Light floral and tea scents, with notes of spice, herb, anise, and flowers on the palate. A quiet, delicate wine. **85** *(11/1/2004)*

Brooks 2002 Pinot Noir (Oregon) $20. Pretty and fruit driven, tasting of sweet, jammy preserves, this is very clean, polished, and expressive with- out relying on excessive new oak. Well-structured, with plenty of acid, it is well-matched to food and balanced for long-term aging. **88** *(11/1/2004)*

Brooks 2002 Janus Pinot Noir (Oregon) $29. Varietal, with lots of vanilla and cherry flavors dominating. Supple and smooth, with good grip and penetration. Velvety finish with a bit of bacon fat. **88** *(11/1/2004)*

Brooks 2002 Amycas White White Blend (Willamette Valley) $13. The odd name is taken from Greek mythology; the grapes are Riesling, Pinot Gris and Gewürztraminer, a very clever blend for Oregon, where all three excel. Fragrant, floral, and fruity, this wine combines the best qualities of the three grapes, and has a lingering, refreshing presence. **90 Best Buy** — *P.G. (12/1/2003)*

BROPHY CLARK

Brophy Clark 2004 Pinot Noir (Santa Rita Hills) $24. The wine comes from one of the most westerly sites in the appellation, a vineyard recently sold by Fess Parker. It has good, crisp acidity, and is very dry, with fine Pinot fruit and herb flavors. It's a stylish Pinot Noir, perhaps not the most powerful exemplar of Santa Rita, but a dashing wine. **89** —*S.H.* *(12/31/2006)*

Brophy Clark 2001 Pinot Noir (Santa Maria Valley) $20. Smells almost Zinny, with big notes of well-ripened wild cherries, pomegranates and pepper. In the mouth, it's very fruity and rich, although completely dry. Quite tasty, although a bit heavy for a Pinot Noir. **84** —*S.H. (12/1/2004)*

Brophy Clark 2000 Pinot Noir (Santa Maria Valley) $22. **86** *(10/1/2002)*

Brophy Clark 1999 Pinot Noir (Santa Maria Valley) $22. Solid and medium in weight, with an aromatic plum-cherry and herb nose that has a com- plex, slightly meaty, funky edge. The earthy black cherry, sour plum, and beet/tomato fruit on the palate rides good acidity onto a somewhat muted finish. Shows dusty tannins; this should improve for another year. **88** *(10/1/2002)*

Brophy Clark 1998 Pinot Noir (Santa Maria Valley) $20. **85** —*M.M.* *(12/15/2000)*

Brophy Clark 1998 Pinot Noir (Arroyo Grande Valley) $18. **89** —*J.C.* *(12/15/2000)*

Brophy Clark 2001 Ashley's Vineyard Pinot Noir (Santa Rita Hills) $24. From a cooler part of this cool appellation, a tart, crisp young wine, sharp with citrusy acids but ripe in bright cherry fruit. It's young and untogether now, but a year or so should bring more complexity and finesse. **87** —*S.H. (12/1/2004)*

Brophy Clark 2004 Sauvignon Blanc (Santa Ynez Valley) $13. Here's anoth- er great Sauvignon that displays Santa Ynez's ripe flavors, crisp acidity, and polished mouthfeel. Bursts with citrus, melon, fig, and spearmint flavors, with a fancy veneer of new French oak. Finishes clean and a little sweet. **87** —*S.H. (12/31/2006)*

Brophy Clark 2000 Valley View Sauvignon Blanc (Santa Ynez Valley) $14. A rich, 100% varietal in which warm sunshine coaxed out ripe notes of figs and white peach, while the region's cool temperatures capture Sauvignon's minty, anise-infused side. The resulting wine is complex and dynamic. High acidity gives this very dry wine a nice bite of tartness. **88** —*S.H. (7/1/2003)*

Brophy Clark 2002 Valley View Vineyard Sauvignon Blanc (Santa Ynez Valley) $13. A crisp, clean wine, high in acidity, with pretty flavors of ripe citrus fruits, figs, and spice. It's a little sweet, and finishes long and honeyed. **85** —*S.H. (9/1/2004)*

Brophy Clark 2001 Syrah (Santa Ynez Valley) $18. This wine shows its cool-climate origins with the peppery edge that dusts the cherry, black- berry flavors and the firm acidity. Finishes with a rich chocolate taste. **85** —*S.H. (9/1/2004)*

Brophy Clark 1999 Syrah (Santa Ynez Valley) $18. Roasted cherry fruit here is light and overridden by gamy brett and metallic notes. The unyielding horsey element will be hard for most people to get past. It has character, but many tasters found the aromas difficult. A retaste con- firmed the panel's initial findings. **83** *(10/1/2001)*

Brophy Clark 1999 Edna Ranch Syrah (Edna Valley) $22. The sour-plum nose sports cedar, leather, and clove accents. Round, even juicy on the palate, it displays a strong, tart cranberry-like element and pepper and oak shadings. Finishes bright, with tart fruit, herbs and leather. Earthy, juicy, a bit herbal, and definitely Syrah. Drink now through 2005. **87** (11/1/2001)

Brophy Clark 2003 Rodney Shull Vineyard Syrah (Santa Ynez Valley) $18. The vineyard is part of the Fess Parker estate, and the wine tastes dry and fruity, with a core of cherries, plums, blackberries, sweet leather, and bitter chocolate flavors that finish a little thin. There's a delicately silky mouthfeel, with firm tannins that call for a nice steak. **86** —*S.H.* (12/31/2006)

Brophy Clark 2002 Rodney Shull Vineyard Syrah (Santa Ynez Valley) $18. Leathery notes and a whole panoply of herbs and spices—cinnamon, pepper, lavender, and fennel—make for a lovely bouquet. In the mouth, however, the wine is not quite as impressive, yielding up tart cherry flavors and a lean mouthfeel. Finishes on dry, herbal notes. **86** (9/1/2005)

Brophy Clark 2000 Rodney's Vineyard Syrah (Santa Ynez Valley) $21. This is a bit riper and sweeter than the Edna Ranch bottling, and certainly less tannic. Blackberry, cherry liqueur, and black raspberry flavors are accessible and sweet. It is, however, a rustic wine, with jagged tannins, while high acidity gives the finish a peppery, hot burn. **85** —*S.H.* (12/1/2002)

Brophy Clark 2001 Lone Oak Vineyard Zinfandel (Paso Robles) $17. A bit sweet and spicy, with jammy raspberry, plum, and blackberry notes. The edges are on the bright side, with some tartness at the end. **85** (11/1/2003)

Brophy Clark 2000 Lone Oak Vineyard Zinfandel (Paso Robles) $17. Light in the nose, with just a hint of red berries and also some tomato. The raspberry and cherry fruit that carries the palate is a bit overcrowded by some potent vanilla oak. And then more of that dominating wood appears on the modest-length finish. **85** —*M.S.* (9/1/2003)

BROWN ESTATE

Brown Estate 2001 Zinfandel (Napa Valley) $32. A classy wine. Sleek, firm, and beautifully structured with lovely bright cherry, spice, chocolate, plum, and anise flavors. Clean and long at the end, the wine comes from a relatively new winery that consistently pumps out high quality. **92** —*J.M.* (3/1/2004)

BRUTOCAO

Brutocao 2003 Cabernet Sauvignon (Mendocino) $20. This is an old-style wine: it's the kind of Cabernet that made Cabernet famous in California. It's a dry, ruggedly tannic wine, filled with rewarding blackberry, coffee, herb, and spice flavors, and finishes with balance and a certain polish. **87** —*S.H.* (12/15/2006)

Brutocao 1996 Bliss Vineyard Cabernet Sauvignon (Mendocino) $16. 87 — *S.H.* (3/1/2000)

Brutocao 1997 Brutocao Vineyards Cabernet Sauvignon (Mendocino) $18. 88 —*P.G.* (12/15/2000)

Brutocao 2001 Estate Bottled Cabernet Sauvignon (Mendocino) $20. Dry, sharp and edgy, this rustic Cab has blackberry and coffee flavors and is fully dry. The sharpness persists through the finish. **83** —*S.H.* (12/15/2005)

Brutocao 2002 Riserva d'Argento Cabernet Sauvignon (Mendocino) $34. Clearly a step up from Brutocao's regular '02, this interesting wine has distinct features of its own. It's very soft and creamy, and intricate in flavors, suggesting macaroons soaked in rum and crème de cassis. But it's dry. **88** —*S.H.* (11/1/2005)

Brutocao 1999 Riserva d'Argento Cabernet Sauvignon (Mendocino) $32. Deep color. Oaky-smoky nose with considerable cassis and black currant. In the mouth, dry, rich, and earthy, with not-too-subtle tannins and a real bite of acidity. Has an herbal, sage and tobacco edge to the fruit, and finishes dry and balanced. **86** —*S.H.* (5/1/2002)

Brutocao 2002 Vineyard Select Cabernet Sauvignon (Mendocino) $25. Properly made in every respect, this Cab shows its warm origins in the raisiny flavors that accompany the blackberries, cherries and oak. That slightly baked edge could actually make it a good match with a smoky barbecue sauce. **85** —*S.H.* (11/1/2005)

Brutocao 1998 Bliss Vineyard Chardonnay (Mendocino County) $15. 84 (6/1/2000)

Brutocao 1997 Bliss Vineyard Reserve Chardonnay (Mendocino) $23. 86 — *P.G.* (10/1/2000)

Brutocao 1999 Riserva d'Argento Chardonnay (Mendocino) $24. From the Sanel Valley, an inland region near Ukiah that produces good, crisp, dry white wines. This one has lemony, buttery, and wildflower aromas, and drinks full and rich. The fruit flavors are bright and buttery in this assertive wine, which has a good structure and is frankly delicious. **90** — *S.H.* (5/1/2002)

Brutocao 2004 Feliz Vineyard Dolcetto (Mendocino) $18. Rustic and ready, this is a wine for spaghetti and meatballs. It's fruity, bold, and ripe, with rich, thick tannins. **83** —*S.H.* (12/15/2005)

Brutocao 2002 Bliss Vineyard Select Merlot (Mendocino) $20. Sharp and raw in acids, with cherry, black raspberry, and white pepper notes, this is a decent, rustic wine. But it seems overpriced for what you get. **84** — *S.H.* (12/15/2005)

Brutocao 2003 Bliss Vineyards Merlot (Mendocino) $20. Tastes like a Cabernet, dry and tannic and fairly sharp, with blackberry, cherry and coffee flavors. A bit rustic. **86** —*S.H.* (12/15/2006)

Brutocao 1996 Brutocao Vineyards Merlot (Mendocino) $18. 90 —*S.H.* (3/1/2000)

Brutocao 2003 Riserva d'Argento Merlot (Mendocino) $34. I like this Merlot for its full-bodied richness and depth of flavor. It's so much better than the '02. With 15% Cabernet, it's almost a full point higher in alcohol than the winery's Bliss Merlot, and it shows in the opulent, fat blackberry, blueberry, and cassis flavors. **90** —*S.H.* (12/15/2006)

Brutocao 2002 Riserva d'Argento Merlot (Mendocino) $34. Ripe to the point of overripe, with chocolate-covered raisin flavors, this soft, rustic Merlot showcases a hot vineyard. Yet it's dry, with only modest alcohol. **84** —*S.H.* (12/15/2005)

Brutocao 1998 Riserva d'Argento Merlot (Mendocino) $32. Very nice, very dry wine, and one that shows Mendocino's promise with this grape. Pronounced aromas of new French oak are sweet and smoky and full of char and vanilla, and complement a rich earthiness in the mouth. The wine is not too fruity but suggest blackberries. The tannins are dry and dusty and provide a chewy mouthfeel. **90** —*S.H.* (5/1/2002)

Brutocao 2004 Pinot Noir (Anderson Valley) $24. Located in central, hot Mendocino, Brutocao reaches into this cool western valley for Pinot, and captures the appellation's terroir with a lightly delicate, silky wine of interest. It's fully dry and crisp in acids, with insistent cola, red cherry, and wood spice flavors. **87** —*S.H.* (7/1/2006)

Brutocao 1998 Feliz Vineyard Pinot Noir (Mendocino) $24. 87 —*P.G.* (12/15/2000)

Brutocao 2003 Riserva d'Argento Pinot Noir (Anderson Valley) $32. This is a super-drinkable Pinot. It's delicately structured, silky, and dry, with complex flavors of cherries, cola, and spices and a rich coat of smoky oak. The finish is long in sweet raisins and cassis. Each sip makes you want another. **91** —*S.H.* (11/1/2005)

Brutocao 2004 Feliz #62 Zinfandel Port (Mendocino) $32. Try this sweet, soft, simple sipper, with its flavors of crème de cassis, rum, and cola, and sugared coffee, with crunchy butter cookies or pound cake. **85** —*S.H.* (7/1/2006)

Brutocao 2003 Contento Vineyard Primitivo (Mendocino) $18. With its sticky sweet finish and raw acidity, this Zin-like wine leaves a lot to be desired. **82** —*S.H.* (11/1/2005)

Brutocao 2002 Contento Vineyard Primitivo (Mendocino) $18. An herbal wine, with flavors redolent of dried thyme and sage. Tart cherry, raspberry, plum, and citrus flavors are also in evidence, unfolding with some length at the end. **86** —*J.M.* (10/1/2004)

Brutocao 2001 Coro Mendocino Red Blend (Mendocino) $35. Bright textured with a zippy cherry core, the wine has an almost tart edge backed by hints of raspberry, cherry, and herbs. Somewhat short at the end. **85** —*J.M. (9/1/2004)*

Brutocao 2003 Hopland Ranches Quadriga Red Blend (Mendocino) $24. A rustic wine that finishes off-dry with sugared blackberry tea and warm cola flavors. Sangiovese, Primitivo, Barbera, and Dolcetto. **81** —*S.H. (11/15/2006)*

Brutocao 2001 Sauvignon Blanc (Mendocino County) $12. A very bright textured wine, redolent of zippy lemons and mineral flavors. Quite clean on the finish, with a flinty, herbal edge. **84** —*J.M. (10/1/2003)*

Brutocao 1997 Bliss Vineyard Sauvignon Blanc (Mendocino) $15. 87 —*S.H. (3/1/2000)*

Brutocao 2003 Bliss Vineyards Sauvignon Blanc (Mendocino) $12. A lemony bright wine that serves up hints of herb and melon. Crisp, simple, and clean. **84** —*J.M. (10/1/2004)*

Brutocao 2005 Feliz Vineyard Sauvignon Blanc (Mendocino) $14. Dry, crisp, and food-friendly, with grapefruit, lime zest, and melon flavors accompanied by quite a bit of acidity. Shows strong Sauvignon character in a clean, bright package. **85** —*S.H. (11/15/2006)*

Brutocao 2004 Feliz Vineyard Sauvignon Blanc (Mendocino) $12. Here's a varietally true wine, correct and simple. It has citrus and lemongrass flavors, and is dry and tart on the finish. **83** —*S.H. (11/1/2005)*

Brutocao 2003 Feliz Vineyard Select Syrah (Mendocino) $25. A bit funky, meaty, and gamy, but also unfurls in the glass to reveal jammy berry scents and a hint of coffee. Full-bodied, yet zips up the finish with citrusy notes. Rustic but enjoyable. **86** *(9/1/2005)*

Brutocao 2002 Zinfandel (Mendocino) $20. Simple cherry and spice flavors hold forth here, while bright acidity carries it along the palate in a fresh manner. Tannins are moderate and the finish is a little short. **84** —*J.M. (10/1/2004)*

Brutocao 2001 Zinfandel (Mendocino) $18. This one's at the limit of brightness, which distracts from otherwise interesting Bing cherry, raspberry, berry, and spice flavors. **80** *(11/1/2003)*

Brutocao 2002 Bliss #3 Vineyard Zinfandel (Mendocino) $20. A full-bodied wine that packs plenty of chocolate, plum, coffee, black cherry, vanilla, and spice flavors. The tannins are fairly smooth, while the finish is a tad short for a wine with this kind of stuffing. Still, quite nice for those who enjoy a rich, sweet Port style. **88** —*J.M. (10/1/2004)*

Brutocao 1996 Bliss Vineyard Zinfandel (Mendocino) $15. 87 —*J.C. (5/1/2000)*

Brutocao 1999 Brutocao Vineyards Zinfandel (Mendocino) $16. From old vines, has deep aromas of coffee, tobacco, cola, plum, black cherry and smoke. It's a big wine, with 15.3 percent alcohol, which it wears well because it's balanced. The fruit is fully ripened and upfront, and surrounded by fairly hefty tannins. **86** —*S.H. (5/1/2002)*

Brutocao 1998 Brutocao Vineyards Zinfandel (Mendocino) $18. Cranberries and watermelon in the nose, leading into a soft, light, pleasant wine. Smooth and simple flavors; the wine needs to be chilled to show its best. This is made for near-term enjoyment. **85** —*P.G. (3/1/2001)*

Brutocao 2003 Estate Zinfandel (Mendocino) $20. Smells like cheddar cheese, tastes sweet, and lacks acidity. **81** —*S.H. (12/15/2005)*

BUCKLIN

Bucklin 2005 Compagni Portis Vineyard Gewürztraminer (Sonoma Valley) $20. The vineyard is in the southern part of the valley, near Carneros, and the wine shows fog-influenced acidity that cleans and refreshes the exotic fruit, flower, mineral, and spice flavors. It's elegant and layered, an Alsatian-style Gewürz that grows more interesting with each sip. **90** —*S.H. (12/15/2006)*

Bucklin 2004 Old Hill Ranch Zinfandel (Sonoma Valley) $34. From an old field blend said to date to the 1880s. The winery states that the wine also includes Grenache, Petite Sirah, Alicante, Carignane, and several other varieties. It's a very complex Zin, with layers of fruits, berries, herbs, and spices, and is full-bodied enough for anything from steak to venison. Minor quibble: too sweet despite high alcohol. **86** —*S.H. (12/15/2006)*

Bucklin 2001 Old Hill Ranch Zinfandel (Sonoma Valley) $30. The fruit flavors are a little lean, with toasty oak at the forefront. Nevertheless, the wine shows good structure. Tannins are ripe, and the anise, plum, black cherry, pepper, and spice notes are well integrated. **88** *(11/1/2003)*

BUEHLER

Buehler 2002 Chardonnay (Russian River Valley) $10. Turning old, tired, and funky, with dried leaf flavors and a tart, rasping finish. This Chard is just too old. **81** —*S.H. (12/15/2005)*

Buehler 2000 Reserve Chardonnay (Russian River Valley) $30. A tight, flinty Chard whose green apple and lime flavors are accompanied by mineral, slate, and chalky notes. Feels streamlined in the mouth despite elaborate oak. The finish is short and spicy. **86** —*S.H. (2/1/2003)*

Buehler 2001 Zinfandel (Napa Valley) $14. Soft and plush, with smooth tannins supporting layers of coffee, currant, chocolate, plum, toast, and tar flavors. Spicy notes add interest to the blend, which finishes a little on the short side. Nonetheless, quite juicy. **88** —*J.M. (9/1/2004)*

Buehler 1997 Estate Zinfandel (Napa Valley) $18. 89 —*P.G. (11/15/1999)*

BUENA VISTA

Buena Vista 2000 Cabernet Sauvignon (Carneros) $20. Great structure here, with super-velvety tannins and firm acids. Feels clean in the mouth, with subtle oak. The flavors suggest blackberries, with a strong overlay of pepper and sage. Cool climate winegrowing has produced a wine that straddles the line between ripe and green. **87** —*S.H. (4/1/2003)*

Buena Vista 2000 Cabernet Sauvignon (California) $9. California Cabernet in at this price? This one tries hard. Has good varietal flavor and pretty tannins, and is dry and balanced. It's a little skimpy in depth and concentration, though. **85 Best Buy** —*S.H. (11/15/2002)*

Buena Vista 1998 Cabernet Sauvignon (Carneros) $17. Made in the international style, the pretty cassis, black currant, and smoky oak aromas lead to a rich, textured wine, deeply flavored and elegantly structured. Lovely tastes of currants and berries are framed in intricate tannins. It's not a blockbuster, but a lovely, limpid, supple wine, perfect for tonight and near-term consumption. **90 Editors' Choice** —*S.H. (11/15/2001)*

Buena Vista 1997 Cabernet Sauvignon (Carneros) $18. Well-made and fancy, this wine is elegant, rather than a blockbuster. They didn't go for enough extract to choke a horse, so the wine is light and airy on the palate, but by no means simple. There's plenty of currant and blackberry fruit and oak. It's a "feminine" wine; not the kind that wins blind tastings, but a food wine you drink with delight. **90 Editors' Choice** —*S.H. (5/1/2001)*

Buena Vista 1996 Cabernet Sauvignon (Carneros) $18. 88 —*M.M. (6/1/1999)*

Buena Vista 1995 Grand Reserve Cabernet Sauvignon (Carneros) $27. 90 —*M.M. (6/1/1999)*

Buena Vista 2004 Chardonnay (Carneros) $20. A plump, medium-bodied Chardonnay with a deft touch of oak, this is what most California Chardonnay drinkers are looking for in an entry-level wine. Slightly nutty, toasty elements frame bold pineapple and citrus flavors. **87** *(10/1/2006)*

Buena Vista 2000 Chardonnay (California) $8. This isn't the greatest wine in the world, but if you're looking for a solid pop-style Chard, this is one. Ripely fruity and spicy, oaky, and smoky, and with a honeyed texture, it will please most everyone without breaking the bank. **86 Best Buy** —*S.H. (12/15/2002)*

Buena Vista 1999 Chardonnay (Carneros) $18. Lush and full-bodied, this is a fruit-driven wine made complex by charry oak and creamy lees. Ripe peach and pear flavors are buoyed by refreshing acidity. Possesses elegance and harmony, making it very drinkable. **88** —*S.H. (2/1/2003)*

Buena Vista 1998 Chardonnay (Carneros) $14. From a perennial value leader, a refreshingly fruity wine with quite a bit of oaky complexities. Its got bold tropical fruit flavor and rich spiciness and full-bodied structure, an assertive wine of distinctive quality. It's the equal of more expensive Chards, and a nice value. **88 Best Buy** —*S.H. (12/31/2001)*

Buena Vista 1997 Chardonnay (Carneros) $15. 89 Best Buy —*S.H.* *(6/1/2000)*

Buena Vista 1996 Estate Chardonnay (Carneros) $14. 87 —*M.M.* *(6/1/1999)*

Buena Vista 1997 Grand Reserve Chardonnay (Carneros) $28. 89 *(6/1/2000)*

Buena Vista 1996 Grand Reserve Chardonnay (Carneros) $26. 91 —*M.M.* *(6/1/1999)*

Buena Vista 2004 Ramal Vineyard Chardonnay (Carneros) $34. Tighter and more citrusy than the regular Chardonnay, with the oak coming across as more restrained, although the proportion of new wood is undoubtedly higher. It's a subtly nutty, textural wine, with apple and lemon notes that linger on the finish. **90** *(10/1/2006)*

Buena Vista 2003 Ramal Vineyard Chardonnay (Carneros) $32. Take either of Buena Vista's clonal bottlings of Chardonnay from this vineyard and kick them down a notch, and you get this wine. It's not quite as complex, but still a rich, supple Chard, a little soft but flamboyant in tropical fruit, oak, and buttercream. **89** —*S.H. (12/15/2005)*

Buena Vista 2004 Ramal Vineyard Clone 17RY Chardonnay (Carneros) $34. What a wonderfully complex, satisfying wine. It combines the steely acidity the vineyard regularly contributes with massively ripe tropical fruit flavors to produce a real stunner. Rich in mango custard, Key Lime pie, pineapple sorbet, vanilla pudding and smoky oak, it has a crispness that makes the flavors sing. Best in its youth, and should hold for a good five years. **94 Editors' Choice** —*S.H. (8/3/2006)*

Buena Vista 2003 Ramal Vineyard Clone 17RY Chardonnay (Carneros) $32. Tasted side by side with the winery's Clone 96 from the same vineyard, this tasty Chard is a bit firmer and denser, although it shares the same qualities of big, exotic fruit and oak, and a rich, leesy creaminess. Both are very fine wines to watch in future vintages. **92** —*S.H. (12/15/2005)*

Buena Vista 2003 Ramal Vineyard Clone 96 Chardonnay (Carneros) $32. From the Sonoma side of Carneros. It satisfies all around, from the rich tropical fruit and spice flavors to the creamy texture and refreshingly crisp mouthfeel to the deliciously long finish. **92** —*S.H. (12/15/2005)*

Buena Vista 2004 Ramal Vineyard Dijon Clones Chardonnay (Carneros) $34. It's fun to compare this to the winery's Ramal Vineyard bottling. This is tighter still, a young, crisp, minerally Chard, racy and elegant in pineapple, mango, and buttered toast, with the high acidity associated with this vineyard. It's a fine, complex wine now, and should hold for at least five years, possibly longer. **93** —*S.H. (8/3/2006)*

Buena Vista 2003 Merlot (Carneros) $25. With its slightly drying tannins and firm finish, this is a steakhouse Merlot, not a soft, easy sipper to drink on its own, yet it's not overpowering in weight. Restrained cherry, tomato, and chocolate flavors form the backbone, while hints of tea and tobacco leaf add more herbal notes. **86** *(10/1/2006)*

Buena Vista 2000 Merlot (California) $9. Lots of value for the money here. Deep and rich, with a fairly complex structure and depth. The flavors veer between dark stone fruits and earthy herbs and tobacco. It's balanced, soft, and supple, a tremendously versatile full-bodied table wine. **88 Best Buy** —*S.H. (11/15/2002)*

Buena Vista 1999 Merlot (Carneros) $22. Not bad, but surprisingly lean and herbal for a '99, with sage and tobacco flavors. It's very dry, rich in tannins and acids, and absolutely clean, with little oak influence. **86** —*S.H. (2/1/2003)*

Buena Vista 1998 Merlot (Carneros) $18. Big, rich, and sturdy, this wine nicely showcases the depth of Merlot's stone-fruit and berry flavors, while the tannins are soft and pretty. Not that it's a slouch. There's a tough backbone of acids and good structure. The finish is rich and interesting. **89 Editors' Choice** —*S.H. (11/15/2001)*

Buena Vista 1998 Merlot (California) $10. Ripe and jammy aromas, with an assortment of wild berry, chocolate, and smoky notes. The flavors are ripe, full, and slightly sweet. Finely meshed tannins and lively acidity produce a harmony. There's a certain lack of finesse, but what can you expect at this price? **86 Best Buy** —*S.H. (5/1/2001)*

Buena Vista 1996 Estate Merlot (Carneros) $19. 85 —*M.M. (6/1/1999)*

Buena Vista 2004 Pinot Noir (Carneros) $22. Like the regular Chardonnay, Beuna Vista's regular Pinot Noir is a medium-bodied, easy-drinking version of the variety. There's enough herbal complexity to keep it interesting, but the cherry-tinged fruit is ripe and the tannins supple. Finishes with a burst of crisp acidity. **87** *(10/1/2006)*

Buena Vista 2000 Pinot Noir (Carneros) $22. A pretty wine, if a little one-dimensional. Has jammy blackberry, cherry, cola, and pepper aromas and flavors, soft, silky tannins and bright acids. Dry and balanced, it fulfills basic Pinot requirements. **86** —*S.H. (2/1/2003)*

Buena Vista 1999 Pinot Noir (Carneros) $17. Reins in that sometimes jammy Carneros fruit with an earthy, mushroomy component and sumptuous tannins. Oak use is judicious. The brilliant Pinot texture is there, silk smooth and highlighted by bright acidity. It seems to change its nature with every sip, surely the mark of a great wine. **91 Best Buy** — *S.H. (12/15/2001)*

Buena Vista 1998 Pinot Noir (Carneros) $17. Cherry and raspberry mark this wine, along with spearmint, slightly herbaceous and tomato notes, and smoky oak. It's varietally correct and more substantial than most Carneros Pinots, with the kind of meatiness you associate with, say, Russian River. The tannins are soft, but complex. For this robust, medium-bodied wine, try high-quality steaks and chops. **89** —*S.H. (5/1/2001)*

Buena Vista 1996 Estate Pinot Noir (Carneros) $16. 87 —*M.M. (6/1/1999)*

Buena Vista 1996 Grand Reserve Pinot Noir (Carneros) $26. 92 —*M.M.* *(6/1/1999)*

Buena Vista 2004 Ramal Vineyard Pinot Noir (Carneros) $38. The tannins and texture are very soft and supple, making this wine glide down all too easily. Delicate dried spice and shiitake perfumes emerge from the glass, while the flavors fold in cherry, plum, and a bit of root beer. Shows a touch of alcoholic warmth on the finish. **89** *(10/1/2006)*

Buena Vista 2003 Ramal Vineyard Pinot Noir (Carneros) $38. Smells gamy, with a smoky, bacon scent that quickly turns fruity in cherries and spice in the mouth. This wine is medium-bodied and dry, with silky tannins and a very smooth, velvety texture. **85** —*S.H. (12/15/2005)*

Buena Vista 2004 Ramal Vineyard Dijon Clones Pinot Noir (Carneros) $NA. Here's a delicious wine, rich and forward in flavor. These Dijon clones produce exceptionally clean, bright fruit, and this Pinot bursts with cherry, pomegranate, rhubarb, and cola flavors. It's fully dry, with subtle complexities from oak. Great now and for the next five years, but don't hold it so long that it loses its fruity youthfulness. **92** —*S.H. (8/3/2006)*

Buena Vista 2003 Ramal Vineyard Pommard Clone 5 Pinot Noir (Carneros) $38. What a pretty Pinot Noir. It's distinctly cool climate, with tangy acidity and a silky texture that frames good varietal flavors of cola, cherries, rhubarb, coffee, and cinnamon spice. Despite the light, airy texture, this wine leaves a seriously fruity aftertaste. **89** —*S.H. (12/15/2005)*

Buena Vista 2004 Ramal Vineyard Swan Selection Pinot Noir (Carneros) $NA. Swan is the old, pre-Dijon clonal selection used by so many wineries. The wine has a youthful character, a little sharp right now, but there's brilliant promise. Crisp in acids, fairly tannic, but loaded with dramatically ripe cherry and pomegranate fruit, this is one to lay down. Best after 2008, but fine now with a rich duck presentation. **92 Cellar Selection** —*S.H. (8/3/2006)*

Buena Vista 2002 Reserve Pinot Noir (Carneros) $15. A bit closed now, but airing reveals strawberry, cherry, and mint notes with a hint of meat and mulch. Clean and dry, showing tea, vanilla, and cherry flavors. Probably best now, but decant it. **86** *(11/1/2004)*

Buena Vista 2001 Sauvignon Blanc (Lake County) $7. This is one of the best Sauvignon Blancs of the year, and at this price, it's a mind-blowing value. Bone dry and crisp, with superb, lusty flavors of gooseberry, lime, and smoke, and beautiful balance. Run, don't walk and buy it by the case. **90** —*S.H. (9/1/2003)*

Buena Vista 2000 Sauvignon Blanc (California) $8. This one's for you if you like dry, tart, acidic, grassy, grapefruit-juice-flavored wines that scour the palate and leave it clean and refreshed. It's an afternoon cocktail wine, perfect for grilled veggies, goat cheese, and garlic bread. **86 Best Buy** —*S.H. (11/15/2001)*

USA

Buena Vista 1999 Sauvignon Blanc (California) $9. Surprisingly rich and layered for this price. Shines with grass, melon, smoke, lime, and butter aromas. Equally tasty in the mouth, with a spicy density that lingers long on the palate. Very flavorful, with ripe, full-bodied lemon-and-lime fruit. Zesty acidity keeps the slight sweetness balanced. One of the year's best Sauvignon Blanc values. **87 Best Buy** —*S.H. (5/1/2001)*

Buena Vista 2004 Syrah (Carneros) $25. Straightforward, uncomplicated but varietally correct, this wine features the bright blueberry and plum notes of Syrah, accented by hints of dried spices and vanilla. Ample in weight, supple in the mouth, but needs a bit more complexity and length to score higher. **86** *(10/1/2006)*

Buena Vista 2004 Ramal Vineyard Syrah (Carneros) $38. Like the regular Syrah, this is fruit-forward, with notes of berry cobbler combining the bold notes of blueberries and boysenberries with vanilla and baking spices. Lovely, soft tannins complement the firmly acidic finish. **89** *(10/1/2006)*

Buena Vista 1998 Harazsthy Collection White Blend (Carneros) $25. Grassy, herbaceous aromas dominate, with smoke, hazelnut, and fig elements. Has powerful flavors of grass and grapefruit, with crisp acidity. Barrel fermentation and lees aging add a sweet creaminess to this bone-dry beauty. **88** —*S.H. (8/1/2001)*

Buena Vista 2001 Zinfandel (California) $9. Quite fruity and pleasant, with bright black cherry, licorice, plum, coffee, cola, and spice flavors that are set on relatively smooth tannins. The finish is a tad short, but the ensemble holds together. **87 Best Buy** *(11/1/2003)*

Buena Vista 2000 Zinfandel (California) $9. Absolutely lovely. Full of pretty raspberry and cherry flavors with peppery spice, and dry. It's not too alcoholic, with tannins that are soft, but intricate and complex. At this price, stock up. **90 Best Buy** —*S.H. (12/1/2002)*

BUFFALO RIDGE

Buffalo Ridge 1999 French Camp Vineyard Chardonnay (Central Coast) $13. Concentrated and intense, it's marked by stylish tropical fruit flavors and quite a dose of smoky oak. There's a mineral streak right down the middle that gives it a steely spine, and refreshing acidity adds to the structural integrity. **87** —*S.H. (11/15/2001)*

Buffalo Ridge 1999 Reserve-Bien Nacido Vnyd. Chardonnay (Central Coast) $20. Much oak here, well-charred and smoky, with pungent vanilla notes that ride high over superripe tropical fruit flavors. If you like these big, rich, extracted, buttery, spicy Chards, with their long, sweet finishes, this one is right up your alley. **88** —*S.H. (11/15/2001)*

Buffalo Ridge 1999 French Camp Vineyard Syrah (Central Coast) $12. Coconut and toast from the very American oaking here predominate, with a hint of mint and faint wild berry flavors peeking through. Still, it's more espresso-like than overtly harsh, though puckery woody tannins rule on the back end. **83** *(10/1/2001)*

Buffalo Ridge 1998 French Camp Zinfandel (Central Coast) $12. Simple fruit and a sweet, almost candied flavor. This wine seems unbalanced. There's an odd hole in the middle, and very little weight or tannin in the finish. It's all forward, sweet fruit, more like candy than berries. **82** —*P.G. (3/1/2001)*

Buffalo Ridge 1999 French Camp Vineyard Zinfandel (Central Coast) $12. The bouquet is promising with aromas of cocoa, spicy cinnamon, and nutmeg, vanilla, butter cookie, and ripe, mixed berries there's so much going on that there's almost too much going on. Dull oak over stewy plum and black berry fruit completes the profile, from palate through to the finish. **84** —*D.T. (3/1/2002)*

BUGAY

Bugay 2003 Cabernet Sauvignon (Sonoma County) $58. From a high mountain vineyard near the Sonoma-Napa border in the Mayacamas, this 100% Cabernet is intense in black currant and spice flavors. The tannins are rich and form a sturdy backbone, and the wine is soft in acids, in the modern style. This is a food-friendly wine, graceful and elegant. **90** —*S.H. (7/1/2006)*

Bugay 2004 Sauvignon Blanc (Dry Creek Valley) $22. This is quite a sophisticated wine, partially barrel fermented and aged *sur lies*, which softens and mellows it. The underlying fruit flavors, of citrus, fig, melon,

and spice, are ripe and juicy in acidity. This is a beautiful accompaniment to grilled shellfish. **90** —*S.H. (7/1/2006)*

Bugay 2003 Syrah (Sonoma County) $48. From a new winery that uses estate grapes that fall outside of any appellation besides the countywide one, this big, dry Syrah is very appealing. It's Northern Rhône in style, with cherry and blackberry flavors laced with leather and herb notes, and the tannins are sizable. This is a wine to watch. Drink now through 2007. **92** —*S.H. (7/1/2006)*

BULLY HILL

Bully Hill 2003 Merlot (New York) $10. Stemmy flavors dominate candied red fruit in this unripe wine that has chalky tannins and a tart feel. **80** —*M.D. (12/1/2006)*

Bully Hill 2003 Pinot Noir (New York) $10. A straightforward and pleasing wine, with red berry, cola and root flavors and aromas on a light-bodied, smooth frame. **84** —*M.D. (12/1/2006)*

Bully Hill 2002 Riesling (New York) $9. A simple, sweet quaff that's surprisingly good, from a winery known more for their wines from French-American hybrids. The peach and superripe apple flavors show a clean, crystalline quality to the fruit. **86** —*J.C. (7/15/2003)*

BUNNELL FAMILY CELLAR

Bunnell Family Cellar NV Vif Red Wine Red Blend (Columbia Valley (WA)) $25. "Vif" is a French word that loosely translates as "vivid, lively, and bright." This proprietary blend includes both red and white Rhône grapes. Bright, chocolaty, grapy, and fresh, with a blast of spicy black pepper. It lives up to its name and then some. **89** —*P.G. (10/1/2006)*

Bunnell Family Cellar 2004 Syrah (Horse Heaven Hills) $40. Soft and fragrant, smooth and showing a pleasing mix of citrus, berry, and plum, this wine has no rough edges. It slides through the palate with the grace of a racehorse, its smooth, ripe tannins leaving a hint of black olive and fresh herb on the finish. **91** —*P.G. (11/15/2006)*

Bunnell Family Cellar 2004 Boushey-McPherson Vineyard Syrah (Yakima Valley) $35. Complete, aromatic, and lively, with a tart, citrusy nose. Layered and precise, this beautifully focused effort sets sparkling acidity against toasty oak. The tart, cool-climate fruit flavors are concentrated and fresh. **92** —*P.G. (10/1/2006)*

Bunnell Family Cellar 2004 Clifton Hill Vineyard Syrah (Wahluke Slope) $37. Forward and dense, this has rich scents of mixed berries, spice, fresh herbs, and toast. The fruit is soft and ripe, and the wine plush, forward, appealing, and open. A bit of citrus rind adds complexity to the long, toasty finish; just a bit of heat also. **90** —*P.G. (10/1/2006)*

BURFORD & BROWN

Burford & Brown 2002 Barbera (Dry Creek Valley) $15. Pours black and dense, a young, tough wine marked with plum and blackberry flavors. You can taste the grape skins in the tannic astringency that numbs the lips. **86** —*S.H. (9/1/2004)*

BURGESS

Burgess 1999 Enveiere Bordeaux Blend (Napa Valley) $70. Here's a wine that doesn't slap you silly, but creeps up sideways, with seductively soft tannins that carry subtle flavors of blackberries and herbs. **91** —*S.H. (10/1/2003)*

Burgess 1997 Cabernet Sauvignon (Napa Valley) $33. 88 *(11/1/2000)*

Burgess 1999 Cabernet Sauvignon (Napa Valley) $38. A solid mid-valley Cab. Well-ripened Cabernet fruit suggests black currants and blackberries, with rich earthy notes of tobacco and dried herbs. It's dry and velvety in the mouth. Tannins are thick, but negotiable. **90** —*S.H. (2/1/2003)*

Burgess 1998 Enveiere Cabernet Sauvignon (Napa Valley) $75. Its bouquet and palate offer loads of blackberry, which is hiding under a charry, smoky-tar cloak. Well-balanced, it closes with oak and a little vanillin sweetness. **90** —*D.T. (6/1/2002)*

Burgess 2002 Vintage Selection Cabernet Sauvignon (Napa Valley) $36. This has been a hit-and-miss wine over the years, and this is one of the misses. It's a dry, fairly tannic wine, with a forward acidity that needs fruit to balance it, but fruit is what the wine lacks. It just isn't rich enough and isn't likely to age well. **83** —*S.H. (5/1/2006)*

Burgess 2001 Vintage Selection Cabernet Sauvignon (Napa Valley) $36. This is a good example of a well-crafted Napa Cab from a great vintage. It's rich and fruity in black currant, sweet herb, and spice flavors, with a good but understated application of oak. Feels sturdy and clean in the mouth, fully dry, with a long finish. **89** —*S.H. (7/1/2005)*

Burgess 2000 Vintage Selection Cabernet Sauvignon (Napa Valley) $39. From this longtime producer, a Cab with modest blackberry and herb flavors that are buried beneath sizable tannins. Not offering much now, so try aging it for a few years and try again. **85** —*S.H. (11/15/2003)*

Burgess 1998 Vintage Selection Cabernet Sauvignon (Napa Valley) $35. Given the difficulties of the vintage this wine achieves elegance and style. It's a wine to drink now while you're aging your '99s. There are light but good berry flavors, negotiable tannins, and soft acids, but there's also a richness that's the hallmark of terroir and lot selection. **89** —*S.H. (9/12/2002)*

Burgess 1998 Chardonnay (Napa Valley) $18. 91 *(6/1/2000)*

Burgess 2000 Triere Estate Vineyard Chardonnay (Napa Valley) $22. Plenty of upfront apple, peach, and pear flavors. Feels supple and opulent, with a silky texture. The finish is ripe and spicy. A bit obvious on the oak: It smacks you with smoke, toast and vanilla. **86** —*S.H. (2/1/2003)*

Burgess 2003 Merlot (Napa Valley) $22. Burgess's Merlots tend to vary in quality, and this is not one of the better ones. It's a soft, dry wine with a rustic mouthfeel, and some bitterness to the finish. The dominant flavors are of cherries and espresso. **83** —*S.H. (5/1/2006)*

Burgess 2002 Merlot (Napa Valley) $20. Dark and fleshy, this is a ripe, extracted Merlot that's big in cherry and cocoa flavors, with a sweet oaky covering. It's quite soft in the mouth, and has rich, dusty tannins. Will be lovely now with a steak, and should improve over the next year or two. **88** —*S.H. (7/1/2005)*

Burgess 2000 Merlot (Napa Valley) $25. Has the luscious tannins and beautiful acids you expect from Napa, and some rich plummy, berry flavors. Also possesses a depth and weight that are appropriate for the price. There's a bit of roughness, though, that detracts. **87** —*S.H. (8/1/2003)*

Burgess 1999 Merlot (Napa Valley) $28. This wine lives up to Merlot's reputation as being "the soft Cabernet." It has deep, rich berry flavors and is very mellow and velvety. It is soft, but retains life and zest. Put it all together and it's an elegant, delicious wine. There are some tannins but it's a wine to drink now or soon. **91** —*S.H. (9/12/2002)*

Burgess 1998 Merlot (Napa Valley) $28. From a dependable producer, a rich, fragrant wine that straddles a nice balance between overt fruitiness and subtle, earthy complexities. The fruits veer toward blackberries, with hints of coffee bean and light oak, and the tannins are modulated and lush. It's drinkable now and probably not a long-term ager. **88** —*S.H. (6/1/2001)*

Burgess 2001 Syrah (Lake County) $19. Spice and anise notes pepper stewed fruit on the nose. The palate delivers straightforward, soft red fruit couched in a dusty blanket. Soft and supple; an easy drinker. **85** *(9/1/2005)*

Burgess 2001 Syrah (Napa Valley) $22. This Syrah's aromas are earthy and dusty, with dried fruit and charred oak bringing up the rear. In the mouth, it offers much the same characteristics, a rustic, woodsy feel principal among them. 1,134 cases produced. **86** *(9/1/2005)*

Burgess 2000 Syrah (Lake County) $22. It's a nice, richly flavored wine, with berry and chocolate flavors and supple tannins. Feels soft and lush in the mouth. **87** —*S.H. (10/1/2003)*

Burgess 2000 Syrah (Napa Valley) $22. There's some real richness in this red, with its plummy, blackberry flavors and deep earthiness. It's dry, with pronounced tannins and feels angular and jagged in the mouth, but a bit of age should soften it. **86** —*S.H. (2/1/2003)*

Burgess 1997 Zinfandel (Napa Valley) $16. 86 —*S.H. (5/1/2000)*

Burgess 2000 Zinfandel (Napa Valley) $22. Cabernet-like with its balance and elegance, and the lush, soft but complex tannins are clearly from Napa. But the flavors are Zinny all the way. Ripe wild blackberries and

black cherries, wild and crazy spices, and white pepper last through the long finish. **90 Editors' Choice** —*S.H. (9/1/2003)*

Burgess 1999 Zinfandel (Napa Valley) $22. From an overlooked winery, a zesty, full-throttle Zin with complex berry and spice fruit and notable oak. There's a density to the flavors that suggests reduced yields and barrel selection of these mountain-grown grapes. It's ripe, velvety, and very easy to drink and enjoy. **90** —*S.H. (9/12/2002)*

Burgess 1998 Zinfandel (Russian River Valley) $18. A core of tart red fruit (particularly plum and cranberry) that runs from start to finish. On the nose, those notes are accented by cashew nut and black olive; in the mouth and on the finish, tangy oak, ink, and stone fruit-pit notes offer more tang. Very lean. **83** —*D.T. (3/1/2002)*

BURRELL SCHOOL VINEYARDS

Burrell School Vineyards 2002 Valedictorian Cabernet Blend (Santa Cruz Mountains) $50. A very nice Bordeaux blend that will complement food rather than overwhelm it. Shows blackberry and herb flavors. A dry, smooth wine with a spicy finish. **87** —*S.H. (10/1/2005)*

Burrell School Vineyards 2002 Estate Pichon Voneyard Cabernet Franc (Santa Cruz Mountains) $30. A lovely wine, maybe a little overoaked, but the cherry flavors are delightful, and the tannic structure is firm. It's light-bodied compared to a Cab Sauvignon, but delightful. **87** —*S.H. (7/1/2005)*

Burrell School Vineyards 2001 Ryan Oaks Vineyard Zinfandel (Amador County) $20. Quite tannic, with a pronounced licorice and leather quality. It's a little dry on the palate, offering hints of plum, coffee, tea, and herbs. **83** *(11/1/2003)*

BUTTERFIELD STATION

Butterfield Station 2000 Cabernet Sauvignon (California) $7. Thin and charmless. There are some watered-down blackberry flavors but basically the wine is weedy and green. Acids are accordingly sharp. **82** —*S.H. (12/31/2002)*

Butterfield Station 2001 Chardonnay (California) $7. Here's an everyday Chard that's simple in its apple and pear flavors, with an overlay of spicy, smoky oak. It's dry and clean, with some richness in the finish. **84** —*S.H. (12/15/2002)*

Butterfield Station 2000 Chardonnay (California) $8. A blend of peach and bright lemon flavors. Short but clean on the finish. **81** —*J.M. (12/15/2002)*

Butterfield Station 2000 Merlot (California) $8. Bizarre, even at this price. Smells like artificially flavored cherry cough drops, and then turns thick and syrupy in the mouth. The finish is cloying. **81** —*S.H. (12/31/2002)*

Butterfield Station 2000 Syrah (California) $7. There are some pretty notes of plum and blackberry in this very dry wine. It opens with a burst of white pepper scents and feels pretty nice and almost lush on the palate. It just lacks depth. **86 Best Buy** —*S.H. (12/1/2002)*

BUTTONWOOD FARM

Buttonwood Farm 1997 Trevin Bordeaux Blend (Santa Ynez Valley) $30. A good Bordeaux blend, rich with tobacco, blackberry, and earthy flavors, with a generous overlay of wood. Feels sharp and pinpointed in the mouth, with a good focus. The finish is dry and dusty with tannins. **87** —*S.H. (4/1/2003)*

Buttonwood Farm 1996 Trevin Bordeaux Blend (Santa Ynez Valley) $26. Dusty, earthy, berry aromas, with a leathery, meaty streak, lead to a dry, berry-rich wine. It has some odd corners. The technical readings probably read correctly, but it's jagged, irregular and rustic. A blend of Merlot, Cabernet Sauvignon and Cabernet Franc, and no challenge to Napa-Sonoma. **84** —*S.H. (12/31/2001)*

Buttonwood Farm 1999 Cabernet Franc (Santa Ynez Valley) $18. A challenging wine. Has some nice notes of ripe blackberry and plum, with tobacco and earthy complexities, and is dry, with rich tannins and good, crisp acidity. Yet there's an astringency that detracts. **85** —*S.H. (5/1/2003)*

Buttonwood Farm 1998 Cabernet Franc (Santa Ynez Valley) $18. Fruity and accessible, it combines wild berry notes with earthy, herbal ones and a meaty, leathery streak. It's dry, with negotiable tannins. Turns sharp and a little green on the finish. **84** —*S.H. (9/1/2002)*

USA

Buttonwood Farm 1995 Cabernet Franc (Santa Ynez Valley) $18. 84 —*S.H. (9/1/1999)*

Buttonwood Farm 1995 Cabernet Sauvignon (Santa Ynez Valley) $18. 84 — *S.H. (7/1/1999)*

Buttonwood Farm 2000 Cabernet Sauvignon (Santa Ynez Valley) $24. They couldn't keep a stubborn streak of green stalkiness out of this wine. But that mintiness is just one flavor in a spectrum of cherries, blackberries, and spices. Easy drinking. **85** —*S.H. (11/15/2004)*

Buttonwood Farm 1998 Cabernet Sauvignon (Santa Ynez Valley) $18. Nice enough, with distinct black currant flavors and good oak integration. Balanced, too, with dry tannins and acidity. The drawback is a sharpness and stubborn herbal streak that probably won't melt with aging. **85**—*S.H. (6/1/2002)*

Buttonwood Farm 1997 Cabernet Sauvignon (Santa Ynez Valley) $18. 86 — *S.H. (12/15/2000)*

Buttonwood Farm 1997 Marsanne (Santa Ynez Valley) $12. 88 —*S.H. (10/1/1999)*

Buttonwood Farm 2002 Marsanne (Santa Ynez Valley) $12. Smooth and polished, with herb, peach, and sweet tobacco flavors and a swirl of spicy oak. Very dry and clean, with a soft, buttercream mouth feel. Try as an alternative to Chardonnay. **86**—*S.H. (12/15/2004)*

Buttonwood Farm 1999 Marsanne (Santa Ynez Valley) $12. A creamy, honeyed wine, with tropical fruit sweetness and spiciness. It has a custardy, lemon-tinged flavor and texture, and a rich, spicy aftertaste. There's something baroque about its layers and myriad flavors. **85**—*S.H. (8/1/2001)*

Buttonwood Farm 1998 Marsanne (Santa Ynez Valley) $12. 87 —*S.H. (11/15/2000)*

Buttonwood Farm 1996 Merlot (Santa Ynez Valley) $18. 90 —*S.H. (12/31/1999)*

Buttonwood Farm 1995 Merlot (Santa Ynez Valley) $18. 88 —*S.H. (9/1/1999)*

Buttonwood Farm 2001 Merlot (Santa Ynez Valley) $18. Ripeness is always the challenge in this southland valley, and this wine displays some minty, stalky notes side-by-side with cherries and chocolate. Soft and gentle in tannins and acids, and nicely versatile at the table. **86**—*S.H. (12/15/2004)*

Buttonwood Farm 2000 Merlot (Santa Ynez Valley) $18. This is the kind of wine that shows better with food than it does on its own. Its modulated balance is understated, but the polished cherry, tobacco, and herb flavors, easy tannins and gentle oak make it perfect for the table. **88**—*S.H. (9/1/2004)*

Buttonwood Farm 1999 Merlot (Santa Ynez Valley) $18. Every year a handful of Santa Ynez vintners tries to play in the Merlot-Cabernet sweepstakes. This entry keeps their game alive, without advancing any closer to the goal line. It's nuanced with soft tannins, but a touch of greens. Needs that North Coast oomph. **86**—*S.H. (4/1/2003)*

Buttonwood Farm 1998 Merlot (Santa Ynez Valley) $18. Packed with candied blackberry fruit and mint, this user-friendly wine drinks nice and easy. It's stylishly dry, with sculpted tannins and good acidity. In fact, it's downright gulpable. Drink early with grilled meats. **88**—*S.H. (6/1/2002)*

Buttonwood Farm 1997 Merlot (Santa Ynez Valley) $18. 82 —*S.H. (11/15/2000)*

Buttonwood Farm 1999 Trevin Merlot (Santa Ynez Valley) $30. A blend of 60% Merlot, 30% Cabernet Franc, and 10% Cabernet Sauvignon, this wine has waited a long time to see the light of day. Smoky rich and fairly smooth, it's got pretty plum, black cherry, chocolate, spice, herb, and mocha notes. **88**—*J.M. (4/1/2004)*

Buttonwood Farm 2001 Devin Pinot Noir (Santa Ynez Valley) $16. Lots of fruit in this pretty white wine, a blend of Sauvignon Blanc and Sémillon. Peach and sweet melon star, but you'll find supporting roles for citrus and fig, as well as oaky notes. It's very ripe, and balanced with refreshing acidity. **87**—*S.H. (4/1/2004)*

Buttonwood Farm 1998 Sauvignon Blanc (Santa Ynez Valley) $12. 86— *S.H. (9/1/1999)*

Buttonwood Farm 2004 Sauvignon Blanc (Santa Ynez Valley) $14. Here's a refreshingly crisp, creamy and complex white wine that seems a lot more expensive than it is. It's dry and rich in citrus, fig, white peach, apricot, and spice flavors that finish long and pure. This is a very good price for a wine of this quality. **89 Best Buy**—*S.H. (2/1/2006)*

Buttonwood Farm 2003 Sauvignon Blanc (Santa Ynez Valley) $14. This is a good price for a dry, crisp, and fairly complex Sauvignon. It has polished flavors of citrus fruit, figs, and melons, and a long finish. **86**—*S.H. (10/1/2005)*

Buttonwood Farm 2002 Sauvignon Blanc (Santa Ynez Valley) $14. From an appellation that's proved itself to be a natural home to this variety and a winery that's clearly mastered it, a terrific white wine. Retains the grape's grass and citrus profile while taming it with Sémillon and oak to create a lush, complex wine. **90**—*S.H. (9/1/2004)*

Buttonwood Farm 2001 Sauvignon Blanc (Santa Ynez Valley) $12. Soft, simple, fruity, and pleasant. That about sums up this carefree wine, with its juicy peach, citrus, and flowery flavors. It drinks just off-dry, with a creamy, honeyed mouthfeel and finish. **86**—*S.H. (3/1/2003)*

Buttonwood Farm 2000 Sauvignon Blanc (Santa Ynez Valley) $12. Always a top producer of this variety, this year's version is even more intense than usual. Opens with a blast of powerful citrus and grass, and turns laser-like in the mouth, with lemon and lime flavors and burning acidity. Finishes with a bit of sugar. **86**—*S.H. (12/15/2001)*

Buttonwood Farm 1999 Sauvignon Blanc (Santa Ynez Valley) $12. 87 — *S.H. (11/15/2000)*

Buttonwood Farm 2001 Devin Sauvignon Blanc-Sémillon (Santa Ynez Valley) $16. A mild-mannered wine that sports a subtle, mineral-like core framed in hints of citrus, melon,.- and herbs. Moderate length at the end, with a tangy edge. **86**—*J.M. (6/1/2004)*

Buttonwood Farm 2000 Devin Sémillon-Sauvignon Blanc (Santa Ynez Valley) $16. Heavier and denser in every respect than the regular Sauvignon Blanc, this wine, a 60-40 blend with Sémillon, is also strongly leesy. The citrus flavors hit the palate with a strong dose of rich sour cream notes. The wine is dry and practically cries out for garlicky dishes. **89**—*S.H. (7/1/2003)*

Buttonwood Farm 2001 Syrah (Santa Ynez Valley) $22. Earthy and lean, with tobaccoey flavors, but there are some pretty cherry notes. This dry wine may soften and improve with a year or two of bottle age. **85**—*S.H. (12/15/2004)*

Buttonwood Farm 1998 Syrah (Santa Ynez Valley) $22. Meat and black pepper meet beets and cola in this velvety, medium-weight wine. Turns earthier on the palate, with leather and coffee notes joining in to provide some complexity. Finishes woody, with chocolate and dried spices. **87** *(11/1/2001)*

Buttonwood Farm 2003 Rosé Syrah (Santa Ynez Valley) $16. What a pretty copper-onion skin color. Opens with a blast of raspberry, vanilla, and smoky aromas leading to a medium-bodied, dry wine with strawberry-raspberry flavors and crisp acidity. Has some real complexity and nuance. **86**—*S.H. (12/15/2004)*

Buttonwood Farm 1997 Syrah-Cabernet (Santa Ynez Valley) $30. The addition of 44% Cabernet Sauvignon adds needed backbone and steel to Syrah's soft fruitiness. Actually, the Cab aromas of black currants are so strong they tend to overpower the wine. In the mouth, it's incredibly rich and dense, but it's also velvety and creamy. It's so succulent, you find yourself admiring the flavors a minute after the last swallow. **92 Editors' Choice**—*S.H. (8/1/2001)*

Buttonwood Farm 1999 Devin White Blend (Santa Ynez Valley) $16. Oakier than the regular bottling, with smoky, woodsy sap and vanilla highlights underlying citrus and crisp pippin-apple flavors. It's full-bodied, dense, a wine more suitable for food than a cocktail. Finishes stylishly dry. **88**—*S.H. (12/15/2001)*

Buttonwood Farm 1997 Devin White Blend (Santa Ynez Valley) $16. 88 — *S.H. (9/1/1999)*

BUTY

Buty 2002 Columbia Rediviva Cabernet Sauvignon-Syrah (Columbia Valley (WA)) $40. Blends of Cabernet and Syrah are blackberry juiciness of the

Syrah. This is still knitting together and should continue to improve for many years. **91** —*P.G. (4/1/2006)*

Buty 2001 Columbia Rediviva Cabernet Sauvignon-Syrah (Columbia Valley (WA)) $40. Not to be confused with the Walla Walla Syrah-Cabernet Sauvignon blend called Rediviva of the Stones. This wine is made from Champoux Cab and Boushey Syrah, rather than all Cailloux, as with its sibling. It's a good effort, well made, but the component parts seem to leave a hole in the mid-palate. There is some nice berry-flavored fruit and espresso-flecked tannins. **87** —*P.G. (6/1/2005)*

Buty 2002 Conner Lee Chardonnay (Columbia Valley (WA)) $25. An excellent Washington Chardonnay, whole cluster pressed, barrel fermented, unfined, and naturally stabilized. Minimum intervention winemaking, giving extra nuances of crisp citrus, rind, pear, and blossoms. Fragrant and food friendly. **89** —*P.G. (11/15/2004)*

Buty 2004 Conner Lee Vineyard Chardonnay (Columbia Valley (WA)) $28. Zelma Long consults with winemaker Caleb Foster, and this beautifully detailed wine shows her distinctive stamp. Barrel fermented in used Burgundy barrels, with no acid or water additions. Lees stirring adds creamy, light flavors of butterscotch, balanced against crisp green apple and pink grapefruit. **91** —*P.G. (4/1/2006)*

Buty 2002 Roza Bergé Chardonnay (Yakima Valley) $25. This is prime old-vine fruit, planted in 1972, and previously showcased in Woodward Canyon's great Chardonnays. Ripe, buttery, and round, this is perfect for those who love lush tropical fruit flavors and plenty of butterscotchy oak. **89** —*P.G. (11/15/2004)*

Buty 2002 Merlot-Cabernet Franc (Columbia Valley (WA)) $35. For some years now, Caleb Foster and Nina Buty have been quietly crafting delicious, powerful, and personable wines at their Walla Walla boutique. This supple, lush Merlot profits from the 10% Cab Franc added to the blend, which gives it a tannic spine laced with roasted espresso. Big, thick, and mouthcoating, yet it retains its focus and length. **90** —*P.G. (11/15/2004)*

Buty 2003 Merlot-Cabernet Franc Red Blend (Columbia Valley (WA)) $35. Not the catchiest name for this superb red blend, but Buty doesn't go for flash. They go for sleek, sophisticated, terroir-driven style. This is a smooth and substantial wine that opens slowly but surely. From a stiff start, with acid and tannin driving the bus, the wine's cassis and cherry and wild berry fruit begins to show, along with hints of stone, coffee, anise, and green tea. The French oak is used subtly and the winemaking is spot on. **91** —*P.G. (12/15/2005)*

Buty 2004 Sémillon-Sauvignon Blanc (Columbia Valley (WA)) $21. Wonderfully ripe, rich, and lush with peaches and cream flavors. The Sémillon, which comprises 72% of the blend, is from a warm site on the Wahluke Slope. It is fermented and matured in neutral French Oak barrels. The Sauvignon Blanc is Yakima Valley fruit, tank-fermented. Exceptionally polished and deeply flavorful, this is one of Washington's very best white Bordeaux blends. **93 Editors' Choice** —*P.G. (4/1/2006)*

Buty 2002 Sémillon-Sauvignon Blanc (Columbia Valley (WA)) $18. Interesting and flavorful, taking the best from both grapes. The Sémillon half of the blend lends extra texture, with flavors of fig dominating. There is just a hint of bread dough from the S,émillon's barrel fermentation. The Sauvignon provides racy green apple and green berry flavors. **88** —*P.G. (11/15/2004)*

Buty 2002 Rediviva of the Stones Syrah (Walla Walla (WA)) $40. One of those interesting Syrahs that seems to blend ripe and underripe fruit—in this case, herbal, wiry flavors and jammy, black cherry and chocolate fudge notes.There's also a hint of funk to the aromas that will intrigue some tasters and put off others. **85** *(9/1/2005)*

Buty 2001 Rediviva of the Stones Syrah-Cabernet (Walla Walla (WA)) $35. A sort of Super-Walla Wallan blend of Syrah (55%) and Cabernet Sauvignon (45%), all from Christophe Baron's Cailloux vineyard. Cailloux's fabled cobblestones lend a distinct minerality to this tour-de-force blend. Fat, plump Syrah provides most of the fruit power, with the Cab, on the racy side, adding proportionality. Plenty of roasted barrel flavors on the finish. **90 Editors' Choice** —*P.G. (11/15/2004)*

Buty 2000 Sémillon-Sauvignon Blanc White Blend (Columbia Valley (WA)) $18. This new Walla Walla winery premieres with a toasty, soft,

barrel-fermented Bordeaux blanc blend that's 70% Sém, 30% Sauv Blanc. The fruit is ripe and packed with rich flavors, without being too fat and tropical. Its lightly herbal, grassy nuances combine with plenty of well-managed, pleasantly spicy, toasty oak. **88** —*P.G. (9/1/2002)*

BYINGTON

Byington 1995 Santa Cruz Mountains Cabernet Sauvignon (Santa Cruz County) $23. 91 —*S.H. (7/1/1999)*

Byington 2001 Smith-Riechel Vineyard Cabernet Sauvignon (Alexander Valley) $29. Softly fruity and rather herbal, with a pleasant mixture of cherry and dill flavors and gentle tannins. This dry, balanced wine has lots of finesse, and will accompany food without overshadowing it. **86** —*S.H. (10/1/2004)*

Byington 1998 Chardonnay (Santa Cruz Mountains) $20. 87 *(6/1/2000)*

Byington 1997 Chardonnay (Santa Cruz Mountains) $17. 83 —*L.W. (11/15/1999)*

Byington 2002 Chardonnay (Santa Cruz Mountains) $22. A very fine Chard with special features that come from the appellation. The fruit is a mélange of Key Lime pie and white peach, drizzled with vanilla and cinnamon, with hints of smoky oak. These mountains always seem to develop a firm, steely acidity that makes the wines ultraclean. **90** —*S.H. (12/1/2004)*

Byington 2002 Chardonnay (Sonoma County) $22. Soft and easy, with some complexity, a pretty Chard with peach and mango flavors and a generous dollop of oak. It's the kind of wine that appeals across the board. **86** —*S.H. (12/1/2004)*

Byington 1997 Santa Cruz Mountains Chardonnay (Santa Cruz Mountains) $20. 90 —*S.H. (7/1/1999)*

Byington 2002 Hastings Ranch Pinot Noir (Paso Robles) $24. Consistent scores for this problematic wine. It's medicinal, with a syrupy texture. **81** *(11/1/2004)*

Byington 2002 Van der Kamp Vineyard Pinot Noir (Sonoma Mountain) $30. Correct but not inspiring, with earthy, coffee, and cherry notes. Finishes with some roughness and astringency. **84** *(11/1/2004)*

Byington 2002 Alliage Red Blend (Sonoma County) $24. This year Byington blended in some Syrah with the Cabernet Sauvignon, to good effect. I wish the wine were crisper and better structured, but there's no denying the deliciousness factor. The black currant pudding, cherry pie, and vanilla-sprinkled mocha flavors are irresistible. **87** —*S.H. (12/1/2005)*

Byington 2002 Hastings Ranch Zinfandel (Paso Robles) $24. Softly luscious in cherry pie and milk chocolate flavors, this pretty wine finishes with a taste of cassis. It's gentle and easy, with an edge of tannin. Totally dry, but rich in fruity essence. **85** —*S.H. (12/15/2004)*

BYRON

Byron 1998 Chardonnay (Santa Maria Valley) $20. 87 *(6/1/2000)*

Byron 1997 Chardonnay (Santa Maria Valley) $19. 91 —*L.W. (11/15/1999)*

Byron 2003 Chardonnay (Santa Maria Valley) $25. Byron's regular Chardonnay has historically been a very good wine. This continues that tradition, rich in tropical fruits, but extremely dry, with a stony minerality and high acids that stimulate the taste buds and call for rich fare. **88** —*S.H. (5/1/2006)*

Byron 2002 Chardonnay (Santa Maria Valley) $25. A lovely Chardonnay brimming with tropical fruits, roasted hazelnut, sweet buttercream, and gingery spices, with a good framework of oak. For all the flavor, there's a streamlined sleekness to the acids that keeps the mouthfeel clean and refreshing. **90** —*S.H. (12/15/2004)*

Byron 2001 Chardonnay (Santa Maria Valley) $24. This is a rich Chardonnay brimming with fruity flavors, and it is also very lavishly oaked. The fruit is tropical, including pineapple and mango, and the elaborate oak contributes buttered toast, smoke, and vanilla. Acidity provides a bracing backbone; one minor quibble is that all the makeup is on the surface. **89** —*S.H. (12/15/2003)*

Byron 1997 Byron Vineyard Chardonnay (Santa Maria Valley) $32. This Chard has always been dependably rich, and here's another tasty offering, with powerful scents of tropical fruits and Oriental spices, and leesy-smoky notes of butter and vanilla. You'll especially enjoy the creamy texture, accented with peach, pineapple, and spicy-buttery flavors. The finish is long and rich, too. **90** —*S.H. (2/1/2001)*

Byron 1996 Estate Chardonnay (Santa Maria Valley) $32. 91 —*S.H. (7/1/1999)*

Byron 1999 Nielson Vineyard Chardonnay (Santa Maria Valley) $40. From Santa Barbara's oldest (1964) commercial vineyard, an extravagant wine marked by scads of toasted oak and creamy lees. Yet these winemaker bells and whistles marry perfectly to the rich tropical fruit flavors. Intense and complex, this is a real beauty. **93** —*S.H. (12/15/2002)*

Byron 1998 Nielson Historic Vines Chardonnay (Santa Maria Valley) $75. The ripe bouquet shows rich banana, butter, and pineapple aromas. Full-bodied, yet bright with lively acidity, the palate displays bright citrus, butterscotch, pineapple, green plum, and vanilla flavors. There's slight heat, but also nice vanilla and citrus notes on the long finish. **91** *(7/1/2001)*

Byron 2002 Nielson Vineyard Chardonnay (Santa Maria Valley) $35. What a string of successes Byron's Nielson Chard has had over the years. As always, this is a high acid, mineral-filled wine, with a taste of lighter fluid riding over the pineapple, pear, and kiwi fruit. Very dry, it should be considered for the cellar, if you're into aging the handful of California Chards that can handle it. **92 Cellar Selection** —*S.H. (5/1/2006)*

Byron 2001 Nielson Vineyard Chardonnay (Santa Maria Valley) $30. Continues the Nielson tradition of lushly ripe, opulently textured Chards. It's rich in papaya and pear flavors that are swimming in toasty oak, with a creamy texture. Smooth and long, and completely satisfying. **92** —*S.H. (2/1/2005)*

Byron 2000 Nielson Vineyard Chardonnay (Santa Maria Valley) $30. Textbook Santa Maria Chard, with its rich flavors of mango, papaya, and pineapple. The acidity is high, making for a tartness through the finish, but oak softens and adds smoky cream and vanilla and a smooth roundness. Satisfying and pleasant all the way through. **90** —*S.H. (12/31/2003)*

Byron 1998 Nielson Vineyard Chardonnay (Santa Maria Valley) $35. One of two Byron bottlings from this source; this one should be less difficult to find in stores. The dry apple and pear fruit flavors are bolstered by crisp acidity, refreshing mineral accents, and earthy elements. This is a chewy, mouthfilling wine with richly textured palate feel. The long finish is tangy with citrus, cinnamon, and mineral components. **90** *(7/1/2001)*

Byron 1996 Reserve Chardonnay (Santa Maria Valley) $24. 90 —*S.H. (7/1/1999)*

Byron 2000 Sierra Madre Chardonnay (Santa Maria Valley) $30. Tastes like the lemon zest. There are pineapple flavors, too, and smoky oak. Coastal acidity brings a steely mineral spine. A magnificent food wine. **91** —*S.H. (9/1/2004)*

Byron 1998 Sierra Madre Chardonnay (Santa Maria Valley) $35. From a cool climate vineyard, a lushly textured wine with a full range of flavors, ranging from spiced apples to peaches and tropical fruits. It's well-oaked, dryish, and finishes with honeyed length. Has that edge of complexity that earns extra points. **92** —*S.H. (9/1/2002)*

Byron 1999 Sierra Madre Vineyard Chardonnay (Santa Maria Valley) $35. A very elaborately detailed wine, as intricate as a Renoir. The fruit runs the gamut from green apples through pears all the way to pineapple, and is set off by really nice acidity. Toasty, plush oak contributes to the complexity of this deliciously rich wine. **93** —*S.H. (12/15/2002)*

Byron 1997 Pinot Blanc (Santa Maria Valley) $16. 88 —*S.H. (9/1/1999)*

Byron 2004 Pinot Blanc (Santa Maria Valley) $20. The grapes are from Bien Nacido. The wine was made Burgundy-style, and it shows in the creamy, oaky complexities. The flavors range from Chardonnay-like peaches and tropical fruits to sautéed bananas, but it's the acidity that really makes this wine work. **89** —*S.H. (7/1/2006)*

Byron 2004 Pinot Noir (Santa Maria Valley) $25. A blend of grapes from two vineyards, including Bien Nacido, this polished Pinot shows the crushed hard spices and deep, black cherry flavors typical of the appellation. It's still a young wine, brimming with acids and tannins, and is drinkable now, but has the stuffing for medium-term aging. It's a good

value for a Santa Barbara Pinot of this quality. **90 Editors' Choice** —*S.H. (11/1/2006)*

Byron 2003 Pinot Noir (Santa Maria Valley) $25. Byron can always be counted on to come up with interesting, terroir-driven wines. This Pinot, clearly from a cool climate, is dry and tart in acids, with a silky texture and ripe, pleasing cherry, cola, and mocha flavors, as well as a complex woodspice taste that lasts through the long finish. **89** —*S.H. (12/15/2005)*

Byron 2002 Pinot Noir (Santa Maria Valley) $25. A very pretty wine, with complex notes of root beer, oak, vanilla, brown sugar, cinnamon, and smoke. The fruity flavors suggest well-ripened cherries and black plums. Polished and supple, with a long, spicy finish. **89** *(11/1/2004)*

Byron 2000 Pinot Noir (Santa Maria Valley) $25. A disputed wine that opens with caramel, tree bark, peat, and some lightly skunky aromas. This has a sweet, mature quality, and to some tasters it seems a lot older than a 2000 should. Others found appeal in the baked apple and toasty flavors, but most found it "soft" and "going downhill." Tasted twice, with consistent notes. **83** *(10/1/2002)*

Byron 1998 Pinot Noir (Santa Maria Valley) $25. This is a light wine—light in fruit, acid and tannins, and light in body. That doesn't mean it doesn't offer a lot of pleasure. It does. It has complex herbal, berry, and spice flavors, and it's nicely dry, with a certain richness. It's a great wine for early drinking. **89** —*S.H. (7/1/2002)*

Byron 1997 Pinot Noir (Santa Maria Valley) $20. 88 *(10/1/1999)*

Byron 2002 Bien Nacido Vineyard Pinot Noir (Santa Maria Valley) $40. Here's a ripe, lush wine, clearly from California. Shows bigtime blackberry, roast coffee, cherry, and high-char oak notes. Full-bodied and dramatic, with a good tension of tannins and acids. Finishes lush and appealing. **89** *(11/1/2004)*

Byron 1996 Byron Estate Vineyard Pinot Noir (Santa Maria Valley) $40. 89 *(10/1/1999)*

Byron 2003 Nielson Vineyard Pinot Noir (Santa Maria Valley) $40. What a track record Byron has achieved with this single-vineyard wine, despite the hassles of ownership change. The '03 continues the tradition. It's rich and complex in cola, black cherry, coffee, cocoa, and cinnamon spice flavors, with the silky elegance you want in a Pinot Noir. Drink now. **92** —*S.H. (7/1/2006)*

Byron 2002 Nielson Vineyard Pinot Noir (Santa Maria Valley) $40. Where Byron's regular '03 Pinot is all about immediate gratification, this single-vineyard release, a year older, is a darker, brooding wine. Instead of red cherries, you get black ones. Cassis, too, and sautéed mushrooms with a splash of balsamic. Still there's a delicious core of mocha. It's an exquisite, silky Pinot Noir, firm and classic, and addictively drinkable. **94 Editors' Choice** —*S.H. (12/15/2005)*

Byron 2001 Nielson Vineyard Pinot Noir (Santa Maria Valley) $40. Dark in color, immense in structure, deep in flavor, this is a blockbuster. The deep color only hints at the intense flavors of sweet black cherry, mocha, roasted coffee, smoky oak, sweet tobacco, and Oriental spices. As big as it is, it's a silky wine that glides across the palate. With Chinese roast duck, a marriage made in heaven. **93** —*S.H. (12/15/2004)*

Byron 2000 Nielson Vineyard Pinot Noir (Santa Maria Valley) $40. Extremely ripe, with succulently sweet black cherry flavors that verge on kirsch. Yet it's not cloying due to good acidity and the sharp woody tang of new oak. Feels delicate yet assertive in the mouth, but is a bit light in body. **89** —*S.H. (12/1/2004)*

Byron 1999 Nielson Vineyard Pinot Noir (Santa Maria Valley) $45. The complex cherry, smoke, cola, and leather bouquet opens to a mildly dusty palate. Wood and fruit are finely meshed here; the ripe cherry-raspberry flavors offset by vanilla and herb accents. **90** *(10/1/2002)*

Byron 1999 Sierra Madre Pinot Noir (Santa Maria Valley) $45. There's plenty of flavor packed into this light, supple wine. Tasters uniformly liked its finely balanced sweet and sour elements. Tart cherry, rhubarb, and beet flavors are offset by butterscotch, caramel, and licorice. It finishes long and even, with caramel, anise, and pepper notes. Drink now–2005. **88** *(10/1/2002)*

Byron 1997 Sierra Madre Vineyard Pinot Noir (Santa Maria Valley) $32. 90 —*S.H. (12/15/2000)*

Byron 1999 IO Red Blend (Santa Barbara County) $60. This Rhône blend from Robert Mondavi-owned Byron contains 80% Syrah and smaller amounts of Grenache and Mourvèdre from the Santa Maria and Santa Ynez valleys. It's a dark, young, brooding wine. There are impressive berry and dark stone-fruit flavors encased in thick but fine tannins, although the wine is a little soft. It possesses elegant complexity. 92 —*S.H. (12/1/2002)*

C.G. DI ARIE

C.G. di Arie 2004 Rosé Blend (Sierra Foothills) $13. Simple, rustic, and slightly sweet in the finish, with vanilla, char, raspberry, and cherry flavors and decent acidity. 83 —*S.H. (12/1/2005)*

C.G. di Arie 2003 Syrah (Sierra Foothills) $30. Smells inviting, but in the mouth, it's sickly sweet, like toothpaste. 80 —*S.H. (12/1/2005)*

C.G. di Arie 2002 Syrah (Sierra Foothills) $25. Harsh, hot, and rather medicinal, with astringent tannins. 82 —*S.H. (4/1/2005)*

C.G. di Arie 2003 Zinfandel (Shenandoah Valley (CA)) $25. Everything about this Zin is fine except the sweetness. It has a lush, rich texture and delicious blackberry liqueur-infused coffee flavors with a dusting of white pepper and cocoa. Unfortunately, the finish turns sugary and cloying. 83 —*S.H. (6/1/2006)*

C.G. di Arie 2002 Zinfandel (Shenandoah Valley (CA)) $25. Hot and dry, with a rough mouth feel and jammy cherry-coffee flavors. 83 —*S.H. (4/1/2005)*

C.G. di Arie 2002 Zinfandel (Shenandoah Valley (CA)) $25. Rich and ripe in blackberry, pudding, and chocolate flavors, with a briary, peppery edge. This mountain Zin wisely avoids both excessive alcohol and residual sugar. Sit back and enjoy the fruit. 87 —*S.H. (8/1/2005)*

C.G. di Arie 2001 Zinfandel (Shenandoah Valley (CA)) $25. What a nice Zin. It's focused and intense in Zinny flavors, with ripe, chocolatey flavors of wild berries, and despite the sweetness, it's totally dry. Balanced and silky, it's a great example of its terroir. 90 —*S.H. (12/15/2004)*

C.G. di Arie 2003 Southern Exposure Zinfandel (Sierra Foothills) $30. This Zin satisfies for its fruit-forward character and smooth, gentle texture. It's very soft for a mountain Zin, with a velvety feel that carries rich flavors of wild cherries and berries, milk chocolate, licorice, and vanilla. 86 —*S.H. (12/1/2005)*

C.R. SANDIDGE

C.R. Sandidge 2002 Tri*Umph Red Wine Bordeaux Blend (Yamhill County) $39. The winery's top wine is a blend of 64% Cabernet Sauvignon, 26% Malbec, and the rest Merlot. Supple and flavored with preserved fruits, it suggests mincemeat pie and blueberry jam. Nicely balanced, mellow, and textured although the finish is a bit short. 89 —*P.G. (12/1/2006)*

C.R. Sandidge 2002 Boushey Vineyard Syrah (Yakima Valley) $18. Light and tart, sappy and fresh, this is a much lighter style of Syrah than one usually associates with the Boushey vineyard. This is burger and pizza wine, simple and refreshing, very clean winemaking with no frills, bells, or whistles. 87 —*P.G. (12/31/2006)*

C.R. Sandidge 2002 Klingele Vineyard Syrah (Yakima Valley) $28. Good color, and a fresh and zippy palate, showing bright berry flavors. It seems almost claret-like, with taut acids and barrel notes suggesting cedar, coffee, and licorice. Substantial, mouth-cleaning tannins. 89 —*P.G. (10/1/2006)*

C.R. Sandidge 2000 Klingele Vineyard Syrah (Yakima Valley) $28. The second Sandidge Syrah is a thick, spicy wine, with ultraripe, even jammy fruit. Power takes the place of purity; there is a distinct earthiness, and more than a whiff of barnyard. Tannins are tough and chewy, but what it lacks in subtlety it makes up for in big flavor. 474 cases made. 87 —*P.G. (12/31/2002)*

C.R. Sandidge 2000 Minick Vineyard Syrah (Yakima Valley) $28. Ray Sandidge is the talented winemaker for Kestrel; for his own label he specializes in Syrah, sourcing fruit from top Yakima Valley sites, such as

Minick. This delicious bottle showcases young, sappy fruit, plenty of tart acid, well-managed tannins, and a light touch with the oak. 486 cases made. 89 —*P.G. (12/31/2002)*

C.R. Sandidge 2004 Stone Tree Red Syrah-Grenache (Columbia Valley (WA)) $34. This 70 percent Syrah/30 percent Grenache blend mixes bright, tangy red berry flavors with an undercoat of white chocolate. Very smooth, very stylish, and very good. 90 —*P.G. (10/1/2006)*

C.R. Sandidge 2004 Viognier (Yakima Valley) $19. Fragrant and intensely fruity, this thick and slightly hot Viognier is loaded with fascinating flavors. Stone fruits galore, and then it morphs into a more buttery, Chardonnay-like creature, only keeping the lime rind highlights. Long and rich. 89 —*P.G. (10/1/2006)*

CA' DEL SOLO

Ca' del Solo 2004 Albariño (Monterey County) $15. Intensely dry in acids and sour lemonpeel flavors, this wine is for the fierce of heart. There's nothing like it in all of California. Shellfish is an obvious pairing, particularly raw oysters. 86 —*S.H. (11/15/2005)*

Ca' del Solo 2002 Barbera (Monterey) $15. Tough and gritty, this robust wine plays the same workhorse role here as in Italy. It's tannic and dry, with earthy flavors. Yet it has a balance and cleanness that's admirable. 85 —*S.H. (10/1/2004)*

Ca' del Solo 2001 Fresia Frizzante Champagne Blend (Monterey County) $15. This fuchsia elixir offers an aromatic blitz of berry candy and wispy, fresh watermelon. A clean, low-acid palate complements the sticky-sweet strawberry flavor. A unique treat that will be welcome for brunch or dessert. 85 —*K.F. (12/1/2002)*

Ca' del Solo 2001 La Farfalla Charbono (California) $15. They used to make Charbono fruity, dry (when "dry" meant dry) and tannic. It lived forever, softening and sweetening in the bottle. Nowadays, no one feels like aging a wine for a dozen years, but if you've got the time, this one will entertain you. 88 —*S.H. (6/1/2004)*

Ca' del Solo 1997 La Farfalla Charbono (California) $15. 86 —*J.C. (10/1/1999)*

Ca' del Solo 2000 Freisa (Frizzante) Freisa (Monterey County) $15. Redolent of strawberries and raspberries, this slightly sweet, very fruity sparkler is made of Freisa, a little-known Piedmontese grape. From veteran envelope-pusher Randall Grahm, it's overtly juicy—so much so you'd swear it was infused with berries—but downright delicious. The soft mouthfeel makes it eminently drinkable. Believe the label, which warns of the potential for uninhibited behavior after drinking. 87 Editors' Choice —*M.M. (12/1/2001)*

Ca' del Solo 2003 Malvasia Bianca (Monterey) $13. Super-lemon-and-limey and absolutely dry, with enough tart green gooseberry that will remind you of a Marlborough Sauvignon Blanc. This wine, which should be well-chilled, is thoroughly palate-cleansing. 85 —*S.H. (10/1/2004)*

Ca' del Solo 2002 Malvasia Bianca (Monterey) $13. A unique interpretation of a unique varietal in California, this wine brims with the aromas of apricots, orange blossoms, peaches, and buttery vanilla. You expect it to explode in sweetness in the mouth, but it doesn't. It is very dry and intense, and very tart with acidity, so that after the initial shock wears off, you find yourself savoring it, right through the long finish. 88 —*S.H. (3/1/2004)*

Ca' del Solo 2000 Malvasia Bianca (Monterey) $12. 88 Best Buy —*S.H. (6/1/2002)*

Ca' del Solo 2005 Malvasia Bianca Malvasia Bianca (Central Coast) $13. Always interesting, Randall Grahm's Malvasia is dependably dry and tart in cool-climate acidity. This vintage is all that and more, with an intensity of flavor ranging from grapefruits to gooseberries. But dryness and acidity really are the hallmarks. Good with raw clams and mussels. 88 Best Buy —*S.H. (10/1/2006)*

Ca' del Solo 2004 San Bernabe Vineyard (Monterey) $13. From this big vineyard in the southern part of the Salinas Valley, a wine amazingly high in acidity, with bright lime, grapefruit, passionfruit, melon, and hay flavors. The alcohol is well under 13 percent, but the wine is absolutely dry. Try as an alternative to Sauvignon Blanc. **89** —*S.H. (11/15/2005)*

Ca' del Solo 2000 Moscato del Solo Moscato (Monterey County) $15. A blend of three Muscats (Canelli, Greco, and Orange) the appealing aromas suggest orange blossoms, vanilla, butter and smoke. It's overtly sweet, with orange flavors and a rich, creamy texture. Bright acids keep it clean and lively. **86** —*S.H. (12/1/2001)*

Ca' del Solo 2003 Big House Red Red Blend (California) $10. This brawling, tannic red might have come from Uncle Luigi's basement. It's mainly Syrah, with Petite Sirah, Zin, Carignane, and at least six other varieties, and will love anything slathered in marinara sauce. **85** —*S.H. (11/15/2005)*

Ca' del Solo 2003 Big House Red Red Blend (California) $10. This is the kind of wine you'd happily drink with almost any fast food and make an upscale dinner of it. It's ridiculously fruity in cherries, with rich tannins and good acidity. **85 Best Buy** —*S.H. (10/1/2005)*

Ca' del Solo 2002 Big House Red Red Blend (California) $10. Syrah dominates this blend, with its peppery, plummy flavors that have an edge of grilled meat, and full-bodied tannins. Yet there are 11 other varieties in the mix that add all sorts of interesting nuances. This dry wine is a fantastic value from Bonny Doon. **88 Best Buy** —*S.H. (5/1/2004)*

Ca' del Solo 2001 Big House Red Red Blend (Santa Cruz County) $10. 90 Best Buy —*S.H. (11/15/2002)*

Ca' del Solo 2000 Big House Red Red Blend (California) $10. A blend of six varietals including Cabernet Franc and Syrah, this wine is utterly distinctive. The raspberry liqueur aroma has a meaty edge complemented with things like ground coffee, violets, and white chocolate. All these flavors mingle in the mouth, and yet the wine is dry. The supple, silky texture is notable. **89 Best Buy** —*S.H. (9/1/2002)*

Ca' del Solo 1999 Big House Red Red Blend (California) $10. I've been drinking this long enough to know that this vintage is better than it has been in the past-it's hard to explain, but this year the wine seems to aspire to be more than it has been. Bouncy red fruit, vanilla and anise dominate the bouquet. The palate offers smooth red berries smothered in vanilla bean, nutmeg and the powdery bubble gum that you find in trading cards. Even and medium-bodied in the mouth, it finishes with anise and pencil-eraser notes. **86** —*D.T. (11/15/2001)*

Ca' del Solo 2004 Big House Pink Rosé Blend (California) $10. A Rhônish blend, with Barbera and Zinfandel, it showcases three of Randall Grahm's signatures, namely, it's refreshingly dry, invigorating in acids, and minerally-herbal-subtle in flavor instead of the intensely ripe fruit that usually marks California. This is a complex wine that will stand up to complex fare. **90 Best Buy** —*S.H. (10/1/2006)*

Ca' del Solo 2003 Big House Pink Rosé Blend (California) $10. Quite diluted, almost watery, with just a trace of strawberry. Bone dry, and the acidity is clean. **83** —*S.H. (10/1/2004)*

Ca' del Solo 2002 Big House Pink Rosé Blend (California) $10. Compared to the winery's Vin Gris de Cigare, Ca' del Solo's "other" blush wine is fuller-bodied, sweeter, and more coarse. It contains everything from Barbera to Charbono to Carignane. **84** —*S.H. (11/15/2005)*

Ca' del Solo 2003 Sangiovese (Monterey) $15. An unbalanced wine, high in alcohol, with some residual sugar, and sharp in acids. Should not have been released. **81** —*S.H. (10/1/2005)*

Ca' del Solo 2002 Il Fiasco Sangiovese (Monterey) $15. Take the purest extraction of cherry fruit sap, blend in some alcohol, add some citrus zest and a sprinkling of tarragon and make it all very dry, and this is what you get. It's a good, clean, unpretentious wine. **86** —*S.H. (10/1/2004)*

Ca' del Solo 1997 Il Fiasco Sangiovese (California) $15. 87 —*M.S. (10/1/1999)*

Ca' del Solo 2003 White Blend (Monterey County) $18. Randall Grahm calls this a Ligurian blend of Pigato, Albario, Treixadura, and Loureiro, from his vineyard in the cool Salinas Valley, but it tastes rather like a blend of Pinot Grigio and Reisling. Clean, dry, and minerally-floral, this refreshing wine has good acids. **86** —*S.H. (12/1/2004)*

Ca' del Solo 2003 Big House White White Blend (California) $10. Tastes Sauvignon Blanc-like, with citrus and mineral flavors framed by crisp

acidity, and a bone-dry finish. There are also subtle nuances of orange pekoe tea and sweet cinnamon. **87 Best Buy** —*S.H. (10/1/2005)*

Ca' del Solo 2003 Big House White White Blend (California) $10. Too many varieties to mention went into this wine, but Sauvignon Blanc contributes acidity and grassiness, Riesling a floral note, and Chenin Blanc a melony, wax-bean quality. The wine seems slightly off-dry. **84** —*S.H. (11/15/2005)*

Ca' del Solo 2002 Big House White White Blend (California) $10. Randall Grahm took eight different varieties from the cool Central Coast, carefully blended them together with no oak, and finished the wine dry. The result is amazingly nuanced despite the mélange of tree fruit, melon, and floral flavors. **87** —*S.H. (2/1/2004)*

Ca' del Solo NV Club Montonico White Blend (California) $12. 84 —*J.C. (12/31/1999)*

CA'BELLA

Ca'Bella 2004 Pinot Grigio (Willamette Valley) $17. This is an attempt to make an Italian-style Pinot Grigio out of Willamette Valley fruit. That's a bit of a challenge, because the wines of Italy are ripened at different levels and show a wholly different range of flavors. Here you will find a mix of austere, citric fruit with a dash of lemon rind in the finish. **85** —*P.G. (2/1/2006)*

CA'NA

Ca'Na 2001 Syrah (Contra Costa County) $30. Shows decent concentration and a creamy, syrupy mouthfeel, but the aromas and flavors are dominated by an excessively vegetal streak reminiscent of green beans. **82** *(9/1/2005)*

Ca'Na 2000 Syrah (Contra Costa County) $29. Opens with a huge burst of cassis, cherry, and sweet toasty oak aromas, rich as sin, with a decadent streak of milk chocolate candy. The flavors are similarly big, although robust tannins smother them. Acidity from this warm inland county is soft, so aging is a gamble. **86** —*S.H. (12/15/2003)*

Ca'Na 1999 Syrah (Contra Costa County) $21. Mulling spices, cedar, and faint blackberry aromas kickoff this oakfest that nevertheless charmed our panel. The toasty, spicy oak flavors go down smooth and easy. **86** *(11/1/2001)*

CADENCE

Cadence 2002 Bel Canto Bordeaux Blend (Red Mountain) $60. The winery's selection of its best barrels, excluding Cabernet Sauvignon. This is 48% Ciel Cab Franc, 48% Tapteil Merlot, and 4% Petit Verdot. Firm and laden with the coffee and espresso scents of Cab Franc. Smoke, liqueur, cherries, and tobacco leaf scents lead into a plummy, yummy, big and broad-shouldered wine that finishes with butterscotchy barrel flavors. **90** —*P.G. (12/15/2005)*

Cadence 2001 Bel Canto Bordeaux Blend (Red Mountain) $50. Everything fits together beautifully in this "Right Bank-styled" Bordeaux blend, a mix of Cabernet Franc (45%), Merlot (45%), and Petit Verdot (10%) from Red Mountain vineyards. Scents of clove, star anise, cardamom, and mushroom wrap around ripe fruits; there is an elegance that belies the high (14.9%) alcohol. Textured and long, it is the most complete and sensuous of the winery's current releases. **92** —*P.G. (5/1/2004)*

Cadence 2003 Coda Bordeaux Blend (Columbia Valley (WA)) $22. About 300 cases were made of this satiny red blend, roughly two-thirds Cabernet Franc and the rest Cabernet Sauvignon. A pretty, softly fruity nose is accented with barrel scents of toasted coconut. It has all the charm and vibrant fruit flavor of a young wine, nicely wrapped in new oak. **89** —*P.G. (12/15/2005)*

Cadence 2003 Bel Canto Red Blend (Red Mountain) $50. The winery's selection of its best barrels makes a fascinating wine, showing mixed Asian spices, supple fruit, and beautiful fine-grained tannins. Muscular and detailed, it has a bit of an alcoholic kick to the finish. Powerful and very well-crafted. **94** —*P.G. (4/1/2006)*

Cadence 2001 Camerata Red Blend (Red Mountain) $50. Cadence winemaker Ben Smith introduced two new wines this year. This is the "Left Bank" Bordeaux blend, Cabernet Sauvignon dominated, with spicy black fruits and early hints of pencil lead, earth, and herb. Right now it is young and tight, the fruit hard and compact, and its long term development difficult to evaluate. **89** —*P.G. (5/1/2004)*

Cadence 2003 Ciel du Cheval Vineyard Red Blend (Red Mountain) $38. Gorgeous, elegant, and refined, this opens into wonderfully aromatic scents of dusty coffee, cocoa, and mocha. There are streaks of chalk, limestone, gravel, and pencil lead, mixed fruits and hints of expressive spice all beautifully layered throughout. Cellar this for at least five years to pull everything together. **94** —*P.G. (4/1/2006)*

Cadence 2001 Ciel du Cheval Vineyard Red Blend (Red Mountain) $35. A whiff of sweaty saddle in the nose, followed by this exemplary vineyard's beguiling mix of stone, mineral, earth, and tart blueberry flavors. The complexity and elegance come through despite the huge (14.9%) alcohol; but perhaps this is pushing the ripeness just a bit too far. The distinctive character of the vineyard is close to being masked. **91** —*P.G. (5/1/2004)*

Cadence 2002 Ciel du Cheval Vineyard Red Wine Red Blend (Red Mountain) $37. Released in November, has opened up nicely since. Breathes well in the glass; a hefty, aromatic, plummy wine showing nicely integrated soft cherry and tobacco notes, along with seductive streaks of citrus, clove, and graphite. It's smooth but not at all flabby, displaying the hints of minerality that mark Ciel fruit. **92** —*P.G. (12/15/2005)*

Cadence 2003 Klipsun Red Blend (Red Mountain) $35. Dark and roasted, with espresso, toffee, and tar flavors right up front, this thickly tannic wine features big, plummy fruit with the concentration of strawberry preserves. A bit of heat, and the massive tannins that are typical from Klipsun vineyard fruit. **90** —*P.G. (4/1/2006)*

Cadence 2001 Klipsun Vineyard Red Blend (Red Mountain) $35. The penetrating bouquet of raspberries, blackberries, and bitter chocolate, and a purple inkiness that seems to stain the glass, suggest the power in this wine, a Merlot-dominated Bordeaux blend. It reminds me of some of the very best Ridge wines; intensely sappy fruit, powerful, and alcoholic, dominates, while the presence of oak is minimized. **90** —*P.G. (5/1/2004)*

Cadence 2003 Tapteil Vineyard Red Blend (Red Mountain) $38. Intense and sappy, this focused and brilliant young wine tastes like condensed berry juice. Despite it's raw power, it retains a sleek, elegant mouthfeel, like a ride in an especially well-built sports car. **92** —*P.G. (4/1/2006)*

Cadence 2001 Tapteil Vineyard Red Blend (Red Mountain) $38. The "home" vineyard for this exciting young winery, this Bordeaux blend shows intense dusty, spicy black fruits and some chalky, mineral tannins. Good grip, but it's still very tight and unyielding. The sense is that it will unwrap some layers over time; right now it feels a bit awkward and rough. **89** —*P.G. (5/1/2004)*

Cadence 2002 Tapteil Vineyard Red Wine Red Blend (Red Mountain) $37. Chunky, solid effort showing aggressive whiskey barrel scents and some heat in the finish. Young, tannic, and chewy. At this point the Ciel shows more elegance and integration, but the Tapteil is distinctive and ageworthy. **88** —*P.G. (12/15/2005)*

CAERNARVON CELLARS

Caernarvon Cellars 1999 Pinot Noir (San Lucas) $26. Quite rich and viscous, with a full-blown core of bright cherry and herb flavors. Spice-like cinnamon and nutmeg also find expression here, framed in very soft tannins. Good acidity holds it together, while the finish is pleasingly long. **89** —*J.M. (7/1/2003)*

Caernarvon Cellars 2002 Rio San Lucas Vineyard Pinot Noir (San Lucas) $25. This wine is quite dry, with a good grip of dusty tannins and a silky mouthfeel. It has cherry-berry and cocoa flavors and a long, fruity finish. Drinking well now, it should be consumed in the next year to preserve vibrancy. **86** —*S.H. (6/1/2005)*

Caernarvon Cellars 2001 Rio San Lucas Vineyard Pinot Noir (San Lucas) $25. The only Pinot I've ever tasted from this appellation, which is in the warmish to hot southern Salinas Valley. Seems a little flat. Has earthy flavors and easy tannins. **83** —*S.H. (10/1/2004)*

Caernarvon Cellars 1999 Cuvée Frank Zinfandel (Monterey) $23. Bright cherry flavors are the hallmark of this zippy wine, which also serves up spice, anise, and briary blackberry notes. Its focus is moderate, but it's still quite enjoyable. **85** —*J.M. (2/1/2003)*

Caernarvon Cellars 2002 Cuvée Frank Zinfandel (Paso Robles) $20. So ripe in berries, it veers into raisins, but they add a note of interest to the cherry, cocoa, and blueberry flavors. The wine is fully dry, at the cost of high alcohol, but that's Zin for you. **87** —*S.H. (10/1/2005)*

Caernarvon Cellars 2001 Cuvée Frank Zlahtina Zinfandel (Paso Robles) $NA. A richly textured, viscous wine, with big, deep black plum, smoke, toast, cherry, licorice, and spice flavors. It falters a bit on the palate, as it finishes a bit short and a touch tannic. Nonetheless, it offers plenty of pleasure. **88** —*J.M. (10/1/2004)*

CAFARO

Cafaro 1997 Cabernet Sauvignon (Napa Valley) $39. **92** *(11/1/2000)*

Cafaro 2000 Syrah (Napa Valley) $32. Deeply colored in a black and purple hue, the wine smells young, with oak and grape aromas dominating. It's obviously in need of age. The flavors are New World ripe, suggesting plums and blackberries, and the tannins are rich enough for cellaring. A more troubling note is the excessively soft mouthfeel. It lacks life and vibrancy and feels flat and syrupy on the tongue. **85** —*S.H. (12/1/2002)*

CAIN

Cain 1997 Cain Five Bordeaux Blend (Napa Valley) $75. **91** *(11/1/2000)*

Cain 2001 Concept Bordeaux Blend (Napa Valley) $46. This blend is very tannic and disagreeably harsh at the moment, unlike many '01s that are so soft and chocolatey. It's a good bet for the cellar because it's balanced and streamlined and has a full well of berry and cherry fruit. Try beyond 2010. **89** —*S.H. (5/1/2005)*

Cain 1997 Concept Bordeaux Blend (Napa Valley) $42. **89** *(11/1/2000)*

Cain NV Cuvée NVO Bordeaux Blend (Napa Valley) $24. Herbal and lean in fruit, with earthy, tobacco flavors and a hint of blackberries and cherries. But the tannin-acid balance gives it a nice structure that will assist good food. A blend of 2000 and 2001. **84** —*S.H. (10/1/2004)*

Cain 2001 Cain Five Cabernet Blend (Napa Valley) $90. This is a tremendous Cabernet, the kind that screams its importance from the first sniff, but it's really too young to drink now. It's powerful in black currant and new oak, with suggestions of herbs and spices, but once those youthful tannins kick in, the wine shuts down. It should begin to come around by 2008 and hold for long after. **92** Cellar Selection —*S.H. (10/1/2005)*

Cain 1999 Cain Five Cabernet Blend (Napa Valley) $85. This blend of five Bordeaux varieties is lean and tight, opening with flavors of earth, tobacco, and sage. The winemaker has crafted a dry, tannic mountain wine built for the cellar. There is a solid core of blackberry fruit, and the wine should age effortlessly for 10 years. **88** —*S.H. (5/1/2003)*

Cain 2002 Concept Cabernet Blend (Napa Valley) $50. Concept seems to be a junior Cain Five. This latest vintage has major problems. It's extremely dry and tannic, with lackluster fruit that just emphasizes the tart acids. Not going anywhere or offering much pleasure. **82** —*S.H. (2/1/2006)*

Cain 2001 Five Cabernet Blend (Napa Valley) $90. What to make of this wine? It's young, with rich, soft, fine tannins framing powerful fruit, backed by a grip of acidity. Cherries, especially, but also black raspberries, with potent Asian spices. There's a trace of raisining, which makes me wonder if it's good for the long haul. But it's certainly very good now. **89** —*S.H. (11/1/2005)*

Cain 1999 Concept Cabernet Sauvignon (Napa Valley) $46. Sort of a junior Cain Five, a Cabernet Sauvignon and Franc blend with a dash of Syrah. Very rich and provocative. There's a ton of lush cassis fruit but even with just 5 percent Syrah, a strong white pepper note, and even a little bit of leather. Very dry, pretty oaky, with the best tannins money can buy, this wine has elegance and finesse. What it needs is substance. **88** —*S.H. (11/15/2002)*

Cain 1996 Cuvée Cabernet Sauvignon (Napa Valley) $24. **89** —*L.W. (7/1/1999)*

Cain 2002 Ventana Vineyard Musqué Sauvignon Blanc (Arroyo Seco) $23. With this vintage, Cain announces the end of their Musqué bottling, after 14 years, and consumers are the losers. This wonderful wine always is crisp and clean, dry and intricately detailed with lime and gooseberry flavors. **91** —*S.H. (6/1/2005)*

Cain 2001 Ventana Vineyard Musqué Sauvignon Blanc (Arroyo Seco) $23. From this distinct varietal clone, a remarkably New Zealand-like wine. It's tart and rich in citrus, gooseberry, and fir aromas and flavors, and so dry and acidic, it practically burns the palate. Which makes it a great aperitif wine to stimulate the palate. This is one of the best California Sauvignon Blancs in years. **92** —*S.H. (9/1/2003)*

Cain 1998 Ventana Vineyards Musqué Sauvignon Blanc (Monterey County) $20. 89 —*M.S. (2/1/2000)*

Cain 1997 Ventana Vineyards Musqué Sauvignon Blanc (Monterey) $20. 90 —*L.W. (9/1/1999)*

CAKEBREAD

Cakebread 2002 Cabernet Sauvignon (Napa Valley) $55. Cakebread's workhorse Napa Cab is soft, dry, and ripe in cherry, blackberry, and chocolate flavors, with rich, sweet tannins. It combines the upscale quality of fine Napa Cab with a rustic, jagged texture. Drink now. **85** —*S.H. (6/1/2006)*

Cakebread 1997 Cabernet Sauvignon (Napa Valley) $37. 93 *(11/1/2000)*

Cakebread 2001 Benchland Select Cabernet Sauvignon (Napa Valley) $95. The big '01s are still rolling out. This one's very fine and Oakville-y, showing well-oaked, lush black currant, and cassis fruit, with a cocoa finish. It has soft, intricately sweet tannins. It's quite delicious now, but seems balanced enough to age through the medium term. Drink before 2010. **92** —*S.H. (11/15/2005)*

Cakebread 2000 Benchland Select Cabernet Sauvignon (Napa Valley) $90. Shows what a good winery can do in a challenging vintage. This wine is elegant rather than profound, opening with beautiful scents of cedar, toast, herbs, and cherries. It's light-bodied, and finishes with a gentle scour of tannins. **88** —*S.H. (11/15/2004)*

Cakebread 1999 Benchland Select Cabernet Sauvignon (Napa Valley) $90. Elegant, with silky tannins and lovely cherry, violet, cassis, chocolate, anise and herb flavors. The wine is focused and sleek, with a long finish. **92** —*J.M. (2/1/2003)*

Cakebread 1999 Three Sisters Cabernet Sauvignon (Napa Valley) $90. Plush and smooth, with round, ripe tannins that frame a core of black currant, blackberry, plum, herb, coffee, and vanilla flavors. The wine is balanced, supple, and long on the finish. **92** —*J.M. (2/1/2003)*

Cakebread 1999 Vine Hill Ranch Cabernet Sauvignon (Napa Valley) $90. Smells terribly musty and bretty, with barely a whiff of fruit or oak. If you can get past that, you'll find thick, astringent tannins coating blackberry and cherry fruit. Tasted twice, with consistent results. **82** —*S.H. (4/1/2004)*

Cakebread 1997 Vine Hill Ranch Cabernet Sauvignon (Napa Valley) $70. Kicks off with ripe plum and earth tones. The wine is fairly plush, with velvety tannins supporting a weave of blackberry cassis and plum flavors. There's a strong herbal core here—unusual but also interesting. Toasty, smoky oak frames the ensemble, which finishes long. **90** —*J.M. (9/10/2003)*

Cakebread 1999 Chardonnay (Russian River Valley) $32. A seductive nose of pineapple, pear, vanilla, and buttered toast leads, followed by a nicely knit, well-fruited, but not-at-all sweet palate. Here, pear, melon, pineapple, and tangerine is offset by light toast and vanilla accents. Balanced and smoothly textured, it shows graceful restraint that suggests it will improve over the next year or two. **91** *(7/1/2001)*

Cakebread 1996 Merlot (Napa Valley) $35. 87 *(3/1/2000)*

Cakebread 2002 Merlot (Napa Valley) $48. There's a firm structure of tannins and acids to this wine, which lends architecture to the black cherry and cocoa flavors. It has additional complexities from oak and all sorts of spices and herbs. It's really a very fine Merlot, powerful, yet pliant. **91** —*S.H. (11/15/2005)*

Cakebread 2002 Pinot Noir (Carneros) $44. Tasters had exactly the same score across the board for this medium-bodied, dry wine. It's rich in cherries and blackberries, with hints of mocha, and has tangy, zesty acids. A wine of more power than finesse. **88** *(11/1/2004)*

Cakebread 1998 Sauvignon Blanc (Napa Valley) $16. 86 *(3/1/2000)*

Cakebread 2004 Sauvignon Blanc (Napa Valley) $21. Richer and more refined than in the past, this refreshingly dry wine is dynamic in lemon and lime, fig, and melon flavors leading to an amazingly long, satisfying finish. It has a tingly acidity that's perfect for goat cheese and grilled veggies. **89** —*S.H. (6/1/2006)*

Cakebread 2003 Sauvignon Blanc (Napa Valley) $22. Semiaromatic, with notes of grapefruit peel, white pepper, and peach. Not that intense but full bodied, with traces of vanilla, spice and bitterness. Finishes soft, with only a whimper of zest. Tasted twice with fairly consistent results. **85** *(7/1/2005)*

Cakebread 2002 Sauvignon Blanc (Napa Valley) $17. This nice, stylish wine offers up lots of ripe flavors of figs, spearmint, and peaches, softened and mellowed with oak. It's a little bit sweet, with enough acidity to offset the fruity lushness. Should be great with pork or chicken with a fruity salsa topping. **86** —*S.H. (12/15/2003)*

Cakebread 2002 Syrah (Carneros) $43. Luscious New World Syrah, with obvious toast and vanilla framing ripe cherry-berry fruit. Lush and creamy-textured, with a supple finish and a touch of caramel. Easy to drink and easy to like. **88** *(9/1/2005)*

Cakebread 2000 Syrah (Carneros) $45. Sleek and velvety, with a spicy edge to its bright, brambly flavors. Bing cherry, blackberry, currant, earth, and herb notes are at the fore, while a hint of cedar and pencil lead adds interest. The finish is clean. **92** —*J.M. (2/1/2003)*

Cakebread 1998 Syrah (Napa Valley) $40. Rubbery, meaty notes accent the sour blueberry and black olive flavors. Has good complexity and a smooth mouthfeel, but lacks zip and excitement. **83** *(11/1/2001)*

CALAFIA

Calafia 2003 Meritage (Napa Valley) $38. This Cabernet-based Meritage also contains a significant amount of Malbec. It's a big, mouth-filling, dry blend, young in chewy, hard tannins, with a stubborn green edge to the cherry-berry flavors. Needs age, but may not have the balance for the long haul. Drink now–2010. **87** —*S.H. (12/15/2006)*

CALCAREOUS

Calcareous 2003 Cabernet Sauvignon (York Mountain) $26. The appellation is near the western, cooler part of Paso Robles, and the wine's rich chocolate fudge and creamy cherry and cassis flavors have the requisite acidity and tannins needed to temper them. Almost sweet on the finish, the wine redeems itself with elegance. The high alcohol isn't really a problem, in terms of balance. **88** —*S.H. (12/15/2006)*

Calcareous 2002 Cabernet Sauvignon (Paso Robles) $24. Opens with a strong Cabernet nose of ripe black currants, with a hint of raisins, then turns soft and rich in the mouth. The gentle texture carries flavors of blackberry marmalade, chocolate, and oak. This polished wine has a long, sweet finish. **90 Editors' Choice** —*S.H. (8/1/2005)*

Calcareous 2002 Reserve Cabernet Sauvignon (Paso Robles) $28. Paso Cabernets are expected to be soft. This one is, but it's also complex and delicious. It lacks the structural elegance of the North Coast, but compels with ripe blackberry, chocolate, anise., and spice flavors. They attract immediately and last through a long finish. **87** —*S.H. (12/31/2005)*

Calcareous 2004 Pinot Noir (York Mountain) $28. Lots of delicious Pinot flavor in the cherry, cola, tea, mocha, rhubarb, and pomegranate fruit. The wine is a bit simple, with a peppery, spicy finish. **85** —*S.H. (12/1/2006)*

Calcareous 2004 Roussanne (Paso Robles) $24. Jammy and fresh, with ripe, rich fruit. Apricot, Fig Newton, peach cobbler, crème caramel, honey, vanilla, and toast flavors all mingle into a complex, spicy finish. The price of dryness is high alcohol, but the wine never tastes hot. **88** —*S.H. (12/1/2006)*

Calcareous 2003 Syrah (Paso Robles) $24. Tremendously forward in fruit, this soft, dry wine has black cherry, blackberry, and chocolate flavors wrapped in smooth, rich tannins, and a peppery aftertaste. **87** —*S.H. (12/31/2005)*

Calcareous 2002 Syrah (Paso Robles) $24. Richly fruity aromas of blackberries and currants are accented by lovely pepper, spice, and herb notes.

Even seems a bit floral on the nose, then turns creamy and supple on the palate, before picking up a hint of alcohol on the finish. **88** *(9/1/2005)*

Calcareous 2004 Viognier (Paso Robles) $24. Here's a tasty, tangy Viognier with lots of nice fruit and wildflower flavors, a richly creamy texture and an oaky veneer. It's very well balanced, and strikes just the right tone for this often exotic variety. **87** —*S.H. (12/31/2005)*

Calcareous 2002 Zinfandel (Paso Robles) $24. Fairly rich in tannins, with well-ripened fruit that runs the gamut from cherries through blackberries to raisins, this is a big Zin. It's dry and high in alcohol, and a great accompaniment to stews and barbecue. **85** —*S.H. (8/1/2005)*

CALE

Cale 1998 Sangiacomo Vineyards Chardonnay (Carneros) $24. 88 *(6/1/2000)*

Cale 1997 Vintner's Reserve Merlot (Sonoma Valley) $NA. 89 Best Buy *(12/31/1999)*

CALERA

Calera 1996 Chardonnay (Mount Harlan) $38. 93 —*S.H. (10/1/1999)*

Calera 2004 Chardonnay (Central Coast) $15. Calera raised their price a buck over last year, though this is still a pretty good buy. It's quite an acidic wine, in a day and age when so many Chards are meltingly soft, and while it's not complex, it is dry and fruity, with a firm minerality supporting the Meyer lemon, nectarine, and vanilla-rich oak flavors. **86** —*S.H. (12/31/2006)*

Calera 2003 Chardonnay (Central Coast) $14. Fruity enough, with white peach and pineapple flavors enriched with a dollop of smoky oak and a chalky minerality in the finish. This is a fine everyday Chardonnay with some real complexity and elegance. **86** —*S.H. (7/1/2006)*

Calera 2002 Chardonnay (Mt. Harlan) $34. Few would hold a Chardonnay more than four years before release. Why does Josh Jensen? The acidity, apparently. His wines do start out on the tart side. Now, this one off the estate has passed its youth and is picking up that baked peach pie, coconut macaroon, dried autumn leaf thing. It's interesting, but drink fast before it slides into senescence. **87** —*S.H. (12/31/2006)*

Calera 2002 Chardonnay (Central Coast) $14. Full-bodied and dry, this 3-year-old Chard is picking up dried fruit notes, although it's still rich in peaches and pineapples. The high acidity has carried the wine this far, but it should be consumed now. **86** —*S.H. (12/15/2005)*

Calera 2001 Chardonnay (Central Coast) $14. A longtime restaurant favorite, this wine mixes its peach and citrus flavors with minerally, stony notes and a kiss of smoky oak. It's very dry, with crisp acids. **85** —*S.H. (12/15/2004)*

Calera 2000 Chardonnay (Central Coast) $18. Getting old and tired, and the fruit, which once must have been all peaches and cream, is fading. So is the acidity. There's still plenty of oak, though. **82** —*S.H. (10/1/2004)*

Calera 2000 Chardonnay (Mount Harlan) $34. You'll find lots of acidity and oak in this wine. In between is the fruit, a mélange of apples, peaches, pineapples, and mangoes. Despite being five years old, it's still fresh and vital, but you should probably drink it now before it loses its polished youthfulness. **89** —*S.H. (12/15/2005)*

Calera 1999 Chardonnay (Mount Harlan) $34. I am at a loss to explain why this wine has been held back so long. It's no longer fresh, but hasn't developed interesting bottle qualities either. Instead, it's a tired, old wine. Tasted twice. **83** —*S.H. (11/15/2004)*

Calera 1999 Chardonnay (Central Coast) $22. Pretty peach and tropical fruit aromas, enveloped in smoky oak, are accompanied by leesy notes. Drinks easy and soft, with plenty of fruity flavors and vanilla-oaky contrasts. The polished finish is pleasant. **86** —*S.H. (12/1/2001)*

Calera 1997 Chardonnay (Mount Harlan) $38. Fermented with native yeast, this estate wine from Chardonnay and Pinot Noir pioneer Josh Jensen is classy, earthy, and firm. Apple and yellow plum flavors mingle with mineral elements on the palate. It finishes nutty and tart, with good length and a solid acid spine. One of the few California wines that are Burgundian in spirit, this is still tight. Although it was one of the oldest wines we tasted, it can still use a few years to fully unfold. **89** *(7/1/2001)*

Calera 2005 Pinot Noir (Central Coast) $23. Nice everyday Pinot that shows true Central Coast character in the light color, big, bright acids, long hangtime, and ripe cherry and raspberry fruit. There's nothing complicated or hard to get about this wine, just an easy silkiness that leads to another sip. **85** —*S.H. (12/31/2006)*

Calera 2003 Pinot Noir (Central Coast) $21. A good introduction to the Calera style. It's a complex, lush wine, despite the light color and light body, with a myriad of cherry, pomegranate, cola, coffee, and vanilla spice flavors. Drink now through 2007. **88** —*S.H. (7/1/2006)*

Calera 2002 Pinot Noir (Central Coast) $20. Right up there with Calera's single-vineyard Pinots, this perennial value showcases a perfect Central Coast sensibility. It's a lightly colored, dry, silky wine, with bright acids that frame cola and cherry fruit. Impressive for its overall elegance. **89** —*S.H. (12/15/2005)*

Calera 2001 Pinot Noir (Central Coast) $20. Decent, with a light, silky texture and good acidity framing modest cherry and spice flavors. Finishes dry. **84** —*S.H. (12/1/2004)*

Calera 2000 Pinot Noir (Central Coast) $24. 80 *(10/1/2002)*

Calera 1999 Pinot Noir (Central Coast) $20. For Calera's least expensive Pinot, this is pretty darned nice stuff. It's packed with true varietal character, from the pale color to the spicy, fruity, tomato-infused flavors to the silky tannins and crisp acids. It's what people want in a delicate yet assertive wine, and defines Central Coast Pinot in a general sense. **87** —*S.H. (7/1/2002)*

Calera 2002 Jensen Vineyard Pinot Noir (Mt. Harlan) $53. Enormously aromatic, endlessly complex, this is one of the best Calera Pinots. It feels full and complete, despite the elegantly light silkiness in the mouth, and the crisp acids and dusty tannins that frame cherry, cola, rhubarb, pomegranate, coffee, and vanilla spice flavors. Enjoyable now, this wine thankfully strikes a different direction from today's heavy, overly ripe Pinots. Drink now through 2012. **95 Editors' Choice** —*S.H. (7/1/2006)*

Calera 2001 Jensen Vineyard Pinot Noir (Mt. Harlan) $50. As usual, this is a wine that doesn't show well in youth. Compare it to some of the flashier coastal bottlings, and it comes across as heavy and earthy. It's thick in tannins, but the core of rich cherry fruit and lively acidity bode well. This is probably a wine to cellar through this decade. **89** —*S.H. (8/1/2005)*

Calera 2000 Jensen Vineyard Pinot Noir (Mount Harlan) $50. This is one tough wine to evaluate. It's not showing much of anything now beyond an oaky earthiness with hints of spicy cherry pie. A hit of tannins numbs the palate. Tasted twice, with consistent result. **84** —*S.H. (12/1/2004)*

Calera 1999 Jensen Vineyard Pinot Noir (Mt. Harlan) $50. Earthy and light in color, with oaky sawdust aromas that pick up steam with airing. Very intense, with plum and raisin flavors coming in front of a dry, firmly tannic finish. In fact, the tannins on this wine are as hard as they come for California Pinot, so it's a tough-edged but tasty ride. **89** —*M.S. (12/1/2003)*

Calera 1997 Mélange Pinot Noir (Mount Harlan) $40. A blend of lots left over from Calera's three prime vineyards, it's an intriguing combination of delicacy and power. The color is pale, the aroma is cola-like and it's light on the palate. But the depth of fruit is great, and so is the complexity. This wine will age well. **90** —*S.H. (7/1/2002)*

Calera 2000 Mills Pinot Noir (Mt. Harlan) $40. My preference over Calera's Selleck. It's more typical and not as eccentric, with lush cherry, coffee, cocoa, and spice flavors balanced with vital acidity. Turns astringently tannic in the finish, but this is a classically structured Pinot that should mature. Drink now through 2008. **91** —*S.H. (12/15/2004)*

Calera 2002 Mills Vineyard Pinot Noir (Mt. Harlan) $43. The vintage was a very good one for Calera, offering the heat needed for ripeness but the cool nights for acidity. Mills is a ripe, delicious wine with blackberry, cherry, cola, mint, and spice flavors resting on a complex, multi-layered palate that finishes firm and dry. Supple now, it should drink well for ten years. **92** —*S.H. (12/1/2006)*

Calera 2001 Mills Vineyard Pinot Noir (Mount Harlan) $40. The oak dominates now, with vanilla, char, and wood sap flavors covering the underlying fruit. Tannins, too. This is a dry, shut-down Pinot Noir,

USA

although rich meats will tickle it into life. Try aging through 2008. **90** — *S.H. (12/15/2005)*

Calera 1997 Mills Vineyard Pinot Noir (Mount Harlan) $55. Sometimes a young Pinot is deceptive. This wine is young and silky, supple, and fruity and has some sharp acidity, but it doesn't overwhelm. It's the kind of wine that doesn't overshadow food. But it's excellent Pinot. The depth of flavor and long finish suggest aging possibilities, but there's no reason not to drink and enjoy it now. **91** —*S.H. (7/1/2002)*

Calera 2002 Mt. Harlan Cuvée Pinot Noir (Mt. Harlan) $28. There's a deliciously earthy richness that suggests Portobello mushrooms sautéed in balsamic and soy. That's not all. Cherries hit mid-palate, then lead to sweet oak and Asian spice. It's a dry, balanced, elegant, and complex young Pinot that drinks well now. Made from mainly new grapes planted on the estate. **88** —*S.H. (12/31/2006)*

Calera 2002 Reed Vineyard Pinot Noir (Mt. Harlan) $48. There are Pinots that are darker in color and fuller in body in California, but few approach this bottling in complexity or apparent ageability. The airy, silky texture holds a wealth of flavors, ranging from red cherries, pomegranates, rhubarb, and espresso to cola and vanilla spice. This is a Burgundian-styled wine that will improve through 2012. **93 Cellar Selection** —*S.H. (7/1/2006)*

Calera 2001 Reed Vineyard Pinot Noir (Mt. Harlan) $45. Similar to Calera's Jensen bottling, a youthful, tough wine with cherry, cola, and oak flavors and high acids and tannins. Not showing well now, although it has plenty of finesse. Best to age it for a few years. **88** —*S.H. (8/1/2005)*

Calera 2000 Reed Vineyard Pinot Noir (Mount Harlan) $45. Maybe not showing its best now, this wine drinks simple and pleasant. It has cherry, orange rind, oak, vanilla, and spice flavors and a light, silky body, with considerable length on the finish. **86** —*S.H. (12/1/2004)*

Calera 1999 Reed Vineyard Pinot Noir (Mt. Harlan) $45. Dry and dusty, with raspberry aromas and lots of terroir-driven spice and verve. This wine feels mature and developed on your palate, surely a result of its age. Flavors of red fruit and cocoa coat your mouth, followed by a smooth, herbal finish. Very complex and a Pinot apart from the crowd. **91** —*M.S. (12/1/2003)*

Calera 2003 Ryan Vineyard Pinot Noir (Mt. Harlan) $40. As good as this wine is now, and it's very satisfying, it possesses enough integrity for the long haul. It's light in color, like a Burgundy, and silky, with complex cherry, mocha and oak flavors that are edged with fine, dusty tannins. It will hold and improve for a decade, peaking around 2009. **92 Cellar Selection** —*S.H. (7/1/2006)*

Calera 2002 Ryan Vineyard Pinot Noir (Mount Harlan) $40. Dry, fairly tough in tannins, and closed down now, this wine isn't an in-your-face charmer. But there's a fantastically rich core of cherry fruit that shows up in the middle and lasts through the finish. All bets are that this Pinot will come into its own in several years, but a nice cut of beef will complement it now. **90** —*S.H. (12/15/2005)*

Calera 2000 Selleck Pinot Noir (Mt. Harlan) $55. A challenge. It's huge and extracted, with massive aromas of black-cherries, cocoa, and slightly sweet cured meat. In the mouth, it's thick as honey, bursting with bitter cherry and unsweetened cocoa flavors, and with good acidity. But it's disjointed and tannic now. Clearly built for the long haul, and the odds are slightly in its favor. Try after 2006. **88** —*S.H. (12/15/2004)*

Calera 2002 Selleck Vineyard Pinot Noir (Mt. Harlan) $58. This is the palest and lightest of Calera's '02 Pinots, but paradoxically it's enormously concentrated in flavor and possible the most ageworthy. It explodes with cherry cola, cherry pie filling, raspberry, blueberry, cocoa-dusted latte, and cinnamon-nutmeg spice. But it has the depth and balance for the long haul. Best now through 2012. **93 Cellar Selection** —*S.H. (12/1/2006)*

Calera 2001 Selleck Vineyard Pinot Noir (Mount Harlan) $55. This is the most accessible of Calera's current single-vineyard releases, a real charmer with its creamy cherry, mocha, and oaky vanilla flavors. But don't be misled, it's an ager. Acidity is big, tannins are sturdy, balance is fine. As with all Calera Pinots, this wine is elegantly structured. **91** —*S.H. (12/15/2005)*

Calera 1996 Selleck Vineyard Pinot Noir (Mount Harlan) $80. 91 *(10/1/1999)*

Calera 2005 Vin Gris of Pinot Noir Pinot Noir (Central Coast) $14. You'll find lots of flavor and interest in this dry blush. Don't be put off by the screwtop; it's a complex wine, with strawberry and raspberry cream, thyme and vanilla flavors. Too bad there aren't more rosés like this. **87** — *S.H. (6/21/2006)*

Calera 1997 Viognier (Mount Harlan) $30. 93 —*S.H. (10/1/1999)*

Calera 2003 Viognier (Mt. Harlan) $36. The first great California Viognier I ever had was Calera's, and I've admired it ever since. The tight acids do a good job of controlling the flamboyant, tropical fruit, white peach and wildflower side. Like a combination of a rich Chardonnay and a crisp Sauvignon Blanc, elegant and delicious. **91** —*S.H. (8/1/2005)*

Calera 2001 Mt. Harlan Estate Viognier (Mt. Harlan) $36. Shows exotic aromas but some restraint as well. Peach, melon, apple, and spice notes form the core, with a mineral edge. Sleek and elegant. **89** —*J.M. (12/15/2002)*

Calera 2005 Thirtieth Anniversary Vintage Dessert Viognier (Mt. Harlan) $30. Very sweet, with masses of pineapple custard, honeysuckle, lemon sorbet, apricot honey, and vanilla spice. This is one delicious dessert wine, and while it may lack complexity, it's a satisfying finish to a great dinner. **87** —*S.H. (12/1/2006)*

CALISTOGA CELLARS

Calistoga Cellars 2003 Cabernet Sauvignon (Napa Valley) $34. Ripe in blackberry, cherry, and coffee flavors, with a sharp, angular mouthfeel due to acids and green tannins, this is a wine you might call rustic. **84** — *S.H. (12/15/2006)*

Calistoga Cellars 2002 Cabernet Sauvignon (Napa Valley) $30. Fairly tannic, but there's a smooth, milk-chocolate texture that flatters the palate. The blackberry fruit is a bit thin in the middle through the finish, but the wine has lots of elegance. **86** —*S.H. (6/1/2005)*

Calistoga Cellars 2000 Louer Family Vineyard Cabernet Sauvignon (St. Helena) $26. Another of the new crop of Cabs, and a very good wine. Meets Napa standards of rich, ripe blackberry, and currant fruit, and perfectly soft tannins, and is well oaked. Misses by a shade or two the owners' expectations of greatness, but it's at the top of the heap in this price range. **91 Editors' Choice** —*S.H. (11/15/2003)*

Calistoga Cellars 2004 Chardonnay (Napa Valley) $22. This has a rich earthy quality, suggesting sweet heaps of mulch and herbs, in addition to fruitier flavors of apples and peaches. It's also somewhat soft and well-oaked. If you're looking for an example of Napa Chard, for better or worse, this is a good one. **85** —*S.H. (5/1/2006)*

Calistoga Cellars 2003 Merlot (Napa Valley) $29. The entry is luscious, with rich black cherry and mocha flavors and smooth, thick tannins. Then oak hits, hard, and it doesn't feel integrated. The wine is so nice on its own, it doesn't really need all that vanilla and char. **84** —*S.H. (5/1/2006)*

Calistoga Cellars 2002 Merlot (Napa Valley) $26. Lots to like about the smooth, tannic structure, and the way the sweet black cherry fruit spreads across the palate. But it could use greater concentration and density. **85** —*S.H. (6/1/2005)*

Calistoga Cellars 2005 Sauvignon Blanc (Napa Valley) $18. Semi-sweet, with candied lemon and lime flavors and good balancing acidity, this is a simple, everyday wine. **83** —*S.H. (12/15/2006)*

Calistoga Cellars 2004 Blossom Creek Vineyard Sauvignon Blanc (Napa Valley) $17. From an estate vineyard in Calistoga comes this dry white wine. It has flavors of apricots, citrus fruits, figs, and peaches, and is obviously very ripe, with no trace at all of cool climate greenness. Good acidity makes it clean and vibrant. **85** —*S.H. (5/1/2006)*

Calistoga Cellars 2003 Zinfandel (Napa Valley) $26. I loved the 2001. This one seems a little obvious, and not quite as complex. It's all about fruit, straightforward blackberries, cherries, coffee, chocolate, and smooth, fine tannins, although it has the same nice dryness and balance. **87** —*S.H. (5/1/2006)*

Calistoga Cellars 2002 Zinfandel (Napa Valley) $22. A superfine Zin, lush, fruity, and balanced, and with extra richness and finesse. Really shows off its ripe blackberries, cherries, and mocha, in a dry package with smooth tannins. **91** —*S.H. (6/1/2005)*

Calistoga Cellars 2001 Zinfandel (Napa Valley) $22. Dark and richly structured, this is a classy style of Zin that features velvety tannins supporting a layered array of black cherry, plum, licorice, toast, vanilla and spice flavors. It's smooth and ripe to the very end, quite elegant and long. **90 Editors' Choice** *(11/1/2003)*

CALIX

Calix 2003 Masked Man Vineyard Syrah (Napa Valley) $33. From a vineyard between St. Helena and Calistoga, this is a good Syrah, but nowhere near as good as the winery's Sonoma bottling, probably because the location is too hot. The wine is soft and melted, although the fruit and chocolate flavors are delicious. **87** —*S.H. (12/31/2005)*

Calix 2003 Parmalee-Hill Vineyard Syrah (Sonoma County) $33. A new discovery for me, and a fabulous one, for with this wine Calix enters the ranks of super-Syrah players. The vineyard is southwest of Sonoma Town, by the Carneros and thus not too hot. Good acidity backs up the black cherry flavors. The wine is balanced, complex, and totally delicious. **92** —*S.H. (12/31/2005)*

CALLAWAY

Callaway 1997 Cabernet Sauvignon (California) $10. 85 Best Buy *(12/31/1999)*

Callaway 1999 Coastal Cabernet Sauvignon (California) $11. There's real varietal character here, with blackberry fruit that persists in the finish. It has well-crafted tannins and a kiss of oak. Full-bodied and dry. Some overripe aromas and flavors of raisins, but overall it's a nice, inexpensive wine. **84** —*S.H. (11/15/2001)*

Callaway 1998 Coastal Cabernet Sauvignon (California) $10. 84 —*S.H. (12/15/2000)*

Callaway 2000 Coastal Winemaker's Reserve Cabernet Sauvignon (Paso Robles) $35. Okay drinking, average in quality and acceptable for its berry-cherry flavors and dry tannins. Feels rather rugged in the mouth and on the finish, where it turns a bit thin. **83** —*S.H. (11/15/2003)*

Callaway 1998 Chardonnay (Temecula) $10. 84 —*L.W. (12/31/1999)*

Callaway 2000 Coastal Chardonnay (California) $11. Pleasant and refreshing with nice varietal character and good structure. Apple and peach flavors are clean and pure, backed by crisp acids. Little, if any, oak detracts from the pretty fruit. **86 Best Buy** —*S.H. (12/15/2002)*

Callaway 1999 Coastal Chardonnay (California) $10. With this wine, Callaway takes a step away from its longtime Temecula appellation and toward the increasingly well-regarded Coastal designation. The wine is a little oakier than Callaway's previous bottlings and the fruit is lean, tending toward grapefruit and green apple. It's crisp and ultraclean, and a good value. **86** —*S.H. (2/1/2002)*

Callaway 2000 Coastal Reserve Chardonnay (Santa Maria Valley) $16. On the herbal side, with tobacco and sage flavors alongside peaches and apples. Dry and tart, it's a refreshing and versatile wine. **85** —*S.H. (5/1/2003)*

Callaway 1999 Reserve Coastal Chardonnay (California) $15. Starts with classic California Chardonnay aromas, including ripe peach and tangerine, smoke, honey, buttered toast and a nice burst of creamy lees. It's very fruity (as you'd expect from this vintage) and sharp, with good acidity cleansing the palate. A very pleasant wine and well worth the price. **87** —*S.H. (5/1/2001)*

Callaway 1998 Chenin Blanc (California) $8. 86 Best Buy —*S.H. (9/1/1999)*

Callaway 2001 Coastal Chenin Blanc (California) $7. Smells intensely floral, an armload of gardenia and forsythia, with additional scents of peaches and kerosene. Has that strong Chenin flavor that always reminds me of hot sealing wax, but there are also apple, mint, and peach notes. Just this side of off-dry, a nice, crisp wine with its own distinct personality. Good value. **86** —*S.H. (9/1/2003)*

Callaway 2000 Coastal Chenin Blanc (California) $8. Herbaceous, wax-bean, and grapefruity aromas introduce this soft, fruity, slightly sweet wine. The citrus and apple flavors are upfront and tasty, and it's very clean. **83** —*S.H. (11/15/2001)*

Callaway 1996 Dolcetto (Temecula) $11. 88 Best Buy —*S.H. (10/1/1999)*

Callaway 1997 Special Collection Dolcetto (Temecula) $15. 85 *(11/1/1999)*

Callaway 1997 Merlot (California) $13. 86 —*L.C. (12/31/1999)*

Callaway 1999 Coastal Merlot (California) $11. Has everything you want in a good red table wine; Good color, nice fruity-berry aromas, fine, ripe flavors, a dry, rich texture, and creamy tannins to cut through sturdy foods. This likeable wine makes for good everyday drinking and won't break the bank. **85** —*S.H. (11/15/2001)*

Callaway 1998 Coastal Merlot (California) $10. A light, earthy wine, with violet, berry, and tea flavors and a sharp, herbal note verging on grassiness or wet hay. It's very dry and the tannins are soft, but crisp acidity keeps it lively in the mouth. **82** *(2/1/2001)*

Callaway 1999 Coastal Reserve Merlot (California) $16. Merlot is the toughest red wine to make interesting in California, not that that stops people from trying. This version highlights the difficulties. It's just too herbaceous and even vegetal, despite some blackberry flavors. The extremely dry tannins and acidity add to the palate impression of earthy austerity. **84** —*S.H. (9/1/2003)*

Callaway 1998 Reserve Coastal Merlot (California) $15. Although basically an earthy wine that was most likely produced from vineyards where the yields were stretched to the max to keep the price down, it does have its charms. You'll find enough black cherry flavors to satisfy, and the tannins are soft and firm. It's dry as dust. The right foods (perhaps roast pork) will coax out its inherent sweetness. **83** —*S.H. (5/1/2001)*

Callaway 1998 Special Collection Pinot Gris (Temecula) $14. 86 —*S.H. (3/1/2000)*

Callaway 1998 Sauvignon Blanc (Temecula) $9. 85 —*L.W. (9/1/1999)*

Callaway 2000 Coastal Sauvignon Blanc (California) $8. Fresh and grassy, a pretty wine with true varietal aromas of hay and citrus fruits. But it drinks richer than you'd think, with pleasant peach flavors and a round, creamy texture. Great value. **86** —*S.H. (9/1/2003)*

Callaway 1999 Coastal Sauvignon Blanc (California) $9. This is the kind of wine people call "cocktail": very dry and a little tart, ultracrisp and clean, and with the lemon-and-lime flavors that are palate wake-up calls. Some riper, fuller peach flavors emerge, but it turns citrusy and dry again on the finish. Sure, it's simple, but it's good. **85 Best Buy** —*S.H. (8/1/2001)*

Callaway 1999 Coastal Syrah (California) $12. In this Syrah, dark blackberry fruit meets cough syrupy sweetness on the nose; in the mouth, sweet berry notes are concealed by cocoa, green apple, and caper flavors. Mouthfeel is round, but the fruit tastes a little underripe and leaves you with a tart finish. **84** *(10/1/2001)*

Callaway 1999 Coastal Reserve Syrah (San Luis Obispo) $16. Aromas of bacon, blackberry, cassis, and smoke are rich and inviting and make your mouth water in anticipation. The flavors don't disappoint. It's not a big wine, but a pretty one, with assertive fruity, peppery flavors silhouetted by richly textured tannins and acids and a dry, smooth finish. **87** —*S.H. (12/1/2002)*

Callaway 2000 Coastal-Reserve Viognier (California) $15. Opens with floral, citrus aromas enriched with a streak of smoky honey. Smooth and crisp, with peach and spiced-apple flavors. Finishes with a spicy, rich aftertaste. **85** —*S.H. (11/15/2001)*

Callaway 2001 Coastal Reserve Viognier (California) $15. Unusual interpretation of Viognier, a wine with strong and tart lemony flavors, like a crisp Sauvignon Blanc, but with floral and nectarine notes with a hint of dried thyme. Bone dry with good acids, a palate-cleansing wine that's a nice cocktail sipper. **85** —*S.H. (3/1/2003)*

Callaway 1998 Special Collection Viognier (Temecula) $15. 85 —*S.H. (11/1/1999)*

USA

CAMARADERIE CELLARS

**Camaraderie Cellars 2001 Grace Bordeaux Blend (Columbia Valley (WA))
$32.** The winery's Bordeaux blend (66% Cabernet Sauvignon, 22%
Merlot, and 12% Cab Franc), it's full, seamless and complete, with rich,
satiny fruit layered into chocolatey oak. This is almost Napa-like, but
with raspberry/cherry fruit that has the acid structure of Washington
grapes. **90** —*P.G. (12/31/2003)*

Camaraderie Cellars 2003 Cabernet Franc (Washington) $25. A very fine
Cab Franc; smooth, polished and showing its varietal character. The cof-
fee ground flavors, mixed with green tea tannins, give it a defining edge.
It's an earthiness that sets it apart from Cabernet Sauvignon. Inside you'll
find plenty of plush blueberry and plum fruit. Good winemaking. **91
Editors' Choice** —*P.G. (11/15/2006)*

**Camaraderie Cellars 2001 Cabernet Sauvignon (Columbia Valley (WA))
$25.** This is the winery's first pure Cabernet since 1996. Despite its
youth, it's already a very complete wine, balanced and expressive, with
pure, vivid cassis and plummy fruit. Focused and compact, it's classic
Washington Cab. **92 Cellar Selection** —*P.G. (12/31/2003)*

Camaraderie Cellars 1999 Cabernet Sauvignon (Washington) $22. This is a
stylish effort, scented with cassis, blackberries, mint, licorice, and coffee.
Dark, tannic and delicious already, it is beginning to show complex layers of fruit flavor as it breathes. Definitely a wine to lay down for the
next 8–10 years. **91 Cellar Selection** —*P.G. (6/1/2002)*

Camaraderie Cellars 2001 Merlot (Columbia Valley (WA)) $25. Substantial
black cherry fruit is married to big, chewy tannins, with more obvious
oak flavors than the other Camaraderie wines. Juicy and big, with some
heat in the finish. **89** —*P.G. (12/31/2003)*

Camaraderie Cellars 1998 Grace Red Blend (Washington) $22. The blend
is 65% Cabernet Sauvignon, 20% Merlot, and 15% Cab Franc, and it
adds up to a sweetly fruity wine limned with chocolatey new oak.
Balanced and structured like Bordeaux, it has substantial tannins and
dominant oak, and seems likely to continue to develop well for another
6-8 years. **91 Cellar Selection** —*P.G. (6/1/2002)*

Camaraderie Cellars 2002 Sauvignon Blanc (Washington) $10. From Red
Mountain fruit, this includes 25% barrel-fermented Sémillon in the
blend. It's a good, melony wine, accented with some unusual fennel
notes. **87 Best Buy** —*P.G. (12/31/2003)*

Camaraderie Cellars 2000 Sauvignon Blanc (Washington) $12. Good fruit,
sourced from an excellent Red Mountain vineyard, starts things off right.
The fresh nose is scented with hay, herb and sweet grass, and leads into a
lovely wine with 25% barrel fermented Sémillon blended in for extra
pizzazz. **90 Best Buy** —*P.G. (6/1/2002)*

CAMBRIA

Cambria 2000 Bench Break Vineyard Chardonnay (Santa Maria Valley) $25.
Much leaner than the '99 vintage. This release shows mineral, slate, and
citrus fruit flavors and high acidity, and is very dry. Feels like liquid steel
gliding over the palate, ultra-clean and tart. No crème brûlée this year,
but nonetheless a distinguished wine. **87** —*S.H. (8/1/2003)*

Cambria 1999 Bench Break Vineyard Chardonnay (Santa Maria Valley) $30.
A winning nose offers aromas of créme brûlée, smoked bacon, pears,
peaches, and toasty vanilla that just keep coming on in this stylish, full
wine. The palate shows similar flavors. The big mouthfeel continues on
the long, slightly sweet finish with its toasty, smoky oak. Strong already,
but it should be even better in six months. From the maker of the fine
affordable and widely available Katherine's Vineyard Chardonnay. Top
Value. **91 Best Buy** *(7/1/2001)*

Cambria 1999 Experimental Clone 4 Chardonnay (Santa Maria Valley) $40.
Fred Holloway's first full vintage started off with a bang. This big, complex Chardonnay has aromas of tropical fruit underscored by
butterscotch and mint. The flavors burst with pineapple and a touch of
menthol, while the long, buttery finish is perfectly complemented by
racy acidity. **91** *(10/1/2002)*

**Cambria 2001 Katherine's Estate Bottled Chardonnay (Santa Maria Valley)
$22.** Big, ripe, rich, and well-oaked. That pretty much says it all about
this show-off wine, with its bold, tropical fruit flavors, crisp coastal

acidity and sleek structure. The tart taste of minerally gunmetal adds
complexity. **89** —*S.H. (8/1/2003)*

Cambria 2004 Katherine's Vineyard Chardonnay (Santa Maria Valley) $16.
This cool-climate wine needs a warm vintage to show its best, and it certainly got heat in 2004. The result is a big, opulent wine with masses of
tropical fruit flavors slathered in spicy oak. Yet it retains crisp, citrusy
acidity, and has an elegant streak of minerality. **88** —*S.H. (12/1/2006)*

Cambria 1999 Katherine's Vineyard Chardonnay (Santa Maria Valley) $22.
87 *(10/1/2002)*

Cambria 1998 Katherine's Vineyard Chardonnay (Santa Maria Valley) $21.
84 *(6/1/2000)*

Cambria 1997 Katherine's Vineyard Chardonnay (Santa Maria Valley) $20.
91 —*S.H. (7/1/1999)*

Cambria 2000 Rae's Chardonnay (Santa Maria Valley) $44. A flamboyant
Chard, packed with tropical fruit flavors and with a lavish overlay of
smoky oak. Drinks crisp and clean in the mouth, with a creamy texture
and a long, spicy finish. Could use a bit more finesse and subtlety, but
glamorous and enticing. **90** —*S.H. (8/1/2003)*

Cambria 1999 Rae's Chardonnay (Santa Maria Valley) $41. Another ele-
gant wine from Cambria. This one has a vanilla, smoke, and grapefruit
nose. Medium-weight, it is crisp in the mouth, though somewhat leaner
than the Bench Break. This cuvée nicely melds green apple fruit with
menthol and vanilla accents. The bouquet is a reprise of the long, sweet-
tart, butterscotch, and tangy oak finish. **91** *(7/1/2001)*

Cambria 1995 Reserve Chardonnay (Santa Maria Valley) $32. 92 —*S.H.*
(7/1/1999)

Cambria 2002 Tepusquet Vineyard Pinot Gris (Santa Maria Valley) $16.
This single-vineyard beauty is made in the full-bodied, oaky-leesy style
that California wines labeled "Gris" usually are. With time, it has mel-
lowed into something marvelous, a totally dry, acidic wine of unusual
finesse and balance. **90** —*S.H. (2/1/2006)*

Cambria 1999 Bench Break Vineyard Pinot Noir (Santa Maria Valley) $42.
Strong caramel, butter, and brown sugar aromas. Flavors of vanilla,
licorice, and tree bark come ahead of some sturdy plum fruit. The finish
is arguably a bit hot and woody. **86** *(10/1/2002)*

Cambria 1999 Experimental 4-2A-115 Pinot Noir (Santa Maria Valley) $50.
Plum, pepper, spicy oak, earth, and coffee on the nose. Flavors include
blackberries, cherries, and mushrooms, but also a hint of celery. The
structure here is impeccable; it's very well built, somewhat like a fortress,
but one with a wide-open door. **90** *(10/1/2002)*

**Cambria 2000 Experimental Clone 115 Pinot Noir (Santa Maria Valley)
$50.** Our favorite of the experimental clones. The smoked bacon and
underbrush aromas turn to a big mouthful of juicy black cherries and
licorice, accented with a dusting of earth. It's a big, lush Pinot that finishes with chocolate-covered cherries. **93** *(10/1/2002)*

Cambria 2000 Experimental Clone 23 Pinot Noir (Santa Maria Valley) $50.
The density of this wine is surprising. Not a wine for the meek, the rich,
heady flavors of plum pudding and spice cake integrate well with dark
fruits and earth. **92** *(10/1/2002)*

Cambria 2000 Experimental Clone 2A Pinot Noir (Santa Maria Valley) $50.
Much meatier than the 115 bottling, 2A also folds in portobello mushroom aromas. The candied, dark cherry flavors are so rich there is a
perception of sweetness. This wine finishes with great length and a touch
of tea. **92** *(10/1/2002)*

Cambria 2000 Julia's Pinot Noir (Santa Maria Valley) $22. From the
coolest corner of the estate, a tough young wine that shows some aging
possibilities. Currently, it is drinkable for its silky, easy tannins and gentle mouthfeel. But the flavors are stubbornly herbal. Seems a victim of
the vintage, but could soften and develop in a few years. **87** —*S.H.*
(8/1/2003)

Cambria 1999 Julia's Pinot Noir (Santa Maria Valley) $26. The bouquet is
sharp: cranberry and sawdust leads into creamy vanilla. Tart red berries
dominate the flavors, and the feel is a bit shrill, aided by strong acidity.
Dusty tannins keep the finish alive. **83** *(10/1/2002)*

Cambria 2004 Julia's Vineyard Pinot Noir (Santa Maria Valley) $19.
Crisply elegant wine with ripe cherry cola fruit, spices, and a silky

smooth texture. A fair amount of new oak adds vanilla and cream. This is a good price for a Pinot of this complexity and charm. **87** —*S.H. (12/1/2006)*

Cambria 1999 Rae's Pinot Noir (Santa Maria Valley) $50. One whiff of the powerful hickory smoke and menthol announces that this was given full oak treatment. Some herbaceous notes mix on the tongue with plum, tomato, and creamy vanilla. It's fairly soft in feel but not in flavor, especially on the finish, where espresso-like coffee comes on full force. **87** *(10/1/2002)*

Cambria 2000 Rae's Estate Bottled Pinot Noir (Santa Maria Valley) $50. A selection of the best estate barrels, this year's Rae's is considerably richer than the Julia's bottling. Cherry, espresso, and herb flavors are framed in voluptuously soft tannins, with a rich mouthfeel and a distinctive silky texture. Has the stuffing and style to elevate it into the realm of excellence. **92** —*S.H. (12/1/2003)*

Cambria 2002 Tepusquet Vineyard Syrah (Santa Maria Valley) $20. Interesting notes on this wine, with one reviewer admiring the lovely fruit and pretty aromas of licorice, blackberry, and spice, while another found the oak unintegrated and distracting. **87** *(9/1/2005)*

Cambria 1999 Tepusquet Vineyard Syrah (Santa Maria Valley) $22. Jammy berries—sweet and sour—and smoky oak open this even, smooth, and well-structured wine. Shows nice weight without being heavy. Has good length and moderate tannins on the close, along with a reprise of jammy fruit and smoke. **87** *(11/1/2001)*

Cambria 1999 Tepusquet Vineyard Syrah (Santa Maria Valley) $50. **87** *(10/1/2002)*

Cambria 1997 Tepusquet Vineyard Syrah (Santa Maria Valley) $22. **89** —*L.W. (2/1/2000)*

Cambria 2000 Tepusquet Vineyard Viognier (Santa Maria Valley) $16. **85** *(10/1/2002)*

Cambria 1997 Tepusquet Vineyard Viognier (Santa Maria Valley) $16. **91 Best Buy** —*S.H. (6/1/1999)*

CAMELLIA

Camellia 2000 Lencioni Vineyard Cabernet Sauvignon (Dry Creek Valley) $40. Heavy on the palate, with a thick texture and harsh tannins. There are some blackberry flavors, but also a veggie streak and a medicinal taste on the finish. **82** —*S.H. (8/1/2004)*

Camellia 1999 Lencioni Vineyard Cabernet Sauvignon (Dry Creek Valley) $45. Dark, with aromas of cardboard, mint, and earth. If you swirl it hard, some blackberry notes emerge. In the mouth, it's dense and dull, stuffed with bitter tannins. The finish is acidic and sharp. **81** —*S.H. (11/15/2002)*

Camellia 1998 Lencioni Vineyard Cabernet Sauvignon (Dry Creek Valley) $35. There's alot of character and punch to this wine, with proper aromas and flavors of well-ripened blackberry and cassis fruit. Be warned, the tannins are hefty, not quite numbing but big, so drink it with rich foods. There's a roughness that might mellow out with some age. **87** —*S.H. (12/31/2001)*

Camellia 2001 Diamo Grazie Red Wine Cabernet Sauvignon-Sangiovese (Dry Creek Valley) $42. Dry, tannic and ungenerous in fruit, leaving behind a puckery, astringent feeling in the mouth. Sangiovese, Cabernet Sauvignon, and Petite Sirah. **82** —*S.H. (8/1/2004)*

Camellia 1999 Diamo Grazie Red Table Wine Red Blend (Dry Creek Valley) $42. Cabernet Sauvignon dominates and brings lush blackberry fruit and rich tannins. Sangiovese contributes acidity, tartness and a lean but vital quality. There's also the kind of dusty tannins that make your tongue stick to your palate. It's very dry and might improve with mid-term aging. **87** —*S.H. (12/15/2001)*

Camellia 2001 Merlo Vineyards Sangiovese (Dry Creek Valley) $24. Smells like bacon frying in the pan, and if there's fruit in this wine, it's effectively buried, so what you get is heat and tannins. **81** —*S.H. (8/1/2004)*

Camellia 2000 Merlo Vineyards Sangiovese (Dry Creek Valley) $28. What is California Sangiovese? This winery answers the question with a

bone-dry wine with very soft tannins and acids and earthy flavors of cherry and tobacco. The taste is fine. The problem is the body, which is so soft it's practically nonexistent. **84** —*S.H. (12/1/2002)*

Camellia 1999 Merlo Vineyards Sangiovese (Dry Creek Valley) $28. From a warm part of the appellation comes this soft, simple and dry table wine. Smell like crushed berries, tobacco, and earth, with a waft of vanillin-tinged oak. Drinks very dry and soft. The finish is tart enough to cut through olive oil and cheese. **86** —*S.H. (12/15/2001)*

Camellia 2001 Lencioni Vineyard Zinfandel (Dry Creek Valley) $22. Funky, with a definite aroma and taste of bacon grease that could be brett. Underneath that is a dry, fairly tannic wine, with cherry flavors. **82** —*S.H. (8/1/2004)*

Camellia 1999 Lencioni Vineyard Zinfandel (Dry Creek Valley) $22. Smells fruity and big, with briary aromas accompanied by chocolate and mint. Tastes big, too. The mélange of berry flavor explodes across the palate, delivering waves of spicy fruit. Very dry. It's a little too soft, and could use more structure, but that's a minor quibble. **86** —*S.H. (12/15/2001)*

CAMELOT

Camelot 2002 Cabernet Sauvignon (California) $8. There's a lot of rich cherry, blackberry, and coffee fruit in this dry Cab. It's not too tannic, with just enough of a grip for balance. Very nice value. **85 Best Buy** —*S.H. (12/1/2005)*

Camelot 2001 Cabernet Sauvignon (California) $7. Fruity-earthy, with pleasant blackberry and cherry flavors diffused with herbs and tobacco. A little sharp in acidity, and very dry. **84** —*S.H. (10/1/2004)*

Camelot 1999 Cabernet Sauvignon (California) $10. Here's a perfectly acceptable sipper that's uncomplicated but clean and affordable. It's also dry. Some ripe berry flavors sit next to stemmier, greener ones, and the tannins are smooth. With nearly 40,000 cases produced, it should be easy to find this value wine. **85** —*S.H. (6/1/2002)*

Camelot 1997 Chardonnay (California) $13. **87** —*L.W. (10/1/1999)*

Camelot 2003 Chardonnay (California) $7. Clean, dry, and oaky, with modest flavors of peaches and pears, and a good finish. A good value. **84 Best Buy** —*S.H. (6/1/2005)*

Camelot 2000 Chardonnay (California) $10. Here's a simple, everyday Chard with apple and peach flavors and soft acids, and oaky components. It satisfies the basic requirements for the varietal. The finish is noticeably sugary. From Kendall-Jackson. **82** —*S.H. (5/1/2002)*

Camelot 1996 Merlot (California) $13. **85** *(3/1/2000)*

Camelot 2001 Merlot (California) $7. This is a wine to stock up on by the case if you like a pretty good, full-bodied red at this price—and who doesn't? It's polished with cherry, tobacco, and spice flavors, and is dry and balanced. **85 Best Buy** —*S.H. (12/15/2004)*

Camelot 1998 Merlot (California) $10. Opens with thin aromas and drinks thin and tart, with just the slightest suggestion of fruit, although there's plenty of acidity. It's a very dry wine with no faults. The finish is extremely dry and rasping. **82** —*S.H. (12/31/2001)*

Camelot 1997 Merlot (California) $10. A soft, round quaffer filled with warmth. Slightly cooked berries are tinged with a hint of wood and dusty earth flavors **82** *(2/1/2001)*

Camelot 2003 Pinot Noir (California) $7. Rather raw and harsh: a hot, dry wine with oak and cherry-berry flavors that turn medicinal on the finish. **82** —*S.H. (6/1/2005)*

Camelot 2002 Pinot Noir (California) $7. A little overripe and pruny, but dry and decently made. Shows some plump fruit, and also some herbal, coffee notes, leading to a finish of bitter tannins. **84 Best Buy** *(11/1/2004)*

Camelot 2001 Pinot Noir (California) $10. Light in color, with strawberry aromas and notes of oak. A bit reedy and discombobulated in the mouth, with aggressive acids and tannins. Very hot and somewhat chemical tasting on the finish. **83** —*M.S. (12/1/2003)*

Camelot 2000 Pinot Noir (California) $10. Well, you can't expect Romanee-Conti for 10 bucks, but this is a pleasant, easy-drinking wine with enough Pinot Character to satisfy. It's silky smooth, with some rasberry, beet, and tomato notes, and dry, with a clean, spicy finish. **84** —*S.H. (12/15/2001)*

Camelot 1997 Pinot Noir (California) $10. Some raspberry fruit in the aroma, but things turn rapidly earthy and herbal, suggesting dried tomato, rhubarb, and oregano. The flavors are simple and uninspiring. Soft, mild, rustic, and thin are other words that come to mind. **82** —*S.H. (2/1/2001)*

Camelot 2004 Sauvignon Blanc (California) $8. Picture perfect Sauvignon Blanc, and at a nice price, too. It seems to come from coastal grapes, to judge from the lime-tart crispness. The tangy flavors are of spiced figs and vanilla, and finish a bit sweet. **85 Best Buy** —*S.H. (12/1/2005)*

Camelot 2003 Sauvignon Blanc (California) $7. There is lots of ripe, fruity flavor in this pleasant, slightly sweet wine. It tastes of lemons and limes, melons, and figs, and is crisp and clean. **85 Best Buy** —*S.H. (6/1/2005)*

Camelot 2002 Shiraz (California) $7. A nice wine, especially for the price. Dark, full-bodied and dry, with rich, spicy flavors of plums and blackberries, and a sweet coating of oak. **86 Best Buy** —*S.H. (6/1/2005)*

Camelot 1999 Syrah (California) $9. Overtly grapey aromas are joined by scents of fresh weed-whacker trimmings. Seems very soft in the mouth, with sour notes of camphor and toast joining in on the palate. Finishes short. Try slightly chilled, as you would a Beaujolais nouveau. **83** *(10/1/2001)*

Camelot 2002 Zinfandel (California) $7. Sweet oak and sweet raspberry merge to create a drink resembling a candy confection, with a sugary finish. **83** —*S.H. (6/1/2005)*

CAMERON

Cameron 2003 Red Wine Cabernet Blend (Napa Valley) $50. This label, from the fine Napa winery, Fisher, is reserved for young vines. It's a classic Médoc blend, based on Cabernet Sauvignon with smaller amounts of other varieties. The winemaker's description is apt: powerful and precocious. Floods the mouth with blackberry tart and chocolate flavors that finish dry, with smooth, supple tannins. Drink now–2010. **91** —*S.H. (9/1/2006)*

Cameron 1997 Clos Electrique Chardonnay (Willamette Valley) $35. **92** *(11/15/1999)*

CAMERON HUGHES

Cameron Hughes 2003 Lot 15 Cabernet Sauvignon (Napa Valley) $15. Looking for a good, moderately priced Napa Cab? Check this one out. It's dry and balanced, with firm tannins and acids framing sweetly ripe Cabernet fruit flavors and a nice touch of oak. The grapes are mostly from Rutherford. **86** —*S.H. (12/31/2006)*

Cameron Hughes 2004 Lot 16 Cabernet Sauvignon (Stags Leap District) $16. Pretty good price for a genuine Stags Leap Cab. It's got plenty of blackberry, cherry, cocoa, and oak flavors, with a good structure of edgy tannins and crisp acids. Might improve for a few years, but good now for its chewy deliciousness. **86** —*S.H. (12/31/2006)*

Cameron Hughes 2002 Lot 7 Cabernet Sauvignon (Knights Valley) $10. This winery has generated buzz in California for its value wines, and this is certainly a nice Cabernet for the price. It's not the smoothest ride, but it's plenty ripe in flavor, with rich tannins and a dry finish. **85 Best Buy** —*S.H. (5/1/2006)*

Cameron Hughes 2003 Lot 8 Pinot Noir (Monterey County) $10. Dry and tart, with fruit so thin it accentuates the alcohol, this wine shows how hard it is to produce a good, inexpensive Pinot Noir. It's properly silky. If only they could have figured out a way to boost the flavors. **82** —*S.H. (5/1/2006)*

CAMPION

Campion 2001 Pinot Noir (Edna Valley) $35. Interesting and complex, and delicious to drink. Cherries, raspberries, and blackberries are spiced up with toasty oak and vanillins, while the mouthfeel is silky, seductive, and crisp. The light, airy texture is enjoyable. **87** —*S.H. (3/1/2004)*

Campion 2000 Pinot Noir (Santa Lucia Highlands) $32. Light in color and in body, almost ethereal, with a smooth, silky texture and bright acids. The pretty flavors include cola and rhubarb, and sweeter notes of raspberries and cherries. **86** —*S.H. (4/1/2004)*

Campion 2000 Pinot Noir (Carneros) $32. This pretty, stylish wine is elegantly silky in the mouth, with hardly any tannins at all, although the

acids are fine. Flavors are on the jammy side, with raspberry, tea, cola, and spice. **86** —*S.H. (4/1/2004)*

Campion 2001 Firepeak Vineyard Pinot Noir (Edna Valley) $45. Silky and elegant, a light-bodied wine that gently speads raspberry, cherry, and smoky spice flavors across the palate. Easy to drink, with some pretty layers of complexity. Hardly any tannins at all, except in the dusty finish. **88** —*S.H. (4/1/2004)*

CAMPUS OAKS

Campus Oaks 1998 Cabernet Sauvignon (Mendocino) $12. This is a modest little wine, on the rough and ready side, with some berry and fruit flavors and a dry finish. Don't look for nuances here, just a clean ordinary wine. **82** —*S.H. (6/1/2002)*

Campus Oaks 2002 Chardonnay (California) $7. The fruit flavors drink thin, but it's a clean, crisp wine that's serviceable at an everyday price. **82** —*S.H. (5/1/2004)*

Campus Oaks 1999 Chardonnay (California) $8. Varietal enough, with smoky, vanilla aromas, a hint of peach and apple flavors and a creamy mouthfeel. It's also dry, with a cut of tartness in the finish. The problem is a funky earthiness and a watery thinness that reduce its attractiveness. **83** —*S.H. (5/1/2002)*

Campus Oaks 2001 Merlot (California) $9. Nice drinking in an everyday Merlot. Has pretty flavors of cherries, cola, and plums that are ripe and juicy. Finishes with a ripely sweet, tannic flourish and a long, fruity aftertaste. A very good value. **85** —*S.H. (5/1/2004)*

Campus Oaks 1998 Merlot (California) $9. Tastes like a store-bought cherry pie with an herbal edge of cranberry. The soft acidity and limpid mouthfeel have just enough acidity to support the ripe fruit. This is a simple, uncomplicated jug-style wine, not bad and not good, and honestly priced. Long, sweet finish. **84** —*S.H. (6/1/2002)*

Campus Oaks 2001 Pinot Noir (Mendocino County) $9. Tastes just like a good coastal Pinot with a little water added. Cherry-raspberry flavors, vanilla, smoke, and cinnamony spices have silky tannins and crisp acids. A nice junior version of the variety. **84** —*S.H. (5/1/2004)*

Campus Oaks 1999 Syrah (California) $9. Stewed fruit, Play-Doh and herb-meets-kelp notes lead into an equally bizarre blend of vegetal, rhubarb, and soy flavors. Mouthfeel is tart, as is the finish. **82** *(10/1/2001)*

Campus Oaks 2001 Old Vine Zinfandel (Lodi) $15. This nice expression of Lodi Zin has concentrated flavors of plums, blackberries, herbs, and peppery spices, and rustic tannins. It's very dry. There's a trace of bitterness as you swallow, but it's the perfect pizza wine. **85** —*S.H. (5/1/2004)*

Campus Oaks 1999 Old Vine Zinfandel (California) $10. There's good, ripe berry fruit here but the wine can't shake off a rustic, homemade quality. The aromas include baked cherry pie and asphalt, while there's a wild, uncontrolled aspect in the mouth. This is not a wine to mull over, but to drink with just about anything and not worry about. **84** —*S.H. (7/1/2002)*

CANA'S FEAST

Cana's Feast 1999 Bordeaux Blend (Red Mountain) $30. This blend of Cab Sauvignon, Cab Franc, and Merlot is young, rambunctious and tight, but also very interesting. The aromas of chocolate, clove, pepper, and black plum do the trick: you are drawn in. Intense flavors of cherry, plum, cassis, and pepper, and a finish of piquant spices and oak are equally satisfying. Based on how this wine responded to air we say give it a few years to settle down. **90** —*M.S. (6/1/2003)*

Cana's Feast 2000 Del Rio Vineyard Bordeaux Blend (Rogue Valley) $30. Southern Oregon, unlike the northern Willamette Valley, is warm and conducive to growing Bordeaux varieties, as evidenced by this hearty, tannic blend of Merlot, Cabernet Sauvignon, and Cab Franc. Right away you get kirsch and cassis from this heavyweight, and that's followed by a ripe palate that blasts loudly with plum and chocolate. Along the way there are some drying tannins and pulsating acids, so either lay it down for a couple of years or decant and serve with grilled meats. **89** —*M.S. (8/1/2003)*

Cana's Feast 1999 Cuvée G Pinot Noir (Willamette Valley) $30. Meaty and rock solid, with a heavily oaked, dark-fruit nose that's sure to please lovers of big Pinot Noir. The palate is sweet and rich, with lots of oak and black plum, while in the end it turns spicy and offers several dimensions of flavor and texture. While it remains a bit simple and straightforward, it scores points for its modern profile and probable mass appeal. Made by Cuneo. **90** —M.S. (9/1/2003)

Cana's Feast 2002 Meredith Mitchell Vineyard Pinot Noir (Willamette Valley) $40. Done in a very sweet, juicy, slightly over-ripe mode, it offers varietally correct flavors in a smooth, everyday style. A couple of extra years in bottle should soften up the tannins sufficiently. **87** (11/1/2004)

CANEPA

Canepa 1998 Gauer Vineyard Chardonnay (Sonoma County) $30. Helen Turley's Chardonnay shows nice complexity, particularly on the nose, where nuanced oriental spice, tobacco, nectarine, floral, and yellow fruit aromas play with the senses. The palate is mild and balanced, with melon, stone fruit, and nut flavors, and a smooth texture to boot. Just a touch of heat shows on the long, dry yet spicy finish. **89** (7/1/2001)

CANOE RIDGE

Canoe Ridge 2003 Cabernet Sauvignon (Columbia Valley (WA)) $20. Soft fruit flavors suggestive of plum and cranberry. The tannins are thick and chocolatey, with streaks of espresso and smoke. Right now most of the flavor seems to come from barrels rather than grapes. **87** —P.G. (4/1/2006)

Canoe Ridge 2001 Cabernet Sauvignon (Columbia Valley (WA)) $20. Broad and roughly tannic, this chewy Cab really needs grilled meat to soften it up and bring out the cherry fruit. That said, it offers a clean, firm slice of Horse Heaven Hills Cabernet Sauvignon terroir, with a long, appealing finish. **87** —P.G. (7/1/2004)

Canoe Ridge 1999 Cabernet Sauvignon (Columbia Valley (WA)) $28. This rich, ripe wine explodes with juicy cassis fruit. It shows fine concentration and plenty of spicy oak. Masterful winemaking; there's a beautiful sense of balance and just flat-out gorgeous fruit. Canoe Ridge is on a roll, and wines of this caliber are rare at this price. **88 Editors' Choice** —P.G. (5/1/2002)

Canoe Ridge 1998 Cabernet Sauvignon (Columbia Valley (WA)) $25. The nose jumps from the glass, promising ripe, black cherry, and cassis fruit, black pepper spice, and some high-toned "lift." Round and succulent, it's a deep-colored, still grapey, sweet and lingering wine with nice pepper spice accents. Much more power than the winery's '97, it shows the strengths of the vintage, drinks well right now, and has the stuffing to cellar well for another half decade. **89** —P.G. (6/1/2001)

Canoe Ridge 1997 Cabernet Sauvignon (Columbia Valley (WA)) $25. **87** —P.G. (11/15/2000)

Canoe Ridge 1996 Cabernet Sauvignon (Columbia Valley (WA)) $25. **91** —S.H. (7/1/1999)

Canoe Ridge 2002 Chardonnay (Columbia Valley (WA)) $19. Crisp apple and citrus fruits highlight the nose and forward palate, with interesting, peppery spices and just a hint of new oak finishing out the back end. Well balanced and interesting. **87** —P.G. (5/1/2004)

Canoe Ridge 2001 Chardonnay (Columbia Valley (WA)) $19. Here you get the whole fruit bowl. Melon, pear, and apple aromas with some fresh floral notes are followed by banana, cantaloupe, and pear flavors. Some light oak spreads across the finish. All in all the feel is a touch flat; brighter acidity would give it an extra boost that it could use. **87** —M.S. (6/1/2003)

Canoe Ridge 2000 Chardonnay (Columbia Valley (WA)) $18. Canoe Ridge is on a roll, with perhaps the best lineup of new releases in their history. This is a subtle, textured, silky Chardonnay, elegantly layered with nuances of stone, herb and leesy fruit. Its subtle pleasures take a minute to explore, but they linger in the mouth like a sweet kiss. **90** —P.G. (2/1/2002)

Canoe Ridge 2000 Chardonnay (Columbia Valley (WA)) $19. **86** —J.M. (5/1/2002)

Canoe Ridge 2000 Oak Ridge Gewürztraminer (Washington) $12. Canoe Ridge delivers a classic bottle, with lychee, honeysuckle, and rosewater mingling in the nose, pears, and pineapple in the mouth. The wine feels soft and sensual, with plenty of balanced power. **88** —P.G. (12/31/2001)

Canoe Ridge 2002 Oak Ridge Vineyard Gewürztraminer (Washington) $13. The winery always does well with this tricky grape, somehow walking the line between floral and oily, sweet and dry, and coming up with intensity that doesn't tire out the palate. Complex and lingering, it's perfect for southeast Asian cuisine. **90 Best Buy** —P.G. (5/1/2004)

Canoe Ridge 1999 Oak Ridge Vineyard Gewürztraminer (Washington) $12. **90 Best Buy** —P.G. (11/15/2000)

Canoe Ridge 2003 Merlot (Columbia Valley (WA)) $20. Light strawberry and cherry candy fruit lays under fairly aggressive new oak. The barrel flavors of toast and butterscotch dominate; but give it a bit of air and out comes the supple, though light, fruit. **87** —P.G. (4/1/2006)

Canoe Ridge 2001 Merlot (Columbia Valley (WA)) $15. This is a transition wine for Canoe Ridge, whose talented winemaker, John Abbott, did the crush but left before finishing it. It's a good effort, but not as lush as previous vintages. The fruit is pretty and the wine balanced, with nice flavors of plum and dried cherries, and intriguing hints of tobacco leaf in the finish. **88** —P.G. (9/1/2004)

Canoe Ridge 1999 Merlot (Columbia Valley (WA)) $14. Herbal aromas mix with field greens and a touch of raspberry jam. The mouthfeel is soft and even, with flavors of endive, arugula, and chocolate-covered cherries. **86** —C.S. (12/31/2002)

Canoe Ridge 1999 Merlot (Columbia Valley (WA)) $25. Though still young and tight, this lovely wine will open up over the course of several hours to reveal ripe, varietal fruit, full-bodied with tannins and acids balanced and integrated. It shows textbook flavors, and a sure hand at the tiller. **89** —P.G. (12/31/2001)

Canoe Ridge 1998 Merlot (Columbia Valley (WA)) $25. **88** —P.G. (11/15/2000)

Canoe Ridge 1997 Merlot (Columbia Valley (WA)) $19. **90** —S.H. (11/1/1999)

Canoe Ridge 1998 Reserve Merlot (Columbia Valley (WA)) $45. **90** —P.G. (11/15/2000)

Canoe Ridge 1999 Reserve-Lot No. 10 Merlot (Columbia Valley (WA)) $45. This is the second time Canoe Ridge has released a reserve, lot-selection Merlot (in 1998 it was Lot No. 16). This wine is still wrapped up tight as a drum, with very young, very compact fruit that suggests depth and power. Like its predecessor, it's serious and dense, but this one needs a lot of breathing time. **91** —P.G. (6/1/2002)

Canoe Ridge 1998 Reserve Lot No. 16 Merlot (Columbia Valley (WA)) $45. This is a special selection of estate-grown grapes, with four percent Cabernet blended in for backbone and zip. The first-ever reserve from Canoe Ridge, it's serious and dense, with a bouquet of red and black fruits, smoke, coffee, and bitter chocolate. In the mouth, it's both open and deep, with good, juicy cherry and berry fruit matched to toasty oak. **93 Cellar Selection** —P.G. (12/31/2001)

Canoe Ridge 1998 Red Table Wine Merlot-Cabernet Sauvignon (Columbia Valley (WA)) $14. **87** —P.G. (11/15/2000)

Canoe Ridge 2000 Red Table Wine Red Blend (Columbia Valley (WA)) $14. An earthy and herbal offering, one that borders on having tomato aromas. Below that you'll find cherry, raspberry, and chocolate prior to a rich, cooling finish that both spicy and long. If only there was some additional ripe fruit flavor here; then you'd have a sure thing. **86** —M.S. (6/1/2003)

CANON DE SOL

Canon de Sol 2000 Meritage (Columbia Valley (WA)) $28. Dark to the point of inky; fragrant with dense fruits, wood, earth. There is a pleasing softness to the scent that invites sipping. This is a very attractive wine with plenty of concentration and deep, dark, tarry, smoky flavors running through the finish. Good value for this style of wine. **88** —P.G. (9/1/2003)

USA

Canon de Sol 2000 Merlot (Columbia Valley (WA)) $24. Fresh, lush ripe red fruits are displayed against some barrel flavors of cracker and vanilla wafer. Forward, plump, and quite pleasant. **87** —*P.G. (9/1/2003)*

Canon de Sol 1999 Merlot (Columbia Valley (WA)) $24. Some high-toned fruit with scents that suggest nail polish. A highly extracted, dark, and heavy wine, with chalky tannins, and a smoky, tarry finish. **86** —*P.G. (9/1/2003)*

CANTIGA WINEWORKS

Cantiga Wineworks 2000 Cabernet Sauvignon (El Dorado) $18. A country-style wine, sharp in the mouth, with herb, coffee, and berry flavors that finish dry. **84** —*S.H. (3/1/2005)*

Cantiga Wineworks 2000 Cabernet Sauvignon-Shiraz (Central Coast) $18. The wine starts off with pleasing cherry, herb, coffee and spice flavors. But it falters with excessive acidity and a tartness on the finish, which is short. **84** —*J.M. (4/1/2003)*

Cantiga Wineworks 2000 Chardonnay (Monterey) $20. Toasty and rich, with pretty butterscotch, apricot, pear, hazelnut, citrus, melon, and spice flavors. Round and full on the finish. **89** —*J.M. (2/1/2003)*

Cantiga Wineworks 2000 Oakless Chardonnay (Monterey) $20. Fruity, with hints of peach and pear framed in tangy, lemony acidity, and cinnamon spice. The wine is showing a touch of oxidation, which gives it a nutty edge. **85** —*J.M. (2/1/2003)*

Cantiga Wineworks 2001 Shiraz (Monterey) $24. Has some baked fruit aromas, and drinks hard and dry, with a core of spice, coffee, and plums. Will open up and sweeten with rich fare **84** —*S.H. (3/1/2005)*

Cantiga Wineworks 2000 Shiraz (Monterey) $24. A pleasant wine, with smoky, toasty aromas and black cherry, raspberry, herb, and spice flavors. **86** —*J.M. (2/1/2003)*

Cantiga Wineworks 2001 Ryan Oaks Vineyard Zinfandel (Sierra Foothills) $16. Pruny, caramelly, and Porty, except that it's dry, at the cost of monster alcohol. Not my style, but a good example of its type. **84** —*S.H. (3/1/2005)*

CANYON ROAD

Canyon Road 2003 Cabernet Sauvignon (California) $9. This is a great price for an everyday Cab that offers lots of pleasure. It's dry and fairly tannic, with good blackberry flavors and a long finish. **85 Best Buy** —*S.H. (10/1/2005)*

Canyon Road 2002 Cabernet Sauvignon (California) $10. Offers a mixture of ripe cherry flavors with some herbal, stemmy notes and sharp acids, in a dry wine with smooth tannins. A hamburger will fall in love with it. **84** —*S.H. (12/31/2004)*

Canyon Road 2001 Cabernet Sauvignon (California) $10. Tastes like it came from overcropped vines, with thin, watery berry flavors and a distinct earthiness. Alcohol, acidity, and tannins take front and center, offering little in the way of pleasure. **83** —*S.H. (6/1/2004)*

Canyon Road 2000 Cabernet Sauvignon (California) $10. What great fruit! It has the stuffing and fruity ripeness of plenty of other costly Cabernets, at a fraction of the price. Maybe that's because they didn't drench it in expensive oak barrels. Don't look for char or vanilla or smoke, just terrific blackberry flavor in a dry package, with $50 tannins. **87 Best Buy** —*S.H. (6/1/2002)*

Canyon Road 1998 Cabernet Sauvignon (California) $8. 87 *(11/15/1999)*

Canyon Road 2004 Chardonnay (California) $8. Don't be misled by the price into thinking this is some simple little Chard, because you'd miss a great deal. It's packed with peach, apple, mango, and spice flavors, with the rich creaminess you want in a good Chardonnay. Cayon Road, owned by Peak Wines, has long been known for value. This wine is partially barrel fermented and aged on the lees—in other words, using fancy Burgundian techniques. Perfect with salmon, roast chicken, or by itself. **87 Best Buy** —*S.H. (11/15/2005)*

Canyon Road 2003 Chardonnay (California) $10. Has all the elements of a top Chard, from the ripe fruit to the oak. It's just a little more modest, and a lot less expensive. **84** —*S.H. (12/31/2004)*

Canyon Road 2002 Chardonnay (California) $10. Has real interest value for the array of apple, peach, and spice flavors and the kiss of oak that adds

vanilla and smoke. Refreshing acidity gives lift and brightness. Good value in an everyday Chard. **85** —*S.H. (6/1/2004)*

Canyon Road 2001 Chardonnay (California) $9. A perennial value wine from Geyser Peak, this vintage the wine is crisp and flinty. You'll get the suggestion of apples and peaches and oaky smoke, but it's a tight, clean wine that goes down easy. **86** —*S.H. (12/15/2002)*

Canyon Road 1999 Chardonnay (California) $8. 84 —*S.H. (10/1/2000)*

Canyon Road 1998 Chardonnay (California) $8. 84 Best Buy —*J.C. (10/1/1999)*

Canyon Road 2003 Merlot (California) $9. Another great value from Canyon Road for its bountiful cherry and blackberry fruit and overall balance. Finishes with an oaky sweetness. **85 Best Buy** —*S.H. (10/1/2005)*

Canyon Road 2002 Merlot (California) $10. A very well-behaved Merlot that offers plenty of sprightly, jammy blackberry and cherry flavors. It's a bit rough and ready, but that bright fruit and clean, dry finish make it a good value. **85** —*S.H. (9/1/2004)*

Canyon Road 2001 Merlot (California) $10. Well-made, with some clean blackberry flavors wrapped in rich tannins, and a dry finish. Not particularly varietal, but a pleasant, easy-drinking wine, and a pretty good value. Should be easy to find, with 60,000 cases produced. **85** —*S.H. (12/1/2003)*

Canyon Road 2000 Merlot (California) $10. Young, sharp, and rude, with that new-wine character that's like a slap across the face. The berry fruit is impertinent and impatient and wants to be drunk now, which suggests a lack of subtlety, but the youthful zest is refreshing. **86 Best Buy** —*S.H. (6/1/2002)*

Canyon Road 1999 Merlot (California) $8. This young wine needs time in a decanter or vigorous swirling in the glass to dissipate some residual sulfur aromas, but it comes around to reveal lean black cherry fruit accented by slightly bitter wood. It's better than it sounds and would make for a decent bar pour or airline offering. **83** —*J.C. (6/1/2001)*

Canyon Road 1998 Merlot (California) $8. 81 —*S.H. (12/31/1999)*

Canyon Road 2004 Sauvignon Blanc (California) $8. A dependable Best Buy almost every year because of its juicy, bone-dry citrus, fig, passion fruit, and spice flavors and zippy acids. Finishes ultraclean and brisk. Buy it by the case. **86 Best Buy** —*S.H. (10/1/2005)*

Canyon Road 2003 Sauvignon Blanc (Alexander Valley) $9. Another in a series of fresh, clean wines with citrus zest, grassy, eau de chat (get it?) and pepper flavors. It gets the job done with its easy appeal. **84** —*S.H. (9/1/2004)*

Canyon Road 2002 Sauvignon Blanc (California) $9. Fans of this wine will not be disappointed. It has the usual intensely grassy, citrusy flavors, and if anything, they're even richer, with a honeyed finish. Once again, very dry and penetrating, with stark acids. **85** —*S.H. (7/1/2003)*

Canyon Road 2001 Sauvignon Blanc (California) $9. Stays true to its house style, with intensely grassy, herbal flavors of mint, citrus, and hay. Extremely dry with bright acidity, it's a zesty clean wine, very refreshing and invigorating, and a good value. **86 Best Buy** —*S.H. (9/1/2002)*

Canyon Road 2000 Sauvignon Blanc (California) $8. Canyon Road is the second label for Geyser Peak, but that's all that's second about it. The product of no malolactic fermentation and no oak, the wine's deep scents of citrus, melon, and passion fruit jump from the glass. Crisp acids provide a lively palate feel and extend the long finish, which duplicates the initial flavors. **88** —*M.N. (11/15/2001)*

Canyon Road 1999 Sauvignon Blanc (California) $8. 86 —*S.H. (9/1/2000)*

Canyon Road 1998 Sauvignon Blanc (California) $NA. 84 —*S.H. (9/1/1999)*

Canyon Road 2002 Shiraz (California) $10. Oozes cherry-cocoa flavor, with rich oaky-vanilla overtones. This dry, soft wine is as ripe as they come, but balanced. **84** —*S.H. (12/31/2004)*

Canyon Road 2001 Shiraz (California) $10. Sharp, tannic, and earthy. You want to find something along the lines of blackberries or plums yet there's not much going on. Still, this dry wine is clean and will do in a pinch. **83** —*S.H. (6/1/2004)*

Canyon Road 2000 Shiraz (California) $10. They call it Shiraz instead of Syrah because it fits the stereotype of a young, jammy Aussie red. It's

USA

 feociously youthful, with blueberry and black cherry flavors that taste like they're fresh from the fermenting vats. A wine like this is sharp and edgy. But it's dry, and has a lot to like. **85** —*S.H. (9/1/2002)*

Canyon Road 2001 Zinfandel (California) $10. A medium-bodied Zin that shows a good blend of bright cherry, tea, plum, spice, herb, and vanilla notes. Fresh and clean on the finish, framed in moderate tannins. **86** *(11/1/2003)*

CAPAROSO

Caparoso 2001 Cabernet Sauvignon (Central Coast) $10. Mainly from Paso Robles, a super-lush, soft wine with 5% Syrah. Drinks jammy and fruity, with black cherry, blackberry, and raspberry flavors. So ripe, it's almost sweet, but it's technically dry. Good value. **86** —*S.H. (11/15/2003)*

Caparoso 2001 Pinot Noir (San Luis Obispo) $17. A delicious Edna Valley wine that drinks soft and luscious; cherry-raspberry flavors are spiced up with cinnamon, clove, and allspice. Not terribly deep or complex, but silky and succulent, and the price isn't bad for a quality Central Coast Pinot. **89** —*S.H. (12/1/2003)*

CAPAY VALLEY

Capay Valley 2000 Syrah (California) $16. On the simple, watery side, with thinned-down cherry flavors and a scour of tough tannins. Way too expensive for what you get. **83** —*S.H. (12/1/2004)*

Capay Valley 1999 Syrah (California) $21. This medium-weight blend of blackberry, leather, and dried spices comes from a California region that doesn't even have an AVA of its own yet. Exotic spice notes hint at Indian or Persian cuisine, with cocoa playing a role, too. Chewy texture, and has some tannins to lose. Try in 2003. **88** *(11/1/2001)*

Capay Valley 2002 Tempranillo (California) $15. Tastes raw, sharp, and herbal, a thin, tough wine that seems to have mostly tannins going for it. **82** —*S.H. (12/15/2004)*

Capay Valley 2004 Viognier (Capay Valley) $15. Upfront wildflower, apricot, peach, sweet citrus, and spice flavors star in this rather simple, tart wine. Good for everyday occasions. **83** —*S.H. (10/1/2005)*

Capay Valley 2003 Viognier (California) $15. From a very warm appellation, a wine soft in acidity but high in sweet, ripe fruity flavor. Swarms of lemon and lime, melon, fig, and even pineapple cover the palate. If easy fruit is your thing, this one's got plenty of it. **84** —*S.H. (11/15/2004)*

CAPELLO

Capello 1999 Cabernet Sauvignon (California) $9. A rugged, country-style wine, with some berry flavors and lots of herbal, earthy notes. Tannins are jagged and rough. Turns a bit sweet on the finish. **84** —*S.H. (6/1/2003)*

Capello 1999 Chardonnay (California) $9. A broad, obvious Chardonnay, with appley flavors and a hit of oak. Good acids provide life and freshness to this otherwise simple, one-dimensional wine. **84** —*S.H. (6/1/2003)*

Capello 1999 Merlot (California) $9. Deep red-purple color, and strong aromas of plums, straw, mushroom, and coffee. Big in the mouth, with rugged berry flavors and tannins. Very dry, and the sticky tannins show up on the finish. **84** —*S.H. (9/1/2003)*

CAPIAUX

Capiaux 2000 Pisoni Vineyard Pinot Noir (Santa Lucia Highlands) $45. If there's a single common element in the wine's from the Pisoni Vineyard, it's a hint of the untamed woods—underbrush, or in this case a peppery mushroominess—accompanied by lush fruit. Creamy, supple, and richly textured in the mouth, this microproduction wine (127 cases) is worth seeking out. **90** *(10/1/2002)*

Capiaux 2000 Widdoes Vineyard Pinot Noir (Russian River Valley) $36. This wine's winning nose had wide appeal, with tea, leather, rose, cinnamon, and root beer accents on lively cherry fruit. But tasters differed about the rest: Some felt the wine failed to deliver on the promise, turning dry and lean, too leathery and tangy. To others the ripe feel, handsomely-accented sweet fruit and long finish were excellent. **88** *(10/1/2002)*

CARABELLA

Carabella 2002 Dijon 76 Clone Chardonnay (Willamette Valley) $23. Light style, that hints at butterscotch, with clean and transparent flavors. The fruit is elegant and pleasant, but seems overmatched by the alcohol. **85** —*P.G. (2/1/2005)*

Carabella 2003 Pinot Gris (Willamette Valley) $14. Big fruit, fleshy and round, dotted with apple-pie spices. It's reasonably soft, a gentle, warm and fuzzy lapdog of a wine, that finishes with noticeable heat. **87** —*P.G. (2/1/2006)*

Carabella 2003 Pinot Gris (Willamette Valley) $14. A crisp, citric wine from estate-grown grapes. Fleshy flavors of grapefruit and ripe pear flavors come through, with some high-toned tropical notes that reach into bubble gum territory. **87** —*P.G. (2/1/2005)*

Carabella 2002 Pinot Gris (Willamette Valley) $14. A concentrated, pear-scented wine that tastes quite ripe and fleshy, with ripe pear flavors coming through, and a hint of honey. Enough tannin to be felt. **87 Best Buy** —*P.G. (2/1/2004)*

Carabella 2000 Pinot Gris (Willamette Valley) $14. An unusual style, with light scents of fennel leading into intriguing flavors of caraway, arugula, and pear. However, after a promising start, the wine fades quickly into a light, tart finish. **86** —*P.G. (2/1/2002)*

Carabella 2002 Pinot Noir (Willamette Valley) $35. This is a good example of Willamette Valley Pinot, with strong flavors of tomato mixed with pretty plum/cherry fruit. Medium ripe, good tannic grip, and a little bit of heat in the finish. Simple but tasty. **86** —*P.G. (2/1/2005)*

Carabella 2001 Pinot Noir (Willamette Valley) $33. This is a good example of Willamette Valley Pinot, with pretty plum/cherry fruit, smooth vanilla, and a little bit of heat in the finish. Simple but tasty. **88** —*P.G. (2/1/2004)*

Carabella 1999 Pinot Noir (Willamette Valley) $33. Earthy and hard, with tart, cranberry-cherry fruit. The time in barrel has added some pretty roasted coconut scents, and there's a lot of smokiness in the nose and in the flavor. Still quite young and tight. **86** —*P.G. (12/31/2001)*

Carabella 1998 Pinot Noir (Willamette Valley) $30. 87 —*M.S. (12/1/2000)*

Carabella 2001 Les Meres Pinot Noir (Willamette Valley) $19. Aging quickly, drinking well, with round, slightly oxidized flavors that show soft cherry fruit and lots of smooth vanilla. Good value and ready to go. **87** —*P.G. (2/1/2004)*

CARDINALE

Cardinale 1997 Cabernet Sauvignon (Mount Veeder) $125. 95 *(11/1/2000)*

Cardinale 2000 Cabernet Sauvignon (Napa-Sonoma) $120. Opens with nice aromas of currants, mint, and smoky oak, and then turns plush in the mouth, with flavors of blackberries, olives, and dried herbs. After that, the tannins kick in, and last through the finish with a puckery astringency. Not likely to age well, because the fruity concentration just isn't there. **89** —*S.H. (12/31/2003)*

CARHARTT CELLARS

Carhartt Cellars 2001 Merlot (Santa Ynez Valley) $30. Brims with blackberry and black cherry flavors. The mouthfeel is angular, not smooth, the finish is tough, and the opulence you want, especially at this price, isn't there. Still, it's a tasty drink. **86** —*S.H. (2/1/2004)*

CARHARTT VINEYARD

Carhartt Vineyard 2002 Estate Merlot (Santa Ynez Valley) $29. There's a note of chocolate peppermint alongside the blackberry and oak aromas that's intriguing, and it's echoed in the mouth. This is a deliciously flavored wine, but it's rather soft in both acids and tannins. **84** —*S.H. (6/1/2005)*

Carhartt Vineyard 2003 Syrah (Santa Ynez Valley) $28. While Tasting Director Joe Czerwinski was a big fan of this wine, finding it smoky, tannic and cellarworthy, our other tasters found it less appealing, calling it vegetal in one instance and muted in another. Partisans will find a dense, creamy-textured wine with flavors of chocolate and blackberries. **86** *(9/1/2005)*

USA

Carhartt Vineyard 2001 Syrah (Santa Ynez Valley) $30. A dark, full-bodied and very extracted wine with powerful fruit flavors. The currant, blackberry, plum, and cherry flavors have a peppery note, especially in the aroma, and the texture is dry and lush. This young wine has lots of baby fat, but is charming now for its opulence. **90** —*S.H. (3/1/2004)*

Carhartt Vineyard 2002 Estate Syrah (Santa Ynez Valley) $29. A strange wine. It smells slightly unripe, with green pepper and oak aromas, then turns unexpectedly sweet in the mouth. Finishes with tough tannins. **84** —*S.H. (6/1/2005)*

CARINA CELLARS

Carina Cellars 2001 Syrah (Santa Barbara County) $16. The peppery aroma tells you this is a cool-climate Syrah. The tannins are rich and dense, with a mouthful of blackberry flavors. Delicious and complex. **89 Editors' Choice** —*S.H. (10/1/2003)*

Carina Cellars 2004 Viognier (Santa Barbara County) $18. Awkward, with tropical fruit aromas that show a burnt toast edge. In the mouth, the wine is dry, tart, and thin. **82** —*S.H. (7/1/2006)*

Carina Cellars 2001 Viognier (Santa Barbara County) $16. Fruit salad in a glass! Everything from mandarin orange to ripe peach, apricot, grapefruit, and even some pineapple. Acidity makes it bright. Simple and easy, a tasty wine meant to be quaffed ice cold. **85** —*S.H. (6/1/2003)*

CARLISLE

Carlisle 2001 Petite Sirah (Dry Creek Valley) $36. Always a leader in "Pet," this vintage is concentrated and intense, with lush flavors of cassis, blackberry, blueberry, anise, and toast. It's a big, full-bodied wine, with firm tannins and a bit soft, but it's oh, so drinkable! There's a bit of heat in the finish. **89** (4/1/2003)

Carlisle 2002 Two Acres Red Blend (Russian River Valley) $36. This Mourvèdre, Petite Sirah, Valdepenas, and Alicante Bouschet field blend shows its roots in the complex structure and mélange of flavors. Totally dry and pretty tannic, it will stand up to strong dishes, such as short beef ribs. Might gain softness and complexity with some time in the cellar. **87** —*S.H. (8/1/2005)*

Carlisle 2001 Two Acres Red Blend (Russian River Valley) $36. Another stunning release from Mike Officer, made from an old field blend. The aroma is gorgeous, with show-stopping wild berry fruit, grilled meat, high-toned lacquer, smoke, and Oriental spice. Once you sip it, you're addicted. Massive fruity-spicy flavors, unbelievably rich and delicious, and bone dry, with superb, complex tannins and fresh, young acids. This wine is wonderful now but clearly has the bones to improve in the cellar. **93** —*S.H. (12/31/2003)*

Carlisle 2000 Two Acres Red Blend (Russian River Valley) $36. An amazing wine, made from old vines near Olivet Lane. The grapes were mistaken for Zinfandel for decades and sold as such, until recently identified as Petite Sirah, Valdepenas, Mourvèdre, and Alicante Bouschet. This is as authentic a field blend as I have ever seen—and the best. Impossible to exaggerate the purity, depth, and concentration. Magnificent, lush texture, fabulous tannins, this wine is world class in every sense. **96 Cellar Selection** —*S.H. (11/15/2002)*

Carlisle 2001 Three Birds Rhône Red Blend (Sonoma County) $23. Pretty aromatics of strawberry, raspberry, and a waft of vanilla and smoke. Drinks delicate and refined, very fruity-jammy, with sleek, silky tannins. This racy wine is made from Grenache, Mourvèdre, and Syrah. **89** — *S.H. (12/1/2003)*

Carlisle 2001 Syrah (Dry Creek Valley) $40. From a warmer part of the appellation, a very ripe wine with lots of distinction. Enormous alcohol, 16.5%, but who cares? The aroma is decadent, suggesting cassis, cherry liqueur, mocha, and vanilla. Flamboyant flavors of ripe, sweet blackberries are wrapped in smooth, dry tannins. **91** —*S.H. (12/1/2003)*

Carlisle 2000 Syrah (Dry Creek Valley) $40. From a young vineyard, a dark, exuberant wine consciously built along Barossa Valley Shiraz lines. Right off the bat, it's brilliant. Huge, concentrated, with gobs of cassis and chocolate-toffee flavors, but completely dry. Wonderfully rich, soft, complex tannins, with soft acids. Captivates the mouth. and handles its enormous alcohol well. **93 Editors' Choice** —*S.H. (6/1/2003)*

Carlisle 2000 Syrah (Dry Creek Valley) $46. Brutally good—in fact, fabulous—Syrah. Has the class, depth, and richness of the best Northern Rhônes. The density of texture is like molten lead, with a quicksilvery mouthfeel that spreads delicious fruit across the palate. Yet despite all this power, the wine feels light and feathery. It combines elegance with mass in an extraordinary way. **95** —*S.H. (12/1/2002)*

Carlisle 2001 Zinfandel (Sonoma County) $23. Bright edged in texture, the wine offers a toasty frame of Bing cherry, cinnamon, raspberry, spice, and herb flavors. Cola and coffee also hold sway, held in moderate tannins. The finish is also moderate in length. **88** (11/1/2003)

Carlisle 2002 Carlisle Vineyard Zinfandel (Russian River Valley) $36. Has some green peppercorn, minty notes in this very dry, tannic wine that lead you to believe not all the berries were fully ripe. That said, there's enough berry flavor to stand up to a rich Italian dish. **86** —*S.H. (8/1/2005)*

Carlisle 2001 Carlisle Vineyard Zinfandel (Russian River Valley) $35. Licorice and spice lead off here. The wine continues with a bright-edged note, showing spicy cherry, berry, cola, chocolate, and herb flavors. A little hot on the finish, it is nonetheless quite pleasing. **89** (11/1/2003)

CARMEL

Carmel 2002 Cabernet Sauvignon (Monterey County) $40. If extract were everything this wine would be okay. Unfortunately the currant and blackberry flavors are encased in an overly soft, almost gluey texture. Beyond that, there's a medicinal taste to the finish. **82** —*S.H. (3/1/2006)*

Carmel 2003 Vintner's Selection Chardonnay (Monterey County) $23. Monterey Chards often exhibit this aroma, which makes you think you could pick them out in a blind tasting. The wine smells fresh and juicy, with Key Lime pie and tropical fruit notes. In the mouth, it's rich, fruit-forward and oaky. This Chard is designed to dazzle. **90** —*S.H. (5/1/2006)*

CARMEL ROAD

Carmel Road 2004 Chardonnay (Monterey) $16. Has most of the elements of a fine Monterey Chard. Keen acids and a lively, clean finish stimulate the tastebuds. The problem is a lack of fruit. The wine teases with peaches, then pulls back and fails to deliver. **82** —*S.H. (10/1/2006)*

Carmel Road 1999 Chardonnay (Monterey) $50. A winning combination of pear, apple, ripe melon, and butterscotch flavors, spiked with spicy clove and tart citrus accents. Lavishly oaked for a mid-weight wine, there's sufficient depth of fruit here to support the wood, and the elements mesh and hold nicely. An easy, lush mouthfeel means it's best enjoyed over the next year or so—if you can keep it around that long. **91** (7/1/2001)

Carmel Road 2004 Pinot Noir (Monterey) $20. Likeable for its silky texture and dry finish, this Pinot also offers high acidity and earthy, cherry, cola, and coffee flavors. It's an elegant, food-friendly wine with a great deal of spicy richness and the silky texture that makes Pinot Noir so distinctive. **90 Editors' Choice** —*S.H. (10/1/2006)*

Carmel Road 2003 Pinot Noir (Arroyo Seco) $35. The appellation is a distinct bench on the west side of the Salinas Valley, and this fine Pinot has benefited from the cool winds and long hang time. Marked by bright acidity and intense cherry, cola, and spice flavors, it's a dry, rich wine, with a silky texture and enough complexity to age through this decade. **92** —*S.H. (10/1/2006)*

CARMENET

Carmenet 1995 Moon Mountain Estate Reserve Bordeaux Blend (Sonoma) $40. 89 —*S.H. (7/1/1999)*

Carmenet 2000 Cabernet Franc (Sonoma Valley) $18. There are some pretty cherry and blackberry flavors wrapped in very thick, astringent tannins. You'll also find a tough earthiness that lasts through the dry, gritty finish. **84** —*S.H. (5/1/2004)*

Carmenet 2001 Cabernet Sauvignon (Lake County) $18. The cherry-berry flavors and oaky notes are backed by firm, tough tannins. Finishes with a gritty scour. May soften with a year or so of bottle age. **84** —*S.H. (5/1/2004)*

Carmenet 2001 Cellar Selection Cabernet Sauvignon (California) $9. Simple and innocent, a wine that neither offends nor stuns. It has pleasant blackberry flavors and is dry, with a good texture and soft tannins. **84** —S.H. (6/1/2004)

Carmenet 2000 Cellar Selection Cabernet Sauvignon (California) $8. Shows proper Cabernet character, namely a full-bodied dry wine with black currant and chocolate flavors framed in oak. No special problems or flaws, but correctly made, and not bad for this price. **84** —S.H. (11/15/2003)

Carmenet 1998 Dynamite Cabernet Sauvignon (North Coast) $20. 86 —S.H. (9/1/2000)

Carmenet 1997 Dynamite Cabernet Sauvignon (North Coast) $20. 88 —S.H. (7/1/1999)

Carmenet 1999 Moon Mountain Reserve Cabernet Sauvignon (Sonoma Valley) $65. Smoky, tarry, licorice notes are firmly in evidence in this dark, rich, and smooth wine. Black currant and cherry flavors are at the core. On the finish there is a hint of bitterness. **89** —J.M. (5/1/2002)

Carmenet 1997 Moon Mountain Reserve Cabernet Sauvignon (Sonoma Valley) $48. 93 (11/1/2000)

Carmenet 1996 Moon Mountain Reserve Cabernet Sauvignon (Sonoma Valley) $40. 90 (11/1/1999)

Carmenet 2002 Chardonnay (Napa Valley) $16. This wine is fresh and clean, with bright acids that cleanse the palate. It's not especially powerful in fruit, with suggestions of citrus, apple, and peach, and snaps to an abrupt finish. **84** —S.H. (2/1/2004)

Carmenet 2002 Cellar Selection Chardonnay (California) $9. You'll get a lot of value for the money with this flavorful wine. It's true to the variety, with good flavors of peaches and cream, while oak adds the usual toasty, spicy overlay. **85** —S.H. (6/1/2004)

Carmenet 2001 Cellar Selection Chardonnay (California) $8. Simple and inoffensive, offering up pleasant peach and apple flavors backed up with decent acids. Even tastes like there's a little oak around the edges. Recognizably Chard-like, at an everyday price. **84** —S.H. (12/1/2003)

Carmenet 1997 Sangiacomo Vineyard Chardonnay (Carneros) $18. 87 —S.H. (10/1/1999)

Carmenet 2001 Merlot (Sonoma County) $20. This solid Merlot pleases for its ripe blackberry, and chocolate flavors and sweetly rich tannins. It's a big wine, but easy to drink, especially with a perfectly grilled ribeye steak. May even benefit from a year or two in the cellar. **87** —S.H. (5/1/2004)

Carmenet 2001 Cellar Selection Merlot (California) $9. Pleasant and clean, an easy sipper with berry and cherry flavors and hints of thyme and sweet tobacco. Although it's light in body and texture, there's a real persistence of ripe fruit through the finish. **85** —S.H. (6/1/2004)

Carmenet 2000 Cellar Selection Merlot (California) $8. You'll be surprised at how much fruit you get in this affordable wine. It has pleasant flavors of plums, blackberries, and cherries, but is dry, with nice tannins. Extremely oaky, maybe too much; sappy-sweet vanillins take over and dominate the finish. **85 Best Buy** —S.H. (12/31/2003)

Carmenet 2002 Pinot Noir (Sonoma County) $20. A ripe smooth, deeply flavored wine. Offers lots of black cherries, cranberries, vanilla, and smoky oak in the mouth. A smooth, polished texture; and a succulent, spicy finish. **88** (11/1/2004)

Carmenet 2002 Cellar Selection Sauvignon Blanc (California) $8. If you like your Sauvignons grassy and citrusy, this one's for you. Tastes like the rinds of limes and grapefruits, with bright acidity. **86 Best Buy** —S.H. (10/1/2003)

Carmenet 2002 Hanson Vineyard Sauvignon Blanc (Lake County) $17. From a region making a major play in Sauvignon Blanc. The fruit got beautifully ripe, moving beyond citrus into rich peach and pear. Yet the cool nights have preserved fresh acidity. Distinctive and compelling. **87** —S.H. (4/1/2004)

Carmenet 1999 Paragon Vineyard Reserve Sauvignon Blanc (Edna Valley) $16. Always an interesting wine, this year it showcases floral and melon notes in addition to the usual grassy-citrusy ones. It's tart enough for dry palates and salty foods but has a round fruitiness and even a little

sweetness that make it nice in its own right. Ten percent Sémillon adds a nutty, figgy element. **88** —S.H. (8/1/2001)

Carmenet 1997 Paragon Vineyard-Reserve Sauvignon Blanc (Edna Valley) $16. 82 —M.M. (9/1/1999)

Carmenet 1999 Evangelho Vineyard Zinfandel (Contra Costa County) $25. From 109-year-old vines, an old-style field blend with It's robust, full of body and flavor, rich and powerful. Runs wild with fruity flavors and stains the glass with thick syrupy cathedrals. **90** —S.H. (9/1/2002)

Carmenet 2001 Evangelho Vineyard Old Vine Zinfandel (Contra Costa County) $20. Distinctly warm-country Zin, with its strong flavors of cassis, plum pudding, and chocolate that come close to raisiny Port but successfully avoid it. As a result, it's a rich and complexly delicious wine. It's also very dry, and the alcohol is controlled. **89** —S.H. (5/1/2004)

Carmenet 1997 Evangelho Vineyard Old Vines Zinfandel (Contra Costa County) $17. 85 —S.H. (5/1/2000)

CARMICHAEL

Carmichael 2000 Sa Vini Red Blend (Monterey County) $18. Soft, fruity, and rich in plummy cocoa and black cherry, but basically dry and robust. Will be a nice accompaniment to pasta with tomato sauce and sausage. Sangiovese, Syrah, and Cabernet Sauvignon. **84** —S.H. (4/1/2005)

Carmichael 2002 Sur le Pont Rhône Red Blend (Monterey County) $18. This blend of Syrah, Mourvèdre, Carignane, and Grenache, which comes from California's Côtes-du-Rhône in southern Monterey as it approaches Paso Robles, is soft, fruity, and simple. It will be good with a rich bouillabaisse or lamb stew. **86** —S.H. (2/1/2005)

Carmichael 2005 Grigio e Bianco White Table Wine White Blend (Monterey County) $14. Clean, zesty, and refreshing, this is a blend of Pinot Grigio and Sauvignon Blanc with a dollop of barrel-fermented Chardonnay. It's unusual, but it works really well. The wine has intriguing flavors of citrus, green apples, peaches, and kiwis, and then a long, spicy, satisfying finish. **89 Best Buy** —S.H. (12/1/2006)

Carmichael 2003 Grigio e Bianco White Table Wine White Blend (Monterey County) $15. This likeable wine is a blend of Pinot Grigio, Sauvignon Blanc, and Chardonnay. It has a myriad of flavors ranging from dry, grassy citrus fruits through riper peaches to wildflowers and apricots. It shows real flair in the zesty acidity, rich finish, and overall balance. **89** —S.H. (12/1/2005)

CARMODY MCKNIGHT

Carmody McKnight 1997 Chardonnay (Paso Robles) $15. 85 (6/1/2000)

Carmody McKnight 1998 Millennium Celebration Chardonnay (Paso Robles) $17. 86 (6/1/2000)

CARNEROS CREEK

Carneros Creek 2001 Gavin Vineyard Chardonnay (Carneros) $20. The apple and pear flavors drink a little on the sweet side, as if a teaspoon of cane sugar were dissolved in the glass. There's also a lot of oak that brings smoky vanilla notes. **84** —S.H. (12/31/2003)

Carneros Creek 1997 Palombo Vineyard Chardonnay (Carneros) $18. 81 (6/1/2000)

Carneros Creek 2000 Pinot Noir (Carneros) $24. Rich in the nose, with smoke, toast, chocolate, and licorice aromas. The palate is quite fruity, as it's dominated exclusively by black fruit with only a slight hint of mocha. The finish is creamy if a bit on the warm side. **90 Editors' Choice** (10/1/2002)

Carneros Creek 2002 Carneros Signature Reserve Pinot Noir (Carneros) $20. Tasty and easy, with a very light body and silky texture. The flavors run the gamut from cherries to spices, beets, cola, and rhubarb. Finishes dry and clean. **84** —S.H. (11/1/2004)

Carneros Creek 2000 Cote de Carneros Pinot Noir (Carneros) $17. Red berries, cocoa, vanilla, and tea grace the nose of this easy drinker. The palate is fruity but balanced, offering some strawberry, cherry and plum—a mixed bag of red fruits. **87 Best Buy** (10/1/2002)

Carneros Creek 1997 Estate Grown Pinot Noir (Carneros) $18. 87 (5/1/2000)

Carneros Creek 2002 Grail Pinot Noir (Carneros) $40. This wine is rather earthy, austere, and dry, but who knows, it could surprise in a few years. **86** —*S.H. (10/1/2005)*

Carneros Creek 2001 Las Brisas Vineyard Pinot Noir (Carneros) $40. Quite pale in color, a translucent garnet hue, this is a delicate, feminine wine, with an ethereal body of silk and satin. It's not light in flavor, though, with raspberry, black cherry, oriental spices, and oaky-smoky vanillins. Polished, pretty, and fully ripe. **89** —*S.H. (2/1/2004)*

Carneros Creek 2002 Los Carneros Reserve Pinot Noir (Carneros) $25. The acidity is high here, leading to a citrus peel tartness partially enriched with oak, cherry, and tobacco flavors. Silky in texture, soft in tannins, this dry, gentle wine is uncomplicated and versatile at the table. **85** —*S.H. (11/1/2004)*

Carneros Creek 2001 Los Carneros Reserve Pinot Noir (Carneros) $25. This is a light-bodied Pinot with Lifesaver fruit flavors, not one of your rich, thick versions, but it's so delicious you have to love it. The raspberry and cherry flavors are wrapped in a silky smooth texture that caresses the palate all the way through the spicy finish. **90** —*S.H. (3/1/2004)*

Carneros Creek 2001 Mahoney Vineyard Pinot Noir (Carneros) $40. This is a bigger wine than the Las Brisas bottling, by a hair. It shares many of the same qualities, like raspberry and cherry cola flavors, soft tannins, and a silky texture. Quite dry, and finishes with a flourish of sweet fruit, oak, and spice. **90** —*S.H. (2/1/2004)*

Carneros Creek 1999 Signature Reserve Pinot Noir (Carneros) $48. Cola and root beer at first, but after that the dense nose is a bit closed. Rich, warm blackberry flavors offer a touch of anise, which comes across almost like black licorice. The finish is all fruit, but with a driving, racy feel spurred on by healthy acidity. **89** *(10/1/2002)*

CAROL SHELTON

Carol Shelton 2002 Cox Vineyard Old Vines Wild Thing Zinfandel (Mendocino County) $28. Only in California. 16-1/2 percent alcohol, and fully dry. So rich, so ripe in berry fruit it's turned into chocolate decadence with a drizzle of cassis. For all the size it's balanced and even harmonious. Yummy with ribs or vanilla ice cream. **90** —*S.H. (12/31/2004)*

Carol Shelton 2001 KarmaZin, Old Vines Zinfandel (Russian River Valley) $30. Plush and smooth, with a fine array of pretty cherry, herb, toast, and spice flavors. The tannins are a bit powdery, but the flavors are good, finishing with a hint of licorice, bright cherry, and spice. **89** *(11/1/2003)*

Carol Shelton 2002 Lopez Vineyard Old Vines MongaZin Zinfandel (Cucamonga Valley) $24. Tannic, full-bodied, and very dry. The blackberry, coffee and spice flavors are rewarding, and the wine is nicely balanced with acidity. This is a classic warm country California Zin, and will likely age. **87** —*S.H. (12/31/2004)*

Carol Shelton 2001 MongaZin, Lopez Vineyard Zinfandel (Cucamonga Valley) $24. Pretty plush, with a racy blend of black cherry, blackberry, cola, cassis, anise, and herb flavors. They're couched in tangy acidity and smooth, rich tannins. Big yet elegant—really ripe, really good. **90 Editors' Choice** *(11/1/2003)*

Carol Shelton 2002 Rock Pile Ridge Vineyard Rocky Reserve Zinfandel (Dry Creek Valley) $32. Shelton shows a deft hand in balancing Zin's over-the-edge tendencies with a more elegant approach. This wine is big in wild berry and spice flavors, and rather alcoholic, but never loses its sense of proportion. **88** —*S.H. (12/31/2004)*

Carol Shelton 2001 Rocky Reserve, Rockpile Ridge Vineyard Zinfandel (Dry Creek Valley) $32. Sleek, plush, and supple on the palate, with plenty of lush chocolate, plum, coffee, vanilla, black cherry, and spice flavors. Elegant and velvety to the end, the wine shows good length and integration. **91** *(11/1/2003)*

Carol Shelton 2002 Rue Vineyard Old Vines KarmaZin Zinfandel (Russian River Valley) $30. This is one big Zin. It's dark as night and full of weight and fruit, and dry as dust. Yet the tannins are sweet and ripe, and they frame intense blackberry, coffee, and chocolate flavors. Try this balanced wine with short ribs or a roast chicken. **89** —*S.H. (12/31/2004)*

Carol Shelton 2001 Wild Thing, Old Vines Zinfandel (Mendocino County) $28. Smooth and creamy textured, with lovely blackberry, black cherry,

coffee, chocolate, spice, toast, and vanilla flavors, all blended with elegance and finesse. On the palate it finishes long and lush. **90** *(11/1/2003)*

CARPE DIEM

Carpe Diem 2004 Chardonnay (Edna Valley) $26. Younger and a bit more raw than the '03, and the oak is sticking out more boldly, but this should be a fine bottle in much the same fashion as its predecessor in a year or so. There's a purity throughout that's outstanding. **90** —*S.H. (11/1/2006)*

Carpe Diem 2003 Firepeak Vineyard Chardonnay (Edna Valley) $26. Notable for high, stimulating acidity and purity of flavor, this lovely Chard brims with lime, mineral, white peach, and apricot flavors, wrapped into a lush, creamy texture. It's an elegant, classy wine that improves as it breathes in the glass. **90** —*S.H. (10/1/2006)*

Carpe Diem 2002 Firepeak Vineyard Chardonnay (Edna Valley) $25. Here's a crisp and elegantly structured wine. The citrus and apple flavors have an earthy, mineral edge and are accompanied by good acidity, leading to a clean and vibrant mouthfeel. There is, however, an almost excessive dryness. **87** —*S.H. (8/1/2004)*

Carpe Diem 2001 Firepeak Vineyard Chardonnay (Edna Valley) $25. Not as rich or concentrated as the previous vintage, and the acidity is low, making for a mushy texture. Still, the peach and tropical fruit flavors are good. Turns hot with alcohol on the finish. **85** —*S.H. (8/1/2003)*

Carpe Diem 2000 Firepeak Vineyard Chardonnay (Edna Valley) $25. A very distinctive wine, rich and powerful. Marked by well-ripened flavors of pears and tropical fruits, dense, and concentrated, with near-perfect acids. A lovely coating of oak adds spicy, smoky complexities. **92 Editors' Choice** —*S.H. (12/15/2002)*

Carpe Diem 2004 Firepeak Vineyard Pinot Noir (Edna Valley) $31. There's a sweaty, leathery note to this Pinot, or something suggestive of the rich, mushroomy undergrowth in a dark forest. The wine is full-bodied and bold in cola, coffee, and cherry flavors. Very dry, with racy acidity so typical of the valley. Might develop complexity with a few years in bottle. Tasted twice. **88** —*S.H. (11/15/2006)*

Carpe Diem 2002 Firepeak Vineyard Pinot Noir (Edna Valley) $29. A nicely drinkable Pinot that shows its cool-climate origins in the crisp acids, light, silky texture and pleasant flavors of cherries, strawberries, and Oriental spices. Totally dry, but there's a fruity sweetness throughout. **86** —*S.H. (11/1/2004)*

Carpe Diem 2001 Firepeak Vineyard Pinot Noir (Edna Valley) $31. A smooth, complex Pinot whose silky texture is nicely balanced with rich flavors. Raspberries and cherries, Oriental spices, smoke, vanilla, and toast coalesce into a gently fruity impression backed up by soft, ripe tannins. Perfect with roast chicken. **90** —*S.H. (3/1/2004)*

Carpe Diem 2000 Firepeak Vineyard Pinot Noir (Edna Valley) $23. The nose is toasted, almost roasted, and therefore fruit aromas are hard to find. But once you get to the palate there's ample cherry along with earthy, leathery accents. The finish is lively, even juicy. The acidity really shows itself late in the game, indicating that the wine could be cellared for several years. **87** *(10/1/2002)*

CARPENTER CREEK

Carpenter Creek 2002 Chardonnay (Washington) $14. Simple, tart, green apple fruit awkwardly married to hard, tannic oak. Nothing comes together; the fruit seems thin and the oak tags a bitter, woody finish onto it. **83** —*P.G. (1/1/2004)*

Carpenter Creek 2002 Riesling (Washington) $10. A distinct scent of garlic rises from the glass; not a good beginning. This is sugary sweet, awkward, and disjointed. **80** —*P.G. (1/1/2004)*

Carpenter Creek 2002 Sauvignon Blanc (Washington) $13. Grassy and herbaceous style, showing light, lemony fruit and mouth-puckering acid. **83** —*P.G. (1/1/2004)*

Carpenter Creek 2002 Syrah (Washington) $38. Already showing some signs of oxidation, which has softened but not integrated the flavors. This is a disjointed wine, tannic, spicy, with a sweet cracker flavor that falls off into an empty mid-palate before heading into very dry, very chalky tannins at the finish. **81** —*P.G. (11/15/2004)*

Carpenter Creek 2002 Signature Series Syrah (Yakima Valley) $38. Clearly an ambitious effort, but one that's raisiny and roasted, with pruny, burnt flavors and a healthy dose of astringency. **82** *(9/1/2005)*

CARR

Carr 2004 Pinot Grigio (Santa Rita Hills) $18. A mostly dry wine, with high Santa Rita acidity that frames complex flavors of green apples, white peaches, figs, sweet tobacco, and crushed, baked Asian spices. The finish is sweeter than I'd prefer, though. **86** *—S.H. (2/1/2006)*

Carr 2005 Turner Vineyard Pinot Gris (Santa Rita Hills) $18. This cool-climate variety loves it in the Sta. (formerly Santa) Rita Hills. High acidity creates a cool, cleansing feel, while the wine brims with citrus zest, pineapple meringue, mineral, and vanilla flavors. This will send chefs into food-pairing heaven. **90** *—S.H. (11/15/2006)*

Carr 2004 Ashley's Vineyard Pinot Noir (Santa Rita Hills) $30. If you're tired of sweet, soft California reds, turn here. The wine is dry and acidic. It's also a bit hot, with a baked fruit, raisiny edge to the cherry fruit, but it does have an elegant complexity. Drink now. **85** *—S.H. (7/1/2006)*

Carr 2003 Ashley's Vineyard Pinot Noir (Santa Rita Hills) $35. This is a deeper, earthier style of Pinot, clearly from a cool climate. You'll find plenty of cherries, but there are mulchy, mushroomy notes, veering into rhubarb, as well as some tannins. The mouthfeel is silky and light, and the wine is very dry. **90** *—S.H. (10/1/2005)*

Carr 2002 Ashley's Vineyard Pinot Noir (Santa Rita Hills) $NA. Identical scores from all tasters for this big, dark, rich wine, which is filled with oaky, blackberry and mocha flavors. It's big, tannic and dense now, heavy in the mouth, but is likely to soften and turn supple with a few years in the bottle. **87** *(11/1/2004)*

Carr 2004 Clos Pepe Vineyard Pinot Noir (Santa Rita Hills) $40. I called the '04 Santa Barbara Pinot vintage "a challenge" due to harvest heat waves, and this wine seems to have been a victim. Although fully dry, it suffers from pruny, raisiny flavors that are far from pleasant. **82** *—S.H. (7/1/2006)*

Carr 2003 Three Vineyards Pinot Noir (Santa Rita Hills) $40. A very fine Pinot. Medium-bodied and dry, it hits with tremendous spice and ripe red cherry flavors that are succulent. Although it's a silky wine, it has a great grip of tannins and acids that cry out for food. Achieves real complexity through the long finish. **92** *—S.H. (10/1/2005)*

Carr 2004 Turner Vineyard Pinot Noir (Santa Rita Hills) $35. Considerably more balanced than Carr's Clos Pepe bottling, this Pinot is very dry and filled with youthful acidity, but it shows the vintage's heat in the intensely ripe stone fruit and berry flavors. It hasn't knit together yet, with the individual parts at odds. Try holding for three years and see what happens. **88** *—S.H. (7/1/2006)*

CARREFOUR

Carrefour 2003 Cabernet Franc (Napa Valley) $30. Soft, fleshy, and opulent, with delicious cherry preserve flavors and a sprinkle of dusty cocoa and cinnamon. Feels elegant and upscale in the mouth. **86** *—S.H. (12/15/2006)*

Carrefour 2003 Cabernet Sauvignon (Napa Valley) $40. Superripe and jammy in cherry pie filling, raspberry, chocolate, blackberry, and lots of oak, this wine has a little bite of raisins in the finish. Drink now–2009. **86** *—S.H. (12/15/2006)*

Carrefour 2003 Merlot (Napa Valley) $25. Here's a nice Merlot that's drinking well now. It has soft, fine tannins and a crisp spine of acidity, while the flavors run to ripe blackberries, coffee, cocoa and smoky leather. **86** *—S.H. (12/15/2006)*

Carrefour 2003 Pinot Noir (Carneros) $28. This wine is very fresh at three-plus years. It's lightly structured, with an elegant, silky mouthfeel and flavors of cola, red cherries, peppery spices, and oak. Don't be surprised if it shows modest improvement with four or five years in the bottle. **87** *—S.H. (12/15/2006)*

Carrefour 2005 Sauvignon Blanc (Napa Valley) $18. If you're sensitive to cat pee, go elsewhere, because this wine reeks of it. That's not all, of course. There's citrus, gooseberry, date nut, white pepper, and zingy, zangy acidity. **84** *—S.H. (12/15/2006)*

CARTER

Carter 2002 Beckstoffer To Kalon Vineyard Cabernet Sauvignon (Oakville) $75. Like other '02s following on the heels of the hedonistic '01s, this wine is less generous, not as immediately seductive because it's not as lush. It is, however, more tannic, and still quite a fine Cab. Hold for five or more years. **90** *—S.H. (2/1/2006)*

Carter 2001 Beckstoffer Vineyards Cabernet Sauvignon (Oakville) $75. Made from grapes grown in the Tokalon Vineyard, this Cab showcases both its terroir and the amazing vintage. It's dry, ripe in currants and cherries, lush in tannins yet expressive and forward. Very drinkable now, with good grip, a dry finish and plenty of elegance. **93** *—S.H. (8/1/2005)*

Carter 1998 Coliseum Block Cabernet Sauvignon (Napa Valley) $50. Big, bright and beautiful, with bing cherry, blackberry, chocolate, vanilla, spice, cedar, and herb flavors, all seamlessly integrated. The acidity is a bit bright—the result of a cool year—but the wine is still a top-notch first release for Eureka hotelier Mark Carter. **92** *—J.M. (12/31/2001)*

Carter 1999 Fortuna Block Cabernet Sauvignon (Napa Valley) $60. Plush-textured, with ripe, firm tannins and plenty of classy blackberry, black cherry, cassis, vanilla, spice, herb, and cinnamon notes. The wine is complex, yet disarmingly easy to enjoy now. Should do well in the cellar, too. **92** *—J.M. (11/15/2002)*

Carter 2002 Truchard Vineyards Merlot (Carneros) $45. Ripeness obviously wasn't a problem here, to judge by the spectacularly forward cherry and cassis flavors. The winemaker put a lot of oak on top. The result is a huge wine that lacks a bit of finesse. After all, size isn't everything. But it could surprise with a few years in the cellar. **90** *—S.H. (8/1/2005)*

Carter 2001 Truchard Vineyards Merlot (Napa Valley) $38. A sleek, smooth wine that serves up plenty of cinnamon and spice flavor backed by a core of blackberry, raspberry, anise, herb, and coffee flavors. It's complex and elegant, showing good length on the finish. **90** *—J.M. (8/1/2004)*

CARTLIDGE & BROWNE

Cartlidge & Browne 2004 Cabernet Sauvignon (California) $13. Minty and sharp, with a menthol edge to the cherries, but the wine is crisp and has a polished, silky texture, so it's pretty good. **83** *—S.H. (12/31/2006)*

Cartlidge & Browne 2000 Cabernet Sauvignon (California) $10. Opens with scents of cherries and chocolate, with a dusty, earthy streak. Turns fruity and overly sweet in the mouth, with flavors of cassis liqueur. The tannins and acids are rustic. **83** *—S.H. (11/15/2002)*

Cartlidge & Browne 2000 Chardonnay (California) $10. Napa and Sonoma fruit shares the spotlight with Lodi grapes to produce this soft, simple wine. Filled with summery, appley sweetness, it's spicy-peppery clean, with a honeyed finish that tastes like vanilla custard. **85** *—S.H. (12/15/2002)*

Cartlidge & Browne 2004 Merlot (California) $13. This wine is rustic, but it's fully dry, has great fruit and rich tannins, and the bottom line is that it's fun. A good example of the fine art of blending cool and warm places. From Clarksburg, Monterey, Mendocino, and Paso Robles. **85** *—S.H. (12/31/2006)*

Cartlidge & Browne 2001 Merlot (California) $10. This is as good as many Merlots that cost much more. The fruity flavors are nicely set off by rich tannins, and the mouthfeel is expressive. **86 Best Buy** *—S.H. (10/1/2003)*

Cartlidge & Browne 2000 Merlot (California) $10. This is a wine that will surprise you. It's amazingly rich and complex for the price. Just packed with fresh, young blackberry, and cherry flavors, and drinks dry, with yummy acidity. It is a bit aggressive, but is a fine Merlot for the price. **86 Best Buy** *—S.H. (12/31/2002)*

Cartlidge & Browne 2005 Pinot Noir (California) $13. Wine lovers who want to figure Pinot out but are on a limited budget would do well to buy this one. It's properly dry and silky, with cherry, strawberry, cola, tea, and cinnamon clove flavors. The wine, made from components from Mendocino to Santa Barbara, is a testament to the fine art of blending. **86** *—S.H. (12/31/2006)*

Cartlidge & Browne 2005 Pinot Noir Rosé Pinot Noir (Sonoma County) $13. You won't see it on the label, but the grapes for this dry blush come from such esteemed cool-climate vineyards as Parmalee, Durell, and Saralee's.

USA

The terroir imparts refreshing acidity, while the wine shows fine dryness, at a time when so many rosés finish sweet. Pinot flavors of cherries and rose petals combine with spicy vanilla to produce a polished, Provencal-style wine. Amazingly, the wine was entirely fermented and aged in stainless steel. **88 Best Buy** —*S.H. (11/15/2006)*

Cartlidge & Browne 2001 Syrah (California) $10. From Delta grapes, an affordable wine that offers plenty of body and flavor. Big, jammy tastes of plums and blackberries wrapped in a rich, thick texture. Sure, it's a country-style wine, but it's an honest, good one. **85** —*S.H. (12/15/2003)*

Cartlidge & Browne 2001 Zinfandel (California) $10. Simple and to the point, with pretty cherry, berry, spice, and toast flavors up front. Tannins are modest, as is the finish, which ends on a toasty note. **85** *(11/1/2003)*

Cartlidge & Browne 1998 Zinfandel (California) $10. Tight as a drum, but a little cherry fruit escapes from the nose. It opens up into a sweet, lovely bottle of wine, with a bit of cocoa and coffee in the finish. Well-balanced, with sweet, clean fruit. **87 Best Buy** —*P.G. (3/1/2001)*

CARVALHO

Carvalho 2003 Chardonnay (Clarksburg) $18. This odd wine has dill and clove aromas, possibly from American oak, and a flavor like sweet chewing tobacco and peaches. **82** —*S.H. (3/1/2006)*

Carvalho 2004 Late Harvest Chenin Blanc (Clarksburg) $12. Sweet and rustic, with one-dimensional peach, apricot, and vanilla flavors and a clean streak of acidity. **82** —*S.H. (3/1/2006)*

Carvalho 2003 Pinot Noir (Clarksburg) $22. Simple and clean, this Pinot has modest cherry flavors and a burst of sprightly acidity. It finishes dry and swift. **83** —*S.H. (3/1/2006)*

Carvalho 2004 Dantone Vineyards Sauvignon Blanc (Clarksburg) $15. Soft and slightly sweet, this is a rustic wine with flavors of grapefruit juice and a touch of oak. **82** —*S.H. (3/1/2006)*

Carvalho 2002 Old Vine Zinfandel (Dry Creek Valley) $22. Fruity and simple, with a slightly sweet, medicinal finish, this Zin has cola and black cherry flavors. The tannins and acids stick around long after the fruit is gone. **82** —*S.H. (3/1/2006)*

CARVER SUTRO

Carver Sutro 1999 Palisades Vineyard Petite Sirah (Napa Valley) $92. Not nearly as good as the 2000, this wine has bizarre aromas and flavors of dill pickles, lead pencils, syrupy cola, and sulfur. It's also so oaky, it hurts the palate. Finishes hot and rough. **82** *(12/31/2003)*

Carver Sutro 2000 Palisades Vineyards Petite Sirah (Napa Valley) $38. This rather famous wine was very good, but did not place among the very top wines, perhaps due to the vintage. It has pretty flavors of black raspberries and cherries, and was framed in well-toasted, high-end oak. Some tasters found its jammy extraction overdone. But overall, quite pleasant drinking. **87** *(4/1/2003)*

CASA BARRANCA

Casa Barranca 2003 Craftsman Red Cabernet Sauvignon (Central Coast) $15. Rather tough and rustic, this Cab has a raw, sharp mouthfeel, although the fruit is very ripe and almost sweet in blackberries, cherries, and mocha. **83** —*S.H. (12/1/2005)*

Casa Barranca 2004 Chardonnay (Santa Rita Hills) $20. It's refreshing to find this kind of high acidity in a California Chard, but that doesn't mean that this is a rich, fruity wine. It's tart in mineral and lime flavors, with a very dry finish. Try with mussels or oysters. **87** —*S.H. (7/1/2006)*

Casa Barranca 2004 Pinot Noir (Santa Rita Hills) $20. Showing plenty of Santa Rita character at a fair price, this wine sure did get ripe during this hot vintage. It's showing powerfully extracted cherry pie, rosehip tea, and coffee-cola flavors that flood the mouth, yet is dry and silky, with an elegant delicacy. **91 Editors' Choice** —*S.H. (7/1/2006)*

Casa Barranca 2003 Pinot Noir (Arroyo Grande Valley) $25. This wine opens with leather, berry, and baked pie crust aromas, and turns very fruity in the mouth. It's kind of heavy and thick for a Pinot Noir. **82** —*S.H. (12/1/2005)*

Casa Barranca 2003 Bungalow Red Syrah-Grenache Rhône Red Blend (Santa Barbara County) $15. Kind of rustic in style, with an edgy, sharp mouthfeel and a finish that's too sweet. But there's plenty of tasty wild berry and red stone fruit flavor. **83** —*S.H. (12/1/2005)*

Casa Barranca 2003 Reserve Sémillon (Santa Barbara County) $15. An earthy wine with flavors of peaches and herb. It's dry, with a scour of acidity and a touch of oak. **83** —*S.H. (12/1/2005)*

Casa Barranca 2003 Barrel Select Syrah (Central Coast) $15. Full-bodied and dry, this nice Syrah has a streak of ripe plum and blackberry fruit, with a spicy finish. It will be good with lamb or steak. **85** —*S.H. (7/1/2006)*

Casa Barranca 2003 Reserve Syrah (Santa Barbara County) $19. Opens with intriguing aromas of intense white pepper, freshly picked blackberries and mocha, but in the mouth, the wine turns overly soft and a bit cloying. **83** —*S.H. (12/1/2005)*

Casa Barranca 2004 Bungalow Red Syrah-Grenache (Santa Barbara County) $15. A Syrah-Grenache blend that's dry and rustically tannic, with a gritty, chewy feeling, and explosively ripe cherry, plum, and cocoa flavors. This is a country-style wine that's looking for country-style stews and roasts. **84** —*S.H. (8/1/2006)*

CASA CARNEROS

Casa Carneros 2001 Pinot Noir (Carneros) $30. Pale in color, and richly perfumed with smoky, cherry, and cola scents. The flavors are similar, with a blast of peppery, cinnamon spice. This is a nice, light Pinot. **86** —*S.H. (12/1/2004)*

CASA CASSARA

Casa Cassara 2001 Burning Creek Vineyard Pinot Noir (Santa Rita Hills) $46. A little pruny or raisiny, and also hot, although there are some succulent black cherry flavors in the middle. But there's something tough and rugged about this wine, and it does leave a burn behind. **85** —*S.H. (12/1/2004)*

Casa Cassara 2001 Estate Pinot Noir (Santa Rita Hills) $28. Smells a little musty and mushroomy, but airing brings out the underlying cherry flavors. In the mouth, this wine is fairly tannic and tight, but once again, those cherries reveal themselves after you swallow. Likely to improve with six months or a year of aging. **85** —*S.H. (12/1/2004)*

Casa Cassara 2001 Syrah (Santa Ynez Valley) $24. Very dry, rather tart and acidic, but the polished cherry and blackberry flavors are juicy and enjoyable, and are sweetened with a dash of oak. This wine desperately needs a big, thick cut of meat to tame it. Try with a sirloin steak. **86** —*S.H. (12/1/2004)*

CASA DE CABALLOS

Casa de Caballos 2000 Forgetmenot Cabernet Blend (Paso Robles) $24. Tastes like any anonymous red wine from anywhere in the world that's hot. Flavors are of burnt blackberry, and are very dry, with an astringent, rough finish. **82** —*S.H. (11/15/2003)*

Casa de Caballos 2002 Choclate Lily Cabernet Sauvignon (Paso Robles) $30. Soft in tannins, but sharp in acidity, with a raw, sandpapery flavor. **82** —*S.H. (2/1/2005)*

Casa de Caballos 2002 Forgetmenot Cabernet Sauvignon-Merlot (Paso Robles) $30. Drinks very soft in tannins, yet has a strong bitterness that detracts. **82** —*S.H. (12/31/2004)*

Casa de Caballos 2002 Ultra Violet Merlot (Paso Robles) $26. There's good, ripe fruit flavor here, but the wine hits the mouth with a raw feeling. Finishes sharp and disagreeably harsh. **83** —*S.H. (2/1/2005)*

Casa de Caballos 2000 Ultra Violet Merlot (Paso Robles) $24. Tastes hot and strong, a heavy wine with earthy, tobacco flavors softened with a hint of briary berry. Totally dry, with an astringent finish. **83** —*S.H. (8/1/2003)*

Casa de Caballos 2000 Maggie May El Nino Red Pinot Noir (Paso Robles) $17. 82 *(10/1/2002)*

Casa de Caballos 2000 Periwinkle Pinot Noir (Paso Robles) $20. Slight hints of barnyard and dirty leather add interest to the nose of this lightweight Pinot. It's juicy and tart but a bit thin, with a chalky mouthfeel and modest cherry fruit. **84** *(10/1/2002)*

CASA NUESTRA

Casa Nuestra 2000 Reserve Chenin Blanc (Napa Valley) $22. Expensive for this varietal, and also for Napa Valley. Pippin apple and spearmint aromas lead to apple and citrus flavors. It's very dry, with somewhat high acidity, a steely wine with similarities to Fumé Blanc. There's a tart, sour finish that suggests sushi. **88**—*S.H. (9/1/2002)*

Casa Nuestra 1999 Merlot (Napa Valley) $38. Enjoyable and plush, this wine packs a fruity punch yet manages to stay elegant. Blackberry, plum, chocolate, coffee, and olive aromas and flavors are accompanied by a soft, velvety texture and dry, dusty tannins. It's rich, and calls to mind a standing rib roast and similar fare. **90**—*S.H. (9/1/2002)*

CASS

Cass 2004 Rockin' One Rhône Red Blend (Paso Robles) $34. Soft and generous in fruity flavor, this has pronounced new oak that accents cherry, raspberry, smoky vanilla, and peppery spice flavors. It's mainly Grenache, with a little Syrah, from the Templeton Gap area of Paso. **87**—*S.H. (12/15/2006)*

Cass 2005 Viognier (Paso Robles) $24. Has all the hallmarks of Viognier, namely lots of tropical fruit, wildflower, vanilla, and spicy aromas and flavors, and finishes thoroughly dry. Could use more brightness and zest, though, as it's a bit flat. **83**—*S.H. (12/15/2006)*

CASTALIA

Castalia 2003 Rochioli Vineyard Pinot Noir (Russian River Valley) $45. Rochioli's winemaker has crafted a fine, silky Pinot. The flavors veer toward red cherries and cola, with an edge of sweet oak, while acidity is tart. The wine finishes sharp, but should soften and improve with five to seven years in the cellar. **90**—*S.H. (12/1/2005)*

CASTELLETTO

Castelletto 2000 Cortese (Temecula) $18. Try this as a dry alternative to Chardonnay next time you want a clean, fruity white wine. The citrus flavors are long on tart acidity, but there's a creaminess that makes it very enjoyable. From Mount Palomar Winery. **87**—*S.H. (4/1/2002)*

Castelletto 1997 Trovato Red Blend (Temecula) $15. Dark, with black cherry and smoke aromas, this deeply flavored wine is sweetly fruity, with ultrasoft tannins. Some overripe notes of raisins and chocolate don't disturb the pretty balance. A Super Tuscan blend of Sangiovese with smaller amounts of Bordeaux varieties. **90 Best Buy**—*S.H. (11/15/2001)*

Castelletto 1999 Sangiovese (Temecula) $16. This very nice wine startles the palate with a peppery assault, then calms down and spreads tart red cherry flavors over the tongue. Dusty tannins show up in the aftertaste. This is pretty good stuff, and it would be interesting to try it with rich Italian cuisine. **87**—*S.H. (12/1/2002)*

Castelletto 1999 Trovato Sangiovese (Temecula) $15. Another super-Tuscan blend of Sangiovese, Cabernet Sauvignon, Merlot, and Cabernet Franc, this darkly tinted wine opens with black cherry and smoke aromas, and turns silky and plush on the palate. The solid structure is locked into place with dry tannins. **90**—*S.H. (4/1/2002)*

CASTELLO DA VINCI

Castello Da Vinci 2003 Cabernet Sauvignon (Napa Valley) $25. A new wine, from a winery started by a retired 4-star general, that shows real command of the genre. It's classically structured, with ripe black currant fruit framed in sturdy, rich tannins. Could develop additional complexity with up to 10 years of age, but it's a good Cabernet right now. **90**—*S.H. (5/1/2006)*

CASTELLO DI BORGHESE

Castello di Borghese 2000 Meritage Bordeaux Blend (North Fork of Long Island) $48. 84—*J.C. (10/2/2004)*

Castello di Borghese 2001 Ovation Private Reserve Bordeaux Blend (North Fork of Long Island) $75. 82—*J.C. (10/2/2004)*

Castello di Borghese NV Petit Château Bordeaux Blend (North Fork of Long Island) $10. A lightweight bordeaux style blend that's best slightly chilled as a stand-in for Beaujolais or Bourgeuil. Berry fruit, with some light tannins that turn a bit green on the finish. **83**—*J.C. (4/1/2001)*

Castello di Borghese 1998 Hargrave Vineyard Cabernet Franc (North Fork of Long Island) $17. A berry scented wine that's loaded with fresh mint aromas and accented by toasty oak. The tannins are ripe and soft; the acidity bright. **85**—*J.C. (4/1/2001)*

Castello di Borghese 1998 Hargrave Vineyard Reserve Cabernet Franc (North Fork of Long Island) $22. Simultaneously softer and richer than Borghese's regular bottling, this wine shows dark berry flavors and only a touch of mint. Some smoky notes add a meatiness that further sets this wine apart. **88**—*J.C. (4/1/2001)*

Castello di Borghese 1998 Hargrave Vineyard Reserve Cabernet Sauvignon (North Fork of Long Island) $32. Cedar- and menthol-scented oak complementweedy cassis fruit, Full bodied, shows a touch more greenness in the finish. **86**—*J.C. (4/1/2001)*

Castello di Borghese 1998 Hargrave Vineyard Chardonnay (North Fork of Long Island) $14. This wine shows some of the less appealing aspects of American oak: overt spice and vanilla flavors and a slick, oily mouthfeel. **82**—*J.C. (4/1/2001)*

Castello di Borghese 2001 Hargrave Vineyard Barrel Fermented Chardonnay (North Fork of Long Island) $22. 83—*J.C. (10/2/2004)*

Castello di Borghese 2000 Hargrave Vineyard Barrel Fermented Chardonnay (North Fork of Long Island) $22. Toast aromas complement delicate notes of grilled nuts and ripe peaches. It's barrel fermented but not overly woody, instead focused on peach and citrus fruit, caressed by filberts. Nicely balanced. **88**—*J.C. (3/1/2002)*

Castello di Borghese 1998 Hargrave Vineyard Reserve Chardonnay (North Fork of Long Island) $18. What a difference from Borghese's regular Chardonnay. This one is loaded with class and refinement, from the delicate aromas of light toast, pear, and hazelnut through the nearly weightless palate that somehow carries a great deal of flavor. **88**—*J.C. (4/1/2001)*

Castello di Borghese 1998 Meritage (North Fork of Long Island) $45. Fruit is totally lacking in this starched out, lean wine that is obviously striving for more, given its price tag. The flavor profile is all cranberry, tomato and bitter greens and while the feel in the mouth is good, the finish is cloying and herbal. **80**—*M.S. (3/1/2003)*

Castello di Borghese 2001 Hargrave Vineyard Merlot (North Fork of Long Island) $20. From the oldest vineyard on Long Island comes this well-oaked wine. Fruit is missing from the bouquet, which has mint and spice but also nail polish and horsey notes. The flavors are on the weedy side, with tomato and sweet oak trying to cover. Still an okay wine, light-bodied and smooth, with high acidity. But definitely less ripe than better vintages. **83**—*M.D. (12/1/2006)*

Castello di Borghese 2000 Hargrave Vineyard Merlot (North Fork of Long Island) $19. 81—*J.C. (10/2/2004)*

Castello di Borghese 1998 Hargrave Vineyard Merlot (North Fork of Long Island) $18. Strong mint and menthol aromatics give way to intense fresh-cut cedar flavors. There's just too much wood for this woodchuck to chuck. **82**—*J.C. (4/1/2001)*

Castello di Borghese 2000 Hargrave Vineyard Reserve Merlot (North Fork of Long Island) $25. Tree bark, bell pepper, and alcohol mar the nose on this offering, which has some good points but also some things that hold it back. For instance, there is some fresh strawberry on the flavor profile but also a hindering note of green. Then there's the finish, which is round and creamy but also hot and clumsy. **84**—*M.S. (1/1/2004)*

Castello di Borghese 1998 Hargrave Vineyard Reserve Merlot (North Fork of Long Island) $25. A huge step up from the overoaked regular bottling, this wine offers aromas of smoked meat and bacon fat. The berry-flavored palate is rich and dense and flows smoothly into a finish that's marked by earth and coffee notes. **88**—*J.C. (4/1/2001)*

Castello di Borghese 1999 Hargrave Vineyard Pinot Blanc (North Fork of Long Island) $10. Starts off strong, with pleasant tangelo aromas and flavors. But somewhere along the line the flavors turn varnishy, finishing with a strong note of lacquer. **82**—*J.C. (4/1/2001)*

Castello di Borghese NV Fleurette Pinot Noir (North Fork of Long Island) $10. A lightweight Pinot that's actually marketed as a rose, this wine nevertheless manages to pack in decent flavors of apple skin, red berries, and cinnamon, capped off by some leathery, meaty notes. **83** —*J.C. (4/1/2001)*

Castello di Borghese 1998 Hargrave Vineyard Pinot Noir (North Fork of Long Island) $35. The dominant aromas are smoke, toast, and cinnamon, which ride over tart-cherry fruit. Turns quite stemmy and tough on the finish. Drink young—with a piece of rare beef to help tame the tannins. **84** —*J.C. (4/1/2001)*

Castello di Borghese 2002 Hargrave Vineyard Reserve Pinot Noir (North Fork of Long Island) $38. Woody on the nose, but with decent red berry and a touch of rhubarb, this wine has a drier, heavier feel and tannins than most Pinots but still delivers modest red berry and cola flavors. Finishes chalky. **84** —*M.D. (12/1/2006)*

Castello di Borghese 1999 Hargrave Vineyard Sauvignon Blanc (North Fork of Long Island) $11. Picked quite ripe, the resulting wine features mainly melon and fig aromas and flavors, with very little grassiness in evidence. Crisp acidity on the finish provides the vivacity needed to pair with oysters or clams. **85** —*J.C. (4/1/2001)*

Castello di Borghese NV Chardonette White Blend (North Fork of Long Island) $7. A blended white, but predominantly-you guessed it-Chardonnay. The soft, sweet pear aromas and flavors are simple and clean, making this a decent quaffer on a hot summer day. **83** —*J.C. (4/1/2001)*

CASTLE

Castle 1998 Cabernet Sauvignon (Sonoma Valley) $25. Because of the difficult vintage, the wine struggles to achieve ripeness and fruitiness. Instead, herbs dominate. That aside, it's balanced and elegant, and gets an A for effort. Rich meats will coax out whatever sugars are hiding in there. **86** —*S.H. (12/31/2001)*

Castle 1998 Chardonnay (Sonoma Valley) $18. 84 *(6/1/2000)*

Castle 1998 Chardonnay (Carneros) $22. 88 *(6/1/2000)*

Castle 1999 Chardonnay (Sonoma Valley) $17. Very ripe, with lots of tropical fruit and a generous dusting of crushed oriental spices such as ginger and cinnamon. Oak overlays add vanilla and smoke notes and a creamy, smooth texture. This is a very complete, satisfying wine. Try with grilled shrimp. **89 Best Buy** —*S.H. (12/31/2001)*

Castle 1999 Chardonnay (Carneros) $20. From the Sonoma side of appellation, this is a ripe, fruity wine brimming with polished peach and breadfruit flavors. Some may find the lees dominating the aroma and palate. Give it six months or so and let it calm down. **87** —*S.H. (12/31/2001)*

Castle 2000 Merlot (Sonoma Valley) $20. Soft and tired, with leathery, funky smells and flavors. Not going anywhere. **82** —*S.H. (5/1/2005)*

Castle 1999 Merlot (Sonoma Valley) $17. Lots of rich cherry and blackberry flavor in this wine, which, approaching five years of age, has softened into a mellow sipper. It's very dry and soft in acids, too. The spicy fruit is really the star here. **87** —*S.H. (12/15/2004)*

Castle 1998 Merlot (Sonoma Valley) $20. Plush and warming, this lovely wine has earthy, dark stone fruit aromas and flavors, and a dollop of smoky oak. It's bone dry, with lush, intricate but melted tannins, and a very nice structure. Has that elusive quality known as elegance. **90** —*S.H. (12/31/2001)*

Castle 1998 Merlot (Sonoma Valley) $20. Plush and warming, this lovely wine has earthy, dark stone fruit aromas and flavors, and a dollop of smoky oak. It's bone-dry, with lush, intricate but melted tannins, and a very nice structure. Has that elusive quality known as elegance. **90** —*S.H. (12/31/2001)*

Castle 1999 Sangiacomo Vineyard Merlot (Carneros) $24. Time has not helped this vegetal wine, which smells and tastes of canned asparagus. Whatever fruit there was is largely gone. **82** —*S.H. (5/1/2005)*

Castle 1997 Sangiacomo Vineyard Donnel Ranch Merlot (Carneros) $25. Dark, young, and rich, with massive stuffing. A big, exuberant, fruity wine, it has juicy berry fruit flavors. Too big to drink now, the finish is dry and fairly tannic, so it's best cellared a few years. **90 Editors' Choice** *(8/1/2001)*

Castle 2001 Pinot Noir (Carneros) $24. Cola, cherry, mocha, and vanilla flavors, in a light-bodied, silky wine, with pronounced acidity. Finishes dry. A bit rustic, but offers good Pinot character. **85** —*S.H. (5/1/2005)*

Castle 2000 Pinot Noir (Carneros) $24. Despite some cherry, raspberry, and cola flavors, this Pinot drinks a bit thin and tart in acidity. It has sharp elbows and even some jagged tannins. It's a good regional wine. **85** —*S.H. (8/1/2004)*

Castle 1999 Pinot Noir (Carneros) $24. You can smell, plummy, blackberry notes on the nose, along with what seems to be well-charred oak. It's a big wine, full-bodied and dense. Not for fans of delicacy, but its brawny size will appeal to some. **86** —*S.H. (12/15/2001)*

Castle 1999 Durell Vineyard Pinot Noir (Carneros) $35. Leathery aromas, along with wood-driven spice, caramel, and chocolate notes. The palate doesn't disappoint, delivering spiced cherries and creamy vanilla. The finish is mellow, with more tasty chocolate and coffee as well as juicy berries. **89** *(10/1/2002)*

Castle 1997 Durell Vineyard Pinot Noir (Carneros) $30. 90 *(10/1/1999)*

Castle 2001 Estate Pinot Noir (Carneros) $32. Despite its silky mouthfeel, there's a toughness to this wine. It's extracted, with jammy stone-fruit flavors, and an earthy edge of coffee and dried herbs. Offers a robust contrast to Castle's regular '01 Pinot. **86** —*S.H. (5/1/2005)*

Castle 1999 Sangiacomo Vineyard Pinot Noir (Carneros) $30. The nose is loaded with stewed plum and roasted tomato. Raspberry, plum, and chocolate flavors get a helping hand from fresh herbal notes, while the tail end is all black fruit, bitter chocolate, and espresso. A bit of warning: This is sweet stuff, a thoroughly modern California wine. **90 Editors' Choice** *(10/1/2002)*

Castle 1997 Sangiacomo Vineyard Pinot Noir (Carneros) $30. 90 *(10/1/1999)*

Castle 2001 Syrah (Sonoma Valley) $24. Rich and ripe, maybe a bit over-oaked, but that doesn't stop the plum, blackberry, hung meat, rum, and coffee flavors from running all over the palate. Finishes firmly dry, with a long aftertaste of spice. **89** —*S.H. (8/1/2004)*

Castle 1999 Syrah (Sonoma Valley) $22. Hickory smoke, tart red fruit and a stemmy-herbal note open this Sonoma Valley Syrah. In the mouth, you'll get your fill of blackberry, leather, and more herbal flavors. Mouthfeel is complex and medium-full; finishes long, with chalky tannins. Yum. Top Value. **90** *(11/1/2001)*

Castle 2001 Port Syrah (Carneros) $28. This country-style wine sure is sweet in chocolate and cassis, but it lacks distinction and balance, and feels rough. **83** —*S.H. (5/1/2005)*

Castle 2002 Viognier (California) $16. Bright and perky with a jolt of wildflower, tropical fruit, and buttery vanilla flavors, this wine also is a bit flat and earthy. It's a middle-of-the-road Viognier. **84** —*S.H. (8/1/2004)*

Castle 2000 Viognier (California) $19. Another fruit-driven wine, showing bright peach, apple, and pineapple aromas and flavors. It's clean, swiftly tart, and a little bit sweet, and finishes with lots of ripe nectary fruit. **86** —*S.H. (12/15/2001)*

Castle 2002 Ripkin Vineyards Late Harvest Viognier (Lodi) $20. Sweet and honeyed, with apricot nectar, peach custard, and vanilla flavors. Could use more acidity. **85** —*S.H. (5/1/2005)*

Castle 2001 Zinfandel (Sonoma Valley) $19. black cherry, plum, and spice notes are the focus here, with hints of coffee and chocolate in the background. Tannins are somewhat powdery, while the acidity is brisk enough to carry the flavors on the palate for a long time. **88** —*J.M. (11/1/2003)*

Castle 1999 Zinfandel (Sonoma Valley) $19. From one of the Zin's natural homes, a classic example. Begins with those wildberry aromas called "brambly," with earthy, peppery notes, and drinks richly fruity-spicy. You'll like the dry-as-dust mouthfeel, with it's complex tannins, and long finish. This well-made wine is a perfect match for rich, grilled meats. **90 Editors' Choice** —*S.H. (12/15/2001)*

Castle 1998 Zinfandel (Sonoma Valley) $19. Ripe, strawberry/raspberry preserves, with a pleasing, jammy, fruity, luscious richness. Ten percent Petite Sirah adds color and punch. There's a fair amount of tannin, but overall a nice balance, and the plush fruit is the highlight. **89** —*P.G. (3/1/2001)*

Castle 1998 Zinfandel (Russian River Valley) $16. Firm, tannic, and fruity, with some nice tropical fruit flavors, wrapped around stiff tannins and some green, slightly stemmy flavors. The finish is hard and rough. **85** —*P.G. (3/1/2001)*

Castle 1997 Zinfandel (Sonoma Valley) $18. 90 —*S.H. (5/1/2000)*

Castle 2001 Parmelee-Hill Vineyards Zinfandel (Sonoma County) $25. Bright and cherry-like up front. But the tannins are astringent and shut down the flavors a bit. As a result, the wine is also short on the finish, ending with drying spice tones. Castle's non-vineyard designate is better. **82** —*J.M. (11/1/2003)*

CASTLE ROCK

Castle Rock 2003 Cabernet Sauvignon (Columbia Valley (WA)) $11. Though Castle Rock is a California winery, this is a Columbia Valley wine; they purchase the juice in Washington and bottle in California. Despite the generic feel to the package, this is the real deal: Smooth and appealing plum and pie cherry fruit is distinctly marked with cinnamon and light cocoa. Substantive and seamless, it carries well into a lingering finish of fine-grained tannins. **88 Best Buy** —*P.G. (4/1/2006)*

Castle Rock 2002 Cabernet Sauvignon (Sonoma County) $11. Clean and varietally correct, this is an inexpensive Cabernet with pleasant flavors of blackberries and oak. It's thoroughly dry, and easy to drink. The sturdy tannins will stand up to rich meats and cheese. **84** —*S.H. (8/1/2005)*

Castle Rock 2002 Cabernet Sauvignon (Napa Valley) $11. Not bad at all for the price. A bit rough in tannins, but you get nice blackberry and cherry flavors and a dash of oak. **84** —*S.H. (2/1/2005)*

Castle Rock 2000 Cabernet Sauvignon (Columbia Valley (WA)) $10. A bouquet of sweet plum, black cherry, oak, and bread flour is a preview of what comes later in the mouth. Medium-bodied, it closes with more of the same (though the fruit's a little blacker, and there's a cashew-nuttiness to boot). Rather tasty, if not a wine whose changing flavors and nuances are things to ponder. **87 Best Buy** —*D.T. (12/31/2002)*

Castle Rock 2004 Reserve Cabernet Sauvignon (Napa Valley) $18. Pretty good Cab for the price, a little soft, but ripe enough, with upfront blackberry and cherry flavors and that chocolate fudge note that marks so many modern Cabs. It's a pleasantly dry wine with some real complexity. **85** —*S.H. (12/15/2006)*

Castle Rock 2003 Reserve Cabernet Sauvignon (Napa Valley) $15. Seems like it was rushed to market, and is thus sharp and acidic now, with tart blackberry and blueberry jam flavors. But this is a wine that could well benefit from cellaring. **86** —*S.H. (8/1/2005)*

Castle Rock 2003 Reserve Chardonnay (Napa Valley) $15. This is one of those earthy Chards, the kind that bring to mind dusty brown spices. It's got appley and smoky, woody flavors, and is dry. **84** —*S.H. (8/1/2005)*

Castle Rock 2002 Merlot (Napa Valley) $11. Super ripe, and so filled with fruity, fructosy cherry sweetness that it's hard to tell if it has residual sugar or not. The tannins are ultra soft, but there's cola-like acidity that gives balance. Pretty good for the price. **85** —*S.H. (2/1/2005)*

Castle Rock 2003 Reserve Petite Sirah (Napa Valley) $15. Rich and soft in blackberry, mocha, and sweet leather flavors, with lots of oak and a long aftertaste. As much as I like this wine, it is too sweet. The finish turns as sugary as a chocolate truffle, although the wine is no doubt technically dry. **87** —*S.H. (8/1/2005)*

Castle Rock 2003 Pinot Noir (Mendocino County) $11. A weird and disturbing aroma suggesting a chemical flaw ruins this wine's otherwise decent flavors and texture. **82** —*S.H. (2/1/2005)*

Castle Rock 2003 Pinot Noir (Carneros) $11. Simple, and a good example of a regional Pinot, with good color clarity, silky tannins, and flavors of cherries and coffee. Has a bit of an off-smell, but otherwise okay. **84** —*S.H. (2/1/2005)*

Castle Rock 2002 Pinot Noir (Russian River Valley) $11. Strictly average, showing tomato, cherry, and oaky aromas and tastes. Feels soft and a little tough in tannins. **84** *(11/1/2004)*

Castle Rock 2002 Pinot Noir (Napa Valley) $11. The same odd smell of barnyard spoilage I found in this winery's Mendocino bottling afflicts this one. Too bad, because it tastes pretty good. **82** —*S.H. (2/1/2005)*

Castle Rock 2002 Pinot Noir (Sonoma Coast) $11. Lots to like about this wine. It's got delicious flavors of black cherries, mocha, white pepper, and various dusty spices, and the creamiest tannins. Almost melts in the mouth with flavor. Rather too soft, but it sure is tasty. **87 Best Buy** —*S.H. (10/1/2005)*

Castle Rock 2001 Pinot Noir (Russian River Valley) $10. Full and harmonious smelling, with berry fruit and leathery spice notes. Sweet and rich, with black cherry and chocolate flavors and a long, warm finish. This popular restaurant wine is rewarding but a bit sweet. Maybe that's what people like so much about it…that and the cost. **87** —*M.S. (12/1/2003)*

Castle Rock 2003 Sauvignon Blanc (Napa Valley) $9. I tasted this wine with a range of other Sauvignon Blancs, all of which cost far more, and it had nothing to be ashamed of. Shows a nice balance of crisp acids and slight oak with well-ripened flavors of citrus fruits, melons, and figs. A splash of Sémillon adds a nutty complexity. At this price, from this appellation, it's a steal. Shouldn't be too hard to find, with 5,600 cases produced. **86 Best Buy** —*S.H. (11/15/2004)*

Castle Rock 2003 Syrah (Central Coast) $9. This cool-climate Syrah brims with bright white pepper, cassis, and coffee flavors, while the tannins are rich, ripe, and fine. It's a bone-dry wine with plenty of style and complexity. **87 Best Buy** —*S.H. (8/1/2005)*

Castle Rock 1998 Syrah (California) $10. At first it seems so easygoing: lots of fruit; a rich, dark, chocolaty wine. But underneath there is a fair amount of structure that will carry it along for a couple of years. I love this style of Californian wine. There's a slight sweetness to the fruit as well as ripe tannins that never intrude. **87** —*S.H. (6/1/2003)*

Castle Rock 1999 California Cuvée Syrah (California) $10. Red berry and cocoa aromas and flavors that have real appeal are undone by a vegetal, green-olivey element. It's a red that's just too green, as noted elsewhere here. Decent palate texture and black and white pepper on the back end just can't overtake the basic tart, green character. **82** *(10/1/2001)*

Castle Rock 2003 Zinfandel (Dry Creek Valley) $9. Here's a drinkable everyday sort of Zin, offering fresh fruity flavors and rich tannins. Finishes with enough acidity to cut through pizza or greasy BBQ. **84** —*S.H. (8/1/2005)*

Castle Rock 1999 California Cuvée Zinfandel (California) $10. The mixed-berry bouquet is muted by a coating of white baking flour. More berry, plus black plum and oak flavors lead to any oaky-ashy finsh, punctuated by a light peppery twinge. **83** —*D.T. (3/1/2002)*

CASTORO

Castoro 2002 Ventuno Anni Bordeaux Blend (Paso Robles) $22. This Bordeaux blend, plus Zinfandel, is a fine example of how this appellation can produce rich, dry and balanced red wines of substance and harmony. It's full-bodied, with earthy, berry flavors and a finish of chocolate. The Zin brings pepper and a feral quality. **87** —*S.H. (2/1/2005)*

Castoro 2003 Cabernet Blend (Paso Robles) $26. Castoro's tried really hard to perfect Cabernet in Paso, and this one, from a hotter part of the appellation, shows typically ripe fruit and softness that make it appealing. It's dryish to slightly sweet, and rich in blackberry and cherry pie filling, melted chocolate and licorice, with a cinnamon spice flourish. **86** —*S.H. (12/31/2006)*

Castoro 2003 Cabernet Sauvignon (Paso Robles) $15. Shows good Cabernet character in the full-bodied flavors of black currants, coffee, and cocoa, and also shows Paso structure in the softness and low acids. Paso struggles to define its own style and Castoro is trying hard. **85** —*S.H. (12/1/2005)*

Castoro 2002 Cabernet Sauvignon (Paso Robles) $15. Soft and smooth, from grapes that grew ripe and fat under the summer sun. The sweet cherry and blackberry flavors have been framed in smoky oak. Fully dry and balanced, this is an easy, sophisticated sipper. **87** —*S.H. (4/1/2005)*

USA

Castoro 2000 Cabernet Sauvignon (Paso Robles) $14. Smells earthy and tobaccoey, although there are blackberry notes below, and drinks typically warm country. Tannins and acids are very soft, and the berry flavors veer into mixed notes of raisins and herbs. For all that, it's a pleasant sip. **85** —S.H. (6/1/2003)

Castoro 2004 Chardonnay (Central Coast) $13. This pleasant wine shows all the usual Chardonnay features of well-ripened tropical fruit and peach flavors, toasty oak, and a creamy, buttery mouthfeel. It's clean and brisk, with a long, fruity finish. **85** —S.H. (12/1/2005)

Castoro 2003 Chardonnay (Central Coast) $13. Here's a dry Chard marked by creamy lees, oak, and an array of yellow and red tree stone fruits. It's a little soft, with a creamy texture. Will go well with food. **85** —S.H. (2/1/2005)

Castoro 2005 Fumé Blanc (Paso Robles) $10. From the spearmint gum aroma, you can tell this wine finishes slightly sweet, and so it does. But the clean acidity keeps it balanced. Would be nice with a salad of mixed greens and smoked trout. **85 Best Buy** —S.H. (7/1/2006)

Castoro 2005 Fumé Blanc (Paso Robles) $9. Loads of citrus, fig, melon, and vanilla flavors mark this slightly sweet wine. Fortunately, crisp acidity balances. Try with roasted eggplant and garlic soup. **84** —S.H. (11/15/2005)

Castoro 2005 Gewürztraminer (Paso Robles) $16. Fruity, spicy and just off-dry, with pleasant tropical fruit, wildflower, honey, and ginger-cinnamon flavors. Nice low alcohol on this pretty wine. **85** —S.H. (12/15/2006)

Castoro 2001 Due Mila Tre Meritage (Paso Robles) $33. Harsh and tannic, with burnt-coffee and plum flavors that finish dry and astringent. **82** —S.H. (5/1/2005)

Castoro 1997 Merlot (Paso Robles) $15. **83** —J.C. (7/1/2000)

Castoro 2002 Merlot (Paso Robles) $14. You'll find cherry-berry flavors mingled with herbs and tobacco in this dry wine. It has a balance of acids and tannins and will pair with rich red meats. **85** —S.H. (12/15/2004)

Castoro 2000 Merlot (Paso Robles) $13. Making Merlot in Paso Robles is a challenge. This effort has flavors of sun-warmed berries and coffee, and the strong tannins are rough-edged and baked. Finishes with a scour of acids and tannins. **84** —S.H. (12/15/2003)

Castoro 2003 Late Harvest Muscat Canelli (Paso Robles) $17. Sweet in orange blossom and apricot flavors, with a good balance of acidity, this is a basic California late-harvest wine, satisfying due to its sweet fruit. Good with vanilla ice cream topped with peaches, with a sugar cookie. **85** —S.H. (12/1/2005)

Castoro 2003 Reserve Petite Sirah (Paso Robles) $18. An interesting wine. It has a certain rustically tannic mouthfeel. Part of the attraction is the fruit, deeply massive in blackberries and coffee, and part is the fine dry finish. Cries out for gorgeous, well-charred lamb chops. **87** —S.H. (12/31/2006)

Castoro 1999 Reserve Petite Sirah (Paso Robles) $16. Here's a classic Paso Robles red wine, big and fruity-sweet, with soft, gentle tannins and easy acids. Has a nice streak of cherry-berry flavor and a lush, supple mouthfeel. As tasty as it is, the panel felt it lacks spark and "fades too quickly on the finish." **85** (4/1/2003)

Castoro 2002 Stone's Throw Reserve Petite Sirah (Paso Robles) $18. Smells disturbingly funky or bretty, and seems shut down. Barely acceptable. **80** —S.H. (5/1/2005)

Castoro 2004 Oakenshield Wineworks Pinot Grigio (Paso Robles) $20. This easy-drinking wine has some superripe apricot flavors that are unusual, but tasty. Otherwise the wine has good varietal character of dryness and tartness. **84** —S.H. (2/1/2006)

Castoro 2004 Bien Nacido Vineyard Pinot Noir (Santa Barbara County) $20. Paso Robles-based Castoro reaches to this famous vineyard for Pinot Noir. The wine is a little hot and rustic by Bien Nacido standards, but satisfies for dryness, silkiness, and jammy black cherry flavors. **87** —S.H. (11/15/2006)

Castoro 2002 Reserve Pinot Noir (Central Coast) $18. Known more for Paso Robles wines, Castoro has reached to the cool South Coast to craft this delicate, silky Pinot. It has rich flavors of cherries and spices, and is dry and balanced. **87** —S.H. (2/1/2005)

Castoro 2000 Reserve Pinot Noir (Central Coast) $18. **82** (10/1/2002)

Castoro 2000 Reserve-Blind Faith Vineyard Pinot Noir (Central Coast) $18. **85** (10/1/2002)

Castoro 2003 Venti Due Anni Red Blend (Paso Robles) $27. A blend of four Bordeaux varieties with 25% Zinfandel, this wine shows its origin in the soft texture and raisiny midpalate. It's a plushly pleasant, full-bodied, tannic wine with Cabernet-esque qualities, while that Zin adds a wild, brambly, spicy note. **88** —S.H. (5/1/2006)

Castoro 2005 Rosato di Paso Rosé Blend (Paso Robles) $20. I liked the '04, a Rhône blend, for its richness, and this one, a Bordeaux blend with one-quarter Zinfandel, is its equal in savoriness. It has slightly sweet cherry and cassis flavors, with a body that's almost a red wine, but with light, silky tannins. Excellent chilled. **86** —S.H. (12/31/2006)

Castoro 2004 Rosato di Syrah Rosé Blend (Paso Robles) $20. This is one of the darker, more full-bodied rosés you'll ever have, but it's a pretty good one. It's likeable for its ultradryness, and the delicate flavors of rose petal, strawberry and thyme that lead to a complex finish. **87** —S.H. (6/1/2006)

Castoro 2000 Syrah (Paso Robles) $18. A tough, gritty wine with tannins to shed, it opens with aromas of earth, blackberry jam, and tobacco. Turns earthy-fruity in the mouth, with a tart hit of acidity in the finish. **84** —S.H. (6/1/2003)

Castoro 2004 Reserve Syrah (Paso Robles) $18. Picture perfect Paso red wine. It's not particularly Syrah-esque, but is a pretty wine, soft, clean and dry, with cherries and chocolate, some smoky oak, and a nice little bite of acidity. **84** —S.H. (12/31/2006)

Castoro 2003 Reserve Syrah (Paso Robles) $18. Here's a lush, juicy Syrah, rich in black currant, cherry, blueberry, chocolate, and coffee flavors that are so long and deep, you just can't help liking it. The wine is soft in texture, and achieves real deliciousness and complexity. **90** —S.H. (5/1/2006)

Castoro 2002 Reserve Syrah (Paso Robles) $18. The aroma is pungent and sweaty, while the cherry flavors are a bit charred and roasted; leathery. Likely brett-affected but richly textured, finishing with dark chocolate notes. **85** (9/1/2005)

Castoro 2001 Reserve Syrah (Paso Robles) $18. Opens with a super-leathery, funky note that could be brett or a clonal attribute. Once past the odor, it's dry, soft and herbal-plummy. **84** —S.H. (5/1/2005)

Castoro 1999 Reserve Syrah (Paso Robles) $18. A berry-filled fruit bomb that offers mouthwatering blackberries and blueberries galore, punctuated by fleeting glimpses of licorice. Picks up some coffee and espresso notes on the finish, where the slight bitterness provides needed structure. **87** (10/1/2001)

Castoro 2004 Reserve Tempranillo (California) $20. Dry and simple, but clean, crisp, and balanced. This has a light-bodied elegance, with silky tannins and cherry, green olive, and herb flavors. Try with grilled flank steak or bacon-wrapped pork. **85** —S.H. (11/15/2006)

Castoro 2002 Reserve Tempranillo (California) $16. Fully dry and medium-bodied, this is quite a good wine for a varietal no one really knows how to make in California. It has a mélange of berry, herb, spice, and coffee flavors, and is drinkable now. Try as an alternative to Zinfandel. **87** —S.H. (4/1/2005)

Castoro 2003 Viognier (Paso Robles) $18. The fruit in this wine is really stunning, considering how dry and balanced it is. It's an explosion of the ripest peaches and tropical fruits, with a buttery, honey-vanilla edge. Firmly in Viognier's exotic style, and tasty. **87** —S.H. (12/15/2004)

Castoro 2004 Stone's Throw Vineyard Viognier (Paso Robles) $18. Displays all the exotic wildflower and tropical fruit aromas and flavors Viognier is famous for, in a dry, soft wine with a honeyed finish. It could be a little more concentrated, though. **85** —S.H. (12/1/2005)

Castoro 2005 Tango White Blend (Central Coast) $20. A little sweet and simple, this blend of Pinot Blanc, Viognier, and Chardonnay offers ample peach and nectarine flavors. **83** —S.H. (12/31/2006)

USA

Castoro 2002 Zinfandel (Paso Robles) $14. Smells and tastes a bit burnt and raisiny, but otherwise a good Zin. Smooth, ripe tannins and pretty flavors of wild berries and coffee. If you like that super ripe note, this is your Zin. 84 —S.H. (2/1/2005)

Castoro 2001 Zinfandel (Paso Robles) $14. A solid effort from a southland appel lation, fully ripened with brambly wild blackberry and cherry-pepper flavors, but balanced in alcohol and without any residual sweetness. A distinctly California wine. 87 —S.H. (4/1/2004)

Castoro 2000 Zinfandel (Paso Robles) $14. This is a fine Zin, on the rough or rustic side, but the price isn't bad, and it's true to the varietal and appellation. Juicy flavors of berries and tobacco, with a hint of raisins, totally dry, and on the hot side, a wine to gulp with barbecue slathered with rich sauce. 85 —S.H. (9/1/2003)

Castoro 2004 Cobble Creek Zinfandel (Paso Robles) $25. Tastes like there's enough residual sugar to bake a pie. There's no doubting the deliciousness of the cherry, raspberry, and chocolate flavors, but that sweetness is off-putting. 82 —S.H. (11/15/2006)

Castoro 2001 Cobble Creek Zinfandel (Paso Robles) $20. Fairly lightweight, with pleasant, though mild, cherry, tar and anise notes. Tannins are a little astringent, and the finish is short. 82 —J.M. (11/1/2003)

Castoro 2003 Cobble Creek Vineyard Zinfandel (Paso Robles) $25. Soft and flat, with sugary-sweet flavors of coffee and gritty tannins. 80 —S.H. (12/1/2005)

Castoro 2000 Giubbine Zinfandel (Paso Robles) $18. A nice Zin with blackberry and cassis flavors and a fine, dry mouthfeel. If there's a fault, it's a streak of overripe raisins that grows stronger through the finish. 85 —S.H. (4/1/2004)

Castoro 2001 Giubbini Zinfandel (Paso Robles) $19. Bright cherry and spice kick off here, with zippy raspberry and plum following up. Tannins are moderately astringent and the finish is bright. 87 (11/1/2003)

Castoro 2001 Late Harvest Zinfandel (Paso Robles) $16. Cherry and plum jam aromas lead to a sweet, unctuous wine, with prickly spices through the finish. The texture is pleasing and smooth. 85 —S.H. (12/1/2003)

Castoro 2004 Oakenshield Wineworks Zinfandel (Paso Robles) $20. With a semi-sweet, medicinal cherry taste, this Zin shows the rustic side of Paso Robles. It feels manipulated, stripped of authenticity. 81 —S.H. (12/31/2006)

Castoro 2002 Reserve Zinfusion Zinfandel (Paso Robles) $19. Dry, tannic, and featureless, with slight berry flavors. 83 —S.H. (5/1/2005)

Castoro 2001 Vineyard Tribute Zinfandel (Paso Robles) $19. On the bright side, with ultra-zippy Bing cherry, raspberry, spice, toast, and chocolate at the fore. Smooth tannins add good texture. 86 (11/1/2003)

Castoro 1998 Vineyard Tribute Zinfandel (Paso Robles) $18. This is a slightly more intense version of the regular Castoro bottling, with an extra punch to the berries and a little more zip in the finish. A clean, bright, focused wine, precise and polished, with a natural elegance. Good balance throughout. 89 —P.G. (3/1/2001)

Castoro 2004 Zinfusion Zinfandel (Paso Robles) $19. Richer and more balanced than the two previous vintages, with opulent cherry pastry filling, blackberry, blueberry, cocoa, and spice flavors that are superripe, but essentially dry. Good tannins and acids, too. A wine to watch. 86 —S.H. (12/15/2006)

Castoro 2003 Zinfusion Reserve Zinfandel (Paso Robles) $19. Here's a rustic, country-style Zin with ripe berry flavors that are good enough to accompany a pizza or cheeseburger. It's dry, with a fruity finish. 83 — S.H. (12/1/2005)

CATACULA

Catacula 2003 Cabernet Sauvignon (Napa Valley) $34. Tough, weedy, and tannic, with a dry, astringent mouthfeel and faint cherry flavors fading back into tannins. Not a very rewarding Cab, and not going anywhere. 81 —S.H. (12/31/2006)

Catacula 2002 Cabernet Sauvignon (Napa Valley) $22. Opens with a Porty aroma, a baked brown sugar, and pie-crust scent that turns dry in the mouth, with flavors of rum-soaked raisins and cocoa. 83 —S.H. (12/15/2005)

Catacula 2001 Napa Valley Cabernet Sauvignon (Napa Valley) $19. Very ripe and opulent in fruit. Has flavors of black currant and cassis; so rich and extracted, it's almost a liqueur. Fortunately, adequate acidity brings life, and oak adds nuances of vanilla and toast. 88 —S.H. (10/1/2004)

Catacula 2000 Rancho Cuvée Cabernet Sauvignon-Merlot (Napa Valley) $19. A Cabernet–Merlot blend with flavors of currants, tobacco, and herbs, and a rich overlay of toasty oak. Bone dry, with smooth tannins. Turns bitter on the finish. 86 —S.H. (11/15/2003)

Catacula 2005 Sauvignon Blanc (Napa Valley) $14. Candied and simple, with candied flavors of pineapple, lemon, lime, and vanilla, this pleasant wine finishes a little sweet, but is balanced by crisp, citrusy acids. It's notable for the clean, richly fruity finish. 84 —S.H. (12/31/2006)

Catacula 2004 Sauvignon Blanc (Napa Valley) $12. Green-grassy and citrusy, with spearmint, alfalfa, and fig flavors, this wine finishes a little sweet and cloying, with a honeyed aftertaste. 83 —S.H. (12/15/2005)

Catacula 2001 Sauvignon Blanc (Napa Valley) $11. Smells sweetly figgy, with enticing waves of smoky vanilla, citrus, and wildflowers. This delicate, gentle wine is rich in fruity flavor, and crisp in acidity. It's a great value in a Sauvignon Blanc from a great appellation. 88 —S.H. (9/1/2004)

Catacula 2000 Sauvignon Blanc (Napa Valley) $11. A straightforward wine that goes the extra mile to achieve richness and finesse. The citrusy flavors are expressive and intense. One of the best Sauvignon Blanc values you'll find. 86 —S.H. (7/1/2003)

Catacula 2003 Late Harvest Sauvignon Blanc (Napa Valley) $25. This is a very, very sweet wine, smacking of honeyed apricots and vanilla custard. As delicious as it is, it could use greater acidity for balance and crispness. 85 —S.H. (12/15/2005)

Catacula 2001 Zinfandel (Napa Valley) $15. Superripe, almost raisiny, with soft tannins and acidity. The softness accentuates the cherries, blackberries, chocolate, and raisins and makes the wine drink syrupy, but it sure does tastes good. 85 —S.H. (9/1/2004)

Catacula 2000 Zinfandel (Napa Valley) $15. Marred by the faults that can and do plague Zin. Uneven ripening resulted in green, stalky aromas and flavors that are lean and tannic on the finish. Meanwhile, a cloying residue of sweetness marks the middle palate. Unbalanced and awkward. 82 —S.H. (9/1/2003)

Catacula 2004 Estate Old Vine Zinfandel (Napa Valley) $22. Sweet and chocolaty, with a soft, melted feel, this simple Zin offers spicy layers of blackberry pie filling and cassis liqueur flavors. Drink now. 83 —S.H. (12/31/2006)

CATANA

Catana NV Reserve Quintetta Port (California) $26. This California Port, made with traditional varieties, is from Calaveras County, and you can taste the sun in the super ripe chocolate, cassis, and blackberry pie flavors. It's gooey and lip-smackingly delicious, with enough acidity to cut through the sweetness. 91 —S.H. (12/1/2004)

CATERINA

Caterina 1999 Cabernet Sauvignon (Columbia Valley (WA)) $20. All Cabernet, as this winemaker likes pure varietals. The nose is quite chocolatey, and the wine carries medium fruit flavors, firm and varietal, with fairly stiff tannins. 88 —P.G. (12/31/2002)

Caterina 1998 Cabernet Sauvignon (Washington) $24. This very much emulates the style of the Merlot, with forward fruit, a hint of spice, and some coffee and clove in the finish. It's a bit heftier, darker, and more tannic than the Merlot, but equally approachable and well-balanced. 87 —P.G. (10/1/2001)

Caterina 1997 Cabernet Sauvignon (Columbia Valley (WA)) $19. 84 —S.H. (11/15/2000)

Caterina 1999 DuBrul Vineyard Cabernet Sauvignon (Yakima Valley) $28. DuBrul is a rising star vineyard whose grapes have found their way into a dozen or more boutique winery bottlings; this is the first from Caterina. Tasty and sweetly scented with plum, cherry, and red fruits, it's deceptively simple, a bit unfocused at first. Yet hours later, it has gathered itself together into a deeper, more satisfying wine. 208 cases made. **89** —*P.G.* *(12/31/2002)*

Caterina 1999 Willard Family Vineyard Cabernet Sauvignon (Yakima Valley) $28. This exceptional bottle features fully ripe, compact fruit, with classic cassis and black cherry flavors at its core. Streaks of earth and iron suggest that the vineyard has a distinctive terroir, and the wine has the muscle to age well for a decade or more. **91** —*P.G.* *(12/31/2002)*

Caterina 1998 Willard Family Vineyard Cabernet Sauvignon (Columbia Valley (WA)) $30. Here's the dark, concentrated intensity one looks for in the best Washington Cabernets, yet it also retains an elegance, a lightness on its feet, that is often sacrificed in the pursuit of pure power. Smooth, almost silky, it's a ripe, fruity wine, bolstered with just the right acid/tannin counterweight, and finished with lush, layered flavors of plum, clove and spice. **90** —*P.G.* *(10/1/2001)*

Caterina 2000 Chardonnay (Columbia Valley (WA)) $13. Still young, raw and a bit oaky, this well-balanced wine just needs some more time to smooth itself out. All the right elements are there, from the polished fruit to the tangy acids to the toasty oak (slightly more than half is barrel fermented). This is a firm, fruity style, well-made and lively. **88 Best Buy** —*P.G.* *(7/1/2002)*

Caterina 1999 Merlot (Columbia Valley (WA)) $20. This is 100% Merlot, smooth and high toned, showing ripe cherry, chocolate, and tobacco flavors. There are definite nail-polish scents and flavors, but they burn off a bit. Pretty and sweet, it's fairly high in tannin, which gives it a somewhat chewy finish. **88** —*P.G.* *(12/31/2002)*

Caterina 1998 Merlot (Columbia Valley (WA)) $24. The nose is open and inviting, with soft scents of coffee and chocolate complementing the pretty cherry/berry fruit. It follows through in the mouth with lightly spicy fruit and a generous plumpness; pretty and engaging. Not a big, powerful wine, but delicious. **87** —*P.G.* *(10/1/2001)*

Caterina 1997 Merlot (Columbia Valley (WA)) $19. **86** —*S.H.* *(11/15/2000)*

Caterina 1999 DuBrul Vineyard Merlot (Yakima Valley) $30. A lot to like here. Firm, tart cherry, and cassis fruit sets the tone. It's still packed and a bit reticent, but opens beautifully into a wine of layered elegance, with firm, age-worthy tannins. **91** —*P.G.* *(9/1/2002)*

Caterina 1999 Willard Family Vineyard Merlot (Yakima Valley) $28. A powerful wine, built upon ripe, fat berry-cherry fruit. It's nicely framed with oak; juicy and delicious, yet certainly ageworthy. 190 cases made. **89** —*P.G.* *(12/31/2002)*

Caterina 1998 Willard Family Vineyard Merlot (Columbia Valley (WA)) $30. This wine has a promising, deep black cherry color to it, and it's scented with dark, roasted coffee, tobacco, and spice. The fruit seems perfectly ripe and balanced, though not jammy or raisiny in any way, and it includes nuances of herb and leaf that add a lot of flavor interest. Classy winemaking, with texture and depth in a drink-now style. 227 cases produced. **90** —*P.G.* *(10/1/2001)*

Caterina 1999 Rosso Red Blend (Washington) $15. A blend of Merlot and Cabernet Sauvignon, the Rosso is a hearty wine with a big, coffee-scented nose showing rich, textured fruit and interesting, gamey, "country" flavors. A lot of rich, textured fruit for such a humble blend. **88** —*P.G.* *(6/1/2002)*

Caterina 2002 Sauvignon Blanc (Columbia Valley (WA)) $15. Quite dry, all stainless fermentation, with plenty of herbal components as the wine rounds into maturity. It develops some pretty cotton candy scents as it warms in the glass also. **89** —*P.G.* *(4/1/2006)*

Caterina 2001 Sauvignon Blanc (Columbia Valley (WA)) $10. This is all Sauv Blanc, all stainless steel-fermented fruit from the Willard and Gordon Brothers vineyards. It offers bracing grapefruit scents and flavors that make it a perfect oyster wine as we head into winter. Crisp and steely, the emphasis is on the racy, vivid fruit. **88 Best Buy** —*P.G.* *(12/31/2002)*

Caterina 2000 Sauvignon Blanc (Columbia Valley (WA)) $10. Made in a crisp, clean style, this lovely wine mixes ripe, round fruit with firm acids. Balanced and brisk, there is a spicy elegance that carries into the lingering finish, with just the merest hint of sweetness. **88 Best Buy** —*P.G.* *(6/1/2002)*

Caterina 2003 Willard Family Vineyard Viognier (Washington) $20. This is fragrant and very pretty with lime/tangerine orange peel citrus scents. On the palate it is soft and smooth, without the bitterness that Viognier can show. Very nice effort, a bit light in the back end, but clean and very aromatic all the way through, with flavors of rose petals and orange peel. Delightful bottle, just 13.5% alcohol. **90** —*P.G.* *(4/1/2006)*

CATHY MACGREGOR

Cathy MacGregor 1998 MacGregor Vineyard Chardonnay (Edna Valley) $30. Smoky, heavy toasted oak complements mild tropical fruit, nuts and coconut on the nose. The toasty flavor and a decidedly earthy note reads big against the pineapple, citrus, and rich vanilla notes showing in the palate of this even, medium-weight wine. Finishes dry, brisk, and slightly tart. **88** *(7/1/2001)*

Cathy MacGregor 1998 Benito Dusi Vineyard Zinfandel (Paso Robles) $26. Waaaaaay big in the mouth, this limited-release Zin (we're talking 198 cases) has a metallic-grapefruit note that cuts into tart blackberry and oak on the palate. Closes with tart grape skin, oak, ink, and molasses flavors. Linger over the bouquet's lilac, lavender, and stewy blackberry nose. **84** —*D.T.* *(3/1/2002)*

CAVE B

Cave B 2002 Famiglia Vineyards Cabernet Sauvignon (Columbia Valley (WA)) $30. Cherry fruit and a strong herbal, earthy component tells the story here. The fruit shows some concentration, but at the expense of rough tannins and a bit of heat in the finish. **85** —*P.G.* *(12/15/2005)*

Cave B 2003 Janine's Vineyard Chardonnay (Columbia Valley (WA)) $20. Light and buttery, with baked apple fruit and notes of cinnamon; it sounds more like a breakfast pastry than a wine but the flavors are soft and pleasant and it all hangs together well. **87** —*P.G.* *(12/15/2005)*

Cave B 2001 Janine's Vineyard Chardonnay (Columbia Valley (WA)) $30. A very soft, approachable wine with plenty of oak flavor behind light tropical, banana-flavored fruit. Only 25 cases produced. **85** —*P.G.* *(1/1/2004)*

Cave B 2002 Famiglia Vineyards Merlot (Columbia Valley (WA)) $30. This wine shows some stuffing, with black cherry/black olive flavors and thick, rough tannins. Notes of moist earth, barnyard, and alcohol burn through the finish. Though the label says 14% alcohol, it feels higher. **85** —*P.G.* *(12/15/2005)*

Cave B 2000 Jersey's Vineyard Merlot (Columbia Valley (WA)) $45. Strong earthy scents of black olive and barnyard dominate the nose. The flavors mix black cherry fruit with earth and stem; tannins are quite firm and a bit green. **85** —*P.G.* *(1/1/2004)*

Cave B 2002 Cuvée du Soleil Red Blend (Columbia Valley (WA)) $35. The best of the winery's new releases, this 45% Cab, 45% Merlot, 10% Cab Franc blend has more nuanced fruit, mixing black cherry, plum, ripe hints of raisin and prune with whiffs of spice and smoke. The rough edges have been smoothed, and the long finish includes pleasing streaks of vanilla. **88** —*P.G.* *(12/15/2005)*

Cave B 2003 Kimberley's Vineyard Sémillon (Columbia Valley (WA)) $25. This 100% Sémillon was barrel fermented in French oak, 60% new. Soft and showing flavors of roasted nuts mixed with honey-coated figs, it is a very good effort, soft and pleasing to the palate. Ready right now. **87** —*P.G.* *(12/15/2005)*

Cave B 2001 Kimberley's Vineyard Sémillon (Columbia Valley (WA)) $35. Lots of brash new oak evident here, masking the light, melony fruit with big, toasty graham cracker flavors. Just 173 cases produced. **85** —*P.G.* *(1/1/2004)*

CAYALLA

Cayalla 2004 RTW Red Blend (Columbia Valley (WA)) $13. A blend of Cab Sauvignon and Franc, Merlot, and Syrah from the makers of Firesteed wines. This clean, accessible Columbia Valley red wine includes mixed red and blue fruits, soft tannins and a medium to light palate weight. It's smooth and fruit-driven, with consistent follow-through flavors that are well integrated. The finish carries the slightest suggestion of oak. **88 Best Buy** —*P.G.* *(6/1/2006)*

CAYMUS

Caymus 1997 Cabernet Sauvignon (Napa Valley) $70. **91** *(11/1/2000)*

USA

Caymus 2003 Cabernet Sauvignon (Napa Valley) $70. This extraordinary wine possesses an enormous wealth of black cherry, blueberry, cassis, and espresso flavors, wrapped in fine, well-toasted oak. Has that rare quality of elegance, in which all the parts work together in harmony. Thoroughly dry, it's marked by a firm, astringent tannic structure now, but is a certain cellar candidate. Should begin to blossom by 2008 and hold through 2015. **94 Cellar Selection** —*S.H. (6/1/2006)*

Caymus 2002 Cabernet Sauvignon (Napa Valley) $70. Manages to feel both soft and tannic at the same time, which means it's fine now but should age for a few years. The black currant and smoky oak flavors are harmonious, with sweet fruit lasting through a long finish. **90** —*S.H. (3/1/2005)*

Caymus 2000 Cabernet Sauvignon (Napa Valley) $70. Smooth, sleek texture supports this balanced wine, redolent of blackberry, black currant, licorice, toast, and herbs. On the finish, it's plush, long, and well crafted, ending with a bright cedary note. **91** —*J.M. (4/1/2003)*

Caymus 1999 Cabernet Sauvignon (Napa Valley) $70. Dense, dark, and deep—it's the three Ds of Napa Cabernet on full display. Aromas of plumcake and bacon get it going, followed by kirsch and blueberry flavors. The smoky, woody finish has essences of campfire, chocolate, and espresso. This packs a ton of flavor and it's highly recommended for fans of powerful California wines. **93** —*M.S. (11/15/2002)*

Caymus 1998 Cabernet Sauvignon (Napa Valley) $70. Creamy black cherry aromas layered with fresh brussel sprouts and spicy arugula flavors of red plums and toasted oak. **89** *(6/26/2002)*

Caymus 2003 Special Selection Cabernet Sauvignon (Napa Valley) $136. Young and dense, almost misleading in its soft fruitiness, but there's tremendous power, and despite the appearance of approachability, it would be a mistake not to cellar this wine. It's explosive in fruit and berry flavors, and the tannins are so melted, you could easily open it tonight. But this is a wine with proven ageability. Should begin to mature by 2010 and drink well through 2020, at least. **93 Cellar Selection** —*S.H. (9/1/2006)*

Caymus 2002 Special Selection Cabernet Sauvignon (Napa Valley) $136. This young wine is fairly tough now, and the fruit is hiding behind the oak and tannins. Like many keepers, it's in a trough, and will go through its ups and downs. Eventually, the cherries and blackberries should emerge, but it doesn't seem like one of the great Special Selections. **91** —*S.H. (10/1/2005)*

Caymus 2001 Special Selection Cabernet Sauvignon (Napa Valley) $136. A lush textured wine that shows gobs of blackberry, cherry, plum, coffee, spice, herb, and anise flavors, all framed in firm, ripe tannins. The finish is long, with a spicy edge. Quite intense and full-on. **93** —*J.M. (12/31/2004)*

Caymus 2000 Special Selection Cabernet Sauvignon (Napa Valley) $136. A bright-edged wine, redolent of Bing cherry, raspberry, blackberry, anise, spice, cedar, and herb flavors. Tannins are powdery, firm, and ripe. They frame the wine in a toasty embrace, ending with a plush finish. Consistently a benchmark from the heartland of California Cabernet. **93** —*J.M. (12/15/2003)*

Caymus 2003 Conundrum White Blend (California) $24. Lots of fresh grapefruit, apricot, peach, wildflower, and spice flavors in this crisp, clean wine. The complex mélange of flavors keeps it fun. **85** —*S.H. (10/1/2005)*

Caymus 2001 Conundrum White Blend (California) $24. Rich and lush, full bodied yet silky on the palate. This unusual blend of Chardonnay, Sauvignon Blanc, Sémillon, Viognier, and Muscat grapes lives up to its name. Nonetheless, it's well integrated, with peach, pear, apple, toast, and spice flavors. **89** —*J.M. (2/1/2003)*

CAYUSE

Cayuse 2003 Camaspelo Bordeaux Blend (Walla Walla (WA)) $55. Cayuse's Bordeaux blend shows remarkable complexity and detail for such a young red wine. Earthy undergrowth, autumnal fungus, some sweetness in the fruit, some brown sugar; it's got so much going on. Long and lingering, it's a fascinating mix of herb, mushroom, cranberry, rock, all interwoven with some pretty, spicy sweet oak. **92** —*P.G. (4/1/2006)*

Cayuse 1999 Syrah (Walla Walla (WA)) $40. The lavish oak provides vanilla and coconut shadings on the tart dark-berry fruit. Its even, polished palate offers plum, coffee, and cocoa flavors. Finishes a touch short, with espresso and bitter chocolate. It's very dark, perhaps a bit one-dimensional, but good of this type. **85** *(11/1/2001)*

Cayuse 2003 Cailloux Vineyard Syrah (Walla Walla (WA)) $55. Incredible fruit intensity. Cranberry, pomegranate, and cherry meet rock, gravel, and pepper. Lovely focus and purity; it's concentrated and tight, with a minerality that is compelling and distinctive. The best yet from Cailloux. Syrah is co-fermented with 4 or 5% Viognier. It's a world-class effort, still quite young and tight, but built for beautiful aging. **95 Cellar Selection** —*P.G. (4/1/2006)*

Cayuse 2002 Cailloux Vineyard Syrah (Walla Walla (WA)) $55. Even more herbal, and more tart, than the winery's En Cerise bottling. Offers peppery aromas and sour red fruit and chocolate flavors, and is streaked with green through and through. Mouthfeel is creamy, but the finish is tart. **85** *(9/1/2005)*

Cayuse 2003 En Cerise Vineyard Syrah (Walla Walla (WA)) $55. The En Cerise is all Syrah; very dark, young, and toasty. It already shows streaks of smoke, pepper, grilled meat, cassis and pomegranate. There's baby fat—bacon, wood spice—but terroir behind it. Herbs, grainy fruit, nuances of grain and herb and wood and earth, all very clean. **93 Editors' Choice** —*P.G. (4/1/2006)*

Cayuse 2002 En Cerise Vineyard Syrah (Walla Walla (WA)) $55. Has aromas of hickory smoke and blueberry, and flavors of red berries. An herbal/rhubarby undercurrent was a detraction for some, and a bonus for others. Medium-weight and creamy in the mouth, this Syrah closes long and mouthwatering. 285 cases produced. **88** *(9/1/2005)*

Cayuse 2000 Cailloux Vineyard Viognier (Walla Walla (WA)) $28. Cayuse is really on a roll, as the inspired fanatic Christophe Baron methodically plants small plots of rock-strewn Walla Walla vineyard. Cailloux (formerly Cobblestone) was his first, and the single acre of Viognier yielded just 120 cases of wine in 2000, but what a wine! Succulent, glorious, peach-scented fruit mingles with butterscotch rum and a distinct impression of the stony, mineral "terroir" that makes the vineyard exceptional. Full malolactic fermentation and aging in neutral French oak render a Condrieu-styled Washington Viognier that ranks with the best in the country. **92** —*P.G. (10/1/2001)*

Cayuse 2004 Cailloux Vineyard Viognier Viognier (Walla Walla (WA)) $21. Beautifully fragrant with citrus blossom and beeswax, lime, and Meyer lemon. In the mouth it is wonderfully full with white peaches, apricot, citrus rind, hints of gooseberry, some honey and tea flavors also. Long, silky, persistent, clean, and pure. In the glass it seems to gain flesh as it smoothes and rounds out; truly a wonderful, silky, voluptuous wine—as good as it gets. **93 Editors' Choice** —*P.G. (4/1/2006)*

CE2V

CE2V 2001 Meritage Cabernet Blend (Napa Valley) $75. A big, big Cab blend, lush and opulent in well-ripened cherries and cassis, with oak doing its vanilla and toast thing. The tannins are soft, smooth, and almost fully resolved, making this wine drink well now. **90** —*S.H. (8/1/2005)*

CE2V 2000 Meritage (Napa Valley) $75. A soft, cuddly sort of wine. A core of ripe fruit nestles inside layers of toast, caramel, and dried spices; it's supple and easy from start to finish. **88** —*J.C. (5/1/2004)*

CE2V 2000 Estate Bottled Sangiovese (Napa Valley) $30. From Mitch Cosentino's estate vineyard, a wine whose aroma is dominated by the perfume of well-charred oak, with vanilla overtones. Beneath is a burst of black cherry and raspberry fruit, and a rich scent of dark honey. In the mouth, the wine is overly sweet, almost sappy, and lacks delicacy and charm. **84** —*S.H. (9/1/2003)*

CE2V 2000 Sauvignon Blanc (Napa Valley) $25. Spicy fruit marks this deliciously drinkable wine, with apple, melon, and citrus veering into tropical fruit flavors. It's crisply round and polished, and slightly sweet, with a degree of complexity. The palate is especially packed with dusty Asian spices and quince. **87** —*S.H. (12/1/2001)*

CE2V 2001 Estate Bottled Sauvignon Blanc (Napa Valley) $25. Smells simple, with vague notes of citrus fruits, but just the opposite in the mouth.

USA

Takes control of the palate with big, oaky flavors of citrus jam, wood, and lots of peppery spices, and finishes rather sweet. A bit over the top. **84** —*S.H. (7/1/2003)*

CEAGO VINEGARDEN

Ceago Vinegarden 2001 Camp Masut Cabernet Sauvignon (Mendocino) $32. Here's a wine that strikes you as pretty good as far as it goes, but the palate yearns for greater complexity. It's dry and polished, with rich tannins and a fine balance, but those cherry and blackberry flavors finish a tad thin, especially considering the price. **84** —*S.H. (12/15/2005)*

Ceago Vinegarden 2000 Clone 337 Cabernet Sauvignon (Mendocino) $38. From Jim Fetzer, a wine from biodynamically grown grapes, and a study in progress. There is some real complexity here, with those telltale cassis and currant flavors associated with Napa, and rich, fine tannins. Has a few rough edges, but clearly a label to watch. **88** —*S.H. (11/15/2003)*

Ceago Vinegarden 2005 Del Lago Chardonnay (Mendocino) $18. The vineyard is in inland Hopland, and the wine has that warm-climate fruitiness. It shows tremendous peach, apricot, pineapple, and pear flavors, with a slightly rustic, sweet finish. **84** —*S.H. (12/1/2006)*

Ceago Vinegarden 2004 Jeriko Vineyard Chardonnay (Mendocino) $18. This powerfully flavored Chardonnay is laserlike in the intensity of its fruit. Mangoes, pineapples, and lemon custard assault the palate, wrapped in a creamy smooth texture. Not particularly subtle, and not for the faint-hearted, this is a quintessentially ripe California wine. **87** —*S.H. (12/15/2005)*

Ceago Vinegarden 2000 Camp Lema Merlot (Mendocino County) $30. Starts off with scents of black currants and smoky oak, with pretty notes of vanilla, violets, and chocolate. Lives up to its promise on the palate, where flavors of currants, chocolate, and herbs are wrapped in some astringent tannins. **88** —*S.H. (2/1/2004)*

Ceago Vinegarden 2001 Camp Masut Merlot (Mendocino) $25. This ambitious brand continues to struggle, in its organic-biodynamic way, to master its Mendocino terroir. This Merlot is clean, dry, and very pure, with cherry flavors, yet it needs greater intensity and complexity, and a longer finish. **84** —*S.H. (12/15/2005)*

Ceago Vinegarden 1999 McNab Ranch Merlot (Mendocino County) $39. A brilliant, rich wine, packed with full-bodied flavors but oozing with finesse and elegance. The tastes veer to plums, blackberries, and chocolate, and the finish is dry and complex. The tannins are thick but soft. This delicious wine was made by Jim Fetzer with organically-grown grapes. **91** —*S.H. (8/1/2003)*

Ceago Vinegarden 2005 Del Lago Muscat Canelli (Clear Lake) $22. Lots of crisp acidity in this pleasantly sweet dessert wine. The acids help make it tangy and clean, while the tangerine, peach, mango, vanilla, spice, and honey flavors are just delicious. And with 8% alcohol, it's easy to drink. **87** —*S.H. (12/1/2006)*

Ceago Vinegarden 2000 Petite Sirah (Mendocino County) $30. Pours dark and gives off inviting aromas of plums, currants, herbs, earth, smoky bacon, pepper, and rich, toasty oak. As good as these are, the flavors are better. They are huge, and spread black currants, olive tapenade, chocolate, and sweet vanillins all over the palate. The tannins are significant, but they are ripe and easy to deal with, in this delicious, dry, classic "Pet" wine. **92** —*S.H. (12/31/2003)*

Ceago Vinegarden 2005 Kathleen's Vineyard Sauvignon Blanc (Clear Lake) $18. The owners, a branch of the Fetzers, make a big deal about being biodynamic, and the wine does seem to have a laser-like purity of citrus zest and grapefruit sorbet flavor that's so clean and vibrant. The tech notes say there was some new oak, but you can hardly sense it; since the fruit and acidity are so upfront. **86** —*S.H. (12/1/2006)*

Ceago Vinegarden 2002 Kathleen's Vineyard Sauvignon Blanc (Mendocino County) $17. A perky white wine, with flavors of lemons, grapefruits, and figs, and a richer streak of white peach. Drinks very dry, with quite a bit of tingly acidity, and finishes clean and spicy. **85** —*S.H. (12/1/2003)*

Ceago Vinegarden 2001 Kathleen's Vineyard Sauvignon Blanc (Mendocino County) $19. An irresistibly drinkable white wine, filled with the juiciest flavors of citrus fruits, fig, melon, and peach, and just the tiniest bit sweet. Crisp acidity cleanses the palate and leaves it feeling minty fresh on the long, spicy finish. **88** —*S.H. (7/1/2003)*

Ceago Vinegarden 2005 Del Lago Syrah Rosé Syrah (Clear Lake) $18. Rather dark and full-bodied for a blush wine, with candied raspberry and cherry flavors and a spicy, vanilla-sweet finish. I like the flavors, but the heaviness and sweetness are awkward. **83** —*S.H. (12/1/2006)*

CECCHETTI SEBASTIANI CELLAR

Cecchetti Sebastiani Cellar 2000 Pinot Noir (Central Coast) $14. **81** *(10/1/2002)*

Cecchetti Sebastiani Cellar 1999 Pinot Noir (Central Coast) $14. **82** *(10/1/2002)*

Cecchetti Sebastiani Cellar 2000 Viognier (North Coast) $14. Some tangy apricot, litchee, and melon notes, with a mild-mannered backbone of acidity. **85** —*J.M. (12/15/2002)*

CEDAR MOUNTAIN

Cedar Mountain 1997 Duet Bordeaux Blend (Livermore Valley) $22. **86** —*M.S. (9/1/2000)*

Cedar Mountain 1998 Blanche's Vineyard Reserve Cabernet Sauvignon (Livermore Valley) $50. Recognizably Cabernet, with black currant and cassis aromas, but it's a clumsy, disjointed wine. Feels angular and jagged in the mouth, with an odd mélange of herbal and berry flavors. **83** —*S.H. (9/1/2003)*

Cedar Mountain 1999 Blanches Vineyard Cabernet Sauvignon (Livermore Valley) $22. An awkward Cabernet whose Port-like elements make it disagreeable. It opens with aromas of raisins and vinyl, and turns fiery on the tongue. This is perhaps not surprising from a winery whose specialty is Port. **81** —*S.H. (11/15/2003)*

Cedar Mountain 1998 Cabernet Royale Cabernet Sauvignon (Livermore Valley) $25. Pretty good and tasty, a Port-style wine made from Cabernet Sauvignon. It has flavors of chocolate, crème de cassis, and Kahlúa, and is sweet but not cloying. **87** —*S.H. (11/15/2003)*

Cedar Mountain 1999 Estate Reserve Blanches Vineyard Cabernet Sauvignon (Livermore Valley) $50. Just barely acceptable due to its oddly baked, vegetal, stewed aromas, and heavy mouthfeel, with its suggestions of cough medicine. **82** —*S.H. (11/15/2003)*

Cedar Mountain 2000 Blanche's Vineyard Chardonnay (Livermore Valley) $18. A bizarre wine weird-aromas and flavors. Smells smoky-sweet, like cotton candy, with mint and peach puree, and has similar flavors. Hard to tell if it's dry or sweet. **82** —*S.H. (8/1/2003)*

Cedar Mountain 1998 Blanches Vineyard Chardonnay (Livermore Valley) $18. **84** *(6/1/2000)*

Cedar Mountain 1998 Chardonnay del Sol Chardonnay (Livermore Valley) $25. An eccentric late harvest Chardonnay with some interesting qualities. Underlying flavors of peaches, but sweetness and perhaps a touch of botrytis add apicot notes. There's also a taste like fine espresso sweetened with a teaspoon or two of cane sugar. Excellent acidity keeps things lively. **88** —*S.H. (6/1/2003)*

Cedar Mountain 1997 One Oak Vineyard Merlot (Livermore Valley) $21. Held back for five years, but it hasn't done the wine much good. Earthy, with funky aromas. The flavors aren't bad, veering toward blackberries, but it's still pretty tannic. **84** —*S.H. (8/1/2003)*

Cedar Mountain 2004 Del Arroyo Vineyard Pinot Grigio (Livermore Valley) $11. Opens with pretty aromas of honeysuckle, vanilla custard, honey, and tangerines that make you think it's sweet, but this is a bone-dry wine. Crisp acidity brightens the modest orange flavors; an appropriate apéritif-style wine. **87 Best Buy** —*S.H. (7/1/2005)*

Cedar Mountain 1997 Vintage Port (Amador County) $21. Made from true Port grape varieties, this wine shares many characteristics with a vintage-style Port. It's young and fruity, filled with blueberry and chocolate flavors, and is very smooth and velvety. Lacks the finesse of the real thing, but pretty nice. **87** —*S.H. (9/1/2003)*

Cedar Mountain 1998 Port Royale Red Blend (California) $35. This attempt to marry Cabernet Sauvignon and traditional Port grapes is noble, but falls flat. The sweet chocolatey flavors of the Port grapes jar with the herbal notes of the Cabernet, resulting in a clash the sensitive palate recoils from. **83** —*S.H. (12/15/2003)*

Cedar Mountain 2004 Del Arroyo Vineyard Sauvignon Blanc (Livermore Valley) $12. A solid effort in an easy-drinking, cocktail white wine. It's clean in acidity and has proper lemon and lime flavors, and is basically dry, although you'll pick up on some fruity sweetness in the finish. **84** — *S.H. (8/1/2005)*

Cedar Mountain 2003 Del Arroyo Vineyard Sauvignon Blanc (Livermore Valley) $18. A rustic, country-style wine, with citrusy flavors, some sharp edges and a slightly sweet finish. **83** —*S.H. (8/1/2005)*

Cedar Mountain 1999 Zinfandel (Amador County) $18. Awkward and disjointed, from the vegetal aromas to the mouth-numbing tannins. Drinks very dry. There's some blackberry fruit way down deep, but it's hard to find. **83** —*S.H. (9/1/2003)*

CEDARVILLE

Cedarville 2001 Viognier (El Dorado) $20. On the plus side are ripe, exotic flavors of peaches, white chocolate, sweetened coffee, vanilla, and cotton candy. There's also a burst of bright acidity. One quibble is the texture, which is thick and syrupy. Some will find it delicious. **85** —*S.H. (5/1/2003)*

Cedarville 2001 Zinfandel (El Dorado) $22. Light-textured, with simple cherry, spice, and oak tones. Moderate length on the finish. **82** *(11/1/2003)*

Cedarville 2000 Zinfandel (El Dorado) $22. Pretty expensive for a Sierra Foothills Zin. Yes, there are exuberantly ripe flavors of blackberries and cherries, and spices like cinnamon, white pepper, and allspice provide a palate wakeup. But it's a rustic wine, with jagged tannins and a bitter finish. **85** —*S.H. (9/1/2003)*

CEDARVILLE VINEYARD

Cedarville Vineyard 2002 Estate Syrah (El Dorado) $25. A bit funky on the nose, with hints of game and dried herbs alongside pepper, plum and coffee aromas. The mouthfeel is smooth and medium-weight, while the finish turns tannic and a bit rustic. Solid Foothills Syrah. **85** *(9/1/2005)*

CEJA

Ceja 2000 Merlot (Carneros) $32. A good, rather simple red wine. It's rich in cherries and earth, with sturdy tannins. **83** —*S.H. (3/1/2005)*

Ceja 2002 Syrah (Sonoma Coast) $28. Big disagreement over this wine, with West Coast Editor Steve Heimoff lauding it for its balance and ripe black cherry flavors, while Tasting Director Joe Czerwinski found it a bit vegetal (green bean). It does have a supple, creamy mouthfeel and a pleasant finish of coffee and herb. **87** *(9/1/2005)*

Ceja 2001 Syrah (Sonoma County) $28. Complex, with plum, clove, oaky vanilla and grilled meat notes. Drinks very dry, with firm tannins. Shows real style in the overall balance and harmony. **86** —*S.H. (3/1/2005)*

CELADON TV

Celadon TV 2002 Esperanza Vineyard Grenache (Clarksburg) $20. A lovely, fresh and focused white wine that offers a classy blend of melon, peach, apple, apricot, herb, and mineral flavors. These are layered in a complex, yet easy-to-drink manner. Smooth yet firm, it's got great balance and a good finish. **90** —*J.C. (10/1/2004)*

CELLAR NO. 8

Cellar No. 8 2003 Cabernet Sauvignon (California) $10. What a great price. This Cab, with a splash of Petite Sirah and Carignane, shows real depth with ripe blackberry and coffee flavors, subtle oak notes, firm tannins and a long, dry finish. With grapes from Paso Robles, Knights Valley, and Lake County, the wine is a testament to the art of blending. **87 Best Buy** —*S.H. (12/31/2006)*

Cellar No. 8 2002 Cabernet Sauvignon (California) $10. Dry and sharp, this wine is not very good. It has harsh tannins and stemmy green flavors, with a dollop of blackberry. **81** —*S.H. (4/1/2006)*

Cellar No. 8 2001 Cabernet Sauvignon (North Coast) $14. Lots to like in this new brand from Beringer, which was made at the old Italian Swiss Colony winery at Asti. It's filled with ripe, rich black currant flavors that are well-oaked, and backed up with firm, sweet tannins. Finishes a bit astringent. **86** —*S.H. (5/1/2004)*

Cellar No. 8 2004 Merlot (California) $10. The name comes from the old Italian Swiss Colony building in Alexander Valley where the wine is made. It's the kind of dry, tannic, and berry-rich red wine the Colony churned out for decades, to drink with anything and everything from the kitchen. **84** —*S.H. (12/31/2006)*

Cellar No. 8 2003 Merlot (California) $10. A little rough around the edges, but this is a pretty good price if you're looking for a dry, balanced and full-bodied red wine. It has fruity and earthy flavors. **84** —*S.H. (3/1/2006)*

Cellar No. 8 2001 Merlot (North Coast) $14. A nice Merlot with polished flavors of plums, blackberries, and coffee, and a good overlay of smoky oak. It's very dry, but the fruit is ripe and sweet. Finishes with a rich mouthfeel and some acidity. **85** —*S.H. (5/1/2004)*

Cellar No. 8 2004 Zinfandel (California) $10. Tough and country-style, a dry, rugged little wine with upfront wild berry and spice flavors. **82** — *S.H. (12/31/2006)*

Cellar No. 8 2003 Zinfandel (California) $10. Raspingly dry and tannicly astringent, with barely any fruit at all, this Zin is clean, at least. **80** — *S.H. (10/1/2006)*

Cellar No. 8 2002 Zinfandel (North Coast) $14. From the less than ripe aromas of stalky greenness to the thin mouthfeel and astringent finish, this is a pretty common wine. Turns medicinal on the finish. **83** —*S.H. (10/1/2005)*

Cellar No. 8 2001 Zinfandel (North Coast) $14. This is yummy Zin, packed with rich, ripe cherry-berry fruit, tobacco, spice, and chocolate, and it's bone dry and moderate in alcohol. It's a big, flavorful wine, yet has balance and charm. Finishes with a scour of acids and astringent tannins, suggesting barbecued steak or roast lamb. **89 Best Buy** —*S.H. (5/1/2004)*

CENAY

Cenay 2001 Blue Tooth Vineyard Cabernet Sauvignon (Napa Valley) $30. Certainly riper and more extracted than the 2000 vintage, this baby is big and fat, and drinkable now. It has very ripe and extracted blackberry flavors and a solid overlay of oak, and the tannins are sweet and complex. Pair with a rich steak, the best you can get. **91 Editors' Choice** —*S.H. (10/1/2004)*

Cenay 2000 Blue Tooth Vineyard Cabernet Sauvignon (Napa Valley) $30. A fine Cabernet in the international style. Well-ripened black currant and herb flavors, supersmooth, and soft tannins, and a rich but nuanced overlay of smoky oak. Defines the current style in Napa, but it's hard to detect any originality or terroir. **89** —*S.H. (12/15/2003)*

Cenay 1999 Blue Tooth Vineyard Cabernet Sauvignon (Napa Valley) $30. This immensely likeable wine, from the Oak Knoll section of the valley, avoids the overly fat, soft fruit of warmer areas, while preserving vital acidity. There's plenty of cassis fruit, and 50% new oak, but it's wonderfully balanced, with a modest 13.5% alcohol. You might easily mistake it for a fine St.-Julien, it's that good. **93** —*S.H. (6/1/2002)*

Cenay 2000 Rodger's Vineyard Pinot Noir (Napa Valley) $26. Pronounced tobacco and earth notes on the nose and palate give this dark, handsome wine plenty of appeal, though some found it facile and entirely barrel-derived. Shows a rich mouthfeel, meaty, smoky elements on dry yet juicy tart cherry fruit and a long, flavorful finish. Drink now-2007. **88** *(10/1/2004)*

Cenay 2002 Rodgers Vineyard Pinot Noir (Napa Valley) $34. Smells rich and oaky, with spicy, vanilla notes. Pretty hard in tannins now, but this big wine has a rich, ripe core of cherries and raspberries and a sweetly fruity finish. Should improve in a year or two. **87** *(11/1/2004)*

Cenay 2001 Rodgers Vineyard Pinot Noir (Napa Valley) $26. From the cooler Oak Knoll region of southern Napa, a wine with berry-cherry flavors and silky tannins. Yet it feels coarse and heavy, with a density and dullness Pinot Noir should not have. Suggests once again the unsuitability of Napa Valley for Pinot Noir. **84** —*S.H. (7/1/2003)*

Cenay 1999 Rodgers Vineyard Pinot Noir (Napa Valley) $26. A heavy woodiness dominates the nose, which otherwise offers cola, molasses,

USA

and plum. That same plum fruit carries into the mouth, where the acidity is powerful, making a food match a necessity. **85** *(10/1/2002)*

CENTURY OAK

Century Oak 2002 Cabernet Sauvignon (Lodi) $13. Here's a soft, simple Cabernet with decent flavors of cherries, blackberries, and coffee. It's dry and balanced, with a polished finish. **83** —*S.H. (12/31/2005)*

Century Oak 2002 Reserve Cabernet Sauvignon (Lodi) $20. A tedious wine, overly soft and with an acidic sharpness. Not as good as the winery's regular Cabernet. **81** —*S.H. (12/31/2005)*

Century Oak 2001 Reserve Cabernet Sauvignon (Lodi) $20. Nice texture, rich and soft in tannins, yet not offering much in the way of flavor. Drinks very dry, with modest berry and earth notes. **84** —*S.H. (3/1/2005)*

Century Oak 2002 Old Vine Zinfandel (Lodi) $13. The berry, cherry, coffee, and spice flavors are wrapped in a rustically textured wine, with an acidic sharpness that persists into the finish. **82** —*S.H. (12/31/2005)*

CERRO CALIENTE

Cerro Caliente 2001 Cabernet Sauvignon (Paso Robles) $19. Smells like inexpensive Port, with aromas of raisins, warm brown sugar, and blackberry marmalade. Has those distinctive hot country flavors of Port, too, although it's dry. Smooth tannins round out the fruity finish. **83** —*S.H. (12/15/2003)*

Cerro Caliente 2002 White Cabernet Sauvignon (Paso Robles) $12. On the sweet side, with well-ripened flavors of raspberries and strawberries. Good acidity keeps it crisp and clean in the mouth, and then the wine turns sweet again on the finish. **83** —*S.H. (11/15/2003)*

Cerro Caliente 2004 Chardonnay (Edna Valley) $20. Shows the bright acidity and citrus of the appellation, and is clean and dry, but could certainly use more fruity concentration. **83** —*S.H. (10/1/2006)*

Cerro Caliente 2001 Chardonnay (Edna Valley) $18. Drinks rough and ready, with a sandpapery texture and a gritty, peppery finish. There's some nice stone fruit flavor but the rustic style is a letdown. **83** —*S.H. (10/1/2003)*

Cerro Caliente 1999 Barrel Reserve Merlot (Paso Robles) $25. Smells bizarre and unclean, with dill pickle and vegetable notes. Feels awkward in the mouth, too. Syrupy thick, flat in acids, and with the taste of cherry cough medicine. **80** —*S.H. (12/15/2003)*

Cerro Caliente 2005 Pinot Grigio (Edna Valley) $20. This is a nice, easy-to-like PG. It's crisp in acidity, with forward melon, lemon, and lime, and date flavors, and while it's dry, it finishes with a honeyed sweetness. Try with avocado and crab salad or a rich baked ham. **85** —*S.H. (10/1/2006)*

Cerro Caliente 2002 Pinot Grigio (Edna Valley) $16. Opens with fruity, lemon and lime aromas, with a funky edge to them. In the mouth, the wine coats the palate with citrus, apple, and apricot notes. Very dry, with no trace of wood; finishes clean and zesty. **84** —*S.H. (12/1/2003)*

Cerro Caliente 2004 Dixon Ranch Vineyard Pinot Noir (Edna Valley) $24. Has a pretty color, a nice, ruby translucency, and polished aromas and flavors ranging from ripe cherries and cola to deeper notes of pomegranates and spice. The mouthfeel is delicate and lilting, but the high alcohol, 15.2%, is a little hot on the finish. **87** —*S.H. (11/1/2006)*

Cerro Caliente 2001 Syrah (Edna Valley) $23. This wine is inky black and smells like Port, with sweetened black currant jam, caramel, and bubble gum scents. But in the mouth, it's bone dry and sturdily tannic. Buried deep is a solid core of peppery blackberry fruit. **84** —*S.H. (12/15/2003)*

Cerro Caliente 2003 Dixon Ranch Vineyard Syrah (Edna Valley) $24. This is a fine, dry wine that proves how amenable the region's cool climate is for making great Syrah. The fruit is lush, filling the mouth with raspberry, cherry, mocha, and vanilla flavors, with a cedary, leathery complexity. Notable for the smooth, supple tannins. **91** —*S.H. (11/1/2006)*

CHADDSFORD

Chaddsford 2001 Merican Bordeaux Blend (Pennsylvania) $40. Shows its age with its dearth of extract and rusting at the rim. This Bordeaux-style blend has some brett qualities that this reviewer found added character. The wine has an almost creamy feel and moderate tannins, with cassis and blueberry, touched with wet tobacco in the mouth. Finishes with a metallic note. **86** —*M.D. (8/1/2006)*

Chaddsford 2001 Cabernet/Chambourcin Cabernet Blend (Pennsylvania) $15. Youthful and gangly, with plum and cherry aromas followed by black fruit and vanilla flavors. On the finish there is pronounced oak and drying tannins, which gives the wine a lean, starching mouthfeel. While it has some style, in the end it doesn't seem to be striving for much. **83** —*M.S. (3/1/2003)*

Chaddsford 1997 Cabernet Franc (Pennsylvania) $13. 87 —*J.C. (8/1/1999)*

Chaddsford 1999 Cabernet Franc (Pennsylvania) $14. Light to the point of being watery, with hints of cherry and green veggies. Sweet-tasting on the finish. **80** —*J.C. (1/1/2004)*

Chaddsford 2003 Cabernet Sauvignon (Pennsylvania) $15. Earth and underripe red vegetable aromas lead to watery flavors of red berry, cinnamon, and earth. Abnormally light-bodied for a Cab, with Band-Aid pervading throughout. **80** —*M.D. (8/1/2006)*

Chaddsford 1999 Cabernet Sauvignon (Pennsylvania) $17. Tastes dull and muted, with cherry flavors that are tinged with green bean and smoldering leaves. **81** —*J.C. (1/1/2004)*

Chaddsford 1998 Seven Valleys Vineyard Chambourcin (Pennsylvania) $16. 83 —*J.C. (8/1/1999)*

Chaddsford 1999 Barrel Select Chardonnay (Pennsylvania) $NA. A soft, low-acid Chard designed for mass appeal, the standard pear and pineapple fruit is tinged with clove and anise. A bit of alcoholic heat comes through on the finish. **84** —*J.C. (1/1/2004)*

Chaddsford 2000 Philip Roth Vineyard Chardonnay (Pennsylvania) $33. Complex and intriguing in the nose, the wine is weighty on the palate and shows a fine blend of citrus, herb, melon, toast, pear, and spice flavors. It finishes long and clean. **91** —*J.C. (7/1/2002)*

Chaddsford 1997 Philip Roth Vineyard Chardonnay (Pennsylvania) $30. 84 —*J.C. (8/1/1999)*

Chaddsford 2003 Merlot (Pennsylvania) $19. Horsey and earthy in the nose, this wine is a nice effort that falls short. Medium in weight, with a smooth feel and nice tannin, blueberry flavors are overcome by mushroom and red cabbage, turning even weirder on the finish. **80** —*M.D. (8/1/2006)*

Chaddsford 1998 Pinot Grigio (Pennsylvania) $15. 87 *(8/1/1999)*

Chaddsford 2004 Pinot Grigio (New York) $16. Plump in the mouth, this New York Pinot Grigio from a Pennsylvania winery is pretty neutral in flavor, with modest hints of apple and citrus providing just enough interest. Ends with a bit of citrus pith. **83** —*J.C. (2/1/2006)*

Chaddsford 2000 Pinot Noir (Pennsylvania) $16. 80 *(10/1/2002)*

Chaddsford 2002 Barrel Select Pinot Noir (Pennsylvania) $25. Very pale in color and light in body, with pretty tea, rose, cola, and spice flavors that pick up sweet raspberries on the finish. **84** *(11/1/2004)*

Chaddsford 2002 Miller Estate Vineyard Pinot Noir (Pennsylvania) $35. Pale, with delicate aromas of tea, rose, cola, and vanilla. Good acidity, and has some interesting flavors of raspberries and root beer in a creamy texture. **85** *(11/1/2004)*

Chaddsford 1999 Merican Red Blend (Pennsylvania) $35. This full-priced Bordeaux-style blend is a bit light on extract but features plenty of tree bark, leather, and cola aromas. Some raspberry and cherry flavors work well on the balanced palate, and the finish is pleasant, if maybe a bit woody. Quite clean, lean and tangy, but expensive given its shallow depth. **85** —*M.S. (3/1/2003)*

Chaddsford 1997 Proprietors Reserve Red Blend (Pennsylvania) $11. 82 —*J.C. (8/1/1999)*

Chaddsford 2000 Proprietor's Reserve White Blend (Pennsylvania) $10. This blend of hybrid grapes (40% Seyval Blanc, 39% Vidal Blanc, 21% Vignoles) yields scents of lime, tonic, and green corn husks. Sweet corn flavors fight with sour lime elements on the finish. **80** —*J.C. (1/1/2004)*

Chaddsford 1997 Proprietors Reserve White Blend (Pennsylvania) $9. 85 —*J.C. (8/1/1999)*

Chaddsford 1998 Spring Wine White Blend (Pennsylvania) $9. 83 —J.C. (8/1/1999)

CHALEUR ESTATE

Chaleur Estate 2004 Blanc Bordeaux White Blend (Columbia Valley (WA)) $31. DeLille Cellars' Bordeaux white is consistently among the best in the country. Rich and buttery, just this side of unctuous, it is smoothly styled with lingering layers of citrus oils, stone fruits, melon, and nuts. Big but not blowsy, broad yet still focused, it weaves together seamlessly, layering in flavors right through the finish. 91 —P.G. (12/15/2005)

CHALK HILL

Chalk Hill 2001 Cabernet Sauvignon (Chalk Hill) $66. Compared to a lush Napa Cab, this has a distinct green olive and French-cured olive character. It must be the terroir, but oak, toasted and spicy, plays an important part. Finally, there's Cabernet's inherent currant flavor. The wine is thoroughly dry and balanced, with smooth tannins. It's a unique Cabernet, but in its own way, very fine. 90 —S.H. (12/1/2005)

Chalk Hill 2000 Cabernet Sauvignon (Chalk Hill) $54. A first rate Cab, notable for the intensity and persistence of its flavors. They include black currants and cassis and the vanilla and smoke from charred oak. Tannins are rich and creamy. But it's the wonderfully rich flavors that startle. 91 —S.H. (6/1/2004)

Chalk Hill 1999 Cabernet Sauvignon (Chalk Hill) $64. Just over the hill from both Napa and Sonoma valleys, Chalk Hill has similar conditions. This nicely ripened wine brims with pure black currant aromas. Shows fine balance and finesse, coming across as light and complex. 90 —S.H. (2/1/2003)

Chalk Hill 2003 Estate Bottled Cabernet Sauvignon (Chalk Hill) $64. Steve Leveque, the winemaker at Chalk Hill, is doing everything right. Everything he touches is gold, including Cabernet. The '03 is extraordinarily balanced and beautiful, a dry, ripe wine of power and full-bodied substance, but enormous subtlety. The cassis fruit meshes seamlessly with toasty new oak to produce compellingly complex flavors. Drink now through 2010. 94 Editors' Choice —S.H. (12/15/2006)

Chalk Hill 1997 Estate Bottled Cabernet Sauvignon (Chalk Hill) $50. 90 (11/1/2000)

Chalk Hill 2002 Chardonnay (Chalk Hill) $36. A well-behaved Chard with a streak of minerality that uplifts the apple and peach flavors, as well as lees and oak. Finishes a bit rough and earthy, with tobacco leaf acidity. 86 —S.H. (12/1/2005)

Chalk Hill 2000 Chardonnay (Chalk Hill) $42. Rich, with a tangy range of flavors from tart green apples through pears and peaches and a hint of pineapple. Well-balanced with creamy, smoky oak, bracing acidity, and dusty brown spices. Picks up a honeyed, resinous quality in the long finish. 90 —S.H. (12/31/2003)

Chalk Hill 2003 Estate Chardonnay (Chalk Hill) $42. Here's a steely, minerally, sleek Chardonnay. Call it Cali-Chablis, if you will. That doesn't mean it's lean. Quite the opposite, it's an enormously complicated wine, with oak, lees, and underlying peach custard and spicy mango cream flavors that finish long and dry. And what great acidity. Makes your mouth water. Chalk Hill is simply doing an amazing job lately, especially with Chardonnay. 93 Editors' Choice —S.H. (11/15/2006)

Chalk Hill 1999 Estate Bottled Chardonnay (Chalk Hill) $42. Expensive, but worth it for the classy aromas and flavors. The peach, pear, and apple notes are polished, and oak contributes smoky, spicy complexities that don't overwhelm. The round, supple texture is accompanied by refreshing acidity, and the finish is long and clean. 92 —S.H. (12/1/2001)

Chalk Hill 1998 Estate Bottled Chardonnay (Chalk Hill) $40. Long known for their powerful, elegant Chardonnays, Chalk Hill's 1998 offering is impressive for its complex array of aromas and flavors. The toasty, leesy, popcorn elements adorn full, richly nuanced sweet pear, pineapple, and peach flavors. A lovely, smooth mouthfeel with a slight granular quality adds texture and interest. This refined wine exudes finesse and refinement. 91 (7/1/2001)

Chalk Hill 2002 Estate Vineyard Selection Chardonnay (Chalk Hill) $67. This ultraexpensive Chardonnay comes down along mineral, steel, and wet stone flavors. It's well-oaked, although you'll find tropical fruit,

subtly, on the finish. It's extremely elegant, with a long draw of acidity and a classic structure. 90 —S.H. (12/1/2005)

Chalk Hill 1999 Estate Vineyard Selection Chardonnay (Chalk Hill) $67. A smooth-drinking Chardonnay that pushes the envelope for size and opulence. Massive tropical fruit is matched with toasty oak. Waves of flavor sensations unfold on the palate, rich and complex. This is a huge, dramatic Chardonnay, but buyers will have to decide if the high price is worth it. 94 Cellar Selection —S.H. (12/15/2002)

Chalk Hill 2000 Merlot (Chalk Hill) $43. This blend of Merlot, Malbec, Cab Franc, and Petit Verdot is layered with blackberry and Indian pudding flavors, generously laced with oriental spices and coffee. It's dry, but the ripeness of the fruit feels sweet through the finish. Soft in acids and tannins; it's instantly drinkable. 89 —S.H. (12/15/2004)

Chalk Hill 1999 Merlot (Chalk Hill) $51. Consciously built along the lines of cult Cabernets, this is a ripe, extracted wine of gentle acids and elaborate oak. It's filled with berry, chocolate, and coffee flavors, but it's actually quite tannic. That drying feeling on the finish suggests cellaring. 90 —S.H. (2/1/2003)

Chalk Hill 1998 Adele's Merlot (Chalk Hill) $100. Opens with unripe aromas of pepper and oregano, then turns extremely dry and tannic. There are some nicely developed blackberry flavors in the middle palate, but they're quickly drowned out by the tannins. Doesn't seem like it's going anywhere. 86 —S.H. (11/15/2002)

Chalk Hill 2001 Estate Merlot (Chalk Hill) $43. There seems to be a great deal of new oak here, to judge by the fresh, strong aromas of vanilla, cedar, and smoky char, but those scents mesh well with the cassis, mocha, peat, and anise that come from fruit. There's also a leathery thing going on, a little sweaty, but it adds a spicy complexity. 89 —S.H. (12/1/2005)

Chalk Hill 2002 Estate Bottled Merlot (Chalk Hill) $43. Warm summer weather ripened the grapes to black cherry and cocoa perfection, while cool nights preserved vital acidity. The oak tastes new and is in full balance with the wine's size. Despite a touch of raisins, this wine should hold and improve for five years before gradually losing fruit. 92 —S.H. (12/15/2006)

Chalk Hill 2002 Estate Vineyard Selection Pinot Gris (Chalk Hill) $40. This is the future of upscale California PG. Made from good grapes in a cool climate, the wine is barrel fermented, aged *sur lies* and given time in the bottle. The result is a dry, tart, delicate yet complex wine. This may be the most expensive PG ever produced in California, but it is an excellent wine. 92 —S.H. (2/1/2006)

Chalk Hill 2000 Estate Vineyard Selection Pinot Gris (Chalk Hill) $40. Crisp and clean drinking here, with lemony and green apple flavors wrapped in a very dry wine. Lively acidity makes the mouthfeel refreshing and zesty. But it seems ridiculously overpriced. 86 —S.H. (9/1/2003)

Chalk Hill 2004 Sauvignon Blanc (Chalk Hill) $25. Richer than the '03, this wine brims with the most savory Meyer lemon, lime, and tart green-apple flavors, boosted and brightened with crisp, minerally acidity. Winemaker Steve Leveque barrel fermented this non-malolactic wine for the first time, to make it a little rounder and creamier. It was a good step; the wine is luscious. 91 —S.H. (8/1/2006)

Chalk Hill 2003 Sauvignon Blanc (Chalk Hill) $25. On the heavy side, with full aromas of toast, baked fruit, and spice. Stylistically, this falls into the category of barrel influenced; there's vanilla, licorice, and resin accents to the spicy apple and melon fruit flavors. Finishes quite dry and spicy, and here the oak notes take over a bit more than they should. 87 (7/1/2005)

Chalk Hill 2001 Sauvignon Blanc (Chalk Hill) $24. Delicate for a California Sauvignon Blanc, with a lilting, airy texture. The flavors are ripe and lush, suggesting spicy lemon yogurt and figs. Hits the palate with a blast of acidity. Finishes sweet although it's technically dry. 90 —S.H. (10/1/2003)

Chalk Hill 1999 Sauvignon Blanc (Chalk Hill) $29. This is one big wine; and in our opinion it's largely overdone. When butter and burnt toast dominate fruit, it's not going to be perceived as being varietally correct, and most tasters will probably struggle to peg it as SB. From a flavor perspective, it's chock full of banana, baked apples, and wood. The finish is resinous and thick. Call it a ripe case of more being less. 85 (8/1/2002)

USA

Chalk Hill 2003 Estate Sauvignon Blanc (Chalk Hill) $25. Lemony and grassy, this very dry, tart wine is refreshing and zesty. *Sur lie* aging has given it body and structure, while a good proportion of new oak gives complex notes of smoke and vanilla. Totally dry. **88** —*S.H. (12/1/2005)*

Chalk Hill 2000 Estate Bottled Sauvignon Blanc (Sonoma County) $29. A very rich wine, with underlying citrus and apple fruit flavors fattened and sweetened with generous oak and lees. High acidity makes everything tingly in the mouth, and the finish is long and generous in this high-class wine. **91** —*S.H. (9/1/2003)*

CHALONE

Chalone 2004 Chardonnay (Monterey County) $12. Kind of on the sweet side, with the flavor of ripe figs and kiwis accented by oak. Even though there's high acidity, which makes for a steely minerality, this wine still finishes too sugary sweet. **84** —*S.H. (3/1/2006)*

Chalone 2003 Chardonnay (Chalone) $30. Here's a soft, full-bodied Chardonnay that has a distinct tang of minerality to it. It's also rich in green apple and white peach flavors, with a coat of toasty oak and a lingering trace of dried herbs on the finish. **88** —*S.H. (12/1/2005)*

Chalone 2002 Chardonnay (Chalone) $25. Easy to detect the mountain origins of this tightly wound wine. It's big in citrusy acids and even has dusty tannins, but there's a sunburst of spiced peach and papaya flavor that make it rich now. A guaranteed ager, and it will be wonderful to follow this wine through its long evolution. **91 Editors' Choice** —*S.H. (12/1/2004)*

Chalone 2001 Chardonnay (Chalone) $25. Very much a mountain-grown Chard, with its lean, tight structure, firm tannins, high acidity, and sleek flavors of citrus and spiced pear. The inherent hardness is softened and enriched through the judicious use of oak and *sur lie* aging, which create a creamy texture. It's young now, and will improve for many years to come. **91** —*S.H. (12/1/2003)*

Chalone 2000 Chardonnay (Chalone) $28. Firm and focused, with a strong mineral-and-citrus core. Pear and apple flavors follow with fresh finish. Well balanced and elegant. **88** —*J.M. (12/15/2002)*

Chalone 1998 Chardonnay (Chalone) $31. 90 —*S.H. (10/1/2000)*

Chalone 1997 Chardonnay (Chalone) $31. 94 —*L.W. (7/1/1999)*

Chalone 2004 Estate Chardonnay (Chalone) $26. There's a soft, earthy weightiness to this Chard, compared to more coastal bottlings that offer brighter acidity. Yet it's tremendously forward in tropical fruit flavors that are very ripe, almost sweet. A little ungainly now, but could knit together in the next five years. **86** —*S.H. (11/15/2006)*

Chalone 2004 Chenin Blanc (Chalone) $22. Someday I'll figure out why anyone in California makes Chenin Blanc, but having said that, Chalone's is one of the best. Dry and high in acids, almost sour, it has ripe flavors of tree fruits, with the weight of a fine Chardonnay. It's a very well made wine. **87** —*S.H. (2/1/2006)*

Chalone 2003 Chenin Blanc (Chalone) $22. Chalone is one of a handful of California wineries that continues to take Chenin Blanc seriously. This is a dry, young wine, balanced and tart in grapefruit flavors. The acidity is quite high. Try as an alternative to Sauvignon Blanc. **86** —*S.H. (7/1/2005)*

Chalone 2002 Chenin Blanc (Chalone) $22. One of the more complex and elegant Chenins in California. Very dry and sleek, with toasted hazelnut and citrus flavors and an enormously rich finish. You don't usually think of Chenin Blanc as an ager, but this one will. **89** —*S.H. (12/1/2004)*

Chalone 2000 Chalone Chenin Blanc (Chalone) $22. Rich, smooth and lush, yet bright and refreshing. The wine is proof that California Chenin Blanc can make a great, dry wine. This one's loaded with gorgeous pear, grapefruit, lemon, mandarin orange, minerals, and herb flavors. Long and rich to the end. **93** —*J.M. (9/1/2003)*

Chalone 2001 Estate Grown Chenin Blanc (Chalone) $22. Crisp yet richly textured, with a blend of lemon, honey, apple, pear, vanilla, and herb flavors that stimulate the palate. Finishes long, with a hint of almonds at the end. **92 Editors' Choice** —*J.M. (5/1/2003)*

Chalone 2003 Grenache (Chalone) $22. This Rhône variety, when well-made in California, is infused with pure cherry flavors, and so it is here.

Very dry, rather pale in color, and light in texture and body, it's well-acidified, with some herbal complexities. Best with Provençal or Mediterranean fare. **88** —*S.H. (8/1/2005)*

Chalone 2004 Merlot (Monterey County) $15. From warmer southern regions of the county comes this ripely juicy, jammy young Merlot. It's powerful in red and black cherry, blackberry, and mocha flavors that are wrapped in smooth, dusty tannins. **85** —*S.H. (12/15/2006)*

Chalone 2004 Pinot Blanc (Chalone) $22. There's a lot of acidity in this wine. It approaches sourness, and is absolutely bone dry, with a rich, ripe core of peach fruit and a long, deep finish. All the elements are there for cellaring for the better part of a decade. **87** —*S.H. (2/1/2006)*

Chalone 2002 Pinot Blanc (Chalone) $22. There's a ton of fruity, spicy extract in this wine, which floods the mouth with pineapple and cinnamon flavors, as well as oak. But it's lively in acidity, keeping it clean and refreshing. Finishes opulently rich and long. Will develop nutty complexities with 4 or 5 years of age. **90** —*S.H. (12/1/2004)*

Chalone 2001 Pinot Blanc (Chalone) $22. A full-bodied, polished wine, a lot like a big Chard with its creamy, leesy texture and peach and pear flavors. But shows its varietal character with a spicy melon note, and has a nice firm backbone of acidity that makes it an ager. **89** —*S.H. (2/1/2004)*

Chalone 2000 Pinot Blanc (Monterey) $24. An opulent, rich white wine, front loaded with yummy sweet oak, vanilla, and butterscotch and backed by hazelnut, apricot, pear, spice, and citrus overtones. Full and long on the finish. **91** —*J.M. (9/1/2003)*

Chalone 1999 Pinot Blanc (Chalone) $24. Very much in the vein of a super-oaked, ripe Chardonnay, bursting with peach and tropical aromas and flavors, but with a distinctly nutty, minerally, almost steely note and an electric jolt of acidity. Judging from the very long, sweet finish, it's got quite a life ahead of it. **91** —*S.H. (2/1/2001)*

Chalone 2003 Estate Pinot Blanc (Chalone) $22. Ripe in peaches and apples, with a creamy texture, this is a rugged Chard-like wine. It's dry, and the oak isn't intrusive. Has a history of aging well, so might improve. **84** —*S.H. (10/1/2005)*

Chalone 1997 Reserve Pinot Blanc (Monterey County) $22. 92 —*L.W. (3/1/2000)*

Chalone 2004 Pinot Noir (Chalone) $35. Chalone continues with its own style, which is not as ripely hedonistic as most other high-end Pinots. But this is the best since 1997. Notable for its balance and harmony, the wine attains great equilibrium of acidity, tannins, oak and cherry fruit. Start drinking this elegant wine in 2008. **90** —*S.H. (11/15/2006)*

Chalone 2003 Pinot Noir (Chalone) $25. Given the historic ageability of Chalone's Pinots, you might want to give this five years in the cellar. Right now, it's a bit heavy and soft, although fruity enough, with a great big burst of black raspberry, cherry, and vanilla flavor. **86** —*S.H. (12/1/2005)*

Chalone 2001 Pinot Noir (Chalone) $25. Chalone's flagship wine in its youth is dark, dense, heavy and tannic. It doesn't show much finesse, and is almost Rhône-like. The winemaker marches to the beat of a drummer who is out of sync with light, delicate Pinot Noirs, but aficionados will stick it in their cellars anyway and keep their fingers crossed. **86** —*S.H. (2/1/2004)*

Chalone 2000 Pinot Noir (Chalone) $30. Juicy fruit and plenty of cinnamon, clove, and chocolate flavors team up in this solid, dark offering. Manages to be tangy and creamy at the same time, ending with woodsy, dried-cherry and spice flavors and easy tannins. Drink now–2006, possibly longer. **88** *(10/1/2002)*

Chalone 1998 Pinot Noir (Chalone) $35. 85 —*S.H. (10/1/2000)*

Chalone 1997 Pinot Noir (Chalone) $31. 90 *(10/1/1999)*

Chalone 2001 Gavilan Rhône Red Blend (Chalone) $30. It's very closed now, except for a whiff of white pepper and cassis. When it hits the palate it spreads hard tannins all over, and feels dried out, like chewing on bark. **84** —*S.H. (12/1/2003)*

Chalone 2003 Syrah (Chalone) $25. Lushly fruity, with layers of blackberries tinged with pie spices, vanilla, and herbs. Doesn't seem to have much structure, so drink now. **85** *(9/1/2005)*

Chalone 2002 Syrah (Chalone) $25. Starts out with a complex melange of aromas, including smoky oak and bacon, then quickly turns fruity in the mouth. Blackberries and cherries co-star, sweet and ripe and pure. Soft tannins make this interesting wine drinkable right away. **88** —*S.H. (12/31/2004)*

Chalone 2001 Syrah (Chalone) $25. Chalone's second Syrah is, in a word, excellent—rich and concentrated in cassis and herb flavors, with accents of smoke, vanilla, and spice. While it's dry and pretty tannic, there's a sweet ripeness that flatters the palate. It's young and sharp now, but the balance suggests ageability. **90** —*S.H. (12/1/2003)*

Chalone 2000 Syrah (Chalone) $30. The wine is front-end loaded with zippy raspberry, cherry, herb, earth, vanilla, chocolate, and blackberry flavors. It's clean and fresh, yet long on the finish. Really lovely. **91** — *J.M. (12/1/2002)*

CHAMELEON

Chameleon 1998 Barbera (Amador County) $17. **86** *(9/1/2000)*

Chameleon 2002 Barbera (Lake County) $15. This is a rustic wine, country-style in its fairly aggressive tannins, the kind of red to down without being too fussy. It's totally dry, with berry, coffee, and earth flavors. Might improve with age, if you care to cellar it. **84** —*S.H. (8/1/2005)*

Chameleon 1998 Sangiovese (North Coast) $19. **86** —*J.C. (9/1/2000)*

Chameleon 1997 Sangiovese (North Coast) $18. **86** —*J.C. (10/1/1999)*

Chameleon 2003 Syrah (North Coast) $16. Not up to the quality shown by Chameleon's 2002 Napa Syrah, but it is almost $10 cheaper. It's still an elegant, complex Syrah laden with spice, herb, and citrus notes, albeit a trifle lean and lemony on the finish. **85** *(9/1/2005)*

Chameleon 2002 Syrah (Napa Valley) $25. West Coast Editor Steve Heimoff found this wine thin and unripe, but our other reviewers praised its briary, herbal notes balanced by bright cherry fruit, calling it complex and elegant. Picks up hints of bacon and spice on the long finish. **89** *(9/1/2005)*

Chameleon 1999 Syrah (Napa Valley) $31. Starts off with smoky, complex aromas of leather, cedar, coffee, and blackberry, with a touch of mint. Smooth black cherry, blueberry, and plum fruit emerges on the palate, accented by cinnamon and clove. Finishes with some dry wood tannins that should drop away by 2003. **90** *(11/1/2001)*

CHANDLER REACH

Chandler Reach 2000 Monte Regale Bordeaux Blend (Yakima Valley) $22. Already showing an edge of brick/orange; this half Cabernet Sauvignon, 26% Merlot, 24% Cab Franc red blend sports noticeable alcohol and substantial tannins. **86** —*P.G. (9/1/2003)*

Chandler Reach 2002 Parris Cabernet Franc (Yakima Valley) $38. Strong whiffs of barrel, cracker, toast, butterscotch and a hint of leather take off in the beginning, but behind it all is solid, ripe, plentiful black cherry fruit. There is also a strong streak of mint running through the middle, and the wine has good weight and texture across the palate. It's muscular without being clunky; there is substance here but it is elegantly displayed, with particularly good tannin management. **91** —*P.G. (6/1/2006)*

Chandler Reach 2002 Parris Cabernet Sauvignon (Yakima Valley) $42. Estate reserve, the first for this winery. Good fruit, sweet and plump, and a moderate 13.8% alcohol. Nice integration of supple tannins, black tea, ground coffee, toffee, and a bit of pepper. Powerful without being overblown. **90** —*P.G. (12/15/2005)*

Chandler Reach 2003 Monte Regalo Red Blend (Yakima Valley) $22. Youthful, plummy, bright, clear, and very toasty. The new oak jumps out at you, but then the fruit stands up to it. It's hard and tannic, taut, compact, serious Cabernet, with plenty of stuffing for cellaring, and just a hint of leather and leaf. **92** —*P.G. (6/1/2006)*

Chandler Reach 2003 Syrah (Yakima Valley) $26. Spicy and bright, this could almost be Grenache, with its penetrating acid and the lightness to its fruit. The oak flavors—substantial hits of cracker, vanilla, and chocolate—seem rather heavy-handed at this point. On the plus side, the nice spicy fruit carries on admirably into the finish. **88** —*P.G. (6/1/2006)*

Chandler Reach 2001 Syrah (Yakima Valley) $26. Sweet, forward fruit; spicy and grapey, with young flavors that carry a lot of French-tasting

terroir. It's a lot like a southern French wine, even showing some herbs and gamy leather. This is ripened to exactly the right point, not too jammy as to disguise the subtle herbs and leaf and spice elements. **89** — *P.G. (9/1/2003)*

CHANGALA

Changala 1999 Syrah (Paso Robles) $16. From the warmer east side of the appellation, this wine illustrates the area's ability to perfecty ripen Syrah to fat, lush flavors of violets, blueberries, chocolate, and sweet black cherries. The downside of this sunny sweetness is harsh tannins, which make the wine angular and chunky in the mouth. **86** —*S.H. (12/1/2002)*

CHANNING DAUGHTERS

Channing Daughters 1999 Brick Kiln Chardonnay (Long Island) $17. Toasty, perhaps a little overly toasty, with lots of menthol notes. Still, there's an attractive nuttiness to the wine and solid pear and white-peach fruit. **86** —*J.C. (4/1/2001)*

Channing Daughters 1999 Scuttlehole Chardonnay (Long Island) $13. Crisp pear and citrus fruit gets almost aggressively tart in this stainless-steel fermented Chard. Good length; should pair well with oysters on the half-shell. **84** —*J.C. (4/1/2001)*

Channing Daughters 1998 Sculpture Garden Merlot (Long Island) $19. Offers mild berry fruit allied to some green bell pepper and herb aromas. A bit light and tart for a single vineyard wine, but still good. **83** —*J.C. (4/1/2001)*

Channing Daughters 1999 Fresh Red Red Blend (Long Island) $15. Bright cherry aromas and flavors. Light and easy to drink, with a bit of green stemminess on the finish that adds character. **84** —*J.C. (4/1/2001)*

CHANNING PERRINE

Channing Perrine 1998 Mudd Vineyard Cabernet Sauvignon (Long Island) $19. Bright berry and red currant aromas. Lighter in style than Cabs being produced by other LI wineries. The finish turns tough and leathery, not a good match for the delicate fruit. **82** —*J.C. (4/1/2001)*

Channing Perrine 1999 Mudd Vineyard Fleur de Terre Merlot (North Fork of Long Island) $16. Bright red-berry aromas, decent weight and slightly tough tannins in the finish all point to this as a good partner to grilled burgers this summer. 100% Merlot. **83** —*J.C. (4/1/2001)*

Channing Perrine 1998 Oregon Road Riesling (Long Island) $13. Modest green-apple fruit is married to earthy grapefruit and lime flavors in this effort by Channing Daughters winemaker Larry Perrine. **83** —*J.C. (4/1/2001)*

CHANTICLEER

Chanticleer 2001 Cabernet Sauvignon (Napa Valley) $45. A complex wine, brimming with cinnamon and spice flavors and redolent of coffee, chocolate, black cherry, black currant, raspberry, herb, and anise flavors. The tannins are firm but ripe, and the finish is quite long. A first release from winemaker Chris Dearden. **91** —*J.M. (12/31/2004)*

CHAPPELLET

Chappellet 2003 Mountain Cuvée Bordeaux Blend (Napa Valley) $26. You can call this Chappellet's everyday claret, but that's an insult to a wine of this quality. It shows classic Napa structure, with firm tannins and rich acidity, and a deep core of black cherry, black currant, and oak flavors. It's delicious now, and should develop for a couple of years. **90** —*S.H. (10/1/2006)*

Chappellet 1996 Cabernet Franc (Napa Valley) $24. **87** —*M.S. (6/1/1999)*

Chappellet 2002 Pritchard Hill Estate Vineyard Cabernet Sauvignon (Napa Valley) $120. Stands out not just because of its size, but also for its balance. It's a big wine, bursting with flamboyant black currant, cassis, mocha, and smoky oak flavors with rich, thick and sweetly ripe tannins. The finish lasts for a very long time. So good now, you might miss its youthful character if you cellar it too long. **95** —*S.H. (12/15/2005)*

Chappellet 2001 Pritchard Hill Estate Vineyard Cabernet Sauvignon (Napa Valley) $110. Your first impression is how concentrated in black currant and cassis fruit this wine is. It's immense as well in flashy new oak. Then there are the tannins. Gentle and sweet, yet complex as a tapestry, they offer structure to the decadent flavors. This is a real achievement, and as soft as it is, the wine seems balanced enough to do interesting things over the next ten years. **94 Cellar Selection** —*S.H. (12/31/2004)*

Chappellet 1999 Pritchard Hill Estate Vineyard Cabernet Sauvignon (Napa Valley) $110. Big and rich in the mouth, with gorgeous, velvety tannins. Offers a juicy plum and cassis core, with oak, tobacco, and earth accents, and a char and cocoa notes on the back end. As compelling as the flavors are, it'll be the mouthfeel that wins you over (this is one of those Cabs that could taste like Eggs Benedict and still be delicious—its mouthfeel is that good). **92 Cellar Selection** *(8/1/2003)*

Chappellet 2003 Signature Cabernet Sauvignon (Napa Valley) $44. This is a stunning Cabernet, but it's too young to drink now. The tannins are simply too big. You could decant it, even overnight, but better to let it age naturally for four or five years. Tremendous in black currant and chocolate flavors, it's fully dry, and offset with crisp acidity. Has all the class and elegance of the best Napa Cabs. **94 Cellar Selection** —*S.H. (10/1/2006)*

Chappellet 2001 Signature Cabernet Sauvignon (Napa Valley) $42. A young, tight, closed mountain Cabernet that should follow a graceful aging curve. Pours inky dark, giving off muted aromas of oak, forest floor and wild blackberries. Dense and tannic now, with rich fruit just waiting to emerge. This classically proportioned wine should begin to be drinkable after 2010. **91 Cellar Selection** —*S.H. (10/1/2004)*

Chappellet 1997 Signature Cabernet Sauvignon (Napa Valley) $35. 90 *(11/1/2000)*

Chappellet 1997 Chardonnay (Napa Valley) $17. 87 —*J.C. (10/1/1999)*

Chappellet 2004 Chardonnay (Napa Valley) $28. The way the tropical fruit flavors, high acidity, oak, and creamy lees play off each other is just wonderful. There's a density and weight that, combined with balance, make this a truly impressive wine. **92** —*S.H. (2/1/2006)*

Chappellet 2003 Chardonnay (Napa Valley) $28. With apple and pear flavors and some oak, this is a clean Chard with mineral overtones. Nothing really stands out or clobbers you sidewise. It's just a well put-together wine, tasteful and understated. **90** —*S.H. (5/1/2005)*

Chappellet 1998 Chardonnay (Napa Valley) $20. 89 *(6/1/2000)*

Chappellet 2000 Signature Chardonnay (Napa Valley) $35. A distinguished wine, with peach and apple fruit flavors lavishly decorated with smoky oak and lees. Anyone can do that, but here, the pedigree of the fruit and the care of the winemaking are evident. There's an elegance and finesse that makes this wine compelling. **90** —*S.H. (2/1/2003)*

Chappellet 1999 Signature Chardonnay (Napa Valley) $35. A winning wine that displays a vibrantly fragrant tangerine, citrus, and herb-butter bouquet. It opens to a full, dense tropical-fruit palate and shows an almost seamless texture. Tangy oak plays off the lingering fruit nuances on this bottling's lengthy, luxurious finish. **91** *(7/1/2001)*

Chappellet 2003 Dry Chenin Blanc (Napa Valley) $15. This is about as well as Chenin can do in California. This bone dry, medium-bodied wine is tart in acids, and has herbaceous, apple, and wax bean flavors and a clean finish. **87** —*S.H. (12/15/2005)*

Chappellet 1997 Moelleux Chenin Blanc (Napa Valley) $40. 91 —*J.C. (12/31/1999)*

Chappellet 1997 Old Vine Cuvée Chenin Blanc (Napa Valley) $14. This continues to be one of the preeminent California Chenin Blancs and it represents a great value as well as an alternative to more conventional white wines. Mostly from old Chenin vines, it is oak aged and classy, not unlike good Chardonnay. Yet it's floral, slightly sweet and a touch grassy, as good Chenin can be. Superb for seafood paella or poached or grilled fish. Not a Loire-style wine, but overall tasty and terrific. **92 Best Buy** —*M.S. (12/15/2003)*

Chappellet 2003 Merlot (Napa Valley) $30. What a great job Chappellet does. It's a brand that's sometimes overlooked in favor of the new kids, but really deserves recognition. This is a stunningly rich, balanced Merlot, long in cherry, cocoa and oak flavors, yet complexed with fine tannins and rich acidity. It validates the old adage that, in California, Merlot is the soft Cabernet. **93** —*S.H. (10/1/2006)*

Chappellet 2002 Merlot (Napa Valley) $30. Very nice, a smooth, polished wine with palate-flattering flavors of ripe blackberries and cherries, and a subtle overlay of toasty oak. Possesses that indefinable element of elegance that marks an excellent wine. **90** —*S.H. (5/1/2005)*

Chappellet 2001 Merlot (Napa Valley) $28. Not a blockbuster, but absolutely lovely. Well-balanced with sweet tannins and crisp acidity, the flavors veer include cherries and rich, sweet fresh herbs. The dryness is nicely contrasted with a long, sweet oaky-fruity finish. **90** —*S.H. (12/15/2004)*

Chappellet 1997 Sangiovese (Napa Valley) $24. 87 —*S.H. (12/15/1999)*

Chappellet 1996 Sangiovese (Napa Valley) $23. 91 —*S.H. (11/1/1999)*

CHARIOT

Chariot 2000 Dolcetto (Central Coast) $18. Much richer and denser than most Italian Dolcettos, the wine is framed in firm, ripe tannins and backed by ripe, cherry, black currant, spice and vanilla tones. Beautifully balanced, long and lovely at the end. **90** —*J.M. (5/1/2002)*

Chariot 2000 Sangiovese (Central Coast) $15. Smooth and sleek, with ripe cherry, plum, herb and toast flavors. Bright, yet long on the finish. Quite nice—and you really can't beat the price. **88** —*J.M. (5/1/2002)*

CHARLES CREEK

Charles Creek 2001 La Sonrisa del Tecolote Cabernet Sauvignon (Napa Valley) $26. This is a very tannic wine. It hits the palate with a dusty, sandpapery feeling that makes the gums numb. Then the fruit emerges, currants and cherries, blackberries, and plums, and they ride through the finish. It is a classic cellar-worthy Napa Cabernet that will only get better through 2010. **92** —*S.H. (5/1/2004)*

Charles Creek 2001 Hawk Hill Vineyard Chardonnay (Russian River Valley) $22. Tastes lean and tart with acidity, with the flavors of apples and citrus fruits, almost like a Sauvignon Blanc. On the other hand, it's clean and well-made, and very dry. **85** —*S.H. (6/1/2003)*

Charles Creek 2002 La Sorpresa Chardonnay (Carneros) $25. Feels rough around the edges despite some well-ripened peach, pear, and apple flavors. Oak adds cream, vanilla, and buttered toast. Turns sweetly honeyed on the finish. **85** —*S.H. (8/1/2004)*

Charles Creek 2003 Las Abuelas Hyde Vineyard Chardonnay (Carneros) $39. Impresses for the sheer volume of the fruit. Flamboyant tropical pineapple, mango, guava, lots of dusty spices, rich oak, but manages to hold onto balance, dryness and even a sense of finesse all the way through the long finish. **92** —*S.H. (6/1/2005)*

Charles Creek 2002 Las Patolitas Chardonnay (Sonoma County) $20. If you like them rich and oaky, this Chard's for you. Tropical fruit, pear, and peach flavors are mingled with smoke, vanilla, and buttered toast to forge a strong, flashy wine. **88** —*S.H. (2/1/2004)*

Charles Creek 2002 Vista del Halcon Chardonnay (Russian River Valley) $22. Oaky, with a raw, acidic mouthfeel that accentuates the lean, citrusy fruit. The wine's got knuckles. **83** —*S.H. (6/1/2004)*

Charles Creek 2002 Miradero Merlot (Napa-Sonoma) $24. After a successful 2001 vintage, the '02 is bit raisiny for me, with that hot, pruny note of super-maturity that mars an otherwise fine dry red wine. **84** —*S.H. (4/1/2005)*

Charles Creek 2001 Miradero Merlot (Sonoma-Napa) $22. Classic North Coast Merlot, polished and sleek, with elegantly soft tannins and flavors of plums, black cherries, and chocolate. Extra-ripe grapes lead to a honey-sweet finish, but the wine is technically dry. Perfect with prime rib. **90** —*S.H. (12/31/2003)*

Charles Creek 2000 Miradero Merlot (Sonoma County) $18. A rich, well-made wine with good berry fruit character and young, complex tannins. Feels dusty and earthy in the mouth, with lots of chewy blackberry flavors leading to a clean, spicy finish. Will benefit from short-term aging. **87** —*S.H. (6/1/2003)*

CHARLES KRUG

Charles Krug 1996 Generations Bordeaux Blend (Napa Valley) $34. This Bordeaux blend offers a bouquet of cassis fruit with earth, tobacco, and slight herbaceous flavors with a licorice note on the palate flow to an

USA

elegant, tart black cherry, pepper, and earth-tinged finish. Drinkable now, but still taut, it should develop well over the next three to five years. **89** *(4/1/2001)*

Charles Krug 1997 Generations-Reserve Bordeaux Blend (Napa Valley) $34. Very dark in the glass and intense in the nose, with cassis, blackberry, mint, white chocolate, smoke, and plum aromas. The flavors are extravagantly fruity, very forward and ripe, but dry and framed in soft, intricate tannins. This wine, a blend of Cabernet Sauvignon, Cabernet Franc, and Merlot, is weighty and very charming. **92 Editors' Choice** —*S.H. (12/1/2001)*

Charles Krug 2002 Family Reserve Generations Cabernet Blend (Napa Valley) $42. Here's a well-oaked Cab that shows the winery's traditional preference for balance over power. It's not a blockbuster Napa Cab, but a subtle, harmonious one, with an elegant interplay of fruit and tannins. Drink now and over the next several years. **89** —*S.H. (11/15/2005)*

Charles Krug 2002 Limited Release Cabernet Franc (Napa Valley) $60. Despite plenty of vanilla and oak on the nose, this Cab Franc is powerful enough to show plenty of varietal character: scents of tobacco and flowers are accented by just the merest hint of green bean. On the palate, the cassis fruit stands out, shaded by layers of cinnamon and clove, with less weight than a Napa Cabernet Sauvignon. Supple, spicy, and long on the finish. **91** *(4/12/2006)*

Charles Krug 1997 Cabernet Sauvignon (Napa Valley) $17. 87 *(12/15/1999)*

Charles Krug 2002 Limited Release Cabernet Sauvignon (Napa Valley) $70. Charles Krug's Limited Release program sets a new level of quality for this Napa stalwart. This Cabernet Sauvignon boasts plenty of smoky oak on the nose, but also bold cassis fruit and hints of vanilla and tobacco. This is fuller and richer than either the Syrah or the Cab Franc, with soft but plentiful tannins that would make this a solid steakhouse choice over the next 10 years. **92** *(4/12/2006)*

Charles Krug 2002 Limited Release IX Clones Cabernet Sauvignon (Napa Valley) $80. The flagship of Krug's new Limited Release offerings, IX Clones refers to the nine different clones of Cabernet Sauvignon that comprise this wine. The result is more complexity than in the "regular" Limited Release Cab and a firmer, chewier finish that suggests cellaring 4-7 years prior to consumption. It's full and creamy-textured on the palate, with aromas and flavors that hint at smoke, cassis, tobacco, cedar, and a multitude of dried spices. Should be great, starting in 2010. Only problem? Just 75 cases were produced. **93 Cellar Selection** *(4/12/2006)*

Charles Krug 2002 Peter Mondavi Family Cabernet Sauvignon (Napa Valley) $24. World-Class Cabernet, made in the modern style. It's softly textured, with melted tannins and low acidity. Black currants, cassis, cherries, milk chocolate, and spices come together and last through a long finish. **88** —*S.H. (11/15/2005)*

Charles Krug 1999 Peter Mondavi Family Cabernet Sauvignon (Napa Valley) $21. A charming Cab. It's soft and the tannins are completely accessible, while the fruity flavors are complex and savory. The structure is light by Napa standards, but in accord with the Krug style. **87** —*S.H. (11/15/2002)*

Charles Krug 1996 Peter Mondavi Family Cabernet Sauvignon (Napa Valley) $16. 86 —*S.H. (9/1/1999)*

Charles Krug 1996 Vintage Select Cabernet Sauvignon (Napa Valley) $50. Refinement and depth show from the start in aromas of chocolate, raisin, and creamy vanilla. The palate of intense cassis, black cherry, and licorice flavors and the full mouthfeel display style and unrestrained power. Dark sweet-and-sour fruit, plenty of oak and full, dusty tannins play out on the long finish. **90 Cellar Selection** *(4/1/2001)*

Charles Krug 2002 Vintage Selection Cabernet Sauvignon (Napa Valley) $51. A ripe but firm, balanced Cabernet. The black currant and cassis flavors mesh well with the oak and soft tannins, leading to real elegance. Drinks well now, but should hold for a good 10 years, if not longer. **92 Cellar Selection** —*S.H. (11/15/2005)*

Charles Krug 1997 Vintage Selection Cabernet Sauvignon (Napa Valley) $50. Unblended as it's always been, at nearly five years the V.S. is as pure a Cabernet as Krug has ever produced. The mouthfeel is limpid, softly

luxuriant, and the flavor is no slouch. The wine is rich, ripe, and endlessly persistent, right down to the curranty finish. This is a beauty you can age for a very long time. **93** —*S.H. (11/15/2002)*

Charles Krug 1995 Vintage Selection Cabernet Sauvignon (Napa Valley) $47. 89 *(12/15/1999)*

Charles Krug 1998 Chardonnay (Napa Valley) $15. 85 *(12/15/1999)*

Charles Krug 2001 Chardonnay (Napa Valley) $17. Good, rich Chard; nicely packed with ripe flavors of white peach, apple, and pear. A solid overlay of toasty oak adds smoky, spicy notes and a creamy texture. Finishes smooth and polished. **88** —*S.H. (6/1/2003)*

Charles Krug 2003 Family Reserve Chardonnay (Napa Valley) $24. This crowd pleaser is rich in tropical fruit, buttered toast, caramelized oak, and vanilla flavors. It has a spicy, creamy texture, and is thoroughly balanced. It's a flamboyant Chard that doesn't tire the palate. **90** —*S.H. (11/15/2005)*

Charles Krug 1999 Family reserve Chardonnay (Napa Valley) $21. Oak, vanilla, spice, and char aromas pour from the glass, overriding scents of ripe peaches and apples and tropical fruits. Despite the extravagant use of oak, the wine has enough fruit and body to handle it. It drinks dry, rich, and complex. A real crowd-pleaser. **88** —*S.H. (12/1/2001)*

Charles Krug 1999 Family Reserve Chardonnay (Carneros) $21. Oak, vanilla, spice, and char aromas pour from the glass, overriding scents of ripe peaches and apples and tropical fruits. Despite the extravagant use of oak, the wine has enough fruit and body to handle it. It drinks dry, rich, and complex. A real crowd pleaser. **88** —*S.H. (12/1/2001)*

Charles Krug 2002 Peter Mondavi Family Chardonnay (Napa Valley) $17. Tight, with citrus, apple, and pear flavors and high acidity. It's a bracing wine that stimulates the taste buds. Winemaker effects include plenty of sweet oak, but it's still lean and angular. **85** —*S.H. (2/1/2004)*

Charles Krug 2000 Peter Mondavi Family Reserve Chardonnay (Carneros) $21. Quite a bit more focused and polished than Krug's regular Chard, it's a big, thick, oily wine dripping with opulent peach, nectarine, and tropical fruit flavors. Well-charred oak frames the whole in spice and glyceriney sweetness. Semisweet, with a slight almond skin bitterness on the finish. **88** —*S.H. (12/15/2002)*

Charles Krug 1999 Family Reserve Generations Meritage (Napa Valley) $35. Made on the lean side, completely different from the hugely ripe style now prevalent. There are sage, sweet tobacco, leather, and blackberry flavors in this bone-dry wine. The tannin-acid balance is unmistakably Napa, plush and elegant. An ager, but perfect with a good steak or roast. **91** —*S.H. (3/1/2003)*

Charles Krug 1997 Merlot (Napa Valley) $17. 90 *(12/15/1999)*

Charles Krug 1999 Merlot (Napa Valley) $21. This is a really nice dinner wine, posh and elegant, yet with richly ripe flavors. Fully dry, with a complex balance of herbs and fruits, and wonderfully rich tannins. Obviously built for the table, a wine that won't distract from your favorite dishes. **90 Editors' Choice** —*S.H. (8/1/2003)*

Charles Krug 2002 Family Reserve Merlot (Napa Valley) $36. Lots of oak on this ripe wine, and it's new and well-charred, to judge from the aroma. The oak theme reprises in the mouth, where it's joined by blackberries and cherries. Overall impression is of a well-made wine, but an oaky one. **85** —*S.H. (11/15/2005)*

Charles Krug 1997 P.Mondavi Family Reserve Merlot (Napa Valley) $25. Toast and smoke aromas entwine a solid core of blackberry fruit. The mouthfeel is rich and creamy without being soupy, thanks to a strong acid backbone that lends a tart edge to the flavors. **91 Editors' Choice** *(6/1/2001)*

Charles Krug 1997 Reserve Merlot (Napa Valley) $28. 92 *(12/15/1999)*

Charles Krug 1996 Pinot Noir (Carneros) $16. 90 Best Buy —*S.H. (6/1/1999)*

Charles Krug 2000 Pinot Noir (Carneros) $19. Lean and earthy, marked by tobacco and white pepper, tomato and dill aromas and flavors. In the mouth, it's very dry, with easy tannins. There's some tart cherry fruit that shows up in the mid-palate, and the finish turns slightly bitter. **85** —*S.H. (7/1/2003)*

USA

Charles Krug 1999 Pinot Noir (Carneros) $18. Plump and supple, this flavorful, well-balanced midweight Pinot presents ample cherry fruit offset by attractive mocha, forest-floor, and smoke accents. On the palate, the wine turns progressively darker and plummier, closing long with dry, firm tannins. Drink now–2006. **88** *(10/1/2002)*

Charles Krug 1998 Pinot Noir (Napa Valley) $16. A sturdy wine, with a bouquet of dark cherry, cola, toast, and a touch of barnyard. The initial flavors are sweet dried cherry, then turn toward more complex leather, sour plum and toast. Tobacco, and a reprise of the early barnyard note, play on the finish with nice back end aromatics **88** *(4/1/2001)*

Charles Krug 1998 Peter Mondavi Family Pinot Noir (Napa Valley) $17. Opens with aromas of red cherry, honey, tobacco, mushroom, vanilla, and spice, and turns very dry in the mouth, with soft tannins framing fairly ripe cherry and raspberry fruit. There's a sappy, nectary quality to the finish that carries these ripe berry flavors forward. **87** *—S.H. (11/15/2001)*

Charles Krug 2003 Peter Mondavi Family Pinot Noir (Carneros) $20. Nice, light-bodied, fruity, and immediately likeable, the way you want a near-term Pinot to be. It's dry and silky, with flavors of cherry compote, coffee, cocoa, vanilla-oak, and cinnamon spice, and a rich, fruity finish. **87** *—S.H. (11/15/2005)*

Charles Krug 2002 Peter Mondavi Family Pinot Noir (Carneros) $20. Light, silky, and elegant. Has a soft, pliant mouth feel, with pleasant cherry, herb, and cola flavors. **85** *—S.H. (2/1/2005)*

Charles Krug 2001 Peter Mondavi Family Pinot Noir (Carneros) $20. Smells weedy and herbal, with only a trace of the berry notes you expect, and doesn't turn any richer once you taste. It's a dry, acidic wine, with tobaccoey flavors. Disappointing. **83** *—S.H. (5/1/2004)*

Charles Krug 1999 Family Reserve Sangiovese (Napa Valley) $20. A welcome addition to early-drinking reds from this historic winery. The wine is very dry and crisp, with easy tannins. The flavors? Slightly bitter and dusty, bringing to mind less-than-ripe cherries with hints of tobacco and sage. It has a round suppleness that's hard to describe, but will be fantastic with Italian fare. **90 Editors' Choice** *—S.H. (12/1/2002)*

Charles Krug 1998 Reserve Sangiovese (Napa Valley) $18. This attractive Cal-Ital hangs leather and cedar accents on the the tart cherry fruit. Medium-weight, with good texture on the palate, it closes with a softly dry, long finish. The grapes for this wine come from 10 acres right at the winery. **89 Editors' Choice** *(4/1/2001)*

Charles Krug 1998 Sauvignon Blanc (Napa Valley) $13. 88 *—M.S. (11/15/1999)*

Charles Krug 2000 Sauvignon Blanc (Napa Valley) $14. Smells very fresh and fragrant, with pronounced gooseberry, citrus, straw, smoke, vanilla, and peach aromas. This exuberantly spicy, fruity wine is very flavorful and dry, a little soft, but voluptuous and creamy. Most of the grapes come from St. Helena vineyards. **88** *—S.H. (11/15/2001)*

Charles Krug 1999 Sauvignon Blanc (Napa Valley) $13. Round with a full, figgy nose and a harmonious blend of grapefruit, melon, and pear flavors. This medium-weight wine is perked up by a mineral note and spicy tang on the finish. **86** *(4/1/2001)*

Charles Krug 2004 Peter Mondavi Family Sauvignon Blanc (Napa Valley) $16. Crisp and clean, with aromas and flavors that blend nectarine and grapefruit. Shows ample weight on the palate, yet finishes tart and refreshing. **87** *(12/15/2005)*

Charles Krug 2003 Peter Mondavi Family Sauvignon Blanc (Napa Valley) $16. Comes down firmly on the grassy, lime, and gooseberry side, a bone dry, tart wine with high acidity. Very clean and proper, a refreshing apéritif, and will go well with a wide variety of food. **86** *—S.H. (10/1/2004)*

Charles Krug 2002 Limited Release Syrah (Napa Valley) $50. This inky wine barely meets the labeling requirements for Syrah (the balance is Cabernet Sauvignon, Merlot, and Petit Verdot), but still boasts plenty of that grape's varietal character in its slightly peppery scents, meaty flavors and blackberry and mulberry fruit. Soft tannins cushion the mouthfeel, but this wine is surprisingly crisp and focused on the finish. **90** *(4/12/2006)*

Charles Krug 1996 Zinfandel (Napa Valley) $11. 84 *—L.W. (9/1/1999)*

Charles Krug 2001 Zinfandel (Napa Valley) $15. Pretty oaky on the nose. The follow-up offers good fruit, however, with cassis, blackberry, and black cherry at the fore. Tannins are quite firm, and the finish is framed in toasty oak, licorice, and spice. **88** *(11/1/2003)*

Charles Krug 1999 Zinfandel (Napa Valley) $15. This is a Zin as classy as many that cost a lot more. True, it could use a tad more fruity concentration, but that's a minor quibble. It's spicy and round, balanced and harmonious, and the tannins are pretty as a picture. **87 Best Buy** *—S.H. (12/1/2002)*

Charles Krug 1998 Zinfandel (Napa Valley) $12. A lighter style. Mild pepper and leather elements offset red-berry aromas. A nice acid backbone supports the fruit and the tart berry flavors are accented by vanilla and clove notes. The finish shows good length, more berry, and mild pepper. **87** *(4/1/2001)*

Charles Krug 1998 Zinfandel (Alexander Valley) $12. Features a deep bouquet of red currants and strawberries. Green tea and licorice accents add interest and the overall feel is bright yet full. Closes with mineral-chalk and licorice elements. **89 Best Buy** *(4/1/2001)*

Charles Krug 2003 Peter Mondavi Family Zinfandel (Napa Valley) $20. Here's a balanced, warming Zin that shows what the variety can achieve when carefully monitored. While not a blockbuster, the wine's berry and cherry flavors have a hearty finish, with some dusty tannins. **87** *—S.H. (11/15/2005)*

Charles Krug 2001 Peter Mondavi Family Zinfandel (Napa Valley) $14. Nice wild berry, oak and peppery notes to this zesty wine, with a soft, easy mouthfeel. Perfect for pizza, burgers, and similar fare. **84** *—S.H. (2/1/2005)*

Charles Krug 2000 Peter Mondavi Family Zinfandel (Napa Valley) $15. A thin, scraggly Zin, marked with faint berry flavors and dry tannins. Finishes astringent and watery. **82** *—S.H. (5/1/2004)*

CHÂTEAU BENOIT

Château Benoit 2000 Chardonnay (Willamette Valley) $16. Burnished gold in color, with aromas of custard, lemon curd, toast, and baked apples. The flavor profile is an amalgam of dull pear and apple, while the finish is heavy as it deals coconut and tropical fruit. Overall it's a soft, fading Chardonnay that can be summed up in one taste. **84** *—M.S. (9/1/2003)*

Château Benoit 2000 Pinot Noir (Oregon) $18. A tight rather deep nose of cherries, rubber and tea starts this one out; however, herbal flavors overshadow the plum and black cherry fruit. There's a slickness to the mouthfeel, which one of our panelists termed "oily and viscous." **83** *(10/1/2002)*

Château Benoit 2000 Doe Ridge Vineyard Pinot Noir (Willamette Valley) $40. An aromatic blend of Bazooka bubble gum and woodspice is hardly what you'd call common, but the palate of cherry, cinnamon, and broad red fruit definitely works. Overall, this is a simple wine, but a clean, well-made one. It's correct in terms of varietal character and balance. **86** *(10/1/2002)*

Château Benoit 2000 Kestrel Vineyard Pinot Noir (Willamette Valley) $40. This wine offers a pretty nose of cherry, baking spices, leather, and clay. Driving cherry fruit on the palate is followed by earthy coffee notes on the long, supple finish. **87** *(10/1/2002)*

Château Benoit 2000 Yamhill Springs Vineyard Pinot Noir (Willamette Valley) $40. The concentrated nose features maple, leather, and hints of bacon and barbecued meat. The palate has some red plum and cherry, but also a creamy vanilla note. The finish is intense and lively, marked by sharp acidity. **87** *(10/1/2002)*

CHÂTEAU BIANCA

Château Bianca 2000 Barrel Fermented Chardonnay (Willamette Valley) $10. There is little difference between this and the winery's reserve. There simply is no flavor here. It's a watery, sour wine, with a finish that suggests something went wrong somewhere along the line. **81** *—P.G. (8/1/2003)*

Château Bianca 1998 Barrel Fermented Chardonnay (Willamette Valley) $9. Though the label makes a point of saying barrel fermented, there is little in the way of oakiness or leesiness to the flavor. The fruit tends toward ripe apples with a hint of citrus; there are some musty, earthy flavors as well. Overall it's a straightforward, fruity, simple Chardonnay. **83** —*P.G. (11/1/2001)*

Château Bianca 2001 Estate Reserve Chardonnay (Willamette Valley) $20. A real letdown. This is a winery with some wonderful, elegant white wines, but here there is harsh, hot, tannic, raw new oak, and banana-flavored fruit. **83** —*P.G. (10/1/2004)*

Château Bianca 1999 Reserve Chardonnay (Willamette Valley) $20. I prefer this winery's barrel fermented Chard to their reserve, because it integrates the delicious flavors of the barrel into the rich, ripe fruit. Apples and pineapples are dominant here, with good structure and plenty of weight in the mouth. **86 Best Buy** —*P.G. (2/1/2002)*

Château Bianca 2000 Winery Estate Reserve Chardonnay (Willamette Valley) $20. This is a wine the winery has lavished some extra care on: barrel fermentation, 50% new oak, extra time in barrel. But the results are disappointing. A thin, sour wine, it has a bitter edge to it and a finish that suggests that something went wrong in the barrel. **81** —*P.G. (8/1/2003)*

Château Bianca 1999 Gewürztraminer (Willamette Valley) $9. This wine has a bright, spicy attack in the aroma that is unmistakably Gewürztraminer. The fruit is ripe, almost fat, with a strong, spicy flavor in the mid-palate and a heaviness in the finish. There is also a little bit of heat, and a slight impression of sweetness from the fruit. **84** —*P.G. (11/1/2001)*

Château Bianca 2001 Estate Bottled Gewürztraminer (Willamette Valley) $9. Sweet, simple fruit holds sway here; the finish is sugary and slightly bitter. **83** —*P.G. (12/31/2002)*

Château Bianca 1999 Pinot Blanc (Willamette Valley) $12. Pinot Blanc grows well in Oregon, but it doesn't often translate in the bottle into a distinctive style that one could call its own. This Pinot Blanc could easily be taken for a stainless steel-fermented Chardonnay or a light Pinot Gris; it's a crisp, fruity white wine that will go well with a wide variety of foods. **85** —*P.G. (11/1/2001)*

Château Bianca 2002 Estate Pinot Blanc (Willamette Valley) $12. If you don't mind a healthy dose of honey flavor in your Pinot Blanc, this is a wine to admire. The elegant fruit nicely blends white peaches and kiwi, and the kiss of honey smoothes out the middle into a very satisfying finish. **88 Best Buy** —*P.G. (10/1/2004)*

Château Bianca 2000 Estate Bottled Pinot Blanc (Oregon) $12. The citrus fruit has a sweet lemon-drop character, augmented with a spritzy mouthfeel—it's kind of like chewing on a sweet and sour candy. Juicy and tart, it falls apart in the finish, which carries a flat, artificial sweetness. **82** —*P.G. (4/1/2002)*

Château Bianca 2001 Wetzel Family Estate Pinot Blanc (Willamette Valley) $18. Essentially a reserve Pinot Blanc, this wine captures pleasant pear flavors and some extra texture suggestive of extended lees contact. Very limited (60 case) production. **85** —*P.G. (8/1/2003)*

Château Bianca 2001 Wetzel Family Estate-Single Cluster Pinot Blanc (Willamette Valley) $18. This is a pleasant, simple wine with typical pear flavors and some texture from aging on the lees. **85** —*P.G. (12/31/2002)*

Château Bianca 2004 Pinot Gris (Willamette Valley) $12. Solid, fleshy and mouthfilling, this shows nicely ripened pear and white peach flavors, full and smooth, with good concentration. The alcohol clocks in at just 12.5%, making this a wine you can eagerly refill your glass with. **89 Best Buy** —*P.G. (2/1/2006)*

Château Bianca 2002 Pinot Gris (Willamette Valley) $10. Pears leap out of the glass, ripe, round, and softly seductive. This wine shows a lovely balance and a wonderful mouthfeel, with flavor that seems to gather strength through the middle. **88 Best Buy** —*P.G. (10/1/2004)*

Château Bianca 2001 Pinot Gris (Willamette Valley) $10. Once you get past the tanky scents and let the wine breathe, it is a perfectly fine, simple bottle of fruit-forward Pinot Gris. One-dimensional, but sound. **85 Best Buy** —*P.G. (12/31/2002)*

Château Bianca 2001 Pinot Noir (Willamette Valley) $12. There's not much going on here. Pale, with scents of wild strawberry, it slips into a very light, herbal set of flavors and glides quietly away. Soundly made, and for the price, it does the job. **85** —*P.G. (10/1/2004)*

Château Bianca 2000 Pinot Noir (Willamette Valley) $12. Smoked tea leaves, prosciutto, and cola aromas ensure interest. In the mouth, it's extracted and fairly rich, with earth, black plum, and coffee flavors. Firm tannins keep the finish strong. It's muscular yet balanced; full yet drinkable. And it should last for another couple of years **88 Best Buy** *(10/1/2002)*

Château Bianca 1999 Pinot Noir (Oregon) $10. This is a grapey wine with an odd mix of sweet beet and musty earth scents. In the mouth it tastes earthy and a bit stemmy. There is fruit here, but it has a sweetness that's quite reminiscent of grape candy, light and sugary. **83** —*P.G. (4/1/2002)*

Château Bianca 1998 Pinot Noir (Willamette Valley) $10. This light, fruity Pinot suggests strawberries, watermelon, and other summer fruits. It's got a fair amount of tannin, but it is definitely a wine to sip, chilled, with picnic food on a warm spring/summer day. **84** —*P.G. (11/1/2001)*

Château Bianca 2001 Cellar Select Pinot Noir (Willamette Valley) $16. This is clearly, identifiably Pinot, and it displays a broadly accessible palate of varietal flavors. Beetroot, cranberry, some sassafras, and cola, with well-modulated tannins and a nice, svelte, varietal finish. Nothing spectacular, but a very nice effort for the money. **87** —*P.G. (10/1/2004)*

Château Bianca 1999 Estate Reserve Pinot Noir (Willamette Valley) $29. Initially there are inviting scents of cola, beetroot, and a hint of tomato, but once tasted the flavors are still quite hard, and the fruit comes across as thin and unyielding. On the finish, the tannins are harsh and somewhat stemmy. **84** —*P.G. (4/1/2002)*

Château Bianca 1997 Estate Reserve Pinot Noir (Willamette Valley) $25. There is a solid, firm, substantive feel to this wine, and it shows nice black cherry fruit, with an underpinning of tar, leather, and licorice. But it also has some rubbery flavors, that extend into the finish, and it winds up with an unpleasant bitterness that is off-putting. If you like dark, burnt coffee kinds of flavors, this will be just right. **85** —*P.G. (11/1/2001)*

Château Bianca 2000 Winery Estate Reserve Pinot Noir (Willamette Valley) $28. Thin for a reserve. The fruit is watery and tart, with flavors of beetroot and a vegetal finish. Breathing time and food may help. **84** —*P.G. (4/1/2003)*

Château Bianca 2003 Riesling (Willamette Valley) $9. Quite a lovely wine, with a beguiling nose that sends up sweet floral/citrus blossom scents that lead into a core of crisp tangerine/orange peel fruit. There is a very nice grip and concentration to the midpalate, and this is one of those wines that you want to return to again and again. **89 Best Buy** —*P.G. (10/1/2004)*

Château Bianca 1999 Riesling (Willamette Valley) $9. This is a straightforward, off-dry style of Riesling, with ripe fruit and a nice balance of sugar and acids. There's a little bit of a resin scent in the nose, and a hint of soapiness in the mouth. The finish is soft and full. **84** —*P.G. (11/1/2001)*

CHÂTEAU BOSWELL

Château Boswell 2003 Estate Cabernet Sauvignon (St. Helena) $94. From a St. Helena vineyard on the Silverado Trail, a ripe, somewhat rustic Cab that's powerful in cassis and chocolate flavors. It's a bit soft. Might pull together in a year or two. **86** —*S.H. (8/1/2006)*

CHÂTEAU CHEVALIER

Château Chevalier 2003 Cabernet Sauvignon (Spring Mountain) $30. Here's a plush, supple Cab, rich in cassis, cherry, coffee, herb, and spice flavors that are wrapped in lush, sweetly ripe tannins. It's a very dry wine, and balanced enough to benefit from mid-term aging. Hold until 2007, then best through 2011 or so. **89** —*S.H. (12/15/2006)*

Château Chevalier 2005 Sauvignon Blanc (Spring Mountain) $24. Concentrated and intense in fruit and crisp in acids, but too sweet, this clean wine shows powerful citrus essence, fig, white peach, and white apricot flavors. **84** —*S.H. (12/15/2006)*

CHÂTEAU FELICE

Château Felice 2002 Acier Chardonnay (Russian River Valley) $16. Has some ripe peach and pear fruit and an oaky veneer, but can't overcome

USA

its rustic mouthfeel. The tannins are apparent. Finishes bitter. **84** —*S.H.* *(12/1/2003)*

Château Felice 2001 Estate Chardonnay (Chalk Hill) $20. This Chardonnay is distinctive for its extreme full-bodiedness. It's a heavy, dense wine, a bit low in acidity but not unattractive, with scents of cigarette, vanilla, and mango and a full-blown fruity, herbal taste. **84** —*S.H.* *(2/1/2004)*

Château Felice 2001 Syrah (Chalk Hill) $22. Smells odd and vegetal, an unripe scent that is not attractive. Marginally better in the mouth, with berry and herb flavors and sturdy, tough tannins. **82** —*S.H. (12/1/2003)*

Château Felice 2001 Mill Road Vineyard Syrah (Paso Robles) $30. A good wine from the warmer part of the AVA, and it shows in the slightly Porty, raisiny flavor and thick, chocolatey, melted tannins and soft acidity. But it's fresh, tasty, and gentle, with a nice, dry finish. **86** —*S.H.* *(2/1/2004)*

Château Felice 2001 Zinfandel (Chalk Hill) $16. A lighter style, with pretty plum, cherry, vanilla, and toast flavors. Tannins are a bit abrupt. **83** *(11/1/2003)*

CHÂTEAU FRANK

Château Frank 1996 Champagne Blend (Finger Lakes) $20. 85 —*S.H.* *(12/31/2000)*

Château Frank 1995 Blanc de Blancs Champagne Blend (Finger Lakes) $25. Though labeled Champagne, it is in fact a sparkling wine made in the Champagne method (fermented in the bottle). Chardonnay and Pinot Blanc are the grapes, and the wine has effusive, yeasty bubbles, a spicy/steely aroma and good balance. There is a bit of a hole in the flavor, which starts and finishes well but falls off in midpalate. **83** —*P.G.* *(6/1/2001)*

Château Frank NV Célébre Crémant Champagne Blend (New York) $15. 84 *(12/31/2000)*

Château Frank 1996 Blanc de Noirs Red Blend (Finger Lakes) $25. This flavorful sparkler comes from one of upstate New York's most respected producers. Pear, floral, and mild spice aromas open on to herbs and flowers on the palate. The bead is steady, though not terribly fine, and the finish long, with bread and lemon-lime notes. Good for dining as well as toasting. **87** —*M.M. (12/1/2001)*

CHÂTEAU JULIEN

Château Julien 2001 Cabernet Sauvignon (Monterey County) $10. Nice everyday drinking with this very soft, easy wine, with its plummy, berry flavors and velvety mouthfeel. There's a rich aftertaste of cherries, and chocolate on the finish. **84** —*S.H. (10/1/2004)*

Château Julien 1999 Cabernet Sauvignon (Monterey County) $10. This charmless wine brings back memories of those old reds that suffered from "the veggies," aromas and flavors of canned vegetables that come from unripe grapes. With its flabby structure, there's not a whole lot to recommend this barely acceptable wine. **80** —*S.H. (9/12/2002)*

Château Julien 2002 Barrel Aged Cabernet Sauvignon (Monterey County) $10. Southern Monterey is the source of inexpensive, everyday Cabernet, and this is a prime example. It has pretty flavors of blackberries and cherries and is dry, with supple tannins. **84** —*S.H. (4/1/2006)*

Château Julien 2000 Barrel Aged Cabernet Sauvignon (Monterey County) $10. There's a beautiful texture on this modern style wine, with its smooth, velvety tannins and easy acids. The actual flavors veer between earthier ones of tobacco and herbs to blackberries and cassis. **86 Best Buy** —*S.H. (10/1/2003)*

Château Julien 1998 Barrel Aged Cabernet Sauvignon (Monterey County) $10. A juicy, plump wine that's filled with fun flavors, among them blackberry, mocha, vanilla, and dark candied cherries. The tannins are soft; the acidity just fine. Don't turn your nose up because of the price, or because you think Monterey and Cabernet don't mix. This is a darned good value. **87 Best Buy** —*S.H. (5/1/2001)*

Château Julien 1999 Estate Cabernet Sauvignon (Monterey County) $22. Darkly colored, brimming with blackberry aromas and oak that hits you across the head. It's new and well charred, with caramel scents. Tannins are thick and rather aggressive. Ambitious Monterey vintners continue to push against Napa. A wine like this advances the cause, but also shows how much remains to be done. **88** —*S.H. (11/15/2002)*

Château Julien 1998 Estate Vineyard Cabernet Sauvignon (Monterey County) $22. Lots of new French oak on this baby, and it shows in the smoky, vanilla-tinged aromas. Young and flashy, with black currant extract. There's a pretty good dose of gum-sticking tannins; with big foods, it's drinkable now. **86** —*S.H. (12/1/2001)*

Château Julien 1996 Grand Reserve Cabernet Sauvignon (Monterey) $9. 84 —*M.S. (7/1/1999)*

Château Julien 2001 Private Reserve Cabernet Sauvignon (Monterey County) $36. Combines ultraripe black currant, cassis, cherry, and coffee flavors with some oak, wrapped in a tart, dry texture that finishes with a sharp edge of tannins. Best to let this still-young wine sit for a year or two. **85** —*S.H. (12/1/2005)*

Château Julien 2000 Private Reserve Cabernet Sauvignon (Monterey County) $36. Ripe and plump in black currant, black cherry jam, and mocha flavors, and very well oaked, this wine is soft in tannins and acids. Drinkable, but could use a firmer structure. **86** —*S.H. (11/15/2004)*

Château Julien 1999 Private Reserve Cabernet Sauvignon (Monterey County) $36. Launches with a strong scent of well-charred new oak, plus vanilla and buttered toast. Yet the underlying fruity flavors of blackberry and cassis easily handle it. Smooth and long in the mouth. **87** —*S.H. (10/1/2003)*

Château Julien 1998 Private Reserve Cabernet Sauvignon (Monterey County) $36. Herculean efforts went into making this expensive wine rich and complex. They gave it their hearts, but the effort falls short. The vintage didn't help. It's partly ripe, partly unripe. It's rugged in the mouth, with a simple nature, and the finish turns sharp. It's not going anywhere. **84** —*S.H. (11/15/2002)*

Château Julien 1996 Private Reserve Cabernet Sauvignon (Monterey County) $28. 87 *(2/1/2000)*

Château Julien 2002 Chardonnay (Monterey County) $10. Here's a great value. It's as ripe as can be in tropical fruit and spices, and the oak contribution shows up as buttered toast and vanilla. Don't look for subtlety, just pure flavor. **85 Best Buy** —*S.H. (12/15/2004)*

Château Julien 2001 Chardonnay (Monterey County) $10. A little obvious in its broad brush use of toasted oak. Pretty much all you get is smoke, char, vanilla, and other sweet wood things. Underneath all that is fairly simple apple and peach fruit flavors and spice. **85** —*S.H. (2/1/2003)*

Château Julien 1998 Barrel Fermented Chardonnay (Monterey County) $10. 85 *(2/1/2000)*

Château Julien 2000 Estate Chardonnay (Monterey County) $22. Bright, zesty Monterey fruit stars, dressed in elaborate mango and pineapple flavors. Oak adds vanilla, smoke, and an unctuous, sappy texture, while lees contact does its creamy thing. This is a big-boned Chard, slightly sweet and quite spicy. **89** —*S.H. (12/15/2002)*

Château Julien 2001 Estate Vineyard Chardonnay (Monterey County) $22. A heavily oaked wine whose fruit doesn't stand up to all that smoky wood. The underlying flavors of tart citrus and white peach lead to a thin, hot finish. **83** —*S.H. (3/1/2004)*

Château Julien 1999 Estate Vineyard Chardonnay (Monterey County) $22. A round and pleasant wine with melon, toast, and pear aromas and flavors, but a bit on the sweet side. Bright citrus and peach notes add interest, a touch of chalk keeps the sweetness in check, and the oak comes up dramatically on the back end. **88** *(8/1/2001)*

Château Julien 2001 Private Reserve Sur Lie Chardonnay (Monterey County) $30. Opens with pretty aromas of tropical fruits and well-toasted oak, and then turns sturdily acidic in the mouth, with flavors of pineapples and apples. Finishes a bit lean, but it's a nicely structured wine that's versatile at the table. **85** —*S.H. (2/1/2004)*

Château Julien 2000 Private Reserve Sur Lie Chardonnay (Monterey County) $30. Oakier and leesier than the château's regular bottling, with riper fruit that veers into papayas and mangoes. Still, there's something earthy and heavy about the wine. **86** —*S.H. (2/1/2003)*

Château Julien 1998 Private Reserve Sur Lie Chardonnay (Monterey County) $20. 86 *(6/1/2000)*

Château Julien 1997 Private Reserve Sur Lie Chardonnay (Monterey County) $20. 91 Editors' Choice *(2/1/2000)*

Château Julien 1999 Merlot (Monterey County) $10. Clumsy, combining plummy, tarry notes with earthy, mushroomy ones. It's fairly dry, with very soft acids and a viscous mouthfeel, like cough medicine. Not a poorly made wine, but simple, and with rough edges. **83** —*S.H. (9/12/2002)*

Château Julien 2001 Barrel Aged Merlot (Monterey County) $10. A little green and sharp, but clean and dry, with slight cherry-berry flavors and firm tannins. **82** —*S.H. (3/1/2005)*

Château Julien 2000 Barrel Aged Merlot (Monterey County) $10. On the thin side, with earthy, mushroomy flavors joined to riper ones of blackberries. Toasty oak brings sweet tannins and vanilla to the mix. **85** —*S.H. (12/1/2003)*

Château Julien 1998 Barrel Aged Merlot (Monterey County) $10. You might think this was a North Coast Merlot, it's so ripe and round and pleasant to drink. Not complex, but with pretty black cherry flavors and their hint of smoky oak, it's tasty. Plus, the tannins are soft. Loses a bit for some raisiny notes, but otherwise, not bad. **85 Best Buy** —*S.H. (5/1/2001)*

Château Julien 1997 Barrel Aged Merlot (Monterey County) $10. 86 *(2/1/2000)*

Château Julien 1999 Estate Merlot (Monterey County) $22. Starts off with oaky aromas floating over cassis and blackberry, and turns exceptionally tannic in the mouth. Numbing, stunning, it's a palate shocker, and doesn't have the fruit to balance the tannins out. Superrich foods, like a leg of lamb, will fare best. **85** —*S.H. (11/15/2002)*

Château Julien 2000 Estate Bottled Merlot (Monterey County) $22. Barely ripe fruity flavors mingle with green, stalky notes, with astringent tannins and a slightly sweet finish. Awkward. **82** —*S.H. (2/1/2004)*

Château Julien 2002 Estate Vineyard Merlot (Monterey County) $20. Raspingly dry, with tough, hard-edged tannins, and disagreeable sweet and sour Chinese sauce flavors that finish astringent. **81** —*S.H. (11/1/2006)*

Château Julien 2001 Estate Vineyard Merlot (Monterey County) $22. Smells and tastes a little hot and overripe, as if some shriveled berries ended up in the hopper. Beyond that, dry and soft, with blackberry and cocoa flavors. **84** —*S.H. (3/1/2005)*

Château Julien 1998 Estate Vineyard Merlot (Monterey County) $22. Very dark, and it coats the inside of the glass with glycerine. The aromas also are strong, suggesting berries, plums, and spices. It drinks round, full-bodied and flavorful, with a fruity extract that only sunny, warm conditions can provide. Moderate tannins suggest short-term aging possibilities. **86** —*S.H. (12/1/2001)*

Château Julien 2001 Private Reserve Merlot (Monterey County) $36. Soft, fruity, and simple, with cherry-chocolate flavors, this dry red wine simply lacks vivacity. **82** —*S.H. (12/1/2005)*

Château Julien 2000 Private Reserve Merlot (Monterey County) $30. Lots of mint and dill in this unripe wine. It's very dry, with some sharp tannins that lead to an astringent finish. **82** —*S.H. (3/1/2005)*

Château Julien 1999 Private Reserve Merlot (Monterey County) $30. Smells inviting, with fancy oaky smoke and vanilla that mingles with underlying cassis and black currant. Then it turns quite tannic in the mouth, so it's hard to find the blackberry flavors. Drink with a juicy steak, or cellar for a few years. **86** —*S.H. (12/31/2003)*

Château Julien 1998 Private Reserve Merlot (Monterey County) $30. There are some plum and blackberry notes in this dry, rather soft wine. There are also numbing tannins, but they're negotiable. It struggles to achieve richness because, after all, the vintage was lousy, and Monterey (outside Carmel Valley) has yet to make the case for Bordeaux reds. **85** *(11/15/2002)*

Château Julien 1997 Private Reserve Merlot (Monterey County) $20. An interesting wine here: some decent blackberry and cassis aromas and flavors and a strong note of anise or licorice. It's not unpleasant, but it is

atypical. Once you get past that, it's pretty good. Some high-toned tannins that suggest mid-term ageability. **86** —*S.H. (5/1/2001)*

Château Julien 1996 Private Reserve Merlot (Monterey County) $20. 87 *(2/1/2000)*

Château Julien 2004 Pinot Grigio (Monterey County) $10. Simple and dry, this fruit-forward wine has peach, nectarine and ripe green apple flavors that are boosted by palate-cleansing Central Coast acidity. **85 Best Buy** —*S.H. (2/1/2006)*

Château Julien 2003 Pinot Grigio (Monterey County) $10. Juicy and refreshing, a nice afternoon apéritif. You'll relish the ripe fig, melon, and spice flavors and crispness. **84** —*S.H. (12/15/2004)*

Château Julien 2000 Pinot Grigio (Monterey County) $10. There's not much to the aroma except for thin lemon notes, but it picks up some pretty citrus and peach flavors in the mouth. Finishes with a nice, clean, slightly off-dry spiciness. **83** —*S.H. (11/15/2001)*

Château Julien 2002 Barrel Aged Pinot Grigio (Monterey County) $10. A fun wine with lemon-and-lime flavors, grassy hay, and a flourish of ripe fig. Very, very dry, with a crisp, tart acidity that cleanses the palate and prepares it for food. **85** —*S.H. (2/1/2004)*

Château Julien 2001 Barrel Aged Pinot Grigio (Monterey County) $10. Fruity and simple, a wine that will give pleasure if you're not looking for complexities. Peaches, melons, and figs, a little sweet, a bit soft. **84** —*S.H. (9/1/2003)*

Château Julien 1997 Sangiovese (California) $13. 87 *(2/1/2000)*

Château Julien 1999 Sangiovese (Monterey County) $10. Smoky, brown-sugar and black cherry aromas lead to a soft, berry-fruity wine that goes down nice and easy. Dry, with a spicy finish. This simple, likeable wine will go well with a wide variety of foods. **84** —*S.H. (11/15/2001)*

Château Julien 2001 Barrel Aged Sangiovese (Monterey County) $10. An easy-drinking wine marked by cherry, herb, and tobacco flavors, a silky texture, and crisp acidity. Has just a tiny too much sweetness, which gives it a cough-mediciney note, but offers pretty good bang for your buck. **85** —*S.H. (3/1/2004)*

Château Julien 2000 Barrel Aged Sangiovese (Monterey County) $10. Think of this as a great by-the-glass red at an inexpensive, family-style restaurant. It's pale in color and soft in tannins, with pretty cherry flavors. Good acidity perks it up, and helps make it a value. Perfect with pizza and lasagna. **86** —*S.H. (12/1/2002)*

Château Julien 2001 Sauvignon Blanc (Monterey County) $9. This is a soft wine, light in body and flavor. It's clean and fruity, with candy tastes and some sweetness. Should do just fine for an affordable, modest wine with no obvious faults. **84** —*S.H. (9/1/2003)*

Château Julien 2000 Sauvignon Blanc (Monterey County) $9. The lemon and grapefruit aromas are thin; the flavors suggest slightly sweetened grapefruit juice. Soft acidity and supple tannins complete the picture. **83** —*S.H. (11/15/2001)*

Château Julien 1998 Barrel Aged Sauvignon Blanc (Monterey County) $8. 84 *(2/1/2000)*

Château Julien 2002 Barrel Fermented Sauvignon Blanc (Monterey County) $9. Very dry, a wine whose alcohol and acidity stand out because the flavors are thin. There are hints of lime and grapefruit, but this is really a modest little wine with few pretensions. **83** —*S.H. (12/31/2003)*

Château Julien 2002 Syrah (Monterey County) $22. Must come from a warmer part of the county, because the fruit is very ripe and elaborate. Delicious in peppery blackberry, leather, and plum flavors, and dry, with rich, complex tannins. A wine to watch. **89** —*S.H. (10/1/2004)*

Château Julien 2000 Syrah (Monterey County) $10. There's a ton of true varietal character in this fun wine. It's very dark in color, and has the nicest aromas of white pepper and blackberries. Tastes just great, rich and filled with berry flavors, bone dry, with smooth tannins. No, it's not a wine of great complexity. But it's still a very good wine. **88 Best Buy** —*S.H. (12/1/2002)*

Château Julien 1999 Syrah (Monterey County) $15. Some of our tasters found this Monterey offering tart and shrill, with strawberry and rhubarb flavors; others praised it for its dark fruit, olive, and anise

USA

flavors. In the end, it's a solid California red that might improve with a year or two of cellaring. **85** *(10/1/2001)*

Château Julien 2003 Estate Vineyard Syrah (Monterey County) $22. This wine has some rough spots, mainly a sharp greenness in the mouth, but it's smooth and velvety in tannins, and very dry. The next step is to get the fruit riper. **84** —*S.H. (3/1/2006)*

Château Julien 2001 Estate Vineyard Syrah (Monterey County) $22. Aromas of smoke, leather, blackberry, and cherry, with oaky nuances. The flavors are very ripe and provide a sunburst of cherry and blackberry that spreads across the palate. The texture is soft and velvety, leading to a mildly astringent finish. **87** —*S.H. (2/1/2004)*

Château Julien 2000 Barrel Aged Zinfandel (Monterey County) $10. Kicks off with pretty toast and oak notes, followed by hints of blackberry, spice, plum, and anise flavors. It's a bit tart on the finish, however. **85** *(11/1/2003)*

Château Julien 1999 Barrel Aged Zinfandel (Monterey County) $10. The words "Zinfandel" and "Monterey" on a label raise eyebrows. The region is cold, and Zin requires heat. This wine aims high but can't overcome its rugged, herbal nature. There are some ripe berry flavors side by side with vegetal ones. The giveaway price is only fair. **83** —*S.H. (11/1/2002)*

Château Julien 2003 Private Reserve Zinfandel (Monterey County) $36. So easy to drink due to the soft, velvety texture and mouthfilling flavors of cherry compote, blackberry jam, and mocha flavors that are finished with the smoky, vanilla accents of smoky oak. This rich Zin even shows blueberry cobbler on the finish. **87** —*S.H. (6/1/2006)*

CHÂTEAU LAFAYETTE RENEAU

Château Lafayette Reneau 2002 Cabernet Sauvignon (Finger Lakes) $NA. Starting to fade at the rim of the glass, this wine has nice aromas of mushroom, balsam, and blueberry pie. It lacks body, though, and the cinnamon and red berry flavors are moderate at best. Finishes with some nice spicy notes. **82** —*M.D. (8/1/2006)*

Château Lafayette Reneau 1999 Owner's Reserve Cabernet Sauvignon (Finger Lakes) $45. If you can handle the pounding aromas of barrel char and spice, which is akin to southern BBQ, then you should like this ripe, well-balanced Cabernet from New York. The palate is substantial, with plum and cherry flavors and a chewy mouthfeel. The finish is multilayered and spicy, and diggers will find some depth and secondary characteristics. **86** —*M.S. (3/1/2003)*

Château Lafayette Reneau 1997 Blanc de Blancs Champagne Blend (Finger Lakes) $30. **87** —*M.M. (12/1/2000)*

Château Lafayette Reneau 2000 Barrel Fermented Chardonnay (Finger Lakes) $13. A pleasant wine, with moderate body, bright acidity and a pear, melon, apple, citrus, and spice flavors. The finish is a bit short and quite lemony. **84** —*J.M. (1/1/2003)*

Château Lafayette Reneau 2000 Proprietor's Reserve-Barrel Fermented Chardonnay (Finger Lakes) $19. Quite viscous and bright, with lots of lemon, orange, pear, melon, and spice flavors. Toasty oak and vanilla also are in evidence, as well as a slight hint of sweetness on the finish. Still, crisp and clean at the end. **89** —*J.M. (1/1/2003)*

Château Lafayette Reneau 2005 Johannisberg Riesling (Finger Lakes) $15. Semisweet, with lemon verbena and honeysuckle aromas and lychee, citrus, and spice flavors. Lacks acidity, to match the sugar and has a gritty mouthfeel ending with sweet bubble gum. **83** —*M.D. (8/1/2006)*

Château Lafayette Reneau 2001 Johannisberg Riesling (Finger Lakes) $12. Sweet and honeyed, but with enough tongue-tingling acidity to keep it almost in check, this is a well-made sweet table wine. Aromas and flavors blend tangerines and ripe apples. **85** —*J.C. (8/1/2003)*

Château Lafayette Reneau 2002 Pinot Noir (Finger Lakes) $20. A rusty color belies this wine's age, but it's still enjoyable, with firm flavors of cola and barnyard. Light yet viscous, with soft tannins. This should be drunk now. **84** —*M.D. (12/1/2006)*

Château Lafayette Reneau 2001 Cuvée Rouge Red Blend (Finger Lakes) $9. Somewhat strange at first, with ultra-bright texture and a riotous array of canned cherry, menthol, blueberry, and herb flavors. Tannins are rustic and the finish is a bit longer than you bargained for, with a touch of sweetness at the end. **80** —*J.M. (3/1/2003)*

Château Lafayette Reneau 2005 Dry Riesling (Finger Lakes) $15. Despite its "dry" label, this Riesling has a touch of sweetness. A Gewürz-like nose of spicy lychee and rose petal dominates, with some aromatic mint notes. In the mouth, the fruit is more generic and candied, but has nice hints of mineral. Finishes with spice and citrus pith. **86** —*M.D. (8/1/2006)*

CHÂTEAU MONTELENA

Château Montelena 2003 Cabernet Sauvignon (Napa Valley) $40. Too young to enjoy now. The tannins and acids are such that they lock the wine down. The fruit tastes sharp and jammy, and the alcohol, even though it isn't high, sticks out. But it's all there, including oodles of blackberries, cherries, licorice, and spice. Needs time. Give it until 2009. **90 Cellar Selection** —*S.H. (12/1/2006)*

Château Montelena 2002 Montelena Estate Cabernet Sauvignon (Napa Valley) $95. Right now this wine is strutting its stuff, showing dense, fudge-like scents of tobacco, cassis, and whiffs of vanilla and coconut and flavors of blackberry with lashings of vanilla and cocoa. But like many vintages of Montelena, expect this one to shut down in another year only to reemerge as a beauty around age 10 or 12. Another classic. **93 Cellar Selection** —*J.C. (9/1/2006)*

Château Montelena 1998 Chardonnay (Napa Valley) $30. The historic estate's 1998 is characteristically lean, angular, and fairly closed. The bouquet of apple cider, anise, and fragrant jasmine-like notes opens to a trim palate of green apple and toast flavors, and a taut mouthfeel. Tart apple and oak, plus a flinty, mineral element play on the finish. Notoriously tight when young, this wine often opens incredibly with cellaring. **87** *(7/1/2001)*

Château Montelena 1997 Chardonnay (Napa Valley) $29. **86** *(6/1/2000)*

Château Montelena 1996 Chardonnay (Napa Valley) $29. **90** —*S.H. (6/1/1999)*

Château Montelena 2001 Riesling (Potter Valley) $15. A nice example of a crisp, tart, and bone-dry Riesling, from a little-known region of Mendocino. Lime, diesel, and flowery tastes finish smooth and clean. Try this as an alternative to Sauvignon Blanc. **85** —*S.H. (12/31/2003)*

Château Montelena 2000 Zinfandel (Napa Valley) $25. Montelena's first Zin since 1994, from estate grapes. Fully ripe and exuberant, a robust wine with cherry and spice flavors that is dry and balanced. Possesses Zin's inherently wild and briary character, but brings as much elegance as the varietal is capable of. **87** —*S.H. (9/1/2003)*

CHÂTEAU MORRISETTE

Château Morrisette 2002 Chardonnay (Virginia) $16. The scents of toasted nuts and lemon furniture polish don't mesh all that harmoniously, but this wine still boasts enough crisp, lemon, and grapefruit flavors to make up for it. Slightly oily in the mouth, with a finish that veers back toward the oaky side. **83** —*J.C. (9/1/2005)*

CHÂTEAU POTELLE

Château Potelle 1997 V.G.S. Cabernet Sauvignon (Mount Veeder) $63. **92** *(11/1/2000)*

Château Potelle 2001 VGS Cabernet Sauvignon (Mount Veeder) $60. Dry and tannic, a real mountain wine that's tight and astringent now, but impeccably structured for the long haul. It has deep flavors of blackberries and plums, with a spiciness throughout, and needs time. Best 2007–2011. **90 Cellar Selection** —*S.H. (9/1/2006)*

Château Potelle 2000 VGS Cabernet Sauvignon (Mount Veeder) $40. A touch of green herbs accompanies the blackberry flavors, and the finish is sharp in acids. However, the tannins are fine and soft. Blame it on the vintage. **86** —*S.H. (2/1/2005)*

Château Potelle 2002 VGS Chardonnay (Mount Veeder) $35. This huge wine captures the essence of mountain fruit. Dense and concentrated in ripe pear, tropical fruit, and spice flavors, it also oozes elaborate honey, marzipan, and buttered toast from oak. Has the weight and intensity of a great white Burgundy. **93** —*S.H. (5/1/2005)*

Château Potelle 1999 VGS Chardonnay (Mount Veeder) $39. Has the lean and tight structure of a mountain wine, with crisp acids framing citrus and peach flavors, but it's also notable for its creamy, lush texture and rich finish. This wine changes constantly in the glass and should improve with age through 2005. **93** —*S.H. (5/1/2003)*

Château Potelle 1998 VGS Chardonnay (Mount Veeder) $39. This wild yeast wine has emerged as one of California's most consistently interesting and concentrated Chards. The dense overlay of oak doesn't just mask watery fruit. These spicy, peachy flavors are massive. Waves of palate sensations roll over the tongue, even in this weak vintage. The wine is also an ager. **94** —*S.H. (9/1/2002)*

Château Potelle 1997 VGS Chardonnay (Mount Veeder) $45. Tasters pegged apples, anise, crème brûlée, and cinnamon in the lively nose of this rich wine—one that also sparked some controversy. The straight-ahead flavor profile is appealing, with solid apple, clove, and butterscotch offset by the attractive anise streak. But is it native yeast or heavy malolactic fermentation that's responsible for the mixed feelings some panelists expressed? Concerns were noted about a dairy-like note on the nose and also a slick, yet gummy texture. Nevertheless, the winning aromas and flavors kept the overall take positive. **87** *(7/1/2001)*

Château Potelle 2002 Riviera Red Blend (Paso Robles) $15. Almost like a nouveau-style wine, fresh and young. Delicate flavors of strawberries drink very dry, although rich foods will coax out the hidden sweetness. A Syrah–Zinfandel blend. **85** —*S.H. (11/15/2003)*

Château Potelle 2001 Riviera Red Blend (Paso Robles) $16. A Syrah-Zinfandel blend that's deep in color, and deep in dark stone fruit flavors. It's full-bodied for a rose, although the tannins are very airy and light. Very dry, this wine has some complexity. **86** —*S.H. (9/1/2003)*

Château Potelle 2004 Sauvignon Blanc (Mendocino) $15. This Sauvignon shows ripe citrus, fig, and melon flavors, while oak and lees add toasty buttercream and vanilla highlights. Best of all is the mouthfeel, which is bright and clean in acidity. **87** —*S.H. (12/1/2006)*

Château Potelle 2001 Sauvignon Blanc (Napa Valley) $15. Distinctive and delicate in the mouth, with crisp acids and very nice flavors, including spearmint, citrus fruits, peaches, and sweet oak. **90 Best Buy** —*S.H. (10/1/2003)*

Château Potelle 2000 Sauvignon Blanc (Napa Valley) $15. Made in a pop style, with spearmint and peach flavors that smack of a tiny little bit of sugar. Yet the acidity and the varietal's underlying citrus character qualify it as a dry wine. This is an easy drinking, uncomplex wine that offers plenty of pleasure. **86** —*S.H. (9/1/2003)*

Château Potelle 2001 Syrah (Paso Robles) $24. Made in the firm, grippy style typical of Potelle's reds, this Syrah could use a couple of years to settle down. But once it does, it'll be fine, with herbal, pepper, and meat accents to the chewy berry fruit. **88** *(9/1/2005)*

Château Potelle 2002 VGS Syrah (Mount Veeder) $75. Dense and structured, this rating may look conservative in a few years' time when this wine comes into its own. Right now, it displays some coffee and blackberry notes against a backdrop of toasty oak and chewy tannins, but the long finish bodes well for the future. **87** *(9/1/2005)*

Château Potelle 2001 Zinfandel (Paso Robles) $22. Quite plush, with charry, smoky, chocolate, coffee, plum, black cherry, vanilla, spice, and toast flavors. The tannins are ripe and smooth, framing a full-bodied wine that offers plenty of spice and richness on the long finish. **90 Editors' Choice** *(11/1/2003)*

Château Potelle 2000 Zinfandel (Paso Robles) $22. This fine Napa producer has set up a Paso Robles operation and here is the result. This is a soft, hot country Zin, with plummy, raisiny flavors, considerable alcohol, and nonexistent tannins. The wine is dry, with a fruity finish. **85** —*S.H. (12/1/2002)*

Château Potelle 2004 Mount Veeder Estate Zinfandel (Napa Valley) $55. Potelle has quietly been crafting one of California's greatest Zins for many years now, from grapes on their mountain estate. There's always a claret-like balance, with beautifully pronounced fruit, near-perfect tannins, and balancing acids without the high alcohol that plagues other Zins. **92** —*S.H. (12/15/2006)*

Château Potelle 1999 Old Vines Zinfandel (Amador County) $18. No mistaking the brambly, wild-berry character of this rugged but likeable wine. It's ripe and fruity and dry, with the sappy fructose of black raspberries and loganberries. Jagged tannins and crisp acidity make it perfect for barbecue. **87** —*S.H. (7/1/2002)*

Château Potelle 1997 Old Vines Zinfandel (Amador County) $21. **85** —*S.H. (5/1/2000)*

Château Potelle 1999 V.G.S. Zinfandel (Mount Veeder) $50. A claret-style Zin in its delicacy, harmony, and racy balance, but there's nothing reserved about the flavors of this mountain wine. Drinks brightly rich and fruity, with gorgeous tannins. There's a graceful femininity to this wine despite somewhat high alcohol. **90** —*S.H. (9/1/2002)*

Château Potelle 1997 V.G.S. Zinfandel (Mount Veeder) $43. **86** —*J.C. (2/1/2000)*

Château Potelle 1997 V.G.S. Zinfandel (Mount Veeder) $35. **91** —*S.H. (6/1/1999)*

Château Potelle 2002 V.G.S. Zinfandel (Mount Veeder) $53. Always among the most elegant and claret-like Zins, this mountain beauty seems to express the French attitude of Potelle's owners. Graceful and harmonious despite the power: the plum, blackberry, and herb flavors have been crafted into a taut, ageable wine. **93** —*S.H. (5/1/2005)*

Château Potelle 2000 V.G.S. Zinfandel (Mount Veeder) $53. Striking for its color, nearly black, suggesting that these mountain grapes are extremely concentrated. Well-toasted oak dominates the aroma, although there are underlying notes of blackberries. Drinks big and massive, with blackberry flavors. A hit of acid shows up on the finish. Cellar material. **91** —*S.H. (3/1/2003)*

CHÂTEAU RODIN

Château Rodin 1999 Zinfandel (El Dorado) $15. Ripe enough grapes, filled with blueberry and black raspberry and pepper flavors, and on the smooth and mellow side. That said, there's a rustic quality, jagged and earthy, and a hint of bitterness in the finish that detracts. **83** —*S.H. (9/1/2002)*

CHÂTEAU SOUVERAIN

Château Souverain 1996 Cabernet Sauvignon (Sonoma County) $17. **91** *(11/15/1999)*

Château Souverain 2002 Cabernet Sauvignon (Alexander Valley) $22. The winery's regular Alexander Valley Cab has not been getting better over the years. They seem to be stretching the vines, producing lean wines that no amount of oak can improve. A decent sipper. **83** —*S.H. (12/31/2005)*

Château Souverain 2001 Cabernet Sauvignon (Alexander Valley) $20. Shows the balance and elegance this winery and region are known for, with modest cherry-blackberry flavors and a touch of smoky oak. Very dry, with a good grip of tannins, this is a nice restaurant wine. **86** —*S.H. (3/1/2005)*

Château Souverain 2000 Cabernet Sauvignon (Alexander Valley) $20. This dependable winery tried hard this poor vintage, and has turned out a beautiful, small wine. It feels as lush and velvety and has some polished cassis and black currant flavors, but is disappointingly thin, especially in the middle palate. **85** —*S.H. (11/15/2003)*

Château Souverain 1999 Cabernet Sauvignon (Alexander Valley) $20. Has the soft, easy but complex tannins that made the appellation famous, and bracing acidity underpinning blackberry, olive, and herb flavors. Feels good and rich in the mouth. Try cellaring it for a few years. **87** —*S.H. (8/1/2003)*

Château Souverain 2001 Winemaker's Reserve Cabernet Sauvignon (Alexander Valley) $40. A very fine wine that showcases what Souverain can do, and also the vintage and the appellation. Well-ripened black currant and cassis flavors are wrapped in a smooth, creamy wine, with good acidity. The mouth experience is rich and classy. **91** —*S.H. (10/1/2005)*

Château Souverain 2000 Winemaker's Reserve Cabernet Sauvignon (Alexander Valley) $35. Offers lush, intricate flavors of blackberries, cassis, roasted coffeebean, sweet milk chocolate, and toasty oak in a soft, gentle wine that has complexity and interest. Not an ager, but a real beauty. **91** —*S.H. (11/15/2004)*

Château Souverain 1999 Winemaker's Reserve Cabernet Sauvignon (Alexander Valley) $35. Luscious, long, full-bodied and rich, a wonderful wine that showcases its appellation. Has well-ripened flavors of black currants and cassis that drink long and deep, although there's some hollowness, which costs it a few points. The flavors are wrapped in soft, easy but complex tannins. Fully dry and nicely oaked, this wine is immediately enjoyable. **90** —S.H. (11/15/2003)

Château Souverain 1997 Winemaker's Reserve Cabernet Sauvignon (Alexander Valley) $35. Makes you want to shout—it's that good. Pure Alexander Valley all the way, with well-ripened cassis and blackberry-infused fruit and soft, luscious, but intricately detailed tannins. A blast of new oak contributes vanilla, toast, and mint. The finish is very dry and complex. **92 Editors' Choice** —S.H. (12/1/2001)

Château Souverain 1996 Winemaker's Reserve Cabernet Sauvignon (Sonoma County) $35. **88** —S.H. (12/15/2000)

Château Souverain 2004 Chardonnay (Sonoma County) $17. Sweet in fruit, almost sugary but staying just dry, this well-oaked wine has ripe flavors of apricots, pineapples, and bananas sautéed in butter. It's a tasty sipper meant to satisfy, and it does. **85** —S.H. (3/1/2006)

Château Souverain 2003 Chardonnay (Sonoma County) $14. Lots to like in this wine. It has ripe peach and pear flavors, with a blast of smoky oak, buttered toast, and lees. Finishes rich in honeyed fruit. **86** —S.H. (3/1/2005)

Château Souverain 2002 Chardonnay (Sonoma County) $14. Loads of mango and papaya, peach, pear, and spice in this delicious wine. Oak adds intricate notes of vanilla and smoke, but the best thing is the bright burst of acidity that keeps it clean. **89 Best Buy** —S.H. (2/1/2004)

Château Souverain 2001 Chardonnay (Sonoma County) $14. Boldly assertive with full-throttle flavors of pears and apples, with a lot of sweet, smoky oak thrown in. Dryish and smoothly textured, a creamy wine that feels good and round in the mouth. Not a lot of depth, but clean and flavorful. **86** —S.H. (6/1/2003)

Château Souverain 2000 Chardonnay (Sonoma County) $14. Flamboyant is the word here. Huge aromas and flavors of tropical fruit, butterscotch, vanilla, smoke, and oriental spices are lavishly oaked. The wine drinks rich and creamy and slightly sweet, and will be fabulous with cream sauce and lobster. And look at that price! A super-value. **91** —S.H. (5/1/2002)

Château Souverain 1999 Chardonnay (Sonoma County) $14. From a value leader, another rich, creamy, toasty Chard, loaded with peach, apple, and pear flavors and a lot of oak. Good acidity and a long finish, but it has a little too much sugar to be considered dry. **85** —S.H. (5/1/2001)

Château Souverain 1997 Reserve Chardonnay (Russian River Valley) $25. **88** (6/1/2000)

Château Souverain 2003 Winemaker's Reserve Chardonnay (Russian River Valley) $30. This barrel fermented wine was aged in 76% new French oak. The Chardonnay has a spicy vanilla character of its own. That double whammy drowns out the tropical fruit, making the wine all toast and sweet vanilla. **82** —S.H. (11/15/2005)

Château Souverain 2001 Winemaker's Reserve Chardonnay (Russian River Valley) $25. Superripe and gooey with tropical fruit. Bursting with mango, pineapple, guava, orange, roasted hazelnut, buttered toast, vanilla, and smoke, in a custardy texture that's smooth and refined. Finishes dry, with a lingering flavor of orange and spice. **90** (12/31/2003)

Château Souverain 2000 Winemaker's Reserve Chardonnay (Alexander Valley) $25. Lush, with butterscotch, vanilla, apple, pear and peach overtones. A tangy mineral edge adds balance, albeit perhaps too brightly. Clean at the end. **87** —J.M. (12/15/2002)

Château Souverain 1999 Winemaker's Reserve Chardonnay (Russian River Valley) $25. Size defines this well-oaked full-bodied wine, which starts with creamy, leesy aromas and turns richly oaky and fruity in the mouth. It's a bit jagged now, and the parts need a little time to knit together, but should make for fine drinking after 2002. **86** —S.H. (12/1/2001)

Château Souverain 1997 Merlot (Sonoma County) $17. **87** —J.C. (7/1/2000)

Château Souverain 2002 Merlot (Alexander Valley) $18. Easy and soft, as befits the variety and appellation, and has extra layers of complexity that make it very good. Rich in blackberries and flowers, with subtle oak and a good backbone of acidity to cut through that steak or lamb. **87** —S.H. (6/1/2005)

Château Souverain 2000 Merlot (Alexander Valley) $18. From a long-time value producer, an immensely rich wine with significantly ripe, big fruit. Has layers of flavors ranging from blackberries and plums to chocolate, and is very dry. But the tannins are great, plush and thick and easy. Might benefit from a year or so in the bottle. **89** —S.H. (8/1/2003)

Château Souverain 1999 Merlot (Alexander Valley) $17. Here's a wine to celebrate, one that reeks with class at a comparatively fair price. It's sleek, combining cassis, sage, and plum flavors with a dose of smoky oak. Dry and a bit tannic, it's a fine dinner wine rivalling some that cost twice as much. **89** —S.H. (9/1/2002)

Château Souverain 1997 Sauvignon Blanc (Sonoma County) $9. **87 Best Buy** —S.H. (9/1/1999)

Château Souverain 2005 Sauvignon Blanc (Alexander Valley) $14. This everyday wine starts with a blast of cat pee, then offers more generous fig, honeydew, apricot, and citrus fruit flavors that finish dry, or nearly so. Zingy acidity makes it all clean and vibrant. **84** —S.H. (12/1/2006)

Château Souverain 2004 Sauvignon Blanc (Alexander Valley) $14. Bone dry and crisp, with some of that raw, feline character, this white is complexed with notes of citrus fruits and just-ripe figs. This pretty cocktail-style wine turns super-spicy on the finish. **85** —S.H. (11/15/2005)

Château Souverain 2002 Sauvignon Blanc (Alexander Valley) $14. Grassy, citrusy, and tart, but those who like this slightly aggressive style will love it. It's dry as dust, with big acids. The winemaker barrel fermented it in order to bring sweeter, softer features, and has succeeded. **87** —S.H. (2/1/2004)

Château Souverain 2001 Sauvignon Blanc (Alexander Valley) $12. Fresh and lively, with lots of melon, citrus, fig, and herb flavors. Zippy clean on the finish. **87** —J.M. (9/1/2003)

Château Souverain 2000 Sauvignon Blanc (Sonoma County) $12. This Sauvignon Blanc stays true to the grassy, citrusy expression of this variety, with bright, focused aromas and flavors of lemons, although a small amount of Chardonnay adds an apply note. It's not quite dry, and a soft roundness adds to the impression of sweetness. **84** —S.H. (11/15/2001)

Château Souverain 2002 Syrah (Alexander Valley) $20. Shows real classy Syrah character in the peppery, meaty aromas and flavors, and plenty of ripe, fruit, and berry complexities. Also demonstrates the balance this winery is known for. Actually more of an old-style field blend, with other Rhône varieties. **87** —S.H. (6/1/2005)

Château Souverain 2000 Syrah (Alexander Valley) $20. Young and jammy, made Aussie Shiraz-style with black stone fruit and berry flavors and strong, immature acids. Very dry, although the tannins are soft. Try with short ribs of beef or similar fare. **87** —S.H. (2/1/2003)

Château Souverain 1999 Syrah (Sonoma County) $20. A blackberry and toast profile marks this quite dark but appealing wine. The mouthfeel is even, but some tasters thought it a bit narrow, and maybe too structured for the depth of fruit. Licorice and tar and moderate tannins close of this inky, mid-weight cruiser. **86** (10/1/2001)

Château Souverain 1997 Zinfandel (Dry Creek Valley) $13. **86** —J.C. (5/1/2000)

Château Souverain 2002 Zinfandel (Dry Creek Valley) $18. Picture perfect Zin from this appellation. It's dry, with flavors of wild berries, briary nettles, and coffee, with a slight raisiny note that adds pleasure. The dusty tannins are fine. Finishes with a slight rusticity that cries out for food. **88** —S.H. (4/1/2005)

Château Souverain 2001 Zinfandel (Dry Creek Valley) $18. Tannins are plush, though the wine is bright. Chocolate, coffee, plum, black cherry, and spice run through the core. It's toasty on the finish, with a green tea edge. **87** (11/1/2003)

Château Souverain 1999 Zinfandel (Dry Creek Valley) $13. From old vines, a fruity wine brimming with wild berry flavors and earthy, spicy notes.

It's dry and soft, although there's a sturdy backbone of tannins to stand up to barbecue. **84**—*S.H. (11/15/2001)*

Château Souverain 1998 Winemaker's Reserve Zinfandel (Dry Creek Valley) $25. This is 100% Zinfandel, unlike the regular bottling, from specially selected barrels. 300 cases made. There's concentrated raspberry fruit in the nose, good intensity on the palate, with a good, rich mouthfeel and full, soft tannins in the finish. **89**—*P.G. (3/1/2001)*

CHÂTEAU ST. JEAN

Château St. Jean 1998 Cinq Cepages Cabernet Blend (Sonoma County) $70. 90—*D.T. (6/1/2002)*

Château St. Jean 2001 Estate Vineyard Cabernet Franc (Sonoma Valley) $50. As good as this wine is, in my opinion Cabernet Franc by itself cannot make a great wine. It's certainly delicious, with cherry, currant, pecan pie, and vanilla flavors, and the tannins are soft, sweet, and complex. But it lacks the depth that a darker varietal, like Cabernet, brings to the table. **88**—*S.H. (3/1/2005)*

Château St. Jean 2002 St. Jean Estate Vineyard Cabernet Franc (Sonoma Valley) $50. As a component wine, this brings a rich cherry aromatic to a Cab blend. On its own, the wine is fairly simple, with red cherry and mocha flavors, and plenty of oak. The wine is dry and elegant. Drink now. **87**—*S.H. (4/1/2006)*

Château St. Jean 2003 Cabernet Sauvignon (Sonoma County) $27. The grapes came from the county's warmer regions, and you can taste the sunshine. Blackberry jam, black currant, cherry, French olive, Provençal herb, and spice flavors are boosted by smoky oak, resulting in a generous, complex wine that has a rich tannic edge but is ready to drink now. **89**—*S.H. (11/15/2006)*

Château St. Jean 2003 Cabernet Sauvignon (California) $15. It may have a statewide appellation, but this wine showcases the winery's skill in crafting complex Cabs at all price levels. With blackberry, cassis, coffee, and oak flavors and long, dry finish, it's a fine, very drinkable wine. **85**—*S.H. (12/15/2005)*

Château St. Jean 2002 Cabernet Sauvignon (Sonoma County) $27. Easy, gentle and soft, this is a simple, fairly thin Cab that's balanced and harmonious. The blackberry and currant flavors, accented by oak, will go well with a juicy steak. **84**—*S.H. (12/31/2005)*

Château St. Jean 2002 Cabernet Sauvignon (California) $15. Rough and ready, but decent in berry-cherry fruit, with easy tannins. This is an everyday Cab with lots of good qualities. **84**—*S.H. (2/1/2005)*

Château St. Jean 2001 Cabernet Sauvignon (Sonoma County) $27. Here's a big, bold wine, made with superripe grapes that achieved intense, although varietally correct, flavors. It's also very oaky. Dry, with a creamy texture and a very long finish in which the cassis sinks into the tongue and stays there. It will develop nicely through 2007. **89**—*S.H. (8/1/2004)*

Château St. Jean 2000 Cabernet Sauvignon (Sonoma County) $27. With some caramelized oak and lots of black fruit, the bouquet isn't snazzy but it doesn't falter. The palate is fresh, lively and loaded with cherry and plum fruit, while the finish is broad, with soft tannins. Very much a mass-market Cab, but one with just enough power and complexity. **87**—*M.S. (11/15/2003)*

Château St. Jean 1996 Cinq Cepages Cabernet Sauvignon (Sonoma County) $33. 92—*J.C. (2/1/2000)*

Château St. Jean 2002 Cinq Cepages Cabernet Sauvignon (Sonoma County) $75. Aloof and tannic now. It's very dry, and those tannins lock in and cry out for something to melt them. It's best to decant this wine many hours in advance of drinking it, but it should develop well over the next eight to ten years. **90 Cellar Selection**—*S.H. (4/1/2006)*

Château St. Jean 2001 Cinq Cepages Cabernet Sauvignon (Sonoma County) $75. A lovely Cab, elegant and harmonious. Strikes an even balance between cherry and blackberry flavors, smoky oak, sweet herbs, cocoa, and spice. The tannins are beautifully ripe and soft. Of all these qualities, balance is foremost. **93**—*S.H. (3/1/2005)*

Château St. Jean 2000 Cinq Cepages Cabernet Sauvignon (Sonoma County) $70. This fine wine, which is at its best now, offers polished flavors of currants, blackberries, and herbs, with smoky nuances from oak.

It is smooth and polished in the mouth, with a good balance of acids and tannins. Not an ager, but complex and elegant. **90**—*S.H. (5/1/2004)*

Château St. Jean 1999 Cinq Cepages Cabernet Sauvignon (Sonoma County) $70. Chunky aromas of red and black fruit mixed with copious oak start it off. The next phase is a spicy clove-tinged, sweet-plum palate that is downright chewy. While it's undeniably rich throughout, it doesn't quite hit the highest marks, and there's a slight green note at the core. **88**—*M.S. (3/1/2003)*

Château St. Jean 1998 Cinq Cepages Cabernet Sauvignon (Sonoma Valley) $70. The wine's cherry aromas are almost stewy, thanks to the toast and eucalyptus notes that envelop them; expect more cherry, soy, and some herbal complexity in the mouth. Medium-weight; closes with tart red fruit and full-on tannin. **90** *(6/1/2002)*

Château St. Jean 2001 Reserve Cabernet Sauvignon (Sonoma County) $90. This top-of-the-line Cab surely must be one of the last 2001s to be released. It's an exquisite wine. New oak dominates, with caramelized vanilla and char. But it's appropriate given the size of the fruit. The black currant, Hoison sauce, crème de cassis, milk chocolate, and licorice flavors are completely satisfying. Best now and for the next ten years. **93 Cellar Selection**—*S.H. (12/1/2006)*

Château St. Jean 2000 Reserve Cabernet Sauvignon (Sonoma County) $90. At this price, you have a right to demand ageability. Will it or won't it? The wine is extracted in blackberry and currant fruit. It's very dry, and the tannins are thick. It's very good, but I do not think it has the stuffing for the long haul. Best now–2010. **88**—*S.H. (10/1/2005)*

Château St. Jean 1999 Reserve Cabernet Sauvignon (Sonoma Valley) $90. Oh, how tough this wine is now. It's like a mummy, wrapped in tannins. It would be easy to pass it by until you notice the intensity of cherry-blackberry fruit. Despite its age, the wine is still aggressively young. Will it soften and improve with cellaring? Probably. Try in 2009. **90**—*S.H. (11/15/2004)*

Château St. Jean 1995 Reserve Cabernet Sauvignon (Sonoma County) $70. 89—*M.S. (9/1/2000)*

Château St. Jean 1998 Chardonnay (Sonoma County) $12. 88—*L.W. (3/1/2000)*

Château St. Jean 2004 Chardonnay (Sonoma County) $14. You'll find some tasty apricots, peach, and vanilla-oak flavors in this soft, creamy wine. It's a nice California Chardonnay, slightly sweet in the finish, and a great accompaniment to salmon or pork. **85**—*S.H. (12/1/2005)*

Château St. Jean 2003 Chardonnay (Sonoma County) $14. Rich and intricate, a Chard that satisfies with its array of white peach, pineapple, mango, buttercream, and spice flavors. Finishes with a slightly sweet, vanilla ice cream flavor. **86**—*S.H. (5/1/2005)*

Château St. Jean 2001 Chardonnay (Sonoma County) $16. A wine of considerable interest and depth. The flavors are lemon-and-limey, with notes of fig and cinnamon and smoky scents from oak. Drinks tart in acids, with some bitterness in the finish. However the balance and elegance are attractive. **88**—*S.H. (6/1/2003)*

Château St. Jean 2000 Chardonnay (Sonoma County) $14. A pretty wine, with tangy apple and pear flavors that are backed by a core of citrus and herb notes. **87**—*J.M. (12/15/2002)*

Château St. Jean 2002 Belle Terre Vineyard Chardonnay (Alexander Valley) $22. Here's a Chard that combines elegance and sophistication with great depth of flavor. It shows its terroir in the soft texture and well-ripened tropical fruit and peach flavors. There's a pretty coating of oak leading to a long, fruity-spicy finish. **89**—*S.H. (12/1/2005)*

Château St. Jean 2001 Belle Terre Vineyard Chardonnay (Alexander Valley) $24. Very rich and compelling, a beautiful wine with layers of tropical fruit, pear, buttered toast, vanilla, and spicy aromas and flavors that mingle on the palate. The creamy texture leads to a honeyed finish. **90**—*S.H. (2/1/2004)*

Château St. Jean 2000 Belle Terre Vineyard Chardonnay (Alexander Valley) $22. Sleek and elegant, with a fine blend of melon and citrus flavors. A mineral core adds complexity. It's toasty, smooth, and long at the finish. **91 Editors' Choice**—*J.M. (12/15/2002)*

Château St. Jean 1999 Belle Terre Vineyard Chardonnay (Alexander Valley) $22. Concentrated and oaky, this wine features superripe tropical fruit and spice aromas and flavors, bolstered by woody vanilla and smoke. Drinks rich and leesy, with well-etched peach, mango, and guava flavors. Crisp acidity provides freshness and zest, while the finish is clean and spicy. **89** —*S.H. (12/1/2001)*

Château St. Jean 2000 Durell Vineyard Chardonnay (Carneros) $25. Rich and buttery, with gobs of butterscotch, plum, peach, pear, vanilla, and spice flavors. A fleshy, lush example of full-bodied California Chardonnay. **91** —*J.M. (12/15/2002)*

Château St. Jean 1997 Durell Vineyard Chardonnay (Carneros) $24.89 — *L.W. (11/1/1999)*

Château St. Jean 2003 Reserve Chardonnay (Sonoma County) $45. What a roll St. Jean has been on with Chardonnay. This wine was made from a majority of Robert Young and Belle Terre vineyard fruit, and is two-thirds new French oak. The combination is mind-blowing. The vineyards contribute concentrated spicy, tropical fruit flavors and perfect acid balance, while the oak provides elaborate seasoning. Absolutely delicious. One of the most satisfying Chards of the vintage. **96 Editors' Choice** —*S.H. (12/1/2006)*

Château St. Jean 2001 Reserve Chardonnay (Sonoma County) $45. It's a pleasure to taste a Chardonnay that's big but not blowsy or overwrought. The wine has been generously oaked and put through its leesy paces, but retains pure articulation of pear and mango flavors. Part of the excellence, undoubtedly, is due to the high percent of Robert Young grapes. **93** —*S.H. (9/1/2004)*

Château St. Jean 1998 Reserve Chardonnay (Sonoma County) $45. Crème brûlée creaminess combines with tart citrus fruitiness in this wine, which displays great balance and richness. A nice oak frame holds it all together and provides a handsome framework for the lime-orange-tangerine citrus core. The palate has buttery caramel and wintergreen accents. Long, serene finish. **91** *(7/1/2001)*

Château St. Jean 2004 Robert Young Vineyard Chardonnay (Alexander Valley) $25. Lots of fancy footwork in this single-vineyard Chard. Really pleases with its deft arrangement of fine, toasty oak, ripe tropical fruit, creamy lees and refreshing acids. Displays poise and finesse, from a producer with long experience working with this vineyard. **90** —*S.H. (12/31/2006)*

Château St. Jean 2002 Robert Young Vineyard Chardonnay (Alexander Valley) $25. This single-vineyard wine has been produced for a long time. Its longevity is explained by the balance and harmony it usually shows. Soft and dry, the wine has pear, peach and buttercream flavors that finish with elegance and finesse. **90 Editors' Choice** —*S.H. (12/1/2005)*

Château St. Jean 2001 Robert Young Vineyard Chardonnay (Alexander Valley) $25. From this famed vineyard, an exciting wine. It's lush in ripe tropical fruit, peach, crème brûlée, and Oriental spice flavors, with a firmly mineral spine. The texture is rich and creamy. Brisk acidity perfectly counterpoints the fruit. **92** —*S.H. (12/15/2004)*

Château St. Jean 2000 Robert Young Vineyard Chardonnay (Alexander Valley) $25. Has all the hallmarks of lush fruit, plus soft but adequate acidity, with a rich coat of oak. Flatters the palate with a creamy intensity and a long, fruity finish. **90** —*S.H. (10/1/2003)*

Château St. Jean 1999 Robert Young Vineyard Chardonnay (Alexander Valley) $25. Silky and rich, with a bright core of herb, melon, citrus, pear and mineral flavors. The wine offers a clean, refreshing edge while lingering long on the finish. **90** —*J.M. (12/15/2002)*

Château St. Jean 1997 Robert Young Vineyard Chardonnay (Sonoma County) $24.90 *(6/1/2000)*

Château St. Jean 1996 Robert Young Vineyard Reserve Chardonnay (Sonoma County) $24.88 *(6/1/2000)*

Château St. Jean 2004 Fumé Blanc (Sonoma County) $13. A serviceable Sauvignon that fulfills the variety's duties of being dry and elegant. It serves up crisp flavors of lemons and limes, with sweet vanilla in the finish. **85** —*S.H. (12/1/2005)*

Château St. Jean 2003 Fumé Blanc (Sonoma County) $13. This is a very nice wine, rich and fruity, but crisp and clean all the way through the

long finish. Brims with ripe lemon and lime, fig, and vanilla flavors. **87** —*S.H. (5/1/2005)*

Château St. Jean 2002 Fumé Blanc (Sonoma County) $13. This is a pleasant sipper, not especially intense, but offering up refreshing citrus and peach flavors. It's nicely dry, with a crisp cut of acidity, making it a nice partner with food. Finishes with a bit of sweet oak. **85** —*S.H. (2/1/2004)*

Château St. Jean 2001 Fumé Blanc (Sonoma County) $13. A pleasant wine, with mild melon, mineral, citrus, peach, and herb flavors. Light textured, medium bodied, and quite refreshing. Clean on the finish. **87** —*J.M. (7/1/2003)*

Château St. Jean 2001 La Petite Etoile Fumé Blanc (Russian River Valley) $20. This very dry wine pushes Sauvignon Blanc into interesting territory. The spicy, citrusy fruit has a rich overlay of oak, and those smoky, vanilla flavors blend in with the lemon and lime to add complexity. It also has refreshingly crisp acidity for balance. **88** —*S.H. (2/1/2004)*

Château St. Jean 2004 La Petite Etoile Vineyard Fumé Blanc (Russian River Valley) $20. Always a rewarding wine, this year's Etoile is particularly rich. It floods the palate with complex fruit spanning the gamut from lemons and limes to pineapples and guavas. Barrel fermentation lends a creamy texture, while the cool climate gives the wine the acidity it needs for balance. **92 Editors' Choice** —*S.H. (8/1/2006)*

Château St. Jean 2003 La Petite Etoile Vineyard Fumé Blanc (Russian River Valley) $20. In every vintage you can predict one thing about this wine: that it will be extremely oaky. Here the aromas are so toasted they almost cover the peach and melon lurking below. The palate offers lots of spice and white pepper along with peach, apple, and herbs. The intensity of the fruit and the natural acidity save it from falling into the category of "severely overoaked." **87** *(7/1/2005)*

Château St. Jean 2002 La Petite Etoile Vineyard Fumé Blanc (Russian River Valley) $20. Showy stuff. It starts off with grassy aromas modulated with vanilla and smoke. In the mouth, the citrus, sweet fig, melon, and spice flavors are delicious, and are balanced with firm, citrusy acids. Made Chard-style, with a full-bodied oakiness, this is a wonderful wine. **92** —*S.H. (12/15/2004)*

Château St. Jean 2000 La Petite Etoile Vineyard Fumé Blanc (Russian River Valley) $20. This is the liquid version of buttered toast. It's that oaky. In the nose there's almost no fruit at all, but in the mouth, once you cut through the layers of wood and butter, there's some melon, pear, and vanilla. But wood overrides that, too. In the finish it's all oak-driven spice and resin. If this all sounds like a lumberjack's special, it is **84** *(8/1/2002)*

Château St. Jean 2005 Gewürztraminer (Sonoma County) $15. Varietally pure and true. This is a crisp, elegantly structured wine with tropical fruit flavors, honeysuckle, vanilla, and masses of dusty crushed brown spices. Finishes really powerful in fruit. **86 Editors' Choice** —*S.H. (12/1/2006)*

Château St. Jean 2004 Gewürztraminer (Sonoma County) $15. Simple, fruity, and a little sweet, with good varietal character, this Gewürz has flowery, spicy flavors, with a sweet apricot and nectarine finish. **83** — *S.H. (12/1/2005)*

Château St. Jean 2003 Gewürztraminer (Sonoma County) $15. Fans of the variety will cheer the intense oriental spiciness that seasons the flowery, fruity flavors. Made Alsatian style, the wine is pretty dry, with a hint of honey on the finish. **84** —*S.H. (10/1/2004)*

Château St. Jean 2000 Gewürztraminer (Sonoma County) $15. Brimming with pretty litchee, melon, peach, pear, spice, and citrus notes, the wine is eminently quaffable, but also serves up a complex and interesting blend of flavor and spice. Really nice. **90** —*J.M. (9/1/2003)*

Château St. Jean 2004 Johannisberg Riesling (Sonoma County) $15. Watery and sweet, this wine isn't offering much, especially at this price. It has simple syrup flavors and is low in acids. **81** —*S.H. (12/1/2005)*

Château St. Jean 2003 Johannisberg Riesling (Sonoma County) $15. Here's a slightly sweet, nicely fruity wine that refreshes the palate with good acidity. It has apricot, peach, honeysuckle, and vanilla flavors that finish with a spicy aftertaste. **84** —*S.H. (10/1/2004)*

USA

Château St. Jean 2002 Johannisberg Riesling (Sonoma County) $15. Despite 12.4% alcohol, this wine still has a healthy dose of residual sugar. The fat mouthfeel and sweet fruit flavors scream California, from the ripe apple and peach flavors to the squeeze of lemony acidity on the finish. **87** —*J.C. (8/1/2003)*

Château St. Jean 2001 Johannisberg Riesling (Sonoma County) $15. Quite fruity, with lush peach, melon, guava, and spice flavors that are balanced by a bit of citrus and an mildly sweet finish. **87** —*J.M. (9/1/2003)*

Château St. Jean 1995 Belle Terre Vineyards Special Selec Johannisberg Riesling (Sonoma County) $30. 90 —*J.C. (12/31/1999)*

Château St. Jean 2001 Estate Vineyard Malbec (Sonoma Valley) $50. Here's a dark, chunky wine that has an aroma of peppered, grilled meat, and a chewiness like meat. It's rather tannic, in the way of some Petite Sirahs, with delicious blackberry flavors. Best after 2006. **90** —*S.H. (3/1/2005)*

Château St. Jean 2002 Reserve Malbec (Sonoma County) $60. This may be the most expensive Malbec in California, but it's a really good wine that is full-bodied and deeply flavored. Like a great Cabernet, it shows polished black currant, spicy plum, and new-oak flavors, with wonderfully rich, sweet tannins and soft acids. So easy to drink, so delicious now, but you might try cellaring it through 2010. **92** —*S.H. (12/1/2006)*

Château St. Jean 2001 Reserve Malbec (Sonoma County) $55. Decent, but you'll do way better in Argentina, and save lots of bucks. Semi-unripe, with green, herb, and cherry flavors. **83** —*S.H. (7/1/2005)*

Château St. Jean 2002 St. Jean Estate Vineyard Malbec (Sonoma Valley) $50. You're struck by the darkness of this wine. Also it's aroma, which is deep and brooding, like something from a vault. In the mouth, the wine is dry and tannic, intended for the cellar. And with its vast core of black cherry and pomegranate fruit and clean balance, it seems destined to ride out the years. Best after 2009 and beyond. **90 Cellar Selection** —*S.H. (4/1/2006)*

Château St. Jean 2003 Merlot (Sonoma County) $25. Ripe, soft, and juicy. An uncomplicated wine that nonetheless shows a good deal of sophistication and style. It has cherry, blackberry, anise, and oak flavors, with rich tannins. **87** —*S.H. (11/15/2006)*

Château St. Jean 2003 Merlot (California) $15. This is a rewardingly supple and above all balanced Merlot. It has a Cabernet-like structure, but lighter, and is marked by delicious cherry and cedar flavors and rich tannins. **86** —*S.H. (12/15/2005)*

Château St. Jean 2002 Merlot (Sonoma County) $25. This red wine is a little thin and short on the finish, but it keeps faith with Merlot's promise of softness and a gentle full-bodiedness. The wine is ripe in cherries, with a touch of smoky oak, and is nicely dry and balanced. **85** —*S.H. (12/31/2005)*

Château St. Jean 2002 Merlot (California) $15. Ripe, with cherry and blackberry flavors and a dose of smoky oak. Finishes dry. Shows some elegance in the smooth texture and balance. **85** —*S.H. (2/1/2005)*

Château St. Jean 2001 Merlot (Sonoma County) $25. Balanced, graceful, and elegant, a wine with smooth, dusty tannins that's easy to drink, but has complexity and style. Has polished flavors of blackberries, green olives, dried herbs, and vanilla. Rich and satisfying. **88** —*S.H. (8/1/2004)*

Château St. Jean 1999 Merlot (Sonoma County) $25. Staggeringly delicious, with white chocolate, cherry and roasted coffeebean aromas and flavors wrapped in sturdy but delicate tannins. It's on the soft, mellow side, with great depth of flavor and a long, sweet, spicy finish. This has to be one of the best Merlots of the vintage. **92 Editors' Choice** —*S.H. (12/1/2001)*

Château St. Jean 1997 Merlot (Sonoma County) $18. 92 *(11/15/1999)*

Château St. Jean 2001 Estate Vineyard Merlot (Sonoma Valley) $50. Here's a Merlot with the sexy texture Merlot is supposed to show. Wrapped into this plushness are delicious flavors of red cherries, spiced plums, and cocoa, with a rich, mushroomy earthiness. It's a seductive wine, probably at its best right now. **91** —*S.H. (3/1/2005)*

Château St. Jean 2001 Reserve Merlot (Sonoma County) $90. There can't be too many 2001 Merlots waiting to be released, and St. Jean must have waited to let the tannins soften. They have. Still a bit hard, the wine

drinks beautifully now, with lush cherry, cocoa, spice, and lavender flavors. The oak is 100% new French, and it works. Drink with the best steak you can find. **93** —*S.H. (12/1/2006)*

Château St. Jean 2000 Reserve Merlot (Sonoma County) $90. Held back unusually long for a Merlot. The tannins are still big and dusty. Yet there's a core of black cherry fruit, and a softness that makes the wine beguiling. Probably best now, with lamb. **89** —*S.H. (10/1/2005)*

Château St. Jean 1999 Reserve Merlot (Sonoma County) $90. Starts off super-oaky, unleashing the telltale scent of rich, charred wood, and its vanilla and spicy notes. Only in the mouth does the fruit generously reveal itself, in fat cascades of blackberries, mocha and sweet herbs. It's very complex, but also very hard now. Drink 2006+. **93** —*S.H. (9/1/2004)*

Château St. Jean 1997 Reserve Merlot (Sonoma County) $100. A huge, full-on, ripe and supple red wine that is buttery smooth on the palate yet offers the structure to support a rich flavor profile including chocolate, plum, cassis, vanilla, coffee, herb, and spice. Very long and velvety on the finish. **93 Cellar Selection** —*J.M. (11/15/2002)*

Château St. Jean 2002 St. Jean Estate Merlot (Sonoma Valley) $50. If this wine were any riper it would be over the top. It's a big, effusive Merlot, bursting with cherry jam and mocha flavors that are wrapped in velvety tannins. It's too soft for aging, but is delicious now. **88** —*S.H. (4/1/2006)*

Château St. Jean 2004 Pinot Noir (Sonoma County) $22. Nothing complicated here, just a Pinot with some real class and varietal distinction. You don't age a wine like this, you savor it with real food. Dry and silky, with cherry, black raspberry, and cola flavors ending with a swirl of dusty brown spice. **87** —*S.H. (11/15/2006)*

Château St. Jean 2003 Pinot Noir (Sonoma County) $19. Light-bodied and ample in cherry, vanilla, and smoky flavors, this wine finishes with a suggestion of cinnamon sugar. Soft with silky tannins. **85** —*S.H. (5/1/2005)*

Château St. Jean 2002 Pinot Noir (Sonoma County) $19. A textbook Pinot that tastes like it has plenty of Russian River Valley grapes inside. Light and silky in texture, but with rich, complex varietal flavors of cherries, cola, rhubarb, vanilla and mocha. **88** —*S.H. (11/1/2004)*

Château St. Jean 2000 Pinot Noir (Sonoma County) $19. 86 *(10/1/2002)*

Château St. Jean 2002 Durell Vineyard Pinot Noir (Sonoma Valley) $45. All tasters praised this wine for its plushness of flavor, delicate body, and long, complex finish. Heaps of ripe cherries, toffee, vanilla, and chocolate wrapped in a smooth, creamy-crisp texture. **88** *(11/1/2004)*

Château St. Jean 2000 Durell Vineyard Pinot Noir (Carneros) $38. Sweet and rich aromas of black cherry, soy, molasses, and smoke signal a full-bodied wine. The mouthfeel is layered and complex; red fruit is followed by herbs, berries then oak. The finish is very dark, featuring coffee, bitter chocolate, and pepper. Sturdy tannins make it solid as a rock. **88** *(10/1/2002)*

Château St. Jean 1999 Durell Vineyard Pinot Noir (Carneros) $38. Toasty oak, smoked meats and black cherries make up the pure, attractive nose. Earthy flavors feature plum and red cherries, and the oak, while definitely there, isn't overwhelming. But you can taste the barrel influence in the finish, where there's a flow of espresso and burnt toast flavors. **87** *(10/1/2002)*

Château St. Jean 1997 Durrell Vineyard Pinot Noir (Carneros) $30. 90 *(10/1/1999)*

Château St. Jean 2005 Riesling (Sonoma County) $15. Easy and simple, with pleasant peach pie, citrus, mango, spiced pear, and vanilla flavors that finish a little sweet and soft. **83** —*S.H. (12/1/2006)*

Château St. Jean 1997 La Petite Etoile Sauvignon Blanc (Sonoma) $13. 84 —*M.M. (9/1/1999)*

CHÂTEAU STE. MICHELLE

Château Ste. Michelle 1996 Cold Creek Vineyard Cabernet Franc (Columbia Valley (WA)) $28. 82 —*J.C. (4/1/2000)*

Château Ste. Michelle 2003 Cabernet Sauvignon (Columbia Valley (WA)) $16. A solid effort, much improved from the sub-par offerings of recent vintages. Soft and plump, it will please many consumers who want something easy and ready to drink with tonight's burger. **87** —*P.G.* (10/1/2006)

Château Ste. Michelle 2002 Cabernet Sauvignon (Columbia Valley (WA)) $16. Odd, disjointed, and chalky, It tastes as if it's been softened up a bit, but nothing knits together and there is neither depth nor definition to the fruit. The unusual blend includes 6% Sangiovese and 2% Syrah. **84** —*P.G.* (12/15/2005)

Château Ste. Michelle 2001 Cabernet Sauvignon (Columbia Valley (WA)) $16. This is 100% Cabernet Sauvignon, so the tart, tight, cassis and berry fruit flavors ring true, and are not softened with something "friendlier." Here is a good shot of true Cab, Washington style, which is to say sharp, tannic, with moderate alcohol and nothing overblown. Perfect food wine. **88** —*P.G.* (7/1/2004)

Château Ste. Michelle 1999 Cabernet Sauvignon (Columbia Valley (WA)) $15. A straight-ahead, no-frills effort that shows herb-tinged cassis and cherry fruit and tight, dry tannins. A hint of tobacco and green tea enlivens the finish. This wine surely will prove cellar-worthy; it may not reach its peak for at least a decade. **87** —*P.G.* (6/1/2002)

Château Ste. Michelle 1998 Cabernet Sauvignon (Columbia Valley (WA)) $15. This has long been the standard-bearer for value-priced Washington Cabernet. Some of the early Ste. Michelle Cabernets have been remarkably long-lived, still tasting rich and complex some 30 years after being released. You can see why. This is a perfectly structured wine, with sleek, tight fruit, firm acids, and no-nonsense oak that buttresses the tannins. It's fine with food and certainly capable of aging indefinitely. **88 Best Buy** —*P.G.* (10/1/2001)

Château Ste. Michelle 2002 Canoe Ridge Cabernet Sauvignon (Columbia Valley (WA)) $22. Soft, light strawberry/cherry flavors suggest a much cheaper wine. Beyond the simple fruit it turns tart and astringent, with very little midpalate. **85** —*P.G.* (12/15/2005)

Château Ste. Michelle 2003 Canoe Ridge Estate Cabernet Sauvignon (Columbia Valley (WA)) $22. Nice, plummy, strawberry and black raspberry fruit anchors this smooth, forward Cabernet. There's a slap of tangy cranberry in there also; it isn't softened to the point of being spineless. The finish is a bit chalky. **87** —*P.G.* (10/1/2006)

Château Ste. Michelle 2001 Canoe Ridge Estate Cabernet Sauvignon (Columbia Valley (WA)) $24. Tart, tight, and stubbornly unyielding, this sharp-edged, berry-flavored wine is not easy to evaluate at this stage of the game. The tannins are thick and chalky, overmatched to the fruit. **86** —*P.G.* (12/15/2004)

Château Ste. Michelle 2000 Canoe Ridge Estate Vineyard Cabernet Sauvignon (Columbia Valley (WA)) $24. This vineyard has some very pretty, cherry-flavored fruit, and fairly soft tannins for a Cab, smooth and almost silky. Not a big wine, but complex, with black cherry, tobacco, and cassis. 5,500 cases made. **89** —*P.G.* (12/31/2003)

Château Ste. Michelle 1998 Canoe Ridge Estate Vineyard Cabernet Sauvignon (Columbia Valley (WA)) $24. This is a tight, tough Cabernet, which has the structure to age well. It's 100% Cabernet from the Canoe Ridge vineyard, and it shows brilliant black cherry fruit, crisp acids, and a healthy undercoat of dark tannins. Young, tough, and bursting with flavor, it's from a great vintage and clearly has a long life ahead, but you can drink it now with anything grilled and meaty and it will make you very happy. **91** (10/1/2001)

Château Ste. Michelle 1999 Canoe Ridge Estates Cabernet Sauvignon (Columbia Valley (WA)) $24. Pretty scents of cinnamon start things off; the flavors show cherry pipe tobacco and plenty of black cherry and cassis fruit. Firm and tannic, it wraps its Bordeaux-style flavors in leaf and leather. **90** —*P.G.* (9/1/2002)

Château Ste. Michelle 2003 Cold Creek Vineyard Cabernet Sauvignon (Columbia Valley (WA)) $25. This wine retains some of the vineyard's firm, taut black cherry fruit, but its edges seem sanded down, smoothed over. It feels oddly soft in the mouth, but rough in the finish, somehow manipulated. This exceptional vineyard is capable of much more. **88** —*P.G.* (10/1/2006)

Château Ste. Michelle 2002 Cold Creek Vineyard Cabernet Sauvignon (Columbia Valley (WA)) $25. Very tight and quite tannic, the venerable (30-year-old) vineyard is not in character here; surely the best grapes

went into the Artist Series and Reserve bottlings. The spare fruit is wrapped in chalky tannins that fall away quickly and fracture into an odd, disjointed finish. **85** —*P.G.* (12/15/2005)

Château Ste. Michelle 2001 Cold Creek Vineyard Cabernet Sauvignon (Columbia Valley (WA)) $29. From one of Washington's best vineyards, this is a complex, Bordeaux-like wine that mixes fruit, mineral, and barrel flavors with an even hand. Lightly spiced with fresh herbs, back-loaded with cocoa/espresso flavors, this is well-defined, with firm, ripe but not at all unctuous fruit. Hold 6–10 years. **91 Cellar Selection** —*P.G.* (12/15/2004)

Château Ste. Michelle 2000 Cold Creek Vineyard Cabernet Sauvignon (Columbia Valley (WA)) $29. Cold Creek may be the most Bordeaux-like vineyard in the Columbia Valley; it holds tightly to its charms, and slowly opens with time. This year's model is a bit more open than last, with tart cassis/cherry fruit, chewy tannins, and some hints of mineral and earth. **89 Cellar Selection** —*P.G.* (12/31/2003)

Château Ste. Michelle 1999 Cold Creek Vineyard Cabernet Sauvignon (Columbia Valley (WA)) $29. This vineyard's Cabs have a way of fooling you; very young and tightly wound upon release, they often unfold into glorious Bordeaux-like wines after a decade or so. This is true to form: compact cassis and cherry fruit, hard tannins, and some nice espresso highlights exist, but need a lot more time to age. **88** —*P.G.* (12/31/2002)

Château Ste. Michelle 1998 Cold Creek Vineyard Cabernet Sauvignon (Columbia Valley (WA)) $32. I confess, I love this vineyard. It's not the jammiest, most opulent in the state, but it consistently delivers vivid, perfectly balanced wines, with amazing aging potential. The latest Cabernet has a wonderful bouquet, blending plush fruits, spice, chocolate, coffee, mineral, tea, and cedarbox. It's complex and delicious, as well as structured to age, without excess oak or overripe fruit. **92** —*P.G.* (12/31/2001)

Château Ste. Michelle 1996 Cold Creek Vineyard Cabernet Sauvignon (Columbia Valley (WA)) $25. 91 —*L.W.* (2/1/2000)

Château Ste. Michelle 2003 Indian Wells Cabernet Sauvignon (Columbia Valley (WA)) $17. The first vineyard-designated Cabernet from Indian Wells, this is much softer than recent vintages of the winery's Cabernets, but in this instance the wine feels stripped. The fruit and core are like shadows seen through a veil, and despite their softness, the tannins still outweigh the rest. There is nothing bad or off here; it just tastes flattened. **85** —*P.G.* (6/1/2006)

Château Ste. Michelle 2002 Reserve Cabernet Sauvignon (Columbia Valley (WA)) $36. A success in the still-improving red wine lineup, the 2002 reserve is built upon grapes from the winery's Cold Creek vineyard—its most substantial, ageworthy grapes—and has a welcome precision and focus missing from the rest of the lineup. Good acid and a fine-tuned nerve structure, the tart fruit carries notes of leaf, anise, and gravel, with green tea tannins through the long finish. 1,000 cases made. **88** —*P.G.* (12/15/2005)

Château Ste. Michelle 2001 Reserve Cabernet Sauvignon (Columbia Valley (WA)) $33. Thin and aggressively tannic, this wine does not seem to have to fruit intensity to overcome its stubbornly hard, tough tannins. **86** —*P.G.* (4/1/2005)

Château Ste. Michelle 1998 Reserve Cabernet Sauvignon (Columbia Valley (WA)) $33. The Château's reserve is held an extra five months in barrel, and represents a selection of the winery's top 1 percent of Cabernet. It's a big, thick, juicy effort loaded with ripe, lip-smacking berry and cassis fruit. Firm acids and a sheath of spice—anise, fennel, tobacco, and coffee—complete the picture. **90** —*P.G.* (6/1/2002)

Château Ste. Michelle 2004 Chardonnay (Columbia Valley (WA)) $13. Very soft and buttery, made in a style sure to reach out to a broad base of consumers looking for accessible flavors with lots of oak and tropical fruit. The style feels more Australian than Washington, but it fits in nicely with the winery's expanding lineup of single-vineyard and reserve Chardonnays. **87** —*P.G.* (8/1/2006)

Château Ste. Michelle 2003 Chardonnay (Columbia Valley (WA)) $12. Pleasing pear and light vanilla aromas lead into a nicely textured, lively and distinctly un-flabby Chardonnay. This is the least expensive of five Chardonnays from Ste. Michelle that all showcase winemaker Bob

Bertheau's elegant, light touch. Happily, there is no reliance on buttered popcorn flavors or excessive new toasty oak to make the flavors pop; this is a great food wine, way ahead of most budget bottles from California. **88 Best Buy** —*P.G. (11/15/2005)*

Château Ste. Michelle 2002 Chardonnay (Columbia Valley (WA)) $13. Ripe apple and light tropical fruit is swathed in Bourbon-barrel and vanilla flavors; the finish comes on like a dessert dish of bananas flambéed in whiskey. Exuberant, to say the least. **87** —*P.G. (7/1/2004)*

Château Ste. Michelle 2000 Chardonnay (Columbia Valley (WA)) $13. A big and friendly wine, with plenty of forward fruit mingling flavors of citrus, apples, and pears. There is a nice blast of vanilla too, the only obvious sign of new oak aging, but the impression overall is of crisp, clean elegance. **89 Best Buy** —*P.G. (7/1/2002)*

Château Ste. Michelle 1998 Chardonnay (Columbia Valley (WA)) $13. 86 —*P.G. (11/15/2000)*

Château Ste. Michelle 1999 Barrel Fermented Chardonnay (Columbia Valley (WA)) $13. Intense aromas of apples and pears start things off, and in the mouth the wine strikes just the right balance between intensity, crispness and full-flavored opulence. Good fruit, good acids, a pleasing creaminess, and an extended finish that lingers cleanly through flavors of toast and butter. **90 Best Buy** —*P.G. (6/1/2001)*

Château Ste. Michelle 1997 Barrel Fermented Chardonnay (Columbia Valley (WA)) $13. 87 *(2/1/2000)*

Château Ste. Michelle 2004 Canoe Ridge Estate Chardonnay (Columbia Valley (WA)) $20. The vineyard's characteristic green apple and light melon flavors are here, though lighter and more ephemeral than in the over-the-top 2003. Nice hints of cinnamon are scattered throughout, and the finishing oak flavors carry an impression of slightly burned crème brûlée. **89** —*P.G. (8/1/2006)*

Château Ste. Michelle 2003 Canoe Ridge Estate Chardonnay (Columbia Valley (WA)) $20. This explodes with full-flavored fruit. A big boy, juicy and concentrated with ripe apple/citrus fruits, and well-integrated streaks of vanilla, hazelnut, and butterscotch. **92 Editors' Choice** —*P.G. (12/15/2005)*

Château Ste. Michelle 2000 Canoe Ridge Estate Chardonnay (Washington) $20. Balance is the key. Firm, fully ripe fruit, still tart and tight enough to provide a steely through-line, is nuanced with lightly spicy oak. Perfectly balanced, polished, and delicious. **91** —*P.G. (9/1/2002)*

Château Ste. Michelle 1999 Canoe Ridge Estate Vineyard Chardonnay (Columbia Valley (WA)) $20. This is a well-made, balanced effort with green apple fruit enhanced with hints of honey and allspice. Still quite young and tight, it is just beginning to soften up and show some nice toasted, roasted nuts in the finish. It isn't quite as intense as the Barrel Fermented Chardonnay from CSM; this is a slightly softer, more approachable wine. **87** —*P.G. (6/1/2001)*

Château Ste. Michelle 2004 Cold Creek Chardonnay (Columbia Valley (WA)) $22. Big, oaky, and extremely bright, with refreshing acids and crisply defined fruit. As is usually the case with this spectacular vineyard, the flavors carry extra intensity; they seem to drill down into the heart of the palate. Though released young, this is a wine that could certainly benefit from another 6–12 months in the bottle. **90** —*P.G. (6/1/2006)*

Château Ste. Michelle 2003 Cold Creek Chardonnay (Columbia Valley (WA)) $22. Winemaker Bob Bertheau lays back on the new oak and gives this great vineyard its due. A classic spine of juicy acid, with ripe—but not fat—citrus and apricot flavors. Long, balanced, and tightly focused. **93 Editors' Choice** —*P.G. (12/15/2005)*

Château Ste. Michelle 2001 Cold Creek Vineyard Chardonnay (Columbia Valley (WA)) $26. This young wine is still assimilating its considerable new oak scents and flavors; but peeking out is a tightly built wine with pretty tropical fruit flavors and a lip-licking finishing smack of creamy caramel. Good now, better in another six months. 5,500 cases made. **91** —*P.G. (12/31/2003)*

Château Ste. Michelle 2000 Cold Creek Vineyard Chardonnay (Columbia Valley (WA)) $28. Cold Creek, which is actually quite a warm site in the Columbia Valley, mixes a crisp, acid-driven backbone with lightly tropical flavors of pineapple and mango. In the middle is a streak of fat butterscotch, leading to a silky finish. **90** —*P.G. (12/31/2002)*

Château Ste. Michelle 1998 Cold Creek Vineyard Chardonnay (Columbia Valley (WA)) $25. Cold Creek is one of the best vineyards in Washington, and does especially well with Chardonnay. This is a laid-back style, a bit coquettish even, that requires a little probing on the part of the consumer. But it rewards your efforts with layers of subtle flavors, beautifully balanced and aromatic. New French oak and sur lie aging help to define the contours and add creaminess, but it is the exceptional Cold Creek fruit that really shines. **91** —*P.G. (10/1/2001)*

Château Ste. Michelle 2004 Ethos Chardonnay (Columbia Valley (WA)) $30. Wonderfully leesy and complex, the second vintage of the top-of-the-line Ethos Chardonnay has intriguing streaks of orange peel and citrus zest, along with buttered nuts, toast, and hazelnut flavors. All the different elements are threaded through the palate and continue into the long, silky finish. The only off notes, perhaps due to the youth of the wine, are some high-toned volatile scents and a bit of alcoholic heat in the back of the palate. **91** —*P.G. (6/1/2006)*

Château Ste. Michelle 2003 Ethos Chardonnay (Columbia Valley (WA)) $30. A brilliant effort, sophisticated and modern. Leesy, textured, long, and elegant, the winemaker's light touch balances hints of herb, yeast and hints of new oak against gorgeous fruit. No reliance on buttered popcorn flavors or excessive new toasty oak. **94** —*P.G. (8/1/2005)*

Château Ste. Michelle 2004 Indian Wells Chardonnay (Columbia Valley (WA)) $17. Beautifully defined fruit flavors—peaches, pineapple, and mango—are supported with buttery, nutty oak and rather firm skin tannins. **89** —*P.G. (8/1/2006)*

Château Ste. Michelle 2003 Indian Wells Chardonnay (Columbia Valley (WA)) $17. Peaches and apricots fill the mouth. The wine has a supple, rich midpalate, and a nice smack of butterscotch to finish. **89** —*P.G. (12/15/2005)*

Château Ste. Michelle 2000 Indian Wells Vineyard Chardonnay (Columbia Valley (WA)) $21. A wonderful new release from this premier producer. Tasted with the winery's Cold Creek Vineyard Chardonnay, it made an interesting contrast. Both were excellent, but the Indian Wells reached for richer, toastier, rounder, and more generous flavors. It's a sure-fire palate pleaser, with a beguiling mix of pink grapefruit, pineapple, mango, and apricot flavors. **91 Editors' Choice** —*P.G. (12/31/2002)*

Château Ste. Michelle 1999 Indian Wells Vineyard Chardonnay (Columbia Valley (WA)) $22. This wine gets the royal treatment despite its modest price: fermentation in new French oak, sur lie aging and a final blending of only the best barrels. It is everything a Columbia Valley Chardonnay can be, forward and fruity, bursting with crisp green apples and buttery pie crust flavors. Delicious right now, but another year or two will take the edges off. **88** —*P.G. (10/1/2001)*

Château Ste. Michelle 2002 Reserve Chardonnay (Columbia Valley (WA)) $30. A brilliant success, with concentrated, multi-layered flavors that let the crisp, structured fruit stand out against the tastefully used new French oak. This is as good as Washington Chardonnay gets, and clearly deserves its reserve status. **93** —*P.G. (4/1/2005)*

Château Ste. Michelle 2001 Reserve Chardonnay (Columbia Valley (WA)) $29. Not much differentiates this from its "Cold Creek" brother; both show new oak scents and flavors, so much so that the fruit is buried. Here the alcohol is a moderate 13%. Moderate levels of acid and the light, pleasant fruit suggest near-term drinking. **89** —*P.G. (5/1/2004)*

Château Ste. Michelle 1999 Reserve Chardonnay (Columbia Valley (WA)) $31. The Château's reserve is not their best Chardonnay (that honor belongs to the Cold Creek) but it's their most accessible, made in a powerful, lush style with softer fruit and more obvious new oak. Fleshy, full-bodied and showing lively spice, it's a drink-me-now pleasure. **90** —*P.G. (7/1/2002)*

Château Ste. Michelle 1997 Reserve Chardonnay (Columbia Valley (WA)) $29. 87 *(4/1/2000)*

Château Ste. Michelle 2003 Gewürztraminer (Columbia Valley (WA)) $9. Very much a food wine, it minimizes the floral oiliness of the grape in

USA

favor of citrus rind and spice. Crisp and fresh, with a touch of sweetness, it makes a perfect partner for crab cakes, Asian noodle dishes, or summer salads. **87** —*P.G. (9/1/2004)*

Château Ste. Michelle 2001 Gewürztraminer (Columbia Valley (WA)) $8. A popular style, fruity and forward, with the emphasis on citrus, grapefruit, and apricot, rather than floral qualities. Sweet fruit set against tangy acid makes it a versatile food wine too. **87** —*P.G. (9/1/2002)*

Château Ste. Michelle 2003 Johannisberg Riesling (Columbia Valley (WA)) $9. The workhorse wine for the Château, 375,000 cases strong. Consistently shows a nice mix of flavors revolving around grapefruit, white peaches, and apricots, with freshness and well-managed off-dry sweetness. Never sugary, never cloying, it has almost as much character as the Eroica for half the price. **88 Best Buy** —*P.G. (9/1/2004)*

Château Ste. Michelle 2001 Johannisberg Riesling (Columbia Valley (WA)) $8. Fresh and pure up front, with aromatic notes of peach, apricot, and petrol. The palate is like nectarines and citrus, with a pure shot of lemon peeking through. The light, refreshing finish cements it as a proper and satisfying cocktail-party wine. **85** —*M.S. (12/31/2003)*

Château Ste. Michelle 2000 Art Series Meritage (Columbia Valley (WA)) $48. With each new vintage, the Ste. Michelle Artist Series honors a particular glass artist; this year it is Italo Scanga of Calabria. Yeah, but how's the wine? Well, it's pretty darn good. Smooth and tannic, it has soft, seductive flavors obtained by blending Bordeaux grapes from top Stimson Lane vineyards. Not quite as precisely defined as the Château reserve wines, it is a very drinkable blend, good, but somehow less than the sum of its parts. **89** —*P.G. (12/31/2003)*

Château Ste. Michelle 2003 Artist Series Meritage (Columbia Valley (WA)) $48. Not a total success. It tastes both soft and hard at the same time; the fruit is tight, tart, and tapers off quickly. Tannins are softened to the point of being inconsequential. The wine lacks grip. **86** —*P.G. (10/1/2006)*

Château Ste. Michelle 2002 Artist Series Meritage (Columbia Valley (WA)) $48. This Meritage blend includes 10% Merlot and 20% Malbec. It is a soft, chocolatey wine with bright raspberry/cherry fruit and plenty of new oak flavors. The oak is still tough and bitter; it has not had sufficient time to soften. 1,500 cases made. **88** —*P.G. (12/15/2005)*

Château Ste. Michelle 2001 Artist Series Meritage Red Wine Meritage (Columbia Valley (WA)) $48. This Meritage blend includes 16% Merlot and 16% Malbec, but does not reflect the diversity on the palate. It seems simple and slightly green, with acidic cherry flavored fruit and a bitter chocolate finish. **86** —*P.G. (4/1/2005)*

Château Ste. Michelle 1997 Merlot (Columbia Valley (WA)) $18. 87 *(4/1/2000)*

Château Ste. Michelle 1996 Merlot (Columbia Valley (WA)) $16. 89 *(11/15/1999)*

Château Ste. Michelle 2002 Merlot (Columbia Valley (WA)) $16. Dark and plum-colored, the aromas suggest green, herbal fruit. In the mouth it tastes soft, stripped, over filtered; yet finishes with awkward, astringent green tannins and a lingering bit of alcoholic heat. **84** —*P.G. (12/15/2005)*

Château Ste. Michelle 2001 Merlot (Columbia Valley (WA)) $16. A crafted, restrained, elegant Merlot, which does not show the softness and fruitiness we normally associate with domestic versions of that grape. Here the fruit flavors run to berries and plums, somewhat straightjacketed in layers of firm mineral and green, earthy tannin. **87** —*P.G. (7/1/2004)*

Château Ste. Michelle 2000 Merlot (Columbia Valley (WA)) $16. Clearly this Merlot is an important part of the winery's portfolio; there are 153,000 cases of this "regular" bottling looking for love. Not as big and lush as its brother in arms from Columbia Crest, this is a more restrained, more elegant wine, with soft and precise fruit flavors that run to berries and plums. Nice hint of cedar in the finish. **88** —*P.G. (12/31/2003)*

Château Ste. Michelle 1999 Merlot (Columbia Valley (WA)) $18. The scent is pure Bordeaux, potent and loaded with black cherry, cedar, and coffee. The wine hits the palate very soft and quite dry, with a smooth, seamless mouthfeel. It's very tasty, never overbearing, and surprisingly rich in this price range. **88** —*P.G. (6/1/2002)*

Château Ste. Michelle 2002 Canoe Ridge Estate Merlot (Columbia Valley (WA)) $24. Lots of chocolatey oak over light cherry fruit; here again the dry, abrasive tannins stick out and give the wine a disjointed mouthfeel, despite the good fruit. **87** —*P.G. (4/1/2005)*

Château Ste. Michelle 2001 Canoe Ridge Estate Merlot (Columbia Valley (WA)) $24. Merlot is Canoe Ridge's main calling card, and this is a lean, cherry-flavored wine with an herbal tannic edge. Despite the hefty (14.4%) alcohol, it is not a heavy wine, but the tannins are rather stiff and abrasive right now. Best drinking should be in 3-5 years. **88** —*P.G. (5/1/2004)*

Château Ste. Michelle 1999 Canoe Ridge Estate Merlot (Columbia Valley (WA)) $23. From an exceptional vineyard site high above the Columbia River, this wine is a dark, potent, and heady mix of toasty, earthy aromas and forward fruit. Flavors of licorice, mocha, and cedar mix into the sassy finish. Overall it's a user-friendly, open and powerful style. **90** — *P.G. (6/1/2002)*

Château Ste. Michelle 1998 Canoe Ridge Estate Vineyard Merlot (Columbia Valley (WA)) $22. Fragrant and forward, this is an appealing Merlot with tart, raspberry fruit married to chocolatey oak. It's a high acid, rich tannin style, and the wine does a good job of scraping the palate clean. It would make a very nice match for an oily fish such as salmon or ahi. Young, tight, tar,t and very tannic at this stage of the game, it feels just a bit thin in the finish. Give it some serious breathing time. **87** —*P.G. (10/1/2001)*

Château Ste. Michelle 1996 Canoe Ridge Estate Vineyard Merlot (Columbia Valley (WA)) $32. 89 —*L.W. (9/1/1999)*

Château Ste. Michelle 2001 Cold Creek Merlot (Columbia Valley (WA)) $33. The winery's top vineyard shows its fragrant side here, with whiffs of tart black fruits and mineral and early hints of leather. It is almost Cab-like in its tight muscularity, and the addition of 5% Syrah adds a hint of pepper to the finish. **90** —*P.G. (5/1/2004)*

Château Ste. Michelle 2002 Cold Creek Vineyard Merlot (Columbia Valley (WA)) $33. Thin, watery, and acidic, this is not at all representative of what this outstanding vineyard can produce. Uncharacteristically lean and unyielding, this is a disappointment. **85** —*P.G. (4/1/2005)*

Château Ste. Michelle 1999 Cold Creek Vineyard Merlot (Columbia Valley (WA)) $32. Not quite as dense as recent vintages, this is nonetheless sharply defined, with tart red berries and cherries underscored with baker's chocolate. The tannins are hard and the wine, as is generally true with this vineyard, needs considerable aging to reveal its full pleasures. **88** —*P.G. (6/1/2002)*

Château Ste. Michelle 1998 Cold Creek Vineyard Merlot (Columbia Valley (WA)) $32. Cold Creek is one of Stimson Lane's premier properties, and this vineyard selection, from a wonderful Washington vintage, shows it at it's best. Sweet, plump fruit, vivid and forward, is married to medium acids and soft tannins, with a smooth, chocolatey finish. **91** —*P.G. (12/31/2001)*

Château Ste. Michelle 2002 Indian Wells Merlot (Columbia Valley (WA)) $17. This wine, from Wahluke Slope (warm site) vineyards, nonetheless retains a distinct herbal flavor, married to very hard, tough, green tannins. Decanting it will help smooth it out. **87** —*P.G. (4/1/2005)*

Château Ste. Michelle 2001 Indian Wells Merlot (Columbia Valley (WA)) $18. Formerly one of the winery's single-vineyard bottlings, Indian Wells is now part of a new "District Series" from CSM. Here are smooth, cherry-dominated flavors, with a bit of cocoa and a finishing edge of acid. Simple and a bit formulaic, but good nonetheless. **87** —*P.G. (5/1/2004)*

Château Ste. Michelle 1999 Indian Wells Vineyard Merlot (Columbia Valley (WA)) $32. The Indian Wells Merlot is oakier and a bit rougher than the Cold Creek. Instead of high acid red fruits, here are blackberries and dusty cocoa, with thick tannins and a generous amount of toasty new oak. **88** —*P.G. (6/1/2002)*

Château Ste. Michelle 1998 Indian Wells Vineyard Merlot (Columbia Valley (WA)) $31. This smooth, seductive wine recalls the superb '94 from this vineyard. There's plenty of fruit, but it's already well blended into the toasty oak, with some cinnamon spice and herbal highlights for added interest. Delicious right now, it will improve with a little bit of bottle age as the hard tannins soften a bit. There are some nice, dark, toasty undercurrents that add a great deal of depth, and a lingering, vanilla custard sweetness in the finish that makes for a very attractive style. **90** —*P.G. (10/1/2001)*

Château Ste. Michelle 2002 Reserve Merlot (Columbia Valley (WA)) $36. Straightforward blackberry and black cherry over dark, chocolatey tannins. Simple, astringent and a bit stripped. **86** —*P.G. (12/15/2005)*

Château Ste. Michelle 2001 Reserve Merlot (Columbia Valley (WA)) $37. Surprisingly tough and chewy, the tannins at this point overwhelm the fruit, which itself seems hard and impenetrable. The tight, unyielding core of cherry/berry fruit is ensconced in rough, ragged tannins that will need some years to smooth out. **87** —*P.G. (12/15/2004)*

Château Ste. Michelle 2000 Reserve Merlot (Columbia Valley (WA)) $37. A selection of the best lots of Merlot from Cold Creek, Horse Heaven, Canoe Ridge, and Indian Wells. The 2000 lacks the profound depth of the '99, but it is still a very classy wine, with a mix of red and blue fruits, defining acids and smooth tannins. The oak barrels add well-integrated notes of black tea, smoke and spice. **90** —*P.G. (12/31/2003)*

Château Ste. Michelle 1999 Reserve Merlot (Columbia Valley (WA)) $37. Just 1,800 cases of this powerful, profound wine are made, from the same three vineyards that go into the winery's vineyard designates: Cold Creek, Canoe Ridge and Indian Wells. Thick, rich fruit is set off with substantial, chocolatey tannins. Still a bit restrained, but give it a few hours and interesting notes of black tea, smoke, leaf, and leather emerge. **92 Cellar Selection** —*P.G. (9/1/2002)*

Château Ste. Michelle 1998 Reserve Merlot (Columbia Valley (WA)) $37. Scented with an intriguing mix of herbs and chocolatey spices, this wine is a deep, dark version of Washington Merlot from Château Ste. Michelle's best vineyards. The fruit is solid cherry; there's lots of toasty oak, and the big tannins are smoothed out so that they find the proper balance. There's plenty of acid to keep the wine lively, and all it needs at this point is time to blend together. **91** *(10/1/2001)*

Château Ste. Michelle 2004 Pinot Gris (Columbia Valley (WA)) $9. Light and zesty, showing hints of lemon and lime, along with sharp, tart grapefruit. It's clean and straightforward. **86** —*P.G. (2/1/2006)*

Château Ste. Michelle 2003 Pinot Gris (Columbia Valley (WA)) $13. A perfect marriage of fresh-cut pears, cinnamon, orange, and a finishing kiss of honeysuckle. Lingers deliciously on the finish. **88 Best Buy** —*P.G. (9/1/2004)*

Château Ste. Michelle 2001 Pinot Gris (Columbia Valley (WA)) $13. This is the newest wine in the Château's ever-expanding lineup, and it shows the rising importance of Pinot Gris in Washington. Perfect varietal flavors set on the border of apple and pear, along with fresh acids and a nice lift from the natural spice of the grape. **89** —*P.G. (9/1/2002)*

Château Ste. Michelle 1998 Artist Series Meritage Red Wine Red Blend (Columbia Valley (WA)) $50. This is as close to Bordeaux as you'll find in Washington, which is to say, darn close indeed. Cassis and earth, leaf and barrel mingle in the seductive nose. The wine, rich and ripe and deep, slowly opens to reveal layer upon layer of fruit, amplified with darker, mineral accents. Defining acids and a subtle hint of oak complete the experience. **91** —*P.G. (12/31/2001)*

Château Ste. Michelle 2005 Riesling (Columbia Valley (WA)) $8. Château Ste. Michelle makes more Riesling than any winery in the country, and this bottling, at 553,500 cases, may qualify as the largest single Riesling production in the world. It's a great bottle of wine, priced for everyday consumption, yet loaded with fresh fruit flavors of peach, pear, and melon. Washington state built its white wine reputation on Riesling, and Riesling is more popular than ever before (statewide it is the third most planted grape, and production is up 23 percent in the past two years). This version is off-dry, lightly spiced, and perfectly framed by vibrant acids. **89 Best Buy** —*P.G. (8/1/2006)*

Château Ste. Michelle 2000 Cold Creek Riesling (Columbia Valley (WA)) $14. The same vineyard provides grapes for the winery's "Eroica" Riesling project with Ernst Loosen. The differences are subtle, but the single vineyard version tastes a bit drier, more citric, and includes lovely hints of orange blossom and honey. **89 Best Buy** —*P.G. (6/1/2002)*

Château Ste. Michelle 2003 Cold Creek Vineyard Riesling (Columbia Valley (WA)) $14. There is a lovely textural quality to Cold Creek Vineyard Riesling, which supports the flavors of grapefruit and white peaches with a minerality through the back half. Offers good grip and a racy, tangy finish, despite its off-dry rating. **91** —*P.G. (9/1/2004)*

Château Ste. Michelle 2002 Cold Creek Vineyard Riesling (Columbia Valley (WA)) $11. **89** —*R.V. (8/1/2003)*

Château Ste. Michelle 2001 Cold Creek Vineyard Riesling (Columbia Valley (WA)) $14. A top vineyard for Riesling, and the source of much of the winery's high end Eroica Riesling fruit. The '01 is medium-dry and leesy, with flavorful richness accented by peach blossom, jasmine, and a hint of stone. **90 Best Buy** —*P.G. (12/31/2002)*

Château Ste. Michelle 1998 Cold Creek Vineyard Riesling (Columbia Valley (WA)) $12. **86** *(2/1/2000)*

Château Ste. Michelle 2001 Dr. Loosen Eroica Riesling (Columbia Valley (WA)) $20. For the first time this Ste. Michelle/Ernst Loosen collaboration is sourced predominantly from Yakima Valley vineyards. It is drier, more minerally than past vintages, with crisp, elegant pineapple, white peach, and green apple fruit. Tight and beautifully structured, it shows surprising power through the long, crystalline finish. Cellar Selection. **92 Cellar Selection** —*P.G. (9/1/2002)*

Château Ste. Michelle 2003 Dry Riesling (Columbia Valley (WA)) $8. Dry but not bone dry, this agreeable wine shows the warmth of the '03 vintage, with its semi-tropical fruit flavors, full-on finish, and sharp, alcoholic edge. Nicknamed "Baby Eroica" because it is an assemblage of lots that didn't quite make the cut for that wine. **87** —*P.G. (9/1/2004)*

Château Ste. Michelle 2001 Dry Riesling (Columbia Valley (WA)) $8. This is a limited edition (about 7000 cases) wine that is mainly sold in the Northwest. The aromas are of lemon wax, light blossom, and apricot. Lots of flavor springs from a textured, almost creamy mouthfeel. Very fresh and inviting. **90** —*P.G. (9/1/2002)*

Château Ste. Michelle 2005 Eroica Riesling (Columbia Valley (WA)) $22. The winery's flagship Riesling collaboration with Ernst Loosen has tweaked the vineyard sources and developed some new approaches to vine management in an ongoing effort to make Eroica more Germanic. This is a tight, high acid wine, that carries its 1.6% residual sugar with the grace of a Spatlese. It briskly walks the line between crisp apple/citrus and off-dry honeyed sweetness, with tremendous length across the palate. **92 Editors' Choice** —*P.G. (8/1/2006)*

Château Ste. Michelle 2003 Eroica Riesling (Columbia Valley (WA)) $20. A collaborative effort with Ernst Loosen, of the Dr. Loosen estate. Bright, intensely flavored grapes are given special handling (night harvest, no crusher/destemmer, slow-fermenting yeasts) and deliver a complex, fleshy, and layered Riesling. This bottling is a bit more forward and juicy than past vintages have been. **89** —*P.G. (9/1/2004)*

Château Ste. Michelle 2002 Eroica Riesling (Columbia Valley (WA)) $20. This is consistently the most concentrated, complex, and stylish Riesling made in Washington. In this excellent year it shows ripe pineapple, white peach, and lime fruit, set up beautifully with crisp, defining acids. Balanced and intensely fragrant; with only 12% alcohol. 10,000 cases made. **91** —*P.G. (12/31/2003)*

Château Ste. Michelle 2005 Indian Wells Riesling (Columbia Valley (WA)) $17. This 2005 is the first vintage for this new single vineyard Riesling from the Indian Wells vineyard in the Wahluke Slope AVA. Ripe and juicy, it's a more tropical style than the others from Ste. Michelle, but still maintains the acid backbone to qualify as racy. The finish is particularly rich and resonant. **90** —*P.G. (8/1/2006)*

Château Ste. Michelle 1998 Sauvignon Blanc (Columbia Valley (WA)) $10. **87** —*P.G. (4/1/2000)*

Château Ste. Michelle 2004 Sauvignon Blanc (Columbia Valley (WA)) $15. Creamy and smooth, mixing citrus, apple, pear, and fig flavors with a dusting of light toast. This is not soft, nor is it too acidic; it's a ripe, round, very approachable wine enhanced with the addition of 5%

Sémillon. Roughly half was barrel fermented, half done in stainless steel, creating a polished mix of richness and precision. **89** —*P.G. (12/31/2006)*

Château Ste. Michelle 2003 Sauvignon Blanc (Columbia Valley (WA)) $10. More stainless steel fermentation than in previous vintages brings out the bright, round, fruity character. Winemaker Bob Bertheau shows his California palate, shying away from the grassy, pungent side of the grape, building instead a crisp, fragrant, and lightly spiced white wine with popular appeal. **88 Best Buy** —*P.G. (12/15/2005)*

Château Ste. Michelle 2002 Sauvignon Blanc (Columbia Valley (WA)) $10. Right down the middle of the road, with safe, simple flavors of stone fruits and hints of hazelnut and almond. Good grip and moderate alcohol (13%) makes it a nice match for chicken, halibut, clams, and pastas in white sauce. **86** —*P.G. (7/1/2004)*

Château Ste. Michelle 2000 Sauvignon Blanc (Columbia Valley (WA)) $10. You can't miss the fruit, which ranges from citrus and melon to apricot and quince. This flavor burst is highlighted by decent acidity, and finishes with spicy zest. The nicest part is that it's mostly dry. Fun stuff, and a good value. **85** —*S.H. (9/12/2002)*

Château Ste. Michelle 1997 Sauvignon Blanc (Columbia Valley (WA)) $10. 88 Best Buy —*L.W. (9/1/1999)*

Château Ste. Michelle 2004 Horse Heaven Vineyard Sauvignon Blanc (Columbia Valley (WA)) $15. This is the designated vineyard for the winery's top Sauvignon Blanc, but here it is merely good, not great. Half barrel fermented, half stainless steel is the approach, but somehow the fruit seems a bit dried out compared with the other bottling. Dried peas and green apple flavors, perhaps a whiff of cardboard, show; overall it's a stony, bone-dry wine despite the addition of 15% Sémillon. **87** —*P.G. (12/31/2006)*

Château Ste. Michelle 2003 Horse Heaven Vineyard Sauvignon Blanc (Columbia Valley (WA)) $15. Nicely crafted and a bit riper than the regular Sauvignon, this fruit-driven wine adds light butterscotch and hints of wood spice to the basic citrus and apple flavors. The acids taste like fresh-squeezed Meyer lemons. **88** —*P.G. (12/15/2005)*

Château Ste. Michelle 2002 Horse Heaven Vineyard Sauvignon Blanc (Columbia Valley (WA)) $15. Huge production (up to 23,000 cases) has diluted the impact of this wine. Still a very tasty, tight and tart style, but it no longer has the pinpoint focus and penetrating depth of previous vintages. **87** —*P.G. (5/1/2004)*

Château Ste. Michelle 2000 Horse Heaven Vineyard Sauvignon Blanc (Columbia Valley (WA)) $14. Another beautiful rendering of succulent Sauvignon Blanc from this premier vineyard, offering fresh, ripe fruit, scents of grapefruit, citrus peel, melon, and lemon wax. There's a nice, spicy lift to the palate, though the finish is not quite as rich and extended as the incredible '99. **90** —*P.G. (2/1/2002)*

Château Ste. Michelle 1999 Horse Heaven Vineyard Sauvignon Blanc (Columbia Valley (WA)) $14. The Horse Heaven vineyard has been producing exceptional Sauvignon Blancs for the past decade. In this unusual vintage, which started very cool and lasted through an extended, late harvest, the grapes ripened to perfection. Ripe, lush fruit gets some added creaminess from barrel fermentation and aging sur lie. There are scents of lime, citrus peel, wet stone and spice, leading to a wonderfully full, focused panoply of flavors in the mouth. The finish goes on forever. **92 Best Buy** —*P.G. (6/1/2001)*

Château Ste. Michelle 1997 Horse Heaven Vineyard Sauvignon Blanc (Columbia Valley (WA)) $14. 88 —*L.W. (9/1/1999)*

Château Ste. Michelle 1997 Sémillon (Columbia Valley (WA)) $10. 86 — *L.W. (9/1/1999)*

Château Ste. Michelle 2003 Sémillon (Columbia Valley (WA)) $9. A mirror image of the Sauvignon Blancs; here the proportions reversed (the Sauv Blanc is at 24%) and consequently the wine has a bit of the woody/woolly mid-palate reediness of Sémillon. Balanced and crisply ripe. **87 Best Buy** —*P.G. (12/15/2005)*

Château Ste. Michelle 2002 Sémillon (Columbia Valley (WA)) $9. Some people think that Sémillon is Washington's (and America's) great undiscovered white wine grape. This 100% varietal bottle displays some of the woolly texture, the hints of lanolin, and the gooseberry green fruit that makes the grape distinctive. **87 Best Buy** —*P.G. (7/1/2004)*

Château Ste. Michelle 1998 Sémillon (Columbia Valley (WA)) $8. 85 — *P.G. (11/15/2000)*

Château Ste. Michelle 1997 Late Harvest Sémillon (Columbia Valley (WA)) $23. 90 —*P.G. (11/15/2000)*

Château Ste. Michelle 2002 Syrah (Columbia Valley (WA)) $15. Has some interesting herbal, peppery overtones to the nose, but the flavors are simple and fruity, a blend of blackberry and cherry, finishing short. **84** *(9/1/2005)*

Château Ste. Michelle 2001 Syrah (Columbia Valley (WA)) $13. An engaging, quaffable style, which sports pretty berry/cherry fruit and a nice peppery middle. It doesn't overpower the palate with fruit or oak, but shows good varietal character. Taste this and you will see why Syrah is the most exciting new red wine in the Columbia Valley these days. **88 Best Buy** —*P.G. (12/31/2003)*

Château Ste. Michelle 2000 Syrah (Columbia Valley (WA)) $15. Light and immaculate fruit lifts up this pleasant, pretty red wine. Immediately enjoyable and fresh, it is a fine choice for drinking with poultry and lighter winter meals. **88 Best Buy** —*P.G. (12/31/2002)*

Château Ste. Michelle 2003 Ethos Syrah (Columbia Valley (WA)) $29. This very limited (600 cases) companion to the winery's Ethos Chardonnay marks a turnaround for Ste. Michelle's red wine program, as Bob Bertheau came on board just before the 2003 crush. The style is seductive, sharp, and spicy; the tart fruits tumble out in a pile of mixed berry and cherry. Chocolate and baking spices add more flavors; the wine is seamless, smooth, and long; the oak beautifully integrated. **94** —*P.G. (6/1/2006)*

Château Ste. Michelle 2003 Ethos Syrah (Columbia Valley (WA)) $29. This very limited (600 cases) companion to the winery's Ethos Chardonnay marks a turnaround for Ste. Michelle's red wine program, as Bob Bertheau came on board just before the 2003 crush. The style is seductive, sharp, and spicy; the tart fruits tumble out in a pile of mixed berry and cherry. Chocolate and baking spices add more flavors; the wine is seamless, smooth and long; the oak beautifully integrated. **94** —*P.G. (12/31/2006)*

Château Ste. Michelle 2002 Reserve Syrah (Columbia Valley (WA)) $29. Smoky and toasty, accented by hints of sour herbs and spice. Crisp acidity brings the lavish oak and ample blackberry fruit into sharp focus. Lacks a bit of texture, but still very good overall. **88** *(9/1/2005)*

Château Ste. Michelle 2001 Reserve Syrah (Columbia Valley (WA)) $29. Spicy, tart, smooth, and polished, with roasted coffee accents that fall just a tad to the green side. Augmented with hints of citrus peel, it centers on penetrating raspberry/black cherry fruit, finishing with licorice and substantial tannins. **89** —*P.G. (12/15/2004)*

Château Ste. Michelle 2000 Reserve Syrah (Columbia Valley (WA)) $29. A pretty wine, scented with orange and chocolate. Very smooth and elegant, it isn't bogged down with massive fruit or too much alcohol. It's stylish in the French way, yet still powerful with layers of flavors that unwrap like Christmas packages. Superior winemaking. Only 2,000 cases made. **90** —*P.G. (12/31/2003)*

Château Ste. Michelle 1999 Reserve Syrah (Columbia Valley (WA)) $29. This has a beautiful nose, with pepper, light balsamic, and green tea scents. The tannins are also tea-like, and the compact fruit mixes red and black flavors. Smoky, tannic, and tight, with strong herb, tea and tobacco flavors. Just 1,800 cases available. **90** —*P.G. (9/1/2002)*

Château Ste. Michelle 1998 Reserve Syrah (Columbia Valley (WA)) $29. A "nice, though understated" cedar, cinnamon-clove, brine, and coffee bouquet psyches you up for an equally intriguing palate—and, in that respect, we were a little disappointed. Its blackberry and heavy oak flavors are pleasant; still, reviewers noted a lack of depth on the palate. Finishes with more wood. **87** *(11/1/2001)*

CHÂTEAU WOLTNER

Château Woltner 1997 Private Reserve Bordeaux Blend (Howell Mountain) $50. 85 *(11/1/2000)*

CHATFIELD

Chatfield 1998 Clements Vineyards Chardonnay (California) $15. 85 *(6/1/2000)*

CHATOM

Chatom 1999 Cabernet Sauvignon (Calaveras County) $18. Asian spice notes grace modest black cherry and herb flavors in this lightweight offering from the Sierras. Finishes short, with some charred-wood notes. **83** *(9/1/2002)*

Chatom 2003 Chardonnay (Calaveras County) $14. Unoaked, and with no malolactic fermentation, this clean, refreshing wine is bright in apple, peach and pear flavors. It has a rich vein of acidity. **88** —*S.H. (3/1/2005)*

Chatom 2002 Chardonnay (Calaveras County) $14. Everyday Chard, with peach and apple flavors, dry and spicy, and an angular mouthfeel. Has a density and weight that may come from mountain vines. **84** —*S.H. (12/1/2003)*

Chatom 2002 Gitano Sangiovese (Calaveras County) $12. Mixed with some Merlot, a tough, young wine with considerable tannins and a punchy, tart mouthfeel, like an old-fashioned jug blend. What you see is what you get, an affordable wine that will go well with pizza or burgers. **84** —*S.H. (9/1/2003)*

Chatom 2003 Sauvignon Blanc (Calaveras County) $18. Ripely sweet in fig, melon and the prettiest white peach, with vanilla and smoky notes. Drinks rich and creamy, with a long, spicy finish. Contains some Sémillon. **87** —*S.H. (2/1/2005)*

Chatom 2002 Sauvignon Blanc (Calaveras County) $14. Smells like lemon-scented floor polish, and tastes like sweetened lemonade. Okay in a pinch. The grapes are probably fine. What is needed here is some Winemaking 101. **83** —*S.H. (12/15/2003)*

Chatom 2002 Sémillon (Calaveras County) $11. Not bad, with clean, pleasant opening aromas of vanilla, cashew, peach and honey. Drinks fruity and dry, with peach flavors and just enough acidity for balance. **84** —*S.H. (12/1/2003)*

Chatom 2001 Syrah (Calaveras County) $23. This is a big, meaty wine, filled with the flavors of plums, blackberries, boysenberries and other very dark bush and tree fruits. It's also firmly tannic. Makes up in strength what it lacks in finesse. **85** —*S.H. (12/1/2003)*

Chatom 1999 Syrah (Calaveras County) $18. A great quaff if we've ever tasted one: Its mouthfeel is medium-weight and soft; it shows a little restraint on the nose, but eventually reveals cherry, cedar and blackberry accents. More cherry shows up on the palate, hand-in-hand with dark berry, tobacco and cinnamon notes. Finishes with wood and a bit of tang—some called it metallic, others minty. **88** *(10/1/2001)*

Chatom 2001 Esmeralda Syrah (Calaveras County) $28. Fruity, filled with succulent cherry, black raspberry and mocha flavors and even blueberries, in a fully dry wine. Soft and gentle texture, long spicy finish. **87** —*S.H. (2/1/2005)*

Chatom 2001 Zinfandel (Calaveras County) $16. Modest flavors of black cherry, plum and spice are framed in mild-mannered toast. Modest at the end as well. **84** *(11/1/2003)*

Chatom 2000 Zinfandel (Calaveras County) $16. Strong and briary, a wine with little finesse and plenty of power. This is country-style mountain Zin at its rawest, with wild berry flavors, punchy tannins and dry, firm acids. Will overwhelm gentle foods, so it's best drunk with barbecue and similar fare. **85** —*S.H. (9/1/2003)*

CHATOM VINEYARDS

Chatom Vineyards 2002 Syrah (Calaveras County) $22. Polished and smooth, with fancy cocoa, blackberry, cherry and coffee flavors that are well-ripened and long-lasting. The tannins are gentle, with good acidity. Turns candy sweet on the finish. **86** —*S.H. (8/1/2005)*

Chatom Vineyards 2002 Esmeralda Syrah (Calaveras County) $34. Smoky and meaty, but balanced by brooding black fruit and dark, earthy flavors. The fruit is ripe and round on The midpalate, then turns a bit tart and attenuated on the finish. **85** *(9/1/2005)*

Chatom Vineyards 2002 Zinfandel (Calaveras County) $16. Try this charmingly rustic wine with almost anything that calls for a very dry red wine. It has earthy, fruity flavors, and the tannins are firm and dusty. **84** —*S.H. (8/1/2005)*

CHATTER CREEK

Chatter Creek 2002 Bordeaux Blend (Columbia Valley (WA)) $16. 105 cases of this Bordeaux blend were produced, and the wine is soft and fruity, with a nice mix of red berry, black cherry, and some smoke and toast. Expansive and lingering, it has a pleasing, almost plush palate feel. Good all-purpose red. **87** —*P.G. (6/1/2005)*

Chatter Creek 2003 Alder Ridge Vineyard Cabernet Franc (Columbia Valley (WA)) $20. Clean and ripe, with young, grapy fruit taking center stage. The wine has the firm, tannic grip of the Cab Franc grape, but the tannins are well managed, smooth and unencumbered with new oak. **88** —*P.G. (6/1/2005)*

Chatter Creek 2002 Alder Ridge Vineyard Cabernet Franc (Columbia Valley (WA)) $20. A light, supple and generous effort, with good pie cherry and plum-flavored fruit, highlighted with hints of coffee grounds. A bit like a Chinon in terms of structure and balance. **87** —*P.G. (6/1/2005)*

Chatter Creek 2000 Alder Ridge Vineyard Cabernet Franc (Washington) $18. There is a distinctive bell pepper/asparagus element here, often found in some Washington Cabernet. But it's soundly made, and the underlying fruit is true to varietal, with a bit of coffee and toast in the tannic finish. **86** —*P.G. (6/1/2002)*

Chatter Creek 1998 Cabernet Sauvignon (Washington) $20. A rich, ripe nose rushes from the glass, redolent with cassis, black cherries and other, darkly mysterious spices. Some classic Washington bell pepper and dill adds interest, and the finish is thick and coats the palate with tannins tasting of coffee and chocolate. **87** —*P.G. (10/1/2001)*

Chatter Creek 2002 Alder Ridge Vineyard Cabernet Sauvignon (Columbia Valley (WA)) $30. With its medium body and supple tannins, this seems destined to be consumed young. Vanilla and pastry-crust notes accent raspberry fruit on the nose, while on the palate, chocolate and caramel shadings frame tart red berries, turning cedary on the finish. **89** —*P.G. (8/1/2006)*

Chatter Creek 1999 Alder Ridge Vineyard Cabernet Sauvignon (Washington) $20. This is a tannic, sleek style of Cabernet, still tightly wound up and closed down. There is good juice here, with bright berry/cherry flavors, just waiting for some additional bottle time to let it loose. Plenty of acids, good tannin management, and a stylish effort that will reward cellaring. **88** —*P.G. (10/1/2001)*

Chatter Creek 2001 Alder Ridge Vineyard Cabernet Sauvignon-Merlot (Columbia Valley (WA)) $22. Excellent vintage, and the blend includes 12% Merlot and a pinch of Syrah. The wine displays a European sense of balance, with just a bit of spicy new oak adding nuance and resonance to the finish. **88** —*P.G. (6/1/2005)*

Chatter Creek 2003 Pinot Gris (Columbia Valley (WA)) $12. This is clean and crisp, a bit softer and rounder than many from Washington, with varietal flavors of pear and cut apple. **87** —*P.G. (6/1/2005)*

Chatter Creek 2000 Pinot Gris (Washington) $12. Washington Pinot Gris is seldom seen—the bragging rights having been claimed by Oregon—but this appealing wine makes a good argument for more. Full, fleshy, pear-flavored fruit is perfectly balanced with refreshing acids. It's a big, bold style that finishes with a hint of bitter rind. **86** —*P.G. (10/1/2001)*

Chatter Creek 2002 Clifton Hill Vineyard Syrah (Columbia Valley (WA)) $30. A young, spicy Syrah, this shows unusually bright and intense fruit, a mix of purple plums and blackberries. There are unusual candied citrus highlights, hints of herb and spice. Top-shelf juice. **91** —*P.G. (6/1/2005)*

Chatter Creek 2003 Jack Jones Vineyard Syrah (Columbia Valley (WA)) $22. Despite its youth it's ready to rock, with appealing varietal fruit, sparked by a nose that says this is what Syrah should be, very pretty and forward. It's a bright and snappy wine, spiced up with plenty of pepper. **88** —*P.G. (6/1/2005)*

Chatter Creek 2000 Jack Jones Vineyard Syrah (Washington) $20. No, it's not that Jack Jones. But it's a fine bottle of wine, with tight, hard fruit that opens slowly into a lovely mélange of plums and cherries. Tangy and tannic, this one needs some more time to come together, but all the components are right there. **89** —*P.G. (6/1/2002)*

USA

Chatter Creek 2003 Lonesome Spring Ranch Syrah (Yakima Valley) $22. Young, big-boned, raw and still grapy, but all the right ingredients are there for a solid, varietal and chewy Syrah, perfect for the barbecue season. **88** —*P.G. (6/1/2005)*

Chatter Creek 2000 Lonesome Spring Ranch Syrah (Yakima Valley) $20. The winemaker, Gordy Rawson, spent years at Columbia Winery, and learned a thing or two about Syrah. A pretty nose shows ripe berry fruit and sweet toast. This is really good juice, varietal and lip-smackingly tart, with a generous amount of fat, flavorful new oak. **91 Editors' Choice** —*P.G. (6/1/2002)*

Chatter Creek 2004 Viognier (Columbia Valley (WA)) $20. Fragrant with lime, citrus, tangerine and grapefruit. The flavors are taut, tart, spiked with cilantro and anise, in a lively, fresh style. Just 12.5 percent alcohol. **88** —*P.G. (4/1/2006)*

Chatter Creek 2003 Viognier (Yakima Valley) $15. From the Lonesome Spring Ranch vineyard, this is very fresh, with juicy citrus and orange peel flavors. **87** —*P.G. (6/1/2005)*

CHEAPSKATE

CheapSkate 2003 Miser Cabernet Blend (California) $8. With Cab Franc added to the Cab Sauvignon, this wine is soft and cherryish, with a fine dusting of dry tannins and a clean, spicy finish. It's not terribly complex, but is a really good value. **84 Best Buy** —*S.H. (11/1/2005)*

CheapSkate 2003 Cabernet Sauvignon (California) $8. There are some fine, ripe blackberry and cherry flavors in this Cab, and although it's rustic and a bit sharp, at this price it's a pretty good house pour. **84 Best Buy** —*S.H. (11/1/2005)*

CheapSkate 2002 Pinot Noir (California) $8. Pretty rude stuff, a harsh, hot wine that's recognizably Pinot Noir with its silky structure and cherry flavors, but that's about it. **82** —*S.H. (11/1/2005)*

CheapSkate 2004 SkinFlint Rosé Blend (California) $8. There's lots to like in this blush wine, made from Bordeaux grapes. It shows spicy cherry and sweet anise flavors, and has enough crisp acidity to make it bright and clean. **84 Best Buy** —*S.H. (11/1/2005)*

CHEHALEM

Chehalem 2000 Chardonnay (Willamette Valley) $19. Another beautifully crafted wine from Chehalem, this combines inviting citrus, melon and papaya fruit with just the right amount of buttered popcorn flavors from new oak. Silky and elegant, it is delicious now but will cellar well. **90** *(8/1/2002)*

Chehalem 2000 Ian's Reserve Chardonnay (Willamette Valley) $32. Young and sassy, this wine is already showing lovely nuances of toast, spice, lees and mineral. Complex, vivid and beautifully balanced, with a lot of fresh leesy texture and the tangy fruit riding on top. Classy winemaking, elegant and sophisticated. **91** —*P.G. (7/1/2002)*

Chehalem 1999 Ian's Reserve Chardonnay (Willamette Valley) $32. This is their top cuvée, from 100% Dijon clones, and it's made in a fresh, clean style without excessive oak or alcohol. There's a good-flavored fullness in the mouth, that keeps the balance among juicy, sweet fruit, toasty barrel and evenhanded acid. This is the rare Oregon Chardonnay that will continue to improve over several years. **89** —*P.G. (2/1/2002)*

Chehalem 2004 INOX Chardonnay (Willamette Valley) $17. Stainless steel fermented and aged, to bring bright, acid-driven fruit to the forefront. Full-bodied and flavorful, with nicely mixed stone fruits, pineapple, green berries and lemony citrus. It sets up sharply on the palate and holds true, just waiting for some fresh shellfish. **90** —*P.G. (5/1/2006)*

Chehalem 2003 Pinot Gris (Willamette Valley) $16. Very fine, showing classic pear and apple flavors, set off in a very pretty, balanced style. There's a little bit of SO2 from recent bottling, but give it a good swirl and this wine rewards you with layers of finesse. **89** —*P.G. (12/15/2004)*

Chehalem 2001 Pinot Gris (Willamette Valley) $15. Here is a solid, Oregon style Pinot Gris, with lots of rich, ripe pear and apple-flavored fruit. There is a sweet butterscotch tilt to the back end, making for an unusually rich, almost tropical finish. **89 Best Buy** —*P.G. (12/31/2002)*

Chehalem 2000 Pinot Gris (Willamette Valley) $15. Chehalem aims for a crisp, Alsatian style of Pinot Gris, blending fruit from all three estate

vineyards, then fermenting in stainless steel. There's an elegant balance here, with palate-refreshing acid. A natural fit with food. **88** —*P.G. (2/1/2002)*

Chehalem 1997 Pinot Gris (Willamette Valley) $19. **80** *(8/1/1999)*

Chehalem 2004 Reserve Pinot Gris (Willamette Valley) $21. Thick, weighty and ripe, with unctuous pear and stone fruit flavors. It's blended from the three estate vineyards—Ridgecrest, Stoller and Corral Creek. The result? A classic Willamette Valley Pinot Gris, creamy and dotted with lively spice. **90** —*P.G. (2/1/2006)*

Chehalem 2003 3 Vineyard Pinot Noir (Willamette Valley) $25. A beautiful wine, exceptionally smooth, supple and silky. It has youthful spice and fine, mixed red fruit and berry flavors. Harmonious, interesting and lively with a perfect blend of baking spices and crisp acids. **90 Editors' Choice** —*P.G. (5/1/2006)*

Chehalem 2000 3 Vineyard Pinot Noir (Willamette Valley) $25. One of the strongest entry-level Oregon Pinots in our 1999 World Series, this year's version again gives a solid performance. Smoke-tinged cherry and cranberry fruit, vanilla, tea and herb accents, and a velour-like mouthfeel provide plenty of pleasure. The long chocolaty finish has supple tannins. Drink now–2005. **88** *(10/1/2002)*

Chehalem 1998 3 Vineyard Pinot Noir (Willamette Valley) $25. **90** —*M.S. (12/1/2000)*

Chehalem 2000 Corral Creek Pinot Noir (Willamette Valley) $39. Smells of black fruit, toasted wood and forest floor. Meaty on the palate, with rich, dense and layered plum and cherry fruit. The finish is smooth, with ample but balancing tannins; nicely integrated and structured. **88** *(10/1/2002)*

Chehalem 2002 Corral Creek Vineyard Pinot Noir (Willamette Valley) $39. This bottle showed some signs of reduction. Stubbornly closed down, with some funky rubber ball aromas, its core of black cherry fruit was virtually invisible. Grainy tannins and some bitter chocolate marked the finish. Should improve with bottle age. **84** *(11/1/2004)*

Chehalem 1998 Corral Creek Vineyards Pinot Noir (Willamette Valley) $39. **93** —*M.S. (12/1/2000)*

Chehalem 2002 Reserve Pinot Noir (Willamette Valley) $50. It almost tastes like a Beaujolais, with grapy, spicy, whole-cluster flavors out in front, but nothing substantial following. Balanced, clean and fruity. **84** *(11/1/2004)*

Chehalem 2002 Ridgecrest Vineyard Pinot Noir (Willamette Valley) $39. Though it feels just a little light, this is nicely made, with a sharp focus, interesting quinine spice, and an elegant, graceful finish. Not a heavyweight, but quite charming. **87** *(11/1/2004)*

Chehalem 2000 Ridgecrest Vineyards Pinot Noir (Willamette Valley) $39. This wine displays a gamut of Pinot aromas: plum, raspberry, bacon, tree bark and dried spices. A touch of earth adds appeal to the palate, which goes heavy on the cherry as well as on the oak. The finish has full yet supple tannins and good length. **87** *(10/1/2002)*

Chehalem 1999 Ridgecrest Vineyards Pinot Noir (Willamette Valley) $39. One look at this violet bomber and you'd think it's Shiraz, not Oregon Pinot. It's rich and loaded with popcorn and Bourbon aromas, sweet black cherry flavors and firm, starching tannins. The distinct flavor of carob can be found on the muscle bound finish. **86** *(10/1/2002)*

Chehalem 2000 Rion Reserve Pinot Noir (Willamette Valley) $50. This is a beauty, with deep, sweet aromas of black cherry, mincemeat pie, vanilla and buttered toast. The palate is full of cherry, plum and vanilla, with charred oak supplying the foundation—too much char for one of our tasters. But the finish is smooth as silk. **92 Editors' Choice** *(10/1/2002)*

Chehalem 1999 Rion Reserve Pinot Noir (Willamette Valley) $50. Some earthy, dense, terroir-driven aromas start this one off, followed by a mouthful of plum, cola and smoked meat. The color is dark as is the overall profile of the wine; it's powerful and richly fruited. Very modern and offering more bulk, intensity and hedonism than elegance. **89** *(10/1/2002)*

Chehalem 2002 Stoller Vineyard Pinot Noir (Dundee Hills) $39. Quite dark and dense, with heavy tannins. Strong scents of tomato leaf and beetroot

USA

give the wine a tough, herbal set of flavors; ungenerous and unyielding, at least for now. **85** *(11/1/2004)*

Chehalem 2000 Stoller Vineyards Pinot Noir (Willamette Valley) $39. This wine has heavy aromas of black coffee and burnt toast. It's hearty plum and black cherry fruit is on the sweeter side, but it's overshadowed by butter and oak. If oak is not your bag, you might be better off with some of Chehalem's other 2000 Pinots. **85** *(10/1/2002)*

Chehalem 1997 Stoller Vineyards Pinot Noir (Willamette Valley) $28. **86** *(10/1/1999)*

Chehalem 2002 Three Vineyards Pinot Noir (Willamette Valley) $39. A bit slow out of the starting gate, this rewards patience with pretty, pale cherry and cranberry fruit, elegantly styled. This is high acid, vibrant, and conspicuously light on the new oak. **88** *(11/1/2004)*

Chehalem 1997 Three Vineyards Pinot Noir (Willamette Valley) $18. **90** *(10/1/1999)*

Chehalem 2001 Corral Creek Reserve Dry Riesling (Willamette Valley) $19. Chehalem makes a number of excellent, single vineyard white wines in a true Alsatian style. This vineyard-designated dry Riesling, creamy and fresh with vibrant flavors of melon, lime and pineapple, stands head and shoulders above most domestic efforts. **90** *—P.G. (12/31/2002)*

Chehalem 2004 Reserve Dry Riesling (Willamette Valley) $21. For those who love the austere, steel and stone flavors of bone-dry Riesling, this will be a welcome discovery. It has plenty of power, citrus rind flavors of fruit and skin, a persistent minerality and a clean, fresh finish. **89** *—P.G. (5/1/2006)*

CHELAN ESTATE

Chelan Estate 2002 Cabernet Sauvignon (Columbia Valley (WA)) $25. A Cab/Merlot blend from Red Mountain grapes, this young wine has great color and good, tart, tight fruit. Flavors run to cranberry, sour cherry and more, done in a firm, tannic, herbal style. **87** *—P.G. (9/1/2004)*

Chelan Estate 2004 Chardonnay-Viognier (Columbia Valley (WA)) $16. A roughly 50-50 blend that comes across with firm, melon-flavored fruit—honeydew, green apple, Asian pear. Brief aging in new 500-liter puncheons gives it just a kiss of toast. 223 cases were made. **88** *—P.G. (4/1/2006)*

CHERRY HILL ESTATE

Cherry Hill Estate 2002 Pinot Noir (Willamette Valley) $27. Comes out ripe and pruney, with smoke and chocolate. Root beer, beetroot, tomato leaf notes make for a distinctly herbal style, spicy and pungent, with good length. **87** *(11/1/2004)*

CHESTER KIDDER

Chester Kidder 2002 Red Blend (Columbia Valley (WA)) $50. It's 45% Merlot, 28% Cabernet Sauvignon, 8% Syrah and 19% Cab Franc, adding up to a somewhat amorphous blend that lacks a bit of focus. There is, on the other hand, plenty of juicy, ripe raspberry fruit, some coffee/espresso scents and a slight whiff of VA. This is the first red wine release from Allen Shoup's Long Shadows collective. **88** *—P.G. (4/1/2006)*

CHEVAL SAUVAGE

Cheval Sauvage 2002 Ashley Vineyard Pinot Noir (Santa Rita Hills) $50. This full-bodied, round Pinot boasts distinctive cola, coffee and roasted meat aromas, then follows up with flavors of black cherries, earth and a hint of wintergreen. Finishes with supple tannins; drink now–2010. **90** *(10/1/2005)*

CHEYANNA

Cheyanna 2004 Zinfandel (Napa Valley) $15. Rustic, a simple Zin with a mixture of superripe raisiny fruit and less ripe mint. The middle is cherries, and the wine is dry and tannic. From Catacula Lake. **82** *—S.H. (12/31/2006)*

CHIARELLO FAMILY VINEYARDS

Chiarello Family Vineyards 2002 Felicia Old Vine Zinfandel (Napa Valley) $45. Lush and powerful, yet balanced and elegant, too. This wine offers a core of rich, ripe plum, black cherry, blackberry, chocolate and spice

flavors that course gracefully along the palate. It's plush, full-blown and long, with a velvety finish. **93** *—J.M. (10/1/2004)*

CHIMERE

Chimere 2002 Angelica Orange Muscat (Santa Barbara County) $14. Sweet in apricot, orange honey and vanilla flavors, and with a gooey texture, this dessert wine nonetheless is balanced with crisp acidity, and is very refreshing. The flavors are addictively good, especially after a rich meal. **92** *—S.H. (3/1/2005)*

Chimere 1996 Pinot Noir (Edna Valley) $23. **89** *(11/15/1999)*

Chimere 2002 Paragon Vineyard Pinot Noir (Edna Valley) $30. Smells Porty and caramelized, and drinks hot and dry. **82** *—S.H. (3/1/2005)*

Chimere 1999 Paragon Vineyard Pinot Noir (Edna Valley) $22. The color here is rusty; its luster is fading. The nose is dry and mellow, offering talc, baking spices and dried red fruit. Flavors of orange peel and clove accent the dry, woody palate, which has a touch of sharpness to it. Drink now or wait for a new vintage. **85** *(10/1/2002)*

Chimere 1997 Paragon Vineyard Pinot Noir (Edna Valley) $22. **84** *—J.C. (12/15/2000)*

Chimere 1999 Santa Maria Hill Vineyard. Pinot Noir (Santa Barbara County) $26. Woody and smoky at first, with aromatic hints of ink, beets, cola and lavender. The palate offers less than the nose, primarily toast and black fruit. Dark coffee and moderate tannins dominate the stern finish. **87** *(10/1/2002)*

CHIMNEY ROCK

Chimney Rock 2003 Elevage Bordeaux Blend (Stags Leap District) $75. This Bordeaux-style blend is complex, mingling cherry, blackberry and cassis fruit with notes of violets, dried spices and black olives. It's full-bodied and supple, with rich, fine tannins that taper off gently on the finish. Drink now–2015. **91** *(9/1/2006)*

Chimney Rock 1997 Elevage Bordeaux Blend (Stags Leap District) $52. **89** *(11/1/2000)*

Chimney Rock 1998 Dionysus Cabernet Blend (Stags Leap District) $74. This blend of 80% Cabernet Sauvignon and 20% Merlot is more elegant and lean than rich. The nose offers meaty brown-sugar and blackberry aromas. Bright raspberry and cherry flavors are enveloped in oak and vanilla in the mouth; finishes with intense woodsy-vanilla notes. 259 cases made. **90** *—D.T. (6/1/2002)*

Chimney Rock 2002 Elevage Cabernet Blend (Stags Leap District) $76. If Tchelistcheff were still here, he might describe this Cab as an iron fist in a velvet glove. It's inviting in rich cassis, blueberry and chocolate flavors, with a soft mouthfeel. But the softness is deceptive; this is a big, deeply structured wine. Drink now through 2012. **92** *—S.H. (12/1/2005)*

Chimney Rock 2003 Rose Cabernet Franc (Stags Leap District) $21. A nice blush wine with a fancy address. It's medium- to ull-bodied, with lush raspberry and cherry flavors, and Provençal-style herbs. Totally dry. **88** *—S.H. (12/15/2004)*

Chimney Rock 2005 Rosé of Cabernet Franc Cabernet Franc (Stags Leap District) $21. Dark in color, full in flavor, this is a big, strong, almost heavy blush wine. Black raspberries, apricot sorbet, red cherry purée, even a hint of tangerine zest, with nice acidity. **85** *—S.H. (11/15/2006)*

Chimney Rock 2004 Rosé of Cabernet Franc Cabernet Franc (Stags Leap District) $21. This is a Beaujolais-like California rosé. It's light in body, aromatic, clean and zippy in acids and fruity, with raspberry, strawberry, vanilla cream and nutmeg flavors. Chill it and then watch how it changes as it warms up on the table. **89** *—S.H. (12/1/2005)*

Chimney Rock 1997 Cabernet Sauvignon (Napa Valley) $40. **91** *(11/1/2000)*

Chimney Rock 1996 Cabernet Sauvignon (Napa Valley) $30. **90** *—M.S. (6/1/1999)*

Chimney Rock 2003 Cabernet Sauvignon (Stags Leap District) $52. This is bigger, bolder and less supple than the Elevage Rouge, with more monochromatic cassis flavors framed by oaky notes of vanilla and cinnamon. Turns a bit chocolaty on the finish. While the Elevage will match roasts, this is more of a steak wine. **90** *(9/1/2006)*

USA

Chimney Rock 2003 Cabernet Sauvignon (Stags Leap District) $52. Your first impression is of a rich, well-structured, important Cabernet. It impresses with ripe, cassis-laced fruit and lush, sweet tannins. Oak provides seasoning, but doesn't dominate this dry, elegant Cab. Drink now through 2010. **90** —S.H. (9/1/2006)

Chimney Rock 2002 Cabernet Sauvignon (Stags Leap District) $49. Very soft, but with enough structure from acids and tannins, this wine is also extremely ripe and extracted. It has flavors of sweetened coffee and blackberry liqueur, as well as oak. Exemplifies the modern, international style. **87** —S.H. (11/15/2005)

Chimney Rock 2002 Cabernet Sauvignon (Napa Valley) $49. A little rough in texture, and with plenty of tannins, this Cab nonetheless satisfies with lots of ripe blackberry and cherry flavors. It's totally dry. Calls for powerful steaks and chops. **87** —S.H. (10/1/2005)

Chimney Rock 2001 Cabernet Sauvignon (Stags Leap District) $49. Seductively sweet, with ripe currant and cherry fruit framed by fancy oak, yet the underlying tannins kick in midway. Nowhere near its maximum integration; best left alone through 2008 to develop nuance. **93** —S.H. (10/1/2004)

Chimney Rock 2000 Cabernet Sauvignon (Stags Leap District) $45. Has those textbook Napa tannins, soft and luxurious but complex, and a pretty edge of fine oak, but can't quite overcome a hollowness in the middle. The first flavor of cassis leads to high expectations, but the finish turns thin and tannic. **86** —S.H. (11/15/2003)

Chimney Rock 1999 Cabernet Sauvignon (Stags Leap District) $45. Aromas of dried earth, wet stone and chocolate prep you for the flavors of fresh plums, chocolate and cedar. The mouthfeel is rich and the tannins finish like a fine emery board. **88** —C.S. (11/15/2002)

Chimney Rock 2002 Reserve Cabernet Sauvignon (Stags Leap District) $100. Expensive, yes, but this is a wine of very high quality. The Cabernet Sauvignon shines through, showing enormous black currant flavor, and then there are the wonderfully ripe, smooth tannins that make the wine glide like velvet. It seems to be best now, but should hold for some years. **93 Editors' Choice** —S.H. (12/1/2005)

Chimney Rock 2001 Reserve Cabernet Sauvignon (Stags Leap District) $107. A great Cab showcasing everything good about Napa's fabulous '01 Cabs. It's rich, vibrant and complex, with layers of cassis, cocoa and roasted coffee flavors, and a deft touch of smoky oak. The tannins are sweet, ripe and subtle. Doesn't clobber you sideways with fruit, but offers elegant, sophisticated drinking. **93** —S.H. (7/1/2005)

Chimney Rock 1999 Reserve Cabernet Sauvignon (Stags Leap District) $90. The first impression is a bit strange; there are some milky notes to the nose that don't really work. But with time that evaporates and what's left is a typically sweet Napa Cab with tons of cassis, black cherry and coffee flavors. On the downside, a buttery, oaky note might be off-putting to some. **88** —M.S. (11/15/2002)

Chimney Rock 1997 Reserve Cabernet Sauvignon (Stags Leap District) $80. 88 (11/1/2000)

Chimney Rock 2003 Fumé Blanc (Napa Valley) $20. A stylishly dry white wine that's a little thin in fruit, but satisfies for its streamlined crispness and acidity. You'll find some flavors of citrus rind and vanilla. **86** —S.H. (12/15/2004)

Chimney Rock 2000 Fumé Blanc (Napa Valley) $18. Strange aromas of chewing gum, silly putty, green beans and turnip make for an unconventional bouquet. The palate is rather vegetal and dilute, with hints of sweet gum and pepper. The finish is light and simple, with just a smidgen of grapefruit. While hard to peg, there's an off quality to this wine that holds it back. **85** (8/1/2002)

Chimney Rock 2001 Elevage Red Blend (Stags Leap District) $72. In 2000 the grapes for this wine struggled to get ripe. No problem in '01. Massive in blackberry, cherry, chocolate and oak flavors, with smooth but firm tannins, it's drinkable tonight, but possesses the balance to develop bottle complexity through 2010. **91** —S.H. (4/1/2005)

Chimney Rock 2000 Elevage Red Blend (Stags Leap District) $60. A blend mostly of Merlot and Cabernet Sauvignon, this wine is very good, but shares the trademark of this deficient vintage. It is graceful and elegant,

for immediate enjoyment. The blackberry and cherry flavors are backed by soft, easy tannins. **88** —S.H. (11/15/2003)

Chimney Rock 1998 Elevage Red Blend (Stags Leap District) $60. "Red table wine," as it's called on the bottle, means "Bordeaux blend" to you and me. This is not a weighty wine. Instead, expect understated blueberry, anise, dried herb and fleshy-peach flavors on the palate. Opens with muted cherry and oak flavors. Very feminine, and very good. **89** —D.T. (6/1/2002)

Chimney Rock 2004 Elevage Blanc White Blend (Napa Valley) $36. This blend of Sauvignon Blanc and Sauvignon Gris is all barrel-fermented— the trick is that only 30% of the barrels are wood, the rest are stainless steel. The result is a complex, multifaceted Sauvignon that's meant to pay homage to white Graves. Subtle toasted nut and vanilla shadings frame melon and peach fruit, while the mouthfeel is creamy and rich, balanced by a bit of grapefruity tang on the finish. **88** (9/1/2006)

CHINOOK

Chinook 2003 Cabernet Franc (Yakima Valley) $20. This little-sung (outside of Washington) winery makes an eagerly-awaited rosé of Cabernet Franc each spring, but here is the real deal. One hundred percent varietal, it puts the lie to the notion that Cabernet Franc must be tannic and tough. Here it is fragrant, firm and tart, with spicy apple, plum, date, fig and even golden raisin flavors. Interested, complex and beautifully crafted, without obvious oak and just 13 percent alcohol. **89** —P.G. (6/1/2006)

Chinook 2003 Chardonnay (Yakima Valley) $17. Solid, fresh with succulent fruit hinting at white peaches and a dusting of cinnamon and sweet spice. Finishes with good length and hints of honey, tea and apricot. Nice effort. **88** —P.G. (12/15/2005)

Chinook 1998 Merlot (Yakima Valley) $28. Always a favorite and highly allocated, this nicely aged wine showcases beautifully ripe, not overripe, Yakima Valley fruit. Sweet scents of Bing cherry, cocoa and spice open softly into a generous but elegant palate, balanced and smooth. **90** —P.G. (9/1/2002)

Chinook 2005 Sauvignon Blanc (Yakima Valley) $17. Leesy and crisp, an immaculate style, with flavors that are translucent, yet layered and substantial. It finishes with an elegant wash of stone, melon and citrus that will give your palate, your meal and your conversation a welcome lift. **88** —P.G. (12/31/2006)

Chinook 2000 Sauvignon Blanc (Yakima Valley) $15. Bright, spicy fruit is handsomely underscored with sweet new oak. This is flat-out classy winemaking, with food-friendly acids and the wine's citrus/melon fruit playing well against the toasty oak. **90** —P.G. (9/1/2002)

Chinook 2004 Sémillon (Yakima Valley) $17. Tart and sharp, with a pleasing tang and snap. The complex, clean and crisp flavors layer fig, citrus rind and clove with high notes of candied orange and citrus blossom. Great varietal character, cool-climate acidity; this is very sophisticated winemaking with spot-on flavors. **90** —P.G. (6/1/2006)

Chinook 2000 Sémillon (Yakima Valley) $14. This wine shows a lot of Bourbon-barrel oak flavor, underscoring fruit that has plenty of apple and melon intensity, enlightened with pleasing herbal accents. **88** —P.G. (9/1/2002)

CHOUINARD

Chouinard 2001 Joan's Vineyard Orange Muscat Ice Wine (Paso Robles) $16. A rich, wickedly sweet dessert wine. From the golden amber color to the sticky texture, this is like honey. But it's delicate and refined, and the orange essence, apricot, vanilla and white chocolate flavors are addictive. **93 Best Buy** —S.H. (12/1/2003)

Chouinard NV Brut Sparkling Blend (California) $13. An average-quality bubbly that's a bit rough around the edges, with sharp bubbles and brisk acidity, but perfectly adequate for ordinary times. The Chenin

Blanc-based flavors are neutral at first, then turn peachy. **84** —S.H. (12/1/2003)

CHRISTINE WOODS

Christine Woods NV Pinot Noir (Anderson Valley) $20. An absolutely middle-of-the-road Pinot that's varietally true. It's silky and high in acids, with lean cranberry flavors, and one-dimensional. Anderson Valley may well be a good home for Pinot Noir, but a wine like this leaves the case to be made. **85** —S.H. *(5/1/2002)*

CHRISTOPHE

Christophe 2000 Pinot Noir (Monterey) $10. 82 *(10/1/2002)*

CHRISTOPHER CREEK

Christopher Creek 1999 Petite Sirah (Russian River Valley) $28. Tasters found overripe notes ranging from prunes and raisins to blackberry compote, wrapped in the sweet vanilla, char and smoke. The tannins are pretty gritty and pronounced. One taster called them chunky, but not painful. **84** *(4/1/2003)*

Christopher Creek 2001 Zinfandel (Dry Creek Valley) $22. Plush aromas yield to tangy bright raspberry and strawberry flavors. There's a lot of spice and heat here as well. Bright on the finish. **84** *(11/1/2003)*

CHUMEIA

Chumeia 2002 Partridge-Leigh Vineyard Barbera (Paso Robles) $25. Robust, full-bodied and bone dry, with baked cherry pie, black currant and mocha flavors accented by sweet toasty oak, this wine is wrapped in thick, jagged tannins. The best thing about it is the rich, ripe, deeply fruity flavors. **85** —S.H. *(6/1/2006)*

Chumeia 2003 Cabernet Sauvignon (California) $13. Raw in acids, chocolaty and ripe in blackberries to the point of raisins, yet dry, this is a country wine meant to be consumed with gusto over barbecued ribs and chicken. **83** —S.H. *(12/31/2005)*

Chumeia 2002 Cabernet Sauvignon (California) $12. Smells burnt, and tastes sharp in tannins and herbaceousness. Unpleasant. **81** —S.H. *(2/1/2005)*

Chumeia 2000 Cabernet Sauvignon (Central Coast) $25. Decent and drinkable, with flavors of blackberries, green olives and sage, and a nice overlay of oak. Very dry, with a good balance of dusty tannins and acidity. Finishes just a bit rough and earthy. **85** —S.H. *(8/1/2003)*

Chumeia 2000 Cabernet Sauvignon (California) $10. Not bad for everyday quaffing, with some rich blackberry flavors and nice, dry tannins. It has a country-style edge of roughness to it, but all in all, this is a pretty good value in Cabernet. **85 Best Buy** —S.H. *(8/1/2003)*

Chumeia 2000 Chardonnay (Central Coast) $16. A little light in fruit, with hints of green apples and spice. Crisp acidity helps to cleanse the palate. This is an okay, everyday drinking Chard. **84** —S.H. *(6/1/2003)*

Chumeia 2004 Simpson Vineyard Chardonnay (Madera) $11. Soft, simple and rather sweet, this Central Valley Chard has flavors of canned peaches and apricots. **82** —S.H. *(12/31/2005)*

Chumeia 2003 Simpson Vineyard Chardonnay (California) $10. Heavy and thick, like canned peach syrup, with too much oak and sweetness. **83** —S.H. *(2/1/2005)*

Chumeia 2001 Simpson Vineyard Chardonnay (California) $10. Pretty rich for an inexpensive Chard, and a single vineyard one at that. Pleasant flavors of peaches and pears are framed in oak. There's a slight burn in the finish, but it's not too hot. **85** —S.H. *(6/1/2003)*

Chumeia 2003 Merlot (California) $13. There's a leathery, sweaty aroma and taste here that's not very pleasant. The wine is also disagreeably sharp. **80** —S.H. *(12/31/2005)*

Chumeia 2002 Simpson Vineyard Merlot (California) $12. A full-bodied, rich wine for those looking for a value. The blackberry, blueberry and cherry-chocolate flavors are melded into soft tannins, and finish long and spicy. **86 Best Buy** —S.H. *(12/31/2004)*

Chumeia 2001 Pinot Blanc (Monterey County) $14. Earthy-fruity, with bizarrely exaggerated oak on the finish. **82** —S.H. *(3/1/2005)*

Chumeia 2000 Pinot Blanc (Monterey County) $14. Smells fragrant and inviting, with aromas of peach, vanilla, smoke and a pretty wildflower streak. In the mouth, the wine seems dominated by high acidity and lees, making it rather tart and sour despite the fruity flavors. **84** —S.H. *(3/1/2004)*

Chumeia 2003 Pinot Noir (Central Coast) $16. Dark, soft and thick, this Pinot brings to mind certain far more expensive Pinots that critics wow as ageable. I don't think so. It's more like a simple Syrah, tasty, but lacking delicacy, with a sweetish finish. **83** —S.H. *(2/1/2006)*

Chumeia 2002 Pinot Noir (Central Coast) $16. A nice, easy Pinot, with tart cherry, coffee and oak flavors that drink dry. You'll find a silky texture and crisp, balancing acids. **86** —S.H. *(2/1/2005)*

Chumeia 2001 Pinot Noir (Santa Lucia Highlands) $28. I preferred this winery's less costly Central Coast bottling to this one, which has an odd, raw meat smell and is too oaky. Although it has polished cherry flavors and good acids, it's odd. **84** —S.H. *(2/1/2005)*

Chumeia 2000 Pinot Noir (Santa Lucia Highlands) $28. This soft and inviting wine seduces with suede, caramel, cinnamon and vanilla aromas and flavors, then turns harsh and a bit metallic on the finish. It's schizophrenic, much like the panel was regarding this wine, with one reviewer liking it more than the score indicates. **85** *(10/1/2002)*

Chumeia 2003 Silver Nectar Muscat-French Columbard Red Blend (California) $10. Okay for an everyday sweetie, with canned fruit and honey flavors and some brightness. **84** —S.H. *(2/1/2005)*

Chumeia 2000 Simpson Vineyard Syrah (California) $10. Opens with a burst of white pepper, leather and blackberry in the aroma, then turns extremely soft in the mouth because of low acidity. But the berry-cherry flavors are pretty good. Innocent stuff, and not a bad price. **84** —S.H. *(12/15/2003)*

Chumeia 2000 Viognier (California) $10. Rustic, with flavors ranging from fruits and flowers to tobacco and toffee. It's dry and crisp, but could use more finesse. **83** —S.H. *(5/1/2003)*

Chumeia 2000 Zinfandel (Paso Robles) $22. If you like Paso Zin, and a lot of people do, this one's for you. It has the requisite flavors of wild berries and tobacco, with a rich streak of herbs and peppery spices, and is very dry and balanced. Drinks a bit hot but not enough to worry about. **87** —S.H. *(9/1/2003)*

Chumeia 2001 Dante Dusi Vineyard Zinfandel (Paso Robles) $22. Rich and plush on the nose, with a blend of earth and black cherry notes. Full bodied and showing ripe black cherry, licorice, raspberry, herb, spice and cedary notes. Tannins are round and the finish is moderate in length. **89** —J.M. *(11/1/2003)*

CHURCHILL

Churchill 2004 Pinot Noir (Russian River Valley) $35. It's all about flavor in this tremendously fruity Pinot, a blend of various vineyards in the appellation. Huge flavors of cherry cola, raspberry, pomegranate, licorice and rhubarb pie with the buttery, baked crust flood the mouth. Only detraction is that there's not a lot of depth. **87** —S.H. *(12/31/2006)*

Churchill 2004 Bella Luna Vineyard Pinot Noir (Russian River Valley) $39. Here's a riper style of Pinot. It's rich in gooey pastry-filling cherry, raspberry, cinnamon and vanilla flavors, and there's not much acidity, but there sure is a lot of smoky new oak. The challenge is to get complexity and nuance. The winemaker is Anthony Austin, who studied with Tchelistcheff and was founding winemaker at Firestone. **87** —S.H. *(12/31/2006)*

CILURZO

Cilurzo 1998 Barrel Fermented Chardonnay (Temecula) $16. 81 *(6/1/2000)*

CINERGI

Cinergi 2000 Red Blend (Napa Valley) $18. This unusual blend of six varietals is dominated by Cabernet Sauvignon. It's a dark, youthful wine marked by oak and black currant aromas and flavors and is extremely dry, with a lean, herbal profile and structured tannins. A bit austere now, it will benefit from cellaring. **86** —S.H. *(12/1/2002)*

CINNABAR

Cinnabar 2001 Mercury Rising Bordeaux Blend (California) $18. This is a Bordeaux blend of great charm and elegance. It's soft all through, like butter or velvet, with pure, restrained flavors of berries, dark stone fruits, cola, and earthier tones of sweet pipe tobacco and soy. Leaves behind a very satisfying mouthfeel and a sense of class. **90 Editors' Choice** —S.H. *(12/1/2004)*

Cinnabar 2000 Mercury Rising Bordeaux Blend (California) $17. A tasty, easy-drinking Bordeaux blend assembled from three very different regions, the Santa Cruz Mountains, Sierra Foothills and Lodi. Very flavorful, almost exotic with cassis, cherry, chocolate, and ripe breadfruit and guava, framed in quite a bit of smoky oak. The tannins are soft. This is a wine that everyone will like. **88** —*S.H. (8/1/2003)*

Cinnabar 2003 Mercury Rising Cabernet Blend (California) $18. Blackberries, cherries, French cured olives, anise and toasty oak are the flavors of this dry, stylish Cab. It has a nice balance and rich tannins, and is close to the quality of more expensive wines. **87** —*S.H. (11/1/2006)*

Cinnabar 2002 Mercury Rising Cabernet Blend (California) $18. This is a pretty good Bordeaux blend. It's balanced in tannins and acids, with a little oak to season the ripe blackberry and cherry flavors. **84** —*S.H. (11/1/2005)*

Cinnabar 2001 Estate Cabernet Sauvignon (Santa Cruz Mountains) $40. A beautiful Cab showcasing flamboyant cassis, cocoa and smoky oak flavors, enhanced by firm, sweetly ripe tannins and a touch of oak. It's delicious, but has enough firmness and complexity to make it noteworthy. **90** —*S.H. (2/1/2005)*

Cinnabar 1998 Chardonnay (Central Coast) $17.85 *(6/1/2000)*

Cinnabar 2003 Chardonnay (Monterey) $18. Unusually tropically, even for California Chard. Big time flavors of ripe, juicy papayas and mangoes that are well oaked. Tasty, but a little syrupy-soft. **86** —*S.H. (2/1/2005)*

Cinnabar 2002 Chardonnay (Santa Cruz Mountains) $25. Rich and oaky, this is one of those Chards that's so good right out the gate, it washes down just about anything. Ripe in tropical fruits, peaches and apples, with a buttery, creamy texture, it's got clean, juicy acids. **90 Editors' Choice** —*S.H. (11/1/2005)*

Cinnabar 2001 Chardonnay (Santa Cruz Mountains) $25. This mountain wine is taut with crisp acidity and a minerally spine. It's also well-oaked and leesy, and the oak has lots of char. This firm structure frames flavors of citrus fruits. It's a good wine, but could possess more fruity opulence. **86** —*S.H. (8/1/2004)*

Cinnabar 1999 Chardonnay (Santa Cruz Mountains) $25. Austere, lemony fruit, with a hefty mineral component, wrapped in considerable oak. The wood contributes expected buttered toast notes and a round, creamy mouthfeel, while the fruit is long and penetrating. The earthiness holds your attention. **90** —*S.H. (9/1/2002)*

Cinnabar 1999 Quicksilver Chardonnay (Central Coast) $18. A tightly structured wine marked by apple and peach flavors, but there's a young earthiness that keeps it from being a mere fruit-fest. Lush, creamy and complex, with real density and weight. Lots to like here. **89** —*S.H. (5/1/2001)*

Cinnabar 1997 Saratoga Vineyard Chardonnay (Santa Cruz Mountains) $25. **84** *(6/1/2000)*

Cinnabar 2000 Sleepy Hollow Vineyard Chardonnay (Santa Lucia Highlands) $25. A really good, complex Chard, at the forefront of this varietal's development in California. Combines ripe flavors of sweet, spicy tropical fruits with cool-climate acidity and structure to produce an addictively drinkable, delicious wine. The oak is thickly applied, but perfectly in balance. A desert island wine: If you could bring only one with you . . . **92** —*S.H. (8/1/2003)*

Cinnabar 2003 Merlot (Paso Robles) $20. Here's a nice, dry red wine whose firm tannins, clean acids and subtle earth, coffee and blackberry flavors would make it a fine partner to a range of food. It's an easy but elegant sipper that won't detract from that delicious steak or rib roast. **86** —*S.H. (10/1/2006)*

Cinnabar 2002 Merlot (Paso Robles) $19. A soft, gentle, easy Merlot, with cherry-cocoa flavors. It's dry and balanced. **84** —*S.H. (2/1/2005)*

Cinnabar 2001 Merlot (Paso Robles) $19. Blended from both sides of Highway 101. Warmer eastside fruit lends voluptuously ripe berry flavors, while the cooler west adds structure. However, acidity and tannins remain quite low and soft. A classic example of a Paso Bordeaux wine with high ambitions. **87** —*S.H. (12/1/2003)*

Cinnabar 2003 Pinot Noir (Santa Cruz Mountains) $35. A very nice Pinot made in a lighter style. Shows cherry, blackberry, mocha and spice fla-

vors encased in a delicate structure, and is dry and silky, with a clean, fruity finish. **87** —*S.H. (11/1/2005)*

Cinnabar 1999 Pinot Noir (Santa Cruz Mountains) $38. From northeast-facing vineyards that catch morning sun at 1,200 feet, this is micro-terroir grapegrowing at its most extreme. Cool weather has yielded crisp acidity and fruit that runs the razor's edge between raspberry ripeness and mint-and-tomato earthiness. Very fine barrels add smoke, spice, vanilla and oak-modulated roundness. It seems to lack depth, but then so do certain Burgundies in their youth. **89** —*S.H. (9/1/2002)*

Cinnabar 1999 Gary's Vineyard Pinot Noir (Santa Lucia Highlands) $42. Smoky, with mildly funky game and earth notes over sweet, briary fruit on the nose. On the palate, toasty oak-driven espresso and bitter chocolate flavors come on strong. The wine finishes a bit muted, as the wood really takes over. **86** *(10/1/2002)*

Cinnabar 1999 Watts-Borden Ranch Syrah (Lodi) $17. Expect wonderful drinking from this ripely juicy, nectary wine, which starts with plummy, peppery aromas and turns richly fruity in the mouth. It's serious red wine, thick and weighty, but somehow delicate and elegant. Dry, but the finish is sweet and spicy, and very long. **91** —*S.H. (11/15/2001)*

CK MONDAVI

CK Mondavi 1998 Cabernet Sauvignon (California) $8. You'll recognize the aromas right off the bat: blackberries, cassis, smoke, vanilla, anise and oak. The flavors are of the pop variety, jammy and candied, but they are tasty. The tannins are very soft and silky, and the acidity is low. It all adds up to a very drinkable wine, one-dimensional to be sure, but a good value for the money. **86 Best Buy** —*S.H. (5/1/2001)*

CK Mondavi 2002 Wildcreek Canyon Cabernet Sauvignon (California) $10. Sure is ripe, with its flood of blackberries and cherries, and it's also dry and rich in tannins. It's rather sharp, though, in jammy acids. An affordable sipper at a fair price. **84** —*S.H. (11/15/2004)*

CK Mondavi 2003 Chardonnay (California) $6. Will satisfy bargain hunters seeking an inexpensive Chard with some good peach and honeysuckle flavors, and a hit of toasty oak. Finishes clean and brisk. **84 Best Buy** —*S.H. (10/1/2004)*

CK Mondavi 1999 Chardonnay (California) $8. Looking for an inexpensive Chard with true varietal character and nutty, spicy, vanilla-tinged flavors from oak? Here's one. It's strictly no-frills, but it does offer a lot to like, and at a decent price. **84** —*S.H. (5/1/2001)*

CK Mondavi 1997 Merlot (California) $9. **81** —*J.C. (7/1/2000)*

CK Mondavi 1999 Merlot (California) $9. This is a simple, soft wine with a good deal of charm. It's well made and easy to drink, with pretty black-cherry flavors that spread over the palate. The only drawback is an herbaceous quality that pervades both the aroma, where it's green and stalky, and the palate, where it's positively sharp. But at this price, these are minor quibbles. **84** —*S.H. (5/1/2001)*

CK Mondavi 2002 Wildcreek Canyon Merlot (California) $10. A good everyday wine, quite dry and balanced and with some ripe blackberry, herb and coffee flavors. The tannins are rich and gripping. Represents a fair value. **85 Best Buy** —*S.H. (12/15/2004)*

CK Mondavi 2001 Merlot-Cabernet Sauvignon (California) $8. This is a nice drinking wine, ripely fruity, with sturdy but soft tannins. It's rich enough to accompany grilled meats, and also good by itself. **86 Best Buy** —*S.H. (5/1/2003)*

CK Mondavi 2002 Wildcreek Canyon Merlot-Cabernet Sauvignon (California) $10. Rich and vibrant in blackberry and cherry fruit, with a sleek overlay of toasty oak, this dry wine will go well with a wide variety of foods. It's a good price for a nice everyday wine. **84** —*S.H. (11/15/2004)*

CK Mondavi 2003 Sauvignon Blanc (California) $6. Rather vegetal, and dry and tart in acidity. Finishes with some black currant flavors. **82** —*S.H. (10/1/2004)*

CK Mondavi 1998 Shiraz (California) $8. Shows some Syrah character in its initial aromas of smoke and boiled beef, but then takes on a grassy, herbal edge that refuses to yield. The medium-weight red berry fruit is overshadowed by rhubarb and herbs. **83** *(10/1/2001)*

CK Mondavi 2001 Zinfandel (California) $7. Good basic Zin drinking, a super-fruity wine in a slightly rough-around-the-edges package. Wild berry flavors have an edge of pruny overripeness, but the wine is dry and not too heady. And what a pretty mouthfeel, soft and velvety. **86** —*S.H. (9/1/2003)*

CK Mondavi 2003 White Zinfandel (California) $7. I would not hesitate to enjoy this wine with simple seafood fare. It's rich and fruity in strawberry, raspberry and vanilla flavors, with a sweet hint of vanilla. **84** —*S.H. (11/15/2004)*

CK Mondavi 2002 Wildcreek Canyon Zinfandel (California) $10. Rather lean and sharp, with an edge of overripe raisins. Fine for everyday occasions and gatherings. **82** —*S.H. (12/15/2004)*

CL

CL 2000 Madonna Vineyard Gewürztraminer (Carneros) $15. People don't think of California Gewurz as a serious wine, but this one is. From old, stressed grapevines on the Napa-Sonoma border, the flavors are dense and incredibly concentrated, suggested lychee, peach, honeysuckle, and all sorts of fruity nectars. Despite the massive size, it's on the dry side. This is a big wine that should not be served too cold. **90** —*S.H. (9/1/2003)*

CL 2000 Armagh Vineyard Pinot Noir (Sonoma Coast) $35. This vineyard is located in one of the coldest sections of Sonoma County, where the fog is unbarred by coastal hills. The wine shows that chilly, maritime influence in its sage and cherry tomato flavors. You either like this kind of earthy Pinot or you don't. I like the dryness and tart, acidic structure. **90** —*S.H. (2/1/2003)*

CL 2000 Kanzler Vineyard Pinot Noir (Sonoma Coast) $40. Dense and concentrated, this Pinot achieves great complexity of structure while maintaining the requisite silkiness. Alongside deep blueberry and black cherry flavors, there's also a tomatoey streak. **90** —*S.H. (2/1/2003)*

CLAAR

Claar 1999 White Bluffs Estate Grown & Bottled Cabernet Sauvignon (Columbia Valley (WA)) $21. A bit weedy in the nose, with notes of pepper and salsa. The flavor profile runs sour, with rhubarb and pie cherries sticking out. The mouthfeel is where the wine suffers most; it's hard and aggressive, with piercing tannins and acids that combine forces to starch out your palate and cheeks. **82** —*M.S. (8/1/2003)*

CLAIBORNE & CHURCHILL

Claiborne & Churchill 2002 Dry Gewürztraminer (Central Coast) $14. Made Alsatian style, quite dry and crisp, with bright acidity. What's great about it is the fully ripened flavor, which ranges from peaches to tropical fruits, wildflowers, spices and honey. A wonderful sipper that will be great with spicy Asian fare. **87** —*S.H. (2/1/2004)*

Claiborne & Churchill 2000 Dry Gewürztraminer (Central Coast) $14. It's a little misleading to call it Òdry.Ó The floral, fruity flavors taste like a fig newton or a peach cobbler, with an intense spiciness that's partly varietal, partly the result of excellent acidity. That steely quality supports the fruitiness. The wine is balanced and quite delicious. **88** —*S.H. (9/1/2003)*

Claiborne & Churchill 2000 Pinot Gris (Edna Valley) $18. This up-and-coming varietal triangulates between Sauvignon Blanc's citrusy, acidic sleekness and the richer, fruitier flavors you find in Alsatian whites. It's a pretty wine, crisp and oak-neutral. **86** —*S.H. (9/1/2003)*

Claiborne & Churchill 2005 Alsatian Style Pinot Gris (Arroyo Grande Valley) $18. Here's one of the more fruit-forward PGs, offering an orchard's worth of peach, apricot, apple, pineapple and lemon flower flavors. For all that, the wine really is Alsatian in its dryness and balancing fresh acidity. This is tasty and likeable. **87** —*S.H. (10/1/2006)*

Claiborne & Churchill 2004 Pinot Noir (Edna Valley) $18. Simple, with cherry, cola and coffee flavors, this wine is a bit sweet, with a harsh, hot finish. **82** —*S.H. (11/1/2006)*

Claiborne & Churchill 2002 Pinot Noir (Edna Valley) $16. What a lovely wine. It showcases the success that Edna Valley enjoyed this vintage. Rich, oaky forest floor, mushroom, hard spice and tomato notes. Red stone fruits also star in the complex flavors. Fairly tannic and bone dry,

with great balance, this is a wine that will benefit from mid-term aging or decanting. **90** *(11/1/2004)*

Claiborne & Churchill 2000 Pinot Noir (Edna Valley) $20. Bright strawberry-rhubarb fruit, toast, orange and pine aromas open this light but flavorful wine. The almost candied cherry fruit wears a black oak veil, but is strong enough to not be completely buried by it. Finishes long, with coffee and cocoa accents. **88** *(10/1/2002)*

Claiborne & Churchill 2000 Runestone Pinot Noir (Edna Valley) $29. **82** *(10/1/2002)*

Claiborne & Churchill 1999 Runestone Pinot Noir (Edna Valley) $29. There is an unmistakable scent of rubber on the nose, but also cinnamon and forest floor. The dusty palate is broad and characterized by some animal qualities, raspberry and vanilla. The finish is redolent with charred oak, which makes it seem heavy. **86** *(10/1/2002)*

Claiborne & Churchill 2002 Runestone Barrel Select Pinot Noir (Edna Valley) $26. A pretty good wine and an easy sipper. It's a little overripe, with notes of stewed prunes, but they add interest to the cherry and tea flavors. Very dry and rather tannic. Try decanting for several hours before serving. **86** *(11/1/2004)*

Claiborne & Churchill 2003 Twin Creeks Pinot Noir (Edna Valley) $30. These Alsatian specialists turn their hand to Pinot, with mixed results. The wine is clean, but thin in flavor, which emphasizes the acidity and makes the mouthfeel and finish overly tart. **83** —*S.H. (11/1/2006)*

Claiborne & Churchill 2002 Twin Creeks Pinot Noir (Edna Valley) $33. A real success story for its delicate, refined structure and lovely flavors of cola, sassafras, orange peel and tart red cherries. Very dry, with some firm tannins, the wine is closed now, and will benefit from hours of decanting. **90** *(11/1/2004)*

Claiborne & Churchill 2002 Dry Riesling (Central Coast) $14. One of the nicer Rieslings in California, from specialists in the Alsatian style. It's fully dry, yet with ripe, delicious flavors of crisp apples and peaches, and a tangy aftertaste of minerals and petrol. Bright acidity makes this wine clean and zesty. **87** —*S.H. (2/1/2004)*

Claiborne & Churchill 2000 Dry Riesling (Central Coast) $14. Made Alsatian style, with beautifully etched peach and apricot fruit and zesty acidity. The residual sugar is a modest 0.2% but there's a rich, honeyed feeling to this dry wine. Finishes spicy and clean. **87** —*S.H. (9/1/2003)*

CLARK-CLAUDEN

Clark-Clauden 2003 Ten-Year-Anniversary Cabernet Sauvignon (Napa Valley) $90. Lots of new-oaky char and unintegrated wood sap in this dry, tannic wine, with ripe black currant, cherry and chocolate flavors. It's not particularly drinkable now, such are the astringent tannins, so try cellaring it. **86** —*S.H. (9/1/2006)*

Clark-Clauden 1997 Cabernet Sauvignon (Napa Valley) $78. **92** *(11/1/2000)*

Clark-Clauden 2002 Cabernet Sauvignon (Napa Valley) $90. From lower Howell Mountain, this 100% Cab has bigtime tannins and tremendous authority. It's dry, shut down and slightly rustic now, with an edgy feel, but the core of ripe Cabernet fruit suggests that it will blossom and improve by 2008, and then hold until at least 2015. **91 Cellar Selection** —*S.H. (8/1/2006)*

CLAUDIA SPRINGS

Claudia Springs 2000 Pinot Gris (Anderson Valley) $14. An awkward interpretation of this up-and-coming varietal. Starts with eccentric aromas of white chocolate and rum, and actually drinks a little sweet. There are peach flavors that taste like they were drizzled with honey. Not a bad wine, but strange for Pinot Gris. **83** —*S.H. (5/1/2002)*

Claudia Springs 2004 Klindt Vineyard Pinot Gris (Anderson Valley) $17. A wonderfully dry, crisp and refreshing wine, this PG has flavors of pink grapefruit, lime and hints of tropical fruit. The bright, natural acidity makes it zesty and clean. **90** —*S.H. (2/1/2006)*

Claudia Springs 1999 Pinot Noir (Anderson Valley) $25. From Boonville vineyards. A big, precocious Pinot, this doesn't offer subtlety, but hits the palate with extracted, jammy flavors, and feels a bit thick. Fortunately, good acidity provides structural balance. Other features include dryness and silky tannins. Judging by size, it may be a cellar candidate. **87** —*S.H. (5/1/2002)*

Claudia Springs 1998 Pinot Noir (Mendocino) $18.91 —*P.G. (12/15/2000)*

Claudia Springs 1998 Clone 115 Vidmar Vineyard Pinot Noir (Mendocino) $25.90 —*P.G. (12/15/2000)*

Claudia Springs 2001 Syrah (Mendocino) $20. Has a certain degree of sur-maturité to its aromas, which turned off one reviewer and turned on two others. The fruit is a bit wild and over the top with stone fruit (apricots?) and berry flavors, but the mouthfeel is creamy and ripe, the finish long and supple. **89** *(9/1/2005)*

Claudia Springs 2000 Lolonis Vineyard Viognier (Redwood Valley) $24. This is the most intensely flavored and concentrated Viognier I've ever tasted from the U.S. It opens up fragrant and sensual, a soft, seductive blend of sweet fruits, blossoms, pollen and perfume. It explodes in the glass into a rich, vivid wine highlighted with polished fruit, concentrated aromas and lipsmacking acids. Ethereal. **93** —*P.G. (5/1/2002)*

Claudia Springs 1998 Eagle Point Ranch Zinfandel (Mendocino) $20. Zin with a Pinot sensibility; it's bright, spicy and forward. Sweet, delicious fruit, with accents of cinnamon, cardamom and anise. This is an elegant and subtle wine, but unusually long and complex, with wonderful structure. Enticing, enchanting wine. **93 Editors' Choice** —*P.G. (3/1/2001)*

Claudia Springs 2000 Eaglepoint Ranch Zinfandel (Mendocino) $20. Harbors a distinctive menthol and toast nose. On the palate it's still quite oak driven, but also offering pretty cherry, blackberry, herb and spice flavors. A little short on the finish. **88** *(11/1/2003)*

Claudia Springs 2000 Rhodes Vineyard Zinfandel (Redwood Valley) $26. Quite juicy, with bright cherry and spice flavors at the lead. Vanilla and toast frame it, while firm tannins give it structure. Moderate length at the end. **86** *(11/1/2003)*

Claudia Springs 1999 Rhodes Vineyard Zinfandel (Redwood Valley) $26. Strides down the road to Port, with raisiny, jammy-chocolate and woody scents that turn viscous and sweet in the mouth. An astounding 17.1 percent of alcohol, nearing the legal limit for an unfortified wine, creates heat. Good acidity keeps things from getting flabby. **86** —*S.H. (5/1/2002)*

Claudia Springs 1998 Rhodes Vineyard Zinfandel (Redwood Valley) $24. A juicy, jammy, alcoholic style, tannic and young. This is gutsy, high-toned wine, with fat, extracted fruit. Very dry tannins, good balance. This wine needs time; it's a very different style from the other Claudia Springs Zins. But it shows the same attention to detail, intense fruit, and stylish, sensitive winemaking. **93** —*P.G. (3/1/2001)*

Claudia Springs 1997 Rhodes Vineyard Zinfandel (Redwood Valley) $24. 86 —*S.H. (5/1/2000)*

Claudia Springs 1999 Vassar Vineyard Zinfandel (Redwood Valley) $20. How do they get such a beautifully balanced, dry wine when the alcohol is—gasp—16%? The answer is, perfect balance between fruit, tannins, sugar and alcohol. The wine heats the palate, but not excessively. This is a lesson in how to control Zin when the sugar at harvest runs away. **88** —*S.H. (5/1/2002)*

CLAY STATION

Clay Station 2003 Malbec (Lodi) $13. This is a junior version of those big, rich Argentine Malbecs. It's something like a California Zinfandel, medi-um- to full-bodied and dry, with brambly berry flavors and a robust, gritty mouthfeel. **83** —*S.H. (12/15/2005)*

Clay Station 2002 Malbec (Lodi) $13. Jammy in dark stone fruits and espresso, sharp in acids and tannins and rough, but clean and focused. Best with rich meats and strong cheeses. **83** —*S.H. (12/15/2004)*

Clay Station 2004 Petite Sirah (Lodi) $13. The tannins of this dry, red wine will happily grapple with the fats of cheese and beef, and the acids will match tomatoes. From Delicato. **83** —*S.H. (12/31/2006)*

Clay Station 2005 Pinot Gris (Lodi) $13. Good, drinkable vin ordinaire here, but nothing to get worked up about. It's just a clean, fruity, vibrant house white. **84** —*S.H. (12/1/2006)*

Clay Station 2004 Pinot Gris (Lodi) $13. Simple and clean, this wine is dry and acidic, with the flavor of grapefruit juice. It's a good sipper with grilled veggies and goat cheese, or by itself. **84** —*S.H. (2/1/2006)*

Clay Station 2001 Cabernet-Petite Sirah Red Blend (Lodi) $13. This fruity wine has some rough tannins and is a bit jagged, but the blackberry, coffee and chocolate flavors are delicious. Fully dry, but finishes with lots of ripe fruit. **84** —*S.H. (12/15/2004)*

Clay Station 2003 Shiraz (Lodi) $13. This is a very dry wine, and full-bodied. It has blackberry, pepper, spice and herb flavors, and some firm tannins. The finish is clean and fruity. From Delicato. **85** —*S.H. (3/1/2005)*

Clay Station 2005 Viognier (Lodi) $13. A little sugary, but otherwise you'll find a powerhouse of ripe tropical fruit, peach, honeysuckle and vanilla spice flavors in this smooth, clean wine. **83** —*S.H. (12/15/2006)*

Clay Station 2004 Viognier (Lodi) $13. Planted as a bit of a fluke—the only vines available to plant the last 40 acres were Viognier—but the results have been just fine. The wine is a bit floral and peppery, like nasturtium blossoms, rounded out with ample pear and peach fruit. Low acidity and a hint of sweetness mark the finish. **86** *(8/1/2006)*

Clay Station 2004 Viognier (Lodi) $13. This is one of those almost over-the-top Viogniers that has every fruit flavor you can think of. It drinks soft in texture and honeyed sweet on the finish, and is a simple quaffer. **83** —*S.H. (12/15/2005)*

Clay Station 2003 Viognier (Lodi) $13. A nice, balanced Viognier that showcases the variety's exotic edge. Mango, cantaloupe, honeysuckle, coffee and vanilla flavors finish a little sweet. **84** —*S.H. (12/15/2004)*

Clay Station 2004 Old Vine Zinfandel (Lodi) $13. Dark, jammy, thick on the tongue and bursting with fresh fruit, this Zin is likeable from the get go. It's not subtle about the way it delivers its no-holds-barred blueberry, blackberry and cherry flavors, wrapped in rich tannins. **85** —*S.H. (12/15/2005)*

Clay Station 2004 Old Vine Zinfandel (Lodi) $12. This and the Gnarly Head bottling exemplify the kind of wine we've come to expect from the Indelicato family. Ripe berry fruit leads the way, but picks up enough earthy complexity along the way to show real character. Shows a bit of heat on the finish, but also some welcome spice. **86** *(8/1/2006)*

CLAYHOUSE

Clayhouse 2003 Estate Petite Sirah (Paso Robles) $20. There's some great flavor here, rich black cherry and blackberry fruit, and the wine is totally dry, but compromised by astringency, which gives it a sharp, rustic character. **83** —*S.H. (12/31/2005)*

Clayhouse 2004 Sauvignon Blanc (Paso Robles) $12. A dry, tartly acidic, citrusy wine. There's a strong greenness to it, a peppery, chlorophylly taste that gets those tastebuds going. **84** —*S.H. (12/31/2005)*

Clayhouse 2003 Syrah (Paso Robles) $13. Rustic, country-style, call it what you will, this is a dry, rugged, fairly tannic wine with cherry-berry, coffee and earth flavors. **83** —*S.H. (12/31/2005)*

CLAYTON

Clayton 1999 Estate Vineyard Old Vine Petite Sirah (Lodi) $29. All of the tasters enjoyed this wine for its easy quaffability and layers of complexity. It's enormously extracted and rich in dark stone fruit and berry flavors; it also has a note of bacon, with a warm, velvety mouthfeel and soft tannins. The finish goes on forever. **89** *(4/1/2003)*

Clayton 1999 Estate Vineyard Old Vine Block SC Petite Sirah (Lodi) $29. A wine that tasters disagreed on. Some found it odd. with a cooked quality. Others liked the raspberry and cherry flavors and long finish. Readers will probably also be split in their reactions. **86** *(4/1/2003)*

Clayton 2000 Zinfandel (Lodi) $19. Rich, ripe, lush and jam-packed with black cherry, plum, licorice, spice, chocolate and coffee flavors. This is a fun wine, but also serves up layers of complexity for added interest. Can't beat the price for flavor like this. **91 Editors' Choice** —*J.M. (9/1/2003)*

CLEMENTS HILLS

Clements Hills 2002 Syrah (Lodi) $12. The nose is quite nice, offering blackberry, blueberry and coffee notes. The panel found meaty, pruny elements to the palate of this lighter-sized wine. Supple tannins are a plus. 600 cases produced. **85** *(9/1/2005)*

CLIFF LEDE

Cliff Lede 2002 Claret Bordeaux Blend (Stags Leap District) $32. It's not made in the flashy, fleshy New World style, but has an earthy, herbal flavor, with a hint of blackberry. Oak is not at all prominent in this dry, balanced wine. **90** —*S.H. (12/15/2005)*

Cliff Lede 2002 Cabernet Sauvignon (Stags Leap District) $50. It was fun comparing this Cab with the winery's '02 Claret. Two more different wines couldn't be imagined. This one, with considerably more Cabernet, is harder and firmer in tannins, with an impressively ripe core of black currants. Tastes oakier, too, but can easily handle it. Drink now through 2007. **93** —*S.H. (12/15/2005)*

Cliff Lede 2001 Cabernet Sauvignon (Stags Leap District) $50. From S. Anderson, of sparkling wine fame, this wine has that seductively lush Stags Leap quality of a velvety mouthfeel and mouth-filling warmth. But then those iron-fist-in-a-velvet-glove tannins kick in, lending astringency to the polished blackberry flavors. Will develop gracefully for years. **92** —*S.H. (10/3/2004)*

Cliff Lede 2004 *Barrel Sample* Cabernet Sauvignon (Stags Leap District) $NA. Polished, rich, elegant and supple, with rich cherry and blackberry flavors and a long, spicy finish. Has got to be the result of careful selection. **92** —*S.H. (8/1/2004)*

Cliff Lede 2001 Poetry Cabernet Sauvignon (Stags Leap District) $100. A stunning wine that shows off the excellence of its origin and the vintage. Long and deep in cherry, currant and mocha, with a round, creamy texture and plenty of smoky oak. The spicy finish lasts for a long time. So polished and delicious, it's hard to resist now, but will age gracefully for many years. Note, though, that the Cliff Lede name appears only on the back of the label. **94** —*S.H. (10/1/2004)*

Cliff Lede 2001 Merlot (Stags Leap District) $38. An almost decadent wine, with superrich, softly sweet chocolate, plum and vanilla flavors and velvety mouthfeel. Saved by good acidity, it shows how Merlot really can be the soft Cabernet. **90** —*S.H. (12/15/2004)*

Cliff Lede 2004 Sauvignon Blanc (Napa Valley) $18. Rich in fig, gooseberry, lemon and lime, chamomile and spice flavors, this bone-dry wine is impressively deep. It displays an elegance and finesse, as well as a power seldom found in California Sauvignon Blanc. **90** —*S.H. (12/15/2005)*

Cliff Lede 2003 Sauvignon Blanc (Napa Valley) $18. Here's an upscale wine that's bright in citrusy, grass, peach and fig-infused fruit and a layering of toasty oak. It's full-bodied like a Chardonnay, but tart and crisp, with a long, spicy finish. **90** —*S.H. (12/15/2004)*

CLINE

Cline 2005 Ancient Vines Carignan (Contra Costa County) $16. Cherries, cherries, cherries—the fruit goes on and on in this dry, soft, velvety wine. It's nothing complicated, but entirely pleasant, so easy to like with, say, penne and sausage. **85** —*S.H. (12/15/2006)*

Cline 1998 Marsanne (Carneros) $18. 89 —*S.H. (6/1/1999)*

Cline 2004 Ancient Vines Mourvèdre (Contra Costa County) $15. Pretty good price for an old-vine Mourvèdre wine of this quality. It's dry and medium-bodied, with a rich array of cherry, mu shu plum sauce, coffee and tamari flavors. The more you sip, the more you like it. **87** —*S.H. (12/31/2006)*

Cline 2003 Ancient Vines Mourvèdre (Contra Costa County) $18. What's puzzling about this wine is why, given the pedigree of the vines, it was so quickly made and rushed to market. It is not a distinctive wine, but a rustic one, dry and berryish. Cline could have done better. **84** —*S.H. (4/1/2005)*

Cline 1997 Ancient Vines Mourvèdre (Contra Costa County) $18. 87 —*S.H. (10/1/1999)*

Cline 2003 Small Berry Mourvèdre (Contra Costa County) $35. This is a subtle wine. Your first impression is of softness, dryness and pretty flavors of cherries and sweet fresh garden herbs. Then you return to find added levels of interest. This wine is best now, and will happily support most lamb dishes. **89** —*S.H. (11/1/2005)*

Cline 1997 Small Berry Mourvèdre (Contra Costa County) $24. 91 —*S.H. (10/1/1999)*

Cline 2004 Pinot Grigio-Chardonnay (California) $10. Here's a nice, fresh, fruity white wine. It opens with a blast of peach, apricot and vanilla flavors, and has good balancing acidity and a richly creamy finish. **84 Best Buy** —*S.H. (11/1/2005)*

Cline 2003 fiveREDS Red Blend (California) $9. Cline makes interesting, offbeat red blends, and this composite of Syrah, Zinfandel, Petite Sirah, Alicante Bouchet and Mourvèdre comes from vineyards scattered all over California. It's a hearty, lusty wine, expressive in peppery cherry and mulberry flavors, and nicely dry. You'll be surprised at how rich it is at this price. **85 Best Buy** —*S.H. (12/15/2006)*

Cline 2002 Oakley Five Reds Red Blend (California) $11. A rather exotic blend of Mourvedre, Grenache, Carignane, Zinfandel and Syrah, and a nice dry red. Smooth and polished, with cherry, herb and earthy flavors. Shows real finesse. **86 Best Buy** —*S.H. (4/1/2005)*

Cline 1998 Roussanne (Carneros) $18. 89 —*S.H. (6/1/1999)*

Cline 1997 Syrah (Carneros) $20. 88 —*S.H. (6/1/1999)*

Cline 2004 Syrah (California) $10. Here's a simple, jammy wine, packed with ripe blackberry, cola, coffee and peppery spice flavors, with a dry, tart finish. Most of it comes from the Sonoma Coast appellation. **84** —*S.H. (12/15/2006)*

Cline 2003 Syrah (California) $10. Although this wine is a little astringent, this is a decent price for a Syrah with a good chunk of Sonoma Coast and Carneros fruit. The wine is totally dry, with rich tannins and a finish that's elegant and food-friendly. **86 Best Buy** —*S.H. (12/31/2005)*

Cline 2002 Syrah (California) $11. Here's a rustic, country-style wine that's very well made, and offers lots to like. It's a bit rough in the mouth, but has flavors of dark stone fruits. Finishes dry and balanced. **85** —*S.H. (4/1/2005)*

Cline 2002 Syrah (Carneros) $20. Here's a big, big Syrah. It's explosive in cherry, blackberry, coffee and chocolate cream pie flavors that have been folded into ripe, smooth tannins. Almost a food group in itself, and best matched with strongly flavored and spiced meats. **87** —*S.H. (6/1/2004)*

Cline 2001 Syrah (Sonoma County) $14. Lusciously sweet, a deeply colored wine saturated with ripe flavors of plums, blackberries and mocha. There are some well-etched tannins and a crisp streak of acidity to help it cut through a well-marbled steak or prime rib. **87** —*S.H. (6/1/2004)*

Cline 2001 Syrah (California) $10. There's a great deal of rich flavor in this Syrah. It's packed with sweet black cherry and blackberry flavors, with hints of mocha and gingersnap. The tannins are a little rough, but it's really a great value. **86 Best Buy** —*S.H. (6/1/2004)*

Cline 2000 Syrah (Sonoma County) $15. 87 —*S.H. (12/1/2002)*

Cline 2000 Syrah (California) $8. Plump, juicy and sweet fruity flavors are packed into this simple wine. The tannins are rich and dusty. Don't look for depth or sophistication beyond the lipsmacking flavors, just enjoy its everyday price. **83** —*S.H. (12/1/2002)*

Cline 2000 Syrah (Carneros) $22. Smells great, bursting with smoky oak, black cherry, dark chocolate, herb and truffle aromas that make your mouth water. The flavors are less flamboyant, though, wrapped in dusty, sticky tannins that coat the palate. Underneath is a deep core of cherry fruit. **90** —*S.H. (12/1/2002)*

Cline 1999 Syrah (California) $10. On the nose and the palate of this black beauty, dried spice and mulchy-cedar flavors envelope a caramel-cherry backbone. Has decent balance, and finishes with dry wood, minerals, hot spices and plenty of black pepper. **85** *(10/1/2001)*

Cline 2004 Cool Climate Syrah (Sonoma Coast) $16. High in acids and dry, this wine has a sharp bite. It's big in blackberry jam and cherry jelly flavors, with a smooth, velvety texture and a rustic finish. **84** —*S.H. (12/15/2006)*

Cline 1999 Los Carneros Syrah (Carneros) $23. This hearty wine delivers lots of anise-accented sour berry fruit on a full, creamy mouthfeel. Dark and tart, earthy and spicy, it has an elegantly rustic quality, showing spice and leather shadings. Finishes long, with peppery deep fruit flavors and full tannins. Hold 2–4 years or decant to drink now. **88** *(11/1/2001)*

Cline 1998 Viognier (Carneros) $18. 89 —*S.H. (6/1/1999)*

USA

Cline 2004 Viognier (Sonoma County) $10. At this price, fans of Viognier's exotic side will stock up by the case. Shows an array of tropical fruit, wildflower and spice flavors that finish in a crisp, honeyed aftertaste. Drink very cold. **85 Best Buy** —*S.H. (11/1/2005)*

Cline 2001 Viognier (Sonoma County) $16. Simple and fruity, but a bit deficient in vibrancy, with ripe peach, pear and fig flavors. Finishes with some sweetness, and would be okay with fruits, Asian food, or by itself. **84** —*S.H. (5/1/2003)*

Cline 2000 Viognier (Sonoma County) $18. Kind of earthy and lemony, with some simple melon and peach characteristics. A bit weedy at the end. **80** —*J.M. (12/15/2002)*

Cline 2002 Four Whites White Blend (California) $11. Fun to figure out which grape contributed what. Fresh peaches, apricots, sweet figs, lemons and limes and vanilla are just this side of off-dry. Sauvignon Blanc, Viognier, Palomino and Gewurztraminer. **85** —*S.H. (2/1/2005)*

Cline 2000 Oakley Vin Blanc White Blend (California) $9. A pleasant enough wine, with melon and apple flavors at its core. Round and smooth on the finish **84** —*J.M. (11/15/2001)*

Cline 2003 Zinfandel (California) $10. I like this Zin a lot for its exuberant varietal character. It's jam-packed with bright cherry, raspberry and peppery spice flavors, with good acids and tannins, and is nicely dry and balanced. Great price, too. **86 Best Buy** —*S.H. (11/1/2005)*

Cline 2001 Zinfandel (California) $10. Pleasantly firm-textured, with toasty oak framing the plum, berry and spice flavors. On the finish it hints at tea and herbs. **86 Best Buy** *(11/1/2003)*

Cline 1999 Zinfandel (California) $10. Full dark berry aromas and flavors and classic pepper accents mark this very likeable wine. Cocoa and meaty elements add a bit of complexity not necessarily expected at this price. Kept lively by its brisk, but not sharp acidity, it finishes peppery with a tart-sweet profile. This straightforward, delicious wine exemplifies how competitive California can still be, despite the trend to priciness. **87 Best Buy** *(3/1/2001)*

Cline 2005 Ancient Vines Zinfandel (Contra Costa County) $16. Cline has access to some pretty old vineyards in Contra Costa, the "opposite coast" from San Francisco, and they do a nice job of crafting the grapes into easy, relatively inexpensive wines. This one is upfront in jammy cherry, blueberry and chocolate fruit, and finishes dry and spicy. **85** —*S.H. (12/15/2006)*

Cline 2004 Ancient Vines Zinfandel (California) $18. From vineyards in Lodi and Contra Costa County, an enormously enjoyable Zin that shows its hot climate origins, but maintains balance and integrity. The cassis, cherry, chocolate and oatmeal-raisin cookie flavors finish in a swirl of acidity and dusty tannins. **90** —*S.H. (11/1/2005)*

Cline 2003 Ancient Vines Zinfandel (California) $18. Rather sweet in fruity extract, with upfront cherry, chocolate, cassis and sweet anise flavors. The texture is sensationally soft and beguiling. Try with pork tenderloin in plum sauce. **87** —*S.H. (4/1/2005)*

Cline 1999 Ancient Vines Zinfandel (California) $23. Stiff tannins and a fair amount of acid on the palate make the black plum and smoke flavors in the mouth and on the finish that much more dark and sturdy. Opens with peppery heat layered with soil and red berry. **84** —*D.T. (3/1/2002)*

Cline 1998 Ancient Vines Zinfandel (California) $23. Big, toothsome wine, chewy and assertive. Cline fans will recognize the style: brambly, peppery, with enormous vitality and punch. Bright, spicy fruit backed with good acids and just enough toast. **89** —*P.G. (3/1/2001)*

Cline 1997 Ancient Vines Zinfandel (Contra Costa County) $18. 89 —*S.H. (9/1/1999)*

Cline 2003 Big Break Zinfandel (Contra Costa County) $25. Compared to Cline's Bridgehead, this Zin is softer and much simpler. There's not much going on, except for high alcohol and a Zinny, berry character. **83** —*S.H. (11/1/2005)*

Cline 2001 Big Break Zinfandel (Contra Costa County) $28. Spicy and rich, with zippy licorice, plum, blackberry and cinnamon notes. Fairly smooth tannins give firm, supple structure. The finish is toasty and bright, moderate in length. **88** *(11/1/2003)*

Cline 1997 Big Break Zinfandel (Contra Costa County) $25. 90 —*S.H. (9/1/1999)*

Cline 1998 Big Break Vineyard Zinfandel (Contra Costa County) $28. A blast of spice, mint, bramble and pepper explodes from the glass. The wine is dense, dark, deep and mysterious; the flavors pungent, penetrating and persistent. Tannic, layered with herbs and spices, powered with big, punchy fruit. This is classic Cline. **93** —*P.G. (3/1/2001)*

Cline 2003 Bridgehead Zinfandel (Contra Costa County) $25. This Zin is almost Port, with its hot, high alcohol, chocolate and raisin flavors and creamy-smooth mouthfeel. It's quite delicious, though, a peculiarity of the hot, dry summers that dominate this inland county. **86** —*S.H. (11/1/2005)*

Cline 2001 Bridgehead Zinfandel (Contra Costa County) $28. Plush, ripe and concentrated, the wine shows complex black cherry, coffee, chocolate, cedar, blackberry, spice and herb flavors that are beautifully couched in ripe, velvety tannins. The wine carries on with good length to the finish. **90** *(11/1/2003)*

Cline 1999 Bridgehead Vineyard Zinfandel (Contra Costa County) $28. Very subtle blackberry notes on the nose preface deeper, more tannic blackberry flavors—plus some charred barrel and metallic notes—on the palate. Full and dry in the mouth with a tannic, gravelly texture; the Bridgehead's finish is equally dry and tannic, with green herb and black pepper flavors at the end. It's dark and dry, but boy, does that finish go on and on. It would go well with a thick, medium-rare marbled steak. May soften in a year or two. **86** —*D.T. (3/1/2002)*

Cline 1999 Fulton Road Vineyard Zinfandel (Russian River Valley) $28. Dark berry (black seedless grapes, perhaps), earth and a briny note lead into tart yet bright and concentrated blackberry and raspberry flavors. Medium-bodied with bright acid, it finishes with taut red fruit, a little chalk and a flash of hot black pepper at the very end. **87** —*D.T. (3/1/2002)*

Cline 2003 Live Oak Zinfandel (Contra Costa County) $25. For some reason, this seems to be the oakiest of Cline's current trio of Zins. It's also the highest in alcohol, at 16%. The wine shows little beyond char and vanilla, except for a sweet cherry finish. Disappointing. **83** —*S.H. (11/1/2005)*

Cline 2001 Live Oak Zinfandel (Contra Costa County) $28. A smoky, toasty, almost bacon-like edge precedes the pretty ripe fruit here. Lush black cherry, plum, strawberry, licorice, vanilla and spice flavors carry forth on the finish, which is long yet fresh—ending with a menthol edge. **89** *(11/1/2003)*

Cline 1999 Live Oak Zinfandel (Contra Costa County) $28. The nose takes a little while to open, but when it does, you'll be entranced by the fresh mint, nutmeg, cinnamon and chalk dust aromas that coat underlying black cherry and red berry notes. In the mouth, the blueberry and blackberry fruit is big, but not to worry—it's two steps shy of tasting overextracted, and the fruity intensity lets up after a few minutes in the glass. Caramel-oak flavors add a rich, velvety texture; finishes with a zippy white-pepper flash, and some chalkiness. Beware: It's yummy, but may bowl you over. **90** —*D.T. (3/1/2002)*

Cline 1998 Live Oak Vineyard Zinfandel (Contra Costa County) $28. There's a lovely sweetness to the fruit, which tastes like ripe, just-picked blackberries. Old vines, 100+ years, deliver sweet, supple, sexy fruit. The wine has very dry tannins, and it might profit from some blending, but with a vineyard this special you have to admire the single-vineyard approach. **93** —*P.G. (3/1/2001)*

Cline 1997 Live Oak Vineyard Zinfandel (Contra Costa County) $28. 92 —*S.H. (5/1/2000)*

CLINTON

Clinton 1999 Seyval Blanc (Hudson River Region) $13. Features unusual aromas of white root vegetables. Dry, sour-earth flavors of parsnips and rutabagas finish crisp and lemony. Try with oysters on the half shell. **83** —*J.C. (1/1/2004)*

Clinton NV Jubilee Seyval Blanc (Hudson River Region) $30. Pleasantly yeasty and with fine scents of burnt toast, but also odd aromas reminiscent of roasted cashews—or maybe peanut brittle. Soft and nutty on the palate, with a short finish. **83** —*J.C. (12/1/2001)*

CLOCKSPRING

Clockspring 2003 Zinfandel (Amador County) $8. From Mountain View, a good producer of Amador Zins, a sort of junior version of their single-vineyard wine. It's light in color and body, and dry, with cherry-berry flavors and a good grip of tannins and acids. Good value. **84 Best Buy** —*S.H. (3/1/2006)*

CLONINGER

Cloninger 1998 Quinn Vineyard Cabernet Sauvignon (Carmel Valley) $18. Carmel Valley is a little pocket of sunny warmth in cool Monterey County, and it's been known as a good source of Cabernet for years. This example got ripe and expressive, with forward berry flavors and a hint of oak. It's too soft and so drinks a little flabby. That's its biggest problem, along with a weak finish. **86** —*S.H. (5/1/2001)*

Cloninger 1999 Chardonnay (Santa Lucia Highlands) $16. Classic Highlands Chard, with very bright, pure, focused aromas and flavors of tropical fruits and spices. The flavors are strong and clean. Oak adds shadings of smoke, vanilla and buttered toast, and there's something creamy and leesy in the texture. A fine wine of some complexity, at a fair price. **87** —*S.H. (5/1/2001)*

Cloninger 2000 Estate Grown Chardonnay (Santa Lucia Highlands) $16. Here's a good, rich Chardonnay, distinctive for its ripe array of tropical fruits, pears, peaches and oriental spices. It feels crisp and clean in the mouth, and finishes rich and spicy. **88** —*S.H. (5/1/2003)*

Cloninger 1999 Pinot Noir (Monterey) $23. The briar-packed, smoky nose is attractive. The fruit is light and features characteristics akin to strawberries and cherries, with a touch of chocolate. The finish carries a note of tobacco; it's kind of rustic. It's weight, which is medium at best, ensures that it will work lighter fare. **87** *(10/1/2002)*

Cloninger 1997 Jardini Vineyard. Pinot Noir (Monterey County) $22. **81** *(10/1/1999)*

CLOS DU BOIS

Clos du Bois 1999 Marlstone Bordeaux Blend (Alexander Valley) $39. Always classy, this blend of Cabernet Sauvignon, Merlot and Malbec shows richness and complexity. The flavors change constantly, suggesting blackberries, sweet plums, espresso, herbs and chocolate. The tannins are a wonder, soft and gentle. **91** —*S.H. (10/1/2003)*

Clos du Bois 1996 Marlstone Vineyard Bordeaux Blend (Sonoma County) $30. **84** *(7/1/2000)*

Clos du Bois 2003 Marlstone Cabernet Blend (Alexander Valley) $50. Marlstone is an old, historic, proprietary wine, but it's been under-performing for some years now. A Cabernet-based blend of all five Bordeaux varieties, this wine is good but has a rustic edge to the very ripe berry and cherry flavors. It should be better. **85** —*S.H. (12/15/2006)*

Clos du Bois 2002 Marlstone Cabernet Blend (Alexander Valley) $50. I like this Cabernet blend for its fruitiness, but it's way too soft for balance. There's no spine, no backbone to the cherry, cassis and oak flavors. It lacks not only acidity but tannins. **83** —*S.H. (12/1/2005)*

Clos du Bois 2001 Marlstone Cabernet Blend (Alexander Valley) $50. After two years in French oak, the tannins are soft, but the acids still evident. Has pretty aromas and flavors of vanilla, tobacco, smoke and cassis, just seems a bit hard-edged on the finish. A blend of 75% Cabernet Sauvignon, 14% Merlot, 8.5% Malbec, 1.5 % Cabernet Franc and 1% Petit Verdot. **87** *(6/1/2005)*

Clos du Bois 2001 Cabernet Sauvignon (Sonoma County) $17. A little raw, with sharp elbows of tannins and acids. Don't be too fussy, just enjoy the plummy, grapy flavors. **84** —*S.H. (6/1/2005)*

Clos du Bois 2000 Cabernet Sauvignon (Sonoma County) $17. Nice, simple Cabernet, with proper varietal flavors and a dusting of oak. Dry, balanced and supple in the mouth, without much depth or complexity. **85** —*S.H. (4/1/2003)*

Clos du Bois 1999 Cabernet Sauvignon (Sonoma County) $17. Like a good Cabernet in slow motion, it makes all the right moves. Pretty blackberry and cassis fruit, good oak, a bit soft but fine enough, and dry, with some

real elegance and character. It could just use a bit more concentration. **84** —*S.H. (12/31/2001)*

Clos du Bois 1996 Cabernet Sauvignon (Sonoma County) $15. **83** —*S.H. (7/1/1999)*

Clos du Bois 2002 Briarcrest Cabernet Sauvignon (Alexander Valley) $36. One hundred percent Cabernet Sauvignon, this wine has well-ripened black currant and cherry flavors, but it's far too soft. Tannins and acidity are still needed, in this age of superripeness. **83** —*S.H. (12/1/2005)*

Clos du Bois 2001 Briarcrest Cabernet Sauvignon (Alexander Valley) $40. Solid California Cabernet, with textbook aromas of toast, cassis, cigar box and vanilla. It's medium- to full-bodied in the mouth, with the vanilla and cassis flavors easily flowing across the palate. **89** *(6/1/2005)*

Clos du Bois 1999 Briarcrest Cabernet Sauvignon (Alexander Valley) $36. Always anticipated, this Cabernet shows particular elegance and finesse this vintage. Not a blockbuster, it doesn't slam you with fruit, but instead offers up soft, smooth tannins that are wrapped around blackberry, coffee and herb flavors. **89** —*S.H. (10/1/2003)*

Clos du Bois 2002 Reserve Cabernet Sauvignon (Alexander Valley) $22. This Cab is dry, fruity, soft and gentle, with extra nuances of complexity. It's deep in blackberry and chocolate flavors, and an intricately detailed balance of acids, tannins, alcohol and oak. Not an ager, but absolutely delicious from the get-go. **90** —*S.H. (12/1/2005)*

Clos du Bois 1999 Reserve Cabernet Sauvignon (Alexander Valley) $22. From a longtime producer of Alexander Valley Cabs, another in a series of successful wines. Stays true to its terroir, a soft wine with melted tannins and round, ripe fruity flavors. Instantly appealing, and versatile at the table. **88** —*S.H. (6/1/2002)*

Clos du Bois 1997 Reserve Cabernet Sauvignon (Sonoma County) $20. **87** —*S.H. (2/1/2000)*

Clos du Bois 1997 Winemaker's Reserve Cabernet Sauvignon (Alexander Valley) $50. Defines it's appellation with soft, velvety tannins and low acids, along with well ripened, pure blackberry and cassis fruit. Of course, there's a good deal of flashy, aromatic oak. Deliciously fruity, it offers plenty of near-term pleasures. **87** —*S.H. (12/1/2001)*

Clos du Bois 1995 Winemaker's Reserve Cabernet Sauvignon (Sonoma County) $50. **88** —*J.C. (7/1/1999)*

Clos du Bois 2004 Chardonnay (North Coast) $12. Plays it right down the middle, with enough fruit, oak and creamy vanilla to satisfy the public clamor for Chardonnay. **83** —*S.H. (12/1/2005)*

Clos du Bois 2003 Chardonnay (North Coast) $12. This white has nice, ripe flavors of peaches and tropical fruits, and good oak. Rich and creamy, this Chard offers lots of pleasure at a good price. **85** —*S.H. (5/1/2005)*

Clos du Bois 2002 Chardonnay (Sonoma County) $14. A crowd-pleasing wine, with its oaky flavors of vanilla, smoke and buttered toast, and ripe fruity flavors of pears and tropical fruits. The texture is creamy smooth, with a rich edge of smoky honey. A nice value. **87** —*S.H. (12/15/2003)*

Clos du Bois 2001 Chardonnay (Sonoma County) $14. Strikes a middle-of-the-road profile, with just enough peach and pear fruit and spicy oak to satisfy. The finish is honeyed and long. **86** —*S.H. (12/15/2002)*

Clos du Bois 2000 Chardonnay (Sonoma County) $14. Continues the CDB tradition of ripe, full-flavored Chards at a good price. Flavors of pear, apple, vanilla, smoke and dusty spices cascade off the palate, in a richly textured wine that's oaky-sweet. Finishes soft, with dusty tannins. **86** —*S.H. (11/15/2001)*

Clos du Bois 1999 Chardonnay (Sonoma County) $14. **86** —*S.H. (11/15/2000)*

Clos du Bois 1998 Chardonnay (Sonoma County) $14. **86** —*S.H. (12/31/1999)*

Clos du Bois 1998 Chardonnay (Sonoma County) $16. **87** —*L.W. (12/31/1999)*

Clos du Bois 2003 Calcaire Chardonnay (Russian River Valley) $22. This first vintage of Calcaire made from Russian River Valley shows a hands-on wine much like when it hailed from Alexander Valley. Still the same heavy oak, with rich lemondrop and tropical fruit flavors. And still very tasty and drinkable. **89** —*S.H. (12/1/2005)*

USA

Clos du Bois 2000 Calcaire Chardonnay (Alexander Valley) $22. Distinctive and individualistic, with mineral, apricot, citrus and wildflower notes—not your typical Chardonnay. This is possibly the result of clonal variations. The wine drinks smooth, creamy, dry and complex, with a peppery finish. **90** —*S.H. (2/1/2003)*

Clos du Bois 1998 Calcaire Vineyard Chardonnay (Sonoma County) $20. 87 *(6/1/2000)*

Clos du Bois 1999 Flintwood Chardonnay (Dry Creek Valley) $22. Big, bold and buttery, a full-bodied Chard that takes over the mouth with great assertiveness. There's a ton of oak and lees, and the wine underwent total malolactic fermentation. The underlying flavors are citrusy, especially limes. This is a very fine Chardonnay, built for big, rich white meat entrées. **91 Editors' Choice** —*S.H. (2/1/2003)*

Clos du Bois 1997 Flintwood Vineyard Chardonnay (Dry Creek Valley) $22. 86 *(6/1/2000)*

Clos du Bois 2004 Reserve Chardonnay (Russian River Valley) $20. Here's a nice, fairly complex Chard that's ripe and toasty and full of peach, pear, green apple and cantaloupe flavors. Finishes dry and spicy-clean. **87** —*S.H. (12/1/2006)*

Clos du Bois 2003 Reserve Chardonnay (Russian River Valley) $16. All of this is barrel-fermented, 45% in new French oak, and it shows in the toasty, nutty scents. Buttery and creamy on the palate, with a plump mouthfeel and layered flavors of ripe pears and dried spices. Long and pineapple-y on the finish. **87** *(6/1/2005)*

Clos du Bois 2000 Reserve Chardonnay (Alexander Valley) $16. A rich, oaky wine easily as good as Chards that cost far more, it has aromas and flavors of ripe white peaches and Delicious apples, and scads of oriental spice. Avoids excessive sweetness, although oak tannins and glycerin make it round and soft. **88** —*S.H. (9/1/2002)*

Clos du Bois 1999 Reserve Chardonnay (Sonoma County) $16. From a dependable producer and a fine vintage comes a problematic wine. The fruit is nicely ripe and suggestive of apples and peaches, and it's balanced and dry. Acidity is adequate. The only jarring note is a strongly toasted character, almost like charcoal, which you can both smell it and taste. Even the finish is marred by this burnt flavor. **84** —*S.H. (2/1/2001)*

Clos du Bois 1998 Reserve Chardonnay (Sonoma County) $16. 85 —*S.H. (2/1/2000)*

Clos du Bois 2000 Merlot (Sonoma County) $18. A pleasant and tasty Merlot, with polished flavors of plums, blackberries, chocolate and green olives. Tannins are soft and fine, and the finish is dry. This is a well-crafted red wine, and very balanced. **87** —*S.H. (4/1/2003)*

Clos du Bois 1999 Merlot (Sonoma County) $18. Soft tannins and light acids make this go down like water. It's docile stuff, easy to drink, but it's pretty thin in the mouth. Your palate wants to find berries or fruit, but there's precious little of either. They stretched the vines to the limit here. **82** —*S.H. (7/1/2002)*

Clos du Bois 1998 Merlot (Sonoma County) $17. Savory dried herbs accent the otherwise soft and simple black cherries that dominate this wine. Closes with some sweet cola and chocolate notes. A solid by-the-glass offering. **84** —*J.C. (6/1/2001)*

Clos du Bois 1997 Merlot (Sonoma County) $17. 83 *(3/1/2000)*

Clos du Bois 2002 Reserve Merlot (Alexander Valley) $22. Like many of the Clos du Bois wines, this is textbook. There's everything you expect in a Merlot—black cherries, vanilla, toast, dried herbs, coffee. On the other hand, also like a textbook, it lacks the drama and excitement to push it into the next class. **87** *(6/1/2005)*

Clos du Bois 1998 Reserve Merlot (Sonoma County) $22. The aromas mingle black cherry and dark chocolate with mint, plus modest oak. In the mouth, it really comes alive with deeply satisfying flavors and soft velvety tannins. **89** —*S.H. (6/1/2001)*

Clos du Bois 1997 Reserve Merlot (Sonoma County) $22. 85 —*S.H. (3/1/2000)*

Clos du Bois 2005 Pinot Grigio (California) $14. Lots of juicy fruit and zesty acidity in this wine. It's PGs like this that are driving the variety in America. Apples, nectarines, peaches, peppery spices and wildflowers all mingle into a fruity, slightly sweet finish. **85** —*S.H. (11/1/2006)*

Clos du Bois 2004 Pinot Grigio (California) $12. Clos du Bois may be jumping on the Grigio bandwagon, but at least winemaker Erik Olsen has turned out a solid example. Effusively fruity on the nose, bursting with ripe pear and melon flavors, this round, easy-drinking wine should be a summertime hit. **85** *(6/1/2005)*

Clos du Bois 2003 Pinot Noir (Sonoma County) $16. Light and crisp, this tart little Pinot boasts just enough cola and black cherry flavors to make it a worthwhile match with roast chicken, or perhaps grilled salmon. **85** *(6/1/2005)*

Clos du Bois 2001 Pinot Noir (Sonoma County) $17. A simple, soft, fruity and one-dimensional Pinot that offers up slight flavors of raspberries, pepper and tobacco. Fully dry, with silky tannins and bracing acids, but it's hard to get over the anorexic profile. **84** —*S.H. (7/1/2003)*

Clos du Bois 2000 Pinot Noir (Sonoma County) $17. There's a raw earthiness to this wine's beet, rasberry , mushroom scents, with their smoky nuances, but it turns richly fruity and spicy in the mouth. Has lovely Pinot texture—all silk and satin. **86** —*S.H. (12/15/2001)*

Clos du Bois 1999 Pinot Noir (Sonoma County) $17. This wine captures Pinot's silky, spicy qualities, although it's thin, light and basic. Some pretty notes of raspberry, smoke, sun-dried tomato, mushroom and chocolate and a nice, spicy intensity on the palate. The tannins are soft and light, and it snaps to a quick finish. **86** —*S.H. (5/1/2001)*

Clos du Bois 2003 Reserve Pinot Noir (Sonoma Coast) $22. Plump and smooth, with piquant briary, herbal accents to the strawberry and raspberry flavors. Picks up coffee and chocolate on the finish, along with just a hint of bitterness. A promising effort. **88** *(6/1/2005)*

Clos du Bois 2003 Sauvignon Blanc (North Coast) $12. Grassy on the nose, but also with hints of nectarine, this is a light, herbal wine fine for picnics or other casual get-togethers. It's plump on the midpalate and tangy on the finish. **84** *(6/1/2005)*

Clos du Bois 2001 Sauvignon Blanc (North Coast) $10. Very dry, tart and grassy, a cool-climate white wine with flavors veering to grass and grapefruit. Refreshing acidity makes the palate feel very clean through the finish. **85** —*S.H. (3/1/2003)*

Clos du Bois 2000 Sauvignon Blanc (North Coast) $10. Grassy, grapefruit and melon aromas, with hints of apples and smoke, lead to dry, tart, citrus flavors in the mouth. The acidity is adequate to make things lively and refreshing in this clean, balanced wine. **85** —*S.H. (11/15/2001)*

Clos du Bois 1998 Sauvignon Blanc (Sonoma County) $9. 84 —*S.H. (9/11/1999)*

Clos du Bois 2003 Shiraz (Sonoma County) $15. A lighter-weight, commercial Shiraz, with a bit of cotton candy or bubblegum to its aromas, that then settles down to deliver juicy blackberry flavors. Finishes with firm tannins, making it fine for cutting through a fatty steak off the grill. **85** *(9/1/2005)*

Clos du Bois 2002 Shiraz (Sonoma County) $12. This is a rather light, bouncy Syrah, made in American oak. Pretty berry and vanilla notes on the nose turn slightly herbal—almost dill-like—by the finish. **85** *(9/1/2005)*

Clos du Bois 1996 Shiraz (Sonoma County) $16. 87 —*S.H. (6/1/1999)*

Clos du Bois 1998 Reserve Shiraz (Sonoma County) $16. This refined blend of dry smoky toast and sweet strawberry fruit shows complex meaty flavors before an abbreviated finish. This is solid stuff from a region that is coming to be identified with California Shiraz. **85** *(10/1/2001)*

Clos du Bois 1997 Reserve Shiraz (Sonoma County) $16. 88 —*S.H. (2/1/2000)*

Clos du Bois 2002 Reserve Tempranillo (Alexander Valley) $22. Winemaker Erik Olsen says the Tempranillo needs really careful tannin management—he even blends in Cabernet Sauvignon to soften this wine. The result is a medium-bodied wine filled with tobacco, vanilla and blackberry nuances and boasting a tart, juicy finish. **88** *(6/1/2005)*

Clos du Bois 1999 Zinfandel (Sonoma County) $14. This wine is so fresh, it's almost rude. It slaps you with vivacity, young acids, and a youthful brashness. It's also very dry, with gentle tannins. Maybe the fruit's a little thin, but with burgers and dogs in the backyard, who cares? 84 —*S.H. (7/1/2002)*

Clos du Bois 1997 Zinfandel (Sonoma County) $14. 84 *(2/1/2000)*

Clos du Bois 2000 Reserve Zinfandel (Dry Creek Valley) $22. What a classic Dry Creek Zin. Good, rich color leads to aromas of of wild berries, herbs and that telltale aroma of brambles, like sun-warmed berry bushes in a thorny patch on a hot day. Brilliant and pure in the mouth, lush and ripe in flavor and dry tannins, but keeps Zin's wild, succulent edge. 90 —*S.H. (2/1/2003)*

Clos du Bois 1999 Reserve Zinfandel (Dry Creek Valley) $22. Made claret style, the fruit and alcohol are restrained, and the wine drinks dry and balanced. Dark cherry and wild berry flavors are mouth-filling and the tannins are complex but approachable. This is a fine example of its appellation and terroir. 90 —*S.H. (7/1/2002)*

CLOS DU LAC

Clos du Lac 2001 Estate Petite Verdot (Amador County) $20. Dark and dry, with plum, espresso and tart blackberry flavors. Big in tannins but soft in acids, so it's easy to drink. Best with ribs and such. 84 —*S.H. (10/1/2004)*

Clos du Lac 2001 Sangiovese (Amador County) $14. Dry and rough, with a burn on the finish, this wine has cherry and earth flavors. 83 —*S.H. (12/15/2004)*

Clos du Lac 2001 Sauvignon Blanc (Amador County) $20. Packs a punch with its strong, zesty flavors of citrus fruits, melon, dried herbs, and anise, and has a nice, delicate structure. Finishes dryish, with good acidity. This is a nice sipper. 85 —*S.H. (10/1/2003)*

Clos du Lac 1997 Syrah (California) $12. 88 Best Buy *(5/1/2000)*

Clos du Lac 2001 Syrah (Amador County) $12. Ripe berry-cherry flavors are wrapped in sturdy tannins. Finishes very dry, with good acidity. 84 —*S.H. (12/15/2004)*

Clos du Lac 2001 Ghirardelli Vineyard Zinfandel (Calaveras County) $20. Deeper, richer and more delicious than the Kane bottling, with great heaps of blackberries and black raspberries wrapped in dry, soft tannins. You'll like this fresh, vibrant wine for its youthful fruitiness and easy drinkability. 87 —*S.H. (12/15/2004)*

Clos du Lac 2001 Kane Vineyard Zinfandel (Amador County) $20. Sturdy and mouth-filling, a balanced, flavorful Zin smacking of wild blueberries and blackberries and herbs. It's very dry, and the tannins are nice and smooth. Nice drinking. 86 —*S.H. (3/1/2004)*

Clos du Lac 2002 Potter Vineyard Zinfandel (Shenandoah Valley (CA)) $20. Good Zin character, with brambly berry flavors and smooth tannins, but a little too sweet 84 —*S.H. (3/1/2005)*

Clos du Lac 1998 Potter Vineyard Zinfandel (Shenandoah Valley (CA)) $18. Nice cherry fruit, in a big, bold, forward, friendly style. The fruit is perfectly ripened, balanced, full and nicely handled, with nothing obscuring the clean, ripe flavors. Well-made wine, with no unnecessary frills. 89 —*P.G. (3/1/2001)*

Clos du Lac 2001 Reserve Blend Zinfandel (Amador County) $16. Unmistakably California Zin, with its briary, brambly flood of wild berry and peppery spice flavors that finish dry and tannic. It's not a heavy wine, but has a silky lightness that makes it super-drinkable. 87 —*S.H. (12/15/2004)*

CLOS DU VAL

Clos du Val 2001 Ariadne Bordeaux Blend (Napa Valley) $32. This is a generous, gorgeous blend of Sémillon and Sauvignon Blanc. Very tight and crisp in youth, with flamboyant acids and scattered tannins that frame a mélange of flavors, especially lime, fig, tobacco and dried herbs. Finishes racy and elegant. 91 —*S.H. (10/1/2003)*

Clos du Val 2001 Reserve Cabernet Franc (Stags Leap District) $85. Polished in red cherry, cocoa, vanilla, cinnamon and oaky smoke, with smooth tannins and a long finish, this wine is medium-bodied and gentle. Its delicacy suggests veal or pork, not beef. 89 —*S.H. (12/31/2004)*

Clos du Val 1997 Cabernet Sauvignon (Stags Leap District) $48. 90 *(11/1/2000)*

Clos du Val 1995 Cabernet Sauvignon (Napa Valley) $24. 85 —*S.H. (6/1/1999)*

Clos du Val 2003 Cabernet Sauvignon (Napa Valley) $30. Soft and seductively fruity, this is a good Cab to drink now, although it will hang in there for a decade. It has forward flavors of cherry pie and blackberry jam, and a fine, elegant structure. 87 —*S.H. (11/1/2006)*

Clos du Val 2002 Cabernet Sauvignon (Napa Valley) $28. Here's a gentle Cab with some sophistication. Although it's not terribly complex, it has interesting flavors of cassis, green olives and toasty oak, and is not too tannic. Might even develop for a year or two. 85 —*S.H. (10/1/2005)*

Clos du Val 2001 Cabernet Sauvignon (Napa Valley) $28. Like its companion '01 Merlot release, this Cab needs time to come together, but when that happens, it will be a lovely drink. The firm, chunky tannins will hold the black currant and herb flavors through this decade. 90 —*S.H. (11/15/2004)*

Clos du Val 2000 Cabernet Sauvignon (Napa Valley) $28. Young and tight and not showing its best now, a cellarworthy wine that's the opposite of today's flamboyant, drink-me-now style. Possesses elegance and finesse with its curranty flavors and dry, subtle tannins. Drink after 2006. 89 —*S.H. (8/1/2003)*

Clos du Val 1999 Cabernet Sauvignon (Napa Valley) $29. Still tight, but showing focused blackberry, cassis, herb, spice and cola flavors. Tannins are sleek andsmooth. The wine is moderate on the finish with a tangy edge. 88 —*J.M. (6/1/2002)*

Clos du Val 1998 Cabernet Sauvignon (Stags Leap District) $55. The style of this winery has changed over the years. The Cabs used to be somewhat tight and austere in their youth, but this puppy is pure velvet, with gobs of sweet blackberry fruit and, of course, quite a bit of oak. It's limpid, pure, soft, intense and immediately drinkable. 90 —*S.H. (12/1/2001)*

Clos du Val 2002 Oak Vineyard Cabernet Sauvignon (Stags Leap District) $62. Seems slightly dry and raisiny, rather than showcasing the opulence of its Stags Leap terroir, but it still shows pleasant notes of cassis, cedar, tobacco and earth. It's a wine that reflects owner Bernard Portet's Bordeaux-influenced sensibilities. 85 *(9/1/2006)*

Clos du Val 2001 Oak Vineyard Cabernet Sauvignon (Stags Leap District) $62. Clos du Val continues to march to a different drummer. It's always been a youthfully shy, dry wine that stresses elegance over flamboyance. This wine has great black currant and herb flavors, but stresses its structure with an acidic, tannic emphasis. It should age for many years. 91 —*S.H. (10/3/2004)*

Clos du Val 2000 Oak Vineyard Cabernet Sauvignon (Stags Leap District) $62. Stays true to the CDV style of crafting wines that tend to be tough in their youth, but are solidly built for the long haul. Good, rich blackcurrant fruit is folded into thick tannins. Stick it in your cave and come back to it in a few years. 91 —*S.H. (11/15/2003)*

Clos du Val 1999 Palisade Vineyard Cabernet Sauvignon (Stags Leap District) $62. The aromas are smoky and earthy, with a touch of game. Concentrated flavors of cassis and green olive boast great acid-tannin balance. The wine finishes rich and smooth. Drink now 'til 2015. 92 —*C.S. (11/15/2002)*

Clos du Val 2002 Reserve Cabernet Sauvignon (Napa Valley) $95. All the parts aren't even close to coming together yet on this immature Cabernet. You have strong, dusty tannins, prickly acids, lots of toasty new French oak, and fine cherry and blackberry fruit. All they need is six to 12 years to figure out how to get along with each other. When they do, the wine should be a beauty. 92 Cellar Selection —*S.H. (12/15/2006)*

Clos du Val 2001 Reserve Cabernet Sauvignon (Napa Valley) $95. With just 13.5% alcohol, this Cab marches to its own beat. In an era of gooey, late-picked wines, this one's dry, tight and tannic, obviously designed for the cellar. Clos du Val always has celebrated their Cab's ageworthiness, and such are the wine's fruity cherry flavors that it should do interesting things after 2008 and beyond. 90 Cellar Selection —*S.H. (12/15/2005)*

Clos du Val 2000 Reserve Cabernet Sauvignon (Napa Valley) $95. Clos du Val fans always have appreciated the elegance and ageability of its Cabs, and this release continues the tradition. It's been getting riper and softer

USA

every year, yet still has that edge of herbs and tannins, and in this vintage, a hint of smoked meat. Now through 2015. **91** —*S.H. (12/31/2004)*

Clos du Val 1999 Reserve Cabernet Sauvignon (Napa Valley) $95. Another classic wine from this fine Napa producer, and one that will live for a long time in your cellar. It is young and tight now, but through the tannins and acids the palate detects gobs of lush, ripe blackcurrants and plums, herbs and tobacco. The tannins are a wonder—rich, thick and intricate, and fully ripe. As good as it is now, this lovely wine will get better through 2009. **94 Editors' Choice** —*S.H. (11/15/2003)*

Clos du Val 1998 Reserve Cabernet Sauvignon (Napa Valley) $95. This is a lovely, tasteful Cabernet that emphasizes elegance and finesse. The currant flavors are pure and framed in rich new oak. Shows all the signs of superior pedigree and breed from a lighter vintage. For the next several years it will be a beautiful wine. **91** —*S.H. (11/15/2002)*

Clos du Val 1997 Reserve Cabernet Sauvignon (Napa Valley) $90. Someone called Stags Leap Cabernets "an iron fist in a velvet glove" and this is a textbook example. All the elements are there: Blackberry and cassis fruit, fine smoky new oak, and gentle tannins. It doesn't hit you over the head. But then you notice the dense middle palate, the enormous finish. This beautiful wine is an ager. **92** —*S.H. (3/1/2003)*

Clos du Val 1995 Reserve Cabernet Sauvignon (Napa Valley) $65. 92 — *L.W. (10/1/1999)*

Clos du Val 1998 Vineyard Georges III Cabernet Sauvignon (Rutherford) $55. This is a lovely, supple 100% Rutherford Cabernet, made in a controlled style. It's stylish, with great flavors and class. The oak is plush. Balance and harmony characterize it all the way, from the brilliant aromas to the clean, thoroughbred aftertaste. **94** —*S.H. (12/1/2001)*

Clos du Val 1997 Vineyard Georges III Cabernet Sauvignon (Rutherford) $48. 94 *(11/1/2000)*

Clos du Val 2004 Chardonnay (Napa Valley) $22. Shows the softness and earthy, herbal character that mark so many Napa Chards. Good new French oak adds flash, and you'll find some nice peach and pear custard flavors, but the wine wants more zest. **84** —*S.H. (11/1/2006)*

Clos du Val 2003 Chardonnay (Napa Valley) $21. Seems riper and juicier than past CDV Chards. Brims with polished apple, peach and pear flavors, and is very spicy. Turns clean and oaky on the finish. **91 Editors' Choice** —*S.H. (10/1/2005)*

Clos du Val 2002 Chardonnay (Napa Valley) $21. Lots of apple, pear and tropical fruit flavors are bathed in toasty oak, and the texture is rich and creamy. For me, the drawback of this wine is that it lacks crispness and so has a syrupy taste and feeling. **85** —*S.H. (11/15/2004)*

Clos du Val 2001 Chardonnay (Napa Valley) $21. This isn't a big, blowsy wine, but a balanced and elegant one, with everything in its proper place. Apple and peach flavors are restrained, and so is the oak. The wine is dry, and crisp acids leave the palate clean and ready for food. **88** —*S.H. (6/1/2003)*

Clos du Val 2000 Chardonnay (Napa Valley) $23. Toasty pear, apple and citrus flavors are prevalent in this bright, textured, refreshing wine. A mineral edge adds complexity and interest, finishing bright and fresh. **88** —*J.M. (5/1/2002)*

Clos du Val 2001 Carneros Vineyard Reserve Chardonnay (Carneros) $46. Made in Clos du Val's restrained style, this is a sleek, tight young wine. It has intense and concentrated flavors of citrus fruits that veer into apples and not-quite-ripe peaches, and is well oaked, with bright acidity. Seems designed to be a food wine, and may develop with a few years in the bottle. **87** —*S.H. (12/15/2003)*

Clos du Val 2004 Reserve Chardonnay (Carneros) $42. Here's a rich Chardonnay with tropical fruit pastry flavors that have a dusty, dried herb edge, and lots of creamy oak. The wine is a bit soft. The fruit and spice flavors reprise on the long-lasting finish. **87** —*S.H. (12/15/2006)*

Clos du Val 2000 Reserve Chardonnay (Carneros) $39. Made in the house style, which emphasizes elegantly restrained fruit and higher acids. Still, this is a big, lush wine. The flavors veer toward peaches, while the oak-and-lees overlay is powerful and creamy. The finish is long and spicy. **92** —*S.H. (12/15/2002)*

Clos du Val 1998 Single Vineyard Chardonnay (Carneros) $21. 88 *(6/1/2000)*

Clos du Val 2003 Merlot (Napa Valley) $25. This classic Napa Merlot is instantly appealing. It's very ripe, exuding black cherry pie, violet, chocolate and leather aromas and flavors, and the structure is impeccable. The smooth, intricate tannins, partial new oak and balancing acidity are just right. This is a great price for a Merlot of this quality. **90** —*S.H. (11/1/2006)*

Clos du Val 2002 Merlot (Napa Valley) $25. This is an elegant, sexy wine, softly luxurious and velvety, with impressive flavors of blackberries, chocolate, plums and oak. It's fairly tannic, and should improve over the next five years. **88** —*S.H. (10/1/2005)*

Clos du Val 2001 Merlot (Napa Valley) $25. You need to age this lovely and complex wine because the considerable oak and fruit have not knit together yet. The well-charred, vanilla-scented barrels dominate the aroma, while rich blackberry fruit and tannins rule in the mouth. Will improve through 2006 or so. **90** —*S.H. (12/15/2004)*

Clos du Val 2000 Merlot (Napa Valley) $25. Made in a restrained, elegant style, with modulated blackberry, currant and herb flavors balanced with oak. Dry, supple and polished, this young wine needs a year or two in the cellar to gain complexity. **88** —*S.H. (8/1/2003)*

Clos du Val 1999 Merlot (Napa Valley) $25. Supple-textured with pretty cherry, smoke, spice and herb flavors. The wine is medium-bodied with mild tannins and a moderate finish. **87** —*J.M. (6/1/2002)*

Clos du Val 2004 Pinot Noir (Carneros) $24. Heavy and soft, with syrupy berry and fruit flavors, this Pinot seriously lacks acidity. What a disappointment. **82** —*S.H. (11/1/2006)*

Clos du Val 2003 Pinot Noir (Napa Valley) $24. There are some good features in this wine, namely the pretty cherry flavor, gentle mouthfeel and light dusting of oak. There's also a cloying sweetness throughout that diminishes the score. **84** —*S.H. (10/1/2005)*

Clos du Val 2002 Pinot Noir (Napa Valley) $24. Pleasant cherry, raspberry and smoky vanilla flavors make this wine polished and easy to sip. It's medium-bodied in weight, and while it could use a bit more delicacy for a Pinot Noir, it's quite delicious. **86** —*S.H. (11/1/2004)*

Clos du Val 2002 Pinot Noir (Carneros) $24. Very oaky, with cherry, raspberry, cranberry and toasty vanilla aromas. Turns lively and elegant, a fruity wine with clove and pepper highlights. Snaps to a quick finish. **86** *(11/1/2004)*

Clos du Val 2000 Pinot Noir (Carneros) $38. Beautifully balanced, this juicy Pinot is supple yet structured. A complex nose, a solid core of ripe cherry-berry and plum fruit, plus tea, spice, cocoa and bacon accents combine to create a well-integrated whole. The long finish, with its elegant, refined tannins, augurs a fine future for this class act. Drink now–2008. **91 Editors' Choice** *(10/1/2002)*

Clos du Val 2001 Carneros Vineyard Pinot Noir (Napa Valley) $38. A pleasant Pinot that takes its well-ripened cherry and raspberry flavors and saturates them with oaky seasonings of vanilla, smoke and sweet tannins. Silky in the mouth, with a short finish. **86** —*S.H. (2/1/2004)*

Clos du Val 2003 Reserve Pinot Noir (Carneros) $42. This is the winery's first Reserve Pinot, the result of frustrating years of trying to figure out this fickle variety, and it's the best Pinot they've ever produced. Dry, rich, ripe and full-bodied, it shows cherry pie filling, herb tea, cola and chocolate flavors. Should hold well and even improve through 2009. **92** —*S.H. (12/15/2006)*

Clos du Val 1998 Single Vineyard Pinot Noir (Carneros) $26. 89 —*M.M. (12/15/2000)*

Clos du Val 2002 Ariadne Sémillon-Sauvignon Blanc (Napa Valley) $32. A creamy, smooth blend of Sémillon and Sauvignon Blanc. The wine serves up hints of melon, hay, mineral, herbs and citrus flavors. Acidity is a bit low for these varieties, but the wine shows elegance, finishing long. **89** —*J.M. (10/1/2004)*

Clos du Val 1999 White Blend (Napa Valley) $25. Fragrant, with well-ripened citrus, melon and peach aromas framed by smoky oak. It's dry, with some crisp tartness, and finishes on a fruity note. Elegant on the surface, with lots of flash and pizazz. **87** —*S.H. (12/1/2001)*

Clos du Val 2000 Ariadne White Blend (Napa Valley) $32. Just delicious. Its one-third Sauvignon Blanc dominates, with grassy, lemony flavors and a dry, tart mouthfeel. The other two-thirds is Sémillon, which adds nutty, figgy notes. Oak softens and fattens. The result is a dry white wine of unusual complexity and density. This would be terrific with spicy Thai food. **90** —*S.H. (12/15/2002)*

Clos du Val 1997 Zinfandel (Napa Valley) $17. 84 —*M.S. (5/1/2000)*

Clos du Val 1999 Palisade Vineyard Zinfandel (Stags Leap District) $28. A single-vineyard Zin bursting with ripe, jammy red and black rasberry fruit and sweet , vanilla-tinged, smoky aromas from French oak. Stresses elegance rather than weight or size, with pretty, melted tannins and a soft, velvety mouthfeel. **88** —*S.H. (12/15/2001)*

Clos du Val 1998 Palisade Vineyard Zinfandel (Stags Leap District) $25. 87 —*S.H. (12/1/2000)*

Clos du Val 1997 Palisade Vineyard Zinfandel (Stags Leap District) $17. 80 —*P.G. (11/15/1999)*

Clos du Val 2001 Reserve Zinfandel (Stags Leap District) $55. Smooth textured, with silky, round tannins, this wine offers finesse on the palate. But the fruit flavors take a back seat with toasty oak up front, and lighter strains of black currant, blackberry, tar and coffee on the follow up. **87** *(11/1/2003)*

CLOS LA CHANCE

Clos La Chance 2000 Cabernet Franc (Central Coast) $35. Modern winemaking techniques come together in this exceedingly ripe, softly tannic wine. Pours dark, with fancy aromas of oak, berries and chocolate. On the palate, fully extracted cherry-berry flavors flood the mouth and last through the finish. But there's a certain simplicity of structure. **86** —*S.H. (11/15/2003)*

Clos La Chance 1997 Cabernet Franc (Santa Cruz Mountains) $32. Cabernet Franc, used in Bordeaux blends and on its own in the Loire, is difficult to make into a complex wine in California. This bottling starts with aromas of black raspberry and spearmint, and drinks soft and fruity. It's a good wine, but on the simple side. **85** —*S.H. (2/1/2001)*

Clos La Chance 1997 Cabernet Sauvignon (Santa Cruz Mountains) $21. 91 —*S.H. (7/1/2000)*

Clos La Chance 2002 Cabernet Sauvignon (Napa Valley) $25. Green olives dominate the aroma of this streamlined wine. It's elegant rather than exuberant, with sturdy tannins, and finishes very dry. Best now. **85** —*S.H. (5/1/2005)*

Clos La Chance 2001 Cabernet Sauvignon (Napa Valley) $25. Simple and rather hot, with a thick, heavy texture that conveys jammy cherry flavors through a slightly sweet finish. Lacks the breeding you expect from this appellation. **84** —*S.H. (6/1/2004)*

Clos La Chance 2000 Cabernet Sauvignon (Napa Valley) $23. There's lots of pretty flavor in this ripe wine, with blackberry and currant notes and a rich overlay of oak. Tannins are dry and fine, with a round, supple texture. On the minus side is an herbal greenness that comes from stalks or unripe berries. **86** —*S.H. (4/1/2003)*

Clos La Chance 2003 Ruby-Throated Cabernet Sauvignon (Central Coast) $17. This is a somewhat harsh wine, edgy in both acids and tannins. However it has polished blackberry and cherry flavors, and will stand up well to rich, oily cheeses and meats. **85** —*S.H. (3/1/2006)*

Clos La Chance 1998 Chardonnay (Santa Cruz Mountains) $19. 87 *(6/1/2000)*

Clos La Chance 1998 Chardonnay (Napa Valley) $18. 88 *(6/1/2000)*

Clos La Chance 1997 Chardonnay (Santa Cruz Mountains) $19. 90 —*J.C. (11/15/1999)*

Clos La Chance 1997 Chardonnay (Napa Valley) $18. 90 —*J.C. (11/15/1999)*

Clos La Chance 2004 Chardonnay (Santa Cruz Mountains) $18. Simple and fruity, with peach and pear flavors that finish with spicy oak, this Chard is fully dry. It has a bracing acidity that provides balance. **84** —*S.H. (11/1/2006)*

Clos La Chance 2003 Chardonnay (Santa Cruz Mountains) $19. This is a very hands-on winemaker wine. It's strong in lees and oak, and feels a bit manipulated. The underlying wine seems very cool-climate, suggesting green apples and cinnamon-laced coffee, with tart acids. **85** —*S.H. (11/15/2005)*

Clos La Chance 2002 Chardonnay (Santa Cruz Mountains) $18. Ripe and concentrated, in the way of mountain wines, with intense lemondrop, honeydew and papaya flavors. Scads of oak add layers of smoke, vanilla and wood spice notes. At the same time, there's a thick, heavy quality to the texture that costs a few points. **86** —*S.H. (6/1/2004)*

Clos La Chance 2001 Chardonnay (Santa Cruz Mountains) $18. A focused, crisp Chard that impresses with finesse rather than size. Comes down on the mineral side, with flavors of peaches and slate and a steely backbone of acidity. Oak is used judiciously, adding nuances of vanilla, smoke and buttercream. **91 Editors' Choice** —*S.H. (10/1/2003)*

Clos La Chance 2000 Chardonnay (Santa Cruz Mountains) $19. Has compact and intense flavors of peaches and pears, wrapped in a lush coating of oak. Notable for the pretty balance of acids, fruit, alcohol and wood. This is a distinguished wine, firm and elegant. **90 Editors' Choice** —*S.H. (5/1/2003)*

Clos La Chance 2000 Chardonnay (Napa Valley) $18. This wine has all the usual elements of ripe, oaky Chardonnay, including a fat, unctuous texture and big, bright peach and pear flavors. However, it has the added plus of elegance that many big wines lack. The finish is especially nice, turning peppery and spicy and lasting for a long time. **90 Editors' Choice** —*S.H. (12/15/2002)*

Clos La Chance NV Amber's Cuvée Chardonnay (Santa Cruz Mountains) $30. This is actually a blanc de blancs, and as you'd expect, it's very light and elegant. There's just a trace of citrus in the nose, and a hint of peaches on the tongue. Dry and crisp. Could use a touch more finesse in the bubbles, but it's a beautiful wine. **90** —*S.H. (12/1/2002)*

Clos La Chance 2005 Glittering Throated Emerald Chardonnay (Monterey County) $15. This Chard tastes like the juice you get in canned apricots and peaches, although it's properly dry, with good acidity. It's a simple sipper that will work in most everyday situations. **83** —*S.H. (11/15/2006)*

Clos La Chance 2002 Vanumanutagi Vineyard Chardonnay (Santa Cruz County) $30. Lemondrop candy, fresh ripe papaya, sun-ripened peach, toasted and sweetened coconut, cinnamon spice—there's enough flavor to go around a dozen wines. There's also lots of oak. This flashy, flamboyant wine has all that, but it's a little soft and one-dimensional. **87** —*S.H. (6/1/2004)*

Clos La Chance 2001 Vanumanutagi Vineyard Chardonnay (Santa Cruz Mountains) $30. Super-delicious, a mouthful of Chardonnay perfection. Really notable for the pure concentration of its flavors, such as fresh ripe white peach, mango, and spicy fig. Elaborately oaked, but not too much to support the huge fruit. The rich and creamy texture is a delight. **92** —*S.H. (6/1/2003)*

Clos La Chance 1999 Vanumanutagi Vineyard Chardonnay (Santa Cruz Mountains) $30. Toasty oak and earth tones form a baseline here, with pear, apple, lemon, melon and herb flavors issuing forth on the palate. The wine's a bit cloudy, and is slightly astringent on the palate, but still offers complexity and finesse to the end. **89** —*J.M. (5/1/2002)*

Clos La Chance 2000 Vanumanutagi Vineyards Chardonnay (Santa Cruz Mountains) $30. A nutty, leesy wine that takes those positive attributes to the limit, resulting in a mix of flavors that range from peanut brittle to lemon custard. The delicate melon and citrus fruit ends up getting a little overwhelmed. **86** —*J.C. (9/1/2002)*

Clos La Chance 2003 Grenache (Central Coast) $29. Showcases Grenache's cherry flavors very well, with the fruit standing front and center in this soft, dry wine with an edge of sweet oak. It could use greater structure, but sure is a tasty sipper. **86** —*S.H. (12/31/2005)*

Clos La Chance 2002 Grenache (Central Coast) $20. This is a light-bodied, soft wine that glides like silk in the mouth. It has a nice balance of cherry-blueberry flavors and earthy, coffee bean notes, and is very dry and tart with acids. **85** —*S.H. (3/1/2005)*

Clos La Chance 1997 Merlot (Central Coast) $17. 88 —*M.M. (3/1/2000)*

USA

Clos La Chance 2002 Merlot (Central Coast) $18. The softly tannic wine has flavors of slightly sweet cherry and black raspberry Lifesaver candy. It's rather rough in texture, and finishes with some heat. **84** —*S.H. (6/1/2004)*

Clos La Chance 2001 Merlot (Central Coast) $18. This Merlot is loaded with plush flavors of dark stone fruits, cola, herbs and violets, and has wonderfully rich tannins. **91 Editors' Choice** —*S.H. (10/1/2003)*

Clos La Chance 2000 Merlot (Central Coast) $18. Primarily Paso Robles fruit, this wine brims with plush blackberries and black cherries. Dry, soft and stylish, it's a worthy table companion that turns a bit thin on the finish. **86** —*S.H. (11/15/2002)*

Clos La Chance 2003 Violet-Crowned Merlot (Central Coast) $17. Young and tart in citrusy acids, and very dry. Has vibrant blackberry, cherry and coffee flavors. It's a well-structured wine that needs time to breathe. **86** —*S.H. (3/1/2006)*

Clos La Chance 2003 Petite Sirah (Central Coast) $35. Soft, super-fruity and dry, this is built along Cabernet lines, with ripe flavors of blackberries, cherries and blueberries, and deliciously sweet oak. The tannins are lush, the acids are soft, and the finish has wild herbs sprinkled with white pepper. **88** —*S.H. (12/31/2005)*

Clos La Chance 2002 Pinot Noir (Santa Cruz Mountains) $25. A little light in body and fruit, but achieves complexity with the rich acids and myriad of flavors. They include cherries, leather, root beer, spices and oaky smoke and vanilla. Good acids, and a silky texture. **87** —*S.H. (2/1/2005)*

Clos La Chance 2001 Pinot Noir (Santa Cruz County) $28. Tasty enough, a deliciously drinkable wine with mouthwatering flavors of cherries and raspberries and a tangy sprinking of cinnamon, nutmeg and pepper. Very dry, but the fruity flavors are so ripe, the wine coats the palate with a honeyed richness. This is a jammy Pinot meant for early drinking. **88** —*S.H. (7/1/2003)*

Clos La Chance 1999 Pinot Noir (Santa Cruz Mountains) $28. Almost Bourbon-like aromas, along with caramel and menthol, open this offering. Toasty oak and cocoa, dark fruit and a fairly full, smooth mouthfeel flow into a black coffee-and-bitter chocolate fade. Drink now–2004. **86** *(10/1/2002)*

Clos La Chance 1997 Pinot Noir (Santa Cruz Mountains) $24. **93** *(10/1/1999)*

Clos La Chance 2002 Biagini Vineyard Pinot Noir (Santa Cruz Mountains) $35. A light and easy Pinot, with cherry, cola and coffee flavors, and a long, dry, spicy finish. Drink now. **88** —*S.H. (11/15/2005)*

Clos La Chance 2001 Erwin Vineyard Pinot Noir (Santa Cruz Mountains) $35. Forward in new oak, this wine opens with a burst of vanilla and toast, but it's big enough to shoulder all that wood. The ripe cherry, pomegranate and coffee flavors are dry, wrapped in soft, silky tannins. You find yourself wishing it had more concentration, though. **89** —*S.H. (2/1/2005)*

Clos La Chance 1997 Erwin Vineyard Pinot Noir (Santa Cruz Mountains) $50. **89** *(10/1/2000)*

Clos La Chance 2005 Pink-Throated Brilliant Rosé Wine Rosé Blend (Central Coast) $14. Rosés make sense for barbecues and the beach. This Grenache-Syrah blend is a pleasant sipper at a decent price. It's dry, crisp and delicate, with subtle raspberry, cherry, herb and vanilla flavors. **85** —*S.H. (11/1/2006)*

Clos La Chance 2004 Rose Wine Rosé Blend (Central Coast) $14. Here's an easy, Rhône-style blush wine that's dry enough to have with a bouillabaisse-type dish, or grilled sausages and veggies. It has polished strawberry, cherry and pepper flavors, boosted by bright acids. **85** —*S.H. (11/15/2005)*

Clos La Chance 2003 Sauvignon Blanc (Central Coast) $16. Drinks kind of bitter and sharp in acids, with lemony flavors and a richer stream of spicy melon. Very dry finish. Nice with salty tapas. **84** —*S.H. (2/1/2005)*

Clos La Chance 2005 Estate Sauvignon Blanc (Central Coast) $16. Comes down on the thin, herbaceous side, with bell pepper flavors and a hint of lime. Acidity is high and cleansing, and the finish is bone dry. **83** —*S.H. (11/15/2006)*

Clos La Chance 2004 Estate Sauvignon Blanc (Central Coast) $16. Textbook coastal Sauvignon Blanc, a bone dry wine with brisk acidity, and flavors of grapefruit, lime, fig and honeydew melon. There's a fine, peppery note on the finish. **87** —*S.H. (11/15/2005)*

Clos La Chance 2002 Syrah (Central Coast) $18. Very soft, very dry, and with a tannic edge, but drinkable right away. Shows an earthy, pepper and leather profile, with hints of blackberries and plums. There's elegance in the overall balance. **85** —*S.H. (2/1/2005)*

Clos La Chance 2001 Syrah (Central Coast) $20. Smells promising, with young Syrah aromas of plum, pepper, blackberry, tobacco and subtle oak. But in the mouth it turns rather simple and even tart. The blackberry flavors finish with a sharp bite of acidity, and it doesn't seem like age will work wonders. **85** —*S.H. (12/15/2003)*

Clos La Chance 2000 Syrah (Paso Robles) $20. This Santa Cruz winery turns southward in search of ripe Syrah. The grapes certainly achieved high sugars, which winemaker Jeff Ritchey vinified to 14.5%, basically bone dry, leaving behind all sorts of fruity, berry flavors. It's a sumptuous wine, built along Cabernet's lines, yet softer and richer, with a sappiness that cries out to be matched food. **90 Editors' Choice** —*S.H. (12/1/2002)*

Clos La Chance 2003 Black-Chinned Syrah (Central Coast) $17. Opens with an inviting blast of white pepper, with overtones of refined toasted oak, cassis and leather. Unfortunately the taste isn't as good as the aroma. The wine turns soft and sweet in the mouth, with a cloying finish. **83** —*S.H. (3/1/2006)*

Clos La Chance 2003 Viognier (Central Coast) $18. Kind of earthy and a bit disjointed, with herb, tobacco and peach flavors and fairly high acidity. It's also a very dry wine. Almost Sauvignon Blanc-like in dryness and tartness; unusual for Viognier, but a good, crisp drink. **85** —*S.H. (8/1/2005)*

Clos La Chance 2005 Estate Viognier (Central Coast) $19. Simple and watery in citrus and flower flavors, this very dry wine also has high acidity. Clean and vibrant, but could use greater concentration of fruit. **83** —*S.H. (11/15/2006)*

Clos La Chance 2004 Estate Viognier (Central Coast) $18. Showing good varietal character, this cool-climate Viognier expresses powerful acidity framing peach, apricot, quince and mango flavors that finish dry and clean. The acids really star, stimulating the palate. **86** —*S.H. (11/15/2005)*

Clos La Chance 2002 Zinfandel (El Dorado County) $18. Very ripe in berry fruit, but dry, with a firm, tannic texture, and turns sweetish on the finish, like the aftertaste of a cherry tart. A bit rough overall, but a good Zin with extra features. **87** —*S.H. (5/1/2005)*

Clos La Chance 2001 Zinfandel (El Dorado County) $20. Toast and vanilla frame the modest fruit, which speaks of cherries and plums. A light and easy quaff; simple. **82** *(11/1/2003)*

Clos La Chance 1997 Zinfandel (El Dorado County) $17. **88** *(5/1/2000)*

Clos La Chance 2003 Buff-Bellied Zinfandel (Central Coast) $17. Smells minty, with a suggestion of Port, an odd combination that suggests unevenly ripened grapes, and this impression is confirmed with the first sip. This is an unbalanced wine, with sweet and sour Chinese sauce flavors. **82** —*S.H. (3/1/2006)*

Clos La Chance 2000 Twin Rivers Zinfandel (El Dorado County) $20. If you want to taste a single-vineyard Sierra Zin with a distinct personality, try this one. The rocky, well-drained mountain soils have concentrated the fruit into intense blackberry liqueur and cherry flavors, heavily spiced with pepper and nutmeg. The tannins are silky. **89** —*S.H. (11/1/2002)*

CLOS MIMI

Clos Mimi 2001 Bunny Slope Vineyard Syrah (Paso Robles) $50. Do we just not get this wine? Aromas are nice enough, starting with floral, minty scents and then delivering some mushroomy notes later on, but the flavors are sour and lean, finishing tangy and herbal. **83** *(9/1/2005)*

Clos Mimi 2000 Bunny Slope Vineyard Syrah (Paso Robles) $50. Here's a big, plummy wine with hints of dark chocolate, roasted coffee bean and grilled meat. It's soft in the mouth, but not flabby, with decadently rich flavors of wild berries, cassis and chocolate. Very dry, but high alcohol creates sweet heat on the finish. **90** —*S.H. (12/1/2003)*

Clos Mimi NV Nini Syrah (California) $13. Pretty rustic, with sweet-and-sour cherry-candy flavors and a sharp, acidic mouth-feel. But with the right meats and cheeses, it will do fine. **83** —*S.H. (3/1/2006)*

Clos Mimi 2004 Petite Rousse Syrah (Paso Robles) $18. Excessive sweetness in the finish mars this otherwise fine wine, with its plum, cherry and leather flavors and rich, sticky tannins. **82** —*S.H. (3/1/2006)*

Clos Mimi 2003 Petite Rousse Syrah (Paso Robles) $17. Smells pretty Rhônish, with peppery, floral and meaty notes layered over blackberry fruit. Winemaker Tim Spear's entry-level Syrah boasts 16% alcohol but it's not all that noticeable, balanced by just enough raspberry, blackberry and vanilla flavors. **85** *(9/1/2005)*

Clos Mimi 2002 Petite Rousse Red Wine Syrah (Paso Robles) $16. A beautiful Syrah, complex and delicious, with lots of finesse, from Clos Mimi. Impresses for the depth of its plum, currant, chocolate, coffee, oak and spice flavors, and rich, sweet tannins. Right up there with the best of them, at a fair price. **91** —*S.H. (4/1/2004)*

CLOS PEGASE

Clos Pegase 1997 Cabernet Sauvignon (Napa Valley) $30. **90** *(11/1/2000)*

Clos Pegase 1996 Cabernet Sauvignon (Napa Valley) $30. **88** —*M.M. (10/1/1999)*

Clos Pegase 2002 Cabernet Sauvignon (Napa Valley) $33. Clos Pegase's regular Cab, as opposed to the single-vineyards and Hommages, succeeds in the very best vintages, of which this was not one. The wine smacks of fabulous technique and is very good, but would score higher if it had greater depth and length. **87** —*S.H. (5/1/2006)*

Clos Pegase 2001 Cabernet Sauvignon (Napa Valley) $32. So ripe, it's gooey in currant, cocoa and cassis flavors that have been lavishly oaked. This is a soft, smooth wine, with velvety tannins, and has enough complexity and nuance to merit its score. **91** —*S.H. (3/1/2005)*

Clos Pegase 1999 Cabernet Sauvignon (Napa Valley) $33. A rich and distinguished Cabernet with well-ripened flavors of blackcurrants and cassis. There's a depth that impresses. The tannins are fairly thick and suggest mid-term cellaring. **89** —*S.H. (6/1/2003)*

Clos Pegase 2001 Graveyard Hill Cabernet Sauvignon (Carneros) $60. The winery's Calistoga Cabernet is lush and opulent. This one is much firmer in acids and tannins, a more structured wine, although equally oaky, but it needs cellaring to show its best. Explodes with black currant and chocolate flavors, and should improve for quite a few years. Drink 2008–2015. **91 Cellar Selection** —*S.H. (12/15/2006)*

Clos Pegase 2000 Graveyard Hill Cabernet Sauvignon (Carneros) $60. You can smell the new oak a mile away, powerful in char and smoky vanilla. Then the cassis hits you and the mind thinks, Great Cab. Rich, ripe and intense, dripping with blackcurrants and chocolate, but with firm tannins. Should be a keeper for years, but hard to resist its immediate charms. **92** —*S.H. (3/1/2005)*

Clos Pegase 1999 Graveyard Hill Cabernet Sauvignon (Carneros) $60. Despite the gloomy name, this is a young and vibrant wine, full of life and future. The cassis flavors are generously wrapped in thick tannins, demanding cellaring. Far too young to drink now, put it away until 2006 and try again. **92 Cellar Selection** —*S.H. (5/1/2003)*

Clos Pegase 2002 Hommage Cabernet Sauvignon (Napa Valley) $75. Clos Pegase has turned into one of the most dependably exciting, multi-varietal wineries in Napa Valley. The very fine '01 Hommage now is followed by an equally good '02. It's ripe and juicy in black currant, cherry and chocolate, with rich, velvety tannins. A minor quibble is that the wine doesn't really need all that new oak; it almost overshadows the beautiful fruit. **91** —*S.H. (12/15/2006)*

Clos Pegase 2001 Hommage Cabernet Sauvignon (Napa Valley) $75. Clos Pegase has really hit its stride in recent years, as this fine Cabernet shows. It's true to the vintage, being supremely ripe and balanced, with pure, intense black currant flavors and quite a bit of new oak. I would cellar this wine for a good five years to let it all come together, and it should hold for several years. **91** —*S.H. (11/15/2005)*

Clos Pegase 1998 Hommage Cabernet Sauvignon (Napa Valley) $75. Sweet chocolate notes counter sour red fruit on the palate; the nose offers the textbook blackberry-and-oak combo. Less than lush in the mouth; oak is

a big player on the finish. Label features Dubuffet's Nu Chamarre painting—yes, the one with a little full-frontal. Whew. **84** —*D.T. (6/1/2002)*

Clos Pegase 2001 Palisades Vineyard Cabernet Sauvignon (Napa Valley) $60. The vineyard is in Calistoga. The wine, 100% varietal, has lots of new French oak. Seriously good, it shows all the hallmarks of a flashy, important Napa Cab, with rich, perfectly sculpted tannins, a deeply impressive structure, and intense, long-lasting black currant, spice and toasty oak flavors. Just terrific now, and should hold and soften through 2012, at least. **94 Editors' Choice** —*S.H. (12/15/2006)*

Clos Pegase 1999 Palisades Vineyard Cabernet Sauvignon (Napa Valley) $60. From this Calistoga vineyard, a first rate Cabernet, sumptuous and elegant. The fruit straddles an interesting line between herbaceous, green olive notes and riper ones of blackberries. Feels just great in the mouth, plush and sensual. Unquestionably an ager. **91** —*S.H. (6/1/2003)*

Clos Pegase 2003 Artist Series Reserve Mitsuko's Vineyard Chardonnay (Napa-Carneros) $36. As good as Clos Pegase's 2003 regular Chardonnay was, this is richer, more complex and more satisfying. It's an oaky wine, with buttered toast and caramel layers on top of tropical fruit flavors. Somehow, acidity pulls it all together, and the wine is balanced. Best now through 2007. **92** —*S.H. (7/1/2006)*

Clos Pegase 1999 Hommage Artist Series Reserve Mitsuko's Chardonnay (Carneros) $36. Possibly the longest name of a Chardonnay in California, and an extraordinary one at that. There is tremendous winemaker influence in the massive oak and lees, but the fruit is huge, an atomic blast of peaches and mangoes. Feels rich, weighty and sensual on the palate. The long finish smacks of vanilla and cinnamon. **94 Editors' Choice** —*S.H. (12/15/2002)*

Clos Pegase 2001 Hommage Mitsuko's Vineyard Chardonnay (Carneros) $36. Enormously oaky, but it sure is delicious. Dominated by the taste of sweet caramelly char, honey and vanilla. Underneath you'll find ripe flavors of sauteed banana, spicy mango and peach cobbler. This flamboyant wine is heady. Try with scallops in a coconut milk and curry sauce **92** —*S.H. (3/1/2005)*

Clos Pegase 2004 Mitsuko's Vineyard Chardonnay (Carneros) $21. Past Chardonnays from this vineyard have been more opulent, and it's a curiosity why the winemaker shied away from ripeness this vintage, when it should have been easy. The absence of richness makes the acidity and alcohol stand out. It's a good wine, just something of a disappointment. **84** —*S.H. (5/1/2006)*

Clos Pegase 2003 Mitsuko's Vineyard Chardonnay (Carneros) $21. This winery continues to turn out some of the most consistently good wines in California. Here's a Chard that lets the terroir shine, rather than overwhelming with bells and whistles. It's clean in acids and dry, with complex citrus, peach, spiced apple and meringue flavors. **90** —*S.H. (12/31/2005)*

Clos Pegase 2002 Mitsuko's Vineyard Chardonnay (Carneros) $21. Tutti-frutti and jammy flavors mingle with plenty of toasty oak to provide for a rich, satisfying Chard. You'll find peaches and pears, apples and pineapples and lots of spices, especially in the long, crisp finish. **88** —*S.H. (4/1/2004)*

Clos Pegase 1997 Mitsuko's Vineyard Chardonnay (Carneros) $19. **91** —*S.H. (11/15/1999)*

Clos Pegase 2002 Mitsuko's Vineyard Hommage Chardonnay (Carneros) $36. Everything about this Chard is brilliantly crafted, but the parts haven't come together. It's all fine charred oak, creamy, yeasty lees and primary peach, pear and tropical fruit, battling it out. But it's a very fine wine, and simply needs a while to coalesce. Try in a few months. **92** —*S.H. (12/15/2005)*

Clos Pegase 1998 Mitsuko's Vineyard Chardonnay (Carneros) $19. **86** *(6/1/2000)*

Clos Pegase 2002 Mitsuko's Vineyard Merlot (Carneros) $25. A soft, voluptuous Merlot. The velvety texture frames ripe, juicy blackberry, cherry jam and milk chocolate flavors, with a flowery, violet note. But the wine is too soft, and the tannins melted. **86** —*S.H. (12/15/2006)*

Clos Pegase 2001 Mitsuko's Vineyard Merlot (Carneros) $25. This is the kind of Merlot that shows how well Carneros can ripen the variety. It's a big, rich wine, almost fat in gooey black cherry, mocha and anise flavors, but is fortunately balanced with rich, furry tannins. It's a bit soft, but very tasty. **87** —*S.H. (12/15/2005)*

Clos Pegase 1999 Mitsuko's Vineyard Merlot (Carneros) $25. A first-rate wine, totally flattering in the mouth, and addictively delicious. It's not big, but restrained and stylish, reining in the blackberry fruit to match a rich overlay of oak. The texture is a marvel, smooth and complex, all the way through the long, distinguished finish. **94 Editors' Choice** —*S.H. (11/15/2002)*

Clos Pegase 2000 Mitsuko's Vineyard Merlot (Carneros) $25. Not as rich as in the past, a wine marked with lean herbal flavors and tough, green tannins. The new French oak helps to provide sweet, fancy notes, but the final impression is astringent and short. **85** —*S.H. (5/1/2004)*

Clos Pegase 2004 Mitsuko's Vineyard Pinot Noir (Carneros) $30. Tastes kind of obviously new oaky, with all that vanilla and char framing cherry pie flavors. It's a flattering, seductive Pinot, with a silky texture and firm acids, but it's basically one-dimensional. Drink now. **85** —*S.H. (11/1/2006)*

Clos Pegase 2003 Mitsuko's Vineyard Pinot Noir (Carneros) $30. Built more along the lines of the '02 than the massive '01, this Pinot is elegant and streamlined. It's polished now in black cherry, pomegranate, rhubarb, coffee and vanilla flavors, and nice and silky, providing a complex, thoroughly satisfying Pinot experience. **89** —*S.H. (5/1/2006)*

Clos Pegase 2002 Mitsuko's Vineyard Pinot Noir (Carneros) $30. Clean and fruity, with light, silky tannins and nice supporting acids, this is a gentle Pinot that flatters with cherries, cola, smoke and vanilla flavors and a smooth texture. It's easy to like. **86** —*S.H. (12/15/2005)*

Clos Pegase 2001 Mitsuko's Vineyard Pinot Noir (Carneros) $30. Polished and delicious, just starting to come into its own. Has shed its youthful tannins to reveal a silky, fleshy wine of charm and nuance. Raspberry, cherry, nutmeg, cola, cocoa and smoky oak flavors unfold in waves, leading to a soft, spicy finish. **92** —*S.H. (3/1/2005)*

Clos Pegase 2001 Mitsuko's Q Block Sauvignon Blanc (Carneros) $18. There's something about this wine that's really likeable. It has standard lemongrass and hay flavors and is bone dry with crisp acidity. The finish is rich and sweet, perhaps due to less aging. More indefinable is a finesse and elegance that make you reach for a second glass. **88** —*S.H. (9/1/2003)*

Clos Pegase 2005 Mitsuko's Vineyard Sauvignon Blanc (Carneros) $19. Strong, powerful in green grass, gooseberry and nettle flavors, a very dry, highly acidic wine with a minerally streak. No malolactic fermentation occurred and no oak was involved. This is a user-specific wine. You either love this style, or can't drink it. **87** —*S.H. (12/15/2006)*

Clos Pegase 2004 Mitsuko's Vineyard Sauvignon Blanc (Carneros) $19. Gooseberries, juniper and lemon rind—those are the sorts of things that come to mind with this intensely dry wine. Yet it has an elegant balance, an inherent finesse that lifts it out of the ordinary into the realm of complexity. Try with shellfish in cream sauce. **90** —*S.H. (12/31/2005)*

Clos Pegase 2003 Mitsuko's Vineyard Sauvignon Blanc (Napa-Carneros) $19. Here's a fruit-forward, jazzy wine that's juicy in honeydew, lime, peach, apple and oak. With all that fruit, it seems on the sweet side, but it's dry, and the acids are perky and mouth-cleansing. Really nice, and bravo to owner Jan Shrem for putting it in a screwtop. **88** —*S.H. (5/1/2005)*

Clos Pegase 2002 Mitsuko's Vineyard Sauvignon Blanc (Carneros) $18. Aromas of peach, pear, citrus and vanilla-smoke lead to a rich, complex wine, filled with lovely fruit flavors and spices. The texture is creamy smooth, with bright acids that make the wine lively and fresh. Long on the finish, and perfect with grilled shrimp. **88** —*S.H. (2/1/2004)*

CLOS PEPE

Clos Pepe 2001 Estate Barrel Fermented Chardonnay (Santa Rita Hills) $20. The fruit here is on the lean side, suggesting citrus fruits and apples, with notes of lusher peaches, and the wine has been fattened up through the use of smoky oak. Feels creamy smooth in the mouth, with a buttery texture, and turns oaky again on the finish. **89** —*S.H. (4/1/2004)*

Clos Pepe 2002 Homage to Chablis Chardonnay (Santa Rita Hills) $25. A big, bracing, exotic Chard with a gunmetal and mineral spine plus, tangy flavors of candied grapefruit, mango and papaya. High in acidity, yet well oaked. Very companionable for food; should age gracefully for several years. **91** —*S.H. (9/1/2004)*

Clos Pepe 2002 Pinot Noir (Santa Rita Hills) $35. Dark and extracted, with scads of blackberries and cherries, and a flourish of Oriental spices, but seems to lack balance and charm. Too big for Pinot, hard and dense, and not likely to improve. Drink now. **85** *(11/1/2004)*

Clos Pepe 2000 Pinot Noir (Santa Rita Hills) $35. Opens strong, with a complex nose of strawberry, cherry, pipe tobacco, menthol, soy, rubbing spices and wheat. A slightly chalky feel along with black tea and herb accents show on the plummy, midweight palate. It closes tasty but tight, with herb and tobacco shadings. While appealing now, best 2004–2008. **89** *(10/1/2002)*

CLOS TITA

Clos Tita 1997 Cabernet Sauvignon (Santa Cruz Mountains) $22. 91 —*S.H. (2/1/2000)*

CLOUD 9

Cloud 9 2001 Composition Red Blend (California) $35. Dramatically rich and smooth, with very ripe flavors of black cherries, red plums, mocha and sweet herbs, this complex wine also has supple tannins that are thick, but gentle. The finish is long and harmonious. Definitely one of the best "California" appellation reds out there. **91** —*S.H. (11/15/2005)*

Cloud 9 2000 Composition Tempranillo Blend (California) $65. This unusual Tempranillo-based blend, with Cabernet Sauvignon, Syrah, Barbera and other grapes, is soft and easy. It has an array of berry-cherry and chocolate flavors, and a sweetish aftertaste. **86** —*S.H. (12/15/2004)*

Cloud 9 2003 Seity Zinfandel (Amador County) $35. The winery claims the wine comes from "the oldest Zinfandel vines on earth." Certainly this is an intensely flavored, densely structured Zin. The flavors go beyond cherry, raspberry and cocoa fruit into the area of dessert pastries, with toasted pie dough and meringue. But the wine is fully dry, at the price of high alcohol, 15.4%. **90** —*S.H. (12/31/2005)*

Cloud 9 2001 Seity Zinfandel (Amador County) $35. Containing a little Barbera, this wine is tremendous in mocha and blackberry flavors. Wines just don't get much more flavorful than this. It's as rich as a fine Port, except that it's dry, without excessive alcohol or stewed fruit. It's also very soft. **88** —*S.H. (12/15/2004)*

CLOUD VIEW

Cloud View 2001 Red Wine Bordeaux Blend (Napa Valley) $60. Smoky and tarry at first, later opening into black cherry and tobacco notes. Long, intense and tannic on the finish; needs time. Try around 2010. A blend of 57% Merlot and 43% Cabernet Sauvignon. **91** *(6/6/2005)*

Cloud View 2002 Estate Red Blend (Napa Valley) $60. There's lots to like in this ripe, flashy, fleshy Cab-based wine. The cassis and chocolate flavors are rich, and so are the tannins. However, it's a little too soft, and could benefit from additional depth and complexity. **87** —*S.H. (12/31/2005)*

COASTAL RIDGE

Coastal Ridge 2003 Cabernet Sauvignon (California) $7. A straightforward sipper with upfront cherry pie and cocoa flavors. Rustic and sweet, this Cab will do in a pinch. **82** —*S.H. (9/1/2006)*

Coastal Ridge 2001 Cabernet Sauvignon (California) $7. Take a good '01 Cab, thin it down, and that's what you get with this affordably drinkable wine. It's dry and balanced, with pleasant berry flavors. **84 Best Buy** —*S.H. (4/1/2005)*

Coastal Ridge 2000 Cabernet Sauvignon (California) $7. Impresses for its pretty flavors and smooth texture. Blackcurrant, blackberry jam, cola and smoky oak mingle to create a rich impression. A bit simple on the finish, but good value. **86 Best Buy** —*S.H. (11/15/2003)*

Coastal Ridge 1999 Cabernet Sauvignon (California) $7. There's a rough, edgy quality to this affordable wine, with sharp acids and tannins, but it's dry and clean and will satisfy unless you're really picky. In fact the dryness is downright refreshing, when so many Cabernets these days drink sweet. **85 Best Buy** —*S.H. (6/1/2002)*

Coastal Ridge 1998 Cabernet Sauvignon (California) $7. Smells herbaceous and weedy, with lots of green, stalky notes and just the barest trace of berry fruit. The flavors are pretty much the same, thin and austere, with a solid dose of tannins. It's well made, but there's not a whole lot to like here. **81** —S.H. (5/1/2001)

Coastal Ridge 2004 Chardonnay (California) $7. Ripe in fruit and a bit soft and thick in texture, this is a decent country-style Chard that offers what consumers want: Peachy, tropical fruit flavors, oak notes and a creamy texture. **83** —S.H. (8/1/2006)

Coastal Ridge 2002 Chardonnay (California) $7. Drinks rustic in texture and sharp, with citrus and peach flavors and an edge of oak. If you need something quick to serve at your next block party, it's a good candidate. **83** —S.H. (11/15/2004)

Coastal Ridge 1999 Chardonnay (California) $6. Anything remotely resembling true Chardonnay at this price is rare, but here's one that succeeds, if at the most elemental level. It's got proper apple and peach fruit and the requisite amount of vanilla-tinged oak, although probably not from new French barrels. It's a tiny bit sweet, but hey, that's the way people like it. And it's very clean. All of which makes it a great value in Chardonnay. **85 Best Buy** —S.H. (5/1/2001)

Coastal Ridge 2000 Barrel Aged Chardonnay (Napa County) $7. Simple and fruity, with peach and apple flavors and a touch of oak. Basically dry, but the finish is very ripe and honeyed. Acids are okay, making this a nice, inexpensive sipper. **84** —S.H. (12/15/2002)

Coastal Ridge 2004 Gewürztraminer (California) $7. Shows good Gewürz character, with its spicy, ginger and cinnamon-flavored notes of white peaches, vanilla and honey. There's good acidity, too, with a semisweet finish. **84 Best Buy** —S.H. (12/1/2005)

Coastal Ridge 2004 Johannisberg Riesling (California) $7. This is the kind of semisweet wine that vast numbers of Americans enjoy. It's clean, fruity and affordable, with peach and honey flavors. **83 Best Buy** —S.H. (12/1/2005)

Coastal Ridge 2003 Merlot (California) $7. I'm giving this wine a qualified recommendation because the fruit is so pretty. It's all black cherries. Yes, it's rustic, but you can't beat the price. **84 Best Buy** —S.H. (10/1/2005)

Coastal Ridge 2002 Merlot (California) $7. Jammy, juicy and a little sweet, but easy enough, with cherry and cola flavors. **83** —S.H. (4/1/2005)

Coastal Ridge 2001 Merlot (Napa Valley) $7. This is a very likeable wine for its deep flavors of blackberries, plums and mocha, and rich texture. Doesn't have a lot of depth, but you'll be pleasantly surprised at what you get for the price. A fantastic value. **86 Best Buy** —S.H. (12/1/2003)

Coastal Ridge 1998 Merlot (California) $7. It's pretty pale for Merlot and light in aroma, too, with a trace of black cherry or blackberry and oak. The flavors are similarly light and modest. It's very dry and clean and well-made. At this price, it's a good value in Merlot. **84 Best Buy** —S.H. (5/1/2001)

Coastal Ridge 2004 Pinot Grigio (California) $7. I want to like this wine, and it's okay for simple drinking, but it's really kind of watery. Still, if you're not fussy, it's dry, tart and clean. **83** —S.H. (7/1/2005)

Coastal Ridge 2003 Pinot Noir (California) $7. If you like Pinot's dry, silky elegance, this is a good everyday wine. It has a delicate mouthfeel, with crisp acids framing modest cherry, berry and spice flavors in a creamy, oak-tinged texture. **84 Best Buy** —S.H. (12/31/2005)

Coastal Ridge 2003 Shiraz (California) $7. Nilla Wafers or graham crackers accent candied raspberry fruit in this lightweight but enjoyable quaffer. Not complex or concentrated, just good, everyday wine at a bargain price. **85 Best Buy** (9/1/2005)

Coastal Ridge 2001 Shiraz (California) $7. Smells pleasant, with plum, blackberry and oak notes, but turns rather thin and tannic in the mouth. Very dry, with some fruit and herb flavors. **83** —S.H. (12/1/2004)

Coastal Ridge 2000 Shiraz (California) $7. A good wine. It's nicely dry, with crisp acids and adequate tannins. There's a pretty good balance between plum and berry flavors and earthy, herbal ones. It's rough around the edges, with a burnt-rubber quality, but okay drinking for everyday occasions. **84 Best Buy** —S.H. (9/1/2002)

Coastal Ridge 1999 Shiraz (California) $7. This simple, Chianti-like Shiraz shows cedar, blackberry and leather from start to finish. It's medium-weight, and has a dusty-cocoa bouquet, and a sweet, dried-spicy finish. **83** (10/1/2001)

COBBLESTONE

Cobblestone 2002 Cabernet Sauvignon (Napa Valley) $39. A very rich Cabernet, with blackberry, cassis and coffee flavors streaked through with vanilla and smoky oak notes. Dry with fairly thick tannins, this wine is just what you want with broiled steak or lamb chops. **90** —S.H. (6/1/2006)

Cobblestone 2001 Cabernet Sauvignon (Napa Valley) $65. Overripe, with raisiny aromas and a soft texture. Otherwise, there are tasty currant and chocolate flavors. **84** —S.H. (10/1/2004)

Cobblestone 1997 Chardonnay (Arroyo Seco) $23. 87 (6/1/2000)

Cobblestone 2004 Chardonnay (Arroyo Seco) $29. A fresh, clean wine with lively acidity. This Chardonnay has lifted tangerine and pineapple flavors, plus a rich coat of oak that adds vanilla and buttered toast flavors. Drink now. **88** —S.H. (6/1/2006)

Cobblestone 2003 Chardonnay (Arroyo Seco) $34. Creamy smooth, dry and crisp with acids, this wine shows modest peach and coffee flavors, accented with a touch of smoky oak. **85** —S.H. (2/1/2005)

Cobblestone 1999 Chardonnay (Arroyo Seco) $22. Here's a very deeply scented wine. Fruit aromas are peach, ripe pear and tropical fruit, accented by oriental spices. The flavors are massive and persistent. It's as fruity as wine gets, but the balance of crisp acidity, fine tannins and integrated oak creates harmony. It's a bit sweet in the finish. **87** —S.H. (12/31/2001)

Cobblestone 1998 Chardonnay (Arroyo Seco) $23. 86 —S.H. (11/15/2000)

CODORNÍU NAPA

Codorníu Napa NV Grand Reserve Sparkling Blend (Carneros) $45. The aroma's fresh, clean and yeasty on this young nonvintage, brut-style sparkler. In the mouth, it's a little rough in texture, with forward flavors of peaches and limes. Give it a few years to begin softening. **87** —S.H. (6/1/2006)

COEUR D'ALENE CELLARS

Coeur d'Alene Cellars 2003 Syrah (Washington) $28. Solid winemaking delivers a fresh, clean Syrah loaded with blackberry and black cherry fruit. The midpalate is elevated by a streak of tart, citrus peel flavors, then leads into the mother lode of barrel toast, chocolate and roasted coffee. **90** —P.G. (6/1/2006)

Coeur d'Alene Cellars 2002 Syrah (Washington) $25. Blackberries and blueberries on the nose, but not a simple fruit bomb, as it picks up greater depth and spice on the palate, adding layers of pepper and anise to the mix. Full-bodied, yet supple, with hints of coffee on the long finish. **90 Editors' Choice** (9/1/2005)

Coeur d'Alene Cellars 2004 Viognier (Washington) $18. A very good effort with this tricky grape. Along with the stone-fruit flavors are sweeter streaks of cotton candy and marshmallow. But the candied fruit is lively and not cloying or artificial. The finish is long and clean, with a twist of buttered nuts and creamy vanilla. **90** —P.G. (6/1/2006)

Coeur d'Alene Cellars 2004 Sarah's Cuvée Viognier (Washington) $22. This limited cuvée has just a bit more plumpness and roundness than the regular 2004, with good varietal spice and the persistence of an exceptional wine. Peach, apricot, sour lemon candy and even a bit of cinnamon strike the palate, with good balance throughout. **89** —P.G. (6/1/2006)

COL SOLARE

Col Solare 2003 Red Table Wine Bordeaux Blend (Columbia Valley (WA)) $70. This wine, though a step up from recent vintages, continues the brand's reputation as an underperformer. This is a well-made, Cabernet-dominated blend with black cherry, sweet chocolate, soft tannins and a streak of licorice down the middle. **89** —P.G. (12/31/2006)

Col Solare 1999 Red Blend (Columbia Valley (WA)) $70. This partnership between Chateau Ste. Michelle and Antinori is always a quality wine. The '99 is a blend of 70% Cabernet Sauvignon, 25% Merlot, 3% Syrah

USA

and 2% Malbec. The classic cassis and chocolate aromas have an accent of caramel. Flavors include intense black currants and a touch of spice. The wine is as elegant as it is deep, with a long, complex finish. **92 Editors' Choice** —C.S. (12/31/2002)

COLD HEAVEN

Cold Heaven 2001 Le Bon Climate Viognier (Santa Barbara County) $25. Nothing heavenly about this wine. It's too old. Smells vegetal, tastes flat, end of story. **81** —S.H. (8/1/2005)

Cold Heaven 2005 Sanford & Benedict Vineyard Viognier (Santa Barbara County) $35. Sometimes lean, elegant wines appeal to specific tastes, and this is that kind of wine. It's very dry, very acidic, with a steely minerality undergirding fresh pineapple and honeysuckle flavors. This is a carefully calibrated wine, not one of those over-the-top Viogniers. **90** —S.H. (11/15/2006)

Cold Heaven 2002 Sanford & Benedict Vineyard Viognier (Santa Barbara County) $NA. Nose is fairly closed, revealing light hay aromas with some airing. Its size is impressive—muscular, even—but showcases more wood than fruit. One reviewer found noticeable alcohol on the finish. **86** (11/15/2004)

Cold Heaven 2000 Sanford & Benedict Vineyard Viognier (Santa Ynez Valley) $25. Pretty and elegant, though not typically forward like many Viogniers. The wine shows off hints of melon, peach, apricot and spice. Silky and lean on the palate, with a clean finish. **88** —J.M. (12/15/2002)

Cold Heaven 2002 Young Vine Sanford & Benedict Vineyard Viognier (Santa Rita Hills) $18. On the palate, this wine has crisp acids, a minerally feel and a pleasant pear-flavored core. Finishes with good length, and minerally, nutty flavors. **87** (11/15/2004)

COLE BAILEY

Cole Bailey 2003 Sesquipedalian Cabernet Sauvignon (Mendocino) $30. A solid effort. It hits all the correct varietal notes of dryness, full-bodiedness and balanced flavors of black currants, green olives and dried herbs. Has a tannic, sandpapery quality that will play well against lamb. **89** —S.H. (3/1/2006)

Cole Bailey 2004 Sesquipedalian Sauvignon Blanc (Mendocino) $18. Showing great varietal character, this wine is bone dry, high in acids and clean, with intense, long-lasting flavors of lemongrass, fig, melon and vanilla-spice. It's a refreshing sipper and shows California Sauvignon near its best. **90** —S.H. (3/1/2006)

COLEMAN

Coleman 2004 Pinot Gris (Willamette Valley) $14. A fruit forward Pinot Gris, almost lush in the mouth. Pears, sliced orange and hints of tropical fruit are nicely blended, with a soft and fresh finish. **88** —P.G. (2/1/2006)

Coleman 2002 Estate Pinot Noir (Willamette Valley) $19. A strong cinnamon scent, along with orange peel and citrus, stands out. The fruit is juicy blackberry, with a smooth, somewhat lean, tannic finish. **87** (11/1/2004)

Coleman 2002 Estate Reserve Pinot Noir (Willamette Valley) $32. Again, cinnamon dominates the nose, like red-hot candies. The flavors recall a mix of sharp candies: wintergreen, cola, and sassafras; all heat and spice. **86** (11/1/2004)

COLGIN

Colgin 2003 Cariad Bordeaux Blend (Napa Valley) $225. A Bordeaux blend based on Cabernet Sauvignon and Merlot, the grapes for this stunning wine came from David Abreu's vineyard in the St. Helena foothills. It's very complex, softer, more open and approachable than Colgin's 100% Cabs, with a flamboyant spectrum of cherries, framboise, cocoa, violets, gingerbread and spices framed in supple, fine tannins. Beautiful, a feminine wine of great beauty. Drink now through 2015. **95** —S.H. (9/1/2006)

Colgin 2003 IX Estate Red Wine Bordeaux Blend (Napa Valley) $175. From the winery's estate vineyard, high up on Pritchard Hill above the Silverado Trail, comes this spectacular Cab-based masterpiece. The color is purple-black, and massively saturated. Very intricate, complex, totally enjoyable, almost perfect. Like a great Pauillac, this monumental wine announces cassis, blackberry, cigar box, pencil lead, spice and cedar flavors that go on and on. Very tannic, but so beautiful, and amazingly rich. Decant if you're drinking now, or open anytime through 2020. **98 Cellar Selection** —S.H. (9/1/2006)

Colgin 2003 Herb Lamb Vineyard Cabernet Sauvignon (Napa Valley) $225. Almost black in color. Flavors are of blackberry, cassis, Provençal herbs; the 100% new oak adds rich toast and char notes. Tannins are brilliant, dense and fluffy. Grown at the base of Howell Mountain, this is classic mountain Cab, beautiful now, fleshy and fat, but with a 20-year lifespan. **95** —S.H. (9/1/2006)

Colgin 1999 Herb Lamb Vineyard Cabernet Sauvignon (Napa Valley) $150. Aromas lean toward black cherry, chocolate and herbs, which sally forth on the palate serving up more dense fruit, licorice, coffee and beautiful toast flavors. Tannins are smooth, supple and ripe. Long, lush and decadent on the finish. **96** —J.M. (6/1/2002)

Colgin 2003 Tychson Hill Vineyard Cabernet Sauvignon (Napa Valley) $250. Like Colgin's great Herb Lamb Cabernet, this is 100% varietal, 100% new oak. It's a unique, different sort of Cab, opening with an iodine, Islay Scotch, sea-salt scent that turns surprisingly rich and fruity in the mouth, sweet in chocolate and extraordinarily ripe black currants. This very young wine needs time to show its best. Drink 2009–2015. **93 Cellar Selection** —S.H. (9/1/2006)

Colgin 2003 IX Estate Syrah (Napa Valley) $125. Colgin's first Syrah, and the first from winemaker Mark Aubert, the wine is very dark and glyceriney, suggesting massive extract. Opens with an exciting blast of white pepper leading to baked cherry pie, leather, truffle and complex earthy scents. In the mouth, it's very fruity and chocolaty, with tons of toasty new oak. Yet there is something dramatic here. This is a Syrah to carefully watch in future vintages. **92** —S.H. (11/15/2006)

Colgin 2002 IX Estate Syrah (Napa Valley) $125. Not that explosive in flavor, but what a mouthfeel. Tannic and richly textured, yet lush at the same time, this is a densely packed wine that should blossom in time to reveal more of its blackberry, tar and spice flavors. A great first effort from owner Ann Colgin and winemaker Mark Aubert. **91** (9/1/2005)

COLLEGE CELLARS

College Cellars 2003 Minick Vineyards Syrah (Yakima Valley) $18. Some tasters will dislike this wine, while others will enjoy it. You might find it the proper blend of herb and spice to go with the tart red berries, or you might find it overtly vegetal—it will depend on your tolerance for green stuff in your wine. **85** (9/1/2005)

COLLIER FALLS

Collier Falls 2001 Hillside Estate Cabernet Sauvignon (Dry Creek Valley) $36. Gritty tannins mark this young wine. It has a sandpapery feel, but underneath all that are impressive flavors. Blackberries, cherries and coffee really shine on the finish. Good now; better in a few years. **88** —S.H. (10/1/2004)

Collier Falls 2000 Hillside Estate Cabernet Sauvignon (Dry Creek Valley) $36. Brilliantly flavored, with lush flavors of blackcurrants and cassis, clearly a classic Cabernet Sauvignon. Tannins are opulent and thick and should hold the wine for several years. There is a youthful, peppery bitterness throughout that will soften in time. **89** —S.H. (12/31/2003)

Collier Falls 2002 Zinfandel (Dry Creek Valley) $26. One of the fruitier Zins around, or maybe the light tannins let the fruit shine through. Either way, it's a flavorful wine, showing blackberry, plum and cherry flavors, with dry, plum skin-bitter tannins. This is a good, all-purpose Zin. **87** —S.H. (11/1/2005)

Collier Falls 2002 Zinfandel (Dry Creek Valley) $26. Made claret style, which is to say, balanced and harmonious despite high alcohol, with no one-element dominating. Pretty cherry, blackberry and cocoa flavors are wrapped in smooth tannins, and the wine is perfectly dry. **89** —S.H. (12/31/2004)

Collier Falls 2000 Zinfandel (Dry Creek Valley) $26. 86 —S.H. (11/1/2002)

Collier Falls 2001 Private Reserve Zinfandel (Dry Creek Valley) $28. Light-textured with bright acidity that highlights the cherry, berry, citrus and herb center. **83** (11/1/2003)

Collier Falls 2000 Private Reserve Zinfandel (Dry Creek Valley) $26. Quintessential old-vine Zin, a rich, thick, concentrated wine oozing with all kinds of flavors and palate impressions. Blackberry, cherry, tobacco, white pepper, cinnamon and rich, decadent chocolate mousse drink fully dry. But the tannins are like wild horses, beautiful and untamed. **89** — S.H. (9/1/2003)

Collier Falls 1998 Private Reserve Zinfandel (Dry Creek Valley) $21. Well-made, with clean, bright fruit and lots of pretty new oak. The wine is beautifully balanced, elegant with a long, rich, toasty finish. Fairly light fruit in this vintage, but well handled and perfectly showcased. **91 Editors' Choice** —P.G. (3/1/2001)

COLUMBIA CREST

Columbia Crest 1996 Reserve Bordeaux Blend (Columbia Valley (WA)) $25. 90 —P.G. (6/1/2000)

Columbia Crest 2001 Walter Clore Reserve Red Bordeaux Blend (Columbia Valley (WA)) $35. This sophisticated blend offers complex flavors of mixed red fruits, nicely textured and layered. You can pick out distinct pomegranate, cranberry, red berry and cherry flavors; there's nothing monolithic about it. There are also some hints of olive and herb, and substantial tannins. **90** —P.G. (4/1/2005)

Columbia Crest 2000 Reserve Cabernet Blend (Columbia Valley (WA)) $30. Fat, open and forward, this is a very accessible wine, with friendly fruit, easy tannins, and plenty of coffee-flavored toasty new barrel. But the juice itself does not rise to the level of the previous reserves; beneath the broadly friendly flavors is a fairly light wine. **88** —P.G. (1/1/2004)

Columbia Crest 1997 Cabernet Sauvignon (Columbia Valley (WA)) $9. 88 Best Buy —P.G. (6/1/2000)

Columbia Crest 1996 Cabernet Sauvignon (Columbia Valley (WA)) $11. 89 (11/15/1999)

Columbia Crest 1996 Estate Series Cabernet Sauvignon (Columbia Valley (WA)) $15. 88 —P.G. (6/1/2000)

Columbia Crest 2003 Grand Estates Cabernet Sauvignon (Columbia Valley (WA)) $11. Firm and slightly chalky, this features light plum, blueberry and mocha components. There's a hint of soapiness, and some herbal roughness in the finish. 150,000 cases. **87** —P.G. (12/31/2006)

Columbia Crest 2002 Grand Estates Cabernet Sauvignon (Columbia Valley (WA)) $11. Bigger, chewier than the Two Vines, this shows more concentrated cassis and very firm tannins; there are some early hints of herb and olive. Overall there is simply power and punch. **89 Best Buy** —P.G. (4/1/2005)

Columbia Crest 2001 Grand Estates Cabernet Sauvignon (Columbia Valley (WA)) $11. A lovely blend of fruit from the Wahluke Slope, which lends aromatics and steely structure, and the Horse Heaven Hills, which gives it a broad, sweet core of jammy preserves. Very smooth, accessible and surprisingly focused, this wine is perfectly aged and blended for near-term enjoyment. **87** —P.G. (7/1/2004)

Columbia Crest 1999 Grand Estates Cabernet Sauvignon (Columbia Valley (WA)) $11. This has really ripe blackberry and cherry flavors, soft tannins, a nice fat mouthfeel and hints of darker roasted stuff. Big, smooth and lush, it gathers power and finishes with a big swoop of meaty, fruity, fat flavor. Not heavy, but delicious and beautifully balanced. **89 Best Buy** —P.G. (9/1/2002)

Columbia Crest 2003 Reserve Cabernet Sauvignon (Columbia Valley (WA)) $30. Firm, chewy and tannic, this newly released wine takes a while to open up. It shows a pleasing sweet cocoa and berry core of fruit that expands into coffee, toast, black tea and even a bit of cola. The finish feels like a bit of fresh, rain-soaked earth—not unpleasant. Overall, though very young, the wine shows good potential. **89** —P.G. (12/31/2006)

Columbia Crest 2002 Reserve Cabernet Sauvignon (Columbia Valley (WA)) $30. Aromatic with black olive, herb and cocoa wrapped around tight raspberry/cassis fruit. The fruit is nicely concentrated, then splays into a broad, chocolaty, softly tannic midpalate. At this stage of life the wine remains angular, woody and unintegrated; with another six to twelve months in bottle it could improve its score by a point or two. **89** —P.G. (12/15/2005)

Columbia Crest 2001 Reserve Cabernet Sauvignon (Columbia Valley (WA)) $30. This shows a remarkable Bordeaux like structure, with dry tannins, some well-balanced herbal/leaf elements, hints of tobacco and spice, and a lingering, complex finish. This really resonates with leafy cut tobacco aromas. **91** —P.G. (4/1/2005)

Columbia Crest 1999 Reserve Cabernet Sauvignon (Columbia Valley (WA)) $28. The nose is big, fat and forward, showing plenty of plush vanilla and sweet cream, matched with ripe black cherry fruit. Oodles of rich fruit, fat, creamy, buttery oak and a silky, unctuous mouthfeel coat the palate. This is a consumer-friendly, forward, ripe and luscious style of wine. **92** —P.G. (9/1/2002)

Columbia Crest 1998 Reserve Cabernet Sauvignon (Columbia Valley (WA)) $28. The price to quality quotient of this winery never fails to amaze. Here is top of the line treatment for a mid-level price. Supple, silky and delicious, the wine smells and tastes of mint, chocolate and vanilla, wrapped around seamless red fruit. Spicy and crisply defined, it is long and satisfying. **91** —P.G. (12/31/2001)

Columbia Crest 2003 Two Vines Cabernet Sauvignon (Columbia Valley (WA)) $8. Smooth and very pretty with plenty of mouth-pleasing cherry, blueberry and raspberry fruit. The tannins are beautifully managed, showing hints of baking chocolate; the flavor mix, palate weight and overall balance are great for an $8 dollar Cabernet. **88 Best Buy** —P.G. (6/1/2006)

Columbia Crest 2002 Two Vines Cabernet Sauvignon (Columbia Valley (WA)) $8. In keeping with the Two Vines style, this shows plenty of bright cherry fruit; but that's not the end of it. In fact it is surprisingly deep, polished and supple with good, juicy fruit and real concentration. There's nothing vegetal, or earthy, or rough; it's a smooth and polished effort but not at all spineless. Where else in the world can they make an $8 cab this good? **88 Best Buy** —P.G. (4/1/2005)

Columbia Crest 2001 Two Vines Cabernet Sauvignon (Columbia Valley (WA)) $8. This is a very nice bottle, firm and showing moderately plump plum and cassis fruit. There is a sense of layering, and hints of anise and mineral and mocha through the midpalate. Finishes clean and surprisingly lengthy. **86 Best Buy** —P.G. (7/1/2004)

Columbia Crest 1999 Cabernet Sauvignon-Merlot (Columbia Valley (WA)) $30. It's made from small lots, cordoned off in the winery and ultimately selected for the final blend, in this year 51% Cabernet and 49% Merlot. The nose has a pleasing texture; along with the fruit, there are hints of mineral, sandalwood, anise and a suggestion of cilantro. Seamless and surprisingly soft, it's back-loaded with fruit flavor and plenty of oak. **92** —P.G. (9/1/2002)

Columbia Crest 2000 Walter Clore Private Reserve Red Cabernet Sauvignon-Merlot (Columbia Valley (WA)) $35. Well made, with sweet fruit flavors accenting berries and hints of cherry preserves. The wine is balanced and even, and hints at tobacco/herbal notes, though it lacks the depth of the '99. It's definitely made for near term consumption as this was a friendly but fairly light vintage. **89** —P.G. (1/1/2004)

Columbia Crest 2000 Chardonnay (Columbia Valley (WA)) $8. A strong, spicy nose opens into a clean and bracing wine, with a firm structure, full flavors and ripe, fresh fruit. It's not as over the top and user-friendly as the enormously popular 1998 and 1999 versions, but it's a darn fine every day go-to bottle. **87** —P.G. (2/1/2002)

Columbia Crest 1999 Chardonnay (Columbia Valley (WA)) $12. Columbia Crest makes three Chardonnays, of which this is the least expensive. It boasts assertive, somewhat herbaceous aromas of peach and spice; the fruit is clean, forward and zesty. It displays a lot of character in a vivid style that showcases Washington's intense fruit and lip-smacking acids. **86** (6/1/2001)

Columbia Crest 1998 Chardonnay (Columbia Valley (WA)) $8. 87 Best Buy —P.G. (6/1/2000)

Columbia Crest 2003 Grand Estates Chardonnay (Columbia Valley (WA)) $12. Big, bright and round, with a buttery, oaky mix of tropical fruits and plenty of sweet, toasty oak. Very well made in a rich, round, approachable style. **88 Best Buy** —P.G. (6/1/2006)

Columbia Crest 2002 Grand Estates Chardonnay (Columbia Valley (WA)) $11. This is a blocky, chiseled, mainstream style, with big, chunky fruit and toasty oak. Still rough around the edges, it has more weight and concentration than the less expensive but oh-so-buttery "Two Vines" bottling. **87** —*P.G. (7/1/2004)*

Columbia Crest 2002 Grand Estates Chardonnay (Columbia Valley (WA)) $11. Bigger, with more obvious oak than the CC "regular", this gets special treatment (hand-stirred for nine months once a week) and 1/4 new oak. It's nicely integrated, big and buttery, with pleasing layers of caramelized sugar and baked apple. A home run. **90 Best Buy** —*P.G. (4/1/2005)*

Columbia Crest 2000 Grand Estates Chardonnay (Columbia Valley (WA)) $11. The Grand Estates lineup from Columbia Crest is always a leader in the Chardonnay and Merlot categories. This offers intense fruit and a decent amount of new oak, bundled into a big, ripe wine with plenty of pineapple/butterscotch power, and enough firm acid to knit it all together. **89 Best Buy** —*P.G. (2/1/2002)*

Columbia Crest 1999 Grand Estates Chardonnay (Columbia Valley (WA)) $13. The Grand Estates is CC's midpriced offering, and the Chardonnay sees plenty of oak and sur lie aging. Rich, toasted-nut aromas underscore firm apple and pear fruit. The custardy texture is a treat. **89 Best Buy** —*P.G. (6/1/2001)*

Columbia Crest 2004 Reserve Chardonnay (Horse Heaven Hills) $30. This is big, round and creamy—a California style of Chardonnay—with a dusting of spice and baker's chocolate. The sweet, appealing barrel flavors include toast and buttery caramel; the fruit seems quite secondary. The difference that Washington fruit makes is the natural acid that lifts the wine and keeps it from getting top-heavy with oak. **89** —*P.G. (12/31/2006)*

Columbia Crest 2003 Reserve Chardonnay (Columbia Valley (WA)) $30. Soft and broad, with rich flavors of butter cookie, toasted coconut, baked pear and light citrus. Just 500 cases were made. **88** —*P.G. (12/15/2005)*

Columbia Crest 2002 Reserve Chardonnay (Columbia Valley (WA)) $30. The biggest and richest of the three CC chards, this is decadently rich, supple and smooth. It tastes lightly of butter; more of butterscotch. Powerful and expressive. **90** —*P.G. (4/1/2005)*

Columbia Crest 1998 Reserve Chardonnay (Columbia Valley (WA)) $18. This top-of-the-line Chardonnay from Columbia Crest gets extra time in barrel and bottle, and comes from the much-heralded 1998 vintage. It's a rich, creamy style, with less obvious buttery oak than the Grand Estates, but more complexity and a thicker, more complex feel to it. Flavors mix fruit, wood, spice and herb evenly. It has a comforting feeling of weight to it; it's not just up-front, aggressive flavors. **90 Editors' Choice** —*P.G. (6/1/2001)*

Columbia Crest 1997 Reserve Chardonnay (Columbia Valley (WA)) $18. **88** —*P.G. (6/1/2000)*

Columbia Crest 2003 Two Vines Chardonnay (Columbia Valley (WA)) $8. Whoa! 400,000 cases of this wine are being released, an enormous production for a Washington wine. Better yet, it's good. Smooth, plump and quite fruity, just soft enough (from partial malolactic fermentation), not too buttery, but just a hint of butterscotch. In short, it tastes like real wine, not microwave popcorn, and has some lasting power. **88 Best Buy** —*P.G. (6/1/2006)*

Columbia Crest 2002 Two Vines Chardonnay (Columbia Valley (WA)) $9. Yet another re-tool for this winery; Two Vines replaces the Columbia Valley tier. Smooth and flavorful, this Chardonnay sports citrus/tropical fruit, suggestions of oak, and medium acids. Plenty of flavor in a balanced, forward, easy-drinking yet meaty effort. **88 Best Buy** —*P.G. (5/1/2004)*

Columbia Crest 2002 Two Vines Chardonnay (Columbia Valley (WA)) $8. Fruity and soft and approachable, a mass-produced wine that still shows hand-crafted flavors. For the price this may well be the country's top chardonnay. **88 Best Buy** —*P.G. (4/1/2005)*

Columbia Crest 2002 Two Vines Chardonnay (Columbia Valley (WA)) $8. Aggressive scents of buttered popcorn lead into a soft, buttery, forward and vanilla-drenched Chardonnay. A popular style at a great price; this is a sure crowd pleaser. **87 Best Buy** —*P.G. (7/1/2004)*

Columbia Crest 2000 Gewürztraminer (Columbia Valley (WA)) $8. This wine walks the line between sweet and tart, showing pumped up fruit in front and vivid, spicy highlights following. The fruit flavors run from pears to pineapple, and overall it's a balanced and juicy bottle, perfect for Pacific Rim cooking. **87** —*P.G. (12/31/2001)*

Columbia Crest 1999 Gewürztraminer (Columbia Valley (WA)) $8. 86 Best Buy —*P.G. (11/15/2000)*

Columbia Crest 2004 Two Vines Gewürztraminer (Columbia Valley (WA)) $8. Off-dry and spicy, with underlying peach and grapefruit flavors. There's plenty of acid; maybe just a bit too much unless that's your style. Only a somewhat thin, chalky finish keeps the score from ratcheting up a notch or two. **86 Best Buy** —*P.G. (6/1/2006)*

Columbia Crest 2003 Two Vines Gewürztraminer (Columbia Valley (WA)) $8. Fragrant yet tangy, with flat-out lovely fruit that showcases the candied citrus side of the grape. Penetrating and long. **88 Best Buy** —*P.G. (6/1/2005)*

Columbia Crest 2001 Johannisberg Riesling (Columbia Valley (WA)) $7. A wonderfully fragrant nose mixes scents of fresh fruits and blossoms, with a sweet and tart flavor profile. These are very user friendly flavors, ripe and round, with more fatness than most Washington Rieslings, especially at this price. **87 Best Buy** —*P.G. (9/1/2002)*

Columbia Crest 1997 Merlot (Columbia Valley (WA)) $11. 88 Best Buy —*P.G. (6/1/2000)*

Columbia Crest 1998 Merlot (Columbia Valley (WA)) $11. Ripe aromas and flavors of blackcurrants, roasted coffeebean, mocha and polished, smoky oak dominate this elegant, supple wine. It's powerful, but understated. Dry, with dusty tannins, it's drinkable now. **89 Best Buy** —*S.H. (12/31/2003)*

Columbia Crest 1996 Estate Series Merlot (Columbia Valley (WA)) $16. Flavors of plum, cherry, cassis, chalky earth, smoke and bell pepper. Still tight and chewy, with suggestions that the fruit from this difficult vintage didn't attain full ripeness. A good effort from a subpar year, marked by a hint of brett on the finish. **87** —*P.G. (8/19/2003)*

Columbia Crest 2003 Grand Estates Merlot (Columbia Valley (WA)) $11. With 200,000 cases produced, this is the benchmark Merlot for the state, if not the country. The newest release needs a bit more time in the bottle; it has been stiffened up with the addition of Cabernet Sauvignon and a dash of Cab Franc, and it is showing its tannic, herb and olive components currently. Some cherry and strawberry fruit is lurking below, along with green tea flavors in the finish. **86 Best Buy** —*P.G. (12/15/2005)*

Columbia Crest 2001 Grand Estates Merlot (Columbia Valley (WA)) $11. Smooth, supple, full and ripe, with a classic chocolate/cherry character. The merlot hits the palate a bit broader than the cab, which is more precise but not as weighty. It is unquestionably is a very seductive wine, broad yet medium deep, with dark berry and chocolatey flavors wrapped together, finishing with a very French hint of herb. **89 Best Buy** —*P.G. (4/1/2005)*

Columbia Crest 2000 Grand Estates Merlot (Columbia Valley (WA)) $11. You'll find this on wine lists all over America and for good reason; it's ripe and sweet and slides down easily, yet offers substantial flavors of plum and sour cherry fruit. Not a blockbuster, but solid and very flavorful, with a meaty, spicy finish. **87 Best Buy** —*P.G. (1/1/2004)*

Columbia Crest 1999 Grand Estates Merlot (Columbia Valley (WA)) $11. This budget wine has sweet fruit and soft tannins, along with surprising concentration and length. Offsetting a hint of stemminess are generous, varietally true flavors, and a rich, meaty nose that suggests beef and coffee. **87 Best Buy** —*P.G. (9/1/2002)*

Columbia Crest 2003 Reserve Merlot (Columbia Valley (WA)) $30. This is barely Merlot—just 75%—and the rest is filled in with Cab Sauvignon, Cab Franc, Petit Verdot and Syrah. This definitely bumps up the tannins and brightens the natural berry flavors. Tart fruit and creamy vanilla finish with softly astringent tannins. Nothing spectacular, but very smooth drinking. **88** —*P.G. (12/31/2006)*

Columbia Crest 2002 Reserve Merlot (Columbia Valley (WA)) $30. A substantial, impressive Merlot, tannic and oaky. The palate impression is thick, smoky and well-endowed with oak. The fruit is dark and meaty, black cherry with hints of herb, chocolate and spice. Big and well-balanced, this may be the best of all the Ste. Michelle group's 2002 Merlots. **90** —*P.G. (12/15/2005)*

Columbia Crest 2001 Reserve Merlot (Columbia Valley (WA)) $30. Tight, dry, and tannic, the flavor mixes good, clean, well-ripened fruit and lots of woodsy, leafy nuances. There are some darker streaks of smoke and char, and beautiful tannin integration. **91** —*P.G. (4/1/2005)*

Columbia Crest 2000 Reserve Merlot (Columbia Valley (WA)) $30. This is a ripe, chocolatey wine with broad flavors and even broader appeal. It coats the mouth with tart cherry and berry flavors, and the tannins, smooth and chocolatey, have a pleasing graininess that suggests ground espresso. **88** —*P.G. (1/1/2004)*

Columbia Crest 1999 Reserve Merlot (Columbia Valley (WA)) $28. This is just the second vintage for the winery's new, high-end reserve wines, and reflects the vintage. Tight, compact and muscular, it is packed with dark black cherry and blackberry fruit, hard tannins and a robust structure. At the moment it is still recovering from its recent bottling; the score could rise substantially. **90** —*P.G. (9/1/2002)*

Columbia Crest 2002 Two Vines Merlot (Columbia Valley (WA)) $8. This is the gold standard for $8 Merlot from anywhere in the world. Pretty fruit is highlighted by bright raspberry scents. Smooth and creamy in the mouth, with lovely flavors of sweet cherry and milk chocolate. **88 Best Buy** —*P.G. (6/1/2006)*

Columbia Crest 2001 Two Vines Merlot (Columbia Valley (WA)) $8. Bright raspberry scents, with a fresh and lifted aspect that adds to its immediate appeal. The blend includes 10% Cab Franc and 10% Cab Sauvignon, a lot of complexity in an $8 wine. This is substantial, layered, with a plummy, herbal, fairly tannic middle and plenty of weight in the follow-through. **88 Best Buy** —*P.G. (12/15/2004)*

Columbia Crest 1999 Merlot-Cabernet Sauvignon (Columbia Valley (WA)) $10. The blend is half Merlot, 35% Cabernet Franc and 15% Cabernet Sauvignon. A rich nose shows sweet, black cherry fruit; the wine has got big flavors that are nonetheless pretty, with soft, understated tannins and high acids. It adds up to a very accessible, delicious bottle of red. **87 Best Buy** —*P.G. (6/1/2002)*

Columbia Crest 2002 Two Vines Merlot-Cabernet Sauvignon (Columbia Valley (WA)) $8. How amazing it is to find a wine of this caliber, with some nice age on it, selling at this price. There is plenty of color, and scents of bramble, cherry, tobacco, ash, bark and smoke. In short, this is a party wine, smooth and delicious, with generous cherry, blueberry and raspberry fruit, ripe tannins and perfectly balanced acids. Put this into a blind tasting with some $30 Bordeaux blends from elsewhere, and you are sure to amaze your friends. 250,000 cases produced. **88 Best Buy** —*P.G. (11/15/2006)*

Columbia Crest 2001 Two Vines Merlot-Cabernet Sauvignon (Columbia Valley (WA)) $8. Time was when cheap Washington Cab-Merlot blends rarely escaped the "veggies", but those days are happily over. There's plenty of sweet cherry fruit here, with some herbal and dill notes to be sure, but overall delivering a lot of ripe flavor for the price. **85** —*P.G. (7/1/2004)*

Columbia Crest 2005 Grand Estates Pinot Grigio (Columbia Valley (WA)) $11. Light, crisp and bracing, this classy effort sets the standard for affordable Columbia Valley Pinot Grigio. The vivid nature of Washington fruit comes through in the fresh flavors of pear and apple, juicy and lucid. Hints of citrus blossom can be found in the nose, and the restrained, 12.5% alcohol gives this elegant wine an almost European polish. Vibrant acidity is the key to the Washington style, bright and juicy and inviting. 5,000 cases produced. **87** —*P.G. (12/31/2006)*

Columbia Crest 1997 Reserve Red Blend (Columbia Valley (WA)) $24. The blend here is 39% Cabernet Sauvignon, 39% Merlot and 22% Cabernet Franc. The wine is dark, dense, what some call "brooding." It is firm and tart up front, but stuffed with layers of oak and herb and cherry/berry flavor. It's too clean to be Bordeaux, too tart to be Californian; it's a classic, Columbia Valley style Washington Cabernet, built to last. **90** —*P.G. (6/1/2001)*

Columbia Crest 1998 Reserve Red Wine Red Blend (Columbia Valley (WA)) $32. The top of the line for Columbia Crest, this powerful, classy blend

is a very polished effort. It leads with rich, textured scents of ripe red and black fruits, accented with toast and vanilla. There are some lovely spices—pepper and fines herbes—that add welcome interest. Overall it's lush and mouth-filling, built to age but delicious right away. **92 Editors' Choice** —*P.G. (12/31/2001)*

Columbia Crest 2003 Walter Clore Private Reserve Red Blend (Columbia Valley (WA)) $35. Warm and fruity, the Walter Clore bottling delivers soft flavors of berry, cherry and vanilla cream, from a blend that is roughly two-thirds Cabernet, one-third Merlot. The pretty fruit seems to hit a wall of tannin, leaving an impression of a two-part wine that lacks the satiny seamlessness of its better peers. **88** —*P.G. (12/31/2006)*

Columbia Crest 2002 Walter Clore Reserve Red Blend (Columbia Valley (WA)) $35. The house style is readily apparent here: red fruits, whiffs of cocoa, light herb and a hint of pickle barrel. Tastes good, comes together well, but hard to distinguish from the reserve cab, which seems to have just a bit more stuffing. **88** —*P.G. (12/15/2005)*

Columbia Crest 2005 Grand Estates Riesling (Columbia Valley (WA)) $11. This is the mid-tier Riesling for Columbia Crest, a sensational wine that captures everything that is distinctive and noteworthy about Washington fruit. Fragrant and loaded with floral aromatics, it carries persistent orange blossom and lemon candy scents and flavors into a lush mid-palate that touches on tropical papaya and mango. The off-dry residual sweetness plumps it up but is mostly masked by the natural acids, keeping this very food-friendly. 5,000 cases produced. **89 Best Buy** —*P.G. (12/31/2006)*

Columbia Crest 2005 Two Vines Riesling (Columbia Valley (WA)) $8. A tangy, green apple flavored Riesling, with some light melon fruit also. It shows more varietal character than the '04 and has a nice juicy pop to the midpalate, despite the relatively high residual sugar. **87 Best Buy** —*P.G. (10/1/2006)*

Columbia Crest 2004 Two Vines Riesling (Columbia Valley (WA)) $8. This is a nice, entry-level Riesling, with fairly broad, light flavors of peach and apricot. It veers close, however, to tasting like generic grape juice, while most Two Vines wines, despite their budget pricing, are solidly varietal. **86** —*P.G. (6/1/2005)*

Columbia Crest 2003 Two Vines Riesling (Columbia Valley (WA)) $8. A new line for value leader Columbia Crest, this exceptionally fragrant, off-dry Riesling bursts with honeysuckle scents and tropical fruit flavors. There's enough crispness to support the residual sugar and keep the wine poised and vivid. **89 Best Buy** —*P.G. (7/1/2004)*

Columbia Crest 1998 Sauvignon Blanc (Columbia Valley (WA)) $6. 88 Best Buy —*P.G. (6/1/2000)*

Columbia Crest 2005 Grand Estates Sauvignon Blanc (Columbia Valley (WA)) $11. Crafted to showcase, not hide, the grape's lightly grassy herbaceousness, this bracing Sauvignon Blanc manages the clever trick of being both restrained and penetrating. The complex mix of grapefruit, lemon, lime and pineapple fruit flavors is set against racy acids and that hint of grassiness. A small portion of the final blend was aged in oak, adding complexity and softening the edges. You won't find a better match for goat and sheep cheeses. 5,000 cases produced. **88 Best Buy** —*P.G. (12/31/2006)*

Columbia Crest 2004 Two Vines Sauvignon Blanc (Columbia Valley (WA)) $8. There is nothing subdued here, no effort to make a sweet, tropical, California-style Sauvignon Blanc. Grassy and penetrating, this is more like New Zealand than Napa, a snappy effort with green apple, lime, citrus and gooseberry. A great seafood wine. **88 Best Buy** —*P.G. (6/1/2006)*

Columbia Crest 2002 Two Vines Sauvignon Blanc (Columbia Valley (WA)) $8. Crisp and clean, nice and refreshing, with plump, tangy green and yellow fruits. Apples and limes up front, while good crisp acids keep it lifted and great with food. **87 Best Buy** —*P.G. (4/1/2005)*

Columbia Crest 1999 Sémillon (Columbia Valley (WA)) $9. Columbia Crest always does a fine job with this budget grape. The accent is on green-apple and green-berry fruit, with suggestions of herb and spice filling in the flavor interest. It's a high acid, food-ready wine that will accompany a wide variety of shellfish, oily steakfish and some cream-sauced pastas. **86** —*P.G. (6/1/2001)*

Columbia Crest 1998 Reserve Ice Wine Sémillon (Columbia Valley (WA))
$28. 92 —P.G. (6/1/2000)

Columbia Crest 1997 Reserve Late Harvest Sémillon (Columbia Valley (WA)) $23. 84 —P.G. (6/1/2000)

Columbia Crest 2000 Sémillon-Chardonnay (Columbia Valley (WA)) $6.
The blend, 70/30, favors Sémillon over Chardonnay. A good thing, which makes for a distinctive, refreshing wine, not just a watered-down Chardonnay. There's a strong streak of fennel running through the clean, lemony fruit. Best enjoyed chilled, with shellfish. 87 —P.G. (2/1/2002)

Columbia Crest 2002 Two Vines Sémillon-Chardonnay (Columbia Valley (WA)) $8. Borrowing a trick from the Australians, Washington's biggest winery takes one of this state's strengths—the always overlooked Sémillon—and marries it to some high-acid Chardonnay, to the benefit of both. Clean, fresh, untampered with, this is content to display good fruit, crisp acids and a polished, immaculate, mouth-cleaning finish. 87 Best Buy —P.G. (12/15/2005)

Columbia Crest 2002 Grand Estates Shiraz (Columbia Valley (WA)) $11.
Very fruity, youthful and packed with brambly berry flavors. Tart, tangy and loaded with berries and cherries, this racy, snappy effort shows surprising depth and weight for its modest price point. There's a nice lick of vanilla in the soft, lush finish. 90 Best Buy —P.G. (10/1/2006)

Columbia Crest 2003 Two Vines Shiraz (Columbia Valley (WA)) $8. Slightly candied, bright cherry fruit and a healthy dose of vanilla give this easy-to-drink Shiraz all the prerequisites for commercial success. The creamy mouthfeel shows very little tannin, while the juicy, mouthwatering finish picks up enough hints of complexity to keep it interesting. With 100,000 cases made, should be plenty easy to find. 85 Best Buy (9/1/2005)

Columbia Crest 2002 Two Vines Shiraz (Columbia Valley (WA)) $8. Opens with a big nose and classic varietal fruit scents of blackberry and pepper. The sweet fruit tastes like fresh-picked, ripe berries; clean and polished, forward and expressive, but in a lighter vein. Vanilla and blueberries light up the finish. 88 Best Buy —P.G. (4/1/2005)

Columbia Crest 2002 Grand Estates Syrah (Columbia Valley (WA)) $11.
Delicious boysenberry fruit dominates this wine, but it doesn't carry through very far. It needs breathing time; when given a few hours, it does seem to expand. Overall, it's a pure and sweet and delicious expression of syrah, giving lots of flavor for the price. 88 Best Buy —P.G. (4/1/2005)

Columbia Crest 2001 Grand Estates Syrah (Columbia Valley (WA)) $11.
This lovely, spicy wine seamlessly mixes bright berry fruit and smooth chocolate, with hints of earth and pepper. There are better Syrahs made in Washington (including CC's own reserve), but you'll have to pay three times as much. 88 Best Buy —P.G. (5/1/2004)

Columbia Crest 2004 Reserve Syrah (Columbia Valley (WA)) $30. Perhaps a bit bottle-shocked from its recent transportation, this Reserve Syrah resisted my attempts to pry open its fruit. Soft and pleasantly oaky, it hinted at cocoa and mocha over orange peel and blueberry fruit, but the fruit remained dumbed down and so the score must remain dumbed down as well. 87 —P.G. (12/31/2006)

Columbia Crest 2003 Reserve Syrah (Columbia Valley (WA)) $30. A bit of a disappointment after the exceptional 2002, this young, hard wine brings scents of citrus, white pepper and green coffee beans into play, with rather aggressive notes of American oak. The pickle-barrel character is a bit of a detraction, and the wine is tart, chewy and still awkward with unresolved tannins. Needs time. 87 —P.G. (12/15/2005)

Columbia Crest 2002 Reserve Syrah (Columbia Valley (WA)) $30. Dense, deep and delicious. Among a fine group of CC reserves, this gets my vote for the best of all. Inky, tannic yet beautifully, classically varietal. Really dense, it delivers concentrated boysenberry and black fruit flavors, and the co-fermentation with viognier adds aromatic orange peel/citrus rind notes. Lively, perfumed and complex. 91 —P.G. (4/1/2005)

Columbia Crest 2001 Reserve Syrah (Columbia Valley (WA)) $30. Much more concentrated and powerfully fragrant than the previous vintage, this is a keeper. It's sinfully dark and bursting with pepper, coffee and berry scents. In the mouth it explodes with vivid fruit intensity, yet

retains an elegance, keeping alcohol at a sensible 14%. 90 Editors' Choice —P.G. (1/1/2004)

Columbia Crest 2000 Reserve Syrah (Columbia Valley (WA)) $28. This is the sixth or seventh vintage of their Syrah, and it hits the palate with tangy, tart red berry fruit. The spice and pepper suggest Syrah; otherwise it is a dead ringer for Dry Creek Zin. The blend includes about 8% Grenache, which adds to the forward fruit intensity. But it's not just fresh and forward and fruity, it is also balanced and lingers into a chocolatey farewell. 89 —P.G. (9/1/2002)

Columbia Crest 1999 Reserve Syrah (Columbia Valley (WA)) $28. The reserve from this well-known winery is, as you would expect, a textbook version of Washington Syrah, the state's newest love affair. Dense and dark, with smooth cherry/chocolate flavors across the palate, it comes on full and soft, seductive. There are spicy berry highlights, very dry tannins, and lots of chocolatey oak. 89 —P.G. (6/1/2002)

Columbia Crest 1998 Reserve Syrah (Columbia Valley (WA)) $28. Jammy, with blueberry, cream and soy notes, the nose of this ripe, dark wine is a veritable creme de Syrah. It's full-bodied, with good structure and grape, cedar and dried-spice flavors. Ripe for drinking now, this will hold through mid-decade, maybe longer. 91 Editors' Choice (11/1/2001)

Columbia Crest 1997 Reserve Syrah (Columbia Valley (WA)) $25. 80 —P.G. (9/1/2000)

Columbia Crest 1996 Reserve Syrah (Columbia Valley (WA)) $20. 92 —P.G. (9/1/2000)

Columbia Crest 1998 White Blend (Columbia Valley (WA)) $8. 85 —P.G. (11/15/2000)

COLUMBIA WINERY

Columbia Winery 2001 Alder Ridge Barbera (Washington) $20. Bold and fruit-filled, this new bottling from Columbia also boasts a soft, creamy mouthfeel that contrasts nicely with tart acids on the finish. Bouncy berry-cherry fruit and hints of milk chocolate provide a high "yum factor" without a lot of complexity. 88 (1/1/2004)

Columbia Winery 1996 Millennium Bordeaux Blend (Columbia Valley (WA)) $75. 89 (4/1/2000)

Columbia Winery 1997 Peninsula Bordeaux Blend (Yakima Valley) $60.
This is Columbia's top of the line Bordeaux blend—49% Cabernet Sauvignon/31% Merlot/20% Cabernet Franc. Although its release has been held back for six years—extraordinary by American standards—it still feels unresolved and incomplete. There is steely black fruit, some earthy tannins, firm acids and rough oak, but it's all in parts, and needs still more time in bottle to pull together. 88 —P.G. (12/31/2003)

Columbia Winery 2001 Red Willow Cabernet Franc (Yakima Valley) $23.
The stiff tannins and earthiness of this wine is underlaid with very soft, very vanilla oak; the effect is startling and disjointed. With more time in the bottle, it may all meld together, but right now it's unclear where this wine is going. 85 —P.G. (12/31/2003)

Columbia Winery 1999 Red Willow Vineyard Cabernet Franc (Yakima Valley) $23. This David Lake Signature Series wine includes 23% Merlot from the same vineyard. There are definite scents of dill and bell pepper along with the expected cherry and blackberry fruits, and a hint of sweet oak as well. Restrained and supple, but not quite as ripe as one would hope for. 86 —P.G. (12/31/2002)

Columbia Winery 1997 Red Willow Vineyard Cabernet Franc (Yakima Valley) $24. Red Willow is Columbia's showplace, and the relationship between winemaker David Lake and winegrower Mike Sauer is symbiosis at its best. The Cab Franc is a tight, tannic, earthy wine, with layers of mineral digging deep into the wine. The fruit is hard and the acids firm; it seems to want more time to display its depth and elegance. 88 —P.G. (6/1/2001)

Columbia Winery 1996 Red Willow Vineyard Cabernet Franc (Yakima Valley) $22. 87 —J.C. (9/1/1999)

Columbia Winery 1998 Signature Series Red Willow Vineyard Cabernet Franc (Columbia Valley (WA)) $22. The Cabernet Franc has been released each year since 1991, and it is consistently fine. Less tannic than most examples of varietal Franc, it has a pretty cherry/berry bouquet, aug-

USA

mented with chocolate shavings and cedar. Tart, with good grip and high acids, it's a wine to age and enjoy with rich meats. **89** —*P.G. (12/31/2001)*

Columbia Winery 2001 Cabernet Sauvignon (Columbia Valley (WA)) $15. There are distinct herbal scents mixed in with the flavors of cassis, blueberry and plum, which makes this rather lean Cabernet feel a bit French. It's nicely balanced and long, with nuances of coffee, green tea, meat fat and vanilla. Complex and layered. **89** —*P.G. (4/1/2005)*

Columbia Winery 2000 Cabernet Sauvignon (Columbia Valley (WA)) $15. Columbia styles its reds on a European model, with lower alcohol and more earthy flavors than most West Coast wineries. This has a rich mix of plants, herbs and spices in the nose, and a good center of plum and mushroom, with a finishing kick. **87** —*P.G. (12/31/2003)*

Columbia Winery 1999 Cabernet Sauvignon (Columbia Valley (WA)) $15. This is classic juice, hard and packed with power, showing dark fruits laced with mocha and spice. The chalky tannins are the only quibble, but this wine will improve for at least a decade in your cellar. **88** —*P.G. (9/1/2002)*

Columbia Winery 1998 Cabernet Sauvignon (Columbia Valley (WA)) $15. This is a fine representation of straightforward, Washington state Cabernet, from an excellent vintage, with no frills. There's a whiff of watermelon, then clean cherry fruit in the mouth, accented with some mocha and cocoa from the barrels. It's forward, balanced and eminently drinkable. **85** —*P.G. (10/1/2001)*

Columbia Winery 2000 Otis Vineyard Cabernet Sauvignon (Yakima Valley) $25. A relatively round, fruity and approachable wine with good cherry/plum flavors when first released, it has recently turned tight and dryly tannic. Shows the classic black pepper and dried sage character of the Otis vineyard. Otis Cabs are best cellared for a number of years in order to reveal their subtlety. **89** —*P.G. (12/15/2005)*

Columbia Winery 1999 Otis Vineyard Cabernet Sauvignon (Yakima Valley) $23. Otis includes the oldest Cabernet vines in Washington state, dating back to the 1950s, and has been a Columbia vineyard-designate since 1981. Black pepper and dried sage are its imprints, and Otis always makes a tight, ageworthy wine, not in the currently fashionable ultraripe mode. Lean and herbal, but deep and ageworthy. **91 Cellar Selection** — *P.G. (4/1/2005)*

Columbia Winery 1998 Otis Cabernet Sauvignon (Yakima Valley) $29. The Otis is fragrant and sensual, with open-knit red berry flavors and hints of mocha and cedar. Not a big wine, but balanced and accessible, with interesting, complex, spicy highlights. **89** —*P.G. (12/31/2003)*

Columbia Winery 1997 Otis Vineyard Cabernet Sauvignon (Yakima Valley) $26. The winery holds back the Otis bottling, which has proven itself an exceptionally long-lived wine over the past two decades. This is now beginning to integrate the distinctive Otis range of herbs, spices and old viney fruit. Tart, leafy and minerally, it has a persistent, elusive power that unfolds over time. **89** —*P.G. (12/31/2002)*

Columbia Winery 1996 Otis Vineyard Cabernet Sauvignon (Yakima Valley) $29. This is the current release. Columbia Cabs age for decades, but need extra time up front. Credit the winery with giving these wines that time. Still youthful and tight, this shows true varietal character, along with the pepper and herbs characteristic of the Otis vineyard. A hint of smoky chipotle creeps into the finish. **88** —*P.G. (6/1/2002)*

Columbia Winery 1998 Red Willow Cabernet Sauvignon (Yakima Valley) $29. This is a blend of 85% Cab Sauvignon, 9% Cab Franc and 9% Merlot, and benefits from the mingling of the three. It is nicely woven together, with supple cassis, berry and mineral streaks, and nice tannins. **90 Cellar Selection** —*P.G. (12/31/2003)*

Columbia Winery 1997 Red Willow Cabernet Sauvignon (Yakima Valley) $29. Starts off cedary and toasty, but picks up more cassis with air, along with an intriguing note of menthol. The black currant flavors are sturdy and almost plum-like, yet possess a soft, supple mouthfeel. Dry tannins on the finish provide the structural framework to age. Drinkable now, better in 2005. **89** *(1/1/2004)*

Columbia Winery 2000 Red Willow Vineyard Cabernet Sauvignon (Yakima Valley) $23. Lots of ripe boysenberry, cranberry and sour cherry fruit to start, with a strong foundation of tar, espresso and bitter chocolate. This could pass for a Super Tuscan in a blind tasting. It unfolds slowly, with

an interesting herbal/olive edge to it, and will reward additional cellaring. **91 Cellar Selection** —*P.G. (4/1/2005)*

Columbia Winery 1996 Red Willow Vineyard Cabernet Sauvignon (Yakima Valley) $29. The blend includes about 6 percent Cabernet Franc, and this is the current release. Bracing, and straightforward, with clean fruit, austere tannins and a bit of chalkiness on the finish. Crisply rendered, but lacking in flesh and a sense of terroir. **87** —*P.G. (6/1/2002)*

Columbia Winery 1999 Sagemoor Vineyard Cabernet Sauvignon (Columbia Valley (WA)) $29. **89** —*P.G. (6/1/2002)*

Columbia Winery 1998 Sagemoor Vineyard Cabernet Sauvignon (Columbia Valley (WA)) $29. Sagemoor is one of the state's oldest vineyards; this wine, the last in the state to be released from the hot, ripe '98 vintage, is now heading into adolescence. Soft, ripe flavors of berry preserves are folded into tart acids and hints of chocolate. **88** —*P.G. (12/31/2003)*

Columbia Winery 1997 Sagemoor Vineyard Cabernet Sauvignon (Columbia Valley (WA)) $29. This is drinking very well already, with a nicely evolved, meaty nose leading to sweet cassis and blackberry fruit. Dusty, spicy and complex, it displays a Bordeaux profile with less funk and more sweet fruit character. **89** —*P.G. (6/1/2002)*

Columbia Winery 1996 Sagemoor Vineyard Cabernet Sauvignon (Columbia Valley (WA)) $24. **89** —*P.G. (4/1/2000)*

Columbia Winery 1999 Otis Vineyard Chardonnay (Yakima Valley) $24. The Otis vineyard is best known for its textured, herbal Cabernets, but it makes a fine Chardonnay as well. The '99 is still lean and taut, with fresh fruit and a few rough edges to the new oak. Partly the vintage, and partly the vineyard, it needs considerably more cellar time than the Wyckoff. **88** —*P.G. (10/1/2001)*

Columbia Winery 1998 Otis Vineyard Chardonnay (Yakima Valley) $50. **89** —*P.G. (11/15/2000)*

Columbia Winery 1999 Otis Vineyard Block 6 Chardonnay (Columbia Valley (WA)) $40. This block has made a wine more austere and yet more complete than the regular Otis Vineyard bottling. Firm fruit mixes melon and pineapple, nuanced with pepper, mineral and a dusting of oak. Balanced and muscular; a classy effort. **89** —*P.G. (7/1/2002)*

Columbia Winery 2001 Otis Vineyard Block 6 Chardonnay (Yakima Valley) $40. From Dijon clones, which are well-suited to the Willamette valley, but less common in Washington. Taut, almost racy, this wine is packed with green berries and citrus flavors, nicely finished with lightly toasted oak. **88** —*P.G. (9/1/2004)*

Columbia Winery 1999 Woodburne Cuvée Chardonnay (Columbia Valley (WA)) $14. The name honors one of the founders of the original winery, and the wine generally mixes buttery fruit with a blast of oak flavor. It's burly, bold and aggressive; subtlety is not its strong suit. But in this price range, for the oak-lover in the crowd, it's a great choice, ready to drink right now. **86** —*P.G. (6/1/2001)*

Columbia Winery 1997 Woodburne Cuvée Chardonnay (Columbia Valley (WA)) $14. **86** —*M.M. (11/1/1999)*

Columbia Winery 2003 Wyckoff Vineyard Chardonnay (Yakima Valley) $19. Tropical fruit flavors of pineapple, banana and melon initiate this young, nicely focused, rather toasty/buttery effort. Some of the vines are almost 30 years old. Though not as over-the-top with the new oak as some past vintages, the '03 will benefit from further bottle time and may well have the complexity and the composition to age nicely for six to eight years. **89** —*P.G. (12/15/2005)*

Columbia Winery 2002 Wyckoff Vineyard Chardonnay (Yakima Valley) $19. Butterscotch, vanilla and spicy anise light up this Burgundian-style chardonnay. Its not-too-ripe fruit flavors of melon and citrus keep it crisp and well-defined, and winemaker David Lake has added just the right amount of toasty new oak. **90** —*P.G. (4/1/2005)*

Columbia Winery 2001 Wyckoff Vineyard Chardonnay (Yakima Valley) $19. A severe, tart wine, its green apple/lemon fruit offset with sharp accents of oak and vanilla. Decanting would be helpful, or set it aside for another 4-5 years bottle age. **87** —*P.G. (9/1/2004)*

Columbia Winery 2000 Wyckoff Chardonnay (Yakima Valley) $19. This gets the full-blown barrel treatment (fermented and aged in French oak, lees-stirring, full malolactic fermentation), and it shows rather more than the fruit. Buttery, richly textured and spice-scented (clove and cinnamon), with only modest levels of yellow fruit flavors that include hints of pineapple and Golden Delicious. **87** *(1/1/2004)*

Columbia Winery 1999 Wyckoff Vineyard Chardonnay (Yakima Valley) $19. Columbia makes several different Chardonnays, and this one always seems to showcase more oak than the rest. Firm citrus and green apple fruit is wrapped in oak and butterscotch, finishing with a hint of anise. **88** —*P.G. (12/31/2002)*

Columbia Winery 1998 Wyckoff Vineyard Chardonnay (Yakima Valley) $19. This David Lake Signature Series Chardonnay combines ripe, green apple fruit with interesting herbal notes. It shows off pretty, precise new oak in a crisp framework of supporting acids. In short, it's deft, balanced, elegant and rewarding. **89** *(10/1/2001)*

Columbia Winery 1997 Wyckoff Vineyard Chardonnay (Yakima Valley) $21. **88** —*P.G. (4/1/2000)*

Columbia Winery 2005 Gewürztraminer (Columbia Valley (WA)) $8. Another spectacular effort, though they've bumped up the price significantly. This is beautifully varietal, mixing floral, bath powder, apple and grapefruit components in both the nose and the mouth. There is an elegant intensity that powers the wine through an exceptionally long, brilliant finish; the residual sweetness keeps the alcohol down to 11.5% without making the wine either soft or sugary. 14,500 cases produced. **90 Best Buy** —*P.G. (11/15/2006)*

Columbia Winery 2004 Gewürztraminer (Columbia Valley (WA)) $9. Quite a perfect match for the 2003, this delightful wine remains bracingly fresh and crisp despite its 3.1% residual sugar. Rich and intense, it shows lovely flavors of pink grapefruit, melon and citrus rind. Some stony crispness underlies the fruit, which captures its sweetness without losing its edge. One of the best Gewürzes in the state, if not the country. **90 Best Buy** —*P.G. (12/15/2005)*

Columbia Winery 2003 Gewürztraminer (Columbia Valley (WA)) $9. This is a real success for the winery, made bracingly fresh and crisp despite its 3% residual sugar. Bright flavors of pink grapefruit dominate the palate, filling out a pristine, crisp and deliciously fresh finish. **90 Best Buy** —*P.G. (4/1/2005)*

Columbia Winery 2001 Gewürztraminer (Columbia Valley (WA)) $7. This is one of Columbia's strengths, turning out perfectly crafted white wines at budget prices. The Gewürz is off-dry, rich and roundly fruity, loaded with mouthfilling, lipsmacking flavors. Chill it to cut the sweetness and you have the perfect wine for spicy noodle dishes. **87** —*P.G. (9/1/2002)*

Columbia Winery 2000 Merlot (Columbia Valley (WA)) $15. Columbia's mainline (17,250 cases) Merlot mixes tart, black cherry fruit with layers of mushroom and earth. Good grip, good length, and some depth as well, though it tails off on the finish. **87** —*P.G. (12/31/2003)*

Columbia Winery 1999 Merlot (Columbia Valley (WA)) $15. The oak jumps out a bit, with plenty of vanilla and a bit of dill, too. A medium-bodied Merlot, still young and tannic and not yet unwrapped. Additional cellar time will help. **87** —*P.G. (9/1/2002)*

Columbia Winery 1998 Merlot (Columbia Valley (WA)) $15. The blend includes 12% Cabernet Sauvignon, 11% Cabernet Franc and even 1% Syrah (!) The nose shows a fair amount of wood and some herbal scents; the flavors are earthy, with hints of root and bark and leaf. But overall it's a well-balanced, hearty wine which, like the Covey Run, delivers the goods at a fair price. **84** —*P.G. (10/1/2001)*

Columbia Winery 1997 Merlot (Columbia Valley (WA)) $15. **88** —*P.G. (4/1/2000)*

Columbia Winery 1999 Red Willow Milestone Merlot (Yakima Valley) $29. Good, ripe, smooth and quite toasty, this shows classic black cherry fruit wrapped in sweet, chocolaty tannins. It needs more time to integrate the wood into the fruit, but it is balanced and well-crafted, and given adequate air time, drinking well already. **89** —*P.G. (12/31/2003)*

Columbia Winery 1997 Red Willow Vineyard Milestone Merlot (Yakima Valley) $24. Ripe fruit wafts out of the glass. This is classy juice, with red and black berry flavors, stiff tannins, and a fine balance. It finishes with a complex, herbal set of flavors. The barrel aging has lent some dark notes of toasted coffee beans and bitter chocolate. This is a complete, interest-

ing wine from an excellent vineyard, well-suited to long-term aging. **89** —*P.G. (10/1/2001)*

Columbia Winery 2004 Pinot Gris (Columbia Valley (WA)) $10. Columbia was the first to produce Pinot Gris in Washington, and this creamy, round and flavorful wine mixes green apples, pears and a hint of cantaloupe. The only failing is a lack of length on the finish. **86** —*P.G. (2/1/2006)*

Columbia Winery 2002 Pinot Gris (Yakima Valley) $10. As is usually the style with David Lake's white wines, this is taut, clean and very crisp, showing light mixed fruit flavors of fig and melon. Just a slight taste of cardboard shows up in the finish. **86 Best Buy** —*P.G. (12/1/2004)*

Columbia Winery 2000 Pinot Gris (Yakima Valley) $10. Pinot Gris is starting to have a presence in Washington, and the straightforward, citrus-flavored fruit shown here suggests a middle-of-the-road style. It's a tart, palate-cleaning wine with a hint of citrus-rind bitterness in the finish. **86** —*P.G. (9/1/2002)*

Columbia Winery 1998 Pinot Gris (Yakima Valley) $9. **84** —*P.G. (11/15/2000)*

Columbia Winery 2000 Cellarmaster's Riesling (Columbia Valley (WA)) $7. Yellow in color and thick in the bouquet. The nose is hard to peg, but there are notes of mustard and asparagus. The palate offers some orange and apple flavors, but also something similar to canned peas. It seems overripe and past its prime. **82** —*M.S. (8/19/2003)*

Columbia Winery 2002 Red Willow Vineyard Sangiovese (Yakima Valley) $25. This wine, though done in the understated style of winemaker David Lake, has an immensely appealing bouquet of spicy red fruits enhanced with cinnamon and toast. A firm, confident entry, that shows fruit that is ripe, not at all jammy, and focuses in on a clean core of pretty cherry. The back palate features a nice mix of cocoa, cinnamon and baking spices. **90** —*P.G. (12/1/2004)*

Columbia Winery 2001 Red Willow Vineyard Sangiovese (Yakima Valley) $20. Part of the "Signature Series" from Columbia, this is a rather tart wine, with green tomato flavors and the barest hints of cherry fruit. **84** —*P.G. (12/31/2003)*

Columbia Winery 1999 Red Willow Vineyard Sangiovese (Yakima Valley) $25. Softly fragrant, with nice hints of dusty cocoa. In the mouth the young fruit is crisp and tastes lightly of tomato and cherry, with a finish that brings in tobacco, earth, dark chocolate and coffee. **88** —*P.G. (6/1/2002)*

Columbia Winery 1998 Red Willow Vineyard Sangiovese (Yakima Valley) $18. **90** —*P.G. (11/15/2000)*

Columbia Winery 2001 Sémillon (Columbia Valley (WA)) $8. This is a rarity—100% Sémillon, showing the woolly, woody side of the grape, with bone-dry styling and nice, creamy hints of bean and vanilla. Complex and suited to shellfish, this is a sleek, textural, very fine effort. **90 Best Buy** —*P.G. (12/31/2003)*

Columbia Winery 1998 Sémillon (Columbia Valley (WA)) $7. **86 Best Buy** —*P.G. (11/15/2000)*

Columbia Winery 1997 Syrah (Yakima Valley) $14. **90** —*P.G. (4/1/2000)*

Columbia Winery 2004 Syrah (Columbia Valley (WA)) $13. This is stylish and clean, just 13.5 alcohol, so nothing about it is overblown or jammy. Winemaker David Lake pioneered Syrah in Washington state almost two decades ago, and still makes one of the most balanced and restrained versions. The polished fruit flavors do not stray into the realm of jam or preserves, but offer true-blue blueberry, currant and cherry, with silky tannins. Though young, this satisfying wine has good aging potential over the near term. 16,000 cases produced. **89 Best Buy** —*P.G. (11/15/2006)*

Columbia Winery 2001 Syrah (Columbia Valley (WA)) $15. Columbia pioneered syrah in Washington state, and still leads the pack at this price point. Smooth and varietal, it mixes ripe (not raisiny) fruit in a sleek, muscular wine laced with vanilla, smoked meat and tar. **90 Best Buy** —*P.G. (4/1/2005)*

Columbia Winery 2000 Syrah (Columbia Valley (WA)) $15. This is the budget Syrah bottling from Columbia, and in this forward, fruity vintage it is a real deal. The sweet and supple core of fruit is limned with toasty oak, and the wine remains muscular and strong through the finish. Don't look for complexity—but full, ripe, balanced flavors are here in abundance. **88 Best Buy**—*P.G. (12/31/2002)*

Columbia Winery 1999 Syrah (Columbia Valley (WA)) $18. There's decent depth of fruit in the inky darkness of this Washington state contender. Black as it is, it reads a touch sweet, with strong vanillin oak and ripe blackberry flavors. Licorice and espresso accents, an even mouthfeel, and a moderate finish with pepper and toast wrap it up. **87** *(10/1/2001)*

Columbia Winery 1998 Syrah (Yakima Valley) $15. 88—*P.G. (11/15/2000)*

Columbia Winery 1999 Red Willow Syrah (Yakima Valley) $35. Despite being a bit closed aromatically, a thick, velvety mouthfeel and dense blackberry and vanilla flavors confirm this wine's quality. With airing, burnt caramel and fleshy berry scents emerge. The finish brings a hint of pepper and some drying tannins—enough to suggest cellaring two or three years. **90** *(1/1/2004)*

Columbia Winery 2000 Red Willow South Chapel Block Syrah (Yakima Valley) $50. Red Willow Vineyard owner Mike Sauer and Columbia winemaker David Lake pioneered Syrah in Washington state. This is Columbia's best. Young, tightly woven, with spice and leather and a gamy edge to it, it has the necessary raw materials, but needs more time. **89**—*P.G. (12/31/2003)*

Columbia Winery 2000 Red Willow Vineyard Syrah (Yakima Valley) $35. Red Willow was one of the first vineyards in the Northwest to grow Syrah. Subsequently, other parts of Washington have proven quite adept with the grape, but Red Willow retains its own unique personality. Reticent, textured, lightly herbal and hinting at smoke and tobacco, it's a wine that will develop gently over time and surprise with its depth and wealth of flavors. Cellar Candidate (8-10 years) **88 Cellar Selection**—*P.G. (9/1/2004)*

Columbia Winery 1998 Red Willow Vineyard Syrah (Yakima Valley) $35. Cedar, meat and saddle-leather aromas open this even, creamy, but not particularly deep, wine. Wood envelops the red-berry and blackberry fruit, with chocolate and vanilla from the toasty oak showing more than the fruit. Finishes long, with spice, pepper, and tangy tannins. Lovers of lavish oak will relish this. **86** *(11/1/2001)*

Columbia Winery 1996 Red Willow Vineyard Syrah (Yakima Valley) $29. 87—*S.H. (11/1/1999)*

Columbia Winery 1997 Reserve Syrah (Columbia Valley (WA)) $32. 92—*S.H. (11/1/1999)*

Columbia Winery 2001 Red Willow Viognier (Yakima Valley) $40. This wine carries scents of fennel, lime and citrus blossom, elegantly expressed in pretty, tangy fruit that drives to a long, crisp finish. **88**—*P.G. (12/31/2002)*

Columbia Winery 2000 Red Willow Viognier (Yakima Valley) $23. Viognier can do well in Washington, but this bottle, despite its David Lake Signature Series pedigree, seems to miss the mark. The fruit is buried in new oak, which reduces its flavors to citrus and buttered popcorn, and leaves the finish hard and tannic. **85**—*P.G. (12/31/2001)*

Columbia Winery 2001 Alder Ridge Vineyard Zinfandel (Columbia Valley (WA)) $20. One of the few non-California Zins tasted for this report, the wine offers a pleasing blend of licorice, plum and black cherry flavors, couched in toasty oak and finishing with a spicy lilt. Tannins are slightly drying. **87**—*J.M. (11/1/2003)*

COLVIN VINEYARDS

Colvin Vineyards 2001 Allégresse Bordeaux Blend (Walla Walla (WA)) $36. This Bordeaux blend includes a small amount of carmenère, for which this winery has built a reputation, and it is done in a style that has garnered a lot of positive attention. This reviewer finds that the overwhelming presence of brettanomyces, which lends a very horsey, leathery scent and flavor, detracts from everything else. It almost completely kills the fruit. **85**—*P.G. (12/1/2004)*

Colvin Vineyards 2002 Cabernet Sauvignon (Walla Walla (WA)) $26. More Yakima than Walla Walla, this tight, stylish Cab shows plenty of leaf and herb, but nothing stemmy or bitter. Sleek and sporting cassis and black cherry fruit, it remains concentrated and balanced into a long, gliding finish tasting of astringent black tea. **89**—*P.G. (4/1/2006)*

Colvin Vineyards 2002 Patina Vineyard Syrah (Walla Walla (WA)) $23. Though fairly light, as are many Walla Walla wines, this delicious effort has such pretty strawberry, raspberry and cherry fruit that it seduces rather than overpowers. Just the right touch with oak adds the slightest finish of cocoa powder. **90**—*P.G. (6/1/2005)*

Colvin Vineyards 2003 Spofford Station Vineyard Syrah (Walla Walla (WA)) $23. Spiced up with tobacco, mint and a bit of pepper, this light, herbal Syrah shows that you don't need 15% alcohol levels of ripeness to make a flavorful, complex wine. The flavors are compact and layered, and they linger beautifully on the palate. This is a wine that should knit together very nicely over the next 6–8 years. **88**—*P.G. (4/1/2006)*

COM E BELLA

Com e Bella 2000 Cabernet Sauvignon (Calaveras County) $30. Sulfury, soft and sweet. **82**—*S.H. (3/1/2005)*

Com e Bella 2001 Cabernet Sauvignon-Syrah (Calaveras County) $24. Fruity in cherries and vanilla, with a note of wintergreen mint, this simple blend is likeable. **84**—*S.H. (3/1/2005)*

COMPASS

Compass 2000 Merlot (Napa Valley) $12. An easy-drinking wine with much of the charm of a pricier Merlot. Has tasty plum, blackberry and chocolate flavors wrapped in rich, smooth tannins. The competition at this price range is fierce, and this wine is holding its own. Good value. **86**—*S.H. (12/31/2003)*

Compass 1998 Merlot (California) $10. Starts out with Cabernet-like aromas of black currants and an undercurrent of something leaner: unsweetened chocolate, anise, and smoky, oaky notes. This wine accomplishes what many inexpensive Merlots don't: a rich, fruity smoothness. Which makes it a good Merlot value, even though the score isn't very high. **84**—*S.H. (2/1/2001)*

COMTESSE THÉRÈSE

Comtesse Thérèse 2002 Cabernet Sauvignon (North Fork of Long Island) $25. For those of you who don't mind brettanomyces, this wine has a nice mouth feel with mild tannins and underlying red fruit. But if horsey is not your thing, stay away. This wine is riding the brett train, and there's no getting off. **82**—*M.D. (8/1/2006)*

Comtesse Thérèse 2004 Russian Oak Chardonnay (North Fork of Long Island) $18. The oak, although prominent in the name, isn't so obvious on the nose of this wine. Instead there's underripe peach and melon, followed by flavors that are more like apples and pears. It's a pleasant, medium-bodied wine with a slightly custardy texture and strong pencilly oak overtones showing through only on the finish. **86**—*J.C. (3/1/2006)*

Comtesse Thérèse 2001 Chateau Reserve Merlot (North Fork of Long Island) $25. 88—*J.C. (10/2/2004)*

Comtesse Thérèse 2003 Hungarian Oak Merlot (North Fork of Long Island) $17. Starts with scents of rhubarb and strawberries and stays right there, offering crisp berry flavors and a tart, lean finish. **82**—*J.C. (3/1/2006)*

Comtesse Thérèse 2003 Traditional Merlot (North Fork of Long Island) $18. Light-medium bodied, and smooth in the mouth, this wine would be fine if not for a strong brett presence, manifesting itself with strong horsey/metallic flavors and aromas. Underneath there is some decent red fruit, but it's too far under to rate higher. **82**—*M.D. (8/1/2006)*

Comtesse Thérèse 2001 Traditional Merlot (North Fork of Long Island) $18. 84—*J.C. (10/2/2004)*

CONCANNON

Concannon 2002 Reserve Assemblage Red Cabernet Blend (Livermore Valley) $24. Dry, soft and a little rustic, with earthy, berry and coffee flavors. Finishes rough in acids and tannins. **84**—*S.H. (6/1/2005)*

Concannon 2003 Limited Release Assemblage Cabernet Sauvignon (Central Coast) $14. Brusque in texture, with jagged tannins, this is a simple, clean wine. It's also high in acidity. **83**—*S.H. (3/1/2006)*

Concannon 2003 Reserve Cabernet Sauvignon (Livermore Valley) $24. Dry, astringent and thin. Even though the alcohol is modest, it has so little in the way of fruit. All you get is prickly heat. **80**—*S.H. (9/1/2006)*

Concannon 2001 Reserve Cabernet Sauvignon (Livermore Valley) $24. How ripe the grapes got during this warm vintage. The glass is filled with lush, plump blackberry and cassis flavors that are easily able to support considerable oak. This fine wine is very soft. **87** —S.H. (12/31/2004)

Concannon 2000 Reserve Limited Release Cabernet Sauvignon (Livermore Valley) $24. This wine will strike some as impossibly tannic and earthy, and it's true it's not particularly fruity. But it's like a fresh young Bordeaux, a Cabernet that needs time. There's a sweet core of blackberry and cherry flavor that's best cellared until 2008. **88** —S.H. (6/1/2004)

Concannon 2003 Selected Vineyard Cabernet Sauvignon (Central Coast) $10. Cherries and green herbs slug it out for primacy in this dry, full-bodied, tannic wine. The cherries win out, dominating the finish along with sweet oak. Pretty good stuff, and not a bad price. **84** —S.H. (12/31/2005)

Concannon 2002 Selected Vineyard Cabernet Sauvignon (Central Coast) $12. Tough and tannic, this wine tastes cooked. It has flavors of grapes that burnt and shrivelled in the heat, with a raisiny finish. **81** —S.H. (12/1/2005)

Concannon 2001 Selected Vineyard Cabernet Sauvignon (Central Coast) $12. What a nice value in an inexpensive Cab. It has plenty of sweet blackberry and cherry flavors, and is dry and balanced. There's a smidgen of oak and a finish of grippy tannins. **85** —S.H. (10/1/2004)

Concannon 2004 Reserve Chardonnay (Edna Valley) $18. Shows the distinctly high acidity and laser-pure lemon and lime flavors that are so typical of this chilly appellation. You'll also find enriching oak and lees influences in this clean Burgundian-style wine. **87** —S.H. (5/1/2006)

Concannon 1997 Reserve Chardonnay (Central Coast) $20. **83** (6/1/2000)

Concannon 1996 Reserve Chardonnay (Livermore Valley) $19. **84** —M.S. (10/1/1999)

Concannon 2002 Reserve Limited Release Chardonnay (Edna Valley) $18. The grapes struggled to get ripe, and you can taste the ocean climate in the green, citrusy flavors that just barely veer into white peach. Acidity is high, and oak has been kept strictly as a light seasoning. **86** —S.H. (6/1/2004)

Concannon 2004 Selected Vineyard Chardonnay (Central Coast) $10. The winery's lowest tier, among four, is watery-thin, with almost no flavor at all. You'll find oak, acidity, alcohol and a drop of pineapple. **82** —S.H. (11/15/2006)

Concannon 2002 Selected Vineyard Chardonnay (Central Coast) $12. Here's a simple, dry wine with lots of perky acids to boost up the apple and citrus flavors. There's some spicy richness and smoky oak in the finish. Pretty good value in a coastal Chard. **85** —S.H. (12/1/2004)

Concannon 2003 Selected Vineyards Chardonnay (Central Coast) $12. A zesty, vibrant Chard, filled with acids, with flavors ranging from ripe citrus to peach. There's very little oak, so the fruit and crispness star. Long, spicy finish, and terrifically food-friendly. **86** —S.H. (2/1/2005)

Concannon 2003 Reserve Merlot (Livermore Valley) $24. Concannon's Merlots have been variable. This latest offering is dry and tart, with red cherry and coffee flavors that finish in a scour of acidity. It needs the softening, enriching presence of fatty meats and cheeses. **85** —S.H. (5/1/2006)

Concannon 2002 Reserve Merlot (Livermore Valley) $24. A modest Merlot, a bit short in fruit, but good for its balance and softness. **83** —S.H. (12/31/2004)

Concannon 2001 Reserve Limited Release Merlot (Livermore Valley) $24. Red Bordeaux varieties can do very well in this appellation if they' re well cared for, and Concannon has done a terrific job with this ripe, fancy Merlot. It has some big tannins, but they're the soft, dusty kind that are drinkable now with rich foods. The blackberry flavors break out into currants and cassis. **91** —S.H. (6/1/2004)

Concannon 2001 Selected Vineyard Merlot (Central Coast) $12. This amazing value wine has many of the attributes of a far costlier Merlot. It's ripe in plum, blackberry and dark chocolate fruit, with complex but fine tannins and a rich overlay of smoky oak. Hard to believe they can release it at this price. **88 Best Buy** —S.H. (12/15/2004)

Concannon 2003 Selected Vineyards Merlot (Central Coast) $10. From cool-climate vineyards comes this hearty country red. It gets the job done with cherry-berry and earthy-spicy flavors, in a nicely dry and balanced package. Has the personality for everything from cheeseburgers to a sizzling steak. **85 Best Buy** —S.H. (12/31/2005)

Concannon 2002 Selected Vineyards Merlot (Central Coast) $12. There sure is plenty of ripe fruit in this wine. It's stuffed with cherries, blackberries and cocoa, and is soft and gentle in the mouth. **84** —S.H. (12/31/2004)

Concannon 2000 Petite Sirah (Central Coast) $12. From this longtime Petite Sirah producer, quality wine with flavors veering between blackberry and cherry, and earthier ones of tar. Some tasters objected to bitterness and so-so depth, but others praised the delicious lively fruit. **86** (4/1/2003)

Concannon 1997 Petite Sirah (Central Coast) $24. What pretty aromas. Sweet oak accents, blackberry, currant, vanilla and smoky notes. The flavors suggest blackberry liqueur, and there's noticeable sugar. Velvety smooth tannins and soft acidity complete this wine. **86** —S.H. (12/1/2001)

Concannon 2001 Heritage Petite Sirah (Livermore Valley) $40. From the winery that claims to have introduced Petite Sirah as a varietal wine comes this dynamic bottling. It's full-bodied, dry and tannic, with a deep undertow of blackberry, cherry, plum and coffee flavors, and has a complex structure. Will be beautiful with a grilled steak, but this is a wine you can stash away for at least a decade. **92 Cellar Selection** —S.H. (12/1/2005)

Concannon 2000 Heritage Petite Sirah (Livermore Valley) $36. So deficient in lively acidity that it just collapses on the palate, making it hard to appreciate the pretty flavors of dry, tart cherries and espresso. Just disappears on the finish. **84** —S.H. (2/1/2005)

Concannon 2003 Reserve Petite Sirah (Livermore Valley) $24. This is one of those old-fashioned Pets that will last for many years. But it's fully drinkable now because of the upfront blackberry, cherry and spicy plum fruit. If you do pop it, you'll find a very dry wine with firm tannins and brisk acidity. If you like well-aged Petite Sirah, feel free to cellar until 2020. **88** —S.H. (11/15/2006)

Concannon 2002 Reserve Petite Sirah (Livermore Valley) $30. Classic Pet, tough in tannins, bone dry, full-bodied, and with a big, hearty core of cherries, black-berries, leather and spices. You can drink it now, but it should soften and sweeten through the decade. **90** —S.H. (6/1/2005)

Concannon 1999 Reserve Petite Sirah (Livermore Valley) $25. Tasters enjoyed the solid credentials of this vibrantly fruity wine. We found a melange of blackberry, cherry and plum flavors, with some earthy, herbal undertones, as well as supple tannins. A few reviewers said a stubbornly vegetal streak kept the wine from scoring higher. **86** (4/1/2003)

Concannon 1995 Reserve Petite Sirah (Central Coast) $23. **90** —J.C. (11/1/1999)

Concannon 2000 Reserve Limited Release Petite Sirah (Livermore Valley) $24. From a Petite Sirah pioneer, a very nice, full-bodied wine that will age. But it's fine now, with deep flavors of plum and herbs, and thick, dusty tannins. Earns extra points for balance and harmony. **91** —S.H. (12/31/2003)

Concannon 2002 Selected Vineyard Petite Sirah (Central Coast) $12. Quintessential Pet, inky black, rich in thick, dusty tannins, absolutely dry, and bursting with blackberry, plum, dark chocolate and spicy, peppery flavors. Beautiful in its own way, and a super value. **88 Best Buy** —S.H. (11/15/2004)

Concannon 2003 Selected Vineyards Petite Sirah (Central Coast) $12. Good, rich flavors, ranging from blackberries and dried herbs to bitter espresso, but way too soft. Like a Dali watch, it just melts without coming to life. **83** —S.H. (2/1/2005)

Concannon 2005 Limited Release Pinot Gris (Central Coast) $14. Entirely produced in stainless steel from this long, cool vintage, the wine shows how lusciously ripe PG can get. Few wines in the world can achieve these enormous levels of pineapples, limes, apricots, mangoes, peaches, apples, wild tropical flowers and vanilla. There's a trace of residual sugar, but the acidity is high, which combined means that the finish is slightly sweet, but beautifully crisp and clean. **87** —*S.H. (12/31/2006)*

Concannon 2004 Limited Release Pinot Noir (Central Coast) $14. Silky and in the style of a coastal Pinot, with cherry cola and spice flavors. Finishes a bit thin, but it shows true varietal character. Not a bad price for the quality. **85** —*S.H. (11/15/2006)*

Concannon 2002 Limited Release Pinot Noir (Edna Valley) $24. Hard to like this difficult wine. It's partially unripe, with herbal notes veering toward vegetal. **82** —*S.H. (6/1/2005)*

Concannon 2002 Selected Vineyards Pinot Noir (Central Coast) $12. A solid Central Coast effort, displaying crisp acids and a light body. The flavors range from red cherries and coffee to citrus fruits. Easy and elegant. **85** *(11/1/2004)*

Concannon 2004 Limited Release Assemblage Red Wine Red Blend (Central Coast) $14. Hard to find much to like with this dry, harsh wine. It's as acidic as coffee, and tannic to boot, with not much fruit. Merlot, Petite Sirah and Petit Verdot. **81** —*S.H. (12/31/2006)*

Concannon 2002 Stampmaker's Red Wine Rhône Red Blend (Livermore Valley) $24. Very fruit forward in cherries and pomegranates, with rich tannins that grip the palate. Feels dry all the way to the finish, when it turns cough-mediciney sweet. **84** —*S.H. (6/1/2005)*

Concannon 2003 Limited Release Sauvignon Blanc (Monterey) $18. Showing sophisticated melon, gooseberry, lime and peach flavors accompanied by tart acidity and a lively mouthfeel. This is an elegant wine, balanced and with plenty of flair. **86** —*S.H. (6/1/2005)*

Concannon 2004 Limited Release Assemblage White Wine Sauvignon Blanc (Central Coast) $15. So dry, so tart is this citrusy, high-acid wine that the palate begs for some morsel to soften it. Goat cheese will do exactly that, or grilled veggies, or a nice halibut sautéed in butter and olive oil. A heck of a good food wine. **87** —*S.H. (12/15/2005)*

Concannon 2005 Reserve Sauvignon Blanc (Monterey County) $18. You'll find a bit of cat pee, so if that turns you off go elsewhere. Fortunately, there are richer notes of citrus fruits, figs and melons. The wine is high in acids and very clean. Unoaked. **85** —*S.H. (12/1/2006)*

Concannon 2004 Reserve Sauvignon Blanc (Monterey County) $18. One of the most distinctive Sauvignon Blancs of the year, this one's very bright, almost searing, in acidity. The acids boost the gooseberry, citrus, fig and vanilla flavors, leading to a long, intensely clean and fruity finish. A wine to watch in future vintages. **90** —*S.H. (12/1/2005)*

Concannon 2002 Reserve Limited Release Sauvignon Blanc (Monterey) $18. This beautiful white wine has a dollop of Chardonnay added for richness, and it shows in the scent of white peach that accompanies the citrus notes. The texture is especially creamy and smooth, and it finishes with a trace of sweet lime. **89** —*S.H. (12/1/2003)*

Concannon 2002 Selected Vineyard Sauvignon Blanc (Central Coast) $12. Here's a nice value. It's clean and fruity, with good acidity, and is just a little tart. Lemon and lime flavors, with a splash of vanilla and wildflower. **85** —*S.H. (12/1/2004)*

Concannon 2004 Selected Vineyards Sauvignon Blanc (Central Coast) $10. Bone dry and acidic, with lemon-and-lime and mineral flavors enriched with a lush streak of nectarine, this is not only a fun Sauvignon, but quite an elegant one. It's hard to imagine a dry white wine more versatile with food. **86 Best Buy** —*S.H. (12/15/2005)*

Concannon 2003 Selected Vineyards Sauvignon Blanc (Central Coast) $12. A nice, dry wine, crisp and tart with acids, clean as a whistle, and bone dry. It features fresh citrus and honeydew flavors, with a hint of peppery spice on the finish. **85 Best Buy** —*S.H. (2/1/2005)*

Concannon 1997 Syrah (Livermore Valley) $20. This wine's exotic character led to widely varying reactions. Some panelists loved its ripe, intense, darkly fruited flavors, others found it pruney and overripe. Likewise, the viscous mouthfeel was dubbed rich and sensuous by some, heavy and leaden by others. Anise and chocolate shadings provide nice accents, either way…this one you'll have to try and decide for yourself. **86** *(10/1/2001)*

Concannon 2004 Limited Release Stampmaker's Syrah (Central Coast) $14. There's not much to like in this dry, harsh, acidic wine. It's thin and

minty, with an astringent finish. The wine tastes like the vines were overcropped. **81** —*S.H. (12/31/2006)*

Concannon 2003 Limited Release Stampmaker's Syrah (Central Coast) $14. Harsh and clumsy, a soft wine with sweet and sour, Chinese sauce flavors. Syrah, Grenache, Petite Sirah, Counoise, Cinsault, Mourvedre. **82** —*S.H. (3/1/2006)*

Concannon 2003 Reserve Syrah (Livermore Valley) $24. Concannon has struggled to get Syrah right for many years, and this is actually their best release in a while. It's a dry, full-bodied, robust wine, rich in tannins and fruit, with some potential for development. The blackberry, coffee and spice flavors will play well against a nice steak. **89** —*S.H. (5/1/2006)*

Concannon 2001 Reserve Syrah (Livermore Valley) $24. Way too soft and flabby, a wine that needs zest to boost the ripe blackberry and coffee flavors. **83** —*S.H. (2/1/2005)*

Concannon 2003 Selected Vineyard Syrah (Central Coast) $10. There's plenty of fruit in this country-style wine. It's jam-packed with blackberries, cherries, plums and roasted coffee flavors, and is thoroughly dry, with full-bodied tannins and tart acidity. **84** —*S.H. (12/31/2005)*

Concannon 2002 Selected Vineyard Syrah (Central Coast) $12. Impressive for its dark color and complex aroma, this wine strikes your palate as pretty good stuff. It's bone dry, with finely ground tannins, a good hit of acidity, and deep flavors of plums, blackberries, coffee and spice. It's one of the best Syrahs you'll find in this price range. **89 Best Buy** —*S.H. (12/1/2005)*

Concannon 2001 Selected Vineyard Syrah (Central Coast) $12. A good everyday wine that scores with its nice, dry tannins and good balance. A bit thin in fruit, but you'll find some plummy, blackberry flavors with a touch of smoked meat. **85** —*S.H. (12/1/2004)*

Concannon 1999 Viognier (Central Coast) $15. Opens with strong aromas of apricot jam, vanilla, honey and wildflower notes, and turns fruity-spicy on the palate. There's the rich texture and flavor of smoky honey, and the finish is spicy and just a little sweet. **85** —*S.H. (11/15/2001)*

Concannon 2004 Limited Release Stampmaker's Viognier (Central Coast) $15. If you're looking for an exotic, lush Viognier, this isn't the one. It's a tight, crisp, cool-climate wine, with citrus flavors and especially well-ripened limes, set off by mouthwatering acidity. It's also a very elegant, well-tailored wine. **87** —*S.H. (12/15/2005)*

Concannon 2003 Stampmaker's White Wine White Blend (Central Coast) $18. Rather raw in the mouth, with a certain rustic nature. It is saved by rich tropical fruit, cashew and oaky flavors, and crisp, mouth-cleansing acidity. **85** —*S.H. (6/1/2005)*

CONIGLIO

Coniglio 2002 Cabernet Franc (Napa Valley) $35. The grapes are from north of St. Helena, on the valley floor. They were fully ripened in this hot vintage, and have fleshy, forward flavors of red and black cherries, coffee, orange zest and cocoa. This is an interesting wine, lighter in body than Cabernet Sauvignon, but with depth, complexity and quite a bit of elegance. **91** —*S.H. (6/1/2006)*

Coniglio 2002 Cabernet Sauvignon (Atlas Peak) $45. The winemaker emphasizes artisanal techniques on mountain fruit, and this 100% Cabernet certainly has an authentic, handmade quality. It's dry, fairly soft and rich in ripe, thick tannins. The fruit is fully ripened, suggesting cherry and blackberry jam with a hint of olive tapenade. Try it now. A wine to watch. **91** —*S.H. (6/1/2006)*

CONN CREEK

Conn Creek 1996 Anthology Bordeaux Blend (Napa Valley) $44. **91** *(7/1/2000)*

Conn Creek 2002 Anthology Cabernet Blend (Napa Valley) $54. This year's Anthology, a blend of all five Bordeaux varieties, is not up to more recent vintages. The wine is a little slipshod, with an overly soft, gluey mouthfeel and a simple structure to the ripe fruit. Drink now. **83** —*S.H. (7/1/2006)*

Conn Creek 2001 Anthology Cabernet Blend (Napa Valley) $54. Made from all five major varieties, this Napa blend seems built for early drinking; the soft finish does not suggest ageability. At the same time, it's quite pleasant and complex now, with well-developed flavors and a classic mouthfeel. **88** —*S.H. (12/1/2005)*

Conn Creek 2000 Anthology Cabernet Blend (Napa Valley) $54. Absolutely delicious, a fat, sumptuous wine that flatters the palate from beginning to end. Smells plush, brimming with currants and fancy oak trimmings, and turns lush and complex with fruit in the mouth. Best to drink it soon, in the fullness of youth. **92** —*S.H. (6/1/2004)*

Conn Creek 2002 Limited Release Cabernet Franc (Napa Valley) $28. The winery has focused on Cab Franc, with mixed results, as the variety is tough to master. This bottling is very dry and astringently tannic, but it has a rich core of cherry fruit. Such is the balance that it might soften and sweeten after 2008. **87** —*S.H. (6/1/2006)*

Conn Creek 2001 Limited Release Cabernet Franc (Napa Valley) $28. Earth and cherry flavors mark this soft, dry wine, with some background notes of leather, hung meat and spice. Turns vanilla-oaky on the long finish. Shows harmony throughout. **88** —*S.H. (5/1/2005)*

Conn Creek 1999 Limited Release Cabernet Franc (Napa Valley) $25. Showcases this varietal's sweetly limpid, berry side. Raspberry liqueur flavors are rich and long on the palate, accompanied by crisp acids and the heat of alcohol. Delicious from the soft texture through the full-bodied, ripe finish. **93 Editors' Choice** —*S.H. (9/1/2002)*

Conn Creek 2002 Hozhoni Vineyard Cabernet Sauvignon (Rutherford) $60. Young and appealing now for its vibrant, upfront cherry and oak flavors, this supple Cab has a lush, fine array of dusty tannins, as well as fine acidity. It's beautifully balanced, a tremendously fruity wine that's has a classic structure and elegance. **91** —*S.H. (12/15/2005)*

Conn Creek 2002 Limited Release Cabernet Sauvignon (Napa Valley) $28. Owned for many years by Washington State's Ste. Michelle Wine Estates, Conn Creek has struggled to regain its early reputation for Napa Cabernet. This bottling is very tannic and astringent, with a rusticity that's unlikely to age away. But the fruit is ripe and polished. **86** —*S.H. (6/1/2006)*

Conn Creek 2001 Limited Release Cabernet Sauvignon (Napa Valley) $28. This is a tight young wine, a little closed in with tannins, but with ripe blackberry and cherry flavors, and a chocolaty finish. It's probably giving all it has now, but is polished enough for a nice dinner. **87** —*S.H. (10/1/2005)*

Conn Creek 2000 Limited Release Cabernet Sauvignon (Napa Valley) $28. A good wine that pleases for its jammy currant and cherry flavors and delicious overlay of vanilla, smoke and char from good oak. The flavors are so rich and broad they flood the mouth and persist long after you swallow. It's a little soft, though. **87** —*S.H. (6/1/2004)*

Conn Creek 1998 Limited Release Cabernet Sauvignon (Napa Valley) $25. Walks a perfect middle road between fine winemaking artisanship and what the vintage brought. The wine is feminine, with delicate Cabernet flavors and a lightness and elegance that make it tableworthy. Not an ager, but possesses grace and harmony. Drink now and until 2004. **90** — *S.H. (6/1/2002)*

Conn Creek 2001 Limited Release Merlot (Napa Valley) $28. Ultraripe and quite oaky, but for all the intensity this big wine maintains balance and harmony. The fruit is a blast of blackcurrants and vanilla, rich and fat in the middle palate and long in the finish. Near-perfect tannins lend structure to this fine Merlot. **91 Editors' Choice** —*S.H. (6/1/2004)*

Conn Creek 1999 Limited Release Merlot (Napa Valley) $25. A very nice wine with lots of personality and charm. Black cherry, tobacco and sage flavors drink fruity and pure, with dry, supple tannins and a richness that lasts into the spicy finish. There's a lightness, delicacy and suppleness that make you reach for more. **91** —*S.H. (6/1/2002)*

CONN VALLEY

Conn Valley 1997 Eloge Bordeaux Blend (Napa Valley) $80. **89** *(11/1/2000)*

Conn Valley 1997 Estate Reserve Cabernet Sauvignon (Napa Valley) $55. **90** *(11/1/2000)*

Conn Valley 1998 Fournier Vineyard Chardonnay (Carneros) $40. Crème brûlée and baked apple aromas on the nose open to a smooth palate of mild apple, pineapple and spice flavors with citrus accents. The flavors

aren't vibrant, though, and the intensity of the oak rendered the faint fruit nearly invisible. **85** *(7/1/2001)*

Conn Valley 1999 Dutton Ranch Pinot Noir (Russian River Valley) $48. The color is rusty and the nose hints at premature aging. Cinnamon and spice aromas mix with tomato and wood, and the result isn't all that pleasing. In the mouth, tired fruit is overrun by caramel and cooked brown sugar notes. **83** *(10/1/2002)*

Conn Valley 1999 Valhalla Pinot Noir (Napa Valley) $60. Black cherry and dried spice aromas share the stage with oaky, cedary notes. Once in the mouth, this fruity offering provides chocolate, cherries and red licorice. Bold, bright acidity creates a racy feel on the finish, and all the while there's a bold undercurrent of toasty wood. **86** *(10/1/2002)*

Conn Valley 1997 Valhalla Vineyard Pinot Noir (Napa Valley) $45. **87** *(10/1/1999)*

CONSILIENCE

Consilience 2001 Petite Sirah (Santa Barbara County) $22. A rich, lush wine that sports a firm framework of ripe, supple tannins surrounding its core of black cherry, blackberry, currant, plum, spice, anise and herbs. Complex yet smooth and sleek. Long, elegant finish. **90** —*J.M. (10/1/2004)*

Consilience 2000 Petite Sirah (Santa Barbara County) $21. Simple and likeable, with cola and black cherry tea flavors wrapped in a light, easy texture. Both the tannins and acids are soft, making for a nice quaff. **86** *(4/1/2003)*

Consilience 2001 Pinot Noir (Santa Barbara County) $30. Lush in ripe cherry fruit, powerfully spiced, crisp in acids, nicely oaked, and with a fine, silky texture, this is a picture perfect South Coast, cool-climate Pinot Noir. It also has a rich earthiness, and retains the delicacy and elegance that varietal demands. **90** —*S.H. (12/1/2004)*

Consilience 2003 Ashleys Vineyard Pinot Noir (Santa Rita Hills) $39. This is a delicious, rich Pinot Noir, although it's a little too soft, full-bodied and heavy for a Pinot. There's a Grenache-like cherry flavor, with chocolate overtones, and the wine is dry. Drink now. **87** —*S.H. (3/1/2006)*

Consilience 2002 Roussanne (Santa Barbara County) $22. Here's a rich, full-bodied wine with the weight and density of an oaky Chard. Has flavors of ripe white peaches, bananas and tapioca, with a trace of white chocolate on the finish, but it's dry. **86** —*S.H. (5/1/2005)*

Consilience 2002 Syrah (Santa Barbara County) $19. Seems a bit reduced upon first opening, with rubbery, meaty notes that gradually give way to smoke and cherries. In the mouth, there's mouthfilling sweet fruit, followed by spice and a hint of warmth of the finish. **85** *(9/1/2005)*

Consilience 2001 Syrah (Santa Barbara County) $17. Very good wine, with cherry-berry-mocha fruit and a dusty tinge of spice. It's the quality of the tannins and the overall balance that lend this wine harmony and power. **91** —*S.H. (9/1/2004)*

Consilience 1998 Syrah (Santa Barbara County) $19. Deep, but sour berry fruit, herbs and garden-earthy aromas open this balanced, light- to medium-bodied wine. Dark berry fruit persists on the palate, in tandem with tobacco, sour herbs and black pepper. Finishes with dry fruit and tangy pepper notes. **88** *(10/1/2001)*

Consilience 2002 Great Oaks Vineyard Syrah (Santa Barbara County) $28. This is a young, immature Syrah you'll want to have with something big and rich, to help tame the somewhat woody-tasting tannins. Berry, coffee and vanilla flavors are mouthfilling and intense, but will they measure up to the tannins in the long run? **86** *(9/1/2005)*

Consilience 2002 Hampton Vineyard Syrah (Santa Barbara County) $38. Shows that it is possible to bottle a high-alcohol wine (16%, in this case) that's still reasonably balanced. Blackberry, coffee and molasses notes are intense and tasty, while the mouthfeel is richly textured. Blackberry fruit powers through some chewy tannins on the finish, suggesting that a few years of aging isn't out of the question. **88** *(9/1/2005)*

Consilience 2001 Rodney Shull Vineyard Syrah (Santa Barbara County) $24. Perplexing wine, with promising hints of smoke, chocolate, plums and blackberries, but also a distressing lack of depth and texture. **82** *(9/1/2005)*

Consilience 2000 Rodney's Vineyard Syrah (Santa Barbara County) $22. This tremendous wine is from Fess Parker's estate vineyard in the northeastern Santa Ynez Valley. It is very ripe in black cherry and blackberry fruit. Yet its smoked meat and white pepper notes give it a distinct Rhônish quality. It's a big, flamboyant wine, but the soft sweetness of the tannins makes it drinkable now. **92** —*S.H. (9/1/2004)*

Consilience 2000 Rodney's Vineyard Syrah (Santa Barbara County) $30. A deep, dark and impressive wine made from Fess Parker's estate, in the Santa Ynez Valley. It has opening aromas of blackberry, dark plum, smoke and oak and a note of cheddar, and drinks intense in fruity flavor and tannins. It's a young, firm wine but a pliant one, and will be beautiful now with a grilled T-bone steak. **90** —*S.H. (2/1/2004)*

Consilience 2002 Star Lane Vineyard Syrah (Santa Barbara County) $36. Boasts concentrated ripe cherries and berries, but also enough volatility to deter a couple of our tasters. Pepper and earth flavors are savory, but the wine finishes a bit hot and sweet-tasting. **82** *(9/1/2005)*

Consilience 2002 Viognier (Santa Barbara County) $21. There may be some botrytis here, it's so unctuous and sweet with apricot and honey flavors. It's good, crisp stuff, but it's not a dry table wine. **84** —*S.H. (5/1/2005)*

Consilience 2001 Viognier (Santa Barbara County) $21. An effusively fruity wine that's delicious and fun to sip. It offers up a burst of ripe peach, pineapple, honeysuckle, vanilla and cinnamony flavors that last for a long time, accented by good acidity. Defines the floral, fruit-salad approach to a good Viognier. **88** —*S.H. (12/31/2003)*

Consilience 2000 Viognier (Santa Barbara County) $21. Quite complex, with effusive fruit. Mineral and earth tones add interest, with pretty peach and melon on the follow-up. Texture is balanced and mellow, while the finish is long. **90** —*J.M. (12/15/2002)*

Consilience 2002 Rhodes Vineyard Zinfandel (Redwood Valley) $30. Dark, hot in alcohol and very low in acids, with chocolate, blackberry and blueberry flavors, but at least it's dry. Will be pleasant with a backyard barbecue. **84** —*S.H. (5/1/2005)*

Consilience 1999 Rhodes Vineyard Zinfandel (Redwood Valley) $30. Smells like a ripe and juicy jamball, and that's just what you get on the palate, too. Big berries burst from the bouquet, sweetened by some creamy oak. Ditto for the palate and the medium-long finish, where vanilla sweetens the fruit even more. Lacks richness in the midpalate, says one reviewer; another calls it at once one-dimensional but utterly quaffable, particularly for novices. **84** —*D.T. (3/1/2002)*

Consilience 1998 Rhodes Vineyard Zinfandel (Redwood Valley) $27. The ripe berry flavors wear a veil of deeply toasted oak in this smooth and supple wine, but does it with finesse. Flavorful, smooth and not weighty, it has a pleasing, even texture on the tongue and displays good persistence with berry, pepper and dark toast flavors lingering on the back end. Perhaps over-oaked, but suavely so. **88** *(3/1/2001)*

CONSTANT

Constant 2002 Claret Bordeaux Blend (Diamond Mountain) $50. Soft, cherried and voluptuous. It is three-quarters Merlot, with the balance Cabernet Sauvignon. The cherry, chocolate and cassis flavors make it instantly appealing, but it has a tannic intensity that will hold it for a good five years. **92** —*S.H. (7/1/2006)*

Constant 2001 Diamond Mountain Vineyard Cabernet Franc (Napa Valley) $45. Imagine a rich, ripe mountain Cabernet without the edgy tannins and spicy currant flavor of the Sauvignon. Complex in cherry and oak flavor, with a smooth texture and an explosion of spice. It has a chocolaty finish, and is lip-smackingly delicious. **90** —*S.H. (12/15/2004)*

Constant 2002 Diamond Mountain Vineyard Cabernet Sauvignon (Diamond Mountain) $85. Constant produces intense red wines that are destined to age, and this one is no exception. It drinks well now despite sizable tannins because it's so soft and sophisticated, but easily has the balance for the long haul. With its tremendously ripe black currant fruit, it should develop bottle complexities through 2015. **94 Cellar Selection** —*S.H. (7/1/2006)*

Constant 2000 Diamond Mountain Vineyard Cabernet Sauvignon (Napa Valley) $75. This is quite a success for a 2000 Cab, probably due to the extreme mountain growing conditions. Although it is strong and even astringent in tannins, there is a sweet, flattering richness of cherry and blackberry fruit that is particularly evident on the long finish. It is an obvious cellar candidate. Drink 2008 and beyond. **90** —*S.H. (11/15/2004)*

Constant 2001 Estate Cabernet Sauvignon (Napa Valley) $85. A massive wine that floods the palate with ripe flavors of blackberries and chocolate and sweet, smoky oak. Ripe, sweet tannins make for a good grip. Finishes lush and opulent, and a little soft. **89** —*S.H. (10/1/2004)*

Constant 2002 Diamond Mountain Vineyard Syrah (Sonoma County) $48. It's not just the inviting scents of white pepper and roasted meat, or the well-ripened blackberry, cherry, blueberry and cocoa flavors that make this wine so good. It's also the fine tannin-acid balance. The wine is lushly fruity, yet structured at the same time, finishing with echoes of pepper and meat. Should drink well for 5–10 years. **92 Cellar Selection** *(9/1/2005)*

CONTRADA

Contrada 2003 Cabernet Sauvignon (Napa Valley) $16. There's lots to like about this dry, balanced Cab that showcases the way Napa ripens grapes while retaining lush, complex tannins. There's a touch of raisining in the finish, but it's seasoning, like salt on a steak. **86** —*S.H. (4/1/2006)*

Contrada 2004 Sauvignon Blanc (Napa Valley) $12. This is a new brand for me, and with this wine they're providing a crisp, fruity Sauvignon Blanc, filled with ripe fig, lime, white peach and vanilla flavors. It's very nice, but would be better if it were a little less sweet. **84** —*S.H. (4/1/2006)*

COOK'S

Cook's NV Blush Champagne Blend (California) $7. **82** —*S.H. (12/15/1999)*

Cook's NV Brut Champagne Blend (California) $7. **82** —*S.H. (12/15/1999)*

Cook's NV Brut Champagne Blend (California) $7. Pleasant enough, with simple apple and citrus notes. **82** —*J.M. (12/1/2002)*

Cook's 2000 Collector's Series Brut Champagne Blend (California) $7. This straightforward sparkler has a hay and lemon nose. The flavors are fruity but not cloying, and turn drier on the finish. The creamy texture and soft fizziness of this likeable bubbly hit all the right notes for mass appeal, including a lively, jazzy bottle. **84** *(6/1/2001)*

Cook's NV Grand Spumante Champagne Blend (California) $7. Sweet and spicy, with honey, clove, apricot and peach notes. Fun, like Asti Spumante. **84** —*J.M. (12/1/2002)*

Cook's NV Grand Spumante Champagne Blend (California) $7. **84 Best Buy** —*J.M. (11/15/2002)*

Cook's NV Spumante Champagne Blend (California) $7. Forward, emphatic aromas of candied peaches, raspberry jam, vanilla and smoke turn overtly sweet in the mouth. There's plenty of ripe, jammy fruit, and just enough acidity to keep it from being overly mushy. The finish is clean. **84** —*S.H. (6/1/2001)*

Cook's NV White Zinfandel Rosé Blend (California) $7. Simple and short, with light cherry, citrus and herb notes. **80** —*J.M. (12/1/2002)*

COOKE CELLARS

Cooke Cellars 2000 Sangiovese (Paso Robles) $24. A bizarre wine. Smells sweet and Porty, with chocolate, stewed prune and tobacco aromas, and turns tart in the mouth, with cranberry flavors and a bitter finish. **82** —*S.H. (2/1/2003)*

COOPER

Cooper 2001 Zinfandel (Lodi) $20. A little raisiny, not too much, and a little sweet, but again, not too much. Straddles the line on both. Raspberries, cherries, and an earthiness. Lots of personality here. **89** —*S.H. (3/1/2005)*

COOPER MOUNTAIN

Cooper Mountain 1999 Chardonnay (Willamette Valley) $12. Clean and tart, with crisp green apple fruit and a nice richness through the mid-palate. It's well integrated, with balanced acids and oak complementing the ripe fruit in a food-friendly style. **88 Best Buy** —*P.G. (4/1/2002)*

USA

Cooper Mountain 1999 Estate Bottled Pinot Blanc (Willamette Valley) $14. Made from 100% organically grown grapes, this Willamette Valley wine has a butterball nose, with lots of cream and caramel, overlaid with freshly cut grass. In the mouth, it's on the acidic side, with a bizarre flavor profile of hay, corn husks and tamales. Minerally finish. **82** —*D.T. (11/1/2001)*

Cooper Mountain 2004 Cooper Hill Pinot Gris (Willamette Valley) $10. Herbal up front, with some prickly aromas of tarragon on top of apple cider. Pear and melon flavors have a citrusy edge, while the finish is decent but a touch dull; there's even a banana note that we detected. Sort of a mish-mash that is decent but challenged. **84** *(2/1/2006)*

Cooper Mountain 2000 Estate Bottled Pinot Gris (Willamette Valley) $15. Cooper Mountain grows organic grapes and does well by them, as this fresh, ripe Pinot Gris shows. There's a hint of vitamin pill and waxy lemon in the bouquet, then it's all about vivid pear and green apple fruit. Plenty of weight and texture fill the mouth, and acid buoys the finish. **87** —*P.G. (4/1/2002)*

Cooper Mountain 2004 Reserve Pinot Gris (Willamette Valley) $14. Clean and inviting, with some citrus on the nose. Apple, lime and melon flavors are just rich and sweet enough to justify the reserve designation. Satisfying, with good balance. **86** *(2/1/2006)*

Cooper Mountain 1999 Pinot Noir (Willamette Valley) $17. Here is a well-made, even-tempered effort, with no rough edges. It shows simple fruit flavors that display pure Pinot character, but add little in the way of texture or spice. In other words, it's perfect for slugging down with something from the grill. **86** —*P.G. (4/1/2002)*

Cooper Mountain 1998 20th Anniversary Pinot Noir (Willamette Valley) $25. 88 —*M.S. (12/1/2000)*

Cooper Mountain 2002 Meadowlark Vineyard Pinot Noir (Willamette Valley) $27. Big but not heavy, balanced and forward, this engaging wine holds your interest with initial cranberry/raspberry flavors, that somehow open up into a more ripe, lightly pruney middle. It's got a pure, clean, long line, racy and nuanced with tea and smoke. **89** *(11/1/2004)*

Cooper Mountain 2002 Reserve Pinot Noir (Willamette Valley) $18. Unpleasant aromas lead into a light, grapy, simple and tannic wine. **84** *(11/1/2004)*

COOPER-GARROD

Cooper-Garrod 1996 Cabernet Franc (Santa Cruz Mountains) $18. 89 — *S.H. (2/1/2000)*

Cooper-Garrod 1995 Cabernet Sauvignon (Santa Cruz Mountains) $28. 92 —*S.H. (2/1/2000)*

Cooper-Garrod 1997 Gravel Ridge Vineyard Chardonnay (Santa Cruz Mountains) $20. 92 —*S.H. (2/1/2000)*

COPAIN WINES

Copain Wines 2001 Eaglepoint Ranch Syrah (Mendocino County) $35. A fantastic mountain wine, distinct and compelling. Wonderfully rich aromas of tangerine rind and blueberry ride high over cassis, plum and the smoky vanillins of fine oak. Tastes as rich as it smells, a dense, lush wine with a huge mouthburst of sweet fruit, smooth, ripe tannins, and a long, spicy-peppery finish. Needs a few years to knit together. **93 Editors' Choice** —*S.H. (12/1/2003)*

COPELAND CREEK

Copeland Creek 2002 Chardonnay (Sonoma Coast) $18. At three-plus years of age, this Chard doesn't taste quite fresh anymore. It seems like it used to have vibrant fruit, but it's losing it. It's dry and tart but not a bad wine, just different. **84** —*S.H. (3/1/2006)*

Copeland Creek 2001 Meritage (Sonoma Coast) $30. This is a hard, tannic, acidic wine showing little charm now despite being more than four years old. It doesn't seem like it has the structure, fruit or balance to age. **81** —*S.H. (3/1/2006)*

Copeland Creek 2002 Pinot Noir (Sonoma Coast) $30. Pale, delicate and light-bodied, and very crisp in acids, with tea, cola, clove, sassafras and oak flavors, and quite dry. From one of the coolest parts of the AVA. **87** —*S.H. (11/1/2004)*

Copeland Creek 2001 Pinot Noir (Sonoma Coast) $30. Awful, with garbagey smells and no flavor. **81** —*S.H. (2/1/2005)*

CORBETT CANYON

Corbett Canyon 1997 Cabernet Sauvignon (Napa Valley) $10. 81 —*S.H. (9/1/1999)*

Corbett Canyon 1997 Reserve Chardonnay (Santa Barbara County) $10. 84 *(10/1/2000)*

Corbett Canyon 1999 Reserve Merlot (California) $7. Generic red wine with lots of plummy fruit, spice, alcohol and dryness. It's clean and proper and gets the job done at an everyday price. **83** —*S.H. (7/1/2002)*

Corbett Canyon 1997 Reserve Merlot (North Coast) $10. 84 *(11/15/2000)*

Corbett Canyon 1999 Reserve Syrah (California) $7. Drinks hot and fruity, with the flavors of spiced blackberry punch. It's not the most delicate wine to ever come down the pike, but it is dry, rich and tasty, with that big, bright, jolting fruitiness that only warm sun can make. **84** —*S.H. (7/1/2002)*

CORE WINERY

Core Winery 2001 Rhône Red Blend (Santa Barbara County) $24. From 3,200 feet up in the Sierra Madre Mountains, a first-release Rhône blend of Mourvèdre, Syrah and Grenache from a promising new vintner. Very good extraction, lots of focus and intensity in the ripe fruit, but balanced, without being overly hot. Delicate tannins and firm acidity provide great structure. **90** —*S.H. (3/1/2004)*

Corey Creek 2001 Chardonnay (North Fork of Long Island) $16. 83 —*J.C. (10/2/2004)*

Corey Creek 1999 Chardonnay (North Fork of Long Island) $15. A thick, buttery and smoky style that may be too much for some tasters. Overripe and grilled peaches lack a bit of depth, yet finish long, lemony and tart, with buttered-popcorn overtones. **85** —*J.C. (1/1/2004)*

Corey Creek 1998 Chardonnay (North Fork of Long Island) $15. Here's a crisp pear- and citrus-scented Chard that has just a kiss of lightly buttered toast and roasted hazelnuts for complexity. A natural for roasted chicken seasoned with lemon. **85** —*J.C. (4/1/2001)*

Corey Creek 2001 Reserve Chardonnay (North Fork of Long Island) $21. 87 —*J.C. (10/2/2004)*

Corey Creek 1999 Reserve Chardonnay (North Fork of Long Island) $18. Whoa. The oak on Corey Creek's regular Chardonnay is near the limits, the Reserve goes over the top. It's heavy, and features butterscotch, sweet caramel and wood, with just a dash of Golden Delicious apples and lots of ground clove on the finish. **82** —*J.C. (1/1/2004)*

Corey Creek 2002 Gewürztraminer (North Fork of Long Island) $23. 83 — *J.C. (10/2/2004)*

Corey Creek 1998 Merlot (North Fork of Long Island) $18. There's plenty of toasty oak, but it only serves to accent the mixed berries and dried herbs that form the core of this juicy wine. Finishes with complex espresso, mocha and chocolate flavors that carry a slight bitter note. **87** —*J.C. (4/1/2001)*

Corey Creek 1998 Rosé Blend (North Fork of Long Island) $11. Peach and faint berry flavors in a light, crisp rosé with just a hint of residual sugar. A versatile picnic wine that's a cheerful copper hue to boot. **83** —*J.C. (4/1/2001)*

CORISON

Corison 1997 Cabernet Sauvignon (Napa Valley) $50. 93 *(11/1/2000)*

Corison 1996 Cabernet Sauvignon (Napa Valley) $45. 94 —*S.H. (2/1/2000)*

Corison 2003 Cabernet Sauvignon (Napa Valley) $65. Cathy Corison brings her deft touch to this blend from various Napa vineyards. It's a soft, comforting wine, classic Napa Cab, with black currant and smoky oak flavors edging into chocolate. It's opulent and proper rather than exciting. **89** —*S.H. (12/15/2006)*

Corison 2002 Cabernet Sauvignon (Napa Valley) $60. This flavorful Cab has some fairly hard tannins, but it's also very soft and melted in acids. The fruit is bigtime, all lush, ripe cassis. A bit disjointed, it's a wine that might improve over the next two years. **88** —*S.H. (3/1/2006)*

Corison 2001 Cabernet Sauvignon (Napa Valley) $58. Napa veteran Cathy Corison has crafted a blended wine of beauty and power. Compared to her Kronos bottling, this Cab is for immediate consumption, although it should hold well for some years. It's lush and gentle in tannins, with upfront flavors of blackberries, cocoa and green olives, and possesses great balance and charm. **91** —*S.H. (12/1/2005)*

Corison 2002 Kronos Vineyard Cabernet Sauvignon (Napa Valley) $100. The vineyard is on benches between Rutherford and St. Helena. The wine is immaculate Cabernet in the modern style, soft and rich in blackberries and cherries that are so ripe, they veer into melted chocolate. This yumminess is complexed with smoky oak, and balanced with just enough dusty tannins to keep it all from collapsing. **90** —*S.H. (12/15/2006)*

Corison 2001 Kronos Vineyard Cabernet Sauvignon (Napa Valley) $90. This single-vineyard beauty is Corison's cellar bet. Tasted beside her regular '01 Napa Cab, it's much deeper, darker and more brooding. It's also far more tannic. It's a big, flavorful wine, packed with plums, blackberries, currants and mocha, as well as a coating of sweet oak. This classic Cab should begin to soften in a few years and will drink well through 2012. **94** —*S.H. (12/1/2005)*

CORLEY

Corley 2003 Proprietary Red Wine Bordeaux Blend (Napa Valley) $50. A Bordeaux blend based on Cab Franc, this is a little lighter in body than traditional Cabernet Sauvignon, but shows the hallmarks of great Napa wine in the soft, rich, sweet tannins and ultraripe cherry purée and milk chocolate flavors, compounded with rich toasty oak. **92** —*S.H. (12/15/2006)*

Corley 2002 Proprietary Red Wine Bordeaux Blend (Napa Valley) $50. Really good claret, in a Napa-Bordeaux sense. It's based mainly on Cab Franc and Merlot, and is soft and polished, with a cherry-chocolate core. A splash of Cabernet Sauvignon adds a touch of deeper structure. This beguiling wine is like Fred Astaire and Ginger Rogers in consummate artistry. **92** —*S.H. (12/15/2005)*

Corley Reserve 2002 Cabernet Sauvignon (Napa Valley) $65. Where Corley's '02 Proprietary Red Wine is all elegance and harmony, this Cab is pure, unalloyed power. What an excellent wine it is, a detonation of cassis—rich, full-bodied and dry. Despite the great intensity, there's balance, which is a real achievement. **94 Editors' Choice** —*S.H. (12/15/2005)*

Corley Reserve 2003 Estate Grown Chardonnay (Oak Knoll) $50. Oak Knoll is in the southern Napa Valley, and this wine reflects its warmish origins in its softness. Although there are polished flavors of apples and peaches and a rich coating of oak, the wine could have greater brightness and a brisker mouthfeel. Still, it's pretty darned flavorful. **87** —*S.H. (12/15/2005)*

CORNERSTONE

Cornerstone 2002 Cabernet Sauvignon (Howell Mountain) $80. From the get-go this wine has disturbing notes. The aroma is raw, and once in the mouth, the wine turns astringently tannic and harsh. Despite a core of blackberry fruit, it's not likely to improve. **82** —*S.H. (5/1/2006)*

Cornerstone 2002 Cabernet Sauvignon (Napa Valley) $60. Although the official alcohol reading is 14.5%, this wine has pronounced flavors of raisins and dessicated berries that mar it. There's a hot, harsh feeling throughout. **82** —*S.H. (12/31/2005)*

COSENTINO

Cosentino 2005 The Novelist Meritage White Bordeaux White Blend (California) $18. Sourced from Napa, Lake County and Lodi, this is a complex white wine with quite a bit of sophistication. Mainly Sauvignon Blanc with some Sémillon, it shows citrus, peach, flower petal, mineral and vanilla flavors, with crisp acidity and a long, spicy finish. **86** —*S.H. (12/15/2006)*

Cosentino 2003 The Poet Meritage Red Wine Cabernet Blend (Napa Valley) $65. When Mitch Cosentino chooses to, and the weather gods allow, he makes a great Napa red. This Cabernet-based blend is very good. It lacks the elegance of the finest vintages, but shows a classic structure and a deep core of blackberry, coffee, olive and new oak flavors. But it's very tannic; if you open before 2009, decant. Otherwise, the wine should develop through 2015. **90** —*S.H. (12/31/2006)*

Cosentino 2002 Reserve Cabernet Franc (St. Helena) $45. If Cabernet Sauvignon isn't careful, Cab Francs like this are going to elbow it aside. This wine has fine dryness and complexity. It's an elegant, velvety wine that's not as heavy as a Cab Sauvignon, but in the same vein. It's oaky and cherryish and frankly delicious. **91** —*S.H. (10/1/2006)*

Cosentino 2003 Cabernet Sauvignon (Napa Valley) $45. There's a lot of pedigree in this Cab. It's beautifully dry, with a fine structure in which fruit, wood, acidity and tannins play well off each other. The tannins, though, are very strong, to the point of astringent lockdown. But there's no reason not to cellar this wine until 2010, at the earliest. **86** —*S.H. (10/1/2006)*

Cosentino 2004 Gewürztraminer (Yountville) $22. Napa Gewürz is a rare bird these days, especially an estate bottling from a winery as fine as Cosentino. The wine is worth the investment for the streamlined, Alsatian-style purity of its spicy fruit and flower flavors, and crisp acidity. **87** —*S.H. (12/15/2006)*

Cosentino 2002 Reserve Merlot (Napa Valley) $42. A rich, dense Merlot, dry and full-bodied. Despite its sizable tannins, it's balanced and forward in tasty cherry, blackberry and smoky oak flavors. Has a lot of style and finesse, and should hold and improve for five years. **90** —*S.H. (10/1/2006)*

Cosentino 2005 Kirschenmann Vineyard Pinot Grigio (Lodi) $18. Sweetish and simple, with the flavors of canned apricots and peaches, with lots of tangy spice. Fortunately the sweetness is balanced by juicy acidity. **84** —*S.H. (11/1/2006)*

Cosentino 2004 Il Chiaretto Sangiovese (California) $18. Not bad for a dessert wine, but the overt sugariness is a turnoff. **81** —*S.H. (11/15/2006)*

COSTA DE ORO

Costa de Oro 1998 Reserva Dorada Cold Coast Vineyard Chardonnay (Santa Maria Valley) $30. 89 *(6/1/2000)*

Costa de Oro 1999 Reserva Dorada Gold Coast Vineyard Chardonnay (Santa Maria Valley) $30. Tasty hazelnut overtones to the apple and cinnamon aromas mark the nose of this elegant wine. Toasted almond, pear and caramel flavors work in harmony. Good acidity and all-around stylish restraint make it a great food wine. **89** *(7/1/2001)*

COSTA DEL SOL

Costa del Sol 2003 Red Wine Red Blend (Napa Valley) $15. I liked this wine two years ago, and this new vintage is equally appealing. A blend of Sangiovese, Zinfandel and Bordeaux grapes, it's dry and rich, with complex berry, earth, herb and spice flavors and some oak influence. From Benessere. **88** —*S.H. (12/1/2006)*

Costa del Sol 2001 Red Wine Red Blend (Napa Valley) $15. A smooth, lovely, easy-drinking red wine that offers a fine blend of smoky, toasty, plum, chocolate, coffee and spice flavors. Soft tannins offer enough structure to hold it together. Moderate length at the end. Made from Sangiovese, Zinfandel and Merlot. **88** —*J.M. (10/1/2004)*

COTTONWOOD CANYON

Cottonwood Canyon 2000 Bistro Classic Chardonnay (Santa Maria Valley) $20. A robust blend of toasty oak, melon, citrus and spice flavors. Tangy and bright, but quite fruity, too. **86** —*J.M. (12/15/2002)*

Cottonwood Canyon 2000 Pinot Noir (Santa Maria Valley) $36. There's certainly a lot going on here, flavor-wise. You discover cherries above all, with currents of blackberry, cola, sugared rosehip tea and plenty of spices. Texturally, there's a certain rusticity and simplicity of structure. Finishes dry, with peppery acids. **86** —*S.H. (8/1/2004)*

Cottonwood Canyon 1999 Estate Pinot Noir (Santa Maria Valley) $32. Caramel and vanilla aromas signal strong oak. The raspberry fruit in the mouth is underscored by a bold streak. **86** *(10/1/2002)*

Cottonwood Canyon 2000 Sharon's Vineyard Barrel Select Pinot Noir (Santa Maria Valley) $64. A very concentrated wine. It's bursting with cherries, blackberries, root beer and chocolate, flavors that feel sweet on the palate, although the wine is bone dry. Hard to criticize, except that it's all on the surface, and at this price, you expect a little more depth. **89** —*S.H. (8/1/2004)*

Cottonwood Canyon 2000 Blanc de Blanc Sparkling Blend (Santa Maria Valley) $48. Expensive, yes, but aims high and largely succeeds in finesse and elegance. Drinks long, smooth and rich, with layers of citrus, vanilla, lees, toasted coconut and smoky wood that finish complex. This is the first sparkling wine from this winery I've tasted, and it's a quite impressive. **90** —*S.H. (12/31/2006)*

Cottonwood Canyon 2001 Blanc de Noir Sparkling Blend (Santa Maria Valley) $48. This is one of the reddest BdNs I've ever seen, and the wine is correspondingly full-bodied and varietally rich. It shows frank strawberry and raspberry flavors, yet maintains a dry elegance and even a light silkiness. Should be fabulous with Ahi tuna, especially tartare. **90** —*S.H. (12/31/2006)*

COTURRI WINERY

Coturri Winery 2001 Zinfandel (Sonoma Mountain) $20. Hot and spicy, this is an over-the-top Zin that features ultra-bright cherry, berry flavors. It's got a canned fruit quality, too. Not for everyone. **82** *(11/1/2003)*

COUGAR CREST

Cougar Crest 2001 Hangartown Select Merlot (Walla Walla (WA)) $26. Dark, deep, extracted to the point of being liqueur-like, with oily, sweet, alcoholic flavors. Plenty of very ripe fruit; not too much oak. This is a style that has its fans, but it's not a food wine, not an aging wine, not a varietal wine. For the aficionados. **87** —*P.G. (9/1/2003)*

Cougar Crest 2001 Syrah (Walla Walla (WA)) $30. Big wine, big fruit, and really big oak. This is very young and showing a lot of power; it sort of bludgeons you with flavor, but the style has its fans. **87** —*P.G. (9/1/2003)*

Cougar Crest 2002 Stellar Vineyard Reserve Syrah (Walla Walla (WA)) $45. Very toasty new oak overrides the fruit scents; in the mouth the flavors are light strawberry and rhubarb, with some surprising sweetness and a soft, approachable finish. Strikes this taster as too much oak for the light fruit. **86** —*P.G. (12/15/2005)*

COUGAR RIDGE

Cougar Ridge 1999 Cabernet Sauvignon (Paso Robles) $18. Rough going here. Opens with earth, cardboard and Port-like blackberry aromas, and turns tannic and tart in the mouth. Might soften with age. **82** —*S.H. (4/1/2003)*

Cougar Ridge 1999 Chardonnay (Central Coast) $13. Smells super-oaky, with charcoal and smoke aromas dominating the underlying fruit. Those flavors are pretty thin, suggesting peaches and apples. Extremely dry and tart, with hefty acids, but it's clean and refreshing. **84** —*S.H. (2/1/2003)*

Cougar Ridge 1999 Merlot (Paso Robles) $18. The raisiny, pruny aromas are almost Port-like, and it's thick and soft. Completely dry, with rasping tannins and tart acids. **83** —*S.H. (4/1/2003)*

COULSON ELDORADO

Coulson Eldorado 2000 Kipp Vineyard Mataro (El Dorado) $15. Soft and jammy, with black and red wild berry flavors and low acidity. It's so soft and sweetly fruity it's almost like raspberry syrup, although it does have some structure and heat from alcohol. Fans of sweet wines will like it a lot. **85** —*S.H. (9/1/2002)*

Coulson Eldorado 2001 Koel Vineyard Mataro Mourvèdre (El Dorado) $15. You say Mataro, I say Mourvèdre. Either way, this is a country wine, rustic and honest. It has fruity flavors of berries and dried herbs. Its fierce tannins won't age out, but the wine will be fine with cheese, red meats and such. **85** —*S.H. (12/1/2003)*

Coulson Eldorado 2000 Vintners Blend Red Blend (El Dorado) $16. Awkward and simple, because the acids are tart and the fruit is too light and there isn't much else in the way of flavor. It's a light wine with very soft tannins. Might wake up with food. **82** —*S.H. (5/1/2002)*

Coulson Eldorado 1999 Johnson Vineyard Syrah (El Dorado County) $16. Though the nose displays interesting smoke, game and nutty notes, there's also a skunky element that put off many tasters. The very dark, narrow palate shows faint black cherry and licorice notes, but is more espresso than anything else. There's just not enough fruit. **81** *(10/1/2001)*

Coulson Eldorado 2000 Safari Vineyard Zinfandel (El Dorado) $18. Dark, dry, tannic and acidic, this is a wine that needs big, rich foods, or else a good deal of time in the cellar. Doesn't offer much now beyond heft. **83** —*S.H. (11/1/2002)*

COURTNEY BENHAM

Courtney Benham 2002 Cabernet Sauvignon (Sonoma County) $25. The winery released their '02 Napa Cab almost a year ago and is only now releasing this one. Was it the tannins? It's still a pretty gritty wine. But it has lively and appealing blackberry and cherry flavors that make it a good partner for barbecued steak or chicken, or just a decadent cheeseburger. **87** —*S.H. (12/31/2005)*

Courtney Benham 2002 Cabernet Sauvignon (Napa Valley) $25. Feels rich in the mouth, with ripely sweet tannins and lots of cherry, blackberry and chocolate flavor, as well as pronounced oak. It's too soft and sugary to age, so drink up now **85** —*S.H. (5/1/2005)*

Courtney Benham 2005 Chardonnay (Napa Valley) $16. Good everyday Chard, with pronounced peach, apple and pear flavors and more exotic notes of tropical fruits. Oak adds the smoke, vanilla and cream that round the wine off. **84** —*S.H. (12/15/2006)*

Courtney Benham 2005 Sauvignon Blanc (Napa Valley) $12. Good price for a Napa Valley wine of this quality. Crisp and fruity, the wine is slightly oaked, and shows forward, ripe flavors of fresh green grapes, apples and pineapples. Contains a little Chardonnay and Columbard. **85** —*S.H. (12/15/2006)*

Courtney Benham 2004 Sauvignon Blanc (Napa Valley) $14. Soft and slightly sweet, with a taste of grapefruits, apricots and peaches, this simple Sauvignon has the benefit of being clean, with a touch of oak for seasoning. **84** —*S.H. (7/1/2006)*

Courtney Benham 2003 Sauvignon Blanc (Napa Valley) $14. Dry, clean and crisp, this is a refreshing, lemon-cream wine that will go well with a wide variety of foods. **85** —*S.H. (6/1/2005)*

Courtney Benham 2004 Zinfandel (Stags Leap District) $25. Showing a translucent ruby color and a silky texture, this Zin is elegantly structured, with spicy blackberry, cherry and pomegranate flavors before a slightly raisiny finish. It's not especially complex, but it is easy to drink now. **84** —*S.H. (12/1/2006)*

COVEY RUN

Covey Run 1997 Newhouse Vineyard Aligoté (Yakima Valley) $14. 88 —*M.S. (11/1/1999)*

Covey Run 2003 Cabernet Sauvignon (Columbia Valley (WA)) $9. Relatively concentrated, tannic, slightly rustic, this earthy, smoky Cabernet offers fair value and varietal flavors with a finish of herbs and moist earth. **86 Best Buy** —*P.G. (4/1/2006)*

Covey Run 2002 Cabernet Sauvignon (Washington) $9. Like the '01, this beautifully structured wine is supple and racy, with tart zippy fruit. It shows classic Washington berry flavors, with cassis, bright acid and a hint of licorice. Absolutely clean and varietal, with the extra dimension rarely found in wines at this price. **89 Best Buy** —*P.G. (11/15/2004)*

Covey Run 2001 Cabernet Sauvignon (Washington) $9. Supple and structured, this wine is a very pleasant surprise. Red meat and coffee spice light up the nose; the midpalate is firm and anchored in clean, varietal cassis fruit, lightly hinting at raspberry. It has good grip and a medium-long finish; this could actually cellar for 6–8 years. **88 Best Buy** —*P.G. (9/1/2004)*

Covey Run 1999 Cabernet Sauvignon (Washington) $9. Simple and slightly earthy, Covey's budget Cab is not as appealing as their Merlot, but it's a good effort nonetheless. Black cherry and cassis speak to the variety, and the stiff tannins suggest some staying power. **86** —*P.G. (9/1/2002)*

Covey Run 1997 Cabernet Sauvignon (Washington) $13. 83 —*P.G. (11/15/2000)*

Covey Run 1998 Barrel Select Cabernet Sauvignon (Yakima Valley) $15. Light cherry and prune fruit. This is simple, soft and round, with sweet, pruny fruit and a little coffee/spice on the finish. **85** —*P.G. (12/31/2001)*

Covey Run 1996 Whiskey Canyon Vineyard Cabernet Sauvignon (Yakima Valley) $29. 84 —*P.G. (11/15/2000)*

USA

Covey Run 2002 Winemaker's Collection Cabernet Sauvignon (Columbia Valley (WA)) $13. Unblended, this is sourced from three different vineyards, half from the famous Champoux vineyard above the Columbia River in the Horse Heaven AVA. Chewy, dusty and aromatic, its herbal notes, offset with clean red fruits, suggest a Bordeaux more than a Napa style. **87** —*P.G. (12/15/2005)*

Covey Run 1997 Cabernet Sauvignon-Merlot (Washington) $8. 87 —*J.C. (11/15/1999)*

Covey Run 2002 Cabernet Sauvignon-Merlot (Columbia Valley (WA)) $9. Pleasant, not too stemmy, with good color and well-managed tannins. The addition of 15% Cab Franc gives it a more substantial, dry, slightly dusty finish. 31,350 cases made. **86 Best Buy** —*P.G. (12/15/2005)*

Covey Run 2001 Cabernet Sauvignon-Merlot (Washington) $9. Cabernet Sauvignon is 43% of the blend, Merlot another 42%, and (surprise!) there's 15% Cab Franc in this budget bottle. As in virtually all inexpensive Bordeaux blends, a certain amount of weediness is present, but you can find that in a $50 Pauillac. This is stiff, textured, surprisingly full, and shows some pretty cherry fruit at the core. **87 Best Buy** —*P.G. (12/31/2003)*

Covey Run 2000 Cabernet Sauvignon-Merlot (Washington) $9. This blend consists of 42% Cabernet Sauvignon, 41% Merlot and the rest Cab Franc. Spicy and peppery, it has the telltale bell pepper scents of not-quite ripeness. But good value nonetheless, and structured for hearty foods. **85** —*P.G. (9/1/2002)*

Covey Run 1999 Cabernet Sauvignon-Merlot (Washington) $11. This classic Bordeaux blend of Cabernet Sauvignon (43%), Merlot (42%) and Cabernet Franc (15%) shows a dusty, earthy nose with hints of lead pencil and black raspberries. Caramel and blackberry flavors balance soft tannins for a velvety finish. This wine has enough acidity to match with Salmon and enough richness for grilled meats. **87 Best Buy** *(5/1/2002)*

Covey Run 1997 Chardonnay (Washington) $10. Best Buy —*M.M. (11/1/1999)*

Covey Run 2004 Chardonnay (Columbia Valley (WA)) $9. Very fruity, with bright melon, pineapple and red apple flavors. It's a step up from the well-made 2003, with crisp fruit and a bit more complexity. A second taste reveals a tart, racy, fruit-forward food wine with fine balance; a great choice for seafood or chicken salad. **87 Best Buy** —*P.G. (10/1/2006)*

Covey Run 2003 Chardonnay (Columbia Valley (WA)) $9. The blend includes 2% Viognier, presumably for bouquet. A measure of the classy winemaking that exemplifies this value brand. The nose indeed shows pretty citrus blossom fragrances, and light green apple fruit. Not showing residual sugar or fake vanilla flavors. Simple, straightforward and perfectly pleasant. **86 Best Buy** —*P.G. (12/15/2005)*

Covey Run 2002 Chardonnay (Washington) $9. Another wonderful effort from Covey Run, showing bright, spicy fruit from mostly Yakima Valley vineyards. A portion was barrel fermented and left on the lees, adding unusual complexity and pushing the wine past "simple, fresh and fruity" status. This is genuinely complex and delicious. **88 Best Buy** —*P.G. (11/15/2004)*

Covey Run 2001 Chardonnay (Yakima Valley) $9. Covey makes a clean, simple version of this wine, with the lightest hints of butter and toast, and a good, clean finish. **85** —*P.G. (5/1/2004)*

Covey Run 2000 Chardonnay (Washington) $9. Here is a soft, smooth, pretty wine that delivers the sort of tropical fruit and caramel flavors that make Chardonnay taste like an ice cream sundae. Pleasant and accessible. **86 Best Buy** —*P.G. (12/31/2003)*

Covey Run 1999 Chardonnay (Columbia Valley (WA)) $12. Starting with a creamy, toasty, tropical-fruit nose, this 50% barrel-fermented Chardonnay has flavors of honeydew and oranges layered with hazelnuts and vanilla cream. There is a lush mouthfeel that finishes smooth but clean. Drink by itself or with chicken and lighter foods. **87** *(5/1/2002)*

Covey Run 1998 Chardonnay (Columbia Valley (WA)) $10. 88 Best Buy —*P.G. (11/15/2000)*

Covey Run 2000 Barrel Select Chardonnay (Yakima Valley) $13. Covey's barrel select wines are given significantly more time in oak, and taste that way. This is not particularly well integrated; the oak is laid on thick, smells like lumber, and has a bitter, roughly tannic edge to it. **86** —*P.G. (12/31/2003)*

Covey Run 2003 Reserve Chardonnay (Columbia Valley (WA)) $22. Rich and intense, it's packed with buttery toasty scents of roasted hazelnuts, floral highlights (jasmine) and clean apple, citrus and pear fruit. Despite the big oak flavors, it keeps its acidity front and center and its flavors lifted. **89** —*P.G. (10/1/2006)*

Covey Run 2002 Reserve Chardonnay (Yakima Valley) $22. Rich, oaky, barrel- fermented flavors accent sweet/tart fruit. Nicely done, soft and round, but avoiding the over-the-top heat and heaviness of comparable California bottlings. **88** —*P.G. (9/1/2004)*

Covey Run 1998 Reserve Chardonnay (Yakima Valley) $15. This can only be described as thick—an unctuous, oaky style that tastes of ultra-ripe tropical fruits and bourbon-infused barrels. Though the alcohol is listed at just 13.5%, it feels bigger, and finishes with some definite heat in the back of the palate. Best drunk young and chilled. **87** —*P.G. (10/1/2001)*

Covey Run 2004 Winemaker's Collection Chardonnay (Columbia Valley (WA)) $13. Rich and round, this young wine is still showing the edges of its new oak, but offers crisp apple and pear flavors along with the vanilla, toast and hazelnut of the wood, and balanced acidity. The sharpness should smooth out with additional bottle age. **88 Best Buy** —*P.G. (12/15/2005)*

Covey Run 2004 Chenin Blanc (Columbia Valley (WA)) $8. A superior Chenin that doesn't denigrate the floral elegance of the grape. Juicy with melons, tangerines and sweet pear. A lovely wine with a hint (1.4%) of residual sugar. **89 Best Buy** —*P.G. (12/15/2005)*

Covey Run 2002 Chenin Blanc (Washington) $7. Chenin gets little respect in the U.S., and has all but disappeared as a serious wine. But it's still a good starter grape, especially when made in a fruity, juicy style as it is here. Off-dry, clean and bracing when chilled. **86 Best Buy** —*P.G. (12/31/2003)*

Covey Run 2000 Chenin Blanc (Washington) $7. Almost no one makes a dry chenin anymore. This is off-dry, fruity and simple, showing nothing of the complexity this grape can achieve if treated right. Citrusy fruit, slightly sugary finish. **85** —*P.G. (8/20/2003)*

Covey Run 1997 Fumé Blanc (Washington) $7. 89 Best Buy —*M.S. (9/1/1999)*

Covey Run 2002 Fumé Blanc (Washington) $9. Just a hint of sweet citrus boosts the forward thrust, making this a rounder, fruitier, somewhat more accessible wine than the previous austere vintage. The light, tart, lemony fruit is simple and pleasant. **85** —*P.G. (5/1/2004)*

Covey Run 2001 Fumé Blanc (Washington) $9. Steely, austere style, with tongue-tingling acids and light, tart, lemony fruit. Modestly herbaceous. **85** —*P.G. (12/31/2003)*

Covey Run 2000 Fumé Blanc (Washington) $12. Aromas of green apples and lime peel are accentuated by a lovely floral note that the 12% Sémillon brings to this mostly Sauvignon Blanc wine. A smidge of Chenin Blanc helps round out the wine. The grassy herbaceous flavors touched with citrus finish simply, with crisp acidity. A perfect match for shellfish. **86** *(5/1/2002)*

Covey Run 1998 Gewürztraminer (Washington) $7. 80 *(4/1/2000)*

Covey Run 2004 Gewürztraminer (Columbia Valley (WA)) $7. Yet another standout effort from this value producer. Clean, penetrating and varietal with layered, spicy fruit—lemon, lime, mint, anise, stone and earth in a marvelously complex array of flavors. 20,500 cases. **90 Best Buy** —*P.G. (12/15/2005)*

Covey Run 2003 Gewürztraminer (Washington) $7. Fresh and bracing, a nice mix of floral and citrus rind aromas, with spicy, semi-tropical fruit flavors. There's a splash of Muscat Canelli in the blend to bring out the orange blossom and tangerine notes. **86** —*P.G. (7/1/2004)*

Covey Run 2002 Gewürztraminer (Washington) $7. Fresh and forward, bursting with floral and citrus scents and ripe, semi-tropical flavors. A splash of Muscat Canelli in the blend brings up the orange blossom and tangerine flavors. **88 Best Buy** —*P.G. (12/31/2003)*

Covey Run 2000 Gewürztraminer (Columbia Valley (WA)) $8. A floral nose with lychee nuts and citrus fruits leads to a similarly-flavored, semisweet

USA

palate. Blending in 11% Muscat Canelli enhances the natural fruitiness of this wine, which is a very pleasant quaffer by itself or with spicy Asian food. Drink over the next year. **86** (5/1/2002)

Covey Run 2005 Quail Series Gewürztraminer (Columbia Valley (WA)) $8. Though not quite up to the exalted standard of the awesome 2004, this excellent aromatic white wine deftly mixes floral scents with dusty talcum powder and spicy citrus. A seamless blend of grapefruit, citrus and green apple fruit is lifted with varietal spice and perfume; the wine has good body too. Sounds like a hot date, which it is, ready for any kind of saucy Asian noodle dish you care to throw at it. Just not up to the overall elegance and polish of the '04. **87 Best Buy** —P.G. (12/31/2006)

Covey Run 2002 Lemberger (Washington) $7. Once marketed as "Washington's Zinfandel," Lemberger is not that interesting, but it has a place as a lusty, grapey, broad-flavored pizza-and-burger red. This is light, with very pretty raspberry fruit, and the rustic tannins are under control. **87 Best Buy** —P.G. (12/31/2003)

Covey Run 2000 Lemberger (Yakima Valley) $7. A popular favorite in the Northwest, Lemberger is a rustic, grapey, Zin-wannabe that offers pleasingly soft, fruity flavors well-suited to summer. This contains 24% Merlot, which adds weight to the fruit. Its soft tannins and light chocolate flavors make this a great go-to wine for the backyard barbecue. **87 Best Buy** —P.G. (9/1/2002)

Covey Run 1999 Lemberger (Yakima Valley) $7. Lemberger is a soft, rustic, grapey red wine that has long been a favorite of Washington winemakers. It's prolific, undemanding and reliable, and can make for a fine, juicy bottle that's just perfect for picnicking. This is one such wine; the bright fruit has enough acid to keep it from feeling flabby, and if you chill it and pack it on your next picnic, you'll be happy. **85 Best Buy** (6/1/2001)

Covey Run 2003 Merlot (Columbia Valley (WA)) $9. Bone dry, tannic, herbal and earthy at first, it benefits from airing, revealing appealing flavors of strawberry, plum and cherry with light licorice, black olive and herbes de Provence. The innovative blend includes a splash of Malbec. **87 Best Buy** —P.G. (10/1/2006)

Covey Run 2002 Merlot (Columbia Valley (WA)) $9. Covey's baseline Merlot is more authoritative than you would expect at this price. Tannic and chewy, it carries some real weight on the palate and delivers strong, herbal flavors that taste like wine, not watered-down punch. **87 Best Buy** —P.G. (6/1/2005)

Covey Run 2001 Merlot (Washington) $9. A nice effort at this price, with mixed dried herb, sweet cracker and sour plum flavors. There's enough bracing acid to give it body, and enough weight to the tart fruit to lift it well above the soda-pop style of most of its peers. **86** —P.G. (9/1/2004)

Covey Run 1999 Merlot (Washington) $9. Soft vanilla flavors counterpoint pretty cherry/berry fruit. This is a well-balanced, complete effort, with no hint of weediness despite its everyday price. **88 Best Buy** —P.G. (9/1/2002)

Covey Run 2001 Barrel Select Merlot (Columbia Valley (WA)) $13. It's easy to see why this was held back; it is not nearly as good as the other '01 Covey Merlots. Still hard and herbal, it slips over into the stemmy side of earthy, with a rough finish. **83** —P.G. (6/1/2005)

Covey Run 2000 Barrel Select Merlot (Washington) $13. A blend that includes some Cabernet Sauvignon (11%) and Cab Franc (3%), which add a little muscle to a somewhat soft, forward Merlot vintage. Definitely aging quickly, and probably drinking its best right now. Soft cherry fruit with tomato leaf/herbal notes, and a chocolaty finish. **87** —P.G. (9/1/2004)

Covey Run 1998 Barrel Select Merlot (Columbia Valley (WA)) $15. Washington Merlot has gotten pretty pricey lately, so it's a pleasure to find a solidly-made version from an excellent vintage such as this at a good price. Red fruit preserves highlight the nose; there is a slight earthiness to the mouthfeel, and some rough tannins, but the wine satisfies and delivers the Merlot goods. Not a keeper, but a fine bottle to showcase the everyday quality that Washington can deliver. **85** —P.G. (10/1/2001)

Covey Run 2001 Reserve Merlot (Columbia Valley (WA)) $22. A serious effort, with stiff tannins over firm fruit. Tightly wrapped in layers of tar,

smoke and espresso, the fruit has a piercing cranberry/cherry character that will pair well with grilled meats. **88** —P.G. (9/1/2004)

Covey Run 2002 Winemaker's Collection Merlot (Columbia Valley (WA)) $13. A very pretty nose to begin, promising some lushness and showing a mix of sweet fruit and a whiff of smoke. In the mouth there are peppery highlights, dry tannins, flavors of strawberry and light melon, and a hint of herb. **88 Best Buy** —P.G. (12/15/2005)

Covey Run 2002 Morio Muskat (Washington) $7. What on earth, you may wonder, is Morio Muskat? Not a Muscat at all—it's a hybrid cross of Sylvaner and Pinot Blanc. Off-dry and full of ripe peachy fruit flavors, it rises above plodder status with a sweet, lifted honeysuckle finish. Pair with soft cow's cheese and a hot summer day. **85** —P.G. (9/1/2004)

Covey Run 1999 Morio Muskat (Yakima Valley) $18. **84** —P.G. (11/15/2000)

Covey Run 2004 Pinot Grigio (Columbia Valley (WA)) $7. This blows away everything in its price range. Plump flavors of pear, peach, citrus and green apple show persistence, grip and mouth-cleaning tartness. **88 Best Buy** —P.G. (2/1/2006)

Covey Run 2004 Riesling (Columbia Valley (WA)) $7. There is an embarrassment of riches in Oregon and Washington when it comes to crisp, seductive Rieslings, but most of the good ones cost double this amount. Wonderfully fresh, lively and fruity, it delivers surprising complexity, with some sweetness (2.7% residual) but nothing sugary or cloying. 57,750 cases were made. The winery also markets (regionally) a limited-edition "Dry Riesling" which still clocks in at an off-dry-ish 1.5% residual. The regular version is the better of the two. **89 Best Buy** —P.G. (11/15/2005)

Covey Run 2003 Riesling (Washington) $7. Covey does a fine job with mainstream Washington Riesling, showing fresh citrus and orange flavors. They lead into a solid, fresh midpalate, and the light touch of sweetness is more than balanced with bright acids. **88 Best Buy** —P.G. (9/1/2004)

Covey Run 2000 Riesling (Washington) $7. This is beautifully sweet and fragrant in the glass, redolent of citrus blossom and a hint of talcum powder. Off-dry with a distinctive spicy streak, it seems to gain concentration through the finish. Big apricot and tangerine fruit extends into a soft, spicy landing. **89 Best Buy** —P.G. (12/31/2001)

Covey Run 1999 Riesling (Washington) $7. **85** —P.G. (11/15/2000)

Covey Run 2004 Dry Riesling (Columbia Valley (WA)) $7. Floral, fragrant and smelling of peaches and apricots, accented with honeysuckle. The addition of just 1% Gewürz may have lifted the nose a bit. Though it's labeled dry, it is in fact off-dry, at 1.5% residual sugar. Full-bodied, flavorful and blessed with a long finish of mint, flowers and lime. **88 Best Buy** —P.G. (12/15/2005)

Covey Run 2003 Dry Riesling (Washington) $7. Very nice effort, tart and bracing, with citrus peel adding an edgy bitterness to the finish. Fragrant and easy-drinking. **87** —P.G. (9/1/2004)

Covey Run 2002 Dry Riesling (Washington) $7. It says "dry" right there on the label, but it's got a lot of fruit sweetness to it. A juicy, generous, spicy wine that ought to be served well-chilled, with noodle dishes and hot stuff. **88 Best Buy** —P.G. (12/31/2003)

Covey Run 1998 Ice Wine Riesling (Yakima Valley) $22. Yum. I didn't know whether to start or finish with this word. The unctuous apricot and peach flavors touched by a spicy botrytis nose make the rich, oily mouthfeel an enjoyable experience. The acids clean up the heavy sugars as the wine closes. This wine is picked and pressed frozen to concentrate the sugars and flavors. Yum. **89** —P.G. (5/1/2002)

Covey Run 2003 Late Harvest Riesling (Washington) $9. A nicely balanced wine that might compare to a particularly ripe spätlese, with just a hint of honeyed botrytis. A balanced palate mixing citrus blossom, apples and lightly roasted almonds. **87 Best Buy** —P.G. (11/15/2004)

Covey Run 2002 Late Harvest Riesling (Yakima Valley) $9. **87** —P.G. (8/1/2003)

Covey Run 2005 Quail Series Riesling (Columbia Valley (WA)) $8. A real step down from the '04. It's still better than the winery's "Dry" Riesling, but it carries a bitter edge, like lemon rind. Fair value, good acids to balance out the residual sugar. There is nothing at all wrong with this excellent, citrusy Riesling, but it is simple, slightly sweet and fruity, without the nuances of the previous vintage. **86** —P.G. (12/31/2006)

Covey Run 2005 Quail Series Dry Riesling (Columbia Valley (WA)) $8. Though labeled dry, it still carries almost 1% residual sugar. This is not their best bottle; it actually seems a bit soft and flabby in the mouth. Some light honeysuckle, weak orange and apple flavors characterize the fruit, but the finish is simple and light. **85** —P.G. (12/31/2006)

Covey Run 2004 Winemaker's Collection Late Harvest Riesling (Columbia Valley (WA)) $13. There is not much botrytis character in 2004, but this is a solidly made late harvest wine whose 5.6% residual sugar is neither sugary nor jagged. Substantial and lined with citrus zest, the round, peachy fruit holds down the center and finishes with a smooth, not fat, lick of sweetness. **88 Best Buy** —P.G. (12/15/2005)

Covey Run 2004 Sauvignon Blanc (Columbia Valley (WA)) $8. Solidly made, in a light, tart, true-to-varietal style. There are pleasant herbal accents and the tangy citrus fruit is lifted with some palate-scraping, clean, leesy acids. **87 Best Buy** —P.G. (6/1/2006)

Covey Run 2003 Sauvignon Blanc (Washington) $9. Another in a series of outstanding efforts for this producer, clearly staking a claim to making Washington's best budget wines. This Sauv Blanc is pungent, flinty and crisp. Lemongrass and citrus fruits are set in a steely, rather than herbaceous frame. **88 Best Buy** —P.G. (11/15/2004)

Covey Run 2002 Sémillon-Chardonnay (Washington) $7. The blend is 60-40; the figgy flavors and slightly woolly texture of the Sémillon matches nicely to the crisp Chardonnay green apple fruit. A pleasant, soundly made quaffer. **85** —P.G. (9/1/2004)

Covey Run 2000 Sémillon-Chardonnay (Washington) $7. A dry style, tightly wound with hints of herb and spice. Simple, crisply rendered, and very fresh, with citrus-flavored fruit. **86** —P.G. (9/1/2002)

Covey Run 2003 Syrah (Columbia Valley (WA)) $9. A bit candied, but not bad for the price, with bubblegum and raspberry flavors joined by lashings of vanilla. No structure to speak of, so drink now. **83** (9/1/2005)

Covey Run 2002 Syrah (Washington) $9. This outstanding effort bursts with bold, dark fruits, laced with herb and earth, and fleshed out with manly tannins. Firm, puckery and balanced, it's got the juicy blackberry core and the hints of toast that let it compete with wines three times the price. **89 Best Buy** —P.G. (11/15/2004)

Covey Run 2001 Barrel Select Syrah (Columbia Valley (WA)) $13. This starts off well, with deep, saturated colors and scents of blood and beef. Not much flavor though; it's a tart, thin wine, tannic and unyielding. **85** —P.G. (7/1/2004)

Covey Run 2000 Barrel Select Syrah (Columbia Valley (WA)) $13. Most Washington Syrahs are in the $25 and up range, so a $13 one is a welcome find, at least in principle. In practice, it's a tart, hard wine, with raw, unintegrated oak. **85** —P.G. (12/31/2003)

Covey Run 1998 Barrel Select Syrah (Yakima Valley) $15. The Syrah grape seems to be finding a niche in Washington. The hot days and cool nights emulate those of the Rhône Valley, retaining acids in the grapes. Plums, currants and fresh-vegetable aromas lead into a mouthful of fleshy dark fruits, leather and a slight gamy quality. Full but well integrated tannins balance the juicy acidity to provide a rich, enjoyable finish. **89 Best Buy** (5/1/2002)

Covey Run 1998 Barrel Select Syrah (Yakima Valley) $15. From beginning to end, the Covey Run shows dark espresso-leather-soil and lots of sour cherry and blueberry flavors. It's a bit thin with moderate acidity, and has a dry, toasty espresso-like finish. **84** (10/1/2001)

Covey Run 2002 Winemaker's Collection Syrah (Columbia Valley (WA)) $13. Pungent and assertive with spice, pepper, juniper and lemon oil, this is a potent style of Syrah, lifted and high toned, that may not have universal appeal. Distinctive, tannic and clearly showing its Viognier and Roussanne components, this leaves a lingering impression of orange peel and white pepper. **88 Best Buy** —P.G. (12/15/2005)

Covey Run 1998 White Blend (Columbia Valley (WA)) $7.83 —P.G. (11/15/2000)

COVINGTON CELLARS

Covington Cellars 2003 Tuscan Red Sangiovese (Walla Walla (WA)) $28. Just 38 cases produced. The fruit is sourced from the Seven Hills vineyards, and the blend is a "super-Walla-Wallan" with 60% Sangiovese, 20% Cabernet Sauvignon and 20% Cab Franc. Light and somewhat unfocused, it has some characteristic high tones, a suggestion of anise and a bit of toasty oak in the finish. **86** —P.G. (6/1/2006)

Covington Cellars 2003 Starr Syrah (Walla Walla (WA)) $25. Just 40 cases produced. It's 78% Syrah, the rest Sangiovese, aged in all new Hungarian oak. Predictably, the oak wins. There's plenty of bacon and smoked meat scents and flavors, but not much going on fruit-wise. **86** —P.G. (6/1/2006)

COYOTE CANYON

Coyote Canyon 2002 Chenin Blanc (Santa Lucia Highlands) $15. Bitter in acidity and bone dry, this wine has lemon and lime, vanilla and herb flavors. Finishes acidic and clean. Needs food. **84** —S.H. (12/31/2004)

Coyote Canyon 2001 Chenin Blanc (Santa Lucia Highlands) $21. One of the better California Chenins of recent years, a clean, dry and crisply acidic wine with citrus, tobacco and dried herb flavors, and a sweet-and-sour finish. Built along Sauvignon Blanc lines, but richer. **87** —S.H. (12/15/2003)

Coyote Canyon 2002 Pinot Noir (Santa Lucia Highlands) $18. Pale in color, with delicate but spicy aromas of cola, gingerbread, cherries and smoky oak, this is really a pleasant wine. It's silky and light in texture, with good flavors of red berries and spices, and is dry and crisp. Finishes with an elegant flourish of spicy oak. **87** —S.H. (11/1/2004)

Coyote Canyon 1999 Garys' Vineyard Pinot Noir (Santa Lucia Highlands) $55. My, how pricy wines from this vineyard have become. This release is rather herbal and earthy, with mushroomy, beet and black cherry flavors with an edge of sweet dried tomato. It's very dry and well-balanced, with considerable oak. Brims with young, firm acids and is a hopeful cellar candidate. **88** —S.H. (8/1/2003)

Coyote Canyon 2002 Reserve Pinot Noir (Santa Cruz Mountains) $32. A lovely Pinot, lightly colored, delicate, silky and elegant. You'll find pretty flavors of cherries, cola, peppery spices and herbs, with gentle oak shadings. **87** —S.H. (11/1/2004)

Coyote Canyon 2001 The Big Pond Pinot Noir (Santa Lucia Highlands) $42. This is an elaboration of the winery's regular Santa Lucia bottling, being darker, oakier and fuller-bodied. The red berry flavors have more intense suggestions of black fruits and coffee. Yet the wine maintains a crisp delicacy and elegance. The finish alone is worth extra points. **91** —S.H. (12/1/2004)

Coyote Canyon 2001 Sangiovese (Russian River Valley) $30. If you can open the faux-wax capsule—no easy task!—you'll find a lovely wine. Drinks dry, supple and light-bodied, like a fine Pinot, with black cherry, earth, tobacco and dried herb flavors that are balanced with crisp acids. Bone dry, it's a delicate but assertive wine. It's hard to imagine a more versatile red to have with everything from roast lamb to pizza. **90** —S.H. (9/1/2003)

Coyote Canyon 2002 Syrah (Arroyo Seco) $32. Ripe in blackberry and coffee flavors, and completely dry, this is a good dinner wine that is searching for a varietal identity. It has nice, even tannins and acids, and no particular personality. **85** —S.H. (12/31/2004)

COYOTE CREEK

Coyote Creek 1999 Syrah (Paso Robles) $17. There's fruit on the nose, but it's more sweet Hawaiian Punch than complex berry. Bright raspberry plus a vanilla extract note on the palate confirmed tasters' initial juicy impressions. It incongruously finishes rather dry, with cedar and metal notes. **81** (10/1/2001)

Coyote Creek 1999 Zinfandel (Paso Robles) $19. Right out of the bottle, this Zin's bouquet is rife with tin-can and weedy-herbal aromas, plus a little pepper; once you're on your second glass, though, those aromas burn off to reveal oaky dark fruit underneath. In the mouth, oak, metallic and sweet powder cover black berry fruit. Lean with slightly elevated acidity, it finishes with stout berry fruit doused in more tangy oak and metallic notes. Tastes more like a French Syrah than a California Zin. **84** —*D.T. (3/1/2002)*

CRANE BROTHERS

Crane Brothers 2002 Syrah (Napa Valley) $40. A controversial wine, with one reviewer calling it polished and easy to drink, while another downgraded it for hints of volatility and brett. Worth trying, as you might find its herbal, peppery notes accenting blackberry fruit appealing and its long finish to pick up vanilla and spice notes, or just simple and watery, as another reviewer did. **86** *(9/1/2005)*

CRANE FAMILY

Crane Family 1999 Merlot (Napa Valley) $37. From a new winery, an interesting first effort. The fruit is on the earthy, tannic side, with high acidity, although there are plummy notes. Yet the structure is impeccable. Oak highlights rather than dominates. Probably not meant to be aged, but keep an eye on this winery. **87** —*S.H. (12/31/2001)*

Crane Family 2000 Don Raffaele Estate Merlot (Napa Valley) $39. A very strong wine of superior tannic and acid structure. You can feel the pedigree in your mouth, smooth, elegant and luscious. The fruit is as ripe as it might be. The flavors are earthy and tobaccoey, and the wine turns astringent on the finish. **86** —*S.H. (8/1/2003)*

Crane Family 2000 Hilltop Selection Merlot (Napa Valley) $52. Terrific structure on this well made wine. You'll be impressed by the rich tannins and fine acids. Caresses the palate with gentle smoothness. But be forewarned, this wine is lean on fruit. It's herbal and earthy. But it shows that a Napa red doesn't have to be fruit bomb to be elegant and delicious. **89** —*S.H. (8/1/2003)*

CRANE LAKE

Crane Lake 2003 Chardonnay (California) $5. Clean, with apple, tangerine and peach flavors and an overlay of oak. Has a pleasantly spicy finish. **84 Best Buy** —*S.H. (12/15/2004)*

Crane Lake 2004 Merlot (California) $5. This is a good price, but be forewarned, this is a very rustic wine. It's dry, sharp in acids and jammy in blackberry flavors, with the unfinished feeling of a wine still in the fermenter. **82** —*S.H. (4/1/2006)*

Crane Lake 2003 Merlot (California) $5. Good five-buck wine. Dry, full-bodied and juicy in youthful berry jam flavors, and even a kiss of smoky oak. **84 Best Buy** —*S.H. (8/1/2005)*

Crane Lake 2004 Pinot Grigio (California) $5. From the Two Buck Chuck folks, a real bargain. Dry and crisp in acidity, and pleasant in bright spearmint, melon and fig flavors. It's the kind of wine that'll go with a wide variety of food. **84 Best Buy** —*S.H. (11/15/2006)*

Crane Lake 2005 Sauvignon Blanc (California) $5. Not much going on with this thin, watery wine. It's dry and tart, with a splash of citrus flavor. **82** —*S.H. (11/1/2006)*

Crane Lake 2004 Sauvignon Blanc (California) $5. Like pungent green grass and cat pee in your white wines? Then buy this one. It's dry and acidic, but has a ripe, long-lasting, citrusy finish. **83 Best Buy** —*S.H. (3/1/2006)*

Crane Lake 2004 Shiraz (California) $5. It isn't Hermitage, but it's clean, fruity and pleasant, in a rustic sort of way. Five dollars is the suggested retail price, but you can probably find it for even less. Sharp in grapey-jammy black cherries and mocha, and fully dry, it's the kind of inexpensive house red that millions of Americans depend on. Kudos to Bronco Wine Co., which makes this and other value brands, including Two Buck Chuck. **84 Best Buy** —*S.H. (11/15/2006)*

CRAWFORD

Crawford 2003 Sauvignon Blanc (Napa Valley) $22. Bright, crisp, fresh and lemony. This zippy wine also serves up a fine core of melon, herb and grapefruit flavors, while finishing with a clean, mineral ending. **88** —*J.M. (10/1/2005)*

CRICHTON HALL

Crichton Hall 2003 Chardonnay (Napa Valley) $28. This wine captures a certain style of Napa Chard, namely an appley, earthy quality that's very

dry, and that shows dusty tannins and soft acids. Drink now. **84** —*S.H. (3/1/2006)*

Crichton Hall 2001 Chardonnay (Napa Valley) $28. You'd almost think this was apple cider, so pure in sweet green and red apple flavors is it. Whether that's due to oak, glycerine or sugar, it's too sweet, and low in acidity to boot. **85** —*S.H. (11/15/2004)*

Crichton Hall 1998 Chardonnay (Napa Valley) $26. **88** *(6/1/2000)*

Crichton Hall 1997 Chardonnay (Napa Valley) $22. **91** —*M.S. (6/1/1999)*

Crichton Hall 1996 Chardonnay (Napa Valley) $22. **91** —*M.S. (6/1/1999)*

Crichton Hall 2001 Merlot (Napa Valley) $32. Very extracted and jammy, just oozing with sweet cherry, plum and blackberry flavors. The smoky, vanilla-packed oak also is pronounced. As tasty as this wine is, it could use more balance and restraint of these powerful elements in order to achieve harmony. **87** —*S.H. (12/15/2004)*

Crichton Hall 1996 Merlot (Napa Valley) $26. **90** —*M.S. (6/1/1999)*

Crichton Hall 1995 Merlot (Napa Valley) $26. **93** —*M.S. (6/1/1999)*

Crichton Hall 2001 Reflexion Merlot-Cabernet Sauvignon (Napa Valley) $75. This stunningly rich and good Merlot-Cabernet blend has a splash of Cab Franc and Syrah, but it's very tannic. Yet beneath the tannins is a solid vein of black cherry, currant, plum, chocolate and spice flavors. Enjoy it now in its youth, or age past 2010. **93** —*S.H. (11/15/2004)*

Crichton Hall 2000 Pinot Noir (Carneros) $32. Very inviting, displaying unique, appealing orange-clove, even peach-like aromatics over a cherry fruit core. Clove, anise, caramel and earth accents show on the smooth, structured palate. Good focus and an even mouthfeel give this lanky wine great appeal all the way through its long, smoke and anise-tinged finish. **89** *(10/1/2002)*

Crichton Hall 1996 Pinot Noir (Napa Valley) $26. **89** —*M.S. (6/1/1999)*

Crichton Hall 1995 Pinot Noir (Napa Valley) $26. **88** —*M.S. (6/1/1999)*

Crichton Hall 2003 Truchard Vineyard Pinot Noir (Carneros) $32. This is a fine vineyard and this is a very good Pinot. It's dry and full-bodied, and flamboyant in cherry pie flavors enriched with vanilla and toast from oak. There's a rich inner structure of acidity and tannin. Good now with a nice steak, but should develop well over the next five years. **89** —*S.H. (3/1/2006)*

Crichton Hall 2001 Truchard Vineyard Pinot Noir (Carneros) $32. You can tell from the pale color that this is a delicate, light-bodied wine, and it is. It's silky and crisp, and feels weightless on the palate. The flavors? Ripe cherries and raspberries, drizzled with vanilla. The sweetness of the fruit creates weight of its own. **89** —*S.H. (12/1/2004)*

CRINELLA

Crinella 2004 Marino Vineyard Sauvignon Blanc (Russian River Valley) $22. Clean, dry and crisp in acidity, this wine has citrus and fig flavors, with an edge of tangy gooseberry. It's nice and elegant, but finishes a little thin. **84** —*S.H. (10/1/2006)*

CRISTOM

Cristom 2003 Pinot Gris (Willamette Valley) $16. This is the winery's first estate-grown pinot gris, a soft, yeasty wine that tastes of white peaches sprinkled with cinnamon. There's a nice lift to the back palate, and a refined elegance through the finish. **87** —*P.G. (2/1/2005)*

Cristom 2004 Estate Pinot Gris (Willamette Valley) $17. High density plantings, select clones, native yeasts—Steve Doerner is as dedicated a winemaker as you will ever meet. This wine validates his efforts; it's a delicious, textural, varied and satisfying effort. The wine plays with the palate, offering layers of stone, fruit, acid, herb, spice and skin that mix and mingle easily. **92 Editors' Choice** —*P.G. (2/1/2006)*

Cristom 1998 Oregon/Washington Pinot Gris (Oregon) $15. About 22% of the fruit is from the Celilo vineyard in Washington, hence the dual appellation. Despite the carpetbagger grapes, or maybe because of them, this is superb wine. Intense, ripe and concentrated with a beautiful blend of citrus and mineral elements. The finish, which adds nuts and smoke to the above, is a dead ringer for good French Chablis, and the finish goes on for miles. **92 Editors' Choice** —*P.G. (11/1/2001)*

USA

Cristom 2003 Eileen Vineyard Pinot Noir (Willamette Valley) $45. The youngest of Cristom's estate vineyards, Eileen is also at the highest elevation. Flavors follow: it is perhaps the most "Oregonian" of the lineup, with noticeable touches of tomato leaf and wet soil, along with tart blackberry and vanilla. Finishing tannins are quite dry and austere. **89** —P.G. (5/1/2006)

Cristom 2002 Eileen Vineyard Pinot Noir (Willamette Valley) $45. This young (planted 1997) vineyard delivers bright, tight fruit tasting of raspberries and currants. There are sweet scents of new oak, hints of blueberry, and plenty of alcohol, though it seems balanced and nicely structured. Needs more time to pull itself together. **90** —P.G. (2/1/2005)

Cristom 2000 Eileen Vineyard Pinot Noir (Willamette Valley) $39. Cristom is into whole-cluster fermentation, and in this case we smelled the stems in the form of green beans and tobacco ash. The mouth is both herbal—like Chartreuse—and sweet, like sugar beets. The finish is layered, earthy and thick. **86** (10/1/2002)

Cristom 2003 Jessie Vineyard Pinot Noir (Willamette Valley) $45. The biggest, brawniest wine in the lineup, the Jessie is also the most hard and severe upon opening. A luscious blend of red, blue and black berries, it is shot through with mineral, earth, leaf and bark as well. **91** —P.G. (5/1/2006)

Cristom 2000 Jessie Vineyard Pinot Noir (Willamette Valley) $39. The nose begins slightly prickly and hot before opening to deliver cherry, smoke and flowers. The fruit borders on pruney, but the wine toes the line of balance to remain stylish and friendly. The palate features soft tannins; it's luxurious rather than hard or racy. **89** (10/1/2002)

Cristom 2000 Louise Vineyard Pinot Noir (Willamette Valley) $39. Cristom has a handful of single-vineyard estate wines, but it's usually the Louise that stands out. It begins with inky black fruit aromas, soy and wintergreen. The palate issues waves of black cherry, plum, mocha, espresso and char. The round, spicy finish is glorious; the total package is solid. **91 Editors' Choice** (10/1/2002)

Cristom 1998 Louise Vineyard Pinot Noir (Willamette Valley) $39. 88 (12/1/2000)

Cristom 1997 Louise Vineyard Pinot Noir (Willamette Valley) $32. 90 (10/1/1999)

Cristom 2003 Marjorie Vineyard Pinot Noir (Willamette Valley) $45. These are lighter, less ripe flavors—pomegranate, rhubarb, salmonberry—but nicely turned in this warm vintage. Some cinnamon spice sweetens the naturally earthy, green tea tannins. **90** —P.G. (5/1/2006)

Cristom 2000 Marjorie Vineyard Pinot Noir (Willamette Valley) $39. The bouquet is soft, with notes of milk chocolate and sweet, ripe black plum. Black cherry is the dominant flavor, with nuances of bacon and vanilla playing supporting roles. Charred oak and black coffee define the finish. **89** (10/1/2002)

Cristom 1997 Marjorie Vineyard Pinot Noir (Willamette Valley) $32. 89 —P.G. (9/1/2000)

Cristom 1998 Marjorie Vineyards Pinot Noir (Willamette Valley) $39. 92 —M.S. (12/1/2000)

Cristom 2000 Mt. Jefferson Cuvée Pinot Noir (Willamette Valley) $24. Strawberry fruit and dried spice hints weren't enough to overcome this light wine's major herb/vegetal notes. There are attractive smoky notes here, but overall it's lean and just too green. **83** — (10/1/2002)

Cristom 2003 Mt. Jefferson Cuvée Pinot Noir (Willamette Valley) $25. This cuvée, also a blend of nine vineyards, is just slightly less rich and ripe and seductive than the lineup-leading reserve. There's a ton of varietally pure, very pretty cherry scents and fruit flavors; then more meaty elements—blood and earth, tea and tannin—start to show through. Wild raspberries fill out the finish. **91 Editors' Choice** —P.G. (5/1/2006)

Cristom 2002 Mt. Jefferson Cuvée Pinot Noir (Willamette Valley) $25. A very fine effort in this price range. It opens with a soft, varietally pure, very pretty nose, scents of cherries and vanilla lightly kissed with herbal spices. The wine tightens up in the mouth, and shows some spine and near-term aging potential. **89** —P.G. (2/1/2005)

Cristom 1998 Mt. Jefferson Cuvée Pinot Noir (Willamette Valley) $25. 87 (12/1/2000)

Cristom 1997 Mt. Jefferson Cuvée Pinot Noir (Willamette Valley) $20. 82 (10/1/1999)

Cristom 2003 Reserve Pinot Noir (Willamette Valley) $35. Cristom's 2003 reserve is a blend of grapes from nine different vineyards. Supple and concentrated, it beautifully mixes raspberry, blackberry and cherry flavors with hints of earth and chewy, tea-leaf tannins. Excellent grip, weight and length; slowly but surely some pretty mocha flavors suffuse the finish. **92** —P.G. (5/1/2006)

Cristom 2002 Reserve Pinot Noir (Willamette Valley) $35. Cristom's reserve is a blend of 11 different vineyards, and makes a strong case for this approach over the single vineyard mania that has gripped Oregon for years. This is a big, concentrated wine, still hard and tight, with raspberry/blackberry fruit focused and lifted by tart acids. Just a light touch of oak balances it out. **91** —P.G. (2/1/2005)

Cristom 2000 Reserve Pinot Noir (Willamette Valley) $39. The nose offers graham cracker and toast, and just a little bit of green. There's tons of plum and cherry on the palate as well as coffee and chocolate—just what you want in terms of complexity and hedonism. Solid tannins drive the broad, oaky finish. **89** (10/1/2002)

Cristom 1998 Reserve Pinot Noir (Willamette Valley) $36. 91 (12/1/2000)

Cristom 1997 Reserve Pinot Noir (Willamette Valley) $30. 88 —P.G. (9/1/2000)

Cristom 2003 Viognier (Willamette Valley) $25. From 100% estate-grown fruit, this barrel-fermented viognier proves that Oregon has real potential with the grape. This is a big, thick wine, lusciously packed with lime and citrus fruit and rind. Big, alcoholic and fruit-driven, it's definitely a drink-now style. **88** —P.G. (2/1/2005)

CRISTOPHE

Cristophe 2000 Pinot Noir (Monterey) $10. 82 (10/1/2002)

CROCKER & STARR

Crocker & Starr 2003 Sauvignon Blanc (Napa Valley) $23. Clean and pretty with some weight to the stone-fruit dominated nose. Clearly from the meaty, ripe-fruit school of thought, with honeysuckle, spiced pear, citrus and minerality molding the palate. Lengthy and large on the finish, with anisette and a hint of alcohol. **89** (7/1/2005)

CROOKED VINE

Crooked Vine 2001 Chardonnay (Livermore Valley) $30. Opens with a strongly oaky, leesy note, and then it turns flamboyantly oaky and fruity in the mouth. The citrus and tropical fruit flavors are accompanied by a caramel taste that comes from well-charred oak barrels. A bit obvious in opting for a blowsy style. **85** —S.H. (12/15/2003)

Crooked Vine 2001 Sangiovese (Livermore Valley) $30. Made in a heavier, full-bodied style, with extracted, ripe fruit suggested plum, blackberry and espresso. Dry, with thick but soft tannins, it needs a little more delicacy. **85** —S.H. (12/1/2003)

CROSSPOINT

Crosspoint 2001 Cabernet Sauvignon (Paso Robles) $12. Opens with an aroma of cheese, under which are green olives, blackberry and coffee. Flavors include blackberries and herbs, and the tannins are very rugged and numbing. Finishes with a gritty astringency. From J. Lohr. **84** —S.H. (12/31/2003)

Crosspoint 2002 Pinot Noir (Monterey County) $12. Starts out with cherry candy aromas and some funky, leathery notes, then turns very fruity in the mouth. Red and black cherries, smoky oak and orange peel flavors drink supple and long, with good acidity. **88 Best Buy** (11/1/2004)

CROZE

Croze 1999 Cabernet Sauvignon (Napa Valley) $35. Dark in color, but it opens with clumsy aromas of vegetables, and the flavors are lean and alcoholic. Seems more like an unripe 1998 than a '99. The austerity merely accentuates the acids and tannins. **82** —S.H. (11/15/2002)

Croze 2004 Rosé of Cabernet Sauvignon (Suisun Valley) $14. Dark for a rose, full-bodied and very dry, with flavors of rosés and blackberry tea. There's a rich, intense finish of berries. **85** —S.H. (11/1/2005)

USA

Croze 2001 Sweetwater Ranch Cabernet Sauvignon (Oak Knoll) $28. This full-bodied wine has a taste of wild herbs, especially lavender, and a robust, silky texture. It's dry, with brambly flavors, and more Rhône-like than a Napa Cab. Has the balance and complexity for fine foods. **89** — S.H. (11/1/2005)

CRYSTAL BASIN CELLARS

Crystal Basin Cellars 2001 Reserve Mourvèdre (El Dorado) $25. A lovely wine, rich and supple. Just shows how well this varietal can do up in the Foothills. Ripe blackberry with a hint of tangerine and peach, and a delicate waft of milk chocolate. Despite the richness the wine is fully dry, with great tannins that are silky smooth. A real find. **90** — S.H. (12/1/2003)

Crystal Basin Cellars 2001 Reserve Syrah (El Dorado) $22. Opens with a pretty aroma that's clean and complex, suggesting violets, cassis, vanilla and smoky spice. Drinks quite rich and supple, with a firm body and a gritty mouthfeel due to the tannins. There's a good amount of sweetly ripe fruit that is pleasant through the finish. **88** — S.H. (12/1/2003)

CRYSTAL VALLEY CELLARS

Crystal Valley Cellars 2003 Cabernet Franc (California) $18. There's tons of upfront fruit in this exuberant, easy drinking wine. Red and black cherries star, with notes of black raspberries and chocolate. Finishes with a sweet, sugary flourish. **83** — S.H. (7/1/2005)

Crystal Valley Cellars 2002 Cabernet Sauvignon (California) $16. A nice, easy drinking wine with some extra features that make it worth your while. Soft in texture, it's loaded with ripe black currant, dark chocolate and oak flavors. Makes you want to keep on sipping. **88** — S.H. (10/1/2005)

Crystal Valley Cellars 2000 Cabernet Sauvignon (Yountville) $16. Has a lot in common with far more expensive Cabernets. The dark color promises a richness that's confirmed with a sniff revealing ripe cassis fruit and smoky oak. In the mouth, it's quintessentially fine California Cabernet, rich and dry, balanced and delicious. Lacks the extra dimensions of the best stuff, but not by much. Impressive, and a great value. **91** — S.H. (12/31/2002)

Crystal Valley Cellars 2002 Chardonnay (California) $14. Part of the huge wave of statewide appellation Chards now hitting the market. This one is strictly down the middle, offering modest peach and apple flavors and a good texture. **84** — S.H. (8/1/2004)

Crystal Valley Cellars 2001 Chardonnay (California) $14. Seriously overpriced, a thin, boring wine with little to recommend it. Tastes like pure alcohol, with nothing going on but acidity. At least it's clean. **81** — S.H. (10/1/2003)

Crystal Valley Cellars 2000 Chardonnay (California) $14. Ripe, polished and pretty, this charming wine has full-throttle apple and pear flavors and tasty spice. It's refreshingly crisp and well-structured, with a long, rich finish. Mainly Lodi grapes, from Cosentino. **87** — S.H. (11/15/2001)

Crystal Valley Cellars 2000 Reserve Chardonnay (California) $16. Dont' be misled by the California appellation: This is a well-made, attractive wine with lots of virtues. The pear flavors veer toward melon, melon and there's a little sweetness, with a dollop of smoky oak and the rich, creamy texture people like. **85** — S.H. (12/31/2001)

Crystal Valley Cellars 2004 The Chard Chardonnay (California) $16. Made primarily from Delta and Lodi grapes, this is an innocently good Chardonnay, rustic in character, but likeable for its fruit, touch of oak and thoroughly dry character. It finishes with a rich streak of vanilla-drizzled peaches and cream. **85** — S.H. (12/15/2005)

Crystal Valley Cellars 2003 Merlot (California) $18. Here's a good, veryday Merlot, with some complexity. It's dry and balanced, with a good array of black cherry, blackberry and toasty oak flavors. Has the flash of a very fine wine, without quite the depth, but the price is fair. **87** — S.H. (3/1/2006)

Crystal Valley Cellars 2002 Reserve Merlot (California) $16. Plenty of jammy black cherry fruit here, really easy to drink and to like for its soft texture. Wears a light jacket of oak that adds seasoning. **86** — S.H. (10/1/2005)

Crystal Valley Cellars 2001 Reserve Merlot (California) $16. There's a very smooth texture in this wine, so velvety are the tannins. There are also some likeable plum and blackberry flavors. A touch of bitter astringency, however, lowers the points. **84** — S.H. (12/31/2003)

Crystal Valley Cellars 2000 Reserve Merlot (California) $16. There's lots of elegance to this ripe, fruity wine. The plum and blackberry flavors are nicely offset by rich, soft tannins and a kiss of oak. Balanced and harmonious, this Merlot is easily as good as many costing far more. **90** — S.H. (11/15/2002)

Crystal Valley Cellars 1999 Reserve Merlot (California) $18. A nice all-purpose red, dry and stylish. It has hot country aromas of plums and raisins, but drinks smooth and fruity. Dry, but with lusciously extracted fruit and soft, pretty tannins. The finish is very long and spicy. A nice, gulpable wine, from Cosentino. **84** — S.H. (12/31/2001)

Crystal Valley Cellars 2001 Pinot Noir (California) $16. Not badly made, just thin and wanting in flavor. The yield on these Solano and Napa county vines must have been enormous. The mouth sensation is of heat and acidity, with a bit of green strawberry thrown in for good measure. **82** — S.H. (7/1/2003)

Crystal Valley Cellars 2000 Pinot Noir (California) $16. Smoky, cedary opening notes set the stage for a wood-dominated performance. It's possible to discern some tart cherry fruit, but the focus is dry, toasted oak. Our panel found this lean and one-dimensional, but fans of oak may lap this up. **84** (10/1/2002)

Crystal Valley Cellars 2002 Sauvignon Blanc (California) $14. A winning wine that charms you with its upfront and honest flavors of well-ripened fruit. Sweet, lemony citrus, figs, melon and spices are wrapped in a creamy texture that finishes with a honeyed richness. **86** — S.H. (8/1/2004)

Crystal Valley Cellars 2000 Mohr-Fry Ranch Sauvignon Blanc (California) $13. From a celebrated Lodi grower; turned into wine by Napa Valley's Mitch Cosentino. A zesty wine with lemongrass, mint and smoke aromas. The fresh, clean flavors are of citrus fruits and spearmint, slightly sweet, with crisp, juicy acidity. **86** — S.H. (11/15/2001)

Crystal Valley Cellars 2001 Mohr-Fry Vineyards Sauvignon Blanc (Lodi) $14. Crystal Valley is a Cosentino brand, and this single-vineyard wine is fruity and tasty, with the rich, honeyed texture of a fully ripe wine. Has a kiss of oak and a nice, long, citrusy finish. **85** — S.H. (7/1/2003)

Crystal Valley Cellars 2002 Syrah (Lodi) $16. Smells raw and minty, and tastes tart in green tannins and acids, turning cherryish on the finish. Perhaps the winemaker was trying to avoid superripeness, but this wine is too sharp to enjoy. **82** — S.H. (9/1/2005)

Crystal Valley Cellars 2001 Syrah (California) $16. A darkly plump, juicy wine, a little on the rustic side with its edgy tannins and rough mouthfeel. But the flavors are nice and ripe, showing peppery plum and blackberry and sweet smoked meat, like prosciutto. **86** — S.H. (12/1/2003)

Crystal Valley Cellars 2000 Syrah (California) $16. There's a ton of varietal character in this fnely crafted wine, from the pepper and plum flavors to the rich, full-bodied texture. It's big and dense but never loses sight of elegance and finesse. The velvety texture is a delight. Great value compared to some of these superpremium prices. **91** Best Buy — S.H. (12/1/2002)

Crystal Valley Cellars 1999 Syrah (California) $15. A lean but smooth, herb-tinged red cherry and ripe tomato profile marks this distinctive wine. In some ways a bit Pinot-like, it has a lively mouthfeel. Finishes tart, with leather and oregano accents on the moderately long finish. **85** (10/1/2001)

Crystal Valley Cellars 2004 Cigar Zin Zinfandel (California) $27. Maybe a few puffs on a cigar would make this taste better, but it seems herbal, hot and flat to me. There's a core of Zinny cherry-berry, but the finish is uninteresting. **83** — S.H. (12/15/2005)

CUNEO

Cuneo 1999 Cabernet Sauvignon-Merlot-Cabernet Franc Bordeaux Blend (Columbia Valley (WA)) $15. Heavily oaked, with aromas of marshmallow, cherry and rubber. The palate is firm and tannic, with spicy flavors and cherry-style fruit. The finish is tart and tight, but very ripe and pure. This wine needs some time to lose its tannic fierceness; just an hour of airing did it wonders. **88 Editors' Choice** —*M.S. (6/1/2003)*

Cuneo 2001 Two Rivers Bordeaux Blend (Washington) $25. This is interesting: a 55% Oregon/45% Washington Bordeaux blend from top vineyards in both states (the two rivers being the Columbia and the Rogue). I like the concept, but both the Red Mountain and the Rogue Valley fruit create similarly tough, chewy tannins, so neither side modulates the other. Very tannic and hard, it's tough sledding. **85** —*P.G. (9/1/2004)*

Cuneo 2000 Two Rivers Bordeaux Blend (Oregon) $18. Inky and dense, with plum-cake aromas along with nuances of tree bark and nutmeg. The more time you give this ripe, tannic red, the more it'll offer. The fruit is pure and ripe, and the tannins are anything but meek. On the finish, root beer, chocolate and vanilla notes add some complexity and sweetness. The fruit is 61% Columbia Valley (Wash.) and 39% southern Oregon, and the whole is a fine yet brawny offering. **90 Best Buy** —*M.S. (8/1/2003)*

Cuneo 2003 Pinot Noir (Willamette Valley) $25. Firm, ripe and very solid: a chunkier, more muscular style of Pinot Noir, somewhat reminiscent of Cabernet. There's good black cherry and boysenberry fruit, some milk chocolate and vanilla bean barrel flavors, and plenty of ripeness. Perfectly enjoyable right now, this is a good effort at this price point. **88** —*P.G. (5/1/2006)*

Cuneo 2002 Pinot Noir (Willamette Valley) $25. Cuneo's Willamette Valley bottling is one smooth customer, classically styled with cherry-flavored fruit and lots of oaky vanilla. Solid, simple, and leans just a bit to the alcoholic side. **87** *(11/1/2004)*

Cuneo 2000 Pinot Noir (Willamette Valley) $15. Rustic and spicy at first, and then it fills out nicely. The fruit is on the rich side, leaning more toward blackberry and Bing cherry than anything red and lean. The finish is smooth and creamy, and ultimately very pleasant. The texture and density are just right, while potent yet restrained acidity keeps it fresh at all points. **89 Best Buy** —*M.S. (9/1/2003)*

Cuneo 2000 Ciel du Cheval Vineyard Sangiovese (Red Mountain) $30. Herbal and earthy, with aromas of pepper and barbecue sauce. The plum and strawberry fruit is tight and dry, while the overall impression is of a sharp, lean red that's a bit hot and sour. This Sangiovese has little in common with the wines of Tuscany, and in this case that's not a good thing. **82** —*M.S. (6/1/2003)*

Cuneo 2001 Del Rio Vineyard Syrah (Rogue Valley) $25. Rich and extracted, with a purple color and nutty, maple-based aromas. There's no denying the power here, and with flavors of sugar beets, smoked meats and kirsch, it's quite the bruiser. Despite that heft, the finish is balanced, with chocolate and dried herb flavors. Some hard tannins make it a bit tough now; maybe time will tame it. **86** —*M.S. (9/1/2003)*

CURTIS

Curtis 2003 Heritage Cuvée Rhône Red Blend (Santa Barbara County) $14. This is a very good wine, and this everyday price makes it a real bargain. A blend of Grenache, Syrah, Mourvèdre and Cinsault, it's more proof of California's ability to produce complex Rhône blends. **89 Best Buy** — *S.H. (6/1/2006)*

Curtis 2002 Heritage Cuvée Rhône Red Blend (Santa Barbara County) $14. A bit rustic in texture and structure, with herb and berry flavors, and very dry. This is a good everyday wine. **84** —*S.H. (10/1/2005)*

Curtis 2001 Heritage Cuvée Rhône Red Blend (Santa Barbara County) $12. Here's a well-ripened, juicy red wine that's full-bodied and rich in fruit, but retains balance and harmony. It's jam-packed with blackberry, cherry, raspberry and all sorts of other berry and red tree fruits, with an overlay of sweet toasty oak. Stylish and delicious, this is a blend of Mourvedre, Syrah and Grenache. **90 Best Buy** —*S.H. (12/1/2004)*

Curtis 2000 Heritage Cuvée Rhône Red Blend (Central Coast) $14. Distinctive for its depth of flavor and smooth, velvety tannins. Carries some polished plum, tobacco, black cherry and tart flavors through the finish. A blend of Mourvedre, Syrah, Grenache, and Counoise. **88** — *S.H. (6/1/2003)*

Curtis 1999 Heritage Cuvée Rhône Red Blend (Central Coast) $12. Smells rustic, with dried herb aromas, like sage and oregano although there are some pretty blueberry and black cherry flavors. There's also a tart, acidic streak that persists into the finish, and it's very dry. A Rhône-style blend of Syrah, Grenache, Mourvèdre and Counoise. **84** —*S.H. (9/1/2002)*

Curtis 2003 Heritage Cuvée Rhône Red Blend (Santa Barbara County) $14. This is a very good wine, and this everyday price makes it a real bargain. A blend of Grenache, Syrah, Mourvèdre and Cinsault, it's more proof of California's ability to produce complex Rhône blends. **89 Best Buy** — *S.H. (6/1/2006)*

Curtis 2003 The Crossroads Rhône Red Blend (Santa Barbara County) $20. Co-released with Curtis's Best Buy Heritage Cuvée, this wine, a blend of Grenache and Syrah, is very similar in its dry construction and forward fruit. Yet it's a little more tannic, and the oak seems more prominent. The flavors explode with cherries, blackberries, pomegranates, plums and mocha. **90** —*S.H. (6/1/2006)*

Curtis 2005 Heritage Blanc Rhône White Blend (Santa Barbara County) $14. Lots of fruit in this easy, everyday wine, but it's dry and crisp, so all that peach, pineapple and honeysuckle is balanced. Roussanne and Viognier from the Santa Ynez Valley. **85** —*S.H. (11/15/2006)*

Curtis 2001 Heritage Blanc Rhône White Blend (Santa Barbara County) $14. An easy to like wine bursting with all sorts of fresh, fruity flavors, especially peaches. There's also a rich, smoky taste of wildflowers and honey. A creamy texture and smooth finish round off this blend of Viognier, Roussanne and Chenin Blanc. **86** —*S.H. (2/1/2004)*

Curtis 2003 Roussanne (Santa Barbara County) $18. Tremendous in fruit, just explodes with apricots, peaches, even bananas, and all sorts of summery wildflowers. There's a butteriness that's probably from oak, and the wine is soft in acids, almost too soft. **84** —*S.H. (10/1/2005)*

Curtis 2003 Ambassador's Vineyard Syrah (Santa Barbara County) $25. The vineyard is in the Santa Ynez Valley. The wine is dry, and offers some complexity with firm tannins and espresso, blackberry, lavender and peper flavors. There's a rustic edge, including a hot finish, that lowers the score. **84** —*S.H. (10/1/2006)*

Curtis 2002 Ambassador's Vineyard Syrah (Santa Barbara County) $25. Another love-it-or-hate-it wine whose reviewers' disparate ratings get turned into a middle-of-the-road score. Tasting Director Joe Czerwinski liked this wine's bold blackberry flavors and supple tannins, which he admitted bordered on being overripe, while the other reviewers criticized it for being jammy and overripe. **85** *(9/1/2005)*

Curtis 1999 Ambassador's Vineyard Syrah (California) $22. A pleasing blend of briary blackberry, plum, tar, herb, toast and smoke flavors, all couched in reasonably smooth tannins. **87** —*J.M. (12/1/2002)*

Curtis 1998 Ambassador's Vineyard Syrah (Santa Barbara County) $20. Cedary, with smoke and tobacco aromas mingling delicately with red berries and dried spices. Nutmeg, leather and raspberries are graced with a healthy dollop of vanilla cream that provides a smooth, rich mouthfeel. **87** *(10/1/2001)*

Curtis 2003 Crossroads Vineyard Syrah (Santa Barbara County) $30. This is a very young wine. It's strong in acids and harsh tannins, with a bitterness in the finish. It doesn't really offer much now because it's so closed. Yet it has a nice core of cherry and blackberry fruit, and could hang in there. Hold through 2007, and try again. **85** —*S.H. (10/1/2006)*

Curtis 2002 Crossroads Vineyard Syrah (Santa Barbara County) $30. Lifted black- and blueberry flavors star on the palate, but beyond that, this wine is all about its oak-derived aromas and flavors: charred toast, smoke, hickory, vanilla and charred barrel are all descriptors that panelists used. Soft on the palate (though to continue the oak theme, one taster called the texture pulpy), with a dry finish. **85** *(9/1/2005)*

Curtis 2000 Crossroads Vineyard Syrah (Santa Ynez Valley) $32. This wine is very varietal, with strong and pronounced notes of white pepper and blackberries. These strong flavors are wrapped in dry, soft tannins and adequate acidity. Has everything but nuance and breed, which may come in future vintages. A winery to watch. **87** —*S.H. (6/1/2003)*

Curtis 1998 Reserve Syrah (Santa Ynez Valley) $30. This South Central Coaster's tart cherry-rhubarb fruit wears a lot of wood and an odd briney (to some), wet-furry (to others) veil. The palate shows cedar and choco-

USA

late notes, but in this case the whole is less than the sum of its parts. Slightly syrupy, it finishes short, a mix of parts that don't cohere that well **84** *(11/1/2001)*

Curtis 2000 Vogelzang Vineyard Syrah (Santa Ynez Valley) $18. Very similar in flavor and texture to the much more expensive Crossroads bottling, but much thinner and less ripe. Marked by tobacco and pepper flavors and tart acids. Still, there's something likeable and authentic, a quality that individual vineyards often interestingly provide. **86** —*S.H. (6/1/2003)*

Curtis 1997 Viognier (Santa Ynez Valley) $18. 87 —*S.H. (10/1/1999)*

Curtis 2005 Viognier (Santa Ynez Valley) $20. A little one-dimensional, but clean and crisp in acids, with the exotic floral and spice flavors the variety is noted for. Try with Asian fare. **84** —*S.H. (12/1/2006)*

Curtis 2003 Viognier (Santa Barbara County) $18. Nothing shy about this wine. It's all about peaches, mangoes, spicy pears, and even cotton candy with a minty taste. It's also oaky and almost sweet. **84** —*S.H. (10/1/2005)*

Curtis 2002 Viognier (Santa Barbara County) $18. This flavorful wine brims with sweet lemon custard, vanilla pudding and crème brûleé flavors, which makes it sound sweet, but it's dry. **87** —*S.H. (11/15/2004)*

Curtis 2001 Viognier (Santa Barbara County) $18. Fruit salad, with a melange of peach, pear, pineapple, grapefruit, maraschino cherry and just about every other fruit you can think of. Drinks rather syrupy and simple, with a hint of residual sugar. **85** —*S.H. (6/1/2003)*

Curtis 2000 Viognier (Santa Barbara County) $18. Zippy acidity and full apricot, peach and spice flavors make this a front-loaded wine. Lots of fun, though hardly subtle in its charms. **87** —*J.M. (12/15/2002)*

CUVAISON

Cuvaison 2003 Cabernet Sauvignon (Mount Veeder) $38. This impressive young mountain Cab follows Cuvaison's very fine '02. It's dense and classically structured, showing well-ripened blackberry, cassis and chocolate flavors and firm, hard tannins. Seems sweeter and softer than the '02; maybe not as ageable, but a fancy Cab. **90** —*S.H. (12/31/2006)*

Cuvaison 2002 Cabernet Sauvignon (Mount Veeder) $40. This dense Cab shows the power of a true mountain wine, with intensely concentrated fruit and a thick coating of tannins. Yet those tannins are finely ground and the texture is as smooth as velvet, making for instant drinkability. The flavors are of black currants, mocha, green olives and spicy oak. Drink this stylish Cab now and through 2012. **92** —*S.H. (11/1/2006)*

Cuvaison 2001 Cabernet Sauvignon (Napa Valley) $38. The fabulous '01 Napa Cabs just keep on coming. This one, a blend from various parts of the appellation, is extraordinarily rich in black currants, wrapped in the finest, smoothest tannins. It offers pure Cabernet pleasure, not a blockbuster, but defining elegance. Drink in the near term to enjoy its youthful beauty. **93 Editors' Choice** —*S.H. (12/15/2005)*

Cuvaison 1999 Cabernet Sauvignon (Napa Valley) $40. Powerful and dramatic, packed with polished flavors of blackcurrants and cassis, sweet roasted pepper, and dried herbs. Tannins are thick and there's a bite of acidity in the finish, suggesting that this delicious young wine will age. But it's drinkable now. **90** —*S.H. (8/1/2003)*

Cuvaison 1997 Cabernet Sauvignon (Napa Valley) $32. 91 *(6/1/2000)*

Cuvaison 2004 Chardonnay (Carneros) $25. Crisp and elegant, with pineapple and peach flavors enhanced by smoky oak. Finishes dry, with a spicy aftertaste. Nice but could use more intensity. **84** —*S.H. (11/15/2006)*

Cuvaison 2003 Chardonnay (Carneros) $22. From a winery that's excelled at Chardonnay for many years comes this impressive wine. It's explosive in tangerines, mangoes, pineapples, cinnamon, vanilla, buttercream and toast, with a long finish of roasted hazelnuts and smoky honey. Absolutely delicious. **92 Editors' Choice** —*S.H. (12/1/2005)*

Cuvaison 2002 Chardonnay (Carneros) $24. A very pretty wine. It's not particularly rich or intense, but rather strives for elegance and finesse, which it achieves. The peach and pineapple fruit flavors are accented by vanilla, buttered toast and cinnamon. Impresses for its sense of harmony and balance. **91** —*S.H. (8/1/2004)*

Cuvaison 2001 Chardonnay (Carneros) $22. Always a nice, rich Chard with oaky nuances but not too much. This year the wine is especially full-bodied, packed with fruity flavors and a spicy, cinnamon and pepper aftertaste. Cuvaison has held its prices down and this wine is actually a value in its class. **91** —*S.H. (6/1/2003)*

Cuvaison 2000 Chardonnay (Napa Valley) $20. Somewhat tightly wound, the wine nonetheless shows fine integration of its complex flavors, redolent of lemon, melon, pear, grapefruit, herb and toast. On the finish, it's bright, fresh and long. **90** —*J.M. (5/1/2002)*

Cuvaison 1998 Chardonnay (Carneros) $19. 88 *(6/1/2000)*

Cuvaison 1997 Chardonnay (Carneros) $17. 93 —*S.H. (12/31/1999)*

Cuvaison 2002 ATS Chardonnay (Carneros) $50. Here's a big, extravagant, unctuous Chard that leaves little to the imagination. Everything's oversized and upfront: the massive tropical fruit and spice flavors, the toasty, caramelized oak, the creamy, leesy texture, the finish. It's flashy, but seems to pall after a few sips. **87** —*S.H. (12/1/2005)*

Cuvaison 1996 ATS Selection Chardonnay (Carneros) $43. 93 —*S.H. (6/1/1999)*

Cuvaison 1999 Carneros Reserve Chardonnay (Napa Valley) $32. A pale gold color belies the full, deep aromas and flavors this wine offers. The lively, multifaceted nose highlights orange, pear, ginger snaps, anise and caramel notes. It opens to a rich, even palate that shows similar flavors and a smooth, buttery feel. The pleasing finish displays plenty of toast, vanilla and spice, and an impressive dry, leesy aftertaste. **89** *(7/1/2001)*

Cuvaison 2004 Estate Selection Chardonnay (Carneros) $36. Smoky-oaky and crisp, with pleasant peach, pineapple and buttercream flavors. This is an easy-to-enjoy Chard with elegance and charm. **86** —*S.H. (11/15/2006)*

Cuvaison 2000 Estate Selection Chardonnay (Carneros) $34. Crisp and bright, yet smooth and creamy, too. The wine serves up pretty orange, lemon, herb, toast, pear and melon flavors, finishing clean. **88** —*J.M. (12/15/2002)*

Cuvaison 1998 Reserve Chardonnay (Carneros) $32. 90 *(6/1/2000)*

Cuvaison 1997 Merlot (Napa Valley) $32. 90 *(6/1/2000)*

Cuvaison 2003 Merlot (Carneros) $31. Cuvaison always does a nice job with Merlot, and this one, from Napa Carneros, shows well-ripened cherry, black raspberry and mocha flavors that have been folded into gentle, sweetly soft tannins. Fully drinkable now. **87** —*S.H. (12/31/2006)*

Cuvaison 2001 Merlot (Carneros) $32. Rich and chocolaty, but goes beyond candied simplicity with real complexity of structure. There are cross-currents of the ripest cherries and black raspberries, and a dash of coffee. That structure is built of ripe, smooth tannins, edgy acids and oak shadings, all kept in balance. **91** —*S.H. (12/15/2004)*

Cuvaison 2000 Merlot (Carneros) $29. Fruity, with pleasant berry-cherry flavors and a dry edge of tobacco and sage. Doesn't have much stuffing in the middle, and powerful tannins make it a bit ponderous. Drink now. **86** —*S.H. (12/15/2003)*

Cuvaison 2003 Pinot Noir (Carneros) $25. There's extracted overripeness here, in the chocolate-coated raisiny edge that com-pletes the cherry fruit and oak flavors, but the wine has a nice Pinot Noir silkiness. Try with grilled lamb. **85** —*S.H. (12/15/2005)*

Cuvaison 2002 Pinot Noir (Carneros) $25. You'll find a cocoa, chocolatey aroma here, and pretty flavors of cherry Lifesaver, vanilla and white pepper. One taster praised the wine's meatiness, while most found it ultimately a little simple. **85** *(11/1/2004)*

Cuvaison 2001 Pinot Noir (Carneros) $29. Delicious and delicate in structure and tannins, with a classic, silky mouthfeel that caresses the palate. Red and black cherry, raspberry, tangerine peel, cola, sweet rhubard, rose hip tea and oaky notes of smoke and vanilla contribute intricate detail. **89** —*S.H. (7/1/2003)*

Cuvaison 2000 Pinot Noir (Carneros) $29. Opens with creamy, fleshy aromas over dark fruit. Juicy and tangy on the tongue, this offers sweet-tart black cherry and plum flavors, very good fruit-acid balance. Showed slight heat to some, but the long, coffee and pepper back end is a handsome close to this solid, spicy Pinot. **87** *(10/1/2002)*

Cuvaison 1998 Eris Vineyard Pinot Noir (Carneros) $20. 90 *(6/1/2000)*

Cuvaison 2003 Estate Selection Pinot Noir (Carneros) $42. Cuvaison's regular '03 Pinot is a little overripe and unbalanced. So is this wine, although it's richer and more concentrated. It's a big, thick wine, too soft, with cocoa and cherry-berry flavors. Simply lacks the flair and finesse you expect at this price. **86** —*S.H. (12/15/2005)*

Cuvaison 2002 Estate Selection Pinot Noir (Carneros) $42. A pretty wine, showing bigtime black cherry, plum and chocolate flavors in a fresh, young body with good acidity and tannins. Finishes a bit hot. **84** *(11/1/2004)*

Cuvaison 2003 Mariafeld Pinot Noir (Carneros) $28. There are absolutely delicious flavors in this Pinot. It explodes with rich cherry pie, mocha and vanilla flavors, with a drizzle of creme de cassis and cinnamon. However, the wine is so soft, almost flat, that it tastes syrupy instead of lively. **84** —*S.H. (12/1/2005)*

Cuvaison 2004 Sauvignon Blanc (Carneros) $19. What a refreshing wine. It's a little sweetish in lemon and lime Lifesaver flavors, but crisp and clean in balancing acidity. Turns rich in vanilla and peppery spice on the finish, with a reprise of the ripe citrus fruit. **88** —*S.H. (12/1/2005)*

Cuvaison 2003 Syrah (Carneros) $30. Cuvaison invested in Carneros early on, and that effort has paid off with this handsome Syrah. It's clearly cool-climate, with thick tannins and peppery, meaty, leathery flavors, but most notable is the balance. This is a wine that combines complexity with sheer deliciousness, marrying blueberry and blackberry notes with hints of coffee, vanilla and black olives. Drink now-2010. **91 Editors' Choice** *(11/8/2006)*

Cuvaison 2002 Syrah (Carneros) $28. The 2002 Syrahs from Carneros hit a sweet spot with our panel and this wine was no exception. Dried spices, black pepper and toast accent mouthfilling blackberry fruit. The tannins are ripe to the point of creaminess, the texture smooth and supple. Finishes a touch warm, but long and spicy. **88** *(9/1/2005)*

Cuvaison 2001 Syrah (Carneros) $29. I love this wine, it's so balanced and easy. Flows like silk and velvet, with sweetly rich tannins and wonderfully modulated plum, blackberry and coffee that mingle in a complex swirl of flavor. Firmly in the Cuvaison style of harmony, balance and elegance. **91** —*S.H. (8/1/2004)*

CYCLES GLADIATOR

Cycles Gladiator 2004 Cabernet Sauvignon (Central Coast) $10. This is a new line from Hahn Estates. The wine is soft, fruity and a little sweet, with cherry, blackberry and chocolate flavors and lush, dusty tannins leading to a pleasant finish. **84** —*S.H. (11/15/2006)*

Cycles Gladiator 2004 Chardonnay (Central Coast) $10. Soft and simple despite rich pineapple and tapioca flavors. The wine has a heaviness it can't quite overcome, but it does finish dry and clean. **83** —*S.H. (11/15/2006)*

Cycles Gladiator 2004 Merlot (Central Coast) $10. The aromas are of mint and blackberries, while the taste is sweet and sour, like a Chinese fruit-based sauce. Finishes with an astringent scour. **81** —*S.H. (11/15/2006)*

Cycles Gladiator 2005 Pinot Grigio (California) $11. Simple and slightly sweet, with grapefruit, peach and a streak of minerally acids. This is a decent everyday wine. **83** —*S.H. (11/15/2006)*

Cycles Gladiator 2004 Syrah (Central Coast) $10. Lots to like in this soft, flavorful Syrah. Paso Robles grapes give it lots of upfront blackberry and chocolate flavors, while cool Monterey lends acidity and white pepper. Loses points, though, for turning sweet and medicinal on the finish. **83** —*S.H. (11/15/2006)*

CYPRESS

Cypress 2002 Cabernet Sauvignon (California) $10. A little light, but juicy in blackcurrant, cherry and cocoa flavors, with firm, sweet tannins. Balanced and harmonious finish. **84** —*S.H. (3/1/2005)*

Cypress 2001 Cabernet Sauvignon (California) $10. Blackberry and herb flavors are wrapped in tough tannins, and the wine is dry. Finishes with a throat-scratching astringency, but at this price, you can serve it by the case at your next block party. From J. Lohr. **84** —*S.H. (12/31/2003)*

Cypress 2003 Chardonnay (California) $10. An easy, everyday Chard, with apricot and peach flavors and a little oak. Finishes creamy and dry. **84** —*S.H. (3/1/2005)*

Cypress 2002 Merlot (California) $10. Unripe, with canned asparagus aromas and a raw mouthfeel to the modest cherry flavors. **82** —*S.H. (3/1/2005)*

Cypress 2003 Sauvignon Blanc (California) $10. Watery, with a squeeze of lime juice and acidity. But it's very clean. **83** —*S.H. (3/1/2005)*

Cypress 2002 Shiraz (California) $10. There's a flood of well-crafted wines such as this these days that are giving consumers the best values in history. This one's juicy and full-bodied, with plumy, spicy flavors and a hint of bacon. **85 Best Buy** —*S.H. (4/1/2005)*

CYRUS

Cyrus 1995 Bordeaux Blend (Sonoma County) $35. 84 —*L.W. (12/31/1999)*

Cyrus 1998 Bordeaux Blend (Alexander Valley) $50. Loaded up front with bright fruit redolent of blueberry, plum and black cherry. An attractive tangy edge gives lift, while toasty oak rounds things off. Though light-textured, the wine still carries plenty of weight and is lovely and long to the end. A blend of Cabernet Sauvignon, Merlot, Cabernet Franc and Malbec from Alexander Valley Vineyards. **91** —*J.M. (6/1/2002)*

Cyrus 1999 Wetzel Family Estate Bordeaux Blend (Alexander Valley) $50. Profoundly rich and complex, a blend of all five Bordeaux varietals. This results in a melange of flavors including blackcurrants and cassis, olives and sweet roasted peppers, dried herbs, and cured tobacco. The tannins are soft, but there is a boost of firm acidity that suggests ageability. **92** —*S.H. (8/1/2003)*

D'ANBINO

D'Anbino 2002 Syrah (Paso Robles) $24. Unusually light in color and body for a Syrah, almost a dark rose. Yet its very distinctive in the dry complexity of the Provencal wild herb, licorice, tart cherry and olive tapenade flavors. **90** —*S.H. (12/1/2004)*

D'ARGENZIO

D'Argenzio 2002 Merlot (Napa Valley) $38. There are lots of ripe, juicy cherry flavors in this wine, and a chocolaty finish. You'll also find a sharpness of acidity and tannins that provides structure. The firmness and fruity sweetness suggest a nice char-broiled steak. **86** —*S.H. (8/1/2005)*

D'Argenzio 2002 Pinot Noir (Russian River Valley) $32. Rich, intricate and rather heavy, like a Persian carpet, with a tapestry of cherry, cola, spice and mocha flavors that are really quite delicious. This wine would benefit from greater acidity, to make all this richness shine, but it's a nice drink. **86** —*S.H. (8/1/2005)*

D'Argenzio 2001 Pinot Noir (Russian River Valley) $29. This is a superrich Pinot. It offers exuberant flavors of cherries, cola, cocoa and even pecan pie, but in this case the acidity is great enough to balance. Fortunately, it maintains delicacy and lightness despite the depth of flavor. **90** —*S.H. (8/1/2005)*

D'Argenzio 2001 Dutton Ranch Pinot Noir (Russian River Valley) $30. Displays classic RRV characteristics of cola, rhubarb, tart pomegranate and cherry, with firm acidity and a silky texture, without showing a whole lot of depth. Still, the ride is a jazzy one. **86** —*S.H. (12/1/2004)*

D-CUBED CELLARS

D-Cubed Cellars 2001 Zinfandel (Napa Valley) $25. Firm textured, with ripe tannins supporting a blend of plum, blackberry, spice, herb and coffee flavors. The wine has a vanilla and herb edge at the finish. **88** *(11/1/2003)*

D-Cubed Cellars 2001 Zinfandel (Howell Mountain) $35. Smooth-textured, elegant and plush, the wine serves up a fine balance of blackberry, cocoa, tea, plum, spice, raspberry and herbal notes, neatly framed in fine, ripe tannins. The finish has a hint of anise and toast, lingering nicely. **91** *(11/1/2003)*

D-Cubed Cellars 2001 Black Sears Vineyard Zinfandel (Howell Mountain) $45. Smooth, ripe texture frames this classy blend of anise, blackberry, black cherry, plum, coffee, tea and herb flavors. It's pretty toasty on the finish, ending broadly on the palate. **90** *(11/1/2003)*

D.R. STEPHENS

D.R. Stephens 2000 Moose Valley Cabernet Sauvignon (Napa Valley) $90. Stylish and plump, a delicious Cab with polished flavors of red stone fruits and berries, and a sweet veneer of toasty oak. Well-balanced, this charmer finishes with complexity. **90** —*S.H. (11/15/2004)*

D.R. Stephens 2003 Moose Valley Estate Cabernet Sauvignon (Napa Valley) $100. From St. Helena. Ultrasoft and ultraripe in the modern style, a cassis and chocolate- flavored wine marked by melted tannins and a soft texture. The wine is voluptuous and very good, but would benefit from better structure. **87** —*S.H. (8/1/2006)*

D.R. Stephens 2000 Walther River Block Cabernet Sauvignon (Napa Valley) $75. This young Cab is a bit tense with acids, and the parts haven't knit together, but it should develop for a few years. Smooth tannins frame black cherry and plum fruit, with a layer of sweet oak. **88** —*S.H. (11/15/2004)*

DAEDALUS

Daedalus 2004 Pinot Gris (Oregon) $16. Another beauty from Oregon, this detailed (almost pointillist) effort is like a tapestry woven of citrus, grapefruit, pears and spice, then soaked in wet stones. Subtle and penetrating. **90** —*P.G. (2/1/2006)*

Daedalus 2003 Pinot Noir (Willamette Valley) $24. Daedalus is a very talented young winery making brilliant wines at sensible prices. The sources for this wine include Carabella, Momtazi, Maresh and Seven Springs, all superior vineyards. Winemaker Aron Hess is one of Oregon's rising stars. Sweet fruit, dried herbs, sandalwood and spice in a clean, silky, seductive, well-rounded and seamless wine. **90 Editors' Choice** — *P.G. (5/1/2006)*

Daedalus 2003 Labyrinth Pinot Noir (Willamette Valley) $39. The Labyrinth bottling is made from older vines than the regular Pinot from Daedalus, and it is saturated with color and scents of mixed flowers. Rich, complex and textural, it adds unusual notes of mineral, hay and herb to the explosion of raspberry and cherry fruit. **90** —*P.G. (5/1/2006)*

Daedalus 2003 Syrah (Columbia Valley (OR)) $24. This is eastern Oregon Syrah, a completely different (and to my taste, far superior) style than the better-known southern Oregon Syrahs. Aromatically rich with smoked meat, tobacco, thyme, sage, berries and a dash of Kahlúa, it is nonetheless balanced and not too alcoholic. The tobacco scents translate into a lovely streak of flavor that runs through the wine. **91 Editors' Choice** —*P.G. (5/1/2006)*

DALLA VALLE

Dalla Valle 2001 Cabernet Sauvignon (Oakville) $100. What a treat. This is the quintessence of Oakville Cab, with an impressively firm structure, ripe tannins, smooth, supple mouthfeel and long, spicy finish. And what fruit! Scads of rich cassis, chocolate and oak, yet thoroughly dry. Drink now through 2012. **94** —*S.H. (11/1/2005)*

Dalla Valle 1999 Cabernet Sauvignon (Napa Valley) $100. Ripe, rich and elegant, this wine is brimming with black plum, strawberry, cassis, chocolate, spice and herb notes. It's smooth-textured and seamlessly integrated, even at this early stage. Firm, plush tannins and just the right amount of toasty oak frame the ensemble. **94** —*J.M. (6/1/2002)*

Dalla Valle 1999 Maya Red Blend (Napa Valley) $120. Plush, smooth and packed tight with complex flavors. Blackberry, anise, black cherry, tar, coal, spice, earth and herbs remain tightly wound, waiting patiently to reveal their full charm in time. Supple, smooth tannins and beautiful balance give this wine classic elegance. **96** —*J.M. (6/1/2002)*

Dalla Valle 1997 Pietre Rosse Sangiovese (Napa Valley) $30. 93 —*L.W. (10/1/1999)*

DANCING BULL

Dancing Bull 2003 Cabernet Sauvignon (California) $12. An awkward, slightly sweet and soft Cab with syrupy cherry cough medicine flavors. The puckery tannins make your tongue stick to the gums. **82** —*S.H. (11/15/2006)*

Dancing Bull 2004 Chardonnay (California) $12. Can't recommend this wine because it's just too thin. It's pretty much watery alcohol, with a few drops of Chard essence. **82** —*S.H. (12/1/2006)*

Dancing Bull 2004 Merlot (California) $10. Loaded with bright, ripe cherry, raspberry, blackberry, chocolate and wintergreen flavors, and seasoned with a touch of oak, this young wine is dry, with a zesty sharpness that calls for food. The grapes are largely from Gallo's Paso Robles vineyard, Sunnybrook, and the wine was made by Rancho Zabaco's team, led by Eric Cinnamon, who describes Dancing Bull as "the lighter side of Rancho Zabaco." Easy to find, with 42,000 cases. **85 Best Buy** —*S.H. (11/15/2006)*

DANIEL GEHRS

Daniel Gehrs 2000 Cabernet Sauvignon (Santa Ynez Valley) $24. Blows off its sulfury fumes to reveal aromas of berries, herbs, olives and oak. A fundamentally simple wine, with modest berry-cherry flavors that turn herbal and tannic into the finish. **85** —*S.H. (11/15/2003)*

Daniel Gehrs 2000 Pinnacles Chenin Blanc (Monterey County) $13. Much like a good Sauvignon Blanc with fresh apple and citrus flavors and tart dryness, it has a rich, complex sappiness that places it head and shoulders above most Chenins. Classy and fun; try it with grilled veggies. **87** —*S.H. (11/15/2001)*

Daniel Gehrs 2004 Gewürztraminer (Central Coast) $15. Straddling the line between dry and off-dry, this crisp, acidic wine is filled with citrus, peach and wildflower flavors that finish in a tremendous swirl of Oriental spice. It has great structure, and is complex enough to accompany racy, Asian-inspired fare. **87** —*S.H. (3/1/2006)*

Daniel Gehrs 1999 Merlot (Santa Ynez Valley) $20. Dry and delicious, this elegant wine straddles the line between ripe blackberry and plum flavors and earthier, peppery ones. The finish is distinguished and prolonged. Notable for its balanced structure. The wine's firm tannins suggest shortterm aging. **90 Editors' Choice** —*S.H. (11/15/2001)*

Daniel Gehrs 2001 Pinot Noir (Santa Barbara County) $20. A lightweight Pinot with lots to like. The raspberry, mocha and vanilla flavors are easy and satisfying, and the wine is silky in the mouth. Finishes dry and peppery. This is a versatile by-the-glass choice. **86** —*S.H. (2/1/2004)*

Daniel Gehrs 2000 Careaga Pinot Noir (Santa Barbara County) $25. 86 *(10/1/2002)*

Daniel Gehrs 1999 Careaga Pinot Noir (Santa Barbara County) $26. Mature, but showing an attractive nose with a spicy, saddle quality. However, the thin fruit seems cedary or burnt and the wine closes with some astringency. Seems tired already. **83** *(10/1/2002)*

Daniel Gehrs 2000 Goodfellow Pinot Noir (Santa Maria Valley) $25. This is a distinctive wine that projects tea, mushroom, smoke, rhubarb and roasted vegetable aromas and flavors. Solid, tart cherry fruit rides a lightto medium-weight frame. It may sound weird, but it holds together well, showing unique character in a field of too many clones. **87** *(10/1/2002)*

Daniel Gehrs 2004 Dry Riesling (Central Coast) $15. A fine Riesling that's made in the Alsatian style. It's not only dry, it's tart in acids, with bright, ripe apple, honeysuckle, citrus and spice flavors. Alcohol is a modest 12.2%. **85** —*S.H. (3/1/2006)*

Daniel Gehrs 2001 Shiraz (Santa Ynez Valley) $20. A lavishly oaked but tasty wine. Aromas are of vanilla, nuts and smoke; coconut and vanilla is piled on mixed berry fruit on the palate. Lush and supple feel; closes with a reprise of the earlier notes. **89** *(9/1/2005)*

Daniel Gehrs 2001 Syrah (Paso Robles) $20. Almost the perfect restaurant wine for big, flavorful lamb or beef dishes. It's rich and jammy, packed with blackberry and cherry flavors that go on forever. Has enough acidity to cut through the fat. **88** —*S.H. (5/1/2004)*

Daniel Gehrs 2001 Syrah (Santa Barbara County) $25. There are some tough acids and tannins framing the cherry and blackberry flavors in this elegant, well-crafted wine. If you're into food pairing, it suggests butter, olive oil, fatty lamb and cheese. Under those softening influences, this will be a fabulous partner. **88** —*S.H. (5/1/2004)*

Daniel Gehrs 1999 Syrah (Paso Robles) $20. Plummy fruit supported by nice acids and a chewy mouthfeel give this Paso Robles offering great appeal. A sweet-and-sour quality marks the fruit, and some intriguing

USA

spicy notes add to the package. Nicely structured, it has positive tension but isn't hard, and closes with lots of spice and even, dusty tannins. **89** *(10/1/2001)*

Daniel Gehrs 1999 Syrah (Santa Ynez Valley) $25. Cherry and plum fruit wears clove, and even curry, accents in this solid, heavily cedar-tinged wine from South Coast veteran Daniel Gehrs. Smoothly textured, toasty and chocolatey in the mouth, it turns sweet and sour, with tangy tannins and white pepper on the long back end. Top Value. **90** *(11/1/2001)*

Daniel Gehrs 2001 Harmon Syrah (Santa Ynez Valley) $25. A medium-weight, good wine, but one whose primary flavors are of the cedar/cigar box/vanilla ilk. Has similar aromas; overall, we wish that fruit played more of a starring role here. **85** *(9/1/2005)*

Daniel Gehrs 2000 Harmon Syrah (Santa Ynez Valley) $25. This is a young and likeable Syrah. It opens with a blast of white pepper, cherry and raspberry aromas and turns fruity in the mouth. The rich, dry tannins and spicy flourish lend it an edge of interest. **89** *—S.H. (3/1/2004)*

Daniel Gehrs 2000 Viognier (Santa Ynez Valley) $18. Spicy and rich, with hints of melon, mandarin orange and lemon. It strikes a nice balance, with good body and acidity. A versatile wine for many occasions, from sipping to serious eating. **88** *—J.M. (11/15/2001)*

Daniel Gehrs 1998 Stolpman Vineyard Viognier (Santa Barbara County) $19. 90 *—S.H. (10/1/1999)*

DARCIE KENT VINEYARDS

Darcie Kent Vineyards 2001 Merlot (Livermore Valley) $18. There's a good wine in here somewhere, with the fine dusty tannins and underlying flavors of plum and blackberry, but the wine is marred by a musty aroma that carries through a taste of mushrooms sauteed in soy sauce. **84** *—S.H. (2/1/2004)*

DARIOUSH

Darioush 2000 Signature Cabernet Sauvignon (Napa Valley) $64. Really smooth textured. Quite elegant as well, with sleek, complex layers of black currant, blackberry, plum, black cherry, herb, chocolate, coffee, spice, toast and a beguiling hint of tar. The wine is incredibly complex and inviting, framed beautifully in velvety tannins. Long and lush on the finish, it's blended from grapes grown on Mt. Veeder, Atlas Peak and the Napa Valley floor. **94** *—J.M. (6/1/2003)*

Darioush 1999 Chardonnay (Napa Valley) $34. This is sensuous Chardonnay that provides plenty of texture and depth without being heavy. The bouquet is robust and complex, with pear, smoke, vanilla, cumin and an appealing oatmeal-graham cracker-like note. A full spectrum of similarly ripe fruit flavors coats the mouth, bolstered by good acidity, and you can almost sink your teeth into the full, chewy mouthfeel. This very impressive bottling finishes long and complex, with grainy pear, spice and buttery notes. **93 Editors' Choice** *(7/1/2001)*

Darioush 2001 Signature Chardonnay (Napa Valley) $38. Crisp acidity blends easily with creamy smooth texture here. This is a fine juxtaposition of mineral, apple, pear, spice and citrus flavors, neatly layered for complexity and eleganty structured. Long and bright at the end. **90** *—J.M. (6/1/2003)*

Darioush 2000 Merlot (Napa Valley) $44. Rich and lush, with smoky, charry overtones and pretty blackberry, plum, chocolate, coffee, herb and toast flavors. The wine shows moderate body and silky tannins. Long, rich and enticing on the finish. **91** *—J.M. (6/1/2003)*

Darioush 2000 Shiraz (Napa Valley) $64. The wine starts of with intriguing bacon and earth tones that are followed up by rich, ripe raspberry, black cherry, spice, licorice, herb and toast flavors. It's beautifully balanced, with supple tannins and a flashy, robust character that remains enticing and long at the end. Look for more of this varietal from Darioush as its Shiraz vineyards mature. **92** *—J.M. (6/1/2003)*

Darioush 2002 Signature Shiraz (Napa Valley) $64. Tasty if a bit over-priced, with bright cherry and mint flavors accented by toast, coffee and earth nuances. Seems a bit tough and hard on the finish, but one reviewer felt it would soften nicely in a year or two. **86** *(9/1/2005)*

Darioush 2001 Viognier (Napa Valley) $28. Has the weight, creamy texture and oak of a bigtime Chardonnay, but the flavor profile is entirely different. Here, you get a mélange of tropical fruit, wildflowers and dusty spices. The flavors are massive, but the wine's acids and tannic structure corral these wild horses and keep them from running wild. **89** *—S.H. (12/1/2003)*

DARK STAR

Dark Star 2001 Ricordati Cabernet Blend (Paso Robles) $20. Dry, rough and earthy, with an astringent mouthfeel. Decanting overnight will bring out the cherries and berries, and the wine is good with barbecue. **84** *—S.H. (6/1/2005)*

Dark Star 2001 Cabernet Sauvignon (Paso Robles) $20. Dry, raw and simple, with pruny flavors and a hot feeling through the finish. **83** *—S.H. (6/1/2005)*

Dark Star 1997 Cabernet Sauvignon (Paso Robles) $20. 87 *—S.H. (7/1/2000)*

Dark Star 1999 Ricordati Cabernet Sauvignon (Paso Robles) $24. Simple, with berry flavors and low acids and tannins. The finish picks up a bit of sweet fruit. It's tricky making a good Bordeaux blend in a warm climate. The danger is that, despite the best efforts, the wine will be flat and one-dimensional. **83** *—S.H. (9/12/2002)*

Dark Star 2001 Anderson Road Cabernet Sauvignon-Syrah (Paso Robles) $15. Nice and fruity in cherries, plums and blackberries, and with drier, more complex notes of roasted coffeebean and Asian spices. Overall, this is a dry, layered wine, with a fair amount of gritty tannins. **86** *—S.H. (6/1/2005)*

Dark Star 2001 Merlot (Paso Robles) $18. This score is perhaps charitable for this wine. It has vegetal-berry aromas, and is very dry and herbaceous in the mouth, with rough tannins. But it's clean. **83** *—S.H. (6/1/2005)*

Dark Star 1999 Merlot (Paso Robles) $18. From warm country, and tastes like it. The first thing you notice is how soft it is. The ripe berry flavors are accented with some sharp tannins, but it's not an ager. It's a simple wine, perfectly serviceable for most occasions. **84** *—S.H. (9/12/2002)*

Dark Star 1997 Merlot (Paso Robles) $18. 83 *—S.H. (7/1/2000)*

Dark Star 1997 Ricordati Red Blend (Paso Robles) $24. 83 *—S.H. (7/1/2000)*

Dark Star 2001 Meeker Vineyard Syrah (Paso Robles) $10. A dry, tough wine, with funky notes. **80** *—S.H. (6/1/2005)*

Dark Star 1999 Meeker Vineyard Syrah (Paso Robles) $22. An oddly vegetal wine, considering the appellation and vintage, it has aromas of bell peppers, and similar herbaceous flavors. On the other hand, it's very soft and finely textured. Not going anywhere, so drink now. **84** *—S.H. (9/12/2002)*

Dark Star 2001 Zinfandel (Paso Robles) $18. There are some lovely cherry and coffee flavors and rich tannins in this wine, but it suffers from a raisiny, Porty aroma. Best with ribs or chicken smothered in a slightly sweet barbecue sauce. **84** *—S.H. (6/1/2005)*

Dark Star 1997 Zinfandel (Paso Robles) $19. 86 *—S.H. (10/1/2000)*

DASHE CELLARS

Dashe Cellars 2000 Merlot (Potter Valley) $26. From a little-known appellation in Mendocino County that has warm days and cool nights comes this wonderfully rich wine. Feels lush and brilliant in the mouth, with ripe berry flavors balanced with herbs and olives. Dry and balanced, with just a kiss of oak, this is a stylish drink with great complexity. **91 Editors' Choice** *—S.H. (4/1/2003)*

Dashe Cellars 2003 Iron Oak Vineyard Merlot (Potter Valley) $26. Simple, soft and dry, with cherry cough drop flavors and some pretty fierce tannins. Decant it for a while to let it breathe. **83** *—S.H. (12/1/2006)*

Dashe Cellars 1999 Sangiovese (Sonoma County) $18. A light-bodied red that's dry and balanced. Has supple, silky tannins and crisp acids framing flavors of tobacco, cherries and pepper. Perfect with roast chicken. **87** *—S.H. (2/1/2003)*

Dashe Cellars 2003 Zinfandel (Dry Creek Valley) $22. A bit grapey and simple, with confected berry fruit flavors and a smooth mouthfeel that lacks weight and richness. **83** *(12/18/2006)*

Dashe Cellars 2002 Zinfandel (Dry Creek Valley) $22. A blend of several vineyards, this is a generous Zin, and very ripe, to judge from the blast of sun-warmed wild berry and cocoa flavors that spread over the palate. It's quite soft in the mouth, and finishes a bit sweet. **87** —*S.H.* *(11/1/2005)*

Dashe Cellars 2001 Zinfandel (Dry Creek Valley) $20. Pretty, plush tannins frame a patchwork of black cherry, plum, cassis, chocolate and coffee flavors. The finish is long and smooth, with a rich creaminess at the end. Less oak-driven than the single-vineyard releases. **89** *(11/1/2003)*

Dashe Cellars 2000 Zinfandel (Dry Creek Valley) $20. This bold, muscular Zin boasts overpowering flavors of wild berries and high alcohol. It's strong, assertive and dry. There's something old-fashioned about it, like great-grandpa made it, and did a pretty good job. **86** —*S.H.* *(2/1/2003)*

Dashe Cellars 1999 Zinfandel (Dry Creek Valley) $20. This is classic Dry Creek fruit, fragrant and spicy, redolent of fresh, ripe berries. Lots of vivid acidity keeps it fresh and polished, and a bit of Carignane and Petit Sirah are in the blend for added texture. Concentrated and lovely wine. **89** —*P.G.* *(3/1/2002)*

Dashe Cellars 2003 Big River Ranch Zinfandel (Alexander Valley) $28. Creamy-smooth in texture, this almost syrupy Zin features smoke, vanilla and maple syrup shadings from oak and dark chocolate and blackberry fruit. The finish shows a touch of heat, not much spice or complexity. **84** Cellar Selection *(12/18/2006)*

Dashe Cellars 2001 Big River Vineyard Zinfandel (Alexander Valley) $28. Bright, plush and brimming with black cherry, blackberry, toast, coffee, anise and spice notes. The tannins are supple and firm, while the finish is silky and long. Really good wine. **90** *(11/1/2003)*

Dashe Cellars 2003 Louvau Vineyard Old Vines Zinfandel (Dry Creek Valley) $28. Smells caramelly and Port-like, with raisiny fruit backed by drying tannins. **80** *(12/18/2006)*

Dashe Cellars 2001 Louvau Vineyard, Old Vines Zinfandel (Dry Creek Valley) $28. Pretty oaky, with a follow up that shows plum, blackberry, black cherry and spice flavors. Tannins are silky and the finish is nonetheless long and lush. **89** *(11/1/2003)*

Dashe Cellars 2001 Todd Brothers Ranch Zinfandel (Alexander Valley) $25. Somewhat oak-driven, the plum, raspberry, blackberry and herb flavors take a backseat. Still, the wine shows well, with fine tannins framing the flavors, which finish with a chocolatey edge. Long and well balanced. **90** *(11/1/2003)*

Dashe Cellars 2000 Todd Brothers Ranch Zinfandel (Alexander Valley) $25. Rich and nuanced, the flavors range from blackberries and blueberries through spiced plums and white chocolate. Best of all is the texture: rich, velvety, supple and flattering. It's a big wine, but wears its size well. **92** Editors' Choice —*S.H.* *(2/1/2003)*

Dashe Cellars 1999 Todd Brothers Ranch Zinfandel (Alexander Valley) $25. The second vintage of this wine, from dry-farmed, 52-year-old vines is a big 'un, with plenty of backbone and muscular tannin. The same sweet, floral, grapey nose identifies it as Todd Brothers, and Dashe used just 18% new oak, keeping the fruit up front where it belongs. 900 cases made. **91** —*P.G.* *(3/1/2002)*

Dashe Cellars 1998 Todd Brothers Ranch Zinfandel (Alexander Valley) $25. Winemaker Michael Dashe singled out this old-vine fruit for special handling, and it pays off in a very fragrant, sweetly grapey wine with an enticing, intoxicating bouquet. Herbs and wildflowers and mixed red fruits explode in a profusion of scents and delicious layers of flavors. **91** —*P.G.* *(3/1/2002)*

Dashe Cellars 2003 Todd Brothers Ranch Old Vines Zinfandel (Alexander Valley) $28. Soft and broad, marked by chocolate fudge flavors and fruit that's more like dates or prunes than fresh berries. **83** *(12/18/2006)*

DAVID BRUCE

David Bruce 2001 Petite Sirah (Central Coast) $18. Dr. Bruce typically produces big, extracted wines. One taster called this super-ripe, and most found flavors of raspberries, blackberries and cherries. But there were also notes of cola and a simple, one-dimensional structure that make it a lightweight. **86** *(4/1/2003)*

David Bruce 1997 Pinot Noir (Chalone) $35. **88** *(11/15/1999)*

David Bruce 2000 Pinot Noir (Central Coast) $20. **86** *(10/1/2002)*

David Bruce 2000 Pinot Noir (Santa Cruz Mountains) $35. A heavy charcoal-toast profile doesn't always work with Pinot Noir, but it's fine in this chewy, dark offering. Deep cherry fruit, leather and smoked meat accents plus a long, espresso-tinged finish perform harmoniously. **89** *(10/1/2002)*

David Bruce 2000 Pinot Noir (Russian River Valley) $35. Lovely deep dusty rose and violet aromas open this light and fresh, yet velvety, offering. Cinnamon, mint, chocolate and tobacco accents keep the palate lively, while a ripe, easy feel makes it eminently drinkable. Drink now–2006. **90** *(10/1/2002)*

David Bruce 2000 Pinot Noir (Sonoma) $25. This soft, slightly creamy wine's berry and cherry aromas and flavors simply lacked life. Though wrapped in smoky oak, and offset by earth, cedar and brown sugar accents, the wine comes off as simple and even a bit dull. **83** *(10/1/2002)*

David Bruce 1997 Pinot Noir (Santa Cruz Mountains) $35. **90** *(10/1/1999)*

David Bruce 1997 Pinot Noir (Sonoma County) $24. **91** *(10/1/1999)*

David Bruce 2000 Truchard Vineyard Pinot Noir (Carneros) $35. There is an intriguing undercurrent of maple and wheat to the otherwise chunky, woody bouquet. Flavors of black cherry and tea sit atop an oaky, vanilla underlay that also brings with it some coconut. **88** *(10/1/2002)*

DAVID COFFARO

David Coffaro 2001 Zinfandel (Dry Creek Valley) $22. Spicy bright, with pleasant cherry, herb, plum, vanilla and toast flavors. Tannins are modest and the finish is a bit short. **85** *(11/1/2003)*

David Coffaro 2003 Bernier's Zinfandel (Dry Creek Valley) $22. Very dry, with finely ground tannins framing delicate flavors of berries and herbs, this Zin is made in a lighter, easier style. **85** —*S.H.* *(11/1/2005)*

David Coffaro 2003 My Zin Zinfandel (Dry Creek Valley) $22. A nice interpretation of Dry Creek Zin, showing pepper, herb, tobacco and cherry flavors that are fully dry and not overly alcoholic. Gives pleasure while showing some real complexity. **87** —*S.H.* *(11/1/2005)*

DAVID GIRARD

David Girard 2004 Grenache (El Dorado) $16. How tasty this fresh wine is. It's all about cherries and raspberries, with overtones of chocolate, vanilla, sweet licorice and pepper. Yet the wine is thoroughly dry, and balanced with rich acidity. It's not only delicious, it's complex. Contains a little Malbec, which brings body. **90** Editors' Choice —*S.H.* *(12/15/2006)*

David Girard 2005 Coeur du Terroir Blanc Rhône White Blend (El Dorado) $22. What a complex, delicious wine this is. A blend of five Rhône varieties, mainly Roussanne, it has the richness and mouthfeel of a barrel-fermented Chardonnay, but a very different taste. The peach, citrus, buttercup flower, honeydew and cantaloupe flavors finish with creamy, cashew butter richness. **90** —*S.H.* *(12/15/2006)*

David Girard 2002 Viognier-Roussanne Rhône White Blend (California) $18. Tastes extremely fruity, with peaches, apricots, lemonade, pineapple juice and all kinds of other stone fruit and spice flavors. This wine could use more acidity, though, as it's kind of flabby. **84** —*S.H.* *(12/15/2005)*

David Girard 2003 Syrah (El Dorado) $28. Shows refinement in the well-managed tannins that lead to a soft, richly complex mouthfeel. The flavors are ripe and tasteful, suggesting blackberry tea, wild cherries, cocoa and cinnamon, with a sweet tang of oak. This is an easy wine to savor. **88** —*S.H.* *(12/15/2005)*

DAVID HILL

David Hill 2001 Chardonnay (Willamette Valley) $15. Very soft in the mouth, with popcorn butter flavors and hints of green apple. Tastes as though it all went through malolactic fermentation; if so, it might have been better had they left some higher-acid wine in the blend. **84** —*P.G.* *(12/1/2003)*

David Hill 2002 Gewürztraminer (Willamette Valley) $12. This hard, tart and bitter wine does not seem to have much of anything in common with the varietal flavors of most Gewürztraminers. **81** —*P.G.* *(12/1/2003)*

David Hill 2002 Estate Port Muscat (Oregon) $42. Extremely limited production (75 6-bottle cases) is the only downside to this superb effort, which overflows with ripe, candied orange peel and citrus dessert fruit flavors. Spiced with clove, sweetened with a honeyed richness, it's smooth and buttery and yet not cloying or heavy. Delightful bottle. 90 —*P.G. (11/15/2005)*

David Hill 2002 Pinot Gris (Willamette Valley) $12. Very grassy and soft, with pungent, pine-needle flavors and aromas. It would probably go well with a good goat cheese. 85 —*P.G. (12/1/2003)*

David Hill 2001 Pinot Noir (Willamette Valley) $16. A light style, already rounding out and heading for an early finish. Good choice with seafood or something spicy. 84 —*P.G. (12/1/2003)*

David Hill 2002 Cuvée Anna-Lara Pinot Noir (Willamette Valley) $18. Odd, stalky, smelling of grass, herbs and orange pekoe tea. This is exceptionally thin, and non-varietal. 83 *(11/1/2004)*

David Hill 2002 Estate Pinot Noir (Willamette Valley) $15. Odd, stalky, smelling like raw celery. Hints of rhubarb are as ripe as it gets, with some sassafras, tomato, and assorted, weak, tea-like flavors. 83 *(11/1/2004)*

David Hill 2002 Estate Reserve Pinot Noir (Willamette Valley) $30. Very light and leafy, with a pale brick color and tart, tea-like flavors. Tannic and earthy, yet insubstantial, and lacking sweet fruit. 84 *(11/1/2004)*

David Hill NV Estate Tawny Port (Oregon) $42. This is solera-aged, going back to 1997 and made from Pinot Noir. Not all that tawny Port-like, it's more of an oxidized, rancio-style dessert wine, but made from Pinot of all things. 86 —*P.G. (11/15/2005)*

David Hill 2002 Late Harvest Riesling (Willamette Valley) $15. Flavors of buttery apple and apricot run through this smooth, pleasant-drinking wine with 8.1% residual sugar. Good length and a sweet, honeysuckle finish. 85 —*P.G. (12/1/2003)*

David Hill 1992 Brut Sparkling Blend (Oregon) $14. A darn good sparkling wine, well-aged and heavily scented with ripe apples, honey and clover. It's made from 100% Pinot Noir, and it's got a whole lot of rich, yeasty flavor for the price. 87 Best Buy —*P.G. (12/1/2003)*

DAVIS BYNUM

Davis Bynum 1997 Hedin Vineyard Cabernet Sauvignon (Russian River Valley) $30. 92 *(11/1/2000)*

Davis Bynum 1999 Chardonnay (Russian River Valley) $25. An intriguing wine, with honeyed-lemon and orange aromas backed up by spicy citrus, pear, apple, melon and floral notes. Long, bright, light, clean and minerally on the finish. 92 —*J.M. (12/31/2001)*

Davis Bynum 1998 Limited Edition Chardonnay (Russian River Valley) $25. 90 *(6/1/2000)*

Davis Bynum 2004 Fumé Blanc (Russian River Valley) $15. Thin and watery, with diluted citrus flavors and lots of raw acidity. 81 —*S.H. (12/15/2005)*

Davis Bynum 1999 Westside Road Meritage (Sonoma County) $35. A Merlot-dominated Bordeaux blend, and clearly grown in a cooler area. Flavors tend toward olives and tobacco, and are totally dry, with expressive acids. Tannins are soft, lush and complex, and coat the palate. A worthy companion for roast beef or lamb. 87 —*S.H. (11/15/2003)*

Davis Bynum 1999 Laureles Merlot (Russian River Valley) $28. Almost inky black, one whiff tells you this is a hugely extracted wine. It's chock full of blackberry and cassis, plum, white chocolate, anise and smoky aromas and flavors. In the mouth, it's a big, tannic wine with soft acids, concentrated blackberry flavors and lots of flashy oak. Very high class, but tannic. Age for a few years. 91 Editors' Choice —*S.H. (2/1/2003)*

Davis Bynum 1997 Laureles Merlot (Russian River Valley) $28. This is a wine made for the cellar. It's dark, and smells rich, with ripe blackberry and plum fruit and a hefty dose of vanilla-scented, smoky oak. Full-bodied, but the tannins are hefty now, and the acidity is high. Probably best to put it away for four or five years and see what happens. 89 —*S.H. (6/1/2001)*

Davis Bynum 2002 Pinot Noir (Russian River Valley) $28. Simple and clean, this Pinot has good qualities and offers pleasure without being

complex. It's light-bodied, dry and silky, with cherry, cola and rhubarb pie flavors. 85 —*S.H. (12/15/2005)*

Davis Bynum 2001 Pinot Noir (Russian River Valley) $28. A nice Pinot with good black cherry, spice and earthy-coffee flavors and a bright burst of acidity. Smooth tannins complete the ride. 86 —*S.H. (10/1/2004)*

Davis Bynum 2000 Pinot Noir (Russian River Valley) $30. Key descriptors from our tasters' notes for this wine include such words as "supple," "balanced," "lingering" and "seamless." It's not a blockbuster, but it is so seductively easy to drink, with its luscious cherry, leather and dried-spice flavors, that it scored unanimously well with our panel. 90 Editors' Choice *(10/1/2002)*

Davis Bynum 2001 3 Vineyards Pinot Noir (Russian River Valley) $50. Silky and very dry, an austere Pinot that has some tannins to resolve. The flavors suggest earth, tobacco and bitter cherry, with just a hint of blueberry. Oak plays a supporting role. Might improve in a few years. 86 —*S.H. (10/1/2004)*

Davis Bynum 2000 Allen Pinot Noir (Russian River Valley) $45. This is full-throttle Pinot, with a bouquet redolent of cherries, plums, graham crackers, coconut, smoke, cinnamon and licorice. It's big yet balanced, with a plush, creamy texture and deep cherry fruit. Caramel, mocha and spices accent the finish. 92 *(10/1/2002)*

Davis Bynum 2001 Allen Vineyard Pinot Noir (Russian River Valley) $50. The winery seems to be picking earlier than most, so that the wine from this celebrated vineyard, in this wonderful vintage, is tough and tannic. You can taste the underlying cherry fruit, but it's hard. The gamble is on ageability. Giving it the benefit of the doubt, try after 2006. 88 —*S.H. (10/1/2004)*

Davis Bynum 2001 Bynum & Moshin Vineyards Pinot Noir (Russian River Valley) $50. Tough, austere and tannic, although the palate senses the underlying quality. Just the faintest impression of cherry fruit rises to the surface, and a good deal of oak. Needs serious time. Try after 2006. 87 —*S.H. (10/1/2004)*

Davis Bynum 1999 Bynum & Moshin Vineyards Pinot Noir (Russian River Valley) $45. Here's a great wine that can be drunk now or held for up to five years. The nose is packed with mocha, smoked meat and crystalline red fruit. Moderate but healthy tannins frame the immensely flavorful palate, while coffee and cool earth creep onto the stylish finish. 91 *(10/1/2002)*

Davis Bynum 1999 Le Pinot Rochioli Vineyard Pinot Noir (Russian River Valley) $75. Is this wine is just too sweet and rich for its own good? You be the judge. The majority of our panel found it to be thumping with rich, very ripe blackberries, but also a medicinal, syrupy quality akin to liqueur. The tannins seem soft and fail to provide the structure this ultra ripe wine needs. 86 *(10/1/2002)*

Davis Bynum 2002 Lindley's Knoll Pinot Noir (Russian River Valley) $55. Oaky, tannic and somewhat twiggy and minty to start, this Pinot has modest cherry and cola flavors. It's not showing particularly well, with some tightness, but gets fruitier and more charming as it breathes. 85 —*S.H. (12/15/2006)*

Davis Bynum 2001 Lindley's Knoll Pinot Noir (Russian River Valley) $50. Very dry, pretty tannic, a Pinot that's too young to fully enjoy now, although a good lamb chop will soften it. Those tannins shut down the palate, barely allowing the cherry-berry flavors to emerge. Best after 2005. 87 —*S.H. (10/1/2004)*

Davis Bynum 2000 Lindley's Knoll Pinot Noir (Russian River Valley) $45. A bit lean and herbal, and certainly not in the same league as the luscious 1999. Just manages to break out into cherry fruit, but mainly consists of sage, cranberry and tobacco flavors. Big acids and fine tannins still combine to make this a compelling wine, despite its leanness. 87 —*S.H. (4/1/2003)*

Davis Bynum 1999 Lindleys' Knoll Pinot Noir (Russian River Valley) $45. Bright cherry, strawberry, spice and herb flavors make a very enjoyable blend in this fresh, young Pinot. Smooth and long on the finish. 90 —*J.M. (5/1/2002)*

Davis Bynum 1999 Lindley's Knoll Best 4 Barrels Pinot Noir (Russian River Valley) $90. Dense aromas of plum, cherry and blackberry, along with complex bacon, oak, saddle-leather and nut accents, set the stage for a strong performance. The plummy fruit, plush mouthfeel and hints of smoke, tobacco and stable notes pack in plenty of palate-tickling pleasure. Closes long and juicy. Just 90 cases made. **91** *(10/1/2002)*

Davis Bynum 2001 Rochioli Vineyard Le Pinot Pinot Noir (Russian River Valley) $80. There's a good Pinot in here waiting to get out, and three or four years may do it. Young and angular, with ripe cherry fruit and a rich earthiness suggesting sweet pipe tobacco, this well-oaked wine is dry, with an elegant, silky texture. **89** —*S.H. (6/1/2005)*

Davis Bynum 2000 Rochioli Vineyard Le Pinot Pinot Noir (Russian River Valley) $NA. Pretty tannic still, and very dry, but with some deep red cherry flavors, this wine may benefit from a few more years, but it's not an ager. It shows an angular structure that will stand up well to beef or lamb. **87** —*S.H. (6/1/2005)*

Davis Bynum 1999 Rochioli Vineyard Le Pinot Pinot Noir (Russian River Valley) $NA. A little too porty and raisiny for my tastes. Drinking dry and somewhat tannic, although the alcohol is a modest 13.9 percent. Drink now. **86** —*S.H. (6/1/2005)*

Davis Bynum 2004 Rosé Blend (Russian River Valley) $15. There's very little fruit in this watery, tart wine. It has trace amounts of cherries and rose petals, and is totally dry. It would be pretty nice if it had more concentration. **83** —*S.H. (12/15/2005)*

DAVIS FAMILY

Davis Family 2001 Cabernet Sauvignon (Napa Valley) $40. Shows the hallmarks of a fine Napa Cab, with ripe black currant and black cherry fruit. It also offers elaborately soft, integrated tannins, fine acidity and a solid overlay of good oak. Drinks dry, round and polished, with a milk chocolate finish. **89** —*S.H. (8/1/2005)*

Davis Family 2003 Dutton Ranch Chardonnay (Russian River Valley) $35. What Dutton Ranch Chards share is a crisp, appley crunchiness, edging into the tropics in a good vintage. In this case, it adds rich new oak and a creamy, leesy mouthfeel, and the flavors approach decadent guava and nectarine. **91** —*S.H. (12/15/2005)*

Davis Family 2002 Dutton Ranch Chardonnay (Russian River Valley) $30. This ripe and oaky Chard shows crisp acids and subtlely charred oak, with flavors of apples and pears and a leesy finish. It's classically New World, with its obvious likeability and uncomplicated drinking. **87** —*S.H. (8/1/2005)*

Davis Family 2004 Pinot Noir (Russian River Valley) $38. Starts with a strong burst of charry, caramelized new wood, then in the mouth it turns very ripe, dense and oaky, with primary Pinot fruit and some dusty tannins. On airing, more complex notes of mushrooms and soy emerge. **88** —*S.H. (12/1/2006)*

Davis Family 2002 Pinot Noir (Russian River Valley) $30. A wonderfully polished and supple wine that pleases with oodles of rich, smoky, cherry flavors and a smooth, chocolatey mouthfeel. The silky texture and crisp acidity make it complex and rewarding. Really a winner. **91** *(11/1/2004)*

Davis Family 2001 Zinfandel (Russian River Valley) $25. Firm textured and well structured, with moderate plum, cherry, spice and herb flavors. A smoky edge runs through it, with hints of licorice and tobacco on the finish, which is moderate in length. **88** *(11/1/2003)*

DE LA MONTANYA

De La Montanya 2003 Syrah (Russian River Valley) $32. Features an elegant interplay of raspberry fruit and herbal (dried thyme, oregano) notes, picking up hints of bittersweet chocolate on the finish. Supple and creamy in the mouth, ending with soft tannins. **88** *(9/1/2005)*

DE LOACH

De Loach 1998 Los Amigos Ranch Cabernet Sauvignon (Russian River Valley) $22. From estate vineyards. Don't look for plush, luxurious Napa softness and melted tannins here. This is a sturdy, tart wine, with punchy herbal, minty, peppery flavors that cut over underlying blackberry notes. It's a muscular wine, but not a tannic one. It won't benefit from age. The strong favors are what they are, and suggest lamb with, say, mint sauce. **87** —*S.H. (9/1/2003)*

De Loach 2003 O.F.S. Cabernet Sauvignon (Russian River Valley) $30. Made in a ripe style, this Cab bursts with jammy black currant, plum

and coffee flavors that finish rich and sweet. But it's also got a firm texture, with fine-grained tannins and a keen edge of acidity. The result is a balanced and stylish Cab that should hold for at least seven years. **90** —*S.H. (10/1/2006)*

De Loach 2000 O.F.S. Cabernet Sauvignon (Russian River Valley) $30. A nice Cab that mingles its polished berry-cherry flavors with earthy tobacco and mocha to make for a dry, very drinkable wine. **87** —*S.H. (11/15/2004)*

De Loach 1998 O.F.S. Cabernet Sauvignon (Russian River Valley) $50. Good, but disappointing. Blackberry, mint, chocolate and black cherry flavors are pretty, but thin, and the weight on the palate, the way the wine feels, is light and watered down. This absence of depth lets the alcohol and tannins star. It's obviously well-made, but is not a wine for the cellar. **87** —*S.H. (8/1/2003)*

De Loach 1997 O.F.S. Cabernet Sauvignon (Russian River Valley) $40. **90** *(11/1/2000)*

De Loach 2004 Chardonnay (Russian River Valley) $16. The problem here is a lack of fruit. Except for a hint of Chardonnay peaches and cream, you get little beyond alcohol and acidity. But it's a clean wine. **82** —*S.H. (10/1/2006)*

De Loach 2002 Chardonnay (Russian River Valley) $16. Rather light in weight, but pretty, with delicate, smoke-tinged pear and citrus flavors that gather focus on the crisp finish. **86** *(8/1/2005)*

De Loach 2001 Chardonnay (Russian River Valley) $16. A nice, somewhat earthy Chard. The fruit doesn't star here, although there are some polished apple and peach flavors. Rather, it's the structure. Good acidity and a touch of dusty tannins make this a natural for food. **85** —*S.H. (12/1/2004)*

De Loach 2000 Chardonnay (Russian River Valley) $18. Oaky, peachy, appley, tropical fruity, vanilla-y, spicy, creamy, honey, toasty—what else can you say? Another good California Chardonnay that gives the people what they want, at a price that, these days, is fair. **86** —*S.H. (12/15/2002)*

De Loach 1999 Chardonnay (Russian River Valley) $21. The understated pear and pineapple flavors of this medium-weight Chardonnay have pleasant spice accents. It finishes stylishly with slightly tart pineapple and citrus notes. **87** *(8/1/2001)*

De Loach 1998 Chardonnay (Russian River Valley) $18. **91** —*S.H. (2/1/2000)*

De Loach 1997 Chardonnay (Russian River Valley) $18. **92** —*S.H. (11/1/1999)*

De Loach 2004 O.F.S. Chardonnay (Russian River Valley) $30. This is a balanced, easy to drink Chardonnay, with citrus, peach and green apple flavors that have been finished with a veneer of smoky oak. It's totally dry. Do not overchill it, as it's a delicate wine that needs some warmth to open up. **88** —*S.H. (5/1/2006)*

De Loach 2003 O.F.S. Chardonnay (Russian River Valley) $26. Smoke, pear and citrus notes dominate this wine's nose, while the palate features flavors that lean more toward apple and pineapple. It's not a heavy, thick California Chardonnay, but rather one that exhibits good balance and a sense of elegance to its lemon-curd finish. **89** *(8/1/2005)*

De Loach 1998 O.F.S. Chardonnay (Russian River Valley) $30. Pear, pineapple and citrus aromas with spearmint accents comprise the bouquet of this Russian River favorite. The wine is round and soft with tea, lemon, tropical fruit and buttercream flavors. It's light- to medium-weight, but with enough complexity to hold the taster's interest, and a persistent, tangy, sweet and sour back-end fade. **89** *(7/1/2001)*

De Loach 1999 Olivet Ranch Chardonnay (Russian River Valley) $22. The lees that the wine was aged on dominate the aromas, with that curiously appealing sour-cream scent that promises a richly creamy texture. And so it is, wrapped gently around delicious apple fruit flavors and dusty oriental spices. It's a dry wine, with great structure, and a zesty acidity that's high by Sonoma standards. **90** —*S.H. (12/15/2002)*

De Loach 1998 Olivet Ranch Chardonnay (Russian River Valley) $20. **89** *(6/1/2000)*

De Loach 2000 Fumé Blanc (Russian River Valley) $14. You get a lot for your money with this wine, which has extra dimensions of creamy complexity. The apple and citrus fruit flavors are exquisite, and wonderfully spiced up with oaky nuances, resulting in a rich, full-bodied white wine that's great on its own, or with food. Good value. **87** —S.H. (9/1/2003)

De Loach 2004 Early Harvest Gewürztraminer (Russian River Valley) $14.
One of the first wines from De Loach after the Boisset takeover, this dry Gewürz is a good portent for the future. It's ultraclean and crisp, with very deep and satisfying flavors of Asian spices, peaches, lychee and citrus. **87** —S.H. (12/1/2005)

De Loach 2000 Early Harvest Gewürztraminer (Russian River Valley) $14.
Fun to sniff, with fragrances of orange blossom, vanilla, citrus and cashew, and fun to drink, too. The blossomy, flowery flavors are lush and forward, and offset by residual sugar that drinks off-dry. Crisp acidity adds brightness and life. **86** —J.M. (6/1/2002)

De Loach 2002 Merlot (Russian River Valley) $19. Dark and saturated in fruity extract, a boldly flavored wine whose plum, blackberry, cured tobacco and smoky oak flavors finish dry. The tannins are rich and thick, but drinkable now. **87** —S.H. (5/1/2005)

De Loach 1999 Estate Bottled Merlot (Russian River Valley) $20. Inland warmth teased out red and black raspberry flavors in these grapes. Ocean fog and chill not only kept acids bright, but held down ripening, yielding earthier notes of tobacco and garden herbs. The complex balance is terrific. Oak adds just the right notes. **89** —S.H. (11/15/2002)

De Loach 1997 Estate-Bottled Merlot (Russian River Valley) $19. **89** (11/15/1999)

De Loach 2001 Pinot Gris (Sonoma County) $14. Rich and creamy, a big wine bursting with wild berry, white stone fruit, flower and spice aromas and flavors. Tastes candied and ripe, with dry tannins and good acidity. A touch of oak adds vanilla and smoky notes. **87** —S.H. (9/1/2003)

De Loach 2004 Pinot Noir (Russian River Valley) $18. De Loach's 30th Anniversary Pinot, from the same vintage, was a stupendous wine, and while this isn't as rich, it's in the same vein. It's very ripe in cherry pie, cocoa puff, cola and oak flavors, with a honeyed finish. Yet it's dry, and maintains balance and harmony throughout. If you like lots of fruit in your Pinot, this is a good pick. **88** —S.H. (10/1/2006)

De Loach 2002 Pinot Noir (Sonoma County) $18. Light and tart, with crisp, authentic Russian River flavors of beet, spice and cola. Perhaps overly polite and polished, but pleasant enough. **85** (8/1/2005)

De Loach 2000 Pinot Noir (Russian River Valley) $18. This lean and focused offering from De Loach showed better than the winery's flagship O.F.S. in our tastings, displaying tart strawberry and rhubarb aromas and flavors uncluttered by lashings of new oak. A bit of oak does show through on the finish, just enough to impart a pleasant caramel sensation. **87** (10/1/2002)

De Loach 2004 30th Anniversary Cuvée Pinot Noir (Russian River Valley) $45. This shows winemaker Greg LaFollette's master touch in the way he's balanced the wine and kept it harmonious. It's a huge mouthful of cherry pie and cassis flavor, with the most delicate notes of raspberries, toasted meringue and vanilla, subtly spiced and dry. A gorgeous Pinot Noir that superbly combines power with elegance. **96 Editors' Choice** — S.H. (8/1/2006)

De Loach 2000 Balletto Ranch Pinot Noir (Russian River Valley) $25.
Clearly a step in quality above the winery's regular release. A slight cloudiness suggests an unfiltered wine—whether or not this is true—but it has the stuffing of flavor and texture that make it interesting. Pale in color, delicate of body, with intensely spicy, raspberry and tobacco flavors and perky acids. Catch it in its youth for flamboyance and spirit. **88** —S.H. (8/1/2003)

De Loach 2001 Estate Pinot Noir (Russian River Valley) $18. A fine communal wine, with its pretty flavors of cherries and raspberries and an edge of cinnamon-spiked coffee. With its delicately silky mouthfeel, it's a versatile food wine. **86** —S.H. (12/1/2004)

De Loach 1999 Estate Bottled Pinot Noir (Russian River Valley) $21. A solid foundation of ripe dark-cherry fruit adds vanilla, toast and cinnamon accents that work to create a full bouquet and palate. This Pinot has character and complexity. Finishes long, with licorice and mineral elements playing off the dry cherry flavors. **87 Editors' Choice** (8/1/2001)

De Loach 1997 O.F.S Pinot Noir (Russian River Valley) $32. **87** (11/15/1999)

De Loach 2003 O.F.S. Pinot Noir (Russian River Valley) $29. Nicely perfumed on the nose, with gentle notes of cinnamon and clove accenting black cherries and plums. It's medium in body, with that elusive Pinot suppleness and velvety mouthfeel, finishing with a bit of cola and spice. **90** (8/1/2005)

De Loach 2002 O.F.S. Pinot Noir (Russian River Valley) $29. Finely scented, with cherries, raspberries, rose petals and smoky oak, and nicely delicate, dry and light in the mouth. Could use more intensity, though. **85** —S.H. (5/1/2005)

De Loach 2000 O.F.S. Pinot Noir (Russian River Valley) $50. After some unusual aromatics described variously by tasters as cheese, brine or shoe polish, this settles down to a lean, angular offering. It shows a tart, slightly bitter profile with sour plum and cranberry flavors, herb and chalk accents. Focused but not rich, it closes a bit narrow and astringent. Tasted twice, with consistent notes. **85** (10/1/2002)

De Loach 1999 O.F.S. Pinot Noir (Russian River Valley) $44. Deeper and darker than the Estate bottling, this shows black cherry, meat and leather nuances. It's sexy, but a touch hot as well. Offers depth and complexity, especially on the finish, where interesting chocolate notes emerge. **88** (8/1/2001)

De Loach 1998 Splendo Blendo 1 Red Blend (Russian River Valley) $80.
Dried cherry, cedar-toast and cumin notes mark the nose of this Sangiovese-Cabernet Sauvignon-Merlot blend. It has a decidedly Tuscan cast to its sour-cherry-and-leather profile, and finishes dry, even and long, with hints of chocolate and plenty of toasty oak. **89** (8/1/2001)

De Loach 2000 Los Amigos Ranch Sangiovese (Russian River Valley) $28.
California struggles to produce great Sangiovese. This worthy effort holds the line of scrimmage. It's a pretty piece of winemaking, with upfront berry and tobacco flavors, soft tannins and mouthwatering acidity, a good foil for olive oil or beef. Yet it's clearly a work in progress. **87** —S.H. (12/1/2002)

De Loach 2003 Sauvignon Blanc (Russian River Valley) $16. Refreshing in acids and citrus zest, this wine finishes semi-sweet with flavors of spearmint, fig and melon. It's a nice cocktail wine, or try one to with a honey-baked ham. **85** —S.H. (5/1/2005)

De Loach 2004 O.F.S. Sauvignon Blanc (Russian River Valley) $20. Wow. This is one big, impressive Sauvignon Blanc. It's the grass and gooseberry, and the acidity. The wine hits the palate like a bomb, dry and crisp and explosive. Mid-palate, the fruit emerges, peaches, figs, melons, limes, kiwi. This is De Loach's first O.F.S. Sauvignon and it's worthy of the designation. **91 Editors' Choice** —S.H. (5/1/2006)

De Loach 2001 Viognier (Russian River Valley) $20. This is a big, rich, ripely fruity wine, filled with gigantic flavors of white peach, apricot, lime zest, white chocolate, fig, raspberry, and lots of other flavorful things. It's been drenched in toasty oak and seems to have a bit of lees in there to boost the creamy texture. For all the flavor, it's pretty dry. **88** — S.H. (3/1/2003)

De Loach 2003 Zinfandel (Russian River Valley) $18. Offers lots to like in a dry, intensely fruity Zin, whose blackberry, cherry, cocoa and tart cranberry flavors explode on the palate. Such a wine could be ordinary, but the balance is impeccable. **88** —S.H. (10/1/2006)

De Loach 2002 Zinfandel (Russian River Valley) $18. Like the Pinot, this wine is a touch light in weight. The briary, peppery berry flavors are true to the appellation, they just need to be amped up. **85** (8/1/2005)

De Loach 2001 Zinfandel (Russian River Valley) $20. Toasty-rich with a mild plum and black cherry core. The oak is quite forward, but the fruit stands up to it. Tannins are smooth and fat, supporting the wine nicely. **86** (11/1/2003)

De Loach 2000 Zinfandel (Russian River Valley) $20. This winery's basic Zinfandel tastes, well, basic. It has clove and tobacco notes and some nuances of riper berries, but you get the feeling they put everything good into the single-vineyard wines. This isn't bad stuff, but you can get a whole lot more for your money elsewhere. **84** —S.H. (11/1/2002)

USA

De Loach 1999 Zinfandel (Russian River Valley) $20. This is a classic California Zin, with ripe, exuberant aromas of strawberry, red raspberry, blueberry, bramble and peppery dust and smoke. Opens with a big burst of spicy berry fruit, round and rich and very dry. Accessible tannins add complexity and structure. **90 Editors' Choice** —*S.H. (11/15/2001)*

De Loach 1999 Zinfandel (California) $13. This attractive entry level Zinfandel has good varietal character with dark berry aromas and flavors offset by cocoa accents. The palate shows good fruit, decent acidity; the wine finishes with sweet-tart berry and mild pepper flavors. **85** *(8/1/2001)*

De Loach 2001 Barbieri Ranch Zinfandel (Russian River Valley) $25. Dark, lush and magnificent Zinfandel, but be warned, the tannins pack a punch. Opens with youthfully earthy aromas that suggest cassis and black cherries, and turns luscious and fruity in the mouth. Perfect now with ribs and such, but best to cellar it for four years or so. **92** —*S.H. (3/1/2004)*

De Loach 2000 Barbieri Ranch Zinfandel (Russian River Valley) $28. How ripe these grapes got. You can taste sunny sugar in every sip: black raspberries, black cherries and blueberries, with all kinds of wonderful crushed brown spices. As sweet as it sounds, the wine is bone-dry, an impression heightened by sticky tannins and excellent acids. This is Zin, pure and simple. **92 Editors' Choice** —*S.H. (11/1/2002)*

De Loach 1999 Barbieri Ranch Zinfandel (Russian River Valley) $30. "Black is Black" went the old song, and this Zin does too, with blackberries, black-pepper and dark-chocolate aromas and flavors galore. An impressive wine that shows full mouthfeel, and a long finish with dusty tannins. **90 Editors' Choice** *(8/1/2001)*

De Loach 1998 Barbieri Ranch Zinfandel (Russian River Valley) $22. 93 —*S.H. (2/1/2000)*

De Loach 1997 Barbieri Ranch Zinfandel (Russian River Valley) $20. 88 —*P.G. (11/15/1999)*

De Loach 2000 Doe Mill Ranch Zinfandel (Sierra Foothills) $28. Hard to believe the grapes were picked in August—but they got really ripe under the intense mountain sunlight. There's a purity of wild berry flavors that's attractive. It has nowhere near the depth or stuffing of coastal bottlings, though—despite the pretty flavors, that's a problem. **85** —*S.H. (11/1/2002)*

De Loach 1997 Estate Zinfandel (Russian River Valley) $18. 87 —*P.G. (11/15/1999)*

De Loach 1999 Estate Bottled Zinfandel (Russian River Valley) $21. Aromas of red berries with thyme and anise accents also show a whiff of acetone that bothered some tasters. After that, this wine is on very comfortable ground. Smooth and evenly textured, it has a balanced, even graceful quality often lacking in Zinfandels. Good length and mild pepper and spice mark the finish. **88** *(8/1/2001)*

De Loach 1998 Estate Bottled Zinfandel (Russian River Valley) $18. 90 —*S.H. (2/1/2000)*

De Loach 2003 Gambogi Ranch Zinfandel (Russian River Valley) $27. De Loach says this has the "broadest shoulders of the single-vineyard designates," but while it may seem slightly burly, it never reaches massive. Instead it nicely balances berry and chocolate flavors and adds a tangy, peppery note to the finish. **88** *(8/1/2005)*

De Loach 2001 Gambogi Ranch Zinfandel (Russian River Valley) $25. An excellent Zin that testifies to the greatness of the vintage for this varietal. Huge flavors of black raspberries, chocolate and wild blackberries are wrapped in beautiful tannins. In fact the tannins don't get much better, rich, soft, dusty and complex. Feels just great in the mouth. But it has a youthful pertness, so drink with red meat or cellar. **92** —*S.H. (3/1/2004)*

De Loach 2000 Gambogi Ranch Zinfandel (Russian River Valley) $28. Old vines (1909) yielded intensely concentrated fruit. Straddles the riper notes of Pelletti with the drier, earthier Papera grapes, yielding brambly flavors cut through with mint. As in many old vine Zins, the texture is lush and complex, but vibrant acidity lends balance and drinkability. **89** —*S.H. (11/1/2002)*

De Loach 1999 Gambogi Ranch Zinfandel (Russian River Valley) $30. Reserved, but with lovely aromatics, this Zin has tart dark-berry fruit

and a slight nuttiness. Quite structured, this will benefit from a couple of years of cellaring. **88** *(8/1/2001)*

De Loach 1998 Gambogi Ranch Zinfandel (Russian River Valley) $22. 88 —*S.H. (2/1/2000)*

De Loach 1997 Gambogi Ranch Zinfandel (Russian River Valley) $20. 89 —*P.G. (11/15/1999)*

De Loach 2001 O.F.S. Zinfandel (Russian River Valley) $40. Medium-bodied with moderate tannins, the wine shows hints of cherry and menthol flavors. Toasty and smoky on the finish. **85** *(11/1/2003)*

De Loach 1998 O.F.S. Zinfandel (Russian River Valley) $35. 93 —*S.H. (2/1/2000)*

De Loach 2003 O.F.S. Zinfandel (Russian River Valley) $29. Spice and chocolate notes gradually give way to more plum and berry flavors as the wine sits in the glass. Ripe, berryish fruit on the palate, finishing a touch warm and tannic. **89** *(8/1/2005)*

De Loach 2000 O.F.S. Zinfandel (Russian River Valley) $50. The winery's finest stuff is varietally intense, with brambly, wild berry and tobacco flavors accented by pepper and clove. It's also quite tannic, with a raisiny roughness that time may soften. At 15% alcohol, the finish is hot. **87** —*S.H. (9/1/2003)*

De Loach 1999 O.F.S. Zinfandel (Russian River Valley) $44. Cuts an elegant profile, with its ripe blackberry fruit and judicious use of oak. Supple and even, it shows good balance. The pepper, chocolate and licorice-tinged finish is long, with fine tannins. It's a big wine, but not awkward, showing depth and style. **90** *(8/1/2001)*

De Loach 2001 Papera Ranch Zinfandel (Russian River Valley) $25. Another fine single-vineyard Zin from De Loach. It's more tannic than the others and is palate-numbing, but there's a rich, thick core of blackberry fruit that wants to come out. Very fine wine, but cellar through 2005. **90** —*S.H. (3/1/2004)*

De Loach 2000 Papera Ranch Zinfandel (Russian River Valley) $28. Said to be from 68-year-old head-pruned vines, the wine is packed with intense flavors, some of them unusual for Zin. The wild berries are there, and so is white chocolate, sweet peppermint and rhubarb pie. It hangs onto Zin's wild character, that edge of barely contained wildness. **87** —*S.H. (11/1/2002)*

De Loach 1999 Papera Ranch Zinfandel (Russian River Valley) $30. Dark cherries, plums, olives and licorice, as well as an edgy, chemical note. Lean in style, the palate's mixed berry flavors have olive accents. Finishes long, with firm tannins and tart acidity. **88** *(8/1/2001)*

De Loach 1998 Papera Ranch Zinfandel (Russian River Valley) $22. 90 —*S.H. (2/1/2000)*

De Loach 2000 Pelletti Ranch Zinfandel (Russian River Valley) $28. Kudos to De Loach for keeping all these vineyards separate. These vines, planted in 1928, have a distinctive blueberry flavor. (Dan Cedarquist, the winemaker, calls it mulberry.) It's a very good Zin, thick and heady, with 15% alcohol, and vinified dry. **91** —*S.H. (11/1/2002)*

De Loach 1999 Pelletti Ranch Zinfandel (Russian River Valley) $30. A bouquet of full, sweet fruit with attractive spice and earth accents and a rich creamy mouthfeel make this large-scale wine a real winner. Despite its plush qualities it has structure and some tannins to resolve. Already delicious, this should shine in three years. Cellar Selection. **91 Cellar Selection** *(8/1/2001)*

De Loach 1998 Pelletti Ranch Zinfandel (Russian River Valley) $22. 91 —*S.H. (2/1/2000)*

De Loach 1997 Pelletti Ranch Zinfandel (Russian River Valley) $20. 92 —*P.G. (11/15/1999)*

De Loach 2001 Saitone Ranch Zinfandel (Russian River Valley) $25. Inky purple and black, a youthful wine with gorgeous aromas of plums and blackberry pie, dark chocolate, mincemeat, sweet compost, and white pepper. Drinks as complex as it sounds, bone dry, with beautiful tannins that are firm and complex but completely accessible. This is terrific, classic Zinfandel. **93 Editors' Choice** —*S.H. (3/1/2004)*

De Loach 2000 Saitone Ranch Zinfandel (Russian River Valley) $28. The vines were planted in 1895. The wine is inky black, and even though the alcohol reads a moderate 14.5%, it seems hot and strong. Jammy fruit is intense. I find a bothering note of clove or sharp mint that may be the result of American oak, or of unripe grapes. Either way, it's a tart, knife-like stab that may mellow out with age. **86** —*S.H. (11/1/2002)*

De Loach 1999 Saitone Ranch Zinfandel (Russian River Valley) $30. Decidedly lighter in color and weight than the Barbieri Ranch wine, the Saitone shows a bouquet of tart cherries, strawberries and herbs. Anise-tarragon notes add interest on the textured palate. Closes with dry, talc-like tannins. **88** *(8/1/2001)*

De Loach 1998 Saitone Ranch Zinfandel (Russian River Valley) $22. 87 —*S.H. (2/1/2000)*

De Loach 1997 Saitone Ranch Zinfandel (Russian River Valley) $20. 90 —*P.G. (11/15/1999)*

DE PONTE CELLARS

De Ponte Cellars 2002 Pinot Noir (Willamette Valley) $28. Nice and firm, with full, bright flavors of black cherry. Still quite tangy and wiry, yet it packs the impression of considerable power. Polished and well made. **88** *(11/1/2004)*

DE SANTE

De Sante 2001 Calder Cabernet Sauvignon (Napa Valley) $40. Largely Howell Mountain Cabernet Sauvignon, this is a tough, young bruiser. It's very tannic now, but very fruity, with balancing acidity. Should purr along nicely for 10 years or so. **87** —*S.H. (5/1/2005)*

De Sante 2004 Sauvignon Blanc (Napa Valley) $20. Quite dry and firm, without the sweet fruitiness that marks so many others. This one's citrusy and minty, but has deeper layers of cream that make it complex. **87** —*S.H. (5/1/2005)*

De Sante 2001 Sauvignon Blanc (Napa Valley) $18. A first wine from this winery, a rich and tasty wine that's right up there with California's best. The lemony, grassy side of Sauvignon Blanc is paired with the nutty, figgy profile of Sémillon to produce a complex, stylish wine. It's so ripe, it tastes sweet, but it's a dryish wine. **90** —*S.H. (10/1/2003)*

DE TIERRA

De Tierra 2003 Merlot (Monterey) $30. Riper than the '02, but still has an herbal, coffee taste that accentuates the alcohol, making for a chili-pepper burn on the finish. **83** —*S.H. (12/1/2006)*

De Tierra Vineyards 2002 Syrah (Monterey) $NA. Smells rather vegetal, and tastes too sweet. Flavors are of blackberries and coffee. **82** —*S.H. (6/1/2005)*

DEAVER

Deaver 2002 Zinfandel (Amador County) $25. Starts with a beautiful aroma that's dramatically chocolatey and oaky, then reveals layers of cherries and black raspberries. Lush, creamy, long in the mouth, with a claret-like balance, but the power of mountain Zin. **92** —*S.H. (3/1/2005)*

DECOY

Decoy 2003 Red Blend (Napa Valley) $28. Mostly Cabernet Sauvignon, with a little Franc, this blend has rich but soft tannins and lush, super-ripe fruit. The blackberry jam, cassis, black cherry and cocoa flavors are wrapped in a creamy texture, and finish impressively long. **89** —*S.H. (2/1/2006)*

DEERFIELD RANCH

Deerfield Ranch 2001 Cabernet Sauvignon (North Coast) $30. Here's a full-bodied Cab that's pretty tannic and dry, but those tannins frame ripe flavors of black currants that will wake up with a good steak. Has good structure and balance, as well as firm acids. **87** —*S.H. (8/1/2005)*

Deerfield Ranch 2000 Cabernet Sauvignon (Napa Valley) $50. There's a firm structure to the fruit, which is elaborate in plummy, blackberry and mocha flavors. Will hold for a few years, but it's best to drink it in its youthful freshness. **87** —*S.H. (11/15/2004)*

Deerfield Ranch 2000 Cabernet Sauvignon (Sonoma County) $35. Very pretty, a softly luxurious, gentle wine whose easy mouthfeel disguises lots of complexity. It's very dry, but filled with ripe, sweet blackcurrant and

spicy plum fruit that's nuanced with green olives, dried herbs and plush oak. **90** —*S.H. (4/1/2004)*

Deerfield Ranch 2002 Chardonnay (Sonoma Valley) $25. Tastes a bit old for a Chard, with the fruit fading. It's still lively in acids, and has enough pear and apple flavors to satisfy. Finishes quick, and overall, it's not what it should be. **84** —*S.H. (8/1/2005)*

Deerfield Ranch 2001 Chardonnay (Carneros) $20. Smells very oaky and leesy, with smoky vanillins, buttered toast and a sweet-and-sour cream aroma that masks the fruit. In the mouth, the oak also dominates, although there's some good underlying white peach and tropical fruit. Give it another six months to knit together. **87** —*S.H. (4/1/2004)*

Deerfield Ranch 1999 Labbe Vineyard Chardonnay Chardonnay (Sonoma Valley) $30. Barrel fermentation yields creamy, smoky aromas and a rich texture. Lees aging boosts the thick mouthfeel. On the other hand, the actual fruit flavors are restrained. No massive guavas and breadfruit here. Think apples, crisp and clean and spicy. This is likely to age well. **91** —*S.H. (9/1/2002)*

Deerfield Ranch 2000 Begin Vineyard Gewürztraminer (California) $16. You have to admire anyone with the courage to make a Gewürz these days, especially a semisweet one. It brims with honey, smoky, jasmine, quince and spice aromas, and drinks with noticeable sugar. Would be nice with fresh fruit. **85** —*S.H. (6/1/2002)*

Deerfield Ranch 1999 DRX Meritage (North Coast) $100. A good but not great wine. Good flavors, nice oak, smooth, polished tannins, but soft, almost flat in acids, and without special features. **85** —*S.H. (11/15/2003)*

Deerfield Ranch 2000 Ladi's Vineyard Meritage (Sonoma County) $75. Not showing much now. It's muted in both aroma and flavor, with the oak and tannins dominating. There are plum, chocolate and blackberry flavors, but this wine's long-term future is doubtful. **86** —*S.H. (11/15/2004)*

Deerfield Ranch 2000 Roumiguiere Vineyard Merlot (Clear Lake) $24. There's plenty to like in this Merlot from Lake County. It's very dry and fairly tannic, but not unduly so. The underlying flavors are of plums, espresso, and blackberries. Drink this sturdy wine with roasted chicken or beef. **87** —*S.H. (9/1/2003)*

Deerfield Ranch 2000 Russian River Vineyards Merlot (Russian River Valley) $30. Opens and finishes with a blast of new oak. The underlying flavors suggest red cherries and herbs. Dry, with some dusty tannins. **85** —*S.H. (12/15/2004)*

Deerfield Ranch 1999 Russian River Vineyards Merlot (Russian River Valley) $32. Said to be from Sonoma County's oldest Merlot vineyards, there's a density and weight that suggest low yields of small, intense berries. Focused flavors of blackberries, cassis, tobacco, black cherry and licorice candy, wrapped in wonderful tannins, and bone dry. This is elegant stuff, if a bit soft. **90** —*S.H. (9/1/2002)*

Deerfield Ranch 2001 Pinot Noir (Sonoma Valley) $30. Smells a bit musty and earthy, with hints of mint and a whiff of cherries. The texture is lovely, just what you want in a Sonoma Pinot: silky, soft and seductive. If only there were more going on with the flavors besides oak. **85** —*S.H. (4/1/2004)*

Deerfield Ranch 2001 Pinot Noir (Carneros) $25. Nice and silky in texture, with soft, gentle tannins balanced by crisp acids. The flavors veer toward cola, rhubarb and cherry, and they're a bit simple. Oak helps, especially in the smoky, spicy aftertaste. **85** —*S.H. (4/1/2004)*

Deerfield Ranch 2002 Cohn Vineyard Pinot Noir (Russian River Valley) $48. Smells young and fresh, with jammy cherry, vanilla and peppery aromas. Drinks a bit hot and sharp, but you'll find some good flavors. A nice example of the variety, Russian River-style. **87** *(11/1/2004)*

Deerfield Ranch 2000 Cohn Vineyard Pinot Noir (Russian River Valley) $48. Grown in the warmer northeastern corner of the valley, this ambitious wine has raspberry, smoke, tobacco and coffee aromas. It's richly soft in tannins and acids, with berry flavors. Yet the finish is a little dilute. **86** —*S.H. (2/1/2003)*

Deerfield Ranch 2002 Jemrose Vineyard Pinot Noir (Bennett Valley) $40. From this newish AVA, a polished wine with tart cherry, beet and oak notes, and quite crisp acidity. You'll find good penetration and length. Finishes with astringency, but nice with meats or cheeses. **87** *(11/1/2004)*

Deerfield Ranch 2002 Jemrose Vineyard Pinot Noir (Bennett Valley) $25. From this Sonoma appellation, a dry, full-bodied Pinot, with plenty of cherry, coffee, cocoa and spice flavors, and a nice overlay of toasty oak. A bit big for a Pinot, almost like a Syrah, but easy to drink. **86** —S.H. (8/1/2005)

Deerfield Ranch 2001 Super Rex Red Blend (North Coast) $40. This highly unusual blend of Sangiovese, Cabernet Franc, Cabernet Sauvignon and Dolcetto starts off with some blackcurrant scents, but the aroma is really pretty earthy. In the mouth, it has vague flavors of berries and tree fruits, but lacks a center. Finishes with a tannic scour. **85** —S.H. (12/31/2003)

Deerfield Ranch 2002 Super T Red Blend (North Coast) $40. A blend of Sangiovese, Cab Franc, Cab Sauvignon and Dolcetto. Rustic, dry and tannic, with earthy-berry flavors. **84** —S.H. (8/1/2005)

Deerfield Ranch 1999 Gold Orion Vineyard Late Harvest Botrytis Riesling (Napa Valley) $50. This deeply colored, golden wine is very sweet and hyperbotrytized, with apricot, Grand Marnier and honey flavors, and the smoothest texture imaginable. It just glides over the tongue and down the throat with a viscous purity. It wants higher acidity, but that's quibbling—it's delicious. **92** —S.H. (9/1/2002)

Deerfield Ranch 2001 Roumiguiere Vineyard Sangiovese (Clear Lake) $22. There's something nicely attractive about this dry, crisp red wine, with its flavors of cherries and tobacco. It shows a balance and harmony you don't always find in California Sangioveses. Has some real complexity. **84** —S.H. (8/1/2005)

Deerfield Ranch 1999 Roumiguiere Vineyard Sangiovese (Lake County) $22. A tantalizing wine, at once rigid and austere, then yielding and generous. It's pale in color, with earthy smells of sun-warmed red brick, dust and an elusive hint of black cherry. Remarkably light in the mouth, like air, with silky tannins. Firm acids scream out for Italian food. **89** —S.H. (9/1/2002)

Deerfield Ranch 2002 Sauvignon Blanc (North Coast) $18. A little bit on the sweet side, with the taste of a stick of spearmint chewing gum and pineapple juice. But there's some good, crisp acidity to make it bright and clean. Perfect for a late afternoon aperitif. **85** —S.H. (4/1/2004)

Deerfield Ranch 2003 Peterson Vineyard Sauvignon Blanc (Sonoma Valley) $20. Solid enough, with forward aromas of grapefruit, lime and river stones. Despite the fact that it was barrel fermented, it isn't an oaky wine. Just the opposite; there's tart, fresh citrus at all check points and nary a wood note except for some faint butter. **87** (7/1/2005)

Deerfield Ranch 2001 Peterson Vineyard Sauvignon Blanc (Sonoma Valley) $18. A very good white wine, perfectly dry, with streamlined flavors of grapefruit, fig and lime, and creamy, vanilla complexities from barrel fermentation. Appealing in the mouth, and near as good as California Sauvignon Blanc gets. **89** —S.H. (7/1/2003)

Deerfield Ranch 2000 Peterson Vineyard Sauvignon Blanc (Sonoma Valley) $18. Kicks the palate with a roundhouse of grass, hay, gooseberry and lime, softened by wood and a hint of lees. This is a distinctive white wine. It shares the crisp, herbal nature of Sauvignon Blanc and adds enough interesting notes to make it complex and stylish. **88** —S.H. (9/1/2002)

Deerfield Ranch 2002 Ladi's Vineyard Syrah (Sonoma County) $40. Brutal at first, with aromas variously described as stinky, murky, and burnt shrimp shells. Thankfully, the stinks do seem to lessen with air, revealing a dry, cedary Syrah with modest cherry-vanilla flavors. **82** (9/1/2005)

Deerfield Ranch 2001 Ladi's Vineyard Syrah (Sonoma County) $40. Take a sip and you get hit broadside by a hugely flavorful, delicious wine. The plum, blackberry and chocolate flavors are ripe and sweet, the tannins rich and soft, and the acids are refreshing. This opulent wine is great on its own, but try with roast leg of lamb studded with plenty of garlic. **91** —S.H. (4/1/2004)

Deerfield Ranch 2000 Ladi's Vineyard Syrah (Sonoma County) $40. Must be unfined or unfiltered, because it's already throwing a heavy sediment. Inky black. Intense, bold aromas of crushed white pepper suggest Northern Rhône Syrah. Deep, concentrated flavors of blackberries and violets, lush, complex tannins, fabulous structure and mouthfeel. You might mistake this for a fine young Hermitage—it's that good. **94** —S.H. (9/1/2002)

Deerfield Ranch 2001 Buchignani Vineyard Old Vine Zinfandel (Dry Creek Valley) $40. What a great Zin. Amazing how these old vines produce such intensity of flavor and perfect tannins. Blackberries, cherries, blueberries, mocha, pecan pie and a splash of sweet Tawny, yet not a trace of residual sugar. It all comes at the cost of high alcohol, however. **93** — S.H. (1/1/2004)

Deerfield Ranch 2000 Old Vine Buchignani Vineyard Zinfandel (Dry Creek Valley) $40. What a terrific Zin, one able to stand beside many a Cabernet or Merlot in terms of richness and tableside elegance. Brimming with blackberry, tobacco, pepper and herb flavors wrapped in soft, luscious tannins, and bone dry. The alcohol is a whopping 16.4%, but it's balanced. **91** —S.H. (9/1/2003)

Deerfield Ranch 1999 Old Vine Buchignani Vineyard Zinfandel (Sonoma County) $40. From 50-year-old vines in an appellation that deserves its reputation as Zin country. The wine has the weight, body and concentration of good Cabernet Sauvignon with a plush mouthfeel and overlay of fine oak. But there's no mistaking the variety: brambly fruit, pepper and jam, and spices aplenty cry "Zinfandel" all the way. **91** — (11/1/2002)

DEHLINGER

Dehlinger 1997 Chardonnay (Russian River Valley) $26. 91 —J.C. (11/1/1999)

Dehlinger 1998 Chardonnay (Russian River Valley) $30. Deep pineapple and orange fruit is wrapped in a deep, toasty oak envelope in this Russian River classic. There are complex nutty, leesy, burnt sugar and even vaguely meaty notes on the nose. These open to a big-bodied but earthy and stony palate where bright, citrusy fruit and vanilla accents also vie for attention. Tightly wound, the burnt-toast and mineral finish is long and tasty, with more vanilla, smoke and apple accents. **92 Top Value** (7/1/2001)

Dehlinger 1999 Goldridge Vineyard Pinot Noir (Russian River Valley) $40. Very pretty, sweet fruit evoked "baked apple," "strawberry pie" and "cherry-chocolate" descriptors from our panelists. Bright acidity shows with a modest tang. Intriguing sandalwood and citrus notes add interest on the long finish. Has unique elements and a solid fruit platform. Drink now–2006. **89** (10/1/2002)

Dehlinger 1997 Goldridge Vineyard Pinot Noir (Russian River Valley) $35. 89 (10/1/1999)

Dehlinger 1998 Syrah (Russian River Valley) $35. Hoo-boy, was the Dehlinger a tasting panel-pleaser. A "complete wine" that "should drink well from now until 2010," it has loads of spice and black-pepper aromas (plus earth, cocoa and graham cracker) and a full, even mouthfeel. Meaty, mixed-berry flavors on the palate are even more complex with dried spices, anise and saddle-leather accents. Finishes long, tart and peppery. "Stellar" and "one of the best of show." **94 Editors' Choice** (11/1/2001)

DEL BONDIO

Del Bondio 1999 Cabernet Sauvignon (Rutherford) $38. This 100% varietal is very ripe and jammy. The cassis flavors drink pure and intense and coat the palate through the long finish. There are underlying flavors of kirsch and mocha. A flamboyant, decadent wine, and a little sweet. **90** — S.H. (11/15/2003)

DELECTUS

Delectus 2000 Stanton Vineyard Merlot (Oakville) $42. Starts off fruity and rich, with thick, jammy cherry, blackberry and chocolate flavors that coat the palate. Feels soft and round in the mouth, like liquid velvet. Yet there's an herbal note that strikes midway and lasts into the finish, where the wine turns astringent with green tannins. **86** —S.H. (5/1/2004)

Delectus 2000 Petite Sirah (Napa Valley) $45. A heady, rich blend, lush yet textured. Dark in color and redolent of blackberry, black cherry, spice, chocolate, coffee and herbs. A tangy finish and powdery tannins add interest at the end, which finishes long. **91** —J.M. (12/31/2003)

Delectus 2000 Argentum Red Blend (Napa Valley) $20. A schizy wine, with cherry aromas joined to weedy, stalky ones. Drinks thin in fruity flavor, although there's a core of cherry and an overlay of smoky oak. Drink now. **84** —S.H. (6/1/2004)

Delectus 2001 Terra Alta Vineyard Syrah (Lodi) $25. Dark, rich and syrupy, a big, thick wine filled with blackberry and cherry flavors. As sweetly ripe as it tastes, the wine is fully dry, with rich tannins. Acids are low, though, making for a flabby mouthfeel. **86** —*S.H. (5/1/2004)*

Delectus 1999 Terra Alta Vineyard Syrah (California) $29. Dark from beginning to end, from aromas of espresso and bitter chocolate to a finish of black pepper and earth. In between there's roasted plummy fruit tinged with leafy tobacco and herb notes. **87** *(11/1/2001)*

DELICATO

Delicato 2004 Cabernet Sauvignon (California) $7. I wanted to like this wine more, but in the end, the sharpness, minty green herbaceousness and raw acidity mute the pleasure. It's clean, simple and inexpensive. **82** —*S.H. (12/15/2006)*

Delicato 2001 Vine Select Monte Rosso Vineyard Cabernet Sauvignon (Sonoma County) $70. A step outside the company's comfort zone, and it shows. While this is better than much of what Delicato sells, it's not that much better to warrant the extra price. A hint of shoe polish mars the cassis-scented nose, while the palate delivers standard chocolate and black currant flavors and a lean, sculpted mouthfeel. This limited-production bottling is available only at the tasting room. **87** *(8/1/2006)*

Delicato 2005 Chardonnay (California) $7. Here's a wine that could win a place as your house Chard. With the majority of the grapes from the hot Sacramento Delta and cool Monterey, it's balanced, with plenty of peach, pear, pineapple and creamy vanilla flavors. The numbers tell the story: Alcohol, at 13.9%, is modest. Residual sugar of only .15 means the wine is bone dry. Meanwhile, acidity of .70 gives the wine a bright, crisp mouthfeel. Another good value from a winery that routinely produces. **85 Best Buy** —*S.H. (11/15/2006)*

Delicato 2003 Chardonnay (California) $7. Has lots in common with more expensive Chards, such as ripe pear and tropical fruit flavors, dusty spices, smoky oak and a creamy texture. Finishes a little sweet. This is a great price. **85 Best Buy** —*S.H. (3/1/2005)*

Delicato 1998 Chardonnay (California) $6. 84 Best Buy *(9/1/2000)*

Delicato 2005 Merlot (California) $7. Clean and properly varietal, but it's a rustic, country-style wine with some rough edges. **80** —*S.H. (12/15/2006)*

Delicato 2004 Merlot (California) $6. Outside of the vineyard, wines like this are what built the company's production to reach 12 million cases per year. Plump and low in acid, with baked black-cherry flavors accented by earth and dried herbs, it just may be the Merlot poured by the glass at your neighborhood hangout. **84 Best Buy** *(8/1/2006)*

Delicato 2004 Merlot (California) $7. There's a depth of fruity flavor and soft richness of texture that make this a very fine value Merlot. You're struck by the way the plum, cherry and blackberry flavors flood the palate, and instead of turning gooey-chocolaty-ripe, there's a white pepper note that makes the wine savory and more companionable with food. Alcohol is a modest 13.5%. **86 Best Buy** —*S.H. (11/15/2005)*

Delicato 2003 Merlot (California) $7. Clean, dry and fruity, an easy drinking wine with cherry and oak flavors that will go with a wide variety of food. **83** —*S.H. (3/1/2005)*

Delicato 2002 Merlot (California) $18. Wine in a box, and a great value for its succulent flavors of sweet black cherries, at the equivalent of $4.50 a bottle. This soft, friendly wine has a voluptuous texture and a spicy finish. **86** —*S.H. (5/1/2004)*

Delicato 1998 Merlot (California) $6. 83 *(9/1/2000)*

Delicato 2003 3 Liter Merlot (California) $18. At $4.50 the equivalent of a regular bottle, this wine in a box is a good deal. It's dry, with cherry and oak flavors, and smooth tannins. Supposedly the wine will keep for a long time once it's opened. **84 Best Buy** —*S.H. (3/1/2005)*

Delicato 2001 Monterey Vine Select San Bernabe Vineyard Merlot (Monterey) $30. This is a plump, succulent Merlot that exhibits plenty of that variety's trademark dried herb shadings. Tobacco and vanilla fill out the midpalate, while the finish features dry, silky tannins. **87** *(8/1/2006)*

Delicato 2001 San Bernabe Vineyard Monterey Vine Select Merlot (Monterey County) $25. This vast vineyard, in the southern Salinas Valley,

has proven itself increasingly capable of producing fine wines from most varieties. Now it shows its hand at Merlot. More work is needed, but this wine is ripe, dry and complex, although a little too oaky. **86** —*S.H. (11/15/2005)*

Delicato 2004 Pinot Grigio (California) $7. Bone dry and crisp, with fairly intense grapefruit and lime flavors, it's a nice sipper that shows some real complexity in the balanced and long finish. **86 Best Buy** —*S.H. (2/1/2006)*

Delicato 1998 Sauvignon Blanc (California) $5. 81 *(9/1/1999)*

Delicato 2005 Shiraz (California) $7. Sure, it's sharp and rustic, but it explodes in fresh cherry, blackberry jam and chocolate flavors, with a white pepper edge, and is smooth and mostly dry. At this price, let it wash down lasagna, cheeseburgers and gravy-smothered fried chicken. **84 Best Buy** —*S.H. (12/31/2006)*

Delicato 2004 Shiraz (California) $7. Soft and medium-bodied in the mouth, this Calfornia Shiraz has tarry, earthy notes on the nose that join plum fruit on the palate. A good, simple, easy drinker. **85 Best Buy** *(9/1/2005)*

Delicato 2004 Shiraz (California) $6. Like the Merlot, this is varietally correct, in this case balancing blackberry and white pepper flavors. Supple tannins make it go down smooth and easy, without a second thought. **84 Best Buy** *(8/1/2006)*

Delicato 2003 Shiraz (California) $7. Fresh and jammy, with youthful acidity, and very dry. Full-bodied and clean. Try with pizza, burgers and BBQ chicken. **84 Best Buy** —*S.H. (12/15/2004)*

Delicato 2002 Shiraz (California) $6. The grapes for this impressive Aussie-style Shiraz, from Lodi and Clarksburg, are ripe; the palate boasts has rich flavors of cherries, black raspberries, blueberries and plums. Feels succulent, with a smooth texture and a long, sweetish finish, but it's perfectly dry. At this price, you can't go wrong. **90 Best Buy** —*S.H. (11/15/2003)*

Delicato 2001 Shiraz (California) $8. On the nose, jammy black fruit, particularly black grapes, shines out from under oak and nut accents. Medium-full on the palate, with chewy plum and blackberry fruit, and an undercurrent of herb that continues on through the finish. A perennial good-value wine. **85 Best Buy** *(12/1/2002)*

Delicato 2003 3 Liter Shiraz (California) $18. What a great value this boxed wine is. It's dry and balanced, with rich tannins and blackberry, cherry, cocoa and spice flavors. Perfect for a large occasion when you don't want to spend a lot of money. **85 Best Buy** —*S.H. (3/1/2005)*

Delicato 2000 Syrah (California) $8. The family name is Indelicato, the wine is called Delicato and the juice is certainly delicious, if not necessarily delicate. Big-time growers, they won Monterey's San Barnabe Vineyard-the world's largest continuous vineyard. Grape suppliers to many California brands, they are well-equipped to deliver value, as in this creamy flavorful Syrah. This star quaffer pushes the pleasure button hard with its sweet dark fruit and attractive price. **87 Best Buy** *(10/1/2001)*

Delicato 1998 Syrah (California) $6. 84 Best Buy *(2/1/2000)*

DELICATO MONTEREY VINE SELECT

Delicato Monterey Vine Select 1998 San Bernabe Vineyard Chardonnay (Monterey) $35. 89 *(9/1/2000)*

Delicato Monterey Vine Select 1998 San Bernabe Vineyard Merlot (Monterey) $40. 88 *(9/1/2000)*

Delicato Monterey Vine Select 1998 San Bernabe Vineyard Petite Sirah (Monterey) $40. 86 *(9/1/2000)*

Delicato Monterey Vine Select 1998 San Bernbe Vineyard Syrah (Monterey) $40. 89 *(9/1/2000)*

DELILLE CELLARS

DeLille Cellars 2002 Chaleur Estate Bordeaux Blend (Columbia Valley (WA)) $29. A classic Bordeaux-style blend of Sauvignon Blanc (56%) and Sémillon (44%). Rich, creamy new wood sets up a very lush wine tasting of ripe citrus, Mandarin orange and apricots. Still young, the tannins are edgy and the wine will definitely benefit from another year or two in the bottle. **90** —*P.G. (7/1/2004)*

USA

DeLille Cellars 2001 Chaleur Estate Bordeaux Blend (Red Mountain) $60. One of Washington's best wines in vintage after vintage, the 2001 Chaleur Estate blends four classic Bordeaux grapes in a complex, layered, spicy red wine. Disarmingly soft and approachable, yet layered with mixed red fruits and lovely hints of leaf and herb. **92** —*P.G. (9/1/2004)*

DeLille Cellars 1997 Chaleur Estate Bordeaux Blend (Yakima Valley) $40. **93** *(6/1/2000)*

DeLille Cellars 2001 D2 Bordeaux Blend (Yakima Valley) $32. This is DeLille's second-tier Bordeaux blend. Still, the list of contributing vineyards reads like a who's who of Washington viticulture. The Merlot-based wine delivers classic black cherry and plum fruit, hints of herb, and plenty of power. Most wineries would kill for a flagship wine this good. **90** —*P.G. (7/1/2004)*

DeLille Cellars 1997 D2 Bordeaux Blend (Yakima Valley) $25. **88** —*P.G. (6/1/2000)*

DeLille Cellars 1997 Harrison Hill Bordeaux Blend (Yakima Valley) $40. **92** —*P.G. (6/1/2000)*

DeLille Cellars 2003 Chaleur Estate Bordeaux White Blend (Columbia Valley (WA)) $31. DeLille Cellars' Bordeaux blended white wine is the best of its type in Washington, if not on the entire West Coast. Broadly fruity yet nuanced with notes of tangerine, citrus and melon, it adds hints of sweet hay, herb and toast to the complex mix. Excellent focus and weave makes for an unusually expressive white wine, which continues to develop new flavors right through the finish. **91** —*P.G. (6/1/2005)*

DeLille Cellars 2003 Doyenne Aix Cabernet Sauvignon-Syrah (Columbia Valley (WA)) $35. This 75% Cabernet, 25% Syrah shows some interesting hints of wild fruits and light, spicy herbs. Young, tight and closed up a bit, it will certainly benefit from another year or two in the bottle. **89** —*P.G. (4/1/2006)*

DeLille Cellars 2002 D2 Merlot (Columbia Valley (WA)) $36. This is the winery's Merlot-driven second wine, generally composed of barrels not used in the flagship Chaleur Estate. In this vintage it comes out a bit on the funky side, with scents that might be interpreted as reminiscent of truffles, leather and earth. Cedar, lead pencil and black fruits suggest its pedigreed sibling. Very tannic, earthy and substantial compared with previous vintages of D2. **89** —*P.G. (6/1/2005)*

DeLille Cellars 2003 Chaleur Estate Red Blend (Columbia Valley (WA)) $68. Powerful, youthful and still a bit raw, the newest release of DeLille's signature red blend shows a range of fruit from cherry and blackberry to dark notes of raisin and balsamic. It's still melding together its aggressive barrel toast, showing good structure and balance for long-term aging. Despite its almost 15% alcohol, it is balanced and even. **92** —*P.G. (8/1/2006)*

DeLille Cellars 1999 Chaleur Estate Red Blend (Yakima Valley) $55. This is DeLille's ultra-premium Bordeaux blend, a dense, complex, luxurious red wine composed of fruit from Klipsun, Ciel du Cheval and Boushey—three of the best vineyards in Washington. A lush bouquet of fresh fruits, spices, chocolate, coffee, leather and sweet vanilla gets things rolling. The wine is generous to a fault, with layers of expressive, tangy fruit, smoky oak and soft tannins. Not quite as ripe as the '98, it is perfectly balanced and cellar-worthy for at least a decade. Cellar Selection. **91 Cellar Selection** —*P.G. (6/1/2002)*

DeLille Cellars 1998 Chaleur Estate Red Blend (Yakima Valley) $45. Though it has been on the market for some weeks, this wine is wrapped up tight as a drum. Firm fruit suggests black cherry, blackberry and cassis, and it shows underlying streaks of dark, mineral-saturated Red Mountain terroir. The weight and dimension of this wine, borne out in past vintages, is not immediately apparent in this latest release—give it time to breathe and it begins to open gradually, revealing layers of smoke, tar, spice and coffee underneath the tight fruit. **91** —*P.G. (6/1/2001)*

DeLille Cellars 2003 D2 Red Blend (Columbia Valley (WA)) $35. The '03 vintage is a particularly good year for D2. The warm, ripe vintage means that this second wine of DeLille has unusual sweetness and richness across the palate. Toasty and laden with cherry/berry flavors, good weight and concentration, and enough stuffing to hang in there through a long, satisfying finish. **90** —*P.G. (4/1/2006)*

DeLille Cellars 1999 D2 Red Blend (Yakima Valley) $32. The D2 is the second label for the winery's Chaleur Estate red, and includes juice from many of the state's top vineyards, about half on Red Mountain. Forward fruit runs to strawberry/raspberry/cherry, with hints of leaf and herb. There is also some subtle oak and just a hint of bacon fat and smoke in the light finish. **89** —*P.G. (6/1/2002)*

DeLille Cellars 1998 D2 Red Blend (Yakima Valley) $30. The name refers to the French highway designation for the Bordeaux wine route. DeLille's D2 is the second label for their flagship Chaleur Estate red. In recent years, it has included not only declassified Chaleur Estate, but some extra juice from Harrison Hill as well. It's always a lovely wine, forward, fruit-filled, warm and generous. The '98 is ripe and forward, with a little bit of heat in the finish. Clean and straightforward, without the extra layers of depth one finds in the Chaleur Estate. **89** —*P.G. (6/1/2001)*

DeLille Cellars 1992 D2 Red Blend (Yakima Valley) $32. **89** —*P.G. (6/1/2002)*

DeLille Cellars 2003 Harrison Hill Red Blend (Yakima Valley) $68. Apart from Columbia's Otis Cab, this is Yakima's (and Washington's) oldest Cabernet vineyard. Newer plantings of Merlot and Cab Franc enhance the blend. The wine is marked by its finesse and exceptional grace. Silky and sensuous, it's a wine that warrants the old-fashioned term "breed"— suggesting manapricot-scented lemon and lime flavors are tinged with peaches, wildflowers and nered elegance. Cherry, bramble berry, plummy fruit and exotic spices light up the finish. **93** —*P.G. (8/1/2006)*

DeLille Cellars 2001 Harrison Hill Red Blend (Yakima Valley) $60. This single-vineyard wine from DeLille is a rare evocation of old-vine, classic Washington fruit. Perfectly ripe, plummy fruit is backed with layers of iron and earth; the fruit has mixed elements of herb and tart red fruits. This is special. **91** —*P.G. (9/1/2004)*

DeLille Cellars 1999 Harrison Hill Red Blend (Yakima Valley) $55. This single vineyard blend includes 65% Cabernet Sauvignon, 25% Merlot and 10% Cab Franc. It is a distinctive wine, salty, linear and slightly metallic in its terroir. The vineyard's cool site, gives the wine lovely extra dimensions, though this is not a style one would describe as fat. Still a bit unresolved at this point in time, it's a more subtle, soil-driven effort than big brother Chaleur Estate. **90** —*P.G. (6/1/2002)*

DeLille Cellars 1998 Harrison Hill Red Blend (Yakima Valley) $45. Harrison Hill includes a small amount of the second oldest Cabernet Sauvignon plantings in Washington state, which form the backbone of this blended red wine. Merlot (25%) and Cabernet Franc (11%) from the same vineyard complete the mix. Soft, plummy scents, reminiscent of old vine Zinfandel, rise from the glass. Harrison Hill is a cool site, and the grapes are often not harvested until November. The gentle flavors of plums, pie cherries, rose petals and anise reflect the extra hang time. Elegant, light and seductive. **90** —*P.G. (6/1/2001)*

DeLille Cellars 2004 Doyenne Roussanne (Columbia Valley (WA)) $26. Lovely and creamy, with thick, juicy flavors of citrus peel, honey, lemon and white peach fruits. Graham cracker and oatmeal flavors coat the finish; overall a very fleshy mouthful of wine. Just 200 cases produced. **90** —*P.G. (4/1/2006)*

DeLille Cellars 2003 Doyenne Syrah (Columbia Valley (WA)) $46. Though still a dense, chalky mouthful of wine, the 2003 Doyenne is a bit more restrained than the over-the-top 2002. Dark streaks of smoke, earth, tar, roasted meat and barrel spices dominate; it takes a lot of breathing time to bring out the underlying fruit. **90** —*P.G. (4/1/2006)*

DeLille Cellars 2002 Doyenne Syrah (Columbia Valley (WA)) $46. DeLille Cellars has now made Doyenne a separate brand, and inaugurated the change with a massively thick bottle and an artist label. Despite its top-notch vineyard sources, this Doyenne seems to lack synergy; it's tight and chewy, with heavy tannins and an abundance of dark, roasted, espresso flavors. At the moment, the chalky tannins threaten to outrun the fruit. **88** —*P.G. (6/1/2005)*

DeLille Cellars 2001 Doyenne Syrah (Yakima Valley) $40. Smooth, supple and ripe, this lovely wine combines power and elegance in one concentrated package. Aromas of berries and jam, white pepper and bacon fat, along with floral notes. Complex and potent. **92** —*P.G. (7/1/2004)*

USA

DeLille Cellars 1999 Doyenne Syrah (Yakima Valley) $38. Here is what all the excitement is about: a Washington Syrah bursting with dense, thick, textured, rich, ripe fruit, yet not too "jammy." The acids are there to support all that weight, along with generous amounts of oak. The zippy, berry-laden fruit shines through, then the oak kicks in with an abundance of smoke, coffee and licorice notes. Big, sappy, sensuous and flat-out sensational wine. **93 Editors' Choice** —*P.G. (6/1/2002)*

DeLille Cellars 1998 Doyenne Syrah (Yakima Valley) $38. This ripe, lush Syrah boldly expresses itself with shiny, saturated colors and bright, spicy, assertive fruit. It's a full-bodied, sappy wine, forward and plump, and the deep core of blackberry fruit is enhanced with pepper, citrus peel, clove and other spices. Young and still grapey, it's delicious right now but can be cellared for some years. **93** —*P.G. (6/1/2001)*

DeLille Cellars 1997 Doyenne Syrah (Yakima Valley) $28. 89 *(6/1/2000)*

DeLille Cellars 2000 Chaleur Estate White Blend (Columbia Valley (WA)) $25. In this new vintage there is a bit more Sauvignon Blanc (69%) than usual; the rest is Sémillon. Rich, oaky and expansive, it is an oak and texture-driven style, with the fruit—clean, slightly herbaceous, spicy and tart—playing second fiddle. Which is no criticism, because the delicious, over-the-top flavors, with layer upon layer of creamy complexity, and the rich, buttery finish just beg for lobster in a cream or butter sauce. Who can argue with that? **92 Editors' Choice** —*P.G. (6/1/2002)*

DeLille Cellars 1998 Chaleur Estate White Blend (Columbia Valley (WA)) $23. 91 *(6/1/2000)*

DeLille Cellars 1999 Chaleur Estate White Wine White Blend (Columbia Valley (WA)) $28. This is a 60/40 blend of Sauvignon Blanc and Sémillon, barrel fermented in 100% new French oak and aged on the lees with occasional batonnage. This rich, expansive, elegant, bone-dry white wine has wonderful intensity and layer upon layer of subtle spice. Polished fruit, light herbs, a seamless mouthfeel and a creamy, structured finish make this wine just about perfect. It's built for medium term aging, but why wait? **93** —*P.G. (6/1/2001)*

DELORIMIER

DeLorimier 1999 Mosaic Bordeaux Blend (Alexander Valley) $30. This Bordeaux-style blend of Cabernet Sauvignon, Merlot, Malbec and Cabernet Franc is soft, plush and elegant, which marks it as a classic representative of its appellation. It possesses a feminine voluptuousness, with velvety tannins that melt on the palate. Yet there's real authority. The sturdy tannins that show up on the finish suggest midterm ageability. **91** —*S.H. (11/15/2002)*

DeLorimier 2001 Mosaic Meritage Cabernet Blend (Alexander Valley) $35. Primarily Cabernet Sauvignon, this blend hits with black currant flavors and is very dry. Has a good backbone of tannins and acidity, and enough of a balance to cellar for a few years. **88** —*S.H. (10/1/2005)*

DeLorimier 2003 Chardonnay (Alexander Valley) $16. High in sweet, toasty oak, with peach, pear and apple flavors that persist in the long finish, this pleasant Chardonnay has lots to like. **84** —*S.H. (11/1/2005)*

DeLorimier 2002 Clonal Select Chardonnay (Alexander Valley) $24. A good, honest and earthy Chardonnay that smacks of terroir. Shows apple, pear and herb flavors, with soft acids and a long, oaky-sweet finish. Finishes balanced and elegant. **90 Editors' Choice** —*S.H. (11/1/2005)*

DeLorimier 2000 Malbec (Alexander Valley) $20. A dark, young wine, rich in sharp acids and fresh youthful fruit, with deep flavors of dark stone tree fruits and berries, such as plums and loganberries. It's very dry, and the tannins, while vigorous, are negotiable. Will mellow with a few years of bottle age. **87** —*S.H. (8/1/2003)*

DeLorimier 2000 Mosaic Meritage (Alexander Valley) $30. Despite some pretty blackberry flavors, the wine comes across as tough and a little weedy. There are green, stalky notes and some angular tannins in the finish. Oak adds softening elements. **85** —*S.H. (11/15/2003)*

DeLorimier 2001 Merlot (Alexander Valley) $20. After a good 2000 vintage, DeLorimier's '01 Merlot is a letdown. It's sharp and oaky, and the cherry fruit tastes unnaturally sweetened. **83** —*S.H. (8/1/2005)*

DeLorimier 2000 Merlot (Alexander Valley) $20. Plump as a baby with its layers of blackberry, cherry and coffee flavors, a rich, round wine with enough weight to accompany big roasted meats. Yet the tannins are fine

enough for the wine to feel light and airy on the palate. The long, extracted finish suggests mid-term aging, but it's gorgeous now. **91 Editors' Choice** —*S.H. (12/15/2003)*

DeLorimier 2003 Sauvignon Blanc (Alexander Valley) $10. Simple and fruity, with spearmint, peach and fig flavors that drink slightly sweet, although there's good balancing acidity. Good for everyday fare. **84** — *S.H. (8/1/2005)*

DeLorimier 2002 Sauvignon Blanc (Alexander Valley) $10. Here's a very nice value in a coastal Sauvignon Blanc. It's very fruity, with flavors of ripe green apples, figs and spearmint, and finishes a bit sweet. Good acidity keeps it clean and refreshing. **85** —*S.H. (6/1/2004)*

DeLorimier 2001 Sauvignon Blanc (Alexander Valley) $10. Tart and thin, an everyday wine with flavors of lemons and spearmint and lots of peppery, gingery spices. Very dry, with decent acidity. Not bad for the price if you're looking for a cocktail sipper. **84** —*S.H. (10/1/2003)*

DeLorimier 2002 Lace Sauvignon Blanc (Alexander Valley) $20. This late-harvest Sauvignon Blanc is very pale in color, though very sweet. Like drinking honey infused with apricots, with delicious suggestions of sweetened coconut, meringue and smoky caramel. Finishes a little quick, but try with a dessert with vanilla and lots of butter. **89** —*S.H. (6/1/2004)*

DeLorimier 2001 Spectrum Reserve Sauvignon Blanc (Alexander Valley) $16. A little thin in fruit, with modest citrus and melon flavors encased in proper acidity, with a touch of oak. Picks up steam on the finish, but could use a bit more concentration. **85** —*S.H. (2/1/2005)*

DeLorimier 2000 Spectrum Reserve Sauvignon Blanc (Alexander Valley) $16. Very flavorful, with a melange of citrus, peach, apricot, apple and bubblegum flavors and a rich, honeyed finish. A bit soft in acidity and basically one-dimensional. A blend of Sauvignon Blanc, Sémillon and Viognier. **85** —*S.H. (10/1/2003)*

DEMUTH

Demuth 2002 Chardonnay (Anderson Valley) $32. An interesting wine for its dryness, leesy character, acidity and streamlined personality. Doesn't hit you with fruit, but nice for the balance and food-friendliness of the apple, peach and mineral flavors. **87** —*S.H. (12/31/2004)*

Demuth 2002 Pinot Noir (Anderson Valley) $40. Deliciously ripe in cherry, mocha and spice flavors, and balanced in good acids and smooth tannins. Not only tasty, but also complex and nuanced. Best now. **90** —*S.H. (5/1/2005)*

DEROSE

DeRose 2002 Special Reserve Cardillo Vineyard Cabernet Franc (Cienega Valley) $19. Kind of tannic now, with flavors suggesting cherries, herbs and sweet pipe tobacco. Very dry, with good acidity. A versatile red wine at the table. **84** —*S.H. (11/15/2004)*

DeRose 2002 Vintner's Reserve Merlot (Livermore Valley) $23. Ultra-dry, tart with acids and tannic, this tough wine has herb and coffee flavors just barely nudging into cherries. **83** —*S.H. (10/1/2004)*

DeRose 2001 Negrette (Cienega Valley) $20. Tastes like a little country wine you came across while traveling the back roads. Rough in texture, with berry flavors, and very dry, it's a little like a rustic Cabernet. **83** — *S.H. (8/1/2003)*

DeRose 2002 Miller Family Vineyard Negrette (Cienega Valley) $23. Firmly tannic, very dry, and rugged in the way of country wines. Offers up ripe plum, coffee and sweet oak flavors, rather like a Barbera. **84** — *S.H. (11/15/2004)*

DeRose 1995 Port (Cienega Valley) $26. Sweet, rich in tannins, high in peppery alcohol and with a chocolatey, blackberry richness, this dessert wine is fun on its own, or beside a perfect espresso after a big, late night dinner. **85** —*S.H. (12/1/2004)*

DeRose NV Hollywood Red Red Blend (Cienega Valley) $18. Rough in texture, with chocolaty, cherry flavors that finish sweet. **83** —*S.H. (12/15/2004)*

DeRose NV Hollywood Red Red Blend (Cienega Valley) $16. Bizarrre and funky, with unacceptable aromas and thick, unpleasant flavors. **81** —*S.H. (5/1/2003)*

DeRose 2002 Al DeRose Vineyard Viognier (Cienega Valley) $26. Rich, juicy and as intricate as a tapestry, with ripe mango, breadfruit, white peach, butterscotch and vanilla flavors interwoven with smoky oak. A crisp spine of acidity provides a clean finish. **88** —*S.H. (11/15/2004)*

DeRose 2002 Cedolini Family Vineyard Zinfandel (Cienega Valley) $24. Smooth as velvet despite the tannins, this softly plush wine features wild berry, mocha and pepper flavors. It's totally dry, with alcohol above 15%. Best with very rich meats and cheeses. **85** —*S.H. (11/15/2004)*

DeRose 2002 Nick DeRose Sr. Vineyard Zinfandel (Cienega Valley) $21. Very dry and rather tannic, with a burst of Zinny wild berry, pepper and earth flavors. A fun wine that will go well with anything Italian. **84** —*S.H. (11/15/2004)*

DESERT WIND

Desert Wind 1997 Ruah Bordeaux Blend (Columbia Valley (WA)) $50. The blend is 46% Cabernet Sauvignon, 38% Merlot and 16% Cabernet Franc. It opens up softly, with fragrant, plummy fruit. Once tasted it turns firm to the point of tough, and the fruit seems constrained, or overpowered, by the rough, earthy tannins. **86** —*P.G. (12/31/2001)*

Desert Wind 2004 Cabernet Sauvignon (Wahluke Slope) $15. Like the merlot, it is earthy, green, stemmy and vegetal, with little or no suggestion of ripe fruit. **80** —*P.G. (6/1/2006)*

Desert Wind 1999 Cabernet Sauvignon (Columbia Valley (WA)) $13. Charred, horsey scents of burnt leather dominate the attack. This is a dark, tannic wine, chewy and mouth-scraping dry; inside is a core of black cherry fruit, but it's overwhelmed by all the tar and smoke. **84** —*P.G. (9/1/2004)*

Desert Wind 1998 Desert Wind Vineyard Cabernet Sauvignon (Columbia Valley (WA)) $20. This is very ripe, perhaps too ripe, with pruney, raisiny fruit, and a dead leaf, slightly decayed quality. It's easy to drink, forward and soft, with very dry tannins and a lot of herbs, tobacco and earth flavors. A style for immediate drinking with foods (steaks!) that need something to cut the fat. **85** —*P.G. (12/31/2001)*

Desert Wind 2004 Bare Naked Chardonnay (Wahluke Slope) $15. The core of this no-oak wine is medium-ripe fruit in the apple/pineapple mode. But a bitter, harsh aftertaste throws it off course, and it never recovers. **84** —*P.G. (6/1/2006)*

Desert Wind 2004 Merlot (Wahluke Slope) $15. Stemmy, green and harsh, with flavors of earth, stem and pip. The watery, dilute flavors barely suggest fruit. **80** —*P.G. (6/1/2006)*

Desert Wind 1999 Desert Wind Vineyard Merlot (Columbia Valley (WA)) $20. A new winery, owned by the Fries family of Dundee, Oregon, with a lovely ppackage and a new entry into the ever-expanding Washington Merlot sweepstakes. The wine is soft and chalky in the mouth, with flavors of berries and cream, but it feels increasingly disjointed and a bit manipulated as the finish wears on. **85** —*P.G. (12/31/2001)*

Desert Wind 2002 Sémillon (Columbia Valley (WA)) $13. An aggressive, alcoholic wine, it shows unusual dark gold tones and smells of hay and oak barrels. Spicy, oaky and hot, its 14.5% alcohol is felt as a burning sensation all the way down the throat. **84** —*P.G. (9/1/2004)*

Desert Wind 2000 Desert Wind Vineyard Sémillon (Columbia Valley (WA)) $20. This premiere effort feels a bit forced; the fruit dry and slightly hot in the mouth, with sharp acids. Missing is the lushness of Sémillon; in its place a tight, alcoholic, slightly bitter wine. **83** —*P.G. (12/31/2001)*

Desert Wind 2005 Bare Naked Viognier (Wahluke Slope) $15. Simple peach flavors sum it up, with a flat, dead mouthfeel and a watery, dilute finish. **82** —*P.G. (6/1/2006)*

DESOLATION FLATS

Desolation Flats 2000 Cabernet Sauvignon (San Lucas) $17. A good, rustic wine with blackberry flavors and firm tannins. It's nicely dry, and has firm acidity. A very nice Cab for everyday drinking. **84** —*S.H. (7/1/2005)*

DETERT FAMILY VINEYARDS

Detert Family Vineyards 2002 Cabernet Franc (Oakville) $35. Explosively fruity but refined. Tastes of the quintessence of black cherries, with nuances of anise and mocha. Rich in tannins, but softly drinkable now, and exquisitely detailed. These grapes used to go into Opus One. **92** —*S.H. (11/15/2004)*

Detert Family Vineyards 2000 Cabernet Franc (Oakville) $30. A first vintage for this longtime grower, tucked into the hillside behind Robert Mondavi winery. Briary black cherry and anise notes are at the fore, backed by tea and herb flavors for added interest. Modest tannins and firm acidity give good structure, with a medium-length finish. **87** —*J.M. (12/1/2002)*

Detert Family Vineyards 2002 Cabernet Sauvignon (Oakville) $45. Rich, dense and concentrated, with juicy currant, cherry, mocha and sweet fresh herb flavors. Well-oaked, this wine is impeccably made and generous in the mouth, and maintains a firm structure. **92** —*S.H. (11/15/2004)*

DEUX AMIS

Deux Amis 2002 Vyborny Vineyards Petite Sirah (Alexander Valley) $25. Petite Sirah at its best aspires to be rich, full-bodied and opulent. This is that kind of wine. It has flavors of red stone fruits and berries, thick, dusty, ageworthy tannins, and is bone dry. It also can't quite shake its basically rustic nature, which this wine celebrates instead of trying to hide. **88** —*S.H. (12/31/2005)*

Deux Amis 2002 Zinfandel (Sonoma County) $19. Fifteen percent is the new 13 percent of alcohol in Zinfandel, but if you can handle the headiness, this is a good choice. Rich and earthy, with the taste of fresh berries picked from bushes at the height of summer, this Zin is perfect for barbecue. **88** —*S.H. (12/31/2005)*

Deux Amis 2001 Zinfandel (Sonoma County) $21. Firm-textured, with the flavors framed in ripe, but powdery, tannins. Plum, cherry, toast and spice are at the center, hiding a bit, but pleasantly in evidence nonetheless. **86** *(11/1/2003)*

Deux Amis 1999 Zinfandel (Sonoma County) $19. Pretty much what you'd expect from a blend of Alexander and Dry Creek Valleys, it starts with dusty, wild-berry aromas leading to a fruity, spicy wine encased in substantial tannins and moderate acids. It will age, but losecharacter. Drink it now or soon in its bright, exuberant, wild youth. **86** —*S.H. (7/11/2002)*

Deux Amis 2002 Belle Canyon Vineyards Zinfandel (Dry Creek Valley) $25. If you're looking for elegance, look elsewhere. But if you like hefty, big-shouldered Zins, pick up this one and try it with a grilled pork chop. It's a dry, tannic, balanced wine, with a classically feral Zin profile. **89** —*S.H. (12/31/2005)*

Deux Amis 2002 Halling Vineyard Zinfandel (Dry Creek Valley) $25. Dry Creek Zins, at their best, like this one, show a rich earthiness, in addition to the expected array of ripe berry flavors. This vineyard, on the western side of the valley, has a balance and harmony that belie the wine's very high alcohol content. **90** —*S.H. (12/31/2005)*

Deux Amis 2001 Rued Vineyard Zinfandel (Dry Creek Valley) $20. Spicy rich on the nose, with zippy cedar, blackberry, cherry, cinnamon, plum, coffee and chocolate flavors throughout. Quite toasty at the end, which is long and bright, though with a touch of bitterness. **89** *(11/1/2003)*

Deux Amis 1998 Rued Vineyard Zinfandel (Dry Creek Valley) $24. This is a very dry, intensely flavored, single-vineyard wine, which is its strength and its drawback. It's all about blackberry, tobacco and espresso, plus a very soft mouthfeel. It has soul, but it's a little one-dimensional, with a tart finish. Yet, it will elevate a humble hamburger into a fancy meal. **85** —*S.H. (7/11/2002)*

Deux Amis 1997 Rued Vineyards Zinfandel (Dry Creek Valley) $24. **90** —*P.G. (11/15/1999)*

DI FRONZO

Di Fronzo 2003 Syrah (Arroyo Grande Valley) $42. Difficult to assess. It's soft and a bit syrupy, but the texture isn't bad, and the cassis and chocolate flavors are impressive for their ripe lushness. A bit eccentric and kind of hot, but there's something about it that's likeable. **87** —*S.H. (12/1/2006)*

DI STEFANO

Di Stefano 1998 Sogno Cabernet Franc (Columbia Valley (WA)) $25. Very much right-bank Bordeaux, with rich aromas of damp humus and tobacco. Then it turns smooth and plush in the mouth with a degree of ripeness that's decidedly New World. Finishes with a touch of toasty oak and decent acidity, but not much tannin. Drink over the next few years. **88** —*J.C. (6/1/2001)*

Di Stefano 1999 Cabernet Sauvignon (Columbia Valley (WA)) $NA. An excellent Cabernet from the superb '99 vintage. It shows the steely, bound-up strength of the vintage, and will need cellar time to unwrap. But the balance between physiological (not sugar) ripeness and ageworthy acids and tannins is there; the wine is going to improve and last for many years. **88** —*P.G. (9/1/2004)*

Di Stefano 1999 Cabernet Sauvignon (Columbia Valley (WA)) $25. A straightforward, simple Cabernet. There are varietal flavors of cassis and black cherry, and some stiff tannins. 515 cases made. **85** —*P.G. (12/31/2002)*

Di Stefano 1998 Cabernet Sauvignon (Columbia Valley (WA)) $25. Seems a little leaner and more compact than DiStefano's other '98s. Leafy cassis aromas coupled with toasty cedary oak are classic Cab, as are the acids and firmly tannic backbone that should permit this wine to age well for 7-8 years. **87** —*J.C. (6/1/2001)*

Di Stefano 2000 Merlot (Columbia Valley (WA)) $NA. This is a full-bodied wine, with very ripe (14.7% alcohol) fruit and a liberal dose of oak. The result is a hot, vanilla-flavored wine that will appeal to those who like the California style. **86** —*P.G. (9/1/2004)*

Di Stefano 1999 Merlot (Columbia Valley (WA)) $28. Light, soft and plummy fruit, with some pretty pie cherry tartness. There is a whiff of spice—sandalwood?—but the overall impression is fairly neutral; hard to find a distinctive point of view. **85** —*P.G. (12/31/2002)*

Di Stefano 1998 Merlot (Columbia Valley (WA)) $25. Shows a lot of toasty oak, with hints of menthol and cedar, married to supple black-cherry fruit. Some dark earthy nuances add complexity, and the finish is long, if a bit toasty **88** —*J.C. (6/1/2001)*

Di Stefano 2000 Meritage Red Blend (Columbia Valley (WA)) $NA. A strange wine that doesn't knit together. The high alcohol, super ripe fruit and nutty, oxidized flavors suggest that it will have a brief lifespan. Flavors of preserves, raisins, prunes and carmelized sugars. **86** —*P.G. (9/1/2004)*

Di Stefano 2003 Sauvignon Blanc (Columbia Valley (WA)) $10. Fresh, creamy, big and bold, this big, delicious wine is fleshed out with 17% sémillon (note to winery: not semillion!). It has a lifted, spicy freshness which, despite the 14+% alcohol, keeps it on the elegant side, and food friendly. **91 Best Buy** —*P.G. (12/1/2004)*

Di Stefano 2000 Sauvignon Blanc (Columbia Valley (WA)) $12. Fresh scents mix melon, tangerine, citrus blossom and honey. The wine is smooth and sappy, with a good backbone of fresh acid. The fruit, though slightly candied, is quite satisfying, and despite the 14.3% alcohol, there is nothing overwrought here. 1,200 cases produced. **87** —*P.G. (12/31/2002)*

Di Stefano 2002 Syrah (Columbia Valley (WA)) $28. A bit understated but admirably balanced, DiStefano's regular Syrah artfully blends blackberries, coffee, herbs and pepper into a medium-bodied, supple wine. Finishes with an emphasis on tangy berries. **86** *(9/1/2005)*

Di Stefano 2002 R Syrah (Columbia Valley (WA)) $32. Restrained on the nose, with subtle herb and spice accents and understated blackberries. Classic, elegant and similarly restrained on the palate, finishing with soft tannins and hints of caramel and minerals. Pretty, but lacks the intensity to score higher. **87** *(9/1/2005)*

DIABLO CREEK

Diablo Creek 2001 Cabernet Sauvignon (California) $10. Tons of ripe, rich fruity flavor in this gentle wine of silky tannins and soft acids. The blackberry, cherry and raspberry flavors finish dry and svelte. **85** —*S.H. (5/1/2004)*

Diablo Creek 2002 Chardonnay (California) $10. The apple and peach flavors have an oaky undercurrent of vanilla and smoke, wrapped in a nice texture. Fine with easy foods. **83** —*S.H. (2/1/2004)*

Diablo Creek 2001 Merlot (California) $10. This gentle, easy Merlot has ripe flavors of cherries and raspberries, with a nice edge of dried herbs and violets. Fully dry, with a silky mouthfeel. **84** —*S.H. (5/1/2004)*

DIAMOND CREEK

Diamond Creek 2002 Gravelly Meadow Cabernet Sauvignon (Napa Valley) $175. Tremendous aromatics on this young wine: a blast of refined cassis, cedar, pine cone, green olives and even roasted meat. Rich and forward in ripe fruit character, and the bigtime tannins are polished. This is an excellent but very young wine. Should peak in 5–7 years. **93** —*S.H. (8/1/2006)*

Diamond Creek 2000 Gravelly Meadow Cabernet Sauvignon (Napa Valley) $175. Smooth and elegant, with a fine tuned core of black cherry, raspberry, blueberry, cedar, spice, coffee, chocolate, herbs and licorice notes. Tannins are firm yet delicate, supporting a long, bright finish redolent of cocoa, vanilla, toast and tangy berries. This is an elegant wine, neatly balanced and downright delicious to the end. **93** —*J.M. (4/1/2004)*

Diamond Creek 2002 Red Rock Terrace Cabernet Sauvignon (Napa Valley) $175. The most complete and compelling of Diamond Creek's trio of '02s, combining the opulent accessibility of Gravelly Meadow with the power and authority of Volcanic Hill. The aromas of cassis, red currants, cedar, tobacco and cigar box lead to massively packed Cabernet flavors wrapped in huge, dusty tannins. The wine is so balanced, so distinguished and complete. Decant now if you must drink it, but it should start to mellow by 2008, and then peak and hold through 2015 at least. **97 Cellar Selection** —*S.H. (8/1/2006)*

Diamond Creek 2000 Red Rock Terrace Cabernet Sauvignon (Napa Valley) $175. Rich, ripe and fragrant, with the essence of spice, cedar, black cherry, black raspberry, cola, strawberries, herbs, licorice, tar and tobacco—all wrapped up in a neatly bound, yet generous package that delivers mounds of pleasure. Muscular with firm acidity, it's got a punch that will keep it long-lived for the cellar. **92** —*J.M. (4/1/2004)*

Diamond Creek 2002 Volcanic Hill Cabernet Sauvignon (Napa Valley) $175. Starts off as a closed, tight wine, aromatically speaking, and needs plenty of decanting to breathe, but once it starts to open, there's an eruption of the most refined cassis and cedar aromas. In the mouth, this is an immense Cabernet, profoundly deep in blackberry, roasted coffee and dark chocolate flavors. It is also enormously tannic, and is effectively locked down. Nowhere near ready, although decanting will help it, but it's best to hold this magnificent wine until 2007, when it should start to open, and then for at least 10 additional years. **95 Cellar Selection** —*S.H. (8/1/2006)*

Diamond Creek 2000 Volcanic Hill Cabernet Sauvignon (Napa Valley) $175. Rich, ripe aromas of black cherry, spice, vanilla and smoke lead the way here. On the palate, it's dark and sleek, with blackberry, tar, more smoke, licorice, cassis, raspberry and herb notes that give it great complexity. The tannins are ripe and smooth, supporting the wine with fine, lush structure. **94** —*J.M. (4/1/2004)*

Diamond Creek 2004 Volcanic Hill *Barrel Sample* Cabernet Sauvignon (Napa Valley) $NA. Opens with fabulous blackberry jam, mocha, cinamonny spice, oak, vanilla and sweet herb aromas. Then turns intense and concentrated, with cherry-blackberry and chocolate flavors smothered in big, smooth tannins. Really high quality. **94** —*S.H. (8/1/2004)*

DIAMOND OAKS

Diamond Oaks 2002 Pinot Noir (Carneros) $21. A solid effort, with consistent scores. Quite extracted in black cherries and plums, but balanced in tannins and acids, with a silky texture. This pleasant wine will go well with roasted meats. **87** *(11/1/2004)*

DIAMOND OAKS DE MANIAR

Diamond Oaks de Maniar 2001 Chardonnay (Chalk Hill) $32. Tarter, drier and leaner than this winery's Carneros bottlings, with apple and peach flavors that blossom across the palate. The oak supports but doesn't overwhelm, while acidity provides crispness. Turns tart and short on the finish. **87** —*S.H. (12/15/2003)*

Diamond Oaks de Maniar 2001 Chardonnay (Carneros) $14. Well-oaked, with apple and tropical fruit flavors and earthier notes of sage and

USA

oregano. It has a creamy texture and spicy-oaky finish that turns sweet and lemony. **85** —*S.H. (12/15/2003)*

Diamond Oaks de Maniar 2000 Reserve Chardonnay (Carneros) $47. Lots of extracted fruit in this spicy, oaky wine, including mango, papaya and pineapple, with notes of ripe pear and banana. Oak barrels and malolactic fermentation add a creamy, buttery texture. Lavish, although it could use more complexity. **88** —*S.H. (12/15/2003)*

Diamond Oaks de Maniar 2002 Merlot (Carneros) $19. Rough in texture, with a combination of overripe and unripe flavors. **83** —*S.H. (5/1/2005)*

Diamond Oaks de Maniar 2002 Hira Ranch Merlot (Carneros) $35. Dry and smooth, but marred by unripe, green flavors, which carry minty eucalyptus flavors through the finish. **83** —*S.H. (5/1/2005)*

DIAMOND RIDGE

Diamond Ridge 2000 Merlot (Russian River Valley) $20. There's a tough streak of herbs and tomato that overshadows the blackberry fruit here, and despite fine tannins and a nice, velvety mouthfeel, that vegetal tone persists through the finish. Rich, oily foods will help to soften and sweeten it. **85** —*S.H. (11/15/2002)*

DIAMOND TERRACE

Diamond Terrace 2002 Cabernet Sauvignon (Diamond Mountain) $55. So sweet, it's almost like a dessert wine, suggesting a cup of sugared cappuccino and cocoa mixed with creme de cassis, sprinkled with nutmeg and vanilla. Almost like something you'd get at Starbucks, instead of a dry table wine. **83** —*S.H. (12/1/2005)*

Diamond Terrace 2001 Cabernet Sauvignon (Diamond Mountain) $50. An intense and concentrated Cabernet that's dominated now by its sheer tannic power. Tight and young, it has a rich, sweet core of black currant fruit modulated by dried herbs and sweet oak. Best after 2008 and beyond. **91 Cellar Selection** —*S.H. (10/1/2004)*

DICKERSON

Dickerson 1999 Limited Release Reserve Zinfandel (Napa Valley) $30. From Joel Peterson—200 cases made, but worth the search. It's a near-perfect expression of its terroir. Shows first-growth status in the racy fruit and Cabernet-like balance. Well-charred oak frames it in sweet vanillin and spices. **93** —*S.H. (9/1/2002)*

DIERBERG

Dierberg 2004 Pinot Noir (Santa Maria Valley) $38. The vineyard has been a source to designations from the likes of Tantara, Foley and Fess Parker. Now they're making their own wine, and it's really good, with loads of crushed brown spices and masses of red stone fruit pie filling and chocolate flavors. It has Pinot's silky delicacy, but is powerful, with a long finish. One of the best Santa Maria Valley Pinots of the year. **93** —*S.H. (12/15/2006)*

Dierberg 2002 Pinot Noir (Santa Maria Valley) $33. Tasters all praised this wine's clean, polished black cherry, beet and vanilla flavors and polished, supple mouthfeel. Could use more strength mid-palate, but the cherry and raspberry finish turns rich with charcoal and vanilla. **87** *(11/1/2004)*

DILIBERTO

Diliberto 2002 Tre Bordeaux Blend (North Fork of Long Island) $25. Nearly purple in the glass, this wine has aromas of cherry and cranberry with touches of olive and leather. Lighter-bodied than many Bordeaux blends, with acidity putting it on the tart side, it is nevertheless enjoyable and a good match for chicken dishes and Italian fare. Tart cherry and darker berry flavors come with spice and leather. A good showing from a more difficult vintage, this winery's second. **85** —*M.D. (12/1/2006)*

DILLIAN

Dillian 2001 Zinfandel (Shenandoah Valley (CA)) $22. A lovely, elegant Zin, made claret style. Medium-bodied, soft and rich in tannins, with crisp acids and good cherry and herb flavors. Classy. Drink now. **90** —*S.H. (3/1/2005)*

DOBBES FAMILY ESTATE

Dobbes Family Estate 2002 Black Label Pinot Noir (Willamette Valley) $50. A big, forceful wine, which comes on strong with powerful aromas of

earth, root, herb and cherry. Plenty of black cherry fruit at the core, along with spicy, resiny, pine-needle pungency. The flavors are complex, long and sustain beautifully through the finish. **90** *(11/1/2004)*

Dobbes Family Estate 2002 Grand Assemblage Cuvée Pinot Noir (Oregon) $22. Candied, simple, with an artificially sweetened flavor. Good but weak. **83** *(11/1/2004)*

Dobbes Family Estate 2002 Skipper's Cuvée Pinot Noir (Rogue Valley) $35. Despite some initial VA, this offers bright cherry fruit flavors and nuances of fresh-cut tobacco. Forward, flavorful and well rounded, its tannins are nicely managed and it shows good balance all around. **88** *(11/1/2004)*

Dobbes Family Estate 2003 Fortmiller Vineyard Syrah (Rogue Valley) $45. Dark and plum-colored, with scents of roasted coffee, toast and black fruits. Blackberry and black cherry fruit is lifted by some lemony acids. The challenge for these Rogue Valley Syrahs is to flesh out the midpalate fruit and keep the tannins in check. This is a good effort, though not up to the outstanding 2002. Just 95 cases were made. **88** —*P.G. (9/1/2006)*

Dobbes Family Estate 2002 Fortmiller Vineyard Syrah (Rogue Valley) $45. Winemaker Joe Dobbes has grabbed hold of southern Oregon Syrah's untapped potential and is clearing a path for everyone else to follow. This is exciting wine, varietal and bold, with flesh and finesse. The rough tannins are largely tamed and the fruit is ripened enough to take on a healthy dose of oak toast. Give it a couple of years to round out and it'll be even better. **90** —*P.G. (8/1/2005)*

Dobbes Family Estate 2003 Grande Assemblage Syrah (Rogue Valley) $24. Strongly scented with orange peel and orange juice, the citrusy opening gives way to some light raspberry fruit. There's a bit of a hole in the middle; then in come the chalky tannins. **87** —*P.G. (9/1/2006)*

Dobbes Family Estate 2002 Grande Assemblage Syrah (Rogue Valley) $26. This wine has an earthy, sensual nose that mixes leather, barnyard, pepper and dense, concentrated dark fruits. Rhône-like and potent, it promises a bit more than it delivers, but for the price it's a heckuva good bottle. Lots of toast, smoke and barrel flavors sweep through the finish. **88** —*P.G. (8/1/2005)*

Dobbes Family Estate 2003 Sundown Vineyard Syrah (Rogue Valley) $48. This is a softer, fruitier Syrah than the Fortmiller, with somewhat better balance. The opening layer of round, cherry-flavored fruit is spiced up with citrus and scented with pepper, smoke and black coffee. The middle lags, then it picks up again with an earthy, tannic finish. Just 2 barrels (48 cases) were made. **88** —*P.G. (9/1/2006)*

Dobbes Family Estate 2002 Sundown Vineyard Syrah (Rogue Valley) $48. This is a fruitier, juicier style than the Fortmiller but equally powerful and confident. Deep purple, saturated and fragrant with pepper, smoke and black cherry. It lacks just a bit of weight on the palate, but may just be young and tight. Give it a lot of breathing time. **89** —*P.G. (8/1/2005)*

DOCE ROBLES

Doce Robles 1999 Syrah (Paso Robles) $20. A brawny, rugged wine with berry and plum flavors and overripe notes of prunes, raisins and stewed tomatoes. This honest country wine suffers from a few flaws and seems overpriced for the quality. **83** —*S.H. (12/1/2002)*

DOG HOUSE

Dog House 2002 Checker's Cab Cabernet Sauvignon (California) $9. Nice and tasty in gooey cherry-chocolate flavors, with a rich cassis finish, but a little too sweet. **84** —*S.H. (11/15/2005)*

Dog House 2004 Charlie's Chard Chardonnay (California) $9. Amazing how they get wines this nice out at this everyday price. While not a blockbuster, this easy sipper has the peach and pineapple fruit, spice and yummy cream you want in a Chard. **86 Best Buy** —*S.H. (11/15/2005)*

Dog House 2002 Maxie's Merlot Merlot (California) $9. Dog's House is on a roll with good, affordable wines. This ohne's dry, soft and smooth, with lip-smacking cherry flavors that turn just a little sweet on the finish. **86 Best Buy** —*S.H. (11/15/2005)*

DOG TAIL

Dog Tail 2005 Cabernet Sauvignon (California) $9. A rustic, drinkable wine, not without its innocent charms. Lodi brings cherried ripeness.

USA

Monterey provides the acids. It's a good marriage at a fair price. **83** —S.H. (12/15/2006)

Dog Tail 2005 Chardonnay (California) $9. Great price for a Chard of this quality. Dry, crisp and amply flavored in peaches and cream, tangerines and buttered toast, it has the richness of more costly wines. **86 Best Buy** —S.H. (12/15/2006)

Dog Tail 2005 Merlot (California) $9. With that sharp, raw aroma and juicy, freshly picked berry flavor that young rustic red wines often have, this dry Merlot cries out for a juicy burger. Both the food and the wine will be elevated. **84 Best Buy** —S.H. (12/15/2006)

Dog Tail NV Fire Hydrant Red Red Blend (California) $9. Sharp, dry and rustic, this is a blend of Cabernet, Cab Franc and Souzao, grown in Lodi and Monterey. It's the kind of wine created to wash down simple fare. **83** —S.H. (12/15/2006)

Dog Tail 2005 Watchdog White White Blend (California) $9. With mostly Chardonnay and a little of the Symphony grape, this is a fruity, deliciously gulpable wine showing intense peach, pear, apple and vanilla-cinnamon flavors. **85 Best Buy** —S.H. (12/15/2006)

DOGWOOD

Dogwood 2003 Meritage Bordeaux Blend (Mendocino County) $38. Rustic and jagged in acids and tannins, with a green, minty streak that won't age out, this Merlot-based Bordeaux blend needs food to mellow it. A soft, runny cheese will echo the sweet blackberry fruit, but on its own, the wine is tough. **84** —S.H. (12/31/2006)

Dogwood 2003 Cabernet Sauvignon (Mendocino) $36. This wine is dry and smooth, with some nice berry-cherry fruit and chocolate. Yet there are some green unripe notes and a sharpness to the tannin-acid structure that detract. **84** —S.H. (12/31/2006)

Dogwood 2004 Zinfandel (Mendocino County) $28. Tough and weedy, a minty, hot wine with some sweet, medicinal cherry cough drop flavors. It's an old-style wine from Brutocao. **82** —S.H. (12/31/2006)

Dogwood 2003 Zinfandel (Mendocino) $28. This is one of those high-alcohol, Porty Zins. With nearly 16% alcohol, it's like a mocha chocolate drink infused with cassis, black cherries and raspberries, then sprinkled with cinnamon and nutmeg. Thankfully it's dry, which makes it worthy of recommendation. **86** —S.H. (12/15/2005)

DOLCE

Dolce 2002 Late Harvest Wine Sémillon-Sauvignon Blanc (Napa Valley) $80. Over many years Dolce has established itself as one of the top dessert wines in California, and the '02 doesn't disappoint. Enormously rich in apricot, tangerine and roasted coconut flavors, with plenty of botrytis notes, the wine was aged in 100% new French oak, and oozes in sweet vanilla char and crème brûlée. **96 Editors' Choice** —S.H. (12/15/2006)

Dolce 1998 White Blend (Napa Valley) $75. Ripe hay, vanilla, and apricot mark the nose; deep orange flavors with cinnamon spice notes and a very smooth mouthfeel are the already promising attributes of this infant. All the right elements are there, and in good balance. Best cellared for three to five years. **93** (2/1/2001)

Dolce 2001 Late Harvest White Blend (Oakville) $75. This Sémillon and Sauvignon Blanc blend continues the Dolce tradition of being among the finest dessert wines in California. The wine as usual is rich and unctuous, a glyceriney sweetie packed with apricot, peach, honey, vanilla and crème brûlée flavors offset by crisp acidity. It's sweet, but not too sweet. **93** —S.H. (10/1/2005)

Dolce 1999 Late Harvest Table Wine White Blend (Napa Valley) $75. Oh, how good this sweetie is. If you have just one white dessert wine this year, make it this rich, thick, unctuous wine, with its fabulous flavors of apricot marmalade, orange honey, pineapple, chutney, smoke, vanilla, toast, toasted hazelnut, the list goes on and on. Fills the mouth with velvety opulence, and finishes very long. A special wine of great distinction. **97 Editors' Choice** —S.H. (12/1/2003)

Dolce 2000 Late Harvest Wine White Blend (Napa Valley) $75. This flamboyant wine is drenched in new oak the way Hollywood stars used to wrap themselves in mink. It's fabulous, gooey-sweet in apricots, honey,

vanilla, peaches and cream and ripe, sweet bananas sautéed in butter. It's all folded into the most unctuous, butter cream texture. Thank goodness for the acids. Deliriously addictive. Mostly Sémillon, with Sauvignon Blanc. **96 Editors' Choice** —S.H. (2/1/2005)

DOMAINE ALFRED

Domaine Alfred 2004 Chamisal Vineyards Chardonnay (Edna Valley) $24. With racy acidity, this palate-cleansing Chard shows a firm minerality undergirding Key lime pie filling and oaky, vanilla flavors. Fully dry, it's a good food Chard. Try with a creamy mushroom risotto. **88** —S.H. (11/1/2006)

Domaine Alfred 2003 Chamisal Vineyards Chardonnay (Edna Valley) $24. Edna Valley presents near-perfect conditions for Burgundian varieties. This Chardonnay has superb acidity, and the fruit has ripened brilliantly. The wine shows explosive tropical fruit, lime pie, vanilla and smoky oak flavors, in a rich and creamy texture that finishes dry. **91** —S.H. (11/15/2005)

Domaine Alfred 2004 Chamisal Vineyards Califa Chardonnay (Edna Valley) $38. The winery's reserve Chard has a richly satisfying buttercream texture that frames ripe flavors of limes, peaches and pineapples, ending in a spicy, honeyed finish. Crisp acidity makes the wine bright and clean. **92** —S.H. (7/1/2006)

Domaine Alfred 2003 Chamisal Vineyards Califa Chardonnay (Edna Valley) $38. I tasted this alongside the winery's regular Chamisal Chard, and actually preferred the latter. They seem to have applied more oak to this wine, which doesn't make it better, only oakier. Not only that, but the oak takes away from the beautiful fruit. **89** —S.H. (11/15/2005)

Domaine Alfred 2000 Chamisal Vineyards, Estate Bottled Chardonnay (Edna Valley) $22. Lean and appley in flavor profile, with crisp acidity. This is a sleek, tight wine, well structured, with standard oak and leesy notes. Does the job without any particular complexity. **85** —S.H. (6/1/2003)

Domaine Alfred 2005 Chamisal Vineyards Pinot Gris (Edna Valley) $25. Here's a nice, easy PG. It's dry and delicate, with pleasant citrus and wildflower flavors and very brisk acidity that uplifts the fruit through a clean, spicy finish. **86** —S.H. (11/1/2006)

Domaine Alfred 2002 Califa Chamisal Vineyard Estate Bottled Pinot Noir (Edna Valley) $48. This winery's Califa bottling is richer and more sophisticated than its regular Chamisal, and showcases the strengths of its Central Coast terroir. Vibrant acidity and a light, silky texture frame cola, cherry, cranberry, rhubarb and coffee flavors. Bone-dry, with some astringency on the finish. Probably best now. **91** —S.H. (8/1/2005)

Domaine Alfred 2000 Califa Chamisal Vineyards Pinot Noir (Edna Valley) $42. Caramel and toasted marshmallow mark the big, charred nose. Some of those sweet, candied notes carry onto the palate, which otherwise offers full-force black cherry. The finish is incredibly dark, like espresso and charcoal. **88** (10/1/2002)

Domaine Alfred 1999 Chamisal Pinot Noir (Edna Valley) $28. Dust, pepper and black cherries on the nose. Ripe black cherries and plums make the palate a joy. It's an incredibly round wine that's properly acidic and very easy to drink. Some toasty oak and a good dose of coffee on the finish close things out the right way. **89** (10/1/2002)

Domaine Alfred 2003 Chamisal Vineyard Pinot Noir (Edna Valley) $28. A little sharp, but this Central Coast Pinot is saved by big, bright flavors of cherries and a Pinotesque texture that's silky and smooth. The cherry theme reprises on the finish, where it's joined by rich notes of vanilla and smoke. **86** —S.H. (11/15/2005)

Domaine Alfred 2000 Chamisal Vineyard Pinot Noir (Edna Valley) $28. A smoky, meaty nose opens to tart plum-skin flavors. Roasted meat and caramel hints play off the fruit, creating palate tension. Supple on the tongue, it closes with more tart fruit and dusty, woody accents. **87** (10/1/2002)

Domaine Alfred 2003 Chamisal Vineyards Califa Pinot Noir (Edna Valley) $48. This is a better wine in every sense than the winery's regular Pinot. It's darker and richer in fruit, with waves of cherry, pomegranate, cola, mocha, vanilla and smoke flavors cascading over the palate. Despite the size, it's silky and elegant. **92** —S.H. (11/15/2005)

USA

Domaine Alfred 1999 Chamisal Vineyards Califa Pinot Noir (Edna Valley) $42. There's nothing not to like about this round, delicious wine. There are classy toast and charcoal aromas on top of red berries and some yeast. The palate offers the right blend of tart, snappy cherry and richer black plum. Healthy tannins help drive the finish. **91 Editors' Choice** *(10/1/2002)*

Domaine Alfred 2002 Chamisal Vineyards Estate Bottled Pinot Noir (Edna Valley) $28. This is a subtle Pinot, elegantly light in body, with a rich melange of flavors suggesting cola, red cherries, cranberries, vanilla and peppery spices. It's also quite high in acidity, which makes it refreshingly clean. Drink now. **89** —*S.H. (8/1/2005)*

Domaine Alfred 2004 Da Red Red Blend (Edna Valley) $18. Domaine Alfred's been on a roll with Pinot Noir and Syrah. Now, they've blended the varieties into a wine of considerable interest. It's dry and robust, with complex cherry, leather and spice flavors leading to a long, rich finish. **88** —*S.H. (6/1/2006)*

Domaine Alfred 2003 Da Red Red Blend (Edna Valley) $18. The winery doesn't say what the blend is, but this wine is very dry, thick and dusty in tannins, with cherry and chocolate flavors. It's perfectly fine, a nice everyday sort of semi-fancy table wine **86** —*S.H. (11/15/2005)*

Domaine Alfred 2005 Chamisal Vineyards Rosé Rosé Blend (Edna Valley) $22. Made from Grenache and Syrah, this is a simpler, sweeter rosé than the winery's Vin Gris. It has raspberry, nectarine and slightly sugared tea flavors, while crisp acidity makes it clean. **85** —*S.H. (11/1/2006)*

Domaine Alfred 2005 Chamisal Vineyards Vin Gris Rosé Blend (Edna Valley) $22. Just delicious, with full-bodied raspberry and cherry-vanilla flavors that finish with dusty cinnamon spice. Tastes a bit off dry, but the acidity gives it a firm tang. **88** —*S.H. (11/1/2006)*

Domaine Alfred 2003 Chamisal Vineyard Syrah (Edna Valley) $28. From one of California's coolest regions comes this dark, very dry, intense Syrah that has Northern Rhône aspirations. It's extremely well balanced, with rich, thick, smooth tannins and a complex profile of white pepper, cassis, sweet leather, coffee, hung meat and oak. It's a stunner that gets better as it sits in the glass. **92 Editors' Choice** —*S.H. (4/1/2006)*

Domaine Alfred 2003 Chamisal Vineyard Califa Syrah (Edna Valley) $42. This winery's regular '03 Syrah is a sensation. The Califa bottling is clearly a different wine, more tannic, deeper, darker and more brooding. It's also sweeter, although it's not clear if that comes from riper fruit or more new oak. Either way, this taster prefers the regular Syrah. **90** —*S.H. (4/1/2006)*

Domaine Alfred 2002 Chamisal Vineyards Estate Bottled Syrah (Edna Valley) $28. Opens with a blast of white pepper, with nuances of cherry pie, leather, and smoky oak. In the mouth, bone dry, fairly hefty in dry tannins, and with good acidity. The overall impression is of a lean, tough, rather tannic wine that needs time. Hold until after 2007. **88** —*S.H. (8/1/2005)*

Domaine Alfred 2004 Chamisal Vineyards Rosé of Syrah (Edna Valley) $24. Opens with an inviting aroma of raspberry purée, white pepper and cocoa powder, then turns very fruity and crisp in the mouth. It's definitely on the sweetish side, but that nice acidity provides balance. **85** —*S.H. (11/15/2005)*

DOMAINE BECQUET

Domaine Becquet 2002 Cabernet Sauvignon-Shiraz (Lodi) $22. Dry, balanced, rich in earthy, cherry and blackberry flavors with a touch of smoky oak. Has a nice claret-like elegance to the smooth, polished tannins. **87** —*S.H. (3/1/2005)*

DOMAINE CARNEROS

Domaine Carneros 1999 Brut Champagne Blend (Carneros) $24. This rich and yeasty sparkler is very much like the wines of Champagne that it's modeled after. The nose is yeasty and full of pear aromas, while the palate is defined by orange and apple flavors. The finish is smooth and comes in a couple of layers, and overall the it is mouthfilling and pure. **88** —*M.S. (6/1/2003)*

Domaine Carneros 1997 Brut Champagne Blend (Napa Valley) $22. Has pretty aromas of toast, vanilla, and spice, with peach, apple, smoke and buttery notes. Not much evidence of yeast or lees. It drinks rich and fruity. Very much in the California style of forward fruit, with good acidity. **89** —*S.H. (6/1/2001)*

Domaine Carneros 1994 Brut Champagne Blend (Carneros) $20. **90 Best Buy** —*J.C. (12/1/1999)*

Domaine Carneros 1998 Brut Cuvée Champagne Blend (Carneros) $23. There's lots of finesse in this dry, elegant wine, with its bready, citrusy aromas and flavors. A crunchy bite of acidity leads to a short, dry finish. A consistent performer in this price range. **87** —*S.H. (12/1/2002)*

Domaine Carneros 1995 Brut Cuvée Champagne Blend (Napa Valley) $20. **89** —*S.H. (12/15/1999)*

Domaine Carneros NV Frivolites Champagne Blend (Carneros) $90. Elegant, with an intriguing spice edge, this wine shows hints of mineral, strawberry and herbs framed in bright, lemony acidity. Toasty, creamy notes extend along the palate, ending in a long, clean finish. **90** —*J.M. (2/1/2003)*

Domaine Carneros 1996 La Reve Champagne Blend (Carneros) $55. This tête de cuvée is a vintage blend that's almost entirely Chardonnay. Very light and airy, with dry citrus and straw flavors and a hit of yeast. Very good, but at this price it could use more finesse. **89** —*S.H. (12/1/2002)*

Domaine Carneros 1994 La Rêve Brut Champagne Blend (Napa Valley) $55. **86** —*S.H. (12/1/2000)*

Domaine Carneros 1993 Le Rêve Champagne Blend (Carneros) $55. **91** —*S.H. (12/15/1999)*

Domaine Carneros 1997 Pinot Noir (Carneros) $35. **90** *(10/1/1999)*

Domaine Carneros 2003 Pinot Noir (Carneros) $28. This lovely wine showcases how well beautifully Carneros's terroir can develop Pinot Noir. The wine is gentle and soft, with a silky texture that carries waves of cherry, cola and spice flavors through a satisfying finish. **90** —*S.H. (12/15/2005)*

Domaine Carneros 2001 Pinot Noir (Carneros) $27. A delicate, enjoyable wine, light in color and weight, fragrantly aromatic, with silky tannins and crisp acids. The cherry, rhubarb and cola flavors are nuanced with vanilla and herbs. Best now through 2005. **86** —*S.H. (4/1/2004)*

Domaine Carneros 2000 Pinot Noir (Carneros) $34. A traditional package of Pinot aromas and flavors such as cedar and tobacco are well-offset on the nose by golden raisins, toasted marshmallow and baked apple pie and on the palate by radicchio and tart cherries. Finishes round and toasty. **85** —*K.F. (2/1/2003)*

Domaine Carneros 1999 Pinot Noir (Carneros) $34. Healthy fruit combined with full-force oak creates a nose of toast, wood and smoked meat atop plum and berries. Raspberry fruit and vanilla dominate the palate, which should appeal to most Pinot drinkers. It's warm and flavorful, if a bit oaky. **87** —*S.H. (10/1/2002)*

Domaine Carneros 2002 Avant Garde Pinot Noir (Carneros) $18. Four identical scores on this simple, light wine. It's delicately structured, with pleasant flavors of strawberry, root beer and vanilla. **84** *(11/1/2004)*

Domaine Carneros 2000 Avant Garde Pinot Noir (Carneros) $18. Shows some complex mushroom and gamy notes on bright, tart cherry-rhubarb-strawberry fruit. Displays what one taster (and Burgundians) called a "good stink." Still, there were some mixed notes, ranging from "thin and a bit dull," to "tart and focused," with a positive majority. Closes with chocolate, dried-spice and lemon accents. Drink now–2005. **88** *(10/1/2002)*

Domaine Carneros 2001 The Famous Gate Pinot Noir (Carneros) $50. This pretty wine is light in body, almost ethereal, but so rich and intricately detailed. Like a medieval tapestry, it has interwoven notes of cherry, mocha, oriental spices, smoky oak and a foresty, pine-nut sharpness. Probably not an ager, but beautiful now for its refinement and complexity. **91** —*S.H. (12/1/2004)*

Domaine Carneros 2000 The Famous Gate Pinot Noir (Carneros) $45. In a split decision, this wine was smooth, but a bit thin and lifeless to some, yet tasty and tart-sweet with juicy fruit, toast and dried spice notes to others. The yeas have it, finding this medium-weight, licorice-accented wine long and interesting. Drink now– 2006. **88** *(10/1/2002)*

Domaine Carneros 2002 Brut Cuvée Sparkling Blend (Carneros) $25. A little rough and scoury around the edges, but gets the job done with some nice doughy, citrus fruit flavors and a dry, crisp finish. Drink now. **85** —S.H. (12/31/2005)

Domaine Carneros 2000 Brut Cuvée Sparkling Blend (Carneros) $24. A lovely blend of lemony-fresh aromas that introduce well-balanced toasty, bread-like notes. The wine shows more fine balance on the palate, with a sparkling array of green apple, grapefruit, pear, melon and honeyed flavors. Long on the finish. **90** —J.M. (12/1/2003)

Domaine Carneros NV Brut Rosé Cuvée de la Pompadour Sparkling Blend (Carneros) $34. Crisp and clean, with a fresh lemony edge that perks up the palate. It's followed by hints of toast, mineral and light strawberry flavors. Bright, yet slightly creamy on the finish. **88** —J.M. (12/1/2003)

Domaine Carneros NV Brut Rosé Cuvée de la Pompadour Sparkling Blend (Carneros) $34. The aromas and flavors of this bubbly are great. Sweet vanilla, smoky char, and yeast, and the cherries and raspberries are ripe and delicious. The wine is a little rough and scoury, though. **86** —S.H. (12/31/2004)

Domaine Carneros 1999 La Reve Blanc de Blancs Sparkling Blend (Carneros) $59. At five years, this bubbly is drinkable, but it needs further cellaring. The acidic texture roughhouses the mouth, creating that pins and needles sensation. The wine is balanced enough to stick away in a cool cellar through 2008, by which time it ought to be smooth and approachable. **90** —S.H. (12/31/2005)

Domaine Carneros 1996 Le Reve Sparkling Blend (Carneros) $55. Bright and fresh, yet also richly textured, the wine offers an elegant blend of citrus, honey, toast, melon, green apple and hazelnut flavors. It's a classy example of New World bubbly that leaves a long, crisp finish and a desire for more. **91** —J.M. (12/1/2003)

Domaine Carneros 1997 Le Rêve Brut Sparkling Blend (Carneros) $55. Basically a blanc de blancs, this 100% Chardonnay is delicate, fine and delicious. It is pale straw in color, with a storm of small, fine bubbles and pretty aromas of lime, smoke, yeast and vanilla. In the mouth, you'll find rich flavors of lime and peach, in a dry wine that's light and clean. It's also firm and crisp enough to warrant a decade in the cellar. **92** —S.H. (12/31/2004)

DOMAINE CHANDON

Domaine Chandon NV 396 Champagne Blend (Carneros) $15. 91 Best Buy —S.H. (12/15/1999)

Domaine Chandon NV Blanc de Noirs Champagne Blend (California) $17. A full-bodied version of Chardon's Brut Classic, except that the color is darker and there are slight hints of strawberries. It's very dry, with slightly rough bubbles and a clean, yeasty finish **86** —S.H. (12/1/2002)

Domaine Chandon NV Blanc de Noirs Champagne Blend (California) $17. Big and rather angular in texture, a full-bodied wine with suggestions of cherries, smoke and vanilla. There's a bit of sweetness. It's an easy sipper that can stand up to steaks and similar fare. **86** —S.H. (12/31/2004)

Domaine Chandon NV Brut Classic Champagne Blend (California) $17. Heads right down the middle, a popular style of bubbly with a little something for everyone. Dry, with suggestions of lime, dough and sweet oak, and nicely effervescent. Finishes with a clean, racy acidity. **87** —S.H. (12/31/2004)

Domaine Chandon NV Brut Classic 196 Champagne Blend (Carneros) $15. 89 Best Buy —S.H. (12/15/1999)

Domaine Chandon NV Brut Classic 198 Champagne Blend (California) $16. This medium-to full-bodied sparkler has a mouthfeel that is at once gravelly and richly smooth-go figure. Granny Smith apples and granite-slate aromas play on the nose; on the palate, the same Granny Smith notes are swathed in dusty-earthy flavors. Though the back palate shows a little toast and cream, the wine's finish is more zippy, tangy citrus-and-metallic than oaky. **87** —D.T. (12/1/2001)

Domaine Chandon NV Brut Classic 198 Champagne Blend (California) $16. Fairly full on the palate, with a core of lemon, herb, toast and nut flavors. **86** —J.M. (12/1/2002)

Domaine Chandon NV Etoile Champagne Blend (Napa County) $35. Pale in color, light in aroma and flavor, and quite tart, this bubbly is citrusy, with sharp acids and a rough mouthfeel. It strives for elegance, but could use more body, flavor and finesse. **85** —S.H. (12/1/2002)

Domaine Chandon NV Etoile Champagne Blend (Napa-Sonoma) $35. Subtle herbs show on the nose of this elegant, tangy blend of Napa and Sonoma fruit. The bright, crisp citrus fruit is offset by a subtle, complex mushroomy hint that adds dimension. Light on the palate, it closes with tart citrus flavors and good length. **88** (12/1/2001)

Domaine Chandon NV Étoile Brut Champagne Blend (Napa County) $35. Subtle herbs show on the nose of this elegant, tangy blend of Napa and Sonoma fruit. The bright, crisp citrus fruit is offset by a subtle, complex mushroomy hint that adds dimension. Light on the palate, it closes with tart citrus flavors and good length. **88** (12/1/2001)

Domaine Chandon NV Étoile Brut Champagne Blend (California) $35. 93 —S.H. (12/1/2000)

Domaine Chandon NV étoile Brut Sur Lees 1999 Champagne Blend (Napa-Sonoma) $35. Drier than the '96 brut, and the better for it. This is an austere, tight wine of finesse. It displays citrus, herb, smoke and yeast flavors, and good acidity. It is very elegant, the kind of wine made for toasts. **90** —S.H. (12/31/2004)

Domaine Chandon NV Étoile Rosé Champagne Blend (Napa Valley) $40. Quite delicate up-front, with hints of toast and citrus. The core is pretty and focused, showing lots of elegant cherry, melon and spice. Full bodied, yet balanced by tangy acidity and a fine lemony finish. **90** —J.M. (2/1/2003)

Domaine Chandon NV Étoile Rosé Champagne Blend (California) $40. 92 —S.H. (12/1/2000)

Domaine Chandon NV Étoile Rosé Champagne Blend (California) $40. Pale copper, with a nose full of berries and yeast, this is an attractive rose that turns slightly sweet on the finish. It's soft and creamy in the mouth, and should prove to be a real crowd pleaser despite it's lack of acidic cut and length. **85** —J.C. (12/1/2001)

Domaine Chandon 2000 Étoile Rosé Champagne Blend (Mendocino-Napa-Sonoma) $45. Rich and full-bodied, this Pinot Noir-dominated wine has a cherry and strawberry flavor along with the doughy yeast and vanilla. It's also a little sweet, but crisp, tingly acidity balances that. Bottom line: deliciously drinkable. **88** —S.H. (12/31/2005)

Domaine Chandon 1999 Étoile Rosé Champagne Blend (Napa-Sonoma) $40. There's a good wine in here and it should emerge in some years. Right now, it's full-bodied, rough and acidic, with suggestions of cherries, limes and yeasty smoke. It would be a shame to drink it now. Best after 2007. **90** —S.H. (12/31/2004)

Domaine Chandon NV Extra-Dry Riche Champagne Blend (California) $17. This mostly Pinot Noir, which has a gold-pink color, is indeed extra dry. The quality of the fruit is not dampened by the extra sweetness, rather, it's rich and zesty, with a hint of raspberry and pepper. Good acids, rich bubbles and if it's a little rough, it cleanses the palate and prepares it for food. **87** —S.H. (12/1/2002)

Domaine Chandon NV Reserve Blanc de Noirs Champagne Blend (Sonoma-Napa) $24. Full-bodied and brisk, a big sparkler that showcases its strawberry-raspberry flavors. Fundamentally dry, although you'll detect some sweetness on the finish. **87** —S.H. (12/31/2004)

Domaine Chandon NV Reserve Brut Champagne Blend (Napa County) $24. 89 —S.H. (12/1/2000)

Domaine Chandon NV Reserve Brut Champagne Blend (California) $24. Mature, with anise and bark-like aromas. Medium to full-bodied, it has a melange of subdued fruit flavors and modest effervescence. The citrus- and peach- tinged finish is medium length. **85** (12/1/2001)

Domaine Chandon NV Reserve Brut Champagne Blend (Napa-Sonoma) $24. Delicate, refined and very dry. This is one of the more elegant bruts around, with a silky mouth feel and very fine texture. Seems to float in the mouth, with gentle lime and vanilla flavors. **92 Editors' Choice** —S.H. (12/31/2004)

Domaine Chandon NV Reserve Brut Champagne Blend (Sonoma-Napa) $24. Brings the quality factor up a notch from the regular brut, with a smoother mouthfeel, riper flavors, and a touch more Pinot Noir, which adds to the impression of size. This is a dry wine, young and clean, with a tart, yeasty finish. **87** —S.H. (12/1/2002)

Domaine Chandon 1996 Vintage Brut Champagne Blend (Sonoma-Napa) $50. Very fine and silky in texture, a little sweet for a brut, but the acidity helps. Intricate flavors of citrus fruits, raspberries, yeast and smoke leading to a smooth finish. **88** —S.H. (12/31/2004)

Domaine Chandon 1995 Vintage Brut Champagne Blend (California) $50. A lime-herb-bread bouquet opens this vintage brut, and a medium-weight green-apple palate with mature accents follows. Lacks zip and sparkle, though, which detracts from the enjoyable flavors. Finishes fairly long with a chalky note. **86** (12/1/2001)

Domaine Chandon 2004 Chardonnay (Carneros) $18. With peach custard, pineapple and smoky, oaky tastes, this is a good, satisfying Chard. It's dry and balanced in acidity, with a nice spiciness. **85** —S.H. (10/1/2006)

Domaine Chandon 2003 Chardonnay (Carneros) $19. Compared to those fat, rich Chards that are hard to pair with food, this one's Chablisian. It's tart in acids and tangy in minerals and stones, with a richly controlled taste that's part apple-citrus fruit and part oak. **90** —S.H. (12/15/2005)

Domaine Chandon 2002 Chardonnay (Carneros) $19. Tart and refreshing for its clean acids and silky mouth feel. You'll find mineral, lime sorbet and plenty of oaky, vanilla and smoke flavors. This balanced, elegant wine is a natural for food. **87** —S.H. (12/31/2004)

Domaine Chandon 2001 Chardonnay (Carneros) $19. Lots of oak has drenched this wine, and it's good oak, too, filled with vanilla, smoky custard and meringue aromas and flavors. The fruit? It's on the citrusy side, although you'll find a pretty aftertaste of white peach. **87** —S.H. (5/1/2004)

Domaine Chandon 2000 Chardonnay (Carneros) $19. Buttered toast, yeast and a hint of nut wrap around warm fruit aromas. A creamy blend of peach and citrus brighten this viscous, full-bodied wine that closes with a clean flinty zip. It is this acidity that well pairs the wine to any summertime fare. **87** — (9/1/2002)

Domaine Chandon 1996 Blanc de Blancs Mt. Veeder Ranch Chardonnay (Mount Veeder) $60. Somewhat closed, the nose has appealing toast and candied apple aromas. It's quite tangy, with substantial acidity, have caramel and toast accents soften the tart pear and lemon flavors a bit. Finishes austerely, with a very dry lime and mineral notes. **88** (12/1/2001)

Domaine Chandon 2003 Pinot Meunier (Carneros) $29. Like a Pinot Noir without the noble structure, this pretty red is medium-bodied and dry, with silky tannins and cola, cherry and mushroom flavors. It has an especially nice, long and spicy finish. **87** —S.H. (12/15/2005)

Domaine Chandon 2002 Pinot Meunier (Carneros) $29. A bit shy in aroma, but airing reveals tea, cola, root beer and cocoa notes. The flavors are of tart cranberries, cherries and vanilla. Very dry, and a nice finish. Give it a year to mellow. **87** (11/1/2004)

Domaine Chandon 2001 Pinot Meunier (Carneros) $29. Similar to Pinot Noir, with the same silky tannins and light body. But the cherry flavors veer in an herbal direction, suggesting oregano and sage. This wine is very dry and a bit austere, although it's elegant. **86** —S.H. (5/1/2004)

Domaine Chandon 2000 Pinot Meunier (Carneros) $29. Dried spices, dusty earth and steely red fruit mesh well in this wine, which closes with enticing cherry and bitter chocolate notes. This wine is toasty, oh-so-smooth, and undeniably plush and seductive. Share this with someone special. **89** — (9/1/2002)

Domaine Chandon 2002 Pinot Noir (Carneros) $29. Another crowd-pleaser for its ripely sweet fruit and smooth, polished mouthfeel. Lots of black cherries, currants and anise, in addition to smoke and vanilla. Really dry, balanced and elegant. Finishes clean and vibrant in youthful acids. **89** (11/1/2004)

Domaine Chandon 2000 Pinot Noir (Carneros) $29. Sweet scents of molasses, cherry, and leafy dried herbs pair classically with cedar and pepper. A sip reveals tobacco and dark plums. Lightweight and big on flavor, this wine is a natural for barbeque with its herbaceous, charred finish. **89** — (9/1/2002)

Domaine Chandon NV Blanc de Noirs 398 Pinot Noir (Carneros) $15. Opens with a faint pinkish hue and apple-herb aromas one taster found

reminiscent of shampoo. There's a cherry edge to the flavors and the wine is only mildly effervescent. It fills out on the close, with a slight nuttiness. The three-digit code, on this and other Chandon wines, refers to the date of disgorgement. **85** (12/1/2001)

Domaine Chandon 2003 Ramal Road Reserve Pinot Noir (Carneros) $45. The winery's regular Pinot, which was released at the same time, is a light, fruity wine. This one's darker, deeper, more ominous. It's a controlled explosion of black cherry, mocha, spice and char in the mouth, enormously attractive and sensual. **92** —S.H. (12/15/2005)

Domaine Chandon 2002 Ramal Road Reserve Pinot Noir (Carneros) $45. All tasters liked this wine for its pleasant flavors of raspberries, vanilla and smoky oak and round, supple mouthfeel. It's graceful and silky in the mouth, with plenty of elegance and finesse. **87** (11/1/2004)

Domaine Chandon NV Blanc de Noirs Sparkling Blend (California) $18. A classic blend of Pinot Noir, with Pinot Meunier and Chardonnay, this is really a terrific sparkler. It's soft and round and elegant, a true bubbly rosé that offers rich strawberry, peaches and cream and vanilla flavors that are subtle and complex. **89** —S.H. (12/31/2006)

Domaine Chandon NV Blanc de Noirs Sparkling Blend (California) $18. Pale in color despite a majority of Pinot Noir, but full-bodied, those cherry and strawberry flavors leap right out of the glass on this bubbly. The wine is dry and a little rough in texture. **85** —S.H. (12/31/2005)

Domaine Chandon NV Blanc de Noirs Sparkling Blend (California) $17. Not a bad price for a full-bodied sparkler of this quality. It's fully dry and balanced, with a bubbly mouthfeel, rich in young acids, that carries cherries and blackberries. Just a bit rough on the finish, but a lovely sipper. **88** —S.H. (12/1/2003)

Domaine Chandon NV Brut Classic Sparkling Blend (California) $17. Chandon's basic brut is balanced and harmonious, with flavors of citrus, pear, raspberry and vanilla, and an engaging edge of dough and smoky oak. Basically dry, but with a sweetly ripe dosage that makes it round and creamy. Best of all, it avoids sharpness, and is smooth. **88** —S.H. (12/1/2003)

Domaine Chandon NV Brut Classic Sparkling Blend (California) $18. On the sweet side, but so nicely acidified and delicious in fruit that you hardly notice the sugar, which just gives the wine a round softness. Beautiful hazelnut, peaches-and-cream and vanilla flavors, with a touch of raspberry zest. **90 Editors' Choice** —S.H. (12/31/2006)

Domaine Chandon NV Brut Classic Sparkling Blend (California) $18. Just a little sweet, which will make it perfect for wedding cake or a fruit tart, this bubbly has wonderfully crisp acids and a nice, doughy Champagne character. The vanilla-infused finish is delightful. **86** —S.H. (12/31/2005)

Domaine Chandon NV Etoile Sparkling Blend (Napa-Sonoma) $35. Stylish and elegant, a full-bodied brut with plenty of Pinot Noir and Chardonnay character in the fruity, peach and lime flavors. Nice integration, with intensity and balance. The finish is dry and clean, with a hint of hazelnut. **90** —S.H. (12/1/2003)

Domaine Chandon 2000 Etoile Sparkling Blend (Napa-Sonoma) $29. This is Chandon's vintage brut. It is a blend of 75 percent Chardonnay and Pinot Noir. The wine has been aged on the lees, and is quite dry. You'll notice right away how silky it is, how it caresses the palate. The flavors are subtle, suggesting the faintest cherries, raspberries, peaches, vanilla, smoke. The finish is elegant. The price is entirely fair. **90** —S.H. (12/31/2006)

Domaine Chandon NV Etoile Rosé Sparkling Blend (Napa-Sonoma) $40. Creamy, with citrus, cherry, herb and mineral flavors on the palate. It's fresh, clean and focused, though a bit reserved for a wine with this much lees contact. Classy nonetheless. **91** —J.M. (12/1/2003)

Domaine Chandon 2001 Etoile Rosé Sparkling Blend (Mendocino-Napa-Sonoma) $34. Released at the same time as Chandon's 2000 Etoile, this is built along the same elegant, classic lines, but it's younger, fresher and, being a rosé, quite a bit richer in fruit. In fact, it's extraordinarily delicious, a mélange of sorbets ranging from raspberry, cherry and peach to lime and vanilla. The finish is crisp and clean. Should hang in there through the decade. **92** —S.H. (12/31/2006)

Domaine Chandon NV Extra-Dry Riche Sparkling Blend (California) $17. Whatever "extra-dry riche" means, this is a slightly sweet brut-style wine, with flavors of peach, raspberry and citrus. The bubbles are on the big size, but on the whole it's a pleasant wine. **87** —*S.H. (12/1/2003)*

Domaine Chandon 1999 L'Etoile Brut Sparkling Blend (Napa-Sonoma) $37. Years of lees contact have made this bubbly soft, creamy and complex, although it still has a crisp spine of acidity. The flavors are rich and doughy, with a ripe finish of strawberries and peaches. It's a little sweet, and should hold well for several years. **87** —*S.H. (12/31/2005)*

Domaine Chandon 2000 Mt. Veeder Single Vineyard Blanc de Blancs Sparkling Blend (Mount Veeder) $45. Rich as sin, and packed with white peach and vanilla flavors, this dry wine shows the finesse, lightness and elegance of a Chardonnay-based sparkling wine. The mousse is creamy, the finish long and decadent. Will be lovely with cracked crab and sourdough bread. **92 Editors' Choice** —*S.H. (12/31/2005)*

Domaine Chandon NV Red Sparkling Blend (California) $19. Fans of Aussie sparkling Shiraz will get off on this dark red, fruity wine. It's has intense flavors of raspberries and cherries that straddle the dry-sweet line, but it's basically dry, clean and balanced. Pinot and Zin. **86** —*S.H. (12/31/2004)*

Domaine Chandon NV Reserve Sparkling Blend (Sonoma-Napa) $24. Way smoother and creamier than Chandon's other nonvintage bubblies, this is a Pinot Noir-based brut with elegance and finesse. The delicate flavors carry hints of limes, strawberries and roasted nuts, accented with leesy dough and smoky oak. **91 Editors' Choice** —*S.H. (12/1/2003)*

Domaine Chandon NV Reserve Brut Sparkling Blend (Napa-Sonoma) $25. Odd, but Chandon's Reserve is rougher and more scouring in the mouth than their less expensive Brut Classic. Maybe it's the dosage. This is drier. But it's also not as smooth or rich. The flavors are deep and long, but the texture is like a Spanish cava, brusque and angular. **86** —*S.H. (12/31/2006)*

Domaine Chandon NV Reserve Brut Sparkling Blend (Napa-Sonoma) $25. Fuller, richer and considerably drier than Chandon's regular Brut Classic, and also more scoury in the mouth, this bubbly could soften and smoothen with a year or two of age. It's doughy and clean, with a rich core of fruit and crisp, citrusy acidity. **87** —*S.H. (12/31/2005)*

Domaine Chandon NV Riche Sparkling Blend (California) $17. If you like your bubbly a little sweet, this is for you. The peach, vanilla, lime, smoke and raspberry flavors are offset with good acidity. Finishes a bit rough. **85** —*S.H. (12/31/2004)*

Domaine Chandon NV Riche Extra Dry Sparkling Blend (California) $18. It's silly to call your sweetest release "extra dry," but that's the convention. Whatever, this is a pretty good bubbly. It's certainly off-dry to overtly sweet, but very acidy, with raspberry, peach and yeasty dough flavors. **85** —*S.H. (12/31/2006)*

Domaine Chandon 1997 Vintage Brut Sparkling Blend (Napa-Sonoma) $50. Still young, acidic and rough, this bubbly isn't showing its best now. But all indications are in favor of cellaring for five years. The wine has a solid core of peach and strawberry fruit, a fine, clean doughy taste, brilliant acidity, a long, powerful finish and the balance and finesse to develop bottle complexity. **91 Cellar Selection** —*S.H. (12/31/2005)*

DOMAINE COTEAU

Domaine Coteau 2002 Pinot Noir (Yamhill County) $27. This comes across as somewhat disjointed, with sweet grapy fruit and some sweaty mushroom aromas that segue into charred, meaty notes. The balance is off, and the oak is tilted heavily to the charred, smoky side. **84** *(11/1/2004)*

Domaine Coteau 2002 Reserve Pinot Noir (Yamhill County) $34. The cola scents characteristic of Oregon Pinot dominate the nose, leading into firm, plummy fruit with interesting layers of black raspberry and black cherry. Turns thin and tannic. **87** *(11/1/2004)*

DOMAINE DANICA

Domaine Danica 2000 Chardonnay (Anderson Valley) $28. Smooth textured, with a silky mouthfeel. The wine is complex, with its hazelnut, pear, melon, herb and spice notes framed in toasty oak nuances. Bright, clean and long on the finish. **91** —*J.M. (12/15/2002)*

Domaine Danica 2002 Heintz Ranch Chardonnay (Sonoma Coast) $25. This Chard is over the top. It's got exceptionally high alcohol and the apricot

flavors taste so baked, they're almost stewed. The wine is dry and oaky, and represents an exaggerated style. **83** —*S.H. (3/1/2006)*

Domaine Danica 1999 Pinot Noir (Carneros) $32. Fruity, silky and simple, with jammy flavors of raspberries and red cherries, tobacco and spice. Feels light and pleasant in the mouth, but could use more stuffing. **85** —*S.H. (7/1/2003)*

Domaine Danica 1999 Zinfandel (Sonoma County) $33. Everyone who tasted this wine with me was drawn to the sexy, comforting nose—think hickory smoke and ham-bone stewiness layered with deep blackberry and brown sugar. On the palate, its black fruit is a little tangy, but is tempered by charred oak and caramel flavors. Well balanced, it closes with oak, green herb and a bit more caramel. Very dark and a bit tight—could use a year or two in the cellar. **89** —*D.T. (3/1/2002)*

Domaine Danica 2000 Salzgeber Vineyard Zinfandel (Russian River Valley) $32. It's all a matter of taste, but to me this wine is too hot, at 15% alcohol, and too sweet. The earthy, berry flavors are rich, and the tannin structure is complex, but it's out of balance. **84** —*S.H. (7/1/2003)*

DOMAINE DE LA TERRE ROUGE

Domaine de la Terre Rouge 1996 Mourvèdre (Amador County) $16. **87** —*S.H. (6/1/1999)*

Domaine de la Terre Rouge 2003 Mourvèdre (Sierra Foothills) $22. Soft in acids and thick in tannins, this wine is fully dry. It's sort of generic, with its berry and cocoa flavors and streak of oak. It's well made, but could be almost any medium-bodied red. **84** —*S.H. (6/1/2006)*

Domaine de la Terre Rouge 2002 Mourvèdre (Sierra Foothills) $22. An interesting and complex wine, dry and medium-bodied, and with soft, sweet tannins. The flavors suggest raspberries, cherries, chocolate and herbs, and there's a soft sweetness to the finish, as opposed to the harder feel of Syrah. **87** —*S.H. (8/1/2005)*

Domaine de la Terre Rouge 2000 Mourvèdre (Sierra Foothills) $20. Earth, herbs, and plums mark this dry wine, with pretty hefty tannins and soft acids. It's a bit one-dimensional but earns extra points for the rich texture and smooth, spicy finish. **86** —*S.H. (5/1/2003)*

Domaine de la Terre Rouge 2000 Muscat a Petits Grains Muscat (Shenandoah Valley (CA)) $15. Inspired by the sweet white wines of southern France, this fruit-filled wine has flavors of peaches and pears, crisp acidity, and is sweet but not terribly so. It brings to mind berry-filled tarts or perfectly ripe tree fruits. **87** —*S.H. (12/1/2002)*

Domaine de la Terre Rouge 2004 Muscat-a-Petits Grains Vin Doux Naturel Muscat (Shenandoah Valley (CA)) $15. This is quite a delicious wine. It's not supersweet, and has long, deep flavors of ripe apricots, white chocolate and vanilla, with a crème brûlée richness that seems equal parts fruit and smoky oak. The acidity is keen, providing balancing relief to the sweetness. Fabulous with a butter cookie or shortbread and vanilla ice cream. **92 Best Buy** —*S.H. (6/1/2006)*

Domaine de la Terre Rouge 2001 Noir Rhône Red Blend (Sierra Foothills) $25. Light to medium in body, and perfectly dry, this Châteauneuf-style wine is explosively ripe in berry fruit, with a pronounced edge of raisins. The charm of this softly rustic wine is all in the flavor. **84** —*S.H. (6/1/2006)*

Domaine de la Terre Rouge 2000 Noir Rhône Red Blend (Sierra Foothills) $25. This blend of Grenache, Mourvèdre and Syrah is interesting and complex, in its own soft, understated way. It's a gentle wine, light in color and body, and easy to mindlessly enjoy, until you notice how complex the cherry, leather, cocoa and oak flavors play off against the smooth tannins. **89** —*S.H. (8/1/2005)*

Domaine de la Terre Rouge 1998 Noir Rhône Red Blend (Sierra Foothills) $22. This blend of Grenache, Mourvedre and Syrah is a little sharp, although the tannins are resolved. At nearly five years, it's showing its age with a loss of fruit and a pickup of herbs and tobacco. **87** —*S.H. (6/1/2003)*

Domaine de la Terre Rouge 1999 Noir Grande Annee Rhône Red Blend (Sierra Foothills) $25. A Châteauneuf-style wine, ultraripe in fruity extract from the hot, thin-air sun of the mountains. Bursts upon the palate with cherry and black raspberry fruit flavor in soft, gentle tannins,

USA

with a long, spicy finish. Grenache, Mourvèdre and Syrah. **88** —*S.H. (6/1/2004)*

Domaine de la Terre Rouge 1995 Noir Grande Année Rhône Red Blend (Sierra Foothills) $20. 91 —*S.H. (10/1/1999)*

Domaine de la Terre Rouge 2003 Tete-a-Tete Rhône Red Blend (Sierra Foothills) $13. Here's a country-style wine, rough and ready for consumption. It's rugged in texture, with jagged tannins framing superripe berry flavors leading to a finish that's almost sweet in raisins. **83** —*S.H. (6/1/2006)*

Domaine de la Terre Rouge 2002 Tete-a-Tete Rhône Red Blend (Sierra Foothills) $13. This is a good, rich Provençal-style Rhône blend, savory in cherry, cocoa and spice flavors, with suggestions of lavender and sweet thyme. It's very dry and has firm tannins, with a satisfyingly complex finish. **88 Best Buy** —*S.H. (8/1/2005)*

Domaine de la Terre Rouge 2001 Tete-a-Tete Rhône Red Blend (Sierra Foothills) $13. A Cheateuneuf-style blend of Grenache, Mourvedre, Syrah, and a few others that's friendly to drink. Fully dry, with some pretty berry flavors and easy tannins, it's a good buy. **86 Best Buy** —*S.H. (6/1/2003)*

Domaine de la Terre Rouge 2004 Enigma Rhône White Blend (Sierra Foothills) $20. This is a delicious white Rhône-style wine, and you might try it as an alternative to Chardonnay. It's quite soft and silky, with a rich array of apricot, peach, honeysuckle and buttercream flavors that finish in a swirl of spicy complexity. **90 Editors' Choice** —*S.H. (6/1/2006)*

Domaine de la Terre Rouge 2001 Enigma Rhône White Blend (Sierra Foothills) $20. This blend of Marsanne, Viognier and Roussanne has a myriad of fruity, berry, and floral flavors. It's very dry and finishes with a honeyed coating of the palate. It's a bit one-dimensional, though. **85** —*S.H. (9/1/2003)*

Domaine de la Terre Rouge 2004 Vin Gris d'Amador Rosé Blend (Sierra Foothills) $13. Shares many of the same qualities as the winery's Rhône reds. You'll find subtle cherry, raspberry, rose petal, vanilla and cinnamon flavors in this delicately structured, dry blush wine. It has a rich complexity that makes it perfect for bouillabaisse. **88 Best Buy** —*S.H. (6/1/2006)*

Domaine de la Terre Rouge 2003 Vin Gris d'Amador Rosé Blend (Sierra Foothills) $13. This enjoyable blush wine is dry, crisp and stylish. It shows subtle flavors of cherries, orange zest, rosehip tea and dried herbs. Fairly full-bodied. Try with bouillabaise, herb-rubbed roast chicken. **85** —*S.H. (8/1/2005)*

Domaine de la Terre Rouge 2001 Vin Gris d'Amador Rosé Blend (Sierra Foothills) $12. Sometimes a dry rose like this just hits the spot, with its pretty raspberry and tobacco flavors and silky mouthfeel. It's light and airy, but full-bodied enough to stand up to veal. A Rhone-style blend of Mourvedre, Grenache and Syrah. **88** —*S.H. (9/1/2003)*

Domaine de la Terre Rouge 2004 Roussanne (Sierra Foothills) $22. The winery began bottling a Roussanne only in 2001. Marching to its own distinct beat, this interesting wine is soft and full-bodied, with a creamy texture framing flavors of apricots, peaches and kiwi. It's dry and balanced. **90** —*S.H. (6/1/2006)*

Domaine de la Terre Rouge 2001 Roussanne (Sierra Foothills) $22. Here's a big, fruity puppy of a wine, filled with life and zest and wagging a friendly tail. You'll love the rich lime and peach flavors, with their hint of spearmint and vanilla and long, dry finish. **87** —*S.H. (6/1/2003)*

Domaine de la Terre Rouge 2002 Syrah (Sierra Foothills) $24. Ripe and accessible now for its detailed flavors of cherries, blackberries, coffee and herbs, and firm, supportive tannins, this Syrah is dry and balanced. The intense cherry flavors reprise on the finish. **88** —*S.H. (8/1/2005)*

Domaine de la Terre Rouge 2000 Syrah (Sierra Foothills) $24. Beautiful dark color, with rich aromas of berries, plums, smoke, meat and white pepper. Drinks lush and full-bodied, a very fine wine. Perfect with short ribs. **90** —*S.H. (6/1/2003)*

Domaine de la Terre Rouge 2003 Ascent Syrah (Sierra Foothills) $75. Terre Rouge's most expensive Syrah, a best barrel selection, fortunately avoids the raisiny overripeness of the other Syrahs, although it's still a very ripe

wine. The flavors are of berries and fruits that have been cooked into a pie. Dry and tannic, it seems best now, although the winemaker feels it's an ager. **87** —*S.H. (6/1/2006)*

Domaine de la Terre Rouge 2002 Ascent Syrah (Sierra Foothills) $75. By far the most tannic and closed of the winery's Syrahs, this wine takes the Northern Rhone for its model. Peppery and leathery, with a core of blackberry and chocolate flavors, it's very dry, rich and balanced. Good now with robust foods, but should soften and sweeten for 3 or 4 years. **92** —*S.H. (8/1/2005)*

Domaine de la Terre Rouge 2000 Ascent Syrah (Sierra Foothills) $75. Only eight barrels of this totally wonderful stuff were produced. This young, immature Syrah is massive and splendid. Huge in fruit, pepper, smoke, and earthy flavors, swaddled in rich tannins and smart oak. Great now, but will improve over the next 4 years. **94 Cellar Selection** —*S.H. (6/1/2003)*

Domaine de la Terre Rouge 2003 High Slopes Syrah (Sierra Foothills) $35. There must have been a great many overripe, shriveled grapes, to judge from the rasiny edge in this wine. It's also kind of rough, but it is very dry, with a nice fruity finish. **84** —*S.H. (6/1/2006)*

Domaine de la Terre Rouge 2002 High Slopes Hautes Cotes Syrah (Sierra Foothills) $35. Dry, firm in tannins, this young Syrah is currently a bit tight. It's showing lots of flair, though, in the suggestion of red and black cherry fruit, sweet grilled meat, cassis and cocoa flavors, and will benefit from a few hours of decanting. Very fine and detailed. **90** —*S.H. (8/1/2005)*

Domaine de la Terre Rouge 2003 Les Cotes de L'Ouest Syrah (California) $15. One taster found this wine a bit herbal, but the others found it a pleasant mix of berry and cherry fruit, tinged with vanilla and savory, meaty notes. Drink now–2010. **85** *(9/1/2005)*

Domaine de la Terre Rouge 2002 Les Cotes de L'Ouest Syrah (California) $15. Right up there in ripe power with the Domaine's other fabulous '02 Syrahs, but even more intense in concentrated black cherry and cocoa fruit, with a strong note of smoked meat or leather. Totally dry, this is a big, impressive young wine with compelling flavors. **93** —*S.H. (8/1/2005)*

Domaine de la Terre Rouge 2001 Les Cotes de l'Ouest Syrah (California) $15. Opens with a disturbing note of green stalks and mint, suggesting unripeness, an impression confirmed with the first taste. Thin in berry-cherry flavors, and a burst of dry tannins shows up on the tart finish. **84** —*S.H. (12/15/2003)*

Domaine de la Terre Rouge 2003 Sentinel Oak Vineyard Pyramid Block Syrah (Shenandoah Valley (CA)) $35. The hot vintage took its toll on this wine, which has raisiny flavors and a cooked fruit flavor. It's bone dry and tannic, although soft in acidity, but there are rich berry and coffee flavors on the finish. **84** —*S.H. (6/1/2006)*

Domaine de la Terre Rouge 2002 Sentinel Oak Vineyard Pyramid Block Syrah (Shenandoah Valley (CA)) $35. A good Syrah, well-balanced in rich tannins and with a subtle interplay of oak, acids and cherry and black raspberry fruit. Loses a few points for some unripe flavors tha suggest green juniper berries, though. **86** —*S.H. (8/1/2005)*

Domaine de la Terre Rouge 2001 Sentinel Oak Vineyard Pyramid Block Syrah (Sierra Foothills) $35. This is a dramatic Syrah, concentrated in blackberries, cassis, black cherries, woodsap, spices and vanilla flavors that flood the palate, sinking in deep and lasting through the finish. The wine is totally dry and balanced. It's young and flashy now, and should be best over the next two or three years. **93** —*S.H. (3/1/2006)*

Domaine de la Terre Rouge 2000 Sentinel Oak Vineyard Pyramid Block Syrah (Shenandoah Valley (CA)) $35. Dynamic, intense, and complex, a massive wine that explodes with blackberry, plum, dark chocolate and herb aromas and flavors. Terrific texture, thick and smooth, and totally drinkable tonight. **92 Editors' Choice** —*S.H. (6/1/2003)*

Domaine de la Terre Rouge 1997 Viognier (Shenandoah Valley (CA)) $25. 90 —*S.H. (6/1/1999)*

Domaine de la Terre Rouge 2004 Viognier (Amador County) $30. From Shenandoah Valley and Fiddletown grapes, Terre Rouge has crafted a rich, exotic Viognier. It captures the variety's lush tropical fruit and wildflower flavors, but maintains balance with crisp acidity and barrel fermentation, which makes the wine creamy smooth. **90** —*S.H. (6/1/2006)*

Domaine de la Terre Rouge 2003 Viognier (Shenandoah Valley (CA)) $30. Lots of toasty, spicy richness in this flamboyantly fruity wine. Shows big, juicy flavors of peach tart, pineapple custard, tapioca and butterscotch, making it almost sweet. Fortunately, the fresh acidity gives it flair and balance. **88** —*S.H. (8/1/2005)*

Domaine de la Terre Rouge 2001 Viognier (Shenandoah Valley (CA)) $28. A tricky, subtle wine, not for everyone. High acidity lends a punch to the citrus and wildflower flavors, and there's a slightly sour taste to the finish, probably from extended lees aging. **86** —*S.H. (6/1/2003)*

Domaine de la Terre Rouge 2003 Enigma White Blend (Sierra Foothills) $20. Made from white Rhône grapes, this is a flashy, fleshy blend that's as rich as a fruity dessert wine, yet it's dry and balanced. The creamy texture carries vanilla, banana cream pie, peach and mocha flavors. **87** —*S.H. (8/1/2005)*

Domaine de la Terre Rouge 1997 Enigma White Blend (Sierra Foothills) $16. **89** —*S.H. (6/1/1999)*

Domaine de la Terre Rouge 1996 Vin Gris d'Amado White Blend (California) $9. **88** —*S.H. (6/1/1999)*

DOMAINE DES MONDES

Domaine des Mondes 2005 Sanford & Benedict Vineyard Saints and Sinners Viognier (Santa Barbara County) $30. New oak bursts forth in an immediate blast of smoky char, while airing reveals lemonddrop, honeysuckle, buttercream and fresh spice notes. The wine is marvelously complicated, zesty in acidity, with all kinds of fruit, flower and spice flavors. Represents a whole new dimension in California Viognier. **93 Editors' Choice** —*S.H. (11/15/2006)*

DOMAINE DROUHIN

Domaine Drouhin 2000 Chardonnay (Oregon) $40. Unlike 1999, this year half of the wine was fermented in stainless steel. Stylish and truly "Burgundian" character, with bright flavors of citrus and stone, buoyant on lively acids, unencumbered by heavy oak. Young and seductive, with a finishing kiss of toast and butter. **92** —*P.G. (7/1/2002)*

Domaine Drouhin 2004 Arthur Chardonnay (Willamette Valley) $27. DDO's Chardonnay comes as close to white Burgundy as you will find in Oregon. Amazing finesse, with crisp, detailed aromas mixing flowers, peaches, melon and almonds. Impressive texture and a long, elegant and precisely-detailed path across the palate. **92 Editors' Choice** —*P.G. (5/1/2006)*

Domaine Drouhin 2002 Pinot Noir (Willamette Valley) $40. The regular DDO has plump, ripe fruit, bright and vivid, and the fresh, simple appeal of Beaujolais. What is missing is the midpalate, which falls off precipitously and never quite recovers. **86** *(11/1/2004)*

Domaine Drouhin 2000 Pinot Noir (Willamette Valley) $40. The panel had differing views of this wine. Some of us liked the cola, pepper and leather aromas; others found hints of horsehide, thistle and char. The palate offers plum, black cherry and chocolate, but also a sweet beet-like undercurrent. Finishes hard, and, some say, bumpy and discordant. **84** *(10/1/2002)*

Domaine Drouhin 1999 Pinot Noir (Oregon) $45. Even in ripe, jammy vintages such as 1998, Domaine Drouhin keeps a sleek, polished profile. In 1999, everyone made tight, lean wines, and this one takes that ageworthy style to an extra dimension. Clear and bright, young and hard, it suggests rather than showcases layers of mineral, earth and red fruit. Firm and elegant, but give it lots of cellar time. **90** —*P.G. (12/31/2001)*

Domaine Drouhin 2000 Laurene Pinot Noir (Oregon) $55. Tight and muscular, the new Laurene opens with a hard, earthy nose that shows more stem and leaf than fruit. Should open up and reveal its complexity as it ages. **89** —*P.G. (2/1/2004)*

Domaine Drouhin 1999 Laurene Pinot Noir (Willamette Valley) $55. The black cherry fruit on the nose is nicely framed in oak. Chocolate, ginger and green tobacco notes over deep, black cherry fruit dance on the supple palate, which shows fine fruit-to-acid balance. It's impressive, but kept from an even higher rating by ascendant oak, under which the

handsome fruit struggles to maintain balance. This will be top-notch if the wood recedes in time. **88** *(10/1/2002)*

Domaine Drouhin 1998 Laurene Pinot Noir (Oregon) $50. This is essentially DDO's reserve bottling, and is released later than the regular, so the '98 is current. Dark and fleshy, it has an open, earthy nose redolent of barnyard, leaf and blossom. It is borderline rustic, smelling of forest floor. The finish is quite rough and tannic. **88** —*P.G. (12/31/2001)*

Domaine Drouhin 1996 Laurene Pinot Noir (Willamette Valley) $45. **85** *(10/1/1999)*

Domaine Drouhin 2002 Laurène Pinot Noir (Oregon) $55. Though DDO is known for its light, elegant touch, the Laurène bottling, which is a reserve, comes across as pruney, hot and simply too ripe in this vintage. **85** *(11/1/2004)*

Domaine Drouhin 1999 Louise Drouhin Pinot Noir (Oregon) $45. This is the best Pinot Noir yet from the Drouhin estate; immensely concentrated and rich. The fruit is complex and penetrating, focused and long, layered throughout a generous and extended finish. Cherries and chocolate linger on the palate, resonating long after the wine has been swallowed. **95 Cellar Selection** —*P.G. (8/1/2002)*

DOMAINE LAURIER

Domaine Laurier 2001 Reserve Pinot Noir (Sonoma County) $13. An easy, likeable Pinot of a kind that used to be impossible to find at this price. The silky texture and crisp acidity frame pleasant flavors of cherries, raspberries and coffee, sweetened with a dash of smoky vanilla. This is a real value for Pinot Noir. **86** —*S.H. (12/1/2004)*

DOMAINE M

Domaine M 2001 Cabernet Sauvignon (Napa Valley) $25. Rich and fruity in blackberry, cherry and chocolate flavors, with a very soft texture and slight sweetness on the finish that's almost medicinal. Still, offers immediate drinking pleasure. **85** —*S.H. (8/1/2005)*

DOMAINE MERIWETHER

Domaine Meriwether 1998 Captain Wm Clark Cuvée Brut Champagne Blend (Oregon) $25. This new brand previously released their second label brut (Discovery), but this is the more "serious" offering. It's a 100% barrel-fermented blend of Pinot Noir (60%) and Chardonnay (40%). Youthful and fresh, it sports generous, tiny bubbles and a yeasty vitality. Green apples and a hint of apricot lead into an elegant, toasty finish. **90 Editors' Choice** —*P.G. (12/1/2001)*

Domaine Meriwether 2002 Pinot Noir (Willamette Valley) $28. There is a lot of smoky, charred new wood here, layered upon tangy cherry and cranberry fruit. An astringent, crisp style that drew mixed reviews from our panel. Should improve with time. **88** *(11/1/2004)*

Domaine Meriwether NV Discovery Cuvée Sparkling Blend (Oregon) $16. Fresh and clean, with scents and flavors of ripe apples and a beery, leesy note. This blend of 58% Pinot Noir and 48% Chardonnay boasts an aggressive bead that gives it a brash, in-your-face quality ideal for casual summer sipping, less so for elegant, formal occasions. **84** —*J.C. (8/1/2003)*

Domaine Meriwether 1998 Fort Clatsop Cuvée Blanc de Blancs Sparkling Blend (Oregon) $25. Admirably toasty, but seems a bit soft and unfocused on the palate, with modest flavors of mushroom and earth. **81** —*J.C. (12/1/2003)*

Domaine Meriwether 1998 Olivia's Cuvée Brut Rose Sparkling Blend (Oregon) $27. Boasts a reddish-copper color and a fine bead, but doesn't give up a lot on the nose—just hints of berries and toast. Tastes more earthy and mushrooomy, with a creamy mouthfeel but a short finish. **84** —*J.C. (12/1/2003)*

DOMAINE SAINT GREGORY

Domaine Saint Gregory 1999 Pinot Blanc (Mendocino) $13. Clove, peach and smoky-vanilla aromas lead to peach and citrus flavors that drink excessively sweet, almost off-dry in the sugar department. The flavors are pretty and the wine is crisp, but would be better if it were dry. **83** —*S.H. (5/1/2002)*

USA

Domaine Saint Gregory 1997 Pinot Noir (Mendocino) $18. 90 —*J.C.* (5/1/2000)

Domaine Saint Gregory 1999 Pinot Noir (Mendocino) $18. Fruitier and more full-bodied than you want in a Pinot Noir, although it's a tasty wine with its own merits. Seems likely it was grown inland, in hot weather. Very extracted and rather sweet flavors of cherries, cola and berries are wrapped in silky tannins. Finishes hot and sweet. 84 —*S.H.* (5/1/2002)

Domaine Saint Gregory 1999 Reserve Pinot Noir (Redwood Valley) $28. Overly ripe grapes have given this wine unbalanced aromas of stewed prunes and make it taste hot and ponderous. Cool nights preserved vital acidity but the fruit tastes cooked. You might almost think this was Syrah except for the tannins. The dry finish reprises the pruny theme. 82 —*S.H.* (5/1/2002)

Domaine Saint Gregory 1998 Reserve Pinot Noir (Anderson Valley) $28. 85 —*P.G.* (12/15/2000)

DOMAINE SANTA BARBARA

Domaine Santa Barbara 2005 Chardonnay (Santa Barbara County) $15. You hardly notice the mild oak and lees elements in this Chard because it's so tart with acids and pure in green apple, Meyer lemon and yellow apricot fruit. There's also a flinty minerality, making this quite Chablisian. 85 —*S.H.* (11/15/2006)

Domaine Santa Barbara 2004 Chardonnay (Santa Barbara County) $15. Here's a friendly Chardonnay with bold flavors of peaches and tropical fruits, with a spicy dusting of oak. It has that nice, bright coastal acidity that balances the richness. 85 —*S.H.* (12/1/2005)

Domaine Santa Barbara 2002 Chardonnay (Santa Barbara County) $15. Simple and one-dimensional, this Chard offers sweet fruit flavors. Finishes rough. 82 —*S.H.* (5/1/2005)

Domaine Santa Barbara 1999 Chardonnay (Santa Barbara) $15. Another flavorful Chard from a fine region and vintage. Aromas of tropical fruits, spices, oak, smoke and lees. Rich and fine in the mouth. The structure is particularly elegant, with crisp acidity, smooth tannins and alcohol all well integrated with the fruit. Gets extra points for harmony and balance. 88 —*S.H.* (5/1/2001)

Domaine Santa Barbara 2002 Pinot Gris (Santa Barbara County) $12. Richer and fuller-bodied than your average California Pinot Gris, this one's got full-throttle flavors of spiced apples and figs, and whistle-clean acidity. It's delicious and complete, a fine complement to poached salmon with a fruity salsa topping. 87 —*S.H.* (9/1/2004)

Domaine Santa Barbara 1999 Pinot Gris (Santa Barbara County) $16. More floral, tropical-fruit notes than usual in a Pinot Gris. Quite flowery and rich in the mouth, with flavors of butter, honey and apricot. It's on the dry side, with a hefty jolt of acidity that keeps things clean. Nice cocktail-style wine. 86 —*S.H.* (5/1/2001)

Domaine Santa Barbara 1999 Pinot Noir (Santa Barbara County) $17. The bouquet here is funky, no doubt about it. Modest cherry, earth and leather combine with wood notes on the palate. On the finish, bold acidity triggers an electric mouthfeel 83 (10/1/2002)

Domaine Santa Barbara 1998 Pinot Noir (Santa Barbara County) $17. Definitely comes down on the gamy side, with an aroma of bacon or sweaty saddle wafting over black raspberry fruit. Oak adds vanilla and charred-smoky elements. In the mouth it's fruity, soft and a little simple. A mere 120 cases produced. 85 —*S.H.* (5/1/2001)

Domaine Santa Barbara 2003 Great Oaks Ranch Syrah (Santa Barbara County) $25. Heavy, soft and tannic, this wine shows black cherry, blackberry flavors and coffee, and is very dry. The cherry finish is attractive, though. 84 —*S.H.* (5/1/2005)

Domaine Santa Barbara 2002 Great Oaks Ranch Syrah (Santa Barbara County) $25. There are lots of interesting things going on in this cool-climate wine. It echoes the Northern Rhône with white pepper and blackberry aromas that are complex and inviting. In the mouth, it turns bone dry, with cherry-berry flavors that are swamped by firm tannins. Try after 2006. 87 —*S.H.* (8/1/2004)

DOMAINE SERENE

Domaine Serene 2003 Clos du Soleil Vineyard Chardonnay (Willamette Valley) $40. Chewy, minty and firm, with full-bodied flavors of apricot and peach. The fleshy fruit is enhanced with sur lies aging in 40% new French oak barrels. 90 —*P.G.* (5/1/2006)

Domaine Serene 2000 Clos du Soleil Vineyard Chardonnay (Willamette Valley) $35. Dijon clone again. This has just the vaguest hint of onion, but otherwise is much improved over this property's '99. There is good, juicy, crisp fruit mixing apple/apricot and light citrus. Balanced acids and a well integrated middle that leads into a somewhat hot, stiff finish. Young and edgy, but well made. 88 —*P.G.* (8/1/2002)

Domaine Serene 1999 Clos du Soleil Vineyard Chardonnay (Willamette Valley) $35. This is a ripe year, but this vineyard designation isn't quite as tropical as their Côte Sud. It's more of a precise style, but there are also some hints of grass, onion and herb. Interesting, but very slightly off. 86 —*P.G.* (8/1/2002)

Domaine Serene 2000 Cote Sud Chardonnay (Willamette Valley) $38. Made from Dijon clones, this is an aggressively oaky wine that needs still more time to soften the bitter oak tannins. Good, smooth, even silky citrus/apple fruit is here, and the overall balance is an improvement over the huge '99. 87 —*P.G.* (12/1/2003)

Domaine Serene 1999 Cote Sud Vineyard Chardonnay (Willamette Valley) $35. This seems a bit overripe in the nose; definitely an ultraripe style, with flavors of peach, apricot and mango. Real tropical, still has decent acids, but the fruit went a bit too far, and there is a definite sweetness too, along with some breakfast toast oak. 87 —*P.G.* (8/1/2002)

Domaine Serene 2003 Evenstad Reserve Pinot Noir (Willamette Valley) $52. Big, thick and brawny, this shows a substantial streak of vanilla over firm, ripe, tasty mixed black fruits. Clean, rich and powerful, with substantial oak spices, it's the most masculine of the three Domaine Serene Pinots in the current lineup. 91 —*P.G.* (9/1/2006)

Domaine Serene 2000 Evenstad Reserve Pinot Noir (Willamette Valley) $47. This is substantial Pinot, with streaks of earth, chocolate, vanilla and herb mixed through sweet fruit. Tannins and acids are well-handled, and the 13.5% alcohol keeps it food friendly. 88 —*P.G.* (12/1/2003)

Domaine Serene 1999 Evenstad Reserve Pinot Noir (Willamette Valley) $47. Oak-wrapped black cherry fruit is a solid foundation, but this elegant wine also sports a prominent green tobacco (or lima bean) element that many panelists found distracting. Bright acidity and an inky, dark, tannic finish complete the package. Is it underripe, or just underage? Try 2004– 2007. 87 (10/1/2002)

Domaine Serene 2003 Fleur de Lis Vineyard Pinot Noir (Dundee Hills) $75. Very soft and approachable, but perhaps a bit too soft—it's almost pillowy, with a mouthfeel like marshmallow. Good black cherry fruit dominates the core. But the wine seems a bit light, lacking in grip and conviction, at least compared with the Grace vineyard bottling. 89 —*P.G.* (9/1/2006)

Domaine Serene 2002 Fleur de Lis Vineyard Pinot Noir (Willamette Valley) $47. The first impression is of a very attractive mix of dusty cocoa, earth, tar and vanilla. Fruit flavors are clean, precise and tart, with youthful vitality and lots of acid. More time could flesh it out and up the score. 88 (11/1/2004)

Domaine Serene 2003 Grace Vineyard Pinot Noir (Willamette Valley) $90. Oregon Pinot at the top of its game; firm and tannic, with a complex mix of berry-driven fruits and lively spices. There is plenty of midpalate concentration, power and length, as the fruit unwinds with blackberry, plum, anise and hints of herb. Dry, green-tea flavored tannins wrap it all into a tidy bundle. 93 —*P.G.* (9/1/2006)

Domaine Serene 1999 Grace Vineyard Pinot Noir (Willamette Valley) $75. Lavish cedar cloaks tart plum and cherry fruit on the nose of this substantial but controversial wine. The dark fruit is offset by licorice and pine, but also by green herbaceous notes, and the wine displays high, even sharp, acidity. Has depth, but it's tight now (and for some, way too green), and closes hard, dark and ashy. Hold for two or three years, best 2004–2008. 88 (10/1/2002)

Domaine Serene 2003 Jerusalem Hill Vineyard Pinot Noir (Willamette Valley) $75. The winery continues its string of successes in the difficult 2003 vintage, with another dense, soft, lush and elegant single vineyard release. Intense and sweetly fruity, it shows strong raspberry and cherry character that is nicely integrated with the toast and caramel of new French oak. Ripe and drinking well, it nonetheless has the structure to age a while. **91** —*P.G. (9/1/2006)*

Domaine Serene 1999 Mark Bradford Vineyard Pinot Noir (Willamette Valley) $75. Quite dark and opaque, this full-bodied Pinot is handsomely toasty and smoky, with a layered black cherry and blackberry fruit foundation. Though youthful and closed, it still feels velvety and deep, showing lots of finesse, and stylish vanilla and herb accents. Finishes long and rich; needs two to three years to unfold. Best 2005–2010. **90 Cellar Selection** *(10/1/2002)*

Domaine Serene 2003 Winery Hill Vineyard Pinot Noir (Willamette Valley) $75. Classic Oregon Pinot from a ripe vintage, the extra heat gives the fruit a sweet dimension without sacrificing the herbal/ leafy/piney character that defines the region. Solid and tight, with lots of fresh herb—tarragon, thyme and sage—and stiff tannins. **90** —*P.G. (9/1/2006)*

Domaine Serene 2000 Yamhill Cuvée Pinot Noir (Willamette Valley) $30. The earthy, meaty nose is sweetened by some bubble gum and cherry cola. It's a fruit-forward Pinot, with bouncy cherry fruit, black plum and sweet oak-driven vanilla. The finish offers chocolate-covered cherries and coffee, and the overall feel is nice due to bright acidity and firm but modest tannins. **88** *(10/1/2002)*

Domaine Serene 2002 Yamhill Cuvée Pinot Noir (Willamette Valley) $33. Though one-dimensional, this is a powerful wine with black cherry fruit and generous oak, expressed as roasted coffee scents and espresso flavors. **85** *(11/1/2004)*

DOMAINE ST. GEORGE

Domaine St. George 2001 Cabernet Sauvignon (Sonoma County) $10. Dark, fruity and thick, a rustic wine with ripe berry flavors. Serviceable, with a good, dry structure and a clean finish. **83** —*S.H. (5/1/2004)*

Domaine St. George 2001 Barrel Reserve Cabernet Sauvignon (Sonoma County) $10. There are some pretty blackberry and olive tapenade flavors alongside a streak of greenish bell pepper. Drinks sharp in acidity and a little thin, but fundamentally sound and serviceable. **84** —*S.H. (6/1/2004)*

Domaine St. George 2001 Coastal Cabernet Sauvignon (California) $8. Simple, earthy and clean. Some Cab character. Dry finish, with blackberry and oak flavors. **83** —*S.H. (10/1/2004)*

Domaine St. George 2000 Coastal Cabernet Sauvignon (California) $7. Simple blackberry and cherry flavors drink rough and ready. It's fully dry. With takeout pizza or a quick burger, it's fine. **83** —*S.H. (3/1/2004)*

Domaine St. George 2001 Wells Vineyard Cabernet Sauvignon (Dry Creek Valley) $15. This is a nice, middle of the road Cabernet, with black cherry, blackberry and herb flavors that are wrapped in chunky, firm tannins. It's a bit sharp in acids, but that will take care of itself with the right foods. **85** —*S.H. (5/1/2004)*

Domaine St. George 2000 Chardonnay (Chalk Hill) $14. Tastes raw and acidic, a tough wine that has traces of citrus fruit flavors. You might think it was a Sauvignon Blanc, it's so dry and tart. **82** —*S.H. (5/1/2004)*

Domaine St. George 2001 Barrel Reserve Barrel Aged Chardonnay (Sonoma Valley) $10. Smells a little funky, with a meaty, raw beef aroma on top of scents of green apples. Tastes thin and watery, with a suggested of appley citrus fruit flavor. The finish turns tart and dry. **82** —*S.H. (9/1/2003)*

Domaine St. George 2003 Coastal Chardonnay (California) $8. Way too sugary, with cloying, candy flavors. **81** —*S.H. (6/1/2005)*

Domaine St. George 2001 Coastal Chardonnay (California) $8. A bit on the watered down side, with faint traces of peach and apple, and a brisk finish that has traces of fruity richness. Enjoy it without being fussy. **84** —*S.H. (2/1/2004)*

Domaine St. George 2000 Coastal Chardonnay (California) $7. An odd, bizarre wine that tastes like the syrup in canned peaches, although the wine is fully dry. Feels gluey and flabby because of low acids. The finish is weak and watery. **81** —*S.H. (6/1/2003)*

Domaine St. George 2003 Merlot (Sonoma County) $10. A good price for a very nice Merlot, from a winery with an increasingly respectable track record. The wine is dry and balanced, with a smooth texture and blackberry, coffee and chocolate flavors. **86 Best Buy** —*S.H. (12/1/2005)*

Domaine St. George 2001 Merlot (Sonoma County) $10. Good, serviceable Merlot, with ripe flavors of cherries and blackberries that last through the swallow. It's dry and soft, and has accents of oak. **84** —*S.H. (5/1/2004)*

Domaine St. George 1999 Merlot (California) $13. Red and black berry fruit, in addition to rougher earth, tobacco and herb notes, and in the mouth it drinks fruity and tart. This is a simple, everyday red wine, dry and clean. **83** —*S.H. (7/1/2002)*

Domaine St. George 2001 Coastal Merlot (California) $8. This easy-drinking wine is full bodied, with flavors of cherries and a touch of chocolatey Kahlúa. It offers plenty of pleasure in a dry, balanced red wine, and is fairly priced. **84** —*S.H. (6/1/2004)*

Domaine St. George 2000 Coastal Merlot (California-Washington) $7. You'll find lots of jammy cherry, blackberry and chocolate flavors in this clean wine. It feels round and supple in the mouth, and finishes dry, with an aftertaste of berries. A nice value at this everyday price. **85** —*S.H. (3/1/2004)*

Domaine St. George 2002 Sauvignon Blanc (California) $6. Smells like dried hay and grapefruit juice, and is completely watery. Acceptable but not recommended. **81** —*S.H. (5/1/2004)*

Domaine St. George 2001 Coastal Syrah (California) $8. The good cherry and blackberry fruit drinks a bit earthy and one-dimensional, and finishes thin. Still, this wine has lush, sweet tannins and a good mouthfeel. **84** —*S.H. (5/1/2004)*

Domaine St. George 2002 White Zinfandel Zinfandel (California) $5. Apricot and strawberry aromas drink fruity and zesty. Not much more to say except that it's dry. **83** —*S.H. (5/1/2004)*

DOMAINE STE MICHELLE

Domaine Ste Michelle NV Champagne Blend (Columbia Valley (WA)) $11. **83** *(12/15/1999)*

Domaine Ste Michelle NV Blanc de Blanc Champagne Blend (Columbia Valley (WA)) $11. Here is a soundly made, attractively packaged and priced, lightweight bubbly. Subtle cinnamon spice enhances the green apple and aromas. Nice weight and clean mouthfeel, with a refreshing, bone-dry finish, capped off with lots of beery bubbles. **86 Best Buy** —*P.G. (12/1/2001)*

Domaine Ste Michelle NV Blanc de Blancs Champagne Blend (Columbia Valley (WA)) $11. Light and elegant, with a trace of citrus and peach flavor. Extremely dry and tart, but with finesse and elegance. A wonderful everyday sparkler. **87 Best Buy** —*S.H. (12/1/2002)*

Domaine Ste Michelle NV Blanc de Noir Champagne Blend (Columbia Valley (WA)) $11. DSM delivers the most reliable, attractive and downright cheap bubbly in the Northwest, and this is their best bottle. Pale salmon, with Pinot-scented light cherry and strawberry fruit, it is technically off-dry but tastes more like a brut. Good concentration through a crisp, yeasty finish. **86 Best Buy** *(12/1/2001)*

Domaine Ste Michelle NV Cuvée Brut Champagne Blend (Columbia Valley (WA)) $11. The richest and finest of this winery's series of value bubblies. This Chardonnay-Pinot Noir blend is delicately scented with raspberry, peach, smoke and yeast, and it's smooth on the palate. So elegant and complex, it's hard to believe it costs so little. **90 Best Buy** —*S.H. (12/1/2002)*

Domaine Ste Michelle NV Cuvée Brut Champagne Blend (Columbia Valley (WA)) $11. **82** *(12/15/1999)*

Domaine Ste Michelle NV Cuvée Brut Champagne Blend (Columbia Valley (WA)) $11. This is straightforward and likeable; dry, but with plenty of fruit. A tad sweeter and much juicier than the Blanc de Blanc, its bright fruit creeps into the tropical zone with hints of pineapple and papaya.

There's nice effervescence in the mouth and the cleansing finish is crisp and tart. **86 Best Buy** *(12/1/2001)*

Domaine Ste Michelle NV Cuvée Brut Champagne Blend (Columbia Valley (WA)) $12. Bigger and more obviously fruity than the Blanc de Blancs, it is a simple, clean, pleasant but nondescript bubbly. **86** —*P.G. (12/31/2004)*

Domaine Ste Michelle NV Extra Dry Champagne Blend (Columbia Valley (WA)) $12. This is significantly sweeter than the rest of the lineup from Domaine Ste. Michelle, and the sweetness has a sugary character that is a bit too reminiscent of cheaper, bulk-fermented bubblies. **85** —*P.G. (12/31/2004)*

Domaine Ste Michelle NV Extra Dry Champagne Blend (Columbia Valley (WA)) $11. 82 *(12/15/1999)*

Domaine Ste Michelle NV Extra Dry Champagne Blend (Columbia Valley (WA)) $11. Has the same fruity flavors as Ste. Michelle's brut, but slightly jagged, angular acids show through, and the finish is a little tart. Needs food, but is a very good wine. **88 Best Buy** —*S.H. (12/1/2002)*

Domaine Ste Michelle NV Blanc de Blancs Chardonnay (Columbia Valley (WA)) $12. Soundly-made, attractively packaged, lightweight bubbly. Crisp green apple aromas lead into a clean and refreshing sparkler, with some citrusy tang. **86** —*P.G. (12/31/2004)*

Domaine Ste Michelle 1998 Luxe Chardonnay (Columbia Valley (WA)) $23. This is the winery's first vintage cuvée, and it's a nice, toasty, creamy wine that has been given extra care from fermentation onward. Some tropical flavors underlie the toast, and it's very full bodied for an all-chardonnay bubbly. The finish tastes of ripe bananas. **89** —*P.G. (12/31/2004)*

Domaine Ste Michelle NV Blanc de Noirs Pinot Noir (Columbia Valley (WA)) $12. This is one of the Ste. Michelle Estates brands, and the only producer of inexpensive sparkling wines in the region. They make four at the $12 price point: a Blanc de Blancs, a Brut, a Blanc de Noirs and an Extra Dry. All are non-vintage and 100% méthode Champenoise. The Blanc de Noirs is consistently the best of the lineup; some of the others can be excessively foamy and a bit chalky through the finish. But the Blanc de Noirs is a pretty, pale copper; lightly Pinot-scented, and a good quaffer that really works well with turkey. **85** —*P.G. (11/15/2005)*

Domaine Ste Michelle NV Blanc de Noirs Pinot Noir (Columbia Valley (WA)) $12. The Blanc de Noirs is the best bottle of the lineup, year in and year out. Creamy and complex, it's a pretty, pale copper, with Pinot-scented hints of cherry fruit. **87 Best Buy** —*P.G. (12/31/2004)*

Domaine Ste Michelle NV Blanc de Blanc Sparkling Blend (Columbia Valley (WA)) $11. Fresh, young and aggressive, with notes of apple and ginger backed by crisp acidity. Clean and refreshing, a well-made bubbly at a price that makes it a solid choice for holiday parties. **84** —*J.C. (12/1/2003)*

Domaine Ste Michelle NV Cuvée Brut Sparkling Blend (Columbia Valley (WA)) $11. Another reliable and affordable release from Domaine Ste. Michelle, this year's brut shows hints of Red Delicious apples and berries wrapped around a core of tart acids. **83** —*J.C. (12/1/2003)*

Domaine Ste Michelle NV Extra Dry Sparkling Blend (Columbia Valley (WA)) $11. Boldly flavored, with massive doses of tart green apples pumped up by bubbles and a trace of sweetness. Simple and a bit sugary, it' would be a good base for "Champagne" cocktails. **83** —*J.C. (12/1/2003)*

DOMENICO

Domenico 2004 Cabernet Franc (Amador County) $22. High in alcohol, frankly sweet, this wine was a victim of the excessive heat of this record hot vintage. Too bad, because the cherry flavors and polished tannins are really nice. **83** —*S.H. (12/15/2006)*

Domenico 2004 Cabernet Sauvignon (Napa Valley) $35. A Bordeaux blend with all five varieties. The vineyard is in the cooler Oak Knoll region. But coolness is relative; the vintage was blazingly hot everywhere, and the wine is almost Porty. **83** —*S.H. (12/15/2006)*

Domenico 2004 Syrah (Amador County) $30. Soft and fairly sweet in what tastes like residual sugar, this wine has blackberry, cola, clove and vanilla

flavors. Everything about it is nice, except that sugary finish. The alcohol level isn't really a problem in terms of balance. **83** —*S.H. (12/15/2006)*

DOMINARI

Dominari 2002 Cabernet Sauvignon (Napa Valley) $75. The '01, reviewed last year, lost a few points for a cut of sharp acidity. This one does, too. There are deliciously full flavors of blackberries and cassis, and great, rich tannins, but that acidity really prickles the palate. **86** —*S.H. (12/31/2005)*

Dominari 2001 Cabernet Sauvignon (Napa Valley) $75. Very young, with a cut of acidity that has yet to be integrated into the oaky, rather flamboyant flavors of cassis and blackberries. It's all there, including lush tannins, but needs a few years to come together. Best after 2005. A new label from Atlas Peak. **88** —*S.H. (10/1/2004)*

Dominari 2002 Merlot (Napa Valley) $45. Unbalanced, with superripe raisin-and-chocolate flavors but also some green peppercorn notes. The tannins are strong, and there's a burn of acid in the finish. **82** —*S.H. (12/31/2005)*

Dominari 2001 Merlot (Napa Valley) $45. This complete and fulfilling Merlot has lots of stuffing. The flavors run toward ripe plums and blackberries, with an undertow of green olive, coffee and chocolate. Oak brings smoky vanillins and adds its own sort of sweetness. But the real wonder are the tannins, which are rich, ripe and complex. **92** —*S.H. (9/1/2004)*

DOMINUS

Dominus 2003 Bordeaux Blend (Napa Valley) $109. The grapes are from the estate in Yountville, just south of Oakville, and young Dominus always seems tight and austere. So it is here. Astringent tannins, youthful acids and new oak are upfront, raising the question of ageability. It's a roll of the dice. The wine is balanced and harmonious, but aggressive now. **87** —*S.H. (9/1/2006)*

Dominus 2002 Estate Bordeaux Blend (Napa Valley) $109. On the border between cool and warm Napa, Dominus really needs a good vintage to shine. It was stellar in 2001, less so this year. The wine is elegant, displaying finesse, balance and taste, yet it's not a blockbuster. Still, so poised is it that you find yourself reaching for a second, or third, glass. Drink now. **89** —*S.H. (12/15/2005)*

Dominus 2001 Estate Bottled Bordeaux Blend (Napa Valley) $109. As good as the 2001 Napanook is, this wine is more intense. The fruit is lusher, the oak newer, the control more complete, but the kicker is the tannins. They're powerful and dusty, and conceal the flamboyance, for now. Needs time; hold until 2010 and beyond. **94 Cellar Selection** —*S.H. (10/1/2004)*

Dominus 1997 Estate Bottled Bordeaux Blend (Napa Valley) $100. 93 *(11/1/2000)*

Dominus 2000 Estate Bottled Red Wine Bordeaux Blend (Napa Valley) $95. Christian Mouiex lowered the price this year. The glut or the vintage? This Dominus is almost as good as the' 99. It's not a lavish blockbuster, but the cassis and herb flavors are delicious, and well oaked. The prettiest part is the mouthfeel, all soft and velvety. Shows plenty of class and elegance. **90** —*S.H. (12/10/2003)*

Dominus 2000 Napanook Bordeaux Blend (Napa Valley) $39. Thin, herbal and tart, with sage, dill and bell pepper flavors accented with hints of cherry and blackberry. The best part is the texture, which is complex and smooth. Not going anywhere, so drink up. **85** —*S.H. (11/15/2003)*

Dominus 1996 Napanook Bordeaux Blend (Napa Valley) $30. 91 —*L.W. (7/1/1999)*

Dominus 1997 Napanook Vineyard Bordeaux Blend (Napa Valley) $30. 90 *(11/1/2000)*

Dominus 2002 Napanook Cabernet Blend (Napa Valley) $39. There's a hardness, a tannic greenness to this Cab-based wine that time may or may not address. It's hard to tell. Meanwhile, the flavors of cassis, blackberries, black cherries, blueberries and smoky oak finish with a dry, peppery spiciness. **85** —*S.H. (12/31/2005)*

Dominus 2001 Napanook Cabernet Sauvignon (Napa Valley) $39. Very dry, and young in its fresh tannins and acids framing ripe, grapy currant flavors, mocha, vanilla and sweet dill. Very fine and balanced, with a powerful finish. Beautiful now, but should develop through this decade. **91** —*S.H. (10/1/2004)*

Dominus 1999 Red Blend (Napa Valley) $117. Opens with herbal aromas of sage, dill and tobacco, with a vanilla, oaky note, so it's surprising how rich it drinks. Sweet cassis is on the palate, framed in soft but intricate tannins. The wine is young and needs decanting or mid-term aging. **91** —*S.H. (11/15/2002)*

Dominus 1999 Napanook Red Blend (Napa Valley) $42. This isn't the Dominus, but a sort of junior to it. Rich and thick, with ripe blackberry and mocha flavors generously accented with oak. Lush and smooth, it's really a complete Napa Cabernet. Even at this price, when you compare it to so many other expensive, ho-hum Cabs, it's a value. **91** —*S.H. (11/15/2002)*

DOÑA SOL

Doña Sol 2002 Cabernet Sauvignon (California) $5. There's a lot of bulk grapes and wine out there, or there was three years ago, and this brand is taking advantage. The Cabernet is rich in fruit, pretty dry, light-bodied and rustic. It will nicely accompany ham, pork or chicken. **84 Best Buy** —*S.H. (6/1/2006)*

Doña Sol 2001 Cabernet Sauvignon (California) $5. Lots of Cabernet character, with ripe black currant, spice and oaky aromas and flavors and a dry finish. Drinks easy, with firm tannins. **84 Best Buy** —*S.H. (10/1/2004)*

DONEDEI

Donedei 2000 Merlot (Columbia Valley (WA)) $37. This shows some very ripe, jammy fruit flavors, with some stemmy notes creeping into the finish. You're left with the flavor impression of slightly decayed fruits and leaves. Just 140 cases were made. **86** —*P.G. (9/1/2003)*

DONUM ESTATE

Donum Estate 2002 Pinot Noir (Carneros) $60. Tasting this wine brings visions of the foggy, wind-swept, rolling hills of the appellation. The coolness has yielded an intensely herbal wine, with flavors of dried herbs such as sage and oregano. The acidity is vibrant, the tannins dusty. It's a well-tailored wine, but I wish there was more fruit. **88** —*S.H. (6/1/2004)*

Donum Estate 2003 Estate Grown Pinot Noir (Carneros) $60. Lots of new oak here, so much that the wine is dominated by it. Beyond the vanilla and char are slightly sweetened cherry pie filling flavors, with soft acids and a peppery finish. Good, but needs work. **86** —*S.H. (12/15/2006)*

DOUGLAS HILL

Douglas Hill 1997 Chardonnay (Napa Valley) $17. 84 *(6/1/2000)*

Douglas Hill 1997 Chardonnay (Napa Valley) $16. 82 —*M.S. (10/1/1999)*

DOVER CANYON

Dover Canyon 2001 Bone Blend Rhône Red Blend (Paso Robles) $24. A likeable, country-style wine, plump and juicy. The tannins are angular and rough, and the finish is hot and tarry, but the cherry pie-crust flavors are deep and satisfying. A blend of Mourvèdre, Syrah and Grenache. **84** —*S.H. (11/15/2002)*

Dover Canyon 1998 Chequera Vineyard Roussanne (Central Coast) $19. 83 —*S.H. (10/1/1999)*

Dover Canyon 1999 Fralich Vineyard Cuvée Syrah (Paso Robles) $28. 88 *(6/1/2003)*

Dover Canyon 1999 Reserve Syrah (Paso Robles) $35. Youthful, grapey aromas precede candied cherry and rhubarb flavors. Seems almost sweet, but folds in some black-pepper notes on the finish. **85** *(11/1/2001)*

DOWNING FAMILY

Downing Family 1999 Cabernet Sauvignon (Napa Valley) $38. Smooth-textured, with toasty oak nuances upfront. The wine serves up a complex blackberry, currant, chocolate, spice and herb pastiche that spreads out wonderfully on the palate, finishing long. **91** —*J.M. (2/1/2003)*

Downing Family 2001 Zinfandel (Oakville) $30. Quite ripe and rich in the nose, with hints of cherry, cedar and spice. On the palate it shows fine-tuned cherry, strawberry, chocolate, tar, toast, vanilla, spice and herb flavors. The tannins are silky and the finish long. **90** *(11/1/2003)*

DR. KONSTANTIN FRANK

Dr. Konstantin Frank 1999 Limited Release Cabernet Franc (Finger Lakes) $25. Herbal aromas stray dangerously close to green bean vegetal in this offering. Chocolate and damp leaves round out the bouquet, while sweet cherries come to the fore in the mouth. Soft tannins and good length on the finish. **85** —*J.C. (1/1/2004)*

Dr. Konstantin Frank 1999 Reserve Cabernet Sauvignon (Finger Lakes) $40. This wine is no bargain, especially when you go searching for ripe Cab fruit and come up empty. The nose is like cherry jello, while the flavors run toward underripe plum and apple skin. And the finish, despite some fleshy roundness, is also overtly tannic. **83** —*M.S. (3/1/2003)*

Dr. Konstantin Frank 1999 Chardonnay (Finger Lakes) $13. Toast and butterscotch flavors lead the way in this relatively full-bodied wine, featuring a fine array of crisp apple, peach, pear, melon and citrus notes. Long and full on the finish. **90 Best Buy** —*J.M. (7/1/2002)*

Dr. Konstantin Frank 2001 Gewürztraminer (Finger Lakes) $16. A lemony, mineral-like opening leads to a spicy, viscous mid-palate that supports melon, pear and apple notes. The finish is moderate in length. **86** —*J.M. (1/1/2003)*

Dr. Konstantin Frank 2001 Dry Johannisberg Riesling (Finger Lakes) $13. 84 —*J.C. (8/1/2003)*

Dr. Konstantin Frank 2000 Dry Johannisberg Riesling (Finger Lakes) $12. Dilute flowery scents and pink-grapefruit, lemon and green apple flavors mark this wine. It's light and clean, but disappointingly short on the finish. **83** —*J.C. (3/1/2002)*

Dr. Konstantin Frank 2001 Reserve Johannisberg Riesling (Finger Lakes) $25. 81 —*J.C. (8/1/2003)*

Dr. Konstantin Frank 2001 Semi Dry Johannisberg Riesling (Finger Lakes) $13. 83 —*J.C. (8/1/2003)*

Dr. Konstantin Frank 2000 Semi-Dry Johannisberg Riesling (Finger Lakes) $12. The heavy aromas and flavors of green apple and unripe pears and peaches are just too sweet and unbalanced—particularly on the finish, which turns cloying. **82** —*J.C. (3/1/2002)*

Dr. Konstantin Frank 1999 Limited Release Merlot (Finger Lakes) $20. Toasted marshmallow and toffee aromas lead into a supple wine that's pillowy soft. The midpalate boasts meat, coffee and black cherry flavors that turn caramel-sweet on the finish. **84** —*J.C. (3/1/2002)*

Dr. Konstantin Frank 1999 Reserve Merlot (New York) $35. The dense nose offers some berry fruit along with char and saline. With some airing, plum and blackberry flavors emerge, but they seem sweet and artificial. And although the finish is mellow and full of licorice and vanilla, the wine seems awkward and flawed. **84** —*M.S. (1/1/2004)*

Dr. Konstantin Frank NV Fleur de Pinot Noir Pinot Noir (Finger Lakes) $12. This pleasant, light red features varietally true aromas of underbrush, cherries and strawberries and simple, bright fruity flavors. The finish brings in an interesting tree-bark note. Try slightly chilled to add needed grip. **84** —*J.C. (3/1/2002)*

Dr. Konstantin Frank 1999 Old Vines Pinot Noir (Finger Lakes) $25. Despite this wine's light color, it carries a lot of flavor intensity. Cherry cola aromas gradually give way to coffee, caramel and bitter chocolate notes. Crisp acidity brings all the flavors together, forming a firm backbone—it will be interesting to see if this is one Finger Lakes Pinot that can age. **85** —*J.C. (1/1/2004)*

Dr. Konstantin Frank 1996 Old Vines Pinot Noir (Finger Lakes) $19. 82 *(10/1/1999)*

Dr. Konstantin Frank 2001 Rkatsiteli (Finger Lakes) $19. A lemony, melony blend—quite bright but with a touch of sweetness. Crisp and clean on the finish with hints of peach and minerals at the end. **86** —*J.M. (1/1/2003)*

Dr. Konstantin Frank 2000 Limited Release Rkatsiteli (Finger Lakes) $15. Made from an old Georgian (think Caucasus, not peach trees) grape variety, the waxy paraffin-scented aromas give way to pear and quince, tinged with red apple skin and lemony acids. There's a certain crystalline quality to the fruit that's very appealing. **86** —*J.C. (3/1/2002)*

USA

DREW

Drew 2004 Gatekeepers Pinot Noir (Santa Rita Hills) $36. A ripe, spicy wine, jammy in red cherry, blueberry and blackberry fruit. This is one of the fruitier Pinots from this appellation, a bit one-dimensional, but it sure does taste good. The name refers to the two vineyards that contributed to the fruit, from either side of the appellation. **88** —*S.H. (3/1/2006)*

Drew 2003 Rio Vista Vineyard Pinot Noir (Santa Rita Hills) $32. Rich, ripe, fleshy and fat, this single-vineyard Pinot is a little soft, but very delicious in gooey red cherry and mocha flavors. Finishes clean and supple, and slightly sweet. **87** —*S.H. (3/1/2006)*

Drew 2003 Hearthstone Vineyard Syrah (Paso Robles) $35. Darkly fruited, with flavors of plums, blackberries and blueberries accented by hints of herbs and chocolate. A medium-bodied wine that finishes softly tannic, with mouthwatering acidity. Youthful; give it 1–2 years. **86** *(9/1/2005)*

Drew 2003 Morehouse Vineyard Syrah (Santa Ynez Valley) $40. Crisp and medium-weight in the mouth, Drew's Morehouse has a profile in which herbal notes and tart cherry and berry flavors are front and center. Another reviewer remarked on the wine's black peppery accents. Distinctive, tight, tart and not for everyone. **87** *(9/1/2005)*

Drew 2003 Old Westy-Alisos Vineyard Syrah (Santa Barbara County) $30. A potent, blackberried-to-the-max wine, its berry aromas taking on a liqueurish warmth and its blackberry flavors accented with just enough spicy complexity. Creamy in the mouth and long on the finish (though one reviewer remarked that the wood on the back end was a bit too heavyhanded). **90 Editors' Choice** *(9/1/2005)*

Drew 2003 Rodney's and Larner Vineyards Syrah (Santa Ynez Valley) $32. Panelists applauded this Syrah's herbal-peppery aromas and flavors, and its tight, blueberry-black cherry fruit core. As mouthfilling and enjoyable as it is, all panelists mentioned that the texture was not quite as rich or complex as we'd have liked. Very good; has potential for excellence. **88** *(9/1/2005)*

Drew 2003 Six-Sense Syrah (Santa Barbara County) $27. A very good Syrah, and a nicely proportioned one. Displays fruit-sweet blackberries at its heart, jazzed up with spicy, black-peppery notes on both the nose and the palate. Finishes woody, though elegantly enough. 320 cases produced. **88** *(9/1/2005)*

DREYER SONOMA

Dreyer Sonoma 1998 Cabernet Sauvignon (Sonoma County) $14. 88 Best Buy —*S.H. (12/15/2000)*

Dreyer Sonoma 1998 Chardonnay (Sonoma County) $10. 84 *(10/1/2000)*

Dreyer Sonoma 2001 Chardonnay (Sonoma County) $10. An exceptionally rich and delicious Chardonnay for the money, and a great value. Oodles of peach, pear and tropical fruit flavors cascade over the palate; the wine is sturdy enough to support the substantial oak with which it has been lavished. **89 Best Buy** —*S.H. (12/1/2003)*

Dreyer Sonoma 2000 Chardonnay (Sonoma County) $10. Very ripe apple and peach fruit stands out in this nice wine. It's got a honeyed richness that extends through the clean, spicy finish. Dry and crisp, it's a great value in a complex, varietally true Chardonnay. **87** —*S.H. (5/1/2002)*

Dreyer Sonoma 1999 Chardonnay (Sonoma County) $10. If you didn't know the price and had to guess, you'd probably figure this wine would cost about $18. It's enormously ripe and fruity, with bright peach, tropical fruits and spices and quite a bit of oak. The technical notes say it was partially barrel-fermented. A wine of enormous charm and a great value in Chardonnay. **86** —*S.H. (2/1/2001)*

DRY CREEK VINEYARD

Dry Creek Vineyard 1997 Bordeaux Blend (Sonoma County) $25. 90 —*S.H. (11/1/1999)*

Dry Creek Vineyard 1998 Meritage Bordeaux Blend (Sonoma County) $28. Always a bit herbaceous, this year the underlying leanness shows in rather green fruit, veering into bell pepper, dill, mint and oregano. All the oak in France and America can't really make the fruit any riper. But the oak does add smoky, creamy, vanilla notes and sweetness, too. There is some pretty fruit—notably blackberry—in the finish, but still, this is a

wine of structure. It's fantastically well made, a classy quaff, and it will pair well with rich red meats, especially beef. **90** —*S.H. (2/1/2001)*

Dry Creek Vineyard 2002 Meritage Cabernet Blend (Dry Creek Valley) $28. The winery has done a good job at their Meritage in the past. This vintage is something of a letdown. The wine suffers from a tart, acidic dryness that lacks generosity of fruit. Yet it retains elegance and balance. Drink now. **84** —*S.H. (7/1/2006)*

Dry Creek Vineyard 1997 Cabernet Sauvignon (Sonoma County) $20. 88 —*S.H. (2/1/2000)*

Dry Creek Vineyard 2003 Cabernet Sauvignon (Dry Creek Valley) $21. Dry Creek Vineyard keeps turning out the most drinkable, delicious Cabernets, at such a good price, and hardly anyone notices. Why? Because it's not from Napa. This wine is soft and rich, with briary blackberry, dark chocolate, coffee and spice flavors that finish completely dry. A sophisticated wine. **90 Editors' Choice** —*S.H. (11/15/2006)*

Dry Creek Vineyard 2002 Cabernet Sauvignon (Dry Creek Valley) $19. This is DCV's first Cab made entirely of Dry Creek fruit. It's a big, dark, dry wine, rich in dusty tannins, with an astringent finish. Doesn't seem drinkable now, but such is the core of dark stone fruits, I suspect it has a great future. Hold beyond 2007. **91** —*S.H. (11/15/2005)*

Dry Creek Vineyard 2000 Cabernet Sauvignon (Sonoma County) $21. I have seldom tasted a Dry Creek Valley Cabernet (the appellation, not the winery) that didn't have a woolly edge to it. This wine is an excellent example. It's briary, with pushy tannins and the succulent flavor of wild blackberries. Oak adds a sheen of vanilla and smoke. **90 Editors' Choice** —*S.H. (11/15/2003)*

Dry Creek Vineyard 1999 Cabernet Sauvignon (Sonoma County) $21. The problem with Dry Creek Cabernets is also their strength. The grapes in this warm valley get dependably ripe, with brambly blackberry flavors. Oak, in whatever form, is a perfect complement. That said, Dry Creek Cabernets don't develop depth or complexity. They're beautiful on the surface but lack those nuances that make for great Cabernet. **87** —*S.H. (11/15/2002)*

Dry Creek Vineyard 2002 Endeavor Cabernet Sauvignon (Dry Creek Valley) $55. This is a huge Cabernet, very soft in the modern manner, and very ripe. It's a blast of cherry jam and milk chocolate, with plenty of toasty oak, and the tannins are firm and complex. Good now, it should hold well for the next ten years. **89** —*S.H. (12/15/2006)*

Dry Creek Vineyard 1999 Endeavour Cabernet Sauvignon (Dry Creek Valley) $55. They must have held this wine back for five years to let the tannins soften. They have, a little, but it's still a tough, hard-edged wine, with blackcurrant, herb and oak flavors. It's a gamble, but could do interesting things over the next ten years. **86** —*S.H. (3/1/2005)*

Dry Creek Vineyard 1998 Endeavour Cabernet Sauvignon (Dry Creek Valley) $50. A big, rich, viscous wine, with pure aromas of cedar and black currant followed by flavors of cassis, earth and tobacco. Tannic and chewy on the finish. A blend of 84% Cabernet Sauvignon and 16% Cabernet Franc. **91** *(12/31/2003)*

Dry Creek Vineyard 1997 Endeavour Cabernet Sauvignon (Dry Creek Valley) $50. A new label from Dry Creek Vineyard, a Cabernet Sauvignon-based wine released at five years of age. Opens with a blast of vanilla-scented smoky oak, with underlying fruity notes of currants, white chocolate, plum preserves and mint. It's still very tannic, its solid core of cherry-berry fruit suggests aging through 2007. **90** —*S.H. (12/31/2002)*

Dry Creek Vineyard 1997 Epoch II Millenium Cuvée Cabernet Sauvignon (Dry Creek Valley) $60. Opens with blackberries and spices; fruity, forward and polished. Dry, with good tannins and balance, but just can't break through a certain ceiling. **87** —*S.H. (2/1/2001)*

Dry Creek Vineyard 1999 Reserve Cabernet Sauvignon (Dry Creek Valley) $35. The flavors are classic Dry Creek Cabernet, ranging from blackberries to tobacco and herbs, with a finish that doesn't let up. The tannic structure suggests time in the cellar, although the wine is fine now with rich foods. **92 Editors' Choice** —*S.H. (10/1/2003)*

Dry Creek Vineyard 1998 Reserve Cabernet Sauvignon (Dry Creek Valley) $35. Defines what makes this appellation great for Cabernet, but also why it won't rival Napa anytime soon. Brilliantly ripe fruit, lovely balance, such a pretty taste of the earth and, in this case, expensive oak. But there's that extra something it aspires to and doesn't quite achieve. It has to do with complexity of tannins. 88 —*S.H.* (7/1/2002)

Dry Creek Vineyard 1997 Reserve Cabernet Sauvignon (Dry Creek Valley) $35. 89 (11/1/2000)

Dry Creek Vineyard 2004 Chardonnay (Russian River Valley) $18. I like the dryness and crispness of this food-friendly wine, but it's not the fruitiest Chard to come down the pike. It's an earthy wine, with herb flavors veering into peaches, and enough oaky-leesy creaminess to add interest. 85 —*S.H.* (7/1/2006)

Dry Creek Vineyard 2003 Chardonnay (Russian River Valley) $16. There's an earthy, herbal quality to the entry of this wine that make you wish it had more fruit. It's dry, oaky and soft, with moderate peach and spice flavors that show up midpalate. 84 —*S.H.* (12/1/2005)

Dry Creek Vineyard 2001 Chardonnay (Sonoma County) $16. Refreshing and on the oaky side, with wood sap, smoke and vanilla notes framing tart apple flavors. There's a spicy pepperiness through the short, dry finish. Good with roasted chicken. 85 —*S.H.* (12/15/2003)

Dry Creek Vineyard 2000 Chardonnay (Sonoma County) $16. Clearly well made, with ultraripe grapes whose sugar was pushed way up by California sunshine; shows crowd-pleasing oak and a creamy, tangerine sorbet flavor and texture. If anything, a bit too flamboyant and obvious. Can you fault a wine for being so made-up that it lacks subtlety? 86 —*S.H.* (12/15/2002)

Dry Creek Vineyard 1999 Chardonnay (Sonoma County) $16. Lees and oak dominate the nose of this very ripe wine. The result is size: A big, rich, oaky, fruity quaff, it fills the mouth with flavors and palate impressions. At the same time, it's a one-dimensional wine; it assaults the senses, but on one plane. Finishes semi-sweet. 85 —*S.H.* (5/1/2001)

Dry Creek Vineyard 1998 Barrel Fermented Chardonnay (Sonoma County) $16. 87 (6/1/2000)

Dry Creek Vineyard 2000 DCV4 Chardonnay (Dry Creek Valley) $22. On the lean side, with apple and citrus flavors typical of the appellation. Acidity is sharp and mouth-watering. This is not a big, fat Chardonnay but it is a well-structured, foodworthy wine, with oaky influences. This tight structure is very clean. 87 —*S.H.* (5/1/2003)

Dry Creek Vineyard 2000 Reserve Chardonnay (Russian River Valley) $22. Big, bold and rich from start to finish. They got the tropical fruit, pear and peach flavors ultraripe and then lavished it with what tastes like lots of new oak and lees. I kind of wish it was a little more elegant and balanced, though. 87 —*S.H.* (12/15/2003)

Dry Creek Vineyard 1999 Reserve Chardonnay (Dry Creek Valley) $22. A lush wine, with deliciously lip-smacking peach and tropical fruit flavors generously accented in oak. The texture has a buttery smoothness that leads to a rich finish. It's not a big blockbuster, but balanced and tasteful. 88 —*S.H.* (12/15/2002)

Dry Creek Vineyard 1998 Reserve Chardonnay (Dry Creek Valley) $22. 89 (6/1/2000)

Dry Creek Vineyard 2003 Saralee's Vineyard Chardonnay (Russian River Valley) $30. The entry on this single-vineyard Chard is strangely neutral. It's not until the middle palate that a blast of sweet, vanilla-y toasty oak hits, and also pear, mango and spice flavors. From then on, it's a satisfying wine, rich and elegant. 87 —*S.H.* (12/1/2005)

Dry Creek Vineyard 2002 Saralee's Vineyard Chardonnay (Russian River Valley) $25. Walks a tightrope. Starts with a tease of ripe pineapple and mango, and then the acids and alcohol take over, leaving an impression of tart leanness. You can't quite decide if it's a big wine, or just well balanced. The right food, such as sea bass seared in butter and served with a fruit salsa, will be perfect. 89 —*S.H.* (12/31/2004)

Dry Creek Vineyard 2005 Dry Chenin Blanc (Clarksburg) $11. Dry Creek Vineyard is one of the few remaining California wineries serious about Chenin Blanc. The wine is similar to a dry Sauvignon Blanc, citrusy and tart, but richer in the finish, with a flourish of apricot and sweet hazelnut. 86 Best Buy —*S.H.* (7/1/2006)

Dry Creek Vineyard 2004 Dry Chenin Blanc (Clarksburg) $10. You can count the number of wineries who specialize in Chenin Blanc on one hand. Dry Creek is one, and this is a giveaway price. The wine is dry, crisp in acids, with a minerally citrus profile that contains tantalizing hints of honey and wildflowers. Try as an alternative to Sauvignon Blanc. 87 Best Buy —*S.H.* (7/1/2005)

Dry Creek Vineyard 2003 Dry Chenin Blanc (Clarksburg) $9. Always a benchmark for bone-dry Chenins, this year's release is fragrant with peach, wildflower and vanilla, and a slightly sour flavor of lemondrop. It's so high in acidity, it practically tingles. 85 Best Buy —*S.H.* (10/1/2004)

Dry Creek Vineyard 2002 Dry Chenin Blanc (Clarksburg) $9. You have to give the winery credit for keeping this knocked-down varietal alive. It's always hard for me to decide if I like it or not. Nicely dry, with crisp acids and lots of fruity flavors of citrus, and a ton of peppery spice. But there's something low-down about Chenin Blanc, like it comes from the bad side of town. 85 —*S.H.* (12/15/2003)

Dry Creek Vineyard 2001 Dry Chenin Blanc (Clarksburg) $9. This may be a simple country wine, but it's got a lot of personality. Bright, forward fruity flavors are accompanied by good acidity, and the wine is indeed dry. The theme is citrus and apple. Try as an alternative to Sauvignon Blanc. 85 —*S.H.* (9/1/2003)

Dry Creek Vineyard 1998 Dry Chenin Blanc (Clarksburg) $9. 82 —*L.W.* (11/1/1999)

Dry Creek Vineyard 2004 Fumé Blanc (Sonoma County) $13. This winery understands Sauvignon Blanc in their bones, and here's another good bottling. It's very crisp, with powerfully clean, vibrant lemon and lime flavors that finish a little sweet in ripe, fruity essence. 86 —*S.H.* (4/1/2006)

Dry Creek Vineyard 2003 Fumé Blanc (Sonoma County) $13. Crisp and clean, this wine refreshes with its bright citrus and fig flavors and acidity. It has a good body and a touch of cream. 85 —*S.H.* (5/1/2005)

Dry Creek Vineyard 2003 Fumé Blanc (Sonoma County) $13. A good job from Sauvignon specialist Dry Creek, although one wishes it were a little drier. Still, the citrus, fig, melon and oak flavors are tasty, and firmed up with crisp acidity. 84 —*S.H.* (10/1/2005)

Dry Creek Vineyard 2002 Fumé Blanc (Sonoma County) $13. This winery's Fumés are always as dry and grassy as the gold hills themselves. Offers citrus, straw and wheaty flavors. Oak adds richer notes of cream and vanilla, but underneath it's a tart, racy wine, bristling with acid. 86 —*S.H.* (12/15/2003)

Dry Creek Vineyard 2001 Fumé Blanc (Green Valley) $13. 89 Best Buy —*S.H.* (11/15/2002)

Dry Creek Vineyard 1999 Fumé Blanc (Sonoma County) $12. 84 —*S.H.* (11/15/2000)

Dry Creek Vineyard 2003 DCV3 Fumé Blanc (Dry Creek Valley) $25. Ripe and creamy, with fleshy peach and melon aromas brought to attention by notes of jalapeño and grass. Like the nose, the palate deals mostly ripe melon and peach flavors with touches of grass, white pepper and greens. Bulky and full. 87 (7/1/2005)

Dry Creek Vineyard 2002 DCV3 Fumé Blanc (Dry Creek Valley) $18. DCV3 is the totally unromantic vineyard name. Only fruit from Stare's original Sauvignon Blanc plantings go into this wine, which sees no oak at all, yet does show a hint of smokiness on the nose. Melon and passion fruit aromas and flavors are lean and light, finishing crisp and clean. 86 (12/31/2003)

Dry Creek Vineyard 2001 DCV3 Fumé Blanc (Dry Creek Valley) $18. A sharp, smart wine, elegantly put together. Flavors are lemons and herbs, which are balanced by crisp acids and smooth tannins. Does just what you want a dry, tart white to do: wake up the palate with clean, fresh flavors. 90 —*S.H.* (3/1/2003)

Dry Creek Vineyard 2004 DCV3 Estate Fumé Blanc (Dry Creek Valley) $25. Seems hollow and watery, especially compared to recent vintages. The '01 scored 90 points. Is this because of the intense heat of the vintage? Whatever, the wine is citrusy and spicy, but you wish it was more intense. 84 —*S.H.* (12/15/2006)

Dry Creek Vineyard 1998 Limited Edition -DCV3 Fumé Blanc (Dry Creek Valley) $16. 90 (2/1/2000)

Dry Creek Vineyard 2000 Limited Edition DCVIII Fumé Blanc (Dry Creek Valley) $18. Wheat grass and hot peppers make for an intriguing if odd bouquet. A fair amount of vegetal flavor carries onto the palate—mostly green beans and some pickle. Fortunately, there is also a light tropical fruit background to the flavor profile, something reminiscent of papaya. Ultimately, however, this wine is characterized more by its vegetal character than bright, clean fruit. **86** (8/1/2002)

Dry Creek Vineyard 2001 Reserve Fumé Blanc (Dry Creek Valley) $18. Thick and custardy in texture, thanks to barrel aging and lees contact that have imparted a soft plumpness to the wine. Starting with ripe fruit doesn't hurt either, adding figs and melons to the mix, while 6% Viognier adds an intriguing floral note to the aromatics. **88** (12/31/2003)

Dry Creek Vineyard 2000 Reserve Fumé Blanc (Dry Creek Valley) $18. The fruity flavors are of lemons and limes, but there's a lot of French oak and lees on top of this barrel-fermented wine. It drinks full-bodied and rich, with a creamy mouthfeel. Very elegant, almost thick through the finish. **86** —S.H. (3/1/2003)

Dry Creek Vineyard 1999 Reserve Fumé Blanc (Dry Creek Valley) $18. The nose of smoke and sweet creamed corn doesn't exactly reel you in. Then a vegetal palate featuring mostly green beans and toasty oak is way off the mark, given the variety we're talking about. The finish is heavy, mouth coating and mildly bitter. **82** (8/1/2002)

Dry Creek Vineyard 1998 Reserve Fumé Blanc (Dry Creek Valley) $18. 88 —S.H. (11/15/2000)

Dry Creek Vineyard 1997 Reserve Fumé Blanc (Dry Creek Valley) $16. 90 —L.W. (2/1/2000)

Dry Creek Vineyard 2000 Meritage (Dry Creek Valley) $26. Approximately 70% Merlot, and the flavors follow suit: black cherries, plums and hints of dried herbs, picking up notes of coffee and chocolate. It's supple and easy to drink, finishing with some soft tannins. **89** (12/31/2003)

Dry Creek Vineyard 1999 Meritage (Sonoma County) $28. There's something quintessentially Dry Creek Valley in this wine, with its lean earthiness and sweet, rich tannins. You'll never get opulent Cabs from this appellation. They veer in the direction of tobacco and sage despite considerable oak. But the wine is layered and very well constructed. **90** —S.H. (11/15/2002)

Dry Creek Vineyard 1997 Merlot (Sonoma County) $20. 85 (3/1/1999)

Dry Creek Vineyard 2003 Merlot (Dry Creek Valley) $18. It's not clear that Dry Creek Valley is the ideal home for Merlot. This winery's bottlings have been good but earthy, tannic and dry in the past. This one represents a step foward. There's something elegant about it, and the cherry and mocha-tinged flavors certainly are pleasurable. Drink now. **88** —S.H. (7/1/2006)

Dry Creek Vineyard 2002 Merlot (Sonoma County) $19. Showing the balance and elegance this winery is known for, this Merlot is earthy, with coffee, herb, blackberry and cherry flavors that finish in a swirl of dry, rather sticky tannins. It's not an ager, but will be fine now with richly marbled meats and hard cheeses. **87** —S.H. (12/15/2005)

Dry Creek Vineyard 1999 Merlot (Sonoma County) $19. This is an example of wonderful winemaking on fruit that's been spread too thin. It has splendid tannins, wonderfully supportive acidity and a fine overlay of spicy, toasty oak, but the fruit has been diluted, possibly due to over-cropping. The blackberry flavors are thin and watered down. **84** —S.H. (12/31/2002)

Dry Creek Vineyard 1998 Merlot (Sonoma County) $21. Aromas of sun-dried tomatoes, coffee, cinnamon, toast, blackberries and currants introduce a wine that drinks light and fruity. Some pretty flavors here, with lots of spice and soft tannins. Nothing to write home about, but nice enough for a dry red table wine. **85** —S.H. (2/1/2001)

Dry Creek Vineyard 1999 Reserve Merlot (Dry Creek Valley) $30. This lovely wine is big and bold, but like an operatic tenor, it possesses elegance and grace. Black currants, coffee, bitter chocolate, violets, French olives and dried herbs are a few of the flavors that mingle in the mouth, framed in ripe tannins. **91** —S.H. (2/1/2004)

Dry Creek Vineyard 1998 Reserve Cuvée Merlot (Dry Creek Valley) $35. A Merlot that aims for the fences and manages a single. The fruit just can't

get it up. Herbaceous, even vegetal notes are tarted up by oak, but even after nearly four years of age, the wine maintains its lean, hard, acidic edge. **84** — (11/15/2002)

Dry Creek Vineyard 2000 Limited Bottling Petite Sirah (Dry Creek Valley) $21. Nice balance here between black fruit (plum, berry) and tobacco and herb flavors. Gritty Dry Creek tannins are very dry, and acidity is good. Feels good in the mouth, if a bit rustic, and the finish is a bit astringent. Looks to be an ager. **86** (4/1/2003)

Dry Creek Vineyard 1999 Pinot Noir (California) $20. Kind of big for a Pinot, almost the size of a lighter Zinfandel. Of course, it's enormously fruity, with raspberries and powdered spices, earthy nuances and herbal and tomato notes. The tannins are mild and the acids low, which makes things soft. It's pleasant drinking, if not especially varietal. **86** —S.H. (5/1/2001)

Dry Creek Vineyard 1997 Pinot Noir (Sonoma Valley) $24. 90 (10/1/1999)

Dry Creek Vineyard 2003 Soleil Late Harvest Sauvignon Blanc (Sonoma County) $25. Very sweet, with powerful apricot, tangerine, pineapple and creme brulee flavors and good acidity to balance out the sugar. Vanilla ice cream would be a good match. **87** —S.H. (5/1/2006)

Dry Creek Vineyard 2000 Soleil—Limited Edition Sauvignon Blanc (Sonoma County) $20. Peachy Canyon NV Mustang Springs Ranch Port (Paso Robles); $40. What you need in a Port-style wine is sugary, caramelized sweetness, the deep, strong taste of fruit, high alcohol and crisp acidity. This wine has them all. But it lacks that extra depth and complexity that a Port wants, especially at this price. Still, a solid effort. **86** —S.H. (9/1/2002)

Dry Creek Vineyard 2004 Taylor's Vineyard Musqué Sauvignon Blanc (Dry Creek Valley) $25. Tasted alongside the winery's DCV3 bottling, this one's considerably more focused in fruit, altogether a more interesting wine. It's also much higher in alcohol. The wine shows polished Meyer lemon, sweet green grass and vanilla flavors, and although it has no oak, it tastes like it does. **88** —S.H. (12/15/2006)

Dry Creek Vineyard 2003 Taylor's Vineyard Musqué Sauvignon Blanc (Dry Creek Valley) $25. A bit smoky and spicy. The bouquet offers soft citrus and stone-fruit aromas, while the palate is on the weighty side, without much acid. Flavors of smoky peach and ballpark franks are not exactly commonplace, but they're fine. Finishes with hints of white pepper. **86** (7/1/2005)

Dry Creek Vineyard 1998 Vintner's Selection Syrah (Dry Creek Valley) $25. There's good deep fruit and licorice and smoke accents in this wine, but they are overrun by rampant oak that shows early and continues full-blown across the palate and onto the finish. There's weight, but not the depth or dimension we wanted. Tart raspberry flavors and smoked-meat accents strive to hold their own against the toasty oak tide through the long close. **86** (11/1/2001)

Dry Creek Vineyard 2003 Beeson Ranch Zinfandel (Dry Creek Valley) $30. Here's a well-behaved young Zin, dry and fruity, with firm tannins and acids that will cut through barbecue. The cherry, blackberry, cola and peppery pomegranate flavors will play beautifully against a rich, savory barbecue sauce. **89** —S.H. (12/15/2006)

Dry Creek Vineyard 2002 Beeson Ranch Zinfandel (Dry Creek Valley) $30. This is a Cab-like Zin. It has a nice balance, lush but easy tannins, good acidity and instant credibility, but never loses Zin's woolly, wild, feral quality. Demands rich fare, like beef short ribs. **89** —S.H. (10/1/2005)

Dry Creek Vineyard 2001 Beeson Ranch Zinfandel (Dry Creek Valley) $30. The Beeson Ranch vines, from the western side of Dry Creek, are 100 or more years old. The flavors are very different from the Somers Ranch Zin, instead offering mint and fresh strawberries layered over a base of chocolate. Quite firm on the finish, this could also be held up to five years. **89** (12/31/2003)

Dry Creek Vineyard 2003 Heritage Zinfandel (Sonoma County) $15. Dry Creek Vineyard knows Zin, and it shows in this dry, balanced and attractive wine. It has Zin's briary, brambly berry richness, with smooth tannins and a complex mouthfeel. As good as it is, it would be even better with greater intensity of fruit. **87** —S.H. (12/31/2005)

Dry Creek Vineyard 2001 Heritage Clone Zinfandel (Sonoma County) $15. A well-made wine that features plush, supple tannins and a classy blend of plum, coffee, chocolate, toast and spice flavors. The finish is smooth and long. Terrific value. **88** *(11/1/2003)*

Dry Creek Vineyard 2000 Heritage Clone Zinfandel (Sonoma County) $15. Pretty much as classic as Sonoma Zin gets, with ripe, fruity wild berry flavors and a peppery taste in the mouth. Bone-dry with fine, rustic tannins, it's distinctive and individualistic, and not too alcoholic. **86** —*S.H. (11/1/2002)*

Dry Creek Vineyard 1999 Heritage Clone Zinfandel (Sonoma County) $15. More forward and jammy than Dry Creek's reserve bottling, this fruity wine also has some pretty firm tannins and crisp acidity. Doesn't seem to be age worthy, so drink now or in the next year. **86** —*S.H. (11/15/2001)*

Dry Creek Vineyard 1998 Heritage Clone Zinfandel (Sonoma County) $15. **85** —*S.H. (12/1/2000)*

Dry Creek Vineyard 1997 Heritage Clone Zinfandel (Sonoma County) $15. **90** —*P.G. (11/15/1999)*

Dry Creek Vineyard 2003 Late Harvest Zinfandel (Dry Creek Valley) $30. Harsh in texture, this Port-style wine has strong flavors of mocha and sweet blackberry and cherry marmalade. As attractively sweet as it is, there's a sharp roughness that detracts. **83** —*S.H. (5/1/2006)*

Dry Creek Vineyard 1999 Limited Edition Late Harvest Zinfandel (Dry Creek Valley) $NA. Smells hot and sugary and plummy, like an overheated saute of fruit jam. The flavors are of sweet berries and alcohol. Unbalanced despite the richness, it combines hot, awkward flavors with richer, softer ones. **83** —*S.H. (9/12/2002)*

Dry Creek Vineyard 2003 Old Vine Zinfandel (Sonoma County) $25. The primary source of this Zin is from Dry Creek Valley. It's rare to find this quality and quantity of upfront fruit in a Zin that's so balanced, but here it is. Massive raspberry, cherry, blackberry, mocha and Asian spice flavors, with buttery, smoky oak notes. Just delicious. Drink now. **93** **Editors' Choice** —*S.H. (11/15/2006)*

Dry Creek Vineyard 2002 Old Vine Zinfandel (Sonoma County) $25. From century-old vines, mainly in Dry Creek Valley, this is a big Zin, jam-packed with purple- and black-skinned stone fruits and berries. The wine is certainly tannic now, and extremely dry. It will be okay now with rich meats and cheeses, but probably better by 2006. **90** —*S.H. (11/15/2005)*

Dry Creek Vineyard 2001 Old Vines Zinfandel (Sonoma County) $21. Toast, vanilla and spice kick off here, followed by pretty cherry, plum, blackberry and herb flavors. Tannins are smooth and the finish offers a smoky rich edge. **88** *(11/1/2003)*

Dry Creek Vineyard 2000 Old Vines Zinfandel (Sonoma County) $21. Dark purple-black in color, this is a young wine brimming with jammy blackberry, espresso, dark chocolate and pepper aromas and flavors. Big in the mouth, filled with juicy acids and fine tannins, although it's dry. **87** —*S.H. (2/1/2003)*

Dry Creek Vineyard 1999 Old Vines Zinfandel (Sonoma County) $21. This is the Zin to show those European visitors who don't understand the varietal. It has the lush texture and depth of a fine wine, with sumptuous tannins, but with that roguish quality that characterizes California's own grape. If a serious wine can be fun and not take itself too seriously, this it it. **91** —*S.H. (3/1/2002)*

Dry Creek Vineyard 1998 Old Vines Zinfandel (Sonoma County) $19. **86** —*S.H. (12/1/2000)*

Dry Creek Vineyard 1997 Old Vines Zinfandel (Sonoma County) $18. **88** —*J.C. (5/1/2000)*

Dry Creek Vineyard 1999 Reserve Zinfandel (Dry Creek Valley) $30. Here's a Zin that makes you think. What is Zin? Does it have an upper price limit? This wine is very dry and ripe, although the fruity, berry flavors are deeply buried under the tannins. It's as velvety smooth as a cult Cabernet, without offering the immediate pleasure and depth. Will it age? This is new style Zin at its best, an experiment in the making. **90** —*S.H. (3/1/2004)*

Dry Creek Vineyard 1998 Reserve Zinfandel (Dry Creek Valley) $30. Gentle but firm, pliant but powerful, this dry, spicy Zin combines opposites. Briary fruit is packed under fairly substantial tannins, but there's enough

there for mid-term aging. Otherwise drink it with substantial foods like barbecued chicken. **90** —*S.H. (12/15/2001)*

Dry Creek Vineyard 1997 Reserve Zinfandel (Dry Creek Valley) $30. Lovely, sweet plummy fruit, leads into a soft, rich, mouth-pleasing wine. Beautiful bouquet, tons of flavor in an elegant style. Leafy, old-viney finish. **90** —*P.G. (3/1/2001)*

Dry Creek Vineyard 2003 Somers Ranch Zinfandel (Dry Creek Valley) $30. Tastes a bit rough and ready, with a Porty edge, although the wine is dry and the official numbers record only moderate alcohol. There's also high acidity that seems out of place for such a ripe wine. **83** —*S.H. (12/15/2006)*

Dry Creek Vineyard 2002 Somers Ranch Zinfandel (Dry Creek Valley) $30. Here's a dark, dry, brooding wine, with plenty of tannins, but it's soft enough to open now. The flavors veer toward coffee, milk chocolate and blackberries. Has good balance and a nice grip to offset a steak. **86** —*S.H. (10/1/2005)*

Dry Creek Vineyard 2001 Somers Ranch Zinfandel (Dry Creek Valley) $30. Both single-vineyard Zins are more tannic and less immediately accessible than Dry Creek Vineyard's other Zins. The Somers Ranch vines are only 20 years old, but in 2001, they've yielded intense aromas of licorice, plum, chocolate and black pepper backed by similarly sturdy flavors. Drink now, or hold up to five years. **90** *(12/31/2003)*

DRYTOWN

Drytown 2002 Zinfandel (Sierra Foothills) $15. Nice and dry, fairly tannic and a bit austere in flavor, with coffee and cherry fruit. Finishes a little hot and astringent, but should soften and sweeten up with grilled meats. **85** —*S.H. (3/1/2005)*

DUCK POND

Duck Pond 1997 Cabernet Franc (Columbia Valley (WA)) $95. From a single vineyard in a warm part of the valley, a massive wine. It's hard to put into words how fruity it is without using the word "bomb," but that's not a pejorative in this case. It's huge, but balanced, dry, harmonious, dramatic and very oaky. Drink it now with full-flavored foods. **90** —*S.H. (12/31/2003)*

Duck Pond 1997 Cabernet Sauvignon (Columbia Valley (WA)) $12. **85** —*P.G. (6/1/2000)*

Duck Pond 2002 Cabernet Sauvignon (Columbia Valley (WA)) $12. There's a deadness in the mouth; the main impression, rather than the fruit you would hope to find in an inexpensive Cabernet, is of rubber, tar and some alcoholic heat. **83** —*P.G. (6/1/2006)*

Duck Pond 2000 Cabernet Sauvignon (Columbia Valley (OR)) $12. The Wahluke slope, where these grapes are grown, is an up-and-coming growing region in Washington state. But this hard, tough, tannic, green wine reveals few of the reasons why. It's Cabernet the way Washington vintners made it 20 years ago. **83** —*P.G. (12/1/2003)*

Duck Pond 2004 Chardonnay (Columbia Valley (WA)) $10. Flat, disjointed and aggressively oaky flavors all but cover up the hints of tropical/pineapple fruit. There's an undertone of gummy plastic through the finish. **83** —*P.G. (6/1/2006)*

Duck Pond 2000 Chardonnay (Willamette Valley) $8. You get plenty of power for the price in this very ripe, fruity wine. It's filled with apple and peach flavors and finishes sweet and spicy, with a rich, honeyed texture. Nice acids offset the richness. **86** —*S.H. (12/31/2002)*

Duck Pond 1998 Chardonnay (Oregon) $10. **87 Best Buy** —*S.H. (9/1/2000)*

Duck Pond 1999 Fries' Desert Wind Vineyard/Wahluke Chardonnay (Columbia Valley (WA)) $9. At first this seems like a simple, pleasant effort, but it comes apart in the finish. As the wine hits the back of the palate it gathers sweetness, and an artificial, brown sugar flavor—along with a flat, disjointed mouthfeel—linger. **81** —*P.G. (2/1/2002)*

Duck Pond 1997 Merlot (Columbia Valley (WA)) $12. **82** —*P.G. (6/1/2000)*

Duck Pond 1998 Fries' Desert Wind Vineyard Merlot (Columbia Valley (WA)) $11. Though it's an Oregon winery, the vineyard is in Washington's Columbia Valley. It's value-priced and soundly made, with ripe cherries leading off a chocolate and coffee nose. Dry, chalky tannins complete the picture, with plenty of spice and wood flavors behind soft cherry fruit. **87 Best Buy** —*P.G. (6/1/2001)*

Duck Pond 1997 Pinot Grigio (Oregon) $9. 85 *(8/1/1999)*

Duck Pond 2005 Pinot Gris (Willamette Valley) $12. Light and lemony, this graceful wine shows an elegant, northern Italian personality rather than the meaty, fleshy style more often found in Oregon Pinot Gris. Pear drop scents and fresh pear flavors dominate the entry, and at this price deliver plenty of clean flavor. Mostly estate-grown fruit, with an average yield of just over two tons per acre, the wine's moderate alcohol levels and firm acids make it a perfect match for shellfish, pasta in cream sauce and herb-infused poultry. 16,000 cases available. **87 Best Buy** —*P.G. (11/15/2006)*

Duck Pond 2003 Pinot Gris (Oregon) $12. Pale, salmon-colored and scented with spicy rhubarb and cut pears, this is a thin, tart, simple wine with a lemon-water finish. Not much going on here. **82** —*P.G. (10/1/2004)*

Duck Pond 2002 Pinot Gris (Oregon) $12. This has a sharp, grassy edge to it, much like Sauvignon Blanc. The flavors are tart, tangy and tight, with a bite to the finish. **86** —*P.G. (12/1/2003)*

Duck Pond 2000 Pinot Gris (Willamette Valley) $9. Duck Pond produces inexpensive wines that are generally estate grown. This is a simple, tart Pinot Gris, with a sugary nose, and it falls a bit flat in the mouth. Though the wine is made quite dry, there is an impression of sweetness in the finish. **82** —*P.G. (2/1/2002)*

Duck Pond 2003 Pinot Noir (Oregon) $12. Earthy scents of wet stem and soil lead into light flavors of rhubarb and wild strawberry. Very light and simple. **83** —*P.G. (10/1/2004)*

Duck Pond 2002 Pinot Noir (Willamette Valley) $9. Inexpensive Oregon Pinot is a rare commodity, and this delivers the flavor goods. Cherries and toast are the main components, with some pretty tough tannins on the back end. **86 Best Buy** —*P.G. (12/1/2003)*

Duck Pond 1998 Pinot Noir (Willamette Valley) $9. 83 —*J.C. (12/1/2000)*

Duck Pond 1997 Syrah (Columbia Valley (WA)) $15. 82 —*P.G. (9/1/2000)*

Duck Pond 2003 Syrah (Columbia Valley (WA)) $12. This begins to show varietal scents of spice, pepper and citrus, but once in the mouth it turns thick, charred, flat and burnt. The fruit tries to fight its way through, but there's a hole in the mid-palate and it leaves a bitter finish. **83** —*P.G. (6/1/2006)*

Duck Pond 2002 Syrah (Columbia Valley (WA)) $12. Great color, dense purple/garnet, and thick scents of blackberries tell you this is a heckuva good $12 wine. Hits the palate with a solid grip, the dense blackberry fruit perked up with white pepper and toast, and finishes big and smoky, with tarry tannins. **88 Best Buy** —*P.G. (11/15/2004)*

Duck Pond 2001 Syrah (Columbia Valley (WA)) $35. Thin, hard and tannic, with green tannins and flavors of light ground coffee. The tannins, earthiness and rough, stemmy finish obscure the fruit or any varietal character. **82** —*P.G. (9/1/2004)*

Duck Pond 2002 Desert Wind Vineyard Syrah (Columbia Valley (WA)) $35. Thin, hard, stemmy and dilute; an odd showing for the estate vineyard fruit and a wine priced at triple the cost of the regular syrah. Green, harsh tannins and a rubbery, acidic impression in the mouth. **81** —*P.G. (6/1/2006)*

Duck Pond 1999 Fries' Desert Wind Vineyard Syrah (Columbia Valley (WA)) $35. Grape, blueberry and blackberry aromas, wrapped in a creamy-butter coating, waft from the bouquet. The palate shows less fruity flavors—instead, it's chock-full of charcoal, smoke and wood flavors, with some dark berry fruit buried underneath. Full but a little tangy in the mouth, it finishes tannic, with stem and lemon flavors. **85** *(11/1/2001)*

Duck Pond 1998 Wahluke Slope Frei's Desert Wi Syrah (Columbia Valley (WA)) $22. 84 —*P.G. (9/1/2000)*

DUCK WALK

Duck Walk 1997 Cabernet Sauvignon (North Fork of Long Island) $19. The leafy cassis and dried spice notes on the nose create a distinctive bouquet that is immediately attractive. Not heavily extracted, this is a Cab built for current consumption. **85** —*J.C. (4/1/2001)*

Duck Walk 1997 Reserve Cabernet Sauvignon (North Fork of Long Island) $29. Weedy, with some bell pepper and herb aromas, cassis and tobacco. Elegantly lean and graceful in the mouth, the wine ends in a long, spicy finish. You might rate it even higher if you don't mind some herbaceousness. **87** —*J.C. (4/1/2001)*

Duck Walk 1997 Reserve Chardonnay (Long Island) $13. Smoky and meaty, with nut, white-peach and clove notes. Firm acidity allowed 100% barrel fermentation without the wine becoming overly soft. **87 Best Buy** —*J.C. (4/1/2001)*

Duck Walk 1998 Aphrodite Late Harvest Gewürztraminer (North Fork of Long Island) $15. Shows good varietal character in its bouquet of roses, ripe pears and lychees. As far as dessert wines go, this is a lightweight, at only 6% residual sugar, but it's certainly flavorful enough. Low acidity suggests it should be drunk over the short term. The only quibble is a shorter than expected finish. **86** —*J.C. (4/1/2001)*

Duck Walk 1997 Reserve Merlot (North Fork of Long Island) $19. Slightly creamy vanilla-oak scents vie with jammy black cherries on the nose. Cherries predominate on the medium-weight palate. Turns a bit drying on the finish, so drink with a rare steak for best results. **86** —*J.C. (4/1/2001)*

Duck Walk 1998 Pinot Grigio (The Hamptons, Long Island) $15. Something of a misnomer, as this wine tastes more like many Alsatian Pinot Gris than the often-insipid Grigios of Italy. Honey and apricot aromas, big and buttery on the palate; the only drawback is the lack of length to the finish, possibly a function of young vines. **87** —*J.C. (4/1/2001)*

Duck Walk 1997 Pinot Meunier (The Hamptons, Long Island) $9. Bright, tart candied cherry aromas are dusted with saddle leather and cinnamon. Light-bodied; gets tarter on the finish, where the fruit becomes more cranberryish. **87 Best Buy** —*J.C. (4/1/2001)*

DUCKHORN

Duckhorn 2003 Cabernet Sauvignon (Napa Valley) $60. The tannins star here. They're Tony Soprano to everyone else's supporting role, including the delicious cherry and blackberry flavors and sumptuous oak. It's all very good, but "voluptuous" is not a word to describe this wine. Drink over the next three years. **87** —*S.H. (9/1/2006)*

Duckhorn 2002 Cabernet Sauvignon (Napa Valley) $60. This wine is markedly sweet in blackberry, cherry and chocolate flavors, an impression heightened by sweet oak. The tannins and acids that counterbalance palate sweetness are notably absent. The result is an international-style wine, soft and sweet, that fails to inspire. **84** —*S.H. (12/1/2005)*

Duckhorn 2000 Cabernet Sauvignon (Napa Valley) $55. Polished and supple, with good currant and cherry flavors backed up by smooth tannins. A very nice Cabernet, although not in the same league as Duckhorn's single-vineyard or estate Cabs. **87** —*S.H. (8/1/2004)*

Duckhorn 1999 Est Grown Cabernet Sauvignon (Napa Valley) $80. Loaded with pretty fruit flavors of cassis, plum and jammy berries, with an earthy, olive-y note and plenty of spicy, charred oak. Layered and complex, with gritty tannins and a rich, slightly hot finish. This Cab is distinctly Napa Valley. **91** —*S.H. (11/15/2002)*

Duckhorn 2001 Estate Cabernet Sauvignon (Napa Valley) $85. The most immediately drinkable of Duckhorn's '01s. It's soft and juicy, with smooth tannins and accessible flavors of cassis-infused cocoa and spices, with good lift from acidity. Dramatic now, and should age well through 2010. **92** —*S.H. (5/1/2005)*

Duckhorn 2002 Estate Grown Cabernet Sauvignon (Napa Valley) $90. I have criticized past Duckhorn top-tier Cabs for excessively tough tannins, and this wine continues in that tradition. The supposition is ageability, but the wines are not pleasant on release. The mid-palate fruit is huge, and the wine may well do interesting things after 2010. **89** —*S.H. (2/1/2006)*

Duckhorn 2000 Estate Grown Cabernet Sauvignon (Napa Valley) $80. Stunningly rich and attractive, just oozing with decadent flavors of cassis, chocolate and spiced plum. Creamy, smooth and long on the palate, with spicy, oaky shadings. Supersoft tannins lead to a long, sweet finish. **90** —*S.H. (8/1/2004)*

USA

Duckhorn 1998 Estate Grown Cabernet Sauvignon (Napa Valley) $80. . It's "a wine that screams California," noted one reviewer, meaning that the Golden State's textbook caramel-jammy blackberry-toast profile is in full effect here. Medium-full in the mouth, with a little heat. It closes with bitter coffee and a little char. Would have been excellent if it had a little more richness. **89** *(6/1/2002)*

Duckhorn 2002 Monitor Ledge Vineyard Cabernet Sauvignon (Napa Valley) $95. Marching to their own beat, Duckhorn's winemakers continue to plow the firmly tannic line, as opposed to the soft, lush modern style. This is a sound decision, but the question is, where is the line? This wine is too tough to enjoy now. **90** —*S.H. (2/1/2006)*

Duckhorn 2001 Monitor Ledge Vineyard Cabernet Sauvignon (Napa Valley) $90. All of Duckhorn's '01 Cabs share much in common. This one's rich and firm in ripe, sweet tannins that are finely ground, and carry intense black currant, cherry, vanilla and toast flavors. It's a powerful wine, but very beautiful. Fully drinkable now, and should hold through 2010. **93** —*S.H. (5/1/2005)*

Duckhorn 2000 Monitor Ledge Vineyard Cabernet Sauvignon (Napa Valley) $90. Rich, nervy and intense yet generous. Slowly unfolds well-oaked flavors of blackberries, cassis and chocolate across the palate. There's also a minerality that adds tang and firmness. Gorgeous extract, amazingly long finish, with near-perfect balance and harmony. **92** —*S.H. (8/1/2004)*

Duckhorn 1999 Monitor Ledge Vineyard Est Grown Cabernet Sauvignon (Napa Valley) $90. Sweetly strong aromas feature anisette toast, dark chocolate, sweet red plums, earth and meat. In the mouth, smooth black fruit, milk chocolate, vanilla and dusty smokiness meld with a soft kiss of full, creamy-soft tannins. **91** *(2/1/2003)*

Duckhorn 2001 Patzimaro Vineyard Cabernet Sauvignon (Napa Valley) $90. Similar to the Stout bottling, a rather dry, tannic wine, filled with dark stone fruit flavors. Grips the palate with dusty astringency now, but aging should soften and release the underlying sweetness and fruit. Nice overall balance and concentration. Hold beyond 2010. **92** —*S.H. (5/1/2005)*

Duckhorn 2000 Patzimaro Vineyard Cabernet Sauvignon (St. Helena) $90. A great wine. It's a bit more herbaceous than Duckhorn's Monitor Ledge, but it still has a rich core of cassis fruit that seems almost dessert-sweet, although the wine is dry. Limpid, elegant and beautifully structured, this complex wine will age for at least a decade. **91** —*S.H. (8/1/2004)*

Duckhorn 1999 Patzimaro Vineyard Est Grown St. Helena Cabernet Sauvignon (Napa Valley) $90. Black currants and cherries on the nose are complemented by sooty char. Black fruit, ash and toast flavors highlight sweet blueberry and anise notes. Fine, dusty tannins add structure. **90** *(2/1/2003)*

Duckhorn 2001 Stout Vineyard Cabernet Sauvignon (Napa Valley) $90. More tannic than Duckhorn's Monitor Ledge, with more darkly skinned fruit flavors and chocolate. Perfectly balanced in flamboyant new oak and acids, rich and supple, long in the finish. Should hold and improve beyond 2010. **92** —*S.H. (5/1/2005)*

Duckhorn 1997 Merlot (Napa Valley) $36. **90** *(3/1/2000)*

Duckhorn 1995 Merlot (Howell Mountain) $42. **92** *(3/1/2000)*

Duckhorn 2003 Merlot (Napa Valley) $50. Here's a wonderfully rich, rewarding Merlot. It's as soft and creamy as melted chocolate mixed with blackcurrant jam and a sprinkle of creme de cassis, with a rich sprinkling of oaky vanilla, but fortunately, it has the acidic backbone needed for structure. This is a sexy wine. **92** —*S.H. (2/1/2006)*

Duckhorn 2002 Merlot (Howell Mountain) $70. There are tannins here, but they're so soft, polished and sweet that they help the wine glide down, adding a textural dimension to the cherry, blackberry essence, cola, coffee and oaky vanilla flavors. It's an expensive wine, but a really fancy one. **92** —*S.H. (12/1/2006)*

Duckhorn 2001 Merlot (Howell Mountain) $70. Wow, what a wine. Tremendous, focused and intense. This Merlot is massive in cassis and black currant flavors, and very well-oaked. Most notable are the tannins. They're powerful and insistent, yet so smooth, so finely knit that they're totally drinkable now, although you may want to give the wine until 2006 to settle down. **93 Editors' Choice** —*S.H. (12/1/2005)*

Duckhorn 2001 Merlot (Napa Valley) $48. Blackberry, white chocolate, flowery violets, toast, licorice and vanilla are just some of the notes that tickle the palate in this complex, oaky wine. For all of its mass, it never loses a sense of harmony and balance. Richly tannic now, and smooth as velvet. **92** —*S.H. (8/1/2004)*

Duckhorn 2000 Merlot (Napa Valley) $46. This wine starts off with dark, funky earth scents that blend well with coffee and medicinal notes. The palate is full of rich, red fruit, accented by arugala and dark chocolate. Overall, a hint lean with cherry and cinnamon lingering on the long finish. **90** —*K.F. (4/1/2003)*

Duckhorn 2002 25th Harvest Merlot (Napa Valley) $48. This is a Merlot for the cellar. Rich, dramatic and creamy, it throws a thick carpet of tannins across the palate that spread the ripest cherries and blackberries, assisted by scads of toasty oak. Fully dry, perfectly balanced, sensual and satisfying, it should improve for at least five years. **94 Cellar Selection** —*S.H. (5/1/2005)*

Duckhorn 2001 Estate Merlot (Napa Valley) $82. Graceful, delicious, complex and drinkable. Super-oaky, with vanilla, toast and wood spice, but the massive cherry and blackberry fruit easily absorbs it. The tannins are rich and ripe, forming a dusty coating that carries sweetness through the finish. Beautiful, extraordinary Napa Merlot. **94** —*S.H. (8/1/2004)*

Duckhorn 1996 Estate Merlot (Napa Valley) $53. **93** *(3/1/2000)*

Duckhorn 2003 Estate Grown Merlot (Napa Valley) $85. Pretty tannic for a Merlot. It's a dusty, super-dry, tight young wine with a fair amount of astringency. But the fruit is something else. The huge cherry pie and toasty, vanilla oak flavors are just delicious. Hard to tell if it will soften before the fruit drops out, though. **87** —*S.H. (12/1/2006)*

Duckhorn 2002 Estate Grown Merlot (Napa Valley) $85. Hits the palate with obvious fruit, sweet in blackberries, espresso and blueberries, with a melted milk chocolate note. The impression of sweetness dominates, despite the firm tannins. Note to winemaker: Rachet that sweetness down next year. Doesn't matter what the lab readings are, the wine tastes sugary. **84** —*S.H. (3/1/2006)*

Duckhorn 2000 Estate Grown Merlot (Napa Valley) $80. Concentrated and muscular, showing more structure than many Cabernets from this challenging vintage. Black cherries, toast and mocha sweep across the palate in slightly monolithic waves; this wine needs some time in the bottle to develop additional complexity and soften the firm finish. Try after 2008. **90 Cellar Selection** *(5/1/2004)*

Duckhorn 1999 Estate Grown Merlot (Napa Valley) $80. Black fruit and portabello aromas mesh with those of mulch and hummus. Sweet fruit and baking spices characterize the palate, which is uplifted by flavors of apple peels and licorice straps. Well balanced with good acidity, this finishes long, strong, and dark. **91** —*K.F (4/1/2003)*

Duckhorn 1997 Estate Grown Merlot (Napa Valley) $65. Features a complex mix of oak and fruit, with aromas and flavors ranging from cedar, cinnamon and cocoa to mocha, black cherries and dried herbs. Fine tannins and crisp acidity complete the package. Drink now or age up to five years. **89** —*J.C. (6/1/2001)*

Duckhorn 1999 Howell Mountain Merlot (Howell Mountain) $65. The least accessible of Duckhorn's Merlot lineup is shut down now by strong, astringent tannins and firm acids. Letting it breathe reveals a fabulous core of ripe cherry and raspberry fruit that is so intense, it's like Framboise. Utterly good, almost gooey in sheer flavor. Will age for a very long time, and best to decant many hours in advance. **93** —*S.H. (8/1/2004)*

Duckhorn 1998 Howell Mountain Merlot (Napa Valley) $50. Animal aromas blow off to leave a nose full of dark earth, ash and black plums. On the palate, there are mushroom, coffee, pepper and char flavors over delicate black fruit. Leafy greens carry to the finish, with menthol and eucalyptus.—K.F. **89** —*K.F. (4/1/2003)*

Duckhorn 1996 Howell Mountain Merlot (Napa Valley) $50. Smoky and tough-skinned, with loads of espresso and heavy toast hiding black fruit. Cedar and dark chocolate round it out. This is a big, brooding wine that still needs some time to come together despite the late release. A Merlot that should rival many Cabernets for longevity. Cellar Selection. **92 Cellar Selection** *(6/1/2001)*

Duckhorn 1999 Three Palms Merlot (Napa Valley) $70. Warm base aromas of driftwood, cinnamon and a thread of toffee are topped by juicy cherries and ripe plums. The fruit carries well to the palate, beginning with red raspberry at entry, and leading to menthol, tobacco and tar flavors. Fruit that can be described as a black apple tempers the charred finish. Lush, ripe fruit and firm tannins, melded by mellow acidity make for an indulgent offering. **92** —*K.F. (4/1/2003)*

Duckhorn 2003 Three Palms Vineyard Merlot (Napa Valley) $80. Reminds me of the '97, a very ripe but very tannic wine that didn't offer much early on. The tannins on the '03 are bigtime astringent, locking down the palate, but oodles of ripely sweet cherry and cedar flavors tease. Best after 2008. **88** —*S.H. (12/1/2006)*

Duckhorn 2002 Three Palms Vineyard Merlot (Napa Valley) $80. This wine shows the usual thick, firm tannins of this vineyard, although they're a lot finer than they used to be. It's also a bit sweetish for a red wine that should be dry. There's a cloying, syrupy taste to the finish. **84** —*S.H. (12/1/2005)*

Duckhorn 2001 Three Palms Vineyard Merlot (Napa Valley) $77. Tannic as usual from this single vineyard near Calistoga, but with a great heart of cherry and blackberry fruit and wonderful suggestions of herbs and nettles. Bone dry, but ripe in sweet fruit, the quintessence of cherry. An obvious cellar candidate that will hold through the decade. **93** —*S.H. (8/1/2004)*

Duckhorn 2000 Three Palms Vineyard Merlot (Napa Valley) $75. Shows some interestingly perfumed herb or floral aromas that add complexity to the cherry and mocha underpinnings. It's a big wine, more supple than Duckhorn's estate bottling, with a smoother, richer finish that makes it come across as flashier and more open, but not necessarily better. **90** *(5/1/2004)*

Duckhorn 1997 Three Palms Vineyard Merlot (Napa Valley) $60. Very cedary and dry, this is built more like a Cabernet than a traditional Merlot. Dusty tannins coat the mouth on the finish, reducing its current pleasure but presaging a long life ahead, when the buried black-cherry fruit is sure to come to the fore. Hold for five years and drink til 2010. **88** —*J.C. (6/1/2001)*

Duckhorn 1996 Three Palms Vineyard Merlot (Napa Valley) $47. 91 —*M.S. (3/1/2000)*

Duckhorn 2001 Decoy Red Blend (Napa Valley) $26. A dry and distinguished Bordeaux blend, with smooth, rich tannins and good character. Black currants and cherries, herbs and cocoa, and toasted oak mingle on the palate, leading to a fine finish. **88** —*S.H. (5/1/2005)*

Duckhorn 2005 Sauvignon Blanc (Napa Valley) $25. I love this wine. Duckhorn has been on a roll with Sauvignon Blanc, and this is the best yet. It's dry and refreshingly crisp in acidity, with delicious citrus, fig, honeysuckle, green apple and spice flavors. A bit of barrel fermentation makes it even richer. The price is creeping up, but this is a seriously good wine. Easy to find with 22,000 cases produced. **91 Editors' Choice** —*S.H. (12/1/2006)*

Duckhorn 2004 Sauvignon Blanc (Napa Valley) $25. Dry and tart, with citrus, kiwi, fig and herb flavors and a creamy texture, this food-friendly wine has some real complexity that need breathing. Try decanting a few hours before serving. **88** —*S.H. (2/1/2006)*

Duckhorn 2003 Sauvignon Blanc (Napa Valley) $23. Crisp and delicately structured, with a clean, brisk mouthfeel, this wine packs a flavor punch. Essence of lemony lime, sweet green grass, vanilla and rich honey lead to a long, fruity, spicy finish. One of the better SB's lately. **89** —*S.H. (5/1/2005)*

Duckhorn 2002 Sauvignon Blanc (Napa Valley) $22. Supple and harmonious with refreshing acidity. Handles the juicy citrus, fig and melon flavors with finesse, showing a real mastery of the variety. **88** —*S.H. (8/1/2004)*

Duckhorn 2000 Sauvignon Blanc (Napa Valley) $21. Muscular, mildly sweaty aromatics make this a little tough to get into, but the flavors are really elevated and complex. There's layered citrus, slate, licorice and spice all working together. The texture is nice, with spiciness coming on late. A bit of sweetness properly offsets the spicy, peppery quality to the finish. **88** *(8/1/2002)*

DUKE

DUKE 2001 Merlot (California) $9. An example of how the grape glut is resulting in good wines below $10. Has polished plum and berry flavors, and is dry, with firm but yielding tannins. Not complex, but with enough finesse to serve with fine foods. **85 Best Buy** —*S.H. (12/31/2003)*

DUKE 2001 Shiraz (California) $9. Briary and peppery, a wine that smells like scads of freshly ground white pepper sprinkled over a blackberry tart just out of the oven. Bone dry, with some hefty tannins, but will succeed with the right foods—roast lamb, for example. **85 Best Buy** —*S.H. (2/1/2004)*

DUNCAN PEAK

Duncan Peak 2002 Cabernet Sauvignon (Mendocino County) $25. Drinks kind of hard and raw now, a very dry, tannic wine. You'll find pretty flavors of blackberries and cherries, but it seems to need time to throw some sediment and chill. Try holding for a few years. **85** —*S.H. (10/1/2006)*

Duncan Peak 1998 Cabernet Sauvignon (Mendocino County) $35. I have admired this property for many years. It comes from a mountain in Mendocino that should have its own appellation. In this dismal vintage the vineyard ripened the grapes enough to evoke blackberries, although the olive flavors are strong. The tannin-acid balance is exciting and suggests mid-term aging. A winery to watch. **90** —*S.H. (6/1/2002)*

Duncan Peak 2001 Reserve Cabernet Sauvignon (Mendocino County) $35. Be warned: This is a very tannic wine. It's so dry and astringent, it makes your mouth pucker, which begs to the question, will it age? The answer is a provisional yes. It's balanced and feels good and rich, and if you chew, there's a lot of blackberry fruit. Best to hold until 2008. **89** —*S.H. (10/1/2006)*

Duncan Peak 2003 Petite Sirah (Mendocino County) $25. There are structural similarities here with Napa Cabernet. The wine is dry, lush in tannins, balanced in acidity, with ripe but controlled black currant and cherry flavors. Yes, there's a certain briary, wild character, but this is really one heck of a good wine. Drink now through 2009 for its youthful fruit. **90** —*S.H. (10/1/2006)*

DUNDEE SPRINGS

Dundee Springs 1999 Pinot Blanc (Oregon) $16. Has a slight cheddar note from lees, riding over apple and lemon aromas. It drinks fruity and citrusy, and quite acidic, with a long, lemonade-flavored aftertaste. A clean, delightful wine. **86** —*S.H. (8/1/2002)*

Dundee Springs 1999 Pinot Gris (Oregon) $12. Smells very bright, with alluring lemon, cocoa and grass aromas. The flavors veer to citrus fruits, apricots and sweet white chocolate, and linger through the longish finish. Yet it's basically a dry wine. **85** —*P.G. (8/1/2002)*

DUNHAM

Dunham 2001 Trutina Bordeaux Blend (Columbia Valley (WA)) $28. This is Dunham's Bordeaux blend, but not their top wine. It's a well-crafted mix of 70% Cabernet Sauvignon, 17% Merlot and 13% Cab Franc, with medium-bodied, mixed berries and red fruits. Barrel flavors of mocha and toast are layered in, and there are some definite traces of herbs and earth—very Bordeaux-like. **88** —*P.G. (12/15/2004)*

Dunham 1999 Cabernet Sauvignon (Columbia Valley (WA)) $45. A bit greener than the '98, with fresh herbs, arugula and bitter chocolate. Lean but not aggressive tannins finish soft. **88** —*C.S. (12/31/2002)*

Dunham 2002 Lewis Vineyard Cabernet Sauvignon (Columbia Valley (WA)) $75. From the winery's favorite vineyard, this limited (242 cases) production, 100% Cabernet is inky black, dense and tannic. Tight layers show many different berries, black cherry, pomegranate and mint. The tannins are ripe and firm, with black tea and graphite flavors. Very fine effort, big but not showy, nor is it a palate-fatiguing high-alcohol fruit bomb. Great fruit from a top vineyard, handled with extreme care and sensitivity. Decant this. **93** —*P.G. (4/1/2006)*

Dunham 2001 VII Cabernet Sauvignon (Columbia Valley (WA)) $45. This is Dunham's top wine, and it is 100% Cab, aged in a 50/50 mix of French and American oak. Firm and compact, with black cherry and cassis, licorice and new leather, it shows good length and balance. The black cherry fruit, not too sweet, is not at all jammy, heavy or hot; but it is supple and deliciously nuanced with espresso and smoke. Cellar 8–12 years. **91 Cellar Selection** —*P.G. (12/15/2004)*

Dunham 2002 VIII Cabernet Sauvignon (Columbia Valley (WA)) $45. It's 100% Cabernet, sappy, supple, silky and lush. It coats the palate and saturates the tongue with wild berries and black cherries. The oak is well-integrated and the extra time in bottle has melded it all together. Some lovely spice comes into the finish, along with coconut, vanilla cream and chocolate. Thoroughly delicious. **92** —*P.G. (4/1/2006)*

Dunham 2005 Lewis Estate "Shirley Mays" Chardonnay (Columbia Valley (WA)) $35. Soft and buttery, this is thickly flavored with caramel, traces of pineapple, and loads of rich, tropical fruit. It's big, delicious, spicy, round and full, and it resonates nicely if you give it a little chill before pouring, to sharpen up the acids. Distinctive and appealing, as are all Dunham wines. **91** —*P.G. (10/1/2006)*

Dunham 2003 Shirley Mays Sémillon (Walla Walla (WA)) $35. Sémillon may well be the best white wine made in Washington, and Dunham's is right at the top of the list. Barrel fermented, estate grown, and showing plenty of toasty new wood, it's deliciously ripe and sweetly fruity, like succulent peaches and fresh citrus. **91** —*P.G. (11/15/2004)*

Dunham 2003 Syrah (Columbia Valley (WA)) $45. While two of our tasters found this wine raisiny and overripe, the other lauded it for its supple tannins, bright acidity and blackberry pie flavors. There's also a heavy overlay of toasty, vanilla- and cinnamon-laden oak, which will please some and turn off others. A love-it-or-hate-it wine. **84** *(9/1/2005)*

Dunham 2002 Syrah (Columbia Valley (WA)) $45. The first thing you notice, apart from the density and magnificent color of this wine, is the perfume. Floral, complex and inviting with spicy citrus scents, it sets up the wine with an elegant, inviting entry that brings nuance and subtlety to a variety that can sometimes behave like an overblown Zinfandel. Here it is world class. **92** —*P.G. (11/15/2004)*

Dunham 2001 Syrah (Columbia Valley (WA)) $45. Saturated with jammy raspberry/black cherry fruit, smoky/peppery scents, and baking spices, this is a seductive, ripe, tart and effusive wine that can't help but tickle the palate. Young, tart and grapy, it needs more time to soften up, but it is really delicious. **91** —*P.G. (11/15/2004)*

Dunham 2000 Syrah (Columbia Valley (WA)) $45. The second Syrah for this cult winery, and again it is bursting with rich, black fruit flavors. A lovely, sweet nose shows mixed berry, gingerbread and vanilla scents, which lead into sweet, appealing fruit. Maybe not quite as big and powerful as the '99, but it's a beautifully balanced and thoroughly delicious effort. **92** —*P.G. (9/1/2002)*

Dunham 2004 Lewis Vineyard Syrah (Columbia Valley (WA)) $75. Winemaker Eric Dunham was the first to latch onto the fruit coming from this exceptional site in the Rattlesnake Hills, and this is as good as any Syrah made in Washington. An awesome nose with spectacular intensity spills out of the glass, carrying superb raspberry scents. The wine is crisp and focused, intense and nuanced. Flavors float from raspberry into the cherry cola realm, heading for a lingering, elegant finish. **94** —*P.G. (11/15/2006)*

Dunham 2002 Lewis Vineyard Syrah (Columbia Valley (WA)) $60. Vivid and potent, the ultraripe fruit maintains its poise, despite the almost 15% alcohol, with high-altitude flavors that seem to etch the fruit in fierce relief. Bright raspberry, strawberry and cherry flavors mingle in a blend that is still elegant, still balanced, though immensely powerful. **93** —*P.G. (11/15/2004)*

Dunham 1999 Lewis Vineyard Syrah (Columbia Valley (WA)) $45. Reviewers loved the Dunham's bouquet—especially its "gobs of fleshy blackberry fruit," toasty oak, and "sugar- cookie" elements. A blackberry, blueberry, white pepper and toasty-vanilla palate and a medium-weight, velour-textured mouthfeel will please even discerning palates. Finishes with more lush berry fruit and charred oak. Will improve through 2004. **92 Cellar Selection** *(11/1/2001)*

DUNNEWOOD

Dunnewood 2000 Cabernet Sauvignon (Mendocino County) $9. What a good job this winery does with Mendocino grapes. This wine has plenty of black currant flavors packed into a smooth, elegant wine. **85 Best Buy** —*S.H. (10/1/2003)*

Dunnewood 1998 Cabernet Sauvignon (North Coast) $8. Has some real varietal Cabernet notes of currant and blackberry, with oaky nuances. It's supple and well-made, although of average quality, and a bit thin in the mid-palate. But it's dry and clean. **83** —*S.H. (5/1/2001)*

Dunnewood 1995 Dry Silk Reserve Seven Arches Cabernet Sauvignon (Sonoma County) $13. **86** *(7/1/2000)*

Dunnewood 1996 Dry Silk Seven Arches Vineyard Rese Cabernet Sauvignon (Sonoma County) $13. **86** *(7/1/2000)*

Dunnewood 1998 Signature Clara's Vineyard Cabernet Sauvignon (Mendocino County) $15. Here's a wine that will surprise you. It has real richness and varietal flavor, and is dry and balanced, with the weight you want in a nice Cabernet. Might even get a little better in another year or two. **87** —*S.H. (8/1/2003)*

Dunnewood 1997 Signature Clara's Vineyards Cabernet Sauvignon (Mendocino) $13. Hits the nail on the head, with ripe, juicy Cabernet aromas and flavors. There's great fruity extraction, with cassis, black-currant and plum flavors, complex with smoky oak. Despite the depth and concentration, the wine is deft, elegant and very dry. **89 Best Buy** —*S.H. (5/1/2001)*

Dunnewood 1995 Dry Silk Reserve Charbono (Napa Valley) $14. **86** *(7/1/2000)*

Dunnewood 2001 Chardonnay (Mendocino County) $9. There's lots of ripe, pretty flavor in this affordable wine. Peaches, apples, and pears are mingled with oak notes through the spicy finish. **84** —*S.H. (6/1/2003)*

Dunnewood 2000 Chardonnay (Mendocino County) $9. It's hard to find much to like here. There are watered-down aromas and flavors of apples, leaving the mouth feeling little but the cold temperature and sting of acids and alcohol. You could say it's clean, and inexpensive, but there's not much more here. **82** —*S.H. (5/1/2002)*

Dunnewood 1998 Chardonnay (North Coast) $8. **83 Best Buy** —*S.H. (7/1/2000)*

Dunnewood 2002 Signature Chardonnay (Anderson Valley) $13. Pretty sweet in vanilla creme and tapioca, with a melange of tropical fruits. Clean acidity keeps it crisp and vibrant. Almost like a dessert wine, except it's dry. **86** —*S.H. (12/15/2004)*

Dunnewood 2000 Signature Chardonnay (Carneros) $13. There's a nice wine in here someplace, but it's hard to find under the heavy hand of excessive oak (chips? extract?). But the peach and apricot flavors are good. **84** —*S.H. (6/1/2003)*

Dunnewood 1997 Dry Silk Reserve Dolcetto (Napa Valley) $14. **85** *(7/1/2000)*

Dunnewood 1999 Merlot (Mendocino County) $9. Pretty common stuff here. They stretched the Merlot with almost the legal limit of Carignane. Possesses full-bodied red wine character, with berry flavors, thick tannins, telltale Mendocino acids and the earthy one-dimensionality of country wines worldwide. **84** —*S.H. (5/1/2002)*

Dunnewood 1998 Merlot (North Coast) $8. Good, dark color indicates full ripening and the aromas back it up, with black-cherry, cherry-tomato, plum, anise and oak notes. It's well made and drinkable, although not particularly varietal. Has that generic red wine personality. Still, the solid dose of fruit, soft tannins and acidity and round, supple texture make it a good buy. **84** —*S.H. (5/1/2001)*

Dunnewood 1997 Reserve Merlot (Napa Valley) $13. **84** *(7/1/2000)*

Dunnewood 2000 Pinot Noir (Mendocino County) $9. Dull and insipid, with little Pinot character beyond some modest berry flavors and easy tannins. Turns gluey and thick on the dry finish. **82** —*S.H. (7/1/2003)*

Dunnewood 1999 Pinot Noir (North Coast) $9. **80** *(10/1/2002)*

Dunnewood 1998 Pinot Noir (North Coast) $8. What a pretty aroma on this soft, likeable wine. Very forward, full of black cherry, black tea, caramel, smoke, mushroom and oak, and yet it's delicate and rather "feminine." A little light in flavor, with black cherry and spices. The texture is creamy, the tannins are soft; yet it manages to retain a firm grip

USA

on the palate. Very fine value in Pinot Noir. **86 Best Buy** —*S.H. (5/1/2001)*

Dunnewood 1997 Barrel Select Coastal Series Pinot Noir (North Coast) $9. 84 Best Buy *(7/1/2000)*

Dunnewood 2002 Signature Pinot Noir (Mendocino County) $9. Pleasant and polished, a pale-colored wine, with sharp acids and pretty flavors of candied cherry and vanilla. Silky and delicate; charming and elegant. **86** *(11/1/2004)*

Dunnewood 1997 Reserve Sangiovese (Mendocino County) $14. 84 *(7/1/2000)*

Dunnewood 1999 Signature Mendocino Sangiovese (Mendocino County) $13. The Signature series is Dunnewood's play for premium status, and a wine like this shows that there's plenty of work to be done. It's rough and earthy and hot, with mouth-curdling acids and a good dose of hard tannins. What flavor there is veers toward generic berry. Needs more tinkering. **84** —*S.H. (5/1/2002)*

Dunnewood 2000 Sauvignon Blanc (Mendocino County) $7. Has pretty flavors, slightly sweet, of peaches and citrus fruits, with hefty acidity, the kind that scours the palate. Smells like freshly mowed hay. This is a likeable, simple wine, at a very good price. **84** —*S.H. (5/1/2002)*

Dunnewood 1999 Sauvignon Blanc (Mendocino) $7. One of those wines that smells so good, you could just sniff and swirl. There's lemongrass, vanilla, spearmint, butter and toast and a honeyed sweetness. Rich and flavorful, with melon and citrus flavors and a round, creamy texture. A slight touch of sweetness makes it fat, but it's basically a dry wine. This is a super value. Buy it by the case for your house white. **87 Best Buy** —*S.H. (5/1/2001)*

Dunnewood 1998 Vintner's Select Coastal Serie Sauvignon Blanc (Mendocino County) $8. 83 *(7/1/2000)*

Dunnewood 2002 Syrah (Mendocino County) $9. Great value in a dry, full-bodied red wine, with its dry flavors of cherries and plums and smooth, supple tannins. Has enough style and class to stand up to a nice leg of lamb. **85 Best Buy** —*S.H. (12/15/2004)*

Dunnewood 2002 Zinfandel (Mendocino County) $9. This is the kind of Zin that goes well with just about anything, from salmon to burgers. It's dry and balanced, with good flavors of berries, coffee and spices. **85 Best Buy** —*S.H. (2/1/2005)*

Dunnewood 2001 Zinfandel (Mendocino County) $9. Tea and herb notes are the watchwords here, with hints of cherry and citrus on the finish. Short at the end. **80** *(11/1/2003)*

Dunnewood 1998 Zinfandel (Mendocino County) $9. Simple in jammy cherry flavors and firmly tannic, this is a wine that strives to be more than it manages to be—which isn't bad. It certainly lacks the stuffing to be a big wine. But it takes a big swing with absolute dryness and high acidity and a rich, mealy mouthfeel, and you have to give credit to the winery for keeping the price this low. **85** —*S.H. (5/1/2002)*

DUNNING VINEYARDS

Dunning Vineyards 2003 Westside Cabernet Sauvignon (Paso Robles) $24. Lots of richness in this dry, slightly tart wine, with its furry coat of tannins. It shows cherry, blackcurrant, herb and coffee flavors that finish with a nice, cocoa-infused complexity. **87** —*S.H. (7/1/2006)*

Dunning Vineyards 2004 Westside Chardonnay (Paso Robles) $16. From the cool side of Paso Robles comes this Chard, which nonetheless shows its warm appellation in its earthiness, which resembles some Napa Chards. The fruit veers toward apples, and the wine is totally dry. **84** —*S.H. (7/1/2006)*

Dunning Vineyards 2003 Westside Merlot (Paso Robles) $24. Dry, tart and modestly fruited, this Merlot has an herb and tobacco edge to the cherry flavors. It's also fairly tannic, but not likely to improve. Drink now with robust fare. **84** —*S.H. (7/1/2006)*

Dunning Vineyards 2003 Westside Syrah (Paso Robles) $28. A weird one, with aromas and flavors that range from soy sauce to meat to mint and pepper. Aggressively tannic, and not likely to age gracefully, so drink 'em if you got 'em. **82** *(9/1/2005)*

Dunning Vineyards 2002 Westside Syrah (Paso Robles) $24. A big, ripe, exuberant Syrah, quite high in alcohol and long on jammy cherry-blackberry fruit, dusted with mocha. Finishes dry and long in fruity concentration. **87** —*S.H. (12/1/2004)*

Dunning Vineyards 2003 Westside Zinfandel (Paso Robles) $32. There's lots of alcohol and heat in this wine, but it's fully dry, and the robust fruit and coffee flavors will appeal to fans of warm-climate, country-style Zins. **84** —*S.H. (7/1/2006)*

Dunning Vineyards 2001 Westside Zinfandel (Paso Robles) $24. The wine has good plum, cherry and raspberry flavors, though the acidity is a bit pronounced. On the finish, there's a nice toast and vanilla edge to round things out. Moderate in length at the end. **85** *(11/1/2003)*

DURNEY

Durney 1993 Estate Bottled Cabernet Sauvignon (Carmel Valley) $25. 85 —*S.H. (7/1/1999)*

Durney 1996 Estate Bottled Chardonnay (Carmel Valley) $23. 86 *(6/1/2000)*

Durney 1998 Heller Estate Merlot (Carmel Valley) $26. A warm microclimate means that reds from Carmel Valley are typically less herbal than those from other portions of Monterey. This wine boasts a nice mix of cedar and black cherries upfront before turning tough, with a bitter edge to the tannins on the finish. Drink it young, with food to tame its rough edges. **86** —*J.C. (6/1/2001)*

DUSTED VALLEY

Dusted Valley 2004 Old Vine Chardonnay (Yakima Valley) $20. Old-vine Kestrel Vineyard fruit delivers; this is excellent juice. Concentrated and lush, it's packed with pineapple, green apple, hints of pear and light tropical fruits. A fruit-driven, powerful wine, with cracker and oatmeal flavors showing up in the finish. **89** —*P.G. (4/1/2006)*

Dusted Valley 2003 Old Vine Chardonnay (Columbia Valley (WA)) $20. Somewhat blocky, with round fruit flavors that show just enough crisp green apple to keep from getting mushy. Fresh, uncomplicated effort. **87** —*P.G. (11/15/2006)*

Dusted Valley 2003 Barrel Thief Red Red Blend (Columbia Valley (WA)) $20. A kitchen sink mix of Sangiovese, Cabernet and Merlot. It offers light fruit and lots of barrel toast. It's not a dense or demanding wine, but certainly a pleasant quaff. **86** —*P.G. (4/1/2006)*

Dusted Valley 2004 Reserve Syrah (Columbia Valley (WA)) $32. A big wine, deep and dense, scented with violets, toast and vanilla. Vanilla dominates the palate, but there is good, concentrated fruit lurking right below, suggesting that this very young wine will come together well in the months ahead. Juicy, jammy and ripe, with a good peppery finish. **89** —*P.G. (4/1/2006)*

Dusted Valley 2004 Stained Tooth Syrah (Columbia Valley (WA)) $24. Very young and grapy, but there's good fruit and it's well managed. It's all about the fruit right now, showing lots of cherry and berry flavors, with a hint of toast and caramel. This may be one of those wines best enjoyed in its first blush of youth. **87** —*P.G. (4/1/2006)*

Dusted Valley 2004 Viognier (Yakima Valley) $20. Perfumed, substantial and potent, this shows the typical varietal flavors of orange peel and citrus fruits, with noticeable heat in the finish. **88** —*P.G. (4/1/2006)*

Dusted Valley 2003 Viognier (Columbia Valley (WA)) $20. Starts with a piercing nose of citrus and pineapple, that leads into a welcome burst of fresh, round, pretty fruit flavors of peach and apricot. No rough edges here, and no heat, just a plump, smooth, pleasing wine. **88** —*P.G. (11/15/2004)*

DUTCH HENRY WINERY

Dutch Henry Winery 2001 Chafen Vineyards Cabernet Sauvignon (Napa Valley) $42. A lighter style of Cabernet, and very pretty, with smoky cherry and spice flavors that are softly oaked. Easy tannins and acids make it instantly drinkable. **87** —*S.H. (10/3/2004)*

Dutch Henry Winery 2001 Argos Meritage (Napa Valley) $38. Light and a bit herbal, with easy tannins and a streak of red cherries and spice. Finishes very dry and somewhat astringent. Good with steak. **85** —*S.H. (10/3/2004)*

DUTCHER CROSSING

Dutcher Crossing 2002 Nevins Vineyard Cabernet Sauvignon (Alexander Valley) $32. Earthy and soft, this Cab shows subtle layerings of herbs, cherries and roast coffee, with a sweet, caramelly coating of oak. It's dry, and the tannins aren't a problem at all. **86** —*S.H. (8/1/2005)*

Dutcher Crossing 2003 Chardonnay (Russian River Valley) $22. Here's a good, all-purpose Chard when you want one that's oaky, ripe, dryish-sweetish and creamy. It has pretty peach, apple and vanilla flavors, and a slight roughness to the finish. **85** —*S.H. (8/1/2005)*

Dutcher Crossing 2003 Stuhlmuller Vineyard Chardonnay (Alexander Valley) $30. Lack of oak is not the problem here. There's scads of it, dripping with vanilla, buttered toast, caramelly char, the works. The fruit? Appley and pineapply, with a creamy texture and a hit of acids. **88** —*S.H. (8/1/2005)*

DUTTON ESTATE

Dutton Estate 2004 Dutton Palms Vineyard Chardonnay (Russian River Valley) $45. From the coolest part of Green Valley, this wonderfully rich Chardonnay has a steely crispness that hits the palate like a laser. The pineapple, apple, kiwi and lime flavors, enhanced with smoky oak, are complex and satisfying. This is a high-class wine that deserves to be served with gourmet fare. **94 Editors' Choice** —*S.H. (7/1/2006)*

Dutton Estate 2002 Dutton Palms Vineyard Chardonnay (Russian River Valley) $40. Smooth and supple, a rich Chard with forward flavors of ripe white peaches, pears and tropical fruits. Picks up buttered toast and smoky vanilla notes midway. Finishes firm with crisp acidity. **91** —*S.H. (12/31/2004)*

Dutton Estate 2004 Dutton Ranch Chardonnay (Russian River Valley) $35. The grapes got so ripe in this vintage, the wine bursts with peach, pineapple, green apple, lime and apricot fruit that tastes like it was baked and caramelized into pie filling. Yet the finish is dry. Just the right amount of new oak gives that fancy edge of buttered toast. **93 Editors' Choice** —*S.H. (12/31/2006)*

Dutton Estate 2004 Dutton Ranch Pinot Noir (Russian River Valley) $35. With an acidity that titillates the tastebuds and pure flavors of red cherries, cola, mocha and woodspice, this dry Pinot is very food friendly. It's not particularly oaky, nor is it complex, but offers plenty of satisfaction. Drink now. **87** —*S.H. (7/1/2006)*

Dutton Estate 2004 Dutton-Thomas Road Vineyard Pinot Noir (Russian River Valley) $45. How translucently light this Pinot is. You just know from the color it's not one of those heavy, superripe wines. In fact, it's as delicate and airy as the fog that visits the vineyard every night. Dry, too, with complex cola, rosehip tea, strawberry, cinnamon and toasty oak flavors. So nice, so elegant, not a big and probably not an ageable wine, but polished. **90** —*S.H. (12/31/2006)*

Dutton Estate 2004 Jewell Block Vineyard Pinot Noir (Russian River Valley) $52. You'd never expect such nice flavor from such a lightly colored wine. Nonetheless, this single-vineyard Pinot is fresh and dry in rosehip tea, strawberry and cinnamon spice, with a bracing coat of toasty oak. It's not a blockbuster, but defines elegance. **88** —*S.H. (12/31/2006)*

Dutton Estate 2003 Thomas Road Pinot Noir (Russian River Valley) $40. I was struck by how pale this Pinot pours. It's a classic chilly-climate wine, light-bodied and elegant but complex, with cherry, raspberry, cola, rhubarb and cranberry sauce flavors that have been sweetened and vanilla-ized with oak. It's also superbly spicy, dusting the palate with cinnamon and dusty cocoa through a long, complete finish. Absolutely delicious. **93 Editors' Choice** —*S.H. (12/1/2005)*

Dutton Estate 2005 Dutton Ranch Cohen Vineyard Sauvignon Blanc (Russian River Valley) $35. The vineyard is in the cool, far western part of Green Valley, and the wine, which never saw oak, has very high acidity, nearly 7.7 g/L. You might expect it to be lean, even feline, but the Duttons, among the best growers in the country, have produced a rich, fruity wine, dry and complex in apricot, citrus, herb and mineral flavors. This is simply a tremendous food wine. **93 Editors' Choice** —*S.H. (8/1/2006)*

Dutton Estate 2003 Cherry Ridge Vineyard Syrah (Russian River Valley) $34. Displays a vaguely Rhônish quality in its herbal, near-rhubarb and white pepper aromatics. Placed alongside flavors of tart berries and a relatively light mouthfeel, you might mistake this wine for a modest Crozes-Hermitage. **86** *(9/1/2005)*

Dutton Estate 2003 Gail Ann's Vineyard Syrah (Russian River Valley) $35. There's so much to like with this small-production Syrah that it's a pity it has flaws. It's a smooth, velvety wine, voluptuous in texture, with plenty of oak-infused blackberry and mocha flavors. Yet there's a sharpness, a green acidic harshness that not even 100% malolactic can eliminate. **85** —*S.H. (12/31/2006)*

Dutton Estate 2002 Gail Ann's Vineyard Syrah (Russian River Valley) $34. Herbal and grassy, this Syrah seems distinctly underripe, with pepper and herbal notes that dominate the modest cherry fruit. Thin and tart. **82** *(9/1/2005)*

DUTTON-GOLDFIELD

Dutton-Goldfield 2004 Dutton Ranch Chardonnay (Russian River Valley) $35. Made mainly from vineyards in Green Valley, the wine was barrel fermented and underwent complete malolactic fermentation. The French oak barrels were 50% new. This level of intervention was appropriate to the underlying wine, which is massive in tropical fruit, pear, fig and melon flavors. The result is complex and lush. **94 Editors' Choice** — *S.H. (6/1/2006)*

Dutton-Goldfield 2003 Dutton Ranch Chardonnay (Russian River Valley) $30. Shows great class and finesse with its well-ripened fruit that's controlled with a clean minerality and high acidity. Oak and lees are both there, in supporting roles. The finish is ultraclean and citrusy, in this complex, dry white wine. **91 Editors' Choice** —*S.H. (10/1/2005)*

Dutton-Goldfield 2002 Dutton Ranch Chardonnay (Russian River Valley) $30. There's an earthy, sweet herbaceousness surrounding the citrus and apple fruit flavors in this very dry wine, which is also generously oaked. It's not flamboyant or hedonistic, but it is balanced, with acidity that cries out for food. **87** —*S.H. (10/1/2004)*

Dutton-Goldfield 2001 Dutton Ranch Chardonnay (Russian River Valley) $30. Starts with inviting aromas of Bosc pears and green apples, and a perfume of smoky caramel and vanilla. Yet it's tight and taut in the mouth, and on the austere side. The flavors veer toward hazelnuts and hard peaches, and finish dry and tart, with steely acids. **86** —*S.H. (12/15/2003)*

Dutton-Goldfield 2000 Dutton Ranch Chardonnay (Russian River Valley) $35. From the cool Green Valley, a wine that didn't get quite ripe this year. There are citrus flavors alongside bell pepper ones and the taste of various herbs. Plenty of oak and lees makes things more complex, but it's still a lean wine that demands foods to wake it up. **87** —*S.H. (12/15/2002)*

Dutton-Goldfield 1998 Dutton Ranch Chardonnay (Russian River Valley) $28. **87** *(3/1/2000)*

Dutton-Goldfield 2004 Dutton Ranch Rued Vineyard Chardonnay (Russian River Valley) $45. Four things define this wine. Extraordinarily ripe fruit, high acidity, a terroir-driven minerality, and lots of new French oak. The flavors are of tropical fruits, the ripest white peaches and vanilla cream, baked into spicy pastry crust. The impression is of impossible richness, California Chardonnay at its most opulent, flamboyant limit. **95 Editors' Choice** —*S.H. (12/15/2006)*

Dutton-Goldfield 2002 Dutton Ranch Rued Vineyard Chardonnay (Russian River Valley) $40. From chilly Green Valley, this wine was released at the same time as the winery's regular Dutton Ranch bottling. It's a shade richer, infused with a streak of mango that fattens and sweetens the earthy, herbal flavors. Marked by bright acids. **88** —*S.H. (10/1/2004)*

Dutton-Goldfield 2000 Rued Vineyard Chardonnay (Russian River Valley) $45. A single-vineyard wine from a part of the Dutton Ranch that capitalizes on east-facing slopes to produce a riper wine than the regular release. It's elaborated with lees and oak but is still a tight, lean wine, barely nudging from citrus and apple into peach. The pedigree shows in the finesse. **90** —*S.H. (12/15/2002)*

Dutton-Goldfield 2003 Rued Vineyard Dutton Ranch Chardonnay (Russian River Valley) $40. The Dutton-Goldfield style is to emphasize acidity and minerality, then to lavish winemaker interventions in the form of oak and lees. This is a Chablisian wine, if you will, dry and crisp, with complex flavors ranging from lemons and cinnamon to gun metal and pineapples. It's very elegant and food-friendly. **92** —*S.H. (12/15/2005)*

Dutton-Goldfield 2001 Rued Vineyard Dutton Ranch Chardonnay (Russian River Valley) $40. Brilliant, intense, nervy and dense are just a few words to describe the feeling and texture of this heavyweight wine. The flavors veer toward bright citrus fruits and pineapple, with complex overlays of toast, lees and vanilla, while the acids are mouthwatering high. **91** —*S.H. (12/15/2003)*

Dutton-Goldfield 2000 Devil's Gulch Pinot Noir (Marin County) $50. Handsome pine, saddle-leather and beet accents adorn dark cherry fruit in this well-balanced welterweight. Oak and tart fruit are married nicely, and the finish, if a touch light, has a smooth, seamless feel along with mocha and herb notes. **89** *(10/1/2002)*

Dutton-Goldfield 2002 Devil's Gulch Ranch Pinot Noir (Marin County) $48. This wine's cool-climate origins show in the intense, lemony acidity that undergirds the cherry, blueberry and spicy-clove flavors. Drinks smooth and elegant, a dry, powerful wine with some tannins to shed. Drink now through 2006. **90** *(11/1/2004)*

Dutton-Goldfield 2003 Devil's Gulch Vineyard Pinot Noir (Marin County) $48. From one of the coldest grape-growing regions in California comes this extremely dry, tart Pinot. There's a green tomato and rhubarb edge to the cherry flavors. **86** —*S.H. (2/1/2006)*

Dutton-Goldfield 2001 Devil's Gulch Ranch Pinot Noir (Marin County) $48. From north of the Golden Gate, in essentially the same terroir as the Sonoma Coast, a cool-climate Pinot marked by freshness and acidity. It straddles the knife's edge between cherry fruit ripeness and earthy tobacco and leather. Very dry, this wine is elegant and firm. **87** —*S.H. (2/1/2004)*

Dutton-Goldfield 2004 Dutton Ranch Pinot Noir (Russian River Valley) $35. Pours lightish in ruby color, smells rich and detailed in Pinot aromas, and drinks dry and elegant, with ripe Pinot fruit. What's not to like? Cherries, cola, rosehip tea and cinnamon spice flavors mingle into a wonderfully long finish, in a texture marked by silk and satin. Drink now. **92** —*S.H. (10/1/2006)*

Dutton-Goldfield 2003 Dutton Ranch Pinot Noir (Russian River Valley) $35. With a tomato-skin bitterness that considerable oak treatment can't quite diminish, this Pinot is saved by a finish of sweet, ripe cherries. Still, it's a study in contrasts. It shows elegance and harmony one minute, then that rustic note emerges. **86** —*S.H. (12/15/2005)*

Dutton-Goldfield 2002 Dutton Ranch Pinot Noir (Russian River Valley) $35. Quite oaky, with smoky, vanilla and buttered toast aromas, but the fruit is big and able to handle it. Cherries, clove, mocha flavors and a full, complete mouthfeel that's polished and refined. Really a lovely wine. **90** *(11/1/2004)*

Dutton-Goldfield 2001 Dutton Ranch Pinot Noir (Russian River Valley) $35. Equal parts cherry-berry fruit and earthier notes of tobacco, cola and rhubarb comprise this dry, complex wine. It's young, with dusty tannins and firm acids, and possesses a balanced elegance that make it an ideal partner to lamb or beef. **91** —*S.H. (4/1/2004)*

Dutton-Goldfield 2000 Dutton Ranch Pinot Noir (Russian River Valley) $40. Supple, with a slight chalkiness to its rich texture, this medium-weight Pinot is reserved yet appealing. Displays stylish smoky notes; the latent high acidity shows in lemony accents to the cherry, cedar and leather flavors. Finishes with solid, dry tannins; try after 2003. **87** *(10/1/2002)*

Dutton-Goldfield 1999 Dutton Ranch Pinot Noir (Russian River Valley) $40. Fabulous, fun wine. The aromas are beautiful: cola, black raspberry, dark tea, vanilla, smoke and dusty spices. On the palate, it's limpid, delicate. It seems to float, yet there's powerful fruit. Wonderful now and through 2003. **93** —*S.H. (7/1/2002)*

Dutton-Goldfield 1998 Dutton Ranch Pinot Noir (Russian River Valley) $33. **90** —*M.S. (5/1/2000)*

Dutton-Goldfield 2000 Dutton Ranch Maurice Galante Vineyard Pinot Noir (Russian River Valley) $55. Juicy and tangy—even racy—this shows vibrant black cherry, cream and dried spice aromas and flavors. On the tongue the wine is medium-weight, with toast and anise accents on tart

plum fruit. The tangy tannins on the close can use a year or two to resolve, but make it a fine food complement even now. **90** *(10/1/2002)*

Dutton-Goldfield 2004 Dutton Ranch Sanchietti Vineyard Pinot Noir (Russian River Valley) $55. Here's one of the bigger, more dramatic Russian River Pinots of the vintage. Dark, medium- to full-bodied and fairly tannic, the wine needs time to throw off some weight and reveal its pretty cherry fruit. Hold until 2008; should drink well through 2012. **90 Cellar Selection** —*S.H. (12/15/2006)*

Dutton-Goldfield 2000 Dutton-Freestone Hill Pinot Noir (Russian River Valley) $55. Dry, smoky, yet richly complex, opening with a potent bouquet of tart cherry, earth, fern, stable and bacon fat aromas. The palate was leaner than expected, showing very brisk acidity and cranberry, cherry-vanilla and toast flavors. Still, it's quite attractive in a bright, angular manner, closing with tart, tangy tannins. **89** *(10/1/2002)*

Dutton-Goldfield 1999 Freestone Hill Vineyard Pinot Noir (Russian River Valley) $55. Only 120 cases of this wine from the Sonoma Coast, where cool weather limits ripeness. There are Burgundian aromas of grilled meat, raw meat and mushroom, with dark berries. Very dry, but with a glyceriney sweetness, it's light and supple on the palate. Might age; might not. This is still unexplored territory for Pinot Noir. **92** —*S.H. (7/1/2002)*

Dutton-Goldfield 2004 McDougall Vineyard Pinot Noir (Sonoma Coast) $52. What a wonderful Pinot Noir, a joy to sip as it warms and changes in the glass. It's a very young wine, dry, sappy and acidic, with a tremendous depth of cherry preserves, licorice, cocoa, oaky spice and something wild and mushroomy that comes from the earth. As good as it is now, it should improve for a decade. **95 Editors' Choice** —*S.H. (12/15/2006)*

Dutton-Goldfield 2002 McDougall Vineyard Pinot Noir (Sonoma Coast) $48. Very full-bodied and rich, and bone dry, this polished wine has plenty of extracted cherry-berry fruit with hints of mocha. Big overay of oak, and rich, thick tannins and firm acids. Very polished and well-made, and should develop nicely for a few years. **89** *(11/1/2004)*

Dutton-Goldfield 2002 Sanchietti Vineyard Pinot Noir (Russian River Valley) $52. A real beauty. Shows complex notes of black cherry, tree bark, cocoa, chocolate and smoky oak throughout, with a supple, delicate mouthfeel. Crisp acidity and a long, spicy finish make it extra attractive. **90** *(11/1/2004)*

Dutton-Goldfield 2003 Sanchietti Vineyard Dutton Ranch Pinot Noir (Russian River Valley) $52. Showing classic Russian River notes of cola, rhubarb and cherry fruit, this Pinot is also dry and tart, with a medium body. It's austere and elegantly structured, and could develop additional complexity in the next 3–4 years. **89** —*S.H. (2/1/2006)*

Dutton-Goldfield 2002 Cherry Ridge Vineyard Syrah (Russian River Valley) $35. Few wineries have explored the cool climate possibilities of Syrah more than this one. This peppery red wine is rich in blackcurrant, coffee and tobacco flavors, and is quite complex. It's also dry and fairly tannic. Drink now. **91** —*S.H. (3/1/2005)*

Dutton-Goldfield 2003 Dutton Ranch Cherry Ridge Vineyard Syrah (Russian River Valley) $35. The winery specializes in cool-climate wines, and this Syrah is patently from a chilly place. It has white pepper and oak aromas, and in the mouth teases with a suggestion of red cherries. But it's a very dry, very tannic wine. Aging is a gamble, but it should develop over the next five years. **89** —*S.H. (2/1/2006)*

Dutton-Goldfield 2001 Dutton Ranch Cherry Ridge Vineyard Syrah (Russian River Valley) $35. Wickedly, sinfully good. This is fruit detonation in the mouth, a blast of pure, sweet cassis, currant, plum and chocolate. The tannins are a velvety wonder, the oak lavish and thick, but perfectly in balance to the size. Opulent and hedonistic, it's best in its sensual, seductive youth. **93 Editors' Choice** —*S.H. (6/1/2004)*

Dutton-Goldfield 2000 Dutton Ranch Cherry Ridge Vineyard Syrah (Russian River Valley) $35. From Green Valley, this vigorous Syrah shows distinct cool-climate character in its white pepper, blackberry and smoky oak aromas. Rich and full-bodied, it's firmly tannic but smooth and velvety. Delicious now, and will age well through at least 2007. **92 Editors' Choice** —*S.H. (2/1/2003)*

Dutton-Goldfield 2004 Zinfandel (Russian River Valley) $30. There's a rusticity here that's partly a function of Zin's wild, brambly nature, and partly due to a raisiny sweet finish. On the plus side is a rich, round mouthfeel and delicious cherry, cranberry and mocha fruit and spice. The September harvest heat wave must have been a huge challenge, even for talented grapegrowers such as the Duttons. **85** —*S.H. (10/1/2006)*

Dutton-Goldfield 2004 Dutton Ranch Morelli Lane Vineyard Zinfandel (Russian River Valley) $40. This is quite a mouthfilling Zin. From old vines, it's rich in flavor, with notes of blackberry jam, cassis, espresso, dark bitter chocolate and anise. It's on the soft side. A hefty amount of new French oak contributes sweet tannins and toast to this full-bodied, zesty wine. **90** —*S.H. (6/1/2006)*

Dutton-Goldfield 2002 Dutton Ranch Morelli Lane Vineyard Zinfandel (Russian River Valley) $35. A well structured, elegant Zinfandel that's framed in silky tannins and marked by focused acidity. Flavors are layered to reveal black cherry, licorice, tar, herbs, spice, chocolate and a hint of coffee as well. Long and fairly lush at the end. **91** —*J.M. (12/31/2004)*

Dutton-Goldfield 2001 Dutton Ranch/Morelli Lane Vineyard Zinfandel (Russian River Valley) $35. A smooth, elegant style, with just the right amount of bright acidity to highlight the plum, cherry, chocolate, cassis, tea and spice flavors. Pretty, ripe, lush and long on the finish. **90** *(11/1/2003)*

Dutton-Goldfield 2000 Morelli Lane Vineyard Zinfandel (Russian River Valley) $35. An astonishing Zin, easily among the best of the vintage, and all the more exciting due to its vineyard, in cold, foggy Pinot Noir country on the far west edge of the appellation. Hard to exaggerrate the quality of the fruit and tannins. Dry and complex, this has quality of a fine Napa Cabernet, with Zin's quintessentially wild personality. But only 240 cases were produced. **94 Cellar Selection** —*S.H. (12/1/2002)*

DUXOUP

Duxoup 2002 Syrah (Dry Creek Valley) $19. You'll enjoy this smooth, supple Syrah for its light texture and silky mouthfeel. The pleasant flavors are of blackberries and coffee, and they finish bone dry, with dusty tannins. **86** —*S.H. (11/1/2005)*

DYNAMITE VINEYARDS

Dynamite Vineyards 2002 Cabernet Sauvignon (North Coast) $17. Ripe and juicy in currant and chocolate flavors, with a good backbone of tannins and acids. Turns a bit raw on the finish, but will be nice now with rich meats. **85** —*S.H. (2/1/2005)*

Dynamite Vineyards 2001 Cabernet Sauvignon (North Coast) $17. This very dry wine has dusty, somewhat astringent tannins. Tastes herbal at first, and then cherry-berry fruit hits the palate. Finishes simple and clean, with some polish. **84** —*S.H. (5/1/2004)*

Dynamite Vineyards 2000 Red Hills Cabernet Sauvignon (Lake County) $25. From hill 2,000 feet above sea level, an amazingly ripe and supple Cab. Filled with oodles of cherry and blackberry fruit, with a long, rich chocolatey finish. Very smooth tannins help this delicious, soft wine go down like velvet. **87** —*S.H. (12/31/2003)*

Dynamite Vineyards 2004 Chardonnay (Mendocino County) $15. A soft, simple wine, with canned fruit flavors and a thick texture. It finishes dry, with notes of oak spice. **82** —*S.H. (3/1/2006)*

Dynamite Vineyards 2002 Merlot (North Coast) $17. This is a dark, young and impressively fruity wine. It's massive in plum, cherry and chocolate flavors, but has subtle nuances of dried herbs and flowers that make it complex. Very dry and stylish, with soft, lush tannins that make it instantly drinkable. **89** —*S.H. (10/1/2005)*

Dynamite Vineyards 2001 Merlot (North Coast) $17. This wine is big and rich, and feels plush and smooth in the mouth. You'll find flavors of cherries, plums, herbs and coffee, and thick but ripe tannins. It's nuanced in its appeal. **87** —*S.H. (5/1/2004)*

Dynamite Vineyards 2000 Merlot (North Coast) $18. Richly textured, though packing a burned-toast framework on the palate. Hints of cassis, blackberry and herb show through as well. Tangy on the finish. **86** —*J.M. (11/15/2002)*

Dynamite Vineyards 2005 Sauvignon Blanc (Lake County) $13. Lots of fruit in this slightly sweet but balanced wine. It's bursting with lemon

and lime, peach, fig and honeydew flavors, with just enough acidity to finish clean and zesty. **84** —*S.H. (12/15/2006)*

Dynamite Vineyards 2002 Sauvignon Blanc (Lake County) $11. A pleasant quaffer, with mild melon and citrus flavors, finishing with moderate length. **84** —*J.M. (4/1/2004)*

Dynamite Vineyards 2004 Kelsey Creek Sauvignon Blanc (Lake County) $11. There's a lovely aroma and flavor of figs in this delicate wine, along with notes of pineapples and sweet lemongrass. It's very dry, with crisp, uplifting acidity. A pleasant wine at a good price. **85** —*S.H. (3/1/2006)*

Dynamite Vineyards 2003 Kelsey Creek Sauvignon Blanc (Lake County) $11. I love the way this wine smells, all full of come-hither fruit and vanilla, but it turns disappointingly watery and acidic in the mouth. **83** —*S.H. (10/1/2005)*

Dynamite Vineyards 2004 Zinfandel (Mendocino County) $17. Nice Zin, rich in wild blackberry, cherry, blueberry, chocolate and coconut candy flavors, with a briary, peppery finish. There's an appealing fat, round softness in this wine. **86** —*S.H. (12/15/2006)*

Dynamite Vineyards 2003 Zinfandel (Mendocino County) $17. This is a bone-dry, slightly overripe Zin, with dusty, briary aromas and flavors of raisins, bitter dark chocolate and ripe plums. It's a serious Zin, a little hot but with plenty of sophistication. **88** —*S.H. (10/1/2005)*

E & J GALLO

E & J Gallo 1999 Barelli Creek Vineyard Barbera (Sonoma County) $19. A good California Barbera, with medium weight, classic tart cherry flavors offset by leather and herb accents, and zingy, almost sharp acidity. Has good body and mouthfeel, and cries out for hearty food like big pasta dishes or cassoulet. **86** *(7/1/2001)*

E & J Gallo 1998 Estate Chardonnay (Northern Sonoma) $50. This is everything a flagship wine should be, with its rich mouthfeel, palate-coating flavors and long finish. The flavors are on the apple side of the Chardonnay spectrum, with toasty oak galore, but would you expect otherwise? The long finish has lots of finesse and style despite its considerable heft. **92** *(7/1/2001)*

E B FOOTE

E B Foote 1997 Bordeaux Blend (Columbia Valley (WA)) $18. **83** —*P.G. (6/1/2000)*

E B Foote 1999 Cabernet Sauvignon (Columbia Valley (WA)) $16. An astoundingly low 12.9% alcohol may account for why it feels so light in the mouth. Out-of-the-bottle volatility on the nose subsides and reveals strawberry and oak aromas. Light red fruit, mushroom, soy and oak flavors are hardly typical of Cabernet, but it's generic enough to be a decent party pour. **84** —*D.T. (12/31/2002)*

E B Foote 1998 Cellar Reserve Cabernet Sauvignon (Columbia Valley (WA)) $32. Dill and bell pepper smells and flavors dominate. This type of Cabernet was quite common in Washington 15-20 years ago. Very tannic, herbal and dry. **82** —*P.G. (6/1/2002)*

E B Foote 1998 Chardonnay (Columbia Valley (WA)) $12. **85** —*P.G. (6/1/2000)*

E B Foote 2001 Chardonnay (Columbia Valley (WA)) $12. Aromas of match stick along with pears and apples get it started. Citrus, mostly lemon, carries the palate, which is fresh and properly weighty courtesy of bracing acidity. The finish is long, with some vanilla notes. Best served well chilled. Once the wine warms it loses some of its freshness. **86** —*M.S. (6/1/2003)*

E B Foote 1999 Chardonnay (Columbia Valley (WA)) $12. This is very simple, very neutral white wine, acidic and plain, with no defining varietal character. **82** —*P.G. (7/1/2002)*

E B Foote 2000 Merlot (Columbia Valley (WA)) $16. With intense cedary aromas along with hints of campfire and Christmas spices, this rock-solid, tannic Merlot shows more wood notes than pure fruit. The palate has ample berry and cherry flavors, but also a strong dose of penetrating oak, as indicated before. And on the finish that wood turns sweet: you get a strong taste of marshmallow and vanilla. **84** —*M.S. (6/1/2003)*

E B Foote 1998 Merlot (Columbia Valley (WA)) $16. Some good fruit gives this wine a solid foundation. It's dark and rough, with black cherry and blackberry flavors, along with toasty coffee and some earthy ash. The tannins are on the rough and rugged side, and the wine has plenty of power. It finishes with hints of chocolate and tannin. **87** —*P.G.* (6/1/2001)

E B Foote 2001 Pinot Gris (Columbia Valley (WA)) $10. Where's the fruit? Where's the substance? Lemon and citrus is all you get, that and some tangy grapefruit on the finish. The acidity is piercing but there's no flesh or bulk to offset it. Consequently the wine is thin and harsh. **80** —*M.S.* (1/1/2004)

E B Foote 2001 Syrah (Columbia Valley (WA)) $18. With a color akin to Beaujolais Nouveau, and sweet berry and bubble gum aromas, you should proceed with caution. The palate is full of tart, heavy raspberry fruit, while the plump finish has some cheek-grabbing tannins and an odd buttery flavor. This wine is slightly strange and unlike your average Syrah. **82** —*M.S.* (6/1/2003)

E B Foote 2000 Syrah (Columbia Valley (WA)) $18. There's a slight note of volatile acidity, so if you are sensitive to it, steer clear. That said, the other aromas and flavors are solid: Black pepper and mixed berries play out across the palate into a long, tart finish. Its crisp acids will cut easily through a fatty burger or grilled steak **88** (10/1/2001)

E. B. Foote 2003 Syrah (Columbia Valley (WA)) $16. A step up from the last time we reviewed an E.B. Foote Syrah, this version combines bright berry flavors with peppery notes in a plump, mouthfilling wine that turns tart on the finish. **86** (9/1/2005)

EAGLE & ROSE ESTATE

Eagle & Rose Estate 1999 Cabernet Sauvignon (Napa Valley) $34. From the eastern side of the appellation, a dark, tannic, dry wine stuffed with plump, fat blackberry fruit. It's youthful and forward, too sharp to enjoy now. Best to cellar for three years. **86** —*S.H.* (11/15/2002)

Eagle & Rose Estate 1998 Cabernet Sauvignon (Napa Valley) $NA. There are some proper currant and blackberry aromas along with hot, rubbery elements in this full-flavored, full bodied wine. Sizeable tannins obscure berry fruit, and the finish is dry and clean. **84** —*S.H.* (12/1/2001)

Eagle & Rose Estate 2000 Merlot (Napa Valley) $24. A bit chunky, with modest cherry, tobacco and earthy flavors. This dry, fairly tannic wine needs food to coax out the berry sweetness. **85** —*S.H.* (12/15/2004)

Eagle & Rose Estate 1999 Merlot (Napa Valley) $24. Gorgeous aromas of well-smoked oak and cassis are a delight. The entry is strongly flavored with black cherry and blackberry, with finely ground tannins, and the wine is very dry and refined. **87** —*S.H.* (11/15/2002)

Eagle & Rose Estate 1998 Merlot (Napa Valley) $24. Ripe, juicy aromas of cassis and blackcurrants start things off; bouquet also has a hefty dose of smoky oak. The flavors veer towards peppery blackberries and plums, but be forewarned: This wine is very tannic. Your tongue sticks to the roof of your mouth. Not likely to improve with age, so drink up with big, rich foods. **85** —*S.H.* (12/1/2001)

Eagle & Rose Estate 1999 Sangiovese (Napa Valley) $24. Thin and tannic. You have to use your imagination to find a bit of fruity flavor in this dry, boring wine. It's clean and scours the palate, but that's about it. **81** —*S.H.* (11/15/2002)

Eagle & Rose Estate 1998 Sangiovese (Napa Valley) $24. Dry and tannic, with good grip on the palate, this austere wine screams for olive oil, butter, gorgonzola cheese or beef. The red berry flavors are not particularly ripe, but there is sweetness hidden deep down in the core. The wine needs food to wake it up. **87** —*S.H.* (12/1/2001)

Eagle & Rose Estate 2000 Sauvignon Blanc (Napa Valley) $16. From the eastern hills of Pope Valley, a somewhat soft, candied wine that has just enough grassy, citrusy flavors to satisfy. Yet it's thin in the finish, leaving a scour of acidity and not much else. **84** —*S.H.* (9/1/2003)

Eagle & Rose Estate 1999 Sauvignon Blanc (Napa Valley) $16. The aroma of wood dominates, with green, juicy notes and quite a bit of smoky char. Underneath all that is some citrus fruit, but not much. It drinks thin, especially in the middle palate, where it's watery. Picks up citrus flavors and tart acids on the finish. **84** —*S.H.* (11/15/2001)

Eagle & Rose Estate 1998 Sauvignon Blanc (Napa Valley) $16. **88** —*S.H.* (11/15/2000)

EAGLE'S DOMAIN

Eagle's Domain 2000 Reserve Chardonnay (Napa Valley) $7. I'll bet there are 2000 Chards out there from famous, expensive wineries that are already getting tired, but this giveaway is full of life and zest. Eagle's Domain is a Rutherford négociant. This wine has peach and pear flavors wrapped in a creamy texture, and a rich veneer of oak. Your friends won't believe it didn't cost a lot more. **86 Best Buy** —*S.H.* (11/15/2004)

EAGLEPOINT RANCH

Eaglepoint Ranch 2004 Grenache (Mendocino County) $18. The ranch is way up in the Mayacamas range, and its red wines are always concentrated. This Grenache is surprisingly light in structure, almost like a Beaujolais, but rich in sweet cherry pie fruit, dry and elegant. **87** —*S.H.* (12/31/2005)

Eaglepoint Ranch 2003 Grenache (Mendocino) $16. I love this wine, not only because it's so good, but also so different. Has the light color and silky body of Pinot Noir, with flavors of cherry liqueur, vanilla and toast, but also has weight and complexity. Try with penne with sausage and mushrooms. **90** —*S.H.* (3/1/2005)

Eaglepoint Ranch 2001 Grenache (Mendocino County) $14. On the light-bodied side, with silky tannins. It's structured like a Pinot Noir, with cola, raspberry, cranberry and rhubarb tea flavors that are a little thin, but nice and different. **86** —*S.H.* (5/1/2004)

Eaglepoint Ranch 2003 Petite Sirah (Mendocino County) $26. Size matters in Petite Sirah, and this is one big wine. Black in color, bone dry and raspingly tannic, it has a rich heart of blackberry and black cherry fruit. Best with barbecued ribs now, but should age effortlessly for a decade or two. **91 Cellar Selection** —*S.H.* (12/31/2005)

Eaglepoint Ranch 2002 Petite Sirah (Mendocino County) $24. After all the soft red wines lately, it's almost a relief to gag on some real tannins. Dry and spicy, with big-time black cherry pie flavors, complete with the baked, buttery crust. **87** —*S.H.* (3/1/2005)

Eaglepoint Ranch 2001 Petite Sirah (Mendocino County) $24. Big and extracted, in the Eaglepoint style of huge mountain red wines. The blackberry and plum flavors have a peppery edge, with notes of leather and dried herbs. It's a nicely dry wine, and the thick tannins call for stick-to-the-ribs meats, or cellaring through 2010. **88** —*S.H.* (5/1/2004)

Eaglepoint Ranch 2001 Coro Mendocino Red Blend (Mendocino) $35. Firm and focused on the palate, the wine shows off a blend of black cherry, coffee, spice, toast and herb notes that are neatly framed in ripe tannins. The finish is moderate in length, ending with a clean edge. **89** —*J.M.* (9/1/2004)

Eaglepoint Ranch 1999 Sangiovese (Mendocino County) $18. You can tell from the dark color this is a big wine, and one whiff confirms it. Blackberries and plums, smoke, pepper, leather and anise are just some of the complex scents. It's big and fleshy in the mouth, but seems too extracted, especially for this varietal, which wants a certain austere delicacy. This could easily be a big Merlot. **86** —*S.H.* (5/1/2002)

Eaglepoint Ranch 2000 Syrah (Mendocino) $22. Grown at 1,800 feet in the eastern Mendocino hills, a densely textured wine with many attributes of a mountain red. Big, chunky and concentrated, with plum, coffee, chocolate and blackberry flavors and rich but softly modern tannins. **88** —*S.H.* (12/1/2003)

Eaglepoint Ranch 1999 Syrah (Mendocino) $24. From longtime growers, now vintners, on the western slopes of the Mayacamas comes this impressive and huge wine. It's dark as night, with brilliantly complex aromas of berries, leather, sage, smoke and white pepper. It's also mouth filling, and has so many facets, it's hard to keep track. The depth of flavor is stunning, while dusty tannins provide structure. A remarkable Syrah with obvious ageability. **94** —*S.H.* (5/1/2002)

EARTHQUAKE

Earthquake 2003 Cabernet Sauvignon (Lodi) $28. Simple and soft, with well-ripened flavors like those chocolate-covered cherry candies. Fortunately the wine is fully dry, but at the cost of very high alcohol, so be forewarned. **83** —*S.H.* (7/1/2006)

Earthquake 2004 Petite Sirah (Lodi) $28. Rustic and hot, with what seems like residual sugar in addition to high alcohol, this Pet tastes like a blackberry-cherry candied confection. In its favor is vibrant acidity and a clean finish. **83** —*S.H. (7/1/2006)*

Earthquake 2004 Syrah (Lodi) $28. The winemaker swung for the fences with this one, letting the grapes get ultraripe, adding a dash of Cabernet Sauvignon, and aging it in what tastes like lots of fancy, toasty new oak. The results show in the wine's opulence. Gooey and soft, it tastes almost sweet in baked blackberry and cherry pie filling, vanilla, milk chocolate and caramel flavors that go on and on. **89** —*S.H. (12/31/2006)*

Earthquake 2003 Syrah (Lodi) $25. West Coast Editor Steve Heimoff liked this wine a lot more than the two other tasters, so if you normallly follow his suggestions, you may want to give this wine a try. He found it very ripe and extracted, with rich, sweet tannins. Our other reviewers found it less appealing, even a little unrefined and alcoholic. **87** *(9/1/2005)*

EAST VALLEY

East Valley 2002 Cabernet Sauvignon (Santa Ynez Valley) $33. If you're used to Napa Cabs, this will come as a surprise. It's earthier, with dried cherry and herb flavors and lots of spices. The tannins don't try to hide themselves, but are in your face. Finally, the wine is dry and modest in alcohol. It's really interesting. **89** —*S.H. (11/1/2006)*

East Valley 2004 Pinot Noir (Santa Barbara County) $36. This is a soft, thick Pinot. It's fully dry, but has the texture of jelly, with cooked cherry flavors. Nothing technically wrong, just kind of awkward. **83** —*S.H. (10/1/2006)*

East Valley 2003 Sangiovese (Santa Barbara County) $26. This single-vineyard wine comes from the Santa Ynez Valley. It's an awkward wine, hot, with raisiny, Porty flavors. It's totally dry. **82** —*S.H. (10/1/2006)*

East Valley 2002 Syrah (Edna Valley) $22. This wine is dominated by acids and tannins that numb the mouth, although the blackberry and cherry flavors are so ripely powerful, they come through unscathed. Feels rustic now, but it's thoroughly dry, and could be more interesting in a year or two. **85** —*S.H. (10/1/2006)*

EASTON

Easton 2003 Barbera (Shenandoah Valley (CA)) $22. Shows an unusually controlled approach to Barbera, with a balanced texture more like a fine Merlot. The blackberry, coffee, leather, grilled meat and slight oak flavors finish rich and complex, and totally dry. Best now and through 2010. **88** —*S.H. (6/1/2006)*

Easton 2002 Barbera (Shenandoah Valley (CA)) $20. Really harsh in tannins and acids, with coffee and berry flavors, this wine might improve after many years, but it's not offering much now. **83** —*S.H. (8/1/2005)*

Easton 2001 Barbera (Shenandoah Valley (CA)) $20. Fruity, tannic and full-bodied, a workhorse grape and wine that strives for elegance and finesse, and comes close. Cherries, leather, lots of herbs and a finish of slightly sweetened coffee suggest robust foods. The high acidity will cut right through fats **86** —*S.H. (6/1/2004)*

Easton 2000 Barbera (Shenandoah Valley (CA)) $20. A strongly flavored wine bursting with red cherry, tobacco, smoke, bacon fat, pepper and spice notes. It's very dry, with rich but easy tannins. Pretty good drinking, and a reminder that this workhorse varietal can make a darn good bottle. **87** —*S.H. (5/1/2003)*

Easton 2000 Cabernet Sauvignon (California) $15. Surprisingly rich and complex for this price and the statewide appellation, a full-bodied wine with glorious flavors of blackcurrants. Coats the mouth and lasts through a long finish. The tannins are soft and intricate and add to the enjoyment. **90 Best Buy** —*S.H. (6/1/2003)*

Easton 2002 Estate Cabernet Sauvignon (Shenandoah Valley (CA)) $30. One of the best Sierra Foothills Cabs I've tasted, this wine is soft and lush in fruit, with rich, intricate tannins framing well-ripened cassis and blackberry pie flavors. The wine is dry and balanced, with just a hint of rusticity. **88** —*S.H. (6/1/2006)*

Easton 2001 Estate Bottled Cabernet Sauvignon (Shenandoah Valley (CA)) $30. Lots to admire in this dry, balanced Cab. It shows plenty of harmo-ny in the way it pulls together the complex berry and spice flavors, smooth tannins, subtle oak and acid-alcohol balance. Easy to drink, yet has style and finesse. **89** —*S.H. (8/1/2005)*

Easton 2004 Sauvignon Blanc (Sierra Foothills) $16. Dry, crisp in acidity and balanced, with citrus flavors, this is a refreshingly clean wine. It could use more fruity concentration, though, as it's thin and watery in the finish. **83** —*S.H. (6/1/2006)*

Easton 2003 Sauvignon Blanc (Sierra Foothills) $16. This is a fairly dry wine, tart in acids and citrus fruits, but enriched with highlights of figs and melons that give it some sweetness in the finish. It seems to have a little smoky oak in there, too. Easy to like, and the slight sweetness will pay well against fruits or sole sautéed in butter sauce. **85** —*S.H. (8/1/2005)*

Easton 2004 Zinfandel (Amador County) $13. If you're looking for a classic Foothills Zin, briary and brambly, with the tannic strength to cut through lamb or short ribs, try this one. It's bone dry and fruity, with a rich sweetness to the finish. **86** —*S.H. (6/1/2006)*

Easton 2003 Zinfandel (Amador County) $13. A good example of a robust mountain Zin that retains a bit of rusticity. It's dry and warming, with earthy, cherry and spice flavors, and rich but negotiable tannins. **85** —*S.H. (4/1/2005)*

Easton 2002 Zinfandel (Amador County) $13. Blackberries and cherries coexist side by side with Porty, raisiny flavors in this rough-and-ready mountain Zin. There seems to be a little residual sugar, to judge by the sweetness. It'll be fine with a pizza pie. **85** —*S.H. (6/1/2004)*

Easton 2002 Zinfandel (Fiddletown) $25. Considerably drier and more tannic than Easton's estate Zin, and maybe more characteristic of the Sierra Foothills. Showing cherry, plum and mocha flavors, with a dusty, astringent finish. Great with beef. **89** —*S.H. (8/1/2005)*

Easton 2001 Zinfandel (Fiddletown) $25. So rich in flavor, it's like liquid candy, a purée of raspberries, cherries and blueberries, with a little brown sugar thrown in for good measure. But it's technically dry, with lush, smooth tannins. Distinctive, concentrated and intense. **90** —*S.H. (6/1/2004)*

Easton 2001 Zinfandel (Amador County) $13. Basic, fundamental Zin, with its wild berry, tobacco and white pepper flavors, brawny tannins and full-bodied texture. A bit rustic. Enjoy with burgers or spaghetti. **84** —*S.H. (9/1/2003)*

Easton 2001 Zinfandel (Shenandoah Valley (CA)) $30. Distinctly briary in its aromas, with overtones of nougat and pine, but in the mouth it really comes alive. Massive, decadently ripe cherry and blackberry flavors are meshed with big, thick, smooth tannins. While it's dry, it finishes like a dessert wine, and a little hot in alcohol. **90** —*S.H. (6/1/2004)*

Easton 2000 Zinfandel (Shenandoah Valley (CA)) $30. One of the best Zins of the year, a near perfect refinement of Sierra Foothills Zin. Estate bottled, it's incredibly soft, rich, and delicious. Caresses the palate with sumptuous blueberry, black cherry, fig, pepper, and white chocolate flavors. Hard to believe it has 15.2 percent alcohol because it's so balanced. Addictive stuff. **93 Editors' Choice** —*S.H. (9/1/2003)*

Easton 2000 Zinfandel (Shenandoah Valley (CA)) $22. Evocative and expressive, this is an in-your-face Zin, with its big flavors of wild dark berries, tobacco, and earth. Yet it's balanced and harmonious, with good tannins and acids, and is completely dry. The alcohol is a relatively modest 14.5%. **88** —*S.H. (9/1/2003)*

Easton 2000 Zinfandel (Amador County) $13. Concentrated and juicy, this Zin packs solid blueberry and other wild berry and spice flavors into a complex package that's dry, but filled with sunny ripeness. From the lush entry through the jammy flavors to the long, peppery finish, it's a heckuva wine. **89 Best Buy** —*S.H. (3/1/2002)*

Easton 2000 Zinfandel (Fiddletown) $25. Lively and zesty, with wild berry and pepper flavors. Suffers from a sharpness that lasts through the finish, and turns syrupy-sweet in the aftertaste. **84** —*S.H. (9/1/2003)*

Easton 1999 Zinfandel (Fiddletown) $25. Here's a wine that defines a distinct style of Sierra Foothills Zin, namely, the wild, brambly kind that seduces with sheer power and exuberance. It's a mouthpunch of blueberry, boysenberry and other berry flavors, wrapped in just enough tannins

USA

and acids to provide balance. There's something woolly about it, especially in the peppery finish. **91** —*S.H. (3/1/2002)*

Easton 1999 Zinfandel (Shenandoah Valley (CA)) $30. This is an extraordinarily interesting wine, because it reeks of personality and terroir, with luscious black raspberry fruit and a rich espresso-and-chocolate dimension. It's a soft, velvety, round wine of great charm. You could get addicted to this stuff. **83** —*S.H. (3/1/2002)*

Easton 1997 Zinfandel (Shenandoah Valley (CA)) $20. Lots of sharp-edged oak around a soft, plummy, chocolate-covered cherry of a wine. Smooth and easy-drinking, up to a fairly tannic finish. The acids keep everything in balance. **87** —*P.G. (3/1/2001)*

Easton 2003 Estate Zinfandel (Shenandoah Valley (CA)) $30. Ultrarich, with a velvety, silky texture despite the sizable tannins, this is a pure Foothills Zin. It's superripe, with blackberry and espresso flavors veering into raisins and cooked fruit, but never loses control and balance. **86** —*S.H. (6/1/2006)*

Easton 2002 Estate Bottled Zinfandel (Shenandoah Valley (CA)) $30. This is a delicious Zin, easy to drink, but it's far from simple. With the elegant mouthfeel of a soft Merlot, it offers rich, almost decadent flavors of black raspberries and cherry mocha, candied ginger, creme de cassis and white pepper. **90** —*S.H. (8/1/2005)*

Easton 2002 Late Harvest Zinfandel (El Dorado) $18. Should be either sweeter or drier. It straddles the line, offering coffee and cassis flavors and astringent tannins. **84** —*S.H. (8/1/2005)*

Easton 2003 Old Vine Zinfandel (Fiddletown) $25. Shows a greater elegance and finesse than Easton's other current Zins, reflected in the smooth, ripe tannins, balancing acids and dry finish. Then there are the flavors, extraordinarily rich in blackberry pie, espresso and peppery spice. This is classic California mountain Zin. **88** —*S.H. (6/1/2006)*

EASTON HOUSE

Easton House NV Lot No. 0102 Red Blend (California) $10. Rustic, thickly textured and fruity, but soft and easy, this honest country wine is clean and satisfying. It has strong berry flavors that most people will appreciate. **84** —*S.H. (8/1/2005)*

EASTWOOD

Eastwood 2004 Cabernet Sauvignon (California) $9. Here's a wine that brings to mind thoughts of easy backyard steaks. It's dry and rich in cherry, blackberry and blueberry fruit flavors, with thick, brisk tannins and a veneer of sweet oak. **84** —*S.H. (6/1/2006)*

Eastwood 2004 Chardonnay (California) $9. Nicely dry, crisp in acidity, and with apple flavors streaked with a stony minerality, this Chard offers clean, everyday pleasure. **84** —*S.H. (6/1/2006)*

Eastwood 2004 Merlot (California) $9. Rustic in country-style tannins, with a hint of raisins, this dry Merlot features cherry and cocoa flavors backed up by firm acids. It's an everyday, versatile red wine. **84** —*S.H. (6/1/2006)*

EBERLE

Eberle 2002 Sauret & Steinbeck Vineyards Barbera (Paso Robles) $18. A nice rendition of this country-style varietal. It's full-bodied and rich in plummy, earthy flavors. There are some tough tannins, but the acids balance. **86** —*S.H. (12/15/2004)*

Eberle 2001 Sauret Vineyard Barbera (Paso Robles) $18. From a well-known vineyard, a dark, rich wine that does not display the harsh acids and tannins of coastal Barberas. The tannins are thick but soft and melted. Flavors include plums, blackberries and chocolate, but it's a little on the soft side. **86** —*S.H. (12/1/2003)*

Eberle 2004 Steinbeck and Sauret Vineyards Barbera (Paso Robles) $20. Classic California Barbera, black in color, bone dry, big in rasping tannins, and rich in fruit. Blackberries, cherries, plums, soy, leather, coffee, the list goes on. Curiously combines rusticity with refinement, and will age for twenty years. **88** —*S.H. (11/15/2006)*

Eberle 2003 Steinbeck and Sauret Vineyards Barbera (Paso Robles) $18. Let's face it: Barbera will never be anything but a workhorse wine. This one, from two famous vineyards, is heavy and dull in texture, with

mocha, blackberry and herbal flavors that finish very dry. It will probably age forever, getting lighter and sweeter. **84** —*S.H. (11/15/2005)*

Eberle 2000 Cabernet Sauvignon (Paso Robles) $23. A supersoft Cabernet whose excellent blackberry and cassis flavors are not supported by tannins or acidity. The taste is so pleasant, the grapes so rich in ripe fruitiness, you wish for a firmer structure. But it's not there. **85** —*S.H. (11/15/2003)*

Eberle 1999 Cabernet Sauvignon (Paso Robles) $28. Consistently one of the best Cabernets made south of the Bay Area, this year the wine is especially tasty. Not too ripe, with suggestions of blackberry and cassis and herbs, and some good, old-fashioned tannins. **91** —*S.H. (7/1/2002)*

Eberle 2002 Estate Cabernet Sauvignon (Paso Robles) $27. Eberle's estate Cab is a seriously attractive wine, due mainly to its soft, velvety tannins and delicious blackberry and cherry flavors. A hint of raisins is there, but adds seasoning to the finish. **91** —*S.H. (11/15/2005)*

Eberle 2001 Estate Cabernet Sauvignon (Paso Robles) $25. A pleasant, easy-drinking Cab with some special qualities, namely the velvety soft texture that feels so plush on the palate. It carries ripe blackberry and cherry fruit flavors. **86** —*S.H. (10/1/2004)*

Eberle 2003 Estate Bottled Cabernet Sauvignon (Paso Robles) $29. Take your average oaky Napa cult Cab, strip away the bells and whistles that make it, rather than food, the star at the table, and what you get is this balanced, elegant Cab. Gary Eberle has spent a lifetime figuring out how to make a wine like this, and food-loving wine drinkers are the beneficiaries. **90** —*S.H. (11/15/2006)*

Eberle 1997 Estate Bottled Cabernet Sauvignon (Paso Robles) $30. **86** *(11/1/2000)*

Eberle 2001 Estate Bottled Reserve Cabernet Sauvignon (Paso Robles) $65. Gary Eberle brings his deft touch to Cabernet, resulting in this smooth wine with soft tannins and an elegant dryness. It's forward in plummy, blackberry fruit, with an earthy, coffee edge. A minor quibble is the taste of raisins or shrivelled prunes are a detraction. **88** —*S.H. (9/1/2006)*

Eberle 1999 Reserve Cabernet Sauvignon (Paso Robles) $75. Quite a fine Cab, and to judge by its freshness, tannins and very long, fruity finish, it's still only in its infancy. It will be interesting to follow its development, but now, it's lively and complex in blackberry and oak flavors. **90** —*S.H. (11/15/2004)*

Eberle 2003 Vineyard Selection Cabernet Sauvignon (Paso Robles) $17. Dry, strong, flavorful, tannic, earthy and balanced. That in a nutshell describes this wine. It's the kind of Cab folks used to drink when they wanted something good with food, but without fuss. **87** —*S.H. (11/15/2006)*

Eberle 2002 Vineyard Selection Cabernet Sauvignon (Paso Robles) $17. Showing good Cabernet character, this pleasant wine has blackberry, currant and cocoa flavors, wrapped in soft, gentle tannins. It's nicely dry, and finishes with a bite of pepper. **86** —*S.H. (11/15/2005)*

Eberle 2001 Vineyard Selection Cabernet Sauvignon (Paso Robles) $17. This softly luscious Cab glides across the palate like velvet, although it finishes with a good grip of tannins. The polished flavors suggest blackberries, currants and coffee, while oak is kept judiciously in the background. **88** —*S.H. (10/1/2004)*

Eberle 2002 Cabernet Sauvignon-Syrah (Paso Robles) $24. Fancy, plush fare from this veteran South Coast producer. Floods the palate with ripe blackberry, cherry, mocha and peppery spice flavors wrapped in soft, luxuriously sweet tannins. The finish is long and reprises the cherry-and-spice theme. **91** —*S.H. (12/15/2004)*

Eberle 2001 Cabernet Sauvignon-Syrah (Paso Robles) $24. Opens with the beautiful scent of well-ripened Cabernet grapes, with intense aromas of blackcurrants and cassis, as well as a pretty overlay of toasty vanilla from oak. The flavors are impressively deep and ripe, but the wine suffers from excessive softness. **85** —*S.H. (11/15/2003)*

Eberle 2004 Chardonnay (Paso Robles) $16. The heat of Paso hasn't given this Chard much acidity, but in its place you'll find beautifully ripened fruit. It tastes like peaches floating in natural cream, drizzled with honey and vanilla and just a dash of creme de cassis. It's really quite an impressive wine. **90** —*S.H. (11/15/2005)*

Eberle 2002 Chardonnay (Paso Robles) $16. A pleasant sipper whose flavors range from citrus fruits through tropical fruits, indicating a regional blend. The other elements are similarly well balanced, with good acidity and a nice overlay of creamy oak and vanilla. **85** —*S.H. (12/1/2003)*

Eberle 2003 Estate Chardonnay (Paso Robles) $16. Lots of toasty oak, plenty of ripe tropical fruit in this polished, friendly wine. The creamy texture and long, spicy finish bring it all together. **87** —*S.H. (12/15/2004)*

Eberle 1998 Estate Chardonnay (Paso Robles) $15. 85 *(6/1/2000)*

Eberle 2005 Estate Bottled Chardonnay (Paso Robles) $18. Dry and crisp, with mineral, ash and slate flavors relieved by a dash of grapefruit. A wine like this doesn't win competitions, but it has its place on the table with tapas or alone as an apéritif. **85** —*S.H. (11/15/2006)*

Eberle 2005 Muscat Canelli (Paso Robles) $14. Always one of Eberle's most pleasant wines. Rich in apricot jam, peach cobbler and spicy vanilla flavors, the wine is overtly sweet but with enough acidity for balance. **84** —*S.H. (12/1/2006)*

Eberle 2004 Muscat Canelli (Paso Robles) $12. The first time I ever had Eberle's Muscat, I thought it was the perfect garden sipper. It still is. Redolent with aromas of flowers and orchard fruits, it's semisweet and clean, with a long, spicy finish. **87 Best Buy** —*S.H. (11/15/2005)*

Eberle 2003 Muscat Canelli (Paso Robles) $12. An old favorite from Eberle, this release is fragrant with orangey butter, smoky honeysuckle and vanilla aromas that lead to impressively ripe tangerine and vanilla flavors. It's frankly sweet, with good balancing acidity. **87** —*S.H. (12/15/2004)*

Eberle 2003 Cabernet Sauvignon-Syrah Red Blend (Paso Robles) $24. As rich as Eberle's Cabernets are, Syrah seems to bring an added dimension of decadent cherry-berry liqueur to the blend. The wine is velvety soft in tannins, and so fruity, it finishes with a honeyed sweetness. **88** —*S.H. (11/15/2005)*

Eberle 1997 Cotes-du-Robles Red Blend (Paso Robles) $14. 88 Best Buy —*S.H. (6/1/1999)*

Eberle 2003 Roussanne (Paso Robles) $22. Deliciously drinkable for its soft, creamy texture and juicy flavors of peaches and cream, exotic tropical fruits, vanilla and honey. This dry wine is great all by itself. **87** —*S.H. (12/15/2004)*

Eberle 2005 Cass Vineyards Roussanne (Paso Robles) $22. While everyone else is picking superripe, Eberle prefers a high- acid, lower-fruit wine. This doesn't have particular Roussanne character as it's too dry and citrusy. But it's a clean wine with a brisk mouthfeel. **85** —*S.H. (11/15/2006)*

Eberle 2004 Cass Vineyards Roussanne (Paso Robles) $22. Almost dessert-like in apparent sweetness, but balanced with crisp acidity, this luscious wine is filled with honey, baked apple, peach, apricot and vanilla flavors. **86** —*S.H. (11/15/2005)*

Eberle 2003 Sangiovese (Paso Robles) $16. With 15% alcohol, this wine's hot, with a prickly, peppery finish. But that's part of its personality, which also includes plummy, black cherry and coffee flavors. It's very dry, and should be good with beef grilled as the sun goes down. **85** —*S.H. (11/15/2005)*

Eberle 2002 Sangiovese (Paso Robles) $16. Tough tannins frame the berry, cherry and herb flavors, leading to a dry finish in this food-friendly wine. Perfect with short ribs. **85** —*S.H. (12/15/2004)*

Eberle 2001 Filipponi & Thompson Vineyard Sangiovese (Paso Robles) $16. Sangiovese likes the warmth of Paso Robles, which ripens it to black cherry flavors, but this seems overcropped. The fruitiness is thin, and is overshadowed by astringent tannins. **84** —*S.H. (12/1/2003)*

Eberle 2002 Lonesome Oak Vineyard Syrah (Paso Robles) $16. Lush and opulent in blackberry and coffee fruit, with a heated, peppery scour of alcohol. This wine is totally dry and balanced, with a long finish. Will be great with barbecue to soften it. **87** —*S.H. (12/15/2004)*

Eberle 2001 Reid Vineyard Syrah (Paso Robles) $20. Like Eberle's Steinbeck Syrah, the flavors here are excellent, suggesting spicy plums and blackberries, with a rich edge of ground coffee and a melange of spices and dried herbs. The tannins also are good and rich. Once again, the problem is excessive softness. The mouthfeel is weak and lacks grip. **85** —*S.H. (2/1/2004)*

Eberle 1999 Reid Vineyard Syrah (Paso Robles) $20. Tart red berries, black pepper and tangy oak aromas lead into a structured, dry blackberry-caramel-oak palate. It's uncomplicated, with an even mouthfeel and a dry mineral-and-metal finish. **85** *(10/1/2001)*

Eberle 1997 Reid Vineyard Syrah (Paso Robles) $18. 88 —*S.H. (6/1/1999)*

Eberle 2003 Rose Syrah (Paso Robles) $14. There's lots of complexity in this polished blush wine. It's rich in spicy blackberry, ginger and vanilla flavors, and is dry and balanced. Full-bodied enough to stand up to steak or chops. **86** —*S.H. (12/15/2004)*

Eberle 2002 Rosé Syrah (Paso Robles) $14. Eberle has a way with rose wines, and this one is very pleasant. It has flavors of strawberries and raspberries and spices that are richly ripe, but the wine is dry. It has a good boost of acidity and will be refreshingly cool on a hot afternoon. **85** —*S.H. (3/1/2004)*

Eberle 2004 Rose of Syrah (Paso Robles) $14. If you're barbecuing and looking for a wine everyone will like, try this dry, fruity blush Syrah. It's got peppery raspberry, cherry and vanilla flavors, and the rich burst of acidity will play well against meats and cheeses. **86** —*S.H. (11/15/2005)*

Eberle 2003 Steinbeck Vineyard Syrah (Paso Robles) $24. What great aromas start things off here. It's all about chocolate and cassis, roasted coffeebeans and smoky vanilla.Then things fall off. The wine turns overly flabby, almost flat in the mouth. But it is dry. **84** —*S.H. (11/15/2005)*

Eberle 2002 Steinbeck Vineyard Syrah (Paso Robles) $20. Drier and more tannic than Eberle's Lonesome Oak Syrah, this wine is also earthier. Flavors of sweet, dried herbs frame dark berries and oak. There's real complexity in the finish. **87** —*S.H. (12/15/2004)*

Eberle 2001 Steinbeck Vineyard Syrah (Paso Robles) $20. A little chewy, with big tannins framing the charry, smoky-edged plum, blackberry and black cherry flavors. Toasty oak and vanilla notes add a framework that finishes with moderate length. **87** *(2/1/2004)*

Eberle 1997 Steinbeck Vineyard Syrah (Paso Robles) $18. 87 —*S.H. (6/1/1999)*

Eberle 2002 Steinbeck Vineyard Reserve Syrah (Paso Robles) $45. Eberle has built more tannic structure into this reserve wine than into their regular Steinbeck Syrah. That seems to have come at the cost of some fruity ripeness, however. At the same time, there's a curious sweetness. It adds up to an awkwardness that's unlikely to change with age. **84** —*S.H. (11/15/2005)*

Eberle 2005 Syrah Rosé Syrah (Paso Robles) $16. A very nice rosé, the kind that wineries should make more of. It's very dry and fruity, not a bomb, with subtle raspberry, tobacco, vanilla, spice and herb flavors, and a bright, crisp spine of acidity for balance. **87** —*S.H. (11/15/2006)*

Eberle 2002 Glenrose Vineyard Viognier (Paso Robles) $22. Unctuously rich in texture, almost like half-and-half, with aromas and flavors of ultraripe peaches, white chocolate, vanilla and honeysuckle. Finishes long and rich. **87** —*S.H. (12/1/2003)*

Eberle 1998 Glenrose Vineyard Viognier (Paso Robles) $20. 87 —*S.H. (10/1/1999)*

Eberle 2004 Mill Road Viognier (Paso Robles) $18. Although it's a rather soft wine, this Viognier has such beguiling flavors that it offers real pleasure. Those flavors include caramelized peach, lemon custard, buttered popcorn, vanilla fudge and honey, and while that makes it sound sweet, it's actually rather dry. **89** —*S.H. (11/15/2005)*

Eberle 2005 Mill Road Vineyard Viognier (Paso Robles) $20. Soft and easy, with fruity, flowery flavors that have an earthiness to them, like soy-sautéed mushrooms. Don't serve it too cold, as it gets more interesting as it warms up. **85** —*S.H. (11/15/2006)*

Eberle 2003 Mill Road Vineyard Viognier (Paso Robles) $18. Filled with fruity flavors ranging from ripe white peaches to papayas, this pleasantly crisp wine also has a spicy, floral finish that lasts for a long time, and leaves behind a taste of honey. **85** —*S.H. (12/15/2004)*

Eberle 2002 Mill Road Vineyard Viognier (Paso Robles) $18. Firmer and more taut than Eberle's Glenrose Viognier, with a sleek backbone of vibrant acidity. But the wine is no slouch when it comes to flavor, offering up gobs of mango, papaya, pineapple and peach, spiced generously with cinnamon and pepper. A very fine wine, and just shows how good Viognier from Paso Robles can be. **89** —*S.H. (12/1/2003)*

Eberle 2001 Mill Road Vineyard Viognier (Paso Robles) $18. Quite smooth and creamy on the palate, with plenty of spice, apricot, melon, peach and pear flavors. Lush on the finish, it lingers nicely. **90** —*J.M. (12/15/2002)*

Eberle 2003 Zinfandel (Paso Robles) $16. Classic Paso Zin, soft, dry, and long on blackberry, cherry, chocolate and spice flavors that flood the palate and last into the finish. There's something soul-soothing about this wine. **87** —*S.H. (11/15/2005)*

Eberle 2004 Remo Belli Vineyard Zinfandel (Paso Robles) $22. Here's a lusty glass of Zin, and quite a bit better than the '03. This time around the wine is robust in berry, coffee, tobacco and herb flavors, and the tannins are rich and thick. Just the thing for a nice steak. **87** —*S.H. (12/1/2006)*

Eberle 2003 Remo Belli Vineyard Zinfandel (Paso Robles) $22. There seems to be too much residual sugar in this soft Zin. Too bad, because it's smooth, with yummy blackberry, cherry and chocolate flavors. **84** —*S.H. (11/15/2005)*

Eberle 2002 Remo Belli Vineyard Zinfandel (Paso Robles) $18. An ultra-fruity style, packed with black cherry, chocolate, raspberry, plum, spice and licorice flavors. The tannins are moderate, as is the finish, which leaves an equally fruity impression. **88** —*J.M. (12/31/2004)*

Eberle 2001 Remo Belli Vineyard Zinfandel (Paso Robles) $18. Bright and spicy in the nose, with zippy, jammy raspberry, cherry, blackberry and plum flavors. Acidity is quite bright, but the tannins are mellow enough to handle it. Fun and zingy to the end. **88** *(11/1/2003)*

Eberle 1997 Sauret Vineyard Zinfandel (Paso Robles) $20. 91 —*J.C. (9/1/1999)*

Eberle 2004 Steinbeck Vineyard Zinfandel (Paso Robles) $18. Nice and fruity, with wild berry, spice, tobacco, pepper and coffee flavors wrapped into fine, silky tannins. The wine is entirely dry. It's a bit prickly due to 16% alcohol, but feels balanced. **85** —*S.H. (11/15/2006)*

Eberle 2002 Steinbeck Vineyard Zinfandel (Paso Robles) $16. You can taste the sun in every chocolaty, wild berry and cassis-infused sip, and thankfully the wine is fully dry. Perfect with barbecue, and delicious all by its lonesome. **90** —*S.H. (12/15/2004)*

Eberle 1997 Steinbeck Vineyard Zinfandel (Paso Robles) $16. 87 —*J.C. (9/1/1999)*

ECHELON

Echelon 2003 Cabernet Sauvignon (Hames Valley) $13. Echelon gets into the Cab game with this bottling from a southernmost, warm region of Monterey, by Paso Robles. The wine is juicy in jammy cherry and blackberry fruit, and dry, with soft acids and smooth tannins. **84** —*S.H. (5/1/2006)*

Echelon 2002 Cabernet Sauvignon (Hames Valley) $12. This is a good everyday red wine, clean and with some richness. It's full-bodied, with blackberry-cherry and earth flavors, and a pretty finish of currants. **84** —*S.H. (8/1/2005)*

Echelon 2001 Cabernet Sauvignon (California) $12. Chalone's second label has produced a nice little Cab with enough body and flavor to satisfy, even at this price. It's certainly no blockbuster, but the blackberries and currants are joined with smoky oak and drink with some richness and finesse. **84** —*S.H. (11/15/2003)*

Echelon 2000 Cabernet Sauvignon (California) $13. Mild-bodied, with hints of blackberry, cherry, herb and spice notes. Easy to quaff. **83** —*J.M. (12/31/2002)*

Echelon 1998 Chardonnay (Central Coast) $15. 85 *(6/1/2000)*

Echelon 2003 Chardonnay (Central Coast) $12. Soupy-soft, simple and cloying, with the flavor of sweetened apricot and peach syrup. **81** —*S.H. (12/1/2005)*

Echelon 2002 Chardonnay (Central Coast) $10. They managed to get a lot of flavor and oak into this wine. It has flavors of peaches and sweet honeydew, with layers of smoke, vanilla and spice. Very clean and satisfying, and a good value. **86** —*S.H. (5/1/2004)*

Echelon 1997 Merlot (Central Coast) $15. 84 —*S.H. (7/1/2000)*

Echelon 2002 Merlot (Central Coast) $12. Here's a dry, fairly tannic wine, chewy and rich in blackberry, chocolate and coffee flavors. It has some bitterness on the finish. This is a fair price for a wine of this balance. **84** —*S.H. (8/1/2005)*

Echelon 2001 Merlot (Central Coast) $12. Here's a decent, everyday sipper in a full-bodied red wine. It's dry enough to accompany a steak or roast, with modest berry flavors that turn astringent on the finish. Perfect for backyard gatherings where barbecue is the theme. **84** —*S.H. (2/1/2004)*

Echelon 1999 Merlot (California) $13. From Chalone's second label. A perfectly acceptable wine with lots of up-front fruity flavors and quite a bit of elegant structure for this price. It's dry, round and supple, and has a surprising edge of quality and depth. You have to hand much of the credit to the excellent vintage, which aids all wines, not just expensive ones. **85** —*S.H. (5/1/2001)*

Echelon 2001 Pinot Grigio (Central Coast) $11. Quite peachy and lemony, with moderate body and a clean finish. Simple and pleasant. **84** —*J.M. (9/1/2003)*

Echelon 2004 Esperanza Vineyard Pinot Grigio (Clarksburg) $10. Simple and off-dry, this lemon and lime flavored wine has overtones of vanilla and peaches, and good acidity. **83** —*S.H. (2/1/2006)*

Echelon 2003 Esperanza Vineyard Pinot Grigio (Clarksburg) $11. With its light, clean mouthfeel, zesty flavors of sweet apple and lime, and swift acidity, this is almost the perfect inexpensive cocktail wine. Fine with fresh fruits or shrimp cocktail, or just on its own. **84** —*S.H. (9/1/2004)*

Echelon 2004 Pinot Noir (Central Coast) $13. Moderately priced Pinot is getting better, as this crisp, fruity wine shows. It has proper varietal character in the silky tannins, keen acids and polished cherry-vanilla flavors, with an edge of smoke oak. **85** —*S.H. (5/1/2006)*

Echelon 2003 Pinot Noir (Central Coast) $10. The Chalone Wine Group created the Echelon brand in 1997 to offer a range of inexpensive wines to complement Chalone's single-vineyard bottlings. This Pinot Noir certainly tastes much better than its price would have you believe. With fruit coming mainly from growers in the cool-climate Santa Lucia Highlands above California's Salinas Valley, the wine is packed with sweet strawberry and cherry flavors, layers of wood, and soft tannins. **86 Best Buy** —*R.V. (11/15/2004)*

Echelon 2002 Pinot Noir (Central Coast) $10. Who would have thought a few years ago you could buy a good Pinot at this price? Sure, it's one dimensional, but satisfies with its silky texture, crisp acids, and cherry, cola and herb flavors. Nice value from the Chalone Wine Group. **85 Best Buy** —*S.H. (5/1/2004)*

Echelon 2001 Pinot Noir (Central Coast) $12. Probably best at first, as it goes a little weedy upon further inspection. In its support there's some leather and cherry as well as creamy berry flavors. It feels good on the palate and isn't sour. But the fruit loses focus with each minute the wine is open. **84** —*M.S. (12/1/2003)*

Echelon 2000 Pinot Noir (Central Coast) $14. A fleshy-textured, mild-mannered Pinot that offers pleasant cherry, plum and herb flavors up front and a moderate finish. **87** —*J.M. (5/1/2002)*

Echelon 1997 Pinot Noir (Central Coast) $NA. 83 — *(10/1/1999)*

Echelon 2003 Shiraz (Central Coast) $12. Super-young and jammy, with high, fresh acidity framing cherry and blackberry flavors, this wine has the merit of being dry and balanced. It's a nice country-style wine, easy to savor with simple fare. **84** —*S.H. (5/1/2006)*

Echelon 1999 Syrah (California) $14. In this lightweight but nicely textured wine, decent complexity shows in the tart berry, rhubarb and cocoa aromas and flavors. Mild smoke and leather accents provide palate interest while the tart-sweet close has gentle peppery notes. **86** *(10/1/2001)*

Echelon 2002 Esperanza Vineyard Syrah (Clarksburg) $10. This lovely Syrah could be one of your basic house reds. It's dry and smooth, with

USA

pure flavors of blackberries, pepper, cocoa and oak. Firm and acidic enough to stand up to rich meats. **85 Best Buy** —*S.H. (4/1/2005)*

Echelon 2001 Esperanza Vineyard Syrah (Clarksburg) $10. There are some pretty plum, blackberry and coffee flavors in this dry wine. It's full-bodied and assertive enough for a steak or a rich beef stew, which will give the rough tannins something to work against. Second label of Chalone. **85** —*S.H. (2/1/2004)*

Echelon 2000 Esperanza Vineyard Syrah (Clarksburg) $10. 84 Best Buy —*J.M. (11/15/2002)*

Echelon 2001 Esperanza Vineyard Viognier (Clarksburg) $13. Spice and peach flavors are at the core of this wine. It's got moderate body, some pleasant mineral overtones and a crisp, clean finish. **85** —*J.M. (9/1/2003)*

Echelon 2003 Driving Range Vineyard Zinfandel (Contra Costa County) $13. Hits all the wrong buttons for me, with its porty, cooked berry aroma and dry, harsh tannins. **82** —*S.H. (8/1/2005)*

ECKERT

Eckert 2000 Eckert Acres Cabernet Sauvignon (Livermore Valley) $18. Average-quality Cab, with flavors of blackberries and herbs and supple tannins. The smooth, complex texture carries the flavors through to a ripe finish. Pretty good for the vintage. **85** —*S.H. (11/15/2003)*

Eckert 2000 Petite Sirah (Lodi) $18. A heavy wine, and Porty too, with aromas of caramelized wood, sweet raisins, and pie crust. It's fruity-rich in very ripe blackberry flavors that are carried in a syrupy texture. **83** —*S.H. (3/1/2004)*

EDEN CANYON

Eden Canyon 2002 Cabernet Sauvignon (Paso Robles) $25. Luscious and soft, with chocolaty blackberry, cassis and cherry flavors. Drinks dry and elegant, with under 14% alcohol. A very nice wine, from California's first Filipino-American winery. **87** —*S.H. (12/31/2006)*

Eden Canyon 2003 Estate Cabernet Sauvignon (Paso Robles) $30. This is quite a good Cabernet. It's from the eastern part of Paso Robles, grown at 1,800 feet of elevation, which modulates the heat. While it shows very ripe Cabernet flavor, it possesses a good acid-tannin structure. **88** —*S.H. (12/31/2006)*

EDGEFIELD

Edgefield 2002 Chukar Ridge Vineyard Syrah (Columbia Valley (WA)) $22. This medium-weight Syrah turns a bit drying on the finish but seems to have the requisite fruit to age well. Mixed berries mingle with coffee and herbs on the nose, while the palate picks up more coffee and vanilla flavors from new oak. Try in 2008. **86** *(9/1/2005)*

Edgefield 1998 Chukar Ridge Vineyard Syrah (Columbia Valley (WA)) $11. Well-structured, this is a fairly serious Syrah for a modest price. Dry cherry, leather, licorice and toast show on a lean, almost claret-like frame. Finishes dry with firm, moderate tannins. A value-cellar choice, this will benefit from one to three years aging. **88 Best Buy** *(10/1/2001)*

EDGEWOOD

Edgewood 2000 Tradition Bordeaux Blend (Napa Valley) $35. Opens with blackberry and herb flavors and scents of smoky oak, and then turns firm in the mouth, with thick but soft tannins. There are notes of blackberries and cherries, and when you swallow, the tannins and acids take over. Could age mid-term, but probably at its elegant best now through 2005. **88** —*S.H. (5/1/2004)*

Edgewood 1995 Tradition Bordeaux Blend (Napa Valley) $30. 88 *(3/1/2000)*

Edgewood 2001 Cabernet Sauvignon (Napa Valley) $26. This is a gentle Cabernet, with a feminine delicacy to it, although it's firm in tannins. The flavors are not powerful, suggesting herbs, cherries and oak, and the finish is totally dry. There's a balance and harmony that's easy to enjoy, but also some real complexity. **88** —*S.H. (11/15/2004)*

Edgewood 2000 Cabernet Sauvignon (Napa Valley) $24. This is a delicious regional Cabernet. It has ripe, gentle tannins, supportive acidity, a pedigreed mouthfeel and succulent oak. The blackcurrant and cassis flavors are a little thin in the middle. **88** —*S.H. (2/1/2004)*

Edgewood 2000 Estate Vineyard Cabernet Sauvignon (Napa Valley) $35. This wine has a good, dark color, rich aromas of currants and toasty oak,

blackberry flavors and fine, dry tannins. It merits a high score because of all these qualities, and yet it would score higher except for a certain absence of depth of flavor. Defines the deficiencies of this vintage. **90** —*S.H. (12/31/2003)*

Edgewood 2000 Frediani Vineyard Cabernet Sauvignon (Napa Valley) $40. This single-vineyard Cab from Edgewood is quite different from their other wines. This is the mintiest of the current releases, with a scent of menthol and eucalyptus that may come from nearby trees. It's also minty in the mouth, but that doesn't stop the blackberry flavors a bit. It's ready to drink now, with sturdy tannins. **90** —*S.H. (2/1/2004)*

Edgewood 2000 Lewelling Vineyard Cabernet Sauvignon (Napa Valley) $35. Feels fancy and plush in the mouth, with pretty tannins that are ripe and dusty, and quite a thick slathering of oak. The flavors are on the thin side, suggesting blackberries; really though, it's more herbal and tobaccoey than fruity. **88** —*S.H. (12/31/2003)*

Edgewood 2000 Reserve Cabernet Sauvignon (Napa Valley) $50. Lots to admire in this fancy Napa Cab, with its focused currant and cassis flavors, elaborate but balanced overlay of toasty oak and sweet, rich tannins. There's also a scour of acidity that prickles on the finish. Doesn't overwhelm, but is easily able to stand up to fine cuisine. **91** —*S.H. (5/1/2004)*

Edgewood 1999 Reserve Cabernet Sauvignon (Napa Valley) $50. A puckery, tannic wine with a real bite of tartness that lasts through the astringent finish, but there's a core of blackberry and cherry fruit that bodes well. The finish reprises the currant-and-berry theme. **89** —*S.H. (2/1/2004)*

Edgewood 2002 Chardonnay (Napa-Sonoma) $20. This fun wine is loaded with spicy pear, tangerine, tropical fruit and citrus flavors that have been lavished with smoky oak. It's long and deep in the mouth, with a crisp burst of acidity. **89** —*S.H. (2/1/2004)*

Edgewood 2000 Chardonnay (Napa Valley) $24. Well structured, with classy toast and vanilla notes framing the core of melon, pear and citrus flavors. Bright and fresh on the finish. **88** —*J.M. (5/1/2002)*

Edgewood 2001 Malbec (Napa Valley) $20. One of the few varietal Malbecs in California, this wine is inky black in color, and very heavy and dense in the mouth. It has flavors of the darkest stone fruits veering into chocolate and peat, and is absolutely dry. A curiosity, it may develop with longterm cellaring. **86** —*S.H. (9/1/2004)*

Edgewood 2000 Malbec (Napa Valley) $20. An interesting wine very similar to a classic Napa Cabernet. Has those lush, smooth tannins, gorgeous, velvety texture and long finish, accented with oaky vanillins and smoke. The flavors are distinctive, like a gooey black cherry pie whose rich sweetness lasts for a long time. **87** —*S.H. (3/1/2004)*

Edgewood 2000 Emmolo Vineyard Malbec (Napa Valley) $40. As good as Edgewood's regular Malbec is, this almost black wine is better. The gooey cherry-pie flavors are riper and sweeter, the tannins are thicker and softer, and the oak is more notable. This is one of those wines whose flavors are so powerful they startle. It's a killer with babyback ribs. **91** —*S.H. (3/1/2004)*

Edgewood 2000 Reserve Malbec (Napa Valley) $50. Normally a blending grape, but here on its own, extracted to the nth degree. This inky black wine is filled with lush blackberry flavors. The tannins are also big, but they're of the soft, mellow type. Drinks a little one-dimensional, but you'll have fun creating the perfect recipe for it. **88** —*S.H. (5/1/2004)*

Edgewood 1999 Reserve Malbec (Napa Valley) $50. Not as likeable as the winery's other two Malbecs, with thick, astringent tannins and a very dry, puckery finish. The theory seems to be ageability, but there isn't enough fruit for the long haul. **86** —*S.H. (3/1/2004)*

Edgewood 1998 Reserve Malbec (Napa Valley) $65. From a winery specializing in this rare Bordeaux variety, comes this sexy wine, rich and full-bodied. It spreads over the palate like velvet, spreading massive flavors of sweet cherry and chocolate. The tannins are soft and fully resolved. **93 Editors' Choice** —*S.H. (12/1/2002)*

Edgewood 1996 Merlot (Napa Valley) $20. 88 —*M.S. (3/1/2000)*

Edgewood 2001 Merlot (Napa Valley) $26. This dependable winery has produced another richly textured, smooth wine. It's marked by cherry, chocolate, olive and herb flavors set off by polished, supple tannins. Displays restraint in the balance of its elements. **91** —*S.H. (9/1/2004)*

Edgewood 2000 Merlot (Napa Valley) $24. Hits all the right notes, with its splendid flavors of blackcurrants, cassis, chocolate, ripe plums, herbs and smoky vanilla. Glides across the palate with the softest imaginable tannins, like butter, but the structure is firm. Close your eyes and enjoy the long finish. **91** *(2/1/2004)*

Edgewood 1999 Merlot (Napa Valley) $24. Fairly sharp and thin, especially for the price, with earthy, coffee and tobacco flavors relieved a bit with hints of blackberry. The tannins are nicely rich and dry, but there should be more stuffing, considering the appellation and the glorious vintage. **86** —*S.H. (12/15/2003)*

Edgewood 2000 Nepenthes Vineyard Merlot (Napa Valley) $40. Only 182 cases were produced of this spectacularly ripe, juicy Merlot, which floods the palate with enormous flavors of blackberries, cherries, chocolate fudge, caramel and vanilla. The soft tannins are a wonder, the smoky oak perfectly applied. **93** —*S.H. (2/1/2004)*

Edgewood 2001 Pinot Noir (Carneros) $24. Heavy, dull and devoid of flavor, a wine that could be any red varietal grown in California. It's thick and flat in the mouth, with hard tannins. **80** —*S.H. (7/1/2003)*

Edgewood 1999 Tradition Red Blend (Napa Valley) $35. A gorgeous blend of Cabernet Sauvignon and Malbec. The latter grape contributes lush, gooey black-cherry notes, while the Cab contributes familiar blackcurrant and cassis flavors. The result is a complex wine further accented with the smoke, wood spice and vanilla of fine oak barrels. **92** —*S.H. (12/31/2003)*

Edgewood 2003 Sauvignon Blanc (Napa Valley) $15. Very dry, with pronounced flavors of gooseberry, lime, grapefruit, kiwi and vanilla, and the acidity is so high, the wine is tingly on the palate. You can really taste the "sauvignon" in this wine, which has a sweet herbal edge to it. Shows real complexity and finesse. **89** —*S.H. (12/1/2004)*

Edgewood 2002 Sauvignon Blanc (Napa Valley) $15. Refreshing and zesty, with flavors of lime, ripe white peach and sweet fig, with spicy notes and crisp acidity. There's a lush, creamy texture, but for all the delicious fruitiness, it's dry. **86** —*S.H. (12/15/2003)*

Edgewood 2001 Sauvignon Blanc (Napa Valley) $20. Beautiful, delicious fruit, cold fermented to bring out the fresh young flavors of kiwi, lime and gooseberry. The long, clean finish is spicy, with a hint of honey. **89** —*S.H. (9/1/2003)*

Edgewood 2000 Sauvignon Blanc (Napa Valley) $20. Hay, cabbage and pickles in the nose? That's not what most of us are seeking. The palate is overtly grassy, bordering on weedy. A slight spritz to the mouthfeel neither helps nor hinders it. Beyond that, there's not much else to say. **81** *(8/1/2002)*

Edgewood 2001 Syrah (Napa Valley) $20. Heavy, dense and peppery, with a sryupy texture smacking of blackberry fruit flavors with a trace of sweetness. This is a big wine that stains the sides of the glass. Finishes with thick tannins. **84** —*S.H. (12/15/2003)*

Edgewood 1996 Zinfandel (Napa Valley) $14. 87 Best Buy —*J.C. (5/1/2000)*

Edgewood 2001 Zinfandel (Napa Valley) $20. The grapes got nice and ripe in this excellent vintage, and give this charming wine concentrated flavors of blackberries, raspberries and even a hint of blueberries. It has Zin's wild and woolly, peppery appeal, but the smoothly ripe tannins lend it a Cabernet-like elegance. **89** —*S.H. (5/1/2004)*

Edgewood 2000 Zinfandel (Napa Valley) $20. Awkward, overripe and too sweet, a textbook wine that falls prey to Zin's traditional pitfalls. There are ripe berry flavors but they are out of balance with everything else. A syrupy, cough-medicomey texture frames it all. **82** —*S.H. (9/1/2003)*

Edgewood 2001 Butala Vineyard Zinfandel (Napa Valley) $35. This terrific Zin impresses for its concentrated flavors and ultrarich tannins. Blackberries, cherries, plums and chocolate cascade in waves across the mouth, wrapped in the prettiest texture. It's soft and firm at the same time. Drinks as smoothly rich as a good Cab, yet hangs onto Zin's unique profile. **91** —*S.H. (5/1/2004)*

EDIZIONE PENNINO

Edizione Pennino 2003 Zinfandel (Rutherford) $38. From Coppola's Rubicon Estate winery, a Zin that's nicely dry, and under 15% alcohol. It possesses real elegance and class, with a streak of blackberry, chocolate and leather flavors wrapped in rich, thick, ripe tannins. **87** —*S.H. (6/1/2006)*

EDMEADES

Edmeades 2000 Chardonnay (Anderson Valley) $18. 91 —*S.H. (5/1/2002)*

Edmeades 1999 Eaglepoint Ranch Petite Sirah (Mendocino) $25. This is the kind of muscular but gentle wine inland Mendocino is betting on. Deep flavors of plums, berries and herbs, extracted and bold, but the wine is well balanced and not too alcoholic. It's fun to taste such rich flavor without having the wine be ponderous. A fine wine, and one that captures Petite's scrappy character. **90** —*S.H. (5/1/2002)*

Edmeades 1996 Eaglepoint Vineyard Petite Sirah (Mendocino) $20. 89 —*S.H. (5/1/2000)*

Edmeades 1997 Pinot Noir (Anderson Valley) $20. 89 —*J.C. (5/1/2000)*

Edmeades 2000 Pinot Noir (Anderson Valley) $20. Let this wine breathe for a little while because there's a dustiness that hides the underlying cherry and blueberry aromas. Once in the mouth, it's fruity and delicate, with cherry-berry flavors enhanced by mocha, vanilla and cinnamon. Feels silky on the palate, with a very crisp streak of acidity. **87** —*S.H. (3/1/2004)*

Edmeades 1999 Pinot Noir (Anderson Valley) $20. 90 —*S.H. (5/1/2002)*

Edmeades 1998 Pinot Noir (Anderson Valley) $16. A heavy wine, atypical of the appellation, which usually produces light-bodied and elegant Pinots. There's something earthy and thick about this one, almost rustic. The flavors are fruity but it lacks the delicacy an Anderson Valley Pinot Noir ought to have. And there's an unpleasant sting of acidity. **83** —*S.H. (2/1/2001)*

Edmeades 1996 Zinfandel (Mendocino) $18. 85 —*S.H. (5/1/2000)*

Edmeades 2003 Zinfandel (Mendocino) $19. A big, brawny, high-alcohol Zin, dry and fairly tannic, and balanced in cherry, tobacco, herb and cocoa flavors. There's nothing subtle about this exuberant wine, which will be great with a big piece of red meat. **88** —*S.H. (8/1/2005)*

Edmeades 2001 Zinfandel (Mendocino) $19. Edmeades's Zins are not noted for modest alcohol, and this one, at 15.6 %, is hot, but oh so good. You can taste the sun in every sip of black currant and sweetened espresso. It's balanced, though, with good acidity and is totally dry. **87** —*S.H. (11/15/2004)*

Edmeades 2000 Zinfandel (Mendocino) $19. Here's a big, superripe Zin, with explosive flavors of cherries and raspberries and a full-throated mouthfeel. It's filled with ripe, sweet fruit, but is dry. It's also quite high in alcohol, and finishes hot. **86** —*S.H. (3/1/2004)*

Edmeades 1999 Zinfandel (Mendocino Ridge) $25. Certainly a step down from Edmeades's single-vineyard Zins from the Ridge, but not by much. Rich and earthy and dry, with berry and tobacco flavors and a spicy finish that lasts for a long time. The wine has a plush, smooth mouthfeel that's sheer pleasure. **90** —*S.H. (11/1/2002)*

Edmeades 1998 Zinfandel (Mendocino Ridge) $25. More of that mountain intensity, with very ripe fruit buttressed with spicy, mineral elements. Brambly, briary, and spicy, leading into a fleshy, round, ripe, soft middle and a long, fruity finish. Good right now. **90** —*P.G. (3/1/2001)*

Edmeades 1999 Alden Ranch Zinfandel (Mendocino Ridge) $25. Longtime winemaker Van Williamson has crafted a late-harvest style wine, with 16.5% alcohol. The rich berry flavors drink on the sweet side, but the wine is saved from flabbiness by firm acids. Zinfandel from these fog-free ridgetops ripens to high sugars, and the winemaker's challenge is to make the wine balanced. **85** —*S.H. (5/1/2002)*

Edmeades 2002 Alden Vineyard Late Harvest Zinfandel (Mendocino) $16. With their Zin grapes approaching Port levels anyway, Edmeades is a natural for a dessert wine. But this one should be richer and sweeter. It's as if the decision were made to keep it off-dry, blurring the line between it and the regular Zins. **85** —*S.H. (11/15/2004)*

Edmeades 2000 Alden Vineyard-Late Harvest Zinfandel (Mendocino Ridge) **$25.** When Zin gets this ripe, all you can do is make a strong, heady, sweet wine. Here, 16.9% alcohol and 2.8% residual sugar make for a powerful, warming brew, distinctive in its own right, and one that has many fans. **84** —*S.H. (5/1/2002)*

Edmeades 1999 Ciapusci Zinfandel (Mendocino Ridge) $25. They say these vines are 121 years old, and certainly, the wine they produce is concentrated. The winemaker, Van Williamson, finds nutmeg, fir, white pepper, tobacco, raspberry and strawberries, which sounds about right. It's also a little more tart than the magnificent Zeni bottling. **92** —*S.H. (11/1/2002)*

Edmeades 2002 Ciapusci Vineyard Zinfandel (Mendocino Ridge) $29. Here's a wine that got so ripe, they had to let the alcohol reach an astonishing 16.5% for it to be dry. With all that heat, it really deserves much richer fruit, for the cherries and blackberries basically abandon the mid-palate. **86** —*S.H. (11/15/2004)*

Edmeades 2001 Ciapusci Vineyard Zinfandel (Mendocino Ridge) $25. A fruity wine redolent of cherry, blackberry and plums. The oak, however, is a bit heavy handed here-as is the acidity. It's still a pleasant quaff, but could use better integration. **84** *(11/1/2003)*

Edmeades 1998 Ciapusci Vineyard Zinfandel (Mendocino Ridge) $25. Head-trained, century-old vines, provide intense scents with old vine herbal, herbaceous accents. Watermelon, hay and strawberries, intensely extracted and 17.5% alcohol. This is over-the-top winemaking, with powerful old vine fruit, and a big, extracted finish, with lingering toasty, hazelnut and vanilla highlights. **92** —*P.G. (3/1/2001)*

Edmeades 1997 Ciapusci Vineyard Zinfandel (Mendocino Ridge) $36. 88 —*S.H. (5/1/2000)*

Edmeades 1998 Eagle Point Vineyard Zinfandel (Mendocino) $24. There's 19% Syrah and 5% Petite Sirah blended in, making for a succulent wine, with spicy, lively fruit leading the charge. There's enough acid to give it structure and balance, but not so much that the wine seems edgy or sour. Full bodied, mouthfilling, flavorful and distinctive. **92** —*P.G. (3/1/2001)*

Edmeades 1999 Eaglepoint Ranch Zinfandel (Mendocino) $25. Very different in character from the Zeni and Ciapusci bottlings, reflecting another terroir. From the slopes of the Mayacamas Mountains, a brambly, jammy wine with clove and tobacco notes, and a rough-and-tumble mouthfeel. Finishes a bit earthy and sharp. Contains 23% Syrah and Petite Sirah. **86** —*S.H. (11/1/2002)*

Edmeades 2002 Piffero Vineyard Zinfandel (Mendocino) $29. From old vines inland in the Redwood Valley, a wine that smells rich in peppery cherry, but doesn't quite follow through on the promise. High alcohol, but low on fruity intensity. **85** —*S.H. (11/15/2004)*

Edmeades 2001 Piffero Vineyard Zinfandel (Mendocino) $25. Less sweet than this winery's Zeni Vineyard bottling. But this one doesn't serve up the same ripe fruit. It's a little tart, with toasty oak framing hints of bright cherry and raspberry flavors. **84** *(11/1/2003)*

Edmeades 1998 Zeni Zinfandel (Mendocino Ridge) $30. Tannic, alcoholic nose, with a softer, rosier color tending toward brick. Old vines, soft, sweet, ancient flavors. The wine feels a little bit pushed—the alcohol is too high, and the finish is harsh, tannic and hot. **86** —*P.G. (3/1/2001)*

Edmeades 2002 Zeni Vineyard Zinfandel (Mendocino Ridge) $29. Would you believe 17.5% alcohol, and there's still residual sugar? That's what these old mountain vines did in 2001's heat waves. Berry, chocolate and Porty flavors and firm tannins. **86** —*S.H. (11/15/2004)*

Edmeades 2001 Zeni Vineyard Zinfandel (Mendocino Ridge) $25. A Port-like style, fruity and sweet, with sharp acidity that adds more shock value than balance. Cherries, blackberries, plums and spice are at the core. Try this with a cigar or Stilton. **86** *(11/1/2003)*

Edmeades 1999 Zeni Vineyard Zinfandel (Mendocino Ridge) $25. An extraordinary wine, and not just because it wears its 16.4% alcohol so well. The raspberry and cassis flavors are rapturously delicious. It seems almost a crime for wine to taste this good. At the same time, the round, soft mouthfeel and dry, dusty tannins are textbook perfect. From 90-year-old vines. **93 Editors' Choice** —*S.H. (11/1/2002)*

Edmeades 1996 Zeni Vineyard Zinfandel (Mendocino) $25. 92 —*S.H. (9/1/1999)*

EDMUNDS ST JOHN

Edmunds St John 2000 Los Robles Viejos Rozet Red Blend (Paso Robles) $28. 87 —*S.H. (11/15/2002)*

Edmunds St John 1997 Rocks and Gravel Red Blend (California) $18. 90 —*S.H. (6/1/1999)*

Edmunds St John 1996 Durell Vineyard Syrah (Sonoma Valley) $25. 91 —*S.H. (6/1/1999)*

Edmunds St John 1997 Fenaughty Vineyard Syrah (El Dorado County) $30. 93 —*S.H. (6/1/1999)*

Edmunds St John 1999 Wylie-Fenaughty Syrah (El Dorado) $32. Decidedly grapey aromas and flavors abound here—it's wine, yes, but somehow the grapiness got to us. Aromas are so sweet and fruity that they are almost liquerish; mouthfeel is full, though slightly hot. Stemmy, citrusy and metallic flavors also make appearances on palate and finish. **84** *(11/1/2001)*

Edmunds St John 1997 Alban-Durell Vineyards Viognier (California) $20. 87 —*S.H. (6/1/1999)*

Edmunds St John 1998 Alban/Durell Vineyards Viognier (California) $20. 93 —*S.H. (10/1/1999)*

Edmunds St John 2000 Los Robles Viejos Rozet White Blend (Paso Robles) $24. This Rhône-inspired blend of Viognier and Roussanne certainly has a lot of fruit, filling the mouth with white peaches, sweet green apples and honeyed spearmint flavors, yet it's quite dry and crisp, and finishes with a lively, clean aftertaste. **87** —*S.H. (12/15/2002)*

EDNA VALLEY VINEYARD

Edna Valley Vineyard 2004 Paragon Chardonnay (Edna Valley) $15. This wine shows those crisp, bright, mouthwatering Central Coast acids. They perk up the lime and tropical fruit flavors enhanced with a touch of vanilla and smoke from barrels. Finishes spicy and dry. **85** —*S.H. (12/1/2005)*

Edna Valley Vineyard 2003 Paragon Chardonnay (Edna Valley) $14. Lots of smoky, caramelized oak has been applied to the underlying peach and pear flavors. Has a nice, creamy texture and finishes a little sweet. **85** —*S.H. (4/1/2005)*

Edna Valley Vineyard 2002 Paragon Chardonnay (Edna Valley) $14. Sure, it's super oaky. But it's good, delicious oak, and all that smoky vanilla and buttercream blend in just fine with the tropical fruit. The buttery, creamy texture seems soft, because it could have more acidity, but it sure tastes good, and is a value in a big, sweet Chard. **89 Best Buy** —*S.H. (6/1/2004)*

Edna Valley Vineyard 2001 Paragon Chardonnay (Edna Valley) $13. This is a very dry, austere wine, marked by lemon and lime flavors and brisk, bright acids. It is like a Sauvignon Blanc, with a creamier texture. Fine now with the right foods, but it might even improve with a year or two in the cellar. **85** —*S.H. (12/15/2003)*

Edna Valley Vineyard 2000 Paragon Chardonnay (Edna Valley) $17. A good, everyday Chard from a cool climate, with apple flavors and quite astringent. Oak softens the high acidity, and the wine comes across as somewhat tart and lean. Good, for those looking for an alternative to the fat, blowsy style. **86** —*S.H. (6/1/2003)*

Edna Valley Vineyard 1998 Paragon Chardonnay (Edna Valley) $19. 90 *(12/31/1999)*

Edna Valley Vineyard 1997 Paragon Vineyard Chardonnay (Edna Valley) $17. 92 —*L.W. (7/1/1999)*

Edna Valley Vineyard 2004 Merlot (San Luis Obispo County) $15. The grapes got plenty ripe in the sunny side valleys of SLO county. Blackberries, cherries, blueberries, plums, chocolate, it's all there, wrapped in dry, finely ground tannins. Good now with steak, roasts, lamb. **86** —*S.H. (12/15/2006)*

Edna Valley Vineyard 2004 Paragon Pinot Gris (Edna Valley) $18. Tart, clean and elegant, this dry, cool-climate PG has a purity of flavors and high acidity that make it a delight. Figs, kiwis, sweet limes, pineapples, tangerines, it's like a trip to the fruit stand. **88** —*S.H. (2/1/2006)*

Edna Valley Vineyard 2003 Paragon Pinot Gris (Edna Valley) $18. So juicy in fresh fruits, it's like drinking an orchard. Pears, apples, figs, spearmint and other spicy flavors have a spine of fresh, citrusy acidity. **89** —*S.H. (10/1/2004)*

Edna Valley Vineyard 2004 Paragon Pinot Noir (Edna Valley) $20. A quintessential Edna Valley Pinot. It's bone dry, with an elegant texture that's pure silk and satin. High acidity frames cherry, cola, pomegranate and coffee flavors that finish in a swirl of dusty Asian spices. **90 Editors' Choice** —*S.H. (10/1/2006)*

Edna Valley Vineyard 2003 Paragon Pinot Noir (Edna Valley) $20. This is the kind of Pinot that you can drink everyday without flinching at the price. It's representative of the coast, a light-bodied but full-flavored wine with tremendous cherry fruit, cola, spice and oak, and a dry finish. **87** —*S.H. (10/1/2005)*

Edna Valley Vineyard 2002 Paragon Pinot Noir (Edna Valley) $15. This is a textbook example of a relatively inexpensive, cool, coastal Pinot Noir, the kind that used to be hard to find. It has cherry and herb flavors, silky tannins, crisp acidity, a nice overlay of toasty oak, and the feeling of a rich, expensive, dry red wine. **87** —*S.H. (6/1/2004)*

Edna Valley Vineyard 2000 Paragon Pinot Noir (Edna Valley) $23. Cherry and plum flavors are backed by complex earth and herb tones. This richly textured Pinot finishes with depth and grace. **89** —*J.M. (5/1/2002)*

Edna Valley Vineyard 1998 Paragon Pinot Noir (Edna Valley) $19. **86** —*S.H. (10/1/2000)*

Edna Valley Vineyard 1997 Paragon Pinot Noir (Central Coast) $20. **86** *(11/15/1999)*

Edna Valley Vineyard 2004 Paragon Sauvignon Blanc (Edna Valley) $14. That brilliant Edna Valley acidity is hard at work here, etching the figgy, pineapply fruit flavors to purity. What a long, powerful finish. This is one fantastically tasty wine, and this is a good price for it. **89** —*S.H. (3/1/2006)*

Edna Valley Vineyard 2003 Paragon Sauvignon Blanc (Edna Valley) $14. Bursting with clean, zesty acids, like biting into a lemon, except the flavors are of ripe figs, lime and white pepper, and some smoky oak. The beautiful acidity underscores the flavors, boosting and brightening them. Finishes dry and stylish. **90 Best Buy** —*S.H. (2/1/2005)*

Edna Valley Vineyard 2002 Paragon Sauvignon Blanc (Edna Valley) $14. A bright, refreshing style that's packed with grapefruit, gooseberry and lemon flavors. It's quite grassy, fairly complex and really delicious. Long and fresh at the end. **89** —*J.M. (9/1/2004)*

Edna Valley Vineyard 2003 Paragon Syrah (Central Coast) $14. This disappointing Syrah seems shallow and superficial, with candied berry and herb flavors that finish sharp and a little green. **82** *(9/1/2005)*

Edna Valley Vineyard 2001 Paragon Syrah (Central Coast) $14. Strikes the palate with a certain fierceness of tannins and rough, briary texture, then calms down to offer modest fruit. **84** —*S.H. (6/1/2004)*

Edna Valley Vineyard 1999 Paragon Syrah (Central Coast) $17. The full, dark berry and cocoa aromas and flavors are winning, and the mouthfeel is smooth and solid. There's a ripe sweetness to the fruit and a creamy, round mouthfeel. A pleasing wine that finishes softly, with a blackberry-chocolate fade and an herb-metallic accent. **88 Editors' Choice** *(10/1/2001)*

Edna Valley Vineyard 1998 Fralich Vineyard Viognier (Paso Robles) $18. **88** —*S.H. (10/1/1999)*

EHLERS ESTATE

Ehlers Estate 2003 Cabernet Franc (Napa Valley) $33. Forward in rich, toasty new French oak, this 100% varietal wine flatters the palate with cherry pie, vanilla and cassis flavors with a dusting of tangerine rind. It's soft, silky and absolutely delicious, a voluptuous wine that hails from Ehlers' St. Helena estate. **91** —*S.H. (8/1/2006)*

Ehlers Estate 2003 Cabernet Sauvignon (Napa Valley) $33. This winery's '03 1886 reserve-style Cab was a monster, and this Cab, though smaller, treads the same waters. It's a ripe, balanced wine that shows a wealth of Cabernet flavors that turn sweet on the finish. **90** —*S.H. (12/1/2006)*

Ehlers Estate 2001 Cabernet Sauvignon (Napa Valley) $28. Dark and dense, a heavy wine shrouded in tannins. Not offfering a whole lot now, although there are some deeply buried cherry flavors. This bone-dry wine may develop nuance in a few years. **85** —*S.H. (10/1/2004)*

Ehlers Estate 2000 Cabernet Sauvignon (Napa Valley) $28. Chock full of smoky, toasty, licorice and herb flavors. The wine also shows hints of cassis and blackberry, all couched in modest tannins, finishing with moderate length. **87** —*J.M. (4/1/2004)*

Ehlers Estate 2003 1886 Estate Cabernet Sauvignon (St. Helena) $75. This A very serious Cab, huge in black currant and cocoa flavors that are generously oaked. Yet it possesses a classic acid and tannin structure and feels ultrarefined and elegant all the way down. This 100% Cabernet really makes you take notice; a wine to linger over and consume with your very best steaks and chops. **94 Editors' Choice** —*S.H. (8/1/2006)*

Ehlers Estate 2003 Merlot (Napa Valley) $30. Nice and supple in chocolaty, cherry pie flavors, and with a good tannic structure that lends balance, despite high alcohol. This is a fun-serious wine from estate vineyards in St. Helena. **89** —*S.H. (8/1/2006)*

Ehlers Estate 2001 Merlot (Napa Valley) $25. Very ripe and well-oaked, this is a big, ambitious wine that trades finesse for sheer volume. It's extracted and jammy in blackberry and cherry fruit, and the tannins are sweet and lush. Drink now through 2005 **85** —*S.H. (10/1/2004)*

Ehlers Estate 2005 Sauvignon Blanc (Napa Valley) $20. This is an elegant Sauvignon Blanc that shows off the variety's versatility. Only a small amount of oak has been added, allowing the bright citrus zest, fig and mineral flavors to shine through. Made from Oakville and Pope Valley grapes. **89** —*S.H. (12/1/2006)*

EHLERS GROVE

Ehlers Grove 1998 Chardonnay (Carneros) $30. **88** *(6/1/2000)*

Ehlers Grove 1998 Dutton Ranch Chardonnay (Russian River Valley) $25. **88** *(6/1/2000)*

EL ALACRAN

El Alacran 2002 Mourvèdre (Amador County) $34. Dry, simple and berryish, with rustic tannins. **83** —*S.H. (4/1/2005)*

EL MIRADOR

El Mirador 2000 Merlot (Walla Walla (WA)) $20. Some dill, herbal, lacquery notes to start, then this big, substantial Merlot broadens out into big, plummy, roasted flavors mixing barrel and ripe grape, with some volatile aromas. Full, bold and fleshy, it is on its way to peak maturity. **86** —*P.G. (9/1/2004)*

EL MOLINO

El Molino 2004 Chardonnay (Rutherford) $42. Napa Cabs can suffer from a soft earthiness, but El Molino has succeeded in producing a wine of real substance and style. It shows fine pear, apple and nut bread flavors, along with a figgy, raisiny quality, and has good enough acidity for balance. The finish is very dry. This complex wine should age well over the next five years. **92** —*S.H. (6/1/2006)*

El Molino 2003 Chardonnay (Rutherford) $40. Chardonnay in Rutherford? Yes, and a very good one. It has polished peach and apple flavors as well as a sweet, rich coat of oak, and is balanced, crisp and dry. **89** —*S.H. (12/15/2005)*

El Molino 2002 Chardonnay (Rutherford) $40. In all objectivity, there is a problem growing Chardonnay in Rutherford. It's simply too hot. This is a good wine, even an interesting one, but it is not great and not worth the price. It has apple and pear flavors, soft acids, and an oaky, creamy finish. **87** —*S.H. (4/1/2005)*

El Molino 1999 Chardonnay (Rutherford) $40. The graceful, subtle nose of pears, apples and hazelnuts don't prepare you for the richness of this old-guard Napa producer's 1999 offering. A full and intense palate of toast, honey, spice and pineapple comes on strong. The flavors are supported by bright acidity, and they linger on the long and lively finish. **90** *(7/1/2001)*

El Molino 2003 Pinot Noir (Rutherford) $52. I haven't been a fan of the winery's Pinot Noirs, and this release doesn't change my mind. It's simple and slightly sweet-tasting, with baked cherry pie and coffee flavors and a heavy overlay of toast. **84** —*S.H. (5/1/2006)*

El Molino 2002 Pinot Noir (Rutherford) $52. Despite the dark color, this Pinot is soft and one-dimensional. It shows ripe flavors of cherries, mocha and cola, with a quick finish. **83** —*S.H. (2/1/2006)*

El Molino 2001 Pinot Noir (Napa Valley) $51. There are lovely flavors and rich textures in this soft, beguiling wine. It shows ripe cherries and black raspberries, with hints of mocha and peppery spice, as well as smoky vanillins from oak. It's a pretty wine. **87** —*S.H. (4/1/2005)*

El Molino 1999 Pinot Noir (Napa Valley) $51. Pepper and plum, slightly candied raspberry fruit plus a full, velour-like texture show in this ripe Napa offering, but panelists still had mixed opinions. To some, the berry and vanilla flavors and rich feel had great appeal, while othersound the wine cedary and a bit hot, with wood and alcohol to spare. **87** *(10/1/2002)*

ELAINE MARIA

Elaine Maria 2002 Merlot (Alexander Valley) $19. This is a wine that aims for lean elegance. It shows a balance of cherry, herb and leather flavors, and is pretty tannic. Drink now. **85** —*S.H. (5/1/2005)*

Elaine Maria 2002 Reserve Merlot (Alexander Valley) $28. Riper than the regular Merlot, with a good core of red and black cherry fruit, and finishes dry and herbal. Full-bodied and fairly tannic, but balanced and complex. A new winery started by a member of the Foppiano family. **88** —*S.H. (5/1/2005)*

Elaine Maria 2003 Sauvignon Blanc (Alexander Valley) $16. Tart and crisp, with refreshing acidity and grassy, gooseberry flavors. Barrel fermentation adds creamy, yeasty notes. Elegant finish. **87** —*S.H. (5/1/2005)*

ELAN

Elan 1997 Cabernet Sauvignon (Atlas Peak) $45. 88 *(11/1/2000)*

Elan 2002 Cabernet Sauvignon (Atlas Peak) $47. This is the best Cabernet I recall ever having from the Atlas Peak appellation. It's a deeply satisfying wine, dry and full bodied, with thick, but fine, tannins and rich flavors of black currants and oak. Best now and through 2007. **92** —*S.H. (3/1/2006)*

Elan 2001 Cabernet Sauvignon (Atlas Peak) $45. Tough, stemmy and unripe, with hard, green tannins and coffee flavors. **83** —*S.H. (12/31/2004)*

Elan 2000 Cabernet Sauvignon (Atlas Peak) $42. A very dense, chocolaty wine, with jammy currant and blackberry fruit. The new oak hasn't yet been fully integrated. Below all that are firm but polished tannins and fine acidity. A few years of aging should lighten it. **88** —*S.H. (11/15/2004)*

Elan 1999 Cabernet Sauvignon (Atlas Peak) $45. The grapes are grown in an appellation that has had difficulty establishing itself in Napa Valley, but this wine is a promising development. With its snappy cassis flavors and soft tannins and acids, it has interest and complexity. **91** —*S.H. (11/15/2002)*

ELARA

Elara 2000 Tollini Vineyard Petite Sirah (Mendocino County) $27. As good as Mendocino Petite Sirah gets, this is a big, robust wine of heroic proportions. Monster extraction of blackberry and plum flavors, rich, thick, dry tannins, and a lipsmackingly good finish that coats the palate with flavor. Preternaturally perfect with barbecue, a match made in heaven. **89** —*S.H. (12/31/2003)*

Elara 2000 Sherwin Vineyard Sangiovese (Mendocino County) $24. From a hilly vineyard. The winemaker says he wants to recreate Chianti, but it's hard to imagine a Chianti with this much sweetness. Tastes like raspberry jam straight out of the jar, with soft tannins to give it a bit of structure. Awkward. **84** —*S.H. (9/1/2003)*

Elara 2000 Syrah (McDowell Valley) $32. From an appellation long noted for Syrah, a dark, dense, richly textured wine, with big flavors of blackberries, tobacco and herbs, and earthy but smooth tannins. It's bone dry with good acids, an immature wine that needs ribs or similar fare to accompany it. Should age well. **87** —*S.H. (12/15/2003)*

ELEMENTAL CELLARS

Elemental Cellars 2004 Croft Vineyard Pinot Gris (Willamette Valley) $15. Assertive, tight and concentrated, with firm mixed stone fruits and a rather hard, unyielding core. This seems likely to evolve well, but it's good right now and offers more grip and weight than most. **91** —*P.G. (2/1/2006)*

ELEVEN

eleven 2003 Cowan Vineyard Cabernet Sauvignon (Yakima Valley) $21. A good effort crafting a moderate, Yakima Valley Cab. There's a bit of the herbal stuff here, but it's done well, balanced and appropriate. The tannins are slightly green but smooth, and there are no bitter edges. Smooth and interesting. **87** —*P.G. (10/1/2006)*

ELIAS

Elias 2000 Pinot Noir (Russian River Valley) $40. No mistaking the tomato, mushroom, red raspberry and cinnamon aromas, or the red berry flavors and silky texture. It's classic Pinot, and while it's not a big wine or an ageable one, it's very well-crafted, with enough elegance to grace white tablecloths. **89** —*S.H. (5/1/2002)*

ELIZABETH

Elizabeth 1998 Sauvignon Blanc (Redwood Valley) $14. 87 —*S.H. (5/1/2000)*

Elizabeth 1998 Zinfandel (Redwood Valley) $18. 85 —*S.H. (5/1/2000)*

Elizabeth 1997 Zinfandel (Redwood Valley) $18. 81 —*P.G. (11/15/1999)*

ELK COVE

Elk Cove 2005 Pinot Blanc (Willamette Valley) $18. There's a nice, melony center to this wine, with suggestions of lightly spiced pears and green apples. The fruit is lively and pure, and the wine has a nice lift to it. The spices kick in at midpalate and carry through a long and thoroughly satisfying finish. Very good winemaking in an elegant style; the alcohol clocks in at a sensible 13%. **89** —*P.G. (9/1/2006)*

Elk Cove 2004 Pinot Blanc (Willamette Valley) $17. What a lovely effort! Clean, concise and brilliantly defined, this could pass for a particularly elegant Pinot Gris, and far outshines the winery's PG in this vintage. Ripe, not fleshy, flavors of Bartlett pear, with a firm through line. **89**—*P.G. (8/1/2005)*

Elk Cove 2005 Pinot Gris (Willamette Valley) $18. Elk Cove makes one of the most refreshing, crisp and nuanced Pinot Gris in the state. This is an excellent bottle, lively and clean, with mixed fruit flavors of pear, melon, kiwi and white peach. It is concentrated but not heavy or thick; the magic of Adam Campbell's winemaking is his ability to perfectly balance and showcase the exact ripeness of his fruit, leaving in the subtle grace notes. This is a perfectly balanced, nuanced and delicious wine. **91 Editors' Choice** —*P.G. (9/1/2006)*

Elk Cove 2004 Pinot Gris (Willamette Valley) $17. Hits with a bit of sharpness and a high-toned edge. The fruit is ripe but the wine seems a bit disjointed. Some breathing time, maybe even decanting, is a good idea. **86**—*P.G. (8/1/2005)*

Elk Cove 2002 Pinot Gris (Willamette Valley) $15. This is lovely, a balanced, complex wine with layers of fruit nicely entwined. It shows just the right mix of acid, tannin and racy texture from whole-cluster pressing. 9,000 cases made. **91 Best Buy** —*P.G. (12/1/2003)*

Elk Cove 2001 Pinot Gris (Willamette Valley) $15. Pinot gris as it should be—ripe and full-bodied, with expressive flavors of fresh pears, spiced with cinnamon. Rich and satisfying, yet tangy enough to accompany even delicate seafood. This is a home run, with just enough of a hint of barrel to give it a finishing kiss of butterscotch. **91 Editors' Choice** —*P.G. (8/1/2003)*

Elk Cove 2000 Pinot Gris (Willamette Valley) $15. Elk Cove wines usually lead with the fruit, and this is no exception. Fleshy and ripe, there is an unusual, pine-scented edge that gives it definition in the mouth, though it adds some nonvarietal flavors to the mix. **86** —*P.G. (2/1/2002)*

USA

Elk Cove 1998 Pinot Gris (Willamette Valley) $15. 88 Editors' Choice (8/1/1999)

Elk Cove 2004 Pinot Noir (Willamette Valley) $25. Fragrant, aromatic, open, and wonderfully accessible, this smells like fresh-cut roses and violets, and tastes of cherries and chocolate. It's a broad, smooth effort that is open and drinking well right now. **89** —P.G. (9/1/2006)

Elk Cove 2003 Pinot Noir (Willamette Valley) $24. Soft, open and wonderfully accessible, this broad, smooth effort has a bit of California styling, thanks to an exceptionally hot vintage. Ready to enjoy right now. **88** —P.G. (8/1/2005)

Elk Cove 2002 Pinot Noir (Willamette Valley) $24. It takes a moment for the SO2 to burn off, but there is nice black cherry fruit waiting underneath, and hints of leather. Tannic and a bit rough through the finish. **86** (11/1/2004)

Elk Cove 2001 Pinot Noir (Willamette Valley) $20. Pure and inviting, with entirely typical and welcome aromas of cherry and smoky wood. The palate is mostly cherry fruit, with simple but appropriate pepper and oak shadings. The finish is just right in terms of flavor and feel, and while the wine is round enough, it retains an acid-based, streamlined character that makes it fine and dandy. **89** —M.S. (9/1/2003)

Elk Cove 2000 Pinot Noir (Willamette Valley) $20. You don't find much $20 Oregon Pinot this good. Forward and bright, it still has a fresh, grapey quality to the fruit, which hits the palate crisp and spicy. Hints of juniper, earth and brown sugar add interest, and the wine retains its focus though a long, satisfying finish. **89** —P.G. (4/1/2003)

Elk Cove 1999 Pinot Noir (Willamette Valley) $18. Purplish and youthful, this Pinot only grudgingly reveals scents of beet, root, earth and fresh-picked tomatoes. Despite several hours of airing, the flavors remain stubbornly closed, with hard tannins and an earthy finish. Needs considerable time. **85** —P.G. (4/1/2002)

Elk Cove 1998 Pinot Noir (Willamette Valley) $18. 90 Best Buy —M.S. (12/1/2000)

Elk Cove 2001 La Boheme Pinot Noir (Willamette Valley) $32. This is high-elevation Pinot, from the northern Willamette, and shows a different flavor set than the superripe, tannic, Zinny wines made further south. But it is very well made, firm and varietal, with a complex mix of herb, leaf and tart fruits, and will prosper with 5–7 years of cellaring. **90** —P.G. (12/1/2003)

Elk Cove 2000 La Boheme Pinot Noir (Oregon) $34. A good La Boheme, which seems to have lost its footing in recent vintages. Juicy, young and quite tart, it shows plenty of bright berry fruit and a bit of concentrated cassis. There is a distinct scent of resin or diesel. Could improve with time. **88** —P.G. (4/1/2003)

Elk Cove 1998 La Boheme Pinot Noir (Willamette Valley) $28. 89 —M.S. (12/1/2000)

Elk Cove 2002 La Bohéme Pinot Noir (Willamette Valley) $36. Though this is Elk Cove's premier vineyard, its appeal is not for all. If you like smoke, leather and tannin, this is your style. Chocolate, burnt coffee and smoked meat are here in abundance, but where's the fruit? **86** (11/1/2004)

Elk Cove 2004 Mount Richmond Pinot Noir (Willamette Valley) $36. Cuttings from the winery's Roosevelt Vineyard were used to plant the Mount Richmond site in 1996. Scents of root, leaf and herb are typical of the terroir. The tart, tight fruit tastes of cranberries and red currants. Stiff, earthy, green tannins. **88** —P.G. (9/1/2006)

Elk Cove 2003 Mount Richmond Pinot Noir (Willamette Valley) $36. Cuttings from the winery's Roosevelt vineyard were used to plant the Mount Richmond site in 1996. Unfined and unfiltered, it is deeply saturated with purple/garnet shades and offers up bright, racy flavors that are almost Grenache-like in their grapy exuberance. The acids are the only awkward note; jagged and a bit chalky. **89** —P.G. (8/1/2005)

Elk Cove 2002 Reserve Pinot Noir (Willamette Valley) $60. Highly enjoyable and distinctive, with a soft, supple palate that smoothes together rich plum, blackberry and black cherry fruit. It's lean but not sour, subtle and lingering, with good grip and a hint of underbrush. **90** (11/1/2004)

Elk Cove 2002 Roosevelt Pinot Noir (Willamette Valley) $48. A difficult wine to evaluate, as the bottle smelled and tasted of burnt match from recent bottling with SO2. Nonetheless, there is a solid core of firm, ripe, polished fruit, and nice smoky, meaty flavors that mingle fruit and barrel. Give it lots of swirling to shake off the sulfur. **88** (11/1/2004)

Elk Cove 2001 Roosevelt Pinot Noir (Willamette Valley) $32. Soft and seductive, the nose is redolent of primary fruits, with leafy, earthy undertones. Good balance and focus, with a sense of gathering strength as it rolls down the throat. Elk Cove is showing significant improvement from vintage to vintage, and is quickly moving into Oregon's top ranks. **90** —P.G. (12/1/2003)

Elk Cove 2000 Roosevelt Pinot Noir (Oregon) $48. Consistently the winery's finest Pinot, the Roosevelt simply outperforms the rest of its siblings. There's plenty of meat on these bones, with more than a hint of iron and mineral flavors. It is compact, clean and persistent. Like the rest of this brand's lineup, it needs more time to really show well. **90** —P.G. (4/1/2003)

Elk Cove 1999 Roosevelt Pinot Noir (Oregon) $48. The dark, plummy purple color announces a "serious" wine, and right now it is pretty tightly wound and closed up. Considerable breathing time begins to reveal rich, black cherry fruit with darker notes of coffee and tar, along with hints of bark and stone. There's a whiff of pickle barrel in the tannic finish. It's a bit of a mystery, but with plenty of potential. **89** —P.G. (4/1/2002)

Elk Cove 1998 Roosevelt Vineyard Pinot Noir (Willamette Valley) $48. 89 —J.C. (12/1/2000)

Elk Cove 2003 Shea Pinot Noir (Willamette Valley) $36. The blackberry and blueberry fruit flavors are a Shea Vineyard signature. In this hot year the juice is sweet and the wine soft and tannic, broadly flavorful, but the awkward acids suggest that some acidification was necessary. Needs a little time. **88** —P.G. (8/1/2005)

Elk Cove 2004 Windhill Pinot Noir (Willamette Valley) $38. Fragrant, aromatic and penetrating, it sends up lively aromas of spice, herb and pine needles. The scents are nicely threaded into the fruit, which mixes raspberry, cherry and crabapple with the spicy, leafy character of Oregon Pinot. **88** —P.G. (9/1/2006)

Elk Cove 2003 Windhill Pinot Noir (Willamette Valley) $36. These vines are now in their 30th vintage (planted in 1974) and reward you with exceptionally sweet fruit flavors of black cherry and blackberry. Soft and tannic, its loose, easy flavors are a reflection of this extra-warm vintage. This is a wine to embrace and enjoy. **90** —P.G. (8/1/2005)

Elk Cove 2002 Windhill Pinot Noir (Willamette Valley) $30. This pleasant, fruity effort falls squarely in the middle of the Elk Cove lineup, showing fresh, clean red fruits and a broad, accessible palate. **88** —P.G. (2/1/2005)

Elk Cove 2001 Windhill Pinot Noir (Willamette Valley) $32. Smoky aromas kick start things, and then comes a blast of tar, char and pure red fruit. The deep, structured, properly acidic palate is pure and healthy as can be, with cherry, raspberry and chocolate flavors coming together perfectly. And the rich, oaky finish is just as it should be. With zest, style and class, this is a fine domestic Pinot. **91** —M.S. (9/1/2003)

Elk Cove 2000 Windhill Pinot Noir (Oregon) $34. Here is a young, forward Pinot bursting with flavors of fruit preserves, chocolate and cola. Still a bit hard and tannic, with a rough, grainy, tannic finish. But the power and muscle of this beast suggests it will improve with some time in the cellar; there is plenty of good raw material here. **89** —P.G. (4/1/2003)

Elk Cove 1998 Windhill Pinot Noir (Willamette Valley) $28. 88 —M.S. (12/1/2000)

Elk Cove 1997 Windhill Pinot Noir (Willamette Valley) $28. 86 (11/15/1999)

Elk Cove 2004 Riesling (Willamette Valley) $17. Oregon Riesling can be as complex and textural as any made in America. When it's done right, as this is, it is the sort of sappy, appley, pleasure-loaded wine that you won't be able to resist. Nice hints of citrus and pear add complexity. **90** —P.G. (8/1/2005)

Elk Cove 2001 Riesling (Willamette Valley) $12. A tart, flinty and apple-y rendition of Riesling, one that's lean and light, one that leaves your mouth feeling clean and fresh after swallowing or spitting. One that would make a particularly pleasant aperitif. **86** —*J.C. (8/1/2003)*

Elk Cove 2000 Estate Riesling (Willamette Valley) $18. 84 —*J.C. (8/1/2003)*

Elk Cove 1999 Brut Sparkling Blend (Oregon) $22. Yeasty and proper in the nose, with a hint of apple blossom. The palate features healthy fruit in the standard pears-and-apples realm, and then some welcome nuances of nutmeg and cinnamon. The finish is dry, long and solid, and overall it delivers the full Champagne experience with no flaws. All in all, a good bubbly effort out of the Northwest. –M.S. **89** —*M.S. (6/1/2003)*

Elk Cove 2001 Del Rio Vineyard Syrah (Rogue Valley) $28. An admirable Syrah, with inky color and sweet fruit. What needs to improve is the tannin management; the finish is hard, green and chalky, when what you really want is for the wine to slip away gracefully. **87** —*P.G. (12/1/2003)*

Elk Cove 2001 Del Rio Viognier (Rogue Valley) $22. The melon, apple and pear aromas aren't as distinctively Viognier as one might expect, but the wine itself is solid and satisfying. The flavor profile is spicy and melony, and feel-wise there's lots of size. (This whopper weighs in at 14.9%, so it should seem big.) A large, chewy yet mildly buttery finish seals the package as full bodied and rich. **88** —*M.S. (8/1/2003)*

ELKE

Elke 2000 Donnelly Creek Vineyard Pinot Noir (Anderson Valley) $24. 80 *(10/1/2002)*

Elke 1997 Donnelly Creek Vineyard Pinot Noir (Anderson Valley) $24. 89 *(10/1/2000)*

Elke 1999 Donnelly Vineyards Pinot Noir (Anderson Valley) $24. Pale and tart, as befits this chilly appellation, the wine has tomato, cola, beetroot and herb aromas and drinks acidly tight and austere. There are hints of strawberries, but it's an herbal, earthy wine, although the tannins are silky soft. May soften and mellow with five plus years in the cellar. **87** —*S.H. (5/1/2002)*

ELKHORN PEAK

Elkhorn Peak 2000 Fagan Creek Merlot (Napa Valley) $18. A nice, easy-drinking Merlot, with herb, blackberry and coffee flavors a a full-bodied mouthfeel. A little rough around the edges, but a pretty good value for a Napa Merlot. **85** —*S.H. (11/15/2004)*

Elkhorn Peak 2002 Fagan Creek Vineyard Pinot Noir (Napa Valley) $30. Dry and earthy, this wine has a silky texture and very modest fruit flavors. It's a nice introductory Pinot Noir but too expensive. **83** —*S.H. (10/1/2005)*

Elkhorn Peak 1999 Fagan Creek Vineyard Pinot Noir (Napa Valley) $30. Rather heavy for a Pinot Noir, and soft, too. The flavors veer toward coffee, cherry and cola. Finishes simple and dry. **83** —*S.H. (8/1/2005)*

ELLISTON

Elliston 1998 Cabernet Sauvignon (Livermore Valley) $30. Opens with a baked, burnt smell, as if a blackberry pie had been singed by a flame and the crust and fruit were caramelized. The blackberry flavors also veer toward excessively ripe, Porty notes, although the wine is fully dry. **84** —*S.H. (11/15/2003)*

Elliston 1997 Sunol Valley Vineyard Pinot Grigio (Central Coast) $10. 87 Best Buy *(8/1/1999)*

ELVENGLADE

ElvenGlade 2004 Pinot Gris (Yamhill County) $15. Round, ripe and polished. The pear and apple flavors are bright and sassy, lined with skin flavors, persistent and well defined. This wine is balanced, harmonious, penetrating and beautifully crafted. It?s a template for all that is good about Oregon Pinot Gris. **91 Best Buy** —*P.G. (2/1/2006)*

ELYSE

Elyse 2001 Morisoli Vineyard Cabernet Sauvignon (Rutherford) $65. This wine is a bit too young now. All the parts haven't come together. The smooth, ripe tannins, black currant and cocoa flavors, polished oak and crisp acids should mesh by 2007. **89** —*S.H. (10/1/2005)*

Elyse 1999 Morisoli Vineyard Cabernet Sauvignon (Napa Valley) $57. Sweet oak and ripe fruit lead off. The follow-up features bright blackberry, currant, sage, thyme and toast flavors. Tannins are firm and fairly ripe, though slightly drying on the finish. **89** —*J.M. (2/1/2003)*

Elyse 2003 Tietjen Vineyard Cabernet Sauvignon (Napa Valley) $65. Seems made in a less ripe style, a minty, wintergreen wine with hints of barely ripened blackberries and some briary wild berries. Drinks bone dry and fairly tannic. If you're into an earthier, more French Bordeaux style, try this one. Will benefit from a decade of aging. **89** —*S.H. (12/15/2006)*

Elyse 2002 Tietjen Vineyard Cabernet Sauvignon (Rutherford) $65. There's lots of vanilla, toast and wood sap in the aroma, with notes of clove and mint beside riper red cherry. Drinks sweet in cherry fruit, but turns sharp on the finish. **85** —*S.H. (12/15/2005)*

Elyse 2001 Tietjen Vineyard Cabernet Sauvignon (Napa Valley) $65. Shows some good black cherry and blackberry flavors, with an earthier, herbal and leathery side, and the tannins stand out. Should soften in a few years. Drink now through 2008. **86** —*S.H. (5/1/2005)*

Elyse 2000 Tietjen Vineyard Cabernet Sauvignon (Napa Valley) $57. This ultrasmooth Cabernet is velvety, with soft, round, sweet tannins. That luscious texture carries flavors of blackcurrants, cherries, anise, dark chocolate, dried herbs and vanilla. It's so good, it makes you wish it were just a bit longer on the finish. **90** —*S.H. (2/1/2004)*

Elyse 2003 Petite Sirah (Rutherford) $36. About as fancy as Petite Sirah gets. Has the bones and authority of a great Cab. Lush, smooth tannins and full-bodied, with powerful, intense flavors of blackberries, plums, espresso, peppery spices and subtle notes from oak barrels. **92** —*S.H. (10/1/2005)*

Elyse 2003 Nero Misto Red Blend (California) $26. Described as a Cal-Ital blend, this wine is very soft and a little sweet in blackberries. It's a rustic, country-style wine, and overpriced. **83** —*S.H. (10/1/2005)*

Elyse 2002 D'Adventure Rhône Red Blend (California) $25. Smells closed and alcoholic, and turns tough and gritty in acids and tannins in the mouth. The flavors veer toward cherries, coffee and tobacco. Rhône blend. **85** —*S.H. (5/1/2005)*

Elyse 2001 Syrah (Napa Valley) $32. Lovely mouthfeel to this wine, with rich, soft but intricate tannins, and lots of ripe blackberry and cherry fruit. It is a little too sweet, though. **85** —*S.H. (5/1/2005)*

Elyse 1999 Syrah (Napa Valley) $35. Bright plum and spice flavors are supported by firm tannins and good acidity. Strong herb and oak components linger on the finish. **87** —*J.M. (2/1/2003)*

Elyse 2003 Korte Ranch Zinfandel (Napa Valley) $28. Looks rich from the dark purple-black color, and it is deep in blackberry and roasted coffee flavors. There are tantalizing hints of white pepper and fresh green herbs. Finishes too sweet for my taste, however, which limits the score. **84** —*S.H. (10/1/2005)*

Elyse 2002 Morisoli Vineyard Zinfandel (Napa Valley) $35. From a Rutherford vineyard, a smooth Zin with an excellent mouthfeel: velvety yet firm. It's fully dry but very high in alcohol. Flavor-wise, the berries are compromised by stalky, green notes.by stalky, green notes. **85** —*S.H. (5/1/2005)*

Elyse 2000 Morisoli Vineyard Zinfandel (Napa Valley) $32. Pretty plum flavors are at the core of this wine. Black cherry, sage, smoke and toast also add interest. Moderate length on the clean, bright finish. **88** —*J.M. (2/1/2003)*

EMERALD BAY

Emerald Bay 1997 Cabernet Sauvignon (California) $7. 83 *(2/1/2000)*

Emerald Bay 1997 Chardonnay (Central Coast) $7. 84 *(2/1/2000)*

Emerald Bay 1997 Merlot (California) $7. 85 Best Buy *(2/1/2000)*

EMERIL'S

Emeril's 2000 Classics Red Blend (California) $13. Here's a big, rich wine, exuberantly fruity and spicy. It's packed with ripe berry and stone fruit flavors, and is very dry. The tannins are nice and intricate. It's not a layered, complex wine, but a fine one, with a lot of character. Cabernet Sauvignon, Syrah and Zinfandel. **86** —*S.H. (12/1/2002)*

USA

EMILIO'S TERRACE

Emilio's Terrace 1999 Estate Cabernet Sauvignon (Napa Valley) $45. From a 4.5-acre vineyard directly behind To Kalon, this is only the winery's third vintage. Sleek and plush, it's loaded with dark plum, black cherry, chocolate, cola, blackberry and spice flavors. The tannins are supple, and the finish is long. **93 Editors' Choice** —*J.M. (2/1/2003)*

Emilio's Terrace 2002 Reserve Cabernet Sauvignon (Oakville) $50. The vineyard is in the foothills above Mondavi, and the wine is marked by the authoritative tannic structure that usually marks Cabs from this neighborhood. Rich in pure cassis, there's a dusty, locked-down quality and a sandpapery astringency that suggests aging. This is a very fine wine and should drink well in a few years and then hold through 2014 or so. **91 Cellar Selection** —*S.H. (8/1/2006)*

Emilio's Terrace 2001 Reserve Cabernet Sauvignon (Napa Valley) $50. Young, taut and dense now, with edgy tannins that will reward cellaring. With its core of cherry, blackberry and cedary cassis, it's likely to hold and improve for a decade. **91** —*S.H. (5/1/2005)*

EMMOLO

Emmolo 2000 Rutherford Sauvignon Blanc (Napa Valley) $16. More oak than the wine can handle is what you get here, from the woody, buttery overtoasted nose through the soft, clumsy, creamy body. It's a real challenge to find any fruit, so you had better like a fully wooded wine if you're going to take a crack at this one. **85** *(8/1/2002)*

ENCORE

Encore 2004 San Bernabe Vineyard White Medley White Blend (Monterey County) $18. Four varieties comprise this blend, and all contribute a little something. The overall impact is an intensely fruity, rather simple wine, with nice acids. It straddles the dry-off dry line. **84** —*S.H. (12/1/2005)*

Encore 2002 San Bernabe Vineyard White Medley White Blend (Monterey) $18. From Monterra, a delicious blend of Sauvignon Blanc, Pinot Blanc, Muscat Canelli and Viognier. Each variety contributes a different fruity flavor. Smooth and a little sweet, with a nice cut of acidity. **87** —*S.H. (12/15/2004)*

ENGELMANN

Engelmann 2000 Cabernet Sauvignon-Shiraz (California) $16. From a winery in the Central Valley town of Fresno, this is a light-bodied wine with faint tastes of berries. The tannins are soft to the point of nonexistence, and acidity is low. **82** —*S.H. (12/1/2002)*

Engelmann 2000 Sangiovese (California) $12. Pretty harsh going. This is a rough-edged bruiser, with tart acids and what tastes like too much residual sugar for a red wine that should be dry. The flavors are thin. **81** —*S.H. (12/1/2002)*

Engelmann 2000 Very Old Vine Zinfandel (California) $12. Whatever "very old vine" means, and there's no legal definition, this is not very good Zin. It's hot and harsh, with awkward acids and tannins. **82** —*S.H. (12/1/2002)*

ENJOIE

Enjoie 2005 Dry Rose Wine Rosé Blend (California) $13. Dry like the name says, and also freshly acidic like a young Beaujolais; and pleasantly silky. The flavor is modest in cherries and spice. **83** —*S.H. (12/1/2006)*

ENLACE

Enlace 2002 Cabernet Sauvignon (Napa Valley) $26. A smooth, supple, easy-drinking but complex wine that shows many of the same qualities of the Cabernets of the parent company, Liparita. The wine is dry and balanced, with firm but pliant tannins supporting tiers of cassis and oak. Should hold well for five years. **90** —*S.H. (3/1/2006)*

Enlace 2002 Merlot (Napa Valley) $25. This wine shows great balance. It is smooth and sumptuous, with blackberry, herb, mocha and cola flavors. Oak plays a supportive, not an intrusive, role. It's a dry wine, with layers of complexity. An upscale second label from Liparita. **89** —*S.H. (3/1/2006)*

Enlace 2004 Sauvignon Blanc (North Coast) $15. If you're looking for a pleasantly fruity, dry white wine with plenty of acidity to stand up to goat cheese and grilled veggies, this is it. It has powerful but elegant fla-

vors of citrus rind and honeydew, with a complexing minerality. Notable for its balance and harmony. **90 Best Buy** —*S.H. (4/1/2006)*

ENOTRIA

Enotria 1999 Arneis (Mendocino) $14. From this Italian variety comes a light, pleasant wine, with floral, citrus and vanilla aromas. It's pretty rich, with an explosion of citrus fruits and a thick, glyceriney texture. **84** —*S.H. (8/1/2001)*

Enotria 1999 Arneis (Mendocino) $15. Soft, simple and slightly sweet, with highly extracted lemon-and-lime flavors and a limpid, supple mouthfeel. It's a nice, clean wine with pretty flavors. **85** —*S.H. (5/1/2002)*

Enotria 1999 Barbera (Mendocino) $13. Smells great, with plummy, dusty, earthy notes that are clean and inviting, but then shocks the palate with a high degree of sugar. Not clear if this was a stuck fermentation or deliberate. Either way, the wine is awkward and almost insipid. Barbera should be dry. **81** —*S.H. (5/1/2002)*

Enotria 1998 Riserva Barbera (Mendocino) $NA. Lots of oak in the nose, with black cherry, earth, stewed tomato, plum and other components. Drinks bitter and sharp, with high acidity. The austere plum and earth flavors finish with a tannic sour. This is a wine that cries out for olive oil. **85** —*S.H. (12/1/2001)*

Enotria 1999 Dolcetto (Mendocino) $16. This is an earthy wine with indeterminate berry flavors, very dry tannins and good acidity, and a rather rough edge to the mouthfeel. It's an old-fashioned wine, a big, old-country red of the kind great-grandpa might have drunk, or made in the basement. **84** —*S.H. (5/1/2002)*

Enotria 1998 Dolcetto (Mendocino) $16. Soft, fruity and dry, it has some pretty flavors of red raspberries, spices and white chocolate. This is a wine for immediate consumption with simple foods like pizza and pasta. **84** —*S.H. (8/1/2001)*

EOLA HILLS

Eola Hills 1998 LBV Port Style Cabernet Sauvignon (Oregon) $18. Port-like, with dried cherry, prune, toast, licorice, coffee and chocolate flavors. Somewhat sweet and bright. **86** —*J.M. (12/1/2002)*

Eola Hills 2000 Chardonnay (Oregon) $10. Here is a big, forward, friendly fruit bomb, which hits you with bold, lemon/apple fruit flavors and a generous amount of toasty, buttery oak. There's nothing complex here, but it's all in scale, big-boned, user-friendly and altogether quite likeable. **88 Best Buy** —*P.G. (4/1/2002)*

Eola Hills 1998 Merlot (Oregon) $12. 85 —*C.S. (12/31/2002)*

Eola Hills 2004 Pinot Gris (Oregon) $10. This has a strong floral component, like body powder, but it is a substantial, meaty wine, with ripe pear and white peach flavors. Intense and focused in the midpalate, it gets a bit hot on the finish. **88 Best Buy** —*P.G. (2/1/2006)*

Eola Hills 1997 Pinot Gris (Oregon) $10. 83 *(8/1/1999)*

Eola Hills 1999 Pinot Noir (Oregon) $12. Cherry, mocha and soy aromas are the clearest part of an otherwise muddled nose. Basic plum and black cherry flavors are not terribly focused, but the dry, moderately tannic finish is clean. Recommended for newcomers to Oregon and Pinot Noir. **84 Best Buy** *(10/1/2002)*

Eola Hills 2001 La Creole Pinot Noir (Oregon) $20. Pale and pretty, with sharp, cranberry-flavored fruit. A wine to drink young—to quaff, if you will—with fried chicken or calamari or some other comfort food. **86** —*P.G. (10/1/2004)*

Eola Hills 1999 La Creole Reserve Pinot Noir (Oregon) $25. 81 *(10/1/2002)*

Eola Hills 1998 La Creole Reserve Pinot Noir (Oregon) $25. 89 —*J.C. (12/1/2000)*

Eola Hills 2002 La Creole Vineyard Pinot Noir (Eola Hills) $20. Notes of cabbage, plum tomato and green bean give this a somewhat medicinal, pungent character. Tannic, thin and difficult. **84** *(11/1/2004)*

Eola Hills 2002 Oak Grove Pinot Noir (Oregon) $13. Pungent, earthy and showing common aromas of beetroot and bark, suggesting marginal ripeness. **84** *(11/1/2004)*

Eola Hills 2001 Wolf Hill Vineyard Pinot Noir (Oregon) $40. This is a tangy, food-friendly style, with tart fruit that suggests cranberries and pomegranate. There is also a distinctive minty quality that's almost eucalyptus (but I don't know that eucalyptus grows in Oregon). Right at the finish line some sweet cherry slips in. **87** —P.G. (10/1/2004)

Eola Hills 2002 Wolf Hill Vineyard Reserve Pinot Noir (Oregon) $40. Fresh and fruity, lightly dusted with cocoa, and balanced to show off some pleasant cranberry/cherry fruit flavors. Some bitter, green tannins come through in the finish. **87** (11/1/2004)

Eola Hills 1999 Wolf Hill Vineyard Reserve Pinot Noir (Oregon) $40. Woody aromas dominate the nose, which otherwise tosses up cherry and toast along with a touch of heat. Black plums, cherry and vanilla compete on the palate, with each taking a bit of first prize. Coffee and burnt toast flavors dot the finish of this overt, bruising wine that could use another year or three in the bottle. **88** (10/1/2002)

Eola Hills 2000 Sauvignon Blanc (Applegate Valley) $10. Aromas of jalapeno peppers, thistle and pine needles raise questions about ripeness while not exactly rolling out the welcome mat. That said, the wine is surprisingly sweet, with orange and lemon flavors. Finally, a thick texture runs in contrast to the lean nose, ultimately leaving one confused and asking: Is this really Sauvignon Blanc? **81** —M.S. (8/1/2003)

Eola Hills 2000 Syrah (Oregon) $12. With aromas of char, toast and charcoal there's too much toasted oak for the fruit on this wine. There are some cassis flavors but they're covered by more char and burnt toast. There is nice acidity on the finish. Give this one time to settle, and hope there's still some fruit. **85** —R.V. (12/31/2002)

Eola Hills 1999 Applegate Valley Syrah (Oregon) $20. Plum skin, milk chocolate and black pepper aromas are satisfying in this Syrah. The tannins are big and there's acidity to match, which prepares your palate for the next sip. **88** —C.S. (12/31/2002)

Eola Hills 2000 Reserve Syrah (Columbia Valley (OR)) $20. Unusual but compelling to some reviewers, but one thing is for sure: This wine is no fruit bomb. The nose has red fruit doused in tons of fragrant spice (cinnamon, clove, curry). Dry on the palate, with red berry and cherry fruit, unsweetened chocolate and cedar flavors. Toast and menthol on the finish. **85** (9/1/2005)

Eola Hills 1998 Reserve Syrah (Applegate Valley) $18. The tart-sweet cherry and blueberry fruit is enveloped in oak, with cedar-sauna aromas and flavors prevailing. Hints of espresso and cinnamon add interest— and the wine never gets sweet or sappy. Closes with a slight tartness and just a hint of meat and spice. **85** (10/1/2001)

Eola Hills 1999 Old Vines Zinfandel (Lodi) $25. Caramel and cream notes throughout make this Lodi wine an easy drinker. On the nose, sweet black berry fruit plus oak and burned caramel set the stage for more oak-derived flavors (plus sweet raspberry and red plum) on the palate. Finishes with more raspberry, smoke, cedar and a little green herb in the back of the throat. **86** —D.T. (3/1/2002)

EOS

EOS 2002 The French Connection Bordeaux Blend (Paso Robles) $20. Rather soft and edgy in tannins, but there's reward in the fresh, lively berry, cherry and herb flavors. Finishes a bit too sweet. **83** —S.H. (11/1/2005)

EOS 2000 French Connection Cabernet Blend (Paso Robles) $20. Here's a Bordeaux blend with some good, rich flavors and fine tannins. Has none of those annoying raisiny notes you sometimes get from the appellation, and the alcohol is a modest 13.2%. **86** —S.H. (5/1/2003)

EOS 1999 The French Connection Cabernet Blend (Paso Robles) $20. Handsomely balanced by herb, cocoa and earth accents to the sweet-tart blackberry fruit, this Bordeaux blend (60% Cabernet Sauvignon, 30% Cabernet Franc and 10% Merlot) is medium weight, with good acidity and supple tannins. This will pair well with a wide range of foods and may be drunk from now through 2005. **88** —M.M. (4/1/2002)

EOS 2002 Cabernet Sauvignon (Paso Robles) $14. Soft in acids, bone-dry and kind of raw-feeling in the mouth, this is an earthy Cab with traces of red and black cherry fruit. **83** —S.H. (3/1/2006)

EOS 2001 Cabernet Sauvignon (Paso Robles) $18. Rich, soft and juicy in blackberry, cherry, raisin and chocolate fruit, with such a sweetly luscious feeling in the mouth. There's a firm structure of dusty tannins that suggests pairing with a barbecued lamb chop. **89** —S.H. (2/1/2004)

EOS 2000 Cabernet Sauvignon (Paso Robles) $18. This dark wine opens with aromas of mint and cassis and suggestions of raisins. The flavors are similar, with hints of dark chocolate, tobacco and herbs. It's fully dry, with soft acids and tannins. It's a gentle Cabernet from the warm part of Paso. **87** —S.H. (11/15/2002)

EOS 1999 Cabernet Sauvignon (Paso Robles) $15. If this doesn't present quite the depth of the Reserve, it's almost as tasty, displaying a similar but scaled-down profile. The black cherry core is complemented by toast and anise notes atop an easy mouthfeel. Finishes with more of the same, turning a bit firmer, with modestly drying tannins. Drinking now until 2004. **88** —M.M. (4/1/2002)

EOS 1996 Hyperion Vineyard Cabernet Sauvignon (Paso Robles) $16. **89** (11/15/1999)

EOS 1999 Reserve Cabernet Sauvignon (Paso Robles) $24. Medium weight and tasty, with a nose of blackberries accented by earth and toast. In the mouth, the wine is ripe and flavorful, with chocolate and dark toast elements offsetting sweet fruit. Shows more structure than the regular bottling, and closes longer, too. Drink now through 2005+. **89** —M.M. (4/1/2002)

EOS 1998 Chardonnay (Paso Robles) $15. **88** (6/1/2000)

EOS 1997 Chardonnay (Paso Robles) $15. **88** (11/15/1999)

EOS 2003 Chardonnay (Paso Robles) $12. Simple and fruity, with canned peach and pear flavors that drink a little heavy, and finish a bit sweet. Okay for everyday fare. **83** —S.H. (11/1/2005)

EOS 2002 Chardonnay (Paso Robles) $15. Opens with the aromas of baked apples and tapioca, and has apple custard flavors in a heavy texture, although it's dry. Very full-bodied, and a little bitter on the finish. **84** —S.H. (6/1/2004)

EOS 2001 Chardonnay (Paso Robles) $15. Soft, fruity and pretty sweet, with very ripe flavors of peach, apple and pear. A honeyed softness coats the palate and makes the wine drink with sorbet-like richness. **84** —S.H. (12/15/2002)

EOS 2000 Chardonnay (Paso Robles) $14. **85** —M.M. (4/1/2002)

EOS 2002 Cupa Grandis Chardonnay (Paso Robles) $40. From EOS, a bells and whistles Chard, with lavish French oak, lees, ripe fruit, malolactic fermentation, the works. For all that, it's pleasant rather than grand, with smoky, appley flavors and a creamy texture. **86** —S.H. (6/1/2004)

EOS 2003 Cupa Grandis Grand Barrel Reserve Chardonnay (Paso Robles) $40. This flavorful Chard puts its fruit upfront. The flavors include apples, pears and dusty brown Asian spices. It's been fairly heavily worked, and is a bit soft in acids, and very creamy. Will be nice with lobster bisque. **89** —S.H. (11/1/2005)

EOS 2003 Reserve Chardonnay (Paso Robles) $20. Bright in apple and citrus flavors, this pleasant Chard shows a crispness that's more akin to a coastal wine than an inland one. It's dry and rich on the finish. **87** —S.H. (11/1/2005)

EOS 1999 Reserve Chardonnay (Paso Robles) $24. Smoky oak and restrained fruit mark the nose of this smooth yet tangy offering. The nut and dried fruit flavors are understated—even reserved—and wrapped in spicy oak. Though tasty, it wants a little for integration and stuffing in the midpalate. Still, it has all the right parts, and it's not about sweetness. Drink now through 2003. **87** —M.M. (4/1/2002)

EOS 2002 Fumé Blanc (Paso Robles) $18. Kicks off with honey and toasty almond tones backed by lush fig, pear, grass, lemon, grapefruit and herb flavors. The finish is long with a distinct and complex mineral edge. Full and round but with good acidity. Long and lush on the finish. **90** —J.M. (6/1/2004)

EOS 2003 Brothers Ranch Vineyard 4, Block 8 Fumé Blanc (Paso Robles) $20. Dusty sawdust aromas run heavy on the nose, with peach and nectarine aromas sitting in reserve. Fairly reserved in terms of flavors, with light fruit duking it out with the more aggressive wood notes. Where it does its best is in the area of balance: citric acids even out any wood and weight. **86** *(7/1/2005)*

EOS 2001 Reserve Fumé Blanc (Paso Robles) $18. Intensely flavorful, a delight on the palate, just brimming with bright citrusy, smoky flavors and a honeyed finish. Young, fresh acidity makes the wine drink clean and juicy. This is first-rate Fume, and a testament to its appellation. **89** *—S.H. (9/1/2003)*

EOS 2000 Reserve Fumé Blanc (Paso Robles) $19. Talk about an assorted but attractive bouquet: this has lemon, peach, dried herbs—even some honey. The flavors veer mostly toward citrus—predominantly lemon and orange. But there's a touch of sweet pineapple in there, too. The finish is spicy and maintains the citrus from the palate, but it does tail off a bit heavy and hot. **88** *(8/1/2002)*

EOS 2002 Merlot (Paso Robles) $15. Unpleasantly sharp in acids, and burdened with residual sugar, this is a hard wine to like. **80** *—S.H. (11/1/2005)*

EOS 2000 Merlot (Paso Robles) $18. Here's an ultrasoft wine whose acids were whittled away by the hot sun, and with tannins that are also soft and melted. Yet there's something delicious and gentle about the plummy, peppery flavors, and it's nice that the wine is dry without being too alcoholic. **87** *—S.H. (11/15/2002)*

EOS 1999 Merlot (Paso Robles) $22. 85 *—M.M. (4/1/2002)*

EOS 2000 Tears of Dew Late Harvest Moscato (Paso Robles) $20. They let a few rows of Muscat Canelli raisin up under the blazing September sun, and here's the result. Intensely sweet, like an apricot tart drizzled with clover honey. Fortunately, high acidity sets it off nicely. Clean, vibrant and a dessert in itself. **90** *—S.H. (12/1/2002)*

EOS 1999 Tears of Dew Late Harvest Moscato (Paso Robles) $17. If you like oranges you'll go wild for this rich, fat overtly orange-tasting dessert wine. Honeysuckle notes enhance the nose, and apricot-leather and mild spices show up on the palate. It's soft but not sloppy—a sweet tooth's delight and a perfect foil for fruit tarts and the like. **86** *—M.M. (4/1/2002)*

EOS 2001 Tears of Dew Late Harvest Moscato (Paso Robles) $20. Seductively delicious, an unctuously thick wine that opens with decadent aromas of apricot jam, sweet fig, tangerine, vanilla and meringue. Feels oily-rich on the palate, with sweet flavors and crisp acids and a clean, honeyed finish. **93** *—S.H. (12/1/2003)*

EOS 1997 Tears of Dew Late Harvest Moscato (Paso Robles) $15. 91 Best Buy *(11/15/1999)*

EOS 2004 Tears of Dew Late Harvest 375ml Moscato (Paso Robles) $22. This dessert wine has pushed itself to the front of the line of California sweeties, and the '04 is a great bottling. It's enormously sweet in late-harvest character, with apricot liqueur, pineapple tart and vanilla cream flavors that are brightened and boosted with cleansing acidity. So addictively delicious you just can't help yourself. **95 Editors' Choice** *—S.H. (12/1/2006)*

EOS 2003 Tears of Dew Late Harvest Moscato Muscat Canelli (Paso Robles) $20. It's time to admit this wine into the elite of California dessert sippers. It's always dependably rewarding in apricot, wild honey and vanilla flavors, unctuously sweet, and well-balanced in acids. This year's offering is true to form. **93 Editors' Choice** *—S.H. (11/1/2005)*

EOS 2002 Petite Sirah (Paso Robles) $13. There's much to like about this wine, namely the full-bodied richness and the smooth tannins, but it's just too sweet. The lovely dark stone fruit tastes like it was sprinkled with sugar. **83** *—S.H. (3/1/2006)*

EOS 2002 Cupa Grandis Grand Barrel Reserve Petite Sirah (Paso Robles) $40. If you like your Pets awesomely dark and extracted, with enormous fruit and lavish oak, you'll enjoy this only-in-California wine. Tastes like a rum-soaked blackberry and chocolate cake, sprinkled with cinnamon, with a peppery edge. But it's dry and soft. **92** *—S.H. (11/1/2005)*

EOS 2001 Cupa Grandis, Peck Ranch Vineyard Block P7 Petite Sirah (Paso Robles) $40. With this thick, dark wine, the folks from EOS have pumped up the volume. It's super soft and supple, with velvety tannins and lots of black cherry, coffee, chocolate, herb, spice, vanilla, toast and

earth flavors. The wine also has some high-toned qualities that bright up on the finish. **92** *—J.M. (6/1/2004)*

EOS 2001 Peck Ranch Vineyard Reserve Petite Sirah (Paso Robles) $20. Despite 15-1/2 percent alcohol, this wine still has residual sugar! Think what the brix must have been at harvest. Drinks like a Port, which is a major fault for a dry table wine. Tasted twice, with consistent results. **80** *—S.H. (11/1/2005)*

EOS 2000 Reserve Petite Sirah (Paso Robles) $25. From a rising star of Paso Robles, a wine with good, ripe fruity flavors that's a bit rough around the edges. The tannins are chewy and grip the palate, and the finish is dry and earthy. **85** *(4/1/2003)*

EOS 1999 Reserve Petite Sirah (Paso Robles) $22. Big and inky, with a brawny flavor profile and feel, this solid Petite Sirah delivers deep blackfruit flavors with attractive meat, earth and herb accents. It's weighty, with good acidity and a full, long finish that possesses substantial tannins—this is not a sipping wine. Best 2004–2010+. **90 Editors' Choice** *—M.M. (4/1/2002)*

EOS 1996 Zephyrus Vineyard Petite Sirah (Paso Robles) $17. 88 *(11/15/1999)*

EOS 2001 French Connection Red Blend (Paso Robles) $20. EOS's complex Bordeaux blend is a big, sturdy wine with a skeleton of firm tannins that finish with a dry astringency, suggesting cellar time. They frame a generous core of blackberry and black cherry fruit. Enjoy now with rich foods, or be patient. **90** *—S.H. (12/31/2003)*

EOS 1999 Torre del Gobbo Red Blend (Paso Robles) $22. Dark cherry, plum and smoky oak aromas open this smooth welterweight. It's a super Tuscan blend made of 25% Sangiovese and 75% Bordeaux grapes. The ripe, plummy fruit shows leather notes and an herb note. Fills out and shows dusty tannins on the finish. Drink now through 2005. **86** *—M.M. (4/1/2002)*

EOS 1997 Sauvignon Blanc (Paso Robles) $14. 87 *(11/15/1999)*

EOS 2002 Sauvignon Blanc (Paso Robles) $15. Fresh and lively, with pretty herb, spice, lemon, grapefruit, pepper, grass and mineral notes. The wine is light textured, yet hangs in there with a clean finish. **88** *—J.M. (6/1/2004)*

EOS 2001 Sauvignon Blanc (Paso Robles) $15. A bit soft, but with some pretty apple and citrus flavors and a pleasant spicy peppery taste. Fully dry, with a round, smooth texture. This is an easy sipping white wine. **85** *—S.H. (3/1/2003)*

EOS 2000 Estate Bottled Sauvignon Blanc (Paso Robles) $14. 87 *—M.M. (4/1/2002)*

EOS 1997 Zinfandel (Paso Robles) $16. 89 *(11/15/1999)*

EOS 2003 Zinfandel (Paso Robles) $18. Softly tannic, rustic and kind of earthy, with ground coffee, nutmeg and cola flavors nudging into blackberries. Ribeye steak will perk it up. **84** *—S.H. (12/1/2006)*

EOS 2002 Zinfandel (Paso Robles) $15. An awkward wine that keeps its alcohol moderate at the cost of residual sugar. Some will like this old-fashioned, jug-wine style. **82** *—S.H. (11/1/2005)*

EOS 2001 Zinfandel (Paso Robles) $16. Bright and fresh, with pretty spice, black cherry, sage, blackberry and coffee flavors. With moderate body and smooth, firm tannins, it makes a satisfying quaff at a good price. Much better than previously reviewed. **88** *—J.M. (2/1/2004)*

EOS 2000 Zinfandel (Paso Robles) $16. No doubt about this being Paso Zin. It's filled with cherry-berry flavors, is very soft in acids and tannins and contains plenty of alcohol. Feels gentle and limpid, and goes down nice and easy. **86** *—S.H. (12/1/2002)*

EOS 2002 Brothers Ranch Vineyard 5 Block 5A Late Harvest Zinfandel (Paso Robles) $20. Alas, the long name can't compensate for the deficiencies here. While it's very sweet, it's also sharp and hot, with a cloying, syrupy mouthfeel. **82** *—S.H. (11/1/2005)*

EOS 1999 Estate Bottled Zinfandel (Paso Robles) $15. This baby goes down easily, particularly if you are not sensitive to oak. Big, lively aromas of caramel and ripe red fruit play on the nose; stewed red berry and more oak flavor the palate. Medium-weight in the mouth but for the prickly tannins that pop up just before the finish; ends with oak, caramel and herb. **87** —*D.T. (3/1/2002)*

EOS 2001 Port Zinfandel (Paso Robles) $28. Lush and sweet, with jammy black cherry, blackberry, coffee, chocolate, licorice and plum flavors. Finishes smoky and long. **90** —*J.M. (6/1/2004)*

EOS 1999 Port Zinfandel (Paso Robles) $27. Inky colored, with extracted blackberry, pepper and tarragon aromas and flavors. Rich and smooth, nutty elements show on the palate and open to a cassis, grilled nut and cracked pepper finish of medium length. Packaged with an interesting mock-engraved pewter label that will get people talking, as will the 19.9% alcohol. **88** —*M.M. (4/1/2002)*

EPIPHANY

Epiphany 1999 Chardonnay (Santa Barbara County) $19. Smells fresh and clean, with vibrant aromas of sun-ripened summer peaches drizzled with vanilla and cream. The fruity flavors are very bright and sharp, underlaid with a rich honeyed sweetness. A long, spicy finish completes the picture. **90** —*S.H. (12/15/2002)*

Epiphany 2005 Grenache Rosé Grenache (Santa Barbara County) $14. This is a dark, powerful rosé, almost a red wine, with the weight and silky texture of a light Pinot Noir. But the flavors are all Grenache, namely, cherries, cherries, cherries. It's a dry wine, with a long, rich, spicy finish. **86** —*S.H. (12/15/2006)*

Epiphany 2005 Camp 4 Vineyard Grenache Blanc (Santa Barbara County) $18. Rich in honeyed wildflower and ripe tropical fruit flavors, with a smoky, pastry pie crust, buttery sweetness, this soft, creamy wine is just delicious. Finishes just a little bit sweet. **86** —*S.H. (12/15/2006)*

Epiphany 2003 Rodney's Vineyard Petite Sirah (Santa Barbara County) $24. With 16.7% alcohol, all kinds of things could have gone wrong with this wine. Somehow, though, it works. It's quite dry, with no trace of raisiny or stewed fruit. Instead it shows bitter chocolate and cassis flavors wrapped in rich tannins. Not for the faint-hearted; an eccentric wine. **88** —*S.H. (11/15/2006)*

Epiphany 2002 Rodney's Vineyard Petite Sirah (Santa Barbara County) $25. One of the blacker wines of the year, and also one of the more alcoholic, with 15.9%. Massively fruited, just explodes with blackberry and cherry marmalade, dusted with chocolate and cinnamon. It sure is tasty, but is it a dry table wine? **87** —*S.H. (11/1/2005)*

Epiphany 1999 Pinot Blanc (Santa Barbara County) $19. Showing a bit of age, with underlying peach fruit beginning to pick up baked pie crust, coconut and meringue notes. Complex and layered in the mouth and very dry, with fruity, mineral flavors. **88** —*S.H. (2/1/2003)*

Epiphany 1999 Pinot Gris (Santa Barbara County) $18. This wine has pretty flavors of lemons, apricots and peaches, and is just a little sweet on the tongue, although crisp natural acidity creates balance. There's an oily, glyceriney smoothness to the mouthfeel that adds interest. A new line from Fess Parker. **87** —*S.H. (9/1/2003)*

Epiphany 2004 Ashley's Vineyard Pinot Gris (Santa Rita Hills) $17. From Fess Parker, this distinctive white wine smacks of terroir. The aroma, dominated by white pepper, adds notes of ripe peaches and tropical citrus fruits, and the flavors are rich and interesting, balanced by high acids. **90** —*S.H. (2/1/2006)*

Epiphany 2005 Goodchild Vineyard Pinot Gris (Santa Maria Valley) $18. Nice and crisp, with rich peach, citrus, guava, honeysuckle, vanilla and spice flavors, this PG has real complexity. It must be the terroir, which has given the wine enormous concentrated ripeness but also beautiful acidity. **90** —*S.H. (12/15/2006)*

Epiphany 2002 Revelation Red Blend (Santa Barbara County) $34. Smells and tastes rather vegetal, although there are equally strong fruity flavors. It's as though someone fell asleep at the sorting table. A rustic wine. **83** —*S.H. (11/1/2005)*

Epiphany 2003 Revelation Red Wine Rhône Red Blend (Santa Barbara County) $32. Big, thick, soft, gooey, delicious, a little hot, that begins to describe this Rhône blend, which is Syrah, Grenache and a dash of Petite Sirah. It's all essence of cherries, melted chocolate, coffee, vanilla, cinnamon. **89** —*S.H. (12/15/2006)*

Epiphany 1999 Rodney's Rhône Red Blend (Santa Barbara County) $36. A Rhone blend dominated by 60% Grenache. The remaining Syrah comes from the same vineyard as Fess Parker's amazing Ô99 Syrah, but it's overshadowed by the Grenache's cranberry, mint and camphor side, the result of the varietal's tendency to overcrop. An obvious touch of residual sugar makes for a sweetish finish. This wine is unfinished, a work in progress. **85** —*S.H. (9/1/2003)*

Epiphany 2004 Camp 4 Vineyard Roussanne (Santa Ynez Valley) $18. Exotic in peach custard, honeysuckle and tapioca flavors, with a rich, creamy, full-bodiedness, this is a nice alternative to Chardonnay. It will be especially attractive with a firm-fleshed white fish, sauteed in butter and EVOO, with a fruity-salsa topping. **89** —*S.H. (5/1/2006)*

Epiphany 2003 Hampton Vineyard Syrah (Santa Barbara County) $35. Almost dessert in a glass, so rich and chocolaty, with such powerful baked blackberry and cherry pie flavors, and a gooey, honeyed softness. Just look at those glycerine stains. The wine may have some residual sugar, but it's dry enough to wash down the best steak you can grill. **90** —*S.H. (12/15/2006)*

Epiphany 2002 Hampton Vineyard Syrah (Santa Barbara County) $35. From Fess Parker, this deeply flavored and richly textured Syrah impresses for its dry elegance. It's fairly tannic now, but if you chew, you'll discover the fine blackberries, plums and unsweetened chocolate along with black olive and coffee. Try aging until 2007. **89** (*9/1/2005*)

Epiphany 2003 Starlane Vineyard Syrah (Santa Barbara County) $35. Not a success, and it had to be heat spells at harvest. The alcohol is a kick-in-the-butt 15.9%, and the wine is semi-sweet in cherry coughdrop flavors. **82** —*S.H. (11/15/2006)*

Epiphany 1999 Stonewall Vineyard Syrah (California) $45. Imagine a sweaty horse crashing through a briar patch—the comingled aromas might smell like this wine. Horsey, leathery notes and blackberries, together with a leafy, untamed side mark this as a unique California experience. **89** (*11/1/2001*)

EPONYMOUS

Eponymous 2002 Cabernet Sauvignon (Napa Valley) $50. From Bob Pepi, a classically structured wine that showcases how beautifully ripe Napa Cab can get, and how rich the tannins can be, grown in the right terroir and made by the right hands. The wine is dry and powerful in cassis and currant flavors that are well-oaked, and it has the body and firmness to age. Drink now through 2012. **92 Cellar Selection** —*S.H. (3/1/2006)*

Eponymous 2001 Cabernet Sauvignon-Merlot (Napa Valley) $50. A nice Cab from a great vintage. Ripe and juicy in currant, cherry, cocoa and oak flavors, with lush, complex tannins that make for a creamy mouth feel. From veteran Bob Pepi, mostly Cab, with a splash of Merlot. **88** —*S.H. (2/1/2005)*

Eponymous 2000 Red Wine Cabernet Sauvignon-Merlot (Napa Valley) $50. A new wine from Robert Pepi, and an ambitious one. The veteran winemaker has crafted an aromatic, rather tannic wine of great structure and potential. Shows ripe blackberry and cherry flavors that are elaborately oaked, with fresh acidity. Drink after 2006. Mostly Cabernet with a splash of Merlot. **90** —*S.H. (10/1/2004)*

EQUINOX

Equinox 2002 Merlot (Oakville) $75. Very fine, filled with beautiful cherries and blueberries, really ripe, and reined in with sweet oak and lush tannins. Elegant and refined, this beautiful wine drinks well now. **92** —*S.H. (3/1/2005)*

EQUUS

Equus 1999 James Berry Vineyard Grenache (Paso Robles) $18. Pleasant drinking fare, light in body and tannins, with a silky mouthfeel and soft acids. Notable for the persistance and intensity of its raspberry flavors. Long, sweet and delicious through the slighty hot finish, the result of high alcohol. **86** —*S.H. (2/1/2003)*

Equus 1999 Mourvèdre (Paso Robles) $18. This is a young, jammy wine, despite the light body and the fact that it's three years old. Raspberry, tobacco and vanilla aromas lead to berry flavors and soft acids, although the tannins are apparent and it finishes with a rough earthiness. **85** —*S.H. (5/1/2003)*

Equus 2000 Roussanne (Paso Robles) $16. A fruity white wine, with the rich peach and pear flavors of Chardonnay, but the lean, crisp citrus character of Sauvignon Blanc. Seems to straddle the two profiles. The finish is dry and spicy. **85** —*S.H. (3/1/2003)*

Equus 1999 Syrah (Paso Robles) $18. Delicious and complete, with lush, ripe fruit suggesting red raspberries and cherries harmonizing with white chocolate and various spices. Very dry, with soft but fine tannins and acids. Smooth and seductive. **90** —*S.H. (2/1/2003)*

Equus 1998 Syrah (Paso Robles) $22. "Nice" to one reviewer, but "a tough customer" to others, the Equus opens with cherry, smoke and tomato aromas and a touch of heat. We can thank oak, coffee and sour cherry pie flavors for the tartness in the mouth; finishes long and dry, with mineral and soft cherry flavors. **86** *(11/1/2001)*

Equus 2000 Viognier (Central Coast) $16. Lots of forward fruit notes of white peach, with floral scents like buttercups and spicy vanilla. Very flavorful, dry and rich, just filled with ripe fruit. Good acidity balances it out. The finish snaps to a quick end, leaving behind a clean palate. **86** — *S.H. (3/1/2003)*

ERATH

Erath 1997 Niederberger Vineyard Reserve Chardonnay (Willamette Valley) $35. 91 —*S.H. (12/31/1999)*

Erath 1998 Pinot Blanc (Willamette Valley) $12. 87 —*S.H. (12/31/1999)*

Erath 2005 Pinot Blanc (Willamette Valley) $14. Solid and unspectacular, this all-stainless, lean-style Pinot Blanc is just this side of innocuous. It's a good, moderately ripe style for those seeking a simple quaffer without too much alcoholic punch; otherwise, not much going on here. **84** —*P.G. (12/1/2006)*

Erath 2003 Pinot Blanc (Willamette Valley) $13. Pretty, pale straw, with nuanced scents and flavors straddling the pear/melon axis. The alcohol is a sensible 13%, and the wine has a lovely balance without sacrificing complexity. **88 Best Buy** —*P.G. (2/1/2005)*

Erath 1998 Pinot Gris (Willamette Valley) $13. 85 —*S.H. (12/31/1999)*

Erath 2005 Pinot Gris (Oregon) $13. This is an accessible, middle-of-the-road style, clean and lightly fruity, with pleasant citrus rind, melon and white peach fruit. Erath, one of the founding wineries of the Willamette valley, was recently acquired by Ste. Michelle Wine Estates, and the Pinot Gris, along with the winery's substantial production of Pinot Noir, can be expected to bolster the two most obvious holes in the company's portfolio. There's a nice streak of minerality that creeps into the finish, which adds a bit of substance to what is a rather light effort. **86 Best Buy** —*P.G. (11/15/2006)*

Erath 2004 Pinot Gris (Oregon) $14. Reliable and fruit-driven, Erath's Pinot Gris is a solid, fruity, tangy wine that shows nice citrus and tangerine flavors. Crisp and lively, great food wine, especially for spicy Asian dishes. **88** —*P.G. (2/1/2006)*

Erath 2003 Pinot Gris (Oregon) $13. Erath's pinot gris is a tart, lemony wine, with a slightly waxy, muted flavor, and a hint of sweatiness to the nose. It takes a distant second to the winery's excellent pinot blanc. **85** —*P.G. (2/1/2005)*

Erath 2000 Pinot Gris (Oregon) $12. A winning effort from this budget producer. It starts with a fine-tuned, lightly spicy bouquet, leading into appealing apple/pear flavors. Crisp and spicy, with good fleshy fruit and a lingering flavor of cinnamon, nicely set off with just the right amount of acid. **88 Best Buy** —*P.G. (4/1/2002)*

Erath 2002 Pinot Noir (Oregon) $16. Concentrated and ripe, perhaps just a bit stewed, but textured and lively, with plenty of front-loaded flavor. Though slightly raisiny, the flavors are inviting and fruit-driven. Ready to drink right now. **87** *(11/1/2004)*

Erath 2001 Pinot Noir (Oregon) $15. Scents of barn, leather, cherry, cola and spice, with a deep streak of mineral, soil and earthy tannin. Interesting wine, especially for this price range, with real depth to it. **87 Best Buy** —*P.G. (12/1/2003)*

Erath 2000 Pinot Noir (Oregon) $15. Black cherry and rubbery aromas yield to a clean, red-fruit palate that also features dried spices and mod-est tannins. This is a wine that has good balance and mouthfeel. Oak comes on strong on the grainy finish. **86 Best Buy** *(10/1/2002)*

Erath 1999 Pinot Noir (Willamette Valley) $24. 82 *(10/1/2002)*

Erath 1998 Pinot Noir (Willamette Valley) $16. 87 Best Buy —*M.S. (12/1/2000)*

Erath 2000 30th Anniversary Reserve Pinot Noir (Oregon) $30. You have to love the back label, an anagram of Erath that reads "Earth Heart Erath." For his 30th anniversary wine, Dick Erath has made a generous, open, flavorful and food-friendly Pinot. Not a blockbuster, but a lovely bottle to simply sip and enjoy. **88** —*P.G. (12/1/2003)*

Erath 2004 Estate Selection Pinot Noir (Dundee Hills) $30. Luminous and plum-colored, this wine seduces from the start. The aromas suggest perfectly ripened but not raisined or jammy fruit; there's a pleasing mix of sweet strawberry and cherry candy highlighted with streaks of fresh earth and leaf. Beautifully proportioned, this wine is selected from the best barrels of the oldest estate vineyards. **90 Cellar Selection** —*P.G. (12/1/2006)*

Erath 2002 Estate Selection Pinot Noir (Willamette Valley) $30. Elegant, classy, in a lighter style, but nuanced with subtle suggestions of meat, mixed fruits and cinnamon. This is not a big wine, nor does it overreach itself. Balanced and clean, with the sort of supple tang that suggests it will improve in the cellar. **87** *(11/1/2004)*

Erath 2002 Leland Pinot Noir (Willamette Valley) $40. Not much to hang your hat on here; it's simple, hard and tannic, with a chewy, rustic grapy flavor. **83** *(11/1/2004)*

Erath 1999 Leland Pinot Noir (Willamette Valley) $45. All elements work together in harmony in this lithe, racy wine. It opens with an inviting nose of tart fruit accented by plenty of spice and smoke. The mouth offers fleshy plum and cherry flavors, earth and leather notes, and a bright, even feel. Closes long and dry, with taut, zingy fruit and tangy charred oak notes. Drink now–2006. **89** *(10/1/2002)*

Erath 2002 Prince Hill Pinot Noir (Willamette Valley) $40. The style might be called feminine for its light, somewhat lean profile. Fairly simple and balanced, with hints of dried spice, forest floor and mushroom. **86** *(11/1/2004)*

Erath 1996 Prince Hill Pinot Noir (Willamette Valley) $35. 85 *(10/1/1999)*

Erath 1999 Reserve Pinot Noir (Yamhill County) $25. This lean, angular wine's cherry, smoke and birch beer aromas open to a tangy palate of strawberry, herb and cocoa flavors. It's dry and structured, with brisk acids that show on the cherry-citrus close. A decent mid-weight to some, it was deemed too light or too bright by other tasters. **84** *(10/1/2002)*

Erath 1998 Reserve Pinot Noir (Willamette Valley) $34. 89 —*J.C. (12/1/2000)*

Erath 1998 Vintage Select Pinot Noir (Willamette Valley) $24. 89 —*M.S. (12/1/2000)*

ERIC ROSS

Eric Ross 1999 Klapp Pinot Noir (Russian River Valley) $40. Is it overripe? After tasting it we're not entirely sure, but we detected aromas and flavors common to Port: mostly raisins, cough syrup and chocolate. Brighter-than-expected acidity, however, manages to balance off those heavy characteristics. **85** *(10/1/2002)*

Eric Ross 2004 Poule d'Or Pinot Noir (Russian River Valley) $35. Light in color, with refined aromatics showing cola, rosehip tea, leather, floral and Asian spice notes. This delicately structured wine is on the light-bodied side, but it's complex and could be exciting with some bottle age. Best now through 2012. **90** —*S.H. (12/1/2006)*

ERRAZURIZ

Errazuriz 1999 La Nuit Magique Pinot Noir (Willamette Valley) $60. The handsome nose of deep cherry with smoke, leather, eucalyptus and cinnamon accents is promising but the palate fails to follow through in this top-end offering from an Oregon pioneer. Smooth and supple in the mouth; finishes dark and toasty, with a mildly chalky feel. Tasted twice, with consistent results. **86** *(10/1/2002)*

ESHCOL RANCH

Eshcol Ranch 2001 Cabernet Sauvignon (California) $10. Everything's right about this nice Cab, from the ripe blackberry and mocha flavors to the smooth tannins, dry balance and fruity finish. It could use a little more concentration, though. **84** —*S.H. (12/15/2005)*

ESSER CELLARS

Esser Cellars 2003 Cabernet Sauvignon (California) $9. Decent everyday Cab, a little rough, but dry and fruity. Has a hit of blackberry essence on the finish. **83** —*S.H. (6/1/2005)*

Esser Cellars 2001 Cabernet Sauvignon (California) $8. Here's a fruity wine brimming with strong blackberry and cherry flavors, and a rich, spicy earthiness like cinnamon espresso. There are some raisiny notes but they add complexity to this dry, softly complex wine. **87 Best Buy** —*S.H. (6/1/2003)*

Esser Cellars 2005 Chardonnay (California) $10. Manfred Esser ran Cuvaison, so he knows Chardonnay. This wine is mainly from Clarksburg, and shows good ripeness, but is balanced by firm acidity. Barrel fermented and aged sur lie, it's crisp and fruity, with freshly picked apple, pineapple, peach, mango and vanilla flavors that finish dry and spicy. The acidity really is racy. At 19,000 cases, it is widely available. **85 Best Buy** —*S.H. (11/15/2006)*

Esser Cellars 2003 Chardonnay (California) $9. Rather vegetal in aroma, although it has simple, fruity flavors. **82** —*S.H. (6/1/2005)*

Esser Cellars 2002 Chardonnay (California) $9. Smells artificially oaky, with vanilla extract aromas, and tastes like oak, too. There are some peach and citrus flavors, but they're pretty thin. **82** —*S.H. (12/31/2003)*

Esser Cellars 2001 Chardonnay (California) $8. A rich, opulent wine at an unbelievable price, this Chard has layers of ripe peaches, pears and tropical fruits, and a lush overlay of toasty oak. The wonderfully creamy texture leads to a long, spicy finish. Despite the statewide appellation, this is as good as many regional Chardonnays. **90 Best Buy** —*S.H. (6/1/2003)*

Esser Cellars 2005 Merlot (California) $10. Tons of ripe cherry fruit flavors mark this soft, slightly sweet wine, along with herbal tastes of wild thyme and rosemary. Calls for roasted leg of lamb, with butter-sautéed baby potatoes. **84** —*S.H. (12/31/2006)*

Esser Cellars 2001 Merlot (California) $8. This dry wine has a clean, swift mouthfeel, dominated by fresh acidity and firm young tannins. There's just enough berry-cherry flavor to stand on its own or accompany a good steak. **85** —*S.H. (4/1/2004)*

Esser Cellars 2002 Pinot Noir (California) $12. Simple, but gets the Pinot job done. Delicate and dry, with cola, cherry and spice flavors and a touch of oak. **84** —*S.H. (6/1/2005)*

ESTANCIA

Estancia 2003 Meritage Cabernet Blend (Paso Robles) $33. With a little Merlot and Petit Verdot, this wine displays soft acids and round, melted tannins to harmonize with the superripe fruit—blackberries, cherries and mocha, along with sweet vanilla and spice flavors from judicious oak. Drink now. **86** —*S.H. (12/15/2006)*

Estancia 2002 Red Meritage Cabernet Blend (Paso Robles) $35. Estancia's Paso experiment with Cabernet-based wines has been problematic. How do you get balance and complexity with all that heat? This blend of Cabernet Sauvignon, Merlot and Petit Verdot is good but rustic, with chocolate-coated raisins the dominant flavor. **84** —*S.H. (5/1/2006)*

Estancia 1997 Cabernet Sauvignon (California) $15. 84 —*S.H. (7/1/2000)*

Estancia 2002 Cabernet Sauvignon (Paso Robles) $15. Dark, soft and rich in fruit, this is an easy Cab with some extra qualities. Low in tannins and acids, effusive in blackberry, cherry, cocoa and coffee, it flatters the palate with flavor and the lush, velvety texture. **86** —*S.H. (12/31/2004)*

Estancia 2002 Keyes Canyon Ranches Cabernet Sauvignon (Paso Robles) $16. This is a young, taut red wine. It's quite dry, and the tannins shut it down a bit. But you'll find intense flavors of blackberries and cherries, and a tasty coating of oak. Drink over the next year. **86** —*S.H. (8/1/2005)*

Estancia 2001 Paso Robles Cabernet Sauvignon (Paso Robles) $15. Kind of hot, with almost Port-like aromas and flavors of chocolate-covered raisins and sweet cassis. Yet the wine is fully dry, with soft, easy tannins. It's a good wine that will have its fans, but it's definitely a hot country Cabernet. **85** —*S.H. (10/1/2004)*

Estancia 2002 Pinnacles Chardonnay (Monterey) $12. A bit lean in fruity flavor, but not bad for the price. You get some polished peach and apple flavors, oaky, vanilla notes and that crisp Central Coast acidity. **84** —*S.H. (11/15/2004)*

Estancia 2000 Pinnacles Chardonnay (Monterey) $13. Ripe pear, melon, citrus and apple form the core of this robust Chardonnay. It's full-bodied, somewhat toasty, and tangy-rich at the end. A mineral edge adds balance. **88** —*J.M. (5/1/2002)*

Estancia 1998 Pinnacles Chardonnay (Monterey County) $12. 89 Best Buy —*S.H. (5/1/2000)*

Estancia 2004 Pinnacles Ranches Chardonnay (Monterey) $12. Estancia owns some impressive vineyards in the Pinnacles region, but you'd never know it from this wine. It's watery, tasting of alcohol and acidity. **81** —*S.H. (10/1/2006)*

Estancia 2003 Pinnacles Ranches Chardonnay (Monterey) $12. I tasted this alongside a Chard costing more than twice as much, and it held its own. The fruit, acids, oak, spice and creamy texture come together in an appealingly balanced package. Finishes dry, long and complex, but just a tad thin. **86** —*S.H. (12/1/2005)*

Estancia 1998 Single Vineyard Reserve Chardonnay (Monterey County) $20. 87 *(6/1/2000)*

Estancia 2001 Meritage (Alexander Valley) $35. This Merlot-dominated blend is very soft and lush, with upfront chocolate fudge and black cherry flavors. It's an almost sweet wine, although it's basically dry and has good acids. **86** —*S.H. (8/1/2005)*

Estancia 2000 Red Meritage Meritage (Alexander Valley) $35. Well-charred oak dominates now, with its toasty vanillins, but underneath lurks a very pretty wine. The blackcurrant and cherry flavors are sweetly delicious, and the tannins are soft and lush. This appealing wine is easy to fall in love with. Give it a few years to knit together. **90** —*S.H. (1/1/2005)*

Estancia 2000 Merlot (California) $16. Generic Merlot, good, rich and full-bodied, without any noteworthy complexities. Berry and plum flavors drink dry, with pretty substantial tannins that need rich foods to cut through. **85** —*S.H. (4/1/2003)*

Estancia 2004 Pinot Grigio (California) $15. This off-dry wine brings gardens to mind. It is one of those perfectly adaptable, all-purpose white wines that goes with just about anything. It tastes of tree-ripe peaches, gardenias and honeysuckle, and has pleasant acidity to offset the sweetness. **84** —*S.H. (7/1/2005)*

Estancia 2003 Pinot Grigio (California) $15. Extremely tart, almost bitter with citrusy acidity, and the flavors are of just slightly sweetened lemon juice. As dry and mouth puckering as it is, it's clean, and the sharpness will work well with shellfish. **85** —*S.H. (11/15/2004)*

Estancia 2002 Pinot Grigio (California) $15. This crisp, delicate charmer is a perfect wine to end the workday with. It's got light flavors of citrus and melon, and is high in acidity and very clean. It's also bone dry. **87** —*S.H. (2/1/2004)*

Estancia 2001 Pinnacles Pinot Noir (Monterey) $15. A bit light, and on the jammy side, but offers pretty flavors of raspberries and cherries in a silk-textured easy drinker. There are some dusty Oriental spices that titillate the palate through the dry finish. **86** —*S.H. (4/1/2004)*

Estancia 2000 Pinnacles Pinot Noir (Monterey) $16. A pleasant Pinot that harbors pretty cherry, herb and licorice flavors framed in charry oak. The finish is on the bright side. **87** —*J.M. (5/1/2002)*

Estancia 1997 Pinnacles Pinot Noir (Monterey County) $14. 88 *(11/15/1999)*

Estancia 2003 Pinnacles Ranches Pinot Noir (Monterey) $15. It's awfully hard to make a really good Pinot Noir for less than, say, $30. This wine tries hard. It shows true Pinot character in the dry, silky mouthfeel, crisp acids and pleasant fruit flavors, which finish with coffee and cocoa. **86** —S.H. (12/1/2005)

Estancia 2002 Pinnacles Ranches Pinot Noir (Monterey) $15. Classy, light in body, with crisp acidity and a silky texture. The flavors veer toward tart red cherries and oak. Finishes dry and balanced. Drink now. **87** (11/1/2004)

Estancia 2000 Proprietor's Selection Pinot Noir (Monterey) $10. Bargain hunters have long known Estancia as a haven for values, and this lovely wine continues the tradition. It shows true Monterey terroir in the translucent color, delicately silky structure, bright, citrusy acids and flavors of cherries, cola, sassafras and sweet tea. You'll also find an overlay of smoky oak. This classic cool-climate Pinot Noir is the perfect food wine, and a terrific everyday one for Pinotphiles. **87 Best Buy** —S.H. (11/15/2004)

Estancia 1997 Reserve Pinot Noir (Monterey County) $22. 89 —J.C. (5/1/2000)

Estancia 2003 Stonewall Vineyard Pinot Noir (Santa Lucia Highlands) $25. This vineyard is in the tenderloin of the appellation, where most Pinots cost far more. This is a pretty good wine that needs tinkering; it could be far better. It's rich in fruit, but is heavy, and could use more finesse. **85** —S.H. (12/1/2005)

Estancia 2002 Stonewall Vineyard Reserve Pinot Noir (Santa Lucia Highlands) $22. A very good wine, at a fair price for a single-vineyard Pinot of this caliber from this appellation. It shows the well-ripened cherry fruit and good acidity that characterize the Highlands, with a nice overlay of toasty oak and vanilla, and is dry and balanced. Lacks the complexity of its famous neighbors, but is worthy of praise on price alone. **88 Editors' Choice** —S.H. (8/1/2005)

Estancia 2002 Stonewall Vineyard Reserve Pinot Noir (Santa Lucia Highlands) $25. A nice example of the variety from a cool climate, with sour cherry, rhubarb and citrusy aromas and flavors. Feels clean and elegant, with lots of jammy cherry fruit. Not a big wine, though, and finishes with a scour of acids and tannins. **86** (11/1/2004)

Estancia 1997 Duo Sangiovese (Sonoma County) $22. 88 —S.H. (9/1/2000)

Estancia 1996 Duo Sangiovese (Sonoma County) $22. 90 —S.H. (11/1/1999)

Estancia 2004 Syrah (Central Coast) $16. Here's a wine that aspires to complexity and only just manages to get there. It's full-bodied and dry, with a smoothly tannic texture, and the earthy, coffee and blackberry flavors cry out for food. Decant it a little before serving. **85** —S.H. (12/31/2006)

Estancia 2003 Lucia Range Ranches Syrah (Central Coast) $15. It doesn't look like any grapes actually came from the Santa Lucia Highlands, so don't be fooled. The wine is dry and earthy, with strong tannins, puckery acids and bitter coffee flavors relieved by a dash of blackberry. **84** —S.H. (10/1/2006)

Estancia 2002 Keyes Canyon Ranches Zinfandel (Paso Robles) $12. Here's a big, rich, tannic Zin, the kind that kicks butt in youth and will age. It's astringent with tannins now, but the core of blackberry and cherry fruit is powerful. Perfectly dry, this wine should develop nicely over the next several years. **88 Best Buy** —S.H. (8/1/2005)

ESTATE RAFFAELE

Estate Raffaele 2002 Clareta Red Blend (California) $22. This blend of Cabernet Sauvignon, Tempranillo and Grenache is forward in ripe berry flavors, and is soft in acids and tannins. Smacks of the warm sunshine and is dry. **84** —S.H. (10/1/2005)

Estate Raffaele 2004 Century Old Vines Zinfandel (California) $NA. Simple, soft and flat, and rather sweet, with cola, cherry and peppery spice flavors. This Zin is said to come from 100-year old vines in Lodi. **82** —S.H. (11/15/2006)

ESTERLINA

Esterlina 2000 Cabernet Sauvignon (Alexander Valley) $35. Ripe and expressive in blackberry, currant and coffee notes, with toasty oak and spice nuances. Rather soft in texture, and easy on the palate, with a long,

fruity finish. NOTE: This wine received a higher score than in a previous tasting. **87** —S.H. (10/1/2004)

Esterlina 1999 Chardonnay (Anderson Valley) $20. This wine may have the highest acidity of any California Chardonnay on the market, to judge by the mouthfeel. Boom—a real blast of tartness. The fruit is lean, even austere, and from the aroma to the finish there's a steely, mineral note. Call it Chablis-like. It's well made and clean and needs the right foods. **87** —S.H. (5/1/2002)

Esterlina 2003 Tres Appellations Chardonnay (Anderson Valley, Sonoma County, Cole Ranch) $18. Made from three different appellations, this Chardonnay's cool-climate origins show in the citrusy acidity and rich, tropical fruit flavors that suggest guava and mango. There's also some toasty oak in this tasty wine. **87** —S.H. (12/1/2005)

Esterlina 2001 Merlot (Cole Ranch) $18. From one of the tiniest AVAs in California, a Mendocino wine that straddles the balance between cherry-infused ripeness and earthier, more tannic dryness. Those tannins reprise on the finish, leaving behind a dusty astringency. **85** —S.H. (10/1/2004)

Esterlina 2001 Pinot Noir (Anderson Valley) $35. Very dry and tart, with good acidity and a sprinkling of tannins that shout out for food. It has a subtle interplay of cherry, coffee, earth and mushroom flavors with a peppery edge. **85** —S.H. (10/1/2004)

Esterlina 1998 Pinot Noir (Anderson Valley) $35. Defines what's wrong and right about Anderson Valley. Right: High acidity, silky tannins, good upfront raspberry flavors nuanced with mushroom and tomato, and tons of spice. What disappoints is one-dimensionality. The wine turns watery in the middle palate, and snaps to a finish. Needs more stuffing and depth. **85** —S.H. (5/1/2002)

Esterlina 2002 Estate Pinot Noir (Anderson Valley) $35. Rustic, with a raisiny edge, this Pinot also is rather rough and sharp in the mouth, with extracted flavors of cherries and coffee. **82** —S.H. (12/1/2005)

Esterlina 2004 Riesling (Cole Ranch) $16. Frankly off-dry to semi-sweet, but with pronounced acidity to balance, this is a Spätlese-style Riesling. It's rich in garden fruit and flower flavors, with a savory spiciness and a long, clean aftertaste. **86** —S.H. (12/1/2005)

Esterlina 2002 Riesling (Cole Ranch) $16. Try this as an alternative to Sauvignon Blanc. It's bone dry and tart, with lime rind flavors and just a hint of mineral. The crisp acidity pulls it all together. Finishes clean and swift. **85** —S.H. (10/1/2004)

Esterlina 1999 Ferrington Vineyards Sauvignon Blanc (Anderson Valley) $18. The danger of trying to ripen Sauvignon Blanc in a cool area, especially in a cool, late vintage, is underripeness. This wine has leafy, vegetal aromas, and the fruity flavors are thin despite an overlay of sweetness. **84** —S.H. (5/1/2002)

Esterlina 2003 Janian Vineyard Syrah (Sonoma Mountain) $25. From the minute you sniff this wine, you like it, an impression that grows stronger from the first sip through the finish. It's dry, peppery-fruity and firm in acids and tannins, with a distinguished mouthfeel. Not an ager, but a brilliant, evocative expression of cool-climate Syrah. **92** —S.H. (12/1/2005)

Esterlina 1999 White Riesling (Mendocino) $13. This is one of the best California Rieslings around. Let's start with acidity, which is crisp and steely. The flavors are exotic and racy, suggesting wildflowers, apples, and an oily, lighter-fluid element. It floats in the mouth because of the light texture, but is serious stuff, and will likely age well. Defines finesse and elegance. **90** —S.H. (5/1/2002)

ESTRELLA

Estrella 2002 Proprietor's Reserve Shiraz (California) $6. A light-bodied Syrah, but one that delivers a surprising amount of complexity for the price. Elements of dried spices and plum mingle with tarry, rubbery notes. A bit short on the finish, but what do you expect for $6? **85 Best Buy** (9/1/2005)

ETUDE

Etude 2002 Cabernet Sauvignon (Napa Valley) $90. The backbone of this wine is from Oakville and Rutherford. It's a classic Napa Cab from what has turned out to be a fine vintage. There's the velvety cassis and chocolate fruit ripeness you expect, and the lavish oak, but good tannins and acids prevent the decadent flavors from turning flabby. Still, the wine's approachability argues for early consumption. **93** —*S.H. (12/1/2005)*

Etude 2001 Cabernet Sauvignon (Napa Valley) $90. This is a great Cab that showcases the ageability of certain Napa Cabs. It's tightly wound now, with acids and rich tannins overshadowing the pure, sweet black-berry, black cherry and cassis flavors. Impressive for its intensity, power and harmony. Drink tonight, or cellar it for a decade. **95** —*S.H. (5/1/2005)*

Etude 2000 Cabernet Sauvignon (Napa Valley) $80. Not really at its best now, a subdued, shy wine offering little beyond serious tannins and an earthiness infused with cassis. The finish is very astringent and sticky, yet the intense, lingering taste of cherries and currants suggests cellaring through 2008, if not longer. **90** —*S.H. (6/1/2004)*

Etude 1999 Cabernet Sauvignon (Napa Valley) $80. Plush tannins and spicy black fruit on the palate leaven the whipped vanilla cream, straw-berry, and cocoa aromas. A beam of currant fruit shines on the full, softly tannic finish. **90** *(2/1/2003)*

Etude 2002 Merlot (Napa Valley) $48. It's hard to imagine a more volup-tuous wine, but it's also powerful and complex, offering up endlessly changing palate impressions. The primary flavor is ripe, juicy blackber-ries, while fine oak does its thing. The tannins are wonderfully soft and refined. With no Cabernet Sauvignon, and just a little Cab Franc and Petit Verdot, this wine restores my belief in Merlot as the seductive, sen-sual alternative to Cab. **95 Editors' Choice** —*S.H. (4/1/2006)*

Etude 1998 Pinot Blanc (Carneros) $25. Starts off with rich, fragrant aro-mas of ripe peaches, mangos and flowers, with vanilla and buttery-oaky notes. There's lots of buttercream in the mouth, along with ripe, forward tropical fruit and spice flavors and a high acidity level that creates a sear-ing, mouthwatering quality. Good stuff. **91** —*S.H. (2/1/2001)*

Etude 2005 Pinot Gris (Carneros) $24. Like the great '04, this wine has a structural integrity and sheer mouth-filling deliciousness that puts it above most other California PGs. It shows high acidity and powerful but subtle flavors of citrus rind, fig and white peach. You could get addicted to this stuff. **91** —*S.H. (12/1/2006)*

Etude 2004 Pinot Gris (Carneros) $24. From an ocean of indifferent Pinot Gris/Grigios, this beauty emerges. The wine is so rich and creamy, it's hard to believe it's never seen oak. It's dry, crisp and enormously com-plex, offering waves of citrus, fig, apricot, white peach and wildflower flavors that are not only broad, but deep and long. **91 Editors' Choice** — *S.H. (2/1/2006)*

Etude 2003 Pinot Noir (Carneros) $40. Tony Soter is at the top of his game, consistently turning out wines that outperform the competition. His '03 Pinot isn't quite as monumental as the '02 Heirloom, but is a fabulous wine, fresh and complex, utterly drinkable now but with a probable life ahead. It's dry and tart in beef bouillon, cherry tomato fla-vors, with a sweet cherry-raspberry and spicy oak edge, and a transparent, elegant quality. Best now through 2008. **93 Editors' Choice** —*S.H. (12/1/2005)*

Etude 2002 Pinot Noir (Carneros) $40. Rather herbal and spicy, bursting with anise, Asian spicebox aromas. Cherries and sweet herbs in the mouth, with a spicy finish. The soft tannins make it instantly drinkable. **89** *(11/1/2004)*

Etude 2001 Pinot Noir (Carneros) $40. Dark for a Pinot, suggesting great extraction, and vibrantly fruity. The flavors are rich and sweet with cher-ry and black raspberry, accented by Oriental spices and oak. Silky and elegant in the mouth, but a firm backbone of acidity lends structure. **90** —*S.H. (5/1/2004)*

Etude 2000 Pinot Noir (Carneros) $40. Deep, with prune and blackberry aromas. This is another big wine from Etude, weighing in at 14.6%, but if you like 'em large, it's your ticket. The mouth oozes black plum and cherry, and the finish is toasty, with creamy chocolate notes. With dry tannins and healthy acids, it manages to hold the line on balance. **90** —*M.S. (12/1/2003)*

Etude 2004 Estate Pinot Noir (Carneros) $42. Fresh and vibrant, showing berry-cherry cola, tea, clove, vanilla and smoky flavors that are just deli-cious. The wine is accented by youthful acidity. If you like your Pinots young, this is for you. However, it should knit together and improve with some cellaring. Best 2007–2010. **91** —*S.H. (12/1/2006)*

Etude 2002 Heirloom Pinot Noir (Carneros) $80. This wine stands out. It's very dry, with a full, firm texture of tannins and acidity, but most notable are the flavors. They are extraordinarily rich, mingling red and black cherries, mocha, cola and spice with toast, caramel and smoke from fine oak. Despite the wine's density, it possesses lightness and ele-gance that make it uplifting. Drink now and over the next several years. **95 Editors' Choice** —*S.H. (12/1/2005)*

Etude 2001 Heirloom Pinot Noir (Carneros) $80. This tiny-production wine (only 480 cases were made) is luscious and opulent. It compels for the sheer intensity of the red and black cherry, rosehip tea, cola and spicy flavors. Goes beyond mere flavor in its balance and harmony, and defines a light-bodied, silky style of great refinement and finesse. **92** —*S.H. (12/1/2004)*

Etude 2000 Heirloom Pinot Noir (Carneros) $80. Everything about this modern, high-extract, high-alcohol wine is of the moment, which is why the Heirloom name seems questionable. What's not at issue is the lush-ness and overt beauty of this 14.9% poster boy for big wines. Chocolate, mint and hickory comprise the nose and the palate is all about pulsing blackberry, blueberry and fudge. A primo heavyweight for the new American palate. **94** —*M.S. (12/1/2003)*

Etude 2005 Rosé Pinot Noir (Carneros) $20. Dry, crisp and lavendery, like a Provençal rosé, but distinctly California due to the ripe, forward cherry and strawberry flavors. This blush wine is really fun to drink. It's as easy as a summer afternoon, yet has the complexity to stand up to a rich, ample bouillabaisse. **88** —*S.H. (12/1/2006)*

EUGENE WINE CELLARS

Eugene Wine Cellars 1999 Melon (Oregon) $14. A few years ago there was a bit of a tempest in a wine barrel when Oregon's winemakers discovered that the Pinot Blanc they had been buying from California was actually Melon, the grape of France's Muscadets. It all made for a lot of confu-sion, but Oregonian Melon is an interesting wine, which has a lot of fat tropical fruit when it's young, and can be quite appealing. The wine does not age; in fact, it falls apart. So drink it young, when the ripe fruit sug-gests mangoes and papayas and swaying palms. **85** —*P.G. (11/1/2001)*

Eugene Wine Cellars 1999 Pinot Gris (Oregon) $14. Pinot Gris has really caught on with consumers, because it can be delicious with so many dif-ferent foods, but particularly with Pacific Northwest halibut and salmon. This is a well-crafted, straightforward version, with the characteristic pear fruit and a certain "graininess" in the mouth. The price seems a lit-tle ambitious, given the competition. **85** —*P.G. (11/1/2001)*

Eugene Wine Cellars 1999 Pinot Noir (Oregon) $15. Here is a pretty Pinot, at least from the smell of it. It's scented with bread and sassafras and lightly hued, as is proper with Pinot. In the mouth it feels young, even spritzy, and the fruit is buoyed on a weightless, watery base that leads nowhere. Somehow the promise of the nose fails to deliver. **82** —*P.G. (11/1/2001)*

Eugene Wine Cellars 1999 Syrah (Oregon) $23. Syrah is the flavor of the month on the West Coast, but Oregon Syrah is a rarity. This wine tastes as if it is from very young vines; there is no depth or texture to the fruit. There is plenty of color, and forward flavors of spice and black cherry. But it lacks weight and finishes with a watery, generic flavor. **83** —*P.G. (11/1/2001)*

Eugene Wine Cellars 1999 Viognier (Oregon) $18. There's a surprising amount of tannin and a hard, almost bitter edge to this wine, rather than the floral scents and elegance one associates with Viognier. The fruit def-initely carries a citrus kick, with plenty of acid, perhaps too much. But with the right food—fresh Northwest oysters spring to mind—it could be just right. **84** —*P.G. (11/1/2001)*

EVERETT RIDGE

Everett Ridge 1997 Cabernet Sauvignon (Dry Creek Valley) $22. **86** —*S.H. (12/31/1999)*

Everett Ridge 1999 Cabernet Sauvignon (Dry Creek Valley) $28. Sure is extracted with thick, syrupy blackberry and plum flavors, and the tannins are soft and melted. But this dry wine needs a little crispness and life to make it come alive. **84** —*S.H. (12/15/2003)*

Everett Ridge 2002 Pinot Noir (Russian River Valley) $30. Pretty, with some complexity to the sassafras, cherry, tomato, cranberry and oaky aromas and flavors. Supple, dry and polished, with soft tannins and nice harmony. **87** *(11/1/2004)*

Everett Ridge 2004 Sauvignon Blanc (Dry Creek Valley) $15. This dry white enters the mouth on the grassy, feline side, then finishes rich in figs and pineapples. It has excellent acidity that leaves the palate feeling clean and refreshed. Will be versatile with a wide range of fare. **87** —*S.H. (8/1/2006)*

Everett Ridge 2003 Powerhouse Vineyard Sauvignon Blanc (Mendocino County) $15. Very dry and tart with acids, but with a rich sweetness from well-ripened citrus fruits, figs and honeydew melon. Shows real flair and style. **86** —*S.H. (12/15/2004)*

Everett Ridge 2002 Powerhouse Vineyard Sauvignon Blanc (Mendocino County) $14. Opens with a delicate aroma of lemon custard, smoke and vanilla, but turns impossibly thin in the mouth. There's almost no flavor at all, like a glass of clear, cold water. **82** —*S.H. (3/1/2004)*

Everett Ridge 2000 Powerhouse Vineyard Sauvignon Blanc (Mendocino) $13. Some lemon and distant notes of anise and tarragon can be found on the nose. The sharp palate tastes a bit like hard candy, offering just a modicum of apple and orange. The finish is thin, bordering on watery. This does not taste bad, but it's more like fruit juice or lemonade than it should be. **85** *(9/1/2003)*

Everett Ridge 2002 Nuns Canyon Vineyard Syrah (Sonoma Valley) $24. This wine earned very different impressions among the panelists. Where one person found it mouthfilling and balanced, another found it flat. One complained that all of the wine's plummy, spicy flavor was concentrated on the front palate, but another lauded its long, peppery finish. **87** *(9/1/2005)*

Everett Ridge 2001 Nuns Canyon Vineyard Syrah (Sonoma Valley) $28. Big, thick and heavy in plummy, chocolate and white pepper flavors, with sturdy tannins. You can taste the heat in the finish, where the wine turns prickly, with a note of raisins. Drink with barbecue seasoned with garlic. **85** —*S.H. (12/15/2004)*

Everett Ridge 2000 Nuns Canyon Vineyard Syrah (Sonoma Valley) $26. A single-vineyard wine, and a very good one. Stylish from the start, with polished tannins framing plummy, berry flavors, and a super-smooth mouthfeel. Nice and dry. Rich foods will cut through the thick tannins. **88** —*S.H. (12/15/2003)*

Everett Ridge 1999 Nuns Canyon Vineyard Syrah (Sonoma Valley) $26. Gamey, menthol-and-leather notes envelope the creamy blackberry aromas on the nose of this Syrah. Strong toast and mint notes bolster the sour blackberry fruit on the palate. The wine's tart, dry chalk-berry finish and dry tannins prompted one taster to say, "Water…now. I need water." **89** *(11/1/2001)*

Everett Ridge 2001 Zinfandel (Dry Creek Valley) $28. Spicy plum and black cherry notes lead the way, followed by a pleasing blend of blackberry, cassis, coffee, chocolate and vanilla. Tannins are firm and focused, giving supple strength to the whole. Quite nice. Elegant to the end. **90** *(11/1/2003)*

Everett Ridge 2000 Zinfandel (Dry Creek Valley) $28. Some nice berry flavors, but the wine feels gritty and awkward in the mouth, with sharp tannins and acidity. The finish is tart, almost sour. **83** —*S.H. (9/1/2003)*

Everett Ridge 2002 Estate Zinfandel (Dry Creek Valley) $22. Here's a Zin that gives Zinfanatics plenty of pleasure. Dry Creek Valley brings harmony to this difficult variety, and while the wine retains Zin's briary, wild profile, it retains a dry balance. Enjoy it now for its flashy, youthful fruit. **87** —*S.H. (10/1/2006)*

Everett Ridge 1998 Old Vines Zinfandel (Dry Creek Valley) $22. Very pretty nose, with plenty of raspberry-focused fruit, and a nice creamy mouthfeel. Delicious, mouth-filling, concentrated wine, with a lot of finesse and a wonderful ripeness. Smooth tannins, long finish, with a touch of toast. **90** —*P.G. (3/1/2001)*

Everett Ridge 1997 Old Vines Zinfandel (Dry Creek Valley) $20. **89** —*S.H. (2/1/2000)*

EVESHAM WOOD

Evesham Wood 1998 Pinot Noir (Willamette Valley) $15. **87 Best Buy** — *J.C. (12/1/2000)*

Evesham Wood 1997 Estate Vineyard Pinot Noir (Willamette Valley) $21. **84** *(10/1/1999)*

Evesham Wood 1998 Le Puits Sec Cuvée J Pinot Noir (Willamette Valley) $36. **86** —*M.S. (12/1/2000)*

Evesham Wood 1997 Shea Vineyard Cuvée 'J' Pinot Noir (Willamette Valley) $27.5. **86** *(10/1/1999)*

Evesham Wood 1998 Temperance Hill Vineyard Pinot Noir (Willamette Valley) $24. **89** —*M.M. (12/1/2000)*

EXP

EXP 2000 Syrah (Dunnigan Hills) $14. This winery has been tinkering with Rhône varietals in this San Francisco Delta region and has yet to make a convincing case that this is the magic spot. It's a rugged wine, with notable tannins and earthy flavors, and very dry. **83** —*S.H. (12/1/2002)*

EXP 1999 Syrah (Dunnigan Hills) $14. On nose, a core of ripe berry and black cherry fruit provides plenty of aroma and flavor. It struggles, though, with the heavy toast regime that ultimately holds it down. Good juice with herb shadings and plenty of grip, that regrettably closes woody and a bit drying. **85** *(10/1/2001)*

EXP 1999 Tempranillo (Dunnigan Hills) $25. Fewer than 1,000 acres of this varietal are planted in California, but it's Spain's best native red grape. This version is so dry, it makes the tongue stick to the palate, and has some notable tannins. But the blackberry flavors are rich and long. The dense, glyceriney wine will age effortlessly and could gain interest. **88** —*S.H. (12/1/2002)*

EXP 2002 Viognier (Dunnigan Hills) $14. There's just a ton of flowery fruit in this dry wine, including the ripest peaches, savory pineapple and nectarines, not to mention smoky vanilla. Ripe, balanced and crisp. **87** —*S.H. (6/1/2004)*

EXP 2001 Viognier (Dunnigan Hills) $14. An awkward wine despite its flavorsome profile. Tastes like cotton candy, with sugary strawberry notes, and has a thick texture, like cream, but insufficient acidity to support it. **82** —*S.H. (12/15/2002)*

EXP 2003 Estate Bottled Viognier (Dunnigan Hills) $14. Nothing shy about this fruity in-your-face wine. It's bold in rich mango, peach and vanilla flavors. May have a little residual sugar, but it's crisp and clean enough to quality as dryish. **84** —*S.H. (8/1/2005)*

EYRIE

Eyrie 2003 Pinot Gris (Willamette Valley) $16. Eyrie's David Lett planted the first Pinot Gris in the country, and after 34 vintages still makes one of the most distinctive. Scents of dried grass, herbs and honeysuckle lead into a crisp, elegant, restrained wine. **89** —*P.G. (2/1/2006)*

FAGAN CREEK

Fagan Creek 2002 Horsley Vineyards Syrah (Dunnigan Hills) $16. While one taster found this wine "delicately herbal," another pegged that element of the aromatics as "rhubarb." Strawberry and cherry flavors flesh out this full-bodied wine that finishes spicy and tannic but fruit-filled. **88** *(9/1/2005)*

FAILLA

Failla 2003 Estate Vineyard Syrah (Sonoma Coast) $48. Round and lush, this Sonoma Cost Syrah has peppery, meaty nuances to its ballsy, lush blackberry flavors. Finishes long, with soft tannins. **92 Editors' Choice** *(9/1/2005)*

Failla 2003 Phoenix Ranch Syrah (Napa Valley) $38. Tastes like the real Rhône thing, from its meaty and coffee-tinged aromas to its peppery, blackberry flavors. But the structure is more Californian, soft and full, if a tiny bit lacking in texture. Peppery notes reprise on the long finish. Drink now–2012. **90** *(9/1/2005)*

FAILLA JORDAN

Failla Jordan 2000 Keefer Ranch Chardonnay (Russian River Valley) $32. From Green Valley, the coolest part of the appellation, a wine with the most wonderful opening scents of ripe pears and the smoky perfume of oak. Perfectly delicious in the mouth, with pronounced pear flavors and a sleek note of minerality. A touch of lees adds a creamy texture but doesn't overwhelm. As opulent and lush as this wine is, it's delicate and elegant. **93 Editors' Choice** —S.H. (7/1/2003)

Failla Jordan 2001 Hirsch Vineyard Pinot Noir (Sonoma Coast) $48. A big, juicy wine. Opens with young, almost jammy aromas of black cherry and black raspberry highlighted with earthier notes of tobacco. Turns long and persistent on the palate, as the fruity flavors are joined by those of grilled meat and tomato. Firm tannins hold it all together. This young, dense wine seems likely to improve for at least five years. **91** —S.H. (7/1/2003)

Failla Jordan 2001 Keefer Ranch Pinot Noir (Russian River Valley) $38. A nice Russian River Pinot from Green Valley, it is marked by berry-earthy flavors, firm tannins and supportive acids, and is very dry. The particular flavors are of cherries with a rich streak of sweet tobacco and herbs. Marked by a bouyancy of texture and a silkiness that glides over the palate, although it finishes quick and may not be an ager. **90** —S.H. (7/1/2003)

Failla Jordan 2000 Estate Syrah (Sonoma Coast) $48. Ultrarich on the palate, muscular and beautifully structured, with gobs of meaty black cherry, black currant, coffee, tea, leather, earth and herb tones. Ripe tannins frame it, with a long, lush finish. **92 Editors' Choice** —J.M. (12/1/2002)

Failla Jordan 2000 Que Syrah Vineyard Syrah (Sonoma Coast) $45. Bright spice and raspberry aromas lead off. Rich and viscous on the palate with complex layers of herb, earth and blackberry. Long and bright on the finish. **90** —J.M. (12/1/2002)

FALCONE

Falcone 2002 Mia's Vineyard Syrah (Paso Robles) $28. This Syrah shows Paso's warm climate in the soft texture and ripe blackberry, cherry and spice flavors, but it has a hint of green beans and roasted coffee that either add complexity or detract from the jammy fruit, depending on your viewpoint. **85** (9/1/2005)

Falconer 1997 Late Disgorged Blanc de Noir Champagne Blend (Sonoma) $22. This is a rough, slight bubbly that needs a bit of work in future vintages. It's bone-dry and very acidic, with barely any flavor at all. It tastes like seltzer or carbonated water. **83** —S.H. (12/1/2002)

Falcor 2002 Le Bijou Bordeaux Blend (Napa Valley) $38. This Merlot-based Bordeaux blend comes from both cooler and warmer parts of Napa, including mountains. It's a very fine wine that will probably hold, although year by year it will lose its gorgeous babyfat deliciousness. More tannic than Falcor's '02 Cabernet, it has similar blackberry, cherry, cassis and chocolate flavors that have been well-oaked in new barrels. **92** —S.H. (12/31/2006)

Falcor 2002 Cabernet Sauvignon (Napa Valley) $48. Decadent and complex, this wine just oozes pastry-filling flavors of blackberries, cherries, chocolate and sweet oak. Such pretty tannins, such balancing acidity. **93** —S.H. (12/31/2006)

Falcor 2001 Chardonnay (Napa Valley) $35. Oak stars in this wine, with its toasty, wood and vanilla aromas and flavors. It's a good wine, but could use greater freshness and intensity, especially at this price. **85** —S.H. (5/1/2005)

Falcor 2003 Bacigalupi Vineyard Chardonnay (Russian River Valley) $38. The 65% new oak is not balanced. Hard to say why. The fruit's there, all gooey pineapple tart and sweet vanilla buttery pie crust, and the alcohol doesn't bother me a bit, but the wine loses points for that toothpick taste. **86** —S.H. (12/31/2006)

Falcor 2003 Genny's Vineyard Chardonnay (Napa Valley) $35. There's an earthiness to this Chard, and a softness despite high (.65) acidity. The flavors veer toward peaches and pineapples, with sweet, fresh green thyme and lots of toasty new oak. Pretty good, with an oaky, honeyed finish. **86** —S.H. (12/31/2006)

Falcor 2001 Merlot (Napa Valley) $32. Rather rustic, with berry and earth flavors inside some pretty edgy tannins. Finishes dry and astringent, with a touch of cherry. **84** —S.H. (5/1/2005)

Falcor 2005 Rosé Rosé Blend (California) $15. Pretty and polished, but you wish this Provençal-style blush had a little more substance. It's a simple wine, with strawberry tea and rose petal flavors that finish dry, crisp and watery. **83** —S.H. (12/31/2006)

Falcor 2003 Sangiovese (Napa Valley) $29. Dry, tannic, acidic and alcoholic, with a drop of cherries. Sangiovese is probably the hardest grape in California to get right. **82** —S.H. (12/31/2006)

Falkner 2000 Chardonnay (South Coast) $8. Awful, and just barely acceptable as a table wine. Starts with vegetable aromas of canned asparagus, and turns sharp and acidic in the mouth, without a trace of fruity flavor. **80** —S.H. (10/1/2003)

FALKNER

Falkner 2000 Reserve Chardonnay (South Coast) $18. Just like the barely drinkable regular release, only with an overlay of oak. Smells vegetal, and the thin flavors veer toward grapefruit. **81** —S.H. (8/1/2003)

Falkner 2002 Meritage (Temecula) $30. This wine is kind of lean, with an astringent dryness framing thin fruit flavors. It's surprising, because Falkner's '02 Merlot is really a very good wine. **83** —S.H. (12/15/2005)

Falkner 2002 Merlot (Temecula) $20. There's something addictive about this polished Merlot, with its succulent cherry flavors and that rich finish of cinnamon-dusted mocha. The wine is dry and velvety, although it could use a bit more acidity. **87** —S.H. (12/15/2005)

Falkner 2000 Muscat Canelli (South Coast) $12. A unique wine, not a bad one, that marches to a different beat. Smells sharply of cigarette tobacco and orange honey, with a dusting of white pepper. In the mouth, it's not sweet at all, but clean and zesty, with the taste of tangerines and cinnamon. **85** —S.H. (12/15/2003)

Falkner 2002 Amante Red Blend (South Coast) $25. Based on Sangiovese, this super Tuscan wine offers lots to like. It's absolutely dry and very soft, with cherry, tobacco and currant flavors that swirl together into a clean finish complexed with dusty tannins. **86** —S.H. (12/15/2005)

Falkner 2001 Riesling (Temecula) $13. A pleasant, fruity wine, with nice flavors of apricot, peach, honeysuckle and green apple. A bit of residual sugar makes the wine off-dry. Finishes swift and fruity. **84** —S.H. (12/31/2003)

Falkner 1999 Amante Sangiovese (South Coast) $16. A terrific super-Tuscan blend of Sangiovese, Cabernet Sauvignon, Merlot and Cabernet Franc. Rich and full-bodied, with obvious pedigree, it features great balance of ripe fruit, soft, dusty tannins and refreshing acidity. This is a first-rate wine that amply shows how good grapes can be in Temecula. **93 Editors' Choice** —S.H. (4/1/2002)

Falkner 2001 Sauvignon Blanc (Temecula) $11. Unattractive, from the slightly moldy, grapefruity aroma to the weak flavors. The fruit tastes diluted, without flavor. Soft acidity makes it all flabby. **81** (10/1/2003)

Falkner 2000 Sauvignon Blanc (South Coast) $10. Starts off a bit musty and earthy, with citrus flavors veering into riper peaches and mangoes. Turns dry and crisp in the finish. A pleasant wine at a good price. **86** —S.H. (4/1/2002)

Falkner 2001 Viognier (Temecula) $13. Smells a bit musty, although there's an undercurrent of fresh peaches. Flavors are dull, leaving behind the heat of alcohol and prickly acidity. **82** —S.H. (12/1/2003)

FALL CREEK VINEYARD

Fall Creek Vineyard 2002 Meritus Cabernet Sauvignon (Texas) $30. Behind a wall of vanilla and toast, there is some bright, red-berried fruit; only time will tell if it will emerge from the shadows and better integrate with the copious wood. For now, this 95% Cab Sauvignon remains cloaked in dry, woody tannins. **84** —J.C. (9/1/2005)

FALLBROOK

Fallbrook 2001 Reserve Cabernet Sauvignon (California) $16. Simple and soft to the point of flatness. Despite the pretty blackberry and cocoa flavors, the wine lacks life. **83** —S.H. (10/1/2005)

USA

Fallbrook 2002 Special Selection Cabernet Sauvignon (South Coast) $25. Sharp in acidity and a little green, this wine is relieved by modest cherry flavors. It's bone dry, and not going anywhere. **83** —S.H. (10/1/2005)

Fallbrook 2000 Special Selection Cabernet Sauvignon (California) $25. There are some good blackberry and currant flavors here, as well as sturdy, supportive tannins, but the wine is a little on the sweet side. There's also a sharpness in the finish. Drink now. **84** —S.H. (10/1/2005)

Fallbrook 2002 Chardonnay (California) $14. This Chard has lots of well-toasted oak framing nice pear and peach flavors. It's dry, spicy and a little rough on the finish. **84** —S.H. (10/1/2005)

Fallbrook 2002 Sleepy Hollow Vineyard Chardonnay (Monterey) $20. A little bitter in acidity, but that's by itself. A nice buttery lobster will certainly complement it. Otherwise, it has rich tropical fruit and a zesty minerality, and a long finish. **87** —S.H. (10/1/2005)

Fallbrook 2002 Reserve Merlot (California) $16. Dry, with berry and earth flavors and a hint of wintergreen. Has a good hit of tannins mid-palate that will play off well against rich fare. **84** —S.H. (10/1/2005)

Fallbrook 2000 Special Selection Merlot (California) $25. You'll find some tannins and herbaceous aromas and flavors in this Cab, which actually give it good grip, and makes it easier to pair with complex foods. It's very dry, with plummy, blackberry flavors. **86** —S.H. (10/1/2005)

Fallbrook 2004 Yakut Vineyard Sauvignon Blanc (South Coast) $12. A good, basic dry white wine, with well-ripened fruit and a touch of oak. Has a creamy texture, and some interesting, lemon and butterscotch flavors in the finish. **84** —S.H. (10/1/2005)

FANTESCA

Fantesca 2002 Cabernet Sauvignon (Spring Mountain) $60. This new brand, from veteran winemaker Nils Venge and friends, is excellent despite the awful name. It achieves that elusive goal of joining bigtime, ripe fruit with subtlety and charm to produce a wine of complexity. The cassis, cherry and oak flavors hit strong, then settle down and let the balance take over. **92 Editors' Choice** —S.H. (12/15/2005)

FANUCCHI

Fanucchi 2003 Trousseau Gris (Russian River Valley) $15. This is a very aromatic wine, reminiscent of Riesling with its peach, apple and flowery flavors and hint of minerality. It's dry and quaffable. **84** —S.H. (10/1/2004)

Fanucchi 2001 Old Vine Zinfandel (Russian River Valley) $29. A smooth-textured wine that tops out with some bright acidity. Nonetheless, it offers a pleasing blend of black cherry, raspberry, cola, coffee and spice notes. Zippy to the end. **87** (11/1/2003)

Fanucchi 2000 Old Vine Zinfandel (Russian River Valley) $29. A good wine, and an honest effort, but something didn't cooperate. There's a green, stalky edge to the berry fruit, and an astringent finish. Drink now, with rich meats and cheeses. **85** —S.H. (12/15/2004)

Fanucchi 1998 Old Vine Zinfandel (Russian River Valley) $29. This is some Zin. Big, textbook Sonoma County, filled with huge jammy young blackberry and boysenberry fruit and a solid dose of pepper. It's dry, with rich tannins and that wild, brawny character only Zinfandel has. The alcohol is a modest 14.1%. **88** —S.H. (12/1/2002)

Fanucchi 1997 Old Vine Zinfandel (Russian River Valley) $24. 90 —S.H. (5/1/2000)

Fanucchi 1996 Old Vine Zinfandel (Russian River Valley) $35. 91 —S.H. (9/1/1999)

FAR NIENTE

Far Niente 2003 Cabernet Sauvignon (Oakville) $115. In the wine's youth, the aroma of new oak dominates, with that smoky, minty, spicy-char note. But in the mouth the fruit explodes in intensely ripe black currants and milk chocolate. The tannins are rich and softly complex. A complete Cabernet that is luscious now, but has the balance to develop, if you can keep your hands off it. **94** —S.H. (12/15/2006)

Far Niente 2001 Cabernet Sauvignon (Oakville) $100. Well made and classic, a wine that combines potency of fruit and firm tannins with a graceful harmony that makes it easy to drink tonight. Oak adds smoky

vanillins as an additional theme. As fine as it is now, the wonderful balance ensures longterm aging through the next decade. **91** —S.H. (10/1/2004)

Far Niente 1997 Cabernet Sauvignon (Napa Valley) $100. 93 (11/1/2000)

Far Niente 2002 Estate Cabernet Sauvignon (Oakville) $110. Before you spend this much, you should know this isn't a wine to enjoy now or even soon. It's too tannic, too closed in. But chew on it and discover a rich core of blackberry, blueberry and cherry fruit. I don't think it's a classic Oakville Cab, but it should reward cellaring. Drink 2008 and beyond. **92** —S.H. (10/1/2005)

Far Niente 1998 Chardonnay (Napa Valley) $44. 91 —S.H. (2/1/2000)

Far Niente 1997 Chardonnay (Napa Valley) $44. 90 —S.H. (10/1/1999)

Far Niente 2002 Chardonnay (Napa Valley) $52. The winemaker notes that this wine has undergone no malolactic fermentation, which is rare in an expensive Chard because you don't get that big, fat, rich buttery softness. What you do get is pure pear and tropical fruit that is elaborately oaked in really good barrels. It is fancy and detailed but not blowsy. **91** —S.H. (11/15/2004)

Far Niente 2000 Estate Bottled Chardonnay (Napa Valley) $52. Expectations for this wine are always high. But this year brings some disappointment. The winemaker has concentrated the spicy peach and pear flavors and framed them generously in oak. Yet it lacks the subtlety and complexity to justify the price. **89** —S.H. (9/1/2002)

Far Niente 1999 Estate Bottled Chardonnay (Napa Valley) $52. This Napa Valley aristocrat sheds its normally understated demeanor and shows lively, pear, apple and melon fruit plus a vanilla-custard richness. There's toasty oak and a lively acid backbone that will help it evolve over the next few years. It's well-balanced, with a toasty, poised finish that's long and has bright lime overtones. **90** (7/1/2001)

FARALLON

Farallon 1997 Merlot (North Coast) $10. 84 Best Buy —J.C. (7/1/2000)

FARELLA-PARK

Farella-Park 1997 Cabernet Sauvignon (Napa Valley) $32. 91 (11/1/2000)

Farella-Park 1996 Cabernet Sauvignon (Napa Valley) $32. 91 —S.H. (7/1/2000)

Farella-Park 1996 Merlot (Napa Valley) $24. 90 —S.H. (7/1/2000)

FAT CAT

Fat Cat 2005 Chardonnay (California) $10. The promotional material for this wine says it's to celebrate "the indomitable spirit and culture of the Big Easy," New Orleans. It's not only a bad wine, it's an insult to the victims of Hurricane Katrina, and a cynical attempt to play off the public's sympathy. If Bronco Wine Co., which owns the brand, donated any of the profits to relief efforts, it would be one thing. But they're not. Shame. **80** —S.H. (12/31/2006)

Fat Cat 2004 Merlot (California) $10. This is a Merlot for people who want one doesn't cost much. It's okay, your basic cherries and cocoa. The winery's suggestion of lamb shanks as a pairing will work well. **83** —S.H. (12/31/2006)

FATTORIA ENOTRIA

Fattoria Enotria 1997 Dolcetto (Mendocino) $16. 84 (9/1/2000)

FEATHER

Feather 2003 Cabernet Sauvignon (Columbia Valley (WA)) $55. Napa's Randy Dunn is making this 100% Cab with Long Shadows winemaker Gilles Nicault. Soft, ripe and plummy, it shows a good mix of red and blue fruits, amplified with lots of toast, chocolate, coffee and cinnamon highlights. Definitely a Napa-meets-Washington style. **91** —P.G. (6/1/2006)

FENESTRA

Fenestra 2003 Silvaspoons Vineyard Alvarelhão (Lodi) $18. This is a robust, rustic wine, rich in dark berry and fruit flavors, thick in tannins and a bit sweet. It's the kind of wine to drink with easy fare. **84** —S.H. (12/1/2006)

Fenestra 2001 Chardonnay (Contra Costa County) $14. Thin and simple. Nothing going on except a dollop of lemon juice. **81** —S.H. (4/1/2004)

Fenestra 2001 Chardonnay (Livermore Valley) $16. Like a drink of cold water with a squirt of lemon juice. Dry and acidic. **81** —S.H. (4/1/2004)

Fenestra 2000 Merlot (Livermore Valley) $19. Smells a little baked, with raisiny, pruny aromas, and this impression is confirmed on tasting. The flavor is rather like raisins that have been soaked in espresso, with a splash of blackberry liqueur. Give it a little chill to offset the heat. **84** — S.H. (6/1/2004)

Fenestra 2000 Merlot (Santa Lucia Highlands) $17. This is a cool appellation best for Pinot Noir, and this Merlot is unripe. It smells just like canned asparagus, and is harsh and acidic. **81** —S.H. (6/1/2004)

Fenestra 2003 Estate Mourvèdre (Livermore Valley) $17. Kind of simple, thin, dry, delicately structured wine with tart cherry and tea flavors, almost like a Pinot Noir. Gets better as it warms up in the glass. **83** — S.H. (12/1/2006)

Fenestra 1999 Petite Sirah (Lodi) $17. An easy-drinking quaffer, with pleasant flavors of blackberry and cherry. So soft and velvety, one taster called it cherry-vanilla ice cream, although it's totally dry. Not a complex, deep wine, but likeable and almost flamboyant in its flavors. **86** (4/1/2003)

Fenestra 2003 Pinot Noir (Livermore Valley) $22. Light in body, with cherry, cola and spice flavors. This Pinot has considerable acidity; and it's certainly not a big wine but has a delicate, tea-like complexity that makes it the best Livermore Pinot I've ever had. **86** —S.H. (12/1/2006)

Fenestra 2002 Silvaspoons Vineyard Port Port (Lodi) $17. Here's a really nice Port-style wine, sweet but not too sweet, with crisp acidity and chocolate, raspberry tart and cassis flavors. A blend of traditional Port varieties with a splash of Syrah, it's delicious now with chocolate. **90** — S.H. (12/1/2006)

Fenestra NV True Red Lot 16 Rhône Red Blend (Lodi) $9. This blend of a bunch of Rhone varietals is heavy and full, with generic berry flavors. It's decently made and dry, and is serviceable with your less demanding culinary creations. **83** —S.H. (6/1/2004)

Fenestra 2002 Dry Rose Rosé Blend (California) $8. A Rhône-style blend. It's one of the darker rosés, and rather heavy-bodied too, with extracted, jammy flavors of fresh black raspberries and cherries. It's dry, with enough power to stand up to a big, juicy cheeseburger. **83** —S.H. (6/1/2004)

Fenestra 2000 Sangiovese (Lodi) $14. An awkward wine that, despite the silky smooth texture that's like a light Pinot Noir and some nice cherry flavors, has a hot, rubbery streak that suggests burnt asphalt. **82** —S.H. (6/1/2004)

Fenestra 2002 Sauvignon Blanc (Livermore Valley) $16. This wine has barely more flavor than tap water. Impossible to recommend, except that it is clean and without technical flaws. **81** —S.H. (3/1/2004)

Fenestra 2002 Sémillon (Livermore Valley) $9. Watery and thin, with citrusy flavors and acids. Even at this price, it's no value. **82** —S.H. (3/1/2004)

Fenestra 2002 Semonnay Sémillon-Chardonnay (Livermore Valley) $13. Blend of Sémillon and Chardonnay, and if anything, even more watery than this winery's varietals. A drag and ripoff. **81** —S.H. (3/1/2004)

Fenestra 1999 Syrah (Livermore Valley) $20. Very dark and dense, and opens with intriguing aromas of pepper, bacon, blackberry and smoke. Turns rich in tannins in the mouth, with a complex, lush texture, but seems too light in fruit for the weight. Could just be me. **85** —S.H. (2/1/2004)

Fenestra 2000 Estate Syrah (Livermore Valley) $15. Intensely peppery, enough to turn off some tasters but turn on others, depending on your individual stylistic preferences. Besides pepper, there's some lavender-like floral notes and a decent helping of red berry fruit along with a supple, easygoing mouthfeel. **88 Editors' Choice** (9/1/2005)

Fenestra 2000 Reserve Syrah (Livermore Valley) $18. West Coast Editor Steve Heimoff found this wine too sweet for his palate, while our other tasters enjoyed its intensely peppery flavors. Cherry-berry fruit forms the smooth core of the wine, while white pepper and cured meat notes add nuance. Finishes long. **87** (9/1/2005)

Fenestra 2003 Silvaspoons Vineyard Tempranillo (Lodi) $19. Take a wine with Pinot Noir's delicate, silky texture and cross it with Zinfandel's robust, rustic quality, and you get this Temp. It's dry and easy in the mouth, with cherry and Kahlua flavors and lots of anise and nutmeg. **85** —S.H. (12/1/2006)

Fenestra 2003 Silvaspoons Vineyard Touriga Franca (Lodi) $22. More California wineries should tinker with this Port variety. This wine is fruitily complex, with a medium body, silky texture and oodles of spice. While it's rustic, it shows real promise. **85** —S.H. (12/1/2006)

Fenestra 2002 Viognier (Contra Costa County) $17. A little rough in texture, with some well-integrated peach, kiwi and vanillas that are accompanied by good acidity. Despite the ripe flavors, this is a fully dry wine. **85** —S.H. (6/1/2004)

Fenestra 1999 Zinfandel (Livermore Valley) $17. Very Zinny with its briary, brambly flavors of newly picked wild blackberries, black raspberries and cherries, and a streak of earthy tobacco and pepper. Drinks dry and full-bodied, with rich, fine tannins and a long, spicy finish. Distinctive. **87** —S.H. (3/1/2004)

FERNWOOD

Fernwood 2002 Redwood Retreat Vineyards Cabernet Sauvignon (Santa Cruz Mountains) $40. Too ripe and raisiny for my tastes, this wine nonetheless is very dry, with smooth tannins. But the raisiny, stewed fruit flavors persists all the way through. **82** —S.H. (4/1/2006)

Fernwood 2003 Redwood Retreat Vineyards Syrah (Santa Cruz Mountains) $33. This is a big, ripe, fruity Syrah, but it has an underlying balance and finesse that give it first-class status. It's a well-oaked, dry wine, with thick but smooth tannins that frame intense blackberry, mulberry and cocoa flavors. Best enjoyed in its youth. **90** —S.H. (4/1/2006)

Fernwood 2002 Zinfandel (El Dorado) $27. Porty and notably sweet, with lots of fruit. **82** —S.H. (2/1/2005)

Fernwood 2002 Redwood Retreat Vineyards Zinfandel (Santa Cruz Mountains) $27. Porty and insipid with sweetness, and soft to the point of collapse. **82** —S.H. (2/1/2005)

FERRARI-CARANO

Ferrari-Carano 2000 Eldorado Noir Black Muscat (Russian River Valley) $25. Having the right amount of tannic structure and acidity, this wine is not cloying, but rather light, simple and quite pleasant. The sensory package includes rose petals, tangerines, blueberries, figs, candied fruit and gruyère cheese. **86** (11/1/2002)

Ferrari-Carano 1999 Trésor Bordeaux Blend (Sonoma County) $45. A Bordeaux blend of all five varieties, but it's extremely tannic and requires age (or a very rich cut of meat) to soften it. Dense, ripe and still youthfully tough at four and one half years, with a rich core of black cherry and blackberry fruit that will gain complexity through this decade. Could improve significantly. **90** —S.H. (8/1/2004)

Ferrari-Carano 1999 Trésor Red Table Wine Bordeaux Blend (Sonoma County) $32. All 5 Bordeaux varieties comprise this complex but young wine. It's sharp in fresh tannins, with a rich core of sweet black cherry fruit. Needs some big, greasy steak to match it, but should develop gracefully for some time. **92** —S.H. (12/1/2004)

Ferrari-Carano 1994 Tresor Reserve Bordeaux Blend (Sonoma County) $65. **87** —S.H. (3/1/2000)

Ferrari-Carano 2001 Trésor Cabernet Blend (Alexander Valley) $45. With fruit sourced from everywhere from Dry Creek to Carneros, this Cabernet-based wine is a good, blended effort, with true varietal character if no particular complexity. It's balanced, fruity and tannic, but too expensive for what you get. **86** —S.H. (12/1/2005)

Ferrari-Carano 2003 Cabernet Sauvignon (Alexander Valley) $30. Made with a drop of Syrah, this is a stylish, rich Cab, with the herbal flavors and soft tannins of Alexander Valley. The cherry fruit mingles with sweet tobacco and thyme, resulting in a restrained but complex, food-friendly wine. **88** —S.H. (12/31/2006)

USA

Ferrari-Carano 2002 Cabernet Sauvignon (Alexander Valley) $34. This soft Cab seems dialed in. There's nothing wrong with it, it's just formulaic in the well-ripened black currant flavors, standard smoky oak, and smooth texture. **84** —*S.H. (12/1/2005)*

Ferrari-Carano 2001 Cabernet Sauvignon (Sonoma County) $28. Very oaky. The enormity of char, vanilla and toast, has not yet integrated with the wine it frames. The underlying flavors are ripe and opulent, spreading over the palate with cherry pie, crème de cassis and chocolate. Give this beautiful wine until 2005 or beyond. **91** —*S.H. (8/1/2004)*

Ferrari-Carano 1999 TreMonte Cabernet Sauvignon (Alexander Valley) $38. Firm textured, with smoky oak, black currant, licorice and herb highlights. Medium weight, medium length. **86** —*J.M. (11/15/2002)*

Ferrari-Carano 1998 Tremonte Cabernet Sauvignon (Alexander Valley) $38. Don't let the orangish rim color fool you. Aromas of cedar and mint followed by flavors of leather and cassis last on a dry, dark-earth finish. A lack of hangtime for the fruit made for a hard wine. **86** *(11/1/2002)*

Ferrari-Carano 1998 Chardonnay (Sonoma County) $25. 87 *(6/1/2000)*

Ferrari-Carano 1997 Chardonnay (Sonoma County) $22. 92 —*M.S. (7/1/1999)*

Ferrari-Carano 2004 Chardonnay (Alexander Valley) $28. Has aromas of buttered toast and peaches a nd cream, but once it the mouth, it turns kind of harsh, with lemon skin and puckery acidity. There's a lot of new oak, which is nice, but it's out of balance with the underlying thinness of the fruit. **83** —*S.H. (12/31/2006)*

Ferrari-Carano 2003 Chardonnay (Alexander Valley) $28. This gentle, balanced and very fine wine displays consummate artistry in winemaking. It has enough fruit, oak and creaminess to satisfy that Chard craving, without any one element sticking out, and manages to be big while retaining finesse and elegance. **90** —*S.H. (12/1/2005)*

Ferrari-Carano 2001 Chardonnay (Alexander Valley) $23. Soft, ripe and oaky, with leesy flavors and notes of apples and tropical fruits. The creamy texture fans out over the palate, finishing with a honeyed smoothness. **86** —*S.H. (8/1/2004)*

Ferrari-Carano 2000 Chardonnay (Alexander Valley) $25. A toasty, buttery nose is the result of 70% new, medium-toast Vosges oak, but the fruit is all California Chardonnay, with Golden Delicious apple and tropical fruit flavors. This wine is medium- to full- bodied and slightly oily in texture. **87** *(11/1/2002)*

Ferrari-Carano 2003 Reserve Chardonnay (Napa-Sonoma) $42. The Reserve has always been oaky, but this may be the oakiest yet. That toasty, caramelly vanilla thing hits hard. Fortunately, the underlying tropical fruit stands up to all the wood. I like this wine, but this is about as far as a winemaker should push oak. **89** —*S.H. (12/1/2005)*

Ferrari-Carano 2001 Reserve Chardonnay (Carneros) $32. Lavish and bold, almost over the top in ripeness, and all those winemaker bells and whistles. Sweet mango and pineapple, vanilla custard, buttered toast and roasted hazelnut flavors swim in an opulently creamy texture. Yet it's fully dry and well balanced. **92** —*S.H. (6/1/2004)*

Ferrari-Carano 2001 Reserve Chardonnay (Carneros) $32. All the bells and whistles are here, from the malolactic fermentation that makes the wine soft and buttery to the heavy lees contact to barrel fermentation with lots of new oak. The result is creamy and complex, framing modest flavors of apples, tangerines and peaches. **89** —*S.H. (8/1/2004)*

Ferrari-Carano 2000 Reserve Chardonnay (Carneros) $32. Ultrabuttery, with butterscotch at the fore. The wine is richly textured, but strikes a pose that is perhaps more influenced by barrel than by fruit. Pretty melon, pear and citrus notes take a back seat. Spicy on the finish. **89** —*J.M. (12/15/2002)*

Ferrari-Carano 1999 Reserve Chardonnay (Napa County) $32. With its 90% Napa and 10% Sonoma lineage, this wine serves up mild lime, butterscotch and green apple aromas and a nicely weighted palate with tropical fruit, peach and caramel flavors. The mouthfeel is soft, with a caramel custard quality. The long, creamy and toasty finish will win raves from lovers of both the full malolactic and well-oaked styles. **89** *(7/1/2001)*

Ferrari-Carano 2004 Tre Terre Chardonnay (Russian River Valley) $34. Vineyard sources for the winery's reserve tier of Chardonnay have bounced around over the years. Now, it's Russian River, but this Chard is far from Ferrari-Carano's best. It has decent peach and apple fruit, but with a thin brittleness inappropriate for this price, and all that new oak doesn't really help. **84** —*S.H. (12/31/2006)*

Ferrari-Carano 2000 TreMonte Chardonnay (Alexander Valley) $32. Clean flint and citrus qualities sit behind a smoldering curtain of heavily toasted oak. Finishes warm, with a white-pepper zing. **87** *(11/1/2002)*

Ferrari-Carano 1998 Fumé Blanc (Sonoma County) $12. 89 Best Buy — *S.H. (3/1/2000)*

Ferrari-Carano 1996 Fumé Blanc (Sonoma County) $11. 88 Best Buy — *S.H. (9/1/1999)*

Ferrari-Carano 2005 Fumé Blanc (Sonoma County) $16. Half-fermented in stainless steel, half in older oak, which is a common approach this day. This 100% varietal wine keeps Sauvignon's fresh, tart citrus fruit and acids, but adds just a little cream and softness. It's not a complicated wine, but it's a refreshing one, with some aspirations to complexity. **85** —*S.H. (12/31/2006)*

Ferrari-Carano 2004 Fumé Blanc (Sonoma County) $16. A fruit-forward, slightly sweet and zesty-clean Sauvignon Blanc. The lemon, lime, fig and melon flavors are tasty. **84** —*S.H. (12/1/2005)*

Ferrari-Carano 2003 Fumé Blanc (Sonoma County) $15. Always a solid wine for the focused flavors, deft oak and clean winemaking. Citrus, fig and spice flavors in a dry, creamy texture, with bright acidity. Wonderful on its own, or with a wide range of food. **89** —*S.H. (12/31/2004)*

Ferrari-Carano 2002 Fumé Blanc (Sonoma County) $15. Fruit's a bit thin, tending to tart green apples, grapefruit and lime, and oak plays a leading role, lending notes of smoke and vanilla and a creamy texture. Very well structured. You find yourself wishing there was more depth of flavor. **85** —*S.H. (7/1/2003)*

Ferrari-Carano 2001 Fumé Blanc (Sonoma County) $15. With 60% Alexander Valley fruit contributing distinct melon, pear and grapefruit aromas and flavors, the usually grassy, herbal qualities of the remaining 40% Dry Creek Valley fruit offer only a pleasant hint of green pea. This easy-drinking wine has a medium-weight body and a short, lime-tinged finish. **88 Best Buy** *(11/1/2002)*

Ferrari-Carano 2000 Fumé Blanc (Sonoma County) $15. Pretty peach, melon, fig and citrus flavors are framed in distinct herb and earth tones here. The wine is quite assertive, with plenty of grassy character. It's a style that may not be for everyone, but is nonetheless appealing in its genre. **87** —*J.M. (11/15/2001)*

Ferrari-Carano 1998 Reserve Fumé Blanc (Sonoma County) $18. 89 —*S.H. (3/1/2000)*

Ferrari-Carano 2003 Merlot (Sonoma County) $25. I liked this better than the winery's more expensive Oakville Merlot because it's not overripe. There's a wealth of chocolate and blackberry flavors, finished with sweet cassis and wrapped in smooth tannins. But it's balanced, soft and dry. **87** —*S.H. (12/31/2006)*

Ferrari-Carano 2002 Merlot (Sonoma County) $25. Merlot has not been the winery's strong suit over the years, but with this vintage, something has changed. The wine is lush and complex. There are enormously deep cherry, mocha and oak flavors, with the rich tannic structure Ferrari-Carano's reds always have the classic finish. **91** —*S.H. (12/1/2005)*

Ferrari-Carano 2001 Merlot (Sonoma County) $25. Rich, soft, sweet and decadent, with black cherry flavors, smooth tannins and a chocolatey finish. The bottle I opened seemed a little bretty and off. Finishes with a scour of tannins. **86** —*S.H. (12/31/2004)*

Ferrari-Carano 1999 Merlot (Sonoma County) $23. This glass-tinter has 6-8% Malbec blended in. The lightweight package is full of black cherry, vanilla and a bit of greenness on the finish. Well-suited to a casual gathering on the patio. **87** *(11/1/2002)*

Ferrari-Carano 1999 TreMonte Merlot (Alexander Valley) $32. This wine has a thin veneer of green herb and string bean. Further evaluation yields chocolate, apple peel, figs and bright cherry fruit. Closes a bit tight with char, pepper and some mint. **86** *(11/1/2002)*

Ferrari-Carano 1997 Vineyards of TreMonte Merlot (Sonoma County) $28. The aromas are herbal, flirting dangerously with green pepper before eventually settling somewhere between oregano and tea. The juicy black cherries on the palate compensate somewhat, and the oak is understated. Best with herb-laced beef or lamb to help accentuate the fruit. **86** —*J.C. (6/1/2001)*

Ferrari-Carano 2000 Siena Red Blend (Sonoma County) $24. Beautiful and soft as an Impressionist painting. Flavors of cherries, black raspberries, spices and herbs are wrapped in rich, easy tannins, coating the palate and finishing ripe but dry. Delicious on its own and immediately drinkable. A blend of Sangiovese, Cabernet Sauvignon and Merlot. **92 Editors' Choice** —*S.H. (11/15/2003)*

Ferrari-Carano 1999 Siena Red Blend (Sonoma County) $28. "Siena" refers to the color of Sonoma soil, but this Sangiovese-based wine points to the winery's Italian heritage. Typical varietal characteristics of dry earth and green herbs are well matched with juicy strawberry, cherry and blackberry flavors. **91** *(11/1/2002)*

Ferrari-Carano 1997 Tresor Reserve Red Blend (Sonoma County) $45. Although extremely dry and tannic, tasters were able to derive sweet blackberry, cherry and plum skin qualities. In the final analysis, some tasters wondered why it was somewhat awry, while others found lots to love. You decide. **86** *(11/1/2002)*

Ferrari-Carano 1996 Siena Sangiovese (Sonoma County) $28. 90 *(10/1/1999)*

Ferrari-Carano 1997 Vineyards of Tremonte Sangiovese (Alexander Valley) $28. Complex aromas of smoke, vanilla, blackberry, citrus rind and earth start things off. On the palate, it's thick with lively berry fruit, and very dry. High acidity keeps it lively and crisp, while fairly hefty tannins provide structure. This fleshy, 100% Sangiovese is ready to drink now. **88** —*S.H. (12/1/2001)*

Ferrari-Carano 1996 Vineyards of TreMonte Sangiovese (Sonoma County) $35. 87 —*M.S. (10/1/1999)*

Ferrari-Carano 1998 Storey Creek Vineyard Sauvignon Blanc (Russian River Valley) $15. 90 —*S.H. (3/1/2000)*

Ferrari-Carano 1997 TreMonte Syrah (Sonoma County) $32. Opening very dark with a candied cherry-grape and licorice nose, this doesn't deliver the weight it sets you up for. The tart fruit bears lots of herb, almost geranium, shadings; it finishes lean and black with tangy tannins, not unlike many well-oaked Tuscan wines. **86** *(11/1/2001)*

Ferrari-Carano 1996 Zinfandel (Sonoma) $16.88 —*S.H. (9/1/1999)*

FESS PARKER

Fess Parker 1998 Chardonnay (Santa Barbara County) $16. 87 *(6/1/2000)*

Fess Parker 2004 Chardonnay (Santa Barbara County) $18. Parker's basic county Chardonnay shares the same features as his upper tier, namely a wonderful balance of acids, fruit, oak and alcohol. The flavors are of tropical fruits, although the wine is necessarily not as rich or concentrated as the single vineyards. **85** —*S.H. (5/1/2006)*

Fess Parker 2001 Chardonnay (Santa Barbara County) $18. Fresh and fruity, with big, clean flavors of apples, peaches and oriental spices. It's also pretty oaky, with telltale vanilla, smoke and char. Drinks fully dry, although the fruit makes it feel sweet and honeyed through the finish. **86** —*S.H. (12/15/2002)*

Fess Parker 1996 American Tradition Reserve Chardonnay (Santa Barbara County) $22. 91 —*S.H. (7/1/1999)*

Fess Parker 2004 Ashley's Vineyard Chardonnay (Santa Rita Hills) $28. Brilliant exposition of Chardonnay from a cool climate. There's a brisk, clean, minerally moutheel, brimming with acidity, that frames exotic flavors of ripe tropical fruits, spices, peaches and vanilla-infused cream, and a finish that turns to pure apricot nectar. Just delicious. **93 Editors' Choice** —*S.H. (10/1/2006)*

Fess Parker 2003 Ashley's Vineyard Chardonnay (Santa Rita Hills) $26. Ashley's is one of the cooler vineyards in this part of Santa Barbara, and you can taste the chilly winds in the brilliant acids. They tingle the taste buds and perk up the rich and pure tropical fruit flavors, leading to a

clean, vibrant finish. This complex Chard is addictively good. **93 Editors' Choice** —*S.H. (11/1/2005)*

Fess Parker 1997 Santa Barbara County Chardonnay (Santa Barbara County) $15. 89 —*S.H. (7/1/1999)*

Fess Parker 2004 Pinot Noir (Santa Barbara County) $25. Here's Parker's basic county bottling. It's a rustic wine, rough and jagged in tannins and a little heavy, with cherry jam and oak flavors. Could soften and improve in a year or two. **83** —*S.H. (5/1/2006)*

Fess Parker 2002 Pinot Noir (Santa Barbara County) $22. Here's your basic Pinot 101. It's dry, with a silky texture, soft tannins and crisp acids that frame cherry, cola and herb flavors. Easy and uncomplicated. **85** —*S.H. (11/1/2004)*

Fess Parker 2000 Pinot Noir (Santa Barbara County) $20. This starter-kit Santa Barbara Pinot has flavors of cherries, blackberries, tomatoes and fresh hard spices, with silky tannins and crisp acids. **86** —*S.H. (2/1/2003)*

Fess Parker 1999 Pinot Noir (Santa Barbara County) $18. Here's a nice example of cool climate, South Coast Pinot, with its tomato, hard spice, mushroom and raspberry aromas, and limpid, silky texture. The berry flavors are delicate, dry, and tasty, and well-integrated oak complements them well. **88 Best Buy** —*S.H. (12/15/2001)*

Fess Parker 2000 American Tradition Reserve Pinot Noir (Santa Barbara) $45. Attractive strawberry, spice, smoke and meaty aromas open this tangy wine. But an overt woody element moves to the fore, taking charge and overriding cherry and chocolate flavors. Closes somewhat astringently, with more cocoa and tart cherry notes. Flavorful, but edgy. **85** *(10/1/2002)*

Fess Parker 1999 American Tradition Reserve Pinot Noir (Santa Barbara County) $32. Fine varietal Pinot, bursting with cherry and spice fruit. The powerful aromas promise a sturdy, big-boned wine, and don't disappoint. In the mouth, waves of cherry-berry fruit and oriental spices drink dry and complex, with intricately detailed tannins. There's an oaky, glyceriney sweetness that lasts through the finish. **92** —*S.H. (12/15/2001)*

Fess Parker 2004 Ashley's Vineyard Pinot Noir (Santa Rita Hills) $50. There's lots of harsh acidity and tannins in this Pinot, which makes it tough at this time. It's a scoury, astringent wine and the best it can offer is a very dry, acidic rosehip tea flavor. Will it age? It's anyone's guess, but I'd say no. **84** —*S.H. (10/1/2006)*

Fess Parker 2003 Ashley's Vineyard Pinot Noir (Santa Rita Hills) $45. If you had to take one red wine to that proverbial desert island, this might be it. It's simply delicious. The cherry, black raspberry, cocoa, coffee, cola and spice flavors are enormously deep and long, yet such is the acidity that the wine is filled with life and zest. Just marvelous, and probably best now and over the next year or two. **94 Editors' Choice** —*S.H. (11/1/2005)*

Fess Parker 2002 Ashley's Vineyard Pinot Noir (Santa Rita Hills) $45. The most complex of this winery's current offerings. It shows a remarkable similarity to the Santa Maria Valley bottlings, with a dense texture and blackberry-cherry flavors. But there's a juicy streak of acidity that creates life and zest. **90** —*S.H. (11/1/2004)*

Fess Parker 2001 Ashley's Vineyard Pinot Noir (Santa Barbara County) $45. A monumental Pinot that showcases the potential of the Santa Rita Hills area. This wine impresses with the depth and complexity of its raspberry, cherry, spicebox, tobacco and vanilla flavors that coat the palate with delicious intensity. For all its size, the acids and tannins are fine and balanced, keeping the mouthfeel silky and refined. **93** —*S.H. (3/1/2004)*

Fess Parker 2004 Bien Nacido Vineyard Pinot Noir (Santa Barbara County) $50. You can taste the shrively raisins all the way through. That's the result of the vintage's excessive heat. This is still a delicious wine. Drink now. **88** —*S.H. (12/1/2006)*

Fess Parker 2002 Bien Nacido Vineyard Pinot Noir (Santa Barbara County) $45. Impresses for its lush, sweet fruit, reminiscent of fully ripened blackberries, black cherries and pomegranates. Those savory flavors are amplified by smoky oak. Dry and crisp in acids, this lovely wine has a medium-full body. **88** —*S.H. (11/1/2004)*

Fess Parker 2000 Bien Nacido Vineyard Pinot Noir (Santa Barbara County) $45. Aromas of tart cherry, plum, mushroom and earth. The mouthfeel is rich and smooth, but the flavors show a dry, earthy note. Finishes long, tinged with pepper, coffee and molasses notes. **85** *(10/1/2002)*

Fess Parker 1999 Bien Nacido Vineyard Pinot Noir (Santa Barbara County) $45. Huge, extracted, a giant wine. There's an explosion of fruit, great weight and depth of flavor, with masses of berries and tree fruits, tomatoes, and herbs. Despite the size, it maintains a subtle harmony and finesse. Defines its terroir, and will soften and mellow with time. **93** —*S.H. (12/15/2001)*

Fess Parker 2000 Dierberg Vineyard Pinot Noir (Santa Barbara) $45. Some appealing woodsy and decay elements go with tart cherry fruit, cola and earth flavors that fail to flesh out and offer the requisite generosity. It's a rather hard, unyielding wine that needs time but may never truly blossom. **85** *(10/1/2002)*

Fess Parker 2002 Marcella's Vineyard Pinot Noir (Santa Barbara County) $45. Almost a carbon copy of Parker's Bien Nacido bottling, this is a dry, dense wine with ripe fruity flavors and a rich overlay of smoky oak. There are some tannins that coat the palate with a dusty astringency, but a good steak will resolve those. **88** —*S.H. (11/1/2004)*

Fess Parker 2000 Marcella's Vineyard Pinot Noir (Santa Barbara County) $45. An angular, appealing mid-weight, with tangy raspberry fruit, leather, cinnamon and clove accents and a dark, charred-oak veneer. Thin and one-dimensional to some, but most found it juicy and appealing, with bright fruit peeking through the dark veil. Drink now–2006. **88** *(10/1/2002)*

Fess Parker 1999 Marcella's Vineyard Pinot Noir (Santa Barbara County) $45. Captures the essence of South Coast Pinot in its fantastic concentration and depth. Berry, smoke, tomato, chocolate and spice mingle together in a silky package that defines harmony, elegance, power and finesse. Only 300 cases made. **94 Editors' Choice** —*S.H. (12/15/2001)*

Fess Parker 1997 Santa Barbara County Pinot Noir (Santa Maria Valley) $18. 90 *(10/1/1999)*

Fess Parker NV Lot 22 Frontier Red Rhône Red Blend (California) $10. You don't have to be old enough to remember Parker's Davy Crockett (whose picture is on the front label) to enjoy this red Rhône blend. It has Syrah's peppery aroma, followed by deep, earthy and berry flavors. Finishes dry and tannic. **87 Best Buy** —*S.H. (5/1/2003)*

Fess Parker 1997 Syrah (Santa Barbara County) $18. 89 —*S.H. (10/1/1999)*

Fess Parker 1996 Syrah (Santa Barbara County) $17. 92 —*S.H. (10/1/1999)*

Fess Parker 2002 Syrah (Santa Barbara County) $18. Two of our reviewers found this wine overly tannic and rough on the finish, while the other praised its supple tannins and creamy texture. All agreed on the ample blackberry fruit and heavyhanded oak, which make the wine somewhat obvious. We just couldn't agree on where this wine is headed in the future. **84** *(9/1/2005)*

Fess Parker 2000 Syrah (Santa Barbara County) $20. Has the characteristic peppery aromas and flavors, and lush, soft tannins with supportive acids, that have long marked this wine. But it seems thin in fruit. A wave of plummy blackberry washes over the tongue and then instantly disappears. Oak is not an adequate replacement. **85** —*S.H. (12/1/2002)*

Fess Parker 1999 Syrah (Santa Barbara County) $20. Starts with an explosion of crushed white pepper and roasted, charred notes, with a suggestion of blackberries. Drinks round, soft and flavorful, a full-bodied red with velvety tannins and fresh acidity. This flattering, dry wine is versatile and easy to drink. **87** —*S.H. (7/1/2002)*

Fess Parker 2002 American Tradition Reserve Syrah (Santa Barbara County) $30. Two tasters picked up pickled asparagus on the nose of this wine, enough to keep it firmly out of the ranks of the high scorers. That said, it still has a pleasant, soft mouthfeel and decent flavors of red berries and spice; one of our reviewers felt it was much better than reflected in the average score. **83** *(9/1/2005)*

Fess Parker 2000 American Tradition Reserve Syrah (Santa Barbara County) $32. The plummy, peppery flavors are dominated by sturdy tannins. It's one of those young, tough wines that needs rich fare. Great texture, slippery and smooth. **88** —*S.H. (10/1/2003)*

Fess Parker 2000 Mackie's Blend Syrah (Central Coast) $13. Decent everyday fare in a big, dry red wine that's laced with thick tannins and some okay plummy, berry fruit flavors. Has a velvety, supple texture that feels good, although the tannins are a bit rude. **84** —*S.H. (12/15/2003)*

Fess Parker 2002 Rodney's Vineyard Syrah (Santa Barbara County) $36. Clearly astringent, but this wine may have a good future. The flavors of ripe, sweet blackberries and smoky espresso are dramatic, and so is the vibrant, lemony acidity. Hold until 2007 while you wait for the components to come together. **86** *(9/1/2005)*

Fess Parker 2000 Rodney's Vineyard Syrah (Santa Barbara County) $36. This is a connoisseur's wine. Its white-pepper aromas are undergirded by blackberry, smoke and tar, and the berry flavors are wrapped in dried herbs, accompanied by some fairly astringent tannins. It has depth and interest, and will be fantastic with a rich cut of lamb or beef. **90** —*S.H. (3/1/2004)*

Fess Parker 1999 Rodney's Vineyard Syrah (Santa Barbara County) $30. Toasty, nutty aromas vie with earthy, horsey scents, but underneath this sideshow there's gobs of blackberries, prune plums and licorice. Finishes long and tangy, with complex notes of coffee, black pepper and smoked meat. **89** *(11/1/2001)*

Fess Parker 2003 The Big Easy Syrah (Santa Barbara County) $35. This wine, from the Parker vineyard in Santa Ynez Valley, shows the voluptuous mouthfeel that's made Syrah so popular. The flavors are of the ripest blackberries cooked into a tart, and then sprinkled with butter, vanilla, cocoa and cinnamon. How good is that? A pointed reminder that high alcohol does not necessarily equal heat. **93 Editors' Choice** —*S.H. (12/1/2006)*

Fess Parker 2002 The Big Easy Syrah (Santa Barbara County) $36. The aroma came across as vegetal to some tasters, suggesting canned asparagus. To others it was more herbal, and followed by structured flavors of coffee, olives and earth. A bit lean perhaps, and a bit oaky as well, but a solid effort. **85** *(9/1/2005)*

Fess Parker 1997 Viognier (Santa Barbara) $18. 91 —*S.H. (6/1/1999)*

Fess Parker 2004 Viognier (Santa Barbara County) $22. Delivers just what consumers want in a Viognier, namely, vibrantly exotic and powerful fruity flavor. Mangoes, papayas, anything your heart desires can be found, in a rich, dry, creamy texture. White chocolate even shows up in the long, delicious finish. **90** —*S.H. (5/1/2006)*

Fess Parker 2001 Viognier (Santa Barbara County) $20. This is a delicious wine, more flavorful than most. Explodes in the mouth with peach, kiwi, sweet pear, buttercream, vanilla and spice. It's rich, yet dry. **88** —*S.H. (5/1/2003)*

Fess Parker 2000 Viognier (Santa Barbara County) $20. Unusually complex and layered for a Viognier, it starts with powerful aromas of peaches, honeysuckle, smoky butter, coconut and a mineral note. Very rich and full, long on fruit and spice; crisp and dry. This harmonious wine has lots of finesse. **90 Editors' Choice** —*S.H. (11/15/2001)*

Fess Parker 1997 Melange du Rhône White Blend (Santa Barbara County) $15. 91 —*S.H. (6/1/1999)*

Fess Parker 2001 White Riesling (Santa Barbara County) $12. Fans will appreciate the vibrant cleanliness and pure flavors of lime, apricot, honey, nectarine and vanilla that mark this slightly sweet wine. It's pleasant on its own as an aperitif, and even better with freshly picked ripe tree fruits. **85** —*S.H. (9/1/2003)*

FETZER

Fetzer 1998 Barrel Select Cabernet Sauvignon (North Coast) $17. Rather rich for a Õ98, especially at this price, but this winery has control over vast acreage and can afford to pick the very best. Has good blackcurrant aromas with a smoky meatiness, and drinks dry and rich. It's a very supple wine, one that flatters the palate with velvety smoothness. **87** —*S.H. (9/5/2002)*

Fetzer 1997 Barrel Select Cabernet Sauvignon (North Coast) $15. 88 Best Buy —*P.G. (12/15/2000)*

Fetzer 1996 Barrel Select Cabernet Sauvignon (North Coast) $15. 88 —*S.H. (2/1/2000)*

Fetzer 1999 Five Rivers Ranch Cabernet Sauvignon (Central Coast) $13. Berry and smoke aromas veering toward cassis and earth lead to a clean, well-balanced, dry wine of considerable character and finesse. Very dry, with a good depth of flavor and gutsy tannins to cut through food. **87** (11/15/2001)

Fetzer 1999 Reserve Cabernet Sauvignon (Napa Valley) $30. The full bouquet displays impressive depth to its blackberry, mint, tobacco and herb scents. The palate is dense, with cassis, chocolate and licorice flavors accented by plenty of spicy oak. Long and spicy, the finish is even, with dark berry and tobacco notes. Has appeal now, but will be better if cellared two to five years. **90** (5/1/2001)

Fetzer 1998 Reserve Cabernet Sauvignon (Napa Valley) $40. Here's a very good wine meant for early drinking. It's well-structured, with fine tannins, smoky oak and good acidity. The underlying flavors, which are pleasant but light, suggest sage, tobacco, cola and blackberries. They turn thin on the midpalate and finish. **87** — (11/15/2002)

Fetzer 1996 Reserve Cabernet Sauvignon (Napa Valley) $30. 88 —P.G. (12/15/2000)

Fetzer 2004 Valley Oaks Cabernet Sauvignon (California) $9. Decently made and properly varietal, this Cab is dry and fruity, with a good backbone of thick tannins. There's a minty streak throughout. **83** —S.H. (5/1/2006)

Fetzer 2003 Valley Oaks Cabernet Sauvignon (California) $9. From this consistent value producer, a nice everyday Cab, with good flavors of blackberries and herbs, and fine, dusty tannins. It turns even richer on the finish, with a lingering taste of oak. **85 Best Buy** —S.H. (12/15/2005)

Fetzer 1999 Valley Oaks Cabernet Sauvignon (California) $10. Here's an herbal, minty Cab with some true varietal notes. It's very dry and clean in the mouth, with melted tannins. Everyday-style price, but with some real elegance, especially in the velvety texture. **86 Best Buy** —S.H. (6/1/2002)

Fetzer 1998 Valley Oaks Cabernet Sauvignon (California) $13. The cherry and smoke aromas wear an attractive olive-herb note, but the fruit could use more weight and definition. Feels like many Merlots, with its very soft, plummy mouthfeel, although the flavor range is darker, showing more blackberry and cassis. Feels a little slick or sappy, but the cassis and licorice flavors on the back end pull this beginner's Cab through. **83** (5/1/2001)

Fetzer 1997 Valley Oaks Cabernet Sauvignon (California) $10. 87 (11/15/1999)

Fetzer 2000 Barrel Select Chardonnay (Mendocino County) $13. Lean and spare, it feels like the grapevines were overcropped, or made to produce too much fruit. You can taste alcohol, and heat and acidity, but what fruit there is just barely falls within citrus territory. Yet it's clean and vibrant. **84** —S.H. (5/1/2002)

Fetzer 1999 Barrel Select Chardonnay (Mendocino County) $14. This well-known, widely-distributed wine offers round apple-toast aromas and a rich, soft mouthfeel. Apple, caramel and orange-tea flavors play on the palate and into the creamy finish, with its big, spicy oak. It's solid and satisfying in a very mainstream manner. **85** (5/1/2001)

Fetzer 2003 Five Rivers Ranch Chardonnay (Monterey County) $13. Has some fruity flavors and a smattering of oak. Finishes with cloying sweetness. **82** —S.H. (5/1/2005)

Fetzer 2000 Five Rivers Ranch Chardonnay (Mendocino County) $14. A new line from Fetzer. This wine has what consumers want, with pretty peach and apple fruit, crisp acidity, lots of toasty, spicy oak and a tiny bit of sweetness. It's a solid delivery at an affordable price. **85** (11/15/2001)

Fetzer 1999 Sundial Chardonnay (California) $9. 81 —S.H. (10/1/2000)

Fetzer 1998 Sundial Chardonnay (California) $9. 86 Best Buy —M.S. (10/1/1999)

Fetzer 2005 Valley Oaks Chardonnay (California) $9. Sweet and sour Meyer lemon flavors dominate this sleek, crisp wine, which shows nuances of tart green apples and a hint of pineapple-laced crème brûlée. It's a little simple, but pretty rich, especially for this price. **85 Best Buy** — S.H. (11/15/2006)

Fetzer 2004 Valley Oaks Chardonnay (California) $9. Has the most delectable fragrance of white peaches and vanilla. In the mouth, the peach flavors are joined by powerful kiwi and pineapple. For all the fruit, the wine is dry, crisp and balanced. **87 Best Buy** —S.H. (12/1/2005)

Fetzer 1998 Gewürztraminer (California) $8. 80 —J.C. (11/1/1999)

Fetzer 2001 Echo Ridge Gewürztraminer (California) $8. I think of summer gardens in full bloom, wicker baskets of perfectly ripened peaches and strawberries, plates of honey and almonds and crushed spices. This clean, semi-sweet wine is like all of them in a glass. **87** —S.H. (9/1/2003)

Fetzer 2000 Echo Ridge Gewürztraminer (California) $10. Sometimes it seems that our white wine industry could become a Chardonnay monoculture. It's good to see that Fetzer isn't abandoning their efforts with other varietals. Sweet peach, mild lychee and spice aromas open this unabashedly sweet and easy wine, with its tangerine flavors and slight spritz on the round palate. Not very complex or sophisticated, but broadly appealing **84** (5/1/2001)

Fetzer 2005 Valley Oaks Gewürztraminer (California) $9. Shows real Gewürz character in the ripe peach, apricot, pineapple and vanilla flavors and blast of cinnamon-nutmeg spice. High acidity balances the sweetness, making the wine pleasantly clean and refreshing. Very nice as a pre-dinner drink, or with Asian food. **85 Best Buy** —S.H. (7/1/2006)

Fetzer 2004 Valley Oaks Gewürztraminer (California) $9. Take an explosion in a fruit store, sprinkle it with dusted cinnamon and nutmeg, then add some white sugar. That's this semisweet wine, which fortunately has good balancing acidity. **83** —S.H. (12/1/2005)

Fetzer 1998 Johannisberg Riesling (California) $8. 83 —J.C. (11/1/1999)

Fetzer 2002 Echo Ridge Johannisberg Riesling (California) $6. Count on Fetzer to have good wines at giveaway prices. This appealing Riesling is delicate in body and very fruity, with ripe flavors of apples, peaches and apricots. It has a spritzy, almost Champagne-like zest, and slight sweetness. It's also easy to drink, with a low 12% alcohol. **87 Best Buy** —S.H. (11/15/2003)

Fetzer 2001 Echo Ridge Johannisberg Riesling (California) $8. Opens with scents of honeysuckle, vanilla, nectarine and smoke, and turns fairly sweet in the mouth, with fruity-berry flavors. Very high-tech clean, with a scour of acidity on the finish. **85** —S.H. (12/31/2003)

Fetzer 1999 Echo Ridge Johannisberg Riesling (California) $10. The sweet grapey aromas on the nose don't mislead, but rather lead to concord-grape and pears-in-syrup flavors. A touch of spritz on the palate adds a little life, and it's at its best well chilled. **82** (5/1/2001)

Fetzer 2003 Merlot (California) $9. Coffee, cherry, earth and herb flavors mark this country-style red wine. It's fully dry, with good supporting acids and tannins. **84** —S.H. (12/15/2005)

Fetzer 2001 Barrel Select Merlot (Sonoma County) $14. Another nice, inexpensive value from this winery. The plum and currant flavors are joined with sage to make a dry wine with character and charm. There's a weightiness in the midpalate that's like more expensive Merlots. **85** — S.H. (4/1/2004)

Fetzer 1999 Barrel Select Merlot (Sonoma County) $13. Round, soft, sweet and supple, this has all the plush berry fruit you'd expect, with a rich overlay of oak. Dry and balanced. This is a super value, and will even benefit from short-term aging. **88** —S.H. (9/1/2003)

Fetzer 1998 Barrel Select Merlot (Sonoma County) $13. The initial aromas of barrel-aging cellar—sweet, dusty wood mixed with plummy, grapey fruit—give way to flavors of black cherries and toast that extend through the supple finish. **85** —J.C. (6/1/2001)

Fetzer 1997 Barrel Select Merlot (Sonoma County) $15. 86 —J.C. (3/1/2000)

Fetzer 2000 Eagle Peak Merlot (California) $9. Black cherry flavors mark this pretty wine, which also has a distinctive herbal edge. The tannins are soft, but good acidity keeps it lively in the mouth, and it finishes clean, fruity and spicy. Nice everyday drinking at a great price. **86 Best Buy** — S.H. (6/1/2002)

Fetzer 1999 Eagle Peak Merlot (California) $13. This entry-level Merlot offers correct plum, black-cherry, toast and smoke aromas. Similar flavors follow, with a soft mouthfeel, but it's not a rich wine. There are no hard tannins, but tangy acids seem to come up on the back end, where it finishes dry, with a dusty cocoa note **84** *(5/1/2001)*

Fetzer 1998 Eagle Peak Merlot (California) $9. 82 —*S.H. (7/1/2000)*

Fetzer 1999 Five Rivers Ranch Merlot (Central Coast) $13. Starts with deep scents of mint, cassis, plum and smoke, with nuances of chocolate and earth. Subtle oak adds spicy notes. The fruit is really forward and ripe. It's a big wine, but the dry, delicate tannins help make it supple and round. **86** *(11/15/2001)*

Fetzer 2004 Valley Oaks Merlot (California) $9. How Fetzer can produce 300,000 cases of this wine, at this price, is a testament to the fine art of blending. This is a smooth, polished, dry Merlot with cherry, vanilla and spice flavors. It's easy to drink and is a nice everyday or party type wine. **85 Best Buy** —*S.H. (11/15/2006)*

Fetzer 2003 Valley Oaks Merlot (California) $9. Fetzer as much as anyone in America is responsible for quaffable, inexpensive vin ordinaire, and this fine Merlot is the latest example. It's dry and balanced, with a polished richness that belies the everyday price. **85 Best Buy** —*S.H. (12/31/2005)*

Fetzer 2000 Reserve Petite Sirah (Spring Mountain) $30. Aims for the fences, swings—and misses. Has some decent, jammy, fruity-berry flavors, and a certain brightness to the mouthfeel, but loses points for the overly simple texture and short, snappy finish. Hard to square with the price. **82** *(4/1/2003)*

Fetzer 2004 Pinot Grigio (California) $9. This wine will appeal to fruit-forward fans who like their whites crisp and ever so slightly sweet. It's rich in apple, citrus, honeysuckle and vanilla flavors, and leaves a pleasant tingle on the palate. **84** —*S.H. (2/1/2006)*

Fetzer 2005 Valley Oaks Pinot Grigio (California) $9. Here's a smooth sipper that shows why PG is so popular lately, and the price is a bargain. It's a dry wine, with complex, tart green apple, citrus and spice flavors. High acidity really makes those tastebuds whistle. **86 Best Buy** —*S.H. (7/1/2006)*

Fetzer 2000 Barrel Select Pinot Noir (Sonoma County) $15. 81 *(10/1/2002)*

Fetzer 1999 Barrel Select Pinot Noir (California) $19. This blend of fruit from Russian River Valley, Carneros and Santa Barbara shows plenty of dark-cherry, spice, and leather Pinot character. Not weighty and very even on the tongue, the flavors show an almost caramel and cola quality. Finishes with even tannins. **86** *(5/1/2001)*

Fetzer 1998 Barrel Select Pinot Noir (California) $15. 87 —*P.G. (12/15/2000)*

Fetzer 1997 Barrel Select Pinot Noir (California) $15. 85 *(11/15/1999)*

Fetzer 1999 Bien Nacido Reserve Pinot Noir (Santa Barbara County) $28. A strong South Coast Pinot filled with spicy flavors and mouth-tingling acids. Very ripe conditions push the tomato fruit toward black cherry, but it still has a bit of herbal, vegetable character. It's dry, and had smooth tannins that make it drinkable now. **91** —*S.H. (12/15/2001)*

Fetzer 2000 Bien Nacido Vineyard Pinot Noir (Santa Maria Valley) $40. Plump, almost slick, this Pinot offers plenty of satisfaction in its dark berry, tar, nut and toasted oak flavors. The palate's black plum, caramel, spice and cedar have great appeal, as do the pepper and spice on the long finish. **88** *(10/1/2002)*

Fetzer 2000 Bien Nacido Vineyard Blocks G + Q Winemaker's Reserve Pinot Noir (Santa Maria Valley) $40. Smoky, meaty and bacony, with a dash of wintergreen, the aromas are bold and intense. The flavors, too, are showy and dramatic, with black cherry and plum blending with leather and mint. Overall, it's a big-boned, heavily extracted wine that just lacks a bit of plushness to the midpalate. **89** *(10/1/2002)*

Fetzer 1998 Bien Nacido Vineyard Reserve Pinot Noir (Santa Barbara County) $28. 87 —*S.H. (12/15/2000)*

Fetzer 2001 Five Rivers Ranch Pinot Noir (Santa Barbara County) $7. You get some real Pinot character in this light and delicately fruity wine. It's very dry, with flavors of raspberries, cherries and blueberries, and is smooth on the palate. **85 Best Buy** —*S.H. (2/1/2004)*

Fetzer 2000 Five Rivers Ranch Pinot Noir (Santa Maria Valley) $13. It's hard to find good Pinot at this price, but here's one. Shows real character

in its raspberry, cherry, tomato, mushroom and smoke aromas and flavors. Silky smooth tannins frame the delicate fruit, and it finishes dry. There's some real elegance and harmony here. **87 Best Buy** *(11/15/2001)*

Fetzer 2000 Five Rivers Ranch Pinot Noir (Central Coast) $14. This plump, low-acid Pinot adds hints of leather to basic strawberry and cinnamon flavors. Toasty notes gather intensity on the finish. It's simple but decent. **84** *(10/1/2002)*

Fetzer 2002 Coro Mendocino Red Blend (Mendocino County) $35. Winemaker Dennis Patton has crafted a dark, dry, solidly tannic wine that's vaguely Zinny, but lusher and rounder, influenced by Grenache's cherry notes. It's a nice barbecue wine now, but will certainly hold and soften for 10 if not 20 years. **90 Cellar Selection** —*S.H. (2/1/2006)*

Fetzer 2001 Coro Mendocino Red Blend (Mendocino) $35. Smooth textured, with ripe tannins that give it good structure. The wine serves up a fairly dense blend of black cherry, raspberry, toast, herb and spice flavors that finish with moderate length at the end. **89** —*J.M. (9/1/2004)*

Fetzer 2005 Valley Oaks Riesling (California) $9. What an aromatic wine this is. It's brimming with wildflower, honey, tropical fruit and vanilla scents, and those flavors reprise in the mouth. The wine is slightly spritzy and off-dry. **84** —*S.H. (7/1/2006)*

Fetzer 2004 Valley Oaks Riesling (California) $9. There's enough residual sugar here to qualify it as a dessert wine, although it's not labeled as such. The flavors are of peaches and vanilla, with good acidity. **82** —*S.H. (12/1/2005)*

Fetzer 2001 Echo Ridge Sauvignon Blanc (California) $8. Clean as a whistle, but on the thin side. Your mouth will easily detect the heat of alcohol, prickly strength of acids and some grassy, citrus flavors, but it's watery in the middle, as possibly you'd expect from an inexpensive wine with 90,000 cases produced. **84** —*S.H. (9/1/2003)*

Fetzer 1999 Echo Ridge Sauvignon Blanc (California) $10. Crisp, grass, mint and mild citrus aromas open this clean, fresh Sauvignon Blanc. It shows mild grapefruit flavors with medium weight, an even texture, and a lightly chalky feel. Not at all sharp or extreme. Finishes short, but brightly. **85** *(5/1/2001)*

Fetzer 1998 Echo Ridge Sauvignon Blanc (California) $8. 86 *(3/1/2000)*

Fetzer 2005 Valley Oaks Sauvignon Blanc (California) $9. Want a solid Sauvignon Blanc at a good price? This one's dry, tart in acidity, and forward in citrus, fig and spicy melon flavors that finish rich and long. What a nice value. **86 Best Buy** —*S.H. (7/1/2006)*

Fetzer 2004 Valley Oaks Sauvignon Blanc (California) $9. Here's a nice wine that's easy and clean, but has some real nuances that make it a repeat sipper. It's dryish, with just a hint of sweetness to the citrus, peach and apple flavors, and balanced with fine acids. **85 Best Buy** —*S.H. (12/1/2005)*

Fetzer 2003 Shiraz (California) $9. Country-style all the way, from the rustic mouthfeel to the earthy and berry flavors. It's a dry wine, clean and well made, and fine for standard Italian fare. **83** —*S.H. (12/31/2005)*

Fetzer 2001 Valley Oaks Shiraz (California) $9. Light, fruity and simple, here's a Shiraz to match up against similar versions from Australia. Minty notes accent crisp red berry flavors, finishing tart and supple. **85 Best Buy** *(9/1/2005)*

Fetzer 1999 Barrel Select Syrah (Mendocino County) $20. Typically dark in color, and what an aroma! You could smell this all day and be happy. Freshly ground coffeebeans, dark unsweetened chocolate, blackberries, pepper, and a wheat-like, barley note: Does that entice you? The flavors are even better. This wine is lush, fruity, ripe, elegant, balanced, soft, rich and long in the finish and sheer pleasure to sip. **92** —*S.H. (5/1/2002)*

Fetzer 1999 Valley Oaks Syrah (California) $9. Good color, and the kind of flavor that many countries would kill for in so inexpensive a wine. It's ripely fruity, with firm tannins and dry acidity. Well-rounded and supple, this is an excellent value in an elegant dinner wine. **86 Best Buy** —*S.H. (9/1/2002)*

Fetzer 1998 Valley Oaks Syrah (California) $11. Very grapey, sweet, jammy berry aromas open this wine, but in the mouth it seems to change identities. There's more tartness and green-herb elements than the nose would indicate. Medium in weight, this wine has a smooth mouthfeel and moderate acidity. The finish offers blackberry and licorice flavors, but with the persistent tartness. **84** *(5/1/2001)*

Fetzer 2004 Valley Oaks Rosé Syrah (California) $9. Dark for a rosé, and full-bodied, this blush Syrah is long and strong in raspberry flavors that finish with a touch of vanilla and white pepper. It's a tasty sipper, nice and dry, almost as robust as Pinot Noir. **86 Best Buy** *—S.H. (12/1/2005)*

Fetzer 2002 Winemaker's Reserve Syrah (Mendocino) $25. Opens with minty, herbal aromas, but also black cherry, coffee and chocolate notes. Tannins are ripe and smooth, yielding a fat, easygoing texture. A solid wine that just comes up a little short on the finish. **85** *(9/1/2005)*

Fetzer 2001 Barrel Select Zinfandel (Mendocino County) $14. Starts off with sweet oak, plum, tar and toast aromas. The wine is medium bodied with pretty blackberry, herb and coffe notes on the follow-up. Tannins are a little rustic and the finish is moderate in length. **87** *—J.M. (11/1/2003)*

Fetzer 1999 Barrel Select Zinfandel (Mendocino County) $12. There are some high-quality vineyards represented in this blend, which includes small amounts of grapes from Sonoma and Amador. It's a succulent and juicy wine. Big, bright jammy berry flavors drink young and assertive and dry, while alcohol and pepper create a bit of a sting through the finish. If you're looking for an inexpensive Zin to show off to foreigners, choose this one. **86** *—S.H. (11/1/2002)*

Fetzer 1998 Barrel Select Zinfandel (Mendocino County) $12. If Springsteen sang about American Zinfandel, this is the wine he'd be drinking. Has those brawny, wild berry flavors, with their edge of pepper and herbs, that define the varietal. Acidity kicks, tannins are well-scrubbed and negotiable. This is rock and roll in the mouth, and downright fun. **90** *—S.H. (5/1/2002)*

Fetzer 1997 Barrel Select Zinfandel (Mendocino County) $14. **88** *—S.H. (12/1/2000)*

Fetzer 1999 Echo Ridge Zinfandel (California) $7. The strawberry and Play-doh—even bubble gum—aromas are actually sweeter than this wine is on the palate, where mild berry and just slightly tart rhubarb emerge. Finishes short and clean; maybe a little less sweet than expected. Serve well chilled. **82** *(5/1/2001)*

Fetzer 1997 Home Ranch Zinfandel (California) $9. **82** *—S.H. (12/1/2000)*

Fetzer 1996 Home Ranch Zinfandel (California) $8. **83** *—S.H. (9/1/1999)*

Fetzer 2004 Valley Oaks Zinfandel (California) $9. A little sharp and rustic, but with simple fare it'll do just fine. Lots of berry-chery flavors, with a rich cocoa edge and smooth tannins, leading to a clean, dry finish. **84** *—S.H. (11/15/2006)*

Fetzer 2003 Valley Oaks Zinfandel (California) $9. Plan a neighborhood fundraiser. Serve pizza, nachos, that sort of thing. Then buy a few cases of this Zin. With its dry tannins and acidity, it will go down easy with Parmesan and olive oil. **84** *—S.H. (12/31/2005)*

Fetzer 2002 Valley Oaks Zinfandel (California) $9. Shows Zin's briary, brambly side, and is intensely dry and a little thin, with moderate alcohol. Ultimately simple, this is a decent simple for pizza or BBQ. **83** *—S.H. (10/1/2005)*

Fetzer 1999 Valley Oaks Zinfandel (California) $10. Sprightly and clean, with full-throttle fruit and spice and a softly tannic texture. The pepper and wild-berry flavors are distinctive and delicious, and nicely dry. Try with pizza, or pasta with spicy sausages. **86 Best Buy** *—S.H. (7/1/2002)*

Fetzer 1998 Valley Oaks Zinfandel (California) $11. This Zinfandel doesn't show either the flavor or mouthfeel it should. There are some indistinct tart-berry flavors, but also a leathery element that needs more fruit to complement it. It's smooth on the palate, but ends a bit woody, and seems tired already. **81** *(5/1/2001)*

FIDDLEHEAD

Fiddlehead 2000 Pinot Noir (Santa Barbara) $50. A amazing wine from this new Santa Barbara appellation. Shows fully ripened blackberry and cherry compote combined with grilled meat, crushed herbs and a hint of tomato. The tannins are as soft as a feather's touch. With delicacy of body matched with full-impact fruit, this wine is a winner. **92 Editors' Choice** *—S.H. (12/31/2002)*

Fiddlehead 1998 Pinot Noir (Willamette Valley) $36. Combines Pinot's silky, sensual quality with forthright flavors that bring to mind cherries, blackberries, tobacco and peppery, earthy spices, with a slight scour of acidity. It's a big, full-bodied wine, but with easy tannins. **87** *—S.H. (12/31/2002)*

Fiddlehead 2001 Fiddlestix Seven Twenty Eight Pinot Noir (Santa Ynez Valley) $38. I got excited smelling this wine. Dramatically toasted oak, mint, cherry compote, mocha, spice aromas, complex and powerful. It's still young now, altogether, a gawky puppy, but in 5 years the lush fruit, oak, brilliant acidity and tannins will meld. Shows great structure. **93** *—S.H. (5/1/2005)*

Fiddlehead 2004 Fiddlestix Vineyard Lollapalloza Pinot Noir (Santa Rita Hills) $50. This is one of the top vineyards in the appellation, sought by anyone who can get the grapes. Co-owner Kathy Joseph has crafted a voluptuous, sensual Pinot that's soft, beguiling and superrich in cherry pie, smoky char and cinnamon-spicy vanilla flavors. It's the kind of Pinot everyone wants to make but usually can't. **94** *—S.H. (11/15/2006)*

Fiddlehead 2001 Lollapalooza Fiddlestix Pinot Noir (Santa Ynez Valley) $50. Pinot that dramatically illlustrates the potential of the Santa Rita Hills. Succulent, intense flavors of black cherries and blueberries, sweet and ripe, are complexed with mocha and dusted with pepper and other spices. All this is encased in a dry silky mouthfeel. **92** *—S.H. (3/1/2004)*

Fiddlehead 1999 Oldsville Reserve Pinot Noir (Willamette Valley) $40. This Burgundian-style baby is a big, dense, chewy wine. It's like a mouthful of grilled meat, ripe beefsteak tomatoes, blackberries and pepper, with a dash of soy. In other words, complex. It's also very dry and fairly tannic, an obvious cellar candidate. **91** *—S.H. (12/31/2002)*

Fiddlehead 2005 Pink Fiddle Rosé Pinot Noir (Santa Rita Hills) $15. Doesn't say so on the label, but the wine comes from Kathy Joseph's Fiddlestix Vineyard, and the wine shows the property's clarity of acidity and wealth of berry and spice flavors. It's very dry, a fun wine yet a serious one too, and certainly among the best California rosés of the vintage. **91** *—S.H. (11/15/2006)*

Fiddlehead 2000 Sauvignon Blanc (Santa Ynez Valley) $22. Drinks soft and gentle, like Pinot Noir, but with assertively attractive flavors of grass, hay, citrus and juniper berry. Crisp, bright acidity adds a kick. This complex, dry white wine comes from the warmer east end of the valley. **88** *—S.H. (9/1/2003)*

FIDDLEHEAD CELLARS

Fiddlehead Cellars 2003 Goosebury Sauvignon Blanc (Santa Ynez Valley) $32. Open knit and plump. The nose offers peach and a bit of banana/vanilla bean. Fairly fruity and citrusy, however, when it comes to the palate. The flavor profile is largely made up of grapefruit, lemon-lime and orange. Finishes with ample power and more citrus. **87** *(7/1/2005)*

Fiddlehead Cellars 2002 Happy Canyon Sauvignon Blanc (Santa Ynez Valley) $22. Buttery and lactic, without much verve. Maybe it's over the hill, or maybe it just isn't as good as what we expected from this label. A flabby wine with sweet, mealy flavors. **81** *(7/1/2005)*

Fiddlehead Cellars 2001 Honeysuckle Sauvignon Blanc (Santa Ynez Valley) $22. Blends floral, buttercup aromas with some stoniness to create an attractive bouquet. Citrusy and zesty, with flavorful accents of gooseberry and lemon. Still lively, but starting to turn south. Get to it quickly. **88** *(7/1/2005)*

FIDELITAS

Fidelitas 2003 Optu Bordeaux Blend (Columbia Valley) (WA) $40. The Optu blends grapes from Conner-Lee, Stillwater, Klipsun, Red Mountain vineyard and a bit of old vine Cabernet from Gamache—all excellent sites. It's two thirds Cabernet, the rest mostly Merlot with 4% Cab Franc. Some nice sweet blackberry and black cherry fruit sails up from the glass; there is a touch of coffee/espresso in the nose also. It's a very pretty wine, accessible and balanced, with light fruit, nicely ripened but with an elegant, feminine personality. **90** *—P.G. (12/31/2006)*

Fidelitas 2003 Cabernet Sauvignon (Walla Walla) (WA) $40. This is 100% Cabernet Sauvignon from old vines. I love the purity of this wine, the way it captures the elegance and the Cabernet character that is so impor-

USA

tant, particularly the black olive and light herb. It seems to be the right combination of New World ripeness and French varietal character; and it comes in at a modest 13.5% alcohol. Sturdy and tart, displaying cranberry and strawberry fruit, lightly spiced with pepper, it finishes with the tannins showing dry, green tea flavors. **89** —*P.G. (12/31/2006)*

Fidelitas 2003 Cabernet Sauvignon (Columbia Valley (WA)) $30. Great vineyard sources (Gamache, Klipsun) start things right, and this pure-blooded, 100% Cab, though pushed to the point of showing some volatile high tones, compensates with saturated flavors of ripe berries, complemented with buttery oak. The silky finish can't help but win your heart. **90** —*P.G. (12/15/2005)*

Fidelitas 2003 Champoux Vineyard Cabernet Sauvignon (Columbia Valley (WA)) $55. The Champoux is muscular, supple and laced with flavors of earth, iron filings, hints of tobacco and dark cherry fruits. It is the deepest and most concentrated of the Fidélitas lineup, with more substance and weight. **91** —*P.G. (12/31/2006)*

Fidelitas 2002 Red Table Wine Cabernet Sauvignon-Merlot (Columbia Valley (WA)) $18. Very well done, this is an almost 50/50 Cab-Merlot mix, showing plenty of sweet/tart berry and red apple flavors. There is a sharp, palate-scrubbing attack, suggesting that this is truly a food wine, but the structure and length speak of a much pricier blend. **88** —*P.G. (12/15/2004)*

Fidelitas 2001 Meritage (Columbia Valley (WA)) $35. A 61% Cab, 25% Merlot, 7% Cab Franc, 7% Malbec blend, it opens with a lovely, inviting nose and shows layered fruits buttressed with chocolate and baking spices. A soft entry and a silky, chocolaty mouthfeel; not a blockbuster, but delicious and beautifully balanced. **89** —*P.G. (12/15/2004)*

Fidelitas 2000 Meritage (Columbia Valley (WA)) $40. A 62% Cab/38% Merlot blend with a dark side. Winemaker Charlie Hoppes goes after the licorice/smoke/tar/toast elements, but matches them to perfectly ripe fruit that is balanced with acid and tannin. Alcohol comes in at a sensible 14.1%, proving that big wines need not be hot and raisiny. Drink this one young. **90** —*P.G. (11/20/2003)*

Fidelitas 2003 Merlot (Columbia Valley (WA)) $25. Sweet and tangy, with clean, pretty cherry and blackberry fruit. This is nicely balanced, with the oak pulled back a bit and the fruit taking the spotlight. A young, supple, silky and well-crafted 100% varietal Merlot. **88** —*P.G. (12/15/2005)*

Fidelitas 2002 Optu Red Blend (Columbia Valley (WA)) $35. The meritage blend is now christened Optu, which recalls an old sci-fi movie but means "best" in Latin. Great vineyard sources include Champoux, Conner Lee and Milbrandt, and the wine, still tight as a drum, mixes herbal Cabernet and Merlot flavors beautifully. It sails along into the midpalate, then seems to hit a wall; perhaps with a bit more bottle edge it could edge up into a higher score. **89** —*P.G. (12/15/2005)*

Fidelitas 2005 Sémillon (Columbia Valley (WA)) $20. All barrel-fermented in used French oak. This is an elegant sipping wine, and the Sémillon shows fig and green plum flavors; it's much less herbal than Sauvignon Blanc. It's a gentle white, not oaky but hinting at toast, and persistent in an appealing style. Perfect for halibut and other seafood; nice with sushi for sure. **89** —*P.G. (12/31/2006)*

Fidelitas 2004 Sémillon (Columbia Valley (WA)) $18. Rich straw-gold, it already is showing signs of oxidation, with scents of wheat, clover, lemon and apple. Rich, round and full-bodied, this drink-now wine offers citrus fruits, figs and melon, with a lovely ripeness. **89** —*P.G. (12/15/2005)*

Fidelitas 2003 Sémillon (Columbia Valley (WA)) $15. Yet another remarkable Sémillon from Washington State; this one is from winemaker Charlie Hoppes, who owns Fidelitas but consults for a half dozen other properties. This is a total wow! wine, packed with flavors of big, plump pear, blood orange, Meyer lemon and Macintosh apple. It puts most Chardonnays to shame for the sheer pleasure it delivers at this price **92 Best Buy** —*P.G. (12/15/2004)*

Fidelitas 2003 Syrah (Columbia Valley (WA)) $35. The are hints of volatility and oxidation, but it makes for a more immediately drinkable Syrah, with plenty of berries and preserves, light touches of toast, and a nice finish of butter and caramel. Drink soon. **89** —*P.G. (12/15/2005)*

Fidelitas 2002 Syrah (Columbia Valley (WA)) $40. A serious, smoky Syrah with herbal and floral nuances, beautifully melded to rich, almost fat varietal fruit. As it breathes there is spicy black pepper and the flavor of roasted meat, all framed by a palate-cleansing lick of tart acid, and a light touch with the oak. Seductive today but measured for medium-term aging. **90** —*P.G. (12/15/2004)*

Fidelitas 2001 Syrah (Yakima Valley) $35. Serious juice. This is perfectly ripened Washington syrah, revealing the bright fruit, vivid acid and spicy concentration that the grape can achieve in eastern Washington. Winemaker Charlie Hoppes has added some attractive dark, licorice and roasted barrel flavors, making a wine that is seductive today but measured for medium term aging. **91** —*P.G. (11/20/2003)*

FIELD

Field 2003 Katarina Cabernet Sauvignon (Alexander Valley) $39. This relatively new brand has sold fruit to established wineries for many years. Now, they're on their own, with grand ambitions. This first, 500-case Cabernet is soft and herbal, with cherry flavors and a good overlay of oak. **84** —*S.H. (12/31/2005)*

FIELD STONE

Field Stone 2003 Cabernet Sauvignon (Alexander Valley) $24. Simple, rustic and raw in acids, with semi-sweet blackberry and cherry jam flavors. **82** —*S.H. (12/1/2006)*

Field Stone 2000 Cabernet Sauvignon (Alexander Valley) $22. Lean and awkward, with thin, cherry-berry flavors and a bit of residual sugar that makes it cloying. That sweetness emphasizes the tough, hard tannins. **82** —*S.H. (5/1/2004)*

Field Stone 2002 Staten Family Reserve Cabernet Sauvignon (Alexander Valley) $40. Lovely young Cab, with that softly tannic, earthy, dried herb and cherry thing that so distinguishes Alexander Valley. The wine has an elegance and refinement that make it fine now for upscale food, but it should age well and improve for a decade. **90 Cellar Selection** —*S.H. (12/1/2006)*

Field Stone 1997 Staten Family Reserve Cabernet Sauvignon (Sonoma County) $38. **93** *(11/1/2000)*

Field Stone 1998 Chardonnay (Sonoma County) $16. **86** *(6/1/2000)*

Field Stone 2000 Staten Family Reserve Chardonnay (Russian River Valley) $22. Extracted and bold, a big wine with ripe flavors of spiced green apples and sweet pears. Spices are Asian, plus some nutmeg and cinnamon. Dry and rich, with a strong overlay of oak. **89** —*S.H. (5/1/2003)*

Field Stone 2003 Merlot (Alexander Valley) $20. Overripe and raisiny, with a sweet-and-sour sharpness. Not a bad wine, but rustic. **82** —*S.H. (12/15/2006)*

Field Stone 1999 Staten Family Reserve Petite Sirah (Alexander Valley) $30. Disappointing, given the vintage and pedigree of the grapes. Opens with tons of smoky oak covering blackberry, cocoa, black cherry and mint aromas and flavors. Loses points for coarseness and a short finish **84** *(4/1/2003)*

Field Stone 2005 Sauvignon Blanc (Alexander Valley) $16. Gets the job done with gooseberry, grapefruit and fig flavors and mouth-cleansing acidity. Basically dry, but there's a honeyed, fruity finish. **85** —*S.H. (12/1/2006)*

Field Stone 2002 Sauvignon Blanc (Alexander Valley) $14. A bit of grass and straw, some lemony citrus, a riper streak of pear and melon and some spices make up this easy, spicy wine. It's dry and brisk with acids, and has some spritziness. **86** —*S.H. (2/1/2004)*

Field Stone 2003 Syrah (Alexander Valley) $22. Cedary and savory on the nose, then delivers cherry-berry fruit accented by leather and more cedar. It's relatively structured for a California Syrah despite not being a heavyweight, so hold it 2–3 years, then drink it over the next five. **86** *(9/1/2005)*

FIELDING HILLS

Fielding Hills 2004 Cabernet Franc (Wahluke Slope) $28. This is lighter, more approachable than the other Fielding reds, with strawberry and cherry fruit and good acidity. Though it does not quite carry the weight of the others, it has wonderful balance, and it is perhaps the most approachable of the new releases, drinking beautifully, with a satiny smooth finish that slides across the palate. Absolutely seamless and poised. **91** —*P.G. (12/31/2006)*

Fielding Hills 2003 Cabernet Franc (Columbia Valley (WA)) $26. The Cab Franc anchors a blend that includes equal parts of Cab Sauvignon, Merlot and Syrah. Here's a quick list of what's going on in this amazing wine: smoke, coffee, spice, currant, cinnamon, chalk, earth, tobacco, cherry, graphite, butter and toast. It is just a flat out beautiful effort. **94 Editors' Choice** —*P.G. (12/15/2005)*

Fielding Hills 2004 Cabernet Sauvignon (Wahluke Slope) $30. Dark, tannic and smoky, this has more tarry tobacco flavor than the other two reds in this series. Muscular, dense and tight, it offers cassis, raspberry and sappy, delicious red fruits. This is very young, very tight, but already nuanced with extraordinary notes of leaf and clean herb. It'll be interesting to see where it goes in 5–10 years. **95** —*P.G. (12/31/2006)*

Fielding Hills 2003 Cabernet Sauvignon (Columbia Valley (WA)) $30. Dark, tannic and saturated, this deeply colored Cabernet shows ripe tannins and dense fruits, dominated by cassis, berry and plum. The oak regimen adds layers of smoke, tar, licorice, and it's all wrapped up in a long, chewy, earthy finish. **93 Editors' Choice** —*P.G. (12/15/2005)*

Fielding Hills 2002 Cabernet Sauvignon (Columbia Valley (WA)) $28. Tight, confident and built upon well-ripened, berry-flavored fruit, this complex, impeccable Cab mixes in notes of iodine, smoke and iron. It suggests what the British call "breed"—a mixture of power and elegance. **90** —*P.G. (6/1/2005)*

Fielding Hills 2002 Cabernet Sauvignon-Syrah (Columbia Valley (WA)) $28. Fairly light, with simple fruit flavors that are a bit overshadowed by the new oak. Perhaps a pullback from 100% new barrels would be worth considering. Nonetheless, this is a very pleasant and good-tasting effort. **88** —*P.G. (11/1/2005)*

Fielding Hills 2004 Merlot (Wahluke Slope) $32. Ripe, tangy berries, consistent with the house style—a tight spine of firm tannin and bright acid. There's a good meaty quality in the midpalate, and plenty of vanilla. I think there is a lot of compact flavor in hiding, right now it's showing a lot of spice (from the 12% Syrah blended in?) and vanilla (from the barrel). **94** —*P.G. (12/31/2006)*

Fielding Hills 2003 Merlot (Columbia Valley (WA)) $28. A phenomenally brilliant effort from this emerging superstar winery. The Merlot is enhanced with 17% Cabernet, 5% Syrah and 2% Cab Franc. You wonï¿?t find Merlot from anywhere else in the country that shows so much supple power and structure. Vibrant fruit is polished to a fine luster with perfectly applied oak ï¿?seasoningï¿? that adds toast, butter, coconut, cedar and smoke, lifted with scents of tobacco, citrus and leaf. You run out of superlatives for this wine. **95 Editors' Choice** —*P.G. (12/15/2005)*

Fielding Hills 2002 Merlot (Columbia Valley (WA)) $28. A new winery, in Washington's emerging Columbia Cascade wine region, whose early releases have been superb. This well-handled Merlot mixes pleasing oak with bright, black cherry fruit, and hints of stone. **91** —*P.G. (6/1/2005)*

Fielding Hills 2004 RiverBend Red Blend (Wahluke Slope) $28. Great color, plush aromas and mouthfeel. It sets up in the mouth with intense, varied flavors including blackberry, black cherry, black licorice and more. The young berry fruit scents are sensational, wrapped tight, and the oak is gently applied (76% new) and lends a pleasing milk chocolate smoothness to the finish. Keeps its focus thanks to acrobatic balance and simply beautiful fruit. **93** —*P.G. (12/31/2006)*

Fielding Hills 2003 Riverbend Red Red Blend (Columbia Valley (WA)) $28. The blend is 40% Cab, 40% Merlot, 15% Syrah and 5% Cab Franc. Supple, juicy, firm and generous all at once, it mixes ripe, plush berries with spicy tannins. Big yet impeccably balanced, despite the mish-mash blending it holds down a firm focus, anchored by exceptional fruit. **93 Editors' Choice** —*P.G. (12/15/2005)*

Fielding Hills 2002 Riverbend Red Red Blend (Columbia Valley (WA)) $28. An emerging trend in Washington is to spice up the standard Bordeaux Cab-Merlot mix with a splash of Syrah; in this instance, 6%. The wine is dark and smoky, yet taut and nervy rather than jammy. Clean fruit and well-managed oak contribute to a lovely, balanced, lively and textured red blend. **90** —*P.G. (6/1/2005)*

Fielding Hills 2004 Syrah (Columbia Valley (WA)) $32. This is classic Washington Syrah; the nose explodes the glass, and it has all the marks of what makes Washington the best in the country. It's big, it's loaded with intense spicy notes, and there are plenty of grace notes of meat and smoke and some of the French stuff going on. Young and packed with flavor, hinting at gravel and soy and a bit of earthy funk. **94** —*P.G. (12/31/2006)*

Fielding Hills 2003 Syrah (Columbia Valley (WA)) $32. A stunning leap forward in quality from the pleasant 2002. This Syrah includes a bit of Cabernet and Merlot; they fill and smooth it out. The wine is supple, silky and plump, with luscious fruit that is wrapped in powerful, toasty/buttery new oak. It makes a big statement; the kind of wine you can't stop reaching for. Absolutely riveting. **94 Editors' Choice** —*P.G. (12/15/2005)*

FIFE

Fife 1997 Cabernet Sauvignon (Napa Valley) $30. **88** *(11/1/2000)*

Fife 2000 Cabernet Sauvignon (Napa Valley) $37. The winemaker swings for the fences and hits a double. This wine, with 25% Cabernet Franc, is unbalanced. There's something awkward about the tannins, which stick out like a sore thumb, and the fruity acids, which leave a bitterness on the finish. May improve with age. **85** —*S.H. (12/15/2003)*

Fife 2001 10th Anniversary Reserve Cabernet Sauvignon (Napa Valley) $32. Dennis Fife brings his talent for rich, gutsy reds to this Cab, a blend of Atlas Peak and St. Helena fruit. It's a big, powerful wine, but elegant and controlled every step of the way. Ripe black currant flavors and substantial oak shadings combine with firm, intricate tannins to produce ageable wine. Drink now through 2013. **92 Cellar Selection** —*S.H. (11/15/2006)*

Fife 1999 Reserve Cabernet Sauvignon (Spring Mountain) $45. Re-released at nearly six years of age. One sniff is all you need to know there's a lot of new, toasted oak here. It's a big, dark, extracted wine, and also a very tannic one, with a deep core of ripe blackberry and blueberry flavors. Despite its age, it still needs time. Best to let it come around by, say, 2008. **91** —*S.H. (10/1/2005)*

Fife 1997 Reserve Cabernet Sauvignon (Spring Mountain) $45. **91** *(11/1/2000)*

Fife 1997 Redhead Vineyard Carignane (Redwood Valley) $19. **90** —*S.H. (3/1/2000)*

Fife 2000 Petite Sirah (Mendocino) $20. Most tasters enjoyed the roasted black fruits, with their hints of spice and solid overlay of smoky oak. The wine is full-bodied and dry in the mouth, with pronounced tannins. It's balanced and rich, but could use extra layers of complexity. **85** *(4/1/2003)*

Fife 1997 Redhead Petite Sirah (Redwood Valley) $24. **89** —*S.H. (10/1/1999)*

Fife 2002 Redhead Vineyard Petite Sirah (Redwood Valley) $24. Beautiful Pet, among the best in California. Stuffed with bigtime berry, plum, cocoa, lavender and coffee flavors, with sturdy tannins, and very dry, it's a wine that will age, although it's approachable now with rich meats and cheeses. **92** —*S.H. (11/1/2006)*

Fife 2000 Redhead Vineyard Petite Sirah (Redwood Valley) $24. A shocker, given this wine's fame. Most tasters faulted it for being overly tart and too oaky, although the fruity-berry flavors are quite tasty and ripe. There was a funky, leathery quality that bothered some. **83** *(4/1/2003)*

Fife 2000 L'Attitude Rhône Red Blend (Mendocino) $20. There are some delicious and complex flavors in this Rhône-style blend, including blackberry, cherry, coffee, chocolate, grilled meat and pepper. For all that, the acidity is low, and the wine could use more uplift and brightness. **86** —*S.H. (12/1/2003)*

Fife 1999 L'Attitude Rhône Red Blend (Mendocino) $20. A Rhône blend, and the wine that best exemplifies the Châteauneuf-style blend that inland Mendocino is hoping will put it on the map. This is magnificent stuff, lusty and full-bodied, with mixed berry flavors that are dominated by the aroma of white pepper. It's dry, with complex, dusty tannins and a round, smooth mouthfeel. Lighter than Cabernet but denser than Pinot

USA

Noir, it strikes a balanced note, and may be one of the most versatile wines around. Cellar Selection. **94 Cellar Selection** —*S.H. (5/1/2002)*

Fife 1997 L'Attitude Rhône Red Blend (Mendocino) $18. 93 —*S.H. (3/1/2000)*

Fife 2001 L'Attitude 39 Rhône Red Blend (Mendocino) $18. Fascinating to taste this alongside Fife's 2002 Redhead Red. Both wines have pretty much the same Southern Rhône blend, although they're from different vintages. L'Attitude is a bigger, more complex wine, thicker and perhaps softer, but everything is deeper and more intriguing. It's one of the best Carignane-based wines I've ever had. **93 Editors' Choice** —*S.H. (11/1/2006)*

Fife 2001 Max Cuvée Rhône Red Blend (Napa Valley) $38. This is the most ageworthy of Fife's current wines, the one to put your money on. Even at this age, it's still drily tough and tannicly astringent. But it's a fine wine, and there is no doubt it has yet to show its stuff. Buried deep is a solid core of blackberry and cherry fruit yearning to get out. This is a wine to buy in multiple bottles, and begin opening in 2009, one by one. Petite Sirah and Syrah. **93 Cellar Selection** —*S.H. (11/1/2006)*

Fife 2002 Redhead Red Rhône Red Blend (Mendocino) $12. Here's Fife's basic Southern Rhône blend. It's a clean, interesting and basically delicious wine, rich in red and black stone fruit flavors that have a chocolaty edge. The more you sip it, the more you like it. **87 Best Buy** —*S.H. (11/1/2006)*

Fife 2005 Redhead Rosé Blend (Mendocino) $12. What a nice rosé this is, elegant, full-bodied and dry. Made from Carignane, it's not especially complex, but shows an array of rose petal, strawberry, Provençal herb, vanilla and spice flavors, wrapped into a silky, crisp texture. 86 —*S.H. (11/1/2006)*

Fife 2000 Redhead Rosé Blend (Redwood Valley) $14. Quite fragrant, with raspberry and strawberry aromas. Fruity, yet dry, and fresh on the palate, it makes a terrific summer quaff. 87 —*J.M. (11/15/2001)*

Fife 2002 Syrah (Mendocino) $20. Seems a bit thinly fruited, but still boasts enough raspberry and cherry fruit to get the job done. It's a lean, focused style, and it finishes with a dry astringency that may or may not improve with age. 83 *(9/1/2005)*

Fife 2002 Syrah (Mendocino) $18. A bit tough and tannic, but noble enough in structure, this Mendocino mountain Syrah has bold plum, blackberry, mocha and herb flavors, and is very dry. It scores high on the deliciousness factor, and is at its best now and for a year or two. 87 —*S.H. (11/1/2006)*

Fife 2001 Syrah (Mendocino) $20. A nice, chewy Syrah with sweet wood-smoked bacon, clove, spicy plum and cherry flavors. The tannins are rich and sweet, and there's a long, fruity finish. 88 —*S.H. (12/1/2004)*

Fife 2001 Max Vineyard Syrah (Napa Valley) $32. Rhône specialist Dennis Fife turns to a vineyard between St. Helena and Calistoga for this Syrah, and the warm vintage has yielded a ripe wine. But Fife has complete control, keeping the rich cherry-chocolate flavors while maintaining a balance of acidity, tannins and dryness. 91 —*S.H. (11/1/2006)*

Fife 1999 Max Vineyard Syrah (Napa Valley) $35. Starts off smelling oaky and spicy, then reveals rich waft of spicy gingerbread and blackberry marmalade aromas and flavors. At nearly five years, the tannins are turning gentle and soft, although there's still some good acidity. 89 —*S.H. (12/1/2004)*

Fife 1999 Old Yokayo Ranch Vineyard Syrah (Mendocino) $35. From warm western slopes over Ukiah Valley, a powerhouse combining audacious fruit with impeccable balance. Concentrated flavors of red and black berries, chocolate, white pepper, bacon, tobacco and coffee are rich, yet with only 13.5 percent alcohol, the wine is balanced and gentle. The mouthfeel is stunning. **95 Editors' Choice** —*S.H. (5/1/2002)*

Fife 2002 Old Yokayo Rancho Vineyard Syrah (Mendocino) $24. This is the Portiest of Fife's Syrahs, in fact the only one with that telltale note of raisiny caramel, which is offputting. The wine is also quite astringent in tannins. It could develop, but it's a tough little puppy right now. 85 —*S.H. (11/1/2006)*

Fife 2000 Old Yokayo Rancho Vineyard Syrah (Mendocino) $30. Has a bit of a reductive character that blows off to reveal sweet cherry and black

raspberry fruit. Finishes very dry, with some firmly gritty tannins. 86 —*S.H. (12/1/2004)*

Fife 1997 Old Yokayo Rancho Vineyard Syrah (Mendocino) $40. Another of our split decisions—tasters couldn't agree on this one. To some it was solid and complex with dark cherry and saddle-leather aromas and flavors, a metallic herb-accented long finish and good grip. Others found it too tart and dry, even thin. Still others found it complex and textured, with game, smoke and chocolate, yet overly woody. You'd best try this yourself. 87 *(11/1/2001)*

Fife 2003 Mendocino Uplands Zinfandel (Mendocino) $18. Soft, slightly heavy and on the hot side, with high alcohol, this burly Zin contains Petite Sirah and Carignane, making it more like those old-fashioned field blends. It has impressively ripe flavors of red and black cherry pie filling, cocoa and spice. 86 —*S.H. (11/1/2006)*

Fife 2001 Mendocino Uplands Zinfandel (Mendocino) $17. A pretty blend of ripe, bright cherry, blackberry, cola, coffee, spice and anise flavors that are couched in good acidity and smooth textured tannins. The finish is moderate in length. 89 *(11/1/2003)*

Fife 2003 Old Vines Zinfandel (Napa Valley) $24. From grapes in the warmer area north of St. Helena comes this soft, polished Zin. It's melted in acids and tannins, but maintains enough balance for the forward, ripe blackberry and cherry pie, coffee and spice flavors. Finishes dry, with some complexity. 88 —*S.H. (11/1/2006)*

Fife 2003 Redhead Vineyard Zinfandel (Redwood Valley) $24. This is the most balanced and enjoyable of Fife's current crop of Zins, a wholesome, complete wine that captures Zin's wild side and tames it. It has the sophisticated structure of a Merlot, with Zin's wild berry, coffee, and spice flavor profile, and is thoroughly dry, without being too alcoholic. 91 —*S.H. (11/1/2006)*

Fife 2001 Redhead Vineyard Zinfandel (Redwood Valley) $24. A leaner style, with smoky, charry, black cherry, licorice, spice, plum, toast, vanilla and herb flavors that weave a measure of complexity. Tannins are firm, and the finish is moderate in length. 87 *(11/1/2003)*

Fife 1997 Redhead Vineyard Zinfandel (Redwood Valley) $24. 91 —*S.H. (5/1/2000)*

Fife 2000 Uplands Zinfandel (Mendocino) $17. Fabulous, absolutely true to its terroir and grape, the wine is the perfect marriage of sun-warmed hillside vineyards and Zin. Round, full-bodied and luscious, filled with juicy flavors of cranberry, black raspberry, black pepper and bitter chocolate. Liquid velvet, this wine will grow with time in the glass. 92 —*S.H. (5/1/2002)*

Fife 2000 Whaler Vineyard Zinfandel (Mendocino County) $20. From benchlands above the Russian River, a gentle giant of a wine. From the dark color to the brooding, peppery aromas, you know it's a big wine. Ripe, full-bodied and extracted, its berry flavors are rich and heady. What's suprising is the balance. Soft, round, mellow and supple, it goes down (as the Burgundians used to say) like Jesus in velvet pants. 92 —*S.H. (5/1/2002)*

FILSINGER

Filsinger 2000 Special Reserve Chardonnay (Temecula) $10. A light and fruity wine. Ripe apple and peach flavors are accented by peppery ginger and cinnamon, and the wine feels round and supple in the mouth. This likeable wine is clean and refreshing, with real varietal character. **87 Best Buy** —*S.H. (4/1/2002)*

Filsinger 1999 Fumé Blanc (Temecula) $7. Combines dry lemon and grapefruit with sweet, extracted fruit-juice flavors that turn apricot-like on the finish. The noticeable sugar defines this thick, syrupy wine. 83 —*S.H. (4/1/2002)*

FIRE STATION RED

Fire Station Red 2003 Shiraz (California) $15. The grapes are from hot areas, like Lodi and Amador, and although the official residual sugar reads dry, the wine tastes very sugary, with cherries. Go figure. From Sonoma Coast Winery. 82 —*S.H. (11/15/2006)*

FIREFALL

Firefall 2000 Lone Meadow Vineyard Rosato di Sangiovese Sangiovese (Fair Play) $10. From a newish appellation in El Dorado County, this is a copper-colored wine with richly sweet strawberry flavors and a peppery streak that lasts into the finish. It's dry enough for the dinner table. Try with cioppino. **85** —*S.H. (9/1/2002)*

Firefall 1999 Lone Meadow Vineyard Syrah (El Dorado) $20. This is a very interesting Syrah and is one to watch in California. The plum, blackberry and rich earth flavors are extremely dry, framed in dusty tannins. It's not a fat, plush wine, but it is complex and layered, a wine that will support foods without stealing the starring role. **90** —*S.H. (12/1/2002)*

Firefall 1998 Lone Meadow Vineyard Syrah (El Dorado) $20. A little austere in the aroma, with earthy, cherry notes. It turns rich, soft and velvety in the mouth, with gentle tannins. There are some pretty cherry-berry flavors, and it's very dry and clean. Will drink well with a wide variety of foods. **85** —*S.H. (7/1/2002)*

FIRESTEED

Firesteed 2004 Pinot Gris (Oregon) $14. Next to the ripe, juicy 2003, the new vintage of Firesteed seems a bit less endowed. Fruit flavors suggest melon and Asian pear, followed by a light note of cinnamon spice. **86** —*P.G. (2/1/2006)*

Firesteed 2003 Pinot Gris (Oregon) $10. Firesteed goes from strength to strength; this is their best Gris to date, enhanced perhaps by the unusually warm vintage. Its ripe fruit tastes like biting into a juicy pear picked right off the tree. Succulent, round and sweetly spicy, with noticeable residual sugar but very appealing semi-tropical flavors. **88 Best Buy** —*P.G. (11/15/2005)*

Firesteed 2000 Pinot Gris (Oregon) $11. Here is a fine effort, widely available (12,000 cases) and well-priced. Stainless steel fermented, it shows crisp, varietal flavors of ripe pear, augmented with a hint of cinnamon. Good focus and length. **88 Best Buy** —*P.G. (2/1/2002)*

Firesteed 2003 Pinot Noir (Oregon) $10. A fine alternative to simple, sweet blush wines is this value Oregon Pinot. The color suggests it is older than an '03, but that just makes it more approachable. Yes it's light, but it's not generic. It offers round varietal flavors of sweet strawberries, hints of herbs and a dash of vanilla. **87 Best Buy** —*P.G. (8/1/2005)*

Firesteed 2002 Pinot Noir (Oregon) $18. Consistent and straightforward, this value brand's mainstream Pinot offers clean, sassy cherry fruit flavors, followed with distinctly herbal notes and some stemmy tannins in the close. **86** *(11/1/2004)*

Firesteed 2001 Pinot Noir (Oregon) $10. Firesteed's 10th vintage shows the consumer-friendly budget brand in top form. Here are tart, varietal flavors, mixing strawberry and sweet cherry fruit. Tannins tend slightly toward earthy, and there is a hint of unripe beet in the finish. But at the price, this is a solid, even fleshy, bottle of good juice. **87 Best Buy** —*P.G. (4/1/2003)*

Firesteed 2001 Pinot Noir (Willamette Valley) $19. Firesteed's mid-tier Pinot benefits from an extra couple of years of bottle age, delivering mature flavors of red fruits, textured with pine resin, herb, lemon oil and a hint of tomato leaf. Elegant and balanced, it's a great choice for those who prefer some age on their Pinot. **88** —*P.G. (8/1/2005)*

Firesteed 1999 Pinot Noir (Oregon) $10. Pale in color, with delicate Pinot-like aromas of strawberry, beetroot, coffee and hard spices. Drinks lightly fruity, spicy and dry. It's a simple, one-dimensional wine, but a very pretty one, and notable for its polished flavors. **84** —*S.H. (8/1/2002)*

Firesteed 1998 Pinot Noir (Oregon) $10. 83 —*M.S. (12/1/2000)*

FIRESTONE

Firestone 2002 Vintage Reserve Bordeaux Blend (Santa Ynez Valley) $32. Raw in acids and tannins, with thin fruit that lets the alcohol poke through, this dry, austere wine just manages to suggest cherries. **82** — *S.H. (12/31/2005)*

Firestone 2001 Vintage Reserve Bordeaux Blend (Santa Ynez Valley) $30. Firestone made real progress with Bordeaux-style wines. This beauty, which is primarily Cab Franc, brims with lush blackberry, sweet cherry

and dark chocolate flavors. While the oak is strong, it's balanced. Feels soft and round, with an ultra-long finish. **90** —*S.H. (10/1/2004)*

Firestone 2003 Cabernet Sauvignon (Santa Ynez Valley) $18. Here's a nice, balanced Cab showing ripe black currant and herb flavors and a bit of oak. Shows some elegance and complexity. **86** —*S.H. (12/1/2006)*

Firestone 2002 Cabernet Sauvignon (Santa Ynez Valley) $18. Simple, dry and fruity, with blackberry, plum, olive, thyme and oak flavors backed up by firm but smooth tannins. Drink now. **84** —*S.H. (11/1/2005)*

Firestone 2001 Cabernet Sauvignon (Santa Ynez Valley) $18. Polished, plump and pretty in cherry and blackberry fruit, this stylish Cab has plenty to like. It's balanced and medium-bodied, with sweet tannins and a clean, easy mouthfeel. **86** —*S.H. (11/15/2004)*

Firestone 2000 Cabernet Sauvignon (Santa Ynez Valley) $18. Stumbles where Santa Barbara Cabs have historically fallen, with green, unripe flavors and tannins and a dry, bitter finish. This wine was not helped by the cool vintage. **83** —*S.H. (8/1/2003)*

Firestone 2001 Chardonnay (Santa Barbara County) $16. Simple and fruity, with fruit cocktail flavors dominated by peaches and sweetened citrus fruits, especially grapefruit. **86** —*S.H. (10/1/2003)*

Firestone 2000 Chardonnay (Santa Barbara) $16. Bright citrus flavors team up with peach, apple and mineral notes. The wine is a bit racy on the finish; overall, it's sleek and lean. **87** —*J.M. (12/15/2002)*

Firestone 2002 Reserve Chardonnay (Santa Ynez Valley) $25. Oodles of flavor just ooze all over the palate, flooding it with tropical fruits, tangerine, spices, smoky oak and vanilla. It's wrapped inside a rich, creamy texture. As sweet as a gooey dessert, yet it's totally dry. **89** —*S.H. (12/15/2004)*

Firestone 2002 Santa Barbara Chardonnay (Santa Barbara County) $16. Citrusy and acidic, with background flavors of peaches and tropical fruits. This is a varietally correct Chard, clean and balanced. It will go fine with scallops or shrimp. **85** —*S.H. (8/1/2004)*

Firestone 1997 Santa Ynez Valley Chardonnay (Santa Ynez Valley) $12. 87 Best Buy —*S.H. (7/1/1999)*

Firestone 2004 Gewürztraminer (Santa Barbara County) $11. Here's a Gewürz that should be easy to identify blind. It's richly aromatic in honeysuckle, lime, cinnamon and spice flavors, with a smoky edge, and drinks fruity and slightly sweet. Good acidity keeps it clean and sharp. **85** —*S.H. (11/1/2005)*

Firestone 2003 Gewürztraminer (Santa Ynez Valley) $10. You'll like the fruity flavors and rich Oriental spices in this dry, crisp wine. It brims with sweet white peach, honeysuckle and cinnamon sugar. A very nice value in Gewürz. **85** —*S.H. (9/1/2004)*

Firestone 2001 Gewürztraminer (Santa Barbara) $9. 87 Best Buy —*J.M. (11/15/2002)*

Firestone 2000 Gewürztraminer (Santa Barbara County) $8. Opens with explosive Gewürz aromas of mingled spices, wildflowers, citrus (especially tangerine rind), and vanilla. The flavors are strong and pronounced, suggesting peaches, sweet lemon, gingery spices and grapefruit. A modest touch of sweetness makes it round and soft. **88** —*S.H. (11/15/2001)*

Firestone 2005 Carranza Mesa Vineyard Gewürztraminer (Santa Ynez Valley) $12. Fermented in stainless steel, and dry, this Gewürz's problem is a lack of fruit. It needs more concentration. **82** —*S.H. (10/1/2006)*

Firestone 2002 Estate Bottled Gewürztraminer (Santa Ynez Valley) $9. Pretty thin sledding here, a watery wine with faint traces of citrus fruits that finish sugary. Hard to find much to praise about it. **82** —*S.H. (3/1/2004)*

Firestone 2003 Merlot (Santa Ynez Valley) $18. Polished and supple, with well-ripened cherry, pomegranate, chocolate, herb and spicy oak flavors wrapped in a soft, mouth-filling texture. Here's a wine to drink tonight. **86** —*S.H. (12/1/2006)*

Firestone 2001 Merlot (Santa Ynez Valley) $18. Equal parts olives and cherries comprise this light-bodied, rather delicately structured Merlot. It's elegant and feminine, and very dry, with a veneer of oak. The cherry theme reprises on the sweet finish. **85** —*S.H. (12/15/2004)*

USA

Firestone 2000 Merlot (Santa Ynez Valley) $18. Smells good and rich, with waves of plum, blackberry, tar and smoke aromas, and the flavors are very similar. Drinks dry and tasty in the mouth, but loses a few points for a gritty tartness through the finish. **85** —*S.H. (8/1/2003)*

Firestone 2001 Reserve Merlot (Santa Ynez Valley) $30. A lovely wine, and the warm vintage conditions ripened the fruit to near perfection. It's succulent in sweet cherry, mocha, leather and oaky, vanilla-spice flavors, and the tannins are rich and soft but complex. A bit soft, and might even benefit from a few minutes in the fridge. **90** —*S.H. (12/15/2004)*

Firestone 1997 Winemaker's Reserve Merlot (Santa Ynez Valley) $25. 84 —*J.C. (7/1/2000)*

Firestone 1997 Riesling (Santa Barbara County) $7. 86 Best Buy —*S.H. (9/1/1999)*

Firestone 2002 Riesling (Central Coast) $8. Light and fresh, with hints of peach, citrus, melon, spice and slate. The wine serves up a refreshing mix for spring and summertime sipping. Fruity on the finish. **86 Best Buy** —*J.M. (8/1/2003)*

Firestone 2001 Late Harvest Riesling (Santa Barbara) $13. 88 Best Buy —*C.S. (11/15/2002)*

Firestone 2005 Vineyard Select Riesling (Central Coast) $10. Semi-sweet in vanilla, honeysuckle and peach fruit, with decent acidity, this wine is a blend of Santa Ynez Valley and Monterey County. **83** —*S.H. (10/1/2006)*

Firestone 2004 Vineyard Select Riesling (Central Coast) $10. This is a nice interpretation of an Alsatian-style Riesling. It's off dry, with ripe peach and wildflower flavors and crisp acids and minerals. Thoroughly clean and vibrant through the finish. **84** —*S.H. (10/1/2005)*

Firestone 1997 Sauvignon Blanc (Santa Ynez Valley) $8. 87 Best Buy —*S.H. (9/1/1999)*

Firestone 2005 Sauvignon Blanc (Santa Ynez Valley) $13. We know that this appellation is friendly to Sauvignon Blanc, and the template is here for a fine one. But this wine's flavors are pretty dilute. **82** —*S.H. (10/1/2006)*

Firestone 2004 Sauvignon Blanc (Santa Ynez Valley) $12. Here's a nice summer white that offers up plenty of fruity flavor, and won't break the bank. Shows spearmint, lemon and lime, peach and vanilla fruit that drinks pretty dry, with a good backbone of acidity. **84** —*S.H. (11/1/2005)*

Firestone 2003 Sauvignon Blanc (Santa Ynez Valley) $12. Bright edged and tangy on the palate, this serves up plenty of fresh gooseberry, lemon, grapefruit and herb flavors. It's fresh and light, with a minerally finish. **87** —*J.M. (9/1/2004)*

Firestone 2002 Sauvignon Blanc (Santa Ynez Valley) $12. A thin, acidic wine smelling and tasting of nail polish and grapefruits, with a scouring mouthfeel. It has a little richness, but there are hundreds of wines at the same price, or less, that are better. **83** —*S.H. (12/15/2003)*

Firestone 2001 Sauvignon Blanc (Santa Ynez Valley) $12. Fresh and lively, with bright-edged lemon/lime flavors and a zingy, citrus finish. Crisp and clean at the end. **87** —*J.M. (9/1/2003)*

Firestone 2000 Sauvignon Blanc (Santa Barbara County) $10. Smells like sweetened lemonade, a combination of honey and citrus fruits with a sprinkling of cinnamon and vanilla. Tastes like lemonade, too—the unsweetened variety—with refreshing acidity. The finish is clean and zesty. An apéritif-type wine. **85** —*S.H. (11/15/2001)*

Firestone 2003 Reserve Sauvignon Blanc (Santa Ynez Valley) $25. Clean and lemony, with custard and butterscotch to the nose. Pretty and citrusy if not particularly deep or complex, with blasts of grapefruit and fresh peach peeking through. Quite easy to like, but limited, with pineapple and citrus taking you home. **87** *(7/1/2005)*

Firestone 2003 Syrah (Santa Ynez Valley) $18. Here's a good, honest country-style wine. It feels handmade, with a ruggedness and slightly sweet finish, but the fruit is polished and ripe and the finish is smooth and clean. **83** —*S.H. (7/1/2006)*

Firestone 2002 Syrah (Santa Ynez Valley) $18. Briary, herbal notes accent sweetly ripe notes of black cherries in this bouncy, medium-weight quaffer. Bright acids provide zest, making the wine finish crisp and clean. **85** *(9/1/2005)*

Firestone 2001 Syrah (Santa Ynez Valley) $18. A dark, intense Syrah that stains the sides of the glass, and smells and tastes as rich as it looks. Bursts of white pepper shoot out, with underlying notes of blackberry and plum, smoky oak, sautéed mushrooms, espresso and herbs. It's dry, but complex and assertive. **90** —*S.H. (2/1/2004)*

Firestone 2000 Syrah (Santa Ynez Valley) $18. Inky-dark, a big, thick wine that erupts with white pepper and tobacco aromas, and is quite tannic at the moment. There's some good blackberry fruit way down deep. The wine is very dry and well made, with a refined mouthfeel. It demands rich foods like spicy lamb. **88 Best Buy** —*J.M. (11/15/2002)*

FISHER

Fisher 2002 Cameron Bordeaux Blend (Napa Valley) $50. An odd wine. It's one of the most overtly sweet Bordeaux blends from Napa I've had in quite some time. Seems to have residual sugar, and also a slightly Porty note. **84** —*S.H. (5/1/2005)*

Fisher 2002 Coach Insignia Cabernet Sauvignon (Napa Valley) $70. This is a tremendous young wine, enormous in fruity stuffing. It's fairly tannic, but the Grenache-like cherry, cassis, plum and fudgy chocolate flavors are so powerful, so evocative, nothing could mask them. Grilled steak will tame it, but this is a good cellar candidate to open between 2008 and 2015. You can also decant for a few hours. **94 Cellar Selection** —*S.H. (12/15/2006)*

Fisher 2001 Coach Insignia Cabernet Sauvignon (Napa Valley) $65. Opens with complex aromas of cassis and new smoky oak, and turns lush and smooth when it hits the palate, yet at times seems almost too ripe. Gorgeous now, and should improve through 2015. **90** —*S.H. (5/1/2005)*

Fisher 2000 Coach Insignia Cabernet Sauvignon (Napa Valley) $75. The question about this wine is, will it age? Now it's firm and hard with tannins and acids, and not too pleasant. But you'll find rich, sweet blackberry and cherry fruit on the finish. Then there's the fine balance of tannins, acids and oak. My hunch is, it's a keeper. **90** —*S.H. (4/1/2004)*

Fisher 2001 Coach Insignia Chardonnay (Sonoma County) $32. This very complex wine is a blend of grapes from various parts of the county. It shows a myriad of flavors ranging from tropical tree fruits to limes and crisp, green apples, and has been well-oaked. The texture is creamy and opulent. Don't chill it too much, because you'll lose some of the high-end nuances. **93** —*S.H. (4/1/2004)*

Fisher 1998 Coach Insignia Chardonnay (Sonoma County) $25. 88 *(6/1/2000)*

Fisher 1997 Coach Insignia Chardonnay (Sonoma County) $25. 89 —*S.H. (11/15/1999)*

Fisher 2003 Mountain Estate Chardonnay (Sonoma County) $45. This is a very peculiar Chard. The new oak is powerful, acidity is high despite partial malo, and there's a strong impact from sur lie aging. All this manipulation has resulted not in complexity but in a heavy-handed wine. **84** —*S.H. (11/1/2005)*

Fisher 2004 Mountain Estate Vineyard Chardonnay (Sonoma County) $56. Napa-based Fisher has a new Chardonnay vineyard in Sonoma, 1,300 feet up, and these Dijon clones have produced an intense wine. The grapes were picked very ripe, and the wine is huge in pear and crème brûlée flavors, with zesty acidity. Impressive for its size and interest. You keep reaching for another glass. **92** —*S.H. (11/1/2006)*

Fisher 1999 Paladini Vineyards Chardonnay (Carneros) $45. Ripe orange and papaya, spice, graham cracker and smoke are a few of the adjectives tasters used to describe the nose of this delightful wine. Though rich and open on the palate, it never gets loose or sloppy. A great chalk element and spice accents nicely offset the rich fruit foundation. Buttered toast and nutty, leesy notes mingle with pineapple on the long, finely balanced back end. **92** *(7/1/2001)*

Fisher 1997 Whitney's Vineyard Chardonnay (Sonoma County) $45. This estate vineyard wine's complex nose melds mineral, spice and lime aromas with herb and floral notes. It handles the disparate elements gracefully, showing body but not weight, and has a soft, almost tender mouthfeel. There's a touch of floral sweetness in the mouth—as on the nose—offset by earthy, mineral flavors on a lithe frame. This wine shows real subtlety, but leaves us wishing for more depth. Finishes light, dry and flinty. **88** *(7/1/2001)*

Fisher 1997 RCF Merlot (Napa Valley) $28. 89 —*S.H. (12/31/1999)*

Fisher 1996 Coach Insignia Red Blend (Napa County) $30.90 —*S.H.* *(2/1/2000)*

FISHEYE

Fisheye 2004 Cabernet Sauvignon (California) $8. A bit minty and tart, but with enough cherries and spices to satisfy. There's something easy and fun about this wine. It's almost as gulpable as Beaujolais. **84** —*S.H. (12/1/2006)*

Fisheye 2005 Pinot Grigio (California) $8. A country-style wine that drinks nice and clean, with brisk acidity framing slightly sweet grapefruit juice flavors. For everyday sort of fare. **84 Best Buy** —*S.H. (12/1/2006)*

Fisheye 2005 Sauvignon Blanc (California) $8. You'll find lots of ripe fig, grapefruit and melon fruit in this crisply acidic wine, and while there's a hit of vanilla and honey on the finish, it's basically dry. Nice and refreshing apéritif. **84 Best Buy** —*S.H. (12/1/2006)*

Fisheye 2004 Shiraz (California) $8. Rough and ready wine here. Call it country style, with a big, exuberant burst of cherry, raspberry, cola, cocoa and pepper flavors. Fine with everyday fare. **83** —*S.H. (12/1/2006)*

FITZPATRICK

Fitzpatrick 1999 Grenache (El Dorado County) $17. There are intense black cherry aromas, pure and simple, in this very dry and fairly tannic wine. Your tongue sticks to the palate while picks up a solid core of that cherry fruit. Doesn't seem like an ager, so its best to consume it early, with big, rich foods, and let those tannins and acids cut through the fats and oils. **85** —*S.H. (12/15/2001)*

Fitzpatrick 1999 Tir Na Nog Red Blend (El Dorado) $20. An unusual blend of Sangiovese, Zinfandel and Nebbiolo, the name is Celtic for a mythological town under the sea. Unfortunately the wine has some very real problems, among them unevenly ripened grapes that put tea-like, green flavors right next to super-extracted fruity ones. It's also awkwardly sweet. **81** —*S.H. (5/1/2002)*

Fitzpatrick 2000 Syrah (Fair Play) $20. A decent, common wine, the kind that's kept the world going since time immemorial. Plenty of ripe cherry-berry flavors, clean, and meant for immediate consumption. Turns a bit rough and jagged in the finish. **85** —*S.H. (6/1/2003)*

Fitzpatrick 2001 Zinfandel (Fair Play) $21. Coffee, toast, tea, raspberry, black cherry and spice are all up front here in this pretty, yet robust, Zin. It's spicy bright, zippy on the palate and serves it all up on smooth tannins. **87** *(11/1/2003)*

FIVE RIVERS

Five Rivers 2003 Cabernet Sauvignon (Paso Robles) $10. Soft and flavorful, with cocoa, sage and blackberry flavors, this Cab has the merit of being dry and moderate in alcohol. It's a nice sipper at a fair price. **84** —*S.H. (3/1/2006)*

Five Rivers 2002 Cabernet Sauvignon (Paso Robles) $10. This textbook Paso Cabernet is soft, although fairly tannic, with very ripe flavors of blackberries, chocolate and coffee. It's simple, but so balanced and clean, it's just yummy. **85 Best Buy** —*S.H. (12/1/2005)*

Five Rivers 2001 Cabernet Sauvignon (Central Coast) $10. It's soft and smooth, with leafy, herbal accents to the mixed berry and tomato fruit. On the light side, but easy to drink and a good value. **85 Best Buy** *(12/16/2005)*

Five Rivers 2004 Chardonnay (Monterey County) $10. Lots of oak flavoring on this modestly fruity wine. It's dryish, with the flavor of canned peaches and vanilla. **82** —*S.H. (12/1/2005)*

Five Rivers 2003 Chardonnay (Monterey County) $10. A very nice Chard, especially at this price. Smooth and creamy, with good acids framing intensely ripe flavors of pineapple, marzipan and cinnamon spice, leading to a long finish. **85 Best Buy** —*S.H. (10/1/2005)*

Five Rivers 2003 Merlot (Central Coast) $10. Jammy, rough and tannic in the way of a country wine, but there's no doubting the powerfully ripe

black cherry and blackberry fruit that stars here. It's a simple, everyday sipper that's priced fairly. **84** —*S.H. (4/1/2006)*

Five Rivers 2002 Merlot (Central Coast) $10. This simple wine opens with plum sauce and oak aromas, then turns soft, dry and heavy in the mouth. It's fully dry. Not bad for less demanding occasions. **83** —*S.H. (12/1/2005)*

Five Rivers 2005 Pinot Grigio (Monterey County) $10. Tastes like a cool-climate SB with the grapefruit and gooseberry flavors, but the acidity is higher than you'll generally find in that varietal, and there's a tangy, clean dryness that absolutely scours the palate. A lovely cocktail sipper, or try with mussels. **84** —*S.H. (8/1/2006)*

Five Rivers 2005 Pinot Noir (Central Coast) $13. There are some really good vineyards in the blend, including Bien Nacido and Laetitia, but somehow the wine doesn't do them justice. It tastes simple and one-dimensional, with jammy, semi-sweet cherry and cola flavors. **82** —*S.H. (12/31/2006)*

Five Rivers 2004 Pinot Noir (Santa Barbara County) $11. This is a simple wine, but there's some good stuff going on at this price. The aroma's just great, although it falls off in the mouth, turning a little thin. A nice, dry Pinot. **83** —*S.H. (12/1/2005)*

Five Rivers 2003 Pinot Noir (Santa Barbara County) $10. A little hot and rubbery, with earthy, coffee flavors that turn cherryish on the finish. Dry and silky texture. **83** —*S.H. (10/1/2005)*

FIVE STAR CELLARS

Five Star Cellars 2003 Syrah (Walla Walla (WA)) $28. Unanimous agreement among our panel regarding this wine: It's good, serviceable Syrah, with tart blackberry fruit outlined in oak. Has some coffee and leafy notes, but lacks a great deal of complexity. **84** *(9/1/2005)*

FLEMING JENKINS

Fleming Jenkins 2005 Victories Rose Wine Rosé Blend (San Francisco Bay) $20. Nice and refreshing in acidity. A delicately structured, clean blush wine whose black cherry, apricot, licorice and spice flavors emerge as the wine warms in the glass. 100% Syrah; it's rich enough to have with steak or beef. **86** —*S.H. (12/1/2006)*

Fleming Jenkins 2005 Syrah Rosé Syrah (San Francisco Bay) $17. Simple and tasty A delicately structured wine with good acidity and a silky texture. The raspberry, strawberry and spicy vanilla flavors finish very fruity. **85** —*S.H. (12/1/2006)*

FLOODGATE

Floodgate 2000 Pinot Noir (Anderson Valley) $30. This sturdy, opaque wine opens with aromas of dark fruits, offset by herb and smoky oak. It's dark all the way through, with earth and bitter chocolate accents. This shows good structure, closes with smooth tannins and should improve over the next couple of years. **87** *(10/1/2002)*

FLORA SPRINOOGS

Flora Springs 1997 Trilogy Bordeaux Blend (Napa Valley) $45. 93 *(11/1/2000)*

Flora Springs 2003 Trilogy Cabernet Blend (Napa Valley) $60. Trilogy used to be made from three Bordeaux varieties; hence the name. The '03 is all five, dominated by Cab Sauvignon. The wine is a little hard now, keeping itself aloof due to the tannins. Yet it has deep, blue and black fruit flavors and a Margaux-like elegance and harmony, and should develop quite well over the next 10 years. **91 Cellar Selection** —*S.H. (9/1/2006)*

Flora Springs 2002 Trilogy Cabernet Blend (Napa Valley) $60. No longer made from just three varieties, this Trilogy has all five Bordeaux grapes. It's complex but young in cassis and oak, with a dry, dusty spread of tannins. Those tannins will play well now with well-marbled smoky, grilled beef, but the wine should hold through 2010. **91** —*S.H. (12/1/2005)*

Flora Springs 2003 Cabernet Sauvignon (Napa Valley) $30. Here's a good Napa Cab at a decent price that will take some cellar age. Mainly from Rutherford grapes, it's showing some stiff tannins, but, with polished cherry, herb and oak flavors, it drinks well now, and should develop for five years. **87** —*S.H. (12/15/2006)*

Flora Springs 2002 Cabernet Sauvignon (Napa Valley) $30. Flora Springs has a lot of vineyard acreage, but they also have many special Cabernet bottlings. This is a good wine, but seems to have been made from the leftovers. Simple, dry and fruity. **84** —*S.H. (12/1/2005)*

Flora Springs 2001 Cabernet Sauvignon (Napa Valley) $30. Nice and easy Cabernet, with a real touch of class. This wine is dry and balanced and a little tannic, and the herb and currant flavors are splashed with a sweet perfume of oak. **86** —*S.H. (10/1/2004)*

Flora Springs 2000 Cabernet Sauvignon (Napa Valley) $30. Opens with tight, young aromas of herbs and oak. Feels smooth and velvety going in, but once the taste hits the palate, it's lean and herbal. Tannins take over and dominate through the dry finish. Not going anywhere, but well-made. **85** —*S.H. (11/15/2003)*

Flora Springs 2002 25th Anniversary Cabernet Sauvignon (Napa Valley) $150. This is certainly a good wine, ripe and delicious in cherry, black currant and chocolate flavors, with rich, intricate tannins and a long, rich finish. It's luscious, but very soft, and doesn't seem likely to age. **87** —*S.H. (12/31/2005)*

Flora Springs 2000 25th Anniversary Celebration Cabernet Sauvignon (Napa Valley) $300. Yes, you read it right. Three hundred bucks a magnum. What you get is a rather soft, simple wine, not without its charms, but a major disappointment. Flavors of blackcurrants, cassis and dried herbs are framed in plenty of toasty oak. Falls flat on the palate, with lackluster acidity and tannins. Not likely to age well. **85** —*S.H. (12/15/2003)*

Flora Springs 2002 Holy Smoke Vineyard Cabernet Sauvignon (Napa Valley) $85. Marches to a different beat. Something about the aroma brings to mind dry, hot summer days when the hills smell of dust and eucalyptus. Turns a lot fruitier in the mouth, with cherries and blackberries and firm, sturdy tannins. Elegant now, and should develop beyond 2010. **91** —*S.H. (10/1/2005)*

Flora Springs 2001 Holy Smoke Vineyard Cabernet Sauvignon (Napa Valley) $85. A plump, sensual wine, so pretty and voluptuous, it's impossible not to love. Just oozes sweet, desserty black currant and Indian pudding flavors, lavishly spiced with toasty vanilla. Best enjoyed in its precocious youth. **91** —*S.H. (10/1/2004)*

Flora Springs 2002 Out-of-Sight Vineyard Cabernet Sauvignon (Napa Valley) $85. The least of Flora Springs' impressive single-vineyard '02s, a tannic, rather herbacous wine suggesting blackberries, but still a very good wine. It's bone dry, showing an austerity now that might soften after five or six years. **88** —*S.H. (10/1/2005)*

Flora Springs 2001 Out-of-Sight Vineyard Cabernet Sauvignon (Napa Valley) $85. This is a tannic, acidic puppydog of a wine. It's not showing its best now, coming off as rather tight and tense. The question is, will it age? The best evidence is a rich core of blackberry and cherry fruit that hits midpalate and really kicks in on the finish. Best after 2008. **89** —*S.H. (10/1/2004)*

Flora Springs 2002 Rutherford Hillside Reserve Cabernet Sauvignon (Napa Valley) $100. Showing the best structure of Flora Springs' impressive quartet of '04 vineyard desigated Cabs, this is a firm, well-sculpted wine whose pedigree stands out, but it needs time. It's a big, tannic, closed wine, dry and astringent. But there's a gigantic heart of blackberry fruit, and I would be surprised if this wine doesn't turn into a real beauty by 2010. **94** —*S.H. (10/1/2005)*

Flora Springs 2001 Rutherford Hillside Reserve Cabernet Sauvignon (Napa Valley) $100. The winery's most expensive Cab is its most tannic and complex. Clearly designed for long-term cellaring, it highlights oak, acids and youthful tannins. Even so, the massive black currant and cherry fruit erupts, seizing control and lasting through a long finish. Despite the size, the balance and harmony guarantee aging. Drink now through 2020. **94** —*S.H. (10/1/2004)*

Flora Springs 1999 Rutherford Hillside Reserve Cabernet Sauvignon (Napa Valley) $100. Ripe and fruity, with intense and penetrating black-currant flavors and a spicing from toasty oak. Quite dry, and a bit acidic, leading to a tart finish. A bit austere now, sort of a Johnny-one-note, but could gain in complexity down the road. **87** —*S.H. (12/31/2002)*

Flora Springs 1997 Rutherford Hillside Reserve Cabernet Sauvignon (Napa Valley) $65. 89 *(11/1/2000)*

Flora Springs 1996 Trilogy Cabernet Sauvignon (Napa Valley) $45. 94 *(11/15/1999)*

Flora Springs 2002 Wild Boar Vineyard Cabernet Sauvignon (Napa Valley) $85. Perhaps even more closed and tannic than the Hillside Reserve, a big wine with a good future. Oozes ripe, pure black currant flavors, well-oaked, and is totally dry. Give it until 2008, then try again. **92** —*S.H. (10/1/2005)*

Flora Springs 1999 Wild Boar Vineyard Cabernet Sauvignon (Napa Valley) $60. This vineyard is in the Pope Valley section, a warm, eastern part of Napa. The wine is delicious and impeccably made, but a little heavy, with notes of raisins, especially in the aroma, and a finish dominated by sweet dark chocolate. The oak overlay is elaborate, if a trifle obvious. Seems expensive for the quality. **87** —*S.H. (11/15/2002)*

Flora Springs 1998 Wild Boar Vineyard Cabernet Sauvignon (Napa Valley) $60. Light, elegant and sweet, as succulent as a chocolate cherry bonbon. It has the lip-smacking quality of a fine candy, a blast of stone fruit that coats the mouth in unguent sweetness and then lingers there for a while. **89** —*S.H. (6/1/2002)*

Flora Springs 1996 Wild Boar Vineyard Cabernet Sauvignon (Napa Valley) $40. 89 *(9/1/2000)*

Flora Springs 2001 Wild Boar Wineyard Cabernet Sauvignon (Napa Valley) $85. A study in balance from the warm Pope Valley region. Shows flamboyant blackberry and chocolate fruit, but has a masculine, firm edge from the tannins and acids, and is also well oaked. In fact, those tannins are big enough to age it for a decade or more. **91** —*S.H. (10/1/2004)*

Flora Springs 2000 Poggio del Papa Cabernet Sauvignon-Sangiovese (Napa Valley) $35. A lush super Tuscan blend from hilly Pope Valley vineyards. Smells very ripe, like sun-warmed wild berries just picked, and turns velvety smooth and flavorful in the mouth. The tannins are considerable, and the wine needs aging through 2005, or to be drunk with rich Italian fare. **88** —*S.H. (5/1/2003)*

Flora Springs 2002 Chardonnay (Carneros) $25. Here's a great food Chard. It's not one of those overblown, oaky wines, but has apple and white peach flavors with overtones of stony minerals and dried herbs. Finishes with a scour of tart acidity. **88** —*S.H. (12/15/2004)*

Flora Springs 2004 Barrel Fermented Chardonnay (Napa Valley) $25. Flora Springs has made this wine for many years, keeping the price pretty much the same. It's still a sophisticated bottle of Chardonnay, dry and fruity and, as the designation suggests, rich in toasty oak notes. **87** —*S.H. (7/1/2006)*

Flora Springs 2003 Barrel Fermented Chardonnay (Napa Valley) $22. A nice Chard, with lively acidity and a modest coating of oak that frames peach and apple flavors. Easy to drink, and fine by itself or as a backup to fresh-cracked crab. **85** —*S.H. (10/1/2005)*

Flora Springs 2001 Barrel Fermented Reserve Chardonnay (Napa Valley) $26. Still oaky, leesy and delicious, this perennial fave is richly packed with spicy citrus, apple, peach and pear fruit this vintage. It feels round and creamy in the mouth, with a tingle of acidity. The finish has the taste of sweetened lemons. **90** —*S.H. (12/15/2002)*

Flora Springs 2000 Barrel Fermented Reserve Chardonnay (Napa Valley) $25. Flora Springs leaped to the top with this wine back in the 1980s, and it's still one of Napa's best, at a decent price. It's super-lush, just packed with apple, peach and tangerine fruit and an overlay of smoky oak. The lush, creamy mouthfeel is highlighted by nice, crisp acidity. **92** —*S.H. (5/1/2002)*

Flora Springs 1998 Barrel Fermented Reserve Chardonnay (Napa Valley) $23. 85 *(6/1/2000)*

Flora Springs 1998 Lavender Hill Vineyard Chardonnay (Napa Valley) $30. 85 *(6/1/2000)*

Flora Springs 2002 Select Cuvée Chardonnay (Napa Valley) $35. Big, bold and delicious, a full-throttle Chard that's drenched with new oak notes of vanilla, spice and smoky char. Below that, the pear and pineapple flavors float in a creamy texture that's enhanced with good acidity. Give it a year to knit together. **90** —*S.H. (5/1/2004)*

USA

Flora Springs 2003 Select Cuvée Chardonnay (Napa Valley) $35. From the pretty golden color, to the powerful aromas of tropical fruits and toasty oak, to the full-throttle flavors and creamy texture, this is a wonderful Chard. It has complexities that unravel as the wine warms in the glass. **91** —*S.H. (10/1/2005)*

Flora Springs 2000 Trilogy Meritage (Napa Valley) $60. When this wine was first produced it was a blend of three Bordeaux varietals, but long-time winemaker Ken Deis has since expanded his palate. This year's version is mainly Cabernet Sauvignon and Merlot, with some Cabernet Franc and Malbec. A young, dense wine with significant tannins, it is marked by an overlay of well-charred oak, but the core of cassis suggests ageability. **91** —*S.H. (11/15/2003)*

Flora Springs 2003 Merlot (Napa Valley) $25. Dry and balanced, this Merlot has blackberry, mocha and anise flavors and well-developed tannins, with a bite of acidity in the finish. Drink now and for the next two years. **86** —*S.H. (12/1/2005)*

Flora Springs 2002 Merlot (Napa Valley) $25. A lovely Merlot, a bit on the light side, with pure flavors of cherries complexed with smoky oak. Feels rich in tannins in the mouth. Clean and balanced. **87** —*S.H. (9/1/2004)*

Flora Springs 2001 Merlot (Napa Valley) $22. Seems kind of ordinary, a fruit-driven wine that's good without being exciting. Tasty and dry, with ripe tannins. The blackberry flavors fall off in the middle palate, but the fruitiness is reprised on the finish. **86** —*S.H. (12/1/2003)*

Flora Springs 2000 Merlot (Napa Valley) $22. Dark, rich and juicy, this wine goes the extra mile to achieve real depth and complexity. It's easy to get big, ripe fruit in California, and this wine has it in spades. What's hard is adding layers of flavor and texture. Dry, with finely ground tannins, this is a white-tablecloth wine. **91** —*S.H. (11/15/2002)*

Flora Springs 1999 Windfall Vineyard Merlot (Napa Valley) $50. This is a weighty wine of early drinkability and charm, with the mouthfeel of a good Cabernet, but with silkier, more accessible tannins. There's a rich, peppery earthiness to the sweet blackberry fruit. Not a blockbuster, it exhibits class, finesse and that elusive quality called style. **91** —*S.H. (6/1/2002)*

Flora Springs 2001 Pinot Grigio (Napa Valley) $12. Made Alsatian style, which is to say dry, but the ripe fruit is distinctly Californian. It suggests fresh green apples, drizzled with lemon and lime zest, and notes of honey and smoke. But there's no oak at all here. The wine could benefit from higher acidity, to give it backbone. **85** —*S.H. (9/1/2003)*

Flora Springs 2000 Pinot Grigio (Napa Valley) $12. Here's a delicious summer sipper that's affordable, too. It's brimming with rich floral, citrus and vanilla aromas. Very bright and fruity, with soft tannins and a pretty bite of crispness. **85** —*S.H. (11/15/2001)*

Flora Springs 2000 Lavender Hill Pinot Noir (Napa Valley) $35. Like 'em juicy but not simple? The cherry, cola, toast and licorice profile of this solid medium-weight Pinot is flavorful and dense. Smoky accents and herb notes add complexity, and the wine finishes full with blackberry and espresso notes. A bit bulky, but there's a lot going on here. **87** *(10/1/2002)*

Flora Springs 1998 Lavender Hill Pinot Noir (Napa Valley) $33. **87** *(10/1/2000)*

Flora Springs 1999 Lavender Hill Vineyard Pinot Noir (Napa Valley) $33. Here's a wine with great bones: nicely structured with firm tannins and good supportive acidity. It's not light and flabby, but it is very drinkable. Flavors? Think of cola laced with black-cherry juice with a dash of Worcestershire. It's very dry, and the long finish turns spicy. **88** —*S.H. (2/1/2001)*

Flora Springs 2001 Trilogy Red Blend (Napa Valley) $60. Comes down on the tough side, with tannins that bury the fruit. Clearly a young, rather aggressive wine, but one whose deep core of black cherry and blackberry fruit has good potential. Cellar for a good six years. **90** —*S.H. (9/1/2004)*

Flora Springs 1999 Trilogy Red Blend (Napa Valley) $60. Trilogy used to be a formula blend of three varietals, but this year it's Cabernet Sauvignon, Merlot, Cabernet Franc and Malbec. This is Flora Springs' flagship wine, and a very good one. It's a flashy wine. The fruit is ripe, the oak is notable, the tannins testify to the best vineyard practices. **92** —*S.H. (11/15/2002)*

Flora Springs 1998 Sangiovese (Napa Valley) $17. **90** —*S.H. (12/15/1999)*

Flora Springs 1999 Sangiovese (Napa Valley) $16. This winery has always taken a light-handed approach to Sangiovese, preferring a delicate, drinkable wine to a ponderous one. The trend continues with this appealing release. It's deeply flavored with berry and spice, in a dry, airy package with just enough weight to qualify as a serious wine. Try it with almost anything, it's that versatile. **90** —*S.H. (7/1/2002)*

Flora Springs 1999 Poggio del Papa Sangiovese (Napa Valley) $35. California has struggled to produce a super-Tuscan that was at once deeply flavored and classically structured. With this wine, Flora Springs raises the bar. It has all the fruity flavors you expect from the vintage, with the architecture of a fine Napa red. The tannins and acids are softly intricate. Mainly Sangiovese and Merlot, with a dollop of Cabernet Sauvignon. **91** —*S.H. (7/1/2002)*

Flora Springs 1998 Sauvignon Blanc (Napa Valley) $12. **89** —*S.H. (3/1/2000)*

Flora Springs 2004 Soliloquy Sauvignon Blanc (Oakville) $25. Soliloquy was a hit from the very start and the wine has become steadily more interesting and complex as the sourcing shifted to Oakville. Now 100% single-vineyard Sauvignon Blanc from the Musqué clone, it's dry, elegant and crisp, with a ripe finish to the fig, Key lime and white peach flavors. Sur lies aging adds a mouthwatering creaminess. **93 Editors' Choice** —*S.H. (7/1/2006)*

Flora Springs 2003 Soliloquy Sauvignon Blanc (Napa Valley) $25. Soft and almost lactic, with vanilla, sweet melon and borderline asparagus aromas. This one sits on the brink of overripeness, where oak and honey flavors vie with creamy fruit to make a full-bodied whole. Finishes with a spot of butterscotch, melon and floor polish. **88** *(7/1/2005)*

Flora Springs 2002 Soliloquy Sauvignon Blanc (Napa Valley) $25. A bright textured, medium-bodied wine that serves up a pleasing blend of lemon, melon, herb and grapefruit flavors. A bit steely edged, it's clean and fresh on the finish. **88** —*J.M. (9/1/2004)*

Flora Springs 2001 Soliloquy Sauvignon Blanc (Napa Valley) $25. One of the first proprietarily-named Meritage whites, and always interesting. This year's version, which is 100 percent Sauvignon Blanc, showcases rather citrusy, grassy fruit and tart acids, courtesy of the Musque clone. Softening comes from oak and lees aging, which lends a creamy roundness to the penetrating flavors. Finishes with a clean, elegant flourish. **88** —*S.H. (10/1/2003)*

Flora Springs 2000 Soliloquy Sauvignon Blanc (Napa Valley) $22. One of the first, and still one of the best, white Meritages, the wine is rich and complex. The dry flavors are of citrus fruits and grassy hay with richer notes of fig and melon. No oak at all, and good acidity provides freshness and brightness. There used to be Sémillon in the blend, but for now, the wine is 100% Sauvignon Blanc. **90** —*S.H. (9/1/2003)*

Flora Springs 1999 Soliloquy Sauvignon Musqué (Napa Valley) $18. Fragrant, with aromas of pear, pink grapefruit and wet stones. Similar flavors carry onto the palate, which also tosses out some banana and melon. The finish is thinner than might be expected given the fact that this has a soft, big body. **87** *(8/1/2002)*

FLOWERS

Flowers 2002 Andreen-Gale Cuvée Chardonnay (Sonoma County) $44. Fabulous intensity of flavor, all lemon custard, vanilla and oak. It is rich and mouthfilling, but with a good, hard minerality and tartness to the finish. **90** —*S.H. (5/1/2005)*

Flowers 2001 Andreen-Gale Cuvée Chardonnay (Sonoma Coast) $44. This is an intense, brilliantly focused wine that displays near perfect balance. The flavors are of fresh, savory lemondrop veering into spicy mango and are well oaked, while the acidity is superb, lending a steely tang to the richness. The finish lasts a full minute. This classic coast Chardonnay will hold and slowly become nutty and complex through the decade. **94** —*S.H. (8/1/2004)*

Flowers 2002 Andreen-Gale Cuvée Pinot Noir (Sonoma Coast) $49. Very ripe, in fact, shows signs of overripeness in the raisiny notes accompanying the plums and coffee. The mouthfeel is heavy and Syrah-like, but

USA

with a silky texture. Good wine but needs more delicacy and breed. **87** —*S.H. (5/1/2005)*

Flowers 2001 Andreen-Gale Cuvée Pinot Noir (Sonoma Coast) $48. Big, extremely ripe, a bit hot in alcohol, definitely full-bodied for a Pinot, with humungous fruit and a scour of tough tannins. It was very hot in the coastal hills this vintage and the wines were bigger than usual. If you can get past the size, this wine is luscious. **92** —*S.H. (8/1/2004)*

Flowers 1999 Camp Meeting Ridge Pinot Noir (Sonoma Coast) $50. Full-bodied, with loads of earth, smoke and tomato. The color is nearly violet and the flavors match: There's an unmistakable sweetness to it, from the welcoming front end through to the warm, kirsch-packed finish. For anyone who loves a sweet, jammy California-style Pinot, look no further. **91** *(10/1/2002)*

Flowers 2000 Keefer Ranch Pinot Noir (Green Valley) $44. Opens with rich aromas of plum, oak, cocoa and green hay. Medium-weight and balanced with fine acidity and good tannic structure, this has potent, palate-filling plum, chocolate and spice flavors. The finish shows deep fruit and plush tannins. Best from 2004–2009+. Cellar Selection. **92 Cellar Selection** *(10/1/2002)*

FLYING GOAT CELLARS

Flying Goat Cellars 2000 Pinot Noir (Santa Maria Valley) $30. Spicy, raspberry and cherry aromas lead off in this full-bodied Pinot. It's loaded with exotic cinnamon, clove and nutmeg flavors. Quite viscous, with a tangy edge on the finish. **88** —*J.M. (6/1/2004)*

Flying Goat Cellars 2003 Dierberg Vineyard Pinot Noir (Santa Maria Valley) $34. Tannic, heavy and a bit hot, and not offering much pleasure now, although it's properly dry, and there's a solid core of black cherry fruit. Finishes with a grapeskin bitterness. **84** —*S.H. (8/1/2005)*

Flying Goat Cellars 2004 Rancho Santa Rosa Vineyard Pinot Noir (Santa Rita Hills) $40. The vineyard is Foley's, and whether or not it's due to superior viticulture, this is the best of Flying Goat's current trio of Pinots. It has the acidity to balance the ultraripe, almost sweet, cherry pie filling and cocoa flavors. Still, the extreme heat of the vintage seems to have impacted the wine, which would benefit from greater delicacy. **87** —*S.H. (11/1/2006)*

Flying Goat Cellars 2003 Rancho Santa Rosa Vineyard Pinot Noir (Santa Rita Hills) $36. Nice silky, elegant mouthfeel to this wine, with its practically nonexistent tannins but crisp acidity. It's not quite ripe, offering a mélange of cherry tomato, rhubarb and cola flavors in addition to deeper cherry ones, but it has complexity and style. **87** —*S.H. (8/1/2005)*

Flying Goat Cellars 2004 Rio Vista Vineyard Pinot Noir (Santa Rita Hills) $42. This is a ripe, superextracted, ponderous Pinot Noir. The massive cherry pie filling, raspberry tart, root beer and cola flavors are so big and sweet, they exceed the limit of what Pinot should be, losing balance in favor of power. **84** —*S.H. (11/1/2006)*

Flying Goat Cellars 2003 Rio Vista Vineyard Pinot Noir (Santa Rita Hills) $38. Very dark, and rather heavy in texture, this is an earthy wine. The flavors suggest coffee and black cherries. **84** —*S.H. (8/1/2005)*

Flying Goat Cellars 2004 Rio Vista Vineyard 2A Pinot Noir (Santa Rita Hills) $38. Made from the old Wadenswil clone, this is a heavy, soft Pinot. It's very ripe in cherry, raspberry and chocolate flavors, and could use greater acidity to lift and brighten it. **84** —*S.H. (11/1/2006)*

FLYNN

Flynn 1998 Pinot Noir (Willamette Valley) $16. **83** —*M.S. (12/1/2000)*

Flynn 1998 Cellar Select Clos d'Or Pinot Noir (Oregon) $10. **81** —*M.S. (12/1/2000)*

FOG MOUNTAIN

Fog Mountain 2000 Chardonnay (California) $8. Nice wine for the price, with plenty of rich apple and lime flavors. Balanced and harmonious, the acids make it clean and refreshing. The finish is long and citrusy. **86 Best Buy** —*S.H. (5/1/2003)*

FOLEY

Foley 2001 Chardonnay (Santa Maria Valley) $35. A smooth textured wine, with pretty caramel, apricot, peach, melon, butterscotch, herb and citrus flavors. Fairly rich, yet clean on the finish. **88** —*J.M. (2/1/2004)*

Foley 2004 Barrel Select Chardonnay (Santa Rita Hills) $38. Racy acidity characterizes this ripely fruity, oaky wine. It's strong in pineapple, apricot and tangerine cream flavors, while plenty of new French oak contributes a spicy, vanilla-infused smokiness. A bit obvious, but certainly a delicious, captivating Chardonnay. **91** —*S.H. (11/1/2006)*

Foley 1999 Barrel Select Chardonnay (Santa Barbara County) $38. One of a back-to-back pair of strong performances from Foley, this wine opens with well-defined herb, caramel and cream nose. Ripe apple and toasted oak flavors round out the rich, buttery palate. The citrus and peach finish goes on forever. Shows complexity, but with a straight-ahead style that make it a real pleaser. Great now. **91** *(7/1/2001)*

Foley 2000 Barrel Select Bien Nacido Vineyard Chardonnay (Santa Barbara County) $27. Toasty oak, creamy lees and citrusy acidity are the stars of this bracing wine, although there is a deep current of papaya underneath. It is very dry, and the taste of earth and mushroomy herbs shows up on the finish. On the lean side, but not without interest. **89** —*S.H. (12/1/2003)*

Foley 1999 Bien Nacido Vineyard Chardonnay (Santa Maria Valley) $35. This is a full, round and juicy wine, with pronounced orange, tangerine and pineapple aromas and flavors. Wonderful hints of vanilla and spice accent the bright tangy core of citrus fruit. A wine that's big and packed with fine ripe fruit, but isn't over the top. **91** *(7/1/2001)*

Foley 2004 Clone 76 Chardonnay (Santa Rita Hills) $35. There's massive flavor in this wine, made from young Dijon clone vines. It's a real bomb blast of juicy apricot, pineapple custard, white peach nectar, tapioca and honeysuckle, with a tangy mineral flourish. Almost too rich for its own good, but retains balance, with good acidity. **90** —*S.H. (11/1/2006)*

Foley 1999 Dierberg Vineyard Chardonnay (Santa Maria Valley) $35. This very rare, single-vineyard Chardonnay has distinct vanilla, golden delicious apple, banana and peach flavors—a nice mix of sweet and sour, but some tasters found searing acidity and a sharp metallic note. Finishes tart, dry and long with a bracing edge capable of cutting right through your fried calamari and spicy sauce. Only 132 cases produced. **87** *(7/1/2001)*

Foley 2004 Rancho Santa Rosa Chardonnay (Santa Rita Hills) $30. From this large vineyard in the heart of the appellation comes this tight, young Chard. It's high in acidity, creating a tart mouthfeel containing mineral, Meyer lemon, green apple, apricot, kiwi and oak flavors. Don't drink it too cold, because it grows more complex as it warms in the glass. **90** —*S.H. (10/1/2006)*

Foley 2003 Rancho Santa Rosa Chardonnay (Santa Rita Hills) $30. Brilliant in acids, with tremendous, explosive fruit flavors, this Chard can easily handle its coating of toasty new oak. Pineapple custard, mango, nectarine, peach pie, lime zest, vanilla and Asian spice flavors come together in a deliciously creamy texture. This massive, magnificent wine showcases the proven terroir of its appellation for Chardonnay. **94 Editors' Choice** —*S.H. (12/15/2005)*

Foley 2002 Rancho Santa Rosa Chardonnay (Santa Rita Hills) $30. There's an earthy tightness to this wine (as well as high acidity and a mineral-laden stoniness) that will not appeal to fans of big, ripe Chards. Consumers need to know that before buying. That said, it is elegant. **88** —*S.H. (5/1/2005)*

Foley 2001 Pinot Noir (Santa Maria Valley) $38. This fabulous young wine is just beginning to hit its prime. You can taste the freshness in the citrusy acids that underlie subtle hints of pomegranates, cherries and oak. It's an elegant, delicate and complex wine. **92** —*S.H. (5/1/2005)*

Foley 2004 Rancho Santa Rosa Pinot Noir (Santa Rita Hills) $38. Ripe, rich and silky, with black cherry, cranberry, cola, leather, cocoa, heirloom tomato, balsamic and spice flavors, this is a heck of a good Pinot. It's dry and balanced, a fine showcase of its celebrated terroir. The juicy acidity is a bit raw, but the wine should mellow by 2007. **91** —*S.H. (11/1/2006)*

USA

Foley 2003 Rancho Santa Rosa Pinot Noir (Santa Rita Hills) $38. Sort of a junior version of Foley's block designations, this wine nonetheless is complex and delicious. It's broad and ripe in cherry, cola, spice and oak flavors, with a nice, silky mouthfeel and brisk acidity. **87**—*S.H. (12/15/2005)*

Foley 2002 Rancho Santa Rosa Pinot Noir (Santa Rita Hills) $38. This Pinot shares much in common with Foley's Barrel Select. It's ripe in cherries one minute, then stalky green hits. Silky, dry and firm, but the green fruit reprises on the finish, and turns bitter. **85**—*S.H. (5/1/2005)*

Foley 2003 Rancho Santa Rosa Barrel Select Pinot Noir (Santa Rita Hills) $50. If you want to know why Santa Rita Hills Pinot is so celebrated, just take a sip. Dry, elegant, complex and totally satisfying, the wine has a myriad of cherry, black raspberry, cola, rhubarb, coffee and spice flavors and the silkiest, most satiny texture imaginable, with crisp acids. Beautiful now and through 2007. **93**—*S.H. (12/15/2005)*

Foley 2002 Rancho Santa Rosa Barrel Select Pinot Noir (Santa Rita Hills) $50. There's a touch of less-than-ripe green flavors in this wine, but it's still a pretty Pinot, with enough cherries to satisfy. Balanced, complex and silky, with a lush mouthfeel. It's a beauty. **90**—*S.H. (5/1/2005)*

Foley 2003 Rancho Santa Rosa Block 4A Clone 2A Pinot Noir (Santa Rita Hills) $45. Co-released with the '03 Barrel Select, this Pinot is more fruit-forward, more immediately accessible and a little sweeter in cherries and vanilla. It is, in a word, fabulous. If you're looking for a Pinot that's flashy right now, this is the one. Defines the world-class status of Santa Rita Pinot. **93**—*S.H. (12/15/2005)*

Foley 2003 Rancho Santa Rosa Block 4D Pommard Clone Pinot Noir (Santa Rita Hills) $45. Compared to Foley's unbelievable Dijon Clone bottling, this one's more tannic and less immediately flashy. It's a dry, full-bodied wine with an elegantly silky texture, but the cherry flavors are a little locked down, although the wine softens and sweetens with airing. A good charbroiled steak should be a fine partner. **92**—*S.H. (12/15/2005)*

Foley 2002 Rancho Santa Rosa Block 4D Pommard Clone Pinot Noir (Santa Rita Hills) $45. Among the brilliant expressions of this terroir-based appellation is this old-clone Pinot. It's complex and deep in earthy, mushroomy essence, with a dry grip, and needs time to express its sweet cherry-cocoa core. This compelling wine will improve through 2010. **94**—*S.H. (5/1/2005)*

Foley 2003 Rancho Santa Rosa Block 5C Dijon Clone Pinot Noir (Santa Rita Hills) $45. This is really good wine, fabulously rewarding from first sniff to last sip. It defines coastal California Pinot, and it possesses that appellation's brisk acids and balanced flavors. Cherries, cranberries and mulberries vie for position against mushrooms, fresh garden herbs and earth, with oak playing a supporting role. What's hard to get across is the wine's complexity and sheer deliciousness. Drink over the next two years. **95 Editors' Choice**—*S.H. (12/15/2005)*

Foley 2002 Rancho Santa Rosa Block 5C Dijon Clone 667 Pinot Noir (Santa Rita Hills) $45. I like this wine for its delicate texture and silky mouthfeel, and the interplay of complex earth, mushroom, coffee, rhubarb and bitter tea flavors. It's not a fruit bomb, and that's the whole point. It's unrelievedly dry except for a finish of sweetness from fruit and oak. **92**—*S.H. (5/1/2005)*

Foley 2004 Rancho Santa Rosa Clone 2A Pinot Noir (Santa Rita Hills) $45. Forward and jammy in blackberry, cherry, pomegranate and coffee flavors, this is certainly a rich, ripe wine, dry and balanced. As good as it is, this single-clone Pinot seems a bit one-dimensional. **87**—*S.H. (11/1/2006)*

Foley 2004 Rancho Santa Rosa Pommard Clone Pinot Noir (Santa Rita Hills) $45. Earthier than Foley's Clone 2A Pinot, with rich mushroom and soy notes underneath the coffee and sweet red cherry flavors, this is a dry wine, with good acidity to balance out all that fruit. It's a little raw and juicy now, a young wine that needs some bottle time to pull itself together. Best 2007 through 2010. **89**—*S.H. (11/1/2006)*

Foley 2000 Santa Maria Hills Pinot Noir (Santa Maria Valley) $31. Opens with aromas of cherries, cranberries, beets, sautéed mushrooms, dried herbs and raw meat, along with the smoke and vanilla of oak barrels. The palate impression is tart, with underlying black cherry flavors and a silky mouthfeel. Drink now. **91**—*S.H. (2/1/2004)*

Foley 2003 Sauvignon Blanc (Santa Barbara County) $16. A raw, juicy, brisk and utterly delightful wine. Acids hit big-time, and the lemon and gooseberry flavors wake the taste buds up. **90 Editors' Choice**—*S.H. (5/1/2005)*

Foley 2000 Sauvignon Blanc (Santa Barbara) $17. This big-bodied wine is full of smoke, toast and custard in the nose, sure signs of barrel fermentation or aging. The mouth is packed with thick, custardy citrus fruit, which renders it a bit like orange-tinged flan. Fortunately, it retains its acids, which keeps it well balanced despite the heavy oaking it went through. **89** *(8/1/2002)*

Foley 2003 Rancho Santa Rosa Syrah (Santa Rita Hills) $30. Mixed berries, sprinkled with white and black pepper, are carried along on a smooth, creamy texture and linger delicately on the finish. Delicious, but it almost seems too clean. **88** *(9/1/2005)*

Foley 2002 Rancho Santa Rosa Syrah (Santa Rita Hills) $30. Here's a wine that went wrong somewhere. It's dark, dry and full-bodied, but is unexpectedly earthy and green in the mouth, and while it has smooth tannins, it's not going anywhere. **84**—*S.H. (5/1/2005)*

FOLEY & PHILLIPS

Foley & Phillips 2005 Rose Wine Rosé Blend (Santa Ynez Valley) $12. This is from the talented team at Foley, a Rhône blend of Syrah, Cinsault and Grenache. Pale in color, the wine is extremely dry, with high acidity and nuanced flavors of rose petals, dried herbs, grapefruit zest and dusty white pepper. One of the best rosés of the vintage, it's terrific with bouillabaisse. **90 Best Buy**—*S.H. (11/1/2006)*

FOLIE A DEUX

Folie a Deux 1999 Harvey Vineyard Barbera (Amador County) $8. This is a deeply fruity, smooth wine with some nuance, without necessarily being complex, if that make any sense. It's aromatic, bone-dry and tart, with lip-smacking black cherry flavors, and some hefty but negotiable tannins. **88**—*S.H. (12/15/2001)*

Folie a Deux 1997 Cabernet Sauvignon (Napa Valley) $24. **89**—*S.H. (7/1/2000)*

Folie a Deux 2000 Cabernet Sauvignon (Napa Valley) $26. Quite good for the vintage, a dense, concentrated wine with beautifully soft, complex tannins. Blackberry and cassis flavors drink dense and dry, with balanced acidity. Possesses that elusive but unmistakable quality of elegance and finesse. This is a big, flamboyant wine, but skillfully vinified; good acidity keeps things bright and crisp. **90**—*S.H. (11/15/2003)*

Folie a Deux 2000 Cabernet Sauvignon (Napa Valley) $26. Unripe and tough, with weedy, herbaceous flavors and hard tannins. **83**—*S.H. (2/1/2005)*

Folie a Deux 1999 Cabernet Sauvignon (Napa Valley) $26. Intensely varietal, with black currant aromas and flavors edged with smoky oak. Dry, rich and complex. The tannins temporarily hide the fruit, but the chewy core shows up in the middle palate. A big wine meant for the cellar. Try after 2006. **91**—*S.H. (11/15/2002)*

Folie a Deux 1998 Cabernet Sauvignon (Napa Valley) $24. **83**—*S.H. (12/15/2000)*

Folie a Deux 2000 Private Reserve Cabernet Sauvignon (Napa Valley) $45. Tough, herbal and hard in the mouth, this tannic wine offers modest blackberry flavors and a dose of oak. It turns syrupy-sweet on the finish. **84**—*S.H. (2/1/2005)*

Folie a Deux 1999 Private Reserve Cabernet Sauvignon (Napa Valley) $40. Expensive, but the equal of the cults. One whiff and you're in heaven, with its gorgeous aromas of cassis and blackcurrants, fine smoky oak and vanilla, and chocolaty mint. The flavors don't disappoint. Hard to describe the density and concentration of fruits and herbs. This is great Cabernet, superb now but an obvious cellar candidate. **94 Editors' Choice**—*S.H. (11/15/2003)*

Folie a Deux 1998 Reserve Cabernet Sauvignon (Napa Valley) $36. **84**—*S.H. (12/15/2000)*

Folie a Deux 1997 Reserve Cabernet Sauvignon (Napa Valley) $36. **87** *(11/1/2000)*

Folie a Deux 1997 Champagne Blend (Napa Valley) $18. 88 —*S.H.* (9/1/2000)

Folie a Deux 1995 Brut Champagne Blend (Napa Valley) $18. 90 Best Buy —*S.H.* (12/15/1999)

Folie a Deux 1997 Chardonnay (Napa Valley) $18. 84 (6/1/2000)

Folie a Deux 2000 Chardonnay (Napa Valley) $22. The underlying fruit suggests flavors of citrus and peaches, but the wine is so oaky, it floods the palate with woody spice, smoke, vanilla and caramel, and the creamy, nutty notes of barrels and sur lie aging. The finish is steely enough to support the richness. 87 —*S.H.* (12/15/2002)

Folie a Deux 2001 Chenin Blanc (Napa County) $18. Here's a rarity, a high-end Chenin Blanc made Burgundian style. Drinks rich, creamy and layered, with broad flavors of white peaches and honeydew melon. This is a good alternative to Chardonnay. 86 —*S.H.* (9/1/2003)

Folie a Deux 1999 Frost Glacon du Raison Gewürztraminer (Mendocino) $31. Thick, viscous—almost oily—and so rich it makes a fine dessert on its own. The wine offers lush peach, apricot, vanilla, spice, tangerine and toast flavors, finishing long. 91 —*J.M.* (12/1/2002)

Folie a Deux 1997 Merlot (Napa Valley) $24. 88 —*S.H.* (7/1/2000)

Folie a Deux 2003 Menage a Trois Red Blend (California) $12. This blend of Zinfandel, Merlot and Cabernet sure is fun. It's gentle in body, with ripe, polished berry-cherry and cocoa flavors and a smattering of smoky oak. A great house red. 86 Best Buy —*S.H.* (12/31/2004)

Folie a Deux 1999 Sangiovese (Napa Valley) $18. There's something about this wine that suggests tarter sauce. Maybe it's the peppery-hot fruitness in the crisp acidity or the dry tartness. Whatever, its a saucy little wine, clean as a whistle. It will go well with any sort of tomato based dish. Drink it young. 86 —*S.H.* (12/15/2001)

Folie a Deux 2001 Sémillon (Amador County) $18. Ripe and juicy, with forward flavors of white peach, lemon and spicy green apple. Nice acids frame the pretty fruit flavors, and the wine finishes swift and clean. 85 —*S.H.* (12/15/2002)

Folie a Deux 1999 Lani's Vineyard Syrah (Amador County) $26. Deep sweet-tart fruit, smoke and spices enliven the nose of this bright, mid-weight Sierra Foothills wine. Cedar accents the cherry fruit, and the chewy mouthfeel has good texture. Woody tannins come on a bit strong on the finish. Best cellared for a couple of years, this is a good case for the future of Syrah in them thar' hills. 88 (11/1/2001)

Folie a Deux 2003 Menage a Trois White Blend (California) $12. Bright and forward in fruit, with orange peel, ripe peach, sweet lime and figgy flavors. Nice and balanced, with good acidity. Moscato, Chardonnay and Chenin Blanc. 86 Best Buy —*S.H.* (12/31/2004)

Folie a Deux 1997 Zinfandel (Amador County) $18. 87 (9/1/1999)

Folie a Deux 2001 Zinfandel (Amador County) $17. The feral mountain grapes manage to keep their personality despite the attempts of this fine Napa producer to bring a Cabernet-like balance to the wine. It's like a Cab in the rich, soft tannins and balance, but those wild, brambly notes win out. 86 —*S.H.* (2/1/2005)

Folie a Deux 2000 Zinfandel (Amador County) $18. Styled with the weight of a fine Cabernet, with modulated alcohol and tannins and a full-bodied but elegant texture. But it's Zin all the way, with the blast of briary, wild berry flavors, pepper and other spices. Seems to have a little bit of residual sugar in the finish that makes it ideal for sauce-slathered barbecue. 88 —*S.H.* (9/1/2003)

Folie a Deux 1999 Bowman Zinfandel (Amador County) $26. Wow, is this good Zin, packed with lip-smacking cherry, white chocolate and tobacco flavors. It's technically dry, but the ripe sweetness of Sierra sunshine fills every sip. The alcohol is high, but this cheerful wine is so good and pure, you hardly notice. Great vineyard, great winemaking, great California wine. 91 —*S.H.* (11/1/2002)

Folie a Deux 1999 Bowman Vineyard Zinfandel (Amador County) $26. A beautiful Zin, among the best ever, with its near perfect balance of fruit, alcohol and tannins. Gorgeous flavors burst on the palate, black cherries, blackberries, cassis, white chocolate, espresso and cinnamon, to name a few. The wine is totally dry, but so ripe, it tastes sweet. Completely addictive, a joy for lovers of dry, balanced Zins, and a triumph for the winemaking team. 94 —*S.H.* (3/1/2004)

Folie a Deux 1997 Bowman Vineyard Zinfandel (Amador County) $24. 88 (9/1/1999)

Folie a Deux 1998 D'Agostini Vineyard Old Vine Zinfandel (Amador County) $22. Full, textured nose mixes cherries and herbs, very clean and complex. The vines are almost 80 years old, and yield a briary, wild berry quality to the fruit. Balanced and complex wine, which unfolds in lingering layers through a long, satisfying finish. 90 —*P.G.* (3/1/2001)

Folie a Deux 1997 D'Agostini Vineyard Old-Vine Zinfandel (Amador County) $20. 86 (9/1/1999)

Folie a Deux 1999 DeMille Vineyard Old Vine Zinfandel (Amador County) $24. Fruit, fruit, fruit all the way, and loads of it. Blackberry, black cherry, plum and even loganberry. Spice, too. Cinnamon, tobacco, anise, clove, pepper. It's balanced, rich, harmonious, about as fine as Sierra Foothills Zin gets. That's saying a lot. 90 —*S.H.* (12/15/2001)

Folie a Deux 1998 Eschen Vineyard Old Vine Zinfandel (Fiddletown) $24. Lots of juicy, jammy aromas here, with earthy tobacco notes, and clove accents from American oak. It's rich and extracted, with wild berry and spice flavors, but quite high—almost searing—acidity. The finish is raspy, thanks to those acids and some tough, dry tannins. 84 —*S.H.* (8/1/2001)

Folie a Deux 1997 Eschen Vineyard Old Vine Zinfandel (Fiddletown) $22. 88 (9/1/1999)

Folie a Deux 1997 Harvey-Binz Vineyard Zinfandel (Amador County) $28. 90 —*S.H.* (9/1/2000)

Folie a Deux 1998 La Grande Folie Old Vine Zinfandel (Amador County) $44. A fair amount of the cuvée is from the 130-year-old Grandpère vineyard, which lends a soft, herbal, grassy undertone to the wine. From elsewhere comes bright cherry fruit, and the wine seems a little disjointed, though it may come together in time. Some nail polish in the nose carries through to the finish. 87 —*P.G.* (3/1/2001)

Folie a Deux 2000 The Wild Bunch Vineyard Old Vine Zinfandel (Amador County) $22. Dense and concentrated, a brilliant Zinfandel that stuns with its beautiful array of flavors and near perfect balance. Dry, with soft but luscious tannins, and amazing flavors, including black cherry liqueur and a core of Belgian chocolate that lasts forever on the finish. A bit hot on the finish, with 15 percent alcohol, but who cares? 93 —*S.H.* (3/1/2004)

Folie à Deux 2004 Ménage à Trois Rosé Blend (California) $12. This rosé is an easy-drinking bottling that has enough fruity complexity and bright acidity to recommend it. A blend of Merlot, Syrah and Gewürztraminer, it's a creamy melange of raspberries, cinnamon, rose petal and tobacco, and very dry. 85 —*S.H.* (11/1/2005)

Folie à Deux 2004 Ménage à Trois White Blend (California) $12. Muscat seems to dominate this three-variety blend, giving an orange blossom aroma. Chenin Blanc adds an appley ripeness, while Chardonnay gives the peaches and cream. The result is a slightly sweet, simple wine that's easy on the palate and wallet. 84 —*S.H.* (11/1/2005)

FOPPIANO

Foppiano 2001 Cabernet Sauvignon (Russian River Valley) $17. Nice, ripe and balanced, a Cab that's easy to drink for its delicious blackberry and cherry flavors and smooth tannins, yet holds extra layers of nuance and interest. 86 —*S.H.* (5/1/2005)

Foppiano 2000 Cabernet Sauvignon (Russian River Valley) $17. This lovely wine, from Sonoma's oldest family-owned winery, continues the Foppiano tradition of excellent value. It has correct flavors of blackberry liqueur, with an olive-y streak, and is very dry and balanced. Shows plenty of grace and harmony. 89 —*S.H.* (11/15/2002)

Foppiano 2001 Riverside Collection Cabernet Sauvignon (California) $7. Overripe and pruny, with a burnt, Porty smell. Harsh and astringent. 82 —*S.H.* (10/1/2004)

Foppiano 2003 Riverside Collection Chardonnay (California) $7. A simple, everyday kind of Chard at a modest price, with apple and pear flavors and some oak. Finishes clean and a little sweet. 84 —*S.H.* (10/1/2004)

USA

Foppiano 2001 Merlot (Russian River Valley) $15. There's some good cherry fruit here, and the tannins are soft and intricate, but the wine has an overtly unripe green stemminess that detracts. **84** —S.H. (5/1/2005)

Foppiano 1999 Merlot (Russian River Valley) $17. **85** (8/1/2003)

Foppiano 1997 Petite Sirah (Sonoma County) $17. **91** —M.S. (5/1/2000)

Foppiano 2003 Petite Sirah (Russian River Valley) $18. Foppiano is a leader in the Petite Sirah movement, with a long history of producing this dark, dry, full-bodied wine. This one's powerful in coffee and blackberry fruit, and scoury in acids and tannins. It will easily ride out the next 15 years, but will never lose its rusticity. **87** —S.H. (3/1/2006)

Foppiano 2001 Petite Sirah (Paso Robles) $15. Pretty nice drinking, with full-throttle fruity-berry flavors raning fom blackberry to mint, with an intriguing tarry, smoky note. Has a rich, creamy texture, almost syrupy, ut saved from flatness by refreshing acidity and charry oak. A simple quaffer, but will age well. **86** (4/1/2003)

Foppiano 2000 Petite Sirah (Sonoma County) $23. From a family that pioneered "Pet" in Sonoma, and one that clearly still understands what to do with it, comes this dense, layered wine. It's young, brooding and tannic. This isn't a wimpy drink-me-now wine. It's built to last, and Foppiano Petite Sirahs age gracefully and improve in the bottle for many years. **90** —S.H. (12/1/2002)

Foppiano 2003 Bacigalupi Vineyard Petite Sirah (Russian River Valley) $17. This is an intricate, detailed Pet that's not as heavy or tannic, and considerably more complex, than most. It has the weight of a fine Zin, with rich flavors of spiced plums, blackberries, espresso, clove and anise, and a brambly finish of fresh, wild berries and pepper. **91 Editors' Choice** —S.H. (12/15/2005)

Foppiano 2002 Bacigalupi Vineyard Petite Sirah (Russian River Valley) $17. This vineyard is in the warmest part of Russian River Valley, and that extra heat shows in the flavors of dark stone fruits, such as plums and pomegranates. The wine also is very tough in tannins, numbing the palate through the bone-dry finish. It will take a dozen years to soften this bruiser, but it's a fine example of its genre. **87** —S.H. (8/1/2004)

Foppiano 2001 Bacigalupi Vineyards Petite Sirah (Russian River Valley) $18. Tasters found a range of flavorful fruits and berries, chocolate and herbs here, although there were overly-ripe raisins as well. The wine impressed for its youthful, bouncyquality, showing almost a spritzy feeling, but it's also one-dimensional. **83** (4/1/2003)

Foppiano 2002 Estate Petite Sirah (Russian River Valley) $23. Nobody in California tries harder than Foppiano, and it's dry, robust, tannic and well-made, with a core of sweet blackberry fruit that should hold it well for a long time. Could be great with a rich sirloin steak in a dark reduction sauce. **90** —S.H. (8/1/2005)

Foppiano 2000 Estate Millenium Selection Reserve Petite Sirah (Russian River Valley) $48. From a Petite Sirah pioneer, a very ripe, extracted wine brimming with black cherry, raspberry and blackberry fruit, with a hint of orange rind. It's pretty tannic, although the wine retains its balance and charm. Undoubtedly an ager, but perfect now with roasts. **87** (4/1/2003)

Foppiano 2004 Pinot Noir (Russian River Valley) $23. Green and weedy, with mint and cherry aromas leading to lean cherry flavors. Finishes dry and tart. **82** —S.H. (11/15/2006)

Foppiano 2002 Pinot Noir (Russian River Valley) $23. A dry, medium-bodied Pinot that shows very ripe fruit, easy tannins and a crisp bite of acidity. The flavors are delicious, all black cherries, sweet rhubarb tea, cola, vanilla and cinnamon. It's a wine you'll find yourself reaching for a second and a third time. **90** —S.H. (12/15/2005)

Foppiano 2000 Pinot Noir (Russian River Valley) $23. A well-behaved Pinot, just what you want in a light, delicate wine. It has subtle flavors of cherry, cola, earth, rhubarb and mushroom, and is framed in silky tannins. The finish is dry, with some astringency. **85** —S.H. (6/1/2004)

Foppiano 2002 Sangiovese (Alexander Valley) $17. Here's a wine that will even please those who say they don't like red wine. It's nice and light but with delicious flavors of ripe red stone fruits and spicy red berries and a touch of vanilla. Feels silky and clean through the spicy finish. **86** —S.H. (8/1/2005)

Foppiano 2001 Sangiovese (Alexander Valley) $18. **87** (8/1/2003)

Foppiano 2002 Zinfandel (Dry Creek Valley) $15. Absolutely easy to drink, a soft, silky wine with pleasantly ripe berry and cherry flavors. Has a rich Asian spiciness throughout, and is dry and balanced. **84** —S.H. (8/1/2005)

Foppiano 2001 Zinfandel (Dry Creek Valley) $15. A robust and spunky Zin, with firm texture and tannins that support a core of black cherry, plum, licorice, spice and herb flavors. It's moderate in length on the finish. **86** —J.M. (4/1/2004)

Foppiano 2000 Zinfandel (Dry Creek Valley) $15. This is a fine example of a winery that takes an elegant approach to Zin, vinifying the grapes to make a wine lighter than many in tannins and in fruit. The winemaker understands that wine is meant to go with food. Berry and herb flavors finish dry and the texture is smooth. **86** —S.H. (12/1/2002)

Foppiano 1998 Zinfandel (Dry Creek Valley) $15. Gamy flavors distinguish this wine, giving it a Rhônish flair. There's a good, meaty mouthfeel, red berries and cherries, with lots of tang. The finish falls off quickly though, making for a fairly light impression overall. **84** —P.G. (3/1/2001)

FORCHINI

Forchini 2004 Proprietor's Reserve Pinot Noir (Russian River Valley) $26. Drinks fairly heavy and flat for a Pinot, with cooked cherry and cola flavors. Needs more life. **83** —S.H. (12/1/2006)

Forchini 2000 Proprietor's Reserve Pinot Noir (Russian River Valley) $24. **86** (10/1/2002)

Forchini 1998 Papa Nonno Old Vine Clone Zinfandel (Dry Creek Valley) $20. **93** —S.H. (5/1/2000)

Forchini 2001 Proprietor's Reserve Zinfandel (Dry Creek Valley) $24. Light-textured and a little bright. Rustic tannins frame spicy cherry and toast notes. **82** (11/1/2003)

FOREFATHER'S

Forefather's (CA) 1999 Cabernet Sauvignon (Alexander Valley) $35. Licorice, blackberry and herb notes are framed in smoky, pine-like oak. Tannins are firm but ripe, while the moderately long finish has an herbal edge. **86** —J.M. (2/1/2003)

FOREFATHERS

Forefathers 2000 Cabernet Sauvignon (Alexander Valley) $32. From long-time Simi winemaker Nick Goldschmidt, now with Allied Domecq, the wine he really wants to make. It is ripe and rich, with flavors of blackcurrants and cassis, and the velvety soft tannins the appellation is famous for. This is a wine to watch, especially in a better vintage like 2001. **92 Editors' Choice** —S.H. (11/15/2003)

FOREST GLEN

Forest Glen 1998 Cabernet Sauvignon (California) $10. Rough, earthy and young, with the sharp acidity of youth and ripe, jammy fruit flavors. The tannins are soft and round, and it finishes sweet and a little awkward. **82** —S.H. (5/1/2001)

Forest Glen 2002 Oak Barrel Selection Cabernet Sauvignon (California) $10. A well-behaved, rustic Cab, with pleasant blackberry, cherry and oak flavors. Very dry, with good varietal character, and a country-style personality. **85 Best Buy** —S.H. (6/1/2005)

Forest Glen 1999 Oak Barrel Selection Cabernet Sauvignon (Sonoma) $10. Typical young, fresh, inexpensive Cabernet, with its jammy blackberry aromas and flavors. It's juicy and sharp in the mouth, with a dry bite of green, unripe grapes and raw finish. **84** —S.H. (3/1/2003)

Forest Glen 2001 Reserve Cabernet Sauvignon (Sonoma County) $34. Forest Glen's first ever reserve bottling is very dark, very dry and very tannic, to the point of palate-searing astringency. It also seems to have high acids, creating a sour taste and burn on the finish. **82** —S.H. (11/15/2005)

Forest Glen 2001 Chardonnay (Sonoma) $12. Plenty of flavor packed into this modest little blush, which smacks of ripe peaches and strawberries. A bit of sugar balances out the high acidity, leading to a soft, semi-sweet aftertaste. **84** —S.H. (9/1/2003)

USA

Forest Glen 2000 Chardonnay (California) $10. True to its word, oak rules, with burnt wood aromas and toasted oak flavors. There's not a lot of fruit, but it's a dry, clean wine, with the round, apple-like character that consumers want. **84** —S.H. (12/15/2002)

Forest Glen 1999 Chardonnay (California) $11. Begins with aromas of peaches and citrus fruits and a vegetal, herbaceous note. Fruity and rough, with good acidity. **82** —S.H. (8/1/2001)

Forest Glen 1999 Forest Fire Chardonnay (California) $8. White Merlot? Why not? It's actually a deep rose color, with fresh, exuberant aromas of raspberries and wildflowers. Drinks fruity and clean, with nice strawberry and raspberry flavors and just a tad of sugar. The finish is pretty. **84** —S.H. (2/1/2001)

Forest Glen 2004 Oak Barrel Fermented Chardonnay (California) $10. Nice and dry, with clean, crisp acidity, but the main problem is a lack of flavor. Tastes very thin and stripped, with watery orange and green apple fruit. Last year's bottling seemed richer. **83** —S.H. (11/15/2006)

Forest Glen 2003 Oak Barrel Fermented Chardonnay (California) $10. A solid Chardonnay that will please fans of well-ripened fruit, creamy textures, and accents of vanilla and smoke. The finish is long, clean and distinctive. **87 Best Buy** —S.H. (10/1/2005)

Forest Glen 2002 Oak Barrel Fermented Chardonnay (California) $10. There is indeed some barrel-fermented character here, including vanilla, smoky aromas and a creamy texture. It's modestly flavored with apples and peaches. **84** —S.H. (6/1/2004)

Forest Glen 2001 Oak Barrel Fermented Chardonnay (California) $10. Simple, fruity, dry, and, yes, oaky, with a note of smoky char and vanilla from beginning to end. The flavors are of peaches, apples and dried herbs. **84** —S.H. (6/1/2003)

Forest Glen 1999 Oak Barrel Fermented Chardonnay (California) $10. Soft and easy to drink, with pronounced fruity-spicy flavors and a solid dose of smoky oak. Quite sweet and soda-like, with a sugary finish. **82** —S.H. (5/1/2001)

Forest Glen 2002 Reserve Chardonnay (Sonoma County) $22. Forest Glen, until now an inexpensive wine, goes upscale with its first-ever reserve bottlings. It's an auspicious launch. This wine is fruity, crisp and well-oaked, and maintains balance and elegance without over-the-top winemaker intervention. **89** —S.H. (11/15/2005)

Forest Glen 2000 Merlot (California) $10. Decent, with ripe flavors of cherries and spice, dry tannins and good acidity. Yes, it's a common wine, made for everyday consumption, but you can't drink expensive stuff every day. This will do in a pinch, or for your next block party. **84** —S.H. (8/1/2003)

Forest Glen 1999 Merlot (California) $11. This is a nice, easy-drinking wine. It's ripe and well-made, from the berry-infused aromas to the soft, round, fruity flavors. Dry, and even sophisticated, you can serve this with fine dinners and save a few bucks. **86 Best Buy** —S.H. (8/1/2001)

Forest Glen 1998 Merlot (California) $10. 83 —S.H. (11/15/2000)

Forest Glen 2004 Oak Barrel Selection Merlot (California) $10. Gets the job done with minty cherr-berry flavors and a clean mouthfeel. The wine is dry, with a good balance of acidity and velvety tannins. **83** —S.H. (11/15/2006)

Forest Glen 2003 Oak Barrel Selection Merlot (California) $10. Simple and jammy, with cherry and blackberry flavors and a rustic mouthfeel. Finishes dry. **83** —S.H. (6/1/2005)

Forest Glen 2002 Oak Barrel Selection Merlot (California) $10. You get lots of bang for your buck in this modest wine. It's fully dry, with smooth tannins, a refreshing bite of acidity, and flavorful notes of blackberries and dark chocolate. All that fruit persists through the long finish. **85** —S.H. (6/1/2004)

Forest Glen 2001 Oak Barrel Selection Merlot (California) $10. Tastes like an inexpensive Aussie Shiraz, with a big burst of jammy blackberry fruit and youthful acidity. This is a dry, full-bodied table wine and it's a good value in an everyday dinner wine. **84** —S.H. (12/15/2003)

Forest Glen 2004 White Merlot (California) $10. There's a rich cherry and vanilla flavor to this wine, with enough residual sugar to make it off-dry.

Fortunately, there's also a nice, clean backbone of acidity to make it balanced. **84** —S.H. (11/15/2005)

Forest Glen 2005 Pinot Grigio (California) $10. Easy to imagine millions of people liking this, and thinking it's easy on the wallet. What's not to like? Crisp and ripe in peach, pear and pineapple flavors, with an obviously sweet finish, it's got instant appeal. **84** —S.H. (12/15/2006)

Forest Glen 2002 Pinot Grigio (California) $10. One of the first new wines of the vintage, a fresh, vibrant and fruity wine that tastes like grapes just picked off the vine. Of course there is alcohol, but the citrus, peach and flowery flavors are delicate and easy. **84** —S.H. (12/1/2003)

Forest Glen 2001 Pinot Grigio (Sonoma) $10. Clean, thin, bone dry, and crisp. That about says it all for this simple, inexpensive wine. It's quite tart and lemony-chalky, and will do just fine with shellfish, appetizers, or as an aperitif. **84** —S.H. (9/1/2003)

Forest Glen 2000 Pinot Grigio (California) $10. Fruity, clean, and on the sweet side, this is an everyday quaffer whose sugary flavors are just fine for a sunny afternoon with ripe peaches or apricots. It's Cailfornia soft, a country style wine that will appeal to those who find some whites tart or sour. **83** —S.H. (9/1/2002)

Forest Glen 1999 Pinot Grigio (California) $11. Fresh, young and strong, with citrusy flavors, this is very dry. You'll notice the acidity, too. It's a refreshing, crisp wine that scours the palate clean. **84** —S.H. (8/1/2001)

Forest Glen 2003 Oak Barrel Selection Sangiovese (California) $10. Here's a pretty little glass of red wine, silky and supple, with a brisk mouthfeel revealing ripe cherry and tobacco flavors with a hint of cocoa. It's dry, tart in acids and superversatile at the table. **85 Best Buy** —S.H. (6/1/2006)

Forest Glen 1999 Shiraz (California) $11. Aromas of red and black berries are mingled with herbal, earthy ones. Earthy, simple and dry, but with nice structure. A good everyday wine for simple meals. **84** —S.H. (10/1/2001)

Forest Glen 2002 Oak Barrel Selection Shiraz (California) $10. A decent quaff, featuring modest cherry-berry fruit and an earthy, herbal undercurrent. Smooth in the mouth, then thins out a bit on the finish. **84** (9/1/2005)

Forest Glen 2000 Oak Barrel Selection Shiraz (California) $10. Rustic and rough, with earthy, jammy berry flavors and harsh tannins. Finishes hot and tarry. Tailgate party special. **84** —S.H. (2/1/2003)

Forest Glen 2005 White Zinfandel Zinfandel (California) $10. Still a popular wine, white Zin appeals for its racy fruit and sweetness, and this Forest Glen bowls a perfect score in that respect. More of a rosé than a white, it shows raspberry, cherry and vanilla flavors, offset by zesty acids. **84** —S.H. (12/15/2006)

FORESTVILLE

ForestVille 1999 Cabernet Sauvignon (California) $6. Smells hot and vegetal, with aromas suggesting canned asparagus, although there are some riper blackberry flavors in the mouth. Very dry and properly structured, with a dusty finish. **84** —S.H. (11/15/2002)

ForestVille 2000 Sonoma Reserve Cabernet Sauvignon (Alexander Valley) $12. A little fruity, a little weedy, a bit tannic, totally dry, and an easy sipper. What's not to like? Will do just fine with that steak, and it's a great price for a Cabernet from this top appellation. **85** —S.H. (6/1/2003)

ForestVille 2002 Chardonnay (Sonoma County) $6. Nothing going on in this deficient wine except alcohol. Not a trace of fruit. **81** —S.H. (11/15/2004)

ForestVille 2000 Chardonnay (California) $6. Aromas and flavors of apples and peaches, with a dose of spicy, smoky oak, characterize this easy-drinking wine. It's dry enough to accompany a wide variety of foods, and at this price, you can stock up by the case. **83** —S.H. (12/15/2002)

ForestVille 1997 Chardonnay (California) $6. 81 —J.C. (10/1/1999)

ForestVille 2002 Sonoma Reserve Chardonnay (Russian River Valley) $12. This reserve-style wine, which is richer than the winery's regular release, offers lots of bang for your buck. Ripe and juicy in peach and apple flavors that are well oaked, with a long, spicy finish. **85** —S.H. (12/15/2004)

ForestVille 2003 Gewürztraminer (California) $6. Lots of true varietal character in this versatile, tasty wine, with ripe fruit, crisp acids and loads of tingly cinnamon and nutmeg spice. Technically dry, but sweet in peaches and wildflowers. A nice value. **85 Best Buy** —*S.H. (10/1/2005)*

ForestVille 2003 Merlot (California) $6. Here's a clean, fruity red wine that offers lots of blackberry and cherry flavor with a zingy edge of fresh, juicy acidity. It's totally dry and balanced, and a great value. **84 Best Buy** —*S.H. (12/1/2005)*

ForestVille 2000 Merlot (California) $6. Lots of plump, ripe, juicy fruit in this dry red wine, at an affordable price. The flavors range from plums and currants to tobacco, and there's a racy edge of oak. **84** —*S.H. (11/15/2002)*

FORESTVILLE

ForestVille 2000 Sonoma Reserve Merlot (Alexander Valley) $12. A Julia Roberts of a Merlot, pretty and innocent, maybe a little clueless. But who cares? It's fruity, dry, and fun, and even has some layers of complexity. Best of all, it doesn't cost too much. Drink up! **85** —*S.H. (8/1/2003)*

ForestVille 2004 Pinot Grigio (California) $6. Another good value from a brand known for them. This wine is dryish to just off-dry, with zesty acidity that frames citrus, melon and peach flavors. It's the perfect everyday picnic wine. **84 Best Buy** —*S.H. (7/1/2006)*

ForestVille 2003 Reserve Pinot Noir (Sonoma County) $16. Shows restraint in the reined-in cherry and herb flavors and modest oak, but it's not a simple wine. It has layers of interest that drink dry and balanced. **85** —*S.H. (5/1/2005)*

ForestVille 2004 Sauvignon Blanc (California) $6. Don't think that the price means this isn't a good wine. Lots of fruity finesse and satisfaction. It's dry and crisp, with long, ripe citrus and fig flavors and such a nice, clean mouthfeel. **85 Best Buy** —*S.H. (10/1/2005)*

ForestVille 1997 Sauvignon Blanc (California) $8. **82** *(3/1/2000)*

ForestVille 2003 Shiraz (California) $6. Surprisingly good for the price; here's a domestic Syrah to take on the hordes of Aussie imports. Light in body, but features the things consumers seem to be looking for in a basic red: cherry fruit accented by caramel and vanilla. Notes of chocolate, cedar and herb chime in on the finish. **85 Best Buy** *(9/1/2005)*

ForestVille 2002 Shiraz (Sonoma County) $6. Kind of sharp and acidic at first, but then the ripe, jammy black cherry flavors spread over the mouth and last through the finish. A nice, simple wine for everyday occasions—and look at the bargain price. **84 Best Buy** —*S.H. (12/1/2004)*

ForestVille 2000 Shiraz (California) $6. Fresh and sharp, a wine marked by upfront acids that make it taste like it's right out of the fermenter. Has pretty flavors of blackberries, with a peppery edge, an everyday sort of wine at an everyday price. **83** —*S.H. (10/1/2003)*

ForestVille 1999 Shiraz (California) $6. Creamy vanilla, sweet caramel and candied berries add up to a wine designed for mass appeal and priced accordingly. It's smooth and goes down easy. **83** *(10/1/2001)*

ForestVille 2003 Zinfandel (California) $6. At this price, you can't go wrong. It's a good quaffing wine, fruity in blackberries and blueberries, spicy and dry. **83 Best Buy** —*S.H. (8/1/2005)*

ForestVille 2002 Zinfandel (California) $6. Fresh, jammy and sharp in acids, this good-value Zin features berry flavors with an earthy edge. It's very dry. Good for pizza. **83** —*S.H. (10/1/2004)*

ForestVille 2001 Zinfandel (California) $6. A smoky, toasty blend that features a simple, bright cherry and spice core. Bright and short on the finish. **83** *(11/1/2003)*

FORGERON

Forgeron 2002 Cabernet Sauvignon (Columbia Valley (WA)) $30. Reductive, closed down and musty. Possibly slightly corked, but a second bottle showed the same musty, closed down flavors. The wine simply falls off a cliff in the midpalate. **84** —*P.G. (12/15/2005)*

Forgeron 2001 Cabernet Sauvignon (Columbia Valley (WA)) $29. Dark and juicy, with powerful, polished blackberry and black cherry fruit. Spice and hints of black pepper help frame the wine, which is structured, confident and tannic. Exceptional winemaking shows throughout. **90** —*P.G. (9/1/2004)*

Forgeron 2004 Chardonnay (Columbia Valley (WA)) $22. Lots of vanilla, spice and buttered nuts, set in a tight, stylish frame. Clean citrus and apple fruit, made in a fresh, crisp and penetrating style. **90** —*P.G. (4/1/2006)*

Forgeron 2003 Chardonnay (Columbia Valley (WA)) $19. This tasty effort, sourced mostly from the outstanding DuBrul Vineyard, brightly combines crisp, lime-edged acidity with moderate tropical fruit flavors of pineapple, green apple and pear. Plenty of barrel spice gives it a fresh-baked apple-pie finish. **88** —*P.G. (6/1/2005)*

Forgeron 2002 Vinfinity Red Blend (Columbia Valley (WA)) $46. Forgeron's prestige offering is rather nondescript, showing toasty oak, other barrel flavors, and a mix of Cab, Merlot and Syrah fruit. It never seems to snap into focus; it's a pleasant red wine that doesn't have the sort of grip and depth one expects in this price range. **86** —*P.G. (4/1/2006)*

Forgeron 2002 Syrah (Columbia Valley (WA)) $30. This is a plump, mouthfilling Syrah that just lacks any extra dimension of depth or richness. The blackberry and charred toast flavors are pleasant, finishing crisp and clean. **86** *(9/1/2005)*

Forgeron 2001 Syrah (Columbia Valley (WA)) $29. Dense, dark color, scented with meaty fruit, smoke, toast and tar, this is quintessential Washington Syrah. It simply delivers, in spades, everything you want: sweet berries, spicy, toasty oak, and highlights of cinnamon and pepper. **91** —*P.G. (9/1/2004)*

Forgeron 2001 Zinfandel (Columbia Valley (WA)) $25. There is nothing wimpy about this delicious Zin from a rising star winery in Walla Walla. Dried fruit, brown sugar and tart cherries fill the mouth with rich flavors. They're underscored by bourbon barrel highlights from aging in American oak. **88** —*P.G. (1/1/2004)*

Forgeron 2003 Alder Ridge Zinfandel (Columbia Valley (WA)) $27. Lots of cinnamon, coffee grounds and spice in both the nose and mouth. Lght and pretty, with baked, spicy cherry cobbler, brown sugar and chocolate flavors. There's plenty of acid to cut through any red meat you might wish to try with it. **87** —*P.G. (4/1/2006)*

FORIS

Foris 2000 Chardonnay (Rogue Valley) $11. All barrel fermented; about half went through malolactic. This is a very light, green appley wine, with firm acids and clean, lightly cinnamon-spiced fruit. **86** —*P.G. (8/1/2004)*

Foris 1996 Siskiyou Terrace Chardonnay (Rogue Valley) $20. **87** —*L.W. (12/31/1999)*

Foris 2000 Gewürztraminer (Rogue Valley) $11. Oregon rarely gets credit for how good its Gewürztraminers can be. This is a perfect example: a classic, varietal nose shows citrus blossom, baby powder and lychee; it's both fragrant and slightly exotic. Clean and creamy in the mouth, its floral flavors have elegant textures and surprising length. **91 Best Buy** —*P.G. (4/1/2002)*

Foris 1997 Klipsun Meritage (Washington) $29. **88** —*P.G. (4/1/2002)*

Foris 1998 Merlot (Rogue Valley) $18. Southern Oregon red wines don't attain the richness of either northern California or Washington state efforts, but they have their own charms. This wine, soft and scented with cranberries, vanilla and eucalyptus, offers pleasing berry/plum-fruit, plenty of firm acid, and a hard, tannic finish. **85** —*P.G. (4/1/2002)*

Foris 1998 Pinot Blanc (Rogue Valley) $11. **89 Best Buy** —*L.W. (12/31/1999)*

Foris 2000 Pinot Blanc (Rogue Valley) $13. Made in a tart, tangy, refreshing style, this tastes of immaculately ripe green apples. No hint of wood, just bracing fruit in a straight-forward, food-ready style. **87** —*P.G. (4/1/2002)*

Foris 2004 Pinot Gris (Rogue Valley) $12. A dark straw color, with a nose of pears, citrus skin and yeast. Very dry and firm, with streaks of steel, petrol, mineral and lime. This is a taut wine, with less assertive fruit than many Oregon Pinot Gris. Some troubling bitterness lingers on the finish. **85** —*P.G. (2/1/2006)*

Foris 2000 Pinot Gris (Rogue Valley) $13. Whatever magic Foris works with its Pinot Gris is wonderfully captured in this near-perfect effort.

Vibrant and fruity, clean and forward, it is softly scented with fragrant pears and citrus zest. Somehow it is both big and rich, yet still elegant and balanced, with true varietal character. **91 Best Buy** —*P.G. (2/1/2002)*

Foris 1999 Pinot Noir (Rogue Valley) $16. Pretty scents of violets and cherries characterize this young Pinot. It's not a big style, but it has a lovely balance and it doesn't overreach. It's complete, light, and flavorful, with well-managed tannins and a hint of pleasing spice in the finish. **87** —*P.G. (4/1/2002)*

Foris 1998 Maple Ranch Pinot Noir (Rogue Valley) $30. First planted in 1988, the Maple Ranch Pinot has a soft sweetness and a generous, open profile derived partly from the vintage and partly from an additional year of bottle time. Lush berry and chocolate flavors coat the palate; the wine finishes sweet, round and full-bodied. **87** —*P.G. (4/1/2002)*

FORT ROSS VINEYARD

Fort Ross Vineyard 2002 Chardonnay (Sonoma Coast) $32. Made in the same style as the Reserve. Shows a cool-climate profile of stones, minerals, cold metal and high acidity, and is dry, elegant and ageworthy. Softening notes from oak provide sweetness. Distinct. **91** —*S.H. (5/1/2005)*

Fort Ross Vineyard 2002 Reserve Chardonnay (Sonoma Coast) $40. What a wine! Only the second release from this winery, and a really good one. Call it Chablisian for its intense mineral, metallic flavors and mouthfeel, and vibrant acidity. It also has lots of oak and lees, and is bone dry, offering tantalizing hints of lime zest, white peach and honey. **93** —*S.H. (5/1/2005)*

Fort Ross Vineyard 2001 Pinot Noir (Sonoma Coast) $34. Aromas offer less than ripe rhubarb, mint and cola alongside riper cherries and cocoa, but in the mouth, it explodes in sweet fruit and smoke. Light in body, delicately acidic, yet incredibly complex. A beautiful Pinot. **92** —*S.H. (5/1/2005)*

Fort Ross Vineyard 2001 Reserve Pinot Noir (Sonoma Coast) $39. Riper and sexier than the regular '01 Pinot, offering a blast of red cherry compote, smoky oak, nutmeg, cinnamon, dry cocoa. Just fabulous quality, dry, complex, all taffeta and silk. Delicate but potent, with great complexity. Has a slight earthiness that should melt away in a few years. **94 Editors' Choice** —*S.H. (5/1/2005)*

FORTH

Forth 2002 Cabernet Sauvignon (Dry Creek Valley) $28. This is one of the ripest, least earthy Dry Creek Cabs I've ever had. It's quite a lush wine, forward in juicy black cherry and cassis flavors, yet complex, with real depth and length to the finish. Drink now. **88** —*S.H. (5/1/2006)*

Forth 2001 Cabernet Sauvignon (Dry Creek Valley) $30. Actually a single-vineyard Cab. Doesn't merit as good a score as Forth's less expensive '02 All Boys Cab because of the astringent tannins, which rob it of instant appeal. Might age, but it's a gamble. **87** —*S.H. (10/1/2004)*

Forth 2000 Cabernet Sauvignon (Dry Creek Valley) $28. Smells a bit funky—brett?—with bacon grease and Band-aid aromas that verge on vegetal. The flavors are an improvement, but the wine is very tannic and rough in texture. **82** —*S.H. (11/15/2003)*

Forth 2003 All Boys Cabernet Sauvignon (Dry Creek Valley) $18. Far simpler, less ripe and altogether less pleasing than Forth's '02 Cab, also just released, this is an earthy, thin wine. Alcohol is the main feature. **82** —S.H. (5/1/2006)

Forth 2002 All Boys Cabernet Sauvignon (Dry Creek Valley) $18. Here's a nice Cab that's easy to like for its ripe berry, chocolate, olive and herb flavors and rich, smooth texture, yet it has a fancy complexity that will translate to a fine dinner. Drink now for the sheer exuberance of youth. **90** —*S.H. (10/1/2005)*

Forth 2004 Sauvignon Blanc (Mendocino) $14. Follows the pattern of ripe fig, melon, citrus and peach flavors that finish reliably dry, but the acids here are distinctively prickly. It's almost going through a secondary fermentation. **84** —*S.H. (10/1/2005)*

Forth 2002 Syrah (Dry Creek Valley) $25. With the extra heat it gets in warm Dry Creek, this Syrah is very ripe in blackberry, black cherry and

even blackstrap molasses flavors, although it's totally dry. The fine structure gives it balance and finesse. **87** —*S.H. (9/1/2005)*

Forth 2001 Syrah (Dry Creek Valley) $25. From an estate vineyard on the west side, this is a jammy wine, sweet in cherry and blackcurrant fruit, with a subtle overlay of toast. It's quite dry, and finishes with a scour of tannins. Good now, in a robust way, and should hold for 5-7 years. **88** —*S.H. (5/31/2005)*

FORTRESS

Fortress 2004 Musqué Clone Sauvignon Blanc (Lake County) $21. These Lake County Sauvignons sure are getting interesting. This one is an amazing wine, bone dry, tingly-tart and filled with gooseberry, grapefruit and minerals. It stimulates some feral instinct in the mouth, living up to its savage, wild name. **90** —*S.H. (11/1/2005)*

FOUNTAIN GROVE

Fountain Grove 1997 Cabernet Sauvignon (California) $10. **84** —*L.W. (12/31/1999)*

Fountain Grove 1998 Chardonnay (California) $10. **83** —*L.W. (12/31/1999)*

Fountain Grove 1997 Merlot (California) $10. **84** —*L.W. (12/31/1999)*

Fountain Grove 1998 Sauvignon Blanc (North Coast) $10. **86** —*L.W. (5/1/2000)*

FOUNTAINHEAD

Fountainhead 2003 Morisoli Borges Vineyard Cabernet Sauvignon (Rutherford) $45. Dry, oaky and balanced, this Cab shows the grace and balance that come from really good terroir. It's superripe, flooding the mouth with rich Cabernet flavors of blackberries, cassis and chocolate, yet maintains harmony. Grown on the true Rutherford bench, west of Highway 29. **89** —*S.H. (12/15/2006)*

FOUR SONS

Four Sons 2002 Cabernet Sauvignon (Stags Leap District) $30. There's lots of rich varietal character in this fresh wine. It's full-bodied and dry, with black currant and cherry flavors and a hit of oak. Finishes with firm tannins, but best consumed now. **86** —*S.H. (12/15/2005)*

Four Sons 2002 Merlot (Carneros) $25. Drinks a bit simple and rustic, with chewy tannins and dried herbs, but there's no denying the plethora of ripe blackberry, plum, cherry and mocha flavors. **84** —*S.H. (12/15/2005)*

FOUR VINES

Four Vines 2002 Bailey Vineyard Syrah (Amador County) $25. There are some ripe berry-cherry flavors in this mountain wine, which contains raw tannins. It's also a little sweet in residual sugar. **84** —*S.H. (12/1/2004)*

Four Vines 2002 Old Vine Cuvée Zinfandel (California) $10. Here's a country-style wine with nice Zinny flavors of berries and mocha and smooth, ripe tannins. Loses a point or two for a sharp, weird sweet-and-sour note on the finish. **83** —*S.H. (12/15/2005)*

FOX BROOK

Fox Brook 1998 Ceãga Vinegarden Merlot (Mendocino) $32. From a biodynamic vineyard owned by a member of the Fetzer family, this is one of the more aromatic '98 Merlots, with lovely black cherry and blackberry in the nose, topped with smoke and vanilla. It's extremely rich, with complex tannins. **88** *(8/1/2001)*

FOX CREEK

Fox Creek 1997 Ceago Vinegarden Chardonnay (Santa Ynez Valley) $35. **88** —*M.M. (10/1/1999)*

FOX RUN

Fox Run 1997 Cabernet Franc (Finger Lakes) $13. **88 Best Buy** —*L.W. (12/1/1999)*

Fox Run 1999 Cabernet Franc (Finger Lakes) $20. If you like wood, you'll like this wine. There's a slight acrid note, but mostly it's very toasty and oaky, with sweet caramel flavors and a tangy finish. **83** —*J.C. (1/1/2004)*

Fox Run NV Blanc de Blancs Champagne Blend (Finger Lakes) $14. **88** *(11/15/1999)*

Fox Run 1999 Chardonnay (Finger Lakes) $9. A pleasant, mild-bodied wine that shows pretty citrus, melon and apple notes at itscore. A fresh, lemony edge on the finish is clean and bright. **87 Best Buy** —*J.C. (7/1/2002)*

Fox Run 2000 Reserve Seneca Lake Estate Grown Chardonnay (Finger Lakes) $13. A well balanced wine that shows good body, modest but adequate acidity, and a good blend of citrus, pear, apple, melon, herb and spice flavors. The finish is moderate in length, and shows a veiled honeyed note at the end. **88 Best Buy** —*J.M. (1/1/2003)*

Fox Run 2002 Pinot Noir (Finger Lakes) $15. A nice, light-bodied wine with some pretty flavors of cherries, vanilla and leather. Has a smooth, creamy texture and an elegant mouthfeel that's almost Burgundian. **86** *(11/1/2004)*

Fox Run 1999 Pinot Noir (Finger Lakes) $12. Marred by acrid aromas of burning vegetation, but otherwise acceptable, with bitter chocolate and caramel oak joining cola and earth. **81** —*J.C. (1/1/2004)*

Fox Run 1997 Estate-grown Reserve Pinot Noir (Finger Lakes) $20. **85** *(10/1/1999)*

Fox Run 2002 Reserve Pinot Noir (Finger Lakes) $25. Smells herbal and peppery, with leather and meaty scents. On the palate it is tart, with simple cranberry and cherry flavors. **83** *(11/1/2004)*

Fox Run 2000 Sable Seneca Lake Estate Grown Red Blend (Finger Lakes) $13. Somewhat herbal in the nose, with moderate body and mild tannic structure. The wine serves up earth tones followed by tea, sage, anise, sour cherry, toast and spice flavors. Clean on the finish. **85** —*J.M. (3/1/2003)*

Fox Run 2002 Riesling (Finger Lakes) $10. Green apples and pears combine harmoniously in this tart, mostly dry offering. Elements of vegetable oil and mineral add complexity. **85** —*J.C. (8/1/2003)*

Fox Run 1999 Riesling (Finger Lakes) $9. Maybe I'm cheerleading for my home state, and maybe I'm preachy about Riesling, but if I could get this delightful wine into enthusiasts' mouths, it might change their minds about both Riesling and New York State wines. This is a rounder, fatter rendition of riesling, with petrol-diesel aromatics over the apple-grape fruit. It has Chardonnay-like weight, but a decidedly different flavor range, with honey-apricot shadings and a long, appley close. **86** *(11/15/2001)*

Fox Run 2001 Dry Riesling (Finger Lakes) $10. **84** —*J.C. (8/1/2003)*

Foxen 1998 Chardonnay (Santa Maria Valley) $20. **92** *(6/1/2000)*

FOXEN

Foxen 1997 Chardonnay (Santa Maria Valley) $20. **85** —*S.H. (7/1/1999)*

Foxen 2003 Tinaquaic Vineyard Chardonnay (Santa Maria Valley) $24. They put the words "dry farmed" on the label to indicate, I suppose, extra concentration, and indeed, this is an intense Chard. It's bone dry, well-oaked, high in acidity and intricately layered in tropical fruit and orange custard flavors. Combines elegance, style and power in the glass. **93 Editors' Choice** —*S.H. (12/15/2005)*

Foxen 1998 Tinaquaic Vineyard Chardonnay (Santa Maria Valley) $30. The pleasant nose of nuts, green apples and caramel also shows an odd whiff that mattered more to some tasters than others. Light apple fruit, spice, earth and butterscotch notes play on the full, but vaguely sour milk-tinged palate. Finishes tart and dry with slight mineral notes, in the manner of some white Burgundies. We've been big fans of Foxen's wines in the past, but this one left us scratching our heads. **86** *(7/1/2001)*

Foxen 1997 Tinaquaic Vineyard Chardonnay (Santa Maria Valley) $30. **90** *(6/1/2000)*

Foxen 2005 Tinaquiac Vineyard Chardonnay (Santa Maria Valley) $28. The vineyard is in the southern Santa Maria, near the Santa Ynez Valley line and probably a warmer part of the AVA. The wine is beautifully ripe in pineapple, apricot, peach, vanilla cream and cinnamon spice flavors, and despite a rich voluptuousness, it has good acidity. This is a worthy followup to the great 2003. **93 Editors' Choice** —*S.H. (12/31/2006)*

Foxen 1996 Tinaquiac Vineyard Chardonnay (Santa Maria Valley) $30. **89** —*S.H. (7/1/1999)*

Foxen 1999 Chenin Blanc (Santa Barbara County) $14. Starts with muted aromas of buttercream, ginger and toffee, with peach scents that emerge as the wine warms up. It's extremely rich and extracted, not at all like Chenins of old. It's also dry, although the ripe fruit tastes sweet. A little soft, but pleasant; sort of a cross between a fruity Riesling and a crisp Sauvignon Blanc. **86** —*S.H. (5/1/2001)*

Foxen 2004 Ernesto Wickenden Vineyard Chenin Blanc (Santa Maria Valley) $18. Winemaker Bill Wathan loves making this wine, which is the best Chenin Blanc in California. Made from 40-year old vines, barrel fermented, bone dry and aged in older French oak, it will change your mind about this variety. Long in lemongrass, kiwi and licorice flavors, with bracing acidity, it has a rich, creamy mouthfeel, great complexity, and a long, interesting finish. **93 Editors' Choice** —*S.H. (12/31/2006)*

Foxen 2003 Ernesto Wickenden Vineyard Old Vines Chenin Blanc (Santa Maria Valley) $18. This is the best California Chenin Blanc I've ever tasted. Bill Wathan gave the wine full Burgundian treatment, which accounts for the rich creaminess, while the grape itself lends high acidity and a sweet-sour lemon flavor with notes of camphor and tumeric. With the vines dating to 1966, this is an extraordinarily complex, bone-dry wine. **93 Editors' Choice** —*S.H. (8/1/2006)*

Foxen 1998 Mourvèdre (Santa Ynez Valley) $25. V**92** —*S.H. (10/1/1999)*

Foxen 2000 Pinot Noir (Santa Maria Valley) $24. Hints of strawberry accent smoke, beet and cinnamon aromas. Then tart red berries take over in the mouth, mingling seductively with notes of clove and cinnamon, before turning peppery. Chocolate and espresso add a dark, emphatic bass note to the finish. **90 Editors' Choice** *(10/1/2002)*

Foxen 2000 Bien Nacido Vineyard Pinot Noir (Santa Maria Valley) $40. This wine's charred-oak veneer is nearly impenetrable. The espresso-caramel cocoon is wound so tightly, the black cherry fruit core is almost completely veiled. May come into better balance and show more fruit with time. **84** *(10/1/2002)*

Foxen 1997 Bien Nacido Vineyard Pinot Noir (Santa Maria Valley) $30. **89** *(10/1/1999)*

Foxen 2003 Bien Nacido Vineyard Block 8 Pinot Noir (Santa Maria Valley) $42. Rich in fruit and soft, this is a Pinot that seems to be giving its best now. It's dry and elegant, with cola, cherry, mocha and spice flavors, and a silky texture. Finishes with enough grippy tannins to enjoy with rich fare, like lamb. **88** —*S.H. (12/15/2005)*

Foxen 2004 Bien Nacido Vineyard Block Eight Pinot Noir (Santa Maria Valley) $42. Bright and acidic as Pinots from this vineyard always are, with crushed hard-spice aromas and ripe cola and cherry compote flavors. The wine is fairly full-bodied and dry, with a polished silk and velvet mouthfeel. Fine now, but has the stuffing to improve for a few years. **90** —*S.H. (11/15/2006)*

Foxen 2004 Julia's Vineyard Pinot Noir (Santa Maria Valley) $42. Soft and elegant, with cherry pie, cola and mocha flavors, this single-vineyard Pinot is a little one-dimensional but offers lots to like. It has a silky, satiny texture. Drink now. **85** —*S.H. (11/15/2006)*

Foxen 2003 Julia's Vineyard Pinot Noir (Santa Maria Valley) $42. This is a very fruity Pinot, and also a tannic one. It's youthful now, with those sharp, fermenty acids and primary cherry fruit flavors that signal the need for time to knit together. **90** —*S.H. (12/15/2005)*

Foxen 2000 Julia's Vineyard Pinot Noir (Santa Maria Valley) $40. Big, bulky and slightly warm, this wine nevertheless delivers copious amounts of mouthfilling fruit. The Port-like plum and spice cake flavors are lush and hedonistic, the mouthfeel layered and rich. If you like big Pinots, jump on it. **89** *(10/1/2002)*

Foxen 1997 Julia's Vineyard Pinot Noir (Santa Maria Valley) $30. **91** *(10/1/1999)*

Foxen 1997 Sanford & Benedict Vineyard Pinot Noir (Santa Ynez Valley) $30. **90** *(10/1/1999)*

Foxen 1994 Sanford & Benedict Vineyard Pinot Noir (Santa Ynez Valley) $NA. Alcohol 13.6%. Brilliantly clear. Darker that the '93. Blast of dusty spices, sweet char, vanilla, oodles of red cherries. Terrifically sweet cherry and raspberry fruit, enormous middle palate. Flamboyant, hedonistic.

USA

Medium-bodied, with good acidity and firm tannins. Beautiful now–2012. **94 Editors' Choice** —*S.H. (6/1/2005)*

Foxen 1993 Sanford & Benedict Vineyard Pinot Noir (Santa Ynez Valley) $NA. Alcohol 13.6%. Beautiful color, brilliant ruby, bricky at the rim. Delicate, understated aromas of cherries, cinnamon, nutmeg, rosehip tea, cola. Light in body and flavor. Very dry, elegant and refined. Long, long finish, crisp acids. Lovely now. **91** —*S.H. (6/1/2005)*

Foxen 2003 Sea Smoke Pinot Noir (Santa Rita Hills) $60. Beautiful aromatics mark this luscious wine. It's bursting with sappy, cherry jam and cocoa notes, and tastes very ripe, almost sweet, with a fleshy, fat roundness. It's a late-picked wine, a little over the top and high in alcohol. **89** —*S.H. (3/1/2006)*

Foxen 2004 Sea Smoke Vineyard Pinot Noir (Sta. Rita Hills) $62. Huge Pinot, dark and extracted, with enormously ripe flavors of baked cherry pie, blackberry jam, cola and chocolate. As delicious as this may sound, the wine suffers from being too soft. Finishes with white sugary sweetness. **82** —*S.H. (11/15/2006)*

Foxen 2003 Sea Smoke Vineyard Pinot Noir (Santa Rita Hills) $60. Foxen has co-released three single-vineyard Pinots, and to my mind this is the best. It's the most closed, tannic and complex, a dark, brooding wine whose depths have swirls of black stone fruits, sweet leather, mocha, spice and oak. It drinks rich and satisfying now, and should develop well over the next five years. **92** —*S.H. (12/15/2005)*

Foxen 2003 Cuvée Jean Marie Red Table Wine Red Blend (Santa Ynez Valley) $30. This Syrah-Mourvèdre blend is soft, smooth and polished, with chocolate and cherry flavors. It is an easy wine with some sophistication and complexity. **86** —*S.H. (3/1/2006)*

Foxen 2000 Foothills Reserve Red Blend (Santa Ynez Valley) $40. A Cab Franc and Merlot blend. There are some rich aromas and flavors of blackcurrants, and of course the oak is very good. But the tannic structure is rugged and unbalanced, and the fruit is too thin. **86** —*S.H. (11/15/2003)*

Foxen 2004 Williamson-Dore Vineyard Cuvée Jeanne Marie Rhône Red Blend (Santa Ynez Valley) $34. The heat during harvest was just horrible, and seems to have impacted this Grenache-Mourvèdre blend. This has never been Foxen's premier red wine anyway; the previous vintage was good, but not great. This year, there's just too much heat. **83** —*S.H. (12/1/2006)*

Foxen 2000 Carhartt Vineyard Syrah (Santa Ynez Valley) $30. A richly fruity wine that offers up plush blackberry, cherry, bitter chocolate and herb flavors that are dry and crisp, plus a smooth, velvety mouthfeel. The tannins are kind of tough, though. **88** —*S.H. (3/1/2004)*

Foxen 2002 Cuvée Jeanne Marie Syrah (Santa Ynez Valley) $35. Only 71% Syrah, but we let it sneak into the tasting (oops—the rest is Mourvèdre and Viognier). The Mourvèdre gives it a gaminess that sets it apart, while the dominant notes are blackberry and toast. Crisp on the finish. **85** *(9/1/2005)*

Foxen 1999 Morehouse Vineyard Syrah (Santa Ynez Valley) $35. Fans of Foxen that we are, we're not sure what went wrong here. The off-putting mineral-chemical-vinyl aromas are hard to get past. When you do, there's scant reward in the thin, sour, red-berry fruit and sharp mineral flavors. Smoke and leather notes are barely redeeming, the rampant volatile acidity just unpleasant. **81** *(11/1/2001)*

Foxen 1997 Morehouse Vineyard Syrah (Santa Ynez Valley) $35. **91** —*S.H. (10/1/1999)*

Foxen 2002 Tianquaic Vineyard Syrah (Santa Maria Valley) $30. If anything, even more serious and complex than Foxen's Santa Ynez bottling. Shows a distinctive cool-climate character with its aromas and flavors of white pepper, raw meat, cola and cassis, and the wonderfully rich, thick, sweet tannins. The blockbuster is of awesome quality, and will age through the decade if you can keep your hands off of it. **84** —*S.H. (12/1/2004)*

Foxen 2004 Tianquaic Vineyard Syrah (Santa Maria Valley) $42. The '03 was so good, but the '04 is a big step down, and you have to blame it on the vintage. Week after week of unrelenting September heat caused problems statewide, and you can taste a hot, stewed-fruit quality in this otherwise fine wine. **84** —*S.H. (12/1/2006)*

Foxen 2003 Tinaquiac Vineyard Syrah (Santa Maria Valley) $35. High in acidity and lush in fruit and oak, with fleshy, richly complex tannins, this beautiful Syrah is delicious now. It's made Northern Rhône style, with a blast of white pepper framing the intense blackberry and mocha flavors. Totally dry, the wine should hold well through 2007. **93 Editors' Choice** —*S.H. (3/1/2006)*

Foxen 2003 Williamson Dore Vineyard Syrah (Santa Ynez Valley) $30. The flavor profile of this single vineyard wine is almost identical to Foxen's Tinaquiac bottling, but this is a much softer wine, without the brilliant acidity marking its cool-climate cousin. The blackberry, cherry, mocha and oak flavors finish long, smooth and very satisfying. **90** —*S.H. (3/1/2006)*

Foxen 2004 Williamson-Dore Vineyard Syrah (Santa Ynez Valley) $40. Lush tannins, ripe cassis, plum and espresso flavors, and nicely dry. The problem is a prickly heat throughout. Even for someone who isn't particularly bothered by high alcohol, it's hard to get past. **85** —*S.H. (12/1/2006)*

Foxen 2002 Williamson-Dore Vineyard Syrah (Santa Ynez Valley) $35. A "wow!" wine. Starts with a stupendous aroma that perfectly integrates toasty, caramelly oak with rich Indian pudding, gingerbread, sweet plum, cherry and spicy clove. The tannins are rich and ripe. **93** —*S.H. (6/1/2005)*

Foxen 2000 Williamson-Dore Vineyard Syrah (Santa Ynez Valley) $30. Dinstinctly peppery, although there are underpinnings of blackberry, smoke and oak. Feels quite posh and suave in the mouth, with smooth, rich tannins and crisp acids that spread blackberry and cherry flavors across the palate. Could use some depth, but otherwise a tasty wine. **89** —*S.H. (3/1/2004)*

Foxen 1997 Rothberg Vineyard Viognier (Santa Ynez Valley) $25. **87** —*S.H. (6/1/1999)*

FOXGLOVE

Foxglove 2001 Chardonnay (Edna Valley) $13. Smells like peaches-and-cream dessert, with sweet vanilla cookies soaking up the cream. The flavors are sweetly fruity and simple, with an edge of herbs and dust. This will please undemanding fans of oaky Chard. **84** —*S.H. (6/1/2003)*

FOXRIDGE

FoxRidge 1997 Chardonnay (Carneros) $12. **82** —*M.S. (10/1/1999)*

FoxRidge 1997 Merlot (Northern Sonoma) $11. **84** —*J.C. (7/1/2000)*

FoxRidge 1997 Merlot (Northern Sonoma) $11. **84** —*J.C. (7/1/2000)*

FRALICH

Fralich 2002 Harry's Patio Red Blend (Paso Robles) $15. Just barely good. Raspingly dry, with a sharp cut of acid and some green flavors, but it'll be fine with a cheeseburger. **83** —*S.H. (8/1/2005)*

Fralich 2003 Claret of Syrah Rosé Blend (Paso Robles) $16. Not really a claret, more of a blush wine, and a dry one at that. There are pleasant cherry-berry, earthy flavors, and a touch of spice on the finish. **84** —*S.H. (8/1/2005)*

Fralich 2003 Fralich Vineyard Viognier (Paso Robles) $22. Strong flavors in this easy-drinking wine. Lots of white peaches, bananas, butter and honey, in a creamy texture that's soft on the finish. **85** —*S.H. (8/1/2005)*

Fralich 2003 Harry's Menage a Trois White Blend (Paso Robles) $18. This is a friendly wine that's easy to drink and to like. It's lush in all sorts of ripe, forward fruity, berry flavors, but has good acidity and a clean finish. **87** —*S.H. (8/1/2005)*

FRANCIS COPPOLA

Francis Coppola 1998 Black Label Bordeaux Blend (California) $17. **82** —*S.H. (7/1/2000)*

Francis Coppola 2000 Diamond Series Black Label Claret Cabernet Sauvignon (California) $17. This is young Cabernet, dark purple in color, with the aroma dominated by the smoke and vanilla of fine oak. It's as rich as blackberry pie, juicy and fat, yet nicely dry. Balanced, with fine tannins, this is a nice glass of red wine. **90** —*S.H. (11/15/2002)*

Francis Coppola 2000 Director's Reserve Cabernet Sauvignon (Napa Valley) $30. A junior cousin to Rubicon, this is made in the same mold, with rich aromas of cassis, sage and smoked oak, and similar flavors. It's a flavorful wine, with dry, fine tannins. But it's kind of soft and flabby. **86** —S.H. (12/31/2002)

Francis Coppola 2002 Sofia Blanc de Blancs Champagne Blend (California) $19. Light in aroma, flavor and body, almost insubstantial except for the bubbles and alcohol, and probably by design. This blend of Pinot Blanc, Sauvignon Blanc and Muscat Canelli has the barest suggestion of peaches, and a hint of sweetness. But it's basically tart, neutral and dry. **86** —S.H. (12/1/2002)

Francis Coppola 1998 Diamond Series Chardonnay (California) $15. 88 (6/1/2000)

Francis Coppola 2000 Diamond Series Blue Label Merlot (California) $17. A tough, punchy wine, young and strong, with rugged tannins and a bite of acid. It has earthy-berry flavors enriched with a bit of Syrah. **84** —S.H. (11/15/2002)

Francis Coppola 2001 Rosso Red Blend (California) $9. Leave it to director Coppola to manage an ensemble cast of Zinfandel, Syrah, Cabernet Sauvignon, Petite Sirah and Sangiovese and come out with a smashing success. Forward fruit flavors mesh with earthier notes of herbs and tobacco wrapped in a silky texture; the finish is complex and long. Serve it with chops or even a simple pasta with cheese. **89 Best Buy** —S.H. (11/15/2003)

Francis Coppola 2004 Diamond Collection Yellow Label Sauvignon Blanc (Napa Valley) $16. Easy to like for its fig and citrus flavors and fresh, clean acids, though it could stand more richness. **85** —S.H. (10/1/2005)

Francis Coppola 2001 Director's Reserve Sauvignon Blanc (Napa Valley) $18. Lots of rich fruit here, ranging from grass and lemons to peaches and pineapple. Feels rich and honeyed, with vibrant acidity. **88** —S.H. (10/1/2003)

Francis Coppola 2004 Rosso Shiraz (California) $11. Soft, rich and ripe with blackberry tart, chocolate and coffee flavors. This rustic, easy Syrah benefits from uncomplicated tannins. **84** —S.H. (12/1/2006)

Francis Coppola 2003 Rosso Shiraz (California) $11. Here's your basic house red, dark, dry and jammy in cherry-berry fruit. It has that fresh, young acidity that tastes like it's straight out of the fermenting tank. **84** —S.H. (12/31/2004)

Francis Coppola 2003 Diamond Collection Green Label Syrah-Shiraz Syrah (California) $16. Bright cherry-berry flavors tinged with a healthy dollop of vanilla and a soft, creamy mouthfeel give this wine easy accessibility and mass appeal. No, it's not profound, but it's a nice mouthful of red wine at an affordable price. **85** (9/1/2005)

Francis Coppola 1999 Diamond Series Green Label Syrah (California) $17. Solid fruit and decent texture mark this offering from the stable of the noted director. Deep berry, black pepper and animal notes open to a pleasing berry-earth-plum palate here. The wine finishes dry with grape and spicy herb notes. **86** (10/1/2001)

Francis Coppola 2004 Diamond Collection Red Label Zinfandel (California) $16. Rustic and easy, with chewy, briary berry and spice flavors, this Zin is a blend from such warm Zin areas as Amador, Paso Robles and Dry Creek. **84** —S.H. (12/15/2006)

Francis Coppola 1997 Diamond Series Zinfandel (California) $14. 82 —J.C. (2/1/2000)

FRANCISCAN

Franciscan 2003 Oakville Estate Magnificat Cabernet Blend (Napa Valley) $45. I've always been partial to Magnificat, not only because it's such a grand wine, but because the price is moderate for Napa, and they haven't raised it for years. A Cabernet-based blend, it's rich, soft, complex and chocolaty, with tiers of cassis and smoky oak. **92** —S.H. (12/15/2006)

Franciscan 2001 Cabernet Sauvignon (Napa Valley) $27. A modest Cabernet that's thin for the vintage. You can taste the underlying quality of blackberry flavor, smooth tannins and elegant acidity, and there's a generous dollop of oak, but in the context of the vintage, it's disappointing. **85** —S.H. (10/3/2004)

Franciscan 1998 Cabernet Sauvignon (Napa Valley) $25. Blach cherry, blackberry, smoky oak and tangy acidity drive this somewhat lean version of Napa Cabernet. The finish is moderate and bright. **86** —J.M. (12/31/2001)

Franciscan 2003 Oakville Estate Cabernet Sauvignon (Napa Valley) $28. Ripe in blackcurrant and cherry fruit, with a rustic edge to the texture, this dry wine is at its best now. Despite the edgy mouthfeel, it does show fine Napa tannins and acids. **84** —S.H. (7/1/2006)

Franciscan 2002 Oakville Estate Cabernet Sauvignon (Napa Valley) $27. Tasted alongside Cabs costing far more, this wine held its own, as it usually does. It's rich in currant, cedar and vanilla flavors, yet dry and superbly balanced. Keeps its harmony through a long, satisfying finish. Drink now. **91 Editors' Choice** —S.H. (12/1/2005)

Franciscan 2002 Oakville Estate Cabernet Sauvignon (Napa Valley) $25. Exemplifies its terroir and vintage with its impeccable balance, and the way the ripe, sophisticated tannins wrap around the fleshy black currant, olive, chocolate and herb flavors. Finishes with some sweetness from charry oak. **91** —S.H. (8/1/2005)

Franciscan 1999 Cuvée Sauvage Chardonnay (Napa Valley) $35. Plush toast and butterscotch aromas kick this one off, with a deep, rich follow-up of melon, citrus, apple, peach, pear, herb and mineral flavors. Quite luscious and compelling, with a substantial finish. **91** —J.M. (5/1/2002)

Franciscan 2001 Cuvée Sauvage Chardonnay (Carneros) $35. This year's release is young, tight and oaky. Hard to smell much beyond well toasted oak, lees and roasted hazelnut, but there's a suggestion of tropical fruits. In the mouth, the flavor of sweet, smoky oak dominates. Hard to tell where it's going. Give it a few months in the cellar to knit together. **88** —S.H. (12/15/2003)

Franciscan 1996 Cuvée Sauvage Chardonnay (Napa Valley) $35. 89 —L.W. (10/1/1999)

Franciscan 2003 Oakville Estate Chardonnay (Napa Valley) $17. This pleasant quaffer offers up good Chard character. The apple, peach and pear flavors have a creamy texture, and just a touch of smoky oak. Turns a bit tart on the finish. **84** —S.H. (12/1/2005)

Franciscan 2002 Oakville Estate Chardonnay (Napa Valley) $16. Fruity and oaky, a likeable Chard that satisfies for its array of peach, pear, spice, smoke and vanilla aromas and flavors and creamy texture. But it could use more oomph. **85** —S.H. (11/15/2004)

Franciscan 1999 Oakville Estate Chardonnay (Napa Valley) $18. 87 —J.M. (5/1/2002)

Franciscan 1998 Oakville Estate Chardonnay (Napa Valley) $18. 90 (6/1/2000)

Franciscan 1997 Oakville Estate Chardonnay (Napa Valley) $17. This opens with intense tropical fruit, marked by an especially large serving of pineapple, with a side of mango. The center is tight and somewhat lean, but the finish opens up into layers of fruit flavors, with an added dash of green apple. **91** —L.W. (6/1/2003)

Franciscan 1996 Oakville Estate Chardonnay (Napa Valley) $18. 88 —M.S. (6/1/1999)

Franciscan 2000 Oakville Estate Cuvée Sauvage Chardonnay (Carneros) $35. Incredibly rich and toasty. Opens with a blast of charry oak, vanilla and caramel. Underlying fruit aromas range from lemons to apples, to peaches and tropical fruits. Drinks full-bodied and powerful, with a creamy texture and vibrant fruit. A sweet-sour note of lees shows up on the finish. **92** —S.H. (2/1/2003)

Franciscan 2000 Oakville Estates Chardonnay (Napa Valley) $17. 91 Cellar Selection —J.M. (5/1/2002)

Franciscan 2001 Merlot (Napa Valley) $22. So filled with sweet cocoa, it's almost like liquid milk chocolate, poured over ripe black cherries and sprinkled with vanilla. Oak adds a toasty edge. This dry wine is as luscious as the California sun could make it. **87** —S.H. (12/15/2004)

Franciscan 1997 Oakville Esate Merlot (Napa Valley) $18. 91 (11/15/1999)

Franciscan 2003 Oakville Estate Merlot (Napa Valley) $22. A little angular and sugary sweet, but it's soft enough, with a creamy, velvety texture and some ripe blackberry jam and chocolate candy flavors. **84** —S.H. (12/1/2006)

Franciscan 2002 Oakville Estate Merlot (Napa Valley) $22. Fruity and very easy to drink for its soft, rich texture and polished finish. Offers flavors of black cherries and cassis, with a chocolaty undertow. Like velvet, and finishes with a kick of tannin. **88** —S.H. (8/1/2005)

Franciscan 2000 Oakville Estate Merlot (Napa Valley) $22. Lush, rich tannins and soft acids lead to a great mouthfeel, round and plush as velvet. The problem is fruit intensity: There are some plum and blackberry flavors but they're thin, and the wine turns watery and a bit harsh on the finish. An oaky overlay is no substitute for ripe flavors. **85** —S.H. (4/1/2003)

Franciscan 1999 Oakville Estate Merlot (Napa Valley) $22. Spicy blackberry and cherry notes are framed in smoky, tarry oak. Tannins are ripe and smooth, though the finish is a little tart. **92** —J.M. (5/1/2002)

Franciscan 2001 Magnificat Red Blend (Napa Valley) $45. Surprisingly tannic and closed for an '01 Napa, but this may be a stylistic decision. It's a very fine wine, well balanced and rich in oak and blackberry-cherry fruit. Totally dry, but those tannins really lock up the flavors. Best after 2010. **90** —S.H. (3/1/2005)

FRANK FAMILY

Frank Family 2002 Cabernet Sauvignon (Napa Valley) $40. Here's a nice glass of Cab, rich and dry and ripe. It has forward flavors of jammy blackberries, black cherries and cassis, with very rich, thick, complex tannins, but it's so sweet in fruit and so velvety, it's instantly drinkable. **90** —S.H. (9/1/2006)

Frank Family 2001 Cabernet Sauvignon (Rutherford) $65. Polished, supple and well-balanced. The cherry, herb and oak flavors are held by sturdy but pliant tannins and a good volume of acidity. Epitomizes a classic Rutherford interpretation. **90** —S.H. (10/1/2004)

Frank Family 2003 Reserve Cabernet Sauvignon (Rutherford) $70. Dark, ripe and tannic, it's an ager, but there's something about it now that's instantly appealing. It is a dry wine but with a honeyed sweetness and glyceriney richness. Oozes blackberry, lead pencil, currant, cedar and mocha flavors leading to a long, balanced finish. **92** —S.H. (12/15/2006)

Frank Family 2002 Reserve Cabernet Sauvignon (Rutherford) $70. Soft, ripe and totally voluptuous, showing gorgeously ripe fruit and tannins. Seductive and delicious. Doesn't seem built for the long haul, but defines Rutherford's red stone fruit, and slightly earthy appeal. **92** —S.H. (9/1/2006)

Frank Family 2000 Reserve Cabernet Sauvignon (Rutherford) $65. Excellent due to the sheer fabulosity of its flavors, which are rich and opulent in black currant, blackberry and roast coffee. But this is a young wine, with sharp acids, and the tannins leave a drying sensation after you swallow. It hasn't all knit together yet. **90** —S.H. (2/1/2004)

Frank Family 1999 Reserve Cabernet Sauvignon (Rutherford) $65. Black as night, with massively oaky aromas and equally powerful black-currant notes, this is clearly a big, young Cabernet. It delivers fresh, complex flavors ranging from blackberries to coffee, dark chocolate, tobacco and sage. Feels fabulously rich in the mouth now, although solid tannins suggest aging through 2008. Cellar Selection. **94 Cellar Selection** —S.H. (12/31/2002)

Frank Family 1998 Reserve Cabernet Sauvignon (Rutherford) $65. It does not seem unreasonable, at this price, to expect a wine to be among the best of its class. This wine is not. Certainly, it is drenched in the best oak money can buy, and drips with the sweet, smoky char of toasted barrels. Beyond that, there are some modest berry flavors and rather nice tannins. **85** —S.H. (6/1/2002)

Frank Family 2004 Chardonnay (Napa Valley) $32. Earthy and dusty flavors of tobacco and herbs accompany the peach fruit in this dry, somewhat soft wine. Oak fills in the thin spots, lending sweet woodsap, vanilla and buttered toast. **85** —S.H. (3/1/2006)

Frank Family 2000 Chardonnay (Napa Valley) $29. Well-toasted oak dominates the aromas, hauling along the usual vanilla and crushed-spice notes. It's oaky in the mouth, too, full of new-barrel sweetness floating above tropical fruit flavors. Dryish and soft in acids, it has a buttery, creamy mouthfeel. **90** —S.H. (9/1/2002)

Frank Family 2004 Zinfandel (Napa Valley) $35. You can't help but taste the harvest heat in this wine, which brims with blackberry and cherry flavors that verge, not on raisins, but what happens when pie filling spills over into the pan and bakes. The wine is very high in alcohol and thus it's soft as chocolate pudding. **87** —S.H. (12/1/2006)

Frank Family 2003 Zinfandel (Napa Valley) $35. There's a lot of alcohol in this Zin, but the wine handles it well, showing a clean balance of fruit, tannins and acids. It's dry, with cassis, cherry and mocha flavors and a hint of raisins. Try it with Chinese beef dishes or grilled steak smothered in onions. **87** —S.H. (3/1/2006)

FRANUS

Franus 2000 Cabernet Sauvignon (Napa Valley) $25. This well-made wine has polished flavors of currants, herbs and spices, elaborated with smoky oak. The tannins are lush and sweet. It's so well structured that you wish it were more concentrated. **86** —S.H. (5/1/2004)

Franus 1999 Rancho Chimiles Cabernet Sauvignon (Napa Valley) $40. Here's a generous Cab that offers ripe blackcurrant, plum, herb and mocha flavors, and a good amount of toasty oak. It's very dry, with smooth, dusty tannins. Finishes with a bit of astringency, but may soften up in a few years. **89** —S.H. (5/1/2004)

Franus 2002 Brandlin Vineyard Zinfandel (Mount Veeder) $32. Mount Veeder has shown itself to be one of the greatest homes of Zin, and this stunning wine is proof. Has the most amazing blackberry, blueberry and black cherry fruit, held in check by firm but smooth tannins. Completely dry, at the cost of high alcohol, but remains balanced and flashy. **93 Cellar Selection** —S.H. (5/1/2005)

Franus 2001 Brandlin Vineyard Zinfandel (Mount Veeder) $22. Starts off with bright raspberry notes in the nose. On the palate, it's fruity and spicy, with a blend of cherry, plum, cinnamon, toast and vanilla flavors. **88** —J.M. (4/1/2004)

Franus 2001 Planchon Vineyard Zinfandel (Contra Costa County) $18. A bit rustic in texture, this wine offers a smoky blend of black cherry, spice, mocha and smoke flavors, finishing with a hint of dryness. **86** —J.M. (4/1/2004)

FRAZIER

Frazier 2003 Cabernet Sauvignon (Napa Valley) $55. It's been several years since I last tasted a Frazier Cab, but this '03 brought back memories of the excellent '99. It's not quite as rich, but is classically structured. From a cooler part of the valley, it blends dried herbs in with the black currants. **90** —S.H. (9/1/2006)

Frazier 1999 Lupine Hill Vineyard Cabernet Sauvignon (Napa Valley) $45. Well-ripened, with pronounced cassis flavors. There are also notes of chocolate, cherries and sweetened espresso. Tannins are very soft, in the modern style, and the wine is dry, with O.K. acidity. Yet there's a one-dimensional simplicity to the structure. The flash is all on the surface. **86** —S.H. (11/15/2002)

Frazier 1997 Lupine Hill Vineyard Cabernet Sauvignon (Napa Valley) $45. **90** (11/1/2000)

Frazier 1996 Lupine Hill Vineyard Cabernet Sauvignon (Napa Valley) $36. **86** —M.S. (12/31/1999)

Frazier 2000 Memento Cabernet Sauvignon (Napa Valley) $75. Ripe and delicious, with blackcurrant and cassis flavors that finish with a citrusy, orange-zest edge. This may come from the French oak, which also brings lush vanilla, cream and smoky notes. Sweet tannins and soft acids make it instantly appealing. **92** —S.H. (2/1/2004)

Frazier 2003 Merlot (Napa Valley) $40. Voluptuous and sensual, this is an exotically ripe style of Merlot that joins lush fruit and toasty oak with a fine tannin-acid structure. They used to call Merlot the soft Cabernet, and in this case it really is true. At its best now. **88** —S.H. (12/1/2006)

Frazier 1999 Lupine Hill Merlot (Napa Valley) $35. This is a first-rate Merlot, smooth and dry, with a good balance of black-cherry and green-olive flavors, and a rich overlay of spicy, smoky oak. It feels light and

USA

delicate on the palate, and yet has the weight of a serious red. **93** —*S.H.* *(11/15/2002)*

Frazier 1997 Lupine Hill Vineyard Merlot (Napa Valley) $35. **87** —*J.C.* *(7/1/2000)*

FREEMAN

Freeman 2004 Pinot Noir (Russian River Valley) $35. Rich and forward in spicy fruit, with a sweet rhubarb edge veering into cola and cocoa. Finishes with an elegant flourish of oak-infused fruit. A complex, multi-layered wine that will handle some years of bottle age. **91** —*S.H.* *(12/1/2006)*

Freemark Abbey 1996 Cabernet Sauvignon (Napa Valley) $27. **85** —*S.H.* *(7/1/2000)*

Freemark Abbey 1995 Cabernet Sauvignon (Napa Valley) $23. **88** —*S.H.* *(6/1/1999)*

FREEMARK ABBEY

Freemark Abbey 2002 Cabernet Sauvignon (Napa Valley) $35. A very nice Cabernet with an opulence and balance and true varietal character, this multi-vineyard blend offers cassis, plum sauce, cocoa, herb and oak flavors. It should drink well for five years. **87** —*S.H. (12/15/2006)*

Freemark Abbey 2001 Cabernet Sauvignon (Napa Valley) $35. Dry and tannic in youth. It's not a particularly ripe wine, but subtle in meshing blackberry fruit flavors with sweet dried herbs and bitter coffee. They strove for balance and harmony, and succeeded. Now through 2010. **89** —*S.H. (3/1/2005)*

Freemark Abbey 2000 Cabernet Sauvignon (Napa Valley) $34. This distinguished Cab shows its pedigree with its ripely sweet blackcurrant and cassis flavors and lovely tannins. The wine caresses the palate, now gentle and soft, now firm. It thins down for a moment in the middle, courtesy of the vintage, and then returns to impress with the long, spicy finish. **90** —*S.H. (5/1/2004)*

Freemark Abbey 2002 Bosché Cabernet Sauvignon (Napa Valley) $65. The winery's flagship single-vineyard Cab, from Rutherford, is extraordinarily rich and opulent, offering tiers of classic Cabernet flavors that don't stop. Cassis, intense cherry, espresso, cocoa, dill, sweet anise, the list goes on and on. Marked by wonderful depth and balance, this long-lived wine is beautiful now and should improve through this decade before slowly winding down. **94 Cellar Selection** —*S.H. (12/15/2006)*

Freemark Abbey 2001 Bosché Cabernet Sauvignon (Napa Valley) $65. One of the best Cabs of the vintage. It's still a young wine, all primary black currant and plum fruit flavors and toasted oak, with complex notes of coffee and mocha. This wine is extraordinarily rich and finely balanced, displaying power, elegance, finesse and an unreal depth of fruit along with great length. Drink now through 2015. **96 Editors' Choice** —*S.H. (12/15/2005)*

Freemark Abbey 2000 Bosché Cabernet Sauvignon (Napa Valley) $68. Not drinkable yet—it's too tannic. The cherries may emerge in a few years, but beyond that this isn't a candidate for the long haul. **87** —*S.H. (8/1/2005)*

Freemark Abbey 1997 Bosché Cabernet Sauvignon (Napa Valley) $68. This big, burly Cab is a Napa Valley tradition. The cedar and cassis aromas and flavors are classic, but boast an untamed, briary wildness to them that gives Bosche its own identity. Finishes long but tart, with mouth-drying tannins that need time to resolve. Drink 2007-2012. **90** *(6/1/2003)*

Freemark Abbey 1999 Estate Bottled Cabernet Sauvignon (Napa Valley) $34. Not overly intense or extracted, this California Cabernet Sauvignon relies on blance and smoothness to impress. Mild cedar and cassis aromas and flavors are exactly what you expect, turning slightly herbal and tea-like on the finish. **87** *(6/1/2003)*

Freemark Abbey 2003 Sycamore Vineyards Cabernet Sauvignon (Napa Valley) $55. Very dry, made in a more restrained style for this very ripe vintage. Shows earthy, mushroomy fruit flavors overshadowed by pronounced acids and tannins. Seems designed for the cellar, and should blossom there. Give it until 2009 to begin to open. **87** —*S.H. (12/31/2006)*

Freemark Abbey 2002 Sycamore Vineyards Cabernet Sauvignon (Napa Valley) $60. A bit closed now, locked down by stubborn tannins and a slight mustiness, but it's a very good wine that should begin to open in a few years. It's got rich black cherry, currant and herb flavors. Best after 2008. **87** —*S.H. (12/15/2006)*

Freemark Abbey 2001 Sycamore Vineyards Cabernet Sauvignon (Rutherford) $55. Full-bodied and dense, with an almost liqueurish, syrupy mouthfeel, and extracted in jammy cherry, plum and cassis flavors. Also a little soft. But the tannins are rich and the wine is absolutely dry. Might develop subtlety and greater finesse in 5 or 6 years. **87** —*S.H. (10/1/2004)*

Freemark Abbey 2000 Sycamore Vineyards Cabernet Sauvignon (Napa Valley) $60. This wine is tough and thin in fruit, and very dry. There's a suggestion of cherries, but this is a lot of money to pay for something that isn't a sure thing. **84** —*S.H. (8/1/2005)*

Freemark Abbey 1997 Sycamore Vineyards Cabernet Sauvignon (Napa Valley) $59. A dry-smelling wine, with hints of cinnamon, pine bark, eucalyptus and earth, that unfold slowly on the palate to reveal bright red cherries and berries. It's big and it's structured, yet finishes smooth and silky, blending in coffee and tea notes. Approachable now, but better after 2005. **91 Cellar Selection** *(6/1/2003)*

Freemark Abbey 1994 Sycamore Vineyards Cabernet Sauvignon (Napa Valley) $39. **93** *(11/15/1999)*

Freemark Abbey 1993 Sycamore Vineyards Cabernet Sauvignon (Napa Valley) $35. **94** —*S.H. (6/1/1999)*

Freemark Abbey 1992 Sycamore Vineyards Cabernet Sauvignon (Napa Valley) $85. The complex nose boasts hints of spring flowers, tobacco, maple syrup and cedar. Now into its second decade, this wine is fully mature, with flavors of molasses and mushrooms that have replaced some of the cherry notes of its youth. The mouthfeel is silky and elegant; the finish chocolaty and smooth. Drink up. **90** *(6/1/2003)*

Freemark Abbey 1998 Chardonnay (Napa Valley) $19. **84** *(6/1/2000)*

Freemark Abbey 2003 Chardonnay (Rutherford) $20. Exciting for its control and balance. There's some big fruit here, just bursting with pears and pineapples, but it's kept tight with acids and firm oak. Finishes long and slightly bitter from lees. **90** —*S.H. (3/1/2005)*

Freemark Abbey 1997 Carpy Ranch Chardonnay (Napa Valley) $26. **85** *(6/1/2000)*

Freemark Abbey 2001 Estate Bottled Chardonnay (Rutherford) $18. This plump Napa Chard shows off plenty of ripe fruit, ranging from apples to pears and lemons to limes. A hint of vanilla emerges as it sits in the glass. A fruity, pleasant drink that finishes with food-friendly lean and lemony flavors. **87** *(6/1/2003)*

Freemark Abbey 1997 Napa Valley Chardonnay (Napa Valley) $18. **87** —*S.H. (6/1/1999)*

Freemark Abbey 1997 Merlot (Napa Valley) $28. **87** —*S.H. (7/1/2000)*

Freemark Abbey 1996 Merlot (Napa Valley) $23. **89** —*S.H. (6/1/1999)*

Freemark Abbey 2002 Merlot (Napa Valley) $24. Perfectly dry, with smooth tannins, the disappointing thing about this Merlot is its lack of richness. It's well-made, but thin in fruit, with only a suggestion of cherry and coffee flavors. **84** —*S.H. (12/31/2005)*

Freemark Abbey 2001 Merlot (Rutherford) $27. A distinctive Merlot that shows true terroir. The aromatics include white pepper, raw meat, and exotic herbs such as tarragon, as well as oak. That sounds strange, but familiar cherry and blackberry flavors rule the mouth. Firm in tannins, and totally dry. Earns extra points for its uniqueness. **91** —*S.H. (3/1/2005)*

Freemark Abbey 2000 Merlot (Rutherford) $25. Blackberry and cola aromas mingle with mint and green tea, and then turn fruity in the mouth, with cherry and blackberry flavors. The tannins are firm and a little sharp, and so is the acidity. Best now. **86** —*S.H. (5/1/2004)*

Freemark Abbey 1999 Merlot (Rutherford) $25. Starts off with some stinky burnt-match aromas, but rights itself quickly, folding in smoke, cherry and herbs. Flavors are modest but correct, with ripe cherries and notes of treebark, picking up mocha nuances on the finish. **85** *(6/1/2003)*

USA

Freemark Abbey 2000 Petite Sirah (Rutherford) $28. Almost all tasters picked up on a funky note on the nose and on the palate. There's some pretty berry-cherry fruit, and the tannins are nice and soft, but the wine can't rise above an ordinary level. Tasted twice, with consistent notes. **82** *(4/1/2003)*

Freemark Abbey 2004 Viognier (Rutherford) $27. I loved the '03. This one's right up there. The grapes give opulent flavors of tropical fruits, wildflowers, minerals, spices and honey, while partial barrel fermentation and new oak aging add a Burgundian creamy richness. The winery is at the top of the Viognier game in California. **93 Editors' Choice** *—S.H. (12/15/2006)*

Freemark Abbey 2003 Viognier (Rutherford) $24. Dry white wines don't get much riper or more exotic than this. This full-bodied wine is jammed with tropical fruit, honeysuckle, meringue, crème brûlée and spice flavors that last through a long finish. It's as rich as cream, yet dry and crisp. Compelling and delicious. **92** *—S.H. (12/15/2004)*

Freemark Abbey 2002 Carpy Ranch Viognier (Rutherford) $20. You'll find this drier and leaner than many of the more opulent California Viogniers. It has citrusy flavors, with a suggestion of apricot and peach, and finishes with a burst of acidity. **85** *—S.H. (5/1/2004)*

Freemark Abbey 2000 Carpy Ranch Viognier (Napa Valley) $25. Quite fragrant, with hints of peach, apricot, spice and herbs. Round and viscous on the finish, with a refreshing orange-citrus finish. **87** *—J.M. (12/15/2002)*

Freemark Abbey 1997 Edelwein Gold White Blend (Napa Valley) $40. **91** *—S.H. (6/1/1999)*

FREESTONE

Freestone 1997 Merlot (Napa Valley) $18. **87** *—J.C. (7/1/2000)*

FREI BROTHERS

Frei Brothers 2000 Cabernet Sauvignon (Alexander Valley) $24. Dark as night and still young, with thick, hard tannins. Seems to struggle to put out flavor, with thin notes of black currants. The acids are soft. **85** *—S.H. (10/1/2003)*

Frei Brothers 2000 Redwood Creek Cabernet Sauvignon (California) $8. Only Gallo, who owns the brand, and a few others could pull off a Cabernet this good and affordable. It's got lovely varietal flavors of blackcurrants and a rich, gentle texture, and is well oaked. Dry and balanced, and with 78,000 cases made, it will be easy to find. **87 Best Buy** *—S.H. (3/1/2003)*

Frei Brothers 2002 Reserve Cabernet Sauvignon (Alexander Valley) $24. Smooth and velvety like a good single malt Scotch, with lush, complex tannins, this wine is compromised by excessive sweetness. There's a sugary, malt taste throughout that detracts. **82** *—S.H. (12/1/2005)*

Frei Brothers 1999 Reserve Cabernet Sauvignon (Alexander Valley) $24. This wine pours as black as a young Port, and has a rich, thick texture. Aromas include raisins, chocolate and wood, and it feels dense. Not delicate or for the faint-hearted. **86** *—S.H. (12/31/2002)*

Frei Brothers 2001 Chardonnay (Russian River Valley) $20. A complex and balanced wine that shows green apples, peaches and pears and a nice overlay of oak. You could say that about a lot of wines, but this beauty is so tasteful and nuanced, it's especially likeable. **91 Editors' Choice** *—S.H. (5/1/2003)*

Frei Brothers 2004 Reserve Chardonnay (Russian River Valley) $20. Super-fruity and super-oaky to the point of overwhelming, all this wine needs is some restraint. There's an enormity of peach custard, pineapple cream, vanilla and honey. The grapes are obviously fabulous. **83** *—S.H. (3/1/2006)*

Frei Brothers 2003 Reserve Chardonnay (Russian River Valley) $20. Rich in well-ripened fruit flavors and with a sweet coat of smoky oak and vanilla, this Chard also has a structural integrity based on crispness and vitality. It's not a soft, creamy Chard but a firm one, with exotic fruit. **89** *—S.H. (12/1/2005)*

Frei Brothers 2000 Reserve Chardonnay (Russian River Valley) $17. A pleasant, medium-bodied wine that offers pretty pear, melon, citrus and apple notes. **86** *—J.M. (12/15/2002)*

Frei Brothers 2001 Redwood Creek Merlot (California) $7. Smells a bit briary and minty, but once you take a sip, it delivers plenty of ripe, sophisticated cherry-berry fruit. The tannins are smooth and polished. There's lots to like in this dry, full-bodied dinner wine at a giveaway price. **86** *—S.H. (4/1/2004)*

Frei Brothers 2003 Reserve Merlot (Dry Creek Valley) $20. Somebody picked early, to judge from the slightly green, peppercorn notes. But in a way that adds to the complexity, and makes the wine different. It's not a fruit bomb, it's a coffee, herb and blackberry-flavored dry Merlot with structural integrity. **88** *—S.H. (12/1/2005)*

Frei Brothers 2001 Reserve Merlot (Dry Creek Valley) $20. From Gallo, a young, tannic wine that tastes almost like a barrel sample. The berry-cherry flavors are jammy and juvenile, with youthful acidity that's sharp on the palate. Not at its best now, but should calm down after 2003. **85** *—S.H. (12/1/2003)*

Frei Brothers 2001 Pinot Noir (Russian River Valley) $24. This Gallo brand exploits extensive new Pinot plantings in the appellation to produce a wine that's clean and correct, rather than exciting. The flavors range from cranberries to black cherries, and the tannins are silky. Will improve with a year or so in the cellar. **87** *—S.H. (7/1/2003)*

Frei Brothers 2003 Reserve Pinot Noir (Russian River Valley) $24. Raw in acids, juicy in briary wild berry flavors with a chocolatey finish, this dry wine is a little jagged around the edges. May soften in a year or so. **84** *—S.H. (10/1/2005)*

Frei Brothers 2000 Reserve Pinot Noir (Russian River Valley) $24. Muscular aromas of plum cake, sawdust and smoked meat make for an attractive and complex nose. The flavors are mostly plum and blackberry, indicating a fully ripe California-style wine. Powerful verve and drive ensure that it races through the finish. **88** *(10/1/2002)*

Frei Brothers 2001 Redwood Creek Sauvignon Blanc (California) $8. A nice, clean wine, filled with lemon and grapefruit flavors and refreshing acidity. Scours the mouth with citrusy thoroughness and leaves behind tart feeling. **85** *—S.H. (3/1/2003)*

Frei Brothers 2003 Reserve Syrah (Russian River Valley) $24. Right out there on the border of superripe, in fact almost sweet, but carefully avoids a sugary finish. Still, it's abundantly rich in blackberry and fruity-tea flavors that are dry in the most technical sense. **84** *—S.H. (6/1/2006)*

Frei Brothers 2002 Reserve Syrah (Russian River Valley) $24. Cherries, cranberries and hints of cocoa lay the groundwork for a decent Syrah—albeit one that's not terribly dense or concentrated. Seems to lack a bit of varietal spice, but it's a solid red wine for daily consumption. **83** *(9/1/2005)*

FRENCH HILL

French Hill 2002 Barbera (Sierra Foothills) $39. Expensive, but worth it for the exciting coffee, smoky new oak, cigar box, black cherry and tar aromas and flavors that are very complex. Drinks smooth and clean, rich in tannins, really top rate. One of the best Barberas of recent memory. **92** *—S.H. (3/1/2007)*

French Hill 2003 Grand Reserve Barbera (Sierra Foothills) $39. Harsh and rough, this wine has a dry, unfinished feel, with herbal, coffee flavors. It may improve with time. **82** *—S.H. (12/1/2005)*

French Hill 2001 Grand Reserve Barbera (El Dorado) $39. Isn't this expensive for a Barbera? You bet it is. It's not a bad wine, but not worth the price. Drinks soft and pasty in texture, with monster flavors of plums, blackberries, chocolate, cherries, and so on that finish rather sweet and simple. **85** *—S.H. (12/1/2003)*

French Hill 2003 Grand Reserve Pinotage (Amador County) $32. Tastes thick and gluey, with sweet-and-sour flavors of cherry cough drops. **80** *—S.H. (12/1/2005)*

French Hill 2002 Grand Reserve Pinotage (Amador County) $32. Full-bodied and dry, and softly tannic, with a melange of blackberry, leather, herb and tobacco flavors and a touch of oak. This complex wine is food-friendly. **87** *—S.H. (3/1/2005)*

FREY

Frey 2000 Merlot (Redwood Valley) $15. One of the few truly organic, i.e., sulfite-free, wineries in California, Frey's Merlot is racy enough, with well-etched blueberry and herb flavors, although it has enough tannins to make your tongue stick to your palate. Tastes better than it smells. Smells a little vegetal. **84** —*S.H. (5/1/2002)*

Frey 2000 Petite Sirah (Mendocino) $12. There's a vegetal, canned asparagus note on the nose right next to deeper notes of blackberries. In the mouth, the wine is thick, extremely tannic and acidic, without a whole lot of fruit. In fact, the tannins are downright palate numbing. It might soften with age. **82** —*S.H. (5/1/2002)*

Frey 2000 Syrah (Redwood Valley) $11. Very dark. One sniff alerts you to problems. There's a vegetal note, somewhere between bell peppers and asparagus, that dominates. The wine is dense, tannic and acidic, and a faint core of dark berry frui. **82** —*S.H. (5/1/2002)*

Frey 1999 Butow Vineyards Syrah (Redwood Valley) $11. A forward, fruity wine with a black cherry-and-plum backbone, accented by licorice, dried spices and black pepper. Smooth and supple in the mouth, this organically grown Syrah is ready to drink tonight. **88 Best Buy** *(10/1/2001)*

Frey 2000 Zinfandel (Mendocino) $11. Smells rubbery and cardboardy, with a hint of blackberry. The flavors are juicy, and there's a real richness to the wine in the mouth. Yet it can't quite overcome its rustic nature. More like a homemade wine than a commercial release. **82** —*S.H. (5/1/2002)*

FRIAS

Frias 2002 Cabernet Sauvignon (Spring Mountain) $65. Not as powerful as the '01, this Cab is still an impressive wine. It's dry, with ripe cherry and cassis flavors, smooth, complex tannins and an elaborate overlay of oak. Very dry, and best now and through 2008. **89** —*S.H. (10/1/2005)*

Frias 2001 Cabernet Sauvignon (Spring Mountain) $65. Classic Napa Cabernet, from the clean, varietally pure black currant and cassis aroma to the smooth tannins and ripe currant and cassis flavors. This is a balanced, elegant wine, despite the full body. It goes down gently, leaving behind a long aftertaste of currants. **92** —*S.H. (10/1/2005)*

Frias 1998 Private Reserve Cabernet Sauvignon (Napa Valley) $50. Young Cabernet aromas of cassis and well-smoked oak yield to varietal flavors of blackberries in this dry wine. The tannins are ultrasoft in the modern Napa style. It's a paint-by-the-numbers wine, made worse by fruit so thin it completely disappears on the finish. **83** —*S.H. (11/15/2002)*

Frias 1999 Spring Mountain Cabernet Sauvignon (Napa Valley) $60. This is an austere Cabernet whose price causes sticker shock and is simply not worth it. It's dry, tart, thin and leathery, with suspiciously soft tannins. Hard to find a single flavor that isn't herbal. Makes you wonder what in the world is going on here. **84** —*S.H. (11/15/2002)*

FRICK

Frick 1995 Cinsault (Dry Creek Valley) $15. **85** —*M.S. (6/1/1999)*

Frick 1996 Syrah (Dry Creek Valley) $24. **91** —*M.S. (6/1/1999)*

Frick 1998 Syrah (Dry Creek Valley) $21. Here's another best-try-it-yourself Syrah—each reviewer identified different flavors and aromas in this wine. Aromas ran the gamut from bubble gum and espresso to cedar, licorice and banana; earth, cherry and herbs were named as dominant flavors. All agree, though, that there's a lot going on in the Frick, and that it needs a few years to whip its split personality into shape. **88** *(11/1/2001)*

Frick 2000 Owl Hill Vineyard Syrah (Dry Creek Valley) $23. Despite being nearly five years old, this wine is dry and tannic, without much fruit. It has earthy, herbal and molasses-like flavors that may have limited appeal, but is unlikely to evolve positively. Drink up. **83** *(9/1/2005)*

FRITZ

Fritz 2003 Cabernet Sauvignon (Dry Creek Valley) $35. The thing about Dry Creek Cabs like this is how wonderfully approachable they are at an early age. It's a soft, gentle wine, immaculately rich in pie-filling flavors of blackberries, cherries, cocoa and vanilla wafer, ending in a swirl of dusty spices. Just really fun to drink. **90** —*S.H. (12/31/2006)*

Fritz 2000 Cabernet Sauvignon (Sonoma County) $29. Tough, dry and tannic, with herbal flavors. The wine is a blend from Dry Creek Valley and Rockpile AVAs, regions that need a good vintage to make good Cab. They didn't get one in 2000. **84** —*S.H. (11/15/2004)*

Fritz 2002 Chardonnay (Russian River Valley) $20. A full-bodied, rich Chard that combines ripe tropical fruit, sweet pear, green apple and spice flavors with winemaker interventions, including smoky oak and lees. The creamy texture and long finish are just great. **89** —*S.H. (10/1/2004)*

Fritz 2001 Dutton Ranch Chardonnay (Russian River Valley) $20. The acidity is bright and juicy, lending a citrus edge to the green apple and spiced pear flavors. Oak adds softness and cream, but the acids really star. **89** —*S.H. (6/1/2004)*

Fritz 2000 Dutton Ranch Chardonnay (Russian River Valley) $22. This is a soft, creamy Chardonnay that's reminiscent of baked apples loaded with cinnamon and perked up with a few curls of orange zest. Finishes long, with creamy vanilla supported by orange echoes. **88** —*J.C. (9/1/2002)*

Fritz 1997 Dutton Ranch Chardonnay (Russian River Valley) $20. **92** —*S.H. (11/1/1999)*

Fritz 1997 Dutton Ranch Shop Block Chardonnay (Russian River Valley) $30. **86** —*L.W. (12/31/1999)*

Fritz 1998 Dutton Vineyard Chardonnay (Russian River Valley) $22. A rich, creamy wine, loaded with personality. Spicy, oaky aromas ride over tropical fruit and peach scents, and it drinks crisp and spicy, although the midpalate is a little thin in fruit. The oaky sweetness is very nice, and so is the whistle-clean finish. **87** —*S.H. (2/1/2001)*

Fritz 1997 Poplar Vineyard Dutton Ranch Chardonnay (Russian River Valley) $22. **85** —*S.H. (2/1/2000)*

Fritz 1998 Ruxton Vineyard Chardonnay (Russian River Valley) $27. Strong , complex aromas, with notes of tropical fruit and coconut. In the mouth, it's oaky and spicy, with penetrating, bright, effusive flavors that you might go so far as to call racy. The alcohol content is high and it drinks a little soft, but this is a very seductive wine. A crowd-pleaser, for sure. **89** —*S.H. (2/1/2001)*

Fritz 1997 Ruxton Vineyard Dutton Ranch Chardonnay (Russian River Valley) $26. **90** —*S.H. (10/1/2000)*

Fritz 2000 Shop Block Dutton Ranch Chardonnay (Russian River Valley) $22. From vines planted in 1967, a lush, complex wine, with peach flavors giving way to dried apricot, hazelnut, flowers and herbs, and a suggestion of brittle autumn leaves in the finish. Round, creamy and opulent on the palate, with a smoky, vanilla edge, it's a fascinating wine that shows how good Chard can be with a little bottle age. **90** —*S.H. (12/31/2003)*

Fritz 1998 Shop Block Vineyard Dutton Ranch Chardonnay (Russian River Valley) $30. A very distinctive Chard—full of character and even eccentricity. There are strong, up-front aromas of tangerines, vanilla, butterscotch, smoke, ripe peaches and caramel. It's especially notable for the thick, creamy texture and a penetrating, spicy clove note that follows through on the long, rich finish. A complex, serious wine. **91** —*S.H. (2/1/2001)*

Fritz 1997 Merlot (Dry Creek Valley) $18. **85** —*L.W. (12/31/1999)*

Fritz 2004 Pinot Noir (Russian River Valley) $30. From this hot vintage, the wine is enormously ripe, with a baked-fruit character. Yet it retains classic Russian River cola, cherry and rhubarb pie flavors along with rich tannins and crisp acids. It's a powerful, robust wine. **89** —*S.H. (12/1/2006)*

Fritz 2002 Pinot Noir (Russian River Valley) $29. Starts off a bit leathery and meaty, then airs to reveal sweet cherries, cola and oaky-vanilla notes. Notable for its great structure of smooth tannins and crisp acids. **88** *(11/1/2004)*

Fritz 2000 Dutton Ranch Pinot Noir (Russian River Valley) $29. This shows many interesting accents—anise, porcini mushroom and a Sherry-like note—that have real appeal. Still, the bright fruit has a dry, woody edge that holds the wine's best parts in check. Closes with some tart fruit, earthy notes and dry tannins. **85** *(10/1/2002)*

Fritz 2005 Sauvignon Blanc (Russian River Valley) $18. A bit too much cat pee for me, although the crisp dryness is appealing. Beyond that, you get ripe grapefruit, lemon peel and passion fruit flavors. **84** —*S.H. (12/1/2006)*

Fritz 2002 Estate Sauvignon Blanc (Dry Creek Valley) $16. This savory white wine has well-ripened, almost sweet flavors of citrus fruits, figs and apples, with an edge of peppery spice. It's very bright in the mouth, with zesty acidity, and finishes with a nice, clean aftertaste. **87** —*S.H. (12/1/2004)*

Fritz 1998 Jenner Vineyard Sauvignon Blanc (Dry Creek Valley) $12. 87 — *S.H. (3/1/2000)*

Fritz 1998 Poplar Vineyard Sauvignon Blanc (Russian River Valley) $15. A fine, elegant Sauvignon Blanc, with ultraclean apple, citrus and floral notes. What's really nice about it is the crispness. It's as bright and as clean as stainless steel. **88** —*S.H. (8/1/2001)*

Fritz 2002 Zinfandel (Dry Creek Valley) $23. This fine wine exemplifies Zin's wild and woolly character in this appellation, one of its natural homes. The flavors are of briary berries, dusty herbs and bitter chocolate, and while the tannins are firm, they allow the fruit through. Its astringency calls for rich pasta dishes or hard cheeses. **87** —*S.H. (10/1/2004)*

Fritz 2001 Old Vine Zinfandel (Dry Creek Valley) $24. Skirts the line of overripeness, with just a suggestion of raisins and heaviness, but wisely stays on the side of balance. Ultrafresh, jammy flavors of cherries and blackberries are encased in rich, complex tannins, and the wine is mercifully dry. **88** —*S.H. (6/1/2004)*

Fritz 1999 Old Vine Zinfandel (Dry Creek Valley) $25. Fragrant and fruity on the nose, with rich plum, black currant, tar and smoke overtones. Spicy and licorice-like at the end with a touch of bitterness. **87** —*J.M. (3/1/2002)*

Fritz 1997 Old Vine Zinfandel (Dry Creek Valley) $20. 92 —*S.H. (11/1/1999)*

Fritz 1997 Roger's Reserve Zinfandel (Dry Creek Valley) $30. 88 3 —*L.W. (2/1/2000)*

FROG POND

Frog Pond 2001 Fralich Vineyard Syrah (Paso Robles) $NA. A pretty wine and very drinkable, with its coffee, mocha, cherry flavors and hints of sweet raisins. Gentle and soft, the wine is also very dry. **86** —*S.H. (12/1/2004)*

FROG'S LEAP

Frog's Leap 2000 Rutherford Cabernet Blend (Napa Valley) $65. This blend of the two Cabernets is fantastically concentrated and delicious. The blackcurrant and cured olive flavors are so sweet and deep, the tannins so rich and smooth, the mouthfeel so creamy and mellow, it's almost like sipping melted chocolate infused with creme de cassis. A stunning success for the vintage. **93** —*S.H. (11/15/2003)*

Frog's Leap 1999 Rutherford Cabernet Blend (Napa Valley) $65. This blend of 65% Cabernet Sauvignon and 35% Cab Franc has silky ripe tannins that support black-cherry, raspberry, plum, chocolate, spice, herb and earth flavors. The finish is racy yet in keeping with the style—elegant and supple to the end. **92** —*J.M. (2/1/2003)*

Frog's Leap 1997 Cabernet Sauvignon (Napa Valley) $30. 91 *(11/1/2000)*

Frog's Leap 2003 Cabernet Sauvignon (Napa Valley) $39. This Cabernet's a little too ripe to be completely balanced. It has raisin flavors along with plums and blackberries, and a soft texture leading to a Port-like finish, although it's dry. **84** —*S.H. (3/1/2006)*

Frog's Leap 2003 Cabernet Sauvignon (Rutherford) $75. This beautifully classic Napa Cab plays it straight down the middle, aiming for drinkability and complex ageworthiness. It's ripe but not a fruit bomb, with lovely blackberry, cassis and oak flavors. Feels opulent and complex, yet totally balanced. Good now, and versatile at the table. **91** —*S.H. (12/15/2006)*

Frog's Leap 2002 Cabernet Sauvignon (Rutherford) $65. Seems a bit light for this vintage and appellation. There are minty, wintergreen aromas along with riper cherries and chocolate, and a bitterness or sharpness to the finish. **85** —*S.H. (12/15/2005)*

Frog's Leap 2002 Cabernet Sauvignon (Napa Valley) $39. Gentle and smooth in tannic structure, with a subtle layer of polished oak, this wine

nonetheless is a little light in fruit. Could use more concentration of its cherries and blackberries. **86** —*S.H. (5/1/2005)*

Frog's Leap 2001 Cabernet Sauvignon (Rutherford) $65. This blend of 86% Cabernet Sauvignon and 19% Cabernet Franc is xtraordinarily rich and amazingly balanced for such a big wine. Stands out even in its pedigreed Rutherford neighborhood. Dense in blackberry, cranberry, sour cherry and oaky flavors. Firm in tannins. Great now but will develop through 2010 and beyond. **94** —*S.H. (10/1/2004)*

Frog's Leap 1999 Cabernet Sauvignon (Napa Valley) $35. Blueberry, vanilla and smoky underbrush are the key aromas—those and a touch of green bean or snap pea. Typical cassis and plum flavors run smoothly over the tannic, full palate. As a whole, it's firm but not too difficult to wrap yourself around. It's stylish, somewhat understated and doesn't need a lot of aging. **90** —*M.S. (11/15/2002)*

Frog's Leap 1998 Chardonnay (Napa Valley) $22. 83 *(6/1/2000)*

Frog's Leap 2003 Chardonnay (Napa Valley) $24. Lots of pleasantly ripe pear, peach and apple fruit, with crisp acids and good wood. Easy to drink, with a slight roughness of texture. **85** —*S.H. (5/1/2005)*

Frog's Leap 2001 Chardonnay (Napa Valley) $22. Has correct varietal flavors of apples, peaches and tropical fruits, is dry, and possesses the requisite oaky influences. Beyond that, there's not a whole lot of interest going on. **84** —*S.H. (12/15/2003)*

Frog's Leap 2000 Chardonnay (Napa Valley) $22. Vivaciously bright, with pretty pear, apple, citrus and herb flavors couched in a tangy-edged body. Fresh on the finish. **88** —*J.M. (5/1/2002)*

Frog's Leap 2003 Merlot (Napa Valley) $34. Full-throttle Merlot here, oaky, tannic and dry. It's a young wine now, somewhat sharp and edgy, but with a promising future. The cherry flavors should sweeten and the tannins soften with three or four years of proper cellaring. **87** —*S.H. (3/1/2006)*

Frog's Leap 2002 Merlot (Napa Valley) $34. This is a beautiful Merlot brimming with ripe blackcurrant, cherry and coffee flavors that are folded into soft, sweet tannins. It has some lovely wood. My only quibble is that it could be from anywhere, an international style wine that's proper rather than exciting. **87** —*S.H. (3/1/2005)*

Frog's Leap 1998 Merlot (Napa Valley) $28. Made in a lighter style, but pretty, with toasty oak aromas that enhance the cherry fruit. Expressive cherries and baking spices on the palate and delicate tannins on the finish make this a wine to enjoy over the near term. **86** —*J.C. (6/1/2001)*

Frog's Leap 2004 La Grenouille Rougante Pink Rosé Blend (Napa Valley) $12. There's something fun about this wine, even though it's kind of spare. It's bone dry, and acidic, with modest strawberry flavors. But it has a fancy quality, and at this price, it's a good buy. **85 Best Buy** —*S.H. (10/1/2005)*

Frog's Leap 2005 Sauvignon Blanc (Rutherford) $16. Pretty much as good as Napa Sauvignon gets. This is a dry, elegant wine with polished fruit and the streamlined, zesty cleansing quality you want from this variety. The wine is delicate and steely, with figgy, lemon-drop flavors and a spicy finish. **87** —*S.H. (12/1/2006)*

Frog's Leap 2004 Sauvignon Blanc (Rutherford) $16. Grabs your interest for its intense varietal character and overall balance and harmony. Zesty lemondrop, gooseberry, fig and vanilla flavors dominate, leading to a dry finish that's rich in acids. Has the weight of a Chardonnay. **90 Editors' Choice** —*S.H. (11/1/2005)*

Frog's Leap 2003 Sauvignon Blanc (Rutherford) $17. A pleasant wine, with bright-hued hints of citrus, green apple, hay, melon and herbs. It's got medium body and a light edge, finishing with moderate length. **87** — *J.M. (10/1/2004)*

Frog's Leap 2001 Sauvignon Blanc (Napa Valley) $16. Light and clean in the nose, with attractive hints of nutmeg and other baking spices. It's certainly not dull, what with its fresh grapefruit, nectarine and tangerine flavors. A crisp, refreshing finish is the final act, making it perfect to accompany shellfish. **88** *(8/1/2002)*

Frog's Leap 2002 Syrah (Napa Valley) $25. A lovely Syrah that's lush in texture and plush in ripe fruit. Full-bodied, with a warming mouthfeel, it has blackcurrant, plum and mocha flavors, and is very dry. The tannins are dense and soft. **89**—*S.H. (12/31/2004)*

Frog's Leap 2004 Leapfrogmilch White Blend (Napa Valley) $14. Very tart in acids, and dry as dust. The main problem with this amusingly-named wine is its thinness. It's watery throughout. **82**—*S.H. (10/1/2005)*

Frog's Leap 1997 Zinfandel (Napa Valley) $18. 86—*P.G. (11/15/1999)*

Frog's Leap 2004 Zinfandel (Napa Valley) $25. The wine has a beautiful texture; it's rich, velvety and silky. With some Petite Sirah and Carignan for complexity, it shows wild berry, exotic spice, coffee, leather and cola flavors. My quibble, and it's a fairly substantial one, is the heat and candied sweetness on the finish. **84**—*S.H. (12/1/2006)*

Frog's Leap 2003 Zinfandel (Napa Valley) $25. What a good job Frog's Leap has done in crafting a Zin with all the balance and harmony of a fine Cabernet, yet with Zin's distinctive personality. Wild, briary flavors of blueberries and black raspberries drink spicy and rich in this dry, addictive wine. **91 Editors' Choice**—*S.H. (11/1/2005)*

Frog's Leap 2002 Zinfandel (Napa Valley) $23. A firm-textured Zin, with fairly smooth tannins that frame a core of herb, plum, cherry, coffee and toast flavors. A touch of spice adds to the blend, with a bright, tangy edge giving extra life to the finish. **87**—*J.M. (10/1/2004)*

Frog's Leap 2001 Zinfandel (Rutherford) $22. A bit tight, with oak-tinged strawberry, coffee and chocolate notes at the core. Tannins are a little astringent, and the finish is moderate in length. **86** *(11/1/2003)*

Frog's Leap 2000 Zinfandel (Napa Valley) $22. The bouquet is earthy, maybe bordering on funky. There just isn't much fruit to it. Beyond that, look for jammy berry flavors and plenty of oak, the latter of which is very strong on the tail end. The wine has spunk but it fails to distinguish itself among the wide world of California Zin contenders. **86**—*M.S. (11/1/2002)*

Frog's Leap 1999 Zinfandel (Napa Valley) $22. A soft, floral-talc note coats earth and juicy red fruit on the comforting, almost sexy, nose. On the palate, flat blackberry and strawberry notes take on a bit of tanginess, thanks to the oak. It's medium to light in weight—this is no heavy-hitter—and finishes a little thin, the floral-talc note returning. The nose is the best part; the wine lightens up considerably after that. **85**—*D.T. (3/1/2002)*

FRONTIER RED

Frontier Red 2004 Lot 51 California Red Wine Red Blend (California) $10. This southern Rhone blend tastes like a wine you'd buy in some little Provencal village straight from the barrel, filling up your carafe for that night. It's dry, robust and honest, with good fruit and the kind of tannins to cut through almost anything. From Fess Parker. **85 Best Buy** —*S.H. (5/1/2006)*

Frontier Red NV Rhône Red Blend (California) $10. A Rhône blend of six varieties, the wine has bittersweet, jammy flavors of wild berries, chocolate, cinnamon and tobacco, with a rough-and-ready texture. Bone dry, it's for quaffing now. **83**—*S.H. (12/31/2006)*

FROSTWATCH

Frostwatch 2004 Chardonnay (Bennett Valley) $27. This is a very dry, tart Chardonnay, almost like a Fumé Blanc except that it's richer and creamier. The flavors are of lemons and limes, and papayas that aren't quite ripe. It's a complex wine that will pick up interest as it warms up and plays against food. **89**—*S.H. (7/1/2006)*

FULL CIRCLE

Full Circle 2002 Cabernet Sauvignon (California) $8. So good, you pinch yourself to believe the price. Dry and lush in dusty tannins, with rich flavors of blackberries, cherries and oak. Just misses the Big Leagues, but a fabulous vaue. **86 Best Buy**—*S.H. (3/1/2005)*

Full Circle 2003 Chardonnay (California) $8. Lots to admire here, and not just the price. This is a dry, smooth wine, with good varietal character. The apple and peach flavors are lightly oaked. **85 Best Buy**—*S.H. (3/1/2005)*

Full Circle 2003 Merlot (California) $8. Impressive for the price, in fact a supervalue. Drinks soft but rich, dry and dusty in cherries, with a pleas-

ing earthiness. The firm tannins would love to bit into a juicy steak. **85 Best Buy**—*S.H. (3/1/2005)*

FUSÉE

Fusée 2003 Cabernet Sauvignon (California) $6. At six bucks a pop, you can't go wrong with this rich, smooth, dry Cabernet. It shows appealing flavors of blackberries, blueberries, cherries and chocolate fudge, and although it's a little light, that richly satisfying fruit carries the day. **85 Best Buy**—*S.H. (11/15/2005)*

Fusée 2002 Cabernet Sauvignon (California) $6. Jammy, juicy and fun. Flavor freaks will love the upfront cherry, blackberry and chocolate flavors, wrapped in silky tannins. **84 Best Buy**—*S.H. (4/1/2005)*

Fusée 2005 Chardonnay (California) $6. Nice price, clean wine, and probably unoaked. However, the fruit is kind of thin and watery. **83 Best Buy** —*S.H. (12/1/2006)*

Fusée 2004 Chardonnay (California) $6. Clean and refreshing, this simple Chard has tropical fruit flavors and a creamy texture. The acidity is nice and brisk, while the finish is quick. **84 Best Buy**—*S.H. (4/1/2006)*

Fusée 2003 Chardonnay (California) $6. If you like ripe, fruity Chards with a creamy texture and a touch of smoky oak, this is a super value. It has flavors of peaches, vanilla, buttered toast and honey. **84 Best Buy**— *S.H. (4/1/2005)*

Fusée 2004 Merlot (California) $6. Tons of cherry and Framboise fruit in this wine, but it's a bit unbalanced, with the flavors turning into chocolate syrup, and the texture is too soft. **83 Best Buy**—*S.H. (11/1/2006)*

Fusée 2003 Merlot (California) $6. Along with life's other mysteries is how Don Sebastiani & Sons put out wines of this quality, at this price. This Merlot is dry, rich and fruity, with the balance and harmony of wines costing far more. Enjoy it for its chocolate and blackberry flavors. **87 Best Buy**—*S.H. (11/15/2005)*

Fusée 2002 Merlot (California) $6. How do they do it at this price? This great value is chockfull of delicious cherry, blackberry and mocha flavors. It's dry and smooth, with a long finish. Buy it by the case. **86 Best Buy** —*S.H. (4/1/2005)*

Fusée 2003 Syrah (California) $6. On the palate of this lighter-bodied Syrah, jammy, fruit-sweet flavors of blackberries are offset with briary, chalky accents. Starts off with sandalwood, clove and ripe fruit on the nose; finishes crisp. **86 Best Buy** *(9/1/2005)*

Fusée 2002 Syrah (California) $6. Dark, young and jammy, and so fresh in grapy flavors and acids, it tastes like it came straight from the fermenting tank. Clean, dry and filled with blackberry, cocoa and coffee flavors. Good value in a fun wine. **85 Best Buy**—*S.H. (12/31/2004)*

Fusée 2001 Syrah (California) $6. Drink this young, jammy wine with pizza. It's that kind of sipper, filled with snappy raspberry and pepper flavors. And look at that everyday price. **84**—*S.H. (9/1/2004)*

Fusée 2000 Syrah (California) $5. This Châteauneuf-style wine is jammy, with black stone fruits, berries and dark chocolate, and a sweet black cherry core, but it has body and tannins to lend it weight. The winemaker suggests pairing it with cassoulet. New from Don Sebastiani & Sons. **90 Best Buy**—*S.H. (11/15/2003)*

Fusée 2004 White Zinfandel (California) $6. Kind of sweet, with simple but pretty flavors of strawberries, vanilla and cinnamon, this clean wine is about as good as white Zin gets. **84 Best Buy**—*S.H. (11/15/2005)*

GABRIELLI

Gabrielli 2001 Coro Mednocino Red Blend (Mendocino) $35. A smoky edged wine with a strong licorice center. Coffee and toast are also at the fore, though primary fruit flavors take a back seat. Tannins are moderate—a bit rustic on the palate. **85**—*J.M. (9/1/2004)*

Gabrielli 1999 Sangiovese (Redwood Valley) $NA. 85—*S.H. (5/1/2002)*

Gabrielli 2000 Rosato Sangiovese (Redwood Valley) $28. Although this wine has some flaws, it's also fruity and fun enough to overlook them. The downside is a vegetatal aroma. On the upside are pretty raspberry flavors, just the tiniest bit off-dry, and wonderful acids that just sing and dance on the palate. If only it smelled nicer . . . **85**—*S.H. (5/1/2002)*

USA

Gabrielli 1997 Syrah (Redwood Valley) $18. A dark, earthy style of Syrah that emphasizes bitter chocolate, coffee and cocoa aromas and flavors but cushions that black severity with a soft, plush mouthfeel. Tart blackberries and creamy mocha flavors provide a solid finish. **85** *(10/1/2001)*

Gabrielli 1999 Zinfandel (Redwood Valley) $18. Rough and country-style, with jagged tannins and sharp acids. The flavors are jammy and ripe enough, with black cherry and black raspberry, tobacco, coffee and lots of spice, and it's dry as a tomb. But it is a little ordinary. **84** *—S.H. (11/1/2002)*

Gabrielli 1998 Goforth Vineyard Zinfandel (Redwood Valley) $18. Awkward drinking, with suspect aromas and flavors. One sniff reveals vegetal, cardboard notes, and tasting confirms this. It's lean and earthy, and high acidity makes it even tarter. Thankfully, it's dry. But this lean wine will have to work hard to find fans. **83** *—S.H. (11/1/2002)*

Gabrielli 1997 Goforth Vineyard Zinfandel (Redwood Valley) $20.87 — *S.H. (5/1/2000)*

GAINEY

Gainey 2004 Chardonnay (Santa Rita Hills) $19. Shows real cool-climate character in the brisk acidity that titillates the mouth and the bright, pure kiwi, lime and pineapple flavors, which are enriched with smoky oak. Could have greater depth, but it has plenty of upscale qualities. **87** *—S.H. (11/15/2006)*

Gainey 2003 Chardonnay (Santa Barbara County) $19. A little too thin in fruit, this wine shows its cool-climate acids, with a trace of lemon and lime flavor. It has a nice structure, but needs greater concentration. **83** — *S.H. (12/31/2005)*

Gainey 2002 Chardonnay (Santa Barbara County) $18. Polished and tasty, a nice Chard notable for its bright burst of citrusy acids. The fruit is tangerines, pineapples and mangoes. **86** *—S.H. (11/15/2004)*

Gainey 2001 Chardonnay (Santa Rita Hills) $32. A beautifully sleek and structured wine, due not only to high acidity but a minerally tang. Well-oaked, but rich enough to handle it. Flavors of lemon custard, apples, peaches and mangoes are wrapped in a creamy smooth texture. **91** — *S.H. (10/1/2003)*

Gainey 2000 Chardonnay (Santa Barbara County) $18. Begins with unique, distinctive anise and mint aromas and flavors, along with white pepper and white peach. It's not a superripe, lush wine, but it's a rich, complex one. Streamlined with acid and oak, this baby is full of finesse, depth and harmony. **90** *—S.H. (12/15/2002)*

Gainey 2003 Limited Selection Chardonnay (Santa Rita Hills) $32. This is 100% barrel fermented, with complete malo; a rich, bright, crisp and pure wine. It's enormously flavorful in key lime pie and toasty, smoky notes, and firmly acidic. Finishes with a honeyed sweetness. **92** *—S.H. (3/1/2006)*

Gainey 2001 Limited Selection Chardonnay (Santa Barbara County) $31. Tremendously rich and complex, this wine brims with opulent fruit and smoky oak. The fruit is all about mangoes and pineapples and similar tropical fare, while the oak is strong but in balance. Good southland acidity makes it all clean and vibrant. Finishes sweet and crisp. **91** *—S.H. (11/15/2004)*

Gainey 1999 Limited Selection Chardonnay (Santa Barbara County) $28. Malolactic fermentation, barrel fermentation, intensely oaky, yet it retains an Armani-like balance and breed. The winemaker wisely resisted overripe grapes; the flavors veer to apples and peaches framed in dry, dusty tannins and bright acidity. **92** *—S.H. (12/15/2002)*

Gainey 1997 Limited Selection Chardonnay (Santa Barbara County) $28.91 *(6/1/2000)*

Gainey 1997 Triada Grenache (Santa Ynez Valley) $16.90 *—S.H. (10/1/1999)*

Gainey 2003 Merlot (Santa Ynez Valley) $20. Gainey has long produced one of the best Merlots from this appellation, pushing the wine to juicy ripeness. The '03 shows expressive cherry pie, blackberry liqueur and cinnamon spice flavors, and is dry and balanced. It's a delicious wine that is best now. **88** *—S.H. (12/15/2006)*

Gainey 2002 Merlot (Santa Ynez Valley) $19. Lots of ripe blackberry and cherry fruit framed in a softly tannic, well-acidified wine. There's an earthy, espresso and herb edge. Finishes dry, oaky and distinguished. **88** *—S.H. (10/1/2005)*

Gainey 2001 Merlot (Santa Ynez Valley) $19. Gainey was one of the first Santa Barbara wineries to nail Merlot, and while the Limited Selection is richer, their regular release is no slouch. Deeply extracted in blackcurrant fruit, well-oaked, and balanced in tannins and acids, it has that sumptuous mouthfeel you associate with upscale red wines. **90** *—S.H. (3/1/2005)*

Gainey 1999 Merlot (Santa Ynez Valley) $20. Picked before the grapes reached full maturity, this wine treads a complex line between blackberry and plum flavors and minty, herbal ones. American oak also adds a streak of sharp green mint. The balance works to the wine's advantage. Dry, dusty tannins are rich and refined. **92** *—S.H. (11/15/2002)*

Gainey 2002 Limited Selection Merlot (Santa Ynez Valley) $34. Richer, firmer and more distinguished than Gainey's regular '02 Merlot, this wine shows black cherry flavors and firm, dusty tannins. It's very dry and elegant. Doesn't seem like an ager, so drink up. **90** *—S.H. (10/1/2005)*

Gainey 1999 Limited Selection Merlot (Santa Ynez Valley) $35. Smooth in the mouth, long on oaky char and vanilla, a delicious wine with full-throttle flavors of sweet cassis and herbs. Sturdy tannins and pronounced acidity provide excellent structure. **91** *—S.H. (10/1/2003)*

Gainey 1998 Limited Selection Merlot (Santa Ynez Valley) $35. A pleasing blend of black cherry, chocolate and herb flavors, all couched in powdery tannins that should smooth out nicely in the cellar. This moderate-bodied Merlot is good for drinking now, too. Finishes clean. **88** *—J.M. (7/1/2002)*

Gainey 1996 Limited Selection Merlot (Santa Ynez Valley) $25.95 *—S.H. (9/1/1999)*

Gainey 2003 Limited Selection Pinot Noir (Santa Rita Hills) $48. Here's a rich, young, sappy wine. It's full-bodied, yet silky and elegant. It has delicious, complex flavors of cherries, raspberries and chocolate that are boosted by crisp acidity, with a smooth, satiny finish. Just yummy. **92** — *S.H. (3/1/2006)*

Gainey 2001 Limited Selection Pinot Noir (Santa Barbara County) $35. An enormous, complex, brooding and extraordinary Pinot Noir, a blend of Bien Nacido and Gainey's Santa Rosa Hills vineyards. Opens with a blast of peppery, cherry fruit, with tobacco and minty overtones. The rich berry flavors in a creamy texture, with sweet oak tannins, feel ripe, plush and terrific in the mouth. **93 Editors' Choice** *—S.H. (7/1/2003)*

Gainey 2005 Riesling (Santa Ynez Valley) $13. Here's a refreshingly crisp Riesling whose high acidity makes it a natural for friendly fare. It has subtle flavors of citrus fruits and minerally chalk, while a bit of residual sugar gives it a mellow roundness. **85** *—S.H. (12/1/2006)*

Gainey 2003 Riesling (Santa Barbara County) $13. Refreshingly high in acidity, a mouth-cleaner with forward flavors of peaches, limes, wild-flowers and spices. It's dryish and rich in fruity essence. Try with fish or pork with a fruity salsa topping. **86** *—S.H. (2/1/2005)*

Gainey 2000 Riesling (Santa Ynez Valley) $12. Pleasant and crisp, this easy-drinking wine has apple and peach flavors and just a tad of sugar. Its ripe, pretty flavors will go well with fresh fruits or grilled fish. **84** *—S.H. (11/15/2001)*

Gainey 1998 Limited Selection Late Harvest Riesling (Santa Ynez Valley) $20.90 *—S.H. (12/31/2000)*

Gainey 2004 Sauvignon Blanc (Santa Ynez Valley) $13. Gainey produces one of the most consistent Sauvignon Blancs, and this refreshing wine is a pretty good bargain, too. It's softly creamy, with polished apricot and peach flavors that finish a little sweet. **86** *—S.H. (7/1/2006)*

Gainey 2003 Sauvignon Blanc (Santa Ynez Valley) $14. This wine is fierce in that sauvage character of citrus rind, gooseberry, tart green kiwi and white pepper flavors, but it's very balanced, with a crisp spine of zesty acidity, and the finish turns ripely sweet in fruit. It's a pleasant sipper with some real elegance. **86** *—S.H. (12/15/2005)*

Gainey 2002 Sauvignon Blanc (Santa Ynez Valley) $13. From a winery that stars every year in this variety, a dry, stylish wine, perfect for cocktails or with food. Shows citrus, fig and oak flavors, with a fat nutty quality from Sémillon. Finishes with a hint of honey. **88 Best Buy** —*S.H. (2/1/2005)*

Gainey 2002 Limited Sauvignon Blanc (Santa Ynez Valley) $30. Well oaked. You pick up on the charry smoke and vanilla right away. But then the fruit hits, all ripe figs and sweet green grasses and lemons and limes and even hints of pineapple. With the fresh acidity, it all combines to a big, lush wine, with a clean, food-friendly scour. **91** —*S.H. (2/1/2005)*

Gainey 2004 Limited Selection Sauvignon Blanc (Santa Ynez Valley) $20. Kirby Anderson, Gainey's longtime winemaker, has crafted this wonderfully rich, vibrant and expressive wine. Partially barrel fermented, but with no new oak, it has a creamy texture framing ripe flavors of apricots, peaches, lemons, limes and grapes. Drink it now for its youthful exuberance. **92 Editors' Choice** —*S.H. (7/1/2006)*

Gainey 2003 Limited Selection Sauvignon Blanc (Santa Ynez Valley) $19. A really great Sauvignon from a producer who consistently excels. Spicy and rich in fig and citrus flavors, with a touch of creamy oak; boosted by fine, bright acidity. Finishes long, rich and clean. **90 Editors' Choice** —*S.H. (10/1/2005)*

Gainey 2001 Limited Selection Sauvignon Blanc (Santa Ynez Valley) $21. This year this wine is extremely grassy, with an intense flavor of gooseberries. The winemaker tried his best to tame the aggression by adding 14 percent Sémillon, barrel fermenting it, and aging on the lees. Still, it's a tart, acidic wine, although it has plenty of class and character. **87** —*S.H. (10/1/2003)*

Gainey 2000 Limited Selection Sauvignon Blanc (Santa Ynez Valley) $20. One of the best Sauvignon Blancs of the vintage, and a testament to eastern Santa Ynez's ability to produce the variety. Pure fruit flavors of citrus, spicy green apples, figs and white pepper drink rich and oh, so refined. Very dry, yet with a honeyed sweetness offset by crisp acids. Elegant and refreshing. A touch of Sémillon adds complexity. **90** —*S.H. (9/1/2003)*

Gainey 1998 Limited Selection Sauvignon Blanc (Santa Ynez Valley) $20. 90 —*S.H. (11/15/2000)*

Gainey 1997 Limited Selection Sauvignon Blanc (Santa Ynez Valley) $18. 90 —*S.H. (9/1/1999)*

Gainey 2002 Limited Selection Syrah (Santa Barbara County) $35. I wish this Syrah were a bit riper, or more concentrated, because it's got a very pretty structure. You'll find cherry, pepper, leather and plum flavors, but they're diluted, and snap to a quick finish. **85** —*S.H. (9/1/2005)*

Gainey 2000 Limited Selection Syrah (Santa Barbara County) $32. Unfiltered, and seriously good wine, although it finishes a bit short. But the velvety texture, intelligent oak treatment, and sweet balance of blackberry fruit, tannins and acids is first class. **92** —*S.H. (3/1/2004)*

GALANTE

Galante 2003 Blackjack Pasture Cabernet Sauvignon (Carmel Valley) $60. Just a little too sweet for my taste, this Cab is also soft in acids and tannins. The flavors are of sugared blackberry tea, cherry pie filling and cola. **85** —*S.H. (12/15/2006)*

Galante 2002 Blackjack Pasture Cabernet Sauvignon (Carmel Valley) $60. I've liked Galante's Blackjack Cab for its balanced ageworthiness, one of the few south-of-San Francisco Cabs you can say that about. This vintage, the wine is big in fruit but tight in tannins and acids. Although decanting will soften it and a good steak will improve it, it's best left alone for at least a year, and should hold for the rest of this decade. **91 Cellar Selection** —*S.H. (7/1/2006)*

Galante 2001 Blackjack Pasture Cabernet Sauvignon (Carmel Valley) $60. This is not one of your out-of-the-gate lush Napa treats. It's young and tightly wound, a wine whose tannins and new oak are wrapped around the cherry and cassis fruit like the bandages on a mummy. Balanced and harmonious, this is one of the more solid cellar candidates of this splendid vintage. **92 Cellar Selection** —*S.H. (10/1/2004)*

Galante 2000 Blackjack Pasture Cabernet Sauvignon (Carmel Valley) $50. A very rich wine that clearly has been hand-picked from the best lots, to judge from the extraordinary quality of the flavors and textures. Cassis, herbs, earth and a note of superripe wild blackberry, sweetened to perfection under the sun. Oak adds judicious nuances of smoke and vanilla.

This is one of the best Monterey County Cabernet Sauvignons in recent years. **93** —*S.H. (11/15/2003)*

Galante 1997 Blackjack Pasture Cabernet Sauvignon (Carmel Valley) $40. 93 —*S.H. (2/1/2000)*

Galante 2003 Rancho Galante Cabernet Sauvignon (Carmel Valley) $20. Nicely dry and balanced, this Cabernet, from a warm inland appellation in Monterey County, shows elegantly tailored blackberry and coffee flavors supported by firm tannins and a dusting of oak. Drink now. **87** —*S.H. (7/1/2006)*

Galante 2001 Rancho Galante Cabernet Sauvignon (Carmel Valley) $20. Shows an affinity to Galante's more expensive Cab bottlings, although it's not as rich or ageworthy despite the tannins. There are flavors of blackberries and currants, and the wine is balanced and clean. **86** —*S.H. (10/1/2004)*

Galante 2000 Rancho Galante Cabernet Sauvignon (Carmel Valley) $20. A nice, easy-drinking Cabernet that has some real complexity. Opens with cassis, smoke and herb aromas that turn rich and fruity in the mouth. The tannins are pretty firm now and should protect the wine for a few years, should you choose to age it. **90 Editors' Choice** —*S.H. (11/15/2003)*

Galante 1997 Rancho Galante Cabernet Sauvignon (Carmel Valley) $18. 89 —*S.H. (2/1/2000)*

Galante 2002 Red Rose Hill Cabernet Sauvignon (Carmel Valley) $30. This is a big, soft, extracted and dense Cabernet that's not showing well now because it's so top-heavy with fruit and oak. But it has an underlying dry elegance, and the blackberry liqueur and espresso flavors are big enough for midterm aging. Best 2007 through 2009. **88** —*S.H. (7/1/2006)*

Galante 2001 Red Rose Hill Cabernet Sauvignon (Carmel Valley) $30. It took a while for this wine to open up, because it's closed and brooding at first. Opens with a cigarette ash aroma you sometimes find in terroir-driven wines. Tannic; airing reveals lush cherry and cassis flavors and a rich overlay of fine smoky oak. Seems a natural for the cellar, and could age to greatness by 2010. **90** —*S.H. (10/1/2004)*

Galante 2000 Red Rose Hill Cabernet Sauvignon (Carmel Valley) $30. Brims with strong cassis, blackberry, cherry and herb flavors that are rich and complex. The tannins are a real success story, velvety and soft but rich and complex. Finishes dry, with a tannic bite, suggesting midterm aging possibilities. **92** —*S.H. (11/15/2003)*

Galante 1997 Red Rose Hill Cabernet Sauvignon (Carmel Valley) $28. 91 —*S.H. (2/1/2000)*

Galante 2003 Estate Merlot (Carmel Valley) $35. Not a successful wine, despite Galante's reputation for Cabernet. It's hot and sharp, with simple cherry cough medicine flavors. **80** —*S.H. (7/1/2006)*

Galante 2004 Estate Pinot Noir (Carmel Valley) $30. Galante made their name with estate Cabernets from this warmish appellation, which is maybe not so kind to Pinot Noir. The wine is big, dry and tannic, flavorful enough, but wanting the silky elegance a coastal Pinot needs. **84** —*S.H. (7/1/2006)*

Galante 2000 Sauvignon Blanc (Carmel Valley) $22. From a warm appellation east of Monterey Bay, this is a pleasant white wine that has lots of dried grass, lime and gooseberry flavors. Acids are high and clean, making for a very clean mouthfeel. **87** —*S.H. (12/1/2003)*

GALLEANO

Galleano 1999 Dos Rancheros Zinfandel (Cucamonga Valley) $18. From old vines, this is a sumptuous Zin, packed with wild berry, chocolate, pepper, tobacco and herb aromas and flavors. Bone-dry, it features a scour of tannins that suggests age-ability. This round, balanced wine is soft enough to drink now. **87** —*S.H. (4/1/2002)*

Galleano 2001 Dos Rancheros Old Vines Zinfandel (Cucamonga Valley) $18. An old-style Zin, finished sweet with residual sugar and palate-coating tannins. This is the kind of big red wine people used to like, and it still has its fans, although it's out of touch with modern tastes. **82** —*S.H. (3/1/2004)*

Galleano NV Old Vines Zinfandel (Cucamonga Valley) $6. Tastes like a Central Valley Port, with overripe berry flavors and thick, numbing tannins, although it's not as sweet as Galleano's more expensive Zins. **81** —S.H. (3/1/2004)

Galleano 2000 Old Vines Zinfandel Port Zinfandel (Cucamonga Valley) $20. From one of the pioneering families of this endangered appellation in greater L.A., a true old-style California Port. Smells rich and inviting, with true Port character, and drinks full, lush and rich in the mouth. Hard to exaggerrate how delicious and fine this sweet wine is. Enjoy with your best chocolate dessert, or on its own. **93 Editors' Choice** —S.H. (9/1/2003)

Galleano 2001 Pioneers Legendary Old Vines Zinfandel (Cucamonga Valley) $16. Pretty much identical with this winery's Dos Rancheros bottling, a sweet wine. If anything, even more tannic, and numbs the palate so that sugar is just about the only thing you can taste. **80** —S.H. (3/1/2004)

GALLERON

Galleron 2000 Cabernet Sauvignon (Napa Valley) $45. Smells and tastes classy, with that powerful cassis and new oak one-two punch that's hard to resist. Has ripe flavors of currants, minty chocolate and vanilla, just delicious, wrapped in a super soft texture of sweet tannins. **92** —S.H. (2/1/2005)

Galleron 2001 Morisoli Vineyard Cabernet Sauvignon (Rutherford) $100. Very ripe and classic in the sweet black currant, red cherry, cassis and fine smoky oak flavors and rich, gentle tannins. Very generous in flavor and mouthfeel. A little soft, and drinking well right now. Defines elegance and richness. **90** —S.H. (10/1/2004)

Galleron 2000 Morisoli Vineyard Cabernet Sauvignon (Napa Valley) $100. Starts with that telltale pedigree aroma of perfectly ripe blackcurrant and cassis complexed with fine smoky oak. In the mouth, soft and gentle, immediately likeable, with ripe, forward flavors. Decadent and delicious, but may be too soft for aging. Drink now. **90** —S.H. (2/1/2005)

Galleron 1999 Morisoli Vineyard Cabernet Sauvignon (Napa Valley) $100. From a vineyard in Rutherford, this wine expresses the heart and soul of the appellation. Intensely beautiful aromas of black currants, rich, thick and fine tannins, and soft acids are framed in beautiful oak. Soft and gentle in the mouth, but with an authority that affirms itself on the long, fine finish. Spectacular. **95** —S.H. (12/31/2002)

Galleron 1999 Trio Vineyard Chardonnay (Napa Valley) $40. From the smoky, spicy nose through the spicy apple notes in the mouth, this bottling has an intriguing earth and mineral streak from start to finish. Medium-bodied, the wine offers some lemon and mineral tang and a lot of smoky oak on the finish. **87** (7/1/2001)

Galleron 2000 Jaeger Vineyard Merlot (Napa Valley) $32. Soft and gentle, with herb, coffee and cherry flavors. Oak adds vanilla and smoky notes. The flavors are marvelous, yet you wish the wine had a firmer structure. Finishes dry. **85** —S.H. (2/1/2005)

Galleron 2001 Branham Rockpile Zinfandel (Sonoma County) $32. Shows nice berry and earth flavors, with Zin's brambly edge, and finishes dry and balanced. The texture is soft. **84** —S.H. (2/1/2005)

GALLERON LAINE

Galleron Laine 1998 Lo Vecchio Estate Vineyard Chardonnay (Napa Valley) $35. Citrus, pineapple, white stone fruits and green apple are among the aromas and flavors in this clean, medium-weight offering. The wine has a nice butterscotch streak, but some tasters found it light to the point of insubstantial, while others praised its balance and elegance. **88** (7/1/2001)

Galleron Laine 1997 Merlot (Napa Valley) $35. A heavy cloak of oak can't hide the high alcohol level (15%). Sure, the alcohol provides weight and texture, but also heat on the finish. The black cherry and black pepper flavors need some time to smooth the rough edges, but then the alcohol will likely become more prominent. Drink young for its rustic ebullience, with rare beef to help tame the tannins. **84** —J.C. (6/1/2001)

GALLO FAMILY VINEYARDS

Gallo Family Vineyards 2003 Estate Cabernet Sauvignon (Northern Sonoma) $75. Classic Cabernet, and ageworthy. Shows balanced blackberry, coffee, black olive, Provençal herb and oak flavors. It has complex tannins, and is very dry. This is not a long hangtime, superripe Cab, but strives for balance and elegance and succeeds. Best now–2016. **92** —S.H. (9/1/2006)

Gallo Family Vineyards 2003 Reserve Cabernet Sauvignon (Sonoma County) $15. Full-bodied, soft and approachable, with rich aromas of vanilla, graham cracker and chocolate overlaid on flavors of cassis and cherry. Clove notes accent fine tannins on the finish. **87** (5/1/2006)

Gallo Family Vineyards NV Twin Valley Cabernet Sauvignon (California) $5. For five bucks you get plenty of lush cherry-blackberry, blueberry and milk chocolate flavor, a smooth texture, velvety tannins and a long, spicy finish. The more you sip, the better it gets. **85 Best Buy** —S.H. (12/15/2006)

Gallo Family Vineyards NV Twin Valley Chardonnay (California) $5. This creamy Chard has good varietal character, with pleasant peach, green apple and cinnamon spice flavors. **84 Best Buy** —S.H. (12/15/2006)

Gallo Family Vineyards NV Merlot (California) $5. For five bucks, you get a smooth, dry wine with nice cherry flavors and a polished edge of tannins. What's not to like? **83 Best Buy** —S.H. (12/15/2006)

Gallo Family Vineyards 2003 Reserve Merlot (Sonoma County) $13. Soft and inviting without being flabby. If more mass-market Merlots were this good the variety wouldn't be so maligned. Mint accents the jammy cherry and mocha flavors, finishing with hints of chocolate and coconut. **87** (5/1/2006)

Gallo Family Vineyards 2004 Reserve Pinot Noir (Sonoma County) $15. A bit divisive among our panelists, with one finding it rather light and lacking in intensity, while others found virtue in its understated yet varietally correct nature. Cola and cherry flavors finish clean and fresh. **87** (5/1/2006)

Gallo Family Vineyards NV Hearty Burgundy Red Blend (California) $5. The red that helped build the House of Gallo never really went away. There's a little Pinot Noir here, mixed with Zinfandel, Sangiovese, Syrah and a couple of others. It's what it's always been, dry, balanced and totally easy, with some real full-bodied richness. **84 Best Buy** —S.H. (12/15/2006)

Gallo Family Vineyards NV Twin Valley Sauvignon Blanc (California) $5. When I was getting into wine, Gallo's inexpensive Sauvignon Blanc was my house white. The wine hasn't changed at all over the years, and still offers plenty of polished citrus, melon and fig flavors in a dry, clean package. **84 Best Buy** —S.H. (12/15/2006)

Gallo Family Vineyards 2004 Reserve Zinfandel (Sonoma County) $13. Perhaps because this is a new line and the Gallos are putting their best foot forward, this Zin is far richer than Gallo's Dancing Bull Zin, which is only a dollar less. It's lush in briary wild berry, cherry pie, blueberry, cocoa and coffee flavors, and nicely dry. Good enough to accompany your best Zin-friendly food. **88 Best Buy** —S.H. (10/1/2006)

Gallo Family Vineyards NV Twin Valley White Zinfandel (California) $5. If Gallo is trying to steer white Zin drinkers to reds, they're doing a good job. This is dark for a blush, and medium-bodied, with semisweet cherry flavors and a distinct finish of fresh thyme. **83 Best Buy** —S.H. (12/15/2006)

Gallo Family Vineyards NV Twin Valley White Zinfandel (California) $6. Sweet and simple, this orange-colored blush will satisfy most fans of white Zin. **82** —S.H. (7/1/2006)

GALLO OF SONOMA

Gallo of Sonoma 2000 Barrelli Creek Vineyard Barbera (Alexander Valley) $24. If you're looking for an obvious cellar candidate, here it is. Rich, young and juicy, with bright plum and black raspberry flavors and a fresh bite of youthful acidity. The tannins are easy, but the acids will let this puppy age effortlessly for years. **88** —S.H. (2/1/2003)

Gallo of Sonoma 1999 Cabernet Sauvignon (Sonoma County) $13. Well-made and expressive of its variety, this wine brims with black currant and olive aromas and flavors, and the smoky oak is nicely integrated. It's dry, with dusty, creamy tannins and a good bite of acid. As good as many more expensive wines, but Gallo's economies of scale keep the price modest. **87 Best Buy** —S.H. (11/15/2002)

Gallo of Sonoma 1999 Barelli Creek Cabernet Sauvignon (Alexander Valley) $32. This ageable wine has sturdy tannins and is a shade too young to drink now. A few years of cellaring will open up the blackcurrant and olive flavors and soften the mouthfeel. If you must open it, try with a perfectly grilled lambchop. **88** —*S.H. (8/1/2003)*

Gallo of Sonoma 1997 Barelli Creek Cabernet Sauvignon (Sonoma County) $28. Displaying great fruit and excellent structure, this can be enjoyed now, but it has soon scale and intensity that we suggest aging it for at least another year or two. Barelli seems to yield darkly-fruited wines of depth and structure that read somewhat tighter and harder in their youth. Has classic cassis, toasty oak and tobacco touches, plus a dusty Alexander Valley feel. **91** *(7/1/2001)*

Gallo of Sonoma 1994 Barrelli Creek Cabernet Sauvignon (Sonoma County) $18. 88 —*S.H. (11/1/1999)*

Gallo of Sonoma 1998 Estate Cabernet Sauvignon (Northern Sonoma) $75. This is wonderfully good Cabernet considering the poor reputation of the vintage. Extravagant oak is layered over vibrant cassis and tobacco, while crisp acidity and lush tannins provide a sense of balance and ageability. Lacks the fullness and depth of the best vintages, but sure to charm. **90** *(3/1/2003)*

Gallo of Sonoma 1998 Frei Ranch Vineyard Cabernet Sauvignon (Dry Creek Valley) $30. This excellent and rich wine smells beautiful, and coats the mouth with velvety smoothness. The flavors range from green olives to tobacco and blackberries, with oaky complexities. The finish is dry, spicy and intense. **90** —*S.H. (8/1/2003)*

Gallo of Sonoma 1997 Frei Vineyard Cabernet Sauvignon (Dry Creek Valley) $26. Oversized, with massive berry-cherry flavors that explode in the mouth. In fact, it's too big. The spicy fruity flavors are so powerful they dominate every other feature. That said, it's dry, and the tannins are soft and intricate. Match it with dramatic, boldly flavored dishes. **87** —*S.H. (9/1/2002)*

Gallo of Sonoma 2000 Reserve Cabernet Sauvignon (Sonoma County) $13. A wonderfully drinkable wine, filled with juicy, delicious flavors of currants and blackberries. It's a bit tannic, but perfectly drinkable now. Especially notable for the rich, velvety mouthfeel and elegant balance. **89** —*S.H. (3/1/2003)*

Gallo of Sonoma 1995 Sonoma County Cabernet Sauvignon (Sonoma County) $11. 90 Best Buy —*L.W. (7/1/1999)*

Gallo of Sonoma 1998 Stefani Vineyard Cabernet Sauvignon (Dry Creek Valley) $30. Rich and dense, and feels just great in the mouth. Flavors of black currants spread across the palate—dry and delicious. Additional complexities come from oak. Tannins are soft and layered. **91 Editors' Choice** —*S.H. (5/1/2003)*

Gallo of Sonoma 1997 Stefani Vineyard Cabernet Sauvignon (Dry Creek Valley) $28. The really ripe dark cherry, toasty oak and licorice aromas and flavors here are winning. It has a wonderful sweetness and balance. The fruit here is rounder and more forward than in the Barelli—still, it's big, juicy and has plenty of structure. **91** *(7/1/2001)*

Gallo of Sonoma 2001 Chardonnay (Sonoma County) $11. A bit lean in fruit, with shades of apple and peach, although the oak is very elaborate and stars with vanilla, smoke and creme brulee notes. The wine is fully dry and has crisp acidity, and is very nice for this everyday price. **86 Best Buy** —*S.H. (6/1/2003)*

Gallo of Sonoma 2000 Estate Chardonnay (Northern Sonoma) $45. Yup, this is a 2000, and it's still fresh and zippy in acidity. It's not a big wine, but a complex, subtle one, with a firm minerality undergirding pineapple and oak flavors. It should hold and improve through this decade, and will be instructive for those who don't know what a good, old Chard can do. **92** —*S.H. (3/1/2006)*

Gallo of Sonoma 2002 Laguna Ranch Vineyard Chardonnay (Russian River Valley) $22. Tart, crisp and dry, in fact a minerally wine of considerable streamline and finesse. The flavors subtly suggest limes, with vanilla and smoke. **87** —*S.H. (10/1/2005)*

Gallo of Sonoma 2003 Laguna Vineyard Chardonnay (Russian River Valley) $24. I wish this Chardonnay had greater concentration of fruit, because the individual parts are really nice. Great structure, firm acids, modest alcohol and tasteful oak can't quite boost the watery peach flavors. **83** —*S.H. (3/1/2006)*

Gallo of Sonoma 2000 Laguna Vineyard Chardonnay (Russian River Valley) $24. A big, rich wine, showing classic Russian River notes of fresh green apples and peaches. Liberal use of well-charred oak and substantial lees contact adds vanilla, smoke and a creamy texture. **90** —*S.H. (12/15/2002)*

Gallo of Sonoma 1999 Laguna Vineyard Chardonnay (Russian River Valley) $23. Seems somewhat crisper and less weighty than prior vintages, with the custardy mouthfeel buttressed by lemony acids. You'll also find apples, sweet plums and the obligatory toast and vanilla. **87** —*J.C. (9/1/2002)*

Gallo of Sonoma 2004 Reserve Chardonnay (Sonoma County) $13. This well-priced Chard has rich, bright acidity and a firm minerality that frames ripe peach, mango, apricot and nectarine flavors, with a veneer of smoky, spicy oak. **89 Best Buy** —*S.H. (3/1/2006)*

Gallo of Sonoma 2000 Reserve Chardonnay (Sonoma County) $11. Smells bright, citrusy and clean, but the bouquet is dominated by oak. A charry, penetrating scent of vanilla, with almost a hint of white chocolate, leads to a rich, creamy wine. It's a bit on the sweet side, and tastes strongly of lees. Pretty good stuff—at this price, it's a swell value. **87 Best Buy** —*S.H. (12/15/2002)*

Gallo of Sonoma 1997 Russian River Valley Chardonnay (Russian River Valley) $10. 87 *(11/15/1999)*

Gallo of Sonoma 1999 Stefani Vineyard Chardonnay (Dry Creek Valley) $23. Here's a Chard that has it all. Well-toasted oak, rich vanilla and meringue, oriental spices, and plush, ripe fruits ranging from apples to peaches to papaya. Brings it all together with exceptional balance and harmony. Absolutely delicious. **91** —*S.H. (2/1/2003)*

Gallo of Sonoma 1997 Stefani Vineyard Chardonnay (Dry Creek Valley) $20. 88 —*M.S. (10/1/2000)*

Gallo of Sonoma 2001 Two Rock Vineyard Chardonnay (Sonoma Coast) $28. Quite bright, with zippy acidity. The fruit flavors lean toward melon, peach, pear, lemon and spice flavors. Pretty vanilla aromas are up front, but the style is leaner than this winery's other single vineyard Chardonnays. A first release from this vineyard. -J.M. **88** —*J.M. (6/1/2003)*

Gallo of Sonoma 2002 Merlot (Sonoma County) $11. This is such a wonderful value. It's rich in cherry, blackberry and cocoa flavors, and perfectly dry. Lives up to Merlot's soft, approachable reputation, but there's real complexity. A dollop of Cabernet Sauvignon and Malbec adds depth and structure to this drinkable Merlot. **87 Best Buy** —*S.H. (12/1/2005)*

Gallo of Sonoma 2000 Merlot (Sonoma County) $11. There are some earthy, berry flavors, but the wine is quite soft. The winemaker has woven the fine tannins into a complex element of the wine's mouthfeel, leaving the finish dry and clean. **86** —*S.H. (11/15/2002)*

Gallo of Sonoma 1997 Merlot (Sonoma County) $11. 89 *(11/15/1999)*

Gallo of Sonoma 2001 Reserve Merlot (Sonoma County) $11. What a finewine this is. The plummy, cherry flavors are layered with an edge of sage and other dried herbs, and the tannins are rich but easy. There's real elegance and finesse here. **89** —*S.H. (4/1/2004)*

Gallo of Sonoma 2004 Pinot Gris (Sonoma County) $13. This affordable wine is Exhibit A on why Pinot Gris/Grigio is such a hot variety. It's like a cross between Sauvignon Blanc and Chardonnay, brisk and clean on the one hand, and rich and fruity on the other. **87** —*S.H. (2/1/2006)*

Gallo of Sonoma 2001 Pinot Gris (Sonoma Coast) $13. There sure is a lot of fruitiness in this wine from a cool, ocean-influenced region. Suggests everything from apples and peaches to melons and figs. It's basically dry, with pretty good acids. Could be a bit firmer, but it's juicy and rich. **86** —*S.H. (9/1/2003)*

Gallo of Sonoma 1997 Pinot Noir (Russian River Valley) $12. 87 *(11/15/1999)*

Gallo of Sonoma 2000 Pinot Noir (Sonoma County) $13. Fruity and supple, this young, jammy wine is easy to drink. It has rich, juicy flavors of newly crushed berries and a slight gassiness that freshens it. So rich, it

USA

seems almost sweet, but it's dry, with soft tannins. **87 Best Buy** —*S.H.* (2/1/2003)

Gallo of Sonoma 1999 Pinot Noir (Sonoma County) $13. Earth, plum and cola notes are the opening act, followed by simple yet clean cherry and plum flavors that are touched up by oak. The finish is more of the same; the mouthfeel borders on being too soft. **85** (10/1/2002)

Gallo of Sonoma 1998 Pinot Noir (Sonoma County) $13. Lovely aromas, flavors and a fine mouthfeel define this rare item—a real Pinot Noir value. Appealing black cherry, earth, and tarragon aromas and flavors keep the taster interested, suggesting a broad range of food pairings, from salmon to lamb. It even offers decent body and length, almost unheard of in this price range. **88** (7/1/2001)

Gallo of Sonoma 2003 Reserve Pinot Noir (Sonoma Coast) $13. A terrific wine at a giveaway price, this coastal bottling shows a rich, complex texture and is very dry. The flavors unfold one by one on the palate: cherries, cocoa, cola, plums, blackberries and spices are highlighted by a burst of crisp acids. **89 Best Buy** —*S.H.* (10/1/2005)

Gallo of Sonoma 2001 Reserve Pinot Noir (Sonoma Coast) $8. This is an astonishing value, especially from such a prestigious appellation. Has a silky texture and lush but dry flavors of cherries, raspberries, herbs, mushrooms, coffee and clove that unfold across the palate. Versatile at the table; try with pork tenderloin with plum sauce. With more than 30,000 cases produced, this should be easy to find. **90 Best Buy** —*S.H.* (11/15/2003)

Gallo of Sonoma 2000 Reserve Pinot Noir (Sonoma County) $13. Chunky and full up front, but with grassy, green aromas. Quite tart the moment you taste it; there's cranberry and wild huckleberry flavors, and a short, borderline sour finish. Too much tartness, with almost orange-like acidity. **81** —*M.S.* (12/1/2003)

Gallo of Sonoma 2001 Two Rock Vineyard Pinot Noir (Sonoma Coast) $28. Cherries, cranberries, coffee, cocoa and cola star in this dry wine. It's a little soft in acidity, and feels smooth and polished, with good intensity and a spicy finish. **87** —*S.H.* (12/15/2004)

Gallo of Sonoma 1997 Sangiovese (Sonoma County) $11. 87 Best Buy — *S.H.* (12/15/1999)

Gallo of Sonoma 1998 Sangiovese (Sonoma County) $13. Nice sweet-tart flavors and a medium mouthfeel make this is one of our most-enjoyed California renditions of Tuscany's workhorse red. The tart black cherry, leather and slight mineral notes are on target, the finish smooth and delicious. **89** (7/1/2001)

Gallo of Sonoma 1999 Barrel Aged Sangiovese (Alexander Valley) $13. Reminiscent of a Hugh Grant summer movie: thoroughly enjoyable, a light-hearted romp, just plain fun. Lots of plump berry-cherry fruit, soft tannins and acids, clean as a whistle and dry. As versatile as a red wine gets, it will go with almost anything. **87** —*S.H.* (12/1/2002)

Gallo of Sonoma 2003 Reserve Syrah (Sonoma County) $13. Full-bodied but not terribly lush or tannic, with readily approachable flavors of blackberries and vanilla leading the way. Turns a bit chocolaty on the soft finish. Well made and nicely balanced. **87 Best Buy** (9/1/2005)

Gallo of Sonoma 1996 Zinfandel (Dry Creek Valley) $11. 86 Best Buy — *M.S.* (9/1/1999)

Gallo of Sonoma 1996 Barrelli Creek Zinfandel (Sonoma County) $20. 91 —*S.H.* (11/1/1999)

Gallo of Sonoma 1999 Barrelli Creek Vineyard Zinfandel (Alexander Valley) $22. Nice Sonoma Zin, with briary, brambly flavors of wild red and black berries and tobacco, white pepper and cedar. The tannins are a little tough now, and the acidity is pretty tart. Best to age for 3 or 4 years, but if you must drink it now, have with big, rich barbecue. **88** —*S.H.* (2/1/2003)

Gallo of Sonoma 1996 Chiotti Vineyard Zinfandel (Dry Creek Valley) $18. 86 —*J.C.* (9/1/1999)

Gallo of Sonoma 1999 Frei Ranch Vineyard Zinfandel (Dry Creek Valley) $22. Spectacular Zin. Drinks with the plush class of a great Cabernet, with well-behaved tannins, a fine overlay of oak, and exquisite balance. But it's Zin all the way with its exuberant, untamed flavors of wild

berries. It's a lip-smackingly good wine, a textbook Sonoma Zin. **91** — *S.H.* (2/1/2003)

Gallo of Sonoma 1998 Frei Vineyard Zinfandel (Dry Creek Valley) $20. Opens with an odd chemical-resin-plastic note, which pops up again on the back end. In the mouth, black plum, oak and chalk flavors glide through to the finish. **83** —*D.T.* (3/1/2002)

Gallo of Sonoma 1997 Frei Vineyard Zinfandel (Dry Creek Valley) $19. With its bouquet of black plum, leather and dried herb notes, this lean Zin has good berry fruit. However, its attributes are balanced by a note of volatile acidity on the nose, and it shows some definite heat in the mouth. The narrow, rather angular structure of the wine seems to constrain the blackberry and spice flavors here. Closes with full, fairly even tannins. **84** (3/1/2001)

Gallo of Sonoma 2003 Reserve Zinfandel (Sonoma County) $13. Not the most powerhouse Zin around, but this is a pleasantly dry, soft wine, with cherry, blueberry and coffee flavors and a gentle texture. **84** —*S.H.* (12/1/2005)

GALLUCIO FAMILY WINERIES

Gallucio Family Wineries 2002 Barile Dolce Chardonnay (North Fork of Long Island) $35. 82 —*J.C.* (10/2/2004)

Gallucio Family Wineries 2001 Cru George Allaire Chardonnay (North Fork of Long Island) $22. 80 —*J.C.* (10/2/2004)

GAMACHE

Gamache 2003 GV Reserve Gamache–Champoux Vineyard Select Cabernet Sauvignon (Columbia Valley (WA)) $40. Both of these outstanding vineyards contributed equally to this older (25+ years) vines Cabernet. It's sleek and sappy, and it serves up a full spectrum of berries as only Washington Cab can. Young, primary fruit flavors carry a lot of snap at the moment, and the bright acids suggest that a few more years in bottle will continue to improve this impressive effort. **90** —*P.G.* (11/15/2006)

Gamache 2003 Syrah (Columbia Valley (WA)) $28. Peppery and a bit meaty or leathery on the nose, this wine then moves into briary, berry fruit on the palate. Pleasant enough, but has a rather light, textureless mouthfeel, making it seem a touch dilute. **84** (9/1/2005)

GAMBA VINEYARDS & WINERY

Gamba Vineyards & Winery 2001 Old Vine Zinfandel (Sonoma County) $40. Kicks off with racy, bright cherry and raspberry aromas, then moves on to a plush, well managed array of spicy rich plum, black cherry, coffee, chocolate, herb, raspberry, vanilla and toast flavors. The tannins are massive but ripe. **89** (11/1/2003)

GAN EDEN

Gan Eden 1994 Chardonnay (Sonoma County) $13. Apple-cider and earth aromas open to a simple apple-toast palate. The mouthfeel is even, the finish dry and rather woody. Then again, there are few drinkable California Chardonnays of this age. **82** (4/1/2001)

GANN

Gann 2004 Spring Hill Vineyard Sauvignon Blanc (Alexander Valley) $18. What went wrong in the making of this wine was excessive sugar. It's so sweet, it's off-dry, a serious flaw in a table wine, and a disservice to consumers who expect a Sauvignon Blanc to be dry. **80** —*S.H.* (5/1/2006)

GARGIULO

Gargiulo 2002 Money Road Ranch Cabernet Sauvignon (Oakville) $55. This is a wine that needs some time to show its best. It's dry and dusty with tannins and a bit hard with acids, but there's a solid core of blackberry, cherry and sweet tobacco flavor. Give it until 2006. **87** —*S.H.* (11/1/2005)

Gargiulo 2002 Money Road Ranch Merlot (Oakville) $35. Drinking very dry and pretty tannic now, this Merlot is not at its best. But there's lots of rich, ripe blackberry and cherry fruit. Try cellaring for a few years to let it all come together. **88** —*S.H.* (11/1/2005)

USA

Gargiulo 2004 Pinot Grigio (Oakville) $25. Elegant, crisp and dry, this PG has citrus zest flavors. The texture and weight are lovely and delicate. My main gripe is that the wine turns thin mid-palate and finishes watery. **83** —*S.H. (2/1/2006)*

Gargiulo 2002 Aprile Red Blend (Oakville) $28. This polished wine brings firm acids and a scour of tannins to the cherry fruit flavors. With 96 percent Sangiovese, the 4 percent of Cabernet Sauvignon shows up in the cassis finish, which is a little sweet. **86** —*S.H. (11/1/2005)*

Gargiulo 2000 Aprile Sangiovese (Napa Valley) $25. Firm and focused, with bright cherry, strawberry and herb notes. Soft, supple tannins give good structure and support a long finish. **88** —*J.M. (9/1/2003)*

Gargiulo 2000 Rosato di Sangiovese Sangiovese (Oakville) $13. Kicks off with pretty cherry notes in the nose. Dry and bright on the palate, the wine shows lovely ripe Bing cherry flavors, elegant citrus and clean mineral notes. A refreshing and satisfying rosé. **87** —*J.M. (9/1/2002)*

GARRETSON

Garretson 2003 The Spainnéach Grenache (Paso Robles) $28. Very good on its own, this wine will challenge chefs due to its unique qualities. It's light-bodied, with an array of candied fruit flavors ranging from raspberries and red cherries to white chocolate powder and vanilla. It's probably technically dry, but seems sweet. **88** —*S.H. (10/1/2005)*

Garretson 2002 Hastings Ranch "The Graosta" Mourvèdre (Paso Robles) $25. Dark, alcoholic and Porty, with the flavors of baked fruits and a hot finish. Will have its fans, but it's an unbalanced wine. **82** —*S.H. (12/31/2004)*

Garretson 2003 The Graosta Mourvèdre (Paso Robles) $28. Tasted along with Garretson's other reds, this one's considerably crisper and livelier in the mouth. It's also drier, with a tobacco and roasted coffee bean edge to the cherries and red plums. The finish is long on cherry fruit. **89** —*S.H. (10/1/2005)*

Garretson NV Glimigrim Red Blend (Paso Robles) $12. 86 *(5/1/2000)*

Garretson 2003 G Red Rhône Red Blend (Central Coast) $20. This is Garretson's least expensive, regional wine, but it's quite good. Based on Mourvèdre, it's creamy smooth, with cherry and cocoa flavors and a streak of earthiness. It's not fruit-driven, and is companionable with a wide range of foods. **87** —*S.H. (10/1/2005)*

Garretson 1998 The Celeidh Rhône Red Blend (Central Coast) $16. 88 — *J.C. (8/1/2000)*

Garretson 2004 G White Rhône White Blend (Central Coast) $18. This Rhône white, which contains Viognier and Roussanne, is flavorful and refreshing. It has flavors of white peach, honeysuckle and tropical fruits, and is basically dry, although the fruitiness and glycerine give it a honeyed finish. **87** —*S.H. (10/1/2005)*

Garretson 2004 The Chumhra Rhône White Blend (Central Coast) $20. Far too sweet for what's supposedly a dry table wine, with what tastes like a ton of turbinado sugar on the finish, this Rhone blend would earn a higher score if it were offered as a dessert wine. It's a question of typicity. **83** —*S.H. (10/1/2005)*

Garretson 2003 "The Celeidh" Rosé Blend (Paso Robles) $18. Very robust and full-bodied, jammy and rich in fresh young cherry, berry, vanilla and spice flavors. Drinks almost sweet, but it's a dry wine, and a lot of fun. Syrah, Mourvedre, Grenache, Roussanne. **86** —*S.H. (12/31/2004)*

Garretson 2004 The Celeidh Rosé Blend (Paso Robles) $18. It says "rosé" on the label, but the wine's as dark as a Syrah, and as full bodied. I chilled it, and although it was unusual, it was a rich, satisfying wine, fruity and crisp. **87** —*S.H. (10/1/2005)*

Garretson 2001 "The Aisling" Syrah (Paso Robles) $30. A distinctive, eccentric Syrah, due mainly to the aromatics, which are unusually powerful in dried leather, porcini mushroom and cocoa. You'll find blackberries and black cherries in the mouth, and oak. Bottom line is a soft, dry wine, balanced and complex, showing real terroir. **91** —*S.H. (12/31/2004)*

Garretson 2002 "The Craic" Syrah (Central Coast) $30. This Syrah was obviously late picked. You can tell by the ultra ripe flavors. It's gooey in cherry liqueur, chocolate and cassis, with a meaty, leathery note, while oak adds smoke and vanilla spice. Even though it's soft, it's not flabby. **89** —*S.H. (12/31/2004)*

Garretson 1999 Alban Vineyard The Finné Syrah (Edna Valley) $60. Mat Garretson, formerly at Eberle and Wild Horse, has been a leader in the California Rhône movement for years, so it is no surprise that his top Syrah is an excellent wine, blending thick blackberry-jam aromas and flavors with hickory smoke and folding in some earth, coffee and cedar. **91** *(11/1/2001)*

Garretson 2001 Hoage Vineyard "The Bulladoir" Syrah (Paso Robles) $45. Verges on a Port-style, with shockingly high alcohol, but that's the price of making this ultra ripe wine dry. Flavors of blackberries and coffee sweetened with a dollop of wild honey, rich and long, with wild herbs. Gets better the more you sip. **87** —*S.H. (12/31/2004)*

Garretson 2003 Mon Amie Bassetti Vineyard Syrah (San Luis Obispo County) $50. Thick and syrupy, with a suggestion of sweetness, this Syrah is jammy and simple, finishing with noticeable alcohol (it's labeled at 16.8%). **82** *(9/1/2005)*

Garretson 2001 Rozet Vineyard "The Lusacain" Syrah (Paso Robles) $45. Almost super ripe, displaying intense, soft cherry, cassis, coffee and smoked meat flavors, with a touch of oak. Saved from flatness by a dusty jacket of tannins. An interesting wine, good by itself, better with the right fare. Grilled lamb, filet mignon, with some sweetness in the sauce or topping. **90** —*S.H. (12/31/2004)*

Garretson 2003 The Aisling Syrah (Paso Robles) $30. Combines slightly sweet-tasting cherry fruit with notes of burnt sugar, coffee and chocolate in an angular wine that's firmly tannic. Picks up a hint of pepper on the finish. **83** *(9/1/2005)*

Garretson 1997 The Aisling Syrah (Paso Robles) $25. 87 —*J.C. (2/1/2000)*

Garretson 2003 The Bulladoir Syrah (Paso Robles) $65. Too sweet-tasting for our tasters, whether from residual sugar or just the combination of high alcohol and superripe fruit. **80** *(9/1/2005)*

Garretson 1999 The Corcairghorm Fralich Vineyard Syrah (Paso Robles) $30. From a warm Eastside vineyard, this wine has pretty aromas of plums, pepper, white chocolate and smoke; well-knit and pure. Big in terms of fruit, but well balanced and elegant. The acids and tannins are soft and user-friendly. **88** —*S.H. (7/1/2002)*

Garretson 2003 The Craic Syrah (Central Coast) $30. A bit hot according to some tasters, a bit sweet according to others, this Syrah boasts moderately intense aromas of coffee and berries, flavors of caramel and marshmallow and a tart finish. **83** *(9/1/2005)*

Garretson 2003 The Luascain Syrah (Paso Robles) $45. Garretson's wines were universally criticized by the panel and this one was no exception, although it fared better than some others. Hints of coffee and roasted fruit are followed by medicinal cherry flavors and a slightly hot (alcoholic) finish. **83** *(9/1/2005)*

Garretson 2001 Viognier (Santa Ynez Valley) $30. Quite floral in the nose, with a fresh, yet complex blend of ripe melon, peach, apricot, mineral and herb notes. Sleek and refined through the long finish. **91** —*J.M. (12/15/2002)*

Garretson 2004 The Saothar Viognier (Paso Robles) $30. More like a dessert wine than a dry table wine, this idiosyncratic Viognier tastes quite sweet and honeyed, with potent fruit flavors and high acidity. **85** —*S.H. (10/1/2005)*

GARY FARRELL

Gary Farrell 1998 Encounter Bordeaux Blend (Sonoma County) $60. Light-to medium-weight in the mouth, particularly considering its pedigree, the Encounter is Farrell's limited-production Bordeaux blend. The nose and palate offer lots of black cherry, coupled with powdery-milky aromas on the nose, and chocolate-earth flavors on the palate. Finishes with good length, and spice and coffee flavors. Only 651 cases made. **90** — *D.T. (6/1/2002)*

Gary Farrell 1997 Encounter Pine Mountain Bordeaux Blend (Sonoma County) $42. 92 *(11/1/2000)*

Gary Farrell 1996 Encounter Pine Mountain Bordeaux Blend (Pine Mountain) $42. 89 —*J.C. (11/1/1999)*

Gary Farrell 2001 Encounter Cabernet Blend (Sonoma County) $60. Gary Farrell is indifferent to prevailing trends, and this Cab is a good illustration. Where most '01s are rich and hedonistic, this one's tight and firm in acids and tannins, almost undrinkable now. However, it has good prospects, for there is a tremendous core of fruit. Hold until 2007. **88** —*S.H. (11/1/2005)*

Gary Farrell 2000 Cabernet Sauvignon (Sonoma County) $34. Right now, it shows its tannins and acids strongly, and is relieved only by hints of cherries, plums and currants. Yet the finish turns ripely sweet. Best after 2010. **88** —*S.H. (11/15/2004)*

Gary Farrell 2000 Bradford Mountain Cabernet Sauvignon (Dry Creek Valley) $40. Very dry, this Cab mixes berry-cherry flavors with herbal ones to produce a wine of angularity and a certain tannic austerity. It's the kind of wine that will play a supporting role at the table, rather than insisting on center stage. **89** —*S.H. (11/15/2004)*

Gary Farrell 1999 Hillside Vineyard Selection Cabernet Sauvignon (Sonoma County) $34. Smooth, smoky and stylish. Huge flavors of cassis and plum are rich yet controlled. The tannins are meaty and firm, but they should subside within a year or two. The coffee, toast and vanilla notes on the finish are just about perfect. This wine is right on, a reflection of Sonoma Cab at its best. **92** —*M.S. (11/15/2002)*

Gary Farrell 2002 Chardonnay (Russian River Valley) $30. The winemaker has crafted a tight, minerally, Chablis-style wine that's high in acidity. You won't find cascades of fruit or massive oak here, but tart citrus and green apple flavors and a firm, steely mouthfeel. Yet the wine possesses an undefinable quality of elegance. Cellar this for as long as you like. **89** —*S.H. (11/15/2004)*

Gary Farrell 1999 Chardonnay (Russian River Valley) $30. A presently reined-in wine with exotic elements, showing a ginger, saffron and green apple bouquet. It's well-balanced, with lively apple and citrus flavors. It has good acidity and a firm structure that should hold it together for three or four years. With aging, it may integrate and develop further. **88** *(7/1/2001)*

Gary Farrell 2002 Bien Nacido Vineyard Chardonnay (Santa Barbara County) $34. You'll find an array of fruit flavors but the main one is sweet-sour lemondrop, sweetened with oak. The wine is soft in acids, with an oily, creamy texture and an oriental spice finish. It has class and elegance. **89** —*S.H. (10/1/2004)*

Gary Farrell 1999 Bien Nacido Vineyard Chardonnay (Santa Barbara County) $30. Lean and tautly balanced, this wine has an outdoorsy, mineral-and-hay bouquet and sweet herbal accents. Green apple flavors take over the palate, though hints of lemon and minerals also show up. Tasters didn't find anything terribly wrong here, just a lack of element that would make it more right. Finishes with lingering oaky notes. **85** *(7/1/2001)*

Gary Farrell 1998 Bien Nacido Vineyard Chardonnay (Santa Barbara County) $28. 89 *(6/1/2000)*

Gary Farrell 2004 Cresta Ridge Vineyard Chardonnay (Russian River Valley) $38. A distinctive Chardonnay made in the Farrell style, which leans toward acidic and elegant. But this is not an austere wine, far from it. It has a rich minerality and flavors of lime and pineapple custard, and then an even richer crème brûlée finish. Delicious and complex. **92** —*S.H. (12/1/2006)*

Gary Farrell 2003 Cresta Ridge Vineyard Chardonnay (Russian River Valley) $38. California Chardonnay doesn't get much leaner or tarter than this acid-filled bottling by a vintner known for picking early. The idea is to streamline the wine, so instead of peaches and pineapples, you get minerals, dried herbs and citrus. It's a good food wine. **88** —*S.H. (11/1/2005)*

Gary Farrell 1998 Rochioli Vineyard Chardonnay (Russian River Valley) $34. The bouquet of Farrell's wine is a mixed bag of buttered popcorn, minerals, herbs, citrus fruit, pineapple and melon stuffed in an oak envelope. Similarly attractive flavors mark the palate, which is fairly full and has an almost rustic quality. Has all the body and length you could want, if not quite all the balance and finesse. **87** *(7/1/2001)*

Gary Farrell 2002 Rochioli-Allen Vineyards Chardonnay (Russian River Valley) $38. Farrell likes to pick early, and thus trades opulence for acidity, elegance and possible ageworthiness. Here you'll find a tight, lemony wine, very crisp. The wine is marked by oak and lees, which add flavor and textural nuances, but it remains flinty and austere. **90** —*S.H. (11/15/2004)*

Gary Farrell 2004 Russian River Selection Chardonnay (Russian River Valley) $32. Very clean and dry, high in citrusy acidity, and with a steely minerality. This streamlined Chard aims for structure, not opulence. The flavors are of white peaches and smoky oak. Defines the Farrell style of detailed elegance. **90** —*S.H. (12/1/2006)*

Gary Farrell 2003 Russian River Selection Chardonnay (Russian River Valley) $32. This is a tense, taut Chardonnay. It's high in acids and nerve-penetrating too, with notes of steel and gunmetal. What fruit there is veers toward ripe grapefruit. Needless to say, the wine is bone dry. **86** —*S.H. (11/1/2005)*

Gary Farrell 2003 Starr Ridge Vineyard Chardonnay (Russian River Valley) $38. This interesting Chard strikes Chablisian notes in the mineral flavors that veer into apples, peaches and pineapples, and the high natural acidity. The wine trades opulence for a steely, structural elegance, and a complexity in the finish that fascinates. **91** —*S.H. (12/1/2005)*

Gary Farrell 2003 Westside Farms Chardonnay (Russian River Valley) $38. Compared to the winery's Starr Ridge Chard from the same vintage, this is unassertive. It's thicker in the mouth, and softer, with a malted-custard texture framing peach flavors. **86** —*S.H. (12/1/2005)*

Gary Farrell 2002 Westside Farms Chardonnay (Russian River Valley) $34. Intense in lemon drop, buttercream and smoky, buttered toast, with very high acidity, this is a Chard of elegance and power rather than flamboyance. It finishes with a clean note of minerals and gunmetal. **91** —*S.H. (5/1/2005)*

Gary Farrell 2000 Westside Farms Chardonnay (Russian River Valley) $34. Unbelievably dense, a wine compacted with all sorts of stone and tropical fruits ranging from peaches to papayas. Lavishly oaked and drenched with buttered toast, smoke, vanilla and butterscotch. This is a full-throttle, no-holds-barred Chard, oozing with richness. **93 Editors' Choice** —*S.H. (2/1/2003)*

Gary Farrell 1997 Calypso Vineyard Merlot (Russian River Valley) $32. 88 —*J.C. (7/1/2000)*

Gary Farrell 1997 Ladi's Vineyard Merlot (Sonoma County) $30. Very polite and proper: not too much oak, not too much fruit. All the ingredients are here in proportion, from the cedary, caramelized oak to the black-cherry and plum fruit that carries hints of dark earth and coffee. **87** —*J.C. (6/1/2001)*

Gary Farrell 1998 Pinot Noir (Russian River Valley) $30. 89 *(10/1/2000)*

Gary Farrell 1997 Pinot Noir (Russian River Valley) $24. 86 — *(10/1/1999)*

Gary Farrell 2002 Pinot Noir (Russian River Valley) $32. Straddles the line between ripeness and its opposite, with beet, tomato, mint and cherry flavors. Lean and tart in acids, and light in body, but harmonious. **86** *(11/1/2004)*

Gary Farrell 2000 Pinot Noir (Russian River Valley) $34. Beet and black cherry aromas open this Pinot stalwart's regular offering. But this bottling comes off quite tart and light, with coffee, cocoa and saddle leather notes taking over from the almost ephemeral fruit. A bit chalky on the tongue, finishing with a tangy feel, but modest flavor. **83** *(10/1/2002)*

Gary Farrell 1999 Pinot Noir (Russian River Valley) $34. This long-time Pinot Noir player's standard bottling is appealing, with inviting aromas of cherry, licorice and date-nut bread. The creamy, juicy texture supports black plum, mocha, coffee and molasses flavors. Panelists had different opinions about the finish, some finding it dry and a bit short, others svelte and polished. **89** *(10/1/2002)*

Gary Farrell 1999 Allen Vineyard Pinot Noir (Russian River Valley) $NA. I think this wine has a future, but right now it's in one of those middle-aged funks. It's ripe in cherries, bright in acids, and smooth, but has a certain flatness. It's a gamble, but check it out in another two or three years. **87** —*S.H. (6/1/2005)*

Gary Farrell 1999 Allen Vineyard Pinot Noir (Russian River Valley) $50. The nose is powerful; it exudes graham crackers, earth and toast. The black cherry fruit on the palate is ripe and almost as sweet as berry syrup. The finish, meanwhile, is long and smooth, but once again it's very sweet. **89** (10/1/2002)

Gary Farrell 1997 Allen Vineyard Pinot Noir (Russian River Valley) $NA. Turning brown and orange, and picking up old Pinot notes of dried cherries, potpourri, mocha and spice, in a very dry, silky, elegantly structured wine. Acids are bright. Pleasant, but not profound. Drink up. **88** —S.H. (6/1/2005)

Gary Farrell 1997 Allen Vineyard Pinot Noir (Russian River Valley) $40. 88 (11/15/1999)

Gary Farrell 1994 Allen Vineyard Pinot Noir (Russian River Valley) $NA. From a very big vintage, a wine still with plenty of cherry and blackberry fruit, and even some gritty tannins. Very dry, and a little awkward in texture. Probably at its best now. **87** —S.H. (6/1/2005)

Gary Farrell 2003 Allen Vineyard Hillside Blocks Pinot Noir (Russian River Valley) $60. One of the ripest Farrell Pinots I've ever tasted, this bottling, from the well-known Allen Vineyard, is enormously fruity. It was a very hot, fast vintage, and the fruit here is enormously rich, almost dessert-like in baked cherry pie and rum-soaked currant flavors. It is, however, fully dry. Drink this decadent Pinot with beef tenderloin served in a wine or fruit reduction sauce. **92** —S.H. (8/1/2006)

Gary Farrell 2002 Allen Vineyard Hillside Blocks Pinot Noir (Russian River Valley) $50. Monumental, magnificent. Russian River Pinot hardly gets much better. Huge flavors of blackberries, tart red cherries, coffee, cola, cherry tomato and generous Asian spices, all of it well-oaked, and the acidity is crisp and cleansing. Layered and never stops changing in the glass. This is beautiful now, and should hold and improve through 2008. **94** —S.H. (5/1/2005)

Gary Farrell 1997 Bien Nacido Vineyard. Pinot Noir (Santa Barbara County) $30. 88 — (10/1/1999)

Gary Farrell 2003 Jack Hill Vineyard Pinot Noir (Russian River Valley) $45. Too young now. The wine is tannic and acidic, with cherry-berry flavors. It's not really very interesting; instead it's kind of raw and dry. Maybe it will go someplace. **84** —S.H. (12/1/2006)

Gary Farrell 2000 Olivet Lane Vineyards Pinot Noir (Russian River Valley) $38. This deep wine's cherry fruit has pruny overtones and cedar, earth, toast and dried leaf accents. Medium-weight and even, it's flavorful but seems unrealized. Though not overtly tight, it seems to be in an awkward phase right now. Closes tart and warm, with tart, woodsy notes. Try in 2003. **87** (10/1/2002)

Gary Farrell 2003 Rochioli Vineyard Pinot Noir (Russian River Valley) $38. This wine, with a pedigreed origin, is not providing much pleasure now, because it's a bit tart and austere. But the cherry and oak flavors should broaden out in several months, giving a fuller, sappier mouthfeel. Not a long-term prospect, but tasty for drinking over the next few years. **84** — S.H. (12/1/2005)

Gary Farrell 2002 Rochioli Vineyard Pinot Noir (Russian River Valley) $50. There's a masculinity to this Pinot, with its crisp acids, firm body and stony minerality. It possesses a youthful austerity, but with hidden depths. There's a rich core of ripe blackberry and cherry fruit, and oak plays a supporting role. It will not really show well without cellaring. Best after 2008. **91** —S.H. (11/1/2004)

Gary Farrell 1999 Rochioli Vineyard Pinot Noir (Russian River Valley) $60. The black fruit nose is driving, which should come as no surprise given the dark color of this well-extracted table wine. Sweet black cherries and a full dose of oak make up the hedonistic palate, and while it's ramped up, the ripe fruit seems to welcome the full-out style that Farrell has chosen. **88** (10/1/2002)

Gary Farrell 1997 Rochioli Vineyard Pinot Noir (Russian River Valley) $50. 91 (10/1/1999)

Gary Farrell 2003 Rochioli-Allen Vineyard Pinot Noir (Russian River Valley) $65. You have to wonder if the winemaker, who sold to Allied-Domecq in 2004, decided to make his Pinots fruitier to appeal to changing consumers tastes. Maybe it was the very hot vintage. In any case, this is more in keeping with California's superripe Pinots than Farrell's formerly tight, acidic ones, with excellent results. It's deliciously drinkable, although perhaps not so ageable. **92** —S.H. (7/1/2006)

Gary Farrell 2000 Rochioli-Allen Vineyard Pinot Noir (Russian River Valley) $60. Made in a leaner style without the hedonistic fruit now in favor, but no less elegant or ageworthy for its herbal, tea and tobacco flavors. This wine is high in acids and fairly tannic. It is so well constructed that it would be a shame to drink it now. Best left alone until 2007. **90** —S.H. (7/1/2003)

Gary Farrell 2002 Rochioli-Allen Vineyards Pinot Noir (Russian River Valley) $60. Softer than Farrell's Allen bottling, and not as deeply layered. Displays cherry, cola and baked rhubarb pie flavors, and is dry and bitter on the finish. Balanced and likely to age. **90** —S.H. (5/1/2005)

Gary Farrell 2002 Rochioli-Allen Vineyards Pinot Noir (Russian River Valley) $60. Paler in color, lighter in body than most of his Russian River neighbors, and higher in acidity, this cherry-infused wine, with its voluptuous coating of oak, is more Pinot-like than the Syrah-like Pinots that are currently critics' darlings. In its youth, it seems awkward, even simple, but could be a keeper. **92** —S.H. (6/1/2005)

Gary Farrell 2004 Russian River Selection Pinot Noir (Russian River Valley) $42. Tart in acidity and a bit austere, this Pinot has an early-picked quality and shows some immature tannins. It's an elegant, streamlined wine with good structure, but leaves you wanting more fruit. **86** —S.H. (12/1/2006)

Gary Farrell 2003 Russian River Selection Pinot Noir (Russian River Valley) $34. Although it's a bit one-dimensional, this is textbook Pinot Noir. It's lightly silky and delicate in the mouth, and dry, with crisp acids carrying flavors of cherries, cola and spice. **85** —S.H. (11/1/2005)

Gary Farrell 2000 Starr Ridge Pinot Noir (Russian River Valley) $38. "Very drinkable," "light on its feet," and "lean and tasty" were panelist comments on this juicy, high-toned wine. Strawberry, tart plum and dried spice flavors accent black chocolate, espresso and lemon notes. Drink now–2007. **88** (10/1/2002)

Gary Farrell 2003 Starr Ridge Vineyard Pinot Noir (Russian River Valley) $45. This is the kind of Pinot Noir that is styled in a leaner, tauter, more acidic way meant to complement food and be cellarworthy. Nonetheless the impressive cherry and blackberry flavors are flattering. **90** —S.H. (11/1/2005)

Gary Farrell 1997 Stiling Vineyard Pinot Noir (Russian River Valley) $30. 84 — (10/1/1999)

Gary Farrell 2000 Encounter Red Blend (Sonoma County) $60. True to the house style, this young, dark wine will not wow you immediately. It's tight now, weighed under by tannins and acidity. Yet there's a succulence in the middle palate that suggests just-ripe black cherries and spicy blackberries. It seems balanced and harmonious enough for extended aging. **90** —S.H. (9/1/2004)

Gary Farrell 1999 Encounter Red Blend (Sonoma County) $60. Smoke and leather aromas get this one out of the blocks in fine fashion. The mouth is bursting with juicy berry and cherry fruit and there's tons of length and dark coffee nuances to the finish. It's certainly chunky; some might even call it a "fruit bomb." But it holds onto its racy, fresh side, so despite its power, it's well-balanced and well-made. **91** —M.S. (11/15/2002)

Gary Farrell 2005 Redwood Ranch Sauvignon Blanc (Sonoma County) $20. As in previous vintages, the 2005 is bone dry, high in acidity, and New Zealandy in its mineral, gooseberry and citrus flavors. This streamlined Sauvignon is one of the cleaner ones around. A beautiful companion for all sorts of foods. **90** —S.H. (12/1/2006)

Gary Farrell 2004 Redwood Ranch Sauvignon Blanc (Sonoma County) $24. This Sauvignon Blanc certainly is grassy. It's also intensely feline. Acidity, as you might expect, is high, and the finish is dry. This stylish wine will have its fans. **85** —S.H. (11/1/2005)

Gary Farrell 2003 Redwood Ranch Sauvignon Blanc (Sonoma County) $20. About as good as Sauvignon Blanc gets in California. It's ultraripe, with lemon and lime, gooseberry, apple and pine flavors, and has very crisp acidity, but that makes it sound like lots of other wines. Where it excels is in sheer intensity. **90 Editors' Choice** —S.H. (12/1/2004)

Gary Farrell 2001 Redwood Ranch Sauvignon Blanc (Sonoma County) $20. If you like yours big and burly, then this might be the right wine for you. Applesauce and lemon meringue pie aromas lead the way toward a palate full of lemon, pineapple, tangerine and vanilla. The finish is stony and leaves a custard-like impression. It's clearly from the barrel-fermented school, but for some that may be fine. For others, however, it will feel overoaked and ponderous on the tongue. **87** *(8/1/2002)*

Gary Farrell 1998 Syrah (Russian River Valley) $32. A smoldering toast, coffee, leather and cassis nose opens this "smooth" and "well put-together" medium-weight Syrah. Cherry, cedar and black pepper were the adjectives on all panelists' lips when it came to the palate; finishes dry, with cedar, caramel and chocolate flavors. **90** *(11/1/2001)*

Gary Farrell 2002 Zinfandel (Dry Creek Valley) $24. Here's a Zin that teases with sweet wild berry tart and rhubarb pie flavors, then pulls back at the last minute, leaving behind a peppery scour and acids. Finishes a bit herbal and tannic. **86** *—S.H. (10/1/2004)*

Gary Farrell 1997 Bradford Mountain Zinfandel (Dry Creek Valley) $30. 87 *—J.C. (11/1/1999)*

Gary Farrell 2000 Bradford Mountain Vineyard Zinfandel (Dry Creek Valley) $36. Bramble and leather aromas with piercing blueberry announce it as pure Zin. The palate follows the nose: Blueberry and licorice flavors dominate, with a slight bubble gum nuance thrown in for good measure. The finish is wall-to-wall smooth, with espresso as the aftertaste. Very firm, but not unyielding. **89** *—M.S. (11/1/2002)*

Gary Farrell 2003 Bradford Mountain Vineyards Zinfandel (Dry Creek Valley) $36. The problem here is excessive sweetness. It tastes like there was a lot of residual sugar in the wine when fermentation was stopped. As a result the flavor is of sugared blackberry tea. **80** *—S.H. (7/1/2006)*

Gary Farrell 2000 Dry Creek Valley Zinfandel (Sonoma County) $24. If purple's your color, then dig in. This is a full but well-balanced cruiserweight with pungent boysenberry and spice-box aromas, developed yet sassy berry, plum and vanilla flavors, and a structured, big-tannin finish. Despite all its power, it dances on your tongue and isn't overstuffed. **90** *—M.S. (11/1/2002)*

Gary Farrell 1999 Maple Vineyard Zinfandel (Dry Creek Valley) $30. An outdoorsy bouquet of forest floor, soil and dried spice, plus some blackberry and cocoa, play on the nose. The blackberry, oak and cocoa, plus some black plum, make encore appearances in the mouth and on the finish. Well-balanced with nice tannins in the mouth; finishes with an oak and white pepper tang, and chalky, earthy goodness. **88** *—D.T. (3/1/2002)*

Gary Farrell 1997 Maple Vineyard Zinfandel (Dry Creek Valley) $30. 86 *—J.C. (11/1/1999)*

Gary Farrell 2003 Maple Vineyard Tina's Block Zinfandel (Dry Creek Valley) $36. Big, ripe, voluptuous and mouth-filling are just a few of the descriptors that come to mind with this dry, juicy Zin. It's a rollicking romp through a fruit store, with a raisiny finish, and feels hotter than the 14.4% alcohol the label says it has. **86** *—S.H. (7/1/2006)*

Gary Farrell 2002 Maple Vineyard Tina's Block Zinfandel (Dry Creek Valley) $36. A most interesting Zin for the exciting line it straddles. Just when you think it's one of those over-the-top residual sweeties, it pulls back. There are a few raisiny notes intermingled with ripe blackberries, but the wine is fully dry, with rich tannins and an earthy finish. **89** *—S.H. (10/1/2004)*

Gary Farrell 1997 Old Vine Selection Zinfandel (Sonoma) $24. 89 *—J.C. (11/1/1999)*

Gary Farrell 2000 Rice Vineyard Zinfandel (Russian River Valley) $27. Very bright and jammy, with a racy acidic streak is how to best describe this solid but slightly tart Zin. The palate features intense fruit—mostly juicy red cherry and raspberry. The finish is clean and crisp; it's racy, like the palate. If there's a fault it's that the middle is too acid-driven and tart. **87** *—M.S. (11/1/2002)*

GELFAND

Gelfand 2004 Petite Sirah (Paso Robles) $30. Winner, darkest wine of the year! Winner, highest alcohol table wine of the year! At 17.1%, the wine is incredibly rich, with massive cherry liqueur, cassis, fudgy chocolate and sweet licorice flavors. Hard to know how to deal with something like this, except to say it's really good at what it is. **90** *—S.H. (12/15/2006)*

Gelfand 2004 Cabyrah Red Blend (Paso Robles) $28. You can tell from the name that it's a mixture of (mainly) Cabernet Sauvignon and Syrah. The wine is deeply colored, almost black, and stuffed with ripe black currant, chocolate and olive flavors enriched with sweet oak. It's a soft wine, but with firm tannins. **87** *—S.H. (12/15/2006)*

Gelfand 2004 Quixotic Red Blend (Paso Robles) $35. This is a ripe, lush wine, with high alcohol (16.3%), low acidity, and very forward flavors of blackberry and cherry jam, cocoa and spicy pepper. The fruit really stars in this dry blend of Cab, Syrah, Zin and Petite Sirah. **85** *—S.H. (12/15/2006)*

GENERATIONS OF SONOMA

Generations of Sonoma 2005 Serres Ranch Late Harvest Aleatico (Sonoma Valley) $30. Very sweet but clumsy, with a weird medicinal, Band-Aid smell. The sugary blackberry taste is one-dimensional. **80** *—S.H. (12/1/2006)*

GENNAIO

Gennaio 2002 Sangiovese (Dry Creek Valley) $19. From Duxoup. This is a Chianti-like, single-vineyard wine from the Teldeschi Vineyard, midway up the east side of the valley. It's dry, tart and light-bodied, with flavors of cherries and herbs. **86** *—S.H. (11/1/2005)*

GEORIS WINERY

Georis Winery 2000 Cabernet Sauvignon (Carmel Valley) $34. Not quite ripe, with blackberry flavors side by side with earthy tobacco and mushroom. The tannins are firm and a bit hard. A good wine, but pricey for the quality. **85** *—S.H. (5/1/2004)*

Georis Winery 2002 Sauvignon Blanc (Monterey) $21. A well-ripened Sauvignon Blanc, quite fruity with fig and peach flavors and a bit of toasty oak. It's technically dry, but filled with fruity sweetness that lasts through the finish. As big as a Chardonnay, but with different flavors. **86** *—S.H. (2/1/2004)*

GEYSER PEAK

Geyser Peak 2002 Reserve Alexandre Meritage Bordeaux Blend (Alexander Valley) $49. Compared to the winery's '02 Reserve Cab, this is less tannic, more accessible, due to the dominance of Merlot in the blend. Still, it's a tannic young wine, dry and astringent despite rich cherry and mocha flavors. It is not particularly drinkable now, and is not a longterm bet. Drink 2007–2010. **88** *—S.H. (5/1/2006)*

Geyser Peak 1998 Reserve Alexandre Cabernet Blend (Alexander Valley) $45. One of the older and more distinguished of Meritage wines, this blend of five Bordeaux varietals is leaner this year but there are pretty berry flavors in addition to herbal ones. It's well-oaked, with complex, dusty tannins. It won't age but it has glamour and elegance and breed. **90** *—S.H. (9/1/2002)*

Geyser Peak 1999 Reserve Alexandre Meritage Cabernet Blend (Alexander Valley) $45. The quintessential Alexander Valley Cabernet, always dependably soft, fruity, and complex. This year is one of the best ever. Plush and velvety, with endless nuances, it's like sipping the essence of black cherries steeped in kirsch. Dry, with just enough oak to add smoke and spice. **93 Editors' Choice** *—S.H. (5/1/2003)*

Geyser Peak 1997 Cabernet Franc (Sonoma County) $20. 92 *—S.H. (7/1/2000)*

Geyser Peak 2003 Cabernet Sauvignon (Alexander Valley) $18. This beautiful wine is the quintessential Alexander Valley Cabernet. It's soft and melted in texture, a gentle but complex wine with enormously rich blackberry, cassis, and oak flavors. And this is a great price for the quality. Geyser Peak is at the top of their game. **91 Editors' Choice** *—S.H. (7/1/2006)*

Geyser Peak 2002 Cabernet Sauvignon (Alexander Valley) $18. Although it doesn't have the complexity of the winery's single-vineyard Cab, this blend shows off its terroir with a soft attractiveness and good varietal character. The blackberry, cherry, roasted coffee, grilled bell pepper, herb, and oak flavors are dry, but a little thin. **85** *—S.H. (12/31/2005)*

Geyser Peak 2001 Cabernet Sauvignon (Alexander Valley) $18. Plush and sleek, with black currant, cherry, herb, and coffee flavors that are wrapped in gentle but complex tannins. Oak adds smoke and vanilla accents. **89** —*S.H. (11/15/2004)*

Geyser Peak 2000 Cabernet Sauvignon (Sonoma County) $17. A solid Cab, but one that reveals the difficulties of the vintage in its lean, tart personality and slightly astringent finish. On the upside, you get complex earth, tobacco, and cassis flavors. **86** —*S.H. (11/1/2003)*

Geyser Peak 1999 Cabernet Sauvignon (Sonoma County) $17. Always rock-solid and fairly priced, Geyser Peak's Cab this year is well-structured and firm, with sturdy tannins and bright acidity. It will need a year or so for the black currant and plum flavors to emerge. There's a rich earthy streak that makes this a fine companion with food. **90** —*S.H. (6/1/2002)*

Geyser Peak 1996 Cabernet Sauvignon (Sonoma County) $16. **89** —*M.S. (10/1/1999)*

Geyser Peak 2001 Block Collection Kuimelis Vineyard Cabernet Sauvignon (Alexander Valley) $32. This mountain Cab has a very dark color, and the tannins are intense and scouring. Will the core of black cherry and blackberry fruit outlive the tannins? The jury's out, but it merits this score by virtue of its overall class and distinction. If you open it now, decant for as long as you can. **90** —*S.H. (11/15/2004)*

Geyser Peak 2000 Block Collection Kuimelis Vineyard Cabernet Sauvignon (Alexander Valley) $26. Richly textured and velvety smooth, this effort shows impressively bold cassis flavors that strike a fine balance against hints of smoke and toast. Good price for a wine of this quality. **90 Editors' Choice** *(11/1/2003)*

Geyser Peak 1999 Block Collection Kuimelis Vineyard Cabernet Sauvignon (Alexander Valley) $26. A fine Cabernet, at the high end of its class, with the soft, luxurious tannins and rich fruit you expect from this appellation. Black currants dominate, with a strong herbal, earthy element, and a sharp finish that indicates ageworthiness. **91** —*S.H. (11/15/2002)*

Geyser Peak 1999 Block Collection, Vallerga Vineyard Cabernet Sauvignon (Yountville) $36. Despite its age of nearly five years, this wine hits the palate hard in stinging tannins and acids. Beyond the herbaceousness are some pure flavors of blackberries and cherries. Drink 2008 and beyond. **89** —*S.H. (10/1/2004)*

Geyser Peak 1998 Kuimelis Vineyard Cabernet Sauvignon (Alexander Valley) $28. It's shy in the nose, with suggestions of cassis and smoky oak, while the flavors veer toward berries and spices, swimming in firm tannins and sharp acidity. It's a delicate wine, one of finesse rather than power, but it is very good. A long, sweetly ripe finish suggests ageability, but it's probably at its youthful, fleshy best now. **88** —*S.H. (7/1/2002)*

Geyser Peak 1997 Kuimelis Vineyards Cabernet Sauvignon (Sonoma County) $27. **91** *(1/1/2000)*

Geyser Peak 2002 Kumelis Vineyard Cabernet Sauvignon (Alexander Valley) $42. I've been impressed by this wine for years. Made from a high mountain vineyard in the Mayacamas range, it's dense in black currant, cherry, and herb flavors, and well-structured, with a pretty coat of oak. Firm but pliant tannins and good, crisp acids frame the fruit, lending this Cab elegance and subtlety. Should develop well for 10 years. **92 Cellar Selection** —*S.H. (11/1/2005)*

Geyser Peak 2002 Reserve Cabernet Sauvignon (Alexander Valley) $46. The overwhelming impression is of strong, astringently dry tannins that absolutely limit pleasure. Is it worth cellaring? There's a deep core of black cherry and cassis fruit and adequate acidity. The wine will undoubtedly throw sediment and soften, but that doesn't equate to improvement. Your best bet is to decant and drink with rich, fatty meats and cheeses. **86** —*S.H. (5/1/2006)*

Geyser Peak 2001 Reserve Cabernet Sauvignon (Alexander Valley) $46. Without the drama of, say, a Napa Cab, this wine exemplifies Alexander Valley in its soft complexity and earthiness. The cherry and blackberry fruit has a terroir-driven mushroomy herbaceousness that makes this a perfect companion for cuisine. Best now through 2012. **90 Cellar Selection** —*S.H. (10/1/2005)*

Geyser Peak 2000 Reserve Cabernet Sauvignon (Sonoma County) $40. Sure it's oaky, with smoky, bacony, and chocolaty aromas, but there are gobs of fruit to support it: plums, blackberries, and black currants. It's

what a California Cab should be—big, rich, and powerful, yet marked by soft, chewy tannins. **91** *(11/1/2003)*

Geyser Peak 1999 Reserve Cabernet Sauvignon (Sonoma County) $40. Grapes had no problem ripening and the wine brims with sweet black currant flavors. Generous oak boosts spice and vanilla, while tannins are soft but molded. This is an early drinking wine of charm and finesse. Drink now through 2003. **88** —*S.H. (6/1/2002)*

Geyser Peak 1997 Reserve Cabernet Sauvignon (Sonoma County) $40. **91** —*S.H. (12/15/2000)*

Geyser Peak 1996 Reserve Cabernet Sauvignon (Sonoma County) $32. **88** —*S.H. (11/1/1999)*

Geyser Peak 1998 Vallerga Vineyard Cabernet Sauvignon (Napa Valley) $35. Geyser Peak reaches across the Mayacamas Range to Yountville in search of Napa Cabernet. Low production kept the lots ripe, and lavish use of oak uplifts the aromas and flavors. There's a simpleness to the middle palate, and it's a little flabby, but spicy fruit saves the day. **86** —*S.H. (6/1/2002)*

Geyser Peak 1997 Vallerga Vineyards Cabernet Sauvignon (Napa Valley) $27. **90** *(1/1/2000)*

Geyser Peak 1998 Chardonnay (Sonoma County) $12. **86** —*L.W. (3/1/2000)*

Geyser Peak 2004 Chardonnay (Alexander Valley) $14. There's plenty of oaky richness in this wine, on top of nicely ripe flavors that smack of pineapples and peaches and cinnamon spice. It shares much in common with the best Alexander Valley Chards. **89 Best Buy** —*S.H. (12/31/2005)*

Geyser Peak 2003 Chardonnay (Russian River Valley) $19. Soft and a little thin, with lemondrop flavors and generous oak. This wine is fully dry, and has a pleasant, creamy texture. **85** —*S.H. (10/1/2005)*

Geyser Peak 2003 Chardonnay (Alexander Valley) $19. Light in flavor, this friendly, everyday Chard shows modest peach, spice, and oak flavors and a creamy texture. **84** —*S.H. (5/1/2005)*

Geyser Peak 2002 Chardonnay (Sonoma County) $12. Ripe pear and tropical fruits, a spicy mouthfeel, polished oak, and a touch of lees, a creamy texture, a slightly sweet, fruity finish—it's all here. Designed to appeal to popular tastes at an everyday price. **85** —*S.H. (10/1/2004)*

Geyser Peak 2001 Chardonnay (Sonoma County) $12. Hard to believe the price on this beauty. It's a steal, with the rich peach and pear fruit flavors, lavish oak, and stylish elegance. This is a complex, layered wine, with a long, spicy finish that carries the pretty flavors for a long time. **88 Best Buy** —*S.H. (2/1/2003)*

Geyser Peak 2000 Chardonnay (Russian River Valley) $16. Doesn't seem as concentrated as in previous vintages. There are apple and peach flavors and a pinch of smoke and vanilla but it's a thin wine. **83** —*S.H. (5/1/2002)*

Geyser Peak 2000 Chardonnay (Sonoma County) $12. From a dependable winery, another clean wine with enough flavor to satisfy. It has upfront berry flavors, juicy and candied. The body is creamy, the finish honeyed. Could be a little crisper. **84** —*S.H. (5/1/2002)*

Geyser Peak 1998 Chardonnay (Russian River Valley) $20. **88** *(1/1/2000)*

Geyser Peak 1998 Block Collection Big River Ranch Chardonnay (Russian River Valley) $23. **88** —*S.H. (11/15/2000)*

Geyser Peak 2001 Block Collection Ricci Vineyard Chardonnay (Carneros) $21. A well-ripened and well-oaked wine featuring flavors of sweet citrus, apples, peaches, and pears. Benefits from refreshing acidity and mild, dusty tannins. Lees plays a supporting role. **89** —*S.H. (6/1/2003)*

Geyser Peak 1999 Block Collection Ricci Vnyd. Chardonnay (Carneros) $20. Ripe and racy, this single-vineyard wine has lots of sweet lime, white peach, and kiwi aromas and flavors on top of a steely framework of crisp acidity. Oak adds buttery, creamy notes. A rich, complex combination. **91 Editors' Choice** —*S.H. (5/1/2001)*

Geyser Peak 2003 Reserve Chardonnay (Alexander Valley) $25. Bright, perky fruit stars in this lovely wine. It's ripe in pineapple and tangerine, with a rich, custard and meringue finish, but it's dry and complex. Easy to like. **90 Editors' Choice** —*S.H. (10/1/2005)*

Geyser Peak 2002 Reserve Chardonnay (Alexander Valley) $24. It explodes with vanilla, buttered toast and smoke, but there's a lot of apple and pear fruit, too. The texture is creamy and the finish is spicy on this lovely, complex wine. **88** —*S.H. (11/15/2004)*

Geyser Peak 2001 Reserve Chardonnay (Alexander Valley) $23. This is the epitome of California Chardonnay, in all of its marvelous excess of butter, toast, and richness. It's viscous and creamy on the palate, with modest apple and pear notes on the finish. **87** *(11/1/2003)*

Geyser Peak 2000 Reserve Chardonnay (Alexander Valley) $23. Lush and candied, this wine is like liquid apple pie and peach cobbler. Spicy-sweet fruit hits the palate in a creamy texture, with an edge of cinnamon. Fills the mouth with fruit, with decent acidity and some dusty tannins. **86** —*S.H. (5/1/2002)*

Geyser Peak 1997 Reserve Chardonnay (Sonoma County) $23. 87 *(1/1/2000)*

Geyser Peak 1996 Reserve Chardonnay (Sonoma County) $20. 88 —*J.C. (11/1/1999)*

Geyser Peak 2003 Ricci Vineyard Chardonnay (Carneros) $23. A very distinct single-vineyard Chard marked by an array of toasted spice notes. Chinese five-spice flavors frame citrus, fig, lime peel, and apricot flavors that finish with a sweet-and-sour aftertaste. It's soft, dry, and balanced. **91 Editors' Choice** —*S.H. (11/1/2005)*

Geyser Peak 2000 Ricci Vineyard Chardonnay (Carneros) $21. Well balanced, with firm acidity and a supple yet focused blend of pear, melon, citrus, apple, herb, and toast flavors. **89** —*J.M. (12/15/2002)*

Geyser Peak 1997 Sonoma Valley Chardonnay (Sonoma Valley) $14. 87 Best Buy —*S.H. (7/1/1999)*

Geyser Peak 2001 Gewürztraminer (California) $9. From select cool vineyards, an intensely aromatic wine, with no sign of oak to hide the pretty fruit. Apricot and orange blossom, litchi, candied peaches, crushed brown spices, honey, and vanilla flavors drink off-dry, but the wine is nervy and steely enough to satisfy dry wine fanatics, especially on a warm afternoon. **86 Best Buy** —*J.M. (6/1/2002)*

Geyser Peak 1998 Johannisberg Riesling (California) $8. 85 Best Buy —*S.H. (9/1/1999)*

Geyser Peak 2000 Reserve Alexandre Meritage (Alexander Valley) $45. A good percentage of Merlot has softened and sweetened the Cabernet, resulting in an opulent wine with accessible tannins. It's rich and balanced in black currant, blueberry, and mocha flavors. Not likely to age, but good for filet mignon. **88** —*S.H. (10/1/2004)*

Geyser Peak 2001 Reserve Alexandre Meritage Meritage (Alexander Valley) $49. The '01 Cabs keep rolling out. This Cabernet blend has some tight tannins that make it dry and astringent right now. It's nowhere near ready. But it should reveal its hearty blackberry and coffee flavors by 2007, and for quite a long time after. **90** —*S.H. (11/1/2005)*

Geyser Peak 1997 Merlot (Sonoma) $16. 84 *(3/1/2000)*

Geyser Peak 2002 Merlot (Alexander Valley) $19. Hot, raw, and unbalanced, this is not a successful wine despite good fruity flavor. **81** —*S.H. (11/1/2005)*

Geyser Peak 2001 Merlot (Sonoma County) $18. A fine Merlot for its exuberantly ripe flavors of blackberries, chocolate, and coffee, and the smooth but complex tannins that provide structure. Completely dry, with a spicy finish. **87** —*S.H. (12/15/2004)*

Geyser Peak 2000 Merlot (Sonoma County) $17. A bit lean in fruit, in keeping with this problem vintage. Aromas of damp earth, cigar, and thyme have just a hint of blackberry. The tannins are very finely ground, and soft acidity makes for a pleasant mouthfeel, but it's thin stuff. **85** —*S.H. (8/1/2003)*

Geyser Peak 1998 Merlot (Sonoma County) $17. You get mostly cedar and charred oak at first, with hints of cherries and mocha. This is one affordable Merlot that doesn't lack for structure—it's just that the structure seems largely wood-derived, leaving insufficient fruit flesh to fill in the gaps. **82** —*J.C. (6/1/2001)*

Geyser Peak 1997 Merlot (Sonoma County) $16. 86 —*L.W. (12/31/1999)*

Geyser Peak 1997 Merlot (Sonoma County) $16. 84 *(3/1/2000)*

Geyser Peak 1999 Block Collection Shorenstein Vineyard Merlot (Sonoma Valley) $26. A good effort, with adequate blackberry flavors, soft, intri-

cate tannins, and okay acdity. It's dry, balanced, and not too oaky, with a velevety mouthfeel. Not a blockbuster, but a gentle wine that will show its best paired with the right foods. **87** —*S.H. (11/15/2002)*

Geyser Peak 1998 Block Collection Shorenstein Vineyard Merlot (Sonoma Valley) $26. Starts off with herbaceous aromas, including mint, but plenty of swirling releases riper ones of black cherries and cocoa. There's a pretty texture, with soft but firm tannins and soft acidity. It's not especially fruity, but it's sleek and elegant, and rich foods will certainly wake up some of its sleeping sweetness. **85** —*S.H. (6/1/2001)*

Geyser Peak 2001 Block Collection Shorenstein Vineyard Merlot (Sonoma Valley) $26. The winery seems to have held back this Merlot as long as they dared, for it is still a very dry, tannic wine. That said, there's some rich cherry and black currant fruit. It will play off a good steak, or you can try aging it through this decade. **87** —*S.H. (11/1/2005)*

Geyser Peak 2000 Block Collection Shorenstein Vineyard Merlot (Sonoma Valley) $26. This dark, complex Merlot combines black stone fruit and herb flavors with hints of coffee and tar. It's very dry, with soft tannins and good acidity. Finishes with some astringency. Drink now. **87** —*S.H. (12/31/2004)*

Geyser Peak 2001 Reserve Merlot (Knights Valley) $40. Dry and raspingly tannic, this wine offers little now in the way of fruit. **82** —*S.H. (11/1/2005)*

Geyser Peak 2000 Reserve Merlot (Alexander Valley) $39. An interesting Merlot that makes you wonder where it's going. It's flashy in upfront black currant fruit and oak, and has bright acidity. But it's also quite tannic, and doesn't have the stuffing for the long haul. Drink now. **86** —*S.H. (12/15/2004)*

Geyser Peak 1999 Reserve Merlot (Sonoma County) $40. A stylish red brimming with plum, sweet tobacco, and blackberry flavors. The tannins are wonderfully complex and slippery, and the acidity is soft, so the wine goes down like velvet. **93** —*S.H. (11/15/2002)*

Geyser Peak 1998 Reserve Merlot (Alexander Valley) $40. Soft and velvety in the mouth, this wine defines its terroir. Spicy, blackberry-scented, smoky oak aromas lead to and exuberantly fruity wine, bursting with sweetly ripe berries. It's light at the core and won't age, but it is beautiful now. **90** —*S.H. (12/1/2001)*

Geyser Peak 1997 Reserve Merlot (Sonoma County) $32. 88 —*S.H. (7/1/2000)*

Geyser Peak 2001 Riesling (California) $9. If daffodils were wine, this is what they'd be. Or maybe it's apricot blossoms. Flowery and honey-sweet, but with crisp acids, this tasty wine may be simple, but there's no denying its assets. **86 Best Buy** —*S.H. (6/1/2002)*

Geyser Peak 2000 Late Harvest Reserve Riesling (Mendocino) $19. Spicy and richly honeyed, but also sporting a serious jolt of bright acidity, the wine offers a lush textured, sweet edged blend of peach, orange, and a hint of banana at the end. **88** —*J.M. (12/1/2002)*

Geyser Peak 1998 Reserve Late Harvest Riesling (Dry Creek Valley) $19. 86 —*S.H. (12/31/2000)*

Geyser Peak 2005 Sauvignon Blanc (California) $12. Here's a Sauvignon Blanc that comes down on the grassy, hay, and gooseberry side, with richer lemon and lime notes. The acidity is clean and zesty, and the finish is a little sweet. **84** —*S.H. (7/1/2006)*

Geyser Peak 2004 Sauvignon Blanc (California) $12. When I was a kid I worked on a farm and baled hay, and this wine brought back memories. Fresh, green grass, sweet dried grass, and lemon and lime aromas lead to intensely fruity flavors that finish too sweet. **84** —*S.H. (12/31/2005)*

Geyser Peak 2003 Sauvignon Blanc (Sonoma County) $12. Easy to drink and likeable for its slightly sweet grass, lemon and lime, fig, and melon flavors, and the zesty clean streak of citrusy acids. The wine cuts across the palate and stimulates it. A very nice value in a cocktail-style white wine. **85** —*S.H. (10/1/2004)*

Geyser Peak 2002 Sauvignon Blanc (Russian River Valley) $20. Starts off with smoky, grassy notes that gradually build in impressive passion fruit and pink grapefruit flavors. Finishes spicy and almost peppery. Next vintage, this is slated to become a single-vineyard, "Block Collection" wine in Geyser Peak's lineup; let's hope the price remains stable. 250 cases made. **90 Editors' Choice** *(11/1/2003)*

Geyser Peak 2002 Sauvignon Blanc (California) $10. The Aussies have taken a page from the Kiwis' book, striving for a fresh, grassy and grapefruity wine. It's lean and racy, clean and crisp. Try it by the glass at your local oyster bar. **86 Best Buy** *(11/1/2003)*

Geyser Peak 2001 Sauvignon Blanc (California) $10. Racy and strong, and comes down firmly on the grass, hay and grapefruit side, brimming with bright, tart fruit. A touch of sugar puts it just this side of sweet, with an intriguing taste of white chocolate on the finish. Gets the nod because it's so ultra-clean and zesty. **86** —*S.H. (9/1/2002)*

Geyser Peak 2000 Sauvignon Blanc (Sonoma County) $9. Bright and fruity, with snappy citrus and passion fruit flavors. Zingy on the finish with a refreshing, lemony edge. Terrific for summer sipping. **88 Best Buy** —*J.M. (11/15/2001)*

Geyser Peak 1999 Sauvignon Blanc (Sonoma County) $9. 84 —*S.H. (5/1/2000)*

Geyser Peak 1998 Sauvignon Blanc (Sonoma County) $9. 82 —*S.H. (9/1/1999)*

Geyser Peak 2005 Block Collection River Road Ranch Sauvignon Blanc (Russian River Valley) $21. On the feline side, with lemongrassy, grapefruit flavors accompanied by crisp acids and a peppery finish. Mainly stainless steel fermented, the wine is dry, with just a touch of neutral oak. **84** —*S.H. (12/31/2006)*

Geyser Peak 2004 Block Collection River Road Ranch Sauvignon Blanc (Russian River Valley) $21. Interesting and aromatic. Notes of honey, apricot, and clover aromas. Quite tight and lean in the mouth, but with mouthwatering flavors of crisp green apple, lime, and mineral. Finishes sharp and wet, with piercing acidity. An individual wine. **90 Editors' Choice** *(7/1/2005)*

Geyser Peak 2003 Block Collection River Road Ranch Sauvignon Blanc (Russian River Valley) $19. Raises the standard of feline to new heights, in a positive sense. The gooseberry and cat flavors are there, but enriched and complexed with sweet lime and nutty, smoky, oaky vanillins. The result is a complex, dry wine with a walk on the wild side edge. **88** —*S.H. (12/1/2004)*

Geyser Peak 1997 Shiraz (Sonoma County) $16. 88 —*S.H. (5/1/2000)*

Geyser Peak 2002 Shiraz (Sonoma County) $17. Plump and juicy in plum, blackberry, and coffee flavors, with hints of earth and prune, this Aussie-inspired Shiraz is a bit unstructured and fat but should have enough density of fruit to last a year or two. **85** *(9/1/2005)*

Geyser Peak 2001 Shiraz (Sonoma County) $18. Blackberry, herb, and tobacco flavors drink very dry, and are framed in big, dusty tannins. Might develop with a bit of age. Fine now with short ribs, barbecue. **85** —*S.H. (12/1/2004)*

Geyser Peak 2000 Shiraz (Sonoma County) $17. A blend of grapes from five different parts of the county. The warmer districts lend ripe blackberry notes; cooler ones bring pepper, olives, and herbs. Feels round and supple in the mouth, yet finishes very dry. **88** —*S.H. (2/1/2003)*

Geyser Peak 1999 Shiraz (Sonoma County) $17. Dark cherry and cream cheese-like aromas open onto a palate chock full of tart cherry, tangy oak and mint flavors. It's got moderate acidity, and a tangy, dry finish. **82** *(10/1/2001)*

Geyser Peak 1995 Bin 1 Shiraz (Sonoma County) $100. 92 *(1/1/2000)*

Geyser Peak 2000 Reserve Shiraz (Sonoma County) $46. Soft and supple in tannins, with just a bit of a sandpapery grip, this dry red has sweetly ripe black currant flavors with a coating of spicy oak and hints of soy sauce. Doesn't appear to have the stuff to age, so drink now. **86** *(9/1/2005)*

Geyser Peak 1999 Reserve Shiraz (Sonoma County) $45. At nearly five years, this is still a dark, young and tannic wine, although the palate senses a softening setting in. It has earthy, coffee, plum, and currant flavors that are held together by good acidity. Hold for a few more years. **89** —*S.H. (12/1/2004)*

Geyser Peak 1998 Reserve Shiraz (Sonoma County) $40. The winery calls it Shiraz because it follows an "Australian" style. If that means tons of toasty oak, they've succeeded. Still, there's also a solid core of black-cherry fruit that offers rich texture and dusty tannins on the finish. **86** *(11/1/2001)*

Geyser Peak 1997 Sparkling Shiraz (Sonoma County) $30. Delightfully refreshing, this sparkling wine is dry, yet filled with complex black cherry and bitter almond flavors. Made in an Aussie style, it also serves up pretty licorice, raspberry, and herbal accents for added interest. A dark alternative to standard sparkling fare. **90** —*J.M. (12/1/2003)*

Geyser Peak 2003 Block Collection Preston Vineyard Viognier (Dry Creek Valley) $19. Takes a controlled approach to a variety that is often over the top. You'll find the usual exotic tropical fruit and ripe peach notes, but they're trimmed with sour citrus, and the acidity helps maintain balance. Dry and elegant, this wine defines the possibilities of upscale Viognier. **90** —*S.H. (11/15/2004)*

Geyser Peak 2002 Block Collection Preston Vineyard Viognier (Dry Creek Valley) $19. From an appellation that has long made a play as a Rhône specialist, a delicate wine, despite the opulence of its fruit. Mango, apricot, peach and cantaloupe flavors mingle, enriched with smoky vanilla and oak, but all this is controlled by firm acids, and the wine is fully dry. **88** —*S.H. (12/31/2003)*

Geyser Peak 2000 Block Collection Sonoma Moment Viognier (Alexander Valley) $19. Lush and lively, with clean, clear, crisp apricot, citrus, spice, and herb flavors, all neatly blended to reveal the riotous edge of this intriguingly different varietal. Bright and long at the end. **90** —*J.M. (12/15/2002)*

Geyser Peak 2004 Preston Vineyard Viognier (Dry Creek Valley) $19. This is one of the more interesting Viogniers around due not simply to the complex fruit, wildflower, and honey spice flavors, although they're delicious, but to the structure. There's a bracing mouthfeel and steely minerality that bring life and zest. **91 Editors' Choice** —*S.H. (11/1/2005)*

Geyser Peak 1997 Zinfandel (Sonoma County) $16. 84 *(5/1/2000)*

Geyser Peak 2000 Zinfandel (Sonoma County) $17. This is happy Zin. Everything about it is bright, polished, expansive, easy, and fun. It defines Zin's briary, brambly berry-and-spice character, and the texture is smooth and juicy. It's not a dense, heavy wine, but light and airy, and just delicious. **88** —*S.H. (11/1/2002)*

Geyser Peak 1996 Zinfandel (Sonoma County) $20. 86 *(1/1/2000)*

Geyser Peak 1999 Block Collection Zinfandel (Cucamonga Valley) $23. Veers toward the overripe end, with raisiny aromas alongside the spicy, berry ones, and curranty flavors that finish hot and peppery. Yet with its dry mouthfeel and softly lush texture, it defines a style that many will like. High alcohol makes it heady and strong. **87** —*S.H. (9/12/2002)*

Geyser Peak 2002 Block Collection Lopez Vineyard Zinfandel (Cucamonga Valley) $30. An old-style Zin from this old growing region near L.A. It's rustic, with intense mocha and berry flavors that drink a little sweet. Soft in acids, it's an interesting wine to pair with food. **86** —*S.H. (12/15/2004)*

Geyser Peak 2002 Block Collection Sandy Lane Vineyard Zinfandel (Contra Costa County) $30. Flirts with too much sugar, but dodges the bullet, remaining dry, but lush and powerful in soft, ripe briary fruit. That means lots of alcohol, but this pretty wine is balanced. Addictively delicious for the blackberry, chocolate finish. **90** —*S.H. (12/31/2004)*

Geyser Peak 2001 Block Collection, Sandy Lane Vineyard Zinfandel (Contra Costa County) $30. Almost black in color, with intensely spicy aromatics. On the palate, it doesn't disappoint, with fun, bright cherry, blackberry, currant, and toast flavors. The acidity is a bit on the bright side, maybe to balance the very slight sweetness. **88** *(11/1/2003)*

Geyser Peak 1999 De Ambrogio Ranch Zinfandel (Cucamonga Valley) $28. Pretty expensive for this appellation. It's very typical hot country Zin, chocolately and berryish, alcoholic, soft, and dry. It nicely avoids raisiny notes and overt sweetness but can't quite overcome that flat, rural style. **85** —*S.H. (7/1/2002)*

Geyser Peak 1997 Winemaker's Selection Zinfandel (Cucamonga Valley) $30. 89 *(1/1/2000)*

USA

Geyser Peak 1997 Winemaker's Selection Zinfandel (Cucamonga Valley) $26. 88 —P.G. (11/15/1999)

GIACINTO

Giacinto 1999 Red Blend (Sonoma County) $30. From a single vineyard, Alice's, in the Bennett Valley area, a complex blend of Merlot, Cabernet Sauvignon, Sangiovese, and Cabernet Franc. It's young and big and jammy now, and consequently a bit unbalanced, with biting fruit. But the rich tannins suggest cellaring. Try aging through 2005. **86** —S.H. (12/1/2002)

GINA

Gina 2003 Chardonnay (Napa Valley) $10. Gina is a second label from the esteemed Flora Springs Winery, of Napa Valley. This wine bears much in common with FS's barrel-fermented Chards. It's richly textured, with tropical fruit flavors and a plastering of smoky, vanilla-infused oak. It was even barrel fermented. The texture is as creamy as a milkshake, and there are all sorts of dusty Oriental spices on the finish. It's a little sweet. **86 Best Buy** —S.H. (11/15/2004)

GINO DA PINOT

Gino da Pinot 2005 Pinot Noir (Monterey) $16. Another innovatively packaged wine from Don Sebastiani & Sons, and if you know the Pinots from the east side of Salinas Valley, like Estancia's, this is much in that vein. It's light-bodied and silky, with easy cherry, cola, vanilla, and spice flavors. **84** —S.H. (12/1/2006)

GIRARD

Girard 1999 Bordeaux Blend (Napa Valley) $40. A terrific wine that defines midvalley balance, harmony, and style. Cassis and smoky oak describe the objective characteristics, but can't convey the feeling of plushness and class. Some dusty tannins suggest holding through 2004. A blend of Cabernet Sauvignon, Cabernet Franc, and Merlot. **92 Editors' Choice** —S.H. (11/15/2002)

Girard 1998 Cabernet Blend (Napa Valley) $40. Smooth and supple on the palate, the wine is brimming with ripe black-cherry, blackberry, anise, and cassis flavors that are followed by hints of coffee and herb. The ensemble is framed in rich, silky tannins that taper off with a long, lush finish. **90** —J.M. (5/1/2002)

Girard 2003 Cabernet Franc (Napa Valley) $40. With a lighter structure than Cabernet Sauvignon and flavors veering toward cherries rather than black currants, this fine wine is deliciously drinkable now. It has the authority of Napa Valley in the elegant, refined tannins. Great with broiled steak. **90** —S.H. (12/15/2006)

Girard 2002 Cabernet Franc (Napa Valley) $40. Dry and firm and well-structured, this Cab Franc offers a complex array of fruit, herb, earth, and oak notes, and that elusive drink-me-again quality. **91** —S.H. (7/1/2005)

Girard 2002 Estate Cabernet Sauvignon (Napa Valley) $60. You can tell this is a young wine by the aroma, which is dominated by oak and a tease of cherry. The fruit is shut down. But in the mouth, there is a rich core of blackberries and cherries, and the tannin-acid balance is near perfect. This fine Cabernet is in need of cellaring. Hold until 2010 and try again. **90 Cellar Selection** —S.H. (12/15/2005)

Girard 1997 Chardonnay (Napa Valley) $28. 86 (6/1/2000)

Girard 2004 Chardonnay (Russian River Valley) $20. This Napa winery has been reaching into the Russian River for their Chardonnay, with good results. Dry and crisp in acids, the wine has a minerality behind the green apple, peach, and melon flavors. The firm structure should provide for aging through 2009. **89** —S.H. (5/1/2006)

Girard 2002 Chardonnay (Russian River Valley) $20. This venerable Napa winery turned to a cool Sonoma locale and has crafted a rich, balanced Chardonnay. It has lush flavors of sweet green apples, cinnamon, vanilla, and toast, and zesty, citrusy acids. Smooth drinking, and an excellent food wine that's not too big. **90** —S.H. (6/1/2004)

Girard 2000 Chardonnay (Russian River Valley) $24. Smooth, creamy and sensual on the palate, the wine is redolent of pear, melon, spice, and vanilla, finishing clean and fresh, with subtle, lemony notes. Long at the end. **89** —J.M. (5/1/2002)

Girard 2000 Meritage (Napa Valley) $40. This blend of Cabernet and other Bordeaux varieties is elaborately crafted, with an overlay of sweet, smoky oak. It feels very elegant in the mouth, and the blackberry, cassis, and cherry flavors are lip-smackingly good. Finishes with a scour of acids and tannins. **91** —S.H. (4/1/2004)

Girard 2004 Petite Sirah (Napa Valley) $24. Girard usually brings a Napa Cabernet touch to Petite Sirah, taming the wine's wildness into elegance. They did their best here, but the hot vintage got in the way. Shows good blackberry and cherry fruit along with chocolate, but there's an awkward imbalance between the dry, harsh tannins and the sugary finish. Drink now with barbecue. **85** —S.H. (12/31/2006)

Girard 2003 Petite Sirah (Napa Valley) $24. Classic Petite Sirah, full-bodied, rich, totally dry, very tannic and fruity. So good now with something big, like short ribs, that it will be difficult to cellar, but this is a wine that will soften and sweeten over many years. And what a finish, long in ripe, wild blackberries, cherries, and coffee. **92 Cellar Selection** —S.H. (12/1/2005)

Girard 2002 Petite Sirah (Napa Valley) $24. Pours inky black, and feels big and rich in the mouth, with firm, tough tannins framing flavors of black and purple stone fruits and berries. Manages to develop real character and finesse in a variety that can be overly wild. Drink now through 2010. **90** —S.H. (11/15/2004)

Girard 2000 Petite Sirah (Napa Valley) $24. Black as ink in color, with pronounced aromas of white pepper and blackberries. Tastes fruitier than it smells, with a myriad of berry flavors, and the tannins are rich. Yet it's too young now, with fresh, sharp acidity. Best to lay this puppy down for a good five years. Ten years is even better. **87** —S.H. (12/1/2002)

Girard 1999 Petite Sirah (Napa Valley) $24. This wine sports an inky dark-violet hue, evoking black cherry, plum, blackberry, cocoa, and spice. On the palate, it's plush, bright, and long. Really delicious. **91** —J.M. (5/1/2002)

Girard 2002 Napa Valley Red Wine Red Blend (Napa Valley) $40. A blend of all five Bordeaux varieties, this is a balanced, harmonious wine, although it's light in flavor and soft texture for a Napa Cabernet-based claret. Because it's not all that rich, it will do best against simpler fare, such as a standing rib roast or beef carpaccio. **86** —S.H. (12/31/2005)

Girard 2005 Sauvignon Blanc (Napa Valley) $15. Refreshingly crisp and zesty, this stainless steel-fermented wine is rich and fruity, with no apparent oak. The flavors are of lemons and limes, kiwis, and green apples, with a long, cinnamon-spice finish. **87** —S.H. (7/1/2006)

Girard 2004 Sauvignon Blanc (Napa Valley) $15. Shows upfront lemon, lime, fig, and melon flavors so ripe, they're almost sweet; however, this is a pretty dry wine. It's also well-balanced, with plenty of refreshing acidity. Has an edge of elegance to it. **87** —S.H. (10/1/2005)

Girard 2003 Sauvignon Blanc (Napa Valley) $15. This refreshingly crisp, clean wine comes from one of California's most consistent Sauvignon Blanc producers. It's rich in ripe citrus, juicy green apple, and spicy fig flavors, with a smooth, honeyed finish. **88** —S.H. (12/1/2004)

Girard 2001 Sauvignon Blanc (Napa Valley) $15. Very dry, with tart flavors of lemons and grapefruits. The problems are that the fruity concentration is diluted, and the acidity is soft and flabby. Not a bad wine, but you can do better for the price. **84** —S.H. (9/1/2003)

Girard 2000 Sauvignon Blanc (Napa Valley) $15. Kicks off with passion fruit and citrus aromas, later to reveal a riveting core of bright lemon, lime, melon, fig, and green apple flavors. Sleek and round-textured, the wine is refreshing to the finish. **90** —J.C. (5/1/2002)

Girard 2002 Zinfandel (Napa Valley) $24. Achieves what so many Zin producers want—a balanced, dry wine with moderate alcohol. Yet the fruity flavors haven't been undermined. Dark stone fruits, blackberries, tobacco, bitter chocolate, sweet herbs, and wonderfully ripe, complex tannins. **92 Editors' Choice** —S.H. (11/15/2004)

Girard 2001 Zinfandel (Napa Valley) $24. A firm but supple-textured wine, sporting layers of cassis, black cherry, toast, smoke, spice, herbs and plum flavors. This is a classy Zin, with silky tannins and a complex array of tastes that unfold with smooth elegance. Long and lush at the end. **91 Editors' Choice** (11/1/2003)

Girard 2004 Late Harvest Zinfandel (Napa Valley) $27. Girard makes a good dry Zinfandel, but this is not such a good dessert wine. It's sweet and sugary, and tastes like a wine meant to be dry, but whose fermentation stuck. Awkward. **81** —*S.H. (3/1/2006)*

Girard 2004 Old Vine Zinfandel (Napa Valley) $24. Lush and ripe, brimming with blackberry, chocolate, and coffee flavors, this soft wine finishes with a distinct, cola-soda sweetness. Fortunately, crisp acidity is there for balance. **85** —*S.H. (12/15/2006)*

Girard 2003 Old Vine Zinfandel (Napa Valley) $24. This is a dry Zin that shows its pedigree in the balanced structure and finely ground tannins. It has classic Zin notes of white pepper, wild cherry-berry fruit, and mocha flavors, with a hot, prickly finish. **90** —*S.H. (2/1/2006)*

GIRARDET

Girardet 2000 Reserve Baco Noir (Umpqua Valley) $35. Strong scents of hay and grass; it's a bit like old-vine Zin but with more grapey fruit flavors. Grapey, slightly foxy, there is also some loganberry fruit, lots of acid and a good long finish. **87** —*P.G. (8/1/2002)*

Girardet 1999 Reserve Baco Noir (Umpqua Valley) $32. Baco Noir is a little-known French hybrid, and Girardet does well with it, creating a rich, ripe, rustic red that might pass for an Amador Zin were the alcohol bumped up a notch. Tangy, grapey fruit and loads of bone-dry tannins tell the story. **85** —*P.G. (4/1/2002)*

Girardet 2000 Chardonnay (Umpqua Valley) $12. Partial barrel fermentation in three different types of barrel give some nice leesy, creamy flavors. The modest fruit flavors run to melon and light citrus. It's elegant and nicely balanced, with a fresh, easy finish. **86** —*P.G. (8/1/2002)*

Girardet 2000 Pinot Gris (Umpqua Valley) $12. Crisp and clean, stainless steel-fermented, yet showing a lot of tropical fruit in the nose, and a touch (half a percent) of residual sugar. Banana, mango, and citrus flavors are there, along with plenty of acidity. Interesting, but not particularly varietal. **85** —*P.G. (8/1/2002)*

Girardet 2000 Barrel Select Pinot Noir (Umpqua Valley) $17. Lots of fresh, ripe fruit, mostly cherry flavors, along with a bit of beet and stem and earth. It's a spicy, lively, young wine with tart tannins, but nothing off. **87** —*P.G. (12/31/2002)*

Girardet 1998 Barrel Select Pinot Noir (Umpqua Valley) $16. **82** —*M.S. (12/1/2000)*

Girardet 2000 Petite Cuvée Pinot Noir (Umpqua Valley) $12. This young Pinot shows scents of beetroot and sassafras and forward fruit (from 50% whole-berry fermentation). Ripe cherry flavors and a bit of earth tell the story. In terms of balance, this is an excellent wine for the price. **87 Best Buy** —*P.G. (12/31/2002)*

Girardet 1999 Premiere Cuvée Pinot Noir (Umpqua Valley) $59. The winery feels that this is their best Pinot Noir, and prices it accordingly. Concentrated and balanced, it shows some grassy flavors along with the sweet fruit. Very tannic. Just one barrel—20 cases—was made. **87** —*P.G. (8/1/2002)*

Girardet 1999 Reserve Pinot Noir (Umpqua Valley) $35. Ripe, premium fruit, and fairly high alcohol levels define this wine. A hot year and ripe fruit combine to create complexity in the nose, with an interesting mix of spices (cardamom, clove), lots of tannin, some darker fruit, and hints of smoke and earth. The only down side: it lacks weight and it finishes very tannic. **88** —*P.G. (8/1/2002)*

Girardet 1998 Reserve Pinot Noir (Umpqua Valley) $35. **88** —*J.C. (12/1/2000)*

Girardet 1999 Marechal Foch Red Blend (Umpqua Valley) $15. This is a good, dark, iron-rich wine, with earth and mineral dominating through a tart finish. Interesting change of pace. **86** —*P.G. (8/1/2002)*

Girardet 2001 Estate Riesling (Umpqua Valley) $8. A lot of shale in the soils adds interest to this elegant, light, fairly soft wine. Off-dry and balanced, it represents good value. Flavors of apples, pears, and blossoms lead; a soft finish with a hint of caramel wraps it up. **87 Best Buy** —*P.G. (8/1/2002)*

GLACIER'S END

Glacier's End NV Chardonnay (North Fork of Long Island) $10. This is a light style of Chardonnay, with some peach aromas and a distinct peanutty quality. Finishes lemony and tart; a good candidate to accompany raw oysters. **85** —*J.C. (3/1/2002)*

Glacier's End NV Merlot (North Fork of Long Island) $10. This second label from Martha Clara Vineyards packs in enough superripe fruit (cherries and apricots, with some yellow-fleshed red plums as well) to make it a good value quaff. Not a lot of structure or complexity, but flavorful and pleasing. **85 Best Buy** —*J.C. (3/1/2002)*

GLASS MOUNTAIN

Glass Mountain 2001 Cabernet Sauvignon (California) $8. Dry and rather rough, this is a country-style wine that shows plenty of berry-cherry fruit. Fine for every day. **83** —*S.H. (8/1/2005)*

Glass Mountain 1999 Cabernet Sauvignon (California) $10. **87 Best Buy** — *C.S. (11/15/2002)*

Glass Mountain 2001 Syrah (California) $8. A little raw in acids, but with some jammy cherry and blackberry fruit, and pretty dry. Drink this rustic wine with anything calling for a full-bodied red. **84 Best Buy** —*S.H. (8/1/2005)*

Glass Mountain 1999 Syrah (California) $10. From Markham, this medium-weight effort adds a touch of mint and a creamy, lactic note to blackberry and blueberry fruit. The finish is long, highlighting waves of supersoft tannins and juicy berries. **87** —*J.C. (9/1/2002)*

GLEN ELLEN

Glen Ellen 1999 Reserve Cabernet Sauvignon (Sonoma) $7. Here's a good training wheels Cabernet. It has real varietal character, with black currant aromas and flavors, although they're not concentrated or dense. But this dry, light wine affords plenty of value. **85** —*S.H. (9/12/2002)*

Glen Ellen 1998 Reserve Cabernet Sauvignon (California) $7. **83** —*S.H. (12/15/2000)*

Glen Ellen 1998 Reserve Chardonnay (California) $7. **82** —*S.H. (11/15/2000)*

Glen Ellen 2000 Proprietor's Reserve Gamay (Sonoma) $NA. This awkward wine is youthful and sharp, with a cut of green aromas and flavors. There's some jammy fruit and the body is very light and silky. Beaujolais is supposed to be fresh but this wine is simply tart and acidic. **82** —*S.H. (9/1/2002)*

Glen Ellen 1999 Reserve Merlot (California) $7. Ripe and jammy sipping is what you'll get in this simple, fruity wine. It's not very varietal, but filled with all sorts of berry and fruit flavors in a soft texture. It's dry enough to maintain balance. **83** —*S.H. (9/12/2002)*

Glen Ellen 1998 Reserve Merlot (California) $7. Light berry and cherry aromas pick up hints of rhubarb and tea, then green-berry and sour-cherry flavors kick in on the palate. It's light, and a bit lean but flavorful, and the price is right. **83** —*S.H. (6/1/2001)*

Glen Ellen 2000 Reserve Sauvignon Blanc (Sonoma) $NA. Begins with light aromas of citrus blossom and honey, and the flavors are light and citrusy. It's pretty sweet, with noticeable residual sugar, but there's enough crispness to balance. **84** —*S.H. (9/12/2002)*

Glen Ellen 1998 Reserve White Zinfandel (California) $7. A coppery colored, off-dry-to-frankly-sweet wine that's simple, fruity, and a little cloying. The dominant flavors are peaches and strawberries, with a very spicy finish, but the acidity seems a bit low. Still, at this price, millions of people will find a lot to like. **83** —*S.H. (2/1/2001)*

GLEN FIONA

Glen Fiona 2001 Cuvée Parallel 46 Red Blend (Walla Walla (WA)) $25. Tart and tangy, with mixed red and blue fruit flavors, light acid, and a fairly thin finish. Tasted alongside Jaboulet's Parallele 45, it's not a bad imitation. Very pleasant sipping wine. **86** —*P.G. (7/1/2004)*

Glen Fiona 1998 Syrah (Walla Walla (WA)) $40. **88** —*P.G. (9/1/2000)*

Glen Fiona 2001 Syrah (Walla Walla (WA)) $20. There's nice spice here, and the fruit definitely speaks of Syrah. Plump, fruity, and flavorful, it

USA

shows polished berry, currant, and cherry, set against mixed herbs and streaked with anise and smoke, with a bit of sweaty saddle in the finish. **88** —*P.G. (7/1/2004)*

Glen Fiona 2000 Bacchus Vineyard Syrah (Columbia Valley (WA)) $20. A sweet honeysuckle note on the nose adds an interestingtouch to this mid-weight, reserved wine. The red berry fruit bears tart lemon and herb accents on the palate. High acidity makes this best consumed with food—it's not a quaffer. Closes with a mineral note and a brisk acid sting. **84** *(10/1/2001)*

Glen Fiona 1999 Bacchus Vineyard Syrah (Columbia Valley (WA)) $24. 82 —*P.G. (9/1/2000)*

Glen Fiona 1997 Basket Press Reserve Syrah (Walla Walla (WA)) $55. 93 —*P.G. (11/15/2000)*

Glen Fiona 2001 Basket Press Reserve Cuvée Lot 57 Syrah (Walla Walla (WA)) $40. That's a lot of names for a simple wine; it's pure Syrah, juicy and tart, dressed up with a very spicy, peppery sheaf that wraps it like peppercorns wrap a hunk of beef. Quick finish, but a nice ride. **88** —*P.G. (7/1/2004)*

Glen Fiona 1999 Puncheon Aged Syrah (Walla Walla (WA)) $40. Green herb, Play-Doh, and smoky-oak aromas are good indications of what follows on this Syrah's palate—more wood (some say cedar; others oak), cream, chocolate, and cherry flavors. Medim-bodied and a little high in acid, it finishes long, with chocolate and charred oak notes. There's not a lot of ripe fruit here. **86** *(11/1/2001)*

GLENORA

Glenora 1996 25th Anniversary Cuvée Champagne Blend (New York) $25. Crisp and clean, with bright citrus and toast notes that finish lively on the tongue. Fresh and light. **87** —*J.M. (12/1/2002)*

Glenora 1998 Brut Champagne Blend (Finger Lakes) $15. A pretty wine, with hints of pear, citrus, toast, apples, and herbs. **86** —*J.M. (12/1/2002)*

Glenora 1999 Barrel Fermented Chardonnay (Finger Lakes) $12. Lean, yet smooth textured, with a pretty core of pear, apple, melon, and citrus flavors. The wine is sleek and bright on the finish, showing moderate length. **87 Best Buy** —*J.M. (1/1/2003)*

Glenora 2002 Riesling (Finger Lakes) $21. Soft, easy, and well-made, this wine is quite sweet, but pleasant, with apple blossom and ripe pear aromas and flavors of apples, pears, and apricot. **85** —*J.C. (8/1/2003)*

Glenora 2000 Riesling (Finger Lakes) $9. Green on the nose, with aromas of grasses, mint and lime. Frankly sweet in the mouth, yet still manages to have a tart edge to the finish. Too sweet. **81** —*J.C. (3/1/2002)*

Glenora 2002 Dry Riesling (Finger Lakes) $10. While this wine is labeled "dry," it's technically not. There's some sugar left in it, it just seems dry if you compare it to the winery's regular, semi-dry version. Aromas of spiced pears and musky, evening flowers blend with flavors of pears, peaches, and dried spices. **86** —*J.C. (8/1/2003)*

Glenora 2001 Dry Riesling (Finger Lakes) $10. 82 —*J.C. (8/1/2003)*

Glenora 2000 Dry Riesling (Finger Lakes) $9. Don't be fooled by the label—this is not a dry Riesling, only drier than the winery's regular bottling. Peach, nectarine, and shale aromas turn sweet on the palate, partially balanced by a dose of lime-like acidity. It's a bit heavy, but intensely flavorful. **84** —*J.C. (6/19/2003)*

Glenora 2001 Vintner's Select Riesling (Finger Lakes) $15. 83 —*J.C. (8/1/2003)*

Glenora 2000 Vintner's Select Riesling (Finger Lakes) $15. Made from handpicked fruit from a single vineyard, this wine is a huge step up from Glenora's regular bottling. The bright green-apple aromas and flavors feature delicate touches of diesel and lime and finish crisp and tart. Just off-dry, with a light, lively feel in the mouth that would work well with Asian cuisine. **87** —*J.C. (1/1/2004)*

GLORIA FERRER

Gloria Ferrer NV Champagne Blend (Sonoma County) $17. 89 Best Buy —*S.H. (12/15/1999)*

Gloria Ferrer NV Champagne Blend (Carneros) $35. 88 —*J.M. (12/1/2002)*

Gloria Ferrer NV Blanc de Blancs Champagne Blend (Carneros) $22. Light and lemony, an easy sipper. Feels pleasant and clean in the mouth, with rough bubbles, an uneven texture and a slightly sweet finish. **86** —*S.H. (12/1/2002)*

Gloria Ferrer 2001 Blanc de Blancs Champagne Blend (Carneros) $24. Displays great elegance in the subtle interplay of lime and peach fruit with smoky dough and yeast. Smooth and creamy texture, great acidity, and a dry finish combine to make this a wonderful sparkler. **90** —*S.H. (12/31/2004)*

Gloria Ferrer NV Blanc de Noirs Champagne Blend (Sonoma County) $18. 84 *(12/1/2000)*

Gloria Ferrer NV Blanc de Noirs Champagne Blend (Sonoma County) $18. This pale pink sparkler smells pretty, with it's intriguing scents of oranges, McIntosh apples, vanilla, and cream. But the flavors are simpler and soft, lacking delineation and focus. **83** —*J.C. (12/1/2001)*

Gloria Ferrer NV Brut Champagne Blend (Sonoma County) $17. 86 —*S.H. (12/15/2000)*

Gloria Ferrer NV Brut Champagne Blend (Sonoma County) $18. One of the drier California bubblies in the market. The pretty vanilla, smoke, rasberry, and lime aromas and flavors are set in a very dry package, with good acidity and lively feeling in the mouth. Finishes a bit hot and peppery. **86** —*S.H. (12/1/2001)*

Gloria Ferrer NV Brut Champagne Blend (Sonoma Valley) $18. This is really fun to drink, with its full-throttle peach and strawberry flavors and rich yeasty accents. It's feels great on the palate, all bubbly and dry and clean, with a pleasant finish. **87** —*S.H. (12/1/2002)*

Gloria Ferrer NV Brut Rosé Champagne Blend (Carneros) $35. Creamy and rich, with hints of cherry and strawberry. The wine is backed by citrus, herb, and mineral notes. **88** —*J.M. (12/1/2002)*

Gloria Ferrer 1991 Carneros Cuvée Brut LD Champagne Blend (Carneros) $32. 90 —*P.G. (12/15/2000)*

Gloria Ferrer 1990 Carneros Cuvée Brut LD Champagne Blend (Carneros) $32. 88 —*S.H. (12/15/1999)*

Gloria Ferrer 1992 Late Disgorged Carneros Cuvée Brut Champagne Blend (Carneros) $32. Fresh, rich and toasty smooth, with complex vanilla, pear, apple, citrus, and floral notes. Creamy on the finish. A fine example of what bottle age can do for bubbly. **91 Cellar Selection** —*J.M. (12/1/2002)*

Gloria Ferrer 1991 Royal Cuvée Champagne Blend (Carneros) $20. 89 —*J.C. (12/1/1999)*

Gloria Ferrer 1993 Royal Cuvée Brut Champagne Blend (Carneros) $22. Manages to find a resemblance to Champagne in its toast and chalk-dust aromas allied to lime fruit. The fine bead and creamy mousse result in a lush, silky mouthfeel that's very California-ripe but flows seamlessly into a long finish. Fine texture and excellent balance mark this as one of California's best sparklers. **91 Editors' Choice** —*J.C. (12/1/2001)*

Gloria Ferrer 1992 Royal Cuvée Brut Champagne Blend (Carneros) $22. 88 —*S.H. (12/1/2000)*

Gloria Ferrer 1994 Vintage Reserve-Brut-Royal Cuvée Champagne Blend (Carneros) $22. This vintage wine is much smoother and more complex than the winery's nonvintage releases. It's yeastier and doughy, with citrusy flavors and a round, creamy mouthfeel. The finish leaves the mouth fresh and clean. **89** —*S.H. (12/1/2002)*

Gloria Ferrer 1998 Chardonnay (Carneros) $20. 88 *(6/1/2000)*

Gloria Ferrer 1997 Chardonnay (Carneros) $20. 91 —*L.W. (11/15/1999)*

Gloria Ferrer 2003 Chardonnay (Carneros) $18. Bright acids liven up very ripe papaya, pineapple, and Key lime pie flavors, wrapped in a rich, creamy texture. The wine finishes with lots of spicy, smoky oak. **88** —*S.H. (12/15/2006)*

Gloria Ferrer 2001 Chardonnay (Carneros) $18. A flavorful wine notable for its crispness and acidity, which makes it drink bright in the mouth. Flavors range from citrus fruits through peaches to tropical fruits, while oak adds a nice veneer of smoke and vanilla. The spicy finish continues for a long time. **89** —*S.H. (12/1/2003)*

Gloria Ferrer 2000 Chardonnay (Carneros) $20. This focused wine has elaborately ripe flavors of peaches, pears, and tropical fruits wrapped in spicy, vanilla-tinged oak. But it never loses its focus or its core, thanks to crisp acidity and overall balance. Despite the opulence, there's plenty of finesse. **90** —*S.H. (12/15/2002)*

Gloria Ferrer 1998 Merlot (Carneros) $23. A bit beefy in the nose, the wine has a distinctly herbal quality, with hints of blackberry and cherry behind it. The finish is moderate with a touch of weediness. **81** —*J.M. (12/1/2001)*

Gloria Ferrer 1997 Pinot Noir (Carneros) $20. 85 *(11/15/1999)*

Gloria Ferrer 2004 Pinot Noir (Carneros) $28. Pleasant and correct rather than exciting, this Pinot Noir has flavors of cola, root beer, pomegranates, cherries, and peppery spices. It's totally dry, with an elegantly silky mouthfeel. Drink now. **85** —*S.H. (12/15/2006)*

Gloria Ferrer 2002 Pinot Noir (Carneros) $26. Weak and tart, with cola, herb, and mocha flavors. Finishes watery and diluted. **84** *(11/1/2004)*

Gloria Ferrer 2000 Pinot Noir (Carneros) $24. Oak-derived vanilla, brown sugar, and menthol aromas open yet another wine that's tasty, but doesn't show real vinous depth and intensity. Cherry fruit is hidden behind a powerful oak veneer, so a caramel quality prevails. Finishes tart and dry, with coffee flavors. **85** *(10/1/2002)*

Gloria Ferrer 1999 Pinot Noir (Carneros) $24. This wine is aromatically challenged; it starts off funky, with intense barrel aromas that work against you. In the mouth, sweet candied plum-like fruit is jostled by earth and mushroom notes, while the finish is tight and tannic. **84** *(10/1/2002)*

Gloria Ferrer NV Blanc De Noirs Pinot Noir (Sonoma County) $18. Pretty toast and dough aromas up front. The wine fans out to reveal a broad range of flavors, including pear, apple, citrus, mineral, honey, nut, and floral qualities. Long at the end. **89** —*J.M. (12/1/2002)*

Gloria Ferrer 2002 Etesian Pinot Noir (Sonoma County) $12. Light color, almost orange at the rim, and delicate and simple, this wine shows spicy cola, and cherry soda flavors, with good acidity. **85** *(11/1/2004)*

Gloria Ferrer 2002 Gravel Knob Pinot Noir (Carneros) $40. Now that they're no longer making only bubbly, the winery is trying to identify block selections of dry Pinot Noir. Give them some time. This Pinot is promising, showing cherry, cola and spice flavors in an elegantly silky texture. **86** —*S.H. (12/15/2006)*

Gloria Ferrer 2000 Gravel Knob Vineyard Pinot Noir (Carneros) $40. There are jammy, tutti-fruity flavors but they are deepened with plum pudding, nougat, sweet espresso and mocha, and Asian spices that tingle the palate through the long finish. All this is wrapped in silky tannins. Gorgeous stuff. **91** —*S.H. (2/1/2004)*

Gloria Ferrer 2002 Jose S. Ferrer Selection Pinot Noir (Carneros) $35. Dry and elegant, not really a rich wine, but a well-structured one. It has keen acids and dusty tannins that frame cola and root beer flavors. Give it a little decanting, since it's somewhat rigid right out of the bottle. **87** —*S.H. (12/15/2006)*

Gloria Ferrer 2002 Rust Rock Terrace Pinot Noir (Carneros) $40. This is a good Pinot but it has some problems that keep the score limited. There's a mulchy earthiness, a sharp, dry mintiness, that limits enjoyment of the underlying cherry flavors, and which is unlikely to age out. **85** —*S.H. (12/15/2006)*

Gloria Ferrer 2000 Rust Rock Terrace Vineyard Pinot Noir (Carneros) $40. Great Carneros Pinot. Fabulously ripe fruity flavors range from raspberries through cherries and currants, sprinkled with cinnamon and nutmeg. Sweet and earthy, like espresso with brown sugar. Totally dry, and silky all the way down. **93** —*S.H. (3/1/2004)*

Gloria Ferrer NV Blanc de Blancs Sparkling Blend (Carneros) $24. All Chardonnay, this wine has a dry elegance that makes it taste really upscale. It shows subtle peach, bread dough, smoky char, and vanilla flavors, and is quite acidic. Makes you think of wedding toasts. **87** —*S.H. (12/31/2006)*

Gloria Ferrer 2002 Blanc de Blancs Sparkling Blend (Carneros) $24. A little rough, and with an evidently high dosage, this peach-fruited wine has a cloying quality and a finish that's too sweet, even by California standards. **82** —*S.H. (12/31/2005)*

Gloria Ferrer 2000 Blanc de Blancs Sparkling Blend (Carneros) $22. Rich, smooth, and delicious, a toasty wine with delicate flavors of lime, peach, and almond skin. It's a bubbly that feels luxurious and complete on the palate, with a creamy mousse and a long, vanilla-tinged finish. One of the more elegant nonvintage bubblies around. **90** —*S.H. (12/1/2003)*

Gloria Ferrer NV Blanc de Noirs Sparkling Blend (Sonoma County) $18. What a pretty color, a pale straw with glints of rosy peach skin, and a suggestion of fresh strawberries and cream on the nose. Drinks smooth and rich, a lively, full-bodied sparkler with firm acidity. **87** —*S.H. (12/1/2003)*

Gloria Ferrer NV Blanc de Noirs Sparkling Blend (Sonoma County) $18. There's lots of strawberry and vanilla flavor in this dry wine. It's a bit aggressive in the mouth, with sharp elbows, though. Finishes clean and scouring. **86** —*S.H. (12/31/2004)*

Gloria Ferrer NV Blanc de Noirs Sparkling Blend (Sonoma County) $18. A great big waft of cherries erupts from the glass, signaling a fruity wine, which indeed this bubbly is. Its full-bodied flavors have a nice yeasty, doughy quality, and the wine is fully dry, although somewhat rough in texture. **86** —*S.H. (12/31/2005)*

Gloria Ferrer NV Blanc de Noirs Sparkling Blend (Sonoma County) $18. Pinot Noir has given this bubbly a full-bodied richness that smacks of red cherries. It's a dry wine, a little sharp and angular, but maintains a distinguished creamy mouthfeel. **87** —*S.H. (12/31/2006)*

Gloria Ferrer NV Brut Sparkling Blend (Sonoma County) $18. Pale and delicate, with flavors of lime, straw, and bread dough, and a lively, persistent sparkle. Drinks quite dry, with lots of polish and elegance. Turns nutty and toasty on the finish. **87** —*S.H. (12/1/2003)*

Gloria Ferrer NV Brut Sparkling Blend (Sonoma County) $18. Bread-doughy and acidic, this carbonically rough bubbly has flavors of limes, strawberries, vanilla, and toast. It's a dry wine, but you can taste the sugary dosage on the finish. **85** —*S.H. (12/31/2006)*

Gloria Ferrer NV Brut Rosé Sparkling Blend (Carneros) $35. A delicious rosé that's delicate and rich, rather than full-bodied and heavy like some rosés can be. This golden-hued wine carries pretty scents of strawberries, vanilla, cream, and smoke. In the mouth, it turns fruity in an elegant way, with a round texture and a long, dry finish. **90** —*S.H. (12/1/2003)*

Gloria Ferrer NV Brut Rosé Sparkling Blend (Carneros) $35. A good blush bubbly, fairly full-bodied and showing flavors of cherries, yeast, and smoky vanilla. Drinks quite dry and lively in acidity, with a fruity finish. **88** —*S.H. (12/31/2004)*

Gloria Ferrer NV Brut Rosé Sparkling Blend (Carneros) $35. Twice the price of the winery's nonvintage brut, and what do you get? A much better wine, a lot smoother in mousse, with a great degree of elegance. The raspberry and cherry-tinged flavors have a complex edge of vanilla, toast, and yeasty lees. **92** —*S.H. (12/31/2005)*

Gloria Ferrer 2003 Brut Rosé Sparkling Blend (Carneros) $35. Seriously good sparkler, so rich, smooth and supple, so elegant and refined, yet packed with the most delicious candied strawberry, vanilla cream, smoky char, and even white chocolate flavors. For all that, it's dry and racy. **91** —*S.H. (12/31/2006)*

Gloria Ferrer 1995 Carneros Cuvée Sparkling Blend (Carneros) $50. Very dry, apparently with a low dosage, which makes those bony acids stick out ever more. Pretty austere now, showing little beyond intense citrus, yeast and char. Such is the balance that it's likely to age well. Hold through 2006, then try again. **91** —*S.H. (12/31/2004)*

Gloria Ferrer 1996 Late Disgorged Brut Carneros Cuvée Sparkling Blend (Carneros) $50. The winery's priciest bubbly is easily its best, finessing the roughness of the lesser blends with a smoothness that glides across the palate like silk. It displays peaches and cream Chard flavor, and a wonderful balance and dryness. Finishes with classic Champagne elegance. **94** —*S.H. (12/31/2005)*

Gloria Ferrer 1996 Royal Cuvée Brut Sparkling Blend (Carneros) $24. Beginning to show its age as the fruit drops. Picking up crushed mineral, dried lime, vanilla, and hints of dusty herbs, but still vibrant and fresh.

USA

Should continue to do interesting things over the years. **89** —*S.H. (12/31/2004)*

Gloria Ferrer 1995 Royal Cuvée Brut Sparkling Blend (Carneros) $22. Held back for eight years, this wine tastes like it was bottled yesterday. It's fresh and doughy, with lime and vanilla flavors; the bubbles are still fierce, as are the acids. It's a clean, lean machine of a sparkler, elegant now, but should age flawlessly for years to come. **92 Editors' Choice** — *S.H. (12/1/2003)*

Gloria Ferrer 1997 Royal Cuvée Brut Sparkling Blend (Carneros) $28. The '96 Royal Cuvée has provided years of excellent drinking, and so will this worthy followup. It's a rich, complex bubbly, two-thirds Pinot Noir and the rest Chardonnay, with full-bodied cherry vanilla, egg custard, yeast, smoke, and spice flavors. The tension between the creamy texture and the high acidity is really interesting. **92 Editors' Choice** —*S.H. (12/31/2006)*

Gloria Ferrer NV Sonoma Brut Sparkling Blend (Sonoma County) $18. Tasty bubbly here, a smooth, polished wine with pronounced lime, raspberry, and vanilla flavors complexed with yeast and smoke. Dry and vibrant, this is easy to drink. **86** —*S.H. (12/31/2004)*

Gloria Ferrer NV Sonoma Brut Sparkling Blend (Sonoma County) $18. Vanilla cream and peaches in cream, with lots of pure yeasty dough, mark this bubbly. It has good, crisp acidity and a rough texture that turns a little sweet on the finish. **85** —*S.H. (12/31/2005)*

Gloria Ferrer 2001 Syrah (Carneros) $22. With its green and herbal notes on the nose that pick up hints of mint and spice, this is not a fruit-driven Syrah. Rather, it relies on spice and herb, buoyed along by cherry fruit. Turns a bit hard on the finish. Age and risk the fruit drying out, or drink young and deal with the tannins? **85** *(9/1/2005)*

GNARLY HEAD

Gnarly Head 2005 Old Vine Zinfandel (Lodi) $12. Rustic, soft, and simple, with jammy raspberry and cherry flavors. Contains almost a quarter of Petite Sirah, but it's still a gentle, medium-bodied wine. **83** —*S.H. (12/1/2006)*

Gnarly Head 2004 Old Vine Zinfandel (Lodi) $11. Heady, briary aromas meld easily into flavors of mixed berries, while herbal notes add interest. Supple tannins on the finish make this one to drink now. **86 Best Buy** *(8/1/2006)*

GNEISS

Gneiss 2000 Cabernet Sauvignon (Napa Valley) $25. This Cabernet shows some good character despite a certain lightness of fruit and body. There are pleasant currant flavors, and those pretty Napa tannins are accented by oak. **85** —*S.H. (11/15/2003)*

Gneiss 2000 Reserve Cabernet Sauvignon (Napa Valley) $39. From Reynolds, a third-tier wine that's richer than the Gneiss regular bottling. Possesses some nicely extracted flavors of black currants and earthy herbs. It has polished tannins and the use of oak adds pronounced notes of vanilla and smoke. **87** —*S.H. (11/15/2003)*

GNEKOW

Gnekow 2000 Nies Old Vine Carignane (Lodi) $14. Any century-old vines that remain in California must be paid attention to. This wine celebrates a varietal usually thought of as inferior. But the wine is intense and thought-provoking. It's dark in color and in tone, with flavors of plums, black cherries, and dark chocolate, and very dry. It's too soft in acidity, and would earn extra points if it were crisper. But it's a fascinating character study. **91 Editors' Choice** —*S.H. (12/1/2002)*

GODSPEED

Godspeed 1999 Cabernet Sauvignon (Mount Veeder) $31. Good fruit and oak on this black currant-scented Cab, but the tannins are rough and numbing, even at five-plus years. Doesn't seem likely to soften before the fruit falls out, so drink up. **85** —*S.H. (5/1/2005)*

Godspeed 2001 Chardonnay (Mount Veeder) $20. No malo in this tight, acidic young wine. It's one of those lemony, citrusy, flinty Chards that will reward aging for 5 or 6 years. **87** —*S.H. (5/1/2005)*

GODWIN

Godwin 2004 Floral Clone Chardonnay (Russian River Valley) $28. If you're a fan of big, oaky Chards, you'll like this one. It's rich and unctuous in ripe tropical fruit custard flavors, with the buttered toast, crème brûlée, and smoky char that comes from new French barrels. But it has a perky acidity that lends it an appley, minerally note. **91** —*S.H. (12/15/2006)*

Godwin 2001 Merlot (Alexander Valley) $35. Released at four-plus years, unusual for a Merlot, but the tannins are beginning to melt, although they're still formidable. The underlying flavors are of cherries and oak, and the wine is dry and balanced. This wine is complex enough to drink with your best fare. **87** —*S.H. (5/1/2006)*

Godwin 2000 Moss Oak Vineyard Merlot (Alexander Valley) $35. A Merlot-based blend that's extraordinarily soft and charming. It has lush flavors of chocolate, blackberry pie, coffee, and spicy oak, and smooth, gentle tannins. As sweetly fruity as it is, it could use more structure. **86** —*S.H. (12/31/2004)*

Godwin 1999 Moss Oak Vineyard Merlot (Alexander Valley) $35. This Cabernet blend serves ripe plum and blackberry flavors up front, with a hint of subtle herb essence. The tannins are a bit dry, however, and the finish is on the bright side. **84** —*J.M. (11/15/2002)*

GOLD DIGGER CELLARS

Gold Digger Cellars 2000 Chardonnay (Washington) $15. A thin, light nose leads to modest green apple flavors of no particular distinction. The wine finishes with a gluey, artificial, alcoholic, bitter flavor. **82** —*P.G. (2/1/2002)*

Gold Digger Cellars 2000 Gewürztraminer (Washington) $12. Happily, this wine smells varietal, with the musky, perfumed nose of Gewürztraminer. Sweet fruit follows, with a nice texture and a clean flavor, leading into a solid, convincing finish. **86** —*P.G. (2/1/2002)*

GOLD HILL

Gold Hill 1999 Cabernet Sauvignon (El Dorado) $25. The grapes are real nice and ripe here, offering up flavors of blackberries and cherries that are succulent and mellow. Smoky oak adds the spicy, sweetly woody nuances from barrel aging. A problem is that the wine is too soft and a little flabby. **86** —*S.H. (9/1/2002)*

Golden 2001 Coro Mendocino Red Blend (Mendocino) $35. Quite herbal up front, but fans out to reveal black cherry, anise, raspberry, and coffee notes. Tannins are mildly astringent, framing a finish that is a bit tart but nonetheless clean. **86** —*J.M. (9/1/2004)*

GOLDEN VALLEY

Golden Valley 1997 St. Herman's Vineyard Chardonnay (Willamette Valley) $15. **88** —*P.G. (9/1/2000)*

GOLDENEYE

Goldeneye 2003 Pinot Noir (Anderson Valley) $52. This was a very good vintage for Goldeneye, the best since '01. The fruit got ripe, offering up a big mouthful of jammy cherry and raspberry flavors accented with sweet oak. The tannin-acid balance is just great. It's delicious, yet has all kinds of complex edges and nuances. **93 Editors' Choice** —*S.H. (12/1/2006)*

Goldeneye 2002 Pinot Noir (Anderson Valley) $52. This is a challenging wine. It has much to like, namely the forward cherry fruit, elaborate oak, and silky texture. On the other hand, the wine lacks vibrant acidity, and has a simple, syrupy finish. Not going anywhere, so drink up. **85** —*S.H. (11/1/2005)*

Goldeneye 2001 Pinot Noir (Anderson Valley) $48. What perfume! Delicate but insistent oaky char and vanilla hit first, followed by raspberry, cherry, cola, and cotton candy. The beautifully silky, light texture reveals sweet raspberry and cherry flavors, tinged with vanilla and cinnamon. Uncommonly beguiling and delicious. **92** —*S.H. (8/1/2004)*

Goldeneye 2000 Pinot Noir (Anderson Valley) $48. This Mendocino Pinot carries a fistful of oak, and that wood creates some lemony, sawmill aromas. Within its class, it's a large, vibrant one, and it seems to have bitten off more that it can chew. The wood notes are just too omnipresent.

That said, it has ripe fruit and a large, satisfying mouthfeel. **87**—*M.S. (12/1/2003)*

Goldeneye 1999 Pinot Noir (Anderson Valley) $45. Amazingly vibrant. Begins with oak, smoke, char, and vanilla from barrels, and then the aromas blast into coconut cream pie, black cherry, licorice, and rich spices. It's in the mouth that the wine stuns with spicy intensity. Dry and stylish, this dry, precocious wine will improve with short-term aging. **93**—*S.H. (5/1/2002)*

Goldeneye 2001 Migration Pinot Noir (Anderson Valley) $26. Jammy and rich in flavor, a silky wine with light tannins and a crisp acidity. Raspberry, cherry, and cola flavors mingle with cinnamon and pepper accented with the spice of oak. Easy and versatile drinking. **87**—*S.H. (3/1/2004)*

GOLDSCHMIDT

Goldschmidt 2001 Game Ranch Cabernet Sauvignon (Oakville) $65. Dark, oaky, very dry and tannic in youth, this well-structured Cab needs time. Those tannins sting and shut down the middle palate, but the bright blackberry and cherry fruit shines through. Should hold and improve for five years in a cool cellar. **91**—*S.H. (12/15/2005)*

Goldschmidt 2001 Vyborny Vineyard Cabernet Sauvignon (Alexander Valley) $65. Purity is the word that comes to mind with this single-vineyard Cab. There's a translucence to the cherry and black currant fruit, and the way the complex tannins glide over the palate. The wine finishes dry. Drink now through 2010. **90**—*S.H. (12/15/2005)*

Goldschmidt 2000 Vyborny Vineyard Cabernet Sauvignon (Alexander Valley) $65. This tough vintage presented the difficulty of achieving ripeness with balance. This wine struggles, but does pretty well. It's a wine to drink now, with its edge of black currant, enhanced with oak, that fades fairly quickly. **90**—*S.H. (2/1/2004)*

GOOSE RIDGE

Goose Ridge 2002 Cabernet Sauvignon (Columbia Valley (WA)) $40. This is loaded with mixed fruit flavors, in fact it's a bit of a fruit salad of a wine. But it lacks definition or specificity, tasting more like a good mutt wine than a superpremium Cabernet. It's pleasant and ready to drink now. **86**—*P.G. (6/1/2006)*

Goose Ridge 2001 Cabernet Sauvignon (Columbia Valley (WA)) $27. It opens on a slightly sweaty off-note, then breathes open to show some sweet cassis fruit wrapped in plenty of cocoa and chocolate. Simple and toasty, with a bit of heat at the end. **87**—*P.G. (11/15/2004)*

Goose Ridge 2003 Reserve Cabernet Sauvignon (Columbia Valley (WA)) $27. This racy Cabernet is full of tart red fruits; its flavors are forward and lightly spicy. The wine seems to have been acidified, perhaps to provide some lift. It is a nicely focused effort; I like the way it gathers itself and holds that focus through a smooth, seamless, long finish. **90**—*P.G. (6/1/2006)*

Goose Ridge 1999 Cabernet Sauvignon-Merlot (Columbia Valley (WA)) $39. Game, barnyard, and horse-stall aromas make this not a fruit lover's favorite. A distinct style that has bright acidity and a finish that shows well integrated tannins. **86**—*C.S. (12/31/2002)*

Goose Ridge 2000 Meritage Red Wine Cabernet Sauvignon-Merlot (Columbia Valley (WA)) $28. Pretty basic: a 50-50 blend of Cabernet and Merlot. This is a soft, fruity, broad style of wine, with big, ripe flavors. What it lacks in depth it makes up for in breadth. It's a wine to enjoy now. **87**—*P.G. (9/1/2004)*

Goose Ridge 2002 Chardonnay (Columbia Valley (WA)) $21. This is really heavy on the vanilla-flavored oak. Buttered nuts and popcorn, it's all here, but the fruit gets buried. **85**—*P.G. (11/15/2004)*

Goose Ridge 2001 Chardonnay (Columbia Valley (WA)) $20. A new label with veteran Charlie Hoppes (3 Rivers, Ste. Michelle) at the winemaking helm. Tight, young, and still a bit hard, but bursting with delicious buttery flavors of roasted nuts and fresh apples. Ageworthy but why wait? **90**—*P.G. (1/1/2004)*

Goose Ridge 2001 Chardonnay (Columbia Valley (WA)) $18. Big, buttery aromas fly out of the glass, but behind them you'll find sweet, ripe fruit,

with mixed flavors of apple, banana, and peach. Smooth stuff. **88**—*P.G. (9/1/2004)*

Goose Ridge 2000 Meritage Red Wine Meritage (Columbia Valley (WA)) $28. The blend is 50/50 Merlot/Cabernet Sauvignon—surefire—and the wine displays perfectly proportioned flavors. The Cab props it up with firm, slightly green tannins, while the Merlot fleshes it out with plummy red fruit. **88**—*P.G. (1/1/2004)*

Goose Ridge 2002 Merlot (Columbia Valley (WA)) $40. Red and black fruit flavors are complemented with clove, cinnamon, and roasted barrel scents. The wine hits a bit of a wall in the midpalate, but that may just mean it requires a little extra time (or breathing). It's a good, flavorful effort, and the barrels add nice flavors of bacon and smoke. **89**—*P.G. (6/1/2006)*

Goose Ridge 2001 Vireo Red Wine Red Blend (Columbia Valley (WA)) $30. A third each of Cabernet, Merlot, and Syrah, this challenging wine just fails to shed its tough, chewy, tannic wrapping. There are some pleasant herbal accents, but the rough tannins and unintegrated, slightly bitter barrel flavors don't offer much pleasure. **85**—*P.G. (11/15/2004)*

Goose Ridge 2000 Vireo Red Wine Red Blend (Columbia Valley (WA)) $30. This proprietary blend is roughly 1/3 each of Cabernet, Merlot, and Syrah. The combination works well enough, but nothing stands out; the three grapes seem to neutralize each other. The result is a straightforward, pleasant, drink-now red wine. **87**—*P.G. (1/1/2004)*

Goose Ridge 2002 Syrah (Columbia Valley (WA)) $25. Coffee, cola, and cedar upfront, followed by hints of game and white pepper. Vanilla and caramel notes surge forward on the finish. Dominated by oak, but with just enough savory fruit character to keep it afloat. **88**(9/1/2005)

Goose Ridge 2001 Syrah (Columbia Valley (WA)) $25. Another oaky effort, which shows some juicy berry scents but fades quickly in the mouth. Some tart, light fruit, green tea tannins, and smoky barrel toast. **86**—*P.G. (11/15/2004)*

Goose Ridge 2000 Syrah (Columbia Valley (WA)) $26. A silky, satiny Syrah that seduces with its vivid, powerful fruit and pleasing oak. The entry is soft and sweet, and the wine opens up to fill the palate with juicy ripe fruit leading into flavors of toasted coconut and milk chocolate. **91 Editors' Choice**—*P.G. (1/1/2004)*

Goose Ridge 2004 Reserve Syrah (Columbia Valley (WA)) $40. Dark purple-black, dense, and spicy, this sports some bright, tart fruit flavors of plum and citrus. It's a bracing wine that needs food or time to show what kind of depth is there. Right now it's all about saturated primary fruits. **89**—*P.G. (6/1/2006)*

Goose Ridge 2002 Viognier (Columbia Valley (WA)) $21. Fairly woody, oaky style, dry, and austere, with tart flavors of stone fruits. Lacks the floral character of some Viogniers, but hits the palate with solid, substantial weight and power. **86**—*P.G. (9/1/2004)*

GOOSECROSS

Goosecross 1998 Chardonnay (Napa Valley) $22. **88**(6/1/2000)

Goosecross 2002 Syrah (South Coast) $25. Unanimously liked, this South Coast Syrah from a Napa winery displays an artful blend of less ripe notes (nettles, thyme) with plusher cherry-berry flavors. Smooth on the palate, with hints of pomagranate and strawberry and the suggestion of berry zinger tea. **87**(9/1/2005)

Goosecross 1999 Syrah (California) $25. Really interesting on the nose, with funky aromas of geranium and tomato leaves, smoke, horse stable, and strawberries. The mouthfeel is creamy, but the flavors turn toward tomato and rhubarb, finishing a bit sour and tart. **85**(11/1/2001)

GORDON BROTHERS

Gordon Brothers 2001 Cabernet Sauvignon (Columbia Valley (WA)) $17. Nicely styled, herbal effort. Scents of bell pepper, leather, and coffee grounds circle around some medium-bodied, black cherry fruit. Not a big wine, but supple and lively, with good balance. **87**—*P.G. (11/15/2004)*

Gordon Brothers 1999 Cabernet Sauvignon (Columbia Valley (WA)) $22. There is just a hint of volatile acidity, enough to brighten the nose, which has Bing cherry and chocolate as well. In the mouth, the fruit has some herb and dill to it, an indication of a cooler vintage, and some fairly stiff tannins. **87** —*P.G. (9/1/2002)*

Gordon Brothers 2004 Chardonnay (Columbia Valley (WA)) $13. A clean, high acid style, showing pineapple/citrus fruit flavors and light touches of fresh green herb. **86** —*P.G. (6/1/2006)*

Gordon Brothers 2000 Chardonnay (Columbia Valley (WA)) $16. A sweet nose sends up plenty of toasty oak scents; the fruit is straightforward, middle-of-the-road Chardonnay, with flavors of fresh cut apples. Fairly soft, it finishes with vanilla and more oak. **87** —*P.G. (9/1/2002)*

Gordon Brothers 1999 Estate Grown Chardonnay (Columbia Valley (WA)) $20. This well-made wine features tangy flavors of citrus, nicely mingled with orange rind and a hint of grapefruit. Good texture, bracing acids, a food-friendly balance and some spicy complexity in the finish. **88** —*P.G. (7/1/2002)*

Gordon Brothers 1999 Merlot (Columbia Valley (WA)) $20. Strong cinnamon and mocha scents illuminate this wine, and the fruit shows some pretty cherry qualities. A bit of dill creeps in too, showing the effect of this cooler vintage on a cooler site. **86** —*P.G. (9/1/2002)*

Gordon Brothers 1998 Tradition Red Wine Red Blend (Columbia Valley (WA)) $50. This is a fragrant, very fruity style, a blend of 56% Cabernet Sauvignon, and 44% Merlot. Bright, well-defined cherry-berry fruit carries with it a solid wallop of alcohol. The acids remain high enough to balance it out, and there is just enough new oak to add interest, without dominating. **88** —*P.G. (12/31/2001)*

Gordon Brothers 2001 Katie's Vineyard Sauvignon Blanc (Columbia Valley (WA)) $12. No visible vintage date on the bottle, but the winery says it's a 2001. Tart and lemony, with crisp acids, it tends toward bland, with simple, green apple fruit. **85** —*P.G. (9/1/2002)*

Gordon Brothers 2002 Syrah (Columbia Valley (WA)) $18. Schizophrenic juice, which starts off herbal and green—bordering on asparagus— before settling down and delivering coffee, dill, blackberry, and vanilla flavors on a creamy-textured mouthfeel. Then it thins out on the finish, fading to lemony acids. **84** *(9/1/2005)*

Gordon Brothers 2001 Syrah (Columbia Valley (WA)) $17. The barrel flavors of sweet cinnamon and toast completely overwhelm the fruit.

A pleasant, modest little Syrah is trying to come out here, but it has been clobbered by all the wood. **86** —*P.G. (11/15/2004)*

Gordon Brothers 1999 Estate Syrah (Columbia Valley (WA)) $30. Medium-weight and very dry with some smoky notes, the modest berry fruit here is overshadowed by a stemmy, leafy, vegetal presence our tasters just couldn't enjoy. Finishes tart, with a trail-mix taste and the green thing that won't quit. Riper fruit needed here. **82** *(11/1/2001)*

GORMAN WINERY

Gorman Winery 2004 The Bully Cabernet Sauvignon (Columbia Valley (WA)) $35. "I love the '04s," says Gorman. "It was a pure year." He captures that purity perfectly in this full-bodied Cabernet Sauvignon, a beautifully structured, he-man style that is still balanced and well-defined. Flavors of berries, cherries, licorice, and baking spices lead through a luxurious, long, smooth, silky finish. Just 288 cases were made. **93** —*P.G. (12/31/2006)*

Gorman Winery 2003 The Bully Cabernet Sauvignon (Columbia Valley (WA)) $30. Pure Cabernet, a mix of Kiona and Conner Lee fruit. Chewy, tannic, and grainy, it needs time, but it has great fruit that bursts into full blown flavor as soon as it hits the palate. What follows is an explosion of berries, stewed cherries, baking spice, coconut, cassis, cinnamon, sandalwood, and more. **92** —*P.G. (4/1/2006)*

Gorman Winery 2004 The Evil Twin Red Blend (Red Mountain) $50. Late-picked Red Mountain Syrah and Cabernet Sauvignon are here combined into an exceptionally ripe, round, and rich red wine. The tannins are ripe and smooth, the fruit tilts slightly into the pruny side, and the finish coats the tongue with chalk, tannin, and pencil lead. Just 95 cases were produced. **94** —*P.G. (12/31/2006)*

Gorman Winery 2004 Zachary's Ladder Red Blend (Columbia Valley (WA)) $25. No Zachary's Ladder was made in 2003, but there are 650 cases of this gorgeous 2004. Thick, smoky, and exotic, it's a big and creamy wine with plenty of acid, plenty of spicy red fruit, and the friendly mocha fla-

vors of new oak. Vineyard sources include Boushey, Alder Creek, and Wahluke Slope. **91** —*P.G. (12/31/2006)*

Gorman Winery 2002 Zachary's Ladder Red Table Wine Red Blend (Columbia Valley (WA)) $25. Mixed berries and red fruits, a dollop of spice, streaks of leaf, tobacco, gravel—it's a lovely bottle, and one that improves dramatically with a few hours of breathing time. **90 Editors' Choice** —*P.G. (4/1/2006)*

Gorman Winery 2004 The Pixie Syrah (Red Mountain) $30. From Red Mountain fruit, this tannic, earthy Syrah blends its tart black cherry and raspberry fruit with a wash of ash, graphite, and coffee grounds. Young as it is, you can already sniff out the roasted meats and herbs to come. Just 130 cases were made. **91** —*P.G. (12/31/2006)*

Gorman Winery 2003 The Pixie Syrah (Red Mountain) $30. This is 100% Syrah from Kiona vineyards, on Red Mountain. It pins the meter at 15% alcohol without tiring out the palate. Silky and substantial, with flavors of raspberry, black cherry, and red licorice, and scents of violets, rose petals, and hints of cracked pepper. **89** —*P.G. (4/1/2006)*

Gorman Winery 2003 The Evil Twin Syrah-Cabernet (Red Mountain) $45. Made from the same late-picked Kiona Vineyard Syrah as Mark Ryan's "Bad Lands," here blended with Conner Lee Cab. It's a benign monster; dense, concentrated, packed with berry, cassis, caramel, coffee liqueur, black tea, and butterscotch. **90** —*P.G. (4/1/2006)*

GRAEAGLE

GraEagle 2003 Red Wing Bordeaux Blend (Columbia Valley (WA)) $22. From Nicholas Cole Cellars, this Merlot (74%), Cab Franc (15%), Cabernet Sauvignon (11%) blend is sourced from Klipsun, Champoux, Seven Hills, and DuBrul vineyards. That's great fruit. It's a plummy wine with a raisiny edge that hints at early oxidation, and it's already showing some brick orange at the rim. Soft to the point of being a bit soapy in the mouth, it continues with mature flavors of black cherry, cola, molasses, and chocolate. Drink this one now. **88** —*P.G. (6/1/2006)*

GRAND ARCHER

Grand Archer 2005 Chardonnay (Sonoma County) $16. Lots of flash in this relatively inexpensive Chardonnay, which shares many of the qualities of far more expensive wines. Flamboyantly ripe tropical fruit, opulent oak with creamy buttered toast and vanilla, a rich, voluptuous texture, waves of complexity and crisp, balancing cool-climate acidity—it's all there. **89** —*S.H. (12/15/2006)*

GRAND CRU

Grand Cru 2000 Gewürztraminer (California) $7. This is a tasty wine. It has distinctly varietal notes, such as the aromas and flavors of rose petals and wildflowers, peaches, and apricots, ginger, and cinnamon, and even custard and vanilla. It's just off-dry, but the acidity is fine. Simple in texture, but a good value. **86** —*S.H. (9/1/2003)*

Grand Cru 2002 Sauvignon Blanc (California) $8. Fruity, semi-sweet, and one-dimensional, a wine with citrus and apple flavors with so much sugar, it's almost like dessert. If this is your style, you'll admire the wine and its affordable price. **84 Best Buy** —*S.H. (12/15/2003)*

GRANDE FOLIE

Grande Folie 1998 Harvey Vineyard Old Vine Zinfandel (Amador County) $44. You can taste the earth, heat, and sunshine in this strong and slightly sweet Zin. The peppery, briary aromas lead to a powerfully fruity wine that seems higher in alcohol than the official reading of 13.5%, suggests. The finish is Port-like. This is a typical style from the Sierra Foothills. **85** —*S.H. (12/15/2001)*

GRANDE RONDE

Grande Ronde 2002 Charlotte's Cuvée Seven Hills Vineyard Bordeaux Blend (Columbia Valley (WA)) $40. It's two-thirds Cabernet Sauvignon, the rest split fairly evenly between Cab Franc and Merlot. A selection of the winery's best barrels, it delivers sweet fruit aromas of boysenberry and blackberry, with coffee accents. **87** —*P.G. (4/1/2006)*

Grande Ronde 2002 Pepper Bridge Vineyard Cabernet Sauvignon (Columbia Valley (WA)) $30. Decently ripe, with grape, plum, and blackberry flavors, and some pretty sweetness in the midpalate. Tannic and earthy, it's fruity and good in front but fades quickly. **86** —*P.G. (4/1/2006)*

Grande Ronde 2000 Seven Hills Vineyard Cabernet Sauvignon (Walla Walla (WA)) $40. This is an earthy, herbal wine, with some interesting cinnamon and spice from the barrel aging. On the palate it's soft and earthy, then turns herbal and a bit rough in the finish. **86** —*P.G. (12/31/2003)*

Grande Ronde 2002 Chardonnay (Columbia Valley (WA)) $20. Deep yellow-green, very soft and ripe, this tastes like an oak-drenched wine already moving past its prime. Finishes with a distinctly bitter edge. **83** —*P.G. (7/1/2004)*

Grande Ronde 1999 Seven Hills Vineyard Merlot (Walla Walla (WA)) $40. Soft, pretty fruit, has some herbal scents showing; leaf and spice lead into some pretty hard tannins. Some volatility in the nose. **85** —*P.G. (12/31/2003)*

GRANDS AMIS WINERY

Grands Amis Winery 2001 Graffigna Vineyard Zinfandel (Lodi) $18. A zippy wine that features firm, ripe tannins to support a theme of licorice, blackberry, spice, menthol, cherry, chocolate, plum, and peppery notes. On the finish, it's a bit racy, with bright acidity keeping things lively until the end. **88** *(11/1/2003)*

GRANITE SPRINGS

Granite Springs 1999 Petite Sirah (El Dorado) $20. Dark, thick, and young, with sour cherry Lifesaver flavors and noticeable dusty tannins. It's actually a very pretty wine, very dry and balanced, with good length and a clean finish. Will age, but drinks well now. **88** —*S.H. (9/1/2002)*

Granite Springs 2000 Estate Petite Sirah (Fair Play) $30. Fails to inspire, with lean, herbal fruit and huge, monster tannins. The mouthfeel is simple and rustic. A hot, peppery note shows up in the finish. **82** *(4/1/2003)*

Granite Springs 2000 Syrah (Fair Play) $18. Shows why Syrah can be such a good full-bodied red. Fleshy flavors of blackberries and cherries combine with an olive streak and soft tannins. Feels rich in the mouth, with a satisfying finish. **87** —*S.H. (2/1/2003)*

Granite Springs 1999 Syrah (El Dorado) $16. Country style, with its rough, earthy tannins and brambly berry flavors. Yet it's clean and likeable, with intensely jammy, berry and stone fruit flavors. It also has a nice, round, supple texture. A versatile wine with lots going for it. **86** —*S.H. (7/1/2002)*

Granite Springs 2001 Zinfandel (El Dorado) $30. There's a tutti fruity element here that distracts a bit from the otherwise fine cherry, berry, raspberry, and spice flavors. Tannins are also a bit tough. **84** *(11/1/2003)*

Granite Springs 2000 Zinfandel (Fair Play) $30. Distinctly Zinny, with peppery, dark berry flavors and a brambly character that veers into raisins and cassis. Nearly 15% alcohol makes the wine hot and heady, although there's no residual sugar. This country-style Zin is overpriced. **85** —*S.H. (11/1/2002)*

GRANVILLE

Granville 2000 Holstein Vineyard Pinot Gris (Oregon) $16. Granville has missed the mark with this ultralight effort, which is not just thin, but feels dead flat in the mouth, and bitter to boot. What happened? **80** —*P.G. (2/1/2002)*

Granville 1999 Holstein Vineyard Pinot Noir (Oregon) $30. An interesting wine whose spicy bouquet includes cardamom, celery, earth, and root. It's firm and tart, tannic and herbal to the taste. The finish is a disappointment—sour and artificial, tasting of graham cracker. **86** —*P.G. (12/31/2001)*

GRAVITY HILLS

Gravity Hills 2003 Base Camp Syrah (Paso Robles) $15. The winemaker calls this a "friendly" Syrah, and that just about sums it up. It's a softly gentle wine, with a silky texture almost like Pinot Noir, and jammy flavors of berries and cherries and a dry, fruity finish. **86** —*S.H. (12/31/2006)*

Gravity Hills 2002 Killer Climb Syrah (Paso Robles) $45. This big, solidly built wine's flavors revolve around darker notes of coffee, game, and tar, There's enough dark fruit to flesh out the midpalate with blackberry and plum before the finish turns tannic and drying. Drink young with a rare hunk of steak. **87** *(9/1/2005)*

Gravity Hills 2002 Westside Syrah (Paso Robles) $15. Boasts some controversial aromas and flavors of coffee grounds, cola, smoke, pepper and brettanomyces that turned one taster on and another off. The texture is fine—soft and approachable—so worth trying if those descriptors sound interesting to you. **83** *(9/1/2005)*

GRAYSON

Grayson 2004 Cabernet Sauvignon (Paso Robles) $10. From hottish Paso, a Cab that's ultrasoft in acids, although there are some firm tannins. Easily worth the price for the smooth chocolate, coffee, and blackberry pudding flavors that finish absolutely dry. **85 Best Buy** —*S.H. (10/1/2006)*

Grayson 2003 Cabernet Sauvignon (Paso Robles) $10. Soft in both tannins and acids, this Cab has upfront juicy flavors of black cherries and mocha, and is fully dry. It's a nice, easy-drinking red wine. **84** —*S.H. (12/1/2005)*

Grayson 2002 Cabernet Sauvignon (Paso Robles) $10. This Paso Cab isn't half bad for this price point. It's definitely soft, but the flavors of blackberry jam, cherry marmalade, chocolate-sweetened cappuccino, and vanilla spice are simply delicious, and make the wine oh, so easy to like. **86 Best Buy** —*S.H. (12/1/2005)*

Grayson 2005 Chardonnay (Dry Creek Valley) $10. Very bright and tangy in tangerine, lime, and nectarine flavors, with bright acidity, this wine also boasts a firm, steely minerality. **86 Best Buy** —*S.H. (11/15/2006)*

Grayson 2004 Chardonnay (North Coast) $10. Soft and simple, with decent peach and banana flavors, this Chard has a creamy texture and a dry, spicy finish. **83** —*S.H. (12/1/2005)*

Grayson 2004 Merlot (Paso Robles) $10. I like this wine for its appealing softness and overall lusciousness. It's Paso at its red-wine best, showing cherry and cassis flavors balanced by a rich earthiness. It's totally dry, but so sweet in fruit, it's irresistible. Super value. **89 Best Buy** —*S.H. (12/1/2005)*

GRAZIANO

Graziano 2001 Coro Mendocino Red Blend (Mendocino) $35. Bright and fresh tasting, with moderate tannins that surround a core of blackberry, cherry, coffee, and spice flavors. The finish is moderate in length, with a slightly drying edge. **87** —*J.M. (9/1/2004)*

GREAT WESTERN

Great Western NV Brut Champagne Blend (Finger Lakes) $10. A faint, attractive earthiness adds unexpected complexity to this wine's floral-hay nose and herb-tinged, green-apple palate. A medium-weight blend of approximately one-third Chardonnay, one-third hybrid grapes (like Seyval Blanc and Vidal) and one-third native American grapes. **85 Best Buy** *(12/1/2001)*

Great Western NV Brut Champagne Blend (New York) $10. **81** —*S.H. (12/31/2000)*

Great Western NV Extra Dry Champagne Blend (New York) $10. Foxy, animal aromas begin your experience with this bubbly. It's rough and fruity, with a dose of sugar. It has a low price going for it, but most wine enthusiasts won't find much to like here. **80** —*S.H. (6/1/2001)*

Great Western NV Extra Dry Champagne Blend (Finger Lakes) $10. Flower-shop aromas jump from the glass of this floral, unabashedly sweet sparkler. Soft and even, it has decent length and an almost ginger-ale quality on the back end. Has definite sweet-tooth appeal and is fine for mimosas and the like. **82** *(12/1/2001)*

Great Western NV Chardonnay (Finger Lakes) $10. This soft, 100% Chardonnay sparkler has an attractive, quite creamy, apple, vanilla, and mild spice bouquet. Sweeter than expected, it's a good, easy drinker, with apple and grape flavors, a touch of nuttiness, and a gentle tang on the back end. **84** *(12/1/2001)*

USA

GREEN & RED

Green & Red 1998 Chiles Mill Vineyard Zinfandel (Napa Valley) $22. Spicy black fruit, with bell pepper, black pepper, and toast adding complexity. Partial whole-berry fermentation brings an element of spicy, forward fruitiness to the wine. Lively mouthfeel, with some heat and lift to the finish. If there were more depth and punch to the fruit, this would warrant an even higher rating. **89** —*P.G. (2/1/2001)*

GREENWOOD RIDGE

Greenwood Ridge 2001 Cabernet Sauvignon (Mendocino Ridge) $25. What a nice Cab this is. Intense cherry and currant fruit, and wonderful balance. Tannins, acids, and oak act in harmony, pulling it all together. Will probably age well. **89** —*S.H. (10/1/2004)*

GREENWOOD RIDGE

Greenwood Ridge 1999 Cabernet Sauvignon (Mendocino Ridge) $30. Reminiscent of the old Martini Cabs from Napa Valley. Just oozes the juiciest, sweetest cassis, and drinks velvety-soft even in youth, with beautifully dry, dusty tannins. Not quite up to par with Napa's best in terms of depth and complexity, but getting close. **92** —*S.H. (5/1/2002)*

Greenwood Ridge 1996 Estate Bottled Cabernet Sauvignon (Mendocino Ridge) $24. 88 —*S.H. (2/1/2000)*

Greenwood Ridge 1999 Du Pratt Vineyard Chardonnay (Mendocino Ridge) $24. From a famous, pioneering vineyard on these ridges, a distinctive wine marked by extraordinary acidity, so high that the finish burns. That tartness nicely complements the austere apple fruit. Standard Burgundian winemaking adds the usual rich, creamy complexities. Strives to define its own regional style, and does so with persistent interest. **90** —*S.H. (5/1/2002)*

Greenwood Ridge 1998 Du Pratt Vineyard Chardonnay (Mendocino County) $24. 88 *(6/1/2000)*

Greenwood Ridge 1997 Merlot (Mendocino Ridge) $24. 90 —*S.H. (3/1/2000)*

Greenwood Ridge 1996 Merlot (Mendocino Ridge) $22. 94 *(11/15/1999)*

Greenwood Ridge 2001 Merlot (Mendocino Ridge) $25. From a winery that shows a deft hand at everything it tackles, a concentrated, young Merlot. Distinctive for its rich acids as well as the deep core of blackberry and coffee flavors and firm tannins. **88** —*S.H. (10/1/2004)*

Greenwood Ridge 1998 Estate Bottled Merlot (Mendocino Ridge) $24. From a producer who believes that these sunny ridgetops are amenable to Bordeaux varietals, this offering makes a good case. It easily attained the necessary ripeness, with huge berry flavors. These ridges also develop acids. Doesn't quite hit excellence, but a wine and producer worth watching. **89** —*S.H. (5/1/2002)*

Greenwood Ridge 2003 Pinot Grigio (Anderson Valley) $16. Very dry to the point of tartness, with a lemony, citrusy flavor, but it's enriched with a touch of spicy fig and apricot. After you swallow, the palate feels fresh, with a clean, spicy finish. This is a great cocktail or food wine. **87** —*S.H. (10/1/2004)*

Greenwood Ridge 2002 Pinot Grigio (Anderson Valley) $16. The first PG from this Mendocino winery, and a very good one. Tons of citrus, apple, and peach fruit, a tad sweet but not too much. Crisp, clean, and refreshing, and utterly likeable. Try as an alternative to Chardonnay or Sauvignon Blanc. **88** —*S.H. (12/1/2003)*

Greenwood Ridge 2003 Pinot Noir (Mendocino Ridge) $25. You'll find crisp, bright acids framing very dry flavors of cherries, coffee, cola, and rhubarb in this cool-climate wine. It's not a lush, fleshy Pinot, but one that celebrates its rather austere, elegant structure. **87** —*S.H. (12/31/2005)*

Greenwood Ridge 2000 Pinot Noir (Mendocino Ridge) $30. Even in Mendocino, growing Pinot Noir on these sunny ridgetops is controversial. This one is certainly ripe and fruity enough, filled with gobs of black raspberry and cherry flavors, and telltale silky tannins. The appellation may yet define itself for the varietal. But for now, as tasty as it is, it seems heavy-handed, and lacks the subtlety delicacy Pinot wants. **86** —*S.H. (5/1/2002)*

Greenwood Ridge 2000 Pinot Noir (Anderson Valley) $24. 82 *(10/1/2002)*

Greenwood Ridge 1999 Pinot Noir (Anderson Valley) $24. Light in color and weight, with spicy cherry and cranberry flavors, bright acids and silky tannins. It's a racy wine, quite dry but filled with sunny flavor. It's a bit light in the middle palate. **87** —*S.H. (5/1/2002)*

Greenwood Ridge 2002 Estate Pinot Noir (Mendocino Ridge) $25. This is a dark, fairly tannic Pinot, with flavors of blue and black stone fruits and berries, and neutral oak. It's acidic and very dry. Not showing much finesse, but a good wine. **85** —*S.H. (3/1/2005)*

Greenwood Ridge 2001 Eye of the Dragon Pinot Noir (Mendocino Ridge) $25. From estate vineyards, a huge, extracted wine, but one that never loses its poise. Jammy cherry-raspberry fruit flavors have overtones of chocolate, spices, and white pepper; the tannins are soft and subtle. Lip-smackingly good. **90** —*S.H. (12/1/2003)*

Greenwood Ridge 2000 Riesling (Mendocino Ridge) $12. 91 Best Buy —*S.H. (5/1/2002)*

Greenwood Ridge 1999 Late Harvest Riesling (Mendocino Ridge) $24. Gosh, this is as good as most southerly appellations, including Napa, get in a botrytis-infected wine. Intense flavors of apricots and wild honey and vanilla, and super acidity for it to bounce off. Pretty darned sweet, beerenauslese level. One sip is not enough. **93** —*S.H. (5/1/2002)*

Greenwood Ridge 1998 Sauvignon Blanc (Anderson Valley) $12. 89 Best Buy —*L.W. (11/1/1999)*

Greenwood Ridge 2004 Sauvignon Blanc (Anderson Valley) $16. Hard to imagine a zestier, more refreshing dry white wine than this. It's brilliant in zingy acids, with richly textured flavors of lemons and limes, gooseberries and pineapples. A little oak adds enough smoky vanilla and buttery wood spice to round this wine off. **92 Editors' Choice** —*S.H. (12/31/2005)*

Greenwood Ridge 2002 Sauvignon Blanc (Anderson Valley) $16. Refreshing and delicious, a crisp, delicate wine that's not too grassy. Has pleasant lime, apple, and vanilla flavors that drink pure and refined. A distinctive, superior Sauvignon Blanc that shows off its terroir. **90** —*S.H. (12/15/2003)*

Greenwood Ridge 2000 Sauvignon Blanc (Anderson Valley) $13. Everything about this wine is pretty good except for one thing: It's too sweet. There just has to be a limit to the amount of sugar or fructose or whatever it is that can find its way into a wine that ought to taste dry. The apple and spearmint flavors taste like they had a few teaspoons of honey stirred in. Fortunately, acidity is high. **84** —*S.H. (5/1/2002)*

Greenwood Ridge 2004 Sémillon (Anderson Valley) $16. This variety doesn't have much of an identity in California, and this wine doesn't clarify things. It's very dry and clean and austere in citrus fruits, with a wash of fig, sort of like a Sauvignon Blanc. **86** —*S.H. (12/31/2005)*

Greenwood Ridge 2003 White Riesling (Mendocino Ridge) $15. Winemaker Allan Green has trademarked this style, which is Alsatian in its slight off-dryness, fruity concentration and high, almost fizzing acidity. It has wildflower and peach flavors with a hint of petrol or lighter fluid. **86** —*S.H. (10/1/2004)*

Greenwood Ridge 2002 White Riesling (Mendocino Ridge) $15. Winemaker Allan Green has mastered this difficult variety at his mountain vineyard. This wine is beautiful, delicate, and full of charm. Feels light as a feather in the mouth, with honeysuckle, peach, and apricot flavors that drink just off-dry. Excellent acidity lends balance and freshness. Sip this in a summer garden. **89** —*S.H. (12/31/2003)*

Greenwood Ridge 2001 Estate Bottled White Riesling (Mendocino Ridge) $12. Almost fleshy textured, the wine is broad on the palate yet offers good acidity for balance. Grapefruit, lemon, melon, pineapple, apple, and herb flavors are blended nicely here in a fine-tuned, elegant style. Fruit driven, but not overly sweet. **88 Best Buy** —*J.M. (8/1/2003)*

Greenwood Ridge 1998 Estate Bottled White Riesling (Mendocino County) $NA. 88 *(8/1/2000)*

Greenwood Ridge 2003 Late Harvest White Riesling (Mendocino Ridge) $25. Wonderfully rich and decadent in botrytis and fruit, just bursting with apricot jam, orange liqueur, honey, vanilla, and smoky oak flavors. Pretty sweet, but never cloys due to the refreshing acidity. Totally addictive with vanilla ice cream. **94** —*S.H. (2/1/2005)*

Greenwood Ridge 1998 Zinfandel (Sonoma County) $21. 90 —*S.H. (2/1/2000)*

Greenwood Ridge 2001 Scherrer Vineyards-Eye of the Dragon Zinfandel (Sonoma County) $25. Smooth and plush, with tangy-edged cherry, berry, spice, and toast flavors. Fleshy and bold, the wine remains quite lovely and fun to drink. Long at the end. **90** *(11/1/2003)*

GREY FOX

Grey Fox NV Butte County Cabernet Sauvignon (California) $10. 83 —*S.H. (2/1/2000)*

Grey Fox 1997 Chardonnay (Napa Valley) $10. 86 Best Buy —*S.H. (2/1/2000)*

Grey Fox NV Merlot (Napa Valley) $20. 84 —*S.H. (3/1/2000)*

Grey Fox 2003 Butte County Syrah (California) $16. Delicate and Pinotesque, including a healthy dose of barnyard. Herbal and cherry scents and flavors are pretty, but light and finish with some hard tannins. **84** *(9/1/2005)*

GRGICH HILLS

Grgich Hills 2002 Cabernet Sauvignon (Napa Valley) $58. Very dense, very new-oaky, dry, and tannic, this Cab, whose backbone is from Yountville, is not drinkable at this time. It's just too youthfully astringent. It doesn't seem like a long-term ager, but should improve by 2007 and hold for a while. **87** —*S.H. (9/1/2006)*

Grgich Hills 2001 Cabernet Sauvignon (Napa Valley) $55. You could drink this classic Cab now, tannic as it is, because any wine this balanced and fine can be appreciated. Better to leave it be for five or ten years. It's a dramatic wine, dense in black currants and black cherries, with a crème de cassis-like unctuousness. Oak has been judiciously applied. After all the new kids on the block have come and gone, Grgich Hills still stands. **93** —*S.H. (11/15/2005)*

Grgich Hills 2000 Cabernet Sauvignon (Napa Valley) $50. Pours dark as midnight, unleashing aromas of oak and black currants, and hits the palate with a tannic bite. In other words, a young wine. The blackberry and cherry fruit struggles to find the surface but finally does. Could be an ager. **88** —*S.H. (11/15/2004)*

Grgich Hills 1999 Cabernet Sauvignon (Napa Valley) $50. This dramatic and flamboyant wine is as big as they get, but never loses focus. Gigantic in its black currant flavors and well oaked, yet there's a core in the tannins and acids that keeps this monster on a short leash. Will age for the long haul. **92** —*S.H. (5/1/2003)*

Grgich Hills 2001 Yountville Selection Cabernet Sauvignon (Napa Valley) $135. One of the last releases from the class of '01, this is a cellar candidate. It is a big, rich, unctuous wine, with gobs of black currant flavors wrapped up tight in a blanket of dusty tannins and new oak. You could drink it tonight with a great steak, but it will hold and improve for at least 10 years. **94 Cellar Selection** —*S.H. (2/1/2006)*

Grgich Hills 1999 Yountville Selection Cabernet Sauvignon (Napa Valley) $125. Tough, vegetal, tannic, and raspingly dry, and not going anywhere. A huge disappointment. Tasted twice. **82** —*S.H. (8/1/2005)*

Grgich Hills 1997 Yountville Selection Cabernet Sauvignon (Napa Valley) $95. Despite its age, this wine still is pretty tannic, but the worse problem is a vegetal character. There's a suggestion of canned asparagus despite scads of oak. Not going anywhere. **84** —*S.H. (2/1/2005)*

Grgich Hills 1997 Chardonnay (Napa Valley) $30. 87 *(6/1/2000)*

Grgich Hills 2003 Chardonnay (Napa Valley) $38. There's a tart earthiness to this Chard that distinguishes it from fruitier bottlings. The flavors bring to mind cured tobacco, sweet dried herbs, and apricots. **87** —*S.H. (2/1/2006)*

Grgich Hills 2002 Chardonnay (Napa Valley) $35. Crisp and dry, a minerally wine with earthy, citrus flavors and a firm structure. For a little richness, there's a streak of peach on the finish. **85** —*S.H. (6/1/2005)*

Grgich Hills 2001 Chardonnay (Napa Valley) $33. Drinks lean and citrusy, with grapefruit and lemon flavors marked by sharp acidity. It's also bone dry, and while there's some oak, it stays in the background. The result is a firm, austere Chardonnay that will likely gain some complexity with bottle age. **86** —*S.H. (4/1/2004)*

Grgich Hills 2000 Chardonnay (Napa Valley) $33. After all these years, this is still one of the best and most distinctive Chards in Napa. Eschewing the fat, blowsy style, this wine is tightly wound and nervy, although there's plenty of tropical fruit flavor and enough oak to satisfy. Lemony acidity shows up in the middle palate and lasts through the long finish, suggesting moderate aging possibilities. **91** —*S.H. (12/15/2002)*

Grgich Hills 1998 Chardonnay (Napa Valley) $30. This Napa Valley mainstay's offering shows a firm acid backbone and crisp, bright green apple flavors with lemony accents. Overall a bit on the lean side, but it shows just a hint of butteriness and some tangy new oak spice on the long, tart finish. **87** *(7/1/2001)*

Grgich Hills 2001 Carneros Selection Chardonnay (Napa Valley) $58. Really spectacular for its concentration and the sheer intensity of the way the fruit, oak, and lees flood the palate, yet crisp, balanced and elegant. Mango, papaya, peach, pineapple, vanilla, buttered toast, the works. All comes together in the long, spicy finish. **93** —*S.H. (12/31/2004)*

Grgich Hills 2004 Fumé Blanc (Napa Valley) $24. Grgich Hills has done another fine job with this crisply fruity wine. It's appealing for its powerful citrus, fig, and lemongrass flavors that finish with a slight honeyed note. The wine also has beautiful acids. **89** —*S.H. (11/15/2005)*

Grgich Hills 2003 Estate Dry Fumé Blanc (Napa Valley) $26. After the sulfur blows off, you'll find a clean, crisp wine of great structure and balance. Firmly acidic, with well-ripened flavors of lime, fig, and spicy melon. Picks up rich subtleties through the finish. **88** —*S.H. (12/15/2004)*

Grgich Hills 2002 Estate Grown Dry SB Fumé Blanc (Napa Valley) $18. The first ever estate Sauvignon Blanc from this winery, and a grassy one it is. Has flavors of litchi, citrus, and melon, and is very tart and dry, with mouthwatering acidity. Perfect with goat cheese and grilled veggies. **86** —*S.H. (2/1/2004)*

Grgich Hills 2001 Private Reserve Style Fumé Blanc (Napa Valley) $18. Aggressively grassy and tart, with strong flavors of green pea, grapefruit, and juniper. If this is your style, you'll like its ultradry, crisp cleanliness and zesty mouthfeel. **85** —*S.H. (7/1/2003)*

Grgich Hills 2000 Private Reserve Style Fumé Blanc (Napa Valley) $18. Hardly run of the mill, this offering is just too much like fruit juice and not enough like white wine. Basic lemon and grapefruit flavors are offset by some herbaceous grassiness, and the finish is tart, almost sour. The balance isn't really there. **83** *(8/1/2002)*

Grgich Hills 2002 Merlot (Napa Valley) $38. Dark, soft, and a bit syrupy, this is an indistinct wine, with cherry, coffee, and oak flavors. It's very harsh and astringent in tannins. **83** —*S.H. (4/1/2006)*

Grgich Hills 2001 Merlot (Napa Valley) $46. Ripe, with rich black cherry and mocha flavors, but achieves real complexity and finesse in the structure. Rich acids and lush, sweet tannins provide the underlying architecture. Dry and flamboyant, and drinking well now. **91** —*S.H. (12/15/2004)*

Grgich Hills 2000 Merlot (Napa Valley) $38. Pretty tannic and astringent from the get go, a wine that puckers the palate. There is a core of black cherry and blackberry fruit, with a tobacco and herbal edge. Finishes very dry, with a rasping feel. May soften in a few years. **86** —*S.H. (4/1/2004)*

Grgich Hills 1999 Merlot (Napa Valley) $38. Dense, dark, and lush, an extracted wine made from very ripe grapes that brim with dark berry and black stone fruit flavors. Big in the mouth, with dense, creamy tannins. Has the exuberance of youth, and best to lay away for a few years to develop further complexity. **89** —*S.H. (8/1/2003)*

Grgich Hills 1995 Violetta Riesling (California) $40. 85 —*J.C. (12/31/1999)*

Grgich Hills 2005 Dry Sauvignon Blanc (Napa Valley) $25. From the extreme southern part of Napa Valley, this wine is a bit herbaceous, with traces of green bean and asparagus. Not too much, but enough to detract from the rest of the apricot and melon flavors. **84** —*S.H. (11/15/2006)*

Grgich Hills 2000 Violetta-Late Harvest White Blend (Napa Valley) $50. Opens with a blast of apricot, lemon mousse, vanilla, butterscotch, and smoky cinnamon aromas, and then really takes off in the mouth. It's dessert in a glass, liquid peach cobbler drizzled with honey and vanilla syrup. Very sweet, with 12 percent residual sugar, but a firm spine of acidity provides balance. An unusual blend of Chardonnay, Riesling, and Sauvignon Blanc. The alcohol level is 13.6%. **93 Editors' Choice** —*S.H. (12/1/2002)*

Grgich Hills 2003 Violetta Dessert Wine 375mL White Blend (Napa Valley) $75. This Chardonnay and Riesling blend tastes TBA—totally botrytis affected—which it was, resulting in an intensely concentrated sweet wine. With 10% residual sugar, it has apricot nectar flavors and a dessert pastry, lemon chiffon thing going on. Always one of California's top dessert wines, the '03 is completely delicious. **95** —*S.H. (11/15/2006)*

Grgich Hills 2002 Late Harvest Violetta White Riesling (Napa Valley) $60. Botrytis has done its thing in the residual sugar (9.3 percent) and heavy apricot jam flavors in this wine. The Chardonnay below that expresses itself in super ripe peaches, while Riesling seems to contribute acidity. Merits its high score, and would do even better with a bit more concentration of taste. **92** —*S.H. (2/1/2005)*

Grgich Hills 1996 Zinfandel (Sonoma) $20. 92 —*M.S. (11/1/1999)*

Grgich Hills 2002 Zinfandel (Napa Valley) $28. Two bottles in a row were stubbornly sulfury, and that may have limited my appreciation. Underneath that you'll find bright mulberry and black cherry flavors, in a balanced wine that's dry and fairly tannic. **84** —*S.H. (10/1/2005)*

Grgich Hills 2001 Zinfandel (Napa Valley) $29. Brings a Cabernet-like balance to this often over-the-top variety, with lush tannins framing fully ripened wild berry, pepper, and coffee flavors. Fully dry, with adequate tannins, and soft in acidity, it will make a fine complement to barbecue. **87** —*S.H. (2/1/2005)*

Grgich Hills 2000 Zinfandel (Napa Valley) $25. Dark in color with brooding aromas of plum jam, chocolate, sweet cherry, and a dose of smoky oak. Drinks young and tannic, with rich, ripe flavors. One problem is an overt sweetness that detracts. **84** —*S.H. (9/1/2003)*

Grgich Hills 1998 Zinfandel (Sonoma County) $28. Good, tangy red fruit, with youthful vigor and zest. Nuances of citrus rind, cranberry, and toast; it's compact and sleek, still young and tight, but perfectly balanced and precision-tuned. **88** —*P.G. (3/1/2001)*

Grgich Hills 1998 Zinfandel (California) $23. Somewhat closed, the nose of this offering shows some red berry, currants, and anise. An evenly textures palate, more of the fruits evidenced on the nose with slight pepperiness mark a classic Zinfandel profile. The finish is moderately tannic, and the wine has the potential to evolve for a year or two. **86** *(3/1/2001)*

Grgich Hills 1997 Zinfandel (Sonoma County) $20. 89 —*S.H. (5/1/2000)*

GRIFFIN CREEK

Griffin Creek 2000 Cabernet Franc (Rogue Valley) $28. The clear scent of root beet along with barrel char works, and so does the ripe palate that's full of red raspberry and chocolate. If none of that sounds like Cab Franc from the Loire Valley or elsewhere, it's not. In it's own right, this is a ripe, full-bodied wine that's oaky, tannic, and big—but also quite clean. And the texture is pure new wave. **88** —*M.S. (8/1/2003)*

Griffin Creek 1999 Cabernet Sauvignon (Rogue Valley) $35. Griffin Creek wines are boldly styled, and this intense Cabernet will please fans of high-toned, vibrant reds. Hints of nail polish and tobacco are here, to go with the generous red fruits. A burst of alcoholic heat in the bright, vivacious finish. **87** —*P.G. (4/1/2002)*

Griffin Creek 1999 Chardonnay (Rogue Valley) $23. The nose features apples and pears, but more the syrupy type as opposed to fresh-cut fruit. Flavors of marzipan, banana, papaya, and barrel-driven spice make for a soft, tropical palate, while the finish is somewhat buttery and soft. It seems to be aging quickly; for whatever reason it's short on zip and pizzazz. **85** —*M.S. (9/1/2003)*

Griffin Creek 2000 Merlot (Rogue Valley) $30. Dark and tannic, with a sappy streak of cherry surrounded by strong flavors of herb, tar, licorice, and smoke. A big and strongly flavorful wine in a distinctive style peculiar to southern Oregon. **86** —*P.G. (8/1/2003)*

Griffin Creek 1999 Merlot (Rogue Valley) $35. Dense and minty, this has a satiny mouthfeel and flavors dominated by new oak. Plenty of vanilla, hints of shoe polish and some minty licorice characterize the finish. Still tannic and quite tight, it should improve over the next 2-3 years. **86** —*P.G. (4/1/2002)*

Griffin Creek 1998 Merlot (Rogue Valley) $40. There is a bit of asparagus/green bean in the nose, often a characteristic of Rogue Valley Merlot, and along with the firm cherry fruit and roasted chocolate is an unmistakable flavor of stem and bean. Apart from that this is a substantial, even muscular wine, well built and flavorful. **85** —*P.G. (11/1/2001)*

Griffin Creek 2002 Pinot Gris (Rogue Valley) $18. A little late for a 2002 release, and the wine seems to have lost a good bit of its freshness. The flavors are oxidative, with an odd finish that mixes notes of Band-aid with the lingering taste of overripe pears. **82** —*P.G. (8/1/2003)*

Griffin Creek 2001 Pinot Gris (Rogue Valley) $18. At first the nose is innocuous, but with patience you get some pear and vanilla. But with this wine first impressions are correct; the palate is flat as a board with only distant dried stone-fruit flavors. There's just no life or zip to speak of. Maybe it's too warm for Pinot Gris in southern Oregon. **81** —*M.S. (12/31/2002)*

Griffin Creek 1999 Pinot Noir (Rogue Valley) $35. This is a lovely, solid effort, especially noteworthy for the Rogue Valley, whose Pinots generally don't show as well as those from the northern Willamette. Clean, crisp, and varietal, it displays pure cherry/berry fruit, livened with sassafras and a bit of spice. Balanced and sweet, it conveys a powerful charm. **88** —*P.G. (4/1/2002)*

Griffin Creek 1998 Pinot Noir (Rogue Valley) $35. 87 —*M.S. (12/1/2000)*

Griffin Creek 2000 Syrah (Rogue Valley) $33. The initial bouquet is mostly lemony oak and violets, but then it expands and grows more full. The palate is tangy and mildly sharp, with raspberry and oak on prominent display, while the finish is largely a continuation of the palate, and thus there's a lemony prickle at the end. Finally, some heat and aggressive acidity combine forces to hold things back. **86** —*M.S. (9/1/2003)*

Griffin Creek 1999 Syrah (Rogue Valley) $35. Just 171 cases were made, in a dense, dark style characterized by roasted, toasty flavors from plenty of barrel time. Some sweet fruit peeks through, with pleasing spice, but the overdone oak and a hint of pickle barrel make for a tannic, rough ride. **84** —*P.G. (4/1/2002)*

Griffin Creek 1998 Syrah (Rogue Valley) $35. Though oak and sawdust get top billing on the nose, briny and herbal notes are also waiting in the wings. The palate shows more berry flavors, plus meaty notes. Cedary-pepper finish underscores our initial "wood-dominated" impressions. **87** *(11/1/2001)*

Griffin Creek 2002 Lakeside Vineyard Syrah (Rogue Valley) $48. Plenty of color and a peppery nose that says Syrah all the way. An unusual style, with nuances of citrus, mint, and resin, thick and somewhat ungainly tannins, deep color, and yet a thinnish mouthfeel that suggests that the fruit got ripe, but just barely. **87** —*P.G. (8/1/2005)*

Griffin Creek 2002 Viognier (Rogue Valley) $25. This wine opens with a very appealing bouquet of tropical and citrus scents, highlighted by tangerine and orange peel. The citrus circus continues in the mouth, mixing lemon and lime, orange, and mango, with enough acid to keep it lively and the right note of a tannic edge at the borderline. **88** —*P.G. (2/1/2005)*

Griffin Creek 2000 Viognier (Rogue Valley) $30. The attack is sharp, hot, with an edge of bitter citrus rind; a bit untraditional for Viognier, which so often is floral and softly seductive. This is a big, hard, assertive wine, bracing and flavored with orange peel. Lots of tannin and extract indicate high (over 14%) alcohol. **85** —*P.G. (4/1/2002)*

GRISTINA

Gristina 1998 Cabernet Franc (North Fork of Long Island) $22. A Franc that shows off its herbal character in a big way, with aromas of fresh tarragon and basil. Fresh berry flavors provide a juicy counterpoint to the green herbs. A lighter style than many L.I. Cabernet Francs, but a successful one. **85** —*J.C. (4/1/2001)*

Gristina 1998 Cabernet Sauvignon (North Fork of Long Island) $20. A solid effort for North Fork Cabernet, which has a tendency towards inconsistency. This has dark cassis fruit underlined by a weedy, herbal streak and a dried-fruit nuance as well. **84** —*J.C. (4/1/2001)*

Gristina 1999 Chardonnay (North Fork of Long Island) $20. This 100% barrel-fermented Chardonnay sees only 20% new oak, so although it has plenty of buttered-pear flavors it finishes fresh, with a hint of citrus. A touch of anise adds complexity to the aromas. **85** —*J.C. (4/1/2001)*

Gristina 1999 Andy's Field Chardonnay (North Fork of Long Island) $40. Strikes a nice balance between the buttered toast and delicate pear and peach fruit. Despite being medium-to-full-bodied, there's a hard, stony feel to the flavors, which finish long and lemony. **87** —*J.C. (1/1/2004)*

Gristina 2000 Apaucuck Chardonnay (Long Island) $10. Kicks off with pretty toast and peach aromas, followed by a strong lemony core. Moderate body and bright acidity make this zippy wine refreshing and food friendly. **87 Best Buy** —*J.M. (7/1/2002)*

Gristina 1998 Merlot (North Fork of Long Island) $20. A smooth, harmonious wine that carries plenty of black cherries and plums upfront, laced with coffee and mocha flavors. Good length on the finish is bolstered by a strong undercurrent of acidity. **87** —*J.C. (4/1/2001)*

Gristina 1998 Andy's Field Merlot (North Fork of Long Island) $27. Takes all of the ingredients of Gristina's estate Merlot and "kicks them up a notch"-cherry, plum, coffee, and mocha aromas and flavors show good depth, a thick texture and a lingering finish. To be released 5/01. **89** —*J.C. (4/1/2001)*

Gristina NV Garnet Red Blend (North Fork of Long Island) $15. A light, entry-level red, with fresh berry aromas and a touch of dried herbs. Dry, but with an appealing softness to its texture. **85** —*J.C. (4/1/2001)*

GROTH

Groth 1996 Cabernet Sauvignon (Napa Valley) $40. 92 —*L.W. (11/1/1999)*

Groth 2003 Cabernet Sauvignon (Oakville) $55. A bit too ripe, with the cassis fruit tinged with raisins, and overly soft, this Cab finishes with some tannic astringency. Doesn't seem like it's going anywhere, so drink now. **84** —*S.H. (9/1/2006)*

Groth 2002 Cabernet Sauvignon (Oakville) $50. This is a Cab that wouldn't stand out in a competitive blind tasting, because it's not a bruiser. Instead, it can claim balance, finesse, elegance, and harmony. Everything's understated. But aficionados will savor the beautiful fruit and classic structure. **91** —*S.H. (12/1/2005)*

Groth 2001 Cabernet Sauvignon (Oakville) $50. Tighter and earthier than many '01 Napa Cabs, and not offering as much decadent enjoyment, although its still a pretty good wine. Full-bodied and oaky, with a touch of raisins. **86** —*S.H. (2/1/2005)*

Groth 1995 Reserve Cabernet Sauvignon (Oakville) $125. 93 —*L.W. (7/1/1999)*

Groth 1998 Sauvignon Blanc (Napa Valley) $14. 90 —*L.W. (11/1/1999)*

Groth 2005 Sauvignon Blanc (Napa Valley) $17. This is quite a delicious Sauvignon, notable for its balance and elegance. Everything is understated, like fine tailoring. The flavors are food-friendly citrus zest, lemondrop, figs, melons, and spicy green apples, and the finish totally dry. **90 Editors' Choice** —*S.H. (11/15/2006)*

GROVE STREET

Grove Street 2001 Cabernet Sauvignon (Sonoma County) $10. Here's a great value in Cabernet. It's from a super vintage, and brims with well-ripened aromas and flavors of currants, blackberries, mocha, and smoky oak. Drinks very dry, with smooth tannins and an opulent mouthfeel. Buy this by the case. **86** —*S.H. (6/1/2004)*

Grove Street 2001 Cabernet Sauvignon (Alexander Valley) $12. There's real finesse and flavor in this soft, supple wine. It shows plush blackberry, cherry, and herb flavors wrapped in rich but easy tannins. This is a decent price for a wine of this quality. **86** —*S.H. (10/1/2004)*

Grove Street 1999 Cabernet Sauvignon (Napa Valley) $50. The well-ripened black currant and jammy blackberry pie fruit is delicious, and the wine, at nearly 5 years, shows few traces of its age. Has the lush, ripe tannins that exemplify Napa. A minor quibble is a sharpness on the finish. **88** —*S.H. (11/15/2004)*

Grove Street 2001 Chardonnay (Sonoma County) $7. Why break the bank for everyday occasions? This fruity, oaky Chard will do just fine. It's clean, with the taste of peaches. **84** —*S.H. (6/1/2004)*

Grove Street 1998 Honor Chardonnay (California) $9. 84 —*S.H. (5/1/2000)*

Grove Street 2001 Merlot (Sonoma County) $18. Tired and sweet, with red and black-cherry flavors and a simple structure, this Merlot is just barely serviceable. **80** —*S.H. (7/1/2006)*

Grove Street 2004 Pinot Noir (Napa-Carneros) $18. You'll find plenty of Pinot character in this dry, crisp wine. It shows cola, cherry, rhubarb, and tea flavors and the elegantly silky mouthfeel that Carneros achieves with the variety. Drink now. **87** —*S.H. (7/1/2006)*

Grove Street 2001 Pinot Noir (Russian River Valley) $13. The aroma is a bit musty, but fortunately, there are prettier scents of cherries and spicy vanilla. Tastes a lot richer and cleaner than it smells. **84** —*S.H. (6/1/2004)*

Grove Street 1998 Baker Syrah (California) $9. 86 Best Buy —*S.H. (5/1/2000)*

GRUET

Gruet 1996 Blanc de Blancs Champagne Blend (New Mexico) $22. Lime, green herb earth and burnt-matchstick aromas open to a toasty, nutty palate with pear, gingersnap, and cracker flavors. Medium-weight, with a steady bead and soft mousse. Finishes long, with a citrus-mineral tang. This is complex, tasty bubbly from an unusual address. **88 Editors' Choice** —*M.M. (12/1/2001)*

Gruet 1997 Grand Rosé Champagne Blend (New Mexico) $30. Smells very toasty and doughy, with accents of salt-cured meat. Remains that way on the palate, picking up a dusting of cinnamon and spice along the way to a woody finish. **84** *(12/1/2001)*

Gruet 2004 Barrel Select Unfiltered Pinot Noir (New Mexico) $45. A pleasant perfume of cola, raspberry, and cherry leads to a balanced, hearty wine with smooth, ripe tannins. Mixed berry and raspberry flavors are a bit tart, but overall this is a thoroughly enjoyable wine that doesn't go over the top. **86** —*M.D. (12/1/2006)*

Gruet 2000 Cuvée Gilbert Gruet Pinot Noir (New Mexico) $24. 81 *(10/1/2002)*

Gruet 2004 Cuvée Gilbert Gruet Pinot Noir (New Mexico) $24. Vibrant red, this sparkling wine producer has crafted a silky, fine table wine with rich red fruit and a demure nose of cola and spice. This is more intense than the Barrel Select Pinot, the dark berry and raspberry flavors a bit deeper and the sassafras finish a bit longer. Enjoy now and over the next three to five years. **87** —*M.D. (12/1/2006)*

Gruet 2000 Blanc de Blancs Brut Sparkling Blend (New Mexico) $22. A still-young wine with new oak aromas of buttered toast and caramel. A bit sharp in the mouth, but with plenty of baked apple, cinnamon, and vanilla flavor. Finishes with a dash of apple cider. **87** —*M.D. (12/31/2006)*

Gruet NV Blanc de Noirs Brut Sparkling Blend (New Mexico) $13. Starts off nicely with scents of yeast that pick up white tropical fruits and freshly picked apples. Peachy flavors again have apple tones, while the acidity is high, just what you need to start off your evening. A bit heavy in the bubbles, though. **85** —*M.D. (12/31/2006)*

Gruet NV Brut Sparkling Blend (New Mexico) $13. Bright yellow with fresh lime aromas and flavors of yellow fruit and pear. A bubbly, broad wine that lacks the substance of some of Gruet's other bottlings. **83** —*M.D. (12/31/2006)*

Gruet NV Brut Rosé Sparkling Blend (New Mexico) $13. Light pink and attractively priced, this has light strawberry aromas and more substantial cherry and strawberry in the mouth. Gruet has done a fine job managing the bubbles in this wine so that it tickles the tongue more than overwhelms it. 5,000 cases produced. **87** —*M.D. (12/31/2006)*

Gruet 1999 Gilbert Gruet Grande Reserve Sparkling Blend (New Mexico) $45. Heavily toasted on the nose, with char and vanilla leading the way, then smoth, creamy flavors of apple, pear, and vanilla with crème brûlée accents. High in acidity and meant to last, this is a well-rounded and put-together wine that should be enjoyed until 2010. **90** —*M.D. (12/31/2006)*

Gruet NV Grand Rosé Sparkling Blend (New Mexico) $30. A plump sparkler with plenty of bubbles balanced by big, intense cherry flavors. Aromas of toast and caramel show the presence of oak but the finish is all fruit, picking up strawberry at the end. **88** —*M.D. (12/31/2006)*

GRYPHON

Gryphon 2000 Pinot Noir (Anderson Valley) $50. Here's a challenging Pinot, the kind that some people call intellectual. Hard to tell what to make of the raspberry and cherry tart flavors with their edge of sugary coffee, substantial oak, and scour of hot acidity. You'll either like it or you won't, but it's an honest effort. **86** —*S.H. (8/1/2004)*

Gryphon 2000 Reserve Pinot Noir (Anderson Valley) $65. Quite delicate in structure, a pale wine with light, silky tannins and adequate acidity. The flavors are modulated, suggesting strawberries, cherry cola, rhubarb, root beer, and coffee. It's rather one-sided now, but may surprise with age. **88** —*S.H. (8/1/2004)*

GUENOC

Guenoc 2000 Victorian Claret Bordeaux Blend (North Coast) $20. Soft, slightly sweet, and packed with flavor, this Bordeaux blend offers up plenty of blackberry, cherry, blueberry, and mocha flavors. It has a nice, crisp balance. **84** —*S.H. (12/1/2005)*

Guenoc 2003 Cabernet Sauvignon (Lake County) $14. Lots of ripe, jammy cherry, blackberry, and chocolate fruit in this easy-drinking Cab. Shows some rusticity, though, in the raisiny finish and astringency of the tannins. **83** —*S.H. (12/1/2006)*

Guenoc 2002 Cabernet Sauvignon (California) $11. Green and stemmy, with a sharp cut of acidity, and a cherry medicine finish. **82** —*S.H. (8/1/2005)*

Guenoc 2001 Cabernet Sauvignon (North Coast) $17. You'll find true varietal character in this multi-county blend, with its clean black currant, plum, herb, and gently oaked flavors. It's dry and balanced, an easy sipper that finishes with some polish and flair. **87** —*S.H. (12/1/2005)*

Guenoc 1999 Beckstoffer IV Cabernet Sauvignon (Napa Valley) $55. Smells big and ripe, with a burst of black currant and cassis fruit with a cut of mint, as well as lots of smoky oak. Rich enough in fruit, but extremely tannic, and turns sharp and bitter on the finish. Could improve with age. **84** —*S.H. (11/15/2003)*

Guenoc 1996 Bella Vista Vineyard Reserve Cabernet Sauvignon (Napa Valley) $41. 92 —*L.W. (3/1/2000)*

Guenoc 1997 Reserve Beckstoffer IV Vineyard Cabernet Sauvignon (Napa Valley) $41. 90 *(11/1/2000)*

Guenoc 1997 Reserve Bella Vista Vineyard Cabernet Sauvignon (Napa Valley) $41. 88 *(11/1/2000)*

Guenoc 1998 Chardonnay (North Coast) $16. 87 *(6/1/2000)*

Guenoc 2005 Chardonnay (Lake County) $12. Simple and fruity, this Chard has flavors of canned apricots and peaches, finished with notes of charry oak. It's a soft wine, and a little bit sweet, but it's pleasant and affordable. **84** —*S.H. (12/31/2006)*

Guenoc 2004 Chardonnay (North Coast) $12. Dry, bright in acids, and fruity, with kiwi and lime flavors that finish with a spicy flourish. This is a nicely elegant Chard that won't break the bank. **85** —*S.H. (12/1/2006)*

Guenoc 2004 Chardonnay (California) $12. Kind of soft and thin, but there's a nice, dry Chardonnay character and enough peaches and cream flavors smoky oak and creamy texture to satisfy. **83** —*S.H. (12/1/2006)*

Guenoc 2003 Chardonnay (California) $11. This is your basic dry, ripe California Chardonnay. A little rustic, with decent fruit and a kiss of oak and cream. **83** —*S.H. (8/1/2005)*

Guenoc 1998 Genevieve Magoon Reserve Chardonnay (Guenoc Valley) $30. 86 *(6/1/2000)*

Guenoc 2002 Genevieve Magoon Vineyard Reserve Chardonnay (Guenoc Valley) $26. Lots of extracted, ripe pineapples, pears, and butter-sautéed bananas, as well as dusty oriental spices and good acidity. There's a smoky edge of charcoal from well-toasted oak in this big wine. **87** —*S.H. (3/1/2005)*

Guenoc 1999 Genevieve Magoon Vineyard Reserve Tutu Chardonnay (Guenoc Valley) $40. This Chardonnay reads on the nose and palate like Key lime pie. Sweet and sour citrus notes are offset by graham cracker, vanilla, and ginger snap. This is great juice with plenty of dimension—at once smooth and full, creamy, and spicy. Don't drink it for dessert, though—try it with grilled chicken in a citrus and spice marinade. Top Value. **91** *(7/1/2001)*

Guenoc 1998 Genevieve Magoon Vineyard Reserve Tutu Unfiltered Chardonnay (Guenoc Valley) $40. Tastes like harvest in Hawaii. Toasted marshmallow, coconut, and sunny tropical fruit notes hula on the opulent nose. A medium-weight palate of rich and warm, very comfortable flavors—apple cider, spice, and earth—follows. A tangy, spicy finish makes you wish it were a touch longer. **89** *(7/1/2001)*

Guenoc 2004 Merlot (California) $9. Raw in acidity and sugary sweet, this Merlot has low alcohol. **80** —*S.H. (12/1/2006)*

Guenoc 2003 Petite Sirah (Lake County) $16. Robust and hearty, this is a wine to quaff with short ribs, roast lamb, broiled chicken. It's big, dry and tannic, with full-throttle blackberry, coffee, and sweet plum flavors that finish in a swirl of dusty spices. Try decanting for a few hours before serving. **86** —*S.H. (12/31/2006)*

Guenoc 2002 Petite Sirah (Lake County) $16. Made in the old-fashioned style, namely a bone-dry, astringently tannic wine that's big enough to peel your socks off. You could drink it now, if you don't mind gluing your palate shut, or you can do what should be done: age it in a nice, cool place for a decade or two. **87** —*S.H. (12/1/2006)*

Guenoc 2001 Petite Sirah (North Coast) $18. This Petite Sirah isn't showing well now, unless you're a fan of big, dark, inky, tannic, dry, heavy red wines. It does have deep cherry and blackberry flavors. **83** —*S.H. (12/1/2005)*

Guenoc 1999 Petite Sirah (North Coast) $21. Decent, everyday quality, with thin flavors of berries and cherries, a hint of smoky oak and firm tannis. Has some unripe, stalky green notes, but is pretty decent as a quaffer. **83** *(4/1/2003)*

Guenoc 2000 Serpentine Meadow Petite Sirah (Guenoc Valley) $35. A huge wine, yet balanced and even elegant. Filled with ripe cherries, blackberries, grilled meat, white chocolate, and smoky oak, and sturdy in tannins, although they're soft and sweet. Delicious now, and should age effortlessly through this decade. **92** —*S.H. (3/1/2005)*

Guenoc 1999 Serpentine Meadow Reserve Petite Sirah (Guenoc Valley) $40. What a hefty price for this wine. Some tasters fell in love with the flashy and distinguished balance of ripe fruit, oak, and tannins, but others were put off by the tannins, and heat on the finish. **85** *(4/1/2003)*

Guenoc 2004 Pinot Grigio (California) $9. Nice price for such a tasty wine, and it's the kind that's making PG the hottest white in America. It's dryish and brightly crisp in acids, with polished citrus, fig, peach, green apple, and white pepper flavors. **85 Best Buy** —*S.H. (12/1/2006)*

Guenoc 2000 Vintage Port (Guenoc Valley) $30. A delicious dessert wine, dark ruby in color, and super-aromatic with caramelized wood, black currant, chocolate, and vanilla notes. The chocolate fudge, blackberry tart and spicy gingerbread flavors are intense. Very sweet, yet balanced with acidity. Makes you think of winter fireplaces, chocolate truffles, and someone special. **94** —*S.H. (2/1/2005)*

Guenoc 1998 Sauvignon Blanc (California) $10. 86 —*L.W. (5/1/2000)*

Guenoc 1997 Sauvignon Blanc (North Coast) $13. 85 —*L.W. (9/1/1999)*

Guenoc 2005 Sauvignon Blanc (Lake County) $11. Picture-perfect Lake County Sauvignon, dryish and crisp in acids, with pleasantly ripe Meyer lemon, pineapple, fig, honeydew, and spicy, white pepper flavors. There's no oak, yet boasts buttercream and vanilla. **86 Best Buy** —*S.H. (12/31/2006)*

Guenoc 2005 Sauvignon Blanc (Lake County) $12. Very, very dry, with good acidity, this citrus- and fig-flavored wine scours and cleanses the palate, getting those tastebuds working. It cries out for grilled veggies, goat cheese, and fresh sourdough bread. **86** —*S.H. (11/1/2006)*

Guenoc 2004 Sauvignon Blanc (Lake County) $13. There are some decent fruity flavors in this wine, and it's dry and clean. But it wants more concentration on the palate. **82** —*S.H. (12/1/2005)*

Guenoc 2000 Estate Selection Sauvignon Blanc (North Coast) $15. Interestingly, there are dried fruits and flowers with a touch of petrol on the bouquet. This wine sits really nicely in the mouth, offering a plethora of lemon-lime, melon, and pear flavors. It's rich and ripe, bordering on the heavy side. But it manages to toe that all-important line of balance, and therefore it qualifies as a winner. **90 Editors' Choice** *(8/1/2002)*

Guenoc 2001 Zinfandel (California) $9. Re-released to the market, but age has not helped this wine. It's turned sharp, with medicinal tastes, and is on the way down. **82** —*S.H. (8/1/2005)*

Guenoc 2001 Zinfandel (California) $12. Smooth and bright, with racy raspberry, plum, cherry, spice, and vanilla flavors. Toasty oak frames it, with plush, pretty tannins for added support. **87 Best Buy** *(11/1/2003)*

GUERRERO FERNANDEZ

Guerrero Fernandez 2004 Cabernet Franc (Dry Creek Valley) $28. It's hard to like this wine. Starts with medicinal, porty aromas, then turns sharp and acidic, with cherry flavors. **80** —*S.H. (6/1/2006)*

Guerrero Fernandez 2004 Merlot (Dry Creek Valley) $28. Dry, harsh, and overripe, this wine has cherry, prune, and raisin flavors and an astringent finish. It's not going anywhere. **81** —*S.H. (6/1/2006)*

Guerrero Fernandez 2004 Pinot Noir (Green Valley) $30. It's hard to understand how they got this massively ripe fruit from grapes with only 13 percent alcohol. Theories abound. It tastes late-picked, almost porty, with currant, coffee, and chocolate flavors, and is full-bodied and dry. **84** —*S.H. (6/1/2006)*

Guerrero Fernandez 2004 Zinfandel (Dry Creek Valley) $28. High in alcohol and a little hot and baked in fruit, this single vineyard wine typifies that style from a hot vintage in California. The stewed berry and raisiny-pruny flavors finish fully dry. This Zin will nicely complement a rich beef stew. **85** —*S.H. (6/1/2006)*

GUILLIAMS

Guilliams 1996 Cabernet Sauvignon (Spring Mountain) $28. 92 —*S.H. (2/1/2000)*

Guilliams 2004 *Barrel Sample* Cabernet Sauvignon (Napa Valley) $NA. Starts out intense, nervous, and taut with acidity and tannins, but is very concentrated in fresh blackberry-cherry fruit. Should age well. **92** —*S.H. (8/1/2004)*

GUISEPPE

Guiseppe 2000 Neese Vineyards Zinfandel (Redwood Valley) $17. Here's California sunshine in a bottle, from the pruny raisiny aromas to the full-throttle berry-preserve flavors and the whopping 15.5% alcohol. It's dry, but all that ripe fruit make your palate think it's tasting Port. Distinctive stuff, and defines this style of Zin. **87** —*S.H. (12/15/2001)*

GUNDLACH BUNDSCHU

Gundlach Bundschu 2002 Rhinefarm Vineyard Cabernet Sauvignon (Sonoma Valley) $32. The vineyard is on the border of Sonoma Valley and Carneros, and this complex Cab shows signs of warm and cool influences. The fruit is rich in cassis, currant, and cocoa, but there's a firm tannin and acid structure that gives balance. It's not an ager, so drink now. **89** —*S.H. (12/1/2005)*

Gundlach Bundschu 2003 Rhinefarm Vineyard Chardonnay (Sonoma Valley) $24. This isn't one of your tropical fruit and oak, acidic cool-climate monster Chards. It's soft and earthy, with a dried sage and oregano edge to the green apple and white peach flavors. **86** —*S.H. (12/1/2005)*

Gundlach Bundschu 1998 Rhinefarm Vineyards Chardonnay (Sonoma Valley) $18. 85 *(6/1/2000)*

Gundlach Bundschu 1998 Sangiacomo Ranch Chardonnay (Sonoma Valley) $16. 87 *(6/1/2000)*

Gundlach Bundschu 2003 Rhinefarm Vineyard Merlot (Sonoma Valley) $29. Thick and soft, this wine has simple, sweetish medicinal flavors of cherry and black raspberry Lifesavers. The oak just adds vanilla. **82** —*S.H. (12/31/2006)*

Gundlach Bundschu 1998 Rhinefarm Vineyard Merlot (Sonoma Valley) $26. Fairly rich in the nose, with smoky black-cherry notes at the fore. On the palate it host a blend of bell pepper, herb, and blackberry flavors, all couched in moderate tannins. The ensemble finishes with a touch of tartness **85** —*J.M. (12/1/2001)*

Gundlach Bundschu 2000 Rhinefarm Pinot Noir (Sonoma Valley) $28. 86 *(10/1/2002)*

Gundlach Bundschu 2004 Rhinefarm Vineyard Pinot Noir (Sonoma Valley) $32. The vineyard is right where southern Sonoma Valley meets Carneros, so it's not as hot as you might think. This rewarding wine is very ripe, brimming in cherry pie, cola, vanilla, and cinnamon spice flavors, in a texture that's both silky and meaty, which may be a contradiction, but it means it's complex. What a versatile food wine. **90** —*S.H. (12/31/2006)*

Gundlach Bundschu 1999 Rhinefarm Vineyard Pinot Noir (Sonoma Valley) $26. From one of the older Pinot Noir vineyards in the valley. There's nothing shy about the aromas or flavors. It's got tomato, coffee, mushroom, black- and red-raspberry and peppery-spicy notes that last into the finish. Silky tannins and mild acids make it immediately drinkable. **87** —*S.H. (7/1/2002)*

Gundlach Bundschu 1997 Rhinefarm Vineyards Pinot Noir (Sonoma Valley) $18. 91 *(11/15/1999)*

Gundlach Bundschu 2001 Rhinefarm Vineyard Zinfandel (Sonoma Valley) $32. Smooth textured and sleek on the palate. The wine serves up a tangy-edged blend of black-cherry, raspberry, vanilla, plum, licorice, and herb flavors that stay with you long on the finish. A good wine from an old family winery. **90** *(11/1/2003)*

GYPSY CANYON

Gypsy Canyon NV Ancient Vine Angelica 375mL Mission (Santa Rita Hills) $120. Tastes like a fortified Madeira, for good reason. Fermentation was halted with 190.5 proof grape spirits, when sugar level was 9%. With 18% alcohol, it's quite sweet, with apricot honey, crème brûlée, and reduced tangerine juice flavors, in a thick, dense texture. **92** —*S.H. (9/1/2006)*

Gypsy Canyon 2004 Pinot Noir (Santa Rita Hills) $75. This is the second vintage from this tiny winery. This is a bone-dry Pinot, dark and full-bodied. It's not a fruit bomb, but shows a controlled balance of rhubarb pie, cola, cherry, and coffee flavors, wrapped in rich, sturdy tannins and a velvety texture. A little rustic now, this fine wine should develop further by 2007 and hold for several years. **89** —*S.H. (3/1/2006)*

GYPSY DANCER

Gypsy Dancer 2002 A&G Estate Vineyard Pinot Noir (Oregon) $60. Spicy, briary scents suggestive of dried fruits. The wine is brambly, with assertive cherry and raspberry flavors, a rich, live-wire mouthfeel, and a spicy, resiny wrap-up. **88** *(11/1/2004)*

Gypsy Dancer 2002 Gary & Christine's Vineyard Pinot Noir (Oregon) $34. Not much fruit to be found here, just lots of dried herbs and pungent spices. There are barrel flavors of vanilla and cocoa, and a lean, tannic finish. **83** *(11/1/2004)*

H. GRAY

H. Gray 2000 Cabernet Sauvignon (Yountville) $34. Fate conspired against this wine. It's cool, southerly Napa location joined up with the inclement harvest to keep ripeness away. The wine is well-oaked, but hard and firm, without the core of fruit needed to age. Disappointing. **85** —*S.H. (5/1/2004)*

H. Gray 1999 Cabernet Sauvignon (Yountville) $25. From estate vineyards and winemaker Celia Welch Masyczek, a gorgeous Cabernet with the kind of tannin structure you expect from a great vintage in Napa Valley. Deep, impressive flavors of black currants, but it's pretty tannic now and requires up to a decade to soften. At today's prices, this one is a relative bargain. **92 Editors' Choice** —*S.H. (8/1/2003)*

H. Gray 2000 Bad Boy Red Syrah-Cabernet (Yountville) $18. From this southerly Napa Valley district, a modern field blend of Syrah, Petite Sirah, and Cabernet Sauvignon that has some real pedigree and finesse despite its size. It is a big, young, tannic, dry wine, dark in color, with a deep streak of blackberry fruit. It will age. **86** —*S.H. (3/1/2004)*

H. Gray 2001 Bad Boy Zinfandel (Amador County) $20. If you call your wine "Bad Boy," you'd better back it up with some bad-ass flavor. This is a nice enough wine, but hardly "bad." Somewhat candy-like, with cherry cough syrup and spice up front and hints of smoke and licorice on the finish. A bit cloying at the end. **82** —*J.M. (4/1/2004)*

HACIENDA

Hacienda 1996 Cabernet Sauvignon (California) $8. 82 *(3/1/2000)*

Hacienda 1999 Clair de Lune Cabernet Sauvignon (California) $7. Starts with rustic, earthy-berry aromas with some green notes, then turns simple and lightly fruity in the mouth. Soft acids and dry tannins help this wine finish clean and scouring. **83** —*S.H. (11/15/2002)*

Hacienda 2003 Johannisberg Riesling (California) $7. An easy, fruity sipper, just a little sweet. Makes you think of eating a ham sandwich on a picnic. **84 Best Buy** —*S.H. (12/31/2004)*

Hacienda 2002 Clair de Lune Merlot (California) $7. Lots of juicy, tuttifruity flavor in this dry, easy wine. Blackberries, cherries, cocoa, and even a little dab of smoky oak. **84 Best Buy** —*S.H. (12/31/2004)*

Hacienda 2003 Sauvignon Blanc (California) $7. A nicely drinkable white table wine for its clean, crisp acidity and flavors of citrus and fig. Perfectly dry, but the ripe fruit is succulently sweet. **84** —*S.H. (10/1/2004)*

Hacienda 2002 Clair de Lune Sauvignon Blanc (California) $7. Clean and zesty, an easy wine with lemon and lime flavors spiced up with an edge of pepper. There's a tad of sugary ripeness that makes it mellow. **83** — *S.H. (12/1/2004)*

Hacienda 1999 Clair de Lune Shiraz (California) $7. Dry red-berry fruit, wood and cinnamon-clove aromas carry just a tinge of chalk-powder notes. The palate shows bright but simple blueberry, cherry, and red berry fruit drizzled with a bit of caramel. It may be a bit sweet, but it has a soft mouthfeel, a pleasing price tag and a chocolate-mineral finish. **85 Best Buy** *(10/1/2001)*

HAGAFEN

Hagafen 1999 Cabernet Sauvignon (Napa Valley) $36. This rustic red serves up a blend of blackberry, cedar, and herb flavors that are couched in powdery tannins. Finishes on an herbal note. **84** —*J.M. (7/1/2002)*

Hagafen 2002 Estate Cabernet Sauvignon (Napa Valley) $40. As soon as I poured this wine, I thought, Uh oh. It's dark and lacks brightness. In the mouth, feels heavy and soft, with very ripe berry and chocolate flavors and awkward oak. **83** —*S.H. (4/1/2005)*

Hagafen 2001 Estate Bottled Cabernet Sauvignon (Napa Valley) $40. A nice, user-friendly California Cabernet, with bold cassis, blackberry, and vanilla aromas and similar flavors, underscored by a dose of tobacco. Supple tannins shine on the finish, which features a heavy dose of vanilla. **88** —*J.C. (4/1/2005)*

Hagafen NV Brut Cuvée Champagne Blend (Napa Valley) $24. Mild kirsch and pink-grapefruit aromas open this medium-weight sparkler. The apple flavors and leesy accents have a softness on the palate that will give the wine mass appeal. The long finish has a fragrant, lingering sweet-tartness. **86** *(4/1/2001)*

Hagafen 2004 Chardonnay (Oak Knoll) $18. Has a persistent vegetal smell and taste, despite some flavors of canned peaches. Tasted twice. **80** — *S.H. (4/1/2006)*

Hagafen 2000 Chardonnay (Napa Valley) $18. The flavors in this kosher wine are very rich, comingling tangerines, ripe peaches, and mangoes for a thoroughly mouth-filling experience. Oak adds smoky, spicy notes. It's

a bit sweet, and could use more bright acid because it's too soft right through the finish. **86** —*S.H. (9/1/2002)*

Hagafen 2003 Merlot (Napa Valley) $27. Rough and sharp in the mouth, with a jagged, piercing mouthfeel, despite well-ripened cherry and blackberry flavors. Not going anywhere, so drink up. **82** —*S.H. (7/1/2006)*

Hagafen 1999 Merlot (Napa Valley) $27. Silky on the palate, this wine serves up a blend of black cherry, licorice, and herb flavors that continue on to a moderate finish. **87** —*J.M. (6/1/2002)*

Hagafen 2002 Estate Bottled Merlot (Napa Valley) $27. Intensely oaky, with powerful vanilla aromas and flavors that come close to swamping the modest black cherry fruit. Creamy-textured on the palate, with a touch of dried spices on the finish. **84** —*J.C. (4/1/2005)*

Hagafen 2004 Estate Pinot Noir (Napa Valley) $32. Opens with a vegetal smell, like canned asparagus, and although it tastes fruitier and has a polished texture, it's still a difficult wine to like, especially at this price. **83** —*S.H. (4/1/2006)*

Hagafen 2002 Estate Bottled Pinot Noir (Napa Valley) $24. Its aromas of leather, smoke, herb, and cherry are "très Pinot," but the flavors don't deliver the same grace and elegance, veering toward cherry and chocolate on a slightly warm, low-acid foundation. **84** —*J.C. (4/1/2005)*

Hagafen 2004 Fagan Creek Block 38 Reserve Pinot Noir (Napa Valley) $50. Robust and full-bodied, what this lacks in finesse and delicacy it makes up for in ripe fruit flavor. Cherries, black raspberries, and chocolate mingle on the palate, finishing long and spicy. **85** —*S.H. (7/1/2006)*

Hagafen 2005 Sauvignon Blanc (Napa Valley) $15. This unique Sauvignon Blanc has gooseberry aromas and flavors suggestive of those Marlborough wines from New Zealand, but also a pickleweed note that veers into cat pee. Yet it's not quite dry, but has a honeyed finish. Try with a spinach salad with shrimp and pink grapefruit. **84** —*S.H. (7/1/2006)*

Hagafen 2004 Sauvignon Blanc (Napa Valley) $15. Opens with a great big burst of freshly sliced grapefruit sprinkled with cinnamon and nutmeg, and tastes just as crisply refreshing. The citrusy fruit and bright acidity clean the palate, preparing it for food. **88** —*S.H. (10/1/2005)*

Hagafen 2000 Sauvignon Blanc (Napa Valley) $13. Light in color, almost translucent. There's just a touch of grapefruit in the otherwise mute nose. In the mouth, the weight is nice, as is the acidity. If you search hard, some grapefruit and apple flavors emerge, but also some asparagus. It finishes clean enough. **83** —*M.S. (4/1/2002)*

Hagafen 2001 Brut Cuvée Sparkling Blend (Napa Valley) $30. Robust and elegant, this bubbly has Chardonnay flavors of peaches, while Pinot Noir gives it a cherry tinge and a fuller body. It's crisp in acids, and finishes with a fine bread dough taste and pronounced sweetness that's almost off-dry. **86** —*S.H. (12/31/2005)*

Hagafen 2001 Brut Cuvée Late Disgorge Sparkling Blend (Napa Valley) $36. It's a darker-colored wine than the regular 2001 Brut Cuvée, more redolent of cherries and strawberries, and fairly heavy for a bubbly. The slightly sweet finish suggests a high dosage. **84** —*S.H. (12/31/2005)*

Hagafen 2001 Syrah (Napa Valley) $27. Lots of smoky, toasty oak here, with just barely enough cherry-scented fruit to support it. Nice velvety texture on the finish, though. **85** —*J.C. (4/1/2005)*

Hagafen 2000 Syrah (Napa Valley) $27. Fairly dense and viscous. The wine serves up smoky, black-cherry, toast, herb, and chocolate flavors couched in supple tannins. Moderate on the finish. **88** —*J.M. (9/1/2002)*

Hagafen 1999 Syrah (Napa Valley) $NA. Cinnamon, clove, earth, and blackberry flavors, plus a chalky-gravel mouthfeel, are what you'll get on the palate; the long finish shows plenty more blackberry, plus toasty, vanilla oak. Deep cherry, nutmeg, and earth aromas. Kosher for Passover. **90** *(11/1/2001)*

Hagafen 2005 White Riesling (Potter Valley) $16. Sweet, soft, and simple, in fact a little insipid, with a sugary finish that makes the candied fruit cloying. **82** —*S.H. (7/1/2006)*

Hagafen 2004 White Riesling (Potter Valley) $19. Soft and fruity, with apple and peach flavors that finish sweet. **83** —*S.H. (4/1/2005)*

Hagafen 2005 Estate White Riesling (Napa Valley) $21. Overtly sweet and simple, with plenty of white peach, honeysuckle, and vanilla flavors, this Riesling has a refreshing acidity that makes it clean. Alcohol is nice and low, only 11 percent. **84** —*S.H. (7/1/2006)*

HAGEN HEIGHTS

Hagen Heights 2002 Cabernet Sauvignon (Napa Valley) $48. This wine, with some Cabernet Franc, represents a cooler-climate interpretation of Napa Valley Cab. It possesses a juicy acidity and tight tannins that frame and gird bright cherry and blackberry flavors. Now youthful, it should hold and improve for many years. Drink now through 2015. **93 Cellar Selection** —*S.H. (5/1/2006)*

HAHN

Hahn 2002 Meritage Bordeaux Blend (Central Coast) $20. A pretty good blend of all five Bordeaux grapes, dominated by Merlot, and marked by effusively fruity aromas and flavors. The fruit is conjoined with well-toasted oak that adds caramel and smoky, spicy notes. Very satisfying, with enough tannins to warrant a few years of aging. **88** —*S.H. (6/1/2004)*

Hahn 2003 Meritage Cabernet Blend (Central Coast) $20. Dark, ripe, intense in fruit, and meltingly soft, this wine is a hallmark of the international style. It's fantastically rich in cherry and blackberry fruit, with an amazingly long finish. If it had more structural integrity it would be a blockbuster. **85** —*S.H. (11/1/2005)*

Hahn 2004 Cabernet Franc (Santa Lucia Highlands) $14. Supple and appealing for its forward cherry flavors, this wine has crisp acids to cut through rich meats, poultry, and cheese. It's a little on the sweet, candied side, though. **84** —*S.H. (5/1/2006)*

Hahn 2004 Cabernet Sauvignon (Central Coast) $14. It's a little sharp in raw acidity, but so appealing are the fruity flavors and smooth tannins that this Cab is pretty good. Besides, pairing it with food will help balance it. **84** —*S.H. (5/1/2006)*

Hahn 2003 Cabernet Sauvignon (Central Coast) $14. Extremely ripe in cherry, blackberry, currant, and cocoa fruit, this wine is excessively soft, and has a baked cherry sweetness on the finish. Yet it's easy to drink and enjoyable. **83** —*S.H. (11/1/2005)*

Hahn 2002 Cabernet Sauvignon (Central Coast) $14. Tough in tannic astringency, with some burn from acids, this rustic wine has earthy, coffee flavors along with underlying hints of blackberries. **83** —*S.H. (10/1/2004)*

Hahn 2001 Cabernet Sauvignon (Central Coast) $12. Kind of weedy and green, with notes of peppermint, chlorophyll, and tobacco. Has a very rich texture, and good, rich tannins, but could use more depth and ripeness. **84** —*S.H. (6/1/2003)*

Hahn 1998 Chardonnay (Monterey County) $12. **84** —*S.H. (10/1/2000)*

Hahn 2004 Chardonnay (Monterey) $14. This simple Chard has likeable, intense flavors of lemons and limes and other tropical fruits, such as guavas and nectarines. It's very dry, and the finish is rich in clean, bright, palate-stimulating acids. **86** —*S.H. (5/1/2006)*

Hahn 2003 Chardonnay (Monterey) $14. Flamboyant tropical fruit flavors star in this polished, likeable wine. Pineapples, mangos, melons, peaches, and spicy pears, with a dollop of vanilla and buttered toast, all in a creamy texture. **86** —*S.H. (6/1/2005)*

Hahn 2002 Chardonnay (Monterey) $14. Extraordinarily ripe fruit has been joined to lavish oak to make a big, strong Chard. The flavors are opulent mango, papaya, and pineapple, and the oak is forward in spice, vanilla, and buttered toast. There's an undertow of lees, joined to crisp acidity. Yummy stuff. **90** —*S.H. (6/1/2004)*

Hahn 2001 Chardonnay (Monterey) $12. This is a good value in Chardonnay because it's quite rich and layered, with tiers of fruit that wash over the palate. There's a nice, earthy note, and also a good dose of oak. Finishes with a trace of bitterness. **86** —*S.H. (6/1/2003)*

Hahn 2004 Meritage (Central Coast) $20. This is easily Hahn's best red Bordeaux-style wine. It's rich in ripe, attractive blackberry, cherry, and cassis fruit, with complex, smooth tannins, and is dry. The main differ-

ence between it and, say, a Napa bottling is acidity, which this wine has plenty of. **87** —*S.H. (5/1/2006)*

Hahn 2001 Meritage (Central Coast) $18. All the parts here are good. The color is rich and dark, the aromas and flavors are rich and ripe, the tannins are velvety and fine, acidity provides a kick of brightness, and the oak is just right. Somehow though it doesn't come together yet. The palate feels the edges. Time may soften them. **86** —*S.H. (8/1/2003)*

Hahn 1999 Meritage (Santa Lucia Highlands) $18. The Santa Lucia Highlands are quickly becoming known for growing exceptional Pinot Noir, but this wine shows that the region also has potential for Bordeaux varieties. It's weedy, slightly green wine, but that's more than compensated for by the wonderfully lush and smooth texture and mouthfeel. **87** *(9/1/2002)*

Hahn 1997 Merlot (Santa Lucia Highlands) $12. **86** —*L.W. (12/31/1999)*

Hahn 2004 Merlot (Monterey) $14. The wine is clean and fruity, with a rustic mouthfeel and a sugary sweet finish to the blackberry and coffee flavors. The sweetness accentuates the tough tannins. **82** —*S.H. (5/1/2006)*

Hahn 2003 Merlot (Monterey) $14. Rich and oaky, this Merlot features flavors of blackberries, cherries, and chocolate, although it's fully dry and not too powerful in alcohol. This is a good price for a full-bodied red of this class. **88** —*S.H. (11/1/2005)*

Hahn 2002 Merlot (Monterey) $14. Dry and rather raw in acids and tannins, with earthy, plum, and blackberry flavors. A good steak will tease out whatever sweetness is hiding down there. **83** —*S.H. (10/1/2004)*

Hahn 2001 Merlot (Monterey) $12. Smells and tastes a little weedy, with green, stalky notes, but saved from disgrace by the pretty blackberry flavors and rich texture. Dry, with firm but easy tannins and good acids, this is a nice everyday sipper at a fair price. **86** —*S.H. (8/1/2003)*

Hahn 2004 Pinot Noir (Monterey) $18. Delicious in deep, satisfying flavor, this wine tastes like a cherry pie drizzled,, with cassis, sprinkled with cinnamon, and baked into a sweetly buttery baked crust. Yet it's bone dry. Full-bodied for a Pinot, it has a silky texture and is very easy to drink. **87** —*S.H. (5/1/2006)*

Hahn 2004 Syrah (Central Coast) $14. This wine has more overtly new, toasty oak on it than almost anything I've tasted lately, especially on the finish, which is pure caramel. The wine itself is ripe in fruit, dry, acidic and tannic. It's not a bad wine, but an odd, inelegant one. **83** —*S.H. (5/1/2006)*

Hahn 2003 Syrah (Central Coast) $14. Shows its cool-climate origins in the peppery, meaty aroma that erupts from the glass, but once you sip, it's super-fruity, almost jammy in black currants, cherries, chocolate, you get the idea. But it's nice and dry, and smooth in ripe tannins. **88** —*S.H. (6/1/2005)*

Hahn 2002 Syrah (Central Coast) $14. The rough edges are smoothed and softened by the ripeness of the cherry and blackberry fruit and a nice touch of smoky oak. Finishes dry and clean, a good food wine. **84** —*S.H. (10/1/2004)*

Hahn 2001 Syrah (San Luis Obispo County) $12. A delicious, supple Syrah from grapes that come mainly from Paso Robles. Full ripeness shows up as lip-smackingly fat flavors of plums, blackberries, and cherries, yet the wine is very dry and balanced. Tannins are soft and yummy. **90 Best Buy** —*S.H. (6/1/2003)*

HALL

Hall 2003 Cabernet Sauvignon (Napa Valley) $35. Good Cabernet. It's dry and balanced, with blackberry and mocha flavors and a little herbaceousness. Drink now. **85** —*S.H. (11/15/2006)*

Hall 2002 Cabernet Sauvignon (Napa Valley) $35. This is certainly a big wine, almost brawny in blackberry and currant fruit. It's probably laboratory dry, although the ripeness creates the impression of jam. A bit rough in tannins, it may benefit from a few years of cellaring. **86** —*S.H. (10/1/2005)*

Hall 2001 Cabernet Sauvignon (Napa Valley) $35. So good, so balanced and so tasty. Bursting with sweet ripe currant, cherry, and mocha flavors that are complemented with velvety smooth tannins and an elaborate

USA

overlay of good oak. Yet it possesses all-important elegance and finesse. **93 Editors' Choice** —*S.H. (10/1/2004)*

Hall 2003 T-bar-T Ranch Cabernet Sauvignon (Alexander Valley) $38. This Cab comes from the vineyard that Iron Horse had such success with. Hall now owns it, but this 100% Cab is a letdown. It's lean, austere, severely dry, and tannic, with herbaceous, tobacco flavors that only suggest fruit. **82** —*S.H. (11/15/2006)*

Hall 2003 Merlot (Napa Valley) $28. Very dry and somewhat tart in acids, this is a lean, austere Merlot. It shows thin flavors of cherries, with a minty, green edge. **83** —*S.H. (11/15/2006)*

Hall 2002 Merlot (Napa Valley) $28. This Merlot is a little overripe, to judge by the raisiny note that shows up in the finish, but the main core of black cherries and cocoa is delicious. The tannins are thick, soft, sweet, ripe, and easy. **86** —*S.H. (11/15/2005)*

Hall 2001 Merlot (Napa Valley) $28. Seductively good, with delicious plum and blackberry flavors dusted with cocoa and anise. It's almost candied, but crisp acidity and firm tannins lend authority and structure. Perfect with a juicy grilled steak. **90** —*S.H. (9/1/2004)*

Hall 2003 Napa River Ranch Merlot (Napa Valley) $50. Merlot has not been this winery's strong point, but this new wine from a vineyard just north of Napa city is their best yet. Resembling Carneros Merlot, it's dry and rich in acids, with cherry, plum, coffee, and spice flavors that are wrapped in firm tannins. Probably at its best now. **87** —*S.H. (12/15/2006)*

Hall 2005 Sauvignon Blanc (Napa Valley) $20. I love this wine for its acidic dryness, which is Sauvignon Blanc's first duty. The wine has a refreshing tartness, relieved by rich lime zest and green apple flavors, with a scour of grapefruit. With no oak at all, it's one classy sipper. **90** — *S.H. (11/1/2006)*

Hall 2004 Sauvignon Blanc (Napa Valley) $20. You might mistake this for one of those Marlboroughs, so rich is it in gooseberry, green hay, and lemon-and-lime flavors. The acidity isn't at New Zealand levels, but it's fine for this dry, likeable, and super-versatile wine. **86** —*S.H. (11/15/2005)*

Hall 2003 Sauvignon Blanc (Napa Valley) $20. Dry and powerful in green grass, gooseberry, and lime-grapefruit tartness, this wine really gets the taste buds juicing. It's clean and zesty in acidity. **86** —*S.H. (12/31/2004)*

HALLAUER

Hallauer 2002 Syrah (Santa Ynez Valley) $21. Roasted fruit aromas are joined by notes of tar on the nose. The palate deals creamy blueberry and vanilla flavors. One taster found it a little sweet; another indicates the unlikelihood of it lasting too long in the cellar. 350 cases produced. **87** *(9/1/2005)*

HALLCREST VINEYARDS

Hallcrest Vineyards 2001 Clos de Jeannie Red Blend (California) $15. From a historic old winery name, organically grown, and made from "a secret red blend." Tastes like a light-bodied Zin, with jammy berry flavors and soft tannins. It's a simple, fun wine. **84** —*S.H. (11/15/2003)*

HALO

HaLo 1997 Cabernet Sauvignon (Napa Valley) $125. This new Cabernet Sauvignon from Trefethen starts with plenty of fancy, toasted oak (high char to judge from the caramelized note) and ripe blackberry aromas. It turns complex, softly tannic and berry-fruity in the mouth. This wine defines style. Drinkable now, but should age classically. **93** —*S.H. (12/1/2001)*

HAMACHER

Hamacher 2000 Cuvée Forêts Diverses Chardonnay (Oregon) $25. A stellar effort from one of Oregon's brightest young stars. It's made in a soft, creamy style, with a palate-pleasing mix of semi-tropical citrus, anise, and spice. Added richness from lees contact and nice toast from the barrel complete the package. A handmade, textured, tasty, full-flavored and unusually satisfying Chardonnay. **91 Editors' Choice** —*P.G. (9/1/2003)*

Hamacher 1999 Cuvée Forêts Diverses Chardonnay (Oregon) $25. This is a very clean, well-balanced wine, with nice hints of honey but not too much, and a lightly spicy finish. **89** —*P.G. (8/1/2002)*

Hamacher 2002 Cuvée Forêts Diverses Chardonnay (Willamette Valley) $30. Hamacher is one of the founding members of the Oregon Chardonnay Alliance (ORCA), and this wine is a shining example of what heights Oregon Chardonnay can achieve. Smoky and nutty at first, it opens to reveal white peach and melon flavors that gradually supplant the oak notes. Richly textured and full-bodied, it also boasts serious length on the finish. **91** *(9/1/2006)*

Hamacher 1996 Cuvée Forêts Diverses Chardonnay (Willamette Valley) $NA. Hints of smoke and butter accent honey, pear, and apples on the nose, while toastier, grainy notes take the lead on the palate. Nicely textured in the mouth, adding hints of vanilla on the finish. Probably fading a bit; drink up. **88** *(9/1/2006)*

Hamacher 2002 Pinot Noir (Willamette Valley) $40. The best since the 1995, this is a big, round, supple wine loaded with black cherry and plum flavors accented by hints of mint and cola. Despite its size, it's harmonious and balanced, featuring a long, richly textured finish. **92 Editors' Choice** *(9/1/2006)*

Hamacher 2001 Pinot Noir (Willamette Valley) $30. A bit sterner than the 2002, this is a wine that needs 3-4 years to settle down and round off some rough edges. Cherry and beet aromas ease into plum and black cherry flavors. Medium-weight, with a long finish that bodes well for aging. **90** *(9/1/2006)*

Hamacher 2000 Pinot Noir (Willamette Valley) $38. Fresh, forward scents of strawberry, berry, and cherry jam are nicely played against flavors of chocolate, vanilla bean, and even a hint of tea. This is sophisticated, artful winemaking, showing a skillful hand at the tiller. Delicious for near-term enjoyment. **90** —*P.G. (3/11/2003)*

Hamacher 2000 Pinot Noir (Willamette Valley) $NA. One of the more evolved examples, Hamacher's 2000 Pinot Noir should be consumed over the next year or two, although it's possible other bottles may show differently (Hamacher felt there was something "off" with this bottle). Complex cherry, sous bois, and mushroom notes finish on a drying note. **88** *(9/1/2006)*

Hamacher 1999 Pinot Noir (Willamette Valley) $NA. Elegantly combines notes of black-cherries, peppery herbs and smoke on the nose, then smoothly glides into a supple, medium-weight palate. Still shows a bit of tannin on the finish. Drink or hold. **90** *(9/1/2006)*

Hamacher 1998 Pinot Noir (Willamette Valley) $NA. Simultaneously fuller and crisper than the seamless '99, this may be one to hold a little while yet. A bit subdued on the nose relative to other vintages, but packs in plenty of fresh fruit flavors. **90** *(9/1/2006)*

Hamacher 1997 Pinot Noir (Willamette Valley) $NA. Slightly lean and beginning to dry out, but this is still a silky, harmonious glass of mature Pinot Noir, featuring hints of mushroom, dried spices, and tobacco. Drink up. **87** *(9/1/2006)*

Hamacher 1996 Pinot Noir (Willamette Valley) $NA. From another tough vintage, this wine has held up well, still showing some berry-scented fruit to go with spice and mushroom flavors. Drink now. **89** *(9/1/2006)*

Hamacher 1995 Pinot Noir (Willamette Valley) $NA. Fully mature and possessed of a wonderfully silky texture, lucky owners of this wine should drink it up at their next special occasion. Shows great complexity, marrying hints of mint, underbrush, and beets with maraschino cherries and citrus. Drink now. **92** *(9/1/2006)*

Hamacher "2004 H Pinot Noir (Willamette Valley) $20. The winery's second label, the "H," is a medium-bodied, moderately-priced offering with solid fruit and good color. Its tannins are substantial, thick, and chewy, and the fruit hints at, but doesn't quite reach, cherry liqueur flavors. For the price, there's a lot of meat on its bones. **86** —*P.G. (12/1/2006)*

Hamacher 1997 Willamette Valley Pinot Noir (Willamette Valley) $30. 91 *(10/1/1999)*

HAMES VALLEY VINEYARDS

Hames Valley Vineyards 2001 Cabernet Franc (Monterey) $19. The black cherry, cassis, and mocha flavors are wrapped in sturdy tannins, and the finish is dry and puckery. Might soften in a year or two. **84** —*S.H. (10/1/2004)*

Hames Valley Vineyards 2001 Cabernet Sauvignon (Monterey) $19. There are some good black currant, and blackberry flavors here, although the tannins are quite tough and dry. They leave a puckery, hard feeling through the finish. **84** —*S.H. (10/1/2004)*

Hames Valley Vineyards 2001 Merlot (Monterey) $19. Herbal and dry, with astringent tannins. Partially relieved by modest blackberry and cherry flavors. Try aging for a year or so. **84** —*S.H. (10/1/2004)*

Hames Valley Vineyards 2003 Sauvignon Blanc (Monterey) $15. Heavy and full-bodied, with citrus, currant, and herb flavors. Finishes very dry, with a scour of acidity. **84** —*S.H. (10/1/2004)*

Hames Valley Vineyards 2000 Syrah (Monterey) $25. Enjoy this Syrah for its easy drinkability. It's full-bodied and dry, with berry, chocolate and spice flavors and an overlay of toasty oak. Has a tannic edge that will cut through fatty meats. **85** —*S.H. (6/1/2005)*

HANDLEY

Handley 1995 Blanc de Blancs Champagne Blend (Anderson Valley) $30. **86** —*S.H. (12/15/2000)*

Handley 1994 Blanc De Blancs Champagne Blend (Anderson Valley) $25. **88** —*S.H. (12/1/2000)*

Handley 1997 Brut Champagne Blend (Anderson Valley) $29. An excellent young blend of Pinot Noir and Chardonnay. Pleasant, subtle flavors of raspberries are accompanied by brisk acids and nice, scouring bubbles that cleanse the palate. The finish contains notes of bread dough and smoke. Will improve with a year or two of cellaring. **88** —*S.H. (12/1/2002)*

Handley 1996 Brut Champagne Blend (Anderson Valley) $17. A brilliant gold color, with a fine stream of beads leading to dusty, bread dough aromas scented with lime peel. It tastes very dry, with citrus flavors and a sharp bite of acidity. The scoury finish is clean and refreshing. **86** —*S.H. (12/1/2001)*

Handley 1995 Brut Champagne Blend (Anderson Valley) $25. 88 —*S.H. (12/1/2000)*

Handley 1994 Brut Champagne Blend (Anderson Valley) $25. 89 —*L.W. (12/1/1999)*

Handley 1997 Brut Rosé Champagne Blend (Anderson Valley) $28. This fragrant rosé opens with very pleasant aromas of strawberries, candied lemon peel, vanilla, and smoke. The flavors are full, with plenty of earth and yeasty notes around the berry core. It has a rich, creamy texture, like a full soft mousse. Goes down like velvet, and the whistle-clean finish has good length. **89** *(6/1/2001)*

Handley 1996 Brut Rosé Champagne Blend (Anderson Valley) $25. 92 —*S.H. (12/1/2000)*

Handley 1998 Chardonnay (Dry Creek Valley) $20. 85 *(6/1/2000)*

Handley 1997 Chardonnay (Dry Creek Valley) $16. 88 —*S.H. (10/1/1999)*

Handley 2001 Chardonnay (Anderson Valley) $16. Milla Handley's estate wine is firmer and more acidic than her Sonoma bottling. It is a racy wine that brightens the palate with a malic acid edge of mineral. The flavor profile is thoroughly tart green apple. This crisp young wine will pair well with a wide range of food. **88** —*S.H. (8/1/2003)*

Handley 2001 Chardonnay (Sonoma County) $18. Made in an earthier style. Not that there aren't exuberant flavors of apples, pears, and peaches, but they're conjoined with notes of tobacco and herbs. Not especially oaky, but the smoke and vanilla complexities are just right. **86** —*S.H. (8/1/2003)*

Handley 1999 Chardonnay (Anderson Valley) $17. Here's a tightly wound Chard with scads of acidity, so much that it seems to tingle on the tongue. The aromas and flavors are of green apples and buttered toast. Crispy clean wine, and very refreshing. **85** —*S.H. (11/15/2001)*

Handley 2003 Estate Chardonnay (Anderson Valley) $19. Handley's Anderson Valley bottling is always bright in acids, which are so nice and clean in a Chardonnay as fruity and rich as this. The flavors are a complex mélange of pineapples, peaches, and pears. **87** —*S.H. (5/1/2006)*

Handley 2000 Estate Chardonnay (Anderson Valley) $17. Classic cool-climate North Coast Chard, with well-etched flavors of green apples and pears, framed in smoky oak and oriental spices. Bright and acidic, with a long finish marked by cinnamon and honey. On the sweet side, so try with sweetish foods, like mango salsa on chicken or salmon. **86** —*S.H. (12/15/2002)*

Handley 2004 Handley Vineyard Chardonnay (Dry Creek Valley) $19. The big acidity on this wine and the citrus fruit flavors make it kind of austere and minerally. But partial new oak and sur lie aging add some richness. This is a very dry, elegant, structural Chard meant for food. Try with a firm white fish topped with a fruity salsa. **87** —*S.H. (12/15/2006)*

Handley 2003 Handley Vineyard Chardonnay (Dry Creek Valley) $18. Polished and elegant, this Chard has real complexity. Works beautifully to integrate its dry apple, peach, and pineapple flavors, oak-driven cream and crisp acids into a coherent whole. **91** —*S.H. (10/1/2005)*

Handley 2000 Handley Vineyard Chardonnay (Dry Creek Valley) $19. Made in the house style, which emphasizes leanness and varietal flavor. In this case, the flavors are of lemons and limes, very dry and tart. The sharp edges are mouthwatering. If you're looking for a big, oaky Chard, go elsewhere. **84** —*S.H. (12/15/2002)*

Handley 1999 Handley Vineyard Chardonnay (Dry Creek Valley) $19. Austere by current standards, with faint apple and peach aromas and a kiss of oak. It's very clean in the mouth, with apple flavors and bright, crisp acidity. Seems more food-friendly than some of the more over-the-top opulent Chards. **86** —*S.H. (11/15/2001)*

Handley 2004 Gewürztraminer (Anderson Valley) $16. Simple, clean, and proper, with peach, citrus, vanilla, and spice flavors and a dry finish. **83** —*S.H. (12/1/2005)*

Handley 2002 Gewürztraminer (Anderson Valley) $15. A clean, fragrant wine, just a little sweet, and filled with pretty flavors of lychee, grapefruit, peach, wildflowers, and dusky Oriental spices. Contains enough acidity for balance. **85** —*S.H. (12/31/2003)*

Handley 2001 Gewürztraminer (Anderson Valley) $15. Here's a cheerful, clean, honest wine. It's filled with sprightly lemon flavors, and is bone dry, and if there's any oak in it, it doesn't show. It's a shellfish wine, or an apéritif to get you going on a hot afternoon. **88** —*S.H. (9/1/2003)*

Handley 2000 Gewürztraminer (Anderson Valley) $14. Sprightly, with floral, grapefruit flavors and a rich honeyed streak that makes it just off-dry. Very clean, refreshing and zesty. The finish is marked by complex spice and fruit. **85** —*S.H. (11/15/2001)*

Handley 2004 Pinot Gris (Anderson Valley) $16. This is a juicy, crisp wine that has lots of citrus, wildflower, lychee, and white peach flavors. Fills the mouth with fruit, then ends on a dry, spicy finish. **85** —*S.H. (2/1/2006)*

Handley 2002 Pinot Gris (Anderson Valley) $16. This easy-drinking wine is polished and smooth, with the flavor of apples and peaches, and a spicy, peppery finish. It's pretty dry, with adequate acidity, a creamy mouthfeel, and just a hint of smoky oak. **86** —*S.H. (12/1/2003)*

Handley 2001 Pinot Gris (Anderson Valley) $16. A nice, sturdy little drinking wine, fruity and slightly sweet, and sprightly with crisp acids. Especially nice are the richly spicy notes that surround the apricot and citrus flavors. **86** —*S.H. (9/1/2003)*

Handley 2000 Pinot Gris (Anderson Valley) $16. Delightful, with peach, apple, and tangerine aromas and the most luscious honey-smoky note. On the palate, it's rich, spicy, and fruity. The most notable thing is the acidity, very high and crisp, the perfect complement to all that fruit. Treads a delicate balance between dry and just slightly sweet. **88** —*S.H. (11/15/2001)*

Handley 1999 Pinot Gris (Anderson Valley) $16. Clean, swift, and pure are some of the words that come to mind to describe this wine. Others are moderately fruity (citrus, apple), fresh (almost no oak), and sharply clean, with its high acids that are ideal with appetizers like bruschetta. Why more people haven't discovered Pinot Gris is a mystery. **87** —*S.H. (8/1/2001)*

Handley 2000 Pinot Meunier (Anderson Valley) $21. I have never understood Handley's interest in this variety as a still wine, whatever it is, because it's never produced a very interesting wine. This one is earthy, dry, and acidic, and the finish is peppery and hollow. **82** —*S.H. (12/1/2002)*

Handley 1999 Pinot Mystére Pinot Meunier (Anderson Valley) $20. Made from Pinot Meunier, which is widely planted in Champagne, this is a robust, somewhat rustic or country-style wine. This Pinot is full-bodied and packed with red and black wild-berry fruit. It's nicely dry, with soft tannins, and goes down easy. **83** —*S.H. (11/15/2001)*

Handley 2004 Pinot Noir (Mendocino County) $19. Made for early drinking, this is a simple, fairly full-bodied Pinot Noir. It's dry, with a silky texture and forward red cherry compote, cola, spice, and vanilla flavors that finish with a cocoa richness. **84** —*S.H. (7/1/2006)*

Handley 2003 Pinot Noir (Mendocino County) $16. Simple and very dry, this Pinot has cherry, coffee, and tobacco flavors and high acidity, wrapped in a silky-smooth texture. A nice lamb chop will soften and sweeten the tartness. **84** —*S.H. (3/1/2006)*

Handley 2003 Pinot Noir (Anderson Valley) $25. Quite a bit richer than Handley's Mendocino bottling, this Pinot shares the same qualities of tart acidity and extreme dryness. The flavors are of cherries, cranberries, and cola. It's lighter in body than many coastal Pinots, but elegant, silky, and balanced. **87** —*S.H. (3/1/2006)*

Handley 2002 Pinot Noir (Anderson Valley) $23. The polished cherry, blackberry, and blueberry flavors have been seasoned with coffee and sautéed mushroom, and laced with citrusy acids. Finishes dry and astringent. **86** —*S.H. (11/1/2004)*

Handley 2002 Pinot Noir (Mendocino County) $18. A nice little commune-style Pinot, with a bit of polish and complexity. The cherry and spice flavors are dry, with an edge of tannins. **85** —*S.H. (11/1/2004)*

Handley 2001 Pinot Noir (Anderson Valley) $25. This vintage the grapes got nice and ripe, and it shows in the lush cherry and black raspberry flavors. They're enriched with oak, and the bright acids and easy tannins add a firm structural component to this drinkable wine. **87** —*S.H. (4/1/2004)*

Handley 2001 Pinot Noir (Anderson Valley) $13. This is pretty lean stuff. The acids and alcohol are relieved by a trace of raspberry flavor and a tiny amount of residual sugar. There's not a lot going on, but it's ultra-clean, an okay beach wine or ham sandwich wine, and the price ain't bad. **85** —*S.H. (9/1/2003)*

Handley 2000 Pinot Noir (Anderson Valley) $25. Pronounced cinnamon shadings accent complex smoke, earth, and stable aromas that would make a Burgundian proud. On the palate, subtle Asian spice and overt chocolate accents complement the deep black-cherry fruit. The long, juicy, peppery finish has tannins to lose. Drink now–2008. **89 Editors' Choice** *(10/1/2002)*

Handley 1999 Pinot Noir (Anderson Valley) $26. Fuller-flavored and bigger-bodied than usual, this year's release is a big, juicy wine, filled with jammy berry and stone fruit, spicy flavors. It fills the mouth with opulent fruit, yet maintains a delicacy of body and silky lightness that is classic. **88** —*S.H. (7/1/2002)*

Handley 1998 Brut Rosé Pinot Noir (Anderson Valley) $29. A dry wine with a pretty copper color and delicate aromas of rasberries and cherries. Tartly elegant, this is a crisp wine that's a little rough, yet flatters with it's clean, yeasty finish. **86** —*S.H. (12/1/2001)*

Handley 2001 Estate Reserve Pinot Noir (Anderson Valley) $23. Sharp in acids, with dusty tannins and a silky texture, the fruit in this pretty wine reminds you of raspberries and red cherries, along with herbs and pepper. While not particularly complex, it's elegant and food-friendly. **89** —*S.H. (12/1/2004)*

Handley 1999 Estate Reserve Pinot Noir (Anderson Valley) $49. 82 *(10/1/2002)*

Handley 1998 Reserve Pinot Noir (Anderson Valley) $48. Another succulent wine from this producer. The cool climate produced a lightly colored, delicate wine, with spicy, raspberry, pepper, and rhubarb flavors and high acidity. Refined, dry, and elegant, it showcases its terroir. **88** —*S.H. (12/15/2001)*

Handley 2000 River Road Vineyard Pinot Noir (Santa Lucia Highlands) $21. Criticized by the panel for its slightly candied fruit and alcoholic warmth, this wine nonetheless delivers waves of voluptuous cherry flavors spiced by vanilla and toast. Turns tart on the finish. **85** *(10/1/2002)*

Handley 2003 Rosé Pinot Noir (Mendocino County) $NA. Shows its Pinot origins in the body, which is fat and firmly flavored with raspberries and tobacco. Dry and attractive, this blush wine is robust enough to enjoy with lamb chops. **85** —*S.H. (12/1/2004)*

Handley 2004 Rosé Pinot Noir (Anderson Valley) $16. Orange-pink, pretty in fruit, and bone dry, this blush wine has pleasant flavors of strawberries and raspberries, with a peppery tingle of fresh acidity. It will be nice with grilled sausage. **84** —*S.H. (12/1/2005)*

Handley 2002 Riesling (Mendocino) $12. A totally refreshing blend of citrus, apple, peach, and pear flavors, all couched in bright textured acidity. The wine makes a fine apéritif as well as a mealtime beverage. Off dry, but hardly sweet, it's crisp and fresh to the end. **87** —*J.M. (8/1/2003)*

Handley 2000 Rosé Blend (Anderson Valley) $12. A blend of Pinot Noir and Pinot Meunier, and very pale, with the faint pink color of onion-skin, it has delicate aromas of strawberry, rose petal, and vanilla. Packs quite a punch in the mouth, with upfront flavors and a soft, semi-dry creaminess. This is a highly enjoyable and very versatile wine. **87** —*S.H. (11/15/2001)*

Handley 2004 Sauvignon Blanc (Dry Creek Valley) $16. Dry and gulpable, with juicy lemon and lime, apricot, mineral, and crème brûlée flavors balanced with crisp acidity. Shows complexity in the long peppery, toasty finish. **87** —*S.H. (12/15/2006)*

Handley 2001 Ferrington Vineyard Sauvignon Blanc (Anderson Valley) $14. Bites into the palate with upfront acids, but it's not a tart wine because the fruity flavors are so fabulously rich. Lemon meringue, sweet lime, and dusty oriental spices like cinnamon are delicious. Really good wine, and addictive. **90** —*S.H. (3/1/2003)*

Handley 2000 Ferrington Vineyard Sauvignon Blanc (Anderson Valley) $15. Comes down firmly on the herbal side, opening with a blast of lemon and dill, but interventions, including barrel fermentation, soften and fatten it and add notes of butter and vanilla. In the mouth the lemony flavors return, with some residual sugar. The finish is a duet of acidity and sweetness. **86** —*S.H. (9/1/2002)*

Handley 1999 Ferrington Vineyard Sauvignon Blanc (Anderson Valley) $14. A first-ever wine from this winery, and a deliciously drinkable one that's filled with a complex range of fruit, such as peaches, pears, apples, lemons, and melon. In the mouth, it's a tad sweet, but firm acidity gives it a crisp steeliness. **88** —*S.H. (11/15/2001)*

Handley 2003 Handley Vineyard Sauvignon Blanc (Dry Creek Valley) $14. I've always been a fan of this wine, which showcases the Dry Creek terroir in an appealing way. Gobs of sweet citrus, fig, melon, and spice flavors, with crisp acids and a clean finish. **88** —*S.H. (10/1/2005)*

Handley 2002 Handley Vineyard Sauvignon Blanc (Dry Creek Valley) $15. Hews to the profile of previous vintages with its citrus, fig, herb, and green apple flavors, with hints of dried straw. The crisp acids and slight note of honey balance each other out, making it tasty and balanced as well as food-friendly. **86** —*S.H. (2/1/2004)*

Handley 2001 Handley Vineyard Sauvignon Blanc (Dry Creek Valley) $14. Classic coastal California, with its clean flavors of lemons and limes, figs, melon, and grass, and zesty acidity. Basically dry, but the fruit is so ripe and full, it's like drinking nectar. Shows the affinity between variety and appellation. **87** —*S.H. (3/1/2003)*

Handley 2000 Brut Sparkling Blend (Anderson Valley) $32. Always serviceably clean and dry, Handley's Brut is a good everyday sparkler, forward in fruit and bright in cool-climate acidity, while a little rough in texture. **84** —*S.H. (6/1/2006)*

Handley 1998 Brut Sparkling Blend (Anderson Valley) $29. Here's a nice, refreshing bubbly with lots of flavor and some elegance. The subtle strawberry and peach is balanced by notes of dough, yeast, and smoke, backed by firm acids. Feels a bit rough at first, but has a clean, rich finish. A blend of 70% Pinot Noir and 30% Chardonnay. **89** —*S.H. (12/1/2003)*

Handley 2003 Syrah (Mendocino County) $20. Plays it right down the middle, an everyday sort of wine that's good enough for white table-cloths but doesn't shake off its rustic personality. It's nicely dry and rich in the sort of tannins that will cut through big meats and cheeses. 85 — S.H. (7/1/2006)

Handley 2002 Syrah (Mendocino County) $20. Starts with interesting aromas of seared meat, blackberries, and oak, and immediately turns rather tannic and sharp in the mouth. There's some nice purple stone fruit, and the finish is bone dry. 85 —S.H. (2/1/2005)

Handley 2003 Zinfandel (Mendocino County) $20. Simple and rustic, this Zin has high alcohol, which may account for the hotly sweet mouthfeel that tastes and feels like cherries and blackberries dripped in chili-pepper sauce. It'll be fine with barbecued chicken and ribs. 84 —S.H. (7/1/2006)

Handley 2002 Zinfandel (Redwood Valley) $20. This easy, soft Zin gives lots of pleasure. It features berry, candied Lifesaver and spicy flavors, with gentle tannins lasting into a long finish. 86 —S.H. (2/1/2005)

Handley 2001 Zinfandel (Redwood Valley) $20. From inland Mendocino, where daytime high temperatures are balanced by chilly nights, a wine of exuberant, even flamboyant, berry and stone fruit flavors and ideal acids. Thankfully, it's totally dry. It's young and precocious, and needs a year or two to come together, but is fine now with rich foods. 86 —S.H. (3/1/2004)

Handley 2000 Williams Vineyard Zinfandel (Anderson Valley) $26. There's something untamed in this wine. Sturdy and strong, with ripe forest berry flavors and woody notes, it's richly textured, with the feel of a fine wine. A few sweet, raisiny notes mar the finish. 86 —S.H. (5/1/2002)

HANGTIME

Hangtime 2003 Chardonnay (Edna Valley) $15. On the soft and sweet side, with the flavor of extremely ripe white peaches drizzled with vanilla, caramel and buttercream. What this New World Chard lacks in complexity it makes up for in sheer, lip-smacking deliciousness. 85 —S.H. (7/1/2006)

HANNA

Hanna 2001 Two Ranch Red Wine Cabernet Blend (Sonoma County) $22. This rather tough wine hits you with tannins and a thick, chocolatey texture that could use more acidity. It has black currant and oak flavors. Can't quite overcome its rusticity. 84 —S.H. (8/1/2005)

Hanna 1996 Cabernet Sauvignon (Sonoma County) $21. 90 (11/15/1999)

Hanna 2000 Cabernet Sauvignon (Alexander Valley) $26. This medium-weight wine offers cassis, bacon and olive on the nose, with herb notes and flavors of currants, black-cherries and plums. Finishes oaky, with touches of chocolate and coffee, soft tannins, and low acidity. 86 (11/15/2003)

Hanna 1999 Cabernet Sauvignon (Alexander Valley) $25. There's something ponderous about this wine. Yes, it makes all the right moves, from the ripe black currant fruit, the dusty tannins, and the overlay of smoky oak, although it's kind of soft. But there's a heaviness that's hard to ignore. 86 —S.H. (6/1/2002)

Hanna 1998 Cabernet Sauvignon (Alexander Valley) $24. Starts off with smoke and black cherry aromas, then settles down on the palate with a smooth blend of black currant, tar, chocolate, and a strong herbal component. Firm, but ripe tannins give good structure. 88 —J.M. (6/1/2002)

Hanna 2001 Bismark Mountain Vineyard Cabernet Sauvignon (Sonoma Valley) $61. From one of the highest vineyards in Sonoma County, this is a tannic wine, although the tannins, in the modern style, are soft and intricate. It's oaky, soft, and quite extracted, with a black currant syrup mouthfeel. 85 —S.H. (11/1/2005)

Hanna 2002 Estate Grown Cabernet Sauvignon (Sonoma County) $31. This is a decent, everyday red wine. It's sharp and dry, with blackberry flavors and a hit of winey acidity that calls for meat or cheese. 84 —S.H. (10/1/2005)

Hanna 2001 Estate Grown Cabernet Sauvignon (Sonoma County) $27. A bit soft and herbal, with hints of tobacco, dried herbs, cherries, and leather, and dry, easy tannins. That makes it sound like a classic Cab from this Sonoma County appellation. It's easy to drink, but that doesn't mean it doesn't possess some interesting complexities. 88 —S.H. (6/1/2004)

Hanna 1998 Hanna Red Ranch Reserve Cabernet Sauvignon (Alexander Valley) $48. Black currants and berries. Olives and chocolate. Dry. Lavish smoky oak. Dusty, refined tannins. Velvety smooth mouthfeel. Good stuff, but it could use more life. Higher acidity would help. We're supposed to rate regardless of price but sticker shock is a fact of life. This is good but not great wine, and seriously overpriced. 87 —S.H. (6/1/2002)

Hanna 2003 Proprietor Grown Cabernet Sauvignon (Sonoma County) $30. Made from Alexander Valley and Mayacamas Mountain fruit, this is a fairly complex Cab, rich in fruit and tannins, dry and soft. It has lovely blackberry and black cherry fruit, modestly accented by oak. 87 —S.H. (3/1/2006)

Hanna 2004 Chardonnay (Russian River Valley) $19. Ripe, rich, and frankly delicious, this well-oaked Chard shows cool-climate acidity. The peach and pear flavors mesh perfectly with the vanilla and buttered toast from the barrels, creating a lush, complex wine. 88 —S.H. (3/1/2006)

Hanna 2001 Chardonnay (Russian River Valley) $18. Smells great, with just the right mix of upfront green apples and the spicy vanillins of smoky oak. Enters the palate with apple and peach flavors and a rich, creamy texture that has extra weight from lees aging. This friendly, polished Chard is as good as many more expensive ones. 87 —S.H. (12/1/2003)

Hanna 2000 Chardonnay (Russian River Valley) $19. Very ripe and spicy, the fruit dominates all other aspects. Peaches and cream flavors are rich and delicious, while oak contributes spice, sweetness and smoke. A long, semi-sweet finish adds interest. This is a crowd-pleasing Chardonnay made to appeal to the widest possible audience. 87 —S.H. (5/1/2002)

Hanna 2002 Estate Grown Chardonnay (Russian River Valley) $18. Here's a crowd pleaser, with its ripe, almost tropical fruit flavors that burst beyond peaches and pears into papaya and an overlay of smoky oak. Mouthfeel is creamy; it's a complex sipper, and clean as a whistle. 89 — S.H. (6/1/2004)

Hanna 1998 Proprietor Grown Chardonnay (Russian River Valley) $17. 85 (6/1/2000)

Hanna 1999 Merlot (Alexander Valley) $25. The wine is rich, from its dark color through the olive, chocolate, and plum aromas to the thick, fruity mouthfeel. It's also more tannic than many bottles now on the market. You can solve that by drinking it with big foods like roasts. This substantial wine won't age, though, so consume in the next few years. 88 —S.H. (9/1/2002)

Hanna 1999 Bismark Ranch Merlot (Sonoma County) $50. There's lots of creamy, milk-chocolatey goodness packed into this wine, softly cushioning cherry and plum fruit. It's soft, supple, and surprisingly light on its feet for a wine that tips the scales at 14.5% alcohol. 88 (5/1/2004)

Hanna 1997 Proprietor Grown Merlot (Sonoma County) $22. Aromas of toast and cedar blend in a little mint over black cherries. This wine has pretty flavors of cherries, cedar, bitter chocolate, and tea, but possesses a certain austerity and restraint. Finishes with some dry tannins; you could age this wine, but you'd be taking a chance—much better to enjoy it now. 84 —J.C. (6/1/2001)

Hanna 1999 Pinot Noir (Russian River Valley) $22. Starts with an odd aroma of baked, almost burnt pie dough, which is hard to ignore. Thankfully, the flavors are better. Red berries and peppery spices are framed in a lightly tannic, softly acidic, dry wine meant for immediate consumption. It's pretty nice drinking, except for that smell. 85 —S.H. (5/1/2002)

Hanna 2004 Estate Pinot Noir (Russian River Valley) $29. Lots of toast, char, and caramel in the aromas, then it turns somewhat heavy and soft, with stewed fruit and espresso flavors. This wine seems to have suffered from the heat. 84 —S.H. (12/1/2006)

Hanna 2002 Estate Grown Pinot Noir (Russian River Valley) $27. Starts off very oaky, with underlying notes of strawberries, cherries, and earthy mushrooms. Tasters liked its delicate body, creamy texture, and elegant finish. **85** *(11/1/2004)*

Hanna 1999 Bismark Ranch Sangiovese (Sonoma County) $50. Deep, stewy red-berry and brown sugar notes get a little heat (and a little currant) on the nose; in the mouth, it's got similar red-berry and toasty notes, and a creamy, velvety texture. Wants a little more acid to balance the vanillin fullness, but it's sexy nonetheless. Has the same extracted-fruit quality as Hanna's other Bismark Ranch offerings, with a percent or two less alcohol. **91** —*D.T. (6/1/2002)*

Hanna 1998 Sauvignon Blanc (Russian River Valley) $12.85 —*S.H. (11/1/1999)*

Hanna 2004 Sauvignon Blanc (Russian River Valley) $17. An odd wine that started with stubborn sulfur that was slow to blow off, then turns too sweet and still seems to be fizzy with fermentation. Impossible to recommend. **81** —*S.H. (11/1/2005)*

Hanna 1999 Reserve Sauvignon Blanc (Russian River Valley) $24. Starts off with a real blast of grass, hay, anise, and other aggressive notes, with just a hint of softer melon. It's pretty powerful in the mouth, too. Citrus flavors are spicy and penetrating in this dry, structured wine. It has an extra dimension of complexity and elegance that make it a fine dinner wine. **88** —*S.H. (9/1/2002)*

Hanna 2005 Slusser Road Vineyard Sauvignon Blanc (Russian River Valley) $17. From a cool part of the appellation comes this dry, potent wine, rich in gooseberry, pink grapefruit, fig, and lemongrass aromas. Zesty, citrusy acidity makes this fruit-forward wine perfect with a salad of mixed bitter greens, chevre, toasted walnuts, and a creamy raspberry vinaigrette. **88** —*S.H. (7/1/2006)*

Hanna 2002 Slusser Road Vineyard Sauvignon Blanc (Russian River Valley) $16. Starts off with a grassy aroma that makes you think it's going to be very dry and tart, but surprise, it quickly turns rich and honeyed, with spearminty, tropical fruit flavors. Nonetheless the varietal's citrusy acids make it a vibrant, yummy choice. **87** —*S.H. (6/1/2004)*

Hanna 2001 Slusser Road Vineyard Sauvignon Blanc (Russian River Valley) $16. Too much sugar has been left in this wine, so that it tastes almost sweet. A pity, because underneath, it's a richly fruity wine, with spearmint, apple, and citrus flavors and brisk acidity. It would be much better if it was fully dry. **85** —*S.H. (9/1/2003)*

Hanna 2000 Slusser Road Vineyard Sauvignon Blanc (Russian River Valley) $16. Bright and refreshing, this Russian River Valley wine is redolent of passion fruit, citrus, and melon. A vivacious example of the varietal, it is light and crisp to the end. **88** —*J.M. (11/15/2001)*

Hanna 1999 Bismark Ranch Syrah (Sonoma Valley) $48. A disappointing wine that opens with starkly unripe, vegetal aromas and never quite overcomes its tough herbaceousness. It's very dry, with rasping tannins and an astringent finish. Tasted twice. **82** —*S.H. (8/1/2005)*

Hanna 2002 Bismark Mountain Vineyard Zinfandel (Sonoma Valley) $51. There's so much heat in this 16% alcohol Zin. Granted, it's fully dry, with a smooth, voluptuous texture, and quite delicious in berry and mocha fruit flavors. Classic Zin in its own right, but oh, that alcohol! **86** —*S.H. (7/1/2006)*

Hanna 1999 Bismark Ranch Zinfandel (Sonoma Valley) $49. 92 —*S.H. (7/1/2002)*

Hanna 1997 Bismark Ranch Zinfandel (Sonoma Valley) $45. Big, ripe, chocolatey wine, with lots of forward, smooth, oaky flavors. Easy to like, with a plush, creamy mouthfeel, and tons of new oak flavor. **88** —*P.G. (3/1/2001)*

Hanna 2003 Proprietor Grown Zinfandel (Alexander Valley) $20. Well, the grapes baked a bit under the sun during this hot vintage, and the wine has some smoky, pie-crust flavors. But that's Zin for you, and the core flavors of black currants and chocolate are rich and delicious. **86** —*S.H. (11/1/2005)*

Hanna 2001 Proprietor Grown Zinfandel (Alexander Valley) $46. A rich, jammy style that shows off hints of spice, black cherry, blackberry, coffee, chocolate, and herb flavors. Licorice dominates the finish, which is slightly astringent but with good length. **89** —*J.M. (11/1/2003)*

HANZELL

Hanzell 2003 Chardonnay (Sonoma Valley) $65. For decades Hanzell has been making one of California's most (and only) ageworthy Chards. The '03 is one for the cellar, but it comes at the price of being hard in youth. Starts out flinty and tannic, although as it airs, new oak and pineapple emerge. This seems like a very good Hanzell. Best 2009–2015. **92** —*S.H. (11/15/2006)*

Hanzell 2002 Chardonnay (Sonoma Valley) $55. I have tasted a number of bottle-aged Hanzell Chardonnays, and when properly cellared from a good vintage, they are totally amazing. This is likely to be such a wine, but right now, it's tight, tart, and earthy, with hints of peach. It's not a mind blower, but is a Chard for those serious about their cellars. Best after 2010. **90 Cellar Selection** —*S.H. (12/15/2005)*

Hanzell 2001 Chardonnay (Sonoma Valley) $55. A fabulous and exciting Chard. It's a big wine, with powerful pear, tropical fruit, and oriental spice flavors, and well oaked. But it's balanced with clean acidity, and feels elegant all the way through. This is a wine with a history of aging well. Drink now, but will hold and improve for at least ten years. **94** —*S.H. (12/31/2004)*

Hanzell 1999 Chardonnay (Sonoma Valley) $50. The first California winery to create an oak-aged, Burgundian-style Chardonnay, Hanzell's been producing rich, creamy Chards for almost 50 years. This wine continues the tradition. Peach, hazelnut, and crème brûlée notes, considerable acidity, and great focus on the palate. This is a wine with a history of aging well. **93** —*S.H. (9/1/2002)*

Hanzell 1997 Chardonnay (Sonoma Valley) $42. 92 —*S.H. (11/15/2000)*

Hanzell 2002 Pinot Noir (Sonoma Valley) $85. The harvest heat seems like it made things tough for Hanzell. The tannins kind of step on the wine's generosity, making it dry and edgy. Troublesome, too, is a touch of raisin. Still, Hanzell Pinots develop well over time, and can surprise. Decant, or try after 2007. **88** —*S.H. (11/15/2006)*

Hanzell 2001 Pinot Noir (Sonoma Valley) $85. At four years of age, this Pinot is just hitting its stride. It has a youthful side in the still fresh cherry and raspberry fruit and vibrant acidity. But it's turning mellow, as the oak melts into the alcohol, lending a soft, creamy infusion of vanilla bean. It's so good now, it will be hard to keep your hands off it, but it should hold for another three to five years. **95 Editors' Choice** —*S.H. (12/15/2005)*

Hanzell 2000 Pinot Noir (Sonoma Valley) $75. The acids hit you first. They perk up a creamy wine with pleasant flavors of cherries, cola, mocha, and spice. It's dry and balanced. The impression is of a lovely Pinot that combines delicacy and elegance with power. Drink now and over the next four years. **90** —*S.H. (2/1/2005)*

Hanzell 1998 Pinot Noir (Sonoma Valley) $58. This vintage just can't compare to the exquisite '97. It shares the house style of balance, elegance, and harmony. Everything that winemaking could contribute, it has. But Mother Nature rules. This year, the concentration is lacking. **87** —*S.H. (2/1/2003)*

Hanzell 1997 Pinot Noir (Sonoma Valley) $50. Irresistible aromas of blackberries, dark chocolate, kid leather, and smoky oak are pure pleasure. In the mouth, there's great depth of flavor, with juicy plum, pepper, and dark berry notes. The sappy, silky-smooth texture is classic Pinot, while a long, rich, spicy finish indicates a long life ahead for this balanced, wonderful wine. **94 Cellar Selection** —*S.H. (12/15/2001)*

HARBINGER

Harbinger 2002 Chardonnay (Napa Valley) $14. Nice and fruity, with peach, pear, and tropical fruit flavors and an edge of smoky oak. Has a rich, creamy texture boosted by a streak of acidity. **85** —*S.H. (2/1/2004)*

Harbinger 2001 Merlot (Napa Valley) $14. There's lots of plummy richness in this dry, smooth red wine. It also has inviting flavors of cassis, mocha, and cherry, and is finished with oak-barrel notes of spicy vanilla and toast. Acids and tannins show up on the finish. **86** —*S.H. (5/1/2004)*

HARGRAVE

Hargrave 1999 Cabernet Franc (North Fork of Long Island) $17. Now called Castello di Borghese, this winery was still using the Hargrave brand for the 1999 vintage. Light and weedy, with hints of green beans and cherry cough syrup. **81** —*J.C. (1/1/2004)*

Hargrave 1999 Chardonnay (North Fork of Long Island) $14. Despite the winery's rechristening as Castello di Borghese, this is the Hargrave label, which was used for the 1999 vintage. Pear-nectar and clove aromas and flavors turn slightly appley, then lemony on the abbreviated finish. **83** —*J.C. (1/1/2004)*

Hargrave 1998 Chardonnay (North Fork of Long Island) $14. This wine shows some of the less appealing aspects of American oak: overt spice and vanilla flavors and a slick, oily mouthfeel. **82** —*J.C. (4/1/2001)*

Hargrave NV Chardonette/White Blend Chardonnay (North Fork of Long Island) $7. A blended white, but predominantly—you guessed it—Chardonnay. The soft, sweet pear aromas and flavors are simple and clean, making this a decent quaffer on a hot summer day. **83** —*J.C. (4/1/2001)*

Hargrave 1998 Reserve Chardonnay (North Fork of Long Island) $18. What a difference from Borghese's regular Chardonnay. This one is loaded with class and refinement, from the delicate aromas of light toast, pear and hazelnut through the nearly weightless palate that somehow carries a great deal of flavor. **88** —*J.C. (4/1/2001)*

Hargrave 1999 Merlot (North Fork of Long Island) $18. Starts off okay, with black cherries and caramel, but with air, a sour pine-resin note takes over the aromas and flavors. Finishes with more caramel and some dusty cranberries. **81** —*J.C. (1/1/2004)*

Hargrave 1998 Merlot (North Fork of Long Island) $18. Strong mint and menthol aromatics give way to intense fresh-cut cedar flavors. There's just too much wood for this woodchuck to chuck. **82** —*J.C. (4/1/2001)*

Hargrave 1998 Pinot Noir (North Fork of Long Island) $35. The dominant aromas are smoke, toast, and cinnamon, which ride over tart-cherry fruit. Turns quite stemmy and tough on the finish. Drink young, with a piece of rare beef to help tame the tannins. **84** —*J.C. (4/1/2001)*

Hargrave NV Fleurette Rosé Blend (North Fork of Long Island) $10. A light-weight Pinot that's actually marketed as a rosé, this wine nevertheless manages to pack in decent flavors of apple skin, red berries, and cinnamon, capped off by some leathery, meaty notes. **83** —*J.C. (4/1/2001)*

Hargrave 1999 Sauvignon Blanc (North Fork of Long Island) $11. Picked quite ripe, the resulting wine features mainly melon and fig aromas and flavors, with very little grassiness in evidence. Crisp acidity on the finish provides the vivacity needed to pair with oysters or clams. **85** —*J.C. (4/1/2001)*

HARLAN ESTATE

Harlan Estate 2002 Cabernet Blend (Napa Valley) $245. The aroma is deep and inviting, equal parts new oak, Cabernet fruit and dried herbs. Has tremendous weight, with red and black cherry, cola, chocolate, cassis, and roasted coconut flavors. Brilliant now, virtually flawless and totally delicious, yet has the impeccable balance to age and even improve over the years. The listed price is its pre-release price. Drink now through at least 2020. **99 Cellar Selection** —*S.H. (9/1/2006)*

Harlan Estate 2000 Cabernet Sauvignon (Napa Valley) $300. A stupendous wine that epitomizes the Harlan style of grace and power. Shows how the most elaborate vineyard and winery practices can contribute to a near-perfect wine, even in a less heralded vintage. The flavors cascade in endless tiers, black currant, cherry, mocha, Indian pudding, oak, and spice, all coming together in a minute-long finish. Magnificent. **98 Cellar Selection** —*S.H. (11/15/2004)*

Harlan Estate 1999 Red Blend (Napa Valley) $200. An exceptional wine. Fragrant, with plenty of plum, black cherry, cedar, and spice aromas. On the palate, it's silky smooth, elegant, and fresh, yet packed with complex layers of blackberry, cassis, chocolate, coffee, anise, sage, thyme, and cherry flavors. Marked by an exquisite textural elegance and harmonious balance, it displays a fine blend of firm, supple tannins and appropriate acidty that support great length on the finish. **96** —*J.M. (7/1/2003)*

HARLEQUIN

Harlequin 2003 Minick Vineyard Syrah (Yakima Valley) $28. Done in an Australian Shiraz style, like the McCrea Boushey Grande Cote. It's big,

lush, and ripe (14.6% alcohol) and fashioned in a surefire, consumer-pleasing style. Lush, sweet fruit brings on the heat in the finish, but what flavor! **91** —*P.G. (12/15/2005)*

Harlequin 2003 Sundance Vineyard Syrah (Columbia Valley (WA)) $28. A north-facing vineyard gives grapes extended hang time and moderates the high Wahluke heat. It's 100% Syrah, 30% whole cluster fermented in 20% new French oak. Good, juicy, with very tart, snappy cranberry/raspberry flavors. Lovely nuances of wet earth, black tea, and soy. A substantial, ageworthy effort. **91** —*P.G. (12/15/2005)*

Harlequin 2002 Sundance Vineyard Syrah (Columbia Valley (WA)) $30. Features a slightly lifted, floral nose, filled with candied berries and spice. Raspberry and strawberry flavors on the midpalate lack a bit of depth but finish with a charming vanilla flourish. **85** *(9/1/2005)*

HARLOW RIDGE

Harlow Ridge 2003 Coastal Vines Cabernet Sauvignon (Lodi) $10. From the winery formerly known as Napa Ridge comes this modestly priced Cab. It's nicely ripe in all kinds of luscious blackberry, cherry, and cocoa flavors, and although it's from the hot region of Lodi, somehow it manages to have crisp acidity. **84** —*S.H. (12/15/2006)*

Harlow Ridge 2005 Chardonnay (Lodi) $10. Simple, with canned peach and apricot flavors and a slightly sweet finish. **83** —*S.H. (12/1/2006)*

Harlow Ridge 2005 Pinot Grigio (Lodi) $10. Balanced and polished, this easy-drinking PG shows the fruit and zest that are driving the variety's popularity. Crisp acidity offsets ripe pineapple, peach, fig, and honeysuckle flavors that finish just a little sweet but very clean. **85 Best Buy** —*S.H. (12/15/2006)*

Harlow Ridge 2005 Pinot Noir (Lodi) $10. Simple and dry. An acidic wine with thin flavors of cherries, strawberries, and greener, minty notes. **83** —*S.H. (12/1/2006)*

HARMONIQUE

Harmonique 2002 Delicacé Pinot Noir (Anderson Valley) $48. Of Harmonique's two Pinots, this is the more "Burgundian." It's paler in color and ineffably silky, with a mélange of cherry, cola, beetroot, and tobacco flavors, and a nice mushroomy earthiness. Could develop for a few more years. **90** —*S.H. (11/1/2005)*

Harmonique 2002 The Noble One Pinot Noir (Anderson Valley) $48. Harmonique has released two '02 Pinots from Anderson Valley and they display how the terroir varies. This one, from a cooler site, is the darker, more full-bodied. It's exceptionally rich in cherry jam flavors, yet delicate and silky. **92** —*S.H. (11/1/2005)*

HARMONY CELLARS

Harmony Cellars 2002 Diamond Reserve Aria Cabernet Blend (Paso Robles) $38. Softly tannic and far too sweet for a dry table wine, this Bordeaux blend pushes its cherry, blackberry, chocolate, and coffee flavors almost into dessert territory. **80** —*S.H. (7/1/2006)*

Harmony Cellars 2003 Merlot (Paso Robles) $16. Simple and a little hot, with baked cherry pie and raisin flavors, this country-style wine finishes dry, with an espresso bitterness. **82** —*S.H. (10/1/2006)*

Harmony Cellars 2004 Diamond Reserve Pinot Gris (California) $22. This harsh, unbalanced wine tastes burnt and raisiny, with a medicinal finish. **80** —*S.H. (2/1/2006)*

Harmony Cellars 2002 Zinfandel (Paso Robles) $18. Tough, bone dry and gritty in tannins, with astringent berry skin flavors and a hint of leather and raisins on the finish. Drink now. **84** —*S.H. (8/1/2005)*

Harmony Cellars 2001 Zinfandel (Paso Robles) $16. Tea-like at its core, the wine offers simple, bright cherry flavors on the follow-up, finishing short. **81** *(11/1/2003)*

HARRINGTON

Harrington 2002 Hirsch Vineyard Pinot Noir (Sonoma Coast) $54. A lovely wine, pale in color and delicate as silk. It's dry and crisp in acids, with a wonderful array of red cherry, cola, candied ginger, rosehip tea, vanilla, spice, and smoky oak flavors. Feels light as a feather on the palate, yet lingers long and rich on the finish. **93** —*S.H. (8/1/2005)*

HARRIS

Harris 2003 Jake's Creek Vineyard Cabernet Sauvignon (Napa Valley) $75. I preferred this to Harris's more expensive Treva's Cab because it's not as tannic, offering more immediate pleasure in an opulent, classy way. Soft and charming, yet with an intense structure, the wine is beautiful in blackberry, cherry, anise, green olive, and vanilla oak flavors that finish complex and dry. Best now through 2010 for its lush fruit. **93** —*S.H.* *(12/31/2006)*

Harris 2003 Treva's Vineyard Cabernet Sauvignon (Napa Valley) $95. Very fine, but tough at this time, a Cabernet that needs serious cellar time. Is it an ager? Pretty guaranteed, to judge by the big, ripe, lockdown tannins, the savory acids, and the core of sweet, sap-rich black currants. Lots of sweet new oak, too, but a wine of this size needs it. Best 2010–2015. **91 Cellar Selection** —*S.H.* *(12/31/2006)*

HARRISON

Harrison 2001 Estate Reserve Cabernet Sauvignon (Napa Valley) $80. You'll want to cellar this wine. The tannins roadblock everything, leaving behind a hard astringency. Fortunately there's rich currant and blackberry fruit, but it needs at least until 2010 to express itself, and could easily hold twice as long. **91 Cellar Selection** —*S.H.* *(10/1/2004)*

Harrison 1999 Reserve Cabernet Sauvignon (Napa Valley) $100. Another huge '99. It is very dark and lavishly oaked, aged in 100% new French barrels. The immediate aroma is of vanilla and toast, while the palate experience is of oak and dry tannins that numb the palate through the finish. There is a core of blackberry fruit that is solid and dense, the result of very low yields. This pricy wine is not drinkable now, unless you're not fussy. If you buy it, plan on aging for at least five years. **91** —*S.H.* *(11/15/2003)*

Harrison 1997 Reserve Cabernet Sauvignon (Napa Valley) $100. 94 *(11/1/2000)*

Harrison 2000 Reserve Chardonnay (Napa Valley) $45. Harrison seems to have put as much oak on their Chard as they do on their Cabernets. Opens with the powerful perfume of toasted wood, wood sap, caramel, and vanilla cookie. Far below is a good wine with citrusy, appley fruit and good acidity. **85** —*S.H.* *(8/1/2004)*

Harrison 1998 Reserve Chardonnay (Napa Valley) $59. Butter and vanilla wrap around tropical fruit and citrus flavors on the full nose. Baked apples, crème caramel and abundant new oak merge to provide this chard with a slightly viscous, buttery texture. Its rich butter and oak may be a bit too much for some. The tangy finish is long and tasty. **90** *(7/1/2001)*

Harrison 2001 Merlot (Napa Valley) $40. A brilliant Merlot that excites for the way it straddles the line between ultraripe fruit and more subtle, earthy tones. The taste of perfectly ripened cherries is sweet and pure, and mingles with plums, peppery spice and green olives. The oak is heavy, but this wine loves it. Finally, the tannins are fabulously sweet and rich. **93** —*S.H.* *(8/1/2004)*

Harrison 2000 Merlot (Napa Valley) $40. From Carneros, a dark, young, meaty wine that's almost a meal in a bottle. What you get is a potpourri of cherry, mushroom, meat, sundried tomato, anise, and dill, with accents of smoky oak. Drinks long and smooth in the mouth, although there's a little place in the middle palate that's hollow, and tough tannins kick in on the finish. **90** —*S.H.* *(12/31/2003)*

Harrison 2001 Claret Red Blend (Napa Valley) $37. Olives, oak, cassis, and cocoa star in the aroma. Turns a bit tough in the mouth, with cherry, blackberry and earthy flavors. The tannins and sweet fruit in the finish suggest age worthiness. Important to decant well in advance if you drink it now. **89** —*S.H.* *(3/1/2005)*

Harrison 2000 Claret Red Blend (Napa Valley) $37. A dark wine that opens with earthy aromas of wild forest berries, grilled meat, and anise and other herbs, and turns fruity and earthy in the mouth. It is very dry, with rich currant and berry flavors, and a rich overlay of oak. **89** —*S.H.* *(11/15/2003)*

Harrison 2001 Syrah (Napa Valley) $33. The Northern Rhône is the model here. Opens with a burst of white pepper and blackberry flavors, well oaked, and turns rich, big and long in the mouth, with powerful blackberry, cherry, and oak flavors. The tannins are pronounced and negotiable. Probably best now. **91** —*S.H.* *(3/1/2005)*

Harrison 2001 Zebra Zinfandel (North Coast) $23. Serves up sweet fruit on the nose, with cherry, black plum, berry, and toast flavors framed in smooth-textured tannins. The wine shows a measure of elegance. Moderate length on the finish. **88** *(11/1/2003)*

HART WINERY

Hart Winery 2002 Syrah (South Coast) $24. One of the most pleasant surprises of this tasting was how well the wines from Hart, a small winery located in Temecula, performed. This effort boasts wonderfully complex aromas of cedar, bacon fat, and cherries, round, mouthfilling flavors and a long, crisp finish. **89** *(9/1/2005)*

Hart Winery 1999 Syrah (Temecula) $24. An amazing wine, with an impenetrable color, that begins with a burst of freshly ground black pepper sprinkled over blackberries, blueberries, and rum-soaked plums, and rich scents of grilled, smoked meat. The flavors are dramatic and bold, all cherries, berries, chocolate, and spices that change with every swirl. This dry, richly balanced wine is sheer heaven. **94** —*S.H.* *(4/1/2002)*

Hart Winery 1998 Syrah (Temecula) $24. Aromas of black pepper and smoke, along with creamy raspberries indicate promise, but the barrel regime takes over on the palate, where caramelized wood continues through the finish as burnt coffee. **85** *(11/1/2001)*

Hart Winery 2002 Volcanic Ridge Vineyard Syrah (Temecula) $32. This is a big, burly Syrah (15.4% alcohol) that just manages to hold onto a sense of balance. Black pepper and meaty aromas burst from the glass, followed by earthy, spicy notes and layers of rich plum and blackberry fruit. Chewy tannins mark the finish, but don't be deceived into thinking that means this wine will age. It might, but it might be better in its rambunctious youth. **90 Editors' Choice** *(9/1/2005)*

HARTFORD

Hartford 2004 Chardonnay (Sonoma Coast) $25. Part of the Jess Jackson empire of wineries, Hartford has a stellar record over the years across everything it produces, and this Chardonnay doesn't disappoint. It's bone dry and high in acidity, with a stony minerality that frames controlled peach, pear, and mango fruit. The wine has that hard-to-define quality of elegant class. **92 Editors' Choice** —*S.H.* *(5/1/2006)*

Hartford 2000 Chardonnay (Sonoma Coast) $22. A blend of lots that didn't make it into the single-vineyard Chardonnays, the Sonoma Coast bottling offers a representative introduction to the Hartford Chardonnay style. Oily-textured melons and peaches are framed by toasty, nutty, buttery accents. **90** *(7/1/2002)*

Hartford 2000 Laura's Chardonnay (Sonoma Coast) $54. 93 *(8/1/2003)*

Hartford 1999 Laura's Chardonnay (Sonoma Coast) $54. An intensely fragrant floral, ginger, peach, lemon-lime, and orange-spice bouquet ushers in this smooth, well-structured wine. The palate shows intricately meshed orange, butterscotch, and toasted nut flavors, offset by angular, racy mineral accents. Finishes long and crisp, with refined pineapple, citrus, and stony flavors. Enjoyable now but still tight, this should offer even more in two years. **93** *(7/1/2001)*

Hartford 2000 Seascape Vineyard Chardonnay (Sonoma Coast) $50. 91 *(8/1/2003)*

Hartford 1999 Seascape Vineyard Chardonnay (Sonoma County) $46. The full fresh-bread aromas of yeast, honey, and oats promise much body, but the palate delivers a dry citrus-mineral mouthful of flavors. Mouthfeel is dry and briskly acid—but with a nice chalky note, too. Chalk shows again on the finish, where it somewhat checks the sharp lemony-metallic notes. **87** *(7/1/2001)*

Hartford 2000 Stone Côte Vineyard Chardonnay (Sonoma Coast) $29. 90 Editors' Choice *(8/1/2003)*

Hartford 1999 Stone Côte Vineyard Chardonnay (Sonoma County) $33. Lots of spice along with a veritable fruit cocktail of complex flavors open this understated performer. From green apple and bosc pears to melon and mint, it has an elegant integration of fruit and spicy, vanillin oak. Tangy acidity keeps it lively, and the wine finishes crisp and dry. Still tight, this could use a year to knit itself together. **91** *(7/1/2001)*

Hartford 1999 Three Jacks Vineyard Chardonnay (Russian River Valley) $33. Four different clones are separately fermented and then blended to make this unique bottling. An expansive nose shows vibrant pineapple, peach, and orange fruit with lemondrop and butterscotch accents. It's rich and mouthfilling, like a bite of banana cream pie, and turns maybe a bit orangey-sweet. Shy on subtlety, it packs in a lot of juicy flavor. **89** *(7/1/2001)*

Hartford 2004 Pinot Noir (Sonoma Coast) $30. Hartford is a high-aiming, small winery that's part of the Jess Jackson empire. The single-vineyard Pinots are outstanding, this regional bottling somewhat less so. Still, it catches the cool Sonoma Coast qualities of acidity and elegance. You'll find cherry and green tea flavors, and the wine should develop over the next five years. **90** —*S.H. (5/1/2006)*

Hartford 2000 Pinot Noir (Sonoma Coast) $25. 89 *(8/1/2003)*

Hartford 2000 Arrendell Vineyard Pinot Noir (Green Valley) $65. 91 *(8/1/2003)*

Hartford 1999 Arrendell Vineyard Pinot Noir (Russian River Valley) $65. Aromas of dark fruit, anise, smoke, and dried herbs morph into flavors of stone fruits (plums, cherries) in the mouth, with a strong undercurrent of pomegranate. This thick, almost syrupy wine is almost steroidally concentrated, but stays focused thanks to lemony acids that might be too much for some tasters. **92** *(7/1/2002)*

Hartford 1999 Dutton Ranch-Sanchietti Vineyard Pinot Noir (Russian River Valley) $50. Pure, seductive Pinot aromas combine floral, rose-petal aromas with dark fruit and brown sugar. Rich flavors of blackberries and boysenberries cascade across the palate in a fall of velvet. Moderate acidity makes it approachable now, but there's enough tannin to preserve it for a few years. A wine that can stand up to steak but still retains a sense of Pinot elegance. **94 Editors' Choice** *(7/1/2002)*

Hartford 2000 Dutton-Sanchietti Pinot Noir (Russian River Valley) $50. 93 *(8/1/2003)*

Hartford 2004 Hailey's Block Pinot Noir (Russian River Valley) $55. The grapes seem like they were picked earlier than others, making for a lean-style Pinot Noir that's high in acids and minerality. It's almost austere, although maybe "restrained" is a better word. Dry and tannic, but with a deep core of cherry compote fruit, the wine needs a little time. Should begin to blossom by 2007 and drink well through 2012. **91 Cellar Selection** —*S.H. (12/15/2006)*

Hartford 2000 Marin Pinot Noir (Marin County) $50. 92 Cellar Selection *(8/1/2003)*

Hartford 1999 Marin Pinot Noir (Marin County) $50. The most Burgundian of the '99s from Hartford, this cool-climate single-vineyard wine smells of leather, clove, even slightly of barnyard. Some green herbaceousness on the palate balances bright cherry fruit—the interplay of elements gives this wine a multifaceted character that changes from sip to sip. Give it 2–3 years for the tannins to smooth out. **92 Cellar Selection** *(7/1/2002)*

Hartford 1999 Sevens Bench Pinot Noir (Carneros) $50. Toastier and smokier than the other bottlings, with clove and coffee accents dressing up sturdy plum and earth flavors. Finishes long, with hints of tart plum skin and dusty tannins. Seems as if rare duck breast would be a perfect match. **91** *(7/1/2002)*

Hartford 2000 Sevens Bench Vineyard Pinot Noir (Carneros) $50. 92 Cellar Selection *(8/1/2003)*

Hartford 1999 Velvet Sisters Pinot Noir (Anderson Valley) $50. An apt name for this richly fruited and supple wine, which features high-toned green grass, stem, and herb aromas over earthy, black-cherry flavors. The finish is long, spicy and briary. If you enjoy the herbal aspect of Pinot Noir, you may rate it even higher. **90** *(7/1/2002)*

Hartford 2000 Velvet Sisters Vineyard Pinot Noir (Anderson Valley) $50. 91 *(8/1/2003)*

Hartford 2001 Zinfandel (Russian River Valley) $25. Quite lush. Richly textured and elegant, with a solid center featuring black-cherry, plum, raspberry, chocolate, coffee, spice, and herbs. Velvety tannins frame the plush layers of fruit that extend long on the finish. **90 Editors' Choice** *(11/1/2003)*

Hartford 1999 Zinfandel (Russian River Valley) $34. Hartford's blended Zin is filled with exuberant aromas of jammy "Zinberry" fruit, baking spices like cinnamon and clove, bittersweet chocolate and black pepper. The vibrant mixed-berry flavors are rich and satisfying, finishing with a touch of warmth and softness. **91** *(7/1/2002)*

Hartford 2001 Dina's Vineyard Zinfandel (Russian River Valley) $34. Full bodied, rich, and beautifully textured. Plush chocolate, coffee, plum, vanilla, licorice, black-cherry, spice, cedar, and herb notes co-mingle here in a fine showing of an elegant, powerful Zinfandel. Long and lush at the end. **91** *(11/1/2003)*

Hartford 2001 Fanucchi-Wood Road Vineyard Zinfandel (Russian River Valley) $34. This supple, smooth style is a winner with us. Velvety tannins frame a core of black-cherry, blackberry, plum, licorice, sweet oak, herbs, toast, tea, coffee, and spice flavors. The finish is elegant, long, and lush, with just enough brightness on the finish. **92** *(11/1/2003)*

Hartford 2001 Hartford Vineyard Zinfandel (Russian River Valley) $34. Inky black in color and densely rich on the palate. This is one of five fine Zins from this winery—plush, silky, sexy, and complex, with a broad array of black-cherry, plum, cola, coffee, chocolate, spice, and herb flavors. Velvety smooth and long on the finish. **93 Editors' Choice** *(11/1/2003)*

Hartford 1999 Hartford Vineyard Zinfandel (Russian River Valley) $34. From the old vineyard in back of Don Hartford's house, this 15.7% alcohol Zin is big—but it's no brute. It's full of dark, rich blackberries, layered with chocolate and black pepper. The velvety texture carries through the long finish, picking up hints of black licorice. **93 Editors' Choice** *(7/1/2002)*

Hartford 2001 Highwire Vineyard Zinfandel (Russian River Valley) $34. Sleek and smooth, jam packed with solid fruit redolent of black-cherry, plum, chocolate, cassis, coffee, herbs, licorice, spice, and cola. Quite complex, elegant, and long on the finish. An excellent wine from a top-notch producer. **92** *(11/1/2003)*

Hartford 1999 Highwire Vineyard Zinfandel (Russian River Valley) $34. Spicier than the other Hartford Zins, with the accent on black pepper and clove. Brambly blackberry and chocolate provide a solid foundation for spice complexities. Hints of crushed nettles provide yet another layer of flavor, and the wine finishes with zippy acids and peppery spice. **93** *(7/1/2002)*

HARTWELL

Hartwell 2002 Cabernet Sauvignon (Stags Leap District) $115. If you enjoy cellaring Cabs, this is probably a good candidate. It's fine to drink now, with forward cassis and cherry flavors that are liberally oaked, and dry. But the tannins are straightforward. They require something big and greasy, like lamb. Drink now through 2012. **92 Cellar Selection** —*S.H. (10/1/2005)*

Hartwell 2000 Cabernet Sauvignon (Stags Leap District) $100. Gorgeous, beautiful wine, so strongly delicious on its own that it will be a challenge to pair it with food. A myriad of flavors cascades over the palate: cassis, black currants, black-cherries, white chocolate, spiced plums, and dried herbs. So rich and decadently ripe, it's almost a dessert wine. The tannins are completely soft and melted. **93** —*S.H. (11/15/2003)*

Hartwell 1998 Cabernet Sauvignon (Stags Leap District) $100. There's some pretty blackberry fruit and spice here, while plenty of fancy oak provides woody spices and sweet vanillins as well as a smoky quality. The texture is smooth and polished. The fruit isn't very dense or concentrated, but this elegant, soft wine drinks well now and will improve in the next year or two. **90** —*S.H. (6/1/2002)*

Hartwell 2001 Estate Grown Cabernet Sauvignon (Stags Leap District) $115. Rich, creamy and lush on the palate, with loads of cassis that just roll on and on through the velvety finish. But is no simple fruit bomb—it also delivers plenty of dried herb and tobacco complexity wrapped in toast and vanilla. Drink now—2015. **93** —*J.C. (10/1/2004)*

Hartwell 1999 Estate Grown Cabernet Sauvignon (Napa Valley) $100. A dense, rich wine with a strong herb-and-spice edge. It fans out, however, to reveal more fruit; blackberries, cassis, and plums come to mind. Anise and chocolate flavors are also in evidence. Cedary edged tannins offer a fine framework in this complex wine, which should age beautifully. **93** —J.M. (11/15/2002)

Hartwell 1997 Sunshine Vineyard Cabernet Sauvignon (Stags Leap District) $95. 93 (11/1/2000)

Hartwell 2002 Merlot (Stags Leap District) $65. This expressive Merlot showcases Napa's ability not only to ripen the variety but to give it pleasurable complexity, no easy task. The cherry, blackberry, and cocoa flavors are replicable elsewhere, as is the oak plastering, but this wine has depth and nuance comparable to a fine Cabernet. **92** —S.H. (8/1/2005)

Hartwell 2000 Merlot (Stags Leap District) $60. Spicy and rich—redolent of bright-edged cherries, blackberries, raspberries, chocolate, and licorice. Smooth tannins give good structure. This top-notch California Merlot finishes long and lush. Really lovely. **91** —J.M. (11/15/2002)

Hartwell 2001 Estate Grown Merlot (Stags Leap District) $60. This gorgeous Merlot brims with pronounced flavors of cherries, blackberries, cassis, coffee, and chocolate, with a pleasant edge of dried herbs. The flavors deeply penetrate the palate and last for a long time on the finish. Ripe, sweet tannins and fresh, grapey acidity provide a firm mouthfeel. Best now through 2005. **91** —S.H. (4/1/2004)

Hartwell 2005 Sauvignon Blanc (Napa Valley) $30. Best known for Cabernet, Hartwell planted Sauvignon Blanc close to San Francisco Bay, and this is their inaugural release. It's a great wine, reminiscent of the best of Marlborough. Enormously rich, it's absolutely dry and high in acids, with a flood of gooseberry, grapefruit zest and white peach flavors. One-quarter new French oak adds a brilliant touch of vanilla and smoky buttercream. With this wine, Hartwell joins the Sauvignon Blanc short list in California. **92 Editors' Choice** —S.H. (12/31/2006)

HARVEST MOON

Harvest Moon 2003 Cabernet Sauvignon (Dry Creek Valley) $32. This Cab is dry and tart in acids. It shows polished blackberry jam, coffee and cocoa flavors, finishing with spicy licorice and Hoisin sauce. A good expression of Dry Creek Valley Cabernet. Drink now. **88** —S.H. (12/1/2006)

Harvest Moon 2005 Estate Dry Gewürztraminer (Russian River Valley) $18. Spicy and fruity and, as the label says, dry. It shows crisp acids and a bright, delicately clean mouthfeel. Kind of like a Sauvignon Blanc except for the exotic tropical fruit and Asian spice flavors. **85** —S.H. (12/1/2006)

Harvest Moon 2003 Estate Zinfandel (Russian River Valley) $32. Here's a big, ripe, juicy Zin that's rustic and a little sweet but enjoyable for its purity. Has powerful flavors of raspberry and cherry purée, with a streak of cocoa and peppery spices. It's lighter in body than others, and not very tannic. It packs a punch of acidity. **86** —S.H. (12/1/2006)

Harvest Moon 2002 Pitts Home Ranch Zinfandel (Russian River Valley) $28. What a beauty. Soft and lush, yet firm in the mouth, with a lovely mélange of wild black cherry, cocoa, pepper, and leather flavors. Finishes with a ripe note of sweet raisiny cassis. For all the sweetness, it's dry and balanced. **93** —S.H. (8/1/2005)

HATCHER

Hatcher 2002 Syrah (Calaveras County) $24. A wonderful wine, big and punchy in blackberry and cherry fruit and a hint of meat and herbs. Smooth, ripe tannins, complex and layered, with a long, rich finish. **90** —S.H. (3/1/2005)

Hatcher 2002 Estate Zinfandel (Calaveras County) $18. Nice Zin, balanced and dry, with an easy, sillky mouth feel. Shows upfront spice, berry, cherry, and coffee flavors. Notable for its harmony. **88** —S.H. (3/1/2005)

HAUER OF THE DAUEN

Hauer of the Dauen 1998 Pinot Noir (Willamette Valley) $14. 85 —M.S. (12/1/2000)

Hauer of the Dauen 1998 Estate Bottled Pinot Noir (Willamette Valley) $14. 81 —J.C. (12/1/2000)

HAVENS

Havens 2004 Albariño (Carneros) $24. This wine, made from one of the great Spanish and Portuguese white grapes, is rare in California. In cool Carneros, it has produced a very dry, flinty, acidic wine, almost sour in grapefruit sensations, with an intriguing minerality and a long, clean, prickly finish. It contains only 12% alcohol. **90 Editors' Choice** —S.H. (11/1/2005)

Havens 2003 Albariño (Carneros) $24. Sort of Pinot Grigio-like, with its tart, lemon, and apple flavors and crisp acidity. Seems a bit simple at first blush, but that zesty acidity makes the mouth water and long for food, like chevre or grilled veggies. **85** —S.H. (10/1/2004)

Havens 2001 Bourriquot Cabernet Blend (Carneros) $35. This is a Bordeaux blend, but it's feminine and delicate, almost evanescent. There's no Cabernet Sauvignon to weigh down the Cabernet Franc and Merlot, and the tannins are light and airy. Yet it's complex and nuanced, with cherry, pomegranate, crème de cassis, and coffee flavors leading to a dry, smooth finish. **93 Editors' Choice** —S.H. (11/1/2005)

Havens 2001 Merlot (Napa Valley) $24. This is a full-bodied Merlot, dark and fairly tannic, with young acids undergirding flavors of currants, black-cherries, and dark bitter chocolate. It's hard now, and will wake up with a good piece of meat, but should soften with a few years of age. **87** —S.H. (6/1/2005)

Havens 2000 Merlot (Napa Valley) $24. A seductive wine made in the Napa Big Red style, which means ultrasoft, velvety tannins, extracted fruit and a lavish overlay of oak. Achieves complexity through the mélange of berries, herbs, and spices that wash over the palate in waves. A bit flaccid, though, and there's a thinness in the center that finishes hot. **88** —S.H. (12/31/2003)

Havens 2000 Reserve Merlot (Carneros) $32. This fine Merlot has many interesting features. The flavors are very complex, mingling fruits, berries, spices, herbs, and oak. It's a tannic, dry wine, but balanced and harmonious. It lacks the stuffing for aging, and will be best over the next few years. **88** —S.H. (10/1/2004)

Havens 2000 Bourriquot Red Blend (Carneros) $35. This blend of Cabernet Franc and Merlot is unusual, and seems designed to fit the cool climate and clay soils of Carneros. The result is a study in progress. It's sweet in chocolatey, plummy fruit and toasty oak, but is seeking finesse and elegance. **86** —S.H. (10/1/2004)

Havens 2002 Syrah (Napa Valley) $24. Creamy and full-bodied, with lush coffee notes accented by blackberries and pepper, finishing on a wiry, herbal note. One reviewer found some rubbery, meaty notes that detracted from the overall experience. Drink now. **87** (9/1/2005)

Havens 2001 Syrah (Napa Valley) $24. This wine has considerable tannins, the tough kind that hit midpalate and last all the way down. But it's notable for the explosive dark-stone fruit flavors way down deep. Dry and acidic; should be best after 2006. **91** —S.H. (6/1/2005)

Havens 2000 Syrah (Napa Valley) $24. Opens with powerful aromas of white pepper, accented with blackberry and new oak. Clearly a young and vibrant wine, with blackberry and spice flavors and some pretty strong tannins. If you drink it now, do so with lamb, rib roasts, and similar fare. Otherwise, let it settle down for a few years. **90** —S.H. (12/1/2003)

Havens 1999 Syrah (Napa Valley) $26. This is the real stuff, with pepper, blackberry, smoke, and an earthy note. Drinks lush and complex. Sheer heaven, with impeccable precision and cohesion of blackberry liqueur, oak, and lush tannins. **91** —S.H. (7/1/2002)

Havens 1999 Hudson T Reserve Syrah (Napa Valley) $45. From a vineyard near Carneros, this inky, dark wine bursts with blackberry, clove, and smoke aromas. Fantastic concentration of fruit; deep, plush, and opulent. The depth of flavor is enormous, yet it's so supple and balanced. Very fine now. Try it with game. **93** —S.H. (7/1/2002)

Havens 2001 Hudson Vineyard Syrah (Carneros) $45. There is excessive softness here. This wine is properly dry, with smooth, complex tannins and a nice balance of berry, herb, and oak flavors, but it collapses in the mouth, and doesn't seem to have the stuff to age. **85** —S.H. (11/1/2005)

Havens 2000 Hudson Vineyard Syrah (Carneros) $45. This is a good wine from a less-than-successful vintage. The blackberry flavors have a raw, unfinished edge that liberal oak cannot sweeten. There's also a streak of tart acidity that leads to a dry, puckery finish. **86** —S.H. (5/1/2004)

HAWK CREST

Hawk Crest 1997 Cabernet Sauvignon (California) $12. 86 —*S.H.* *(3/1/2000)*

Hawk Crest 1996 Cabernet Sauvignon (California) $9. 83 —*S.H.* *(11/1/1999)*

Hawk Crest 2003 Cabernet Sauvignon (California) $14. Easy, tannic, and kind of rough, this Cab offers dry, earthy, coffee-infused flavors. The fruit has been de-emphasized, but it still possesses some finesse. **83** — *S.H. (10/1/2006)*

Hawk Crest 2001 Cabernet Sauvignon (California) $14. There's some nice berry-cherry stuff going on, but this wine would be more likeable if not for the harsh tannins and bitter coffee flavors. **83** —*S.H. (6/1/2004)*

Hawk Crest 2000 Cabernet Sauvignon (California) $14. Tastes and smells hot, with a burnt rubber note that persists through the tart, peppery finish. The wine is very dry, with little fruit. **82** —*S.H. (8/1/2003)*

Hawk Crest 1996 Reserve Cabernet Sauvignon (California) $16. 83 —*L.W. (7/1/1999)*

Hawk Crest 2004 Chardonnay (California) $11. Here's a good, everyday Chard with plenty of fruit and cream flavor and a tangy, crisp mouthfeel. It does the California Chard thing at a fair price. From Stag's Leap Wine Cellars. **84** —*S.H. (10/1/2006)*

Hawk Crest 2002 Chardonnay (California) $11. Okay Chard for everyday purposes, with decent fruit flavors. It's dry, clean, and tart on the finish. **83** —*S.H. (6/1/2004)*

Hawk Crest 2001 Chardonnay (California) $11. Kind of soft and flabby, with well-ripened flavors of peaches and pears, and an overlay of oak that seems too heavy for the wine's weight. On the other hand, it's pretty inoffensive at this price. **83** —*S.H. (10/1/2003)*

Hawk Crest 1998 Chardonnay (California) $10. Here's a nice everyday drinking wine with some real richness from ripe Chardonnay grapes and a touch of toasty oak. It will satisfy that craving for apple and peach-flavored fruit. Dry and spicy, with the creamy texture of a good wine, but it won't break the bank. **83** —*S.H. (2/1/2001)*

Hawk Crest 1997 Reserve Vineyard Selection Chardonnay (California) $14. **84** —*S.H. (7/1/1999)*

Hawk Crest 1998 Vineyard Selection Chardonnay (California) $15. 88 *(6/1/2000)*

Hawk Crest 1997 Merlot (California) $12. 87 Best Buy —*S.H. (3/1/2000)*

Hawk Crest 2003 Merlot (California) $14. Dry, fruity, and rustic in feeling, with edgy tannins and jammy cherry, berry and cocoa flavors, this is a decent everyday sipper. **83** —*S.H. (10/1/2006)*

Hawk Crest 2001 Merlot (California) $14. You get a lot for your bucks with this dry, full-bodied red wine. It has pleasant flavors of plums, cherries, and herbs, with rich, supportive tannins and a fruity, oaky finish. **85** —*S.H. (6/1/2004)*

Hawk Crest 2000 Merlot (California) $14. Rough and awkward, with some cherry flavors and greener ones of stems and herbs. Drinks dry and fairly tannic. Perfectly acceptable as an inexpensive chugger. **83** —*S.H. (8/1/2003)*

Hawk Crest 1996 Vineyard Select Reserve Merlot (California) $16. 82 — *L.W. (9/1/1999)*

HAWLEY

Hawley 2002 Cabernet Sauvignon (Dry Creek Valley) $27. Extremely ripe fruit stars here, with intense black currant flavors. The wine is totally dry, and pretty tannic, with a grippy, sandpapery finish. It may soften and smooth out with a year of bottle age. **85** —*S.H. (12/31/2005)*

Hawley 2001 Cabernet Sauvignon (Dry Creek Valley) $28. Opens with a sulfury smell that's slow to blow off, masking the underlying blackberry aroma. In the mouth, it's quite extracted and jammy in berry fruit, yet the tannins are tough and astringent. Drinks like a simple country wine. **84** —*S.H. (5/1/2004)*

Hawley 1999 Cabernet Sauvignon (Dry Creek Valley) $28. You can smell the cassis and blackberry fruit a mile away. The oak, too. Dry and full-bodied, with a rich earthiness. Soft tannins make it immediately drinkable. **90** —*S.H. (11/15/2002)*

Hawley 2004 Chardonnay (Russian River Valley) $21. There's plenty of ripe fruit in this wine, but it tastes kind of aggressive in oak, with scads of toast and vanilla-woodsap flavors that aren't really needed, since the pineapple, pear, and peach flavors are delicious by themselves. It would be interesting to try this unoaked. **84** —*S.H. (12/31/2005)*

Hawley 2003 Foppoli Ranch Chardonnay (Russian River Valley) $20. Here's a ripe Chard that detonates the palate with tangerine, pineapple, peach, and green apple, and a spicy seasoning of oak. It has a creamy texture and a sweet, fruity intensity that finishes with a scour of orange peel. Delicious. **88** —*S.H. (12/15/2004)*

Hawley 2001 Bradford Mountain Merlot (Dry Creek Valley) $26. This interesting wine takes your basic berry-cherry Merlot flavors and boosts them with more complex notes of sweet sweaty leather, olives, and violets. There's also an elaborate layering of smoky oak. I wish the wine were a little firmer in acidity, but it's very nice. **86** —*S.H. (11/1/2005)*

Hawley 2000 Bradford Mountain Merlot (Dry Creek Valley) $20. This interesting Merlot seesaws between ripe flavors of black currants and cassis and a delicious earthiness that suggests green olives. It's very dry, with lusciously ripe tannins and soft acids. Not an ager, but a plump, meaty wine for early consumption. **90** —*S.H. (5/1/2004)*

Hawley 1999 Bradford Mountain Merlot (Dry Creek Valley) $24. Bradford Mountain is in Dry Creek Valley. The wine is tough and young, but very good. With its brambly, peppery flavors and sturdy tannins, it could easily be mistaken for Zinfandel. Don't hold that against it. Enjoy it for its lusty, zesty self. **88** —*S.H. (11/15/2002)*

Hawley 2003 Pinot Noir (Russian River Valley) $32. It's easy drinking with this silky, delicate Pinot, with its flavors of rhubarb, beet, cola, and cherry, and cinnamon-spice finish. This dry wine is probably at its best now. **85** —*S.H. (11/1/2005)*

Hawley 2002 Oehlman Vineyard Pinot Noir (Russian River Valley) $32. Rather earthy and wanting fruit. Lots of leather and cedar, a tough, chewy wine that reveals cherries on the finish. **84** *(11/1/2004)*

Hawley 2000 Oehlman Vineyard Pinot Noir (Russian River Valley) $28. Beautiful structure here, with good acids and supple, complex tannins, and a fine overlay of oak. But there's a lot of unripe or green fruit, offering mint and oregano aromas and flavors, and the finish is lean. **85** —*S.H. (2/1/2003)*

Hawley 2004 Viognier (Placer County) $20. This Sierra Foothills wine is fruity enough, even semi-sweet in flowery peach and vanilla flavors, but there's a rough-hewn edge that tells you it's a rustic wine. **83** —*S.H. (11/1/2005)*

Hawley 2003 Viognier (Placer County) $20. So ripe in fruit, so honey-rich, and so creamy in oak, it's practically a dessert wine. That's the strength and the weakness. Delicious, but not really a dry table wine. **85** —*S.H. (12/31/2004)*

Hawley 2001 Viognier (Placer County) $21. Pleasantly fruity, with flavors of mangoes and aromatic flowers, peaches, apples, citrus fruits, and spearmint. It's a little sweet and a little soft and a little simple. Best drank very cold. **85** —*S.H. (12/15/2002)*

HAYMAN & HILL

Hayman & Hill 2003 Reserve Selection Cabernet Sauvignon (Napa Valley) $14. Briary and brambly, this Zin has an exotic, peppery personality all its own. Fortunately, the wine is thoroughly dry and balanced, and will be good with barbecued chicken slathered in a rich, spicy tomato sauce. **86** —*S.H. (12/15/2005)*

Hayman & Hill 2004 Reserve Selection Chardonnay (Russian River Valley) $14. Lots of toasty oak on this very dry wine, and a big burst of citrusy acids. In fact the fruit veers toward lemons, limes, and grapefruits, just nudging into riper green apples and peaches. **85** —*S.H. (12/15/2005)*

Hayman & Hill 2003 Reserve Selection Chardonnay (Russian River Valley) $14. This is quite a sophisticated Chard, showing the quality of wines that cost far more. It's rich, with toasty oak that frames flavors of pineapples, buttered toast, spicy mango, and ripe white peach. Feels creamy through a long, spicy finish. **87** —*S.H. (7/1/2005)*

Hayman & Hill 2003 Reserve Pinot Noir (Edna Valley) $14. This Pinot is a good value. It shows lots of panache in the elegantly silky mouthfeel, dryness, crisp acids, and subtle flavors of cherries, spices, and oak. Feels classy in the mouth, and is a good ambassador of its cool-climate appellation. **86** —*S.H. (7/1/2005)*

Hayman & Hill 2002 Reserve Selection Shiraz-Viognier (Monterey County) $14. The 7% Viognier goes a long way. The big, bright boost of citrus and acidity dominates. The Syrah itself is soft and plummy-chocolatey, with a smear of tannins. **84** —*S.H. (12/15/2005)*

Hayman & Hill 2002 Reserve Selection Shiraz-Viognier (Monterey County) $14. Viognier lends a bright, floral note and citrusy acidity to this Syrah's plums and blackberries. Still, this is a medium-bodied, dry red with a firmly tannic finish. **86** —*S.H. (7/1/2005)*

Hayman & Hill 2003 Reserve Selection Zinfandel (Dry Creek Valley) $14. Lean, herbal, and austerely dry, this Zin offers little in the way of fruit, although it's perfectly clean and decent. If you concentrate, you'll find modest cherry-berry flavors. **83** —*S.H. (12/15/2005)*

Hayman & Hill 2001 Reserve Selection Zinfandel (Dry Creek Valley) $15. Smooth textured, with toasty rich oak framing a center of black currant, black-cherry, blackberry, anise, vanilla, and mild spice flavors. The finish is velvety and moderate in length. **88** *(11/1/2003)*

HAYWOOD

Haywood 1999 Vintner's Select Cabernet Sauvignon (California) $10. A thin, simple wine, with some berry flavors. Very dry, with somewhat sharp tannins and acidity, it finishes on a harsh green note. **81** *(8/1/2001)*

Haywood 1999 Vintner's Select Chardonnay (California) $10. Smells citrusy and oaky, with a distinct melon note. This is a simple, somewhat rough wine that expresses the most basic Chardonnay characteristics, but offers little beyond affordability. **82** —*S.H. (8/1/2001)*

Haywood 1999 Vintner's Select Merlot (California) $12. Walks a tight line between a sharp, thin, herbaceous profile, and juicier, riper, more focused berry aromas and flavors. Finishes dry, with moderate tannins. **84** —*S.H. (8/1/2001)*

Haywood 1998 Vintner's Select Merlot (California) $10. 82 —*M.S. (7/1/2000)*

Haywood 1996 Los Chamizal Estate Zinfandel (Sonoma Valley) $16. 91 —*S.H. (11/1/1999)*

Haywood 1996 Los Chamizal Estate Rocky Terr Zinfandel (Sonoma Valley) $23. 92 —*S.H. (11/1/1999)*

Haywood 1998 Los Chamizal Vineyard Zinfandel (Sonoma Valley) $20. Deep briary, wild-berry, and pepper aromas. In the mouth, it's ripe and sweetly fruity, with soft tannins and pepper-spice notes. It's bone dry, with adequate acidity. Classic Sonoma Zin in its expressive exuberance and unpolished likeability. **88** *(8/1/2001)*

Haywood 1998 Los Chamizal Vineyard Zinfandel (Sonoma County) $20. Deep briary, wild-berry, and pepper aromas. In the mouth, it's ripe and sweetly fruity, with soft tannins and pepper-spice notes. It's bone dry, with adequate acidity. Classic Sonoma Zin in its expressive exuberance and unpolished likeability. **88** —*S.H. (8/1/2001)*

Haywood 1998 Morning Sun Zinfandel (Sonoma County) $30. Opens with aromas of wild berries, white pepper, earth, and a trace of leather. Tough and unyielding tannins coat the palate, and you'll need some meat to break through this gridlock, but underneath it all is a core of ripe dark-berry fruit. This could use 3–6 years of aging. **86** —*S.H. (8/1/2001)*

Haywood 1998 Rocky Terrace Zinfandel (Sonoma County) $35. This is a challenging Zin. It's fruity but it's also earthy and mushroomy, with a blast of vanilla oak. Right now it's pretty tannic, but beneath that roughness is a core of fruit. It's austere now—difficult even—but some time in the cellar could soften and open it. **86** —*S.H. (8/1/2001)*

HDV

HdV 2003 Napa Valley Red Wine Bordeaux Blend (Carneros) $60. A huge disappointment, given the pedigree of the ownership (Romanée-Conti) and vineyard (Hyde). The wine isn't fully ripe, showing a green mintiness, yet is also raisiny, too ripe. In other words, it's clumsy. **82** —*S.H. (12/31/2006)*

HdV 2004 Chardonnay (Carneros) $55. Made from the Hyde Vineyard, (although it's not designated on the front label), this is as good as Carneros gets. It's soft and opulently layered, offering waves of pineapple, mango, guava, nectarine, peach, and new oak flavors in a rich, creamy-leesy texture. The warmth of the vintage worked for this Chardonnay, keeping the Carneros fog away and elevating the wine to perfect ripeness. **93** —*S.H. (12/31/2006)*

HdV 2003 Chardonnay (Carneros) $55. Over the years, my impression of this wine has not varied. It's obviously more acidic, tarter, and less ripe than comparable Chards in its price range, with an eye toward Chablis. It's a praiseworthy wine, with intense lemon cream and pineapple flavors, but would score higher if it had greater richness. **89** —*S.H. (12/31/2005)*

HdV 2002 Chardonnay (Carneros) $55. This is an elegant, minerally Chard, whose primary features are lime, green grapes, and steel flavors, and brisk, tangy acids. Its leanness is partially alleviated by oak, which brings cream and smoke. The finish is elegant and penetrating. **89** —*S.H. (5/1/2005)*

HdV 2001 Chardonnay (Carneros) $48. A solid effort that's missing out on the richness for a better score. It's well structured, with juicy, citrusy acidity, and there's certainly some pretty oak. The flavors also veer toward citrus fruits, with suggestions of tart green apple. Turns peppery-astringent on the finish. Give it a few hours to breathe, and it will soften up. **89** —*S.H. (5/1/2004)*

HdV 2001 Red Blend (Carneros) $65. They pulled out all the stops, starting with fully ripened grapes that give huge blackberry, cassis, cherry, and plum flavors. Elaborate oak adds even more sweet notes, and modern tannin management results in a very soft, elaborate mouthfeel. This stylish Merlot-Cabernet blend has lots of appeal. **91** —*S.H. (5/1/2004)*

HdV 2002 Proprietary Red Red Blend (Carneros) $60. This is a wine rich in oak, flavorful berry-cherry flavors and sturdy tannins. It's young now, with a rather rasping mouthfeel, but is balanced. Turns a bit sharp on the finish, but should improve in the short haul. Drink now through 2006. **88** —*S.H. (6/1/2005)*

HdV 2004 Syrah (Carneros) $60. From the Hyde vineyard comes this viscous wine, dripping with blackberry cola, cherry pie, chocolate, cappuccino, and vanilla crème brûlée flavors. How delicious is that? Still, the wine is dry, with ripe, smooth tannins that make you want another sip. Would score higher if there were more concentration and depth. **90** —*S.H. (12/31/2006)*

HdV 2002 Syrah (Carneros) $48. This is a dark, dense wine that smells better than it tastes. Aromas are of dusty black pepper, pure cassis, wild blackberry, smoky oak, and a hint of smoked meat or leather. The opulent flavors are of intense cassis and cherry, and the tannins are beautifully soft and complex. My gripe, and it's a big one, is a sugary sweetness that makes the wine almost cloying. **86** —*S.H. (9/1/2004)*

HdV 2001 Syrah (Carneros) $48. This interesting wine showcases the continuing promise of Carneros Syrah. In this warm vintage, the grapes became very ripe, and give blackberry, cassis, and cherry flavors. They're wrapped in soft, complex, sweet tannins that coat the palate with a creamy smoothness. The flavors sink last forever. **90** —*S.H. (5/1/2005)*

HEALDSBURG

Healdsburg 2001 Cabernet Sauvignon (California) $8. Smells simple, with plum, berry, and earth aromas. Picks up some richness in the mouth, with well-ripened blackberry flavors. Finishes dry. **84** —*S.H. (11/15/2003)*

Healdsburg 2001 Chardonnay (California) $8. Rough around the edges, with dull flavors and an overly sweet finish. Sure, the price is right, but you can do better. **82** —*S.H. (12/1/2003)*

Healdsburg 2001 Merlot (California) $8. Rugged and tannic, with alcohol and acidity taking center stage on the palate. There are some very dry cherry-berry and herb flavors. Not bad for this everyday price. **84** —*S.H. (12/1/2003)*

Healdsburg 2001 Shiraz (California) $8. What it has in common with Aussie Shiraz is strong, jammy berry fruit, crisp acids, and dry tannins.

But this wine has a rough edge to it, and finishes rustic and simple. **83** —S.H. (12/15/2003)

Healdsburg Viticultural Society 2002 Reserve Cabernet Sauvignon (Dry Creek Valley) $13. Defines a style entirely separate from Napa's. Has those rustic Dry Creek tannins and even a briary edge to the blackberries and cherries, and is totally dry. Well-made and elegant. **88** —S.H. (11/15/2004)

Hedges 1998 Bordeaux Blend (Columbia Valley (WA)) $11. **88 Best Buy** (4/1/2000)

Hedges 1997 Three Vineyards Bordeaux Blend (Columbia Valley (WA)) $21. **90** —S.H. (4/1/2000)

Hedges 1996 Three Vineyards Bordeaux Blend (Columbia Valley (WA)) $20. **90** (11/15/1999)

Hedges 1999 Red Mountain Reserve Cabernet Sauvignon (Columbia Valley (WA)) $42. Hedges is one of a handful of Washington wineries producing top-caliber wines in significant quantities. This is their best deeply colored, elegant, and Bordeaux-like in style and substance. Powerful, muscular black cherry fruit blends with dense, firm tannins, highlighted with elements of iron and earth. The wine, though young and compressed, is a perfect expression of Red Mountain Cabernet. About 20% Merlot is also in the blend. 2,100 six-bottle cases made. **94 Editors' Choice** —P.G. (6/1/2002)

Hedges 2002 Two Vineyards Reserve Cabernet Sauvignon (Red Mountain) $52. This is a bit bigger than the "regular" 2003 Two Vineyards red wine, but doesn't have the same level of complexity and finesse. Ripe, tannic, hearty, and a bit chalky, this 95% Cab Sauvignon gets the "reserve" tag due to its size rather than its subtlety. **88** —P.G. (4/1/2006)

Hedges 1997 Red Mountain Reserve Cabernet Sauvignon-Merlot (Columbia Valley (WA)) $45. **92** —P.G. (11/15/2000)

Hedges 2001 Three Vineyards Red Wine Cabernet Sauvignon-Merlot (Red Mountain) $18. An estate grown (56%) Merlot (44%) blend, from the winery whose efforts spearheaded the successful campaign to certify Red Mountain as an AVA. Big, dark, and toasty, with roasted flavors, like black-cherries soaked in bourbon, augmented with pepper and barrel spice. Flavorful and balanced, with pretty scents of orange peel. **90 Best Buy** —P.G. (12/1/2004)

Hedges 2003 Two Vineyards Cabernet Sauvignon-Syrah (Red Mountain) $40. A limited (350 case) selection of Bel'Villa and Hedges vineyard fruit, this 80-20 Cab-Syrah blend is focused, young, tight and full of promise. Cranberry, cherry, and currant fruits are married to light chocolate, black tea, and that gravelly Red Mountain minerality. **91** —P.G. (4/1/2006)

Hedges 1999 Fumé Chardonnay (Columbia Valley (WA)) $9. **88 Best Buy** —P.G. (11/15/2000)

Hedges 1998 Fumé Chardonnay (Columbia Valley (WA)) $9. **88 Best Buy** —S.H. (2/1/2000)

Hedges 2003 Fumé-Chardonnay (Columbia Valley (WA)) $10. The Chardonnay, which comprises about a third of the blend, adds a lovely fullness to the palate, and brings in some stone fruit flavors as well. The wine is nicely integrated, tasting neither like a Sauv Blanc or a Chardonnay, but rather a flavorful hybrid, lightly scented with white peach, lavender, and pineapple. **87 Best Buy** —P.G. (12/1/2004)

Hedges 2001 C-M-S Red Blend (Columbia Valley (WA)) $10. The blend is half Cab and half Merlot and a splash of Syrah; hence the moniker C-M-S. A full 20% of the fruit comes from the winery's vineyards in the Red Mountain AVA. It captures the complexity of far more expensive red blends, with a succinct mix of red fruits, mineral, and fresh-roasted coffee-bean flavors. This and the winery's superb blended white wine may be the two best bargains in Washington. **89 Best Buy** —P.G. (11/15/2003)

Hedges 2004 CMS Red Blend (Columbia Valley (WA)) $11. Classic, rich and supple; this tastes like a far more expensive wine. It has a European polish, mixing plum, berry and cherry fruit with darker streaks of tar, coffee and smoke. The 13.5% alcohol is perfectly ripe and stylish, and

the wine has good length, precision and complexity. **88 Best Buy** —P.G. (10/1/2006)

Hedges 2000 CMS Red Blend (Columbia Valley (WA)) $11. CMS stands for Cabernets, Merlot and Syrah, the components of this fragrant, fruit-loaded, immensely popular blend. Ripe red and blue berries, tart and tangy, are the stars of this show. No oak here, just plenty of well-defined fruit flavor. The wine is in good supply (28,000 cases); hence the bargain price. **89 Best Buy** —P.G. (6/1/2002)

Hedges 2002 CMS Red Wine Red Blend (Columbia Valley (WA)) $12. Cabernet, Merlot, Syrah and Cab Franc are the C, M and S in the name. Strong roasted coffee scents set off the brisk entry; the Syrah seems to juice up the fruit while the Cabs punch up the tannins. There are a lot of smoky, roasted flavors, and the wine has a good solid grip. Very tasty and appealing. **89 Best Buy** —P.G. (12/1/2004)

Hedges 1999 Columbia Valley Red Blend (Washington) $11. For years Hedges produced a popular, inexpensive Cabernet-Merlot; with the addition of Cabernet Franc and Syrah, the wine has evolved into something more complex, though the price still screams "bargain." Scented with cherries and grapes, underscored with dark, toasty aromas, and wrapped in some pretty tough tannins, it's a serious effort that could stand a bit of cellaring. A third of the fruit comes from reserve caliber vineyards. **88 Best Buy** —P.G. (10/1/2001)

Hedges 1998 Red Mountain Reserve Red Blend (Columbia Valley (WA)) $45. This is the winery's flagship blend, all estate-grown fruit, and built to age. Intense color, perfume, and flavors highlight a focused, concentrated wine. It carries powerful cherry fruit into a compact, extended finish. The wine is so young and compressed that it doesn't yet show the nuances of terroir and barrel that are built into it; let it breathe for several hours, or give it another five years. **92** (10/1/2001)

Hedges 2003 Three Vineyards Red Blend (Red Mountain) $22. Concentrated and supple, this meaty and tannic blend of 56% Merlot, 40% Cabernet Sauvignon and a smattering of Cab Franc and Syrah comes from estate vineyards on Red Mountain. Broad-shouldered and powerful, it shows excellent cassis and red currant fruit and plenty of concentration. 9,700 cases. **89** —P.G. (4/1/2006)

Hedges 1999 Three Vineyards Red Blend (Red Mountain) $18. The price is certainly right for this elegant, stylish blend (58% Cabernet Sauvignon, 39% Merlot, 3% Cabernet Franc) of Red Mountain fruit. All estate grown, the price and production (7,800 cases) belie the commitment to quality. Here is a vivid, racy wine, impeccably balanced and tightly wound. Thirteen months in barrel, of which 20% was new. **92** —P.G. (6/1/2002)

Hedges 1998 Three Vineyards Red Blend (Columbia Valley (WA)) $22. The three vineyards are all on Red Mountain, the newest viticultural appellation in Washington state, and headquarters for Hedges Cellars. This is an elegant, stylish Cabernet/Merlot blend, the fruit clean and lean. The tight, youthful structure is beautifully balanced, compact, and precise. Time, air, bottle age, and food will all help it show its full potential. **91 Editors' Choice** (10/1/2001)

Hedges 1998 Syrah (Columbia Valley (WA)) $32. **87** —P.G. (11/15/2000)

Hedges 2002 Bel Villa Estate North Block Syrah (Red Mountain) $75. On the leaner, more structured side of things, which might have penalized it in our tasting format, but which also may bode well for future development. Smoke, vanilla, and toast accent bright raspberry and mineral shadings, finishing with some dry, astringent tannins. **86** (9/1/2005)

Hedges 2001 White Blend (Columbia Valley (WA)) $9. Another stunning success for Hedges. This 52/48 blend of Sauvignon Blanc and Chardonnay explodes from the glass with a heavenly bouquet of fresh, succulent pineapple/pear fruit. Intense and powerful, it continues with a gorgeous mouthfeel, creamy and bright, into a polished, rich finish. **91 Best Buy** —P.G. (6/1/2002)

Hedges 2000 White Blend (Columbia Valley (WA)) $9. A near 50/50 blend of Chardonnay and Sauvignon Blanc, this perennially popular wine is a perfect match for seafood, pasta, light cheeses, and salads. It's an elegant, stylish wine, with clean, green apple flavors, a strong scent of lime, and a hint of pear. Gorgeous mouthfeel, with creamy, intense fruity, bright acids, and a polished, rich finish. **90 Best Buy** —P.G. (10/1/2001)

Hedges 2005 CMS White Blend (Columbia Valley (WA)) $11. It's mostly C (Chardonnay) and S (Sauvignon Blanc) with a splash of Marsanne providing the "M" that complements the well-established CMS Red. Each of the grapes adds something special and the whole seems to be more than the sum of its parts. The Sauv Blanc lifts it, giving it vivid acid and bright herb; the Chardonnay fills in round apple and pear flavors, and the little bit of Marsanne adds peach to the fruit. **88 Best Buy** —*P.G. (10/1/2006)*

Hedges 2004 CMS White White Blend (Yakima Valley) $11. You may know the CMS red, always a popular blend from this Red Mountain winery. Now they've added a CMS white, replacing their Fumé-Chardonnay with a too-hip-for-words Chardonnay/Marsanne/Sauvignon Blanc blend. There is just a bare hint of summery sweetness; be sure to keep it chilled and it will make you happy. **88** —*P.G. (8/1/2005)*

HEITZ

Heitz 2000 Cabernet Sauvignon (Napa Valley) $35. Big and rugged, with blackberry and herb flavors that finish very dry and tannic. A blend from various parts of Napa Valley. **84** —*S.H. (11/15/2004)*

Heitz 1999 Martha's Vineyard Cabernet Sauvignon (Napa Valley) $120. Opens with powerful aromas of cedar, toasty oak, and vanilla perfume framing ripe black currant and mocha. Turns wonderfully smooth in the mouth. Plump and ripe in cherry and currant fruit, it's beautiful now, but has the tannins and balance to last forever. **94** —*S.H. (11/15/2004)*

Heitz 1994 Trailside Cabernet Sauvignon (Napa Valley) $49. 89 *(3/1/2000)*

HELIX

Helix 2004 Aspersa Chardonnay-Viognier (Columbia Valley (WA)) $16. This 75-25 blend shows interesting bacon fat aromas and a lot of sweet cinnamon spice. The blend really works, as the Viognier adds lift and precision to the Chardonnay, which softens and smoothes out the Viognier's rough edges. **90** —*P.G. (6/1/2006)*

Helix 2003 Merlot (Columbia Valley (WA)) $20. The Merlot in Reininger's Helix line has flavors of toasty oak, and satiny red and black fruits. The blend, mostly Merlot, also includes 14% Cab Franc and 1% Cab Sauvignon. Substantial, slightly hot, with moderately rough tannins but a lot of flavor for the price. **88** —*P.G. (6/1/2006)*

Helix 2003 Syrah (Columbia Valley (WA)) $20. This is 100% Syrah, dark and sappy, with sweet primary fruit flavors. It is a good indication of the quality and style of mainstream Washington Syrah, unblended and seemingly unoaked. Tastes of blue plum and spicy cherry fruit, with perfectly balanced acids and surprising density for its price. It's even got a finishing lick of licorice. **89** —*P.G. (6/1/2006)*

HELLER ESTATE

Heller Estate 2001 Estate Bottled Cabernet Sauvignon (Carmel Valley) $35. Has the weight, texture and polished tannins of a fine Napa Cab, and the same flavor profile, with intense cassis, black currant, and cocoa flavors. There's also some pretty oak, and a sweet, cassis-infused finish. Shows the potential for Cabernet in this tiny appellation. **88** —*S.H. (8/1/2005)*

Heller Estate 2003 Estate Chardonnay (Carmel Valley) $22. From a warmish Monterey County appellation comes this soft, creamy Chard. It has pretty flavors of very ripe white peaches and apricots, drizzled with vanilla, and seems a little sweet. **85** —*S.H. (11/1/2005)*

Heller Estate 2004 Estate Chenin Blanc (Carmel Valley) $20. Semisweet, with a lemon tart flavor, this Chenin also has some good, crisp acidity that makes it balanced and clean. **83** —*S.H. (11/1/2005)*

Heller Estate 2002 Toby's Vintage Merlot Port (Carmel Valley) $35. Drinks very sweet, with caramel, fudge, cherry marmalade, and vanilla flavors. The balance is a little off, but with a wedge of double chocolate cake, no one will care. **87** —*S.H. (11/1/2005)*

HELVETIA

Helvetia 1998 Pinot Noir (Willamette Valley) $18. 82 —*M.S. (12/1/2000)*

HENDRY

Hendry 2003 Hendry Vineyard Red Wine Bordeaux Blend (Napa Valley) $33. Hendry, known for Zinfandel, also produces dependable Bordeaux blends, of which this one, which contains all five classic varieties, is a good example. It's pretty tannic now, but the sweetness in the finish may prove to be a limiting factor. Best now with rich fare. **88** —*S.H. (7/1/2006)*

Hendry 2001 Red Wine Bordeaux Blend (Napa Valley) $30. A delicious and balanced wine that suggests the greatness of this vintage. It hits the mouth with firm, dusty tannins, and then the flavors explode. You'll find blackberries, cherries, and currants, intensely sweet and concentrated, and lavish but appropriate new oak. Finishes with an acidic verve that suggests aging. A blend of all five classic Bordeaux varieties. **93** —*S.H. (5/1/2004)*

Hendry 2002 Block 8 Cabernet Sauvignon (Napa Valley) $49. A Napa winemaker told me that "olive" is not a fashionable word to use with Cabernet. Maybe, but the olives here are beautiful. They're the black, French-cured type, enriched with cassis and flashy new oak, and the flavors are balanced with wonderfully rich tannins and fine acids. What a fabulous job Hendry is doing with these Block 8 Cabs. Drink now–2010. **93** —*S.H. (12/15/2006)*

Hendry 2001 Block 8 Cabernet Sauvignon (Napa Valley) $48. After a disappointing 2000, Hendry's Block 8 returns to form with this ultrarich, super-fruity Cab. It's massive in black cherry pie flavor, drizzled with crème de cassis and sprinkled with cinnamon sugar, and finishes very long and dry. However, the tannins remain sizable at four-plus years. Best now through 2010. **92** —*S.H. (6/1/2006)*

Hendry 2000 Block 8 Cabernet Sauvignon (Napa Valley) $40. There's a burst of white pepper that escapes just after you pop the cork, although it airs to blackberry pie. This is a young, tannic wine, too tight to drink now. The peppery, herbal side suggests against long-term cellaring, but it should soften and sweeten by 2006. **89** —*S.H. (11/15/2004)*

Hendry 1999 Block 8 Cabernet Sauvignon (Napa Valley) $40. Exceedingly dark, and starts off closed and mute, a difficult wine to evaluate in its youth. If you open it now, give it plenty of airing. Currently gives of aromas of dill, cured olives, and earth, although there is a tremendous core of sweet blackberry buried under the tannins, which are soft and fine. **90** —*S.H. (11/15/2003)*

Hendry 1998 Block 8 Cabernet Sauvignon (Napa Valley) $40. An amazing wine, given the vintage. Huge, rich, mouthfilling blackberry and cassis flavors coat the palate and go on forever. They went the extra mile to isolate the ripest blocks in this spotty vintage. The wine is thick and vibrant, a lip-smacking experience if ever there was one. **94 Editors' Choice** —*S.H. (12/31/2002)*

Hendry 2002 Blocks 19 & 20 Chardonnay (Napa Valley) $25. This soft wine has an earthiness to it, with nuances of yellow stone fruits, but it's more about herbs. Finishes quick. **85** —*S.H. (12/15/2004)*

Hendry 2001 Blocks 19 & 20 Chardonnay (Napa Valley) $25. Fruity and oaky, this pretty wine has flavors of ripe pears and figs, and a rich, creamy texture. It's clean and vibrant in the mouth, with just a slight trace of almond-skin bitterness in the finish. It's softer than the Blocks 9 & 21 bottling. **90** —*S.H. (2/1/2004)*

Hendry 2003 Blocks 19 & 20 Dijon Clones Chardonnay (Napa Valley) $25. Never effusively fruity, Hendry Chards are characterized by polished herb and mineral notes, although there are underlying peach flavors. This ultradry wine is crisp and earthy, with a complex balance that makes you like it more and more as you sip. **89** —*S.H. (5/1/2006)*

Hendry 2000 Blocks 19 and 20 Chardonnay (Napa Valley) $25. This is really a different kind of California Chardonnay. It offers apples and pears, with expressive acidity and a powerful dose of lees. The oak is there, in the smoke and vanilla, but plays a subsidiary role. It possesses those undefinable qualities of elegance and complexity. **92** —*S.H. (12/15/2002)*

Hendry 2003 Blocks 9 & 21 Chardonnay (Napa Valley) $25. There's real consistency to Hendry's array of block-designated Chardonnays. This one shares those qualities of earthy, herbal, even tobaccoey notes along with apple and peach flavors. It shares also the dryness and softness. These are very distinct wines, and they have their place in the menu of California Chardonnay. **88** —*S.H. (6/1/2006)*

Hendry 2002 Blocks 9 & 21 Chardonnay (Napa Valley) $25. Bright and lively in acidity and pure fruit, brimming with ripe peach, lime, and

USA

quince flavors. Oak forms a seasoning, with suggestions of vanilla and toast. A well-balanced wine that will go well with food. **89** —*S.H. (4/1/2006)*

Hendry 2001 Blocks 9 & 21 Chardonnay (Napa Valley) $25. A great success, rich and firm, and notable for bright acidity and a stony, mineral quality. Yet it turns lush and opulent in the mouth, with deep, ripe flavors of pears. The spicy finish is so sweet in oaky spice, it's almost like white chocolate. A fascinating study in contrasts. **92 Editors' Choice** —*S.H. (2/1/2004)*

Hendry 2000 Blocks 9 and 21 Chardonnay (Napa Valley) $25. Very close in profile to Blocks 19 and 20, although a tad leaner. Apple and pear flavors are joined with herbs, with rich lees and a balanced overlay of smoky oak. These two Block wines are so similar, only an expert could tell them apart. **91** —*S.H. (12/15/2002)*

Hendry 2005 Unoaked Chardonnay (Napa Valley) $17. No oak here, so what you get is upfront acidity that makes for a direct, tart mouthfeel that frames ripe lime, apple, and peach flavors veering into pineapples. This is a simple, clean wine. **84** —*S.H. (10/1/2006)*

Hendry 2004 Unoaked Chardonnay (Napa Valley) $17. Hendry's vineyard, located west of Napa city, is in a cool location, and vital acidity marks this wine. It has green apple and cinnamon spice flavors, while oak adds the usual smoke and vanilla complexities. **87** —*S.H. (12/31/2005)*

Hendry 2005 Pinot Gris (Napa Valley) $19. Entirely made in stainless steel, this is a fresh tasting, vibrant young wine. It has zingy acids, and forward flavors of citrus fruits, melons, and white pepper. This dry wine is nice as an apéritif. **85** —*S.H. (10/1/2006)*

Hendry 2003 Blocks 4 & 5 Pinot Noir (Napa Valley) $30. This wine confirms my observation that Hendry's Pinots, however well made, do not meet today's expectations. It's dry and herbal, but devoid of aging potential. **85** —*S.H. (2/1/2006)*

Hendry 2001 Blocks 4 & 5 Pinot Noir (Napa Valley) $27. This is a big, rich wine, with substantial tannins and quite a bit of body. It feels like it was grown in a warmer climate, with its plummy, black and blue fruit flavors. But it has a velvety softness that makes it enjoyable now. **86** —*S.H. (4/1/2004)*

Hendry 2002 Hendry Ranch Pinot Noir (Napa Valley) $27. There are certainly some rich flavors in this full-bodied wine, such as chocolate-covered cherries, and it has a nice, silky texture. However one must fault it for being too big for a Pinot Noir and lacking delicacy. Whatever the case, its still a tasty wine. **86** —*S.H. (8/1/2005)*

Hendry 1999 Hendry Vineyard Pinot Noir (Napa Valley) $27. **92** —*S.H. (9/1/2003)*

Hendry 2002 Block 24 Primitivo (Napa Valley) $28. For California Primitivo this wine advances the argument a mile. It's rich and ripe in berry, cocoa, and coffee flavors, with a fabulously delicious finish. What it has in common with Zinfandel is a briary exuberance, but it's really closer in quality to a fine Napa Cab. **91** —*S.H. (8/1/2005)*

Hendry 2002 Hendry Ranch Red Blend (Napa Valley) $30. This Bordeaux blend is firm in the mouth, exhibiting rich tannins and a full-bodied dryness. However the flavors are spectacularly upfront, featuring ripe cassis and black currant, milk chocolate, vanilla, and a toasted smokiness from oak. Addictively good wine. **91** —*S.H. (8/1/2005)*

Hendry 2005 Rosé Blend (Napa Valley) $13. Made from Cab Sauvignon and Zin, this is pretty full-bodied for a rosé, with jammy raspberry and cherry pie filling and spice flavors. It's basically dry, with a honeyed finish. **84** —*S.H. (10/1/2006)*

Hendry 2002 Block 28 Zinfandel (Napa Valley) $31. With nearly 16% alcohol, the wine is dry, although it does have heat. It's forward in berry-cherry, mocha, and peppery spice flavors, with a trace of raisins. Obviously, with a wine of this size, you'll want to be careful both drinking it and matching it with food. **88** —*S.H. (5/1/2006)*

Hendry 2001 Block 28 Zinfandel (Napa Valley) $28. A leaner but still classy style for this winery. Tannins are a tad rustic, framing a layered core of black cherry, blackberry, herb, spice, and tobacco notes, finishing with moderate length. **88** —*J.M. (12/31/2004)*

Hendry 2000 Block 28 Zinfandel (Napa Valley) $28. This terrific Zin marries Napa's gorgeously rich tannins and perfect balance with Zin's wild berry flavors to produce a delightful wine. It's elegant enough to accompany fine foods, like a grilled T-bone steak, but it will also be perfect with pizza, lasagna, and barbecue. **91** —*S.H. (9/1/2003)*

Hendry 1999 Block 28 Zinfandel (Dry Creek Valley) $28. What a difference a block makes. This is good Zin, but not as fruity as Block 7. It's tighter and leaner, with tobacco and sage flavors, although there's a rich core of blackberry and the oaky notes add additional sweetness. The ultralong finish, which is breathtaking, suggests ageability. **92** —*S.H. (12/1/2002)*

Hendry 2004 Block 7 Zinfandel (Napa Valley) $29. When Hendry Zin is good, which it usually is, it's very good, and so it is with this ripe, flashy but balanced wine. Block 7, in particular, is as dependable as Zin gets. It's so delicious in jammy cherry, blackberry, and cocoa flavors, yet dry and crisp, with that sip-me-again quality that quickly empties the bottle. **91** —*S.H. (12/15/2006)*

Hendry 2003 Block 7 Zinfandel (Napa Valley) $29. After years of 90-plus scores for Block 7 Zin, this wine doesn't rise to the occasion. It's a good wine, with pleasant cherry flavors and rich, dusty tannins, but lacks that extra edge of intensity to merit an excellent score. **87** —*S.H. (2/1/2006)*

Hendry 2002 Block 7 Zinfandel (Napa Valley) $27. A rich, lush, round wine that's quite fruit forward, showing plenty of black-cherry, plum, strawberry, chocolate, herb, spice, and blueberry flavors. Extremely soft textured, yet structured. A sexy, plush style that's long on the finish. **90** —*J.M. (12/31/2004)*

Hendry 2001 Block 7 Zinfandel (Napa Valley) $27. Sleek and elegant, with zippy chocolate, tea, coffee, spice, black cherry, and plum flavors that are framed in toasty, sweet oak. The wine is long, lush and ripe on the finish, showing great style. **91** *(11/1/2003)*

Hendry 2000 Block 7 Zinfandel (Napa Valley) $20. A terrific Zin, concentrated and focused, with enormous fruit but also possessing the qualities of balance and finesse. All the more surprising given the 15% of alcohol. Huge flavors of berries, tobacco, and dark chocolate drink fully dry. **91** —*S.H. (9/1/2003)*

Hendry 1999 Block 7 Zinfandel (Napa Valley) $20. What a nice Zin. It's very forward-fruity. You'll get off on the endlessly rich blackberry, cherry and boysenberry flavors, spiced up with pepper, tobaco, tobasco and sweet oak. On the other hand, the acids and tannins are dry. Feels just great in the mouth, massaging the palate with soft, creamy tannins. **92** —*S.H. (12/1/2002)*

Hendry 1997 Block 7 Zinfandel (Napa Valley) $20. **83** —*P.G. (11/15/1999)*

HENEHAN HILLS

Henehan Hills 2001 Syrah (Dry Creek Valley) $19. Lots of complexity to this wine, although it's soft and easy enough to drink tonight. It has firm tannins and well-ripened flavors of mocha, black and red cherries, currants, and toast. Brims with ripe, sunshiney sweetness through the fruity finish. **87** —*S.H. (8/1/2005)*

Henehan Hills 2001 Zinfandel (Dry Creek Valley) $19. Solidy rustic, the kind of country wine you fall in love with at that B&B, then discover it's not as good as when you drank it gazing over the vineyard. Dry, earthy-fruity, and acidic. **84** —*S.H. (8/1/2005)*

HENRY ESTATE

Henry Estate 1998 Barrel Fermented Chardonnay (Umpqua Valley) $15. This is a straightforward, buttery, barrel-fermented style of Chardonnay. Butterscotch and roasted nuts rule the day, with some very soft hints of ripe apple as a nod to the fruit. If you really like oak, this is the Chardonnay for you, at a fair price. **84** —*P.G. (11/1/2001)*

Henry Estate 1999 Gewürztraminer (Umpqua Valley) $10. A distinct scent of burnt match spoils the entry, and the harsh flavors of SO2 can be felt in the mouth as well. This is fermented dry, and it's a simple, fruity effort, which could be any one of a number of generic white wine grapes. **82** —*P.G. (11/1/2001)*

Henry Estate 1999 Merlot (Oregon) $18. Henry Estate, Scott Henry explains, "is more Alsace/Burgundy country, but we feel we are on the ragged edge of pulling these Bordeaux guys off." A fair and candid assessment. This is a lean, but not too green, Merlot. It shows dark cherry fruit, some stem and wood, and fairly stiff tannins. **85** —*P.G. (8/1/2002)*

Henry Estate 2001 Müller-Thurgau (Umpqua Valley) $9. This is a quaffable (about 10% alcohol), off, dry white wine, with intense, clean, lovely floral flavors. Citrus and citrus blossom mingle, making it almost like a still version of Prosecco. There is a surprisingly long finish with spicy floral flavors, intense and flavorful. **88 Best Buy** —*P.G. (8/1/2002)*

Henry Estate 2004 Pinot Gris (Umpqua Valley) $13. Dusty, pale coppery color and scents of pears and bubble gum. Ripe, round and fruity, with lots of tropical flavors and some perceptible sweetness. **88 Best Buy** — *P.G. (2/1/2006)*

Henry Estate 1999 Pinot Gris (Umpqua Valley) $16. Henry Estate is not known for its Pinot Gris because this is only the second year they have produced any significant quantity. It's a light blush-colored, musk-scented wine, with plenty of pear fruit and spice, good flesh, and a crisp follow-through. **88** —*P.G. (2/1/2002)*

Henry Estate 2002 Pinot Noir (Umpqua Valley) $18. Smoky, beet, and bark, with some vanilla. Light, dry, thin. **83** *(11/1/2004)*

Henry Estate 2000 Pinot Noir (Umpqua Valley) $13. Here is an unusual mix of scents: pine needle, barnyard, and earthy, cherry fruit. A good-value wine, with plenty of cherry flavor, augmented by a hint of chicken coop. Balanced, soft tannins finish it out. About 3000 cases made. **86 Best Buy** —*P.G. (12/31/2002)*

Henry Estate 1999 Pinot Noir (Oregon) $51. Medium-weight, with solid, red cherry, black plum, cedar, and cinnamon aromas and flavors. Though a bit too woody and dry for some panelists, others praised the soy and dry-rub spiced fruit on the palate. The very dark close shows lingering toasty oak, pepper, and espresso notes. Drink now through 2006. **87** *(10/1/2002)*

Henry Estate 2002 Barrel Select Pinot Noir (Umpqua Valley) $28. Earthy, with herb and tomato, and tart cranberry fruit. Lean but supple, with some soft, woodsy notes. **84** *(11/1/2004)*

Henry Estate 1998 Barrel Select Pinot Noir (Umpqua Valley) $25. This is a reserve style wine that is made in non-reserve years. A step up from their "Umpqua" bottling, with more texture, firm fruit, and it moves past light cherry flavors into some tart berry. **87** —*P.G. (8/1/2002)*

Henry Estate 1996 Barrel Select Pinot Noir (Umpqua Valley) $20. 87 *(11/15/1999)*

Henry Estate 2001 Umpqua Cuvée Pinot Noir (Umpqua Valley) $39. Borderline translucent in color, and equally light in the nose. The aromas are of cranberry and chlorine. The palate is all strawberry and some bitter oak, and while it picks up steam and fills out with time, the initial impression is hard to overcome. **82** —*M.S. (8/1/2003)*

Henry Estate 1999 Henry the V Red Blend (Umpqua Valley) $23. You've got to love the name (there have been Henry II, III and IV's made, with different blends of grapes). This is 43% Cabernet Sauvignon, 24% Merlot, 19% Cabernet Franc, 9% Syrah, and 5% Malbec. The nose shows earth and stem first, with some sweet grape and red fruits underneath. Balanced and fruit forward, with plenty of tart acids. **86** —*P.G. (8/1/2002)*

Henry Estate 2000 Muller Thurgau White Blend (Umpqua Valley) $9. Muller-Thurgau can be a delight in Oregon, but it can also easily miss the mark. This spritzy, sweet wine seems to dance to its own drummer, and should probably be chilled and enjoyed as an apéritif rather than with a meal. It's clean, fresh, and tastes of melon and pears. **84** —*P.G. (11/1/2001)*

HERINGER

Heringer 2004 Chardonnay (Clarksburg) $13. Clarksburg, in the warm Delta region, is better known for Chenin Blanc. This Chard shows its origins in the softness and earthiness that accompanies the apple flavors. It's a perfectly decent everyday sipper. **84** —*S.H. (7/1/2006)*

Heringer 2003 Petite Sirah (Clarksburg) $21. This wine enters dry, then turns raisiny sweet on the finish. It's big, voluptuous, and soft in acidity, with furry tannins. **83** —*S.H. (7/1/2006)*

HERMAN STORY

Herman Story 2004 Larner Vineyard Grenache (Santa Ynez Valley) $32. Super-rich in cherries, with even richer chocolate fudge and coffee notes. This flavorful wine is balanced with lively acidity and a minerality that undergirds it. It's a bit obvious and forward, but those flashy flavors are just yummy. **90** —*S.H. (11/15/2006)*

Herman Story 2004 Syrah (San Luis Obispo County) $30. A blend of two great vineyards, Shadow Canyon and Laetitia, this wine is notable for its delicacy and charm. But that doesn't mean it's wimpy. It's tremendously rich in cherry preserves, kirsch, cassis, and spices, but maintains a crisp balance and freshness. Very fine and dry finish. **93 Editors' Choice** —*S.H. (11/15/2006)*

Herman Story 2004 Larner Vineyard Syrah (Santa Ynez Valley) $28. Exotically rich, with sun-sweetened blackberry and cherry pie flavors accented with deeper, darker notes of plums, leather, licorice, and coffee. The wine is soft and oaky, and for all the lusciousness, it's not exhibiting particular terroir. **86** —*S.H. (11/15/2006)*

HERMANN J. WIEMER

Hermann J. Wiemer 1997 Cuvée Brut 2000 Champagne Blend (Finger Lakes) $23. 84 *(12/31/2000)*

Hermann J. Wiemer 1997 Chardonnay (Finger Lakes) $12. 88 *(11/15/1999)*

HERON

Heron 2002 Cabernet Sauvignon (California) $11. Smells pleasantly interesting and complex, with a delicate interplay of blackberry, oak, and white pepper, but there's a letdown in the mouth. There, the wine turns sharp and acidic, although dry. Drink now. **83** —*S.H. (12/15/2005)*

Heron 2001 Cabernet Sauvignon (California) $12. Good everyday drinking at a decent price. Dry and fairly tannic, with grippy blackberry, cherry, and sage flavors, and balancing acidity. **84** —*S.H. (8/1/2005)*

Heron 2003 Chardonnay (California) $11. A great value in Chard at this price for its ripe, upfront flavors of pineapples and pears, creamy smooth texture and spicy finish. There's a lot of oak, too. **85 Best Buy** —*S.H. (8/1/2005)*

Heron 2001 Chardonnay (California) $11. Simple and one-dimensional, although there are decent apple flavors and the wine is very clean and swift. Drinks dry, with light notes of smoke and vanilla. Turns watery and a bit hot on the finish. **84** —*S.H. (6/1/2003)*

Heron 2003 Merlot (California) $11. This Merlot is simple and a little thin, but it satisfies because it's so clean and dry. The tannins are rich and dusty, while the cherry-berry flavors pick up steam on the finish. **84** —*S.H. (12/15/2005)*

Heron 2002 Merlot (California) $12. A very nice and drinkable wine. Ripe in jammy plum and blackberry fruit, with crisp acidity and a touch of oak. **84** —*S.H. (12/15/2004)*

Heron 1999 Merlot (California) $13. A spicy clove-and-barbecue nose leads the way to a palate full of red berries. However, there's so much chalky dust on the palate, and all the way through to the finish, that you don't get as much full flavor as you might otherwise. **83** —*D.T. (2/1/2002)*

Heron 2003 Pinot Noir (California) $11. This simple little Pinot is dry, with cherry cola flavors, a nice, silky texture, and a clean, fruity finish. At this price, it's a good way to ease into an appreciation of this red-hot variety. **84** —*S.H. (12/15/2005)*

Heron 2002 Pinot Noir (California) $12. Many of the grapes from this statewide appellation wine must have come from cool coastal regions: it's crisp, delicate, and well-flavored, with cola, cherry, and spice notes. **85** —*S.H. (8/1/2005)*

Heron 2003 Syrah (California) $11. In France, this would be a vin de pays. It's a simple little country wine, dry and bracing, with good cherry-berry flavors and a rich earthiness. It'll be fine with a grilled flank steak you might even find yourself reaching for a third glass. **85** —*S.H. (12/15/2005)*

Heron 2002 Syrah (California) $12. Kind of heavy and rough in texture, but decently dry, with a range of blackberry, cassis, coffee, and earth flavors. A red wine to drink with food, not ponder over. **84** —S.H. (8/1/2005)

Heron 1999 Syrah (California) $13. Though reviewers were quick to recognize big berry, grape, and rhubarb flavors on the nose, they were just as quick to identify a greenness that followed through to the palate. (Cilantro? Green pea? You decide.) Add chalky, smoky, metallic flavors and a sharp, prickly finish, and, well, that's that. **83** (10/1/2001)

HERON HILL

Heron Hill 2003 Ingle Vineyard Johannisberg Riesling (Finger Lakes) $25. A medium-full wine with an oily roundness broken by spice and citrusy acids. Flavors of lemon and citrus pith are tart and dry, but lychee, mineral, and petrol round them out, matching the nose. Finishes with a tart orange aftertaste. **88** —M.D. (8/1/2006)

Heron Hill 2003 Icewine Riesling (Finger Lakes) $100. Medium body and good acidity set the tone, while flavors of tropical fruits keep this wine grounded, even if they don't vault it to the next level. A musky nose has plenty of citrusy fruit with a hint of sawdust. **86** —M.D. (8/1/2006)

Heron Hill 2004 Ingle Vineyard Icewine Riesling (Finger Lakes) $50. Mint graces the nose, along with vanilla, citrus, and pineapple. The palate delivers tropical fruits and baked apple, while mouthwatering acids form a solid structure, with just enough sugar to match. **88** —M.D. (8/1/2006)

Heron Hill 2004 Late Harvest Riesling (Finger Lakes) $36. Nice aromas of mint and golden raisin transfer to the mouth, where tropical fruit, especially pineapple, joins the fray. Medium-bodied with good sweetness and decent acidity, and a finish that could be longer. **86** —M.D. (8/1/2006)

Heron Hill 2002 Reserve Riesling (Finger Lakes) $25. A dry, Alsatian-style Riesling with aromas of petrol, meat, and a hint of fruit. Despite its dryness the wine comes across as oily, with spicy, minerally flavors, including petrol. Not for fruit seekers, but should impress those looking for mineral-laden wines. **85** —M.D. (8/1/2006)

HERRERA

Herrera 2003 Cabernet Sauvignon (Napa Valley) $125. Big, soft and lush, this Cabernet tastes like melted chocolate fudge laced with crème de cassis and a splash of espresso. It's as rich as a dessert pastry, but with sturdy tannins and plenty of toasty oak it defines power. What it needs is subtlety and complexity. **90** —S.H. (12/1/2006)

HERZOG

Herzog 2002 Special Edition Warnecke Vineyard Cabernet Sauvignon (Chalk Hill) $70. Here's a Cab with extreme dryness, sturdy tannins, and tart acids. It's not offering much now, but will it improve? Probably in the short run, as the cherry and blackberry fruit is there. Drink from 2006–2008. **86** —S.H. (12/31/2005)

Herzog 2000 Special Edition Warnecke Vineyard Cabernet Sauvignon (Chalk Hill) $52. As good as Herzog's Special Reserve Cab is, this one is better. It has the same ripely fruity currant and cassis flavors, with fine tannins and a luxurious coating of oak that has been judiciously applied. But it goes the extra mile in finesse and balance, and is simply superb. Right up there with the best, and a considerable success for the vintage. **93** —S.H. (11/15/2003)

Herzog 1997 Special Edition Warnecke Vineyard Cabernet Sauvignon (Chalk Hill) $42. **89** (11/1/2000)

Herzog 2002 Special Reserve Cabernet Sauvignon (Napa Valley) $34. There's a dry bitterness and a green unripeness that make this Cab disappointing. Tannic and acidic, with a bare suggestion of cherry fruit. **82** —S.H. (12/31/2005)

Herzog 2000 Special Reserve Cabernet Sauvignon (Napa Valley) $35. A very fine Cabernet, the kind you like to think you'd instantly identify in a blind tasting as superior Napa. It has ripe flavors of cassis and black currants, and fabulously rich, dry, complicated tannins that glide across the palate with velvety smoothness. Oak contributes the usual vanilla and smoke to this delectable kosher wine. **91 Editors' Choice** —S.H. (11/15/2003)

Herzog 1997 Special Reserve Cabernet Sauvignon (Sonoma County) $32. **86** (11/1/2000)

Herzog 2001 Special Reserve Chardonnay (Russian River Valley) $27. This Chardonnay is impressive. It's power-packed with ripe pineapple fruit that tastes as if it has been grilled in the barbecue, sprinkled with brown sugar, drizzled with vanilla and honey and then liquified. The fusion of strong oak with fruit is impressive, as are the rich, creamy texture and long, spicy aftertaste. **94** —S.H. (8/1/2005)

Herzog 2000 Special Reserve Chardonnay (Russian River Valley) $27. Great grapes have given a lush, fruity wine, filled with ripely sweet flavors of pears and tropical fruits, girded with crisp acidity, and finishing with powerful fruit and spice. Good winemaking has added creamy, smoky oak, and the deft touch that makes this a beautiful Chardonnay. **92 Editors' Choice** —S.H. (12/15/2003)

Herzog 2003 Late Harvest Chenin Blanc (Clarksburg) $16. Okay dessert wine, with plenty of honeyed sweetness and apricot, orange, and honeysuckle flavors. Could use more acidity. **84** —S.H. (7/1/2005)

Herzog 2002 Special Reserve Merlot (Alexander Valley) $30. The fruit is way too thin in this wine, which is a major disappointment as Herzog has been on such a roll with reds. You get alcohol and oak and not much else. **82** —S.H. (12/31/2005)

Herzog 2002 Special Reserve Cabernet/Zinfandel/Syrah Red Blend (California) $40. A nice enough wine, with all sorts of juicy berry and stone fruit flavors that finish ripely sweet. But it lacks varietal identity. Between 3 grape types coming from 3 counties, it's just another fresh, New World red wine. **87** —S.H. (8/1/2005)

Herzog 2003 Special Reserve Syrah (Edna Valley) $30. From one of California's coolest appellations, this Syrah is inky dark and fairly acidic. It's tannic, but the tannins are rich and fine and drinkable now. The wealth of flavors include blackberries, mocha, the sweet, caramelly vanilla of oak, and peppery spices. **92** —S.H. (12/31/2005)

Herzog 2002 Special Reserve Syrah (Edna Valley) $30. A wonderfully easy wine to drink, due to its softness and fruitiness, yet with complex nuances that merit this high score. Pours dark, and shows briary, pepper, blackberry, and coffee aromas. They lead to a balanced, dry wine that exudes cassis and sweet oak flavors. **91** —S.H. (8/1/2005)

Herzog 2001 Special Reserve Syrah (Edna Valley) $30. This is beautiful Syrah, a joy to drink. It pours dark and glyceriney, and while it's a bit mute in aroma, it explodes in the mouth, with flavors of cassis, spicy plum, chocolate, roasted meat, vanilla, and smoke. Hard to describe the smooth mouthfeel, or the fancy aftertaste. For all the flamboyance, it's a dry, controlled wine, assured of itself and in perfect balance. Kosher **94** —S.H. (1/1/2002)

Herzog 2003 Late Harvest White Riesling (Monterey) $19. Sweet, apricotty and crisp, with a lemon-custard note. Not complex, and snaps to a quick finish. **84** —S.H. (8/1/2005)

HESS

Hess 2002 Small Block Series Syrah (Napa Valley) $32. Despite a warm, inviting nose of brandied cherries and blackberries, the mouthfeel doesn't display much richness or texture and the finish shows a touch of alcoholic heat. **83** (9/1/2005)

HESS COLLECTION

Hess Collection 2003 Mountain Cuvée Bordeaux Blend (Mount Veeder) $35. Lovely claret. It's softer and more forward than most Napa mountain Cabs you'll find, with gentle but complex tannins and rich blackberry, cherry, cocoa, and toasty, new-oak flavors. Has real elegance and finesse. **88** —S.H. (12/1/2006)

Hess Collection 2001 Cabernet Blend (Napa Valley) $115. Tough and tannic now, and not yielding much, this 96% Cabernet Sauvignon was grown in Mayacamas Mountains vineyards. Yet there's a tremendous core of cherry and blackberry fruit, and a rich spine of acidity to hold the wine for aging. Designed for 10 years in the cellar. **92 Cellar Selection** —S.H. (12/15/2005)

Hess Collection 2002 Cabernet Sauvignon (Mount Veeder) $40. Here's an outstanding Napa Cab, notable not just for its lush black currant and mocha flavors, but the outstanding tannic structure. Firm as two-by-fours, yet soft as velvet, the tannins lend this wine a great internal

USA

architecture. Drink now through 2010. **94 Editors' Choice** —*S.H. (3/1/2006)*

Hess Collection 2001 Cabernet Sauvignon (Mount Veeder) $40. Very, very tannic and closed now, which isn't surprising given its mountain appellation, this young Cab needs time in the cellar. But it should develop well. It's balanced, and there's a core of sweet blackberry and cherry fruit that should emerge by 2010. **90 Cellar Selection** —*S.H. (11/1/2005)*

Hess Collection 1995 Cabernet Sauvignon (Mount Veeder) $27. 87 —*M.M. (6/1/1999)*

Hess Collection 1995 Cabernet Sauvignon (Napa Valley) $25. 91 *(10/1/1999)*

Hess Collection 2000 Estate Cabernet Sauvignon (Napa Valley) $34. From a winery with a good track record, here's a full-bodied, flavorful red dinner wine. It has currant, blackberry, and oak flavors and intricate tannins, and is very dry. It's the sort of elegantly formulated Cabernet that Napa seems to produce so effortlessly. **89** —*S.H. (11/15/2004)*

Hess Collection 1999 Estate Cabernet Sauvignon (Napa Valley) $20. Smells ripe and oaky, with tons of black currant and blackberry fruit. Almost sweet in the mouth with rich oak and ripe fruit, but quite dry, with firm tannins that turn almond-skin bitter on the finish. **90 Editors' Choice** —*S.H. (11/15/2003)*

Hess Collection 2001 Hess Select Cabernet Sauvignon (California) $15. Juicy and filled with fruity flavors, with lots of blackberry, cherry, and ripe currant flavors. The tannins are on the rugged side, with jagged edges, but this is a pretty nice sip. **86** —*S.H. (4/1/2004)*

Hess Collection 2000 Select Cabernet Sauvignon (California-Washington) $15. This is a young and easy drinking red wine with enough character to stand up to a good roast. It has jammy flavors of blueberries and cherries that have been baked into a pie, and the wine finishes with a gritty feel of dry tannins. **85** —*S.H. (2/4/2003)*

Hess Collection 1997 Chardonnay (Napa Valley) $18. 83 *(6/1/2000)*

Hess Collection 2004 Chardonnay (Napa Valley) $19. Against a background of dusty earth and herbs, there's bright peach, pear, and pineapple flavors and a rich tangerine streak that meshes with the sweet new oak. It's all on the surface, but what a deliciously polished surface it is. **87** —*S.H. (12/1/2006)*

Hess Collection 2003 Chardonnay (Napa Valley) $19. This is a fairly simple wine that has been rather heavily oaked. It has pleasant flavors of peaches, mangoes, cinnamon, and cream, with lots of vanilla and char. **86** —*S.H. (11/1/2005)*

Hess Collection 2002 Chardonnay (Napa Valley) $18. Rich and ripe, this Chard brims with tropical fruit and Oriental spice flavors. It's pretty oaky, with splashy vanilla and toast notes that are perfectly in keeping with the size of the fruit. **87** —*S.H. (11/15/2004)*

Hess Collection 2001 Chardonnay (Napa Valley) $19. A lush, opulent Chard marked by oaky aromas and flavors. The underlying flavors are of tropical fruits, enhanced with vanilla, buttered toast, and smoky spices. Drinks very rich and flamboyant; a show-off wine. **90** —*S.H. (12/1/2003)*

Hess Collection 1997 Select Chardonnay (California) $11. 87 *(11/15/1999)*

Hess Collection 2002 Mountain Cuvée Red Blend (Mount Veeder) $35. A successful wine that shows its mountain origins in the density and concentration of tannins and flavors, yet it's so soft, in the modern way, it's immediately drinkable. Dry, robust flavors of black-cherries, chocolate, and wild herbs. **90** —*S.H. (10/1/2005)*

Hess Collection 2001 Select Syrah (California) $13. As fruity as can be, an explosion of blackberry, currant, plum, cherry, and stone fruits. For all the flavor, the wine is totally dry, with easy, rich tannins. Has an aggressive edge of acidity that marks some very young red wines. **85** —*S.H. (3/1/2004)*

Hess Collection 1998 Select Syrah (California) $13. Most reviewers found the inky, sulphury, onion-ring aromas "hard to get past," but once they did, they were glad to get to the deep, sweet blackberry juice that's topped by a dusty-soy note. Finishes with bitter chocolate and toast. It's sweet, though somewhat simple. **84** *(10/1/2001)*

Hess Collection 2001 Zinfandel (Dry Creek Valley) $27. Light-textured up front, the wine serves up modest black-cherry, toast, and herb flavors. Tannins are mild, as is the finish. **84** *(11/1/2003)*

HESS ESTATE

Hess Estate 2002 Cabernet Sauvignon (Napa Valley) $20. Hess almost always nails the vintage, and this is a nice example of a good, not great, Cab. It tastes mountainy, to judge from the tannins and fruit concentration. Will be good now with rich, well-marbled beef, but should develop for a few years. **87** —*S.H. (11/1/2005)*

Hess Estate 2001 Cabernet Sauvignon (Napa Valley) $20. This is a good wine that can hold its own among some far more expensive bottlings. It's ripe in currants and cassis, and well-oaked, with elaborate tannins. The mouth impression is of elegance, intensity, and balance. **91** —*S.H. (5/1/2005)*

HESS SELECT

Hess Select 2003 Cabernet Sauvignon (California) $15. Ripe in blackberry, cherry, cassis, and coffee flavors, with a dollop of oak, this Cab is dry and a bit edgy in tannins. Might soften and gain complexity in a year or two. **85** —*S.H. (2/1/2006)*

Hess Select 2002 Cabernet Sauvignon (California) $15. Polished and ripe, this softly tannic wine shows ripe black currant, cherry, and smoky oak flavors. It has just enough acidity to make it lively. **85** —*S.H. (6/1/2005)*

Hess Select 2004 Chardonnay (California) $10. This will tickle your Chardonnay tastebuds. It's a rich, creamy, oaky wine, with flamboyant pineapple custard, tangerine, tapioca, and spicy flavors that swirl into a long finish. **85 Best Buy** —*S.H. (2/1/2006)*

Hess Select 2003 Chardonnay (California) $10. Very oaky, with a blast of char and caramel. Under that is light fruit suggesting pineapples and pears, in a creamy texture. **84** —*S.H. (6/1/2005)*

Hess Select 2003 Syrah (California) $14. A decent value, the 2003 Hess Select Syrah starts off with scents of black-cherries and blackberries, then turns earthier on the palate, finishing with flavors of coffee and some rustic tannins. **86** *(9/1/2005)*

Hess Select 2002 Syrah (California) $13. Here's an everyday red wine, dry and fruity, with a simple structure. It's sweet throughout, from ripeness and oak. **84** —*S.H. (6/1/2005)*

HEWITT

Hewitt 2002 Cabernet Sauvignon (Rutherford) $75. Sumptuously intense fruit, fine toasted oak, and lush, smooth tannins all come together in this dramatic wine. It's a wonder of modern Napa Valley, offering delicious cassis, chocolate, and cherry flavors, with enough acidity for balance. Doesn't seem like an ager, but it sure is good now. **92** —*S.H. (12/15/2005)*

Hewitt 2001 Cabernet Sauvignon (Rutherford) $75. An inaugural release from Chalone Wine Group, and an important one. Possesses the hallmarks of greatness, from the subtle but complex mingling of cassis, cherry, herb, tobacco, mint, and dark chocolate flavors to the fabulously ripe, sweet tannins. Big and sturdy yet nuanced, this wine is gorgeous now and should last many years in the cellar. **95 Cellar Selection** —*S.H. (10/1/2004)*

Hewitt 2003 Estate Grown Cabernet Sauvignon (Rutherford) $80. Ripe, soft and polished, this is one of those Cabernets that feels fancy and upscale in the mouth. Mainly that comes from the quality of the tannins, which are refined and sweet, and the flavors, which are a combination of blackberry, ripe grapes, and new oak. Probably at its best now and for the next five years. **91** —*S.H. (12/15/2006)*

HEY MAMBO

Hey Mambo 2004 Red Malbec (Napa Valley) $14. Very dry and full-bodied, with gritty tannins that cry out for grilled meats, cheeses, and olive oil. It's rustic, but refined rustic, and a great value. **87** —*S.H. (8/1/2006)*

HIDDEN CELLARS

Hidden Cellars 1996 Cabernet Sauvignon (Mendocino) $15. 87 —*S.H. (3/1/2000)*

Hidden Cellars 1998 Eaglepoint Ranch-Mendocino Heritage Petite Sirah (Mendocino) $25. Looks so dark, you could fill a fountain pen with it. They take "Pet" seriously in these parts and vinify it the way the red soil grows it: fiercely strong and pushy. This is an enormous wine, massive in berry flavor, bone dry, sappy, and juicy. It will probably age forever. The most amazing thing is the alcohol, a modest 13.5%, which makes it balanced. **93** —S.H. (5/1/2002)

Hidden Cellars 2002 Alchemy Sauvignon Blanc (Mendocino) $13. Really too lean and watery to recommend, although it's clean and dry. **82** —S.H. (12/1/2004)

Hidden Cellars 1997 Syrah (Mendocino) $15. **88** —S.H. (5/1/2000)

Hidden Cellars 1998 Syrah (Mendocino) $15. The nose is promising, with big, jammy berry fruit, vanilla, and licorice aromas. The palate and finish, though, show a lot of tart berries, dry wood, and dried spices. Finishes with a coffee-meets-lemon-peel bite. **86** (10/1/2001)

Hidden Cellars 1997 Deep Valley Zinfandel (Mendocino) $30. A medium-full wine, with an appealing mix of nut, cocoa, anise, oak, and black fruit on the palate. Opens with paprika and cinnamon, plus cocoa aromas; closes with a definitive vanilla-anise-oak tang. **87** —D.T. (3/1/2002)

Hidden Cellars 1997 Medocino Heritage Zania-Hitzma Zinfandel (Mendocino County) $28. **90** —S.H. (9/1/1999)

Hidden Cellars 1996 Mendocino Heritage Eaglepoint Zinfandel (Mendocino County) $28. **90** —S.H. (9/1/1999)

Hidden Cellars 1997 Mendocino Heritage Pacini Vine Zinfandel (Mendocino County) $28. **89** —S.H. (9/1/1999)

Hidden Cellars 2000 Old Vines Zinfandel (Mendocino) $13. Not a very interesting wine, and evidence that this once unique and interesting winery has lost its cutting edge. This is an earthy wine with flavors of blackberries and plums. Turns watery on the finish. **84** —S.H. (9/1/2003)

Hidden Cellars 1998 Old Vines Zinfandel (Mendocino) $13. After being purchased by Parducci, this winery continues to craft big, bold, brawny reds from inland county. This release, from vines averaging 35 years of age, is less ripe than in warmer, drier vintages, but is still a kicker. Some sharp clove flavors accompany richer berry notes. It's dry and strong and has lots of Mendocino personality. **86** —S.H. (5/1/2002)

Hidden Cellars 1997 Sorcery Zinfandel (Mendocino) $28. **90** —S.H. (5/1/2000)

Hidden Cellars 1996 Sorcery Zinfandel (Mendocino County) $28. **90** —S.H. (11/1/1999)

HIDDEN MOUNTAIN RANCH

Hidden Mountain Ranch 1997 Chardonnay (San Luis Obispo) $11. **84** —S.H. (2/1/2000)

Hidden Mountain Ranch 1997 Zinfandel (California) $16. **83** —S.H. (2/1/2000)

Hidden Mountain Ranch 1998 Dante Dusi Vineyard Zinfandel (Paso Robles) $20. **85** —S.H. (2/1/2000)

HIGH PASS

High Pass 1998 Pinot Noir (Willamette Valley) $16. **83** —J.C. (12/1/2000)

High Pass 1998 Reserve Pinot Noir (Willamette Valley) $25. **87** —J.C. (12/1/2000)

HIGH VALLEY

High Valley 2003 Cabernet Sauvignon (Lake County) $25. This Cab tastes like it comes from a hot climate. It's soft in acids and tannins, with slightly sweet flavors of cherry liqueur. **83** —S.H. (11/1/2005)

High Valley 2004 Sauvignon Blanc (Lake County) $15. Here's another successful Lake County Sauvignon Blanc. It's zingy in refreshing lemon custard flavors, with a rich, butteriness brightened by citrusy acids. Finishes a little sweet. **86** —S.H. (11/1/2005)

High Valley 2003 Sauvignon Blanc (Lake County) $18. A bit thin in lemony flavor, with crisp acids and an edge of vanilla and sweet clover on the finish. Very dry and clean. Fine with picnic fare. **84** —S.H. (12/15/2004)

HIGHLANDS

Highlands 2002 Beatty Ranch Cabernet Sauvignon (Howell Mountain) $80. This is a big, tough, gritty powerhouse of a Cabernet. It's probably an ager, tannic and very dry, packed with jammy cherry and blackberry fruit. Hold until 2009. **88** —S.H. (3/1/2006)

Highlands 2002 Hozhoni Vineyard Syrah (Napa Valley) $30. Overtly sweet in residual sugar, which in my book is a sin in a wine that's supposed to be a dry table wine. Avoid. **80** —S.H. (3/1/2006)

Highlands 2002 Zinfandel (Howell Mountain) $30. Tasted alongside the winery's Beatty Ranch bottling, or at least less fruity, which lets the tannins dominate. The wine is fully dry, with coffee, dried herb, and pomegranate flavors. **85** —S.H. (3/1/2006)

Highlands 2002 Beatty Ranch Zinfandel (Howell Mountain) $30. There's a big, sturdy spine of tannins in this wine, as you'd expect from the origin, but acids are soft. So lush is the blackberry and coffee fruit that it's drinkable now. Thoroughly dry, this single-vineyard Zin is elegant and balanced. **89** —S.H. (3/1/2006)

HIGHTOWER CELLARS

Hightower Cellars 2003 Cabernet Sauvignon (Red Mountain) $50. This is a 90/10 Cab/Merlot blend, dense and oaky. The bourbon barrel flavors and hint of heat on the finish keep it from a higher score, but the dark streaks of mineral, espresso, and caramel add interest. The core cherry/cassis fruit is ripe and focused. **89** —P.G. (11/15/2006)

Hightower Cellars 2002 Cabernet Sauvignon (Columbia Valley (WA)) $31. Firm and balanced, Hightower's Columbia Valley Cab includes 7% Cabernet Franc. It's a bit grapy, with raspberry the dominant fruit, and young-vine flavors. Though light and fruity, it's well made and buoyed with bracing natural acids. **88** —P.G. (10/1/2006)

Hightower Cellars 2001 Cabernet Sauvignon (Columbia Valley (WA)) $28. I like the firm core of cassis, cherry, and plum; it says Cabernet loud and clear. A bit monolithic, but it transitions cleanly to well-managed tannins and makes a smooth landing. **88** —P.G. (11/15/2004)

Hightower Cellars 2000 Cabernet Sauvignon (Columbia Valley (WA)) $31. This is an interesting mix of fruit from Walla Walla, Red Mountain and Columbia Valley vineyards. Scents of alfalfa and spice lead into a loose-knit, engaging wine with a chalky, tannic finish. Another year or two will help smooth it out. **88** —P.G. (9/1/2004)

Hightower Cellars 2003 Pepper Bridge Vineyard Cabernet Sauvignon-Merlot (Walla Walla (WA)) $25. This is a 50/50 Cab/Merlot blend, all from Pepper Bridge vineyard. It tastes young and a bit dilute; there is an impression of herb and mushroom on the finish, but not enough overall punch to merit a higher score. **87** —P.G. (11/15/2006)

Hightower Cellars 2003 Merlot (Columbia Valley (WA)) $28. Smooth, hard, and glossy, with tightly wound fruits dappled with light herbs. The mix of plum, cherry, coffee, and earth is perfectly balanced, and the wine shows good density and extract. Grapes are from Red Mountain, Walla Walla, and Horse Heaven. **92** —P.G. (10/1/2006)

Hightower Cellars 2001 Merlot (Columbia Valley (WA)) $25. A smooth, full-bodied wine that really showcases what Washington Merlot is all about. Plummy and sweet, the fleshy fruit hints at raspberry preserves, leading to a silky, chocolate and vanilla finish. **89** —P.G. (11/15/2004)

Hightower Cellars 2000 Merlot (Columbia Valley (WA)) $28. Good vineyard sources and adept handling make for a tight, muscular Merlot that succeeds in a lackluster vintage. This shows some muscle, with firm, plump fruit and solid underpinnings of smooth tannin. Black olive/herbal notes add complexity. **89** —P.G. (9/1/2004)

HIGHWAY 12

Highway 12 2004 Serres Ranch Field Blend Bordeaux Blend (Sonoma Valley) $24. This Bordeaux blend comes from the Carneros-Sonoma Valley border, a cool area. But the vintage was extraordinarily hot, and the wine benefited. It's ripe in Cabernet character with rich, fine tannins and sweet oak. A lush, complex experience. **89** —S.H. (12/1/2006)

USA

HILL FAMILY ESTATE

Hill Family Estate 2002 Cabernet Sauvignon (Napa Valley) $38. Really too dry and tannic to enjoy now, this dark, young wine may do interesting things in four or five years. It has cassis and cherry flavors and enough supportive acidity to develop. **87** —*S.H. (12/15/2005)*

Hill Family Estate 2001 Origin Cabernet Sauvignon-Merlot (Napa Valley) $38. Kicks off with a velvety texture of ripe smooth tannins. They support a fine-tuned blend of cocoa, black cherry, herb, toast, plum, and chocolate flavors. Quite elegant, with a smooth, silky finish. Great price for this kind of quality. **91 Editors' Choice** —*J.M. (10/1/2004)*

Hill Family Estate 2002 Beau Terre Vineyard Merlot (Napa Valley) $30. You'll find a pretty good hit of dry, sticky tannins in this single-vineyard wine. They enclose a solid core of ripe blackberry and cherry fruit flavors that have been well-oaked. Try now with a good steak, or cellar for three to five years. **88** —*S.H. (12/15/2005)*

Hill Family Estate 2001 Beau Terre Vineyard Merlot (Napa Valley) $32. Smooth textured and framed in rich, ripe tannins, this classy Merlot serves up a lush, complex blend of black-cherry, cassis, blackberry, sage, thyme, and coffee flavors. Silky sleek on the long finish. **91** —*J.M. (9/1/2004)*

Hill Family Estate 2002 Pinot Noir (Carneros) $38. This is a ripe and full-bodied Pinot. It has cherry, tobacco, coffee, and herbal flavors, and a dusting of dry tannins. Drink now through 2006. **84** —*S.H. (12/15/2005)*

HINMAN

Hinman 1999 Chardonnay (Oregon) $10. The aroma and taste of this simple wine is completely dominated by artificial butter; it's like a mouthful of microwave popcorn. Many people like microwave popcorn, but not necessarily to drink. Apart from that, it's light, watery, and lacking any distinct varietal character. **82** —*P.G. (4/1/2002)*

Hinman 2001 Pinot Gris (Oregon) $11. The sweet, pleasant nose has plenty of citrus and tropical fruit. One whiff gets you excited. But the palate is nonexpressive, offering just the basics in terms of apples and spice. The finish, meanwhile, turns round and heavy, with no acid backbone to speak of. In the end you wind up wondering what happened to the promise of the bouquet. **84** —*M.S. (12/31/2002)*

Hinman 1999 Pinot Noir (Oregon) $13. Kudos for the clear lucidity of this simple little wine, with its fragrant bouquet of chocolate and sweet cherry. In the mouth there are flavors of stem and earth, cranberries and tart acids, with a hint of bitterness in the tannins. **86** —*P.G. (4/1/2002)*

Hinman 2000 Rogue Red Red Blend (Rogue Valley) $13. "Rogue" is right—there's Cabernet, Merlot, Syrah, Grenache, and Malbec in here. It's a good wine, but its components keep it from having much of a discernible style of its own. Roasted red berries and cherries dominate the palate; finishes with oak and a little acid. **86** —*D.T. (12/31/2002)*

Hinman 2002 Riesling (Oregon) $8. A big mouthful of tangy grapefruit, with a nice, crisp citrus-rind tang on the finish. **87** —*P.G. (12/1/2003)*

HIP CHICKS

Hip Chicks 2003 Reserve Pinot Noir (Willamette Valley) $35. A very tannic, rustic, earthy wine, whose burnt sugar, raisined fruit suggests grapes left to hang a bit too long. This rough, rugged style may suit some palates, but it seems a bit brutal for Pinot Noir. **85** —*P.G. (9/1/2006)*

HIP CHICKS DO WINE

Hip Chicks do Wine 2004 Pinot Gris (Willamette Valley) $15. Volatile, high-toned, peardrop aromas; the wine follows with acidic, pear-flavored fruit and some burn in the finish. **83** —*P.G. (2/1/2006)*

Hip Chicks do Wine 2002 Pinot Noir (Willamette Valley) $18. Medicinal, cherry fruit. Oak and mocha. Lean finish. **83** *(11/1/2004)*

HITCHING POST

Hitching Post 1988 Benedict Vineyard Pinot Noir (Santa Ynez Valley) $NA. Note the "Benedict Vineyard" label, from a time when Sanford had lost control. Alcohol 13.5%. Good color, cloudy with sediment. Rich red cherry aroma, anise, sweet beet, smoky char, spice. Dry, full-bodied, rich

in dark cherry fruit. Still tannic, should develop. Now-2010. **90** —*S.H. (6/1/2005)*

Hitching Post 2003 Cargasacchi Pinot Noir (Santa Rita Hills) $40. A bit too dry, acidic and tannic for my tastes, although it could age out. This wine has exotic spice, leather, coffee, and cherry-blackberry flavors. It's an interesting Pinot, from a great vineyard, yet difficult and challenging. Was it picked too early? **86** —*S.H. (11/15/2006)*

Hitching Post 2003 Fiddlestix Pinot Noir (Santa Rita Hills) $50. I tasted this wine with Kathy Josephs' Fiddlestix bottling, from her Fiddlehead label, and the wines are very different. This seems less ripe, harder in tannins, and stronger in acids. That is a stylistic choice, of course, but this wine is not as lush or immediately likeable, although it's still very good. Give it three to five years in the cellar. **89** —*S.H. (11/15/2006)*

Hitching Post 2003 Rio Vista Vineyard Pinot Noir (Santa Rita Hills) $40. The vineyard is from the warmer, eastern end of the appellation, yet this is still a dry, acidic, hard wine that's showing significant tannins. It's not offering a lot of pleasure now, although a rich steak will play well. A core of cherry-blackberry fruit suggests aging. Hold for a few years. **87** —*S.H. (11/15/2006)*

Hitching Post 2001 Sanford & Benedict Vineyard Pinot Noir (Santa Rita Hills) $40. A luscious Pinot with lip-smacking flavors of black-cherries, coffee, and herbs that earns extra points for its fine balance and mouthfeel. It's not a powerhouse but it's suave and has great finesse. **90** —*S.H. (2/1/2004)*

Hitching Post 2001 Santa Rita's Earth Pinot Noir (Santa Rita Hills) $30. Defines Pinot from this AVA, with its succulent cherry, raspberry, and blackberry flavors and clean acidity. For all the deliciousness it's a tad obvious, as if all the beauty were a veneer of sweet fruit. The challenge is to develop depth and substance. **89** —*S.H. (3/1/2004)*

Hitching Post 2000 Purisma Mountain Syrah (Santa Ynez Valley) $25. A voluptuously smooth, full-bodied Syrah that feels as plush as velvet on the palate. The fruit is elaborately layered, sending waves of blackberry, plum, and blueberry across the palate. Has a nice spicy edge that carries the fruity flavors into a long finish. **92** —*S.H. (3/1/2004)*

HOGUE

Hogue 1998 Bordeaux Blend (Columbia Valley (WA)) $10. 88 Best Buy —*P.G. (6/1/2000)*

Hogue 1997 Genesis Cabernet Franc (Columbia Valley (WA)) $18. 84 —*P.G. (9/1/2000)*

Hogue 2004 Cabernet Sauvignon (Columbia Valley (WA)) $9. Firm, tannic, and earthy, this budget-priced Cabernet mixes grapes from three different AVAs—Horse Heaven Hills, Yakima Valley, and Wahluke Slope. Though there are some sharp, green tannins, the juice shows no green bean or asparagus character, and there are some interesting highlights of anise and graphite. **85 Best Buy** —*P.G. (8/1/2006)*

Hogue 2002 Cabernet Sauvignon (Columbia Valley (WA)) $9. This is a fine effort in this price range. It has some real muscle, firm, stiff tannins and tight, herbal fruit. Nicely rounded at the end, with toasty, smoky oak filling in for the finish. **87 Best Buy** —*P.G. (7/1/2004)*

Hogue 1996 Columbia Valley Barrel Select Cabernet Sauvignon (Columbia Valley (WA)) $15. 89 —*L.W. (7/1/1999)*

Hogue 2001 Genesis Cabernet Sauvignon (Columbia Valley (WA)) $17. Hogue has a light touch with this accessible, well-blended Cab, which includes 9% Cab Franc, 7% Merlot and splashes of Syrah and Lemberger. For all that, it shows simple, strawberry-flavored fruit, with more tannin than power, and an earthy finish. **84** —*P.G. (11/15/2004)*

Hogue 2000 Genesis Cabernet Sauvignon (Columbia Valley (WA)) $16. Heavy toast in the aroma leads to emerging notes of blackberry, pencil lead, cassis, and pepper. Drinks full-bodied and rich and extracted with lots of jammy blackberry fruit, but it's very dry. A big wine, and a great value at this price. **91** —*S.H. (1/1/2002)*

Hogue 1999 Genesis Cabernet Sauvignon (Columbia Valley (WA)) $17. Has all the correct elements for Cabernet, including a rich, dark color, cassis and blackberry flavors, dry tannins, and a full-body. But it can't quite overcome a rustic tendency in the mouthfeel, which is rough and jagged. **85** —*S.H. (12/31/2002)*

Hogue 2001 Reserve Cabernet Sauvignon (Columbia Valley (WA)) $30. Hogue may have overreached here. Great new package, and they've got some ripe (14.6% alcohol) fruit. But the tannins are over the top, chalky, and still slightly green. The fruit, pretty and showing Bing cherry and blackberry flavors, can't quite muster the muscle to keep up. **87** —*P.G. (9/1/2004)*

Hogue 2000 Reserve Cabernet Sauvignon (Columbia Valley (WA)) $30. Magnificent, dense, compelling, a huge wine with so much flavor, it threatens to break right out of the bottle. Blackberry, cassis, currant, plum, dark chocolate, black cherry, peppery spices, and smoky oak and vanilla, but this is no mere fruit bomb. Kept under control by firm tannins and crisp acids. Hogue proves it can play with the big boys. **93** —*S.H. (1/1/2002)*

Hogue 1996 Reserve Cabernet Sauvignon (Columbia Valley (WA)) $30. 87 —*J.C. (4/1/2000)*

Hogue 1999 Vineyard Selection Cabernet Sauvignon (Columbia Valley (WA)) $17. Hogue's mid-level Cab is very well-made, with firm cassis fruit set against a backdrop of slightly chalky tannins. Showing a nice mix of cherry, cranberry, sandalwood, and earth, it gives more complexity than usual at this price. **87** —*P.G. (6/1/2002)*

Hogue 1998 Vineyard Selection Cabernet Sauvignon (Columbia Valley (WA)) $16. There is an appealing, loose-knit openness to this wine, which is labeled Cabernet Sauvignon but includes 15% Merlot and some Cabernet Franc and Lemberger as well. Lemberger, you say!? Well, it adds a touch of grapey insouciance to the wine, which is fruity, forward, nicely balanced, and easy to enjoy. **87** —*P.G. (6/1/2001)*

Hogue 1997 Cabernet Sauvignon-Merlot (Columbia Valley (WA)) $9. 88 Best Buy —*S.H. (7/1/1999)*

Hogue 2000 Cabernet Sauvignon-Merlot (Columbia Valley (WA)) $10. Hogue has been hit or miss lately, and this young, thin wine is more miss than hit. Hard and tannic, it seems almost weightless, offering little in the way of depth or fruit. **83** —*P.G. (6/1/2002)*

Hogue 1999 Cabernet Sauvignon-Merlot (Columbia Valley (WA)) $10. Hogue's low-cost red is a roughly 50/50 blend, with surprising ripeness and sweetness for a wine in this price range. There's just a bit of the bell pepper quality of inexpensive Washington Cabernet, but not enough to be off-putting. The wine is reasonably ripe, full, and well-balanced, with fruit, acids, and tannins in equal proportion. **85** —*P.G. (6/1/2001)*

Hogue 1998 Chardonnay (Columbia Valley (WA)) $10. 86 —*P.G. (6/1/2000)*

Hogue 2002 Chardonnay (Columbia Valley (WA)) $10. Nothing flashy here, just straightforward, tart fruit flavors leaning to apple, white peach, and other cool-climate fruit. **86** —*P.G. (9/1/2004)*

Hogue 2000 Chardonnay (Columbia Valley (WA)) $10. A crisply rendered, well-crafted effort from this reliable producer, this is a "fruit-forward" (as the winery likes to say) mix of citrus, apples, and spicy oak. Young and somewhat tight, it has the balance and the acid support for further aging. **87 Best Buy** —*P.G. (2/1/2002)*

Hogue 1999 Chardonnay (Columbia Valley (WA)) $10. Hogue makes a full line of Chardonnays and calls this least expensive bottling their "fruit forward" version. Although that's true, there's more to this wine than simple fruit. There's fruit aplenty, to be sure, but other layers of flavor interest as well: vanilla cream, caramel, and cinnamon spice. **88 Best Buy** —*P.G. (6/1/2001)*

Hogue 1998 Barrel Select Chardonnay (Columbia Valley (WA)) $15. 87 —*P.G. (6/1/2000)*

Hogue 2002 Genesis Chardonnay (Columbia Valley (WA)) $16. This is mainstream Chardonnay. Light pineapple fruit is smothered in the buttered popcorn scents and flavors of French oak and malolactic fermentation. **87** —*P.G. (11/15/2004)*

Hogue 1999 Genesis Chardonnay (Columbia Valley (WA)) $15. This is classic New World Chard, with its rich and spicy peach, pear, and even tropical-fruit flavors, and the elaborate overlay of spicy, smoky oak barrels. It's opulent and supple, with a creamy texture and a long, spicy finish. **88 Best Buy** —*S.H. (12/31/2002)*

Hogue 2002 Reserve Chardonnay (Columbia Valley (WA)) $22. This is for fans of the big, oaky style. It has plenty of sweet oak, wrapped around pineapple/tropical fruit. What Washington adds to the equation is acid, which gives the wine a solid underpinning that lifts it on the palate, and keeps it food friendly. **88** —*P.G. (9/1/2004)*

Hogue 2001 Reserve Chardonnay (Columbia Valley (WA)) $22. Oak, anyone? Wood sap, vanilla, smoky char, and all those indescribable oaky aromas and flavors dominate, to the wine's detriment. Somewhere in here is a nicely ripe wine with peach and pear flavors and crisp acids. Message to the winemaker: Lighten up. **85** —*S.H. (1/1/2002)*

Hogue 1999 Vineyard Selection Chardonnay (Columbia Valley (WA)) $14. This is a fine companion wine to Hogue's less-expensive "regular" Chardonnay. It shows the same luscious, tropical/citrus fruit flavors, the added layers of caramel and vanilla, the spicy finish. Just a bit more punch and power to it, and along with all that, a certain youthful tightness that suggests another half-year of cellar time is in order. **89** —*P.G. (6/1/2001)*

Hogue 1999 Chenin Blanc (Columbia Valley (WA)) $7. Hogue built its reputation with stunningly fruity, crisp, bright white wines such as this, and no one in America does a better fruit-forward Chenin. Delicious, like a New World Vouvray, with the same sweet/sour seduction and food-friendly acids. **87 Best Buy** —*P.G. (8/19/2003)*

Hogue 1998 Fumé Blanc (Columbia Valley (WA)) $8. 88 Best Buy —*L.W. (11/1/1999)*

Hogue 2003 Fumé Blanc (Columbia Valley (WA)) $9. Snappy, lemony, and clean, this refreshing wine gives you bracing green apple/lemon flavors through and through. Perfect for summer salads, shellfish, and pasta. **86** —*P.G. (9/1/2004)*

Hogue 2001 Fumé Blanc (Columbia Valley (WA)) $10. Young and crisp, this intensely spicy wine goes down nice and easy. Citrus, fig, and melon flavors are long and rich, showing some complexity. A pleasure to sip on a warm day. **86** —*S.H. (12/31/2002)*

Hogue 2000 Fumé Blanc (Columbia Valley (WA)) $10. Hogue pulls together a well-balanced, zesty wine with definite herbal nuances and stainless steel styling. It's crisp and precise, sleek and tart, a perfect wine to serve chilled with fresh winter oysters. **87 Best Buy** —*P.G. (12/31/2001)*

Hogue 1999 Gewürztraminer (Columbia Valley (WA)) $7. 85 —*P.G. (6/1/2000)*

Hogue 1998 Gewürztraminer (Columbia Valley (WA)) $7. 84 *(4/1/2000)*

Hogue 2003 Gewürztraminer (Columbia Valley (WA)) $10. Neat new red label for Hogue, and a further extension of their fruit-forward style. A lush, broad, accessible wine with tropical fruits displayed against a sweet, lightly spicy backdrop. **86** —*P.G. (7/1/2004)*

Hogue 2001 Gewürztraminer (Columbia Valley (WA)) $10. The Hogue style is "fruit forward" and so it is with this simple, off-dry, quite fruity Gewürz. The fruit runs to pear and citrus, and the finishing impression is of a sugary tartness. **85** —*P.G. (6/1/2002)*

Hogue 2000 Gewürztraminer (Columbia Valley (WA)) $8. Hogue emphasizes the fruit in their white wines, and this lip-smacking Gewürz is a good example of their style. Forward, fresh, and flavorful, its simple pleasures are easy to appreciate and enjoy. There's plenty of grapefruit and apricot fruit flavors, firm acids, and a tart, full finish. **87 Best Buy** — *P.G. (6/1/2001)*

Hogue 1999 Johannisberg Riesling (Columbia Valley (WA)) $7. 87 Best Buy —*P.G. (6/1/2000)*

Hogue 1998 Johannisberg Riesling (Columbia Valley (WA)) $NA. 86 — *L.W. (9/1/1999)*

Hogue 2002 Johannisberg Riesling (Columbia Valley (WA)) $9. Drinks a bit thin and watery, although there are pleasant flavors of white peaches, apricot, and citrus. At this price, you don't expect super concentration. Meanwhile, there's a refreshing tartness, and the wine, while basically dry, has a honeyed edge. **85** —*S.H. (1/1/2002)*

Hogue 2000 Johannisberg Riesling (Columbia Valley (WA)) $8. There's plenty of peachy punch to this off-dry Riesling, fresh off the excellent 2000 vintage in the Columbia Valley. It's meant to be served chilled—a

USA

good idea, which emphasizes the acids and takes the sweet edge off. Flavors of orange candy dominate the finish. **86** —*P.G. (6/1/2001)*

Hogue 1997 Genesis Blue Franc Lemberger (Yakima Valley) $14. 85 —*P.G. (9/1/2000)*

Hogue 2001 Terroir Lemberger (Columbia Valley (WA)) $20. Hogue has always done well with this oddball, Austrian grape, and this ramps it up a flavor notch or two, with the addition of 20% Syrah. Spicy, grapey, and loaded with black-cherry flavors, it finishes with broad, smooth tannins. **88** —*P.G. (1/1/2004)*

Hogue 2004 Merlot (Columbia Valley (WA) $9. Hogue's wines have been spotty of late, and the constant change in label design makes the wines difficult to track on the shelf. But this latest Merlot shows a marked improvement over recent vintages, a hopeful sign that this important producer is back on track. It's got a nice, soft entry, with black-cherry candy dominating the palate. There's a slightly burnt, raisiny flavor running through the finish, as if the grapes were a bit roasted, but the tannins are smooth and for the price it drinks well and delivers an extra dollop of intensity. **86 Best Buy** —*P.G. (8/1/2006)*

Hogue 2003 Merlot (Yakima Valley) $10. No wimpy Merlot here; Hogue pumps it up by adding generous amounts of Syrah and Lemberger to the blend. This has more texture, color and weight than any ten buck California Merlot, and enough muscular tannin to stand up to whatever you're throwing on the grill. **87** —*P.G. (8/1/2005)*

Hogue 2002 Merlot (Columbia Valley (WA)) $9. Hogue's striking new label and comfortable $9 price point seem to be aimed at bringing in loyal, long term customers. This is the right sort of wine for that; simple, pleasant, fairly generic but soundly made and, one suspects, reliably consistent year in and year out. **85** —*P.G. (7/1/2004)*

Hogue 2001 Merlot (Columbia Valley (WA)) $10. As always, this is very young, fresh, and jammy. Blatant acids push black-cherry marmalade flavors that are dry and rich. Has some real depth; a rich, creamy wine that makes up in power what it lacks in finesse. **87 Best Buy** —*S.H. (12/31/2002)*

Hogue 2000 Merlot (Columbia Valley (WA)) $10. This is the first time Hogue has made a varietally designated Merlot for their budget line, and it's a solid effort. Sweet, pretty fruit is played against tart tannins, with just a hint of cinnamon and mocha spice. Good for the price. **85** —*P.G. (6/1/2002)*

Hogue 1997 Barrel Select Merlot (Columbia Valley (WA)) $15. 87 —*P.G. (6/1/2000)*

Hogue 2001 Genesis Merlot (Columbia Valley (WA)) $17. A cool climate style of Merlot, with firm, herbal fruit dominating, despite the inclusion of some juice from warmer Wahluke Slope vineyards. Hints of volatile acidity and some hard, rough tannins make this a wine that can benefit from extended aeration. **84** —*P.P. (11/15/2004)*

Hogue 1998 Genesis Merlot (Columbia Valley (WA)) $17. Lots of juicy flavors here. Packed with jammy plum, blackberry, and cherry tastes that ooze over the tongue, and it's nicely dry, with no hint of sugar. But those meddlesome tannins are jagged, making for a rough ride. **85** —*S.H. (1/1/2002)*

Hogue 2001 Reserve Merlot (Columbia Valley (WA)) $30. Smooth and silky, it shows plenty of black-cherry fruit, with a pleasing roundness and a very soft, plush landing. Very drinkable. **87** —*P.G. (9/1/2004)*

Hogue 1996 Reserve Merlot (Columbia Valley (WA)) $30. 87 —*J.C. (4/1/2000)*

Hogue 1999 Vineyard Selection Merlot (Columbia Valley (WA)) $17. Hogue has three tiers of its red wines; this is the middle Merlot, showing fragrant, sweet fruit in the nose, along with hints of mocha and vanilla. It's actually a complex blend that includes Lemberger, Syrah, Cabernet Franc, and Sangiovese, though Merlot is the mainstay. It's a tart, tannic, vividly fruity, forward-drinking wine, ready right now. **87** —*P.G. (6/1/2002)*

Hogue 1998 Vineyard Selection Merlot (Columbia Valley (WA)) $16. Hogue puts bright, black-cherry fruit in the nose, even though the wine is still a bit tight in the glass. It's not a big or bold style, but a very well-made, one should say well-crafted, wine and a fine value. It shows good

structure and true varietal flavors, with a pleasing finish and dark, toasty tannins. **87** —*P.G. (6/1/2001)*

Hogue 2003 Pinot Grigio (Columbia Valley (WA)) $10. Friendly, fruity, likeable wines such as this may steal some of Oregon's thunder when it comes to affordable Pinot Gris. Fresh flavors of pear and apple are softly cushioned in a spicy wine with hints of citrus rind adding interest to the finish. **87** —*P.G. (7/1/2004)*

Hogue 1998 Pinot Gris (Columbia Valley (WA)) $8. 86 Best Buy —*S.H. (11/1/1999)*

Hogue 2001 Pinot Gris (Columbia Valley (WA)) $10. A fine example of why this fresh, fruity variety is gaining new fans. Apple and melon flavors are round and supple, with a creamy texture. Crisp acids make everything perky. **86 Best Buy** —*S.H. (12/31/2002)*

Hogue 2000 Pinot Gris (Columbia Valley (WA)) $10. Nice effort, with fresh, snappy stone fruits, augmented with a bit of spice and a hint of honey. This is a firm, tart, food-friendly wine, with a clean, lemony finish. **87 Best Buy** —*P.G. (2/1/2002)*

Hogue 1998 Genesis Pinot Gris (Yakima Valley) $13. 89 —*L.W. (2/1/2000)*

Hogue 2001 Riesling (Columbia Valley (WA)) $10. Riesling has long been a mainstay of Hogue—the winery makes some 52,000 cases and says they can't make enough—and it is a fruity, clean, standard-issue Washington style. Crisp and easy to enjoy, it's a "chill it and swill it" surefire summer sip. **86 Best Buy** —*P.G. (6/1/2002)*

Hogue 1997 Genesis Schwartzman Vineyard Riesling (Yakima Valley) $13. No oak here, thank you; just pure and delicious Riesling fruit with a hint of botrytis to add complexity to the apple-pear range of flavors. This dry-finished wine can hang with powerful chili-based dishes and is delightful as an apéritif. **90** —*L.W. (8/19/2003)*

Hogue 2001 Late Harvest Riesling (Columbia Valley (WA)) $12. Though the label says "late harvest" don't look for unctuous sweetness here; it's a laid-back, off-dry style which still has plenty of acid underpinning a generous core of peach/apricot fruit. Nuances of tea and just the barest hint of honey make it ideal for pairing with fruit-based desserts. **88** —*P.G. (6/1/2002)*

Hogue 2002 Terroir Riesling (Columbia Valley (WA)) $13. Very ripe, even hot for Riesling, this wine can only be described as unctuous. Packed with fat, tropical fruit, it tastes like a big fruit salad. Mango, papaya, and other flavors contribute plenty of big pleasure. **88 Best Buy** —*P.G. (11/15/2004)*

Hogue 2001 Genesis Sangiovese (Columbia Valley (WA)) $13. Pale in color, a delicate wine, with tea, cola, and smoky aromas. Turns fruity in the mouth, with light flavors suggesting black raspberries and red

cherries. Nicely dry, with crisp acidity. Clean and vibrant, if not very complex. **85** —*S.H. (6/1/2003)*

Hogue 2001 Terroir Sangiovese (Columbia Valley (WA)) $25. This limited-production (137 cases) wine is made primarily of Walla Walla Seven Hills Vineyard fruit, which lends a soft, pleasantly fruity cherry pie character. Four other red grapes are blended in, which gives it a generic red, rather than varietal, palate. **87** —*P.G. (9/1/2004)*

Hogue 1998 Genesis Burgess Vineyard Sauvignon Blanc (Columbia Valley (WA)) $15. 88 —*L.W. (2/1/2000)*

Hogue 1998 Sémillon (Columbia Valley (WA)) $7. 86 Best Buy —*2/1/2000*

Hogue 1999 Sémillon (Columbia Valley (WA)) $8. This distinctive wine, loaded with personality, is full of green-apple flavors, with wax, flint, and lime notes chiming in. It's not a hugely complex wine, nor an oversized monster, but it offers terrific flavors that will no doubt sing with oysters or clams this summer. **88 Best Buy** —*P.G. (6/1/2001)*

Hogue 1999 Genesis Sémillon (Columbia Valley (WA)) $13. About a third of this wine is fermented in oak, and it's enough to give it some vanilla in the nose to go with the fig and melon fruit. There are hints of grass and even anise as well, with the wine developing a bit of asparagus as it opens. **85** —*P.G. (12/31/2001)*

Hogue 2002 Syrah (Columbia Valley (WA)) $9. How do you make a Syrah this good at this price? Simple—you add 22% Lemberger

USA

(Blaufränkisch) and ramp up the boysenberries. This is tangy, loaded with bright fruit, and clean as a whistle. **87 Best Buy** —*P.G. (7/1/2004)*

Hogue 1997 Barrel Select Syrah (Columbia Valley (WA)) $15. **86** —*P.G. (9/1/2000)*

Hogue 1997 Barrel Select Syrah (Columbia Valley (WA)) $15. **87** —*S.H. (11/1/1999)*

Hogue 2001 Genesis Syrah (Columbia Valley (WA)) $16. Complex and inviting on the nose, with aromas of ripe blackberries, toasty oak, and pepper. Loses a little steam on the palate, where it shows less fruit and more herbal, rhubarby notes. Still, very good in a somewhat herbal idiom. **87** *(9/1/2005)*

Hogue 1999 Genesis Syrah (Columbia Valley (WA)) $25. A dark, tight, and tannic wine, reflecting the character of the vintage. Tart, earthy fruit firms up the center, making it chewy and concentrated. Time will open it up and do a bit to smooth out the hard, green tannins. **87** —*P.G. (12/31/2002)*

Hogue 1997 Genesis Syrah (Columbia Valley (WA)) $25. **88** —*P.G. (9/1/2000)*

Hogue 1996 Genesis Syrah (Columbia Valley (WA)) $15. **87** —*P.G. (9/1/2000)*

Hogue 2001 Terroir Syrah (Columbia Valley (WA)) $25. The opening scents are of black-cherry with a bit of nail polish, and the wine hits the palate in a disjointed way. Perhaps the addition of Lemberger should be re-thought; it makes the finish tart and grapy, and devalues the Syrah. And how can a wine from three completely different growing regions be called "terroir"? **85** —*P.G. (9/1/2004)*

Hogue 1999 Vineyard Selection Syrah (Columbia Valley (WA)) $18. Briary berry, herb, and vanilla aromas and flavors define this medium-weight, balanced wine. There are almost Port-like notes and white pepper accents on the palate, with a soft mouthfeel. On the back end, the wine turns leaner and more angular, showing some structure and a more serious metallic-herb note. **86** *(10/1/2001)*

Hogue 2003 Genesis Viognier (Columbia Valley (WA)) $16. Crisp and citric, this steely style of Viognier tastes of green apples, lime, and gooseberry. Some slightly bitter citrus skin flavors add interest to the finish, which is lively and hints at oak. But what's the story on the weird little cartoon character on the label? **87** —*P.G. (4/1/2005)*

Hogue 2001 Genesis Viognier (Columbia Valley (WA)) $15. Ripe and bold, here's a wine with plenty of flavor. Sweet tropical fruits and Lifesavers, you name it. It's in there, backed with bracing acids and a firm, steely structure. This is very rich, so consume it with the right foods. **87** —*S.H. (12/31/2002)*

Hogue 2000 Vineyard Selection Viognier (Columbia Valley (WA)) $16. Apricot and orange blossoms, flowers and ginger brighten up the nose, and the ripe, fruity flavors follow through in the mouth. The Columbia Valley is far enough north to allow the grapes to ripen without sacrificing the acids, avoiding the flabbiness that mars some California Viogniers. **88 Best Buy** —*P.G. (10/1/2001)*

HOLBROOK

Holbrook 2001 Syrah (Central Coast) $16. Here's an easy-drinking, everyday Syrah that pleases for its good fruit, dryness, and balance. It has enough punchy cherry and blackberry flavors to stand up to everything from pizza to steak. **84** —*S.H. (9/1/2005)*

HOLDREDGE

Holdredge 2004 Pinot Noir (Russian River Valley) $32. Too sweet by a mile, this Pinot, made from a variety of Dijon clones and older selections, tastes like it has residual sugar. The alcohol, which at 13.9% is relatively low for California, may explain that. **82** —*S.H. (7/1/2006)*

Holdredge 2002 Pinot Noir (Russian River Valley) $30. An easy, one-dimensional Pinot, with simple flavors of cola, coffee, and cherries, in a dry, very light wine. **84** —*S.H. (11/1/2004)*

Holdredge 2004 Wren Hop Vineyard Pinot Noir (Russian River Valley) $36. Right now this single-vineyard Pinot is a little gawky. It may be too young, and it's hard to tell where it's going. The individual parts are good but they haven't come together. There's a lot of primary cherry and

cola fruit, adequate acidity, dusty tannins, and rich oak. Try stashing it in a cool cellar for three or four years. **88** —*S.H. (7/1/2006)*

Holdredge 2002 Lovers Lane Vineyard Syrah (Russian River Valley) $28. Smells leathery and bacony, and has a rough, dry texture with tough tannins and a hint of cherry fruit. Try decanting. **84** —*S.H. (12/15/2004)*

Holdredge 2004 Zinfandel (Dry Creek Valley) $24. The winery's tech sheet describes this wine, made from very old vines, as having no residual sugar, but it certainly tastes a little sweet. There's a sugary edge to the wealth of cherry compote, black raspberry tea, and vanilla flavors. Try with barbecue smothered in sauce. **85** —*S.H. (7/1/2006)*

Holdredge 2004 Zinfandel (Alexander Valley) $24. Pours dark and heavy looking, and the aroma suggests Port, which the first sip confirms. Despite official descriptions as dry, the wine tastes sweet and hot, thanks to nearly 16 percent of alcohol. **80** —*S.H. (7/1/2006)*

HOLLY'S HILL

Holly's Hill 2000 Chardonnay (El Dorado) $15. Very lean and crisp, almost steely in the mouth. The fruit is thin, suggesting watered-down peach flavors. Yet there's something likeable about the intense citrusy cleanliness, the crisp, earthy acidity, the way the wine washes across the palate and stimulates the taste buds. **85** —*S.H. (12/15/2002)*

Holly's Hill 2003 Grenache (El Dorado) $17. Light in color, and soft and simple in the mouth, with cherry and raspberry flavors. Finishes clean and fruity. **84** —*S.H. (12/15/2004)*

Holly's Hill 2003 Rosé Traditionnel Grenache (El Dorado) $12. Quite full-bodied for a blush, and strong in fruity, spicy flavors. The tastes of strawberries, raspberries, and cinnamony pepper flood the mouth, perked up by good acids. Fully dry, it's a great food wine, and a great value. **87 Best Buy** —*S.H. (12/15/2004)*

Holly's Hill 2002 Mourvèdre (El Dorado) $18. Gritty, with raisiny flavors and soft acids. **82** —*S.H. (12/15/2004)*

Holly's Hill 2003 Tranquille Blanc Rhône White Blend (El Dorado) $16. Easy drinking, with peach and vanilla flavors and a creamy texture. Finishes dry. A white Rhône blend of Viognier and Roussanne. **84** —*S.H. (12/15/2004)*

Holly's Hill 1999 Sangiovese (California) $17. Lightish in color, it opens with earthy, tobacco aromas, a hint of mint and, if you really concentrate, blackberries. It's very limpid in the mouth, light as a feather, but the fruit is great. The concentrated blackberry taste is dry and flavorful, with wonderful acids. This is a very individualistic wine, and fun to drink. **87** —*S.H. (7/1/2002)*

Holly's Hill 2000 Syrah (El Dorado) $22. Dark and ripe, with brawny aromas and flavors of blackberries, chocolate, coffee, and leather. Dry, with good, rich tannins, but loses points because of a rough earthiness that makes it awkward and jagged in the mouth. **84** —*S.H. (6/1/2003)*

Holly's Hill 1999 Syrah (El Dorado) $20. Here's an edgy wine, a walk on the wild side. Explosive aromas of blueberries, crushed white pepper, earth, and smoke lead to slightly sweet wild-berry flavors, packaged in very silky tannins, although the acids are fine. It's a big wine, making up in chutzpah what it lacks in finesse. **85** —*S.H. (7/1/2002)*

Holly's Hill 2002 Wylie-Fenaughty Syrah (El Dorado) $22. A little sharp in acids, and a bit rough around the edges. This country-style wine has good fruit and a little residual sweetness. **83** —*S.H. (12/15/2004)*

Holly's Hill 2000 Viognier (Amador County) $15. Quite spicy, with a toasty, herbal edge. Citrus, peach, and melon notes add a fruity theme. Clean at the end. **87** —*J.M. (12/15/2002)*

Holly's Hill 2000 Vin Doux Viognier (California) $18. Bizarre. Tastes very sweet and chocolatey, with a candied gooey thickness; the acids are clean and sharp and nicely balance the sugar. But the wine smells like cardboard, with a faint apricot note. If you can get past the aroma, it's not bad. **82** —*S.H. (12/31/2001)*

Holly's Hill 2001 Zinfandel (Sierra Foothills) $17. Somewhat earthy and meaty, but also offering hints of bright cherry and spice. Oak and moderate tannins frame it all, finishing with a toasty edge. **85** *(11/1/2003)*

Holly's Hill 1999 Zinfandel (Amador County) $17. There's always a sense of anticipation in opening a new Sierra Foothills Zin, and this one lives up

USA

to the reputation. It's very strong and fruity, with huge aromas and flavors of wild berries, and it also has those raisiny, Port-like notes so common to this area. Despite the 15% alcohol, it drinks bone dry, with the silkiest tannins imaginable. **87** —*S.H. (7/1/2002)*

HOLLYWOOD & VINE

Hollywood & Vine 2000 Cabernet Sauvignon (Napa Valley) $78. Smooth, silky tannins frame a complex tier of bright cherry, cassis, blackberry, sage, anise, and toast flavors. The wine is elegantly structured, well balanced, and shows good balance, acidity, and length. A Napa Valley Cabernet with great finesse. **91 Cellar Selection** —*J.M. (9/1/2003)*

Hollywood & Vine 1999 Cabernet Sauvignon (Napa Valley) $75. Richly textured and lush on the palate, this smooth, complex wine offers a fine taste of what Napa Cabernet can achieve. Black-cherry, cassis, blackberry, tar, chocolate, herb, and earth notes are well integrated and layered. Firm, ripe tannins frame the ensemble, which finishes long. **92** —*J.M. (6/1/2002)*

Hollywood & Vine 2001 Chardonnay (Napa Valley) $40. Smooth and creamy textured, with lovely toast and spice notes up front. Melon, pear, apple, mandarin orange, and lemon flavors are evenly balanced. The wine is crisp and clean on the finish, yet also long and fresh. **91** —*J.M. (6/1/2003)*

HOME HILL

Home Hill 2002 Pinot Noir (Carneros) $30. Smells white peppery and hits the palate with a raw quality of acidic espresso, cola and oak, although sweet black-cherry flavors emerge after a while. Drink now. **84** —*S.H. (4/1/2004)*

HOMEWOOD

Homewood 1997 Merlot (Napa Valley) $25. Here's a rough, earthy wine, with some nicely ripe berry fruit and sturdy tannins. There are real jammy flavors in the mouth, suggesting blackberry marmalade, although it's dry. A little soft, it's round and full, and the finish turns hot and rough. **84** —*S.H. (12/1/2001)*

Homewood 1997 Kunde Vineyard Zinfandel (Sonoma Valley) $16. Dark purple in color, this wine begins with earthy, cardboard aromas and turns dense and Port-like in the mouth. The palate sensations are of tannins, acidity, weight and heat. The finish is thin and alcoholic. **82** —*S.H. (11/15/2001)*

HONIG

Honig 1996 Cabernet Sauvignon (Napa Valley) $22. 90 —*M.S. (10/1/1999)*

Honig 2001 Cabernet Sauvignon (Napa Valley) $30. Ripe in blackberry fruit, with chocolate, root beer, and currant notes, and well oaked, this dry wine shows plenty of polish and flair. It drinks well now, and has soft, velvety tannins. **87** —*S.H. (12/15/2004)*

Honig 2003 Sauvignon Blanc (Rutherford) $20. A bit of sweaty rawness accompanies the aromas of pineapple, grapefruit, and peach, while the palate is adequately citrusy but still a bit flat and low-acid. Good flavors but the mouthfeel is chunky. Ultimately the wine just tastes good. **87** *(7/1/2005)*

Honig 2001 Sauvignon Blanc (Napa Valley) $14. 90 Best Buy —*J.M. (11/15/2002)*

Honig 1999 Sauvignon Blanc (Napa Valley) $13. A pleasing, fruity blend of melon, citrus, fig, and herb flavors that finishes long and bright with a mineral edge. **88** —*J.M. (12/15/2001)*

HOODSPORT

Hoodsport 1998 Cabernet Franc (Yakima Valley) $20. 82 —*S.H. (9/1/2000)*

Hoodsport 1998 Chardonnay (Yakima Valley) $11. 82 —*S.H. (11/15/2000)*

Hoodsport 1998 Reserve Chardonnay (Yakima Valley) $17. 88 —*S.H. (11/15/2000)*

Hoodsport 1998 Chenin Blanc (Yakima Valley) $9. 81 —*S.H. (11/15/2000)*

Hoodsport 1998 Gewürztraminer (Yakima Valley) $9. 83 —*S.H. (11/15/2000)*

Hoodsport 1998 Lemberger-Cabernet (Yakima Valley) $11. 85 —*S.H. (9/1/2000)*

Hoodsport 2002 Pinot Noir (Oregon) $27. Simple, with a soft, creamy, mint and vanilla aroma. Tart rhubarb flavors, or perhaps strawberries and cream, fill up the middle. **85** *(11/1/2004)*

Hoodsport 1998 Sémillon (Yakima Valley) $9. 81 —*S.H. (11/15/2000)*

Hoodsport 2002 Syrah (Yakima Valley) $27. Ultraripe blackberries carry a suggestion of briary-brambly stemminess in addition to the jammy fruit flavors. Creamy and supple in the mouth, ending on a soft, easy note. **88** *(9/1/2005)*

HOOK & LADDER

Hook & Ladder 2003 Third Alarm Reserve Cabernet Sauvignon (Russian River Valley) $30. This is Cecil De Loach's brand, since he sold his winery to Boisset USA, and it's a nice Russian River Cab of which there aren't many. It shows a cool-climate delicacy and silkiness, but is tasty, with ripe flavors and bright acidity. **86** —*S.H. (12/1/2006)*

Hook & Ladder 2003 Chardonnay (Russian River Valley) $16. A decent everyday Chard, well-oaked, with solid peach, pear, and pineapple flavors, in a creamy texture. **84** —*S.H. (10/1/2005)*

Hook & Ladder 2003 Third Alarm Reserve Chardonnay (Russian River Valley) $25. Harsh and unrewarding, this thin Chard has a bitter, tobaccooey quality, and a medicinal finish. **81** —*S.H. (12/31/2005)*

Hook & Ladder 2004 Pinot Noir (Russian River Valley) $20. Here's a solid effort that shows great Russian River character in the silky, velvety texture and fine acids that frame the red cherry, cola and mocha fruit. The flavors are powerfully forward, yet the wine has both elegance and subtlety. It wouldn't hurt to decant it for a few hours. **88** —*S.H. (3/1/2006)*

Hook & Ladder 2003 The Tillerman Red Blend (Russian River Valley) $16. A sort of Super-Tuscan, although a rustic one, dry and acidic, with flavors of fresh berries. Cab Sauv, Cab Franc, and Sangiovese. **83** —*S.H. (11/1/2005)*

Hook & Ladder 2004 Zinfandel (Russian River Valley) $22. Cecil De Loach was famous for his Zinfandels when he owned De Loach Winery, and he shows his deft hand with this wine. It's not one of those kick-butt Zins, but instead it is balanced and medium-bodied, just a little heavier than Pinot Noir, with fine fruit and spice. What a great food wine. **87** —*S.H. (12/1/2006)*

Hook & Ladder 2003 White Zinfandel (Russian River Valley) $8. A typical white Zin, pale pink in color, with strawberry and vanilla aromas that drink off-dry. It's clean and crisp in acids. **83** —*S.H. (10/1/2005)*

HOOPES

Hoopes 2003 Cabernet Sauvignon (Oakville) $60. Opens with a lovely perfume, that sharp, recognizable whiff of ripe Cabernet fruit and toasty new oak. Cherries, cassis, wintergreen, spice, and anise in the mouth. Made in a more delicate, elegant style than many others, and so appealing for its silk and satin texture. **90** —*S.H. (9/1/2006)*

Hoopes 2002 Cabernet Sauvignon (Oakville) $60. Graceful and decadent, this wine is made by longtime growers now with their own brand. It's ripe and gooey in black currant, cassis, and chocolate, and beautifully structured, with fine, crisp acids and dusty tannins. As good as it is now, it should hold and improve for several years. **94 Editors' Choice** —*S.H. (11/1/2005)*

HOP KILN

Hop Kiln 1997 Chardonnay (Russian River Valley) $18. 88 —*S.H. (11/1/1999)*

Hop Kiln NV Big Red Red Blend (California) $13. This unusual blend is effusively fruity. You can find just about any flavor you want, but the cherries stand out. It's also dryish-sweetish, with the accent on dry, and well-structured. **85** —*S.H. (11/1/2005)*

Hop Kiln NV Rushin' River Red Red Blend (California) $15. Rich, ripe, and lush, this wine could only be from a warm climate in the New World. It's super-fruity but dry, with smooth, intricate tannins. The flavors range from red cherries and succulent forest blackberries to mocha and cinnamon spice. **87** —*S.H. (12/31/2005)*

Hop Kiln 2004 A Thousand Flowers White Blend (North Coast) $12. Tastes like all of its constituent varieties, with a complex array of peaches, apricots, grapefruits, apples, and figs. There's good acidity and what seems to be some residual sweetness. I'd love to see this wine completely dry. **84** —S.H. (11/1/2005)

Hop Kiln 2005 Thousand Flowers White Blend (California) $14. Fruit-forward and savory in peach, pineapple, apricot, melon, and spice flavors, this blend of five varieties is mainly Sauvignon Blanc and Chardonnay, which gives it some nobility. It's a dry, refreshing, friendly wine. **84** —S.H. (11/15/2006)

Hop Kiln 2004 Old Windmill Zin Zinfandel (Russian River Valley) $22. If you like your Zins overtly sweet, this one's for you. It's soft and silky, with upfront blackberry, cherry, raspberry, cola, and chocolate flavors. Almost sweet enough for a dessert wine. **82** —S.H. (11/15/2006)

Hop Kiln 2001 Turtle Creek Vineyard Zinfandel (Russian River Valley) $16. Fairly woody, with bright acidity and hints of cola, smoke, herb, black-cherry and spice flavors. The finish is a tad short, with mild tannins. **84** (11/1/2003)

HOPKINS VINEYARD

Hopkins Vineyard 1999 Estate Bottled Cabernet Franc (Western Connecticut Highlands) $16. Herbal, green aromas are surrounded by leather, barrel char, and some berry syrup. The mouth is sharp, featuring mostly pie cherry and cranberry fruit, and while the finish broadens out somewhat, it's still a linear, hollow wine without much richness. **83** —M.S. (3/1/2003)

Hopkins Vineyard 1999 Estate Bottled Chardonnay (Western Connecticut Highlands) $15. Hints of vanilla and hazelnut dominate here, while the fruit takes a back seat. Some nice apple and pear notes come through, nonetheless. Toasty, clean, but a bit short on the finish. **84** —J.M. (7/1/2002)

HOPPER CREEK

Hopper Creek 2002 Merlot (Napa Valley) $35. From Yountville, an elegant wine with a dollop of Cabernet for complexity. It's delicious in pure, cassis-laced cherry kirsch and blueberry flavors, with fine oak seasoning. The texture is soft and velvety, with vibrant acidity accompanying lush tannins. **92** —S.H. (8/1/2006)

HOURGLASS

Hourglass 2003 Cabernet Sauvignon (St. Helena) $115. This supple Cabernet feels gentle and soft on entry, then stuns with hidden power and depth. Fully ripe, with chocolatey cassis, and cherry flavors. Marked by firm tannins, it is generous now, yet should hold for a good 10 years. **93** —S.H. (8/1/2006)

Hourglass 2001 Cabernet Sauvignon (St. Helena) $90. The oak jumps out—think char, vanilla, and new barrels. But this magnificent wine is much more than that. It's intensely ripe with cassis, pure and focused. It has sweet tannins and fine, good acidity and perfect balance. Superb right out of the bottle, but should hold through the decade. **94** —S.H. (10/1/2004)

Hourglass 2000 Cabernet Sauvignon (Napa Valley) $85. This is gorgeous. Smooth, rich, ripe, and loaded with complex flavors. Black-cherry, blackberry, plum, cloves, coffee, spice, chocolate, licorice, anise, menthol, and eucalyptus all weave a kaleidoscope of taste for a tantalizing, heady, and satisfying wine. Velvety tannins frame it all, leaving it long and lush at the end. Just when you think it's over, a new wave of plum, chocolate, toast, and vanilla teases the palate for an even longer finish. **95 Editors' Choice** —J.M. (12/15/2003)

Hourglass 1998 Cabernet Sauvignon (Napa Valley) $75. A gloriously concentrated wine, filled with black-cherry, plum, blackberry, chocolate, licorice, raisin, and herb flavors. Plush, velvety, complex, elegant, and voluptuous all the way to its long, long finish. Unfortunately, only 48 cases were made. The good news is that we'll see as much as 800 cases for the 2000 vintage. **95 Cellar Selection** —J.M. (5/1/2002)

Hourglass 1997 Cabernet Sauvignon (Napa Valley) $125. **95** —J.M. (12/31/2001)

HOWELL MOUNTAIN VINEYARDS

Howell Mountain Vineyards 2001 Cabernet Sauvignon (Howell Mountain) $60. This wine is very tannic now, but it's a cellar candidate. Under that blanket of tannins is a fabulously ripe well of blackberry, cherry, and dusty cocoa fruit. Drink 2009 and beyond. **91** —S.H. (6/1/2005)

Howell Mountain Vineyards 2000 Cabernet Sauvignon (Napa Valley) $36. Thin and unimpressive despite a lavish overlay of oak. The label reads HMV, not Howell Mountain Vineyards, and you get the feeling it's a sort of second label for lesser quality wines. Hard to find any charm at all, and it's certainly not an ager. **84** —S.H. (12/15/2003)

Howell Mountain Vineyards 2001 Beatty Ranch Cabernet Sauvignon (Howell Mountain) $75. What a special wine this is. It blasts forth with the pencil lead, cedar, and black currant aromas of a great Bordeaux, and boasts the tannins that this mountain appellation is famous for. You could drink it now with a big steak, but this ageable Cab will be looking quite nice after 2010. **94** —S.H. (6/1/2005)

Howell Mountain Vineyards 2001 Black Sears Vineyard Cabernet Sauvignon (Howell Mountain) $75. Black as midnight and tough in tannins. Don't touch this baby for a long time! Dry, balanced, and oaky, it shows tremendous blackberry and currant fruit that should begin to reveal itself by 2010. **93** —S.H. (6/1/2005)

Howell Mountain Vineyards 2001 HMV Cabernet Sauvignon (Napa Valley) $36. Young and impressive for its size and balance, despite some hefty tannins, this wine won't come into its own for a while. The ripecore of blackberry and black-cherry fruit is big enough to suggest cellaring. Hold until 2007 and beyond. **89** —S.H. (10/1/2005)

Howell Mountain Vineyards 2003 Beatty Ranch Zinfandel (Howell Mountain) $38. Compared to the winery's Black Sears Zinfandel, also off Howell Mountain, this is earthier and less compelling. It's comparably high in alcohol, with ripe fruity flavors and powerful tannins, but it doesn't have the depth and complexity. Drink now. **85** —S.H. (5/1/2006)

Howell Mountain Vineyards 2002 Beatty Ranch Zinfandel (Howell Mountain) $38. How big this wine is, but how drinkable now. It's not just the fruit, which ranges from blackberries to cherries and cocoa, it's the tannic structure. Somehow it's soft and intense at once. Totally dry, and not overly alcoholic, this Zin picks up even more power on the finish. **93** —S.H. (10/1/2005)

Howell Mountain Vineyards 2001 Beatty Ranch Zinfandel (Howell Mountain) $34. Rich and round on the palate; texture is this wine's strong point. The flavors range from licorice to plum, cherry, chocolate, herb, and spice. On the finish, it's fresh and lively, with pretty toast to frame it. Quite nice. **90** (11/1/2003)

Howell Mountain Vineyards 1997 Beatty Ranch Zinfandel (Howell Mountain) $NA. **90 Best Buy** —S.H. (6/1/1999)

Howell Mountain Vineyards 2003 Black Sears Vineyard Zinfandel (Howell Mountain) $38. This is a huge (16% alcohol) decisive, clearly Californian Zin. The flavors are massively rich and fruity and the wine is, in its own eccentric way, addictingly good. Just be sure to bring a designated driver. **90** —S.H. (5/1/2006)

Howell Mountain Vineyards 2002 Black Sears Vineyard Zinfandel (Howell Mountain) $38. An eccentric, difficult, complex Zin. It smells of intense white pepper, although in the mouth, cherries and blackberries show up. Then the tannins close in like a stranglehold. Cellar this interesting wine for a few years. **90** —S.H. (10/1/2005)

Howell Mountain Vineyards 2001 Black Sears Vineyard Zinfandel (Napa Valley) $34. Smooth and sleek, with a finely crafted mesh of dark plum, blackberry, cassis, chocolate, coffee, cedar, raspberry, and toast flavors. Beautifully balanced and layered, it serves up plenty of interest and pleasure. Long and lush on the finish. **92** (11/1/2003)

Howell Mountain Vineyards 1997 Black Sears Vineyards Zinfandel (Howell Mountain) $NA. **88** —S.H. (6/1/1999)

Howell Mountain Vineyards 2003 Old Vine Zinfandel (Howell Mountain) $26. At 15-3/4% alcohol, this wine is a little hot, but that's in keeping with the enormity of fruit. The blackberry tart and chocolate-covered cherry flavors are so enormous, they seem to require a package of equal size. The result is dry, balanced, and delicious. **90** —S.H. (5/1/2006)

Howell Mountain Vineyards 2001 Old Vine Zinfandel (Howell Mountain) $24. Firmly structured and focused, with a core of blackberry, tar, spice, cherry, and herb flavors. Toasty oak frames the layers of flavor, while ripe tannins give good support, though it's a little dry on the finish. **87** (11/1/2003)

Howell Mountain Vineyards 1997 Old Vine Zinfandel (Howell Mountain) $24. 91 —S.H. (6/1/1999)

Howell Mountain Vineyards 2002 Old Vines Zinfandel (Howell Mountain) $26. Kind of tough in the mouth at this time, with aggressive tannins that effectively bury the blackberry flavors. There's also a streak of hung meat or smoky leather that adds dimension. Best to let it soften for a few years. **87** —S.H. (10/1/2005)

HRM REX GOLIATH

HRM Rex Goliath NV Cabernet Sauvignon (Central Coast) $9. Good, fruity flavors and rich tannins here, but the wine finishes sweet in sugary cherries. Will do for folks who like that sort of thing. **83** —S.H. (6/1/2005)

HRM Rex Goliath NV Cabernet Sauvignon (Central Coast) $8. 80 —J.M. (6/1/2003)

HRM Rex Goliath NV Cabernet Sauvignon (California) $9. Dry, smooth, and rustic, this Cab offers berry and oak flavors in a full-bodied wine, with clean, rich tannins. It'll be fine for everyday purposes. **84** —S.H. (12/15/2005)

HRM Rex Goliath 2004 Chardonnay (Central Coast) $9. This Chard is kind of thin in fruit and top heavy in oak. It tastes of alcohol mildly flavored with peach essence and slathered in toast and vanilla. **82** —S.H. (12/15/2005)

HRM Rex Goliath 2003 Chardonnay (Central Coast) $9. Decent, with fruity flavors and a spicy coat of toasty oak. Finishes clean and simple. **83** — S.H. (6/1/2005)

HRM Rex Goliath 2001 Free Range Chardonnay (Central Coast) $8. This is the kind of modest little wine you can serve in the backyard at your next block party. It will satisfy most Chard drinkers with its pretty array of tropical fruit flavors and smoky overlay of oak. Finishes dry and spicy. **84** —S.H. (12/31/2003)

HRM Rex Goliath NV Merlot (Central Coast) $9. Can't really recommend this tough, vegetal wine, but it does have a fruity, cherry flavor on the finish, and is dry. **82** —S.H. (6/1/2005)

HRM Rex Goliath NV Merlot (Central Coast) $8. Tangy cherry flavors are framed in smoky, oaky flavors. Licorice-like at the end. **82** —J.M. (9/1/2003)

HRM Rex Goliath NV Merlot (California) $9. Fruity, tart, and simple, this wine has some awkward edges. There's a rustic feeling in the mouth that leads to a medicinal finish. **82** —S.H. (12/15/2005)

HRM Rex Goliath 2004 Pinot Grigio (California) $9. This deliciously gulpable PG shows why the varietal is so popular in America. Beautifully dry and crisp, full flavored in lemon, lime, peach, and pepper notes, and clean through the finish, and you can't beat that everyday price. **85 Best Buy** —S.H. (12/15/2005)

HRM Rex Goliath NV Pinot Noir (California) $9. Light and simple, with pleasant cola, rhubarb, and sage flavors and a delicate, silky mouthfeel. Turns dry and clean on the finish. **83** —S.H. (12/15/2005)

HRM Rex Goliath 2001 Free Range Pinot Noir (Central Coast) $8. Weird name, simple wine, but not a bad one. It's awfully hard to get distinction in Pinot Noir at this price. The wine is dry, and there are some berry flavors wrapped in silky tannins. **84** —S.H. (7/1/2003)

HRM Rex Goliath 2003 Free Range Shiraz (Central Coast) $9. Gets the nod for its upfront, juicy flavors of cherries, blackberries, raspberries, plums, chocolate, you name the fruit, it's in there. Yet it somehow maintains dryness and crispness. Yummy stuff. **85 Best Buy** —S.H. (6/1/2005)

HUBER

Huber 2004 Chardonnay (Santa Rita Hills) $25. From an estate in the appellation's tenderloin, an intensely minerally, high-acid wine with bright citrus flavors and lots of sweet, flashy oak that adds a vanilla-cream richness. This is unusually food-friendly and versatile for a Chardonnay. **90** —S.H. (3/1/2006)

Huber 2005 Estate Grown Chardonnay (Santa Rita Hills) $21. Very crisp in zesty acidity, bone dry, and with exotic flavors. This stony, minerally

Chardonnay impresses for its firm structure. Flavorwise, it's explosive in lemons, limes, crunchy pears, Asian spices, and buttery vanilla, even though it's unoaked. Showcases its terroir in a fine way. **90** —S.H. (11/15/2006)

Huber 2004 Dornfelder (Santa Rita Hills) $25. How dark this wine pours, with a purple glycerine that stains the glass. Aromatically, it's a powerhouse with heaps of violets, blackberry jam, raw meat, and caramelly vanilla. In the mouth, acidity hits first, then fruit, and then the tannins lock everything down. Powerful but immature. Hold until 2010. **89 Cellar Selection** —S.H. (12/1/2006)

Huber 2004 Pinot Noir (Santa Rita Hills) $34. This is a good regional wine, with tasty cherry pie, smoke, and spice flavors. It has good acidity and an intense, spicy finish. Drink now. **88** —S.H. (3/1/2006)

HUG

Hug 2003 Bassetti Vineyard Syrah (San Luis Obispo County) $40. This crisp, medium-weight wine starts off with scents of rubber and smoke that give way to bright berry fruit. Very vibrant and tart on the finish, where it picks up hints of coffee and plum. **86** (9/1/2005)

HUMANITAS

Humanitas 2001 Chardonnay (Edna Valley) $15. This is the "expensive" one on my list, but all net proceeds are donated to charity. In Latin, "humanitas" means "philanthropy," and winery founder Judd Wallenbrock has made giving back through fine wine his mission. A fragrant, melony front gives way to vanilla and spice overtones. It fans out to reveal hints of orange, lychee, grapefruit, and lemon flavors, and finishes with moderate length. **87** —J.M. (11/15/2003)

HUNDRED ACRE

Hundred Acre 2000 Cabernet Sauvignon (Napa Valley) $100. Redolent of rose petals and black-cherry in the nose, it fans out into a silky-smooth texture that supports elegant black currant, blackberry, plum, anise, and spice flavors with just a hint of chocolate and herbs. A lengthy finish leaves a velvety impression on the palate. This is an auspicious debut made exclusively from the owner's estate vineyard. Barrel samples from 2001 show it's no flash in the pan. The next Napa cult Cab? **95 Cellar Selection** —J.M. (11/15/2002)

HUNNICUTT

Hunnicutt 2001 Cabernet Sauvignon (Napa Valley) $37. Has all the hallmarks of Napa Cab, from the cassis fruit to the expensive oak and the smooth, ripe tannins and good acids. It's very good, and would merit a few extra points with additional fruity concentration. But it's dry and elegant. **89** —S.H. (12/31/2004)

Hunnicutt 2003 Zinfandel (Napa Valley) $29. Packs a wallop with classic Zin personality, a big, rich, likeable wine filled with thrillingly ripe blackberry, cherry, and chocolate flavors, and thick, gooey tannins. It's in your face, but has a subtlety and grace that belie the size. **88** —S.H. (3/1/2006)

Hunnicutt 2002 Zinfandel (Napa Valley) $28. This Zin has the classic structure of a fine Cabernet, with firm, dusty tannins, a full-bodied mouthfeel and flavors of dark stone fruits and blackberries. What makes it altogether Zinny is the brambly, peppery fruit. Should be great with a grilled steak. **91** —S.H. (12/31/2004)

HUNT CELLARS

Hunt Cellars 1999 Reserve Rhapsody Meritage Cabernet Blend (Central Coast) $29. This Bordeaux blend offers blackberry, plum, and cassis and a hint of tobacco. The tannins are considerable and gritty, and the finish is bone dry. **84** —S.H. (5/1/2003)

Hunt Cellars 1998 Cabernet Sauvignon (Paso Robles) $40. Smells raisiny and pruny, and flavors of overripe, dehydrated grapes show up in the mouth. Fully dry, with soft tannins and acids. The alcohol is a modest 13.5 % but the wine feels hot and prickly. **84** —S.H. (5/1/2003)

Hunt Cellars 2000 Destiny Vineyards Bon Vivant Cabernet Sauvignon (Paso Robles) $34. This is a plump and juicy Cabernet whose softness typifies Paso Robles reds. Despite the cherry flavors, this is an earthy wine, with suggestions of dill and sweet oregano. **86** —S.H. (10/1/2005)

Hunt Cellars 2000 Destiny Vineyards Mt. Christo Block Cab-Ovation Cabernet Sauvignon (Paso Robles) $60. Pungently dry, this earthy wine has tobacco and herb flavors that finish with a suggestion of cherries. It's not a fruity wine, although it is a fairly tannic one. **86** —*S.H. (10/1/2005)*

Hunt Cellars 2001 Destiny Vineyards Mt. Christo Block Cab-Ovation Reserve Cabernet Sauvignon (Paso Robles) $48. Hunt's 2001 Duets, a Cab-Syrah blend, is a very good wine. This wine, oddly, is not. It has a metallic sharpness that seems almost like artificial acidity, and feels awkward and harsh in the mouth. Too bad, because the flavors are pretty. **83** —*S.H. (12/1/2005)*

Hunt Cellars 2000 Moonlight Sonata Chardonnay (Central Coast) $24. This is hot-country Chard spiced up with strong oak that makes it awkwardly flamboyant. Peach syrup and nectarine flavors are tarted up with ginger, cinnamon and pepper, wrapped in rustic tannins. The flavors are tasty but it lacks balance and harmony. **84** —*S.H. (12/15/2002)*

Hunt Cellars 1999 Harmony Reserve Merlot (Central Coast) $27. Opens with aromas of freshly baked cherry pie crust, tar, licorice, and ginger-snap, with similar flavors. Feels big and rich in the mouth, with a thick, dense texture. Clearly not a classic Merlot, but interesting in its own right. **86** —*S.H. (12/15/2003)*

Hunt Cellars 1997 Petite Sirah (Central Coast) $35. Petite Sirah is enjoying a comeback, and here's one reason why. This is a deeply fruity, well oaked, balanced wine. It's rich and intricately detailed, with a myriad of spicy berry flavors. Combines the light softness of Pinot Noir with Cabernet's fullness of body to produce a food-worthy wine that's delicious on its own. **90** —*S.H. (12/1/2002)*

Hunt Cellars 2001 Zinfandel Port Port (Paso Robles) $45. This is a super-sweet wine, and who doesn't like fabulously sweet flavors of cherries, gingerbread, toffee, caramel, white chocolate, and plum pudding? Fortunately, there's good acidity for balance. It's a little rustic, but the decadence ultimately rules. **88** —*S.H. (12/31/2005)*

Hunt Cellars 2001 Destiny Vineyards Duet Red Blend (Paso Robles) $32. This Cab-Syrah blend, from a winery that's worked very hard on its reds over the years, is rewarding for its big, upfront surge of blackberry, cherry, and cocoa flavors that last through a long, spicy finish. It's balanced in alcohol, and dry. **89** —*S.H. (12/1/2005)*

Hunt Cellars 1997 Rhapsody in Red Red Blend (California) $50. A blend of Sangiovese, Merlot, and Pinot Noir that is profoundly overpriced. It's soft and flabby, with dry, indeterminate berry and cardboard aromas and flavors. Goes through the mouth with little body and little finish except heat. **82** —*S.H. (9/5/2002)*

Hunt Cellars 2000 Destiny Vineyards Rhapsody Sangiovese (Paso Robles) $20. Starts off with raisiny, pruny aromas of dessicated grapes, with earth and tobacco notes, and then turns sharp in the mouth, although the tannins are light and silky. Flavors veer toward dark berries, with angular tannins and a jagged mouthfeel. **84** —*S.H. (9/1/2002)*

Hunt Cellars 2002 Starlight Concerto Destiny Vineyards Sauvignon Blanc (Paso Robles) $34. Nobody says Paso Robles is white wine country, as evidenced by this unbalanced hulk that weighs in at 15.7%. One reviewer refused to rate it, calling it a "strange brew of heat and chemicals," while our other two panelists found it barely acceptable but loaded down with oak, butterscotch and vanilla. **80** *(7/1/2005)*

Hunt Cellars 2005 Afternoon Delight Syrah Rosé Syrah (Paso Robles) $22. Pale in color, simple in structure and on the slightly sweet side, this blush has delicate flavors of strawberries, rose petals, and herb tea. **83** —*S.H. (12/31/2006)*

Hunt Cellars 1997 Calif Syrah (California) $25. Woody and floury, marked by herbs and licorice (maybe the herb is tarragon?) and a tart, old-wood, dusty quality that finishes with some bitter-chocolate notes. **84** *(11/1/2001)*

Hunt Cellars 2001 Destiny Vineyards Hilltop Serenade Reserve Syrah (Paso Robles) $32. Flavorful and full-bodied, this Syrah with the long name has rich cherry and black raspberry flavors that are balanced with fine tannins. It's fully dry, with a long finish, and should accompany fancy fare. **90 Editors' Choice** —*S.H. (9/1/2005)*

Hunt Cellars 1999 Serenade Syrah (California) $22. A sturdy, structural wine where tannins, oak, acidity, and alcohol play starring roles. The fla-

vors veer towards earth, sage, plums and tobacco, and are underscored by sizable tannins. This wine will soften and become richer in time. Drink now with barbecue, or cellar. **87** —*S.H. (12/1/2002)*

Hunt Cellars 1998 Zinfandel (Paso Robles) $24. 90 —*S.H. (5/1/2000)*

Hunt Cellars 2001 Old Vines Zinfandel (Paso Robles) $28. Quite spicy and smoky, framed in vanilla and toast notes. Blackberry, licorice, and herbal notes are on the follow-up. The wine has a resiny edge on the finish. **85** *(11/1/2003)*

Hunt Cellars 2001 Outlaw Ridge Vineyard Zinfandel (Paso Robles) $27. Black-cherry, blackberry, licorice, coffee, and herb flavors blend nicely here. Tannins are a little powdery, with the finish moderate in length and somewhat resiny at the end. **86** —*J.M. (11/1/2003)*

Hunt Cellars 2001 Outlaw Ridge Vineyard, Lower Bench Zinfandel (Paso Robles) $30. A bright-edged wine with peppery black-cherry, blackberry, clove, anise, coffee, herb, and spice flavors. Tannins are modest, with just a touch of astringency. **87** —*J.M. (11/1/2003)*

Hunt Cellars 2000 Outlaw Ridge Zinphony #1 Zinfandel (Paso Robles) $30. The brawniest of Hunt's releases, it borders on Port-like, with 14.7% alcohol and a burst of plummy, raisiny fruit. Other notes include char, smoke, and a caramelized, pie-crust scent. Drinks big, slightly sweet, hot and peppery. **85** —*S.H. (9/1/2002)*

Hunt Cellars 1999 Zinphony Zinfandel (Paso Robles) $20. Marred by excessively raisiny aromas and flavors. Zinfandel is notoriously uneven to ripen, and this crop seems to have been marked by overripe grapes that made their way into the blend. It's dry, with soft Paso tannins and acids, but the balance is off. **84** —*S.H. (11/1/2002)*

Hunt Cellars 2000 Zinphony #2 Old Vines Zinfandel (Paso Robles) $28. If anything, more concentrated than this winery's Reserve. It's hard to imagine denser, more powerful fruit. Explosively berried, yet dry, supple, balanced, and not overly alcoholic. Defines Paso Zin in its lushness, soft tannins, and low, polished acidity. **92** —*S.H. (9/1/2002)*

Hunt Cellars 1999 Zinphony #2 Reserve Zinfandel (Paso Robles) $24. Soft and plump as a big baby, and filled with succulent, juicy blobs of blueberries and raspberries, this dry Central Coast wine makes up for the lack of tannic structure with delicious flavors. **91** —*S.H. (9/1/2002)*

HUNT COUNTRY VINEYARDS

Hunt Country Vineyards 2002 Dry Riesling (Finger Lakes) $10. This wine starts slowly, but a little bit of air really loosens it up, yielding aromas of vegetable oil, apples, and spring flowers. In the mouth, it's light in body yet crisply flavored, with Granny Smiths dominating. Enough floral elements persist on the palate to provide moderate complexity. **87 Best Buy** —*J.C. (8/1/2003)*

Hunt Country Vineyards 2001 Late Harvest Riesling (Finger Lakes) $15. 83 —*J.C. (8/1/2003)*

Hunt Country Vineyards 2002 Semi-Dry Riesling (Finger Lakes) $10. 80 —*J.C. (8/1/2003)*

HUNTER HILL VINEYARD & WINERY

Hunter Hill Vineyard & Winery 2001 Old Vine, Schulenburg Vineyard Zinfandel (Lodi) $17. The texture here is smooth and elegant, but the flavors don't follow in the same vein, with olive, herb, and tart citrus leaving a somewhat bitter finish. **81** *(11/1/2003)*

HUNTINGTON

Huntington 2000 Cabernet Franc (Alexander Valley) $18. From an up-and-coming winery, a nice wine with berry and earth flavors, and some rich chocolate and tobacco notes. Very dry, but it's pretty tannic. Might soften and gain some complexity with a few years in the cellar. **87** —*S.H. (6/1/2003)*

Huntington 2003 Cabernet Sauvignon (California) $12. A full-throttle Cab, rich and ripe in intense cherry, plum, blackberry, and coffee flavors, although fully dry. A little on the soft, simple side, though. **84** —*S.H. (11/15/2005)*

Huntington 2002 Cabernet Sauvignon (Napa Valley) $20. Comes down on the earthy side, with a streak of herbal, stemmy flavors framing the

USA

blackberries and cherries. Very dry, with firm tannins. The astringent finish suggests rich meats and cheeses. **85** —*S.H. (11/15/2004)*

Huntington 2001 Cabernet Sauvignon (Napa Valley) $18. Classic Napa Cab, and very pretty. Opens with pure, strong aromas of black currants and oak, with similar flavors, plus a streak of cherries and chocolate. Not a blockbuster, but delicately structured, a lovely wine with brisk but soft tannins and a dry, fruity finish. **89** —*S.H. (11/15/2003)*

Huntington 2005 Chardonnay (Sonoma County) $14. Here's a good every-day Chard, offering immediate pleasure in the ripe tropical fruit and peach flavors, creamy texture and smoky oak influence. It's a blend of Russian River and Alexander Valley. **85** —*S.H. (12/15/2006)*

Huntington 2004 Chardonnay (Sonoma County) $12. Generically ripe and oaky, with a taste of canned apricot and peach syrup. Will do for every-day occasions. **82** —*S.H. (11/15/2005)*

Huntington 2002 Chardonnay (Russian River Valley) $15. Simple, with fruity flavors and oak shadings that finish dry. **83** —*S.H. (12/31/2004)*

Huntington 2001 Chardonnay (Russian River Valley) $15. This is a likeable Chard brimming with citrus and green apple flavors and tart Russian River acids. Has a little oak, not much, just enough to lend some vanilla and cream notes. **85** —*S.H. (12/1/2003)*

Huntington 2000 Chardonnay (Russian River Valley) $15. Ripe, oaky, and rich, a good example of Russian River Chard with its green apple, mineral and spicy flavors, crisp acids, ripe tannins, and firm, polished structure. Balanced and clean, a very pretty wine. **88** —*S.H. (5/1/2003)*

Huntington 2002 Merlot (California) $12. Rather earthy and sharp in acids, with a raw, stalky streak, although there's enough cherry fruit and oak to satisfy. Finishes dry and balanced. **84** —*S.H. (11/15/2005)*

Huntington 2005 Sauvignon Blanc (Sonoma County) $14. For those who like their Sauvignons dry, tart, and a little aggressive. Mainly from Dry Creek Valley, the wine has strong lemongrass and grapefruit flavors, with riper notes of figs. The low alcohol and crisp acidity make it especially drinkable. **85** —*S.H. (12/15/2006)*

Huntington 2004 Earthquake Sauvignon Blanc (Sonoma County) $12. Here's a pleasant SB, unchallenging with its upfront fig, gooseberry, citrus and melon flavors and crisp acids. Has some pretty levels of spicy complexity in the finish. **85** —*S.H. (11/15/2005)*

Huntington 2003 Earthquake Sauvignon Blanc (Sonoma County) $14. A nice white wine with a little of Sauvignon's aggressive, cat pee scent, but it's softened with citrus and fig notes. Maintains very crisp acidity that makes this ideal for tart goat cheese, grilled veggies, and similar fare. **85** —*S.H. (12/1/2004)*

Huntington 2002 Earthquake Sauvignon Blanc (Napa County) $12. A good, clean, white wine, with upfront flavors of citrus fruits and spearmint, boosted by acidity. Fills the mouth with juicy tartness that lasts through a spicy finish. **86** —*S.H. (12/15/2003)*

HUSCH

Husch 2002 Cabernet Sauvignon (Mendocino) $21. Doesn't taste quite ripe, with a wintergreen flavor to the cherries, and lots of tough acids and tannins. Bone dry, this is a wine that makes your gums tingle with astringency. **83** —*S.H. (3/1/2006)*

Husch 2001 Cabernet Sauvignon (Mendocino) $18. Although this Cab was grown in the warmer area inland from Anderson Valley, it's still not quite ripe. There's something vegetal in the aroma, although it's considerably sweeter in cherry fruit, not to mention oak, in the mouth, which saves it. **84** —*S.H. (11/1/2005)*

Husch 2000 La Ribera Vineyards Cabernet Sauvignon (Mendocino) $18. Here's a good, enjoyable wine not without minor deficiencies. You'll find some hearty flavors of cherries, blackberries, and toast, as well as notable tannins. There's an astringent coarseness throughout that may soften in time. **86** —*S.H. (8/1/2004)*

Husch 2002 Old Vines La Ribera Vineyards Carignane (Mendocino) $15. Cabernet-like in weight, tannins, and full-bodiedness, but without the elegance and finesse. The blackberry, cassis, and coffee flavors are ripe, while the wine is totally dry. A bit coarse, but has an earthy charm. **85** —*S.H. (8/1/2004)*

Husch 2004 Chardonnay (Mendocino) $14. Lots of ripe, rich Chardonnay character in this wine, with its strong flavors of peaches and cream, spicy woodsap, vanilla, and buttered toast. It's a nice, dry wine with refreshing acids. **85** —*S.H. (3/1/2006)*

Husch 2004 Chardonnay (Anderson Valley) $18. Intense and focused in peach, pineapple, and lime fruit, with a liberal coating of smoky oak and a creamy, leesy texture, this Chard has bright, high acidity that cleanses the palate. It finishes with powerfully ripe fruit. **88** —*S.H. (3/1/2006)*

Husch 2003 Chardonnay (Mendocino) $14. When I think of Husch wines I think of acidity, and this wine has lots of it. It's perfectly dry and tart, with ripe green-apple flavors and a pleasant spiciness. **87** —*S.H. (11/1/2005)*

Husch 2001 Chardonnay (Mendocino) $14. Fresh and appley, an easy drinking Chard with all the basic features of oak, creamy texture and refreshing acids. Not especially layered or complex, but friendly and clean. **85** —*S.H. (6/1/2003)*

Husch 1998 Estate Bottled Chardonnay (Mendocino County) $13. **87** —*S.H. (5/1/2000)*

Husch 2001 La Ribera Vineyards Chardonnay (Mendocino) $18. I love the juicy acidity in this wine. It lifts and brightens the lime, pineapple, and breadfruit flavors and makes them shine. An edge of oak adds a pretty polish of smoky vanilla and toast. The combination of freshness and ripe fruit is delicious. **90** —*S.H. (8/1/2004)*

Husch 2000 Special Reserve Chardonnay (Anderson Valley) $25. One hundred percent new French oak has given this wine splinters. It blasts out smoky char and vanilla, and you can even taste oak on the sappy-sweet finish. Underneath all that are peach and tropical fruit flavors, but you have to search for them. Sometimes, less is more. **85** —*S.H. (12/1/2003)*

Husch 1999 Special Reserve Chardonnay (Anderson Valley) $25. Lean and tight, this is an appley wine with high acidity. The minerally, steely texture is firm and just the right match for fish. The oaky overlay adds richness but does not overwhelm this young, vivacious wine. **89** —*S.H. (2/1/2003)*

Husch 1998 Special Reserve Chardonnay (Anderson Valley) $25. From a pioneer of this appellation, a full-throttle wine involving lots of new French oak. The flavors veer toward ripe peaches and apples and the acidity is predictably high, given its origins. There's a lovely, creamy mouthfeel. One criticism: Excessive sweetness. Tastes like it has some residual sugar that doesn't belong there. **85** —*S.H. (5/1/2002)*

Husch 2005 Chenin Blanc (Mendocino) $11. Cool climate acidity and long hangtime ripeness mark this expressive wine. It's filled with tart green apple, peach, pineapple, pine cone, and rich honeyed flavors, with that distinctive waxed bean note of Chenin Blanc. **86** —*S.H. (12/15/2006)*

Husch 2002 Chenin Blanc (Mendocino) $10. A good value for its crisp flavors of tart green apples, peaches, lime, and even riper ones of pear and tropical fruit. Drinks off-dry, with a honey-sweet finish. Notable for its balance and subtle harmony. **86** —*S.H. (12/15/2003)*

Husch 2005 Gewürztraminer (Anderson Valley) $14. Anderson Valley is one of the best homes to the aromatic whites in California, as evidenced once again by this dry, delicately structured Alsatian-style Gewürz. It's not a strong wine, but a lively, crisp one, with polished citrus, peach, apple, floral, and spice flavors. **85** —*S.H. (12/15/2006)*

Husch 2002 Gewürztraminer (Anderson Valley) $12. Pleasantly crisp and zingy, a sharply acidic wine with just enough residual sugar to round it out and make it mellow. The flavors veer toward grapefruit, peach, fig, nutmeg, orange zest, and white pepper. **85** —*S.H. (12/31/2003)*

Husch 2001 Gewürztraminer (Anderson Valley) $12. A big, bold wine, packed with flavor. Like drinking a bakery dessert: Peppermint, lime, white chocolate, ginger, peach tart, honeysuckle, and apricot jam, but the wine is basically dry, with shining acidity. From one of the best Gewürztraminer districts in California. **86** —*S.H. (9/1/2003)*

Husch 2000 Gewürztraminer (Anderson Valley) $11. Defines this varietal with its gingersnap flavors, and a crisp backbone of steely acidity, courtesy of cool growing conditions. It's dryish, and very clean. A bit one-dimensional, though. **85** —*S.H. (5/1/2002)*

Husch 2003 Late Harvest Gewürztraminer (Anderson Valley) $18. This is a sweet wine, with fruity flavors of apricots, and notes of wildflowers, honey, and spice. It has balancing acidity and a smooth texture. **85** — *S.H. (11/1/2005)*

Husch 2001 La Ribera Vineyards Merlot (Mendocino) $25. Thin, astringent and mouth-puckeringly dry, this wine offers little relief in the way of fruit. The palate searches for cherries and berries and encounters alcohol and harshness. Strange, considering the ripe vintage. **83** —*S.H. (8/1/2004)*

Husch 2005 Muscat Canelli (Mendocino) $14. The official residual sugar is 6%, but the wine tastes just off-dry to slightly sweet. It's a refreshing sipper, with pretty flavors of honey, freshly squeezed tangerines, and peaches and cream, all boosted by bright, zingy acids. **84** —*S.H. (12/15/2006)*

Husch 1997 Pinot Noir (Anderson Valley) $19. 83 *(11/15/1999)*

Husch 2003 Pinot Noir (Anderson Valley) $21. This is a very pure, clear Pinot Noir. It doesn't have a lot of alcohol, extract or oak. It's ripe in cherries and blueberries, but not overripe. The acidity is bright and the mouthfeel is silky. In other words, it's super-drinkable. **90 Editors' Choice** —*S.H. (11/1/2005)*

Husch 2001 Pinot Noir (Anderson Valley) $18. This awkward wine smells overripe and pruny, and turns weirdly sweet and tart in the finish, like cough medicine. **82** —*S.H. (12/15/2004)*

Husch 2000 Pinot Noir (Anderson Valley) $18. Here's an easy drinking, well-made Pinot with pleasant flavors of cherries, raspberries, and strawberries. It's nice and crisp with acidity. Not very complex, but clean and dry, with some tannins on the finish. **85** —*S.H. (12/1/2003)*

Husch 1999 Pinot Noir (Anderson Valley) $19. 81 *(10/1/2002)*

Husch 2000 Apple Hill Vineyard Pinot Noir (Anderson Valley) $35. This opens with plum, stable, and stewed-fruit aromas. Tasters were impressed by the black and red fruit, meat, smoke, red earth, caramel, and cinnamon flavors packed into the palate. The long chewy finish shows off intense fruit and pepper-clove accents. Best after 2003. **90** *(10/1/2002)*

Husch 1999 Knoll Vineyard Pinot Noir (Anderson Valley) $35. Candied strawberry and cherry aromas come in a clear second to intense woodiness. In the mouth, tangy, juicy cherry and plum fruit vies with popcorn-like oak. This is forward and fruity, but ultimately quite simple. **85** *(10/1/2002)*

Husch 2004 Sauvignon Blanc (Mendocino) $12. The high acidity that marks Husch's Chards also is found in this wine, which makes it super clean and vibrant. It's bone dry, with zesty citrus and fig flavors, and is a great example of this style in California. What a great value. **88 Best Buy** —*S.H. (3/1/2006)*

Husch 2003 Sauvignon Blanc (Mendocino) $12. Nicely drinkable for its firm acids, steely backbone, and fig and grapefruit flavors sweetened with a touch of oak. Try with seared halibut with a fruity salsa topping. **85** — *S.H. (11/1/2005)*

Husch 2002 La Ribera Vineyards Sauvignon Blanc (Mendocino) $12. Bright and irresistibly zesty, a white wine with apple, fig, peach, and sweet lime flavors. Rich acidity highlights the fruit, creating balance and cleanliness. Finishes with a long, delicious aftertaste of fig, lime, and honey. What a nice value. **87** —*S.H. (8/1/2004)*

Husch 2001 La Ribera Vineyards Sauvignon Blanc (Mendocino) $12. Lots to like in this simple, flavorful wine, with its pretty citrus and apple flavors and crisp bite of acidity. Could use more concentration and depth, but the wine is versatile and friendly. **86** —*S.H. (3/1/2003)*

Husch 1998 La Ribera Vineyards Sauvignon Blanc (Mendocino) $12. 88 **Best Buy** —*S.H. (5/1/2000)*

Husch 2004 La Ribera Vineyards Renegade Sauvignon Blanc (Mendocino) $18. Made with native yeast and barrel-fermented, this Sauvignon is not very high in acidity, and so the edge of sweetness isn't balanced with tartness, which is a fault. The flavors are of apricots, peaches, apples, and pineapples. **84** —*S.H. (3/1/2006)*

Husch 2005 Late Harvest Sauvignon Blanc (Mendocino) $20. Simple and sweetly sugary, with high acids framing apricot, tangerine, butter-sautéed banana and honey flavors. **84** —*S.H. (12/15/2006)*

Husch 2003 Renegade Sauvignon Blanc (Mendocino) $18. Made from wild yeasts, hence the name, this wine is twice the size of Husch's regular '03 Sauvignon Blanc. It's rich and intense in fig, apple, grapefruit, honeydew, and spice flavors, with a creamy texture brightened by firm acids and sweetened with considerable oak. One of the more rewarding Sauvignon Blancs I've had in a while. **91 Editors' Choice** —*S.H. (11/1/2005)*

Husch 2003 Syrah (Mendocino) $28. I love the structure of this wine, but wish it were richer in fruit. It's very dry and balanced, with a creamy mouthfeel and deft, ripe tannins. The cherry flavors finish quick, leaving behind alcohol, tannins, and acidity. **85** —*S.H. (3/1/2006)*

HYATT

Hyatt 1998 Ice Wine Black Muscat (Yakima Valley) $25. 92 —*M.S. (11/15/2000)*

Hyatt 1997 Bordeaux Blend (Yakima Valley) $11. 84 —*P.G. (6/1/2000)*

Hyatt 1997 Cabernet Sauvignon (Yakima Valley) $15. 87 —*P.G. (6/1/2000)*

Hyatt 1997 Reserve Cabernet Sauvignon (Yakima Valley) $25. 88 —*P.G. (6/1/2000)*

Hyatt 1999 Cabernet Sauvignon-Merlot (Yakima Valley) $11. Cabernet Franc (50%) rules, with Merlot (30%) and Cabernet Sauvignon (20%) following along. Scents of strawberry preserves, earth and mocha mingle; the wine has simple, tangy cranberry flavors and an earthy finish. **85** — *P.G. (6/1/2002)*

Hyatt 1998 Chardonnay (Yakima Valley) $11. 89 Best Buy —*P.G. (6/1/2000)*

Hyatt 2000 Chardonnay (Yakima Valley) $10. This is a whole different critter than the winery's quaffable '99. It is tart and resiny, with a strong scent of licorice. The rustic flavors are earthy and rough, with a bitter, alcoholic finish. **83** —*P.G. (9/1/2002)*

Hyatt 1999 Chardonnay (Yakima Valley) $10. Interesting scents of spice, herb, and pine mix with tropical pineapple fruit. It all leads into a buttery finish, delivering a lot of flavor for the price. Barrel-fermented, malolactic, and sur lie aging—the full monty. **86** —*P.G. (9/1/2002)*

Hyatt 2000 Reserve Chardonnay (Yakima Valley) $18. The reserve is not particularly oaky; rather it puts the emphasis on straightforward, well-rendered green apple fruit flavors, augmented with some balanced flavors of licorice and vanilla. **87** —*P.G. (9/1/2002)*

Hyatt 1998 Fumé Blanc (Yakima Valley) $11. 87 —*P.G. (6/1/2000)*

Hyatt 1997 Merlot (Yakima Valley) $14. 85 —*P.G. (6/1/2000)*

Hyatt 1999 Merlot (Yakima Valley) $12. The Hyatt is tight, hard, and chewy. Its stiff tannins are calling the shots, and leaving an earthy impression strongly tasting of roots and stems through a somewhat bitter finish. **84** —*P.G. (9/1/2002)*

Hyatt 1998 Reserve Merlot (Yakima Valley) $19. The fruit here is certainly more ripe and powerful than in the winery's regular bottlings. But it is offset by rugged tannins, and an earthiness that borders on rusticity. **85** —*P.G. (9/1/2002)*

Hyatt 1997 Reserve Merlot (Yakima Valley) $25. 86 —*P.G. (6/1/2000)*

Hyatt 1997 Syrah (Yakima Valley) $20. 87 —*S.H. (9/1/2000)*

Hyatt 2001 Syrah (Yakima Valley) $13. While one taster found this wine disturbingly close to vegetal, others were more enthusiastic, calling it soft and expansive. There's some red fruit on the nose, but the flavors are darker, more akin to blackberry according to this wine's proponents. **86** *(9/1/2005)*

Hyatt 1998 Estate Grown Syrah (Yakima Valley) $25. Lean, with a dried fruit and cedar-sandalwood-pine profile offset by earthy accents. A mineral note adds interest to the dark cherry fruit. More weight could move it up to the next level of quality, but it has appeal as a lighter, almost Burgundian-style Syrah. **85** *(11/1/2001)*

Hyatt 2000 Reserve Syrah (Yakima Valley) $18. Reserve it may be, but it is a thin wine nonetheless, with hard, green flavors and a stemmy, tannic finish. **83** —*P.G. (9/1/2002)*

USA

USA

HYDE VINEYARD

Hyde Vineyard 2001 Chardonnay (Carneros) $48. A solid effort that's missing out on the richness for a better score. It's well structured, with juicy, citrusy acidity, and there's certainly some pretty oak. The flavors also veer toward citrus fruits, with suggestions of tart green apple. Turns peppery-astringent on the finish. Give it a few hours to breathe, and it will soften up. **89** —S.H. (5/1/2004)

Hyde Vineyard 2001 Merlot-Cabernet Sauvignon (Carneros) $65. They pulled out all the stops, starting with fully ripened grapes that give huge blackberry, cassis, cherry, and plum flavors. Elaborate oak adds even more sweet notes, and modern tannin management results in a very soft, elaborate mouthfeel. This stylish Merlot-Cabernet blend has lots of appeal. **91** —S.H. (5/1/2004)

Hyde Vineyard 2001 Syrah (Carneros) $48. This interesting wine showcases the continuing promise of Carneros Syrah. In this warm vintage, the grapes became very ripe, and give blackberry, cassis, and cherry flavors. They're wrapped in soft, complex, sweet tannins that coat the palate with a creamy smoothness. The flavors sink into the tongue and last forever. **90** —S.H. (5/1/2004)

I'M

I'M 2004 Chardonnay (Sonoma County) $17. Made in a different style from most Sonoma Chards, this wine is less about fruit than minerals. It has a steely mouthfeel, with mouthwatering acidity and hints of citrus zest. Could almost be a Sauvignon Blanc. **86** —S.H. (11/1/2006)

I'M 2003 Chardonnay (Sonoma) $17. This oddly named wine captures the spirit of Sonoma Chard. It's crisp and fruity, with a dollop of oak and dry finish that includes some dusty tannins. **84** —S.H. (3/1/2006)

I'M 2004 Rosé Blend (Napa Valley) $13. This is one of the drier blush wines out there, with an interesting mélange of herb, apple, peach, and tobacco flavors. Try it with bruschetta, grilled veggies, or a nice grilled salmon steak. **84** —S.H. (7/1/2006)

ICARIA CREEK

Icaria Creek 1997 Cabernet Sauvignon (Alexander Valley) $45. Yes, 1997 is the current vintage. Reviewers gave this wine's bouquet two thumbs up—it has lovely aromas of wheat biscuit, mint, and cassis. Our biggest gripe here was the wine's weight—which, for a Cabernet from a good vintage, was pretty light. Still, it had some pleasant cherry, red plum, and earth flavors. **87** (8/1/2003)

Icaria Creek 2002 Estate Cabernet Sauvignon (Alexander Valley) $38. This Cab is a little soft, and not all that fruity, so the dry tannins stick out, but it's so balanced and understated that it's a natural to accompany good food without overshadowing it. The cherry, cassis, herb, and coffee flavors are lightly seasoned with oak. Drink now. **88** —S.H. (12/15/2005)

Icaria Creek 2001 Estate Hillside Cabernet Sauvignon (Alexander Valley) $38. Soft and surprisingly herbaceous for the vintage, with blackberry and cherry flavors edged with dill. Feels rather flat, too. Would benefit from greater concentration and acidity. **84** —S.H. (10/1/2004)

Icaria Creek 1998 Cabernet Sauvignon-Barbera (Alexander Valley) $45. One of the last '98s to be released, and still dark in color. The tannins are hefty, although they're of the soft, pliant kind, and acidity is low. Oak overshadows the fruit. Not offering much now, and doesn't seem to be an ager. **84** —S.H. (8/29/2003)

ICI/LA-BAS

Ici/La-Bas 1998 Philippine Chardonnay (Mendocino County) $35. Complex leesy, smoky, nutty aromas adorn the nose of this racy wine. It displays a citrusy tartness and lime, green apple, vanilla, and wintergreen accents that linger refreshingly. Finishes with unusual apple, nut and burnt sugar aromas and flavors. A Mendocino appellation wine from Jim Clendenon, the notorious 'Mind Behind' Santa Barbara County's Au Bon Climat Winery. **89** (7/1/2001)

Ici/La-Bas 1997 Les Revelles-Mendocino Elke Vy Pinot Noir (Anderson Valley) $50. **85** (10/1/1999)

Ici/La-Bas 1997 Les Revelles-OR/CA Vineyard Se Pinot Noir (Willamette Valley & Anderson Valley) $35. **88** (10/1/1999)

IDYLWOOD

Idylwood 1999 Pinot Noir (Willamette Valley) $14. Tart red fruit wears forest-floor and smoke accents on this light wine's nose. Subdued cherry flavors, prominent saddle leather and earth accents mark the slightly chalky palate. Narrows on the tangy, almost lemon-oaky finish. **84** (10/1/2002)

Idylwood 1999 Corral Creek Vineyard Pinot Noir (Willamette Valley) $25. There is already some evidence of brick coloring around the edges of this wine, which opens with an aromatic mix of dark fruits, tobacco, leather, and barnyard smells. It's open and tangy, somewhat rustic, but distinctly Burgundian for all that, and fun to drink. **87** —P.G. (4/1/2002)

Idylwood 1998 Founder's Reserve Pinot Noir (Willamette Valley) $25. **86** —J.C. (12/1/2000)

IL CUORE

Il Cuore 1996 Rosso Classico Red Blend (California) $11. **85** —J.C. (10/1/1999)

Il Cuore 1996 Zinfandel (California) $10. **81** —J.C. (5/1/2000)

IL PODERE DELL'OLIVOS

Il Podere Dell'Olivos 1998 Tocai (Central Coast) $12. An intriguing wine, fresh and inviting, with complex aromas of ripe peaches, minerals, vanilla, spice, smoke, and buttery toast. Ricj and deliciously fruity in the mouth, with a great velvety texture. It finishes nicely dry and long. **88** —S.H. (12/1/2001)

Il Ponte 1999 Fra Due Terre Sangiovese (California) $35. Dark raspberry and cherry flavors are wrapped in licorice and toasty oak. The finish is spicy and bright with a hint of tar and herbs. **87** —J.M. (5/1/2002)

ILONA

Ilona 1999 Meritage (Napa Valley) $70. This tribute wine opens with a seductive, intense chocolate-tinged dark berry fruit bouquet. Layered flavors and a deep velvety texture provide pleasure galore in Catherine Eddy's homage to her mother. You can cellar this through 2007, but you don't have to—this single-vineyard blend from one of Napa's most desirable neighborhoods is supple and delicious now. **92** —M.M. (11/15/2002)

ILSLEY

Ilsley 2002 Cabernet Sauvignon (Stags Leap District) $48. Dense, delicious, and dry, this Cab comes from between the Silverado Trail and the Vaca Mountains. It's quite impressive, with a deep structure and complex, layered flavors of currants, plums, chocolate, and herbs. Thick, furry tannins suggest aging. Best after 2008, and should hold and improve for another 10 years afterward. **92 Cellar Selection** —S.H. (11/1/2006)

IMAGERY

Imagery 2003 Artist Collection Barbera (Sonoma Valley) $31. Dark, robust, dry, full bodied, tannic, and acidic. That pretty much sums up this old-fashioned, young wine. It's a serious cellar candidate, stuffed with blackberry jam, leather, and coffee flavors. Best after 2010 and for years beyond. **88 Cellar Selection** —S.H. (6/1/2006)

Imagery 2001 Artist Collection Barbera (Sonoma Valley) $31. One of the more interesting Barberas out there. This dry, full-bodied wine has rich but soft tannins, making it drinkable now. The flavors veer toward blackberries, coffee, leather, and grilled meat. **88** —S.H. (4/1/2005)

Imagery 2000 Artist Collection Barbera (Sonoma Valley) $31. Big, dark, and thick with tannins, a tough young wine with a core of berry, cherry, and chocolate flavors. Hefty acidity lends it a scour. It's far from a hedonistic monster, but has integrity. Try with rich game or lamb. **89** —S.H. (12/1/2003)

Imagery 1999 Wildwood Vineyard Barbera (Sonoma Valley) $31. Pricey, but worth it for the young, fresh, jammy aromas and great flavors. Bursting with blueberry, black-cherry, bay leaf, and smoke, yet pretty tannic and bitter, it's a tough punchy wine that calls out for great food. **90** —S.H. (12/1/2001)

Imagery 1997 Rancho Salina Vineyard Bordeaux Blend (Sonoma Valley) $35. **87** (11/1/2000)

Imagery 1996 Cabernet Franc (Sonoma) $22. Floral and herbal aromas intertwine with scents of toasty oak and bright raspberry-cherry fruit in this delicious offering from the Rancho Salina and Blue Rock vineyards. Benziger's Imagery Series always offers distinctive flavors, some more successfully than others, but this one is a hit—and ready to drink as well. **88** —J.C. (6/1/2003)

Imagery 2002 Artist Collection Cabernet Franc (Sonoma County) $34. The main problem with this wine is that it's excessively soft. Despite the delicious flavors of cherries, cocoa, and mint, and the rich, thick, sweet tannins, it falls flat in the mouth, and lacks vibrancy. **84** —S.H. (12/15/2005)

Imagery 1999 Artist Collection Cabernet Franc (Alexander Valley) $27. An interesting wine from a variety normally used for blending. Shows up with a burst of cherry and currant flavors, with a complex streak of bacon. The texture is sheer delight, dry, soft and caressing. Try as an alternative to Merlot. **87** —S.H. (11/15/2003)

Imagery 1998 Artist Collection Cabernet Franc (Sonoma Valley) $27. Sautéed mushrooms, leather, and hung meat aromas introduce this deeply colored wine, which seems exceptionally soft, with low tannins. The berry flavors veer toward blackberries and black raspberries. It;s very dry. Try with barbecue or roasted chicken. **85** —S.H. (12/1/2001)

Imagery 2001 Ash Creek Vineyard Cabernet Sauvignon (Alexander Valley) $40. The appellation says Alexander Valley, but this is a high mountain vineyard, and this Cab has some hefty tannins. It's dry and delicious, with intense black currant flavors and elaborately smoked oak. Drink now with a good steak. It may be a little too soft to endure aging. **90** —S.H. (12/15/2005)

Imagery 1999 Ash Creek Vineyard Cabernet Sauvignon (Alexander Valley) $35. Simple and earthy, with coffee and spiced plum flavors. Curiously lean and one-dimensional for such a great vintage. The tannins are soft and melted and acids are also easy. **85** —S.H. (8/1/2003)

Imagery 1998 Ash Creek Vineyard Cabernet Sauvignon (Alexander Valley) $50. Deep cassis fruit wears strong earth and leafy, herbal notes in this balanced, medium-weight wine. There's good concentration, but the green note seen in many 1998's detracts. It's more vegetal than herbal to some tasters. Closes with firm, drying tannins, an earthy note and decent length. **87** (12/1/2001)

Imagery 1999 Sunny Slope Vineyard Cabernet Sauvignon (Sonoma Valley) $35. A good, richly flavored Cabernet that shows proper varietal character without any special qualities. Flavors of black currants drink dry, wrapped in smooth tannins. May improve a bit with a few years in the cellar. **86** —S.H. (8/1/2003)

Imagery 1998 Sunny Slope Vineyard Vineyard Collection Cabernet Sauvignon (Sonoma Valley) $50. A roasted fruit, tar, and pungent pepper nose opens this tangy welterweight. Stewed berry and plum flavors follow, but the wine is a bit thin and to some, slightly hot. Toasty oak and anice accent the red fruit flavors on the modest finish. **85** (12/1/2001)

Imagery 2002 Vineyard Collection Ash Creek Vineyard Cabernet Sauvignon (Sonoma Valley) $40. This Cab is just a little too superripe, with raisin and cooked grape flavors, although there are lots of superb blackberry and cassis notes also. They must have let some shrivelled grapes get through the sorting process, and the wine has suffered. **84** —S.H. (4/1/2006)

Imagery 2000 Vineyard Collection Ash Creek Vineyard Cabernet Sauvignon (Alexander Valley) $35. After struggling with this vineyard for a number of years, Joe Benziger seems to have gotten a handle on this finicky mountain fruit. Even in this so-so vintage, the wine is complex and pleasurable, although tannic. Hold until 2008. **92** —S.H. (4/1/2005)

Imagery 2001 Vineyard Collection Sunny Slope Vineyard Cabernet Sauvignon (Sonoma Valley) $35. Imagery's wines, across the board, keep getting better and better, and this single-vineyard Cab is the latest example. It's dry and complex, with cassis and black currant flavors that are seasoned with toasty oak. Finishes balanced and elegant. **92** —S.H. (4/1/2005)

Imagery 1999 Ricci Vineyard Chardonnay (Carneros) $25. This wine opens with aromas of anise, green apples, and white peaches, plus plenty of leesy and oaky notes, including vanilla, smoke, and buttered toast. The spicy flavors are full throttle, the texture round and creamy. Picks up some leesy bitterness in the finish. **87** —S.H. (12/1/2001)

Imagery 2002 Artist Collection Lagrein (Paso Robles) $33. Made from a Northern Italy grape, this is a wine to cut through olive oil, cheese, and tomato sauce. It's dry and very tannic, with plum and blackberry flavors. You might try it as an alternative to Zinfandel. **86** —S.H. (12/15/2005)

Imagery 2001 Malbec (North Coast) $33. This dark, heavy wine is fully dry, but has ripe flavors of blackberries, blueberries, and black-cherries that are so sweet, they verge on chocolate. It's a big wine that calls for roasts and similar fare. **86** —S.H. (10/1/2004)

Imagery 1999 Malbec (Alexander Valley) $33. Lovely aromas of mint and blackberry are penetrating and individualistic. In the mouth, it tastes strong and powerful, with persistent spicy, peppery blackberry flavors, jammy and delicious. Sleek tannins and crisp acidity add body to this elegant wine. **88** —S.H. (12/1/2001)

Imagery 2000 Artist Collection Malbec (North Coast) $33. A disappointment, given winemaker Joe Benziger's success with individual Bordeaux varieties. Smacks of underripe grapes, with stalky, green, vegetal aromas and flavors, although there's a streak of blackberry. The tannins kick in mid-palate and turn astringent through the dry finish. **84** —S.H. (4/1/2004)

Imagery 1998 Artist Collection Malbec (Alexander Valley) $33. Dark, with oaky, plummy aromas and a touch of earthy, mushroomy funk. Drinks fairly tannic, although the acidity is low, with sunny, ripe, fruit and berry flavors. Nicely dry. The finish picks up the tannic theme again. **87** —S.H. (12/1/2001)

Imagery 2002 Sunny Slope Vineyard Merlot (Sonoma Valley) $35. Good as it is, this wine is having acidity problems, meaning it's overly soft and melted. Yes, it has delicious flavors of black-cherries, chocolate, and oak, and the tannins are smooth and luxurious, but what about balance? **85** —S.H. (12/15/2005)

Imagery 2001 Sunny Slope Vineyard Merlot (Sonoma Valley) $29. Imagery has worked hard with this vineyard, and in this near-perfect vintage has crafted a very good wine. It's young, thick, and juicy, with elaborate fruit flavors and oak, and a touch of brashness. Best to leave it alone for a few years. **90** —S.H. (10/1/2004)

Imagery 1999 Sunny Slope Vineyard Merlot (Sonoma Valley) $29. Dark and extracted, with jammy berry flavors and a strongly earthy component, including tobacco, sage, and tree bark. In the mouth this wine is very dry and pretty tannic, although the acidity is soft. A bit awkward, and not likely to improve in the cellar. **85** —S.H. (8/1/2003)

Imagery 2000 Vineyard Collection Sunny Slope Vineyard Merlot (Sonoma County) $29. A remarkably rich and dense wine, considering the poor reputation of the vintage. It's stuffed with blackberry and cherry fruit that is well oaked, with vanilla, spice, and smoky nuances. It's lush and supple, with the texture of velvet. You almost hate to swallow, but the finish is long and suave. **92** —S.H. (4/1/2004)

Imagery 2001 Petite Sirah (Paso Robles) $35. Bigtime Pet here, an enormously ripe and extracted wine. It's huge in chocolate and cassis flavors that are almost sweet, although the wine is totally dry and balanced. The tannins are smooth enough to drink tonight with appropriately sized chow. **89** —S.H. (10/1/2004)

Imagery 2002 Artist Collection Petite Sirah (Paso Robles) $36. Big, dark, tannic, dry and fruity, yet balanced in all its parts, this gentle giant actually shows elegance. It's packed with cherry, tobacco, mint, and oak flavors that drink well now, and should hold and improve for many years. **91 Editors' Choice** —S.H. (10/1/2005)

Imagery 2000 Artist Collection Petite Sirah (Paso Robles) $35. Dramatically dark, staining the glass with glycerine streaks, this wine unabashedly celebrates its hot country origins. Considerable tannins frame a core of berry fruit, with a zingy, peppery note that stimulates the taste buds, but acidity is soft. At the same time, it retains a rustic character typical of the varietal. **86** —S.H. (8/1/2003)

Imagery 1998 Artist Collection Petite Sirah (Paso Robles) $32. Opens with blackberry aromas complexed with smoky oak, white chocolate, and roasted coffeebean. In the mouth, sumptuous fruitiness. It's a jammy wine, with wild berry flavors framed with oak and soft tannins. This likeable wine is ideal with roasts. **87** —S.H. (12/1/2001)

Imagery 1999 Shell Creek Petite Sirah (Paso Robles) $35. Showcases this California variety nicely, with a rich dark color and powerfully fruity, peppery, plummy aromas. There's a rich mouthfeel to the blackberry and plum flavors, as well as solid tannins and good acidity. This is a super Barbera, and a fine expression of terroir. **90** —*S.H. (12/1/2001)*

Imagery 2001 Petite Verdot (Sonoma County) $33. A blending grape, on its own this very dark wine is super-fruity and somewhat one-dimensional. Shy in aroma, the major impacts are the plummy flavor and thick tannins. **85** —*S.H. (12/1/2004)*

Imagery 2003 Artist Collection Petite Verdot (Sonoma Valley) $38. This is a black, dry, tannically astringent wine that doesn't seem to merit its own bottling. It might soften and sweeten in ten or fifteen years, but why bother. Still, it's clean and balanced. **83** —*S.H. (4/1/2006)*

Imagery 2000 Artist Collection Petite Verdot (Sonoma County) $33. A big, darkly colored wine, Hulk-sized in its mouthfilling flavors. They range from very ripe, jammy summer blackberries, plums, and blueberries to dark chocolate and coffee, and are very dry. There's a dusty sprinkling of tannins in the mouth that demands rich foods, such as duck, steak, or lamb. **90** —*S.H. (4/1/2004)*

Imagery 2000 Artist Collection-Bien Nacido Vineyard Pinot Blanc (Santa Maria Valley) $18. Impressive for the tart tangerine rind and mango flavors that hit the palate like a sledgehammer, backed up with bright acidity. Sears the throat with a long, peppery finish. Considerable oak fattens and softens the texture. **87** —*S.H. (2/1/2004)*

Imagery 1999 Bien Nacido Vineyard Pinot Blanc (Santa Maria Valley) $21. Smells luscious, with tangerine cream, camomile, orange popsicle, smoke, vanilla custard, lees, and spicy aromatics. This round, full, fruity wine is very clean and refreshing, with finely etched fruit and a smooth, lemony finish. **86** —*S.H. (12/1/2001)*

Imagery 2003 Pinot Noir (Carneros) $25. Elegant and clean, this pale wine has modest raspberry flavors with a sweet edge of oriental spice, especially cinnamon. It's very dry, with quite a long fruity finish. **85** —*S.H. (12/1/2004)*

Imagery 1999 Rancho Salina Vineyard Red Blend (Sonoma Valley) $29. Pretty aromas of cassis and violets are framed in oak, with vanilla and cedar notes. Drinks fruity and tannic, very full in the mouth, and finishes dry and spicy. A Meritage blend of Merlot and Cabernet Sauvignon from 1,000 feet in the Mayacamas Mountains. **85** —*S.H. (12/1/2001)*

Imagery 2001 Sangiovese (Dry Creek Valley) $22. This is a big, toughly tannic wine. Deep down inside the astringency are very ripe and exuberant black-cherry flavors. The finish once again turns tannic. The wine is unlikely to age. **85** —*S.H. (11/15/2004)*

Imagery 2003 Artist Collection Sangiovese (Dry Creek Valley) $24. Here's a raspingly tannic, high-acid wine that feels astringently dry at first. Then the cherry flavors kick in, and all sorts of complexing herbs, spices, and oak influences. It's an interesting red, but those tannins and acids call for something rich and Italian, like chicken cacciatore. **89** —*S.H. (6/1/2006)*

Imagery 2002 Artist Collection Sangiovese (Dry Creek Valley) $24. Not Imagery's most successful wine. This red is very soft, with a lifeless mouthfeel and uninteresting flavors of berries and too much oak. **82** —*S.H. (10/1/2005)*

Imagery 2000 Artist Collection Sangiovese (Sonoma County) $22. Black-cherry, herb, spice, and smoky leather notes are framed in a wine that feels silky smooth on the palate, with a nice edge of tannins. It's fully dry. Turns thin in the middle, rough on the finish. From Dry Creek Valley. **85** —*S.H. (4/1/2004)*

Imagery 1999 Artist Collection Sangiovese (Sonoma County) $22. Absolutely delicious for its lipsmackingly rich plummy, blackberry, and smoky, earthy flavors. They flood the mouth with ripe, sweet fruit, and are made lively by fresh acids and wonderfully complex tannins. This wine is made with one-fifth Cabernet Sauvignon and Petite Sirah to add body. **90 Editors' Choice** —*S.H. (9/1/2003)*

Imagery 1996 Imagery Series Sangiovese (Dry Creek Valley) $20. **82** —*J.C. (10/1/1999)*

Imagery 1999 Polesky Vineyard-Red Hill Vineyard Sangiovese (Sonoma County) $21. Earth, tobacco, licorice, and black-cherry aromas lead to a rich, fruity wine in the mouth. It's a bit heavy and quite acidic, with hefty tannins, and finishes very dry and rasping. This is a structured wine that needs food to mellow it. **85** —*S.H. (12/1/2001)*

Imagery 2002 StoneDragon Syrah (Sonoma Valley) $35. Features ripe blackberries, cherries, and creamy cola flavors. The tannins are a bit firm, but the acidity is fine, and Asian spices take over the finish. Drink young, before the fruit fades. **87** *(9/1/2005)*

Imagery 2004 Artist Collection Viognier (Sonoma County) $24. I love this wine for the way the winemaker has reined in Viognier's tendency toward over-the-topness, yet not sacrificed its exotic character. It's characterized by vibrant acids and a clean, cool mouthfeel, with complex notes of white peach, honeysuckle, mango, vanilla, and spice that finish thoroughly dry. **90 Editors' Choice** —*S.H. (12/15/2005)*

Imagery 2002 Artist Collection Viognier (North Coast) $21. Stays true to the popular style of Viognier with its burst of mango, tangerine, honeydew, wildflower, and Oriental spice flavors. Drinks very rich and creamy, so powerful in fruity flavor that it's almost best drunk on its own. **87** —*S.H. (12/31/2003)*

Imagery 1999 Creek Vineyard Viognier (Alexander Valley) $25. Aromas of wildflowers, especially honeysuckle and jasmine, ride next to sweet butter, peach, smoke, and spice. Drinks very forward and ripely fruity, with armloads of berry and stone fruit flavors. On the dry side, but round, mellow and fat. **87** —*S.H. (12/1/2001)*

Imagery 1999 Artist Collection White Blend (Napa Valley) $25. Opens with a trumpet peal of well-toasted oak and sweet vanillins riding over mango and breadfruit aromas. On the palate, the first impression is of high lees, with a rich, creamy texture and plenty of oak covering tropical fruits. Dry and lush. A blend of Chardonnay, Pinot Blanc and Pinot Meunier. **89 Best Buy** —*S.H. (12/1/2001)*

Imagery 2000 Artist Collection White Burgundy White Blend (California) $25. Explosively fruity, with big, bold flavors of peaches, pears, apples, tropical fruits, you name it. Drinks firmly dry, although oak brings a wood-sap sweetness. Lees aging was significant and adds a sour cream note. A blend of Chardonnay and Pinot Blanc. **86** —*S.H. (7/1/2003)*

Imagery 2003 White Burgundy White Blend (Carneros) $27. With Chardonnay, Pinot Blanc, and Pinot Meunier, this is a multi-layered wine, and a welcome alternative in dry whites. There's fresh, pert fruit, but also mineral and herb complexities, and the finish is dry. **90 Editors' Choice** —*S.H. (10/1/2005)*

Imagery 2002 White Burgundy White Blend (North Coast) $25. Chardonnay, Pinot Blanc, and Pinot Meunier comprise this smooth, suave white wine. It's got Chard-like features modulated with a nutty, flowery streak, and is very dry, with an overlay of smoky oak. **86** —*S.H. (10/1/2004)*

Imagery 1997 White Burgundy White Blend (North Coast) $22. **84** —*J.C. (11/1/1999)*

Imagery 2004 Wow Oui White Burgundy White Blend (Sonoma County) $24. I've never had a blend of Sauvignon Blanc and Muscat Canelli, but this delicious wine argues for more. It has Sauvignon's dry, acidic citrusy character, while the Muscat adds a rich orange blossom note. Simply wonderful and refreshingly different. **90** —*S.H. (12/15/2005)*

Imagery 1999 Yountmill Vineyard White Blend (Napa Valley) $25. The aromas are very oaky and spicy, with cinnamon, nutmeg, brown sugar, caramel, smoke, vanilla, and tropical fruit notes. There's lots of oak up front in the mouth, plus peach and citrus flavors and a soft, creamy mouthfeel. A blend of Pinot Blanc, Chardonnay, and Pinot Meunier. **86** —*S.H. (12/1/2001)*

Imagery 2002 Taylor Vineyard Zinfandel (Dry Creek Valley) $40. Imagery continues to bring a full-blown, baroque interpretation to its interesting single-vineyard wines. This Zin is ultraripe, exhibiting chocolate, cherry, and coffee flavors, and is soft in tannins. Yet there's a grip and dryness that make it complex. **90** —*S.H. (10/1/2005)*

Imagery 2000 Vineyard Collection-Taylor Vineyard Zinfandel (Alexander Valley) $35. Excellent, wild, and wonderful Zin. Here's a wine that captures the varietal's cowboy character, with its briary flavors of wild, sun-warmed berries and peppery spices. The dry, firmly tannic mouthfeel is classy. A fabulous homemade pizza, topped with gooey cheese, is the perfect marriage. **91** —*S.H. (9/1/2003)*

INCOGNITO

Incognito 2004 Red Wine Red Blend (Lodi) $19. A blend of eight varietals, kind of a Rhône-Bordeaux blend, this red shows a true Lodi typicity. It's soft in acids and tannins, and just luscious, with a milk chocolate edge to the blueberry, blackberry, cherry, pomegranate and coffee flavors, and there's a rich sweetness on the finish. **87** —*S.H.* *(12/15/2006)*

Incognito 2005 Viognier (Lodi) $19. Easy to like for its fruity, flowery flavors and crisp acidity, this wine has extra layers of complexity. It feels as rich as honey in the mouth, yet is fundamentally dry. Nice with poultry, veal, or fish with a fruity salsa topping. **90 Editors' Choice** —*S.H.* *(10/1/2006)*

INDIAN SPRINGS

Indian Springs 1997 Cabernet Franc (Nevada County) $15. 90 —*S.H.* *(2/1/2000)*

Indian Springs 1999 Cabernet Franc (Nevada County) $15. The Sierra Foothills region has proven its ability to make good Cab Franc, and this one, from 1,800 feet up, is flavored with red-berry fruit. It lacks some body in the middle palate, making it too soft, but it's an easy to like wine, especially at this price. **85** —*S.H.* *(12/15/2001)*

Indian Springs 1997 Cabernet Sauvignon (Nevada County) $13. 84 —*S.H.* *(12/31/1999)*

Indian Springs 1998 Chardonnay (Nevada County) $15. 87 *(6/1/2000)*

Indian Springs 2000 Chardonnay (Nevada County) $14. Here's all the oaky vanilla, ripe peach flavor, and creamy texture that people like in an affordable wine. It's not white Burgundy, but this pretty wine from the Sierra Foothills has plenty of charm and character. **86** —*S.H.* *(12/31/2001)*

Indian Springs 2001 Primavera Rossa Red Blend (Nevada County) $16. Smells raw and unripe, with green, stalky aromas that are weirdly coupled with Port-like notes. In the mouth, it's semi-sweet, with a cough-medicine taste. **81** —*S.H.* *(5/1/2004)*

Indian Springs 1999 Sangiovese (Nevada County) $16. Rough, fruity, and earthy, it has some hot vintage flavors of raisins, and a peppery finish that suggests overripe, pruny grapes. It's a dry wine, with soft acidity and soft tannins. What it has going for it are ripely sweet, sunny fruit and berry flavors that would be nice with barbecue. **85** —*S.H.* *(9/12/2002)*

Indian Springs 2000 Sauvignon Blanc (Nevada County) $12. This wine has good varietal character with citrusy flavors, dry, crisp acidity and a bright, zesty punch that cleans the palate. There's an odd, baked quality in the aroma that keeps it from being as good as it could be. **82** —*S.H.* *(12/15/2001)*

Indian Springs 2000 Sémillon (Nevada County) $10. Call it country style, or rustic. It has some ripe peach and citrus flavors and drinks dryish, with a simple texture marked by adequate acidity. A perfectly decent quaffer at a perfectly acceptable price for the quality. **83** —*S.H.* *(9/12/2002)*

Indian Springs 1996 Syrah (Nevada County) $14. 85 —*S.H.* *(6/1/1999)*

Indian Springs 2001 Syrah (Nevada County) $18. This is a richly fruity, full-bodied wine with lots of sweet blackberry, plum and cherry-chocolate flavors. It's dry and clean, with soft, complex tannins. There's real distinction here, from a part of California you don't hear much about. **87** —*S.H.* *(5/1/2004)*

Indian Springs 1999 Syrah (Nevada County) $16. From the Sierra Foothills, this well-structured, dark wine offers ripe blue- and blackberry fruit, with leather and espresso accents. The palate's lively plum and pepper flavors are nicely integrated with the oak used here, and flow into a dry finish with even, moderate tannins. **86** *(10/1/2001)*

Indian Springs 1997 Viognier (Nevada County) $14. 83 —*S.H.* *(6/1/1999)*

INDIGO HILLS

Indigo Hills 2000 Cabernet Sauvignon (North Coast) $12. One of Gallo's dozens of brands, this is a nice wine from five counties north of the Golden Gate. It has pretty aromas and flavors of black currants. It is dry and clean, with easy tannins, and a nice finish. **86 Best Buy** —*S.H.* *(12/31/2002)*

Indigo Hills NV Champagne Blend (North Coast) $12. 86 Best Buy —*S.H.* *(12/15/1999)*

Indigo Hills 2003 Chardonnay (Sonoma County) $12. The fruit is leaner and thinner on this than most of Gallo's current Chards, but in a way, that works in its favor. The wine is more Chablisian, with moderate peach flavors and a crisp, clean minerality. **85** —*S.H.* *(3/1/2006)*

Indigo Hills 2001 Chardonnay (Central Coast) $12. A simple, innocuous Chard with flavors of peaches and pears and a veneer of oak. Feels lightweight on the palate, and finishes short and a bit sweet. **83** —*S.H.* *(12/1/2003)*

Indigo Hills 2000 Chardonnay (Central Coast) $12. Dust and earth aromas cover underlying apple flavors in this simple, rather sweet wine. Excessively soft acidity makes it drink syrupy. Still, it has basic Chard features and will satisfy most big crowds. **83** —*S.H.* *(5/1/2002)*

Indigo Hills 1997 Merlot (California) $13. 85 Best Buy —*J.C.* *(7/1/2000)*

Indigo Hills 1999 Pinot Noir (Central Coast) $14. Slightly stewed tart-cherry aromas give hints to the grape's character. The fruit isn't very lively, despite some tangy acidity; muted berry, beet, and cocoa shadings add interest. **83** *(10/1/2002)*

INMAN FAMILY

Inman Family 2002 Pinot Gris (Russian River Valley) $24. A lovely wine, partially barrel-fermented and quite rich. Bursts forth with flavors of citrus, pear, and peach in a custardy texture that is dry but feels honey-sweet. Represents a higher class of Pinot Gris in California, with appropriate pricing. Only 70 cases produced. **87** —*S.H.* *(12/1/2003)*

INZINERATOR

InZinerator 2003 Zinfandel (California) $15. Weird name, flashy packaging, and pretty good Zin! It's a nice, easy wine for that home-cooked lasagna or barbecue. Soft and direct, with flavorful cherry, chocolate, coffee, and pepper-spice notes through a dry finish. **86** —*S.H.* *(11/15/2006)*

IO

Io 2000 Red Blend (Santa Barbara County) $60. Not as concentrated as the '99, but an impressive wine. The aroma is especially attractive, with white pepper, cassis, and grilled meat accented with smoky oak. Similar flavors, especially black currant, and rich, fine tannins. Notable for the long finish. Mainly Syrah, with Grenache and Mourvèdre. **90** —*S.H.* *(12/31/2003)*

Io 1996 Rhône Red Blend (Santa Barbara County) $40. 90 *(2/1/2000)*

Io 2002 Rhône Red Blend (Santa Barbara County) $30. This is a big wine, with plum, blackberry, coffee, and dusty spice flavors, with some raisins. The wine is thoroughly dry, and turns sharp on the finish. Mostly Syrah, with Grenache and Mourvèdre and one-third new oak. **86** —*S.H.* *(11/1/2006)*

Io 2001 Rhône Red Blend (Santa Barbara County) $30. With a good track record, this Santa Barbara Rhône blend continues to delight as a full-bodied and dry red wine. As in previous years, the fruit is ripe and upfront, all blackberries accented with white pepper and grilled meat notes. It's fairly tannic and calls for rich, marbled meats. **90** —*S.H.* *(12/15/2005)*

Io 2000 Rhône Red Blend (Santa Barbara County) $60. Pours dramatically dark, staining the sides of the glass with glycerine, suggesting a big, rich wine. And it is, opening with oaky blackberry and meaty aromas that turn robust on the palate with an explosion of fruit. Dense, intense, and concentrated, this dry Rhône blend is best enjoyed in its youthful precocity. **91** —*S.H.* *(12/1/2004)*

Io 2000 Rhône Red Blend (Santa Barbara County) $30. Savory and meaty to some, impossibly brett-ridden to others; this is admittedly gamy—even barnyardy—but if you like funk in your Syrah, bring in dis one. Does have a velvety mouthfeel and some blackberry fruit, so it's not one-dimensional. **85** *(9/1/2005)*

Io 1997 Rhône Red Blend (Santa Barbara County) $40. 94 Editors' Choice —*S.H.* *(11/15/2000)*

Io 1998 Syrah (Santa Barbara County) $60. This blend of 88% Syrah, 6% Grenache, and 6% Mourvèdre smells pretty funky at first, before settling

USA

down into an earthy, peppery, Rhône-like sulk coated with cedary oak. Cinnamon and clove notes, finely tanned leather and mixed berries make for a balanced wine that can be decanted and consumed now or saved another few years. **90** *(11/1/2001)*

Io 2002 Ryan Road Vineyard Syrah (San Luis Obispo County) $35. This wine coats the glass with glycerinery streaks, and throws off amazingly complex aromas ranging from cherry liqueur through smoky oak to mouthwatering grilled lamb. It's that rich, too, offering endless tiers of black stone fruit flavors. The structure is provided by good acidity and firm tannins. **93** —*S.H. (9/1/2004)*

Io 2001 Ryan Road Vineyard Syrah (San Luis Obispo County) $35. It's approachable and drinkable now, with its flamboyant flavors of blackberries and herbs and lush, easy tannins, but is more balanced. Exciting in the mouth; the extremely long, spicy finish suggests aging through at least 2006. **93 Editors' Choice** —*S.H. (10/1/2003)*

Io 2002 Upper Bench Syrah (Santa Maria Valley) $35. Finding the fruit in this tannic, closed wine is like digging down through an archaeological tell. Get deep enough, and you'll hit the cherries and blackberries. But it's so dry and astringent now that it's practically undrinkable. Demands cellaring. Try in 2010 but it still might not be ready. **90** —*S.H. (9/1/2004)*

Io 2001 Upper Bench Syrah (Santa Maria Valley) $35. Heaps of peppery blackberry fruit are wrapped in rich, fine tannins and near-perfect acidity. This is a young wine but it's so drinkable. Fascinating from the first sip through the long, seductive finish. **92 Editors' Choice** —*S.H. (10/1/2003)*

IRIS HILL

Iris Hill 2002 Pinot Noir (Oregon) $16. Round, sweet, and appealing, with black-cherry and lush vanilla wrapped together into a lush, fruity core. The fruit is perfect, and the wine is polished, silky, and delivers a long, drawn-out finish that never tires or turns sour. **90 Best Buy** *(11/1/2004)*

IRISH

Irish 2003 Chenin Blanc (Clarksburg) $16. Apples, spearmint, and ripe white peaches, with refreshing acidity. Very clean, and a bit sweet on the finish. **85** —*S.H. (3/1/2005)*

Irish 2003 Petite Sirah (Lodi) $32. Dark, too soft, Porty, hot with alcohol, and with a slightly sweet finish, this wine is unbalanced. **82** —*S.H. (10/1/2005)*

Irish 2004 Elk Vineyard Petite Sirah (Lodi) $45. If not for the excessive sweetness, this would be a nice wine. It has great tannins, good acidity, and lovely cherry flavors, with hints of licorice and cocoa. But that finish is insipidly sugary. **81** —*S.H. (7/1/2006)*

Irish 2003 Late Harvest Petite Sirah (Lodi) $22. Oozes chocolate fudge, gooey cherry pie and vanilla sprinkle flavors, and drinks pretty sweet, with a soft, velvety mouth feel and crisp, balancing acidity. Delicious, decadent dessert wine. **88** —*S.H. (2/1/2005)*

Irish NV Blarny Red Red Blend (California) $18. Simple and sweet. This wine has candied cherry and coffee flavors. **80** —*S.H. (7/1/2006)*

Irish 2004 Viognier (California) $14. This is a rustic, common wine, a little earthy, with modest flavors of peaches, vanilla, and honeysuckle. It has a honeyed finish but is basically dry. **83** —*S.H. (7/1/2006)*

Irish 2003 Viognier (California) $14. From Madera County, a very fruity wine, with floral, peach, honeysuckle and vanilla notes. Dryish to slightly sweet, with clean acidity and a creamy texture. **85** —*S.H. (2/1/2005)*

IRON HORSE

Iron Horse 1997 T-bar-T Benchmark Bordeaux Blend (Sonoma County) $50. 94 *(11/1/2000)*

Iron Horse 2000 T-bar-T Blend 1 Bordeaux Blend (Alexander Valley) $32. This combination of Cabernet Sauvignon, Cabernet Franc, and Merlot is very good. It has big, bright flavors of cherries and blackberries, infused with the perfume of oak, and is very dry. The tannins are ultra-soft, although they lock in on the finish and suggest aging. **91** —*S.H. (12/15/2003)*

Iron Horse 2003 T-bar-T Benchmark Cabernet Blend (Alexander Valley) $70. This is a gorgeous wine, a blend of Cabernet Sauvignon, Petit Verdot, and Cabernet Franc. It's light and delicate, but powerful, and boasts delicious cherry pie, cassis, cocoa, char, and spice flavors. It possesses the kind of tannins that are soft and sweet now, but firm enough to hold the wine for many years. Best now, or anytime through 2015. **96 Editors' Choice** —*S.H. (12/15/2006)*

Iron Horse 2002 T-bar-T Benchmark Cabernet Blend (Alexander Valley) $70. Stronger, deeper, richer, more impressive in every way than Iron Horse's '02 Cab, this Bordeaux blend is beautiful, powerful, and delicious. Benchmark is the singular wine of this mountainous property, and the '02 is a worthy successor to past vintages. The wine, rich in fruit yet softly voluptuous, showcases the ability of this west wall of the Mayacamas to provide the only serious alternative in California to Napa Valley Cabernet. **94 Editors' Choice** —*S.H. (11/15/2005)*

Iron Horse 1999 T-bar-T Benchmark Cabernet Blend (Alexander Valley) $56. It's clear that winemaker Forrest Tancer is aiming at a California-class Cabernet blend, a complex wine, lush in fruit and herbs, softly tannic and framed in the finest oak. He largely succeeds with this bottling, made only in the best vintages. It lacks the structure of Napa Cabernet, which is unavoidable given its terroir. But it defines Alexander Valley. **92** —*S.H. (7/1/2002)*

Iron Horse 1999 T-bar-T Cabernet Franc (Alexander Valley) $26. Possesses deep flavors of currants and blackberries, and yet you still have to wonder why it merits bottling on its own. It's bone-dry and tannic, and its austerity is a challenge. **86** —*S.H. (9/1/2002)*

Iron Horse 2002 T-bar-T Vineyard Cabernet Franc (Alexander Valley) $30. I've never quite understood why California vintners bottle Cab Franc separately, but this wine shows why the great ones deserve it. Where Cabernet Sauvignon is all black currants, this is cherries, pure and simple. It's got the balance, finesse, complexity, and allure that Iron Horse T-bar-T reds consistently show, with a different flavor profile. **92** —*S.H. (11/15/2005)*

Iron Horse 1996 Cabernet Sauvignon (Sonoma County) $23. 91 *(11/1/1999)*

Iron Horse 1997 T-bar-T Cabernet Sauvignon (Sonoma County) $35. 94 *(11/1/2000)*

Iron Horse 2003 T-bar-T Cabernet Sauvignon (Alexander Valley) $35. A beautiful wine, pure and gentle yet powerful. Softer than Napa, maybe earthier, with lush red cherry and vanilla cream flavors sprinkled with a dash of crème de cassis and dusty cocoa. The sweet, toasty caramel from oak char shows on the finish. Drink now–2009. **93 Editors' Choice** — *S.H. (12/15/2006)*

Iron Horse 2001 T-bar-T Proprietor Grown Cabernet Sauvignon (Alexander Valley) $35. Right up there with the best of Iron Horse's recent Cabs. This one's dry and balanced, with a complex array of blackberry, cherry, herb, and spice flavors that finish long and ripe. There's a scour of tannins that suggests midterm ageability. Now through 2008. **92** —*S.H. (10/1/2004)*

Iron Horse 2002 T-bar-T Vineyard Cabernet Sauvignon (Alexander Valley) $35. Coming off the high hills of the Mayacamas despite the valley designation, this Cab showcases the softness and slight herbaceousness of Alexander Valley Cabs, along with mountain intensity and the power of winemaker Forrest Tancer's low-yield viticulture. It's a beautiful wine, generous and complex, rich in fruit yet dry, balanced, and elegant. **92** — *S.H. (11/15/2005)*

Iron Horse 1991 Champagne Blend (Green Valley) $28. 86 *(12/15/1999)*

Iron Horse 1995 Champagne Blend (Green Valley) $34. At 9 years, still very pale, with good bubbles and crisp acids. However, you begin to pick up on an aged Champagne character. Very dry and complex, clean and satisfying in the mouth, this wine should develop with additional bottle age. **92** —*S.H. (12/31/2004)*

Iron Horse 1993 Blanc de Blancs Champagne Blend (Green Valley) $34. This 100% Chardonnay bubbly has powerful citrus aromas, with a strong dose of dough and charred oak. It's lightly fruity, crisp, and dry. On the whole, this is an elegant, delicate, clean wine, with a long, rich finish. **88** —*S.H. (12/1/2001)*

USA

Iron Horse 1992 Blanc de Blancs Champagne Blend (Sonoma County) $34.
92 —*S.H. (12/1/2000)*

Iron Horse 1994 Brut Classic Vintage Champagne Blend (Green Valley)
$25. 85 *(12/15/1999)*

Iron Horse 1991 Brut LD Champagne Blend (Sonoma County) $60. 93 —
S.H. (12/1/2000)

Iron Horse 1992 Brut LD Champagne Blend (Green Valley) $50. Delicious
and mature, this sparkler was held on its lees for seven years. Lovely
baked bread, vanilla, pear spice, and smoke aromas open to a rich palate
of bread, citrus, dried fruit, and deep earthy flavors. The mouthfeel is
even and round with modest bead and mousse, and it finishes dry and
long. The sparkle is a little faint, but the flavors vibrant and complex. 91
(12/1/2001)

Iron Horse 1991 Brut LD Champagne Blend (Green Valley) $50. 91 —*J.C.*
(12/1/1999)

Iron Horse 2000 Brut Rosé Champagne Blend (Green Valley) $30. Strong
and full-bodied, with raspberry-cherry, dough and vanilla flavors and a
rich, creamy texture. A little sharp in acids, with irregular mousse, and
with a lovely, rich finish. 89 —*S.H. (12/31/2004)*

Iron Horse 1997 Brut Rosé Champagne Blend (Sonoma County) $30. Fairly
dark for a rosé, this Pinot Noir-based bubbly is overtly fruity. Raspberry
and strawberry aromas and flavors are complemented by yeast and bread
dough. Full-bodied and rich, with a spicy, fruity finish. 90 —*P.G.*
(12/1/2002)

Iron Horse 1996 Brut Rosé Champagne Blend (Green Valley) $30. Starts off
with aromas of fresh cherries tinged with meat and mushrooms, then
takes on a bit of almond butter with airing. Flavors are tart cherry and
bitter chocolate, finishing swiftly. 84 *(12/1/2001)*

Iron Horse 1994 Brut Rosé Champagne Blend (Green Valley) $28. 90 —*J.C.*
(12/1/1999)

Iron Horse 1995 Brut Rosé Champagne Blend (Sonoma County) $30. 90
(12/1/2000)

Iron Horse 1994 Brut Russian Cuvée Champagne Blend (Green Valley) $24.
83 —*J.C. (12/1/1999)*

Iron Horse 1994 Brut Vrais Amis Champagne Blend (Green Valley) $29. 90
—*L.W. (12/1/1999)*

Iron Horse 1996 Brut Wedding Cuvée Champagne Blend (Green Valley)
$22. 86 —*J.C. (12/1/1999)*

Iron Horse 1999 Classic Vintage Brut Champagne Blend (Green Valley)
$28. Similar to the Wedding Cuvée but finer, a smooth wine with sug-
gestions of lime, vanilla, lees, and dough, that's dry, with just a hint of
sweet dosage. There's a rich creaminess and elegance to the structure that
showcase the wine's pedigree. 90 —*S.H. (12/31/2004)*

Iron Horse 1997 Classic Vintage Brut Champagne Blend (Sonoma County)
$28. This is Iron Horse's signature bubbly. Opens with delicate aromas
of lime, vanilla, and smoke, and when you taste it, strawberries kick in.
The mouthfeel is especially nice, light as air and soft as silk, despite the
crisp acids. 90 —*P.G. (12/1/2002)*

Iron Horse 1996 Classic Vintage Brut Champagne Blend (Green Valley)
$28. Starts with classic bubbly aromas, yeasty and bready, with a notice-
able streak of raspberries and cherries. It's very dry and clean—on the
elegantly austere side—and a bit rough. There's a core of cherry fruit,
but it's best consumed young and fresh. 87 —*S.H. (12/1/2001)*

Iron Horse 1995 Classic Vintage Brut Champagne Blend (Sonoma County)
$26. 89 —*S.H. (12/1/2000)*

Iron Horse 1998 Good Luck Cuvée Champagne Blend (Sonoma County)
$24. Fairly broad on the palate, with a touch of sweetness. Melon, apple,
and toast flavors come to the fore. 86 —*J.M. (12/1/2002)*

Iron Horse 1997 Russian Cuvée Champagne Blend (Sonoma County) $28.
This is the same Pinot Noir-Chardonnay blend as the Classic Vintage
Brut, and is very similar to it in taste. The technical notes say that it's the
sweetest of the bubblies, and it does have a soft, round, honeyed finish.
87 —*P.G. (12/1/2002)*

Iron Horse 1996 Russian Cuvée Champagne Blend (Green Valley) $26.
Opens with delicate, fine-Champagne aromas, tinged with smoke and

vanilla, and turns creamy in the mouth. There's a trace of citrus fruit in
this dry, full-bodied wine. The finish is succulent, filled with flavor and a
little bitter. 86 —*S.H. (12/1/2001)*

Iron Horse 1995 Russian Cuvée Champagne Blend (Sonoma County) $26.
89 *(12/1/2000)*

Iron Horse 1995 Vrais Amis Champagne Blend (Sonoma County) $26. 90
(12/1/2000)

Iron Horse 2000 Wedding Cuvée Champagne Blend (Green Valley) $29.
Dry and clean, if a bit rough in acidity and sharp bubbles, with bready,
yeasty flavors hinting at limes, vanilla, and a tart bite of half green strawberry. Finishes long and rich. 87 —*S.H. (12/31/2004)*

Iron Horse 1999 Wedding Cuvée Champagne Blend (Sonoma County) $28.
An approachable, easy-to-like wine. Majority Pinot Noir lends sweet
raspberry flavors, while Chardonnay contributes limes. The rest is all
dough and acidity and lees. It's a bit rough and scoury on the palate. 87
—*P.G. (12/1/2002)*

Iron Horse 1998 Wedding Cuvée Champagne Blend (Green Valley) $28.
Very forward in the nose, with spicy raspberry and lime aromas accompanied with yeasty, baked-bread notes. It's delicious and ripe, with a real
blast of fruity flavors. Dry and robust, it's a bit rough on the peppery finish. 87 —*S.H. (12/1/2001)*

Iron Horse 1997 Wedding Cuvée Brut Champagne Blend (Green Valley)
$28. 90 —*S.H. (12/1/2000)*

Iron Horse 1997 Chardonnay (Green Valley) $22. 92 —*S.H. (7/1/1999)*

Iron Horse 2000 Chardonnay (Green Valley) $26. Iron Horse hits pay dirt
with a brilliantly evocative wine that's very rich. It strikes a fine balance
with the ripe tropical fruit flavors, deft touch of smoky oak, and a sleek,
acid-tinged mouthfeel that finishes with flavors of minerals and steel. 92
—*S.H. (12/15/2002)*

Iron Horse 1994 Blanc de Blancs Chardonnay (Sonoma County) $34. This
100% Chardonnay has strong scents of lime, smoke, freshly baked
bread, and vanilla. It's lemon-and-limey and rich, but delicate. Feels light
and fresh on the palate, with a clean finish. 88 —*P.G. (12/1/2002)*

Iron Horse 1993 Blanc De Blancs Chardonnay (Green Valley) $34. This
100% Chardonnay bubbly has powerful citrus aromas, with a strong
dose of dough and charred oak. It's lightly fruity, crisp, and dry. On the
whole, this is an elegant, delicate, clean wine, with a long, rich finish. 88
—*S.H. (12/1/2001)*

Iron Horse 2003 Corral Vineyard Chardonnay (Green Valley) $35. Here's a
reserve that really merits the extra price. As good as the regular Chard is,
this single-vineyard bottling is even better. It's more intense and concentrated in fruit and oakier, with that same clean, bright acidity. 93 —*S.H.*
(2/1/2006)

Iron Horse 2002 Corral Vineyard Chardonnay (Green Valley) $32. A deeply
satisfying and intense Chard, for its wealth of well-ripened tropical fruit,
pear, Key lime pie, vanilla, and toast flavors and the refreshing acidity
that makes the wine clean and lively. The long, complete finish is
impressive. Defines the sunshine and chill of its appellation. 93 **Editors'**
Choice —*S.H. (7/1/2005)*

Iron Horse 2001 Corral Vineyard Chardonnay (Green Valley) $37. Classic
Russian River Valley Chardonnay, with its flavors of tart green apples
and peppery, cinnamony spices. A spine of steely acidity provides a brilliant counterpoint to the opulent flavors, while a smattering of dusty
tannins kicks in on the finish. A superb Chard, and versatile at the table.
91 —*S.H. (12/1/2003)*

Iron Horse 1997 Cuvée Joy Chardonnay (Green Valley) $30. Intriguing
Asian spice, peanut brittle, pineapple, and butter cream aromas comprise
the bouquet of this round, well-integrated wine from Sonoma County's
tiny Green Valley appellation. Everything flows smoothly into the lingering pineapple, butterscotch, pear, and apple flavors in the finish. Top
Value. 90 *(7/1/2001)*

Iron Horse 1997 Cuvée Joy Chardonnay (Green Valley) $30. 92 —*L.W.*
(3/1/2000)

Iron Horse 2003 Estate Chardonnay (Green Valley) $26. A gorgeously
crisp, balanced Chardonnay from Iron Horse. Those Green Valley acids
dependably boost and brighten the fruit, which in this vintage is ripe

and opulent in green apple, kiwi, lime, and pineapple flavors. Oak and lees make it all creamy and complex. **91** —S.H. (2/1/2006)

Iron Horse 2002 Estate Chardonnay (Green Valley) $26. These high-acid grapes have made for a mouthwateringly crisp wine, with deliciously provocative flavors of high-toned citrus fruits, including oranges, and lots of vanilla and buttered toast. Clean, complex, and satisfying. **90** — S.H. (7/1/2005)

Iron Horse 2001 Estate Bottled Chardonnay (Green Valley) $26. First rate, a winemaker's wine made from grapes with a real smack of terroir. High, citrusy acidity marks the well-ripened mango, tangerine, and smoky-vanilla and leesy flavors that are wrapped in a richly creamy texture. Bold and complex. **90** —S.H. (6/1/2004)

Iron Horse 1998 Estate Bottled Chardonnay (Sonoma County) $24. 88 (6/1/2000)

Iron Horse 2001 Thomas Road Chardonnay (Green Valley) $37. Pretty similar to Iron Horse's Corral bottling, maybe a tad higher in acidity and firmer in structure, but that's splitting hairs. Again, those refreshing flavors of tart green apples sprinkled with white pepper, with an edge of grass and herbs. Its angularity suggests but does not demand aging. **91** — S.H. (12/1/2003)

Iron Horse 1998 T-bar-T Fumé Blanc (Sonoma County) $18. 90 —S.H. (11/1/1999)

Iron Horse 2002 T-bar-T Vineyard Merlot (Alexander Valley) $30. After all the Sideways kicks Merlot took, this wine shows there's a real future for the variety, if vintners will take it seriously. It has the classic structure of a Cabernet, yet is softer and gentler, although no less complex and rewarding. The cherry compote, cocoa, and vanilla flavors are reminiscent of the candies and desserts we grew up with, with sophistication and flair. **92** —S.H. (11/15/2005)

Iron Horse 1998 Pinot Noir (Green Valley) $28. 87 (10/1/2000)

Iron Horse 1997 Pinot Noir (Green Valley) $24. 90 (10/1/1999)

Iron Horse 2002 Pinot Noir (Green Valley) $30. A crisp wine that glides like silk over the palate. It has pretty flavors of cherries, cola, rhubarb, and herb tea, and is very dry, with a long, spicy finish. **87** —S.H. (11/1/2004)

Iron Horse 2000 Pinot Noir (Green Valley) $30. This solidly built wine is big. Cherry, mint, and saddle-leather aromas, a chalky, fine-grained feel and ripe cherry, apple, and tea flavors comprise a fulfilling package. Closes long, with herb and leather accents. Drink now-2007. **91 Editors' Choice** (10/1/2002)

Iron Horse 1999 Pinot Noir (Green Valley) $30. Best-ever from this producer, whose house style mingles pure, ripe black raspberry, and cherry notes with earthier ones of rhubarb, tomato, and dark tea, Fancy oak adds vanilla and smoke nuances. This wonderfully rich, layered wine is dry and complex and a joy to drink. **93 Editors' Choice** —S.H. (12/15/2001)

Iron Horse 2000 Corral Vineyard Pinot Noir (Green Valley) $60. Oak frames the firm, dark cherry fruit of this chewy wine. This offers nutty, smoky, charred-oak and burnt marshmallow flavors to spare, but enough solid fruit shows to assure you this will be worth the wait. The long tannic close sports chocolate, bramble, and tar notes. Try in 2004. **90** (10/1/2002)

Iron Horse 2004 Estate Pinot Noir (Green Valley) $35. This is classic Green Valley Pinot, with cool-climate acidity and a firm, almost mineral cleanliness in youth. Elegant, refined, and ultradry, it should be aged, to let it soften and allow the cherry fruit to express itself. Best 2007–2010. **90 Cellar Selection** —S.H. (12/15/2006)

Iron Horse 2003 Estate Pinot Noir (Green Valley) $35. This Pinot is a little thin and acidic, although the cherry, cola, root beer, and spicy oak flavors are pretty. The palate needs more weight, depth, and length. I'm not a fan of aging Pinot, but this one might surprise. **85** —S.H. (2/1/2006)

Iron Horse 2002 Estate Pinot Noir (Green Valley) $30. The grapes seem to have been picked relatively early in order to preserve lively acidity. The result is a somewhat lean wine, with moderate cherry flavors and a sleek coating of oak. Balanced, dry, silky, and clean, this isn't a big Pinot, but it's an elegant one. **88** —S.H. (10/1/2005)

Iron Horse 2001 Estate Bottled Pinot Noir (Green Valley) $30. This pale-colored Pinot is somewhat lean rather than fleshy, due probably to its

cool location, but it is a wonderful example of how terroir can be exploited by great grapegrowing and winemaking. Crisp and steely in acidity, it is elaborately oaked, with succulent flavors of raspberries, tangerine zest, vanilla custard, and sugared coffee. **90** —S.H. (6/1/2004)

Iron Horse 2004 Q Pinot Noir (Green Valley) $70. This is a new reserve-style bottling, produced at less than 50 cases. It's an unusual Pinot for Iron Horse, being darker, softer, and fuller-bodied, without the crisp acids usually associated with Green Valley. Yet it's immensely complicated. You could criticize it for being Rhône-like, but it's silky, airy, and Pinotesque all the way. The operative word is "fascinating." Every sip is different, and an adventure. **94** —S.H. (12/31/2006)

Iron Horse 2002 Rosé de Pinot Noir Pinot Noir (Green Valley) $15. As easy and tasty as a summer wine gets, this blush also has a lovely coppery-pink color. Flavors of fresh strawberries and spice burst on the palate, and drink just a tad off-dry. **87** —S.H. (7/1/2003)

Iron Horse 2005 Rosé de Pinot Noir Pinot Noir (Green Valley) $15. If you smelled this blind you might think it was Sauvignon Blanc. But swirl it, let it breathe, and the rosehip tea comes along. In the mouth, the wine is crisp with tea, cherry skin, and root beer flavors. **86** —S.H. (12/1/2006)

Iron Horse 2001 Thomas Road Pinot Noir (Green Valley) $60. In this vintage the grapes became very ripe, and the flavors burst on the palate. Raspberry and cherry star, with supporting roles from espresso, earthy mushrooms, and peppery spices. Yet there is some heat from alcohol, and the acidity could be brighter. **89** —S.H. (2/1/2004)

Iron Horse 2000 Thomas Road Pinot Noir (Sonoma County) $60. This beautifully balanced Pinot boasts aromas of dark fruit, leather, and smoked meat. The subtly grained, mid-weight palate shows toast and tea accents over blackberry and plum. Finishes long, but hard and closed, with taut acids and drying tannins, espresso, and black chocolate flavors. Drink 2004–2010. **90** (10/1/2002)

Iron Horse 1998 Thomas Road Vineyard Pinot Noir (Sonoma County) $50. This wine become pretty pricey but that's because consumers recognize its quality; its sheer deliciousness can't be beat. It has all the elements of fine Russian River Pinot—it's dry and has lots o f ripe fruit, pretty oak, toast, and spice—and it puts them all together in a super-elegant package. The vintage is light but the wine doesn't seem to mind. Its class shows. **90** —S.H. (2/1/2001)

Iron Horse 2004 Rosato di Sangiovese Rosé Blend (Green Valley) $10. Here's a light-bodied, silky rosé, with herb, tobacco, and cherry flavors and good, cleansing acidity. It seems a little sweet, but that may be due to the fruity, vanilla-y finish. **85** —S.H. (11/15/2005)

Iron Horse 2004 Rosé de Pinot Noir Rosé Blend (Green Valley) $15. My oh my, is this pink wine tasty. It's pure essence of strawberries, ripe, clean and dry, backed up by firm, cool climate acidity. Try this juicy blush with salmon sautéed in butter and garlic, with a sprinkle of black pepper. **88** —S.H. (11/15/2005)

Iron Horse 1997 Sangiovese (Sonoma County) $19. 91 —S.H. (12/15/1999)

Iron Horse 1996 Sangiovese (Sonoma County) $22. 91 —S.H. (10/1/1999)

Iron Horse 2000 Rosato Sangiovese (Alexander Valley) $15. Here's a summer sipper with lots of enjoyment. It starts with pretty strawberry, cola, and spice aromas, leading to dry, spicy flavors of strawberry and black tea. There's real elegance and charm, and a rich, long finish. **86** —S.H. (11/15/2001)

Iron Horse 2005 Rosato di Sangiovese (Alexander Valley) $12. This is a great price for a blush wine of this quality and complexity. It's very dry, yet with a fruity sweetness of strawberries and cherries. Wonderfully fresh and clean in vibrant acids, it's hard to believe it was unoaked because it's so creamy. **87 Best Buy** —S.H. (12/1/2006)

Iron Horse 2003 Rosato di Sangiovese Sangiovese (Alexander Valley) $10. My one non-Oz wine is this rosé; it falls more into the "light red" than "pink-colored white" category, in terms of weight and flavor. Berry aromas have cream-nutty accents, while on the palate the berries take on earthy nuances. From Iron Horse, who are as adept at big reds as they are at sparklers, and continues to surprise us. **86 Best Buy** —D.T. (11/15/2004)

Iron Horse 2002 Rosato di Sangiovese Sangiovese (Alexander Valley) $15. Thin and simple, with modest strawberry flavors and a watery finish. It's also soft and flabby. Iron Horse's Pinot Noir blush wine, at the same price, is an incomparably better wine. **83** —S.H. (9/1/2003)

Iron Horse 1999 T-bar-T Proprietor Grown Sangiovese (Alexander Valley) $24. Iron Horse seeks a full-bodied, even ageable, wine with this difficult varietal, and has blended in small amounts of Cabernet Sauvignon and Merlot. The wine is tannic, with generic berry flavors, and very dry. It's a nice complement to rich pastas with olive oil and butter. **87** —S.H. (9/1/2003)

Iron Horse 2000 T-bar-T Sangiovese (Alexander Valley) $24. This hard-to-grow variety had a difficult time in 2000, and no less a talented wine-maker than Forrest Tancer struggled with it. The resulting wine is tight and lean, with citrusy acids framing cherry fruit and some scoury tannins. Best with rich cheeses to sweeten it. **86** —S.H. (12/15/2004)

Iron Horse 1997 Cuvée Joy Sauvignon Blanc (Sonoma County) $24. **89** —S.H. (9/1/2000)

Iron Horse 1999 T-bar-T Cuvée R Sauvignon Blanc (Alexander Valley) $19. This 14.5% bruiser contains 20% Viognier, which adds a tropical fruit character to the nose and palate. The mouthfeel is soft, with flavors heavy on banana and melon. Woody characteristics such as nuttiness, particularly almonds, also pop up. To its detriment, the oak and fruit seem to be fighting each other more than complementing one another. **87** (8/1/2002)

Iron Horse 2005 T-bar-T Cuvée R Sauvignon Blanc (Alexander Valley) $24. It's 99% Sauvignon Blanc, with a splash of Viognier. The wine is really a wonderful barrel-fermented style, rich, unctuous, and exotic in citrus, nettle, and wildflower flavors. It's wines like this that are making Sauvignon Blanc a certified superstar. **93** —S.H. (10/1/2006)

Iron Horse 1998 Blanc de Blancs Sparkling Blend (Green Valley) $34. The vintage was a cool one, and the wine shows an acidic, fairly lean profile that is sleekly elegant. It has subtle freshly baked bread and citrus flavors, with an edge of creamy kiwi and lime. The dosage gives it a honeyed, but dry, finish. **90** —S.H. (12/31/2006)

Iron Horse 1997 Blanc de Blancs Sparkling Blend (Green Valley) $34. Interesting that Iron Horse has released this at eight years of age. It's still a young, acidic wine, but is mellowing, with a tantalizingly sweet core of peaches and cream just edging into crème brûlée. This complex bubbly should develop well throughout the decade. **90 Editors' Choice** —S.H. (12/31/2005)

Iron Horse 1994 Blanc de Blancs Sparkling Blend (Green Valley) $34. At nearly 10 years of age, this rich sparkler has developed mature flavors and aromas that take the lime and peach into dried fruit and dusty spice. It is fine and complex, with lively acidity. Will keep for years to come. **91** —S.H. (12/1/2003)

Iron Horse 1996 Blanc de Blancs LD Sparkling Blend (Green Valley) $60. At 11 years, this 100% Chardonnay sparkler has achieved a taffeta softness that just melts in the mouth. With residual sugar of 0.9%, it shows a distinctly honeyed taste. Offers beautifully rich, mature lemondrop, vanilla, and and butterscotchy dough flavors, with keen acidity. As good as it is, let it develop through 2008 and beyond. **93** —S.H. (12/31/2006)

Iron Horse 1996 Blanc de Blancs LD Sparkling Blend (Green Valley) $60. There's more going on in this wine than in a New York minute. It's rich and young, brimming with acid, yeast, and citrus fruit, and with a finish of toast and char. But it has a depth and nobility that make it complex and ageworthy. Should hold easily through 2010. **93 Cellar Selection** —S.H. (12/31/2005)

Iron Horse 1996 Brut LD Sparkling Blend (Green Valley) $50. Almost the quality of great vintage Champagne, in terms of smoothness and texture. This connoisseur's wine is muted in flavor, such that the acids and smooth texture star. But it's an ager. **91** —S.H. (12/1/2003)

Iron Horse 1996 Brut LD Sparkling Blend (Green Valley) $50. A very great success that's picking up some charry, smoky, old yeast notes in addition to the rich lime and white peach, but it's as fresh as can be. Vibrant in acids, with a refined, smooth texture, and very dry, it's the epitome of elegance. Still young. Drink now through this decade. **93** —S.H. (12/31/2004)

Iron Horse 1998 Brut Rosé Sparkling Blend (Green Valley) $30. One of the darker, more extracted blush bubblies, with an orangey-pink color and pronounced flavors of raspberries and herbs. Round and full-bodied in the mouth, the wine is nicely dry, with a clean, spicy finish. **88** —S.H. (12/1/2003)

Iron Horse 1997 Brut Rosé Sparkling Blend (Green Valley) $30. Fairly dark in color, it starts off with a bright cherry core that extends to black-cherry, citrus, and herbs along the palate. It's creamy, fresh, and long on the finish. **89** —J.M. (12/1/2003)

Iron Horse 2001 Classic Vintage Brut Sparkling Blend (Green Valley) $30. A nice, classy bubbly that shows the character of Iron Horse's more expensive sparkling wines, but at a lower price. Mainly Pinot Noir, it's full-bodied and dry, with suggestions of strawberries, yeast, and vanilla. **88** —S.H. (12/31/2006)

Iron Horse 2000 Classic Vintage Brut Sparkling Blend (Green Valley) $30. A little sweet, a little scoury in acids, and strong in yeast and bread, this young, assertive sparkler shows delicate peach and strawberry flavors. It's at its best now, so drink up. **87** —S.H. (12/31/2005)

Iron Horse 1998 Classic Vintage Brut Sparkling Blend (Green Valley) $28. A young, fragrant bubbly that opens with pretty aromas of peaches, limes, smoke, vanilla, and baked bread. It is delicately dry in the mouth, with rich flavors and a silky texture. **87** —S.H. (12/1/2003)

Iron Horse 2000 Russian Cuvée Sparkling Blend (Green Valley) $30. The Russians liked sugar in their Champagne, and this cuvée is one of Iron Horse's sweeter ones. The residual sugar makes it round and mellow despite crisp acidity. But the finish is dry and whistle-clean. **87** —S.H. (12/31/2005)

Iron Horse 1999 Russian Cuvée Sparkling Blend (Green Valley) $28. A bit sweeter than Iron Horse's drier bruts, and very polished, with subtle raspberry, lime, yeast and smoky-vanilla flavors and good acidity. Easy and delicious to drink, but complex and nuanced in all the right ways. **88** —S.H. (12/31/2004)

Iron Horse 1998 Russian Cuvée Sparkling Blend (Sonoma County) $28. A little sweet, a little tart, somewhat rough hewn, this is the most rustic of Iron Horse's line of bubblies. It has flavors of citrus fruits and peaches and the bright, aggressive acidity this cool climate appellation brings. **87** —S.H. (12/1/2003)

Iron Horse 2001 Russian Cuvée Sparkling Blend (Green Valley) $30. Always the sweetest of the winery's brut-style bubblies, in keeping with the Russian Czars' liking for sugared Champagne, this is still fundamentally dry. It has pleasant peach, strawberry, yeast, butter cookie and vanilla flavors offset by cleansing acidity. **87** —S.H. (12/31/2006)

Iron Horse 2002 Wedding Cuvée Sparkling Blend (Green Valley) $34. Maybe it's all marketing, but this does seem to be an ideal wedding-toast bubbly. There's something for everyone. Despite being almost all Pinot Noir, it's light and delicate, with a crisp elegance and a fine mousse, and that effervescent pleasure that only a fine bubbly provides. **91 Editors' Choice** —S.H. (12/31/2005)

Iron Horse 2003 Wedding Cuvée Sparkling Blend (Green Valley) $34. This is always one of Iron Horse's nicest sparklers. It seems softer, rounder, creamier and fruitier than the others it certainly is relatively high in alcohol, yet is no less elegant. Just delicious in strawberry, lime, vanilla and lees flavors, with a clean, uplifting finish. **92 Editors' Choice** —S.H. (12/31/2006)

Iron Horse 1999 Wedding Cuvée Sparkling Blend (Green Valley) $28. Made a little on the sweet side, with forward flavors of raspberries and limes, but it's still a dry wine. Feels lush and round in the mouth, leaving a lively prickle of acidity on the finish. **87** —S.H. (12/1/2003)

Iron Horse 2000 Viognier (Alexander Valley) $17. Full-bodied, round and polished, this wine begins with floral, honey and peach aromas, and similar flavors follow. Barrel fermentation creates a smooth, velvety, buttery mouthfeel, soft and complete. It tastes dry, but rich and honeyed. **90 Editors' Choice** —S.H. (11/15/2001)

Iron Horse 2000 T-bar-T Viognier (Alexander Valley) $24. Fans of intensely flavored Viogniers bursting with wildflower and tropical fruit notes won't be disappointed. This one's got honeysuckle, guava, ripe peach and

USA

mangoes, in a light, unoaky package. Yet it's dry. This is a fun wine, meant for early enjoyment. **89** —*S.H. (9/1/2002)*

Iron Horse 2005 T-bar-T Viognier (Alexander Valley) $24. Easy to ripen, hard to achieve balance and elegance. That's Viognier, and Iron Horse does one of the better jobs. That's because in addition to tropical fruit, citrus, flower, and spicy flavors, the wine is very dry and acidic. In this case there's a bit of oak but just enough to add a touch of cream. **87** — *S.H. (12/15/2006)*

Iron Horse 2002 T-bar-T Viognier (Alexander Valley) $24. Retains Viognier's exotic personality of tropical fruits, wildflowers, and other intense aromatics, but does so in a stylish way. With its steely center and just-right veneer of oak, this wine gushes richness balanced by control. **90** —*S.H. (12/1/2003)*

Iron Horse 2004 T-bar-T Late Harvest Viognier (Alexander Valley) $25. This sweet wine shows Viognier's wildflower and tropical fruit flavors, with an intensely honeyed texture. The alcohol is remarkably low, below ten percent, which is why the acidity, which is not high, seems so dominant. With no oak, the wine is a study in fruity purity. **89** —*S.H. (2/1/2006)*

Iron Horse 2001 T-bar-T Proprietor Grown Viognier (Alexander Valley) $24. No one has worked harder to tame Viognier's over the top flavors than Iron Horse. This release has peach, citrus, and pear flavors and is very dry, with mouthwatering acidity. Bright and clean, it's a nice alternative to Sauvignon Blanc. **87** —*S.H. (3/1/2003)*

Iron Horse 2004 T-bar-T Vineyard Viognier (Alexander Valley) $24. Some Viogniers are exotically fruity. Not this one, which is elegantly crisp and refined. Its lemon and lime flavors just barely nudge into wildflowers. Has a rich, honeyed finish. **90** —*S.H. (7/1/2006)*

Iron Horse 2001 T-bar-T Cuvée R White Blend (Alexander Valley) $19. This blend has 80% Viognier, which adds a peach and apricot streak that adds interest to the lemony, grapefruity flavors. Drinks tart, bone dry and clean, with sleek acidity. A terrific, elegant wine, perfect for a first course, and a great offering from this top producer. **90 Editors' Choice** —*S.H. (7/1/2003)*

Iron Horse 2000 T-bar-T Cuvée R White Blend (Alexander Valley) $17. Here's a lovely white wine that emphasizes Sauvignon Blanc's tart, lemony fruit and crisp structure, and Viognier's floral, honeyed notes. Rich and complex, with waves of bright berry fruit and spice and a long, delightful finish. **88** —*S.H. (11/15/2001)*

Iron Horse 2002 T-bar-T Cuvée R White Blend (Alexander Valley) $19. Another refreshing and distinctive Cuvée R, crisp and citrusy enough in Sauvignon Blanc character to stimulate the palate. Viognier gives the flavor an exotic, flowery edge. The lilting, silky mouthfeel is especially nice. **90** —*S.H. (12/1/2003)*

Iron Horse 2004 T-bar-T Cuvée R White Blend (Alexander Valley) $24. Always elegantly sleek and dry, this year's Cuvée R, a blend of Sauvignon Blanc and Viognier, shows citrus and flower flavors. Smooth and lively in the mouth, with crisp acidity. Barrel fermentation and sur lies aging make this wine unusually rich. **91 Editors' Choice** —*S.H. (7/1/2006)*

IRONSTONE

Ironstone 1994 Crown Jewel Bordeaux Blend (California) $30. **89** *(11/15/1999)*

Ironstone 2003 Cabernet Franc (California) $10. Dryish to slightly off-dry, very soft and velvety, with ripe cherry, cocoa, and plummy-blackberry flavors. This is a nice, easy-drinking wine. It's the kind of by-the-glass sipper you order with pizza or burgers. **84** —*S.H. (11/15/2006)*

Ironstone 1999 Cabernet Franc (California) $10. This Loire varietal, also used in blending in Bordeaux, faces challenges on its own in California. Here, it's simple and dry, with appealing but light berry flavors and dusty tannins. Perfectly honest and forthright, it's okay as a red table wine. **83** —*S.H. (12/1/2002)*

Ironstone 1997 Cabernet Franc (California) $11. **88 Best Buy** *(11/15/1999)*

Ironstone 2002 Reserve Cabernet Franc (Sierra Foothills) $20. I've long thought Cab Franc is a secret strength of the Foothills. This bottling is dry, balanced, and complex, with a rich earthy, coffee streak to the cher-

ry flavors. It's a bit sharp, and could soften with a year or two of aging. **87** —*S.H. (6/1/2006)*

Ironstone 1999 Reserve Cabernet Franc (Sierra Foothills) $18. Considerably richer than the regular release, this wine has plenty of fresh, sappy berry fruit, wrapped in a velvety, plush texture. It feels opulent in the mouth, and the finish reveals interesting, even complex flavors. **89** —*S.H. (12/1/2002)*

Ironstone 2003 Cabernet Sauvignon (California) $10. Many inexpensive Cabs smell this inviting, but then fall apart in the mouth. This one holds together. It's explosive in cherry, blackberry, and chocolate flavors, yet dry and balanced and long on the finish. **86 Best Buy** —*S.H. (2/1/2006)*

Ironstone 1999 Cabernet Sauvignon (California) $10. A nice Cabernet at a nice price, this pleasant wine offers rich varietal character in a straightforward way. The blackberry and cassis flavors are enhanced with smoky oak notes, and it's dry and clean. **84** *(11/15/2002)*

Ironstone 1998 Cabernet Sauvignon (California) $9. Dry, even, and light, this slightly sweet, straightforward wine offers cassis, blueberry and toast aromas and flavors. Soft and pleasant on the palate, it tightens up just a bit on the back end, showing mild tannins. A solid bar-pour and entry-level Cab, easy to enjoy. **86 Best Buy** *(8/1/2001)*

Ironstone 2002 Reserve Cabernet Sauvignon (Sierra Foothills) $30. Ironstone's 2002 Bordeaux reds all are very good, and it's clear what they're aiming at. This Cabernet, the current release, is packed with black currant, cocoa, and oak flavors that drink deep and long. Yet it retains a trace of the rustic sharpness that marks most Sierra Foothills wines. The next step is elegance. **87** —*S.H. (7/1/2006)*

Ironstone 1999 Reserve Cabernet Sauvignon (Sierra Foothills) $25. Here's one of the most serious bids in the Sierras for a Cabernet that rivals coastal versions. It comes close. Pretty flavors of currants and blackberries, a nice overlay of fancy oak and soft, intricate tannins are a pleasure in the mouth. It needs more depth and finesse, but this is a wine to watch. **88** *(11/15/2002)*

Ironstone 1997 Reserve Cabernet Sauvignon (Sierra Foothills) $24. This is a soft, full wine, with good depth of flavor. Ripe blackberry and cassis fruit mark the palate, offset by attractive cedar notes. Clean, elegant, and complex. Easy tannins and modest acidity make it approachable now. **88** *(8/1/2001)*

Ironstone 2004 Chardonnay (California) $10. There's an edge of green mintiness to this Chard, which adds complexity to the apple and peach flavors. The texture is smooth and creamy, perked up by fine acids. Try with grilled sole in butter sauce. **85 Best Buy** —*S.H. (2/1/2006)*

Ironstone 2000 Chardonnay (California) $10. Clean and simple, with peach and apple flavors and a solid dose of oak. It has a rich, creamy mouthfeel, and the finish is spicy and ripe. Satisfies the basic requirements for California Chardonnay. **83** —*J.M. (12/15/2002)*

Ironstone 1999 Chardonnay (California) $9. Vanilla, ripe pear, and dry citrus aromas and flavors highlight this featherbed of a wine. The palate's soft, almost sappy feel, round melon fruit and mild spices are easy to like. It's not cloying or tacky, just don't look for spine or structure. **85** *(8/1/2001)*

Ironstone 1997 Chardonnay (California) $10. **86** *(11/15/1999)*

Ironstone 2003 Reserve Chardonnay (Sierra Foothills) $18. All the bells and whistles have been applied to this elaborately crafted wine. There's lots of oak, and the mouthfeel is smooth and creamy, offset by crisp acids. There could be more fruit intensity, though. **85** —*S.H. (2/1/2006)*

Ironstone 2003 Reserve Chardonnay (Sierra Foothills) $18. Soft and well-oaked, this Chard has some good fruit, and there's a leesy flavor and creaminess, but the acidity is too low for balance. **83** —*S.H. (3/1/2006)*

Ironstone 1998 Reserve Chardonnay (California) $16. This wine's deep gold color is in line with its ripe-apple and butterscotch flavors. There's plenty of oak, and a round mouthfeel. Sophisticated palates may find this package just too obvious, but tangy oak over overtly sweet fruit is a bulls-eye if you're not seeking nuance. **87** *(8/1/2001)*

Ironstone 2001 Meritage (Sierra Foothills) $35. A rich, balanced Cab-based blend of all 5 classic Bordeaux varietals. Understated and elegant, polished and fruity. Feels harmonious and balanced through the finish. **90** —*S.H. (2/1/2005)*

Ironstone 2002 Reserve Meritage (Calaveras County) $35. Few Foothills wineries are making a more serious play at Cabernet than Ironstone. This new release shows progress. It's dry and balanced, with some complexity, although there's a slightly rustic note to the tannins and acids. **87** —*S.H. (2/1/2006)*

Ironstone 2000 Merlot (California) $10. From the largest winery in the Sierra Foothills, this fine value offers up plenty of juicy cherry and berry fruit, with gentle tannins. Easy drinking, with a long, rich finish. Perfect with grilled lamb chops. **87 Best Buy** —*S.H. (11/15/2002)*

Ironstone 1999 Merlot (California) $9. The fragrant aromas of soft red berries, black-cherries and cocoa are inviting. A bit simple, but this soft and fruity wine actually smells and tastes like Merlot. Finishes a little drier than the palate shows, with supple tannins. **85** *(8/1/2001)*

Ironstone 1997 Merlot (California) $11. **85** *(11/15/1999)*

Ironstone 2002 Petite Sirah (California) $10. Full-bodied and rustic, a big, dry, chewy wine with coffee, plum, and macaroon flavors. Dry, but filled with fruity ripeness. Perfect with barbecue. **86 Best Buy** —*S.H. (2/1/2005)*

Ironstone 2005 Expression Red Blend (California) $6. I accidentally refrigerated this red wine. Voila! It's great cold. Just goes to show that the conventional wisdom doesn't always hold. A blend of Shiraz and Cab Franc, the wine is rich in cherry-filled chocolate, with a dash of lavender, licorice, and pepper, and the finish is dry. Easy to find, with 25,000 cases produced. Ironstone is really doing a great job in making varietally true, inexpensive wines. **86 Best Buy** —*S.H. (11/15/2006)*

Ironstone 2003 Xpression Red Blend (California) $8. A little sweet, silky and light in body, with raspberry-cherry flavors. Darker than a rosé. Try chilling before you drink. **85 Best Buy** —*S.H. (2/1/2005)*

Ironstone 2003 Sauvignon Blanc (California) $10. Fresh and grassy, with a background of lemons and figs. Drinks clean and vibrant in acids, and finishes dry and clean. **87 Best Buy** —*S.H. (2/1/2005)*

Ironstone 2003 Shiraz (California) $10. You're having pizza or a cheeseburger or ham sandwich. The pleasure is simple and real. You want a red wine to go with it, not too expensive. This is a good choice. It's dry and balanced, and rich in fruit. **84** —*S.H. (2/1/2005)*

Ironstone 2002 Shiraz (California) $10. A good wine at a good price. Though the mouthfeel is a bit flat, with baked-fruit flavors and powdery feel, its starts and ends nicely. It smells like black-cherry preserves, and finishes with cinnamon and spice. **85 Best Buy** *(9/1/2005)*

Ironstone 2000 Shiraz (California) $10. Young and jammy flavors offer a burst of red and black-cherry marmalade. This dry wine has some dusty tannins and is pleasurable in a simple way. Drink it with hamburgers, pizza, and other comfort foods. **84** —*S.H. (12/1/2002)*

Ironstone 1999 Shiraz (California) $9. Aussie-like, with big, jammy aromas of fresh wild berries, white pepper, grilled meat, and smoke. Overripe and very fruity, almost candied, with ripe, pure flavors and peppery spice. It's dry, soft, and mellow. **86 Best Buy** *(8/1/2001)*

Ironstone 2005 Obsession Symphony (California) $8. A simple dessert wine that's sweet but not overly so, with ripe apricot, peach, and pear flavors and a floral note of honeysuckle. There's quite a bit of acidity for balance. **84 Best Buy** —*S.H. (12/1/2006)*

Ironstone 2003 Obsession Symphony White Blend (California) $8. Smells like a dessert wine, with the apricot, wildflower, and honey aroma of a sweet Riesling, and drinks on the off-dry side, too. There are modest peach and apple flavors. Notable for the fresh, sharp burst of acidity. **85** —*S.H. (6/1/2004)*

Ironstone 2000 Obsession Symphony White Blend (California) $7. This tastes very sweet, with dense, perfumey Muscat and orange aromas. The slight spritz keeps it from becoming totally cloying, but this could use more spine and less sugar. Like an Italian moscato; unless you've got a sweet tooth, this is over-the-top. Could work poured over strawberries. **84** *(8/1/2001)*

Ironstone 1998 Obsession Symphony White Blend (California) $8. **85** *(11/15/1999)*

Ironstone 2000 Zinfandel (California) $10. Very smooth in the mouth—perhaps a bit mushy—this Zin has loads of distinctive red fruit (especially raspberry) coated with what tastes like maple or molasses. Caramel-cream and blackberry stand out on the finish and in the bouquet. An easy crowd-pleasing quaffer. **85** —*D.T. (3/1/2002)*

Ironstone 1999 Zinfandel (California) $9. Captures Zin's true varietal character, with briary, brambly wild berry fruit, pepper, and soft tannins. Those fruity flavors are exuberant on the palate, carried by firm, dry tannins and adequate acidity. A friendly, easy to like wine, and a good value. **86** *(8/1/2001)*

Ironstone 2005 Old Vine Zinfandel (Lodi) $10. Peppery and briary, with wild berry and peppermint flavors, this crisp Zin finishes just a tad sweet. It makes you think of easy fare, like pasta primavera or roast chicken. **84** —*S.H. (12/15/2006)*

Ironstone 2000 Reserve-Old Vines Zinfandel (Lodi) $18. You can pretend that Zin is Cabernet, or you can let it express its wild, wooly self, in all its glory. This wine does just that. Old vines concentrate flavors to laser-like purity, while retaining that footloose quality. With soft but complex tannins and soft acidity, this wine is quintessential California Zin. **87** —*S.H. (11/1/2002)*

Ironstone 2003 Reserve Old Vine Zinfandel (Lodi) $20. If there's anything Lodi succeeds at, it's old-vine Zin. Of course, it's soft and chocolatey, but it's delicious, with beautifully etched cherry and blackberry flavors. **91** —*S.H. (2/1/2006)*

IRONY

Irony 2002 Cabernet Sauvignon (Napa Valley) $16. Pretty good for the price, with real upscale Napa character. Rich and dry in blackberry, blueberry, and chocolate flavors, the wine has a polish and elegance that make it a good buy. Gets better as it airs, so decant for an hour or so. **87** —*S.H. (12/31/2006)*

Irony 2004 Chardonnay (Napa Valley) $14. Seems tired, and even though it's not an old wine, it just lacks zest. It's a simple little Chardonnay with modest peach flavors and a dry earthiness. **82** —*S.H. (12/31/2006)*

Irony 2002 Merlot (Napa Valley) $16. This is a good approximation of more costly Napa reds. It's rich in cherry, blackberry, and mocha flavors, and dry, with a touch of smoky oak. There's good value for the money. From Delicato. **85** —*S.H. (12/31/2006)*

ISENHOWER CELLARS

Isenhower Cellars 2003 Bachelor's Button Cabernet Sauvignon (Columbia Valley (WA)) $NA. It's 100% Cabernet, from Kiona, Tapteil, and old-vine Bacchus fruit. Very smooth, it sends up whiskey-barrel aromas and spice from the barrel aging. There is satiny fruit, and some alcoholic burn in the finish. **88** —*P.G. (4/1/2006)*

Isenhower Cellars 1999 Merlot (Columbia Valley (WA)) $22. Plump black-cherry fruit stands out, buttressed with firm tannins and flavors of tar, toast, smoke, and coffee. There is plenty of oak, with an appealing hint of bitterness. The fruit is classic Washington Merlot, pure and powerful rather than soft and pretty. **90** —*P.G. (9/1/2002)*

Isenhower Cellars 2003 Red Paintbrush Merlot (Columbia Valley (WA)) $26. Balanced and fresh, with good fruit sources (Milbrandt, Kiona, Tapteil, Bacchus) and Cabernet (20%) and Syrah (5%) providing backbone and spice. Cherry fruit dominates, with a generous slash of vanilla from new American oak. **88** —*P.G. (4/1/2006)*

Isenhower Cellars 2001 Red Paintbrush Merlot (Columbia Valley (WA)) $25. This could be labeled Merlot, but the winery has apparently elected to go with flower names for its wines. By any name it's delicious, with sweet cherry fruit framed in big, dark toasted flavors from new American and French barrels. It's a big wine that keeps the alcohol under 14% and consequently does not fatigue the palate. **89** —*P.G. (9/1/2004)*

Isenhower Cellars 2003 River Beauty Red Blend (Red Mountain) $32. The Syrah is blended with a generous (30%) portion of Mourvèdre. It's a very floral wine, plump and rich. The flower scents lead into ripe flavors of blueberries, cherries, plums, and more. Sophisticated, it has just the right touch of fresh herbs to add interest and complexity. **91** —*P.G. (4/1/2006)*

Isenhower Cellars 2000 Syrah (Columbia Valley (WA)) $25. Another fine effort from this new Walla Walla winery. Half Red Mountain and half Walla Walla fruit, it is smooth and polished, with sweet, spicy, raspberry/strawberry/cherry flavors. Tangy and delicious through a very pretty finish. **91** —*P.G. (9/1/2002)*

Isenhower Cellars 2003 Looking Glass Syrah (Columbia Valley (WA)) $22. Brightly fruity, 100% Syrah, with flavors of mixed berries and some peppery spice. Young, still a bit yeasty and very fresh. This is tasty and unpretentious juice. **88** —*P.G. (4/1/2006)*

Isenhower Cellars 2003 Looking Glass Syrah (Columbia Valley (WA)) $22. Ripe and soft, with a creamy mouthfeel and a finish that slides away rather quickly, this Syrah is almost too facile, too easy to drink; it doesn't require any thought, the coffee and berry flavors just slip down effortlessly. **85** *(9/1/2005)*

Isenhower Cellars 2002 River Beauty Syrah (Columbia Valley (WA)) $32. Starts with some off, vegetal notes, then folds in bright berry flavors and plenty of oak. Smooth and creamy in the mouth, finishing with firm acids and sturdy tannins. Could improve with cellaring. **83** *(9/1/2005)*

Isenhower Cellars 2003 Three Dogs Syrah (Columbia Valley (WA)) $20. Very tart and spicy, with distinct notes of clove and orange peel. Citrus and apple flavors crop up unexpectedly, and the tannins have a hint of green tea about them. **88** —*P.G. (4/1/2006)*

Isenhower Cellars 2001 Wild Alfalfa Syrah (Columbia Valley (WA)) $25. Beautiful fruit is the star here, showing complex flavors of blackberry, brambleberry, and loganberry, nicely set off against sweet oak. Just a perfect balance, with some life ahead, but why wait. It's really a treasure right now. **90 Editors' Choice** —*P.G. (9/1/2004)*

Isenhower Cellars 2004 Late Harvest White Blend (Columbia Valley (WA)) $22. Yeasty, honeyed, aromatic, and rich with floral, citrus blossom, peach, apricot, and spiced orange pekoe tea notes. **90** —*P.G. (4/1/2006)*

Isenhower Cellars 2004 Snapdragon White Blend (Columbia Valley (WA)) $18. This 70-30 Roussanne/Viognier blend is rich and yeasty, a great food wine. Creamy and fresh, it shows light citrus, grapefruit, and a tiny hint of honeyed sweetness. Think Thai, Creole, curry, or seafood with this gem. 530 cases produced. **90** —*P.G. (4/1/2006)*

J VINEYARDS & WINERY

J Vineyards & Winery 1998 Champagne Blend (Russian River Valley) $28. Fresh, light, and focused, with citrus, apple, mineral, and toast flavors. Clean, bright and refreshing on the finish. **88** —*J.M. (12/1/2002)*

J Vineyards & Winery 1997 Brut Champagne Blend (Russian River Valley) $28. Bright lemon-lime aromas and flavors, a fine steady bead and a slight mineral note mark this solid Russian River Valley offering. No longer affiliated with any other winery, J is tasty, medium-weight bubbly that closes with good length and dry citrus flavors. **88** —*M.M. (12/1/2001)*

J Vineyards & Winery 1996 Brut Champagne Blend (Sonoma County) $28. **90** —*S.H. (12/15/1999)*

J Vineyards & Winery 1998 Pinot Gris (Russian River Valley) $16. **90** —*S.H. (11/1/1999)*

J Vineyards & Winery 2004 Pinot Gris (Russian River Valley) $18. A little thin for my tastes, still there's some decent citrus and spearmint fruit, and the wine is dry, tart, and clean on the finish. **85** —*S.H. (7/1/2005)*

J Vineyards & Winery 2002 Pinot Gris (Russian River Valley) $18. Almost addictive with its fresh, clean flavors of sweet lemon, fig, tart green apple and cinnamon, encased in lively acidity. This zesty white wine has extra layers of complexity and depth. It's also one of the most versatile food wines around. **87** —*S.H. (7/1/2003)*

J Vineyards & Winery 2001 Pinot Gris (Russian River Valley) $18. Effusively fruity. It's like taking every fruit in the produce department and making wine from all of them. But tangerine and lime dominate, made bright and crisp with acidity. A tad of residual sugar makes things round and juicy. **87** —*S.H. (12/15/2002)*

J Vineyards & Winery 2000 Pinot Gris (Sonoma County) $NA. A smooth textured wine, reminiscent of fine textured Chardonnay. It's balanced,

clean and fresh, hints of toast, pear, citrus, and herbs. Clean at the end. **88** —*J.M. (9/1/2003)*

J Vineyards & Winery 2002 Pinot Noir (Russian River Valley) $28. Oaky and full. Silky and smooth in the mouth, this wine offers up cherries, strawberries, coffee, and tea. A dry wine that shows zest and interest. **87** —*S.H. (11/1/2004)*

J Vineyards & Winery 2000 Pinot Noir (Russian River Valley) $24. A blend from throughout the valley, this is a lighter-style wine made in a delicious, accessible manner. It offers flavors of raspberries, strawberries, spices, smoke, and vanilla, and is silky on the palate. Finishes with a graceful elegance. **87** —*S.H. (2/1/2004)*

J Vineyards & Winery 1998 Pinot Noir (Russian River Valley) $20. Pale in color, with delicate aromas of raspberries, smoke, vanilla, rhubarb, and black tea. The spice flavors dominate, ranging from pepper and cinnamon to allspice and mint, along with jammy berry fruit. All this is set in an elegant, polished structure, framed by oak. It's light in body, but fullflavored. **88** —*S.H. (11/15/2001)*

J Vineyards & Winery 1999 Estate Bottled Pinot Noir (Russian River Valley) $20. The red cherry aromas and flavors are accented by dusty rose, spice, and leather. Too much oak for the fruit bothered some palates, but others found it fresh, with coffee and herb shadings over sour plum fruit. Finishes tart with prominent wood. **84** *(10/1/2002)*

J Vineyards & Winery 1999 Nicole's Vineyard Pinot Noir (Russian River Valley) $35. This pretty wine has delicate aromas of spiced cherries, smoke, and vanilla, with an edge of violets. It is rich in cherry, rhubarb, tea, cola and herbs, wrapped in a silky texture. The seductive flavors cascade in waves across the palate. **91** —*S.H. (2/1/2004)*

J Vineyards & Winery 2000 Robert Thomas Vineyard Pinot Noir (Russian River Valley) $40. A single-vineyard wine from a warmer part of the appellation. The extra heat and sunshine show in the ripe, fleshy flavors of cherries and raspberries, full-bodied mouthfeel, and soft acids. Finishes with a smoky edge of wood and spice. **89** —*S.H. (4/1/2004)*

J Vineyards & Winery NV Brut Rosé Rosé Blend (Russian River Valley) $32. Pretty copper color; has powerful aromas of strawberries. This fullbodied bubbly has deep flavors of strawberries, vanilla, white pepper, and toast. The fruit is ripe, yet the body is elegant. **91 Editors' Choice** —*S.H. (6/1/2004)*

J Vineyards & Winery 1999 Vintage Brut Sparkling Blend (Russian River Valley) $30. Very refined and smooth in the mouth, with an ultracreamy texture that carries subtle flavors of lemongrass, vanilla, and yeast. Very dry, with crisp acids. This is a bubbly that feels rich and elegant all the way down. **90** —*S.H. (12/31/2004)*

J Vineyards & Winery 2001 Viognier (Alexander Valley) $NA. The aromas suggest Key lime pie topped with whipped cream and a sprinkling of white chocolate, but it's surprisingly soft and featureless in the mouth. There are peach flavors, but ultrasoft acidity turns them syrupy. An aggressive overlay of oak only adds vanilla. Seems like an afterthought by the winemaker. **84** —*S.H. (9/1/2003)*

J Vineyards & Winery 2002 Hoot Owl Vineyards Viognier (Russian River Valley) $28. An excellent Viognier. The tropical fruit, wildflower and spicy flavors are strong and ripe, but they're balanced by bright acids and even some dusty tannins. That makes the wine full-bodied and complex. It's delicious on its own, but will be excellent with pork tenderloin. **90** —*S.H. (12/31/2003)*

J. BENTON FURROW

J. Benton Furrow 2002 Old Vine Zinfandel (Dry Creek Valley) $20. Nice try, with smooth tannins, but there's unappealing medicinal and sweetenedcoffee flavors on the finish. From 70-year old vines. **83** —*S.H. (5/1/2005)*

J. BOOKWALTER

J. Bookwalter 2002 Cabernet Sauvignon (Columbia Valley (WA)) $38. It's 100% Cab, and perfectly captures the uniqueness of great Washington Cabernet Sauvignon. There's power and structure without the jammy thickness of California Cabs; it's sleeker, more tart, more vertically structured than they are. Still quite youthful and compact, with tangy red fruits and a spicy frame; good length finishing with licorice, cedar, tar, and leaf. **91 Cellar Selection** —*P.G. (12/15/2005)*

USA

J. Bookwalter 2001 Cabernet Sauvignon (Columbia Valley (WA)) $32. At first tight and a bit unyielding, it sends up little wafts of scent—cinnamon and spice—before slowly broadening out with classic Bordeaux notes of lead pencil, cedar, and graphite. Lean but not mean, this shows the grip and polish of very skillful winemaking, married to superb fruit. Classic black-cherry and cassis, with the acidity and lean muscularity that distinguishes the best Washington Cabs. **94 Editors' Choice** —*P.G. (11/15/2004)*

J. Bookwalter 2003 Johannisberg Riesling (Columbia Valley (WA)) $12. This may well be the best Riesling being made in Washington at the moment. Off-dry and very lightly carbonated, it explodes with a bouquet of flower flavors that hit you with lilac, citrus blossom, talcum powder, and more. Lively and tight, the flavors gather strength and concentration as they move through a myriad of pretty fruits, finally resolving in a long, slightly honeyed finish. A masterful effort. **93 Best Buy** —*P.G. (11/15/2004)*

J. Bookwalter 2002 Chapter One Meritage (Columbia Valley (WA)) $68. The winery's first Meritage has a hefty bottle but a rather dull, black, and white label. It's layered and complex, quite young with streaks of pencil lead, licorice, and charcoal around dense black fruits and sweet tannins. The wine shows a very strong spine on which the tart fruit hangs; that tartness characterizes optimal Washington ripeness. Full and complete, it hints appropriately at leaf and spice nuances. **93** —*P.G. (12/15/2005)*

J. Bookwalter 2004 Merlot (Columbia Valley (WA)) $38. The clever blend adds 8% Malbec and 8% Petit Verdot; both grapes boost the tannin and color and give the wine a meatiness lacking in most domestic Merlots. The Merlot part ain't shabby either: broad, rich strokes of plum, and cherry fruit, saturated in barrel-infused layers of smoke, baking chocolate and espresso. The sweet cherry in the center gives the wine a chocolate bon-bon character, and the finish, with a bit of liquorous heat, suggests that it will drink at its best in the near term. **90** —*P.G. (12/31/2006)*

J. Bookwalter 2003 Merlot (Columbia Valley (WA)) $36. Predominantly Merlot, the blend also includes Cabernet Sauvignon, Malbec, and Petit Verdot (7% each). Smooth, supple, and silky, it's dense and deeply saturated—inky to the eye and thick against the glass. The flavors show plenty of char and chocolate, with mocha, coffee bean, cherry, and cassis thickly applied. Lip-smacking flavor bolstered with natural acids, sweet tannins, and a long finish. **89** —*P.G. (12/15/2005)*

J. Bookwalter 2002 Merlot (Columbia Valley (WA)) $30. A dead ringer for Napa Merlots costing twice as much, a sensational wine. Beautifully crafted, it displays finesse as well as sheer power, with layers of black-cherry, plum, and cassis, plenty of baking chocolate, good grip through the midpalate and a dusty, delicious denouement. **92 Editors' Choice** —*P.G. (11/15/2004)*

J. Bookwalter 2005 Riesling (Columbia Valley (WA)) $16. Continuing its string of outstanding Rieslings, J. Bookwalter once again has produced an exceptionally fragrant wine absolutely brimming with scents of sweet blossom, citrus, peach, mango, and pear. The mix of fruits is marvelous; equally impressive is the racy acidity that keeps the wine poised, balanced and right on the fence between dry and sweet. **93** —*P.G. (12/31/2006)*

J. Bookwalter 2004 Riesling (Columbia Valley (WA)) $16. Despite its 1.9% residual sugar, this is succulent, not sweet. An exceptionally fragrant wine, lush with blossoms, sweet peach, mango, and pear. Beautifully ripened and concentrated; vibrant so that it seems to shimmer in the mouth, like a wave breaking over the palate. Poised, racy, fruity, and sensuous, it just goes on and on. **92 Editors' Choice** —*P.G. (12/15/2005)*

J. DAVIES

J. Davies 2003 Cabernet Sauvignon (Diamond Mountain) $69. The Schramsberg sparkling wine owners jumped into the Cabernet game a few years ago, and it was an impressive debut. The '03 shows they're in it to stay. It's a tight young mountain Cabernet, pert in chewy tannins and acids, yet beautifully structured, with impressively ripe flavors. Despite the powerhouse fruit, it's elegant. Best now–2020. **94 Cellar Selection** —*S.H. (12/15/2006)*

J. Davies 2002 Cabernet Sauvignon (Diamond Mountain) $65. Only the second Cabernet release from this famous (as Schramsberg) bubbly

house. This is a dense, dry, tannic mountain Cabernet, rich and long in blackberry fruit. It's drinkable and probably at its best now due to soft acids. **90 Cellar Selection** —*S.H. (10/1/2005)*

J. Davies 2001 Cabernet Sauvignon (Diamond Mountain) $65. From this longtime bubbly producer (Schramsberg), a Cab that shows its mountain origins in the noticeable tannins. That doesn't mean it's not drinkable now. It is, because the tannins are ripe and sweet. It does mean that this is a wine to age. Finishes long and harmonious. Now through 2010 and beyond. **92** —*S.H. (12/31/2004)*

J. GARCIA

J. Garcia 2001 Cabernet Sauvignon (Sonoma County) $15. This is a nice regional Cab that amply displays how well this county can ripen the grape, especially in a great vintage. There's a lovely balance of cherry and blackberry fruit with sweet dried herbs and coffee. The finish picks up dusty tannins. **85** —*S.H. (10/1/2004)*

J. Garcia 2001 Merlot (Sonoma County) $15. Drinks rather harsh and jagged, although there's a core of blackberry fruit that hits midway and lasts through the finish. In fact the fruit saves it, but unless you're a hard-core Deadhead, you can do better for the dough. **84** —*S.H. (12/15/2004)*

J. Garcia 2001 Zinfandel (Sonoma County) $15. A robust and hearty Zin with exuberant wild berry flavors and some twiggy herbaceousness. Very dry and acidic. **85** —*S.H. (11/15/2004)*

J. JACAMAN

J. Jacaman 2003 Pinot Noir (Russian River Valley) $35. This winery's '02 Pinot was very good. The '03 is even better. It's richer and more nuanced, offering savory flavors of cherries, coffee, sweet rhubarb pie, cola, cocoa, and spice flavors that unfold in waves in the mouth. Dry and crisp, with some dusty tannins, this wine will be best in its tasty youth. **90** —*S.H. (12/1/2005)*

J. Jacaman 2002 Pinot Noir (Russian River Valley) $35. Dark, full-bodied, and thick, with jammy black-cherry and cocoa flavors, as well as substantial oak. Not particularly delicate, but lip-smackingly good. **88** —*S.H. (3/1/2005)*

J. LOHR

J. Lohr 2002 Cuvée PAU Bordeaux Blend (Paso Robles) $50. Very oaky, with scads of toast, caramel, and smoky vanilla, and the Cabernet Sauvignon fruit stars with its cassis flavors. This is a dark, rich wine, young in tannins, bone dry, and easily on a par with the wonderful '01. This bottling is raising the Cabernet bar in Paso Robles. **91** —*S.H. (9/1/2006)*

J. Lohr 2001 Cuvée Pau Bordeaux Blend (Paso Robles) $50. This hommage to Pauillac is darkly colored and powerful, with flavors of black currants and a decadent, dark chocolate note. There's lots of flamboyant oak. Texturally, it's soft in acids, with melted, smooth tannins, and the finish is dry. It's a delicious, interesting wine, and a testament to J. Lohr's ambitions with Cabernet Sauvignon. Drink now. **91** —*S.H. (4/1/2006)*

J. Lohr 2001 Cuvée POM Bordeaux Blend (Paso Robles) $50. Opens with a blast of caramelized oak, and it's hard to get anything else, but in the mouth, the wine is softly creamy, with delicious cherry, chocolate, anise, and Asian spice flavors that finish dry and long. It's a sensuous wine that's at its best now. **89** —*S.H. (9/1/2006)*

J. Lohr 2000 POM Bordeaux Blend (Paso Robles) $50. Here's what warmish Paso Robles does so well, in the right hands. This Merlot-based blend is fabulously gooey in cassis, chocolate fudge, red currant, and vanilla flavors. The terroir keeps acidity low, so the wine is very soft, but it's so decadently rich, you'll like it anyway. **88** —*S.H. (11/15/2005)*

J. Lohr 2000 PAU Cabernet Blend (Paso Robles) $50. I don't know if there's technical residual sugar in this wine, but it sure tastes like it. Brings to mind sweetened cherry cough medicine, with a flat, syrupy finish. **82** —*S.H. (11/15/2005)*

J. Lohr 2000 St. E Cabernet Blend (Paso Robles) $50. How ripe the grapes got this vintage. This wine is bursting with fudgy chocolate, cassis, raspberry, and coffee flavors. But it's too soft, with almost no structure, and too sweet. The finish tastes like melted brown sugar and butter. **83** —*S.H. (11/15/2005)*

USA

J. Lohr 2001 Carol's Vineyard Cabernet Sauvignon (Napa Valley) $40. A classic Napa Cab from this great vintage. Mesmerizes with new oak, black currant and cassis aromas, and the first sip explodes with blackberries, cherries, and vanilla. The tannins are fine, soft, ripe, and sweet. Completely satisfying all the way. **93** —*S.H. (2/1/2005)*

J. Lohr 2003 Estates Seven Oaks Cabernet Sauvignon (Paso Robles) $15. There's pleasure in this polished, soft wine. It's dry and rich in tannins, with good blackberry, cassis, and black-cherry flavors that are deep and long. The softness gives it a supple, creamy-smooth mouthfeel. **85** —*S.H. (4/1/2006)*

J. Lohr 1999 Hilltop Cabernet Sauvignon (Paso Robles) $32. Quite oaky and charry on the nose, with black-cherry and plum aromas circulating. Drinks soft and round in the mouth, with melted tannins and low acids. A warm-climate Cab that's delicious and easy to like. **90** —*S.H. (11/15/2003)*

J. Lohr 2001 Hilltop Vineyard Cabernet Sauvignon (Paso Robles) $32. Still young, fresh, and vibrant, this Cab also is still dense in tannins, so be forewarned, although it's nothing that rich fare can't handle. It seems to be built for the cellar. The only concern is an overripe raisiny taste that would limit ageability. **88** —*S.H. (4/1/2006)*

J. Lohr 2000 Hilltop Vineyard Cabernet Sauvignon (Paso Robles) $32. Held back nearly five years, this Cab still has some sturdy tannins, but I would drink it now because the fruit's in a precarious position. It's rich and tasty now in black currants and cherries, but too soft to age. **87** —*S.H. (11/15/2005)*

J. Lohr 1997 Hilltop Vineyard Cabernet Sauvignon (Paso Robles) $33. 91 *(11/1/2000)*

J. Lohr 2002 Seven Oaks Cabernet Sauvignon (Paso Robles) $15. While you're waiting for your huge Cabs to age, sustain yourself with this drinkable wine tonight. It's soft and gentle, with pretty flavors of blackberries, black-cherries, and coffee. Has an elegance that belies the affordable price. **88** —*S.H. (5/1/2005)*

J. Lohr 2001 Seven Oaks Cabernet Sauvignon (Paso Robles) $15. This flavorful, soft Cabernet should satisfy your guests, yet won't break the bank. It has pleasant flavors of black currants, cherries, sage, dill, tobacco, and smoky oak, and the tannins are firm and a little tea-like. Finishes with a ripe, fruity flourish. **87** *(12/1/2003)*

J. Lohr 2000 Arroyo Vista Chardonnay (Arroyo Seco) $25. Big, big, big, in every respect. Fruit, acids, oak, body, extract, it's all packed into a huge wine that fills the mouth with citrus, apple, and guava flavors wrapped in a rich, custardy texture. Yet the wine is balanced and elegant. Calls for high-end pairing at the table. **92** —*S.H. (2/1/2004)*

J. Lohr 1999 Arroyo Vista Chardonnay (Arroyo Seco) $25. This is the recipe for expensive Chard in California: Get the fruit good and spicy-ripe. Keep yields low so it's intense. Lavish it with the best oak, and keep it on the lees, stirred frequently for months. There's more of course, but that's the basic outline. This wine follows the rules and is very good. **89** —*S.H. (12/31/2001)*

J. Lohr 2004 Arroyo Vista Vineyard Chardonnay (Arroyo Seco) $25. Some people will think this is too oaky, but I like that buttered toast and caramelized, butterscotchy vanilla, especially when it's married to a wine with this powerful fruit and acidity. Pineapple, mango, nectarine, and cinnamon spice flavors lead to a long, rich finish on this satisfying, creamy wine. **90** —*S.H. (12/31/2006)*

J. Lohr 2003 Arroyo Vista Vineyard Chardonnay (Arroyo Seco) $25. That crisp Monterey acidity accompanies this Chard all the way, boosting and brightening the pineapple custard, coconut cream pie, and vanilla spice flavors. It's a rich, decadent wine that finishes with a honeyed sweetness. **90** —*S.H. (3/1/2006)*

J. Lohr 2002 Arroyo Vista Vineyard Chardonnay (Arroyo Seco) $25. Long in candied lime, papaya, and buttered toast flavors, this lovely sipper is also crisp in acids. All the fruit drinks clean and minerally pure, like mountain water. **90** —*S.H. (5/1/2005)*

J. Lohr 2001 Arroyo Vista Vineyard Chardonnay (Arroyo Seco) $25. This is a big, flamboyant California Chard, with layers of butter, toast, and tropical fruit topped by grace notes of caramel and spice. With all of its size and exuberance, it will thrills fans of the style. **89** *(12/1/2003)*

J. Lohr 1996 Arroyo Vista Vineyard Chardonnay (Monterey) $25. 84 —*L.W. (11/15/1999)*

J. Lohr 2004 Riverstone Chardonnay (Arroyo Seco) $14. This small appellation is a good, but little-known source of wonderfully crisp white wines. This Chard is dry but ripe in pineapple and vanilla cream flavors, with a rich coating of smoky oak. This is a good price for a wine of this complexity. **88** —*S.H. (3/1/2006)*

J. Lohr 2003 Riverstone Chardonnay (Arroyo Seco) $14. One of the best Chards in this price category, this Monterey example is rich in tropical fruit, peach, and spice flavors, and crisp in acidity. It has smoky oak, buttercream, a bit of lees—in other words, the works. **90 Best Buy** —*S.H. (11/15/2005)*

J. Lohr 2001 Riverstone Chardonnay (Arroyo Seco) $14. A rich, New World-style Chard with very ripe, forward fruity flavors of tangerine, apricot, and tropical fruits. Well-framed in oak, and with refreshingly crisp acids, this full-bodied wine is well-priced for the quality. **87** —*S.H. (2/1/2004)*

J. Lohr 1998 Riverstone Chardonnay (Monterey County) $15. 88 *(6/1/2000)*

J. Lohr 2003 Los Osos Merlot (Paso Robles) $15. Nice and rich, this is a layered, complex wine with cassis, cherry, and coffee flavors that finish very dry, with soft but fine tannins. The wine has obvious refinement and pedigree. There's a bit of sharpness that should mellow over the next year or two. **88** —*S.H. (12/1/2006)*

J. Lohr 2002 Los Osos Merlot (Paso Robles) $15. Here's a Merlot that's forward in jammy black-cherry, blackberry, and chocolate flavors. It's soft, in the way of warm country wines, but the firm tannins provide a good structure. **85** —*S.H. (11/15/2005)*

J. Lohr 2001 Los Osos Merlot (Paso Robles) $15. Shows decent Merlot character in its aromas and flavors of black-cherries and herbs. It's a plump, supple wine that finishes with some green-edged tannins—just enough to stand up to your next grilled T-bone. **86** *(12/1/2003)*

J. Lohr 1999 Cuvée PAU Red Wine Red Blend (Paso Robles) $50. The Pauillac-inspired, Cabernet Sauvignon-based cuvée, like the St. E, drew mixed reviews, with some tasters lauding its power and intensity, while another questioned its dusty astringency. Thankfully, there's no denying its bold, black currant fruit and mouth-filling flavors. **89** *(12/1/2003)*

J. Lohr 1999 Cuvée POM Red Wine Red Blend (Paso Robles) $50. This is the Pomerol-inspired member of the Cuvée series trio, with lush coffee and black-cherry flavors surrounding a core of bright acidity. Finishes long, with a mouthwatering quality all of our tasters admired. **90** *(12/1/2003)*

J. Lohr 1999 Cuvée St. E Red Wine Red Blend (Paso Robles) $50. Our tasters' opinions varied on this wine, with some calling it "a bit light," while others lauded its "sophistication." It's smooth and creamy in the mouth, with distinct notes of tobacco and herbs. Modeled after St.-Emilion, Cabernet Franc is the largest portion of the blend. **91** *(12/1/2003)*

J. Lohr 2003 Wildflower Valdeguie Red Blend (Monterey) $7. What is California Valdeguie? Darned if I know. This one's fresh and jammy in cherry fruit, with a piercing cut of acidity, almost like a Beaujolais Nouveau. It's dry and fun. **84 Best Buy** —*S.H. (5/1/2005)*

J. Lohr 2002 Bay Mist Riesling (Monterey) $8. Bright, fresh, fruity, and light bodied, with pretty peach, apple and spice flavors that leave a crisp, clean, and pleasant finish. Fairly sweet, but refreshing. **86** —*J.M. (8/1/2003)*

J. Lohr 2005 White Riesling (Arroyo Seco) $8. The residual sugar is 2.3 grams, which makes this Riesling a little sweet. But it is very acidic and crisp, which gives it that fascinating sweet-tart tension you get in a good German Riesling. At the same time, the wine is enormously flavorful in citrus, honeysuckle, peach, nectarine, apricot, and vanilla flavors. The Arroyo Seco AVA gets credit for that magical combo of ripeness and acidity. Entirely stainless fermented and aged, this Riesling has a low alcohol of only 12.1 percent. **86 Best Buy** —*S.H. (11/15/2006)*

J. Lohr 2005 Carol's Vineyard Sauvignon Blanc (Napa Valley) $18. Simple and grassy, with dry, acidic flavors of lemons, grapefruits, and a hint of feline spray. Try with shellfish, roasted peppers, and chèvre. **83** —*S.H. (12/31/2006)*

J. Lohr 2004 Carol's Vineyard Sauvignon Blanc (Napa Valley) $18. There's a refreshing crispness and minerality in this wine, despite well-ripened pineapple, peach, fig, and melon flavors. It shows rich acids, dry complexity, and a long, satisfying finish that lift it well above the pack. **90** —*S.H. (4/1/2006)*

J. Lohr 2003 Carol's Vineyard Sauvignon Blanc (Napa Valley) $18. This is a crisp, refreshing sipper that's long on fruity flavor. Bright acidity under girds the lemon and lime, grapefruit, peach, and slightly grassy flavors, and the finish is spicy and clean. **87** —*S.H. (2/1/2005)*

J. Lohr 2002 Carol's Vineyard Sauvignon Blanc (Napa Valley) $18. A lovely, ripe style of Sauvignon Blanc, with touches of stone fruit alongside citrus, gooseberries, and a touch of herbaceousness. The ripeness and four months on the lees have imparted a sense of creaminess to the mouthfeel, yet the wine finishes zippy and fresh. **88** *(12/1/2003)*

J. Lohr 2001 Carol's Vineyard Sauvignon Blanc (Napa Valley) $18. A faint perfume of pear can be caught on the otherwise dull nose. The flavors run toward candied pear, honeydew, and peach. There's some spiciness to the finish, but also a watery quality that doesn't do much for the wine. In the end, it doesn't hit the varietal mark squarely. **84** *(8/1/2002)*

J. Lohr 2004 South Ridge Syrah (Paso Robles) $15. Earthy and rustic, but clean and drinkable, this wine has coffee flavors, with plums, tabasco, and some coarse tannins. **83** —*S.H. (12/31/2006)*

J. Lohr 2003 South Ridge Syrah (Paso Robles) $15. A perfectly fine everyday red. You get enough herb, pepper, and floral notes to mark it as Syrah, plus candied cherry-berry fruit and sufficient tannin to give it structure. **84** *(9/1/2005)*

J. Lohr 2001 South Ridge Syrah (Paso Robles) $15. This enjoyable wine is soft and tasty, with black currant, cherry, Indian pudding, and herb flavors. It's round and supple in the mouth, with sweet, easy tannins. Finishes with just a bit of acidity, and will be a perfect match for roast beef. **86** —*S.H. (4/1/2004)*

J. Lohr 1999 South Ridge Syrah (Paso Robles) $15. Jammy blackberries and black currants on the nose show up again on the palate, where they are spiced up with a bit of black pepper and sour berry fruit. Panelists had mixed feelings about this wine's mouthfeel—some called it thick and syrupy, others thought it smooth and full—but all agreed that it finishes quite tart. **87 Editors' Choice** *(10/1/2001)*

J. Lohr 1997 South Ridge Syrah (Paso Robles) $14. 90 Best Buy —*S.H. (2/1/2000)*

J. Lohr 2004 Wildflower Valdeguié (Arroyo Seco) $8. When I sniffed this wine I thought it was a big Beaujolais. It has a carbonic maceration, fresh grapey scent. The flavors are young and zesty, too, suggesting tart red and black-cherries. Highly acidic, it's a wine to savor with gusto and good, comfortable food. **86 Best Buy** —*S.H. (11/15/2005)*

J. Lohr 2001 Bramblewood Zinfandel (Lodi) $15. A pleasant offering of toasty oak nuance and raspberry, cherry, vanilla, and spice flavors. The texture is a bit astringent, but the ensemble is fairly well balanced, ending on a toasty note. **86** *(11/1/2003)*

J. Lynne 2003 Chardonnay (Russian River Valley) $23. Tastes as honeyed as a nougat candy, rich in caramel, vanilla, and buttered toast. Somewhere under all that oak is decent pineapple fruit. **84** —*S.H. (10/1/2005)*

J. Lynne 2002 Chardonnay (Russian River Valley) $18. A very nice Russian River Chardonnay, with those pretty apple, pear, and pineapple flavors, crisp, cool-climate acids, and spicy finish. There's a lot of toasty oak, too. **87** —*S.H. (8/1/2005)*

J. Lynne 2003 Pinot Noir (Russian River Valley) $24. Pretty pale in color, and light and silky in texture, but with some powerful flavors. Cherries, cola, sweet rhubarb pie, Oriental spice and sweet smoky oak mingle together in a pleasant finish. **86** —*S.H. (10/1/2005)*

J. Lynne 2002 Cameron Ranch Vineyard Pinot Noir (Russian River Valley) $22. Simple and easy, with some nice attributes. Starts with smoky, oaky

aromas leading to cherry flavors and an elegant texture. This is a good regional-style wine. **84** *(11/1/2004)*

J. Wilkes 2004 Bien Nacido Vineyard Pinot Blanc (Santa Barbara County) $18. This brilliantly fruity wine shows South Coast Chardonnay-like flavors in the ripe mango, papaya, and peach, and also showcases cool-climate acidity that makes that fruit sing on the palate. It's a young, dry, vibrantly fresh wine that's delicious by itself, but should be fabulous with fish or chicken topped with a tropical fruit salsa. **90** —*S.H. (12/15/2005)*

J. Wilkes 2003 Bien Nacido Vineyard Block Q Pinot Noir (Santa Barbara County) $50. This Pinot is deep, full-bodied, and rich, with a succulent core of black-cherry, mocha, and spice flavors, and is dry despite the ripe fruitiness. **91** —*S.H. (12/15/2005)*

J. Wilkes 2002 Bien Nacido Vineyard Block Q Pinot Noir (Santa Barbara County) $50. Shows cherry, cola, cocoa, and coffee flavors wrapped in nicely balanced acids and tannins, with a pleasant mouthfeel through the finsh. This is a dry, very nice, coastal Pinot Noir, silky and elegant. **89** —*S.H. (12/15/2005)*

J. Wilkes 2004 Bien Nacido Vineyard Hillside Pinot Noir (Santa Barbara County) $38. Classic Bien Nacido Pinot, this low- production wine shows a fine, elegantly silky mouthfeel, with brisk acidity and red cherry and cola flavors that turn massively spicy on the finish. It's captivating right now, a racy young wine of great pedigree and distinction. **92** —*S.H. (11/1/2006)*

J. Wilkes 2004 Solomon Hills Vineyards Pinot Noir (Santa Barbara County) $38. This is a new vineyard from the owners of Bien Nacido, located within sight of the Pacific. The vines are young but promising. This low-production Pinot is dry and racy as the latest clones have given it huge, pure cherry pie, raspberry, cocoa, and Fig Newton flavors. Hard to imagine a more delicious young Pinot. Drink this racy wine now. **92** —*S.H. (11/15/2006)*

J.C. Cellars 1997 St. George Vineyard Petite Sirah (Napa Valley) $35. 84 —*S.H. (6/1/1999)*

J.C. Cellars 1997 Eaglepoint Vineyard Syrah (Mendocino) $25. 87 —*S.H. (6/1/1999)*

J.C. Cellars 1997 Mesa Vineyard Syrah (Santa Barbara County) $20. 89 —*S.H. (6/1/1999)*

J.C. Cellars 1999 Ventana Vineyards Syrah (Monterey) $30. Floral and peppery, with a strong herbaceous note similar to some

Crozes-Hermitages, combined with red-berry fruit and notes of saddle leather. The thick mouthfeel verges on syrupy, carrying the sweet flavors through a bitter-espresso finish. **88** *(11/1/2001)*

J.C. Cellars 1998 Alegria Vineyard Zinfandel (Russian River Valley) $30. 90 —*S.H. (5/1/2000)*

J.C. Cellars 2001 Rhodes Vineyard Zinfandel (Redwood Valley) $26. Smooth and supple on the palate, with plenty of toasty oak that frames a core of pretty black-cherry, berry, coffee, chocolate, plum, and spice flavors. The wine is well balanced and offers moderate length on the finish. **89** *(11/1/2003)*

J.C. Cellars 1998 Rhodes Vineyard Zinfandel (Redwood Valley) $26. 87 —*S.H. (5/1/2000)*

J.J. Mchale 1999 Cabernet Franc (Clear Lake) $27. Darkly purple, this wine smells young, too. Blueberries, earth, and tobacco aromas lead to dry flavors of boysenberries and other dark berries, and soft tannins. Light on the oak, it's not a deeply layered wine, but it's honestly made and likeable, and will come alive with food. **85** —*S.H. (12/1/2002)*

J.J. Mchale 2000 Lolonis Vineyard Chardonnay (Redwood Valley) $33. From the inland Redwood Valley, this is an easy-drinking wine. Flavors of apples and peaches are a little oaky, with adequate acids and a short, clean finish. **84** —*S.H. (12/15/2002)*

USA

USA

J.J. Mchale 2000 Dorn Vineyard Fumé Blanc (Clear Lake) $18. Hailing from an emerging region northeast of Napa Valley, this SB is heavily oaked, and thus features big batches of butter and toast. Yellow apples and cantaloupe flavors are barely detectable under the veneer of thick oak. It's surely full-bodied, bordering on over the top. But it has positive qualities, including a rich and pleasant mouthfeel. **86** *(8/1/2002)*

J.J. Mchale 2000 Pinot Noir (Anderson Valley) $33. 86 *(10/1/2002)*

J.J. Mchale 2000 Dorn Vineyard Sauvignon Blanc (Clear Lake) $18. A first-rate wine that appeals for its lush fruit and gentle balance. Despite underlying lemon and grass flavors, it's enriched with nuances of figs and peaches and a round, creamy, oaky texture. This likeable wine is also a good value. **87** *—S.H. (9/1/2003)*

J.J. Mchale 1999 Syrah (Clear Lake) $29. A very dark wine, inky purple, that stains the glass with glycerine, it opens with powerful aromas of black pepper. The pepper theme reprises on the palate, along with blackberries. The wine is very dry and feels thick and heavy, the result of low acids. Much work remains to be done, but this early result is promising. **86** *—S.H. (12/1/2002)*

J.K. CARRIÈRE

J.K. Carrière 2002 Pinot Noir (Willamette Valley) $36. Plump fruit is sparked with interesting aromas of meat, Mexican chocolate, and citrus. The mid-palate shows good weight and a pleasing mix of plums, cherries, and chocolate/cinnamon highlights. **87** *(11/1/2004)*

J.K. Carrière 2002 Provocateur Pinot Noir (Willamette Valley) $18. Sweet, candied apple fruit. The mouthfeel is light, the flavors simple. There's a pleasant, slightly peppery edge to the finish. **85** *(11/1/2004)*

JACK WILLIAM

Jack William 2005 Sauvignon Blanc (Alexander Valley) $16. Comes down on the slightly soft, slightly sweet side, with spearmint, lemonade, spiced melon, and fig flavors. Maybe a bit too sweet, but a tasty sipper. **84** *—S.H. (11/15/2006)*

JADE MOUNTAIN

Jade Mountain 1999 Caldwell Vineyard Merlot (Napa Valley) $38. Full-bodied and richly textured, the wine sports a spicy blend of black-cherry, blackberry, toast, herb, coffee, and smoke flavors. Slightly astringent on the finish. **89** *—J.M. (11/15/2002)*

Jade Mountain 1997 Caldwell Vineyard Merlot (Napa Valley) $34. 88 *— L.W. (12/31/1999)*

Jade Mountain 1997 Paras Vineyard Merlot (Mount Veeder) $52. 87 *(12/31/1999)*

Jade Mountain 2003 Mourvèdre (Contra Costa County) $18. Mourvèdre is a difficult wine to make. The grapes need heat, which they obviously got in this soft, rich bottling, with grapey, chocolaty flavors. But there's a rough-edged quality the wine-maker believes will evolve with age. I'm not so sure. **87** *—S.H. (11/1/2005)*

Jade Mountain 2002 Mourvèdre (Contra Costa County) $18. They say the vines are 100 years old, and you do seem to taste an extra dimension of the earthy, cherry, mint, and chocolate flavors that seem to have all sorts of herbs and soils mingled in. The wine is dry and soft, and easy to savor. **87** *—S.H. (10/1/2004)*

Jade Mountain 2001 Mourvèdre (Contra Costa County) $18. A light textured, easy drinking wine that nonetheless offers layers of complexity with its fresh raspberry, blueberry, and spice flavors, evenly tempered with good acidity and a fine-tuned herbal edge. Packs the concentration found in old vines. **88** *—J.M. (12/1/2003)*

Jade Mountain 1997 Mourvèdre (California) $20. 84 *—S.H. (10/1/1999)*

Jade Mountain 2004 Evangelho Vineyard Mourvèdre (Contra Costa County) $20. Drinks hot and thick in tannins, and despite some pretty cherry, cured leather, blackberry, and coffee flavors, there's a rusticity the wine can't quite overcome. But it'll be fine with barbecue. **84** *—S.H. (8/1/2006)*

Jade Mountain 2002 La Provençale Red Blend (California) $16. This blend of Mourvèdre, Syrah, Grenache, and Viognier is medium-bodied, dry and rich. It has a Merlot-like mouthfeel, with its soft, lush tannins, but the flavors are all about the Rhône. Spices and chocolate frame intense blackberries, cherry liqueur, coffee, and sweet lavender. **88** *—S.H. (10/1/2004)*

Jade Mountain 2001 La Provençale Red Wine Red Blend (California) $16. A Rhône-style blend of Mourvèdre, Syrah, Grenache, and Viognier that is rich and good, especially considering the price. It has fruity, spicy flavors and is very dry and interesting, and turns ripely sweet on the finish. There's an edge of tannins and acidity that adds complexity. **88** *—S.H. (4/1/2004)*

Jade Mountain 2003 La Provencale Rhône Red Blend (California) $16. I love this 4-variety Rhône blend of Contra Costa, Monterey, and Mount Veeder fruit. It combines warm region jammy fruit with cool climate acids. Just delicious in cherries, raspberries, and milk chocolate, with a silky, crisp, balanced structure. Great price for a wine of this complexity. **89 Editors' Choice** *—S.H. (11/1/2005)*

Jade Mountain 1997 La Provencale Rhône Red Blend (California) $19. 87 *—M.S. (2/1/2000)*

Jade Mountain 2004 Syrah (Monterey County) $15. Hews to an Aussie-style Shiraz, meaning it's a big, young, brightly jammy wine with impertinent blackberry and cherry flavors. You can't call it complex, but it's fun, brash, and easy. **84** *—S.H. (12/1/2006)*

Jade Mountain 2003 Syrah (Monterey County) $15. Jammy and a bit bulky, this attempt at a Monterey Syrah from a brand that made its reputation in Napa is a bit of a disappointment. The big currant, plum, and vanilla flavors are tasty, but lack depth and richness. **83** *(9/1/2005)*

Jade Mountain 2003 Syrah (Napa Valley) $27. Very tannic and dry, this Syrah isn't offering much pleasure now. The question is if it ever will. It's a gamble. There is a solid core of blackberry fruit buried down deep, but it may not survive the aging process. To be fair, Tasting Director Joe Czerwinski felt it would age nicely, but the rating reflects the panel's overall impression. **85** *(9/1/2005)*

Jade Mountain 2002 Syrah (Napa Valley) $27. Super Syrah, just fabulous in blackberry, cherry, milk chocolate, sweet leather, herb, and oak flavors, and with such a lush, smooth mouthfeel. Just oozes quality, from the dramatic first taste to the ultralong finish. **92** *—S.H. (10/1/2004)*

Jade Mountain 2001 Syrah (Napa Valley) $25. Here's a beautiful drinking wine that's rich and smooth. It hits all the right notes, with its well-ripened blackberry, coffee, and chocolate flavors, velvety tannins and grand overlay of oak. It is very dry, but those ripe flavors are sweet in fruitiness and last through the long finish. **90** *—S.H. (3/1/2004)*

Jade Mountain 1999 Syrah (Napa Valley) $25. A spicy, earthy wine that serves up ripe currant, plum, and blackberry flavors. Layers of licorice, mineral, and herbs are also in evidence. The finish is tangy, with firm, supple tannins. **89** *—J.M. (7/1/2002)*

Jade Mountain 1998 Syrah (Napa Valley) $25. Though "heaps of black pepper" show on the bouquet and in the mouth, we were still able to discern earth, black-plum, and cherry flavors. Finishes with spice, anise, and a hint of raisin. **85** *(11/1/2001)*

Jade Mountain 1997 Hudson Vineyard Syrah (Napa Valley) $32. 90 *(2/1/2000)*

Jade Mountain 2001 Paras Vineyard Syrah (Mount Veeder) $50. As good as Jade Mountain's '02 Syrah is, this is considerably better, if complexity and depth are the yardstick. It begins with an impressive burst of white pepper, and then floods the mouth with the plushest blackberry and cherry flavors. Ultimately, it's the tannins that strike you. They're soft as velvet, sweet, and as intricate as an old tapestry. **94** *—S.H. (10/1/2004)*

Jade Mountain 2000 Paras Vineyard Syrah (Mount Veeder) $50. This is a richly textured, lush, complex wine brimming with a well integrated blend of earth tones, black-cherry, raspberry, anise, tea, coffee, chocolate, herb, spice, and toast flavors. Long and seductive to the end, it's hard hold to back and just sip this hedonistic blend. **93** *—J.M. (4/1/2004)*

Jade Mountain 1997 Paras Vineyard Syrah (Mount Veeder) $52. 85 *—J.C. (2/1/2000)*

Jade Mountain 2000 Paras Vineyard P-10 Syrah (Mount Veeder) $75. Still plenty of grippy tannins in this wine, which has some Grenache and Viognier. But the astringency doesn't mask the huge flavors of black-cherries and sweet oak. Displays pure mountain character of intensity and power. Drink now through 2010. **93** —*S.H. (5/1/2005)*

Jade Mountain 2004 Snows Lake Vineyard Syrah (Red Hills Lake County) $17. From a new appellation in Lake County comes this very interesting single-vineyard Syrah. At first it seems like a jammy flatterer, but then more complex layers kick in. It's a big, soft wine with intense blackberry and cassis fruit that turns chocolatey on the finish. **87** —*S.H. (12/1/2006)*

Jade Mountain 2003 Paras Vineyard Viognier (Mount Veeder) $30. This monster Viognier has an entire fruit stand built in. The flavors range from ripe white peach through apricot and pineapple to the most decadent papayas. The oak, however, seems excessive. **88** —*S.H. (11/1/2005)*

Jade Mountain 2001 Paras Vineyard Viognier (Mount Veeder) $30. Rich, lush, peach, and melon flavors are at the heart of this fruity wine. It's loaded with spice, with hints of banana, apple, vanilla, toast and mineral flavors. Best for preprandial sipping. **88** —*J.M. (5/1/2003)*

JAFFURS

Jaffurs 2001 Stolpman Vineyard Grenache (Santa Barbara County) $20. A beautiful and charming wine. The aromas and flavors are exotic, suggesting rhubarb pie, cherry, white chocolate, and smoke. It is gentle and lilting, with a firm spine of acidity, and one of the best Grenaches out there. **91** —*S.H. (3/1/2004)*

Jaffurs 1997 Mourvèdre (Santa Barbara County) $20. 89 —*S.H. (6/1/1999)*

Jaffurs 1997 Cuvée Red Blend (Santa Barbara County) $19. 90 —*S.H. (6/1/1999)*

Jaffurs 1997 Roussanne (Santa Barbara) $19. 87 —*S.H. (6/1/1999)*

Jaffurs 1997 Syrah (Santa Barbara County) $22. 89 —*S.H. (6/1/1999)*

Jaffurs 2004 Syrah (Santa Barbara County) $23. Ripe and forward, with blackberry jam, sweetened espresso, white pepper, and chocolate flavors, this wine shows much the same quality as Jaffurs's more expensive single-vineyard wines. It's just a bit rougher and sharper. **87** —*S.H. (12/1/2006)*

Jaffurs 2003 Syrah (Santa Barbara County) $23. Soft and velvety in the mouth, with striking aromas of mint, pepper, and blackberries, this blended Syrah from Craig Jaffurs represents a solid value. It even firms up a bit on the finish, suggesting that while it is delicious now, it should drink well for at least 4–5 years. **88** *(9/1/2005)*

Jaffurs 2002 Syrah (Santa Barbara County) $23. This winery's least expensive Syrah is a value, because it's pretty much as good as the single-vineyard bottlings. It's rich in blackberry, cassis, mocha, and white pepper, with intricately woven tannins. Great with a barbecued steak. **89** —*S.H. (5/1/2005)*

Jaffurs 2001 Syrah (Santa Barbara County) $23. Craig Jaffurs's most basic Syrah is pretty good stuff. It is rich and dense, with deep flavors of currants, plums, molasses, pepper, and tobacco. The texture is smooth as velvet. This voluptuous wine is a pleasure to sip. **89** —*S.H. (2/1/2004)*

Jaffurs 2004 Ampelos Vineyard Syrah (Santa Barbara County) $42. Actually from Santa Rita Hills, this wine is very young now and needs to be decanted to appreciate its ripe blackberry, cola, spice, and oak flavors. The air will soften the somewhat astringent tannins and let the wine's flash shine through. **91** —*S.H. (11/15/2006)*

Jaffurs 2004 Bien Nacido Vineyard Syrah (Santa Barbara County) $30. Bien Nacido is in cool territory, but '04 was savagely hot, and this Syrah has the taste of blackberry, cherry, and chocolate baked into a smoky, charry pastry crust. Easy now and for the next year or two. **88** —*S.H. (12/1/2006)*

Jaffurs 2003 Bien Nacido Vineyard Syrah (Santa Barbara County) $30. Similar to Jaffurs' Thompson Vineyard bottling, this one's tannins divided the panel, with one taster finding it too astringent, while the others felt a few years' cellaring would bring it around. With lots of pepper and blackberry, it's an atypically powerful, extracted Syrah from Bien Nacido. **89** *(9/1/2005)*

Jaffurs 2002 Bien Nacido Vineyard Syrah (Santa Barbara County) $30. There's not much difference between Jaffurs' three cool-climate, single-vineyard Syrahs (Bien Nacido, Thompson, and Melville). This one's firm, taut and rich in chocolaty-blackberry, roasted coffeebean and spice flavors, with a sweet finish. **90** —*S.H. (5/1/2005)*

Jaffurs 2001 Bien Nacido Vineyard Syrah (Santa Barbara County) $30. Drinks tough and tannic, and the palate searches for happy fruit only to be defeated. Way down there someplace there are blackberry and cherry flavors, but those tannins are numbing. On the other hand, Bien Nacido Syrahs often take five or so years to come around, so age it. **89** —*S.H. (2/1/2004)*

Jaffurs 1999 Bien Nacido Vineyard Syrah (Santa Barbara County) $30. White pepper aroma. Subtle blackberry fruit reveals itself on the palate, as do some tough tannins. Very dry, with an earthy, tannic finish. Needs a few years to soften up. **86** —*S.H. (7/1/2002)*

Jaffurs 2003 Larner Vineyard Syrah (Santa Barbara County) $34. At only 34 cases produced, this review is likely to be more academic than useful, but since Craig Jaffurs sent it in for review, here it is: Our least favorite of his 2003 efforts, with herbal, peppery notes combining with medicinal black-cherry flavors and a mouthfeel that lacks the richness found in Jaffurs's other bottlings. **85** *(9/1/2005)*

Jaffurs 2003 Melville Vineyard Syrah (Santa Barbara County) $38. Our favorite of Craig Jaffurs' 2003 lineup was this coffee-scented offering from the young Melville Vineyard. Blackberry and pepper add varietal spice and California lushness to the mix. This is a big, full-bodied wine, with velvety tannins on the long finish. **91 Editors' Choice** *(9/1/2005)*

Jaffurs 2002 Melville Vineyard Syrah (Santa Barbara County) $38. In a nutshell, pours dark, smells rich, tastes ripe in fruit, with smooth, sweet tannins. Specifically, shares much in common with Jaffurs' other Syrahs, namely, blackberry, cassis, cocoa, and spice flavors that finish fruity-sweet. The quality factor is high. **89** —*S.H. (5/1/2005)*

Jaffurs 2001 Melville Vineyard Syrah (Santa Barbara County) $32. So tannic and astringent, you can barely feel anything else in the mouth. Blackberry? Cherry? Hard to tell. Dry, tough and puckery; not likely to go anywhere. **85** —*S.H. (3/1/2004)*

Jaffurs 2002 Stolpman Vineyard Syrah (Santa Ynez Valley) $38. Rich in blackberry, blueberry, plum, cocoa, and coffee flavors, with good tannins and decent acidity. A very nice wine, showing elegance and finesse. Finishes with a scour of tannins, suggesting short-term aging. **87** —*S.H. (5/1/2005)*

Jaffurs 2001 Stolpman Vineyard Syrah (Santa Barbara County) $32. A deliciously fruity wine despite its somewhat tough tannins. Those tannins are astringent, but the cherry flavor is so ripe and insistent that it lasts through the finish. This dry wine is a very nice sip with a rich cut of beef or lamb, but the future of this bottling is with tannin management. **90** —*S.H. (10/1/2003)*

Jaffurs 1999 Stolpman Vineyard Syrah (Santa Barbara County) $32. Incredibly rich, with ripe cherry, plum, spice, and herb notes at the fore. It's all framed in luscious, broad tannins that are firm but velvety. Long on the finish. **93** —*J.M. (7/1/2002)*

Jaffurs 2004 Thompson Vineyard Syrah (Santa Barbara County) $34. Dark purple in color and stunningly huge, with fresh young fruit, this is a thick, glyceriney Syrah stuffed with blackberry jam, espresso, cinnamon, dark chocolate, and peppery notes. So fruity and so rich, but it's also a tannic wine that will benefit from a few years of age. **92 Cellar Selection** —*S.H. (12/1/2006)*

Jaffurs 2003 Thompson Vineyard Syrah (Santa Barbara County) $34. The nature of this wine's tannins divided the panel, with one taster finding it too tannic, while another felt it would age well. On balance, it's a well-made wine, with ample blackberry fruit and peppery spice, tinged with hints of coffee and cinnamon. **89** *(9/1/2005)*

Jaffurs 2002 Thompson Vineyard Syrah (Santa Barbara County) $34. Perhaps a bit more tannic than the Bien Nacido bottling, but that's splitting hairs. Rich in ripe, sweet blackberry, and mocha fruit, with a long finish. The sweetness calls for something that echoes it, like the char that grilling gives to meat. **90** —*S.H. (5/1/2005)*

Jaffurs 2001 Thompson Vineyard Syrah (Santa Barbara County) $34. This is a young wine, fairly tannic, acidic, and peppery now. It is very clean and well made, and possesses a deep core of cherry-berry fruit. It will improve with a few years in the cellar, but if you drink it now, pair it with roast duck. **91** —*S.H. (2/1/2004)*

USA

USA

Jaffurs 1999 Thompson Vineyard Syrah (Santa Barbara County) $32.
Opens with a nose that's deep and ripe, but not sweet. Full and pleasurable, it shows tangy black-cherry and cedar notes on the soft, fleshy palate. This spicy, oaky Syrah closes with good length, notes of coffee, pepper, and licorice and easy tannins. Fine for immediate consumption. **88** *(11/1/2001)*

Jaffurs 2004 Verna's Vineyard Syrah (Santa Barbara County) $38. I love the rich, chewy texture on this Syrah. It's all velvet and chocolatey fudge. The flavors are very ripe and forward, showing blackberry tart, mocha, and charred oak. There are also some furry tannins and a touch of sweetness from the alcohol and fruit. Needs time. Best 2007–2010. **88** *—S.H. (12/1/2006)*

Jaffurs 1997 Viognier (Santa Barbara) $22. 87 *—S.H. (6/1/1999)*

Jaffurs 2005 Viognier (Santa Barbara County) $23. This full-bodied wine shows off mouth-filling peach, pineapple, and apricot flavors that are creamy, due perhaps to aging on the lees. It's really complex for Viognier—exotic and opulent but never losing control and elegance. **90** *—S.H. (12/1/2006)*

Jaffurs 2003 Viognier (Santa Barbara County) $23. Honeyed in peach, papaya, fig, and pear fruit flavors, with a dusting of brown spices, this wine has good acidity. It's a pleasant, zesty outdoor sipper. **87** *—S.H. (5/1/2005)*

Jaffurs 2002 Viognier (Santa Barbara County) $23. Made in such a way as to preserve its intense fruitiness, this wine brims with delicious flavors of ripe mango and guava, nectarine, pineapple, and vanilla. Oak has been applied modestly, just enough to give it a creamy texture. Beautiful stuff, perfect with crab cakes with a mango salsa topping. **91 Editors' Choice** *—S.H. (12/1/2003)*

JAMES JOHNSON

James Johnson 2002 Bisou Cabernet Sauvignon (Napa Valley) $60. From a tiny vineyard in St. Helena, a soft, superripe, extracted Cab whose currant and cherry flavors are so fruity, they veer into chocolate fudge. The wine is dry, with supportive tannins. **87** *—S.H. (8/1/2006)*

JAMESPORT

Jamesport 2002 Estate Merlot (North Fork of Long Island) $22. A bit sharp on the nose, implying the high acid that is later evident in the mouth. Aromas of green bean, onion, and cranberry lead to cran-/strawberry flavors with hints of oak and earth. Light-to-medium bodied and on the tart side. **84** *—M.D. (12/1/2006)*

Jamesport NV East End Series Merlot (North Fork of Long Island) $16.
With all the Merlot grown on Long Island, it's a shame there aren't more wines like this. Moderately priced, and well worth it, this wine delivers good dark-fruit flavors (blueberry, ripe cherry) and pencil shaving, a nice mouthfeel, and the bouquet of a wine twice the price. There is a touch of barnyard to the nose and palate, but not enough to overpower. A nice job from one of the older vineyards on the East End (1981). **85**
—M.D. (12/1/2006)

Jamesport 2001 Reserve Merlot (North Fork of Long Island) $39. The nose is less than appealing, with green notes meshing with prune and nail polish aromas. High acid and moderate tannins support decent purple fruit and almond skin flavors. A disappointment compared to the East End bottling. **80** *—M.D. (12/1/2006)*

Jamieson Canyon 1999 Cabernet Sauvignon (Napa Valley) $20. Dark as night, and with such a dramatic aroma, you can't wait to taste it. Huge and hedonistic, an Incredible Hulk of a wine bursting with black currants and cassis and smoky oak. Luxurious tannins make for a smooth, gentle mouthfeel. Enjoy this youthful wine now. **91 Editors' Choice** *—S.H. (8/1/2003)*

Jamieson Canyon 2000 Chardonnay (Napa Valley) $15. Smells kind of funky, with earthy, armpitty scents, but tastes a little better. The peach and apple flavors are wrapped in a thick, syrupy texture. **82** *—S.H. (10/1/2003)*

Jamieson Canyon 1999 Merlot (Napa Valley) $17. Superripe and flamboyant, as you'd expect from the vintage, bursting with plum, blackberry, tobacco, sage, and green olive flavors, and the tannins are a

wonder. Velvety soft and luxurious in the mouth. A trace of acidic bitterness in the finish loses a few points. **90 Editors' Choice** *—S.H. (8/1/2003)*

JANA

Jana 2005 Riesling (America) $18. The grapes were grown in the Finger Lakes, then shipped in cold storage to the winemaking facility in Napa. The wine is pleasantly crisp, with off-dry green apple, pineapple, and honeysuckle flavors. Nice with grilled trout or as a cocktail. **85** *—S.H. (12/15/2006)*

Jana 2005 Old Vine Riesling (Napa Valley) $15. Off-dry to semisweet, this wine has appley, honeysuckle, and citrus flavors. Okay, but it lacks the crispness and acidity needed to balance the sweetness. **83** *—S.H. (12/15/2006)*

JANKRIS

JanKris 2005 Westside Estate Chardonnay (Paso Robles) $10. Not a very interesting; a soft, weak wine with aromas and flavors of canned fruits. **81** *—S.H. (12/31/2006)*

JanKris 2003 Estate Merlot (Paso Robles) $10. Rustic and simple, this dry wine has herbaceous, barely-ripened cherry flavors, along with a rough mouthfeel. **82** *—S.H. (12/31/2006)*

JanKris 2003 Crossfire Red Blend (Paso Robles) $9. There are some ripe, lip smacking flavors of sweet blackberries, cherries, chocolate, and licorice here. Drinks dry but a little raw and sharp. Nice with comfort foods. Cab Sauvignon, Syrah, and Merlot. **84** *—S.H. (4/1/2005)*

JanKris 2004 Estate Picaro Red Blend (Paso Robles) $10. Rustic and harsh in green, acidy mint, with a sweeter edge of cherries. Zinfandel, Merlot, and Cabernet. **82** *—S.H. (12/31/2006)*

JanKris 2003 Riatta Red Blend (Paso Robles) $9. A nice, easy drinking, everyday sort of red. It's dry and clean, with berry and tobacco flavors. Sangiovese, Zinfandel, Cabernet Sauvignon. **84** *—S.H. (4/1/2005)*

JanKris 2004 Estate Crossfire Rhône Red Blend (Paso Robles) $10. JanKris is located in the cooler, westside Templeton Gap area of Paso Robles, and their wines are moderately priced. This blend of Cabernet Sauvignon, Syrah, and Merlot is very fruity, with ripe blackberry, cherry, pomegranate, cocoa, tobacco, and coffee flavors that finish softly dry. There's something about the long, rich aftertaste that makes this balanced wine especially impressive, and at this price, it's a great house red. **85 Best Buy** *—S.H. (11/15/2006)*

JanKris 2003 Syrah (Paso Robles) $10. Too stinky for two of our three reviewers, with one going so far as to call it fecal. Too bad about that smell, wrote another. There's some coffee, black pepper, and sour black-cherry, so it's not all bad. **82** *(9/1/2005)*

JanKris 2002 Tres Ranchos Zinfandel (Paso Robles) $9. Ripe and chocolatey, with soft tannins. There's a nice hit of black-cherries and pepper mid-palate. **84** *—S.H. (4/1/2005)*

JANUIK WINERY

Januik Winery 2003 Cabernet Sauvignon (Columbia Valley (WA)) $30. A great lineup of vineyards—sort of a who's who in Washington—contributes to this excellent Cabernet. Champoux, Klipsun, Red Mountain, Seven Hills, and Ciel du Cheval are all in the blend, which is 91% Cabernet Sauvignon, 2% Merlot, 4% Cabernet Franc, and 3% Petit Verdot. Deep, concentrated, and tannic, it mixes dense and earthy black fruit with barrel notes of smoke and char. Full-bodied, seamless, and long. **92** *—P.G. (11/15/2006)*

Januik Winery 2000 Cabernet Sauvignon (Columbia Valley (WA)) $NA. Januik is right on the money with this wine, which takes full advantage of its light, forward, pretty fruit, and accents it with precise, toasty oak and cinnamon spice. Flavorful and appealing, it's not a wine to age, but rather to delight in. **88** *—P.G. (9/1/2004)*

Januik Winery 2003 Seven Hills Vineyard Cabernet Sauvignon (Walla Walla (WA)) $35. From the excellent Seven Hills property, this classic Cabernet (with 10% Merlot) is consistent to the Januik style—plush, tannic, and broadly flavored, with a lush palate of mixed fruits. Aged in new French barrels for 20 months, the ripe, sweet fruit is set against a finish of lightly charred, toasty oak. **90** *—P.G. (11/15/2006)*

Januik Winery 2004 Cold Creek Vineyard Chardonnay (Columbia Valley (WA)) $30. Januik knows this vineyard inside and out and takes full advantage of its strengths. Despite the malolactic treatment, the wine remains firm in structure, with green apple and spiced pear fruit. It feels soft and creamy, but has enough acid to retain its lively finish, with a lick of light butterscotch and hazelnut crème. Full, rich, and seamless. **90** — *P.G. (10/1/2006)*

Januik Winery 2000 Cold Creek Vineyard Chardonnay (Columbia Valley (WA)) $NA. Cold Creek is arguable Ch. Ste. Michelle's premiere vineyard; Januik was their winemaker until recently, and they generously offered him fruit for his new winery. He's taken the crisp, ripe, perfectly defined fruit of the vineyard and ramped it up; new oak adds layers of toast and the grapes seem extra ripe, with a honeyed richness. Exceptional. **91** — *P.G. (9/1/2004)*

Januik Winery 2004 Elerding Vineyard Chardonnay (Columbia Valley (WA)) $25. From an excellent, cool, Yakima Valley vineyard, the Elerding Chardonnay exhibits firm, lightly spicy green apple fruit with pink grapefruit and citrus notes. Aged on the lees for 10 months in new French oak barrels. **89** —*P.G. (10/1/2006)*

Januik Winery 2003 Merlot (Columbia Valley (WA)) $25. Merlot drives the bus here, but onboard are smatterings of Cabernet Sauvignon (6%), Cabernet Franc (3%), and Petit Verdot (3%). The result is a slick, textured, integrated wine, with more character than fruity Washington Merlots. Tight and laced with lead and mineral, it benefits from some air. **90** —*P.G. (10/1/2006)*

Januik Winery 2000 Merlot (Columbia Valley (WA)) $NA. Mike Januik, formerly winemaker with Château Ste. Michelle, is an old hand in Washington, now entering his third decade nurturing and nursing this state's fruit. His wines are understated, elegant, and graceful, proportioned to age but created for near term enjoyment as well. Excellent, fruit-driven, balanced, and restrained. **88** —*P.G. (9/1/2004)*

Januik Winery 2003 Syrah (Columbia Valley (WA)) $30. The Syrah is the superstar of Januik's superb red wine lineup. Saturated, sappy, and brilliantly detailed, it combines the audacious fruit power of perfectly ripened Washington Syrah with the zest of fresh-squeezed citrus and notes of pepper, tar, and graphite. Beautiful definition and elegant power. **93 Editors' Choice** —*P.G. (11/15/2006)*

Januik Winery 2002 Syrah (Columbia Valley (WA)) $30. Former Château Ste. Michelle winemaker Mike Januik has crafted a very approachable, inviting Syrah. Scents of coffee and blackberry jam waft from the glass and are echoed in the flavors, which also pick up a bit of vanilla. Soft and creamy-textured, the tannins are supremely soft on the finish. Drink now. **87** *(9/1/2005)*

Januik Winery 2000 Syrah (Columbia Valley (WA)) $NA. Smooth, forward, and balanced is the style here. Nice highlights of spice, pepper, and herb too. It lacks power, but that's the vintage, not the winemaker. **88** —*P.G. (9/1/2004)*

JARVIS

Jarvis 1999 Reserve Chardonnay (Napa Valley) $58. Lavishly oaked from the first whiff on the nose and palate, dense toasty notes envelope the pineapple and tropical fruit. Plenty of vanilla and both a tangy nuttiness and a creaminess from the oak, provide a nice mouthfeel tension. Panelists had two schools of thought about this wine: The oak totally dominates—certainly now—and how you feel about that determines your take on the wine. Lacking fruit? Or just tight and needing a year or two to open? Only time will tell. **87** *(7/1/2001)*

Jarvis 1999 Reserve Unfined, Unfiltered Chardonnay (Napa Valley) $58. A very ripe tropical-fruit nose is complemented beautifully by an intense smoky-toasty element. Pineapple, mango, and caramel flavors stand out on the full palate: The smoky note resurfaces later, riding out the persistent finish. This is a sleek, stylish, but very solidly built Chardonnay. It pushes all the right sensory buttons, with big body and great lines, like a '56 Buick. **91** *(7/1/2001)*

JEFFERSON VINEYARDS

Jefferson Vineyards 2002 Signature Meritage (Monticello) $24. Nicely structured, but where's the fruit? Despite a rich, dark color, the flavors are of tobacco, earth, and menthol. Drying tannins on the finish. **82** — *J.C. (9/1/2005)*

Jefferson Vineyards 2002 Estate Reserve Bordeaux Blend (Monticello) $30. Tart and crisp, yet with surprisingly supple tannins. Intense tobacco and herb notes alongside red plum flavors in this medium-weight blend of 50% Merlot, 22% Petit Verdot, 18% Tannat, and 10% Malbec. **84** — *J.C. (9/1/2005)*

JEKEL

Jekel 2001 Sanctuary Bordeaux Blend (Arroyo Seco) $NA. This wine's blackberry fruit wears a hearty overlay of chocolate and coffee. The nose follows the same profile, with a dash of anise or eucalyptus. Acids on the finish are firm and crisp. A food-friendly wine; a blend of 59% Merlot, 39% Cabernet Sauvignon, with small parts Petit Verdot, Malbec, and Cabernet Franc. **89** *(9/2/2004)*

Jekel 1999 Sanctuary Bordeaux Blend (Arroyo Seco) $30. On the nose, there's a rustic, cedar-and-herb accent to the cherry and cassis fruit. The wine is medium-weight, with nice, dense cassis and bright cherry fruit right at midpalate. Finishes with firm tannins. **88** *(9/2/2004)*

Jekel 1995 Sanctuary Estate Reserve Bordeaux Blend (Monterey) $26. **86** —*S.H. (7/1/1999)*

Jekel 1999 Sanctuary Cabernet Blend (Arroyo Seco) $28. Offers heaps of blackberry, herb, and tobacco flavors. Oak plays a supporting role. Fairly tannic, and slightly bitter in the finish. Could use more weight in the middle. **86** —*S.H. (5/1/2003)*

Jekel 1997 Sanctuary Cabernet Blend (Arroyo Seco) $28. **91 Editors' Choice** —*S.H. (12/1/2001)*

Jekel 2003 Cabernet Sauvignon (Central Coast) $15. Feels a bit harsh and scoury despite nicely ripe cherry and blackberry flavors and a touch of oak. Fine with everyday fare, but it really could be more mellow. **83** — *S.H. (7/1/2006)*

Jekel 2002 Cabernet Sauvignon (Central Coast) $15. Smells nice and inviting, with good Cab character. But in the mouth, a wave of harsh, dry, green astringency hits. **82** —*S.H. (12/31/2005)*

Jekel 2004 Chardonnay (Monterey County) $13. There's not much going on with this thin Chard. The watery flavors and absence of fruit emphasize the acids and alcohol. **82** —*S.H. (6/1/2006)*

Jekel 1998 F.O.S. Reserve Chardonnay (Monterey) $22. **87** —*S.H. (11/15/2000)*

Jekel 1997 FOS Reserve Chardonnay (Monterey) $21. **88** —*L.W. (11/15/1999)*

Jekel 1999 FOS Reserve Gravelstone Vineyard-Est. Res. Collection Chardonnay (Monterey) $18. Clearly an older wine, picking up a bottle bouquet of dried herbs, lees, and yeast, riding on top of basic peach, pear, and tropical fruits. Drinks very dry and crisp. The fruit is beginning to fade, leaving behind flavors of dried leaves, herbs, minerals, and spice. An interesting wine of considerable nuance and subtlety. **90 Editors' Choice** —*S.H. (8/1/2003)*

Jekel 2003 Gravelstone Chardonnay (Monterey) $11. Kind of sweet and simple, but the very ripe flavors are palate flattering, and it gives nice smoky, vanilla notes from oak. **84** —*S.H. (5/1/2005)*

Jekel 2002 Gravelstone Chardonnay (Monterey) $14. Butter, pear, and cinnamon aromas preface tropical fruit on the palate. Feels round and medium-weight, with oak not so obvious until the finish. Even so, Winemaker Cara Morrison says that future vintages will show even less wood. **86** *(9/2/2004)*

Jekel 2000 Gravelstone Chardonnay (Monterey) $11. From this cool-climate region, a crisp, dry wine that veers toward apple flavors. It feels lively and perky in the mouth, with good acids that come from chilly weather. A touch of oak adds spicy nuances. It's a good value in a lean Chardonnay. **87** —*S.H. (5/1/2002)*

Jekel 1999 Gravelstone Chardonnay (Monterey) $11. All kinds of tropical fruits in the pleasant aroma, plus buttery, creamy notes and smoky, spicy oak. Tastes fat and opulent, with intense tropical fruit flavors and nervy acidity. This is very nice wine and easily the equal of others costing twice as much. **87 Best Buy** —*S.H. (11/15/2001)*

USA

Jekel 1998 Gravelstone Chardonnay (Monterey County) $15. 86 *(6/1/2000)*

Jekel 1997 Gravelstone Chardonnay (Monterey) $15. 88 —*S.H. (10/1/1999)*

Jekel 2002 Gravelstone Winemaker's Collection Chardonnay (Monterey) $11. You'll find apple, peach, and citrus flavors in this bright, clean young wine. It has the crisp acidity of a cool climate, and finishes with an intense taste of spicy white peach. Nice value. 86 —*S.H. (4/1/2004)*

Jekel 2005 Gewürztraminer (Monterey) $13. There's a trace of sweet jasmine-accented pink grapefruit on the finish, but this is basically a dry wine, crisp in acids and cleansing on the palate. The flowery, fruity, spicy mélange of flavors will be nice with Asian food. 84 —*S.H. (8/1/2006)*

Jekel 2000 Sanctuary Reserve Malbec (Arroyo Seco) $NA. It's not often that you find an American Malbec that's so easy to drink. Aromas are of coffee and nut, and maybe some dust or wheat. On the palate it's understated but sturdy, with soft tannins and a wheaty-dusty overlay to its plum plum fruit. A straightforward wine, of solid quality. Drink now–2009. 88 *(9/2/2004)*

Jekel 2003 Merlot (Monterey) $15. Polished cherry, blackberry, and coffee fruit flavors comprise this Merlot. It's bone dry, with rich tannins and a smattering of oak. Has a jagged quality that's not likely to age out, but it's a pretty good wine. 85 —*S.H. (6/1/2006)*

Jekel 2001 Merlot (Monterey) $19. Toasty, herbal aromas; taut plum fruit on the palate takes on herb and coffee flavors, and tealike tannins that persist through the finish. Though this wine shows well, Winemaker Cara Morrison promises that the 2002 and 2003 vintages are even better. 86 *(9/2/2004)*

Jekel 2002 Winemaker's Collection Merlot (Monterey) $15. There's a disagreeable sharpness and bitterness to this wine. Even for a vin de table, it's tough going. 82 —*S.H. (12/31/2005)*

Jekel 2001 Winemaker's Collection Merlot (Monterey) $15. Here's one of the fruitier Merlots of the year. It's a real blast of jammy cherry, blackberry and black raspberry flavor, but for all the richness, it's balanced and dry. The soft, smooth tannins are a delight. 88 —*S.H. (4/1/2004)*

Jekel 1999 Winemaker's Collection Merlot (Monterey) $15. Awkward, although not disagreeable, with earthy, mulchy aromas that veer into spearmint, suggesting unripe fruit; 24,000 cases produced. It's very dry, almost tart. Acidity makes the mouth water, and there's not a whole lot of ripe flavor. Oak notes are minimal. 84 —*S.H. (6/1/2002)*

Jekel 2004 Pinot Noir (Monterey County) $15. Very pale in color, very light in flavor, and tart, this Pinot doesn't offer much in the way of flavor. It has modest cherry flavors. 82 —*S.H. (5/1/2006)*

Jekel 2001 Pinot Noir (Monterey) $19. Sour cherry, tobacco, and herb aromas signal what's to come on the palate: bright cherry and herb, with not a lot of stuffing to fill it out. Shows notable alcohol on the finish. 84 *(9/2/2004)*

Jekel 1999 Pinot Noir (Arroyo Seco) $15. Marked by forward berry-cherry aromas along with smoke, spice, and vanilla. The flavors are direct and blunt, of dark berries and stone fruits, couched in substantial tannins. The after-taste is long and spicy-sweet. Pretty good stuff, but not likely to improve. Drink now. 86 —*S.H. (12/15/2001)*

Jekel 2000 Winemaker's Collection Pinot Noir (Monterey) $15. The nose of this very light wine offers scents of earth, meat, and faint red fruits. Plum cherry and herb flavors follow, but also a sawdust-like woody note. The herb element comes up strongly, turning sharply greener on the thin finish. 83 *(10/1/2002)*

Jekel 1999 Winemaker's Collection Pinot Noir (Monterey) $15. Opens with classic aromas of strawberries and smoke, beefsteak tomatoes, crushed hard spices, and vanilla-infused spices suggesting sweetness, although it's a dry wine. The mouthfeel is silky, with red berry flavors uplifted by spicy acids. It's not especially complex, but it's a pretty wine, and easy to drink. 87 —*S.H. (5/1/2002)*

Jekel 2001 Winemaker's Collection Pinot Noir (Monterey) $19. Rather light in color and in body, and as silky as taffeta. Pure, bright cherry jam, cola, orange zest, clove, and mocha, with crisp acids and a smoky oak veneer. Delicious and sensual. 90 —*S.H. (12/15/2004)*

Jekel 2005 Riesling (Monterey) $12. Like a nice German kabinett. There's lots of fresh, clean acidity framing off-dry peach, citrus, and spice flavors. 83 —*S.H. (12/1/2006)*

Jekel 2002 Riesling (Monterey) $11. Aromas are of light, fresh pineapple and a little petrol, and pineapple flavors persist on the palate. It's crisp and minerally in the mouth, and finishes with a gooseberry-green brightness. 86 *(9/2/2004)*

Jekel 2001 Riesling (Monterey) $10. A lovely wine, teetering on the edge of sweetness. The pretty apple, apricot, and honeysuckle flavors have a crisp, steely edge of acidity, and there's a rich streak of mineral and diesel that adds complexity. 86 Best Buy —*S.H. (8/1/2003)*

Jekel 1999 Riesling (Monterey) $10. A glass of this fruity, slightly off-dry wine at the cocktail hour will wake your palate up and make it sing for whatever follows. It's hard to imagine prettier flavors of peaches, apricots, and strawberries, sprinkled with dusty brown spices. The sugar isn't high enough to make it overtly sweet, and the acidity keeps things crisp and lively. 87 *(8/1/2001)*

Jekel 2004 Winemaker's Collection Riesling (Monterey) $10. Pretty good price for this clean, vibrantly tart wine. It's a little simple, but has pleasant tastes of citrus, flower, orange zest, and litchi, with a spicy, fruity finish. 84 —*S.H. (12/1/2005)*

Jekel 2002 Winemaker's Collection Riesling (Monterey) $9. Another fine JR from this respected Salinas Valley winery. It's strongly flavored, with extracted peach, honeysuckle, gingerbread, and citrus flavors, and a minerally streak suggesting flint. The acids are bright and firm. This dry wine finishes with a ton of spices. 86 —*S.H. (4/1/2004)*

Jekel 2000 Winemaker's Collection Riesling (Monterey) $10. The prettiest aromas are here, all peaches and wildflowers, honey, and oriental spices, and a buttery, smoky note. The flavors are nice, too, suggesting apples and peaches. It's off-dry, and kind of simple, lacking the acids needed to make it shine. 85 Best Buy —*S.H. (6/1/2002)*

Jekel 2003 Winemaker's Selection Riesling (Monterey) $9. Fancy name for a simple wine. It's dryish and crisp, and light in flavor, with traces of peaches and wildflowers. 83 —*S.H. (5/1/2005)*

Jekel 2001 Syrah (Monterey) $15. You'll get tons of upfront cherry, blackberry, and jammy black raspberry fruit in this simple, likeable wine. It's dry, with a nice bite of tannins and good balancing acidity. 85 —*S.H. (6/1/2005)*

Jekel 2000 Syrah (Monterey) $15. A big, thick wine, but not a clumsy one. Filled with plummy, peppery, blackberry flavors and pronounced but easy tannins. 88 Best Buy —*S.H. (10/1/2003)*

Jekel 1999 Winemaker's Collection Syrah (Monterey) $15. There are earthy, coffee, and berry aromas, and generic berry flavors. The wine is extremely dry, although a bit soft. It's not identifiably Syrah. It could be anything. The winemaker added some Riesling to lift it up. The finish is austere and alcoholic. 84 —*S.H. (9/1/2002)*

Jekel 1998 Winemaker's Collection Syrah (Monterey) $16. Both the nose and the palate have a strong blackberry fruit backbone. Reviewers round out the bouquet with toast, walnut, and butter aromas; licorice, caramel, and coffee flavors jazz up the fruit on the palate. A big, smooth feel and a fruit-driven but butterscotchy finish will please both oenophiles and wine neophytes. 88 Editors' Choice *(10/1/2001)*

JENICA PEAK

Jenica Peak 2004 Pinot Grigio (California) $10. Fruity, tart in acids, and just off-dry, this is a clean cocktail style wine. It's good for group gatherings where you want something for everyone. 83 —*S.H. (2/1/2006)*

Jenica Peak 2003 Coastal Syrah (California) $10. Not terribly concentrated or complex, but what this wine does offer are easygoing berry flavors tinged with meat and pepper on the finish. 84 *(9/1/2005)*

JEPSON

Jepson NV Blanc de Blanc Brut Champagne Blend (Mendocino County) $20. This bubbling, fermenting mass of bread dough in a glass packs an aggressive mousse that's rough and rustic. Fresh lime and tonic flavors finish with softer citrus notes of tangerine rind and orange pith. Has a certain raw appeal to it's brashness. 84 —*J.C. (12/1/2001)*

Jepson NV Burnee Hill Vineyard Blanc de Champagne Blend (Mendocino County) $18. 83 —*P.G. (12/1/2000)*

Jepson 1989 Late Disgorged Champagne Blend (Mendocino County) $35. 90 —*L.W. (12/1/1999)*

Jepson 2003 Chardonnay (Mendocino) $15. Way too thin. There may have been a nice, dry, peach-flavored Chard here, but it's been diluted nearly to water and oak. 82 —*S.H. (12/15/2005)*

Jepson 1999 Estate Select Chardonnay (Mendocino) $16. Austere and flinty, a Chablis-like wine of exceptional acidity, rapier texture, and a taste of gunmetal that veers ever so slightly into peach. This is a wine with an edge, a nervy wine that's super-clean. Don't think it's a simple wine. It's not. 91 —*S.H. (5/1/2002)*

Jepson 1998 Estate Select Chardonnay (Mendocino County) $15. 86 *(6/1/2000)*

Jepson 1997 Estate Select Chardonnay (Mendocino) $15. 89 —*L.W. (11/15/1999)*

Jepson 2003 Sauvignon Blanc (Mendocino) $12. This is a satisfying wine, with pleasant citrus, fig, and melon flavors wrapped in a crisp, buttercream texture. It finishes a little sweet, but is basically a dry table wine. 85 —*S.H. (12/15/2005)*

Jepson 2000 Sauvignon Blanc (Mendocino County) $11. Jepson's Sauvignon Blancs have long been lauded as among Mendocino's best. Grown along the Russian River, on the flatlands, it's typically racy and crisp. This version is richer and perhaps oakier than in the past, and emphasizes melon flavors over raw citrus. It has the weight of a Chardonnay, and is clearly designed to go with fine foods. 87 —*S.H. (5/1/2002)*

Jepson 1998 Estate Select Sauvignon Blanc (Mendocino County) $11. 88 Best Buy —*L.W. (2/1/2000)*

Jepson 2002 Syrah (Mendocino) $20. Here's an elegant, full-bodied Syrah that tastes good on the first sip, then gets better as you go along. It has wonderful balance, with firm, dusty tannins and fine acidity framing well-ripened cherry, mocha, and white pepper flavors. 90 —*S.H. (12/15/2005)*

Jepson 2000 Syrah (Mendocino County) $22. The first estate Syrah from this well-regarded property advances the argument for inland-Mendocino Rhônes. Has good color and extract, and fine structure and balance. But it does seem a bit thin. From the flats near the Russian River; it's a wine to watch. 86 —*S.H. (5/1/2002)*

Jepson 2000 Viognier (Mendocino County) $16. From vineyards adjacent to the Russian River bottomlands, a sprightly, tart wine with few of Viognier's exotic floral character, but nonetheless with the lean, zesty flavors of citrus. In fact, it's easy to mistake it for Sauvignon Blanc, and a nice one. The acidity gives the palate a real jolt. You might even try this with shellfish. 86 —*S.H. (5/1/2002)*

Jepson 1998 Feliz Creek Cuvée White Blend (Mendocino County) $9. 89 Best Buy —*M.S. (11/15/1999)*

Jepson 2000 Feliz Creek Cuvée-Estate Select White Blend (Mendocino County) $9. Mainly that old white standby, French Colombard. It will never make a great wine but this one isn't bad. Sort of like Sauvignon Blanc, filled with tart Meyer lemon fruit flavors and very crisp acidity. It's got a touch of sugar that balances it out nicely. 86 —*S.H. (5/1/2002)*

Jepson 2001 Poma Ranch Zinfandel (Mendocino) $18. Quite light in texture and color. Flavors are pretty ephemeral too, with hints of plum, spice, cherry, and herbs. Easy enough to quaff, but where's the beef? 80 —*J.M. (11/1/2003)*

JERIKO

Jeriko 2000 Chardonnay (Mendocino) $19. Extremely ripe fruity aromas and flavors of sweet pear and white peach mark this well-oaked wine, with its smoky vanillins and toasty edge. Feels a bit rough, and the finish has some jagged notes. 85 —*S.H. (6/1/2003)*

Jeriko 2001 Brut Chardonnay (Mendocino) $50. Actually a Blanc de Blancs, since it's 100% Chardonnay, this is a wine of great purity, maybe because of the organic grapes. The bread dough, vanilla, and subtle peach flavors have a very rich, creamy texture, without the

jaggedness of ordinary bubblies. This is an important new addition to California's sparkling wine portfolio. 93 Editors' Choice —*S.H. (6/1/2006)*

JESSIE'S GROVE

Jessie's Grove 2001 Vintners Choice Zinfandel (Lodi) $15. A full bodied Zin, replete with big burly tannins and bright, jammy cherry, herb, blackberry, chocolate, and spice flavrors. Coats the palate in a thick, velvet-like feel. Fun and fruity. 87 —*J.M. (3/1/2004)*

Jessie's Grove 2001 Westwind, Old Vine Zinfandel (Lodi) $20. Densely black in color, though the flavors seem more modest than the color would indicate. Deep, black plum notes are in evidence, along with toasty oak and black-cherry nuance. The finish is a bit astringent and short. 84 *(11/1/2003)*

JESSUP CELLARS

Jessup Cellars 2000 Cabernet Sauvignon (Napa Valley) $45. Smells rather reduced, but that may age out. In the mouth, the cherry-berry fruit is paired with earthy, herbal notes, wrapped in tough tannins. Not likely to improve with age. 84 —*S.H. (10/1/2004)*

Jessup Cellars 1997 Lauer Vineyard Cabernet Sauvignon (Napa Valley) $39. 91 *(11/1/2000)*

Jessup Cellars 2001 Merlot (Mount Veeder) $38. A nice, juicy red wine with some well-ripened cherry, coffee, cocoa, and herb flavors and firm, rich tannins. Dry, and finishes with a mixture of astringency and sweetness. Be careful to decant this wine for several hours. 87 —*S.H. (10/1/2004)*

Jessup Cellars 1999 Port (Napa Valley) $25. Richly textured with plump, ripe, silky tannins. The wine kicks off with a burst of chocolate, then settles down to reveal black-cherry, cassis, backberry, and spice flavors. Long and lush to the end. 90 —*J.M. (3/1/2004)*

Jessup Cellars 1998 Zinfandel (Dry Creek Valley) $28. 88 —*S.H. (5/1/2000)*

Jessup Cellars 2001 Zinfandel (Napa Valley) $28. Starts off with an unattractive smell suggesting sulfur or dirty socks. In the mouth, there's a fine wine, but the odor is impossible. 82 —*S.H. (10/1/2004)*

Jessup Cellars 2000 Reserve Zinfandel (Dry Creek Valley) $28. A bright textured wine, redolent of cherries, herbs, and spice. Tannins are a bit robust, while the finish is a touch hot and short. 85 —*J.M. (9/1/2003)*

JEWEL

Jewel 2002 Cabernet Sauvignon (Lodi) $10. Lots of almost sweet blackberry and cherry fruit in this dryish wine. It's a bit too soft in tannins and acids, and collapses on the finish, except for the intense fruit, which lingers. 84 —*S.H. (11/1/2005)*

Jewel 2001 Cabernet Sauvignon (California) $10. A real value for its heaps of well-ripened blackberry and spicy plum flavors, but it's dry and balanced. 85 —*S.H. (10/1/2004)*

Jewel 2000 Firma Cabernet Sauvignon-Sangiovese (California) $NA. Country-style Super-Tuscan wine here, with berry and herb flavors wrapped in rough tannins, crisp acids, and a bitter, peppery finish. For all that, it has a nice rusticity that will go well with hearty foods like pasta with tomato sauce. A Sangiovese-Cabernet Sauvignon blend, with a dash of Merlot. 86 —*S.H. (3/1/2004)*

Jewel 2002 Chardonnay (Monterey) $10. There's a wealth of rich, flamboyant pineapple and mango flavor here and a softly decadent note of bananas sautéed in butter. The vanilla and toast notes from oak are smoothly integrated. Yet this wine is dry. 87 Best Buy —*S.H. (12/1/2004)*

Jewel 2003 Un-Oaked Chardonnay (Monterey) $10. With no wood, what you get are the pure fruit flavors of sweetly ripe peaches, pineapples, and mangoes in this delightful wine, which has enough brisk acidity to balance. A very good value. 87 Best Buy —*S.H. (11/1/2005)*

Jewel 2002 Merlot (California) $10. A nice, dry Merlot that pleases for its ripe fruity flavors and soft tannins. It's a solid value and will nicely complement meats and cheeses. 84 —*S.H. (12/15/2004)*

Jewel 2002 Petite Sirah (California) $10. Here's a big, dark, peppery wine, rich in plummy blackberry fruit and completely dry. It's modest in alcohol, with a long, rich finish. Hard to imagine anything better with BBQ ribs slathered in sauce. What a great value. **87 Best Buy** —*S.H.* (*12/15/2004*)

Jewel 2001 Petite Sirah (California) $10. 81 (*4/1/2003*)

Jewel 2000 Petite Sirah (California) $10. 81 (*4/1/2003*)

Jewel 2003 Pinot Noir (California) $10. Very soft and velvety in texture, but also very ripe, this Pinot is easy to like. It has exuberant flavors of cherries, chocolate, and spice that linger into the finish. **85 Best Buy** —*S.H.* (*10/1/2005*)

Jewel 2002 Pinot Noir (California) $10. Good value for the pretty flavors of sour cherry, tomato, and toasty oak, and the spicy finish. Feels clean and varietally correct, and turns sweet in oak and spice on the finish. **85** (*11/1/2004*)

Jewel 2003 Firma Red Blend (Lodi) $10. A little rough and rustic, but there are lots of ripe fruit flavors and a good tannic structure in this unusual blend of four varieties. **83** —*S.H.* (*10/1/2005*)

Jewel 2004 Dry Rosé Blend (Lodi) $10. This tasty blush wine tastes like it comes from France. It's filled with the aromas of lavender, wild thyme, and chamomile, with fruity nuances of strawberries. Surprisingly rich and complex, with a full body and a dry finish. Great value. **87 Best Buy** —*S.H.* (*11/1/2005*)

Jewel 2003 Sauvignon Blanc (Lake County) $10. From an increasingly well regarded county for Sauvignon Blanc, an attractively ripe wine. Bursting with sweet fig, spice, and cantaloupe melon flavors, and with a good balance of acids. **86 Best Buy** —*S.H.* (*12/1/2004*)

Jewel 2001 Shiraz (California) $10. You'll find stewed fruit flavors in this everyday wine, but it's nicely dry, with smooth tannins and a rich, plummy finish. **84** —*S.H.* (*12/15/2004*)

Jewel 1999 Syrah (Lodi) $10. Jammy, raspberry, black-cherry, smoke, earth, and pepper aromas leap from the glass, and then it turns fruity in the mouth, with a supple texture. Dry, dusty tannins mask a dense core of dark berry fruit. This is good drinking and a very nice value. **85** —*S.H.* (*7/1/2002*)

Jewel 2004 Viognier (California) $10. Offers lots of juicy flavors, with a creamy texture and a clean spine of acidity. Peaches, apricots, sweet lime, honeysuckle, and honey, with a dry finish. Very nice. **85 Best Buy** —*S.H.* (*11/1/2005*)

Jewel 2003 Viognier (California) $10. Made in the exotic style, with a mèlange of tropical fruit, wildflower, and spice flavors that are rich in ripe, fruity sweetness, although the wine itself is dry. **85 Best Buy** —*S.H.* (*11/15/2004*)

Jewel 2002 Viognier (California) $10. Great aromatics on this wine, which opens with a burst of ripe peach, honeysuckle, apricot, and citrus notes. In the mouth, it's lush and rich with all kinds of stone fruit and floral flavors. Drinks subtly off-dry, a good wine for today's Asian-inspired fare. Great value. **86 Best Buy** —*S.H.* (*6/1/2003*)

Jewel 2002 Old Vine Zinfandel (Lodi) $10. Beautiful aromas in this wine, with its perfume of wild forest blueberries, smoke, earth, and just a hint of raisins. Would be better if it weren't so soft, to the point of collapse. **83** —*S.H.* (*11/1/2005*)

Jewel 2001 Old Vine Zinfandel (Lodi) $10. This lovely Zin has just enough sweetness to satisfy. It also has enough cherry fruit to balance the herbs, white pepper, and coffee flavors. Not too alcoholic and fully dry, it's a great value. **86 Best Buy** —*S.H.* (*11/15/2004*)

Jewel 2001 Old Vine Zinfandel (Lodi) $10. A lightweight Zin that serves up modest plum, blackberry, oak, and tar flavors. Simple and short. **82** —*J.M.* (*11/1/2003*)

JEZEBEL

Jezebel 2003 Pinot Noir (Willamette Valley) $18. This is a lighter, grapey style of Pinot Noir but nonetheless delicious. Moderately ripe, with no vegetal notes, it features mixed blue and red fruits that lead smoothly into a textured, lightly tannic finish. **88** —*P.G.* (*2/1/2005*)

Jezebel 2003 Syrah (Columbia Valley (OR)) $18. A very unusual wine that most folks will either love or find off-putting. There were wildfires near the vineyard right at harvest, and the smoke from the fires can be

smelled and tasted in the wine. That said, Syrah is noted for its smoked bacon flavors, and this wine has them in abundance, along with some rich, plummy fruit. **88** —*P.G.* (*2/1/2005*)

Jezebel 2003 Blanc White Blend (Willamette Valley) $12. Sineann's Peter Rosback and Rex Hill's Aron Hess have teamed up to make this wonderful blend of Gewürztraminer, Riesling, Pinot Gris, Pinot Blanc and Chardonnay. Usually such "mutt" wines are a disjointed mess, but this one keeps its focus. There is a great fruit forward attack that leads into mixed flavors of stone fruits with sweet hints of honey and butterscotch. **89 Best Buy** —*P.G.* (*2/1/2005*)

JM CELLARS

JM Cellars 2000 Columbia Valley Cuvée Bordeaux Blend (Columbia Valley (WA)) $21. This is 50% Cabernet Sauvignon, 44% Merlot, and 6% Cab Franc. Made in a full-throttle, high-alcohol mode, with thick, spicy, tannic flavors. There's nothing subtle here, but it's certainly big, with bold flavors of blackberry jam, toast, white chocolate, and white pepper. **90** —*P.G.* (*9/1/2003*)

JM Cellars 2003 Cuvée Bordeaux Blend (Columbia Valley (WA)) $28. The fourth vintage of this Bordeaux blend (56% Cabernet Sauvignon, 28% Merlot, 10% Malbec, and 6% Cabernet Franc). Tart, fruit-driven, and spiced up with pretty, chocolate barrel flavors, it is a very appealing, consumer-pleasing style. **89** —*P.G.* (*8/1/2006*)

JM Cellars 2003 Tre Fanciulli Cabernet Blend (Columbia Valley (WA)) $35. The winery's signature red features Klipsun Cabernet blended with Merlot and Syrah sourced from a variety of top sites. Interesting cherry tobacco and chocolate streaks marry well to the ripe cherry fruit, and it's got the extra length you look for in this price range. 325 cases produced. **89** —*P.G.* (*8/1/2006*)

JM Cellars 2003 Cabernet Sauvignon (Red Mountain) $35. Klipsun, Ciel, and Red Mountain vineyard grapes comprise this wine, which displays the tannic toughness of the appellation. The barrel flavors, particularly chocolate and coconut, are evident, but the fruit is hard and tight, a bit overwhelmed by the tannins. Just 90 cases produced. **87** —*P.G.* (*8/1/2006*)

JM Cellars 2000 Cabernet Sauvignon (Red Mountain) $30. This is very firm, tight, clearly varietal Cabernet, with black fruits and a bit of cassis. The wine is medium weight and shows good balance. **87** —*P.G.* (*9/1/2003*)

JM Cellars 2003 Merlot (Red Mountain) $32. 100% Merlot from Klipsun and Ciel. Opens tart and hard, than strolls into somewhat grassy, slightly herbaceous territory. Tart acids and green tea tannins keep your lips at attention; it shows good concentration and will taste best with rich foods. **88** —*P.G.* (*8/1/2006*)

JM Cellars 1999 Tre Fancivilli Red Blend (Columbia Valley (WA)) $28. A well put-together blend of Cabernet Sauvignon, Merlot, and Syrah. The tar and blackberry aromas match the flavors with the addition of char and milk chocolate and a long, lingering finish. **90** —*C.S.* (*12/31/2002*)

JM Cellars 2005 Klipsun Vineyard Sauvignon Blanc (Red Mountain) $NA. This is the sixth vintage for this wine, and there is no question that Klipsun's SB is something special. The clean, barrel-fermented effort is quite dry, clean, and toasty. It's been barrel aged sur lie in French oak (half new). Just 5% Sémillon is added, but it gives the mouthfeel a touch of lanolin. **88** —*P.G.* (*12/31/2006*)

JM Cellars 2003 Klipsun Vineyard Sauvignon Blanc (Red Mountain) $18. Crisp and pungent with ripe aromas and flavors of peach, apricot, pear and anise. Barrel-fermented and aged sur lie for six months in 50% new French oak; it retains enough firm acid to keep it lively and balanced, and the fruit shines. **89** —*P.G.* (*12/1/2004*)

JM Cellars 2003 Syrah (Columbia Valley (WA)) $32. This wine begins with lively, juicy, spicy blackberry and raspberry fruits, then adds pepper and vanilla to the mix. The tannins are soft and approachable. **88** —*P.G.* (*8/1/2006*)

JM Cellars 2005 Viognier (Columbia Valley (WA)) $NA. The second vintage of Viognier for JM, it's mostly Stillwater Creek fruit, with 6% Ciel du Cheval Roussanne. A lovely spicy nose starts it off, with sweet apricot, cooked peach, and cinnamon notes. It's a rich, ripe and creamy style of Viognier, spotted with spicy ginger. Unusual but well made and delicious. The gingerbread finish is quite distinctive. **89** —P.G. (12/31/2006)

JOCELYN

Jocelyn 2002 Cabernet Sauvignon (Napa Valley) $32. Here's a very soft, melted Cab, and while the flavors, which are of black currants, chocolate, spiced coffee and oaky vanilla, are delicious, it seems structurally off. It won't age, so drink up. **85** —S.H. (12/15/2005)

JODAR

Jodar 1999 Cabernet Sauvignon (El Dorado County) $18. A tough, gritty wine that's overly soft in acids. The flabbiness makes the tannins harder than they really are. Vague traces of berries and herbs drink very dry. **82** —S.H. (11/15/2003)

Jodar 1999 2,400 Feet Sangiovese (El Dorado) $26. 81 —S.H. (5/1/2002)

JOHN ANTHONY

John Anthony 2003 Cabernet Sauvignon (Napa Valley) $55. The grapes are from Oak Knoll, a southerly, cooler district, and while the wine is very ripe and oaky, it has bright acidity. That makes for a wonderful balance to the lush cherry pie, cassis, and chocolate flavors. So delicious and drinkable now, it will be hard to keep from opening, but should age well for a decade. **92** —S.H. (9/1/2006)

John Anthony 2005 Church Vineyard Sauvignon Blanc (Carneros) $19. The wonderfully bright, citrusy acidity pushes and brightens the citrus, melon, and fig flavors. It's such an expressive wine, so bold and well-structured. No oak seems to have been added, but no matter, the wine is so rich, clean, and fruity that it doesn't need it. Just brilliant California Sauvignon Blanc. **92 Editors' Choice** —S.H. (12/1/2006)

John Anthony 2003 Syrah (Napa Valley) $35. Terrific Syrah. It has plenty of blackberry, cherry, and cocoa flavors, and lots of smoky new oak. Richly sweet in tannins, with good acidity. But that's just the beginning. The wine, from Carneros, also has enormously complex nuances that teasingly reveal themselves sip by sip. **94 Editors' Choice** —S.H. (12/1/2006)

JOLIESSE

Joliesse 2003 Chardonnay (California) $8. A pleasant, easy Chard that's light on fruit but balanced and dry. You'll find modest peach and oak flavors and crisp acids. **84 Best Buy** —S.H. (12/15/2004)

Joliesse 2000 Reserve Chardonnay (California) $7. Some pretty apple aromas, but marred by vegetal smells and a clumsy mouthfeel. Dryish, this is a wine that will do in a pinch if your guests aren't too discriminating. **83** —S.H. (6/1/2003)

Joliesse 2002 Lot 57-Limited Edition Shiraz (California) $9. This rosé boasts slightly meaty aromas, plus a healthy dose of limes and berries. Feels big in the mouth and slightly soft, so maybe it's not totally dry, or maybe it's just an oversized rosé with relatively low acidity. Either way, it'll go down just fine this summer. **85** —J.C. (7/1/2003)

Joliesse 2003 Rosé Shiraz (California) $9. Lots of full-throttle raspberry, smoke, and vanilla flavors in this dry, balanced blush wine. It's crisp in acidity, with a fruity finish. **84** —S.H. (12/15/2004)

Joliesse 2001 Limited Edition Zinfandel (California) $10. Fairly smooth and sleek, with modest cherry, black currant, spice, coffee, and oak tones. On the palate, the smooth tannins give structure to the blend. Moderate toast on the finish. **86** (11/1/2003)

JONES FAMILY

Jones Family 1997 Cabernet Sauvignon (Napa Valley) $75. 95 (11/1/2000)

Jones Family 1999 Cabernet Sauvignon (Napa Valley) $85. Firm, rich and smooth, framed by silky ripe tannins. This plush, muscular wine offers mounds of black currant, blackberry, plum, chocolate, coffee, anise, spice, and herb flavors. Long and sleek on the finish. **94** (11/15/2002)

JORDAN

Jordan 1997 Cabernet Sauvignon (Sonoma County) $45. 86 (11/1/2000)

Jordan 1995 Cabernet Sauvignon (Sonoma County) $38. 91 —S.H. (11/1/1999)

Jordan 1999 Cabernet Sauvignon (Sonoma County) $48. From a mixture of Sonoma and Mendocino grapes, and with 50,000 cases produced, this is an average wine. Fulfills the basic Cab requirements of blackberry fruit and a full body without achieving excitement. **85** —S.H. (11/15/2003)

Jordan 1998 Cabernet Sauvignon (Sonoma County) $45. This is an easy-drinking Cab with pleasant black currant flavors and more than a hint of olives and other green, herbal notes that are a testament to the poor vintage. The tannins are soft, although acidity is sharp, and there's a green tartness all the way through the finish. **85** (11/15/2002)

Jordan 1998 Chardonnay (Sonoma County) $25. 86 (6/1/2000)

Jordan 2000 Chardonnay (Russian River Valley) $26. Jordan's first-ever Russian River Chard is very good. It has the ripe green apple and peach flavors you expect from the appellation, with its crisp, supporting acids. Oak plays an integral, but not a dominating, role. **91** —S.H. (2/1/2003)

JORY

Jory 1998 "El Nino" Chardonnay (Central Coast) $15. 81 (6/1/2000)

Jory 1997 Lion Oaks Ranch Sangre De Dono Syrah (Santa Clara Valley) $50. 85 —J.C. (2/1/2000)

JOSEPH FILIPPI

Joseph Filippi 2001 Blanc Grenache (Cucamonga Valley) $11. This pink-colored wine smells like a pack of Lifesavers. Raspberry, cherry, and strawberry flavors are sweet, while high acidity brings a slight fizziness. Nice hot; weather beach-sipper. **84** —S.H. (4/1/2002)

Joseph Filippi 2001 Zinfandel (Cucamonga Valley) $18. An ultra-ripe style that sports dried fruits and rustic tannins framed in cedary, spicy oak. Chocolate and tea are also prevalent, with hints of black-cherry too. **84** (11/1/2003)

JOSEPH PHELPS

Joseph Phelps 2001 Insignia Bordeaux Blend (Napa Valley) $125. A triumph. Aged nearly two years in all-new French oak, this massive wine stuns with its superb balance. Manages the elusive challenge of reining in hugely ripe black currant, cherry, and oak flavors and sweet tannins while keeping the palate impression soft and alluring, almost feminine. Just gorgeous right out of the bottle, but should develop effortlessly through the decade and beyond. **96** —S.H. (10/1/2004)

Joseph Phelps 1997 Insignia Bordeaux Blend (Napa Valley) $120. 95 (11/1/2000)

Joseph Phelps 2002 Insignia Cabernet Blend (Napa Valley) $142. This celebrated wine is not mind-blowing right now. It's dry, oaky, tannic and soft. There's a wealth of cassis and moo shu pork flavors, and huge new oak. Yet it holds itself back, teasing but withdrawing into its tannic cloak. Collectors, be reassured it's worth stashing. Drink now through 2010, but after that, it's a gamble. **92** —S.H. (12/31/2005)

Joseph Phelps 1997 Cabernet Sauvignon (Napa Valley) $35. 90 (11/1/2000)

Joseph Phelps 2003 Cabernet Sauvignon (Napa Valley) $48. Shows the deft Phelps touch in the softly complex texture whose tannins are just as velvety as they come, and the ripe, pure fruit. The blackberry, cassis, and red cherry flavors are enriched with vanilla and toast from oak. Drink this fine Cabernet now and through 2008. **91** —S.H. (7/1/2006)

Joseph Phelps 2002 Cabernet Sauvignon (Napa Valley) $48. Here's a good Cabernet that satisfies all the basic requirements. It's dry, rich, in blackberry and currant fruit, and sturdy in tannins, with a fine overlay of toasty oak. **87** —S.H. (10/1/2005)

Joseph Phelps 2001 Cabernet Sauvignon (Napa Valley) $65. This is the sort of Cab you sip and immediately like. It's not only rich in currant and oak, with elaborate tannins, but possesses that extra dimension of pedigree due to the balance and harmony. Not for the cellar, but great now for your best foods. **89** —S.H. (10/1/2004)

Joseph Phelps 2000 Cabernet Sauvignon (Napa Valley) $45. A dense, layered wine, marked by pure cassis flavors. Picks up intensity in the middle palate, where it turns rich and compelling. Harmony and elegance, not

USA

to mention ageability, mark this expression of Cabernet. **92 Editors' Choice** —*S.H. (5/1/2003)*

Joseph Phelps 1999 Cabernet Sauvignon (Napa Valley) $42. Impeccably structured. Has those brilliant Napa tannins that are as finely knit as a medieval tapestry, and a bit of a scour from acidity. Oak adds gentle complexities. It's a little light, though. With this weight and density, you want more fruity concentration. **88** —*S.H. (6/1/2002)*

Joseph Phelps 2002 Backus Cabernet Sauvignon (Oakville) $175. Right up there with the best of the '01 Napas. Smooth and polished, with a velvety mouthfeel that conveys cherry and blackberry flavors, without heavy extract. Oak plays a supportive role. The overall impression is of elegance, power, and extreme balance. The tannins are soft enough for immediate drinking, yet should protect this wine through at least 2015. **95** —*S.H. (3/1/2005)*

Joseph Phelps 2001 Backus Cabernet Sauvignon (Oakville) $150. Tasted alongside a bevy of Oakville Cabs, this beauty was the star of the show. It's a huge, masculine wine, authoritative and ageable. Pours dark and drinks tannic and oaky, with a massive core of cassis, cherry and chocolate fruit encased in perfect tannins. What grace and power, what balance. Drink now through 2016, at least. **97 Cellar Selection** —*S.H. (11/1/2005)*

Joseph Phelps 2000 Backus Vineyard Cabernet Sauvignon (Oakville) $150. Attention to detail shows in the intensity of the currant and cassis flavors, the elaborately crafted tannins, and the vibrant edge of acidity. It's not an ager, but is as good a representative of 2000 Napa Cabernet as you'll find. **93 Cellar Selection** —*D.T. (2/1/2004)*

Joseph Phelps 1999 Backus Vineyard Cabernet Sauvignon (Oakville) $150. Even at this price, most of the 400-case production is already snapped up. Nonetheless, this is great Cabernet. Incredibly plush, ultrafeminine, with all the bells and whistles of a hallmark wine. Flavors lean toward cherry, blackberry, plum, strawberry, toast, vanilla, anise, herbs, spice, and chocolate. It's all couched in velvety, smooth tannins and a finish that doesn't stop. **96 Cellar Selection** —*J.M. (2/1/2003)*

Joseph Phelps 2000 Insignia Cabernet Sauvignon (Napa Valley) $125. There are some great black currant, cassis and cherry flavors in this fine wine, but in the end, the stubborn tannins dominate. They're tough and gritty, and finish with a stark astringency. The wine will soften in time, but it doesn't have the stuffing for the long haul. **88** —*S.H. (5/1/2004)*

Joseph Phelps 1998 Chardonnay (Carneros) $22. 90 *(6/1/2000)*

Joseph Phelps 2000 Chardonnay (Carneros) $26. This is a good wine that's weakened by a lack of harmony. The fruit veers toward mangoes and breadfruit. The acids are fine. A gentle overlay of oak and pronounced lees add textural complexity. Yet the parts don't come together smoothly; it feels jagged in the mouth. **87** —*S.H. (9/1/2002)*

Joseph Phelps 2002 Ovation Chardonnay (Napa Valley) $44. Huge, lavish in new smoky oak, vanilla, and caramel, with massive fruit flavors of ripe, sweet green apples and peaches. This wine underwent malolactic fermentation but retains a crisp, juicy acidity. Finishes complex and leesy, with astounding penetration and length. **94** —*S.H. (12/15/2004)*

Joseph Phelps 2002 Ovation Chardonnay (Napa Valley) $48. A controlled explosion best describes this year's Ovation. Always intense and concentrated, it exhibits well-ripened apple, pear, and pineapple flavors with plenty of lees and smoky oak, and finishes with clean acidity. Yet it maintains a steely minerality throughout. **92** —*S.H. (3/1/2005)*

Joseph Phelps 2001 Ovation Chardonnay (Napa Valley) $44. A very fine Chardonnay notable especially for its firm, crisp structure. The bright acids frame apple, pear, and tropical fruit flavors that are well oaked, with a rich, leesy mouthfeel. Has the extra refinement and depth needed for excellence. **92** —*S.H. (12/15/2003)*

Joseph Phelps 2000 Ovation Chardonnay (Napa Valley) $44. Absolutely delicious, first-rate Chard marked by a noble structure. Flavors aren't bad either—think green apples generously sprinkled with oriental spices. Feels crisp and authoritative in the mouth through the long, firm finish. **92** —*S.H. (2/1/2003)*

Joseph Phelps 1999 Ovation Chardonnay (Napa Valley) $45. Joseph Phelps's flagship Chardonnay is a study in sophisticated style. A fragrant peach, pineapple, smoke, and floral bouquet might, in other wines, be overpowering, but here it is subtly seductive. Rich peach, tart orange, and oat flavors ride the velvety palate, and the long, suave finish displays tangerine, peaches and cream aromas and flavors. There are layers of nuance to explore here—savor this one slowly. **91** *(7/1/2001)*

Joseph Phelps 1998 Ovation Chardonnay (Napa Valley) $44. 92 *(10/1/2000)*

Joseph Phelps 1997 Ovation Chardonnay (Napa Valley) $40. 92 —*L.W. (10/1/1999)*

Joseph Phelps 1997 Merlot (Napa Valley) $35. 87 —*M.S. (7/1/2000)*

Joseph Phelps 2002 Merlot (Napa Valley) $40. Take a sip, and you think, Wow, that's good. Dark, deeply aromatic in black currants, mocha java coffee, subtle herbs, green olives and fine oak. Turns sweet but dry in blackberry and cherry flavors wrapped in beautifully ripe, soft, expressive tannins. **92** —*S.H. (10/1/2005)*

Joseph Phelps 2000 Merlot-Cabernet Sauvignon (Napa Valley) $40. Brings a whole new dimension to Merlot by adding flair and nuance to the usual well-ripened plum and blackberry flavors. Here, kirsch, cassis, and dark chocolate mingle together in rich, delicate but complex tannins to forge a wine of interest and longevity. **92** —*S.H. (6/1/2003)*

Joseph Phelps 1999 Le Mistral Red Blend (California) $25. Always balanced and elegant, this blend of six Rhône grapes seems drier than usual, a bit more tannic and less fruity than in past years. That makes it a "food wine," and a very nice one at that. It won't hit you in the head with size, but it's a classy stylish addition to the table. **88** —*S.H. (12/15/2001)*

Joseph Phelps 2003 Le Mistral Rhône Red Blend (Monterey County) $30. Phelps practically owns the patent on red Rhône blends with Mistral, consistently a wine that offers not only immediate pleasure but depth and complexity. Sourcing the grapes from Monterey makes economic as well as terroir sense. The wine is dry, rich, succulent, balanced, and well oaked. **88** —*S.H. (12/31/2005)*

Joseph Phelps 2002 Le Mistral Rhône Red Blend (Monterey County) $30. Combines Syrah's blackberries and Grenache's raspberries to produce an intensely fruity wine. It's dry and smoothly textured, with soft tannins and acids. Delicious with spicy broiled chicken. **90 Editors' Choice** —*S.H. (10/1/2005)*

Joseph Phelps 2001 Le Mistral Rhône Red Blend (Monterey County) $25. Rich and complex in gamy, raw meat aromas, with cherries, lavender, thyme, and a tantalizing hint of white chocolate. This Provencal-style wine is delicious and dry. Syrah, Grenache, Carignane, Petite Sirah, and several others. **91** —*S.H. (12/1/2004)*

Joseph Phelps 2000 Le Mistral Rhône Red Blend (California) $25. Delicious and beguiling, with something for everyone. The mélange of fruity-spicy flavors is touched with subtle herb and oak notes in a silky texture. This Rhône-style blend of Syrah, Grenache, Mourvèdre, and others is the ideal food wine. **91 Editors' Choice** —*S.H. (12/1/2003)*

Joseph Phelps 1997 Le Mistral Rhône Red Blend (California) $25. 91 —*M.S. (2/1/2000)*

Joseph Phelps 1998 Sauvignon Blanc (Napa Valley) $15. 81 *(3/1/2000)*

Joseph Phelps 2003 Sauvignon Blanc (Napa Valley) $22. This is dynamite Sauvignon Blanc. It's strongly flavored in citrus, fig, melon, and vanilla flavors, with a fresh cut of green grass and compelling acidity, and is also dramatically tense and vibrant. Accomplishes that balancing act that most of the competition cannot. **92** —*S.H. (3/1/2005)*

Joseph Phelps 2002 Syrah (Napa Valley) $35. This offering from one of California's Syrah pioneers seems a touch tannic and earthy, but also features sturdy blackberry fruit and a creamy mouthfeel. **85** *(9/1/2005)*

Joseph Phelps 2000 Syrah (Napa Valley) $40. So much flavor, yet such balance and harmony. The richness is in the blackberry and spice flavors that don't let up. The balance lies in the crisp acids, smooth tannins, and impeccable touch of fine oak. Such a wine will age, but it's appealing right out of the bottle. **92** —*S.H. (4/1/2004)*

Joseph Phelps 1999 Syrah (Napa Valley) $NA. Rich and concentrated, with well developed flavors of plums and blackberries and a spicy, peppery streak. Very dry, with stylish, ripe, and fine tannins, and enough acidity for balance. This wine feels distinguished enough for the best tables. **90** —*S.H. (6/1/2003)*

Joseph Phelps 1998 Syrah (Napa Valley) $37. Joseph Phelps was the first in modern Californian wine industry to produce a Syrah, but the flavor and texture here, like so many similarly rated wines, is largely oak-derived. Yes, there's some quite sweet blackberry and red berry, meat, toast, and caramel flavors. Still, our tasters found this decidedly wood-dominated and not well-defined. Not bad, but disappointing. **86** *(11/1/2001)*

Joseph Phelps 1996 Vin du Mistral Syrah (California) $30. **87** —*L.W (10/1/1999)*

Joseph Phelps 2002 Viognier (Napa Valley) $30. From one of the original Rhône Rangers, a wine that captures the flamboyant side of this chameleon grape, with its array of tropical fruit, flower, and spice flavors, but never loses balance. That's because of the near-perfect acids and deft oaking. It's amazing how a Viognier this ripely fruity is also complex. **91** —*S.H. (2/1/2004)*

Joseph Phelps 2001 Viognier (Napa Valley) $35. Bold and striking, a powerfully flavored wine that manages to be balanced despite the size. Big, extracted flavors of apples and peaches and wildflowers drink dry and a little tannic, with a dusty mouthfeel. The finish is long and flavorful, but the lasting impressin is of style and class. **90** —*S.H. (3/1/2003)*

Joseph Phelps 2000 Viognier (Napa Valley) $35. From a pioneer of this variety in California, here's an exotic, strong interpretation. Smells enormously bright and forward, with honey, jasmine, peach, custard, and smoke aromas. The flavors are powerfully fruity, although the wine is dry. Considerable acids make it tart enough for poultry or fish. **86** —*S.H. (12/15/2001)*

JOSEPH SWAN VINEYARDS

Joseph Swan Vineyards 2000 Cuvée de Trois Pinot Noir (Russian River Valley) $20. This lush offering features some Port-like elements—chocolate, dried spices, rich, plummy fruit, and a dense, creamy texture—but has enough acidity to retain its essential Pinot character. The tannins on the finish are so soft and ripe that you hardly notice them. **89 Editors' Choice** *(10/1/2002)*

Joseph Swan Vineyards 2000 Saralee's Vineyard Pinot Noir (Russian River Valley) $25. This lean, racy Pinot's tart plum and cranberry-rhubarb flavors overcame a perceived thinness to make friends. Still it was a split decision among tasters, some finding it sour, with not a lot there; others praised its plummy qualities, finding it harmonious and elegant, finishing with a crisp, refreshing tang. **85** *(10/1/2002)*

Joseph Swan Vineyards 1999 Steiner Vineyard Pinot Noir (Sonoma Mountain) $25. Right off the bat, the murky, rusty color is a red flag. But the aromas are more or less correct, with mushroom, beet, tomato, and woodspice. The flavors are sweet, with marshmallow and brown sugar. **83** *(10/1/2002)*

Joseph Swan Vineyards 2004 Trenton Estate Pinot Noir (Russian River Valley) $45. There's something exuberantly old-fashioned about this Pinot. It's dark, dry, and tannically rustic, with huge, gobby, fresh cherry pie flavors deep inside. Swan Pinots last for a long time; give this one five years to soften and melt those tannins. **89 Cellar Selection** —*S.H. (12/15/2006)*

Joseph Swan Vineyards 1999 Trenton Estate Vineyard Pinot Noir (Russian River Valley) $42. Earth, bramble, mint, and vanilla aromas lead into a sweet, plummy palate that has some candied qualities, as well as more mint. This wine could probably use racier acidity; it seems soft. **85** *(10/1/2002)*

JOSEPH ZAKON

Joseph Zakon NV Kosher Cabernet Sauvignon (America) $9. Understated on the nose, but hits the right notes in the mouth, combining a medium-weight, supple mouthfeel with cherry, plum, and coffee flavors. Turns creamy on the finish, with just enough spice and acid for balance. Drink now. **85 Best Buy** —*J.C. (4/1/2006)*

JOULLIAN

Joullian 2001 Chardonnay (Monterey) $15. Oak and lees add extra layers of complex interest to this smooth wine. It has pretty flavors of apples, peaches, and honeydew, and those Monterey acids are firm and bright. The finish is notable for its rich spices and length. **88** —*S.H. (2/1/2004)*

Joullian 2000 Chardonnay (Monterey) $15. Rich and creamy, this complex, layered wine is packed with white peaches, butterscotch, toast, and honey. Completely dry, with enough acidity to make it lively. Finishes with some spice. **90 Best Buy** —*S.H. (2/1/2003)*

Joullian 1999 Chardonnay (Monterey) $15. This wine seems overly leesy, and very high acidity makes things even tarter, almost sour. The underlying flavors are citrusy and lemony, making the wine taste like a Sauvignon Blanc. It's not very "Chardonnay," but it's clean and vibrant. **85** —*S.H. (12/15/2002)*

Joullian 1996 Family Reserve Chardonnay (Monterey County) $24. **83** *(6/1/2000)*

Joullian 2000 RogerRose Vineyard Chardonnay (Monterey) $23. Smells late-picked and ultraripe, opening with a blast of rich tangerine, lime, and peach sorbet aromas, complexed with smoke and vanilla. Flamboyant in the mouth, too; a big, unctuous wine that's dry and rich at the same time. Crisp Salinas Valley acidity boosts the flavors. **87** —*S.H. (12/1/2003)*

Joullian 2000 Sleepy Hollow Vineyard Chardonnay (Monterey) $27. There are some nice, ripe flavors of peaches and pears here, but also a disagreeable harshness, especially in the finish. It leaves a peppery burn on the palate. There's also a ton of oak, more than the underlying fruit seems to need. **83** —*S.H. (10/1/2003)*

Joullian 1999 Sleepy Hollow Vineyard Chardonnay (Monterey) $27. Hang onto your hat with this fruit-forward, honeyed wine, filled with oak, spices, and sweetness. It's a big, wild kicker, and calls for equally rich foods, like lobster, butter, saffron, or cream. Almost a meal in itself. **90** —*S.H. (5/1/2002)*

Joullian 1999 Merlot (Carmel Valley) $30. Long on flavor, this is a classy wine meant for white tablecloths. The pleasant aromas are of green olives, smoke, white chocolate, and berries, and a hint of bacon fat. Drinks soft and plush, striking a nice balance between herbs and fruit. Some sharpness from acids is okay, and suggests short-term ageworthiness. **89** —*S.H. (6/1/2002)*

Joullian 2000 Sauvignon Blanc (Carmel Valley) $14. A wallop of a wine, packed with flavorful lemon and lime, ginger, pepper, and yellow stone fruits, especially peaches and apricots. There's a nice, creamy mouthfeel that lasts through the long, ripe finish. Good value. **88** —*S.H. (9/1/2003)*

Joullian 2003 Family Reserve Sauvignon Blanc (Carmel Valley) $20. Smoke, hard cheese, melon, and vanilla/pannacotta aromas are friendly enough, while the palate is round and ripe. Arguably a bit too loaded with sweet, ripe flavors of banana, honey, and peaches, but some people might like that. Lots of oak, but acidic enough to handle it. **86** *(7/1/2005)*

Joullian 2002 Syrah (Carmel Valley) $30. Quite a lush Syrah. It's perfectly ripened and brimming with black-cherry, blackberry, and chocolate flavors, but has complexity in the smooth tannins and polished overlay of oak. Finishes dry and long. Try with short ribs. **88** —*S.H. (6/1/2005)*

Joullian 1997 Zinfandel (Carmel Valley) $20. A very interesting wine from a rarely-seen appellation. The fruit is distinctly wild berry—huckleberry maybe—with spice and good acid. But the finish has a bitter, metallic note that lingers unpleasantly. **83** —*P.G. (3/1/2001)*

Joullian 2002 Sias Cuvée Zinfandel (Carmel Valley) $20. Dry and medium-bodied, a different type of Zin. It's more restrained than most, offering berry, leather, and coffee flavors, and while it's smooth in the mouth, the acid-tannin balance is quite complex. Turns increasingly interesting on the finish. **90** —*S.H. (8/1/2005)*

Joullian 2001 Sias Cuvée Zinfandel (Carmel Valley) $20. Recognizably Zinny with its array of wild berry, tobacco, and earth flavors, and peppery mouthfeel, not to mention the dry, somewhat rough tannins. There's some real richness in the middle, and the finish is spicy and clean. **86** —*S.H. (3/1/2004)*

USA

JUDD

Judd 2001 Cranston Vineyard Petite Sirah (California) $26. A ripe, big-boned red wine that's dry and fruity enough to stand up to barbecue or a nice pot roast. It's got chocolatey, blackberry flavors and sturdy tannins. **85** —*S.H. (6/1/2005)*

Judd 2001 Syrah (Napa Valley) $26. Starts with a tough, closed aroma of dust, earth, and dried spices, but there's a heart of cherries and blackberries buried under the tannins. Not showing well now. May improve after 2005. **85** —*S.H. (6/1/2005)*

JUDD'S HILL

Judd's Hill 1999 Estate Cabernet Blend (Napa Valley) $75. Easily deserves its high score due to the ripe cassis flavors and near-perfect tannins. Caresses and seduces the palate with the soft velvety intensity of a fine liqueur. Yet some tough tannins and firm acidity make for a scour on the palate. May or may not age; hard to tell. A blend of Cabernet Sauvignon, Cabernet Franc, and Merlot. **90** —*S.H. (11/15/2003)*

Judd's Hill 1997 Cabernet Sauvignon (Napa Valley) $45. **93** *(11/1/2000)*

Judd's Hill 2002 Cabernet Sauvignon (Napa Valley) $40. Absolutely delicious Cabernet, with rich tannins framing impeccably ripe, jammy cassis and chocolate fruit that's well oaked. The tannins are a wonder, thick and soft and sweet. This is New World Cabernet at its decadent, hedonistic best. **92** —*S.H. (5/1/2006)*

Judd's Hill 2001 Cabernet Sauvignon (Napa Valley) $40. Classic '01 in the perfectly ripened fruit, which shows a balance of cassis, chocolate, and olive flavors, lush, firm tannins, and the overall impeccability. There's great oak here, and it meshes perfectly. Drink now through 2014. **93** —*S.H. (6/1/2005)*

Judd's Hill 1999 Cabernet Sauvignon (Napa Valley) $40. Good and rich and classy, with excellently ripe blackberry, currant and herb flavors and a nice overlay of toasty oak. Tannins are as fine as can be, smooth and complex, although they're young and tend to stun the palate. **91** —*S.H. (8/1/2003)*

Judd's Hill 1999 Merlot (Napa Valley) $26. A well-made Merlot brimming with lush black currant, cherry, and spice flavors. The tannins are velvety smooth but considerable, creating a puckery mouthfeel. If you need to drink it now, do so with rich beef or lamb dishes. Otherwise, stick it in the cellar for a few years. **89** —*S.H. (12/1/2003)*

Judd's Hill 1999 Juliana Vineyards Merlot (Napa Valley) $30. A smooth, polished wine most notable for its intense cherry flavors. Like sipping pure fruit nectar, and made better by the rich tannins. So delicious now, it doesn't seem likely to get better with age. **91** —*S.H. (12/1/2003)*

Judd's Hill 1999 Summers Ranch Merlot (Knights Valley) $30. Not even in the same ballpark as this winery's excellent Juliana bottling, which costs the same. This is a decent wine, but the flavors have a tobaccoey, dried-herb edge, and the tannins are rustic. **86** —*S.H. (12/1/2003)*

JUSLYN VINEYARDS

Juslyn Vineyards 2000 Red Wine Bordeaux Blend (Napa Valley) $50. Here's a wine that has some pleasant features, namely the gentle tannins and fine, oaky veneer. But the fruit is thin, and the wine struggles to impress the palate with depth. Seems seriously overpriced. Mostly Cab Sauv, with Merlot and Cab Franc. **84** —*S.H. (12/1/2004)*

Juslyn Vineyards 2002 Estate Red Wine Cabernet Blend (Spring Mountain) $90. Juslyn's top wine is just under the legal limit to call it Cabernet Sauvignon. It's surprisingly soft and accessible for a Spring Mountain Cab, offering immediate pleasure with its juicy, upfront blackberry liqueur and cocoa flavors. It's certainly a complex, balanced, elegant wine, and quite drinkable now. But it should hold and even improve for a decade. **92** —*S.H. (12/15/2006)*

Juslyn Vineyards 2002 Perry's Blend Cabernet Blend (Napa Valley) $60. This Cabernet-based blend has some pedigreed vineyard fruit in it, including Tokalon and Beckstoffer Georges III. It's extremely soft and complex, but not showing all that well at this moment. Seems a bit closed down, muted. But it's a very fine wine that probably needs time to open. Drink 2008–2010. **91 Cellar Selection** —*S.H. (12/15/2006)*

Juslyn Vineyards 2001 Cabernet Sauvignon (Napa Valley) $55. Ripe and juicy, with black currant, blackberry jam, and cherry flavors and smooth tannins. Lacks a bit of depth, but the richness works. **86** —*S.H. (5/1/2005)*

Juslyn Vineyards 2001 Cabernet Sauvignon (Spring Mountain) $85. Cedar, chocolate, and cassis abound in this surprisingly smooth and creamy mountain Cabernet. Immediately approachable because of its supple texture, yet firms up on the finish, suggesting midterm (5–8 years) aging potential. **90** *(5/1/2005)*

Juslyn Vineyards 2000 Cabernet Sauvignon (Napa Valley) $50. This understated wine doesn't overwhelm with fruit, but creeps up on you subtly. The cherry and herb flavors are delicate, and judiciously balanced with tannins and oak. It's a feminine wine that will marry well with roasts, poultry, and soft cheeses. **89** —*S.H. (4/1/2004)*

Juslyn Vineyards 1999 Cabernet Sauvignon (Napa Valley) $60. Velvety smooth and plush, this intense wine shows complex layers of smoke, blackberry, cassis, licorice and spice. It's all framed in toasty oak and firm, ripe tannins, finishing long and lush. **92** —*J.M. (2/1/2003)*

Juslyn Vineyards 2000 Estate Cabernet Sauvignon (Spring Mountain) $85. A big, dense, sturdy wine, rich in tannins and with the structure to age. It's rather muted now, but buried deep is a solid core of blackberry, cassis, herb, and olive flavors that turn up on the finish. Best after 2006. **91** —*S.H. (4/1/2004)*

Juslyn Vineyards 2002 Vineyard Select Cabernet Sauvignon (Napa Valley) $80. Soft, ripe, and dry, this wine, with a little Merlot and Cab Franc, is largely from Beckstoffer's Tokalon Vineyard, with a dollop from the winery's Spring Mountain estate. The wine is complex, young, and comes together harmoniously, but needs some time to develop. Best from 2008, and should hold well for many years beyond. **93 Cellar Selection** —*S.H. (12/15/2006)*

Juslyn Vineyards 2001 Vineyard Select Cabernet Sauvignon (Napa Valley) $75. This is a good Cabernet but seems pricey for what you get. It's well crafted, ripe, and oaky, and finishes with harsh acids. **85** —*S.H. (5/1/2005)*

Juslyn Vineyards 2000 Vineyard Select Cabernet Sauvignon (Napa Valley) $75. A lighter style of Cab, with pretty black-cherry, blackberry, and herb flavors and softly sweet tannins. Notable for its balance and harmony, this elegant wine will support, not overwhelm, fine food. **90** —*S.H. (4/1/2004)*

Juslyn Vineyards 1999 Vineyard Select Cabernet Sauvignon (Napa Valley) $75. Sleek, smooth, and focused, powerful but elegant, this wine shows vivid blackberry, plum, anise, sage, chocolate, and spice flavors all couched in classy oak. Tannins are firm and fine, providing structure and finesse. **93** —*J.M. (2/1/2003)*

Juslyn Vineyards 1998 Vineyard Select Cabernet Sauvignon (Napa Valley) $75. Aromas of plums, currants, and burnt match are more interesting than the dark berry and earth flavors that have an initial richness. It lacks fullness throughout, finishing fairly thin. Drink soon. **86** —*C.S. (6/1/2002)*

Juslyn Vineyards 2003 Sauvignon Blanc (Napa Valley) $24. Fruity, crisp, and slightly sweet, with pear, citrus, fig, and spearmint flavors, this easy sipper will go well with a variety of foods. **85** —*S.H. (5/1/2005)*

Juslyn Vineyards 2002 Sauvignon Blanc (Napa Valley) $NA. Takes this varietal's citrusy, grassy flavors and lifts them into riper fig, melon, and peach. The bright acidity is balanced by rich, sweet tannins and a creamy texture from barrel fermentation. The result is a charming wine, dry and satisfying. **87** —*S.H. (2/1/2004)*

JUSTIN

Justin 2002 Isosceles Bordeaux Blend (Paso Robles) $55. A bit fudge-like, with thick, soft flavors of chocolate and cassis joined by herbal notes of thyme or tea. Turns a bit drying on the finish. **87** *(6/1/2006)*

Justin 2001 Isosceles Bordeaux Blend (Paso Robles) $55. Cabernet Sauvignon-dominated Bordeaux blend, starting with lush, inviting new oak, cassis, sweet thyme, vanilla, and mushroom aromas, Turns subtle, supple, and elegant in the mouth, powerful and refined. Dry, long, this wine finishes with class and distinction. **92** —*S.H. (12/31/2004)*

Justin 2003 Justification Bordeaux Blend (Paso Robles) $42. Starts off smelling very new-oaky, and as it airs, this Cab Franc-based wine turns aromatic in cherries, cassis, violets, and lavender. It's an interesting wine, a little hot, a little baked, but very dry. It's also fairly tannic. The cherries, oak, and tannins suggest a good grilled steak. **89**—*S.H. (9/1/2006)*

Justin 1999 Isosceles Cabernet Blend (Paso Robles) $48. A smooth, silky texture supports ripe black-cherry, blackberry, cassis, bay leaf, sage, anise, toast, and chocolate flavors. Moderate acidity and firm, ripe tannins provide structure. Long on the finish. **92**—*J.M. (11/15/2002)*

Justin 2003 Cabernet Sauvignon (Paso Robles) $25. A bit overripe, with aromas of dill and raisins, and once in the mouth, the wine has a dried fruit, raisiny taste, although it's dry. It's also quite acidic, and that acidity feels disembodied and not natural. **82**—*S.H. (9/1/2006)*

Justin 2002 Cabernet Sauvignon (Paso Robles) $22. Smells vegetal, and tastes unnaturally sweet. **81**—*S.H. (6/1/2005)*

Justin 1999 Cabernet Sauvignon (Paso Robles) $23. Redolent of black-cherry, blackberry, smoke, anise, coffee, tar, and herbs, this lush, vibrant Cabernet is couched in smooth-textured tannins. It finishes on a bright, almost tart note. **89**—*J.M. (11/15/2002)*

Justin 2002 Reserve Cabernet Sauvignon (Paso Robles) $40. Pretty closed now, showing woody, mulchy notes, but eventually heaves out blackberries and dark chocolate. Rich and refined, and dense, with plush plum, blackberry, and oak flavors. Tannic now, but should develop well in the bottle. **91**—*S.H. (12/31/2004)*

Justin 2000 Chardonnay (Paso Robles) $19. Light and lemony, with a zippy mineral core that leaves the palate bright and refreshed. **87**—*J.M. (12/15/2002)*

Justin 1998 Estate Chardonnay (Paso Robles) $19. **88** *(6/1/2000)*

Justin 2003 Reserve Chardonnay (Paso Robles) $22. Comes across as rather soft and a bit simple, with earth, peach, and apple flavors that have been generously oaked. Could use more liveliness and crispness. **84**—*S.H. (7/1/2005)*

Justin 1998 Reserve Chardonnay (Paso Robles) $23. **87** *(6/1/2000)*

Justin 2002 Justification Merlot-Cabernet Franc (Paso Robles) $40. This Cab Franc and Merlot blend is elegant and refined. Notable for the subtle interplay of dried earth, blueberry, and oak flavors with the rich tannins. It's a wine of enormous charm and finesse. Bone dry, and packing a long, fruity finish. **92**—*S.H. (12/31/2004)*

Justin 2003 Obtuse Port (Paso Robles) $22. Made from Cabernet Sauvignon, and you can taste the blackberry and currant flavors. Fairly sweet, not too much so, with earthy tannins and a chocolatey finish. **84**—*S.H. (7/1/2005)*

Justin 2003 Sauvignon Blanc (Edna Valley) $13. Yes, it's dry and clean, but bitter in lean citrus flavors, and cuttingly acidic. Citrus and acidity are good, but not to this extent. Oysters, however, will pair well. **84**—*S.H. (8/1/2005)*

Justin 2002 Syrah (Paso Robles) $22. Smells refined and oaky, showing aromas of ripe currants, chocolate, herbs, and white pepper. Smooth, polished, and dry, with rich tannins. Drinks well now. **90**—*S.H. (12/31/2004)*

Justin 2000 Syrah (Paso Robles) $22. An interesting wine that showcases how well Syrah can do in so many places. It has much in common with the best Napa bottlings: rich, ripe flavors, smooth and distinguished tannins, and a long, mouthcoating finish that gets better as the wine warms up on the table. It is a little thin in flavor and too soft for aging, but a wine to watch. **89**—*S.H. (12/15/2003)*

Justin 2000 Halter Vineyard Syrah (Paso Robles) $22. Although the flavors are a bit thin, probably as a result of the vintage, the wine shows extraordinary qualities of smoothness, texture, and native pedigree, as well as talented winemaking. It is dry; would be very good with lamb. **91 Editors' Choice**—*S.H. (12/15/2003)*

Justin 1998 Mac Gillivray Vineyard Syrah (Paso Robles) $23. Although this young wine is tough as nails right now, offering little more than espresso, spice, and tart blackberries, it may improve with age. An intense wine that's clearly not for everyone. **84** *(11/1/2001)*

Justin 2002 Reserve Syrah (Paso Robles) $40. This wine is considerably more closed and tannic than Justin's regular release. It's just as fruit-forward, but shows a tight hardness now. Hard to tell where it's going. Now through 2005? **87**—*S.H. (12/31/2004)*

Justin 2002 Reserve Tempranillo (Paso Robles) $30. An unpleasant wine. Not really flawed, just thin, with vaguely bitter cherry flavors, and acidic, offering little pleasure **83**—*S.H. (8/1/2005)*

Justin 2001 Zinfandel (Paso Robles) $23. A plummy, smooth style that serves up good coffee, black-cherry, licorice, and spice flavors. The finish has a slight resiny quality, which shifts to cherries at the end. **86** *(11/1/2003)*

Justin 1999 Zinfandel (Paso Robles) $23. If you do not care for a heavy, syrupy style of Zinfandel, then don't try this. Although it isn't stewed, it's on that cusp in terms of ripeness. Earthy, barnyard aromas signal a deep, prune-driven palate. And the finish is also heavy, but by then the wine's coffee, toffee, and chocolate notes might be growing on you. **85**—*M.S. (11/1/2002)*

K VINTNERS

K Vintners 2003 Ovide–En Cerise Vineyard Red Cabernet Sauvignon-Syrah (Walla Walla (WA)) $55. This Christophe Baron vineyard makes a splendid Cab/Syrah blend, packed with mineral, chalk, pencil lead, and spice. Intense and pinpoint focused, it brings on sharply defined flavors of raspberries and strawberry preserves, wrapping the thick fruit in mineral and dark, slightly bitter tannins. **94**—*P.G. (12/15/2005)*

K Vintners 2003 Roma–En Chamberlin Vineyard Red Cabernet Sauvignon-Syrah (Walla Walla (WA)) $55. An equivalent two-thirds Cab, one-third Syrah blend to the Ovide, this time using En Chamberlin fruit. The wines are strikingly different, equally powerful, but the Roma is perhaps more straightforward with its jammy, full-on cherry/berry fruit parade. Citrus rind lifts the finish, leading into nicely sculpted tannins. **93**—*P.G. (12/15/2005)*

K Vintners 2003 The Creator Cabernet Sauvignon-Syrah (Walla Walla (WA)) $45. Composed of 60% Cabernet Sauvignon from the biodynamic En Cerise Vineyard, and 40% Syrah from Seven Hills. The fruit has a touch of the goop funk the French call gout de merde, and the wine has a big spine of tarry tannin. This is tight and ageworthy; if you drink it soon you'd best decant it early. **92**—*P.G. (8/1/2006)*

K Vintners 2003 Guido Red Blend (Walla Walla (WA)) $30. Seven Hills fruit anchors this mix of Sangiovese (75%) and Syrah (25%). It's strongly scented with tobacco notes and sweet herb notes. Carries the characteristic tartness of Sangiovese but in a flavorful and penetrating style; it tastes bigger than it feels. Notes of violets and pepper add nuance to the blend. **91**—*P.G. (8/1/2006)*

K Vintners 2002 The Boy Red Blend (Walla Walla (WA)) $35. An unusual blend of Grenache, Tempranillo, and Syrah, this is the most forward and voluptuous of the K wines. Sweet, supple, and smooth, it shows lots of midpalate fruit, just this side of jammy. **88**—*P.G. (7/1/2004)*

K Vintners 2002 Cougar Hills Syrah (Walla Walla (WA)) $35. The aromas recall fresh-turned soil, showing leaf, earth, manure, and herb. But it is in no way stemmy; under the scents of earth and twig is some nicely ripened, sweet berry fruit. Young, complex, and fascinating. **91**—*P.G. (7/1/2004)*

K Vintners 2002 End of the Road Syrah (Washington) $28. The name references the winery's location on the east side of Walla Walla, near the state border. Fruit from Cougar Hills, Morrison Lane, and the Seven Hills vineyards is blended to create this intense, dense, smoky Syrah, bursting with tangy berries. Focused, spicy, tart, and complex, the juicy fruit flavors layered and compact. **90**—*P.G. (7/1/2004)*

K Vintners 2003 Lucky No. 7 Syrah (Walla Walla (WA)) $35. The name refers to the Seven Hills vineyard grapes, which deliver exceptional minerality to this sleek, elegant Syrah. Mixed light red fruits show pomegranate, wild berry, and cherry, with refined texture and deceptive intensity. **90**—*P.G. (12/15/2005)*

K Vintners 2003 Milbrandt Syrah (Columbia Valley (WA)) $24. A rich, fat, popular style with bright berries, tart acids, and plenty of spice. It's fruit-powered and warmly accessible, but shows plenty of spine. **88** —*P.G.* *(12/15/2005)*

K Vintners 2002 Milbrandt Syrah (Wahluke Slope) $25. Another aromatic and pure expression of tangy berry fruit, enlivened with scents of smoke, meat, and black olive. Balanced and taut, the wine is still quite young, but is already supple and delicious, with a long life (15-20 years) ahead. **91** —*P.G.* *(7/1/2004)*

K Vintners 2003 Morrison Lane Syrah (Walla Walla (WA)) $45. Thick and jammy, this popular bottling is solid and flavorful, packed with Syrah fruit flavors and plenty of chocolatey oak. A big boy, a bit monolithic but strong. **89** —*P.G.* *(12/15/2005)*

K Vintners 2001 Morrison Lane Syrah (Walla Walla (WA)) $45. Every "K" Syrah has a raison d'etre. In this instance, there is a meaty power under the blocky fruit, mitigated with some pleasant barrel flavors of cracker and cocoa. You can drink it young, or wait for it to pull itself together, with equal enjoyment. **91** —*P.G.* *(5/1/2004)*

K Vintners 2001 Pepper Bridge Syrah (Walla Walla (WA)) $45. A lot of people buy Pepper Bridge fruit, but no one makes a better Syrah from it than Charles Smith. Taut, spicy, young, and aggressive, this bold wine is like a day of windsurfing. You feel as if you are on the edge of something big, barely holding on. It's a breath of fresh air, a slap in the face that wakes up the palate. **92** —*P.G.* *(5/1/2004)*

K Vintners 2002 The Beautiful Syrah (Walla Walla (WA)) $30. The best of a gorgeous lineup from K, this distinctive, extremely floral and complex wine is both profound and elegant. The high-toned floral bouquet leads into flavors that perfectly mix flowers and fruits, with a lingering, fascinating and unforgettable finish. **93** —*P.G.* *(7/1/2004)*

K Vintners 2003 El Jefe–En Chamberlin Vineyard Red Tempranillo-Cabernet Sauvignon (Walla Walla (WA)) $55. Another vineyard owned by Cayuse's Christophe Baron, it delivers intense, focused, concentrated, full-flavored fruit from which this Tempranillo-Cabernet blend is crafted. Dried fruits, citrus, green berries, and notes of candied pineapple, lime slices, and even ham drift across the palate in an amazing progression of delightful surprises. **93** —*P.G.* *(12/15/2005)*

K Vintners 2004 Viognier (Columbia Valley (WA)) $20. A sweet nose of flowers, passion fruit, pears, and perfume leads into a plump, floral/citrus evocation of the grape, kissed lightly with vanilla. **90** —*P.G.* *(12/15/2005)*

KAAT

KAAT 1996 Pisoni Vineyard Pinot Noir (Santa Lucia Highlands) $NA. Has a bit of veggie on the nose, but tastes similar to the '96 Pisoni. Full-bodied and fruity, with black-cherry, sweet tobacco, coffee, cola, and dusty, peppery spice flavors. (Non-commercial bottling) **90** —*S.H.* *(6/1/2005)*

KAHN

Kahn 2001 Avelina Winery Merlot (Santa Ynez Valley) $15. Rustic and heavy, with berry-cherry flavors and some astringency through the finish. Tannins are pronounced and thick. Drinks like a country-style wine, although it has no flaws. **84** —*S.H.* *(12/1/2003)*

Kahn 1999 Cuvée Jacques Red Blend (Santa Barbara County) $20. The aromas are wild berries and smoke, with raisiny, burnt notes. In the mouth, it's light on fruit, but firmly tannic and alcoholic. A pleasant, country-style wine that is a blend of 75% Grenache and 25% Syrah. **83** —*S.H.* *(11/15/2001)*

Kahn 2003 Sauvignon Blanc (Santa Ynez Valley) $18. Utterly without flavor, like watery alcohol with a drop of lemon juice. **82** —*S.H.* *(5/1/2005)*

Kahn 2001 Sauvignon Blanc (Santa Ynez Valley) $15. Rather soft and candied, a ripely fruity wine with semi-sweet Lifesaver flavors of lemon and lime. Feels a bit heavy in the mouth, lacking acidity and zest. **84** —*S.H.* *(10/1/2003)*

Kahn 2000 Sauvignon Blanc (Santa Ynez Valley) $16. Unless you just love oak, this one is way too woody. Buttered toast, creamed corn, and popcorn aromas are seconded on the palate by thick, cloying buttery flavors and very little fruit. Not appealing. **82** *(8/1/2002)*

Kahn 2002 Syrah (Santa Ynez Valley) $30. A very good Syrah, full-bodied and warming, but dry. It shows dark stone fruit and cocoa flavors with a rich earthiness, and is soft enough to drink now. **88** —*S.H.* *(5/1/2005)*

Kahn 2001 Syrah (Central Coast) $13. Plenty of ripe flavors here, ranging from black-cherries and cocoa through coffee, sage, and dill. The structure is simple, with easy tannins and supportive acids. Seems like a pizza sort of wine. **84** —*S.H.* *(12/15/2003)*

Kahn 2000 Syrah (Santa Ynez Valley) $26. Richer and bigger in every way than Kahn's regular Central Coast bottling. Brims with full-throttle flavors of blackberries and herbs dusted with white pepper, and the tannins are rich and fine. Loses a few points due to an astringent finish. **87** —*S.H.* *(12/1/2003)*

Kahn 1999 Syrah (Santa Barbara County) $29. Very nutty on the nose, with chocolate and carob notes reminiscent of trail mix. Medium- to full-bodied blackberry fruit lies at the core, but the focus is elsewhere: leather, cocoa, dried spices, coffee and peanut were among the descriptors tossed around by our panel. **87** *(11/1/2001)*

Kahn 2002 Colson Canyon Vineyard Syrah (Santa Barbara County) $42. Shows more of a cool-climate influence than the regular Syrah with white pepper aromas and thick tannins. Has a rich melange of blackberry, plum, coffee and tobacco flavors that finish long and harmonious. **91** —*S.H.* *(5/1/2005)*

Kahn 2000 Colson Canyon Vineyard Syrah (Santa Barbara County) $38. Marginally richer and finer than Kahn's Santa Ynez Syrah, with knock-your-sox off flavors of cherries and blackberries that flood the mouth. The tannins are quite thick and melted. Feels plush and velvety through the finish. **89** —*S.H.* *(12/1/2003)*

Kahn 2002 Susich Vineyard Syrah (Santa Ynez Valley) $42. Cedary and toasty, with big, mouthfilling flavors of roasted fruit that pick up hints of pepper and dried spices. But we also found hints of nail polish and dry, woody tannins on the finish. **84** *(9/1/2005)*

KALAMAR

Kalamar 2002 Syrah (Yakima Valley) $30. Tarry and meaty, with flavors that run toward coffee, roast beef and gravy. Some plum fruit pokes through, then bitter tannins clamp down on the finish. **83** *(9/1/2005)*

KALI HART

Kali Hart 2002 Chardonnay (Monterey County) $13. This is an everyday sort of Chard that earns extra credit for ripe, tropical fruit flavors, good acidity and veneer of oak. Thin on the finish, but a good value. **85** —*S.H.* *(10/1/2004)*

Kali Hart 2001 Chardonnay (Monterey County) $12. A "winery within a winery" from Talbott vineyards, and a good value. The intensely ripe tropical fruit flavors have a spicy edge, and have been well oaked and aged on the lees. Before the recent glut, you would have paid a lot more money for a wine of this quality. **88 Best Buy** —*S.H.* *(12/1/2003)*

Kali Hart 2001 Pinot Noir (Monterey County) $14. Soft, gentle and a little cooked. The cherry-berry aromas and flavors have an edge of raisins and Port. Yet the wine is fruity and silky and has some good varietal character. **83** —*S.H.* *(5/1/2004)*

KALLICK

Kallick 1997 Bien Nacido Vineyard Pinot Noir (Santa Maria Valley) $22. **84** *(10/1/1999)*

KALYRA

Kalyra 1997 Buttonwood Farm Vineyard Cabernet Sauvignon (Santa Ynez Valley) $30. Six years of age has not made this into a great wine. It is a hybrid of blackberry and vegetal aromas and flavors that wrestle for supremacy in the mouth. The tannins win. **83** —*S.H.* *(11/15/2003)*

Kalyra 2001 La Presa Vineyard Chardonnay (Santa Ynez Valley) $20. This wine has some ripe flavors of peaches and tropical fruits and is well-oaked. Yet it doesn't come together into a harmonious whole, and there is also a bitter, almond-skin taste. **84** —*S.H.* *(12/31/2003)*

Kalyra 2001 Tucker's Run La Presa Vineyard Syrah (Santa Ynez Valley) $20. A rather earthy and closed wine, and pretty tannic, too. There are some blackberry flavors but the mouthfeel is tough, and the finish turns astringent. May benefit from five years of aging. **85** —*S.H. (3/1/2004)*

KAMEN ESTATE

Kamen Estate 2002 Cabernet Sauvignon (Sonoma Valley) $50. Although a very good wine, this bottling is not in the same league as the sumptuous '01. It's more tannic and less fruity, although the cassis and cherry fruit that's there is delicious. This is one to drink now while your agers are in the cellar. **87** —*S.H. (12/15/2005)*

Kamen Estate 2001 Cabernet Sauvignon (Sonoma Valley) $50. This mountain wine stuns with its intensity. You can taste the sunny concentration in every sip of cherry and black currant fruit. The tannins are a work of art, rich and elaborate and flamboyant, while the acids are tight and balancing. Beautiful right out of the gate, but a guaranteed ager. **92** —*S.H. (10/1/2004)*

KARL LAWRENCE

Karl Lawrence 1997 Cabernet Sauvignon (Napa Valley) $40. 89 *(11/1/2000)*

Karl Lawrence 1996 Cabernet Sauvignon (Napa Valley) $30. 95 —*M.S. (10/1/1999)*

Karl Lawrence 2001 Cabernet Sauvignon (Napa Valley) $50. This is a big, dry, plush, ripe, and very fine Cabernet, but it's an infant in serious need of time. There are numbing tannins that frame deliciously sweet black-cherry, blackberry, and herb flavors. Try after 2010. **92 Cellar Selection** —*S.H. (10/1/2004)*

KARLY

Karly 1997 Marsanne (Amador County) $20. 87 —*S.H. (6/1/1999)*

Karly 1996 Syrah (Amador County) $20. 84 —*S.H. (6/1/1999)*

Karly 1997 Buck's Ten Point Zinfandel (Amador County) $15. 88 —*P.G. (11/15/1999)*

Karly 2003 Pokerville Zinfandel (Amador County) $12. I love this wine for its smooth, full-bodied exuberance, the way it just takes over the palate and rules. Flavors of wild berries, bitter dark chocolate, and coffee are fat and fleshy, and best of all, totally dry, without being overly alcoholic. This is one of the best Zin buys of the year. **89 Best Buy** —*S.H. (3/1/2006)*

Karly 2002 Pokerville Zinfandel (Amador County) $12. Earthy and peppery, with grilled meat and dried cherry notes. You'll find pleasant cherry flavors in this dry red wine **85** —*S.H. (3/1/2005)*

Karly 1998 Sadie Upton Zinfandel (Amador County) $22. 90 —*S.H. (5/1/2000)*

Karly 2003 Warrior Fires Zinfandel (Amador County) $24. Isn't it funny how sometimes a winery's more expensive wine isn't as good as its less costly one? That's the case here. This wine is hot in alcohol and overripe in raisiny flavors, while Karly's Pokerville, at half the price, is terrific. **84** —*S.H. (3/1/2006)*

Karly 2002 Warrior Fires Zinfandel (Amador County) $24. Rather disjointed, with the alcohol sticking out like a sore thumb, and a musty, sweaty smell. Turns fruity in the mouth. **83** —*S.H. (3/1/2005)*

Karly 1997 Warrior Fires Zinfandel (Amador County) $25. 87 —*P.G. (11/15/1999)*

KARMERE

Karmere 2002 Empress Hayley's Zinfandel (Shenandoah Valley (CA)) $12. Smells Porty and caramelized, but is bone dry, with astringent tannins and coffee flavors. **83** —*S.H. (3/1/2005)*

KASON

Kason 2002 Barrel Select Pinot Noir (Willamette Valley) $39. Very fragrant, with dried, dusty notes of saddle, barnyard, earth, and fruit leather. Not an elegant wine, but plenty of flavor to it. Drink it up; this one's ready. **87** —*P.G. (8/1/2005)*

KATHRYN HALL VINEYARDS

Kathryn Hall Vineyards 2003 Sacrashe Vineyard Cabernet Sauvignon (Rutherford) $75. What a roll this winery has been on the last several vintages. The '03 is huge, showing masses of forward, classic Cabernet fruit.

Just erupts with dark berry-cherry, plum, boysenberry and coffee flavors with a rich, butterscotchy, gingersnap cookie note. But the tannins bite from this hilly vineyard. Best 2009–2015. **93 Cellar Selection** —*S.H. (12/15/2006)*

Kathryn Hall Vineyards 2002 Sacrashe Vineyard Cabernet Sauvignon (Rutherford) $65. Classic Napa Cabernet, opening with powerful aromas of cherries and cassis, and turning exceptionally lush and long in the mouth. The tremendous fruit flavors and sweet oak come together in a dry, firmly tannic structure that leads to a long, complex finish. Beautiful now and through 2012. **93 Editors' Choice** —*S.H. (12/15/2005)*

Kathryn Hall Vineyards 2001 Sacrashe Vineyard Cabernet Sauvignon (Rutherford) $55. Very big in tannins, a tough, hard wine now, but what fruit! Rich in sweet-sour black and red cherry, plum, milk chocolate, and oak through the long finish. Terrific wine, but should be cellared for maximum enjoyment. Best after 2007. **93 Cellar Selection** —*S.H. (10/1/2004)*

Kathryn Hall Vineyards 2000 Sacrashe Vineyard Cabernet Sauvignon (Rutherford) $50. Big-time Napa Cabernet, delicious and exciting. Fruity aromas of cassis and black currants are swimming in vanilla and spicy smoke from oak aging, and the tannins are soft and ripely sweet. Lacks a bit of concentration and is not an ager, but a beautiful wine now. **90** —*S.H. (3/1/2004)*

Kathryn Hall Vineyards 1999 Sacrashe Vineyard Cabernet Sauvignon (Rutherford) $50. A beautiful, classic wine that showcases the balance and harmony of Rutherford Cabernet. Has a feminine character in the soft, pliant tannins and sumptuous mouthfeel, but there's nothing shy about the currant and olive flavors and the long finish. Big, impressive, and flashy. **94 Editors' Choice** —*S.H. (10/1/2003)*

KATHRYN KENNEDY

Kathryn Kennedy 1997 Cabernet Sauvignon (Santa Cruz Mountains) $120. 90 *(11/1/2000)*

Kathryn Kennedy 1997 Lateral Red Blend (California) $25. 89 —*M.S. (7/1/2000)*

Kathryn Kennedy 2001 Syrah (Santa Cruz County) $36. Cassis and blackberry jam flavors last long on the finish, backed up with thick, hard tannins. Very dry, this is a big, young wine that is drinkable with lamb and other rich dishes but is best left in the cellar for five years. **87** —*S.H. (12/15/2003)*

Kathryn Kennedy 1997 Maridon Vineyard Syrah (Santa Cruz Mountains) $64. 92 —*S.H. (6/1/1999)*

KAUTZ

Kautz 1997 Library Collection Chardonnay (California) $15. 85 *(6/1/2000)*

KAZMER & BLAISE

Kazmer & Blaise 2002 Primo's Hill Pinot Noir (Carneros) $36. Here's a big, bright wine with attractive aromas of pepper, cherry, pine needle, and plums. It's medium-bodied, with vibrant acidity framing spicy, plummy fruit. Finishes long and dry. **89** *(11/1/2004)*

Kazmer & Blaise 2001 Primo's Hill Pinot Noir (Carneros) $42. From Acacia winemaker Michael Terrien, a personal project and a very fine wine. It possesses its appellation's character of silky tannins, crisp acids, and upfront, jammy fruit. Cherries, coffee, tobacco, and herbs flood the palate, with enough body to suggest roast duck or lamb chops. **90** —*S.H. (4/1/2004)*

Kazmer & Blaise 2000 Primo's Hill Pinot Noir (Carneros) $42. Michael Blaise Terrien is the winemaker at Acacia, but this is his private project, with vineyard owner Peter Kazmer Molnar. The wine starts with white pepper, but is distinctly Pinot-esque in the silky mouthfeel. The fruit is very pure, tantalizing, with a come-hither tease, and restates the case for Carneros as serious Pinot country. **92** —*S.H. (2/1/2003)*

KEEGAN

Keegan 1997 Chardonnay (Knights Valley) $28. 90 *(6/1/2000)*

Keegan 2000 Chardonnay (Russian River Valley) $32. Interesting and compelling. Somehow the wine combines unctuous tropical fruit flavors with a crisp minerality. The whole of it is wrapped in rich, toasty oak, and there is quite a bit of acidity. One of the more food-friendly Chardonnays of the vintage. **91** —S.H. (7/1/2003)

Keegan 2002 Buena Tierra Vineyard Chardonnay (Russian River Valley) $38. Richer upfront pineapple and savory white peach flavors than Keegan's Ritchie bottling, and with similar oak, it's a more forward, palate-flattering wine, and a softer one, as well. Made in the popular style, this is a real crowd-pleaser. **90** —S.H. (5/1/2005)

Keegan 2002 Ritchie Vineyard Chardonnay (Russian River Valley) $38. Smoky char, vanilla, and buttered toast flavors flood the mouth. But dried citrus peel, tropical mango, and ripe peach hit midpalate, taking over and lasting through the finish. Very dry and very crisp, this is a beautifully balanced, subtle, food-worthy Chard. **91** —S.H. (5/1/2005)

Keegan 2002 Pinot Noir (Russian River Valley) $34. Nicely captures Pinot's delicacy and silkiness, with easy tannins that carry spicy cherry and oak flavors. This is an elegant wine, although you find yourself wishing it had more stuffing in the middle. **87** —S.H. (5/1/2005)

Keegan 1999 Pinot Noir (Russian River Valley) $48. Deep, sweet almost candied fruit is accented by bacon and saddle leather on the nose of this plump, sensuous wine. Some tasters found the tobacco and horsy notes overbearing, but others praised attractive strawberry and caramel accents. Drink now–2005. **86** (10/1/2002)

Keegan 2002 E Block Pinot Noir (Russian River Valley) $48. The palate impression is of cherries and raspberries baked into pie, with a buttery, flaky, smoky crust and a dusting of cinnamon and brown sugar, all wrapped in silk and satin. Would get a higher score if it had greater intensity and depth of flavor. **89** —S.H. (5/1/2005)

Keegan 1996 Zinfandel (Sonoma County) $24. 93 —M.S. (9/1/1999)

KEENAN

Keenan 2002 Mernet Reserve Bordeaux Blend (Spring Mountain) $79. There's a disconnect between Keenan's '02 Reserve Merlot, a gorgeous wine, and this 50-50 blend of Merlot and Cabernet Sauvignon. The wine has a cooked sweetness that, combined with softness, is rustic. It must have been the Cabernet. Stick with the Merlot. **84** —S.H. (7/1/2006)

Keenan 1995 Cabernet Sauvignon (Napa Valley) $27. 91 —S.H. (2/1/2000)

Keenan 2002 Cabernet Sauvignon (Napa Valley) $40. Keenan is on Spring Mountain, and while it's not clear if the grapes are from there, this Cab tastes mountainy. It's young and tight in tannins, but with an enormously rich core of cassis and cherry fruit. The dry balance suggests ageability. Hold until 2007, and should drink well through this decade. **90** —S.H. (10/1/2006)

Keenan 2000 Cabernet Sauvignon (Napa Valley) $39. This pure, focused wine has class to spare. Fills the mouth with a velvety smoothness that's perfectly balanced. At the same time, it possesses oodles of rich, ripe black currant flavor. Simply yummy. **91** —S.H. (6/1/2004)

Keenan 1998 Cabernet Sauvignon (Napa Valley) $40. Pleasingly focused with smoky cassis and blackberry flavors that are followed by licorice and herb notes. Tangy on the finish, the wine is framed in smooth tannins. **88** —J.M. (6/1/2002)

Keenan 1997 Cabernet Sauvignon (Napa Valley) $36. 92 (11/1/2000)

Keenan 1996 Cabernet Sauvignon (Napa Valley) $36. Chocolate, cedar, plum, and black-cherries come to mind in this firm-textured wine. Powdery tannins are slightly drying on the palate, though the wine shows good structure in general. The finish is moderate, hinting at sage and blackberry. **87** —J.M. (12/1/2001)

Keenan 2001 25th Anniversary Cabernet Sauvignon (Napa Valley) $39. Here's a fruity, soft Cab that shows its vintage conditions in the ripe cassis and currant flavors that ride high over the blackberries, cherries, and herbs. It's well-balanced, with soft tannins and smoky oak. **88** —S.H. (11/15/2005)

Keenan 2002 Reserve Cabernet Sauvignon (Spring Mountain) $89. My first impression was how sweet and soft this wine is. But it's not really sweet, just ripe in jammy fruit and young, caramelly oak. It's also pretty tannic. Keenan's regular '02 is actually more rewarding, and I don't think this rather ungainly Reserve will surpass it. **85** —S.H. (12/1/2006)

Keenan 1998 Chardonnay (Napa Valley) $18. 84 (6/1/2000)

Keenan 1997 Chardonnay (Napa Valley) $18. 87 —S.H. (2/1/2000)

Keenan 2004 Chardonnay (Spring Mountain) $25. Chardonnay from Napa mountains? Yes. The wine is tightly packed and nervy, as far from a fat, opulent Chard as you can imagine. Thoroughly dry, with a minerality behind the citrus flavors, which suggests aging in a cool cellar for a good decade. **90 Cellar Selection** —S.H. (7/1/2006)

Keenan 2003 Chardonnay (Spring Mountain) $24. Simple and earthy, with peach, pear, and sweet oak flavors, and a slightly rough mouthfeel. Finishes with an awkward sweetness. **84** —S.H. (6/1/2005)

Keenan 2002 Chardonnay (Napa Valley) $22. A little on the lean side, but there's enough apple and peach fruit to satisfy. Oak adds the usual notes. This crisp, tart wine is very clean and will be good with shellfish. **86** — S.H. (6/1/2004)

Keenan 1999 Chardonnay (Napa Valley) $22. Quite bright on the palate, with tangy lemon and mineral notes at the fore. This is a bracing Chardonnay, very lean and refreshing, with lime and herb flavors on the clean finish. **87** —J.M. (11/15/2001)

Keenan 1996 Merlot (Napa Valley) $24. 89 —S.H. (3/1/2000)

Keenan 2003 Merlot (Napa Valley) $34. Made mostly from the winery's Spring Mountain estate, with some fruit from Carneros. The cherries, green olives and smoky oak are offset by hefty tannins, leading to a bone-dry, somewhat austere finish. The wine has elegance, but not opulence. Drink now. **85** —S.H. (12/31/2006)

Keenan 2002 Merlot (Napa Valley) $32. Here's a fine Merlot that needs a little while to calm down. Already it's an intense wine, complex in fruit, oak, coffee and dried herb flavors, and as gentle and soft as it is, the tannins keep things firm and edgy. Best through 2007. **88** —S.H. (6/1/2006)

Keenan 1999 Merlot (Napa Valley) $30. A dark, textured wine, with deep seated blackberry, black-cherry, cassis and herb flavors. Tannins are smooth and firm, with a good solid finish. **89** —J.M. (12/31/2003)

Keenan 2001 25th Anniversary Merlot (Napa-Carneros) $25. This wine drinks a bit lean and austere, especially considering the vintage and neighborhood. The primary flavors veer toward herbs, tobacco, plums and coffee, backed up by hefty tannins and an overlay of oak. It's very dry. **85** —S.H. (6/1/2004)

Keenan 2003 Mailbox Vineyard Reserve Merlot (Spring Mountain) $58. A mountain wine, too tannic for early drinking, as it shuts down the palate with dry astringency. But it's all there for aging. With a rich heart of blackberry and cherry fruit, the wine should come into its own after 2009. **91** —S.H. (12/31/2006)

Keenan 2002 Reserve Merlot (Spring Mountain) $56. Keenan's 2002 regular is very good. The Reserve emulates all its fine qualities and far exceeds it in richness. This is a soft yet complex wine, rich in supple tannins, with extraordinary flavors of blackberry-laced espresso and pure, dark unsweetened chocolate. As dry as it is, the finish is as sweet as crème de cassis. **94 Editors' Choice** —S.H. (6/1/2006)

Keenan 2000 Reserve Merlot (Spring Mountain) $48. One of the best Merlots of the vintage, a rich, sumptuous wine that excites due to its impressive components. Complex blackcurrant, cassis, mocha, herb and smoky oak flavors flood the palate, while tannins and acidity rein it all in. An exciting experience, and gets even better with a few hours of air. **93** —S.H. (6/1/2004)

Keenan 1998 Reserve Merlot (Napa Valley) $30. Starts off strong in the nose, with dark plum and smoke aromas. But it falters a bit on the palate with an unusually bright, tangy edge to the blackberry and licorice hues. Tannins are somewhat powdery, with a hint of tartness on the finish. **85** —J.M. (6/1/2002)

Keenan 1999 Mernet Merlot-Cabernet Sauvignon (Napa Valley) $75. This Merlot/Cabernet blend (hence, Mernet) serves up fairly exuberant aromas. It's quite smoky and rich, full-bodied, with big, ripe tannins and layers of cassis, blackberry, anise, toast and coffee flavors. Long at the end. **91** —J.M. (11/15/2003)

Keenan 2000 Reserve Mernet Merlot-Cabernet Sauvignon (Napa Valley) $65. No, a Mernet is not something you trawl for mermaids with, it's Keenan's 50-50 blend, where Merlot's fleshy opulence has been tempered with more tannic Cabernet. The result is a firm wine that will soften and develop complexity by 2006. **89** —*S.H. (4/1/2004)*

Keenan 2001 Mernet Reserve Red Blend (Napa Valley) $75. Easy to drink for its soft richness, yet complex in structure, this well-oaked wine has ripe flavors of cherry liqueur, black raspberries, and white chocolate, with a peppery, spicy finish. The acidity is refreshing. Merlot and the two Cabernets, in case you couldn't figure it out from the proprietary name. **92** —*S.H. (2/1/2005)*

KEEVER

Keever 2003 Cabernet Sauvignon (Yountville) $60. This 100% Cabernet is very pure and elegant in cherry and cassis flavors. The tannins are sturdy and thick, but the mouthfeel is lighter in weight than Cabs from Oakville or Rutherford. In fact, elegance and finesse really are the hallmarks of this wine. Best now and through 2010. **90** —*S.H. (8/1/2006)*

KELHAM

Kelham 2000 Cabernet Sauvignon (Oakville) $45. From an estate vineyard next to Martha's and Opus One and just down the hill from Harlan, this Cab shows the true grace and harmony of its terroir. Well-ripened black currant fruit is framed in rich oak and offset by firm, sweet tannins. **92** —*S.H. (11/15/2004)*

Kelham 1999 Cabernet Sauvignon (Oakville) $45. Rich and nuanced, with ripe black currant and plum flavors. The tannins are dry and refined, accompanied by refreshing acidity. There's great structure and elegance to this wine, which shows its appellation's terroir well. **90** —*S.H. (2/1/2003)*

Kelham 2000 Reserve Cabernet Sauvignon (Oakville) $75. From hillside blocks in a prime Oakville location, this Cab is oakier and considerably more concentrated than Kelham's regular '00. It's loaded upfront with cassis, black currant, red cherry, and oaky flavors, and has rich, firm tannins. Drink now through 2010. **92** —*S.H. (11/1/2005)*

Kelham 1999 Reserve Cabernet Sauvignon (Oakville) $75. Deep, dark, brooding, and delicious, a massive young Cabernet brimming with ripe flavors and superb tannins. A solid dose of toasty oak frames complex flavors of chocolate, herbs, blackberries, coffee, and spice. The long, sweet finish is impressive. **93** —*S.H. (2/1/2003)*

Kelham 2001 Merlot (Oakville) $45. Grapes for this very distinctive Merlot used to go to Duckhorn. The wine is soft and sensual, showing red and black-cherry fruit, with an edge of cocoa, and robust but sweet tannins. Should hold well for six years. **92** —*S.H. (11/1/2005)*

Kelham 1999 Merlot (Oakville) $45. Very dry, with plum, cherry, and blackberry flavors, and hints of green olives, fresh herbs, and tobacco. Has a great, sexy structure, with dusty tannins. Long on the finish. This is a wine for the cellar, although it's beautiful now. **93 Editors' Choice** — *S.H. (2/1/2003)*

Kelham 2000 Sauvignon Blanc (Oakville) $22. A strongly flavored wine, grown in a high-rent Napa district. Fifty percent new French oak shows up in the aromas of toast, caramel, and vanilla. The underlying fruit tastes of citrus and white peach. Finishes dry and clean. **90** —*S.H. (3/1/2003)*

KELLER

Keller 2004 La Cruz Vineyard Chardonnay (Sonoma Coast) $29. Take Keller's unoaked Chard, add some well-toasted new French oak, and you get this rich version. The oak stars, putting out buttered toast, crème brûlée, and vanilla spice flavors. Down under all that is a wealth of tropical fruit, peach, and green apple flavors. **90** —*S.H. (12/31/2006)*

Keller 2005 Oro de Plata Chardonnay (Sonoma Coast) $22. Here's a stainless steel-fermented Chard that features nothing but cool-climate varietal flavor. It's a floral wine, reminiscent of unoaked New Zealand Chardonnay, with overtones of kiwi, lime, nectarine, and vanilla, accented by bright acidity. **88** —*S.H. (12/31/2006)*

KELTIE BROOK

Keltie Brook 1998 Merlot (California) $13. 87 Best Buy —*J.C. (7/1/2000)*

KEMPTON CLARK

Kempton Clark 2001 Zinfandel (California) $10. Smooth textured, with spicy nuances and blackberry, raspberry, cola, tea, and herb flavors. The tannins are ripe and firm and the finish is good. **86 Best Buy** *(11/1/2003)*

Kempton Clark 1997 Lopez Ranch Zinfandel (Cucamonga Valley) $18. 83 —*P.G. (11/15/1999)*

Kempton Clark 1998 Mad Zin Zinfandel (Dunnigan Hills) $10. From this Delta appellation east of San Francisco, a workhorse Zin. Smells sharp, with clove notes, but there are some rich berry flavors in the mouth. It's also dry, low in acids, and with some dusty tannins. Everyday stuff, spirited and clean, at a very nice price. **84** —*S.H. (3/1/2002)*

Kempton Clark 1997 Mad Zin Zinfandel (California) $12. 81 —*P.G. (11/15/1999)*

KEN BROWN

Ken Brown 2003 Bien Nacido Vineyard Pinot Noir (Santa Maria Valley) $30. The scent of this wine is all about Pinot's allure, with rich, ripe notes of cherry tart and rhubarb pie, mouthwatering vanilla and crushed spice, and fine, toasted oak. With the first taste, it doesn't disappoint. With the second, it addicts. It's light-bodied and silky, not an ager, but seriously elegant. **92** —*S.H. (12/31/2005)*

Ken Brown 2003 Syrah (Santa Barbara County) $28. Veteran winemaker Ken Brown, lately of Mondavi-owned Io, has his own new brand. This Syrah is clearly cool-climate, with peppery aromas, thick tannins, and bone-dry flavors of dark stone fruits. It's not an undisputed success, but is a wine worth following. **87** —*S.H. (12/31/2005)*

KEN WRIGHT

Ken Wright 2004 Celilo Vineyard Chardonnay (Washington) $25. Ken Wright is one of more than a dozen winemakers sourcing fruit from this exceptional vineyard. These 30-year-old Chardonnay vines are some of the oldest in the Northwest. Here they display substantial lime and citrus flavors, whiffs of honeysuckle and clover, light peach and some buttery richness in the finish. **90** —*P.G. (5/1/2006)*

Ken Wright 2004 Pinot Blanc (Washington) $25. Rarely does Pinot Blanc generate much excitement in the U.S., but this fragrant, beguiling mix of pears, apples, and white peaches, laced with floral scents and finished with leesy creaminess, is a gem. Excellent concentration and length, along with some noticeable residual sugar—just right for spicy Asian food or pork loin with fruit sauce. **92 Editors' Choice** —*P.G. (5/1/2006)*

Ken Wright 2004 Abbott Claim Pinot Noir (Willamette Valley) $50. Strikingly original, with subtle flavors of citrus, juniper, pine needle, dried herbs, and mint. Harvested at less than one ton an acre, this distinctive, compelling wine is built around tart cranberry fruit. Long, penetrating, and persistent. **94** —*P.G. (5/1/2006)*

Ken Wright 2004 Canary Hill Pinot Noir (Willamette Valley) $50. Forward, tart, and spicy, the Canary Hill's tangy red fruit is lifted with light citrus—lime and grapefruit. Nicely balanced and moderate in length. **90** —*P.G. (5/1/2006)*

Ken Wright 2004 Carter Pinot Noir (Willamette Valley) $50. The Carter has an appealing softness in the mouth; it's almost airy, but not thin or dull in any way. Cranberry/cherry fruit seems to float above pillowy tannins, with just a bare hint of mint in the finish. Light and delicate. **91** —*P.G. (5/1/2006)*

Ken Wright 2004 Freedom Hill Pinot Noir (Willamette Valley) $50. The Freedom Hill is the biggest of all the Ken Wright Pinots, except possibly the Shea. Tannic and leathery, this has a distinct streak of coffee grounds running all through it. Gutsy and potentially the longest lived. **93** —*P.G. (5/1/2006)*

Ken Wright 2004 Guadalupe Pinot Noir (Willamette Valley) $50. Full, rich, and big, with cherries and plums, buttered nuts and vanilla. It's ripe and varietal, beautifully structured and compared with previous vintages, reined in just a bit. **92** —*P.G. (5/1/2006)*

Ken Wright 2004 McCrone Pinot Noir (Willamette Valley) $50. Lovely nose, scented with violets, sweet candy, and rose petals. The flavors balance citrus oil, pineapple, pomegranate, and red cherries, detailed and nicely balanced. But there is a note of plastic or Band-aid that creeps into the finish; otherwise this would be rated significantly higher. **89** —*P.G.* *(5/1/2006)*

Ken Wright 2004 Nysa Pinot Noir (Willamette Valley) $50. Pretty, spicy scents of berry and cranberry mix with sweet plum on the palate. Lovely, aromatic, and sweet, this young wine needs a little more time than its stable mates; it's still a bit yeasty and tight. But very nicely made and balanced. **90** —*P.G.* *(5/1/2006)*

Ken Wright 2004 Savoya Pinot Noir (Willamette Valley) $50. From a Ken Wright-owned vineyard, the Savoya is a lighter style, sprinkled with fresh whiffs of basil, thyme, and rosemary, and hints of pine needle. An elegant, almost delicate, wine. **91** —*P.G.* *(5/1/2006)*

Ken Wright 1999 Shea Vineyard Pinot Noir (Yamhill County) $40. Wright's single-vineyard Pinots are released very young, and rarely show their best for a year or two, but this one scores right out of the starting gate. With its smooth attack of blackberries and chocolate, plump flesh and round, forward fruit flavors, it's instantly likeable. But given the innate balance of the high-acid 1999 vintage, it should have many good years ahead. **92** —*P.G.* *(11/1/2001)*

KENDALL-JACKSON

Kendall-Jackson 2001 Stature Bordeaux Blend (Napa Valley) $95. This Bordeaux blend is certainly an oaky wine. It's made in a fruit-forward style, and seems lusher, softer and more accessible than K-J's other new release, Highlands Estates Cabernets from Sonoma County. Of course, it's also more than four years old now. It's a really good wine, with a flashy opulence that makes it appealing. **90** —*S.H.* *(5/1/2006)*

Kendall-Jackson 2001 Cabernet Sauvignon (California) $15. Rich and fruity, a textbook North Coast Cab. The flavors of black-cherry, coffee, herbs, and a smattering of smoky oak are well balanced with firm tannins and good acidity. **86** —*S.H.* *(10/1/2004)*

Kendall-Jackson 1997 Buckeye Vineyard Cabernet Sauvignon (Sonoma County) $45. **90** *(11/1/2000)*

Kendall-Jackson 1997 Elite Cabernet Sauvignon (Napa Valley) $100. **91** *(11/1/2000)*

Kendall-Jackson 2001 Grand Reserve Cabernet Sauvignon (California) $26. Jess Jackson continues his quest for the perfect blended wine. This combination of Napa, Sonoma, and Mendocino is quite hefty in astringent tannins. Beneath that is a rich core of sweet black-cherry fruit. It seems designed for the cellar. Best after 2007. **90** —*S.H.* *(6/1/2004)*

Kendall-Jackson 1997 Grand Reserve Cabernet Sauvignon (California) $60. **93** *(11/1/2000)*

Kendall-Jackson 1996 Grand Reserve Cabernet Sauvignon (California) $74. **89** *(2/1/2000)*

Kendall-Jackson 2002 Grand Reserve Sonoma-Napa-Mendocino Counties Cabernet Sauvignon (California) $26. Very tannic now, and dusty dry, so you might want to hang onto it for a while, or try with something rich and fatty. The fruit is good, suggesting blackberries and coffee. **85** —*S.H.* *(10/1/2005)*

Kendall-Jackson 1999 Great Estates Cabernet Sauvignon (Napa Valley) $40. Mainly from Rutherford, a beautiful wine. Opens with alluring aromas of black currant and cassis and the lilting perfume of new French oak, with its smoky vanillins. In the mouth, supple and polished, long on Cabernet flavor, with rich, sumptuous tannins. The tannins are already melted, making it drinkable now. **92** —*S.H.* *(11/15/2003)*

Kendall-Jackson 1999 Great Estates Cabernet Sauvignon (Alexander Valley) $40. The flavors are herbal and tobaccoey, with only faint traces of fruit, and the texture is flaccid. Alexander Valley can produce a far better Cabernet. **85** —*S.H.* *(11/15/2003)*

Kendall-Jackson 1998 Great Estates Cabernet Sauvignon (Napa Valley) $49. Darker than the Alexander Valley bottling, and richer in fruit, with powerful black currants blasting from the glass. The structure is better, too, with beautiful Napa tannins that have the deceptive simplicy of the Bauhaus. A notable success for the vintage. **90** —*S.H.* *(12/31/2002)*

Kendall-Jackson 1998 Great Estates Cabernet Sauvignon (Alexander Valley) $49. Beautiful red wine, deep, dark, and juicy. There's drama in the rich aromas of cassis, perfumed with smoky oak, and the sumptuous

texture. It glides like velvet over the palate, carrying black currant flavors. Could use a tad more depth. **88** —*S.H.* *(12/31/2002)*

Kendall-Jackson 1997 Great Estates Cabernet Sauvignon (Alexander Valley) $45. Begins with inviting black currant and cassis aromas and notes of dark chocolate, smoke, and plums. There's a voluptuous, seductive texture with velvety smoothness, and the flavors are of perfectly ripened berries framed in vanilla-tinged oak. Soft and complex with a stylish finish, this beauty is ready to drink now. **92** —*S.H.* *(12/1/2001)*

Kendall-Jackson 2003 Hawkeye Mountain Cabernet Sauvignon (Alexander Valley) $50. From one of the highest vineyards in the Sonoma Mayacamas comes this profoundly structured, deeply tannic Cab, which also is quite oaky. Bone dry and relatively closed and astringent, it's of very fine quality, and desperately needs time. Twenty years isn't out of the question to allow the nuclear core of blackberries and cherries to unfurl. **93 Cellar Selection** —*S.H.* *(5/1/2006)*

Kendall-Jackson 2002 Hawkeye Mountain Estate Cabernet Sauvignon (Sonoma County) $45. From a high mountain vineyard over the Alexander Valley, a wine of extraordinarily tough tannins. The wine is clearly built for the cellar. Deep down you'll find a solid core of well-ripened cherry fruit, but it's basically undrinkable now. It could blossom into greatness, however, after 2010. **91** —*S.H.* *(8/1/2004)*

Kendall-Jackson 2003 Highlands Estate Napa Mountain Cabernet Sauvignon (Mount Veeder) $50. Only 300 cases were made of this serious mountain wine. It's tough as nails now, filled with tannins and acids, and everything's shut down in the driest way. Deep down there is amazing fruit and authority. This 100% Cabernet will live for two decades, but if you must open it anytime soon, it needs serious decanting and the richest, most imperial foods. **92 Cellar Selection** —*S.H.* *(5/1/2006)*

Kendall-Jackson 1999 Stature Cabernet Sauvignon (Napa Valley) $100. Offers a smooth, creamy mouthfeel and a red plum-fruit core, with caramel and tobacco accents. Aromas are of figs and Indian spices; one reviewer found the fruit a bit candied. This is a very good Cab, drinkable in the near term, though not one that necessarily merits such a lofty price tag. Finishes with bitter chocolate. **88** *(8/1/2003)*

Kendall-Jackson 2003 Trace Ridge Cabernet Sauvignon (Knights Valley) $50. From mountain vineyards comes this deep, dark, impressively intense Cab. Opens with a blast of new oaky smoke, char, and vanilla, but once in the mouth, huge waves of flamboyant blackberry and cassis, black-cherry and vanilla oak flavors unfold, with a meaty note. The wine is totally dry and balanced, and while it's drinkable now, it should improve through 2015. **94 Cellar Selection** —*S.H.* *(5/1/2006)*

Kendall-Jackson 2003 Vintner's Reserve Cabernet Sauvignon (Sonoma-Napa-Mendocino) $18. There's plenty of ripe Cabernet flavor in this succulent wine. Cherries, raspberries, and blueberries are supported by fine, expressive tannins and crisp acidity, leading to a dry, spicy finish. **86** —*S.H.* *(11/15/2006)*

Kendall-Jackson 2002 Vintner's Reserve Cabernet Sauvignon (Napa-Mendocino-Sonoma) $16. This is a pretty nice, average Cabernet, dry and balanced, with good fruit flavors. It's a little pricy for what you get, though, and is marred by a bitterness in the finish. **84** —*S.H.* *(12/31/2005)*

Kendall-Jackson 2001 Vintner's Reserve Cabernet Sauvignon (California) $16. There are some nice, smooth tannins in this wine, but it's a little raisiny. Turns hot and sandpapery on the finish. **84** —*S.H.* *(10/1/2005)*

Kendall-Jackson 2000 Vintner's Reserve Cabernet Sauvignon (California) $16. This is a pretty good Cab, with polished flavors of blackberries, cherries, dried herbs, and coffee. The tannins are smooth and chunky, leading to a slightly astringent finish. **86** —*S.H.* *(6/1/2004)*

Kendall-Jackson 1997 Vintner's Reserve Cabernet Sauvignon (Calaveras County) $17. **88** —*S.H.* *(12/15/2000)*

Kendall-Jackson 1996 Vintner's Reserve Cabernet Sauvignon (California) $21. **86** *(2/1/2000)*

Kendall-Jackson 2001 Collage Cabernet Sauvignon-Merlot (California) $10. Marked by exceedingly ripe fruit, this wine explodes with sweet blackberry, cherry, and chocolate flavors. It has a smooth mouthfeel and a soft finish. **84** —*S.H.* *(6/1/2005)*

Kendall-Jackson 2000 Collage Cabernet Sauvignon-Merlot (California) $9. Pretty good for the price. There are some nice, deep berry fruit flavors, and the wine is very dry, with soft, approachable tannins. Drinks rough and country-style, but it's clean and gulpable enough for everyday occasions. **84** —*S.H. (6/1/2002)*

Kendall-Jackson 2000 Collage Cabernet Sauvignon-Shiraz (California) $9. A new, Aussie-style line from K-J, a series of varietal blends. This wine is a little too stewed and overripe, with raisiny, pruny aromas and flavors. The finish is a bit jammy and treacly, but it's not a bad casual sipper. **83** —*S.H. (9/1/2002)*

Kendall-Jackson 1999 Collage Cabernet Sauvignon-Shiraz (California) $9. A brand new line from K-J. This very attractive wine has lush fruit and spice flavors, with maximum extract. Tannins and acids all are adequate. What K-J seems to be aiming for is a new flavor, neither Cabernet nor Syrah but in-between, and they've succeeded. Yes, it's simple and uncomplicated, but there's plenty of pleasure for the money. **86 Best Buy** —*S.H. (5/1/2001)*

Kendall-Jackson 2001 20th Harvest Release Chardonnay (California) $16. The underlying flavors are of tart green apples, with a bite of acidity. Despite barrel fermentation, oak stays in the background of this very dry wine. **87** —*S.H. (12/15/2002)*

Kendall-Jackson 2001 Camelot Bench Chardonnay (Santa Maria Valley) $17. Tropical fruit flavors (particularly papaya) make the wine bright and crisp on the palate. Those same acids prevail over efforts to soften, including barrel and malolactic fermentation and lees aging, so that the wine maintains a steely, hard backbone. It is not lush, but it is intense. **89** —*S.H. (12/1/2003)*

Kendall-Jackson 2002 Camelot Highlands Estate Chardonnay (Santa Barbara County) $25. Leesy and custardy, with melon and lime flavors accented by toast. Rich and weighty; finishes with caramel. **90** *(3/1/2004)*

Kendall-Jackson 2002 Camelot Highlands Estate Chardonnay (Santa Barbara County) $25. Here's a Chard with great interest and distinction. Strikes the mouth with a mineral and steel firmness that's sleek and streamlined, but then a rich tone of sweet tropical fruits, vanilla, and buttered toast bursts on the palate. The pineapple and mango is very intense, and coats the tongue through a long finish. Nervy, balanced, and quite delicious. **91** —*S.H. (8/1/2004)*

Kendall-Jackson 1999 Camelot Vineyard Chardonnay (Santa Maria Valley) $17. From one of the best Chardonnay regions in the state, a cool-climate wine with pronounced peach, apple, and tropical fruit flavors and a blast of zesty, spicy, smoky oak. Clean and crisp, with a creamy, rich texture. Finishes with a vanilla note. The package is marred by too much sugar; consumers love sweetness, but this one takes things a little too far. **85** —*S.H. (5/1/2001)*

Kendall-Jackson 1998 Camelot Vineyard Chardonnay (Santa Maria Valley) $17. **90** *(6/1/2000)*

Kendall-Jackson 2004 Grand Reserve Chardonnay (Monterey-Santa Barbara) $20. A huge, complex wine that flatters the palate with enormously rich, layered flavors of lemondrop, vanilla custard, and butterscotch flavors. Fortunately, there's crisp Central Coast acidity. **90** —*S.H. (4/1/2006)*

Kendall-Jackson 2003 Grand Reserve Chardonnay (California) $20. There are some apple and peach flavors in this wine, and also a strong citrusy note that lends acidic brilliance to the mouthfeel. There's also an earthy, tobaccoey flavor throughout that might play well off grilled winter root vegetables. **85** —*S.H. (10/1/2005)*

Kendall-Jackson 2002 Grand Reserve Chardonnay (California) $20. Very tart in acidity, this wine from the cooler parts of Monterey, Santa Barbara, and Sonoma has a green, minerally edge to its apple pie flavors. It's well oaked, and long on the spicy finish. Good as a cocktail, or perfect with cracked crab. **89** —*S.H. (6/1/2004)*

Kendall-Jackson 2001 Grand Reserve Chardonnay (California) $20. A blend of Santa Barbara, Monterey, and Sonoma in true K-J style, and very good in a generic sort of way. What it lacks in terroir it makes up for in flamboyantly ripe fruit. Impresses for its lush, creamy texture, layers of smoky oak and long, spicy finish. **91 Editors' Choice** —*S.H. (12/1/2003)*

Kendall-Jackson 1999 Grand Reserve Chardonnay (California) $19. From this very noble vintage comes a bottling that is softer than the Camelot bottling but no less rich and fruity. Filled with tremendous fruit flavors—apples and peaches specifically—and ultraspicy, cinnamon notes from both the grape and the oak. Made in the fashionable style, round and sweet, although it's a little flat and lacks added dimensions. **85** —*S.H. (5/1/2001)*

Kendall-Jackson 1998 Grand Reserve Chardonnay (California) $25. **89** *(6/1/2000)*

Kendall-Jackson 1997 Grand Reserve Chardonnay (California) $26. **86** —*S.H. (7/1/1999)*

Kendall-Jackson 2000 Great Estates Chardonnay (Santa Barbara County) $25. A clean Chard exhibiting rich South Coast characteristics of high acidity and tropical fruit. Oak plays a supporting role and provides a creamy texture. The wine is tight, but should improve. **88** —*S.H. (5/1/2003)*

Kendall-Jackson 2000 Great Estates Chardonnay (Monterey County) $25. A wonderful wine showing lemon and green apple flavors framed by high acidity and some dusty tannins. Highlights the cool climate of the appellation. Steely and minerally on the finish. **89** —*S.H. (5/1/2003)*

Kendall-Jackson 2000 Great Estates Chardonnay (Arroyo Seco) $25. A fresh, vibrant wine that displays lemon and tart green apple flavors and a great heap of acid. Steely and clean, it cleanses the mouth. Try cellaring for a year or two and see what happens. **88** —*S.H. (5/1/2003)*

Kendall-Jackson 1999 Great Estates Chardonnay (Arroyo Seco) $35. Bright pear, peach, pineapple, ginger snap and floral notes grace a fresh, fragrant nose. The palate's exotic tropical fruit, ginger, and lychee nut flavors mingle beautifully in a medium-full, though perhaps slightly sweet, package. Elegant and appealingly fresh. **91** *(7/1/2001)*

Kendall-Jackson 1999 Great Estates Chardonnay (Sonoma Coast) $22. Held back probably to tame fierce acidity, and it's still a young, lean, tart wine. Fresh, juicy flavors of lemons drink very clean and vibrant, but it's austere stuff. Try with goat cheese on toast. **88** —*S.H. (8/1/2003)*

Kendall-Jackson 1999 Great Estates Chardonnay (Sonoma Valley) $35. This seductive, creamy Chard wraps smoky, spicy, vanilla-laden oak flavors around a core of lush tropical fruit. There's lively acidity and a lot to like here. The finish shows a slight edge that may smooth out in another three or four months. **90** *(7/1/2001)*

Kendall-Jackson 2004 Highland Estates Camelot Highlands Chardonnay (Santa Maria Valley) $30. Here's an intense, nervy wine, brilliantly acidic, layered and rich. It has enormous lemondrop, mango, and pineapple flavors and lots of smoky, vanilla-accented new oaky notes, and is creamy in the mouth. The finish is long, lush, and spicy. This is a real palate flatterer. **92** —*S.H. (5/1/2006)*

Kendall-Jackson 1997 Paradise Vineyard Chardonnay (Arroyo Seco) $17. **87** *(6/1/2000)*

Kendall-Jackson 2004 Seco Highlands Estate Chardonnay (Arroyo Seco) $30. A little softer than K-J's Camelot Highlands, but no less delicious, with similar lemon drop and custard flavors and a tinge of sweet, ripe pear. The mouthfeel is round, creamy, and full-bodied, with a complex veneer of toasty oak. **92** —*S.H. (4/1/2006)*

Kendall-Jackson 2001 Stature Chardonnay (Santa Maria Valley) $60. I drank this wine throughout an entire four course meal and it made everything, from salad to steak to dessert, better, even as it intensified. It's fabulously rich and dry and acidic and complex. The Santa Maria Valley is famous for the tropical fruits and spices this wine shows in spades. **94** —*S.H. (12/1/2004)*

Kendall-Jackson 1998 Stature Chardonnay (Santa Maria Valley) $60. Taste this wine and you'll agree: It's big. Even fat. A fragrant, buttery apple-floral bouquet opens into a banana, orange, and hay palate. The mouthfeel is creamy, round, and lively—it's full-flavored without being too weighty. Pear and butterscotch linger on the finish. **90** *(7/1/2001)*

Kendall-Jackson 2005 Vintner's Reserve Chardonnay (California) $12. The wine that made America fall in love with Chardonnay is still semi-sweet, with a treasure trove of tropical fruit and spice flavors, boosted with creamy oak barrel influence, that's pretty irresistible at this price. Now sourced exclusively from coastal counties, the wine shows a brisk, citrusy acidity. **85** —*S.H. (12/31/2006)*

Kendall-Jackson 2004 Vintner's Reserve Chardonnay (California) $12. K-J is justifiably proud that all the grapes in the VR Chard now come from Jackson estate vineyards. Another change is the wine seems drier than in past years, more balanced. That's a real step forward. **84** —*S.H. (2/1/2006)*

Kendall-Jackson 2002 Vintner's Reserve Chardonnay (California) $12. The wine that made K-J famous is as good as ever, maybe better. Honeysuckle and pear aromas and a slightly oily, sweet mouthfeel are balanced on the finish by tart green apples. **86** *(3/1/2004)*

Kendall-Jackson 2001 Vintner's Reserve Chardonnay (California) $12. Comes across as very oaky, with a blast of charcoal, vanilla, and sweet wood framing peach flavors that are overtly sweet. Below that the wine is basically simple, although it's clean and well-made. **84** —*S.H. (6/1/2003)*

Kendall-Jackson 1999 Vintner's Reserve Chardonnay (California) $11. A simple but likeable Chard, with pretty apple and peach flavors and lots of crushed hard spices, like cinnamon and nutmeg. Has a touch of smoky oak. The K-J style really hasn't changed much over the years: Pick the grapes ripe, keep things slightly sweet and get some wood notes in. **84** —*S.H. (5/1/2001)*

Kendall-Jackson 1998 Vintner's Reserve Chardonnay (California) $12. 85 —*S.H. (11/15/2000)*

Kendall-Jackson 2003 Vintner's Reserve Chardonnay (California) $12. A clean, correct California Chardonnay, reliable as ever. Pear, peach, and citrus flavors go down easily, buffered by graham crackery spice. **85** *(5/1/2005)*

Kendall-Jackson 2002 Stature Meritage (Napa Valley) $120. 92–94 More vibrant that the '01, with anise and herb notes and a lush, chewy texture. black-cherry and spice flavors; long, velvety finish. **93** *(3/1/2004)*

Kendall-Jackson 2001 Stature Meritage (Napa Valley) $120. Already bottled, this wine isn't scheduled to be released until March 2005. If you like your Cabs big, rich, and chewy (and who doesn't?) it's never to early to start badgering your retailer or wholesaler to try to get you some of the 613 cases produced. Toasty notes accent dark chocolate and plum scents, while intense cassis flavors fill the mouth. Sturdy; try after 2006. **93 Cellar Selection** *(3/1/2004)*

Kendall-Jackson 2002 Taylor Peak Estate Merlot (Sonoma County) $35. Made solidly in the style of Jess Jackson's mountain estate wines, a dark, dense Merlot of great intensity and weight. It possesses a laserlike concentration of sweet cassis and cherry fruit that is wrapped in significant tannins. Meets the challenge with such wines and achieves balance and finesse. **92** —*S.H. (12/15/2004)*

Kendall-Jackson 1996 Buckeye Vineyard Merlot (Sonoma County) $33. 86 —*J.C. (7/1/2000)*

Kendall-Jackson 2003 Grand Reserve Merlot (Sonoma-Napa) $26. A first-rate Merlot at a good price for the quality. Dry and complex, with a soft, velvety texture, this supple wine features blackberry, red cherry, cocoa, and sweet dried herb flavors, finished with toasty oak. **91 Editors' Choice** —*S.H. (4/1/2006)*

Kendall-Jackson 2001 Grand Reserve Merlot (California) $26. With a major component from the Anderson Valley, this wine has big tannins that are a little numbing. They frame some rich blackberry and cherry flavors that have notes of vanilla and mocha. Very full-bodied, this wine needs to be cellared through 2005 or even longer. **89** —*S.H. (6/1/2004)*

Kendall-Jackson 1995 Grand Reserve Merlot (California) $47. 89 —*S.H. (3/1/2000)*

Kendall-Jackson 2002 Grand Reserve Sonoma-Mendocino-Napa Counties Merlot (California) $26. This wine is ultrasoft in both acidity and tannins. The flavors are complex, ranging from cherries and tobacco to sweet herbs and oak. But it loses points because it's too soft and could use greater structure. **84** —*S.H. (10/1/2005)*

Kendall-Jackson 1999 Great Estates Merlot (Sonoma County) $35. Tries, with considerable success, to advance the argument that Sonoma is Merlot's natural home. A ripe, rich, plummy wine, with terrific fruit and

superb tannins, easy enough to drink tonight or age a few years. It's so good, you can't help but reach for another glass. **91** —*S.H. (12/31/2002)*

Kendall-Jackson 1998 Great Estates Merlot (Sonoma County) $35. Aromas of smoke, plum, earth, espresso, and blackberry are pleasant. In the mouth, the flavors are terrifically extracted, with pronounced berry and stone-fruit notes that are very dry. It's on the soft side, with velvety tannins. The lip-smacking finish is deliciously spicy. **88** —*S.H. (12/1/2001)*

Kendall-Jackson 1998 Great Estates Merlot (Alexander Valley) $40. Smells rich and chocolaty, with blackberry and plum scents framed in plush smoky oak. You'll like the richly sweet flavors, offering layers of berries and tree fruits, and the lush structure provided by fine, dust tannins. It's overtly soft, with low acidity and very flattering on the palate. **89** —*S.H. (12/1/2001)*

Kendall-Jackson 2003 Highlands Estate Taylor Peak Merlot (Bennett Valley) $40. Only 500 cases were produced of this thick, tannic, complex wine from Sonoma County. It's cellarworthy and hard, dry and astringent now in dense cherry, cassis and mocha flavors that finish with wonderful length and harmony. You can drink it now, but you must adjust for the tannins. Otherwise, cellar until at least 2008. **92 Editors' Choice** —*S.H. (4/1/2006)*

Kendall-Jackson 2002 Piner Hills Estate Merlot (Sonoma County) $35. 89–91 The most powerful of the Estate Merlot samples, it's also the ripest, with mocha and black-cherry flavors. Structured finish. **90** *(3/1/2004)*

Kendall-Jackson 2002 Sable Mountain Estate Merlot (Mendocino) $25. Tannic; chocolate and plum aromas and flavors, and high-toned red fruit. **87** *(3/1/2004)*

Kendall-Jackson 2000 Stature Merlot (Sonoma County) $60. Everything that money can buy has gone into this wine, but it cannot rise above its vintage. It's rich in oak, with firm, rich tannins, and the winemaker squeezed black currant, plum, and tobacco flavors from the grapes. But there's a thinness that leads to a short, astringent finish. **86** —*S.H. (12/15/2004)*

Kendall-Jackson 2002 Taylor Peak Estate Merlot (Bennett Valley) $35. Herbaceous, with basil and oregano atop a tart cherry base. Crisp. **86** *(3/1/2004)*

Kendall-Jackson 2003 Vintner's Reserve Merlot (Sonoma-Napa-Mendocino) $18. At this price VR is treading into high-priced waters, but quality is keeping up. The wine is rich and lush, with a fine balance of dusty tannins, crisp acids and direct blackberry, coffee, and herb flavors. **85** —*S.H. (12/15/2006)*

Kendall-Jackson 2002 Vintner's Reserve Merlot (California) $16. An easy drinking dinner wine, dry and balanced, with smooth tannins and plum, blackberry and coffee flavors. Has a rich, blueberry-muffin taste on the finish. **85** —*S.H. (5/1/2005)*

Kendall-Jackson 2001 Vintner's Reserve Merlot (California) $15. A nice, plummy wine with some real richness. Round, full-bodied, and firm, with a coffee-earthy finish that sets off the fruit. Fairly tannic and very dry. **86** —*S.H. (10/1/2004)*

Kendall-Jackson 2001 Vintner's Reserve Merlot (California) $16. This blend from various parts of California is dry and medium-bodied. It has modest flavors of plums, black-cherries and coffee, and is lightly oaked. Finishes with some richness and complexity. **87** —*S.H. (6/1/2004)*

Kendall-Jackson 2000 Vintner's Reserve Merlot (California) $16. A pleasant sipper with some real depth and varietal character. The plummy, blackberry flavors have a nice streak of mocha and dried herbs, and are wrapped in fine, easy tannins. Feels good and clean through the spicy finish. **86** —*S.H. (8/1/2003)*

Kendall-Jackson 1997 Vintner's Reserve Merlot (California) $21. 88 —*S.H. (3/1/2000)*

Kendall-Jackson 1999 Great Estates Pinot Noir (Monterey County) $32. This dark and spicy Pinot is built on a solid tart-cherry foundation that's accented by black pepper and cinnamon. Oak is prominent, providing menthol shadings, and the wine finishes long and toasty. **89** *(10/1/2002)*

Kendall-Jackson 2001 Seco Bench Estate Pinot Noir (Monterey) $35. Solid Monterey Pinot, with hints of green herbs adding complexity to black-cherry fruit. Cinnamon, cola, and caramel round out the finish of this medium-weight wine. **90** *(3/1/2004)*

Kendall-Jackson 2004 Seco Highlands Estate Pinot Noir (Arroyo Seco) $35. Opens with a pure, clean, high-toned aroma, powerful yet delicate, of cherries, cola, coffee, cinnamon, and smoky oak. In the mouth, the wine has fantastic density and concentration, rich in fruits and spices, but with a brilliant Pinotesque silkiness. Simply a marvelous wine. **94 Editors' Choice** —*S.H. (5/1/2006)*

Kendall-Jackson 2002 Seco Highlands Estate Pinot Noir (Monterey County) $35. A new wine from K-J. It's high in cool-weather acidity that tingles the mouth, while the flavors are modest, ranging from raspberries, cola, coffee, and vanilla to various dusty herbs and rosehip tea. Could use more fatness and charm, but it's an interesting wine, and one to watch. **88** —*S.H. (11/1/2004)*

Kendall-Jackson 2005 Vintner's Reserve Pinot Noir (California) $14. Shows real Pinot character in the light silkiness, nice acidity, and flavors of cherries, cream, and vanilla spice. If you're just starting to get into the variety, this is a good intro. **84** —*S.H. (12/1/2006)*

Kendall-Jackson 2004 Vintner's Reserve Pinot Noir (California) $14. Here's a Pinot that shows all the classic, cool-climate qualities of the variety, from silky tannins and crisp acids to cherry cola flavors and a spicy finish. It's just too thin in body to merit a higher score. **83** —*S.H. (12/31/2005)*

Kendall-Jackson 2003 Vintner's Reserve Pinot Noir (California) $14. This Pinot is very dry, and it fulfills the basic varietal requirements of a silky texture with crisp acids. You'll find modest flavors of cherries and leather. **84** —*S.H. (6/1/2005)*

Kendall-Jackson 2002 Vintner's Reserve Pinot Noir (California) $14. Light and delicately flavored with subtle cherry, tobacco, and spice flavors, this pleasant wine is suitable for everyday dinners. Has some real length through the finish. **84** —*S.H. (11/1/2004)*

Kendall-Jackson 2001 Vintner's Reserve Pinot Noir (California) $14. From coastal counties between Mendocino and Santa Barbara, a nice, supple wine that has plenty of Pinot character. Don't expect depth or ageability, but this black raspberry-flavored wine has soft, silky tannins and a spicy finish. **85** —*S.H. (7/1/2003)*

Kendall-Jackson 2000 Vintner's Reserve Pinot Noir (California) $14. Pretty cherry and herb aromas and flavors have to first fight their way through a rough earthy overlay. The wine is thickly textured, but a bit heavy, finishing with burnt wood and a tart note. **83** *(10/1/2002)*

Kendall-Jackson 1999 Vintner's Reserve Pinot Noir (California) $12. From six coastal counties, a varietally true Pinot at an everyday price, which is a rare thing. Delicate aromas of beet, mushroom, hard spice, tea, and black-cherry precede a balanced, silky, dry wine, with good berry flavors and a sprinkling of dusty tannins. **86** —*S.H. (11/15/2001)*

Kendall-Jackson 1998 Vintner's Reserve Pinot Noir (California) $17. 87 — *S.H. (12/15/2000)*

Kendall-Jackson 1998 Collage Red Blend (California) $9. Rustic, fruity stuff here, with bold fruity-spicy flavors. A galumphing wine that's big and boisterous; nothing shy about it. A bit rough-edged, it needs meat and pasta and similarly uncomplicated foods to tame it. **84** —*S.H. (5/1/2001)*

Kendall-Jackson 1999 Collage-Zinfandel/Shiraz Red Blend (California) $9. Surprisingly rich and nuanced for such an inexpensive wine, it has balanced aromas and flavors of blackberries, pepper and earth. Has the finesse and complexity of red wines costing a lot more. **87 Best Buy** — *S.H. (9/1/2002)*

Kendall-Jackson 2002 Collage Zinfandel-Shiraz Red Blend (California) $10. Simple, rather sweet and candied, with raspberry and cocoa butter flavors and a soft, fruity finish. Nice with mushroom pizza. **83** —*S.H. (6/1/2005)*

Kendall-Jackson 2000 Late Harvest Riesling (California) $20. Bright lemon and honey notes are at the core of this spicy wine. It moves on to reveal some peach and apple at the end. Enjoyable but lacking balance. **84** —*J.M. (12/1/2002)*

Kendall-Jackson 2005 Vintner's Reserve Riesling (California) $10. Off dry and fruity, this clean wine is balanced by ample acidity. The peach, papaya, honeysuckle, apricot, vanilla, and oriental spice flavors are savory. Good job from K-J. **85 Best Buy** —*S.H. (7/1/2006)*

Kendall-Jackson 2004 Vintner's Reserve Riesling (California) $10. Slightly sweet, especially on the finish, where the citrus and fig flavors turn decidely honeyed. This is a soft, slightly common wine. **83** —*S.H. (10/1/2005)*

Kendall-Jackson 2000 Vintner's Reserve Riesling (California) $10. Peachy clean, with a pleasing fruity quality that is mild and not overpowering. Bright enough to avoid any cloying sensation, with a touch of sweetness at the end. Great for apéritifs and seafood. **86** —*J.M. (6/1/2002)*

Kendall-Jackson 1999 Sauvignon Blanc (California) $10. For fans of grassy, gooseberry-accented wines. Lemon and lime show here, too, with decent acidity. Tiny amounts of Sémillon and Chardonnay add dimension. It's fruity and simple, very clean (as you'd expect), a touch sweet and finishes swiftly. **84** —*S.H. (5/1/2001)*

Kendall-Jackson 2005 Vintner's Reserve Sauvignon Blanc (California) $11. A nice, everyday Sauvignon from K-J, with juicy citrus zest, grapefruit sorbet and spicy flavors. Finishes off-dry and clean. **84** —*S.H. (11/15/2006)*

Kendall-Jackson 2004 Vintner's Reserve Sauvignon Blanc (California) $10. This is one of those Sauvignon Blancs that comes down firmly on the super-dry, grassy, tart side, relieved by lemon and lime fruit. Try this clean, zesty wine with a salad of wilted greens with goat cheese and figs, tossed in a little EVOO and a splash of balsamic. **85 Best Buy** —*S.H. (2/1/2006)*

Kendall-Jackson 2003 Vintner's Reserve Sauvignon Blanc (California) $10. Way sweet, but it's perky with acidity, and there's no denying the lemon, lime and spicy fig flavors. Nice for a cocktail, or with pigs in a bun. **84** —*S.H. (6/1/2005)*

Kendall-Jackson 2002 Vintner's Reserve Sauvignon Blanc (California) $10. Nice and drinkable, a simple wine with slightly sweet flavors of citrus fruits and the acidity you expect from this varietal. It will go with almost anything, so don't be too fussy. **84** —*S.H. (2/1/2004)*

Kendall-Jackson 2001 Vintner's Reserve Sauvignon Blanc (California) $10. Simple and innocent, a small Sauvignon with hints of citrus fruits and figs. Very dry, with crisp acidity and a clean, peppery finish. **84** —*S.H. (7/1/2003)*

Kendall-Jackson 2000 Vintner's Reserve Sauvignon Blanc (California) $9. Sweet and candied, this sipper is like dessert in a bottle. The citrus flavors suggest tartness, but a high degree of residual sugar makes it soft and honeyed. **83** —*S.H. (9/12/2002)*

Kendall-Jackson 1998 Vintner's Reserve Sauvignon Blanc (California) $12. 86 —*S.H. (11/1/1999)*

Kendall-Jackson 1997 Vintner's Reserve Sauvignon Blanc (California) $9. 86 *(9/1/1999)*

Kendall-Jackson 2002 Alisos Hills Estate Syrah (Santa Barbara County) $35. Huge and intense in every respect. Dark and extracted, high in toasty oak, dense in tannins, tingly in acidity, and most of all, enormous in fruit. Waves of plum and blackberry cascade across the palate, ending in a burst of spice and mocha. Drink now through 2010. **92** —*S.H. (8/1/2004)*

Kendall-Jackson 1999 Grand Reserve Syrah (California) $22. Deep raspberry and cherry fruit buttressed by creamy vanillin oak and an earthy, animal element opens this dark, tangy wine. More of the same follows in the mouth where licorice, cocoa, and espresso accents add interest. Rich and burly, it closes with full but supple tannins. **87** *(11/1/2001)*

Kendall-Jackson 2003 Highlands Estate Alisos Hills Syrah (Santa Barbara County) $30. Pours dramatically dark and brooding, with an enormous burst of white pepper, blackberry, and coffee and an edge of smoked meat and leather. Huge in the mouth, with masses of blackberries, plums, espresso. Bone dry, thick in sweet tannins, and long on finish. Drink now— 2012. **93 Editors' Choice** —*S.H.* (5/1/2006)

Kendall-Jackson 2003 Vintner's Reserve Syrah (California) $12. This is a young, sharp, jammy wine but has a depth of fruit and a rich structure that make it awfully likeable. Blackberries, cherries, blueberries, cocoa, coffee, it all adds up to a palate sensation. **86** —*S.H. (4/1/2006)*

Kendall-Jackson 2002 Vintner's Reserve Syrah (California) $14. With KJ's vast grape sourcing, getting ripe fruit obviously wasn't a problem. This wine is ripe and juicy, with somewhat candied berry flavors and sweet caramelly notes. Soft and easy to drink. **87** (9/1/2005)

Kendall-Jackson 2001 Vintner's Reserve Syrah (California) $14. Smells and tastes just like what it is, a young, fresh, and jammy wine, sharp in acidity and vibrant with blackberry and cherry flavors. Extremely dry, but with a nice ripe sheen. **84** —*S.H. (12/1/2004)*

Kendall-Jackson 1999 Vintner's Reserve Syrah (California) $16. Ripe and smooth with a slightly syrupy, extracted quality, this black fruit-and-licorice pleasure ball delivers the goods. Full on the palate with dark chocolate flavors and plenty of toasty oak, it finishes dry, rich, and flavorful; well-fruited to the end. **89 Best Buy** *(10/1/2001)*

Kendall-Jackson 1997 Vintner's Reserve Syrah (California) $17. 88 —*S.H.* (2/1/2000)

Kendall-Jackson 1997 Vintner's Reserve Viognier (California) $16. 85 — *S.H. (6/1/1999)*

Kendall-Jackson 2000 Great Estates Zinfandel (Mendocino) $25. From mountain vineyards, with a touch of Petite Sirah, Grenache, and Carignane, this tastes like an old-fashioned field blend. It has that wild explosion of berries and stone fruits, but the winemaking was very fine, resulting in fine tannins and a soft, dry mouthfeel. **91** —*S.H. (12/1/2002)*

Kendall-Jackson 1999 Great Estates Zinfandel (Dry Creek Valley) $28. Smells forward and ripe, with wild berry, bramble, and blueberry aromas and an array of crushed, dust oriental Spices. On the palate, it's awkward, somewhat hot, with 15% alcohol and some overripe, raisiny flavors that are Port-like. Some, however, will go nuts over this style. **84** —*S.H. (12/15/2001)*

Kendall-Jackson 2004 Vintner's Reserve Zinfandel (California) $12. Does just what VR does across all varieties, offering up a ripe, varietally true Zin that's all about upfront fruit and spice. Finishes with a scour of dusty tannins. **84** —*S.H. (12/1/2006)*

Kendall-Jackson 2003 Vintner's Reserve Zinfandel (California) $12. Easy drinking and balanced, this food-friendly Zin has pleasant cherry and berry flavors and a hint of peppery spice in the finish. It's nice and dry, with a polished mouthfeel. **85** —*S.H. (4/1/2006)*

Kendall-Jackson 2002 Vintner's Reserve Zinfandel (California) $12. Made in a popular style, this jammy wine has cherry, blackberry, and spiced rum flavors that are ripe and pure, with a pleasantly tannic texture. Easy to like. **86** —*S.H. (6/1/2005)*

Kendall-Jackson 2001 Vintner's Reserve Zinfandel (California) $12. Soft and fruity, with good body and a core of black-cherry, plum, cassis, spice and herb notes. A bit bright on the finish, but nice nonetheless. **86** (11/1/2003)

Kendall-Jackson 1997 Vintner's Reserve Zinfandel (California) $17. 83 — *J.C. (2/1/2000)*

KENNETH-CRAWFORD

Kenneth-Crawford 2004 Lafond Vineyard Syrah (Santa Rita Hills) $32. A polished, supple Syrah, light in body and color, with high acidity framing deep, impressively ripe flavors of cherries and spice. This is a Côtes-du-Rhône-ish sort of wine, and very tasty. **88** —*S.H. (3/1/2006)*

KENT RASMUSSEN

Kent Rasmussen 2002 Cabernet Sauvignon (Napa Valley) $28. Dry, crisp, and tannic. It is not a soft, opulent fruit bomb, but a wine of structure. That's not to say it doesn't have fruit, because it does—mainly cherry and blackberry compote. But those authoritative tannins give the heft needed for medium-term aging. Drink now through 2010. **91 Cellar Selection** —*S.H. (3/1/2006)*

Kent Rasmussen 1997 Chardonnay (Napa Valley) $25. 91 —*M.M.* (10/1/1999)

Kent Rasmussen 1996 Reserve Chardonnay (Napa Valley) $45. One of the oldest wines submitted, a deliciously complex crème brûlée, coconut, nutmeg, vanilla, and smoke bouquet opens this classy contender. Full and creamy on the palate, it offers rich, finely nuanced pear and nectarine fruit flavors accented by clove, nutmeg, and coconut. Still feels young, finishing long and bold with intriguing spice and tangy pineapple notes. **92** (7/1/2001)

Kent Rasmussen 2003 Late Harvest Gewürztraminer (Russian River Valley) $16. Even if you're not a huge fan of dessert wines, you might like this one. It's a very sweet, flashy wine filled with brilliantly opulent apricot purée, mango, peach cobbler, vanilla, and cinnamon spice flavors, with bright, good acidity for balance. Absolutely delicious. **94** —*S.H.* (3/1/2006)

Kent Rasmussen 2001 Chavez & Leeds Vineyard Petite Sirah (Rutherford) $30. Here's Petite Sirah near its best. The wine is full-bodied and dry, with the structure of a great Cabernet, but an entirely different profile. Black and red cherry, ripe blueberry, and mocha flavors are finished with sweet toasty oak. Acidity is low, the tannins rich and complex in this delicious wine. **91** —*S.H. (12/31/2005)*

Kent Rasmussen 1996 Pinot Noir (Carneros) $27. 88 —*M.S. (6/1/1999)*

Kent Rasmussen 2003 Pinot Noir (Carneros) $30. This Pinot is so ripe and full-bodied that it's almost Rhône-like. The black-cherry pie and cola flavors veer into milk chocolate. Yet the wine somehow maintains a silky delicacy and dry elegance, and in the end, it's quite a tasty drink. **89** — *S.H. (4/1/2006)*

Kent Rasmussen 2001 Pinot Noir (Carneros) $28. Opens with a blast of smoky, vanilla-tinged new oak, and there's oak in the sharp-sweet tang of the flavors, too. Fairly full-bodied and tannic for the varietal, with underlying black-cherry flavors, this wine finishes with some astringency. **86** —*S.H. (12/1/2004)*

KENWOOD

Kenwood 2003 Cabernet Sauvignon (Sonoma County) $18. Plays it right down the middle. A good quality Cab at a fair price. Shows a rich tannic-acid structure and ripe fruit that has an earthy mushroom and soy edge. Drinking well now and for the next several years. **87** —*S.H.* (12/1/2006)

Kenwood 2002 Cabernet Sauvignon (Sonoma County) $18. Showing some rough, inelegant edges, this Cab doesn't seem fully ripened. The blackberry and cherry flavors finish with a green note, and the wine is fully dry. **83** —*S.H. (12/15/2005)*

Kenwood 2001 Cabernet Sauvignon (Sonoma County) $18. Lush, ripe, and delicious, this is a Cab that everyone will like. It's nicely ripe in sweet black currants, dusted with an edge of herbs and cocoa, and is easy, with fine tannins and a rich overlay of oak. **88** —*S.H. (12/31/2004)*

Kenwood 2000 Cabernet Sauvignon (Sonoma County) $16. Easy-drinking, with flavors of blackberries, cherries, herbs, and a touch of smoky oak. This pretty wine is very dry, with gentle tannins, and can accompany a wide range of meats and cheeses. **86** —*S.H. (11/15/2003)*

Kenwood 1999 Cabernet Sauvignon (Sonoma County) $20. Straddles the perilous border between expensive and affordable Cabernet. It's plush and layered, with softly luxurious tannins and easy acids and a kiss of oak, although it's a bit light on fruit. **86** —*S.H. (12/31/2002)*

Kenwood 1998 Cabernet Sauvignon (Sonoma County) $22. From a reliable producer, an adequate Cab and a relative success for the vintage. Oak contribute flashy spice, vanilla, and sweet tannins, and it's surprisingly ripe and fruity given the 43,000 case production. This is a nice, dry wine that satisfies and offers some complexity. **86** —*S.H. (12/1/2001)*

Kenwood 1997 Cabernet Sauvignon (Sonoma County) $22. 88 —*S.H.* (12/15/2000)

Kenwood 2001 Artist Series Cabernet Sauvignon (Sonoma County) $70. After a string of great vintages, this bottling is a disappointment. After four-plus years, it remains quite tannic, with an acidic astringency. **84** — *S.H. (6/1/2006)*

USA

Kenwood 1999 Artist Series Cabernet Sauvignon (Sonoma County) $70.
The grapes come from high mountain vineyards that yield small berries. This wine is young, tough and tannic. It's not one of your softly opulent '99s that immediately seduces. There is a deep core of blackberry, cherry, and cassis fruit and a lush overlay of oak. This 25th vintage of Artist Series is a serious cellar candidate. Best after 2008. **91** —S.H. (4/1/2004)

Kenwood 1998 Artist Series Cabernet Sauvignon (Sonoma County) $75. So what's this famous, hands-on Cabernet like at four years? In a word, it suffers from its vintage. Although you root for it, it can't overcome a thinness that verges on herbs and veggies. Elaborate oak doesn't help. Makes you realize that every year is not a vintage year in California. **86** —S.H. (12/31/2002)

Kenwood 1997 Artist Series Cabernet Sauvignon (Sonoma County) $75. From one of the largest and most highly touted vintages in a great decade, this is large and fairly fat. The cassis, fruitcake, and menthol nose and sweet blackberry and chocolate palate aim to please…and do just that. It feels a bit low in acidity, making it lush and forward, displaying a bit of heat and a looser structure. Still, this pleasure package is young, and the long, dark finish shows even, well-dispersed tannins. Another winner in a streak, if maybe less of a keeper. Drink now–2009, again probably sooner rather than later. **93** (4/1/2002)

Kenwood 1996 Artist Series Cabernet Sauvignon (Sonoma County) $70. Weighty and supple, this continues the strong mid-90s run with its dark fruit, toast and herb nose. There's a touch of sweet sur-maturité (over-ripeness) here, but there's tangy acidity, too, to keep it together. It's deep and sweet, with blackberry, chocolate, and herb flavors and a lengthy, smooth black pepper and anise-tinged finish. Drink now–2007, probably sooner rather than later. **91** (4/1/2002)

Kenwood 1995 Artist Series Cabernet Sauvignon (Sonoma Valley) $65. The lovely nose of rich briary fruit, licorice, vanilla cream, and anise pulls you in to this luscious and lushly textured wine. It's very smooth and suave on the tongue, offering deep cassis flavors and tobacco accents. Long and dry, the finish shows spicy oak, berries, and espresso. Drink now–2008. **92** (4/1/2002)

Kenwood 1994 Artist Series Cabernet Sauvignon (Sonoma County) $75. A strong performance from a vintage considered among the best; this comes on and stays intense through the close. However, the wine's scale caused some doubts to be registered about its balance—it's pretty hot, and high in alcohol. Still, few argued with the toast, dark berry, and licorice nose, the dark spicy-sweet flavors or rich, even mouthfeel. Closes long and a little hot, with large, mouthcoating tannins. Drink now–2006. **92** (4/1/2002)

Kenwood 1993 Artist Series Cabernet Sauvignon (Sonoma County) $75. Leaner in profile and not quite as deep as the 1992, but nicely structured and attractive. This has a slightly more Bordeaux-like feel and balance and displays a cherry, earth, tobacco, and herb bouquet. Blueberry, plum, and espresso show on the even, smooth palate. It closes long with soft, ripe tannins and the herb notes atop the dark fruit. Drink now–2005. **91** (4/1/2002)

Kenwood 1992 Artist Series Cabernet Sauvignon (Sonoma County) $75. Impressively plummy and chocolatey, the Merlot in this reads strongly, though it's actually 2 percent less than in the 1991. The wine is full and still firm, with copious aromas and flavors of cedar and menthol, raisins and cocoa. Closes fairly long with dark tart-sweet fruit and nice, still slightly tight tannins. This will keep. Drink now through 2008; best after 2004. **91** (4/1/2002)

Kenwood 1991 Artist Series Cabernet Sauvignon (Sonoma County) $75. More ripe and lush, even more aromatically complex than the 1990. The bouquet is intense with toast, earth, mushroom, animal, and mint notes. In the mouth it shows dark, underbrush-like notes with overripe fruit and leather notes. Ends warm, with ripe tannins and more dark fruit. Drink now–2006. **90** (4/1/2002)

Kenwood 1990 Artist Series Cabernet Sauvignon (Sonoma County) $75. Opens darkly sweet with an expressive nose showing clove, chocolate, tobacco, and eucalyptus. This wears its oak more openly on the deep blackberry fruit, offering black licorice and caramel accents. Closes juicy but firm, with good structure and a briary note. Drink now–2003. **89** (4/1/2002)

Kenwood 1989 Artist Series Cabernet Sauvignon (Sonoma County) $75. Though it's no blockbuster, this vintage still offers a charming bouquet of tea, smoke, menthol, and cocoa. It's light compared to most years, with black-cherry, soy, and tobacco flavors. Closes soft yet bright, with mild tannins and acidity. Surprisingly decent for a wine of its age and the so-so vintage. Drink now. **87** (4/1/2002)

Kenwood 1988 Artist Series Cabernet Sauvignon (Sonoma County) $75. The weakest bottling of the vertical, the wine of this tough vintage shows prune, leather, and old leaves on the nose. Dried-out, thin, and woody, it's decidedly past its best. Past its prime. **84** (4/1/2002)

Kenwood 1987 Artist Series Cabernet Sauvignon (Sonoma County) $75. This controversial wine engendered major differences of opinion. Some tasters rated it excellent; others thought it in decline. Notes on this wine range from dumb and minty, thin and drying out, going down fast (from the naysayers) to rich, dry, sweet-tart fruit, a big smooth feel, a long plum-and-prune finish and life through mid-decade (from its proponents). One to try for yourself. Disparate scores. Drink now–2006, or past its best, depending on whom you believe. **88** (4/1/2002)

Kenwood 1986 Artist Series Cabernet Sauvignon (Sonoma County) $75. Browning, with a tobacco, carob, earth, and pine bouquet, this medium-weight bottling wears its age with class. The fruit is fully mature and starting to fade, but there's enough left to support tasty, complex spice and earth notes. Inherently well-balanced, it finishes long, still showing good acids and tannins, with attractive smoke, coffee, and meat notes. Drink now. **90** (4/1/2002)

Kenwood 1999 Jack London Cabernet Sauvignon (Sonoma Valley) $35. How has one of California's oldest vineyard-designated Cabs kept its price so low? The winery, owned by Korbel's Heck family, has maintained the wine's hallmarks of upfront fruit, complexity and early drinkability. The wine doesn't have the depth you'd expect from a '99, but it's very elegant and drinkable. **88** —S.H. (11/15/2002)

Kenwood 2003 Jack London Vineyard Cabernet Sauvignon (Sonoma Valley) $30. Ripe and polished, with intense cassis, plum, spice, and oak flavors enriched by the toast of fine oak. The wine continues the long Jack London tradition of early balance and drinkability, with the promise of midterm aging. **90** —S.H. (12/1/2006)

Kenwood 2002 Jack London Vineyard Cabernet Sauvignon (Sonoma Valley) $30. A bold, almost jammy Cabernet, with vibrant blackberry and cassis flavors that virtually conceal the underlying structure. Seems destined to be enjoyed young. **89** (12/15/2005)

Kenwood 2001 Jack London Vineyard Cabernet Sauvignon (Sonoma Valley) $30. A big, softly tannic wine that can be consumed with pleasure now or held up to 10 years, this shows classic aromas and flavors of smoke, cassis, and vanilla and a long, fruit-driven finish. **90** (12/15/2005)

Kenwood 2001 Jack London Vineyard Cabernet Sauvignon (Sonoma Valley) $30. Tastes like good grapes forced into over-production, to judge from the watery finish. It's still a good wine, with black currant flavors, but you wish it was more intense, especially from this historic label. **85** —S.H. (2/1/2005)

Kenwood 2000 Jack London Vineyard Cabernet Sauvignon (Sonoma Valley) $30. On the leaner, more herbal side of the spectrum, with cherry flavors spiced with a piny or resinous green note. Finishes a bit hard and astringent, but not likely to improve with age, so enjoy it now with rare steak. **85** (12/15/2005)

Kenwood 1999 Jack London Vineyard Cabernet Sauvignon (Sonoma Valley) $NA. Reined in and tight, but with solid potential given another few years of cellaring. Smoke, earth, and herbal notes accent cassis and black-cherry fruit. Crisp and firm on the finish, but should bloom by 2008. **87** (12/15/2005)

Kenwood 1998 Jack London Vineyard Cabernet Sauvignon (Sonoma Valley) $NA. A difficult vintage that should have been drunk in its youth, the '98 shows a strong herbal component, lacks fruit, and features a clipped, high-acid finish. **83** (12/15/2005)

Kenwood 1998 Jack London Vineyard Cabernet Sauvignon (Sonoma Valley) $35. Somewhat lean, with a core of herb, anise, blackberry, and vanilla flavors. A smoky finish marks the end. **86** —J.M. (6/1/2002)

Kenwood 1997 Jack London Vineyard Cabernet Sauvignon (Sonoma Valley) $NA. This Cab, from a vintage that has been criticized for a perceived lack of longevity, is still chugging right along. Smoky and toasty on the nose, it adds flavors of superripe fruit on the palate: dates, figs and prunes. Richly textured, with a long, still-chewy finish. Drink now–2010. **89** *(12/15/2005)*

Kenwood 1996 Jack London Vineyard Cabernet Sauvignon (Sonoma Valley) $NA. An interesting wine, with some green herbal elements on the nose, but also a plump, expansive mouthfeel and ripe flavors of chocolate and plum. Still shows some tannins on the finish. Drink now–2010. **89** *(12/15/2005)*

Kenwood 1995 Jack London Vineyard Cabernet Sauvignon (Sonoma Valley) $NA. Just beginning to drop its fruit, making the focus now on earth and tobacco flavors. This doesn't seem as ripe as the '94, but shows a bit more structure, ending on a slightly astringent note. Drink up. **88** *(12/15/2005)*

Kenwood 1994 Jack London Vineyard Cabernet Sauvignon (Sonoma Valley) $NA. Lovely when first poured, this belted out rich cassis and vanilla scents alongside aged notes of leather and dried spices. Silky and medium-bodied, with a long, elegant finish. Several minutes later, it started to fade. Drink up. **89** *(12/15/2005)*

Kenwood 1993 Jack London Vineyard Cabernet Sauvignon (Sonoma Valley) $NA. On the downhill slide, this still packs in enough tobacco, earth, molasses, and prune flavor to remain pleasurable. **84** *(12/15/2005)*

Kenwood 2000 Jack London Vineyard-25th Anniversary Cabernet Sauvignon (Sonoma Valley) $30. This richly flavorful wine is smoky and lush, with hints of cassis and black-cherry and dusty spices. It is very dry, with soft, easy but complex tannins, and leaves a lingering aftertaste. Excellent, and would score higher except for a bit of thinness in the middle that lavish oak does not cover. **90** —*S.H. (11/15/2003)*

Kenwood 1997 Jack London Vineyard Cabernet Sauvignon (Sonoma Valley) $35. 91 *(11/1/2000)*

Kenwood 2005 Chardonnay (Sonoma County) $15. Lots of oak, lots of upfront ripe peach, pear, and tropical fruit, that's pretty much the story with this widely available Chard. With more than 100,000 cases, it should be easy to find. **84** —*S.H. (12/15/2006)*

Kenwood 2004 Chardonnay (Sonoma County) $15. Peaches and cream, buttered toast, a squeeze of vanilla and a dusting of cinnamon pretty much describes this tasty Chard. It has extra layers of complexity in the balance and long finish. **88** —*S.H. (12/1/2005)*

Kenwood 2003 Chardonnay (Sonoma County) $15. Easy to like for its tropical fruit and pear flavors that are well oaked, and the rich, creamy texture. Fine, crisp acids follow on the long finish, leading to a clean, spicy mouth feel. **87** —*S.H. (12/31/2004)*

Kenwood 2001 Chardonnay (Sonoma County) $15. A nice, easy-drinking Chard, with modulated fruity flavors of peaches and apples, and pretty brisk acidity. The acids make the wine feel tingly on the palate, which stimulates the taste buds. The finish is balanced and dry. **86** —*S.H. (12/15/2002)*

Kenwood 2000 Chardonnay (Sonoma County) $15. There's some pretty apple and peach fruit, and enough oaky influences to bring out smoky, vanilla nuances. The texture is supple, crisp, and creamy. Made in a crowd-pleasing style, and one that won't break the bank. **85** —*S.H. (12/31/2001)*

Kenwood 1999 Chardonnay (Sonoma County) $15. This ripe, lovely wine shows classic Russian River Valley aromas of ripe, sweet, green apples. The winemaking adds smoky, vanilla-scented oak, a creamy, leesy smoothness and a rich softness that owes to malolactic fermentation. What strikes you, though, is the balance. All the parts come together in this super-enjoyable wine. At this price, it's a great value. **89** —*S.H. (2/1/2001)*

Kenwood 1998 Chardonnay (Sonoma County) $15. 84 *(6/1/2000)*

Kenwood 2005 Reserve Chardonnay (Russian River Valley) $20. Richer and tarter than Kenwood's regular '05 Chard, this wine shows the acidity and green apple flavors of the central part of the valley. Bosc pears,

Meyer lemons, and white peaches pleasantly complicate things as you continue to sip. **87** —*S.H. (12/15/2006)*

Kenwood 2004 Reserve Chardonnay (Russian River Valley) $20. This is a good wine, but it doesn't really seem like a reserve. It's a little thin and weedy, although the peach flavors and oak layering is pleasant enough. **84** —*S.H. (12/1/2005)*

Kenwood 2003 Reserve Chardonnay (Russian River Valley) $20. Shows proper Chard character in the peach flavors, oaky overtones, and creamy texture. Could use more concentration, though, as it's rather weak on the finish. **84** —*S.H. (6/1/2005)*

Kenwood 2002 Reserve Chardonnay (Russian River Valley) $20. This refreshing Chard keeps all its elements reined in for balance and charm. You'll find apple and peach flavors, subtle oak, crisp acidity, and a touch of lees, all wrapped in a creamy texture. **85** —*S.H. (9/1/2004)*

Kenwood 2001 Reserve Chardonnay (Russian River Valley) $20. Opens with a blast of well-toasted oak, vanilla, caramel, and char, and oak dominates the palate through the finish. Underneath is some ripe peach and pear fruit. The texture is soft and creamy. **87** —*S.H. (12/15/2002)*

Kenwood 2000 Reserve Chardonnay (Russian River Valley) $20. A very nice complete wine, with something for everyone. Fans of fruit will rejoice in the ripe, spicy peach and pear flavors, oakies will like the woodsy smoke and vanilla. The creamy smooth texture leads to a spicy, leesy finish. **88** —*S.H. (12/31/2001)*

Kenwood 1999 Reserve Chardonnay (Sonoma County) $20. Fresh pear, apple, and citrus flavors are neatly balanced in this delicate, fairly elegant wine. Moderately complex with a bright, clean finish. **88** —*J.M. (11/15/2001)*

Kenwood 1998 Reserve Chardonnay (Sonoma County) $25. 85 *(6/1/2000)*

Kenwood 2002 Shows Vineyard Pedigree Chardonnay (Sonoma County) $15. A wine that is light in texture and weight, but the tropical fruit flavors are ripe and succulent, and rather heavy oak adds a coating of vanillins and toast. Offers plenty of fancy Chard character at a reasonable price. **85** —*S.H. (12/1/2003)*

Kenwood 2005 Gewürztraminer (Sonoma County) $11. Here's a glassful of fruits, flowers, and above all, spices. Just slightly sweet, but with good acids, the wine bursts with white peach, pineapple, vanilla custard, and honeysuckle flavors, and just about every Asian spice you can think of. **84** —*S.H. (11/1/2006)*

Kenwood 2001 Gewürztraminer (Sonoma County) $11. Will appeal to fans of the varietal for its highly aromatic scents of jasmine, fresh white tree fruits, garden flowers, and mélange of oriental spices. The flavors are similarly rich and dense, with just a tiny bit of residual sugar to round and soften the acidity. **85** —*S.H. (9/1/2003)*

Kenwood 2000 Gewürztraminer (Sonoma County) $11. Starts with telltale aromas of wild-flowers, honey, peach, apricot, and spices, and turns very flavorful on the palate. There's a burst of exotic fruit and spices, but it's nicely dry and somewhat soft. **84** —*S.H. (11/15/2001)*

Kenwood 2003 Merlot (Sonoma County) $17. Kind of rough in texture, with sandpapery tannins, and fruit that's a combination of too sweet cherry jam and raw green peppercorns, this is a rustic Merlot. **82** —*S.H. (2/1/2006)*

Kenwood 2002 Merlot (Sonoma County) $17. A lush Merlot, dry and balanced, with smooth tannins that support blackberry and cocoa flavors. Likeable for its harmony and easy drinkability. **86** —*S.H. (10/1/2005)*

Kenwood 2000 Merlot (Sonoma County) $17. What a nice wine. It's a real pleasure to sip this dry, fruity wine, whose flavors are evenly balanced between blackberries and herbs. The weight in the mouth is perfect, full-bodied, and yet easy. A nice bite of acidity undercuts the flavors. **87** —*S.H. (9/1/2003)*

Kenwood 1999 Merlot (Sonoma County) $17. Fans of lush, full-flavored and well-structured red wines will like this one. It has the weight and elegance of a good Cabernet, with plummy, berry flavors, and a kiss of oak. Lacks perhaps depth, but it's a very good wine offering lots of immediate enjoyment. **87** —*S.H. (9/12/2002)*

Kenwood 1998 Merlot (Sonoma County) $17. Enough berry and plum richness and smoky oak to satisfy fussy drinkers, yet dry and compact, with a nice shine of acidity. Not too complex or subtle, but there's plenty to like about it. Should be easy to find with more than 30,000 cases produced. **87** —*S.H. (2/1/2001)*

Kenwood 2004 Jack London Vineyard Merlot (Sonoma Valley) $25. The wine pours midnight black and tastes closed now, the kind of Merlot that hints at cherries and blackberries, then stops short with tannic lockdown. With its inherent balance and integrity, it will drink well now with a rich steak, but decanting for a few hours will help. **87** —*S.H. (12/31/2006)*

Kenwood 2003 Jack London Vineyard Merlot (Sonoma Valley) $25. Awkward and jarring in sharp acids and unresolved green tannins, this dry wine offers few pleasures right now, beyond a trace of barely ripened cherry fruit. It's not likely to improve, so drink up. **83** —*S.H. (2/1/2006)*

Kenwood 2002 Jack London Vineyard Merlot (Sonoma Valley) $25. Rather tough and tannic, and very dry, with modulated berry and herb flavors. By itself this wine isn't showing much. It really needs something rich, like lamb or steak, to stimulate it. **86** —*S.H. (3/1/2005)*

Kenwood 2001 Jack London Vineyard Merlot (Sonoma Valley) $24. Oak dominates this 100% Merlot. The barrels lend vanilla and smoke notes and an oaky sharpness that covers the underlying cherry fruit. Youthful tannins also cover it up. Drink now through 2006. **85** —*S.H. (12/15/2004)*

Kenwood 2000 Jack London Vineyard Merlot (Sonoma Valley) $30. Pretty wine, with lovely texture due mainly to the soft, luscious tannins and crisp acids. There are some good flavors of plum and blackberry, but also a stubborn streak of herbal greenness, suggesting some less-than-ripe grapes. **87** —*S.H. (12/15/2003)*

Kenwood 1999 Jack London Vineyard Merlot (Sonoma Valley) $30. Showing hints of black-cherry, chocolate, anise, and herb flavors, this full-bodied wine is structured with firm, ripe tannins that lead to a supple finish. **88** —*J.M. (9/1/2002)*

Kenwood 1998 Jack London Vineyard Merlot (Sonoma Valley) $30. Cinnamon, herbs, spice and pepper are frontrunners here, backed by nuanced blackberry, cassis, and tar notes. Falters a bit on the finish, however, ending with a touch of tartness. **84** —*J.M. (12/1/2001)*

Kenwood 1998 Massara Merlot (Sonoma Valley) $25. Unfortunately, 1998 was not 1997, when this bottling was very good. This vintage is less ripe, and so the wine has some green aromas and flavors, in addition to blackberry. That makes the tannins stick out more. There's nothing to contain them, but if you pair it with the right, rich foods, it will be just fine. **85** —*S.H. (9/1/2002)*

Kenwood 1997 Massara Vineyard Merlot (Sonoma Valley) $25. Dark, oaky, and fine in every respect. Sonoma Valley, often underrated as Merlot country, lends the fruit a very deep and satisfying blackberry component, which is highlighted, in this case, by toasty oak. The tannins are soft and finely etched. Gorgeous stuff, quite lovely now, but the solid core of fruit indicates mid-term aging potential. **92** —*S.H. (2/1/2001)*

Kenwood 2002 Reserve Merlot (Sonoma Valley) $25. Easily merits its reserve status due to the upscale, velvety texture, rich, oaky fruit flavors and overall balance that, combined, offer impressive pleasure. **90** —*S.H. (9/1/2006)*

Kenwood 2001 Reserve Merlot (Sonoma Valley) $25. Smooth and polished, and very dry, with blackberry flavors and a touch of herbaceousness. Just as good as Kenwood's less expensive '02 Merlot. **86** —*S.H. (10/1/2005)*

Kenwood 2000 Reserve Massara Merlot (Sonoma Valley) $25. Bone-dry and scoury in tannins and acids, with a tart, astringent mouthfeel, but satisfies for the layering of black-cherry, briary berry, pepper, and tobacco flavors. Has enough elegance to pair with a rich cut of beef. **86** —*S.H. (10/1/2004)*

Kenwood 1999 Reserve-Massara Merlot (Sonoma Valley) $25. Very nice, a soft, supple red wine with flair and elegance. Has deep, rich flavors of plums, blackberries, and coffee, and dry, complex tannins, and feels good in the mouth. It will develop for a few years. **89** —*S.H. (10/1/2003)*

Kenwood 2004 Pinot Noir (Russian River Valley) $18. Very ripe in the mouth, with mounds of black-cherry and mocha flavors, this Pinot has a full-bodied, slightly heavy feeling. It's dry and silky, and a nice example of a good Russian River Pinot from a warm vintage. **85** —*S.H. (5/1/2006)*

Kenwood 2003 Pinot Noir (Russian River Valley) $17. Round, smooth, and polished, this Pinot shows jazzy flavors of raspberries, cherries, mocha, vanilla, and smoke. It's a tasty sipper, and has a light, silky mouthfeel. **87** —*S.H. (6/1/2005)*

Kenwood 2002 Pinot Noir (Russian River Valley) $17. Picture-postcard cool-climate Pinot, with young, fresh cherry, strawberry, and mint aromas, a modest overlay of smoky oak, and refreshing acidity. Delicate and feminine, this silky wine is elegant and crisp through the finish. **88** *(11/1/2004)*

Kenwood 2001 Pinot Noir (Russian River Valley) $17. A pale shadow of richer Russian River Pinot, but with plenty of flavor and appellation character. Sort of an introductory Pinot, with pretty cola and cherry flavors and silky tannins. Snaps to a quick finish. **85** —*S.H. (7/1/2003)*

Kenwood 2000 Pinot Noir (Russian River Valley) $17. Creamy and supple in feel, with strawberry, dried cherry, and cola notes, this shows handsome smoke and leather accents. But a strong herbaceous note (to some tasters it was even vegetal) shows a little at first, and expands with time. Closes lean, tart, and green. **85** *(7/1/2003)*

Kenwood 1999 Pinot Noir (Russian River Valley) $17. This wine preserves the region's vital characteristics (well-ripened fruit and spice), although they've been diluted by necessity for commercial purposes, what with 28,000 cases produced. Light and soft, with delicate yet surprisingly delicious black-raspberry, smoke, and cinnamon notes. **86** —*S.H. (5/1/2001)*

Kenwood 2000 Jack London Vineyard Pinot Noir (Sonoma Valley) $20. 80 *(10/1/2002)*

Kenwood 2005 Pinot Noir Rosé Pinot Noir (Russian River Valley) $15. A market glut of Pinot Noir grapes and wine is resulting in more vintners offering the variety as a blush. Consumers are the beneficiaries. This delightful wine is delicate, silky, and dry, with tangy acids framing subtle strawberries and cream flavors. **86** —*S.H. (12/15/2006)*

Kenwood 2004 Reserve Pinot Noir (Russian River Valley) $25. Here's a likeable, complex Pinot, rich in varietal flavor and dry. The silky mouthfeel is elegant, while the cherry, cocoa, rhubarb, and cola fruit is expressive and satisfying through the long, pepper-spicy finish. Drink now. **90** —*S.H. (9/1/2006)*

Kenwood 2000 Reserve Olivet Pinot Noir (Russian River Valley) $30. A charming wine with lots of Pinot character. Flavors range from cherries and berries to rose, tobacco, coffee, and peppery spice. A little on the thin side, it's very light and soft in the mouth, and is not built for age. But it's fun and enjoyable now. **86** —*S.H. (7/1/2003)*

Kenwood 1999 Reserve-Olivet Pinot Noir (Russian River Valley) $30. A handsome wine that blends dark cherries and blackberries with lighter strawberry and even stewed tomato flavors, supported by smoke, cinnamon-clove, and dried herb accents. With its supple, balanced mouthfeel, this is a tasty, attractive wine for the near-term. Drink now–2005. **89** *(10/1/2002)*

Kenwood 2005 Sauvignon Blanc (Sonoma County) $13. Clean as a whistle, brisk in acidity, and tangy in citrus flavors, this county wine satisfies at a fair price. It finishes extremely dry, with a flourish of spice. **85** —*S.H. (11/15/2006)*

Kenwood 2004 Sauvignon Blanc (Sonoma County) $13. Run, don't walk, to buy this by the case. It's California SB at its best, long and deep in gooseberry and alfalfa flavors, but complexed with richer notes of lime, peach custard, and vanilla pudding. But it's not a sweetie. It's dry and crisp in acids. **90 Best Buy** —*S.H. (12/1/2005)*

Kenwood 2003 Sauvignon Blanc (Sonoma County) $11. Lovers of grassy, citrusy and bone-dry white wines will go gaga over this one. It has those hay and gooseberry notes, only lightly touched by oak, that drink so fresh and vibrant, accompanied by crisp acidity. Good value. **86 Best Buy** —*S.H. (12/31/2004)*

Kenwood 2002 Sauvignon Blanc (Sonoma County) $11. A simple, refreshing little wine, with clean, modest flavors of fruits and spices. Bring it to the beach. **83** —*S.H. (12/31/2003)*

Kenwood 2001 Sauvignon Blanc (Sonoma County) $12. Satisfyingly crisp and juicy, with Lifesaver candy flavors of lemon, lime, and peach. The wine is very clean. It's on the sweet side, and will be good with tropical fruit salsas. **85** —*S.H. (9/1/2003)*

Kenwood 2000 Sauvignon Blanc (Sonoma County) $13. Quite tasty, with ripe, bright grapefruit, passionfruit, lemon, and herb flavors. It's light and refreshing; long and clean on the finish. A terrific quaffer. **88 Best Buy** —*J.M. (11/15/2001)*

Kenwood 1999 Sauvignon Blanc (Sonoma County) $12. **85** —*S.H. (11/15/2000)*

Kenwood 1998 Sauvignon Blanc (Sonoma County) $11. **85** —*M.M. (3/1/2000)*

Kenwood 2005 Reserve Sauvignon Blanc (Sonoma County) $15. Green grass, cat pee, gooseberry, and lemons and limes are the flavors that mark this crisp white wine. These strong flavors won't appeal to everyone. Nice with bruschetta with grilled veggies and chèvre. **84** —*S.H. (12/15/2006)*

Kenwood 2004 Reserve Sauvignon Blanc (Sonoma County) $15. Kenwood's regular Sauvignon Blanc was a hard act to top. This one costs two bucks more, and while it's richer in creamy oak and lees, it's really not better, just different. It's a yummy, complex wine, and this is a great price for this quality. **90 Best Buy** —*S.H. (12/1/2005)*

Kenwood 2002 Reserve Sauvignon Blanc (Sonoma County) $15. Smooth and polished, and just happens to be delicious. You'll find clean, soft flavors of lime, orange zest, honeydew melon, and spice, with oaky shadings. **86** —*S.H. (2/1/2005)*

Kenwood 2001 Reserve Sauvignon Blanc (Sonoma County) $15. A nice, easy-drinking sipper that goes right to the soul of Sauvignon Blanc in its lemon and grass flavors, with riper notes of melons and figs. Barrel fermentation softens, and the wine turns slightly sweet on the finish. Perfect with fruity salsa toppings. **86** —*S.H. (9/1/2003)*

Kenwood 2000 Reserve Sauvignon Blanc (Sonoma County) $15. Smells like fresh summer fruit, and tastes like it, too. Watermelon, peach, apple, and a bite of spearmint all come together in a creamy package. Heightened with just enough acidity to make it sing; it finishes slightly sweet. **86** —*S.H. (12/15/2001)*

Kenwood 1997 Reserve Sauvignon Blanc (Sonoma County) $16. **87** —*L.W. (9/1/1999)*

Kenwood 2003 Jack London Vineyard Syrah (Sonoma Valley) $30. Here's a huge wine that trades subtlety for sheer power. It's in your face, an explosion of blackberry and cherry flavors with a cinnamon-sprinkled espresso finish and bigtime tannins, and is thankfully dry. Drink now through 2007. **86** —*S.H. (12/31/2006)*

Kenwood 2003 Zinfandel (Sonoma County) $16. There's an upfront taste of raisins in this dry wine, but it's not distracting. Rather, it's a seasoning to the blackberry, currant, and plum flavors, with their edge of sweet oak and spices. Soft and beguiling, this lovely Zin will be great with beef stew. **87** —*S.H. (3/1/2006)*

Kenwood 2002 Zinfandel (Sonoma County) $16. This is a great example of coastal Zin 101. Dry and balanced, with upfront, sun-ripened wild berry and peppery, spicy flavors, and rich but easy tannins. The acidity is substantial and lasts through the finish. **86** —*S.H. (10/1/2005)*

Kenwood 2001 Zinfandel (Sonoma County) $16. Fairly smooth and round on the palate, with an elegant, lighter-styled array of black-cherry, blackberry, plum, toast, and coffee flavors. The finish is moderate in length, but fairly plush. **87** *(11/1/2003)*

Kenwood 2000 Zinfandel (Sonoma County) $16. An easy, quaffable Zin with pleasant berry and herb flavors and a fine finish. It's very dry and well-balanced, and has good acidity and nice, dusty tannins. **86** —*S.H. (3/1/2003)*

Kenwood 1999 Zinfandel (Sonoma County) $16. Pretty cherry and herb flavors lead the way here. Tannins are a bit rustic and the finish somewhat herbal. **84** —*J.M. (3/1/2002)*

Kenwood 1998 Zinfandel (Sonoma County) $15. Full berry cocoa and pepper aromas on the nose open to solid black-cherry and chocolate flavors. The mouthfeel is big, but there's fairly high acidity, too, and some big tannins with a decided bite on the back end. The elements are there in this dense and chunky wine; only time will tell if they come into greater harmony. **85** *(3/1/2001)*

Kenwood 1997 Zinfandel (Sonoma Valley) $15. **89** —*P.G. (11/15/1999)*

Kenwood 2004 Jack London Vineyard Zinfandel (Sonoma Valley) $23. Nice and forward in jammy wild cherry, blackberry, and root beer flavors, with a peppery, spicy edge, this super-drinkable Zin is a little soft, but dry and balanced. It's as full-bodied as a Cabernet, and finishes with enough complexity to pair with robust meats and full-flavored cheeses. **87** —*S.H. (12/31/2006)*

Kenwood 2003 Jack London Vineyard Zinfandel (Sonoma Valley) $20. I tasted this alongside Kenwood's Reserve Zin, and although it's priced the same, it's not half the wine despite the vineyard designation. This one's raisiny and hot, with a sweetened coffee taste. **83** —*S.H. (12/31/2005)*

Kenwood 2002 Jack London Vineyard Zinfandel (Sonoma Valley) $20. A solid Zin, rich in blackberry, cassis, cherry, coffee, and spice flavors, and dry. It shows a nice balance of fruit, acidity and tannins, with a smooth mouth feel. **88** —*S.H. (4/1/2005)*

Kenwood 2001 Jack London Vineyard Zinfandel (Sonoma Mountain) $20. Lovely, a mountain wine with big, concentrated fruity flavors of cherries, raspberries, and sweet blueberries, and big, firm tannins. Yet those tannins are ripe and sweet. Floods the mouth with fruit, and leaves behind vanilla, oaky shadings. **90** —*S.H. (4/1/2004)*

Kenwood 2000 Jack London Vineyard Zinfandel (Sonoma Valley) $20. More evidence of the spottiness of this vintage. Well-made and with good structural integrity due to a fine pedigree of tannins, but the blackberry flavors are diluted with herbal, green notes veering into chlorophyll. Not likely to improve, so drink now. **86** —*S.H. (3/1/2003)*

Kenwood 1999 Jack London Vineyard Zinfandel (Sonoma Valley) $20. A pretty wine, with subtle cherry and herb notes at its core. Moderate body and a moderate finish wrap it up. **86** —*J.M. (3/1/2002)*

Kenwood 1998 Jack London Vineyard Zinfandel (Sonoma Valley) $20. This solid, mainstream Zinfandel displays blackberry fruit and some creamy notes on the nose. Well-defined, dark berry flavors with white pepper and leather accents mark the palate. The mouthfeel is even and the finish here is brisk, tart, and juicy. A touch less oak might let the fruit shine a bit more. **86** *(3/1/2001)*

Kenwood 1997 Jack London Vineyard Zinfandel (Sonoma Valley) $20. **84** —*P.G. (11/15/1999)*

Kenwood 1999 Mazzoni Zinfandel (Sonoma County) $20. Licorice-like on the palate, with an herbal, smoky follow up. Tannins are ripe and rich thought the finish has a touch of tartness. **88** —*J.M. (3/1/2002)*

Kenwood 1997 Mazzoni Zinfandel (Sonoma County) $20. **87** —*S.H. (12/1/2000)*

Kenwood 1999 Nuns Canyon Zinfandel (Sonoma Valley) $20. Bright, spicy cherry and herb flavors are highlighted in this light-textured Zin. Moderate tannins and body make it an easy quaff. **86** —*J.M. (3/1/2002)*

Kenwood 1997 Nuns Canyon Zinfandel (Sonoma Valley) $20. **88** —*S.H. (12/1/2000)*

Kenwood 1997 Old Vine Zinfandel (California) $16. **85** —*P.G. (11/15/1999)*

Kenwood 2003 Reserve Zinfandel (Sonoma County) $20. Lots of Zinny character in this wine, with its flavors of just-picked wild berries, pepper, and that brambly, briary character that marks the variety. There's a deep juicy character that's simply scrumptious. Best of all, the wine is dry and balanced. **91 Editors' Choice** —*S.H. (12/31/2005)*

Kenwood 2002 Reserve Zinfandel (Sonoma County) $20. Shows real Zinny character with its brambly berry fruit, which tastes of the sun in every ripe taste. Lots of spicy notes, with an edge of espresso. This dry wine is soft in acids and tannins. **85** —*S.H. (2/1/2005)*

Kenwood 2001 Reserve Mazzoni Vineyard Zinfandel (Russian River Valley) $20. This easy Zin has black raspberry and cherry flavors, and a distinctive streak of white chocolate and sweet basil that adds complexity. It's lush and full bodied, with ripe tannins and a burst of juicy acidity. **87** —*S.H. (4/1/2004)*

Kenwood 2000 Reserve Mazzoni Vineyard Zinfandel (Sonoma County) $20. From a warm vineyard in northern Alexander Valley, a dark wine, hot wine. The flavors veer into blackberries and other wild berries with a streak of tobacco and earth. It is very dry and a bit rough. Will benefit from a few years in the cellar. **86**—*S.H. (3/1/2003)*

Kenwood 1997 Upper Weise Zinfandel (Sonoma Valley) $15. 87—*S.H. (12/1/2000)*

Kenwood 1997 Upper Weise Vineyard Zinfandel (Sonoma Valley) $15. Interesting cedar, game, and leather notes accent this wine's blackberry and chocolate aromas and flavors. There's an almost Rhône-like quality to this full-bodied, well-balanced wine. Produced from a certified organic vineyard, the finish displays dark cherry and chocolate flavors with peppery accents. **86** *(3/1/2001)*

KESTREL

Kestrel 2002 Cabernet Sauvignon (Yakima Valley) $20. Dark, roasted barrel scents cover the tart berry fruit. Chocolate and espresso dominate; the actual wine is tart, astringent, and completely overpowered. **83**—*P.G. (12/15/2005)*

Kestrel 1997 Cabernet Sauvignon (Columbia Valley (WA)) $21. The winery held back releasing the wine until this spring, probably to give the tannins extra time to soften up. It's got herbal flavors and the fruit seems to be fading. Drink up. **85**—*P.G. (9/1/2002)*

Kestrel 1998 Old Vine Cabernet Sauvignon (Columbia Valley (WA)) $50. A harvest of just 2 tons/acre from 30-year-old vines created this gem, a lovely companion to the winery's Old Vine Merlot. It's fragrant and lush, a lively mix of mushroom, spice, and gentle fruit. The nose rolls on into a textured, multilayered explosion, with generous and subtle flavors of preserves, leaf, and spice. **92**—*P.G. (9/1/2002)*

Kestrel 2002 Old Vine Estate Cabernet Sauvignon (Yakima Valley) $50. Hard and tannic with scents of old leather. Very slowly the black-cherry fruit emerges, along with moist earth, coconut, and vanilla. Barrel flavors overpower the lightweight fruit, which is simply plowed under with oak. The hot, bitter tannins add a jarring note to the finish. **85**—*P.G. (12/15/2005)*

Kestrel 2002 Merlot (Columbia Valley (WA)) $20. A Bordeaux blend whose oaky nose is leavened with leather and tobacco scents. The cherry and plum fruit flavors are substantial enough to bring the wine into a briefly sweet pie cherry midpalate. Chewy and astringent on the finish. **85**—*P.G. (12/15/2005)*

Kestrel 1999 Merlot (Yakima Valley) $20. Juicy and delicious, this is from the best vintage of the past decade, and it's just now opening up and showing its stuff. Ripe flavors of bright berries give it a Zin-like attack, but the back end is all Washington, with fleshy, chewy fruit and smoky tannins. **88**—*P.G. (12/15/2004)*

Kestrel 2000 Estate "Old Vine" Merlot (Yakima Valley) $50. Thick, heavy and tannic, with chewy, black-cherry fruit with plenty of graham cracker/vanilla from the barrel aging. Powerful but ultimately a simple wine. **87**—*P.G. (12/15/2004)*

Kestrel 1998 Old Vine Merlot (Yakima Valley) $50. "Old Vine" is not a phrase that crops up on many Washington wine labels, but here it is meaningful. The vineyard was planted in 1972; these are among the most venerable Merlot plantings in the state. Thick, rich red, and black fruits are nicely set off in a spicy, toasty, palate-coating wine with rare complexity. **93 Editors' Choice**—*P.G. (9/1/2002)*

Kestrel 2003 Vintners Merlot (Yakima Valley) $20. Good, solid, chunky aromas of berry and chocolate lead into ripe, spicy raspberry and cherry fruit. The wine is loaded with creamy, milk chocolatey oak. Smooth and broad, it coats the palate. Though not a deep or textured effort, the fruit and smooth mouthfeel make for plenty of near-term enjoyment. There is just enough weight to give the impression of extra ripeness, a plus in this price range. **89**—*P.G. (6/1/2006)*

Kestrel 2002 Vintners Old Vine Estate Merlot (Yakima Valley) $50. Dark, almost black-cherry colored, this is an authoritative wine with concentrated layers of red and black fruits. It's thick through the midpalate, then swings into an interesting, minty, lifted, citrusy finish. Spicy and tart, with real meat on its bones. **90**—*P.G. (6/1/2006)*

Kestrel 2002 Estate Sangiovese (Yakima Valley) $20. Sangiovese is showing some promise in Washington state, and the extra care given this wine

includes bleeding off 12% of the juice to intensify color and flavor. Violets and cranberries, cookie dough, and hints of tobacco can be found, along with the puckery acids characteristic of the grape. **86**—*P.G. (4/1/2005)*

Kestrel 2000 Syrah (Yakima Valley) $28. Forward and fruity, this medium-bodied wine shows good balance and varietal spice—white pepper and roasted coffee—along with delicious cherry/berry fruit. **88**—*P.G. (9/1/2002)*

Kestrel 1999 Syrah (Yakima Valley) $28. Jammy berry plus black-pepper and vanilla cake-batter aromas set you up for an overly sweet treat, but that's not what you get on the palate. Instead, heavy cedar, licorice, and smoke envelope blackberry fruit flavors. Mouthfeel is medium-full, though lean enough to make some reviewers wish that it had more dimension. **87** *(11/1/2001)*

Kestrel 2003 Co-fermented Syrah (Yakima Valley) $38. Dark, plummy, and very spicy, this excellent wine shows the lifted streak of citrus that seems to characterize Yakima Valley Syrahs. Penetrating and deep, its compact fruits are loaded with interesting citrus/floral highlights, and hints of exotic perfumes and powders. Long, seductive, and exotic, finishing with a lick of sealing wax. **93**—*P.G. (6/1/2006)*

Kestrel 2002 Estate Syrah (Yakima Valley) $20. There's some nice mixed berry fruit and hints of toast and lavender and a soft, supple mouthfeel, but despite a label showing only 13.8% alcohol, this wine seemed slightly hot to all three of our tasters. **83** *(9/1/2005)*

Kestrel 1999 Estate Syrah (Yakima Valley) $50. A fat, meaty wine, which tastes of very ripe berries and raw steak. Tight, dark, and smoky, it has a ripe earthiness to it that adds power and weight, but comes off a bit rough at the moment. **89**—*P.G. (9/1/2002)*

Kestrel 2002 Signature Edition Co-Ferment Syrah (Yakima Valley) $38. Shows some pretty red berry and violet notes, but they're slathered in vanilla, caramel and cinnamon toast. The lavish oaking gives it a smooth, attractive mouthfeel, but two of our reviewers found this wine too alcoholic. **85** *(9/1/2005)*

KIDDUSH HASHEM CELLARS

Kiddush Hashem Cellars 2001 Great Oaks Ranch Road Syrah (Santa Barbara County) $29. A well-made wine that serves up bright-edged cherry, raspberry, blackberry, sage, thyme, and pepper notes. Tannins are a bit powdery. With moderate body, the wine finishes with good length and just a touch of dryness. Kosher. **89**—*J.M. (4/3/2004)*

KING ESTATE

King Estate 1999 Chardonnay (Oregon) $10. Strikes a firm varietal profile with apple, peach, and vanilla flavors, oaky notes, and a creamy mouthfeel. It's a bit rough around the edges, with a simple, slightly sweet finish. **84**—*S.H. (12/1/2003)*

King Estate 1998 Chardonnay (Oregon) $10. Broad and obvious in its appeal, with peach marmalade and applesauce tastes and saccharine sweetness. There also seems to be a smoky vanilla streak from some kind of oak. It's a country-style common wine and there's not much going on beyond the fruit. **83**—*S.H. (8/1/2002)*

King Estate 1996 Chardonnay (Oregon) $14. 88—*M.M. (12/31/1999)*

King Estate 1998 Reserve Chardonnay (Oregon) $20. Smells oaky, with smoky vanilla and sweet, charred notes riding high over flamboyant tropical fruit aromas, including guavas and breadfruit. This is a big wine, but the pieces aren't all in place. It's like a symphony orchestra playing different tunes. Give it a few months to knit together. **87**—*S.H. (8/1/2002)*

King Estate 1997 Reserve Chardonnay (Oregon) $15. This is much creamier, with much more leesy flavor than the regular bottling, but not as much ripe fruit (perhaps because it is from a different vintage). Various flavors of nuts, honey, spice, and light tropical fruit mingle in a well balanced finish. **89**—*P.G. (8/1/2003)*

King Estate 2004 Pinot Gris (Oregon) $15. A touch sharp, with canned fruit on the nose along with pear and creamsicle. Melon, pear, and lime form a standard palate, although the finish is a bit acidic and stark. Zesty for sure; not that deep or intensely flavored. **85** *(2/1/2006)*

King Estate 2003 Pinot Gris (Oregon) $15. King Estate, more than any other Oregon winery, can claim Pinot Gris as its signature wine. This is pleasantly middle of the road, with flavors of pear and apple, lightly kissed with spice. **86** —*P.G. (8/1/2005)*

King Estate 2001 Pinot Gris (Oregon) $15. Intensely fruity and jammy, just bursts upon the palate with an explosion of white peach, apricot, nectarine, mango, and citrus flavors. Acids are pretty firm, creating balance. There is a strong impression of sweetness. **84** —*S.H. (12/1/2003)*

King Estate 2000 Pinot Gris (Oregon) $14. With its pear-spice profile, hint of petrol and ripe texture, it's no surprise this is a wine list favorite—it delivers positive flavor and feel in a range crowded with anonymous wines. It may be a touch hotter than the label's 13%, making it even more like many of its cousins from Alsace. Full, decidedly more Gris than Grigio in style, it's a winning ATC—alternative to Chardonnay. **88** **Best Buy** *(3/1/2002)*

King Estate 1998 Pinot Gris (Oregon) $14. **88** *(3/1/2002)*

King Estate 1997 Pinot Gris (Oregon) $13. **87** **Best Buy** *(8/1/1999)*

King Estate 2004 Domaine Pinot Gris (Oregon) $25. Pretty and elegant, it mixes detailed notes of pear, melon and light guava fruits, layered and textural. Beautifully balanced and harmonious, it's the second straight success for this new tier of organic, estate-grown wines. **91** —*P.G. (2/1/2006)*

King Estate 2003 Domaine Pinot Gris (Oregon) $25. King Estate's new high end Domaine wines, organically grown and certified, are off to a great start with this exceptional Pinot Gris. Stone fruits and citrus peel flavors dominate, layered and textural. The fruit is fleshy but not fat, with pear, papaya, and mixed tropical highlights, and a crisp, snappy, clean finish. **91** —*P.G. (2/1/2005)*

King Estate 2004 Domaine Vin Glacé Pinot Gris (Oregon) $25. This is one solid, tight nectar with exotic stone-fruit aromas alongside honey, melon, and apricot. It's got just enough complexity to satisfy fans of serious European dessert wines. Long and sweet late, with excellent acidity and a lush texture. **93** **Editors' Choice** *(2/1/2006)*

King Estate 2001 Reserve Pinot Gris (Oregon) $20. Higher in acids and lower in sugar than the regular bottling, and shares most of the same characteristics. Packed with jammy white stone fruit and floral flavors. Lees adds a rich, creamy texture. Still, it's not a dry wine, and is best matched with dishes with some sweetness. **86** —*S.H. (8/19/2003)*

King Estate 2000 Reserve Pinot Gris (Oregon) $20. Flavorful and richly textured with pear, nutmeg, earth, and petrol aromas and flavors. The complex palate expands with melon, peach, citrus, and pepper notes, all supported by good acidity. Strikes a nice textural balance between roundness and crispness. The tangy close of this handsome, large-scaled white shows dry citrus-pear notes. A superb match for veal or pork. **90** **Editors' Choice** *(3/1/2002)*

King Estate 1997 Reserve Pinot Gris (Oregon) $18. **87** *(8/1/1999)*

King Estate 2001 Vin Glacé Pinot Gris (Oregon) $18. A very sweet wine that tastes like the juice of fresh, ripe pears, sweetened with sugar and honey. It's simple but has good acidity. Snaps to a clean finish. **86** —*S.H. (12/1/2003)*

King Estate 2004 Vin Glacé Pinot Gris (Oregon) $18. Straightforward but hedonistic, with pure yet mature apricot and nectarine aromas flowing on an unctuous, fully ripe bouquet. Candied apple, orange, and apricot flavors are committed and easy to grasp; really focuses on freshness and acidity more than complexity. **91** *(2/1/2006)*

King Estate 2000 Vin Glacé Pinot Gris (Oregon) $18. More nutty and buttery than sweet up front, this dessert wine shows almond and dried apricot hints on the nose. Decent acidity holds it together firmly, with the sweetness blossoming on the late-mid and back palate. Closes longer than you first think, as it does a false fade, making a nice reprise with an orange-almond back bouquet. **88** *(3/1/2002)*

King Estate 2001 Pinot Noir (Oregon) $22. Herbal and sharp in acids, with austere, tobacco, and herb flavors that just manage to break into cherries. Finishes dry and tannic. **84** —*S.H. (12/15/2004)*

King Estate 2000 Pinot Noir (Oregon) $20. Here is a good, even-handed Pinot with clean, soft fruit flavors dominating. No hint of stem or earth; light nuances of grass, herb and spice along with soft, plummy fruit and an easy finish. **88** —*P.G. (12/15/2002)*

King Estate 1999 Pinot Noir (Oregon) $22. A stewy red fruit, tomato, meat, toast, and herb bouquet announces this producer's solid, smooth regular bottling. It's undeniably tasty, with cherry, plum skin, earth, and leather flavors, and an even mouthfeel. Very accessible, it closes with tart fruit and spice flavors. Don't wait—drink now–2004. **88** *(10/1/2002)*

King Estate 1998 Pinot Noir (Oregon) $20. Dusty cherry and smoke aromas open this fairly light Pinot Noir. Even and supple in the mouth, it offers red berry and rhubarb flavors and mild herb accent notes. Licorice and tar hints add a little complexity. Finishes smoothly with decent length, but without the substance expected of a 1998. Drink now. **85** *(3/1/2002)*

King Estate 1996 Pinot Noir (Oregon) $18. **84** *(10/1/1999)*

King Estate 1999 Croft Vineyard Pinot Noir (Willamette Valley) $40. Darker than the winery's other single-vineyard Pinot, this one shows intense raspberry/loganberry flavors, and some spice and pepper too. There is good concentration in the midpalate, with tart, tangy, tightly-wound fruit and well-integrated tannins. I would prefer a bit more new oak, but even so there is a pleasant toasty bite to the finish. **91** —*P.G. (8/1/2002)*

King Estate 2003 Domaine Pinot Noir (Willamette Valley) $50. From organically grown (and certified) grapes, this tart, spicy, silky Pinot shows a lot of class and style. The fruit glides onto the palate, with a pleasing mix of cherries, berries, rhubarb, and pomegranate. The acids and tannins are balanced and firm, and there are appropriate herbal components that let you know it's Pinot and not Zinfandel. **90** —*P.G. (9/1/2006)*

King Estate 2002 Domaine Pinot Noir (Oregon) $50. This latest release of King Estate's top-of-the-line Domaine bottling shows that the 2001 was no fluke. A serious effort, juicy and concentrated, it opens with lovely scents of Pinot cherry-berry and plum fruit, layered with earth, wood, leaf, spice, and plenty of tart fruit. The new oak is there but restrained, and the structure suggests that putting this one away for a few years will be very rewarding. **91** **Cellar Selection** —*P.G. (11/15/2005)*

King Estate 2001 Domaine Pinot Noir (Oregon) $50. Most Oregon wineries seem to equate high prices with high extract, high alcohol, and high concentrations of new oak. King Estate's lovely and elegant new Domaine bottling shows a different style to good effect. Powerful scents of Pinot cherry/berry and plum fruit, laced with toast, milk chocolate, vanilla wafer, and creamery butter lead into a firm, supple, silky wine. Graceful and seamless, it's a supremely elegant Pinot that expresses the grape with quiet power. **91** —*P.G. (2/1/2005)*

King Estate 1999 Domaine Pinot Noir (Oregon) $50. Smoky, deep, and darkly fruited, the harmonious nose sets the stage for rich fruit, spices, herbs, and ample oak, which all come together with intensity and style. Then the juicy long finish wraps it up beautifully. Pinot purists might decry a lack of restraint, but to us the potent combination of intensity and complexity is the star. Drink now through 2007 **91** **Editors' Choice** *(10/1/2002)*

King Estate 1998 Domaine Pinot Noir (Oregon) $50. Uniformly well-liked by our panel, the Domaine bottling offers fat, tart-sweet cherry-berry aromas and flavors bearing earth, smoke, and spice accents. The fruit is full and bouncy on the tongue, with interesting mint and cocoa notes. Balanced and elegant, this tasty wine is tempting now and should improve further, drinking well through 2006. **90** *(3/1/2002)*

King Estate 1999 Pfeiffer Vineyards Pinot Noir (Willamette Valley) $40. Sweet fruit, pure and crystal clear defines this single-vineyard effort from King Estate. It's a crisp, tight Pinot with firm fruit and a concentrated, spicy middle. Nothing jammy or over the top, but well made and knit together. This is the third year they have made the wine, though just the second "official" release. **89** —*P.G. (8/1/2002)*

King Estate 1998 Pfeiffer Vineyards Pinot Noir (Willamette Valley) $40. Lean and attractive with chalk, yeast, and anise notes accenting bright fruit aromas. More Burgundian in manner than the other wines, this is light- to medium-weight with a lively mouthfeel. Shows good flavor intensity, with herb and vanilla offsetting the tart cherry flavors. The moderately long close shows more of the same and even tannins. Drink now through 2004. **88** *(3/1/2002)*

King Estate 1999 Reserve Pinot Noir (Oregon) $35. A finesse style, elegant and soft. Smooth, fruit forward, and perfectly balanced. Nothing out of proportion, no hint of stem or harsh or bitter tannins. There is a lovely purity of fruit, mixed red fruits, plum and cherry. A mere hint of chocolate shavings, but the oak is minimal, perhaps too minimal. **90** —*P.G. (8/1/2002)*

King Estate 1998 Reserve Pinot Noir (Oregon) $35. Solid and flavorful, with a bouquet of smoky oak over dry cherry fruit, accented by pepper and spice. The wood is plentiful but handsome, nicely framing the ripe fruit. Earthy forest-floor notes and a supple yet tangy mouthfeel complete the attractive package. It's warm and inviting, finishing with good length. Drink now through 2005. Significantly better than a bottle rated previously. **89** *(3/1/2002)*

King Estate 2003 Signature Pinot Noir (Oregon) $25. King Estate is retooling their Pinot lineup, eliminating the reserve tier. This "Signature" bottling incorporates a higher percentage (almost two thirds) of estate-grown fruit. Firm and tight, it's a nice mix of berries and pomegranate, hard and lightly metallic. There are hints of bark and earth, and the structure to improve over the next 3–5 years. **89** —*P.G. (5/1/2006)*

King Estate 1998 Late Harvest Riesling (Oregon) $18. 87 —*J.C. (12/31/1999)*

KING FISH

King Fish NV Pinot Grigio (California) $6. Easy and rustic, which in this case means lots of user-friendly, uncomplicated fruit. I wish it were drier, but it has good balancing acidity. **83 Best Buy** —*S.H. (12/1/2006)*

KINGS RIDGE

Kings Ridge 2002 Pinot Noir (Oregon) $17. Herbal, with fruit scents of beet and strawberry. This is a simple wine, but pleasant and open, with a fruit-forward style that carries itself lightly. **85** *(11/1/2004)*

Kings Ridge 2000 Pinot Noir (Oregon) $15. This is the second label of Rex Hill, and it's a fine, engaging, Beaujolais-like wine, fruity and forward. Lightly spicy, with zippy acids and lively fruit, it's the perfect quaffing wine while waiting for the Rex Hill single-vineyard wines to evolve. There are very few Oregon Pinots of this quality at this price. **87 Best Buy** —*P.G. (4/1/2002)*

KINTER COLLINS

Kinter Collins 2004 Pacheco Vineyard Chardonnay (Sonoma Coast) $18. Here's a tight, acidic young Chard from this cool-climate appellation. It's showing lots of mineral flavors now, against a background of Meyer lemon, and apricot, and the finish is totally dry. **86** —*S.H. (10/1/2006)*

Kinter Collins 2003 Pacheco Vineyard Chardonnay (Sonoma Coast) $18. The cool climate has accentuated the minerality and tangy acidity of this wine, which is its basic structure. Ripeness contributes tantalizing tastes of lime and mango. To this, the winemaker has seasoned brilliantly with oak, which is smoky, caramelly, vanilla-infused and creamy. What a wonderful wine. It makes you wonder how they sell it at this price. **91 Editors' Choice** —*S.H. (12/1/2005)*

KIONA

Kiona 2001 Cabernet Sauvignon (Washington) $20. A tight, spicy Cab, with a gamy streak running through peppery, sweet black-cherry fruit. Plenty of firm tannins, and some early suggestions of lead pencil and tobacco, along with anise and smoke. **88** —*P.G. (5/1/2004)*

Kiona 1997 Cabernet Sauvignon (Washington) $20. 87 —*P.G. (11/15/2000)*

Kiona 2001 Estate Bottled Reserve Cabernet Sauvignon (Red Mountain) $32. Their reserve Cab, from their own Red Mountain vineyard, is this winery's finest effort. The 2001 is not quite as penetrating and powerful as the magnificent 1999, but it is a stylish, polished, almost steely wine with medium-term aging potential, perfectly ripened fruit, a fine focus and highlights of Red Mountain minerals. **90** —*P.G. (5/1/2004)*

Kiona 1997 Reserve Cabernet Sauvignon (Yakima Valley) $30. 87 —*P.G. (11/15/2000)*

Kiona 1998 Cabernet Sauvignon-Merlot (Washington) $10. 85 —*P.G. (11/15/2000)*

Kiona 2002 Chardonnay (Washington) $10. A soft wine that doesn't try to be more than it is. Pale citrus fruit is given little (if any) oak exposure; this is a plain, but balanced, everyday style of Chardonnay. **86 Best Buy** —*P.G. (5/1/2004)*

Kiona 1998 Chardonnay (Washington) $10. 85 —*P.G. (11/15/2000)*

Kiona 2000 Estate Bottled Reserve Chardonnay (Red Mountain) $20. Deep gold and saturated with nutty, oily scents, this wine seems well on its way to maturity. The fruit flavors—green apple, pineapple—are subsumed to the flavors of early oxidation; roasted nuts, yeast and minerals. **87** —*P.G. (5/1/2004)*

Kiona 1998 Reserve Chardonnay (Columbia Valley (WA)) $18. 86 —*P.G. (11/15/2000)*

Kiona 2003 Chenin Blanc (Columbia Valley (WA)) $8. Light and smooth, with a Vouvray-like hint of honeyed sweetness, this is a perfect springtime sipping wine. Great for decks, docks, and picnics. **87 Best Buy** —*P.G. (5/1/2004)*

Kiona 1998 Chenin Blanc (Columbia Valley (WA)) $6. A ripe, almost thick, peach-laden wine with big, rich fruit and lots of punch. **87** —*P.G. (8/19/2003)*

Kiona 1999 Ice Wine Chenin Blanc (Yakima Valley) $19. 90 —*P.G. (11/15/2000)*

Kiona 2001 Lemberger (Columbia Valley (WA)) $10. At one time, Lemberger (also known as Blaufrankisch) was touted as the Zinfandel of Washington. Now that Washington actually makes Zinfandel, not to mention Syrah, poor old Lem has lost a bit of lustre. Nonetheless Kiona's was, and is, one of the best. Soft, grapy, fruity, simple, and scrumptious. **87 Best Buy** —*P.G. (5/1/2004)*

Kiona 1998 Lemberger (Washington) $10. 89 *(11/15/1999)*

Kiona 1998 Merlot (Columbia Valley (WA)) $20. This is still the current release. A very hot vintage in Washington, it leads with a Portlike nose of raisins and prunes; follows with soft, ripe and roasted flavors. The tannins are deep and earthy. Drink now. **87** —*P.G. (9/1/2002)*

Kiona 1997 Merlot (Washington) $20. 86 —*P.G. (11/15/2000)*

Kiona 2001 Estate Bottled Reserve Merlot (Red Mountain) $30. Soft, plummy, and lightly spiced, this seems a bit thin and green, given the premier vineyard and an exceptional vintage. Somehow the fruit didn't go the extra mile, and the wine doesn't have the weight and complexity of past Kiona reserves. **87** —*P.G. (5/1/2004)*

Kiona 1999 Late Harvest Muscat (Yakima Valley) $7. 88 Best Buy —*P.G. (11/15/2000)*

Kiona 2003 Dry Riesling (Columbia Valley (WA)) $8. A whiff of bottling sulfur blows off quickly, leading into a bold, vivacious, crisply defined, dry and fruit-driven wine. Nicely mixes honeysuckle, Meyer lemon, and hints of pink grapefruit with a textured, mineral finish. **89 Best Buy** —*P.G. (5/1/2004)*

Kiona 2000 Dry White Riesling (Columbia Valley (WA)) $8. Scents of lemon wax and a slightly spritzy mouthfeel are followed by somewhat surprisingly sweet fruit for a wine labeled dry. The flavors favor orange juice and orange candy. If you like a fairly heavy, fruit-forward style, this is just right. **87** —*P.G. (9/1/2002)*

Kiona 2003 White Riesling (Columbia Valley (WA)) $8. This off-dry version is a perfect wine for Thai food. The fruit nicely combines tropical flavors with citrus; there is a hint of sweetness, and the elegant, stylish finish continues indefinitely. Graceful and seductive. **89 Best Buy** —*P.G. (5/1/2004)*

Kiona 1999 Rosé Blend (Columbia Valley (WA)) $6. 85 Best Buy —*P.G. (11/15/2000)*

Kiona 1998 Sémillon (Columbia Valley (WA)) $9. 87 Best Buy —*P.G. (11/15/2000)*

Kiona 2002 Syrah (Red Mountain) $25. One taster noted an odd, pickle-barrel quality to this wine, but as our other reviewers did not, his score was discounted. The tasters who liked the wine praised it for its bright blackberry fruit and peppery spice allied to ripe tannins. **86** *(9/1/2005)*

USA

Kiona 1998 Syrah (Yakima Valley) $30. A split-personality, split-decision wine in which berry fruit and creamy chocolate are offset by a pine-green herb streak. That infuses the wine with a neo-Rhônish, woody, resiny quality that appealed to certain tasters and left others cold. Some enjoyed the unique strawberry-cocoa-raisin flavors, others found the dry, green profile just too much. **85** *(11/1/2001)*

Kiona 1997 Syrah (Yakima Valley) $30. 84 —*P.G. (11/15/2000)*

Kiona 1998 White Riesling (Columbia Valley (WA)) $6. 85 —*P.G. (11/15/2000)*

Kiona 1998 Dry White Riesling (Columbia Valley (WA)) $6. 86 Best Buy —*P.G. (11/15/2000)*

Kiona 1998 Late Harvest White Riesling (Yakima Valley) $7. 88 Best Buy —*P.G. (11/15/2000)*

KIRKLAND RANCH

Kirkland Ranch 1998 Cabernet Sauvignon (Napa Valley) $30. A creamy wine offering berry and black-cherry fruit, offset by licorice and menthol accents. This mid-weight Cab has a soft palate of ripe fruit, licorice, and vanilla. Finishes evenly with smooth, dry tannins and dark fruit. **89** *(9/1/2001)*

Kirkland Ranch 1998 Estate Cabernet Sauvignon (Napa Valley) $36. Opaque and full-scale, this plush wine has deep cassis and tobacco aromas. Yes, there's an intense amount of cedar and vanilla oak, but it's well married to the deep black currant fruit. Finishes long and dense, with firm tannins and chocolate notes. Age for two or three years; should keep for a decade or more. **91 Cellar Selection** *(9/1/2001)*

Kirkland Ranch 2000 Chardonnay (Napa Valley) $20. Lots of oak and ripe apple and peach fruit, with good acids in this dry, creamy wine. The finish is filled with cinnamon, ginger, and other spices. Can't quite overcome a certain simplicity and rusticity, though. **85** —*S.H. (6/1/2003)*

Kirkland Ranch 1999 Chardonnay (Napa Valley) $20. This mid-weight Chardonnay offers some complexity, with spicy and leesy notes accenting the apple-pear fruit. A touch of pineapple on the nose and vanilla on the palate add further interest. The mouthfeel is even, though the wine shows a bit of alcoholic heat. It finishes with good length, showing butter and spice notes. **88** *(9/1/2001)*

Kirkland Ranch 1999 KRV Block #13 Chardonnay (Napa Valley) $30. Aromas of smoke, cream, and herbs atop a ripe pineapple foundation. In the mouth, pineapple prevails again along with apple, toast, and butterscotch notes. It's supple, and though quite fruit-driven, it's not at all sweet. The wine shows complexity and finishes long and light on its feet. Top Value. **90** *(7/1/2001)*

Kirkland Ranch 1998 Merlot (Napa Valley) $24. Vanilla, cocoa, and tobacco highlight the berry fruit of this compact red. The mouthfeel is rich and not overly soft, the fruit ripe, but without the depth of the estate bottling. The finish is slightly hot, but marked by good length and tobacco and toast notes. **87** *(9/1/2001)*

Kirkland Ranch 1998 Estate Merlot (Napa Valley) $30. Toasty oak and tobacco notes frame black plums and cocoa in this nicely balanced wine. The solid black-cherry, berry, and earth flavors are on target; the mouthfeel is smooth and fairly supple. Dry and softly tannic, the finish shows good length, more plum flavors, and licorice-anise notes. **89** *(9/1/2001)*

Kirkland Ranch 2004 Pinot Grigio (Napa Valley) $16. From southern Napa, this wine has good acids and is very dry, with citrus and peach flavors. There's an earthiness, a dried herbal quality that makes it fuller-bodied than most. **83** —*S.H. (2/1/2006)*

Kirkland Ranch 2000 Pinot Noir (Napa Valley) $32. 81 *(10/1/2002)*

KIT FOX

Kit Fox 2001 Cabernet Sauvignon (California) $14. This is the kind of wine people have drunk with enjoyment, if with no particular discernment, forever. It is dry and clean, with berry, earthy flavors, and is also pretty tannic. Has some nice intensity on the finish. **84** —*S.H. (11/15/2003)*

Kit Fox 2002 Sunflower Vineyard Cabernet Sauvignon (California) $14. Hot and awkward, with earthy flavors and a harsh finish. **82** —*S.H. (5/1/2005)*

Kit Fox 2002 Cabernet Sauvignon-Syrah (California) $14. Simple and rustic, with a very dry mouthfeel and coffee flavors. **82** —*S.H. (5/1/2005)*

Kit Fox 2001 Cabernet Sauvignon-Syrah (California) $14. A dark, rough, semisweet wine reminiscent of the old jug wines of yesteryear. It has earthy, berry flavors and rugged tannins. **83** —*S.H. (11/15/2003)*

Kit Fox 2001 Fumé Blanc (California) $12. This is a simple version of Sauvignon Blanc. It has modest lemon and melon flavors, and is dry. Finishes a bit soft. **83** —*S.H. (7/1/2003)*

Kit Fox 2002 Syrah (California) $15. Lots of stubborn sulfur. Earthy, tough flavors, with a dry, rasping finish. **83** —*S.H. (5/1/2005)*

Kit Fox 2001 Syrah (California) $15. A dull, tannic wine with vague berry and herb flavors. Drinks very dry, with a tart, bitter finish. **82** —*S.H. (12/15/2003)*

Kit Fox 2001 Viognier (California) $12. Fruity, soft, and simple. The flavors are of apples, peaches, and wildflowers, and the wine is very dry. Has a nice apricoty taste that lingers through the finish. **84** —*S.H. (7/1/2003)*

KLINKER BRICK WINERY

Klinker Brick Winery 2001 Old Vine Zinfandel (Lodi) $24. A full-bodied wine, with dark, plush plum, black-cherry, tobacco, vanilla, chocolate, spice and anise flavors. Tannins are big, ripe and supple, while the finish is moderate in length. A fine effort from old vines and a relatively new winery. **89** *(11/1/2003)*

KLUGE ESTATE

Kluge Estate 2002 Brut Chardonnay (Albemarle County) $38. Despite its relative youth, this Virginia-made sparkler is pungently toasty on the nose, then moves into green apple and lime flavors. It does show its dosage a little, but finishes with decent flourishes of smoke, toast, and citrus. **86** —*J.C. (6/1/2005)*

Kluge Estate 2001 Brut Albemarle County Chardonnay (Virginia) $38. Shows some good potential, with ginger and toast aromas that develop into meaty, soy, and mushroom flavors on the palate. Creamy mouthfeel, too. Too bad there's a hint of an odd, plastic-like note to the finish. **85** —*J.C. (12/31/2004)*

KNAPP

Knapp 2000 Chardonnay (Cayuga Lake) $11. Bright and lemony, with a hint of minerals, herbs, and toast. Clean and fresh on the finsh. **86** —*J.M. (1/1/2003)*

Knapp 2001 Barrel Reserve Chardonnay (Cayuga Lake) $14. Firm structure, good body, and perky acidity give this wine focus on the palate. It's cloaked in a robe of modest oak that frames pretty melon, pear, orange, and spice flavors. Moderate length on the finish. **88** —*J.M. (1/1/2003)*

Knapp 2002 Dry Riesling (Cayuga Lake) $11. Light in weight, but quite tart and zesty in the mouth, this wine's green apple and lime flavors deliver a touch of sweetness despite the "dry" moniker. **85** —*J.C. (8/1/2003)*

Knapp 2002 Semi-Dry Riesling (Cayuga Lake) $11. Sweet and ripe, with intense flavors of apples and pears. Decent acidity keeps it from becoming cloying, but this comes close to being dessert-sweet. **85** —*J.C. (8/1/2003)*

KOEHLER

Koehler 2003 Sauvignon Blanc (Santa Ynez Valley) $12. Not a bad price for this modest wine, which satisfies for its upfront citrus and fig flavors and bone dry finish. Really cleans out the old palate. **84** —*S.H. (10/1/2005)*

KONGSGAARD

Kongsgaard 1998 Chardonnay (Oakville) $60. Apple, pear, coconut, and chalk mark the bouquet of this smooth yet crisp and brisk wine from the Napa microproducer. Lime, pineapple, and apricot with oak and cinnamon shadings are in play on the rich, viscous palate and flow beautifully through to the finish. Though full, the wine never gets weighty. It closes light on its feet, long and tangy, with lemon, cream, and oak accents. **89** *(7/1/2001)*

KORBEL

Korbel NV Blanc de Noirs Champagne Blend (California) $11. This copper-colored wine is on the fruity side, with upfront strawberry aromas next to smoke, vanilla, and bread dough. This is a very clean, very dry bubbly, full-bodied and fruity in flavor. The bubbles are a bit rough, but it's a good value. **86 Best Buy** —*S.H. (12/1/2002)*

Korbel NV Brut Champagne Blend (California) $11. Crisp, clean, and fruity, with apple and citrus aromas compounded by bread dough, vanilla, and smoke. Drinks bone dry and a bit austere, with sharp edges from acids. But it's saved by the finish, which is richly fruity. **85** —*S.H. (9/1/2003)*

Korbel NV Brut Champagne Blend (California) $11. One of America's best-selling Bruts, affordable and dependable. They score again with a delicately flavored, dry wine with elegance and finesse. **87 Best Buy** — *S.H. (12/1/2002)*

Korbel NV Brut Champagne Blend (California) $11. A nice, dry sparkling wine, showing subtle citrus, cherry, smoke, and yeast flavors. It has a good mouth feel and is balanced and crisp. **86 Best Buy** —*S.H. (12/31/2004)*

Korbel NV Brut Kosher Champagne Champagne Blend (California) $18. 84 *(12/15/1999)*

Korbel NV Brut Rosé Champagne Blend (California) $13. Salmon pink in color, this starts with a burst of raspberry cream and vanilla aromas, and turns rich and creamy on the palate. Has pretty fruit flavors of raspberries and strawberries, it's drier than you expect, more fruity than sweet. Closes with an ultraclean finish. **87** —*S.H. (6/1/2001)*

Korbel NV Chardonnay Champagne Blend (Russian River Valley) $11. Similar to Korbel's Brut, but less full-bodied, this dry, crisp wine is elegant. Finishes with citrus, peach, vanilla, and yeast flavors. **85** —*S.H. (12/31/2004)*

Korbel NV Extra Dry Champagne Blend (California) $11. Not really extra dry, but rather, off-dry. Fairly full on the palate, with a pleasant peach and citrus center. **84** —*J.M. (12/1/2002)*

Korbel 1996 Le Premier Reserve Champagne Blend (Russian River Valley) $25. This vintage Brut is clearly finer than the regular nonvintage brut. Shares the same character of dry elegance and finesse, with subtle flavor. It's very pinpointed and rich, and feels good and satisfying in the mouth. **90** —*S.H. (12/1/2002)*

Korbel 1994 Le Premier Reserve Champagne Blend (Russian River Valley) $22. 90 —*S.H. (12/1/2000)*

Korbel 1997 Master's Reserve Blanc de Noir Champagne Blend (Russian River Valley) $14. 82 —*P.G. (12/31/2000)*

Korbel NV Natural Champagne Blend (Sonoma County) $13. Medium weight, this 60% Pinot Noir and 40% Chardonnay blend boasts dry apple-earth flavors with mild lime hints. Somewhat closed on the nose, it opens a bit on the palate, and throughout displays a fine, even bead. Finishes modestly with a hint of sweet fruit. **85 Best Buy** —*M.M. (12/1/2001)*

Korbel 2000 Natural Champagne Blend (Russian River Valley) $14. A tremendously flavorful wine that showcases beautiful Chardonnay and Pinot Noir flavors. Like sipping the essence of limes and strawberries, with the crisp, scouring bubbles of Champagne. Very dry and clean, with a long, rich finish. **88 Best Buy** —*S.H. (9/1/2003)*

Korbel 1999 Natural Champagne Blend (Sonoma County) $13. Subtle Chardonnay flavors of peaches and apples taste brisk and tart thanks to high acidity, with barely any sweetness at all to soften it. This severe style is very clean, and calls for the right foods. Sushi would be perfect. **87** *(12/1/2002)*

Korbel 1996 Natural Champagne Blend (Sonoma County) $13. 84 —*L.W. (12/1/1999)*

Korbel 1995 Reserve Le Premier Champagne Blend (Russian River Valley) $22. A controversial wine among our panelists, with some praising its "elegant and complex aromas of baked bread" while others called it "woody" and "dull." There are citrus, apple, and toast flavors and a clean finish. Your best bet is to try a bottle for yourself. **87** *(12/1/2001)*

Korbel NV Rouge Champagne Blend (Sonoma County) $13. 80 —*S.H. (12/1/2000)*

Korbel NV Rouge Champagne Blend (Sonoma County) $13. This sparkling red wine opens with deep red berry and slight leathery aromas. Full, yet soft on the palate, with plenty of cherry and vanilla flavor, it's an interesting step off the well-beaten path of mainstream sparklers. The dry cherry and mineral finish shows good length, but this is a somewhat acquired taste. **86 Best Buy** —*M.M. (12/1/2001)*

Korbel NV Rouge Champagne Blend (Sonoma County) $13. Dark in color, almost red, and you might mistake it, blind-smelling, for a Pinot Noir, except for the doughy scent. Drinks rich and full-bodied, with raspberry-strawberry flavors. What's neat about this bubbly is that your mouth can't figure out if it's dry or off-dry. It straddles that mysterious line perfectly. **85** —*S.H. (12/1/2002)*

Korbel NV Chardonnay (California) $11. Basically a Chardonnay-only Brut. It has nice peach and apple flavors and a bit of sugar to soften it, but it's basically dry, and of course a little lighter and more elegant than the regular Brut. **88 Best Buy** —*S.H. (12/1/2002)*

Korbel 1998 Chardonnay (Russian River Valley) $18. 88 *(6/1/2000)*

Korbel NV Brut Champagne Chardonnay (California) $18. 85 *(12/15/1999)*

Korbel NV Chardonnay Champagne Chardonnay (California) $11. Opens with clean and inviting aromas of freshly sliced peaches, vanilla, and bread dough, and turns rather tough in the mouth. The peach flavors are fine and dry. **85** —*S.H. (12/1/2003)*

Korbel NV Blanc de Noirs Sparkling Blend (California) $11. A rich, full-bodied wine with lush flavors of cherries, raspberries, vanilla, smoke, and yeast. It's dry and creamy, with bright acids and a long, satisfying finish. **87 Best Buy** —*S.H. (12/31/2004)*

Korbel NV Blanc de Noirs Sparkling Blend (California) $11. Full-bodied and slightly sweet on the finish, this sparkler has pronounced red cherry and strawberry flavors. It will appeal to those who like a little dosage in their sparkling wine. **84** —*S.H. (12/31/2005)*

Korbel 1998 Blanc de Noirs-Cuvée Pinot Noir Sparkling Blend (Russian River Valley) $14. Kicks off with a blend of pretty peach and citrus flavors. Firm and focused, with zippy lemon, grapefruit, and spice flavors, the wine finishes with a bright, toasty edge. **87** —*J.M. (12/1/2003)*

Korbel NV Brut Sparkling Blend (California) $11. One of Korbel's most consistent wines, this Brut shows a rich elegance and balance, with doughy flavors of peaches and a hint of smoke, vanilla, and cherry. **87 Best Buy** —*S.H. (12/31/2005)*

Korbel NV Brut Sparkling Blend (California) $11. Classic Korbel Brut, elegant, delicate, and inexpensive. Nobody does a better job at this price. The wine is dry, with subtle lime, strawberry, peach, yeast, and vanilla flavors, and a finish of real elegance. Hard to believe they produced 750,000 cases. **87 Best Buy** —*S.H. (12/31/2006)*

Korbel NV Brut Rosé Sparkling Blend (California) $10. Here's a nice, easy-drinking blush bubbly. It's dry and crisp, although a little rough and sharp, with subtle strawberry and yeast flavors. **85** —*S.H. (6/1/2005)*

Korbel NV Brut Rosé Sparkling Blend (California) $11. All of Korbel's new sparklers are good values—when are they not? But this rosé is particularly elegant and delicious. It's not just the strawberries, lemon zest, vanilla, and yeasty dough flavors, which are tasty enough, it's the mouthfeel, which shows real Champagne finesse and silkiness. This blend of Russian River Pinot and Sangiovese, Chenin Blanc and Gamay from the Sacramento Delta is addictively drinkable. **87 Best Buy** —*S.H. (6/1/2006)*

Korbel NV Brut Rosé Sparkling Blend (California) $11. With lots of Pinot Noir and Gamay, this salmon-colored wine is full-bodied. It shows cherry and raspberry flavors alongside the yeast, smoke, and vanilla. Dry, round, and creamy, and easy to inhale. **87 Best Buy** —*S.H. (12/31/2004)*

Korbel NV Brut Rosé Sparkling Blend (California) $11. Pale pink, with pretty apple and cherry flavors at the fore. The wine is fresh, clean, and light textured, offering a lively, toasty finish. **86 Best Buy** —*J.M. (12/1/2003)*

Korbel NV Brut Rosé Sparkling Blend (California) $11. All of Korbel's new sparklers are good values—when are they not? But this rosé is particularly elegant and delicious. It's not just the strawberries, lemon zest, vanilla, and yeasty dough flavors, which are tasty enough, it's the mouthfeel, which shows real Champagne finesse and silkiness. This blend of Russian River Pinot Noir and Sangiovese, Chenin Blanc, and Gamay from the Delta is addictively drinkable. **87 Best Buy** —*S.H. (11/15/2006)*

Korbel NV Chardonnay Champagne Sparkling Blend (California) $11. Tastes like a country-style Chardonnay with bubbles. The flavors of peaches and green apples have a doughy edge, and the wine is elegant and dry. **85** —*S.H. (12/31/2005)*

Korbel NV Extra Dry Sparkling Blend (California) $11. Extra dry, of course, means a little sweet, and so this bubbly is. It has good acidity and modest bread dough, apple, and peach flavors, with a clean finish. **84** —*S.H. (12/31/2005)*

Korbel 1997 Le Premier Sparkling Blend (Russian River Valley) $25. Quite bright and lemony, with a rich, weighty body. Backed by pretty vanilla, toast, and nut flavors, the wine serves up a fresh, clean finish that ends with an interesting mineral edge. **89** —*J.M. (12/1/2003)*

Korbel 2004 Natural Sparkling Blend (Russian River Valley) $14. This is one of the lower dosage Korbel bubblies, and quite dry. It's a blend of Pinot Noir and Chardonnay, and has a very smooth, refined mouthfeel, with delicate flavors of citrus, yeast, honey, and a touch of strawberry. **86** —*S.H. (12/31/2006)*

Korbel 2003 Natural Sparkling Blend (Russian River Valley) $14. This driest of Korbel's lineup also bears a vintage designation. It's crisp and elegant, with bread dough flavors and a hint of lime zest and smoke. It's a great accompaniment to wedding cake. **85** —*S.H. (12/31/2005)*

Korbel 2002 Natural Sparkling Blend (Russian River Valley) $14. With minimum dosage, this is drier than Korbel's other Brut styles, and also rougher in texture. It showcases citrus, bread dough and spicy flavors. **85** —*S.H. (12/31/2004)*

KOSTA BROWNE

Kosta Browne 2002 Pinot Noir (Sonoma Coast) $28. A bit stemmy, with overripe prune and raisin flavors. Feels harsh and hot throughout. **83** *(11/1/2004)*

Kosta Browne 2002 Pinot Noir (Russian River Valley) $34. Most tasters found the aroma dominated by oak, cocoa, and herbs, but there's a deep core of tart cherry and rhubarb fruit that, laced with youthful acidity, is clean and refreshing. **86** *(11/1/2004)*

Kosta Browne 2002 Cohn Vineyard Pinot Noir (Russian River Valley) $48. Aromas and flavors ranged from rich and balanced cherries to overripe raisins and underripe hay and grass. There's a slightly sweet coffee edge to the fruit. Finishes with astringency. **84** *(11/1/2004)*

Kosta Browne 2000 Cohn Vineyard Pinot Noir (Russian River Valley) $48. Rich and ripe on the palate. Plush and full, brimming with plum, cherry, chocolate, spice, herb, and vanilla flavors. Lively and long on the finish. A real treat. **92** —*J.M. (7/1/2003)*

Kosta Browne 2002 Kanzler Vineyard Pinot Noir (Sonoma Coast) $48. Air this young wine to let it show its candied cherry and raspberry flavors. It's smooth and creamy, with some dusty tannins on the finish. Drink now with rich meats. **86** *(11/1/2004)*

KOVES-NEWLAN

Koves-Newlan 2002 Cabernet Franc (Napa Valley) $30. Rather aggressive now in acids and tannins, with lots of oak and cherry and earth flavors. Simple now, but might knit together and improve in a year or two. **84** —*S.H. (7/1/2005)*

Koves-Newlan 1999 Cabernet Sauvignon (Napa Valley) $25. Lush fruit here, all blackberries and cassis and sweet olive tapenade. The tannins are wonderful, at once firm and unyielding, and then turning buttery. Oak provides a smoky, spicy framework. The acidity is odd, though. It doesn't seem integrated. **89** —*S.H. (6/1/2002)*

Koves-Newlan 2002 Estate Cabernet Sauvignon (Oak Knoll) $35. Oak Knoll is a southern Napa Valley appellation, cooler than Oakville or Rutherford or even the mountains, which is maybe why this young wine is so tannically dry and acidic. **84** —*S.H. (12/31/2005)*

Koves-Newlan 2001 Estate Cabernet Sauvignon (Napa Valley) $35. Lush, balanced, and totally delightful, this Cab, from a veteran producer,

showcases ripe grapes bursting with currant, cherry, and oaky flavors. It's dry and elegant through the long finish. **90** —*S.H. (4/1/2005)*

Koves-Newlan 2002 Napa Valley Chardonnay (Napa Valley) $25. Oaky and leesy, from the first whiff to the finish. You pick up on the toast and char and the sweet-sour lees. The problem is the fruit, which is watery. The diluted apple flavors let the acidity dominate the mouthfeel. **84** —*S.H. (9/1/2004)*

Koves-Newlan 1999 Pinot Noir (Napa Valley) $20. Everything about this wine is designed to flatter the palate, from the cherry and black raspberry fruit, dusted with dry crushed spices, to the overlay of richly toasted oak, to the soft, yielding tannins. What's not to like? It ain't grand cru Burgundy, but it sure is nice drinking. **87** —*S.H. (9/1/2002)*

Koves-Newlan 2003 Estate Pinot Noir (Napa Valley) $26. Shows proper varietal character in the light, silky texture, dryness, and acidity, but the flavors are really thin. **83** —*S.H. (11/15/2005)*

Koves-Newlan 2002 Estate Pinot Noir (Oak Knoll) $26. Very dry and earthy, with a scour of acidy tannins, this Pinot isn't showing much fruit. It has coffee flavors, but is most notable for the astringent finish. **83** —*S.H. (11/15/2005)*

Koves-Newlan 2001 Estate Pinot Noir (Napa Valley) $26. Rather soft in texture and a little one-dimensional, but you'll find pleasant cherry, cola, and oak flavors and a rich tannin-oak complex. Finishes dry and elegant. **85** —*S.H. (4/1/2005)*

Koves-Newlan 2002 Reserve Pinot Noir (Oak Knoll) $30. I don't really see any more richness in the winery's Reserve Pinot than in the regular one, released a few months ago. The wine is thin and tart, with bitter cherry flavors, although it's clean enough. **83** —*S.H. (12/31/2005)*

Koves-Newlan 1997 Reserve Pinot Noir (Napa Valley) $26. From the winery's estate vineyard, south of Yountville, a big wine, with an impressive depth of flavor. Cherries and wild berries and all kinds of dry leafy herbs are wrapped in silky tannins, with firm acidity. Overall, the wine feels plush and luxurious all the way down. **89** —*S.H. (9/1/2002)*

Koves-Newlan 2001 Zinfandel (Napa Valley) $25. Plenty of sweet fruity flavor in this savory wine. Wild blackberries, blueberries, and cherries are joined with peppery spices, and the wine is completely dry. Keeps the alcohol nicely balanced, and will be super with barbecue. **86** —*S.H. (9/1/2004)*

KRAMER

Kramer 2002 Estate Pinot Noir (Willamette Valley) $20. Similar to the Rebecca's, with dead leaf/silage aromas. The fruit shows tart cranberry and a bit of bitter chocolate at the end. **84** *(11/1/2004)*

Kramer 2002 Rebecca's Reserve Pinot Noir (Willamette Valley) $35. Quite leafy, with barnyard scents. On the palate there's citrus peel and earthy, less than fully ripe fruit. **85** *(11/1/2004)*

Kramer 2002 Reserve Pinot Noir (Yamhill County) $30. There's a grassy herbal note on top, but the wine is fresh and forward, with mixed, ripe fruits and some root beerish spice in the finish. **86** *(11/1/2004)*

KRUTZ

Krutz 2004 Chardonnay (Santa Lucia Highlands) $30. Not much going on here besides alcohol and acidity. The fruit is thin and citrusy. A little Viognier adds modest floral notes. **82** —*S.H. (10/1/2006)*

KULETO ESTATE

Kuleto Estate 2002 Cabernet Sauvignon (Napa Valley) $60. Kuleto muscles itself into the top ranks with wines like this well-made, serious Cabernet. It's dry and balanced, and shows elegant restraint in how the blackberry and cassis fruit has been reined in but still allowed to express itself. Oak plays a supporting role. Drink now through 2008. **92** —*S.H. (12/15/2005)*

Kuleto Estate 2001 Cabernet Sauvignon (Napa Valley) $50. Like a rich dessert, cherry-centered, drizzled with crème de cassis, vanilla, and oaky caramel, with a cherry-coffee finish. Almost sweet, but not too much. Stylish and tasty. **87** —*S.H. (4/1/2005)*

Kuleto Estate 2002 Pinot Noir (Napa Valley) $40. Very good stuff here, really polished and silky. Shows a burst of jammy blackberry, strawberry,

USA

and rhubarb flavors, and what one taster described as full-on wood. Enormously rich and ripely extracted, but all the parts haven't come together. Drink now–2007. **87** *(11/1/2004)*

Kuleto Estate 2002 Sangiovese (Napa Valley) $25. What a match for dinner: This wine's high acidity will cut through cheese or meat easily, and its bigtime cherry and blackberry flavors would complement garlicky, tomato sauce nicely. Finishes dry, with a dusting of tannin. **88** —*S.H. (12/15/2005)*

Kuleto Estate 2001 Sangiovese (Napa Valley) $22. This wine's a bit thick and heavy for my taste. It sits on the palate, lacking life. Still, the plum, leather, red cherry, and cocoa flavors are pleasant, and the finish is dry. **83** —*S.H. (12/1/2005)*

Kuleto Estate 2002 Estate Syrah (Napa Valley) $40. Features a roasted, smoky nose reminiscent of campfire or toasted marshmallows; a compelling feature. That's followed by meaty flavors, some coffee and earth notes and a plump mouthfeel. Everything is going along smoothly until the finish, which turns excessively tart, adding a discordant note to an otherwise very good wine. **86** *(9/1/2005)*

Kuleto Estate 2003 Zinfandel (Napa Valley) $30. This is a really beautiful example of how Napa ripens Zin so well, especially in a warm vintage. The wine is exuberant in black currant, chocolate, and coffee fruit flavors that are complexed with smooth, firm tannins and a gentle backbone of acidity. **90** —*S.H. (12/1/2005)*

Kuleto Estate 2002 Zinfandel (Napa Valley) $28. Quite successful, with its complex array of pepper, cherry, mocha, and vanilla aromas and flavors and rich, sweet tannins. Has the finesse of a Cabernet, with Zin's wild, spicy edge. The elaborate finish is sweet and very long. **90** —*S.H. (12/15/2004)*

KULETO ESTATE FAMILY VINEYARDS

Kuleto Estate Family Vineyards 2000 Sangiovese (Napa Valley) $24. Versatile and friendly, a rich red wine abounding in cherry, plum, and mocha flavors. It's a bit soft, and may get swamped by a spicy tomato sauce, but it's an easy drink. **86** —*S.H. (5/1/2004)*

Kuleto Estate Family Vineyards 2001 Syrah (Napa Valley) $36. Soft, ripely sweet, filled with fruity flavors, draped with smoky oak, and frankly delicious. It's made in the international style, with long, fat flavors that coat the palate and linger into the finish. It will go with a wide range of foods. **90** —*S.H. (5/1/2004)*

Kuleto Estate Family Vineyards 2001 Zinfandel (Napa Valley) $28. Juicy, rich, and fairly plush on the palate. The flavors are redolent of jammy blackberry, plum, cherry, spice, toast, vanilla, and herbs. Silky tannins hold it together, finishing with good length. **90** *(11/1/2003)*

KULETO VILLA

Kuleto Villa 1998 Naitve Son Sangiovese (Napa Valley) $32. High oak marks this lush wine, with aromas of toast, blackberry, black-cherry, and spice. Dense and full-bodied, with rich fruit and a fat, fleshy mouthfeel. A little soft, but generous and plush. **88** —*S.H. (12/1/2001)*

KUNDE

Kunde 1997 Cabernet Sauvignon (Sonoma Valley) $20. 90 —*S.H. (7/1/2000)*

Kunde 2001 Cabernet Sauvignon (Sonoma Valley) $21. Rich and long in flavor, and wonderfully smooth, this is a gentle Cab that possesses some real complexity. Combines ripe blackberries, cherries, and oak with sweet tannins, and finishes soft, with a rich vanilla flourish. **90** —*S.H. (12/31/2004)*

Kunde 2000 Cabernet Sauvignon (Sonoma Valley) $21. Another well-made wine from Kunde. It has unmistakable Cab flavors of black currants, and it is well-oaked. The tannins are noticeable, dry but ripe. It's a bit soft and thin, though. **86** —*S.H. (11/15/2003)*

Kunde 1998 Cabernet Sauvignon (Sonoma Valley) $20. Softly fruity, with pleasant aromas of blackberries spiced up with a touch of smoky oak. In the mouth, the tannins are fine and melted, the acidity a bit low, creating an easy-drinking wine with plenty of upfront berry flavors. **87** —*S.H. (11/15/2001)*

Kunde 2000 Drummond Vineyard Cabernet Sauvignon (Sonoma Valley) $45. Strikes all the right high-end Cabernet notes. Ripe, plush black currant and cassis fruit, lush, soft tannins, balanced acids and a fine overlay of oak all combine for a rich mouthfeel. The quick finish suggests drinking now. **88** —*S.H. (11/15/2004)*

Kunde 1999 Drummond Vineyard Cabernet Sauvignon (Sonoma Valley) $30. Smells earthy and mushroomy, with modest flavors of blackberries. Feels flat in acidity in the mouth. A disappointment, especially considering the vintage. Tasted twice, with consistent results. **84** —*S.H. (5/1/2004)*

Kunde 1997 Drummond Vineyard Cabernet Sauvignon (Sonoma Valley) $25. This fine wine straddles the border between good and complex. The elements are terrific: pedigreed blackberry and cassis fruit, fine oak nuances, and soft Sonoma tannins. It's just a tad thin in the middle. Drink it with meat. **87** —*S.H. (7/1/2002)*

Kunde 1996 Drummond Vineyard Cabernet Sauvignon (Sonoma Valley) $24. 87 —*S.H. (12/15/2000)*

Kunde 1998 Drummond Vineyard-Estate Bottled Cabernet Sauvignon (Sonoma Valley) $27. A soft, gentle wine that slides down like velvet. The pleasant blackberry and currant flavors are very dry. Fairly rugged tannins kick in on the short finish. **88** —*S.H. (11/15/2002)*

Kunde 2002 Estate Cabernet Sauvignon (Sonoma Valley) $21. This is late for a winery to release an '02 Cab, especially at this price. But the wine has benefited from the extra aging, turning softer and gentler in tannins, yet maintaining complex, fresh cassis and blackberry-tart flavors. **88** —*S.H. (11/1/2006)*

Kunde 2002 Reserve Cabernet Sauvignon (Sonoma Valley) $60. Here's a rich, dense, impressive Cab. It shows soft acids, melted tannins, and beautifully ripe cassis, black currant, black-cherry pie, and milk chocolate flavors, with well-integrated smoky oak notes, and is thoroughly dry. It doesn't seem like an ager, but is delicious now and for the next few years. **91** —*S.H. (9/1/2006)*

Kunde 2001 Reserve Cabernet Sauvignon (Sonoma Valley) $60. Really too young to drink now—it's tannic and acidic, with that primary fruit jamminess of an immature wine. Yet it's an excellent Cabernet. Should only improve over the next two or three years. **91** —*S.H. (8/1/2005)*

Kunde 1997 Reserve Cabernet Sauvignon (Sonoma Valley) $40. This grower-turned-vintner pulls out all the stops. This is as good as the appellation gets. Displays classic Cabernet notes of cassis and olives, framed in gorgeously smoked oak. Dry, luscious tannins, creamy acids. If there's a criticism, it's a little too obvious. Think finesse. Napa has it. So far, Sonoma Valley, even at this level, doesn't. **93** —*S.H. (12/31/2001)*

Kunde 1997 Chardonnay (Sonoma Valley) $15. 88 *(11/1/1999)*

Kunde 2004 Chardonnay (Sonoma Valley) $16. With an oaky edge to the peach, apricot, and orange cream flavors, this Chard is tasty, although a little soft. It sure is ripe, all the way through the spicy finish. **85** —*S.H. (12/31/2005)*

Kunde 2003 Chardonnay (Sonoma Valley) $16. Here's a big, ripe, creamy, oaky Chardonnay. The oak stars, contributing flamboyant vanilla, char, and woody spices, but there's plenty of fruit flavor ranging from apples and peaches all the way to papayas. **86** —*S.H. (8/1/2005)*

Kunde 2001 Chardonnay (Sonoma Valley) $16. A fine young estate Chardonnay from these growers-turned-producers in the heart of the valley. Displays clean and pure apple and peach flavors, and enough oak to season with vanilla and woody spices. Balanced and pretty, and a good match for salmon or crab. **87** —*S.H. (12/1/2003)*

Kunde 2000 Chardonnay (Sonoma Valley) $16. Another sweet, oaky Chardonnay joins the ever-growing line. Not that it's an indifferent wine. This family produces nothing but impeccably tailored wines, and this one is among the best of class at this price point. **87** —*S.H. (9/1/2002)*

Kunde 1999 Chardonnay (Sonoma Valley) $16. Ripe and full-bodied with tiers of fruit flavors ranging from green apples and peaches to pears and mango. None-too-subtle oak adds vanilla, smoke, and butterscotch elements. Just enough residual sugar for it to drink a bit like an orange-vanilla milkshake. **88** —*S.H. (5/1/2001)*

USA

Kunde 1997 C.S. Ridge Chardonnay (Sonoma Valley) $20. 92 *(11/1/1999)*

Kunde 2000 C.S. Ridge Vineyard Chardonnay (Sonoma Valley) $22. Very rich and fruity, stuffed with pear, peach and mango flavors that go on and on. Oak and yielding acids give this Chard a smooth, creamy mouthfeel. **87** —*S.H. (12/15/2002)*

Kunde 1999 C.S. Ridge Vineyard Chardonnay (Sonoma Valley) $22. This is the leanest and tightest of Kunde's trio of single-vineyard offerings. It's laced with citrus flavors, tart and minerally, and it drinks crisply clean and refreshing. The finish is tart and lemony. Try with shellfish, or a grilled trout. **90** —*S.H. (5/1/2002)*

Kunde 2002 Estate Grown Chardonnay (Sonoma Valley) $16. Pretty and polished, a soft and gentle Chard with peach, spice flavors, and a touch of lees. Easy to drink and likeable for the seamless blend of fruit and oak. **86** —*S.H. (12/15/2004)*

Kunde 2001 Estate Grown, C.S. Ridge Vineyard Chardonnay (Sonoma Valley) $22. Bright and pure in tangerine and tropical fruit flavors, with a delicious spiciness and oaky vanilla creaminess. Wish it had a tad more concentration in the middle, but it's still a very good wine. **89** —*S.H. (12/15/2004)*

Kunde 2000 Kinneybrook Vineyard Chardonnay (Sonoma Valley) $22. A bit leaner and earthier by a hair than Kunde's Ridge bottling, but still a richly fruity wine. Spreads sweet oak all over the mouth, with accompanying vanilla and toast notes. Acids and tannins are soft and approachable. **86** —*S.H. (12/15/2002)*

Kunde 1997 Kinneybrook Vineyard Chardonnay (Sonoma Valley) $20. 92 *(11/1/1999)*

Kunde 2003 Reserve Chardonnay (Sonoma Valley) $35. Streamlined, with mineral, Mandarin orange, and oak flavors. This pleasant Chard, from estate vineyards in the warm Sonoma Valley, is dry and balanced. **87** —*S.H. (11/1/2006)*

Kunde 2002 Reserve Chardonnay (Sonoma Valley) $35. Made bells and whistles style, including flown-blown ripe tropical fruits, a creamy, leesy mouth feel, lots of smoky oak and vanilla, and rich, crisp acids. Awfully good, and gets better as it warms in the glass. **89** —*S.H. (12/31/2004)*

Kunde 2001 Reserve Chardonnay (Sonoma Valley) $35. This outstanding Chard is polished and absolutely delicious. The pineapple, peach, pear, and nectarine flavors have been enhanced with charry oak and a dose of lees. Creamy smooth in texture, this flavorful wine is sprinkled with a sweet tang of spice that lasts through the long finish. **91** —*S.H. (2/1/2004)*

Kunde 2000 Reserve Chardonnay (Sonoma Valley) $35. A terrifically flamboyant wine, filled with jazzy flavors that impress for their sheer hedonism. Peaches and pears veer way over to tropical fruits, and there's a lot of oak and lees to boot. The rich, creamy texture leads to a long, spicy finish in this young, delicious wine. **91** —*S.H. (6/1/2003)*

Kunde 1999 Reserve Chardonnay (Sonoma Valley) $35. Fans of spicy, bold Chards will love this one. Huge aromas of ripe peaches and pineapple, cinnamon, buttered toast, and smoke are followed by layered flavors and textures. Dramatic, showy and extravagant, this complex wine finishes with honeyed sweetness. **91** —*S.H. (12/31/2001)*

Kunde 1998 Reserve Chardonnay (Sonoma Valley) $30. 90 —*S.H. (11/15/2000)*

Kunde 1999 Wildwood Vineyard Chardonnay (Sonoma Valley) $22. The aroma is a great burst of mineral and tropical fruit, so good you just have to taste it. Follows through brilliantly, with all sorts of fruit flavors, lavishly oaked and with a steely, stony nerve. The finish is spicy and acidic. This is a distinguished single-vineyard wine, not a me-too, but an authentic product of terroir. For this kind of quality, it's also a good value. **93** —*S.H. (5/1/2002)*

Kunde 1997 Wildwood Vineyard Chardonnay (Sonoma Valley) $20. 89 *(11/1/1999)*

Kunde 2000 Wildwood Vineyard-Estate Bottled Chardonnay (Sonoma Valley) $22. Jam-packed with bright fruit flavors of peaches, pears and tropical fruits, and spiced up with the vanilla and toast notes of oak. This is a rich wine, big and bold, and a real crowd pleaser. **87** —*S.H. (12/15/2002)*

Kunde 1998 Fumé Blanc (Sonoma Valley) $18. 88 —*L.W. (5/1/2000)*

Kunde 1998 Magnolia Lane Vineyard Fumé Blanc (Sonoma Valley) $12. 87 —*L.W. (5/1/2000)*

Kunde 2001 Merlot (Sonoma Valley) $18. With their vineyard holdings, Kunde does a great job at varietally true wines at reasonable prices. This dry red wine has flavors of berries, cherries, and herbs. It's soft and gentle, with good supportive acids, tannins and a complex finish. **87** —*S.H. (8/1/2005)*

Kunde 2000 Merlot (Sonoma Valley) $18. A very expressive and well-made wine. The stylistic decision was made to leave some aggressive but elegant tannins beside the herb and plum flavors, maybe to accentuate its foodworthiness. Finishes tough and gritty, but may soften in a few years. **87** *(11/15/2002)*

Kunde 1999 Merlot (Sonoma Valley) $18. The bouquet begins with weedy, green and cola notes, which is surprising for such a good vintage. Also expect some faint traces of blackberry flavors. The sharpness continues in the mouth. Bone dry, with lovely tannins. **83** —*S.H. (11/15/2001)*

Kunde 2003 Block 4SB20 Sauvignon Blanc (Sonoma Valley) $19. A bit pricy, but a good wine for its crisp, minerally mouthfeel and bone-dry, palate-cleansing finish. Has intense flavors of lemons and grapefruits. **87** —*S.H. (10/1/2005)*

Kunde 2004 Magnolia Lane Sauvignon Blanc (Sonoma Valley) $15. This wine's fresh and zingy in acidity, and bone dry, with richly textured citrus fruit flavors and the tart, mouthwatering spiciness of green juniper berries. This single-vineyard bottling is almost always a winner. **87** —*S.H. (12/31/2005)*

Kunde 2003 Magnolia Lane Sauvignon Blanc (Sonoma Valley) $15. The best Magnolia in recent memory. Rich and sophisticated in gooseberry, fig, and vanilla flavors, totally dry, and with crisp acidity, this wine is clean and refreshing. Cries out for oysters, or just about anything. **88** —*S.H. (12/31/2004)*

Kunde 2002 Magnolia Lane Sauvignon Blanc (Sonoma Valley) $15. Very dry, crisp, tart, and lemony. This is about as good as this style of Sauvignon Blanc gets in California. The addition of a small amount of Sémillon and Viognier enrichens but does not interfere with the varietal's refreshing personality. **87** —*S.H. (12/15/2003)*

Kunde 2001 Magnolia Lane Sauvignon Blanc (Sonoma Valley) $14. This wine has emerged in recent years to be one of the most savory Sauvignon Blancs at this nice price. It's very tart and lemony, with refreshing acidity. Totally dry, it finishes with a clean scour. **86** —*S.H. (9/1/2003)*

Kunde 2000 Magnolia Lane Sauvignon Blanc (Sonoma Valley) $14. Bigtime lemongrass and grapefruit aromas, along with subtler notes of fig and nut, characterize this zesty, clean wine, A bit of sweetness on the finish is offset by high acidity. **86** —*S.H. (11/15/2001)*

Kunde 1999 Magnolia Lane Sauvignon Blanc (Sonoma Valley) $13. Always a good bet, this single-vineyard wine bursts from the glass with grass and hay aromas, citrus fruits, vanilla, and creamy, smoky notes. It's superrich in the mouth, with tons of ripe peach and tangerine flavors and a hint of honeyed sweetness, but it's basically dry. A fine partner for toasted sourdough rounds topped with goat cheese and olive tapenade. **87 Editors' Choice** —*S.H. (8/1/2001)*

Kunde 2000 Syrah (Sonoma Valley) $23. Good grapes, good winemaking, good wine. It's forward in the blackberry, cherry, and sweet chocolate aromas and flavors, but it's not a jammy wine. Sturdy tannins provide structure. **89** —*S.H. (10/1/2003)*

Kunde 1999 Syrah (Sonoma Valley) $23. Opens with an interesting bouquet that combines dark fruit, leather, meat, and ultra-toast aromas with herb and floral notes. Medium- weight and structured, it offers dark cherry with green herbal shadings and a chewy but not hard mouthfeel. The espresso and pepper finish displays a nice back-bouquet. **87** *(11/1/2001)*

Kunde 1998 Syrah (Sonoma Valley) $20. This easy-drinking Syrah shows plenty of upfront blueberry and black-cherry fruit balanced by smoke, toast, coffee, and cocoa shadings. There's a lot to like about this wine's tangy, peppery finish and chewy mouthfeel. **86** *(10/1/2001)*

Kunde 1997 Estate Bottled Syrah (Sonoma Valley) $20. 90 *(2/1/2000)*

Kunde 2001 Estate Grown Syrah (Sonoma Valley) $23. Elegant and harmonious, this dry wine bursts with flavors of blackberries, sweet leather, and coffee. It's so nicely balanced, with firm tannins, acids, and oak perfectly framing the fruit. An excellent dinner wine, with nuance and complexity. **90** —S.H. (12/15/2004)

Kunde 2004 Viognier (Sonoma Valley) $24. Wow, is this wine ever unripe. It has the skunky, cat pee smell of the greenest Sauvignon Blanc, and is raspingly dry and acidic. Weird for a variety famed for its exotic fruitiness. **83** —S.H. (12/31/2005)

Kunde 2003 Viognier (Sonoma Valley) $23. Dry and crisp, a balanced wine that nonetheless showcases Viognier's wildly exotic side. Ripe tropical fruits, honeysuckle, Key lime pie, vanilla, and cinnamon through the finish. **87** —S.H. (12/31/2004)

Kunde 2002 Viognier (Sonoma Valley) $23. Few wineries have a more consistent track record with this rare Rhône white than Kunde. This year, as usual, the wine is brilliant in tropical fruit, apple, peach, honeysuckle, and buttery-vanilla flavors. It's well-balanced with acids and just a touch of oak. **90** —S.H. (2/1/2004)

Kunde 2001 Viognier (Sonoma Valley) $23. Scads of fruits and flowers mark this ripe, rich wine. Peaches, bananas, apricots, honeysuckle, papaya, and lime flavors drink smooth and crisp, thanks to good acids. The wine is dry, clean, and crisp. Lovely by itself, or with spicy, fruity-sweet foods. **88** —S.H. (9/1/2003)

Kunde 2000 Viognier (Sonoma Valley) $23. Peaches, spice, and citrus flavors are at the fore of this zingy wine. It's long and bright to the end. **87** —J.M. (12/15/2002)

Kunde 2001 Zinfandel (Sonoma Valley) $16. Bright cherry and citrus flavors form the core of the wine, though tannins are somewhat astringent. It's a bit weak on the mid-palate, too, finishing a little short. **83** —J.M. (11/1/2003)

Kunde 1999 Zinfandel (Sonoma Valley) $15. Opens with thin, sharp aromas of stalks, earth, and coffee, and turns tart and herbaceous in the mouth. There's not much beyond the heat of alcohol, acidity, and tannins. Disappointing. **82** —S.H. (11/15/2001)

Kunde 1998 Zinfandel (Sonoma Valley) $15. Herbs and spices dominate the nose, and the wine has an intriguing blend of 9% Petite Sirah, 2% Grenache, and 2% Mourvèdre in it. Interesting and flavorful, though not entirely varietal in character. The mix of spices tastes a bit like a Provençal wine, and it's delicious for the price. **89** —P.G. (3/1/2001)

Kunde 2001 Century Vines Zinfandel (Sonoma Valley) $25. A mild mannered wine that serves up pretty plum, cherry, herb, and vanilla flavors. Smooth tannins leave a smoky note at the end. **85** (11/1/2003)

Kunde 2000 Century Vines-Shaw Vineyard Zinfandel (Sonoma Valley) $25. Pretty good Zin, with a lush texture and rich, fine tannins. Pepper and blackberry aromas and flavors, and very dry. Loses a point or two for unripe notes of dill and oregano. **85** —S.H. (12/1/2002)

Kunde 2000 Estate Bottled Zinfandel (Sonoma Valley) $16. Fruity and simple, with plum and pepper flavors and a hard edge of tannins. A dry, drinkable young wine to have with barbecued pork ribs and similar fare. **85** —S.H. (11/1/2002)

Kunde 1997 Estate Bottled Zinfandel (Sonoma Valley) $15. 86 —P.G. (11/15/1999)

Kunde 1997 Robusto Zinfandel (Sonoma Valley) $30. 89 —S.H. (5/1/2000)

Kunde 2002 Shaw Vineyard Century Vines Zinfandel (Sonoma Valley) $30. You could smell this from Mars and know it's Zin. Wild berries, woodsy dust on a hot summer day, roasted coffee bean, white pepper and a hint of raisins mark the aromas. In the mouth the wine is full, dry, and spicy, and wildly fruity. It's a bit hot, but that's Zin for you. **90** —S.H. (12/31/2005)

Kunde 1999 Shaw Vineyard Century Vines Zinfandel (Sonoma Valley) $25. What does "briary" mean? Think about a wild black raspberry bush on a hot summer afternoon. The wood, the bark, the dust, the chlorophyll from the baking leaves and the berries, with that wild, primitive, spicy, fructose-sweet bitterness. This wine is bone dry and finishes with a tannic bite. Drink it now with sturdy chow. **86** —S.H. (7/1/2002)

Kunde 1998 Shaw Vineyard Century Vines Zinfandel (Sonoma Valley) $24. The winery claims the vines date back to 1882; the wine is a stunner, with rich, old vine complexity mixing cherries, leafy old-vine flavors, smooth chocolatey oak. Smooth, seductive, delicious. **90** —P.G. (3/1/2001)

Kunde 1997 Shaw Vineyard Century Vines Zinfandel (Sonoma Valley) $24. 87 —P.G. (11/15/1999)

Kunde 2001 Shaw Vineyard, Century Vines Zinfandel (Sonoma Valley) $28. A moderate-bodied Zin that sports rustic tannins and bright acidity. It's got a briary blend of black-cherry, blackberry, herb and raspberry flavors, finishing with medium length at the end. **87** —J.M. (10/1/2004)

KUNIN

Kunin 2003 Syrah (Santa Barbara County) $28. This SBC Syrah's flavors are very ripe, with accents of coffee and meat. Full and soft in the mouth, it's an all-purpose, enjoyable wine. **87** (9/1/2005)

Kunin 2001 Syrah (Santa Barbara County) $24. Quite ripe and intense, with strong, penetrating aromas and flavors of cassis, blackberry, coffee, toffee, and Oriental spices. Smooth and clean going down, although the tannic structure could use more finesse. **85** —S.H. (12/1/2003)

Kunin 2000 Syrah (Santa Maria Valley) $35. Starts with overtly gamy, leathery aromas, and turns thick and tannic, a wine that numbs the palate and demands rich, oily foods. Underneath the tannins are some lean blackberry and plum flavors. Seems to have been the victim of a late-harvest rainstorm that thinned the fruit. **85** —S.H. (12/1/2002)

Kunin 2000 Syrah (Santa Rita Hills) $35. From this new, cool-climate appellation, a wine of high acidity, with a bony, tannic structure that's lean, with earth, sage, and tobacco flavors. Yet there's an interesting taste of the earth. This is a first-crop wine, and one to watch as the vines mature. **85** —S.H. (12/1/2002)

Kunin 2002 Alisos Vineyard Syrah (Santa Barbara County) $35. A good, though overdone, wine. Intense in the mouth, but it is heavy on the earth, prune, and coffee flavors. A smooth feel segues into a mocha-laden finish; 300 cases produced. **86** (9/1/2005)

Kunin 2001 Alisos Vineyards Syrah (Santa Barbara County) $30. From an easterly, warm part of the Santa Ynez Valley, this wine displays beautiful aromas of finely oaked, ripe Syrah: cassis and violets, lavender and grilled meat, and a hint of raisin. The mouthfeel is full. Finishes a bit hot due to 15.1% alcohol. **89** —S.H. (2/1/2004)

Kunin 2000 French Camp Syrah (Paso Robles) $28. Big, extracted, and jammy, this Aussie-style wine has raspberry, cherry, and blueberry flavors accompanied by soft, slippery tannins and rather low acidity. It all makes the wine slide down the throat with a delicious, fruity finish. It's an easy-going, fun-to-drink wine. **85** —S.H. (12/1/2002)

Kunin 1999 French Camp Vineyards Syrah (Paso Robles) $28. Fresh young cherry-berry aromas, with a kiss of oak, lead to extracted, jammy, full-bodied flavors that explode in the mouth. Soft, luscious, and round, there's lots of immediate pleasure here. **85** —S.H. (7/1/2002)

Kunin 2000 Stolpman Vineyard Viognier (Santa Ynez Valley) $28. Extremely floral up front, then racy and rich on the palate. The wine serves up a serious blend of ripe fruit; apricots, melons, peaches, and pears come to mind. All are couched in a creamy, spicy blend that lingers nicely on the finish. **91** —J.M. (12/15/2002)

KYNSI

Kynsi 2004 Bien Nacido Vineyard Pinot Blanc (Santa Maria Valley) $22. Much like Chardonnay, with a creamy texture framing ripe pineapples, mangoes, apple butter, toast, and caramel. This is a big, powerful wine but one with great control and finesse. **90** —S.H. (12/1/2006)

Kynsi 2003 Bien Nacido Vineyard Pinot Blanc (Santa Maria Valley) $22. Smells dusty, fruity and very young, an impression confirmed in the mouth, which is a jumble of pineapple, apricot, oak and acidity. It doesn't all quite come together, but it will, in a year or so, and could hold for a while after that. **90 Editors' Choice** —S.H. (10/1/2005)

Kynsi 2003 Pinot Noir (Edna Valley) $28. Crafted from a blend of vineyards, Kynsi's approach here is a riper, heavier Pinot, fuller in body than many others from the region. The flavors show the ripeness, suggesting

USA

baked red and black-cherry pie filling and gooey black raspberry jam veering into cocoa-laced coffee. It's a big wine, but very dry, with bracing acidity. **88** —*S.H. (10/1/2006)*

Kynsi 2002 Pinot Noir (Edna Valley) $28. Opens with lots of toasty oak, but as nice as those charry, vanilla accents are, this wine can't quite overcome a certain rustic character, despite scads of well-ripened black-cherry and raspberry flavors. **85** —*S.H. (10/1/2005)*

Kynsi 2003 Bien Nacido Vineyard Pinot Noir (Santa Maria Valley) $36. Shows enormously ripe fruit: baked cherry pie, raspberry tea, cola, coffee, and cocoa, with thyme and oregano accents. But after the flattering fruit, the wine turns kind of soft and one-dimensional. **86** —*S.H. (12/1/2006)*

Kynsi 2002 Bien Nacido Vineyard Pinot Noir (Santa Maria Valley) $36. Lots of Pinot character in the soft, silky mouthfeel, and those cool-climate acids balance out the ripe cherry and mocha fruit. As tasty as it is, seems a bit one-dimensional, especially for the price. **85** —*S.H. (10/1/2005)*

Kynsi 1999 Paragon Vineyard Pinot Noir (Edna Valley) $25. Delicate and complex, a cool climate wine with a mixture of ripe cherry flavors and leaner ones of tobacco, tomato skin, and cranberry. Bone dry with excellent acidity, this somewhat tart wine is well made, and may be an ager. **88** —*R.V. (7/1/2003)*

Kynsi 2003 Stone Corral Vineyard Pinot Noir (Edna Valley) $45. Made in a riper style, a flamboyant wine with tremendous fruit and also significant oak. Will appeal to aficionados of big Pinots, with its muscular cherry pie, black raspberry marmalade, cranberry sauce, mocha, and smoky, toasty flavors. Fortunately, the wine is quite dry, and those wonderful Edna Valley acids sustain balance. Should hold if not improve for a few years before it loses freshness. **91** —*S.H. (10/1/2006)*

Kynsi 2004 Bien Nacido Vineyard Syrah (Santa Maria Valley) $22. Kynsi's Syrahs are small production but worth seeking out. This is a big, opulent Syrah, filled with cassis, chocolate, spiced plum, and coffee flavors, and while it's basically dry, it has that fructosy, glycerineiy finish that very ripe wines can have. **87** —*S.H. (12/15/2006)*

Kynsi 2003 Bien Nacido Vineyard Syrah (Santa Maria Valley) $22. Kynsi's Syrahs are small production but worth seeking out. This is a big, opulent wine, filled with cassis, chocolate, spiced plum, and coffee flavors, and while it's basically dry, it has that fructosy, glyceriney finish that very ripe wines can have. **87** —*S.H. (12/15/2006)*

Kynsi 2002 Bien Nacido Vineyard Syrah (Santa Maria Valley) $46. Bien Nacido Syrahs are usually tannic in youth, and so is this fresh young wine. Starts with hints of coffee, meat, and pepper, and has a wonderfully concentrated heart of blackberry, cassis, cherry, and spice flavors. Great with rich meats and cheeses, but should improve through 2008. **91** *(9/1/2005)*

Kynsi 2003 Edna Ranch Syrah (Edna Valley) $32. Opens with a blast of leather and animal scents, followed by brilliant raspberries and cherries, and then the sweet, spicy oak kicks in. What a sequence. The followup is rich and opulent. A bit on the soft side, but this is a really likeable Syrah. **89** —*S.H. (11/1/2006)*

Kynsi 2002 Edna Ranch Vineyard Syrah (Edna Valley) $28. Edna Valley is one of the coolest prime coastal areas in California, and this wine is fresh in acidity. It starts with a burst of white pepper and black currants, then turns long and juicy in the mouth, showing just how ripe the grapes got. This is beautiful Syrah, balanced, rich, and nuanced. **92 Editors' Choice** *(9/1/2005)*

Kynsi 2003 Kalanna Syrah (Edna Valley) $44. Massive, dense, oaky young Syrah, rich and impressive in ripe fruit. The cherries, raspberries, and sweet milk chocolate are delicious, and complexed with darker, animal notes that, with the tannins, give the wine weight and gravity. **94** —*S.H. (7/1/2006)*

Kynsi 1999 Paragon Syrah (Edna Valley) $28. An intensely gamy or leathery scent opens this deeply fruity wine, which has luscious flavors of kirsch and black-cherries. These rich, jammy flavors coat the palate with syrupy deliciousness and the finish is ripe and long-lasting. **86** —*S.H. (12/1/2002)*

Kynsi 1998 South Ridge Vineyard Syrah (Paso Robles) $25. From a warm vineyard, it has super-ripe aromas of baked cherry pie, with smoky vanil-

la. Made in a rustic style, with berry flavors and soft acidity. **83** —*S.H. (7/1/2002)*

Kynsi 2001 Barn Owl Vineyard Zinfandel (Paso Robles) $30. An interesting, terroir driven wine that combines ripe, fruity blackberry and cherry flavors with a subtle hint of green peppercorn, especially in the aroma. A bit unfocused, though, with a sweetish finish. **86** —*S.H. (10/1/2005)*

L DE LYETH

L de Lyeth 2003 Cabernet Sauvignon (Sonoma County) $11. Smells too green and minty, and tastes too sweet, to merit a higher score. If you're not fussy, there are enough cherry-berry flavors to get by. **82** —*S.H. (5/1/2006)*

L de Lyeth 2003 Merlot (Sonoma County) $11. Here's a soft, plushly textured Merlot, with polished cherry, blackberry, and toast flavors and a dry finish. It's a pleasant sipper, and will benefit from decanting before serving to let it breathe and develop. **85** —*S.H. (5/1/2006)*

L'AVENTURE

L'Aventure 2002 Cuvée Cote a Cote Red Blend (Paso Robles) $70. Quite delicious, and despite the full-bodiedness, it's balanced and elegant. Offers a generous mouthful of black-cherries, blackberries, chocolate, and sweetmeats, wrapped in rich, thick, sweet tannins. Might be a little tricky to pair with foods due to high alcohol. Try something enormously rich. Grenache-Syrah blend. **92** —*S.H. (6/1/2005)*

L'Aventure 2002 Estate Cuvée Red Blend (Paso Robles) $80. A dramatic wine. Huge, almost overwhelming in the volume of cassis, cocoa, grilled meat, and sweet oak flavors, yet elegantly dry and crisp. It has the most wonderful texture, mouthfilling and voluminous, yet somehow light as velvet. Finishes with a scour of tannins, but it's probably not an ager. Drink now through 2007. **93** —*S.H. (6/1/2005)*

L'Aventure 2002 Optimus Red Blend (Paso Robles) $50. This complex Syrah and (with a little Zin) showcases both varieties at their western Paso Robles best. The Syrah is rich in dark berry-cherry and mocha flavors, while the Cabernet adds cassis and a nice tannic structure. I'm not sure what the 4 % of Zin brings, maybe a wild, peppery note. The final impression is of real class and distinction. Drink now and for the next few years. **94 Editors' Choice** —*S.H. (10/1/2005)*

L'Aventure 2001 Optimus Red Blend (Paso Robles) $45. From Rhône-possessed Paso Robles, an adventurous blend of Cabernet Sauvignon, Syrah, Petit Verdot, and Zinfandel. The aroma is subdued now, closed and brooding. On the palate is an explosion of cassis, briar, chocolate, and coffee. Sweet, ripe tannins make for a dusty mouthfeel. Needs a minimum of a year in the cellar. **92** —*S.H. (6/1/2004)*

L'Aventure 2000 Optimus Red Blend (Paso Robles) $45. A blend of Syrah, Cabernet Sauvignon, Zinfandel, and Petit Verdot. Massive berry and fruit flavors, accented with natural spices and 100% new French oak, and wrapped in fancy, smooth tannins. The wine feels important on the palate, and flatters it from entry through the long, delicious finish. It's great to see Paso Robles step up to the plate and produce such world-class wine. **93** —*S.H. (11/15/2003)*

L'Aventure 1999 Optimus Red Blend (Paso Robles) $48. Boasts a fabulous texture marked by really fine, slippery tannins that coat the mouth like velvet. The plum, blackberry, anise, spice, and smoke flavors are beautifully integrated with fine oak. Notable for the balance of all its parts, a textured, nuanced wine that sets the bar higher for West Side Syrah. A Syrah-Cabernet Sauvignon blend. **89** —*S.H. (11/15/2002)*

L'Aventure 2001 Syrah (Paso Robles) $NA. There is certainly some warm weather influence in the sinfully ripe blackberry pie and cherry tart flavors. On the other hand, cooler winds from the Pacific have left intact the citrusy acidity and edgy tannins. The result is elegance and charm, a showcase for this emerging appellation. **91** —*S.H. (6/1/2004)*

L'Aventure 2000 Syrah (Paso Robles) $40. The opening aroma is muted in fruit, dominated by white pepper and a landslide of new oak. You have to slosh it around the mouth to experience the depth and range of fruit, which is big and extraordinarily rich. Tannins are dry and complex. This is a wine obviously meant for the cellar, and it should glide through the next five years and turn into a very interesting drink. **93 Editors' Choice** —*S.H. (12/15/2003)*

USA

L'Aventure 1999 Syrah (Paso Robles) $36. Creamy—almost buttery—and loaded with vanilla and dried spices, yet there's also loads of plum, raspberry, and blueberry fruit, along with complex espresso, pepper, and smoke nuances. The long finish resonates with notes of berries and cream. **90** *(11/1/2001)*

L'Aventure 2002 Estate Syrah (Paso Robles) $65. Not for the faint of heart, with 16.5% alcohol, but that's the price of fermenting this wine to dryness. Robust, with strong cherry and blackberry flavors, decent acidity and dusty tannins. A great slab of meat will deal with it. **90** *—S.H. (6/1/2005)*

L'ECOLE NO 41

L'Ecole No 41 1999 Apogee Pepper Bridge Vineyard Bordeaux Blend (Walla Walla (WA)) $42. The blend here is 50% Cabernet Sauvignon, 46% Merlot, and 4% Cabernet Franc, making a soft, seductive, sweetly fruity red wine that is immediately flat-out delicious. Consumer-pleasing flavors of ripe cherries and berries mingle with plenty of smooth, chocolatey oak, and seamless tannins. Rich, and decadent and really good. **90** *—P.G. (6/1/2002)*

L'Ecole No 41 2004 Ferguson Commemorative Reserve Bordeaux Blend (Columbia Valley (WA)) $45. This wine honors winery founders Jean and Baker Ferguson, and the grapes are sourced from many of the vineyards they used in the early 1980s—Sagemoor, Bacchus, Dionysus, and Klipsun. Still very young, very tight and very nicely structured, it shows good acid, tart fruit mixing berry, cherry, and red licorice; firm tannins, ripe but chewy; and a good spine that is keeping things wrapped up tight. **92 Cellar Selection** *—P.G. (12/31/2006)*

L'Ecole No 41 2000 Pepper Bridge Vineyard Bordeaux Blend (Walla Walla (WA)) $42. L'Ecole's Bordeaux blend feels a bit light in this vintage. The blend favors Merlot (57%), with Cab Sauvignon (39%), and Cab Franc (4%) filling out the rest. Forward and pleasant, it carries scents and flavors of light herb and alfalfa over pale strawberry preserves. **86** *—P.G. (9/1/2004)*

L'Ecole No 41 2003 Pepper Bridge Vineyard Apogee Bordeaux Blend (Walla Walla (WA)) $45. L'Ecole's other Bordeaux blend features Pepper Bridge fruit, divided almost equally between Merlot (45%) and Cabernet Sauvignon (47%), with Cab Franc and Malbec filling out the rest. All the right pieces are in place—scents and flavors of light cherry, pretty chocolate, hints of dill and herb, and a sprinkle of coffee. But it's still jagged and unresolved; give it another year. **90** *—P.G. (8/1/2006)*

L'Ecole No 41 2002 Pepper Bridge Vineyard Apogee Bordeaux Blend (Walla Walla (WA)) $45. L'Ecole's Bordeaux blend is divided equally between Merlot (48%) and Cab Sauvignon (48%), with Cab Franc (4%) filling out the rest. Forward and open, it carries scents and flavors of light cherry, blackberry, and hints of herb. Very smooth and supple, flavorful and easy to drink, but just a bit light for a Meritage-style wine. **88** *—P.G. (4/1/2005)*

L'Ecole No 41 2001 Pepper Bridge Vineyard Apogee Bordeaux Blend (Walla Walla (WA)) $42. L'Ecole's Bordeaux blend evenly matches Merlot (48%), with Cab Sauvignon (49%) while Cab Franc (3%) fills out the rest. Forward and round, it shows herbal scents and more than a whiff of barnyard over fruit flavors of strawberry preserves. **87** *—P.G. (7/1/2004)*

L'Ecole No 41 1998 Pepper Bridge Vineyard Apogee Bordeaux Blend (Walla Walla (WA)) $42. Apogee is L'Ecole's proprietary Bordeaux blend. This Merlot-dominated (60%) wine also includes about one-third Cabernet Sauvignon and a dash of Cabernet Franc; it shows complex aromas of nutmeg, cinnamon, and coffee, with plump, ripe red fruit. It's nicely balanced, big and tart, and it gently cascades into a long, spicy finish. **90** *—P.G. (6/1/2001)*

L'Ecole No 41 2003 Seven Hills Vineyard Estate Perigee Bordeaux Blend (Walla Walla (WA)) $45. L'Ecole's estate Bordeaux blend is a bigger, chewier wine than its companion Apogee, although in this new vintage the two are far closer than the 2002s. Still pulling itself together, this wine hints at lime, stone, and pepper, and features a fair amount of broad, chocolatey oak. The fruit is hiding just a bit, but this is very well made and should round out nicely over the next 3–5 years. **90** *—P.G. (8/1/2006)*

L'Ecole No 41 2002 Seven Hills Vineyard Perigee Bordeaux Blend (Walla Walla (WA)) $45. This is L'Ecole's estate Bordeaux blend, and comes exclusively from the Seven Hills vineyard. A lovely nose suggests violets, truffle, fresh-turned earth, sweet spice, hay, and leather—lots to dive into here! The wine continues with a panoply of exotic, well-matched flavors, and the mix of fruit and leather and tannin and herb is just about perfect. **93** *—P.G. (4/1/2005)*

L'Ecole No 41 2003 Cabernet Sauvignon (Columbia Valley (WA)) $30. A 100% Cabernet, dark and tightly knit with scents of roasted coffee and espresso over red berry, blueberry, and black-cherry fruit. Vineyard sources include Klipsun, Pepper Bridge, Seven Hills, and Milbrandt, and the vines average over 25 years of age. **88** *—P.G. (8/1/2006)*

L'Ecole No 41 2003 Cabernet Sauvignon (Walla Walla (WA)) $37. Warm, lush, and seductive, the winery's Walla Walla Cab includes 6% Cab Franc in the blend. A vibrant mix of boysenberry, blueberry, black raspberry, and black-cherry, it's big, smooth, full, fleshy, and immensely flavorful. **91** *—P.G. (10/1/2006)*

L'Ecole No 41 2002 Cabernet Sauvignon (Columbia Valley (WA)) $30. L'Ecole does a really nice job with this 100% pure varietal wine, which smells of sweet black-cherry fruit, cinnamon, spice, and smoke. Very satisfying on the palate, it is smooth and supple, seems to expand and layer itself seamlessly as it cascades through the mouth, and lasts a good long while. Sweet, ripe fruit and nicely managed tannins, with some potential to age for 8–10 years. **90 Cellar Selection** *—P.G. (4/1/2005)*

L'Ecole No 41 2001 Cabernet Sauvignon (Columbia Valley (WA)) $30. An easy, palate-friendly wine, whose forward, accessible red fruit flavors are wrapped in soft, chocolatey oak. Perfect with pizza, burgers, or weekend cookouts, it is a straightforward blend from seven different vineyards. **87** *—P.G. (7/1/2004)*

L'Ecole No 41 2000 Cabernet Sauvignon (Columbia Valley (WA)) $30. L'Ecole does a really nice job with this friendly wine, which is forward, accessible, and unchallenging. Perfect with pizza, burgers, or Friday night poker games, it captures sweet, ripe fruit and nicely managed tannins. **87** *—P.G. (9/1/2004)*

L'Ecole No 41 2000 Cabernet Sauvignon (Walla Walla (WA)) $36. 100% Cabernet, this is a good wine with which to "dial in" the flavors of Walla Walla valley fruit. There are generous, open, loose knit notes of strawberry and raspberry compote, with an herbal current reminiscent of fresh alfalfa. Nicely balanced by natural acids and well-proportioned tannins. **88** *—P.G. (9/1/2004)*

L'Ecole No 41 1999 Cabernet Sauvignon (Walla Walla (WA)) $36. The nose shows the complexity that makes Walla Walla so interesting. Mixed in with ripe fruit are scents of chilies, bell peppers, and other piquant spices. Full and fleshy, as is the house style, but nuanced as well. A little green-bean flavor can be found in the finish. **87** *—P.G. (12/31/2002)*

L'Ecole No 41 1999 Cabernet Sauvignon (Columbia Valley (WA)) $30. This bottling blends fruit from several premium Columbia Valley vineyards (Portteus, Bacchus, Klipsun, and Seven Hills) into a complex whole. Hints of jalapeño, bell pepper, herb, and pickle barrel underlie sweet cherry and cassis; the wine is firmly tannic and tightly muscled, with a hint of barnyard in the finish. **88** *—P.G. (6/1/2002)*

L'Ecole No 41 1998 Cabernet Sauvignon (Walla Walla (WA)) $36. L'Ecole seems to motor effortlessly from strength to strength, and here is a beautiful blend (81% Cabernet Sauvignon/11% Merlot/8% Cabernet Franc) of Walla Walla fruit that adds up to a lush, forward wine with the accent of rich fruit and plenty of chocolate. Still, the acids are kept high enough to add life; tannins are soft and smooth, and the finish is nothing but sweet fruit. **91** *—P.G. (12/31/2001)*

L'Ecole No 41 1998 Cabernet Sauvignon (Columbia Valley (WA)) $30. Here is a wine with a stellar bouquet, redolent with chocolate-covered cherries, cassis, a bit of "gout de terroir" and other barnyardy stuff best left to the imagination. Complex, lush, and ripe, it overwhelms the palate with silky sensations, all wrapped up in smooth chocolate. There's a mouth-cleansing dryness to the tannins that invites another sip, and another. **90** *—P.G. (6/1/2001)*

L'Ecole No 41 1997 Cabernet Sauvignon (Walla Walla (WA)) $33. Intense and structured, L'Ecole's Walla Walla Cab exhibits welcome complexity

USA

as well. The textbook aromas and flavors of cassis, tobacco, and cedar are paired with enough tannin and acidity to support five years or more of aging. **89** —*J.C. (6/1/2001)*

L'Ecole No 41 1998 Chardonnay (Columbia Valley (WA)) $20. 90 —*P.G. (6/1/2000)*

L'Ecole No 41 2005 Chardonnay (Columbia Valley (WA)) $20. Clean, perfumed and solidly built; it's still a bit blocky but that is its youth showing. It persists nicely into some interesting herbal/spicy nuances in the finish. The fruit is chunky, starring apple and white peach, with a hint of apricot. The finish is clean with a lick of mineral. **90** —*P.G. (12/31/2006)*

L'Ecole No 41 2004 Chardonnay (Columbia Valley (WA)) $20. A firm, structured yet smooth rendition with flavors of melon, red delicious apples, and light tropical fruits. Crisp acidity, creamy lees and light hints of toast. **89** —*P.G. (8/1/2006)*

L'Ecole No 41 2003 Chardonnay (Columbia Valley (WA)) $20. A young, soft and very pleasant wine, with flavors of red delicious apples and suggestions of pear. Broad and smooth, forward and easy-drinking. Nice hints of toast and cinnamon add interest. **87** —*P.G. (4/1/2005)*

L'Ecole No 41 2001 Chardonnay (Columbia Valley (WA)) $20. Sweet and smooth, with broad, simple fruit flavors. Banana and vanilla combine into a flavorful, accessible wine reminiscent of the Aussie style. **87** —*P.G. (9/1/2004)*

L'Ecole No 41 2000 Chardonnay (Columbia Valley (WA)) $19. Soft and supple, this forward, engaging wine is accented with fennel and herb. It's a smooth, polished effort, with barrel-fermented flavors that add creamy depth to the fruit without piling on the oak. **88** —*P.G. (2/1/2002)*

L'Ecole No 41 1999 Chardonnay (Columbia Valley (WA)) $20. This excellent Chardonnay is both crisp and smooth, with ripe, lemony green apples augmented with hints of custard and vanilla. It has both weight and balance, and should cellar well for the near term. But why not enjoy it now? **88** —*P.G. (6/1/2001)*

L'Ecole No 41 2001 Walla Voila Chenin Blanc (Washington) $12. A startlingly intense, grassy nose smells of sweet, new-mown hay. In the mouth follow flavors of peaches, apricots, lemons, and herbs. Starts out sweet and finishes dry, with an ultraripe, flavorful finish. Consume young. **89** —*P.G. (9/1/2002)*

L'Ecole No 41 2004 Merlot (Columbia Valley (WA)) $30. This is a very classy, sophisticated wine, blended from a wide range of Washington vineyards. It's really a Right Bank-styled Bordeaux blend, 80% Merlot, 12% Cab Franc, and a smattering of Cabernet Sauvignon and Petit Verdot. Berries and spice, chocolate and herb, and many other lightly applied nuances make this a pleasure to sip. **90** —*P.G. (10/1/2006)*

L'Ecole No 41 2000 Merlot (Walla Walla (WA)) $33. Mostly Seven Hills Vineyard fruit, this Bordeaux blend is spicier, livelier and more assertive than its sister blend Apogee. The fruit has more vivid berry components, and the wine sets up more astringent and firm. **87** —*P.G. (9/1/2004)*

L'Ecole No 41 2000 Merlot (Columbia Valley (WA)) $29. Big, friendly and wrapped in a lot of chocolatey oak. The fruit is forward and light, and it is just big enough to hang in there with all the barrel flavors. **87** —*P.G. (9/1/2002)*

L'Ecole No 41 1999 Merlot (Columbia Valley (WA)) $30. The blend includes 10% Cabernet Sauvignon, and 8% Cabernet Franc, which adds some nice texture to the nose. It's very ripe and somewhat alcoholic, with straightforward, jammy fruit balanced against firm acids and tannins. Big, bordering on rustic, and delicious. **86** —*P.G. (12/31/2001)*

L'Ecole No 41 1999 Merlot (Walla Walla (WA)) $36. The nose suggests a wine of breeding, elegance and depth, with ripe, blueberry fruit blended with layers of toast, nuts, caramel, and coffee. This is firmer than the other L'Ecole Merlots, and it shows streaks of earth and mineral, along with tight tannins that suggest long-term agind potential, Give it plenty of breathing time or age 6-8 years. **92 Cellar Selection** —*P.G. (12/31/2001)*

L'Ecole No 41 1998 Merlot (Walla Walla (WA)) $36. There are spicy berries aplenty, followed by smooth milk chocolate, and a high-toned edge that propels the aromas out of the glass. Though still young and tight, the

wine opens up and fleshes out as it breathes, which suggests it will do the same as it ages in the bottle. Right now it's a tart, tight, tasty, textured wine that's hard to keep your hands off. **89** —*J.C. (6/1/2001)*

L'Ecole No 41 1998 Merlot (Columbia Valley (WA)) $36. A solid effort that showcases chocolate and cherry flavors in a medium-bodied format. Not a lot of complexity here, but it's clean, well-made and satisfying, hitting all the right flavor buttons. Drink over the next few years. **87** —*P.G. (6/1/2001)*

L'Ecole No 41 2000 Seven Hills Vineyard Merlot (Walla Walla (WA)) $39. The vineyard supplies grapes to many of Walla Walla's best wineries; L'Ecole does a bang-up job, placing dark, rich, roasted coffee flavors from new oak barrels against sweet, open, raspberry/cherry fruit. This new vintage is still angular and jangly; give it a few more months in the bottle and it will smooth out into a luscious delight. **91** —*P.G. (9/1/2002)*

L'Ecole No 41 1999 Seven Hills Vineyard Merlot (Walla Walla (WA)) $40. Anyone that doubts that Merlot is capable of producing a big, lush, seductive and densely flavored wine should try this exceptional bottle from one of Washington's premier red wine producers. "It's the Jayne Mansfield of Washington reds," as one friend described it. A fine, crowd-pleasing wine that shows jammy fruit matched to thick tannins and toasty, coffee-flavored oak. **91** —*P.G. (12/31/2001)*

L'Ecole No 41 1998 Seven Hills Vineyard Merlot (Walla Walla (WA)) $38. Seven Hills is a favored vineyard, and this is a step up from L'Ecole's Walla Walla and Columbia Merlots. There's more fruit, more concentration, more firm flesh, and the wine has an aura of power about it. Yet there's finesse as well, in the soft, spicy nose, and in the smooth, seamless way the wine fills the mouth with ripe flavor. **91** —*P.G. (6/1/2001)*

L'Ecole No 41 2005 Sémillon (Columbia Valley (WA)) $15. Fans of the winery's "Barrel-Fermented" Sémillons, note—this is the one, but that term has been dropped from the label. It's now about 15% new oak, down from 40% in past years. Fourteen percent Sauvignon Blanc is in the blend. It's a very clean, very fresh style; perhaps a bit less creamy and rich than the last couple of years, but absolutely delicious. Consistent flavors of nettle, lime, grapefruit, and melon; lovely balance and a bit of heat in the finish. **90** —*P.G. (12/31/2006)*

L'Ecole No 41 2004 Barrel-Fermented Sémillon (Columbia Valley (WA)) $15. L'Ecole's budget bottling blends in 14% Sauv Blanc, making a brilliant, creamy, rich and textural wine which softly suggests nettle, lime, grapefruit, tangerine, and citrus. **91 Best Buy** —*P.G. (8/1/2006)*

L'Ecole No 41 2003 Barrel-Fermented Sémillon (Columbia Valley (WA)) $15. L'Ecole's other two Sémillons are 100%, but this budget bottling smartly blends in just the right amount (13%) of Sauvignon Blanc, filling in the tart kiwi-flavored fruit and light herbs with hints of creamy, spicy oak. **90 Best Buy** —*P.G. (4/1/2005)*

L'Ecole No 41 2001 Barrel-Fermented Sémillon (Columbia Valley (WA)) $15. Big flavors combine the round, vanillin character of Sémillon with the herbal spice of (11%) Sauvignon Blanc. Delicious and distinctive, this wine makes you wish more wineries focused on this neglected grape. **90 Best Buy** —*P.G. (9/1/2004)*

L'Ecole No 41 1999 Barrel-Fermented Sémillon (Columbia Valley (WA)) $15. Who else besides L'Ecole makes three different Sémillons? Bravo for showing that this much-maligned grape can be made in a wide variety of styles, and can blossom if given the superstar treatment usually reserved for Chardonnay. This low-priced version emphasizes fruit and spice to good effect. It's clean, bracing, and refreshing, and showcases citrus/mineral flavors in a tight, concise style. **89** —*P.G. (6/1/2001)*

L'Ecole No 41 1998 Barrel-Fermented Sémillon (Columbia Valley (WA)) $15. 93 Best Buy —*M.S. (4/1/2000)*

L'Ecole No 41 2000 Barrel-Fermented Sémillon Sémillon (Columbia Valley (WA)) $15. Fresh figs and citrus characterize this blend of 85% Sémillon and 15% Sauvignon Blanc from some top Columbia Valley vineyards. Sur lie aging adds a creamy concentration, and malolactic fermentation cuts the acids. Good winemaking adds up to a beautiful bottle at a fair price. **88 Best Buy** —*P.G. (12/31/2001)*

L'Ecole No 41 2004 Fries Vineyard Sémillon (Wahluke Slope) $20. Not quite up to the ultraripe heights of recent vintages, this is a somewhat lighter version of this Sémillon. Fig and light herb are the dominant flavors, augmented with pretty toasty highlights from the barrel fermentation, and lovely textures from the extended lees contact. **89** —*P.G. (8/1/2006)*

L'Ecole No 41 2003 Fries Vineyard Sémillon (Washington) $20. Another classic edition of L'Ecole's best Sémillon. Big, fresh, and bursting with ripe and delicious fruit. Green apples and pears and bright, toasty tropical flavors are perfectly meshed, and the wine fills out in the mid-palate; then sails into a thoroughly satisfying, lingering finish. **93 Editors' Choice** —*P.G. (4/1/2005)*

L'Ecole No 41 2001 Fries Vineyard Sémillon (Washington) $20. From an excellent source that has traditionally provided L'Ecole's best Sémillon. The wine is so big, so bursting with ripe and delicious fruit, yet perfectly balanced and complex, that it makes you wonder: why doesn't anyone else do this with Sémillon.? It's flat out stunning, revelatory. **93 Editors' Choice** —*P.G. (9/1/2004)*

L'Ecole No 41 2000 Fries Vineyard Sémillon (Wahluke Slope) $20. Once again Marty Clubb has crafted a stunning Sémillon, with an ultraripe nose of figs, kiwi, lime, and apricots. Along with the bonanza of fruit comes a lot of oak, but it keeps its balance and, flashy though it is, never fatigues. The three ring finish includes coconut, vanillla, pineapple, and banana. Who knew Sémillon could do all that?! **92** —*P.G. (6/1/2002)*

L'Ecole No 41 1999 Fries Vineyard Sémillon (Wahluke Slope) $22. This wine is at the extreme end of the spectrum for Sémillon, and has an avid following as a result. Golden yellow in color, it shows ultraripe fruit that smells of apricots, peaches, and pine. The fruit supports a lot of oak. Winemaker Marty Clubb has a great touch with this often-overlooked grape. As good as it is, the '99 still seems less complex than the spectacular '98. **92** —*P.G. (6/1/2001)*

L'Ecole No 41 1998 Fries Vineyard Sémillon (Wahluke Slope) $22. 91 *(4/1/2000)*

L'Ecole No 41 2002 Fries Vineyard-Wahluke Slope Sémillon (Washington) $20. From a source that has traditionally provided L'Ecole's best Sémillon. Consistent year after year, this is a big, bold wine, bursting with ripe and delicious fruit. It's not quite up to the winery's extraordinary 2001, but this vintage tilts slightly towards the hot end of the flavor spectrum, while remaining lush, toasty, and satisfying. **90** —*P.G. (7/1/2004)*

L'Ecole No 41 2003 Seven Hills Vineyard Sémillon (Walla Walla (WA)) $20. A young and lush Sémillon, this shows lush, ripe, rich, round, peachy/citrus fruit. Barrel fermented, it hints at interesting cocoa/nougat flavors also, but the pure, round fruit is what really stands out. Lovely hints of honey streak through the finish. **92 Editors' Choice** —*P.G. (4/1/2005)*

L'Ecole No 41 2001 Seven Hills Vineyard Sémillon (Walla Walla (WA)) $20. Pure Sémillon, with a ripe, honeyed richness to it. This is a soft, luscious wine, round and slightly oxidized, ready to drink and quite flavorful with distinctive streaks of Asian spice, herb and honey. The flavors last and last. **90** —*P.G. (9/1/2004)*

L'Ecole No 41 2000 Seven Hills Vineyard Sémillon (Walla Walla (WA)) $22. Nobody in the country is making better Sémillon than L'Ecole, and this estate bottling is the best of the best. Rich, ripe, and seductive, it layers delicious fruit and herbs in a creamy wine that lingers beautifully. Just the right amount of oak completes it. **91** —*P.G. (12/31/2001)*

L'Ecole No 41 1999 Seven Hills Vineyard Sémillon (Walla Walla (WA)) $22. This is an almost magically delicious, ripe, alcoholic wine which packs plenty of punch but carries its weight with confidence and authority. Walla Walla's great 1999 grapes seem to effortlessly achieve an unbelievable balance of ripe, tropical fruit and firm, bracing acids. Add eight months in a mix of new and second-year French oak and you have a star. **93 Editors' Choice** —*P.G. (6/1/2001)*

L'Ecole No 41 2005 Seven Hills Vineyard Estate Sémillon (Walla Walla (WA)) $20. If there's a better Sémillon in the country, I can't find it. This is 100% varietal, done in a rich style featuring ripe, round, peachy fruit. Barrel fermented, it has some interesting notes of honeysuckle, clover, and sweet apple. The pure, round fruit is what makes this Sémillon a standout. **91** —*P.G. (12/31/2006)*

L'Ecole No 41 2004 Syrah (Columbia Valley (WA)) $25. This is more fruit-driven, whereas the Seven Hills bottling is meatier, more Northern Rhône. Features a vivid, ebullient, young, and grapey nose; while the young, zippy fruit is tight, tart and spicy. There is a good lift to the palate, with firm acids and a layer of citrus rind adding body to the finish. **91** —*P.G. (12/31/2006)*

L'Ecole No 41 2003 Syrah (Columbia Valley (WA)) $30. Winemaker Marty Clubb has crafted a medium-weight wine with smooth tannins and simple coffee and berry flavors. There's nothing out of place here, but neither anything extraordinary. **85** *(9/1/2005)*

L'Ecole No 41 2003 Syrah (Columbia Valley (WA)) $25. Sappy with blackberry, blueberry, and black raspberry fruits, deep enough to suggest cassis also. A fine, dense, clean, and supremely fruity Syrah. **89** —*P.G. (8/1/2006)*

L'Ecole No 41 2004 Seven Hills Vineyard Syrah (Walla Walla (WA)) $37. Very few wineries got Walla Walla grapes in this freeze year, and even L'Ecole, which owns a piece of the Seven Hills vineyard, had to rely on other sources for many of its wines. But this is 100% Seven Hills Syrah, and it delivers wonderful fruit flavors with layers of citrus and tart berries. A green tea streak cuts through the substantial tannins. **89** —*P.G. (11/15/2006)*

L'Ecole No 41 2003 Seven Hills Vineyard Syrah (Walla Walla (WA)) $37. A corpulent Syrah, with lots of dark plum and sweet oak flavors and just enough pepper to keep things interesting. Finishes with a powerful blast of coffee and caramel. **87** *(9/1/2005)*

L'Ecole No 41 2000 Seven Hills Vineyard Syrah (Walla Walla (WA)) $35. L'Ecole is known for making powerful, explosive wines—and that's just the whites. This is a potent blend of black-cherry and cassis, with lots of deep, toasty, roasted espresso flavors reminiscent of Aussie Shiraz **89** —*P.G. (12/31/2002)*

L'Ecole No 41 1999 Seven Hills Vineyard Syrah (Walla Walla (WA)) $34. With a mouthfeel that's this smooth, with this many layers, we could almost forget to mention its long, toast-meets-red berry finish. Whoops, there we go. Jammy blackberry, brown sugar, and chocolate aromas are "so sexy"; the palate echoes the same flavors, but also adds smoke, dried spices, and plum to the mix. Reviewers sum it up as a "sexy fleshpot" and "black as night, but done right!" **92 Editors' Choice** *(11/1/2001)*

L'HOMME QUI RIS

L'homme Qui Ris 1998 Sparkling Wine Champagne Blend (Monterey County) $22. A dry, Brut-style wine that's a little heavy for a bubbly, but with real yeasty Champagne character. Give the wine a bit more elegance and it's a winner. **84** —*S.H. (12/31/2006)*

L'UVAGGIO DI GIACOMO

L'Uvaggio di Giacomo 2001 I Colombi Arneis (California) $16. An Italian variety, similar to Sauvignon Blanc. This is a strong, distinctive wine, with upfront lemon and grapefruit flavors. It has softer, buttery notes from oak and lees. It is not subtle but provides a direct hit of tart, clean flavor. **85** —*S.H. (9/1/2003)*

L'Uvaggio di Giacomo 2000 Il Gufo Barbera (California) $16. Rough and untamed, a dry, fruity wine with berry and tobacco flavors and country style tannins. Hits the palate with an aggressive texture and turns tart on the finish. **84** —*S.H. (2/1/2003)*

L'Uvaggio di Giacomo 1999 La Pantera Barbera (California) $20. Opens with a blast of white pepper, with underlying hints of blackberries. Fruity and dry, with a good dose of tannins. This is a food wine. It is not hedonistic on its own, with a tart, austere finish, but it is a very nice wine with the right foods. **85** —*S.H. (2/1/2003)*

L'Uvaggio di Giacomo 1999 Il Leopardo Nebbiolo (California) $18. Pretty full-bodied, with blackberry and cherry flavors and a dry hit of acids and tannins, especially on the finish. Feels a little thick and heavy. Needs food, the richer the better. **85** —*S.H. (2/1/2003)*

L'Uvaggio di Giacomo 1999 Il Ponte Sangiovese (California) $32. A tough, dry wine, with gritty tannins and pronounced acidity. Flavors veer toward blackberries, tobacco and herbs. Like a decent Chianti, it's tart and austere but clean, a wine that tastes O.K. on its own but will improve with food. **86** —*S.H. (2/1/2003)*

L. PRESTON

L. Preston 2000 2000 Red Blend (Dry Creek Valley) $24. From longtime Rhône specialist Preston, this is a blend of Syrah, Cinsault, Carignane, and Mourvèdre. The wine is kind of featureless, with generic berry flavors and pretty tough tannins. It turns thin and watery on the finish, and doesn't seem to be going anywhere. **84** —*S.H. (12/1/2002)*

LA BETE

La Bete 2002 Pinot Noir (Willamette Valley) $15. Oaky and disjointed, with candied, strawberry fruit also manages to be tart. **84** *(11/1/2004)*

La Bete 1998 Knight's Gambit Vineyard Pinot Noir (Willamette Valley) $40. **92** —*M.M. (12/1/2000)*

La Bete 2002 Momtazi Vineyard Pinot Noir (Oregon) $25. This consistently pleased our tasting panel, which found it substantial and highlighted with scents of flowers and sweet fruits. Balanced and robust, it offers grace notes of sandalwood, mixed citrus and more. **88** *(11/1/2004)*

La Bete 2002 Sélection du Cave Pinot Noir (Oregon) $20. Fairly simple, this is quite tart, citric, and on the edge of unripe. Orange peel and rhubarb are the dominant notes, and it's refreshing, though possibly too tart for some tasters. **86** *(11/1/2004)*

La Bete 2002 Stoller Vineyard Pinot Noir (Oregon) $25. This is a lovely effort, with spicy citrus highlights and a tart, elegant, supple, and polished mouthfeel. The oak is beautifully managed, infusing the aromas with mocha and herb, and the finish lingers seductively. **90** *(11/1/2004)*

LA CREMA

La Crema 2004 Chardonnay (Russian River Valley) $24. Shows lots of polish in the ripe tropical fruit and green apple flavors that have a baked, buttery pie crust edge. Brisk cool-climate acidity perks up these rich flavors and makes the wine clean and balanced. **89** —*S.H. (11/15/2006)*

La Crema 2001 Chardonnay (Sonoma Coast) $16. Hard, lean, and minerally, with mouth-tingling acidity and flavors of stone, herbs and citrus fruits. This is not one of your fat, hedonistic monsters, but will pair better with foods. The finish turns honeyed, with hints of peaches. **87** —*S.H. (8/1/2003)*

La Crema 2000 Chardonnay (Russian River Valley) $24. Quite austere, with citrusy, appley, minerally flavors and tart acids. This is not your usual fruit monster, although oak and lees do their best to add nuance and complexity. A good wine that is versatile at the table. **85** —*S.H. (7/1/2003)*

La Crema 2000 Chardonnay (Sonoma Coast) $20. From this red-hot AVA, this exciting Chard rocks with bold, penetrating fruit. You can taste the cool ocean tang, which coaxed out apples and citrus, while winemaker bells and whistles, such as barrel fermentation and sur lie aging, provide welcome complexities. They completed the malolactic fermentation, which softens the wine a bit but makes it buttery and creamy. **91 Editors' Choice** —*S.H. (12/15/2002)*

La Crema 1999 Chardonnay (Russian River Valley) $30. This appealing Chardonnay is the same wine that carried a reserve designation in prior vintages. It's lushly woven and has aromas and flavors of pear, pineapple, and peach. The fruit is rich but not overly sweet, and sports accents of cinnamon and allspice. This balanced, medium-weight wine finishes long and easy with a nice nuttiness. Top Value. **90** *(7/1/2001)*

La Crema 1999 Chardonnay (Sonoma Coast) $20. Toasty oak and cinnamon aromas team up with lovely pear, apple, citrus, and spice flavors. Fleshy-textured, with a moderate finish. **87** —*J.M. (11/15/2001)*

La Crema 1998 Cold Coast Vineyard Chardonnay (Sonoma Coast) $20. **86** *(6/1/2000)*

La Crema 1997 Cold Coast Vineyards Chardonnay (Sonoma Coast) $16. **90** —*S.H. (11/1/1999)*

La Crema 2003 Nine Barrels Chardonnay (Russian River Valley) $55. Only 200 cases were produced of this extraordinary wine. It just explodes in unfolding waves of lime custard, pineapple tart, ripe white peach, crème brûlée, and Asian spice-box flavors, and a minerality usually found in Chards from the far Sonoma Coast. With that metallic stoniness comes mouthwatering, citrusy acidity leading to a long, dry finish. **95 Editors' Choice** —*S.H. (12/31/2006)*

La Crema 1997 Reserve Chardonnay (Russian River Valley) $27. **90** *(6/1/2000)*

La Crema 1997 Reserve Chardonnay (Russian River Valley) $26. **92** —*S.H. (11/1/1999)*

La Crema 2004 Pinot Noir (Anderson Valley) $29. There's a bit of leathery funk, for those who like that, to the cherry, cocoa, cola, and spice flavors of this dry, silky wine. It's a little soft, with a smooth, polished texture that makes it easy to drink. **87** —*S.H. (11/15/2006)*

La Crema 2004 Pinot Noir (Russian River Valley) $29. The best, most complex of La Crema's three appellation series Pinot Noirs shows true Russian River character. It's medium- to full-bodied, with oak-tinged cherry compote, root beer, and cocoa flavors. Tannic weight could help it improve for a couple of years. **88** —*S.H. (11/15/2006)*

La Crema 2004 Pinot Noir (Carneros) $29. A little one-dimensional, but clean and tasty, with bright cherry and cola flavors and some smoky oak. The silky texture and brisk acidity make it food-friendly, especially with something like grilled wild salmon. **86** —*S.H. (11/15/2006)*

La Crema 2001 Pinot Noir (Sonoma Coast) $18. Rather spare despite the cherry-berry, cola and spice flavors. The tannins are ultralight, and the acidity you'd expect from this cool coastal appellation isn't there. That leaves alcohol and fruit and a certain flabbiness. **84** —*S.H. (8/1/2003)*

La Crema 2000 Pinot Noir (Russian River Valley) $35. Juicy dark fruit, toasty oak, nutmeg, caramel, and pepper elements combine nicely in this substantial wine. It's juicy but structured, and turns more serious on the finish where firm tannins show on the long, tea- and spice-accented fade. Drink now–2007. **88** *(10/1/2002)*

La Crema 2000 Pinot Noir (Sonoma Coast) $25. Dark and earthy, with saddle leather and forest floor aromas, this Pinot has a slightly creamy feel. There are cola and chocolate hints, but overall the flavors are a bit indistinct. Closes soft, with a mocha and dark cherry fade. **85** *(10/1/2002)*

La Crema 2000 Pinot Noir (Carneros) $26. This is deep and earthy, with leather and herbal accents. A powdery quality softens the full-blast cherry and plum fruit, which carries a touch of cola and oaky vanilla. The finish is top-shelf, with citrus peel, tea, dried spices, espresso, and burnt toast. It's simultaneously rustic yet refined; the perfect match. **90 Editors' Choice** *(10/1/2002)*

La Crema 1999 Pinot Noir (Sonoma Coast) $22. Pretty cherry flavors lead the way, framed in subtle herb notes. But the tannins are rough, and the finish a bit short and tart. **82** —*J.M. (12/15/2001)*

La Crema 1999 Pinot Noir (Carneros) $35. With complex aromas of blackberry, mushroom, and beet, and an overlay of smoky oak, this wine tastes young, rich and sappy. It's quite dry—even tart at this young age—but with a core of berry fruit and enough dusty tannins to suggest short-term aging. Try after 2002. **87** —*S.H. (12/15/2001)*

La Crema 1998 Pinot Noir (Russian River Valley) $35. With complex aromas of blackberry, mushroom, and beet, and an overlay of smoky oak, this wine tastes young, rich an sappy. It's quite dry—even tart at this young age—but with a core of berry fruit and enough dusty tannins to suggest short-term aging. Try after 2002. **87** —*S.H. (12/15/2001)*

La Crema 2003 Nine Barrels Pinot Noir (Russian River Valley) $75. With crisp tartness and beautifully ripened fruit, this Pinot Noir shows its cool-climate terroir. Floods the mouth with tiers of cherry, cola, root beer, licorice, spices, and toasty oak, leading to a long, rich and fine finish. It's a bit immature now, although it'll wash down a great steak, but probably better 2007–2010. **92** —*S.H. (12/31/2006)*

La Crema 2002 Syrah (Sonoma County) $24. A very supple, easy-to-drink version of Syrah that showcases cherry-berry fruit carried along on a plush bed of cedary oak. A bit simple. **83** *(9/1/2005)*

La Crema 1999 Syrah (Sonoma County) $24. Dark, earthy notes punctuate smoked-meat and bright cherry aromas. Turns leathery, spicy, and meaty on the full-bodied palate, finishing with firm tannins. Structured, complex, and built to age: drink 2005–2010. Top Value. **91** *(11/1/2001)*

La Crema 2000 Viognier (Sonoma Valley) $24. This is a strange style of California Viognier, but an interesting one. The usual flower and fruit notes are undercut by much drier, tart notes of acidity. It's as if the winemaker wanted to make a leaner style of wine. It succeeds, but at the cost of losing varietal character. It's fresh and clean but easy to mistake for Sauvignon Blanc. **84** —*S.H. (12/15/2001)*

La Crema 1998 Zinfandel (Sonoma County) $19. Smooth style, with lots of vanilla cream and ripe berry fruit. Forward, inviting style of wine, with light tannins and a clean, focused finish. It's well balanced and professionally made, but ultimately unexciting. **86** —*P.G. (3/1/2001)*

LA FAMIGLIA DI ROBERT MONDAVI

La Famiglia di Robert Mondavi 1999 Barbera (California) $19. Mondavi tries to bring refinement to a varietal that is stubbornly rustic. Flavors of grilled meats, plums, and pepper are sharply acidic. This is a zesty wine that you don't want to get too analytical about. It will flatter lasagna and anything with lots of olive oil and butter. **86** —*S.H. (12/1/2002)*

La Famiglia di Robert Mondavi 1998 Barbera (California) $20. An austere, earthy wine, with aromas of plums, roasted coffee bean, and tomato. Sharp and bitter, with high acidity, and very dry. Easy to drink; a nice wine for pasta and tomato sauce. **85** —*S.H. (11/15/2001)*

La Famiglia di Robert Mondavi 1997 Barbera (California) $20. 87 —*S.H. (9/1/2000)*

La Famiglia di Robert Mondavi 2001 Moscato Bianco Moscato (California) $15. Flavors of orange sorbet, tangerine, honeysuckle, vanilla and cinnamon drink slightly off-dry, with an edge of sweetness. The texture is a little fizzy, like a sparkling wine, adding to the pleasure of this delightful, summery sipper. **86** —*S.H. (12/1/2003)*

La Famiglia di Robert Mondavi 1999 Moscato Bianco Moscato (California) $11. 90 —*S.H. (12/31/2000)*

La Famiglia di Robert Mondavi 1997 Pinot Grigio (California) $16. 88 —*M.S. (11/15/1999)*

La Famiglia di Robert Mondavi 1997 Pinot Grigio (California) $16. 87 —*S.H. (10/1/1999)*

La Famiglia di Robert Mondavi 2003 Pinot Grigio (Monterey County) $15. Clean, tart and lemony, with a sweet wildflower edge, this wine, which is really very dry, is refreshing. Nice on its own or with appetizers. **84** —*S.H. (11/15/2004)*

La Famiglia di Robert Mondavi 2002 Pinot Grigio (California) $15. Tastes like the production on this wine was really stretched. The flavors are thin, tasting of lemon and grapefruit juices dissolved in water. There's lots of acidity, too. But it's pleasantly clean. **84** —*S.H. (8/1/2004)*

La Famiglia di Robert Mondavi 2001 Pinot Grigio (California) $18. Kind of blah, a simple wine with lemony, earthy flavors. Clean and very dry, but seems to need more oomph. Just sits there in the mouth without offering much excitement. **85** —*S.H. (9/1/2003)*

La Famiglia di Robert Mondavi 1999 Pinot Gris (Anderson Valley) $16. This flavorful, appetizing wine would be perfect with a wide variety of foods because it's so fruity and clean. The freshest, ripest peaches and nectarines float out of the glass, with similar fruity flavors; meanwhile, crisp acidity makes the wine bright and zingy. No wood mars the bright, pure flavors, which finish with a trace of almond-skin bitterness. **86** —*S.H. (8/1/2001)*

La Famiglia di Robert Mondavi 1997 Colmera Red Table Wine Red Blend (Napa Valley) $40. 89 —*S.H. (9/1/2000)*

La Famiglia di Robert Mondavi 1997 Sangiovese (California) $19. 89 —*S.H. (9/1/2000)*

La Famiglia di Robert Mondavi 1996 Sangiovese (California) $22. 88 —*S.H. (10/1/1999)*

La Famiglia di Robert Mondavi 2000 Sangiovese (California) $20. A comforting and easy-drinking wine that has levels of complexity and interest. Bone dry, with dusty, soft tannins and soft acids that frame flavors of cherry, tobacco, and dried herbs. Delicate in structure, yet authoritative and versatile at the table. **87** —*S.H. (9/1/2003)*

La Famiglia di Robert Mondavi 1999 Colmera Sangiovese (Napa Valley) $45. This blend of Sangiovese, Syrah, and Teroldego is very soft, and glides over the palate like a silk sheet. It is very dry, and has berry and herb flavors. It seems designed by Tim Mondavi for the table, for it is an understated, subtle wine, not an authoritative one. **86** —*S.H. (3/1/2004)*

La Famiglia di Robert Mondavi 1998 Colmera Sangiovese (California) $45. The flagship of La Famiglia, this represents a supreme effort to perfect Sangiovese in California. Dry berry fruit is wrapped in soft acids and low tannins that make for elegant drinking. It's a good wine but struggles to find complexity and nuance. Yet Colmera is a wine to watch. Contains 83% Sangiovese, with 14% Syrah and 3% Teroldego. **88** —*S.H. (5/1/2002)*

LA FERME MARTIN

La Ferme Martin 1998 Chardonnay (Long Island) $13. Very tart and crisp, like biting into a green apple and adding a squeeze of lime. Pure unadulterated Chardonnay fruit that tastes similar to an unoaked Macon or Chablis. From Wölffer. **85** —*J.C. (4/1/2001)*

La Ferme Martin 1998 Merlot (Long Island) $14. Plummy and weedy flavors in a medium-wight format that picks up some chocolate notes on the finish. Soft and easy to drink. From Wolffer. **85** —*J.C. (4/1/2001)*

LA FILICE

La Filice 2003 Petite Sirah (Hames Valley) $30. The appellation is the warmest in Monterey, so this is a warm-climate wine that's soft in acidity and easy in tannins, with ripe blackberry, chocolate, cola, and coffee flavors. Shows real flair and sophistication. **90** —*S.H. (11/15/2006)*

La Filice 2003 Joseph George Cépage Rhône Red Blend (Paso Robles) $30. Ed Filice is the winemaker at Tolosa Winery, in Edna Valley. This Syrah and Cabernet Sauvignon blend is dry, fairly tannic, soft and ripe in dark fruit and milk chocolate flavors, with a nice licorice and pepper edge. At its best now, it shows real complexity and elegance. **90** —*S.H. (11/1/2006)*

La Filice 2003 Syrah (Paso Robles) $20. Postcard Paso Syrah, big and exuberantly ripe in blackberry, chocolate, and licorice flavors and exotic spices. It's soft in acids, with dusty, fine tannins that provide good grip and structure. Made with grapes from the east and west sides. **87** —*S.H. (11/15/2006)*

LA GARZA

La Garza 1999 Cabernet Sauvignon (Oregon) $18. Green peas, asparagus, and arugula make up the nose on this wine. The flavors include more vegetables. Ends thin and watery. **81** —*C.S. (12/31/2002)*

La Garza 1999 Reserve Cabernet Sauvignon (Oregon) $27. Sweet aromas of vanilla and creamy butter are accented by a hint of red pepper. The flavors of raspberry and milk chocolate are lean and finish unevenly. **84** —*C.S. (12/31/2002)*

La Garza 1999 Merlot (Umpqua Valley) $25. This is quite well made, a simple, dry red wine that mimics cru bourgeois Bordeaux. Dried plum fruit and still drier tannins make it a great match for grilled meats. Barnyardy enhance the French connection. **86** —*P.G. (4/1/2002)*

LA JOTA VINEYARD

La Jota Vineyard 2001 Cabernet Franc (Howell Mountain) $62. I know of no Cab Franc that costs more than this, but this is a very good wine. Be forewarned, it's high in alcohol and thick in tannins, so forget about drinking it now. Deep down inside is a teasing core of ripe, sweetly decadent cherry fruit that's yearning to be free. Hold until 2010. **91** —*S.H. (11/15/2004)*

La Jota Vineyard 2001 Cabernet Sauvignon (Howell Mountain) $52. Size does matter on Howell Mountain. This ageless wine is nowhere near ready to drink due to the massive tannins. Yet there's no question it will age for many, many years. If you must open it now, decant for 24 hours. **91** —*S.H. (10/1/2004)*

La Jota Vineyard 2004 *Barrel Sample* Cabernet Sauvignon (Napa Valley) $NA. Gorgeous aromas of blackberry tart, vanilla and oak lead to strong, rich fruity flavors of cherries and blackberries. So ripe, it finishes almost sweet. Rich in tannins, and compelling for its depth and harmony. **93** —*S.H. (8/1/2004)*

La Jota Vineyard 2001 Anniversary Release Cabernet Sauvignon (Howell Mountain) $93. La Jota set out to make a great wine for their 20th, and lucky for them they ran into such a vintage. If it's less dense than the finest 2001s, it's still a great one. As flavorful as sweet Napa black cur-

USA

rants get, and those Howell tannins are the structure that will let this wine develop through 2010. **93** —*S.H. (10/1/2004)*

La Jota Vineyard 2001 Petite Sirah (Howell Mountain) $46. Big, rich in fruit, astringent in tannins, crisp in acids, high in alcohol, and well-oaked. The flavors are the darkest stone fruits. Drink now with short ribs or lamb, or age as long as you want. It will outlive you. **88** —*S.H. (11/15/2004)*

LA ROCHELLE

La Rochelle 2001 La Rochelle Vineyard Chardonnay (Monterey) $16. A well-oaked Chardonnay, brimming with smoky vanilla and buttered toast notes that ride high over ripe fruit flavors ranging from lemon zest to apple, peach, pear, and pineapple. Tastes leesy, with a bright streak of acidity that is mouth-watering. **87** —*S.H. (12/15/2003)*

La Rochelle 2004 Pinot Gris (Arroyo Seco) $24. Insiders know Arroyo Seco as one of the best small appellations on the Central Coast. The whites display firm acids and a brilliant minerality. Varietally, this wine exhibits freshly picked peach, apple, quince, and butterscotch flavors that finish clean and dry. **89** —*S.H. (12/15/2006)*

La Rochelle 2003 Pinot Noir (Monterey) $18. Smells and tastes sharp, but this acidity is expressed in sweet peppermint and wintergreen that adds a piquant, tart touch to the cherry and cocoa flavors. This is a really lovely Pinot, velvety, elegant, and balanced, a wine that some other producers would charge far more for. **90 Editors' Choice** —*S.H. (12/15/2006)*

La Rochelle 2003 Pinot Noir (Santa Lucia Highlands) $34. To me this is the least of La Rochelle's current Pinot lineup. It shows plenty of ripe Pinot fruit and silky tannins, but there's a baked, one-dimensional character to the cherries. The wine is excessively soft. **85** —*S.H. (7/1/2006)*

La Rochelle 2001 Pinot Noir (Monterey) $18. Good example of cool Central Coast Pinot, with its polished, jammy flavors of cherry and raspberry and dusty spices, complexed with smoky oak. Bright acidity and gentle tannins make for an easy drink. A little light, but a pretty good value. **86** —*S.H. (3/1/2004)*

La Rochelle 2003 Classic Clones Pinot Noir (Arroyo Seco) $38. Easily the best of La Rochelle's three Pinots, with a zesty acidity that frames ripe cherries, pomegranates, cola, oak, and citrus zest. The Arroyo Seco is an under-appreciated appellation in Salinas Valley, while the clonal mix of this wine consists of older selections, not today's cleaned-up Dijon specimens. This is a complex, addictive Pinot. Best now and for a few years. **93 Editors' Choice** —*S.H. (7/1/2006)*

La Rochelle 2001 San Vicente Vineyard Pinot Noir (Monterey) $30. An exceedingly fine Pinot, as juicy as they get. Oodles of elaborate cherry, raspberry, root beer, gingerbread, and mocha flavors, oaky and spicy, wrapped in a silky texture, with clean, bright acidity. Shows real complexity and finesse. **92** —*S.H. (12/15/2004)*

La Rochelle 2003 San vincente Vineyard Pinot Noir (Monterey) $34. The vineyard is in the Arroyo Seco, although you wouldn't know that from the label, and the wine shows the ripe, almost sweet fruit from this warm vintage. Strangely, it's not nearly in the same league as the winery's Classic Clones Pinot, also from Arroyo Seco. It has a softness that turns ponderous after the first sip. **85** —*S.H. (7/1/2006)*

LA SIRENA

La Sirena 2001 Cabernet Sauvignon (Napa Valley) $125. Very distinctive, opening with pencil lead and cedar-cigar box aromas. Very fine and pure. Airing coaxes out the deep blackberry, red, and black-cherry and blueberry flavors. Finishes with a sweep of sweet fennel. Well-structured and delicious now, and should age beyond 2010. **93** —*S.H. (11/1/2005)*

La Sirena 2004 Moscato Azul Dry Muscat Canelli (Napa Valley) $28. One of the most distinctive aromatic dry white wines I've ever had from California. Brilliantly acidic and bone dry, with intense orange blossom, peach, floral, and vanilla flavors. The pure transparency of the fruit has not been interfered with by oak. **90** —*S.H. (11/1/2005)*

La Sirena 2002 Syrah (Santa Ynez Valley) $45. Nice nose on this wine, blending graham cracker, marshmallow, and chocolate notes into a veritable smore-gasbord of aromas. Doesn't quite have the same richness on the palate, however, and turns a bit tart on the finish. **86** —*S.H. (9/1/2005)*

La Sirena 2002 Syrah (Napa Valley) $55. More exciting than winemaker Heidi Barrett's Santa Ynez bottling, this smooth, creamy-textured Syrah is packed with ripe plums and blackberries, yet manages to be complex at the same time, adding hints of pepper and dried spices. The long finish echoes with hints of ripe berries and cracked pepper. **90** *(9/1/2005)*

LA STORIA

La Storia 2002 Zinfandel (Alexander Valley) $28. A ton of smoky, charry oak has been slathered on this wine, lending it caramel and butterscotch aromas, but it's also terrifically fruity. Bursting with ripe cherry and black raspberry flavors that drink dry and balanced. From Trentadue. **88** —*S.H. (3/1/2005)*

La Storia 2001 Zinfandel (Alexander Valley) $30. Smooth and sleek, with velvety tannins that frame layers of black-cherry, blackberry, sage, tar, coffee, and hints of chocolate, too. The finish is plush and long, toasty rich. **89** *(11/1/2003)*

LA TOUR

La Tour 2002 Chardonnay (Napa Valley) $18. This deliciously lush and richly textured wine is blessed with a fine blend of ripe, tropical flavors redolent of papaya and mango. It's got good acidity for balance and also shows subtle hints of citrus and melon flavors. In fact, it tastes like it costs twice as much as the suggested retail price. A first release from Tom LaTour, better known as the head of the San Francisco-based Kimpton Hotel Group. The grapes were grown on his Mt. Veeder vineyard. **91** —*J.M. (10/1/2004)*

LABYRINTH

Labyrinth 2002 Bien Nacido Vineyard Pinot Noir (Santa Maria Valley) $28. Shows that Santa Maria cool-climate thing in the beet and slightly tomatoey notes that accompany the cola flavors. Bone dry and pretty acidic, but clean and elegant. Not an ager, so drink now. **85** —*S.H. (10/1/2005)*

LACHINI

Lachini 2002 Pinot Noir (Willamette Valley) $30. Smoky and aggressive, this is a wham-bam style with enough saddle leather to call in the cavalry. Toast, coffee, smoke, and caramel pile on oaky flavors. It's big, rough-hewn, and tannic, but tasty. **88** *(11/1/2004)*

Lachini 2003 "S" Pinot Noir (Willamette Valley) $34. Lachini's "S" label, as they describe it, is the winery's experimentation with different winemaker styles, harvest dates and vineyard management. The same estate grapes go into Lachini's LV Pinot, but the two styles of wine could not be more different. The S is made by Peter Rosback, who grabs the gold ring of extraction, weight, and power without losing sight of varietal character or balance. Succulent, thick, toasty, and laced with coffee and cherry tobacco, this wine is sheer enjoyment. **91 Editors' Choice** —*P.G. (11/15/2005)*

Lachini 2002 Lachini Family Estate Pinot Noir (Willamette Valley) $35. Seductive floral accents make a nice entry, and the wine, tart and juicy, carries aromas and flavors of orange peel, sour cherry, and bitter chocolate. **87** *(11/1/2004)*

Lachini 2003 LV Estate Pinot Noir (Willamette Valley) $36. Lachini winemaker Isabelle Dutarte, who made half a dozen vintages at Domaine Drouhin and trained under Maison Drouhin, definitely has a DDO style going here. Tight, compact, structured, and immaculate, this focused effort rewards breathing time with aromas of wild berry, gravel, and earth. Tart and juicy, it's one of those wines that's even better on the second day. **90** —*P.G. (11/15/2005)*

LADERA

Ladera 2003 Cabernet Sauvignon (Howell Mountain) $68. Ladera's regular Napa Cab is really good. This one's nearly twice the price. What do you get? The wine is higher in alcohol, and tastes woodier, too, with a sugared blackberry tea sweetness. It's a little ponderous now, but you might want to stick it in the cellar for five years or so and see what happens. **87** —*S.H. (12/15/2006)*

Ladera 2003 Cabernet Sauvignon (Napa Valley) $35. Really good Cab here, a blend of mountain and foothills fruit that captures Napa's elegant intensity. It's a fully dry, balanced wine, with hefty, sticky tannins yet an immediate approachability of blackberry and Chinese plum sauce flavors and a rich, chocolatey finish. Good now and over the next ten years. **90** —*S.H. (12/15/2006)*

Ladera 2002 Cabernet Sauvignon (Howell Mountain) $65. Tasted alongside Ladera's '01 Lone Canyon Cab, this is better structured. The acid and tannin ballet is an exciting one, joined by rich smoky oak and a ripe Cabernet expression of black currants and cassis that's delicious. This is a major-league wine that should develop through 2010. **92 Cellar Selection** —*S.H. (12/1/2005)*

Ladera 2001 Cabernet Sauvignon (Howell Mountain) $65. Everyone's tannins are getting softer these days, but Howell Mountain Cabs are hanging in there. Massive, with intense black currant and oak flavors that finish dry. You can tell this is a very fine wine from its balance. Best after 2008, but approachable now. **92** —*S.H. (3/1/2005)*

Ladera 2001 Lone Canyon Vineyard Cabernet Sauvignon (Napa Valley) $65. A lovely Cab. Although it's got some richly dry tannins, it's soft and melted enough to drink now. The flavors of black currants, cassis, and cocoa harmonize perfectly with finely toasted oak. **89** —*S.H. (12/1/2005)*

Ladera 2002 Lone Mountain Vineyard Cabernet Sauvignon (Napa Valley) $65. Ladera has been producing ageworthy Cabernets for the last few years and this is surely one. As rich and dense in tannins as it is, it's shockingly forward in blackberry and cherry fruit flavors, while a plethora of new French oak adds even more sweetness. The result is voluptuous now, but it should age effortlessly for at least 10 years. **93 Cellar Selection** —*S.H. (5/1/2006)*

LADYBUG

Ladybug NV Old Vines Cuvée 11 White Table Wine White Blend (Mendocino) $13. Fruity and off-dry to sweet, this blend of four varieties has flavors of canned pears, peaches, and apricots. **83** —*S.H. (12/1/2006)*

Ladybug NV Old Vines White White Blend (Mendocino) $13. This blend of French Colombard and other white wines is simple and dry, with green grape, white peach, and vanilla flavors that finish clean and fruity. **84** —*S.H. (12/1/2005)*

LAETITIA

Laetitia NV Brut Cuvée Champagne Blend (Arroyo Grande Valley) $20. This unusual sparkler is full in both color and flavor, with earthy, almost matchstick aromas and similar deep, mature flavors. The even bead and full mousse give it an almost chewy mouthfeel, and it finishes long, dry and complex. Has unique character, plenty of flavor and will appeal to a wide variety of tasters. **88 Editors' Choice** —*M.M. (12/1/2001)*

Laetitia 1997 Brut Rosé Champagne Blend (Arroyo Grande Valley) $28. Pretty cherry highlights, with intriguing citrus, sage, and herb flavors on the follow-up. Fresh and clean on the finish, with firm structure and elegance. **90** —*J.M. (12/1/2001)*

Laetitia 1997 Cuvée M Champagne Blend (Arroyo Grande Valley) $28. Bright and fresh, with toasty, ripe aromas and flavors that hint of peach, melon, apple, and citrus. Lemony and clean on the finish, the wine sports tiny bubbles and plenty of finesse. **88** —*J.M. (12/1/2001)*

Laetitia 1994 Cuvée M Champagne Blend (Arroyo Grande Valley) $30. **86** *(12/31/2000)*

Laetitia 2004 Chardonnay (Arroyo Grande Valley) $16. This Chard shows the boldly ripe flavors of tropical fruits, roasted hazelnuts, buttercream, Asian spices, and toast that many California Chards have, but also a distinctively high acidity that pushes those flavors out and makes them sing. **92 Editors' Choice** —*S.H. (12/31/2005)*

Laetitia 2003 Chardonnay (Arroyo Grande Valley) $16. Here's a cool climate Chard with bright, citrusy acidity that boosts its tropical fruit flavors. With a smoky edge of oak, and lots of tangy spices, it's clean and refreshing. **88** —*S.H. (2/1/2005)*

Laetitia 2001 Estate Chardonnay (Arroyo Grande Valley) $18. Here's a rich, full-bodied Chard packed with big, fruity flavors of mangoes and pears. It also has an elaborate overlay of well-toasted oak and good acids. **90 Editors' Choice** —*S.H. (5/1/2003)*

Laetitia 1998 Estate Chardonnay (Arroyo Grande Valley) $18. **88** *(6/1/2000)*

Laetitia 1997 Estate Reserve Chardonnay (Arroyo Grande Valley) $26. **92** —*L.W. (11/15/1999)*

Laetitia 2000 Reserve Chardonnay (Arroyo Grande Valley) $26. Tight and austere, with citrusy flavors, a hint of pear, and a metallic, minerally feel. Lavish oak adds smoke and vanilla. Turns acidic and prickly on the finish. **85** —*S.H. (12/15/2003)*

Laetitia 1998 Reserve Chardonnay (Arroyo Grande Valley) $33. Refined and inviting, the bouquet offers caramel, hazelnuts, and toast. Dark apple, toast, spice, and earth flavors fill the mouth. The mouthfeel is rich and dense, though a touch more fruit would really have it singing. Finishes with spice and faint lime notes, and a toasty oak flavor that really takes over. The former Deutz Champagne estate in San Luis Obispo County, Laetitia is now devoted to producing Chardonnay and Pinot Noir. **89** *(7/1/2001)*

Laetitia 1998 Winemaker's Select Chardonnay (Edna Valley) $18. **88** *(6/1/2000)*

Laetitia 2004 Pinot Blanc (Arroyo Grande Valley) $16. Well structured and totally dry, with very high acidity and intense flavors of citrus fruits, figs, green apples, and slightly unripe peaches. This polished, elegant wine is a natural with a wide variety of food. **88** —*S.H. (12/31/2005)*

Laetitia 2000 Pinot Blanc (Arroyo Grande Valley) $19. Very focused and pure, with bright tangerine peel flavors and crisp acidity. Oak adds the plush, rich nuances of vanilla and a sappy-sweet mouthfeel, while a dollop of lees creates a creamy note. The wine is very dry and tart and clean. **86** —*S.H. (9/1/2003)*

Laetitia 1999 Estate Pinot Blanc (Arroyo Grande Valley) $16. Brilliantly pure tropical fruit joins with jolting acidity and overlays of smoky oak to produce this full-flavored beauty that brims with melon, guava, and peach notes. It's crisp, clean, refreshing, and complex, with a long, spicy finish. **90 Editors' Choice** —*S.H. (11/15/2001)*

Laetitia 2001 Pinot Noir (Arroyo Grande Valley) $25. Absolutely delicious, a wine that is so easy to drink, you don't want to stop. Yet it possesses complexities that raise it above the ordinary. Flavors include jammy raspberries and cherries, Oriental spices, vanilla, smoke, and sweetened coconut, but the wine is thoroughly dry. Smooth on the palate, with bright acidity. **90** —*S.H. (3/1/2004)*

Laetitia 2000 Pinot Noir (Arroyo Grande Valley) $25. Solid, middle-of-the-road Pinot, with dusty, earthy cherry aromas that open up into ripe cherry and chocolate flavors that incorporate a hint of citrus fruit. It's not as if the oak really takes charge. Closes a little short with black coffee and chocolate notes. **87** *(10/1/2002)*

Laetitia 1999 Pinot Noir (San Luis Obispo County) $25. The deep cherry, beet and smoke profile appealed to all of us. It is velvety on the tongue, with round berry, earth and charcoal flavors. It comes off smooth, dark and handsome, even if the flavors are a little indistinct, wrapping up with an attractive espresso finish. **89** *(10/1/2002)*

Laetitia 1999 Pinot Noir (Santa Barbara County) $25. Quite ripe and juicy, serving up a rich blend of black-cherry, plum, and herb flavors. It fans out on the palate to reveal hints of licorice, smoke, and even chocolate. More muscular than your average Pinot, it's plush and smooth on the finish. **91** —*J.M. (7/1/2002)*

Laetitia 2003 Estate Pinot Noir (Arroyo Grande Valley) $25. Here's a Pinot that delivers plenty of upfront cherry fruit to the palate, but maintains a dignified elegance and lightness of body. The fruit flavors are complexed by oak, while high acidity adds a clean minerality. Finishes with a real stamp of quality. **89** —*S.H. (10/1/2005)*

Laetitia 2002 Estate Pinot Noir (Arroyo Grande Valley) $25. Shows rich charcoal, roast coffee, cherry, anise, vanilla, and cola flavors, in a medium-bodied wine that's balanced and dry. There's some real complexity in the flavors and crisp acidity. Powerful tannins suggest aging. Drink now through 2007. **88** —*S.H. (11/1/2004)*

Laetitia 1997 Estate Pinot Noir (Arroyo Grande Valley) $23. **89** *(11/15/1999)*

Laetitia 2000 Estate Reserve Pinot Noir (Arroyo Grande Valley) $35. A lovely, supple wine that's a joy on the palate, with its silky tannins and round, smooth mouthfeel. The flavors veer toward raspberries and cherries and finish off with a peppery, spicy aftertaste. This is a lighter-style, jammy wine. **88** —*S.H. (7/1/2003)*

Laetitia 1999 Estate Reserve Pinot Noir (Arroyo Grande Valley) $47. Ripe—even plump—this almost-too-easy wine shows an oaky, cinnamon, clove, and caramel bouquet. The black-cherry, cocoa, and coffee flavors show still more oaky vanilla and brown sugar. The dusty, slightly tangy back-end tannins indicate that this could stand aging for a few years. Drink now–2005. **88** *(10/1/2002)*

Laetitia 1997 Estate Reserve Pinot Noir (Arroyo Grande Valley) $33. **91** *(10/1/1999)*

Laetitia 2004 La Colline Pinot Noir (Arroyo Grande Valley) $60. Extremely complex, and while it shows powerful red cherry, cola, rhubarb, and tea flavors, it maintains the essential elegance that Pinot requires. The acidity is wonderful. Vey, very dry. So balanced, so layered, so drinkable. **96** —*S.H. (7/1/2006)*

Laetitia 2003 La Colline Pinot Noir (Arroyo Grande Valley) $60. Tasted side by side with Laetitia's Les Galets bottling, this wine is virtually identical. The differences are minute. Colline is perhaps a shade more acidic, a bit leaner, a little drier and more tannic. But like Galets, it is an authentically great, young Pinot Noir, as elegant and complex as any Pinot of the vintage. **95 Editors' Choice** —*S.H. (12/1/2005)*

Laetitia 2002 La Colline Pinot Noir (Arroyo Grande Valley) $60. This is a masculine Pinot, deep in color and muscular, but elegant. Think Armani. The flavors veer toward dark fruits and berries, such as blackberries, spicy blue plums, coffee bean, and even bitter dark chocolate, yet the wine possesses an airy, lilting quality, thanks to soft tannins and brisk acidity. **92** —*S.H. (2/1/2005)*

Laetitia 2001 La Colline Pinot Noir (Arroyo Grande Valley) $60. Silkier and more charming than Laetitia's Les Galets, a wine so delicious and easy to drink that its complexity almost escapes notice. There are layers of spice, cherry fruit compote, raspberry purée, cola, and cinnamony spices that unfold on the palate. Drink now and over the next year. **90** —*S.H. (6/1/2004)*

Laetitia 1999 La Colline Pinot Noir (Arroyo Grande Valley) $60. There's a complex mélange of aromas and flavors that one taster felt incorporated too many citrus, and vegetal notes, but the rest of the panel enjoyed the cherry, herb, cocoa, cinnamon, citrus and olive notes. Smooth and polished, this combines structure and immediate appeal. Good now, but best after 2004. **92 Cellar Selection** *(10/1/2002)*

Laetitia 1999 La Colline Pinot Noir (Arroyo Grande Valley) $NA. Cool coastal conditions make for a wine that straddles the ripeness line, with notes of blackberries and earthy, herbal notes of tobacco, sage, and cranberries. Lavish oak softens and fattens. The wine is very dry, and there are some unresolved tannins that a year or so of aging might soften. **89** —*S.H. (9/1/2003)*

Laetitia 2004 Les Galets Pinot Noir (Arroyo Grande Valley) $60. As full-flavored as this is, it maintains the delicate elegance Pinot should have. It strikes the palate with great balance, a composite of fine acidity, easy but complex tannins, and superb cherry, tea, and oak flavors with an underlying minerality. Showcases the greatness of Arroyo Grande Valley as a source of some of the best Pinots from California. **93** —*S.H. (11/1/2006)*

Laetitia 2003 Les Galets Pinot Noir (Arroyo Grande Valley) $60. This block designate from Laetitia's estate vineyard comes from a warmer, eastern site. It is high in acidity and extremely dry. The flavors and mouthfeel are so complex that it takes several sips to grasp what's going on, by which time the wine has climbed to even higher levels. This is truly great California Pinot Noir. **95** —*S.H. (12/1/2005)*

Laetitia 2002 Les Galets Pinot Noir (Arroyo Grande Valley) $60. Quite a different wine from Laetitia's Colline bottling, although it's not fair to say one's better. This is chunkier, with berry and stone fruit flavors intrigued by a meaty, leathery note. It's also more tannic and, for the moment, less accessible, although a tenderloin of beef will deal with that. Probably an ager. Drink now through 2008. **92** —*S.H. (2/1/2005)*

Laetitia 2001 Les Galets Pinot Noir (Arroyo Grande Valley) $60. Les Galets, from Laetitia's estate vineyard, is a brilliant wine. It's fuller and denser than the companion La Colline bottling, with plum and spicy blackberry flavors and a molasses, Indian pudding note. Tannins are evident but

not intrusive. This serious Pinot Noir is built to improve in the cellar through 2007. **92** —*S.H. (6/1/2004)*

Laetitia 2003 Reserve Pinot Noir (Arroyo Grande Valley) $40. This Central Coast Pinot smells so wonderful, you just know it's going to be great. It's not the blockbuster of the winery's block selections, but is nonetheless elegant, silky, and complex. Totally dry, it's rich in cherries, sweet leather, cola, and toasty oak. Laetitia is on a real Pinot roll. **92** —*S.H. (12/1/2005)*

Laetitia 2002 Reserve Pinot Noir (Arroyo Grande Valley) $40. A beautiful Pinot of considerable power and subtlety. Shows ripe flavors of blackberries, blueberries, and cocoa, with minerals and hard spices. There's a firmness to the mouth feel but also a lusciousness, and the silky finish is polished. **90** —*S.H. (2/1/2005)*

Laetitia 2001 Reserve Pinot Noir (Arroyo Grande Valley) $40. Laetitia's regular '01 Pinot was very good. This silky charmer is even better. It's exuberantly rich in upfront raspberry, cherry, vanilla, roasted coffee, and spice flavors that drink dry and bright, thanks to crisp acidity. Thoroughly enjoyable, with nuance and complexity. **91** —*S.H. (12/15/2004)*

Laetitia 2000 Brut Cocquard Sparkling Blend (Arroyo Grande Valley) $25. The wine shows off rich, toasty aromas up front, followed by lemon and grapefruit notes on the palate. Green apple and herbs line the finish. **87** —*J.M. (12/1/2003)*

Laetitia 2000 Brut Coquard Sparkling Blend (Arroyo Grande Valley) $25. Rich and smooth bubbly, with plenty of high-end refinement. Feels elegant in the mouth, with complex layers of citrus fruits, a hint of peach, and doughy, yeasty flavors. It's absolutely dry, with some scoury acids that may soften with a few years of age. **90** —*S.H. (5/1/2004)*

Laetitia NV Brut Cuvée Sparkling Blend (San Luis Obispo County) $16. Starts out a little sulfury, but it blows off to reveal citrus and dough flavors. Drinks very dry and acidic, a lean, austere bubbly with some elegance. Turns astringent on the finish. **85** —*S.H. (6/1/2004)*

Laetitia NV Brut Cuvée Sparkling Blend (Arroyo Grande Valley) $18. Bone dry and elegantly clean in acidity, this doughy, austere wine is less fruity than most California Bruts, with accents of lime peel and vanilla. **86** —*S.H. (12/31/2005)*

Laetitia NV Brut Cuvée Sparkling Blend (Arroyo Grande Valley) $18. Feels a bit rough and sandpapery, but otherwise it's a nicely dry wine, with good structure and true Champagne flavors of citrus, cherry cream, and yeast. Chardonnay, Pinot Blanc, and Pinot Noir. **86** —*S.H. (12/31/2006)*

Laetitia NV Brut Cuvée (San Luis Obispo/Santa Barbara Counties) Sparkling Blend (Central Coast) $16. Starts out a bit sulfury, but later reveals citrus and dough flavors. Dry and acidic; turns astringent on the finish. **86** —*J.M. (12/1/2003)*

Laetitia 2002 Brut de Blanc Sparkling Blend (Arroyo Grande Valley) $25. This 70% Chardonnay wine is dry, light-bodied, and elegant. It has a vanilla-tinged flavor of peaches, while the Pinot Noir contributes a strawberry taste. **87** —*S.H. (12/31/2005)*

Laetitia 2003 Brut de Blancs Sparkling Blend (Arroyo Grande Valley) $25. Laetitia is one of the best table wine producers in the appellation, and it's no surprise this Chardonnay-Pinot Blanc blend is so good. It's complex, with rich lemon zest, yeasty brioche, and peach-vanilla cream flavors that finish dry and long. Will benefit from a little bottle age to take the edge off. **90** —*S.H. (12/31/2006)*

Laetitia 2001 Brut de Noir Sparkling Blend (Arroyo Grande Valley) $25. This is the fullest-bodied of Laetitia's crop of bubblies. It has a tinge of raspberries and strawberries, but is still an elegantly structured, silky wine, a nice interpretation of Central Coast sparkling wine. **88** —*S.H. (12/31/2005)*

Laetitia 2000 Brut Rosé Sparkling Blend (Arroyo Grande Valley) $25. A bright-edged, steely, mineral-like wine that serves up lots of lemon and grapefruit. The finish is fresh and zippy with a hint of cherries at the end. **87** —*J.M. (12/1/2003)*

Laetitia 2002 Cuvée M Sparkling Blend (Arroyo Grande Valley) $30. This is a really good wine. It has the kind of smooth, elegantly silky texture of a fine Champagne, and is delicate but complex, with brioche, vanilla, custard, peach, strawberry, and lime zest flavors. You can taste the dosage in the honeyed finish. Best now through 2010. **92** —*S.H.* *(12/31/2006)*

Laetitia 2003 Syrah (Arroyo Grande Valley) $25. There aren't many Arroyo Grande Syrahs, this being Burgundian terroir, but this one aspires to Côte Rôtie standards. It's a fine and interesting wine. Shows white pepper and blackberry flavors, quite dry and well-oaked, with intricate tannins. Best now and through 2006. **92** —*S.H.* *(12/31/2005)*

Laetitia 2000 Syrah (Santa Barbara County) $25. A thin wine, with tough tannins and a stubborn mouthfeel. Has some blackberry and cherry flavors, but they're outweighed by dried herbs and tobacco. A ton of new oak does little to enrich it. **85** —*S.H.* *(3/1/2004)*

LAFOND

Lafond 1998 Lafond Vineyard Chardonnay (Santa Ynez Valley) $30. Big and easy with caramel and creamy notes to spare, this has good apple, spice, and toast elements and an appealing nutty-leesy aspect. Still, it seems already quite mature, like it needs to be drunk now. Enjoy it soon for its full mouthfeel and ripe baked apple flavors. **87** *(7/1/2001)*

Lafond 1997 Lafond Vineyard Chardonnay (Santa Ynez Valley) $28. **90** *(6/1/2000)*

Lafond 2004 SRH Chardonnay (Santa Rita Hills) $20. You can't smell acidity, but you can smell fruit so bright, it has to be high in acidity. This Chard is rewardingly pure and sharp in Key lime pie, papaya purée, fresh juicy tangerine, and smoky, vanilla-infused oak flavors, and it grows more interesting with every sip. **92 Editors' Choice** —*S.H.* *(11/1/2006)*

Lafond 1997 Sweeney Canyon Chardonnay (Santa Ynez Valley) $28. **87** *(6/1/2000)*

Lafond 2000 Sweeny Canyon Vineyard Chardonnay (Santa Ynez Valley) $28. Elaborately oaked, and opens with a smooth waft of buttered toast, smoky char, and vanilla. There are hints of fruit in the aroma, but it's on the palate that the flavors really hit. Tropical fruits, mainly, with hints of white peach, and a sleek minerality that's part acidity, part stony terrior. Complex, young, and compelling. **92** —*S.H.* *(10/1/2003)*

Lafond 2003 Lafond Vineyard Pinot Noir (Santa Rita Hills) $48. A little too big and extracted for finesse, this full-bodied wine is almost Rhônesque. It's dark, with cherry jam and mocha flavors, and is a bit soft and hot. Lots of new French oak piles the smoky, vanilla flavors on. **86** —*S.H.* *(11/1/2006)*

Lafond 2000 Lafond Vineyard Pinot Noir (Santa Ynez Valley) $35. A good wine but just a tad simple. The aromas are on the weedy, hay side, with suggestions of forest floor and oak, and in the mouth, coffee and bitter cherry flavors fight their way up through thick tannins. Possibly a victim of its vintage. **86** —*S.H.* *(2/1/2004)*

Lafond 1999 Lafond Vineyard Pinot Noir (Santa Ynez Valley) $35. With its coating of dusty earth, the nose is dense and hard to penetrate. Time in the glass helps, exposing black-cherry, vanilla, herbs, toast, and coffee. some smoky bacon shows up on the finish. Overall it's big, ripe, and raring to go—and it still has a few more years until it peaks. **88** *(10/1/2002)*

Lafond 1997 Lafond Vineyard Pinot Noir (Santa Ynez Valley) $35. A bizarre style of wine. The aromas are Port-like—old Port—with a caramelized, candy-sugar note verging on pie crust. There's also a streak of clove. In the mouth, it's earthy and dense, with tomato flavors and a dash of sweetness from oak. **82** —*S.H.* *(2/1/2001)*

Lafond 2004 SRH Pinot Noir (Santa Rita Hills) $24. A bit heavy and hot, with cooked cherry pie filling flavors and tannins that you might find in a Rhône wine. Could soften with some years in the bottle. **84** —*S.H.* *(11/1/2006)*

Lafond 2000 SRH Pinot Noir (Santa Ynez Valley) $18. Grown in the Santa Rita Hills (SRH) appellation, this dense wine is young, and packed with deep berry-cherry flavors, wrapped in thick tannins. It's a bit rough and gawky now, and may be better in a year or two. **86** —*S.H.* *(2/1/2003)*

Lafond 2000 Joughin Vineyard Syrah (Santa Ynez Valley) $30. From a warmer, inland vineyard, a well-structured Syrah with lush tannins, good acids, and a fancy overall mouthfeel that nevertheless is thin in fruit. The hay, straw, and herb flavors just manage to suggest blackberries. Still, the wine's bones are good. **86** —*S.H.* *(3/1/2004)*

Lafond 2000 Lafond Vineyard Syrah (Santa Ynez Valley) $30. As dark as this wine is, it is thin on fruit flavor. Smells like a bale of hay on a hot summer day, which is a nice, natural smell, but not for Syrah. In the mouth, modest cherry and blackberry flavors are very dry and rather tannic. **86** —*S.H.* *(3/1/2004)*

Lafond 1998 Lafond Vineyard Syrah (Santa Ynez Valley) $28. Mingles ripe blackberry and blueberry flavors with earthy, truffly notes. There are also suggestions of coffee, chocolate, and bouquet garni, as well as solidly smoked oak. Very dry, with soft, supple tannins and good acidity from a cool vintage. Much better than a previous sample. **90** *(11/1/2001)*

Lafond 2000 Melville Vineyard Syrah (Santa Ynez Valley) $30. The wine is astringently tannic and offers little relief by way of flavor, but if you concentrate you'll find a core of black-cherry. Still, the structure is so fine that with a suitably rich dish, the wine would be better. **86** —*S.H.* *(3/1/2004)*

Lafond 2004 SRH Syrah (Santa Rita Hills) $18. Very good Syrah, with tight, astringently young tannins courtesy of the region's cool climate. Impressive for its balance, a big, rich, dry wine with ripe blackberry, coffee, and white pepper flavors and an elegant, upscale mouthfeel. Drink now through 2010. Excellent value for the price. **91** —*S.H.* *(11/1/2006)*

Lafond 2000 SRH Syrah (Santa Ynez Valley) $18. From the new Santa Rita Hills appellation, this inky-dark, purple wine stains the sides of the glass, one indication of how big and young it is. It has the jammy berry flavors and insolent acidity of youth, while oversize tannins make it muscular. Not drinkable now, except with the biggest foods. Try aging until 2006. **89** —*S.H.* *(12/1/2002)*

Lafond 1998 Stolpman Vineyard Syrah (Santa Ynez Valley) $28. Pronounced, sharp cherry-berry aromas, generously enhanced by sweet, smoky oak. In the mouth, it's full bodied, syrupy, and dense, with jammy berry flavors and soft, lush tannins. Very much a Châteauneuf-style wine. **89** —*S.H.* *(7/1/2002)*

LAGIER MEREDITH

Lagier Meredith 2000 Syrah (Mount Veeder) $50. A fine mountain wine, tough and tannic in youth, with a gritty tightness and bite of fresh acidity in the finish. But there's a dense core of cherry-berry fruit and an earth, mushroomy concentration that suggests ageability. **88** —*S.H.* *(2/1/2004)*

Lagier Meredith 1999 Syrah (Mount Veeder) $50. From young vines in this southwest Napa appellation, a dramatic wine, dense and opulent. It's dark and brooding to look at, a purple, glyceriney wine that could easily lose balance, but doesn't. Underlying flavors of plum, blackberry, licorice, and spices are balanced with superb tannins and acids and just-right oak. The finish is incredibly long and satisfying. Only the second commercial release. **93** —*S.H.* *(12/1/2002)*

LAGO DI MERLO

Lago di Merlo 2001 Sangiovese (Dry Creek Valley) $19. This wine is delicate and crisply silky. It has cherry and kirsch flavors that turn a bit hot and burnt in the finish. **84** —*S.H.* *(11/1/2005)*

LAIL

Lail 1997 J. Daniel Cuvée Bordeaux Blend (Napa Valley) $75. **93** *(11/1/2000)*

Lail 2001 J. Daniel Cuvée Cabernet Sauvignon (Napa Valley) $80. Made from Howell Mountain grapes, yet rich and approachable in youth. There are huge, chewy tannins, but they're sweet, and frame black currant and cherry-chocolate fudge flavors. This makes it sound like a dessert wine, but it's dry and balanced and entirely satisfying. **92** —*S.H.* *(10/1/2004)*

Lail 2000 J. Daniel Cuvée Cabernet Sauvignon (Napa Valley) $80. The blackberry, cherry, mocha, and herb flavors are tasty, but are undeniably thinner that the previous two vintages, and are buried under thick, tough tannins. Not likely to improve with age. **86** —*S.H.* *(5/1/2004)*

Lail 1999 J. Daniel Cuvée Cabernet Sauvignon (Napa Valley) $80. High-end stuff, the cutting edge of what Napa is doing with Cab. The fruit is exquisitely ripe, the quintessence of black currants, but this density is balanced by lightness and grace. The mouthfeel is round and soft.

Luxurious tannins will protect the wine as it ages. **95 Editors' Choice** —*S.H. (11/15/2002)*

Lail 1998 J. Daniel Cuvée Cabernet Sauvignon (Napa Valley) $75. Among the better '98s, this wine's vineyard pedigree shows in the polished fruit and supple tannins, the result of great terroir. The aromas suggest black-cherries and blackberries with intense oaky, smoky tones. Particularly notable for the soft, lush mouthfeel, like sipping pure velvet. If the wine were more concentrated it would be classic. **93** —*S.H. (6/1/2002)*

Lail 2003 Blueprint Cabernet Sauvignon-Merlot (Napa Valley) $45. This classy wine is tasty, with voluptuously ripe crème de cassis and blackberry tart flavors enriched with chocolate fudge, vanilla, and spicy, smoky oak. The tannins are superfine, and while the wine is a bit soft, it's dry and balanced. A relative value compared to their pricier J. Daniel Cuvée. **90** —*S.H. (7/1/2006)*

Lail 2002 Blueprint Merlot-Cabernet Sauvignon (Napa Valley) $45. Dominated by Merlot, this is a soft wine with cherry, blueberry, and blackberry flavors. There's an earthiness that keeps it from being a fruit bomb, as well as a sweetness from oak, that will delight chefs figuring out how to prepare duck or lamb. Very dry and complex, with a lingering finish, it is delicious now, and should hold for five years. **93 Editors' Choice** —*S.H. (11/1/2005)*

Lail 2001 Blueprint Merlot-Cabernet Sauvignon (Napa Valley) $45. Smells rather muted, with an oaky earthiness, but if you air it a lot, the cassis and currants show up. One sip is enough to reveal the sharp-edged tannins, but there's a solid core of currant and blackberry fruit. Not showing well now, but seems designed for longterm aging. **87** —*S.H. (10/1/2004)*

LAIRD

Laird 2000 Cabernet Sauvignon (Napa Valley) $60. Four-plus years have not helped this unripe wine. It remains herbal and even vegetal, with a tough, astringent finish, despite some nice oak. **82** —*S.H. (8/1/2005)*

Laird 1999 Laird Family Estate Cabernet Sauvignon (Napa Valley) $65. Full and musclebound, with licorice and leather notes to the nose. The palate is juicy and bright, featuring ample berry fruit and notes of chocolate. The finish is all fruit and little subtlety, hardly different from blackberry jam. Overall this is a creamy mouthful of wine. **88** —*M.S. (11/15/2002)*

Laird 1999 Rutherford Ranch Cabernet Sauvignon (Rutherford) $75. Claret-style and elegant, this Cab's approachable enough to drink now. Dried green herbs and earth coat black and red plum on the nose; red berries, anise, and white pepper shine on the palate. Spicy oak-derived goodness smolders on the finish. Only 275 cases produced. **91** —*D.T. (6/1/2002)*

Laird 2002 Chardonnay (Carneros) $30. Charred oak brings vanilla, buttered toast, spice, and other barrel notes, but can't quite elevate the underlying wine, which has vegetal flavors. It's also high in acids. Not bad, but expensive for what you get. **84** —*S.H. (8/1/2005)*

Laird 1999 Chardonnay (Napa Valley) $40. Smooth and creamy from start to finish, this wine is a dead-on mainstream pleaser. Begins with a nutty and toasty nose that also shows traces of apple and lemon. The palate, buttressed by a healthy dose of oak, also offers a lot of fruit flavor, including pear and lemon, without being overly sweet. The bouquet's creamy and nutty notes reappear on the supple back end. **88** *(7/1/2001)*

Laird 1999 Cold Creek Chardonnay (Carneros) $44. This Carneros Chardonnay shows solid mainstream style. Apple, caramel, and mint aromas on the nose open to apple, coconut, and menthol-oak flavors. The mouthfeel is full, though some tasters thought more big than full. Toasty new oak takes the lead, and a touch of heat shows on the back end. **89** *(7/1/2001)*

Laird 2004 Cold Creek Ranch Pinot Grigio (Carneros) $16. Here's a PG that's considerably drier and more acidic than most. There's a real need for this kind of wine, with its lime zest, fig, and white peppery-spice flavors and cleansing, crisp elegance. **88** —*S.H. (2/1/2006)*

LAKE MISSOULA

Lake Missoula 2002 Deluge Red Wine Cabernet Blend (Yakima Valley) $40. This is two-thirds Cab Sauvignon and one-third Cab Franc. Very well constructed with soft, rich, broad fruit showing ripe raspberry and

cherry flavors. Smooth and satiny through the long, satisfying finish. Despite its ripeness it retains just the right hint of cool-climate herb, adding interest and nuance to the finish. **92** —*P.G. (8/1/2006)*

LAKE SONOMA

Lake Sonoma 2002 Cabernet Sauvignon (Alexander Valley) $22. Soft, simple, and sweet, with cherry jam and mocha flavors that finish sugary, and ample tannins. **82** —*S.H. (10/1/2006)*

Lake Sonoma 2001 Cabernet Sauvignon (Alexander Valley) $22. Still pretty tannic after all these years, and with a sharp bitterness in the finish, this wine is at its peak. It has cherry and cassis flavors and is a little sweet. **82** —*S.H. (12/15/2005)*

Lake Sonoma 2000 Cabernet Sauvignon (Alexander Valley) $22. A wine that wins you over for its balance, harmony and elegance. Modulated blackberry and herb flavors are reined in by rich, thick tannins, while just-right oak adds nuances of smoke and vanilla. Feminine and gentle, and a nice companion for food. **89** —*S.H. (8/1/2004)*

Lake Sonoma 1999 Cabernet Sauvignon (Alexander Valley) $22. A bit rough and tannic around the edges, with a tart, earthy finish, but there's some pretty black currant fruit, and the wine is dry and clean. **86** —*S.H. (10/1/2003)*

Lake Sonoma 1998 Cabernet Sauvignon (Alexander Valley) $21. Dependable year after year for relative value, in this vintage which so many in California flunked, Lake Sonoma delivers a solid effort. Lush cassis is married to green olive and herb, with sumptuous tannins and an overlay of oak. It's not a keeper, but one of the most balanced and food-worthy Cabs of the vintage. **91** —*S.H. (6/1/2002)*

Lake Sonoma 2005 Chardonnay (Russian River Valley) $16. Good everyday Chardonnay, a little stretched for fruit, but offering up pleasant enough peach, pineapple, and apple flavors, with custardy, vanilla, and woodsmoke nuances. Shares the characteristics of the best RRV Chard, although it's not as concentrated. **85** —*S.H. (12/31/2006)*

Lake Sonoma 2004 Chardonnay (Russian River Valley) $16. Too oaky for my tastes, this wine brims with spicy, smoky new-woody flavors and woodsap sweetness that overshadow the fruit. Aren't we past the toothpick stage? **83** —*S.H. (12/15/2005)*

Lake Sonoma 2003 Chardonnay (Russian River Valley) $15. Doesn't show a lot of fruit, with citrus flavors just verging into tart green apples. Very clean and zesty with acidity, with oak shadings, it will be good with broiled salmon. **85** —*S.H. (3/1/2005)*

Lake Sonoma 2002 Chardonnay (Russian River Valley) $15. For the past few years, Lake Sonoma has been crafting intensely oaky, well-ripened Chards that offer lots of drinking pleasure. This wine is redolent of peaches and tropical fruits, and is spicy and smooth. **86** —*S.H. (6/1/2004)*

Lake Sonoma 2001 Chardonnay (Russian River Valley) $15. This fruity-wine has crisp acids and a pretty overlay of toasty oak. Drinks rich in apple, citrus, and pear flavors, with a creamy texture, and is dry. **86** —*S.H. (7/1/2003)*

Lake Sonoma 2000 Chardonnay (Russian River Valley) $15. Sweet oak and butterscotch lead the charge. The wine serves up ripe melon and apple flavors, but is slightly cloying on the finish. **84** —*J.M. (12/15/2002)*

Lake Sonoma 1999 Chardonnay (Russian River Valley) $15. This one shows off hints of butterscotch, vanilla, and citrus in the nose, followed by pretty pear, lemon, and toast notes on the palate. The wine is medium-bodied and quite refreshing. Clean on the finish. **87** —*J.M. (11/15/2001)*

Lake Sonoma 1998 Chardonnay (Russian River Valley) $17. 88 *(6/1/2000)*

Lake Sonoma 2000 Heck Family Cellar Selection Chardonnay (Russian River Valley) $11. A nice, well-rounded wine, with enough ripe, appley fruit and oak to satisfy. Dry and crisp, with a polished structure. **86** —*S.H. (5/1/2003)*

Lake Sonoma 2004 Fumé Blanc (Dry Creek Valley) $16. There's an acidic tartness to this wine that's just perfect to balance the slightly sweet flavors. The figs, citrus, melons, and peaches are so ripe, they need that burst of crispness, which cleanses and stimulates the palate for food. **85** —S.H. (5/1/2006)

Lake Sonoma 2003 Fumé Blanc (Dry Creek Valley) $14. A really beautiful white wine, really distinctive for its flavors of grassy hay and citrus fruits with richer notes of sweet figs, spicy melons and smoky oak. Quite complex, with a creamy texture, and not overly sweet. **88 Best Buy** —S.H. (3/1/2005)

Lake Sonoma 2002 Fumé Blanc (Dry Creek Valley) $14. Takes advantage of Dry Creek's sometimes herbally profile to produce a wine with lime, apricot, and peach flavors enriched by sweet tobacco, sweet roasted bell pepper, and dried sage. It's impressive not just for the flavors but the crisp spine of acidity that makes them shine. **87** —S.H. (2/1/2004)

Lake Sonoma 2005 Sauvignon Blanc (Dry Creek Valley) $16. Classic Sauvignon Blanc, dry and racy, with high, mouthwatering acidity framing ripe citrus, melon, fig, vanilla, and peppery spice flavors. Finishes long in ripe citrus fruit. **85** —S.H. (12/15/2006)

Lake Sonoma 2003 Zinfandel (Dry Creek Valley) $18. Lake Sonoma is one of the most dependable wineries in the county in its price range, and this Zin continues that tradition. It's dry and balanced, with a Cabernet-like structure that frames delicious blackberry, cherry, cocoa, tobacco, spice, and vanilla oak flavors. **88** —S.H. (7/1/2006)

Lake Sonoma 2002 Zinfandel (Dry Creek Valley) $16. Soft and dry, this is a generic, medium-bodied red wine that could be anything. It has berry and chocolate flavors, and a gentle scour of tannins. **84** —S.H. (10/1/2005)

Lake Sonoma 2001 Zinfandel (Dry Creek Valley) $17. A fairly bright-edged, chocolatey blend, backed up by black-cherry, berry, spice, and coffee notes. Smooth tannins frame it. On the finish, it's moderate in length. **87** (11/1/2003)

Lake Sonoma 2000 Zinfandel (Russian River Valley) $22. A fine single vineyard Zin from a cool hillside near Guerneville. Beautiful aromas of wild berries, chocolate, tobacco, and a strong dose of white pepper lead to full-bodied, dry flavors of berries. Especially likeable for its complex tannins and round, gentle mouthfeel. **90** —S.H. (3/1/2003)

Lake Sonoma 2000 Zinfandel (Dry Creek Valley) $17. Good example of a Zin that maintains balance between riper cherry and berry flavors and greener stalky notes. The former yield richness and pleasure. The latter add an herbal, tart element. The wine is fully dry, with good balance and soft tannins. **86** —S.H. (3/1/2003)

Lake Sonoma 1999 Zinfandel (Dry Creek Valley) $15. Toasty, charry plum and black-cherry hold court in the wine, which is medium-bodied and marked by a touch of rustic tannin. **85** —J.M. (3/1/2002)

Lake Sonoma 1998 Zinfandel (Dry Creek Valley) $15. Blackberry aromas with tobacco accents turn slightly barnyardy. Brisk acidity supports the solid, spicy red and black berry fruit here, but the palate feel is rather thin. It's fairly full-scaled, but not particularly graceful, and finishes dry and burnt-toasty, with a briar and tobacco note. **84** (3/1/2001)

Lake Sonoma 1997 Old Vine Zinfandel (Sonoma County) $17. Fat fruit, juicy and ripe, brimming with wonderful fruit flavors. The wine is unctuous, sinfully lush, and still balanced with berries and spice and some good toasty oak. Young and hard, but good stuff with a nice life ahead. **91 Editors' Choice** —P.G. (3/1/2001)

Lake Sonoma 2000 Old Vine Saini Farms Zinfandel (Dry Creek Valley) $20. There sure is some great ripe berry fruit in this old-vine Zin, and the interplay of flavors, tannins, and acidity is fun and complex. But excessive residual sugar gives it an uncomfortably sweet edge for a table wine that's supposed to be dry. **85** —S.H. (9/1/2003)

Lake Sonoma 1999 Old Vine Saini Farms Zinfandel (Dry Creek Valley) $20. Fairly lush, with a creamy smooth texture and thick, meaty tannins that support a blend of spicy black-cherry, chocolate, blackberry, and herb flavors. **89** —J.M. (11/1/2002)

Lake Sonoma 2002 Saini Farms Old Vine Zinfandel (Dry Creek Valley) $20. A tannic wine, and although it's dry, it has overripe, raisiny flavors. Finishes with a rustic roughness and Porty caramel. **84** —S.H. (10/1/2005)

Lake Sonoma 1998 Saini Farms Old Vine Zinfandel (Dry Creek Valley) $24. Bright cherry flavors lead the way, followed by pretty plum and licorice notes. However, the finish is a little short, and the tannins are a bit coarse. Still, very enjoyable. **86** —J.M. (11/15/2001)

Lake Sonoma 2001 Saini-Farms, Old Vine Zinfandel (Dry Creek Valley) $24. A cedary, spicy blend of flavors redolent of bright cherry, plum, blackberry, cocoa, and coffee. The tannins are fairly ripe and the finish is good, though moderate in length. **88** (11/1/2003)

LAMBERT BRIDGE

Lambert Bridge 1998 Crane Creek Cuvée Bordeaux Blend (Dry Creek Valley) $50. A really wonderful wine. It seems classic Dry Creek Valley, in terms of bright, spicy fruit, as polished as marble on the surface, with maybe less stuffing than, say, Napa. But that's not to put it down. Racy tannins and dry acids make it competitive in a worldwide market. **92** —S.H. (6/1/2002)

Lambert Bridge 2002 Crane Creek Cuvée Bordeaux Blend (Dry Creek Valley) $70. Mainly Merlot, this Bordeaux blend is enormously rich in sweet cassis, cherry, and cedar. It's assertive in that way, yet possesses an elegant architecture composed of rich, dusty tannins and crisp acids. Should hold well for at least five years. **91** —S.H. (11/1/2005)

Lambert Bridge 1999 Crane Creek Cuvée Cabernet Blend (Dry Creek Valley) $50. A flavorful wine, with jammy flavors of berries, red stone fruits and oriental spices. Young and fresh, almost brash, with easy tannins, it's drinkable now, but might age short-term. A blend of Merlot, Cabernet Sauvignon and Cabernet Franc. **88** —S.H. (5/1/2003)

Lambert Bridge 2002 Chardonnay (Sonoma County) $20. Ripe in tropical fruit and peaches, and fairly oaky. The rich, creamy texture and long, spicy finish are pleasant. **86** —S.H. (3/1/2005)

Lambert Bridge 2001 Chardonnay (Sonoma County) $20. Despite being clean and well made, there's not a lot of excitement in this earthy wine. It is dominated by acids, some dusty tannins and flavors of citrus and dried herbs. The finish is dry and tart. On its own, doesn't offer a lot of immediate pleasure, although goat cheese and similar fare will show it off. **85** —S.H. (12/1/2003)

Lambert Bridge 2000 Chardonnay (Sonoma County) $20. Moderate body, with pretty grapefruit flavors and hints of pineapple, apple, melon, and herbs that leave a fresh taste on the palate. Mineral notes provide a clean finish. **88** —J.M. (12/15/2002)

Lambert Bridge 1999 Chardonnay (Sonoma County) $20. Starts off with plenty of sweet oak—vanilla and butterscotch come to mind. Then tropical fruits like mango and lemon kick in, with hints of minerals on the bright finish. Quite nice. **89** —J.M. (11/15/2001)

Lambert Bridge 1998 Chardonnay (Sonoma County) $18. 89 (6/1/2000)

Lambert Bridge 1997 Chardonnay (Sonoma County) $18. 87 —S.H. (2/1/2000)

Lambert Bridge 1997 Chardonnay (Dry Creek Valley) $24. 90 —L.W. (10/1/1999)

Lambert Bridge 2002 Merlot (Sonoma County) $26. Made from about 90% Dry Creek fruit, Lambert Bridge's Merlot is very dry and softly scented with red cherry, sweet pipe tobacco, and coffee flavors nudging into cocoa. It has a delicate, refined mouthfeel, showing less power than sheer finesse. **90** —S.H. (11/1/2005)

Lambert Bridge 2000 Merlot (Sonoma County) $24. A nicely modulated wine, with extracted flavors of blackberries, plums, coffee, tar, and dried herbs, and a strong dose of cassis. Pretty oaky, too, and the tannins are young and thick. Very dry and balanced, it will age well for a couple of years. **85** —S.H. (12/15/2003)

Lambert Bridge 1999 Merlot (Sonoma County) $24. Seems very oaky, with in-your-face aromas of vanilla, char, and pepper, but the fruit is able to support it. In fact, the underlying flavors are rich and gorgeous. It shows Cabernet's cassis and blackberry aromatics, with the soft tannins and velvety, drink-me-now texture of Merlot. **92 Editors' Choice** —S.H. (7/1/2002)

Lambert Bridge 1997 Merlot (Sonoma County) $22. 85 —S.H. (3/1/2000)

Lambert Bridge 2000 Old Vine Cuvée, Bacchi Vineyards Red Blend (Russian River Valley) $32. Spicy and smoky, with deep black-cherry, plum, and licorice flavors. This blend of 62% Zin, 38% Petite Sirah has a bright edge, with a zingy finish and rustic tannins. **87** —*J.M. (11/15/2002)*

Lambert Bridge 2003 Sauvignon Blanc (Dry Creek Valley) $16. With a little Viognier to push the fruit up, and made with the Musqué clone, this wine showcases DCV's well-earned reputation for Sauvignon Blanc. Dry, stylish, and balanced, it offers flavors of citrus, fig, melon, and cured tobacco. **87** —*S.H. (11/1/2005)*

Lambert Bridge 2001 Sauvignon Blanc (Dry Creek Valley) $16. Quite tangy, with a bright lemony air. Pleasant melon and herb flavors run through it. Simple and fresh. **85** —*J.M. (9/1/2003)*

Lambert Bridge 1998 Sauvignon Blanc (Dry Creek Valley) $14. 90 Best Buy *(3/1/1999)*

Lambert Bridge 2000 Dry Creek Sauvignon Blanc (Dry Creek Valley) $16. With 6% Viognier in the mix, this wine carries some smoky aromatics as well as the odd note of ball park franks smothered in mustard. The distinct flavor of lemon drops are accented by an assortment of green herbs, while it finishes in a muscular fashion, emphasizing a pronounced oak element. **85** *(9/1/2003)*

Lambert Bridge 2003 Viognier (Placer County) $20. Lots of ripe, opulent peach, tropical fruit, pear, cocoa, and buttercream flavors in this rich, exotic wine. A little soft in acids, but the flavors carry the day. Try with seared sea bass. **87** —*S.H. (12/15/2004)*

Lambert Bridge 2000 Viognier (Placer County) $20. Fragrant and fruity, with hints of peaches and melon. Floral qualities round things out. On the finish, it packs a bright, refreshing, citrus note. Fun to drink. **88** —*J.M. (11/15/2001)*

Lambert Bridge 2001 Damiano Viognier (Sierra Foothills) $20. Pretty peach and spice notes sit on a viscous, velvety platform. A tangy, melony edge round things off. Finishes moderately long. **87** —*J.M. (12/15/2002)*

Lambert Bridge 2003 Damiano Vineyards Viognier (Placer County) $20. Has all the flamboyant tropical fruit, wildflower, spice, white chocolate, and buttery vanilla flavors you could want. This is the type of Viognier that grabs your attention and demands equally exotic fare. Try with duck with a fruity, gingery sauce. **88** —*S.H. (2/1/2005)*

Lambert Bridge 2001 Zinfandel (Dry Creek Valley) $24. A somewhat subdued style that nonetheless serves up plenty of body and finesse. The flavors lean toward blackberry, currant, tar, and anise. Toasty oak frames the ensemble, which finishes with moderate length. **87** *(11/1/2003)*

Lambert Bridge 2000 Zinfandel (Dry Creek Valley) $24. Harvest heat took its toll. The wine suffers from raisiny fruit that shows up in the middle palate and really mars the finish. Too bad, because in all other respects this is a lovely wine: Beautiful tannins, perfect acidity, and really nice blackberry and pepper flavors. Good Zin just shouldn't be raisiny, period. **84** —*S.H. (11/1/2002)*

Lambert Bridge 1999 Zinfandel (Dry Creek Valley) $22. Dark and richly scented, this youthful wine burst with black raspberry and blueberry aromas, mocha coffee with a dash of cinnamon. Drinks supple, round, and ripely fruity, with succulent flavors that last through the spicy, finely tannic finish. **88** —*S.H. (12/15/2001)*

Lambert Bridge 1997 Dry Creek Valley Zinfandel (Dry Creek Valley) $22. 91 —*L.W. (9/1/1999)*

LAMBORN FAMILY VINEYARDS

Lamborn Family Vineyards 2001 The Cork Report Zinfandel (Howell Mountain) $30. Quite earthy in the nose. But on the palate, it's smooth and lush, filled with chocolate, coffee, plum, black-cherry, cola, and toast flavors. It's incredibly velvety, seductive, and fun to drink. **90** *(11/1/2003)*

LAMOREAUX LANDING

Lamoreaux Landing NV Pinot Noir (Finger Lakes) $12. 87 *(11/15/1999)*

Lamoreaux Landing 2000 Pinot Noir (Finger Lakes) $15. 84 *(10/1/2002)*

LANCASTER

Lancaster 1999 Estate Bottled Bordeaux Blend (Alexander Valley) $65. An alluring Bordeaux blend that's smooth and supple, with mocha and char nuances on the black plum fruit. More than one reviewer, however, questioned its longevity and its depth. **89** *(10/1/2003)*

Lancaster 1997 Reserve Bordeaux Blend (Sonoma County) $65. 92 *(11/1/2000)*

Lancaster 2002 Estate Red Wine Cabernet Blend (Alexander Valley) $70. There's a classic Alexander Valley softness and herbaceousness to the cherry, cassis, blueberry, and oak flavors of this Cab, and while it's rich and balanced enough to drink with the best steak you can find, it should age for a while. Best now through 2009. **90** —*S.H. (12/15/2005)*

Lancaster 2001 Red Blend (Alexander Valley) $65. What's likeable about this wine is the velvet-smooth texture and milk chocolatey softness. It melts into the palate, carrying supple tannins and a nice cut of acidity. Flavorwise, it has a rich earthiness with flashes of black-cherries and currants. Might improve after 2006. **89** —*S.H. (5/1/2005)*

LANDMARK

Landmark 2004 Damaris Reserve Chardonnay (Sonoma Valley) $36. Damaris is a wine whose sourcing keeps shifting, from Bien Nacido to Sonoma County. Now it's Sonoma Valley. The wine is dominated by oak, all vanilla and char, but isn't very interesting down below. The flavors are citrusy, just not big enough for a wine with this famous a name. **83** —*S.H. (12/31/2006)*

Landmark 2001 Damaris Reserve Chardonnay (Sonoma) $30. Lush, creamy, and soft, featuring bold flavors of mango, pineapple, and ripe pear framed in plenty of oak. The finish is long and spicy. This opulent Chard is a real crowd-pleaser. **92 Editors' Choice** —*S.H. (2/1/2004)*

Landmark 1998 Damaris Reserve Chardonnay (Sonoma County) $32. 86 *(10/1/2000)*

Landmark 1998 Damaris Reserve Chardonnay (California) $32. This blend of 35% Sonoma, 33% Santa Barbara and 32% Monterey grapes shows the intensity and depth of flavor that careful grape selection and knowledgeable blending can achieve. The wine is full and forward, with mango, pear, pineapple, popcorn, and very toasty oak boldly coating the palate. Just a touch unsubtle, it's still very delicious, and finishes with butterscotch and nutmeg. **89** *(7/1/2001)*

Landmark 2002 Damaris Reserve Bien Nacido Vineyard Chardonnay (Santa Maria Valley) $34. Smells flamboyant and elaborate, with powerful oriental fruits supported by toasty oak and creamy lees. In the mouth, the flavors of pineapples and mangoes explode, leading to a long, spicy finish. **89** —*S.H. (8/1/2005)*

Landmark 2002 Lorenzo Chardonnay (Russian River Valley) $45. This is a nice, rich Chard, with good peach and pineapple flavors and pronounced oak shadings. It's dry, with good acidity and a creamy mouthfeel. **87** —*S.H. (8/1/2005)*

Landmark 2001 Lorenzo Chardonnay (Russian River Valley) $45. Firm in its steely texture, with bright citrusy acids and a mélange of fruity flavors ranging from sweet apples through peaches and pears, with a tease of pineapple purée. This lush wine has a rich, creamy texture, and finishes with butterscotchy caramel. **92** —*S.H. (5/1/2004)*

Landmark 2004 Overlook Chardonnay (Sonoma County-Monterey County-Santa Barbara County) $26. Although the grape sourcing on Overlook has changed, the wine's price has barely nudged over the years, and it still shows the polish and zest of all Landmark's Chardonnays. It's a wonderfully rich wine, finely balanced and rewarding. **91 Editors' Choice** —*S.H. (5/1/2006)*

Landmark 2001 Overlook Chardonnay (Sonoma) $25. Declares itself firmly on the side of minerals, slate, steel, citrus fruits, and acidity. You get the idea. It's on the opposite side of the spectrum from lush, tropical fruity renditions. Reminds you of those old California Chablis, in the best sense, although this wine has an incomparably better pedigree. Seems built for aging. **87** —*S.H. (12/15/2003)*

Landmark 2000 Overlook Chardonnay (Sonoma County) $25. Polished green apple and peach flavors are joined with oriental spices to provide a rich, tasty drink. Oak adds vanilla, smoke, and toast. Very dry, with biting acidity. Earns extra points for complexity and great structure. **91** —*S.H. (2/1/2003)*

Landmark 1998 Overlook Chardonnay (Sonoma County) $22. 85 *(6/1/2000)*

Landmark 2003 Overlook (Sonoma-Monterey-Santa Barbara) Chardonnay (California) $25. High in acids, this is a young wine that impresses with its power and finesse. It's pretty good now, almost Chablisian with its fruity flavors undergirded with sleek minerals. But it might pick up some aged Chardonnay character by 2006. **90 Editors' Choice** —*S.H. (8/1/2005)*

Landmark 1999 Grand Detour Van Der Kamp Pinot Noir (Sonoma Mountain) $45. This defines plump, fat Pinot. There are meaty chocolate and prune aromas in front of spice cake, black plum, and vanilla flavors. The finish offers some mocha, and despite its weight there's plenty of acidity to keep things driving forward. It seems a bit hot despite the modest (by California standards) 13.9% alcohol. **86** *(10/1/2002)*

Landmark 1997 Grand Detour Van der Kamp Vine Pinot Noir (Sonoma Mountain) $34. 91 *(10/1/1999)*

Landmark 2001 Grand Detour Van der Kamp Vineyards Pinot Noir (Sonoma Mountain) $30. Shows classic cool coastal Pinot Noir characteristics of light-bodied, silky smooth tannins, crisp acidity, and delightful flavors of ripe raspberries, red cherries, cola, and spices. A little one-dimensional, but totally drinkable. **88** —*S.H. (10/1/2005)*

Landmark 2001 Kastania Pinot Noir (Sonoma Coast) $45. Rather full-bodied for a Pinot, with black-cherry and mocha flavors that finish dry and spicy. It's not a great wine, but has a satisfying quality. **86** —*S.H. (10/1/2005)*

Landmark 1999 Kastania Vineyard Pinot Noir (Sonoma Coast) $45. At once creamy and angular, a tart-sweet nose offers bright cherry-rhubarb, herb and smoked meat aromas. It's full yet not weighty on the tongue, showing fine balance. Anise, coffee, and charcoal notes add interest, and the tangy close displays ripe tomato and sour cherry flavors with herb accents. Drink now–2007. **89** *(10/1/2002)*

Landmark 2003 Steel Plow Syrah (Sonoma Valley) $25. On the plus side of this ambitious Syrah is an attractive mouthfeel of rich, sweet tannins, accented by sweet oak, that frames blackberry fruit flavors. On the minus is a minty sharpness that seems to come from green stems or unripe berries mixed into the crush. Doesn't seem like an ager. **85** —*S.H. (12/31/2006)*

Landmark 2002 Steel Plow Syrah (Sonoma County) $23. A new wine from Landmark, better known for its Chardonnays. This Syrah starts off a bit reductive, with scents of rubber and asphalt, but blossoms on the palate into a smooth beauty loaded with blackberry and pepper. A bit tannic on the finish, but should develop nicely over the next few years. **90 Editors' Choice** *(9/1/2005)*

LANE TANNER

Lane Tanner 2000 Pinot Noir (Santa Maria Valley) $22. The "least" of Lane Tanner's range of Pinots, but complex and delicious. Ripe berry and spice flavors are rich, and there's a tangy earthiness suggesting sautéed mushrooms. Very dry and crisp, with a silky texture and a long, smooth finish. **87** —*S.H. (7/1/2003)*

Lane Tanner 2002 Bien Nacido Vineyard Pinot Noir (Santa Maria Valley) $28. Plenty of rich, ripe cherry flavors in this Pinot, and also hints of mint, oregano, and cola. Dry, with firm acidity, and the prettiest texture, all silky and smooth. Might do something interesting over the years. Right now, it's pretty good, not great. **88** —*S.H. (10/1/2005)*

Lane Tanner 2000 Bien Nacido Vineyard Pinot Noir (Santa Maria Valley) $28. Lane Tanner makes sexy wines. You're not supposed to say so, but there it is. This wine brings to mind silk and velvet. Something about it shimmers. It's also delicious, so full of opulent berry fruit you want to swirl it around your mouth forever before you swallow. Fortunately, you can always take another sip. **91 Editors' Choice** —*S.H. (7/1/2003)*

Lane Tanner 1999 Bien Nacido Vineyard Pinot Noir (Santa Maria Valley) $25. Dark and ripe, the wine shows typical Bien Nacido aromas of sun-dried tomatoes, sautéed mushrooms, hard spices, and deep notes of plum and blackberry. Oak adds smoky, charred, vanilla elements.

Achieves the impossible by being both big and light at the same time. The size is in the flavors, which are fruity and enormous. Yet there's a lilt, an airiness that is, in a word, elegant. Tannins are pure silk, and the finish is long and spicy. **93** *(12/31/2001)*

Lane Tanner 2003 Julia's Vineyard Pinot Noir (Santa Maria Valley) $30. Hard and resistant, both in acids and in fruit. Suggestions of cherries are offset by green, stalky notes. Finishes very dry. Not going anywhere, so drink up. **86** —*S.H. (10/1/2005)*

Lane Tanner 2000 Julia's Vineyard Pinot Noir (Santa Maria Valley) $30. With its assertive aromas of gingersnaps, coffee, and black-cherries, this wine, like Lane herself, isn't shy. Neither are the flavors: strong dark coffee, cloves, and cinnamon, black-cherry, and plum are intense without being heavy. **89** *(10/1/2002)*

Lane Tanner 2002 Melville Vineyard Pinot Noir (Santa Rita Hills) $25. Long and rich in ripe black-cherry, blueberry, and blackberry flavors, with an exquisite edge of dusty spice, this fully dry wine excites for its balance and seductiveness. Itï¿?s silky and airy, but a serious Pinot Noir. So good now itï¿?s hard to resist, but could actually improve over the next 5 years. **93 Editors' Choice** —*S.H. (10/1/2005)*

Lane Tanner 2000 Melville Vineyard Pinot Noir (Santa Ynez Valley) $25. Plush cherry fruit offset by anise, violet, and smoked meat aromas sets the stage for this juicy Pinot. Deep and sensuous, this offers finely balanced herb, cola, and dark cherry flavors. It finishes long and complex, with jammy fruit, dried spice, coffee and pepper notes. Drink now through 2007. **90 Editors' Choice** *(10/1/2002)*

Lane Tanner 1997 Syrah (San Luis Obispo County) $20. 88 —*S.H. (10/1/1999)*

Lane Tanner 2002 French Camp Vineyard Syrah (San Luis Obispo County) $20. In keeping with Tanner's style, this is a lighter-weight Syrah, with delicate fruit flavors and pleasant cracked pepper and dried spice notes. **84** *(9/1/2005)*

Lane Tanner 2000 French Camp Vineyard Syrah (San Luis Obispo County) $20. Full and rich, with meaty, black pepper and black raspberry flavors, and very dry, it has a nice balance. Tannins are soft but complex, and the acids provide a crisp balance to the rich fruitiness. **89** —*S.H. (9/1/2002)*

Lane Tanner 1997 JK Vineyard Syrah (Santa Ynez Valley) $20. 94 —*S.H. (10/1/1999)*

Lane Tanner 2001 Reserve Syrah (Santa Barbara County) $22. Delicately fruited and tart, with some minty-wintergreen notes and cherry-berry flavors. Built on acidity rather than tannin, as you might expect from a winemaker known for her Pinot Noirs. **84** *(9/1/2005)*

LANG & REED

Lang & Reed 2004 Cabernet Franc (Napa Valley) $22. Delicious and quirky, this wine has a cherried richness and the weight of a fine Chinon, but the silky gentleness of a light, pleasant Beaujolais. It's really a likeable wine, and there's nothing quite like it in California. **89** —*S.H. (11/1/2006)*

Lang & Reed 2003 Cabernet Franc (Napa Valley) $22. Lang & Reed, one of the few Cab Franc specialists in Napa, has produced in this wine a delightful, even complex sipper. It's much lighter in body than a Cab Sauvignon, with a richly herbal edge to the cherry flavors. Notable for its dryness, balance, and harmony. **88** —*S.H. (12/15/2005)*

Lang & Reed 2000 Cabernet Franc (Napa Valley) $21. Chunky, fruity, lots of oak; yes, it's the perfect bistro wine. Raspberry and vanilla aromas, some red licorice on the chewy palate, and then a snappy finish that hangs around for a while. It's Cab Franc Napa-style, and for a youthful wine, it's easy to drink but still offers enough nuance and character to satisfy the discerning wine drinker. **87** —*M.S. (12/1/2002)*

Lang & Reed 2002 Premier Etage Cabernet Franc (Napa Valley) $40. This designation is the winery's reserve bottling. Winemaker John Skupny has the cellar in mind, to judge from the sandpapery tannins. Still, there's a delicate lightness, a red cherried, cranberry flavor underneath that offers immediate appeal yet has the capacity to age for 10 years. **93 Editors' Choice** —*S.H. (12/31/2006)*

Lang & Reed 2001 Premier Etage Cabernet Franc (Napa Valley) $36. Where Lang & Reed's '03 Cab Franc is elegant and light-bodied, this is

USA

fuller and more complex, although it has nowhere near the weight of a Cabernet Sauvignon. The silky texture carries flavors of cherries, tobacco, sweet kid leather, and thyme. Enjoy this dry, slightly tannic wine with grilled veal chops in a wine reduction sauce with mushrooms. **92 Editors' Choice** —S.H. (12/15/2005)

Lang & Reed 2000 Wild Hare Cabernet Franc (Rutherford) $15. Light cherry and herb flavors are couched in moderate body. This is a light, textured wine for simple quaffing. Try it on the rocks or as an apéritif. Seafood and poultry would also make good matches. **84** —J.M. (11/15/2001)

LANGE

Lange 2004 Pinot Gris (Willamette Valley) $16. This is very light, beery, a bit waxy too. Lange has made some excellent Pinot Gris over the years, but this is a rather simple and uninteresting effort. **83** —P.G. (2/1/2006)

LANGTRY

Langtry 1998 Bordeaux Blend (Guenoc Valley) $23. 84 —L.W. (3/1/2000)

Langtry 1996 Bordeaux Blend (Napa Valley) $48. 87 —L.W. (11/1/1999)

Langtry 1997 Meritage Bordeaux Blend (North Coast) $50. 91 (11/1/2000)

Langtry 2000 Meritage Red Blend (North Coast) $40. Rather bitter in green, stemmy herbs and acids, and not showing much beyond modest cherry and oak flavors. Finishes very dry. **84** —S.H. (12/31/2004)

Langtry 2002 Meritage White Blend (Guenoc Valley) $20. Easy drinking, dry white wine, crisp in acids and clean of finish, with earthy, citrus, and peach flavors. It's the kind of wine that seems to go with everything. **85** —S.H. (12/31/2004)

LAPIS LUNA

Lapis Luna 2000 Chardonnay (California) $10. Though it's a 2000, it's still bright, fresh, and dry, with zippy, lemony overtones. The label says "cellared and bottled by"—as opposed to "produced and bottled by." That's usually code for bulk wine. But who cares? With its green apple, melon, and grapefruit flavors, this wine is fun to drink. The finish is clean, but a little short. **85** —J.M. (11/15/2003)

Lapis Luna 2000 Merlot (California) $10. A dry, fairly tannic wine that intrigues with an array of plums, herbs, coffee, and tobacco. Don't turn away because it's not fruity. There's some real complexity and elegance here. **86 Best Buy** —S.H. (12/15/2004)

LARAINE

Laraine 2001 Gerber Vineyards Chardonnay (Sierra Foothills) $14. An interesting Chard showing a bit of age. Picking up a nutty character, very rich and soft in the mouth, with nice oriental spice, butterscotch, and ripe peach flavors. Finishes clean and vibrant. **89 Best Buy** —S.H. (2/1/2005)

Laraine 2002 Gerber Vineyards Syrah (Sierra Foothills) $22. Plummy and chocolatey and a little sweet. Finishes oaky, with some raisiny notes, and very soft. **84** —S.H. (2/1/2005)

LARKMEAD

Larkmead 2001 Cabernet Sauvignon (Napa Valley) $45. A bit light in texture and thin in fruit, with herb and cherry flavors. But it's suave and elegant, a lighter type of Cab that won't fight with your food. **85** —S.H. (10/3/2004)

Larkmead 2001 Merlot (Napa Valley) $35. Smooth and supple, with pretty cherry, smoke, and vanilla flavors and a hint of smoked meat or bacon fat. Drinks easy in tannins, with a dry finish. **85** —S.H. (12/15/2004)

LATAH CREEK

Latah Creek 2001 Cabernet Sauvignon-Merlot (Washington) $20. Most Washington Cab-Merlots are low-end wines, but in this case it is a true reserve, though not labeled as such. Bordeaux-like structure, tight, and herbal and young. I suspect it will age very well, as a recent taste of the winery's stellar 1991 Reserve demonstrated. Here the tannins are nicely managed; the hint of oak is just right. **89 Cellar Selection** —P.G. (12/31/2003)

Latah Creek 2004 Chardonnay (Washington) $11. Still a bit awkward, this young wines has fruit flavors that seem to be hanging between fermentation flavors of banana and green apple, and a more oak-driven toasty/buttery character. At this point it needs more time to see if it will ultimately knit together. **85** —P.G. (4/1/2006)

Latah Creek 2002 Chardonnay (Washington) $11. Winemaker Mike Conway has been using fruit from the same vineyards since 1982, his first vintage. He believes in letting the fruit speak for itself, and it does. This is ripe and delightful, mixing flavors of pineapple and tart tangerine. There's a finishing hint of spice from gently applied oak, and the finish is crisp and refreshing. 11,000 cases produced. **88 Best Buy** —P.G. (12/31/2003)

Latah Creek 2002 Quilomene Hills Vineyard Johannisberg Riesling (Washington) $7. This is classic, old-style Washington Riesling, showing a puckery sweetness. The off-dry residual sugar (about 2.5%) is perfectly balanced with bright acid. Crisp and inviting, it has a very nice presence and palate feel, and it resonates through the clean finish. **88 Best Buy** — P.G. (12/31/2003)

Latah Creek 2002 Moscato d'Latah Moscato (Washington) $14. This is very pretty fruit, with sweet, appealing flavors of Satsuma orange and tangerine. If there were some spritz it would recall a light and refreshing Italian sparkler, but without the bubbles it falls just a bit flat. **86** —P.G. (12/31/2003)

Latah Creek 2004 Muscat Canelli (Washington) $10. Lots of spritz and a forward, peachy, fruit-driven set of flavors; almost like a Prosecco but with a bit more concentration and powerful, peachy fruit. Just under four percent residual sugar, yet it retains enough acid to give it some verve, and clocks in at just 10.5% alcohol. **88** —P.G. (4/1/2006)

Latah Creek 2004 Johannisberg Riesling (Washington) $7. Very classy, and classic, WA Riesling, with just enough residual sugar to offset the zippy acids. Bright, fresh, crisp, and clean, with a wash of honeyed sweetness underlying the ripe peaches and apple-flavored juice. Just a delightful bottle of Riesling. **90 Best Buy** —P.G. (4/1/2006)

Latah Creek 1999 Syrah (Washington) $19. Dark, sour cherry fruit has clove and cardamom accents—but a green, almost seaweedy element comes on, staying too strong and too long. The fruit never really regains control in this lean wine, and it closes with a slightly hard, bitter herb edge. **83** (10/1/2001)

LATCHAM

Latcham 2000 Sauvignon Blanc (El Dorado) $12. What a value. Bright and crisp and eye-opening, with green grass, gooseberry, lemon and lime flavors, and a tangy bite of mineral from the earth. This dry, edgy wine just scours the palate with its tart acids. **89 Best Buy** —S.H. (9/1/2002)

Latcham 1999 Zinfandel (El Dorado) $18. Dark, young, and robust, it's a classic Foothills Zin, with intensely ripe fruit, ultrasoft tannins and acids, and rather rustic mouthfeel. That's not a put-down. The wild berry flavors are delicious and the wine is a joy to drink right through the long, sweet finish. **87** —S.H. (11/1/2002)

Latcham 2001 Special Reserve Zinfandel (El Dorado) $25. Spicy plum and raspberry notes kick off here, followed by hints of licorice, coffee, and herbs. The wine is tangy on the finish, with mildly firm tannins. **86** (11/1/2003)

Latcham 2000 Special Reserve Zinfandel (Fair Play) $25. Inky black, a massive Zin marked by excessive tannins that make the fruit almost impossible to appreciate now. You either have to age this for a long time, or drink it with grilled foods. Big, rustic, a country-style wine, and very dry. **84** —S.H. (11/1/2002)

LATITUDE 46° N

Latitude 46° N 2004 Syrah (Columbia Valley (WA)) $28. A concentrated, young, satiny wine that mixes in 8% percent Grenache. Inky purple, it already is beginning to hint at developing layers of meat, smoke, tar, and licorice, although the primary fruit flavors, sappy and concentrated, dominate. It's very young; give it plenty of air time. **92** —P.G. (6/1/2006)

Latitude 46° N 2004 Clifton Cuvée Red Wine Syrah (Columbia Valley (WA)) $18. At 76% Syrah, this red blend (the balance is Grenache) just squeaked past our tasting censors. It's a bit soft and jammy, also high in alcohol, but boasts loads of ripe cherry-berry fruit backed by a hint of chocolate. **83** *(9/1/2005)*

Latitude 46° N 2003 The Power and the Glory Syrah (Columbia Valley (WA)) $28. Split decision on this wine, with one reviewer liking it for its vibrant blackberry fruit and briary, peppery spice and mouthwatering finish, while our other two reviewers downgraded it for being green. **86** *(9/1/2005)*

LATOUR

LaTour 2003 Chardonnay (Napa Valley) $39. A little too sweet, both in oak and in fruit, for a dry table wine. But the flavors, of white peaches and lime custard, are tasty. **84** —*S.H. (10/1/2005)*

LAUREL GLEN

Laurel Glen 2002 Cabernet Sauvignon (Sonoma Mountain) $55. Classic Laurel Glen, a Cabernet stuffed with dense, thrillingly ripe fruit, yet surrounded by dusty mountain tannins that warrant cellaring. The flavors are as intricate as a tapestry, weaving together black currants, blueberries, plums, cocoa, macaroons, spices, and sweet oak. Thoroughly dry, this is great Laurel Glen. Decant now; drinkable through at least 2015. **95** —*S.H. (9/1/2006)*

Laurel Glen 2001 Cabernet Sauvignon (Sonoma Mountain) $50. High-octane mountain wine. Bone dry, with a big, refined structure that promises long life. The blackberry and cherry flavor is as rich as any Laurel Glen in memory. Bigtime tannins, too, but soft and sweet in the modern style. Drink 2006–2020. **92 Cellar Selection** —*S.H. (10/1/2004)*

Laurel Glen 2000 Cabernet Sauvignon (Mendocino County) $10. Despite being a bit thin in body, this inexpensive wine offers some good, ripe black currant fruit, and a very pretty texture. It's velvety smooth, with plush tannins, and dry but satisfying. This wine, from Patrick Campbell, is a very good value. **87** —*S.H. (6/1/2003)*

Laurel Glen 2000 Cabernet Sauvignon (Sonoma Mountain) $50. In vintages like this, Laurel Glen can be a tough love. This version is extremely dry and raspingly tannic and herbal, with black-cherry and sweet oak shadings. Will it soften and sweeten with age? Roll the dice until 2008. **87** —*S.H. (10/1/2004)*

Laurel Glen 1999 Cabernet Sauvignon (Sonoma Mountain) $50. Owner-winemaker Patrick Campbell calls this "one of our all-time great vintages." He's right. Inky black, tight, young, and tannic, but filled with promise, this wine needs a great deal of time, but will reward patient cellaring. Don't touch it before, say, 2008. By that time, the massive tannins will begin to melt and allow the plush black currant flavors to shine. **92** —*S.H. (11/15/2002)*

Laurel Glen 1997 Cabernet Sauvignon (Sonoma Mountain) $50. Always eagerly awaited, in this difficult year Patrick Campbell has crafted a light wine, but one no less harmonious and enjoyable. Right now oak dominates a rather earthy, closed nose, but there's a dense, chewy core of essential blackberry fruit that bodies well for the future. Try aging until 2005. **89** —*S.H. (12/1/2001)*

Laurel Glen 2002 Counterpoint Cabernet Sauvignon (Sonoma Mountain) $30. This may be a second wine to Laurel Glen's fabulous '02 estate Cab, but it can hold its head high in any gathering. It's soft and rich, with lovely varietal cassis, milk chocolate, and smoky oak flavors that finish with a savory cut of anise. Fine now, and should hold for several years. **91** —*S.H. (11/15/2006)*

Laurel Glen 2001 Counterpoint Cabernet Sauvignon (Sonoma Mountain) $25. What a great junior sibling to the real Laurel Glen. Superripe in black currant and cassis fruit, this dry wine has firm, ripe tannins, and is well oaked. Polished and supple. Drink now. **87** —*S.H. (12/15/2004)*

Laurel Glen 2000 Counterpoint Cabernet Sauvignon (Sonoma Mountain) $25. Laurel Glen's second wine, and no slouch. This vintage brings a richly textured, deeply flavored Cab as good as many costing far more. Ripe flavors of currants are wrapped in toasty oak, with firm but plush tannins. Will age through the decade and improve. A good value. **91 Editors' Choice** —*S.H. (11/15/2003)*

Laurel Glen 1999 Counterpoint Cabernet Sauvignon (Sonoma Mountain) $25. This terroir-driven wine is the second wine of Laurel Glen itself. It is strongly scented with cassis, which also dominates the flavors. Oak

plays a supporting role. There are some tannins, enough to provide a dusty mouthfeel. Try this for a fine alternative to the usual Napa-Sonoma fare. It's distinctive. **91** —*S.H. (9/12/2002)*

Laurel Glen 1999 Reserve Cabernet Sauvignon (Sonoma Mountain) $75. This is the first commercial reserve wine Patrick Campbell has released in more than 20 years of winemaking, and it is indeed something special. Young and dense now, with firm tannins and acidity, and a richly explosive, meaty core of black currant and cassis fruit. Completely authoritative. Campbell is at the top of his game with this marvelous, ageworthy wine. Drinkable now, but best aged through the decade. **94 Cellar Selection** —*S.H. (11/15/2003)*

Laurel Glen 1999 Red Blend (California) $9. Rich, earthy, and dry, this will satisfy barbecue denizens who want something good to wash down ribs and chicken, but it has style and finesse, too. The spicy, wild-berry and plum flavors are appealing. A blend of Zinfandel, Petite Sirah, Carignane, Grenache, Alicante Bouchet, Barbera, and Mourvèdre. **86 Best Buy** —*S.H. (7/1/2002)*

Laurel Glen 2004 Reds Red Blend (Lodi) $10. An old-fashioned field blended-style wine, Reds is almost always a dependably complex, satisfying sipper at a fair price. This year's release is soft and dry, with well-balanced fruit and earth flavors that will go nicely with a good steak or grilled pork chop. **86 Best Buy** —*S.H. (7/1/2006)*

Laurel Glen 2002 Reds Red Blend (Lodi) $9. This blend of Zinfandel, Carignane, and Petite Sirah tastes like one of those regional wines you discovered on vacation. You remember the sweet cherries, how dry it was, and how perfect with that chicken cacciatore. Shows up the promise of Lodi. **89 Editors' Choice** —*S.H. (3/1/2005)*

Laurel Glen 2001 Reds Red Blend (California) $8. This wine has become quite popular with the public, mainly due to its price, but I have often found it stemmy and crude. In its favor it has bigtime fruit and easy tannins, and sloshes around the mouth quite well. Zin, Petite Sirah, and Carignane. **84** —*S.H. (9/1/2004)*

Laurel Glen 2000 Reds Red Blend (California) $8. This year, Patrick Campbell has crafted an unusual blend of Zinfandel, Syrah, Petite Sirah, Grenache, and Barbera, but the basic Reds style remains unchanged. It's still a big, lusty wine. Filled with young, fresh jammy flavors and strong acids, it's dry as dust, and cries out for rustic foods, like pizza or grilled chicken. **87 Best Buy** —*S.H. (12/1/2002)*

Laurel Glen 1999 Old Vine Za Zin Zinfandel (California) $18. Mainly from century-old vines in Lodi, here's a dark, rich, almost syrupy wine, packed with wild-berry flavors. It's big, but the tannins are creamy and soft, and the acidity is low, so it's immediately drinkable. There's a lip-smacking quality to it. It's a saucy wine, delicious. **90** —*S.H. (7/1/2002)*

Laurel Glen 2002 Old Vine Za-Zin Zinfandel (Lodi) $15. Here's a big, full-throttle Zin. It has some well-ripened flavors of wild berries and some not so ripe ones of oregano and thyme, and the tannins are very dry and edgy. It's also hot with alcohol. There's nothing subtle here, just a form of Zinfandel that you'll either like, or not. **85** —*S.H. (3/1/2004)*

Laurel Glen 2000 Za Zin Zinfandel (Lodi) $15. Patrick Campbell sought out old vineyards and found them in Lodi. The wine is big, rough and assaulting with blackberry-blueberry flavors. It is very dry, with the soft tannins and acids you'd expect from a warm climate. A good wine with pizza. **85** —*S.H. (11/1/2002)*

Laurel Glen 2004 Za Zin Old Vine Zinfandel (Lodi) $15. Soft, simple, and a little baked, this Zin has a trace of cooked raisins, and a hot feeling from high alcohol. It will sustain Italian food and barbecue. **82** —*S.H. (7/1/2006)*

LAUREL LAKE

Laurel Lake 1999 Cabernet Sauvignon (North Fork of Long Island) $15. One of the better wines to come from this perennial underachiever, hopefully this is a sign of better things ahead. It has a grassy, herbaceous streak, but its not vegetal, instead showing tart cherry flavors that turn cranberry-like on the finish, where they also pick up some caramel notes. **85** —*J.C. (1/1/2004)*

Laurel Lake 1998 Reserve Cabernet Sauvignon (North Fork of Long Island) $18. Aromas of vanilla and stewed berries lead into a palate that features more of the same: sweet wood and overripe raspberries. Syrupy and simple. **82** —J.C. (4/1/2001)

Laurel Lake 2001 Reserve Chardonnay (North Fork of Long Island) $18. 87 —J.C. (10/2/2004)

Laurel Lake 1999 Reserve Chardonnay (North Fork of Long Island) $15. A lean style, with unripe pear notes married to a pencilly cedar-graphite combination. Very lemony and tart on the finish, this Chard will probably be at its best with shellfish. **87** —J.C. (1/1/2004)

Laurel Lake 1998 Reserve Chardonnay (North Fork of Long Island) $18. Vanilla, butterscotch, and some harsher oak-derived compounds dominate the modest citrus fruit that might have been wine before it was turned into oak juice. For wood lovers only. **80** —J.C. (4/1/2001)

Laurel Lake 2000 Merlot (North Fork of Long Island) $14. 82 —J.C. (10/2/2004)

Laurel Lake 2002 Syrah (North Fork of Long Island) $20. Rather light in color relative to the California and Washington State wines, but intriguingly perfumed, with scents of pepper, herbs, and pie cherries. It's light in body as well, but still flavorful. A pretty wine, with just enough fruit to maintain a precarious balance. **85** (9/1/2005)

LAURIER

Laurier 2000 Chardonnay (Carneros) $15. A nice, easy drinking wine made in the international style. Quite ripe and extracted, with strong apple and peach flavors. Well oaked, with a smoky, creamy texture and a honeyed taste through the finish. A little hollow mid-palate, but that's a minor defect. **86** —S.H. (6/1/2003)

Laurier 1996 Barrel-Fermented Chardonnay (Sonoma County) $19. 84 (6/1/2000)

Laurier 2000 Merlot (Dry Creek Valley) $15. Here's a wine with charm and elegance. Very dry, with cherry-berry flavors and a streak of sweet dill and tobacco. Has a rich, creamy texture and a sweet hit of oak. **85** —S.H. (10/1/2004)

Laurier 2003 Pinot Noir (Carneros) $15. Simple, one-dimensional cherry, cola and oak flavors are wrapped in a tough, gritty texture. Finishes bitter. **83** —S.H. (5/1/2005)

LAUTERBACH

Lauterbach 2001 Pinot Noir (Russian River Valley) $32. A nice Russian River Pinot, with its pretty flavors of sweet cherries, root beer, and spice, and the crisp acidity that cool nights bring. Glides across the palate like silk, but has some overripe raisiny flavors that detract. **87** —S.H. (12/1/2004)

Lauterbach 2001 Syrah (Russian River Valley) $38. Tough, young, and brooding now for its upfront tannins and acids, this wine nonetheless has polished flavors of cherries, cassis and mocha that show up in the middle palate. It's very dry, but ripe in fruity extract. Finishes with oaky, cherry sweetness. **87** —S.H. (9/1/2004)

LAVA CAP

Lava Cap 2000 Granite Hill Reserve Petite Sirah (El Dorado) $30. There's some very pretty blackberry and cassis fruit, but it tastes unnaturally sweet, and most of the tasting panel detected excessive heat in the short finish. **83** (4/1/2003)

Lava Cap 2000 Sémillon (El Dorado) $18. Kind of bizarre, because there are baked custard and sweetened espresso and honeyed spice aromas, and then it turns unnaturally sweet on the palate. It's also flat, with an odd, medicinal aftertaste. Most Sémillons don't have these particular features. **82** —S.H. (9/1/2002)

Lava Cap 2001 Reserve Syrah (El Dorado) $20. Starts promising, with delicate scents of herbs, cherries, menthol, and a hint of citrus peel, but quickly accelerates into jammy, cooked raspberries and lashings of vanilla that turn inexplicably tart and aggressive on the finish. Perplexing. **84** (9/1/2005)

Lava Cap 1999 Reserve Syrah (El Dorado) $40. Look at that price! This is a dark wine, exciting to smell. The word "fiery" comes to mind. Something warm about it: baked cherry tart, blackberry pie fresh from the oven. In the mouth, huge, ripe, and flattering. Floods the palate with

sweet fruity, berry flavors, but bone dry. Tannins are a work of art, soft and intricate. Worth every penny, and one of the best Sierra wines in memory. The high alcohol level is not apparent. **93 Editors' Choice** — S.H. (6/1/2003)

Lava Cap 1998 Reserve Syrah (El Dorado) $20. This medium-weight wine is zippy, lively, and has nice structure. Tart cranberry, fig, and briary-butterscotch aromas don't adequately prepare you for the lush blackberry, caramel, and chocolate flavors. The creamy, though slightly tannic (one reviewer called it "Rhônish") finish fades slowly, with a metallic-mineral note on the back palate. **89** (10/1/2001)

LAVELLE

LaVelle 2004 Vintage Select Pinot Noir (Willamette Valley) $18. Quite earthy, almost to the point of tasting like dirt. Instead of fruit there is tomato, beet, and root; it's a charmless style of Pinot. Hard to understand the "select" part. **84** —P.G. (12/1/2006)

LaVelle 2005 Riesling (Willamette Valley) $14. Hints of nail polish and flavors of hard citrus candy, with grainy honey and sugar. This is not a shy Riesling; it's intense, rich with peach and apricot, and pushed just a bit too far for some tastes. **86** —P.G. (12/1/2006)

LAVENDER RIDGE

Lavender Ridge 2002 Syrah (Sierra Foothills) $28. Jammy red-berry fruit gives this wine the scent of raspberry confiture. Add in a healthy dose of vanilla and the result is a very easily accessible and approachable wine that will probably win friends for Sierra Foothills Syrah. Drink now. **85** (9/1/2005)

LAWRENCE J. BARGETTO

Lawrence J. Bargetto 1998 Chardonnay (Santa Cruz Mountains) $20. 89 (6/1/2000)

Lawrence J. Bargetto 1998 Pinot Grigio (California) $15. 87 (8/1/1999)

LAWSON RANCH

Lawson Ranch 2002 Lockwood Vineyard Chardonnay (Monterey County) $8. This likeable wine gets the basic Chard job done with its creamy texture, veneer of sweet, toasty oak, and flavors of peaches, pineapples, and pears. Nice spices on the finish. **84 Best Buy** —S.H. (7/1/2005)

LAZY CREEK

Lazy Creek 2000 Chardonnay (Anderson Valley) $16. Lean and strongly flavored with a taste of the earth: mineral, slate, and subtle hints of apples. The winemaking was hands-on, with partial barrel fermentation and lees aging, but it's still a wine of austerity, at least for Chardonnay. High acidity adds a scour to the finish. **86** —S.H. (5/1/2002)

Lazy Creek 2000 Gewürztraminer (Anderson Valley) $16. 89 —S.H. (5/1/2002)

Lazy Creek 1999 Gewürztraminer (Anderson Valley) $12. Starts off with pretty litchi, plum, citrus, and melon notes and sports good body and acidity with a well-rounded mouthfeel. Has loads of minerals on the finish. **87** —S.H. (11/15/2001)

Lazy Creek 1999 Barrel #9 Gewürztraminer (Anderson Valley) $27. From a little vineyard in Philo, this wine has been fermented to absolute dryness, which is rare in a Gewürz. Thus, the acidity is unrelieved, and it's high. Fruit? Try hints of peach, with earthy herbs. It's a fierce wine, a connoisseur's wine. Something this dry and intense needs food to soften it. The winemaker recommends foie gras. **87** —S.H. (5/1/2002)

Lazy Creek 2000 Pinot Noir (Anderson Valley) $32. 90 (10/1/2002)

Lazy Creek 1999 Pinot Noir (Anderson Valley) $26. Less is more; you get the feeling the wine was made by a hands-off winemaker. It's understandable why he would want the grapes to speak for themselves. They're amazing, offering up the most generous, sappy flavors you can imagine. You wish it had more of the artist's touch, even more oaky-framing, something to organize this raw talent. But there's no doubting its pedigree—an Anderson Valley Grand Cru. **94** —S.H. (5/1/2002)

Lazy Creek 2000 Puncheon #3 Pinot Noir (Anderson Valley) $62. The question is whether this wine will improve with age, because it's a difficult wine now. Earthy and dense with herbal, cherry flavors, and pretty full-bodied for a Pinot, it's also tannic and tough. Acidity is upfront and tart. Try again in 2005. **87** —*S.H.* (4/1/2003)

LE BON VIN DE LA NAPA VALLEY

Le Bon Vin de la Napa Valley 2003 Cabernet Sauvignon (Napa Valley) $10. This new wine from Don Sebastiani & Sons is a value worth seeking out. It shows real Napa finesse, in the smooth, rich tannins and classic Cabernet black currant and cherry flavors, with a sweet coating of oak. **85 Best Buy** —*S.H.* (12/31/2005)

Le Bon Vin de la Napa Valley 2004 Chardonnay (Napa Valley) $10. This new brand from Don Sebastiani & Sons has got to have the most fun closure in the industry. The wine itself is what this company does so well, just about as good as it gets at this price. Ripe, balanced, and super-drinkable. **85 Best Buy** —*S.H.* (12/31/2005)

Le Bon Vin de la Napa Valley 2004 Merlot (Napa Valley) $14. A new wine from Don Sebastiani & Sons, and it's off-beat and quite good. Dry, soft, and interestingly complex, with cherry, mocha, and spice flavors finished with a touch of raisins. Some of the grapes, which include Merlot, Petite Sirah, and Syrah, come from Lodi. **87** —*S.H.* (11/15/2006)

LE CADEAU VINEYARD

Le Cadeau Vineyard 2003 Pinot Noir (Willamette Valley) $40. What a spectacular effort. Dense and precise, it explodes from the glass with pure varietal scents and crisp, layered flavors. The mix of red fruits seamlessly weaves into barrel flavors of coffee, toast, caramel, and buttered nuts, then adds licorice and spice to the long, clean, lifted finish. A tour de force. **95 Editors' Choice** —*P.G.* (9/1/2006)

LE CUVIER

Le Cuvier 1999 Zinfandel (San Luis Obispo County) $30. A jammy blend of plum, black-cherry, blackberry, spice, and chocolate flavors. The tannins are smooth and firm. Bright on the finish. **88** —*J.M.* (2/1/2003)

LE VIN

Le Vin 2000 Cabernet Sauvignon (Mendocino County) $36. A real find. French in style, dry, rich, and elegant. Hints of cherry and cassis are wrapped in thick, fine tannins, and the mouthfeel is sensual and velvety. Delicious now, but should hold through the decade. Grapes from Yorkville Highlands. The winemaker is the well-known Kerry Damsky. **92** —*S.H.* (11/15/2003)

Le Vin 2000 Chardonnay (Russian River Valley) $19. Loads of sweet pineapple and vanilla mark this richly succulent wine. Super-concentrated fruity flavors blast the palate, leading to a long finish. For all its ripeness, the wine is dry. Strong and tasty stuff! **88** —*S.H.* (8/1/2003)

Le Vin 2000 Merlot (Mendocino County) $28. What a great smell! Strong, clean, and refined, of plums, roasted coffeebean, cassis, cocoa, and smoky oak. Drinks very rich and elaborate, with great stuffing and finesse, and bone dry. **91** —*S.H.* (12/31/2003)

LEAL VINEYARDS

Leal Vineyards 2003 Estate Carnaval Cabernet Blend (San Benito County) $24. Leal is making real progress on its wines, to judge by this dry, balanced Bordeaux blend. It has lush, sweetly ripe fruit and rich tannins, and feels quite elegant and complex in the mouth. Might improve with a year or two in the bottle. **87** —*S.H.* (6/1/2006)

Leal Vineyards 2001 Cabernet Sauvignon (San Benito County) $24. Here's a full-bodied, fruity Cab, rich in blackberries and cherries and all sorts of other berries and fruits. It's a little hot, but easy to drink. **84** —*S.H.* (10/1/2005)

Leal Vineyards 2004 Estate Chardonnay (San Benito County) $24. Nice and crisp in acidity, with ripe peach, apple, and pineapple flavors. There's a bite of green sharpness on the finish, but it's still a good Chard. **85** —*S.H.* (12/1/2006)

Leal Vineyards 2003 Estate Chardonnay (San Benito County) $24. Uncomplicated but clean, this Chard is flat in acids, with sweet greenpea flavors that just break into riper peaches. **83** —*S.H.* (11/15/2005)

Leal Vineyards 2001 Carnivàl Meritage (San Benito County) $24. Fruity, but overly soft and sweet, with a sugary finish. **81** —*S.H.* (11/15/2005)

Leal Vineyards 2003 Estate Merlot (San Benito County) $24. Smells baked and pruny-Porty. And although the flavors are better, and the wine is dry, that aroma detracts. **83** —*S.H.* (11/15/2005)

Leal Vineyards 2003 Estate Grown Threesome Rhône Style Blend Rhône Red Blend (San Benito County) $24. This Rhône blend is rustic and super-fruity, with an astringent, tannic mouthfeel and a semisweet finish. It seems overpriced for what you get. **83** —*S.H.* (12/31/2005)

Leal Vineyards 2004 Threesome Rhône Red Blend (San Benito County) $24. I often find Leal's red wines to be too sweet and rustic in mouthfeel, and so it is with this Rhône blend. It has a roughly tannic texture and a sugary cherry finish. **82** —*S.H.* (12/1/2006)

Leal Vineyards 2003 Estate Syrah (San Benito County) $24. From this county just to the north of Monterey comes this dark, super-fruity Syrah, bursting with cherry, blackberry, mocha, and spice flavors. It has a honeyed sweetness, and a rustic mouthfeel. **84** —*S.H.* (11/15/2005)

Leal Vineyards 2002 Estate Grown Syrah (San Benito County) $24. Lush and creamy, according to one taster, undefined and flabby says another. Both agree on the wine's superripe fruit—akin to blackberry brandy—and ultrasoft tannins. It's just a question of personal preference. **86** (9/1/2005)

LEAPING HORSE

Leaping Horse 2000 Cabernet Sauvignon (Lodi) $5. Shows good varietal character, with black currant flavors, dry tannins and full body. Feels rough around the edges, but it's not a bad glass of wine. **85 Best Buy** —*S.H.* (2/1/2003)

Leaping Horse 2004 Chardonnay (Lodi) $6. There are some very unripe grapes here, to judge from the wintergreen and chlorophyll flavors. The wine is dry and tart on the finish. **82** —*S.H.* (2/1/2006)

Leaping Horse 2001 Chardonnay (Lodi) $5. A little disjointed, but plenty of varietal character in the apple, vanilla, and peach flavors, and even some toasty oak. Dry and smooth. From Ironstone. **84** —*S.H.* (2/1/2003)

Leaping Horse 2000 Merlot (Lodi) $5. Don't be misled by the price, this is a good value. Ripe and rich, with pronounced berry flavors, dry, and supple. Good tannins and a hit of acidity make it clean and refreshing. It's not complex or ageable, but a nice mouthful at a super-value price. **85 Best Buy** —*S.H.* (2/1/2003)

Leaping Horse 2005 Shiraz (Lodi) $NA. Sometimes all you need is an inexpensive red like this one. This Lodi Syrah erupts in white pepper aromas and is tartly crisp in cherry and blackberry flavors. **84** —*S.H.* (12/1/2006)

Leaping Horse 2003 Shiraz (Lodi) $5. A little too soft in acids, and gooey in cassis and oak flavors, but this wine has good, rich tannins and a chocolatey taste on the finish. **84 Best Buy** —*S.H.* (8/1/2005)

Leaping Horse 2001 Shiraz (Lodi) $5. Harsh in tannins, low in fruit, with a rough mouthfeel, this is a good example of a rural wine in need of improvement. **82** —*S.H.* (12/1/2004)

LEAPING LIZARD

Leaping Lizard 2003 Chardonnay (Napa Valley) $10. One of the better values out there right now, this Chard features flavors of juicy yellow peach, green apple, and pineapple, with a touch of spicy, vanilla-tinged oak, housed in a soft, creamy texture. **85 Best Buy** —*S.H.* (11/15/2005)

Leaping Lizard 2003 Pinot Noir (Carneros) $10. So what do you get for ten bucks? A pretty nice Pinot. It's silky and dry, with rich red cherry, raspberry, vanilla, cinnamon, and toast flavors, and a long, spicy finish. **85 Best Buy** —*S.H.* (11/15/2005)

LEDGEWOOD CREEK

Ledgewood Creek 2004 Cabernet Sauvignon (Napa Valley) $16. A little weedy, but offers enough Cabernet flavor to satisfy, in a smoothly tannic texture. The blackberries, cherries, coffee, and herbs finish dry, with some smoky oak. **84** —*S.H.* (12/31/2006)

Ledgewood Creek 2004 Chardonnay (Suisun Valley) $14. Everyday Chard, dry and balanced, with crisp acidity, some creaminess and a touch of new oak barrel to the peaches and citrus. Could be richer and longer in flavor, though. **83** —*S.H.* (12/31/2006)

Ledgewood Creek 2002 Limited Reserve Suisun Valley Chardonnay (North Coast) $18. Ultraripe in all sorts of fruity flavors, notably pear, and with a rich application of smoky oak, this wine will appeal to fans of big, unctuous Chards. It's spicy and long on the finish, too. **85** —*S.H. (6/1/2004)*

Ledgewood Creek 2002 Suisun Valley Chardonnay (North Coast) $13. This very ripe wine has an array of flavors ranging from peaches and pears to tropical fruits. It has a thick, malted mouthfeel that makes it a little heavy, but it's a decent wine. **84** —*S.H. (6/1/2004)*

Ledgewood Creek 2001 Suisun Valley Chardonnay (North Coast) $13. Simple and fruity, with flavors of spiced apples and peaches and a pronounced oakiness. Finishes dry and oaky-spicy. **83** —*S.H. (10/1/2003)*

Ledgewood Creek 2005 Picnique Fumé Blanc (Suisun Valley) $9. Very clean, dry, and zesty Sauvignon Blanc here, a bit light in flavor, but at this price, it offers enough Meyer lemon, apricot, and white pepper flavor for value. **84** —*S.H. (12/31/2006)*

Ledgewood Creek 2001 Suisun Valley Merlot (North Coast) $15. This everyday sort of wine has pleasant berry and herb flavors, and is dry and clean. It's the kind of wine you get by the glass in an inexpensive restaurant. **84** —*S.H. (6/1/2004)*

Ledgewood Creek 2005 Sauvignon Blanc (Suisun Valley) $12. This newish appellation, located in the Delta, has been busy promoting itself lately for inexpensive, sound wines just like this. All stainless steel, it's tasty and balanced, with ripe pink grapefruit, apricot, apple, fig, melon, and spice flavors, offset by refreshing acidity. **85** —*S.H. (12/31/2006)*

Ledgewood Creek 2004 Estate Grown Syrah (Suisun Valley) $12. Perfectly decent everyday red wine, chocolatey, soft and dryish, with pleasant pie filling flavors of cherries dusted with cinnamon and a dash of crème de cassis. **83** —*S.H. (12/31/2006)*

LEDSON

Ledson 2002 Cabernet Franc (Alexander Valley) $48. Here's a very ripe Cabernet Franc whose plummy flavors veer into dried prunes. It's dry, and a little hot, but there's something nice about it. It's honest and forthright, and will support food without overwhelming it. **86** —*S.H. (7/1/2005)*

Ledson 2002 Cabernet Sauvignon (Alexander Valley) $90. Here's a very fine Cabernet, big, ripe, and powerful. It's thoroughly dry, with charming cherry and blackberry flavors, but it's also fairly tannic, although a rich steak will cut right through the astringency. Now–2012. **91** —*S.H. (10/1/2005)*

Ledson 2002 Reserve Cabernet Sauvignon (Alexander Valley) $110. Semisweet and rustic, this cherry and cassis-flavored wine is also soft and flabby. A ton of oak doesn't really help to make it any better than it is. **82** —*S.H. (12/31/2005)*

Ledson 2004 Chardonnay (Carneros) $36. This is a pretty good wine, clearly well made and balanced, with crisp, bright acids, a creamy texture, some nice oak, and restrained tropical fruit flavors. **87** —*S.H. (12/31/2005)*

Ledson 2002 Chardonnay (Russian River Valley) $24. Quite a smooth and polished Chard. It impresses for its upfront apple and pear flavors, and is balanced, dry, and crisp. Fills the mouth with spice through the finish. **87** —*S.H. (8/1/2004)*

Ledson 2001 Chardonnay (Russian River Valley) $24. Has that pure appellation fruit taste of ripe green apples and sweet pears, framed in crisp acids. Feels bright and delicious in the mouth, accented with oak notes of vanilla and smoke. A creamy texture lends allure. This rich, hedonistic wine instantly appeals to the senses. **90 Editors' Choice** —*S.H. (7/1/2003)*

Ledson 2000 Chardonnay (Arroyo Seco) $20. Rather lean, acidic, and bitter, with citrusy, appley flavors and a nice overlay of oak and lees. With only 646 cases produced, seems to be the victim of overly cool growing conditions. **86** —*S.H. (5/1/2003)*

Ledson 2000 Chardonnay (Russian River Valley) $24. Rich and balanced, this big, full-bodied wine is filled with powerful flavors of citrus fruit and apple. Considerable acidity makes for a steely feel; there isn't a lot of oak, just enough to add some sweetness. **89** —*S.H. (2/1/2003)*

Ledson 1999 Reserve Chardonnay (Russian River Valley) $32. Aromas of movie popcorn, hops, and Asian pear open this rather over-the-top wine. It's a decidedly candy-sweet combination of butterscotch, peach, and nut flavors with a soft, round mouthfeel. The light orange finish is easy. If you have good friends who just don't like dry wines, this is a great one to serve them. **88** *(7/1/2001)*

Ledson 1998 Reserve Chardonnay (Sonoma County) $32. This wine's fat, tropical fruit, banana, and toast nose has a pungent, spicy Gewürztraminer quality. The palate is the payoff. It shows the aforementioned elements, plus cinnamon, clove, and vanilla flavors. What you get is a ripe, unctuous wine—big, maybe even a bit overblown, but totally lovable. The long, spicy finish of this unique bottling is impressive. **91** *(7/1/2001)*

Ledson 2000 Johannisberg Riesling (Monterey) $16. From the cool Meador Vineyard in Arroyo Seco, a deliciously fruity wine with an appley bite of acid that washes and comforts the palate. It's filled with true flavors of apples, peaches, and wildflowers, and just off-dry. The finish is tart, with a hint of petrol and flint. **87** —*S.H. (6/1/2002)*

Ledson 2000 Harmony Collection Jeff Bridges Be Here Soon Meritage (Napa Valley) $125. Dry, tough, and astringent, this wine makes you wonder if it will improve with bottle age. It's not offering much pleasure now. It will take a lot of effort for the blackberry fruit to beat out those thick, gritty tannins. **84** —*S.H. (2/1/2006)*

Ledson 1999 Merlot (Sonoma Valley) $36. Quite rich and distinguished, with the full-bodied weight and rich, thick tannins of a fine Cabernet, yet with Merlot's flavors of cherries, plums, and violets, with a white chocolate edge. Impresses for its youthful purity and deliciousness, as well as the refined texture. **91** —*S.H. (8/1/2003)*

Ledson 1998 Merlot (Sonoma Valley) $34. This is one of the most interesting Merlots of the vintage because it combines fruity ripeness with herbal and vegetal notes to create a complex wine. Blackberry and cassis, a bit of stewed tomato and mushroom, grilled meat, green olives, and roasted coffee beans only begin to describe it. Dry and harmonious. **93** —*S.H. (7/1/2002)*

Ledson 2002 Estate Merlot (Sonoma Valley) $38. Very dry, fairly tannic and a little earthy, this red wine is soft and gentle in the mouth. It's easy to drink, but full-bodied enough to stand up to a steak. **87** —*S.H. (10/1/2005)*

Ledson 2003 Petite Sirah (Contra Costa County) $34. Very rich in fruit. A weighty, dense wine of power yet refinement, with ripe black-cherry pie, milk chocolate, and spice flavors wrapped in substantial tannins. So filled with fruity ripeness it tastes sweet. Best with hearty roasts and cheeses. **88** —*S.H. (11/15/2006)*

Ledson 2002 Pinot Noir (Russian River Valley) $36. Starts off a little minty and green, although you'll find an undercurrent of racy red cherry. It's not the most opulent Pinot, but the crisp acids and silky smooth tannins offer lots to like. **85** —*S.H. (11/1/2004)*

Ledson 2003 Primitivo (Napa Valley) $36. Too sweet and pastry-like for me, with cherry and raspberry flavors that taste a bit sugared, like pie filling, then dusted with sweetened cocoa. The wine is also too soft. You'll either love it or you won't. **83** —*S.H. (11/15/2006)*

Ledson 1999 Legend Red Blend (Sonoma County) $36. An unusual blend of Zinfandel and Merlot, this is a softly fruity wine of great charm and appeal. There's lots of upfront spicy fruit, framed in melted tannins, and it's sprightly and refreshing on the palate. It's easy to like and immediately drinkable, yet possesses enough richness and complexity for the best tables. **91** —*S.H. (7/1/2002)*

Ledson 2003 Mes Trois Amours Red Wine Rhône Red Blend (California) $30. This blend of Mourvèdre, Grenache, and Syrah—the three loves, get it?—is dry and fine. It has real complexity, mingling tart cherry skin and blackberry flavors with earthy coffee, tobacco, spices, and herbs. Best now. **90** —*S.H. (11/15/2006)*

Ledson 2000 Rosé Blend (California) $14. Rosés are making a comeback, and it's because of nice wines like this. It's super-fruity, with suggestions of the ripest peaches and apricots. You can taste the sunny sweetness but it's basically a dry wine. Refreshing acidity gives it a clean boost. **87** —*S.H. (9/10/2002)*

Ledson 2003 Sangiovese (Alexander Valley) $34. Dry, thin, and tannic, with low-key cherry flavors, but clean. This acidic wine needs Italian food to balance it. **83** —*S.H. (11/15/2006)*

Ledson 2002 Sangiovese (Alexander Valley) $34. A big, dark, extracted wine, solidly in the modern style. The fruit is massive in blackberries and chocolate, and the tannins are soft, ripe, and smooth. There's far too much oak, though, and the acidity could be firmer. **86** —*S.H. (10/1/2005)*

Ledson 2003 Sauvignon Blanc (Russian River Valley) $20. Polished and clean, a wine whose grassy, citrus flavors are enhanced with notes of melon and smoky oak. Turns thin in the middle, with an oaky, spicy finish. **85** —*S.H. (12/15/2004)*

Ledson 2001 Sauvignon Blanc (Napa Valley) $20. Light, crisp, and refreshing, the kind of wine you can guzzle with fried chicken, but is also elegant enough to set out with a fine dinner. The lemon and honeydew flavors are enriched with spicy oak. Turns slightly sweet on the finish. **87** —*S.H. (10/1/2003)*

Ledson 2000 Sauvignon Blanc (Napa Valley) $18. Soft, almost mute apple and pear aromas are accented by bell pepper and some lima beans. It's a typical bouquet for Napa SB, which is followed by the flavors of white grapefruit, a little citrus pith, and some vanilla. Throughout there's a hint of spicy green veggies, mostly bell pepper and jalapeños. Overall, it offers good balance, just not enough fruit to override the green character. **87** *(8/1/2002)*

Ledson 2000 Michele's Cuvée White Blend (California) $20. 88 —*S.H. (6/1/2002)*

Ledson 2003 Bacigalupi Vineyard Zinfandel (Russian River Valley) $40. This is a big, ripe Zin from a great vineyard in a warm part of the appellation. There's a lot of heat, but it works well with the blackberry pie, cherry tart, and milk chocolate flavors. Nice and dry, if a bit soft. **90** —*S.H. (11/15/2006)*

Ledson 2002 Century Vine Zinfandel (Russian River Valley) $46. Lots of perky acidity here, to offset and balance the superripe black currant and cocoa flavors. There's a spicy note of licorice or anise that adds to the profile. Fancy stuff. Search out the perfect recipe for this one. **90** —*S.H. (10/1/2005)*

Ledson 2002 Old Vine Zinfandel (Russian River Valley) $36. Young and jammy, with sharp, youthful grape acidity and primary dark berry and stone fruit. chocolate, and pepper flavors. Might improve with a year or two of cellaring. **84** —*S.H. (10/1/2005)*

Ledson 2001 Old Vine Zinfandel (Russian River Valley) $30. How close a good Zin gets to great Cab is well illustrated with this complex, plush wine. It's dry, soft and clean, and brimming with ripe, chocolatey fruit. What makes it uniquely varietal is the brambly pepperiness. **89** —*S.H. (12/31/2004)*

Ledson 2001 Old Vine Zinfandel (Dry Creek Valley) $36. Very ripe, very extracted, and pretty oaky, too, but it all works. This is an exuberantly fruity Zin, packed with raspberry, cherry, cocoa and coffee flavors that finish with a spicy, peppery edge. It's youthfully crisp and fresh now, and is a great food wine. **90** —*S.H. (8/1/2004)*

Ledson 1999 Old Vine Zinfandel (Dry Creek Valley) $28. Here's what you look for in old-vine Sonoma Zin: concentrated brambleberry, chocolate, tobacco, and spice flavors; very dry, complex tannins; crisp acids and a certain rustic quality that's charming and easy to drink. This particular baby has it all. It's wild, savage now in youth, but will mellow with time. **87** —*S.H. (7/1/2002)*

Ledson 2000 Old Vines Zinfandel (Lodi) $28. Easy drinking Zin, with good flavors of wild berries and spices wrapped in a creamy texture. Even though the wine is fully dry, it has a softness, almost a butteriness, that is almost sweet. Turns real long on the finish, with a ripe fruitiness that lasts. **88** —*S.H. (3/1/2004)*

Ledson 1999 Old Vines Zinfandel (Russian River Valley) $36. From 50-year old vines, a big, jammy wine stuffed with all sorts of berry and tree-fruit flavors. It's Lifesaver candy, a burst of spicy fruit, but thankfully bone dry, balanced, crisp, and in its own way authoritative. Soft tannins make it immediately drinkable, and probably not an ager. **88** —*S.H. (7/1/2002)*

LEEWARD

Leeward 1996 Edna Valley Reserve Chardonnay (Edna Valley) $16. 85 —*M.S. (10/1/1999)*

Leeward 1998 Reserve Chardonnay (Edna Valley) $16. 85 *(6/1/2000)*

Leeward 1996 Merlot (Napa Valley) $24. 91 —*M.S. (6/1/1999)*

Leeward 1997 Bien Nacido Vineyard Pinot Noir (Santa Barbara County) $20. 86 *(11/15/1999)*

LEGACY

Legacy 1997 Estate Bottled Bordeaux Blend (Sonoma County) $90. 88 *(11/1/2000)*

LEHRER

Lehrer 2002 Syrah (Contra Costa County) $34. Supple and creamy, with roasted fruit and coffee flavors joined by vanilla and caramel notes. Some meat and molasses flavors chime in on the finish, which features a burst of citrusy acidity. **84** *(9/1/2005)*

LEMELSON

Lemelson 2000 Chardonnay (Willamette Valley) $20. This is a firm, even meaty, Chardonnay, with extended lees contact and stirring the dominant flavor. High acid and sharp mineral notes underscore the tight structure, well suited to cellaring. Some subtle, creamy, honeyed notes of pear, melon, and flowers complete the picture. **89** —*P.G. (9/1/2003)*

Lemelson 2000 Wascher Vineyard Chardonnay (Willamette Valley) $26. Low yields, wild yeasts, Dijon clones—this wine is the total package. Better yet, it tastes great, with sweet toasty scents rolling into flavors featuring roasted nuts and caramel candy popcorn. Smooth, flavorful, forward, and bursting with fruit. **90** —*P.G. (9/1/2003)*

Lemelson 1999 Wascher Vineyard Chardonnay (Willamette Valley) $26. This is an oaky, mouthfilling wine which retains enough vibrant fruit and leesy creaminess to compensate for all the new wood. Big, juicy, and balanced, it's nicely put together. **88** —*P.G. (2/1/2002)*

Lemelson 1999 Pinot Gris (Oregon) $18. Though it was barrel-fermented in previously used Burgundian barrels, the flavor of expensive new oak dominates this buttery effort. If rich and toasty is what you want, this is for you. It's well-made, but it could just as easily be a Chardonnay. **88** —*P.G. (2/1/2002)*

Lemelson 2000 Tikka's Run Pinot Gris (Willamette Valley) $18. This is a rich, barrel-fermented style that delivers creamy, layered, textured flavors accented with flower, white pepper, and mineral notes. A smack of butterscotch finishes it beautifully. **90 Editors' Choice** —*P.G. (8/1/2003)*

Lemelson 2001 Pinot Noir (Oregon) $13. Pinot Noir rosé may be something of a rarity, but when it is this good, one wonders why. Dry, spicy flavors that are most reminiscent of French roses make a youthful, refreshing, food-friendly wine. **88** —*P.G. (4/1/2003)*

Lemelson 2003 Chestnut Hill Vineyard Pinot Noir (Willamette Valley) $38. This was Eric Lemelson's first planted vineyard and it's now beginning to show its stuff. Clearly Oregonian in its opening mix of leaf, root, herb and earth scents, it rounds up into some pleasing cherry/plum fruit flavors that resonate as a very pretty core of sweet fruit. Persistent and concentrated, it's still tight and compact but promises great things to come. **92** —*P.G. (5/1/2006)*

Lemelson 2002 Chestnut Hill Vineyard Pinot Noir (Willamette Valley) $33. Big, ripe fruit flavors show blackberry, blueberry, and black-cherry,, hot and unstructured. Burnt toast and coffee flavors suggest over-charred barrels, and it makes for a heavy, tannic wine. **87** *(11/1/2004)*

Lemelson 2003 Jerome Reserve Pinot Noir (Willamette Valley) $44. The Jerome represents the winery's selection of what it considers its best barrels. For me, it falls just a bit short of the single-vineyard bottlings in this hot, ripe year. Delicious to be sure, it's got plenty of sweet, jammy raspberry and cherry fruit, and tell-tale vanilla from new oak barrels. Big, forward, and tannic. **89** —*P.G. (5/1/2006)*

Lemelson 2002 Jerome Reserve Pinot Noir (Willamette Valley) $44. The top of the Lemelson line, this tart, clean, refreshing wine is saturated with the flavors of just-picked berries. An excellent food wine, with bracing acid and a firm grip. **90** *(11/1/2004)*

USA

USA

Lemelson 2000 Jerome Reserve Pinot Noir (Willamette Valley) $44. Lemelson's top bottling, this fragrant, seamless wine is a complex blend of fruit, leaf, spice, and vanilla components, with plenty of new French oak, power, and aging potential. It will improve over the next 6–8 years. **91 Cellar Selection** —*P.G. (4/1/2003)*

Lemelson 1999 Jerome Reserve Pinot Noir (Willamette Valley) $44. This brand-new operation is ambitious and well-funded, and the results show. Of their single-vineyard Pinots, this is the biggest. It's a rugged, chewy wine with unabashed tannins and oodles of jammy blackberry fruit, anise and sassafras. Just 207 cases. **91** —*P.G. (12/31/2001)*

Lemelson 2000 Reed & Reynolds Vineyard Pinot Noir (Willamette Valley) $38. This excellent, 20-year-old, dry-farmed vineyard is one of Oregon's best. Cola scents set off a clean, perfectly ripened, elegant Pinot that clearly demonstrates the varietal character of the grape. Not a block-buster, but a beautiful rendering of the varietal, with extra dimensions that seem to reflect the terroir. Structure to add complexity over time. **91** —*P.G. (4/1/2003)*

Lemelson 2003 Resonance Vineyard Pinot Noir (Willamette Valley) $38. This biodynamically farmed vineyard gives great fruit. Here it is detailed with a full range of floral aromas, candied red fruits, hints of cinnamon, and plenty of balancing tannins. Just the right touch with the new oak, too. Lemelson really nails it in 2003. **93** —*P.G. (5/1/2006)*

Lemelson 2002 Resonance Vineyard Pinot Noir (Willamette Valley) $38. Pretty cherry and plum scents open into richer, sweeter sensations of blackberry pie. Medium weight, soft and accessible, it finishes with sweet, chocolatey oak. **88** *(11/1/2004)*

Lemelson 2003 Stermer Vineyard Pinot Noir (Willamette Valley) $38. Ripe and seductive with cherries and sweet cranberries, this young, tight, stylish Pinot has nothing but clear sailing ahead. There's excellent concentration through the midpalate, a light touch with the new oak, and beautifully textured fruit throughout. Love it now or leave it for later; you can't lose either way. **91** —*P.G. (5/1/2006)*

Lemelson 2002 Stermer Vineyard Pinot Noir (Willamette Valley) $38. Another star in a super lineup from Lemelson, the Stermer is lush with ripe, wild berries saturated in milk chocolate. The middle thickens into fat black-cherry flavors, and it sails into a smooth, polished, satiny finish that tastes like ripe fruit on wet stone. **90** *(11/1/2004)*

Lemelson 2000 Stermer Vineyard Pinot Noir (Willamette Valley) $38. A youthful, compact wine with pure, pleasurable fruit. The flavors run to berries red, blue and black, along with hints of cassis, spice, and even cocoa. It's a balanced, elegant wine that shows careful winemaking and good medium-term aging potential. **89** —*P.G. (4/1/2003)*

Lemelson 1999 Stermer Vineyard Pinot Noir (Willamette Valley) $38. Stermer is the estate vineyard, named for the previous owners, who were prune farmers. Some prunes still shoe up in this tight, dark wine, plus some plums and cherries. A spicy component enlivens the nose and palate, which is soft, smooth and expansive. The finish includes a hint of herb. Just 218 cases. **90** —*P.G. (12/31/2001)*

Lemelson 2000 Thea's Selection Pinot Noir (Willamette Valley) $29. The winery calls this their "most precocious" Pinot, and indeed it is. Forward, fruity, sweetly flavored with grapes and berries, it also carries light spices and enough tannins for short-term cellaring. **88** —*P.G. (4/1/2003)*

Lemelson 1999 Thea's Selection Pinot Noir (Willamette Valley) $29. This wine's style is forward and fruity, perfumed with the scent of strawberry preserves. It shows good concentration in the mouth, with sweet, almost candied, flavors of cherry and strawberry. The finish is ripe, smooth, and a bit syrupy. Only 650 cases made. **89** —*P.G. (12/31/2001)*

Lemelson 2002 Thea's Selection Pinot Noir (Willamette Valley) $29. Very pretty, satiny, creamy, and delicious. Flavors of black-cherry and cream are mixed with sassafras and spice, a very winning combination. **88** *(11/1/2004)*

Lemelson 2001 Adria Vineyard-Dry Riesling Riesling (Willamette Valley) $19. 83 —*J.C. (8/1/2003)*

LENZ

Lenz 1997 Cabernet Sauvignon (North Fork of Long Island) $30. Shows plenty of bright red-fruit flavors of cherry and red currants. Yes, there's a hint of green pepper, but not so much as to be objectionable. It's more than made up for by the lush mouthfeel and ease with which this wine goes down. **88** —*J.C. (4/1/2001)*

Lenz 1994 Cuvée Champagne Blend (North Fork of Long Island) $30. Starts out with aromas of toast, strawberries, and citrus. Tart and dry and very fresh; this should hold well in the bottle for some time. Winemaker Eric Fry only makes between 500 and 600 cases each year and disgorges it in small batches so it's always fresh when released. **90 Editors' Choice** —*J.C. (4/1/2001)*

Lenz 1998 Gold Label Chardonnay (North Fork of Long Island) $25. Ripe and buttery, this reserve Chard from winemaker Eric Fry could hardly be more different from his White Label bottling. Superripe pineapple fruit is marked by plenty of oak-imparted spice. Lush and ready to drink. **87** —*J.C. (4/1/2001)*

Lenz 1998 White Label Chardonnay (North Fork of Long Island) $11. A crisp, zippy wine dominated by tart apple and pear fruit that's tinged with lemon and lime. Lean and citrusy, there's no oak here to clutter up Chardonnay's bright fruit flavors. **86 Best Buy** —*J.C. (4/1/2001)*

Lenz 1998 Gewürztraminer (North Fork of Long Island) $12. Features textbook Gewürz aromas of rose petals and lychee fruit before yielding to a dry, bitter-almond note on the finish. **87 Best Buy** —*J.C. (4/1/2001)*

Lenz 1997 Merlot (North Fork of Long Island) $25. Big, bold black-cherry fruit is accented by a pinch of dried herbs. Cedary oak gives delineation and focus to the rich, smooth palate that's weighty without being heavy. **89** —*J.C. (4/1/2001)*

Lenz 1997 Estate Bottled Merlot (North Fork of Long Island) $55. According to winemaker Eric Fry, the big reason for the quality of this wine is vine age—a venerable (by LI standards) 22 years. This is a big, dense wine pumped full of black-cherries and capped off by hints of cedar and coffee. Right now it's more about potential than pleasure—try to hold a bottle or two for five years. **91 Cellar Selection** —*J.C. (4/1/2001)*

Lenz 1998 Pinot Gris (North Fork of Long Island) $20. A clean, crisp, citrusy wine that lacks the rich texture found in the best Alsatian Pinot Gris, but still packs in a lot of tart, lemony flavors. Good shellfish wine. **85** —*J.C. (4/1/2001)*

LEONARDO FAMILY VINEYARDS

Leonardo Family Vineyards 2001 Cabernet Sauvignon (Lodi) $12. There's lots of good varietal character in this pleasant wine. It has correct flavors of black currants, olives, and herbs, and is wrapped in delicately soft tannins. The finish is dry and fruity. Not a lot of stuffing going on, but will be nice with roast beef. **85** —*S.H. (8/1/2003)*

Leonardo Family Vineyards 2001 Cabernet Sauvignon-Syrah (Lodi) $14. A nice little red blend, easy to drink, with cheerful flavors of blackberries and cherries that are very ripe without being in your face. Entirely dry, with light tannins. Enjoy with everything from sandwiches to steak. **85** —*S.H. (8/1/2003)*

Leonardo Family Vineyards 2002 Pinot Grigio (California) $10. Here's a friendly sipper you can buy by the case and enjoy every day with everything from fried chicken to fruit salad. It has pleasant flavors of lemons and peaches, and is dry and crisp, with a peppery finish. **85** —*S.H. (12/1/2003)*

LEONETTI CELLAR

Leonetti Cellar 2003 Reserve Bordeaux Blend (Walla Walla (WA)) $100. 100% estate grown. More tannic and dense than the Cabernet, this is roughly three-quarters Cabernet, one-sixth Merlot, but replaces that wine's Cab Franc and Carmenère with Petit Verdot. The nose shows hints of mushroom, jasmine, blueberries, raspberries, and dark chocolate. All in all a big but surprisingly subtle, scented, sensuous wine. **95** —*P.G. (10/1/2006)*

Leonetti Cellar 2002 Reserve Bordeaux Blend (Walla Walla (WA)) $95. If any wine can elevate Leonetti's stunning Cabernet to yet another level, it is this astonishing blend of 52% Cabernet Sauvignon, 31% Merlot, and 17% Petit Verdot, all from estate vineyards. Sweet plum, blueberry, and blackberry fruits are seamlessly married to layers of different flavored chocolates. Silky and supple, it uses oak as a sensual enhancement, but the wood flavors of mocha, nuts, butter, and toast are so beautifully smoothed into the fruit that they are never intrusive. **95** —*P.G.* *(12/15/2005)*

Leonetti Cellar 2001 Reserve Bordeaux Blend (Walla Walla (WA)) $95. Reserve is their version of a classic Bordeaux blend; this vintage pencils out as 48% Cabernet Sauvignon, 37% Merlot, the rest split evenly between Cab Franc and Petit Verdot. Sweet black-cherry fruit is married seamlessly to layers of different flavored chocolates; long, silky, seamless, and seductive. Styled for near-term enjoyment. **94** —*P.G.* *(11/15/2004)*

Leonetti Cellar 2000 Reserve Bordeaux Blend (Walla Walla (WA)) $95. It simply says "reserve" on the label, but the blend is 40% Cabernet Sauvignon, 40% Merlot, 10% Cab Frank, and 10% Petit Verdot. Soft, plush, and forward, it envelops the palate in rich red fruits and sweet spice, then finishes with the layers of flavorful oak for which Leonetti is famous. Sophisticated, brilliant winemaking. **94** —*P.G.* *(9/1/2003)*

Leonetti Cellar 2003 Cabernet Sauvignon (Walla Walla (WA)) $70. Here you will find classic Bourbon barrel-vanilla flavors, but with bright, polished fruit showing through. This is firm and substantial—very clean winemaking—crisp, tight, polished, and silky. Already it's showing layers of berries, currants, and blueberries. **94** —*P.G.* *(11/15/2006)*

Leonetti Cellar 2002 Cabernet Sauvignon (Walla Walla (WA)) $65. Leonetti continues to hit the high marks it sets for itself in this, its 25th vintage. The Walla Walla Cab includes 10% Merlot and small batches of Cab Franc and Carmenère. The astonishing, classic Leonetti aromas of penetrating, ripe black fruits, cedar, coffee, and chocolate are there in spades, but the overall impression is that the oak has been pulled back just a bit, or perhaps the fruit is just that much riper. Violets and lead pencil continue the stream of sensuous highlights, as the wine winds into its pungent, densely saturated finish. **94** —*P.G.* *(12/15/2005)*

Leonetti Cellar 2001 Cabernet Sauvignon (Walla Walla (WA)) $65. No longer the biggest or oakiest Cab in the valley, this is a more sinuous, sensuous style, with a citrusy lift to the pretty cherry fruit, perhaps from the inclusion of a tiny bit of Syrah (there's also a bit of Carmenère!). Still young and a bit tannic, this will benefit from three to five years of further bottle age. **91** —*P.G.* *(11/15/2004)*

Leonetti Cellar 2000 Cabernet Sauvignon (Walla Walla (WA)) $65. Bursting with fragrant, powerful berries and spice, this wine still shows the edges of youth, with the new oak a bit jagged and the tannins slightly green and chalky. But all it needs is time (or air!) and there is no denying that this is a jammy, juicy, just plain delicious mouthful of wine with a masterful hand at the wheel. **93** —*P.G.* *(9/1/2003)*

Leonetti Cellar 1999 Cabernet Sauvignon (Walla Walla (WA)) $60. This is the winery's first nonreserve Cabernet from 100% Walla Walla fruit. It's a subtle style shift: more floral qualities, more finesse, a mix of red fruits and a light hint of bell pepper. Tannins are soft but substantial; in the mouth, flavors extend and include interesting herb and leaf nuances. The core of ripe fruit is there and firmly in place; the tannins are showing a bit of stem right now and the oak is hiding. **92** —*P.G.* *(9/1/2002)*

Leonetti Cellar 1998 Cabernet Sauvignon (Columbia Valley (WA)) $60. Here again the 1998 vintage shows its forward, fat, fruity, lip-smackingly luscious qualities right out in front. This is a meaty, oaky Cab, with firm, tongue-lashing tannins, plenty of red berry/cassis fruit and a power-packed profile from top to bottom. It's delicious and strong, with coffee, bitter chocolate, and licorice lining the extended finish. Ideally, you'll give it about two more years of cellar time and then go for it. **95** —*P.G.* *(10/1/2001)*

Leonetti Cellar 1997 Cabernet Sauvignon (Columbia Valley (WA)) $55. 93 —*P.G.* *(11/15/2000)*

Leonetti Cellar 1998 Reserve Cabernet Sauvignon (Walla Walla (WA)) $95. Leonetti's reserve, made entirely from grapes grown in the Walla Walla valley, is a distillation of everything that makes this the quintessential Washington state cult winery. Ripe, classy cassis fruit is seamlessly married to layers of oak; the barrel aging adding dimensions of toast and chocolate, espresso, and cream, butterscotch, and roasted nuts, to the extended finish. The blend is three quarters Cabernet, with the rest a 50/50 split of Merlot and Petit Verdot. In my experience Leonetti's

reserve wines are magnificent upon release, and should be enjoyed while still young. Just 576 cases produced. **96** —*P.G.* *(10/1/2001)*

Leonetti Cellar 2004 Merlot (Columbia Valley (WA)) $60. There was no Pepper Bridge or Seven Hills Merlot in the mix in 2004, but this as good as any other Leonetti Merlot, which is to say as good as it gets, aided by the inclusion of Cold Creek vineyard fruit. Soft, lush, and beautifully aromatic; it's just lightly dusted with chocolate and hints of spicy herb. **92** —*P.G.* *(10/1/2006)*

Leonetti Cellar 2003 Merlot (Columbia Valley (WA)) $55. Intense and concentrated, this puts to rest any ideas that Merlot is incapable of making "real" wine. The flavors are smooth and chocolatey, the mouthfeel liquorous, ripe and lush. High-toned fruits and flowers slide into the mellow tannins, all resolving in a superripe, decadently rich finish. **93** —*P.G.* *(12/15/2005)*

Leonetti Cellar 2002 Merlot (Columbia Valley (WA)) $55. Firm and muscular, this delivers powerful, concentrated red currant, cherry, and berry fruit, tightly wrapped and resonant. Young and compact, the wine just begins to hint at the complexity it contains, with notes of herb, leaf, and barrel spice. Good weight and concentration, plus exceptional length and precision. **92 Editors' Choice** —*P.G.* *(11/15/2004)*

Leonetti Cellar 2001 Merlot (Columbia Valley (WA)) $55. This may be less oaky and more fruit-driven than previous Leonetti Merlots, which means it is more food-ready and probably built for a longer lifetime. The fruit is perfectly ripe, concentrated, and spicy with exceptional length and precision. Very young and compact, this is extraordinary Merlot. World class. **92** —*P.G.* *(12/31/2003)*

Leonetti Cellar 2000 Merlot (Columbia Valley (WA)) $55. Can anything compare with the glorious Leonetti '99? This is a fine effort, with its showy mix of red fruits, berry, and pomegranate flavors dominating. Though immediately delicious, it is less meaty and muscular than the previous vintage. It's all about sweet, forward fruit, backed with soft, pleasing tannins. **91** —*P.G.* *(9/1/2002)*

Leonetti Cellar 1999 Merlot (Columbia Valley (WA)) $55. For more than two decades, Merlot has been the signature wine for Leonetti. This year's version is dense and tannic. The immediate impression is of charcoal, ash, and black-cherries. As the wine opens up there are spices (black pepper, anise, bay leaf), roasted nuts, lush tannins, and more fruits—berries, cherries, and plums. Though young, tight and still tannic, with several hours breathing time this extraordinary Merlot begins to smooth out the rough edges and show its best stuff. **94** —*P.G.* *(10/1/2001)*

Leonetti Cellar 1998 Merlot (Columbia Valley (WA)) $50. 94 —*P.G.* *(11/15/2000)*

Leonetti Cellar 2004 Sangiovese (Walla Walla (WA)) $50. Beautifully crafted, aromatic, high-toned but not over the top. Plummy, pretty cherry fruit, lightly spiced and showing a bit of chocolate as it breathes. In this freeze year the crop was reduced by two thirds; just 289 cases were produced. **91** —*P.G.* *(10/1/2006)*

Leonetti Cellar 2003 Sangiovese (Walla Walla (WA)) $50. Sharp, youthful, tart, and spicy, this fresh, lively Sangio is spiced up with citrus rind and tangy berries. The blend includes 22% Syrah. **89** —*P.G.* *(12/15/2005)*

Leonetti Cellar 2002 Sangiovese (Walla Walla (WA)) $50. Don't let the apparent lightness of this stylish Sangio fool you; its elegant demeanor does not in any way mean it is wimpy. Here is fresh, lively fruit, spiced with citrus rind, showing clean, varietal fruit and a perfect kiss of oak. **91** —*P.G.* *(11/15/2004)*

Leonetti Cellar 2001 Sangiovese (Walla Walla (WA)) $50. Sangiovese is the little-known star of the Walla Walla Valley, where it ripens nicely and acquires some genuine semblance to its Tuscan cousins. Leonetti does it up in the flashy house style, with sweet, spicy fruit wrapped in tasty but still tasteful oak. Forward, soft, and sweetly appealing. **89** —*P.G.* *(9/1/2003)*

Leonetti Cellar 2000 Sangiovese (Walla Walla (WA)) $50. Walla Walla wineries are turning out some pretty delicious Sangiovese these days, and Leonetti always seems to lead the pack. This is plenty tannic, stuffed with rich cherry fruit and nuanced with leather and tobacco. Really pretty with soft tannins and lots of sweet cherry flavor. **91** —*P.G.* *(9/1/2002)*

Leonetti Cellar 1999 Sangiovese (Walla Walla (WA)) $50. Leonetti seems to get more extracted fruit, more depth and power, more flat-out flavor from Sangiovese than virtually anyone else in the country. A lot of it, let's face it, is the same Leonetti magic that is applied to other red wines: rich layers of buttery, nutty, luscious oak underscoring the strawberry/plum flavors of the Sangiovese grapes. About 20% Syrah is included in the blend. The result is an exciting wine, sensuous and sleek. **91** —P.G. (10/1/2001)

Leonetti Cellar 1998 Sangiovese (Walla Walla (WA)) $50. 91 —P.G. (11/15/2000)

LEVERONI

Leveroni 2004 Chardonnay (Carneros) $16. A little earthy and tart, this is a minerally, high-acid Chard with tight flavors of citrus fruits and barely ripened white peach. It has a clean mouthfeel and a swift finish. **84** — S.H. (12/15/2005)

Leveroni 2003 Chardonnay (Carneros) $16. A nice example of a Carneros Chard, balanced in tree fruit flavors, with crisp acidity and a hint of pear liqueur on the finish. It's clean and refreshing. **85** —S.H. (4/1/2005)

Leveroni 2003 Merlot (Sonoma Valley) $18. Pleasing, but basically straightforward. It's all on the surface, but the cherries and oak, vanilla, and woodspice come together in a satisfying swirl of dusty tannins. **86** — S.H. (12/15/2005)

Leveroni 2002 Merlot (Sonoma Valley) $18. What a nice wine this is. It's dry and balanced, and although there's a complex structure of tannins, it's drinkable now. The flavors veer between blackberries, plums, coffee, leather, and dusty spices. **90** —S.H. (4/1/2005)

Leveroni 2001 Merlot (Sonoma Valley) $18. This wine impresses for its smooth mouthfeel. It feels as soft as velvet, and yet the tannins are richly textured and even dense. Polished flavors of plums, blackberries, and dark chocolate linger through a long finish. **89** —S.H. (6/1/2004)

Leveroni 2004 Pinot Noir (Sonoma Valley) $18. One sniff and you know the grapes were baked. Smells like that gummy filling that burbles over the edge of a cherry pie in the oven. In the mouth, it's a little more forgiving, but still finishes with the taste of raisins. **83** —S.H. (12/15/2005)

Leveroni 2002 Pinot Noir (Sonoma Valley) $15. This flavorful wine is eccentrically heavy for a Pinot Noir. It's dark and full-bodied, with blackberry, root beer, and cola flavors, and has some sweet, dense tannins. Yet it retains Pinot's silky texture, and is dry and easily drinkable. **85** —S.H. (11/1/2004)

Leveroni 2003 Syrah (Sonoma Valley) $18. The texture is smooth and fine, the tannins just right, but the fruitiness is too upfront, in your face. There's just unrestrained gobs of cherries and jammy berries. Whatever happened to balance? **83** —S.H. (12/15/2005)

Leveroni 2002 Syrah (Sonoma Valley) $18. Drinks rather cooked, with a baked pie crust aroma and strong, harsh berry flavors wrapped in thick tannins. Drink now. **84** —S.H. (6/1/2004)

LEWIS

Lewis 1997 Reserve Cabernet Sauvignon (Napa Valley) $60. 96 Cellar Selection (11/1/2000)

Lewis 1999 Reserve Chardonnay (Napa Valley) $48. A flamboyant bouquet of pineapple, ripe orange, floral, nuts, and toasty oak opens to a full palate of orange, nectarine, and pineapple flavors. Interesting accents including brown sugar, buttered popcorn, and mineral notes provide great tension against the fruit. Round and full—if a touch soft—it closes with a long, refined spicy-nutty finish. **90** (7/1/2001)

Lewis 2002 Syrah (Napa Valley) $60. In the lush, richly textured and oaky style that seems to becoming typical of Napa Syrah, this wine stands out as an exemplar of the type. Vanilla-infused berries finish long, with a hint of alcohol and a touch of coconut. A touch lacking in typical Syrah-like complexity, but an excellent wine. **90** (9/1/2005)

Lewis 1999 Syrah (Napa Valley) $NA. Yum's the word for the Lewis, another feather in winemaker Paul Hobbs's cap. It's so complex from beginning to end that reviewers had difficulty recording the numerous flavors and aromas that we found. Here's a sampling: We read the mouth as having a combination of prune, plum, smoked meat, toasted coconut,

caramelized onion, and vanilla aromas; the palate offers plum, cream, dried spices (cinnamon and nutmeg, mostly) and nutty-earthy notes. "Long, long" finish is chock-full of red berries, black pepper, peanut shells, and a smidge of powdered sugar. "Wow!" wrote one reviewer. Um, yes. Agreed. **91** (11/1/2001)

LIBERTY SCHOOL

Liberty School 2004 Cabernet Sauvignon (Paso Robles) $14. Lots to like in this Cab. Few regions do a better job of ripening red wines than Paso Robles while keeping prices modest. This one, from the hilly, limestony west side, is softly rich in blackberry and cherry flavors wrapped in fine, sweet tannins. This is a good price for a Cab of this quality. **89 Best Buy** —S.H. (12/15/2006)

Liberty School 2003 Cabernet Sauvignon (California) $12. This is a good price for a Cab that's dry, balanced, and elegant. It's obviously not a blockbuster, but the way the cherry, and blackberry flavors interact with oak and dried herbs makes the wine charming and even complex. **87 Best Buy** —S.H. (12/15/2005)

Liberty School 2002 Cabernet Sauvignon (California) $13. Lots of richness and complexity in this lovely wine, which has flavors of ripe blackberries, cassis, roasted coffee, herbs, and smoky oak. It's quite dry, with a good grip of tannin. **86** —S.H. (11/15/2004)

Liberty School 2004 Chardonnay (Central Coast) $13. With a dash of oak for vanilla and crème brûlée seasoning, this is a very ripe, soft Chardonnay. The fruit flavors veer toward apricots and nectarines, and finish a bit sweet. **84** —S.H. (12/15/2006)

Liberty School 2003 Chardonnay (Central Coast) $12. This Chard has some decent citrus and peach fruit, but it's really too tart and sour to offer much pleasure. **82** —S.H. (12/15/2005)

Liberty School 2002 Chardonnay (Central Coast) $13. This nice, everyday Chard has pleasantly ripe, plump flavors of tropical fruits and peaches. There's a rich veneer of smoky oak that adds spices and vanilla. **85** — S.H. (12/15/2004)

Liberty School 2000 Chardonnay (Central Coast) $14. Bizarre and unripe. Aromas of canned peaches with a strong note of the veggies, especially asparagus. The oaky overlay feels unnatural, with disembodied smoke and char flavors. Tart and acidic, and that vegetal taste returns to haunt the finish. **82** —S.H. (9/1/2003)

Liberty School 2004 Syrah (Central Coast) $13. Jammy, grapey, and fresh, with blackberry and cherry flavors that taste right out of the fermenter. Richness comes from notes of coffee, leather, and spice. So easy to imagine drinking this wine with a cheeseburger. **86** —S.H. (12/15/2006)

Liberty School 2003 Syrah (California) $12. You'll find lots of cool-climate richness in this Syrah. It has an inviting aroma of white pepper, with cassis and coffee flavors that finish dry and balanced. It's a little thin, but dry and interesting, a decent value at this price. **85** —S.H. (12/31/2005)

LIEB

Lieb 1993 Champagne Blend (North Fork of Long Island) $20. Shows extended tirage in its initial yeasty aromas that fold in some yellow apple scents as well. Turns more citrusy toward the finish, which is done in a softer, mass-market style. **86** —J.C. (4/1/2001)

Lieb 1999 Chardonnay (North Fork of Long Island) $15. Rich buttery aromas are quickly supplanted on the palate by crisp flavors of pears and lemons. Shows good persistence on the finish. The combination of butter and citrus seems like a natural to accompany a basic beurre blanc. **86** —J.C. (4/1/2001)

Lieb 2002 Merlot (North Fork of Long Island) $24. Lieb's regular Merlot is a solid effort, showing Long Island flavors in a nicely structured wine. Cranberry, sour cherry and spice have a smooth, chocolaty feel from the nose to the palate, while the tannins suggest aging potential. A good wine from a solid producer. Drink over the next five years. **86** —M.D. (12/1/2006)

Lieb 1997 Reserve Merlot (North Fork of Long Island) $20. A lush, approachable wine that features cherry and tobacco aromas and flavors. Tart acidity spices up the softly tannic finish, giving it a lively feel that would pair well with a variety of foods **88** —J.C. (4/1/2001)

Lieb 1998 Pinot Blanc (North Fork of Long Island) $15. Creamy, spicy aromas show hints of oranges or tangerines. Medium-weight, with a clean finish that would complement virtually any seafood dish. 84 —*J.C.* (4/1/2001)

LIGHTHOUSE

Lighthouse 2002 Crescendo Chardonnay (Central Coast) $15. Offers lime, pineapple, and mango flavors—even a hint of banana—with bright acidity and hints of vanilla and buttered toast. There's nothing subtle about this Chard. 87 —*S.H.* (7/1/2005)

Lighthouse 2002 Cachet Merlot (Central Coast) $16. This is a really nice wine. It's soft and gentle in tannins, but with perky acidity and complex layers of coffee, plum, blackberry, and leather flavors. Feels elegant and polished, a great wine for sophisticated fare. 90 Editors' Choice —*S.H.* (7/1/2005)

LILY

Lily 2002 Chardonnay (Sonoma County) $16. Not showing much beyond a huge, unbalanced plaster of charred oak. Smells and tastes like toothpicks. 83 —*S.H.* (8/1/2005)

Lily 2002 Pinot Noir (Sonoma Coast) $18. Starts with a blast of leathery animal, oak, and cherry cocoa, then turns tough and earthy in the mouth, with a cherry finish. Very dry, with a good, silky mouthfeel. Might develop additional complexities in a year or two. 86 —*S.H.* (8/1/2005)

LIMERICK LANE

Limerick Lane 2003 Collins Vineyard Syrah (Russian River Valley) $28. While this Syrah may not quite reach the heights of the old-vine Zinfandel from this vineyard, the vines are several decades younger. Even now, the results are impressive: bold raspberry fruit is couched in ultra-ripe tannins and framed by hints of vanilla. It even picks up some spice and game notes on the finish. 89 (9/1/2005)

Limerick Lane 2002 Collins Vineyard Syrah (Russian River Valley) $28. Lots to like in this intense, dry red wine. Smells complex and inviting, with bacon fat, leather, chocolate, blackberry, and smoke aromas, and the initial mouthfeel is lush and textured. Turns a bit thin in the middle, but maintains elegance and balance. 87 —*S.H.* (12/15/2004)

Limerick Lane 1999 Collins Vineyard Syrah (Russian River Valley) $36. It is supple and goes down easily, but you'll want to drink the Limerick Lane slowly enough to appreciate its complexity. Vanilla-chocolate aromas, plus earthy, meaty (one reviewer called it "barbecue") notes beef up a sour red-fruit bouquet. Creamy chocolate pops up again on the palate, where it melds with other dark toast, mocha, black-cherry and dried spice flavors. Finishes long, with sweet vanilla and licorice notes. 90 (11/1/2001)

Limerick Lane 2002 Collins Vineyard Zinfandel (Russian River Valley) $26. A great Zin, rich and opulent. Floods the mouth with briary blackberry, blueberry, cherry, chocolate, and pepper flavors that just take over the palate. Yet the wine is dry and balanced, with firm, ripe tannins. One of the best Zins of the year. 92 —*S.H.* (12/15/2004)

Limerick Lane 2001 Collins Vineyard Zinfandel (Russian River Valley) $26. Pleasantly fruity, but with tannins that are not as supple and elegant as the Old Vine version of this wine. Look for toasty oak, plum, black-cherry and spice, with a finish that's moderate in length. 86 (11/1/2003)

Limerick Lane 1999 Collins Vineyard Zinfandel (Russian River Valley) $26. Sugary-earth and anise aromas accent deep blackberry on the nose; in the mouth, this Russian River Valley Zin has bright raspberry and blueberry flavors, kept in check beautifully with oak and dried spice notes. Luscious in the mouth, and sexy overall, it finishes long with loads of blackberry and a little caramel at the very end. Could be even better after a year or two in the cellar. 91 —*D.T.* (3/1/2002)

Limerick Lane 1998 Collins Vineyard Zinfandel (Russian River Valley) $26. All the components of fine Zinfandel are in top form here, from the opening fat, dark berry aromas to the deep, sweet fruit on the smoothly textured palate and the lovely fruit-acid balance. Closes handsomely, with full even tannins and some white pepper on the long back end.

Drinks well now and has the structure to last and improve for a few years as well. 90 (3/1/2001)

Limerick Lane 2001 Collins Vineyard, Old Vine Zinfandel (Russian River Valley) $26. Fresh and plush, with rich, round plum, black-cherry, toast, tar, coffee, herb, and spice flavors that sail nicely over firm, ripe tannins. Fun and easy to appreciate, the wine finishes with moderate length. 89 (11/1/2003)

LINCOURT

Lincourt 2002 La Cuesta Vineyard Cabernet Sauvignon (Santa Ynez Valley) $35. Santa Barbara Cabs continue to have their work cut out for them, but as grapes are sourced from warmer areas, progress is made. This bottling shows fine varietal character, with plum, cassis, and blackberry-tea flavors, and is very dry. It has a tannic angularity that works well with rich meats. 88 —*S.H.* (11/1/2006)

Lincourt 2004 Chardonnay (Santa Barbara County) $18. A combination of Santa Maria and Santa Rita fruit, with the majority from Bien Nacido, this is a dry, crisp Chardonnay. It's more rustic than the Chards from Foley, the parent winery, but shows some interesting qualities. 85 —*S.H.* (11/1/2006)

Lincourt 2002 Chardonnay (Santa Barbara County) $18. Cool-climate Chard, with crisp, outspoken acidity and flinty flavors. A scour of fresh lime and mineral hits in the middle, leading to sweet oak on the aftertaste. 87 —*S.H.* (5/1/2005)

Lincourt 2004 Pinot Noir (Santa Barbara County) $22. Foley's second wine, this is partly from their Santa Rita Hills estate and partly from the new Solomon Hills vineyard, in Santa Maria. It's a fine, dry Pinot, with bitter cherry, unsweetened cocoa, cola, and subtle herb and spice flavors. 85 —*S.H.* (11/1/2006)

Lincourt 2002 Pinot Noir (Santa Barbara County) $22. Shows well-ripened black-cherry and cola fruit, with hints of Heirloom tomatoes and a dose of smoky oak. Dry and silky, but a little heavy in body. 86 —*S.H.* (5/1/2005)

Lincourt 2001 Pinot Noir (Santa Barbara County) $22. Released along with the '02, this wine still tastes young and fresh. It has cool Southland acids and is delicate in structure, with a mélange of herb, rhubarb, and cherry flavors. 87 —*S.H.* (5/1/2005)

Lincourt 2000 Pinot Noir (Santa Barbara County) $31. We like a particular South Central Coast Pinot character that shows in this supple, light- to medium-weight, tart-sweet (accent on tart) candidate. Sour cherry-cranberry fruit—with some tomato-like flavors—is complemented nicely by attractive smoke, herb, and bitter chocolate accents. The long finish is tangy with fine, cocoa powder tannins. Drink now–2006. 88 (10/1/2002)

Lincourt 2004 Sauvignon Blanc (Santa Ynez Valley) $16. Older oak barrel aging as well as stirring on the lees bring softness and creaminess to this fresh, clean wine. It brims with bright acidity, showing tart green apple, papaya, lemongrass, and apricot flavors, and again proves how beautifully this Santa Barbara appellation ripens Sauvignon Blanc. 89 —*S.H.* (11/1/2006)

Lincourt 2004 Syrah (Santa Barbara County) $20. With grapes from both the cool east and warm west part of the county, this attractive Syrah shows ripe, plum, boysenberry, and blackberry fruit backed up with firm acids and tannins. It's very dry, and drinks well now with steak or lamb. 87 —*S.H.* (11/1/2006)

Lincourt 2003 Syrah (Santa Barbara County) $20. Squeaky clean, richly fruity, and perfectly inviting, this ripe, elegant Syrah starts with modest blackberry notes, then opens up to show more raspberry and vanilla shadings. Not a blockbuster, just ripe, creamy, and well crafted. Good value, too. 89 (9/1/2005)

Lincourt 2002 Syrah (Santa Barbara County) $20. Northern Rhône-like, a big, dark and somewhat tannic wine, with grilled meat, pepper, and blackberry flavors and a smooth finish. Not especially complex. 86 —*S.H.* (5/1/2005)

LINDEN

Linden 2001 Glen Manor Bordeaux Blend (Virginia) $29. black-cherry, tobacco, and brown sugar scents start this wine down the right track,

USA

and the mouthfeel is supple and creamy, but things come a bit unglued on the short-lived finish, where the flavors turn tart. **83** —*J.C. (9/1/2005)*

Linden 2001 Hardscrabble Bordeaux Blend (Virginia) $32. This Bordeaux blend has a touch of horse and earth on the nose. It shows some of the ripeness possible in Virginia with rich flavors of blueberry, cassis, and heavy oak that's suited to this full-bodied wine. Sweet fruit mellows the smooth tannins, while acidity shows through on the finish. **85** —*M.D. (8/1/2006)*

Linden 1998 Hardscrabble Red Bordeaux Blend (Virginia) $24. This Cabernet blend has a big, green-bean-and-bell-pepper nose, wrapped in a cloak of cedar. Charred oak marks the palate: It's wearing an oversized oak jacket over undersized black-cherry fruit. **83** —*J.C. (1/1/2004)*

Linden 1997 Reserve Red Bordeaux Blend (Virginia) $28. The barrels seem expensive: the copious flamboyant smoky, toasty oak is soft, forward and tasty. But the fruit doesn't quite measure up, leaving a bit of a hollow in the midpalate. A blend of 65% Cabernet Sauvignon, 27% Cabernet Franc, 5% Petit Verdot, and 3% Merlot. **83** —*J.C. (1/1/2004)*

Linden 2001 Hardscrabble Chardonnay (Virginia) $22. Not afraid of using oak, Linden's Hardscrabble, named after the site in the Blue Ridge Mountains, has toasty vanilla and popcorn aromas that translate to buttery oak in the mouth. It's backed by nice tropical fruit, but the wine's body doesn't quite size up. **85** —*M.D. (8/1/2006)*

Linden 1998 Hardscrabble Chardonnay (Virginia) $20. 84 —*J.C. (1/1/2004)*

Linden 2002 Petite Verdot (Virginia) $24. Brambly dark fruit characterizes this PV, with high acidity playing a leading role, leaving a sour taste on the finish. **83** —*M.D. (8/1/2006)*

Linden 1999 Glen Manor Red Blend (Virginia) $23. This mix of Cabernet Sauvignon, Cab Franc, and Petit Verdot begins with slightly cheesy, animal notes. Once they blow off, there is sweet boysenberry styled fruit and some richness. The finish is round and broad, but ultimately it's quite basic, as is the wine. **84** —*M.S. (3/1/2003)*

Linden 1999 Hardscrabble Red Blend (Virginia) $28. A pungent nose of mint, black-cherry and sweet spice kicks things off in good form, followed by cherry, berry and citrus flavors. On the back end there are some toasty notes, and overall it's friendly warm and well balanced. But there isn't a whole lot of stuffing, which you might expect for close to $30. **84** —*M.S. (3/1/2003)*

Linden 2000 Vidal Blanc (Virginia) $22. A lush, sweet blend of honey, apricot, citrus, kumquat, spice and vanilla notes. Viscous and rich on the palate, the wine makes a very satisfying dessert or dessert accompaniment. **89** —*J.M. (1/1/2003)*

Linden 2003 Late Harvest Vidal Blanc (Virginia) $23. Starts with restrained aromas of fresh pear, clove, and honey, then develops candied pineapple and citrus flavors along with a hint of corn on the cob. Focused, not overly sticky or concentrated, finshing clean and fresh. **89** —*J.C. (9/1/2005)*

LINNE CALODO

Linne Calodo 2003 Nemesis Rhône Red Blend (Paso Robles) $60. Nemesis contains almost 90% Syrah, the highest percentage of Linne Calodo's three current red releases. It's a big, dark wine, saturated with cassis and dark chocolate flavors, with delicious notes of cherries, raspberries, and oak. It has an interesting and complex tannin-acid structure. This compelling, authoritative Rhône blend showcases the brilliance of its terroir. **94 Editors' Choice** —*S.H. (10/1/2005)*

Linne Calodo 2003 Rising Tides Rhône Red Blend (Paso Robles) $42. With a higher percentage of Syrah than Sticks and Stones, Linne's Rising Tides is darker and deeper. It suggests black-cherries veering into black currants, with a rich, dark chocolate note, and a finish of sweet, charry oak. Nonetheless it's a dry wine, and a little soft. **93 Editors' Choice** —*S.H. (10/1/2005)*

Linne Calodo 2003 Sticks and Stones Rhône Red Blend (Paso Robles) $60. With a majority of Grenache, this wine flatters with pure, sweet red and black-cherry flavors. Syrah seems to bring color and depth, while Mourvèdre contributes a delicious chocolate note. The wine is fully dry, high in alcohol, soft in acidity, and utterly delicious. **92 Editors' Choice** —*S.H. (10/1/2005)*

Linne Calodo 2005 Contrarian Rhône White Blend (Paso Robles) $36. What a complex and interesting blend of Roussanne and Viognier. Opens with a honeyed, marzipan and almond cookie bouquet, but turns surprisingly dry and acidically crisp in the mouth, with Meyer lemon, vanilla, gingerbread, and Asian spice flavors. Really impressive for its power, depth, and length. **94 Editors' Choice** —*S.H. (12/1/2006)*

Linne Calodo 2004 Contrarian Rhône White Blend (Paso Robles) $36. This is a distinctive blend of Roussanne and Viognier. It's impressively rich, offering up complex waves of kiwi, vanilla custard, white peach sorbet, and white chocolate flavors. That makes it sound sweet, but it's a dry wine. A little soft, but totally delicious. **92** —*S.H. (10/1/2005)*

LION VALLEY

Lion Valley 1999 Reserve Chardonnay (Willamette Valley) $16. They pulled out all stops on this wine, including barrel fermentation in French oak, and you can smell the smoky, woody notes. There's also something like burnt honey, and the apple and spicy peach flavors seem overtly sweet. Good structure, but it's kind of rustic. **83** —*S.H. (4/1/2002)*

Lion Valley 1999 Estate Pinot Gris (Willamette Valley) $14. The first whiff brings a noseful of sulfur, although most of it blows off on airing. The underlying flavors are lovely, though, suggesting citrus fruits and apple, supported by crisp acidity. Finishes clean and crisp. Would score higher except for the opening smell. **83** —*S.H. (8/1/2002)*

LIPARITA

Liparita 2001 Cabernet Sauvignon (Napa Valley) $38. Assembled from various parts of the valley, this classic Napa Cab showcases well-ripened black currant, French roast coffee, and oak flavors, and a smooth, rich and complex texture. It's bold enough in firm tannins to age through this decade. **92** —*S.H. (5/1/2005)*

Liparita 1999 Cabernet Sauvignon (Napa Valley) $36. Big, big Cabernet, with all the attributes of this unreal vintage. Dark in color, with concentrated, rich aromas of cassis and olive and young, unintegrated smoky oak. Fills the mouth with lush flavors of blackberries and herbs, with distinctive Napa tannins that are fine and dusty. Quite young now, it needs a few years to knit together. **93 Editors' Choice** —*S.H. (11/15/2003)*

Liparita 1997 Cabernet Sauvignon (Napa Valley) $45. 92 *(11/1/2000)*

Liparita 2003 Vineyard Reserve Cabernet Sauvignon (Napa Valley) $65. Soft, ripe, and tasty, this fruit-forward Cabernet offers plenty of palate-pleasing currant, cassis, cherry, and mocha flavors, along with sweet smoky oak. It's a dry wine, but long on the finish in ripe fruit, and the tannins are harmoniously integrated. Drink now. **89** —*S.H. (9/1/2006)*

Liparita 1999 Vineyard Reserve Cabernet Sauvignon (Napa Valley) $50. In a word, massive, a masterpiece of Napa Cabernet from a great vintage. A barrel selection from three vineyards, and a mere 275 cases produced. This wine pours dark and thick, and announces itself with smoky oak aromas riding over cassis. The flavors are rich in blackberries and herbs, framed in rich, thick, dusty tannins. As good as it is, it would be a shame to drink it now. Best after 2004, and for many years afterward. **95 Cellar Selection** —*S.H. (11/15/2003)*

Liparita 1997 Vineyard Reserve Cabernet Sauvignon (Napa Valley) $65. 88 *(11/1/2000)*

Liparita 2000 Chardonnay (Carneros) $24. Creamy smooth, with moderate acidity and a pleasant array of apple, mineral, melon and herb flavors. The finish is clean, with a lemony edge. **87** —*J.M. (10/1/2003)*

Liparita 1998 Chardonnay (Carneros) $33. The bouquet is like an aromatic walk in the woods—it has pine, earth, and floral elements as well as the expected fruit aromas. Red apple and plum flavors are accented by lemon-lime the mouth, and a mineral note asserts itself. It has body but not weight, and closes with a clean citrus-chalk finish. **88** *(7/1/2001)*

Liparita 2001 Merlot (Napa Valley) $29. The aroma's the best part now, alluringly rich and inviting in currants, oak, and cocoa. But in the mouth, its way too tannic. The underlying black-cherry flavors are shut down. Balanced enough to improve, though. Try after 2007. **87** —*S.H. (5/1/2005)*

Liparita 1999 Sauvignon Blanc (Napa Valley) $18. Too bad some people have eyes only for Chardonnay, when a wonderful dry white wine like this is available. Made from the "Musque" clone and farmed by the family that owns Flora Springs, it veers toward citrus fruits and a pleasant splash of buttery, honeyed toast. Elegant and limpid in the mouth. **91 Editors' Choice** —*S.H. (5/1/2001)*

Liparita 2000 Oakville Sauvignon Blanc (Napa Valley) $18. A strong vegetal character mars the nose of this otherwise dry, spicy Napa Valley SB. There is a boatload of asparagus and green pepper to the nose, and in the mouth the fruit element, meaning papaya and mild citrus, gets gobbled up by a potent blast of green flavors. The finish is spicy and dry, but it's also heavy with the taste of green peas. Was ripeness a problem here? Seems like it was. **85** *(8/1/2002)*

LITTLE VALLEY

Little Valley 1999 White Rabbit Cabernet Sauvignon (San Francisco Bay) $18. A country-style Cab with odd notes, although it's still drinkable. The blackberry notes ride next to an aroma like a chocolate candy bar, and the thin flavors are wrapped in rough tannins. **83** —*S.H. (11/15/2003)*

Little Valley 2001 White Rabbit Chardonnay (San Francisco Bay) $13. A rough and ready Chard with peach and apple flavors, a creamy texture and some fairly pronounced oak. It's not a bad wine for the price, and has some nice fruit, but the smoky oak has been applied with a heavy hand. **84** —*S.H. (3/1/2004)*

LIVINGSTON

Livingston 1996 Moffett Vineyard Cabernet Sauvignon (Napa Valley) $50. **88** *(3/1/2000)*

Livingston 1997 Mitchell Vineyard Syrah (Napa Valley) $35. **91** *(3/1/2000)*

LIVINGSTON MOFFETT

Livingston Moffett 2002 Mitchell Vineyard Syrah (Napa Valley) $27. This Syrah receives a split vote from the panel, its fans lauding the rich, jammy aromas and flavors of blackberry and spice, and its soft tealike tannins on the finish. Its detractors found a stalky note on the palate, but could still applaud the wine's mouthfeel. **87** *(9/1/2005)*

Livingston Moffett 2002 Parkinson Vineyard Syrah (Napa Valley) $45. This wine's performance wasn't quite up to the winery's other offering. Its flavor profile—caramel, black-cherry, vanilla, mixed berries—left a sweet, confected taste in some reviewers' mouths. Others still admired the wine's lush but soft feel. **85** *(9/1/2005)*

Livingston Moffett 1997 Gemstone Vineyard Bordeaux Blend (Napa Valley) $75. **90** *(11/1/2000)*

Livingston Moffett 1999 Chardonnay (Napa Valley) $40. Very ripe tropical fruits and appealing pear, apple, and spice notes show well in this nicely balanced wine. Good acidity plays a solid supporting role here. The toasty oak holds the almost overripe fruit in check—it's strong from the mid palate through the handsome butter-and-apple finish. **88** *(7/1/2001)*

Livingston Moffett 1999 Mitchell Vineyard Syrah (Napa Valley) $35. There's plenty of sour herb on the even, dark fruit; soy, bouillon, and leathery notes add real complexity. Medium-weight, with handsome fruit-acid balance, it's slightly tart, a bit herbaceous, but also possesses fine structure and real potential to develop. Closes with tangy tannins, charcoal, and pepper accents. Best held for three years. **89** *(11/1/2001)*

LLANO

Llano 1997 Signature Bordeaux Blend (Texas) $9. **91** *(11/15/1999)*

LLANO ESTACADO

Llano Estacado 1998 Celler Select Cabernet Sauvignon (Texas) $18. What a great color on this ripe, full-flavored wine. It opens with heaps of blackberry and green olive aromas and moderate smoky oak. In the mouth, it has good berry extract, and is most notable for its dry, elegant harmony. Finishes syrupy. **90** —*S.H. (5/1/2001)*

Llano Estacado 2000 Chardonnay (Texas) $12. A fine effort, brimming with bright, clean lemony fruit, as well as spiced apple, pear, and vanilla. It's light on the oak, and drinks very clean and supple, with impressive depth. Low alcohol (12.1%) keeps it light and enjoyable. **88** —*S.H. (5/1/2001)*

Llano Estacado 2000 Cellar Select Chardonnay (Texas) $18. Yummy. Exotically rich, ripe fruit marks this expressive, polished wine. Apple, peach, pear, vanilla, and toast highlight the aroma, and it drinks extravagantly rich without being over the top. The finish is complex and harmonious. **90** —*S.H. (5/1/2001)*

Llano Estacado 1999 Signature Red Red Blend (Texas) $9. This dry, earthy wine succeeds with soft but intricate tannins and bracing acidity, together with a rich, hearty mouthfeel. The fruit could be a little more polished. Nonetheless this wine is complex, and a good companion to a wide range of foods. **88** —*S.H. (5/1/2001)*

Llano Estacado 1999 Passionelle Rhône Red Blend (Texas) $9. A Rhone blend of Carignane, Syrah, and Viognier, it has pretty aromas of spicy raspberries and smoky vanilla, with a rich herbaceousness suggesting rhubarb and fresh tomato. The color is a dark rose, and it drinks fruity and soft. You could put a bit of a chill on it. **84** —*S.H. (5/1/2001)*

Llano Estacado 2000 Sauvignon Blanc (Texas) $8. Primarily from the High Plains and Hill Country, a fruity-citrusy-figgy wine with a nice cut of smoky apricot. Drinks quite full-bodied and rich, and very dry, with pretty acidity, and then turns tartly crisp on the finish. **86** —*S.H. (5/1/2001)*

LOCKWOOD

Lockwood 2004 Estate Cabernet Sauvignon (Monterey) $13. Sourced from the southern Salinas Valley, which grows quickly warm to hot as it approaches Paso Robles, this wine is dry and fruity, with a rustic texture. It has coffee and blackberry tea flavors, and is clean and balanced. **83** —*S.H. (12/15/2006)*

Lockwood 2001 Estate Cabernet Sauvignon (Monterey County) $12. This easy Cab gets the job done with its dry, smooth flavors of blackberries and cherries and a gentle touch of oak. It has enough tannins to cut through a big steak or chop, and finishes clean. **85** —*S.H. (7/1/2005)*

Lockwood 1997 Estate Grown & Bottled Cabernet Sauvignon (Monterey) $16. The dark fruit and cedar nose is a perfect setup for solid berry flavors. Medium weight, a good acid backbone, and a full finish mark this winner. The juicy berry and spice flavors and the solid dusty tannins on the back end are noteworthy. Drink now–2004. **88** *(6/1/2001)*

Lockwood 1999 Estate Grown & Estate Bottled Cabernet Sauvignon (Monterey) $15. Textbook Cabernet, with fresh and vibrant aromas of currants, black olives, and blackberries, and an elaborate perfume of smoky oak. The flavors are similar and very long and extracted. It's kind of soft, and the palate yearns for more structure around all that flavor. **86** *(11/15/2002)*

Lockwood 2004 Chardonnay (Monterey) $11. Clean enough, but not much going on in this dry, thin Chard. It has watery, vaguely Chardonnay-like flavors and is acidic. **82** —*S.H. (12/15/2006)*

Lockwood 1998 Chardonnay (Monterey County) $16. The apple, earth, and mild tropical fruit aromas, good mouthfeel and apple-pear and caramel flavors are all right on target. Lockwood's largest volume bottling, this hits all the right notes. Toasty, spicy oak mingles with apple, spice, and butterscotch on the close. Drink now. **87 Best Buy** *(6/1/2001)*

Lockwood 2000 Estate Grown & Bottled Chardonnay (Monterey) $15. Lean and earthy, a wine with apple flavors and high acidity whose virtue is cleanliness and vibrancy rather than delicious hedonism. Restrained fruit lets the alcohol and acidity star. Try with mussels, clams, or grilled veggies. **86** —*S.H. (2/1/2003)*

Lockwood 1998 Estate Grown & Bottled Chardonnay (Monterey County) $16. **86** *(6/1/2000)*

Lockwood 1998 VSR Chardonnay (Monterey) $35. Apple and tropical fruit aromas accented by mint, grass, and herbal notes open to an equally bright palate of pineapple, mango and citrus flavors. In this classy, medium-bodied Chardonnay, these lively elements meet buttery vanilla notes in the mouth and flow into a long caramel finish with brisk, pepper-oak accents. **90** *(7/1/2001)*

Lockwood 1997 VSR Chardonnay (Monterey) $30. Mature and full bodied, with caramel and crème-brûlée aromas. The even, rich mouthfeel has a creamy texture. Tropical fruit, spice, and caramel flavors on the palate extend into the finish, where a dry, chalky note and the underlying acidity come up. Lovely now. **89** *(6/1/2001)*

Lockwood 1997 VSR Meritage (Monterey County) $45. A complex and delicious Bordeaux blend, with a bouquet of blackberries, herbs, tobacco, and prunes. The nose promises a lot and the palate delivers full, sweet fruit flavors and a rich texture. The finish is long and toasty, with deep fruit and vanilla flavors and solid tannins that indicate good ageability. Best from 2002–2009. **92 Editors' Choice** *(6/1/2001)*

Lockwood 2002 Merlot (Monterey) $13. Good everyday Merlot here, a little on the rustic side, but offering plenty of ripe, tasty plum, blackberry, coffee, and cocoa flavors. The grapes are from the San Lucas appellation, a warmer region on the road toward Paso Robles. **84** *—S.H. (12/15/2006)*

Lockwood 2000 Merlot (Monterey) $12. Plum and berry-cherry flavors mingle with herbal, coffee, and cola notes in this very dry red wine. The firm tannins will easily stand up to barbecue and similar fare. **84** *—S.H. (5/1/2004)*

Lockwood 1997 Merlot (Monterey County) $18. Sweet and sexy, this notable Merlot value offers berry, earth, herb, and cocoa elements knit into a smooth, appealing package. There's a touch of Bordeaux Right Bank complexity in the bouquet, then decidedly New World ripe black-cherries and toasty oak on the palate. Finishes spicy-sweet, with a caramel note from the oak. Drink now–2003. **88 Best Buy** *(6/1/2001)*

Lockwood 2001 Estate Merlot (Monterey County) $12. Round, smooth and supple; this soft, easy red has flavors of blackberries, roast coffee, grilled meat, and mushroom. It's very dry, with gentle tannins. **85** *—S.H. (7/1/2005)*

Lockwood 1999 Estate Grown & Estate Bottled Merlot (Monterey) $15. From vineyards in the warmer southern part of the county, this is a dark, ripe wine that bursts with plum and blackberry flavors enlivened by oak. It's dry and sumptuous, with fine tannins. A raisiny note shows up on the tart finish. **86** *(11/15/2002)*

Lockwood 1997 VSR Merlot (Monterey) $45. This structured Merlot opens with a complex bouquet of well-knit cherry, currant, oak, mocha and leather aromas. Similar flavors and licorice accents follow on the full and supple palate. This large-scaled but evenly-textured and balanced Merlot finishes long, with dark fruit and toast flavors. The sturdy tannins will reward cellaring. Drink now–2007+. **91** *(6/1/2001)*

Lockwood 1998 Pinot Blanc (Monterey) $12. Pear, lemon, butter, and petrol aromas open to a mouthful of understated pear flavors. The full palate balances weight with fairly high acidity. More oak is evident on the finish than on the palate, and it closes with notes of spicy wood and oranges. Drink now. **85** *(6/1/2001)*

Lockwood 2004 Block 7 Pinot Noir (Monterey) $20. Here's a well-behaved Pinot Noir. It's textbook coastal, a delicately structured, silky, high-acid wine with cola, cherry, root beer, rhubarb, and rosehip tea flavors. Really delivers the goods at a fair price for the quality. **88** *—S.H. (12/15/2006)*

Lockwood 2005 Sauvignon Blanc (Monterey) $11. Very dry, very acidic and crisp to the point of tartness, and a little watery, with grapefruit and slightly richer lime and fig flavors, this is a nice everyday wine. It won't win big accolades from the critics, but consumers will appreciate its quality-to-price ratio. **84** *—S.H. (12/15/2006)*

Lockwood 2001 Sauvignon Blanc (Monterey) $9. Fresh citrus fruits, figs, melons, and spearmint chewing gum are the flavors you'll find in this nice sipping wine. It's pleasantly crisp, and finishes with a honeyed richness. **85** *—S.H. (5/1/2004)*

Lockwood 1999 Sauvignon Blanc (Monterey County) $12. This medium-weight Sauvignon Blanc opens with citrus and mild vanilla aromas. Rich on the palate, it's 100% barrel-fermented and contains 5% Chardonnay, but does not undergo malolactic fermentation. Its appealing blend of melon, grapefruit, and fig flavors finishes with good length and more of the citrus/vanilla elements from the nose. Drink now. **87 Best Buy** *(6/1/2001)*

Lockwood 2004 Estate Sauvignon Blanc (Monterey) $10. Classic coastal Sauvignon Blanc, ripe and forward in lemon and lime, honeydew, alfalfa, peppery cinnamon, and vanilla flavors, with a great deal of acidity, although the finish is a little sweet. There's a lot going on here. **86 Best Buy** *—S.H. (12/1/2005)*

Lockwood 1998 Estate Grown Sauvignon Blanc (Monterey) $11. **87** *—L.W. (5/1/2000)*

Lockwood 2000 Estate Grown & Bottled Sauvignon Blanc (Monterey County) $11. This is tasty stuff, not only because it has the prettiest lemon and lime tastes, but the crisp acidity makes it lively on the palate. It's dryish, with a honeyed, ripe sweetness that lasts long into the finish. **87** *—S.H. (7/1/2003)*

Lockwood 1996 Syrah (Monterey County) $15. **87** *—L.W. (2/1/2000)*

Lockwood 2001 Syrah (Monterey) $14. An interesting Syrah, and complex. The cherries and cocoa are married to pepper and sweet tobacco in this dry, rich wine. Nice with grilled lamb chops and scalloped potatoes. **86** *—S.H. (6/1/2005)*

Lockwood 1999 Syrah (Monterey) $16. Some rough, numbing tannins mask the underlying cherry fruit. This is a young wine, with sharp acidity, and it's not offering much pleasure now. Best to cellar it in a cool place for a good two years, when it should soften up. **85** *—S.H. (12/1/2002)*

Lockwood 2001 Estate Syrah (Monterey County) $11. Dry and robust, this is a friendly, full-bodied Syrah. It has some rugged tannins and good earthy, coffee, and cherry flavors, with a hint of blueberries in the finish. Versatile with a wide range of foods. **85** *—S.H. (7/1/2005)*

Lockwood 2002 Shale Ridge Syrah (Monterey) $8. You'll like this fresh, young wine for its jammy blackberry and cherry flavors and rich, full-bodied texture. It's dry and spicy, with a long, fruity finish. **84** *—S.H. (4/1/2004)*

LOGAN

Logan 2002 Sleepy Hollow Vineyard Chardonnay (Monterey County) $18. Big, ripe, and juicy, with concentrated tropical fruit flavors and a rich, creamy texture. Oaky and smoky, this plush wine isn't subtle. **86** *—S.H. (10/1/2004)*

Logan 2001 Sleepy Hollow Vineyard Chardonnay (Monterey County) $18. From vintner Rob Talbott, a less expensive version of his single-vineyard Chard. It's crisp and oaky, with a suggestive leesy mouthfeel, and very dry. The flavors are complex, but highlighted by fresh pineapple and gingery spices. **87** *—S.H. (2/1/2004)*

Logan 1998 Sleepy Hollow Vineyard Chardonnay (Monterey County) $17. **88** *(6/1/2000)*

Logan 2000 Pinot Noir (Monterey County) $18. From Robert Talbott, an easy "Intro to Monterey Pinot Noir" kind of wine. It has earthy cherry, cola, and rhubarb flavors, is very dry, and shows the crisp acidity and silky tannins you expect from the variety. **85** *—S.H. (10/1/2004)*

Logan 2002 Sleepy Hollow Vineyard Pinot Noir (Monterey County) $18. Young, soft, and a bit jammy-syrupy, this Pinot may benefit from a year or two in the cellar. It has a rich, ripe core of black-cherry fruit, with an edge of sweetened coffee, although it's a totally dry wine. **86** *—S.H. (12/15/2005)*

Logan 1999 Sleepy Hollow Vineyard Pinot Noir (Monterey County) $20. From Robert Talbott. This isn't a bad Pinot, although it's pretty tannic and also has some minty, tomatoey notes, in addition to the riper blackberries. Will satisfy Pinotphiles for its soft, silky tannins, crisp acids and complexity. **86** *—S.H. (2/1/2004)*

LOGAN RIDGE

Logan Ridge 2002 Riesling (Finger Lakes) $9. On the sweet side, but it's also crisp, with enough zesty acidity to provide balance. Floral, appley and refreshingly light, this is a fine picnic wine. A chalky note gives added depth to the finish. **87 Best Buy** *—J.C. (8/1/2003)*

LOKOYA

Lokoya 2002 Cabernet Sauvignon (Mount Veeder) $120. There's something almost Zinny about this wine, with its brambly, briary notes of wild blueberries and blackberries and sun-warmed summer bark and dust. It possesses fabulous intensity, but those mountain tannins are palate-numbing, and they shut down the finish. Demands time beyond 2010. **94 Cellar Selection** *—S.H. (5/1/2005)*

LOLONIS

Lolonis 2002 Cabernet Sauvignon (Redwood Valley) $22. This is a Cab with high aspirations. It's ripe in black currant flavors, with a rich layer of oak, and rich, sweet tannins. It can't quite overcome a certain rusticity, but you have to admire the effort. **85** —S.H. (8/1/2005)

Lolonis 2001 Cabernet Sauvignon (Redwood Valley) $22. Long and rich in sun-ripened fruit, just brimming with blackberry jam and sweet chocolate flavors, spiced up with oak. Dry and balanced, an easy-to-drink wine with real complexity and flair. **87** —S.H. (10/1/2004)

Lolonis 2000 Cabernet Sauvignon (Redwood Valley) $22. Smells unusual for a Cab, with cheese, sandalwood, molasses, orange peel, and other aromas suggesting overly ripe grapes. In the mouth, turns quite tannic. **82** —S.H. (11/15/2003)

Lolonis 1999 Private Reserve Cabernet Sauvignon (Redwood Valley) $35. Soft and delicate in structure, a gentle wine that has some pretty flavors of cherries and blackberries. It's a bit tart in acidity, and will be good with a rich steak. **85** —S.H. (3/1/2004)

Lolonis 1997 Private Reserve Cabernet Sauvignon (Redwood Valley) $30. 89 (11/1/2000)

Lolonis 2002 Winegrower Selection Cabernet Sauvignon (Redwood Valley) $32. Superripe to the point of raisiny, this Cab has a soft, melted mouthfeel. It's thoroughly dry, and while the alcohol isn't very high, there's a peppery heat on the finish. **84** —S.H. (3/1/2006)

Lolonis 2001 Winegrower Selection Cabernet Sauvignon (Redwood Valley) $32. A bit overripe, with chocolate-covered raisin flavors beside the fresher ones of blackberries. It's dry and clean, though, with a long, sweet finish. **84** —S.H. (10/1/2004)

Lolonis 2002 Winegrowers Selection Castenon Vineyard Cabernet Sauvignon (Redwood Valley) $32. This is an admirable effort at an upscale Cab, at an upscale price. It's rich in ripe blackberry, cassis, and cherry flavors and well-oaked, and is fully dry. If you compare it to a Napa Cab, the tannic structure is more obvious. The wine has elbows and knees, but it will pair very well with a big, rich meat dish. **88** —S.H. (8/1/2005)

Lolonis NV Carignane (Redwood Valley) $14. They have a lot of old-vine "minor" varietals left in Mendocino, and this wine comes from some of them. It's probably as good as a Carignane can be, rustically tannic and earthy, bone dry, with piercing acidity and peppery-berry flavors. It's an honest California Vin de Pays. **86** —S.H. (5/1/2002)

Lolonis 1998 Chardonnay (Redwood Valley) $16. 86 (6/1/2000)

Lolonis 1997 Chardonnay (Redwood Valley) $21. 86 —S.H. (3/1/2000)

Lolonis 2004 Chardonnay (Redwood Valley) $17. This superripe Chard assaults the palate with massive pineapple, passionfruit, and kiwi flavors. There's also tremendous oak. Somehow it doesn't all mesh together in harmony. Size isn't everything. **84** —S.H. (2/1/2006)

Lolonis 2000 Chardonnay (Redwood Valley) $17. Extracted and a bit clumsy, with grapefruit, stewed peach, and tobacco flavors. Pretty acidic, with dusty tannins and a jagged mouthfeel, and turns tart on the finish. **84** —S.H. (6/1/2003)

Lolonis 2002 Antigone Late Harvest Chardonnay (Redwood Valley) $24. Very sweet, with flavors of peach and apricot shortcake drizzled with vanilla and cinnamon, this wine has good, firm acids. It's complex enough to warrant another glass or two. **88** —S.H. (2/1/2006)

Lolonis 1997 Late Harvest Chardonnay (Redwood Valley) $35. An intensely sweet wine, with an amazing residual sugar level of 18.7 percent. Sweetness covers a multitude of sins. This wine has flavors of apricots and peaches and is clean, with good acids. It has no particular complexity but is delicious anyway. **88** —S.H. (6/1/2003)

Lolonis 2000 Private Reserve Chardonnay (Redwood Valley) $30. A nice, easy drinking Chard with the usual winemaker bells and whistles. Peach and apple fruit is wrapped in plenty of toasted oak, and drinks smooth and creamy. Finishes a bit simple, and the wine is overpriced. **86** —S.H. (6/1/2003)

Lolonis 2003 Fumé Blanc (Redwood Valley) $13. Very dry and crisp, with dusty, palate-stimulating acidity that frames citrus and fig. A good choice for goat cheese and grilled veggies on toast. **85** —S.H. (12/1/2004)

Lolonis 2001 Fumé Blanc (Redwood Valley) $14. From an emerging Mendocino appellation, an engaging, dry wine. Its mouth-cleansing acidity is fresh and clean, highlighting pretty flavors of lime and honeydew, and leads to a tart finish. **87** —S.H. (7/1/2003)

Lolonis 2000 Fumé Blanc (Redwood Valley) $14. Melons come to mind. Sweet honeydew and cantaloupes, spicy and rich, and, a hint of peaches, and something elusively tropical, like breadfruit. Whatever the fruits are, they drink dry, and are suspended in a crisp, clean wine that finishes with just a trace of bitterness. **87** —S.H. (5/1/2002)

Lolonis 1997 Merlot (Redwood Valley) $21. 85 —S.H. (3/1/2000)

Lolonis 2001 Merlot (Redwood Valley) $22. They say the 24-hour temperature shift in this Mendocino appellation swings by a huge amount. In this case, the hot daytime has yielded raisiny flavors, while the cool nighttimes provide the crisp acidity needed for balance. The result is interesting. **85** —S.H. (6/1/2004)

Lolonis 2002 Heritage Vineyards Petros Merlot (Redwood Valley) $40. Opens with the baked brown sugar, caramelly aroma of a Port-style wine, and tastes almost as sweet. This is actually a delicious wine, with good tannins and acids to balance the sugar, but it's not really a dry table wine. **85** —S.H. (12/15/2006)

Lolonis 2001 Petros Heritage Vineyards Merlot (Redwood Valley) $65. Shows real finesse in the rich balance of fruit, oak, acidity, and tannins, and while it's complex, it's also an easy drink. Soft in texture, with sweet tannins, this wine flatters with black currant and cherry flavors. **90** — S.H. (10/1/2004)

Lolonis 1999 Private Reserve Merlot (Redwood Valley) $28. A nice Merlot that drinks rich and satisfying. Notable for the smooth, lush texture, like velvet on the palate, and carrying plum and blackberry flavors. This is a fancy, versatile table wine that could use just an extra edge of depth and complexity. **88** —S.H. (8/1/2003)

Lolonis 1998 Private Reserve Merlot (Redwood Valley) $28. Smells ripe and juicy, with piquant black-cherry marmalade aromas complexed with smoky oak. Tastes fruity, too, and the berry flavors are deep and impressive. The wine is dry, with good acidity, and very clean. It's easy to drink, although it seems a bit overpriced. **82** —S.H. (5/1/2002)

Lolonis 1997 Private Reserve Merlot (Redwood Valley) $28. There's a slightly meaty edge to this wine that may put some people off, but in our view it's simply another layer of complexity, gently spread on top of smoke, cedar, dark chocolate, and maple syrup. Full and creamy, with a long, toasty finish that's prolonged by juicy acids. **88** (6/1/2001)

Lolonis 2000 Petros Merlot-Syrah (Redwood Valley) $70. Pours dark and has closed, earthy aromas with a suggestion of blackberries and toast. This is a very dry, young wine, filled with acids and tannins, with a core of berry fruit. A blend of Merlot and Syrah. **84** —S.H. (5/1/2004)

Lolonis 1996 Orpheus Private Reserve Petite Sirah (Redwood Valley) $20. 89 —M.S. (3/1/2000)

Lolonis 1999 Orpheus-Private Reserve Petite Sirah (Redwood Valley) $35. Tasters jumped on this wine for a variety of flaws ranging from overt sweetness to volatile acidity and a lack of harmony between oak and fruit. It's okay- drinking stuff, with decent flavors. Might improve with a few years of cellaring. **84** (4/1/2003)

Lolonis NV Ladybug Red Cuvée III Red Blend (Redwood Valley) $13. Straddles the fine line between a rustic country-style red and a refined wine. Full-bodied and fairly tannic, with cherry-berry flavors. **85** —S.H. (12/15/2004)

Lolonis 2001 Ladybug Red Old Vines Red Wine Red Blend (Redwood Valley) $13. An enjoyable country wine. It's fruity, dry, and full-bodied, with the simple pleasures a well-made wine brings. **85** —S.H. (6/1/2004)

Lolonis 2000 Old Vines Ladybug Red Blend (Redwood Valley) $12. Intricately detailed, with flavors of blackberries, cassis, cherries, herbs, chocolate, and coffee wrapped in ripely soft tannins. This full-bodied, dry wine is a value in a field blend of Carignane, Merlot, Napa Gamay, and Zinfandel. **87** —S.H. (5/1/2004)

Lolonis NV Old Vines Ladybug Red Cuvée V Red Blend (Redwood Valley) $13. An honest country effort, dry, rugged and fruity. It has some tough

USA

tannins, so drink it with something that has lots of cheese, olive oil or natural meaty fats. **83** —*S.H. (3/1/2006)*

Lolonis 1998 Petros Red Blend (Redwood Valley) $70. A complex red wine that drinks softly fruity and dry, and with quite a bit of style and elegance. The most notable feature is the texture. It's velvety and round, and characterized by soft, dusty tannins. In this environment, fruit, and berry flavors can shine. It's made in the international style: Soft, ripely sweet, extracted, and fruity, and well-oaked. A blend of Merlot, Cabernet, and Petite Sirah. **90** —*S.H. (5/1/2002)*

Lolonis 2002 Eugenia Late Harvest Heritage Vineyard Sauvignon Blanc (Redwood Valley) $32. A very sweet wine, rich in vanilla and spice, with long, deep flavors of apricot jam, peach pie, and a finish of white chocolate-infused coffee. It's a delicious dessert wine. **90** —*S.H. (2/1/2006)*

Lolonis 1998 Fumé Blanc Sauvignon Blanc (Redwood Valley) $12. **86** — *S.H. (5/1/2000)*

Lolonis 2002 Winegrower Selection Syrah (Redwood Valley) $32. I like the underlying wine here. It's rich in cassis and mocha fruit, and has excellently firm tannins and balancing acidity. On the downside, I find the wine overoaked. **86** —*S.H. (12/1/2005)*

Lolonis 1997 Zinfandel (Redwood Valley) $20. 87 —*J.C. (5/1/2000)*

Lolonis 2003 Zinfandel (Redwood Valley) $20. This Zin wine is so ripe, the fruit tastes cooked, like the goo that oozes out from an oven-baked cherry or raspberry pie. There are also chocolate fudge notes, with a cassis finish. It's pretty exotic, but dry. **85** —*S.H. (12/1/2005)*

Lolonis 2002 Zinfandel (Redwood Valley) $18. Dry and full-bodied, with a brambly, wild forest personaility that shows cherry and pepper flavors and a robust mouthfeel. So rich in fruit, it asks for foods equally powerful. **84** —*S.H. (8/1/2005)*

Lolonis 2001 Zinfandel (Redwood Valley) $18. A pleasing, floral style of wine that serves up velvety tannins to support a fine array of tea, blackcherry, toast, vanilla, plum, spice, and herb notes. Chocolatey on the finish, which is long and appealing. **90 Editors' Choice** *(11/1/2003)*

Lolonis 2000 Zinfandel (Redwood Valley) $18. Here's a muscular superhero of a Zin that packs a punch with its big, bold, briary flavors of wild berries. There's also a strong earthiness reminiscent of sweet golden tobacco. Very dry, with smooth tannins and a heady, slightly hot finish due to 14.7% alcohol. **87** —*S.H. (9/1/2003)*

Lolonis 1999 Zinfandel (Redwood Valley) $20. This appellation has some of the older Zin vines left, and those half-century specimens produced this baby. It has telltale briar and pepper flavors and is very dry, but is overly soft, with a medicinal, cough-mediciney finish. **84** —*S.H. (5/1/2002)*

Lolonis 1998 Zinfandel (Redwood Valley) $20. Sweet, spicy fruit, with nicely matched toasty oak framing it. Everything balances out; this actually has the best balance and most seductive fruit of the three Lolonis bottlings, and certainly represents the best value. **88** —*P.G. (3/1/2001)*

Lolonis 1999 Beaucage Vineyard Zinfandel (Redwood Valley) $30. Some people will like this, but it's a lesson in what not to do with Zinfandel, especially from old vines. It's overly soft and too sweet, which makes it unbalanced. You can't appreciate the fine inherent flavors of the grapes. This is a Zin that would benefit from being drier, and more alcoholic. **83** —*S.H. (5/1/2002)*

Lolonis 2003 Late Harvest Zinfandel Port Zinfandel (Redwood Valley) $32. Only 150 cases were produced of this wine. It's a lovely sipper, rich and sweet in cassis, coffee, and chocolate flavors that are wrapped in smooth, velvety tannins. The fruity sweetness really kicks in mid-palate and lasts through a decadant finish. **92** —*S.H. (5/1/2006)*

Lolonis 1998 Private Reserve Zinfandel (Redwood Valley) $30. Chocolate, nut and stewed fruit aromas lead to a mute palate, with reticent blackberry and plum flavors. Flavors peek out more on the finish—oak, blackberry and bitter green herb. It might have been more interesting if the flavors had shown up earlier. **82** —*D.T. (3/1/2002)*

Lolonis 1996 Private Reserve Zinfandel (Redwood Valley) $25. 88 —*J.C. (9/1/1999)*

Lolonis 2000 Tollini Vineyard Zinfandel (Redwood Valley) $32. A bit hot in the nose, but the flavors are pleasant and mild. It features pretty but simple cherry notes at the fore. Cedar, spice, and herbs follow suit. Tannis are a bit astringent, while the wine finishes with moderate zip and a toasty edge. **86** —*J.M. (9/1/2003)*

Lolonis 1998 Tollini Vineyard Zinfandel (Redwood Valley) $28. A lot of wood, still pretty rough, surrounds a thick, tannic, muscular, ripe, rustic, Old World-style Zin. There's nothing elegant about this wine, but it packs a lot of flavor into a sturdy frame. **87** —*P.G. (3/1/2001)*

Lolonis 2001 Winegrower Selection Zinfandel (Redwood Valley) $32. This appellation has made a reputation for Zins of this type. It's very ripe, almost raisiny, yet stays dry. Has all those warm Zin flavors of blackberry pudding, spicy plums, chocolate fudge, and espresso, yet it's dry and balanced. **87** —*S.H. (6/1/2004)*

Lolonis 2002 Winegrowers Selection Tollini Vineyard Zinfandel (Redwood Valley) $32. Clearly huge in fruit, this big wine startles with blackberry, cherry, raspberry, and cocoa flavors. If it was any riper it would have residual sugar, but it's dry. It's also rather rustic in the way the tannins and briary texture stick out, but it's a classic California Zin. **86** —*S.H. (8/1/2005)*

LONDER

Londer 2003 Kent Ritchie Vineyard Chardonnay (Sonoma Coast) $36. High acidity combines with extreme spiciness to make this wine exceedingly prickly on the palate. Thankfully it's filled with yummy flavors of pineapple custard, butterscotch, caramel, and toast, and has a rich, creamy texture. Fabulous with lobster. **90** —*S.H. (8/1/2005)*

Londer 2002 Kent Ritchie Vineyard Chardonnay (Sonoma Coast) $35. Fascinating wine, with a cool edge of minerally acidity that teases the palate with intense green apple and ripe peach flavors, and a lavish overlay of what tastes like new French oak. It all comes together in this fine, plush Chardonnay. **90** —*S.H. (6/1/2004)*

Londer 2003 Dry Gewürztraminer (Anderson Valley) $20. A very nice Gewurz that showcases how well it does in this AVA. Bright and crisp in acidity, with perky, fresh flavors of green papaya, citrus, and dusty spices. Will play nicely off fish or pork topped with fruity salsas. **86** —*S.H. (3/1/2005)*

Londer 2002 Dry Gewürztraminer (Anderson Valley) $20. Has aromas and flavors of a wide array of fruits, spices, and wildflowers. It has very svelte acidity and is fully dry, but could use more concentration. **85** —*S.H. (6/1/2004)*

Londer 2004 Pinot Noir (Anderson Valley) $30. Simple and varietally true, this soft Pinot has a silky texture, with very ripe, forward cherry, cola, spice and oak flavors. It's fairly full and heavy for a Pinot. **84** —*S.H. (11/1/2006)*

Londer 2002 Pinot Noir (Anderson Valley) $28. Light-bodied, silky, and airy, this gentle Pinot nonetheless has complex flavors. Tea, cola, cherries, gingerbread, spice, vanilla, and smoky oak mingle together through the long finish. **87** —*S.H. (2/1/2005)*

Londer 2001 Pinot Noir (Anderson Valley) $28. A rather lean wine that tries to find charm, but can't quite overcome the acidity and tannins. There's not a whole lot of fruit, but the cola and coffee flavors should perk up against a rich, marbled steak. **85** —*S.H. (6/1/2004)*

Londer 2004 Keefer Ranch Pinot Noir (Green Valley) $42. Keefer Ranch has been the source of great Pinots from Failla, Flowers, Tandem, and others. This bottling is enormously ripe and forward in vanilla-accented cherry pie filling, cola and root beer flavors, with a good amount of toasty oak. It's a bit soft and sweet. **86** —*S.H. (11/1/2006)*

Londer 2004 Londer Estate Grown Pinot Noir (Anderson Valley) $46. There's enormously ripe, pure fruit in this Pinot. It floods the palate with red cherry pie, cola, root beer and spice flavors that are undeniably delicious. Yet the wine is too soft and jammily extracted to be balanced. **85** —*S.H. (11/1/2006)*

Londer 2004 Paraboll Pinot Noir (Anderson Valley) $52. This is the winery's reserve blend, and the first thing you notice is the oak that leaps out on the first scent. The wine handles it easily, though, with enormously ripe, deep cherry pie, pomegranate, rhubarb, cola, and spice flavors. It's a bit soft and obvious, but very tasty. **89** —*S.H. (11/1/2006)*

Londer 2002 Paraboll Pinot Noir (Anderson Valley) $45. Like Londer's regular Pinot, this two-vineyard blend is light in body and silky. It's also lusher, with a dense core of cherry, cola, rhubarb tea, and spice flavors. It's a little flabby, but makes up for it in delicacy. **88** —*S.H. (2/1/2005)*

Londer 2001 Paraboll Pinot Noir (Anderson Valley) $42. Lean and herbal, with an Heirloom tomato edge, although there are hints of black-cherry. The spareness only accentuates the acidity and tannins. A generous dollop of oak adds notes of smoke and vanilla. There's an angular elegance, though, and the wine may develop complexities in the bottle. **86** —*S.H. (6/1/2004)*

Londer 2001 Van Der Kamp Vineyard Pinot Noir (Sonoma Mountain) $35. A well-made Pinot from a rather obscure appellation, this wine is very dry and earthy, with flavors of sage and black-cherries. The dryness follows through the finish, which is quite acidic, suggesting rich fare. **88** —*S.H. (6/1/2004)*

LONE CANARY

Lone Canary NV Red Bordeaux Blend (Yakima Valley) $13. A blend of Cab, Merlot, and Syrah, this forward, tasty effort charms with cherries and grapes, then surprises with a solid center core of plump cassis and raspberries, gently leading into a fruit-driven finish. A lot of bang for the buck. **88 Best Buy** —*P.G. (9/1/2004)*

Lone Canary 2003 Rouge Bordeaux Blend (Columbia Valley (WA)) $20. This complements the winery's "Rosso" and "Red" blends; it's the Bordeaux blend in the trio. The color is a bit murky, and the flavors, though pleasant enough, have a certain murkiness also, mixing earth, toast, hazelnut, some indistinct red fruits, and a finishing lick of raspberry preserves. It's a good, all-purpose quaffing wine, but doesn't quite conjure up Bordeaux. **87** —*P.G. (6/1/2006)*

Lone Canary 2002 Rouge Bordeaux Blend (Yakima Valley) $20. Lone Canary does a Red, a Rosso and this Rouge, a classic Bordeaux blend of two Cabs and Merlot. Winemaker Mike Scott shows his European leanings, keeping alcohol levels in check (13.5%) and emphasizing balance and nuance over sheer power. The wine displays some of the herbal nuances and delicate oak influences lost in jammier efforts, but pushes through a long, intriguing finish. **89** —*P.G. (9/1/2004)*

Lone Canary NV Red Red Blend (Yakima Valley) $13. This blend of 68% Cabernet Sauvignon, 23% Merlot, and 9% Syrah is pleasant, accessible and light. Forward fruit, tasting a bit like a young Beaujolais, finishes with a tangy, lively snap. Simple and ready right now. **85** —*P.G. (12/31/2003)*

Lone Canary 2003 Rosso Red Blend (Columbia Valley (WA)) $15. This is 78% Sangiovese; the rest a blend of Merlot and Cabernet Sauvignon. Delicious, round, warm, soft, and nicely touched with leafy, herbal, tobacco-flavored fruit. Unlike most domestic Sangiovese, this very much recalls the soft, leafy flavors of Chianti. The finish has just a bit more heat and tannin, but compensates with distinctly varietal flavors. **89** —*P.G. (4/1/2006)*

Lone Canary 2002 Rosso Red Blend (Yakima Valley) $17. Lone Canary's Rosso is a nod to the super Tuscan style. Sangiovese dominates the blend, bringing tart cherry and plum flavors to the front. Lean and tangy, it's nicely balanced with some interesting flavors: nutmeg, vanilla bean and a hint of leather. **88** —*P.G. (9/1/2004)*

Lone Canary 2005 Sauvignon Blanc (Yakima Valley) $10. Quite young, grassy, and pungent, this has piercingly tart flavors of green berries and lime, much in the New Zealand mode, though not quite as ripe. Some light, appropriate, citrus rind bitterness creeps into the finish. **88 Best Buy** —*P.G. (6/1/2006)*

Lone Canary 2003 Sauvignon Blanc (Yakima Valley) $10. The second vintage from Lone Canary follows right in the footsteps of the '02, with juicy, plump, tangy fruit front and center. Ripe with sweet grapefruit, pineapple, and citrus, it retains enough acid to keep it lively through the finish. **88 Best Buy** —*P.G. (9/1/2004)*

Lone Canary 2002 Sauvignon Blanc (Yakima Valley) $10. Winemaker Mike Scott left Caterina to start Lone Canary. The first release is a sharp,

melony, oyster-friendly Sauv Blanc, steely and refreshing. **88 Best Buy** —*P.G. (12/31/2003)*

LONETREE

Lonetree 1997 Sangiovese (Mendocino) $17. **89** —*S.H. (9/1/2000)*

Lonetree 1998 Syrah (Mendocino County) $20. Earthy, plummy, peppery and bacon-fat aromas start things off. Juicy in the mouth, with rich, jammy berry flavors and a hit of palate-numbing tannins. Drink now with rich foods, or hold for a few years. **85** —*S.H. (11/15/2001)*

Lonetree 1998 Eaglepoint Ranch Syrah (Mendocino) $20. Features berry fruit and toasty oak—with the sexy oak taking the lead. Powdered cinnamon, vanilla extract, and bittersweet chocolate—is this a list of wine descriptors or a dessert recipe? Finishes tart and dry, bringing the oak back under control. **87** *(10/1/2001)*

Lonetree 1997 Eaglepoint Ranch Syrah (Mendocino County) $19. **91** *(5/1/2000)*

Lonetree 1996 Zinfandel (Mendocino) $16. **88** —*S.H. (5/1/2000)*

LONG

Long 1998 Seghesio Vineyard Sangiovese (Sonoma County) $25. **90** —*S.H. (12/15/1999)*

LONG MEADOW RANCH

Long Meadow Ranch 1997 Cabernet Sauvignon (Napa Valley) $50. **90** *(11/1/2000)*

Long Meadow Ranch 1996 Cabernet Sauvignon (Napa Valley) $59. **92** —*M.S. (12/31/1999)*

Long Meadow Ranch 2001 Cabernet Sauvignon (Napa Valley) $55. A very fine wine that showcases Napa's rich, ripe tannins and perfectly ripened cassis fruit flavors. Oak, of course, brings vanilla, smoke, and additional sweetness. Not for the long haul, so best now for a few years. **90** —*S.H. (5/1/2005)*

Long Meadow Ranch 1999 Cabernet Sauvignon (Napa Valley) $60. Dark, heady, and tannic—that pretty much describes this latest release from winemaker Cathy Corison. It's also very French-oaky, packed with smoke and vanilla. In other words, a young wine meant for aging. Seems to have the balance and richness to improve through 2009. **91** —*S.H. (11/15/2002)*

Long Meadow Ranch 1998 Cabernet Sauvignon (Napa Valley) $57. From a single vineyard 1,700 feet in the Mayacamas. It's a bit tough and tannic now, raising the question of whether it has the fruit to soften with age. There are some pretty cherry-berry flavors, but there's a lot of sage and oregano, too. It's obviously well-crafted and with a good pedigree, but not an ager. **87** —*S.H. (11/15/2002)*

LONG RIDGE GROVE VINEYARDS

Long Ridge Grove Vineyards 2001 Cabernet Sauvignon (Central Coast) $10. Rough, rugged, and a bit sour, marked by sharp acids and a vegetal taste. Avoid. **81** —*S.H. (6/1/2004)*

Long Ridge Grove Vineyards 2002 Chardonnay (California) $10. From the vast sea of statewide Chardonnay out there comes this perfectly acceptable wine. It has peach and apple flavors and some oak, and is creamy and dry. **84** —*S.H. (6/1/2004)*

Long Ridge Grove Vineyards 2001 Merlot (Central Coast) $10. Earthy and vigorous, a young wine marked by sharp acids and some vigorous tannins. The dry mouthfeel offers little in the way of fruit. **83** —*S.H. (6/1/2004)*

LONG VINEYARDS

Long Vineyards 1998 Cabernet Sauvignon (Napa Valley) $60. Rich, spicy, plum, anise, chocolate, black currant, herb and distinctive mint notes weave a complex web of flavor in this firm, focused Cabernet. Smooth, plush tannins frame the ensemble, which finishes—like the label says—long. **92** —*J.M. (12/1/2001)*

Long Vineyards 1998 Chardonnay (Napa Valley) $40. Rich, ripe fig, and toast aromas up front are backed by classy pear, melon, citrus, and mineral notes. The wine is well balanced and full-bodied, yet refreshing and quite elegant. Grown high in the hills above Rutherford. **93 Cellar Selection** —*J.M. (12/1/2001)*

Long Vineyards 2002 Laird Family Vineyard Pinot Grigio (Carneros) $18. A tasty, easy wine that brims with spearmint chewing gum and sweet grapefruit flavors that veer into riper tropical fruits. It's crisp in acidity, with a good structure. Versatile at the table, and a great apéritif drink. **86** —*S.H. (2/1/2004)*

Long Vineyards 2000 Laird Family Vineyard Pinot Grigio (Carneros) $20. Bright, textured, and crisp, with zingy lemon flavors and a flinty mineral edge. A classy, refreshing white wine that is long and clean on the finish. **88** —*J.M. (11/15/2001)*

Long Vineyards 1999 Seghesio Vineyards Sangiovese (Sonoma County) $25. Fairly tight at first, but showing pretty cherry and herb flavors at it's core. The wine will probably open and soften within a year. Delicate on the palate with a moderate finish. **85** —*J.M. (12/1/2001)*

LONGBOARD

Longboard 2003 Redgrav Vineyard Cabernet Sauvignon (Alexander Valley) $50. Soft and juicy, with extremely ripe fruit that's almost jammy, this 100% Cabernet is complex and interesting. It immediately flatters with upfront blackberry tea, a honeyed cherry liqueur taste, and plenty of toasty oak, then pulls back and shows a deeper, earthier side. Drink now–2010. **89** —*S.H. (12/15/2006)*

Longboard 2003 Rochioli Vineyard Cabernet Sauvignon (Russian River Valley) $50. World-famous Rochioli doesn't want to use their own Cabernet grapes, so they sell them to former J Wine Co. winemaker Oded Shakked, who carefully crafts this dry, full-bodied 100% Cabernet. It's young, acidic, and tannic, but with its polished core of cherries, should ease well into the next decade. **88** —*S.H. (12/15/2006)*

Longboard 2001 Rochioli Vineyard Cabernet Sauvignon (Russian River Valley) $42. Another polished, succulent release from a vineyard that's not supposed to be warm enough to ripen Cabernet. Of course, the vintage was very good, and this effort shows upfront black currant and leather flavors, with a long, fruity finish. It's generously oaked, and really excellent. **90** —*S.H. (11/15/2003)*

Longboard 1999 Rochioli Vineyard Cabernet Sauvignon (Russian River Valley) $50. Cool-climate grapes from this famed vineyard yielded a tannic wine that shows enormous promise. Brims with peppery, cedar, and cassis aromas and flavors. Bone-dry and austere now, but the solid core of chewy fruit suggests prime aging potential, reminiscent of a young Pauillac. The winemaker, Oded Shakked, is the longtime winemaker at J Wine Co. **93 Editors' Choice** —*S.H. (11/15/2002)*

Longboard 2005 Sauvignon Blanc (Russian River Valley) $24. This refreshing wine has that extra something that pushes it to the next level. Shows deliciously ripe lime, lemon, and sweet grass flavors that show little oak influence, letting the fruit and spice shine. Without malo, the wine is sprightly in mouth-cleansing acidity. **89** —*S.H. (12/15/2006)*

Longboard 2003 Syrah (Russian River Valley) $32. Both of the Longboard Syrahs have a similar pine-resiny quality to their aromas, but this one also boasts luscious blackberries, spice and meaty elements. Supple tannins and a lengthy finish elevate this wine well above the ordinary. **88** *(9/1/2005)*

Longboard 2003 Syrah (Russian River Valley) $32. A bit on the simple side, but likeable for its cherry pie filling, blackberry jam, cola, and spicy coffee fruit that fill the mouth with flavor. Thoroughly dry, the wine is elegantly smooth and balanced. Drink now. **86** —*S.H. (12/15/2006)*

Longboard 2002 Syrah (Russian River Valley) $33. Dark, big, and rich, and very fine. Starts off with elaborate and inviting aromas of smoky oak, blackberries, cocoa, coffee, and spice, and turns super-rich in the mouth, offering oodles of ripe, berry fruit and oak. Dry, with soft, lush tannins and complex, it's a beauty. **91** —*S.H. (12/31/2004)*

Longboard 2001 Syrah (Russian River Valley) $29. Israeli-born winemaker Oded Shakked has specialized in cool-climate Syrah and his passion shows in this evocative wine. It is clearly modeled on the wines of the Northern Rhône, with its peppery aroma, cherry flavors, and thick tannins. **87** —*S.H. (2/1/2004)*

Longboard 2000 Syrah (Russian River Valley) $29. Oded Shakked is the winemaker at J and this is his own label. Wth this wine he shows he likes the peppery Syrahs of the Northern Rhône. The flavors are as good as anything you'll find in California, with plums and white pepper and a just-right overlay of oak. The acidity this vintage is a little too soft, but the elegance almost makes you not notice. **91** —*S.H. (12/1/2002)*

Longboard 1999 Syrah (Russian River Valley) $27. A very fine, young wine that would be a dead ringer for a good Northern Rhône red except for the rather soft acids. Brilliant fruit straddles the borderline between ripe blackberry fruit and drier pepper, sage and tobacco. Upfront tannins pack a punch. Best to let it rest through 2003. A brand to watch. **90** —*S.H. (12/1/2002)*

Longboard 2002 Dakine Syrah (Russian River Valley) $47. Interesting to contrast this to Longboard's regular Syrah [below]. This single-vineyard bottling is darker and considerably more tannic, although the aromatics and flavors are similar. It's elaborately oaked, and too astringent to enjoy now. The regular is the wine to drink in the next few years. Try after 2008. **90** —*S.H. (12/31/2004)*

Longboard 2003 Dakine Vineyard Syrah (Russian River Valley) $45. Owner/winemaker Oded Shakked was until recently the longtime winemaker at J Wine Co. Now he's doing his own thing, and this is his personal vineyard, in prime Pinot Noir country along Westside Road. The wine is softly opulent in blueberry, blackberry, and coffee flavors, with a melted chocolate richness balanced by rich, ripe tannins. Drink now. **90** —*S.H. (12/15/2006)*

Longboard 2003 Dakine Vineyard Syrah (Russian River Valley) $47. Noticeably piny or resinous in both aroma and flavors, but otherwise solid, with bright cherry flavors, decent concentration and a long finish. **85** *(9/1/2005)*

LONGFELLOW

Longfellow 2002 Cabernet Sauvignon (Napa Valley) $50. Last year's Cab was lean and funky. This year, it's too sweet. They kept the alcohol to 14.6%, but the wine tastes like it has residual sugar, with overtly sweet blackberry and cherry pie filling flavors. **83** —*S.H. (9/1/2006)*

Longfellow 2001 Cabernet Sauvignon (Napa Valley) $50. A bit funky in smell and rough in texture, with herbal and berry flavors. Lots of tannins, not much fruit. **83** —*S.H. (5/1/2005)*

Longfellow 2003 Pinot Noir (Sonoma Coast) $35. Located on the southern edge of the appellation, practically within sight of the office towers of San Francisco, this wine has very ripe fruit. The baked cherry pie filling flavor is a little one-dimensional, but it's a delicious dimension. Finishes nicely dry and spicy. **87** —*S.H. (11/1/2006)*

Longfellow 2002 Pinot Noir (Sonoma Coast) $35. Shows real complexity in the array of cola, rhubarb pie, raspberry, red cherry, sweet tobacco, and spicy flavors, with an overlay of toasty oak. Delicate and silky mouthfeel with a long, intensely fruity finish. **90** —*S.H. (5/1/2005)*

Longfellow 2001 Pinot Noir (Los Carneros) $36. A spicy rich wine, packed with bing cherry, raspberry, toast, menthol, and herb flavors. It's got good, but moderate length on the finish, backed by supple tannins and a bit of a licorice edge at the end. **89** —*J.C. (3/1/2004)*

Longfellow 2003 Syrah (Dry Creek Valley) $32. Just delicious, a really fine Syrah notable for its balance and complexity. Dry and smoky, it has plum, blackberry, and coffee flavors, with a streak of sweet anise and leather. Doesn't say so on the label, but the grapes came from the Unti Vineyard. The tannins are rich and thick, but this wine is best in its flashy youth. **93 Editors' Choice** —*S.H. (11/1/2006)*

Longfellow 2002 Syrah (Dry Creek Valley) $32. You'll find ripe blackberry, coffee, and anise flavors in this very dry wine, and also a richly earthy streak that suggests humus and dried autumn leaves. It's smooth and supple, with good length. Distinctive and interesting. **89** —*S.H. (5/1/2005)*

Longfellow 2001 Syrah (Dry Creek Valley) $29. Opens with pretty strong notes of freshly ground white pepper, but turns lusciously fruity in the mouth, with cherry-berry flavors. The tannins are gritty and firm, leaving a dry, slightly scouring finish. A rack of lamb would be the perfect accompaniment. **87** —*S.H. (2/1/2004)*

USA

LONGORIA

Longoria 2005 Clover Creek Vineyard Albariño (Santa Ynez Valley) $26. Granted, there haven't been that many, but this is the best California Albariño I've had. A wonderful wine, crisply acidic, and deeply flavored. Candied citrus zest, peach pie, pink grapefruit, buttery honeysuckle, apricot, nectarine, and no oak because it doesn't need any. A spectacular food wine or just cocktail. Shows the promise of this variety in the right climate. **93 Editors' Choice** —*S.H. (12/15/2006)*

Longoria 2000 Evidence Bordeaux Blend (Santa Barbara County) $35. This Bordeaux blend has some good flavors of black currants, tobacco, and herbs, and has rich, soft tannins and a good grip on the palate. It is very dry, and has layers of complexity. It is a step in the right direction for a region that has been dissed for Cabernet. **89** —*S.H. (11/15/2003)*

Longoria 2003 Evidence Red Wine Bordeaux Blend (Santa Barbara County) $42. Known for his Pinots and Chards, Rick Longoria tried hard with this red, even though Santa Barbara has struggled with Bordeaux. Wisely, Longoria bases the wine on Cabernet Franc and Merlot, which do better in cooler climates than Cabernet Sauvignon. The wine is fine, rich, and promising. **87** —*S.H. (12/15/2006)*

Longoria 2000 Blues Cuvée Cabernet Franc (Santa Ynez Valley) $25. Astringent and herbal, a taut wine marked by tobacco, oregano, and mint notes. But it's not without its charms. Bone dry, with thick, gentle tannins and pronounced acidity, it nonetheless has a taste and individuality that make it interesting. **87** —*S.H. (6/1/2003)*

Longoria 2001 Chardonnay (Santa Rita Hills) $25. Brilliantly flamboyant grapes went into this wine, to judge from the results. Has huge, massive flavors ranging from the ripest pears to succulent tropical fruits. The wine is big enough to support the extensive lees and new oak. **92 Editors' Choice** —*S.H. (12/15/2003)*

Longoria 2000 Clos Pepe Vineyard Chardonnay (Santa Barbara) $32. The winemaker did not let the grapes hang long and get superripe. He picked when the citrusy, appley notes were just beginning to veer into white peach, and so preserved intense acidity. Lees is notable, oak less so, but both are seamless. The result is interesting and balanced—you might even call it Chablisian. **90** —*S.H. (12/15/2002)*

Longoria 2002 Cuvée Diana Chardonnay (Santa Rita Hills) $32. Combines just the right amount of fresh acidity, ripe fruits, and spices, and smoky oak to produce a balanced, delicious wine. Packed with powerful tropical fruits, cinnamon, vanilla, toast, even a white chocolate richness on the finish. **92** —*S.H. (2/1/2005)*

Longoria 2004 Cuvée Diana Chardonnay (Sta. Rita Hills) $36. Don't look for fat, buttery stuff here. This wine is as streamlined as a steel girder. With high acidity and a firm minerality, it hits the palate clean and spicy. But once it warms up, wham! Exotic kiwis, limes, and mangoes take over as well as the buttercream effects of barrel fermentation. Fantastic concentration, and probably good for a decade. **93** —*S.H. (11/15/2006)*

Longoria 1999 Huber Vineyard Chardonnay (Santa Ynez Valley) $32. This wine cuts a racy Chablis-like profile. Green apple and lemon-lime fruit, mild spices and a dry earthiness are all in play here. They ride on brisk acidity through a tart and minerally finish. A thoroughbred wine that, to some, "lacks stuffing." **86** *(7/1/2001)*

Longoria 2000 Mt. Carmel Vineyard Chardonnay (Santa Barbara County) $36. Riper and richer than Longoria's Clos Pepe bottling, but strikes most of the same notes. Lees coat the mouth with sour (in the good sense) flavors, riding over intensely spicy apples and lemons. The wine is dry and acidic, but paradoxically, rich and layered. Don't drink it too cold. Try aging it. **92** —*S.H. (12/15/2002)*

Longoria 1999 Mt. Carmel Vineyard Chardonnay (Santa Ynez Valley) $60. The complex smoke, earth, spice, and mineral aromas that open this wine are followed by subdued tangerine and citrus flavors, dried spice, and mineral accents on an oaky frame. Like the other Mt. Carmel Vineyard offerings, this is a bit tight now but has a promising, good balance. Not a fruit-driven wine, this finishes long with spice and mineral elements. Only 86 cases produced. **88** *(7/1/2001)*

Longoria 1998 Sanford & Benedict Vineyard Chardonnay (Santa Ynez Valley) $28. 88 *(6/1/2000)*

Longoria 1998 Santa Rita Cuvée Chardonnay (Santa Ynez Valley) $25. 87 *(6/1/2000)*

Longoria 1997 Santa Rita Cuvée Chardonnay (Santa Ynez Valley) $25. 89 —*S.H. (7/1/1999)*

Longoria 2000 Santa Rita Hills Chardonnay (Santa Barbara County) $25. Longtime vintner Rich Longoria has crafted an intensely flavored wine whose tastes are exotic, even eccentric. Bosc pears dominate, with their spicy, nutty flavors, augmented by rich oak and the creamy mouthfeel from lees. It's a big, thick wine with good acidity. **92** —*S.H. (9/1/2002)*

Longoria 2004 Alisos Vineyard Grenache (Santa Barbara County) $22. What a pretty wine. It's not complex or anything, just straightforward in cherry, mocha, and violet flavors touched by smoky oak. The texture is soft and voluptuous. **87** —*S.H. (12/15/2006)*

Longoria 1996 Merlot (Santa Ynez Valley) $23. 89 —*S.H. (9/1/1999)*

Longoria 1999 Merlot (Santa Barbara County) $28. Good, dark color, and opens with intriguing aromas ranging from fresh blackberries through coffee, pepper, spiced plums, and herbs. Smooth drinking, but with pronounced tannins and crisp acids. Will benefit from mid-term cellaring, and should be very nice by 2004. **87** —*S.H. (4/1/2003)*

Longoria 1998 Merlot (Santa Barbara County) $28. Roasted coffee aromas are tinged with cedar and cassis, but this is not a fruity wine by any measure. Instead, the focus is on damp earth and humus; the fruit and coffee notes are accents to the earthy whole. Tannins are firm and may outlast the modest fruit, so drink soon for its unconventional charm. **85** —*J.C. (6/1/2001)*

Longoria 2005 Pinot Grigio (Santa Barbara County) $19. The aim here is an unoaked, brisk white wine, and that's exactly what this is. Don't look for nuance. It's an easy sipper that's citrusy and spicy, the kind of wine to toss back with cioppino, broiled halibut or just a simple salad. **85** —*S.H. (12/1/2006)*

Longoria 2004 Pinot Grigio (Santa Barbara County) $19. There's little or no oak on this wine, allowing the pure citrus and fig flavors to shine through. There's a tart, tingly mouthfeel in this dry, fruit-forward, easy PG. **84** —*S.H. (2/1/2006)*

Longoria 2002 Pinot Grigio (Santa Barbara County) $18. As vintners sort out their styles for this increasingly popular varietal, Rick Longoria settles for a cool-climate interpretation. It is Bauhaus-lean and dry in texture and structure, with flowery, lemony flavors and bright acidity, but that does not fully describe its considerable appeal. **88** —*S.H. (12/1/2003)*

Longoria 2003 Bien Nacido Vineyard Pinot Noir (Santa Maria Valley) $42. What an awesomely complex, deep Pinot. It shows ripe berry fruit flavors, but what's so rewarding is the earthy, mushroomy, slightly decadent quality that grounds the wine and gives it depth and soulful interest. That's not to undermine the fabulous black and red stone fruit. Drink now through 2010. **94 Editors' Choice** —*S.H. (8/1/2006)*

Longoria 2002 Bien Nacido Vineyard Pinot Noir (Santa Maria Valley) $NA. Smells pruny and raisiny, suggesting overripeness, and has tea and cherry flavors, but is soft in acidity and almost flat. One taster found it disjointed; another called it syrupy. **84** *(11/1/2004)*

Longoria 2001 Bien Nacido Vineyard Pinot Noir (Santa Maria Valley) $36. A curious wine. On the plus side is a tantalizingly tasty flavor, like fully-ripened raspberries and cherries crushed into a delicious nectar, then sprinkled with honey and white pepper. A good overlay of toasty oak adds richness. Yet there's a syrupy sweetness, like cough medicine, that detracts. **85** —*S.H. (7/1/2003)*

Longoria 1999 Bien Nacido Vineyard Pinot Noir (Santa Maria Valley) $36. Smoky and properly herbal aromas set the stage for an equally smoky palate that features plenty of ripe red fruit. This wine toes the all-important line of balance perfectly. It's thin and racy enough to seem fresh, but there's ample body weight to satisfy those who like a real mouthful from their Pinot Noirs. **89** *(10/1/2002)*

Longoria 2004 Fe Ciega Vineyard Pinot Noir (Sta. Rita Hills) $43. Firm in acids, with some tannins, yet not at all hard. This is a magnificent, masculine Pinot Noir. It floods the palate with cherry pie, cola, and mocha flavors, Asian spices, and a sweet, smoky, buttery phyllo pastry quality.

USA

So technically perfect, with such structure, it seems guaranteed for the cellar. Drink now through 2010, but who knows how long it will last. **95 Editors' Choice** —*S.H. (11/15/2006)*

Longoria 2002 Fe Ciega Vineyard Pinot Noir (Santa Rita Hills) $40. Similar to Longoria's Mt. Carmel bottling, but trades a shade of opulence for greater tannins and an earthy, tobaccoey note beside the cherries, mocha, and oak. Rich and complex, with firm acids and a silky texture. Serious Pinot Noir. **91 Editors' Choice** —*S.H. (11/1/2004)*

Longoria 2001 Fe Cienaga Pinot Noir (Santa Rita Hills) $36. A gorgeous wine that impresses for its early charm, complexity, and ageability. It's delicious now, with the flavor of a black-cherry and cassis tart sprinkled with cinnamon and vanilla, wrapped in a smoky-sweet buttery pie crust. Feels super in the mouth, soft and elegant, while a trace of earthy tannins in the finish will protect it in the cellar. **94** —*S.H. (3/1/2004)*

Longoria 2004 Mt. Carmel Vineyard Pinot Noir (Santa Rita Hills) $85. Longoria makes one of the most balanced Pinots in California, combining power and charm with early drinkability. This beauty is complex in aromatic beetroot, cherry, cola, oakspice, and smoke notes, and drinks dry and supple, with fairly tight tannins. It shows brilliant structure, with a firm, silky texture and brisk acidity. It is a wholesome, completely fulfilling Pinot Noir. **96 Editors' Choice** —*S.H. (3/1/2006)*

Longoria 2002 Mt. Carmel Vineyard Pinot Noir (Santa Rita Hills) $50. A great success, a great wine that seems to epitomize this appellation. Brimming with cool-climate acidity, firm and steely in texture, but lush and seductive. The cherry, mocha, and cinnamon flavors go on forever, massive yet balanced and harmonious. **94** —*S.H. (11/1/2004)*

Longoria 2001 Mt. Carmel Vineyard Pinot Noir (Santa Rita Hills) $50. This dramatic wine is dark, young and closed. It opens with a flourish of black-cherry and currant aromas conjoined with the smoky vanillins of oak, but it hasn't all come together. Yet it impresses with its sheer flashy depth. Give this puppy a few years to knit together. It is a very, very good wine. **92** —*S.H. (10/1/2003)*

Longoria 2000 Mt. Carmel Vineyard Pinot Noir (Santa Barbara County) $50. Rich, ripe cherry-strawberry fruit is accented by leather and chocolate in this spicy, complex wine. Molasses, cinnamon, and anise nuances and a long, dark finish add to its appeal. Still tight, this should reward patience, improve over the next two years and may improve beyond its score. Try in 2004. **88** —*S.H. (10/1/2002)*

Longoria 2002 Sanford & Benedict Vineyard Pinot Noir (Santa Rita Hills) $42. Plush, oaky, and young, but clearly very fine, this Pinot exudes blackberries, cherries, smoky oak, vanilla, and spice, with firm acids. It's so ripe, it's almost jammy. Delicious now, but give it a year or two to knit together. **91** —*S.H. (11/1/2004)*

Longoria 2001 Syrah (Santa Barbara County) $22. An excellent red wine, with nice body and structure. The flavors range from plums and black-cherries to white pepper, and the tannins are voluptuously soft and complex. It's totally dry, a beautiful wine to pair with your finest foods. **92 Editors' Choice** —*S.H. (2/1/2004)*

Longoria 2000 Syrah (Santa Barbara County) $22. Supple, dry, and very light on fruit. Instead, offers earthy, tobacco flavors and the tastes of dried kitchen herbs. Hefty tannins and acids leave your tongue sticking to the roof of your mouth. Obviously not very giving right now. **86** —*S.H. (12/1/2002)*

Longoria 2003 Alisos Vineyard Syrah (Santa Barbara County) $32. A new wine from veteran Rick Longoria. It combines both cool climate and warmer aspects, showing ripe, forward, almost jammy cherry and cassis fruit as well as the acidity and tannins associated with, say, Santa Rita. It's a compelling wine, complex and delicious. **92 Editors' Choice** —*S.H. (12/1/2006)*

Longoria 2001 Alisos Vineyard Syrah (Santa Barbara County) $22. A brilliant and impressive wine whose rich fruit, lush tannins and structure recommend it. A mélange of blackberries and plums, with notes of mushrooms, herbs, and peppery spices. It's fully dry, but the fruit flavors are so ripe, they finish with a delicious sweetness. Drinkable now, but also cellarworthy. **93** —*S.H. (2/1/2004)*

LOOKOUT RIDGE

Lookout Ridge 2000 Chardonnay (Sonoma Coast) $35. At five-plus years of age, this Chard's fruit takes a backseat to stone, mineral, and herb flavors, in addition to its original oak. It's bone dry, with crisp acids. Complex and interesting, it finishes with a dusty earthiness. Drink now. **90** —*S.H. (6/1/2005)*

Lookout Ridge 2001 Keefer Ranch Pinot Noir (Sonoma Coast) $45. Fans of sheer volume will exult, but this wine, good as it is, is a bit overblown. It overwhelms with oak as well as berry flavor so ripe, it approaches chocolate-coated raisins. It is an interesting, well-made Pinot, yet would benefit from greater elegance and a lighter, defter touch. **88** —*S.H. (6/1/2005)*

Lookout Ridge 2001 Alta Coma Sangiovese (Mendocino) $40. Starts with a blast of charry oak, and turns fierce in tannins and acids in the mouth, as well as searingly dry. Somewhere in there is intense black-cherry fruit. Important to decant this young, tough wine well in advance. It's a gamble, but try cellaring for a few years. **88** —*S.H. (6/1/2005)*

LORANE VALLEY

Lorane Valley 1996 Chardonnay (Oregon) $10. 86 —*M.M. (12/31/1999)*

LORCA

Lorca 2004 Pinot Gris (Monterey County) $14. An interesting wine that shows Sauvignon character in the pungent aromas and flavors, and bright Monterey acidity. The wine is enhanced by a rich streak of vanilla spinkled with lime zest. **86** —*S.H. (2/1/2006)*

LORING WINE COMPANY

Loring Wine Company 2004 Brosseau Vineyard Pinot Noir (Chalone) $48. Similar to Loring's other single-vineyard Pinots in the exceptionally ripe fruit, with flavors veering into blackberry and cherry pastry, deep espresso, cocoa, and spice. However there's considerably more tartness here, with a brisk acidic tingle that accentuates the tannins. Best to cellar this young wine for five years and try again. **90 Cellar Selection** —*S.H. (5/1/2006)*

Loring Wine Company 2002 Brosseau Vineyard Pinot Noir (Chalone) $46. The lightest and most elegant of Loring's releases, and for me the most satisfying, although it's still a big, dense wine. Cherry, coffee, root beer, and smoky oak flavors, with good acidity and rich tannins. Feels a bit heavy now, but should soften and develop complexities in time. Drink now through 2010. **88** —*S.H. (11/1/2004)*

Loring Wine Company 2004 Cargasacchi Vineyard Pinot Noir (Santa Rita Hills) $48. So rich and dramatically flavorful, it's practically a new food group. Stuns with the power of its black-cherry, blackberry jam, dark chocolate, coffee, and toast flavors that unfold in waves on the palate and just go on and on. Fully dry, the wine represents a triumph of modern viticulture and enology. But it will take some artful cooking to come up with a dish to pair it with. **91** —*S.H. (5/1/2006)*

Loring Wine Company 2000 Clos Pepe Pinot Noir (Santa Lucia Highlands) $40. Posh and seductive, with black-cherry and cedar aromas, this clean and modern beauty offers intensity without excessive weight. The full feel and mouth-filling brambly berry, vanilla, and spice flavors pushed our pleasure buttons. It closes long and dry, with tea notes and some even tannins. Drink now–2007. **91 Editors' Choice** (10/1/2002)

Loring Wine Company 2004 Clos Pepe Vineyard Pinot Noir (Santa Rita Hills) $48. Masses of extra-ripe cherry pie, currant, cocoa, and blackberry jam flavors flatter the palate in this rich, slightly heavy wine. It's almost sweet, with a creme de cassis and cherry liqueur finish. This is the Loring style, flamboyant and extracted in New World, sun-drenched fruit. **88** —*S.H. (5/1/2006)*

Loring Wine Company 2002 Clos Pepe Vineyard Pinot Noir (Santa Rita Hills) $46. Dark and young now, and thick in the mouth, almost Syrah-like in its density. Rich in chocolate, blackberry, and coffee flavors, and well-oaked. Not typical of Pinot, but will it age? The acids and tannins suggest it will. Hold until 2006 and see what happens. **87** —*S.H. (11/1/2004)*

Loring Wine Company 2004 Durrell Vineyard Pinot Noir (Sonoma Coast) $48. Here's a huge, flamboyant Pinot, dramatically young and vibrant in massive black-cherry, mocha, and cinnamon spice flavors that are wrapped in tannins seemingly made of pure velvet. It's eccentric, and quintessentially Californian. Beware the high alcohol. **91** —*S.H. (5/1/2006)*

Loring Wine Company 2004 Garys' Vineyard Pinot Noir (Santa Lucia Highlands) $48. Deliriously delicious, decadent, stupendously flavorful, words can't describe the impression this massive wine makes. It's an explosion of blackberry pie, cherry marmalade, vanilla fudge, and Oriental spice flavors, all carefully controlled in a dry, crisp, softly tannic package. All Loring's wines possess superripeness, but this one somehow brings balance and sophistication. Wow. **94 Editors' Choice** —*S.H. (5/1/2006)*

Loring Wine Company 2003 Garys' Vineyard Pinot Noir (Santa Lucia Highlands) $46. As delicious as this wine is, it still treads the dangerous line of oversize. It's dark, full-bodied, and dense in sweet blackberry, chocolate and cherry flavors. It was easily ripened to its considerable size but there's something to be said for restraint and subtlety, especially with Pinot Noir. **90** —*S.H. (7/1/2005)*

Loring Wine Company 2002 Garys' Vineyard Pinot Noir (Santa Lucia Highlands) $46. Tart in citrusy acidity, and thankfully so, as the richly dense chocolate, and cherry flavors need a boost of life. Still, this is a heavy wine that doesn't show Pinot's flair, elegance, and silkiness. Hard to know what to make of it, but it's delicious. **87** —*S.H. (11/1/2004)*

Loring Wine Company 2000 Garys' Vineyard Pinot Noir (Santa Lucia Highlands) $40. The dense color is a sure indicator of how rich and intense this Monterey wine is. With plum aromas, hints of cinnamon and nutmeg, it's round, deep and packed to the core with exuberance but also lots of style. **92 Editors' Choice** *(10/1/2002)*

Loring Wine Company 2004 Keefer Ranch Pinot Noir (Green Valley) $48. Thick and dense in the mouth, with candied flavors of chocolate-covered cherries and new oak, this is a delicious wine that could be a little drier and more structured. The acidity is low, making the wine feel soft and melted. **86** —*S.H. (5/1/2006)*

Loring Wine Company 2004 Llama Farm Pinot Noir (California) $48. A blend of various Loring vineyards, this wine is soft and flamboyant in fruity flavor, and a little sweet in the finish, with dramatically ripe black-cherry, chocolate, and coffee flavors encased in soft, velvety but complex tannins. It defines the modern style of cool-climate California Pinot Noir allowed to achieve maximum ripeness. **88** —*S.H. (5/1/2006)*

Loring Wine Company 2004 Naylor Dry Hole Vineyard Pinot Noir (Chalone) $48. Despite its rich ripeness, this wine is a bit lighter in alcohol and tighter than Loring's other releases. The tannins and acids suggest midterm cellaring, but if you drink it now, you'll like the richness of the black-cherry compote, mocha, Oriental spice, and toast flavors. **89** —*S.H. (5/1/2006)*

Loring Wine Company 2004 Rancho Ontiveros Vineyard Pinot Noir (Santa Maria Valley) $48. So syrupy sweet and delicious, you almost want to pour this over a cup of vanilla ice cream. It's fabulously rich in cherry compote and milk chocolate, yet dry and backed up by crisp acids. Defines the extreme of a ripe, extracted, somewhat heavy Pinot Noir style, but there's no denying how good it tastes. **89** —*S.H. (5/1/2006)*

Loring Wine Company 2002 Rancho Ontiveros Vineyard Pinot Noir (Santa Maria Valley) $46. Smells chocolatey and heavy, and this is confirmed in the mouth. Dense, weighty and full-bodied, with a thick, fudgy texture and chocolate and blackberry flavors. **85** —*S.H. (11/1/2004)*

Loring Wine Company 2004 Rosella's Vineyard Pinot Noir (Santa Lucia Highlands) $48. There's a baked, roti quality to the aroma of this wine, suggesting the crust of a fresh cherry pie, with the cherry filling flavors accented by vanilla and cinnamon and even a drizzle of crème de cassis. It's a very decadent beverage. Who could have dreamed California Pinot could taste this good? On the other hand, the very size will intimidate chefs. Where is this monster style of Pinot Noir going? Stay tuned. **93** —*S.H. (5/1/2006)*

Loring Wine Company 2002 Rosella's Vineyard Pinot Noir (Santa Lucia Highlands) $46. Dark, heavy, and chocolatey. You might think you were drinking Syrah, it's so dense. It's a good, in fact a delicious wine, but where is the delicacy and elegance of Pinot Noir? Might age, but who knows? **85** —*S.H. (11/1/2004)*

Lost Canyon 2001 Pinot Noir (Carneros) $38. Simple and jammy, although tasty enough, with lip-smacking, candied flavors of cherries, raspberries, and spicy mocha. Feels light and silky in the mouth, with gentle acids and tannins. **86** —*S.H. (7/1/2003)*

Lost Canyon 2004 Dutton Ranch Morelli Lane Vineyard Pinot Noir (Russian River Valley) $40. Young and strong now, with a dry mouthfeel and firm acidity and tannins, this fine Pinot should develop with age. The cherry, mocha, cola, and rhubarb flavors are deep and long, and together with the silky texture, offer great pleasure. Drink now through 2010. **92** —*S.H. (9/1/2006)*

Lost Canyon 2003 Dutton Ranch Morelli Lane Vineyard Pinot Noir (Russian River Valley) $38. Opens with peppermint, pepper, and oak aromas, and while there are richer cherry and spice flavors, this is still a sharp, eccentric wine. **84** —*S.H. (10/1/2005)*

Lost Canyon 2002 Dutton Ranch Morelli Lane Vineyard Pinot Noir (Russian River Valley) $38. Pale in color, almost translucent. On the palate you'll find cherries and cola, and a simple, acidic structure. **85** —*S.H. (11/1/2004)*

Lost Canyon 2004 Las Brisas Vineyard Pinot Noir (Los Carneros) $40. Dry, delicate, and delicious, this Pinot offers lots of complex pleasure now, and has the stuffing for midterm aging. A compact wine, with youthful acidity and tannins, yet the cherry and cola flavors impact with power. Should hold well through 2010. **91** —*S.H. (9/1/2006)*

Lost Canyon 2003 Las Brisas Vineyard Pinot Noir (Carneros) $38. While technically good, this is not a satisfying wine. It's lean and tart, and not quite ripe, with green flavors partially relieved by red cherries. **83** —*S.H. (10/1/2005)*

Lost Canyon 2002 Las Brisas Vineyard Pinot Noir (Carneros) $38. Easy to enjoy, tasty in rich fruit, and simple in structure, this is a wine most people will like for its ripe flavors of raspberries and cherries, dusted with mocha and cinnamon. It's also easy on the palate, with a silky texture and light body. **87** —*S.H. (11/1/2004)*

Lost Canyon 2004 Saralee's Vineyard Pinot Noir (Russian River Valley) $40. Grown in the cool heart of the valley, but in a hot vintage, this beautifully ripe Pinot combines fruity power with elegant harmony to produce a delicious, complex wine. It's sturdy in acids and tannins, and bone dry. While the alcohol is high, it feels balanced and graceful. Best in its youthful flamboyance. **93 Editors' Choice** —*S.H. (9/1/2006)*

Lost Canyon 2003 Saralee's Vineyard Pinot Noir (Russian River Valley) $38. Smells funky, vegetal, and even a little unclean, although some will call it barnyardy. Acidly sharp and austere in the mouth, and dry. **82** —*S.H. (10/1/2005)*

Lost Canyon 2002 Saralee's Vineyard Pinot Noir (Russian River Valley) $36. This is one of the palest Pinots of the vintage, barely more than a rosé. The flavors, as you might guess, are thin. There's some pretty watermelon and strawberry in there, but it seems like a case of stretching good vines into over-production. **84** —*S.H. (11/1/2004)*

Lost Canyon 2003 Alegria Vineyard Syrah (Russian River Valley) $33. Quite high in acidity, but also pumped full of blackberry fruit, this Syrah comes across as a bit monolithic and tight at this stage of its evolution. Masses of soft tannins give promise for the future, so hold 2–3 years and see what develops. **87** *(9/1/2005)*

Lost Canyon 2002 Alegria Vineyard Syrah (Russian River Valley) $32. This is a tannic young wine. You can taste and feel the astringency of the grape skins and seeds immediately. Coats and numbs the palate, obscuring the underlying blackberry fruit. There's no guarantee that age will soften, but if you're a gambler, cellar for the better part of this decade. **86** —*S.H. (12/1/2004)*

Lost Canyon 2004 Stage Gulch Vineyard Syrah (Sonoma Coast) $35. Not particularly pleasurable at this point. The numbing tannins and high acids completely obscure everything that's going on below, which leaves collectors the option of cellaring it. I do not know where this wine is going, but my money's on ageability, because it's so rich in fruit. Try again in 2010. **88** —*S.H. (10/1/2006)*

USA

Lost Canyon 2003 Stage Gulch Vineyard Syrah (Sonoma Coast) $33. This bottling is similar to Lost Canyon's Trenton Station Russian River Syrah, in the cherry flavors, firm acids and tannins and long finish. It may be a little tarter, but it's in the same ballpark. Drink it now, to best appreciate the fresh, savory fruit. **88** *(9/1/2005)*

Lost Canyon 2002 Stage Gulch Vineyard Syrah (Sonoma Coast) $32. What an interesting wine this is. It's intricate in aromas and flavors, with a range that includes cherry, cola, sweet wild blackberry, and spices, and has complex tannins and crisp acidity. It's obviously a young wine, and very exuberant and expressive in its youth. But it's so balanced, it will probably age gracefully. **90** *—S.H. (12/1/2004)*

Lost Canyon 2001 Stage Gulch Vineyard Syrah (Sonoma Coast) $33. The winemakers sought out a vineyard close to the ocean, in order to produce a cold-climate Syrah. They got a tough, tannic wine, with pepper and blackberry flavors and strong, complex tannins that make the wine undrinkable in youth. May age, but it's really unknown. **87** *—S.H. (12/15/2003)*

Lost Canyon 2004 Trenton Station Vineyard Syrah (Russian River Valley) $35. This is from the cooler, southern portion of the valley, and the climate shows in the notable tannins and acids that put the wine in lockdown. Yet it's a very fine Syrah, rich and classy in meaty blackberry and coffee flavors and a luscious finish of blueberry tart. You could enjoy this single-vineyard wine now, but it should soften and develop additional bottle complexities from 2007 through 2010. **93 Editors' Choice** *—S.H. (10/1/2006)*

Lost Canyon 2003 Trenton Station Vineyard Syrah (Russian River Valley) $35. Bountiful in acids that add zest and perkiness, this wine has the fruit to fill all that structure. The flavors are of blackberries and blueberries, and the finish firm and tannic. Youthful; age 2–3 years. **88** *(9/1/2005)*

LOST RIVER

Lost River 2003 Cabernet Sauvignon (Columbia Valley (WA)) $23. Strongly flavored with smoky, charred oak, the smoke, coffee, and espresso flavors ride roughshod over the pretty raspberry and red currant fruit. The poor fruit is overwhelmed; the winemaking seems better suited to bigger, riper, richer fruit. **86** *—P.G. (6/1/2006)*

Lost River 2002 Cabernet Sauvignon (Columbia Valley (WA)) $23. Good fruit to start, with solid black-cherry and berry notes well-matched to the new oak. But it seems to hit a wall mid-palate and fall off; perhaps it's just a bit of bottle shock. Score could improve with more time in bottle. **88** *—P.G. (4/1/2005)*

Lost River 2002 Merlot (Columbia Valley (WA)) $21. A tiny winery in the backwater burg of Mazama, Lost River is making some of the best, affordable boutique wines in Washington. Don't look for a fancy label, but get a load of the fruit and style in the bottle. This is an elegant Merlot showcase, a perfectly shaped expression of supple berry and cherry flavor, tart, vivid, and racy. Lean, not mean; it's a classic. **91 Editors' Choice** *—P.G. (12/1/2004)*

Lost River 2003 Sémillon (Columbia Valley (WA)) $14. What a score! This is sexy Sémillon, kissed with honey and flowers, and supple with a round core of delicious, intriguing, complex fruits. Pear, apple, blood orange, and more are wrapped in a thoroughly delicious, well-rounded mid-palate, and the wine extends itself effortlessly into a lingering, delicious finish. Light enough to be food friendly, yet complex and wonderfully concentrated. **92 Best Buy** *—P.G. (12/1/2004)*

LOST RIVER WINERY

Lost River Winery 2003 Syrah (Walla Walla (WA)) $21. Panelists found everything from black olive, earth, coffee, and Hershey's syrup on toast here—simply put, this is not a fruit-driven wine. Still, tannins are supple and acids, crisp. Finishes with charred-meat flavors. **87** *(9/1/2005)*

LOUIS M. MARTINI

Louis M. Martini 1995 Barbera (Lake County) $12. 87 Best Buy *—M.S. (9/1/2000)*

Louis M. Martini 2003 Cabernet Sauvignon (Sonoma County) $17. This is a good Cabernet, dry and varietal, with cassis and coffee flavors farmed in rich, fine tannins. There's a rustic edge to the finish, so drink now. **84** *—S.H. (11/1/2006)*

Louis M. Martini 2002 Cabernet Sauvignon (Sonoma County) $15. Subtle notes of toast, vanilla, and chocolate allow the leafy, cassis-driven fruit to shine. It's a medium-weight Cab, not a heavyweight, which makes it easier to pair with food. Finishes lush and chocolatey, with the merest hint of raisins. **86** *(9/1/2005)*

Louis M. Martini 2002 Cabernet Sauvignon (Napa Valley) $24. Here's a Cab made in Martini's old style, which was a dry, fairly tannic wine low in alcohol compared to today, and consequently less ripe, although there are some raisiny notes indicating unbalanced bunches. Drink now. **85** *—S.H. (12/1/2005)*

Louis M. Martini 2001 Cabernet Sauvignon (Sonoma County) $17. A nice Cabernet that has some richness and complexity. It has easy flavors of berries, cherries, olives, and herbs that are framed in thick, dusty tannins. Finishes very dry, with a sprinkling of oak. There's a tough quality that well-marbled beef will tame. **85** *—S.H. (2/1/2004)*

Louis M. Martini 2000 Cabernet Sauvignon (Napa Valley) $24. Earthy and herbal, with sage, dill, and mushroom flavors, and a streak of red cherry that only partly relieves the austerity. The tannins are tough and gritty, and lead to a dry, puckery finish. **84** *—S.H. (2/1/2004)*

Louis M. Martini 1997 Family Vineyard Selection Ghost Pines Vineyard Cabernet Sauvignon (Chiles Valley) $30. This wine begins with very oaky, charry aromas riding high over black currants. An elegant, soft but complex wine with sweet blackberry extract, oak overlays and lush tannins. There's a rough earthiness, however, that keeps it from the top echelon. **87** *(8/1/2001)*

Louis M. Martini 1999 Ghost Pines Vineyard-Family Vineyard Selection Cabernet Sauvignon (Chiles Valley) $30. Strikes all the right Cabernet notes of black currant and cassis flavors, smoky oak overtones, and smooth tannins. But can't quite overcome a one-dimensionality and rough, slightly sweet finish. **84** *—S.H. (11/15/2003)*

Louis M. Martini 2003 Lot No. 1 Cabernet Sauvignon (Napa Valley) $100. Concentrated in cassis, cherry, plum, chocolate, and new oak flavors, this is a young Cabernet, currently showing vibrant tannins and acidity. All the parts haven't come together, so you don't want to drink it now. It shows promise, and should be better after 2008. **89** *—S.H. (9/1/2006)*

Louis M. Martini 2002 Monte Rosso Vineyard Cabernet Sauvignon (Sonoma Valley) $85. Tannic and young and dry. This adolescent Cab is locked down now, but it shows the flash and structure associated with this vineyard. Is it an ager? Hard to tell, because it's more elegant than powerful, and you have to wonder if the fruit will outlive the tannins. The betting is on longevity. Drink 2008–2015. **90** *—S.H. (9/1/2006)*

Louis M. Martini 2001 Monte Rosso Vineyard Cabernet Sauvignon (Sonoma Valley) $50. The 2001 vintage appears to mark a step up in quality for these wines. Lead pencil and dusty berry notes start this wine off, opening to deliver bright cassis flavors and a full-bodied, firmly structured mouthfeel. Long on the finish. Drink 2010–2020. **91** *(9/1/2005)*

Louis M. Martini 2000 Monte Rosso Vineyard Cabernet Sauvignon (Sonoma Valley) $55. Despite the difficulty of the vintage, this is a very good effort. It's bigger, fuller and more-extracted than the '99, with muscular cedar, cassis and graphite aromas and flavors. Drink 2008–2012. **88** *(9/1/2005)*

Louis M. Martini 2000 Monte Rosso Vineyard Cabernet Sauvignon (Sonoma Valley) $55. Martini's flagship Cab is a blockbuster. It is exceptionally ripe, with lush currant and cassis flavors that have a laserlike concentration. There's a good deal of new oak, but the massive flavors are easily able to handle it. The result is a special success for this vintage. **92 Cellar Selection** *—S.H. (12/31/2003)*

Louis M. Martini 1999 Monte Rosso Vineyard Cabernet Sauvignon (Sonoma Valley) $50. Starts off with smoke, toast, chocolate, anise, and herb aromas. Pretty cherry, blackberry, sage, and licorice flavors follow, and the tannins are robust. **88** *—J.M. (11/15/2002)*

Louis M. Martini 1999 Monte Rosso Vineyard Cabernet Sauvignon (Sonoma Valley) $65. With views extending all the way to San Pablo Bay, this vineyard is slightly cooler than most Cabernet spots, and in the '99 vintage, this is reflected in some slight bell-peppery aromas. You still get plenty of cassis and earth flavors, and the tannins are supple, making this a nice wine to drink now–2010. **88** *(9/1/2005)*

Louis M. Martini 1998 Monte Rosso Vineyard Cabernet Sauvignon (Sonoma Valley) $65. Already bricking a little bit at the rim, wines like this gave the '98 vintage a bad rep. The wine is still good, but nowhere what it can be, with fading fruit, green herbs and sharp acidity on the finish. **85** *(9/1/2005)*

Louis M. Martini 1998 Monte Rosso Vineyard Cabernet Sauvignon (Sonoma Valley) $50. Here's a welcome return to the big leagues by this Napa Valley veteran. True to house style, it's modulated, refusing size in favor of finesse. The pretty currant and oak-infused flavors define style and grace. This sumptuous wine has the balance to age for a long time. **93 Cellar Selection** *—S.H. (12/1/2001)*

Louis M. Martini 1997 Monte Rosso Vineyard Cabernet Sauvignon (Sonoma Valley) $40. 93 *(11/1/2000)*

Louis M. Martini 1996 Monte Rosso Vineyard Selection Cabernet Sauvignon (Sonoma Valley) $35. 88 *—L.W. (10/1/1999)*

Louis M. Martini 2003 Reserve Cabernet Sauvignon (Napa Valley) $24. For immediate consumption, this wine has easy Cabernet flavors suggesting blackberries, cassis, and green olives. With a layer of toasty oak, it is dry and balanced. Too bad it doesn't have more concentration, because it's got all the elements of a fine Napa Cab except depth. **85** *—S.H. (11/15/2006)*

Louis M. Martini 2002 Reserve Cabernet Sauvignon (Napa Valley) $24. A bit thick in tannins now, this wine needs more time to settle down, but by 2008 it should be a nice sipper. It has polished cherry and cocoa flavors with a sweet coat of smoky oak. **87** *—S.H. (7/1/2006)*

Louis M. Martini 2001 Reserve Cabernet Sauvignon (Napa Valley) $25. Ripe and juicy in black currant, as befits the vintage; also shows polished, firm tannins. Oak adds sweet vanillins through the lingering finish. **87** *—S.H. (5/1/2005)*

Louis M. Martini 2001 Reserve Cabernet Sauvignon (Alexander Valley) $35. Has a flashy, showy nose of toasty, smoky oak and vanilla, but also plenty of blackberry and cassis fruit. Ripe, lush, and oak-laden, but with enough chewy tannins to suggest cellaring a couple of years. **89** *(9/1/2005)*

Louis M. Martini 2000 Reserve Cabernet Sauvignon (Alexander Valley) $35. A beautifully balanced wine that shows how to make the best of a lesser vintage. The cherry, blackberry, and blueberry flavors are delicately framed in smoky oak, with a lush, smooth texture. **91** *—S.H. (2/1/2004)*

Louis M. Martini 2000 Del Rio Vineyard Chardonnay (Russian River Valley) $22. Marked by extreme oak, with charred, vanilla-infused aromas and spicy wood flavors. The underlying fruit is hard to discern under all that wood, but seems to veer toward peaches. Slightly sweet, with good acidity, it will please those who think oak and Chardonnay are synonymous. **85** *—S.H. (9/1/2002)*

Louis M. Martini NV Family Vineyard Selection Del Rio Vineyard Chardonnay (Russian River Valley) $21. This wine has a flinty, minerally personality, with a full overlay of toasty oak. Don't look for fat, blockbuster fruit here—the flavors tend toward lime and tangerine. The oak adds caramel, vanilla, and smoky notes. It's supple in the mouth but closes strangely flat. **84** *—S.H. (8/1/2001)*

Louis M. Martini 1997 Reserve Chardonnay (Russian River Valley) $18. 85 *(6/1/2000)*

Louis M. Martini 2001 Monte Rosso Vineyard Folle Blanche (Sonoma Valley) $18. Bright and fresh, with pretty grapefruit, lemon, green apple, and herb flavors. Wll balanced and zippy. **87** *—J.M. (9/1/2003)*

Louis M. Martini 2000 Monte Rosso Vineyard Folle Blanche (Sonoma Valley) $17. From a little-known grape sometimes used in French Muscadet, this is a strong, tart wine, with pronounced citrus flavors. The acidity is scouring, with no apparent oak at all, and the finish is slightly sweet and lemony. **84** *—S.H. (12/15/2002)*

Louis M. Martini 2000 Del Rio Vineyard Gewürztraminer (Russian River Valley) $18. Oh, how good this wine smells, like a garden in June, or a basket of freshly picked fruits dusted with spice, or wild honey drizzed over toasted macadamia nuts. This isn't a wine to ponder over, it's to enjoy with grilled shrimp on a skewer with roasted red peppers and onions. **88** *—S.H. (6/1/2002)*

Louis M. Martini 2002 Del Rio Vineyard-5 Nail Selection Gewürztraminer (Russian River Valley) $16. Fragrant and delicate, a wine with polished flavors of green apple, peach, litchi, wildflowers, and Oriental spices. Drinks very dry and quite acidic. Refreshing and flavorful, especially with Asian fusion fare. **85** *—S.H. (12/31/2003)*

Louis M. Martini 1997 Merlot (Chiles Valley) $25. 90 *—S.H. (11/15/2000)*

Louis M. Martini 1999 Del Rio Vineyard Merlot (Russian River Valley) $22. Marks a welcome return to the old Martini style of soft, delicious red wines that are intricate in detail and subtly marked by wood. The flavors spread feather-like over the palate, highlighting black-cherry, pepper, tobacco, and spice; dry and rich. Has an extra layer of nuance that makes each sip different from the last. **90 Editors' Choice** *—S.H. (9/1/2002)*

Louis M. Martini 1999 Ghost Pines Vineyard-Family Vineyard Selection Merlot (Chiles Valley) $27. Pretty sweet for a dry table wine, and rather cloying. Feels flat on the palate despite officially high acidity. The flavors and texture veer toward cherry cough medicine, turning bitter on the finish. **83** *—S.H. (12/1/2003)*

Louis M. Martini 1997 Sangiovese (Dunnigan Hills) $14. 83 *(10/1/1999)*

Louis M. Martini 2001 Monte Rosso Vineyard Sémillon (Sonoma Valley) $18. 87 *—S.H. (12/15/2002)*

Louis M. Martini 1996 Zinfandel (Sonoma County) $12. 85 *—P.G. (11/15/1999)*

Louis M. Martini 1999 Gnarly Vine-Monte Rosso Vineyard Zinfandel (Sonoma Valley) $40. Moderate body and cherry-like flavors blend nicely with plum and herbal notes. An enjoyable Zin from old vines. **87** *—J.M. (12/1/2002)*

Louis M. Martini 1997 Gnarly Vine Monte Rosso Vineyard Zinfandel (Sonoma Valley) $40. 86 *—S.H. (12/1/2000)*

Louis M. Martini 2001 Monte Rosso Vineyard Zinfandel (Sonoma Valley) $20. A bit stark, the wine features powdery tannins that frame smoky oak, with blackberry, coffee, and tar notes on the follow-up. It finishes with a toasty edge. **84** *(11/1/2003)*

Louis M. Martini 2000 Monte Rosso Vineyard Zinfandel (Sonoma Valley) $20. A very pure Zin, with lots of integrity. It has the brambly, wild berry flavors lovers of this varietal expect, wrapped in dry, dusty tannins. The structure and mouthfeel are rich and beautifully balanced. **92 Editors' Choice** *—S.H. (12/1/2002)*

Louis M. Martini 1999 Monte Rosso Vineyard Zinfandel (Sonoma Valley) $30. Dark and powerful, this glass-staining wine explodes with blackberry marmalade and smoke aromas, and fills the mouth with powerful fruity, berry flavors. Despite the size, it's elegant and harmonious, with sweet, oaky tannins. **90** *—S.H. (12/15/2001)*

Louis M. Martini 2002 Monte Rosso Vineyard Gnarly Vine Zinfandel (Sonoma Valley) $35. Very youthful, boasting loads of blackberry aromas accented by briary-herbal-stemmy notes and hints of vanilla. On the palate, you get cherries, chocolate, and soem raisiny notes. Finishes long and velvety, an expression of Monte Rosso Zin as good as any we've tried. **90** *(9/1/2005)*

Louis M. Martini 1998 Monte Rosso Vineyard Gnarly Vine Zinfandel (Sonoma Valley) $40. From low-yielding 120-year-old vines, this is one of the most serious Zins around. It's soft, well-structured and harmonious, with Zin's briary, jammy, peppery, wild berry fruit. The mouth-coating flavors persist on the long delicious finish for a full minute. **91** *—S.H. (12/15/2001)*

LOXTON

Loxton 2002 Reserve Syrah (Sonoma County) $30. Interesting wine, combining intensely gamy notes with assertive fruit and bold peppery accents. It's rich and extracted, too, then turns tart and tannic on the finish. The big question is, will it age well? **85** *(9/1/2005)*

Loxton 2002 Sonoma Hillside Vineyards Syrah (Sonoma County) $24. Grilled meat and ripe berries combine in this medium-weight Syrah blended from five hillside vineyards. Australian winemaker Chris Loxton has crafted an admirably balanced wine that finishes with driving acidity and good length. **86** (9/1/2005)

Loxton 1999 Timbervine Ranch Syrah (Russian River Valley) $26. From hills above the river, a lovely wine, with black-cherry and white-pepper aromas and flavors and sweet vanilla and oak. Rich and spicy in the mouth, with pronounced blackberry and cherry fruit, jammy and sweet. Very balanced, all the way to the long, richly satisfying finish. **90** —S.H. (7/1/2002)

LUCAS & LEWELLEN

Lucas & Lewellen 2001 Cabernet Franc (Santa Barbara County) $22. The cherry fruity sure ripened up, yet there's a sharpness and rusticity to this wine that detract. No obvious faults, though. **83** —S.H. (7/1/2005)

Lucas & Lewellen 2000 Valley View Vineyard Cabernet Franc (Santa Barbara County) $25. The Solvang area is warmish but with chilly nights. This beautiful Cab Franc shows why this variety may be Santa Ynez's best red Bordeaux grape. Aromas of blackberry and cherry lead to sweet berry-cherry flavors that flood the palate and end with a flourish of ripe tannins. Its feminine charm is irresistible. **91** —S.H. (10/1/2003)

Lucas & Lewellen 2001 Cote del Sol Cabernet Sauvignon (Santa Barbara County) $32. Vegetal, unripe, with gluey-sweet flavors. **80** —S.H. (8/1/2005)

Lucas & Lewellen 2000 Cote del Sol Valley View Vineyard Cabernet Sauvignon (Santa Barbara County) $32. Believe it or not, a wine made only from the south-facing side of the vines, which is the warmer side. Smells dramatically ripe and oaky, with a waft of black currant, dark chocolate, caramel, olive, herbs, and a hint of leather. Feels rich and intense in the mouth, long on blackberry and cherry flavor wrapped in a mellow, soft texture. **89** —S.H. (11/15/2003)

Lucas & Lewellen 2002 Valley View Vineyard Cabernet Sauvignon (Santa Barbara County) $25. Semi-sweet and simple, but clean. That about sums up this cherry and raspberry jam-flavored wine. It's fine with burgers, and you can put a chill on it if you want to. **83** —S.H. (9/1/2006)

Lucas & Lewellen 2001 Valley View Vineyard Cabernet Sauvignon (Santa Barbara County) $25. Smells moldy, with berry flavors and a flat texture. **81** —S.H. (8/1/2005)

Lucas & Lewellen 2000 Valley View Vineyard Cabernet Sauvignon (Santa Barbara County) $23. Drinks rich and juicy, with ripe berry, cherry, and herb flavors and a round, smooth, supple mouthfeel. The finish is long and sweet with ripe berries. **87** —S.H. (11/15/2003)

Lucas & Lewellen 2004 Chardonnay (Santa Barbara County) $15. Missing the lushness of the Goodchild Chard, but still a clean, tasty wine showing pineapple and toasty oak flavors. Easy to savor with its zesty acidity. **84** —S.H. (12/1/2006)

Lucas & Lewellen 2003 Chardonnay (Santa Barbara County) $15. Rustic, despite some ripe peach and other stone fruit flavors and what tastes vaguely like oak. **83** —S.H. (8/1/2005)

Lucas & Lewellen 2004 Goodchild Vineyard Chardonnay (Santa Barbara County) $22. Rich in peach, pear, and tropical fruit, with an exotic toasted coconut cream pie taste that's simply delicious. Waves of rich, ripe, flamboyant flavor are what this Chard is all about. **88** —S.H. (12/1/2006)

Lucas & Lewellen 2003 Goodchild Vineyard Chardonnay (Santa Barbara County) $22. It's all here, the ripe, fruity flavors, creaminess, the lees, spices, and oak, in a somewhat countrified Chard that could use a lighter touch and more finesse. **84** —S.H. (8/1/2005)

Lucas & Lewellen 2000 Goodchild Vineyard Chardonnay (Santa Barbara County) $20. An opulently ripe, mouthfilling wine from the Santa Maria Valley. Tropical fruit, apple, pear, smoke, and vanilla flavors have been lavishly oaked, adding a buttered-toast note that lasts through the long, spicy finish. **89** —S.H. (12/15/2003)

Lucas & Lewellen 2000 Goodchild Vineyard Chardonnay (Santa Barbara County) $20. A rough wine, despite the ripe tropical fruit flavors and overlay of oak. There's an earthy, mushroomy undertow that feels heavy and clammy on the palate. **84** —S.H. (12/31/2003)

Lucas & Lewellen 2003 Merlot (Santa Barbara County) $21. Awkward, with sweet-and-sour Chinese food flavors. Now it's cherries, then it's balsamic. Finishes sugary sweet. **82** —S.H. (12/1/2006)

Lucas & Lewellen 2001 Merlot (Santa Barbara County) $21. Raw, with an unclean smell and sweet, medicinal flavors. **81** —S.H. (8/1/2005)

Lucas & Lewellen 2000 Merlot (Santa Barbara County) $18. From the Los Alamos area, a nice lighter-style Merlot, with red and black-cherry, smoke, and minty aromas and flavors, finished with an oaky veneer of vanilla and cream. The easy tannins lead to a finish that's long on the taste of cherries. **87** —S.H. (3/1/2004)

Lucas & Lewellen 2002 Petite Sirah (Santa Barbara County) $26. Dark and very tannic, and as dry as dust, this wine shows the deep core of plummy blackberries that the variety is known for, but could use finesse. **84** —S.H. (8/1/2005)

Lucas & Lewellen 2001 Pinot Noir (Santa Maria Valley) $15. Very dry, with silky tannins and crisp Central Coast acidity. Good varietal character in an everyday Pinot. **84** —S.H. (8/1/2005)

Lucas & Lewellen 2004 Hilltop Pinot Noir (Santa Barbara County) $26. There's lots going on in this Pinot, which comes from the Santa Maria Valley. It shows cool-climate acidity and tiered flavors of red stone fruits, tea, cola, and dried spices. And all of that is packaged into a silky, elegant, refined body. **89** —S.H. (12/1/2006)

Lucas & Lewellen 2001 Vin Gris Pinot Noir (Santa Barbara County) $12. A 100% Pinot Noir from the Santa Maria Valley with ripe flavors of strawberry, rose hip tea, peach, and smoke. Feels dry and fancy in the mouth, with an enjoyable depth and complexity. Finishes with smoke and honey. VALUE. **87** —S.H. (10/1/2003)

Lucas & Lewellen 2003 Sauvignon Blanc (Santa Barbara County) $18. There are some good fruity flavors in this wine, ranging from lemons and limes to tart green apples. It's dry, with a spicy finish. **84** —S.H. (8/1/2005)

Lucas & Lewellen 2001 Sauvignon Blanc (Santa Barbara County) $12. Stainless steel only, from Los Alamos. A crisp, delicate, winsome wine, with good acidity and a steely texture, but there's nothing wimpy about the melon, citrus, and fig flavors, which have a smoky, spicy edge to them. **86** —S.H. (12/31/2003)

Lucas & Lewellen 2003 Syrah (Santa Barbara County) $24. Tastes kind of overripe, with raisin and blackberry flavors. Finishes with a flourish of sticky tannins. Best with meats and cheeses. **84** —S.H. (12/1/2006)

Lucas & Lewellen 2002 Syrah (Santa Barbara County) $20. Divergent opinions on this wine. Proponents will find it creamy and full-bodied, blending cherry, vanilla, and rhubarb flavors. Detractors will call it stewy and flabby. **85** (9/1/2005)

LUCAS VINEYARDS

Lucas Vineyards NV Lucas Blanc de Blancs Chardonnay (Finger Lakes) $15. Button mushrooms, clean compost and hints of toast give this wine an interesting flavor profile, but the wine turns a bit too sweet on the finish. **82** —J.C. (12/1/2003)

Lucas Vineyards 2001 Dry Riesling (Finger Lakes) $10. Lightweight and possessed of brisk acidity, this tart and snappy style might work well with fresh shellfish. Simple sour-apple flavors scour the palate. **85** —J.C. (8/1/2003)

Lucas Vineyards 2002 Semi-Dry Riesling (Finger Lakes) $10. Slightly floral on the nose, with some pear and nectarine as well, this light-bodied wine blends sweet stone-fruit flavors with tart green apples on the palate, giving it a degree of balance. **86** —J.C. (8/1/2003)

Lucas Vineyards NV Lucas Extra Dry Sparkling Blend (Finger Lakes) $12. Offers a simple but enjoyable bouquet of rising bread dough, followed by flavors of pear and apple. The texture combines a hint of creaminess with crisp acidity on the fairly dry finish. **86 Best Buy** —J.C. (12/1/2003)

LUCCA

Lucca NV Vino Rosso di Santa Barbara Red Wine Sangiovese (California) $10. A simple but very likeable blend that shows nice berry, plum, and earth flavors wrapped in sturdy, smooth tannins. It's very dry and balanced, with a tasty finish. Just about the perfect spaghetti wine. **86 Best Buy** —*S.H. (3/1/2005)*

LUCIA

Lucia 2004 Chardonnay (Santa Lucia Highlands) $35. From the Pisoni family, a crisp, fruity Chard that's long and deep in jammy apricot, lemon drop, and guava flavors that are set off by high acids. This is a big, in-your-face wine, but it has some fine complexities. **87** —*S.H. (8/1/2006)*

Lucia 2004 Garys' Vineyard Pinot Noir (Santa Lucia Highlands) $45. Drinks young, crisp in acids and a little impertinent now, but with great charm; this wine is alive with vibrant cherry, mint, and oak flavors that finish in a swirl of chocolate raspberry mousse. That makes it sound sweet, but it's bone dry, just enormously ripe in fruit. It's Santa Lucia Pinot in all its flamboyant glory. Drink soon. **91** —*S.H. (8/1/2006)*

Lucia 2002 Garys' Vineyard Syrah (Santa Lucia Highlands) $38. From Pisoni, a huge, flashy and forward wine, stuffed with cherry-chocolate fruit flavors. It's a little awkward now in the way its youthful tannins, oak and fruit haven't consolidated. Should knit together and improve in the next year or so. **89** —*S.H. (7/1/2005)*

LUCY

Lucy 2005 Rosé of Pinot Noir Rosé Blend (Santa Lucia Highlands) $18. From Pisoni, a slightly sweet, crisp, fun blush wine that's filled with ripe Pinot character. It's all about cherries, strawberries, vanilla, and mint, offset by refreshing acids. **85** —*S.H. (6/21/2006)*

LUNA

Luna 1999 Merlot (Napa Valley) $32. Juicy-fruity wine here, with various berry flavors, full-bodied and ripe, wrapped in a softly tannic, dry wine. It strives for elegance and finesse and comes close, but a rough edge cuts those aspirations short. Merlot remains a difficult wine even in Napa. **88** —*S.H. (9/12/2002)*

Luna 2004 Pinot Grigio (Napa County) $18. This is a richer, oakier style of PG. It aims, not for vibrancy and freshness, but subtlety and complexity. A bit low in acids, it's long in cinnamon-sprinkled yellow peach and apricot flavors, with oak and vanilla seasoning. **86** —*S.H. (2/1/2006)*

Luna 1999 Canto Red Blend (Napa Valley) $60. Expensive, yes, but these guys know what they're doing. This Super-Tuscan blend of Sangiovese, Merlot, and Cabernet Sauvignon defines Napa's virtues: Complexity, deliciousness, and the softest, creamiest tannins, together with the modern penchant for low acidity and, of course, lots of new oak. This wine wows with opulence and impresses with elegance. **95** —*S.H. (9/1/2002)*

Luna 2003 Sangiovese (Napa Valley) $18. Luna's 2002 was a swing and a miss for exaggerated flavors that were practically sweet. This vintage is also very ripe, with a desserty taste, like cherry marmalade. It's not as unbalanced, but the challenge remains dryness. The alcohol is 15.4%. **84** —*S.H. (5/1/2006)*

Luna 2002 Sangiovese (Napa Valley) $18. Some will like the extracted, ripely sweet blackberry and cherry flavors, but not me. There's also that stinging Sangiovese acidity. **82** —*S.H. (12/15/2005)*

Luna 2000 Sangiovese (Napa Valley) $18. Pretty much as good as California Sangiovese gets, combining Pinot Noir's soft, supple tannins and Merlot's full-bodied fruit. Very ripe and spicy, with black raspberry flavors, it's dry, with crisp acidity. This is a gentle but firm wine that will go well with a wide variety of foods. **90** —*S.H. (12/1/2002)*

Luna 1999 Reserve Sangiovese (Napa Valley) $50. Could be the most expensive Sangiovese in California. It's surely interesting and complex. Very dry, with layers of tobacco, pepper, sage and black-cherry flavors, but it's not a fruit-driven wine. Has a dusty layer of strong tannins, but is accessible enough for immediate enjoyment with rich, oily foods. The finish is bitter, tart, and dry. **88** —*S.H. (5/1/2002)*

LYETH

Lyeth 1996 Bordeaux Blend (Napa County) $14. **88** —*M.S. (10/1/1999)*

Lyeth 2003 Meritage Cabernet Blend (Sonoma County) $15. Dry and gritty in texture, with hard-edged, jagged tannins, this wine is very ripe. It has strong black-cherry, blackberry, and coffee flavors, and needs to be decanted before serving. **84** —*S.H. (5/1/2006)*

Lyeth 2002 L de Lyeth Cabernet Sauvignon (Sonoma County) $11. Bone dry, fairly astringent in tannins, and with berry, coffee, and herb flavors, this wine is clean and correct. Fine for most everyday purposes. **83** —*S.H. (10/1/2004)*

Lyeth 2001 Reserve Cabernet Sauvignon-Merlot (Alexander Valley) $32. Beautifully drinkable in the prime of its youth, with subtle blackberry, cherry, herb, and violet flavors folded into soft, dusty tannins. Perfect now with a well-marbled steak, but should age short-term. **88** —*S.H. (2/1/2005)*

Lyeth 2002 Meritage (Sonoma County) $15. Elegant rather than powerful, this Bordeaux blend shows earth, cherry, blackberry, and herb flavors wrapped in gentle oak. It's a bit tannic, just enough to bite into a nice piece of beef. **86** —*S.H. (2/1/2005)*

Lyeth 2001 Meritage (Sonoma County) $15. Comes down on the lean, herbal side despite some polished plum and berry flavors. The tannins kick in with a fierce bite, and turn dry and astringent on the finish. Might soften with a year or two in the cellar. **84** —*S.H. (5/1/2004)*

Lyeth 2002 L de Lyeth Merlot (Sonoma County) $11. A nice, balanced wine, with some good plummy, berry-cherry flavors. It's soft, easy, and very dry, and has an extra edge of complexity that makes it a good value. **85** —*S.H. (10/1/2004)*

Lyeth 2002 L de Lyeth Sauvignon Blanc (Sonoma County) $11. Very clean, very dry, and nicely tart in acids, this wine is delicately structured but strongly flavored with spicy figs, honeydew melon, lime zest, and vanilla. The more you sip, the more you like it. It's a great value. **86** —*S.H. (10/1/2004)*

LYNCH

Lynch 2002 Cabernet Sauvignon (Napa Valley) $60. A tightly wound, good cellar candidate. Balanced in rich tannins and acids, with solid cassis and cherry fruit and a sweet veneer of oak, it's splendid tonight with a steak, but should really hit its stride in a few years. **92** —*S.H. (7/1/2005)*

Lynch 2002 Canis Major, Unti Vineyard Syrah (Dry Creek Valley) $25. Beautifully balanced, with an intensely flavored core of black-cherry, black currant, coffee, spice, herb, and hints of chocolate. Tannins are supple, yet firm, and frame the wine with elegance. Toasty and lush on the finish. Good price; great wine. **90** —*J.M. (9/1/2004)*

Lynch 2002 Lynch Knoll Vineyard Syrah (Spring Mountain) $65. This Syrah aims high. It's dry, rich, and full-bodied, with rich tannins and oak, and is fruity enough for the core of cassis to develop for several years. On the other hand, it has a sharp finish that may crack this wine up before the tannins fall out. **90** —*S.H. (7/1/2005)*

Lynch 2002 Canis Major Zinfandel (Dry Creek Valley) $24. Quite fragrant, with complex aromas of chocolate, black-cherry, raspberry, herbs, and spice. They extend along the palate as well. The wine is fairly full bodied, but serves up good acidity for a balanced quaff. On the finish, it's framed in toasty oak and pretty vanilla, finishing long and lush. From winemaker Brenda Lynch, also of Mutt Lynch. **91** —*J.M. (9/1/2004)*

LYNMAR

Lynmar 2004 Chardonnay (Russian River Valley) $27. A blend of half barrel-fermented wine with half tank-fermented, this is a ripe, fruit cocktail of a wine, blending tropical fruit with smoke, vanilla, and citrus. Soft and easy to drink. **89** *(6/1/2006)*

Lynmar 2003 Chardonnay (Russian River Valley) $22. Too leesy and oaky for my taste, with tough, earthy-lemony flavors underneath. Acidity is tart. **84** —*S.H. (5/1/2005)*

Lynmar 2000 Chardonnay (Russian River Valley) $24. Boy, is this yummy. Ripe and rich as can be, packed with lip-smacking spiced apple, peach, and papaya flavors and an elaborate overlay of smoky oak. A creamy texture and firm acids balance out this irresistible wine. **92** —*S.H. (12/15/2002)*

Lynmar 2002 Quail Cuvée Chardonnay (Russian River Valley) $30. There's a ton of winemaker bells and whistles here, notably oak and lees, but they can't overcome the wine's lean earthiness. The result is unbalanced, although not unpleasurable. **85** —*S.H. (5/1/2005)*

Lynmar 1999 Quail Cuvée Chardonnay (Russian River Valley) $30. Richer and bigger in every respect than the winery's regular release, this is a wine on steroids. The fruit is huge and explosive, and the oak seems toastier and heavier. But size isn't everything. Lynmar's regular Chardonnay is more balanced and harmonious. **89** —*S.H. (12/15/2002)*

Lynmar 2003 Quail Hill Vineyard Chardonnay (Russian River Valley) $38. Completely barrel-fermented, and it shows in the wine's lavish oak, ample weight, and rich, oily texture. It's nutty and leesy, and much less overtly fruity than the winery's Russian River bottling, instead focusing more on weight and texture. **91** *(6/1/2006)*

Lynmar 2003 Pinot Noir (Russian River Valley) $32. Plump and soft, with flavors that closely echo those found in the Quail Hill Vineyard bottling: spice, beet, earth, cola, and cherries. Not as big as the Quail Hill, and not as long on the finish, but an attractive, easy-to-drink Pinot for near-term consumption. **88** *(6/1/2006)*

Lynmar 1999 Pinot Noir (Russian River Valley) $28. This most basic of Lynmar's Pinots satisfies with silky tannins, soft acidity, and pleasant cherry flavors. A dollop of oak adds smoke and char. It's a simple wine, properly made and easy to drink. **86** —*S.H. (2/1/2003)*

Lynmar 2004 Five Sisters Pinot Noir (Russian River Valley) $80. Pours dark and smells youthful, with cherry, raspberry, cola, and spice scents. In the mouth, it's a big wine that's stuffed with cherry pie and oak flavors. It's also fairly tannic, which should enable it to age for a few years. This is a success for the vintage. **90** —*S.H. (12/1/2006)*

Lynmar 1997 Five Sisters Pinot Noir (Russian River Valley) $NA. This selection of five barrels (each representing one of Fritz's five daughters) is still lively, thanks to crisp acids that artfully point up flavors of cola, earth, and black-cherries. Smoke and earth on the nose. Drink now–2010. **89** *(6/1/2006)*

Lynmar 2003 Quail Hill Vineyard Pinot Noir (Russian River Valley) $45. Fairly big and full in the mouth, yet quite silky in texture, with supple tannins that softly frame flavors of cola, earth, raspberries, and beets. Picks up dried-spice notes on the long finish. **90** *(6/1/2006)*

Lynmar 2002 Quail Hill Vineyard Pinot Noir (Russian River Valley) $30. Absolutely lovely. Throws off complex cherry, rhubarb, cola, and oak aromas, and then turns into the quintessence of cherry flavor, rich yet airy and lilting. Best consumed in its flashy, seductive youth. **90** —*S.H. (6/1/2005)*

Lynmar 1994 Quail Hill Vineyard Pinot Noir (Russian River Valley) $NA. Even tasted from magnum, this wine is starting to show its age, revealing smooth tannins and a slightly thinning texture. Meaty notes add spice to the beet and earth aromas and flavors. Drink up. **87** *(6/1/2006)*

Lynmar 2001 Quail Hill Vineyard Quail Cuvée Pinot Noir (Russian River Valley) $35. Gorgeous. The grapes ripened perfectly, yielding lushly sweet cherry, raspberry, and sweet coffee flavors that have been enhanced with smoky, spicy oak. Completely dry, this seductively delicious wine is wonderfully silky, and finishes long. **93** —*S.H. (12/15/2004)*

Lynmar 2002 Quail Hill Vineyard Quail Cuvée Pinot Noir (Russian River Valley) $40. Denser, more tannic and fuller bodied than Lynmar's regular Pinot, which actually makes it less accessible. Showing notes of cherries and plums, as well as considerable oak. Tremendous spice in the finish. The richness, complexity and depth, not to mention tannins, suggest midterm aging. Hold until 2006. **92** —*S.H. (6/1/2005)*

Lynmar 1999 Reserve Pinot Noir (Russian River Valley) $50. 88 —*S.H. (2/1/2003)*

Lynmar 1996 Reserve Pinot Noir (Russian River Valley) $NA. Drinking well now, with smoke and earth aromas that easily slide into cola, black cherry, and plum flavors. Plump in the mouth, but with crisp acids that may take over in another few years. Drink up. **89** *(6/1/2006)*

Lynmar 2005 Vin Gris of Pinot Noir Pinot Noir (Russian River Valley) $24. Pretty expensive for a rosé, but it's a seriously good, crisp wine from a

premier Pinot producer. It features elegant strawberry, rose petal, tea, and dried herb flavors that change with every sip. A dash of Syrah seems to add body and richness. **90** —*S.H. (12/15/2006)*

M. COSENTINO

M. Cosentino 1999 CE2V Bordeaux Blend (Napa Valley) $75. This is a Bordeaux-style blend, primarily Cabernet Sauvignon, from Cosentino. It is from vineyards scattered around Napa Valley. Considerable restraint has been brought to bear, wisely avoiding excessively over-the-top fruit. An herbal, sage-and-pepper note accompanies the blackberry flavors. Dry and full-bodied, with a tannic edge, this wine will benefit from midterm aging. **90** —*S.H. (11/15/2002)*

M. Cosentino 1997 M. Coz Bordeaux Blend (Napa Valley) $100. 88 *(11/1/2000)*

M. Cosentino 1996 M. Coz Bordeaux Blend (Napa Valley) $80. 86 *(3/1/2000)*

M. Cosentino 1998 The Poet Bordeaux Blend (Napa Valley) $65. This blend of five Bordeaux varieties, dominated by Cabernet Sauvignon, is fruity for the vintage, packed with jammy berry flavors further sweetened with sappy oak. It's soft and uncomplicated, light in body and acids, and won't age. Drink now through 2003. **88** —*J.M. (6/1/2002)*

M. Cosentino 1997 The Poet Bordeaux Blend (Napa Valley) $65. 94 *(11/1/2000)*

M. Cosentino 1996 The Poet Bordeaux Blend (Napa Valley) $40. 87 *(2/1/2000)*

M. Cosentino 2002 CE2V Meritage Cabernet Blend (Napa Valley) $100. Cosentino is one of Napa's most consistent Cabernet producers. The CE2V, a vineyard bottling, always shows vintage variation. Based on Cabernet Sauvignon, the '02 is a great success, immensely rich in concentrated cassis fruit, and totally dry. The tannins are extensive, but soft and complex in the modern style. This is a wine to drink now and over the next 15 years. **94** —*S.H. (7/1/2006)*

M. Cosentino 2001 Cabernet Franc (Lodi) $28. Not very Porty, in that it's not terribly sweet, nor is it fruity. There are raisiny notes but it's really an earthy, green herb wine. Will disappoint those expecting richness. **83** —*S.H. (10/1/2004)*

M. Cosentino 2001 Cabernet Franc (St. Helena) $34. This sure is a pretty wine. It's lighter in body than a mid-valley Cab Sauvignon, and veers more toward cherry than blackberry fruit. It's also gussied up with toasty oak. Finishes dry, rich, and harmonious. **90** —*S.H. (3/1/2005)*

M. Cosentino 2000 Cabernet Franc (Napa Valley) $34. Great Napa structure here, with elegant, complex tannins that are soft as brushed velvet, and fine acids. Flavorwise, it was not the best idea to vinify on its own, in this vintage that produced many lean red wines. Herbal and earthy, the wine wants more fruit. **86** —*S.H. (6/1/2003)*

M. Cosentino 1999 Cabernet Franc (Napa Valley) $34. Pretty expensive for a varietal yet to prove itself in California. It's got pretty enough fruit and an elaborate overlay of oak, but no particular depth or complexity. In fact, it's simple and flat. **84** —*S.H. (9/1/2002)*

M. Cosentino 1997 Cabernet Sauvignon (Napa Valley) $28. 88 *(3/1/2000)*

M. Cosentino 2002 Cabernet Sauvignon (Napa Valley) $45. This isn't a wine to cellar. But it's a beautiful young wine now, one of the most attractive '02s around to accompany a fine meal. It's intricate in cassis and oak flavors, with flamboyantly ripe, complex tannins and crisper acidity than Napa usually offers. Seems to improve with every sip. **90** —*S.H. (11/1/2005)*

M. Cosentino 2001 Cabernet Sauvignon (Napa Valley) $38. This dark young wine is tannic and tight now, but it's an obvious cellar candidate. There's a rich core of red and black-cherry and currant, alongside pronounced oak and a delicious chocolatey edge. The finish is extremely long, with sweet ripe fruit. Leave it until 2008 and beyond. **92 Cellar Selection** —*S.H. (10/1/2004)*

M. Cosentino 2000 Cabernet Sauvignon (Napa Valley) $34. The plush and inviting aromas of currants, olives, menthol, and smoky oak do not follow up as richly as you hope. The wine turns tannic and astringent, with blackberry flavors on entry that promise but don't deliver. **85** —*S.H.* *(12/31/2003)*

M. Cosentino 1999 Cabernet Sauvignon (Napa Valley) $34. Why do so many Cabs seem so flabby lately? Maybe because the vintners are striving for super-maturity at the expense of freshness and acidity. This wine has supple berry flavors and some nice oak, but it's curiously lifeless on the palate. Just sits there. Doesn't sing. **85** —*S.H.* *(9/12/2002)*

M. Cosentino 2002 Hoopes Ranch Cabernet Sauvignon (Oakville) $75. What a great job Mitch Cosentino does with Bordeaux varieties. This one continues the tradition. Rich and dramatic in cassis, cherry, and toast, this balanced wine has smooth, polished tannins and a long finish. Remarkably good now, it should develop for many years. **94 Cellar Selection** —*S.H.* *(11/1/2005)*

M. Cosentino 2001 Hoopes Ranch Cabernet Sauvignon (Oakville) $65. Here's a flamboyant, oaky wine that pushes it all to the limit. You can taste the sappy ripeness in the black currant flavors that have a sweet, pecan pie decadence. Dry, with luxuriously soft, fine tannins and perfectly fine acids, this is a real crowd pleaser. **93** —*S.H.* *(10/1/2004)*

M. Cosentino 2001 Reserve Cabernet Sauvignon (Napa Valley) $80. Exceptionally ripe in black-cherries, blackberries, cassis, and chocolate, and sweet in fruit juice essence, although it's technically dry. Polished and smooth, with a nice edge of acids and tannins for grip. Almost too flamboyant in sweet opulence. Anything more in this direction will be excessive. **90** —*S.H.* *(4/1/2005)*

M. Cosentino 2000 Reserve Cabernet Sauvignon (Napa Valley) $80. Dark in color and quite oaky, with lots of smoke and vanilla aromas riding on top of black currants. The blackberry flavors promise richness, then drop off in the middle and turn herbal. Tannins and alcohol show up on the finish. **86** —*S.H.* *(11/15/2003)*

M. Cosentino 1999 Reserve Cabernet Sauvignon (Yountville) $80. This is a very big wine. It's oversized in the purple-black color, in the massive aromas of black currants and oak, and in the mouth. Coats the palate in rich currant fruit and thick, dusty tannins. It's too awkward to enjoy now, which raises the question whether it will mellow with age. **87** —*S.H.* *(11/15/2002)*

M. Cosentino 1997 Reserve Cabernet Sauvignon (Napa Valley) $80. Opens with a solid Cabernet nose of black currants. The tannins here are fine and dispersed, the acidity is a little low in the current fashion, yielding a plush mouthfeel. Finishes long and spicy, but maybe a touch superficially pretty. **90** —*S.H.* *(8/1/2001)*

M. Cosentino 2000 Charbono (Napa Valley) $25. Drink this robust wine with barbecued pork ribs and don't be too fussy. It's dry and tannic enough to slice through grease. **84** —*S.H.* *(10/1/2004)*

M. Cosentino 2004 Chardonnay (Napa Valley) $28. From the Oak Knoll area, this is a super-oaky wine, bursting with vanilla and char. The underlying fruit isn't really big enough to sustain it, though. The wine is earthy and soft, leaving the oak to dominate. **84** —*S.H.* *(6/1/2006)*

M. Cosentino 2003 Chardonnay (Napa Valley) $22. Rich, creamy, and well-oaked, this Chard oozes tropical fruit, caramel, and spicy vanilla flavors. It's sweetish in honey on the finish. **88** —*S.H.* *(10/1/2005)*

M. Cosentino 2002 Chardonnay (Napa Valley) $30. Absolutely huge, a monster wine that's exceedingly ripe and super oaky. It explodes with focused flavors of tropical fruits, buttered toast, vanilla custard, cinnamon, and spice, and the fruity, spicy finish lasts for a very long time. Yet it's balanced and harmonious. **92** —*S.H.* *(9/1/2004)*

M. Cosentino 2002 Chardonnay (Napa Valley) $25. From the cooler Oak Knoll district, a spicy, ripe Chard that's big in everything. Super tropical fruit flavors, lavishly toasted new oak, lots of lees and all the other bells and whistles. **88** —*S.H.* *(12/1/2004)*

M. Cosentino 2001 Chardonnay (Napa Valley) $22. There's plenty of fancy toasted oak lathered over ripe fruity flavors ranging from apple and pear through mangoes, but somehow it doesn't knit together. The result seems heavy-handed, a paint-by-the-numbers Chardonnay. **84** —*S.H.* *(12/31/2003)*

M. Cosentino 2000 Chardonnay (Napa County) $22. Another day, another oaky, rich Chard. Or three. You'll find apples and peaches, you'll find spices and creaminess, and you'll find a broad, delicious Chardonnay that says, drink me. It's easy to comply. If you're curious, the Napa Valley AVA. doesn't cover the entire county; hence the appellation. **87** —*S.H.* *(5/1/2002)*

M. Cosentino 1999 Chardonnay (Napa Valley) $22. Big, rich, and extracted, this wine was partially barrel-fermented, and there's quite a bit of sweet, smoky, vanilla-tinged oak—from the aromas through the long, spicy finish. Despite the bulk, it's elegant and balanced. This full-bodied, no-holds-barred white would be particularly good with barbecued shrimp served in a saffron and coconut-milk sauce. **90** —*S.H.* *(8/1/2001)*

M. Cosentino 1999 Chardonnay (California) $18. Cream and honey aromas highlight this juicy, fleshy wine. With its buttery texture and slightly sweet fruit flavors, it's about pleasure, not complexity, and it finishes long and spicy. **86** —*S.H.* *(8/1/2001)*

M. Cosentino 1998 Barrel-Fermented Chardonnay (California) $20. 86 *(6/1/2000)*

M. Cosentino 2004 CE2V Chardonnay (Napa Valley) $40. Without showing the richness of prior vintages, this year's bottling is earthy and crisp and very dry. It has a steely minerality and modest fruit that suggests green apples and pineapples. **85** —*S.H.* *(7/1/2006)*

M. Cosentino 2003 CE2V Chardonnay (Napa Valley) $40. Ripe in peaches, pineapples, crème brûlée, buttered toast, vanilla, and other big Chard notes, with a super-creamy texture. Finishes a bit hot and peppery. **88** —*S.H.* *(8/1/2005)*

M. Cosentino 2002 CE2V Chardonnay (Napa Valley) $28. Almost overripe, almost too alcoholic, almost overextracted, and flirts with being too oaky, but not quite, all of which makes this a big, fat Chardonnay that tests the limits. Nothing subtle about the blast of flavors and huge mouthfeel. As rich as it is, try with lobster and drawn butter. **90** —*S.H.* *(8/1/2004)*

M. Cosentino 2000 CE2V Chardonnay (Napa Valley) $28. Size matters in this massively structured, hugely fruity wine, with oak to match. The fruits are tropical, with the deeply spicy, intense flavors of mango, guava, and pineapple. Lees complexes but doesn't overwhelm, while the well-charred oak frames it all in toast, vanilla and sweet tannins. It demands big, fancy foods. **93** —*S.H.* *(12/31/2001)*

M. Cosentino 2005 Legends Chardonnay (California) $25. Soft and simple, with one-dimensional Chardonnay flavors of canned peaches. The wine-making notes emphasize that the wine has not undergone malolactic fermentation. Good thing, because there's almost no discernible acidity. **83** —*S.H.* *(12/31/2006)*

M. Cosentino 2001 The Sculptor Reserve Chardonnay (Napa Valley) $30. This wine wins you over by the sheer force of its exuberant personality. It has a range of citrus, peach, and tropical fruit flavors that are tightly wound together by high acidity, while new oak adds aromatic and textural elements. **89** —*S.H.* *(2/1/2004)*

M. Cosentino 2000 The Sculptor Reserve Chardonnay (Napa Valley) $30. Bells and whistles Chard, with good and ripe flavors of peaches and pears elaborately framed in well-toasted oak, which brings vanilla, smoke, and spicy notes. Feels round and creamy in the mouth, and finishes with a honeyed richness. **89** —*S.H.* *(6/1/2003)*

M. Cosentino 1999 The Sculptor Reserve Chardonnay (Napa Valley) $34. The nose here delivers a hefty dose of meaty, smoky, nutty notes paired with mild pear and apple. The palate doesn't show complexity—a pronounced toasted oak rides hard on apple and pineapple fruit. It's balanced and finishes dry, but comes up wanting the desired texture and nuance. **85** *(7/1/2001)*

M. Cosentino 2003 Dolcetto (Lodi) $18. Simple and innocuous, this soft wine has cherry-berry and coffee flavors and tastes slightly sweet, but at least has long length on the finish. **84** —*S.H.* *(5/1/2005)*

M. Cosentino 2002 Dolcetto (Lodi) $18. This inky black, very tannic and dry wine is tough going. There are deeply buried dark stone fruit and herb flavors that may emerge with many years of aging. Meanwhile, it's best with something like short ribs. **84** —*S.H.* *(11/15/2004)*

USA

M. Cosentino 2001 Celle Vineyard Dolcetto (California) $18. Dark, rich, and heavy, a wine with thickly ripe flavors of plums, tomato, and pepper. Feels dense in the mouth, with firm tannins and low acidity. This very dry wine calls for rich foods, such as roast duck or a beef stew. **88** —*S.H. (3/1/2004)*

M. Cosentino 2002 Gewürztraminer (Yountville) $22. Fruity, flowery, intense and enormously spicy. Cinnamon, nutmeg, coriander, cardamom, and white pepper dance on the palate. Finishes nicely dry; a complex table wine. **88** —*S.H. (10/1/2005)*

M. Cosentino 2001 Gewürztraminer (Yountville) $22. Enormously fragrant, a wine that puts out an amazing array of aromatics. Spicy gingerbread, honeysuckle, vanilla, smoky caramel, baked apple, pie crust, you name it. It's as flavorful as it smells, but totally dry, with crisp acidity. Brilliant. **91** —*S.H. (6/1/2004)*

M. Cosentino 2000 Gewürztraminer (Yountville) $22. Yountville is a cooler part of Napa, and you can taste the acid tanginess, but it's also a lush wine that brims with exotic fruit and flower flavors that persist into a honeyed finish. Barrel fermentation will satisfy Chardonnay fans who demand creaminess. Vietnamese food would be a nice match. **86** —*S.H. (6/1/2002)*

M. Cosentino 1999 Gewürztraminer (Yountville) $22. The scent of well made Gewürz always comes as a shock. So much flower, gingery spice, grapefruit and honey, sometimes even a tinge of botrytis. This beauty startle with its aromas, then calms down in the mouth to offer pleasant citrus flavors softened by a honeyed texture. But it's bone-dry. **87** —*S.H. (12/1/2001)*

M. Cosentino 1998 Estate Yountville Gewürztraminer (Napa Valley) $22. 87 —*L.W. (9/1/1999)*

M. Cosentino 2003 Legends Meritage (Napa Valley) $80. When Cosentino's clarets hit the mark, they're darn near as good as anything in the valley. This blend of Cabs Sauvignon and Franc and Merlot is wickedly good. There's a ton of oak, but it's just the perfect touch. Tastewise, it's black currants, crème de cassis, and sweet Asian spices. So soft and forward; drink now. **93** —*S.H. (9/1/2006)*

M. Cosentino 2000 M Coz Meritage (Napa Valley) $100. This Bordeaux blend is, in a word, delicious. It showcases the continued finesse of this fine estate in its dapper, elegant structure and deft touch of oak. It is not a wine to age; it just doesn't have the depth. But the currant and sweet cherry flavors are satisfying and complete. **91** —*S.H. (3/1/2004)*

M. Cosentino 2002 M. Coz Meritage (Napa Valley) $125. Most of the grapes come from Yountville, a coolish Napa region. Buried below the tannins are enormously ripe blackberries, cherries, and red currants. The wine is impeccably balanced. The tannins will cut through a good steak now, but you can age this Cab through the decade. **92 Cellar Selection** —*S.H. (12/31/2005)*

M. Cosentino 2001 M. Coz Meritage (Napa Valley) $120. This fabulous wine stuns in every respect. It's sweet in black currant, plum, mocha, and oak flavors, yet retains a balanced dryness. A stiff backbone of acidity provides life and zest, but the intricate tapestry of tannins has a soft, aged feel. Voluptuous in the mouth; will age and likely improve beyond 2010. **95** —*S.H. (10/1/2004)*

M. Cosentino 1999 M. Coz Meritage (Napa Valley) $100. Looks fierce, with a dark, brooding quality, but is surprisingly open in its youth. Oak dominates the aromas, which include well-ripened blackberry and a meaty, earthy note from Merlot and Cabernet Franc. Very supple in the mouth, with juicy flavors and a drink-me-now appeal, but the telltale dust of tannins in the finish indicates ageability. **92** —*S.H. (11/15/2002)*

M. Cosentino 1999 The Novelist Meritage (California) $16. Primarily Sauvignon Blanc, this wine is tart, dry, crisp, and spicy, with zesty acids that scour the palate and make the tastebuds sing. Sémillon adds richer, nutty, and floral notes. It's a complex wine, with a great depth of flavor that persists into the long finish. Nice job, and a good value for the quality. **89** —*S.H. (12/15/2001)*

M. Cosentino 2000 The Poet Meritage (Napa Valley) $65. There are black currant and cassis flavors and very strong tannins, the kind that make your tongue stick to the gums. It's a big wine but not a concentrated one, and is unlikely to age. Drink now. **87** —*S.H. (5/1/2004)*

M. Cosentino 1999 The Poet Meritage (Napa Valley) $65. Firm, young, and tannic, a tight wine that may improve in the cellar. Pours very dark, with modest flavors of blackberries, plums, and tobacco, but those tough, gritty tannins are pretty strong, and the fruit may not outlive them. **85** —*S.H. (11/15/2003)*

M. Cosentino 1997 Merlot (California) $20. 86 *(3/1/2000)*

M. Cosentino 2002 Merlot (Napa Valley) $34. There's too much oak on this wine. The charry wood and vanilla jumps right out and clubs you. The underlying wine, while pretty, isn't a heavyweight. It's pleasant in cherries, but lacks a middle, which oak can't make up for. **85** —*S.H. (11/1/2005)*

M. Cosentino 2002 Merlot (Oakville) $90. This 100% Merlot is so voluptuous, it reminds you of a great Pomerol. It's big and rich in black-cherry, vanilla, and smoky char, with a nice, peppery finish. Shows great weight and volume, and lots of elegance. **92** —*S.H. (11/1/2005)*

M. Cosentino 2001 Merlot (Oakville) $75. Full-bodied and very dry, with plummy, coffee, and bitter chocolate flavors. There is a scour of tannins and acidity that cuts across the rich fruit and shortens it through the finish. Try cellaring it for a few years. **88** —*S.H. (6/1/2004)*

M. Cosentino 2001 Merlot (Napa Valley) $38. This Merlot contains massive flavors of cherries, with a spicy, figgy streak. The oversized tannins add to the impression of heft, but they're very ripe, sweet and easy. Of course, lots of new oak is in keeping with the fruit. Delicious and succulent, and perfect with a very rich cut of beef. **92** —*S.H. (9/1/2004)*

M. Cosentino 2002 Estate Merlot (Oakville) $75. While this is a good wine, it really costs too much for what you get. This wine is dry, with cherry and oak flavors, but is way too tannic to enjoy now. **85** —*S.H. (12/31/2005)*

M. Cosentino 1999 Estate Merlot (Oakville) $90. Only 350 cases were made of this expensive wine, grown on the winery's estate. It's really very fne. Takes advantage of the vintage's ripeness, overrunning with plush berry flavors, and it's also notable for the velvety texture and complexity of the tannins. It's not an ager, but flatters with the extravagance of youth. **93** —*S.H. (9/12/2002)*

M. Cosentino 2004 Legends Merlot (Napa County) $28. Larry Bird is the legend; Mitch Cosentino made the wine, which is rather one-dimensional and thin. Shows modest cherry and vanilla flavors, but makes you wonder why this high-powered team couldn't come up with something more concentrated and powerful. **83** —*S.H. (12/31/2006)*

M. Cosentino 1997 Oakville Estate Merlot (Napa Valley) $75. 91 *(12/31/1999)*

M. Cosentino 2000 Reserve Merlot (Napa Valley) $38. Tons of smoky, vanilla-tinged oak has been plastered over a wine whose underlying flavors are of black currants and cassis. The result is pleasing to the palate, with a level of complexity enhanced by rich tannins. This supple wine is best consumed early. **90** —*S.H. (4/1/2004)*

M. Cosentino 1999 Reserve Merlot (Napa Valley) $38. Plenty of oak here, in the smoky, charry aromas. Below is a somewhat closed, austere wine. Earthy, mushroomy aromas show now, and there may not be enough fruit to carry it through the long haul. Yet it's beautifully structured, with lush tannins and crisp acids. The right foods will wake it up. **87** —*S.H. (12/31/2001)*

M. Cosentino 2001 Sonoma Valley Nebbiolo (Sonoma Valley) $28. Not much Nebbiolo out there in California, but this is a good and interesting one. It's dark, dense and mouthfilling, oozing sweet plum, black currant, chocolate, tobacco, and pepper flavors that are wrapped in luscious tannins. Finishes dry and firm. **90** —*S.H. (9/1/2004)*

M. Cosentino 2002 Petite Sirah (Lodi) $27. Rich, powerful, and dense, this is classic California "Pet," with its dark color and massively compacted plum, roasted coffeebean, chocolate, and grilled-meat flavors. It's tannic, but soft enough to drink tonight. **90** —*S.H. (5/1/2005)*

M. Cosentino 2003 Knoll Family Vineyard Petite Sirah (Lodi) $27. Lodi produces hearty red wines so easily. This Petite Sirah is very dry and full-bodied, and pretty tannic, too, with ripe cherry, blackberry, coffee, and bitter chocolate flavors that are edged with a little oak. It's a complex wine that's best now in its sheer, unadulterated youth. **90** —*S.H. (6/1/2006)*

M. Cosentino 2001 Knoll Family Vineyard Petite Sirah (Lodi) $24. A real disappointment from this fine Napa Valley winery. Smells like stewed tomatoes and boiled prunes, with Lifesaver candy flavors finished with an unnatural sweetness. The finish is hot and sweet. **80** *(4/1/2003)*

M. Cosentino 2004 Pinot Grigio (Lodi) $18. Basically simple, this is an acidic, almost sour white wine, with lemon and grapefruit flavors, although there's a vanilla sweetness on the finish. A little oak barrel aging has lent some softness. **84** —*S.H. (2/1/2006)*

M. Cosentino 2002 Pinot Grigio (Solano County) $18. A sprightly white wine, quite dry and pert with acids, and with the earthy, herbal flavors of a nice Italian country wine. Has some real complexity. **87** —*S.H. (11/15/2004)*

M. Cosentino 2001 Pinot Grigio (California) $18. Simple, with apple and pear flavors that taste like canned fruit juice. The wine is soft and gentle in the mouth, and could use a bit more life and acidity. **84** —*S.H. (9/1/2003)*

M. Cosentino 2000 Pinot Grigio (Yountville) $16. Sappy, lemon-bright flavors characterize this clean, refreshing wine, along with enough acidity to make it zesty and alive. Barrel fermentation adds creaminess, and there's a long, sweetish spiciness in the finish. **84** —*S.H. (11/15/2001)*

M. Cosentino 2005 Stewart Vineyard Pinot Grigio (Solano County) $18. The brief barrel aging is hardly noticeable on this dry, crisp, fruit-forward wine. The apricot, citrus and white peach flavors have a honeysuckle floweriness, and the finish is long and clean. **84** —*S.H. (11/15/2006)*

M. Cosentino 2002 Pinot Noir (Russian River Valley) $35. In making a lateral move to Pinot Noir, Mitch Cosentino brings a Napa Cabernet sensibility to this variety. This is a big, dark, extracted Pinot, an attractive wine with its chocolate and blueberry flavors, but rather heavy-handed for a wine that should be elegant and crisp. **85** —*S.H. (11/1/2005)*

M. Cosentino 2001 Pinot Noir (Russian River Valley) $25. A very nice Pinot that is drinkable right away, despite weighty tannins. The silky texture carries flavors of spiced strawberries, raspberries, and smoky coffee that are very persistent through the finish. **89** —*S.H. (2/1/2004)*

M. Cosentino 2001 Pinot Noir (Yountville) $34. A fascinating, rich, and complex wine. Starts with jazzy Lifesaver flavors and combines them with warmer notes of baked cherry tart and sweet tobacco. It's all well oaked. Silky smooth in the mouth, dry in sugar but ripe in fruity flavor, and finishes with a wonderful edge of Oriental spice and mocha. **92 Editors' Choice** —*S.H. (5/1/2004)*

M. Cosentino 2000 Pinot Noir (Carneros) $30. The light, brickish color is easily noticeable, as is the bramble and cedar on the nose. Flavors of vanilla and brown sugar work with the dried cherry fruit, which despite having some pop doesn't seem overly fresh. A peppery spice to the finish comes courtesy of some wood tannins. **88** *(10/1/2002)*

M. Cosentino 2000 Pinot Noir (Yountville) $30. Dark and tasty, this solid Pinot has an appealing earthiness. black-cherry fruit, cedar, and leather accents ride a mid-weight, slightly chalky feel. A pepper-licorice finish closes it nicely. Drink now-2006. **87** *(10/1/2002)*

M. Cosentino 1999 Pinot Noir (Yountville) $34. Very ripe and fruity stuff here, a blast of jammy strawberry and black raspberry and spicy cola. Oak adds smoke and vanilla. It's dry, with lusciously complex tannins and soft acids. It's hard to describe how delicious it is. It's not an ager, it's a Lolita of a wine. Fortunately, it's not against the law to enjoy it young. **93 Editors' Choice** —*S.H. (12/15/2001)*

M. Cosentino 1999 Il Chiaretto Red Blend (Yountville) $20. This red wine is an unusual blend of Sangiovese, Cabernet Sauvignon, Cabernet Franc, and Mourvèdre. Not surprisingly, there's no varietal identification here. It opens with indeterminate aromas of berries and oak, and turns richly

berryish and spicy in the mouth. It's dry, with velvety tannins. **88** —*S.H. (11/15/2001)*

M. Cosentino 2003 Med Red Red Blend (Lodi) $16. Simple, pleasant, dry, and fruity, and not much more to say. A mongrel blend of Tempranillo, Charbono, Carignane, Valdiquie, Alicante and Mourvèdre, like Nonno used to make in the basement. **86** —*S.H. (5/1/2005)*

M. Cosentino 2002 Med Red Red Blend (Lodi) $12. This blend of five obscure varieties has generic red and black berry flavors. It's very tannic and dry, a wine that leaves your palate puckering. Okay for pizza. **84** —*S.H. (6/1/2004)*

M. Cosentino NV Ol' Red Red Blend (California) $12. A multivarietal, multivintage blend of various reds going back to 1997, this wine is very dry and, in its own way, complex. The older wines soften it and lend dried fruit notes, the younger ones keep it vibrant with a suggestion of red cherries and sweet tobacco. The end result is really fascinating. **88 Best Buy** —*S.H. (5/1/2006)*

M. Cosentino 2000 Tenero Rosso Red Blend (Lodi) $18. This mixture of Napa Gamay, Mourvèdre, Zinfandel, and Sangiovese feels like a marriage of convenience. The grapes were available, so let's throw them together. The result is awkwardly sweet and hot, a simple wine that finishes with bizarre residual sugar. **82** —*S.H. (12/1/2002)*

M. Cosentino 2001 CE2V Sangiovese (Napa Valley) $30. Big wine, full bodied, but with gentle tannins and crisp acids, and very dry. There's a suggestion of cherries and tobacco. Would go well with rich cheeses or your best tomato sauce. **90** —*S.H. (8/1/2005)*

M. Cosentino 2001 Il Chiaretto Sangiovese (California) $16. Heavy, dark, and dense, with unevenly ripened flavors ranging from sweet blackberry to bitter coffee. There's also excessive residual sugar and sharp tannins. Last year's release was so much better, indicating the difficulties of taming this tricky varietal. **83** —*S.H. (8/1/2004)*

M. Cosentino 2003 Il Chiaretto Sangiovese (California) $18. Unbalanced and rustic, with a sugary, soda-pop taste to the cola flavors. As far from Chianti as you can get. **82** —*S.H. (12/15/2005)*

M. Cosentino 2002 Il Chiaretto Sangiovese (California) $18. Drinks hot and slightly sweet, with cherry-infused coffee flavors, and is deficient in acids. **82** —*S.H. (5/1/2005)*

M. Cosentino 2000 Il Chiaretto Sangiovese (California) $20. Remarkably rich and good for a varietal that can be disappointing. Starts out with big flavors of red cherries, espresso, and sage, and turns velvety and creamy on the palate. Very dry, with crisp acids, this is an excellent and versatile table wine. **90 Editors' Choice** —*S.H. (9/1/2003)*

M. Cosentino 1997 Il Chiaretto Sangiovese (California) $18. **88** —*J.C. (10/1/1999)*

M. Cosentino 2002 CE2V Sauvignon Blanc (Napa Valley) $25. Deals some funky aromas of smoked meat and pickled cabbage, but clears up to show apple, butter, and wood notes. The acidity seems on the low side, but there's ample pineapple and citrus to keep it standing. Pretty good, if soft. **87** *(7/1/2005)*

M. Cosentino 2000 The Sem Sémillon (Napa Valley) $18. There seem to be fewer Sémillons in California these days, but this delicious wine makes you wonder why. It has the texture of a big Chard—creamy, smoky, and viscous—but the flavors are of spicy figs and dates. As rich and honeyed as the wine strikes the palate, it's quite dry and oaky. **90 Editors' Choice** —*S.H. (12/1/2003)*

M. Cosentino 1998 The Sem Sémillon (Napa Valley) $22. **86** —*L.W. (9/1/1999)*

M. Cosentino 2000 The Novelist Meritage Sémillon-Sauvignon Blanc (California) $16. Oak from barrels stars front and center, overshadowing the citrus, melon, and fig flavors underneath. Feels great in the mouth, creamy and lush. By summer 2003, it will be better. A blend of 80% Sauvignon Blanc and 20% Sémillon. **89** —*S.H. (7/1/2003)*

M. Cosentino 2003 Syrah (California) $18. Here's a big, dry, tannic wine that needs rich fare to wake it up. Short ribs of beef will tickle the blackberry and espresso fruit and make it rise up and shine. There's real complexity in the depth of flavor, balance, and long finish. **87** —*S.H. (5/1/2006)*

M. Cosentino 2002 The Temp Tempranillo (Lodi) $18. Almost Port-like in alcoholic level, a heavy, dry wine that, for all the rich array of cherry, chocolate, and blackberry flavors, feels rather dense and molten in the mouth. It's also very tannic, and numbs the lips and the tongue after you swallow. **84** —*S.H. (8/1/2004)*

M. Cosentino 2000 Viognier (California) $22. Mitch Cosentino gathered grapes from around the state, and vinified and aged the wine very dry. The result is a new-style Viognier that allows the varietal's exotic fruit and floral flavors to star. This is one of the more interesting approaches to California Viognier, which is often too oaky and sweet. **87** —*S.H. (12/15/2002)*

M. Cosentino 2000 Vin Doux Viognier Kay Viognier (California) $30. Mitch Cosentino used stainless steel fermentation to preserve the brilliant peach nectar fruit of this vin doux (sweet wine), then aged it in French oak to add a creamy mouthfeel. It's sweet and rich and delicious and shows another face of Viognier. **88** —*S.H. (9/1/2002)*

M. Cosentino 2002 White Blend (California) $12. Smells like a dessert wine, with apricot, smoky honey, and caramel aromas, but quickly turns dry. It has elusive but fascinating flavors, and no small amount of complexity. A blend of five or more grapes including Riesling, Chard, and Viognier. **87** —*S.H. (5/1/2005)*

M. Cosentino 2001 Avant et apres White Blend (California) $16. Slightly sweet, with a bit of botrytis in the aroma. Beyond the sweetness are modest flavors of apples and pears. **84** —*S.H. (6/1/2004)*

M. Cosentino 2001 The Novelist White Meritage White Blend (California) $16. A super-oaky blend of Sauvignon Blanc and Sémillon. It has leanish flavors of lemons and limes and plenty of acidity. There's even a sprinkling of dusty tannins. **85** —*S.H. (2/1/2004)*

M. Cosentino 2002 Cigar Zinfandel (Lodi) $27. Pushes the table wine envelope with nearly 16% alcohol, and while it's fully dry, it strikes the palate as ponderous. Heavy tannins and a tobaccoey herbaceousness smother whatever fruit is in there. **84** —*S.H. (10/1/2004)*

M. Cosentino 2000 Cigar Zin Zinfandel (Lodi) $27. Here's a Port-like Zin to sip late at night as the snow falls and the chestnuts are roasting. Plum pudding, raisin, and dark-chocolate flavors, with slight residual sugar and enough acidity to make it bright and balanced. **86** —*S.H. (7/1/2002)*

M. Cosentino 1998 Cigar Zin Zinfandel (California) $22. 92 —*P.G. (11/15/1999)*

M. Cosentino 2001 Cigar Zin Zinfandel (Lodi) $27. A jammy, plush style that serves up plenty of sweet oak and fruit. black-cherry, blackberry, plum, chocolate, and cassis are represented. Vanilla and spice round things off, leaving a fresh, fruity finish. **89** *(11/1/2003)*

M. Cosentino 2004 The Zin Zinfandel (Lodi) $30. Dark and very dry, with thick, sticky tannins, this Zin has cherry-berry and coffee flavors and a huge, mouthfilling texture. It's a rustic wine, charming in a hearty kind of way. **84** —*S.H. (3/1/2006)*

M. Cosentino 2003 The Zin Zinfandel (California) $30. Drinks almost sweet in cassis and sugared espresso flavors, and seems to have some residual sugar despite 15.2 percent alcohol. Fans of this genre will love it. **84** —*S.H. (10/1/2005)*

M. Cosentino 2002 The Zin Zinfandel (Lodi) $30. Kind of overripe in raisins and prunes, which detracts for me, but it's dry, with a chocolate and cassis finish that flatters the palate. The tannins are soft and sweet. **86** —*S.H. (2/1/2005)*

M. Cosentino 2001 The Zin Zinfandel (Lodi) $30. A fruity, jammy style that serves up black-cherry, blackberry, coffee, cola and spice notes. Tannins are ripe and firm with tea and toast notes at the end. **87** *(11/1/2003)*

M. Cosentino 2000 The Zin Zinfandel (Lodi) $30. Classic late-harvest Zin that packs a real whallop. Wld berries and stone fruits mingle with pruny, raisiny notes in this softly textured, rather alcoholic wine. They couldn't or didn't ferment to dryness, so there's some sugar in the middle palate and finish, where those raisiny flavors reappear. **87** —*S.H. (7/1/2002)*

M. Cosentino 1997 The Zin Zinfandel (California) $22. 93 —*P.G. (11/15/1999)*

M. TRINCHERO

M. Trinchero 1996 Coastal Selection Cabernet Sauvignon (California) $13. 85 —*S.H. (2/1/2000)*

M. Trinchero 1997 Family Selection Cabernet Sauvignon (Santa Barbara County) $13. 86 Best Buy —*S.H. (12/15/2000)*

M. Trinchero 1997 Founder's Estate Cabernet Sauvignon (Napa Valley) $40. 89 *(11/1/2000)*

M. Trinchero 1998 Coastal Selection Chardonnay (California) $12. 86 —*S.H. (12/31/1999)*

M. Trinchero 1998 Founder's Estate Chardonnay (Napa Valley) $25. 90 *(6/1/2000)*

M. Trinchero 1999 Marios Reserve Chardonnay (Napa Valley) $30. This is a seductive pleasure-bomb, with a ripe core of tropical, citrus, and banana fruit flavors wrapped in a toasty-oak and butterscotch cocoon. Lush and creamy, it hits all the right notes; as it pushes the ripeness and vanilla envelopes to the max, it does so with great style and balance. The long, toasty, crème brûlée finish has great appeal. Top Value. **92** *(7/1/2001)*

M. Trinchero 1997 Coastal Selection Merlot (California) $12. 84 —*S.H. (3/1/2000)*

M. Trinchero 1998 Family Selection Merlot (California) $12. From the Sutter Home family, a super value. You'll find sweetly ripe, round berry-cherry fruit flavors in a soft, supple package that's easy to drink. It's delicious and has some real class and elegance. Definitely a best buy in Merlot. **87 Best Buy** —*S.H. (5/1/2001)*

M. Trinchero 2000 Mary's Vineyard Sauvignon Blanc (Napa Valley) $19. Made in the full-blown, barrel-fermented and aged style, this wine shows off the cooper's art in its bold toasty-caramelly-vanilla aromas and flavors. Some peach fruit manages to sneak through the wooden stockade, providing a hint of balance. **84** *(8/1/2002)*

M.G. VALLEJO

M.G. Vallejo 2000 Pinot Noir (Sonoma) $11. Simple and candied, but not unpleasant, this is a perfect "party Pinot." Chill it slightly to accentuate the black-cherry fruit and minimize its slightly syrupy mouthfeel. **83** *(10/1/2002)*

M.G. Vallejo 1996 Red Blend (Sonoma County) $7. 84 *(11/15/1999)*

MACARI

Macari 2000 Alexandra Bordeaux Blend (North Fork of Long Island) $65. Starts with some scents of asphalt and treebark, then clears up to reveal ripe black-cherry aromas. This Merlot-dominated blend (69%) is firmly built but not hard, with notes of tobacco and earth that add welcome complexity. Finishes with good length and crisp acidity. **87** —*J.C. (10/2/2004)*

Macari 2000 Bergen Road Bordeaux Blend (North Fork of Long Island) $36. Despite being 66% Merlot, this wine isn't some soft, easy-drinking quaff. It's firmly structured and a bit lean, with shadings of tart red fruit, tobacco, and vanilla. **85** —*J.C. (10/2/2004)*

Macari 1997 Bergen Road Bordeaux Blend (North Fork of Long Island) $32. A blend of 55% Cabernet Sauvignon, 25% Merlot, 16% Cabernet Franc, and 4% Malbec, this top-end offering from Macari boasts bold aromas of weedy cassis tempered with toast and chocolate. Will be considered overly green by some, pleasantly herbal by others, but no one will deny its lush mouthfeel and appealingly peppery finish. **87** —*J.C. (4/1/2001)*

Macari 1997 Estate Bottled Cabernet Franc (North Fork of Long Island) $19. Sometimes Franc can have a lovely, alluringly floral bouquet; other times it can be downright vegetal and display green-bean characteristics. Unfortunately, this is an example of the latter. The wine has nice weight and texture, so if you don't mind your veggies in liquid form this might be more to your liking. **80** —*J.C. (4/1/2001)*

Macari 2003 Unfiltered Cabernet Franc (North Fork of Long Island) $24. Macari seems to have trouble getting Cabernet Franc ripe, as this wine shows. Tomato and vegetal aromas mix with pickle barrel, while the palate is tart and vegetal. **80** —*M.D. (8/1/2006)*

Macari NV Brut Champagne Blend (North Fork of Long Island) $21. Granny Smith apple, plus the tiniest bit of tropical fruit-pineapple and mango-aromas on the nose. There's more apple in the mouth, but it's more dull and unripe than vibrantly fruity; it finishes medium-long with lemon and apple-peel flavors. **84** —*D.T. (12/1/2001)*

Macari 2000 Chardonnay (North Fork of Long Island) $15. Seems a little sweet and simple on the palate, but does show solid aromatics of pear, herb, and apple. It's medium- weight, with a touch of anise on the finish. **84** —*J.C. (3/1/2002)*

Macari 2003 Early Wine Chardonnay (North Fork of Long Island) $12. Bottled just over a month after harvest, this light, crisp Chardonnay would make a decent shellfish white. Lime, peach, and mineral notes finish clean and fresh, with a zesty, citrusy aftertaste. **84** —*J.C. (10/2/2004)*

Macari 1998 Estate Bottled Chardonnay (North Fork of Long Island) $15. There's some light toast and vanilla flavors layered over modest Bosc-pear fruit, but a lack of intensity holds this wine back despite a generous mouthfeel and ample structure. **83** —*J.C. (4/1/2001)*

Macari 1998 Reserve Chardonnay (North Fork of Long Island) $22. These grapes were pushed hard: first for ripeness and low yields, then with barrel fermentation and plenty of new wood. The result is a rich, but-tery, nutty wine with a core of white-peach flavors that never fully reveal themselves. Drink young before the fruit fades. **85** —*J.C. (4/1/2001)*

Macari 1998 Merlot (North Fork of Long Island) $24. This top-notch effort is toasty from its stay in French oak, but has the rich depth of fruit to retain its balance. Although tight right now, black-cherry and espresso flavors are tinged with dried herbs. The finish is tart and lingering, and slightly tannic. Hold for two or three years, then drink over the next five or so. **88** —*J.C. (2/1/2002)*

Macari 2002 Estate Merlot (North Fork of Long Island) $15. Offers plenty of clove, cinnamon, coffee, and tobacco aromas, then delivers tart, lemo-ny fruit with undercurrents of tobacco. Tannins are supple, and the wine finishes crisp, with lively acidity. **84** —*J.C. (3/1/2006)*

Macari 2001 Reserve Merlot (North Fork of Long Island) $35. A toasty, vanilla-scented Merlot that boasts a plump, appealing mouthfeel, but seems to lack sufficient fruit to carry the weight of all the oak. Finishes with a hint of mocha. **83** —*J.C. (10/2/2004)*

Macari 2004 Sauvignon Blanc (North Fork of Long Island) $16. Nice tropi-cal fruit and citrus aromas waft from the glass, picking up pine along the way. Strong acids put this wine firmly on the tart side, and flavors of lemon/lime gatorade will have your mouth puckering. **80** —*M.D. (8/1/2006)*

Macari 1999 Estate Bottled Sauvignon Blanc (North Fork of Long Island) $10. Only slightly grassy and with strong lemony overtones to the fruit, this near-colorless white is as crisp and refreshing as a sea breeze. Would be perfect with the local oysters or clams on the half-shell. **85 Best Buy** —*J.C. (4/1/2001)*

Macari 2002 Block E White Blend (North Fork of Long Island) $36. This blend of Chardonnay (70%) and Sauvignon Blanc (30%) seems to have seen better days. It smells of roasted corn and butter, and comes across almost sweet and fat in the mouth. **82** —*J.C. (10/2/2004)*

Macari 2000 Essencia White Blend (North Fork of Long Island) $35. Quite honey-like, with a strong apricot component. Lush, rich and velvety on the palate. The wine is intense and focused, and long on the finish. **90** —*J.M. (12/1/2002)*

MACCALLUM

MacCallum 2002 DJ Red Cabernet Sauvignon-Syrah (Yakima Valley) $28. Syrah makes up almost three quarters of the blend; the rest is Cabernet, and the results are spectacular. This tiny winery (50 cases of this were produced) has come up with a meaty, substantial, poised, and polished effort that offers both heft and elegance—a rare combo. Dense, deep blueberry in color, it sends up evocative scents of violets and berries, then smoothes into a silky middle with cedar, sandalwood, lead pencil,

and licorice. Soft, substantial tannins keep it gliding through a long, sat-isfying finish. **93** —*P.G. (12/15/2004)*

MacCallum 2003 Shannon's Reserve Malbec (Columbia Valley (WA)) $28. Their first-ever reserve, this dark and tannic Malbec is densely extracted and shows the intense boysenberry character of the Northwest. Smoky tannins add a meatiness to the finish, along with some fat from new oak. **90** —*P.G. (10/1/2006)*

MacCallum 2003 Pinot Noir (Willamette Valley) $35. This tiny producer makes extraordinary wines. These Pinot vines are over 30 years old, low-yielding, and hand-harvested. New oak is restrained and the wine is left to express itself in a truly Burgundian fashion. The scents have a reveal-ing intensity, the bouquet is build up from many influences of fruit, spice, rock, and barrel. In the mouth it's full but restrained, with concen-trated power and plenty of acid. Exceptional winemaking. **92** —*P.G. (9/1/2006)*

MacCallum 2002 Syrah (Yakima Valley) $25. This is 100% Syrah, just 100 cases produced, and jumps right to the top ranks of Washington's best. Plenty of full frontal oak, but right behind it comes dark, serious, massive fruit. Beautifully layered, from hints of citrus peel, to red and blue berries, into the peppery and smoky finish, it is elegant and seam-lessly integrated through flavors that last a full minute in the mouth. **93** —*P.G. (12/15/2004)*

MACCHIA

Macchia 2001 Barbero Vineyard, Voluptuous Zinfandel (Lodi) $18. A big, jammy style, with plenty of up-front plum, black-cherry, blackberry and spice flavors. Coffee and chocolate line the edges, with bright acidity at the end. **87** *(11/1/2003)*

Macchia 2001 Clock Spring Vineyard Zinfandel (Amador County) $16. Kicks off with vanilla and spice notes. The flavors lean toward ripe cher-ry and plum, though the oak is quite forward and tends to mask the pretty fruit. Tannins are powdery but ripe. **86** *(11/1/2003)*

Macchia 2001 Generous Zinfandel (Lodi) $16. A full-bodied, slightly sweet style that touts a wellspring of tea, coffee and herb flavors at first, then follows with spicy cherry and blackberry notes. Zippy on the end. **86** *(11/1/2003)*

Macchia 2001 Linsteadt Vineyard Zinfandel (Amador County) $20. Toasty oak frames this plummy, spicy wine. The flavors extend to cherry and herbs as well and offer a smoky, beefy quality on the finish. This wine is a bit on the zippy side at the end. **85** *(11/1/2003)*

MACLEAN

Maclean 2002 Cabernet Sauvignon (Napa Valley) $45. This is a better wine than Maclean's '01, riper and richer. It shows blackberry, cassis, and oak flavors, and a good structure. Still, it could use greater concentra-tion. **85** —*S.H. (12/1/2005)*

Maclean 2001 Cabernet Sauvignon (Napa Valley) $50. Surprisingly vegetal for an '01 Napa Cab, this wine has an asparagusy streak that stands out. Finishes tart and earthy. **82** —*S.H. (9/1/2005)*

Maclean 2003 Sauvignon Blanc (Napa Valley) $18. On the sweet side, as if the grapefruit, fig, and apple flavors had some sugar put in, but that's mostly offset by good acidity. Still, it's not a completely dry wine, so be forewarned. **84** —*S.H. (11/1/2005)*

MACMURRAY RANCH

MacMurray Ranch 2004 Pinot Gris (Russian River Valley) $20. None of the MacMurray Ranch wines are shy on flavor, particularly the Pinot Gris, which is broad and mouthfilling. It coats the taste buds with fruity notes of peach, citrus, and strawberry, backing it up with a gentle almondy nuttiness. **87** *(11/1/2005)*

MacMurray Ranch 2003 Pinot Gris (Russian River Valley) $20. This is an elegant white wine, dry, crisp and sophisticated. Shows flashy flavors of citrus fruits, roasted almond and vanilla. Try as an alternative to Sauvignon Blanc. **87** —*S.H. (5/1/2005)*

MacMurray Ranch 2002 Pinot Gris (Russian River Valley) $23. Juicy as an orchard, a great big blast of peach, green apple, apricot, tangerine, and even mango fruit flavors that drink ripely sweet through the finish. A

USA

pretty veneer of crisp acidity powers this delicious wine. **87** —*S.H.* *(2/1/2004)*

MacMurray Ranch 2001 Pinot Gris (Russian River Valley) $23. Tries, like Henry Higgins, to boost Pinot Gris' homely, Eliza Doolittle personality into My Fair Lady, with some success. Has brilliantly upfront melon and citrus flavors, and was given lees aging for additional complexity. It's fun to drink, and fancy-complex, but it is kind of sweet, and displays sugar in the finish, for some reason. **86** —*S.H. (9/1/2003)*

MacMurray Ranch 2003 Pinot Noir (Sonoma Coast) $20. The largest cuvée by far, with 42,000 cases made, this will be the one most often seen on shelves. It features plenty of sweet-seeming upfront toast and caramel, gradually showing crisper, cherry-driven flavors, until it ends on a citrusy note. **87** *(11/1/2005)*

MacMurray Ranch 2003 Pinot Noir (Russian River Valley) $35. A big, full-bodied Pinot, with flavors of cola, black cherry, earth, and mushroom. A heat spike led to high sugars, says winemaker Susan Doyle, but the flavors lagged behind, requiring longer hang time. Slightly tough on the finish, this is a ruggedly masculine wine. **87** *(11/1/2005)*

MacMurray Ranch 2002 Pinot Noir (Sonoma Coast) $15. Crisp and delicate, with coffee and cherry flavors. A little rough around the edges, with dry tannins. Decant before serving. **85** —*S.H. (11/1/2004)*

MacMurray Ranch 2001 Pinot Noir (Sonoma Coast) $15. Kind of unripe and thin, with tobacco, beet and herb flavors, although a touch of black-cherry helps. The texture is smooth, but the finish is a little watery. **83** —*S.H. (7/1/2003)*

MacMurray Ranch 2000 Pinot Noir (Russian River Valley) $32. 87 *(10/1/2002)*

MacMurray Ranch 2003 River Cuvée Pinot Noir Pinot Noir (Russian River Valley) $60. Mainly Dijon clones off Martini's Del Rio property cropped at a measly 1.5 tons per acre, this wine shows good concentration and a full, soft mouthfeel. Cherry and vanilla flavors predominate, with a hint of mint adding some herbal complexity. Ends on dark chocolate and coffee notes; could use a little more length and fruit on the finish. Only 400 cases produced. **89** *(11/1/2005)*

MacMurray Ranch 2003 Winemaker's Block Selection Pinot Noir (Russian River Valley) $50. Too acidic and sweet for my tastes, with well-ripened cherry and mocha flavors that are certainly flattering. The sweetness seems to get stronger as the wine warms up, making it an awkward sip. **83** —*S.H. (5/1/2006)*

MACPHAIL

MacPhail 2004 Pinot Noir (Sonoma Coast) $40. Made from Dijon clones, this Pinot, from two vineyards in Sebastopol, shows classic coastal character in its firm dryness, crisp acidity, elegant mouthfeel and fruity flavors that, while ripe, finish with a rich touch of earthy mushrooms and herbs. It's a first-rate Pinot, at its youthful best now. **90** —*S.H. (9/1/2006)*

MacPhail 2003 Pinot Noir (Russian River Valley) $40. This delicious Pinot shows Russian River at its best. The wine is fully dry and balanced, with a rich, full-bodied mouthfeel that remains silky and smooth. The flavors are wonderful, all cherry marmalade, dusty cocoa, espresso, and sweet oak. **91** —*S.H. (12/15/2005)*

MacPhail 2002 Pinot Noir (Russian River Valley) $40. Delicate and light, showing smoky, hay and herb, coffee, and floral aromas. The flavors of sassafras and citrus peel lead to a spicy finish. Not showing much fruit, though. **86** *(11/1/2004)*

MacPhail 2004 Goodin Vineyard Pinot Noir (Sonoma Coast) $54. The vineyard is in Sebastopol, in the south of the Russian River Valley. Acidity in this wine is very high, almost prickly, while the fruit tends toward cola, rhubarb, just-ripe cherries, rosehip tea, and beef bouillion. It seems like the grapes were picked fairly early to yield a more structured Pinot. Doesn't seem like an ager, but could surprise. The finish is succulent. **92** —*S.H. (9/1/2006)*

MacPhail 2004 Pratt Vineyard Pinot Noir (Sonoma Coast) $56. The vineyard isn't very far from the Goodin Vineyard, which MacPhail also bottles, but the two wines are very different. This is far riper and more alcoholic, with dense flavors of cherry marmalade and melted chocolate,

and a cassis-like liqueur on the finish. It's a glyceriney wine that tastes sweeter than it technically is. Fairly tannic, the wine is best now through 2008. **92** —*S.H. (9/1/2006)*

MacPhail 2004 Sangiacomo Vineyard Pinot Noir (Sonoma Coast) $58. This big, powerful young wine tastes more alcoholic than the 14% that the label claims it is. It's superripe in cherry, blackberry, and cassis flavors, and Grenache-like in the mouth, which means it's a little heavy for a Pinot. If you like this style, you'll love this wine, which came from a vineyard in the county seat, Santa Rosa. **87** —*S.H. (9/1/2006)*

MacPhail 2003 Sangiacomo Vineyard Pinot Noir (Sonoma Coast) $40. This single-vineyard Pinot is distinctive. It has an intense white peppery aroma, but in the mouth shows a cascade of powerful cherry, cocoa and spice flavors, with a rich earthiness suggesting sautéed mushrooms with a dash of soy sauce. The mouthfeel is light and silky but powerful. It's a fascinating wine that changes with every sip. **94 Editors' Choice** —*S.H. (12/15/2005)*

MacPhail 2004 Toulouse Vineyard Pinot Noir (Anderson Valley) $37. The vineyard is in Philo, which isn't as cool as people think, especially when there are harvest heat spells as there were in 2004. The wine is very ripe, weighted down by raisiny, cooked berry flavors that seem more appropriate to Zinfandel. Still, it's a tasty wine, rich and fruity and dry. **86** —*S.H. (9/1/2006)*

MacPhail 2003 Toulouse Vineyard Pinot Noir (Anderson Valley) $35. Pale in color, light in body, this Pinot is elegant. It's dry and acidic, with cola, red cherry, coffee and vanilla flavors that finish in a swirl of spice. **87** —*S.H. (12/15/2005)*

MacPhail 2002 Toulouse Vineyard Pinot Noir (Anderson Valley) $35. Smoky and toasty on the nose, and jammy in candied cherry and cola. Very ripe, almost sweet. But it's easy and silky in the mouth. **84** *(11/1/2004)*

MACROSTIE

MacRostie 2004 Chardonnay (Carneros) $22. Last year, I wrote of this wine that it's firm in acids and minerals, with apple, citrus, and peach flavors and a clean, streamlined finish. The same goes for the '04. It's a totally dry, elegantly steely wine that won't compete with fancy fish or poultry dishes. **89** —*S.H. (7/1/2006)*

MacRostie 2003 Chardonnay (Carneros) $20. Firm in acids and minerals, and with well-oaked apple, citrus, and peach flavors, this streamlined Chardonnay is clean and balanced. It's a good accompaniment to cracked crab. **90 Editors' Choice** —*S.H. (10/1/2005)*

MacRostie 2002 Chardonnay (Carneros) $20. An interesting, complex Chard that straddles the line between steely austerity and fruity complexity and pulls it off well. Has citrus and apple flavors with nuances of more flamboyant peach and pear, and a great burst of fresh acidity. The oak is barely noticeable. Finishes dry and elegant. **90** —*S.H. (11/15/2004)*

MacRostie 1998 Chardonnay (Carneros) $19. 86 *(6/1/2000)*

MacRostie 2000 Reserve Chardonnay (Carneros) $25. This is a tight, young wine, bursting with well-charred oak aromas and flavors that add smoke, vanilla, and buttered toast to the underlying tropical fruit and spice flavors. There's also quite a bit of acidity, making this crisp wine lively and clean. **90** —*S.H. (2/1/2004)*

MacRostie 1998 Reserve Chardonnay (Carneros) $33. A lively citrus tang balances the rounder fig, melon, toast, and dried spice flavors that predominate here. Finishes evenly with medium length. It seems to be at its peak, so drink this round and well-integrated Chardonnay up now. **88** *(7/1/2001)*

MacRostie 2003 Wildcat Mountain Vineyard Chardonnay (Carneros) $30. Although this Chard was put through malolactic, it's quite acidic, stimulating the tastebuds with citrusy brightness. There are richer flavors of pears and smoky, buttered toast. This is the kind of Chard that gets more interesting in the glass as it warms up. **90** —*S.H. (11/1/2005)*

MacRostie 2001 Wildcat Mountain Vineyard Chardonnay (Carneros) $30. Impressive for its taut, tightly knit flavors of apples, peaches, and pears, held together by firm acids and a smattering of dusty tannins. A high percentage of oak also contributes tannins, as well as sweet vanilla and toast. **89** —*S.H. (11/15/2004)*

MacRostie 2002 Merlot (Carneros) $26. Beautiful Merlot, another argument in favor of Carneros as one of the variety's finest homes. Brisk acidity and fine, complex tannins set off lush blackberry jam, cassis, cola, coffee, and new-oak flavors. The wine has a soft, velvety texture. Best now through 2007. **90** —*S.H. (12/1/2006)*

MacRostie 2001 Merlot (Carneros) $26. From the Napa side, a fine Merlot that shows why Carneros has such a well-deserved reputation for the variety. Dark and juicy, with plum, coffee, and herb flavors, this wine has rich tannins and is very dry. It wil likely improve over the next five years. **90** —*S.H. (10/1/2004)*

MacRostie 1996 Merlot (Carneros) $26. **87** —*M.S. (6/1/1999)*

MacRostie 2003 Pinot Noir (Carneros) $26. What a nice Pinot this is. It's not only easy to drink, it's complex in the interplay of fruit, acids and oak. There are black and red cherries, pomegranates, sweet rhubarb pie, mocha, and spicebox flavors, wrapped in an elegantly silky package. The finish is deep and long. **90** —*S.H. (5/1/2006)*

MacRostie 2002 Pinot Noir (Carneros) $24. Starts with enticing aromas of roasted coffee bean, allspice, rhubarb, cola, oak, and a hint of black-cherry. Turns fairly heavy and weighty in the mouth, with some tannins, and finishes dry. **86** —*S.H. (4/1/2005)*

MacRostie 2001 Pinot Noir (Carneros) $24. Light in color and in body, marked by delicate cola, rhubarb, and cranberry flavors. Drinks dry and crisp in acids. Picks up a bit of sweet oaky complexity on the finish. **85** —*S.H. (5/1/2004)*

MacRostie 2001 Beresini Vineyard Reserve Pinot Noir (Carneros) $27. Here's a Pinot Noir that's light, silky, and elegant. You can taste the cool climate in the crisp acidity that undergirds the cherry, cola, and roseship tea flavors, and the finish is dry and clean. Not too much oak stands between the fruit and the palate. **87** —*S.H. (12/1/2004)*

MacRostie 2002 Wildcat Mountain Vineyard Syrah (Carneros) $32. A bit herbal, but those nuances are under control, lending complexity to the black-cherry and plum flavors. The result is a medium-weight wine that brings a boatload of spice and meat notes, even a hint of insecticide, yet stays supple and fruity at the same time. **92 Editors' Choice** *(9/1/2005)*

MacRostie 2001 Wildcat Mountain Vineyard Syrah (Carneros) $39. Here is cool-climate Syrah. There is a white pepper aroma that leaps from the glass, and the acids and tannins are much more pronounced. Yet there are also underlying blackberry and plum flavors that are rich, ripe, and dense. The wonderful structure and finesse is easily worth the price. **93 Editors' Choice** —*S.H. (5/1/2004)*

MADDALENA

Maddalena 2003 Cabernet Sauvignon (Paso Robles) $14. With grilled beef, lamb, or pork, this rugged wine will be fine. It's very dry, fruity, and fairly tannic, with flavors ranging from blackberries and espresso to smoky leather and oak—with a little unsweetened bitter chocolate pudding swirled into the finish. **85** —*S.H. (12/31/2006)*

Maddalena 2002 Cabernet Sauvignon (Paso Robles) $13. Here's a simple, country-style Cab, ripe in black-cherry and chocolate flavors. It's soft in acidity, and finishes slightly sweet. **83** —*S.H. (7/1/2006)*

Maddalena 2001 Cabernet Sauvignon (Paso Robles) $17. Soft and juicy, with plum, blackberry and chocolate flavors. Easy to drink and dry, with a spicy finish. **84** —*S.H. (10/1/2004)*

Maddalena 1999 Cabernet Sauvignon (Central Coast) $13. There's plenty of sweet, ripe blackberry, cherry, and chocolate flavors here, so if big taste is your thing, this is a good everyday wine. The texture is rather rustic, however, and the wine finishes simple. **84** —*S.H. (5/1/2003)*

Maddalena 2004 Chardonnay (Monterey) $12. Crisp in crunchy, mouthwatering acidity, with little or no oak, this Chard shows purely etched flavors of pineapples, kiwis, limes, and dusty spices. It's a fruit-forward, food-friendly wine that's clean and direct. **85** —*S.H. (11/15/2006)*

Maddalena 2003 Chardonnay (Monterey) $12. Tastes like the syrup you get in canned peaches and canned apricots, and is almost as sweet and soft, with clumsily applied oak. **82** —*S.H. (12/1/2005)*

Maddalena 2002 Chardonnay (Monterey) $10. A great value for its great big burst of juicy peach, pear, and tropical fruit flavors and the crisp acidic flair of its mouthfeel. Totally dry and balanced, it shows little oak, but the flavors stand on their own. **86 Best Buy** —*S.H. (11/15/2004)*

Maddalena 2001 Chardonnay (Monterey) $10. Hard to get lushness and complexity into a Chard at this price, but this wine tries hard. It's a cool climate wine, to judge from the crisp, upfront acidity. Flavors veer toward apples and citrus fruits, and if there's any oak, it doesn't show. Finishes clean and lean. **84** —*S.H. (8/1/2003)*

Maddalena 2000 Chardonnay (Monterey) $10. Good varietal character here, with peach flavors veering into tropical fruits, and a solid overlay of smoky oak. Has those pretty Monterey acids that add life and zest. The finish is spicy and peppery. It's a little bitter in the finish, but a perfectly nice wine, and a good value. **85** —*S.H. (6/1/2003)*

Maddalena 2002 Merlot (Paso Robles) $13. If you're fussy, this is an awkward wine, a bit sweet and rustic. Yet it's clean and fruity, and will easily wash down grilled meats and poultry. **83** —*S.H. (7/1/2006)*

Maddalena 2000 Merlot (Central Coast) $12. Smells and tastes like an inexpensive Aussie Shiraz, with jammy raspberry and cherry flavors and a dry, peppery finish. The texture is a little syrupy and thick, but it's a good, easy wine. **85** —*S.H. (8/1/2003)*

Maddalena 2003 Muscat Canelli (Paso Robles) $10. Overtly sweet, with orange and vanilla flavors, and lively acidity. This would be a lovely wine to sip on a summer day, or with fresh fruit. **85 Best Buy** —*S.H. (5/1/2005)*

Maddalena 2005 Pinot Grigio (Monterey) $12. Rustic, with off-dryish lemondrop flavors. Balanced by bright acidity. If you like your white wines a little sweet, this is a good pick. **83** —*S.H. (11/15/2006)*

Maddalena 2004 Pinot Grigio (Paso Robles) $12. Lots of figgy, peach, and citrus fruit in this ripe wine, which has enough tartness to make it clean. It doesn't taste entirely dry, though, with a honeyed richness throughout. Nice by-the-pool sipper. **84** —*S.H. (2/1/2006)*

Maddalena 2003 Pinot Grigio (Monterey) $11. Fruity and lush in vanilla-infused peach, apple, and pineapple flavors, accented with good acidity. A fine value in a dry white wine. **85** —*S.H. (12/15/2004)*

Maddalena 2002 Pinot Grigio (Monterey) $11. Takes an easy approach to the varietal that emphasizes the fresh citrus and white peach flavors and lets the crisp young acids shine. Pretty close to bone dry. **85** —*S.H. (12/1/2003)*

Maddalena 1999 Pinot Grigio (Arroyo Seco) $10. Packaged in a fancy bottle, it stakes a claim to class. Does it succeed? Yes, with pretty apple and spice aromas and rich apple-citrus flavors. Tart acids make it bright, and there are some nice dusty tannins. Doesn't quite achieve complexity, but it's a great drink, and, at this price, one of the year's best values in a white apéritif-style wine. **87 Best Buy** —*S.H. (12/15/2001)*

Maddalena 1998 Loma Vista Vineyard Pinot Grigio (Arroyo Seco) $9. **86 Best Buy** *(8/1/1999)*

Maddalena 2005 Riesling (Monterey) $12. Is it a dessert wine or a table wine? At 4% sugar, it's clearly sweet, but refreshing acidity and a light texture make it clean and vibrant. The mineral-laced apple and floral flavors will be fine with roast chicken, fresh fruit, or alone. **84** —*S.H. (11/1/2006)*

Maddalena 2004 Riesling (Monterey) $11. Overtly sweet in flowery nectarine and peach fruit, this wine needs more acidity for balance. It's soft and honeyed and simple. **82** —*S.H. (12/1/2005)*

Maddalena 2003 Riesling (Monterey) $10. Not really dry, more off-dry, with clean aromas and flavors of petrol, peaches, wildflowers, and vanilla. Enjoy this crisp, pleasant wine with fresh fruit or sautéed trout, or as an apéritif. **85 Best Buy** —*S.H. (12/1/2004)*

Maddalena 2002 Riesling (Monterey) $10. Full bodied and viscous on the palate, the wine is balanced by bright acidity that gives it good focus. Peach, grapefruit, apple, and spice notes are at the core here, followed by a lemony fresh finish. Quite fruity in style and fairly sweet. Try it as an apéritif or with duck and sweet sauces. **87 Best Buy** —*J.M. (8/1/2003)*

Maddalena 2005 Sauvignon Blanc (Paso Robles) $12. Nice and refreshing, with flavors of fig, peach, pineapple, and quince purée, slightly sweetened by honey, but finished with brisk acidity. This is a fine everyday sipper. **84** —*S.H. (12/31/2006)*

Maddalena 2004 Sauvignon Blanc (Paso Robles) $12. Simple and rich in spearmint, peach, fig, and vanilla flavors, this white wine has a semisweet taste, and just enough tartness to keep it from cloying. **83** —*S.H. (12/1/2005)*

Maddalena 2002 Sauvignon Blanc (Paso Robles) $10. A nice, easy-drinking and affordable wine for everyday purposes. Has all you want in an inexpensive white, plenty of savory citrus and lemongrass flavors, zesty acids and a clean, fruity flourish on the finish. A very good value. **85** —*S.H. (12/15/2003)*

Maddalena 2002 Syrah (Central Coast) $13. This is a dry, fruity wine that shows good Syrah character. It's smooth and balanced, with cherry and blackberry flavors and a tannic finish. A blend of Monterey and Paso Robles fruit. **84** —*S.H. (12/31/2005)*

Maddalena 1997 Loma Vista Vineyard Syrah (Arroyo Seco) $15. 86 —*L.W. (2/1/2000)*

Maddalena 2005 Syrah Rosé Syrah (Paso Robles) $12. Simple, soft, and a little sweet, with strawberry and raspberry soda flavors and a spicy, white peppery finish. Nice picnic or beach blush wine. **83** —*S.H. (11/15/2006)*

MADONNA

Madonna 2004 Mont. St. John Pinot Grigio (Carneros) $26. Pricey, but distinctive for its bright, refreshing acidity and dry, complex citrus, kiwi, green apple, and white pepper flavors, with nuances of oak and lees. **91** —*S.H. (2/1/2006)*

Madonna 2001 Due Ragazzi Reserve Pinot Noir (Carneros) $55. Dijon clones seem to give a purity of fruit that leaps out of the glass, and here you'll find focused cherry and cola flavors, with intriguingly complex notes of mint and smoky oak. The wine drinks young, acidic, and tannic now, but should soften and sweeten in a few years. **86** —*S.H. (12/1/2004)*

MADONNA ESTATE

Madonna Estate 2002 Madonna Estate Pinot Noir (Carneros) $20. Very ripe with its chocolate, toffee, and cherry jam aromas. Clean and spicy in the mouth, showing sassafras, cola, and cherry flavors. Finishes with all kinds of spices. **85** *(11/1/2004)*

Madonna Estate-Mont St. John 2000 Chardonnay (Carneros) $16. Way too oaky, like drinking toothpicks. Packs a mouthful of char and smoky spice riding on top of apple and peach flavors. The finish turns spicy and oaky again. **85** —*S.H. (6/1/2003)*

MADRIGAL

Madrigal 1997 Merlot (Napa Valley) $24. 82 —*J.C. (7/1/2000)*

Madrigal 1996 Petite Sirah (Napa Valley) $24. 84 —*M.S. (6/1/1999)*

Madrigal 2001 Petite Sirah (Napa Valley) $35. Starts off with rich aromas that are redolent of chocolate, coffee, and black-cherry. On the palate, it's firm textured, framed in ripe tannins that highlight more cassis, earth, spice, and complex herb flavors. Bright and long on the finish, this is a big, beautiful wine. **93** —*J.M. (9/1/2004)*

Madrigal 2000 Petite Sirah (Napa Valley) $33. Young, fresh, and vibrant, this exuberant wine has appealing raspberry-smoky aromas and flavors, compounded with notes of leather, spice, and sweet espresso. Feels rich and smooth in the mouth, thanks to soft tannins. **88** *(4/1/2003)*

Madrigal 1999 Petite Sirah (Napa Valley) $30. A deep purple hue foreshadows the ripe, rich flavors in this wine. Jammy blackberry, cassis, herb, licorice, and spice all blend nicely. They are framed in supple, firm tannins, and backed by a tangy finish. **91 Editors' Choice** —*J.M. (12/1/2002)*

Madrigal 2001 Zinfandel (Napa Valley) $26. Sleek and smooth textured, this fleshy, velvety wine is packed with lovely plum, black-cherry, cedar,

herb, spice, and chocolate flavors. It's lush, long, and rich, yet offers a good measure of finesse and elegance. Not over the top, just terrific. **91** —*J.M. (8/1/2004)*

MADRONA

Madrona 2000 Gewürztraminer (El Dorado) $10. Opens with beautiful Gewürz aromas like honeysuckle, plum blossom, vanilla, fresh peaches and white chocolate. But this early promise of great taste isn't fulfilled. In the mouth the wine is disappointingly thin. The finish reveals some spicy peach flavors. **84** —*S.H. (9/1/2003)*

Madrona 2002 Malbec (El Dorado) $27. Here's an understated claret-style wine that doesn't overwhelm with any one thing, just satisfies with overall balance and style. It's dry and complex, with a seamless integration of blackberry fruit and oak, and supportive tannins. **90** —*S.H. (7/1/2005)*

Madrona 1999 Marsanne (El Dorado) $15. Exotic and rich, it drinks like a chocolate smoothie, with cocoa and vanilla flavors, a creamy texture and some residual sugar. Good acidity balances things out. There are also some pretty peach and pear flavors. **84** —*S.H. (12/15/2001)*

Madrona 2002 New-World Port (El Dorado) $24. Not quite off-dry, but with a little sweetness, an earthy, chocolatey wine that's neither here nor there. **84** —*S.H. (7/1/2005)*

Madrona 2003 Melange de Trois Rhône White Blend (El Dorado) $16. This Rhône-style blend is a nice, everyday wine. It has apple, peach, and floral flavors. Turns creamy and ripely sweet on the finish. **85** —*S.H. (10/1/2005)*

Madrona 2001 Riesling (El Dorado) $10. Quite viscous, with creamy peach, melon, and pear flavors at its core. An odd mineral note sticks out, though, while the finish could use a touch more acidity. **82** —*J.M. (8/1/2003)*

Madrona 2000 Dry Riesling (El Dorado County) $12. From one of the highest vineyards in California, at 3,000 feet, another dependably dry, complex wine from this specialist. It's leaner than in previous years, with subtle citrus flavors, but very well structured. A real bite of lemony acid makes it perfect for a grilled trout. It's also an ager and a good value. **87 Best Buy** —*S.H. (6/1/2002)*

Madrona 1999 Dry Riesling (El Dorado) $14. A lovely, crisp, light wine that's not really dry, but nearly so. Has finely detailed citrus and wildflower aromas and flavors, and good acidity. **85** —*S.H. (8/1/2001)*

Madrona 2002 Shiraz-Cabernet Sauvignon (El Dorado) $16. Lots of snappy cherry, cocoa, gingerbread, and spice flavors in this gentle wine. It's a little too soft, and is almost as sweet as a dessert wine on the finish. **84** —*S.H. (10/1/2005)*

Madrona 1999 Reserve Syrah (El Dorado) $20. Chunky tannins surround a center of rich black cherry fruit with a strong dose of white pepper. Fully dry and balanced, long on flavor, this wine has mid-term aging possibilities. **87** —*S.H. (2/1/2003)*

Madrona 1998 Zinfandel (El Dorado County) $12. 86 —*S.H. (5/1/2000)*

Madrona 2003 Zinfandel (El Dorado) $15. An interesting and likeable wine. It's dry, but packed with ripe cherry pie flavors and a dusting of powdered sugar and cocoa, and a tiny taste of currants. Would benefit from greater acidity or tannins. **87** —*S.H. (10/1/2005)*

Madrona 2000 Zinfandel (El Dorado) $14. This is a good example of a slightly rustic, mountain-grown Zinfandel. It's dry and powerful in wild, brambly fruit and alcohol, and the tannins are assertive. Has a rough-and-ready character but is clean and balanced and possesses a sense of the earth. **87** —*S.H. (11/1/2002)*

Madrona 2003 30th Anniversary Zinfandel (El Dorado) $38. Madrona does a good job with mountain Zin, and for their anniversary they pulled out all the stops. The wine is exceptionally balanced, showing none of the excess that can mar Foothills Zin. Dry, delicious in spice, cocoa, and berry flavors and rich in fine, smooth tannins, it's drinking well now and should be best in its vibrant youth. Try with a very fine steak. **92 Editors' Choice** —*S.H. (7/1/2006)*

Madrona 1997 Late Harvest Zinfandel (El Dorado) $16. 84 —*S.H. (5/1/2000)*

Madrona 1998 Reserve Zinfandel (El Dorado) $18. Smoke and oak dominate the nose, with some fairly light, pretty fruit underneath. The oak seems mismatched for the weight of the fruit, which is sweet and charming, like cherry Lifesavers. **87** —*P.G. (3/1/2001)*

Madrona 1997 Reserve Zinfandel (Paso Robles) $18. 89 —*S.H. (5/1/2000)*

MAFFEY

Maffey 2000 Zinfandel (California) $24. An assemblage from both cool and warm Northern California regions, and a successful one. Coastal grapes provide the zesty acidity and fine tannins, while Lodi brings lush, rich fruit. The overall effect is dry, rich and full-bodied. **87** —*S.H. (12/1/2002)*

MAHONEY

Mahoney 2002 Mahoney Vineyard Pinot Noir (Carneros) $36. Fairly tannic fare from Carneros Creek's Francis Mahoney, and not showing much now, but it may be a keeper. You'll find a rich and interesting mélange of tobacco, earth and herbs, with a tease of black-cherry and spice. Very dry and crisp on the finish. **86** —*S.H. (11/1/2004)*

MAISON BASQUE

Maison Basque 1997 Black Zinfandel Zinfandel (California) $24. Dark, brick colored wine, heavily oxidized, with nutty, smoky, Madeira-like flavors, and thick, dry tannins. An odd, raisiny approach to Zin. **82** —*P.G. (3/1/2001)*

MAKOR

Makor 2001 Zinfandel (Arroyo Grande Valley) $12. A leaner style that still serves up plenty of pretty, ripe plum, berry and cherry flavors. Tea, coffee and toast bring up the rear, with a finish that shows good length. **87** *(11/1/2003)*

MALIBU

Malibu 2004 Bordeaux Blend (California) $40. Even in the cool Santa Monica Mountains of Malibu the heat waves of this vintage struck, and this wine suffered. It has Porty, raisiny aromas and a stewed-fruit taste, with heat on the finish. **82** —*S.H. (12/1/2006)*

Malibu 2004 Cabernet Franc (California) $30. Pours light in color for a Bordeaux red, and the wine itself is delicate and elegant, without the density of, say, Napa. Yet it's full of fruity flavor, rich in black-cherries, and bone dry. **86** —*S.H. (12/1/2006)*

Malibu 2004 Syrah (California) $30. Dry, with a cooked or stewed-berry flavor and tannic, acidic bitterness on the finish. Considerable French oak just adds oak to an ordinary wine. **82** —*S.H. (12/1/2006)*

MALVOLIO

Malvolio 2002 Laetitia Vineyard Block A Pinot Noir (Arroyo Grande Valley) $56. Huge, dark. Opens with beautifully ripe cherry, cola, rhubarb, oak and plum notes, with a spicy, pine needle scent. It's massive, but brilliantly balanced and opulent, with a lush, silky texture. Has plenty of tannins, and should have no problems holding and even improving over the next several years. **92** *(11/1/2004)*

Malvolio 2001 Laetitia Vineyard Block A Pinot Noir (Arroyo Grande Valley) $48. This wonderful wine trades a bit of Block I's seductive immediacy for a richer, darker structure you may want to cellar for a few years. The flavors suggest plums, blackberries and black-cherries complexed with chocolate and coffee, but that silky Pinot texture remains alluring. **92** —*S.H. (10/1/2004)*

Malvolio 2001 Laetitia Vineyard Block F Pinot Noir (Arroyo Grande Valley) $48. Similar to Block I, but with darker cherry, mocha, spice and oak flavors, and also a leathery, smoked meat note. It's also more tannic, and a bit closed now. Interesting how different these blocks are even in the same vineyard. **91** —*S.H. (10/1/2004)*

Malvolio 2001 Laetitia Vineyard Block I Pinot Noir (Arroyo Grande Valley) $48. Wow, what a delicious Pinot. It's lusciously silky in the mouth, with great acids framing a complex array of flavors ranging from red cherries, black raspberries and oaky vanilla to Asian spices and sweet tobacco. Absolutely addictive and compelling, and shows what this vineyard is capable of. **93** —*S.H. (10/1/2004)*

Malvolio 2002 Laetitia Vineyard Clone 115 Pinot Noir (Arroyo Grande Valley) $48. Opens with dramatic char, obviously lots of good new oak, with complex scents of lavender, clove, cinnamon, bigtime cherry pie, vanilla. Velvety, lush in the mouth. This is a powerful, dense, even brooding wine, plastered with oak, that needs long decanting or aging to show its best. Now through 2010. Another great success from this AVA. **92** *(11/1/2004)*

Malvolio 2003 Laetitia Vineyard Clone 667 Pinot Noir (Arroyo Grande Valley) $48. An extraordinarily rich Pinot, fat and opulent in cherry compote, mocha and root beer flavors. Generously oaked, it offers spicy oak notes and a velvety texture. It's a big, fruit-forward wine, but manages to maintain delicacy and harmony throughout. Best now through 2008. **92** —*S.H. (10/1/2006)*

Malvolio 2002 Laetitia Vineyard Clone 667 Pinot Noir (Arroyo Grande Valley) $48. A big, rich and complex wine. Itï¿?s almost Syrah-like, dark and bold in smoky, meaty, plum and chocolate flavors, but is saved by crisp acidity and a smooth silkiness. Really good, and will get better for a year or two. **89** *(11/1/2004)*

Malvolio 2003 Laetitia Vineyard Clone 777 Pinot Noir (Arroyo Grande Valley) $48. Silky elegance marks this wine, with subtle flavorings of cola, red cherries, tobacco and cinnamon spice. **92** —*S.H. (7/1/2006)*

MANDOLINA

Mandolina 2001 Dolcetto (Santa Barbara County) $12. Opens with intricate and invitingly complex aromas of leather, grilled meat, black raspberries, cherries, and sautéed mushrooms. Turns fruity in the mouth, with cherry and berry flavors and a sprinkling of spice. The tannins are easy. **86** —*S.H. (3/1/2004)*

Mandolina 2005 Pinot Grigio (Santa Barbara County) $14. Forward and ripe in fig, citrus, and tropical fruit flavors, but with a good grip of acidity. It's a little sweet on the finish. **84** —*S.H. (12/1/2006)*

Mandolina 2004 Pinot Grigio (Santa Barbara County) $14. A little sweet on the finish, but otherwise a nice sipper, with citrus, nectarine, and peach flavors balanced with good acidity. If that finish were totally dry, it would be a heck of a wine. **84** —*S.H. (2/1/2006)*

Mandolina 2003 Toccata Riserva Red Blend (Santa Barbara County) $32. More or less a Cal-Ital blend, the wine is aromatically pretty but very sweet in the mouth. It tastes like sugared blackberry tea and chocolate-filled cherry candies. **82** —*S.H. (12/1/2004)*

Mandolina 2002 Rosato Rosé Blend (Santa Barbara County) $12. An uncomplicated and zippy little wine that pours a pretty coppery-red color and smells like freshly picked strawberries. The strawberry and raspberry flavors are peppery-spicy, and there's a tiny amount of sweetness to offset the acidity. VALUE. **85** —*S.H. (3/1/2004)*

MANNING ESTATES

Manning Estates 2001 Cabernet Sauvignon (Central Coast) $8. Drinks rather weedy and herbal, with notes of green stalky wood and bark dominating the modest blackberry flavors. It's dry and clean, with sturdy tannins, and would benefit from a little more fruit. **83** —*S.H. (11/15/2003)*

Manning Estates 2002 Chardonnay (Central Coast) $8. Seven hundred fifty milliliters of the vast ocean of Chardonnay now on the market has been put into a bottle, and this is what it tastes like. It's got peaches and apples and a bit of oak, in a creamy texture. **84** —*S.H. (12/31/2003)*

Manning Estates 2001 Merlot (Central Coast) $8. Modest, with pleasant plum and blackberry aromas and flavors. Drinks dry and clean, with soft tannins. Perfectly acceptable for everyday needs. **83** —*S.H. (2/1/2004)*

MANZONI

Manzoni 2004 Family Estate Vineyard Pinot Noir (Santa Lucia Highlands) $23. This a young, tough Pinot with considerable tannins and acidity. Chew on it, though, and you find cherries, darker blackberries, and bitter chocolate. The question is ageability, and the answer is only a guess. Try holding through 2006. **88** —*S.H. (12/1/2006)*

USA

USA

MARA

Mara 2004 Dolinsek Ranch Reserve Zinfandel (Russian River Valley) $40. Unbalanced, with a hot, Porty mouthfeel and medicinal, sweet-and-sour cherry flavors. **82** —*S.H. (12/15/2006)*

MARAMONTE

Maramonte 2002 Syrage Premium Red Table Wine Red Blend (California) $12. This is a blend of Syrah, Petit Verdot, and Petite Sirah. It's a very good wine. Dry, soft, and polished, it features blackberry pie, cherry-filled chocolate candy, and coffee flavors that are wrapped in soft but complex tannins. Kudos to the winemaker who came up with this interesting blend. **88 Best Buy** —*S.H. (12/31/2006)*

MARCELINA

Marcelina 1995 Cabernet Sauvignon (Napa Valley) $25. 87 —*L.W. (11/1/1999)*

Marcelina 1998 Cabernet Sauvignon (Napa Valley) $30. Basic upscale Cabernet here, with black currant and green olive notes encased in oak. It's dry and soft, but it does have a plush, velvety texture. There's some good fruit in the middle and a nice spiciness that lasts into the finish. **87** —*S.H. (6/1/2002)*

Marcelina 2003 Chardonnay (Carneros) $24. Pretty acidic now, and dry, with the flavor of grapefruit and lime juice and a squeeze of peach syrup. There's a mineral thing going on in the finish. **86** —*S.H. (10/1/2005)*

Marcelina 2001 Chardonnay (Carneros) $25. A Chard that's rich and oaky. Fills the mouth with ripe flavors of apples, peaches, and pears, wrapped in a creamy, smooth texture. Finishes with a delicious array of spices. **89** —*S.H. (5/1/2003)*

Marcelina 1997 Chardonnay (Napa Valley) $22. 88 *(6/1/2000)*

Marcelina 2000 Pinot Noir (Carneros) $32. 87 *(10/1/2002)*

MARGUERITE-RYAN

Marguerite-Ryan 2000 Pisoni Vineyards Pinot Noir (Santa Lucia Highlands) $48. Vividly fragrant, with silky smooth tannins framing the ensemble. The wine features black cherry, blackberry, sage, coffee, spice, anise, clove, and a hint of bright raspberry on the finish. Full-bodied yet balanced and elegant, it is long and lush to the end. **92** —*J.M. (7/1/2003)*

Marguerite-Ryan 2000 Sara Jean's Vineyard Pinot Noir (Santa Lucia Highlands) $45. Pretty cedar, spice, cherry, herb, chocolate, and anise flavors are smoothly integrated. It's rich and dynamic on the palate, a mix of creamy smooth texture and firm acidity that adds interest. Long on the finish. **90** —*J.M. (7/1/2003)*

MARIAH

Mariah 1999 Merlot (Mendocino Ridge) $30. Here's a wine that could teach certain regions to the south a thing or two. Fully ripened fruit contains nary a hint of those bothersome vegetal notes. Instead, plush blackberry flavors are packed into a balanced wine of proper acids and dry, dusty, tannins. this is quite an accomplishment and adds luster to the reputation of its appellation. **93** —*S.H. (5/1/2002)*

Mariah 1998 Merlot (Mendocino Ridge) $28. 93 —*S.H. (5/1/2002)*

Mariah 1999 Syrah (Mendocino Ridge) $30. This Brown-Forman-owned brand succeeded with Zinfandel and now is trying its hand at Syrah, with mixed results. This release, while well-made, lacks stuffing, although the acid and tannin structure is very good. There are some earthy-berry flavors but the wine needs more oomph. More tinkering is called for, probably in the vineyards. **85** —*S.H. (5/1/2002)*

Mariah 1999 Syrah (Mendocino Ridge) $30. This Brown-Forman-owned brand succeeded with Zinfandel and now is trying its hand at Syrah, with mixed results. This release, while well-made, lacks stuffing, although the acid and tannin structure is very good. Ther are some earthy-berry flavors but the wine needs more ooomph. More tinkering is called for, probably in the vineyards. **85** —*S.H. (5/1/2002)*

Mariah 2003 Zinfandel (Mendocino Ridge) $25. Soft, complex, and delicious, this Zin comes from mountain vineyards grown high above the fogs of Anderson Valley, where the sun ripens the grapes well. The wine is lush and complex, with black currant, mocha, and spice flavors that are so ripe they suggest rum-soaked raisins. **90** —*S.H. (11/15/2006)*

Mariah 2002 Zinfandel (Mendocino Ridge) $35. Created as a Zinfandel specialist, Mariah produces exquisitely crafted, although big-boned, Zins from this high-altitude appellation. The wine is dry and balanced, with a rich earthiness to the blackberry, coffee, and tobacco flavors. It's also very tannic, and needs to be served with the right fare. Lamb and duck come to mind. **90** —*S.H. (5/1/2006)*

Mariah 2001 Zinfandel (Mendocino Ridge) $30. Say hello to this marvelously ripe, cheerful Zin. It totally turns you on. The marvelously ripe flavors range from sweet cherries to a baked blackberry tart dusted with cinnamon and cocoa, and finished with a bite of fig. Soft, unctuous tannins, rich acids, total balance. Released simultaneously with the '00, but so much better at the same price. **93 Editors' Choice** —*S.H. (2/1/2005)*

Mariah 2000 Zinfandel (Mendocino Ridge) $30. Black as night, gooey as sweet ice cream syrup, flooded with cherry, blackberry, and mocha flavors, yet totally dry. So filled with fruity richness, so soft in tannins, it's addictively drinkable. **90** —*S.H. (2/1/2005)*

Mariah 1999 Zinfandel (Mendocino Ridge) $31. Dark in color and dense in aroma, with plummy, blackberry, woody notes. Tastes big and rich and deep, a wine to accompany roasted meat and game. This winery is making an attempt to establish itself as a first-growth Zin house, and bears watching. **90** —*S.H. (5/1/2002)*

Mariah 2001 Poor Ranch Vineyard Zinfandel (Mendocino) $35. A very good Zin that's more tannic than Mariah's Mendocino Ridge wines, and a little less concentrated in fruit. Nonetheless, it's dry, big-hearted and warming in berries and spices. **90** —*S.H. (2/1/2005)*

MARICOPA

Maricopa 1999 Shiraz (California) $8. The nose is so cedary it's almost sauna-like, but it works with the cherry fruit. Surprisingly complex flavors of tobacco, earth, and stable leather accent the dark berry foundation. It's balanced and has a long, juicy finish. And, unusual at this price, it may also improve over the next year or two. **87 Best Buy** *(10/1/2001)*

MARILYN REMARK

Marilyn Remark 2003 Grenache (Monterey County) $45. There's lots of rich, ripe cherry flavor in this dry wine, as well as lingering notes of vanilla, cinnamon, and milk chocolate. It goes down easy for the soft, creamy texture and gentle tannins. **87** —*S.H. (12/1/2005)*

Marilyn Remark 2002 Wild Horse Road Vineyard Grenache (Monterey County) $45. From a warmer part of Monterey, but you can taste the herbs and fresh acids that the last of the chilly winds bring. They join tart red cherries, rhubarb, and touches of oak to frame this dry, delicate wine. It possesses subtleties that keep you coming back for more **88** —*S.H. (12/31/2004)*

Marilyn Remark 2001 Wild Horse Road Vineyard Grenache (Monterey County) $45. This Grenache tastes old-viney, with amazingly dense, concentrated flavors of black cherry fruit and nuances of smoky coffee that hit the palate with force and last through a long finish. They're wrapped in rich, sweet tannins, and finish with lively pepper and acidity. **92** —*S.H. (5/1/2004)*

Marilyn Remark 2004 Loma Pacific Vineyard Marsanne (Monterey County) $30. This is a fun wine. It has a rich, creamy texture, and is very flavorful, with white peach, apricot, spice, and sweet oak flavors. The finish is oaky and bright with acidity. **86** —*S.H. (12/1/2005)*

Marilyn Remark 2003 Loma Pacific Vineyard Marsanne (Monterey County) $30. An extraordinarily rich and fruity white wine, dry and crisp, but lavish in peach, papaya, mocha, honeysuckle, vanilla, and smoky flavors, and a butter cream texture. No mere fruit bomb, it has elegance and complexity. **89** —*S.H. (12/31/2004)*

Marilyn Remark 2002 Loma Pacific Vineyard Marsanne (Monterey County) $28. A dramatically good wine from a new winery that bears watching. It has the rich, creamy flair of a top Chardonnay, but with more exotic flavors. They include white peach, guava, wildflowers, and spicy lemon zest. Bone dry, with a sleek, minerally spine of acid. **91** —*S.H. (2/1/2004)*

Marilyn Remark 2003 Petite Sirah (California) $26. Rich and full-bodied, this heartwarming wine appeals for its smooth, dry texture, richly dense tannins, and complex flavors of dark stone fruits, leather, roasted coffee, and spice. It should play well against well-marbled beef. **90** —*S.H. (12/1/2005)*

Marilyn Remark 2004 Rosé de Saignee Rosé Blend (Monterey County) $22. You can smell the cherries in this Syrah and Grenache blend as soon as you pop the cork. Vibrant in red cherry, strawberry, raspberry, rose petal, and vanilla flavors, it's bone dry and crisp. This blush wine shows real class. **87** —*S.H. (12/1/2005)*

Marilyn Remark 2004 Lockwood Valley Vineyard Roussanne (Monterey County) $25. From a warmer part of the Salinas Valley, this is a somewhat simple, heavy wine, with a creamy texture and citrus, apricot, and papaya flavors enhanced with a touch of oak. Finishes dry and full-bodied. **85** —*S.H. (12/1/2005)*

Marilyn Remark 2003 Arroyo Loma Vineyard Syrah (Monterey County) $35. Seems a bit thin on fruit and dominated by toasty oak, picking up a caramelly, toasted marshmallow flavor on the finish. **82** *(9/1/2005)*

Marilyn Remark 2002 Arroyo Loma Vineyard Syrah (Monterey County) $35. Dry, dense, and deeply flavored, this powerful wine might improve with a few years of age. It's tannic now, and laced with cool climate acids, but those black plum, coffee, and Provencal herb flavors are there, waiting to get out. **88** —*S.H. (12/31/2004)*

MARIMAR ESTATE

Marimar Estate 2003 Don Miguel Vineyard Chardonnay (Russian River Valley) $28. Chards are tight, acidic, and minerally in youth, showing a lees-infused structure but offering waves of complexity. With toasty oak, the base flavors are of nectarines, mangoes, peaches, zesty green apples, and dustings of Asian spice. **92** —*S.H. (12/1/2006)*

Marimar Estate 2002 Don Miguel Vineyard Chardonnay (Russian River Valley) $28. I loved Marimar Torres's Dobles Lias Chard, released earlier, for many of the reasons I like this one. First is the brilliant acidity, brisk, bold and palate-stimulating. Then there's the complex palate, full of sweet green apple, pineapple, mango, mineral, vanilla, and buttered toast flavors. **93 Editors' Choice** —*S.H. (11/15/2005)*

Marimar Estate 2005 Don Miguel Vineyard Acero Chardonnay (Russian River Valley) $25. Distinctive; shows the ripe tropical fruits and Fuji apples that mark the appellation, but also a richly exotic streak of apricot. Grown in the cool Green Valley region, the wine is marked by crisp, minerally acids. Amazingly, it's never seen oak, although it has a wonderfully creamy texture. **91** —*S.H. (12/31/2006)*

Marimar Estate 2003 Don Miguel Vineyard Dobles Lias Chardonnay (Russian River Valley) $40. Dobles lías, "double lees," tells you this is a leesy wine, and that slight sour-creamy flavor dominates. This is a wine you love or don't. I find it refreshingly dry and complex, not a fruit bomb, but a dry, elegant Chard, in which new French oak adds enriching notes. **92** —*S.H. (7/1/2006)*

Marimar Estate 2002 Don Miguel Vineyard Dobles Lias Estate Chardonnay (Russian River Valley) $40. I like this wine because it's different. You'll find green apple and pineapple flavors, and various toasted notes of wood, coconut, and hazelnut, not to mention lees and Oriental spice. Those crisp Green Valley acids undergird the richness. Finishes complex and with great finesse. **92** —*S.H. (10/1/2005)*

Marimar Estate 2003 Don Miguel Vineyard Pinot Noir (Russian River Valley) $35. Here's a very dry, stylish Pinot, and while it has plenty of fruit, it has mushroom, balsamic, and soy flavors that deepen and ground the cherries and cola. The overall impression is of a young, complex, fleshy Pinot that should hold and develop for five years. **91** —*S.H. (12/1/2006)*

Marimar Estate 2002 Don Miguel Vineyard Pinot Noir (Russian River Valley) $35. Pours dark, smells strong and clean, showing cherries, vanilla, oak, spices, and herbs. Full-bodied, crisp in acids and with sturdy tannins, but lacks the stuffing for a higher score. **86** *(11/1/2004)*

Marimar Estate 2003 Don Miguel Vineyard Cristina Selection Pinot Noir (Russian River Valley) $47. When our tasting panel team tasted the '02 a few years ago, we found it heavy, but possibly a sleeper. The '03 is in the same vein. While it lacks a certain vibrancy and has tannic weight, the deeply flavored core of cherries is impressive and suggests mid-term aging. **86** —*S.H. (12/1/2006)*

Marimar Estate 2002 Don Miguel Vineyard Cristina Selection Pinot Noir (Russian River Valley) $45. Ripe, oaky, and chocolatey, with hints of cherries and spices, and very dry, but a bit heavy. Seems to want more freshness and charm: it's rather tannic. Could be a sleeper; try after 2006. **85** *(11/1/2004)*

Marimar Estate 2004 Don Miguel Vineyard Earthquake Pinot Noir (Russian River Valley) $47. This is Marimar's reserve-style Pinot. The '04, like the '03, shows authoritative structure in the fine tannins and acids that frame wonderfully ripe fruit. It's a complex, grippy young wine, elaborately gorgeous in blackberry pie, cherry tart, blueberry, cola and vanilla spice flavors, with an earthy undertow of balsamic-dashed heirloom tomato. Great now and through 2007 for its youthful beauty. **94** —*S.H. (12/31/2006)*

Marimar Estate 2003 Don Miguel Vineyard Earthquake Block Pinot Noir (Russian River Valley) $42. Structure defines this superb Pinot Noir. It's dramatic in fruit, with tantalizingly ripe black cherry and cola flavors, and has been generously oaked, but it's the classic acid-tannin balance elevates it. Like all great Pinots, it teases the palate, now one thing, now another. Drink now through 2007. **93** —*S.H. (11/15/2005)*

Marimar Estate 2004 Dona Margarita Vineyard Pinot Noir (Sonoma Coast) $45. This is Marimar's first Sonoma Coast Pinot, and the result is promising. The wine is more acidic and deeper than her estate Pinots, bringing to mind Hirsch Pinots. It's big, rich, complex, and almost Syrah-like. A wine to watch. **90** —*S.H. (12/1/2006)*

MARIMAR TORRES

Marimar Torres 2001 Dobles Lias Chardonnay (Russian River Valley) $40. Creamy and smooth, a wine with the texture of taffeta, and for those who like their Chards toward the citrusy, appley side. The extra lees aging gives it a sour mash flavor that, combined with the brisk acids, is distinctive. **88** —*S.H. (12/15/2003)*

Marimar Torres 2000 Don Miguel-Dobles Lias Chardonnay (Russian River Valley) $40. Tighter and leaner than in the past, with flavors that range between lime, hazelnut, and peach. Very crisp acidity is uplifting and bright. But what really marks this wine is the extended lees contact. The creamy, rich texture feels just great. This is an elegant wine of great complexity. **92** —*S.H. (12/15/2002)*

Marimar Torres 2001 Don Miguel Vineyard Chardonnay (Russian River Valley) $28. There's lots of rich acidity in this wine. It braces the tremendous pear and pineapple fruit and sweet oak, and lends the wine zest and structure. Finishes with a brilliant array of tangy spices. **90** —*S.H. (11/15/2004)*

Marimar Torres 2000 Don Miguel Vineyard Chardonnay (Russian River Valley) $26. This is brilliant Chard because of its superb tropical fruit flavors, the powerful but tasteful oak and the rich, crisp acidity. It takes all three of those components for a big California Chard to work, and this one does. **92** —*S.H. (5/1/2003)*

Marimar Torres 1998 Don Miguel Vineyard Chardonnay (Russian River Valley) $25. **86** —*S.H. (11/15/2000)*

Marimar Torres 1997 Don Miguel Vineyard Chardonnay (Russian River Valley) $25. **85** *(6/1/2000)*

Marimar Torres 1998 Don Miguel Vineyard Dobles Lías Chardonnay (Russian River Valley) $45. This is a unique wine with an unusual and impressive bouquet of peach smoke, cocoa, and hazelnut. Balanced but firm on the palate, it offers robust fruit and spice flavors and mint, toast and nut accents. There's even an intriguing kirsch-like cherry note in here. Full-bodied, it's a wine of real individual character that finishes dense, long and spicy. **90** *(7/1/2001)*

Marimar Torres 2001 Don Miguel Vineyard Pinot Noir (Russian River Valley) $35. The wine is dark and big, as you might expect given the vintage. Feels heavy and earthy, with a mélange of beet, cherry tomato, coffee, cola, and oak flavors, and rich tannins on the finish. Not showing much delicacy or refinement now. Try after 2006. **88** —*S.H. (12/1/2004)*

Marimar Torres 2000 Don Miguel Vineyard Pinot Noir (Russian River Valley) $32. Dark berry fruit, tea, and herb accents and prominent chocolate notes feature in this multifaceted wine. It's plummy and woodsy, full in feel, yet tart and tangy on the long, rich, dark chocolate close. Drink now–2006. **88** *(10/1/2002)*

Marimar Torres 1999 Don Miguel Vineyard Pinot Noir (Russian River Valley) $32. Saturated with rich plum aromas that are accented by cola and root beer, this is a winner in terms of depth and balance. A soft but structured palate offers black fruit and enough wood to satisfy a lumberjack; a touch too much charcoal on the finish holds it back from greatness. **89** *(10/1/2002)*

Marimar Torres 1998 Don Miguel Vineyard Pinot Noir (Russian River Valley) $30. 91 —*S.H. (12/15/2000)*

MARIO PERELLI-MINETTI

Mario Perelli-Minetti 2001 Cabernet Sauvignon (Napa Valley) $21. A little ordinary, but an okay Cab, although at this price you'll do better elsewhere. Berries and herbs, with dry tannins on the finish. **84** —*S.H. (10/1/2005)*

Mario Perelli-Minetti 2000 Miriam Reserve Cabernet Sauvignon (Napa Valley) $75. This is quite a serious Cabernet from a winery that hasn't been too visible for a while. It's intensely concentrated in cassis fruit, and well-oaked, and also fairly tannic and dry. Graceful and elegantly structured, it may well hold for a decade or more. **93** —*S.H. (10/1/2005)*

MARK RIDGE

Mark Ridge 2000 Merlot (California) $9. Smells young and jammy, with newly-fermented aromas of black cherries and raspberries. Tastes like jam, too, oozing with ripe fruity-berry flavors. There's lots to like here, although the wine can't overcome its humble, country-cousin roots. **86 Best Buy** —*S.H. (11/15/2002)*

MARK RYAN

Mark Ryan 2001 Ciel du Cheval Vineyard "Dead Horse" Bordeaux Blend (Red Mountain) $35. The name is a questionable play on "Ciel du Cheval" which loosely translates as Horse Heaven. There is nothing questionable about the wine, a stunning success. Inky, thick with black cherry fruit, wrapped in smoke and iron, it captures the essence of the vineyard. The blend includes 10% Petit Verdot; which adds wonderful complexity, and the judicious new oak seals it with a kiss of butterscotch. **93** —*P.P. (12/1/2004)*

Mark Ryan 2003 Gun Metal Red Bordeaux Blend (Columbia Valley (WA)) $35. This Bordeaux blend is 64% Cabernet Sauvignon, 21% Merlot, and 15% Cab Franc. The cooler region allows the fruit to ripen while keeping its grip and muscle. It's lush but not jammy; showing herb and wood (20 months in French oak), bacon, and smoke. The finish is layered with cedar, leaf, and resonant, plummy fruits. Beautifully long and balanced. 350 cases made. **90** —*P.G. (12/15/2005)*

Mark Ryan 2001 Long Haul Red Bordeaux Blend (Columbia Valley (WA)) $35. A muscular Bordeaux blend that mixes 46% Merlot, 31% Cab Franc, 12% Cab Sauvignon and 11% Petite Verdot. There's nice midpalate concentration, showing black cherry, berry, and currant. Just a hint of rubber ball, but the wine overall has an elegant profile, sleek and well put together. **90** —*P.G. (12/1/2004)*

Mark Ryan 2005 Chardonnay (Columbia Valley (WA)) $35. Grape sources are Conner-Lee and Stillwater Creek, and as befits them, the wine was given first-class treatment: French oak, native yeasts, lees stirring, etc. The results are impressively rich and creamy, packed with tropical fruit, mango, pineapple, apricot—whatever you call it, it's yummy stuff. **91** —*P.G. (12/31/2006)*

Mark Ryan 2003 Bad Lands Red Red Blend (Red Mountain) $45. An intriguing blend of two-thirds Kiona Syrah, one-third Ciel du Cheval Petit Verdot, this textural wine retains its Syrah aromatics but bulks up tannically from the PV, which contributes green herb and eucalyptus spice notes also. Winemaker Mark McNeilly is on to something special here, though a small hole remains right in the midpalate. The finish resonates with an herbal/minty spice note. Just 97 cases made. **89** —*P.G. (12/15/2005)*

Mark Ryan 2004 Dead Horse Ciel du Cheval Vineyard Red Blend (Red Mountain) $42. This wine somewhat inverts the winery's Long Haul label, with Cabernet dominant rather than Merlot. It is the most com-

pact, vertical, and indecipherable of the Mark Ryan wines, and the most potentially expressive of the magnificent Ciel du Cheval fruit. Black cherry, licorice, smoke, and graphite add layers of darkness—a veritable Joseph Conrad wine—and it will require more age to reveal all of its secrets. **94** —*P.G. (12/31/2006)*

Mark Ryan 2003 Dead Horse Red Red Blend (Red Mountain) $39. The winery's "Left Bank" blend is 58% Cabernet Sauvignon, 21% Merlot, 17% Cab Franc, and 4% Petit Verdot, all Ciel du Cheval fruit. The biggest and best wine of a very strong lineup, it captures the rich, silky chocolate flavors of high-end Napa but also showcases the elegant, gravelly minerality of the vineyard. Dense and layered, with extended mixed fruit flavors enhanced with notes of cinnamon toast and mocha. 300 cases made **93 Editors' Choice** —*P.G. (12/15/2005)*

Mark Ryan 2004 Long Haul Ciel du Cheval Vineyard Red Blend (Red Mountain) $39. Also from Ciel du Cheval, this Pomerol-styled red was tasted a few weeks ahead of its planned November release. The black cherry fruit, with a dark mineral and graphite undercurrent, rides on a river of acid into the silky finish of coffee and buttery chocolate. Beautifully structured and—there's no better word for it—hedonistic. **93** —*P.G. (12/31/2006)*

Mark Ryan 2003 Long Haul Red Red Blend (Red Mountain) $37. The Long Haul is the winery's "Right Bank" blend, it's 48% Merlot, 45% Cab Franc, and 7% Petit Verdot. All Ciel du Cheval fruit, it's big but structured, melding buoyant cherry fruit to a gravelly mineral base. It's a meaty, tannic wine, but the minerality keeps it lively and rich without being too heavy. Has some green-tea flavors in the tannins; the whole package is a jump forward in polish and grace from previous vintages. Just 225 cases produced. **92** —*P.G. (12/15/2005)*

Mark Ryan 2004 The Dissident Red Blend (Washington) $25. A tremendous value, this blend of Cabernet, Merlot, and Syrah is named for a Pearl Jam song and matches that band's vigor and raw energy. Thick tannins and scrapey acids suggest why these grapes may have been cut from the final blends for the other wines, but they show plenty of firm, ripe fruit and tarry complexity. **89** —*P.G. (12/31/2006)*

Mark Ryan 2004 Wild Eyed Syrah (Red Mountain) $35. Red Mountain fruit (from Ciel, Hedges and Kiona) creates this delicious Syrah, laced with powerful flavors of coffee liqueur and chocolate. Co-fermented with a dash of Viognier. Satiny and citrusy, it maintains an elegant precision for a wine that offers such richness. **92** —*P.G. (12/31/2006)*

Mark Ryan 2005 Viognier (Red Mountain) $25. This wine goes right to the top of the heap to stand with the best Washington viogniers. The fruit is from Ciel du Cheval on Red Mountain, and winemaker Mark McNeilly has framed it in his own distinctive style. Big but not heavy, lush and textural, it's slathered in flavors of pear and caramel, with a lightly honeyed finish. Just 100 cases were produced. **93** —*P.G. (12/31/2006)*

MARK WEST

Mark West 1997 Chardonnay (Russian River Valley) $14. 88 —*S.H. (11/1/1999)*

Mark West 1999 Gewürztraminer (Sonoma County) $12. An exquisite wine that combines delicacy and harmony with enormously fruity-spicy flavors that fill the mouth. The aromas suggest candied ginger, tropical fruits, vanilla, and wildflowers. The flavors are effusively fruity and on the dry side, with refreshingly crisp acidity. Try it with Asian-Pacific fusion foods. **87** —*S.H. (5/1/2001)*

Mark West 1996 Godwin Family Reserve Merlot (Sonoma County) $NA. 81 —*L.W. (12/31/1999)*

Mark West 2004 Pinot Noir (Central Coast) $9. Lots to like in this simple, varietally proper Pinot. It's light bodied and silky, with a very soft texture and pretty flavors of cola, cherries, blackberries, and toast. Finishes dry and spicy. **84** —*S.H. (12/15/2005)*

Mark West 1999 Pinot Noir (Sonoma County) $18. Light, tasty, and simple, it offers up pretty aromas of red raspberries, smoke, and vanilla. In the mouth it's fruity and soft. There's good extracted fruit and a generous dusting of oak. It can't quite achieve complexity, but it's a nice wine that's thoroughly enjoyable. **85** —*S.H. (5/1/2001)*

USA

MARKHAM

Markham 1996 Cabernet Sauvignon (Napa Valley) $22. 89 —S.H. (2/1/2000)

Markham 2002 Cabernet Sauvignon (Napa Valley) $30. Middling Cab, with cigarette stub and cherry-berry aromas and flavors. The flavors are pleasant and varietally true. **83** —S.H. (9/1/2006)

Markham 2001 Cabernet Sauvignon (Napa Valley) $27. There's something awkwardly disagreeable about this wine. It's soft and gluey, and finishes cloyingly sweet. **81** —S.H. (12/1/2005)

Markham 2004 Chardonnay (Napa Valley) $18. Feels flat and soft, with weak peach and pineapple fruit. Slightly sugary on the finish. Barrel fermentation adds some richness. **83** —S.H. (11/15/2006)

Markham 2002 Chardonnay (Napa Valley) $19. A bells and whistles Chard that pulls out all the stops for richness. Ripe tropical fruit and peach flavors swim in smoky oak with vanilla and spice overtones. The texture is creamy, with crisp acidity. **86** —S.H. (12/1/2004)

Markham 2000 Chardonnay (Napa Valley) $17. Toasty, spicy oak leads the way here, framing pear, apple, and lemon flavors in a medium-bodied mouthfeel. Bright on the finish. **86** —J.M. (12/15/2002)

Markham 1999 Chardonnay (Napa Valley) $17. Quite oaky and bright, with a tangy lemon core. Somewhat simple and lean; clean on the finish. **82** —J.M. (12/15/2002)

Markham 1999 Reserve Chardonnay (Napa Valley) $31. This soft, elegant wine made from select lots shows plush peach, apple, pear, melon, and caramel notes on the nose and in the mouth. The peach is particularly distinct. Not overpowering, it's a sleeper that has plenty of texture, plus butterscotch and coconut flavors playing out on the even finish. **89** (6/1/2003)

Markham 1997 Reserve Chardonnay (Napa Valley) $28. 91 —L.W. (11/15/1999)

Markham 1997 Merlot (Napa Valley) $19. 85 —S.H. (7/1/2000)

Markham 2002 Merlot (Napa Valley) $22. Definitely on the ripe, intense side, with strong flavors of currants and anise-infused chocolate, but keeps its balance and integrity, mainly through the fine acid-tannin balance. Not too oaky, either, and what a great, long finish. **88** —S.H. (8/1/2005)

Markham 2000 Reserve Merlot (Napa Valley) $42. I liked Markham's 2002 Merlot, but this reserve, with which it was co-released, is on a higher plane. It's grittier in tannins and oakier, and shows all sorts of fruit, herb, spice, and oak complexities. Overall, a softly balanced, dry red wine to showcase fine culinary efforts. **92** —S.H. (8/1/2005)

Markham 1998 Reserve Merlot (Napa Valley) $38. Somewhat herbal, with hints of blackberry, cherry, and spice. The tannins are moderate, as is the finish, with a dash of pepper at the end. **85** —J.M. (11/15/2002)

Markham 1997 Reserve Merlot (Napa Valley) $35. Delivers almost everything you could ask for from a California Merlot. Plenty of plush, opulent fruit (blackberry and currant) and high-quality oak, and it tastes terrific. It has that pinpoint, laser-like quality you find in good wine. It's also very tannic: It numbs the palate and dries out on the finish, so it's best now with rich, fatty meats or age it and let it soften. **92 Editors' Choice** —S.H. (6/1/2001)

Markham 1996 Reserve Merlot (Napa Valley) $35. 92 —M.S. (3/1/2000)

Markham 1999 Petite Sirah (Napa Valley) $24. On the plus side are rich blackberry, dark cherry, and earthy flavors, enhanced with full-throttle, toasty oak. But the wine tastes a bit simple. All in all, drinkable, but no complexity. **83** (4/1/2003)

Markham 1998 Petite Sirah (Napa Valley) $24. Markham has been a reliable Petite source over the years, and succeeded even in the difficult '98 vintage. Rich blackberries and blueberries are dusted with black pepper. The one indication of a tough year is the dry, tannic finish, but it should work fine with a rare steak. **88** —J.C. (9/1/2002)

Markham 1998 Sauvignon Blanc (Napa Valley) $10. 87 Best Buy (3/1/2000)

Markham 2004 Sauvignon Blanc (Napa Valley) $14. Classic coastal-style Sauvignon, bright and crisp in acids, yet very ripe and rich in fruit. The figs, melons, sweet white peaches, and pink grapefruit flavors are easy and delicious. **85** —S.H. (11/15/2005)

Markham 2003 Sauvignon Blanc (Napa Valley) $14. Made solidly in the current style of ripely sweet fig, citrus, and spice flavors with a good backbone of acidity. Clean and refreshing. **84** —S.H. (12/1/2004)

Markham 2001 Sauvignon Blanc (Napa Valley) $13. Lemon-lime aromas, flavors of grapefruit, pear, anise, and white pepper, and a medium finish with hints of lemon zest is what you get from this wine. It has what it takes to match a wide variety of food, and served well chilled it can be a good apéritif all by itself. **88** (9/1/2003)

Markham 1999 Sauvignon Blanc (Napa Valley) $10. An easy-to-drink wine with simple but pretty flavors of citrus and wildflower; smoky, honeyed notes add complexity. It's on the sweet side, maybe too much so, but that's the way lots of people like to drink their "dry" white wines. Decent value. **84** —S.H. (5/1/2001)

Markham 2002 Zinfandel (Napa Valley) $20. Easy and gentle, with well-ripened cherry-berry flavors mingled with green peppercorn and dill, this Zin offers pleasure for its soft tannins and long finish. It has a dry, fruity, spicy finish. **85** —S.H. (12/1/2005)

Markham 2001 Zinfandel (Napa Valley) $17. A wine that serves up a moderate array of spicy plum, black cherry, blackberry, and licorice flavors, all framed in mild tannins and finishing with moderate length. **85** (11/1/2003)

Markham 1999 Zinfandel (Napa Valley) $17. Markham makes a straightforward, good-value bottle, emphasizing dark, smoky, tarry scents and big, chunky cherry fruit. There is plenty of weight and heavy tannin, but the wine feels a bit heavy and plodding. **85** —P.G. (3/1/2002)

MARR

Marr 2002 Cuvée Selena Grenache (California) $18. Easy and polished; a silky, delicately structured wine with ripe cherry and spice flavors that are offset by just-right acids and tannins. Likable for its instant appeal and the way the cherry flavors last on the finish. **85** —S.H. (12/1/2006)

Marr 2003 Petite Sirah (Tehema Foothills) $27. Very much in the same vein as the '02, this is a wine intense and concentrated with blackberry jam and coffee flavors. It finishes dry, with some fairly hefty tannins and shows a ruggedness that could soften with bottle age. **86** —S.H. (12/1/2006)

Marr 2002 Petite Sirah (Tehema Foothills) $27. The grapes came from 2,500 feet up on Mount Lassen, and there is indeed power and intensity to the blackberry and coffee flavors as well as a spicy, peppery finish. The wine is pretty tannic and should develop well over the next ten years. **86** —S.H. (12/1/2006)

Marr 2001 Petite Sirah (Tehema Foothills) $24. From the Sierra Foothills, a simple, likeable wine with pleasant berry-cherry flavors and a solid dose of toasty oak. It's very tannic, so be warned, but it's okay to drink now with rustic fare, such as pizza. A few tasters objected to its tart astringency. **86** (4/1/2003)

Marr 2003 Cuvée Patrick Reserve Rhône Red Blend (California) $22. The winemaker sourced Syrah and Petite Sirah from various parts of the state, then threw in a splash of Viognier. The result is a brisk, bright, fairly acidic red wine that's lush in cherry, blackberry, and chocolate flavors. With strong, dry tannins, this is a good wine that shows the fine art of blending. **86** —S.H. (12/1/2006)

Marr 1999 Vine Hill Syrah (Russian River Valley) $25. Made in a jammy, extracted style, with baked apple pie, cinnamon, anise, and black pepper aromas. The tannins are pretty strong now, and so the wine is tough and aggressive. Best to let it sit for a year or two. **85** —S.H. (12/1/2002)

Marr 2003 Zinfandel (Sonoma County) $26. Very black in color with massive black currant flavors and very high alcohol. It's certainly a brawny Zin, and it hardly needs the added Petite Sirah, which makes it even more muscular and youthfully aggressive. But it's a good, sound wine that should age for decades. **88** —S.H. (12/1/2006)

Marr 2003 Mattern Ranch Old Vine Zinfandel (Mendocino County) $23. From a hot, inland part of Mendocino planted in 1930. It has a little

USA

Petite Sirah, and who knows what else. It's a big, thick, wine that's delicious and layered in berry, cherry and chocolate flavors. And it has that high-alcohol prickly heat you either love or hate. Distinctively and proudly Californian. **89** —*S.H. (12/1/2006)*

MARSHALL

Marshall 2004 Duarte Vineyard Barbera (Placer County) $13. Here's an everyday blush with forward flavors of raspberries, strawberries, and vanilla. It's a little sweet. It's the perfect innocent Thanksgiving wine to have with a honeybaked ham and all the trimmings. **84** —*S.H. (11/1/2005)*

Marshall 2001 Cabernet Franc (Napa Valley) $28. Starts with an unpleasant asparagus smell. It's dry, tannic, and simple on the palate. **81** —*S.H. (11/1/2005)*

Marshall 2003 Pinot Noir (Carneros) $28. With its light, silky texture, delicate mouthfeel, and upfront flavors of cherries, mocha, and oak, this delightful Pinot is easy to drink. Its tart acids and dusty tannins will be a nice counterpoint to food. **87** —*S.H. (11/1/2005)*

MARSHALL FAMILY WINES

Marshall Family Wines 2003 Syrah (Napa Valley) $26. Has some dense blackberry and plum flavors but they're buried deep under a blanket of road tar and rubber that never truly dissipates. Oaky, too. **83** *(9/1/2005)*

MARSTON FAMILY

Marston Family 2001 Cabernet Sauvignon (Spring Mountain) $65. A very fine Cab. It's tightly wound and rather closed down now, with sturdy tannins, but chew on it and discover a fantastic core of sweet blackberry fruit. Best after 2008 and long afterwards. By renowned vintner Philippe Melka. **93 Cellar Selection** —*S.H. (10/1/2004)*

Marston Family 2000 Cabernet Sauvignon (Spring Mountain) $60. Somewhat lean and firm textured, with powdery tannins that frame a core of blackberry, cassis, anise, herbs, and spice. The finish is moderate in length, with a hint of astringency. With time, the wine should age quite gracefully. Best after 2006. **88** —*J.M. (2/1/2004)*

Marston Family 1999 Cabernet Sauvignon (Spring Mountain) $60. Opens with aromas of black currants, chocolate, and olives, then adds toasty oak. The mouthfeel is smooth and velvety, and the wine is fully dry. There's an edge of rough earthiness that keeps it from getting a higher score, but it's still a very good wine. **87** —*S.H. (2/1/2003)*

Marston Family 2002 Proprietor Grown Cabernet Sauvignon (Spring Mountain) $80. This Cab flirts with overripeness, and just manages to avoid it. Another day or two on the vine, and those currant and chocolate flavors would have been raisins. Winemaker Philippe Melka has lavished considerable oak on it, and it shows in the raw, cedar, and ash aroma. Drink now. **86** —*S.H. (11/15/2005)*

MARTELLA

Martella 2004 Oleta Vineyard Grenache (Fiddletown) $26. Intensely jammy in red cherry fruit, this likeable, easy wine also shows a crisp acidity that grips the palate and balances the superripeness. There are flavor and texture complexities that lift it out of the ordinary. **86** —*S.H. (10/1/2006)*

Martella 2003 Heart Arrow Ranch Petite Sirah (Mendocino) $35. Tastes both ripe and unripe at the same time, with the prime feature being a tart acidity that makes the palate burn. The flavors are of raisins and mint, and the finish is dry. **82** —*S.H. (10/1/2006)*

Martella 2003 Camel Hill Syrah (Santa Cruz Mountains) $55. This wine might improve with age, but right now the parts are not cooperating. You have ripe blackberry and coffee fruit with an edge of raisins, gritty tannins that make the tongue stick to the gums, and sweet oak that sticks out like a sore thumb. It's all good, but a bit feral. Give it three years. **88** —*S.H. (10/1/2006)*

Martella 2002 Camel Hill Vineyard Syrah (Santa Cruz Mountains) $55. This interesting wine showcases a host of dark, spicy notes beginning to end: coffee, dark chocolate, roasted meat, black pepper, you name it. Medium-bodied and well balanced; 51 cases produced. **87** *(9/1/2005)*

Martella 2003 Fairbairn Ranch Syrah (Mendocino) $45. From the longtime winemaker at Thomas Fogarty in the Santa Cruz Mountains comes this lush fruit bomb from Mendocino. Cedar and vanilla mark the nose, but the palate couches ripe plummy fruit in a cradle of vanilla. Finishes with a touch of heat. The bad news? Only 76 cases made. **88** *(9/1/2005)*

Martella 2003 Hammer Syrah (California) $24. Tough and gritty, this is a country-style wine with ripe berry, cherry, and coffee flavors that finish a little sweet in raisins. It's at its best now, so drink up. **83** —*S.H. (10/1/2006)*

Martella 2002 Hammer Syrah (California) $24. Thick and dark in terms of flavors and aromas, but not in terms of richness or size. On the nose, we found thick, syrupy fruit and chocolate flavors; on the palate, plum fruit. Some call it supple, others, simple. Whatever side we fell on, we all agreed that it was a good, enjoyable quaffer. **86** *(9/1/2005)*

Martella 2000 Hammer Syrah (California) $23. Here's one of the richer Syrahs on the market. It's almost like biting into a cherry-filled chocolate candy, it's that flamboyant in flavor. Sweet fruit spreads over the tongue, coating it with soft tannins and low acids. It's best in its sweet youth. **87** —*S.H. (12/1/2002)*

Martella 1999 Hammer Syrah (California) $NA. The panel was pretty consistent in its comments on the Martella: All agreed that neither the palate nor the bouquet show extraordinarily unusual flavors, but what's here (plenty of blackberry, vanilla, and spices) is rich, set in a velvety texture, and pushes all the right buttons. Smoke, cinnamon, and briary aromas on the nose; slightly hot but raspberry flavors on the finish. Very pleasurable. Only 695 cases produced. Top Value. **91** *(11/1/2001)*

Martella 2004 Zinfandel (Fiddletown) $26. Drinks a little hot and over-ripe, with raisiny flavors, but at least it's fully dry. If these big, ripe, extracted Sierra Foothills Zins are your thing, you'll love it. **84** —*S.H. (10/1/2006)*

MARTHA CLARA

Martha Clara 2000 6025 Bordeaux Blend (North Fork of Long Island) $NA. **84** —*J.C. (10/2/2004)*

Martha Clara 2000 Chardonnay (North Fork of Long Island) $14. A lightweight wine, with modest apple and pear flavors edged out by lima bean and plywood notes. Finishes lemony. **82** —*J.C. (3/1/2002)*

Martha Clara 1999 Chardonnay (North Fork of Long Island) $10. Toast aromas accent ripe pears and golden-delicious apples in this soft, easy-to-like Chard that only lacks a bit of depth. A slightly bitter note on the finish should become less noticeable over the next few months. **83** —*J.C. (4/1/2001)*

Martha Clara 2000 Estate Reserve Chardonnay (North Fork of Long Island) $18. A steely, lean, and focused wine. Quite lovely and made in a fine, Burgundian style. The fruit is subtle but expands on the palate to reveal wonderful pear, apple, citrus, herb, and mineral qualities. Long and fresh on the finish. **90 Editors' Choice** —*J.M. (4/1/2003)*

Martha Clara 1999 Estate Reserve Chardonnay (North Fork of Long Island) $17. A snappy, tangy wine that shows good balance and integration. Its mineral core fans out to reveal pretty pear, apple, citrus, and herb flavors, all couched in moderate toast. **87** —*J.M. (7/1/2002)*

Martha Clara 2004 Gewürztraminer (North Fork of Long Island) $16. A sweet white offering varietally correct aromas of rose, lychee, and spice. Low alcohol and low acid leave the sugar to do the talking, which it does with flavors of lychee and peach. Good for summer sipping, with a spicy finish. **84** —*M.D. (8/1/2006)*

Martha Clara 2001 Gewürztraminer (North Fork of Long Island) $15. Fairly dry, with lemony litchee, melon flavors, wrapped in a mineral-like robe. Very crisp, very clean; and quite light textured. **87** —*J.M. (1/1/2003)*

Martha Clara 2000 Gewürztraminer (North Fork of Long Island) $15. It's spicy, as the grape's name implies, but doesn't have a lot of the rose or lychee scents typical of the variety. Instead, there's baking spices lightly sprinkled over honeydew melon. Nice balance of sweet and tart elements makes the wine easy to drink. **85** —*J.C. (3/1/2002)*

Martha Clara 2000 Merlot (North Fork of Long Island) $16. **84** —*J.C. (10/2/2004)*

Martha Clara 2004 Pinot Grigio (North Fork of Long Island) $16. Starts off with modest pear and pineapple scents, then delivers citrus and underripe pear flavors on the light-bodied palate. Tart and crisp on the finish. **83** —*J.C. (2/1/2006)*

Martha Clara 2002 Five-O Red Blend (North Fork of Long Island) $25. Half Merlot, with the rest Cabernet Sauvignon, Cabernet Franc, and Syrah, this earthy blend offers flavors of tobacco, mushroom, and mixed berry. A zesty nose offers lemon and red fruit, with a touch of funk, while the wine finishes with earthy, plummy notes. **84** —*M.D. (8/1/2006)*

Martha Clara 2004 Riesling (North Fork of Long Island) $15. After the acetone blows off, the aromas are like sticking your nose in a honey jar. Round and sweet in the mouth, but not full, with honeysuckle and animal musk flavors, this lacks acidity to lift it, giving it a heavy feeling. **80** —*M.D. (8/1/2006)*

Martha Clara 2000 Riesling (North Fork of Long Island) $15. This medium-weight Riesling has distinctive oil-shale aromas that meld well with the melon, apple, pear, and lime flavors. The tart finish lingers, bringing in a note of slightly bitter citrus rind. **87** —*J.C. (1/1/2004)*

Martha Clara 2004 Sauvignon Blanc (North Fork of Long Island) $16. With its relativly low alcohol (12.2%) and brisk, citrusy flavors, this would make a solid beach-party wine. Hints of peach help to round it out, but the emphasis is on refreshing acidity. **85** —*J.C. (3/1/2006)*

Martha Clara 2003 Estate Reserve Sauvignon Blanc (North Fork of Long Island) $21. Aromas of metallic fruit conjure memories of canned peaches, and while two of our panelists were forgiving and found likable qualities like mineral, stone fruits and a soft texture, our third taster shot this one down, labeling it "mealy and spread thin." **85** *(7/1/2005)*

Martha Clara 1999 Sémillon-Chardonnay (North Fork of Long Island) $15. An intensely lemony wine that folds in some pear aromatics. Quite full on the palate and yet very fresh, clean and citrusy; tailor-made for the region's shellfish. **84** —*J.C. (4/1/2001)*

Martha Clara NV Brut Methode Sparkling Blend (North Fork of Long Island) $18. Shows some hints of light toast on the nose, followed by pineapples and pears on the palate. It's creamy and smooth in the mouth, but has a suggestion of sweetness that distracts slightly from what should be a crisp, clean finish. **84** —*J.C. (12/1/2003)*

Martha Clara 1999 Viognier (North Fork of Long Island) $15. An absense of the variety's trademark floral and peach aromatics presages the lack of ripeness found on the palate. An angular peppery streak of green fruit runs through the wine from start to finish, despite good palate presence. **81** —*J.C. (4/1/2001)*

Martha Clara 2000 Ciel White Blend (North Fork of Long Island) $26. Honeyed and lush, with hints of apricot, apple, citrus, and peach. Rich and full on the palate. **88** —*J.M. (12/1/2002)*

MARTIN & WEYRICH

Martin & Weyrich 2001 Cabernet Sauvignon (Paso Robles) $40. A fine effort. It was so easy to get ripeness in this long, warm vintage, which shows in the sunburst of blackberry, cherry, and spicy black plum flavors that mark this Cab. It's soft and supple in the mouth, with a pleasingly sweet finish. **86** —*S.H. (10/1/2004)*

Martin & Weyrich 2001 Etrusco Cabernet Sauvignon (Paso Robles) $22. Plump and juicy, with ripe flavors of blackberries, cherries, and herbs that have been well-oaked. Soft and gentle in the mouth, but has some rich tannins and good acids. For early consumption. **86** —*S.H. (10/1/2004)*

Martin & Weyrich 2000 Etrusco Cabernet Sauvignon (Paso Robles) $22. A fruity, dry wine that combines Cabernet's structure and blackberry and herb flavors with Sangiovese's cherries and acidity. Full-bodied and tasty, with easy, complex tannins. **86** —*S.H. (10/1/2004)*

Martin & Weyrich 1997 Etrusco Cabernet Sauvignon (Paso Robles) $18. 84 —*S.H. (7/1/2000)*

Martin & Weyrich 1998 Chardonnay (Edna Valley) $18. 86 *(6/1/2000)*

Martin & Weyrich 2003 Chardonnay (Edna Valley) $18. This Paso Robles-based winery has reached into cool-climate Edna Valley for their Chardonnay, with good results. The wine has good acidity and is dry and minerally, with citrus fruit flavors. Try with cracked crab and a well-buttered sourdough baguette. **90** —*S.H. (6/1/2006)*

Martin & Weyrich 1999 Chardonnay (Edna Valley) $18. Someone is bound to describe this as "Burgundian" because it has a dry, mealy, nutty aroma

and feels very smooth and rich. There's also something earthy and barn-yardy, in a positive way. **90 Editors' Choice** —*S.H. (9/1/2002)*

Martin & Weyrich 1998 Hidden Valley Chardonnay (Paso Robles) $13. 88 Best Buy —*S.H. (5/1/2000)*

Martin & Weyrich 1999 Reserve Chardonnay (Edna Valley) $24. More concentrated than the winery's regular release, this polished version gets right to the point. It shines bright with focused tropical fruit flavors underlaid with tart citric acids. The lees and oak are laid on thick, but are in balance with the fruit. It's a fancy wine, but hard to find, with only 550 cases produced. **92** —*S.H. (9/1/2002)*

Martin & Weyrich 1998 Reserve Chardonnay (Edna Valley) $28. 88 *(6/1/2000)*

Martin & Weyrich 2005 Moscato Allegro Muscat Canelli (California) $12. Extremely low in alcohol, only 7%, this wine is very sweet in apricot and cane sugar flavors. It has a good, crisp spine of acidity for balance. **85** —*S.H. (4/1/2006)*

Martin & Weyrich 1999 Moscato Allegro Muscat Canelli (California) $12. 88 —*S.H. (12/31/2000)*

Martin & Weyrich 1999 Nebbiolo (Paso Robles) $15. Smells rich and alluring, with smoky plum and tea aromas and a whiff of freshly crushed black pepper. In the mouth, it's deeply flavored, with a solid core of plum and blackberry fruit. Fairly substantial tannins make the palate scoury now, and the finish is tannic, too. Try it with barbecue or a rich lasagna. **86** —*S.H. (12/1/2001)*

Martin & Weyrich 2002 Il Vecchio Reserve Nebbiolo (Paso Robles) $19. An interesting wine that shows its warm terroir in the softness and baked fruit quality. The flavors, wrapped in gentle tannins, are of cherry pie, black currants, cocoa, and tobacco, and the finish is dry. The natural acidity makes the wine clean and food-friendly. **86** —*S.H. (6/1/2006)*

Martin & Weyrich 2000 Pinot Grigio (Central Coast) $13. Ripely fruity and polished, the apple and peach flavors stand out in the mouth, framed by adequate acidity. The finish is clean and peppery. This is a light, supple wine; it's very easy to drink. Seems best suited for fresh fruits, with a nice grilled trout, or all by itself. **85** —*S.H. (11/15/2001)*

Martin & Weyrich 2003 Flamenco Rojo Red Blend (Napa Valley) $35. Hard on the heels of the winery's excellent 2002 comes this wine, very much in the same ripe, smooth mold. It's fresher and more youthful in tannins, but has the same blackberry, cassis, cherry, and mocha flavors. **89** —*S.H. (5/1/2006)*

Martin & Weyrich 2002 Flamenco Rojo Red Blend (Napa Valley) $35. Martin & Weyrich, which is based in Paso Robles, has released three consecutive vintages of this red Napa Valley blend, which is comprised of multiple Spanish and Portuguese varieties. This is the best of the trio, rich and dense, filled with extracted berry flavors and sweet tobacco. It's an interesting, complex wine. Try as an alternative to Cab or Zin. **90** —*S.H. (5/1/2006)*

Martin & Weyrich 2001 Flamenco Rojo Red Blend (Napa Valley) $35. At four-plus years, this wine is losing its youthful freshness, and despite the great vintage, is showing early signs of age. It's at its best now, soft and fruity, with traces of dried cherry and sweet leather. **87** —*S.H. (5/1/2006)*

Martin & Weyrich 2002 Insieme Red Blend (Paso Robles) $18. This blend of red varieties is very rich, soft and forward in cherry, red currant, chocolate, and coffee flavors. It's nicely dry, with a persistent finish. **85** —*S.H. (6/1/2006)*

Martin & Weyrich 1999 Insieme Red Blend (Paso Robles) $16. A bright-toned red blend of Sangiovese, Zinfandel, Cabernet Sauvignon, and Nebbiolo. Cherry, strawberry, citrus, and herb are the cornerstones flavors. Tannins are mild, and the finish is zingy. **86** —*S.H. (11/15/2002)*

Martin & Weyrich 2005 Matador Rosé Blend (Central Coast) $12. A lovely rosé, a bit on the sweet side, with luscious cherry and raspberry tea, cola, and vanilla flavors, and crisp acidity for balance. Almost as full-bodied as a Pinot Noir, the wine is made from Tempranillo grapes. **85** —*S.H. (12/1/2006)*

Martin & Weyrich 2002 Il Palio Sangiovese (Paso Robles) $15. While others have abandoned the Sangiovese quest, M&W persists, in this case with a polished, easy wine with plenty of likeable fruit character. It's dry and silky, with cherry and cocoa flavors, and the variety's robust acidity makes it perfect for cutting through Italian food. **86** —*S.H. (6/1/2006)*

Martin & Weyrich 1999 Il Palio Sangiovese (Paso Robles) $16. Fairly dark in color for this varietal, with pronounced aromas of dark stone fruits, red berries and blackberries, alongside earthy, mushroomy notes and some oak shadings. Fairly earthy and herbal on the palate, with tomato juice and plum flavors. Acidity and tannins contribute to a short, tart finish. **84** —*S.H. (11/15/2001)*

Martin & Weyrich 2001 Syrah (York Mountain) $25. Quite firm and tannic, with good acids too. Opens with strong white pepper aromas that air out to reveal luscious cassis and cherry liqueur aromas and flavors. Likely to develop further for a few years. **88** —*S.H. (12/1/2004)*

Martin & Weyrich 2002 Dante Dusi Vineyard Zinfandel (Paso Robles) $25. The vineyard is an old one with a proud name, and the winemaker does it justice in crafting this dry, balanced wine. It's Zin all the way, with wild berry, cocoa, and spice flavors and rich tannins that contribute to the lush, soft mouthfeel. Earns extra points for the sheer exuberance of its varietal personality. **91** —*S.H. (6/1/2006)*

Martin & Weyrich 1997 Dante Dusi Vineyard Reserve Zinfandel (Paso Robles) $22. Some earthy elements mingle with the fruit, which has a ripe tomato edge. Good structure, without the harshness or heat that affects so many '97s. If anything, it's a little underripe, with bell pepper, beet, and earthy flavors. **85** —*P.G. (3/1/2001)*

Martin & Weyrich 2004 La Primitiva Zinfandel (Paso Robles) $14. There's a thick, syrupy mouthfeel to this very ripe, very soft wine. But the fruity flavors are rich and satisfying. It's a decent everyday Zin. **83** —*S.H. (6/1/2006)*

Martin & Weyrich 1997 Ueberroth Vineyard Zinfandel (Paso Robles) $22. Bright, brash fruit sets this off on the right note, with raspberries and strawberries and even a little watermelon in the mix. Fruit defines the middle, and extends through to the full, ripe finish. **87** —*P.G. (3/1/2001)*

MARTIN BROTHERS

Martin Brothers 1998 Moscato Allegro Muscat Canelli (Paso Robles) $12. **86** —*J.C. (12/31/1999)*

MARTIN ESTATE

Martin Estate 2003 Collector's Reserve Cabernet Sauvignon (Rutherford) $110. Made in a tight young style that requires cellaring, the wine opens with a minty, cigarette ash and char aroma, then turns much sweeter in the mouth. Ripe cherries, blackberries, cola, and sweet spicy oak flavors dominate, leading to a tannic finish. Should develop by 2009 and then hold well through 2015. **90 Cellar Selection** —*S.H. (12/15/2006)*

Martin Estate 2002 Collector's Reserve Cabernet Sauvignon (Rutherford) $100. Made in a superripe way that will appeal to some, this Cab has notes of raisins and prunes, as well as pronounced sweet oak. It's fully dry, and turns a bit hot on the finish. **85** —*S.H. (12/15/2005)*

MARTIN FAMILY VINEYARDS

Martin Family Vineyards 1999 Cabernet Sauvignon (Napa Valley) $44. A big, lush and fruity wine, with cherry, plum, coffee, tea, and herb flavors up front. This burly, broad-shouldered Cab is full bodied, with powdery tannins and some length on the finish. **87** —*J.M. (12/15/2003)*

Martin Family Vineyards 2001 Pinot Noir (Russian River Valley) $35. A pleasant enough wine with moderate body and soft tannins. Flavors range from herbal to cherry and plum. An earthy note pervades, however, with a bright finish. **83** —*J.M. (7/1/2003)*

Martin Family Vineyards 1999 Syrah (Alexander Valley) $32. Rich, plummy, earthy notes lead off here. The wine is front-loaded with black cherry, plum, and herb flavors. However, the earthy qualities tend to overshadow the fruit. **85** —*J.M. (12/15/2003)*

Martin Family Vineyards 2001 Crazy Horse Zinfandel (Dry Creek Valley) $32. Cherries and herbs rise to the fore here in this mild mannered wine. Tannins are chewy, and the wine shows moderate length on the finish. **85** —*J.M. (3/1/2004)*

Martin Family Vineyards 2001 Rattlesnake Rock Zinfandel (Russian River Valley) $32. Cola and cherry notes are at the core of this burly Zin. Tannins are soft, and the flavors are framed by mild spice and toast with

hints of black cherry and herbs. It seems a little sweet on the finish. **87** —*J.M. (3/1/2004)*

Martin Family Vineyards 2001 Red Rooster Zinfandel (Dry Creek Valley) $28. The wine has some nice black cherry and berry notes up front, but it's got too much brightness on the palate. Tannins are mild, but the finish is rustic. **80** *(11/1/2003)*

Martin Family Vineyards 2001 The Rooster Zinfandel (Dry Creek Valley) $32. Quite rich and cherry-like. The wine also serves up chocolate, plum, jammy strawberry, and anise flavors. It's got a touch of sweetness too— plus plenty of body and smooth, supple tannins. **87** —*J.M. (3/1/2004)*

MARTIN RAY

Martin Ray 1997 Synthesis Diamond Mountain Vineyard Bordeaux Blend (Napa Valley) $50. 91 *(11/1/2000)*

Martin Ray 2002 Cabernet Sauvignon (Napa-Mendocino-Santa Clara Counties) $20. Ripe in fruity flavor, a bit sharp and rustic, this wine brims with blackberry jam, cola, chocolate, and coffee. The best part is the tannin structure, which is smooth and rich. **84** —*S.H. (12/15/2006)*

Martin Ray 2001 Cabernet Sauvignon (Diamond Mountain) $50. I love this wine for its heft, polish, and sheer razzle-dazzle. It wows with fruity intensity and flatters with decadence, yet never loses elegance and harmony. Rich in ripe, sweet tannins, and succulent in cassis, cocoa, and smoky new oak flavors, it's an ager. Drink now through 2015. **94 Cellar Selection** —*S.H. (4/1/2006)*

Martin Ray 2001 Cabernet Sauvignon (Santa Cruz Mountains) $50. This concentrated and intense mountain Cabernet is an obvious cellar candidate. Its huge tannins fan out across the palate, leaving behind a dusty astringency. Yet it's so sweet in chocolate and black currant fruit that it's drinkable right away. Should easily make it to the 20-year mark. **93** —*S.H. (5/1/2005)*

Martin Ray 2004 Angeline Cabernet Sauvignon (Sonoma County) $14. Rustic, country-style, but ripe in Cabernet fruit, with a rich tannin structure and a long, dry finish. Shows real polish in the upfront blackberry, cherry, and currant flavors. **84** —*S.H. (9/1/2006)*

Martin Ray 2003 Angeline Cabernet Sauvignon (Sonoma County) $14. Shows plenty of coastal Cabernet character at a fair price. Sure, it's a bit rough, but the cherry-berry flavors, smooth tannins, and kiss of oak will nicely accompany foods calling for a dry, full-bodied red wine. **85** —*S.H. (7/1/2006)*

Martin Ray 2002 Angeline Cabernet Sauvignon (Sonoma County) $10. Rustic and simple, with coffee and herb flavors and sharp acids. Turns blackberryish on the finish. **82** —*S.H. (11/1/2005)*

Martin Ray 2001 Napa, Sonoma & Mendocino Counties Cabernet Sauvignon (California) $16. This is a good, rich Cabernet, rather generic in style, which is to say it's dry and ripe in black currant fruit, well-oaked, and with fine, dusty tannins. Drink now. **87** —*S.H. (10/1/2005)*

Martin Ray 2002 Reserve Cabernet Sauvignon (Santa Cruz Mountains) $60. A worthy followup to the 2001, it's not as voluptuous, but is better structured and is likely more ageworthy. The wine is tannic, but balanced and rich in Cabernet fruit. It has that edge of elegant complexity that marks a great wine. Drink now–2015. **93 Cellar Selection** —*S.H. (9/1/2006)*

Martin Ray 2002 Reserve Cabernet Sauvignon (Diamond Mountain) $60. The tannic structure of this Cab is front and center, both anchoring the wine and making it inaccessible now. But there's little doubt about its ageability. The balance is great, and the heart of blackberry and cherry fruit is just bursting to get out. Defines Napa mountain Cab, and needs to be cellared. Should hit its stride in 2011 and hold for another 10 years. **93 Cellar Selection** —*S.H. (9/1/2006)*

Martin Ray 2002 Reserve Cabernet Sauvignon (Sonoma Mountain) $60. The appellation is little known because so few wines bear it, but Cabs from here, notably Laurel Glen's, are notoriously long-lived. This wine is right there in terms of ageability. It's enormously strong in tannins now, and bone dry, offering only hints of what it could be. But it's a powerful, masculine wine that should hit its stride after 2010 and hold for another decade. **91 Cellar Selection** —*S.H. (9/1/2006)*

USA

Martin Ray 2001 Reserve Cabernet Sauvignon (Napa Valley) $25. Smooth, complex, and ageable, this wine has rich tannins that are wrapped around cassis and oak flavors. It's a pleasant Cab that will go well with a steak, but has the balance and stuffing to improve. Now through 2010. **90** —S.H. (12/31/2004)

Martin Ray 2005 Chardonnay (Russian River Valley) $20. Nice and direct in ripe fruit and oak flavors, this is textbook proper Chardonnay. The flavors are of tropical fruits and spice, the texture is creamy, the finish is long and spicy. **86** —S.H. (12/15/2006)

Martin Ray 2004 Chardonnay (Russian River Valley) $16. Simple but drinkable, this Chard has fruit and oak flavors, a creamy texture and crisp acids. It's fully dry. **83** —S.H. (12/31/2005)

Martin Ray 2003 Chardonnay (Russian River Valley) $16. Superripe and super-oaked, with syrupy fruit flavors, this is somebody's idea of the popular style, but it's really an exaggerrated one. Where's the balance? **83** —S.H. (11/1/2005)

Martin Ray 2004 Angeline Chardonnay (Russian River Valley) $10. A little raw and green, but there are some Chardy flavors of peaches, cream, and spices, and the wine is dry and creamy. **83** —S.H. (12/31/2005)

Martin Ray 1999 Mariage Chardonnay (Russian River Valley) $20. From a venerable Burgundian producer comes this earthy, spicy wine, with a body and texture that are unctuous and creamy. There's a whole fruit basket here, with everything from green apples to peaches to tropical fruit. What's harder to express is the wine's power to satisfy. Rich and lush, it swings for the bleachers and just misses, but it's a solid triple. **91 Editors' Choice** —S.H. (5/1/2001)

Martin Ray 1998 Mariage Chardonnay (California) $18. 86 (6/1/2000)

Martin Ray 1997 Mariage Chardonnay (California) $20. 90 —S.H. (10/1/1999)

Martin Ray 2000 Miriage Chardonnay (Russian River Valley) $16. Nowhere near as rich as the sumptuous '99. Leans toward lime flavors, with high acidity and smoke and vanilla from oak. The finish is very clean and refreshing, but this is far from an opulent Chardonnay. **86** —S.H. (5/1/2003)

Martin Ray 2005 Angeline Gewürztraminer (Mendocino County) $14. Not from Anderson Valley, but from warmer inland vineyards. This pleasant Gewürz is sprightly in acidity with exotic passion fruit, Asian pear, kumquat, citrus, and honeysuckle flavors, and a finish of powdered, dusty Asian spice. If you haven't had a great California Gewürz in a while, try this one. **89 Best Buy** —S.H. (11/15/2006)

Martin Ray 2004 Angeline Gewürztraminer (Mendocino County) $10. Opened with some sulfur which was slow to blow off. Below that is a fairly fruity, dry and spicy Gewürz. **84** —S.H. (10/1/2005)

Martin Ray 2002 Merlot (Napa Valley) $16. You won't notice this wine's overripe, raisiny flavors and alcoholic warmth if you just quaff it. **83** —S.H. (11/1/2005)

Martin Ray 2004 Angeline Merlot (Sonoma County) $14. Martin Ray has struggled with this brand, and this wine won't help its reputation. It's not a good Merlot, with sweet-and-sour cherry flavors like Chinese mushu sauce. **81** —S.H. (7/1/2006)

Martin Ray 2002 Angeline Merlot (Sonoma County) $10. Simple, fruity, and medicinal, with semisweet cherry flavors, and a soft feel. **82** —S.H. (11/1/2005)

Martin Ray 2001 Diamond Mountain Merlot (Napa Valley) $40. A beautiful Merlot that lives up to the promise of "the soft Cabernet." It does have a velvety, cushiony mouthfeel, with blackberry and cocoa flavors, and achieves a harmony and balance rare in this varietal. Absolutely first-rate. **92** —S.H. (5/1/2005)

Martin Ray 1997 Diamond Mountain Vineyard Merlot (Napa Valley) $50. 86 —M.S. (3/1/2000)

Martin Ray 1997 Pinot Noir (Russian River Valley) $40. 88 —M.S. (5/1/2000)

Martin Ray 2004 Angeline Pinot Noir (Russian River Valley) $10. Continues this winery's streak of offering a good value under this label.

The wine is dry and silky, with pleasant cola, rhubarb, coffee, and cherry flavors that are offset by crisp acids. **85 Best Buy** —S.H. (4/1/2006)

Martin Ray 2004 Angeline Pinot Noir (Sonoma Coast) $10. A decent, clean Pinot Noir, but the cherry, cola, and coffee flavors lack concentration and finish watery. **83** —S.H. (12/31/2005)

Martin Ray 2003 Angeline Pinot Noir (Russian River Valley) $10. A nice wine with real varietal character, a smooth mouthfeel, crisp acids, and ripe flavors of raspberries, cherries, and mocha. Try this as a first course leading up to the expensive stuff. **86 Best Buy** —S.H. (6/1/2005)

Martin Ray 2004 Reserve Pinot Noir (Russian River Valley) $40. Easily the best Martin Ray Pinot in memory, this wine has hidden depths, and is absolutely delicious right now. It's pale in color, even a little brown at the edge, yet explodes in the mouth with fresh, vibrant cherry pie filling, rhubarb tea, cola, and cinnamon flavors. Despite the power, the texture is delicate and silky. **92** —S.H. (11/1/2006)

Martin Ray 2001 **1 Liter Red Blend (Central Coast) $15.** Shows a myriad of red stone fruit and berry flavors mingled with fresh spices, in the cutest little bottle you've ever seen. But there's sugar in the finish, which lowers the score. **83** —S.H. (11/1/2005)

Martin Ray 2005 Angeline Riesling (Mendocino County) $14. This is one of the more interesting Rieslings out there, and that's because it's very dry, like an Alsatian Riesling. It has crisp acidity and a steely, minerally undertone to the tart green apple, peach, and spice flavors. Very nice, versatile at the table, a real sommelier's wine. **89 Best Buy** —S.H. (11/15/2006)

Martin Ray 2004 Angeline Syrah (Dry Creek Valley) $14. A dry, fruity red wine from a fine appellation. It has sturdy, dusty tannins and bright blackberry and coffee flavors, and enough acidity to cut through any meats or cheeses you can find. **85** —S.H. (8/1/2006)

Martin Ray 2004 Angeline Zinfandel (Dry Creek Valley) $14. Strikes a nice balance of its parts, although it can't quite overcome its rustic nature. Dry and quite tannic, this Zin shows berry flavors with overtones of earth, coffee, and tobacco. **84** —S.H. (10/1/2006)

MARTINE'S

Martine's 2000 Syrah (California) $17. A solid Syrah, with aromas of smoke and herbs layered over berry fruit. Chocolate and berry flavors flow across the palate. Slightly viscous; finishes with spicy, peppery notes. **86** (10/1/2003)

Martine's 2001 Viognier (California) $15. Warm and slightly alcoholic, with a thick, rich mouthfeel that coats the taste buds with flavors of pear and anise. Finishes a touch short and green apple-like. **85** (10/1/2003)

MARTINI & PRATI
Martini & Prati 1999 Tower Hill Pinot Noir (California) $14. 80 (10/1/2002)

MARYHILL

Maryhill 2003 Proprietor's Reserve Serendipity Bordeaux Blend (Washington) $40. This Bordeaux blend (40% Malbec, 35% Cabernet Sauvignon, 20% Merlot, and 5% Cabernet Franc) shows some leathery notes in the aromas, more herb and dusty earth than the single varietal wines, and mixed red fruits. Light hints of cinnamon and cocoa are nicely laid in; the tannins, as with the other reds, are quite astringent. **88** —P.G. (6/1/2006)

Maryhill 2003 Proprietor's Reserve Cabernet Franc (Columbia Valley (WA)) $32. A real success, Maryhill's exceptional Cab Franc shows dark, black fruits laced with licorice and streaks of tarry tannin. Structured and supple, dense, and just hinting at decadence. **90** —P.G. (6/1/2006)

Maryhill 2002 Cabernet Sauvignon (Columbia Valley (WA)) $20. Earthy, dry, and tannic, with roasted earth, dark fruits, and a more herbal, less ripe profile overall. Good, workmanlike, Bordeaux-style Cabernet. **87** — P.G. (6/1/2006)

Maryhill 2003 Proprietor's Reserve Cabernet Sauvignon (Columbia Valley (WA)) $34. This Cab is classically structured, dense and dry, with cedary, black tea flavors circling black cherry and black berry fruit. Astringent, spare, long, and complex, with a sweet, lightly toasty core. **90** —P.G. (6/1/2006)

USA

USA

**Maryhill 2003 Proprietor's Reserve Chardonnay (Columbia Valley (WA))
$18.** Soft and oaky, this is a simple Chardonnay with more than its share
of buttery oak. Flavors are cracker, toast, buttered nuts; there is little
impact from the fruit. **87** —*P.G. (6/1/2006)*

Maryhill 2002 Grenache (Columbia Valley (WA)) $24. This is the winery's
first attempt at this classic Southern Rhône variety, which all but disap-
peared from Washington vineyards in the last decade. It's a good start,
with bright, cranberry/cherry fruit, balancing acids, and a lift at the end
from some cinnamon spice. **86** —*P.G. (9/1/2004)*

Maryhill 2003 Pinot Gris (Willamette Valley) $13. The fruit is from
Oregon, and lacks the crisp authority of the Washington style. Ripe,
loose-knit, and tasting of sweet cracker in the finish, it closes out with a
bit of candy-sweet sugar. **85** —*P.G. (10/1/2004)*

Maryhill 2002 Pinot Noir (Willamette Valley) $18. Fragrant, soft, and sub-
stantial, this Pinot has an interesting roasted chipotle character that would
seem to be perfect for grilled burgers or flank steak. Despite its youth, it
is mature and ready to drink immediately. **87** —*P.G. (11/1/2004)*

Maryhill 2002 Sangiovese (Columbia Valley (WA)) $16. Light and pleas-
antly fruity, but showing little of the varietal character of the grape. The
fruit is tart, with rhubarb and pie cherry, and the finish is notable for
some distinctive smoke and charcoal spice. **86** —*P.G. (9/1/2004)*

**Maryhill 2002 Proprietor's Reserve Sangiovese (Columbia Valley (WA))
$26.** Aging in new French oak (hence the reserve label) has been handled
well, and the tart, sour cherry Sangiovese flavors seem to float on a chassis of light, toasty spice. Hints of pipe tobacco and tea should develop
further with time; only the hot finish keeps it from meriting a higher
score. **87** —*P.G. (9/1/2004)*

Maryhill 2003 Syrah (Columbia Valley (WA)) $16. Smooth, flavorful, and
fairly priced—what else could one want? It's starts off a bit toasty and
smoky, then delivers waves of caramel, smoked meat, and berry flavor,
supple tannins and an elegant finish. **89 Editors' Choice** *(9/1/2005)*

Maryhill 2001 Syrah (Columbia Valley (WA)) $18. Fragrant with blackber-
ries, sandalwood, plum, and toast, this is a very appealing wine that
makes the most of its light fruit. The finish hints at mint and herb, and
there are substantial tannins. May be at its best right now. **87** —*P.G.
(9/1/2004)*

Maryhill 2003 Proprietor's Reserve Syrah (Washington) $36. Not as suc-
cessful as the winery's other reds, this seems overloaded with vanilla
scents and flavors. The oak overpowers the light fruit, and the tannins—
again quite dry–are not set off against anything ripe and sweet to
counterbalance their bitterness. **85** —*P.G. (6/1/2006)*

Maryhill 2001 Reserve Syrah (Columbia Valley (WA)) $28. A substantial
effort, with supple, grapy, black cherry fruit suffused with smoke, pepper, and meaty tannins. Young and relatively hard, it needs a little
breathing time to soften up, but it's a delicious, well-made wine. **90
Editors' Choice** —*P.G. (9/1/2004)*

Maryhill 2003 Viognier (Columbia Valley (WA)) $15. A young, fat, forward
style of Viognier, which fills the mouth with concentrated, intense flavors of tropical mango and Juicy Fruit gum. **86** —*P.G. (9/1/2004)*

Maryhill 2002 Zinfandel (Columbia Valley (WA)) $22. Maryhill is making
more Zin than anyone in Washington, and has proven that there is a
place for it there. The fruit is ripe but not jammy, and the acids stay up
there despite the high 15% alcohol. Bright berries and a kiss of oak set
the style; there's a touch of Mendocino-style incense in the finish. **87** —
P.G. (9/1/2004)

Maryhill 2002 Proprietor's Reserve Zinfandel (Columbia Valley (WA)) $32.
Sweet, very ripe fruit sends up liqueurous flavors of cherry cordial laced
with espresso and dark chocolate. Smooth and palate-filling, with a defi-
nite kick, it shows that Washington can make California-style, close to
late-harvest Zin if it wants to. **88** —*P.G. (9/1/2004)*

MASON CELLARS

Mason Cellars 2004 Sauvignon Blanc (Napa Valley) $16. There's good cat
pee and bad cat pee. This is the good stuff. The complex array of flavors
includes gooseberries, lime zest, sweet green grass, and grapefruit, and
the wine is totally dry, with good acidity. I had this with scallops
wrapped in prosciutto and it was a great match. **91** —*S.H. (3/1/2006)*

MASSET WINERY

Masset Winery 2000 Cabernet Sauvignon (Yakima Valley) $20. Good
color, plenty of very astringent tannins, and hints of some black cherry
fruit, but it's buried in earthy tannins. **83** —*P.G. (1/1/2004)*

Masset Winery 1999 Cabernet Sauvignon (Yakima Valley) $20. This seems
quite light and thin, with watery, green tomato flavors and hard, herbal
tannins. **82** —*P.G. (1/1/2004)*

MASUT

Masut 2003 Pinot Noir (Redwood Valley) $30. This is a dry, charming
wine, a junior partner to Masut's Block Seven bottling. It has ripe, pure
cherry flavors and a chocolatey finish. It's very gentle, with low acids and
tannins. **86** —*S.H. (10/1/2005)*

Masut 2002 Pinot Noir (Redwood Valley) $30. From a growing region with
one of the largest diurnal temperature swings in the state, an eccentric
Pinot. It's heavy with tannins and herbal, coffee, and plum flavors, with
big acidity. Not a bad wine, but atypical for Pinot. **84** —*S.H. (11/1/2004)*

Masut 2001 Pinot Noir (Redwood Valley) $30. Tasty and full-bodied, this
is a wine you might mistake for a Chateauneuf, with its plummy, blackberry and spice flavors. Heavy for a Pinot, with thick but manageable
tannins, but still a good, rich wine. **88** —*S.H. (7/1/2003)*

Masut 2003 Block 7 Pinot Noir (Redwood Valley) $50. Masut is making a
surprisingly strong case for warm-climate Pinot, as evidenced by this very
good wine. No problems getting the fruit ripe in cherries and blackberries, and the balance of alcohol, tannins, acids, and oak is fine. A winery
to watch. **90** —*S.H. (10/1/2005)*

MATANZAS CREEK

Matanzas Creek 2000 Cabernet Sauvignon (Sonoma County) $35. Very
oaky, with burnt aromas that carry a note of cured meat. Plum and cassis
work the palate, and next up is a finish that's starchy and tannic, but also
zippy and forward. **86** —*M.S. (11/15/2003)*

Matanzas Creek 1997 Chardonnay (Sonoma Valley) $31. 91 —*L.W.
(11/1/1999)*

Matanzas Creek 1998 Chardonnay (Sonoma County) $33. This sunny,
medium-gold wine opens with caramel and apple aromas. More candy
apple-like flavors appear in the mouth, accompanied by tropical fruit
and toasty accents with a rich caramel tone. It verges on too-sweet, but
it's nonetheless pleasing in an uncomplicated way. **87** *(7/1/2001)*

Matanzas Creek 1996 Sonoma County Chardonnay (Sonoma County) $30.
86 —*S.H. (7/1/1999)*

Matanzas Creek 2000 Merlot (Sonoma County) $30. A bit muddled and
herbaceous, with roasted black cherries joined by notes of toast and barrel char. **85** *(1/21/2004)*

Matanzas Creek 1997 Merlot (Sonoma Valley) $56. A classy Merlot, sleek
and well structured, with hints of blackberry, chocolate, anise, herb, and
toast that are securely nestled inside. Firm, ripe tannins frame the ensemble, which should really blossom in two to five years. **91** —*J.M.
(12/1/2001)*

Matanzas Creek 2000 Sauvignon Blanc (Sonoma County) $22. From the
get-go it's a big, full grapefruit-driven wine that's laced with smoke and
vanilla. Citrus, mostly lemon, is the taste profile, while good lively acids
power the tight, lemony finish. Serve chilled alongside a platter of tasty
appetizers. **89** *(8/1/2002)*

Matanzas Creek 2002 Syrah (Sonoma County) $25. Boasts a dark flavor
profile, combining well-done toast, black cherries, asphalt, and leather.
Low acidity gives it a smooth mouthfeel, but some drying tannins stick
out on the finish, giving it a rough edge. **85** *(9/1/2005)*

MATCH

Match 2002 Butterdragon Hill Cabernet Sauvignon (St. Helena) $72. This is
an inaugural release, made by Napa veteran Cary Gott, grown on the
western hillsides above Highway 29. It is 100% Cabernet, classic in its
acid and tannin structure, with very ripe cherry compote and cassis flavors. However, it's too sweet for complete balance and enjoyment. **85**
—*S.H. (7/1/2006)*

MATTHEWS

Matthews 2001 Bordeaux Blend (Columbia Valley (WA)) $50. A full-bore Bordeaux blend with all five varieties. Two-thirds Cabernet Sauvignon sets the backbone, and the wine unfolds with plenty of power, dark, plummy fruit and full, roasted espresso-like barrel flavors. If there's a down spot it's the acidic tang to the finish, which seems a bit jagged. **90** —P.G. (6/1/2005)

Matthews 2001 Elerding Vineyard Reserve Cabernet Sauvignon (Yakima Valley) $60. This single-vineyard effort, the top bottle from Matthews, is a comet of a Cab that streaks across the palate with crisp, tart, tightly focused berry fruits. It leaves behind a tail that broadens into a pretty rainbow of flavors—black cherry, mineral, black tea—and keeps its concentration through a long, resonant finish. **93** —P.G. (11/15/2004)

Matthews 2002 Red Blend (Columbia Valley (WA)) $50. This young, dense, saturated, complex, and extremely tight wine is sappy and packed with myriad berries and red/blue fruits. It is wrapped in stiff, hard, thick, dark tannins that add tight layers of moist earth, black tea, roots, and bitter chocolate. This baby needs time. **94** —P.G. (12/15/2005)

Matthews 2004 Klipsun Sauvignon Blanc (Red Mountain) $18. Winemaker Matt Loso dropped Sémillon from the blend a few years ago, then tried fermenting in all stainless, moved to barrels in 2005 and jumped to concrete in 2006. The 2004 Klipsun is yeasty, bone dry, and richly textured. The young, beery yeast flavors are augmented with light, fresh herbs and hints of citrus zest and honey. Lingering, lovely textures. **90** —P.G. (12/15/2005)

Matthews 2003 Hedges Estate Vineyard Syrah (Red Mountain) $50. Ripe and thick is the name of the game here: Aromas are one step away from Porty, and flavors are of very ripe mulberries and blueberries. It's thick and syrupy on the palate, and chewy on the finish, with enough fresh acidity to keep it in good balance. 175 cases produced. **89** (9/1/2005)

Matthews 2004 Hedges Vineyard Syrah (Red Mountain) $50. A step beyond the immense 2003, this actually supercedes the sheer massive power of that wine with a sleeker, more elegant structure. Classy, bright, lifted scents lead into a peppery, red-fruited Syrah annotated with citrus oil. Tart, young, clean, and delineated, it is Matt Loso's immaculate, concise winemaking at its best. This can go a long way; it continues to add depth and layers of mineral and texture as it breathes open. **94 Editors' Choice** —P.G. (11/15/2006)

MAURITSON

Mauritson 2005 Sauvignon Blanc (Dry Creek Valley) $16. Last year's bottling was a hard act to follow, but Mauritson's done it again. The vintage was cooler and this wine seems crisper and zestier but no less flavorful, bursting at the seams with ripe lemon, lime, peach, and wildflower flavors. Turns as rich as honey on the finish, but it's a dry wine. **90 Editors' Choice** —S.H. (12/15/2006)

Mauritson 2004 Sauvignon Blanc (Dry Creek Valley) $16. Made from the old Clone 1, which gives classic grass and citrus flavors, and the Musqué clone, which contributes brighter gooseberry notes. Absolutely dry, and boosted by mouthwatering zesty acidity, it also has low alcohol. This is one of the purest expressions of unoaked, non-malolactic Sauvignon Blanc in California. **91 Editors' Choice** —S.H. (8/1/2006)

Mauritson 2003 Sauvignon Blanc (Dry Creek Valley) $16. No oak, no malolactic, just pure, ripe fruit and plenty of zesty acids mark this delicate wine. It shows flavors of citrus, gooseberry, and alfalfa or hay, and finishes very clean and dry. **88** —S.H. (11/1/2005)

Mauritson 2004 Zinfandel (Dry Creek Valley) $24. The outlines of a great Dry Creek Zin are here in the fleshy texture, polished tannins and ripe, briary flavors of wild red raspberries, cherries and blueberries. The problem is a certain sweet, glyceriney harshness that comes from very high alcohol, courtesy of the extreme vintage conditions. **86** —S.H. (12/15/2006)

Mauritson 2002 Zinfandel (Dry Creek Valley) $24. Made by sixth generation growers, this Zin is rich and extracted, with plum, berry, spice and tobacco flavors. It's built with strong acids and tannins that should pull it through the next ten years, but it's a lovely wine now. **90 Editors' Choice** —S.H. (11/1/2005)

Mauritson 2001 Zinfandel (Dry Creek Valley) $24. Somewhat tight, with smoky licorice, blackberry, coffee, and tar flavors. Could open with time, but for the moment it only hints at what may come. **85** (11/1/2003)

Mauritson 2001 Growers Reserve Zinfandel (Dry Creek Valley) $33. Mainly from hillside grapes, this Zin is far more tannic and concentrated than Mauritson's regular Zin. But it's by no means undrinkable, because the blackberry, blueberry, and pepper flavors are just delicious. Still, it should benefit from a few years of aging. **91** —S.H. (11/1/2005)

MAYACAMAS

Mayacamas 1999 Chardonnay (Napa Valley) $32. After all these years, Mayacamas still marches to a different drummer. Not for them flamboyant fruit or a heavy plaster of oak. You won't find tropical fruits, scads of spices and vanilla. This wine is tight and earthy, and the dryness is not offset with glycerin or other pseudo-sugars. It's earthy and austere. The point is ageability, if you care to cellar it. **87** —S.H. (12/15/2002)

Mayacamas 2002 Sauvignon Blanc (Napa Valley) $20. One of the best Sauvignons of this or any vintage, a brilliant and evocative wine of great style and flair. Powerfully dry, with citrus, fig, apple, and peppery spice flavors and a lush overlay of oak. Compelling for its intensity and complexity. **93** —S.H. (12/15/2004)

MAYO

Mayo 2002 The Libertine Bordeaux Blend (Sonoma County) $15. There are some grapes that shouldn't be mixed. This blend of various Bordeaux varieties, Petite Sirah and Barbera is one such. There are candied, Lifesaver flavors and deeper, darker currant and plum flavors, and the result is a vinous culture clash. **84** —S.H. (6/1/2004)

Mayo 2000 Los Chamizal Vineyard Cabernet Sauvignon (Sonoma Valley) $35. Dark, with earthy blackberry aromas and notes of sautéed mushrooms and oak. Very rich in the mouth, filled with blackberry flavors. The tannins are pronounced and thick in this young, aggressive wine. Try aging for five years. **87** —S.H. (4/1/2003)

Mayo 1997 Los Chamizal Vineyard Cabernet Sauvignon (Sonoma Valley) $35. **89** (11/1/2000)

Mayo 2001 Napa River Ranch Vineyard Cabernet Sauvignon (Napa Valley) $35. Very ripe and extracted, verging on black currant marmalade, although it's technically dry, but lavish oak lends a wood-sap sweetness. The tannins are ripe and gentle, providing a plush mouthfeel. Glamorous and balanced. **90** —S.H. (6/1/2004)

Mayo 1998 Barrel Select Chardonnay (Sonoma Valley) $25. **87** (6/1/2000)

Mayo 2002 Laurel Hill Vineyard Chardonnay (Sonoma Valley) $20. Extraordinarily ripe from a hot vintage, this Chard takes spiced apple flavors and bakes them into a tart, sprinkled with toasted cinnamon and nutmeg. It's also really oaky. Too big for cracked crab, but try with poached salmon in a creamy aioli. **87** —S.H. (6/1/2004)

Mayo 2004 Balletto Vineyards Unwooded Pinot Gris (Sonoma Coast) $20. It's unusual to see a Pinot Gris from this appellation, much less a vineyard-designated one. This wine easily lives up to its address. It's sleek, slick, and clean in high acidity, with a vibrant minerality that explodes with fig, grapefruit, and white pepper flavors. Absolutely yummy. **90 Editors' Choice** —S.H. (12/15/2005)

Mayo 2002 Piner Ranch Vineyard Pinot Noir (Russian River Valley) $30. Very nice, a rich, juicy Pinot that unfolds layers of flavor on the palate. Enters dry, then releases a sunburst of spicy cherry and blackberry fruit with overtones of mocha and white pepper. Quite full bodied, but keeps its silky lightness throughout. **89** —S.H. (11/1/2004)

Mayo 2001 Piner Ranch Vineyard Pinot Noir (Russian River Valley) $30. Has the extra depth of earthy meatiness you want in a Russian River Pinot. This is a big, complex wine whose flavors range from cherries through rhubarb, cranberry, cola, and sweet heirloom tomato to sage, pepper, and oregano. It feels great in the mouth, light and lilting but serious. **91** —S.H. (7/1/2003)

Mayo 1998 Piner Ranch Vineyard Pinot Noir (Russian River Valley) $35. **91** —J.C. (12/15/2000)

USA

USA

Mayo 2000 Sangiacomo Vineyard Pinot Noir (Carneros) $35. Defines the old style of Carneros Pinot, with juicy flavors of raspberries and cherries and the silkiest, smoothest tannins you ever had. Very dry, with the tart, peppery acidity that makes it a natural partner for food. Yet it's fundamentally a light wine with limited aging potential. **85** —S.H. (7/1/2003)

Mayo 1998 Sangiacomo Vineyards Pinot Noir (Carneros) $35. 87 —J.C. (12/15/2000)

Mayo 2004 Emma's Vineyard Unwooded Sauvignon Blanc (Napa Valley) $20. With no wood, all you get is pure fruit. The flavors are young and vibrant, suggesting succulent ripe grapes, grapefruits, and white peaches, set off by keen acids. What a pretty wine this is, bone dry, long on the finish and complex. **89** —S.H. (12/15/2005)

Mayo 2001 Un-Wooded Emma's Vineyard Sauvignon Blanc (Napa Valley) $20. Packs a punch with citrus and grass flavors, with good acids. Bone dry, scours the palate and provides a thoroughly clean, vibrant finish. As the name suggests, no oak at all. What you get is pure Sauvignon character. **86** —S.H. (9/1/2003)

Mayo 2002 Page-Nord Vineyard Syrah (Sonoma Valley) $30. Mayo has struggled in the past with these grapes but this vintage brings them back to form. Lush, ripe, and intense in plum, cherry, violet, and smoky leather flavors, in a dense, complex wine that will develop additional complexities through 2006. **89** —S.H. (6/1/2004)

Mayo 2001 Page-Nord Vineyard Syrah (Napa Valley) $30. There's a lot to praise about this wine, notably the smooth tannins and harmonious mouthfeel. On the downside is a disappointing thinness of fruit. The blackberry, plum, and cherry flavors seem watered down. So rich is the texture that this lack of fruit is a big letdown. **85** —S.H. (12/15/2003)

Mayo 2002 Ricci Vineyard Zinfandel (Russian River Valley) $25. This is a huge wine, so ripe it tastes sweet. Milk chocolate and blackberry jam flavors have a peppery edge, and are wrapped in significant tannins. **86** —S.H. (6/1/2004)

Mayo 2000 Ricci Vineyard-Old Vine Zinfandel (Russian River Valley) $25. From the warmer, northeast corner of the appellation, and vines averaging 45 years of age, a powerful wine that is a victim of its own excess. It's a classic case of too much alcohol (18.5%), too much heat, and residual sugar that tastes sweet and Porty. Very high acidity helps, but there's not enough to create balance. **83** —S.H. (11/1/2002)

Mayo 2000 Ricci Vineyard-Reserve-Old Vine Zinfandel (Russian River Valley) $35. Somebody should pass a law against residual sugar in Zinfandel, especially when it's made from grapes as obviously good as these. Sugar masks the exquisite berry, tobacco, and earth flavors. Sugar also accentuates tannins, making them tougher and grittier. Until there's such a law, all we can do is hope. **83** —S.H. (11/1/2002)

Mayo 2001 Ricci Vineyard Old Vines Zinfandel (Russian River Valley) $25. Really delicious, in that ultraripe, juicy style. Black cherry, plum, blackberry, cassis, spice, pepper, and herbs blend in a bold manner, making this a very satisfying wine. Spicy, bright, and long on the finish, with firm ripe tannins to frame it. **91 Editors' Choice** (11/1/2003)

Mayo 2000 Ricci Vineyard Unfiltered Zinfandel Port Zinfandel (Russian River Valley) $30. Mayo knows how to make sweetish Zins that should be dry. Here's their effort at an outrightly sweet Zin, and it ain't bad. Curranty, raisiny aromas lead to cassis and blackberry jam flavors that are immensely ripe, and the sugar level is dessert-high. It's warmly satisfying. Try with, or over, vanilla ice cream, and be happy. **87** —S.H. (9/1/2002)

Mayo 2001 Ricci Vineyard, Reserve, Old Vines Zinfandel (Russian River Valley) $38. Bright and racy on the palate, with up front chocolate, black cherry, spice, toast, plum, pepper, and herb flavors. The tannins are somewhat astringent, however, but the wine is still quite lovely. **89** (11/1/2003)

Mayo 1998 Ricci Vineyard Zinfandel (Russian River Valley) $25. The nose of this Russian River Valley, single-vineyard offering shows positive dark berry fruit bearing mild meaty accents. Made in a lighter style, the flavors follow the aromatic opening and the wine finishes dry with medium tannins, red berry, and tea notes. **85** (3/1/2001)

MAYO FAMILY

Mayo Family 2003 Laurel Hill Vineyard Unwooded Chardonnay (Sonoma Valley) $15. Strong in ripe apple flavors, with an herbal, earthy character and some tannins, this is a tough wine that finishes with some almond-skin bitterness. It's bone dry. **85** —S.H. (4/1/2005)

Mayo Family 2003 Emma's Vineyard Un-Wooded Sauvignon Blanc (Napa Valley) $20. This single-vineyard wine has lots of complexity and interest value. It mingles hay and grass notes with far richer ones of peach, apple, mint, and anise, in a creamy texture that's boosted by crisp acidity. **88** —S.H. (4/1/2005)

MAYSARA

Maysara 2003 Pinot Gris (Willamette Valley) $15. This is very nice, crisp and fresh, with pure fresh cut pear fruit flavors, and hints of pear skin and citrus rind. There's good texture, mouthfeel and body, with crisp minerality setting off the ripe fruit. A nice, smooth, unwooded finish. **88** —P.G. (2/1/2005)

Maysara 2001 Pinot Gris (Willamette Valley) $15. This is very nice, crisp and fresh, with pure pear fruit, highlighted by some pear skin and citrus rind. The tannins give some nice definition to the finish; there is just the barest hint of residual sugar. **89** —P.G. (12/1/2003)

Maysara 2002 Delara Pinot Noir (Willamette Valley) $45. A proprietary name for a barrel select reserve. Round and sweetly fruity, it's easy to see why these 12 barrels stood out from the pack. Yet this forward, ripe wine may be at its best sooner than the more layered estate cuvée. Two thirds new oak lends a tasty vanilla element to the finish. **89** —P.G. (2/1/2005)

Maysara 2002 Delara Pinot Noir (Willamette Valley) $45. Caramel and brown sugar scents, leading into a rich, likeable midpalate showing some complexity. Caramel, mocha, coffee, and chocolate, with blackberry fruit. Oak-dominated but lush. **86** (11/1/2004)

Maysara 2002 Estate Cuvée Pinot Noir (Willamette Valley) $32. From a blend of very low-cropped pinot clones, this expressively fruity wine jumps with strawberry, raspberry, cherry, and plum fruits, hints of mineral and a tight streak of tannic beetroot. Complex, youthful and engaging effort. **90** —P.G. (2/1/2005)

Maysara 2002 Estate Cuvée Pinot Noir (Willamette Valley) $32. Pleasing, well-integrated scents show herb, leaf, bacon, and much more. There's a delicate balance to the way the dried herbs and pretty fruit flavors mix, and a velvety mouth feel that finishes off with a dab of cocoa. **89** (11/1/2004)

Maysara 2001 Estate Cuvée Pinot Noir (Willamette Valley) $32. Bigger, darker, bolder, and more alcoholic than the winery's reserve, this is another fine effort. Depending upon your preference (power v. elegance) you may or may not prefer it over the more restrained reserve. Full, fleshy, youthful, and structured to age. **89 Cellar Selection** —P.G. (12/1/2003)

Maysara 2003 Reserve Pinot Noir (Willamette Valley) $22. Maysara's track record for affordable, well-made Pinot Noir continues with this young and juicy Willamette valley reserve. Tangy blackberry/black cherry fruit—still evolving into full wine-hood—is at the center of a tight, tarry, still tannic wine that delivers plenty of power and complexity for the modest tab. **88** —P.G. (2/1/2005)

Maysara 2001 Reserve Pinot Noir (Willamette Valley) $22. This lovely debut should be a signal to other new Oregon producers that affordable, very well-made Pinot Noir is here. This has a balanced blend of herb and fruit flavors; and offers the layered, textured pleasures of real Burgundy. **89 Editors' Choice** —P.G. (12/1/2003)

Maysara 2002 Willamette Reserve Pinot Noir (Willamette Valley) $22. Varietal, but weak. Cedar and cherry, coffee, oak, and spice. Smooth, delicate, a bit shallow and simple. **85** (11/1/2004)

MAZZOCCO

Mazzocco 1999 Matrix Bordeaux Blend (Dry Creek Valley) $40. This charming wine is probably drinking at its peak now. It's a little light in body, but nearly five years of bottle age has mellowed the tannins. You'll find pleasant cherry-berry flavors leading to a gently sweet finish. **87** —S.H. (12/1/2004)

Mazzocco 1995 Matrix Bordeaux Blend (Dry Creek Valley) $30. 86 *(12/31/1999)*

Mazzocco 1995 Cabernet Sauvignon (Sonoma County) $18. 88 —*L.W. (12/31/1999)*

Mazzocco 2000 Cabernet Sauvignon (Sonoma County) $20. A bit tough and gritty with dry tannins, but there's a core of cherry-berry fruit that shows up on the finish. This is a wine of structure, leanly elegant and balanced, that will be content to play a supporting role at the dinner table. 87 —*S.H. (4/1/2004)*

Mazzocco 1999 Reserve Cabernet Sauvignon (Dry Creek Valley) $50. Still bruising in tannins. Will this wine ever mellow out? The answer is yes, to judge by the still-fresh blackberry and cherry fruit that doesn't seem to have aged at all. Hold for another five years. 87 —*S.H. (12/31/2004)*

Mazzocco 1997 Stone Ranch-Old Vine Carignane (Sonoma County) $14. 88 —*L.W. (11/1/1999)*

Mazzocco 1998 River Lane Chardonnay (Sonoma County) $15. 87 *(12/31/1999)*

Mazzocco 2001 River Lane Vineyards Chardonnay (Sonoma County) $15. Ripe and fruity, this tasty wine is filled with flavors of pears and pineapples, apples, and peaches and a sprinkling of Oriental spices. It is well oaked and creamy smooth, with a long, fruity finish. 87 —*S.H. (2/1/2004)*

Mazzocco 2000 River Lane Vineyards Chardonnay (Sonoma County) $18. A lean, sleek Chard, with citrus flavors veering into green apples, and bright, firm acids. Oak fattens and adds sweet creamy notes. Turns dry on the finish, with oriental spices. 86 —*S.H. (6/1/2003)*

Mazzocco 1997 Winemaker's Select Chardonnay (Sonoma County) $20. 90 —*L.W. (12/31/1999)*

Mazzocco 1996 Merlot (Dry Creek Valley) $20. 83 *(12/31/1999)*

Mazzocco 2001 Pinot Noir (Russian River Valley) $28. Delicate in texture, and in flavors, too. Modest cola, herb tea, and black cherry flavors go down easy in this silky, dry wine. 84 —*S.H. (12/31/2004)*

Mazzocco 2002 Sauvignon Blanc (Russian River Valley) $14. You'll find a dry, crisp white wine, with modest citrus and figgy-melon flavors. But there are intriguing notes of fresh herbs sprinkled throughout, like lavender, thyme, anise, and dill, which make this ideal for food pairing. 87 —*S.H. (2/1/2005)*

Mazzocco 1997 Viognier (Dry Creek Valley) $24. 88 —*L.W. (10/1/1999)*

Mazzocco 2001 Bevill Vineyards Viognier (Dry Creek Valley) $24. Nice spicy fruit in this clean, crisp wine. It has flavors of peach, mango, pineapple, and citrus fruits, and an almost Gewürz-like spiciness. A touch of oak brings smoky vanilla. 86 —*S.H. (2/1/2005)*

Mazzocco 1997 Bevill Vineyards Viognier (Dry Creek Valley) $24. 90 —*S.H. (11/1/1999)*

Mazzocco 1996 Zinfandel (Dry Creek Valley) $18. 88 —*L.W. (9/1/1999)*

Mazzocco 1995 Zinfandel (Sonoma County) $22. 90 —*L.W. (9/1/1999)*

Mazzocco 2001 Zinfandel (Dry Creek Valley) $16. Tea and herbs lead the way here, followed by briary blackberry, herb, and spice flavors. The finish is zippy yet smooth, moderate in length. 86 *(11/1/2003)*

Mazzocco 1997 Zinfandel (Dry Creek Valley) $16. There's some old-vine juice included in the blend, and it shows. The nose is lushly scented with plums, raisins, pie cherries, and ripe red fruits, with some of that distinctive new mown hay quality that old vines send up. A little barnyard aroma too, in a good way. Very extracted and intense. 89 —*P.G. (3/1/2001)*

Mazzocco 2001 Cuneo & Saini Zinfandel (Dry Creek Valley) $22. A spicy, bright blend of raspberry, cherry, chocolate, licorice, vanilla, spice, and coffee flavors. Bright acidity stands out, while the smooth tannins keep it supple. Moderate in length on the finish. 87 *(11/1/2003)*

Mazzocco 2001 Cuneo & Saini Vineyard Zinfandel (Dry Creek Valley) $22. Light in color and in body. This is a good vineyard and you wish they'd achieved greater concentration. Cherries and other red berries, dry, fairly tannic. Drink now. 84 —*S.H. (10/1/2005)*

Mazzocco 1997 Cuneo & Saini Vineyard Zinfandel (Dry Creek Valley) $22. Made from 80-year-old vines, the Cuneo Saini is lively and medium-bodied in the mouth. Oak, brown sugar, and cocoa stand out on the nose, and are followed on the palate by blackberry coated with a healthy dose of black pepper. Fresh herbal flavors meld the palate with the finish, where chalky-cocoa powder flavors linger. 89 —*D.T. (3/1/2002)*

Mazzocco 1995 Cuneo Sani Vineyard Zinfandel (Dry Creek Valley) $22. 87 —*L.W. (9/1/1999)*

Mazzocco 2001 Quinn Vineyard Zinfandel (Dry Creek Valley) $22. Bright and cherry-like, with vanilla and spice notes framing it. The texture is zippy, with cedar, herb, and toast finishing up. 85 *(11/1/2003)*

Mazzocco 2001 Quinn Vineyard Zinfandel (Dry Creek Valley) $22. Light and earthy, this wine seems overcropped, given the vintage and the single vineyard sourcing. It's thin in black cherry and coffee flavors, and very dry. 84 —*S.H. (10/1/2005)*

Mazzocco 1997 Quinn Vineyard Zinfandel (Dry Creek Valley) $22. Deep red berry dusted with cocoa powder, cinnamon-spice and eucalyptus, comprise the tantalizing bouquet. The Quinn is well-balanced, with tannins to spare that give it plenty of texture. On the palate, the red berry is tarter than what the bouquet offers, but it's rounded out with layers of of bitter chocolate and black pepper. Stewy red berry and a black pepper-and-mineral zing complete the picture. 91 —*D.T. (3/1/2002)*

Mazzocco 2001 Somers Vineyard Zinfandel (Dry Creek Valley) $22. Dry, tannic, and hot, this Zin has definite notes of overripeness in the raisiny aromas and flavors. If you like this style, fine, but it's out of balance. 83 —*S.H. (10/1/2005)*

Mazzocco 2001 Stone Ranch Zinfandel (Alexander Valley) $22. A polished, Merlot-style Zin, soft and velvety in body. The cherry and earth flavors are dry, and dusty tannins show up in the finish. 85 —*S.H. (10/1/2005)*

Mazzocco 1999 Stone Ranch Vineyard Zinfandel (Alexander Valley) $22. This great wine proves that Zinfandel is a noble variety. It has the huge, rich density of a fine Cabernet, with Zin's distinctive wild berry flavors. The tannins are big and sweet, but the finish astounds. 92 —*S.H. (11/15/2004)*

MCCRAY RIDGE

McCray Ridge 2000 Two Moon Vineyard Merlot (Dry Creek Valley) $30. There are some gritty tannins to this wine that make it chewy, almost like a food. It has pretty cherry and blackberry flavors and good acidity that balance the tannins out. Has extra layers of complexity that add interest. 89 —*S.H. (9/1/2004)*

McCray Ridge 1999 Two Moon Vineyard Merlot (Dry Creek Valley) $29. This is a very good Merlot, with near-perfect fruit, balanced between blackberries and olives. The oak adds complexity but isn't plastered on. The wine has the elusive quality of elegance. The depth of flavor and the rich texture are really nice. 93 —*S.H. (9/1/2002)*

McCray Ridge 2000 Two Moon Vineyard Luna Miel Merlot-Cabernet Sauvignon (Dry Creek Valley) $32. There's some good cherry-berry fruit here, with a solid overlay of oak, and the wine is completely dry. Feels rough and sharp, though, with acidity and tannins. Merlot-Cabernet blend. 84 —*S.H. (11/15/2004)*

MCCREA

McCrea 2001 Elerding Vineyard Chardonnay (Yakima Valley) $32. Rich and oily, it's a blockbuster, with big pineapple and tropical fruit, wrapped in nutty buttery oak and finishing with a blast of alcohol. 88 —*P.G. (12/31/2003)*

McCrea 2000 Elerding Vineyard Chardonnay (Yakima Valley) $30. This is the third year McCrea has made an Elerding Chardonnay, fermented on wild yeasts in stainless tanks, then aged sur lie in fairly neutral oak. Complex, textured, and loaded with banana and butterscotch flavors, it's a rich wine that retains enough elegance to go down easily with food. 90 —*P.G. (7/1/2002)*

McCrea 1998 Elerding Vineyard Chardonnay (Yakima Valley) $28. 92 —*P.G. (6/1/2000)*

McCrea 2004 Ciel du Cheval Counoise (Red Mountain) $32. The vines are Beaucastel material sourced from Tablas Creek in 1999. The wine is

USA

scented and flavored with blue plum, tart pie cherry, and blackberry. It is reminiscent of Sangiovese, with bracing acidity and a lightness in the midpalate. McCrea has worked in nice notes of spice, light chocolate, and a whiff of soy, making this a perfect salmon wine. **90** —*P.G. (10/1/2006)*

McCrea 2004 Grenache (Washington) $32. Grapy and bright, this is the quintessential fruit-driven red wine, with bright red cherry and raspberry flavors lifting the palate. Persistent and focused, it carries the flavors through a very clean and substantial finish, ending with roasted nut-skin tannins. **90** —*P.G. (10/1/2006)*

McCrea 2004 Ciel du Cheval Mourvèdre (Red Mountain) $32. Now in its third vintage, this Mourvèdre (with 11% Syrah in the blend) is better than ever. More than just a fruity, spicy-sweet red wine, it's got a luscious, smoky, gamy quality now showing for the first time. Dark and powerful, with flavors of graphite running through the tannins, superb definition, and appealing minerality. **92** —*P.G. (10/1/2006)*

McCrea 2004 Sirocco Rhône Red Blend (Washington) $35. This Grenache-based, southern Rhône-style red wine includes 30% Mourvèdre, 25% Syrah, and 5% Counoise. The fruit is sourced from several Yakima valley vineyards, and overall this is brilliantly fruit-driven, racy and precise. The Grenache dominates, an explosion of raspberries, plenty of buoyant acid, and a tart and nervy mouthfeel. Long, clean, very concentrated; it's a joy to drink. **91** —*P.G. (12/31/2006)*

McCrea 2005 Ciel du Cheval Vineyard Roussanne (Red Mountain) $25. The cuttings came from Tablas Creek's Beaucastel vines and were planted on Red Mountain in 1999. They are just now coming into their flavor years. This is young, yeasty, and fleshy with flavors of citrus and stone fruits. I like the texture and balance, the vivid acids underpinning the clean fruit, and the hint of butterscotch wrapping up the finish. **88** —*P.G. (12/31/2006)*

McCrea 2004 Syrah (Washington) $28. Pure Syrah sourced from Ciel du Cheval and Destiny Ridge vineyards, with a wash of blue/purple fruits, light pepper and herb. As it opens out a mix of wild berry flavors emerges, propelled by crisp acids, and leading into a peppery, tannic finish, nudged with smoke and ash. Not the biggest of McCrea's Syrahs, but nicely made and balanced. **88** —*P.G. (12/31/2006)*

McCrea 2000 Syrah (Yakima Valley) $35. The fruit comes primarily from Ciel du Cheval and Boushey vineyards, and delivers intense, spicy cherry and pungent grape scents and flavors. There are hints of tobacco and wild fruits, too, and the forward style favors early drinking. **88** —*P.G. (9/1/2002)*

McCrea 1999 Syrah (Yakima Valley) $35. Aromas are meaty and bacon fat, with tons of spicy white pepper and blackberry notes. Drinks dense and young, jammy, with oodles of freshly crushed blackberries. Gentle but firm tannins give it great structure. **87** —*S.H. (6/1/2002)*

McCrea 1998 Syrah (Yakima Valley) $28. 90 —*P.G. (6/1/2000)*

McCrea 2004 Amerique Syrah (Yakima Valley) $45. McCrea's Amerique bottling uses one and two-year-old American oak and tries for an Australian Shiraz flavor. I'm not sure it wouldn't be better just being what it is— a crisp, oaky, cool climate Syrah from Washington state, which in this vintage is almost one quarter Mourvèdre. The plummy fruit carries a lot of toasty, nutty cracker flavors from the barrel aging, overlaid with zesty citrus, one of the hallmarks of Washington Syrah. **89** —*P.G. (12/31/2006)*

McCrea 2001 Amerique Syrah (Yakima Valley) $40. The Amerique bottling of McCrea Syrah uses American, rather than French, oak, much of it neutral. Flavors are ripe and forward, with the fruit tasting of strawberries and other red fruits. **87** —*P.G. (12/31/2003)*

McCrea 2000 Amerique Syrah (Yakima Valley) $40. McCrea makes five different Syrahs, and the style here, which he calls "our Shiraz," uses American oak barrels to imitate the big, smoky flavors of Australian wines. This is a powerhouse, tannic and young, packed with ripe black fruits set against delicious, toasty oak. **90** —*P.G. (9/1/2002)*

McCrea 2001 Boushey Grand Cote Syrah (Yakima Valley) $45. From a cooler site, the Boushey shows more of the roasted, smoky character of Syrah. It's harvested a month later than the Ciel du Cheval Syrah, so it's

a rougher, fleshier wine with some alcoholic heat in the finish. But man, what a riot of flavors! **90** —*P.G. (12/31/2003)*

McCrea 1999 Boushey Grande Cote Vineyard Syrah (Yakima Valley) $42. From a hillside vineyard; starts with refined but closed aromas of blackberry, pepper, and smoky oak. There's a polished structure, with silky, intricate tannins and good acids. Has a core of round, sweet berry fruit flavors that lead to a lingering finish. **91** —*S.H. (6/1/2002)*

McCrea 2003 Boushey Vineyard Syrah (Yakima Valley) $52. As with the Ciel bottling, this is pure Syrah from a single vineyard. As usual, the Boushey is more forward and opulent and this vintage is packed with flavors and scents of smoked meat, herb, red fruits, and chocolate. Despite its heft it remains precise, focused, and beautifully defined. No blast of new oak; it's got wonderful balance. **94 Editors' Choice** —*P.G. (11/15/2006)*

McCrea 2002 Boushey Vineyard Syrah (Yakima Valley) $55. Reductive aromas of burnt matchstick and rubber gradually fade to reveal the coffee, molasses, and meat notes that dominate this wine. Creamy and full-bodied, but lacking obvious fruity character. Finishes with soft tannins. **87** *(9/1/2005)*

McCrea 1998 Boushley Vineyards Syrah (Yakima Valley) $35. 90 —*P.G. (9/1/2000)*

McCrea 2003 Ciel du Cheval Syrah (Red Mountain) $52. This pure Syrah from a great Red Mountain vineyard is a classic in every respect. Deep, succulent black fruits are underscored by tart acid, bone-dry tannins, and the vineyard's typical mineral streak. Hints of pepper are sprinkled throughout, and the tight, concentrated layering promises good aging potential. 197 cases made. **93 Editors' Choice** —*P.G. (11/15/2006)*

McCrea 2001 Ciel du Cheval Syrah (Yakima Valley) $45. From a superb Red Mountain vineyard, this is the best of all of the McCrea Syrahs. Generously layered with blue and black fruits, it hints at iron and gunmetal, extends broadly through the palate, and finishes with cassis and violets. **91 Cellar Selection** —*P.G. (12/31/2003)*

McCrea 2002 Ciel du Cheval Vineyard Syrah (Red Mountain) $55. One of Washington's Rhône pioneers, McCrea is still one of the best. The Ciel du Cheval bottling boasts a smoky, hickory-like note alongside hints of game and a supersized dollop of blackberry fruit. The texture is rich and velvety, the flavors satisfying. **89** *(9/1/2005)*

McCrea 1998 Ciel du Cheval Vineyard Syrah (Yakima Valley) $35. 90 —*P.G. (9/1/2000)*

McCrea 1999 Ciel du Cheval Vineyard Syrah (Yakima Valley) $45. Because the nose is a bit tight, it may be difficult to pick up more than light berry, toasty oak, and black-pepper aromas. More toasty oak pops up in the mouth, where there are also some black-cherry and sour-chocolate flavors. A bit hot in the mouth (or is that a bit of volatile acidity?) and on the finish. **86** *(11/1/2001)*

McCrea 1999 Cuvée Orleans Syrah (Yakima Valley) $50. This is McCrea's top-of-the-line Syrah, a lush and deeply expressive wine that includes about 7% Viognier. Black fruits, vivid acids, and plenty of roasted new oak flavors kick the finish into high gear. **92** —*P.G. (9/1/2002)*

McCrea 2003 Cuvée Orleans Syrah (Yakima Valley) $60. Fruit from both Boushey and Ciel du Cheval goes into this special reserve. Always a blockbuster, it is perhaps a touch too ripe in this warm vintage. Dark, jammy, minced pie/fruit compote flavors mix with baked apple, cherry, and plum. There are tasty baking spice flavors also, and the wine is ready to be consumed now. The blend includes 12% Mourvèdre and a touch of Viognier. **91** —*P.G. (11/15/2006)*

McCrea 2002 Cuvée Orleans Syrah (Yakima Valley) $60. Normally winemaker Doug McCrea's top wine, this year we gave the nod to his Ciel du Cheval bottling, which seemed to have a bit more tannin. The Cuvée Orleans boasts lush blackberry and cassis flavors, hints of meat and pepper, but falls off just a bit on the finish. **87** *(9/1/2005)*

McCrea 2000 Cuvée Orleans Syrah (Yakima Valley) $50. This is the fourth edition of this Côte-Rotie-inspired bottling, which combines fruit from both Ciel du Cheval and Boushey vineyards. In classic Rhône style, some Viognier (7%) is also included in the blend. This cuvée is the biggest and spiciest of all the McCrea Syrahs, and needs a bit more time to unwrap, hence the later release date. **91** —*P.G. (12/31/2003)*

McCrea 2001 Yakima Valley Syrah Syrah (Yakima Valley) $38. The most forward and immediately drinkable of McCrea's Syrah lineup, this wine is comprised of lots that were selected out of the Boushey Grand Côte bottling. It shows plenty of toast and smoky power, at a slightly better price. **88** —*P.G. (12/31/2003)*

McCrea 2001 Viognier (Yakima Valley) $22. Makes a strong case for being the best Viognier in Washington. It's not easy to hit the mark with this grape, but here it shows its best. Fragrant with fresh, racy citrus blossom and tangerine scents, lively acidity, and a nice hint of citrus rind on the persistent finish. **92 Editors' Choice** —*P.G. (12/31/2003)*

McCrea 2000 Viognier (Yakima Valley) $23. Viognier is rarely so perfectly balanced, intensely flavored without becoming too sweetly perfumed, rich but not so ripe as to lose its subtle elegance. **91** —*P.G. (9/1/2002)*

McCrea 1998 Viognier (Yakima Valley) $20. 89 —*P.G. (6/1/2000)*

McCrea 2005 Ciel du Cheval Vineyard Viognier (Red Mountain) $25. This Viognier seems much more balanced than previous vintages, and though it packs a lot of fruit power into its mid-palate, the flavor details are what elevate it into the 90-point range. Spice, rind, pear skin, and even a whiff of fresh cut tobacco can be found in the lovely bouquet. The fruit suggests white peach and citrus, and the finish never becomes hot or clumsy. **90** —*P.G. (12/31/2006)*

McCrea 2000 La Mer White Blend (Yakima Valley) $18. This is 58% Viognier and 42% Chardonnay, making a crisp, clean, dynamic white with plenty of lime and citrus flavor. Delicious and refreshing, it's a perfect food wine. **89** —*P.G. (9/1/2002)*

MCDOWELL

McDowell 2003 Grenache (McDowell Valley) $12. Watery, with trace amounts of raspberries on the finish. **82** —*S.H. (6/1/2005)*

McDowell 1997 Grenache Rosé Grenache (Mendocino) $9. 88 Best Buy —*S.H. (6/1/1999)*

McDowell 2000 Rosé Grenache (California) $9. This Rhône blend drinks candied and off-dry, with ripe berry, fruit, and spice flavors, and on the soft side. Strives to combine the freshness and lightness of a white with the weight of a red, and does a pretty good job of it. **86** —*S.H. (9/1/2002)*

McDowell 2001 Marsanne (Mendocino) $16. Rich and fruity, a flavorful wine tasting like white chocolate, peaches, cheesecake, and lime, with nuances added from oak. Feels thick and heavy in the mouth, as this variety often does in California. Almost syrupy. Could benefit from more finesse and lightness. **85** —*S.H. (6/1/2003)*

McDowell 1997 Marsanne (Mendocino) $16. 87 —*S.H. (6/1/1999)*

McDowell 2000 Reserve Petite Sirah (Mendocino) $20. The panel was unanimous in calling this wine a solid average in quality. It has decent flavors of red and black stone fruits, and the tannins are gritty through the tart finish. It's a big, thick wine, best with meat dishes. **83** —*S.H. (4/1/2003)*

McDowell 2002 Syrah (Mendocino County) $25. Pours dark and extracted, with rich, ripe chocolate and blackberry preserve flavors. Pretty tannic now, and finishes dry and fruity. Good with chops, steak. **85** —*S.H. (6/1/2005)*

McDowell 2000 Syrah (Mendocino County) $12. Here's a nice, smooth wine from a veteran Rhône specialist, and one that's always one of the best values in California. In a good vintage, McDowell's Syrahs age gracefully. This release, while soft and charming, has an unripe, stalky note that suggests early drinking. **85** —*S.H. (12/1/2002)*

McDowell 1999 Syrah (Mendocino) $14. Sour briny, fishy aromas open onto a palate with light berry fruit and dusty earth flavors. Finishes dry, with some peppery notes. Very simple, and very dull. **80** *(10/1/2001)*

McDowell 1997 Syrah (Mendocino) $12. 88 —*M.G. (11/15/1999)*

McDowell 1997 Mendocino Estate Syrah (Mendocino) $22. 89 —*S.H. (6/1/1999)*

McDowell 1999 Reserve-McDowell Valley Syrah (Mendocino) $24. Raspberry aromas and flavors dominate the McDowell—in the bouquet, they're bolstered by blueberry and linseed aromas and, on the palate, chocolate, earth, and walnut flavors. Medium-weight and a little tart on the palate and on the long, toasty finish. Top Value. **90** *(11/1/2001)*

McDowell 2003 Viognier (Mendocino County) $16. From this Rhône pioneer, a delicately fragrant, crisp, dry wine that's rich in fruity flavor, yet balanced and sophisticated. Shows persistent peach flavors. **87** —*S.H. (6/1/2005)*

McDowell 2000 Viognier (Mendocino) $16. Lots of smoke and butterscotchy tapioca in the nose, and a spicy, peaches-and-cream sweetness. Drinks very fruity, with ripe peach and citrus flavors and spices, but is very dry and searing with high acids. **87** —*S.H. (5/1/2002)*

McDowell 1997 Viognier (Mendocino) $16. 90 Best Buy —*S.H. (6/1/1999)*

MCILROY

McIlroy 1999 Salzgeber Vineyard Cabernet Franc (Russian River Valley) $24. Rare are the places that Cabernet Franc produces a distinctive wine. In fact, no savory Russian River Valley examples come to mind. This wine suggests the difficulties. Very tannic and raw, highly acidic, and although it's dark in color, lacking fruity extract. Nor is it a wine to age. It's barren now, and not going anywhere. **83** —*S.H. (9/1/2002)*

McIlroy 2000 Aquarius Ranch Chardonnay (Russian River Valley) $21. Textbook RRV Chard reveals green apple and intense spice, white peach and honey flavors, generously wrapped in smoky oak. Has a real richness and creaminess to the texture. Finishes too sugary, but has a lip-smacking quality many will admire. **87** —*S.H. (9/1/2002)*

McIlroy 2000 Aquarius Ranch Late Harvest Gewürztraminer (Russian River Valley) $13. Pretty decadent stuff here. Bursting with sweet apricot and spice flavors, and 0.8% residual sugar makes it taste decidedly sweet. There's an oily, unguent texture—you can see the glycerin lines stain the side of the glass. It could use a little more acidity. **89 Best Buy** —*S.H. (9/1/2002)*

McIlroy 1999 Aquarius Ranch Merlot (Russian River Valley) $21. A wine that elicits mixed feelings. On the plus side, subtle fruit and oak, with a rich earthiness and sleek tannins. Does a good job of keeping Merlot fat and plump, while maintaining an herbal character. On the other hand, there's pronounced acidity and a sharpness that shows up on the finish. Doesn't seem likely to age well, but you never know. **87** —*S.H. (9/1/2002)*

McIlroy 1999 Aquarius Ranch Pinot Noir (Russian River Valley) $24. Bone dry and light, with cranberry, cola, and tomato flavors in a silky package. This is a wine that seems to be an expression of its vineyard. It's not a rich wine, nor one to age beyond a year or so. But it possesses an earthy honesty. **86** —*S.H. (9/1/2002)*

McIlroy 1998 Porter-Bass Vineyard Zinfandel (Russian River Valley) $18. Very good, not great Zinfandel. Makes all the right moves, with spicy, peppery berry fruit, dry, thick tannins, good acidity and a nice roundness from oak that does not overpower. Offers plenty of pleasure, and finishes with a bite of acidity. Could use more depth, though. **88** —*S.H. (11/1/2002)*

MCINTYRE VINEYARDS

McIntyre Vineyards 2003 Chardonnay (Monterey County) $13. Drinks rather rough and syrupy, with the flavor of canned peaches and an oaky veneer. **82** —*S.H. (12/1/2005)*

McIntyre Vineyards 2002 Force Canyon Vineyard Pinot Noir (Monterey County) $31. Here's a medium-bodied, silky wine that shows the classic elegance of cool-climate winegrowing. Fully dry, with complex flavors of cherries, cola, rhubarb, coffee, and spice, it has a touch of smoky oak. It's an irresistibly yummy Pinot Noir. **92 Editors' Choice** —*S.H. (12/1/2005)*

McIntyre Vineyards 1998 L'Homme Qui Ris Sparkling Blend (Monterey County) $22. Rather lemony and simple, with tart, crisp flavors and a clean finish. Sort of like lemonade with bubbles (sans sugar). **84** —*J.C. (12/1/2003)*

MCKENZIE-MUELLER

McKenzie-Mueller 2001 Cabernet Franc (Napa Valley) $28. Nice and ripe, with black cherry and vanilla flavors and a mouth-warming feel that's partly the result of the body, partly due to soft tannins and acids. Brings to mind those luscious, likeable wines of Chinon. **86** —*S.H. (7/1/2005)*

USA

McKenzie-Mueller 2001 Cabernet Sauvignon (Napa Valley) $40. Harsh and difficult, with dry tannins and a gluey mouthfeel that makes the blackberry flavors taste medicinal. **83** —*S.H. (7/1/2005)*

McKenzie-Mueller 2002 Malbec (Carneros) $30. Clean and decent, but hard to recommend. Bone dry, astringent, and heavy in coffee and cherry flavors. **83** —*S.H. (7/1/2005)*

McKenzie-Mueller 2001 Merlot (Carneros) $28. Comes down on the rustic side, but offers pleasant flavors of cherries, roast coffee, and cocoa, in a dry wine. **84** —*S.H. (7/1/2005)*

McKenzie-Mueller 2003 Pinot Grigio (Carneros) $16. Crisp, clean, and a little sweet, with figgy, lemon and lime flavors. An enjoyable wine that refreshes the palate. **84** —*S.H. (7/1/2005)*

McKenzie-Mueller 2004 Reserve Pinot Grigio (Carneros) $16. There's no oak at all in this wine, so what you get is pure lime, kiwi, and nectarine fruit flavor and high, bright acids. It's bone dry, with absolutely no sugar on the finish. What a refreshing wine. **87** —*S.H. (2/1/2006)*

McKenzie-Mueller 2001 Pinot Noir (Carneros) $28. Harsh, with burnt cherry notes that make the tannins and acids stick out. No major flaws, but it's hard to like. **82** —*S.H. (7/1/2005)*

McKenzie-Mueller 2001 Reserve Pinot Noir (Carneros) $35. Flawed. Smells and tastes dirty and funky, with medicinal cherry flavors. **82** —*S.H. (7/1/2005)*

MCKINLEY SPRINGS

McKinley Springs 2002 Syrah (Columbia Valley (WA)) $24. This new winery has a first release that is tough to peg. It is so incredibly dense and Port-like in color and aroma that you expect it to slam into the palate like a tropical storm, but it doesn't hit quite that hard. Oxidized and showing more baking spices than fruit, it nonetheless is a flavorful effort that will bring some enjoyment in the near term. **86** —*P.G. (12/15/2004)*

MCMANIS

McManis 2005 Cabernet Sauvignon (California) $10. Pretty good for this price, a balanced red wine, brimming with blackberry and cherry flavors, smoky oak, and the full-bodied richness you want in a Cab. Easy to find, with 76,000 cases produced. **84 Best Buy** —*S.H. (12/31/2006)*

McManis 2004 Cabernet Sauvignon (California) $10. Simple and fruity, this everyday wine will please Cab lovers who don't want to shell out big bucks. It's dry and balanced, with blackberry, currant, and plum flavors and an oaky coating. **84** —*S.H. (12/31/2005)*

McManis 2003 Cabernet Sauvignon (California) $10. A little sweet in residual sugar, but otherwise a nice wine, with soft tannins and ripe flavors of cherries and chocolate. **84** —*S.H. (12/31/2004)*

McManis 2002 Cabernet Sauvignon (California) $10. Offers some pleasant berry, cherry flavors in a soft package with easy tannins and acids. Finishes dry and fruity. Will do fine with a light picnic or café lunch. **84** —*S.H. (2/1/2004)*

McManis 2001 Cabernet Sauvignon (California) $9. Very dark in color, with weak aromas of currants and coffee. It's soft and simple to taste, but the big problem is residual sugar. It's too sweet and cloying. **82** —*S.H. (12/31/2002)*

McManis 2000 Cabernet Sauvignon (California) $10. 80 —*S.H. (11/15/2002)*

McManis 2005 Chardonnay (River Junction) $10. Rich in apricot, peach, and pineapple flavors that finish a little sweet and oaky. This is the kind of inexpensive Chardonnay that California so effortlessly produces, all to the benefit of consumers. **85 Best Buy** —*S.H. (12/1/2006)*

McManis 2004 Chardonnay (River Junction) $10. With its easy flavors of apples and peaches and touch of spicy oak, this everyday Chard is a pretty good buy. It's soft, but that fruit is ripe and pretty. **84** —*S.H. (11/15/2005)*

McManis 2001 Chardonnay (California) $9. A drinkable, simple wine, with appley-fruity flavors and oaky notes. It's a little sweet and soft, and feels thick in the mouth. **84** —*S.H. (12/15/2002)*

McManis 2000 Chardonnay (California) $9. From a new winery, an earthy, fruity wine with some pretty flavors. The fruit is obviously ripe, displaying pear and spice notes, overlaid with spicy oak and vanilla. It's soft and a bit sweet and medicinal but a good buy. **84** —*S.H. (5/1/2002)*

McManis 2003 River Junction Chardonnay (Central Coast) $10. Peach and tropical fruit flavors highlight this soft wine, with oaky notes. It has a creamy texture and finishes dry. **84** —*S.H. (12/1/2004)*

McManis 2005 Merlot (California) $10. Dark, dry and fruity, this Merlot is a little heavy and simple, but has a tasty array of blackberries, black cherries, plums, pomegranates, and savory spices. Nice everyday red, with a bit of fanciness. **84 Best Buy** —*S.H. (12/31/2006)*

McManis 2004 Merlot (California) $10. This rustic wine is soft and velvety, with ripe cherry and coffee flavors, but seems just a little too sweet on the finish to qualify as truly dry. **83** —*S.H. (5/1/2006)*

McManis 2003 Merlot (California) $10. Earthy, with cherry cough medicine flavors and a sharp finish. **82** —*S.H. (12/15/2004)*

McManis 2002 Merlot (California) $10. This label continues the value game with another rich, flavorful wine at an everyday price. It floods the mouth with juicy, sweet flavors of cherries and blackberries, with a round, opulent texture. Buy this beauty by the case, not the bottle. **90 Best Buy** —*S.H. (2/1/2004)*

McManis 2001 Merlot (California) $9. Smells and tastes like a decent inexpensive Cabernet, with black currant flavors and soft, easy tannins. It's also soft in acids, but the flavors are pretty and the wine is pleasant to sip. **85** —*S.H. (12/31/2002)*

McManis 2000 Merlot (California) $9. 81 —*S.H. (11/15/2002)*

McManis 2004 Petite Sirah (California) $11. Ultra-dry, tannic, full-bodied, strong and red, this country-style wine is something you'd drink with barbecued ribs. The flavors of blackberries and coffee are enriched by some oak. **83** —*S.H. (12/31/2005)*

McManis 2003 Petite Sirah (California) $10. Lovely, complex flavors of blackberries sprinkled with pepper, balsamic, and vanilla, and gentle, lush tannins. Fully dry, but would earn a few extra points if it wasn't so soft. **84** —*S.H. (12/31/2004)*

McManis 2005 Pinot Grigio (California) $10. Apricots, grapefruits, apples, figs, peaches, melons—there's a whole orchard in this dry, crisp PG. It has a particular savory character from the citrusy acids. What a great price for this wine. **86 Best Buy** —*S.H. (10/1/2006)*

McManis 2004 Pinot Grigio (California) $10. Plenty of ripe, semi-sweet fig, citrus, and cantaloupe flavors in this crisp wine. It has a fizziness that's not unpleasant. **84** —*S.H. (7/1/2005)*

McManis 2003 River Junction Pinot Grigio (Central Coast) $10. From a tiny Delta appellation, a soft, easy wine with lemony, fruity flavors. It finishes with a tart, citrus aftertaste, and is dry. **83** —*S.H. (11/15/2004)*

McManis 2005 Syrah (California) $10. The wine is green and thin in fruit, and bone dry. There are some blackberry and cherry flavors, but they're drowned out by the acids and tannins. Okay in a pinch. **83** —*S.H. (12/31/2006)*

McManis 2004 Syrah (California) $10. Smells and tastes sweet, like a baked cherry tart, with the gooey filling and the sweet, smoky crust. This is a serious deficiency in a table wine. **81** —*S.H. (6/1/2006)*

McManis 2003 Syrah (California) $10. Rather soft and thick in texture, a low tannin, low acid wine with flavors of sweetened coffee, cherry compote, and rhubarb pie. Easy and gentle. **84** —*S.H. (12/31/2004)*

McManis 2002 Syrah (California) $10. The black cherry and black raspberry flavors are fruity and ripe, and have an edge of smoky tobacco and white pepper. Although it's easy to drink now, the tannins are finely etched. Delicious with duck with a dark fruit sauce. **86 Best Buy** —*S.H. (2/1/2004)*

McManis 2001 Syrah (California) $9. A dark, fruity wine, very ripe, packed with blackberry, plum, pepper, and tobacco flavors. Dry, and a little soft, but with adequate acids. Would get a higher score but for its immature, rustic tannins. **84** —*S.H. (12/1/2002)*

McManis 2005 Viognier (California) $10. Smells citrusy like a Sauvignon Blanc, but once in the mouth, wham! All those fruits and flowers erupt in a cascade of peaches, apricots, pineapples, and honeysuckle. The wine

USA

is rich in acidity, and dryish, with a finish that's long in fruity essence. **85 Best Buy** —*S.H. (10/1/2006)*

McManis 2004 Viognier (California) $10. Big and fruit forward in pineapples, apricots, and peaches, with a good spine of acidity and a nice, creamy texture; this dry, balanced wine is a great value. **86 Best Buy** —*S.H. (10/1/2005)*

McManis 2003 Viognier (California) $10. Run, don't walk, to stock up on this by the case. If you have a hankering for a fruity, spicy dry white wine, balanced with crisp acidity and with plenty of finesse, this is it. Tropical fruits, wildflowers, peaches, vanilla, you name it. **88 Best Buy** —*S.H. (12/15/2004)*

MCNAB RIDGE

McNab Ridge 1997 Reserve Cabernet Sauvignon (Mendocino County) $18. This is the kind of wine that farmers have drunk for centuries. It's red and full-bodied. It's dry and balances dark berry and stone fruit flavors with earthy tones. It's fairly tannic, with a crisp backbone of acidity, and it will probably age forever because it's so balanced. And it's rustic. **85** —*S.H. (5/1/2002)*

McNab Ridge 2000 Meritage (Mendocino County) $20. What's likeable about this Bordeaux blend is its dryness. It doesn't slam you with over-the-top, extracted fruit, but is controlled in its herb and blackberry flavors and smooth but firm tannins. **90** —*S.H. (11/15/2004)*

McNab Ridge 1999 John H. Parducci Signature Series Mendotage Meritage (Mendocino) $35. A a lip-smackingingly good, limited edition Bordeaux blend from a veteran producer. It's as ripe as can be, very gentle and filled with juicy berry flavors. The upfront fruit is packaged in soft tannins, while acids seem stronger than Napa-Sonoma. The wine has real bite. **87** —*C.S. (5/1/2002)*

McNab Ridge 1998 Merlot (Mendocino County) $15. A newish label from veteran Mendocino producer Parducci. I want to praise it, but it fails to rise above an average rustic level, and harkens back to an rough, old style of red wine. Smells earthy and plummy, and turns fiercely tannic and dry, and not particularly varietal. **84** —*S.H. (5/1/2002)*

McNab Ridge 1999 Muscat Canelli (Mendocino County) $12. 89 —*S.H. (5/1/2002)*

McNab Ridge 2000 Petite Sirah (Mendocino County) $18. Tasters tried in vain to find fruit in this thin, vapid wine. Despite the lack of flavor, the tannins are big and rasping, and the wine is drenched in unnatural oak. **81** *(4/1/2003)*

McNab Ridge 2002 Napoli Vineyard Pinotage (Mendocino) $18. Dry, with ripe cherry and black plum flavors and rich tannins that turn dryish on the finish. Has the weight, although not the distinction, of a fine Merlot. **84** —*S.H. (12/15/2004)*

McNab Ridge 2004 Sauvignon Blanc (Mendocino) $12. Pleasant in ripe peach, citrus, vanilla, and spice flavors, this dry, fruity wine is furnished with excellent acidity that makes it clean and bright. It's an easy charmer at a fair price. Great with roasted chicken. **85** —*S.H. (4/1/2006)*

McNab Ridge 2003 Sauvignon Blanc (Mendocino) $12. Sweet, fresh grass, lemon and lime, fig, and vanilla mark this dry wine. It has a pleasantly clean streak of acidity to offset the fruity flavors. **85** —*S.H. (12/15/2004)*

McNab Ridge 2003 Zinfandel (Mendocino) $18. Enormously high in alcohol, nearly 16 percent, with a hot, Porty mouthfeel and raisiny tastes, this is certainly an eccentric Zin. Not my style, but some will like it. **83** —*S.H. (4/1/2006)*

McNab Ridge 2002 Zinfandel (Mendocino) $18. Sweet enough in jammy cherry and wild berry fruit, with a wild, peppery edge. There is, however, a heavy, syrupy mouthfeel that detracts. **83** —*S.H. (12/15/2004)*

MCPRICE MYERS

McPrice Myers 2002 Larner Vineyard Syrah (Santa Ynez Valley) $25. Here's a beautiful, lush aromatic mélange of pepper, smoky vanilla, cassis, gingerbread, and bacon. Really complex and compelling, and it drinks as fine as it smells. Just delicious, with soft, rich tannins and a long, mellow finish. **92** —*S.H. (12/1/2004)*

MEADOR

Meador 2000 Maverick Syrah (Arroyo Seco) $50. Another major success from Ventana. Starts with complex aromas of meat, smoky oak, and cassis, then turns wonderfully flavorful in the mouth, with an explosion of currant, cherry, plum, chocolate, and spice. Feels dense and lush. Finishes very dry, with tannins to shed. **92** —*S.H. (9/1/2004)*

Meador 1998 Maverick Syrah (Arroyo Seco) $50. The bouquet of black-cherry and cranberry fruit wears a weedy, vegetal mantle that appears early. There's some nice pepper, caramel and clove notes on the palate, even a ripe, figgy quality to fruit, but ultimately they're done in by the tart green shadow. Our panel found the wine hard to warm up to. **83** *(11/1/2001)*

Meador Estate 2003 Block 9 Chardonnay (Arroyo Seco) $30. To this taster, there's so much high-char new oak on this Chard that it goes beyond toast all the way to burnt ash. Too bad, because the underlying wine is crisp and ripe in polished tropical fruit. **84** —*S.H. (12/15/2006)*

Meador Estate 2001 Maverick Syrah (Arroyo Seco) $50. Polished and supple yet young and even immature, this wine flatters now for its rich blackberry, cherry, meat, and oak flavors. It's very dry, with sturdy, dusty tannins and a bite of acidity on the finish. Dramatic now for its overall balance, and best with rich fare. Drink now through 2005. **90** —*S.H. (6/1/2005)*

MEANDER

Meander 2003 Cabernet Sauvignon (Napa Valley) $65. This ambitious effort doesn't succeed due to a sharpness throughout, a tart, wintergreen note that detracts. Everything else, the oak, the tannins, is fine. **84** —*S.H. (12/31/2005)*

MEDLOCK AMES

Medlock Ames 2002 Bell Mountain Ranch Red Bordeaux Blend (Alexander Valley) $25. Not only is this a deliciously drinkable wine, it has lots of complexity and should even improve for a couple of years. It's a big, soft, dry Merlot-based Bordeaux blend, juicy in cherry pie and succulent blueberry flavors and a rich, honeyed, toasty oak finish. Best now–2010. **91** —*S.H. (12/15/2006)*

Medlock Ames 2002 Bell Mountain Vineyard Cabernet Sauvignon (Alexander Valley) $42. Here's a young Cabernet that's rich in complex, sweet tannins. The fruit shows all the hallmarks of the vintage, wonderfully ripe in blackberry, cherry, blueberry, and chocolate flavors with an extravagant coating of toasty new oak. It's awfully good now, and should be opened by 2010 or so because of the softness. **92** —*S.H. (12/15/2006)*

Medlock Ames 2004 Bell Mountain Vineyard Chardonnay (Alexander Valley) $20. Here's a big, rich, mouthfilling Chard. It's superoaky, super-ripe and just delicious, offering up a wealth of mango, guava, pineapple custard, and peach pie fruit, with the crème brûlée, buttercream, and buttered toast from new oak. Really good Chardonnay. **92** —*S.H. (10/1/2006)*

Medlock Ames 2001 Bell Mountain Vineyard Merlot (Alexander Valley) $35. Let this one breathe for an hour or two. At first it tastes a bit tired, but oxygen perks it up and restores vivacity to the fruit. Ultimately, it's a very softly structured, very dry wine, with complex cherry, coffee, herb, cola, and tea flavors. Drink now. **87** —*S.H. (12/15/2006)*

MEEKER

Meeker 1997 Eighth Rack Zinfandel (Sonoma County) $14. Forward, fruity and clean, with a jokey label showing a moose, an elk and a sheep playing pool. This wine would make a great house Zin if the price were just a tad lower. **86** —*P.G. (3/1/2001)*

Meeker 1997 Gold Leaf Cuvée Zinfandel (Dry Creek Valley) $18. Plummy, ripe, beginning to oxidize. Ready to drink right now, it's got a leafy, tomato flavor to it. Unusual. **82** —*P.G. (3/1/2001)*

MELROSE

Melrose 2002 Parker's Pinot Noir (Umpqua Valley) $24. Truly Burgundian in its soft, silky elegance. It offers sweet, delicious, seductive fruit, seamless and extended, substituting finesse for sheer power. Subtle, intense. **89** *(11/1/2004)*

Melrose 2002 Reserve Pinot Noir (Umpqua Valley) $26. Very spicy, with a tart entry and some sour cherry fruit. Elegant, feminine, and plush through the middle. **88** *(11/1/2004)*

MELVILLE

Melville 2000 Chardonnay (Santa Rita Hills) $20. Superextracted and ripe, a big candy bar of a wine filled with sweet peach liqueur and nectarine flavors. Spicy oak adds additional sweet, sappy vanilla and oak elements. Big and lush, but could use more balance and harmony. **86** —*S.H. (12/15/2002)*

Melville 2002 Clone 76-Inox Chardonnay (Santa Rita Hills) $28. An entirely unoaked wine designed to showcase its terroir, which it does in the tartly crisp acidity and streamlined citrus and apple flavors. The wine drinks severe and steely sharp. The bottle I tasted was also a little fizzy. **86** —*S.H. (12/15/2003)*

Melville 2004 Estate Chardonnay (Santa Rita Hills) $26. A nice, basic Santa Rita Chard, very high in acids, with complex citrus peel, mineral, and oak flavors. It's a clean, refreshing and balanced wine. **88** —*S.H. (3/1/2006)*

Melville 1999 Pinot Noir (Santa Rita Hills) $24. Aims for the middle of the road: not flamboyant or oaky, just the right balance of sweet berry fruit, acidity and wood. This lightly tannic wine will go with a range of foods. **89** —*S.H. (2/1/2003)*

Melville 2001 Carrie's Pinot Noir (Santa Rita Hills) $40. Darker in color than the estate, and riper too, with black cherries that veer into blackberries. There are fascinating bursts of tangerine rind, roasted coffee, cinnamon, and cola that add complexity. Feels a bit hot, with a slightly heavy sweetness toward the finish. **90** —*S.H. (10/1/2003)*

Melville 2001 Estate Pinot Noir (Santa Rita Hills) $25. Young and jammy at the moment, bursting with bright, fully ripe flavors of black cherries. The fruit is wrapped in rich tannins that are ripe and sweet, and a streak of vibrant acidity cuts through everything. Not fully knit together at this stage; and calls for short-term cellaring. **89** —*S.H. (3/1/2004)*

Melville 2000 Syrah (Santa Rita Hills) $24. Bright, jammy fruit is plump and juicy in this likeable wine, which is most notable for the balance of its parts. It's a full-bodied, rich wine, with earthy-berry flavors, dry and tart with fresh young acidity. Made by Greg Brewer, of Brewer-Clifton, from 100% estate grapes. **86** —*S.H. (12/1/2002)*

Melville 2004 Donna's Syrah (Santa Rita Hills) $30. Opens with a gorgeous mélange of white pepper, cherry, and raspberry fruit, and hints of cocoa, leather, coffee, smoky oak, and dusty brown spices. So pure, refined and delicious. Easy to drink yet complex and powerful. **92** —*S.H. (11/15/2006)*

Melville 2003 Estate Syrah (Santa Barbara County) $20. So pretty and polished, with such an attractive aroma. Light, delicately structured, yet powerful in raspberry and cherry fruit, gingerbread, and vanilla. Just a lovely glass of red wine to drink now. **89** —*S.H. (11/15/2006)*

Melville 2005 Verna's Viognier (Santa Barbara County) $18. Super aromatic, with powerful lemondrop, apricot pit, and wildflower scents leading to lots of rich, fruity-flowery flavors. Great acidity makes it crisp and clean, with a firm minerality. Finishes with a honey and citrus flourish. **88** —*S.H. (11/15/2006)*

MENDELSON

Mendelson 1999 Muscat Canelli (Mendocino County) $35. Spice and mineral notes frame a honey-like core in this zingy dessert wine. The finish has a menthol kick. **87** —*J.M. (12/1/2002)*

Mendelson 1999 Dessert Wine Pinot Gris (Napa Valley) $35. A pleasant, sweet wine, with moderate body and nutty, spicy, melon, and peach notes. A bit more acidity would provide needed focus. **85** —*J.M. (12/1/2002)*

Mendelson 2002 Pinot Noir (Santa Lucia Highlands) $38. Smells caramelly and oaky, and tastes overly sweet. **82** *(11/1/2004)*

Mendelson 2001 Pinot Noir (Santa Lucia Highlands) $38. Redolent of black cherries and cola in the nose. On the palate, it fans out to reveal spice, more cherry, strawberries, bacon, cedar, tea, and spice flavors.

Tannins are powdery but ripe, while the finish is bright. **89** —*J.M. (2/1/2004)*

MENDOCINO COLLECTION

Mendocino Collection 1997 SketchBook Collection Merlot (Mendocino) $23. 84 *(11/1/1999)*

MENDOCINO GOLD

Mendocino Gold 2000 Cabernet Sauvignon (Mendocino County) $12. A nice Cabernet, proper and pleasant, it tastes of black currants and oak and is very dry and balanced. No doubting that it comes from a good vineyard and has been made in a competent style. **86** —*S.H. (8/1/2003)*

Mendocino Gold 2001 Chardonnay (Mendocino County) $10. A bright, zesty wine, long on flavor and easy on the wallet. Has pretty flavors of sweet ripe peaches, framed in toasty oak, and a rich, creamy texture. This good wine is a value. **86 Best Buy** —*S.H. (6/1/2003)*

MENDOCINO HILL

Mendocino Hill 1999 Sangiovese (Mendocino County) $18. The winery is quite proud of this wine, and with good reason. Some coastal Sangioveses are light and jammy, but not this one. It's a big, sturdy, rich wine, and the fruity-berry flavors are outstanding. Strikes a nice balance between fruit and herbal-tobacco notes. Upfront tannins suggest short-term aging. **89** —*S.H. (5/1/2002)*

Mendocino Hill 1999 Syrah (Mendocino County) $20. From a small family winery and vineyards in Hopland, a good example of this sun-ripened, full-bodied varietal. It's a big, inky wine with aromas of blackberry jam and freshly crushed black peppercorns. The flavors are enormous and extracted and jammy, but it's a dry wine, with 14.5 percent alcohol. It's a fine, robust wine and a quintessential Mendo big red. **88** —*S.H. (5/1/2002)*

MEOLA VINEYARDS

Meola Vineyards 2002 Unfiltered Cabernet Sauvignon (Alexander Valley) $60. Offers everything that Alexander Valley's famous for: a soft, easy texture, slightly herbaceous flavors of cherries and cassis, and lots of elegance. This unfiltered Cab is totally dry and nicely balanced. **89** —*S.H. (12/15/2005)*

Meola Vineyards 2002 Venezia Cabernet Sauvignon (Alexander Valley) $60. Very ripe and extracted, with bigtime blackberry, cherry, blueberry, cassis, and vanilla-oaky flavors, this Cab has a slightly rustic mouthfeel. It's so fruity, it tastes almost semi-sweet, although it's technically dry. **85** —*S.H. (12/15/2005)*

MER SOLEIL

Mer Soleil 2003 Chardonnay (Central Coast) $42. Another interesting Chard from this Santa Lucia Highlands estate; why the Wagners don't put that appellation on the label is a mystery. The wine seems even higher in acidity than usual, with greater ageworthiness, and experience shows this is one for the cellar. The tropical fruit flavors are well oaked, and finish absolutely dry. Best after 2008. **90 Cellar Selection** —*S.H. (6/1/2006)*

Mer Soleil 2002 Chardonnay (Central Coast) $42. Classic Mer Soleil, which is to say it's a small nuclear explosion in the mouth. Don't drink it too cold, or you'll minimize the rich tropical fruit and vanilla cream flavors. This big Chard should be enjoyed with food that's buttery and slightly sweet, like broiled lobster. **92** —*S.H. (5/1/2005)*

Mer Soleil 2001 Chardonnay (Central Coast) $42. Hard to figure why the Wagners of Caymus don't put the fine Santa Lucia Highlands AVA on the front label, but there's no questioning the quality of this wine. It's brilliant in tropical fruit and pear flavors, with a lavish overlay of smoky oak and a very long, sweet finish. Has those citrusy, minerally Monterey acids that perk up the flavors, making them even richer. **92** —*S.H. (2/1/2004)*

Mer Soleil 2000 Chardonnay (Central Coast) $42. Fabulously rich and complex, this wine stuns the palate with its ever-shifting flavors, which range from citrus through apples, peaches, and tropical fruits. Spicy and cinnamony, with an elaborate oak overlay that is perfectly suited for fruit this big. Lush and opulent, right through the long finish. **93** —*S.H. (2/1/2003)*

Mer Soleil 1999 Chardonnay (Central Coast) $40. Lush and ripe, with a heady collection of tropical fruit flavors that ranges from mango, coconut, and pineapple to lemon, melon, and orange. Hints of spice and vanilla add interest, while a subtle earthy quality contributes complexity. Dense and long at the end. **93** —*J.M. (12/15/2002)*

Mer Soleil 1998 Chardonnay (Central Coast) $40. This plush Chardonnay's bouquet shows an ultraripe botrytis note in its vanilla, peach, clove, and caramel aromas. Dried fruits, caramel, and honey flavors massage the palate: the mouthfeel is full and viscous—even voluptuous. A must for lovers of larger-than-life Chards. **90** *(7/1/2001)*

Mer Soleil 2000 Late Harvest White Wine White Blend (Santa Lucia Highlands) $36. **92** —*J.M. (9/1/2003)*

MERIDIAN

Meridian 2003 Cabernet Sauvignon (California) $10. There are some nice cherry-berry notes in this somewhat tannic wine. It's very soft, almost syrupy, which makes the fruit taste sweeter and more candied than it really is. **82** —*S.H. (5/1/2006)*

Meridian 1996 Coastal Reserve Cabernet Sauvignon (California) $22. **83** —*S.H. (12/15/2000)*

Meridian 2005 Chardonnay (Santa Barbara County) $10. Smells and tastes raw and rustic, with a sharp mintiness on the finish that detracts from the tropical fruit flavors. The quality of Meridian's Chards has varied recently. **83** —*S.H. (11/15/2006)*

Meridian 2004 Chardonnay (Santa Barbara County) $10. It's rich in Chardonnay character, with tropical fruit, peach, pear, and oak flavors set in a richly creamy, honeyed texture that's highlighted by brisk, South Coast acidity. **87 Best Buy** —*S.H. (12/31/2005)*

Meridian 2003 Chardonnay (Santa Barbara County) $10. Started in the early 1980s by veteran winemaker Chuck Ortman, Meridian hit the big-time after it was bought by Beringer, when it became a dependably value-oriented winery. This Chard benefits from Beringer's extensive vineyard acreage in the county. Winemaker Signe Zoller chose lots that combine balance and complexity with lush pineapple, peach, tangerine, and honeysuckle flavors, set in a creamy texture. **86 Best Buy** —*S.H. (11/15/2005)*

Meridian 2002 Chardonnay (Santa Barbara) $10. The price is right, but this wine is rather skimpy in fruit, over-oaked and too sweet. **83** —*S.H. (2/1/2005)*

Meridian 2001 Chardonnay (Santa Barbara County) $11. Usually a good value, but this year the fruit is thinner than in past vintages. Has tropical fruit flavors and quite a bit of smoky oak, with mouthwatering acidity. Because of the weak fruit, oak, and alcohol dominate. **84** —*S.H. (6/1/2003)*

Meridian 2000 Chardonnay (Santa Barbara County) $11. Meridian strikes again with this spiffy Chard packed with well-ripened tropical fruits and spices, and a solid dose of smoky oak. It's clean, crisp, and intense, with a honeyed texture and long finish. **87 Best Buy** —*S.H. (12/31/2001)*

Meridian 1998 Chardonnay (Santa Barbara County) $10. **89 Best Buy** —*M.M. (11/15/1999)*

Meridian 1999 Limited Release Chardonnay (Santa Barbara County) $22. Focus is what this wine is all about. The tropical fruit flavors are pinpointed. The acids are bright and sharp. The oaky overlay is spicy and pungent, and the finish is long and clean. **89** —*S.H. (12/15/2002)*

Meridian 2002 Reserve Chardonnay (Santa Barbara County) $16. Super oaky, and this time the smoke, char, vanilla, and wood sap outweigh the fruit. There are hints of pineapple and mango, but that barrel influence is overwhelming. **84** —*S.H. (11/15/2004)*

Meridian 1999 Reserve Chardonnay (Edna Valley) $14. Meridian does it again. A big, bold wine with well-etched tropical-fruit flavors, pronounced but balanced oak, and crisp, lively Central Coast acidity. This easy sipper offers plenty of flavor, and is a good value in oaky Chardonnay. **88 Best Buy** —*S.H. (12/15/2002)*

Meridian 1998 Reserve Chardonnay (Edna Valley) $15. **89** *(6/1/2000)*

Meridian 2002 Gewürztraminer (Santa Barbara County) $8. A perky wine with lots of upfront flavors, including honeysuckle, lychee, peach, vanilla, honeydew, and dried spices. Very crisp and clean, with a suggestion of sweetness lasts through the finish. Good value if you like California Gewürz. **85** —*S.H. (12/31/2003)*

Meridian 1999 Limited Release Petite Sirah (Paso Robles) $18. Average to good in quality, with hot country notes of plums and roasted fruits veering into raisins. Feels a bit thin on the palate, with the flavors obscured by hefty tannins. Too one-dimensional to merit a higher score, but decent enough. **84** *(4/1/2003)*

Meridian 2005 Pinot Grigio (California) $10. Little or no oak masks the citrus, tart green apple, and spicy fig flavors in this very dry, likeable wine. Tastes like it has lots of cool coastal grapes in it, to judge from the crisp acids that make it so clean. **85 Best Buy** —*S.H. (10/1/2006)*

Meridian 2004 Pinot Grigio (California) $10. As refreshingly crisp and clean as California PG gets, with brilliant acidity boosting vibrant flavors of kiwi, fig, and pineapple. Best of all, the wine is totally dry. **90 Best Buy** —*S.H. (2/1/2006)*

Meridian 2003 Pinot Grigio (California) $11. A very refreshing wine, clean and zesty, with fig, peach, lime, pineapple, and buttercream flavors. Pretty complex for this price. **85** —*S.H. (7/1/2005)*

Meridian 2002 Pinot Grigio (California) $11. Citrus and apple flavors drink dry and fruity, with a spine of acidity that carries into the finish. A little touch of oak adds smoothness and vanilla. **85** —*S.H. (2/1/2004)*

Meridian 2005 Pinot Noir (Central Coast) $11. Hits you with a sharp, acidic jamminess and an almost Beaujolais-like carbonic tingle, but it's a dry wine that could settle down in a year or so. Cherries, cola, and spice flavors. **84** —*S.H. (11/15/2006)*

Meridian 2004 Pinot Noir (Central Coast) $10. I happened to taste this right after a Pinot that cost five times as much, and this one wasn't shamed. In fact, it stood up quite well. No, it didn't have the concentration, but the purity of fruit, crisp acids and silky texture make for a lovely Pinot Noir. **86 Best Buy** —*S.H. (5/1/2006)*

Meridian 2003 Pinot Noir (Central Coast) $11. Decent, with cherry and cocoa flavors, and dry through the finish. There's a burnt element that makes it harsh, though. **83** —*S.H. (7/1/2005)*

Meridian 2000 Pinot Noir (Santa Barbara County) $12. **82** *(10/1/2002)*

Meridian 1999 Pinot Noir (Santa Barbara County) $11. Lots to like in this everyday wine, with its strawberry, spice, beet, and cola flavors and dry, silky-smooth mouthfeel. The tannins are light and airy. It has enough body and flavor to stand up to rich foods, yet maintains delicacy and elegance. **86 Best Buy** —*S.H. (12/15/2001)*

Meridian 1998 Pinot Noir (Santa Barbara County) $13. From a winery that doesn't ever seem to do anything wrong comes this fine, almost complex wine. It would probably be fantastic from a better vintage. As it is, it's good, with some density to it, and spicy, aromatic fruit that satisfies despite thinness in the middle palate. Considering how hard it is to find good Pinot at this price, you have to consider it a great value. **86** —*S.H. (5/1/2001)*

Meridian 1996 Coastal Reserve Pinot Noir (Santa Barbara County) $22. **90** *(10/1/1999)*

Meridian 2002 Reserve Pinot Noir (Santa Barbara County) $16. Comes down on the thin side, although it has that light, silky texture you expect from Pinot. There are some cherry and raspberry flavors, and the finish is very dry. **84** —*S.H. (11/1/2004)*

Meridian 1998 Reserve Pinot Noir (Santa Barbara County) $22. **88** —*S.H. (12/15/2000)*

Meridian 2005 Sauvignon Blanc (Central Coast) $10. A bit simple, but bone dry and very clean, with zesty acidity that frames keen flavors of pink grapefruit. This is a good choice for a cocktail style wine if you're on a budget and have a crowd to entertain. **84** —*S.H. (10/1/2006)*

Meridian 2004 Sauvignon Blanc (Central Coast) $10. What a nice cocktail sipper this is, perfect for the first wine of the evening. It's crisp in cool-climate acids that push out ripe pineapple, fig, and melon flavors. The finish is honeyed and long-lasting. **85 Best Buy** —*S.H. (5/1/2006)*

Meridian 2002 Sauvignon Blanc (Central Coast) $8. Not much going on in this thin wine, beyond a trace of lemon and watered-down peach flavor. It's dry, with a creamy texture and bright acidity. **83** —*S.H. (12/31/2003)*

Meridian 2000 Sauvignon Blanc (California) $8. Largely from Paso Robles fruit, the grapes got ripe enough under the hot sun to produce spearmint, citrus, and honeydew flavors, ripe and apparently sweet, with enough acids to make it drink bright. It's flashy on the surface, a wine that appeals to the senses, with richness, cleanliness, and a long, honeyed finish. Good value. **86** —*S.H. (9/12/2002)*

Meridian 1998 Syrah (Paso Robles) $15. Briary, wild berry fruit bears deep horsey, game, leather and pine accents in this full wine. The nose's somewhat funky notes may challenge some, but add real complexity. A palate of blackberry, cocoa, anise, and earth offers plenty of flavor and a pleasing roundness. Closes handsomely, with dusty tannins and an earthy note. **87 Editors' Choice** *(10/1/2001)*

Meridian 2002 Reserve Syrah (Santa Barbara County) $16. Pretty tannic in its adolescence, and would probably have benefited from additional time before release. Underneath the bitter astringency are blackberry and coffee flavors. As tough as it is on its own, it will greatly benefit from a big, greasy leg of roasted lamb. **86** —*S.H. (12/1/2004)*

MERRIAM VINEYARDS

Merriam Vineyards 2003 Jones Vineyard Cabernet Franc (Dry Creek Valley) $35. Starts with a nose that's slow to open. In the mouth, the wine is dry and medium-bodied, with herb and tart red-cherry flavors. Decant it— once you do, you'll see that it's a good, dry, complex wine. **88** —*S.H. (3/1/2006)*

Merriam Vineyards 2003 Cabernet Sauvignon (Dry Creek Valley) $35. Very soft to the point of melted, this gentle wine has chocolate, blackberry pie, cherry jam, and smoky flavors that are fundamentally dry, but finish with an almost liqueur-like sweetness. Good with everything from a smoky charbroiled steak to vanilla ice cream. **86** —*S.H. (12/15/2006)*

Merriam Vineyards 2001 Cabernet Sauvignon (Sonoma County) $35. Here's an easy Cab that has well-ripened blackberry and currant flavors and is dry and fairly tannic. There's a rusticity to the mouthfeel. Will play well against a steak. **85** —*S.H. (10/1/2005)*

Merriam Vineyards 2000 Cabernet Sauvignon (Dry Creek Valley) $35. How dark this wine is. It opens with a brambly, dusty aroma, like wild berries on a hot summer day, as well as hints of dried leather and toast. In the mouth, there's a burst of black currant that quickly disappears into the tannins. Best after 2006. **86** —*S.H. (6/1/2004)*

Merriam Vineyards 2002 Windacre Merlot (Russian River Valley) $35. Harsh and vinegary, this wine is dry, with medicinal cherry flavors. The acidity creates a really unpleasant mouthfeel. **80** —*S.H. (10/1/2005)*

Merriam Vineyards 2001 Windacre Merlot (Russian River Valley) $35. A great Merlot that completely satisfies for its dryness, its firm, ripe tannins, and its lush interplay of blackberry, cherry, tobacco, and dark chocolate flavors. The finish goes on forever. As tannic as it is, it will be fine with a nice steak, or you can stick it in the cellar for a few years and let it soften. **93** —*S.H. (12/15/2004)*

Merriam Vineyards 2000 Windacre Vineyard Merlot (Russian River Valley) $34. A first-rate wine, with well-ripened flavors of blackberries, espresso, cola, tea, and bitter chocolate, but made more interesting by fresh acidity not often seen in today's better Merlots. This cool-climate wine also has sturdy tannins that suggest mid-term aging. **88** —*S.H. (7/1/2003)*

MERRY EDWARDS

Merry Edwards 2003 Pinot Noir (Sonoma Coast) $29. Displays classic cool climate character in the stimulating acids and brisk tannins. Is it a cellar-worthy wine? Probably not. There's blackberry and cherry fruit, but this dry, elegant wine isn't built for the long haul. **87** —*S.H. (12/1/2005)*

Merry Edwards 2002 Pinot Noir (Sonoma Coast) $27. A mellow, smooth wine with soft tannins that frame savory flavors of cherries, vanilla, cinnamon, and mint. It's racy and stylish, with good length to the finish. Drink now. **88** *(11/1/2004)*

Merry Edwards 2002 Pinot Noir (Russian River Valley) $32. This is an easy, all-purpose Pinot despite some fairly hefty tannins. It glides over the tongue carrying cola, cherry, rhubarb, heirloom tomato, and smoky flavors, and finishes dry. **86** —*S.H. (4/1/2005)*

Merry Edwards 2001 Pinot Noir (Russian River Valley) $32. A lovely Pinot that rises above everyday status to achieve real depth and complexity, although it's not on a par with Merry's single-vineyard releases. It's light and silky, with spicy flavors of cherries, rhubarb, tea, vanilla, and toast. **87** —*S.H. (6/1/2004)*

Merry Edwards 2001 Pinot Noir (Sonoma Coast) $27. Very similar in profile to Merry Edwards's Olivet Lane bottling, with the same pomegranate, cherry, rhubarb, and tobacco flavors. It is a little leaner and sharper, although that same dryness is there. That makes it a relative value. **91** —*S.H. (4/1/2004)*

Merry Edwards 2000 Pinot Noir (Russian River Valley) $32. Big Pinot, opening with a blast of black cherries, truffle, smoke, new kid leather and a thousand other scents. Rich, dense, and fruity—a delight packed with pure cherry flavors. Yet it feels light as a feather, soft as silk. **93 Editors' Choice** —*S.H. (2/1/2003)*

Merry Edwards 2003 Klopp Ranch Pinot Noir (Russian River Valley) $48. The aromatics on this wine are so inviting. This is a huge Pinot, young, dry, and sappy at this time, with grape, cola, rhubarb, black cherry, and rosehip tea flavors, set off by crisp acids and silky tannins. Despite the size, it maintains a complex elegance. It's very good now, but will benefit from a few years in the bottle. **93** —*S.H. (7/1/2006)*

Merry Edwards 2002 Klopp Ranch Pinot Noir (Russian River Valley) $48. Dark, super-extracted in fruit, and rather hot and heavy, with some complexity. It has a rich mélange of blackberry, black cherry, cola, espresso, briar, sweet leather, and spicy flavors, and is fairly tannic and bone dry. A cellar candidate, it will pair well with lamb or beef. **89** —*S.H. (4/1/2005)*

Merry Edwards 2001 Klopp Ranch Pinot Noir (Russian River Valley) $48. From the southern, cooler part of the valley, but on a sunny ridge above the fog, a fascinating study in contrasts. It has brilliantly crisp, citrusy acidity, but is a fat, fleshy wine, with mouthwatering flavors of black cherries, cola, mocha, and gingersnap. The scour of dusty tannins on the finish suggests this wine will hold for several years. **92** —*S.H. (6/1/2004)*

Merry Edwards 2000 Klopp Ranch Pinot Noir (Russian River Valley) $48. Dark as night, clearly a concentrated wine. Brooding aromas are dominated by smoky oak, although under that are cherry, chocolate, olive, and herb scents. Explodes in the mouth, filling the palate with richness and authority. Tannic and acidic now, but with a core of cherry fruit worth aging. **92** —*S.H. (2/1/2003)*

Merry Edwards 2003 Meredith Estate Pinot Noir (Sonoma Coast) $48. After years of buying grapes, Merry Edwards finally has her own vineyard in the Sonoma Coast. This young wine is high in acidity that offsets the ripe red and black cherry, mocha, cola, and cinnamon spice flavors. It's elegant and complex now, and changes as it warms and breathes in the glass. There's a sugary sweetness on the finish. **91** —*S.H. (7/1/2006)*

Merry Edwards 2001 Meredith Estate Pinot Noir (Sonoma Coast) $45. From one of the coolest parts of the appellation, a brilliant, joyous wine the palate celebrates for its lush flavors and brilliant acidity. It's hard to exaggerate the way the cherry, mocha, gingery spice and smoky oak flavors mingle to produce a Renoiresque complexity. **91** —*S.H. (6/1/2004)*

Merry Edwards 2000 Meredith Estate Pinot Noir (Sonoma Coast) $45. Dark and thick, it stains the glass. Opens with powerful aromas of olives, espresso, white chocolate, cherries, smoke, and vanilla. Enormously complex, a cool-climate wine with pronounced but fine tannins and crisp acids. **91** —*S.H. (2/1/2003)*

Merry Edwards 2004 Olivet Lane Pinot Noir (Russian River Valley) $57. A glorious success, for this or any vintage. It shows classic Russian River balance and refinement, with exquisitely ripe berry and stone fruit flavors counterbalanced with earthier mushroom and funky leather notes. The acids, tannins and silky mouthfeel are textbook Pinot. Best now–2012. **94** —*S.H. (12/15/2006)*

Merry Edwards 2001 Olivet Lane Pinot Noir (Russian River Valley) $48. A firm, focused wine, with some tannic bite. Smoky, herb notes give way to black cherry, raspberry, anise, and tea. Somewhat charry and bright on the end, yet still intriguing to the taste. This is a wine that should unfold nicely in the cellar. **89** —*J.M. (4/1/2004)*

Merry Edwards 2000 Olivet Lane Pinot Noir (Russian River Valley) $48. Fabulous depth and complexity, from the lush cherry flavors to the rich, velvety texture to the long, fascinating finish. The fruit is wonderfully set off against smoky oak. It's the kind of wine you'd drink at your last meal. **94** —*S.H. (2/1/2003)*

Merry Edwards 2003 Olivet Lane Methode a L'Ancienne Pinot Noir (Russian River Valley) $54. The Edwards style is big, ripe, and rich, and this wine displays it in bold face. Although dry, it's massive in blackberries and cherries, melted milk chocolate, coffee, and vanilla flavors. It has the richness of Syrah, without the tannins. This is a silky, complicated, and enjoyable wine. **90** —*S.H. (12/1/2005)*

Merry Edwards 2002 Olivet Lane Methode a la Ancienne Pinot Noir (Russian River Valley) $51. A somewhat controversial wine for its earthy complexities of rhubarb, tomatoes, beets, and oak, and cinnamon and clove overlay. Delicate in structure, with strong acids and tannins, some will find it Burgundian while others will find it thin. **86** *(11/1/2004)*

Merry Edwards 2003 Windsor Gardens Pinot Noir (Russian River Valley) $57. This is a wine that need some age. Not a lot, but a few years for the edges to soften. It has some tannins and youthful acids, and an oaky veneer, that haven't integrated yet with the cherry and coffee fruit. A good sleep in a good cellar through 2007 or 2008 will do wonders. **89 Cellar Selection** —*S.H. (12/1/2005)*

Merry Edwards 2000 Windsor Gardens Pinot Noir (Russian River Valley) $54. Pretty similar to the Klopp bottling, with herbal notes suggesting coffee, earth, mushrooms, and tobacco, and fruitiness just veering into cherry. Has much the same tannic and acidic structure, firm and masculine. A trace of bitterness calls for the richest possible foods. **92** —*S.H. (2/1/2003)*

Merry Edwards 2001 Windsor Gardens Methode a l'Ancienne Pinot Noir (Russian River Valley) $54. An impressive wine for its compelling interest. It's fruit-rich, suggesting cherries and pomegranates, with notes of rhubarb, black tea, and dried herbs that ride in waves across the palate. Oak contributes nuances but is not strong. Extremely dry, with bright acidity, this wine will develop additional complexities for a few years. **92** —*S.H. (4/1/2004)*

MERRYVALE

Merryvale 1997 Beckstoffer Vineyard Bordeaux Blend (Napa Valley) $45. 93 *(11/1/2000)*

Merryvale 2000 Profile Bordeaux Blend (Napa Valley) $79. This blend is marginally better than Merryvale's Reserve Cabernet, but it's not a rich wine. The mouthfeel is dominated by dry tannins and acids that lead to a tart, astringent finish. There are some blackberry and black cherry flavors along with herbs and earth, and the texture is supple and rich. May soften and sweeten in time. **87** —*S.H. (3/1/2004)*

Merryvale 1998 Profile Bordeaux Blend (Napa Valley) $90. Sleek, smooth, and elegant, with fine tannins that frame a wine that's flush with plum, cassis, anise, herb, and chocolate flavors. Plush and velvety on the palate, it's got a finish that doesn't quit. Cabernet doesn't get much better, anytime or anywhere. **96 Cellar Selection** —*J.M. (12/1/2001)*

Merryvale 1997 Profile Bordeaux Blend (Napa Valley) $85. 92 —*S.H. (12/15/2000)*

Merryvale 1996 Profile Bordeaux Blend (Napa Valley) $75. 86 *(7/1/2000)*

Merryvale 1997 Cabernet Sauvignon (Napa Valley) $20. 90 —*M.S. (2/1/2000)*

Merryvale 1999 Cabernet Sauvignon (Napa Valley) $26. Textbook Napa Cabernet. Aromas of freshly baked blackberry pie, olives, green peppers, and smoky oak, although the wood does not overwhelm. Bone-dry, with those great Napa tannins. This is not a wine with great depth or complexity, but it has an elegance that will never disappoint. **88** —*S.H. (6/1/2002)*

Merryvale 1998 Cabernet Sauvignon (Napa Valley) $25. 87 —*S.H. (12/15/2000)*

Merryvale 2002 Beckstoffer-Clone Six Cabernet Sauvignon (Rutherford) $88. Exceptionally ripe and expressive even among the flamboyant 2002 Rutherfords, with a pleasing note of vanilla and char from oak, this Cab is rich in cherry fruit flavors. The tannins are sweet and fine, and sturdy enough to carry it through 2010. **90** —*S.H. (12/15/2005)*

Merryvale 2001 Beckstoffer Clone Six Cabernet Sauvignon (Rutherford) $90. Mint, cedar, and a bit of tomato leaf accent lovely cassis fruit. Full-bodied, with a slightly dusty mouthfeel, like finely ground cinnamon or cocoa, and picking up hints of those flavors as well. Finishes clean and crisp, with soft tannins. **91** *(7/1/2005)*

Merryvale 2003 Beckstoffer Vineyard Clone Six Cabernet Sauvignon (Rutherford) $95. Very ripe and aromatic, throwing out cascades of inviting scents. New toasty oak dominates, with undercurrents of blackberry jam, blueberry, mocha, and anise. In the mouth, huge, lush, powerful, an explosively fruity young wine, yet maintains balance and elegance. Really good. Best now–2015. **94** —*S.H. (12/15/2006)*

Merryvale 2002 Beckstoffer Vineyard X Cabernet Sauvignon (Oakville) $75. The first impression of this Cab is that it's way too young. It has plenty of flash in the ripe Cabernet fruit, rich oak, dense tannins, and crisp acidity, but those tannins hold the wine in lockdown, and the parts are far from coming together. In serious need of cellaring, this dynamic young wine should begin to be approachable by 2008. **91 Cellar Selection** —*S.H. (8/1/2006)*

Merryvale 2001 Beckstoffer Vineyard X Cabernet Sauvignon (Oakville) $75. From a vineyard just behind Brix restaurant, this is a soft-textured, full-bodied Cab with dark plum and earth flavors. Picks up hints of tobacco and chocolate on the finish. **90** *(7/1/2005)*

Merryvale 2001 Beckstoffer Vineyards Clone Six Cabernet Sauvignon (Rutherford) $88. Built for the cellar, with its tannins and oak dominating. Bone dry and taut, there's little relief now through the rasping finish. The betting is on the chewy core of cherry and blackberry fruit, but a well-marbled steak will make for a good pairing. **90** —*S.H. (10/1/2004)*

Merryvale 2000 Beckstoffer Vineyards Clone Six Cabernet Sauvignon (Rutherford) $75. There must have been severe vineyard selection for this wine, for it rises above the vintage to achieve real intensity and concentration. Cassis, black currants, and cherry flavors are enhanced with a touch of menthol and a lot of oak to produce a lavish, complex mouthfeel. The tannins are a work of art, lush and soft. **91** —*S.H. (11/15/2003)*

Merryvale 2001 Beckstoffer Vineyards Vineyard X Cabernet Sauvignon (Oakville) $75. This is a very dry and well-balanced Cab with some very pedigreed origins. Not a blockbuster but oozes class. It provides elegant drinking now despite its tannins, yet seems destined to improve. **91** —*S.H. (10/1/2004)*

Merryvale 2000 Beckstoffer-Vineyard X Cabernet Sauvignon (Oakville) $75. Rich and plush, with sweet oak and ripe plum, black cherry, black currant, earth, cedar, and spice flavors that offer a certain measure of hedonistic complexity. The tannins are fine-tuned and the finish is long. **92** —*J.M. (12/15/2003)*

Merryvale 2002 Reserve Cabernet Sauvignon (Napa Valley) $40. Tannic and tough now, with a sandpapery mouthfeel, this Cab has flavors of blackberry, cherry, and cassis fruit. It's bone dry, with good acidity. Hard to tell where it's going. Probably best now and for the next five years. **86** —*S.H. (5/1/2006)*

Merryvale 2001 Reserve Cabernet Sauvignon (Napa Valley) $35. A beautiful Cab, soft and luscious, with nuances that keep you coming back. Black currant, cassis, coffee, green olive, and smoky oak flavors are wrapped in easy tannins that finish smooth and gentle. Delicious. Drink now. **91** —*S.H. (2/1/2005)*

Merryvale 2000 Reserve Cabernet Sauvignon (Napa Valley) $35. A good wine, but a disappointment considering this winery's track record. Tries to achieve opulence, but the herbal, tobaccoey edge and astringent tannins rule. Finishes dry and puckery, and there's not enough stuffing to warrant much aging. **86** —*S.H. (12/31/2003)*

Merryvale 1999 Reserve Cabernet Sauvignon (Napa Valley) $39. Plush, stylish, and classy, this Cab displays a beautiful balance of parts that together spell elegance. Blackberry and cassis flavors, framed by smoky oak, are set off by crisp acids and dusty, accessible tannins. Doesn't possess the stuffing for long-term aging, but should provide pleasant drinking now through 2006. **92** —*S.H. (11/15/2002)*

USA

Merryvale 1998 Reserve Cabernet Sauvignon (Napa Valley) $39. Spicy and complex, with blackberry, herb, spice, and cassis notes. It's a classy wine, though a bit short on the finish. Perhaps a little more bottle time will open things up. **88** —*J.M. (12/1/2001)*

Merryvale 1997 Reserve Cabernet Sauvignon (Napa Valley) $39. 89 *(11/1/2000)*

Merryvale 2002 Starmont Cabernet Sauvignon (Napa Valley) $25. Ripe, full-bodied, and dry, this Cabernet has tons of forward fruit flavor wrapped in heavy tannins, but the acidity is low, and the wine feels soft. It's a bit one-dimensional, but elegant enough. Drink now. **85** —*S.H. (8/1/2006)*

Merryvale 2001 Starmont Cabernet Sauvignon (Napa Valley) $24. I love this wine for the effortless way it charms. Everything's restrained, from the currant and cherry flavors to the oak, while the softly sweet tannins create a smooth, mellow mouthfeel. It's a feminine Cab that will support, not compete with, the best foods. **91 Editors' Choice** —*S.H. (6/1/2004)*

Merryvale 2000 Starmont Cabernet Sauvignon (Napa Valley) $25. An easy-drinking Cab with cassis and blackberry flavors and moderate oak. Feels rich in the mouth, with soft, dusty tannins and bracing acids. **86** —*S.H. (10/1/2003)*

Merryvale 2001 Dutton Ranch Chardonnay (Russian River Valley) $29. Solidly in the Merryvale style, featuring exuberantly ripe fruit and lavish oak balanced with acidity. The intense flavors veer toward spicy pears, pineapple, and white peach, and last through a long finish. **91** —*S.H. (2/1/2004)*

Merryvale 2000 Dutton Ranch Chardonnay (Russian River Valley) $29. A smooth, classy Chardonnay, this wine strikes a fine balance between elegance and strength. Framed in toasty oak, it shows off plenty of pretty citrus, pear, apple, and herb flavors, finishing clean and long with a mineral edge. **90** —*J.M. (7/1/2003)*

Merryvale 1999 Dutton Ranch Chardonnay (Russian River Valley) $35. Smooth and silky, with subtle pear, melon, vanilla, mineral, and herb flavors that are polished and integrated. Finishes long, with a classy citrus edge. **91** —*J.M. (12/15/2002)*

Merryvale 1998 Dutton Ranch Chardonnay (Russian River Valley) $35. 88 —*S.H. (11/15/2000)*

Merryvale 2003 Reserve Chardonnay (Carneros) $29. Here's a compact, young Chard that's tight in minerals and acidity, riding high over well-oaked tropical fruit and peach flavors. It's closed now, and should be allowed to breathe for a while. Drink now through 2009. **88** —*S.H. (5/1/2006)*

Merryvale 2002 Reserve Chardonnay (Carneros) $30. Bigger and richer than the Starmont bottling, with correspondingly heavier oak. Lots of toast and grilled pineapple and peach notes on the nose, followed by a mouthfilling wine laced with smoky accents. Echoes of butter and dark toast on the finish. **90** *(7/1/2005)*

Merryvale 2001 Reserve Chardonnay (Carneros) $29. This is an elegant Chard with apple, pear, and toasted coconut flavors spiced with liberal doses of smoky oak and lees. It has very crisp, citrusy acids that make it clean and lively. Will be a good companion to a wide range of foods. **90** —*S.H. (10/1/2004)*

Merryvale 2000 Reserve Chardonnay (Carneros) $29. A good, not great, and refreshing wine, with flavors ranging from citrus fruits to peaches. Has a good overlay of oak and crisp acids. Very clean and balanced, but lacks expected richness, and snaps to an early finish. **86** —*S.H. (6/1/2003)*

Merryvale 1999 Reserve Chardonnay (Napa Valley) $35. Firm and rich textured, with bright acidity that keeps it fresh. This wonderful wine is loaded with complex pear, apple, herb, and citrus notes that just keep on singing throughout its long finish. **93** —*J.M. (12/1/2001)*

Merryvale 2002 Silhouette Chardonnay (Napa Valley) $50. Even at three-plus years, this Chard still tastes young and tight. It's perfectly dry, with high acidity and an earthiness that covers citrus and peach flavors. It will never be a big, over-the-top wine, but it's a fine one that should develop additional complexities over the next five years. **88** —*S.H. (8/1/2006)*

Merryvale 2001 Silhouette Chardonnay (Napa Valley) $45. Lots of new oak and lees lend this wine toasty, yeasty, creamy notes, with vanilla on the finish. The fruit? It's green apples and papayas, with liberal acids. Feels a bit tight now, and could develop for a few years. **92** —*S.H. (12/31/2004)*

Merryvale 2000 Silhouette Chardonnay (Napa Valley) $45. Made from best barrels, this wine offers more richness and satisfaction than Merryvale's Reserve bottling, although it's far from a big wine. Flavors of peaches and apples are restrained. Oak plays a vital role here in enriching and fattening the wine. **88** —*S.H. (6/1/2003)*

Merryvale 1999 Silhouette Chardonnay (Napa Valley) $49. Pulls out all the stops to create a big, massively complex wine. Despite the flamboyant tropical fruit flavors and rich spiciness supplied by oak, the wine never loses control of itself. It's a tame lion. Fills the mouth with creamy flavors and sensations that roll on and on. The finish returns to the spicy-fruity theme with a hint of smoky honey. **93** —*S.H. (5/1/2002)*

Merryvale 1997 Silhouette Chardonnay (Napa Valley) $48. 89 *(10/1/2000)*

Merryvale 2002 Starmont Chardonnay (Napa Valley) $19. A bit over-oaked, with those buttery, caramelly aromas and flavors dominating the underlying apple tart fruit. But it's rich and complicated, offering up an array of oriental spices that pack a real punch on the finish. **87** —*S.H. (6/1/2004)*

Merryvale 2001 Starmont Chardonnay (Napa Valley) $19. The real deal for fans of big, full-blown Chards. Starts with richly ripe, super-extracted flavors of peaches, pears, mangoes, and other tropical fruits, and it's all generously wrapped in oak. The texture is creamy, the finish polished and rich. **92 Editors' Choice** —*S.H. (12/1/2003)*

Merryvale 2000 Starmont Chardonnay (Napa Valley) $20. Here's a wine that is marked by smoky oak and the creamy effect that comes from lees aging. But the underlying fruit is lean and citrusy. You can taste lemons and grapefruits as the liquid sloshes across the palate. It's a very dry wine, the kind that makes you want to put food into your mouth. **86** —*S.H. (5/1/2002)*

Merryvale 1999 Starmont Chardonnay (Napa Valley) $20. Made with fully ripened grapes, this is a lush, complex, thoroughly enjoyable wine. It's fairly dry by California standards, but offers up masses of sweet fruit and oak extract. The balance is especially nice; all parts are in harmony. **90 Editors' Choice** —*S.H. (5/1/2001)*

Merryvale 1998 Starmont Chardonnay (Napa Valley) $20. 89 *(6/1/2000)*

Merryvale 2001 Beckstoffer Las Amigas Vineyard Merlot (Carneros) $35. Mint, black cherries, and graham crackers all mingle elegantly in this bright, medium-weight wine. The crisp acids keep the wine focused, ending on a citrusy note. **87** *(7/1/2005)*

Merryvale 2002 Beckstoffer Vineyard Las Amigas Vineyard Merlot (Carneros) $43. Carneros is a cool-climate source of Merlot, but the harvest was hot in 2002, and this is an exceedingly ripe wine. The blackberry and cherry flavors are tinged with the taste of raisins. There are also some hefty tannins in this dry, somewhat astringent wine. **84** —*S.H. (8/1/2006)*

Merryvale 2001 Beckstoffer Vineyards Las Amigas Vineyard Merlot (Carneros) $39. The tannins and acids hit the palate broadside, leaving it dry and rasping. There are some cherry flavors deep inside, and of course oak. Not likely to age. **85** —*S.H. (12/15/2004)*

Merryvale 2000 Los Amigos Vineyard Merlot (Carneros) $39. Starts off with ripe cherry and strawberry aromas. It's full bodied and spicy upfront, with firm, supple tannins that frame licorice, blackberry, chocolate, coffee, tea, and herb flavors. A touch bright on the long finish. **90** —*J.M. (12/1/2003)*

Merryvale 2001 Reserve Merlot (Napa Valley) $32. An easy to like Merlot, with the weight of Cabernet. Smooth, ripely soft tannins, lots of smoky new oak, and true varietal flavors of ripe cherries, black raspberries, cocoa, and vanilla. Finishes soft and fruity. **88** —*S.H. (2/1/2005)*

Merryvale 2000 Reserve Merlot (Napa Valley) $32. This is a well-oaked wine with plenty of smoky vanilla and sweet wood tannins designed to sex up the fairly lean wine that lurks beneath. There are some cherry-berry flavors that are swamped by dry tannins, and the finish is short, but it has a lean elegance to it. **87** —*S.H. (2/1/2004)*

USA

Merryvale 1999 Reserve Merlot (Napa Valley) $39. A dark, young, chewy wine, obviously capable of aging. Shows iodine, earth, herb, and blackberry-tart aromas, and is a bit tough in the mouth. Yet it's very classy and stylish. Dry tannins coat the palate, masking rich fruit. This is a wine of structure rather than hedonism. **92** —*S.H. (11/15/2002)*

Merryvale 1998 Reserve Merlot (Napa Valley) $39. Dark-hued and richly textured, this striking Merlot show gobs of complex blackberry, cassis, chocolate, licorice, and herb flavors. Fat and long on the finish, it's a fine example of what this variety can really do when handled properly. **91** —*J.M. (12/1/2001)*

Merryvale 2002 Starmont Merlot (Napa Valley) $24. Opens with red plum, berry, toast, and a whiff of fresh tomato. Arguably a bit sharp in the mouth, but the overt acidity only emphasizes the brightness of the cherry, raspberry, and plum flavors. Jumpy and juicy on the finish. Definitely not heavy. **86** —*M.S. (12/31/2006)*

Merryvale 2001 Starmont Merlot (Napa Valley) $22. Another winning red wine from Merryvale. It goes beyond the ripe berry-cherry, herb, and oak-infused flavors to achieve real class and distinction. Those rich, sweet tannins are really classy. **90** —*S.H. (6/1/2004)*

Merryvale 2000 Starmont Merlot (Napa Valley) $29. In the mouth, this wine has the plushest, smoothest tannins you can imagine, soft and furry and fine as fur. Oak barrel aging adds sweet oak and more smoothness. Yet the underlying fruit lacks intensity for all this structure. The plum flavors turn earthy on the finish. **86** —*S.H. (4/1/2003)*

Merryvale 1998 Beckstoffer Vineyard Merlot-Cabernet Sauvignon (Napa Valley) $60. Smooth and elegant, yet also powerful, with ripe blackberry, chocolate, currant, and herb notes, all couched in rich, firm tannins and sweet oak nuances. Long and lush at the end. A blend of 52% Merlot, 48% Cabernet. **92** —*J.M. (12/1/2001)*

Merryvale NV Antigua Muscat Canelli (California) $30. **91** —*J.C. (12/31/1999)*

Merryvale 2003 Pinot Noir (Carneros) $40. This is a plump, corpulent Pinot with soft tannins and loads of plum, black cherry, and cola flavors. Has some cinnamon and clove notes as well, and a warm, velvety finish. **89** *(7/1/2005)*

Merryvale 2002 Pinot Noir (Carneros) $29. A lovely wine that benefits from its cool climate origins. Bright, fresh acidity accompanies cherry, sweet funky leather, and spice flavors, and the mouthfeel is delicate and fine. This is a beautiful, complex food wine. **90** —*S.H. (11/1/2004)*

Merryvale 2000 Pinot Noir (Sonoma Coast) $44. The first-ever Pinot from a winery well-known for Bordeaux-style wines, it's a study in clonal selection and terroir. This wine just manages to achieve berried ripeness while maintaining crisp acidity. It's definitely a wine to watch in future vintages. **92** —*S.H. (2/1/2003)*

Merryvale 2001 Profile Red Blend (Napa Valley) $85. An amazingly delicious and complex wine. Dark and rich, filled with black currant, cocoa, and new oak flavors and lush, sweet tannins. Finishes with a scour of fresh acidity. Made from some of Napa's greatest vineyards, such as To-Kalon and Georges III, this is a wine with a great future. Now through 2012. **93** —*S.H. (12/31/2004)*

Merryvale 1999 Profile Red Blend (Napa Valley) $90. A blend of four varieties dominated by Cabernet, grown in seven vineyards, this represents current tastes in Napa. It's extremely rich in ripe blackberry and cassis flavors, made up with richly smoked oak. The tannins are ultrasoft, and so are the acids. **90** —*S.H. (12/31/2002)*

Merryvale 2000 Sauvignon Blanc (Napa Valley) $17. Sweet fig and melon notes are highlighted here, balanced by tangy citrus and spice. Long and lush, the wine remains refreshing and clean on its classy finish. **88** —*J.M. (11/15/2001)*

Merryvale 2004 Juliana Vineyard Sauvignon Blanc (Napa Valley) $22. Smells juicy and succulent, with inviting citrus, kiwi, and vanilla spice aromas. The flavors are very similar, back up by firm, bright acidity. There's a ripe, tangy lime flavor in the finish that tastes a little sweet. **87** —*S.H. (5/1/2006)*

Merryvale 1999 Juliana Vineyard Sauvignon Blanc (Napa Valley) $22. **87** —*S.H. (11/15/2000)*

Merryvale 2003 Juliana Vineyards Sauvignon Blanc (Napa Valley) $22. Definitely full of peach aromas, and on the side you'll find accents of smoke, caramel, and lemon curd. If that sounds heavy, it's not. In fact, this wine shows excellent balance. The palate is pure, with sweet pineapple and nectarine. And the finish is flattering; the mineral, chalky quality is just right. Purity is this wine's first, middle and last name. **90 Editors' Choice** *(7/1/2005)*

Merryvale 1998 Reserve Sauvignon Blanc (Napa Valley) $22. **86** *(3/1/2000)*

Merryvale 2003 Starmont Sauvignon Blanc (Napa Valley) $15. A great and interesting white wine whose price belies its excellence. It's ripe and lush in citrusy, fig, and honeydew melon flavors and has a rich layering of toasty oak. The finish is long and pleasing. **91** —*S.H. (10/1/2004)*

Merryvale 2002 Starmont Sauvignon Blanc (Napa Valley) $16. Fresh and lively on the palate, the wine is redolent of lemon, lime, grapefruit, and herbs. It's got good structure, leaving a clean, fresh taste on the palate and finishes with moderate length. **87** —*J.M. (2/1/2004)*

Merryvale 2001 Starmont Sauvignon Blanc (Napa Valley) $17. Here's a wine with tart grass and citrus flavors enriched with oak. A small percent of Sémillon adds richer notes of melons and figs. Earns extra points with a creamy texture and long, spicy finish. **88** —*S.H. (9/1/2003)*

Merryvale 2002 Syrah (Napa Valley) $30. A bit peppery and herbal, but with plenty of crisp, tangy fruit at its core. The overall impression is of a wine that's a bit rustic and rough but solid and well made. **85** *(9/1/2005)*

MESSINA HOF

Messina Hof 2000 Angel Johannisberg Riesling (Texas) $15. **81** —*J.C. (8/1/2003)*

METHVEN FAMILY

Methven Family 2004 Pinot Gris (Willamette Valley) $23. There's plenty of spicy fruit here, ripe to the point of tasting baked, like apple pie or a pear compote. It's rich and flavorful, but needs to be drunk now, as the nose is already showing a Sherry character. **86** —*P.G. (12/1/2006)*

Methven Family 2004 Pinot Noir (Willamette Valley) $33. This new winery has put out a first release that is juicy, sweet and loaded with concentrated raspberry and strawberry fruit. It's so fruity, in fact, that it tastes more like fruit concentrate than wine! If it had a bit more tannin and some of the bones of a bigger wine, the fruit could certainly carry it to a higher score. **86** —*P.G. (12/1/2006)*

Methven Family 2004 Reserve Pinot Noir (Willamette Valley) $55. Though not from the estate vineyard, this is a well-done reserve from this new and substantial Eola Hills vintner. Sweet and juicy, it's like the concentrate of blackberry, raspberry, and boysenberry. Good tannic structure supports the fruit. **88** —*P.G. (12/1/2006)*

Methven Family 2004 Riesling (Willamette Valley) $21. Baked apple pie is what this wine smells like, and the flavors are astonishingly the same, like an apple tart right out of the oven. It's not a particularly sweet wine, but the fruit carries with it a suggestion of sweetness, and there's a strong cinnamon spice component also. Might make a great companion to a non-sweet fruit tart. **87** —*P.G. (12/1/2006)*

METTLER FAMILY VINEYARDS

Mettler Family Vineyards 2002 Cabernet Sauvignon (Lodi) $25. There's a stewed quality to the fruit, and heat in the finish. that make this Cab not worth the price. Will work with simple fare. **83** —*S.H. (11/1/2005)*

Mettler Family Vineyards 2001 Cabernet Sauvignon (Lodi) $26. An honest, country-style Cab marked by excessively ripe blackberry flavors that veer into raisins, but it's dry. The tannic structure is fierce, leaving a puckery feeling in the aftertaste. **85** —*S.H. (6/1/2004)*

Mettler Family Vineyards 2000 Cabernet Sauvignon (Lodi) $24. Full around the edges but leaner at the core. Nonetheless, this has ripe fruit flavors, nuances of orange peel and even a bit of bitter chocolate. It's juicy, fruity, and sizable, exactly what most folks seek in California Cabernet. **87** —*M.S. (11/15/2003)*

Mettler Family Vineyards 2003 Petite Sirah (Lodi) $25. Intense and concentrated in fruit, fully dry, and with lush, thick tannins, this Petite Sirah aims for the front of the pack and succeeds. Flavorwise, it's rich in blackberries, plum pudding, espresso, and spice flavors that finish long and impressively complex. Great now, and should hold and develop over the next decade. **90 Editors' Choice** —*S.H. (5/1/2006)*

Mettler Family Vineyards 2002 Petite Sirah (Lodi) $25. This Petite Sirah seems ripe and unripe at the same time. It has a veggie aroma, yet some almost sweet raisiny flavors. **82** —*S.H. (11/1/2005)*

Mettler Family Vineyards 2001 Petite Sirah (Lodi) $26. Pretty nice wine, a full-bodied, dry red with pleasant berry-cherry flavors and dusty tannins. Pricey for what you get. May age well. **85** —*S.H. (6/1/2004)*

MI SUEÑO

Mi Sueño 2003 Cabernet Sauvignon (Napa Valley) $60. Rich and almost overpowering in ripe fruit, this is a wine that doesn't pull its punches. Masses of jammy blackberry, cassis, cherry, mocha, and smoky pie-crust flavors, with significant tannins and a dry finish. Nothing subtle here, just pure, spectacular New World red wine. **92** —*S.H. (12/1/2006)*

Mi Sueño 2004 Chardonnay (Carneros) $35. On the soft side, but the limpid mouthfeel packs plenty of flavor, including well-ripened apple, peach, pear, and pineapple. Oak plays a dominant role, bringing vanilla, buttered toast, and spice. **89** —*S.H. (12/1/2006)*

Mi Sueño 2004 Pugash Vineyard Chardonnay (Sonoma Mountain) $45. Well oaked, with a toasty, vanilla-infused cream and caramel edge, this polished Chard has peach custard flavors dusted with cinnamon, nutmeg and candied ginger. It's delicious and complex. The word "rich" doesn't begin to do it justice. **92** —*S.H. (12/1/2006)*

Mi Sueño 2004 Ulises Valdez Vineyard Chardonnay (Russian River Valley) $38. Tastes like there's lots of toasty, charry, smoky oak on this big, ripe wine, but the papaya, nectarine, and hazelnut croissant flavors are sizeable and can shoulder the wood. The finish is long, spicy, and impressively rich. **90** —*S.H. (10/1/2006)*

Mi Sueño 2004 Ulises Valdez Vineyard Pinot Noir (Russian River Valley) $42. Earthy, with cherry pie filling, cola, rhubarb, nutmeg, and cinnamon flavors. This dry wine is a little soft and one-dimensional, but has a silky mouthfeel. **85** —*S.H. (10/1/2006)*

Mi Sueño 2003 El Llano Red Wine Red Blend (Napa Valley) $35. Based on grapes from Coombsville, a cooler southerly part of Napa, this is a blend of 80% Cabernet Sauvignon and 20% Syrah. It's almost superripe, but it wisely avoids sweetness, offering a huge mouthful of cherry pie, cassis, chocolate fudge, and vanilla oak flavors in a softly tannic package. Drink now. **89** —*S.H. (12/1/2006)*

Mi Sueño 2003 Syrah (Napa Valley) $40. An interesting, complex wine with the peppery aroma of a fine Northern Rhône. But the softness and forward fruit are all California. Tastes like blackberry tea with a shot of cassis followed by a shot of cocoa. Sweet oak is there, too. **89** —*S.H. (12/1/2006)*

MIA'S PLAYGROUND

Mia's Playground 2003 Cabernet Sauvignon (Alexander Valley) $16. Young and jammy, this is a Cab that tastes like it just came out of the fermenter. It's all grapy, primary fruit blackberries and cherries, with an undertow of smoky vanilla. **86** —*S.H. (12/1/2005)*

Mia's Playground 2002 Cabernet Sauvignon (Alexander Valley) $16. A simple, kind of rough and earthy Cab, thin in fruit, which accentuates the tannins. It's dry and spicy on the finish. **83** —*S.H. (5/1/2005)*

Mia's Playground 2003 Chardonnay (Russian River Valley) $16. This is a pretty good wine. It has the ripe peach, tropical fruit and oaky flavors, creamy texture and oak of top Chards, although there's a homespun rusticity that shows. **85** —*S.H. (5/1/2005)*

Mia's Playground 2002 Merlot (Dry Creek Valley) $16. Simple, fruity, and soft, with an easy tannic structure, this Merlot is at its best now for the rich berry and cherry flavors, with a hint of chocolate. **83** —*S.H. (12/1/2005)*

Mia's Playground 2002 Pinot Noir (Sonoma Coast) $16. Gentle and soft, with modest flavors of cherries and cola that are dry, with zesty acidity. This is a nice, everyday Pinot. **84** —*S.H. (12/31/2004)*

Mia's Playground 2003 Zinfandel (Dry Creek Valley) $16. Super-tasty in blackberry, cherry, and chocolate flavors, this Zin couldn't possibly be

riper or fruitier. On the other hand, it could be crisper. Those flavors, while delicious, feel a bit syrupy, due to insufficient acidity. **85** —*S.H. (12/1/2005)*

Mia's Playground 2002 Zinfandel (Dry Creek Valley) $16. Racy and irresistible, a Zin that sings out with bright flavors of cherries, blackberries, and raspberries, fresh as the summer sun. Soft, sweet tannins and a smidgen of oak add interest. **87** —*S.H. (12/31/2004)*

MICHAEL CHIARELLO

Michael Chiarello 2000 Eileen Cabernet Sauvignon (Napa Valley) $45. One of the darker Cabs of the year, and dominated by tough, numbing tannins. Will it age? There are deliciously sweet blackberry and cherry flavors that emerge after you swallow. Not really ready, but with a big T-bone, will be enjoyable. **87** —*S.H. (5/1/2004)*

Michael Chiarello 2000 Petite Sirah (Napa Valley) $45. Inky black. This smooth-textured wine is amply supported by ripe tannins that frame a solid core of blackberry, cherry, plum, licorice, and spice flavors. Densely structured with fine aging potential. **91** —*J.M. (12/31/2003)*

Michael Chiarello 2001 Roux Old Vine Petite Sirah (Napa Valley) $45. This is an old-style Pet, black as night, and the mouthfeel is dominated by massive tannins that sting with toughness. A deep core of cherry fruit is buried now; by 2011, this wine will soften and sweeten. **88** —*S.H. (5/1/2004)*

Michael Chiarello 2000 Zinfandel (Napa Valley) $45. Quite dark, thick, and lush. The wine benefits from bright acidity and complex earth tones as well. Primary flavors range from black cherry, to plum and strawberry. It finishes with tangy, bright spice at the end. **90** —*J.M. (9/1/2003)*

Michael Chiarello 2001 Felicia Old Vine Zinfandel (Napa Valley) $50. Full, rich and bright, this wine serves up a complex array of raspberry, cranberry, chocolate, spice, coffee, and herbs. A lush and hedonistic expression of Napa Valley old-vine Zin that covers the palate in a velvety embrace. It's long, smooth, and packed with character to the very end. **92** —*J.M. (9/1/2004)*

Michael Chiarello 2000 Giana Young Vines Zinfandel (Napa Valley) $28. Quite intense, with a pronounced spicy character. The wine is smooth, rich, ripe, and filled with herb, plum, raspberry, black cherry, and licorice flavors. Fat and lively right up to the end. **89** —*J.M. (9/1/2003)*

Michael Chiarello 2001 Giana Zinfandel (Napa Valley) $30. This wine carries its zippy acidity well. The bright edge highlights a dense core of cherry, raspberry, and cola flavors, all framed in toasty oak with hints of vanilla. Spice and herb notes add interest, while the finish is long and lush. **90** —*J.M. (9/1/2004)*

MICHAEL POZZAN

Michael Pozzan 2002 Annabella Special Selection Cabernet Sauvignon (Napa Valley) $15. A fine Cab whose balance and slight earthiness will enhance, not swamp, food. Delicately structured, with cherry, cassis, oak, and tobacco flavors, and rich tannins. **87** —*S.H. (3/1/2005)*

Michael Pozzan 2003 Annabella Special Selection Chardonnay (Napa Valley) $12. Super-oaky, just oozing high char and sweet caramel. Underneath is ripe tropical fruit, with a sweet finish. If you like this style, it's a good value. **84** —*S.H. (3/1/2005)*

Michael Pozzan 2002 Annabella Special Selection Merlot (Napa Valley) $14. An easy drinking Merlot that's a little sweet, but not too much. It has oak and cherry-chocolate flavors, and the tannins are smooth and polished. **84** —*S.H. (3/1/2005)*

Michael Pozzan 1997 Reserve Red Blend (Napa Valley) $13. 88 *(11/15/1999)*

Michael Pozzan 2005 Sawyer Vineyards Sauvignon Blanc (Lake County) $10. Pozzan is an Oakville-based brand, a négociant, really, that frequently offers value. This single-vineyard wine is rich and dry in citrus, apricot, and fig flavors, with a refreshing minerality leading to a tartly clean finish. It shows why Lake County has a reputation for Sauvignon Blanc. The wine has a modest 12.5 percent of alcohol, and is one-quarter Sémillon. **87 Best Buy** —*S.H. (11/15/2006)*

Michael Pozzan 2003 Special Reserve Sauvignon Blanc (Napa Valley) $9. One of the more surprising aspects of the glut is the quantity and quality of inexpensive Napa Valley wines. Michael Pozzan, whose forebears began growing grapes in California in the 1800s, has his own 50,000-case winery in Oakville. The Reserve line represents value across several varieties. This dry, stylish Sauvignon is citrusy and figgy, with great elegance, flair, and nuance. Dry and crisp, it's as good as many wines costing far more. **87 Best Buy** —*S.H. (11/15/2004)*

MICHAEL SULLBERG

Michael Sullberg 2001 Cabernet Sauvignon (California) $9. A nice little country-style Cabernet, with some plummy flavors along with earth, tobacco, and herb. Drinks very dry, with easy tannins. Perfectly okay for that next backyard barbecue for the relatives. **85** —*S.H. (11/15/2003)*

Michael Sullberg 2001 Merlot (California) $9. A nice, drinkable Merlot at a fair price for the quality. Pleasant berry and plum flavors are wrapped in sturdy but accessible tannins. The finish is dry and fruity, with a nice edge of tobaccoey spice. **85** —*S.H. (12/31/2003)*

MICHAEL-SCOTT

Michael-Scott 2001 Balliet Vineyard Cabernet Sauvignon (Napa Valley) $35. Black currant, herb, and chocolate flavors are wrapped in dry tannins with elbows. They scour the mouth, giving a rustic mouthfeel. The finish is fruity, very dry, and puckery. **85** —*S.H. (6/1/2004)*

Michael-Scott 2001 Zinfandel (Sonoma County) $24. A very attractive Zin with big flavors of wild blackberries and sweet little cherries dusted with black pepper, clove, and allspice. It's a dry wine, but big and rich in ripe, sunny fruit. Made from older vines scattered around the county. **89** —*S.H. (6/1/2004)*

Michael-Scott 2001 Stagnaro Vineyard Zinfandel (Napa Valley) $22. A fruity style that's backed up with lots of sweet oak. Plum, cherry, blackberry, vanilla, spice, and hints of raspberry come to mind, framed in firm but ripe tannins. **87** *(11/1/2003)*

MICHAUD

Michaud 2000 Chardonnay (Chalone) $40. From high in the mountains above Monterey, crisp, steely acidity frames appley, peachy flavors. Most notable are the winemaker additions of flashy French oak and lees, which make for a creamy, rich mouthfeel. **90** —*S.H. (5/1/2003)*

Michaud 2002 The Pinnacles Chardonnay (Chalone) $35. I like the oak on this wine, also the crispness, the tropical fruit flavors, but the creamy mouthfeel, and the way the fruit is yielding to a sweet nutty character. It's just beginning a slow down and should remain interesting through 2007. **88** —*S.H. (12/1/2006)*

Michaud 2000 Pinot Noir (Chalone) $45. A plump but graceful wine, brimming with sour plum and cherry flavors. Finishes tart and lemony, but with coffee and chocolate accents as well. It's slow out of the blocks, so give it a brisk decanting prior to serving. **85** —*S.H. (7/1/2003)*

Michaud 2000 Sangiovese (Chalone) $25. Seems like a work in progress, a stubbornly dry, acidic wine with flavors of black cherries, tar, tobacco, and dried herbs. Yet there's a likeable finesse and taste of the earth, and the wine could easily improve over the next decade. **86** —*S.H. (9/1/2003)*

Michaud 2000 Syrah (Chalone) $35. This is a wonderful Syrah that brings to mind the rich Hermitages of the Northern Rhône. It's dense in the mouth, with layers of cherry-berry fruit accented with peppery spices. Brilliant and evocative. **92 Cellar Selection** —*S.H. (10/1/2003)*

MICHEL LAROCHE

Michel Laroche at Rutherford Hill 1999 Chardonnay (Napa Valley) $50. Sleek and clean on the palate, this elegant wine offers pretty pear, apple, citrus, and mineral flavors, all well-integrated, and classically styled. Long and elegant on the finish, it is a first release by Burgundian Michel Laroche and Rutherford Hill's Anthony Terlato. Only 200 cases made. **89** *(12/1/2001)*

MICHEL-SCHLUMBERGER

Michel-Schlumberger 2001 Cabernet Sauvignon (Dry Creek Valley) $32. Cabs from this appellation, no matter how ripe they are, always seem to have a brawny, briary edge to them, and this wine is no exception. The blackberries might have been picked in a dusty, thorny patch. Something about the acidy, tannic structure is appealing. **91** —*S.H. (12/31/2004)*

Michel-Schlumberger 1998 Cabernet Sauvignon (Dry Creek Valley) $27. Earthy, with dusty tannins, there's some pretty blackberry fruit. But it's a light wine that turns thin in the middle palate. Not a keeper, but it's polished for near term consumption. **85** —*S.H. (12/1/2001)*

Michel-Schlumberger 1997 Benchland Cabernet Sauvignon (Dry Creek Valley) $27. 87 —*S.H. (9/1/2000)*

Michel-Schlumberger 1997 Reserve Cabernet Sauvignon (Dry Creek Valley) $62. Pronounced blackberry and cedar-scented fruit is kept in check by sturdy but elegant tannins and a kiss of toasty oak in this balanced wine. It's round and supple, and very dry. The blackberry and black cherry flavors pick up again on the finish. **89** —*S.H. (12/1/2001)*

Michel-Schlumberger 1997 Chardonnay (Dry Creek Valley) $20. 92 —*S.H. (11/1/1999)*

Michel-Schlumberger 2000 Chardonnay (Dry Creek Valley) $23. Lean and earthy, a tart wine with lime and grapefruit flavors and powerful acidity. There's little apparent oak or lees. If you like austere, flinty Chards, this one is made for you. **86** —*S.H. (5/1/2003)*

Michel-Schlumberger 1999 Chardonnay (Dry Creek Valley) $20. Ripe and polished apple and peach fruit is joined by smoky oak notes in this easy-to-like wine. Zesty, fresh acidity makes the fruity flavors bright and alive. The finish is spicy, with a smattering of dust and tartness. **86** —*S.H. (11/15/2001)*

Michel-Schlumberger 2001 La Brume Chardonnay (Dry Creek Valley) $30. Dry Creek Chards ask for a certain indulgence. They're never opulent or over the top, and have rather earthy flavors that bring to mind sweet, cured tobacco. This wine, which is a fine example, features winemaker interventions, like lees and oak, and finishes with some tannins. If you're adventurous, try aging it. **87** —*S.H. (8/1/2003)*

Michel-Schlumberger 1998 Merlot (Dry Creek Valley) $21. Soft and pretty, with black cherry and smoke aromas and cherry-berry flavors. The bone dry tannins are accompanied by crisp acidity, resulting in a feeling if elegance and harmony. **89** —*S.H. (12/1/2001)*

Michel-Schlumberger 1997 Benchland Merlot (Dry Creek Valley) $27. 87 —*S.H. (11/15/2000)*

Michel-Schlumberger 2003 Pinot Blanc (Dry Creek Valley) $21. An interesting wine with an array of citrus, peach, and tart pineapple flavors, very high acidity, and a super-long finish. It tingles on the palate, and is refreshing and ultra-clean. Has some complexity, and is a natural for food. **87** —*S.H. (12/1/2004)*

Michel-Schlumberger 1999 Benchland Wine Syrah (North Coast) $20. The tart red cherry fruit on the nose bears a green tobacco-herb note that garnered mixed reviews. Darker on the palate, the wine shows black plum flavors and a chalky note. Finishes with decent length and modest tannins. **86** *(10/1/2001)*

MIDLIFE CRISIS

Midlife Crisis 2004 Pinot Grigio (Paso Robles) $16. There?s a caramel and butterscotch aroma, and then the wine turns a bit thin in the mouth, with modest citrus flavors that finish dry and tart. **82** —*S.H. (2/1/2006)*

MIDNIGHT CELLARS

Midnight Cellars 2000 Mare Nectaris Reserve Bordeaux Blend (Paso Robles) $35. Quintessential Paso Cab blend, rich, dry, and soft. You'll find cherry and coffee flavors, with an herbal edge, wrapped in gentle but richly textured tannins and low acidity. **88** —*S.H. (2/1/2005)*

Midnight Cellars 1997 Mare Nectarus Reserve Bordeaux Blend (Paso Robles) $31. This impressive Paso Robles Bordeaux blend is a plush, opulent wine. The fruit is ripe and sweet, the tannins fine, and it has balance and harmony. The glycerine in this unctuous wine oozes down the sides of the glass. Firmer tannins and higher acidity would make it more "serious," but it's a pleasure-fest as it is. **90** —*S.H. (8/1/2001)*

Midnight Cellars 1999 Mare Nectaris Cabernet Blend (Paso Robles) $35. All five of the prime red Bordeaux varieties comprise this rich and deep wine that drives on with persistence even if it has some hollowness at the core. Aromas of currants and raspberry make for a nice nose. The palate is bold with the taste of cherries, the finish sharply focused and herbal. **88** —*M.S. (5/1/2003)*

Midnight Cellars 1998 Mare Nectaris Reserve Cabernet Blend (Paso Robles) $34. With 70% Cabernet Sauvignon, you might expect this five-varietal Bordeaux blend to taste pretty much like Cabernet, and it does. Although there's plenty of toasty, cedary oak, the cassis fruit shines through, dressed up by vanilla and chocolate notes. Not as deep as in the best of vintages, but a classy crowd-pleaser nonetheless. **88** (9/1/2002)

Midnight Cellars 2001 Mare Nectaris Reserve Red Wine Cabernet Blend (Paso Robles) $38. Tasted blind, you'd identify this as a hot climate Cab, for the softness of acids and tannins and rather baked, raisiny fruit flavors that finish like Port. People must like it, or else the winery wouldn't charge so much, but there are scores of better Cabs at this price. **84** —S.H. (2/1/2006)

Midnight Cellars 2001 Moonlight Cabernet Franc (Paso Robles) $22. Heavy, soft, and dry, with some sharp tannins framing the cherry and coffee flavors, but it'll do with a juicy cheeseburger. **83** —S.H. (5/1/2005)

Midnight Cellars 2001 Estate Cabernet Sauvignon (Paso Robles) $28. Dense, tannic, and dry, this wine has a vegetal note and finishes with a harsh burn. **82** —S.H. (5/1/2005)

Midnight Cellars 2001 Nebula Cabernet Sauvignon (Paso Robles) $19. Tannic, soft, dry, and uninteresting, with a caramelly, Porty smell. **81** — S.H. (5/1/2005)

Midnight Cellars 1999 Nebula Cabernet Sauvignon (Paso Robles) $22. Sappy, grapey fruit is joined by strong herbal overtones reminiscent of dried oregano and parsley. While some panelists felt it had potential to develop over the next couple of years, others dismissed it for saline aromas that they termed "fishy." **83** (9/1/2002)

Midnight Cellars 1997 Nebula Cabernet Sauvignon (Paso Robles) $22. Everything seemingly went right for this wine: The vintage yielded ripe grapes that produced full, deeply attractive blackberry flavors with a sunny sweetness. There's a nice kiss of toasty oak; the wine is balanced and harmonious. It's a little soft and low in acidity. **88** —S.H. (8/1/2001)

Midnight Cellars 2000 Capriccio Italien Cabernet Sauvignon-Sangiovese (Paso Robles) $30. This is a blend of Sangiovese, Merlot, and Cabernet Sauvignon. It is very dry. There are some rich flavors of berries and herbs. It is a good, somewhat rustic red wine. The tannins are considerable and last through the finish. **85** —S.H. (5/1/2003)

Midnight Cellars 1997 Chardonnay (Paso Robles) $18. **84** (6/1/2000)

Midnight Cellars 2004 Equinox Chardonnay (Central Coast) $16. This wine offers powerful fruit, strong acids, strong oak, and a creamy texture. It's dry, but almost desserty in the peach and pineapple custard, vanilla-drizzled flavors. **85** —S.H. (4/1/2006)

Midnight Cellars 2000 Equinox Chardonnay (Paso Robles) $18. Very ripe and very oaky, this is a big wine filled with the flavors of sweet summer peaches, figs, vanilla, and cream. It has a little bit of residual sugar and finishes with a honeyed, custardy aftertaste. **86** —S.H. (12/15/2002)

Midnight Cellars 1999 Equinox Chardonnay (Paso Robles) $18. Melon, peach, and vanilla aromas lead to a refreshingly fruity wine in the mouth. The flavor is peach, and creamy soft. It's a little earthy on the finish, with a trace of orange-rind bitterness. **86** —S.H. (11/15/2001)

Midnight Cellars 1997 Capricorn Merlot (Paso Robles) $22. **88** —J.C. (7/1/2000)

Midnight Cellars 1999 Eclipse Merlot (Paso Robles) $22. There's lots to like in this rustic but pretty wine, infused with blackberry and cassis aromas and flavors. Softly fruity in the mouth, the finish picks up the ample tannins. Try it with robust foods like barbecue. **86** —S.H. (12/1/2001)

Midnight Cellars 2001 Estate Merlot (Paso Robles) $18. Heavy and soft, with Port, raisin, cherry, and caramel aromas. Dry wine finishes with a scour of tannins. **83** —S.H. (5/1/2005)

Midnight Cellars 1999 Estate Merlot (Paso Robles) $23. Plum, raisin, and blackstrap molasses aromas proceed this fruity wine. There are plenty of berry flavors, but they're buried under numbing tannins. The acids are low, so it's not going anywhere. **84** —S.H. (12/1/2001)

Midnight Cellars NV Gemini Port (Paso Robles) $23. Very sweet and chocolatey, with plenty of smoky oak. Cherries, blackberries, and spicy plum pudding in a rustic package. Syrah and Zinfandel. **84** —S.H. (2/1/2005)

Midnight Cellars 2000 Full Moon Red Blend (Paso Robles) $10. Starts with overripe aromas of raisins and prunes, and turns hot in the mouth, with raisiny flavors alongside berry and stone fruit. Tannins and acids are soft and melted. A blend of Zinfandel, Syrah, and Cabernet Sauvignon. **83** —S.H. (11/15/2002)

Midnight Cellars 2001 Full Moon Red Wine Red Blend (Paso Robles) $13. Rugged and tasty, a rustic wine that's easy to drink. Earthy berry flavors and firm tannins. Zin, Syrah, and Cab Sauvignon. **84** —S.H. (3/1/2005)

Midnight Cellars 2002 Gemini Red Blend (Paso Robles) $32. This blend of Syrah and Zinfandel is soft and pleasant. It has flavors of cherries, cocoa, and vanilla cream. **84** —S.H. (4/1/2005)

Midnight Cellars 2000 Starlight Sangiovese (Dry Creek Valley) $19. The bouquet is light and snappy, with touches of chocolate. The mouthfeel is equally racy, but it's also high toned and borderline tart. The finish is fresh and it's here that the wine's acids do their thing. Depth isn't its calling card, but it should do well with food given its zippy profile. The 14.4% alcohol, meanwhile, seems kind of high for Sangiovese. **87** —M.S. (5/1/2003)

Midnight Cellars 1999 Starlight Sangiovese (Paso Robles) $22. Once tannic, always tannic? If so, this tough wine will remain rasping, and will need to be drunk with rich, oily foods to help tame the tannins. Underneath, it has some briary flavors and soft acidity, and is as dry as a desert summer wind. **85** —S.H. (9/1/2002)

Midnight Cellars 2001 Starlight Reba Sangiovese (Paso Robles) $19. This awful wine is barely reviewable. It's raspingly dry and bitter, with unripe cherry flavors. **80** —S.H. (2/1/2006)

Midnight Cellars 2000 Starlight Reba Sangiovese (Dry Creek Valley) $19. Feels raw and sharp, with cherry flavors that finish slightly sweet. **82** — S.H. (4/1/2005)

Midnight Cellars 2002 Nocturne Syrah (Paso Robles) $19. There's plenty of fruit in this country-style wine. The fruit consists of all sorts of black and red berries and stone fruits, with an edge of espresso and oaky caramel. The country is in the rugged texture, which calls for a good steak. **85** —S.H. (12/1/2005)

Midnight Cellars 2001 Nocturne Syrah (Paso Robles) $24. A rustic wine with strong, edgy tannins and modest cherry and coffee flavors. It's very dry and astringent, but will soften with beef. **85** —S.H. (3/1/2005)

Midnight Cellars 2000 Nocturne Syrah (Paso Robles) $26. Gentle and soft, this warm country wine offers generous flavors of plums and blackberries and black pepper. It's dry and balanced, yet a little rough around the edges. There are some raisin notes that show up in the finish. **85** —S.H. (12/1/2002)

Midnight Cellars 1999 Nocturne Syrah (Paso Robles) $24. Out of the bottle, the Nocturne shows stemmy cinnamon flavors. After a few minutes, though, expect a sumptuous sour-cherry, raspberry, and toast bouquet. More of the same bright red fruit surfaces on the palate, where they are met with menthol and vanilla-cream flavors. Our tasters were especially keen on the minerally, almost chewy mouthfeel and finish. Drink now—it'll be the easiest thing you've ever had to do. Top Value. **90** (11/1/2001)

Midnight Cellars 2001 Vineyard Select Syrah (Paso Robles) $48. Heavy, with a raw mouthfeel to the black cherry flavors. Finishes dry and astringent, but clean. **83** —S.H. (3/1/2005)

Midnight Cellars 2001 Zinfandel (Paso Robles) $18. Smoky, bright raspberry, cherry, licorice, and spice flavors lead the way here. The wine offers firm tannins as a framework and finishes with a racy edge, showing moderate length on the finish. **88** —J.M. (11/1/2003)

Midnight Cellars 2000 Zinfandel (Paso Robles) $18. The bouquet is a mish-mash of tomato, barrel char, plum, and pine, and together it doesn't exactly sing. The palate is jammy and sweet, and oak comes up aggressively on the back end. By the time the wine finishes, all you have is mouth full of spicy oak, which some folks weaned on this flavor might very well enjoy. **83** —M.S. (9/1/2003)

Midnight Cellars 1998 Zinfandel (Paso Robles) $21. Good color, tight, firm fruit, with some heft to it. There's cassis as well as cherry, and the wine has the weight of a Sonoma Zin, with good acids to give it lift. This is the first estate bottling from this exciting new winery. Unfortunately, just 28 cases made. **90** —*P.G. (3/1/2001)*

Midnight Cellars 2003 Crescent Zinfandel (Paso Robles) $26. This represents everything I don't like in Zin. Sorry! Very high alcohol, nearly 16 percent, with Porty, raisiny flavors, it's more like a dessert wine. **82** —*S.H. (2/1/2006)*

Midnight Cellars 1999 Crescent Zinfandel (Paso Robles) $22. Sturdy blackberry and oak flavors, plus a little earth, run from palate to finish; on the nose, there's more of the same, plus a slight Sweet Tart note. **87** —*D.T. (3/1/2002)*

Midnight Cellars 2002 Estate Zinfandel (Paso Robles) $24. A little raisiny, a little sweet. Feels velvety smooth in the mouth, with pleasant cherry and cocoa flavors. Good hot climate Zin. **85** —*S.H. (3/1/2005)*

Midnight Cellars 1999 Estate Zinfandel (Paso Robles) $26. Okay, so they only made 125 cases—but don't say we didn't warn you. This Zin's nose balances powdered sugar, ripe mixed berries, and hickory and cedar; you'll encounter loads of chalk and dust over oak and tart red plum on the palate. Medium-weight, it closes with more tart red-berry fruit and powder. **88** —*D.T. (3/1/2002)*

Midnight Cellars 1999 Reserve Zinfandel (Paso Robles) $28. Blackberry and plum-preserve aromas mingle with earthy, minty notes leading to a big, rich, jammy Zin packed with flavor and heat. High alcohol packs a punch, but absolute dryness keeps it balanced. **85** —*S.H. (12/15/2001)*

MIDSUMMER CELLARS

Midsummer Cellars 2003 Cañon Creek Vineyard Cabernet Sauvignon (Napa Valley) $45. Here's a lovely, dry Napa Cab, less flashy and more tannic than some others, but perhaps more balanced and ageworthy. It has equal shares of blackberry and cherry fruit, with earthy, tobacco, and coffee notes. New, sweet oak imparts extra richness. Should improve for the next six years or so. **90 Cellar Selection** —*S.H. (4/1/2006)*

Midsummer Cellars 2003 Mann Vineyard Cabernet Sauvignon (Napa Valley) $35. You'll want to cellar this young Cab because presently it's too tannic and closed in for pleasure. Yet it has the stuffing to age. There's a big core of black currant fruit, and the wine's balance should allow it to effortlessly come together by 2010. **91 Cellar Selection** —*S.H. (4/1/2006)*

Midsummer Cellars 2001 Hickok Traulsen Zinfandel (Napa Valley) $22. Toasty, smoky, and spicy, this Zin serves up a moderate blend of bright cherry, plum, blackberry, and herb flavors. The finish is bright and moderate in length. **85** *(11/1/2003)*

MIGRATION

Migration 2004 Pinot Noir (Anderson Valley) $30. The best Migration I've had. It's rich in Pinot fruit, silky and complex. With cherry, cola, and licorice flavors and a generous dollop of oak it deals an elegant balance, highlighted by refreshingly crisp acidity. **88** —*S.H. (12/1/2006)*

Migration 2003 Pinot Noir (Anderson Valley) $28. From the Duckhorn and Goldeneye family, this is a soft, juicy Pinot. It's very flavorful, suggesting a freshly baked red cherry tart, with accents of mocha, vanilla, and cinnamon, but it's basically dry. **85** —*S.H. (12/1/2005)*

Migration 2002 Pinot Noir (Anderson Valley) $26. Pretty dark and rich, a big, full-bodied wine with complex flavors of cherry, tobacco, earth, coffee, mint, and cola, and some sweet chocolate in the finish. This is a muscular, fruit-driven wine, but could use more subtlety and elegance. **87** *(11/1/2004)*

MILES

Miles 1999 Pinot Noir (Finger Lakes) $16. Toast and cedar frame delicate cherry and cranberry fruit. Light but pretty—and the oak comes on a bit strong on the finish. **84** —*J.C. (3/1/2002)*

MILL CREEK

Mill Creek 2002 Kreck Family Vineyards Cabernet Sauvignon (Sonoma County) $25. Ripe and juicy, with intense blackberry jam and mocha flavors, this smoothly textured wine has rich tannins, perhaps from a majority of Dry Creek Valley grapes. With some sweetness on the finish, it's ready to drink now. **85** —*S.H. (12/1/2006)*

Mill Creek 2005 Estate Chardonnay (Dry Creek Valley) $16. Nice peach and apple pie flavors, along with fresher honeydew define this friendly, soft, somewhat earthy wine. A bit of lees and oak and complexity. **86** —*S.H. (12/1/2006)*

Mill Creek 2005 Estate Gewürztraminer (Dry Creek Valley) $14. Just what the doctor ordered for warm nights and fusion fare. Dry, crisp, and wonderfully flavorful, with oodles of tropical fruit, wildflower, and, most of all, oriental herbs and spice flavors like cinnamon, nutmeg, ginger, and lemongrass. Just a really nice California Gewürz. **86** —*S.H. (12/1/2006)*

Mill Creek 2002 Estate Merlot (Dry Creek Valley) $20. Ripe and juicy. with forward blackberry, cherry jam, mocha, plum, and smoky oak flavors. This Merlot is dry, with crisp acids and soft tannins. **84** —*S.H. (12/1/2006)*

Mill Creek 2005 Estate Sauvignon Blanc (Dry Creek Valley) $16. The main characteristics in this food-friendly wine are citrus, melon, and fig, while partial barrel fermentation adds a creamy richness. Fresh, citrusy acidity makes it all clean and vibrant. **85** —*S.H. (12/1/2006)*

Mill Creek 2001 Zinfandel (Russian River Valley) $22. Marked by deep, rich licorice and black cherry flavors, the wine also serves up an array of lovely plum, raspberry, coffee, cola, and spice flavors. Tannins are smooth yet firm, and the finish is moderate in length. **89** —*J.M. (11/1/2003)*

Mill Creek 1998 Zinfandel (Dry Creek Valley) $18. Soft, plum and cherry fruit scents, augmented with hints of rose petal and cranberry. In the mouth it's lean and insubstantial, with a hard, tannic finish. **83** —*P.G. (3/1/2001)*

MILLBROOK

Millbrook 2000 Cabernet Franc (New York) $18. The nose is meaty, with smoky black-fruit notes. But it's also overtly vegetal, as is the palate, which struggles to deliver plum and berry fruit amid a field's worth of green. Texture-wise, it's smooth and fulfilling, but it doesn't rank at the next level due to its strong herbal core. **83** —*M.S. (2/27/2003)*

Millbrook 2000 Chardonnay (New York) $14. A blend of pear, peach, and banana flavors is followed by a citrus-like finish. The wine is zippy on the finish, but a little short. **81** —*J.M. (2/27/2003)*

Millbrook 1999 Proprietor's Special Reserve Chardonnay (Hudson River Region) $16. Somewhat viscous, yet searingly bright, with orange, clove, peach, pear, apple, and lemon flavors at the fore. Zippy bright to the end, it's fun to drink, but lacks balance. **85** —*J.M. (2/27/2003)*

Millbrook 2004 Pinot Noir (New York) $20. The color is more brown than would be expected at this age, but flavors are still young, albeit candied. Red cherry and root beer aromas lead to sweet, tart cherry flavors. **81** —*M.D. (12/1/2006)*

Millbrook 2001 Tocai Friulano Estate Bottled Tocai (Hudson River Region) $12. A pleasing, light textured wine that shows lovely peach, pear, floral, mineral, and spice notes. Fresh and clean on the palate, it would be a fine match for picnics or seafood. **88 Best Buy** —*J.M. (2/27/2003)*

MILLIAIRE

Milliaire 1997 Clairmont Cabernet Sauvignon (Sierra Foothills) $22. Shows good varietal character in its blackberry-cassis aromas; there's also a strong note of charred, smoky oak. Tastes ripe and sweet, with rich, extracted blackberry flavors, modulated tannins and moderate alcohol. Dry and elegant, with a sweet finish. **87** —*S.H. (8/1/2001)*

Milliaire 2002 Eagle's Nest Petite Sirah (Lodi) $18. Very peppery and fruity, a big, dark wine loaded with blackberries. Soft, and finishes a little sweet. **84** —*S.H. (2/1/2005)*

Milliaire 2001 Syrah (Sierra Foothills) $20. Dark, thick with tannins, a sturdy wine with plenty of fleshy blackberry and coffee flavors. Bone dry, and can probably age for a few years. **85** —*S.H. (2/1/2005)*

Milliaire 2001 Clockspring Zinfandel (Sierra Foothills) $18. Dramatic in the power and intensity of its ripe brambly, briary berry flavors, with touches of earth, tobacco, and sweet ground spices. Despite the flamboyance, remains balanced and controlled. Defines these ancient Foothills Zins. **91 Editors' Choice** —*S.H. (2/1/2005)*

Milliaire 1997 Clockspring Zinfandel (Sierra Foothills) $18. Lovely nose, with coconut and hazelnut scents augmenting the cherry/berry fruit. Not an ordinary set of scents and flavors, but enticing and distinctive. The fruit is intense and perfumed, and the accents of coconut seem just right. **90** —P.G. (3/1/2001)

Milliaire 2001 Ghirardelli Zinfandel (Sierra Foothills) $18. From old head-pruned vines, a big, kick-butt Zin crammed with jammy wild berry and spicy flavors. Dry and balanced, very long in the finish, rich, and bold. **90** —S.H. (2/1/2005)

Milliaire 1997 Ghirardelli Zinfandel (Sierra Foothills) $18. The chocolate family bought the vineyard in 1900. The wine is made in open-top fermenters, and the fruit is sweet and flavorful, with a pleasing intensity. Pretty and seductive style, leading to a cocoa-infused finish with soft tannins. Distinctive and appealing. **89** —P.G. (3/1/2002)

MILONE

Milone 1996 Bells Echo Vineyard Echo Bordeaux Blend (Mendocino) $25. **91** —S.H. (3/1/2000)

Milone 1997 Sanel Valley Vineyard Sanel Bordeaux Blend (Mendocino County) $48. A Bordeaux blend from inland Mendocino, with an interesting aroma. It's like raspberry and peppermint, or cotton candy with a dollop of smoky oak and vanilla. That minty, cedary flavor persists in the month. It's nice to taste such high acidity in a California wine, but the eccentric flavors are puzzling. **85** —S.H. (5/1/2002)

Milone 1997 Hopland Cuvée Chardonnay (Mendocino) $10. **88 Best Buy** —S.H. (3/1/2000)

Milone 1999 Sanel Valley Vineyard Chardonnay (Mendocino) $18. Organically grown, with a woody, peachy smell. It tastes of peaches and apples, although citric acidity gives it a lemony feel. Finishes crisp, with a Meyer lemon flavor. Good drinking, and the oak barely shows. **85** —S.H. (5/1/2002)

Milone 1997 Bells Echo Vineyards Echo Red Blend (Mendocino County) $30. A different blend from the Sanel, this one marries Petite Sirah to Cabernet Sauvignon and Merlot. It smells hot and overripe. There are some berry flavors, but it's tannic, acidic, and scours the mouth with heat and roughness. It will probably mellow with age, but now it's rustic. **83** —S.H. (5/1/2002)

Milone 1999 Sanel Valley Vineyard Zinfandel (Mendocino County) $15. From 40-year-old vines, this is an odd wine, with cherry cough-medicine, herbal aromas and a sharp taste. The acidity seems very high, making the wine tart, and there isn't enough berry flavor to offset it. If you can get past the rustic nature, it's okay. **83** —S.H. (5/1/2002)

Milone 1997 Sanel Valley Vineyard Zinfandel (Mendocino County) $15. **88** (5/1/2000)

MINER

Miner 2002 The Oracle Cabernet Blend (Napa Valley) $50. Similar to Miner's '02 Cab, this wine shares the same rusticity. The tannins overcome the fruit, which struggles to express itself, and the wine seems unlikely to age well. A lighter style Bordeaux blend that has some elegance. **85** —S.H. (12/15/2005)

Miner 2003 Cabernet Sauvignon (Oakville) $54. Miner's estate Cabs have the tannins that mark the best of Oakville. They contribute to the complex structure that stars in this wine. The ripe cherry and cassis fruit can be achieved anywhere it's hot enough, but those tannins are a wonder. One quibble is that the wine finishes too sweet. **88** —S.H. (7/1/2006)

Miner 2002 Cabernet Sauvignon (Oakville) $50. A little earthy and rustic, this Cab has a tobacco-and-herb edge to the blackberry and coffee flavors. It's very dry and fairly tannic, with pronounced oak. Has some elegance, but doesn't seem to be an ager, so drink now. **85** —S.H. (12/15/2005)

Miner 2001 Cabernet Sauvignon (Oakville) $50. A great success that showcases its origins in the rich, sweet tannins that support the well-ripened fruit. Black currants, cassis, white chocolate, and oaky vanilla flavors drink extraordinarily deep and long, in this soft wine. It's almost a dessert, except it's dry. **93** —S.H. (12/31/2004)

Miner 2000 Cabernet Sauvignon (Oakville) $50. Starts off with a classic Napa nose of pure cassis, vanilla, and smoke. In the mouth, the wine is very plush in its smooth, dry tannins and creamy, oaky texture. Yet there is a thinness to the black currant flavors that disappoints, and will prevent longterm aging. **87** —S.H. (11/15/2003)

Miner 1999 Cabernet Sauvignon (Oakville) $60. The huge currant and dark fruit aromas are typical of Napa Valley-floor wines. The flavors are surprisingly complex with plum, black olive, and leather. The mouthfeel is rich and powerful with a velvet-like finish. **92** —C.S. (11/15/2002)

Miner 1997 Cabernet Sauvignon (Oakville) $60. **86** (11/1/2000)

Miner 1998 Chardonnay (Napa Valley) $28. **87** (6/1/2000)

Miner 2004 Chardonnay (Napa Valley) $30. Here's a superripe Chard, huge in all sorts of fruit. The apple, peach, pear, pineapple custard, lime pie, and vanilla flavors are just delicious. If the acidity were higher, it would be a fabulous wine. Still, it's pretty tasty. **88** —S.H. (3/1/2006)

Miner 2003 Chardonnay (Napa Valley) $28. I actually like this wine more than Miner's more expensive '02 Wild Yeast Chard, with which it was simultaneously released. It's not as overwrought. Here, the tasty fruit takes over, with good results. **87** —S.H. (7/1/2005)

Miner 2002 Chardonnay (Napa Valley) $25. Everything's on steroids in this big, big Chard. For starters, the tropical fruit and spice flavors are enormously ripe and concentrated. So is the oak, which has been liberally applied so that the wine bursts with vanilla and buttered toast. Fortunately, there's good acidity to keep everything balanced. **90** —S.H. (11/15/2004)

Miner 2000 Chardonnay (Napa Valley) $30. Well-oaked, with plenty of toasty, smoky, charry flavors. The underlying fruit veers toward peaches and pears. This is a pleasant wine, not very complex, but well made. Turns very oaky again on the finish, with sweet woody tannins. **85** —S.H. (6/1/2003)

Miner 2000 Oakville Ranch Chardonnay (Napa Valley) $35. Silky smooth, with pear, apple, toast, spice, and vanilla notes at the fore. The wine has good weight on the palate and a long, clean, supple finish. **90** —J.M. (2/1/2003)

Miner 2004 Wild Yeast Chardonnay (Napa Valley) $50. Dry and a bit soft, with baked apricot and peach pie flavors, this Chardonnay is very oaky. Made from Oakville grapes, it just doesn't have the freshness you want in a white wine. **84** —S.H. (11/15/2006)

Miner 2002 Wild Yeast Chardonnay (Napa Valley) $50. There's certainly a lot of flashy oak and lees here, contributing pretty vanilla and caramel flavors. But there's something disjointed about the underlying wine, which lacks vibrancy. **86** —S.H. (7/1/2005)

Miner 2002 Merlot (Napa Valley) $30. They don't get much riper than this wine, with powerful, almost over-the-top black currant and black cherry flavors. It's a big wine, but nicely balanced, with rich, complex, smooth tannins and very nice acids. Oak plays a supporting, not dominant, role. The finish is dry. Drink now. **90** —S.H. (4/1/2006)

Miner 2001 Oakville Ranch Vineyard Merlot (Oakville) $28. Picked a little earlier than most? Yes, to judge by the healthy dose of herb and tannin that accompanies the berry and cherry fruit. Great bones, though, and great structure, a versatile food Cab. **88** —S.H. (12/15/2004)

Miner 2003 Stagecoach Vineyard Merlot (Napa Valley) $35. Ripe, with blast-in-your-mouth cherry pie, blackberry jam, dark chocolate, cassis, and rum-soaked raisin flavors that go on forever, not to mention lots of rich, sweet new oak. All this flavor is balanced by fine acidity and an intricate overlay of dusty tannins, resulting in a delicious Merlot. Drink now. **91** —S.H. (11/15/2006)

Miner 2001 Stagecoach Vineyard Merlot (Napa Valley) $28. Red wines don't get much riper than this. It's just bursting with essence of red and black cherry, black raspberry, and white chocolate flavors, and is dry. But it really needs structure. The wine feels collapsed, melted on the palate. **84** —S.H. (12/1/2005)

Miner 2001 Stagecoach Vineyard Merlot (Napa Valley) $28. From a famed vineyard, a strong and pedigreed wine. The structure immediately alerts you that it's an excellent wine, with its firm, sweet tannins, ripe fruit and crisp acids, not to mention the fine oak. Rather astringent now, but the flood of cherry and blackberry flavor suggests cellaring until 2006. **92** — *S.H. (12/15/2004)*

Miner 2000 Stagecoach Vineyard Merlot (Napa Valley) $35. Great Merlot, one that rises above the ordinary to achieve real distinction. Has aromas and flavors of blackberry, cassis, plum, chocolate, coffee, violets, and smoky oak, and drinks dry and smooth. The tannins are wonderfully thick, soft, and complex, and the finish impresses with its intensity. So rich, it's almost its own food group. **93 Editors' Choice** —*S.H. (12/1/2003)*

Miner 2002 Petite Sirah (Napa Valley) $40. Exuberant and lusty. This is a big red wine, dry and full-bodied and not at all reticent. Ripe, almost jammy flavors of blackberries, cassis, cherries, and cocoa, with a sweet covering of oak, and rich, thick, ripe tannins. Drink now. **92** —*S.H. (8/1/2005)*

Miner 2004 Garys' Vineyard Pinot Noir (Santa Lucia Highlands) $50. Big and bold in baked cherry pie flavors, with lots of new oak, this mouth-filling Pinot certainly appeals for its enormous fruit and silky texture. It's distinctly New World, fruit-forward and vibrantly clean, if a bit one-dimensional. **86** —*S.H. (11/15/2006)*

Miner 2002 Garys' Vineyard Pinot Noir (Santa Lucia Highlands) $50. Paler in color than Miner's Rosella's bottling, and more delicately structured, but there's nothing shy about the flavors. They're richly intricate, a tapestry of red cherry, cola, rosehip tea, cinnamon, mocha, vanilla, and smoky oak. Simply delicious, and so smooth, so fine in the mouth. **93** —*S.H. (11/1/2004)*

Miner 2000 Garys' Vineyard Pinot Noir (Santa Lucia Highlands) $50. Tight, leathery, and toasty describes the nose of this heavyweight. Raspberry fruit is prominent, and so is wood spice and cinnamon. Oak plays a big role in this wine, especially on the finish: Toast and espresso are all over the long, dark fade. Fortunately, potent acidity keeps things clean. **90** *(10/1/2002)*

Miner 2004 Rosella's Vineyard Pinot Noir (Santa Lucia Highlands) $50. As is typical of Pinots from this appellation, the wine is fruit-driven. We're talking a huge mouthfeel of cherry-rhubarb pie and oak-influenced cocoa-dusted peanut brittle flavors, but fortunately the wine is totally dry, and maintains a keen, acidic silkiness. Drink this big Pinot with strongly flavored food. **92** —*S.H. (10/1/2006)*

Miner 2002 Rosella's Vineyard Pinot Noir (Santa Lucia Highlands) $50. This classic cool-climate Pinot Noir shows the crisp acids, silky texture and lush, intricate flavors induced by nighttime fog and daily sunshine. Those flavors run to cherries, with nuances of cola, rhubarb, oaky vanilla, and peppery spice. Not only a fun wine, but a complex one that distinguishes the appellation. **92** —*S.H. (11/1/2004)*

Miner 2004 Rosato Rosé Blend (Mendocino) $15. Rich and fruity in cherries, rose flower, and vanilla, yet a little simple, this blush wine is dry and balanced. **83** —*S.H. (12/1/2005)*

Miner 2000 Rosato Rosé Blend (Mendocino) $13. Bright raspberry flavors lead the way here in this tangy, crisp rosé. It finishes moderately with a citrus-like flair and serves up enough intensity to pair well with an array of dishes from lobster to pasta to burgers on the grill. **87** —*J.M. (11/15/2001)*

Miner 1997 Sangiovese (Mendocino County) $20. 89 —*S.H. (12/15/1999)*

Miner 2002 Syrah (Napa Valley) $28. A soft-textured, easy-drinking Syrah that one reviewer called a nice everyday, by-the-glass wine. Slightly candied cherry-berry fruit is accented by dried spices that seem to fade rapidly on the finish. **84** *(9/1/2005)*

Miner 2001 Syrah (Napa Valley) $28. Still young and sharp in acids and tannins, but what a mouthful of fruit you get. Pure, sweet black currant and black cherry fruit, with a spicy, peppery finish and generous oak. Cellar this for a few years to soften. It should develop softness and complexity by 2006. **92** —*S.H. (12/15/2004)*

Miner 2004 Simpson Vineyard Viognier (California) $20. Viognier's fruity, floral aspects are toned down with an herbal, earthy note. There's some good, firm acidity. From Madera County, in the Central Valley. **84** — *S.H. (12/1/2005)*

Miner 2003 Simpson Vineyard Viognier (California) $20. This single-vineyard wine shows ripe flavors that are reminiscent of tree fruits, wildflowers, vanilla, and spice. It has a creamy texture and finishes semi-sweet. **85** —*S.H. (11/15/2004)*

Miner 2002 Simpson Vineyard Viognier (California) $20. A heavy, dull wine due to the syrupy mouthfeel that lacks acidity and zest. There are some nice flavors of peaches and apples, but the palate longs for crispness. From Madera, in the Central Valley. **84** —*S.H. (12/1/2003)*

Miner 2002 Zinfandel (Napa Valley) $28. A good, balanced Zin, properly dry, with the weight and texture of a fine Cabernet. The flavors veer toward sour cherries, and there's a fine dusting of gritty tannins throughout. Drink now with rich cheeses and tomato sauces. **86** —*S.H. (8/1/2005)*

MIRABELLE

Mirabelle NV Brut Champagne Blend (North Coast) $16. Even and medium-weight, this Schramsberg-owned sparkler has a citrus (but not all biting) palate, with traces of caramel and Jolly Rancher candy on the back palate. It's bouquet shows pear-tart aromas enveloped in dusty, "grandmother's attic" notes (or, as one reviewer put it, "mature, not fruity"). The mouthfeel is even and lively, and not too effervescent. Finishes with stony-mineral notes. **85** —*D.T. (12/1/2001)*

Mirabelle NV Brut Champagne Blend (North Coast) $16. Sporting a rich, doughy aroma, this pretty bubbly serves up broad peach, pear, and toast flavors that are highlighted by a tangy citrus finish. **87** —*J.M. (12/1/2002)*

MIRAMONT

Miramont 2002 Celestial Cabernet Sauvignon (Lodi) $19. Dry and rich in blackberry, cocoa, coffee, herb, and oak flavors, this Cab has a finish of ripe raisins and cassis. It's a soft, full-bodied wine that will benefit from a year or so in bottle. **86** —*S.H. (4/1/2006)*

Miramont 2002 Vintners Reserve Celestial Cabernet Sauvignon (Lodi) $25. Deeper and slightly more tannic than the winery's regular Cab, this bottling is very dry. With soft acids, it shows well-developed flavors of blackberries and mocha and a deep, ripe black plum taste on the finish. It should hold and improve for several years. **87** —*S.H. (4/1/2006)*

MIRASSOU

Mirassou 2003 Cabernet Sauvignon (California) $10. Now owned by Gallo, and the game plan seems to be to make simple, clean varietal wines with a California appellation—at least for now. Cherries, blackberries, slightly sweet and simple. **83** —*S.H. (11/1/2006)*

Mirassou 2002 Cabernet Sauvignon (California) $10. Rather unripe, with green mint and cherry flavors and a sharpness through the finish. **82** — *S.H. (11/1/2005)*

Mirassou 2001 Cabernet Sauvignon (California) $10. Has some herbal, tomatoey notes, but overall this is a satisfying mouthful of Cabernet, with plummy fruit and supple tannins. Sourced mainly from Paso Robles and Lodi. **85 Best Buy** *(11/15/2004)*

Mirassou 1999 Coastal Selection Cabernet Sauvignon (Central Coast) $11. They called this a miracle vintage in the Central Coast, and here's why. At this price, to get fruit this opulent is unbelievable. The black currant quality is the equal of anything made in California. Of course, they don't get the tannins or acid structure of finer North Coast vineyards. **87 Best Buy** —*S.H. (11/15/2002)*

Mirassou 2004 Chardonnay (Monterey County) $11. A little thin on the finish, but bright in perky acidity. The fruit on this dry wine veers toward Key lime, lemons and vanilla. **83** —*S.H. (9/1/2006)*

Mirassou 2003 Chardonnay (Central Coast) $11. This is an everyday sort of Chard, one that offers plenty of fruit, oak, and cream without complicating things. **84** —*S.H. (4/1/2005)*

Mirassou 2002 Chardonnay (California) $10. Shows its cool coastal origins (according to Mirassou, it could be labeled Monterey County) in its tight, citrusy fruit and crisp acids. There's hint of butter to go with notes of sweet corn and custard. **84** *(11/15/2004)*

Mirassou 2000 Coastal Selection Chardonnay (Monterey) $11. Opens with intense, explosive notes of ultraripe tangerines, orange custard, baked meringue, vanilla, and toast. This is clearly a ripe, oaky wine, and it holds its size well, thanks to zesty acidity. It's flamboyant and delicious. **88 Best Buy** —*S.H. (12/15/2002)*

Mirassou 1999 Coastal Selection Chardonnay (Monterey County) $13. Juicy peach and spicy lime fruit is joined by herbal notes and a whiff of lees in this dry, fairly tart wine. A burn of acidity piques the middle palate, and then the citrus flavors kick in on the crisp, clean finish. **85** —*S.H. (11/15/2001)*

Mirassou 1998 Coastal Selection Chardonnay (Monterey County) $12. 83 —*S.H. (10/1/2000)*

Mirassou 1998 Harvest Reserve Chardonnay (Monterey County) $16. 88 *(6/1/2000)*

Mirassou 1996 Harvest Reserve Chardonnay (Monterey County) $16. 87 — *S.H. (7/1/1999)*

Mirassou 1998 Mission Vineyard Chardonnay (Monterey County) $24. 91 —*S.H. (2/1/2000)*

Mirassou 1998 San Vicente Vineyard Chardonnay (Monterey County) $24. 88 *(6/1/2000)*

Mirassou 1999 Showcase Selection Chardonnay (Monterey County) $30. The rich bouquet shows buttery, creamy vanilla notes with hints of tarragon and sweet hay. Golden apple and pear wears sweet butterscotch on the medium-weight, soft palate. Shows a bit of alcoholic heat as well as good intensity and impressive weight, but a one taster found it too controlled by vanillin oak qualities at the expense of the fruit. **89** *(7/1/2001)*

Mirassou 1998 Showcase Selection Chardonnay (Monterey County) $30. 85 *(6/1/2000)*

Mirassou 2002 Merlot (California) $10. Pretty basic fare, raw and harsh, but with some redeeming berry flavors that finish dry. **82** —*S.H. (11/1/2005)*

Mirassou 2001 Merlot (California) $10. Seems a trifle raisiny, with dark, plummy notes that come across as sun-baked rather than fresh. Still, it offers a mouthful of fruit and a nice, plump texture. **83** *(11/15/2004)*

Mirassou 1999 Coastal Selection Merlot (Monterey) $11. It's hard to find inexpensive Merlot that's good, but here's one. True, it's tannic. There's a numbing quality that stuns the palate. But there are pretty blackberry flavors, and it's very dry, with good acids. With the right foods, it will do just fine. **84** *(11/15/2002)*

Mirassou 1997 Coastal Selection Merlot (Monterey County) $13. 81 —*S.H. (11/15/2000)*

Mirassou 1998 Harvest Reserve Merlot (Monterey County) $18. Simple and cola-like, it has bright flavors of strawberry and raspberry jam, with peppery, alcoholic heat, although it's basically dry. The weight is more like a rosé than a red, but it's pure and tasty. **85** —*S.H. (7/1/2002)*

Mirassou 1996 Limited Bottling Merlot (Monterey County) $18. 85 —*J.C. (7/1/2000)*

Mirassou 1999 Mirassou Harvest Reserve Merlot (Monterey County) $18. Displays nice tension between ripe, jammy blackberry fruit and earthier notes of bell pepper and tobacco, and the tannins are rich and deft. If the wine has a fault, it's excessive softness. Those pretty flavors just sit on the palate; they don't dance. **85** —*S.H. (11/15/2002)*

Mirassou 1997 Harvest Reserve Dedication Bot Petite Sirah (Monterey County) $18. 89 *(11/1/1999)*

Mirassou 2000 Coastal Selection Pinot Blanc (Monterey County) $12. Smells and tastes like a good Chardonnay, with peaches-and-cream, tangerine and buttered toast notes, and a creamy smooth texture. There's a honeyed richness all the way through the finish that's irresistible. **88** — *S.H. (9/1/2003)*

Mirassou 1999 Coastal Selection White Burgundy Pinot Blanc (Monterey County) $12. From an endangered varietal in California, and it's too bad. Not just a Chardonnay wannabe, Pinot Blanc shows apple, melon, and peach flavors, and it's rounder and fatter. This version is a little sweet, a little okay; all in a nice sipping wine. **84** —*S.H. (12/15/2001)*

Mirassou 1997 Limited Bottling Fifth Generat Pinot Blanc (Monterey County) $16. 87 —*S.H. (9/1/1999)*

Mirassou 2000 Mirassou Mission Vineyard Pinot Blanc (Monterey County) $22. Powerful in fruit and oak, this is a big, gutsy wine. The flavors veer toward tangerine peel, caramel, crème brûlée, ginger, white chocolate, and peach jam, but the wine is quite dry. Turns baked and hot on the finish. This is a good alternative to a fat Chardonnay. **87** —*S.H. (9/1/2003)*

Mirassou 1999 Mission Vineyard Pinot Blanc (Arroyo Seco) $24. Heavily oaked and aged on the lees; the underlying tropical fruit flavors are bright and clean. These winemaker interventions, however, are almost intrusive. That's a matter of taste, and some will find it fancy and complex. **85** —*S.H. (12/15/2001)*

Mirassou 1997 White Burgundy Pinot Blanc (Monterey County) $9. 82 — *M.S. (9/1/1999)*

Mirassou 1997 Pinot Noir (Monterey County) $11. 84 *(11/15/1999)*

Mirassou 2002 Pinot Noir (Central Coast) $10. Cola and root beer notes give complexity to black cherry and cinnamon flavors in this soft, supple wine. Finishes a bit thin and tart, but it is still a great value in Pinot Noir. **85 Best Buy** *(11/15/2004)*

Mirassou 1999 Coastal Selection Pinot Noir (Central Coast) $13. Tastes over-cropped, meaning that they had to produce a huge crop to get the price down this low. The wine is thin, herbaceous, and raspingly dry. with sharp acidity and a watery finish. **82** —*S.H. (12/15/2001)*

Mirassou 1999 Coastal Selection Pinot Noir (Monterey County) $10. The general character here is light and leafy, as advertised by the herbal, cedary bouquet. Toasty oak on the palate helps support the simple but ripe raspberry fruit. And the finish yields dried cherries and coffee as well as some spice. **86 Best Buy** *(10/1/2002)*

Mirassou 1998 Coastal Selection Pinot Noir (Monterey County) $14. Coffee, sugared tea, raspberry, and a hint of smoked bacon lead to watery berry flavors and simple tannins in this tartly acidic wine. It's clean and drinkable but there's no getting around its basic one-dimensionality. **83** —*S.H. (11/15/2001)*

Mirassou 1999 Harvest Reserve Pinot Noir (Monterey County) $15. Aromas of tree bark, root beer, and creamy oak. Plum, cranberry, and cherry all make up the palate, with wood and drying tannins coming on late in the game. The weight, which is medium at best, is pretty nice; it isn't heavier than the wine calls for. **88 Best Buy** *(10/1/2002)*

Mirassou 1997 Harvest Reserve Pinot Noir (Monterey County) $16. 86 *(12/15/1999)*

Mirassou 1997 Limited Bottling Pinot Noir (Monterey County) $18. 86 *(12/15/1999)*

Mirassou 1999 Showcase Selection Pinot Noir (Monterey County) $30. Tasters uniformly liked this bright berry and black cherry wine, the top of the line from this venerable family winery. Dark earthy notes, vanilla oak and herb accents nicely complement the crisp and lively fruit. Drink now through 2006. **89** *(10/1/2002)*

Mirassou 1997 Showcase Selection Pinot Noir (Monterey County) $30. 91 *(10/1/1999)*

Mirassou 2004 Riesling (Monterey County) $11. Simple and off-dry, with all sorts of fruity, flowery and spicy flavors, this wine shows off high, crisp Monterey acidity, which makes it finish clean. The alcohol is a comfortable 13%. **84** —*S.H. (10/1/2006)*

Mirassou 2004 Riesling (Monterey) $10. Frankly sweet, with sugary citrus, peach, and wintergreen flavors, this wine fortunately has decent acidity to make it crisp and clean. **83** —*S.H. (12/1/2005)*

Mirassou 2001 Coastal Selection Riesling (Monterey) $7. Fruity and semisweet, it brings to mind the old Liebfraumilchs many of us cut our teeth on. The pretty apple, peach, and flower flavors are offset by crisp acidity, and the finish is clean and long. **86** —*J.M. (6/1/2002)*

Mirassou 2000 Coastal Selection Riesling (Monterey County) $8. Great vintage, great Riesling vineyard from the chilly Salinas Valley. There are some beautiful floral and fruit aromas, and lovely flavors. The acid-sugar balance is perfect. But the wine isn't concentrated enough to merit a higher score. They must have stretched the vines pretty thin. **85** —*S.H. (6/1/2002)*

Mirassou 1998 Family Selection Riesling (Monterey) $8. 86 Best Buy — S.H. (9/1/1999)

Mirassou 2003 Sauvignon Blanc (Calaveras County) $10. Plump, yet crisp, this fruit-forward Sauvignon has something for everyone: a hint of grassiness, ripe stone fruit, and fig flavors and decent freshness on the finish. 85 Best Buy (11/15/2004)

Mirassou 1999 Harvest Reserve Syrah (Monterey County) $18. Inky black. Shows promise in the aromas, which are filled with blackberry, pepper, and oak notes. But it falls apart in the mouth. After a nice entry, in which you detect perfectly lush tannins, the fruit just isn't there. It turns to water on the midpalate, leaving an impression only of tannins and alcohol. 83 —S.H. (12/1/2002)

MIRO

Miro 2004 Coyote Ridge Vineyard Petite Sirah (Dry Creek Valley) $30. Big and rich. The flavors are blackberries, plums, and coffee so ripe, they touch into black currant and raisin territory. Yet the wine maintains poise and dryness. Drink now–2015, at least. 90 —S.H. (12/31/2006)

Miro 2001 Coyote Ridge Vineyard Petite Sirah (Dry Creek Valley) $35. Stone cold classic Sonoma Petite Sirah, black in color, brooding, dense in body, and brilliantly fruity. The sweet, smooth tannins hold massive flavors ranging from black currants and coffee to grilled meat and plenty of smoky oak. Easy to drink now, but should age well for many years. From a branch of the Trentadue winery. 92 —S.H. (3/1/2005)

MISSION MEADOW

Mission Meadow 2000 Merlot (Santa Barbara County) $25. Opens with pretty aromas of cherries, herbs, and smoky oak. There are some ripe, juicy flavors of berries and cherries and the tannins are easy, although it's a bit simple in structure and in the snappy finish. From Plam, of Napa Valley. 85 —S.H. (2/1/2004)

MISSION PARK

Mission Park NV Artist Series Red Cuvée Red Blend (Central Coast) $8. This is a nice, richly dry Rhône blend with a dash of Cabernet. It's a fruit-forward wine, yet has a complicated tannin-acid structure that reins the fruit in and grounds the wine. Showing a bit of sharpness now that should level off with a year or so of bottle age. 86 Best Buy —S.H. (9/1/2006)

MITCHELL

Mitchell 1999 Reserve Malbec (El Dorado) $21. A seldom-used grape, even in Bordeaux, this version is dark, tannic and aggressive, a tough wine offering little pleasure now and unlikely to improve. There are some plummy flavors. It's dry, and clean, and simple. 82 —S.H. (5/1/2002)

MITCHELL KATZ WINERY

Mitchell Katz Winery 2000 JK's Cabernet Sauvignon (Livermore Valley) $24. A sweet, flavorful Port-style dessert wine. Opens with enticing aromas of cassis, chocolate, caramel, vanilla, and smoke. Rich and chocolatley in the mouth, with ripe flavors of currants that are backed up with bracing acidity. Delicious, with a long, sweet finish. 90 Editors' Choice —S.H. (11/15/2003)

Mitchell Katz Winery 2001 Crackerbox Vineyards Sangiovese (Livermore Valley) $22. Smells funky and tanky, and has a heavy, thick texture with blackberry flavors. 82 —S.H. (12/1/2003)

MIXED BAG

Mixed Bag 2002 Red Wine Red Blend (California) $10. This dry wine has a simple structure, jammy fruit flavors and pert acids. Like some fast foods, it's good and quick, at a good price. 85 Best Buy —S.H. (5/1/2005)

Mixed Bag 2002 White Wine White Blend (California) $10. Dry and rustic, with crisp acids, this earthy wine has some fruity flavors. 83 —S.H. (5/1/2005)

MOKELUMNE GLEN

Mokelumne Glen 2001 Kerner (Lodi) $12. This is a simple, inocuous wine, made from an old, minor German varietal. It's soft and fruity, with

peach flavors and a dollop of acidity, and is a little sweet. 83 —S.H. (3/1/2004)

Mokelumne Glen 2004 Lemberger (Lodi) $14. Dry and heavy, this wine is bitter and astringent, and not going anywhere. 80 —S.H. (4/1/2006)

Mokelumne Glen 2004 Select Late Harvest Dreirebe White Blend (Lodi) $20. A blend of three German varietals, this is a very sweet, but balanced, dessert wine, rich in honeyed apricot, pineapple, and white peach flavors. It's likeable for the creamy texture and the sweet spicy richness of the finish. 87 —S.H. (4/1/2006)

Mokelumne Glen 2001 Zinfandel (Lodi) $12. Kicks off with rich and spicy black cherry and raspberry notes, followed by interesting licorice, plum, tar, smoke, and spice flavors. The texture is a shade astringent, but the wine remains quite nice. 88 Best Buy (11/1/2003)

MONT PELLIER

Mont Pellier 2000 Syrah (California) $7. Dark in color, a big, strong wine. There's a distinct aroma of white pepper to the aroma, but in the mouth, blackberry and plum flavors emerge. Totally dry, with good, accessible tannins. Simple, but at this price, it's an amazing value. 84 —S.H. (12/15/2003)

Mont Pellier 2000 Viognier (California) $7. Simple and fruity, with peach and tropical fruit flavors and high acidity. This is a very dry, tart wine, clean and well made. It's perfectly adequate for nondemanding occasions, especially considering the price. 85 Best Buy —S.H. (12/15/2002)

MONTAGE

Montage 2003 Cabernet Sauvignon (California) $11. Taste this against a great North Coast Cab costing far more, and you'll find profound similarities. The oak-infused cassis flavor, fine tannins, dryness, and balancing acidty are all there. The only difference is depth, but still, this is a great value. 86 Best Buy —S.H. (6/1/2006)

Montage 2002 Cabernet Sauvignon (California) $12. Here's a perfectly drinkable, everyday sort of Cabernet, a little rough around the edges, but dry and balanced. There's some good fruit, and sturdy tannins. 84 —S.H. (11/15/2005)

Montage 2003 Chardonnay (California) $11. Has everything the best Chards have, without quite the same complexity or depth, of course. But's it's a value for the rich pear, peach, and pineapple flavors, creamy smooth texture, and sumptuous overlay of oak. 86 Best Buy —S.H. (5/1/2006)

MONTE LAGO

Monte Lago 2000 Single Vineyard Sauvignon Blanc (Clear Lake) $20. There's a hint of saline or wet dog in the nose, and that keeps the wine from really taking off from the runway. Beyond that, citrus mixes with creamy notes to make up the mouth, and then it ends in a lemony, lush way. It's not a very complex wine, but it has enough zip to keep it going. 86 (8/1/2002)

MONTE VOLPE

Monte Volpe 1996 Barbera (California) $11. 86 (11/15/1999)

Monte Volpe 1999 Montepulciano (Mendocino) $14. Tastes like a homemade wine, with jammy, marmalade aromas and flavors. Seems like a bit of residual sugar found its way into the wine, which is also crisp and somewhat tannic. Brings to mind those old jug red wines. 84 —S.H. (5/1/2002)

Monte Volpe 1997 Pinot Grigio (Mendocino) $12. 87 Best Buy (8/1/1999)

Monte Volpe 2000 Pinot Grigio (Mendocino) $13. Nice fruit, suggesting almonds and lemons and white peaches, and good acidity makes it bracing and clean. This is a likeable, everyday sort of wine that goes down easy. It's sweeter than most examples of this varietal, with a clover honey taste. 85 —S.H. (5/1/2002)

Monte Volpe 1999 Pinot Grigio (Mendocino) $12. This is a light-bodied wine that has lots of crisp acidity, a steely spine that's very clean and refreshing and is bone dry. Strongly citrusy, with lots of lemon and grapefruit. It's a simple apéritif wine that won't break the bank. 84 —S.H. (8/1/2001)

Monte Volpe 1997 Sangiovese (Mendocino) $16. 88 —M.S. (9/1/2000)

MONTEMAGGIORE

Montemaggiore 2002 Superiore Red Blend (Dry Creek Valley) $40. This Cabernet-Syrah blend is obviously very ripe, packed with black cherry and chocolate flavors, with interesting herb and pepper notes. There's a nice edge of tannins and acids. Sophisticated and intricate, it will pair well with lamb or beef. **89** —S.H. (10/1/2005)

Montemaggiore 2003 Paolo's Vineyard Syrah (Dry Creek Valley) $32. A bit too ripe, to judge from the stewed berry and raisin flavors, but other than that, the wine is fully dry, with rich, complex tannins. Drink with roasted meats and hard cheeses. **84** —S.H. (7/1/2006)

Montemaggiore 2002 Paolo's Vineyard Syrah (Dry Creek Valley) $32. A bit tough in tannins, but it seduces with tart plum and ripe cherry flavors, and hints of leather and coffee. It's a full-bodied, thickly textured wine that could use a year or two to come together. **88** (9/1/2005)

MONTEREY PENINSULA

Monterey Peninsula 1997 Sleepy Hollow Vineyardd-Doctor's Rese Pinot Noir (Monterey County) $22. 90 (10/1/1999)

MONTEREY VINEYARD

Monterey Vineyard 1998 Cabernet Sauvignon (Monterey County) $7. 83 —S.H. (12/15/2000)

Monterey Vineyard 1998 Chardonnay (Monterey County) $7. 83 —S.H. (5/1/2000)

Monterey Vineyard 1997 Merlot (California) $7. 82 —J.C. (7/1/2000)

Monterey Vineyard 1997 Pinot Noir (California) $8. 82 (10/1/1999)

Monterey Vineyard 1999 Pinot Noir (Central Coast) $7. 81 —S.H. (12/15/2000)

MONTERRA

Monterra 2000 Encore San Bernabe Vineyard Red Medley Cabernet Blend (Monterey County) $18. Mostly Cabernet Sauvignon and Grenache, and quite ripe and lush. There's an undertow of Cabernet's currant and herb tones, but the fresh, sweet cherry and rose notes of Grenache make it succulent. Finishes long, with a dusty coating of tannin. **87** —S.H. (6/1/2004)

Monterra 2000 Cabernet Sauvignon (Monterey County) $13. Medium-bodied with grapey, plummy fruit—but also enough green vegetable and oak flavors to keep us from liking it more than we did. Finishes with oak and dry tannins. **84** (12/1/2002)

Monterra 2001 Chardonnay (Monterey County) $10. This Chard is fermented on lees for 4–6 months, in both French and American oak, which is more than you can say for most other Chards at this price. Slate, pear, and vanilla aromas don't prepare you for the über-malo toasty flavors that coat pear and apple-skin fruit on the palate. Mouthfeel is resinous, creamy, and full-bodied. **85** (12/1/2002)

Monterra 1998 Chardonnay (Monterey) $9. 87 Best Buy (9/1/2000)

Monterra 2001 Merlot (Monterey County) $10. Young and jammy in blackberry and cherry fruit, with firm acids. Soft in tannins and very dry, it's sturdy enough for ribs. **84** —S.H. (12/15/2004)

Monterra 2000 Merlot (Monterey County) $13. This quaffing Merlot was aged in oak for a year, which is evidenced by spice and caramel aromas on the nose. Plum and blackberry fruit is nice and jammy; mouthfeel is smooth but solid. **86** (12/1/2002)

Monterra 1997 Merlot (Monterey) $9. 85 Best Buy (9/1/2000)

Monterra 1996 Promise Merlot (Monterey) $10. 87 (11/15/1999)

Monterra 1999 Encore Red Blend (Monterey County) $20. A blend of Cabernet, Merlot, Petite Sirah, Zinfandel, and Syrah, it's a unique, love-or-hate wine. The fruit (despite its big-boned components) isn't jammy; rather, the flavors lean more toward cherry and fruit skin than fleshy fruit. Smells like chocolate-covered cherries, with some mint. 1,200 cases produced. **85** (12/1/2002)

Monterra 2001 Encore Rosé Blend (Munterey County) $18. A bizarre blend of Cabernet, Merlot, Syrah, and Pinot Noir; panelists were split as to whether it was likeable or not. Where one reviewer found sweet strawberry taffy aromas, another found spice and chocolate. Where one reviewer noted sour fruit and flat wood flavors, another noted smoke and raspberry notes. Clearly one to try for yourself. 400 cases produced. **85** (12/1/2002)

Monterra 2002 Encore Dry Rosé Medley Rosé Blend (Monterey County) $18. Rather full and heavy for a rosé, with cherry cough drop and orange flavors, and a thick texture. It will be good with a spicy Mediterranean fish stew. Syrah, Merlot, Cabernet Sauvignon, and Pinot Noir. **84** —S.H. (6/1/2004)

Monterra 1998 Sangiovese (Monterey) $9. 83 (9/1/2000)

Monterra 2004 Shiraz (Monterey County) $9. This lighter-sized Shiraz has black cherry flavors and herbal, peppery notes that start up on the nose and don't let go until the last second of the medium-long, tart finish. A fine, by-the-grill wine. **84** (9/1/2005)

Monterra 2001 Syrah (Monterey County) $10. Fruity, rough, and dry. The blackberry-cherry flavors are very ripe, and have a chocolatey finish. **83** —S.H. (12/15/2004)

Monterra 2000 Syrah (Monterey County) $13. Delicato says that this offering is more French-styled than its other offerings. Though you won't exactly mistake this for a Cotes-du-Rhône, there's more of a mineral component here than oak, and the fruit isn't as jammy and sweet as it is in some of the other offerings. **86** (12/1/2002)

Monterra 1998 Syrah (Monterey) $13. Very ripe—some tasters felt overtly overripe—aromas and flavors gave this wine a Port-like character. Prunes, figs, and nuts, a supple, low-acid mouthfeel, and a long sweet-and-sour finish comprise an interesting, but not universally enjoyed package. A split decision, and very much a personal call. **84** (10/1/2001)

Monterra 1997 Syrah (Monterey) $9. 86 Best Buy (9/1/2000)

Monterra 2000 Encore White Blend (Monterey County) $18. A blend of 40% Chardonnay, 26% Viognier, and 24% Pinot Blanc (plus small quantities of Sauvignon Blanc and Riesling), this new addition to the Delicato portfolio spends 12 months in French oak. Its MacIntosh apple-and-oak profile drives this fact home. Ends with an acidic, lemony twinge. 900 cases made. **85** (12/1/2002)

Monterra 2002 San Bernabe Vineyard White Medley White Blend (Monterey County) $18. From an unusual blend, it has an array of fresh fruit and berry flavors, and drinks on the sweet side. Chardonnay, Sauvignon Blanc, Pinot Blanc, Muscat Canelli, and Viognier. **85** —S.H. (6/1/2004)

Monterra 1998 Zinfandel (Monterey) $9. 82 (9/1/2000)

MONTES

Montes 1999 Montes Alpha Merlot (Santa Cruz County) $16. 85 —D.T. (7/1/2002)

MONTEVINA

Montevina 2003 Barbera (Amador County) $10. Pasta with tomato sauce comes to mind when drinking this dry wine, with its berry flavors and thick tannins. It's rustic and easy, a carafe sipper that's clean and easy in price. **83** —S.H. (12/1/2005)

Montevina 2001 Barbera (Amador County) $11. If you've been reluctant to try this old-fashioned variety, this value-priced release is a good place to start. It's dark and dry, with plummy, earth, herb, and tobacco flavors relieved by a rich streak of sweet black currant. Beautifully structured, and a great accompaniment to tomato-based dishes. **88 Best Buy** —S.H. (6/1/2004)

Montevina 1998 Barbera (Amador County) $12. In California, Italy's workhorse red produces a juicy, richly fruity, dry red wine, with some of the highest acids you'll find in the state. Soft tannins are fine, but that crisp tartness demands olive oil, prosciutto, or pizza. Hold the anchovies. **87** —S.H. (11/15/2001)

Montevina 1999 Terra d'Oro Barbera (Amador County) $18. A smooth, rich red wine, without the hefty tannins that can mark this varietal. Beautifully round and ripe, with intense berry flavors. Drinks dry and crisp, and advances an already serious case for Sierra Foothills Barbera. **90** —S.H. (2/1/2003)

Montevina 1996 Terra d'Oro Barbera (Amador County) $18. 84 —S.H. (10/1/1999)

Montevina 2000 Terra d'Oro Barbera (Amador County) $15. Pretty much as good as California Barbera gets, with the smooth, rich tannic texture of a fine Merlot and a good mélange of berry-cherry, tobacco, and herb flavors. Finishes dry and clean, with good acidity. **89 Editors' Choice** —*S.H. (6/1/2004)*

Montevina 2000 Fumé Blanc (California) $7. Light, pleasant, and fruity, with plenty of lemon and honey flavors. It's also nicely dry, with good acidity and balance. **85 Best Buy** *(8/1/2001)*

Montevina 2005 Terra d'Oro Moscato (California) $18. With its honeyed flavors of tangerines, peaches, wildflowers, and vanilla, this is a pleasant sipper if you're looking for something off-dry to frankly sweet. Low alcohol makes it a nice summer beach or picnic wine. **85** —*S.H. (11/15/2006)*

Montevina 2000 Rosato Nebbiolo (Sierra Foothills) $8. Sometimes you just want something fresh, fruity, and cold on a hot summer day. Here's a raspberry-scented wine with dry berry flavors, and it's the prettiest salmon color. A slight effervescence adds zest. **84** —*S.H. (11/15/2001)*

Montevina 2004 Pinot Grigio (California) $10. Slightly sweet, but clean and zesty, this pleasant wine will go well with a nice baked ham. The flavors suggest ripe peaches, lemons, and limes. **84 Best Buy** —*S.H. (12/1/2005)*

Montevina 2002 Pinot Grigio (California) $10. Pleasant vanilla bean and melon aromas lead you to a round, rather rich mouthful of citrus, apple, and banana. Not a thriller, but not bad at all. In a pedestrian way, this white serves a purpose where others fall short. **85** —*M.S. (12/1/2003)*

Montevina 2001 Pinot Grigio (California) $10. Watery and thin, a citrusy wine whose mouthfeel is mainly alcohol and peppery heat. The flavors veer toward grapefruits and lemons, and the finish is dry and watery. **83** —*S.H. (9/1/2003)*

Montevina 2000 Pinot Grigio (California) $10. Pleasant, light, and crisp, it shows pretty aromas of lemons, vanilla, and white peaches. It's pretty dry, although there's some ripe sweet fruit in the middle palate. **86** *(8/1/2001)*

Montevina 2005 Terra d'Oro Pinot Grigio (Santa Barbara County) $18. So much fruit, so much acidity, such a nice PG. It's all about apples, peaches, limes, and wildflowers, dry and delicious, and the most remarkable acidity for balance. This lusty wine is versatile with all sorts of different foods. **87** —*S.H. (11/1/2006)*

Montevina 2001 Freisa Red Blend (Amador County) $13. Dark as a moonless night, dry as dust and earthy, this wine is like a cross between Merlot and Zin. It's plummy, but finishes with a peppery spiciness. The tannins are big and thick, so drink this with very rich fare. **86** —*S.H. (6/1/2004)*

Montevina 1998 Sangiovese (Amador County) $12. There are some nice features about this wine, notably the berry flavors, dry tannins, and clean finish. But there's a green, stalky quality that makes it taste tart and lean. Rich, oily cheeses and meats will enhance it. **85** —*S.H. (9/1/2003)*

Montevina 1997 Sangiovese (Amador County) $12. 85 —*S.H. (11/1/1999)*

Montevina 2002 Terra d'Oro Sangiovese (Amador County) $NA. Soft and silky, with moderate alcohol that seems to have been achieved at the cost of some sweetness. The cherry flavors taste like they were dusted with white sugar. **83** —*S.H. (3/1/2006)*

Montevina 1998 Terra d'Oro Sangiovese (Amador County) $18. Smells simple, with candy-jammy wild-berry and tar aromas and an earthy, stemmy streak. The flavors are sweetly berryish, with a simple structure and soft tannins and acidity. **83** —*S.H. (11/15/2001)*

Montevina 1996 Terra d'Oro Sangiovese (Amador County) $16. 86 —*S.H. (10/1/1999)*

Montevina 2001 Sauvignon Blanc (California) $10. Rich in lime and peach flavors, slightly sweetened with sugar, bu the acidity is fine and the wine straddles the line between dryish and off-dry. Has a pleasantly fruity, clean finish. **85 Best Buy** —*S.H. (3/1/2003)*

Montevina 2002 Syrah (Amador County) $12. Extremely supple, with herbal overtones that add a layer of complexity to the ripe blackberry fruit flavors. Finishes on a note reminiscent of black tea, yet rounded and not overly tannic. Drink this well-priced Syrah over the next year or two. **85** *(9/1/2005)*

Montevina 2000 Syrah (Amador County) $10. Good dark color. Smells a bit stemmy and weedy, with green chlorophyll aromas alongside black cherries. That vegetal note continues in the mouth, where the tannins are notably smooth and refined. If only it had more fruit. **84** —*S.H. (6/1/2003)*

Montevina 1998 Syrah (Sierra Foothills) $18. Berry aromas and lots of toasty oak announce this medium-weight wine. Nicely balanced, the dark berry fruit has appealing coffee and leather accents and the wine shows moderate acidity and even tannins. It's another indication of the real potential of Syrah from the Sierra Foothills. **87 Editors' Choice** *(8/1/2001)*

Montevina 2002 Terra d'Oro Syrah (Amador County) $20. Combines clean berry and vanilla flavors in an easy-to-drink, somewhat light-bodied wine. A bit simple, with a dash of heat on the finish. **83** *(9/1/2005)*

Montevina 2000 Terra d'Oro Syrah (Amador County) $18. A bit on the earthy, tobaccoey side, although there are some pretty flavors of blackberries. Tannins are gritty but soft, and girdle the wine in a dense texture. Notable for the long, intense finish, which coats the palate with cassis. May improve with a few years in the cellar. **85** —*S.H. (2/1/2004)*

Montevina 2001 Terra d'Oro Syrah (Amador County) $15. This Syrah might strike you at first as austere, because the first impression is of moderated plums, herbs, and tobacco. But that doesn't take into account the balance, integrity, and harmony that make it an ideal food wine. **89** —*S.H. (6/1/2004)*

Montevina 2002 Teroldego (Amador County) $16. A dry wine, with pleasant black cherry and cocoa flavors and smooth, rich tannins. Tasted blind, you could mistake it for a soft Syrah. **84** —*S.H. (4/1/2005)*

Montevina NV Zinfandel (Amador County) $15. Heady, with strong aromas of prunes, milk chocolate, caramel, and honey. It's pretty sweet (9.8%), with berry flavors. Lacks the finesse and concentration of the real thing, but it's soft and drinkable, and the price isn't bad. Would be nice with vanilla ice cream. **86** —*S.H. (9/12/2002)*

Montevina 2002 Zinfandel (Sierra Foothills) $10. Simple, with berry-cherry and cocoa flavors and an undertow of pepper, this Zin is soft and smooth. It has a long, fruity finish and isn't too alcoholic or hot. **84 Best Buy** —*S.H. (12/1/2005)*

Montevina 2001 Zinfandel (Sierra Foothills) $11. The winemakers call this a "kinder, gentler Zin," and there is something limpid about the silky tannins and rose petal and blackberry flavors. Yet it's firmly Zinfandel-like, with its burst of bramble and wild scour of peppery spices. **86** —*S.H. (6/1/2004)*

Montevina 1999 Zinfandel (Amador County) $12. Big, bold, and briary, with scads of wild-berry aromas and spices, this wine drinks fruity and soft and very dry, despite its intense, jammy fruit. Ultracrisp acidity makes it lively. Defines Foothills Zin at its countrified best. **88 Best Buy** —*S.H. (11/15/2001)*

Montevina 1998 Zinfandel (Sierra Foothills) $10. 84 —*S.H. (12/1/2000)*

Montevina 1997 Zinfandel (Amador County) $10. 86 —*P.G. (11/15/1999)*

Montevina 2003 Deaver Vineyard 100 Year Old Vines Zinfandel (Amador County) $28. This Zin is full-bodied and rich in fruit, massively packed with blackberry and blueberry jam, chocolate, and coffee flavors finished with cassis and currants. It's bone dry, with a creamy mouthfeel. **90** —*S.H. (3/1/2006)*

Montevina 1998 SHR Field Blend Zinfandel (Sierra Foothills) $14. This is big but not hard, a meaty and dark wine with a positive rustic quality. It's round but with a brambly edge, and shows full mixed-berry fruit, an easy mouthfeel and an even finish with white-pepper notes. **87** *(8/1/2001)*

Montevina 2003 Terra d'Oro Zinfandel (Amador County) $18. With just a trace of raisins, this wine flirts with being overripe, but wisely comes down on the side of balance. It's dry, full-bodied, and rich, with deep chocolate and black raspberry flavors. This beautiful wine is a natural with barbecued beef or chicken. **88** —*S.H. (3/1/2006)*

Montevina 2002 Terra d'Oro Zinfandel (Amador County) $18. Picture perfect Sierra Zin, rich, ripe, and powerful. Showing strong blackberry, cherry, coffee, cocoa, and spice flavors, wrapped in sturdy but soft tannins. High in alcohol, but dry and perfectly balanced, with no overripe notes. **91** —*S.H. (3/1/2005)*

Montevina 1999 Terra d'Oro Zinfandel (Amador County) $18. Ripe, rich, and full-bodied, a wine that excites the palate with a delicious coat of blackberry and chocolate fruit sprinkled with pepper. Dry, with smooth, complex tannins, and Zin's wild, exuberant nature. **89** —*S.H. (2/1/2003)*

Montevina 1997 Terra d'Oro Zinfandel (Amador County) $16. 87 —*S.H. (12/1/2000)*

Montevina 1996 Terra d'Oro Zinfandel (Amador County) $16. 86 —*S.H. (9/1/1999)*

Montevina 2002 Terra d'Oro Deaver Vineyard 100 Year Old Vines Zinfandel (Amador County) $28. A lush, dramatic Zin that's fully ripe yet avoids any hint of raisins or excessive sugar. The mouth filling flavors of sweet cherry tart, crème de cassis, vanilla and peppery spices are wrapped in smooth tannins, with a bite of acidity. Super high in alcohol, though. **90** —*S.H. (4/1/2005)*

Montevina 2003 Terra d'Oro Home Vineyard Zinfandel (Amador County) $25. Although it's slightly rustic, with some sharpness, this is almost the perfect Zin for barbecue or something more prepared, like braised beef or pork ribs. It's a comfort-food red, dry and full-bodied, yet clean, with an honesty that comes from the terroir. **87** —*S.H. (6/1/2006)*

Montevina 2002 Terra d'Oro Home Vineyard Zinfandel (Amador County) $24. Smells and tastes overripe, with suggestions of raisins and stewed prunes. The flavors veer toward chocolate fudge, although it's not an especially sweet wine. It's certainly distinctive, and will have its fans. **85** —*S.H. (4/1/2005)*

Montevina 2001 Terra d'Oro Zinfandel (Amador County) $15. You'll find some raisiny flavors that result in an overcooked aroma and flavor, as well as some rough tannins. It's a rustic Zin whose edges will be rounded out with rich cheeses or meats. **84** —*S.H. (6/1/2004)*

Montevina 2001 Terra d'Oro Deaver Vineyard Old Vine Zinfandel (Amador County) $21. Delicous and rich, with gobs of sweet ripe cherry and blackberry flavor. The tannins are lovely, too, very ripe and soft but intricate as velvet. There's a note throughout of sweetened coffee that adds interest. **89** —*S.H. (6/1/2004)*

Montevina 2000 Terra d'Oro School House Road Zinfandel (Amador County) $21. Concentrated and intense with mountain fruit, this Zin is medium-bodied, with lush, sweet tannins. The myriad of flavors ranges from ripe cherries and pomegranates to mild coffee, leather, and herbs. It's bone dry and not too alcoholic, and a great companion to food. **90** —*S.H. (6/1/2004)*

Montevina 2000 Terra d'Oro Schook House Road Field Blend (Amador County) $24. A very successful Zin, big and brawny and authoritative in its berry and cherry flavors with layers of leather, grilled meat, and herbs. A hint of raisins adds nuance but doesn't detract. Big and lush, a fireplace wine for mid-winter. **90** —*S.H. (3/1/2005)*

Montevina 1999 White Zinfandel (Amador County) $7. With a color akin to the soft pink of ripe peaches, this low-alcohol wine has aromas of peach, apricot, watermelon, and vanilla. Drinks fruity and simple but clean and zesty, too, with adequate acidity. Off-dry, it gives the impression of some sweetness. **83** —*S.H. (2/1/2001)*

MONTHAVEN

Monthaven 2001 Cabernet Sauvignon (Central Coast) $12. Riper than last year, and $2 more expensive, too, but gets the same score because it's too sweet. Nice aromas of smoky currants, and some good, ripe blackberry flavors, but why did they keep so much sugar in? **84** —*S.H. (3/1/2004)*

Monthaven 2001 Coastal Merlot (Central Coast) $12. A serviceable wine, with plummy berry flavors and some fairly rugged tannins, but on the whole it's an easy sip. It's also a bit on the sweet side. **84** —*S.H. (2/1/2004)*

Monthaven 2000 Pinot Noir (California) $10. So what does ten bucks buy in Pinot Noir? A light-bodied wine with tart, green strawberry, cola, and cranberry flavors, plenty of crisp acids and smooth tannins. **84** —*S.H. (7/1/2003)*

Monthaven 2000 Syrah (California) $10. One of a rash of new and inexpensive statewide appellations as a result of the grape glut, this is a decent every sipper. It has berry flavors and is very dry and clean. Acids are out of proportion to the fruit, however, resulting in a peppery tartness. **84** —*S.H. (12/15/2003)*

Monthaven 2000 Zinfandel (California) $10. Here's your basic red wine, the kind drunk around the world. It has berry, earthy flavors, and is bone dry and acidic, with strong tannins. It's a rustic, country-style wine, and you can gulp it down with your next pizza. **83** —*S.H. (9/1/2003)*

Monthaven 2001 Coastal Zinfandel (Central Coast) $8. A pleasing blend of plum, black cherry, smoke, berry, and herb flavors, all couched in firm tannins. Toast and smoke frame the finish which is moderate in length and fairly spicy. **86 Best Buy** *(11/1/2003)*

MONTICELLO

Monticello 2003 Tietjen Vineyard Cabernet Sauvignon (Rutherford) $45. Starts off very oaky, with masses of sweet buttery char, crème brûlée, and vanilla notes. What's under all that? Delicious blackberry pie filling and polished cherry cola. Drinks voluptuously smooth, soft, and slightly sweet. Best now and for a couple of years. **90** —*S.H. (12/15/2006)*

Monticello 2004 Estate Grown Syrah (Oak Knoll) $34. This is the first Monticello Syrah I've had, and it's a very impressive one. Grown in the cooler southern part of Napa Valley, it shows crisp acids and a peppery zest that make the blackberry, cherry, and chocolate flavors extra enjoyable. **91** —*S.H. (12/15/2006)*

MONTICELLO VINEYARDS

Monticello Vineyards 2000 Proprietary Bordeaux Blend (Napa Valley) $50. An unusual blend dominated by Cabernet Franc and Merlot, with only ten percent Cabernet Sauvignon. Very dark, rich, and fruity, with cassis, black currant, anise, and herb flavors that are wrapped in big, sturdy tannins. Too young to drink now, unless it's with an enormous dish like braised short ribs, but best left for four or five years. **91** —*S.H. (8/1/2003)*

Monticello Vineyards 1999 Corley Reserve Cabernet Sauvignon (Napa Valley) $85. A fabulously rich, generous wine that oozes over the palate like nectar, carrying along black currant, cassis, and herb flavors and substantial flavoring from oak. Although it feels soft on the palate, a hit of tannin kicks in on the finish. **91** —*S.H. (2/1/2003)*

Monticello Vineyards 1997 Corley Reserve Cabernet Sauvignon (Napa Valley) $65. 91 *(11/1/2000)*

Monticello Vineyards 2001 Jefferson Cuvée Cabernet Sauvignon (Napa Valley) $34. This wine is sort of a junior sister to Corley's more expensive ones. It's rich in fruit and oak, with wonderful tannins that give a sensual, velvety mouth feel. Drinks smooth and delicious right through the long finish. **91** —*S.H. (2/1/2005)*

Monticello Vineyards 1999 Jefferson Cuvée Cabernet Sauvignon (Napa Valley) $34. This mouthful packs plenty of black currant fruit, plus elaborate oak shadings and soft, rich Napa tannins. Hold it in your mouth, feeling the great texture and letting the flavors change. Turns dry and tannic on the finish. **90** —*S.H. (2/1/2003)*

Monticello Vineyards 2002 Jefferson Cuvée Cabernet Sauvignon (Napa Valley) $34. This is a good, fairly complex Cab that's likeable and balanced. It show fine blackberry and cherry flavors, with a good tannin-acid balance and some nice oak. Drink now. **87** —*S.H. (12/15/2005)*

Monticello Vineyards 2001 Reserve Cabernet Sauvignon (Napa Valley) $75. A very fine wine, rich, full-bodied, and sensationally ripe. Floods the mouth with cassis and oak flavors, and the tannins are sweet and intricate. Feels great just to slosh it around the palate. **92** —*S.H. (2/1/2005)*

Monticello Vineyards 2002 Tietjen Vineyard Cabernet Sauvignon (Rutherford) $45. Opens with complex aromas of cherry pie, sweet oak, peppery wintergreen, and an exotic note of candied ginger and Asian spice. On the palate, it then turns lush and layered, with swirls of fruit and spice leading to a long finish. This wine is best from now through 2012. **90** —*S.H. (12/15/2005)*

Monticello Vineyards 2001 Tietjen Vineyard Cabernet Sauvignon (Rutherford) $45. Dark, almost black. An interesting note of pine tar

USA

floats over the classic blackberry, cherry, and plum aromas, and also lots of sweet, charry oak. Rather hard with tannins now, but what a long, fruity finish. Best after 2008. **91** —*S.H. (10/1/2004)*

Monticello Vineyards 2000 Tietjen Vineyard Cabernet Sauvignon (Napa Valley) $50. Shows some blackberry and cherry fruit aromas and flavors along with dried sage and dill, and the fruity flavors are on the lean side. That lets the dusty tannins and acids dominate the palate. **86** —*S.H. (2/1/2004)*

Monticello Vineyards 1999 Tietjen Vineyard Cabernet Sauvignon (Napa Valley) $55. Tasty single-vineyard Cabernet from Rutherford. You will be zonked by the intensity of flavors. Black currants, plums, coffee, tobacco, and spices are all framed in well-smoked oak. Deep and long, with an impressive finish. One drawback is excessively soft acidity. **89** —*S.H. (12/31/2002)*

Monticello Vineyards 2001 Corley Reserve Chardonnay (Napa Valley) $50. A selection of the better barrels from the Home Ranch, the Reserve is fantastically rich and complex. No mere fruit bomb despite scads of flavors ranging from apples and peaches through pears and mangoes, there's also a sleek backbone of steel, all of it wrapped in a rich, honeyed texture. The finish is long and intricately constructed of dusty brown spices. **93** —*S.H. (8/1/2003)*

Monticello Vineyards 1999 Corley Reserve Chardonnay (Napa Valley) $40. Notes of smoke, toast, lime, and herbs play against guava, pear, and brown sugar scents in the bouquet. A chalk note accents zesty orange, grapefruit, and guava flavors and a soft mouthfeel. Vanilla, clove, and oak highlights mark the wine's creamy, medium-length finish. **89** *(7/1/2001)*

Monticello Vineyards 1997 Corley Reserve Chardonnay (Napa Valley) $30. 88 *(6/1/2000)*

Monticello Vineyards 2003 Estate Chardonnay (Napa Valley) $26. A medium-weight Chard with mainstream attributes: toasty oak, ripe pears, and a plump, custardy mouthfeel. Finishes with a bit of alcoholic warmth. **85** *(5/1/2005)*

Monticello Vineyards 2001 Home Ranch Vineyard Chardonnay (Napa Valley) $45. This is stunningly good single-vineyard wine. The fruit shows well-ripened apples and peaches all the way into pineapples and mangoes, offering up a cascade of flavors that tumble across the palate. Oak shadings are generous, but in balance. Displays a crispness and delicacy of acids more usually associated with cooler regions. Absolutely first class. **92** —*S.H. (8/1/2003)*

Monticello Vineyards 1999 Merlot (Napa Valley) $30. Rich and sumptuous, this is a magnificently decadent Merlot that oozes ripe grapes and elaborate oak. The flavors veer toward blackberries and cassis, with a delicious taste of French olives. The fruit easily handles the oaky overlay. **93 Editors' Choice** —*S.H. (2/1/2003)*

Monticello Vineyards 2002 Estate Merlot (Napa Valley) $30. Smells rather like green olives, with strands of spicy wood. In the mouth, you get tannins, alcohol, and herbs, with a hint of cherry fruit. Strangely muted. **85** —*S.H. (3/1/2005)*

Monticello Vineyards 1997 Corley Family Vineyards Pinot Noir (Napa Valley) $24. 87 *(12/15/1999)*

Monticello Vineyards 2002 Estate Pinot Noir (Napa Valley) $34. Here's a Pinot made for food. It's lightly colored and delicately structured, with a silk and taffeta mouthfeel made firm by crisp acids. The flavors veer toward tart cherries, strawberries, cola, coffee, and mouth-tingling spices. **90** —*S.H. (3/1/2005)*

Monticello Vineyards 2004 Estate Grown Pinot Noir (Oak Knoll) $34. The vineyard is in the cooler southern part of Napa Valley, and it shows in the wine's crispness and silky delicacy. This is an elegant, gentle Pinot that's rich in berry fruit, spice flavors, and complexity. **87** —*S.H. (12/1/2006)*

Monticello Vineyards 2003 Estate Grown Pinot Noir (Oak Knoll) $34. With a deep, mulchy taste of the earth that's reminiscent of cured tobacco, mushrooms, and roasted coffeebean, this full-bodied Pinot also shows plum and blackberry notes that are slightly baked. It's a hearty, soft wine, but not a rustic one. **86** —*S.H. (12/15/2005)*

Monticello Vineyards 2001 Proprietary Red Blend (Napa Valley) $50. Impresses for its ripely sweet flavors that mass in the mouth and wash across the palate in waves. Currants, cassis, cherries, coffee, vanilla, smoky oak, you name it. The texture is luxurious and smooth as velvet. As big as it is, this wine never loses its harmony and balance. **93** —*S.H. (2/1/2005)*

MONTINORE

Montinore 1999 Winemaker's Reserve Chardonnay (Willamette Valley) $18. This is a very oaky style, which is fine if the fruit is up to the challenge, but here it seems insubstantial, thin and simple. There is a slightly bitter, rubbery aftertaste as well. **83** —*P.G. (2/1/2002)*

Montinore 2005 Gewürztraminer (Willamette Valley) $14. A good effort, clearly varietal with a mix of grapefruit and floral flavors. Medium intensity, the fruit is penetrating and tart, and the floral scents have a somewhat soapy character, which is not unpleasant. The wine is technically off-dry, but really shows little sweetness. **85** —*P.G. (9/1/2006)*

Montinore 2004 Gewürztraminer (Willamette Valley) $9. A nice follow-up to the excellent 2003, this is dry, varietal, and beautifully perfumed with classic sweet floral notes. Good concentration and length; it doesn't get so over-the-top it's like swallowing perfume, but it captures that aspect of the grape nicely, with lingering richness. **88 Best Buy** —*P.G. (11/15/2005)*

Montinore 2003 Gewürztraminer (Willamette Valley) $9. A mouthful of fresh grapefruit and lime. The bracing, citrus fruit is backed with some wet stone mineral and enough tannin to give the finish some muscle. Nothing delicate here, but plenty of flavor. **87 Best Buy** —*P.G. (10/1/2004)*

Montinore 2000 Gewürztraminer (Willamette Valley) $9. A very fragrant, inviting wine, with whiffs of ripe pears and apricots, along with a slight hint of baby powder. Nice, spicy, and immediately enjoyable, it carries through to a clean finish with lots of citrus peel and some good acids. **87 Best Buy** —*P.G. (4/1/2002)*

Montinore 2001 Late Harvest Estate Bottled Gewürztraminer (Willamette Valley) $9. The bright gold color and botrytis aromas tell you right off the bat that this is late-harvest juice. In the mouth, the extract and thickness are that of Vendanges Tardives Alsace whites, and flavor-wise, there's quince, peach, and cinnamon, along with more botrytis and white raisins. Quite interesting for the region and a solid take on European-style late-harvest Gewürz. Possibly best with blue cheese or foie gras. **87 Best Buy** —*M.S. (8/1/2003)*

Montinore 2003 Müller-Thurgau (Willamette Valley) $12. Off-dry and chunky, with simple fruit flavors. **83** —*P.G. (11/15/2005)*

Montinore 2000 Müller-Thurgau (Willamette Valley) $7. Cheese, milkweed, and straw make for an unattractive nose, while the mouth is overtly sweet as if made from dried and candied mango and pineapple. The finish fades fast while leaving behind a residue left that isn't that pleasant. **80** —*M.S. (8/1/2003)*

Montinore 2005 Pinot Gris (Willamette Valley) $14. Scents are spicy and herbal, with notes of fresh cut apple, tart pear, and citrus. Light and dilute, it seems to disappear quickly in the mouth, without the weight or ripe fruit flavors that many Oregon Pinot Gris can display. **84** —*P.G. (9/1/2006)*

Montinore 2004 Pinot Gris (Willamette Valley) $10. This winery's Pinot Gris always has a fair amount of color, but sometimes it drifts over from straw to tawny gold, right on the edge of oxidation. Here there is a vegetal/grassy tone that dominates; missing is the fresh pear fruit. **82** —*P.G. (11/15/2005)*

Montinore 2003 Pinot Gris (Willamette Valley) $10. A slight, coppery blush from skin contact can also be detected in the somewhat tannic mouthfeel. Light flavors of pear hold the center of this tart, somewhat underripe effort. **85** —*P.G. (10/1/2004)*

Montinore 2002 Pinot Gris (Willamette Valley) $10. Nice effort, with just the faintest hint of blush to the color. It has pretty pear aromas, and it feels substantial in the mouth, but neither hot nor heavy. Pear fruit flavors are accented with hints of Meyer lemon. **88 Best Buy** —*P.G. (12/1/2003)*

USA

Montinore 2001 Pinot Gris (Willamette Valley) $10. Melon and citrus aromas get this soft, ripe, and round wine going. The palate is full and plump, with bold citrus and tropical flavors and a welcome textural creaminess. The finish is smooth and supple, and as a whole this wine covers all the bases while showing itself to be a more than capable food accompaniment. **88 Best Buy** —M.S. (8/1/2003)

Montinore 2000 Pinot Gris (Willamette Valley) $10. There's a distinctly tawny shade to this wine, a scent of beer, and the flavors show a bit of oxidation. Simple and somewhat watery, it finishes with the tastes of apple and pear tarts, a hint of honey, and a good bit of acid. **84** —P.G. (4/1/2002)

Montinore 2002 Entre Deux Pinot Gris (Willamette Valley) $14. A single-vineyard Pinot Gris (is the world really ready?); with heavy exposure to neutral oak. The wine looks old, already golden with shades of sandy brown; it feels fat and overripe with tropical fruit flavors that finish with a blast of alcohol. **86** —P.G. (12/1/2003)

Montinore 2003 Pinot Noir (Willamette Valley) $14. Tastes like black cherry cola. The ripe, lush style flirts with oxidation, loads in the vanilla flavors, and finishes with a burst of heat. Needs the mellowing influence of food to show its best. **84** —P.G. (11/15/2005)

Montinore 2002 Pinot Noir (Willamette Valley) $13. Grapy, candied, and light, like a cherry Lifesaver. The simple fruit flavors are pleasant, but the body lacks weight and texture, giving it a tired limpness in the mouth. **84** (11/1/2004)

Montinore 2001 Pinot Noir (Willamette Valley) $13. Fragrant and tannic, with scents of plum, dried cherry, and sandalwood. This is tart, tight, and herbal, but well-priced with clear varietal character. **86** —P.G. (12/1/2003)

Montinore 2000 Pinot Noir (Willamette Valley) $12. 82 (10/1/2002)

Montinore 1999 Pinot Noir (Willamette Valley) $13. Opens with a sharp, bitter scent, which might generously be called juniper, herb, and pine. But in the mouth it remains tough and quite tannic. It's hard, chewy, and roughhewn, showing little in the way of fruit. **83** —P.G. (4/1/2002)

Montinore 2003 Graham's Block 7 Pinot Noir (Willamette Valley) $32. It's ripe to the point of being sweet, and the fruit hits the jammy side of strawberry. Simple, raisiny, and pushed to the limits of ripeness. **86** — P.G. (12/1/2006)

Montinore 2000 Graham's Block 7 Pinot Noir (Willamette Valley) $30. Montinore's best single-vineyard Pinot shows elegant flavors of black cherry and plum, softly woven into a smooth, sensuous wine. Good purity and persistence, and a fine, silky finish. Not as robust as the '99, but delicious. **89** —P.G. (12/31/2002)

Montinore 1999 Graham's Block 7 Pinot Noir (Willamette Valley) $30. Montinore has just begun releasing single-vineyard Pinots, and the results so far are promising. This wine sports elegant cherry fruit, soft tannins, and a sensuous, feminine style. Smooth and well-built, it descends into a tight tannic finish that suggests needing some additional time in the cellar. **90 Cellar Selection** —P.G. (12/31/2001)

Montinore 2003 Parson's Ridge Pinot Noir (Willamette Valley) $32. The Parson's Ridge is the best of the multiple offerings from Montinore Estate. The fruit flavors are full and ripe but the wine is already drinking at its best right now. **87** —P.G. (12/1/2006)

Montinore 2000 Parson's Ridge Vineyard Pinot Noir (Willamette Valley) $30. This is a pretty Pinot, showing soft, forward fruit, and good varietal flavors. It feels a bit light in the middle, and the finish, though clean and true, lacks depth. **87** —P.G. (12/31/2002)

Montinore 1999 Parson's Ridge Vineyard Pinot Noir (Willamette Valley) $30. This has immediate appeal, with its jammy, strawberry-cherry nose leading into a ripe, firm wine, set up with crisp acids and stiff tannins. A nice whiff of coffee highlights the somewhat rough, woody finish. **89** — P.G. (12/31/2001)

Montinore 1998 Pierce's Elbow Single Vineyard Pinot Noir (Willamette Valley) $35. Deceptively light in color, this well-balanced wine delivers aromas and flavors on a big scale. A fine cherry, floral, smoke, and anise bouquet pulls you in; the smooth texture and cherry-licorice-chalk flavor

profile follow through with great style. Finishes full with smoky notes and dry, even tannins. Drink now through 2005. **91** —M.M. (11/1/2001)

Montinore 2000 Pierce's Elbow Vineyard Pinot Noir (Willamette Valley) $30. Medium-weight fruit, with cherries and cherry tomatoes mixing it up, along with some pleasant nuances of earth and mineral. The finish is silky smooth and light. **87** —P.G. (12/31/2002)

Montinore 1999 Pierce's Elbow Vineyard Pinot Noir (Willamette Valley) $30. A pretty, pale cherry color, distinctly scented with root beer and cherry cola. The fruit is fairly light, but clean, well-defined by crisp acids, and finished off with well-integrated flavors of bark and stem. **88** —P.G. (12/31/2001)

Montinore 2004 Winemaker's Reserve Pinot Noir (Willamette Valley) $21. Sweaty, flat, and vegetal, it doesn't show much beyond leafy tomato flavors and green, astringent tannins. **84** —P.G. (12/1/2006)

Montinore 2000 Winemaker's Reserve Pinot Noir (Willamette Valley) $19. Fragrant with scents of plum, dried cherry, leaf, and a hint of earth. This is a mix of lots from the three single-vineyard selections, and is markedly improved in this new vintage. Flavors of pie cherries dominate a balanced and pleasant finish. **88** —P.G. (12/31/2002)

Montinore 1999 Winemaker's Reserve Pinot Noir (Willamette Valley) $19. The label says reserve, but the wine fits more comfortably in the "Regular Joe" category. A bit volatile at first, with vinegar and nail polish aromas, it improves in the glass to show vanilla, spice and curry over an earthy core of tart cherry fruit. **87** —P.G. (12/31/2001)

Montinore 2002 Winemaker's Reserve Pinot Noir (Willamette Valley) $19. The reserve is a bigger version of the regular Pinot, with more heat, more tannin, more bite. Sharp, hot, and acidic, with green tannins that seem to thin out the finish. **83** —P.G. (11/15/2005)

Montinore 2001 Late Harvest Riesling (Willamette Valley) $10. At almost 6% residual sugar, this is almost a dessert wine, perhaps best served with foie gras or a cheese course. The aromas and flavors combine elements of preserved lemon rinds, ripe pears, and apricots in a rich, sweet, oily wine. **87** —J.C. (9/1/2003)

Montinore 2005 Semi-Dry Riesling (Willamette Valley) $10. Bracing and tart, with mixed citrus flavors suggesting lime, lemon, and a trace of pineapple. There's a slightly bitter, lemon-rind edge that gives the wine some extra definition and should work wonders with halibut or swordfish. **87 Best Buy** —P.G. (9/1/2006)

Montinore 2004 Semi-Dry Riesling (Willamette Valley) $9. Off-dry and light, this looks to be well on its way to oxidation. Brown apples, slightly baked and flat tasting. **83** —P.G. (11/15/2005)

Montinore 2003 Semi-Dry Riesling (Willamette Valley) $9. This comes across as dry, due to the tart, tangy acids. The fruit is broad and clean, with fresh-cut green apple dominant. Simple and refreshing. **86 Best Buy** —P.G. (10/1/2004)

Montinore 2001 Semi-Dry Estate Bottled Riesling (Willamette Valley) $9. Peach and butter open, with thin grapefruit and lemon on the palate. Notes of lychee and toast throughout. On the palate, there is a slight spritziness. Clean and citrusy on the short finish. **85** —K.F. (12/31/2002)

MONTANA

Montona 2000 Reserve Cabernet Sauvignon (Napa Valley) $50. Here's a well-oaked wine that has some ripe flavors of black currants and cassis, as well as impressive tannins. The fruit sinks into the palate and persists through a long finish. Might even age, but probably best now. From Andretti; Only 243 cases were produced. **91** —S.H. (5/1/2004)

Montona 2000 Reserve Cabernet Sauvignon (Napa Valley) $50. Re-released after an additional two years in bottle, this wine, which was very good in 2003, is on a downhill slide. It's losing fruit, cracking up as the Brits say. From Andretti. **83** —S.H. (12/1/2005)

Montona 2002 Chardonnay (Napa Valley) $30. User-friendly Chard, with pleasant flavors of peaches and pears and enough oak to add a smoky, spicy edge. Has a nice, creamy texture, with crisp acids. Easy-drinking wine with lots of charm. **87** —S.H. (2/1/2004)

Montona 2002 Chardonnay (Napa Valley) $30. Winemaker bells and whistles, such as smoky oak and creamy lees, star in this earthy wine, which has been re-released after two years. It doesn't seem at all old. There's enough peach and apple flavor to make it balanced. **88** —*S.H. (12/1/2005)*

Montona 2001 Merlot (Napa Valley) $40. Like Montona's 2000 Cab, this wine also has been re-released since its debut in 2003, and it, too, has gone downhill. The wine is losing fruit and picking up harsh acidity, although it's still drinkable. **83** —*S.H. (12/1/2005)*

Montona 2001 Merlot (Napa Valley) $40. There's much to praise in this deeply colored, densely structured wine. It's built for the cellar, with its impressively ripe, sweet tannins and crisp acids that frame plum, blackberry, cassis, and chocolate flavors. Yet it's delicious straight out of the bottle, and will be great with lamb. Drink now through 2010. **92** —*S.H. (5/1/2004)*

MONTPELLIER

Montpellier 2003 Merlot (California) $7. There sure is a lot of fruity concentration in this wine. It fills the mouth with black cherry, blackberry, and red plum flavors, with a rich chocolate and coffee note. It's also very dry and balanced, although a little soft and thin on the finish. **84 Best Buy** —*S.H. (12/1/2005)*

Montpellier 2001 Merlot (California) $7. You'll be surprised how much richness there is here. Oodles of sweet black cherry fruit, with a hint of oak, and it's all dry and crisp. Thank the grape glut for this incredible value. **86** —*S.H. (9/1/2004)*

Montpellier 1997 Pinot Noir (California) $8. 83 *(5/1/2000)*

Montpellier 1999 Pinot Noir (California) $8. Wintergreen, toast, and a bit of buttered popcorn are the primary aromas, followed by a palate of chocolatey oak and modest red fruit. The finish is woody and drying. **83** *(10/1/2002)*

Montpellier 2003 Syrah (California) $7. Reviewers detected a host of aromas: blueberry confiture, bacon, even floral notes. The medium-weight palate deals blueberry and cassis. Finishes short. **84 Best Buy** *(9/1/2005)*

Montpellier 1999 Syrah (California) $7. Starts with modest cherry-berry fruit aromas with some cedar and vanilla notes that turn almost caramel-like with air. This is a light, tart Syrah that has enough juicy fruit flavors to carry the sweet oak and still finish fruity, with a slight peppery tang. **86 Best Buy** *(10/1/2001)*

Montpellier 2002 Viognier (California) $7. Rather sweet for a table wine, but some people will like the sugary peach, honeysuckle, and vanilla flavors. Has some nice acids on the finish. **83** —*S.H. (10/1/2004)*

MOON MOUNTAIN VINEYARD

Moon Mountain Vineyard 2000 Cabernet Franc (Sonoma Valley) $30. The essence of black cherries is the taste that floods the palate, with rich overlays of oak. There are sturdy tannins yet they are gentle, making the wine immediately enjoyable. This is a firm, full-bodied red wine that will be delicious with lamb or steak. **90** —*S.H. (5/1/2004)*

Moon Mountain Vineyard 2003 Cabernet Sauvignon (Sonoma County) $16. This is a yummy Cab, gentle in the mouth, insistent in flavor, and rich and balanced. There's a rich herb edge to the blackberry flavors, and the finish is dry, with a dusting of tannins that a good steak will cut right through. **89** —*S.H. (4/1/2006)*

Moon Mountain Vineyard 2002 Reserve Cabernet Sauvignon (Sonoma Valley) $35. This mountain wine is thick in dusty tannins, and too young to fully enjoy now. But it's a guaranteed ager, with its balance of acids and deep, delicious core of black currant, black cherry, cola, and cocoa flavors. It has that extra edge of complexity that makes for a great Cabernet. Drink after 2007. **92 Cellar Selection** —*S.H. (4/1/2006)*

Moon Mountain Vineyard 2001 Reserve Cabernet Sauvignon (Sonoma Valley) $30. A little unripe, with leafy, almost vegetal aromas that turn tough and tannic in the mouth. Dry, too. It's an austere wine, probably not going anywhere. **84** —*S.H. (10/1/2005)*

Moon Mountain Vineyard 2000 Reserve Cabernet Sauvignon (Sonoma Valley) $40. Starts off with pretty black currant and black cherry flavors, and a lush overlay of oak. Fills the mouth with fruit, and then it suddenly turns tough and dry from those stubborn, hard mountain tannins. May age out. **86** —*S.H. (5/1/2004)*

Moon Mountain Vineyard 2004 Chardonnay (Sonoma County) $13. What's likeable about this wine is that it doesn't go for the cheap thrills of super-ripe fruit and form of oak flavoring so common in Chards of this price. What you get is a dry, minerally wine, with a firm spine and just enough peach and oak to make it rich and complex. **88 Best Buy** —*S.H. (4/1/2006)*

Moon Mountain Vineyard 2004 Sauvignon Blanc (Sonoma County) $13. This is a refreshingly crisp, fruity wine that's rich in citrus, fig, and apple flavors. It's not exactly dry, leaving a sweet finish that suggests pairing with broiled fish or chicken topped with a fruity salsa. **85** —*S.H. (3/1/2006)*

Moon Mountain Vineyard 2003 Vadasz Vineyard Sauvignon Blanc (Sonoma Valley) $20. The label points out that this is barrel fermented, but a sniff and sip will tell you that much. The nose pumps petrol at first and then plenty of smoky wood. In the mouth, it's immensely round and chewy, with vanilla, coconut, banana, and peach flavors. Broad but zesty enough, which allows the heavy toast element to work. **87** *(7/1/2005)*

Moon Mountain Vineyard 2002 Vadasz Vineyard Sauvignon Blanc (Sonoma Valley) $20. This single-vineyard release is richer than the winery's Reserve, but it stays true to the house style, which is a citrusy grassiness and extreme dryness. The flavors veer toward grapefruit juice, fig, and melon, with creamier notes from oak barrels. Has sharp acidity. **87** —*S.H. (5/1/2004)*

Moon Mountain Vineyard 2002 Reserve Sémillon-Sauvignon Blanc (Edna Valley) $16. A little Sémillon can't quite cover up the extremely grassy, cat pee aromas of this tart, citrusy wine. As you'd expect, it's super dry, and high in acidity. It will have a place with goat cheese, which will coax out sweetness. **84** —*S.H. (5/1/2004)*

Moon Mountain Vineyard 2002 Monte Rosso Zinfandel (Sonoma Valley) $30. From this famous old mountain vineyard, a dense and concentrated Zin that blows you away with deliciousness. It's very dark and young, with a flair of acidity and sweet tannins, and blackberry, cassis, and mocha flavors that finish with a superripe raisiny note. But that slight Portiness is a seasoning element, and does not distract. **92** —*S.H. (6/1/2004)*

MOOREWOOD

Moorewood 2001 Syrah (Monterey County) $19. Deliciously smooth and full-bodied, this big red wine is plump with flavors of plums, cherries, mocha, tangerine rind, and spicy oak. Although it's fully dry, it tastes sweet in ripe fruit. The tannins are rich and smooth. Could use more concentration, but it's really a good wine. From Testarossa. **90 Editors' Choice** —*S.H. (6/1/2004)*

MORGAN

Morgan 1998 Chardonnay (Monterey County) $20. 87 *(6/1/2000)*

Morgan 2004 Chardonnay (Monterey) $20. Morgan's basic Chardonnay, rushed to market, shows the same vibrant acids and whistle clean mouthfeel in his more expensive bottlings. The flavors are of passion fruit, pineapple juice, and lime zest, with a steely, stony minerality that finishes ultra-dry. **87** —*S.H. (12/31/2005)*

Morgan 2003 Chardonnay (Monterey) $20. Displays all the flair of Monterey's terroir, with tropical fruit flavors and crisp, bright acidity that makes even this rich wine finish clean. Oak adds just the right touch of charry vanilla. **90** —*S.H. (11/15/2005)*

Morgan 2002 Chardonnay (Monterey) $20. A lean, streamlined wine with weak citrus and peach flavors and lots of lees. It's absolutely dry. **84** —*S.H. (12/15/2004)*

Morgan 2000 Chardonnay (Monterey) $20. Peach, melon, citrus, and spice leave a bright and attractive finish here. Honeyed, toasty notes wrap it up. **88** —*J.M. (5/1/2002)*

Morgan 1999 Chardonnay (Monterey) $20. Monterey veteran Dan Lee hits the bullseye with this rich, ripe, leesy wine that drinks fancy and elegant. The peach and tropical fruit flavors are very concentrated and intense, wrapped in a creamy texture, and the finish is long and spicy. **89** —*S.H. (11/15/2001)*

USA

Morgan 2001 Barrel Fermented Chardonnay (Monterey) $20. High acidity adds a metallic, mineral firmness to the peach and pear flavors, while oak and lees contribute softer, creamy notes. This sleek wine is vibrant and perky through the spicy finish. **90 Editors' Choice** —*S.H. (2/1/2004)*

Morgan 2004 Double L Vineyard Chardonnay (Santa Lucia Highlands) $35. Call it Chablisian for its high acidity and dry minerality, with suggestions of herbs and mushrooms that create a deep undertow to the brighter peach and pineapple flavors. This is a powerful, very complex wine, easily able to handle its share of new French oak. **92** —*S.H. (4/1/2006)*

Morgan 2003 Double L Vineyard Chardonnay (Santa Lucia Highlands) $35. This single-vineyard Chardonnay impresses for its taut structure and promise of aging. It's totally dry, and beneath that slate and metal is a core of ripe yellow peach. Fans of blowsy Chards will find it spare, but if you like Chablis, you'll love the complex, stony minerality. Hold until 2007. **91 Cellar Selection** —*S.H. (12/15/2005)*

Morgan 2002 Double L Vineyard Chardonnay (Santa Lucia Highlands) $34. A wonderful Chard. Don't chill it too much or you'll miss the interplay of ripe tropical fruits, oak, creamy lees, butterscotch, and oriental spices. Bright in citrusy acids and elegant, it will be great alone, or try with something hedonistic, like broiled lobster with melted butter. **92 Editors' Choice** —*S.H. (3/1/2005)*

Morgan 2001 Double L Vineyard Chardonnay (Santa Lucia Highlands) $30. From the same appellation as Morgan's Rosella's bottling, but very different, a leaner, crisper wine, although equally fine. Marked by high acids and citrusy flavors, it's been enriched with oak and lots of lees. A bit tight now; may be an ager. **90** —*S.H. (2/1/2004)*

Morgan 2004 Double L Vineyard Hat Trick Chardonnay (Santa Lucia Highlands) $65. Acidity and minerals are the hallmarks of this exciting Chardonnay. Of course, you'll find the ripe tropical fruit and new oak and lees of other Chardonnays, but it's really that tanginess that attracts. Currently the wine shows primary flavors of mangoes and papayas, but it would not surprise me if it ages well beyond five years. **95 Editors' Choice** —*S.H. (12/1/2006)*

Morgan 2000 Double L Vineyard Chardonnay (Santa Lucia Highlands) $36. A bit oily textured, with bright lemon and herb notes that add some balance. Citrus is at the core of this wine, which finishes fresh. **88** —*J.M. (12/15/2002)*

Morgan 2003 Hat Trick Double L Vineyard Chardonnay (Santa Lucia Highlands) $50. This is a best-of selection from this vineyard. It's a concentrated version of the regular Double L bottling. Completely dry, filled with stony minerals smothering ripe yellow peach flavors, it's an immature wine that calls to mind grand cru Chablis. Should develop well through 2008 and possibly beyond. **92** —*S.H. (12/15/2005)*

Morgan 2002 Hat Trick Double L Vineyard Chardonnay (Santa Lucia Highlands) $50. This low production barrel selection from Morgan's Double L Vineyard is one of the best Chards of the vintage. Has everything Double L has, but more. Fabulous weight and density, and tiers of flavors ranging from pineapples through peaches, crème brûlée and butterscotch. Fat, almost meaty, yet dry, elegant, and refined. **96 Editors' Choice** —*S.H. (5/1/2005)*

Morgan 2005 Metallico Chardonnay (Monterey) $20. Morgan has hit its stride with this unoaked Chardonnay. Nothing comes between the intense citrus, pineapple, white peach, apple, and spice flavors and your palate. Cleansing acidity boosts it all and makes the wine star-bright. Morgan leads the pack of California unoaked Chards. **90** —*S.H. (11/15/2006)*

Morgan 2004 Metallico Chardonnay (Monterey) $20. I have enjoyed this unoaked Chard since Morgan started producing it. Made largely from the same fruit as the winery's more expensive bottlings, the wine exhibits bright, crisp Santa Lucia acidity, and lime, Meyer lemon, and papaya flavors. It's compellingly drinkable. **90** —*S.H. (11/15/2005)*

Morgan 2003 Metallico Chardonnay (Santa Lucia Highlands) $20. This will be an education for those who have never tried a totally unoaked Chardonnay made from really good grapes. You get to taste the pure flavors of pineapple, peach, and spice that mark this appellation, as well as the zesty cut of acidity. **86** —*S.H. (12/1/2004)*

Morgan 2002 Metallico Chardonnay (Santa Lucia Highlands) $20. Too sweet. It is unoaked, and captures the ripe, tropical fruit flavors of this appellation, but even the aroma smells like honey. Consumers have a right to expect Chardonnay to be dry, and this isn't. **83** —*S.H. (12/1/2003)*

Morgan 2001 Metallico Chardonnay (Santa Lucia Highlands) $20. Serves up a pleasingly fruity blend of peach, melon, pear, apple, spice, and herb flavors. The confusing "Metallico" designation refers to steel tanks—the wine sees no oak. The finish is equally fruit highlighted, almost sweet. **87** —*S.H. (12/15/2002)*

Morgan 1999 Reserve Chardonnay (Monterey) $30. Slightly odd-scented nose with hints of pipe tobacco, grapefruit, green apple, and herbs. Better on the palate with green pear, faint apple, pineapple, and herbal notes in a tart, lean framework. Pleasant hints of oak show up on the finish. **86** *(7/1/2001)*

Morgan 1998 Reserve Chardonnay (Monterey) $30. 90 *(6/1/2000)*

Morgan 2004 Rosella's Vineyard Chardonnay (Santa Lucia Highlands) $35. I liked Morgan's Double L Chard for its Chablis-like character. This wine is more so. It's drier, more acidic, and more elegant, but there's nothing lean about the power of its core of tropical fruit, which detonates on the palate and doesn't stop. There's fascination with every sip, as the wine slowly changes in the glass. This is a great wine and showcases the infinite possibilities of this appellation. **95 Editors' Choice** —*S.H. (4/1/2006)*

Morgan 2003 Rosella's Vineyard Chardonnay (Santa Lucia Highlands) $35. You can smell the minerals in this tight, compelling wine. It has an aroma suggesting cold metal, even a touch of diesel, floating above the guava, pineapple, nectarine, and peach flavors. Smoky oak and zesty acidity help make this Chard very complex and satisfying. **91** —*S.H. (12/15/2005)*

Morgan 2001 Rosella's Vineyard Chardonnay (Santa Lucia Highlands) $34. Tropical fruit flavors explode in honeyed richness, thrilling the palate with sweet mango and nectarine, but beautiful acidity makes it crisp and clean. Loads of oak, too. Defines this cool-climate appellation for Chardonnay in its pinpoint balance of acid to fruit. **91** —*S.H. (2/1/2004)*

Morgan 2000 Rosella's Vineyard Chardonnay (Santa Lucia Highlands) $34. While the fruit is fairly elegant, offering pretty pear, citrus, and herb flavors, the oak is a little on the woody side, causing the fruit to pull up a tad short. Medium bodied and crisp on the finish. **88** —*J.M. (12/15/2002)*

Morgan 2002 Rosella's Vineyard Chardonnay (Santa Lucia Highlands) $34. So ripe, yet so crisp in acids, a Chard that showcases the Burgundian climate of its appellation. Oozes bright, pure, spicy tropical fruit and mineral flavors that are totally dry. Oak and lees contribute buttered toast, vanilla, and a chewy creaminess. **91** —*S.H. (3/1/2005)*

Morgan 1998 Pinot Gris (Monterey) $18. 87 —*M.S. (3/1/2000)*

Morgan 2005 R&D Franscioni Vineyard Pinot Gris (Santa Lucia Highlands) $16. This brilliant PG has just a bit of older French oak on it, which adds softening cream, but the wine would be great even without it. The flavors of citrus zest, grapefruit sorbet, melons, and figs are enormously rich and strong, and perfectly balanced by crisp acidity and a vibrant minerality leading to a dry, clean finish. What a great price for a wine of this stature. **91 Editors' Choice** —*S.H. (11/15/2006)*

Morgan 2004 R&D Franscioni Vineyard Pinot Gris (Santa Lucia Highlands) $16. I find most California Pinot Gris, or Grigio, simple, soft, and semi-sweet. This commendable wine by contrast is brilliantly structured, with keen acids boosting Key lime, sweet thyme and vanilla flavors. It's easily among the best of its genre. **88** —*S.H. (11/15/2005)*

Morgan 2003 R&D Franscioni Vineyard Pinot Gris (Santa Lucia Highlands) $16. This refreshing wine has pretty flavors of peaches, apples, all sorts of garden fruits and even flowers. It drinks just a tad sweet, and is balanced with rich acids. **85** —*S.H. (11/15/2004)*

Morgan 2002 R&D Franscioni Vineyard Pinot Gris (Santa Lucia Highlands) $16. Offers crisp acids and good structure, which only nature can provide. Flavors range from citrus and apples through ripe peach. Its major flaw is that it's so sweet, it's like a dessert wine. If it were dry, it would be gorgeous. **84** —*S.H. (12/1/2003)*

Morgan 2001 R&D Franscioni Vineyards Pinot Gris (Santa Lucia Highlands) $15. A little soft and simple. The spearmint flavors are long and spicy, and finish with a sugary sweetness that's like lemonade. It's not a bad little wine, nice for summertime sipping. Try with fresh fruit. **84** —*S.H. (9/1/2003)*

Morgan 1997 Pinot Noir (Monterey County) $20. 84 *(11/15/1999)*

Morgan 2001 Pinot Noir (Santa Lucia Highlands) $22. Pinot Noir from this newish appellation is taking on a profile, and it's one of extreme fruitiness combined with fresh acidity. This wine is filled with the flavors of cherries and raspberries, and has been generously oaked. It's crisp and dry and easy to like. **87** —*S.H. (4/1/2004)*

Morgan 2000 Pinot Noir (Santa Lucia Highlands) $22. Textbook Central Coast Pinot, with cherry flavors veering toward tobacco, crushed hard spices, coffee, and cola. Great acid-tannin balance makes for a wonderful mouthfeel, firm and authoritative. Layered, complex, and vibrant. **90 Editors' Choice** —*S.H. (2/1/2003)*

Morgan 1999 Pinot Noir (Santa Lucia Highlands) $38. Bright cherry and spice flavors dominate, followed by racy cinnamon, tea, and pepper notes. Moderate body and silky texture. **88** —*J.M. (12/15/2001)*

Morgan 1999 Pinot Noir (Monterey) $24. Classic Central Coast Pinot, with strawberry-daiquiri, smoke, tomato, exotic hard-spice, and sautéed mushrooms aromas leading to intense, nervy raspberry flavors. Chilly nights provide crisp acidity. Drink now and over the next few years. **88** —*S.H. (12/15/2001)*

Morgan 1998 Pinot Noir (Monterey County) $21. 88 —*M.S. (5/1/2000)*

Morgan 2004 Double L Vineyard Pinot Noir (Santa Lucia Highlands) $55. This is from Dan Morgan Lee's own vineyard. It's in the coolest northwest part of the appellation, near its boundary, and is more acidic and elegant than his purchased Pinots further south. The 2004 vintage was blazingly hot, and the grapes loved it. Big in cherry, cola, leather, and spice flavors, it's a wine to savor. Best now through 2008. **93** —*S.H. (8/1/2006)*

Morgan 2003 Double L Vineyard Pinot Noir (Santa Lucia Highlands) $50. Morgan has released three single-vineyard '03 Pinots, and it's hard, fun work choosing the best. For me, it's the Double L. It's a firm, fairly tannic and dry wine, rich, balanced and intricately structured. Combines the taste of cherries, blackberries, and coffee with smoky oak to offer intensely complex pleasure now. Should develop well over several years. **94 Editors' Choice** —*S.H. (12/15/2005)*

Morgan 2002 Double L Vineyard Pinot Noir (Santa Lucia Highlands) $45. The hardest of Morgan's trio of Pinots, bright in citrusy acidity and dusty tannins, and better able to cut through a serious rack of lamb. Features black cherry, raspberry, vanilla, and smoke notes with herbs, such as rosemary and thyme. Juicy and delicious, and probably at its best now. **92** —*S.H. (3/1/2005)*

Morgan 2001 Double L Vineyard Pinot Noir (Santa Lucia Highlands) $42. There's a wealth of extracted fruit here that astonishes for its sweet ripeness, strength, and complexity. Cherries and raspberries star, along with coffee, mocha, and all sorts of Asian spices. All this flavor is wrapped in a silky, crisp wine with a lilting, airy texture. **92** —*S.H. (8/1/2004)*

Morgan 2000 Double L Vineyard Pinot Noir (Santa Lucia Highlands) $42. Excellent Pinot, not just for its exquisite flavors but for the layers of complexity. Has everything you look for in California Pinot, tons of berry-cherry, earth, tobacco, and spicy herb flavors and a silky texture that caresses the palate. Young and fruity now, this fine wine will develop additional nuances with age. **92 Cellar Selection** —*S.H. (7/1/2003)*

Morgan 2004 Garys' Vineyard Pinot Noir (Santa Lucia Highlands) $50. The color is fairly light, a lovely translucent ruby, so the weight of this wine comes as something of a surprise. Boasts big flavors: ripe black cherry, and tart, concentrated cola, and vanilla flavors enhanced with smoky, spicy oak. Yet the wine is nicely dry, and offset by acidity. Drink now and through 2010. **92** —*S.H. (8/1/2006)*

Morgan 2003 Garys' Vineyard Pinot Noir (Santa Lucia Highlands) $45. Compared to Double L, Garys' is a shade more obvious, but that's a royal comparison. This is a terrific wine in its own right, rich and fruity, wonderfully oaked, complex, and totally satisfying in a Pinotesque way.

It's a firm, masculine, elegant wine, with beautiful acidity, and should hold well for a number of years. **93 Editors' Choice** —*S.H. (12/15/2005)*

Morgan 2002 Garys' Vineyard Pinot Noir (Santa Lucia Highlands) $38. This is the softest of Morgan's current Pinots, and also the palest. It's jammy with cherry Lifesaver, French roast coffee, and cola flavors, and is dry. Finished with an edge of dusty tannins, it will nicely complement a juicy steak. **89** —*S.H. (3/1/2005)*

Morgan 2001 Garys' Vineyard Pinot Noir (Santa Lucia Highlands) $35. Everybody wants grapes from this vineyard for its fabulous terroir, which usually yields wines of impeccable balance and lushness. This wine is light and delicate in structure, with beautifully firm acids and sweetly complex flavors of cherry pie, mocha, and vanilla. It's a pleasure to sip. **93** —*S.H. (8/1/2004)*

Morgan 2000 Garys' Vineyard Pinot Noir (Santa Lucia Highlands) $38. Rich and complex, with an amazing array of flavors. Cherries, blackberries, spices, tobacco, soy, spicy cola, and smoky oak are framed in luxuriously smooth, silky tannins and crisp acids. It will probably develop with a year or two of age. **91** —*S.H. (7/1/2003)*

Morgan 1999 Reserve Pinot Noir (Santa Lucia Highlands) $38. Start with South Central coast aromas of tomato, rhubarb, hard spices, tea, and blackberries, with oaky complexities. These notes follow in the mouth, with blackberry and cherry flavors. The tannins pack a solid punch, but not so much that you can't drink it tonight. **89** —*S.H. (12/15/2001)*

Morgan 2004 Rosella's Vineyard Pinot Noir (Santa Lucia Highlands) $50. Dry, elegantly silky, and bright in acidity, this single vineyard Pinot showcases the appellation's ability to ripen Pinot grapes to a hugeness that somehow stays varietally balanced. The red and black cherry, cola, rhubarb pie and pomegranate flavors are wrapped in a classic tannic-acid structure that's compellingly drinkable. **93** —*S.H. (8/1/2006)*

Morgan 2003 Rosella's Vineyard Pinot Noir (Santa Lucia Highlands) $45. This is the least of Morgan's lineup. Its chief fault is deficient acidity or crispness. It feels soft and melted in the mouth, but its lovely cherry, coffee, and cola flavors are very nice. Would benefit enormously from more structure. **86** —*S.H. (12/15/2005)*

Morgan 2002 Rosella's Vineyard Pinot Noir (Santa Lucia Highlands) $38. Totally aromatic, with cherry, vanilla, spice, cola, gingerbread, and smoky scents leaping out of the glass. It's no less flavorful. Deliciously sippible and dry, with a polished, silky mouthfeel and a crisp finish. **91** —*S.H. (3/1/2005)*

Morgan 2001 Rosella's Vineyard Pinot Noir (Santa Lucia Highlands) $35. A gorgeous wine, sumptuous and compelling. Hits all the right notes, with its silky smooth mouthfeel, dusting of fine tannins, restrained oak, and polished cherry, raspberry, cola, and rosehip flavors. The finish is long, clean, and spicy. **91** —*S.H. (8/1/2004)*

Morgan 2000 Rosella's Vineyard Pinot Noir (Santa Lucia Highlands) $38. A rich and complex Pinot that will need short-term cellaring. Brimming with flavors ranging from blackberries and cherries to earth, tobacco, sun-dried tomato, and Oriental spices. Perfect tannins and acids make a lush, intriguing texture. **91** —*S.H. (7/1/2003)*

Morgan 2004 Twelve Clones Pinot Noir (Santa Lucia Highlands) $30. What I like about Morgan's Pinots is that they avoid the muscularity of certain Santa Lucia Pinots while retaining a ripe opulence. This is a big wine, wealthy in sweet black cherry fruit, but there's real elegance in the high acidity and silky mouthfeel. Best now through 2008. **91** —*S.H. (4/1/2006)*

Morgan 2003 Twelve Clones Pinot Noir (Santa Lucia Highlands) $25. Not in the same league as Morgan's finest, this is still a fine interpretation. Dry, tart in acids, and well-oaked, with a silky texture and cherry and cola flavors veering into riper blackberries, it's a classic Santa Lucia Pinot, at a relatively affordable price. **87** —*S.H. (11/15/2005)*

Morgan 2002 Twelve Clones Pinot Noir (Santa Lucia Highlands) $22. Very ripe and intense in cherry and blackberry fruit, with nuances of beet and tomato and a lavish overlay of smoky oak and vanilla. Drinks fully dry, with some astringent tannins that provide good grip. Finishes with a velvety, fruit-driven aftertaste. **87** *(11/1/2004)*

Morgan 2001 Cotes du Crow's Red Blend (Monterey) $13. A fine Rhône style wine, dry and stylish. It has cherry, coffee, and herb flavors offset by good acids and smooth, dynamic tannins. A blend of Syrah and Grenache. **85** —S.H. (3/1/2004)

Morgan 2004 Cotes du Crow's Rhône Red Blend (Monterey) $18. This is a southern Rhône blend of Grenache and Syrah. It has some new oak and is very ripe, with explosive cherry pie and vanilla spice flavors. It seems to have noticeable residual sugar, making it almost a dessert wine. **84** —S.H. (12/15/2006)

Morgan 2003 Cotes du Crow's Rhône Red Blend (Monterey) $22. Some Rhône blends burst with fruit. This one has cherries, but it's an understated, elegant wine, dry and earthy-herbal, with dusty tannins. This blend of Grenache and Syrah has complexity and style. **89 Best Buy** —S.H. (11/15/2005)

Morgan 2000 Cotes du Crow's Rhône Red Blend (California) $14. A Grenache-Syrah-Petite Sirah blend from a warmer part of the county. Cool nights yield good acids, but the wine isn't fully ripened. You can taste green, stalky flavors alongside the red cherry ones. The mouthfeel is a bit rough. Still, it's not without interest. **86** —S.H. (9/1/2002)

Morgan 1998 Sauvignon Blanc (California) $12. 88 —M.S. (11/15/1999)

Morgan 2005 Sauvignon Blanc (Monterey) $16. Crisp in acidity, this ultra-clean wine shows upfront Meyer lemon and pineapple sorbet, fig, and melon flavors. Oak, some of it new, adds subtle nuances of vanilla and cream. Would score higher except for a bit too much cat pee, an aroma increasingly disagreeable to me. **85** —S.H. (12/1/2006)

Morgan 2004 Sauvignon Blanc (Monterey) $15. The same acidity that permeates all of Morgan's white wines is present here, along with citrus, kiwi, tobacco leaf, and white pepper flavors. The wine is searingly dry, but there's a rich creaminess that softens and elevates it. **87** —S.H. (12/31/2005)

Morgan 2003 Sauvignon Blanc (Monterey) $14. I don't know if this is the Musque clone, but it's all about gooseberries and bright Meyer lemon and lime flavors with mouth-searing acidity. Powerful finish, intensely clean, and a natural for food. Try with a salad of endive, pink grapefruit, and sautéed scallops. **89 Best Buy** —S.H. (11/15/2005)

Morgan 2002 Sauvignon Blanc (Monterey County) $14. Fresh and bright on the nose, with pretty gooseberry and citrus aromas. Crisp on the palate, the wine shows a blend of lemon, herb, and mineral flavors, finishing clean at the end, with moderate length. **87** —J.M. (10/1/2004)

Morgan 2001 Sauvignon Blanc (Monterey) $14. This is an extremely grassy wine. It suggests hay, straw, and juniper berry, with riper notes of honeydew and cantaloupe. It's very dry and tartly crisp. Lots of new, charry oak adds complexity and softening, and the wine has an interesting finish. **88** —S.H. (3/1/2003)

Morgan 2000 Sauvignon Blanc (California) $15. Aggressive stuff here, not for the faint-hearted. Begins with big, brawny aromas of citrus, grass, hay, and gooseberry, with a hint of honey. The flavors are also big and assertive, with lemon, grapefruit, and tangerine. It's very dry and very crisp, with acidity that's on the high side. **85** —S.H. (11/15/2001)

Morgan 1997 Syrah (Monterey) $15. 87 —S.H. (6/1/1999)

Morgan 2003 Syrah (Monterey) $22. I had this wine after tasting good Cornas and St. Joseph, and it has nothing to be ashamed of. Like them, it announces with impressive peppercorn and blackberry aromas, and while it's a bit short in depth and finish, it offers a rich spectrum of dark fruit wrapped in rich, fine tannins. **87** —S.H. (11/15/2006)

Morgan 2002 Syrah (Monterey) $22. On the herbal side, with one taster suggesting the grapes struggled to get ripe, while another admired the wine's balance between pepper, herbs, and berries. Medium-weight, with ample complexity and a dry, spicy finish perfect for steaks and roasts. **87** (9/1/2005)

Morgan 2001 Syrah (Monterey) $22. Grapes from warmer parts of the county lend blackberries and chocolate, while those from cooler ones contribute herbs and acidity. It's a pretty good wine, but there are harsh, twiggy elements and some fierce tannins that are unlikely to wilt with age. **85** —S.H. (12/1/2004)

Morgan 2000 Syrah (Monterey) $20. Big aromas and flavors of blackberry, black pepper, white chocolate, and tobacco, as well as oaky influences. Feels big and lush in the mouth, but the tannins are well-behaved. It's

drinkable now, although it turns a bit harsh on the finish. **87** —S.H. (2/1/2003)

Morgan 2003 Tierra Mar Syrah (Monterey County) $40. Morgan's Tierra Mar bottling has grown interesting over the years, and the '03 continues to spark notice. It's a big wine, with forward cassis, kirsch, and chocolate flavors that are deep and long, with rich but velvety tannins. However, it's a bit soft, so drink now. **87** —S.H. (12/15/2006)

Morgan 2002 Tierra Mar Syrah (Monterey County) $35. Toasty and cedary on the nose, but the oak is more integrated on the palate, where ripe blackberries, plums, and coffee take charge. Nicely balanced, with crisp acids balancing the fruity concentration and supple tannins. **89** (9/1/2005)

Morgan 2001 Tierra Mar Syrah (Santa Lucia Highlands) $35. Stunning concentration and intensity in this Syrah, which is a blend of Rosella's and Paraiso fruit. Offers huge flavors of chocolate, blueberry, cassis, flowers, and minerals. Lush and dense; flatters now, but should soften for some years. **93** —S.H. (7/1/2005)

Morgan 2000 Tierra Mar Syrah (Santa Lucia Highlands) $35. This Syrah goes beyond mere berry-cherry flavors to achieve real richness, depth, and complexity. It also demonstrates the possibilities of this appellation for Syrah. Enormous in the mouth, with endlessly changing fruit, mocha, grilled meat, dried herb, and pepper flavors that are wrapped in fine, soft tannins. Compelling now, but with the stuffing and balance to last through the decade. **94 Editors' Choice** —S.H. (12/1/2003)

Morgan 1999 Tierra Mar Syrah (Monterey) $52. Big in the mouth, though perhaps on the dry side, this Syrah has a smoldering black palate—think black plum, earth, espresso, and licorice. Think that it couldn't get any blacker than that? Add smoke, black-pepper, and toast flavors on the finish to its profile. Cellar for two or three years. **89** (11/1/2001)

MORRISON LANE

Morrison Lane 2003 Barbera (Walla Walla (WA)) $24. A clear winner at Morrison Lane, the Barbera is enhanced with a splash of Carmenère. It carries its beautiful berry flavors into a sharp, tangy, snappy finish. **90** —P.G. (10/1/2006)

Morrison Lane 2003 Cinsault (Walla Walla (WA)) $27. This is a very pretty Pinot Noir color, scented with raspberries and spiced up with a lightly peppery finish. **88** —P.G. (10/1/2006)

Morrison Lane 2003 Counoise (Walla Walla (WA)) $33. Counoise is a surprise winner in Washington, making a deliciously spicy wine with light fruits running from watermelon to strawberry to plum. There's a bit of a hole in the middle, but that's the nature of the grape. **90** —P.G. (10/1/2006)

Morrison Lane 2003 33 1/3 Red Blend (Walla Walla (WA)) $33. This is a three-part blend of Syrah, Counoise, and Viognier, cofermented into a spicy, peppery, citrusy wine. Orange peel and other citrus provide the aromatic highlights, and the fruit has sharp, tart cranberry flavors, with a peppery bite. **90** —P.G. (10/1/2006)

Morrison Lane 2003 Sangiovese (Walla Walla (WA)) $24. Walla Walla is home to quite a few excellent Sangios, but most show a lot of new oak. This puts the pretty strawberry fruit right up front, with plenty of acid and a refreshing finish. **88** —P.G. (10/1/2006)

Morrison Lane 2002 Syrah (Walla Walla (WA)) $NA. Jammy and almost sweet-tasting, with masses of basic blackberry fruit laced with vanilla. Broad and mouthfilling, with a trace of heat on the finish. **86** (9/1/2005)

Morrison Lane 2002 Reserve Syrah (Walla Walla (WA)) $29. Jammy and almost sweet-tasting, with masses of basic blackberry fruit laced with vanilla. Broad and mouthfilling, with a trace of heat on the finish. **86** (9/1/2005)

Morrison Lane 2002 Reserve Syrah (Walla Walla (WA)) $50. From the vineyard's oldest vines (planted 1994) this is the first reserve. Good concentration and Syrah character, dark and peppery, with saturated, fleshy fruit and substantial alcohol—15.9%. **90** —P.G. (11/15/2006)

MOSAIC

Mosaic 2002 Meritage Red Wine Cabernet Blend (Alexander Valley) $40. A little too soft and bland for my taste, although it's nicely dry, with modest alcohol and finely meshed tannins. Tastes surprisingly thin for this excellent Cabernet vintage. **84** —*S.H. (12/15/2006)*

Mosaic 2003 Reserve Cabernet Sauvignon (Alexander Valley) $40. Soft, juicy, and direct, this Cab offers lots of pleasure in its elegant balance of ripe cherry-berry fruit, rich tannins and fine acid-oak integration. It's the kind of Cab made for drinking with food, not worshipping. Should develop well over five years or so. **88** —*S.H. (12/15/2006)*

Mosaic 2004 Chardonnay (Sonoma County) $16. Here's a modest, likeable Chard, a bit soft, with pear, apple, peach, and cream flavors. It's extremely well balanced, and has a satisfyingly long finish. Great with roast chicken or grilled fish with a brown butter sauce. **86** —*S.H. (12/15/2006)*

Mosaic 2002 Reserve Chardonnay (Alexander Valley) $28. At four-plus years, the wine is hanging in there, maintaining fruit and freshness and picking up some aged, dried pineapple and peach character. It's an interesting wine, picking up textural complexities, but needs to be drunk soon. **90** —*S.H. (12/15/2006)*

Mosaic 2004 Malbec (Alexander Valley) $25. If you know those Argentine Malbecs, you know what you're in for. This is a dark, huge, tannic, explosive red wine, with massive blackberry and cherry, cocoa, and sweet leather flavors. It's perfectly dry, but quite a bit softer than those from Argentina. Drink now with barbecued steak. **90** —*S.H. (12/15/2006)*

Mosaic 2002 Merlot (Sonoma County) $20. Here's a nice, everyday sort of Merlot with some extra qualities that make it fine with steaks and chops. It displays firm but finely ground tannins and upfront cherry, coffee, and licorice flavors. **85** —*S.H. (12/15/2006)*

Mosaic 2004 Sauvignon Blanc (Sonoma County) $12. This is a clean and easy Sauvignon Blanc. It's crisp in acidity, with bright, focused lemon, lime, tart green apple, fig, and spicy white melon flavors. A nice sipper at a fair price. **86** —*S.H. (12/15/2006)*

Mosaic 2004 Reserve Sauvignon Blanc (Alexander Valley) $20. Great price for a wine of this complexity and satisfaction. It's dry and crisp in acidity, with a wealth of lemon, lime, and grapefruit citrus flavors and richer notes of peach pie and yellow apricot purée. Almost seems underpriced for what you get. **88** —*S.H. (12/15/2006)*

MOSBY

Mosby 1997 Santa Barbara County Chardonnay (Santa Barbara County) $10. **85** —*S.H. (7/1/1999)*

Mosby 2004 Cortese (Santa Barbara County) $16. Here's something a little different. It's very dry, with interesting tobacco, white pepper, sage, and citrus flavors that have a depth and complexity that makes this wine special. Try as an alternative to Sauvignon Blanc. **88** —*S.H. (5/1/2006)*

Mosby 2003 Cortese (Santa Barbara County) $14. Sort of like a Sauvignon Blanc, this wine has citrusy flavors and is very dry. There's an almond skin bitterness on the finish. Try with clams in a white sauce. **84** —*S.H. (12/1/2005)*

Mosby 2002 Cortese (Santa Barbara County) $14. A simple white wine that opens with flavors of lemon, peach, avocado, and vanilla. The flavors are citrusy, with a soft texture, low in acidity. The finish is very dry and citrusy. **85** —*S.H. (3/1/2004)*

Mosby 2004 Stelline di Cortese Cortese (Santa Barbara County) $16. This is a rough, rustic sparkler, with a jagged mouthfeel that frames dry flavors of bubble gum. **82** —*S.H. (4/1/2006)*

Mosby 2002 Dolcetto (Santa Barbara County) $16. I don't know what California Dolcetto is supposed to taste like, but this likeable wine resembles a light-bodied Zin. It has pleasant berry flavors, is dry, and has silky tannins. **85** —*S.H. (12/1/2005)*

Mosby 2002 La Seduzione Lagrein (California) $26. Very dry, very tannic, not offering much on its own now, but there's a muscle of black cherry fruit that a a long-cooked pork or beef stew could release. Might also age, if you feel like rolling the dice. **86** —*S.H. (10/1/2005)*

Mosby 1994 Rosso di Nebbiolo Nebbiolo (Santa Barbara County) $10. **86** Best Buy —*S.H. (10/1/1999)*

Mosby 1998 Pinot Grigio (Santa Barbara County) $14. **83** —*S.H. (3/1/2000)*

Mosby 1997 Pinot Grigio (Santa Barbara County) $10. **88** Best Buy —*S.H. (10/1/1999)*

Mosby 2005 Pinot Grigio (Santa Barbara) $14. This is easy, zesty, and dry, with high acidity framing mouth-puckering grapefruit, pear, and flowery flavors that finish spicy and clean. **85** —*S.H. (12/1/2006)*

Mosby 2004 Pinot Grigio (Santa Barbara County) $14. Too sweet in sugary flavor, and without the acidity to balance, this wine is cloying, despite some nice citrus, peach, and fig flavors. **82** —*S.H. (2/1/2006)*

Mosby 2003 Pinot Grigio (Santa Barbara County) $14. Fresh and succulent, with ripe flavors of apples, citrus fruits, figs, and spices. Fundamentally dry, with good acids, this is an easy wine to like. **84** —*S.H. (11/15/2004)*

Mosby 2002 Pinot Grigio (Santa Barbara County) $14. Smells earthy and mushroomy, with hints of peaches and wildflowers. Drinks dry and soft, a simple wine with flavors of citrus fruits. Would score higher if it had brighter acidity. The finish is flat. **84** —*S.H. (12/1/2003)*

Mosby 2003 Primitivo (Monterey County) $20. Smells a little funky, and tastes harsh and angular, with gritty tannins and slightly sweet cherry flavors. **82** —*S.H. (12/1/2005)*

Mosby NV Lucca Red Wine Red Blend (California) $10. Hot and rustic, but clean, with earth, coffee, and berry flavors and strong tannins. Drink this dry, tart wine with simple picnic foods, like pizza and cheeseburgers. **83** —*S.H. (10/1/2006)*

Mosby 2001 Roc Michel Red Blend (Monterey County) $18. Smells baked, and is heavy and chocolatey in the mouth. Finishes oaky. Syrah and Mourvèdre. **82** —*S.H. (3/1/2005)*

Mosby 2000 Roc Michel Fremir Rhône Red Blend (Monterey County) $18. A Rhône blend marked by baked, earthy aromas of blackberry tart and coffee, and dry flavors of blackberries. There is a very distinctive taste of chocolatey cassis that persists through the finish, and is very strong, although it is dry. Acids are soft, but the tannins are strong and persistant. A blend of Syrah and Mourvèdre. **87** —*S.H. (3/1/2004)*

Mosby 1995 Sangiovese (Santa Barbara County) $16. **90** —*S.H. (10/1/1999)*

Mosby 2003 Sangiovese (Santa Barbara County) $22. Hot and harsh in texture, this rustic wine shows espresso and blackberry flavors, and is dry, with gritty tannins. **82** —*S.H. (12/1/2005)*

Mosby 2005 Rosato di Sangiovese (Santa Barbara County) $18. Dry and crisp, with raspberry, strawberry, and vanilla flavors in front of a spicy finish. Picks up interest as it goes along, and makes you think how versatile it might be with a wide range of food. **86** —*S.H. (12/1/2006)*

Mosby 2004 Rosato di Sangiovese Sangiovese (Santa Barbara County) $14. Here's a nice blush wine. It's got a pretty salmon color and intense flavors of raspberries and cherries, and is dry. For something offbeat, try with sushi. **85** —*S.H. (10/1/2005)*

Mosby 1996 Vigna della Casa Vecchia Sangiovese (Santa Barbara County) $18. **88** —*S.H. (12/15/1999)*

Mosby 2004 Teroldego (Santa Barbara County) $26. This is a dry, heavy wine, with coffee and tobacco flavors and a hint of cherry. It's very high acid, with an unrelieved bitterness. **81** —*S.H. (4/1/2006)*

Mosby 2003 Teroldego (Santa Barbara County) $26. I don't know what California Teroldego is supposed to be, but this one is dark, full-bodied, dry, tannic, and nicely balanced. It has cherry and blackberry flavors and could age out a bit. **86** —*S.H. (10/1/2005)*

Mosby 2002 Teroldego (Santa Barbara County) $24. Thick and cloying, with the texture and flavor of cherry cough syrup. **82** —*S.H. (3/1/2005)*

Mosby 2005 Traminer (Santa Barbara County) $18. Pretty much a basic Gewürz, but the flavors are on the thin, watery side. Yet this wine is clean and dry. If only it had greater fruity concentration. **82** —*S.H. (10/1/2006)*

Mosby 2004 Traminer (Santa Barbara County) $18. There's scads of fruit and flowers in this wine. Spices, too. It has a rustic, unbalanced astringency, though. **82** —*S.H. (12/1/2005)*

Mosby 2003 Traminer (Santa Barbara County) $16. Very Gewürzty with its spice-accented flavors of lush fruits and wildflowers. It's a dry wine, but almost sweet with ripe honey. Finishes bracing and clean. **85** —*S.H.* *(12/1/2004)*

Mosby 2002 Traminer (Santa Barbara County) $16. Wildflowers, peaches, tart green apples, and opulent oriental spices come together in this richly fruity but very dry wine. The most notable thing about it is the acidity, which is fresh and peppery. Try with Chinese food or salty meats. **86** — *S.H. (2/1/2004)*

MOSHIN

Moshin 2004 Clone 115 Pinot Noir (Russian River Valley) $45. Dry, earthy, and not showing a lot now, this closed wine needs decanting or a bit of bottle age to open up. Presently. a cloud of tannins is hiding ripe cherry, cola and tobacco flavors. Hard to predict where it will end up, but the structure suggests a year or two in the cellar. **87** —*S.H. (12/1/2006)*

MOTIF

Motif NV Classic Champagne Blend (California) $8. The candied aromas here smell like fruity Jello, with a dusting of cocoa. Drinks the same way, with fairly sweet, fruit, chocolate, and vanilla flavors. It's clean and very easy drinking. **83** —*S.H. (6/1/2001)*

MOUNT AUKUM

Mount Aukum 2003 Syrah (El Dorado) $16. Dried herbs make for a tea-like, leafy bouquet, while the palate is crowded with syrupy blackberries. It's a bit of a disconnect that may work for some tasters but not for others. **85** *(9/1/2005)*

Mount Aukum 2003 Syrah (Fair Play) $26. A step up in concentration and ripeness from the winery's El Dorado bottling, but maybe not in overall quality, as some of the wine's alcohol is apparent and the leafy notes so attractive to some in the other bottling are absent in this one. Drying tannins on the finish. **85** *(9/1/2005)*

MOUNT EDEN

Mount Eden 2000 Cabernet Sauvignon (Santa Cruz Mountains) $30. Great structure and balance, among the finest in the world, with all the pedigree that terroir brings to Cabernet. But vintage rules. This harvest, the wine is lean in fruit, with a pepper and sage profile. **87** —*S.H. (8/1/2003)*

Mount Eden 2002 Cuvée Saratoga Cabernet Sauvignon (Santa Cruz Mountains) $24. Here's a really ripe Cab that bursts with cherry, black currant, coffee, and cocoa flavors wrapped in smooth tannins. It's a little obvious, but has some real complexity. It's not an ager, though, so drink up. **87** —*S.H. (9/1/2006)*

Mount Eden 2002 Estate Cabernet Sauvignon (Santa Cruz Mountains) $37. A couple of things about this wine are immediately striking: First is the fruit, which is enormously juicy to the point of jamminess, accented by smoky oak. Second is the smooth, supple texture, mainly due to the wonderful tannins. It's a complex, wholesomely dry wine, delicious now but with the structure to last at least a decade. **93 Editors' Choice** —*S.H. (9/1/2006)*

Mount Eden 2001 Estate Cabernet Sauvignon (Santa Cruz Mountains) $35. This ageable wine is young and tannic now, with an astringent finish. Cherry and blackberry stuffing is down there for the long haul. Best after 2010 and beyond. **90** —*S.H. (6/1/2005)*

Mount Eden 2000 Old Vine Reserve Cabernet Sauvignon (Santa Cruz Mountains) $55. Similar in style to the '99, but a touch more accessible. This young, closed-in wine is still pretty tannic, but there's a rich, thick core of sweet cherry and blackberry fruit that bodes well for aging. Possesses the firm structure of a mountain wine. **91** —*S.H. (5/1/2004)*

Mount Eden 1999 Old Vine Reserve Cabernet Sauvignon (Santa Cruz Mountains) $55. Still a baby, and easy to misunderstand, but this is one serious puppy. Youthful tannins and acids frame juvenile, primary fruit flavors of blackberries, and oak has been tastefully applied. But the rich core of fruit, and overall balance, urge longterm aging for a good ten years. **92 Cellar Selection** —*S.H. (8/1/2003)*

Mount Eden 2002 Chardonnay (Santa Cruz Mountains) $35. This winery's Chardonnays are long-lived, but that means they're tight and hard in youth. Even though this one's more than three years old, it's still high in acids and the fruit is locked down under a straitjacket of steel and miner-

als. Best left alone until 2007, and should hold for 10 years afterward. **90** —*S.H. (9/1/2006)*

Mount Eden 2001 Chardonnay (Santa Cruz Mountains) $35. Try this if you're curious what Chardonnay does when it's just starting to develop bottle complexities. The primary fruit is fading, leaving behind dried apricot, quince, and peach flavors with overtones of herbs and clay. The wine is super-dry and remains high in acidity. Should hang in there through this decade. **90** —*S.H. (9/1/2006)*

Mount Eden 2000 Chardonnay (Santa Cruz Mountains) $45. Big, extracted, rich, and bold, a break with the old style that emphasized leanness and acidity for aging. This beauty will satisfy fans of ripe tropical fruit and lots of oak, made in an accessible style. Doesn't seem like a keeper, and best now for several years. **92** —*S.H. (5/1/2004)*

Mount Eden 1999 Chardonnay (Santa Cruz Mountains) $45. Incredible wine, although some may find it overoaked. Dark gold color. Huge, luscious flavors, oozing with tropical fruits, smoky honey, oriental spices, buttered toast, tangerine, vanilla, and crème fraîche. This decadent wine seems thick in the mouth. **94 Editors' Choice** —*S.H. (2/1/2003)*

Mount Eden 1998 Cottonwood Canyon Vineyard Chardonnay (Santa Maria Valley) $18. **90** *(6/1/2000)*

Mount Eden 1998 Mac Gregor Vineyard Chardonnay (Edna Valley) $18. **87** *(6/1/2000)*

Mount Eden 2001 MacGregor Vineyard Chardonnay (Edna Valley) $16. Way too oaky, like sniffing and tasting toothpicks. Somewhere under all that vanilla and smoke is some nice tropical fruit, good acidity and a rich, creamy texture. **85** —*S.H. (5/1/2004)*

Mount Eden 2000 MacGregor Vineyard Chardonnay (Edna Valley) $18. Brilliant, focused flavors of tangerine, white peach, honey, vanilla, lemon zest, and smoke are delicious and complex. Bright acidity adds flair and life, while oak contributes a rich, creamy mouthfeel. The finish is long and intense. **91** —*S.H. (2/1/2003)*

Mount Eden 2001 West Slope Edna Ranch Chardonnay (Edna Valley) $12. Rich, full-throttle Chard, bursting with tropical fruit flavors and gorgeous acidity. Tastes barrel-fermented and leesy, with layers of sweet cream tapering into a spicy finish. **87 Best Buy** —*S.H. (9/1/2003)*

Mount Eden 2003 Wolff Vineyard Chardonnay (Edna Valley) $17. Showing the high, brisk acidity this region is known for, this dry wine has modest peach and pineapple flavors and some smoky oak. Feels like sur lie aging played a part too, to judge by the creaminess. This pleasant sipper gains complexity as it warms in the glass. **86** —*S.H. (8/1/2006)*

Mount Eden 2002 Wolff Vineyard Chardonnay (Edna Valley) $17. An odd wine, with aromas and lean flavors ranging from vegetal to tart citrus fruits, and austerely dry. Clean, but hard to like. **82** —*S.H. (6/1/2005)*

Mount Eden 2002 Pinot Noir (Santa Cruz Mountains) $35. Showing the big, forward, ripe fruit that is currently in favor in California, this Pinot is high in acidity, with a bracing quality despite rich cherry, cola, rhubarb, and mocha flavors and a hint of sautéed mushrooms. It's bone dry, and has a young, sappy quality that suggests midterm aging. Drink now–2010. **91 Cellar Selection** —*S.H. (9/1/2006)*

Mount Eden 2001 Pinot Noir (Santa Cruz Mountains) $35. Doesn't win your heart immediately. It's in your face in acids and tannins. But it is a very fine Pinot worth cellaring. It's rich in spicy, berry flavors, with a silky texture that will only get silkier. Try after 2008. **90** —*S.H. (6/1/2005)*

Mount Eden 1999 Pinot Noir (Santa Cruz Mountains) $45. Given the intense aromas and flavors, it's hard to believe this wine is light and racy. The balanced, complex, and elegant profile shows cinnamon, anise, and soy accents on bright cherry and tart plum fruit. Who needs weight with this much going on? **92 Editors' Choice** *(10/1/2002)*

Mount Eden 2000 Estate Pinot Noir (Santa Cruz Mountains) $45. This tough mountain wine has coffee and tomato aromas and flavors, and bigtime tannins. It's very well oaked, but can't quite come up with the fruit a wine of its size needs. Finishes lean and tannic. **85** —*S.H. (5/1/2004)*

USA

MOUNT PALOMAR

Mount Palomar 1999 Meritage (Temecula) $18. A well-made wine that shows just how good a Bordeaux-style blend can be from this appellation, especially when made in a great vintage. It's dry and balanced and rich, with a touch of smoky oak and refined tannins. Lacks the acid structure of northerly reds, and needs additional complexities, but a big step forward for Temecula. **89** —*S.H. (11/15/2002)*

Mount Palomar 1997 Meritage (Temecula) $16. Well-crafted, with a good, deep color and classic aromas of black currants, cassis, green olives, and a smoky layer of sweetly charred oak. Drinks rich and ripe, with pronounced berry flavors that are wrapped in dry, dusty tannins. Soft acids make it round and supple in the mouth, but limit its ageability. **90** — *S.H. (4/1/2002)*

Mount Palomar NV Limited Reserve Port (California) $28. Real Portuguese Port-style aromas, with chocolate, blackberry, spice, and sweet vanilla aromas, and a fruity depth of flavor that pleases. It's richly sweet, with a velvety texture and the high acids necessary to make things bright and balanced. A very nice bottle of dessert wine, highly recommended. **90** — *S.H. (9/12/2002)*

Mount Palomar 2000 Shorty's Bistro Red Red Blend (Temecula) $12. As the name implies, this is a wine to quaff with munchies, and its only duties are to be red and dry. It fulfills those amply, with dark berry flavors and enough full-bodiedness to stand up to most anything. This blend of Barbera, Cinsault, and Sangiovese is cheerful and honest. **86 Best Buy** —*S.H. (12/1/2002)*

Mount Palomar 2001 Riesling (Temecula) $9. This wine, which smells as if it has been heavily sulfured, has some nice flavors of apples, wildflowers, and apricots, underscored by a honeyed sweetness. But it's very soft and lacks the vivacity to make it come alive on the palate, where it feels tired. **83** —*S.H. (12/31/2003)*

Mount Palomar 1999 Syrah (Temecula) $16. From this Southern California appellation, a spicy, rustic wine that's very dry and full of charm. Flavors of wild berries are strong and tannins are supple. It's not very varietal, but it's a nice, friendly wine. **84** —*S.H. (7/1/2002)*

MOUNT PLEASANT WINERY

Mount Pleasant Winery 2003 Brut Imperial Sparkling Blend (Augusta) $16. A bit on the heavy side, with faint scents of watermelon and cotton candy, but will have its fans for its attractive light coppery-pink color and amiable, off-dry nature. **83** —*J.C. (6/1/2005)*

MOUNT ST. HELENA

Mount St. Helena 2002 Cabernet Sauvignon (Napa Valley) $25. Good, basic Napa Cabernet; well-ripened, with cassis and chocolate flavors and plenty of oak, and tannins that are completely resolved. Finishes a little sweet and simple. **85** —*S.H. (8/1/2005)*

Mount St. Helena 2003 Rose of Charbono (Napa Valley) $16. Sulfury and awkward, with a strawberry-banana taste and a mawkish finish. **81** — *S.H. (11/1/2005)*

Mount St. Helena 2003 Sauvignon Blanc (Napa Valley) $16. This bone-dry, fairly astringent wine does just what Sauvignon is supposed to. It cleanses the palate, stimulates the taste buds, and offers pleasant citrus and melon flavors with a long, minerally finish. From Origin. **88** —*S.H. (10/1/2005)*

Mount St. Helena 2003 Sauvignon Blanc (Napa Valley) $16. Another enormously fruity Sauvignon Blanc, jam-packed with ripe fig, peach, melon, and citrus flavors, with a spicy finish. Simple and likeable. **84** —*S.H. (11/1/2005)*

MOUNT TAMALPAIS

Mount Tamalpais 1999 Merlot (Marin County) $23. Ripe cherry aromas and flavors come to the fore in this pretty wine. It's medium bodied and elegant, displaying firm, ripe tannins and an interesting herbal edge for added complexity. One of the few wines to emerge from Marin County, better known for surfing and mountain biking. A fine first release. **88** — *J.M. (7/1/2002)*

MOUNT VEEDER

Mount Veeder 1995 Reserve Bordeaux Blend (Mount Veeder) $50. 92 *(11/1/1999)*

Mount Veeder 2002 Reserve Cabernet Blend (Napa Valley) $80. The fruit is ripe and delicious, all about cassis, black currants, and creamy cocoa. The tannins are wonderfully lush and ripe. Oak barrels add fine smoke and spice. The problem is a sugary sweetness that hits midpalate and lasts through the finish. **84** —*S.H. (7/1/2006)*

Mount Veeder 2001 Reserve Cabernet Blend (Mount Veeder) $80. This fabulous mountain Cabernet blend is hefty in tannins, but it's so delicious and balanced, it's totally drinkable now. Massive black currant flavors penetrate the palate and last forever on the finish. Oak adds smoky, spicy complexities. Cellar a case of this wine through 2015 or so, opening one bottle a year to experience its evolution. **95 Cellar Selection** —*S.H. (10/1/2005)*

Mount Veeder 2003 Cabernet Sauvignon (Napa Valley) $40. Very good Cab, creamy, dry, and rich. The flavors are super-upfront, all blackberry and cherry pie, chocolate, and charry vanilla oak, with cinnamon spice in the finish. It's a decadent wine, and fortunately has the crisp acidity and firm tannins for balance. Should be easy to find, with 19,000 cases. Best now–2012. **91** —*S.H. (12/15/2006)*

Mount Veeder 2001 Cabernet Sauvignon (Napa Valley) $40. Oaky and ripe; full of blackberry, cherry, and chocolatey fruit, with complex nuances of green olives and sweet, fresh herbs. You can feel the dusty tannins in your gums on the finish, but they're ripe and fine. Showy now, and should age effortlessly through the decade. **91** —*S.H. (10/1/2004)*

Mount Veeder 2000 Cabernet Sauvignon (Napa Valley) $40. Here's a big, tannic wine that's built solid and tight, and showcases mountain origins. Big, big flavors of black currants, toast, vanilla, smoke, and spices carry through on the long finish. Built for ageability. **89** —*S.H. (11/15/2003)*

MOUNTAIN DOME

Mountain Dome NV Brut Champagne Blend (Columbia Valley (OR)) $15. Mountain Dome has won a faithful following in the Northwest by making accessible, broadly flavorful bubbly that comes as close to a fruit bomb as fizz ever does. This is a clean, fresh, and quite tasty effort, two thirds Pinot Noir and one third Chardonnay. **86** —*P.G. (12/31/2004)*

Mountain Dome NV Brut Sparkling Blend (Washington) $16. This lush, fruity blend is two thirds Pinot Noir, one third Chardonnay, and mostly from the 2001 vintage. It is a delicious, every day, méthode champenoise sparkling wine with crisp, fleshy, green apple flavors. Fruit-driven, it's got good punch and persistence, and a clean and refreshing finish. **87** —*P.G. (4/1/2006)*

Mountain Dome 1998 Brut Sparkling Blend (Washington) $20. The vintage Brut is the same blend and receives the same treatment as the NV, but the best barrels are chosen and it gets an extra three years en tirage. Just 300 cases were made of the '98. It is showing mature flavors of toast and buttered pears. Round and creamy, it's got a bold toastiness but retains enough fruit to remain fresh. **88** —*P.G. (4/1/2006)*

Mountain Dome 1997 Brut Sparkling Blend (Washington) $26. This is about two-thirds Pinot and one-third Chardonnay. Very tart and beery, it's a big, simple, fruity style with outsized bubbles. **84** —*P.G. (12/1/2003)*

Mountain Dome NV Brut Rosé Sparkling Blend (Washington) $26. The cuvée is 85% Pinot, 15% Chardonnay. A pretty, salmon-colored blend made with grapes harvested in '94 and '92. As you might expect there is some nice richness to it, showing aged, caramel, roasted flavors. **86** — *P.G. (12/1/2003)*

Mountain Dome NV Cuvée Forté Sparkling Blend (Washington) $30. This is the winery's reserve cuvée, first produced in 1995 and released for the Millennium. It's half Pinot and half Chardonnay, made from the best of the best grapes and vintages. This is just the second release in the winery's two decade history. Though NV, it is based on the very ripe 1998 vintage. The winery's most elegant sparkling wine, it has a fine, textured mouthfeel and nicely nuanced flavors of pear, apple, and light citrus. The over-the-top fruitiness of the regular Brut is tamed, and it has the grace and texture of a genuine Champagne. **90** —*P.G. (4/1/2006)*

USA

Mountain Dome NV Rosé Sparkling Blend (Washington) $24. The rosé is especially nice; with a pretty cherry core of sweet fruit. Basically it is free run (saignée) juice with a smidgen (two percent of still wine added to brighten the color. Barrel aged and fermented; 300 cases produced. **88** —P.G. (4/1/2006)

MOUNTAIN GATE

Mountain Gate NV Red Wine Red Blend (Lodi) $22. Smells like a sugary confection, high in oaky caramel, and turns a little sweet. Sangiovese, Syrah, and Carignan. **83** —S.H. (3/1/2005)

MOUNTAIN VIEW

Mountain View 2004 Chardonnay (Monterey) $7. Showcases the bright acidity and pure tropical fruit flavors of cool-climate Monterey Chards, with a delicious kiwi and lime taste. This is a super price for a wine of this caliber. **85 Best Buy** —S.H. (3/1/2006)

Mountain View 1997 Pinot Noir (California) $8. 83 (11/15/1999)

Mountain View 1996 Zinfandel (California) $7. 82 —J.C. (5/1/2000)

Mountain View 2002 Clockspring Vineyard Zinfandel (Amador County) $10. Not without its flaws, this is nonetheless a decent wine for things like barbecue, when all you need is something clean, dry, and fruity, at a good price. It's a fairly tannic wine, with coffee and cherry flavors and zesty Zinfandel spice. **84** —S.H. (3/1/2006)

MT. VERNON

Mt. Vernon 2000 Cabernet Sauvignon (Sierra Foothills) $28. Lots of sun-ripened berry fruit, with smooth tannins and a nice, dry finish, but there's a tart edge of acidity that time won't resolve. Tastes almost like an old Chianti, and best consumed with rich, oily fare. **84** —S.H. (8/1/2003)

MUELLER

Mueller 2004 Emily's Cuvée Pinot Noir (Russian River Valley) $38. Aromatically inviting, with clean, focused cherry, pomegranate, cola, and oak scents leading to a full-bodied palate. A little heavy and hot, but otherwise a very nice Pinot that can hold for a few years. **88** —S.H. (12/1/2006)

MUIRWOOD

Muirwood 2001 Syrah (Monterey) $11. Tough and gritty in tannins, with an earthy, rustic mouthfeel. It is saved by ripe, jammy blackberry and cherry flavors, and a sweet coating of toasty oak. **85** —S.H. (6/1/2005)

MUMM CUVÉE NAPA

Mumm Cuvée Napa NV Blanc de Blancs Champagne Blend (Napa Valley) $22. 86 —S.H. (12/15/2000)

Mumm Cuvée Napa 1997 Blanc de Blancs Champagne Blend (Napa Valley) $22. Quite rich for Mumm's annual lineup, with citrus and melon flavors, maybe because a third of the blend is Pinot Gris. It's fully dry, with a crisp mouthfeel and a yeasty finish. Light and elegant through the finish. **88** —S.H. (12/1/2002)

Mumm Cuvée Napa NV Blanc de Noirs Champagne Blend (Napa Valley) $18. Almost a rosé, and quite full-bodied, this rich wine brims with strawberry and cherry flavors and yeasty, bread dough notes. It's very dry. Really easy to sip, and with layers of nuance and subtlety. **89** —S.H. (12/31/2004)

Mumm Cuvée Napa NV Brut Prestige Champagne Blend (Napa Valley) $18. Dry, crisp, and tart in acids, this bubbly offers lots of pleasure. The subtle flavors of citrus fruits, strawberries, yeast, and toasty vanilla drink a little rough in texture, but this is a good price for the quality. **87** —S.H. (12/31/2004)

Mumm Cuvée Napa NV Cuvée M Champagne Blend (Napa Valley) $18. A tiny bit sweet, with lemon and peach flavors and a bit of a rough scour of acidity. Yet the creamy texture and clean yeasty finish make it a good sip of bubbly. **87** —S.H. (12/31/2004)

Mumm Cuvée Napa 1998 DVX Champagne Blend (Napa Valley) $45. A crowd pleasing sparkler for its intricate mélange of Chardonnay and Pinot Noir flavors, rich moussy texture, crisp acids, and just-right dosage. The cherry and lime flavors are edged with smoky vanilla honey and taste just great. Almost addictively good. **92** —S.H. (12/31/2004)

Mumm Cuvée Napa 1996 DVX Champagne Blend (Napa Valley) $50. 89 —P.G. (12/15/2000)

Mumm Cuvée Napa NV XXV Anniversary Reserve Brut Champagne Blend (Napa Valley) $25. A Brut-style, very dry blend that's mainly Chardonnay and Pinot Noir. Offers lots to like with its suggestion of lime and raspberry encased in smoky vanilla and doughy yeast flavors. Crisp acidity makes it clean. **87** —S.H. (12/31/2004)

Mumm Cuvée Napa 1998 Blanc de Blancs Champagne Blend (Napa Valley) $22. Tastes kind of lean and earthy, with dried straw and grapefruit flavors rounded off by a bit of honeyed sweetness from lees and dosage. Strives for elegance, but could use more finesse. **85** —S.H. (12/1/2003)

Mumm Cuvée Napa NV Blanc de Noirs Champagne Blend (Napa Valley) $18. With a pretty copper color and a delicate, complex aroma of dough, yeast, fresh strawberries, and vanilla, this rosé bubbly is a delight. It's bone dry, with a full body and a long, clean finish. **87** —S.H. (12/31/2005)

Mumm Cuvée Napa NV Brut Prestige Champagne Blend (Napa Valley) $18. Drier and rougher than Mumm's Reserve Brut, this is a decent bubbly for the price. It has nice Champagne flavors of baked bread, yeast, and citrus, and is very clean and lively. **86** —S.H. (12/31/2005)

Mumm Cuvée Napa NV Cuvée M Champagne Blend (Napa Valley) $18. With a slightly sweet finish that accentuates the fruit but doesn't cloy, this bubbly is crisp and clean, and despite that edge of sugar, it holds its own in dry country. Primarily Pinot Noir and Chardonnay, it has good acidity. **87** —S.H. (12/31/2005)

Mumm Cuvée Napa 1997 DVX Champagne Blend (Napa Valley) $45. Mumm's top cuvée, and its most French in terms of smoothness and elegance. Smells beautiful, with delicate notes of peach, strawberry, roasted hazelnuts, smoke, vanilla, and dough, and eases over the palate with a creamy grace. It's pretty austere now, showing tart limes, but has the concentration and balance for aging. **91** —S.H. (12/1/2003)

Mumm Cuvée Napa NV Reserve Brut Champagne Blend (Napa Valley) $25. The smoothest and suavest of Mumm's current offerings, this fruit-forward bubbly has a slightly sweet dosage. Fortunately, it's crisp in acidity. The peach, bread dough, vanilla, and cherry flavors are delicious, with a long aftertaste. **89** —S.H. (12/31/2005)

MUMM NAPA

Mumm Napa 2001 Blanc de Blancs Sparkling Blend (Napa Valley) $25. This is a wonderful BdB, so refined and elegant, with such a smooth, satin-and-silk mouthfeel, which is really what you want in an upscale sparkling wine. With one-third Pinot Gris in with the Chardonnay, it shows white and yellow stone fruit, mainly citrus, flavors, with a savory brioche fullness, and a clean and dry finish. **92 Editors' Choice** —S.H. (12/31/2006)

Mumm Napa NV Blanc de Noirs Sparkling Blend (Napa Valley) $18. A little rough in texture, but delicious, with a rich mélange of strawberry parfait, brioche, lime juice, peaches and cream, and toast flavors that finish long and dry. Contains 85% Pinot Noir, with the balance Chardonnay, and is easy to find, with 95,000 cases. **87** —S.H. (12/31/2006)

Mumm Napa NV Brut Prestige Sparkling Blend (Napa Valley) $18. An interesting blend of Pinot Noir, Chardonnay, Pinot Meunier, and Pinot Gris, this bubbly shows complex flavors of bread dough, yellow citrus fruits, and wildflowers, but is subtle and dry. One of the nicer things is the mouthfeel, which is light and refined. Finishes with real elegance. Production is an amazing 300,000 cases. **87** —S.H. (12/31/2006)

Mumm Napa NV Cuvée M Sparkling Blend (Napa Valley) $18. Here's a sweetie. With its vanilla cream, lime sorbet, and raspberry purée flavors balanced by rich acidity, and at an affordable price for good bubbly, it's destined to wash down many a wedding cake. **84** —S.H. (12/31/2006)

Mumm Napa 1999 DVX Sparkling Blend (Napa Valley) $45. Just beautiful, one of the best DVXs ever. The vintage gave this Pinot Noir and Chardonnay blend great ripeness to go with elegant balance. The flavors are enormously complex, offering swirls of brioche, citrus zest, vanilla, roasted almond skin, toasted coconut, and raspberry purée, and the finish is refreshingly crisp and dry, yet also slightly honeyed. Feels classy all the way. **93** —S.H. (12/31/2006)

Mumm Napa NV Reserve Brut Sparkling Blend (Napa Valley) $25. This is the most full-bodied of Mumm's current sparklers and despite the lack of a vintage designation, it has the weight and complexity of a true tête de cuvée. Nearly half Pinot Noir and Chardonnay, with a drop or two of other whites, it's creamy and rich in citrus and peach flavors, with a hint of strawberries. **91** —*S.H. (12/31/2006)*

MURPHY-GOODE

Murphy-Goode 2002 Wild Card Claret Bordeaux Blend (Alexander Valley) $19. Enjoy this brawny wine with a nice steak to soften it. It's a bit tannic, but rich in blackberry, plum, and oak flavors, and thoroughly dry. **85** —*S.H. (2/1/2005)*

Murphy-Goode 2001 Wild Card Claret Bordeaux Blend (Alexander Valley) $19. Tastes like the grapes were picked relatively early, for the tannins are strong, acidity is high, and you don't find lush fruit. There are hints of blackberries, but this is a streamlined wine, perhaps designed for food. **86** —*S.H. (8/1/2004)*

Murphy-Goode 2000 Wild Card Claret Bordeaux Blend (Alexander Valley) $19. This new Bordeaux-style blend from Murphy-Goode is classic Alexander Valley, with its bright, chewy red stone-fruit flavors and tannins that are so soft, they just melt in your mouth. Fortunately, the acidity is sufficient to provide balance. This lip-smacking blend consists of Cabernet Sauvignon, Merlot, and Petit Verdot. **90** —*S.H. (11/15/2002)*

Murphy-Goode 2003 All In Claret Cabernet Blend (Alexander Valley) $45. Murphy-Goode has a history of producing quality Bordeaux blends. But there's way too much new oak here, 100 percent in fact, and that, on top of a residual-sugary finish, pushes this wine into unbalance. **80** —*S.H. (7/1/2006)*

Murphy-Goode 2003 Wild Card Claret Cabernet Blend (Alexander Valley) $20. This is a sort of junior version of the winery's All In Claret, and it suffers from the same sugar problems. The alcohol is moderate, but it's almost as candied sweet as a dessert wine. **81** —*S.H. (7/1/2006)*

Murphy-Goode 2002 Cabernet Sauvignon (Alexander Valley) $24. Very soft in tannins, and acidicly sharp, this Cab is thin in fruity flavors, especially considering the good vintage. A disappointment. **83** —*S.H. (2/1/2006)*

Murphy-Goode 2001 Cabernet Sauvignon (Alexander Valley) $22. Full-bodied and robust even for a Cabernet, with strong tannins that frame blackberry, currant, dill, and earthy flavors. Finishes very dry and prickly with tannic astringency. May soften in a year or two but it's not an ager. **85** —*S.H. (8/1/2004)*

Murphy-Goode 2000 Cabernet Sauvignon (Alexander Valley) $22. A rewarding and satisfying Cab. It may not be in the top tier, but it's close, with voluptuous tannins and classically complex Cab flavors of black currants, olives, and herbs. Lacks a bit of concentration in the center, but the pedigree is so good, you'll hardly notice over a grilled ribeye steak. **91 Editors' Choice** —*S.H. (8/1/2003)*

Murphy-Goode 1999 Cabernet Sauvignon (Alexander Valley) $22. Dark, with plush blackberry and smoke scents, this finely crafted wine has lots to offer. You'll like the polished fruity flavors and velvety texture. Soft acids make it immediately drinkable. **90 Editors' Choice** —*S.H. (12/1/2001)*

Murphy-Goode 2002 Adams Knoll Cabernet Sauvignon (Alexander Valley) $35. Of the three new designated Cabs this winery has out now, this is the most elegant and accessible. It has polished, fine tannins and a silky mouthfeel framing intense blackberry and currant flavors, and is totally dry. But it's a young wine that needs a good five years to show its stuff. **90 Cellar Selection** —*S.H. (3/1/2006)*

Murphy-Goode 1998 Brenda Block Reserve Cabernet Sauvignon (Alexander Valley) $55. Smoky and bacony upfront, with subtle blackberry, cassis, and herb flavors on the follow-up. Moderate body is framed by powdery tannins; however, that may or may not round off in time. On the whole, a very good wine, though the finish is a bit herbal. **87** —*J.M. (12/1/2001)*

Murphy-Goode 1999 Goode-Ready Cabernet Sauvignon (Alexander Valley) $18. Ripe blackberry aromas mingle with greener notes of anise and stalks in this softly drinkable, likeable wine. The polished flavors are pretty. Finishes fruity, with a hint of acidity and tannins. **85** —*S.H. (11/15/2001)*

Murphy-Goode 2002 Sarah Block Murphy Ranch Cabernet Sauvignon (Alexander Valley) $35. Softer and smoother than the winery's Adams Knoll bottling, this wine is dense in plum, blackberry, and roasted coffee flavors. It has young, hard tannins that make it immature now, but you have to wonder if the softness limits its ageability. **87** —*S.H. (3/1/2006)*

Murphy-Goode 2001 Sarah Block Murphy Ranch Cabernet Sauvignon (Alexander Valley) $40. Opinions on this wine ranged all over the board. While one taster found this wine "delicious" and raved over its complex flavors, sturdy tannins, and good supporting acidity, two others were less enthusiastic—with one criticizing it for its herbal notes and hard, tart finish. But all could agree it's best now and over the next few years. **87** *(10/1/2005)*

Murphy-Goode 1997 Sarah Block Swan Song Reserve Cabernet Sauvignon (Sonoma County) $39. **90** *(11/1/2000)*

Murphy-Goode 2002 Terra A Lago #4 Cabernet Sauvignon (Alexander Valley) $45. This block selection combines the richness of the winery's Adams Knoll Cab with the tannic inaccessibility of the Sarah Block. The result is a wine that needs age. It displays its appellation's herbal, tobaccoey personality, with a solid core of cherry and blackberry fruit. Best to cellar until 2008, and should hold well beyond that. **92 Cellar Selection** —*S.H. (3/1/2006)*

Murphy-Goode 2002 Chardonnay (Sonoma County) $15. Dry and acidy-tart, this is a wine of great structure and balance. The flavors veer toward lime custard, mangoes, apricots, vanilla, and slate, with a gentle overlay of toasty oak. It's quite a sophisticated Chardonnay, and a great value. **90 Best Buy** —*S.H. (11/1/2005)*

Murphy-Goode 2001 Chardonnay (Sonoma County) $15. This fine Chard has the steely structure and citrusy acids of a cool climate wine. It's not a lush or hedonistic, but controlled, with its apple and pear flavors and touch of oak and lees. **87** —*S.H. (5/1/2004)*

Murphy-Goode 2000 Chardonnay (Sonoma County) $15. This Chard is light and refreshing, with hints of pear and peach flavors, framed in tangy citrus notes. Simple and clean. **86** —*J.M. (5/1/2002)*

Murphy-Goode 1999 Chardonnay (Sonoma County) $15. Creamy toast and vanilla aromas come to the fore in this elegant Chardonnay. Well balanced, with medium body, it offers moderate acidity and pretty pear, apple, and citrus notes. A fine-tuned example of style and value. **88 Best Buy** —*J.M. (11/15/2001)*

Murphy-Goode 1998 Barrel-Fermented Chardonnay (Sonoma County) $15. **89** *(6/1/2000)*

Murphy-Goode 2003 Island Block Chardonnay (Alexander Valley) $19. This elaborate wine totally satisfies for its rich, creamy texture and forward pineapple custard, kiwi, honeydew, and tangerine flavors. As if that weren't enough, toasty new oak carries it over the finish line. Dry and balanced, lots of quality here for the price. **91 Editors' Choice** —*S.H. (7/1/2006)*

Murphy-Goode 2002 Island Block Chardonnay (Alexander Valley) $19. Very well oaked, this full-throttle Chard features smoky, vanilla-tinged buttered toast aromas leading to a fruity, spicy finish. The flavors suggest golden-skinned tree fruits and honey. **87** —*S.H. (11/1/2005)*

Murphy-Goode 2000 Island Block Estate Chardonnay (Alexander Valley) $21. Grown down on the gravelly banks of the Russian River, this is not a big, rich Chard, but a lean one, with lemon and apple flavors and a sharp bite of acidity. Oak adds softening complexities and a creamy texture, but it's still a tart, clean wine. **86** —*S.H. (6/1/2003)*

Murphy-Goode 1999 Island Block Reserve Chardonnay (Alexander Valley) $21. Vanilla and butterscotch aromas call forth in this surprisingly bright-textured Chardonnay. Zingy lemon notes leave a searingly clean finish, marked by hints of minerals and herbs. **87** —*J.M. (12/1/2001)*

Murphy-Goode 2002 Fumé Blanc (Sonoma County) $12. All the elements of a good summer sipper are here. The citrus and spiced apple flavors, the crisp, minerally acidity and the clean, zesty feeling it leaves behind on the palate. **84** —*S.H. (12/1/2004)*

Murphy-Goode 2001 Fumé Blanc (Sonoma County) $13. A perky little white wine, dry as dust, with lemon and lime flavors that are boosted by bright acidity. Spreads over the palate with a tart pepperiness, an ideal food wine. It's also a good value. **86** —*S.H. (7/1/2003)*

Murphy-Goode 2000 Fumé Blanc (Sonoma County) $13. Quite bright and lemony, with a squeaky-clean finish. This tangy and refreshing wine would be a great match for briny oysters or other seafood. **86** —*J.M. (11/15/2001)*

Murphy-Goode 1997 Reserve Fumé Blanc (Sonoma County) $24. **91** —*S.H. (9/1/1999)*

Murphy-Goode 2003 Merlot (Alexander Valley) $20. The winery's basic Merlot has a sharp, acidic bite, which detracts quite a bit from the lush, soft tannins and ripe, lush plum, blackberry, and cherry flavors. Drink now. **83** —*S.H. (2/1/2006)*

Murphy-Goode 2002 Merlot (Alexander Valley) $19. From a winery that's made a real mark with Merlot, a fine effort, with its blackberry and black cherry flavors mingled with dry, sweet herbs and Indian pudding. It's drinkable now, with a firm grip of dusty tannins. **89** —*S.H. (12/15/2004)*

Murphy-Goode 2001 Merlot (Alexander Valley) $19. Defines its appellation with soft, lusciously sweet tannins, a gentle mouthfeel, and well-ripened cherry and blackberry fruit. As drinkable as it is, it's also a complex wine, with many different nuances. If only it had a bit more concentration. **88** —*S.H. (5/1/2004)*

Murphy-Goode 2000 Merlot (Alexander Valley) $19. Plum and black cherry flavors and marvelously rich tannins. Notable for its balance in the mouth. Drink it young to capture its vibrancy and juicy zest. **90 Editors' Choice** —*S.H. (5/1/2003)*

Murphy-Goode 1999 Merlot (Alexander Valley) $19. Bright and fruity, with pretty cherry and raspberry notes. There's also a certain leafy complexity, with hints of smoke and coffee on the finish. Good wine. Good price. **89** —*J.M. (7/1/2002)*

Murphy-Goode 1998 Merlot (Sonoma County) $19. A blend of black cherry, chocolate, and herb flavors. Moderate body and powdery tannins round it off for a pleasant quaff. **86** —*J.M. (11/15/2001)*

Murphy-Goode 1999 Reserve Robert Young Vineyards Merlot (Alexander Valley) $45. Impressive for its size and richness, but also for its elegance and finesse. Blackberry and olive flavors lead, while generous oak adds vanilla and cream notes. Soft tannins and acids provide a plushness that lasts through the refined finish. **92** —*S.H. (2/1/2003)*

Murphy-Goode 2001 Robert Young Vineyard Reserve Merlot (Alexander Valley) $45. Youthful in acids and tannins, with that slightly raw, feral quality that marks a great young wine. But there's a core of blackberries and cherries, and an overall balance, that suggests ageability. Try holding until 2007. **90** —*S.H. (10/1/2005)*

Murphy-Goode 2000 Robert Young Vineyards Reserve Merlot (Alexander Valley) $45. This concentrated wine almost startles with the richness of its black cherry, currant, olive, chocolate, and spicebox flavors. They flood the mouth, but are well balanced by smooth, polished tannins that have been burnished to a sheen, good acidity and a lush overlay of oak. As extracted as it is, it's balanced and harmonious. **93** —*S.H. (8/1/2004)*

Murphy-Goode 1999 Petite Verdot (Alexander Valley) $32. Not normally bottled on it's own, so this wine might surprise you with its concentrated plum, licorice, and oaky scents and deep berry flavors. The texture is viscous and thick, while both acids and tannins are soft. The dry finish is the best part—long and penetrating. **88** *(12/15/2001)*

Murphy-Goode 2001 Murphy Ranch Petite Verdot (Alexander Valley) $35. Rather hard in tannins now, a tough young wine that will rise up to something like short ribs. Best to leave it alone for 3 or 4 years. Blackberries, rich and intense, form its heart. **90** —*S.H. (10/1/2005)*

Murphy-Goode 2002 Pinot Noir (Russian River Valley) $30. Not particularly complex, but does a nice job with its cola, cherry, spice, and vanilla flavors that drink soft and crisp. It's an easy Pinot that will be good with a wide range of food. **87** —*S.H. (3/1/2005)*

Murphy-Goode 1999 Pinot Noir (Russian River Valley) $35. Starts off with extremely young, jammy flavors and a sharp bite of fresh acidity. If you let air in the glass, the oak shows through, toasty and warming. Underneath is rich, cherry-berry fruit and spice. Tannins are firm but

ripe. Best to age until 2002, or let it breathe for an hour or more. **87** *(12/15/2001)*

Murphy-Goode 1997 Pinot Noir (Russian River Valley) $30. **91** —*M.S. (5/1/2000)*

Murphy-Goode 2000 J&K Vineyard Pinot Noir (Russian River Valley) $35. **87** *(10/1/2002)*

Murphy-Goode 2001 Sauvignon Blanc (Alexander Valley) $18. A smooth, toasty, oaky style of Sauvignon Blanc. Quite viscous and almost chewy on the palate. The flavors run towards melon, fig, more toast, pear, and apple flavors. Hints of butterscotch are at the end, finishing still bright and clean. **88** —*J.M. (10/1/2004)*

Murphy-Goode 1999 Fumé II The Deuce Sauvignon Blanc (Sonoma County) $24. Any SB boasting 14.5% alcohol is going to come across as being real big, and this one does for sure. But beyond its heft, it offers underripe melon, pear, and butter flavors and an odd cheesy quality. There's also a forest's worth of oak here, which makes it heavy rather than balanced. **86** *(8/1/2002)*

Murphy-Goode 2000 Reserve Fumé Sauvignon Blanc (Alexander Valley) $17. A great and versatile food wine. Its polished flavors of lime, fig, and apricot are drizzled with Oriental spices and smoky oak. One of California's most consistent wines, and rich enough to stand in for Chardonnay. **88** —*S.H. (7/1/2003)*

Murphy-Goode 2002 Reserve Fumé Sauvignon Blanc (Alexander Valley) $17. They held this back for a pretty long time, perhaps hoping it would soften, but it hasn't. It's still a tough, acidic, almost sour wine, with gooseberry and grapefruit flavors, and searingly dry. **83** —*S.H. (2/1/2006)*

Murphy-Goode 1999 Reserve Fumé Sauvignon Blanc (Sonoma County) $17. A subtle blend of melon, mineral, herb, and citrus flavors, all couched in a classy, firm yet silky texture. Not opulent, but rather a refined version of this Sauvignon Blanc. **88** —*J.M. (11/15/2001)*

Murphy-Goode 2001 Reserve Fumé Sauvignon Blanc (Alexander Valley) $17. Firm textured, yet plush, with a solid core of bright acidity and flavors redolent of green apple, melon, herbs, grapefruit, and lemon. Clean and fresh on the finish. **88** —*J.M. (2/1/2004)*

Murphy-Goode 2000 The Deuce Sauvignon Blanc (Alexander Valley) $24. Bone dry, it has strong aromas of juniper and gooseberry, with an undercurrent of lime. Crisp acidity leaves the palate cleansed. **87** —*S.H. (10/1/2003)*

Murphy-Goode 2003 Liar's Dice Zinfandel (Sonoma County) $20. Here's a pure expression of one type of Zin. It's brawny, briary, peppery, and rugged in tannins, and totally dry, but fortunately not too high in alcohol. It'll be perfect with barbecue. **86** —*S.H. (11/1/2005)*

Murphy-Goode 2000 Liar's Dice Zinfandel (Sonoma County) $20. A pleasing blend of cherry, cola, and herb flavors that are couched in smooth-edged tannins. **87** —*J.M. (11/1/2002)*

Murphy-Goode 1999 Liar's Dice Zinfandel (Sonoma County) $19. Look no further for jammy, blueberry-scented Zin, bursting at the seams with all sorts of wild berry flavors. It's as fresh as the morning sun, and Beaujolais-like in its seductively youthful beauty and charm. **89 Editors' Choice** —*S.H. (11/15/2001)*

Murphy-Goode 1998 Liar's Dice Zinfandel (Sonoma County) $17. Toasty nose, bright fruit, makes for a classy, creamy, zippy Zin. This is really a pleasure, balanced and forward and full of life. There are some nuances of tar and spice in a balanced, exceptionally lively, seductive wine. **91 Editors' Choice** —*P.G. (3/1/2001)*

Murphy-Goode 1997 Liar's Dice Zinfandel (Sonoma County) $16. **83** —*P.G. (11/15/1999)*

Murphy-Goode 2001 Liar's Dice, TJM Zinfandel (Sonoma County) $20. Starts off with toasty spice notes, then moves on to pretty raspberry, plum, and blackberry flavors. Tangy acidity makes it lively, and toasty oak tops it off. Long at the end. **88** *(11/1/2003)*

Murphy-Goode 2002 Liar's Dice Zinfandel (Sonoma County) $19. Robust and full-bodied, with a sandpapery edge of tannins, this wine features slightly earthy flavors of wild berries, and is bone dry. **86** —*S.H. (11/15/2004)*

Murphy-Goode 2000 Snake Eyes Zinfandel (Alexander Valley) $35. There's nothing subtle about this fruit-driven wine, with its turbocharged flavors of wild berries and stone fruits. But 60-year-old vines give complexity and finesse over and above mere power, and discreet winemaking lets the fruit express itself. **90** —S.H. (2/1/2003)

Murphy-Goode 2001 Snake Eyes Ellis Ranch Zinfandel (Alexander Valley) $35. Pretty and smooth textured, with ripe, elegant plum, cherry, black currant, and vanilla flavors. The wine is plush and long, with additional smoke, toast, coffee, and anise notes that add interest. Smooth at the end. Elegant and well done. **90** (11/1/2003)

Murphy-Goode 2002 Snake Eyes Ellis Ranch Reserve Zinfandel (Alexander Valley) $35. A wonderful Zin that combines lushly ripe fruit with a smooth, velvety mouth feel. Blackberries, cherries, spicy blueberries, and cocoa flavors drink sweet in fruity essence, yet the wine is dry. Has the balance and elegance of a fine Cabernet, with Zin's distinct personality. **92** —S.H. (3/1/2005)

MURRIETA'S WELL

Murrieta's Well 2001 Vendimia Bordeaux Blend (Livermore Valley) $30. A beautiful example of how nice Livermore Bordeaux reds can be when made well. This ageworthy wine is quite tannic now, but the tannins are dried, fine, and drinkable with rich meats. The cassis, plum, and blackberry flavors are impressively deep and long-lasting on the finish. **92 Editors' Choice** —S.H. (11/15/2003)

Murrieta's Well 1999 Vendimia Red Wine Bordeaux Blend (Livermore Valley) $35. Lots to like in this soft and earthy Bordeaux blend, with the tobacco and herb flavors teased by hints of blackberries and cherries. Oak doesn't overwhelm, but adds graceful touches. Has the balance to age. **87** —S.H. (3/1/2004)

Murrieta's Well 2001 White Vendimia Bordeaux Blend (Livermore Valley) $21. Always an interesting Bordeaux blend to taste, this mixture of Sauvignon Blanc, Sémillon, Malvasia Bianca, and Orange Muscat is alive with citrus, orange blossom, mineral, and dried herb aromas and flavors. It's very complex in the mouth, and zesty with fresh acidity. Fun to drink, but also a serious white wine. **90 Editors' Choice** —S.H. (11/15/2003)

Murrieta's Well 1998 Vendimia Sémillon-Sauvignon Blanc (Livermore Valley) $20. Creamy and rich, this blend of Sauvignon and Sémillon provides plenty of upfront citrus and fig flavors in a smooth-drinking dry wine with a lot of finesse. Fairly high char oak provides a smoky, butterscotchy note. **86** —S.H. (11/15/2001)

Murrieta's Well 1998 Zinfandel (Livermore Valley) $27. After nearly five years, this interesting wine's tannins have softened, and are now lush and easy. They support dry, fruity flavors of cherries and plums that are succulent through the last swallow. Pricy, but there's plenty of elegance. Try substituting this for a fine Cabernet. **91** —S.H. (3/1/2004)

Murrieta's Well 1997 Zinfandel (Livermore Valley) $29. From 85-year-old, head-pruned vines; a full-bodied, jammy Zin bursting with the spicy aromas and flavors that make California's own variety so popular. The tannins are soft but intricate, and vibrant acidity provides lively balance. **88** —S.H. (12/15/2001)

MUTT LYNCH

Mutt Lynch 2002 Merlot Over and Play Dead Merlot (Livermore Valley) $20. A sleek style, with smooth, supple tannins that frame a core of black currant, thyme, chocolate, coffee, and spice notes. The finish is long and refined. A fine effort from an often overlooked appellation. **89** —J.M. (9/1/2004)

Mutt Lynch 1999 Merlot Over and Play Dead Merlot (Livermore Valley) $20. Sweer cherry and vanilla flavors come to the fore in this pretty, robust, yet elegant Merlot. Smooth, sleek tannins and a creamy texture mark the finish, which fans out to reveal complex cassis, chocolate and herb notes. **90** —J.M. (12/31/2001)

Mutt Lynch 2001 Canis Major, Perotti Vineyard Zinfandel (Dry Creek Valley) $23. Fairly densely structured, with black cherry, blackberry, licorice, herb, spice, and oak nuances. The tannins are quite firm, but ripe, keeping the wine neatly supported. On the finish it's smooth and ripe. **88** (11/1/2003)

Mutt Lynch 1999 Domaine du Bone Zinfandel (Dry Creek Valley) $20. An elegant style that is made from 50-year-old vines. The wine is made in a refined style. Not effusive, but showing a fine blend of black currant, cherry, herb, and toast flavors. Lovely now, but it should also improve nicely in the cellar. **88** —J.M. (12/15/2001)

Mutt Lynch 2002 Portrait of a Mutt Zinfandel (Sonoma County) $15. Bright and spicy on the nose, with hints of chocolate and raspberries. Pretty fruit continues along the palate, showing cherries, cocoa, coffee, cinnamon, and toast. Fresh and lively to the end. **88** —J.M. (9/1/2004)

Mutt Lynch 2001 Portrait of a Mutt Zinfandel (Sonoma County) $15. Juicy and ripe, this one strikes a fine balance between effusive cherry, blackberry, plum, and anise flavors and ripe tannins that give good structure to the whole. On the finish, it's bright, with coffee and cola notes for good measure. **88** (11/1/2003)

MYSTIC CLIFFS

Mystic Cliffs 1997 Cabernet Sauvignon (California) $7. Starts with nice cassis and black currant aromas with a kiss of smoky oak. It's pretty rich for this price, with some real varietal character. Drinks dry and soft and fruity. This would make a very nice everyday wine or an inexpensive by-the-glass selection in a restaurant. **84** —S.H. (5/1/2001)

Mystic Cliffs 1999 Chardonnay (California) $7. Starts with fruity, lush aromas of honey, apple, butter, and cream, caramel, toast, and smoky oak. Nicely layered flavors of ripe peaches and green apples and spices. A winemaker's wine that's just a tad sweet and soft, but very clean, with a swift, pleasant finish. **84 Best Buy** —S.H. (5/1/2001)

Mystic Cliffs 1997 Merlot (California) $7. A very nice wine at a good price. Starts with a sweet fruit-oaky aroma that is warm and round. In the mouth it's soft and charming, with black cherry and mocha flavors. Simple but satisfying, and a good value. **85 Best Buy** —S.H. (5/1/2001)

Mystic Cliffs 1997 Winemaker's Select Merlot (Monterey County) $11. **83** (3/1/2000)

MYSTIC WINES

Mystic Wines 1999 McDuffee Vineyard Cabernet Sauvignon (Columbia Valley (OR)) $28. Dark and smoky, with green flavors dominating the finish. There's a minty/menthol streak as well, and some very dry, astringent tannins. **83** —P.G. (2/1/2004)

Mystic Wines 1999 Hillside Vineyard Merlot (Columbia Valley (OR)) $24. Very earthy and stemmy in the nose, the fruit buried in scents of bark and soil. The wine is a bit rough and tumble in the mouth, more powerful than many Merlots, but less smooth and sweet than the truly ripe ones. This is tannic, herbal, and quite astringent. **83** —P.G. (2/1/2004)

Mystic Wines 2002 Temperance Hill Vineyard Pinot Noir (Willamette Valley) $24. There's a heavy sniff of earth and saddle leather here, along with raw meat and matchstick. Nonetheless, it's a substantial wine that simply needs breathing time. **88** (11/1/2004)

Mystic Wines 2001 Syrah (Columbia Valley (OR)) $20. Spicy, supple, and silky fruit lights up the front of this excellent wine. Black pepper spice highlights the midpalate, and the wine glides to a smooth, modestly long finish. **87** —P.G. (2/1/2004)

Mystic Wines 2001 Hillside Vineyard Zinfandel (Columbia Valley (OR)) $20. Feels disjointed and incomplete; there is some raisiny fruit in front, then a big hole in the middle, then some burnt sugar and smoke, and finally a drop off into a vaguely leafy finale. **83** —P.G. (2/1/2004)

NADEAU FAMILY VINTNERS

Nadeau Family Vintners 2002 Critical Mass Zinfandel (Paso Robles) $28. This is the softest, richest, and fruitiest of Nadeau's three new Zins. It's dense in cherry and chocolate fudge flavors, with a cherry liqueur finish. Has practically no tannins, and just enough acidity to prevent cloying. **88** —S.H. (11/1/2005)

Nadeau Family Vintners 2002 Home Ranch Zinfandel (Paso Robles) $25. Even though this Zin has raisiny flavors that show some of the berries were too ripe, they're merely a seasoning to what is otherwise a yummy wine. It's soft in acids and tannins, with a cocoa finish. **86** —S.H. (11/1/2005)

Nadeau Family Vintners 2001 Mooney Homestead Zinfandel (Paso Robles) $28. Quite plush, with pretty plum, cassis, black cherry, tar, coffee, toast, and spice up front. The wine sits on the tongue with a velvety edge that tapers off sooner than one would wish, given the tasty fruit flavors. Very nice, nonetheless. **88** (11/1/2003)

Nadeau Family Vintners 2002 The Bouncer Zinfandel (Paso Robles) $25. I don't know why they call it Bouncer, but it may be because the high alcohol has a kick. Drinks hot, soft, and extremely fruity, with cassis, chocolate, and sweet coffee flavors that define warm-climate Zinfandel. **86** —S.H. (11/1/2005)

NAGGIAR

Naggiar 2003 Sangiovese (Sierra Foothills) $19. What you get with this wine is a lot of cherry pie flavor along with a fairly heavy, soft mouthfeel and some gritty tannins. Drink now. **84** —S.H. (12/1/2006)

Naggiar 2003 Syrah (Sierra Foothills) $22. Here's a wine with briary, wild-berry flavors and substantial, somewhat astringent tannins. But the flavors are rich, like very ripe blackberries, raspberries, and logan berries picked on a hot summer day. Very nice, especially with a good steak. **86** —S.H. (12/1/2006)

NALLE

Nalle 2003 Hopkins Vineyard Pinot Noir (Russian River Valley) $38. This wine is less alcoholic, leaner, and higher in acidity than many others. As a result, it's a chiseled wine, showing cola, cherry, clove, and cinnamon flavors, with a lean herbaceousness. It should develop well over the next 6–8 years. **90 Cellar Selection** —S.H. (11/1/2005)

Nalle 2003 Zinfandel (Dry Creek Valley) $26. Here's a young, dark Zin with vibrant tannins and high acids that frame blackberry and cassis flavors. It's quite different from many other Sonoma Zins, with alcohol below 14% and plenty of claret-like elegance. Should develop well in the cellar through this decade. **90** —S.H. (11/1/2005)

Nalle 1999 Zinfandel (Sonoma County) $28. A bright textured Zin, redolent of cherry, blackberry, herbs, and anise. Sleek and tangy to the end. **88** —J.M. (3/1/2002)

NAPA CELLARS

Napa Cellars 1998 Chardonnay (Napa Valley) $22. 83 (6/1/2000)

NAPA CREEK

Napa Creek 2000 Cabernet Sauvignon (Napa Valley) $12. Nice Cab you can enjoy on ordinary occasions, and a pretty good value, especially for the upscale appellation. It has pleasant flavors of ripe blackberries and cherries, and round, sweet tannins. **85** —S.H. (6/1/2004)

Napa Creek 1996 Chardonnay (Napa Valley) $16. 87 (6/1/2000)

Napa Creek 2002 Chardonnay (Napa Valley) $12. Here's a smooth, creamy Chard with flavors of apples, peaches, buttered toast, vanilla, and plenty of oriental spices. The rich flavors last through a long finish. Has enough complexity to stand up to cracked crab, with a sourdough baguette. **87** —S.H. (6/1/2004)

Napa Creek 2000 Merlot (Napa Valley) $12. An everyday sort of wine, with some fruity flavors and thick tannins. Very dry, though a bit of rough throughout. **84** —S.H. (6/1/2004)

NAPA DAN

Napa Dan 2003 Cabernet Sauvignon (Napa Valley) $30. A fine, full-bodied Cab, fleshy and fat in blackberry and cassis flavors and a grilled-meat chewiness. This fully dry wine has rich, sweet tannins and a good finish. It should hold and improve a bit with several years in the bottle. **87** — S.H. (7/1/2005)

Napa Dan 2003 Pool Yard Chardonnay (Napa Valley) $18. A decent Chard with some peach, apple, and oak flavors, and a creamy texture. Turns a bit sharp and spicy on the finish. **84** —S.H. (7/1/2005)

NAPA REDWOODS ESTATE

Napa Redwoods Estate 2000 Alden Perry Reserve Castle Rock Vineyard Red Wine Bordeaux Blend (Mount Veeder) $48. Smooth and velvety drinking, and a very good food wine for its modulated berry and herb flavors and firm acids. This is a wine that does not overwhelm with size,

but it is elegant and balanced and shows its pedigree well. **89** —S.H. (5/1/2004)

Napa Redwoods Estate 1999 Castle Rock Vineyard Alden Perry Reserve Bordeaux Blend (Mount Veeder) $56. A huge, extracted wine, with massive fruit and berry flavors that flood the palate. Framed in thick but soft tannins, it's opulent in the mouth, but a stinging bite of youthful acidity almost demands aging through 2006. **92** —S.H. (10/1/2003)

Napa Redwoods Estate 2001 Castle Rock Vineyard Merlot (Mount Veeder) $38. This well-crafted Merlot has pleasant flavors of plums, blackberries, and coffee that are wrapped in smooth tannins. It is very dry, and feels round and supple in the mouth. There are some less ripe herbal flavors that limit ageability, but it's a good table wine. **90** —S.H. (5/1/2004)

Napa Redwoods Estate 1999 Castle Rock Vineyard Merlot (Mount Veeder) $42. Blackberry, black cherry, violets, pepper, espresso, chocolate, and an array of oriental spices are wrapped in a lush, velvety texture. Despite the massive fruit, the wine is dry, and the tannins are a wonder. **92** —S.H. (10/1/2003)

Napa Redwoods Estate 2001 Alden Perry Reserve Red Blend (Mount Veeder) $48. Cherry, berry, and herb flavors are buried inside bigtime tannins that numb the palate, in this dry, smoothly textured wine. It's questionable whether the wine has enough stuffing for the cellar. **87** — S.H. (11/15/2004)

NAPA RIDGE

Napa Ridge 2003 Cabernet Sauvignon (Napa Valley) $12. You'll find some unripe, green, and briary notes in this everyday Cab, besides the more varietal flavors of blackberries and cherries. It's dry and soft, with rich tannins. **83** —S.H. (4/1/2006)

Napa Ridge 2000 Cabernet Sauvignon (Napa Valley) $12. Pretty darned good Cab, a softly fruity wine with some real class. The cherry flavors have a nice edge of smoky oak, and the velvety texture is easy. **85** —S.H. (11/15/2004)

Napa Ridge 2000 Cabernet Sauvignon (Lodi) $10. A serviceable wine, rugged and simple, with basic Cabernet blackberry flavors. There are also notes of dehydrated berries in the raisin and prune flavors. Simple tannins are soft and easy. **84** —S.H. (4/1/2003)

Napa Ridge 1999 Cabernet Sauvignon (Napa Valley) $12. There aren't a lot of Napa Cabs at this price. Here's one, and it's pretty nice. Has classic blackberry and currant flavors, a hefty dose of oak, and is extremely dry with decent acids. A bit rough around the edges, but it might soften with a year or two in the bottle. **85** —S.H. (11/15/2002)

Napa Ridge 1997 Coastal Vines Cabernet Sauvignon (Central Coast) $11. **87** (11/15/1999)

Napa Ridge 1997 Reserve Cabernet Sauvignon (Napa Valley) $20. Aromas are of cedar, plums, and dried cherries. There are rich berry and chocolate flavors and a creamy, smooth balance that makes this a very drinkable and enjoyable wine. **88** —C.S. (11/15/2002)

Napa Ridge 2003 Chardonnay (Napa Valley) $12. This Chardonnay is showing plenty of well-toasted oak, vanilla, and caramel flavors and some very ripe tropical-fruit flavors. The creamy texture leads to a slightly rough finish. **84** —S.H. (7/1/2005)

Napa Ridge 2000 Chardonnay (Napa Valley) $12. A refreshing, sweet white sipper chock full of juicy pear, peach, tangerine, and apple flavors, and even a little mango for fans of tropical fruit. It's soft and clean, and the oaky nuances last into the finish. **84** —S.H. (12/15/2002)

Napa Ridge 1998 Chardonnay (North Coast) $10. Very ripe, forward fruit characterizes this slightly heavy, somewhat dense wine. It has a kiss of oak and a little sweetness, with good, crisp acidity. **83** —S.H. (8/1/2001)

Napa Ridge 2003 Coastal Vines Chardonnay (North Coast) $10. There's scads of fruit in this dryish wine, everything from pineapple custard and peach cobbler to ripe green apples. It's creamy and oaky. **84** —S.H. (12/31/2005)

Napa Ridge 1996 Reserve Chardonnay (North Coast) $17. **87** —J.C. (10/1/1999)

Napa Ridge 2003 Merlot (Napa Valley) $12. Despite the smooth tannins, delicious blackberry, and cherry fruit and good acidity, this wine finishes

USA

just a little too sweet for comfort, although some wine aficionados will enjoy that burst of sugar. **83** —*S.H. (4/1/2006)*

Napa Ridge 2000 Merlot (Napa Valley) $11. Red berry aromas are accented with field greens and earth. There is a juicy feel to the wine that is simple, yet soft and pleasant. **84** —*C.S. (11/15/2002)*

Napa Ridge 2003 Coastal Ridge Merlot (California) $7. The fruit here is so pretty—it's all black cherries and black raspberries. It's a little rustic, but perfectly drinkable, and you can't beat the price. **84 Best Buy** —*S.H. (11/1/2005)*

Napa Ridge 2002 Coastal Vines Merlot (Lodi) $10. Nice, dry, and fruity in plummy chocolate flavors, this wine also has some well-sculpted tannins. The ripe fruitiness lasts through a long finish. **84** —*S.H. (12/15/2004)*

Napa Ridge 1998 Coastal Vines Merlot (California) $10. Has weird aromas of cooked mushrooms and asparagus, but strangely, it tastes pretty good, with berry flavors and a dry, softly tannic structure. Not a bad wine, except for that odd smell. **81** —*S.H. (8/1/2001)*

Napa Ridge 1997 Reserve Merlot (Napa Valley) $20. Begins with aromas of plums and blackberries and coffee, with very spicy, dusty notes. The flavors are rich and fruity, with an earthy, almost rough edge, and some green accents. Tannins turn sharp on the finish. **84** —*S.H. (6/1/2001)*

Napa Ridge 1999 Pinot Grigio (California) $10. Crushed almonds, earth, and a trace of honey and citrus mark the aromas. Then it turns fruity in the mouth and a tad sweet. It's a nicely balanced, apéritif-style wine for a fair price. **84** —*S.H. (8/1/2001)*

Napa Ridge 2004 Coastal Ridge Pinot Grigio (California) $7. Okay for simple drinking, although it's kind of watery. If you're not fussy, it's citrusy, dry, tart, and clean. **83** —*S.H. (7/1/2005)*

Napa Ridge 2001 Pinot Noir (North Coast) $10. Soft, fruity, and simple, a somewhat bitter wine marked by cherry, cola, and herb flavors. Turns supple and silky on the finish. **84** —*S.H. (7/1/2003)*

Napa Ridge 2003 Coastal Vines Pinot Noir (North Coast) $10. Soft, simple, and jammy, this Pinot has modest cherry and coffee flavors and a light, silky texture. **82** —*S.H. (12/31/2005)*

Napa Ridge 1998 Shiraz (Stanislaus County) $10. Has pretty aromas of black cherry, oak, and earth, and equally pretty berry flavors. It also has a dry earthiness that invites food. **85** —*S.H. (10/1/2001)*

Napa Ridge 2003 Coastal Vines Shiraz (Lodi) $10. Lots of juicy, ripe blackberry and cherry fruit in this wine, with a taste of honeyed espresso in the finish. Shows nice dryness and a good tannic structure. **84** —*S.H. (7/1/2005)*

Napa Ridge 1998 Triad White Blend (North Coast) $9. This unusual blend of Chardonnay, Sauvignon Blanc, and Sémillon has clean aromas of ripe peach, toast, vanilla, and buttered popcorn. It's very fruity and rich, with nice, round, full flavors that are designed to please. **85** —*S.H. (8/1/2001)*

Napa Ridge 1996 Coastal Zinfandel (North Coast) $9. 86 Best Buy —*L.W. (11/1/1999)*

NAPA VALLEY VINEYARDS

Napa Valley Vineyards 2002 Reserve Cabernet Sauvignon (Napa Valley) $17. Soft, simple, and sugary sweet, with black cherry and blackberry pie flavors and a milk chocolate finish. From Gallo. **80** —*S.H. (7/1/2006)*

Napa Valley Vineyards 2003 Chardonnay (Napa Valley) $15. Pretty nasty, with vegetal aromas and medicinal flavors. **81** —*S.H. (10/1/2005)*

Napa Valley Vineyards 2004 Reserve Chardonnay (Napa Valley) $15. Gallo scores with this ripe, creamy Chard. It fills the mouth with tropical fruit, vanilla custard, and woodspice flavors. Not a complex wine, it's a guaranteed crowd pleaser. **85** —*S.H. (7/1/2006)*

Napa Valley Vineyards 2004 Reserve Chardonnay (Napa Valley) $18. Here's a new wine from Gallo. Like many Napa Chards, it has an herbal, earthy quality to the peaches-and-cream flavors. It's also a bit soft, sweet and one-dimensional. **84** —*S.H. (3/1/2006)*

Napa Valley Vineyards 2002 Reserve Merlot (Napa Valley) $15. Slightly sweet, soft, and thick, with cherry Lifesaver flavors and a spicy finish, this everyday wine will be okay with simple fare. From Gallo. **83** —*S.H. (7/1/2006)*

NAPA WINE CO.

Napa Wine Co. 1997 Cabernet Sauvignon (Napa Valley) $32. 90 *(11/1/2000)*

Napa Wine Co. 2001 Cabernet Sauvignon (Napa Valley) $32. Smooth and supple, with ripe black currant and oak flavors framed by polished tannins. There's a good, sandpapery grip to the mouth feel that suggests pairing with rich meats, or you can age this wine through the decade. **91** —*S.H. (3/1/2005)*

Napa Wine Co. 2000 Cabernet Sauvignon (Napa Valley) $32. Doesn't say so, but this wine actually is from a single vineyard in Oakville, and the quality makes it a good value for the appellation. The tannins are fairly harsh while the fruit is muted. Yet there's enough cherry-currant concentrate to survive mid-term aging. If you can't wait, a fabulous steak will eat right through the astringency. **90** —*S.H. (6/1/2004)*

Napa Wine Co. 1999 Cabernet Sauvignon (Napa Valley) $32. Serves up layers of ripe, lush cherry, blackberry, cassis, herb, and spice flavors. Firm, ripe tannins and discreet use of oak make this a winner. **92** —*J.M. (2/1/2003)*

Napa Wine Co. 1998 Cabernet Sauvignon (Napa Valley) $32. Redolent of cassis, blackberry, herbs, anise, smoke, and toasty oak aromas, the wine fans out gracefully on the palate to reveal more layers of equally well-defined fruit. Tannins are soft and round, finishing moderately with a clean freshness **91** —*J.M. (12/1/2001)*

Napa Wine Co. 1999 Pinot Blanc (Napa Valley) $18. Creamy smooth texture supports a core of citrus, mineral, and herb notes that combine with great elegance. The finsh is long and clean. **88** —*J.M. (11/15/2001)*

Napa Wine Co. 1998 Pinot Blanc (Napa Valley) $18. 85 —*L.W. (3/1/2000)*

Napa Wine Co. 1998 Sauvignon Blanc (Napa Valley) $18. 89 —*L.W. (3/1/2000)*

Napa Wine Co. 2003 Sauvignon Blanc (Yountville) $14. A good Sauvignon Blanc from Napa. It's dry and crisp, with grassy, citrus, melon, and fig flavors and subtle but rich oak layerings. Qualitatively, it approaches the complexity of a good Cabernet. **90 Best Buy** —*S.H. (10/1/2004)*

Napa Wine Co. 2001 Sauvignon Blanc (Oakville) $18. Basic grapefruit and white peach aromas give way to a palate that's mostly about lemon and melon. This wine seems to have gone through far too severe a barrel regimen, and to us, popcorn and butter just don't complement most Sauvignon Blancs. **85** *(8/1/2002)*

Napa Wine Co. 2000 Sauvignon Blanc (Yountville) $18. Bright and vivacious in the nose, with gobs of upfront fruit on the palate. Passion-fruit, lemon, lime, and other racy citrus flavors leave a sleek and clean trail on the finish, which is marked by distinct hay and herb notes. **88** —*J.M. (11/15/2001)*

Napa Wine Co. 2001 Zinfandel (Napa Valley) $20. Sleek yet full bodied, with elegant, ripe tannins and a fairly complex array of plum, blackberry, spice, cola, and herb flavors. Toasty oak is well balanced and neatly frames the ensemble, which finishes with good length. **89** *(11/1/2003)*

NAVARRO

Navarro 1994 Cabernet Sauvignon (Mendocino County) $24. 89 —*L.W. (11/1/1999)*

Navarro 1997 Cabernet Sauvignon (Mendocino) $25. I don't think of Navarro as a Cabernet house, but go figure. In fact, go find this wine, if you want a credible alternative to "down there," as they say in these parts. Dry, delicious, and in a league of its own for California Cabernet, and clearly poised to get better. **91** —*S.H. (5/1/2002)*

Navarro 1997 Chardonnay (Anderson Valley) $13. 89 Best Buy —*L.W. (11/15/1999)*

Navarro 2001 Chardonnay (Anderson Valley) $18. A beautiful wine, with perfectly ripe fruity flavors of peaches, apples, and guava that are wrapped in crisp, clean acids. Oak adds a luscious overlay of cream, buttered toast, vanilla, and woody spices. The finish is long and compelling. A great value. **92 Editors' Choice** —*S.H. (12/1/2003)*

Navarro 2001 Chardonnay (Mendocino) $13. Hand it to Navarro to make satisfying wines and keep the prices modest. This is a well-structured

Chard with flavors ranging from citrus through tart green apples to tropical fruits, and has a firm streak of acid. The ginger-cinnamon finish is very long. **88 Best Buy** —*S.H. (12/1/2003)*

Navarro 1999 Chardonnay (Mendocino) $13. Here's something different in Chard. Starts with blunt aromas of green apples, honey, and smoky oak, very clean and penetrating. There's lots of peach and apple fruit in the mouth, accompanied by sharp acidity. This is an angular wine with layers of complexity. **86** —*S.H. (12/31/2001)*

Navarro 2002 Premiere Reserve Chardonnay (Anderson Valley) $19. A really good, interesting Chard that marches to a different beat. Clean and zingy in fresh, bright acids that bite into the palate, carrying pure flavors of lime zest, vanilla, and toast, in a creamy texture. Has a vitality that's especially appealing. **90** —*S.H. (12/31/2004)*

Navarro 1999 Premiere Reserve Chardonnay (Anderson Valley) $18. Has tangerine and smoke aromas, plus hints of oak and lees. It's quite fruity, with brilliant acidity, which makes it more brittle than, say, a Sonoma Chard. It's dryish, with a very long, spicy finish. Enjoy it now with rich, spicy, buttery foods. **87** —*S.H. (12/31/2001)*

Navarro 1997 Gewürztraminer (Anderson Valley) $14. 89 —*L.W. (9/1/1999)*

Navarro 2002 Gewürztraminer (Anderson Valley) $16. This perennial fave is spicier than usual this year. It brims with fresh gingersnap and vanilla aromas, with big, big flavors of spiced apples, nutmeg, and ripe white peach. Versatile and fun. **87** —*S.H. (6/1/2004)*

Navarro 2000 Gewürztraminer (Anderson Valley) $14. Opens with very aromatic scents of ginger, cinnamon, wildflower, peaches, apples, vanilla, and honey. AS befits the appellation, it's very acidic and dryish. The peach and apple flavors aren't as concentrated as in previous years. **84** —*S.H. (12/15/2001)*

Navarro 2002 Cluster Select Late Harvest Gewürztraminer (Anderson Valley) $25. Outrageously sweet and delicious, a wine that blows your mind with the first sip. It's powerful in apricot, banana flambé, and vanilla cream flavors, with a viscous texture that stains the glass with glycerine. Dessert in a glass. **93** —*S.H. (6/1/2004)*

Navarro 1998 Late Harvest Gewürztraminer (Anderson Valley) $12. 90 Best Buy —*S.H. (12/31/2000)*

Navarro 1997 Late Harvest Gewürztraminer (Anderson Valley) $45. 92 —*L.W. (9/1/1999)*

Navarro 2000 Vintage Select Late Harvest Gewürztraminer (Anderson Valley) $25. A beautiful wine, with a good history of aging. Begins with aromas of apricot liqueur, smoke, spices, and vanilla, with maybe a touch of botrytis, and turns rich and dramatic in the mouth. It's sweet but not overwhelmingly so, with a creamy texture and crisp acidity. Fancy and elegant. **90** —*S.H. (12/31/2001)*

Navarro 1999 Mourvèdre (Mendocino) $19. A most interesting wine, and one that has a lot to teach aficionados of overextracted fruit and oak. It doesn't need those props, because it has enough vitality on its own. It's earthy, mushroomy and strawberry-plummy, and tastes like a mélange of those elements sautéed in olive oil. Dry tannins let you appreciate the flavors and structure. **89** —*S.H. (5/1/2002)*

Navarro 2001 Dry Blanc Muscat (Anderson Valley) $14. Refreshing and clean, a tart young wine with bright flavors of orange pekoe, lemon zest, and apricot. As the label states, it is dry, but finishes with a richly honeyed texture. A great summer sipper, or try with a salad of greens and tangerine sections. **87** —*S.H. (3/1/2004)*

Navarro 1999 Dry Muscat Blanc Muscat (Anderson Valley) $18. Usually made sweet, this is unusual interpretation. In fact, it smells sweet, with gingerbread and lime-orange sorbet aromas and similar flavors. Yet it's dryish, not really bone-dry, but straddles the border. This would be good with spicy fusion food. **86** —*S.H. (12/15/2001)*

Navarro 1998 Petite Sirah (Mendocino) $19. You'll love this wine for the sheer voluptuousness of the flavors. It makes love to the palate, caressing it with dry, velvety softness and delivering ripe berry flavors filled with sweetness and purity. It's lipsmackingly good, and a fine example of how good this old California varietal can be, albeit with a sort of ruggedness. **91** —*S.H. (5/1/2002)*

Navarro 2002 Pinot Gris (Anderson Valley) $16. A fresh, zesty, and incredibly aromatic wine that satisfies at every level. The crisp acidity supports bright flavors of extremely ripe peaches, mangoes, figs, vanilla, and smoke. **88** —*S.H. (6/1/2004)*

Navarro 2000 Pinot Gris (Anderson Valley) $16. Just what you want Pinot Gris to be. Tart and apple-lemony, but with enough richness to satisfy. Strike the perfect balance of sugar and acid, with an ultraclean finish that leaves a fresh, spicy feeling on the palate. **87** —*S.H. (12/15/2001)*

Navarro 2001 Pinot Noir (Mendocino) $14. Navarro has held the line on prices, and this Pinot Noir is possibly the best Pinot value on the market. It is not a blockbuster. It is a pleasant wine, with a truly varietal character that includes flavors of ripe cherries, orange zest, and dusty spices and a fine, silky mouthfeel. **88** —*S.H. (2/1/2004)*

Navarro 2000 Deep End Pinot Noir (Anderson Valley) $38. They call the coldest, westernmost part of the valley the deep end, and presumably this wine comes from there. It's pretty good stuff. Robust and silky, to begin with. Feels fine in the mouth. You want to swirl it around and enjoy the raspberry-cherry flavors. A bite of acidity finishes it. Fabulous with crostini and olive tapenade. **90** —*S.H. (5/1/2002)*

Navarro 1999 Methode a l'Ancienne Pinot Noir (Anderson Valley) $19. A cold climate wine brimming with sharp cherry-raspberry aromas and flavors. Oak is not evident here—just that big, brilliant blast of fruit, in a very dry wine of considerable acidity. It's also light as a feather, with airy tannins. The round, supple texture makes it a restaurant favorite. **87** —*S.H. (12/15/2001)*

Navarro 2001 Methode a l'Ancienne Pinot Noir (Anderson Valley) $20. Navarro's Ancienne always seems to produce a fresh Pinot, not an ageable heavyweight, and this one's no exception. It has pretty flavors of cherries, coffee, and smoke, with silky tannins. **86** —*S.H. (6/1/2004)*

Navarro 2000 Navarrouge Red Blend (Mendocino) $9. This wine is rustic and made country-style but there's something lovable about it, like a big old dog. It's friendly and fun. The tastes are juicy and rich, the texture round and mellow, and although it's no match for your top-notch collector's items, it will do just fine most of the time. 32% Valdiguie, 26% Zinfandel, 29% Pinot Noir, and 13% Cabernet Sauvignon. **86 Best Buy** —*S.H. (5/1/2002)*

Navarro 2002 White Riesling (Anderson Valley) $15. A nice example of a California Riesling in the Alsatian style. Quite dry, but rich in fruity essence, with flavors of minerals, peach, citrus, slate, and a pretty jasmine note. Very high in acidity, though, with a sour finish. **86** —*S.H. (12/31/2004)*

Navarro 2002 Rosé Blend (Mendocino) $13. This great wine kind of sneaks up on you. First you think it's just a modest little blush wine, but it's awfully hard not to take another sip. Then you realize how good it is. Raspberries, vanilla, and cinnamon, and bone dry. Made from Grenache and Syrah. Another super value from Navarro. **88** —*S.H. (3/1/2004)*

Navarro 2003 Old Vine Cuvée Rosé Blend (Mendocino) $13. Light in color, aroma, and weight, and pretty thin in flavor, too. There are vague suggestions of strawberries. **84** —*S.H. (12/31/2004)*

Navarro 2002 Cuvée 128 Sauvignon Blanc (Mendocino) $14. Fresh, young, tart, and tasty with fig, melon, citrus, and straw flavors. Bracing acidity makes it clean. Although this wine is very dry, it feels quite rich in the mouth, and finishes long in fruit. **87** —*S.H. (6/1/2004)*

Navarro 2000 Cuvée 128 Sauvignon Blanc (Anderson Valley) $14. If you like crisp, you'll like this high-acid wine, but some might be put off by the intensely aggressive green grass and hay notes. They dominate the aroma and flavor. On the other hand, it's clean, sharply etched, and mouth watering. Try with shellfish. **84** —*S.H. (12/15/2001)*

Navarro 1998 Cuvée 128 Sauvignon Blanc (Mendocino) $13. 91 Best Buy —*S.H. (9/1/2000)*

Navarro 2001 White Riesling (Anderson Valley) $14. Made in the Alsatian style, a very dry wine, rich in bright acidity, with flavors of citrus fruits, honeysuckle, and slatey kinds of minerals. Pleasant enough, with a snappy little finish that smacks of citrus. **85** —*S.H. (12/31/2003)*

Navarro 2000 White Riesling (Anderson Valley) $14. If you're looking for a California Riesling that's a worthy rival to German ones, try this wine.

Clean, zesty aromas of wildflowers, apples and lime lead to racy fruit flavors underscored by very high acidity. There's a tangy minerality that makes it feel steely and firm. It's not bone dry, but close enough. Call it California Spatlese. **88** —*S.H. (5/1/2002)*

Navarro 1997 Late Harvest Cluster Select White Riesling (Anderson Valley) $25. 94 —*S.H. (12/31/2000)*

Navarro 2001 Zinfandel (Mendocino) $19. A very ripe, almost overblown style that emphasizes berry-cherry fruit, cola, and milk chocolate flavors that are almost flamboyant. Totally dry; a bit hot in alcohol. **87** —*S.H. (6/1/2004)*

Navarro 2000 Old Vine Zinfandel (Mendocino) $25. Anderson Valley's premier producer turns to inland for fifty year old vines and the heat to ripen them. They got plenty ripe this vintage, with deep, impressive berry and fruit flavors and accents like chocolate and rum. It's a little soft, but okay. Sixteen percent alcohol is heady, but the wine handles it well, and has been fermented to full dryness. **89** —*S.H. (5/1/2002)*

NEESE

Neese 2000 Nonno Guiseppe Zinfandel (Redwood Valley) $17. Hang onto your hats, here's an Arnold of a Zin, big and brawny, but with star quality. The Mendocino appellation is a little known home to old vine, high quality Zin vines, and this juicy and succulent, but dry, wine is a fine example. **87** —*S.H. (9/12/2002)*

NELMS ROAD

Nelms Road 2000 Cabernet Sauvignon (Columbia Valley (WA)) $25. Nice effort in this value label, showing clean varietal character in the nose, and tight, focused flavors across the palate. It's solid and flavorful, though one-dimensional. **87** —*P.G. (6/1/2002)*

Nelms Road 2000 Cabernet Sauvignon (Columbia Valley (WA)) $19. Firm and tannic, this is a solid, budget Cab with some earthy notes of bark and a core of tight red currant fruit. In the mouth flavors of tart berry dominate, with a tannic bite in the back end. Air it out! **87** —*P.G. (9/1/2003)*

Nelms Road 2001 Merlot (Columbia Valley (WA)) $19. Nelms Road is Woodward Canyon's value label, but what a lovely bottle of wine this is! It puts a lot of insipid California Merlots to shame with its spicy, peppery fruit and clean, lightly herbal persistence through the finish. **88** —*P.G. (9/1/2003)*

Nelms Road 2000 Merlot (Columbia Valley (WA)) $20. Nelms Road is the second label of Woodward Canyon, and shows Rick Small's sure-handed winemaking skills. Young fruit in a forward style, it has hints of greenness, but nothing detrimental, and just enough oaky spice to kick up the flavor interest. **87** —*P.G. (6/1/2002)*

NELSON

Nelson 1998 Cabernet Franc (Sonoma Valley) $32. Starts with mint, earth, and black cherry aromas that suggest some uneven ripening. Very dry, with substantial tannins. The light vintage has tamped down the fruit, leaving a wine of structure and elegance rather than depth. Enjoy this one soon. **87** —*S.H. (12/1/2001)*

Nelson 1997 Cabernet Franc (Sonoma Valley) $24. A clean, well made wine displaying Cab Franc's herbaceous, earthy, and spicy-floral side. Drinks on the lean side, with some spare, delicate berry fruit; it definitely needs food to bring out its best qualities. Very dry. **84** —*S.H. (2/1/2001)*

Nelson 1999 Pinot Noir (Russian River Valley) $28. Intricate, pretty aromas of red cherry, smoke, strawberry, cigar box, and dusty spices are followed by dry but full flavors of berries and fruits. **86** —*S.H. (12/15/2001)*

NERELLI

Nerelli 2004 After Hours Proprietor's Choice Bien Nacido Vineyard White Blend (Santa Maria Valley) $40. A blend of botrytized Pinot Blanc and Chardonnay, with 38.3% residual sugar, this enormously sweet dessert wine is rich and pure in apricot, vanilla, and buttercream flavors. It's a rewarding wine, a rich, complex after-dinner sipper. **91** —*S.H. (8/1/2006)*

NEVADA CITY

Nevada City 2001 Vin Cinq Bordeaux Blend (Sierra Foothills) $16. A Bordeaux blend, it's dry and balanced, with some nice cherry-berry flavors and a touch of oak. Could use a little more ripeness and finesse. **84** —*S.H. (6/1/2004)*

Nevada City 2001 Cabernet Franc (Sierra Foothills) $17. The mountains have produced a pleasantly drinkable wine. It has plummy, cherry, and licorice flavors with an earthy edge of coffee, and soft tannins. Try as an alternative to Merlot. **84** —*S.H. (6/1/2004)*

Nevada City 2000 Cabernet Sauvignon (Sierra Foothills) $16. Rustic and dry, with puckery tannins, this earthy wine blends coffee and herb flavors with a touch of berry. **83** —*S.H. (6/1/2004)*

Nevada City 1999 Cabernet Sauvignon (Sierra Foothills) $16. From Nevada County, this wine is full of black currant flavors and dry tannins. The trick, of course, is to get Cabernet to taste fancy and pedigreed. No sense buying a rustic Cabernet at any price—we have Zin for that. **84** —*S.H. (11/15/2002)*

Nevada City 2000 Petite Sirah (Sierra Foothills) $28. A completely average wine, with jammy flavors of red and black cherry, spice, and a hint of tarry earth. Tastes soft and mellow, with a thick, syrupy texture. There's nothing wrong with it, but it's pricey for what you get. **85** *(4/1/2003)*

Nevada City NV Rough and Ready Red Cask 202 Lirac Red Blend (California) $10. A blend of Syrah, Cab Sauvignon, Charbono, Petite Sirah, and Zinfandel that lives up to its moniker. It's rough in its briary, earthy flavors, and ready to drink. **84** —*S.H. (6/1/2004)*

Nevada City 2001 Syrah (Sierra Foothills) $20. Well-ripened cherry-blackberry fruit is floating in sturdy, rough tannins that make the mouthfeel rugged. It's an honest country-style wine, but seems expensive. **85** —*S.H. (6/1/2004)*

Nevada City 2000 Syrah (Sierra Foothills) $18. Fully ripened fruit, from four vineyards in four counties, comes together seamlessly to to produce this flavorful red wine. It's juicy and filled with berry flavors that taste dry, but finish sweet. This country wine is soft and a little short on finesse. **85** —*S.H. (12/1/2002)*

Nevada City 2000 Zinfandel (Sierra Foothills) $15. A distinctive, old fashioned California mountain Zin. It's strong in alcohol, very ripe in blackberry flavor, and tannic and rustic in texture, with just a touch of Porty raisins. **85** —*S.H. (6/1/2004)*

Nevada City 1999 Zinfandel (Sierra Foothills) $15. Juicy and ripe. You can taste the sun in every sip of the blackberry, blueberry, and black cherry flavors. The wine is balanced and supple, maybe too soft, but that's nitpicking. It's Sierra-esque in its rugged, briary way. **86** —*S.H. (11/1/2002)*

NEVEU

Neveu 2003 Pinot Gris (Siskiyou County) $13. Rustic and thin-flavored, with odd citrus and medicinal flavors. **82** —*S.H. (5/1/2005)*

Neveu 2002 Pinot Noir (Siskiyou County) $15. Smells like chocolate cake frosting, and turns dry and bitter. **81** —*S.H. (7/1/2005)*

NEWELL

Newell 2003 Para Dois Petite Sirah (Monterey County) $36. This is one of those big, inky, juicy Pets that has contributed to the modest boom in variety. Although the sandpapery tannins and acids currently lock down the wine, it has an impressive core of blackberry fruit that bodes well for the cellar. Best 2009–2015. **89** —*S.H. (12/1/2006)*

NEWLAN

Newlan 2000 Cabernet Sauvignon (Napa Valley) $30. A beautiful Cab that cheats the vintage with its plumpy ripe fruit. Pours black, and opens with young, fairly closed aromas of herbs and oak, but the hidden depths of this wine reveal themselves in the black currant, cherry, and chocolate flavors that last through the finish. Should age through the decade, or try now with prime rib. **90** —*S.H. (12/31/2003)*

Newlan 1998 Chardonnay (Napa Valley) $16. 88 *(6/1/2000)*

Newlan 2000 Chardonnay (Napa Valley) $17. This is a hands-on wine filled with everything toasty oak and lees can add. The underlying flavors are fairly lean, suggesting citrus fruits and a hint of green apple. The result is not a big, fat Chard, but a tight, crisp, and elegant one. Perfect with roasted chicken. **87** —S.H. (12/15/2002)

Newlan 1999 Chardonnay (Napa Valley) $18. There's a strong leesy, cheesy note on top of apple and peach fruit, in addition to a moderate dose of oak. That leesy quality returns in the finish, where it turns slightly bitter and spicy. This is a nice, pleasant, mildly complex wine. **86** —S.H. (11/15/2001)

Newlan 1999 Merlot (Napa Valley) $20. An exciting and tastefully made wine that approaches the ultraripe fruit of the vintage with restraint. Young, jammy plum and blackberry flavors are reined in with herbal, olivey notes, and oak has been sparingly applied in this dry, elegant table wine. **90 Editors' Choice** —S.H. (8/1/2003)

Newlan 1998 Merlot (Napa Valley) $20. The nose seems lean and vaguely unripe. You get aromas of chocolate and green olives, and the most distant whiff of meat. Of course there's a great deal of oak, including American, which lends vanillin and smoky notes, but still an impression of leanness carries through in the mouth. It struggles to say the word "fruit." It's also very tannic. That aside, it may soften and improve in time. **85** —S.H. (2/1/2001)

Newlan 2000 Pinot Noir (Napa Valley) $24. A light-bodied, savory Pinot Noir with pleasant cherry and spice flavors and a silky, gentle texture. It has enough complexity to stand up to fancy fare, and will gain by a few hours of decanting. **87** —S.H. (12/1/2004)

Newlan 1999 Pinot Noir (Napa Valley) $20. 87 —S.H. (9/1/2002)

Newlan 1996 Reserve Pinot Noir (Napa Valley) $25. 85 —S.H. (12/15/2000)

Newlan 1997 Reseve Pinot Noir (Napa Valley) $26. 89 —S.H. (9/1/2002)

Newlan 1999 Late Harvest White Riesling (Napa Valley) $25. Fantastically rich and sweet—even decadent—with apricot, crème brûlée, and caramel aromas and botrytis. Deeply opulent and fruity in the mouth with flavors of apricot nectar, it has a zesty, cleansing cut of acidity. Drizzle it on vanilla ice cream on a hot night. **91** —S.H. (12/1/2001)

Newlan 1997 Zinfandel (Sonoma County) $20. 86 —S.H. (5/1/2000)

Newlan 2000 Zinfandel (Napa Valley) $22. With some very old grapes and a goodly proportion of other Rhônish red grapes, this is an authentic, old-style field blend. It's big, rich, dark, and tannic. It's a dry, strong, lusty wine meant to accompany grilled meats and Italian fare. **86** —S.H. (11/1/2002)

Newlan 1998 Zinfandel (Napa Valley) $22. Good, thick, black cherry fruit, dense tannins, with a dark, dense, chalky finish. This is manly Zin—muscular, balanced, and heavy. Great for outdoor grilling. **87** —P.G. (3/1/2001)

Newlan 1997 Zinfandel (Napa Valley) $20. 88 —S.H. (5/1/2000)

Newlan 1997 Wallstrum Family Zinfandel (Sonoma County) $20. Starts out nice, with a good, fruity raspberry nose, but on the palate are tastes of tomatoes, with a dry, astringent, tannic finish. **83** —P.G. (3/1/2001)

NEWSOME-HARLOW

Newsome-Harlow 2001 Meritage (Calaveras County) $28. Chocolate-covered raisins here, real ripe and fruity, with smooth tannnis and a rich, creamy mouthfeel. This is a big, brawny style of Cab, but it's lush and attractive. **88** —S.H. (2/1/2005)

Newsome-Harlow 2004 Big John's Zinfandel (Calaveras County) $25. Soft and chocolatey, with an infusion of cassis, soy, and licorice, this lip-smacking Zin finishes a bit hot and peppery, with a hint of raisiny sweetness. Keeps you coming back due to the rich flavors. **85** —S.H. (12/1/2006)

Newsome-Harlow 2003 Big John's Vineyard Zinfandel (Calaveras County) $24. This is one of those juicily extracted Zins that blasts a hole in the palate. It has big flavors of black, blue, and red wild berries, with a stimulating peppery finish. A dry wine with dusty tannins that will cut through meats and cheeses. **89** —S.H. (10/1/2005)

Newsome-Harlow 2001 Big John's Vineyard Zinfandel (Calaveras County) $24. Big mountain Zin, fruity, briary, and brambly, with rich, sweet tannins, but marred for me with too much residual sugar. **84** —S.H. (2/1/2005)

Newsome-Harlow 2002 Big John's Vineyard Zinfandel (Calaveras County) $24. Clean, balanced, and smooth despite the tannins, because the acidity is low. The wine features berry flavors with an earthy, dill finish. **84** —S.H. (5/1/2005)

NEWTON

Newton 2000 Le Puzzle Cabernet Sauvignon (Spring Mountain) $45. Richly textured and flavorful, this gentle wine has pretty cherry and blackberry notes, as well as eathier ones of tobacco and herbs. Oak adds sweetness, but is not heavy. Some astringent tannins suggest modest aging possibilities. **89** —S.H. (11/15/2003)

Newton 2000 Unfiltered Cabernet Sauvignon (Napa Valley) $41. Soft in acids and buttery in melted tannins, this wine slides its cherry-berry flavors gently across the palate. It is polished and smooth, with a light but delicious mouthfeel. Turns a bit astringent on the finish as those dusty tannins kick in. **88** —S.H. (11/15/2003)

Newton 2002 Chardonnay (Napa-Sonoma) $24. Only a shadow of Newton's fabulous Unfiltered, but contains many similar traits, among them rich, ripe, and opulent tropical fruit flavors that are long and persistent through the finish. There's an oaky creaminess that adds to the richness. **88** —S.H. (8/1/2005)

Newton 1998 Naturally Fermented Chardonnay (Sonoma County) $23. 86 (6/1/2000)

Newton 2002 Unfiltered Chardonnay (Napa Valley) $56. Impressive, delicious, a tremendous wine in every respect. It's powerfully smoky, with spiced oak everywhere, rich in buttered toast and vanilla, but such pretty fruit underneath, it's easily able to support it. Mangoes, pineapples, peaches, ripe Bosc pears, loads of dusty spices, and a rich, full creamy texture. **94** —S.H. (8/1/2005)

Newton 2000 Unfiltered Chardonnay (Napa Valley) $42. The winemaker calls this wine "minerally," and it's true that it's not a ripely opulent Chard, although there are some pleasant tropical fruit flavors along with the herbs and stones. But mainly this is a firm wine, well-oaked, with bracing acidity. Turns a bit sharp on the finish. **90** —S.H. (12/1/2003)

Newton 2000 Epic Merlot (Napa Valley) $42. Firmly in the style of Newton's unfiltered Merlot, but a shade richer and deeper, and oak plays a more apparent role. It is a very fine wine, and had it been from a better vintage would be near-classic. Flavors of blackberries and cherries, chocolate, and herbs mingle in a package that is dry and smooth. The tannins are gorgeous. **93** —S.H. (12/31/2003)

Newton 2000 Unfiltered Merlot (Spring Mountain) $NA. I love this wine, with its plummy, blackberry flavors and hint of grilled meat. The tannins are nice and ripe and dry, resulting in a velvety texture that feels fine. Deep and complex. **91** —S.H. (12/31/2003)

Newton 2000 Special Cuvée Pinot Noir (Sonoma) $66. A lovely, nuanced nose of oriental spices, jasmine, and lilacs opens this seductive wine. Dark plum-berry fruit, leather, and coffee flavors and a supple, balanced feel add to its appeal. Soft and low in acidity to one taster, but to most it was simply succulent. The subtle, chocolate-tinged finish of fine-grained tannins is long and sensuous. Drink now–2007. **90** (10/1/2002)

NEYERS

Neyers 2001 Cuvée d'Honeur Syrah (Napa Valley) $45. From the Hudson Vineyard in Carneros, this is a very dark wine bursting with crème de cassis, chocolate, mint, smoke, vanilla, and toast aromas. The flavors are similarly rich and unctuous, with great weight and a fabulous core of blackberries and spice. For all its size, it never loses its sense of balance and elegance. **94 Editors' Choice** —S.H. (11/1/2003)

Neyers 2001 Pato Vineyard Zinfandel (Contra Costa County) $30. A densely textured wine that serves up a fine blend of black cherry, black plum, coffee, chocolate, toast, sweet oak, spice, raspberry, and vanilla flavors. They're couched in firm but silky tannins that give good structure and lead to a long finish. **90** (11/1/2003)

Neyers 2001 Tofanelli Vineyard Zinfandel (Napa Valley) $35. A bright-edged wine that offers cola, black cherry, spice, toast, vanilla, licorice, cedar, coffee, and chocolate flavors, all well-integrated and supported by firm, ripe tannins. It sits well on the finish, lingering nicely. **91** (11/1/2003)

USA

NICHOLAS COLE CELLARS

Nicholas Cole Cellars 2003 Camille Bordeaux Blend (Columbia Valley (WA)) $48. Tight, tart, racy, and stylish; this Bordeaux blend of 47% Cabernet Sauvignon, 38% Merlot, and 15% Cab Franc is the best yet from this young winery, a neighbor of Leonetti. Tart, primary fruit sets up a foundation that is substantial and tannic. There's plenty of power here; it just needs more time. **91** —*P.G. (10/1/2006)*

Nicholas Cole Cellars 2002 Camille Bordeaux Blend (Columbia Valley (WA)) $48. This is the wine formerly known as Claret. The new vintage is still young, grapey, looser, and more broadly fruity than the sensational '01. But what's interesting are layers of ripe fruits, tar, mineral, dark chocolate, and chalk. The wine just seems to constantly reveal more of itself as it sits in the glass. **91** —*P.G. (4/1/2005)*

Nicholas Cole Cellars 2001 Claret Bordeaux Blend (Columbia Valley (WA)) $46. Half Cab Sauvignon, half Cab Franc, from two top vineyards (Champoux and Klipsun), this wine has improved dramatically since its initial release. Truly Bordeaux-like, it has fascinating streaks of lead pencil, tar, and leather, layered and textured, behind supple, substantial cassis and berry fruit. Balanced and deep. **93** —*P.G. (4/1/2005)*

NICHOLS

Nichols 1997 Central Coast Blend Chardonnay (Central Coast) $30. 88 —*J.C. (3/1/2000)*

NICKEL & NICKEL

Nickel & Nickel 2002 Branding Iron Cabernet Sauvignon (Oakville) $75. Here's a bright, ripe, and juicy Cabernet that impresses for its wealth of flavor and refined structure. It's bold in black currants, cassis, and chocolate, with a rich layering of oak, yet maintains balance and elegance. Dry and soft, this is a wine to drink now and through 2006. **90** —*S.H. (12/1/2005)*

Nickel & Nickel 1997 Carpenter Vineyard Cabernet Sauvignon (Napa Valley) $75. 92 —*(11/1/2000)*

Nickel & Nickel 2002 Dragonfly Vineyard Cabernet Sauvignon (St. Helena) $90. Decadent, hedonistic, all those adjectives don't do credit to the fancy way this Cab hits the mouth. It's Renoir in a glass. Soft but firmly structured and well oaked, the complex flavors range from cassis and vanilla to mocha and gingerbread, and are totally dry. Pure Napa Cab, although it's probably not an ager because of the softness. **94** —*S.H. (12/1/2005)*

Nickel & Nickel 1999 Dragonfly Vineyard Cabernet Sauvignon (Napa Valley) $90. Rarely does a wine with such a mellow, subdued nose shine in the mouth as this does. Below the aromatic veil of boysenberry and chocolate is ripe cassis and berry fruit, which gives way to a tight, clean, structured finish that oozes coffee, character, and class. **92 Cellar Selection** —*M.S. (5/1/2003)*

Nickel & Nickel 2002 John C. Sullenger Vineyard Cabernet Sauvignon (Oakville) $75. This is a big, ripe wine, and fairly tannic too, although the tannins are soft, ripe and sweet. Where N&N's Dragonfly bottling from St. Helena is all immediate gratification, this is more firmly structured, less flashy. But it's soft in acidity, and not a candidate for aging. Drink now and through 2006. **88** —*S.H. (12/1/2005)*

Nickel & Nickel 2001 John C. Sullenger Vineyard Cabernet Sauvignon (Oakville) $75. A stunning Cabernet, rich, pure, and powerful. Blackberries, currants, oak, and sweet fresh herbs flood the palate. It's a tannic wine, with a hard-edged mouthfeel, but the tannins are so sweet, it's tempting to uncork now. Drink right away, or age for 10 years and let it develop magic. **94** —*S.H. (10/1/2004)*

Nickel & Nickel 1999 John C. Sullenger Vineyard Cabernet Sauvignon (Oakville) $75. This smells like Bordeaux, from the cassis and earth all the way to the foresty aromas that some might even call green. The palate is a smooth ride of currant, plum, and bitter chocolate, all with a cool, herbal underbelly. **90** —*M.S. (5/1/2003)*

Nickel & Nickel 1998 John C. Sullenger Vineyard Cabernet Sauvignon (Oakville) $75. Smooth textured with spicy raspberry, cherry, cedar, and herb notes. While it's elegant and supple, it doesn't share the intensity of some of it's Oakville neighbors. Moderate and bright on the finish. **87** —*J.M. (12/31/2001)*

Nickel & Nickel 1997 John C. Sullenger Vineyard Cabernet Sauvignon (Oakville) $65. 92 *(11/1/2000)*

Nickel & Nickel 1997 Rock Cairn Cabernet Sauvignon (Oakville) $75. 90 *(11/1/2000)*

Nickel & Nickel 2001 Rock Cairn Vineyard Cabernet Sauvignon (Oakville) $75. A great Cabernet—the only question is whether to consume it now or later. In favor of now are the rich currant, dark chocolate, and oak flavors, ripe, sweet tannins and overall balance. But it's a big, masculine wine that will easily soften and improve through the decade. **93** —*S.H. (10/1/2004)*

Nickel & Nickel 2002 Stelling Vineyard Cabernet Sauvignon (Oakville) $130. This is the most expensive of N&N's current Cab lineup and also a remarkably good wine. It combines flamboyantly ripe fruit with a fine, rich structure and balance, although it's a little soft. The complex flavors of blackberries, blueberries, and cherries are well-oaked, and the finish is long and spicy. **92** —*S.H. (12/1/2005)*

Nickel & Nickel 2001 Stelling Vineyard Cabernet Sauvignon (Oakville) $125. Impresses with its opulence and decadence. Soft, almost too soft, in texture, with a velvety, melted fudge mouthfeel that carries flavors of chocolate, vanilla, blackberry, cassis, spices, and smoky oak across the palate through a long finish. A bit of a letdown in the middle palate. **93** —*S.H. (10/1/2004)*

Nickel & Nickel 1999 Stelling Vineyard Cabernet Sauvignon (Oakville) $125. 91 —*J.C. (6/1/2003)*

Nickel & Nickel 1998 Stelling Vineyard Cabernet Sauvignon (Oakville) $100. Smoky toast and earth tones offer an enticing aromatic entrée to this silky textured wine. It's marked by elegance and balanced bing cherry, blackberry, raspberry, spice, herb, and cedar notes. Long on the finish. **91** —*S.H. (12/31/2001)*

Nickel & Nickel 1997 Stelling Vineyard Cabernet Sauvignon (Oakville) $95. 93 *(11/1/2000)*

Nickel & Nickel 1999 Tench Vineyard Cabernet Sauvignon (Oakville) $65. 89 —*J.C. (6/1/2003)*

Nickel & Nickel 2002 Vogt Vineyard Cabernet Sauvignon (Howell Mountain) $75. Dark, dry, and firmly tannic, this seems to be one for the cellar, although for how long is a challenge. The fruit is terrifically ripe in black currants and cassis, and the tannins are gorgeously thick, but there's a softness that makes me wonder if the balance is there for very long. **85** —*S.H. (12/1/2005)*

Nickel & Nickel 2001 Vogt Vineyard Cabernet Sauvignon (Howell Mountain) $75. This is a wine to lay away, to judge by the hard tannins that dominate it. But so strong is the heart of fruit that the flavors burst through that straitjacket. They flood the palate with amazingly dense black currant, cherry, and dark chocolate fruit that last through a long finish. As tough as it is now, it will develop gracefully for many years. **93** —*S.H. (10/1/2004)*

Nickel & Nickel 2000 John's Creek Chardonnay (Napa Valley) $50. Steely and firm on the palate, with a marked bend toward citrus and herb flavors. Bright and clean on the finish. **87** —*J.M. (12/15/2002)*

Nickel & Nickel 2003 John's Creek Vineyard Chardonnay (Napa Valley) $50. Very young now, with powerful acids and tightly wound white peach fruit, just nudging into pineapples. Accentuated with oak and lees. Finishes with a punch of minerality. **88** —*S.H. (10/1/2005)*

Nickel & Nickel 1999 John's Creek Vineyard Chardonnay (Napa Valley) $50. Aromas of ripe cantaloupe, vanilla, and tropical fruits plus creamy malolactic notes show on the nose of this limited-production Napa Chardonnay. This offering, a distinct label from the proprietors of Far Niente, has apple, pear, and white peach flavors. Expect caramel and nut accents on a smoothly textured, buttery palate. The finish is long and dry—you'll see a reprise of the nutty elements plus a hint of lime. **89** *(7/1/2001)*

Nickel & Nickel 2004 Searby Vineyard Chardonnay (Russian River Valley) $40. The winery specializes in single-vineyard wines, and this is certainly a unique Chardonnay, but it's not an opulent one. On the contrary, it's flinty, acidic, and raspingly dry, which makes one think it was picked early. It's almost like a Sauvignon Blanc, with its puckery lemon flavors. **85** —*S.H. (10/1/2006)*

Nickel & Nickel 2003 Searby Vineyard Chardonnay (Russian River Valley) $38. My favorite of N&N's three new single-vineyard Chards. Shows broad appeal with its array of peach, apple, and tropical fruit flavors, heightened with touches of oak and lees. Young and crisp in acids, it's full-bodied enough to accompany roast duck. **90** —*S.H. (10/1/2005)*

Nickel & Nickel 2002 Searby Vineyard Chardonnay (Russian River Valley) $35. This great wine manages to be delicate and assertive at the same time. The delicacy lies in the tart citrus, apple, and herb flavors and crisp acidity that make the wine almost weightless. The power is in its tightly coiled intensity. **92** —*S.H. (9/1/2004)*

Nickel & Nickel 2004 Truchard Vineyard Chardonnay (Carneros) $40. The aim here seems to be to avoid ripe, opulent fruit in favor of an elegantly streamlined wine you might call Chablisian. The result is bone dry, high in aciditiy and lean, with mineral and citrus flavors. This is against the grain these days for fruity Chards. **85** —*S.H. (10/1/2006)*

Nickel & Nickel 2003 Truchard Vineyard Chardonnay (Carneros) $38. Banana, peach, papaya, vanilla, toasted oak, and lees all mingle together to make this Chard complex. It also features rich acidity and minerals for extra nuance. May gain added dimensions over the next four years. **89** —*S.H. (10/1/2005)*

Nickel & Nickel 2002 Truchard Vineyard Chardonnay (Carneros) $35. Crafted along leanly tailored, elegant lines, this wine has high acidity and a citrusy, mineral character. It's a wine of great structural integrity, focused and pristine, although it's also oaky. The right foods will coax out the inherent sweetness and Oriental spice. **90** —*S.H. (9/1/2004)*

Nickel & Nickel 2001 Truchard Vineyard Chardonnay (Carneros) $35. A big Chard that will satisfy fans of ripe, oily fruit with a lavish overlay of oak. The flavors range from apples to peaches and sweet tropical fruits, wrapped in a buttercream texture. Finishes dry and spicy. **89** —*S.H. (12/1/2003)*

Nickel & Nickel 2000 Truchard Vineyard Chardonnay (Carneros) $35. Firm and bright, yet round on the palate. The wine shows a fine blend of pear, apple, herb, hazelnut, and citrus flavors. The finish is particularly grape-fruit-like, long, and bright. **89** —*J.M. (12/15/2002)*

Nickel & Nickel 2002 Harris Vineyard Merlot (Oakville) $40. Co-released with N&N's Suscol Ranch Merlot. This one's as ripe in currant, black cherry, and chocolate fruit, and the tannins are as intricate and complex. Seems just a shade less complete, although it's still a dazzling wine. **90** —*S.H. (10/1/2005)*

Nickel & Nickel 2001 Harris Vineyard Merlot (Oakville) $40. This intense and concentrated wine shows a youthful precocity, but it also has the balance and stuffing to age gracefully. The cassis, cherry, smoky oak, mocha, and mint flavors are generous, and the tannins are notable but negotiable. Drink now through the decade. **91** —*S.H. (12/15/2004)*

Nickel & Nickel 2000 Harris Vineyard Merlot (Oakville) $40. Monster Merlot, a wine that kicks butt from first to finish. Pours a deep garnet, and leaves streaky glycerine on the glass. Opening aromas are young and closed, of blackberry, ground coffee, and spice. In the mouth, explodes with rich flavors of cassis, chocolate, and spicy plum pudding. For all its size, this gorgeous wine is balanced and harmonious. **93** —*S.H. (12/31/2003)*

Nickel & Nickel 2002 Sori Bricco Vineyard Merlot (Diamond Mountain) $40. This dry, tannic Merlot has simple flavors that are a bit unripe. There's a green-bean streak that just barely breaks into coffeebean and plum. It's not going anywhere. **82** —*S.H. (12/1/2005)*

Nickel & Nickel 2001 Sori Bricco Vineyard Merlot (Diamond Mountain) $40. An amazingly dense and concentrated mountain wine, young and plucky in youthful tannins and acidity, and a guaranteed cellar candidate. It's tough and gritty now, but there's a powerful undertow of black currant and cherry fruit that will carry it easily for years. **92 Cellar Selection** —*S.H. (12/15/2004)*

Nickel & Nickel 2003 Suscol Ranch Merlot (Napa Valley) $55. From a cool area of the valley comes this very dry, astringently tannic wine, which is not very fruity. The flavors are lean, veering toward dried herbs, leather, and earth, with a cherry core. The texture is rich and complicated. It's a

young wine and if you're a risk-taker, you should lay it down. **86** —*S.H. (10/1/2006)*

Nickel & Nickel 2002 Suscol Ranch Merlot (Napa Valley) $50. A fabulous Merlot that impresses with its instant deliciousness and complexity, yet is likely to hang in there and improve. Dark and full-bodied, with black currant, plum, grilled meat, olive, dark chocolate, and spice flavors. The tannic structure is intricate, soft, and complex. Drink now through 2010. **93** —*S.H. (10/1/2005)*

Nickel & Nickel 2001 Suscol Ranch Merlot (Napa Valley) $50. A gorgeously crafted Merlot that shows bigtime fruit along the lines of blackberries, cherries, cassis, coffee, and sweet green olives, but is remarkably balanced and self-possessed. Fully dry, it's also well oaked. Showcases the terroir of its vineyard and the capability of its winemaking. **93** —*S.H. (12/15/2004)*

Nickel & Nickel 2002 Darien Vineyard Syrah (Russian River Valley) $40. Starts off on the savory side of Syrah, with coffee and meat aromas and flavors taking the lead over the black cherry fruit. But then it picks up brighter berry notes on the long, textured finish. Tannic enough to want rare beef. **87** *(9/1/2005)*

Nickel & Nickel 2002 Dyer Vineyard Syrah (Carneros) $35. Has some gorgeous aromatics reminscent of lavender or mint that add an extra dimension to this wine's tart red plum flavors. On the leaner side, but crisp and elegant. Another fine example of Carneros Syrah. **89** *(9/1/2005)*

Nickel & Nickel 2001 Dyer Vineyard Syrah (Carneros) $35. Young, dark, and brooding, and pretty oaky and tannic now, but all the signs point to an ageable wine. Chew on it and find a rich core of black cherry pie flavors, edged with mocha and white pepper. Best after 2005. **91** —*S.H. (12/1/2004)*

Nickel & Nickel 2000 Ponzo Vineyard Zinfandel (Russian River Valley) $45. The first impression is of a very hot wine. The official label reading is 14.9 percent alcohol, but it feels higher, with a tingly, peppery feeling through the finish. The flavors are of blackberry jam and cassis, white chocolate, and immense spice, and while the wine is dry, it's very rich and expressive. The tannins are soft and lush, in the modern style. **87** —*S.H. (3/1/2004)*

Nickel & Nickel 1998 Ponzo Vineyard Zinfandel (Russian River Valley) $45. After its dark but alluring earth-black, olive-tree, bark-mixed berry bouquet, this Zin's reserved blackberry, charred oak, and maple palate comes as no surprise. Medium-weight, it closes with sweeter blackberry flavors. **88** —*D.T. (3/1/2002)*

NIEBAUM-COPPOLA

Niebaum-Coppola 1999 Rubicon Bordeaux Blend (Rutherford) $100. A wonderfully refined wine, with firm, ripe tannins that fream an elegant blend of rich plum, blackberry, coffee, chocolate, cassis, black cherry, cedar, and spice flavors. The finish is long and smooth, with a bright cherry boost at the end. Francis Coppola's benchmark wine. **94** *(8/1/2003)*

Niebaum-Coppola 1996 Rubicon Bordeaux Blend (Rutherford) $90. Tasting a bit raisiny from this warm, dry year, with gobs of sweet cherries and cocoa. Lush, rich, full, still fairly tannic at the age of 9-1/2 years, the wine should continue to develop for an additional five to ten years. **87** —*S.H. (9/1/2006)*

Niebaum-Coppola 2001 Rubicon Cabernet Blend (Rutherford) $100. An excellent wine, and clearly an ager, but I don't think it's in the league of the magnificent '99. It's too young to enjoy now, to judge from the closed, astringent, oaky, tannic mouthfeel. But there's certainly some powerful cassis fruit. Hold until at least 2008. Eventually, it could stun. **90** —*S.H. (10/1/2005)*

Niebaum-Coppola 2002 Cabernet Franc (Rutherford) $44. One of the best Cab Francs out there, intricately structured and rich in terroir character. It's lighter in body than a Cab Sauv, with cherry, mocha, caramel, vanilla, dusty oriental spice, and anise flavors that unfold in waves. Totally addictive and elegant. **94** —*S.H. (4/1/2005)*

Niebaum-Coppola 2001 Cabernet Franc (Rutherford) $44. Impressive for its sheer size, a dark, muscular wine jammed with juicy cherry and currant flavors. Drinks dry, with firm but sculpted tannins. It's on the tough side. At its youthful best now with a juicy steak. **86** —*S.H. (5/1/2004)*

Niebaum-Coppola 2000 Cabernet Franc (Rutherford) $44. Dark and rich, a young, expressive wine with plummy, spicy flavors and tannins so rich and thick, they're bound to age. It's not clear, however, if Cab Franc is worth vinifying on its own. This wine has a certain one-dimensionality. **86** —S.H. (6/1/2003)

Niebaum-Coppola 2002 Cask Cabernet Sauvignon (Rutherford) $65. Shows quite oaky now, with powerful notes of vanilla, char, and wood sap, but it's also rich in cherry fruit, with a touch of grilled meat. Texturally, this Cab is dense, smooth, fine, and very dry, with substantial tannins. It's too young now, but should be a beauty by 2008 and beyond. **93 Cellar Selection** —S.H. (12/15/2005)

Niebaum-Coppola 2000 Cask Cabernet Sauvignon (Rutherford) $65. Lavishly smoked oak, with its vanilla and aromatic wood-sap, just can't quite overcome the fruit's thinness. As soft and pretty as the texture and tannins are, the wine still leaves you wishing for more, especially at this price. **86** —S.H. (5/1/2004)

Niebaum-Coppola 1999 Cask Cabernet Cabernet Sauvignon (Rutherford) $65. Seductively delicious, a wine that caresses the palate with velvety tannins. Dry and balanced, with cassis, blackberry, tobacco, and herb flavors. Oak adds char, vanilla, and smoke, as well as a woody sweetness. Seems higher in acidity that many other Napa Cabs, which gives it grip and body. **93** —S.H. (2/1/2003)

Niebaum-Coppola 1998 Cask Cabernet Cabernet Sauvignon (Rutherford) $65. This 100% Cabernet Sauvignon celebrates the old Inglenook Cask Cabs, but has to grapple with a thin vintage. It's dry, but excessively soft and low on fruit. Tries to make up for a lack of stuffing with oaky sweetness, and has charm, but no depth. **89** —S.H. (6/1/2002)

Niebaum-Coppola 2001 Estate Cask Cabernet Sauvignon (Rutherford) $110. Dramatic from the get-go, an amazing wine that oozes well-ripened black currant, cassis, mocha, and oak aromas and flavors. Exuberantly, decadently rich, with a chocolate fudge sweetness, although it's totally dry. The tannins are ripe, sweet, smooth, and unctuous. Would score even higher were it not for a softness that could limit its ageworthiness. **93** —S.H. (10/1/2004)

Niebaum-Coppola 2002 Blancaneaux Marsanne (Napa Valley) $30. Quite richly textured, with a strong spice, pear, apricot, and apple core. It's viscous, but carries good acidity for balance. An unusual wine that finishes long and fresh, yet has plenty of weight. **88** —J.M. (9/1/2004)

Niebaum-Coppola 1997 Merlot (Napa Valley) $40. 89 —S.H. (7/1/2000)

Niebaum-Coppola 2000 Merlot (Rutherford) $44. The Godfather would love this dark, rich wine, with its intricate layers of plum and blackberry flavors that coat the tongue. It's very dry and food friendly. The finish lasts for a full minute. Fairly tannic now, although they're soft and creamy, but it will improve through 2005. **91 Cellar Selection** —S.H. (12/15/2003)

Niebaum-Coppola 1999 Merlot (Rutherford) $44. A big, big wine. It's one of the darker wines out there, and the plummy, blackberry aromas suggest deeply ripe flavors. They're there, a solid core of massive fruit, although it's buried now under the weight of oak, alcohol, and tannins. It's a young wine, and a bit awkward. May round out with age. **90** —S.H. (6/1/2002)

Niebaum-Coppola 2000 Dolcetto Red Blend (Napa Valley) $28. The Godfather's hommage to a common Italian varietal is a Zinfandel-like fruity wine, rich in berry flavors suggesting plums and blueberries. It's dry, with distinctly Napa-esque fine dusty tannins. Raises this garden-variety grape to a new level of luxury. **87** —S.H. (12/1/2002)

Niebaum-Coppola 2000 Rubicon Red Blend (Rutherford) $100. Showcases the shortcomings of the vintage as well as the strengths of its terroir and winemaking. The blackberry and cassis flavors are obviously short, and snap to an abrupt finish, but the textural complexity and oaky overlay are very fine. A charming wine meant for early drinking. **90** —S.H. (11/15/2003)

Niebaum-Coppola 1997 Rubicon Red Blend (Rutherford) $100. A master-piece from this near perfect vintage. Completely ripe, classic, and fresh, with oodles of red cherry and black currant flavors that are generously oaked. Amazingly, the wine is still young and tannic. So beautifully structured, so smooth and polished, firm yet soft, just a gorgeous wine.

Hold onto it until at least 2012, if you can. **97 Cellar Selection** —S.H. (9/1/2006)

Niebaum-Coppola 2003 Blancaneaux Rhône White Blend (Rutherford) $40. This Rhône white blend is very dry and bright in acids, with a racy mouthfeel that stimulates the palate. The flavors veer toward wildflowers, apricots, vanilla, and oak, but they thin out and turn oaky and bitter. **86** —S.H. (10/1/2005)

Niebaum-Coppola 2002 Blancaneax Rhône White Blend (Rutherford) $30. Pale in color, and with elusive aromas that suggest wildflowers, peaches, and apricots, this is an exotic blend of Marsanne, Roussanne, Chardonnay, and Viognier. It turns full-bodied in the mouth, and complex in fruity, spicy flavors. **89** —S.H. (9/1/2004)

Niebaum-Coppola 2002 RC Reserve Syrah (Rutherford) $46. It doesn't say Syrah on the front label, but that's what's in the bottle, nicely concentrated and rich, layered with toasty, vanilla-scented oak and imbued with a creamy, supple texture and chewy finish. The flavors are an intricate blend of blueberry-blackberry and vanilla, which should develop more complexity with age. **90** (9/1/2005)

Niebaum-Coppola 2000 RC Reserve Syrah (Rutherford) $56. A new wine from Francis Coppola, named after his son Roman and made from Syrah grapes planted in 1996 on the estate. The high score reflects the amazing extract and beautiful integration of fruit with the tannins and oak. This is pure ambrosia. Clearly New World in origin with its ripeness and softness. Small amounts of Petit Verdot and Merlot round it out. **94 Editors' Choice** —S.H. (12/1/2003)

Niebaum-Coppola 2001 Edizione Pennino Zinfandel (Rutherford) $35. A firm-textured style that shows dark blackberry, coffee, and licorice notes. The tannins are a bit rustic, while the finish is moderate in length, ending with a smoky edge. **87** —J.M. (4/1/2004)

Niebaum-Coppola 2000 Edizione Pennino Zinfandel (Rutherford) $44. Dark, almost black. You just know this is a big wine. Smells a bit one-dimensioanl and earthy, with blackberry notes and an oaky overlay. But it tastes a lot better. Big and thick, it fills the mouth with blackberry flavor, wrapped in soft, intricate tannins. **88** —S.H. (2/1/2003)

Niebaum-Coppola 1999 Edizione Pennino Zinfandel (Rutherford) $40. Blueberry in the mouth, with a little more oak than I'd like, the Edizine Pennino (named for Coppola's maternal grandfather, Francesco Pennino) has sweet earth and luscious blackberry aromas on the nose. Finishes with blue and red fruit, plus a smoldering matchsticky note. This is a sexy, button-pushing wine, however much this note may have simplified it. **89** —D.T. (4/1/2002)

Niebaum-Coppola 1998 Edizione Pennino Zinfandel (Napa Valley) $40. 89 —D.T. (3/1/2002)

NIGHT OWL

Night Owl 2004 San Bernabe Vineyard Chardonnay (Monterey County) $12. To call this Chard "rustic" is no put-down, as it affords some good Chardonnay pleasure at a good price. It's soft in acids, with a thick, creamy mouthfeel and ripe flavors of peach custard and guava. **83** —S.H. (12/15/2005)

Night Owl 2003 San Bernabe Vineyard Pinot Noir (Monterey County) $14. This vineyard in the southern Salinas Valley has been getting really interesting in recent years. This is the first Bernabe Pinot Noir that's captured my attention. It's dry and nicely varietal, scoring well on the deliciousness scale. **86** —S.H. (12/15/2005)

Night Owl 2005 San Bernabe Vineyard Riesling (Monterey County) $12. On the sweet side, like an easy German wine, with apple, honeysuckle, peach, spice, and vanilla flavors balanced by refreshing acidity. **84** —S.H. (12/15/2006)

Night Owl 2004 San Bernabe Vineyard Shiraz (Monterey County) $12. Rustic and likeable, an easy wine to wash down burgers or simple Italian. Has loads of cherries, blueberries, boysenberries, loganberries, and plums, with a dusting of clove and pepper. But for all that fruit, it's totally dry. **84** —S.H. (12/31/2006)

Night Owl 2004 San Bernabe Vineyard Shiraz (Monterey) $12. The 2003 version wowed our tasting panel last year, and this edition is a worthy follow-up, featuring a lovely nose of raspberry and stone fruits. Creamy and smooth in the mouth, with red berry and vanilla flavors, it's not all that complex, but satisfying nonetheless. **86** *(8/1/2006)*

Night Owl 2003 San Bernabe Vineyard Shiraz (Monterey County) $12. Though an herbal note shows on both the nose and the finish, this Shiraz is still very good. It is fairly full and creamy in the mouth, with black cherry and vanilla flavors, and a briary element that adds complexity—and it smells just as it yummy as it tastes. **88 Best Buy** *(9/1/2005)*

NINE GABLES

Nine Gables 2001 Pifari Cedar Vista Vineyard Zinfandel (Shenandoah Valley (CA)) $20. Tasted like sweetened coffee with an astringent finish. **81** —*S.H. (3/1/2005)*

NO

No 2005 Sauvignon Blanc (Lake County) $10. A bit of cat pee, but not too much unless you're sensitive to it, with richer citrus and gooseberry notes that finish dry and zesty. The unusual name refers to no oak, no malo and no cork. **85 Best Buy** —*S.H. (12/1/2006)*

NOAH

Noah 2002 Merlot (Yountville) $25. You might take this for a Cab because of the intensely pure cassis entry. Then in the midpalate, the prettiest cherries show up, along with lots of new-oaky flavors and elaborate tannins. All the parts are pretty in this exceptionally smooth, stylish Merlot. A great price for such a wine. **92** —*S.H. (8/1/2006)*

Noah 2001 Los Chamizal Vineyards Zinfandel (Sonoma Valley) $20. Certain Zin fans will celebrate this wine, which emphasizes Zin's rustic, briary, high-alcohol personality. Brims with the flavors of brambly fruit and pepper, with dry tannins and a little bit of residual sugar. **86** —*S.H. (12/15/2004)*

NOCETO

Noceto 1997 Sangiovese (Shenandoah Valley (CA)) $13. 90 Best Buy —*S.H. (12/15/1999)*

Noceto 1998 Riserva Sangiovese (Shenandoah Valley (CA)) $22. Satrts with smoky, black cherry aromas and a hint of stewed tomato and tobacco. Drinks soft, gentle, and complex. There's a chewy meatiness to the flavors and textures that's appealing. It finishes nicely: dry, elegant, and clean. **87** —*S.H. (12/1/2001)*

Noceto 1998 Riserva Sangiovese (Shenandoah Valley (CA)) $22. Starts with smoky, black cherry aromas and a hint of stewed tomato and tobacco. Drinks soft, gentle and complex. There's a chewy meatiness to the flavors and textures that's appealing. It finishes nicely: dry, elegant and clean. **87** —*S.H. (12/1/2001)*

Noceto 2002 Ferrero Ranch Zinfandel (Shenandoah Valley (CA)) $16. Light in flavor and delicate in texture, a Sangiovese-like Zin from this Sangiovese specialist. Tea, raspberry, and cola flavors. Atypical, but likeable. **85** —*S.H. (3/1/2005)*

NONNE GIUSEPPE

Nonne Giuseppe 2001 Neese Vineyards Zinfandel (Redwood Valley) $15. Extremely high in alcohol, this wine starts with raisiny, stewed prune aromas, but it's totally dry, and actually has some nice berry and coffee flavors. Made in the old style, it will have its aficionados. **84** —*S.H. (12/31/2004)*

NORD ESTATE

Nord Estate 2002 Red Wine Cuvée Bordeaux Blend (Napa Valley) $45. From Rutherford, a Merlot and Cabernet Sauvignon blend that's deep and long in cassis and black cherry flavors. It possesses purity and balance, placing it in the front tier of the appellation. Fine now despite its youth, and should hold and soften through this decade. **92** —*S.H. (3/1/2006)*

Nord Estate 2003 Page Nord Vineyard Cabernet Sauvignon (Napa Valley) $42. Although this vineyard is source to acclaimed Syrahs, the Cab is challenging. It needs serious decanting or aging, being dry and tannic. Then there's the blackberry, cassis, and cocoa core, which begs to be released. But the high alcohol may limit ageability. A bit of a conundrum. **88** —*S.H. (3/1/2006)*

Nord Estate 2003 Page Nord Vineyard Cabernet Sauvignon (Napa Valley) $42. The mouthfeel is fat, fleshy, and opulent in malted cherry, raspberry, and chocolate flavors. Although the wine is probably technically dry, it's one of those Cabs that has a sweet finish, rich in fruity essence. It's also quite high in alcohol. **87** —*S.H. (8/1/2006)*

Nord Estate 2002 Chardonnay (Napa Valley) $24. When Napa Valley Chardonnay doesn't succeed, it can be because the climate is too hot. Although the grapes for this wine were grown in Yountville, the wine is soft in acids and earthy. It's not a bad wine, but lacks brightness to boost the fruit. **84** —*S.H. (3/1/2006)*

Nord Estate 2002 Trio Merlot (Yountville) $30. Cool Yountville is treading the line for Bordeaux reds, and this Merlot shows its risky origins in the tough, acidic mouthfeel and minty, green flavors. It just lacks the richness that Merlot needs. Drink now. **84** —*S.H. (3/1/2006)*

Nord Estate 2003 Green Island Vineyards Pinot Noir (Napa Valley) $24. Has cherry, coffee, and blackberry flavors and a rich tannic structure. It's very dry, and oak contributes vanilla, spices, and char. It's a big wine, not particularly elegant now, but could soften and complex with three or four years in the bottle. **86** —*S.H. (3/1/2006)*

Nord Estate 2001 Diversity Syrah (Napa Valley) $85. Ripe in cassis and cherry flavors, well-oaked and toasty, this dry Syrah has complex flavors of black currants, coffee, white pepper, and other dusty spices. Despite its four years of age, it has a sharpness and heat from high alcohol that detract from the mouthfeel. **85** —*S.H. (3/1/2006)*

NORMAN

Norman 2002 Conquest Cabernet Sauvignon (Paso Robles) $20. Soft and sweetly ripe, this is a Cab with the creamy texture and flavor of milk chocolate, in addition to truer varietal ones of blackberries and cherries. It's so ripe in fruity flavor that it's almost sweet, but good acidity and finely textured tannins keep it dry. **85** —*S.H. (8/1/2005)*

Norman 2003 Reserve Cabernet Sauvignon (Paso Robles) $36. Shows the soft lusciousness of Paso, and also the ultraripe fruit that pushes the blackberries and cherries into baked pie filling territory. The wine is dry and fairly tannic, but not so much that a grilled sirloin won't easily handle it. **85** —*S.H. (12/15/2006)*

Norman 2004 Pinot Grigio (Paso Robles) $15. Strikes the palate as quite sweet, with citrus, melon, and fig flavors. The wine is a bit soft in acidity, which makes it slightly cloying. **83** —*S.H. (2/1/2006)*

Norman 2003 The Vocation Rhône Red Blend (Paso Robles) $32. A blend of Syrah, Grenache, Mourvèdre, and Petite Sirah, this wine shows a rustic but easy drinking quality. It's fairly tannic, with a long finish of cherries, blackberries, and spiced coffee. **85** —*S.H. (12/15/2006)*

Norman 2003 Vino Rosado Dry Rosé Blend (Paso Robles) $15. There are a lot of blush wines on the market these days, and this is a nice one. It's completely dry, with intriguing flavors of raspberries, spices, and herbs. Very delicate and rich, with real complexity. Grenache and Syrah. **86** —*S.H. (12/1/2004)*

Norman 2003 Syrah (Paso Robles) $20. Very youthful and unintegrated, with our panel's question remaining unanswered: Will it come together or fall apart? For now, you get decent materials in the form of ripe raspberry fruit, ample size, and weight, but also a sense of rawness and lack of precision. **84** *(9/1/2005)*

Norman 2002 Syrah (Paso Robles) $20. Strives for class and finesse with its moderate alcohol, dry finish, and delicate balance of plummy, coffee, tobacco, and earth flavors. The tannins are still kind of edgy and rough, but there's a nice fruity sweetness. **85** —*S.H. (12/15/2004)*

Norman 2002 The Vocation Syrah (Paso Robles) $32. Seems to have seen a fair amount of oak, boasting copious vanilla scents and even hints of coconut layered atop ripe cherry and blackberry fruit. Bright acids and firm tannins give the finish a sharp edge. **85** *(9/1/2005)*

Norman 1998 The Monster Zinfandel (Paso Robles) $18. Smells very ripe, almost stewed, and it lives up to its name (The Monster) with big, rustic, extracted, alcoholic flavors. For those who like old-style Zin, with no-holds-barred power. **85** —*P.G. (3/1/2001)*

Norman 2002 Old Vine Zinfandel (Cucamonga Valley) $19. The sweetest and most Port-like of Norman's lineup. This dark wine is dense in tannins and soft in acids. **83** —*S.H. (11/15/2004)*

Norman 2000 Old Vine Zinfandel Port Zinfandel (Cucamonga Valley) $20. Sure is sweet, with a super-sugary blast of late-harvest blackberry, caramel, and toffee-coffee flavors. Yet there's a good cut of acidity to balance. Try with vanilla ice cream. **86** —*S.H. (12/15/2004)*

Norman 2002 The Classic Zinfandel (Paso Robles) $12. I guess they call it classic because it's modest in alcohol, but that comes at the cost of a bit of residual sugar. The flavors are cherries, herbs, and tobacco. **84** —*S.H. (11/15/2004)*

Norman 2002 The Monster Zinfandel (Paso Robles) $20. Don't look for finesse in a wine called "the monster." It's truly Hulkian in wild, brambly berry and pepper fruit and high in alcohol. It's also mercifully dry. **85** —*S.H. (11/15/2004)*

Norman 1997 The Monster Zinfandel (Paso Robles) $18. 84 —*P.G. (11/15/1999)*

NORTHSTAR

Northstar 2003 Merlot (Walla Walla (WA)) $60. Very light, showing strawberry and raspberry fruit, but with little weight or extract. The oak is managed a bit better here than with the Columbia Valley wine, so it feels less imbalanced. But the fruit is less substantial, so it's pretty much a wash between the two bottlings. **87** —*P.G. (11/15/2006)*

Northstar 2003 Merlot (Columbia Valley (WA)) $52. Aggressive, expensive-tasting French oak rules the day here, with moderately ripe, totally generic black cherry fruit flavors. It's all about the barrel, with butterscotch, toast, butter, and more butter. Very tasty, quite drinkable, but extremely simple. **88** —*P.G. (11/15/2006)*

Northstar 2002 Merlot (Walla Walla (WA)) $60. The winery's Walla Walla bottling, though it accounts for less than a tenth of the 9,000- case production, is far more substantial and varietal than the Columbia Valley Merlot. Thick, chalky tannins, chewy blueberry/cherry fruit, good weight, and length bring some power to what is otherwise a straightforward, rather tannic wine. **88** —*P.G. (12/15/2005)*

Northstar 2002 Merlot (Columbia Valley (WA)) $52. Once conceived as a Merlot specialist, Northstar seems to have drifted, well, south, and is now crafting more of a Right Bank Bordeaux blend. A confusing array of vineyard sites are packed into the wine, which seems to have wandered into a kind of mid-life identity crisis. Pleasant strawberry and raspberry fruit anchors a rather simple palate. **87** —*P.G. (12/15/2005)*

Northstar 2001 Merlot (Walla Walla (WA)) $60. This is the second vintage for Northstar's Walla Walla bottling, and the vintage is slightly better, with more substantial weight and tannin. Walla Walla strawberry fruit flavors are here in abundance, with nicely managed oak and a long, smooth mid-palate. **90** —*P.G. (7/1/2004)*

Northstar 2001 Merlot (Columbia Valley (WA)) $52. Medium-bodied, showing cherry and plum fruit and a rather hard structure, with herb, green tea, and tobacco streaks. Not quite up to previous standards. **88** —*P.G. (4/1/2005)*

Northstar 1999 Merlot (Columbia Valley (WA)) $50. Northstar has ramped up production to 2,900 cases, on its way to 15,000 once the new winery (being built in Walla Walla) is operational. Here is flat-out killer fruit, stacked with all the flavors of the rainbow, that finds the silky sweet spot on the palate and goes for a long, long ride. This winery is on a roll. Editors' Choice. **94 Editors' Choice** —*P.G. (9/1/2004)*

Northstar 1998 Merlot (Columbia Valley (WA)) $50. Northstar makes a bold, ultra-premium Merlot. It's soft, satiny, and sexy, with voluptuous black cherry/blackberry fruit, layers of chocolate, and spices suggestive of cinnamon, mint, and more exotic flavors. Powerful and complex, yet open and accessible, it showcases the "serious" side of Merlot. **93 Editors' Choice** *(10/1/2001)*

Northstar 2003 Syrah (Columbia Valley (WA)) $40. The first-ever Northstar Syrah, it's 100% Syrah, yet and fits in perfectly with the house style. Supremely smooth and satiny, the voluptuous mouthfeel focuses on sweet, plummy fruit slathered in chocolate. It's delicious but made in

very limited quantities (sold only at the winery and to winery club members). **91** —*P.G. (6/1/2006)*

NOTA BENE CELLARS

Nota Bene Cellars 2002 Syrah (Washington) $22. Smells of baked berries, cinnamon, and pie crust. In the mouth, it has meat, leather, soy, and briar flavors and a long, drying finish. **84** *(9/1/2005)*

NOVELLA

Novella 2001 Brothers Vineyard 6, Block 5 Cabernet Sauvignon (Paso Robles) $11. Smells young, fresh, and grapy, with plummy, blackberry flavors and mouthwatering acidity. Wash simple foods down with this dry, affordable red wine. **84** —*S.H. (6/1/2004)*

Novella 2005 Chardonnay (Paso Robles) $10. Another unoaked Chard hits the market, and with good results at a good price. Nothing but juicy peach, pear, and pineapple flavors and crisp acidity. Oak probably would have brought it down. **85 Best Buy** —*S.H. (12/1/2006)*

Novella 2001 Chardonnay (Paso Robles) $11. Smells nice, with apple, smoke, and vanilla flavors. Turns modestly flavorful in the mouth, with some pleasant fruit and a spicy finish. **84** —*S.H. (6/1/2004)*

Novella 2002 Merlot (Paso Robles) $10. This is an okay red wine, the kind you can drink with pizza or burgers. It's rustic, fruity, and quaffable. **83** —*S.H. (11/1/2005)*

Novella 2000 Merlot (California) $11. Smells aggressively green and stalky, then turns bizarrely sweet and Port-like. **80** —*S.H. (6/1/2004)*

Novella 2002 Moscato (Paso Robles) $11. Has pleasant flavors of pineapple, apricot, and vanilla. It's fairly sweet, with a good spine of acidity. **85** —*S.H. (6/1/2004)*

Novella 2003 Muscat Canelli (Paso Robles) $10. Paso Robles is making a play for the most congenial home in California to sweet Muscat, under any name, and this wine shows why. It's crisp and acidic, sweet but not cloying, and offers wonderful flavors of mangoes, papayas, and honey-sweetened peach pie. Addictively good, and the alcohol is only 11.5%. **94 Best Buy** —*S.H. (11/1/2005)*

Novella 2000 Petite Sirah (Paso Robles) $13. What a fine job EOS has done with this softly rich, hedonistic wine from Paso Robles. It has flavors of berries, cherries, chocolate, and earth, though they're a little syrupy due to low acids. The wine is still flavorful, with firm tannins holding the center. **88 Best Buy** *(4/1/2003)*

Novella 2002 Brothers Ranch Vineyard Pinot Grigio (Paso Robles) $13. Fresh and fruity, with sweetish flavors of apples, cotton candy, and peaches. Seems like it has a little sugar, but it's nice and crisp with acidity. **84** —*S.H. (6/1/2004)*

Novella 2002 Synergy Red Blend (Paso Robles) $12. This blend of Sangiovese, Zinfandel, and Petite Sirah is okay for quickies like a cheesey pizza. It's dry and hot, with ripe black cherry flavors that last a long time on the finish. **83** —*S.H. (11/1/2005)*

Novella 1999 Synergy Red Blend (Paso Robles) $11. Everything comes together in this handsome Zinfandel, Sangiovese, and Petite Sirah blend. A bouquet of dark raspberry and deep floral notes opens to a full palate of similar flavors with leather and black pepper accents. This has a lively tang on the tongue and a big finish, with mouth-coating but even tannins. This notable value may be consumed now, but will be even better in a year. **90 Best Buy** —*M.M. (4/1/2002)*

Novella 2005 Sauvignon Blanc (Paso Robles) $10. Zesty, clean, and fruity, with ripe grapefruit juice, fig, and melon flavors. This SB finishes with a slightly sweet flourish of honey. From the beach to the patio, it'll be just fine. **84** —*S.H. (12/1/2006)*

Novella 2002 Brothers Vineyard 6, Block 4 Sauvignon Blanc (Paso Robles) $11. Starts off with lively aromas of citrus and gooseberry. On the palate, it's not quite as intriguing, but still refreshing, ending with herbal hints. **85** —*J.M. (6/1/2004)*

NOVELTY HILL

Novelty Hill 2003 Cabernet Sauvignon (Columbia Valley (WA)) $25. A quality Bordeaux blend, nicely fleshed out with Malbec, Merlot, and Cabernet Franc components. Fine spices focus the core of raspberry and

USA

black cherry, and there's a suggestion of cola running through the finish. **90** —*P.G. (11/15/2006)*

Novelty Hill 2001 Cabernet Sauvignon (Columbia Valley (WA)) $20. The Cab is a bit heavier than Novelty's Merlot, but tastes much the same, with young, primary, light cherry fruit flavors that show little concentration or depth. One dimensional and light. **86** —*P.G. (12/15/2004)*

Novelty Hill 2002 Conner Lee Vineyard Chardonnay (Columbia Valley (WA)) $20. Soft and buttery, this will certainly hold great appeal for those who want to smell and taste buttered popcorn and roasted nuts with their Chardonnays. The fruit is light and melony, showing hints of green apple but without the crispness that would give it some lift and relief from all that new oak. **87** —*P.G. (12/15/2004)*

Novelty Hill 2001 Conner Lee Vineyard Chardonnay (Columbia Valley (WA)) $22. The second vintage for this new winery, whose wines are made by the talented Mike Januik. Outstanding fruit anchors this terrific Chardonnay, which is layered with citrus and tropical fruits, streaks of vanilla and mint, and leads into a long, taut finish. **91 Editors' Choice** —*P.G. (9/1/2004)*

Novelty Hill 2003 Merlot (Columbia Valley (WA)) $25. Good, solidly made blend with enough Cabernet Sauvignon and Franc to add coffee aromas and firm up the tannins. It falls away in the finish, getting light and a bit leafy, with echoes of green tea. **89** —*P.G. (10/1/2006)*

Novelty Hill 2001 Merlot (Columbia Valley (WA)) $18. Initially pleasant tasting, though very light, with somewhat dilute flavors of tart pie cherry, and a midpalate that seems almost watery. Young fruit? It turns slightly soapy and thin at the end, leaving little impression. **86** —*P.G. (12/15/2004)*

Novelty Hill 2000 Merlot (Columbia Valley (WA)) $25. This is a good benchmark Merlot, with open, complex flavors of red berries and currants. The fruit is nicely balanced against medium acids and modest hints of oak, making this a restrained, complete, and classy wine for discriminating palates. **89** —*P.G. (9/1/2004)*

Novelty Hill 2003 Stillwater Creek Merlot (Columbia Valley (WA)) $25. Rich, powerful and sappy, with a tarry core packed with fruit. Young, concentrated and spicy with whiffs of anise and plum. **91** —*P.G. (10/1/2006)*

Novelty Hill 2003 Klipsun Vineyard Sauvignon Blanc (Red Mountain) $18. Lots of new oak showing here, with all the attendant flavors of vanilla and toasted coconut. But the firm, tannic Klipsun vineyard fruit stands up nicely, softer in '03 than previously, but still sophisticated, bold, and assertive. **88** —*P.G. (12/1/2004)*

Novelty Hill 2000 Klipsun Vineyard Sauvignon Blanc (Red Mountain) $19. This is the first release from an important new boutique winery. Consulting winemaker Mike Januik was Ste. Michelle's white wine guru for many years; he now runs his own winery. The grapes, from Red Mountain's top site, are superb. A hint of sweetness makes this mouthfilling, fragrant, fruit-loaded wine immensely appealing. **92** —*P.G. (9/1/2002)*

Novelty Hill 2004 Stillwater Creek Sauvignon Blanc (Columbia Valley (WA)) $25. Crisp, authoritative melon and mineral, limned with lime and citrus and pineapple. A lovely wine, concentrated and rich. **90** —*P.G. (10/1/2006)*

Novelty Hill 2003 Syrah (Columbia Valley (WA)) $20. Ripe black fruit and spicy, smoky scents pull you into this smooth and lush gem of a Syrah. Dense and fruit-driven, it's a showcase of the superripe 2003 vintage, which blessed Washington's Syrahs with unprecedented power. **92 Editors' Choice** —*P.G. (10/1/2006)*

Novelty Hill 2002 Syrah (Columbia Valley (WA)) $20. Tight and toasty, with a healthy dose of menthol-scented oak atop bright raspberry fruit. Dense and smooth enough on the palate, finishing on a dry, cedary note. **87** *(9/1/2005)*

Novelty Hill 2002 Stillwater Creek Vineyard Syrah (Columbia Valley (WA)) $28. Following some grassy, hay-like scents, the fruit comes across as a bit raisiny and Port-like in flavor. Turns tart, almost citrusy on the finish, with drying tannins. **83** *(9/1/2005)*

NOVY CELLARS

Novy Cellars 2002 Meritage (Mendocino County) $19. A rich, soft, complex wine, showing blackberry, cherry, oak, cocoa, and sweetened coffee flavors. Almost as sweet as a dessert wine, but it's technically dry. Instantly appealing, and great with a good steak. **88** —*S.H. (2/1/2005)*

Novy Cellars 2000 Syrah (Napa Valley) $22. There's so much to like here, it's hard to know where to start. Begin with the texture and mouthfeel, which is wonderfully rich and velvety. It coats the palate, spreading berry flavors all over and penetrating the taste buds with lively acidity. The finish is as sweet as honey, maybe a little too sweet given the soft acids. **92** —*S.H. (12/1/2002)*

Novy Cellars 2003 Christensen Family Vineyard Syrah (Russian River Valley) $32. Intensely peppery, and while we like pepper in our Syrahs, this one will be close to overwhelming for some tasters. Thankfully, we did find enough blackberry fruit and meaty concentration to help balance out this mouthfilling, spicy wine. **88** *(9/1/2005)*

Novy Cellars 2000 Gary's Syrah (Santa Lucia Highlands) $35. A cool-climate Syrah from a celebrated vineyard, and it does not strike out, with black peppercorn, plum, and blackberry notes, and with fine dried-herb flavors showing up in the long finish. Bone-dry, with thick, fine tannins. If you're familiar with a good Bien Nacido Syrah, this is remarkable similar, and suggests the potential of this area for Northern Rhône-style Syrahs. **90** —*S.H. (12/1/2002)*

Novy Cellars 2003 Gary's Vineyard Syrah (Santa Lucia Highlands) $32. Supple and full-bodied, thanks to admirable fruit extract and high alcohol (15.2%). Supporters lauded its rich mouthfeel and coffee and grilled meat flavors, while detractors lamented its hot finish. **85** *(9/1/2005)*

Novy Cellars 2003 Judge Family Vineyard Syrah (Bennett Valley) $32. Seems almost overripe and underripe at the same time, with jammy blackberry notes vying with herbal, green ones. Touches of caramel give it a sweet-ish tinge on the finish. **84** *(9/1/2005)*

Novy Cellars 2000 Page-Nord Syrah (Napa Valley) $26. The vineyard is in southern Napa, a relatively cool region. The wine is very dark, with a purple color, and it stains the glass. It smells tight, earthy, and young now, offering up just a tease of cassis. But it erupts on the palate with an explosion of berries, spices, and fine tannins. Extraordinarily rich now, but will unquestionably develop. **94 Cellar Selection** —*S.H. (12/1/2002)*

Novy Cellars 2002 Page-Nord Vineyard Syrah (Napa Valley) $30. Interesting to contrast this with Novy's Rosella's bottling. It's much firmer in structure, with sturdier tannins, although they're sweet. It also seems oakier and sweeter all around. Blackberries, coffee, and cocoa are the flavors. **90** —*S.H. (3/1/2005)*

Novy Cellars 1999 Page-Nord Vineyard Syrah (Napa Valley) $34. An intense nose of skunk, toasty oak, and earthy notes veils deeply submerged black fruit. The lushly textured palate carries rich espresso, blackberry, vanilla, and toast flavors. Finishes long, just as it began— opaque, burnt toast over dark, buried fruit and firm tannins. Don't touch now—cellar for three or more years, keep your fingers crossed, and hope for the dense fruit to rise to the top. **87** *(11/1/2001)*

Novy Cellars 2002 Rosella's Vineyard Syrah (Santa Lucia Highlands) $30. This AVA is best known for Pinots that can be Syrah-like in weight. Here's a real Syrah, and it's outstanding. Dark and dense, but fresh in acids, with ripely sweet tannins, it shows an intense peppery note accompanied by flamboyant blackberry and coffee flavors. Finishes dry and smooth. **92** —*S.H. (3/1/2005)*

O'BRIEN

O'Brien 2003 Chardonnay (Napa Valley) $18. Pretty lean and earthy, not showing much fruit beyond tobacco, applesauce, and oak flavors. But it's clean and balanced. **84** —*S.H. (5/1/2005)*

O'Brien 2001 Estate Merlot (Napa Valley) $36. Sturdy and firm in tannins, dry and fairly oaky, with plummy, herb flavors, this wine is pretty closed down now, although a good piece of meat will wake it up. Might soften and improve in a year or so. **86** —*S.H. (5/1/2005)*

O'Brien 2002 Seduction Red Blend (Napa Valley) $25. The winery doesn't identify what the grapes are, but it tastes like a generic red wine, full-bodied and dry, with a rather rustic mouthfeel. **84** —*S.H. (5/1/2005)*

USA

O'REILLY'S

O'Reilly's 2005 Pinot Gris (Oregon) $13. A bit of residual sugar sticks out, rounding out and fruiting up this leesy, fresh wine. It shows the light citrus side of Oregon Gris. **88 Best Buy**—*P.G. (12/1/2006)*

O'Reilly's 2004 Pinot Gris (Willamette Valley) $12. This spicy, fresh, and citrus-flavored wine is at the opposite end of the spectrum from winemaker David O'Reilly's Owen Roe Pinot Gris. But it's just as good, and perhaps more flexible as far as matching food. Finishes with crisp, leesy, mineral flavors. **91 Best Buy**—*P.G. (2/1/2006)*

O'Reilly's 2005 Pinot Noir (Oregon) $15. Light, tannic, leafy, and earthy, which is not entirely inappropriate for a $15 Oregon Pinot. The herbal flavors come with the low-rent territory, but the balance and clean sweep of the wine demonstrate David O'Reilly's sure winemaking hand. A well-made budget bottle. **86**—*P.G. (12/1/2006)*

O'SHAUGHNESSY

O'Shaughnessy 2001 Cabernet Sauvignon (Howell Mountain) $54. Dark, full-bodied and rich, with well-detailed black currant and cocoa flavors and a flamboyant but balanced coating of new oak. Impresses not only for its power, but for the soft luxury of its mouthfeel. Beautiful now, and perhaps best over the next 5 years to capture in its youth. **94 Editors' Choice**—*S.H. (10/1/2005)*

OAK HOLLOW WINERY

Oak Hollow Winery 2001 Zinfandel (California) $5. Bright and cherry-like. This is a simple wine; pleasant enough. **80** *(11/1/2003)*

OAK KNOLL

Oak Knoll 2004 Pinot Gris (Willamette Valley) $11. Light and fresh, tart and marked with spice and mixed citrus fruits. A style well-suited for shellfish or poultry, and more reminiscent of Italian Pinot Grigios than many Oregon bottlings. **87 Best Buy**—*P.G. (2/1/2006)*

Oak Knoll 2000 Pinot Gris (Willamette Valley) $13. A really nice wine, refreshing and light, with delicate lemon-grapefruit flavors complexed with creamy lees. The acidity is very crisp and assertive. No discernible oak at all, and with this pretty fruit and structure, it doesn't need any. **87**—*P.G. (8/1/2002)*

Oak Knoll 2002 Willamette Valley Pinot Gris (Willamette Valley) $11. You'll find lots of charm in this easy-drinking wine, with its citrus and fig flavors and tart acidity. It's dry and balanced and will complement food very well, especially spicy fare that echoes the wines white pepper and lime. Very nice, and a good value. **86**—*S.H. (8/1/2004)*

Oak Knoll 1999 Pinot Noir (Willamette Valley) $15. **82** *(10/1/2002)*

Oak Knoll 1998 Five Mountains Pinot Noir (Willamette Valley) $40. **86**—*M.S. (12/1/2000)*

Oak Knoll 1999 Five Mountains Vineyard Pinot Noir (Willamette Valley) $30. Comes on with an unusual smoky menthol-ash veneer over herb (vegetal, to some) aromas. The fruit is tart, with earth and sawdust accents, while lemony acids amplify the sour edge. Overall, reviewers found it a bit lean and a bit green. **83** *(10/1/2002)*

Oak Knoll 1999 Vintage Reserve Pinot Noir (Willamette Valley) $25. Bing cherry, plum, rhubarb, and cedar elements meld handsomely on the nose of this tasty medium-weight wine. Attractive clove, chocolate, and licorice accents add interest; more than one taster complimented the ripe mouthfeel. Finishes long with modest tannins. Offers a lot to like, and should be even better in one to two years. **88** *(10/1/2002)*

Oak Knoll 1998 Vintage Reserve Pinot Noir (Willamette Valley) $38. **83**—*J.C. (12/1/2000)*

Oak Knoll 2000 Willamette Valley Pinot Noir (Willamette Valley) $NA. Simple and one-dimensional, a wine that has easy flavors of tea, cola, and cherries, and is very dry. Tart acidity makes it prickly, and the finish is swift and clean. **84**—*S.H. (8/1/2004)*

OAKFORD

Oakford 1996 Cabernet Sauvignon (Oakville) $75. **92** *(12/31/1999)*

Oakford 1995 Cabernet Sauvignon (Oakville) $60. **95**—*S.H. (6/1/1999)*

Oakford 2001 Cabernet Sauvignon (Oakville) $85. This Cab is so good, you'll want to drink it now, but it should age well for a decade. Rich and delicious in ripe black cherry, blackberry, cassis, and chocolate, and well-oaked, it's aided by firm tannins and good acidity. **93 Cellar Selection**—*S.H. (11/1/2005)*

Oakford 1998 Cabernet Sauvignon (Oakville) $100. Flashy oak and deep, pure black currants show from the first whiff, and the purple color stains the sides of the glass in this wine with enough glycerine to float the Sixth Fleet. Doesn't disappoint on the palate, with ripe blackberry flavors and gorgeous, velvety tannins. Closes long, with a sweet, richly-fruited finish. **95 Cellar Selection**—*S.H. (8/1/2001)*

Oakford 1997 Estate Grown Cabernet Sauvignon (Oakville) $85. **90** *(11/1/2000)*

OAKSTONE

Oakstone 1999 Estate De Cascabel Vineyard Cabernet Sauvignon (Fair Play) $18. Has its work cut out for it. Fundamentally a one-dimensional, country-style wine, it's clean and soft, with earthy, berry flavors, and dry tannins. Would benefit from extra depth, complexity, and concentration. **82**—*S.H. (9/1/2002)*

OAKVILLE RANCH

Oakville Ranch 2001 Estate Robert's Blend Bordeaux Blend (Oakville) $75. Shows true Cabernet character in the dry, smooth tannins, rich, full-bodied mouthfeel and harmonious flavors of black currants, coffee, and oak. It all comes together to make a polished, soft wine. Drink now through 2008. **88**—*S.H. (12/15/2005)*

Oakville Ranch 2001 Cabernet Sauvignon (Oakville) $50. What a beautiful opening aroma. Cedar, cigar box, and pure smoky oak mingle with ripe cassis and black currants, and an earthy mix of green olives and grilled meat. Drinking ripely sweet in fruit, with beautiful tannins, this smooth Cab drinks well now and should hold through 2015. **93 Cellar Selection**—*S.H. (11/15/2005)*

Oakville Ranch 2000 Cabernet Sauvignon (Oakville) $42. Still quite firm in dry tannins, with bell pepper, herb, and coffee flavors, although there's a core of cherry fruit. Doesn't seem like it's going anywhere. **85**—*S.H. (3/1/2005)*

Oakville Ranch 2000 Reserve Cabernet Sauvignon (Oakville) $101. Shockingly overpriced. Tough, dry, and tannic, with raisiny flavors. Why would anyone buy this wine? **82**—*S.H. (8/1/2005)*

Oakville Ranch 2000 Robert's Blend Cabernet Sauvignon-Cabernet Franc (Oakville) $75. Pretty tough and tannic now, with a bone-dry, mouth-numbingly austere feeling throughout, and doesn't seem to have the fruity stuffing to develop. You'll find traces of blackberries in the gritty finish. **84**—*S.H. (8/1/2005)*

Oakville Ranch 2004 Chardonnay (Oakville) $35. Showing that earthy, dried herb character that so often marks Napa Chardonnays, this Oakville-grown wine is soft in acids and rich in spicy, creamy oak and lees notes. It has pleasantly ripe apple, peach, and pineapple flavors. **87**—*S.H. (7/1/2006)*

Oakville Ranch 2003 Chardonnay (Oakville) $35. Soft, kind of flat, and thin in flavor, with notes of apples, peaches, and oak, and a dry finish. **82**—*S.H. (12/15/2005)*

Oakville Ranch 2001 Vista Vineyard Chardonnay (Oakville) $30. Rather sharp and tart in green apple bitterness, and pretty acidic through the finish, although the oak and cream make up for it. But that structure works in favor of food. **85**—*S.H. (3/1/2005)*

Oakville Ranch 2000 Merlot (Oakville) $33. Vegetal, with aromas of canned asparagus. Drinks dry and herbaceous. Tasted twice. **82**—*S.H. (3/1/2005)*

Oakville Ranch 2003 Field Blend Red Blend (Napa Valley) $30. An old-fashioned blend of Zinfandel, Petite Sirah, and Carignane, this robust wine approximates what the old-timers drank, although they probably didn't pick it this ripe. It's explosive in juicy fruit flavors, with very little oak to get in the way. The tannins are rich and thick, suggesting beef or lamb dishes. **86**—*S.H. (7/1/2006)*

USA

USA

Oakville Ranch 2002 Field Blend Red Blend (Oakville) $30. The blend is Zinfandel, Petite Sirah, and Carignane on this enjoyable mélange. It could be anything, but is awfully good, with its rich, ripe tannins and smooth flavors of berries, cherries, and coffee. Drink whenever you need something dry and full bodied. **88** —*S.H. (12/15/2005)*

Oakville Ranch 2001 Field Blend Red Blend (Oakville) $30. The only field-blended wine to actually call itself a field blend consists of Zinfandel, Petite Sirah, and Carignan. It's very dry and bold in tannins, a rather earthy wine with a deep core of fruit. Should age effortlessly for decades. **88** —*S.H. (3/1/2005)*

OASIS

Oasis 1998 Dry Gewürztraminer (Virginia) $18. 81 —*J.C. (8/1/1999)*

Oasis 2004 Pinot Noir (Santa Barbara County) $22. If you have a friend who doesn't get cool-climate Pinot, turn her on to this. It's dry, balanced, and wonderfully silky, with luscious varietal flavors of cherries, cola, and woodspice, and a hint of rich cassis on the finish. It's a lovely wine. **90** —*S.H. (3/1/2006)*

Oasis NV Dogwood Blush Rosé Blend (Virginia) $10. 80 —*J.C. (8/1/1999)*

OBSIDIAN

Obsidian 2002 Obsidian Ridge Vineyard Cabernet Sauvignon (Lake County) $25. It is no insult to Lake County to say this is the best Cabernet I have ever had from there. It smells importantly ripe and finely oaked, and possesses succulent cassis, cherry, and chocolate flavors, with an earthy edge of fine herbs. From Acacia's Michael Terrien. **90** —*S.H. (11/15/2004)*

Obsidian 2003 Obsidian Ridge Vineyard Syrah (Red Hills Lake County) $25. Seems a bit herbal or grassy at first, then reveals more mixed berries and spice with air. But it turns irretrievably tannic on the finish, with flavors of over steeped berry zinger tea. Probably best consumed young, for its exuberant fruit. **85** *(9/1/2005)*

OJAI

Ojai 2004 Bien Nacido Vineyard Chardonnay (Santa Maria Valley) $28. This enormously ripe wine shines with a purity of tropical fruit and candied citrus flavors that are generously oaked. But for all the richness, a penetrating acidity cuts through and makes the wine finish clean. Drink this Burgundian-style Chardonnay soon for its youthful opulence. **92** —*S.H. (8/1/2006)*

Ojai 2002 Bien Nacido Vineyard Syrah (Santa Barbara County) $40. Big Syrah, and an obvious ager due to the thick, young tannins and relative closedness. But the fruit is so enormous in black cherry compote, chocolate, and cassis, and everything is so balanced and harmonious, that the wine cannot fail to improve. Best by 2008, and will hold for some years beyond. **92 Cellar Selection** —*S.H. (8/1/2006)*

OKANAGAN ESTATE

Okanagan Estate 2004 Pinot Grigio (Washington) $NA. From a site that is actually just on the Washington side of Canada's Okanagan wine region, this light but very stylish wine shows concentrated pear flesh flavors right in the core. Surprising length and texture. **89** —*P.G. (2/1/2006)*

OLD BROOKVILLE

Old Brookville 2000 Gold Coast Reserve Chardonnay (Long Island) $14. A bit weedy and tart, with hints of hazelnut and vanilla up front. Some attractive pear and apple notes are in evidence, however, while the finish is moderate. **81** —*J.M. (9/10/2002)*

OLIVET LANE

Olivet Lane 1997 Pinot Noir (Russian River Valley) $20. 87 *(12/15/1999)*

OLSON OGDEN

Olson Ogden 2003 Syrah (Sonoma County) $22. Grape is the dominant fruit flavor here, jazzed up by spice, graham cracker, and vanilla notes on both the nose and the palate. Has decent grip on the palate, and fades into a grape jelly/lollipop finish. **87** *(9/1/2005)*

Olson Ogden 2003 Unti Vineyard Syrah (Dry Creek Valley) $29. Extremely dry and tart, this wine has a punchy toughness, despite the presence of some pleasant cherry, blackberry, and coffee flavors. Give it two or three years and hope it comes around. **83** *(9/1/2005)*

Olson Ogden 2002 Unti Vineyard Syrah (Dry Creek Valley) $29. There's lots to admire in this dry, complex wine. It starts with a burst of white pepper, grilled meat, and blackberry aromas, then turns ripe in the mouth, with blackberry and Kahlúa flavors. There are some sturdy tannins throughout. **89** —*S.H. (5/1/2005)*

OPOLO

Opolo 2000 Cabernet Sauvignon (Paso Robles) $32. Pretty good red wine here, nice and juicy, with well-etched flavors of blackberries and tobacco. The texture is especially pleasing and limpid. Needs an extra edge of depth and complexity to hit the big time, but it sure is delicious. **89** — *S.H. (8/1/2003)*

Opolo 2001 Estate Cabernet Sauvignon (Paso Robles) $30. Rather vegetal on the opening, and turns only modestly fruity in the mouth. **82** —*S.H. (5/1/2005)*

Opolo 2002 Rhapsody Meritage (Paso Robles) $45. Typically Paso red wine, in the soft, easy tannins, low acid, and powerful blackberry, cocoa, and cherry flavors that are almost sweet in the finish. **85** —*S.H. (5/1/2005)*

Opolo 2002 Merlot (Paso Robles) $26. A solid effort, soft and clean, with likeable cherry and blackberry fruit. Finishes with a dusting of fine tannins. **84** —*S.H. (5/1/2005)*

Opolo 2000 Merlot (Paso Robles) $26. Here's a wine with quite a bit of juicy black cherry jam in it. It's youthful and clean, with nice tannins and a good shot of stimulating acidity. It's fully dry, but ripe and sweet in rich fruit. Good drinking! **88** —*S.H. (12/15/2003)*

Opolo 2002 Pinot Noir (Paso Robles) $24. A little heavy and rough, but the flavorful cherries, cocoa, and spices are tasty, and the wine is clean and balanced. **84** —*S.H. (5/1/2005)*

Opolo 2000 Pinot Noir (Central Coast) $32. From a vineyard in the Santa Lucia Highlands, a young, jammy wine bursting with candied flavors of raspberries and cherries. It drinks very concentrated and intense. There's a caramelly note that may come from well-charred barrels in this dry, full-bodied wine. **87** —*S.H. (7/1/2003)*

Opolo 2003 Roussanne (Central Coast) $20. Okay wine, dry and with good acidity, but kind of generic. Features peach and cashew flavors, and a smoky finish. **84** —*S.H. (5/1/2005)*

Opolo 2000 Syrah (Paso Robles) $28. Here's a juicy, fruit-driven wine that frames blueberry, blackberry, and plum jam flavors in considerable tannins. The wine is kind of mouth-numbing and needs time to soften up, but it should evolve to a richer softness in a few years. Would be great with roasted leg of lamb. **87** —*S.H. (12/1/2002)*

Opolo 2001 Estate Syrah (Paso Robles) $24. This gentle wine does what Paso so effortlessly accomplishes. It's soft, juicy, and filled with forward fruit flavor, but is by no means one-dimensional. Cherries, blackberries, mocha, and peppery spices unfold in waves, and the finish is clean and dry. **90** —*S.H. (5/1/2005)*

Opolo 2003 Viognier (Central Coast) $22. Fruity and clean, with a simple structure that shows fruit, spice, and butter-cream flavors. Doesn't seem varietally correct. **84** —*S.H. (5/1/2005)*

Opolo 2003 Mountain Zinfandel (Paso Robles) $24. You don't have to peek at the label to know this is a high-alcohol wine. The 16.6% burns the palate. It's also deficient in acidity, so while the cassis and chocolate flavors are fine, it's unbalanced. **83** —*S.H. (5/1/2005)*

Opolo 2003 Reserve Zinfandel (Paso Robles) $32. The most concentrated and fruity of Opolo's '03 Zins features powerful black currant and chocolate. Like the others, it's soft in acids and lush in tannins. Finishes rather hot, but a terrific wine for a barbecue on a summer evening. **87** — *S.H. (5/1/2005)*

Opolo 2003 Summit Creek Zinfandel (Paso Robles) $18. Ripe in blackberry and cocoa flavors, smooth in sweet tannins, this very nice Zin showcases Paso's ability to produce soft, immediately drinkable red wines. **85** —*S.H. (5/1/2005)*

OPTIMA

Optima 2001 Cabernet Sauvignon (Alexander Valley) $40. Alexander Valley Cabs can have an earthiness, a dried thyme and dill character. But that doesn't mean a wine like this doesn't have complexity and interest. The entry isn't super-fruity, but the finish is rich in black currants, in this dry, balanced and nuanced wine. **90** —*S.H. (11/15/2005)*

Optima 2003 Rosé of Cabernet Sauvignon (Alexander Valley) $13. Seems like there's a lot of blush wines from major varieties and good appellations out there these days. This dry wine is fairly fruity and simple, with good acidity. **83** —*S.H. (10/1/2004)*

Optima 2003 Zinfandel (Dry Creek Valley) $25. Absolutely delicious, compulsively drinkable. This is quintessential Dry Creek Zin, robust yet fine, packed with sweet wild berry and fruit flavors, spicy and balanced. There's a polish of raisins and chocolate on the finish that make it especially delightful. **92 Editors' Choice** —*S.H. (11/15/2005)*

OPUS ONE

Opus One 2000 Bordeaux Blend (Napa Valley) $125. Made in the Opus style, which is graceful, limpid, and elegant, but with hidden depths of authority and power. The blackberry, cherry, and oak flavors are pretty, but the wine is most notable for its harmony and grace. Tannins play only a supportive role, but they will let this wine age effortlessly for many years. **92** —*S.H. (12/1/2004)*

Opus One 2001 Cabernet Blend (Napa Valley) $160. Starts with tons of rich new oak in the aroma, showing the most inviting notes of cedar, cigar box, and pencil lead that segue to the remarkable fruit. The attack is powerful, with a punch of cassis spreading broadly and deeply across the palate. With its sturdy, clean tannins, this beautiful wine displays classic power, elegance, and balance. **95 Cellar Selection** —*S.H. (11/1/2005)*

ORBIS

Orbis 2000 Chardonnay (Carneros) $19. This new winery is aiming for the fences with its bells-and-whistles Chard. Barrel fermentation and sur lie aging add creamy overlays to ripe tropical-fruit flavors. Crisp acidity makes the flavors shine, and produces a brisk, clean finish. Notable for its balance and harmony. **91 Editors' Choice** —*S.H. (12/15/2002)*

OREANA

Oreana 2005 Sauvignon Blanc (California) $18. Despite the California appellation, the winery says the grapes are from Santa Barbara, and you can taste a cool-climate acidity permeating this dry, citrusy wine. There's a minerally spine to it, and it finishes with a clean, refreshing scour. Very nice. **88** —*S.H. (11/1/2006)*

Oreana 2005 Verdelho (California) $22. An interesting wine, different from anything you've tasted in more familiar varieties. The wine is high in acid, creating a peppery taste behind the smoky, citrus and dried herb flavors. Finishes a bit too sweet to be called dry, though. **84** —*S.H. (11/1/2006)*

ORFILA

Orfila 1997 Ambassador's Reserve Limited B Chardonnay (San Diego County) $15. **87** *(6/1/2000)*

Orfila 2003 Ambassador's Reserve Merlot (San Diego County) $28. A little more work is needed but the promise seems to be there with this wine from south of L.A. It's ripe enough in cherry, blackberry, plum, and coffee flavors, with good tannins and acidity. **85** —*S.H. (12/15/2006)*

Orfila 1997 Ambassador's Reserve Limited B Merlot (San Diego County) $25. **81** —*J.C. (7/1/2000)*

Orfila 2000 Limited Bottling Ambassador's Reserve Merlot (San Diego County) $28. There is some well-ripened berry fruit in this dry wine, yet it loses points for a roughness in the tannins and a tart bitterness that lasts through the finish. A work in progress from California's most southerly appellation. **84** —*S.H. (12/15/2003)*

Orfila 2001 Pinot Noir (Edna Valley) $41. Yes, the vintage is correct. Who else is releasing a 2001 Pinot in 2006? Yet it's a good wine, dry, clean, and silky, with cherry pie, cola, rosehip tea, and spice flavors. That Edna Valley acidity has preserved it well. **87** —*S.H. (12/15/2006)*

Orfila 1999 Pinot Noir (Edna Valley) $35. There are some cherry-berry and pepper flavors here, but the wine is too soft, and drinks fruity and simple. There are also some overripe, pruny tastes, leading to a hot finish. **84** —*S.H. (2/1/2003)*

Orfila 1997 Limited Bottling Pinot Noir (Arroyo Grande Valley) $30. **84** —*J.C. (5/1/2000)*

Orfila NV Lotus Cuvée Lot #123 Rhône White Blend (San Pasqual) $28. This Rhône blend is ripe to the point of off-dry, with flamboyant flavors of ripe white peaches, lime pie, vanilla custard, and smoke. With a creamy texture, it has a long aftertaste. **86** —*S.H. (5/1/2005)*

Orfila NV Lotus Lot #45 Rhône White Blend (San Pasqual) $28. Powerful aromatics lead to powerful fruity flavors in this Rhône-style wine. A blend of Viognier, Marsanne, and Roussanne, it explodes in apricot and peach juice, vanilla bean, and honeysuckle flavors that finish dry and spicy. The high alcohol isn't a problem. **87** —*S.H. (12/15/2006)*

Orfila 1998 Sangiovese (San Pasqual) $20. This is a wine with multiple problems. It's excessively soft, which makes it feel insipid in the mouth. The flavors include a medicinal taste like plastic bandage, which leaves the palate feeling uncomfortable. Much work remains to be done here. **82** —*S.H. (12/1/2002)*

Orfila 2003 Di Collina Sangiovese (San Pasqual) $20. Black cherry fruit stars in this dry, rustic wine. It has strong acids and dusty, astringent tannins, making it worthy of cheese, oil, sausage, tomatoes, that kind of fare. **85** —*S.H. (12/15/2006)*

Orfila 2001 Di Collina Sangiovese (San Pasqual) $20. Very dry, and deficient in acids, this wine has cherry flavors and is rustic. **83** —*S.H. (5/1/2005)*

Orfila 1999 Syrah (San Pasqual) $24. A dense, dark wine, with dark stone-fruit flavors. It feels thick and gluey in the mouth, probably because of excessively soft acidity. There are also some rugged tannins. This is an awkward, country-style wine. **84** —*S.H. (12/1/2002)*

Orfila 1999 Limited Bottling Val de la Mer Syrah (San Pasqual) $25. From a little-known but cool appellation in San Diego County, a pretty good Syrah that has its work cut out for it. Approaches the quality of more northerly regions with pretty blackberry and pepper flavors and smooth tannins, but can't overcome its rustic edge. **85** —*S.H. (12/15/2003)*

Orfila 2003 Val de la Mer Syrah (San Pasqual) $25. Porty and sugary sweet, this blackberry-flavored wine is simple. **80** —*S.H. (12/15/2006)*

Orfila 1998 Val de la Mer Estate Syrah (San Pasqual) $24. Dark aromas and flavors of coffee and cola share center stage with cedar and black cherries. Despite the heavy flavors, the wine is a bit on the light side, but smooth and harmonious. Finishes with hints of espresso and smooth, velvety tannins. **88** *(11/1/2001)*

Orfila 1998 Lotus Cuvée Viognier (San Pasqual) $28. Pricey, but an example of the promise this area shows for this white Rhône variety. It's an interesting wine, dry and crisp, yet rich in fruity extract. The creamy-smooth texture frames the zesty peach, citrus, herb, chocolate, and floral flavors perfectly. **89** —*S.H. (4/1/2002)*

Orfila NV Lotus White Blend (San Pasqual) $28. From San Diego County, a white Rhône-style blend of Viognier, Marsanne, and Roussanne. Smells light, but there's considerable body and flavor, with tropical fruits and figs and further seasoned with well-charred oak. The finish is spicy. **85** —*S.H. (12/15/2002)*

Orfila 2004 Gold Rush Zinfandel (California) $24. Have some warm country Zin. It's black in color, with high alcohol, soft acids, and Porty flavors of blackberry essence, sweetened espresso, and chocolate truffle. **86** —*S.H. (12/15/2006)*

Orfila 2002 Gold Rush Old Vines Zinfandel (California) $24. You'd expect a smaller appellation than "California" given the words on the label. Too sweet. **82** —*S.H. (5/1/2005)*

Orfila 2001 Gold Rush, Old Vines Zinfandel (California) $22. A bit earthy on the nose, while the follow-up is packed with ripe plum, black cherry, spice, and herb flavors. Quite jammy but there's also a weedy, ultra-bright edge that makes this hard to handle. **83** *(11/1/2003)*

ORGANIC VINTNERS

Organic Vintners 2003 California Collection Vegan Cabernet Sauvignon (Mendocino) $15. This clean, dry wine has forward varietal flavors of blackberries and cherries, and a firm backbone of tannins that will cut through a good piece of beef. **85** —*S.H. (8/1/2005)*

Organic Vintners 2003 Vegan Pinot Noir (Mendocino) $15. This is a lightly colored, light-bodied, dry Pinot, with modest cherry, cola, and coffee flavors. It has a pleasantly spicy finish, and will be good with grilled fare and cheeses. **84** —*S.H. (12/1/2005)*

ORIEL

Oriel 2002 Midnight Rambler Cabernet Sauvignon (Rutherford) $30. This ripe, forward Cab is extracted in fruit, and made soft in the modern style. It displays flavors of black cherries and cassis, with vanilla and char from oak, and a sweet herb note. Almost sweet, but fundamentally dry, it's a nice steak wine. **87** —*S.H. (11/1/2005)*

Oriel 2003 Dylan Chardonnay (Russian River Valley) $25. Kind of earthy and mute, and also soft, with the flavor of canned fruit syrup, although it's fairly dry. **82** —*S.H. (11/1/2005)*

Oriel 2003 Jasper Pinot Noir (Russian River Valley) $25. Straightforward, cool-climate Pinot, extracted and jammy in black cherries, cola, and mocha, and fairly heavy on the wood. Also has good acidity and a silky, though fairly full-bodied, texture. **85** —*S.H. (11/1/2005)*

ORIGIN

Origin 2002 Paramount Cabernet Blend (Napa Valley) $65. This most expensive of Origin's trio is also the most tannic and, theoretically, the best and most ageworthy. It's a very good wine, with pronounced black currant, cherry, violet, and oak flavors. There's a sharpness of acidity that calls for rich, fatty fare if you drink it young. **91** —*S.H. (10/1/2005)*

Origin 2002 Family Home Cabernet Sauvignon (Napa Valley) $55. Marginally richer and riper than Origin's Heritage Sites Red Wine, but, costing considerably more, it's a lesser value. This is a somewhat tannic wine with herb and cherry flavors, and a sharpness throughout. **88** —*S.H. (10/1/2005)*

Origin 2002 Heritage Sites Red Blend (Napa Valley) $35. A good example of a less-than-ripe wine that nonetheless offers pleasure and complexity. There's mint and greenness alongside the expected cherries and blackberries, but sometimes you don't want a mouthful of fruit. Possesses an elegance that will play well off a steak with lots of pepper. A blend, but 76% Merlot. **87** —*S.H. (10/1/2005)*

ORIGIN NAPA

Origin Napa 2003 Gamble Vineyard Sauvignon Blanc (Napa Valley) $27. Pungent and ripe, with aggressive citrus and stone-fruit aromas. Tastes a bit like a powder-based fruit drink, with grapefruit and gritty, acid-driven lemon characteristics. Quite zippy and tangy on the finish. **86** *(7/1/2005)*

Origin Napa 2001 Gamble Vineyard Sauvignon Blanc (Napa Valley) $23. This pricey Napa bottling opens with citrusy, grassy aromas mingling with oaky, smoky and leesy notes. In the mouth, the lime, fig, and tobacco flavors are seductive, but the acidity is low. **85** —*S.H. (10/1/2003)*

Origin Napa 2002 Heart Block Sauvignon Blanc (Napa Valley) $50. No, the price isn't a typo. This dry wine brims with lime peel, fig, vanilla, and peppery spice flavors, and possesses a polished elegance in its tart acids and dusting of tannins. It has the creamy texture of a nice Chard, plus a very long finish. **90** —*S.H. (12/15/2004)*

OROGENY

Orogeny 2004 Pinot Noir (Green Valley) $30. You get that Green Valley acidity in the tart, citrusy bite the wine takes on the palate, followed by a spicy followup of red cherries, cola, and pomegranates. The finish is bone dry. This is a well-structured Pinot, elegant and sleek, that should hold and even improve for five years. **88** —*S.H. (11/15/2006)*

Orogeny 2003 Pinot Noir (Green Valley) $30. From this appellation in the southwest corner of Russian River Valley comes this big, dark, extracted, jammy, almost Rhône-style wine. It's super-fruity in black cherry and oak flavors, but so full-bodied, you almost wonder if it is Pinot Noir. Still, it's a very nice, well-balanced wine. **87** —*S.H. (12/1/2005)*

Orogeny 2002 Pinot Noir (Green Valley) $25. Ripe and oaky in vanilla and toast, with a layer of cola and cherries emerging after airing. Tastes very ripe and full, and a bit heavy, with a chocolatey finish. Could benefit from a few years in bottle. **85** *(11/1/2004)*

ORTMAN FAMILY

Ortman Family 2002 Cabernet Sauvignon (Napa Valley) $35. Showcases good vintage Napa character in the refined tannins and blackberry flavors, with a bit of green peppercorn. Oak provides additional richness. Drink now and for the next two or three years. **85** —*S.H. (4/1/2006)*

Ortman Family 2001 Cabernet Sauvignon (Napa Valley) $45. The man who founded the Central Coast's Meridian stretches north to craft a complex, easy-drinking wine. It has ripe, juicy cherry and blackberry flavors, with nuances of oak. Some hard-edged tannins show up in the finish, suggesting rich meats and cheeses. **87** —*S.H. (3/1/2005)*

Ortman Family 2000 Cabernet Sauvignon (Napa Valley) $50. First you notice the gentleness and soothing softness, the way the tannins spread like a Persian carpet across the tongue. Then the purity of the flavors strikes, as the black currants, olives, smoky oak, and dried herbs unfold in waves. This is a classy glass of wine. Drink now, though. **91** —*S.H. (5/1/2004)*

Ortman Family 2004 Chardonnay (Edna Valley) $25. So high in acidity that it creates a tingly burn on the palate, this dry wine is bright and forward in lemon and lime flavors, and a tangy minerality. Finishes fine and clean. **87** —*S.H. (10/1/2006)*

Ortman Family 2003 Chardonnay (Edna Valley) $24. If you love those big, rich, gooey Central Coast Chards, you'll enjoy this one. It's flamboyant in pineapple custard, lime pie, papaya, nectarine, and spice flavors, and super-oaky, too, with the cool-climate acidity this appellation is known for. **89** —*S.H. (12/1/2005)*

Ortman Family 2002 Chardonnay (Edna Valley) $25. This cool Central Coast wine has tropical fruit and lemondrop flavors as well as zesty acidity. Veteran winemaker Chuck Ortman has added a substantial amount of toasted oak. The result is a clean, flavorful wine. **87** —*S.H. (6/1/2005)*

Ortman Family 2001 Chardonnay (Edna Valley) $28. Oaky, ripe, and complex, a real crowd-pleaser of a Chard. Bursts on the palate with pineapple, mango, toasted coconut, buttered toast, vanilla, and spices, wrapped in a creamy texture. **90** —*S.H. (5/1/2004)*

Ortman Family 2004 Pinot Noir (Santa Rita Hills) $30. Seems softer than you expect from this appellation, but there's no denying the delicious cherry pie, raspberry tart, mocha, and vanilla bean flavors that swirl to a spicy finish. Fully dry, the wine is silky and fine. **87** —*S.H. (11/15/2006)*

Ortman Family 2003 Pinot Noir (Willamette Valley) $30. The thick tannins, upfront acids, and deeply buried core of cherry, tobacco, and plum fruit suggest cellaring. Certainly the wine isn't showing a lot now. **84** —*S.H. (12/1/2005)*

Ortman Family 2003 Pinot Noir (Santa Rita Hills) $30. I might have thought this was Santa Maria, for it has that just barely ripe, white pepper, crushed brown spice, and rhubarb profile. In the mouth, it's dry, medium-bodied, and balanced, with a tease of cherry. Probably at its best now. **84** —*S.H. (12/1/2005)*

Ortman Family 2002 Pinot Noir (Santa Barbara County) $34. A lovely Pinot, supple and velvety in the mouth, and loaded with personality. Big, juicy flavors of cherries, black raspberries, and coffee, with toast and vanilla overtones. As rich as it is, this dry wine is elegant and complex. **90** —*S.H. (11/1/2004)*

Ortman Family 2001 Pinot Noir (Santa Barbara County) $34. This is certainly a cool-climate wine, to judge from the mint, rosehip tea, rhubarb, and cola flavors, and the very high acidity that makes the palate tingle. It's extremely dry, with a veneer of tannin. Yet this wine possesses a likeable terroir and a good structure and may even develop in the bottle. **87** —*S.H. (5/1/2004)*

Ortman Family 2004 Fiddlestix Vineyard Pinot Noir (Santa Rita Hills) $40. Chuck Ortman is one of the few to source grapes from this esteemed vineyard. The '04 is a giant step ahead of the '03, suggesting an increasing mastery of the grapes. This inky dark wine is hugely ripe, with red and black fruit-filled pastry flavors, yet dry, silky and balanced. Should develop additional complexities by 2008. **90** —*S.H. (12/15/2006)*

Ortman Family 2003 Fiddlestix Vineyard Pinot Noir (Santa Rita Hills) $40. Bone dry, acidic, and tannic, and seemingly early picked, because there's not a whole lot of fruit, this is a lean Pinot Noir. Finishes with a scour of bitter coffee and cherry skin. **85** —*S.H. (12/1/2005)*

Ortman Family 2005 Syrah Rosé Blend (Paso Robles) $16. This dark pink-colored wine has simple strawberry and vanilla flavors. It's dry and soft, an easy sipper for the summer. **83** —*S.H. (11/1/2006)*

Ortman Family 2002 Sangiovese (Paso Robles) $20. Dry and bitter, this wine has earthy, tobaccoey flavors with a hint of cherries. With its firm acidity, it will be a fine, unobtrusive accompaniment to Italian fare. **85** —*S.H. (11/15/2004)*

Ortman Family 2003 Syrah (San Luis Obispo County) $25. Veteran wine-maker Chuck Ortman (formerly of Meridian) and his family are behind this wine, which boasts intriguing scents of white pepper, raw meat, dried herbs, and mixed berries. On the palate, it's true to the Ortman style of favoring elegance over weight, turning a little tart and lemony on the finish. **86** *(9/1/2005)*

Ortman Family 2002 Syrah (San Luis Obispo County) $25. This Central Coast Syrah shows its cool-climate terroir in the intense blast of white pepper that announces it. It's very tannic now, fiercely so, which inhibits the pleasure factor. Despite the cherry and blackberry fruit that shows up on the finish, I don't think it's an ager. **86** —*S.H. (6/1/2005)*

Ortman Family 2001 Syrah (San Luis Obispo County) $25. Veteran Chuck Ortman took some tough as nails, tannic Edna Valley fruit and tried his best to soften and fatten it with Paso Robles grapes. The cool climate won out. This wine is hard and firm, dry and astringent. If you have the patience, it may reward cellaring for at least 10 years. **86** —*S.H. (5/1/2004)*

OS WINERY

OS Winery 2004 Bordeaux Blend (Washington) $22. Very smooth and chocolatey, the red blend has dumped the Lemberger (thankfully) and is a solid Bordeaux mix of 45% Cabernet Sauvignon, 30% Merlot, and 25% Cab Franc. Smoky, earthy, and substantial, it carries the winery's characteristic roasted coffee and bitter chocolate flavors through the big, tannic finish. **88** —*P.G. (10/1/2006)*

OS Winery 2003 Champoux Vineyard Bordeaux Blend (Columbia Valley (WA)) $30. This Bordeaux blend is three-quarters Cab Franc, the rest Cab Sauvignon and Merlot. It shows some volatility along with berry, tobacco, and espresso scents in the nose. Light fruit flavors of berries, strawberries, and melon can be found; finishing with somewhat rough-and-tumble tannins. **88** —*P.G. (12/15/2005)*

OS Winery 2004 Meek Vineyard Petite Verdot (Yakima Valley) $42. Tight and tannic, this wine is a flavorful mix of plum, cassis, black pepper, black coffee, and smoke. Austere, bone dry, and blackly tannic, it shows excellent length and structure within the confines of the variety. **89** —*P.G. (10/1/2006)*

OS Winery 2003 Red Blend (Columbia Valley (WA)) $20. This high-toned wine is packed with supple, juicy fruit, big and round and ripe. It's almost half Lemberger, Washington's answer to Zinfandel, and it has been vinified in neutral oak for full fruit impact. The vineyard sources—Klipsun, Champoux, and Sheridan—are exceptional for a "mutt" wine. **88** —*P.G. (12/15/2005)*

OS Winery 2004 Sheridan Vineyard Ulysses Red Blend (Yakima Valley) $50. After the terrific 2003 Ulysses this is a come-down. Sweaty and tight, with a tart, unyielding palate, this herbal, peppery wine requires some effort. Released too soon? Most certainly, but it's a good question whether the chocolatey oak will ever smooth into the light, tart fruit flavors of red berry and pomegranate. **87** —*P.G. (10/1/2006)*

OS Winery 2003 Sheridan Vineyard Ulysses Red Blend (Yakima Valley) $50. OS (formerly Owen-Sullivan) has hit a home run with the 2003 Ulysses, a voluptuous red that is 60% Cabernet Franc, 30% Merlot, and 10% Cabernet Sauvignon. Extracted and volatile, it's not a bashful wine, but it has many layers of nuanced flavors that expand in the glass, filling

the nose with dried herbs, mineral, leaf, coffee, and scorched earth. **93** —*P.G. (12/15/2005)*

OS Winery 2005 Champoux Vineyard Riesling (Horse Heaven Hills) $22. I believe this is the first time that a Champoux Riesling has been vineyard designated, by this winery or any other. It's well deserved; this is a succulent, lush bottle of lemon-drop flavors. The 3% residual sugar is snapped up easily by the juicy acids; chunky and loaded with flavor, this is old-school Washington Riesling at its finest. **90** —*P.G. (10/1/2006)*

OS Winery 2004 Dineen Vineyard Syrah (Yakima Valley) $42. An interesting tangle of flavors—silky smooth chocolate and bright citrus, wrapped around cool-climate Syrah fruit. There is a lovely floral element in the nose, and the bright berry core is smoothly melded into lightly toasted, chocolatey barrel flavors. **89** —*P.G. (11/15/2006)*

OSPREY'S DOMINION

Osprey's Dominion 2002 Cabernet Franc (North Fork of Long Island) $22. Herbal flavors dominate the cherry fruit in this light- to medium bodied wine. The tannins are chalky but not green, while the aromas of barnyard, cola, vanilla, and red berry suggest this wine should be drunk now. **84** —*M.D. (8/1/2006)*

Osprey's Dominion 2001 Cabernet Franc (North Fork of Long Island) $18. Kudos to winemaker Adam Suprenant, a New York native, who has done a lot with reds here, even the difficult Cabernet Franc. This version has developed aromas of mushroom, balsam, and chocolate shading plenty of dark berry. Cherry-berry flavors are edged with mushroom, while the smooth tannins meld nicely with moderate acidity. This wine should be enjoyed now and over the next two years. **87** —*M.D. (8/1/2006)*

Osprey's Dominion 2002 Flight Meritage (North Fork of Long Island) $35. Vintage can make all the difference in a wine, as evidenced in this Merlot-dominant Bordeaux blend. Where the 2000 vintage of this wine was tomatoey, this wine has plenty of purple fruit. Grapey plum aromas mix with spice while flavors of blueberry, pencil shavings, and dark spice coat the mouth. Nicely balanced tannins and a spicy, fruity finish round this wine out. **87** —*M.D. (8/1/2006)*

Osprey's Dominion 2001 Flight Meritage (North Fork of Long Island) $35. Still a dark red, this wine is starting to show some age with dried spice-dominated aromas of cola and funk. Light- to medium-bodied, with moderate tannins and acidity just shy of sharp, the flavors consist of mixed berries, tobacco, eucalyptus, and mushrooms, finishing with herbs. Drink now and over the next few years. **85** —*M.D. (8/1/2006)*

Osprey's Dominion 2000 Flight Meritage (North Fork of Long Island) $35. This Merlot-Cab Sauvignon smells and tastes like tomato juice, with balsam and tobacco accents. Smooth tannins offer a creamy feel, but high acid makes it tart. **80** —*M.D. (8/1/2006)*

Osprey's Dominion 2002 Merlot (North Fork of Long Island) $18. More oak is evident in this wine than Osprey Dominion's Reserve, the vanilla shading bright cherry fruit aromas and giving a pie-crust element to the red-berry flavors. Soft and creamy, with tobacco notes that carry through the finish. **87** —*M.D. (8/1/2006)*

Osprey's Dominion 2001 Merlot (North Fork of Long Island) $18. Lavishly oaked, with layers of vanilla and cream wrapped around a core of red berry fruit. Creamy and supple on the midpalate, then turns tangy and lemony on the finish. **85** —*J.C. (3/1/2006)*

Osprey's Dominion 2000 Merlot (North Fork of Long Island) $18. 84 —*J.C. (10/2/2004)*

Osprey's Dominion 2002 Reserve Merlot (North Fork of Long Island) $35. Brick red, with tight, grippy tannins, this medium-bodied wine has mild red-berry and cassis aromas touched with brown leaf. Darker blueberry shows in the mouth, backed by mineral and oak. Hard tannins take over on the finish. **85** —*M.D. (8/1/2006)*

OTTIMINO VINEYARDS

Ottimino Vineyards 2001 Von Weidlich Vineyard Zinfandel (Russian River Valley) $36. Bright and spicy, yet dense and rich, the wine serves up its plum, blackberry, cassis, toast, vanilla, and herb flavors framed in an unusual camphor edge. Fairly bright on the finish, with a long, zippy end. **89** *(11/1/2003)*

OUTPOST

Outpost 2000 Pringle Family Vineyard Zinfandel (Howell Mountain) $45. Everything you want in a Zinfandel without overdoing it. The blueberry fruit is fresh and immense. Layered with spice and cocoa, the wine is big, complex, and elegant all at the same time—something that is hard to achieve with this grape. Made to enjoy now but will last for quite a while. **94** —C.S. (11/1/2002)

OWEN ROE

Owen Roe 2004 Rosa Mystica Cabernet Franc (Columbia Valley (WA)) $36. Citrus and coffee streaks run through the stiff, herbal fruit. It's not quite all the way ripe; there are notes of dill and pickle barrel, also an unusual cola/root beer flavor usually found in Pinot Noir. Not particularly varietal, but still an interesting wine. **88** —P.G. (8/1/2006)

Owen Roe 2003 DuBrul Vineyard Cabernet Sauvignon (Yakima Valley) $60. DuBrul fruit is here taken to the limit, delivering dense, almost syrupy flavors of concentrated blueberry, balsamic vinegar, and moist earth. Big and nicely detailed, this mixes in toasty cracker, vanilla, and tannins tasting of black tea. **90** —P.G. (8/1/2006)

Owen Roe 2004 DuBrul Vineyard Merlot (Yakima Valley) $45. Dusty and light, this sends up scents of pretty rose petals dusted with chocolate powder. The lightly floral quality makes for an elegant and restrained wine, but the chocolatey oak keeps it flavorful and very appealing. **90** —P.G. (8/1/2006)

Owen Roe 2004 Pinot Gris (Willamette Valley) $20. Exceptionally lush and ripe, this broadly tropical Pinot Gris oozes with papaya, mango, banana, and mashed pear flavors. Exotic, soft and totally plush, it's like sinking into the most comfortable chair on the planet. **91** —P.G. (2/1/2006)

Owen Roe 2004 Red Blend (Yakima Valley) $42. The blend is half Merlot, the rest Cabernet Franc and Cabernet Sauvignon, from vineyard sources including DuBrul and Elerding. Smooth and supple, this richly fruity wine shows the lively herb and spice details that characterize the best Yakima Valley sites. Perfectly balanced, elegant, and stylish, it's the perfect example of how Washington combines the best of Old and New World styles. **91** —P.G. (8/1/2006)

Owen Roe 2004 Lady Rosa Syrah (Columbia Valley (WA)) $45. Very solid—it is hard and a bit chunky—this is dark, sensuous Syrah. Streaks of black tar, smoke, and tannin take it to the dark side of the grape, moving into an earthy, smoky finish. **89** —P.G. (8/1/2006)

OWEN-SULLIVAN

Owen-Sullivan 2002 BSH Bordeaux Blend (Washington) $35. The BSH blend is 70% Cab, 13% Cab Franc, and 17% Merlot. Cherry fruit holds down the core here, with good concentration that is highlighted with one-third new French oak. High-toned notes in the nose, and a bit of wet dog in the finish. **87** —P.G. (6/1/2005)

Owen-Sullivan 2000 Champoux Vineyard Cabernet Franc (Columbia Valley (WA)) $25. Though released early, and still showing some sweet, grapey scents, this is a very pretty wine reminiscent of a young Syrah. Berry, cherry, and chocolate mingle with the fruit right out in front. It's a quite drinkable, delicious, forward style. **88** —P.G. (6/1/2002)

Owen-Sullivan 2000 Klipsun Vineyard Merlot (Red Mountain) $25. This very young, grapey, yeasty wine is still pulling itself together, but shows very nice, sweet fruit, augmented with spice and a hint of mint. Light and supple, another few months in the bottle will certainly help. **87** —P.G. (6/1/2002)

Owen-Sullivan 2002 Ulysses Merlot-Cabernet Sauvignon (Yakima Valley) $50. This vintage is vineyard designated (Sheridan Vineyard) and 80% Merlot; the rest Cabernet Sauvignon. A ripe, plumy wine, showing a lifted nose bordering on volatility. Despite the pretty fruit, the finish is somewhat bitter, almost scorched. **87** —P.G. (6/1/2005)

OWL RIDGE

Owl Ridge 2003 Brigden Vineyard Cabernet Sauvignon (Sonoma County) $50. The wine is 100% Cabernet, sourced from a vineyard in the Mayacamas. It's very tannic and dry at this point. Such is the massive fruit core, of cassis and cherries, and the overall balance, that the wine must age well, even though it has no history of doing so. Hold until 2010 and try again. **93 Cellar Selection** —S.H. (9/1/2006)

Owl Ridge 2004 Vineyard Select Cabernet Sauvignon (Sonoma County) $38. A bit on the tannic side, with a slight green, unripe feeling, but there's something nice about the blackberry fruit, with a taste of roasted coffeebean, and the smooth, velvety texture. A satisfying wine. **86** —S.H. (12/31/2006)

Owl Ridge 2004 Vineyard Select Chardonnay (Sonoma Coast) $32. If you like acidity, your salivary glands will love this Chard, which is tart to almost searing. It shows good tropical fruit and new oaky flavors, but that acidity limits what otherwise is an opulent wine. **86** —S.H. (12/31/2006)

PACIFIC ECHO

Pacific Echo 1996 Champagne Blend (Anderson Valley) $27. 85 (12/15/1999)

Pacific Echo 1995 Blanc de Blancs Champagne Blend (Anderson Valley) $27. 89 (12/31/2000)

Pacific Echo NV Brut Champagne Blend (Mendocino County) $22. 87 —P.G. (12/31/2000)

Pacific Echo NV Brut Champagne Blend (Mendocino County) $22. Fresh and toasty, with a creamy texture and pretty melon, citrus, apple, pear, mineral, and nut flavors. Moderate at the end. **88** —J.M. (12/1/2002)

Pacific Echo 1995 Brut Champagne Blend (Anderson Valley) $33. Very Champagne-like in the nose, with earthy-yeasty aromas and underlying notes of citrus, smoke, and mineral. Pretty, inviting. In the mouth, great complexity. The wine has begun its aging cycle and has gorgeous balance and richness, almost opulence. There are baked, aged characteristics, and it finishes dry and long. **93** —S.H. (6/1/2001)

Pacific Echo 1997 Brut Rosé Champagne Blend (Mendocino County) $27. Very pale in color, with a slight coppery sheen and pronounced aromas of strawberry. It's very rich in the mouth, just loaded with fruity, spicy personality. Not quite dry, with just a trace of sugar. There's a nice creaminess to this crowd-pleasing sparkler. **90** —S.H. (6/1/2001)

Pacific Echo NV Crémant Champagne Blend (Anderson Valley) $23. 87 —S.H. (12/31/2000)

Pacific Echo 1995 Private Reserve Brut Champagne Blend (Anderson Valley) $31. 88 —M.M. (12/31/2000)

Pacific Echo 1992 Private Reserve Brut Champagne Blend (Anderson Valley) $32. 91 —M.S. (12/1/2000)

Pacific Echo 1996 Blanc de Blancs Sparkling Blend (Anderson Valley) $27. Toasty, nutty, vanilla, and spice aromas lead off here. A firm-textured wine with pear, apple, hazelnut, lemon, spice, and herb flavors neatly interwoven, it's got muscle and finesse. On the finish, it's lush, showing elegance and lots of staying power. **91** —J.M. (12/1/2003)

Pacific Echo 1998 Brut Sparkling Blend (Anderson Valley) $22. Rich toast and hazelnut aromas lead the way here, with a bright-edged citrus core on the follow-up. The wine is richly textured, serving up tangerine, herb, and mineral flavors on the finish. **88** —J.M. (12/1/2003)

Pacific Echo 1998 Brut Rosé Sparkling Blend (Anderson Valley) $24. Quite fragrant, with hints of peaches, tangerine, and wildflowers. It's creamy on the palate, serving up a lovely blend of toast, green apple, citrus, pear, and grapefruit flavors. Full and rich on the finish. Really lovely. **91 Editors' Choice** —J.M. (12/1/2003)

Pacific Echo NV Cramant Sparkling Blend (Anderson Valley) $22. The wine shows hints of honey and citrus up front, followed by toast and nut flavors. But it's a little flat on the midpalate. **84** —J.M. (12/1/2003)

PACIFIC STAR

Pacific Star 1996 Venturi Vineyard Charbono (Mendocino County) $32. They say there are only 47 acres of Charbono still planted in California, and this wine from 100-year-old vines, proves there should be more of it. Intense, rich, and full-bodied, it has deep flavors of plums and spices, and the most wonderfully mellow tannins. Try it as an alternative to Zinfandel. **89** —S.H. (12/1/2001)

Pacific Star 2000 Pamela's Vineyard Chardonnay (Mendocino County) $NA. 84 —*S.H. (6/1/2003)*

Pacific Star 1999 Liebelt Vineyards Merlot (Lodi) $20. From a warm appellation, a rugged, earthy wine with some distinctly raisiny notes. It's very soft and round, with a low-acid, velvety mouthfeel and outsized fruit. The finish is a bit sweet and Port-like. 83 —*S.H. (7/1/2002)*

Pacific Star 1997 Reserve Merlot (Mendocino County) $22. Pretty and inviting aromas of black cherries, rhubarb, smoke, and a rich earthiness lead to an extracted, slightly jammy wine. It's very dry, and the tannins are approachable now. 84 —*S.H. (12/1/2001)*

Pacific Star 1999 Meadows Vineyard Mourvèdre (Contra Costa County) $20. Light in color, with jammy, smoky aromas and ripe fruity flavors, soft tannins, and low acids. A pleasant, easy-to-drink wine. 84 —*S.H. (11/15/2001)*

Pacific Star 2000 Petite Sirah (Mendocino County) $26. Simple, dull, vegetal, earthy and hollow are a few words tasters used to describe this wine, whose flavors just manage to suggest less than ripe cherries. Finishes short. 82 *(4/1/2003)*

Pacific Star 1999 Reserve Petite Sirah (Mendocino County) $26. 86 —*S.H. (9/1/2003)*

Pacific Star 2001 Coro Mendocino Red Blend (Mendocino) $35. A fairly tart style, that leaves the palate feeling squeaky clean. Flavors run from citrus to bing cherry and herbs. On the finish, it's a little short. 84 —*J.M. (9/1/2004)*

Pacific Star 1999 Dad's Daily Red Red Blend (California) $12. 83 —*S.H. (11/15/2002)*

Pacific Star 2000 Viognier (California) $16. Smells thin and earthy, and with a bothersome streak of chlorophyll, indicating less-than-ripe grapes. This impression is confirmed in the mouth, where it drinks sharp and thin. It's dry and clean, and that's about it. 82 —*S.H. (12/15/2001)*

Pacific Star 1999 Zinfandel (Mendocino County) $14. Young, sharp aromas are stemmy and green, and lead to a thin, sharp wine in the mouth. Acid and alcohol dominate. There's not much fruit to find, but if you concentrate you can conjure up some berries. Dry, acidic, and rasping, it will certainly be better with some rich foods. 82 —*S.H. (12/15/2001)*

Pacific Star 1999 B-Bar-X Ranch Reserve Zinfandel (Mendocino County) $24. Showcases Zin's wild, almost savage side, with that briary, berry profile. But it's very dry, thin, and rasping, with scouring acidity and a lean, lean mouthfeel. This palate-stinging wine needs rich, oily foods to tease out whatever ripe fruit is hiding inside. 83 —*S.H. (12/15/2001)*

PAEONIA

Paeonia 2003 Late Harvest Bien Nacido Vineyard Pinot Blanc (Santa Maria Valley) $30. From the old gold color to the exotic, explosive apricot aromas, this is one sweet dessert wine. Botrytis heavily infected the grapes, which were harvested at enormously high brix. The residual sugar is 27%. The wine could use more intense fruit flavor to justify all that sugar. 88 —*S.H. (8/1/2006)*

PAGE

Page 1999 Bordeaux Blend (Napa Valley) $58. Sleek, smooth, and complex. This impressive wine is supported by firm, ripe tannins. The flavors range from cassis to licorice, coffee, blackberry, plum, spice, and herbs. It's all couched with muscular elegance and backed by sweet oak. Long and lush at the end. 93 **Cellar Selection** —*J.M. (5/1/2003)*

PAGE CELLARS

Page Cellars 2001 Preface Red Wine Bordeaux Blend (Red Mountain) $37. Fragrant and meaty, with hints of barnyard, leather, and herb. Right now the wine has a reductive character, tight and showing scents of rubber, but with airing and swirling it opens into a compact, well-constructed, ageworthy Bordeaux-style wine. 88 —*P.G. (9/1/2004)*

Page Cellars 2002 Preface Cabernet Sauvignon-Cabernet Franc (Red Mountain) $37. A blend of Cabernet Sauvignon and Cabernet Franc, this Red Mountain red suffers from an excess of high-toned, volatile aromas and rough, untamed tannins. The grapes sources are solid but there are too many raw, unpolished edges; it doesn't quite pull itself together. 85 —*P.G. (6/1/2006)*

Page Cellars 2002 Syrah (Columbia Valley (WA)) $37. Very fruity, with sweet, grapey flavors verging on Port. The superripe fruit catches your immediate attention, then hits an odd spot with a gluey back palate that is entirely disconnected from the front. 85 —*P.G. (11/15/2004)*

PAGOR

Pagor 2001 Tempranillo (California) $11. Those of you living outside California might have some difficulty finding this wine, but I've included it because it's rare to find good California Tempranillo at any price. This one's made by winemaker Ed Pagor, who says most of these grapes are grown in the Sierra Foothills, despite the California appellation. The wine is somewhat austere out of the starting block, but it comes around in the glass, sporting cherry, raspberry, spice, and blackberry flavors. The tannins are robust but not out of line, giving it a firm, full texture. 86 —*J.M. (11/15/2003)*

PAIGE 23

Paige 23 2000 Syrah (Santa Barbara County) $21. This is a beautiful, rich wine, impressive for the depth of its violet, lavender, blueberry, and strawberry aromas and flavors. The smoke and char of oak plays a supporting role in creating layers of complexity. Well-known winemaker Heidi Barrett assembled this elegant, subtle, and tasteful wine. 93 **Editors' Choice** —*S.H. (12/1/2002)*

PAINTER BRIDGE

Painter Bridge 2003 Chardonnay (California) $7. Watery, with an odd medicinal flavor along with the peaches. 82 —*S.H. (5/1/2005)*

Painter Bridge 2001 Chardonnay (California) $7. Intensely fruity and spicy, with layers of tropical fruits, peaches, figs, and tapioca. Lavishly oaked, with crisp acids and a long, rich finish. Despite the size, could use more nuance and finesse. 87 **Best Buy** —*S.H. (2/1/2003)*

Painter Bridge 2002 Zinfandel (California) $7. A decently dry and well structured wine, but too thin in fruit to really recommend. 83 —*S.H. (5/1/2005)*

PALMAZ

Palmaz 2002 Cabernet Sauvignon (Napa Valley) $100. I liked the winery's 2001, although it was quite tannic, but this isn't in the same league. This vintage is also numbingly tannic, maybe even more so, but the core of fruit that charmed a year ago isn't there, leading to questions about ageability. If you're a gambler, cellar it for six years and see what's up. 88 —*S.H. (5/1/2006)*

Palmaz 2001 Cabernet Sauvignon (Napa Valley) $100. An inaugural wine from the Palmaz family and winemaker Randy Dunn. Massive, huge, all currant, cassis, and cherry fruit, with an elaborate overlay of smoky oak. The bigtime tannins are thick but softly sweet. Drink now through 2008. 90 —*S.H. (5/1/2005)*

PALMER

Palmer 1997 Select Reserve Bordeaux Blend (North Fork of Long Island) $25. This blend of 55% Cabernet Sauvignon, 39% Merlot, and 6% Cabernet Franc shows why many people like to compare Long Island to Bordeaux. Tastes like a Bordeaux, with dark cassis and coffee flavors. Built like a Bordeaux, to age. 87 *(4/1/2001)*

Palmer 1995 Select Reserve Bordeaux Blend (North Fork of Long Island) $25. 84 —*J.C. (12/1/1999)*

Palmer 2002 Proprietor's Reserve Cabernet Franc (North Fork of Long Island) $19. Sour and lean, with stemmy green flavors and aromas that dominate. The mouth is herbal and chalky with a medium body. 80 —*M.D. (8/1/2005)*

Palmer 1998 Proprietor's Reserve Cabernet Franc (North Fork of Long Island) $18. Aromas of toast and dried herbs—even flowers—mingle on the nose, then give way to juicy black cherry flavors that linger through the finish, where coffee and caramel chime in, adding welcome complexity. 88 **Editors' Choice** —*J.C. (4/1/2001)*

Palmer 1997 Proprietor's Reserve Cabernet Franc (North Fork of Long Island) $18. 88 —*J.C. (12/1/1999)*

Palmer 1998 Cabernet Sauvignon (North Fork of Long Island) $15. Already showing some signs of age in its slightly browning rim, this Cab boasts scents of eucalyptus, vanilla, cinnamon, and red cherries, but it's all overly delicate—almost lacy. There's just not enough there to score higher despite its charms. **83**—*J.C. (4/1/2001)*

Palmer 2002 Proprietors Reserve Cabernet Sauvignon (North Fork of Long Island) $NA. Thin and lean, with moderate flavors of red berry and green weedy notes. **80**—*M.D. (8/1/2006)*

Palmer 2003 5 Acre Block Chardonnay (North Fork of Long Island) $NA. Buttered toast, pear, and citrus aromas show promise, but the crisp lemony flavors don't hold up. Finishes tart. **81**—*J.C. (3/1/2006)*

Palmer 1995 Barrel-Fermented Chardonnay (North Fork of Long Island) $17. **81**—*J.C. (8/1/2000)*

Palmer 1998 Estate Chardonnay (North Fork of Long Island) $12. Very crisp, and loaded with tart green apples and lemons, this would be an ideal match for light fish or shellfish dishes. This is what unadulterated cool-climate Chardonnay tastes like. **84**—*J.C. (4/1/2001)*

Palmer 1997 Estate Chardonnay (North Fork of Long Island) $12. **84**—*J.C. (8/1/1999)*

Palmer 1998 Reserve Chardonnay (North Fork of Long Island) $15. Boasts classic barrel-fermented Chardonnay aromas of toasted hazelnuts and white peaches. Very pretty and very well made; it's on the lighter, more elegant side. Finishes with a welcome touch of citrus. **86**—*J.C. (4/1/2001)*

Palmer 1999 Gewürztraminer (North Fork of Long Island) $15. Very floral aromatics mark this distinctive effort; it's positively overflowing with rose petals. Turns more musky and spicy in the mouth, before fading away a little abruptly. **84**—*J.C. (4/1/2001)*

Palmer 1999 Select Harvest Gewürztraminer (North Fork of Long Island) $30. The characteristic Gewürz aromas of rose petals and lychee are partially masked by honey and apricot, but they're still there, giving this sticky a delightfully exotic edge. Try this moderately viscous sweet wine with a creamy blue-veined cheese for a special flavor/texture match. **89**—*J.C. (4/1/2001)*

Palmer 1997 Merlot (North Fork of Long Island) $18. Strays too far into the kitchen-herb spectrum for this taster. Big and creamy, with a mocha finish that lingers, but the fresh-cut thyme, parsley, and basil make for an eccentric mouthful. **83**—*J.C. (4/1/2001)*

Palmer 2002 Reserve Merlot (North Fork of Long Island) $30. This winery has produced better wines, as this one is tart in acidity and light- to medium-bodied. Flavors are in the unripe spectrum, going from green bean to candied berry to rhubarb. Oak adds a welcome spice, but a pickled finish leaves a last impression. **81**—*M.D. (12/1/2006)*

Palmer 1997 Reserve Merlot (North Fork of Long Island) $30. Heavy oak treatment marries well with this wine's dark, roasted black cherry flavors, turning into chocolate and espresso on the finish. Has the structure to last a few years in the cellar but can be drunk now. **86**—*J.C. (4/1/2001)*

Palmer 1998 Vintner's Cuvée Merlot (North Fork of Long Island) $10. Looks prematurely mature, already browning at the rim. Smells it, too. Slightly acrid tobacco and dried parsley aromas turn into cedary cigar-box flavors in the mouth, and the finish seems to be thinning out. Lean and over-mature, but still has a sense of elegance. **83**—*J.C. (1/1/2004)*

Palmer 1998 Estate Pinot Blanc (North Fork of Long Island) $13. Ripe melons and pears dance a delicate duet on the palate—softly and gently shifting ever so slightly from honeydew to Bosc and back, before turning lean and citrusy on the finish. **83**—*J.C. (4/1/2001)*

Palmer 1997 Lieb Vineyards Pinot Blanc (North Fork of Long Island) $13. **86**—*J.C. (8/1/1999)*

Palmer 2001 White Riesling (North Fork of Long Island) $14. **85**—*J.C. (8/1/2003)*

Palmer 1998 Select Reserve White Blend (North Fork of Long Island) $14. A kitchen-sink blend of Chardonnay, Pinot Blanc, Sauvignon Blanc, and Gewürztraminer, this wine showcases a rich combination of tropical fruit, pear, and pink grapefruit with grassy overtones and just a hint of toast. **86**—*J.C. (4/1/2001)*

Palmer 2000 White Riesling (North Fork of Long Island) $13. The sweet-smelling pear and guava aromas don't carry through to the palate, which

is quite dry and marked mainly by oily kerosene flavors. It's full for Riesling and richly textured, with good length, it's just not a classically fruity New World Riesling. **85**—*J.C. (3/1/2002)*

PALMERI

Palmeri 2002 Stagecoach Vineyard Syrah (Napa Valley) $47. Fruit seems easy to achieve in Syrah, but balance and elegance are more difficult goals. This fine wine is exuberantly fruity—red and black cherries—and adds notes of pecan pie, chocolate, and spice. Full and soft in the mouth, yet tangy and fresh on the finish. **89** *(9/1/2005)*

Palmeri 2003 Van Ness Vineyard Syrah (Alexander Valley) $47. This is an expensive Syrah. It's also a very good one that exhibits its origins in the soft, rich tannins and herbaceousness that accompany the blackberry and cherry fruit flavors. Bone dry, and without overpowering oak, the wine has a firmly tannic structure that calls to mind roast lamb. Drink now through 2006. **93**—*S.H. (2/1/2006)*

PALMINA

Palmina 2004 Alisos Vineyard Pinot Grigio (Santa Barbara County) $22. Nice and whistle-clean in acidity, with a sleek minerality, this wine has ripe flavors of pineapples, nectarines, and crisp green apples. It tastes a little sweet because it's so fruity. Try with southeast Asian fare. **85**—*S.H. (3/1/2006)*

PALOMA

Paloma 2002 Merlot (Spring Mountain) $51. Tasted in a rather tannic flight, this baby was even more tannic. It pours inky black, and reveals nothing in the aroma, save for grapes and oak. Yet there are powerful signs of a magnificent future, especially the long, sweet finish of blackberry syrup. Great now with robust fare, but should hold through the decade. **94 Cellar Selection**—*S.H. (10/1/2005)*

Paloma 1999 Syrah (Spring Mountain) $36. Full-bodied and well balanced; smoke, herb, and tart berry fruit mark the Paloma's palate. Its plum, smoke, saddle-leather, and dried-flower bouquet is similarly distinctive. After a year or two in the cellar, it will probably be even more complex. Finishes long, with black tea and cocoa notes. **90** *(11/1/2001)*

PALOTAI

Palotai 2002 Pinot Noir (Umpqua Valley) $18. Offers plump, candied fruit, with an acidic edge that has an artificial, chalky aftertaste. **85** *(11/1/2004)*

PALUMBO FAMILY VINEYARDS

Palumbo Family Vineyards 2000 Tre Fratelli Bordeaux Blend (Temecula) $28. A Bordeaux blend from this warmish appellation east of L.A. It's a bit musty on opening, with Porty aromas of cooked raisins and caramel. Drinks rich in sweet berry fruit, with some residual sugar on the finish. **82**—*S.H. (4/1/2004)*

PANTHER CREEK

Panther Creek 1993 Brut Champagne Blend (Willamette Valley) $50. Opens with traditional aromas of hay and toast. Pineapple and a hint of apricot waft in to the palate, which has toast and stone fruit flavors. The finish is clean and a bit grassy, with a touch of toast. This is a great pour for celebrating at home. **86**—*K.F. (12/1/2002)*

Panther Creek 2004 Melrose Vineyard Pinot Gris (Oregon) $18. A different cast to the fruit; it's pear but also pineapple, with some caramel laced in from (presumably) barrel time. Some sweetness rounds out the finish. **89**—*P.G. (2/1/2006)*

Panther Creek 2000 Arcus Pinot Noir (Willamette Valley) $60. A sniff reveals smoked meats, bacon, coffee, and leather. The flavors are clean and pure—there's an abundance of inky black cherry and plum. The balance between juicy flavorful fruit and firm mouthcoating tannins is just right. Muscular but not overbuilt. **91 Cellar Selection** *(10/1/2002)*

Panther Creek 1999 Arcus Estate Pinot Noir (Willamette Valley) $60. Fragrant and voluptuous, with beetroot and black cherry aromas spiced with smoky oak. Huge extract, filled with cola and peppery wild berry fruit. Tannins are soft, with fine acidity. The spicy finish goes on forever. This is a limpid, supple, sweetly feminine wine, and immediately drinkable. **92**—*S.H. (11/1/2001)*

Panther Creek 2000 Bednarik Vineyard Pinot Noir (Willamette Valley) $48. Leather, tobacco, and spice aromas yield to flavors of black cherry fruit with vanilla apple skin and charred wood nuances. This is a fiercely tannic wine, so much so that it seems hard as nails on your tongue despite ripe fruit. **86** *(10/1/2002)*

Panther Creek 1998 Bednarik Vineyard Pinot Noir (Willamette Valley) $48. **92** —*J.C. (12/1/2000)*

Panther Creek 2000 Freedom Hill Pinot Noir (Willamette Valley) $48. Dark and woody, with dry cherry fruit under charcoal and caramel aromas. Ample coffee and black fruit flavors show on the palate and the slightly bitter finish. Will appeal more to fans of heavy toast and dry, almost (quipped one taster) Cabernet-like fruit. **86** *(10/1/2002)*

Panther Creek 1999 Freedom Hill Pinot Noir (Willamette Valley) $49. This huge, brooding wine is bound to be controversial. There's nothing silky or elegant about it—yet. Muscular and broad-shouldered, it's packed with massive pepper and berry fruit, and leaves the palate numb with tannins. It's a must for mid- to long-term cellaring. **90** —*S.H. (11/1/2001)*

Panther Creek 1998 Freedom Hill Vineyard Pinot Noir (Willamette Valley) $48. **91** —*J.C. (12/1/2000)*

Panther Creek 2002 Nysa Vineyard Pinot Noir (Willamette Valley) $40. Tight, hard young fruit is overshadowed with big, butterscotch barrel flavors. Pleasant and unexpressive. **85** *(11/1/2004)*

Panther Creek 2000 Nysa Vineyard Pinot Noir (Willamette Valley) $48. Usually Panther Creek's wines are not this charred, but the '00 Nysa is downright burnt. The acrid, burnt-toast nose is just too much for the plummy fruit, which is there but isn't much more than a backdrop to the heavy-handed oak. **84** *(10/1/2002)*

Panther Creek 1999 Nysa Vineyard Pinot Noir (Willamette Valley) $49. Earthy plum, mushroom, and cola notes accent the nose, which features strong scents of wet tree bark. Impressively deep and rich on the palate, dominated by damp earth, but highlighted by a bright beam of acidity and firm tannins on the finish. Better in 2003. **88** —*J.C. (11/1/2001)*

Panther Creek 1998 Nysa Vineyard Pinot Noir (Willamette Valley) $48. **90** —*M.S. (12/1/2000)*

Panther Creek 2000 Red Hills Pinot Noir (Willamette Valley) $60. This winery insists that all of its single-vineyard wines are vinified identically to show off the true nature of the vineyard, but with this wine we detected inordinate barrel char. Beyond the heavy toast, we noted intensity and a strong grip in the mouth, both indications of powerful tannins. Several years of bottle age might permit the oak to fade and the gritty texture to soften. **87** *(10/1/2002)*

Panther Creek 1999 Red Hills Estate Pinot Noir (Willamette Valley) $60. Young aromas of plum concentrate, chocolate, tobacco, pepper, and moderate oak lead to a rather jammy wine. Berry and spice flavors explode in the mouth. The texture is syrupy, thick, dense. Seems to need time for all the parts to knit together. **87** —*S.H. (11/1/2001)*

Panther Creek 1999 Reserve Pinot Noir (Willamette Valley) $40. Intense and structured, firm acidity provides a backbone to flavors of caramel, toast, beets, pie cherries, and pine boughs. Its strength is also its primary drawback; the assertive acidity mutes the other components, and there may not be enough flesh in the long run. Give this backward offering a couple years in the cellar to smooth out. **87** *(11/1/2001)*

Panther Creek 1998 Reserve Pinot Noir (Willamette Valley) $36. **91** —*M.S. (12/1/2000)*

Panther Creek 2002 Shea Vineyard Pinot Noir (Willamette Valley) $40. Mingled red fruits, including cranberry, red currant, and raspberry, are swathed in new oak. Tough, with dry tannins and plenty of vanilla, it needs more time to knit together, but all the right pieces are here. **88** *(11/1/2004)*

Panther Creek 2000 Shea Vineyard Pinot Noir (Willamette Valley) $48. There's an unqualified deepness to the black fruit on the nose, which has accents of bacon and rubber. The fruit is more red than the darker bouquet might indicate; it's actually a bit tangy. The tannins on the finish are nothing if not full, which, combined with zippy acidity, makes the wine a bit hard. **88** *(10/1/2002)*

Panther Creek 1999 Shea Vineyard Pinot Noir (Willamette Valley) $49. Boasts alluring aromas of dusty iron-laced earth, cinnamon, and cumin, but doesn't quite follow through on the palate, where the cherry, berry, and spice flavors come across as tart and hard. May blossom with age or may dry out—our tasters were evenly divided. **89** *(11/1/2001)*

Panther Creek 2002 Temperance Hill Vineyard Pinot Noir (Willamette Valley) $40. Green bean and coffee notes characterize this light, somewhat awkward wine, whose tart, simple fruit is no match for all the snazzy new oak. **85** *(11/1/2004)*

Panther Creek 2000 Winemaker's Cuvee Pinot Noir (Oregon) $35. Toast and smoke, are dominant on the nose, while crisper red fruit follows on the snappy finish, which still carries a distinct hint of oak. The finish is mostly clean and smooth. **87** *(10/1/2002)*

Panther Creek 2003 Winemaker's Cuvée Pinot Noir (Willamette Valley) $20. This is a dark, toasted, roasted, and tannic effort that clearly reflects the heat of the 2003 vintage in the Willamette Valley. Oaky and astringent, it is not for admirers of a silky, seductive style of elegant Pinot Noir, but will certainly speak to those who want some brawn in their reds, whatever the grape. Let it breathe. **85** —*P.G. (11/15/2005)*

Panther Creek 2002 Winemaker's Cuvée Pinot Noir (Oregon) $25. Balanced and light, showing a hint of leathery mustiness. Cherry and plum flavors are sweet and simple, and there's a light touch of chocolate rounding out the tangy finish. **86** *(11/1/2004)*

Panther Creek 2000 Youngberg Pinot Noir (Willamette Valley) $48. Like every Panther Creek Pinot we tasted, there is lots of oak—too much for one of our panelists. But there's also a bounty of pristine black fruit aromas and smoky bacon. In the mouth, it's lush, still with ample barrel char, but with even more lip-smacking plum fruit. **92 Editors' Choice** *(10/1/2002)*

PANZA

Panza 2000 Stag's Leap Ranch Petite Sirah (Napa Valley) $NA. A solid effort that pleased nearly the entire panel, this wine has an array of flavors ranging from cherries and cassis through white pepper, bacon, and smoky plum. Oak adds vanilla and sweet woody tannins. Still young, this rich wine has a long, pretty finish and could improve with age. **88** *(4/1/2003)*

PAOLETTI

Paoletti 1997 Cabernet Sauvignon (Napa Valley) $48. **87** *(11/1/2000)*

Paoletti 1997 Non Plus Ultra Cabernet Sauvignon (Napa Valley) $110. **90** *(11/1/2000)*

PAPAPIETRO PERRY

Papapietro Perry 2003 Pinot Noir (Russian River Valley) $38. The winery's basic appellation wine is full-bodied and heavy, showing very ripe berry, cherry, and mocha flavors. It's almost like Syrah in weight, except for the silky, fine tannins. **85** —*S.H. (3/1/2006)*

Papapietro Perry 2002 Pinot Noir (Russian River Valley) $38. The most important things about this wine are its upfront oak and full-bodied character. The former brings vanilla, toast, and sweet oak shadings to the black cherry and cola fruit. It's soft in acids, which may explain a certain heaviness, but it sure is tasty. **87** —*S.H. (3/1/2005)*

Papapietro Perry 2003 Leras Family Vineyards Pinot Noir (Russian River Valley) $45. There's good acidity in this wine, with fruit that seems too extracted and sweet, like a baked, granulated sugar-infused cherry pie. If you're a fruit freak, this will do it for you. **86** —*S.H. (3/1/2006)*

Papapietro Perry 2003 Peters Vineyard Pinot Noir (Sonoma Coast) $45. Superripe in fruit, this Pinot flatters with cherry pie flavors, with the baked crust and sugary syrup. It has wonderful acidity, but whatever happened to dry, balanced elegance? **85** —*S.H. (3/1/2006)*

Papapietro Perry 2002 Peters Vineyard Pinot Noir (Sonoma Coast) $42. There's a silky, crisp quality that makes this wine vibrant. It carries flavors of raspberries and red cherries dusted with brown sugar and smoky oak, and reveals cinnamon, nutmeg, and other spices on the finish. There's a definite sweetness throughout, which chefs will note. **90** —*S.H. (3/1/2005)*

Papapietro Perry 2003 Pommard Clones Pinot Noir (Sonoma Coast) $58. Shares the same characteristics of the winery's other 2003 Pinots, namely an apparent sweetness that's inappropriate in a dry table wine. There's probably no measurable sugar, but the palate impression is of sweetened cherries. **85** —*S.H. (3/1/2006)*

Papapietro Perry 2003 Zinfandel (Russian River Valley) $30. Classic Russian River Zinfandel, rich, pure, and balanced. The blackberry, blueberry, cherry, cassis, and chocolate flavors are amazingly rich and powerful, spiced with black pepper and the sweet, subtle taste of raisins, although the wine is totally dry. **93** —*S.H. (3/1/2006)*

PAPIO

Papio 2004 Cabernet Sauvignon (California) $6. Fruity and forward, this everyday Cab is dry, with ultraripe blackberry, currant, and blueberry flavors and a rich, creamy texture, with a coat of smoky oak. **83 Best Buy** —*S.H. (12/31/2005)*

Papio 2004 Chardonnay (California) $6. So tart and citrusy, it's more like Sauvignon Blanc. It's an easy sipper with enough lemon and lime fruit and creaminess to make it a value. **84 Best Buy** —*S.H. (12/31/2005)*

Papio 2004 Merlot (California) $6. Acidity and green stemmy flavors dominate, despite some red and black cherry flavors. It's a dry wine, with obvious oak. **82** —*S.H. (12/31/2005)*

PARADIGM

Paradigm 2002 Cabernet Sauvignon (Oakville) $53. Pretty much a copy of last year, maybe a tad less opulent, this is a soft, balanced Cabernet that shows off Oakville's supreme ability to ripen fruit and tannins. It's a gentle, thoroughly dry wine, rich in black currant, cherry, and mocha flavors, with a nice cut of acidity. Best in its youth, but should hold for 10 years. **92** —*S.H. (7/1/2006)*

Paradigm 2001 Cabernet Sauvignon (Oakville) $53. Made by Heidi Barrett, a gracefully soft, impressively balanced wine, with ripe, almost sweet cassis, cherry, and cocoa flavors. Sure is easy to drink, but also has the structural harmony to hang in there for up to 10 years. **91** —*S.H. (11/1/2005)*

Paradigm 1997 Estate Bottled Cabernet Sauvignon (Napa Valley) $48. 92 *(11/1/2000)*

PARADIS

Paradis 1997 Woodbridge Ranch Cabernet Sauvignon (California) $12. Odd, disturbing aromas of sweet rhubarb pie start things off; then it turns medicinal and sweet in the mouth. Clean, with good acids, but seems a combination of overripe grapes and suspect winemaking. Barely drinkable. **80** —*S.H. (11/15/2001)*

Paradis 1999 Woodbridge Ranch Chardonnay (California) $10. Earthy, with peach and apple aromas and a funky component. Light and simple peach flavors, and decent acidity. **81** —*S.H. (11/15/2001)*

Paradis 1997 Woodbridge Ranch Merlot (California) $10. Dusty and earthy, with aromas of slightly raisined fruit, chocolate, and a hint of fresh herbs. The modest dark berry fruit is overwhelmed on the palate by strong earth flavors, but the mouthfeel is generous and smooth. **85 Best Buy** —*J.C. (6/1/2001)*

Paradis 2001 Cask Reserve/Old Vine Zinfandel (Lodi) $12. Tastes like Zin, but the back label says it's Syrah. We'll believe the front label for this pleasant, moderate-bodied red wine that sports ripe raspberry, spice, plum, licorice, toast, and vanilla flavors. Soft tannins keep the finish smooth. **87 Best Buy** —*J.M. (11/1/2003)*

PARADISE RANCH

Paradise Ranch 2002 Rockpile Vineyard Cabernet Sauvignon (Sonoma County) $35. Paradise Ridge has struggled with Cab, and continues to. This one's ripe and juicy in Cabernet fruit, but has a stubborn rusticity and jagged mouthfeel it can't quite overcome. It's a good Cab, but I think this vineyard is simply better for Zinfandel and Petite Sirah. **84** —*S.H. (12/1/2006)*

Paradise Ridge 2000 Cabernet Sauvignon (Sonoma County) $28. On the plus side, well-etched cassis and black currant flavors and rich, fancy tan-

nins. On the other hand, there's a tart, bitter note mid-palate and finish. **85** —*S.H. (10/1/2003)*

Paradise Ridge 1999 Cabernet Sauvignon (Sonoma County) $25. Rough and earthy, it has some well-developed berry-fruit flavors. High acidity scours the mouth. A serviceable wine, dry and austere, with rasping tannins that aren't likely to soften with age. **83** —*S.H. (7/1/2002)*

Paradise Ridge 1998 Cabernet Sauvignon (Sonoma County) $22. Ripe, with blackberry aromas and sweetly smoky oak. In the mouth, blackberry and cassis flavors are joined with raisiny notes and sweet, hot, Port-like nuances. Could use a bit more polish. **82** —*S.H. (12/1/2001)*

Paradise Ridge 2001 Elevation Rockpile Vineyard Cabernet Sauvignon (Sonoma County) $36. From this newish appellation, a Cab that has much in common with Dry Creek examples. It's quite dry, with spicy, wild berry and jam flavors and a certain rustic character. Earns points for sheer concentration. **87** —*S.H. (10/1/2004)*

Paradise Ridge 2002 Ladi's Vineyard Cabernet Sauvignon (Sonoma County) $27. Feels young and gritty in the mouth, with astringent tannins and a core of cherry-berry fruit. This wine is seriously in need of decanting, but it doesn't seem like an ager. **84** —*S.H. (12/1/2006)*

Paradise Ridge 2001 Ladi's Vineyard Cabernet Sauvignon (Sonoma County) $29. You get a combo of ripe blackberry and cherry alongside sharp green tea notes in this wine. It's dry, with smooth tannins and an astringent finish. **85** —*S.H. (2/1/2005)*

Paradise Ridge 1997 Barrel Select Nagasawa Vineyard Chardonnay (Sonoma County) $18. 82 *(6/1/2000)*

Paradise Ridge 2002 Nagasawa Vineyard Chardonnay (Sonoma County) $22. Lots of winemaker influence here in the leesy quality and oaky notes that have been added to an underlying wine tasting of apples and pears. The result is a dry, complex Chard that finishes with a bite of green apple acidity. **87** —*S.H. (2/1/2005)*

Paradise Ridge 2001 Nagasawa Vineyard Chardonnay (Sonoma County) $19. Kind of earthy and funky, with fruity flavors side by side with tobacco and ginger. There's also a bite of tart acidity in this lean wine. Definitely marches to a different beat. **84** —*S.H. (6/1/2003)*

Paradise Ridge 2000 Nagasawa Vineyard Chardonnay (Sonoma County) $18. Ripely fruity, with peach, tangerine, and tropical fruit flavors and a solid dose of spicy, smoky oak. There's also a strong, leesy note. On the palate, it's round and full-bodied, with a rich, honeyed texture and a long finish. **87** —*S.H. (12/31/2001)*

Paradise Ridge 1998 Nagasawa Vineyard Chardonnay (Sonoma County) $16. Odd aromas mark this unbalanced wine, as do musty, grapefruit-juice flavors and sour finish. It's just barely drinkable. **80** —*S.H. (11/15/2001)*

Paradise Ridge 2001 Merlot (Sonoma County) $28. This wine is clean, good, and tasty. It's not especially complex, but shows berry, cherry, spice, and oak flavors that are wrapped in a soft, balanced package. **86** —*S.H. (12/1/2005)*

Paradise Ridge 2000 Ladi's Vineyard Merlot (Sonoma County) $25. Dense and heavy, a young, full-bodied wine that feels thick in the mouth. It may be an ager. For the moment, though, the plum and blackberry flavors lack delicacy and zest, and the finish is syrupy and ponderous. **84** —*S.H. (12/15/2003)*

Paradise Ridge 1999 Ladi's Vineyard Merlot (Sonoma County) $23. This is described as a country-style wine because of its rugged tannins and angular, rough mouthfeel. The deeply plummy flavors are ripe, but very dry. The biggest problem may be the acids, which are very low. You long for more crispness and life, something to offset the fruitiness. **84** —*S.H. (7/1/2002)*

Paradise Ridge 1998 Ladi's Vineyard Merlot (Sonoma County) $22. Some pretty blackberry and smoke aromas mingle with buttery-fudge notes. Unusual for this varietal. Sweet as it smells, it tastes bone dry, with berry flavors and good tannins. **84** —*S.H. (12/1/2001)*

Paradise Ridge 2002 Rockpile Vineyard Merlot (Sonoma County) $30. I have not been a great fan of this winery's Bordeaux reds, and this one also has a countrified thing going on, despite some very ripe and lip-smacking cherry flavors. Half the oak barrels it was aged in were new. **85** —*S.H. (12/1/2006)*

Paradise Ridge 2002 Pinot Noir (Russian River Valley) $29. Opens with jammy cherry fruit, cocoa, roasted meat, and smoky oak, and has plenty of cherry, coffee, and cola flavors, but needs just a little more grace and finesse. Still, this dry wine could soften and come together by 2005. **86** *(11/1/2004)*

Paradise Ridge 2003 Elizabeth and Henry's Vineyard Pinot Noir (Sonoma Coast) $32. Simple, soft, and syrupy, this cola and cherry-flavored wine is dry, with oaky influences and a rustic finish. **82** —*S.H. (12/31/2005)*

Paradise Ridge 2002 Elizabeth and Henry's Vineyard Pinot Noir (Russian River Valley) $29. Dark and glyceriney, a big, extracted wine that's a bit clumsy now, but has potential. Notable for the big cherry and plum flavors and super-sized tannins, and high alcohol. Should benefit from a year or two of bottle age. **87** *(11/1/2004)*

Paradise Ridge 2003 Grandview Vineyard Sauvignon Blanc (Sonoma County) $15. Lemons, limes, spearmint, and green melon flavors, tart and fresh with acidity. A clean, vibrant, and assertive wine, dry and bitter. Nice by itself or with seared halibut topped with fruity salsa. **86** —*S.H. (2/1/2005)*

Paradise Ridge 2001 Grandview Vineyard Sauvignon Blanc (Sonoma County) $14. Here's a crisp, uncomplicated white wine perfect for summer evenings and grilled shrimp over the barbie. It has slightly sweet flavors of apples and peaches and telltale grapefruit and grass, set off by good acidity. Clean and vibrant, it finishes with a hint of herbed honey. **87** —*S.H. (9/1/2003)*

Paradise Ridge 2000 Grandview Vineyard Sauvignon Blanc (Sonoma County) $14. A single vineyard wine showing lots of bright fruit character. Lemon Lifesaver and honey aromas mingle with grassy notes, leading to a round, crisp and dry wine with considerable finesse. It's made in a popular style and will go well with many types of food. **87** —*S.H. (12/15/2001)*

Paradise Ridge 1999 Grandview Vineyard Sauvignon Blanc (Sonoma County) $14. Here's an atypical wine for this variety. It has grapefruit aromas with a hint of banana and chocolate, and a pronounced tingle or sparkle. Bone dry and refreshing. Purists will object, but others will like it. **82** —*S.H. (11/15/2001)*

Paradise Ridge 2002 Garrod Ranch Syrah (Santa Cruz Mountains) $29. Lots to like in this dry, oaky wine. It features upfront cherry, black raspberry, and chocolate flavors in a smooth texture, tinged with vanilla and smoke, and the tannins are smooth and sweetly ripe. **86** —*S.H. (2/1/2005)*

Paradise Ridge 2001 Hoenselaars Vineyard Upper Block Syrah (Sonoma County) $32. From a block within a vineyard, a distinctive wine, with its own style and personality. Flavors span the gamut from blackberries and cassis to tobacco, rhubarb, white pepper, white chocolate, and sage, and the tannins are dry, rich, and complex. Has a youthful bite of acidity, suggesting short-term aging. **90** —*S.H. (12/15/2003)*

Paradise Ridge 2002 Ladi's Vineyard Syrah (Sonoma County) $28. This single-vineyard Syrah shows coffee, red cherry, red plum, pomegranate, and white pepper flavors that are powerful, but subtle. It's drinkable now, with a tart, acidic streak through the finish that calls for rich grills and cheeses. **87** —*S.H. (12/1/2005)*

Paradise Ridge 2001 Ladi's Vineyard Syrah (Sonoma County) $28. This is a clean and well-made Syrah with notes of white pepper and blackberry. It's generous in the mouth, although the tannins are quite pronounced. Very dry and balanced, it will be great with lamb, filet mignon, or roast pork. **87** —*S.H. (12/1/2004)*

Paradise Ridge 2000 Ladi's Vineyard Syrah (Sonoma County) $27. This is a dark, very aromatic wine, brimming with aromas of freshly-crushed white pepper and blackberries. It's filled with fruity sweetness, but is fundamentally dry. The tannins are soft and melted, and the acids are soft, too. This makes it rich and mellow. **87** —*S.H. (12/1/2002)*

Paradise Ridge 1999 Ladi's Vineyard Syrah (Sonoma County) $25. A little disjointed, with pretty, ripe, berry fruit. Yet there are sharp green aromas, and a certain stubbornly tannic, green streak in the mouth. Could use

more concentration, depth, and finesse, especially at this price. **84** —*S.H. (7/1/2002)*

Paradise Ridge 2003 Hoenselaars Vineyard Zinfandel (Russian River Valley) $30. Too soft and syrupy for my tastes, with a viscous texture framing blackberry and coffee flavors. Just lacks life and zest. **82** —*S.H. (12/31/2005)*

Paradise Ridge 2001 Hoenselaars Vineyard Lower Block Zinfandel (Sonoma County) $25. A tasty Zin that flatters the mouth with deliciously ripe, gooey flavors of blackberry and mulberry jam, with a long, spicy finish. The texture is smooth and velvety and the tannins are thick but friendly. You'd never believe it has nearly 16 percent alcohol, it's so balanced. **90** —*S.H. (3/1/2004)*

Paradise Ridge 2002 Hoenselaars Vineyard Upper Block Zinfandel (Sonoma County) $27. Lots to like in this ultra-dry wine, with its soothingly rich tannins and flavors of wild berries, peppery spices, and herbs, and earthy tobacco. Could have a bit more concentration, but it's quintessential Sonoma Zin. **87** —*S.H. (11/15/2004)*

PARADUXX

Paraduxx 2002 Red Blend (Napa Valley) $43. Tasty in blackberry jam and sugared espresso flavors, although technically dry, this wine is pretty tannic, with a slightly rustic edge. It's full-bodied enough to go with big, sturdy roasts and strongly-flavored cheeses. **87** —*S.H. (8/1/2005)*

Paraduxx 1999 Red Blend (Napa Valley) $40. An interesting blend of 60% Zinfandel and 40% Cabernet Sauvignon. There are aromas and flavors of spicy cinnamon and jammy blackberries. The earthy mouthfeel and coarse tannins suggest these two varietals, which aren't used to sharing the same barrel, need some time to integrate. **89** —*C.S. (12/1/2002)*

Paraduxx 2002 Paraduxx Red Blend (Napa Valley) $43. This is a blend of Zinfandel, Cabernet Sauvignon, and Merlot from Duckhorn. It shows its Napa origins in the ripeness of fruit and smooth, rich tannins. The blackberry, cherry, and chocolate flavors turn a bit soft and sweet on the finish. **84** —*S.H. (12/1/2005)*

Paraduxx 2003 Red Wine Red Blend (Napa Valley) $45. Extraordinarily ripe, with baked berry pastry and currant flavors. Zinfandel gives the wine a briary edge, while Cabernet brings elegance. This big wine is tannic now and will benefit from a few years, but not too many, in the bottle. **89** —*S.H. (12/1/2006)*

Paraduxx 2001 Red Wine Red Blend (Napa Valley) $43. This somewhat bizarre marriage of Zinfandel and Cabernet Sauvignon may lack harmony due to the coming together of flavors that don't really work well in tandem, but the exuberant fruit and spice and firm tannins are enjoyable. **88** —*S.H. (8/1/2004)*

PARAISO VINEYARDS

Paraiso Vineyards 2004 Chardonnay (Santa Lucia Highlands) $16. Showing plenty of zesty acidity, this dry Chard has modest flavors of peaches and pineapples, wrapped into a creamy texture. It finishes quick and clean. **84** —*S.H. (10/1/2006)*

Paraiso Vineyards 2003 Chardonnay (Santa Lucia Highlands) $18. I like this smooth, dry wine, although it's rather overworked. The oak and lees are a bit obvious, yet the papaya and peach fruit flavors, and the acidity, are powerful enough to make it all work. **86** —*S.H. (12/1/2005)*

Paraiso Vineyards 2002 Chardonnay (Monterey County) $18. Earthy and simple-fruity, with way too much toasted oak. Will have its fans. **83** — *S.H. (5/1/2005)*

Paraiso Vineyards 2001 Chardonnay (Santa Lucia Highlands) $16. Shows impressive heft and viscosity for a wine that's totally dry, with honeyed Golden Delicious apple and spiced pear notes at the core. Shows a little heat and lots of buttery character on the finish. **86** *(10/1/2003)*

Paraiso Vineyards 2000 Chardonnay (Santa Lucia Highlands) $16. Made in a highly individualistic style that's not for everyone. Tart and lean, with citrus flavors and just a riper hint of peaches. Drinks high acid, leesy and sour, with little to soften the hard, metallic mouthfeel. **85** —*S.H. (6/1/2003)*

Paraiso Vineyards 1999 Chardonnay (Monterey County) $16. A remarkably intense wine from vineyards located in the western hills of Salinas Valley.

Made with grapes ripened enough to veer it into tropical fruit territory, but those telltale Monterey acids are bright as a bell. A solid dose of oak lends smoky vanilla and spice components. The result is a full-throttle wine, strong and flavorful. What it lacks in refinement it makes up in sheer exuberance. **89** —*S.H. (5/1/2001)*

Paraiso Vineyards 1998 Chardonnay (Santa Lucia Highlands) $16. 86 —*S.H. (11/15/2000)*

Paraiso Vineyards 1997 Chardonnay (Santa Lucia Highlands) $16. 85 —*L.W. (7/1/1999)*

Paraiso Vineyards 2003 Eagles' Perch Chardonnay (Santa Lucia Highlands) $30. The best Paraiso Chard I've ever had, this inaugural wine, a low-production block release, is tight and firm. Acidity, minerals, and lees star. But there's also a tremendous core of ripe tropical fruits, roasted hazelnut, marzipan, coconut macaroon, and all sorts of interesting things. Cellar it for a while, then drink from 2007–2010. **91 Cellar Selection** —*S.H. (12/1/2006)*

Paraiso Vineyards 1999 Pinot Blanc (Santa Lucia Highlands) $13. Starts off with powerful aromas of tropical fruits and spices, with buttery notes and oaky-vanilla complexity. Drinks fat and sweet, with very forward tropical fruit flavors and high, biting acidity. Clean, bright, and focused. Drink now, or over the next year. **87** —*S.H. (5/1/2001)*

Paraiso Vineyards 1998 Pinot Blanc (Santa Lucia Highlands) $13. 86 *(3/1/2000)*

Paraiso Vineyards 1997 Pinot Blanc (Monterey County) $13. 83 —*J.C. (11/1/1999)*

Paraiso Vineyards 1997 Reserve Pinot Blanc (Santa Lucia Highlands) $23. 87 —*J.C. (11/1/1999)*

Paraiso Vineyards 2003 Pinot Noir (Santa Lucia Highlands) $22. Showing plenty of Santa Lucia character in the well-ripened black cherry fruit flavors and sturdy structure, Paraiso's Pinot also displays an elegance that makes it immediately drinkable. It's dry, but there's an impression of sweetness from toasty oak and ripe fruit that's irresistibly tasty. **87** —*S.H. (12/1/2005)*

Paraiso Vineyards 2002 Pinot Noir (Monterey County) $20. Tough and earthy, not showing much in the way of fruit. The mouthfeel is sandpapery. **83** —*S.H. (5/1/2005)*

Paraiso Vineyards 2001 Pinot Noir (Santa Lucia Highlands) $20. One of the least expensive SLH Pinots you'll find, and one that shows the cool climate in its briary notes layered over crisp black cherry and plum flavors. Picks up anise, Asian spice, and caramel on the finish. **86** *(10/1/2003)*

Paraiso Vineyards 2000 Pinot Noir (Santa Lucia Highlands) $16. Dry cherry, spice, stewed fruit, and orange tea aromas open this tangy, medium-weight wine. Turns quite tart and charry on the palate, closing peppery–even prickly–on the back end. **83** *(10/1/2002)*

Paraiso Vineyards 1999 Pinot Noir (Monterey) $16. This easy wine's bouquet shows hints of leather and earth. Smooth, even slick, on the palate, its plum fruit, cinnamon, and cocoa elements are attractive, but also communicate a certain dullness. **84** *(10/1/2002)*

Paraiso Vineyards 2003 West Terrace Pinot Noir (Santa Lucia Highlands) $40. Paraiso's West Terrace Pinot is one of the secrets of the appellation. The wine exemplifies Santa Lucia with big, bold cherry pie, cola, mocha, and spice flavors, bright acidity, and voluptuous tannins. Despite the size, it never loses elegance and finesse. **91** —*S.H. (11/15/2006)*

Paraiso Vineyards 2002 West Terrace Pinot Noir (Santa Lucia Highlands) $40. This Pinot may develop additional bottle complexities, but right now it's extremely dry and rather thin in fruit, with a tobacco and herb streak that makes the acids and tannins stick out. It doesn't possess the lushness of the '01, but rather has a lean elegance. **86** —*S.H. (12/1/2005)*

Paraiso Vineyards 2001 West Terrace Pinot Noir (Santa Lucia Highlands) $40. This Pinot achieves effortless ripeness and balance. Shows layers of cherry, black raspberry, mocha, vanilla, and oak flavors, while the texture is fine as silk. Drink now through 2006. **92** —*S.H. (12/15/2004)*

Paraiso Vineyards 2000 West Terrace Pinot Noir (Santa Lucia Highlands) $32. From 30-year-old vines, this is a silky-smooth Pinot with dark fruit

flavors. Plum and black cherries crowd the palate, graced by dried spices and coffee notes. **88** *(10/1/2003)*

Paraiso Vineyards 2005 Riesling (Santa Lucia Highlands) $14. Shows lots of rich, appealing Riesling character in the honeysuckle, citrus, and peach flavors that finish just a tad sweet. Fortunately, that crisp Santa Lucia acidity provides overall balance. **84** —*S.H. (12/15/2006)*

Paraiso Vineyards 2004 Riesling (Santa Lucia Highlands) $14. If I were a restaurateur, I'd buy this by the case, sell it by the glass and make a lot of money. It's Alsatian-style, bone dry, and crisp, opulent in peach and honeysuckle flavors, with a diesel, mineral undertone. The acidity will be brilliant against food. **89 Best Buy** —*S.H. (12/1/2005)*

Paraiso Vineyards 2001 Riesling (Monterey County) $14. A pretty wine, filled with juicy fruit flavors such as peach, apple, and kiwi. Drinks pretty sweet, with a rich, honeyed finish. Fortunately, good acidity is there for balance. **85** —*S.H. (9/1/2003)*

Paraiso Vineyards 2001 Riesling (Santa Lucia Highlands) $13. A pretty wine, filled with juicy fruit flavors such as peach, apple, and kiwi. Drinks pretty sweet, with a rich, honeyed finish. Fortunately, good acidity is there for balance. **85** —*S.H. (9/1/2003)*

Paraiso Vineyards 1999 Riesling (Monterey County) $10. Someday Americans will rediscover the delights of Riesling, and wines like this will help them do it. You hardly notice the slight residual sugar. It's just enough to let the apple, pear, and wildflower flavors dance on the palate. Good acidity helps keep things clean and balanced. Really, there's so much to like about this wine, especially as an accompaniment to, say, fusion dishes, that it's sad to think most people will never experience its pleasures. **88 Best Buy** —*S.H. (5/1/2001)*

Paraiso Vineyards 1998 Riesling (Santa Lucia Highlands) $9. 87 Best Buy —*L.W. (9/1/1999)*

Paraiso Vineyards 2002 Syrah (Santa Lucia Highlands) $20. Slightly herbal and peppery, backed by tart cherry-berry flavors and hints of vanilla and chocolate. Supple, without much apparent tannin, but built instead around crisp acids. Turns slightly cranberryish on the finish, simultaneously picking up a luscious hint of hickory smoke. **87** *(9/1/2005)*

Paraiso Vineyards 2001 Syrah (Santa Lucia Highlands) $20. The better buy of the Paraiso Syrahs is the regular bottling, offering whiffs of black pepper and berries, a rich, thick mouthfeel and a short but pleasant finish. It's from young vines, averaging only 5–6 years old; look for even better things to come in the future. **88** *(10/1/2003)*

Paraiso Vineyards 2000 Syrah (Santa Lucia Highlands) $24. A good, full-bodied red wine built along Cabernet lines. It has flavors of blackberries, plums, and white pepper, with earthy, tobacco notes, and is very dry. Tannins are hefty but negotiable, although short-term aging is recommended for this well-built young wine. **86** —*S.H. (6/1/2003)*

Paraiso Vineyards 1999 Syrah (Santa Lucia Highlands) $24. Faint grape and toast and a barnyardy, brett note show on the nose. In the mouth, it's full-bodied and chewy with brisk acidity, showing blackberry, smoked-meat, and coffee flavors. Still a little rough on the back end, with tannins to lose—best held 3–4 years. Shows promise, though the nose was rather mute. **88** *(11/1/2001)*

Paraiso Vineyards 1997 Syrah (Santa Lucia Highlands) $23. 91 *(11/1/1999)*

Paraiso Vineyards 2001 Wedding Hill Syrah (Santa Lucia Highlands) $45. One of the best Syrahs I've ever had from this appellation, and right up there with California's best. Deep, dark, and complex, it offers dramatic helpings of plum sauce, leather, blackberry, chocolate, coffee, and oak flavors that don't stop. The tannic structure is a wonder. Completely dry, yet with a fruity sweetness, it's totally drinkable now and for the next few years. **95** —*S.H. (12/15/2004)*

Paraiso Vineyards 2000 Wedding Hill Syrah (Santa Lucia Highlands) $40. From a block at the top of the property, named for…you guessed it…this ripe, blackberry-scented Syrah is aged mainly in American oak, imparting a creamy, vanilla note to the fruit flavors. Finishes crisp and even, gradually spreading out over the palate and kept in focus by moderate acidity. **89** *(10/1/2003)*

PARDUCCI

Parducci 2002 Cabernet Sauvignon (Mendocino County) $10. An easy country-style wine, with pleasant berry and herb flavors. Drinks dry and a bit rough. **83** —*S.H. (12/31/2004)*

Parducci 2001 Cabernet Sauvignon (California) $10. Young and grapey, a baby of a wine brimming with juicy flavors of blackberries, cherries, and toast. It has a spine of crisp, citrusy acidity. Exuberant and fresh. **85** — *S.H. (5/1/2004)*

Parducci 2000 Cabernet Sauvignon (Mendocino) $9. This is a country-style Cab, rugged and easy. Provides a pretty good mouthful of blackberry and currant flavor, and is nice and dry. Tough tannins suggest big, rich foods. **84** —*S.H. (8/1/2003)*

Parducci 1999 Cabernet Sauvignon (Mendocino) $9. Made lean, with sage, oregano, and other dried herb aromas and flavors, with a streak of blackberry on the palate. Softly tannic, with a nice overlay of rich oak. This quaffable, balanced wine has moderate alcohol and is well-suited for the table.. **88** —*S.H. (5/1/2002)*

Parducci 1997 Reserve Cabernet Sauvignon (Mendocino) $14. This must have been one tannic wine for Parducci to sit on it for six years. Those tannins have resolved, and the wine is soft and drinkable, but still with a firm enough backbone to stand up to the sweet blackberry and cherry flavors. **85** —*S.H. (4/1/2004)*

Parducci 2002 Chardonnay (Mendocino County) $10. Watery and dry, with the barest suggestion of melons. **82** —*S.H. (10/1/2004)*

Parducci 2001 Chardonnay (Mendocino) $9. Pretty thin going, almost like a Sauvignon Blanc with its tart, citrusy fruit flavors and high acidity. Not a bad wine, but if you're looking for a rich, oaky Chardonnay, shop around. **84** —*S.H. (8/1/2003)*

Parducci 2000 Chardonnay (Mendocino) $9. Tastes like orange cream yogurt, full of rich, bold tangerine, vanilla, honey, and smoke, and creamy-smooth in texture. What's not to like? Made in the popular style, and with grace, style, and finesse.. **87** —*S.H. (5/1/2002)*

Parducci 1998 Largo Ranch Reserve Chardonnay (Mendocino County) $20. 84 *(6/1/2000)*

Parducci 1998 Reserve Chardonnay (Mendocino County) $16. 81 *(6/1/2000)*

Parducci 2003 Vintage White Chardonnay-Sauvignon (North Coast) $4. You won't beat anything out there for a value at this price. It's a fruity, dry blend of Sauvignon Blanc and Chardonnay, and hits the spot with apple and peach flavors. **85 Best Buy** —*S.H. (12/1/2004)*

Parducci 2001 Merlot (California) $9. Lots to like, especially at this price. There are nice, ripe flavors of plums, blackberries, and coffee, and the wine is dry and crisp. The tannins are a bit rugged, and there's a rustically earthy mouthfeel, but this wine is a good value in a full-bodied, everyday red. **85** —*S.H. (12/1/2003)*

Parducci 1999 Merlot (Mendocino) $10. Simply delicious, in that fleshy, supple way Merlot was meant to be ripe, mellow, and soft. A delightful aroma of berries and smoke leads to mingled flavors of blackberries, chocolate, and clove. There's a delicacy of body that complements the upfront flavors of this value wine. **89** —*S.H. (5/1/2002)*

Parducci 2000 Petite Sirah (California) $10. A dark wine, with a thick texture and flavors of plums, berries, and chocolate. Fundamentally simple, with soft, easy tannins, but the flavors are gigantic. This is a super wine for those backyard barbecues where you need an affordable red to wash it down. **85** —*S.H. (12/31/2003)*

Parducci 1998 Reserve Petite Sirah (Mendocino) $14. Smells young and fresh, like blackberry jam, with sharp acids. Long and big on blackberry flavor. Tannins play rope-a-dope, seemingly easy, but then they kick in on the finish. Begs for long-term cellaring. **88** —*S.H. (12/31/2003)*

Parducci 2004 Pinot Grigio (California) $10. Rather sweet in apricot and peach flavors, this wine has a good grip of acidity and a clean finish. **84** —*S.H. (2/1/2006)*

Parducci 2002 Pinot Noir (Mendocino County) $10. Smells a bit musty and earthy, with some pleasant cherry-berry flavors and silky tannins. Not a bad little wine. **83** —*S.H. (11/1/2004)*

Parducci 2001 Pinot Noir (Willamette Valley) $9. So what's this California winery doing in Oregon? Making a nice little Pinot Noir for the masses. Connoisseurs will find it simple, but give Parducci a break. This is a good introduction to Pinot at a price everyone can afford. **84** —*S.H. (8/1/2003)*

Parducci 2001 Pinot Noir (Mendocino) $9. A simple little Pinot, with the requisite soft, silky tannins, and cherry flavors accented with mocha and peppery spice. Drinks dry and clean, with good acidity. **83** —*S.H. (12/1/2003)*

Parducci 2000 Pinot Noir (Mendocino) $9. 80 *(10/1/2002)*

Parducci 1999 Red Blend (Mendocino) $5. Dull, earthy, and unbalanced, with tobacco and green tea flavors and bitter acids. Mainly Carignane from old vines. This could be a far better wine. **83** —*S.H. (11/15/2003)*

Parducci 2001 Coro Mendocino Red Blend (Mendocino) $35. A spicy-edged wine that shows off cinnamon and peppery notes up front. Blackberry and herb flavors dominate on the palate, while the finish is mildly tannic and moderate in length. **86** —*J.M. (9/1/2004)*

Parducci 1997 Sangiovese (Mendocino County) $10. 87 Best Buy —*S.H. (12/15/1999)*

Parducci 2003 Sauvignon Blanc (Lake County) $8. Extremely light in citrusy flavor, leaving a palate impression of alcohol, acidity, and heat. There's a taste of lemons on the finish. **83** —*S.H. (12/1/2004)*

Parducci 2002 Sauvignon Blanc (Lake County) $8. Fulfills the basic requirements of citrusy, grassy fruit, crisp, tart acids, a clean mouthfeel and a bone-dry finish, but has thinned-down flavors. **84 Best Buy** —*S.H. (10/1/2003)*

Parducci 1998 Reserve Syrah (Mendocino) $14. Simple and earthy, with pleasant flavors of blackberries and boysenberries. The tannins are quite soft and supple, while acids are low, making for an easy sipper. **84** —*S.H. (10/1/2003)*

Parducci 2001 White Blend (North Coast) $5. A simple quaffer that has citrus flavors from Sauvignon Blanc and appley, peachy ones from Chardonnay. There's a bitterness throughout, but it's not bad for the price. **83** —*S.H. (7/1/2003)*

Parducci 2000 Zinfandel (Mendocino) $9. Smooth in the mouth, with thinned-down flavors of blackberries and peppery spice, and bone dry. A nice everyday wine that has a degree of elegance and finesse, and will be fine with everything from pizza to grilled meat. **85 Best Buy** —*S.H. (9/1/2003)*

Parducci 1997 Vineyard Select Zinfandel (Mendocino) $10. 83 —*P.G. (11/15/1999)*

Parducci 2003 White Zinfandel (Mendocino County) $5. Gets the job done with slight raspberry flavors and good acids. Dry and spicy. **83** —*S.H. (11/15/2004)*

Parducci 2002 White Zinfandel (California) $5. A pleasantly fruity, copper-colored wine, with raspberry and peach flavors. Straddles the line between dry and slightly sweet, and finishes with a trace of almond-skin bitterness. **84** —*S.H. (3/1/2004)*

PARKER STATION

Parker Station 2003 Chardonnay (Santa Barbara County) $12. Tastes kind of thin and simple, with watery flavors of peaches, alcohol, and oak that finish quick. But it's a clean, balanced wine. **83** —*S.H. (5/1/2006)*

Parker Station 2001 Pinot Noir (Santa Barbara County) $12. From Fess Parker, this blend is true to its South Coast roots, with black cherry, herb, and coffee flavors, soft tannins, and crisp acids. If you're looking for an everyday Pinot Noir, it will do. **84** —*S.H. (4/1/2004)*

Parker Station 2003 Syrah (Santa Barbara County) $12. Here's a Syrah that's rich and full-bodied enough to stand as an inexpensive replacement for something far more costly. It has elaborate flavors of blackberries, cherries, coffee, leather, and white pepper, and is fully dry and balanced, with a long finish. From Fess Parker. **87 Best Buy** —*S.H. (5/1/2006)*

USA

PARKERS ESTATE

Parkers Estate 2003 Private Reserve Old Vine Street Cabernet Sauvignon (Sonoma County) $15. From Sonoma comes this honest, country-style Cab. It shows good varietal character, being dry, smooth, spicy, and full-bodied. A nice pepper steak will be the perfect match. **83** —S.H. (2/1/2006)

Parkers Estate 2004 Private Reserve Blue Ash Road Chardonnay (Sonoma County) $15. Ripe in peach, pear, and apple flavors, with a rich earthiness backed up by firm acids. The finish is dry and creamy. **85** —S.H. (2/1/2006)

Parkers Estate 2002 Private Reserve North Peyton Block Merlot (Sonoma County) $15. Simple and one-dimensional, with cherry flavors that finish slightly sweet, and a soft mouthfeel. **82** —S.H. (2/1/2006)

Parkers Estate 2003 Private Reserve Dillon Ranch Zinfandel (Sonoma County) $15. A rich and pedigreed Zin. It's soft, with a velvety texture and ripe, complex flavors of blackberries, cherries, milk chocolate, and peppery spices that finish totally dry and balanced. **87** —S.H. (4/1/2006)

PARRY CELLARS

Parry Cellars 2002 Cabernet Sauvignon (St. Helena) $48. This is a generic but agreeable Cab. It's a little too soft and flaccid, with collapsed tannins, but the cherry and cassis flavors are ripe and attractive. Drink now. **84** — S.H. (4/1/2006)

Parry Cellars 2001 Cabernet Sauvignon (Napa Valley) $46. Opens with a powerful and appealing scent of cherry and black currant fruit that's dressed up with smoky oak. Impressive for its balance and elegance despite the ripe flavors, and accessible now for its gentle tannins. Will surely age well. **90** —S.H. (10/3/2004)

Parry Cellars 2000 Cabernet Sauvignon (Napa Valley) $40. Opens with a green, herbal smell that suggests mint, but fortunately it tastes better. Spicy blackberry, cherry, and espresso flavors are wrapped in gently soft tannins. The underripe theme reprises on the finish, where it turns sharp. **85** —S.H. (4/1/2004)

PARSONAGE VILLAGE

Parsonage Village 2001 Cabernet Sauvignon (Carmel Valley) $42. Starts off with a disturbing aroma of pickled dill and canned asparagus that makes it hard to enjoy the wine once you taste. There are some polished cherry and berry flavors. **82** —S.H. (8/1/2004)

Parsonage Village 2001 Reserve Cabernet Sauvignon (Carmel Valley) $54. Opens with simple aromas of cherry berry and oaky overtones. In the mouth, it's a bit heavy and tannic, with berry flavors. Finishes hot and astringent. **84** —S.H. (8/1/2004)

Parsonage Village 2001 Chardonnay (Carmel Valley) $36. Dark, somewhat heavy and quite ripe, a wine with a multitude of intense flavors that range from sweet cherries to blackberry pie and Kahlua. There's even a note of blueberries floating in the firm tannins. Finishes dry, with astringency, suggesting aging for a year or so. **86** —S.H. (9/1/2004)

Parsonage Village 2001 Syrah (Carmel Valley) $36. Starts with a sharp, raw scent that gradually airs to reveal layers of currants, cherries, and plums. Drinks rather sharp in acidity and tough, too, but there's a pretty wine in there. Definitely decant this wine in the morning to give it plenty of time to breathe. **86** —S.H. (8/1/2004)

Parsonage Village 2001 Carmelstone Reserve Syrah (Carmel Valley) $54. The model was the Northern Rhône, with its opening blast of white pepper and complex mélange of plummy currants and smoky leather. In the mouth, this wine is dense and full-bodied, dry, fairly tannic, and very rich. On the finish, the currants powerfully return, coating the palate for a long time. A very good and interesting wine. **91** —S.H. (8/1/2004)

PASCHAL

Paschal 2000 Quartet Red Wine Bordeaux Blend (Applegate Valley) $25. This is assembled from ten different vineyards, and is the winery's flagship wine. It's a blend of 44% Cabernet Franc, 34% Cabernet Sauvignon, 13% Merlot, and 9% Malbec. This wine has a good focus to the mid-palate, a decent amount of sweet cassis fruit, and a soft and lingering, though tannic, finish. **86** —P.G. (8/1/2002)

Paschal 1998 Cabernet Sauvignon (Applegate Valley) $28. This new Southern Oregon winery has been growing good grapes for over a decade. Their first release is a solid effort, with broad, sweet smoky flavors, soft tannins, and a drink-now structure. Sweet brown sugar, tobacco, and cedar notes enhance the soft finish. **87** —P.G. (4/1/2002)

Paschal 2000 Reserve Cabernet Sauvignon (Rogue Valley) $28. This might be one of Oregon's best Cabernet efforts to date. Yes, it's firm, with hard tannins, but time should allow that to settle down. In the meantime, there's char, road tar, and caramel on the nose, while plum, cassis, and chocolate dominate the rich, extracted palate. Toward the end it's the tannic structure that makes itself most felt. But again, some time in the cellar is probably all it requires. **89** —M.S. (8/1/2003)

Paschal 1999 Chardonnay (Rogue Valley) $16. All stainless steel fermented using Dijon clones. A clean, delicate style, but with an elegant touch and nuances of honey, clove. Very well balanced and textured, with a light but long progression of flavors. **88** —P.G. (8/1/2002)

Paschal 2000 Estate Chardonnay (Rogue Valley) $18. Their estate Chardonnay is all barrel-fermented. A bigger style, with lots of texture but not too much oak. Leesy, creamy, with buttery, tropical fruit. Again, well-balanced and stylish. **88** —P.G. (8/1/2002)

Paschal 2001 Estate Grown Chardonnay (Rogue Valley) $18. Light and flowery up front, and clean. The palate is more mouthfilling than might be expected; the flavors veer toward apple and pear, and while those flavors are basic, they are persistent and clean, as is the finish. Decent acidity and overall freshness keep this wine vital. It stumbles compared to great Chardonnay, but for Oregon it's not disappointing. **85** —M.S. (9/1/2003)

Paschal 2000 Merlot (Applegate Valley) $25. This is a firm wine, with upfront flavors of plum and berry, enhanced with finishing licks of vanilla and white chocolate. A bit of Cabernet Sauvignon (8%) adds punch. **87** —P.G. (8/1/2002)

Paschal 2000 Pinot Blanc (Rogue Valley) $16. Scents of hay and alfalfa open into an elegant, stylish wine with lovely textures. It is lightly citric, with pretty nuances of grass, hints of honey, and tea. The winemaker has a gentle, delicate touch with all his wines, but this is the best of the best. Just 100 cases were produced. **90 Editors' Choice** —P.G. (8/1/2002)

Paschal 2001 Pinot Gris (Rogue Valley) $18. Maybe southern Oregon is too hot for white wines; at least it appears to be based on this flat, rather lifeless offering. The nose is like applesauce, while the palate is bland and lazy, with only a modicum of grapefruit working in its favor. A little banana and citrus pith on the finish save it from a worse fate. **80** —M.S. (8/1/2003)

Paschal 1999 Pinot Gris (Rogue Valley) $18. This starts off with a creamy, spicy mouthfeel, but leads to somewhat bitter fruit. Once swallowed, the flavors become somewhat chemical, and the wine feels flat and out of balance. Perhaps a bad bottle? **82** —P.G. (2/1/2002)

Paschal 2000 Estate Pinot Noir (Rogue Valley) $24. Very forward, with pretty, medium-ripe cherry flavors. The sweet fruit picks up some vanilla from the barrel, and finishes with smooth tannins. Though at first blush it seems a bit light, sweet and simple, the flavors are persistent, the balance perfect. **86** —P.G. (8/1/2002)

Paschal 2001 Syrah (Rogue Valley) $26. Very different, and not always a seamless package. The nose offers graham cracker, saline, and the purest hit of wet dog you could ever care to inhale. But there's also blueberry and earth aromas. The palate is tannic and tight, with some overt grapey flavor and also a note of plum or blackberry pie. All in all, this is a funky, odd wine, one that will appeal to some people and turn off others. Only 336 cases produced. **85** —M.S. (9/1/2003)

Paschal 1998 Syrah-Cabernet (Oregon) $24. Yes, that is the official name for this tannic blend. It features tart berry fruit; a bit Zin-like; the tannins are substantial but well managed, without the chalkiness often found in southern Oregon. A good summer BBQ wine. **85** —P.G. (8/1/2002)

PATIANNA ORGANIC VINEYARDS

Patianna Organic Vineyards 2005 Sauvignon Blanc (Mendocino County) $18. Patianna has been producing biodynamically-grown Sauvignon

Blanc under the radar, and consumers really should discover it. The '05 is quite as good as the '03, maybe better, a dry, crisp, elegantly balanced wine, with delicately unoaked citrus flavors. It's Sauvignons like this that are weaning wine lovers away from Chardonnay. **91 Editors' Choice** —*S.H. (12/31/2006)*

Patianna Organic Vineyards 2004 Sauvignon Blanc (Mendocino County) $16. Very New Zealandy in the bone-dry flavors of gooseberries, lime peel, and honeysuckle, and the zingy edge of acidity, this fine white wine was grown biodynamically by a member of the Fetzer family. It has a long, rich, spicy finish. **87** —*S.H. (12/15/2005)*

Patianna Organic Vineyards 2003 Estate Grown Sauvignon Blanc (Mendocino) $16. A sensational Sauv Blanc, among the best this year. Filled with clean, vibrant citrus and tropical fruit flavors and juicy acids, and completely without any cloying edge of sweetness. **90 Best Buy** —*S.H. (12/31/2004)*

Patianna Organic Vineyards 2003 Fairbairn Ranch Syrah (Mendocino County) $30. From a winery practicing biodynamic grapegrowing, this is a big, sturdy Syrah, very dry, and pretty tannic. It's also very clean, with strong flavors of roasted coffee and blackberries. The size calls for sturdy, rich, barbecued meats. **90** —*S.H. (11/15/2005)*

PATIT CREEK CELLARS

Patit Creek Cellars 2001 Cabernet Sauvignon (Walla Walla (WA)) $35. Right now this is all about the oak, which over-rides everything else. Given that the vintage is 2001, neither brand new nor an off-year, it's less likely that the balance will change much in the months ahead. Light cherry and strawberry flavors fight to be heard. **86** —*P.G. (4/1/2005)*

Patit Creek Cellars 2003 Merlot (Walla Walla (WA)) $32. This is a good effort, built upon Pepper Bridge and Seven Hills fruit. It stands in the middle ranks of Walla Walla Merlots, quite similar to many other wines from the valley. New oak dominates the nose, with scents of smoke and char. The fruit is sweet cherry, with a hint of tobacco. **88** —*P.G. (6/1/2006)*

Patit Creek Cellars 2000 Merlot (Walla Walla (WA)) $32. A well-made wine, with good fruit, a nice mix of flavors, and just the right application of toasty, expensive new oak. Balanced and sophisticated; Jean François Pellet from Pepper Bridge is the consulting winemaker. **88** —*P.G. (9/1/2003)*

PATRICK M. PAUL

Patrick M. Paul 2000 Merlot (Columbia Valley (WA)) $28. This tiny winery makes just a few hundred cases per year. The Merlot is grapey and rustic, with Grenache-like fruit flavors and some rough, chocolatey oak. **85** —*P.G. (9/1/2002)*

PATTON VALLEY VINEYARD

Patton Valley Vineyard 2002 Pinot Noir (Willamette Valley) $30. Estate-grown fruit is done here in a fresh, bright, citrusy style. Vivid and delicious, with snap and precision, this aromatic Pinot Noir has orange peel highlights and a pungent, tartly fruity palate. Food-friendly and nuanced, and a nice break from the jammy style. **91** —*P.G. (8/1/2005)*

Patton Valley Vineyard 2002 Pinot Noir (Willamette Valley) $30. So young the yeast still carries a slightly beery aroma, this grapy, light style has pretty, cherry candy fruit and some heat on the finish. **86** *(11/1/2004)*

Patton Valley Vineyard 2000 Pinot Noir (Oregon) $28. This is the first release from a new Oregon vintner. Appealing, open, fresh, and fruity, it tags spicy cranberry and strawberry scents onto a well-made, soft, and smooth Pinot. Supple tannins and just a hint of barrel toast complete the wine. **88** —*P.G. (12/31/2002)*

PATZ & HALL

Patz & Hall 2002 Chardonnay (Napa Valley) $33. Loads of well-charred oak covers underlying peach, pear, and tropical fruit flavors in this crisp wine. It's fully dry, but so sweet in ripe fruit, you'd think it had a little honey. **87** —*S.H. (4/1/2004)*

Patz & Hall 2002 Durell Vineyard Chardonnay (Sonoma Valley) $38. Smells and tastes like oak, with opulent vanillins, smoke, and buttered toast. Yet it's thin on fruit. There are suggestions of tart green apples and hints of

white peach. Turns a bit watery on the finish, except for the oak. **86** —*S.H. (4/1/2004)*

Patz & Hall 2002 Woolsey Road Vineyard Chardonnay (Russian River Valley) $38. It's a pleasure to sip this Chardonnay, which is rich and balanced. The sweet peach, pineapple, and spice flavors are offset by crisp acidity, and the texture is lush and creamy. The long finish reprises the spicy, cinnamony theme. **91** —*S.H. (4/1/2004)*

Patz & Hall 1999 Woolsey Road Vineyard Chardonnay (Russian River Valley) $37. Taut and intensely structured, the compact smoke, lime, ginger, and nut bouquet here hints at what's within. The mouth offers lime and chalk, vanilla and apples and a creamy yet firm mouthfeel—it's surprisingly full, with bright acidity. The dry, crisp finish with its spicy, toasty flavors has great length, again showing structure and refinement. Will be at its best in two-plus years. **92 Cellar Selection** *(7/1/2001)*

Patz & Hall 2002 Pinot Noir (Sonoma Coast) $33. Shows bright cranberry, red cherry, and rhubarb flavors, with mouth-puckering acidity and a silky texture. There's complexity and style in the way the flavors, oak, tannins and acids work together. **87** *(11/1/2004)*

Patz & Hall 2002 Alder Springs Vineyard Pinot Noir (Mendocino County) $50. Closed at first, requires decanting to bring out the rich core of black cherry and dried spice aromas, and their template of smoky oak. Thick in youthful tannins now, and oaky, but a very good wine, rich and intense. Best after 2007. **90** *(11/1/2004)*

Patz & Hall 2001 Alder Springs Vineyard Pinot Noir (Mendocino County) $50. Quite ripe in sunny fruit, with gobs of cherry, blackberry, and mocha flavors. It's a bit thick and heavy for a Pinot, with almost the weight and texture of a Syrah. But there's no denying the rich and tasty deliciousness. **87** —*S.H. (4/1/2004)*

Patz & Hall 2002 Hyde Vineyard Pinot Noir (Carneros) $50. Starts off a bit sulfury. A full-bodied wine, balanced and harmonious. Exhibits ripe, big fruit and intriguing herbal notes, and isn't overly alcoholic. Solid, middle-of-the-road Pinot. **86** *(11/1/2004)*

Patz & Hall 2002 Pisoni Vineyard Pinot Noir (Santa Lucia Highlands) $65. A real winner for its complex array of earthy, coffee, smoke, black cherry, and vanilla flavors, and the great balance and charm. Combines power and elegance in one package. Rich and mouthfilling, with a long, attractive finish. **91** *(11/1/2004)*

Patz & Hall 2001 Pisoni Vineyard Pinot Noir (Santa Lucia Highlands) $70. What a price, but what a wine. For starters, it's huge in cherry compote flavors, drizzled with sweet mocha, vanilla, and powdered sugar. That makes it sound like a dessert wine, but it's dry, with rich, ripe tannins and firm acids. What it lacks in subtlety it more than makes up for in sheer decadence. **93** —*S.H. (4/1/2004)*

PAUL HOBBS

Paul Hobbs 2002 Beckstoffer Tokalon Vineyard Cabernet Sauvignon (Oakville) $NA. Young and so tannic, but the fruit is massive and intense, and the balance suggests aging. Blackberries, cassis, and oak mesh perfectly in this dry wine. The alcohol is creeping up there, at 14.8%. Best now with very rich fare, or hold through 2012. **92 Cellar Selection** —*S.H. (6/1/2005)*

Paul Hobbs 2000 Beckstoffer Tokalon Vineyard Cabernet Sauvignon (Napa Valley) $NA. Minty, oaky, coffee, and blalckberry aroma, gingersnap cookie. Tastes big, ripe, boldly tannic. Very dry. Not showing well, could improve after 2008. **85** —*S.H. (6/1/2005)*

Paul Hobbs 2001 Beckstoffer-Tokalon Vineyard Cabernet Sauvignon (Oakville) $185. Young, closed, dense, but fine. Flavors suggest rum-soaked raisins, cassis, sweet oak, and gingerbread. Long, rich, fat, extracted, borders on super-maturity but not quite, maintaining balance and even elegance. Finishes long and fruity. Hold beyond 2008. **94 Cellar Selection** —*S.H. (6/1/2005)*

Paul Hobbs 1999 Chardonnay (Russian River Valley) $38. An intoxicating bouquet of clove, ripe orange, peach, and melon promises a lot, but this wine delivers. The similarly heady palate of creamy, ripe tropical fruit is almost romantic, the richly textured mouthfeel full and lush. Finishes long in the same sensuous manner. Drink now for its exuberant fruit and voluptuous feel. Like Paul, his wines exude style and character. **91** *(7/1/2001)*

Paul Hobbs 1999 Richard Dinner Vineyard Chardonnay (Sonoma Mountain) $47. Like autumn in a bottle, the subdued smoke and pear bouquet is followed by a buttered apple, toast, and vanilla palate. The flavors are more understated than they sound—this wine is all about subtlety and balance. It builds in layers, complex and butter-smooth. The standout finish shows butterscotch and mineral notes in a delightful tension. **90** *(7/1/2001)*

PAUL MATTHEW

Paul Matthew 2002 Pinot Noir (Russian River Valley) $25. Forward in jammy red fruit, cranberry, and watermelon flavors, with a light, delicate mouthfeel, this flavorful wine turns milk chocolatey on the finish. **85** *(11/1/2004)*

PAUL THOMAS

Paul Thomas 1997 Bordeaux Blend (Washington) $9. **83** —*J.C. (11/1/1999)*

Paul Thomas 1999 Cabernet Sauvignon (Washington) $8. Initially there is a hint of sweetness in the nose, strawberries and sweet crackers. But once in the mouth, the wine turns tannic and thin, a simple red wine with an earthy character. **84** —*P.G. (6/1/2002)*

Paul Thomas 1999 Cabernet Sauvignon-Merlot (Washington) $8. Now part of the Canandaigua Wine portfolio, Paul Thomas offers inexpensive varietals and blends such as this, a smoky, earthy take on Washington reds. The fruit shows some strawberry preserve flavors, along with might be called iron or mineral, or maybe simply earth. Coarse and roughly tannic in the finish. **83** —*P.G. (10/1/2001)*

Paul Thomas 1997 Chardonnay (Washington) $7. **83** —*J.C. (11/1/1999)*

Paul Thomas 1999 Chardonnay (Washington) $8. Bone-dry, hard, and crisp, this is a basic, stainless-steel fermented, nonmalolactic style of Chardonnay. Brisk and competent, but neutral. **84** —*P.G. (7/1/2002)*

Paul Thomas 1997 Reserve Chardonnay (Columbia Valley (WA)) $11. **91 Best Buy** —*M.M. (11/1/1999)*

Paul Thomas 1999 Merlot (Washington) $8. The demand for Merlot grapes has left slim pickings for the value brands like Paul Thomas. Earthy, stemmy, and showing bare hints of red fruits, this is a hard, tart red wine giving little of the pleasure of Merlot. **83** —*P.G. (6/1/2002)*

PAUMANOK

Paumanok 2002 Assemblage Bordeaux Blend (North Fork of Long Island) $36. Paumanok's Bordeaux blend, a 53-47 blend of Merlot and Cabernet, is a serious, structured wine that needs time or a couple of years in the cellar to open up. Fairly ripe for a Long Island red, it shows cherry and red berry fruit wrapped in a chocolatey palate with good oak spice. The bouquet is closed, although lemon and cranberry show though. But the wine finishes with good length and flavors of black pepper and pencil shavings. Drink 2008–2012. **88** —*M.D. (12/1/2006)*

Paumanok 2000 Assemblage Bordeaux Blend (North Fork of Long Island) $36. **86** —*J.C. (10/2/2004)*

Paumanok 1998 Cabernet Franc (North Fork of Long Island) $18. The floral nose on this wine is textbook Franc; married to the bright cherry fruit that comes through on the palate, the result is a lighter-style, charming wine that should prove versatile with food. Dangerously gulpable. **88 Editors' Choice** —*J.C. (4/1/2001)*

Paumanok 1998 Cabernet Sauvignon (North Fork of Long Island) $18. Toasty, with a bit of cedar or menthol on the nose; red berries and licorice on the palate. The fruit here is delicate and tart, particularly on the finish, where the flavors are almost lemony. **84** —*J.C. (4/1/2001)*

Paumanok 2001 Barrel-Fermented Chardonnay (North Fork of Long Island) $18. **82** —*J.C. (10/2/2004)*

Paumanok 1999 Barrel-Fermented Chardonnay (North Fork of Long Island) $17. The barrel-fermentation shows in the buttery, toasty aromas that overlay pear and peach fruit. Orange and lemon flavors echo on the finish, so you know it hasn't been over oaked. **85** —*J.C. (4/1/2001)*

Paumanok NV Festival Chardonnay (North Fork of Long Island) $10. The aromas bring to mind buttered cashews and pears poached in vanilla

syrup. The flavors follow suit, in a medium-bodied wine that's soft and easy to drink but tails off a bit on the finish. **84** —*J.C. (4/1/2001)*

Paumanok 2003 Festival Chardonnay (North Fork of Long Island) $10. **83** —*J.C. (10/2/2004)*

Paumanok 2000 Dry Chenin Blanc (North Fork of Long Island) $15. This wine is so clean and fresh, it's like biting into a tart Granny Smith—albeit one with pear, citrus, and even grape overtones. Mouthwatering acidity leaves you craving sip after sip: It's the quintessential apéritif wine. **86** —*J.C. (4/1/2001)*

Paumanok 2002 Merlot (North Fork of Long Island) $18. Dark red, with mushroom, red berry, earth, and green bean aromas. Fairly light, and with high acidity, the wine shows earthy red fruit, blueberry, and rhubarb along with a good dose of oak. **84** —*M.D. (12/1/2006)*

Paumanok 2002 Grand Vintage Merlot (North Fork of Long Island) $36. Wood plays a leading role in this wine, offering brown spice and pickle barrel aromas as well as vanilla, tobacco, and spice flavors. In between there are aromas of glove leather and flavors of sweet red fruit that pick up intensity toward the finish. Medium-bodied, with solid tannins, the wine nevertheless comes across as bulky and without the acidity many Long Island wines have. **85** —*M.D. (12/1/2006)*

Paumanok 2000 Grand Vintage Merlot (North Fork of Long Island) $36. **83** —*J.C. (10/2/2004)*

Paumanok 2003 Dry Riesling (North Fork of Long Island) $18. **85** —*J.C. (10/2/2004)*

Paumanok 2000 Dry Riesling (North Fork of Long Island) $15. Starts off with intriguing aromas of spring flowers (lilacs?) and Asian pear. Crunchy apple and ripe lime flavors linger on the palate. Drink now or age up to five or seven years. **87** —*J.C. (4/1/2001)*

Paumanok 2002 Late Harvest Riesling (North Fork of Long Island) $27. **84** —*J.C. (10/2/2004)*

Paumanok 1998 Late Harvest Riesling (North Fork of Long Island) $27. The aromas feature a sweet blend of honeydew and cantaloupe, with some decidedly floral notes. Round and sweet in the mouth, and marked by a slightly bitter grapefruit-pith note that persists on the finish. **87** —*J.C. (4/1/2001)*

Paumanok 2003 Semi Dry Riesling (North Fork of Long Island) $18. **85** —*J.C. (10/2/2004)*

Paumanok 2000 Semi Dry Riesling (North Fork of Long Island) $15. Starts off with aromas of apple blossoms and ultraripe pears. The pear notes carry through on the palate, where they're joined by a touch of anise. This slightly sweet bottling pales in comparison to Paumanok's Dry Riesling, but offers a well-made, soft alternative. **83** —*J.C. (4/1/2001)*

Paumanok 2004 Sauvignon Blanc (North Fork of Long Island) $20. Some chalk and mineral on the green-apple nose, followed by tart citrus flavors that are propelled by firm acidity. Clean and lean, with scouring lemon to the finish. Potentially too sharp for some folks; others, however, may go for its razor-like personality. **87** *(7/1/2005)*

PAVILION

Pavilion 2003 Cabernet Sauvignon (Napa Valley) $12. Shares some fine Napa Cab quality at a fair price, and although there's a rusticity to the mouthfeel, the fruit is ripe and properly varietal. The cassis and chocolate flavors are wrapped in fine, mature tannins. **85** —*S.H. (9/1/2006)*

Pavilion 2002 Cabernet Sauvignon (Napa Valley) $12. Not a bad wine at all. Has cherry-berry fruit, with gritty, sweet tannins. Totally dry. **84** —*S.H. (5/1/2005)*

Pavilion 2001 Cabernet Sauvignon (Napa Valley) $11. You can thank the grape surplus for this value wine, which has many of the attributes of an expensive Cab. Cassis and black currant flavors are framed in smoky oak, with smooth tannins and good acidity. **86** —*S.H. (10/1/2004)*

Pavilion 2005 Chardonnay (Yountville) $10. It offers up lots of ripe kiwi, peach, pineapple, and spice flavors, brightened by a good cut of acidity. Tastes fresher than some far more expensive Napa Chards. **86 Best Buy** —*S.H. (11/15/2006)*

Pavilion 2004 Chardonnay (Napa Valley) $10. There's lots of richness in this dry Chardonnay. From the peaches and cream, pineapple tart, and smoky oak and vanilla flavors, to the smooth, creamy texture and the long, cinnamon spice finish, it satisfies. And look at that price. **86 Best Buy** —*S.H. (9/1/2006)*

Pavilion 2003 Chardonnay (Napa Valley) $11. A very well-behaved Chard and a good value from this appellation. It's pretty rich in appley flavors, with bright acids and a smoky veneer of sweet oak. **86** —*S.H. (10/1/2004)*

Pavilion 2003 Merlot (Napa Valley) $12. Sometimes all you need is a nice, inexpensive Merlot to go with that steak, and this is a good one. It's dry and fruity, a little rough around the edges, with rich berry-cherry flavors and a full, complete mouthfeel. **85** —*S.H. (10/1/2006)*

Pavilion 2002 Merlot (Napa Valley) $12. Pleasant sipping here, with a rich core of blackberry, coffee, and chocolate flavors that drink very dry, but sweetened with a splash of oaky vanillins. Good structure, too. A good value. **85** —*S.H. (10/1/2004)*

Pavilion 2005 Sauvignon Blanc (Napa Valley) $10. Clean, well-structured and bone dry, this wine has great structure. The only problem is a near-total absence of flavor. It's very weak in grapefruit and lime. But it's a good wine for big parties and such. **83** —*S.H. (11/1/2006)*

Pavilion 2003 Syrah (Napa Valley) $12. Heavy and soft in texture, this Napa Syrah is forward in simple cherry-berry fruit, and finishes sugary sweet. **80** —*S.H. (7/1/2006)*

PAVIN & RILEY

Pavin & Riley 2001 Merlot (Columbia Valley (WA)) $12. Although it has but a tiny percentage of California's production, Washington is not immune to the grape glut. Négociant brands such as this are the result, offering wines like this sound, accessible, soft, and fruity Merlot at a decent price. **86** —*P.G. (12/31/2003)*

PAVONA

Pavona 2001 Chardonnay Blanc Chardonnay (Monterey County) $18. A spicy Chard from cool-climate Monterey. It's packed with pear, pineapple and mango flavors whose sweetness is boosted by smoky oak. Finishes with a long, candied flourish. **85** —*S.H. (9/1/2004)*

Pavona 1997 Paraiso Springs Pinot Blanc (Santa Lucia Highlands) $13. **90** —*L.W. (3/1/2000)*

Pavona 1997 Pinot Noir (Monterey County) $18. **85** *(11/15/1999)*

Pavona 1999 Pinot Noir (Monterey County) $18. Burgundian, with plummy, forest-floor, mushroom, smoke, and slightly funky aromas. Softly fruity and velvety, with a delicacy and finesse that carries through the dry, spicy finish. **88** —*S.H. (11/15/2001)*

Pavona 2001 Coastal Selection Pinot Noir (Monterey County) $20. Delicate all around in body, texture, and flavor. Shows cola, cherry, tobacco, and spice, with silky tannins and those crisp Central Coast acids. **85** —*S.H. (12/1/2004)*

Pavona 1999 Peacock Blue Ltd. Release Syrah (California) $21. The herbal and briny notes in this wine divided our panel, with some tasters relishing its near-vegetal complexities layered over syrupy blackberry fruit, while others condemned it for the same. Try it yourself. **85** *(11/1/2001)*

Pavona 1999 Purple Peacock Syrah (California) $18. Dank, rhubarb-meets-seaweed aromas open onto a blackberry-and-oak palate with a hard mouthfeel. Finish is dry, dull, and tart. **81** *(10/1/2001)*

Pavona 1999 Purple Peacock Syrah (Lodi) $18. A full-bodied wine that rides a bit rough in the mouth, with ripe flavors of cherries, blackberries, and coffee and a bit of raisining. The finish also turns hot. Try with a pepper-rubbed pork tenderloin. **85** —*S.H. (9/1/2004)*

Pavona 1999 Old Vine Zinfandel (Lodi) $18. Classic warm-country Zin, with briary, brambly wild-berry aromas with a hint of raisins, and big, juicy flavors. Finishes hot. Modest tannins and soft acidity make this dry wine immediately drinkable. **86** —*S.H. (11/15/2001)*

PEACHY CANYON

Peachy Canyon 2000 Para Siempre Bordeaux Blend (Paso Robles) $38. Dry, with berry, cherry, sage, and dill flavors and dry, ripe tannins. Clearly from a warmer climate, with a soft texture and low acids. Mostly

Merlot, with some Cabernet Sauvignon and Franc. **86** —*S.H. (11/15/2003)*

Peachy Canyon 1999 Para Siempre Bordeaux Blend (Paso Robles) $38. This is the kind of fat, high-alcohol but plush and soft red wine that Paso is famous for. A Bordeaux blend, it's filled with juicy berry flavors and is round and supple, but heady, with 14.5% alcohol. Yet it's balanced, with nice dry tannins. **89** —*S.H. (9/1/2002)*

Peachy Canyon 2003 Para Siempre Cabernet Blend (Paso Robles) $38. Based on Cabernet Sauvignon, with Merlot and Cab Franc, this is a somewhat rustic wine: Though it has a jagged mouthfeel, it also has deep, wholesome blackberry, blueberry, cherry, and chocolate flavors. With a smoky char-broiled steak, it'll be fine. **86** —*S.H. (12/15/2006)*

Peachy Canyon 2002 Para Siempre Cabernet Blend (Paso Robles) $38. With ultraripe cherry pie filling, blackberry jam, and milk chocolate flavors, this wine manages to stay dry, which is a feat given the relatively modest alcohol. It's soft and velvety smooth. Drink now. **86** —*S.H. (12/1/2006)*

Peachy Canyon 2001 Para Siempre Cabernet Blend (Paso Robles) $38. This is a good, dry wine, with some punchy tannins. It's quite soft in the mouth, with flavors of cherries, herbs, and earth. **86** —*S.H. (7/1/2005)*

Peachy Canyon 2002 Cabernet Sauvignon (Paso Robles) $38. Starts off dry and fairly tannic, with robust flavors of dried cherries, blackberry skin, coffee, and black pepper, then finishes tart and sandpapery dry. For all that, there's elegance and good structure. Grilled pepper steak seems an ideal match. **87** —*S.H. (12/15/2006)*

Peachy Canyon 2000 Cabernet Sauvignon (Paso Robles) $25. This soft, dry Cabernet shows its origins in the pliant tannins and easy acids that frame blackberry and herb flavors. It is a good representative of its terroir, and will be good with roast lamb and similar rich fare. **85** —*S.H. (11/15/2003)*

Peachy Canyon 2000 De Vine Cabernet Sauvignon (Paso Robles) $30. Well-ripened, with some cassis, plum, and black currant flavors, and earthier ones of herbs and dried tobacco. The tannins are low and easy, and the acidity is soft in this easy-to-drink wine. **85** —*S.H. (11/15/2003)*

Peachy Canyon 2003 Devine Cabernet Sauvignon (Paso Robles) $38. After tasting Napa Cabs, it takes an intellectual step sideways to appreciate a Cab like this from Paso Robles. It's totally dry, sharper in acids, and mintier than its northern cousins, but has a cherried flair that makes you want to drink it with a steak. **87** —*S.H. (12/15/2006)*

Peachy Canyon 2001 DeVine Cabernet Sauvignon (Paso Robles) $50. There's lots of richness in this ripe, balanced Cab. It shows elegant notes of currants, blackberries, and smoky oak, wrapped in thick, fine tannins. Achieves real elegance through the satisfyingly long finish. **88** —*S.H. (7/1/2005)*

Peachy Canyon 2000 DeVine Cabernet Sauvignon (Paso Robles) $50. Seems off all down the line, from the dull smell to the overly soft texture. On the other hand there's some pretty cherry-berry fruit. **83** —*S.H. (12/31/2004)*

Peachy Canyon 2003 Old School House Cabernet Sauvignon (Paso Robles) $25. Peachy has long produced an Old School House Zin, but this is the first OSH Cab I know of. Like the Zin, it's a warming, rustic, friendly wine, awash in blackberry, dark chocolate, coffee, and sweet oregano flavors, bone dry and finely tannic. **87** —*S.H. (12/15/2006)*

Peachy Canyon 1999 West Side Cabernet Sauvignon (Paso Robles) $25. West Side, in Paso Robles, means hot, and while the alcohol in this wine is a moderate 13.5%, you can taste the heat in the gentle tannins and soft acids. It's bone-dry, with berry flavors. A nicely crafted young wine. **88** —*S.H. (9/1/2002)*

Peachy Canyon 2001 Merlot (Paso Robles) $23. Soft, dry, and earthy, this is a wine that will benefit from a little decanting, which should bring out the underlying cherry and plum fruit. Has a bitter chocolate note that's appealing. **86** —*S.H. (7/1/2005)*

Peachy Canyon 2000 Merlot (Paso Robles) $23. Middle-of-the-road fare, with pleasant flavors of berries, coffee, and herbs wrapped in firm, heavy tannins. Drinks soft in acids, and finishes dry as dust, leaving the palate a little numb. Rich fare, such as roast lamb, will wake up the hidden fruit. **85** —*S.H. (12/31/2003)*

Peachy Canyon 1999 Merlot (Paso Robles) $23. Dark and soft, with earthy flavors and riper notes of blackberries, but very dry. This is a wine that gets right to the point. It's well-made and meant to be consumed with food. It's not an ager and there's a rough-hewn quality to it, but it's likeable. **86** —*S.H. (6/1/2002)*

Peachy Canyon 2003 Mr. Wilson's Vineyard Merlot (Paso Robles) $23. Merlot is tough to make anywhere, and Paso Robles isn't its best home. It's too hot there. This is a rustic, high alcohol wine, with an edgy texture and sweet-and-sour cherry flavors. **82** —*S.H. (12/15/2006)*

Peachy Canyon 2002 Petite Sirah (Paso Robles) $22. Dark, big, rich, extracted, dry, powerful. So what else did you expect? This is true Pet, with blueberry, blackberry, chocolate, and pepper flavors and voluminous tannins. Drink now with barbecue. **88** —*S.H. (10/1/2005)*

Peachy Canyon 2001 Petite Sirah (Paso Robles) $22. You have the right to elegance and finesse in a Petite Sirah, and you get it here. Dry, soft, and balanced, it retains Pet's big-boned exuberance, while corralling the flavors and tannins to claret levels. **90** —*S.H. (11/15/2004)*

Peachy Canyon NV Zinfandel Port III Port (Paso Robles) $25. Smells cardboardy and unripe, and although there's a lot of sugar, this is a disastrous Port-style wine. **81** —*S.H. (7/1/2005)*

Peachy Canyon 2000 Para Seimpre Red Blend (Paso Robles) $38. Simple, drinkable, but with noticeable flaws, especially the funky smell. Merlot-based blend. **82** —*S.H. (12/31/2004)*

Peachy Canyon 1999 Syrah (California) $19. A soft, generic red with pillowy caramel and vanilla shadings. Jammy blackberry fruit and hints of plums and licorice give it just enough character to make it commendable. **84** *(10/1/2001)*

Peachy Canyon 1999 Zinfandel (Paso Robles) $15. Lovely aromas, like a cherry-filled chocolate-caramel candy, and it's great drinking, too. Complex wild berry fruit and spice fill the mouth in a delightful explosion of flavor. Thankfully, it's dry and balanced, despite hefty alcohol. **89 Best Buy** —*S.H. (12/15/2001)*

Peachy Canyon 1998 Zinfandel (Paso Robles) $17. 87 —*D.T. (9/1/2003)*

Peachy Canyon 1999 Benito Dusi Ranch Zinfandel (Paso Robles) $26. A very fine Zin, with balanced aromas of blackberries, chocolate, and the smell of a warm berry thicket on a hot, dusty summer's day. Big in the mouth, with pungent, spicy fruit flavors and a bite of acid. **91 Editors' Choice** —*S.H. (12/15/2001)*

Peachy Canyon 1998 Benito Dusi Ranch Zinfandel (Paso Robles) $26. 89 —*S.H. (5/1/2000)*

Peachy Canyon 1997 Dusi Ranch Zinfandel (Paso Robles) $26. 89 —*P.G. (11/15/1999)*

Peachy Canyon 2000 Eastside Zinfandel (Paso Robles) $15. Rugged, warm-country Zin, with ripe wild berry and cola flavors and an edge of tobacco and sage. Rugged and woolly tannins are the main features. **86** —*S.H. (2/1/2003)*

Peachy Canyon 1997 Eastside Zinfandel (Paso Robles) $15. 85 —*P.G. (11/15/1999)*

Peachy Canyon 2004 Especial Zinfandel (Paso Robles) $36. I've found variability in Especial, despite its high price. It shows an artisinal, vintage-driven nature that can be beguiling or rough. The '04 is a bit of both. It's not a smooth, seductive Zin. The tannins are too feral. But it is interesting, with complex blackberry, blueberry, cherry, and Asian spice flavors. Try aging, but not too long. You don't want to lose that fresh fruit. **88** —*S.H. (12/1/2006)*

Peachy Canyon 2003 Especial Zinfandel (Paso Robles) $30. Take a whiff of this wine, with its green peppercorn and sage and thyme aromas, and you'd think it was dry. But in the mouth, it's ripe, sweetish and hot, with raisiny flavors. To me, that suggests an imbalance. Some people like this style. I'm just not one of them. **84** —*S.H. (12/1/2005)*

Peachy Canyon 2001 Especial Zinfandel (Paso Robles) $30. Bright-edged and zippy, with bing cherry, cocoa, citrus, licorice, and coffee flavors at the center. A tea-like edge is evident on the finish, which is fairly long. It then reveals a smooth, plush, creamy edge. **91** *(11/1/2003)*

Peachy Canyon 2000 Especial Zinfandel (Paso Robles) $30. A blend of Peachy's best Zins, and it costs a few bucks more, but isn't better. Forward flavors of raspberries and cherries are wrapped in soft tannins and acids. The wine could use more structure. **86** —*S.H. (2/1/2003)*

Peachy Canyon 1997 Especial Zinfandel (Paso Robles) $28. 86 —*P.G. (11/15/1999)*

Peachy Canyon 1999 Estate Bottled Zinfandel (Paso Robles) $30. Sure, there's something wild and wacky about Zin that Europeans don't get. It's not well-behaved. It's rude, aggressive, over the top. It's a blast of wild fruit and spices. It's high in alcohol. It's not a parlor wine, but that's what we like about it! Pulls off Zin's bad-boy act, in spades. **90**—*S.H. (12/15/2001)*

Peachy Canyon 1998 Estate Bottled Zinfandel (Paso Robles) $30. A blend of Peachy Canyon Estate (67%) and Mustang Springs Ranch (33%) fruit. In this vintage the Peachy Zins seem to lack intensity, but this is a well-balanced effort that shows the best of what is there. Clean, forward fruit, with lots of blueberry and a light, toasty framework. Good wine, but pricey. **89** —*P.G. (3/1/2001)*

Peachy Canyon 1999 Incredible Red Bin 110 Zinfandel (California) $NA. Quite fruity, with jammy blackberry and blueberry flavors at the fore. A zingy tartness on the finish keeps it from being cloying, however. Spicy, with toasty oak at the end **86** —*J.M. (11/15/2001)*

Peachy Canyon 2002 Incredible Red Bin 114 Zinfandel (Paso Robles) $12. Balanced and dry, here's a Zin you can have with elegant food. It's dry, and the alcohol is below 14%. The berry and spice flavors are juicy. Good value in a Zin. **86** —*S.H. (11/15/2004)*

Peachy Canyon 2003 Incredible Red Bin 116 Zinfandel (Paso Robles) $12. It's a little hot, but there are some nice features to this Zin. It has an interesting range of flavors, from sage and blackberries to chocolate and raisins, and is very dry, with sturdy tannins. Plus, the price ain't bad. **85** —*S.H. (12/1/2005)*

Peachy Canyon 2004 Incredible Red Bin 119 Zinfandel (California) $12. Shows real Peachy Canyon class in the ripe fruit, spice flavors, and lush tannic structure. The wine is much more rustic and angular than the Paso Robles bottlings, but it's still a fine Zinfandel. **86** —*S.H. (12/1/2006)*

Peachy Canyon 2001 Incredible Red, Bin 113 Zinfandel (Paso Robles) $12. Light on the fruit, showing hints of cherry and berry notes. Tannins are firm and a little overwhelming. **80** *(11/1/2003)*

Peachy Canyon 1997 Lakeview Zinfandel (Paso Robles) $21. 85 —*P.G. (11/15/1999)*

Peachy Canyon 2001 Mr. Wilson's Vineyard Zinfandel (Paso Robles) $26. A smooth-textured wine that sports a pretty core of cherry, plum, coffee, and chocolate flavors. The tannins are firm and ripe and offer a good framework to support the flavors. **88** *(11/1/2003)*

Peachy Canyon 2004 Mustang Springs Zinfandel (Paso Robles) $30. Tastes riper than Peachy's other '04 Zins, with alcohol close to 16%, and some Petite Sirah in the blend. The wine is enormous in blackberry jam, cassis, and blueberry pie flavors. Fabulous, exotic, and just delicious, with gobs of chocolate. **92** —*S.H. (12/1/2006)*

Peachy Canyon 2000 Mustang Springs Zinfandel (Paso Robles) $26. Fruity and big, with black raspberry and black cherry flavors and a hit of spicy pepper. Feels hot and dry in the mouth, with low acids and silky, dusty tannins. There's an herbaceous edge that relieves the purely fruity character. **86** —*S.H. (2/1/2003)*

Peachy Canyon 1999 Mustang Springs Zinfandel (Paso Robles) $26. The real McCoy here. Pretty aromas of red berries and blackberries ride along dusty spices and earth, leading to a rich, round, spicy, fruity wine. It's notable for its dry balance and harmony, with firm but easy tannins and soft acids. **90** —*S.H. (12/15/2001)*

Peachy Canyon 1998 Mustang Springs Zinfandel (Paso Robles) $26. This wine, from a newly acquired property, is tart and young, grapey almost, with the fruit a little reduced. The wine seems to be in hiding. It falls off in the middle and finishes with tannin and little else. This may just need more time in bottle to blossom. **86** —*P.G. (3/1/2001)*

Peachy Canyon NV Mustang Springs Port Zinfandel (Paso Robles) $NA. Quite fruity, with jammy blackberry and blueberry flavors at the fore. A zingy tartness on th finish keeps it from being cloying, however. Spicy, with toasty oak at the end. **86** —*S.H. (11/15/2001)*

Peachy Canyon 2003 Mustang Springs Ranch Zinfandel (Paso Robles) $26. This Zin is very similar to Peachy Canyon's Especial Zin, with aromas suggesting thyme, sage, and spicy white pepper, and rich flavors of wild dark berries and chocolate. But it's more balanced and harmonious. A nice example of Paso Robles Zinfandel. **88** —*S.H. (12/1/2005)*

Peachy Canyon NV Mustang Springs Ranch Port Zinfandel (Paso Robles) $40. 85 —*S.H. (9/1/2002)*

Peachy Canyon 2004 Old School House Zinfandel (Paso Robles) $30. This is the best Old School House in years. It really impresses with its length and depth of its flavors, offering a huge mouthful of blackberry jam, cherry pie, and nutmeggy chocolate cocoa. High in alcohol but perfectly in balance. **91** —*S.H. (12/1/2006)*

Peachy Canyon 2003 Old School House Zinfandel (Paso Robles) $26. This Zin is more balanced than most of Peachy Canyon's others. It's lower in alcohol and not as hot. Still, there's a rustic edge to the ripe berry, cherry, and chocolate flavors. Will be a hit with barbecue. **86** —*S.H. (12/1/2005)*

Peachy Canyon 2001 Old School House Zinfandel (Paso Robles) $26. Smooth and supple, with a strong chocolate and coffee core that extends to reveal plush plum, black cherry, vanilla, and spice flavors. Toasty oak and a seriously viscous texture give this wine a compelling and enjoyable richness. **90** *(11/1/2003)*

Peachy Canyon 2000 Old School House Zinfandel (Paso Robles) $26. Black raspberry and spice flavors emerge from this dry, intense wine that has fairly rough tannins and a tart finish. Could use more structural integrity, and feels a little soft and flat on the palate. **87** —*S.H. (2/1/2003)*

Peachy Canyon 2004 Snow Vineyard Zinfandel (Paso Robles) $30. Better than last year's bottling, which was prickly and hot, the '04 has a coffee and tobacco edge, as well as hints of Provençal herbs and bitter, unsweetened chocolate. In addition, there are cherry and plum skin flavors. **88** —*S.H. (12/1/2006)*

Peachy Canyon 2003 Snow Vineyard Zinfandel (Paso Robles) $26. This is a hot wine, with 15.5% of alcohol, and that heat dominates the pleasant berry, cherry, and mocha flavors. The wine is fully dry, but it's hard to get around the prickly, peppery burn on the palate. **83** —*S.H. (12/1/2005)*

Peachy Canyon 2004 Westside Zinfandel (Paso Robles) $20. What a classic Paso Zin. Even though the vintage was a scorcher, this Westside is balanced and delivers delicious cocoa, raspberry, cherry, and blueberry flavors, and then all kinds of tangy herbs and spices. And such a soft, voluptuous texture, too. Should be easy to find with a case production of 4,795. **90 Editors' Choice** —*S.H. (12/1/2006)*

Peachy Canyon 2003 Westside Zinfandel (Paso Robles) $19. The west side of Paso Robles is the cooler side, and this Zin is crisper than Peachy Canyon's others. That makes it a better wine. That said, there's a briary rustic quality, and an edginess to the mouthfeel, that age is not likely to remove. **86** —*S.H. (12/1/2005)*

Peachy Canyon 2001 Westside Zinfandel (Paso Robles) $19. Velvety smooth and classy, with a fine-tuned core that features black cherry, cocoa, spice, plum, cassis, coffee, spice, and subtle herb notes. Really lovely, with a velvety finish that goes on and on. **90 Editors' Choice** *(11/1/2003)*

Peachy Canyon 2000 Westside Zinfandel (Paso Robles) $19. Refined and elegant, with well-behaved blackberry, black cherry, and pepper flavors that are reined in with fine, controlled tannins. Although the acidity could be higher, this is a lovely, complete Zin. **89** —*S.H. (2/1/2003)*

Peachy Canyon 1999 Westside Zinfandel (Paso Robles) $19. The aroma is almost delicate for a Paso Zin. It's faintly earthy and dusty, with hints of berries. It's also austere in the mouth, with dusty tannins wrapped around soft, berry fruit. This is a wine of structural integrity. Dry and balanced. **87** —*S.H. (12/15/2001)*

Peachy Canyon 1998 Westside Zinfandel (Paso Robles) $19. This wine strikes a perfect balance, showing the jammy, slightly raisiny ripeness of Paso Robles fruit, but keeping enough acid in the mix to buoy it up. Plump and ripe, it gives a lot of flavor for the price, with interesting layers of fruit and earth through the finish. **89** —*P.G. (3/1/200*

PEACOCK FAMILY VINEYARD

Peacock Family Vineyard 2001 Cabernet Sauvignon (Spring Mountain) $60. Some of the grapes got overripe during this remarkably long, dry, warm vintage, to judge from the raisiny aromas. Then, too, the wine has a hot mouthfeel and finish. **84** —*S.H. (12/1/2005)*

PECONIC BAY WINERY

Peconic Bay Winery 2002 Cabernet Franc (North Fork of Long Island) $22. This wine's aromas are all over the place, and few of them entice: funk, lactic, earth, and bramble. Cab Franc character shows through with some cherry flavors on the palate, while rhubarb and tree bark flavors support. Finishes with chalky green tannins. **82** —*M.D. (8/1/2006)*

Peconic Bay Winery 2003 La Barrique Chardonnay (North Fork of Long Island) $17. Light and fresh, with smoky overtones to the citrus and melon aromas. Flavors favor smoky buttered corn, then bright, lemony acids take over on the finish. **83** —*J.C. (3/1/2006)*

Peconic Bay Winery 2001 La Barrique Chardonnay (North Fork of Long Island) $17. 84 —*J.C. (10/2/2004)*

Peconic Bay Winery 2003 Steel-Fermented Chardonnay (North Fork of Long Island) $13. A nose of papaya, white fruit, and lemon verbena is pleasant, while the mouthfeel has nice balance, smooth, and round without being fat. Has cantaloupe and tropical fruit in the mouth, then finishes with a pithy note. **84** —*M.D. (8/1/2006)*

Peconic Bay Winery 2002 Steel-Fermented Chardonnay (North Fork of Long Island) $13. 84 —*J.C. (10/2/2004)*

Peconic Bay Winery 2001 Merlot (North Fork of Long Island) $24. 81 —*J.C. (10/2/2004)*

Peconic Bay Winery 2004 Riesling (North Fork of Long Island) $13. A hint of petrol on the nose designates this as a serious Riesling, while white fruit flavors and spice flavors dance along the medium-bodied palate. A touch of sweetness is balanced with citrusy acids, which will leave your mouth craving more. **87** —*M.D. (8/1/2006)*

Peconic Bay Winery 2003 Riesling (North Fork of Long Island) $13. 83 —*J.C. (10/2/2004)*

Peconic Bay Winery NV Polaris Riesling (North Fork of Long Island) $35. This wine has Muscat-like floral aromas as well as orange liqueur and vanilla, then turns toward honeyed peach nectar in the mouth, with hints of musk. Very sweet, the acidity sometimes pierces while at other times it's distant, giving an uneven feel. **83** —*M.D. (8/1/2006)*

Peconic Bay Winery 2003 Polaris Ice Wine Riesling (North Fork of Long Island) $35. 85 —*J.C. (10/2/2004)*

PEDESTAL

Pedestal 2003 Merlot (Columbia Valley (WA)) $55. Michel Rolland consults on this extraordinary Merlot, part of Allen Shoup's Long Shadows project. Dark, dense, supremely concentrated with a silky, smoky, voluptuous mouthfeel, Pedestal is beautifully ripened, nuanced, and complete. Lovely notes of bacon and smoked meats permeate the thick, juicy fruit. Still tight and young, this is a Merlot to savor, and to save. **93 Editors' Choice** —*P.G. (6/1/2006)*

PEDRONCELLI

Pedroncelli 2003 Three Vineyards Cabernet Sauvignon (Dry Creek Valley) $14. A very nice Cabernet at a fair price. It's a smooth wine with a good grip of tannins framing currant, herb, and smoky oak flavors. Finishes with real complexity and elegance. **86** —*S.H. (12/1/2006)*

Pedroncelli 1997 Fumé Blanc (Dry Creek Valley) $9. 80 —*M.M. (9/1/1999)*

Pedroncelli 2002 Bench Vineyards Merlot (Dry Creek Valley) $14. Dark, dry and earthy, this Merlot has tobacco, herb ,and bitter cherry flavors. It's pretty tannic, too, although low in acids. **84** —*S.H. (3/1/2006)*

Pedroncelli 2002 Petite Sirah (Dry Creek Valley) $14. Take a Dry Creek Cabernet, give it a more robust body, a more rustic mouthfeel, and push the flavors toward plums and leather, and you get this old-style wine. The dry, rasping tannins suggest aging for at least eight years. **86** —*S.H. (12/1/2006)*

Pedroncelli 2000 Petite Sirah (Dry Creek Valley) $15. Another wine with a wide range of scores. Some praised its rich, mouthfilling texture and

USA

complex flavors of berries, stone fruits, and green olives. Others found the tannins rasping, with a too-short finish. This is a wine, though, with a history of improving in the cellar. **85** *(4/1/2003)*

Pedroncelli 2002 F. Johnson Vineyard Pinot Noir (Sonoma County) $15. Dry, elegant, and refined, without too much stuffing. Pleasant for its sour cherry, tea, and dried spice flavors and silky texture. **86** *(11/1/2004)*

Pedroncelli 2000 F. Johnson Vineyard Pinot Noir (Russian River Valley) $NA. Despite being a big, plummy wine from an AVA not known for Pinot Noir, this offering from a winery better known for Zinfandel has uncanny complexity, blending floral (lilac?) aromas with dried spices and ripe cherries and strawberries. The warming finish features a hint of cocoa powder. **88 Best Buy** *(10/1/2002)*

Pedroncelli 2004 East Side Vineyards Sauvignon Blanc (Dry Creek Valley) $10. The east side of the valley is the warm side, since it gets the afternoon sun, and this is certainly a ripe wine. It's huge in pineapple, fig, and melon flavors, and has a crisp edge of clean acidity. Finishes with a hint of sweetness. **86 Best Buy** *—S.H. (3/1/2006)*

Pedroncelli 1997 Zinfandel (Dry Creek Valley) $9. **85** *—M.S. (11/1/1999)*

Pedroncelli 2002 Mother Clone Zinfandel (Dry Creek Valley) $14. A little too sweet for its own good, with sugary, blackberry flavors. This may have been a deliberate decision to keep the alcohol down to a reasonable 14.6 %. Take away the sweetness, and there's a great Zinfandel here. **83** *—S.H. (3/1/2006)*

Pedroncelli 2001 Mother Clone Zinfandel (Dry Creek Valley) $14. A charry, chunky wine that serves up hints of black cherry, anise, and blackberry flavors. The powdery tannins are fairly tough on the tongue. **80** *—J.M. (11/1/2003)*

Pedroncelli 1997 Mother Clone Special Vineyard Sele Zinfandel (Dry Creek Valley) $13. **87** *—J.C. (5/1/2000)*

Pedroncelli 1996 Pedroni-Bushnell Zinfandel (Dry Creek Valley) $14. **84** *—P.G. (11/15/1999)*

Pedroncelli 2005 Zinfandel Rosé Zinfandel (Dry Creek Valley) $10. Simple and dryish to off-dry, with raspberry and vanilla flavors and good acidity. This is a nice little blush wine and the price is fair for what you get. **83** *—S.H. (12/1/2006)*

PEIRANO

Peirano 2003 The Heritage Collection Barbera (Lodi) $12. Tough and gritty in acids and tannins, this wine is okay now with rustic fare, and may benefit from some cellaring. It's stuffed with fruity, berry, and spice flavors, and is totally dry. **84** *—S.H. (6/1/2006)*

Peirano 2002 The Heritage Collection Barbera (Lodi) $13. Typical California Barbera in the sturdy, lumberjack quality, with its rough-hewn tannins and deep flavors of plums and tobacco. Bone dry. **84** *—S.H. (11/15/2004)*

Peirano 2002 Cabernet Sauvignon (Lodi) $10. There are some good Cab qualities in the blackberry fruit and full-bodied firmness, but there's also a rustic edginess to the mouthfeel. Still, it's a good-value Cabernet. **84** *—S.H. (11/15/2004)*

Peirano 1999 Cabernet Sauvignon (Lodi) $10. It's rustic, but there's something balanced and enjoyable in this wine. Combines blackberry and olive notes with some green, stalky flavors that add interest. It's absolutely dry, not just in the official sense, but in the mouth, with a dusting of tannins. **87 Best Buy** *—S.H. (9/1/2002)*

Peirano 2004 Autumn's Blush Cabernet Sauvignon (Lodi) $5. This dry, crisp rosé is 100% Cabernet Sauvignon. It has gentle flavors of strawberries, raspberries, apricots, and vanilla, and is really a pretty wine. **84 Best Buy** *—S.H. (5/1/2006)*

Peirano 2001 Autumn's Blush Cabernet Sauvignon (Lodi) $9. A rosé made from Cabernet Sauvignon, but not showing much varietal character. Delicate peach and apricot flavors drink rather sweet and flabby. **82** *—S.H. (2/1/2004)*

Peirano 2001 Heritage Collection Cabernet Sauvignon (Lodi) $18. Not a great success this vintage due to the baked, Porty aroma, with its suggestion of caramelized raisins, and Port-like, alcoholic flavors. Turns tannic and hot on the finish. Lacks definition and delicacy, and seems to be a

victim of the heat. **84** *—S.H. (11/15/2003)*

Peirano 2004 The Heritage Collection Cabernet Sauvignon (Lodi) $12. Under the warm Lodi sun Cabernet gets as ripe as anywhere in California. The trick is balance, which Peirano dependably achieves. This wine is robust in blackberry jam, cassis, and chocolate flavors, but has good acids and firm tannins, and a soft, voluptuous texture. **88 Best Buy** *—S.H. (5/1/2006)*

Peirano 1999 Chardonnay (Lodi) $11. Here's a good value from an area that's becoming known for affordable wine. It's ripely fruity, round, supple, and dry. Fills the mouth with pretty flavors that are underscored by rich lees. **86** *—S.H. (12/15/2002)*

Peirano 1998 Chardonnay (Lodi) $10. An average wine, from a less than successful vintage and a hot region. Fruity aromas and citrus flavors are one-dimensional, although the wine is clean and tart. It tastes rather like a simple Chablis. **84** *—S.H. (5/1/2002)*

Peirano 2001 The Heritage Collection Chardonnay (Lodi) $15. Dry and tart, a sleek wine that offers a prickly mouthfeel without a whole lot of fruit. The modest flavors are of grapefruit juice with a squeeze of peach. **83** *—S.H. (4/1/2004)*

Peirano 1999 Six Clones Merlot (Lodi) $12. Dark color. Aromas of herbs and medicinal notes. Awkward flavors, mingling berries with odder, almost synthetic ones. But it's dry, with soft tannins and good texture. A bizarre mix. **80** *—S.H. (11/15/2002)*

Peirano 1998 Six Clones Merlot (Lodi) $10. Pretty good for the money, with some fancy blackberry and chocolate flavors and a sumptuous mouthfeel. There are some ruder herbal, green notes that take it down a few notches. The bottom line is, this dry wine is just fine for most occasions. **86 Best Buy** *—S.H. (6/1/2002)*

Peirano 2001 The Heritage Collection Six Clones Merlot (Lodi) $17. This ripe and fruity Merlot has aromas of black currants, plums, herbs, and anise, and drinks dry and velvety. Turns tannic toward the finish. **86** *—S.H. (2/1/2004)*

Peirano 2002 The Heritage Collection Petite Sirah (Lodi) $18. A little thin for my tastes, in the sense that it teases with the suggestion of black cherries but then withholds. In place of the anticipated fruit you get a flush of tannins and acids. **84** *—S.H. (11/15/2004)*

Peirano NV The Other Red Blend (Lodi) $14. Soft, smooth, and ripe in black cherry and coffee flavors, this one-dimensional wine finishes a little sweet, with a good grip of tannins. It's a blend of Syrah, Petite Sirah, and Cabernet Sauvignon. **83** *—S.H. (5/1/2006)*

Peirano 1999 Sauvignon Blanc (Lodi) $9. Just what the doctor ordered in a likeable, affordable white wine. Packs plenty of ripe spearmint and lemon flavors with enough acidity to make it bright and clean. A tiny amount of sugar will satisfy your sweet tooth without compromising the wine's basic dryness. **87 Best Buy** *—S.H. (9/1/2002)*

Peirano 2004 Heritage Collection Sauvignon Blanc (Lodi) $12. Rich in lime and grapefruit flavors with notes of tropical fruits, melons, and figs, this refreshing white wine has the generous acids needed for balance. It's a little sweet on the finish, but not too much. **84** *—S.H. (4/1/2006)*

Peirano 2002 The Heritage Collection Sauvignon Blanc (Lodi) $12. This is quite a fine Sauvignon Blanc, easily as good as many coastal versions costing more. The flavors range from sweet citrus fruits through figs and melons, while a splash of Viognier adds a rich, exotic note. Brilliant too for its crisp acidity, making it clean and refreshing. **87 Best Buy** *—S.H. (12/1/2004)*

Peirano 1998 Shiraz (Lodi) $10. This pretty wine shows how well this variety thrives in Lodi. There's a mushu pork note, with peppery plum aromas and flavors that are delicious, and yet the wine is bone dry. Adequate acids and tannins make for balance. It may not be a complex wine but it's a thoroughly enjoyable one. **87 Best Buy** *—S.H. (9/1/2002)*

Peirano 2002 The Heritage Collection Shiraz (Lodi) $13. Dry, soft, and tannic, with earthy, coffee, and cherry flavors, this clean red wine is rather rustic. It will wash down burgers and beef stew very easily. **83** *—S.H. (5/1/2006)*

Peirano 1999 The Heritage Collection Shiraz (Lodi) $17. With a little bottle age, this soft wine is picking up bottle bouquet of dried violets and

Kahlúa, in addition to the plum, blackberry, and olive tapenade notes. Drinks very rich, dry, and spicy, scattering an array of dusty brown allspice and Chinese spice around the mouth. **89** —*S.H. (3/1/2004)*

Peirano 1999 Viognier (Lodi) $12. From this family-owned winery comes an earthy, spicy wine with floral, passion-fruit and lemongrass aromas that drinks soft and fruity. The flavors suggest honey-baked apples drizzled with citrus juices, although it's basically dry. Lots of fun to drink. **84** —*S.H. (11/15/2001)*

Peirano 2004 Heritage Collection Viognier (Lodi) $12. Inexpensive Viognier can be a disaster because the exotic wine is difficult to control, but Peirano has done a good job with this dry, crisp, balanced bottling. It's rich in mango, apricot, peach, and vanilla flavors, and has a luxuriously creamy mouthfeel. **86** —*S.H. (4/1/2006)*

Peirano 2001 The Heritage Collection Viognier (Lodi) $15. Drinks dry and thin, with citrus and grass flavors that taste more like Sauvignon Blanc. Resembles that variety also with its high acidity and tart, peppery finish. **83** —*S.H. (12/31/2003)*

Peirano 2004 Heritage Collection The Other White Blend (Lodi) $12. With Chardonnay, Sauvignon Blanc, and a splash of Viognier comprising the blend, this is a fruity wine, ripe in peach, pineapple, melon, honeysuckle, and vanilla spice flavors. It's dry and crisp in acids, and is a lot of fun to drink. **86** —*S.H. (4/1/2006)*

Peirano 1999 Old Vine Zinfandel (Lodi) $10. Age has not improved this vegetal wine. It's soft and simple, with the taste of asparagus. **80** —*S.H. (4/1/2006)*

Peirano 1998 Old Vine Zinfandel (Lodi) $14. In 1997 this wine was wonderfully rich. This year, it's not, instead providing less ripe flavors of tobacco, sage, and mint. Those pretty tannins are there, soft and intricate, and the acidity is fine. It's a victim of its vintage. **85** —*S.H. (11/1/2002)*

Peirano 1997 Old Vine Zinfandel (Lodi) $10. A very great value in Zinfandel, this warm-climate wine is filled with ripe berry fruit that only steady sunshine can produce. There are some underlying raisiny flavors but they're overshadowed by the sheer balance. Exquisitely dry, flamboyantly drinkable, with wonderful tannins, this is great Zinfandel, and look at that price. **91** —*S.H. (9/1/2002)*

Peirano 1998 Primo Zinfandel (Lodi) $11. This is a dark, unripe Zin that seems to have been made from grapes not suitable for the main blend. It's herbal to the point of vegetal, with flavors of canned asparagus, although there's a hint of riper berries. **82** —*S.H. (11/1/2002)*

PEJU

Peju 2001 Cabernet Franc (Rutherford) $65. This is among the best Cab Francs ever bottled in California. Normally in need of toning up with other Bordeaux grapes, this 100% varietal wine needs no help. It is profoundly good, with the weight and tannins of Cabernet Sauvignon but a silky, feminine quality all its own. Subtle and nuanced; it doesn't hit you over the head with extraction and oak, but is complex, layered, measured. **93** —*S.H. (8/1/2004)*

Peju 2000 Cabernet Franc (Napa Valley) $30. An extraordinarily dense, rich wine, with huge fruit. Blackcherries, blackberries, nectarines, blueberries, the list goes on and on. This flavor is packed into soft but complex tannins and soft acids. A bit more structure would be nice. **88** —*S.H. (6/1/2003)*

Peju 1999 Cabernet Franc (Napa Valley) $30. It's hard to make Cab Franc stand on its own in California, and this wine does not advance the cause. It's proper rather than special. Dry, wonderfully complex tannins, and adequate acids, but the fruit is thin. Especially at this price, you want hedonism or ageability, and the wine has neither. **85** —*S.H. (12/1/2002)*

Peju 2002 Estate Cabernet Franc (Napa Valley) $40. There's a green edge to this Cab Franc that suggests mint and dill, but those herbs are nicely integrated into the sweet cherry and oak flavors, and help ground the wine. Its tannins will cut beautifully through a roasted duck. **90** —*S.H. (7/1/2005)*

Peju 2002 Reserve Cabernet Franc (Rutherford) $90. Nobody is trying harder to master Cab Franc, and this noble wine continues Peju's streak. It's voluptuously soft, but not too soft, with enough acidity and tannins for structure. Meanwhile, the flavors are a wonder. Black currants, red

and black cherries, white chocolate, sweet vanilla, and an edge of smoky char, to name a few. Drink now. **90** —*S.H. (11/1/2005)*

Peju 1997 Cabernet Sauvignon (Napa Valley) $45. **91** *(11/1/2000)*

Peju 1999 Cabernet Sauvignon (Napa Valley) $48. Overshadowed by its neighbors on Highway 29, Peju is often one of the better wines of the vintage. This classic Napa Cabernet brims with cassis, cigar box, sage, and dark chocolate aromas and flavors. Has more aggressive tannins than many other Cabs, which give it greater structure as well as ageworthiness. **92** —*S.H. (11/15/2002)*

Peju 1998 Cabernet Sauvignon (Sonoma County) $38. Starts with earthy, modest berry and chocolate aromas, then turns into a rather common sip. The berry flavors are okay but don't knock you out, and the acidity is much too soft. **85** —*S.H. (6/1/2002)*

Peju 2003 Estate Cabernet Sauvignon (Napa Valley) $40. Raw and harsh, and even though there's some good blackberry and cherry fruit, not to mention toasty oak, the tannins come across as astringent and minty-green. Not going anywhere, so drink now. **82** —*S.H. (12/31/2006)*

Peju 2001 Estate Cabernet Sauvignon (Napa Valley) $38. Released a full year after the excellent Rutherford Cab, with which it has much in common. It's ample in berry, cherry, and currant fruit, and oak has been applied judiciously. What's harder to convey is its balance and wonderful structure. Has an elegance and sweet harmony throughout. **91** —*S.H. (11/1/2005)*

Peju 2000 Estate Cabernet Sauvignon (Napa Valley) $38. A bit lean, with modest berry flavors, and the tannins are rather sharp and astringent. There's also a cut of acidity that adds to the impression of dryness and astringency. Could certainly use more softness and flesh. **84** —*S.H. (8/1/2004)*

Peju 2002 Estate Bottled Cabernet Sauvignon (Napa Valley) $38. Almost as good as the '02 reserve, which costs three times as much, Peju's estate Cab is rich and complex and showcases Napa at its ripe, decadent best. It's deep and long in cassis and oak flavors and wonderfully balanced. A dry wine of great charm. Drink now through 2008. **92** —*S.H. (7/1/2006)*

Peju 1997 Estate Bottled Reserve Cabernet Sauvignon (Rutherford) $95. **90** *(11/1/2000)*

Peju 2003 Reserve Cabernet Sauvignon (Rutherford) $105. Drinks very soft and forward and is accessible now, with plenty of upfront cherry pie filling, blackberry jam, cocoa, and cola flavors. Tannins are enough to hold the wine for a decade of slow improvement. Notable for its opulence and the polished expressive fruit. Could potentially improve quite a bit. **90** —*S.H. (12/15/2006)*

Peju 2002 Reserve Cabernet Sauvignon (Rutherford) $125. Here's a big, bold, expressive Cab, packed with powerful black cherry, mocha, currant, and spice flavors that are well oaked and very dry. The tannins are strong and fine. Really marvelous for its balance and harmony. Needs time, but good now with a steak. **93 Cellar Selection** —*S.H. (12/31/2005)*

Peju 2000 Reserve Cabernet Sauvignon (Rutherford) $85. I think the philosophy here was to harvest the grapes at lower sugars and higher acids, then plaster the juice with oak, and create an ageable wine. It may well develop later in the decade, but now this is a tough, tannic, astringent wine. There's no guarantee, but try around 2010. **85** —*S.H. (8/1/2004)*

Peju 1999 Reserve Cabernet Sauvignon (Rutherford) $95. It's a close call as to which is better, Peju's regular '99 or this pricy Reserve. This one wins on sheer richness. It's a fabulous wine, thick and juicy, a glyceriney beauty drenched with elaborate oak. Has a depth and beauty of flavor that puts it among the best. Framed in exquisite tannins, it thrills the palate. **94** —*S.H. (11/15/2002)*

Peju 1998 Reserve Cabernet Sauvignon (Rutherford) $85. They must have limited the crop on these vines, because the wine is more concentrated in fruity extract than many '98 Cabs. It's also lavishly oaked. Having said that, there are problems. It's overly soft, even flabby, and lacks life; it's like cola syrup without the carbonation. At this price, it lacks subtlety. **87** —*S.H. (6/1/2002)*

Peju 1998 Chardonnay (Napa Valley) $22. **84** *(6/1/2000)*

Peju 2001 Chardonnay (Napa Valley) $22. Rich enough in fruit and spice, and there's some nice green apple and pear fruit flavors. The oak is very strong and highly charred. Finishes with a dry, slightly bitter earthiness, like swallowing a bit of raw tobacco. **84** —*S.H. (6/1/2003)*

Peju 1998 H.B. Vineyard Chardonnay (Napa Valley) $28. 84 *(6/1/2000)*

Peju 2002 Lianna Late Harvest Chardonnay (Napa Valley) $45. Delicious and savory, an intensely sweet wine, brimming with wild honey and cane sugar, that smacks of ripe apricots and peach sorbet sprinkled with the zest of tangerines. There's an intense vanilla flavor throughout. **90** —*S.H. (8/1/2004)*

Peju 2001 Carnival French Columbard (California) $12. Still the second most widely planted white wine grape in California, but hardly ever seen on its own. This is a fruity wine (peaches, apricots), with fresh acids and quite a bit of sweetness, enough to quality as off-dry. **84** —*S.H. (3/1/2004)*

Peju 2001 Merlot (Napa Valley) $35. The polished tannins, creamy oak and blackberry flavors are all satisfying, yet this wine is marred by an edge of raisins and stewed prunes caused by overripe grapes. The cooked flavor will not age away. **84** —*S.H. (8/1/2004)*

Peju 2000 Merlot (Napa Valley) $35. Picture-perfect Napa Merlot, filled with delicious flavors ranging from ripe black cherries and boysenberries to sweet dark chocolate, olives, and sage. It's not only terrifically flavored, it also has great structure. **92** —*S.H. (10/1/2003)*

Peju 2002 Estate Merlot (Napa Valley) $35. A satisfyingly rich Merlot, soft and feminine, yet showing real character in the fine tannins and gentle acids that frame the fruit. The flavors, of cherries and sweet oak, are flattering to the palate. **87** —*S.H. (11/1/2005)*

Peju 2002 Petite Verdot (Napa Valley) $35. What a roll Peju has been on with Bordeaux wines. This is the first Petit Verdot I've had from them, and it's very good, given the variety's inherent limitations. It's dark, very dry, full-bodied, and intensely tannic, with currant flavors. You could try stashing it away for a decade, or drink it now with a well-marbled steak. **89** —*S.H. (5/1/2006)*

Peju 2001 Rosé Blend (California) $18. Would you believe Cabernet Franc, Merlot, Cabernet Sauvignon, Chardonnay, and French Columbard in a dry rosé wine? It's good, too, with rich berry-cherry flavors and some real depth and complexity. Particularly nice is the long finish, which continues the spicy, fruity flavors. Drink very cold. **88** —*S.H. (3/1/2004)*

Peju NV Provence Rosé Blend (California) $18. The reds give the cherryberry fruit, the dusty tannins and, obviously, the darkish color. Colombard contributes a fresh, grapy tartness. A simple, dry, easy-drinking rosé. **84** —*S.H. (12/31/2005)*

Peju 2001 Sauvignon Blanc (Napa Valley) $16. Totally refreshing and palate cleansing, a New Zealand-type wine with bright lime and gooseberry flavors, boosted by crisp acids. Turns very citrusy and spicy on the long finish. **87** —*S.H. (3/1/2003)*

Peju 2000 Sauvignon Blanc (Napa Valley) $22. Pricey for the variety, especially considering the quality, which is not high. Smells and tastes vegetal, with traces of asparagus, oregano, and mint, and a weird sweetness on the finish. **82** —*S.H. (9/1/2002)*

Peju 2004 Estate Sauvignon Blanc (Napa Valley) $16. This isn't really dry, as it finishes almost as sweet as a dessert wine. Good with fruit salad or as a summery apéritif. **83** —*S.H. (12/31/2005)*

Peju 2005 Estate Bottled Sauvignon Blanc (Napa Valley) $18. There's so much to like here, from the citrus, fig, and melon flavors to the bright acidity and rich creaminess, but the stubborn cat pee aromas are a problem for this reviewer. **83** —*S.H. (12/31/2006)*

Peju 1999 Syrah (Napa Valley) $65. I also did a double-take when I saw the price. This is a very tannic wine, for starters. It plasters the mouth with numbing dust, and is as dry as the grave. But you know what? It doesn't have the core of fruit needed to age. It's earthy and tough and in the absence of flavor, the acidity stands out. **84** —*S.H. (12/1/2002)*

PEJU PROVINCE

Peju Province 2001 Cabernet Franc (Napa Valley) $35. A lovely wine, understated and elegant. It's a feminine wine, with subtle herb, cherry, and oak flavors, and rich, firm tannins. Displays a seamless quality and complexity that make you reach for a second glass. **91** —*S.H. (3/1/2005)*

Peju Province 2001 Reserve Cabernet Sauvignon (Rutherford) $85. Ripe, soft, and hedonistic, an instantly likeable wine for its sheer opulence. Just bursting with sweet cherry, blackberry, milk chocolate, and smoky oak flavors wrapped in sweet, smooth tannins. Drinking absolutely beautiful now and throughout the next ten years. **92** —*S.H. (10/1/2004)*

Peju Province 2002 Syrah (Napa Valley) $32. Simple, clean, and likeable, with blackberry and pepper notes, medium body and supple tannins. Pepper comes on strong on the finish. **85** *(9/1/2005)*

Peju Province 2001 Estate Syrah (Napa Valley) $32. Pretty tannic at this point, but you'll find ripe black cherry and sweet oak flavors poking through. There's also a cocoa note that adds richness. Calls for a good steak, preferably barbecued. **88** —*S.H. (3/1/2005)*

Peju Province 2002 Zinfandel (Napa Valley) $25. From a winery that's doing just about everything right these days, a rich and polished Zin. Floods the mouth with ripe cherry, plum, blackberry, cocoa, and peppery spice flavors. The texture is smooth and complex. **91** —*S.H. (3/1/2005)*

Peju Province 2002 Reserve Zinfandel (Napa Valley) $45. It's tempting to score this wine even higher, because it's so decadently delicious. Just oozes chocolate, cassis, pecan pie, French roast coffee, and vanilla flavors, wrapped in ripe, soft tannins. The quibble is that it finishes as sweet as a dessert wine, although it's probably technically dry. **92** —*S.H. (3/1/2005)*

PELLEGRINI

Pellegrini 1995 Encore Red Table Wine Bordeaux Blend (North Fork of Long Island) $24. 86 —*J.C. (8/1/1999)*

Pellegrini 1997 Vintner's Pride Encore Bordeaux Blend (North Fork of Long Island) $29. The Pellegrini style seems to emphasize extraction. That's great—up to a point. In this wine, the slightly weedy cassis fruit adequately balances the starching tannins, yielding an age-worthy wine that should develop for up to 10 years. **88** —*J.C. (4/1/2001)*

Pellegrini 1997 Cabernet Sauvignon (North Fork of Long Island) $17. Aromas of cedar, earth, and cassis are accented by tobacco. Mediumweight, with fine structure and good balance; weediness comes through on the lingering finish. **87** —*J.C. (4/1/2001)*

Pellegrini 1995 Cabernet Sauvignon (North Fork of Long Island) $35. At over five years of age, this wine still boasts an impressively saturated purple color and dense, rich black-fruit aromas. There's plenty of oak, too. But the tannins are dry and hard; this wine's future development is unclear. Impressive more than pleasurable, and might always stay that way. **87** —*J.C. (4/1/2001)*

Pellegrini 2003 Cloverdale Ranch Cabernet Sauvignon (Alexander Valley) $22. Shows lots of rich varietal character and classy tannins that frame cassis and mocha flavors that finish dry. There's a bit of sharpness midpalate that suggests a few years of age will help the wine work out its kinks. Best 2007–2009. **87** —*S.H. (9/1/2006)*

Pellegrini 1998 Estate Bottled Unfiltered Cabernet Sauvignon (North Fork of Long Island) $17. The color is of a Bordeaux wine with significant age behind it, and the aromas match: It's earthy, with more leather and mushroom than fresh fruit. Still, down deep there is some spiced cherry and coffee, and the acidity is vital enough to keep it alive and kicking. **84** —*M.S. (3/1/2003)*

Pellegrini 2004 Old Vines Carignan (Redwood Valley) $18. From 72-year old vines grown in an interior Mendocino location that has a very wide summer temperature swing. Cool nights have preserved vital acidity, but the heat took its toll, resulting in a sugary sweetness and high alcohol. **82** —*S.H. (11/15/2006)*

Pellegrini 2003 Old Vine Carignane (Redwood Valley) $16. Soft and easy, with flavors of ripe red cherries and earthiness, this wine is very dry. Finishes a bit sharp, but will be fine with cheeses and meats. **84** —*S.H. (3/1/2005)*

Pellegrini 1996 Chardonnay (North Fork of Long Island) $13. 83 —*J.C. (8/1/1999)*

Pellegrini 2001 Chardonnay (Russian River Valley) $10. Tight and lean, a citrusy wine of high acidity that scours the palate and feels clean and refreshing through the tart finish. Unoaked. This austere wine will be good with shellfish or goat cheese appetizers. **85** —*S.H. (6/1/2003)*

Pellegrini 2001 Chardonnay (North Fork of Long Island) $13. 82 —*J.C. (10/2/2004)*

Pellegrini 1998 Chardonnay (North Fork of Long Island) $13. Toasty, with mouthwatering aromas of lemon custard and crème brûlée. Medium-bodied, the oak seems a little less integrated on the palate, manifesting as a slightly bitter spice edge to the otherwise soft, almost pillowy, fruit. 86 —*J.C. (4/1/2001)*

Pellegrini 2004 Olivet Lane Chardonnay (Russian River Valley) $24. Quite a distinguished Chardonnay, with a streak of steely minerality that undergirds the Key lime pie and buttery, smoky oak flavors. The wine is very dry and has bright acidity. 88 —*S.H. (11/15/2006)*

Pellegrini 2005 Unoaked Chardonnay (Russian River Valley) $16. Made with no oak to interfere with the intensely ripe fruitiness, and no malolactic fermentation to soften the bright, crisp acidity. This wine has green apple, nectarine, and papaya flavors and vibrant minerality. It's so clean and fine; really a delicious Chard. 89 —*S.H. (11/15/2006)*

Pellegrini 2000 Merlot (North Fork of Long Island) $18. 84 —*J.C. (10/2/2004)*

Pellegrini 1997 Merlot (North Fork of Long Island) $17. Aromas of smoke and toast over black cherries and mocha, with some dried-herb accents. Full-flavored, but the mouth-drying tannins require cellaring, and only time will tell if this wine will ever come into balance. 87 —*J.C. (4/1/2001)*

Pellegrini 2003 Cloverdale Ranch Merlot (Alexander Valley) $21. Starts with upscale aromas of charry new oak and black currants, always a good sign in a Bordeaux red. Rich, ripe, and chocolatey, the wine picks up blackberry and coffee flavors and finishes dry, with a dusty scour of tannins. Best now through 2009. 88 —*S.H. (11/15/2006)*

Pellegrini 2001 East End Select Merlot (North Fork of Long Island) $13. 80 —*J.C. (10/2/2004)*

Pellegrini 1999 East End Select Merlot (North Fork of Long Island) $12. A juicy, ready-to-drink Merlot for this evening's dinner table. Sweet black-cherry fruit is accented by just a dash of sweet peppers. 84 —*J.C. (4/1/2001)*

Pellegrini 1998 Estate Bottled Unfiltered Merlot (North Fork of Long Island) $17. Smoky and crisp textured, the wine is somewhat bitter, though it carries some pleasant cherry and herb flavors. The finish is tart, with more smoke and licorice overtones. 82 —*J.M. (3/1/2003)*

Pellegrini 2004 Olivet Lane Vineyard Pinot Noir (Russian River Valley) $24. Located in the heart of the valley, hard by such stalwarts as De Loach, this fine Pinot shows cool-climate qualities of brisk acidity and ripe fruit. Cherries, cola, root beer, espresso, cocoa, and tangy spices mingle in front of a clean, dry finish. 89 —*S.H. (11/15/2006)*

Pellegrini 2000 Frank's Steak House Red Unfiltered Red Blend (North Fork of Long Island) $NA. 84 —*J.C. (10/2/2004)*

Pellegrini 1998 Vintner's Pride Encore Unfiltered Estate Grown Red Blend (North Fork of Long Island) $29. Quite herbal and earthy in the nose. On the palate the wine shows bright acidity, but an interesting blend of sage, blackberry, bay leaf, anise, menthol, and tea flavors. Tannins are soft and the finish is moderate in length. 86 —*J.M. (3/1/2003)*

Pellegrini 2005 Rosato Rosé Blend (Redwood Valley) $14. Deeply colored, deeply flavored, and slightly off-dry, this wine has cherry pie filling flavors sprinkled with vanilla and cinnamon. It's a simple blush sipper. 83 —*S.H. (11/15/2006)*

Pellegrini 2005 Leveroni Vineyard Sauvignon Blanc (Lake County) $14. Wines like this advance Lake County's claim to be the Sauvignon Blanc capital of California. With very high acidity, this unoaked wine stimulates the tastebuds with pure citrus zest, apricot, and green grass flavors. 88 —*S.H. (11/15/2006)*

Pellegrini 1996 Finale White Dessert Wine White Blend (North Fork of Long Island) $25. 80 —*J.C. (8/1/1999)*

Pellegrini 2004 Eight Cousins Vineyard Zinfandel (Russian River Valley) $24. Here's a rich, complex, savory Zin from the coolish south-central part of the valley. The vines were planted only in 2000, but the wine has the density of the old vine Zins that border the vineyard. The wild raspberry, coffee, cola, and peppery spice flavors finish thoroughly dry, with rich tannins. 90 —*S.H. (11/15/2006)*

Pellegrini 2003 Eight Cousins Vineyard Zinfandel (Sonoma County) $24. A nice, easy Zin with some special features. It's dry and balanced in alcohol, acids, and tannins, with ripe flavors and a smooth mouth feel. The touch of rusticity should play well against ribs and barbecued chicken. 85 —*S.H. (2/1/2005)*

PEND D'OREILLE

Pend d'Oreille 2001 L'Oeuvre Reserve Red Table Wine Bordeaux Blend (Columbia Valley (WA)) $25. This Bordeaux blend has good, tart, spicy, berry-driven fruit as its focus, and some pleasing, chocolatey tannins wrapping around. It's well made, with streaks of anise and tar adding depth; a middleweight that could age for 5–6 years. 87 —*P.G. (9/1/2004)*

Pend d'Oreille 2001 Cabernet Sauvignon (Columbia Valley (WA)) $16. This comes on like a fairly simple cherry and chocolate Cab, until some herbal (some might say stemmy) flavors kick in midpalate. The finish is oaky, mixing chocolate and coffee streaks. 87 —*P.G. (6/1/2005)*

Pend d'Oreille 2000 Cabernet Sauvignon (Columbia Valley (WA)) $16. Tannic and chewy, the fruit is at the cranberry/pomegranate end of the cabernet spectrum. The tannins are chalky and green, and there seems to be some smoky earthiness, perhaps from older barrels, in the finish. 84 —*P.G. (9/1/2004)*

Pend d'Oreille 1998 Cabernet Sauvignon (Columbia Valley (WA)) $16. A rustic, red-fruited wine that is more reminiscent of an Italian variety than its French name suggests. Medium-bodied in the mouth, the fruit is accessorized with green tobacco and brown earthy flavors. The finish carries a touch of medicinal heat on the very end. 85 —*D.T. (12/31/2002)*

Pend d'Oreille 1999 Bistro Rouge Cabernet Sauvignon-Merlot (Washington) $11. The name fits the wine. This Cabernet-Merlot blend is a nice straightforward bottle of red wine. The milk chocolate and raspberry flavors join smooth tannins and earthy aromas. 87 **Best Buy** —*C.S. (12/31/2002)*

Pend d'Oreille 2000 Bistro Blanc Chardonnay (Washington) $11. This Idaho winery sourced its neighbor state's fruit to create this perfectly quaffable Chardonnay. Pear, orange, and custard aromas yield to flavors of pear and just a hint of coconut. The finish is smooth, yet simple. Ultimately this is a good, clean, straightforward white, albeit an ordinary one. 86 —*M.S. (6/1/2003)*

Pend d'Oreille 2002 Merlot (Columbia Valley (WA)) $20. Soft and oaky, this is an easy-drinking wine that is already showing some brick around the edges. It's not for cellaring, but for right-now chocolatey pleasure it delivers the goods. 88 —*P.G. (6/1/2005)*

Pend d'Oreille 2001 Merlot (Columbia Valley (WA)) $20. There is a distinctly herbal scent, green olive, thyme, and bark, that is often found in cool climate Washington grapes. Some sour cherry and rough tannins suggest that it would be best with spicy, smoky grilled meats. 84 —*P.G. (9/1/2004)*

Pend d'Oreille 1999 Merlot (Columbia Valley (WA)) $20. Aromas of green olives, wet dirt, and a dash of pepper makes one speculate, "Where's the fruit?" Some can be found on the palate in the form of red berries mixed with vanilla, but for the most part this is a soil-driven Merlot that is a bit too tart and tannic on the finish. 84 —*C.S. (12/31/2002)*

Pend d'Oreille 2002 Sauvignon Blanc (Washington) $8. This Idaho winery uses Washington fruit to deliver this light, crisp, pleasant wine. This wine offers pale green berry flavors, lemon zest, and the barest hint of spice on the refreshing finish. 86 —*P.G. (9/1/2004)*

Pend d'Oreille 2000 Syrah (Columbia Valley (WA)) $23. It's a shame there were only 100 cases made of this delicious Syrah. Fleshy black cherry aromas touched with celery burst into layers of red plum fruit on the palate. The tannins are rich, but there's enough acidity here to balance them out. 90 —*C.S. (12/31/2002)*

PENDLETON

Pendleton 2004 Reserve Chardonnay (Santa Lucia Highlands) $35. This is a new winery for me, and it's produced quite an impressive wine. It's big, thick, mouth-filling, with creamy pineapple custard and spice flavors and a firm, acidic minerality that is clearly a function of terroir. Impresses not only for power but finesse. 92 —*S.H. (12/15/2006)*

PENDULUM

Pendulum 2003 Red Blend (Columbia Valley (WA)) $25. Pendulum is a collaboration with Allen Shoup (Long Shadows), and that, plus the fact that this 1,500-case red wine is a mix of eight different varieties, suggests that it is crafted from barrels that did not make the final blend for Long Shadows. There is plenty of expensive, toasty new oak in the nose, cedar and smoke and black olive also, but the wine doesn't really have any focus. Pleasant, especially for the new oak. **87** —*P.G. (12/15/2005)*

PENNER-ASH

Penner-Ash 2000 Pinot Noir (Willamette Valley) $45. A sweet, ripe, soft wine, with chocolate-covered cherry aromas. The plummy palate is rich and easygoing, while black plum and licorice guide the expansive, smooth finish. Low acidity makes it a drink-now Pinot. **90** *(10/1/2002)*

Penner-Ash 1999 Pinot Noir (Willamette Valley) $49. Deep-toned, this mouthfilling Pinot wears clove and vanilla accents on black cherry and plum aromas and flavors. The supple, juicy texture provides plenty of pleasure. Closes firmly, with moderate tannins, coffee, and pepper notes. Tasty and satisfying, though not particularly complex. Drink now–2005. **88** *(10/1/2002)*

PEPI

Pepi 2000 Barbera (California) $14. Barbera can make a good, all-purpose dry wine when grown in warmer regions and yields are limited. The grapes for this wine are from Lodi and Amador counties. It's very dry, sappy, and acidic, with an almond-skin bitterness, and neutral berry flavors. One-dimensional, but might perk up with a little tomato sauce and olive oil. **86** —*S.H. (12/1/2002)*

Pepi 2004 Chardonnay (California) $9. Shows plenty of Chard character in the creamy, buttery texture, with its pleasant flavors of peaches, vanilla, and toast. This is a nice by-the-glass wine for restaurants. **84** —*S.H. (11/15/2005)*

Pepi 2003 Chardonnay (Napa Valley) $8. Pretty thin in fruit, but it's a clean wine with modest peach and apple flavors and oak shadings. **83** —*S.H. (12/1/2004)*

Pepi 2002 Chardonnay (Napa Valley) $14. This is a classic New World Chardonnay, ripe with apple, peach, and tropical fruit flavors, and lavishly oaked with smoky vanillins. It has a creamy texture, a bite of acidity, and a spicy finish. **85** —*S.H. (2/1/2004)*

Pepi 2001 Chardonnay (Napa Valley) $14. The first Chard from this winery in nearly a decade displays very pure, sleek fruit. Stainless-steel fermentation preserved vital apple, kiwi, and lime flavors, set out against refreshing acidity. This bold wine is flavorful and zesty. **88 Best Buy** —*S.H. (12/15/2002)*

Pepi 2002 Merlot (Calaveras County) $8. Dry, fruity, and richly thick in tannins, this fine value is a bit raw, but good for steaks and chops. The blackberry and oaky flavors are plump and juicy. **84** —*S.H. (12/15/2004)*

Pepi 2002 Merlot (California) $8. I always think of wines like this as pizza wines. This one has succulent, jammy cherry-berry fruit. It's dry, and has a good grip of tannin. There's a young, fresh sharpness that will cut right through mozzarella. **84** —*S.H. (10/1/2004)*

Pepi 2004 Pinot Grigio (California) $11. This is not only a great price, it's a nice wine. It's dry and smooth and crisp, with juicy apple, lemondrop, cinnamon, and vanilla flavors that don't stop coming. Great as an apéritif. **86 Best Buy** —*S.H. (11/15/2005)*

Pepi 2003 Pinot Grigio (Oregon) $11. Sometimes you just need a crisp, dry, fruity white wine that doesn't cost too much, and this one fits the bill. It's flavored with the tastes of sweet green apples, figs, and cinnamon. **85** —*S.H. (12/15/2004)*

Pepi 2001 Pinot Grigio (Willamette Valley) $11. Aromas of snap peas and minerals come in front of grapefruit, apple, and lemon flavors. This wine has both a stony, crisp core as well as a plump, chewy texture. The finish is at once tangy and lean, but also fairly driven. Not an easy wine to wrap your arms around and assess, but not bad either. **85** —*M.S. (8/1/2003)*

Pepi 2000 Pinot Grigio (Willamette Valley) $12. This wine is so dry, sharp, and tart, it's like lemon juice. Some will like it, while others more used to ripe, sweet fruit may find it sour. One thing is for sure, it could use some food. One of those wines that's great with shellfish. **84** —*S.H. (8/1/2002)*

Pepi 1998 Colline di Sassi Red Blend (Alexander Valley) $25. This is an elegant wine that will go well on the best tables. It balances plummy, spicy berry fruit and smoky oak with rich tannins and a bite of acidity to create a very dry wine meant for food. It's not a blockbuster and won't win blind tastings, but it's the wine you'll turn to for repeat sips. A blend of Sangiovese, Cabernet Sauvignon, and Merlot. **92 Editors' Choice** —*S.H. (12/15/2001)*

Pepi 2003 Sangiovese (California) $11. This is a generic red wine. It's soft, with berry and coffee flavors and a scour of tannins on the finish, and dryish overall. Versatile with a wide range of things. **84** —*S.H. (6/1/2005)*

Pepi 1999 Sangiovese (California) $14. Blends grapes from the Sierra Foothills and Mendocino to produce a balanced, rich, and harmonious drink with rich flavors of black cherry, tobacco, and spices. In Chianti-like fashion, it's bone dry, light, and delicate of structure, and rather bitter. The color is pale. This is a well-made wine that would be good with a wide variety of foods, especially hard Italian cheeses. **90 Best Buy** —*S.H. (12/1/2002)*

Pepi 1998 Two Heart Sangiovese (California) $14. One of the drier Sangioveses of the year. It comes down firmly on the lean side, and while there are suggestions of black cherry fruit in the aroma, in the mouth it's distinctly acidic, lean and sharp. The struggle to interpret this variety in California continues, but this austere approach will not find favor with consumers. **84** —*S.H. (12/15/2001)*

Pepi 1997 Two Heart Canopy Sangiovese (California) $17. 87 —*S.H. (12/15/1999)*

Pepi 2004 Sauvignon Blanc (California) $9. This wine's a little on the thin side, but for the price, you get some nice fig, lemon, and lime flavors, in a crisp, dryish wine. **84** —*S.H. (11/15/2005)*

Pepi 2003 Sauvignon Blanc (California) $8. A bit aggressive in lemony, gooseberry flavor, but it's clean and tart, and wakes your palate right up. Perfect for seaside snacks, picnics, cocktails. **84 Best Buy** —*S.H. (12/1/2004)*

Pepi 2002 Sauvignon Blanc (California) $13. With its hit of sweetness, this could be almost any varietal, with mango, peach, and lime flavors. Fortunately, there's a spine of crisp acidity that keeps it clean and striking. **85** —*S.H. (2/1/2004)*

Pepi 1999 Two Heart Canopy Sauvignon Blanc (California) $12. Tart and lean, with a low flavor profile but pronounced acidity. They must have picked the grapes very young. You can taste the green lemony flavors, while the wine scours and sears the palate. If you like this style, the wine is a good buy. If you want something fuller, stay away. **84** —*S.H. (12/15/2001)*

Pepi 2000 Two Heart Canopy Sauvignon Blanc (California) $11. A combination of Napa and Lake county grapes, this 100% varietal wine shines with pure aromas of Meyer lemons and cantaloupe. The flavors are similar, packed into a rich, dry, creamy texture. This is a beautiful drinking wine, and an excellent value. **88** —*S.H. (9/1/2003)*

Pepi 2002 Shiraz (California) $8. I was shocked on seeing the price, because this wine is really good. It's far from a blockbuster, but is rich in fruit and spice, with a fine, dry mouthfeel, and minus the grating feeling an inexpensive young Shiraz can have. **86 Best Buy** —*S.H. (12/1/2004)*

PEPPER BRIDGE

Pepper Bridge 2002 Cabernet Sauvignon (Walla Walla (WA)) $50. Fragrant, herbal, and oaky, with light notes of fresh grass and alfalfa coming up into the nose. The fruit is light and lacks density. The winemaking is careful, yet the new oak still outweighs the light fruit, at least for the moment. **87** —*P.G. (6/1/2006)*

Pepper Bridge 2001 Cabernet Sauvignon (Walla Walla (WA)) $50. Good, solid, ripe fruit that shows interesting leather and saddle scents. The wine is concentrated and reasonably long, with new oak flavors of toast and sweet cocoa. Very good winemaking is evident here. **89** —*P.G. (11/15/2004)*

Pepper Bridge 1999 Cabernet Sauvignon (Walla Walla (WA)) $50. Pepper Bridge has supplied fruit too many of Washington State's top wineries, but this is only the second vintage made under their own label. It's a very pretty Cabernet, with soft, ripe fruit tasting of plums and cherries. Fragrant and focused, it shows classy winemaking and a smooth, sophisticated style. **90** —*P.G. (6/1/2002)*

Pepper Bridge 2002 Merlot (Walla Walla (WA)) $45. The winery's oaky-smoky style is well-suited to Merlot in ripe years such as this, and it's a very seductive wine. Nuances of pipe tobacco, dried herb, dust, coffee grounds, and butterscotch complement the strawberry-cherry flavors of Pepper Bridge fruit. Sophisticated and smooth, with plenty of tannic grip. **90** —*P.G. (12/15/2005)*

Pepper Bridge 2001 Merlot (Walla Walla (WA)) $45. The warm, broad, strawberry/cherry flavors of Pepper Bridge fruit are in evidence here. There are also hints of dill and bell pepper, leather, and saddle, and some well-managed herbal notes that add interest and balance. **88** —*P.G. (7/1/2004)*

Pepper Bridge 1999 Merlot (Walla Walla (WA)) $45. Light scents of wild cherry lead into a well-balanced Merlot with an elegant style. Some nice whiffs of mocha augment the medium-weight fruit, and the soft tannins are nicely managed, making this fine for near-term enjoyment. **88** —*P.G. (6/1/2002)*

Pepper Bridge 2003 Seven Hills Vineyard Reserve Red Blend (Walla Walla (WA)) $50. Big, hot, and very liquorous, with definite Bourbon barrel flavors. There's plenty of ripe, full-blown berry-flavored fruit, just this side of jammy, but overall it's a bit of a fruit/oak bomb. **90** —*P.G. (8/1/2006)*

Pepper Bridge 2002 Seven Hills Vineyard Reserve Red Blend (Walla Walla (WA)) $50. It's about 80% Cabernet, 20% Merlot, all from the Seven Hills vineyard. Classy, polished, and nicely balanced, it has plenty of pretty oak, but also some interesting streaks of green coffee and green tea, tobacco, light smoke, and pretty berry fruit, with just a hint of citrus. **90** —*P.G. (12/15/2005)*

PEPPERWOOD GROVE

Pepperwood Grove 1997 Cabernet Franc (California) $7. **85 Best Buy** —*S.H. (7/1/2000)*

Pepperwood Grove 2003 Cabernet Sauvignon (California) $8. This is ripe enough, but tastes too sugary sweet, and has a raw, unfinished edge. **82** —*S.H. (11/15/2005)*

Pepperwood Grove 2002 Cabernet Sauvignon (California) $9. Another great value from this dependable brand. It's rich in ripe black currant, cherry, and cocoa flavors, with smooth, sturdy tannins. **85 Best Buy** —*S.H. (5/1/2005)*

Pepperwood Grove 1998 Chardonnay (California) $7. **84** —*S.H. (5/1/2000)*

Pepperwood Grove 2003 Chardonnay (California) $9. Here's a clean, low oak wine that emphasizes its fresh peach, green apple, and mango flavors. It's dry, with a good grip of acidity. **84** —*S.H. (3/1/2005)*

Pepperwood Grove 2004 Merlot (California) $8. Sometimes all you need in a wine is for it to be dry, fruity, and fun to drink. With a lamb or turkey burger, well-prepared, this is a good companion, jammy and jazzy in fresh cherry and cocoa flavors, with a brisk streak of acids and tannins. **85 Best Buy** —*S.H. (5/1/2006)*

Pepperwood Grove 2003 Merlot (California) $9. Shows the class of a more expensive Merlot in the rich, smooth structure, pure flavors, and overlay of good oak. Finishes sweet with cherries and mocha. **85 Best Buy** —*S.H. (6/1/2005)*

Pepperwood Grove 2001 Merlot (California) $8. So rich in flavor, it's like an orchard meets a candy store. Plums, blackberries, cherries, chocolate, herbs, and spices swim in a richly tannic, dry, and balanced wine. Will go with lots of fare, but try with lamb and rosemary. **88** —*S.H. (3/1/2004)*

Pepperwood Grove 2004 Pinot Grigio (California) $8. This offering from Don Sebastiani & Sons shows why Pinot Grigio is so popular. It shows citrus, peach, and white pepper flavors, accompanied by crisp acids, and finishes a little sweet. Instantly appealing to the palate, it's got a giveaway price. **85 Best Buy** —*S.H. (11/15/2005)*

Pepperwood Grove 1997 Pinot Noir (California) $7. **85** *(5/1/2000)*

Pepperwood Grove 2003 Pinot Noir (California) $9. Easy and enjoyable

Pinot, with real varietal character in the soft, silky texture, crispness, and cherry, cola, cinnamon, and vanilla flavors. **85** —*S.H. (3/1/2005)*

Pepperwood Grove 2002 Pinot Noir (California) $9. Good value in a statewide appellation for the concentrated black cherry, vanilla. and toast flavors and balance. Feels plump and juicy in the mouth, with a delicate structure. **86 Best Buy** *(11/1/2004)*

Pepperwood Grove 2000 Pinot Noir (California) $9. Round, soft, and slightly sweet-tasting, this wine offers a mouthful of vanilla-accented grape and black cherry flavors. Sure it finishes short, but look at the price. **84 Best Buy** *(10/1/2002)*

Pepperwood Grove 2004 Syrah (California) $8. Lots to like in this Syrah with plummy blackberry, cola, dark chocolate, and coffee flavors. It has the sharply acidic jamminess of a youthful wine. **84 Best Buy** —*S.H. (11/15/2006)*

Pepperwood Grove 2002 Syrah (California) $9. Well-ripened, with an almost candied flavor of cherries, raspberries, and peppermint, but it feels dry and crisp. Finishes with a rich, smooth tannic structure. **86 Best Buy** —*S.H. (6/1/2005)*

Pepperwood Grove 2002 Syrah (California) $9. This wine is so stuffed with flavor, it's amazing. The fruits consist of intense cherries, but there's a candied aspect, suggesting vanilla-glazed cinnamon, or oatmeal raisin cookies. Yet it's very dry, and the tannins are rich. A great value in a big, stylish red dinner wine. **89** —*S.H. (6/1/2004)*

Pepperwood Grove 1999 Syrah (California) $7. Some reviewers called the aromas earthy; others called them "wet dog syndrome" and "flea powder." The wine's flavors, though, show that they didn't name this winery Pepperwood Grove for nothing: it's got loads of black pepper, licorice, oak, and espresso flavors. Finishes with requisite black pepper and oak. **83** *(10/1/2001)*

Pepperwood Grove 2005 Viognier (California) $8. Easy and nice, with plenty of tropical fruit and spice flavors wrapped in a crisp package. The peaches, pineapples, and melons linger long into the finish. **84 Best Buy** —*S.H. (12/1/2006)*

Pepperwood Grove 2004 Viognier (California) $8. If you like superfruity Viogniers, you'll love this blast of peaches, papayas, passion fruit, white pepper, and vanilla. It's clean, simple, and refreshing. **84 Best Buy** —*S.H. (11/15/2005)*

Pepperwood Grove 2003 Viognier (California) $9. What a pleasant wine. Fresh and vibrant, with mouth-cleansing acidity backing up ripe flavors of apples, peaches, nectarines, and vanilla honey. Just floods the palate with juicy flavor. **86 Best Buy** —*S.H. (8/1/2005)*

Pepperwood Grove 2002 Viognier (California) $9. A fruity, easy sipper with lots of peach, pear, apricot, and citrus fruit flavors that drink crisp and clean. It's fairly dry, with a ripe, honeyed taste that brings all that fruit together on the finish. **84** —*S.H. (12/31/2003)*

Pepperwood Grove 2001 Viognier (California) $9. Simple and watery, with vaguely fruity flavors of peaches and citrus. Very dry, with adequate acidity. **83** —*S.H. (7/1/2003)*

Pepperwood Grove 1997 Zinfandel (California) $7. **83** —*S.H. (5/1/2000)*

Pepperwood Grove 2004 Zinfandel (California) $8. Easy does it with this simple, jammy Zin. It's full throttle in blackberry, chocolate, and spice flavors, soft, and just a bit sweet. **83** —*S.H. (11/1/2006)*

Pepperwood Grove 2003 Zinfandel (California) $8. If you need a full-bodied red that's clean and inexpensive, this is a good bet. It's a rustic wine, but dry, with fruity charm and a good bite of tannins to cut through a Philly cheesesteak. **84** —*S.H. (11/15/2005)*

Pepperwood Grove 1999 California Cuvée Zinfandel (California) $7. Garden-fresh vegetables, oak, and red berry fruit give way to bouncy, easy red-plum fruit and a finish that adds oak to the fruity mix. A good grocery-store pick. **83** —*D.T. (3/1/2002)*

PER SEMPRE

Per Sempre 1997 Select Reserve Cabernet Sauvignon (Napa Valley) $66. **91** *(11/1/2000)*

Per Sempre 1999 The Lisa Shiraz (Napa Valley) $60. This offers a lot, maybe too much, of everything—supermature pruney fruit, tons of smoky oak, and a jammy mouthfeel. It's fat, and closes long with dense fruit and black pepper accents. It's also over the top—overripe, highly extracted, densely wooded; if you love that style, you'll enjoy this much more than our tasters did. This has potential as a Port, though, consumed at the end of a meal with cheeses and nuts. **85** *(11/1/2001)*

Per Sempre 1998 Wirth Ranch Vineyard Zinfandel (Solano County) $30. This attractive wine opens with a nicely nuanced bouquet of berry, spice, and earth accented by positive gamy and slightly barnyardy notes. The textured palate offers attractive dark fruit and a touch of tar and licorice. Ends with an even, dry, long finish of pepper, earth, and leather. **87** *(3/1/2001)*

PERALTA

Peralta 2001 Cabernet Sauvignon (Central Coast) $10. A nice, juicy Cab with pretty berry-cherry flavors and sweet tannins. It's dry and balanced and a good value. Primarily Paso Robles. **84** —*S.H. (10/1/2004)*

Peralta 2002 Chardonnay (Santa Barbara County) $10. This serviceable Chard has some good fruity, vanilla, and spice flavors and a touch of oak. With its creamy texture, it's a nice value. **84** —*S.H. (12/1/2004)*

Peralta 2003 Sauvignon Blanc (Paso Robles) $8. Thin and bizarre, with vegetal flavors. Avoid. **81** —*S.H. (12/1/2004)*

Peralta 2001 Syrah (California) $8. Sure it's fruity and simple. But it's also cleanly made and easy to drink. Has a fair amount of oak for a wine at this price point—caramel and vanilla notes accent the tannic cherry fruit. **85 Best Buy** *(9/1/2005)*

PERBACCO CELLARS

Perbacco Cellars 2003 Chardonnay (Edna Valley) $22. At three years, this Chard is losing some freshness, and is picking up a dried peach and apricot flavor. It's also softening, which emphasizes the creaminess. It's best to pop the cork on this dry wine now. **85** —*S.H. (10/1/2006)*

Perbacco Cellars 2001 Chardonnay (Edna Valley) $20. Unripe, with vegetal aromas and weak fruity flavors. Also overoaked. **82** —*S.H. (6/1/2005)*

Perbacco Cellars 2000 La Linda Vineyard Chardonnay (Edna Valley) $18. A fresh, lively Chardonnay, filled with juicy flavors of lemons and peaches, enriched by toasty oak and a creamy texture. Long finish. **90 Editors' Choice** —*S.H. (5/1/2003)*

Perbacco Cellars 2005 Laetitia Vineyard Pinot Grigio (Arroyo Grande Valley) $19. PG needs a cool climate to preserve all-important acidity, and this outstanding vineyard, in sight of the chilly Pacific, certainly is cool. The wine is well-structured, with high, biting acidity that frames citrus, peach, and apple flavors. No oak here, just fruit. **87** —*S.H. (12/31/2006)*

Perbacco Cellars 2004 Laetitia Vineyard Pinot Grigio (Arroyo Grande Valley) $18. The vineyard is one of the coolest in California, and that maritime influence shows in the intense, citrusy acidity that really perks up the palate. The flavors are also intense, suggesting Meyer lemon sorbet drizzled with vanilla and a hint of butterscotch. For all that, the wine is totally dry. This is one of the best California PGs of the vintage. **90 Editors' Choice** —*S.H. (10/1/2006)*

Perbacco Cellars 2004 Laetitia Vineyard Pinot Grigio (Arroyo Grande Valley) $14. Brilliantly tart in acids and perfectly dry, this top-flight Pinot Grigio boasts citrus and passion fruit flavors. Truly a fine PG, with the weight and complexity of a fine Fumé Blanc. **90 Best Buy** —*S.H. (2/1/2006)*

Perbacco Cellars 2004 Pinot Noir (Arroyo Grande Valley) $28. Made in a very ripe, almost late-picked style, this Pinot has sweetened coffee, rosehip tea, and blackberry pie filling flavors with an edge of rum-soaked raisins. It's a bit heavy for a Pinot Noir, but very clean and dry, and will do well with a big steak. **84** —*S.H. (11/1/2006)*

Perbacco Cellars 2002 Pinot Noir (Arroyo Grande Valley) $25. Very soft, smooth and rather thick, this is one of those Pinots that flatters with scads of ripe fruit and toasty oak. It's certainly delicious in cherry, cocoa, and spice, but has a certain one dimensionality. **87** —*S.H. (6/1/2005)*

Perbacco Cellars 2003 Dionysus Pinot Noir (Arroyo Grande Valley) $45. Although it's in the same style as the winery's '04 regular Pinot, this is far more sophisticated. It's a big, big wine, very ripe, with strong black cher-

ry pie, cola, chocolate, and rum-drizzled raisin flavors. It has an essential balance and harmony that lend it panache. **90** —*S.H. (11/1/2006)*

PEREGRINE HILL

Peregrine Hill 2003 Cabernet Sauvignon (Texas) $8. Already shows some bricking at the rim, so best to drink this up in the next few months. Dried fruit notes are not unappealing and there are some pleasant meaty, soy-sauce elements as well. **83** —*J.C. (9/1/2005)*

PERFECT 10

Perfect 10 2003 Blonde Chardonnay (Monterey) $10. Good melon, apple, and vanilla aromas precede honey, vanilla, and spice flavors. It's sweet, ripe, and easy to drink, with touches of wood and marshmallow. Where this concept wine scores best is on the tongue: It has generous acidity and enough body to ensure balance. **85 Best Buy** —*M.S. (11/1/2005)*

PERRY CREEK

Perry Creek 1996 Cabernet Sauvignon (El Dorado) $12. 88 —*S.H. (7/1/1999)*

Perry Creek 1999 Estate Bottled Cabernet Sauvignon (El Dorado) $14. It's ripely assertive, with blackberry flavors. What makes it only acceptable is awkwardness everyplace else. The texture is syrupy, and while it's bone dry, it has a cough mediciney flavor. The tannins are rugged and palate-scouring. **82** —*S.H. (11/15/2002)*

Perry Creek 1999 Estate Bottled Cellar Select Cabernet Sauvignon (El Dorado County) $28. Not offering a lot now, with rough-hewn, earthy aromas that verge on vegetal, and thin blackberry flavors. Tannins are pretty nice and the wine has a smooth texture that makes up for the lack of richness. **84** —*S.H. (12/15/2003)*

Perry Creek 2002 Chardonnay (El Dorado) $14. An everyday Chard, with pleasant peach and apple flavors and a bit of oak. Dry and crisp in acids, and easy to drink. **84** —*S.H. (10/1/2004)*

Perry Creek 2001 Chardonnay (El Dorado County) $14. Ripely fruity, with sun-warmed flavors of white peach and nectarine. Acids are fine, and boost the structure. There's also a subtle overlay of oak that adds to the tastes. **86** —*S.H. (8/1/2003)*

Perry Creek 2000 Estate Bottled Merlot (El Dorado) $12. There's pretty blackberry fruit, and some notes of raisins and prunes. This big, rich, and slightly sweet mountain wine from a hot wine region is rustic, honest and, in its own way, likeable. **85** —*S.H. (11/15/2002)*

Perry Creek 1999 Mourvèdre (El Dorado) $16. Generic red wine, with indistinct although ripe berry fruit, smooth tannins, and bright acidity. Drinks rough at the edges, and is very dry, yet clean. **84** —*S.H. (9/1/2002)*

Perry Creek 2003 Estate Bottled Muscat Canelli (El Dorado) $10. A slightly sweet wine with pleasant peach and apricot flavors and refreshing acidity. Low in alcohol, too. **84** —*S.H. (10/1/2004)*

Perry Creek 2000 Cellar Select Petite Sirah (El Dorado) $28. Extremely oaky in new wood, with strong smoky-vanilla notes covering up young, fresh, jammy flavors of blackberry and plum. The tannins are strong, but the wine lacks substance in the middle, and finishes thin. **84** *(4/1/2003)*

Perry Creek 1996 Syrah (El Dorado) $15. 90 —*S.H. (10/1/1999)*

Perry Creek 2002 Syrah (El Dorado) $15. Broad and mouthfilling but lacking depth and complexity, this Syrah offers black cherry and vanilla flavors that turn tough and tannic on the finish. **83** *(9/1/2005)*

Perry Creek 1999 Syrah (El Dorado) $16. Pretty tannic stuff. Dark, inky color, with dense aromas of plums, blackberries, and chocolate. Good dark stone fruit and berry flavors, completely dry, and a little soft on acid, but those tough, gritty tannins call for cheese to bring out sweetness. **85** —*S.H. (6/1/2003)*

Perry Creek 1999 Cellar Select Syrah (El Dorado) $24. Boasts bacon and pepper aromas, along with toast and mixed berries. Rich and chewy on the palate, its dense flavors include hints of blackberries, fruitcake, and chocolate. The flavors and texture are a bit Port-like (but dry) and finish long and tart, with masses of soft, ripe tannins. Hold 2–3 years and drink through 2010. Top Value. **90** *(11/1/2001)*

Perry Creek 1998 Estate Bottled Syrah (El Dorado) $16. A chalky element provides character and offsets this wine's ripe, but not overly sweet, black cherry fruit here. There's a green herb presence, too, that some tasters found very attractive, others less so. This shows some structure and could evolve over a year or two. Closes long with cocoa, oak and a reprise of the chalk note. **85** *(10/1/2001)*

Perry Creek 2000 Estate Bottled Cellar Select Syrah (El Dorado County) $28. Juicy flavors of cherry and blackberry wrapped in soft, elegant tannins and a coat of smoky oak. Drinks dry and stylish, in the modern way, and would be better if it had more depth. **85** *—S.H. (12/15/2003)*

Perry Creek 2002 Wild Turkey Ridge Cellar Select Syrah (El Dorado) $28. Another love-it-or-hate-it wine that ended up with a mid-80s score. Supporters touted the wine's blackberry and blueberry fruit and richly textured tannins that should allow the wine to improve with age, while detractors focused on candied fruit and a finish they found short. **85** *(9/1/2005)*

Perry Creek 2002 Viognier (El Dorado) $18. The flavors star here, with an ensemble of fresh peach, pear, apple, honeysuckle, spice, and vanilla, and a long, ripe finish. But the wine is basically dry. **84** *—S.H. (10/1/2004)*

Perry Creek 2000 Viognier (El Dorado) $16. 86 *—S.H. (12/15/2002)*

Perry Creek 1999 Viognier (El Dorado) $16. Packs a punch with peach, honey, and wildflower aromas and flavors, as well as various spice and vanilla. It's smoothly textured, with good acids and a sprightly mouthfeel, and finishes long and sweetly ripe. **84** *—S.H. (12/15/2001)*

Perry Creek 2001 Estate Bottled Viognier (El Dorado) $16. An odd wine. Has strong and simple aromas of tobacco, ripe peaches, mandarin oranges, and toast, and is fairly sweet and heavy, with Lifesaver candy flavors. **83** *—S.H. (12/15/2002)*

Perry Creek 2002 La Vie Sur Mars White Blend (El Dorado) $16. Clean, crisp and with a swift finish, this wine has flavors of citrus fruits and peaches. It's very dry. A blend of Viognier and Marsanne. **84** *—S.H. (12/15/2004)*

Perry Creek 2001 Zinfandel (El Dorado) $12. Pretty plum and cherry flavors are at the center of this wine. The tannins are smooth and supple, while the finish is moderate in length, showing hints of coffee and spice. **87** *(11/1/2003)*

Perry Creek 2000 Cellar Select Zinfandel (El Dorado) $24. Enormously high in alcohol, nearly 16%, which is the cost of fully fermenting the wine to dryness. Heat buries the wild berry flavors, and the finish picks up a hint of raisins. If you like this style, you'll like this wine. **84** *—S.H. (11/1/2002)*

Perry Creek 2000 Cellar Select Spanish Creek Ranch Zinfandel (El Dorado) $24. Sweet aromas of berry jam and white pepper. In the mouth, it's extracted and jammy, with rich berry flavors. It also has soft acids and tannins, with some residual sugar. Extremely high alcohol makes it hot. You either like this approach, or you don't. **84** *—S.H. (11/1/2002)*

Perry Creek 2004 Cellar Select Potter Vineyards Zinfandel (Amador County) $28. Smells caramelly and Porty, then tastes sweet and hot, with a sugary, blackberry jam finish. Some will like this style. **82** *—S.H. (12/1/2006)*

Perry Creek 2001 Spanish Creek Ranch Zinfandel (El Dorado) $24. A full-bodied wine, framed in impressive tannins that lean a bit toward astringency. Flavors are blackberry and plum, with hints of toast and spice. A bit short on the finish. **86** *(11/1/2003)*

Perry Creek 2004 Zin Man Zinfandel (Sierra Foothills) $14. This is a good, country-style Zin: clean, dry, and balanced. It has flavors of blackberries, root beer, and pepper, while the mouthfeel is silkily tannic. It's a wine to drink with food and not fuss over. **85** *—S.H. (12/1/2006)*

Perry Creek 2001 Zin Man Zinfandel (Sierra Foothills) $12. A blend of floral notes and charry, smoky qualities. The blackberry, cassis, and licorice flavors take a backseat but are in evidence nonetheless. **84** *(11/1/2003)*

Perry Creek 2000 Zin Man Zinfandel (Sierra Foothills) $12. A wine like this makes me sad. Blessed by nature with the ability to ripen Zinfandel to perfection in this warm region, the winemaking is, let us say honestly, imperfect. The wine is syrupy sweet and cloying. The acids are much too low. And 15.5% alcohol makes for a hot mouthfeel with nothing to balance it out. **82** *—S.H. (11/1/2002)*

Perry Creek 1998 Zin Man Zinfandel (Sierra Foothills) $12. A peppery

nose, tart wine, with plenty of acid, perhaps too much acid. The mouthfeel is awkward, unbalanced, and the finish is odd. It tastes over-manipulated. **83** *—P.G. (3/1/2001)*

Perry Creek 1997 Zin Man Zinfandel (Sierra Foothills) $12. 88 Best Buy — *S.H. (9/1/1999)*

PESSAGNO

Pessagno 2001 Sleepy Hollow Vineyard Chardonnay (Santa Lucia Highlands) $25. Fresh honey, peach, toast, mineral, cinnamon, spice, and herb notes give pleasing complexity to this elegant wine. It's packed with flavor, richly textured, yet bright and firm on the finish, which ends with a refreshing citrus note. Great price for a wine of this quality. **93 Editors' Choice** *—J.M. (6/1/2004)*

Pessagno 2000 Sleepy Hollow Vineyard Chardonnay (Santa Lucia Highlands) $30. Fragrant, with hints of butterscotch, vanilla, ginger, and spice. Also richly textured, with pear, peach, apple, orange, and more spice flavors. It finishes clean and long, with a lemony edge. **92** *—J.M. (5/1/2003)*

Pessagno 1999 Sleepy Hollow Vineyard Chardonnay (Santa Lucia Highlands) $35. Gloriously rich on the nose, with toasty butterscotch, spice and hazelnut nuances. Bright fruit on the palate weaves a classy flavor profile of pear, apple, citrus, and herb. Sleek and long on the finish, the wine is an auspicious first release from veteran Monterey winemaker Steve Pessagno. **92** *—J.M. (12/1/2001)*

Pessagno 2001 Central Avenue Vineyard Pinot Noir (Monterey) $18. Aromatic, soft, and delicate, a silky, lean wine with flavors of herbal tea, cola, root beer, and vanilla. Pretty and punchy, with zesty Monterey acids. Finishes a little short. **87** *—S.H. (12/15/2004)*

Pessagno 2000 Central Avenue Vineyard Pinot Noir (Monterey) $25. Light and slightly creamy, this opens with candied cherries, tea, and rhubarb aromas. It picks up earth, cinnamon, and caramel accents on the palate. Though it aims for elegance, it remains a bit too ethereal. **85** *(10/1/2002)*

Pessagno 1999 Central Avenue Vineyard Pinot Noir (Monterey) $65. Smooth and lush, with toasty oak, cherry, and herb flavors. This robust wine has plenty of complexity, although it's still quite young and tight, with firm, ripe tannins framing the ensemble. A good candidate for the cellar, this first release is a fine addition to Monterey's arsenal of Pinot Noirs. **90** *—J.M. (12/15/2001)*

Pessagno 2001 Gary's Vineyard Pinot Noir (Santa Lucia Highlands) $50. Smooth textured, yet with a pleasing bright, spicy edge. The wine shows a complex blend of bing cherry, plum, pepper, spice, coffee, earth, and anise flavors. Soft tannins give it a round mouthfeel. The finish is long and bright. **92** *—J.M. (6/1/2004)*

Pessagno 2000 Gary's Vineyard Pinot Noir (Santa Lucia Highlands) $55. Intense black raspberry aromas with nuances of tea, leather, and rubber get the game rolling, and phase two is a palate loaded with pure, enveloping black cherry fruit. Even at 14.6% alcohol, vital acidity keeps the balance proper. **93 Editors' Choice** *(10/1/2002)*

Pessagno 1999 Gary's Vineyard Pinot Noir (Santa Lucia Highlands) $50. Vividly ripe, sweet fruit here, with a powerful core of spice, wild cherry, and cinnamon. Firm tannins give it good structure, while the finish is long and clean. Drinking well now, but should age nicely over the next 5 to 10 years. **92** *—J.M. (12/15/2001)*

Pessagno 2000 Spring Grove Vineyard Pinot Noir (San Benito County) $28. Opening with a light stewed berry, tea, and mushroom nose, this entry from Monterey veteran Steve Pessagno has tasty elements but is shy on substance. Boasts interesting cola, herb, and caramel accents and lively fruit-acid balance, but could use more meat on its bones as a stronger platform for the flavors. **84** *(10/1/2002)*

Pessagno 2001 Spring Grove Vineyards Pinot Noir (San Benito County) $25. Fresh and refined, with a fine-tuned core of cherry, spice, cola, leather, herb, and earth flavors. The wine is smooth textured and elegant, serving up a long, silky finish. Classy Pinot from the Central Coast. **90** *—J.M. (6/1/2004)*

Pessagno 2000 Hames Valley Vineyard Port (Monterey) $33. A lush, rich Port with a smooth texture and flavors that range from black cherry, blackberry, cassis, cinnamon, anise, chocolate, toffee, butterscotch, and thyme. It's complex yet delightfully easy to drink. **92** —*J.M. (6/1/2004)*

Pessagno 2001 Idyll Times Vineyard Zinfandel (San Benito County) $21. Quite bright and spicy, with briary black cherry, blackberry, plum, tobacco, fig, vanilla, and toast notes. Zippy, fresh, and fullblown. It's bright and fresh until the end. **89** —*J.M. (11/1/2003)*

Pessagno 2000 Idyll Times Vineyard Zinfandel (San Benito County) $21. Fresh, bright plummy fruit aromas lead off. On the palate, the wine is smooth-textured and also spicy and round. Pretty hints of thyme and sage offset ripe cherry and raspberry notes. **89** —*J.M. (11/1/2002)*

PETER MCCOY

Peter McCoy 1997 Clos des Pierres Reserve Chardonnay (Knights Valley) $45. There's still a good and pleasant dose of pineapple and apple fruit accented by vanilla spice in this wine, but a mature and overly soft palate-feel suggests that it's best consumed near-term. Finishes smooth and light, with medium length. Drink up this year. **85** *(7/1/2001)*

PETER MICHAEL WINERY

Peter Michael Winery 2003 Les Pavots Cabernet Blend (Knights Valley) $150. Tannic and closed to the point of inaccessibility, this Cab-based blend, which contains Cabernet Franc, Merlot, and Petit Verdot, comes from low-yielding vines grown 1,700 feet above Knights Valley. It all comes down to a question of ageability. The answer is it will age quite nicely. The balance is superb, and the core of fruit is there. Do not open this wine until 2010; it should continue to develop for another 10 years at least. **93 Cellar Selection** —*S.H. (9/1/2006)*

Peter Michael Winery 2000 Les Pavots Cabernet Blend (Knights Valley) $110. A well-ripened, opulent wine; it's huge in black currant and cassis flavors and elaborate oak. You can taste the barrels in the smoke, vanilla, and spicy flavors. Acidity hasn't been integrated yet, nor have the dusty tannins. It's really good now, but is best left to soften and integrate through 2008. **93** —*S.H. (5/1/2004)*

Peter Michael Winery 2001 Belle Cote Chardonnay (Sonoma County) $60. This opulent, all-too-drinkable wine offers powerful aromas and flavors of ripe Bosc pears that are liberally oaked. It is a big, muscular wine, with a rich texture of buttery cream and fine lees, and a tight spine of acidity. Will hold in your cellar for many years, but it's superb now. **92** —*S.H. (2/1/2004)*

Peter Michael Winery 1999 Belle Côte Chardonnay (Sonoma County) $60. In this fine offering from one of this tasting's most consistent performers, a nutty, pineapple-ginger nose opens to a lively mouth of citrus, hazelnut, and spice. The feel is firm, elegant. This handsomely constructed wine finishes long with subtle white peach notes, with dashes of tangy spice and chalk. **90** *(7/1/2001)*

Peter Michael Winery 1999 Cuvée Indigene Chardonnay (Sonoma County) $85. The flagship of the Peter Michael Chardonnays is a stylish, sexy wine. Opens with a wonderful nose of peach, tropical fruit, nuts, and orange tea; it shows great poise and a classic sense of proportion from bouquet to finish. The wine unfolds and expands in the glass, offering lovely orange, mineral, and tarragon flavors. The engaging finish has great length and subtle aromas and flavors. Impressive for its restraint and attention to detail, this is delicious now but will also reward keeping. **92 Cellar Selection** *(7/1/2001)*

Peter Michael Winery 2001 La Carriere Chardonnay (Sonoma County) $60. This most complete of Sir Peter's Chardonnays combines exquisite acidity with opulence. It is a fresh, young wine, a bit sharp in its bite, but packed with lime, peach, and pear flavors that also possess a flinty, mineral edge. The finish is long, spicy, and impressive. As good as it is now, its precocity suggests aging through 2010. **93** —*S.H. (2/1/2004)*

Peter Michael Winery 1999 La Carriere Chardonnay (Sonoma County) $60. Fine flavor definition and very good acidity. Citrus, apple, and herb aromas sing on the nose. Round apple, anise, and pineapple show on the velvety palate. The wine finishes with a pretty melding of pineapple and vanilla, like an elegant tropical creamsicle. Enticing, but still tight enough to warrant holding it for a year or two. **90** *(7/1/2001)*

Peter Michael Winery 2002 Ma Belle-Fille Chardonnay (Sonoma County) $75. From vineyards 1,900 feet up in the Mayacamas, a heavyweight Chard. The parts haven't knit together yet, but when they do, look out. Ripe pears and apricots, mangoes, and vanilla, all drip with honey, in a

creamy, soft texture. It has a long, dusty spice finish. Start drinking at the end of this year. **93** —*S.H. (5/1/2005)*

Peter Michael Winery 2001 Mon Plaisir Chardonnay (Sonoma County) $60. Rich and tart, a spice-packed wine brimming with flavors of pears and tropical fruits that are tightly wound around a core of fresh young acids. The oak has been lavishly applied. Fine now, but will benefit from a few years of age. **91** —*S.H. (2/1/2004)*

Peter Michael Winery 1999 Mon Plaisir Chardonnay (Sonoma County) $60. A tart pineapple-lemon nose with caramel and smoke accents ushers in a full palate. Apple and pear flavors add body, and a chalky note contributes complexity and texture to the palate. Slight creaminess provides a fat, full feel, but maybe just a bit more softness than some tasters preferred. Still, this is a solid wine with finesse and body. It displays both smoky toast and bright orange-lemon notes on the finish. **90** *(7/1/2001)*

Peter Michael Winery 2001 L'Apres Midi Sauvignon Blanc (Sonoma County) $38. Apple, citrus, and peach flavors commingle in this dry, pretty wine. It has crisp acidity and a nice overlay of oak that adds buttery, smoky, vanilla notes. Best now through 2004. **86** —*S.H. (2/1/2004)*

Peter Michael Winery 2004 L'Apres-Midi Sauvignon Blanc (Knights Valley) $42. As rich as a Chardonnay, yet with Sauvignon's distinctive savory profile, this is great wine. From low-yielding mountain vineyards, the juice was barrel-fermented and aged sur lies, but no malolactic fermentation was permitted. Few Sauvignons in California achieve this level of complexity. The lush, roasted nuts, with a firm, hard minerality throughout. **94 Editors' Choice** —*S.H. (8/1/2006)*

Peter Michael Winery 2003 L'Apres Midi Sauvignon Blanc (Sonoma County) $42. Largely clean, but big-boned and a bit hot. This wines pumps a ton of flavor, which if you like loud, heavy citrus and stone fruits is a good sign. But it's also a touch sticky and grabby. While we liked the wine, we can see others either loving or leaving it. **86** *(7/1/2005)*

PETER PAUL WINES

Peter Paul Wines 2001 Merlot (Napa Valley) $39. Rich, semi-sweet, and heavy, this wine opens with a swampy undertow that competes with the blackberries. Tastes pretty good, though, with ripe berries, cherries, and spices. **84** —*S.H. (10/1/2005)*

PETERS FAMILY

Peters Family 2002 Meritage Cabernet Blend (California) $25. Despite the statewide appellation, this delightful Cab blend shows complexity and finesse. It's big and deep in cassis and blackberry fruit, with a rich overlay of oak, but never loses balance, with a nice tension of acidity and tannins. Best now through 2006. **91** —*S.H. (12/1/2005)*

Peters Family 2002 Gardner Vineyard Cabernet Sauvignon (Sierra Foothills) $34. It's bizarre that this Cab is so much more expensive than Peters' '02 Meritage, which was released at the same time. This isn't nearly as fine. It's rustic and soft, with an edgy mouthfeel. **84** —*S.H. (12/1/2005)*

Peters Family 2001 Gardner Vineyard Cabernet Sauvignon (Sierra Foothills) $40. Nice and ripe, this Cab moves beyond blackberries into lusher cassis and currant notes, with a cedary, spicy edge. It's very dry and balanced in acids, and is soft and creamy in the mouth. Drink now. **86** —*S.H. (10/1/2004)*

Peters Family 2004 Sangiacomo Vineyard Chardonnay (Carneros) $36. This is a lovely Chardonnay, delicately structured, elegantly silky, crisp and authoritative. It doesn't whack you with fruit, but presents subtle peach custard, buttercream, and citrus flavors girded with a hard minerality. Quite a bit of new oak adds complexity. This is a good Chard for foodies who shy away from the fruit bombs. **91** —*S.H. (11/15/2006)*

Peters Family 2003 Sangiacomo Vineyard Chardonnay (Carneros) $30. Richer than the '02, this single-vineyard Chard is crisp and bright in acidic structure, with oak and lees to add complexity. The underlying flavors suggest citrus fruits, peaches, pears, apricots, and mangoes. **90** —*S.H. (12/1/2005)*

Peters Family 2002 Sangiacomo Vineyard Chardonnay (Carneros) $32. Brimming with zesty, citrusy acidity, this Chard is bright and a bit earthy. The underlying flavors of limes and apples are sweetened with toasty oak. Finishes spicy and long. **88** —*S.H. (12/15/2004)*

Peters Family 2001 Meritage (California) $25. Lots of class and distinction in this dry Bordeaux blend. It has aromas of cassis and smoky oak, with currant, cherry, and herb flavors. The tannins are soft and complex. **88** —*S.H. (10/1/2004)*

Peters Family 2004 Dunah Vineyard Pinot Noir (Sonoma Coast) $42. I haven't cared for this winery's Bordeaux wines, but with the Burgundians they're hitting pay dirt. This Dijon-clone Pinot is an excellent dry, silky wine with complex flavors of cherries, black raspberries, cola, licorice candy, and cinnamon spice. Unfiltered and well oaked, the wine offers something new and interesting with every sniff and sip. **92** —*S.H. (11/15/2006)*

Peters Family 2002 Clements Ridge Vineyard Syrah (Lodi) $25. There's a baked, raisiny edge to this wine that detracts, like a bit of burnt crust on an otherwise tasty fruit tart. Good, rich fare might minimize it and accentuate the appealing cherry flavors and rich tannic structure. **85** —*S.H. (12/1/2005)*

PETERSON

Peterson 1998 Agraria Big Barn Red Cabernet Blend (Dry Creek Valley) $52. An intense wine, with cassis flavors wrapped in rich tannins and oak. Smooth and velvety, but turns bitter and simple on the finish, with an herbal, coffee note. **86** —*S.H. (5/1/2003)*

Peterson 1999 Bradford Mountain Cabernet Sauvignon (Dry Creek Valley) $28. Here's a young Cabernet with lots going for it, in the mélange of berry and earth flavors and nice structure. Tannins are firm and fine, and the overlay of smoky oak fits like a glove. Pleasant now, but those tannins suggest rich, well-marbled meat. **89** —*S.H. (6/1/2003)*

Peterson 2000 Bradford Mountain Vineyard Cabernet Sauvignon (Dry Creek Valley) $29. Very tannic; puckers the palate and leaves it dry and brisk. There is a stream of plummy blackberry fruit but it doesn't seem rich enough to warrant aging. Drink soon. **85** —*S.H. (10/1/2004)*

Peterson 1999 Merlot (Dry Creek Valley) $24. From this well-regarded Sonoma County appellation, a ripely fruity wine, brimming with plum, blackberry, tobacco, and spice aromas and flavors. It's rich, but balanced by finely intricate tannins and very nice acids. There's a harmony and balance that make it fun to drink. **90** —*S.H. (7/1/2002)*

Peterson 1999 Floodgate Vineyard Pinot Noir (Anderson Valley) $28. There's nothing delicate about the massive flavor explosion, with mingled notes of raspberries, cherries, and blackberries, with peppery, gingery spices. It's big, bold and brassy, but the tannins are light and silky, which makes it float on the palate despite the fruit. **88** —*S.H. (7/1/2002)*

Peterson 1997 Zinfandel (Dry Creek Valley) $18. 82 —*P.G. (11/15/1999)*

Peterson 1998 Zinfandel (Dry Creek Valley) $18. There's a lively gaminess to the nose; a wild, Rhônish note, perhaps from the Carignane, Mourvèdre, and Petit Sirah blended in. This wine is front-loaded: the flavors lighten up on the palate, and the finish is tight and tannic. **87** —*P.G. (3/1/2001)*

Peterson 2000 Bradford Mountain Zinfandel (Dry Creek Valley) $25. A tasty, juicy Zin whose wild berry, cola, coffee, pepper, and spice flavors are wrapped in rich, sturdy but soft tannins. A little hollow in the middle, though. **85** —*S.H. (10/1/2004)*

Peterson 1997 Bradford Mountain Zinfandel (Dry Creek Valley) $21. Firm, ripe, and fruity, with a nice mix of plums, berries, and earth. The mountain fruit shows good acids, some mineral elements, and a long, complex finish with a fair amount of earth and barnyard. A distinctive, earthy style. **91 Editors' Choice** —*P.G. (3/1/2001)*

PETRONI

Petroni 2000 Cabernet Sauvignon (Sonoma Valley) $55. Very oaky, rather under-fruited, and tannic, this is a tough wine that calls for rich meats and fowl. Finishes scouringly dry and tannic. **84** —*S.H. (12/31/2004)*

Petroni 2000 Poggio Alla Pietra Sangiovese (Sonoma Valley) $55. Extremely dry, rather rugged in tannins, and with unresolved acids, this is a tough wine softened just a bit with a streak of ripe cherry fruit. Will be fine with cheese and tomato sauce. **84** —*S.H. (12/31/2004)*

PEZZI KING

Pezzi King 2000 Cabernet Sauvignon (Sonoma County) $25. There's a wild, brambly note to the blackberry flavors, and a rich streak of cherry-

chocolate candy in the middle palate. It's a little unusual, but there's no denying the deliciousness and class of this wine. **89** —*S.H. (6/1/2004)*

Pezzi King 1998 Chardonnay (Sonoma County) $17. 86 *(6/1/2000)*

Pezzi King 1997 Susie's Reserve Merlot (Dry Creek Valley) $26. 91 *(3/1/2000)*

Pezzi King 2000 Pinot Noir (Russian River Valley) $30. If you enjoy your cherry fruit on the tart side, served on a plank of cedar, then this wine is for you. So call us beavers—we fell for the smooth, toasty aromas. Lean, lemony flavors and hints of black tea and root beer keep the wine interesting. **88** *(10/1/2002)*

Pezzi King 1999 Pinot Noir (Russian River Valley) $30. Leather and rubber aromas, with a touch of green mixing in with strawberries and cream. The palate is full of foresty flavors, most of all oak, but also cola, vanilla, and sweet, ripe, red fruit. With a wall of firm tannins in support, this has good balance and just the right body. **87** *(10/1/2002)*

Pezzi King 2003 Jane's Reserve Sauvignon Blanc (Mendocino County) $27. Lemon is the dominant character of the nose. Flavors of buttery vanilla, likely derived from oak, soften the citrus flavors. On the finish, it's long and citrusy, and here a swath of oak comes on adding cinnamon and spice flavors. **87** *(7/1/2005)*

Pezzi King 1999 Syrah (Dry Creek Valley) $27. One reviewer called this Syrah's bright berry, leather, and milk chocolate aromas "Zin-like"— imagine how pleased he was with himself to find that this Syrah is made by a winery famous for its Zinfandels. A creamy mouthfeel full of cherry, blueberry, licorice, and oak—plus a juicy, medium-long finish—make this a good choice for near-term enjoyment. **87** *(11/1/2001)*

Pezzi King 1997 Estate Zinfandel (Dry Creek Valley) $26. 87 —*P.G. (11/15/1999)*

Pezzi King 2001 Old Vines Zinfandel (Dry Creek Valley) $25. A smoky, fruity style with soft tannins that frame plum, black cherry, herb, and earth tones. Finishes with moderate length. **87** —*J.M. (8/1/2004)*

Pezzi King 2000 Old Vines Zinfandel (Dry Creek Valley) $25. Bright and effusive, with lots of ripe cherry, raspberry, plum, and blackberry flavors. Spice and herbs and interest to the blend, which is framed in ripe, firm tannins and shows a hint of vanilla and toast. Finishes with moderate length. **88** —*J.M. (6/11/2004)*

Pezzi King 1997 SLR Zinfandel (Dry Creek Valley) $24. 88 —*P.G. (11/15/1999)*

PHEASANT VALLEY

Pheasant Valley 2003 Celilo Vineyard Chardonnay (Washington) $15. Fruit from one of the top two or three Chardonnay vineyards in Washington shows its crisp green-apple spine with plenty of toasty oak to add spice. Somehow manages to be both firm and fleshy at once. **90** —*P.G. (6/1/2005)*

PHELAN VINEYARD

Phelan Vineyard 2000 Cabernet Sauvignon (Napa Valley) $75. Rich and bright, with heady aromas of tea, spice, smoke, vanilla, toast, plum, and herb. The wine is smooth, rich, sleek, and plush on the palate, with pretty plum, black cherry, tar, coffee, and more spice flavors. The finish is long. A first release from this new producer. **91** —*J.M. (12/15/2003)*

PHILIP STALEY

Philip Staley 1999 Chardonnay (Russian River Valley) $15. If the grapes were any riper, they'd be doing chin-ups in the glass. A blast of pungent peach, green apple, and cantaloupe notes is accented by new oak. That power carries over to the flavors. It might almost be too ripe for food. Definitely in the California style, like it or not. **87** —*S.H. (5/1/2001)*

Philip Staley 2000 Staley Vineyard Grenache (Russian River Valley) $18. This winery specializes in Rhône-style wines from a warmer, northeastern part of Russian River Valley, almost in Dry Creek. This is a light red, fruity wine with a minty streak, soft tannins, and excellent acidity. It's light but firm, and impressive for the interest it arouses even though it's not a blockbuster. **88** —*S.H. (12/1/2002)*

Philip Staley 1999 Staley Vineyard Grenache (Russian River Valley) $18. Normally used as a blending grape in California, sometimes Grenache is good enough to stand on its own. This one is, with its black cherry, spice, and tobacco aromas and flavors and dry, lacy tannins. It's a soft, young wine, with plenty of jammy character. **89** —*S.H. (7/1/2002)*

Philip Staley 1996 Staley Vineyard Grenache (Russian River Valley) $13. **89** —*L.W. (6/1/1999)*

Philip Staley 1998 Mourvèdre (Russian River Valley) $16. Sprightly and light, this is a feathery wine on the palate, with soft acids and gentle tannins, although the fruit is pure California. Raspberry, tobacco, blackberry, and cinnamon flavors fill the mouth and are delicious to savor. It's very dry and stylish, with a fruity, Lifesaver finish. **87** —*S.H. (7/1/2002)*

Philip Staley 1995 Staley Vineyard Mourvèdre (Russian River Valley) $15. **90** —*L.W. (6/1/1999)*

Philip Staley 2000 Somers Vineyard Petite Sirah (Dry Creek Valley) $24. From a Rhône specialist, a wine the tasters liked for its fruity mix of cherry-berry flavors, although it started off closed and tight and needed considerable airing. Tannins are on the hefty side, which makes the wine feel chewy and rustic. **86** *(4/1/2003)*

Philip Staley 1999 Somers Vineyard Petite Sirah (Dry Creek Valley) $21. Connoisseurs are taking a fresh look at this variety despite its reputation as a common wine. Let's get one thing straight: It will never possess the refined personality of, say, Cabernet. But sometimes this rough-edged, drily tannic wine fits the bill perfectly. I'm thinking game, or bruschetta with peppers and onions. **89** —*S.H. (12/1/2002)*

Philip Staley NV The Coat of the Roan Foal 1 Rhône Red Blend (California) $12. A Rhône-style blend of Syrah, Grenache, Carignan, Mourvèdre, and Petite Sirah, and it's really quite stylish and even complex, despite the modest price. Exceedingly dry, with flavors of dried cherries and all sorts of herbs, and a peppery edge. **89** —*S.H. (8/1/2004)*

Philip Staley 2002 Duet Sauvignon Blanc-Sémillon (Sonoma County) $16. Another solid hit for this wine, one of the best Sémillon and Sauvignon Blanc combos in the state. Very dry and crisp, it has a beautiful structure, and aloof, regal flavors of citrus, mineral, and lime zest. Elegant, beautifully balanced, and versatile with food. **90** —*S.H. (8/1/2004)*

Philip Staley 1998 Syrah (Russian River Valley) $18. Here's a very dry, somewhat tart wine, soft in body but with some firm tannins. The palate impression is austere, with thin flavors of sour cherry and white pepper. It's a light wine but one with charm and style. **86** —*S.H. (7/1/2002)*

Philip Staley 1999 Staley Vineyard Syrah (Russian River Valley) $21. This Rhône specialist makes his wines in the warmest part of the appellation, and the grapes get plush and polished. Here, you'll find distinctive black cherry flavors with a peppery edge. The wine is very dry, with good tannins, and seems designed for food. **90** —*S.H. (12/1/2002)*

Philip Staley 2002 Staley Vineyard Viognier (Russian River Valley) $22. Here's a full-throttle, well-structured wine whose streamlined flavors of lemons and limes, nettles, chamomile, gun metal, and vanilla skirt around the tendency of Viognier to be overly exotic. A great sunburst of acidity backs the flavors up, accentuating the wine's dryness. **89** —*S.H. (8/1/2004)*

Philip Staley 2001 Staley Vineyard Viognier (Russian River Valley) $23. Made in a drier, leaner style, with delicate flavors of minerals and slate, and a suggestion of lemon rind. Crisp in acids and firm in texture. **88** —*S.H. (12/1/2003)*

Philip Staley 2000 Staley Vineyard Viognier (Russian River Valley) $21. Doesn't smell or taste like a typical California Viognier. The grass, hay, and gooseberry aromatics lead you to expect a dry wine. But then it turns almost shockingly sweet in the mouth, with the flavor of pineapple juice. Bizarre and discomforting. **83** —*S.H. (9/1/2003)*

Philip Staley 1997 Staley Vineyard Viognier (Russian River Valley) $16. **88** —*L.W. (6/1/1999)*

Philip Staley 2001 Duet White Blend (Sonoma County) $17. Staley is a Rhône guy but shows a firm hand with this blend of Sémillon and Sauvignon Blanc. It's dry, with flavors of lemons and figs, and a rich streak of smoky oak. Crisp acids make it shine. **90** —*S.H. (12/15/2002)*

Philip Staley 1998 Zinfandel (Dry Creek Valley) $18. From this Rhône specialist, a nice sipping wine with powerfully fruity flavors in a delicately structured, light-bodied wine. The pretty wild-berry and oregano flavors are surrounded by velvety tannins and soft acidity, so it goes down like silk. It's dry as dust. **89** —*S.H. (7/1/2002)*

PHILIPPE-LORRAINE

Philippe-Lorraine 1998 Chardonnay (Napa Valley) $18. **87** *(6/1/2000)*

Philippe-Lorraine 1999 Chardonnay (Napa Valley) $16. Starts with refined aromas of smoke, toast, butter, spice, and tropical fruits; also a nearly vegetal herbal overtone. The creamy texture and tropical fruit flavors are framed by heavy oak. **88** —*S.H. (11/15/2001)*

Philippe-Lorraine 1998 Merlot (Napa Valley) $23. Lighter than the '97, with pretty blackberry and black cherry aromas. Oak shadings add vanilla and smoke. The texture is supple, with flavors of berry and cherry, and it finishes nicely dry and spicy. **88** —*S.H. (12/1/2001)*

PHILLIPS

Phillips 1999 Reserve Chardonnay (Lodi) $20. Awkward and earthy, with off-putting medicinal, herbal aromas and flavors. There are some apple notes but they are drowned in tart, chemically ones. This is a difficult wine to say anything nice about. **80** —*S.H. (12/31/2001)*

Phillips 1997 Reserve Merlot (California) $15. **87** —*J.C. (3/1/2000)*

Phillips 1999 Syrah (California) $16. Welcoming blackberry, anise, smoke, and mustard-seed aromas lead into a tart blueberry-blackberry palate accented by paprika and cranberry notes. Medium-weight and lively, the wine finishes with toasty vanilla, cedar, and cherry flavors. Enjoy it now, while it's young. **87** *(10/1/2001)*

Phillips 1999 Old Vine Zinfandel (Lodi) $20. The Phillips has burnt cracker and gingerbread notes on the nose, plus ripe mixed berries and toast flavors from palate to finish. A lightweight one-trick pony, but absolutely drinkable. **83** —*D.T. (3/1/2002)*

PHILO RIDGE

Philo Ridge 2002 Syrah (Sonoma County) $18. Despite a relatively modest stated alcohol level of 13.6%, one of our tasters downgraded this wine for being a bit hot tasting, or it would have scored even higher. It does have a harmonious bouquet of pepper, herbs, and berries, while the palate consists of a core of red berries covered in layers of spice. It's a leaner, spice-driven style. **88** *(9/1/2005)*

PHOENIX

Phoenix 2000 Cabernet Sauvignon (Napa Valley) $28. Pours inky black, and smells young and backward. Lots of airing reveals blackberry jam, with hints of dark chocolate, vanilla, and toast. Drinks soft, velvety, luscious and complex. Good berry fruit is supported by firm, dry tannins. Lovely now, and best consumed in the next year or so to capture its vibrant youth. **92 Editors' Choice** —*S.H. (11/15/2003)*

Phoenix 2000 Reserve Chardonnay (Napa Valley) $19. Shows typical communal flavors of peach, apple, and tangerine fruit, with dusty spices and an overlay of oak that adds vanilla and toast notes. It's a candied wine, sweetly flavorful but soft and a bit simple. **85** —*S.H. (9/12/2002)*

Phoenix 2000 Reserve Pinot Noir (Napa Valley) $23. Dark and earthy, a wine that might be a Rhône blend, it's that deep in stone fruits and herbs. But the tannins are distinctly Pinot-esque, light and silky. Strange for a Pinot, and lacking varietal delicacy, but a good wine nonetheless, with rich flavors and a long finish. **87** —*S.H. (12/1/2003)*

Phoenix 2000 Blood of Jupiter Sangiovese (Napa Valley) $20. Looks rich in the glass, and smells vibrant and alive, with black cherry marmalade scents spiced up with black pepper. Drinks very light on the tongue, with soft acidity and dry, pliant tannins. The cherry flavors are good, but you wish for a firmer structure. **85** —*S.H. (9/1/2003)*

Phoenix 1999 Blood of Jupiter Sangiovese (Napa Valley) $20. Takes the soft, supple approach to this varietal, with pleasant berry flavors, very low acidity and barely any tannins, and a dry, bitter finish. It's a one-dimensional wine that really needs foods to show best. **84** —*S.H. (9/12/2002)*

PIANETTA

Pianetta 2003 Estate Cabernet Sauvignon (Monterey) $28. Must have been grown in the warmer parts of Monterey, because the wine is soft and candied, with jammy cherry and blackberry flavors veering into chocolate-covered raisins. **84** —*S.H. (3/1/2006)*

Pianetta 2003 Estate Shiraz-Cabernet Sauvignon (Monterey) $24. A marriage of royal peers. Syrah brings its distinctive leathery, animal notes to

Cabernet's classic black currants in this dry, voluptuous wine. The winery's Cabernet was one-dimensional, but the addition of Syrah has given it depth and complexity. **88** —*S.H. (4/1/2006)*

Pianetta 2003 Estate Syrah (Monterey) $28. Dark and very dry, this distinctive Syrah has a leathery note, what the Brits used to call sweaty saddle, on top of ripe black currant, coffee, and sweet vanilla flavors. It's soft in texture and pretty tannic, but voluptuous. **86** —*S.H. (4/1/2006)*

PIEDRA CREEK

Piedra Creek 2004 San Floriano Vineyard Pinot Noir (Edna Valley) $22. The acidity is a bit too high, making for a stinging mouthfeel, and the cherry flavors are out of whack, with some unripe green notes, on this bone-dry, somewhat simple wine. **83** —*S.H. (9/1/2006)*

Piedra Creek 2004 San Floriano Red Blend (San Luis Obispo) $22. This unusual blend, based on Lagrein, is dry and robust, the kind of full-bodied wine you drink in front of a fireplace when you want something warming. It's a tannic wine with lots of earth and cherries. **85** —*S.H. (10/1/2006)*

Piedra Creek 2001 Benito Dusi Vineyard Zinfandel (Paso Robles) $24. Classic Paso Zin, with its ripe, brambly flavors of wild blackberries, raspberries, and blueberries and a raisiny streak that adds a wild edge. For all the fruity flavor, it's bone dry, and the alcohol level is controlled. Delicious with a ragout of beef or game. **90** —*S.H. (4/1/2004)*

PIEDRA HILL

Piedra Hill 2003 Cabernet Sauvignon (Howell Mountain) $40. Piedra Hill is the Cabernet-only brand of former La Jota owner Bill Smith, now better known for his W.H. Smith Pinots from Sonoma Coast. But he hasn't lost his touch for Howell Mountain Cabs. This one's dry, complex, and enormously tannic. Don't even think of opening it until at least 2010, but it should develop well beyond that. **91 Cellar Selection** —*S.H. (10/1/2006)*

PIETRA SANTA

Pietra Santa 2002 Chardonnay (California) $14. Ripe and rich in tropical fruit flavors, and well-oaked, this polished wine offers lots of pleasure. Finishes long and spicy. **86** —*S.H. (12/15/2004)*

Pietra Santa 2001 Chardonnay (Cienega Valley) $13. Light textured, fresh, and lemony, the wine has a subtle touch of toast and herb flavors. Hints of melon, pear, and apple round off the flavors. It finishes with a fresh mineral edge. **88 Best Buy** —*J.M. (6/1/2003)*

Pietra Santa 2000 Dolcetto (Cienega Valley) $25. Dry, raw, and tannic, with a cherry skin bitterness, but there are no obvious flaws. It's just a simple country wine. **83** —*S.H. (6/1/2005)*

Pietra Santa 2001 Merlot (Cienega Valley) $18. Very dry and harsh in the mouth, with a sandpapery texture, this wine has earth, coffee, and cherry flavors. **83** —*S.H. (6/1/2005)*

Pietra Santa 2000 Merlot (Cienega Valley) $18. Oak stars, with its toasty, caramelly notes, but underneath there's not a lot going on. The flavors veer toward blackberries, and the texture is very soft. **84** —*S.H. (12/15/2004)*

Pietra Santa 1999 Merlot (Cienega Valley) $13. The wine shows a blend of cherry, herb, cedar, and spice notes. Tannins are firm but ripe, giving good structure. A bit drying at the end. **86** —*J.M. (12/1/2003)*

Pietra Santa 2002 Pinot Grigio (California) $14. This is a good white wine that satisfies for its total dryness, refreshing acidity, and flavors of Meyer lemons, just-ripened figs, and straw. A dollop of Chardonnay adds distinction. **86** —*S.H. (12/15/2004)*

Pietra Santa 2001 Sacred Stone Red Blend (California) $14. A little of this, a little of that. This red blend sure is sweet in ripe fruit, flooding the mouth with all kinds of berries and fruits, although it's dry. A bit rough, but likeable for the beautiful fruit. **85** —*S.H. (12/15/2004)*

Pietra Santa 2000 Sasso Rosso Red Blend (California) $14. A rustic, country-style wine meant for easy drinking with pasta and beef stew. It's dry and a little tannic. **84** —*S.H. (12/15/2004)*

Pietra Santa 1999 Sasso Rosso Red Blend (Cienega Valley) $12. Raw, harsh, and tannic, with earthy flavors. **82** —*S.H. (6/1/2005)*

Pietra Santa 1998 Sasso Rosso Red Blend (California) $13. This blend of Sangiovese, Dolcetto, Cabernet Sauvignon, and Merlot offers surprisingly complexity for the price. Aromas of sweat, leather, and dried spices are complemented on the palate by flavors of sour cherries and tart rasberries, turning to espresso and caramel on the finish. **87** —*J.C. (12/1/2001)*

Pietra Santa 2001 Sangiovese (Cienega Valley) $24. Tobacco and black cherry flavors drink dry, in a simple, rather rough texture that closes with a scour of tannins. Good with tomato sauce and cheese. **84** —*S.H. (6/1/2005)*

Pietra Santa 2000 Sangiovese (Cienega Valley) $24. Super-dry, acidic, and herbaceous, a rasping wine that makes your gums pucker with astringency. Still, it good for its style. Those acids should cut through a rich pasta primavera. **84** —*S.H. (12/31/2004)*

Pietra Santa 2000 Sassolino Sangiovese (Cienega Valley) $25. A super Tuscan blend that's light and pleasant. It has pretty cherry and herb flavors and is dry and elegant, with soft tannins. **85** —*S.H. (12/15/2004)*

Pietra Santa 2000 Zinfandel (Cienega Valley) $20. Hot with alcohol, and cloying with residual sugar. Unbalanced. **82** —*S.H. (12/31/2004)*

PIÑA

Piña 2000 Cabernet Sauvignon (Howell Mountain) $48. Gigantic fruit stars here. It just explodes in an intense burst of cherries, black currants, and mocha. Hard to believe how ripe and delicious it is. Probably too soft to age for long, so drink this decadent nectar now. **90** —*S.H. (11/15/2004)*

Piña 2001 Estate Cabernet Sauvignon (Howell Mountain) $54. This is a wine that will change your perception of Howell Mountain Cabs as wines that you have to cellar to enjoy. Yes, it's tannic enough for the long haul, but so good now, it's hard not to drink it. Packed with ripe, rich currant, cherry, and sweet tobacco fruit, with vanilla and cocoa seasonings, it's absolutely delicious. Drink now through 2012. **94 Editors' Choice** —*S.H. (11/1/2005)*

PINDAR VINEYARDS

Pindar Vineyards 1997 Reserve Cabernet Sauvignon (North Fork of Long Island) $19. Loaded with new oak, which in this case means it's cedary and very mentholly. Under that is some tobacco and coffee. Very drying tannins clamp down on the finish. **84** —*J.C. (4/1/2001)*

Pindar Vineyards 1995 Cuvée Rare Chardonnay (Long Island) $28. A "rare" example of 100% Pinot Meunier, this crisp sparkler has slight yeasty notes that add nuance to the fresh citrusy fruit. Robust flavors, yet lean and very dry. **86** —*J.C. (4/1/2001)*

Pindar Vineyards 1998 Peacock Chardonnay (Long Island) $9. With 20% barrel fermentation, this wine is surprisingly rich and spicy for a low-end Chard. The aromas and flavors bring to mind pears and golden-delicious apples, before turning tart on the finish. **84** —*J.C. (4/1/2001)*

Pindar Vineyards 1998 Reserve Chardonnay (Long Island) $13. Toasty and buttery on the nose, with an appealing nutty character. Turns more aggressively woody on the palate before finishing with bold buttered-popcorn flavors. **86** —*J.C. (4/1/2001)*

Pindar Vineyards 1998 Sunflower Chardonnay (Long Island) $18. This wine is oaky; it's 100% barrel-fermented and aged in new French oak for 12 months. Despite that, it's not over the top. Aromas of smoke and cured meats lead the way, then sweet pears. The texture is slick—even oily—and definitely viscous. Finishes long, with plenty of oak-imparted spice. **88** —*J.C. (4/1/2001)*

Pindar Vineyards 1999 Ice Wine Johannisberg Riesling (Long Island) $35. Sure, it's made "artificially" in a commercial freezer, but so what? It tastes good. Dried apricots and honey are imbued with layers of flavor and richness. Enough acidity to avoid being cloying, but not so much that you'll want to age it. Drink now. **90** —*J.C. (4/1/2001)*

Pindar Vineyards 1997 Mythology Merlot (North Fork of Long Island) $28. The best Mythology yet, with more lush fruit than previous vintages have possessed. It's still earthy and leathery with tobacco notes, but this year the wine has enough sweet cassis fruit to balance it out. The creamy texture is a treat. **90** —*J.C. (4/1/2001)*

Pindar Vineyards 2003 Reserve Barrel Select Merlot (North Fork of Long Island) $19. Modestly priced for a reserve, Pindar, one of Long Islands largest producers, crafted an old-style wine with balsam, shoe leather,

USA

and cherry aromas. Dusty tannins give it a good if simple mouthfeel, dealing modest cherry, vanilla, and mint. Seems a bit advanced, so drink up. **86**—*M.D. (12/1/2006)*

Pindar Vineyards 1997 Port (Long Island) $25. A blend of Cabernet Franc and Cabernet Sauvignon, fortified with brandy and aged in oak has yielded a young gawky wine that tastes like you would expect: sweet cassis and plum fruit is married to plenty of vanilla and menthol oak. Hints of chocolate emerge on the finish. Light tannins and low acidity make this a Port that's made to drink soon, not for the extended aging of traditional vintage Ports. **86**—*J.C. (4/1/2001)*

Pindar Vineyards NV Pythagoras Red Blend (North Fork of Long Island) $11. Sappy candied-cherry fruit aromas lead into a soft, easy-to-drink blend that's an unpretentious quaff for the backyard grill. **83**—*J.C. (4/1/2001)*

Pindar Vineyards 1997 Syrah (Long Island) $25. Faint smoke notes accent the crisp blackberry fruit. Not a lush wine, but it has just enough flesh to prevent it from being hard. The finish is tart and peppery, as befits cool-climate Syrah. **87**—*J.C. (4/1/2001)*

Pindar Vineyards 1998 Viognier (Long Island) $23. A slightly floral nose leads into a plump wine, filled with rich melony fruit. Traces of heat and spice adorn the finish. **85**—*J.C. (4/1/2001)*

PINE & POST

Pine & Post 2004 Chardonnay (Columbia Valley (WA)) $5. Solid and clean, this well-made Chardonnay includes a generous (20%) proportion of Sémillon, which fleshes it out. The dominant flavors are tangerine and citrus, and the wine sets up crisply in the mouth without feeling stripped or sour in any way. **87 Best Buy**—*P.G. (4/1/2006)*

Pine & Post 2004 Merlot (Columbia Valley (WA)) $5. An excellent Merlot; certainly the best at this price point that I have tasted in the past 15 years. Good, solid black cherry fruit is accented with coffee ground flavors. None of the usual vegetal flavors that plague wines at this price, nor are the tannins anything but ripe and smooth. Best of all, there is real fruit concentration through the midpalate. **87 Best Buy**—*P.G. (4/1/2006)*

PINE RIDGE

Pine Ridge 1999 Andrus Reserve Bordeaux Blend (Napa Valley) $135. **90**—*J.C. (6/1/2003)*

Pine Ridge 2002 Charmstone Bordeaux Blend (Napa Valley) $30. Smells too raisiny and tastes too hot and sweet to merit a higher score. The grapes seem to have gotten away from the pickers during the harvest. **82**—*S.H. (11/15/2006)*

Pine Ridge 2002 Onyx Bordeaux Blend (Napa Valley) $55. One of the few California Bordeaux reds that's predominantly Malbec, this dramatic young wine startles with its richness and complexity. It offer lush, ripe flavors of black currants, cocoa, tobacco, and new oak, and the tannins are as good as Napa gets, soft and luxurious. Drink sooner rather than later. **92**—*S.H. (9/1/2006)*

Pine Ridge 2002 Red Wine Cabernet Blend (Oakville) $60. This wine opens with woody, earthy, bacony aromas and turns oddly sweet in the mouth, like cherry cough medicine. It's not bad, just odd. **83**—*S.H. (10/1/2005)*

Pine Ridge 1997 Cabernet Sauvignon (Howell Mountain) $50. **89** *(11/1/2000)*

Pine Ridge 1997 Cabernet Sauvignon (Rutherford) $26. **85** *(3/1/2000)*

Pine Ridge 1997 Cabernet Sauvignon (Stags Leap District) $50. **95** *(11/1/2000)*

Pine Ridge 2003 Cabernet Sauvignon (Howell Mountain) $80. Huge, just tremendous and authoritative. Aged in new, high-toast oak for 17 months, it bursts with smoky char and caramelized vanilla, while the underlying fruit explodes with spicy plum, wild blackberry marmalade, and chocolate. The tannins are very strong, but ripely sweet and finely meshed. A guaranteed cellar candidate, it should slowly improve for a decade, and last another decade beyond that. **95 Cellar Selection**—*S.H. (12/31/2006)*

Pine Ridge 2003 Cabernet Sauvignon (Rutherford) $40. I had to double-check the price on this brilliant wine because it's much less than other

Napa Cabs. It's a fat, sweet, fleshy wine, instantly appealing for its delicious blackberry, blackstrap molasses, cherry, violet, and sweet oak flavors, yet it's a cellar guarantee. The tannins are finely ground and wonderfully ripe, giving the wine a firm lushness that lasts through a long, satisfying finish. Should be easy to find, with 10,300 cases produced. **94 Editors' Choice**—*S.H. (12/15/2006)*

Pine Ridge 2003 Cabernet Sauvignon (Oakville) $75. Drinks immature and gangly now, a fresh young Cab that needs time to knit together. It's all there, though, from the ripe blackberry, cassis, cherry marmalade, and cappuccino flavors and sweet, vanilla-infused new oak to the firm, sweet young tannins. Very fine, high-class wine. Should blossom by 2009, then evolve for many years. **92 Cellar Selection**—*S.H. (12/31/2006)*

Pine Ridge 2002 Cabernet Sauvignon (Rutherford) $39. Displays a nice balance of ripe cassis fruit and earthy green olives, with rich oak. It's a voluptuous wine, dry and balanced, but probably not an ager. The pairing opportunities are endless. **90**—*S.H. (10/1/2005)*

Pine Ridge 2002 Cabernet Sauvignon (Stags Leap District) $75. The '01 was a hard act to follow. If the '02 lacks a bit of the rich opulence of its predecessor, it may be a more ageable wine. The tannins are thick yet sweet, covering ripe black currant and oaky-mocha flavors that last through an impressively long finish. Drink this dry, balanced Cab now–2014. **93 Cellar Selection**—*S.H. (8/1/2006)*

Pine Ridge 2001 Cabernet Sauvignon (Howell Mountain) $70. If you get off on aging your Cabs, this is more than an even bet. In fact, it's a sure thing, with its rich, thick tannins that shut things down now. But deep down inside is a massive core of sweet blackberry that captures the fabulous sun of this historic vintage. Best from 2010 and beyond. **92 Cellar Selection**—*S.H. (10/1/2004)*

Pine Ridge 2001 Cabernet Sauvignon (Stags Leap District) $70. This luxurious wine flatters the palate with its sumptuous fruit, ripe and big but not overbearing. The black currant, cassis, plum, mocha, smoky oak, and spicy flavors swim in sweet, fine tannins. A spine of acidity keeps it all honest. Gorgeous now, and will age through 2015 or beyond. **94 Cellar Selection**—*S.H. (10/1/2004)*

Pine Ridge 2001 Cabernet Sauvignon (Rutherford) $37. Young and tight, with hard tannins and some citrusy acids that obscure the fruit. Yet there's a dense nucleus of sweet red and black cherry and cassis, and all the elements are balanced and harmonious. Nice now, but if you can, allow it to age for at least seven years. **91**—*S.H. (10/1/2004)*

Pine Ridge 2001 Cabernet Sauvignon (Oakville) $55. A big, exuberant wine, filled with power but a bit wanting in grace at this stage of its life. The fruit is ripe and explosive, the oak similarly sized, and so are the tannins. All the parts aren't working in harmony, but should pull together just fine by 2010. **89**—*S.H. (10/1/2004)*

Pine Ridge 2000 Cabernet Sauvignon (Rutherford) $37. A lighter style of Napa Cabernet, with pretty spice, cherry, cedar, vanilla, plum, and anise notes. Tannins are mild, with medium body. The finish is also moderate in length. **87**—*J.M. (8/1/2003)*

Pine Ridge 1999 Cabernet Sauvignon (Howell Mountain) $50. Heady and big, a tremendously dense, rich wine that packs in plenty of satisfaction. Opens with black fruit, chocolate, plum, coffee, maple syrup, and cassis scents, with a ton of flashy new oak. Turns rich and complex in the mouth, packed with delicious fruity flavors and long, ripe tannins. **92**—*S.H. (11/15/2002)*

Pine Ridge 1999 Chardonnay (Stags Leap District) $40. This light and elegant wine opens with orange and mild tropical fruit aromas. Easy peach and pear flavors bear dry vanilla and toasty oak accents. Even and soft on the palate, the nutty-leesy-chalky finish brings the wine to a pleasing close. **87** *(7/1/2001)*

Pine Ridge 2004 Dijon Clones Chardonnay (Carneros) $33. What's so interesting about this Chardonnay is the dryness and the earthy minerality. There are flavors of dried herbs and dried fruits, such as apricots, lemons, and pink grapefruits. Usually these Dijon clones produce enormously fruity wines, but this fine wine has a sleek, high-acid Chablisian elegance. **90**—*S.H. (8/1/2006)*

Pine Ridge 2003 Dijon Clones Chardonnay (Carneros) $27. It's easy to see what Pine Ridge is trying to do: build a massive, Burgundian

Chardonnay. There's lots of toasty oak and other winemaker complexities, but it's overworked for the fruit. **84**—*S.H. (10/1/2005)*

Pine Ridge 2001 Dijon Clones Chardonnay (Carneros) $25. Kicks off with hints of vanilla, honey, melon, peach, spice, and citrus flavors. The wine is full bodied and viscous. It finishes with moderate length and a touch of spice at the end. **89**—*J.M. (8/1/2003)*

Pine Ridge 2000 Dijon Clones Chardonnay (Napa Valley) $25. Rich, creamy, and enticing, the wine serves up a classy blend of fine-tuned toast nuance and appealing pear, apple, melon, grapefruit, lemon, herb, and honey-like notes. Long and lush at the end. **91**—*J.M. (5/1/2002)*

Pine Ridge 1998 Dijon Clones Chardonnay (Carneros) $25. **88** *(6/1/2000)*

Pine Ridge 2002 Le Petit Clos Chardonnay (Stags Leap District) $50. Brutally good, a wine so powerful in ripe tropical fruits and new smoky oak that it just detonates the palate. Huge, mouth-filling flavors of mango and pineapple, caramelized oak, butterscotch, cinnamon, clove, vanilla, toast, and who knows what else cascade in waves, ending in a super-long, sweet finish. Massive, but balanced and elegant. If it had a slightly denser middle, it would be perfect. **95**—*S.H. (12/31/2004)*

Pine Ridge 2001 Onyx Malbec (Napa Valley) $50. A Malbec-based blend, and wouldn't you know it from the black color. Smells young and hung-meaty, with overtones of herbs and oak, but the suggestion of black currants is irresistible. Turns massive in the mouth, flooded with fruity flavor, and tannic, with a dry, hard finish. Certainly cellar-worthy. Try after 2006. **91**—*S.H. (12/31/2004)*

Pine Ridge 2002 Crimson Creek Merlot (Napa Valley) $27. Tastes kind of soft and thick in jammy cherry and blackberry flavors, with low acidity and some keen tannins that turn astringent on the finish. It's showing its rusticity and is not likely to improve. **84**—*S.H. (8/1/2006)*

Pine Ridge 1997 Crimson Creek Merlot (Napa Valley) $22. **93** *(11/15/1999)*

Pine Ridge 1998 White Blend (California) $11. **89**—*M.S. (11/1/1999)*

Pine Ridge 2004 Chenin Blanc-Viognier White Blend (Clarksburg) $14. Sweet enough to be considered a dessert wine, with honeyed apricot, peach, sweetened herb tea, and vanilla spice flavors. Benefits from crisp acidity. A simple, flavorful sipper. **84**—*S.H. (11/15/2006)*

PINOT EVIL

Pinot Evil 2004 Reserve Pinot Noir (Edna Valley) $15. A bit raw and sharp in acidity, with some minty greenness, this wine also has cherry and cocoa flavors. It's very dry, and is a pretty good buy for a good coastal Pinot. **85**—*S.H. (9/1/2006)*

PIPER SONOMA

Piper Sonoma NV Blanc de Noir Champagne Blend (Sonoma County) $19. This Sonoma standby displays ripe-apple, herb, and hay notes and an even bread. Moderate complexity shows on the palate with its full, soft mousse. Closes with plum and hints of tangy citrus. **87** *(12/1/2001)*

Piper Sonoma NV Brut Champagne Blend (Sonoma County) $19. Dried peach and apple aromas open this round, even sparkler. An earthy note, and an element that seemed herbal to some tasters, leafy or green to others, shows early on and persists throughout. The bead is fine and even, and the wine is soft on the palate. A straightforward Brut, but on the earthy side. **85** *(12/1/2001)*

Piper Sonoma NV Blanc de Noir Pinot Noir (Sonoma County) $20. Full-bodied and rich, yet delicately structured, this bubbly shows raspberry, vanilla, smoke, and bread dough flavors, and is dry. Turns rich in red berry fruit on the finish. **88**—*S.H. (12/31/2004)*

Piper Sonoma NV Blanc de Noir Sparkling Blend (California) $18. Toasty aromas carry a hint of earthiness as well, then the wine turns citrusy and lemon-like through the midpalate. Finishes tangy and surprisingly lean for a Blanc de Noirs. **85**—*J.C. (12/1/2003)*

Piper Sonoma NV Brut Sparkling Blend (Sonoma County) $20. A bit rough in texture, but polished in sweet vanilla, smoke, dough, and subtle peach and citrus flavors. Has just enough dosage to make it finish round. **87**—*S.H. (12/31/2004)*

Piper Sonoma NV Brut Sparkling Blend (California) $18. Kicks off with toast, mushroom, and earth aromas suggestive of a well-aged blend, then delivers a smooth creamy mouthful packed with rich fruit and earth fla-

vors. Assertive enough to pair successfully with many first courses. **88**—*J.C. (12/1/2003)*

PIPESTONE VINEYARDS

Pipestone Vineyards 2001 Zinfandel (Paso Robles) $22. Pretty, bright, cherry and wild berry flavors are the hallmarks here. Light, pleasant, and easy drinking. **85** *(11/1/2003)*

PIROUETTE

Pirouette 2003 Red Blend (Columbia Valley (WA)) $55. The Pirouette from Long Shadows is made by Agustin Huneeus and Philippe Melka. It's 56% Cabernet Sauvignon, 22% Merlot, 10% Syrah, 9% Cab Franc, and 3% Petit Verdot. Dusty, toasty and showing lots of coffee aromas, it hits the palate quite soft, seamless, classy, rich, and luscious in a Napa Valley style. It's silky, with fine tannins, still quite young and nicely nuanced. **90**—*P.G. (4/1/2006)*

PISONI

Pisoni 1996 Pinot Noir (Santa Lucia Highlands) $NA. Another non-commercial bottling. Dark. Opens with lavish layers of cherries, cocoa, brown spices, charcoal. Drinks enormously rich and full-bodied, very forward in cherry and blackberry fruit. Tannins still sturdy. Still young and dramatic, with a sweet Heirloom tomato and balsamic finish. **92**—*S.H. (6/1/2005)*

Pisoni 1994 Pinot Noir (Santa Lucia Highlands) $NA. This non-commercial bottling is still very rich and satisfying. Good dark color. Clean, vibrant in rhubarb, cherry, and cola flavors. Full-bodied and spicy, as well as very dry. Still tannic, should hang in there for some years. **91**—*S.H. (6/1/2005)*

Pisoni 2002 Pinot Noir (Santa Lucia Highlands) $60. Dark and dramatic. This is an enormous wine, superextracted in cherry, blackberry, and mocha flavors, but totally dry. Almost Syrah-like, except for the silky tannins. Not particularly nuanced now, but the gamble is on ageability. Drink now and through the decade. **92**—*S.H. (11/1/2004)*

Pisoni 2001 Estate Pinot Noir (Santa Lucia Highlands) $NA. Smells porty-rich in white chocolate, fudge, vanilla, smoky char, and fruit. Enormously rich, almost decadent flavors of chocolate, cherries, blueberries. So big. Needs time to knit together. Hold until 2008. Earns its points on sheer volume. **93**—*S.H. (6/1/2005)*

Pisoni 2000 Estate Pinot Noir (Santa Lucia Highlands) $NA. Dark. Lovely aromatics of red and black cherry, char, oak. Drinks full-bodied and rich, with some tannins to shed, but not quite the distinction of the '99. **90**—*S.H. (6/1/2005)*

Pisoni 1999 Estate Pinot Noir (Santa Lucia Highlands) $NA. Even better than the '98, an elegant, harmonious wine, long in rich, sweet cherry fruit. Great balance and style. Feels supple and smooth, with great acidity. Char and vanilla stand out on the finish. Dazzling now, and should improve and hold for a decade. **95**—*S.H. (6/1/2005)*

Pisoni 1998 Estate Pinot Noir (Santa Lucia Highlands) $NA. First commercial bottling from Pisoni. Just as fresh as a new wine, really fruity, with ripe cherry, cocoa, cigar box, anise, cinnamon, and pepper notes. Drinks rich and intense. This dry, silky, harmonious wine is just beautiful. **93**—*S.H. (6/1/2005)*

Pisoni 2002 Garys' Vineyard Pinot Noir (Santa Lucia Highlands) $38. A little awkward, with slightly sweet cherry and medicinal flavors, and over-oaked for its modest frame. Yet there's refreshing acidity and a lush texture that are likeable. **86**—*S.H. (11/1/2004)*

PIZIALI

Piziali 2004 Late Harvest 375 mL Sauvignon Blanc (Lake County) $32. With residual sugar of 11.5%, this is a very sweet wine, concentrated in apricot, lime, and pineapple sorbet flavors, and with the high acidity needed for balance. It's a lusciously clean dessert wine. **90**—*S.H. (10/1/2006)*

PLUMPJACK

Plumpjack 1997 Cabernet Sauvignon (Oakville) $44. **94**—*S.H. (2/1/2000)*

Plumpjack 2001 Cabernet Sauvignon (Oakville) $58. Really first rate, fat, fleshy, flashy, and sensual. Hard to exaggerate the beauty of the currant

USA

USA

and cherry fruit, so ripe, polished, and pure, and the sweet finesse of the tannins. In a few years the inherent structure will kick in, tightening the wine and guaranteeing it a long life. **95** —*S.H. (10/1/2004)*

Plumpjack 2003 Estate Cabernet Sauvignon (Oakville) $68. Pickles and dill in the nose, with underlying cherries and blackberries. In the mouth, it enters brawny and rustic, and very tannic. The fruit is locked down. Seems sound, but disappointingly tough. Could develop, but it's a gamble. Tasted twice. **86** —*S.H. (9/1/2006)*

Plumpjack 2002 Estate Cabernet Sauvignon (Oakville) $62. Not in the same ripeness league as the '01, but still an enormously attractive wine. It's just a bit leaner, but perhaps more structured. Shows blackberry, currant, coffee, oak, and herb flavors and some fairly big tannins. Nice now, but should hold and improve through 2010. **90** —*S.H. (10/1/2005)*

Plumpjack 1999 Reserve Cabernet Sauvignon (Napa Valley) $155. Smooth, rich, and lush, with firm tannins that support a wonderfully complex blend of plum, blackberry, black cherry, coffee, anise, chocolate, herb, and earth flavors. Lingers on the finish. **93** —*J.M. (2/1/2003)*

Plumpjack 1999 Reserve Chardonnay (Napa Valley) $40. The nose here shows clean pine and citrus notes, with accents of herb and tropical fruit. Straightforward apple, pear, and nut flavors show on the palate. In some ways, including the nutty finish, the wine is good—in other ways, it's just there. **86** *(7/1/2001)*

PLUNGERHEAD

Plungerhead 2004 Zinfandel (Dry Creek Valley) $14. The latest from Don Sebastiani & Sons continues the tradition of their other brands, offering up a ripe, fruity, spicy Zin that finishes nice and dry. A good price for such authentic Dry Creek Zin character. **85** —*S.H. (7/1/2006)*

POET'S LEAP

Poet's Leap 2004 Riesling (Columbia Valley (WA)) $22. Round and warmly fruity, this is a lovely mix of grapefruit, stone fruits, and light tropical flavors. Nice and spicy, balanced and harmonious, it has almost 2% residual sugar (and has been criticized for it) but it works well to soften and round out the acids. **90** —*P.G. (4/1/2006)*

Poet's Leap 2003 Riesling (Columbia Valley (WA)) $22. Elegant and refined, offering mixed citrus scents, a clean, fresh, and lively mouthfeel built upon a generous core of melon, yellow plum, and sweet citrus fruits. Despite its off-dry sweetness, its firm acids keep it food friendly. This is the first release from Long Shadows, a consortium of boutique wineries. **89** —*P.G. (11/15/2004)*

PONTIN DEL ROZA

Pontin del Roza 1999 Cabernet Sauvignon (Yakima Valley) $18. Nice black cherry fruit powers the nose, with just the barest hints of stem and root. Firm fruit is buttressed by tart acids, and the middle opens up sweetly, adding flavors of cocoa and coffee. **87** —*P.G. (9/1/2002)*

Pontin del Roza 2000 Chenin Blanc (Yakima Valley) $7. A nice bottle of wine, bone-dry and fragrant, with pleasing, simple flavors. **87** —*P.G. (9/1/2002)*

Pontin del Roza 2003 Pinot Grigio (Yakima Valley) $15. A good effort, showing nicely rounded edges with the extra time in bottle. Mixed stone fruits are spiced up with cinnamon and given a finishing lift with tart acids; flavors linger gracefully through the finish. **88** —*P.G. (2/1/2006)*

Pontin del Roza 2000 Pinot Grigio (Yakima Valley) $12. The aromas are clean and varietal, and the fruit follows along with pleasant, light pear and apple flavors, buoyed by tangy acids. **85** —*P.G. (9/1/2002)*

Pontin del Roza 2000 White Riesling (Yakima Valley) $8. Pontin scores with a sweet, lemony, ripe mouthful of fresh and fruity Riesling. Shows the verve and juicy deliciousness of Yakima Valley fruit. **87** —*P.G. (9/1/2002)*

Pontin del Roza 2000 Sangiovese (Yakima Valley) $23. The style can only be called "nouveau" as the soft, forward, very grapey aromas are followed by tart, lightly spicy cranberry fruit and a quick, light finish. **84** —*P.G. (9/1/2002)*

PONZI

Ponzi 1998 Arneis (Willamette Valley) $18. **90** —*M.S. (4/1/2000)*

Ponzi 2004 Arneis (Willamette Valley) $20. It's too bad Ponzi doesn't make more of this gorgeous wine, or inspire someone else in Oregon to plant it. Penetrating scents and flavors show pineapple, citrus, peach, and tropical fruits, and the piercing aromatics blossom on the tongue into a long, seductive, marmalade of a wine. Unique and flavorful. **88** —*P.G. (11/15/2005)*

Ponzi 1997 Chardonnay (Willamette Valley) $18. **87** —*S.H. (12/31/1999)*

Ponzi 1997 Clonal Chardonnay (Willamette Valley) $22. **89** —*S.H. (12/31/1999)*

Ponzi 2003 Reserve Chardonnay (Willamette Valley) $30. Ripe peaches, mango, and citrus jump from the glass; there's no lack of lush fruit in this reserve. Oddly, despite barrel fermentation, the fruit completely overshadows any trace of oak. Juicy and ripe, with some slightly bitter citrus rind in the finish. **88** —*P.G. (5/1/2006)*

Ponzi 2002 Reserve Chardonnay (Willamette Valley) $30. Lots of wood flavor comes out, though the winery says just 20% was new. Barrel-fermented, 100% malolactic, and weekly lees stirring give the wine plenty of lush texture in a semi-tropical fruit context. **90** —*P.G. (8/1/2005)*

Ponzi 1999 Reserve Chardonnay (Willamette Valley) $25. This reserve shows nice lime/citrus scents, hints of honey, and a bit of sandalwood, which is quite interesting. It's an elegant, lightly spicy, complex, and subtle wine, with delicious nuances and a dancer's balance. **92 Editors' Choice** —*P.G. (8/1/2002)*

Ponzi 1998 Reserve Chardonnay (Willamette Valley) $27. In the hot, forward 1998 vintage, more than 1999, Oregon's reserve Chardonnays are so ripe and rich that they may already be at, or even past, their peak. Here are scents of ripe apples and whiskey barrels, plenty of alcoholic heat, and a substantial amount of new oak. Drink soon. **87** —*P.G. (2/1/2002)*

Ponzi 2005 Pinot Blanc (Willamette Valley) $17. A very tasty Pinot Blanc from Luisa Ponzi, who deftly extracts light pear and apple fruit while retaining streaks of lemon and pineapple. This is the sort of elegant, fruit-driven, flavorful white wine that makes Oregon Pinot Blanc such a pleasure. **88** —*P.G. (12/1/2006)*

Ponzi 2001 Pinot Blanc (Willamette Valley) $15. **89 Best Buy** —*M.S. (12/31/2002)*

Ponzi 2005 Pinot Gris (Willamette Valley) $17. This excellent PG has plenty of palate weight and texture besides. It's spicy, with fleshy pear and cinnamon flavors leading into marzipan that's lifted with citrus. Lots going on as it continues to surprise, finishing with a crisp mineral acidity. Might be the best Ponzi PG in the past decade. **90 Editors' Choice** —*P.G. (12/1/2006)*

Ponzi 2004 Pinot Gris (Willamette Valley) $17. This excellent Gris enters the mouth full-on with soft, appealing flavors of cantaloupe, pear, and pineapple. Then it rather quickly slips away. **87** —*P.G. (11/15/2005)*

Ponzi 2001 Pinot Gris (Willamette Valley) $12. **86 Best Buy** —*M.S. (12/31/2002)*

Ponzi 2004 Pinot Noir (Willamette Valley) $35. Complex scents suggest rosewater, dried cherry, raspberry, and baking chocolate. In the mouth, it's tight, compact, and stylish. I love the details, the hints of earth and bark, and the rich vein of berry. The barrel flavors are well integrated and matched to firm tannins. **89** —*P.G. (12/1/2006)*

Ponzi 2003 Pinot Noir (Willamette Valley) $30. Softer in 2003 than in more normal vintages, this shows ripe red fruit flavors, chewy tannins, and spicy tobacco notes. Despite the heat and ripeness, it retains an herbal undertone, and the tannins have a bit of a green edge to them. **88** —*P.G. (11/15/2005)*

Ponzi 2002 Pinot Noir (Willamette Valley) $30. Straightforward and fruity, with ripe, slightly sugary flavors of cherry cola. It has some of the jammy preserved raspberry fruit of California, but without the midpalate weight. **85** *(11/1/2004)*

Ponzi 1998 Pinot Noir (Willamette Valley) $25. **92** —*M.S. (12/1/2000)*

Ponzi 2003 Reserve Pinot Noir (Willamette Valley) $50. Concentrated, tannic, and earthy, the reserve shows dense black cherry fruit, sweet plum, hints of leaf, forest floor, and damp earth. Firm, tannic, and substantial; give it plenty of breathing time. **90** —*P.G. (5/1/2006)*

Ponzi 2002 Reserve Pinot Noir (Willamette Valley) $50. Broad, ripe, and immediately appealing, this well-made wine offers plenty of red fruit flavors, light spice, and new oak toast. What is missing is any special signature from the vineyards that might vault it up a notch or two. **88** —*P.G. (8/1/2005)*

Ponzi 2003 Tavola Pinot Noir (Willamette Valley) $20. Although it is the inexpensive bottle in the Ponzi lineup, the Tavola holds its own, with fragrant varietal aromas of sassafras and cherry. There's a nice lift to it, a pine needle freshness, and additional notes of cocoa, anise, and more. Soft, easy-drinking, yet multi-dimensional. **88** —*P.G. (11/15/2005)*

Ponzi 2005 Riesling (Willamette Valley) $25. This is the first dry Riesling since 1993, though it was a Ponzi hallmark from 1974 until it was dropped. Fashions have brought dry Riesling into play again, and this is a textbook example mixing Meyer lemon, chamomile tea, and even a bit of peppery spice. Unfortunately just 70 cases were made. **92** —*P.G. (12/1/2006)*

POPE VALLEY WINERY

Pope Valley Winery 2001 Chenin Blanc (Napa Valley) $16. Hints of lemon, herb, melon, apple, pear, and anise mark this lovely Chenin Blanc. Not as sweet as a true dessert wine, but fresh and fruity. Try it before dinner as an apéritif. **88** —*J.M. (12/15/2003)*

Pope Valley Winery 2003 Old Vine Meyercamp Ranch Chenin Blanc (Napa Valley) $10. This wine is distinct and interesting. It's dry and intense in citrusy acids, with a softening touch of fig and peach. A well-made, good wine. Try with Waldorf salad. **86 Best Buy** —*S.H. (6/1/2005)*

Pope Valley Winery 2001 Zinfandel Port Zinfandel (Napa Valley) $35. Smells caramelly and rich in blackberries, and then turns semi-sweet in the mouth, with cassis, chocolate, and coffee flavors. The tannins show up on the finish. **84** —*S.H. (6/1/2005)*

PORTER CREEK

Porter Creek 2002 Timbervine Ranch Syrah (Russian River Valley) $36. Divergent views on this wine, with one taster finding it lovely and capable of aging 5–10 years, while other reviewers found it less impressive. Aromas and flavors combine peppery, herbal, meaty notes with riper notes of plum and blackberry, while the tannins clamp down on the finish. **87** —*P.G. (9/1/2005)*

POWERS

Powers 2001 Bordeaux Blend (Columbia Valley (WA)) $30. This Bordeaux blend (62% Cab, 33% Merlot, and 5% Cab Franc) comes from the great Champoux Vineyard in an excellent vintage. Rough, leathery, and tannic, the fruit shines here; it's big enough to take even the hard, stemmy tannins. Notes of tar, smoke, and licorice wrap the blackberry fruit. **88** —*P.G. (4/1/2006)*

Powers 2004 Chardonnay (Columbia Valley (WA)) $10. Already showing signs of oxidation, this dry, dusty Chardonnay tastes mostly of oak. **82** —*P.G. (4/1/2006)*

Powers 1999 Chardonnay (Columbia Valley (WA)) $10. This is a light, unassuming, quite neutral wine, cleanly made, with tart, simple fruit. A hint of herb and plenty of acid complete the picture. **85** —*P.G. (2/1/2002)*

Powers 2004 Pinot Grigio (Columbia Valley (WA)) $12. Despite its youth this wine is already taking on a tawny appearance, and the flavors are dusty, flat, and tired. There's a curious, cotton candy sweetness in the mouth as the wine finishes. **82** —*P.G. (2/1/2006)*

Powers 1999 Pinot Noir (Columbia Valley (WA)) $10. Sharp, acidic, and earthy, this wine shows the underripe side of Pinot Noir, with some sweet oak. The light fruit is encased in a rough, tannic, earthy shell, with an odd, minty finish. **83** —*P.G. (12/31/2001)*

Powers 1998 Parallel 46 Red Blend (Columbia Valley (WA)) $30. There is nothing shy about this blend of 60% Cabernet Sauvignon, 30% Merlot, and 10% Cabernet Franc. Thick and jammy, it showcases juicy, succulent fruit with a tart, youthful grip. It needs more time to soften and open up, but has the balance and the weight for cellaring. **88** —*P.G. (12/31/2001)*

Powers 2004 Riesling (Columbia Valley (WA)) $10. A sweet and sour style, offering tangy pineapple, lime, and citrus with some residual sweetness.

Big and a bit clunky, but the excellent fruit holds your interest. **86** —*P.G. (4/1/2006)*

Powers 1999 Syrah (Columbia Valley (WA)) $16. The complex nutmeg, clove, and meat-accented cherry bouquet is appealing, but on the tongue, the wine turns decidedly harder and less generous. A touch of anise shows, but a taut, lean character prevails with plenty of oak and brisk acidity. Should open more with a year or two of aging. Will work with hearty food, too. **86** *(10/1/2001)*

PRAGER

Prager NV Noble Companion Tawny Port Cabernet Sauvignon (Napa Valley) $45. Pale in color, but everything else is explosive. The cola, espresso, raspberry, vanilla, and meringue flavors are soft in the way of an aged Port, yet firm with bracing acids. This all-Cabernet Sauvignon sweet wine is simply excellent. **93** —*S.H. (12/1/2003)*

Prager 1999 Aria White Port Chardonnay (Napa Valley) $45. This 100% Chardonnay looks and smells like a true late-harvest wine, with its dark golden color and decadent aromas of caramel, vanilla, and meringue. It's very sweet and unctuous, with a thick, syrupy texture that frames flavors of white chocolate and banana, but good acidity keeps it lively. **89** —*S.H. (12/1/2003)*

Prager 1999 Port Petite Sirah (California) $32. A fine, full-bodied vintage Port, ready to drink now, with rich, sweet flavors of cassis, raspberry, and chocolate truffle and a deliciously spicy finish. Completely addictive, a wine to savor after dinner is over and the hour grows late. **93 Editors' Choice** —*S.H. (12/1/2003)*

Prager 2001 Royal Escort Paladini Vineyard LBV Port Petite Sirah (Napa Valley) $65. 100% Petite Sirah. The depth of sweet flavor is stunning. Black cherries, white chocolate fudge, honey, coffee, pecan pie, vanilla, the list goes on and on. So delicious, you can enjoy it now with a rich chocolatey dessert, but the tannins are bold. This wine will age and soften for many years. **93** —*S.H. (12/15/2004)*

Prager 2001 Aria White Port (Napa Valley) $48. Produced from Chardonnay grown in Carneros, this wine has caramel, toast, and baked fruit-pie aromas that are clean and inviting. It's not as sweet as you'd think, and the roasted fruit flavors are offset by good acids. **87** —*S.H. (3/1/2006)*

Prager 2000 Aria White Port (Napa Valley) $48. This Chardonnay is quite sweet, with botritised vanilla and apricot flavors, but it lacks finesse and cleanness. There's a harsh, burnt edge to the finish. **83** —*S.H. (12/15/2004)*

Prager NV Noble Companion Tawny Port (Napa Valley) $45. Turning a delicate tea-brown in color, this lovely wine explodes with aromas of toffee, milk chocolate, dark honey, butterscotch, and coffee. It's very sweet, with an ultrasmooth texture and a wonderful grip of acidity that makes it clean and compelling. Drink now. Made from Cabernet Sauvignon. **92** —*S.H. (12/15/2004)*

Prager 2001 Sweet Clair Late Harvest Riesling (Napa Valley) $27. This late-harvest Riesling has 11.2% residual sugar, meaning it's very sweet. It has flavors of ripe apricots and orange liqueur, and good acidity. Finishes a bit thin. **85** —*S.H. (12/1/2003)*

Prager 2002 Sweet Claire Riesling (Central Coast) $38. This wine is unique. I know of nothing like it in California. It's slatey and appley, with unctuous layers of botrytised apricot, sweet fig, vanilla, and caramel. Despite the honeyed taste, it's crisp with coastal acidity. **90** —*S.H. (12/15/2004)*

PRAXIS

Praxis 2004 Merlot (Alexander Valley) $15. Lots of bang for the buck here. Offers mouth-filling, juicy blackberry, cherry, pomegranate, and coffee flavors in a bone-dry, soft wine, with a fairly complicated tannin structure. Drink now. **87** —*S.H. (12/15/2006)*

Praxis 2003 Pinot Noir (Monterey) $15. Silky and light in texture, with good cool-climate acidity, and earthy, cherry-cola flavors that finish thin. **84** —*S.H. (12/15/2004)*

Praxis 2005 Sauvignon Blanc (Sonoma County) $15. Nice wine. Made from the area where Russian River Valley meets Alexander Valley, the wine shows warm-climate ripeness and cool-climate acidity. Bursts with

USA

juicy lime, fig, and melon flavors leading to a dry, white peppery finish. **85** —*S.H. (12/15/2006)*

Praxis 2003 Syrah (Dry Creek Valley) $14. Shows lots of mixed berries and caramelly oak on the nose, while the flavors veer toward simple cherry and vanilla. Light in body and supple of tannin; an easy-drinking Syrah with mass appeal. **85** *(9/1/2005)*

Praxis 2002 Viognier (Lodi) $15. A fruity quaff that features flavors redolent of apricots, peaches, lemons, and grapefruit. Acidity is bright, giving the finish some balance and freshness. **86** —*J.M. (4/1/2004)*

PREJEAN

Prejean 2001 Dry Riesling (Finger Lakes) $9. **83** —*J.C. (8/1/2003)*

Prejean 2001 Semi-Dry Riesling (Finger Lakes) $9. **84** —*J.C. (8/1/2003)*

PRESIDIO

Presidio 1997 Chardonnay (Santa Barbara County) $12. **86** —*S.H. (7/1/1999)*

Presidio 1999 Merlot (Santa Barbara County) $18. With some Cabernet Franc, and from the east end of Santa Ynez Valley, the two best Bordeaux reds in the appellation combine to make a soft, juicy wine, with ripe berry flavors and some herbal notes, and a smooth finish. **87** —*S.H. (3/1/2004)*

PRESTON

Preston 1995 Platinum Red Bordeaux Blend (Columbia Valley (WA)) $17. **81** —*S.H. (9/1/2000)*

Preston 1998 Cabernet Sauvignon (Columbia Valley (WA)) $12. Forward and strong, with a meaty aroma, this wine tastes more of cherry tomato than sweet cherry, and shows plenty of herbal flavors too. Tart and tannic finish. **83** —*P.G. (6/1/2002)*

Preston 1997 Cabernet Sauvignon (Columbia Valley (WA)) $12. This is what might be called old-style Washington Cabernet. The fruit is mixed liberally with bell pepper and dill; there is plenty of tannin and a distinctly earthy aroma of the barnyard that carries well into the finish. For some, it will be pleasantly reminiscent of cru Bourgeois Bordeaux. **85** —*P.G. (6/1/2001)*

Preston 1998 Chardonnay (Columbia Valley (WA)) $10. **81** —*P.G. (6/1/2000)*

Preston 1998 Reserve Chardonnay (Columbia Valley (WA)) $16. **82** —*P.G. (6/1/2000)*

Preston 1998 Beaujolais Rose Gamay (Columbia Valley (WA)) $10. **82** — *P.G. (6/1/2000)*

Preston 1998 Merlot (Columbia Valley (WA)) $12. The nose promises a potent mix of grassy fruit and earthy barnyard accents, but once in the mouth it all falls apart. The barnyard flavors are out of control, and the nail polish high notes don't help. **82** —*P.G. (6/1/2002)*

Preston 1997 Merlot (Columbia Valley (WA)) $12. Preston releases their red wines relatively late, and the extra time in barrel and bottle softens the tannins, and gives the finished wines a rounded quality. This is a solid effort, true to varietal, with plummy fruit, good balance, and a nice chocolatey, toasty finish that has just a slight taste of bitter banana to it. Good, serviceable Merlot at a fair price. **86** —*P.G. (6/1/2001)*

Preston 1999 Reserve Merlot (Columbia Valley (WA)) $22. The aromas are of tree bark, tea, and cola. Juicy blackberry flavors burst onto your palate touched with spice and full but soft tannins, all of which makes this an enjoyable wine to drink now or through 2005. **89** —*C.S. (12/31/2002)*

Preston 1998 Sauvignon Blanc (Columbia Valley (WA)) $8. **80** —*P.G. (6/1/2000)*

Preston 2002 Preston Vineyard Syrah (Columbia Valley (WA)) $23. The big question for this wine is: Will it ever come into balance? It's got broad, mouthfilling flavors of coffee, caramel, prune, and vanilla, all cut short on the finish by masses of tough, chewy tannins. **84** *(9/1/2005)*

PRESTON OF DRY CREEK

Preston 2003 Cavallo Barbera (Dry Creek Valley) $25. Dense purple in hue, this full-bodied wine has powerful aromas of mushu plum sauce, cherry pipe tobacco, and white pepper. It's tannic, but very soft, with a

dry, cherry-leather finish. Try this assertive wine with bold fare. **89** — *S.H. (11/1/2005)*

Preston 1999 Carignane (Dry Creek Valley) $20. Not considered a noble varietal, Carignane can offer pleasure, and this one does. It's quite rich and smells and tastes Porty, with dark chocolate and raisin notes, although the official alcohol is a moderate 13.6%. The plummy flavors are powerful, the tannins and acids soft. **86** —*S.H. (9/1/2002)*

Preston 1998 Marsanne (Dry Creek Valley) $13. 92 Best Buy —*L.W. (5/1/2000)*

Preston 1999 Mourvèdre (Dry Creek Valley) $22. One of the more interesting of the lesser Rhône grapes, but vintners struggle to give it depth. This one's got flattering red berry fruit flavors and soft acidity and tannins. Drinks dry and velvety, with a spicy finish. **87** —*S.H. (9/1/2002)*

Preston 1997 Mourvèdre (Dry Creek Valley) $16. 90 —*S.H. (2/1/2000)*

Preston 1997 Mas Viejo Mourvèdre (Dry Creek Valley) $16. 85 —*S.H. (10/1/1999)*

Preston 1996 Vineyard Select Mourvèdre (Dry Creek Valley) $20. 86 —*S.H. (6/1/1999)*

Preston 1997 Faux Red Red Blend (Dry Creek Valley) $11. 86 —*S.H. (6/1/1999)*

Preston 2002 L. Preston Red Blend (Dry Creek Valley) $25. Here's a big, dark, rustic red. It's effusive in red stone fruit and berry flavors, framed in vigorous tannins that lend the wine grip and structure. Despite the volume, it's easy to quaff. Syrah, Cinsault, and Mourvèdre. **88** —*S.H. (11/1/2005)*

Preston 1997 Cuvée de Fumé Sauvignon Blanc (Dry Creek Valley) $12. 89 Best Buy —*S.H. (9/1/1999)*

Preston 2001 Hartsock Sauvignon Blanc (Dry Creek Valley) $18. Refreshingly lemony and clean, here's a nice sipper for summer nights. The citrus and spice flavors could be more concentrated, and the acidity a bit firmer, but this dry white wine is fine for most occasions. **86** —*S.H. (9/1/2002)*

Preston 1998 Syrah (Dry Creek Valley) $18. 90 —*S.H. (2/1/2000)*

Preston 1997 Syrah (Dry Creek Valley) $18. 87 —*J.C. (11/1/1999)*

Preston 1997 Estate Grown Syrah (Dry Creek Valley) $18. 86 *(6/1/1999)*

Preston 1997 Estate Reserve Vogensen Bench Syrah (Dry Creek Valley) $28. Ripe and even, this appealing Sonoman delivers a lovely perfume of cassis toast and white pepper. Plenty of oak keeps it dark and tart, but of the type, it's very well done, with an even mouthfeel and long, tangy finish. This should be even better in two or three years. **89** *(11/1/2001)*

Preston 1998 Viognier (Dry Creek Valley) $20. 89 —*J.C. (10/1/1999)*

Preston 2000 Old Vine / Old Clone Zinfandel (Dry Creek Valley) $20. One of the best Zinfandels of the year. It defines Dry Creek Valley in its brambly fruit and soft, dusty tannins, but raises the bar in elegance, complexity, and sheer pleasure. It's a very dry wine, with a trace of bitterness in the finish. Drink this with the finest barbecue and grilled meats you can find. **93** —*S.H. (12/1/2002)*

Preston 2003 Old Vines Old Clones Zinfandel (Dry Creek Valley) $25. Made in a riper, sweeter style than others, with a roasted fruit character suggesting grilled cherries. The texture is smooth, soft, and supple. **85** —*S.H. (11/1/2005)*

Preston 1997 Old Vines/Old Clones Zinfandel (Dry Creek Valley) $15. 89 — *P.G. (11/15/1999)*

Preston of Dry Creek 2001 Cavallo Block Barbera (Dry Creek Valley) $25. Here's the kind of red 19th-century Sonoma immigrants drank with gusto, a strong, rich wine with berry flavors and an in-your-face personality. Dry, tannic, and gutsy, this wine isn't shy about showing its sunny, warm-climate origins. **86** —*S.H. (5/1/2003)*

Preston of Dry Creek 2002 Cinsault (Dry Creek Valley) $20. A simple, country-style wine, with cherry flavors. It's dry and tannic. It's not Cinsault's fault that by itself it can only make an innocent little wine. **83** —*S.H. (10/1/2004)*

Preston of Dry Creek 1999 Petite Sirah (Dry Creek Valley) $36. Preston brings control to this explosive varietal, reining in the berry and fruit flavors to craft a wine that's more like a Cabernet of Merlot. It's still big in flavors, with oodles of blackberry jam and pepper, and very dry. **87** —*S.H. (9/1/2003)*

Preston of Dry Creek 2002 Vogensen Bench Syrah-Sirah Red Blend (Dry Creek Valley) $20. Dark and vigorous, with blueberry and plum flavors and a soft, easygoing mouthfeel. A bit light and simply fruity, but a decent quaff. **86** *(9/1/2005)*

Preston of Dry Creek 2003 Vin Gris Rosé Blend (Dry Creek Valley) $15. The herb, raspberry, and vanilla flavors in this pale wine drink very dry. The good acidity will complement a terrine or chopped liver on crackers. Easy to sip, and with some complexity. Mourvèdre and Cinsault. **85** —*S.H. (10/1/2004)*

Preston of Dry Creek 2000 Vin Gris Rosé Blend (Dry Creek Valley) $11. Check out the pretty onionskin color of this subtle rosé, a blend of Mourvèdre, Cinsault, and Grenache. Starts with delicate but rich aromas of raspberry and smoke, and tastes very dry. There's an austerity to the flavors but also a good degree of complexity in the interplay of dusty tannins, acids, and alcohol. **87 Best Buy** —*S.H. (11/15/2001)*

Preston of Dry Creek 2003 Hartsock Sauvignon Blanc (Dry Creek Valley) $16. Very dry and citrusy-grassy, very crisp in lemony acids, and ultra-clean, this wine turns sweet with figs and cured tobacco on the finish. It's a fine apéritif sipper. **85** —*S.H. (10/1/2004)*

Preston of Dry Creek 2000 Hartsock Estate Reserve Sauvignon Blanc (Dry Creek Valley) $16. Pepper, peppermint, wintergreen, menthol, and spearmint highlight this young, herbaceous, but charming wine. The aggressive grassiness is nicely countered by a rich, creamy texture, although of course it's bone dry. There's a long, peppery, citrusy aftertaste. **87** —*S.H. (11/15/2001)*

Preston of Dry Creek 2000 Late Harvest Sémillon (Dry Creek Valley) $28. A dense, oily wine whose full-bodiedness leaves thick stains of glycerine on the glass. Tastes strongly of apricots and figs, and is very sweet and rich. Would be nice with vanilla ice cream. **89** —*S.H. (12/15/2003)*

Preston of Dry Creek 1999 Estate Syrah (Dry Creek Valley) $20. This big Dry Creek stalwart has fine, deep berry fruit, a slight and attractive meatiness on the nose and olive-garlic accents. Sounds weird, but it works: It has firm structure: the tightly packed fruit needs a few years to open and shed the moderate tannins. **89** *(10/1/2001)*

Preston of Dry Creek 2001 Vogensen Bench Syrah (Dry Creek Valley) $18. Pretty thick with tannins now, and that tough, chewy earthiness you sometimes get in a young red wine. Yet there's a rich core of black cherry fruit that's sweet and pure, accompanied by peppery herbs and spices. Drink with roast lamb or prosciutto. **86** —*S.H. (10/1/2004)*

Preston of Dry Creek 2000 Vogensen Bench Syrah (Dry Creek Valley) $22. Once you get past the tannins, you'll find a rich vein of young, jammy black cherry nectar. This dry wine is polished, supple, and forward in fruit. Be sure to match it that have foods with a sweet edge, like a smoky baked ham with cherry sauce. **87** —*S.H. (12/15/2003)*

Preston of Dry Creek 2003 Viognier (Dry Creek Valley) $25. You'll find Viognier's floral, exotic side in the tropical fruit and wildflower aromas and flavors, but the wine is very dry, with crisp acidity. It's clean and vibrant. **86** —*S.H. (10/1/2004)*

Preston of Dry Creek 2002 Viognier (Dry Creek Valley) $25. Fruit salad in a glass, with big flavors of peaches, limes, apples, and grapefruit. Drier than most of today's Viogniers, with very crisp acids that wash over the palate and stimulate it for food. **87** —*S.H. (6/1/2003)*

Preston of Dry Creek 2000 Viognier (Dry Creek Valley) $18. Here's a chewy wine that combines lush, exotic aromas and flavors with very dry fruit and a graceful elegance. The aroma suggests wild thyme and honey, grapefruit juice, and smoky spices. It drinks rather like a Sauvignon Blanc, with tight, lemony flavors and crispness. **87** —*S.H. (11/15/2001)*

Preston of Dry Creek 2002 Old Vines/ Old Clones Zinfandel (Dry Creek Valley) $24. Fairly full bodied and thick on the palate. The wine shows off some nice spice and cherry flavors, but it also has a bit of an herbal edge to it. Tannins are firm but mild, while the finish is a bit short. **85** — *J.M. (10/1/2004)*

Preston of Dry Creek 2001 Old Vines/Old Clones Zinfandel (Dry Creek Valley) $20. Bright-textured with cherry and berry flavors up front, the

wine offers moderate tannins and tea-like flavors on the finish. **85** *(11/1/2003)*

PRETTY-SMITH

Pretty-Smith 1999 Cabernet Franc (Paso Robles) $18. Normally a blending wine, because on its own this varietal offers sweetness and frangrance without accompanying body and depth, and this wine shows why. It's pretty as a picture, with black raspberry flavors and soft tannins, but it seems to need a center of gravity, especially at this price. **85** —*S.H. (9/1/2002)*

Pretty-Smith 1999 Cabernet Sauvignon (Paso Robles) $18. Here's a classic Paso Cabernet, with its ripe, juicy berry and stone fruit flavors, soft, pliant acids, and rich, velvety tannins. Nicely dry, it's the sort of wine you can play with in your mouth and discover wave after wave of delicious flavors. It's fun but serious, that rarest of things, a versatile Cabernet. **90** —*S.H. (9/12/2002)*

Pretty-Smith 1999 Chardonnay (Paso Robles) $16. Lots of well-toasted oak, brimming with vanilla, covers some awkward fruit. The oak doesn't taste natural, but like chips, or liquid smoke. The fruit is citrusy, although the wine does drink dry. The result is an odd, disagreeable drink. **81** —*S.H. (9/12/2002)*

Pretty-Smith 1999 Fumé Blanc (Paso Robles) $13. Starts with lemon and melon aromas with a nice cut of smoke and mineral, and turns rich and fruity in the mouth. There's a strong dose of spice, and the finish is honeyed and a little sweet. It's a clean drinking wine with charm. **85** —*S.H. (9/12/2002)*

Pretty-Smith 1999 Merlot (California) $18. Once upon a time this would be have a perfectly fine $8 wine. Now, it's an $18 wine, but it's still a nice drink. It's very dry, and balances blackberry flavors with less ripe herbal ones, resulting in some complexity. The finish is dry and fruity-spicy. Soft in acids, but the rich tannins add structure and spine. **87** —*S.H. (9/12/2002)*

PREVAIL

PreVail 2003 Back Forty Red Blend (Alexander Valley) $80. I think that Ferrari-Carano, which created this new label, felt a little left behind in the Cabernet race. They created this Cabernet-based blend, with a little Syrah, in the modern Napa style. It's velvety soft, superripe, and new oaky, with chocolate fudge and blackberry pie filling taste. A delicious modern wine for delicious steaks and chops. **92** —*S.H. (12/31/2006)*

PreVail 2003 West Face Red Blend (Alexander Valley) $50. Very similar to the winery's Back Forty, with a little Syrah added to the Cabernet Sauvignon and Cabernet Franc, this luscious wine has a chewy, cherry, mu shu plum sauce and new oak vanilla deliciousness. The chewiness is from mountain tannins. The wine is soft, but with just enough acidity for balance. Very fine, really tasty. A brand new label from Ferrari-Carano and one to watch. **92** —*S.H. (12/31/2006)*

PRIDE MOUNTAIN

Pride Mountain 2002 Cabernet Franc (Sonoma County) $56. Cab Franc alone rarely makes a great wine in California, and this one's no exception. It's awfully nice in initial raspberry-cherry flavors, but loses substantial power and vitality midpalate, especially given the size of the tannins. **86** —*S.H. (6/1/2005)*

Pride Mountain 2000 Cabernet Franc (Sonoma County) $52. It's easy to make Cab Franc tasty almost anywhere, but difficult to make it great. Pride succeeds in the latter with mountain grapes that concentrate flavors. Lush, opulent blackberry fruit is exquisitely offset with rich oak and dusty tannins. The texture is fabulous, at once light and dense. **95 Cellar Selection** —*S.H. (12/1/2002)*

Pride Mountain 1999 Cabernet Franc (Sonoma County) $52. It's standard these days for any Napa red to be soft, voluptuous, and ripely fruity, with creamy tannins and an overlay of smoky oak. This is such a wine. It's very good, although it lacks depth because Cab Franc on its own is rather shallow. **89** —*S.H. (9/1/2002)*

Pride Mountain 1997 Cabernet Sauvignon (Napa Valley) $36. 92 *(11/1/2000)*

Pride Mountain 2002 Cabernet Sauvignon (Napa Valley) $62. After encountering this tannic wine, you're left wondering if the cellar will be kind to it. Probably, but it's not a slam-dunk. It's tough and gritty, and you have to chew on it to release the black currants from their cage. Hold until 2008 and try again. **86** —*S.H. (6/1/2005)*

Pride Mountain 2000 Cabernet Sauvignon (Napa Valley) $56. Black as midnight, and stains the side of the glass. This is a big, extracted wine with plenty of body. Potent Cabernet aromas of black currants, tar, tobacco, and herbs explode from the glass, along with lots of sweet oak. **93 Editors' Choice** —*S.H. (2/1/2003)*

Pride Mountain 1999 Cabernet Sauvignon (Napa Valley) $56. Dark, plush and elegant, this wine defines style. It's fashionably dry and ripe, with black currant flavors and low acids. Oak adds vanilla and sweet, woody tannins but does not overwhelm. It's what consumers are looking for in an expensive California Cabernet. You could object that it's generically good. It lacks a sense of ground, of individuality, but that's tilting at windmills. **90** —*S.H. (6/1/2002)*

Pride Mountain 1996 Napa Valley Cabernet Sauvignon (Napa Valley) $30. 91 Cellar Selection —*L.W. (7/1/1999)*

Pride Mountain 2001 Chardonnay (Napa Valley) $35. From mountain vineyards, an intense fruit with enormously concentrated apple and peach flavors, generously oaked. The texture is creamy smooth, with sprightly acidity to make it lively and fresh. The long, spicy finish leaves behind a rich mouthfeel. **92** —*S.H. (2/1/2003)*

Pride Mountain 2000 Chardonnay (Napa Valley) $35. A big wine in every way, it manages to combine power with nuance and balance. High-extract tropical fruit is married to lavish oak, while high alcohol adds to the sense of monumentality. But it all hangs together to create a lavishly structured wine. **90** —*S.H. (5/1/2002)*

Pride Mountain 2001 Vintner's Select Mountain Top Vineyard Chardonnay (Sonoma County) $45. A young, tight mountain Chardonnay with a steely mouthfeel and crisp acids. There's a core of peach and apple fruit wound around the dusty tannins, while oak adds cream and vanilla notes. Best to cellar for a year. **89** —*S.H. (6/1/2003)*

Pride Mountain 2002 Merlot (Napa-Sonoma) $52. What a fabulous Merlot. Yes, it's dense in texture, like molten metal, with melted tannins, but it's kept lively with clean acids. Meanwhile, the flavors are sheer mountain fruit: concentrated blackberries and cherries and decadent mocha. Complex, elegant, and addictively good. **93 Editors' Choice** — *S.H. (6/1/2005)*

Pride Mountain 2000 Merlot (Napa-Sonoma) $48. Rich and long in the mouth, with impressively concentrated flavors of blackberries and plums and a delicious note of chocolatey fig. These ripe flavors are fully dry, with the most wonderful velvety tannins. The wine is soft and full of charm. **92** —*S.H. (11/15/2002)*

Pride Mountain 1999 Merlot (Napa-Sonoma) $48. What power and drama have gone into this wonderful wine. Sheer Pomerol, with pencil shaving, black cherry, cedar, chocolate, and gamy-meaty aromas and flavors, tinged with violets, and the most voluptuous mouthfeel. Sheer hedonism right through the long sweet finish. **94 Editors' Choice** —*S.H. (6/1/2002)*

Pride Mountain 1998 Merlot (Napa-Sonoma) $38. Sleek and elegant, the wine is blessed with fine tannins and supple texture, and its blackberry, plum, cassis, chocolate, and herb flavors flood the palate in a rush that finishes long and luxuriously. Top-notch Merlot. **93** —*J.M. (12/1/2001)*

Pride Mountain 2000 Vintner's Select Wind Whistle Vineyard Merlot (Napa County) $65. A success despite a certain leanness, a young wine in need of mid-term cellaring. Notes of of green olives, bacon, unsweetened dark chocolate, and boysenberries are wrapped in sumptuous, lush tannins that melt on the palate. This bone dry wine needs rich meats. **91 Cellar Selection** —*S.H. (8/1/2003)*

Pride Mountain 2000 Petite Sirah (Napa Valley) $40. Another tasting panel favorite, this is a big, extracted wine, but far from clumsy. The plush, jammy flavors include cherry, blackberry, vanilla, coffeebean, and spice; the wine feels round and powerful in the mouth. It never loses sight of elegance and finesse. **90** *(4/1/2003)*

Pride Mountain 2003 Syrah (Sonoma County) $55. Winemaker Bob Foley prefers older barrels for his Syrah, which lets the massive mountain fruit shine through. The result has a savory, meaty quality to the blackberry

fruit, and picks up complex notes of coffee and pepper as well. A bit firm on the finish for current consumption; this is one of the rare California Syrahs that needs 2–3 years of cellaring. **91 Cellar Selection** *(9/1/2005)*

Pride Mountain 2003 Viognier (Sonoma County) $40. Hits the top of the yummy scale. Massive flavors of tropical fruits, peaches, vanilla custard, honeysuckle, butterscotch, all of it smooth and creamy. Impacts the palate enormously; a big wine all the way through. **92** —*S.H. (6/1/2005)*

Pride Mountain 2001 Viognier (Sonoma County) $40. From Pride's estate 2,100 feet up in the Mayacamas, another in a string of impressive Viogniers. Follows the pattern of tempering the varietal's over the top character with barrel fermentation and lees aging. The result is a wine with the density of a big Chardonnay, but with Viognier's rich, yummy array of fruity flavors. **90** —*S.H. (6/1/2003)*

Pride Mountain 2000 Viognier (Sonoma County) $40. Sharply etched garden flower, citrus, butter, smoke, vanilla, and tropical fruit flavors are wrapped in a refined, oily texture of crisp acids and sleek tannins. The result is addictively drinkable and broad enough to be versatile at the table. **93 Editors' Choice** —*S.H. (9/1/2002)*

PRIMOS

Primos 2003 Sangiovese (Redwood Valley) $25. Vintage #1 smells very new-oaky. The wine itself is ripe in cherries, but has the flaw of excessive residual sugar, making it cloying. Let's hope Vintage #2 is dry. **82** —*S.H. (11/1/2005)*

PRINCE MICHEL DE VIRGINIA

Prince Michel de Virginia 1997 Chardonnay (Virginia) $13. 83 —*J.C. (8/1/1999)*

Prince Michel de Virginia 1997 Barrel Select Chardonnay (Virginia) $19. 84 —*J.C. (8/1/1999)*

PROSPERO

Prospero 2000 Cabernet Sauvignon (Sonoma County) $15. Blackberries and cherries and unripe notes of oregano and dill in both the aroma and the flavor. Turns simple and gluey in the mouth, with a sacchariney sweetness. **82** —*S.H. (12/31/2003)*

PROSPERO

Prospero 2001 Chardonnay (Russian River Valley) $18. Simple and fruity, with syrupy flavors of canned peaches and pears and an overlay of oak-like notes. Finishes watery and sweet. **83** —*S.H. (4/1/2004)*

Prospero 2000 Merlot (Sonoma County) $14. Not quite ripe, a bone dry wine with herbal-minerally flavors, stern tannins and notable acidity. Almost Chianti-like in its thin austerity, but it will fare well against a tomato-based pasta dish. **84** —*S.H. (12/31/2003)*

Prospero 1997 Reserve Merlot (Mendocino) $14. An acidic, tannic wine that overwhelms the mouth with tough astringency. It's certainly clean and dry, and is firm enough to stand up to, say, spaghetti with marinara sauce. On its own, it's pretty thin. **83** —*S.H. (2/1/2004)*

Prospero 2002 Syrah (California) $12. Seems a bit overripe, with roasted, caramelized fruit flavors and a hint of volatility, but does have some pleasant allspice and cinnamon notes as well. **82** *(9/1/2005)*

PROVENANCE VINEYARDS

Provenance Vineyards 2002 Cabernet Sauvignon (Oakville) $40. Very dark and young now—this wine needs to be cellared. It's powerfully tannic, with a burst of acidity; the mouthfeel is dusty and astringent. Has enough fruit to last beyond 2008. **89** —*S.H. (6/1/2005)*

Provenance Vineyards 2002 Cabernet Sauvignon (Rutherford) $35. Fascinating to compare this to Provenance's '02 Oakville Cab. The two share many of the same elements, namely big tannins that call for aging, but the Rutherford is marginally softer and less structured. Try after 2006. **88** —*S.H. (6/1/2005)*

Provenance Vineyards 2001 Cabernet Sauvignon (Rutherford) $35. Strives for balance and harmony and achieves both in the way the black cherry and herb flavors play off the tannins, acids and oak. Bone dry, this impeccable wine will develop further complexities for many years. **91 Editors' Choice** —*S.H. (10/1/2004)*

Provenance Vineyards 2001 Cabernet Sauvignon (Oakville) $35. From one of California's greatest Cabernet appellations, a big, rich wine, ripe with black currant, cherry and herb flavors wrapped in distinctively sweet, soft tannins. Reeks of class and elegance, with a cut of acidity that lends balance and firmness. **92** —S.H. (8/1/2004)

Provenance Vineyards 2000 Cabernet Sauvignon (Rutherford) $35. A cedary blend of spicy, licorice-like flavors, laced with blackberry and herb notes. The body is moderate for Napa Cabernet. Tannins are firm but powdery, while the finish is moderate in length. **87** —J.M. (6/1/2003)

Provenance Vineyards 2001 Beckstoffer Tokalon Vineyard Cabernet Sauvignon (Napa Valley) $NA. Dark, ripe, rich, and inviting. Char, vanilla, mocha, blackberry. Very rich and sweet but balanced. Tannins ripe, smooth, satisfying. Now-2012. **92** —S.H. (6/1/2005)

Provenance Vineyards 2003 Merlot (Napa Valley) $35. Robust and full-bodied, this will do well with a nice steak. It's dry, with a softly tannic mouthfeel framing black cherry, blackberry, and coffee flavors. Not likely to improve, so drink now through the end of the year. **87** —S.H. (7/1/2006)

Provenance Vineyards 2002 Merlot (Carneros) $27. Lots to like in this full-bodied, dry wine. It's showing good flavors of blackberries and currants, chocolate, and red cherries, and sweet oak. It finishes with a bit of fiery tannins and acids, though, suggesting very rich fare. **88** —S.H. (6/1/2005)

Provenance Vineyards 2001 Merlot (Carneros) $27. There's a good wine in here but it's disguised now beneath firm, astringent tannins. Chew it a little, and you'll find some plush black cherry and blackberry fruit. The oak also stands out, with edgy char and smoke. Give it a few years to come together. **88** —S.H. (8/1/2004)

Provenance Vineyards 2000 Merlot (Carneros) $28. Top flight Merlot, brimming with ripe black cherry, blackberry, chocolate, smoke, sage, thyme, anise, and pepper notes. It's all framed in silky ripe tannins, smooth, sleek, and lush. The finish is long. **92** —J.M. (8/1/2003)

Provenance Vineyards 2002 Las Amigas Vineyard Merlot (Carneros) $40. Lush in texture and well-oaked, with Merlot's soft, luxurious mouthfeel, this wine has had the best uprbringing imaginable, to judge by the pedigree. There are some beautiful cherry flavors. However, the score is compromised by a sharpness that will not age out. **86** —S.H. (2/1/2006)

Provenance Vineyards 2002 Paras Vineyard Merlot (Mount Veeder) $40. A little on the soft side, this wine charms for the purity of its black cherry, blackberry, and cocoa flavors. It also has a nice scour of tannins that grip the palate and stimulate it for rich foods. **88** —S.H. (6/1/2005)

Provenance Vineyards 2005 Sauvignon Blanc (Rutherford) $19. Fruity and lush, this Sauvignon offers a blast of lemon and lime, pineapple, applesauce, and cinnamon spice flavors, offset by crisp acids. With no oak, the fruit is the real star. **86** —S.H. (12/15/2006)

Provenance Vineyards 2004 Sauvignon Blanc (Napa Valley) $19. There's beautifully ripe citrus and fig fruit and clean, crisp acidity in this wine. It impresses for its balance and elegance, and would score higher if it weren't quite this sweet, almost off-dry on the finish. **84** —S.H. (2/1/2006)

Provenance Vineyards 2003 Sauvignon Blanc (Rutherford) $19. Another Rutherford Sauvignon Blanc. What's going on? This ones crisp in acids and mouthwatering in citrus fruits, enriched with a touch of fig. Completely dry, it's a great food wine, but delicious on its own. **88** — S.H. (12/1/2004)

PROVISOR

Provisor 2003 Syrah (Dry Creek Valley) $30. Drying and tannic, with questionable ageworthiness, but some attractive black cherry and plum flavors and hints of anise, mint, and graphite. Drink young with rare beef to help tame the tannins. **84** (9/1/2005)

Provisor 2002 Syrah (Dry Creek Valley) $30. Dark as a moonless midnight, dry as a desert, and chockful of thick, dusty tannins, but saved by overall balance and complexity and a deep core of black cherry fruit. Almost impossible to drink now except with something huge, like lamb. Should develop nicely through 2010. **90** —S.H. (3/1/2005)

PUCCIONI

Puccioni 2004 Old Vine Zinfandel (Dry Creek Valley) $28. Blended with some Petite Sirah, this Zin is enormously rich in wild berry, coffee, tobacco, and spice flavors, with a honey-ripe sweetness, but it's dry. A little oak adds a pleasant vanilla and caramel richness. **90** —S.H. (12/31/2006)

Puccioni 2003 Old Vine Zinfandel (Dry Creek Valley) $28. Veteran Napa vintner Glenn Proctor turns his sights to old vine Sonoma Zin to craft this robust, effusively fruity wine. It's dry to the palate, laced with rich tannins, and has ripe berry-cherry flavors that veer into raisins. **86** —S.H. (6/1/2006)

Q

Q 2002 Syrah (Sonoma County) $16. Starts off cedary, then expands to deliver toast and vanilla scents. Sound oaky? It is, but it's balanced by bright raspberry fruit. Creamy and supple on the palate, with an easy finish. **86** (9/1/2005)

QUADY

Quady 2001 Elysium Black Muscat (California) $10. "Elysium" in Greek mythology is the afterlife of perfect bliss, and it's not hard to imagine this as its house pour. It is sweet—but not shockingly so—with blackberry, orange, vanilla, and chocolate flavors, and a richly smooth mouthfeel. If you're treating yourself to something chocolatey, especially if it has oranges or strawberries, this will be a seductive companion. **89** —S.H. (11/15/2003)

Quady 1998 Electra Orange Muscat (California) $NA. 87 (12/31/1999)

Quady 1998 Essencia Orange Muscat (California) $18. 81 —J.C. (12/31/1999)

QUAIL CREEK

Quail Creek 1999 Cabernet Sauvignon (California) $10. Young and purple, with strong aromas of cassis, dark chocolate, and smoky vanilla. It's surprisingly rich and dense; a layered wine with lots of interesting flavors. It's also quite tannic, and will be better if aged for a few years. Contains 20% Syrah. **87 Best Buy** —S.H. (8/1/2001)

Quail Creek 1998 Cabernet Sauvignon (California) $10. It hits all the right Cabernet notes of blackberry, plum, cassis, tobacco, mint, and even chocolate. Dry and well structured, with fine acidity and modulated tannins. So why not a higher score? Because everything is very light. Nonetheless, it's good value for the money. **84** —S.H. (5/1/2001)

Quail Creek 1999 Chardonnay (California) $10. A richly fruity, spicy, oaky wine that offers up plenty of what consumers like, in an everyday, affordable package. The fruit veers toward peaches and tropical fruit, and it's a little sweet. Seems flabby around the edges, but not bad for the price. **84** —S.H. (5/1/2001)

Quail Creek 1999 Merlot (California) $10. This is a simple, straightforward, everyday sort of wine, light in aroma and body, but with acceptable black cherry, earthy flavors. It's dry and clean. 20% Syrah adds complexity and notes of currants and meat. **85 Best Buy** —S.H. (5/1/2001)

QUAIL RIDGE

Quail Ridge 2001 Cabernet Sauvignon (Napa Valley) $16. Rough in texture, sharp in vinegary acids, this is a hard wine to like. It's not going anywhere, but the fruity flavors wlll be fine with simple fare. **83** —S.H. (11/1/2005)

Quail Ridge 1999 Reserve Cabernet Sauvignon (Napa Valley) $50. Lush and balanced in the mouth, with dusty tannins, the Quail Ridge offers butterscotch, red berry fruit, herb, and mineral from beginning to end. It's aged in small French oak barrels for 26 months—was I imagining a charred, bourbon-like note on the palate? Worth finding one of the 743 cases made. **91** —D.T. (6/1/2002)

Quail Ridge 1997 Volker Eisele Vineyard Reserve Cabernet Sauvignon (Napa Valley) $45. This dark, brooding young pup is gorgeous now and will only get better. Toasty oak dominates the nose, masking ripe blackberry fruit. It really sings in the mouth, with a blast of fruit and spice, and dry, lacy tannins. It's soft enough to drink tonight, but will hold well. **92** —S.H. (8/1/2001)

USA

Quail Ridge 2003 Chardonnay (Napa Valley) $12. Picnics and Chardonnay: predictable, but perfect. If you're into the dejeuner sur l'herbe thing with, say, salami and pastrami sandwiches with Swiss cheese, roast chicken, potato salad, cream cheese-filled celery sticks, olives, apples, and bananas, this rich, creamy, and fairly-priced Chard will not disappoint. You'll like it even served in little plastic glasses. **86** —S.H. (8/1/2005)

Quail Ridge 2000 Reserve Chardonnay (Mendocino) $24. Made in the style popular today, with rich, ripe flavors of peaches, pears, and tropical fruits, and a generous dose of oak. Feels creamy and very spicy in the mouth and through the long finish. **86** —S.H. (10/1/2003)

Quail Ridge 2002 Merlot (Napa Valley) $14. A bit rough, but once you factor the price in, this is a decent buy. The balanced ripe blackberry flavors will elevate a hamburger. **85** —S.H. (11/1/2005)

Quail Ridge 1998 Volker Eisele Vineyard Merlot (Napa Valley) $40. Very fragrant and alluring, with drink-me aromas of fancy plums, blackberries, currants, smoke, and oak. Quite a big mouthful of fruity extract, yet it's nicely balanced, with elegant tannins and a dry, creamy texture. Contains trace amounts of Cabernet Sauvignon and Malbec. **91 Cellar Selection** —S.H. (8/1/2001)

Quail Ridge 2000 Sauvignon Blanc (Napa Valley) $14. Asparagus and other vegetal aromas are quite strong. Grapefruit and lime flavors are marred by a persistent attack of green. The finish is tangy and tart, raising questions about its ripeness. Too green and flinty to merit higher. **85** (9/1/2003)

Quail Ridge 1997 Reserve Barrel-Fermented Sauvignon Blanc (Rutherford) $15. **85** —M.M. (3/1/2000)

Quail Ridge 1999 Zinfandel (Napa Valley) $23. A bizarre stewed fruit, fresh herb and Asian spice-scented bouquet could not have prepared me for the cloyingly sweet watermelon, bright raspberry, and strawberry daquiri flavors that dominate the palate and the finish. Finishes short, with more of the same, plus oak and smoke flavors. **80** —D.T. (3/1/2002)

QUATRO

Quatro 1997 Cabernet Sauvignon (Sonoma County) $16. **86** —S.H. (2/1/2000)

Quatro 2002 Cabernet Sauvignon (Alexander Valley) $15. A nice Cab with some real distinction. There are ripely sweet cherry, chocolate, and dried herb flavors, and the texture is velvety smooth and soft. A little heavy and dense, though. **85** —S.H. (11/15/2004)

Quatro 1997 Merlot (Sonoma County) $16. **84** (3/1/1999)

QUEEN OF HEARTS

Queen of Hearts 2002 Cabernet Sauvignon (Santa Barbara County) $12. Soft and rustic; very low acidity and simple, semi-sweet cherry cough medicine flavors. **82** —S.H. (9/1/2006)

Queen of Hearts 2004 Chardonnay (Santa Barbara County) $10. As tart in acids and zingy as cool-climate Chard comes, with bright, mouth-stimulating lime and kiwi flavors that finish dry and clean. There's a tiny bit of oak, but the fruit really stars in this tasty, affordable wine. **85 Best Buy** —S.H. (12/1/2006)

Queen of Hearts 2003 Merlot (Santa Barbara County) $12. Upfront cherry, blackberry, and chocolate flavors hit with some nice, furry tannins, and the wine is basically an everyday, by-the-glass sort of Merlot. **84** —S.H. (12/1/2006)

Queen of Hearts 2004 Sauvignon Blanc (Santa Barbara County) $10. Filled with bright, zesty fruit, this Sauvignon offers lots to like, such as forward pineapple, cinnamon, and vanilla flavors that finish just a little sweet. High acidity provides much-needed balance. **84** —S.H. (12/1/2006)

QUILCEDA CREEK

Quilceda Creek 2003 Cabernet Sauvignon (Washington) $95. Lovely color and aromatics, this supremely powerful yet graceful wine sends up a mix of plum, berry, dust, mint, and menthol. It's spicy and young, and surprisingly light on its feet. The concentration here is different from a top-tier Napa Cabernet; the fruit has a pleasing elegance. The acids are firm but unobtrusive, the tannins are ripe, smooth but substantial, giving the wine some weight and power. As good as anything this superb producer has ever done. **97 Cellar Selection** —P.G. (10/1/2006)

Quilceda Creek 2002 Cabernet Sauvignon (Washington) $80. Amazing density; the aromas billow up from the glass and weave together sinuously, taking you on a magic carpet ride before the wine even hits your mouth. This wine has the power of a monster California Cab while retaining the subtlety of a first-growth Bordeaux. It is just a massive blast of dark fruit, incredible viscosity, silky textures, and soft herbs, pepper and spice. The oak—all new, all French—is unobtrusive and perfectly integrated. **97 Cellar Selection** —P.G. (12/15/2005)

Quilceda Creek 2001 Cabernet Sauvignon (Washington) $80. This is an almost-pure, Champoux Vineyard Cabernet, the best of the best. It's extremely aromatic, rich, and textured, tight and dense. As it slowly opens it reveal layer upon layer of black fruits, mineral, salt, and lovely, evanescent hints of herb. It does not show its 14.9% alcohol except for a slight bit of heat in the finish. Very, very young; Quilceda Creek Cabs may be the longest lived in Washington. **95 Cellar Selection** —P.G. (9/1/2004)

Quilceda Creek 1999 Cabernet Sauvignon (Washington) $60. Quilceda makes big, muscular Cabernets, but the power is tightly controlled and never out of whack. Firm cherry fruit is edged with mixed spices from barrel aging. Still young and hard, this is a tannic wine that clearly has the stuffing and structure to age indefinitely, but if drunk now will require many hours of breathing time. **93 Editors' Choice** —P.G. (6/1/2002)

Quilceda Creek 1998 Cabernet Sauvignon (Washington) $60. After "fiddling around," as he puts it, with blends in his '96 and '97 Cabs, winemaker Alex Golitzin decided to go with straight Cabernet in '98, an exceptional vintage for Washington State. This is a tight, focused effort, with powerful black fruits augmented with herbs and spices and a hint of mineral. Young, tart, and tannic, it will continue to improve as it knits together over the years. **95 Editors' Choice** —P.G. (6/1/2002)

Quilceda Creek 2003 Merlot (Washington) $65. Oaky, toasty, and spicy, this thick, massive Merlot is packed with berries, cherries, plums, and chocolate. The Cab Franc adds meaty tannins to the beautiful blueberry, blue plum, and blackberry fruit. A sweet, supple Merlot with hints of coffee, black tea, and earth. Makes you wish Quilceda made more of it. **95** —P.G. (11/15/2006)

Quilceda Creek 2002 Merlot (Washington) $65. Thick, dark, and chewy, this is as good as Merlot gets. The source vineyard is Champoux, and it has also contributed a smattering of Cab Franc to the blend, which also includes 22% Klipsun Cabernet Sauvignon. This is a ripe, chewy wine, loaded with blueberry, blackberry, citrus, and dried herb. Though front-loaded with big, jammy fruit, it continues to develop more subtle and complex strains of herb, tar, and black tea as it unwinds. It has the authority, the density, and the impact of Cabernet. **94 Editors' Choice** —P.G. (12/15/2005)

Quilceda Creek 1999 Merlot (Washington) $60. In this vintage the Klipsun Vineyard Merlot (75%) is blended with Cabernet Sauvignon from Ciel du Cheval (22%) and Cabernet Franc from the Taptiel Vineyard, all prime property on Washington's Red Mountain. Tight and focused, this exceptionally well-structured Merlot mixes red and black fruits with exotic spices. Muscular and built to age, it's an amazing wine. **94** —P.G. (6/1/2002)

Quilceda Creek 1998 Merlot (Washington) $60. This extremely limited-production Merlot (about 250 cases) is Alex and Paul Golitzin's "other" great red. It's all Klipsun Vineyard fruit, 75% Merlot and 25% Cabernet, and its soft, chocolatey tannins envelope the taste buds in a sensual, textured landscape comprised of luscious cherry fruit and laced with hints of anise and roasted coffee. Big and extracted, yet more approachable than the Cabernet. **92** —P.G. (6/1/2002)

Quilceda Creek 2002 Red Blend (Columbia Valley (WA)) $35. Fragrant and inviting with sweet aromas of raspberries and ripe cherries. Not a hint of anything vegetal or off in any way; this is the finest declassified wine I've ever tasted. "If it's not a 95 right out of the barrel," says Alex Golitzun, "it's declassified." The blend is 70% Cabernet Sauvignon, 20% Merlot, and 10% Cab Franc. Medium-light in the mouth, with pretty cinnamon and baking spices, and a clean, crisp palate impression. Reasonably concentrated, it finishes lightly smoky and thoroughly delicious. **93** —P.G. (12/15/2005)

Quilceda Creek 1998 Red Blend (Washington) $40. The wine not used in their primary red wines goes into this modestly named "Red Wine" which is one of the top two or three such second label wines made in Washington. Think Les Forts de Latour and you get the picture. Forward, richly scented, and dense; the only difference from the big Quilceda Cabernet is that this one is front-loaded, and doesn't deliver the power in the finish. **89** —*P.G. (6/1/2002)*

Quilceda Creek 2003 Red Red Blend (Columbia Valley (WA)) $35. A wonderful nose of violets and mixed fruits, with hints of Asian spices. Long and seamless, textural, and detailed, it leads into flavors of boysenberry, blueberry, and cherry. The oak is very nicely applied, and the wine keeps coming at you with flavors of Bourbon barrel, soft soy, balsamic, and moist earth, all beautifully integrated. **93** —*P.G. (10/1/2006)*

Quilceda Creek 2001 Red Wine Red Blend (Columbia Valley (WA)) $35. Quilceda's second wine is gorgeous, supple, and sweet with lovely Cabernet cassis and smooth hints of licorice and chocolate. Though not as concentrated as the Cabernet, it is immediately delicious, and would put to shame most wines in its price category. **92 Editors' Choice** —*P.G. (9/1/2004)*

QUILICI

Quilici 2004 Sangiovese (California) $12. Pours light in color and feels light in body, with pleasant raspberry, cola, and spice flavors, and a dry finish. Despite high alcohol (15.5%) it's not hot. **84** —*S.H. (12/31/2006)*

QUINTA DA SONORA

Quinta da Sonora 2000 Verdelho (California) $12. From 100% Lodi grapes, a fresh, fruity, lively wine with tropical fruit and spice aromas. The flavors are very rich and ripe, suggesting pineapple, guava, cinnamon, and nutmeg. Despite the intense fruitiness, it's dry and balanced. **87** —*S.H. (11/15/2001)*

QUINTANA

Quintana 2000 Cabernet Sauvignon (North Coast) $18. Lots of richness in this pretty red table wine. It's dry and complex, with true varietal flavors of black currants and herbs, and a good overlay of spicy, toasty oak. Tannins are melted, with supportive acids, and the finish is dry and flavorful. **87** —*S.H. (4/1/2003)*

Quintana 1999 Cabernet Sauvignon (North Coast) $18. You can taste the sun of this glorious vintage in every fruity, berry-filled sip. It's bursting with juicy, ripe flavors, wrapped in the sculpted tannins and soft acids, but it's nicely dry. This is a pretty wine, delicious, and uncomplex. From Laurel Glen. **88** —*S.H. (9/12/2002)*

QUINTESSA

Quintessa 1996 Bordeaux Blend (Rutherford) $90. 90 *(9/1/2000)*

Quintessa 2002 Bordeaux Blend (Rutherford) $120. The best Quintessa in years, this huge, rich wine is really too young now. All the parts are beautiful, from the ripe, sweet cherry-blackberry fruit through the fine, dusty tannins to the lush overlay of vanilla-scented oak. This will be a great wine by 2007 and should last for many years afterward. **94 Cellar Selection** —*S.H. (12/15/2005)*

Quintessa 1999 Bordeaux Blend (Rutherford) $100. Displays distinct valley-floor qualities, with its well-ripened black currant fruit and soft, intricately woven tannins. Feels rich and lush in the mouth, and coats the palate through the long finish. Oak provides a context, but doesn't overwhelm. Feels too soft to age, but you never know. **93** —*S.H. (12/31/2002)*

Quintessa 2003 Cabernet Sauvignon (Rutherford) $120. This wonderfully rich young wine is enormously powerful in blackberry preserves, crème brûlée, mocha, and cassis flavors. There's lots of new oak, but it's well integrated, and the tannins are softly gentle, yet ripe and complex. Almost feminine in its opulence, the wine is beautiful now, but has the balance to hold and even improve for many years. Drink now–2020. **94 Cellar Selection** —*S.H. (12/15/2006)*

Quintessa 2001 Cabernet Sauvignon (Rutherford) $110. Quite ripe and oaky, made in a big, impressive style. Knocks you out with the density and concentration of its black currant, dark chocolate, and coffee flavors. Completely dry, and with a tart, espresso-like bitterness, this beauty is guaranteed to age, with its firm tannins. Drink now through 2015. **92** —*S.H. (10/1/2004)*

Quintessa 2000 Red Wine Red Blend (Rutherford) $100. This estate has pulled out all the stops and produced a delicious wine of substance, finesse, and great charm. It floods the palate with flavors of black currants and cassis that carry ripely sweet fruit impressions deep into the taste buds, but it's dry. The oak is elaborate and in keeping with the fruit. For all the size, it's a feminine wine, and best enjoyed in its youth. **92 Cellar Selection** —*S.H. (12/31/2003)*

QUIVIRA

Quivira 2001 Wine Creek Ranch Mourvèdre (Dry Creek Valley) $15. This is a big blush wine, not light and simple like white Zin, but full-bodied and dense. It's very flavorful, with the taste of peaches and cherries a dusty, herbal earthiness. The finish is a little cloying, but overall it's a dry wine. **85** —*S.H. (9/1/2003)*

Quivira 2003 Wine Creek Ranch Mourvèdre (Dry Creek Valley) $14. With some Grenache, this coppery-pink wine is flashy with raspberry, strawberry, cinnamon, vanilla, and coffee flavors. It's very dry, with a good spine of acidity, and will go with a wide variety of appetizers. Nice for a summer cocktail, too. **85** —*S.H. (10/1/2004)*

Quivira 2004 Wine Creek Ranch Rosé Mourvèdre (Dry Creek Valley) $14. Here's a deeply colored, strongly flavored blush wine, but despite the power, it's delicate in structure. The fruit is all cherries and raspberries, and the finish is totally dry. You could almost substitute this pretty wine for Pinot Noir. **87** —*S.H. (11/1/2005)*

Quivira 1997 Cuvée Red Blend (Dry Creek Valley) $13. 85 —*L.W. (6/1/1999)*

Quivira 2000 Dry Creek Cuvée Red Blend (Dry Creek Valley) $18. A Rhône-style field blend that shows why this style of red wine was a favorite of the oldtimers. It's rich, dense, concentrated, and just plain fun to drink. Somehow combines easiness with complexity, making this dry, fruity wine one of the most versatile bottlings of the vintage. Forward tannins in the finish suggest aging possibilities. **91** —*S.H. (12/1/2002)*

Quivira 2003 Steelhead Red Blend (Dry Creek Valley) $18. Tasted beside the 2002, which is soft and flamboyant, this younger wine is tighter and fresher. Both wines are dominated by Grenache, which should release its time-bomb cherriness by the end of 2005. This Châteauneuf-style blend also contains Mourvèdre, Syrah, and Zinfandel. **88** —*S.H. (11/1/2005)*

Quivira 2004 Steelhead Blended Red Wine Red Blend (Dry Creek Valley) $18. Easy and soft, this blend of Grenache, Zin, Syrah, and Mourvèdre has polished cherry, herb, and tobacco flavors, with gentle tannins and a very dry finish. The grapes are from Quivira's estate vineyards. **84** —*S.H. (11/15/2006)*

Quivira 1997 Sauvignon Blanc (Dry Creek Valley) $11. 88 Best Buy —*L.W. (9/1/1999)*

Quivira 2004 Fig Tree Vineyard Sauvignon Blanc (Dry Creek Valley) $16. Made white Bordeaux-style, with barrel fermentation in partially new French oak and aged sur lies, this vineyard bottling is always interesting, but the '04 is one of the best. It's rich and creamy, with complex flavors of Meyer lemon, ripe fig, honeydew, crushed pineapple, and peppery spice. Yet for all that, it's quite dry. Don't overchill, or you'll miss the nuances. **92 Editors' Choice** —*S.H. (7/1/2006)*

Quivira 2003 Fig Tree Vineyard Sauvignon Blanc (Dry Creek Valley) $16. From estate grapes, this intensely flavored wine shows citron, lemongrass, and fig flavors, brightened by acid. Sémillon, barrel fermentation, and sur lie aging all bring a rich, nutty creaminess, and a slight sweetness, to the finish. **87** —*S.H. (8/1/2005)*

Quivira 2000 Fig Tree Vineyard Sauvignon Blanc (Dry Creek Valley) $16. Lemon and lime flavors mark this pleasant wine, grown in one of California's best appellations for the varietal. It's dry and crisp, with a dusty sprinkling of tannins. The citrusy theme picks up again on the tart finish. **87** —*S.H. (9/1/2003)*

Quivira 1999 Fig Tree Vineyard Sauvignon Blanc (Dry Creek Valley) $18. This wine has a dairy note to the nose; i.e., cheese, custard, and yogurt. Lemony flavors are accented by dried baking spices, while the back palate is a touch chalky, offering some good and welcome grip. Overall,

USA

the wine seems a bit heavy. If it were pushing amps, it would be a high-power machine. **87** *(8/1/2002)*

Quivira 1998 Fig Tree Vineyard Sauvignon Blanc (Dry Creek Valley) $14. 89 —*L.W. (2/1/2000)*

Quivira 2002 Wine Creek Ranch Syrah (Dry Creek Valley) $24. Funky on the nose, with sulfury notes that not all tasters will find attractive or have the patience to deal with. But beyond the funk there's a big, full-bodied, impressive wine, loaded with blackberries, vanilla, and pepper. **86** *(9/1/2005)*

Quivira 1998 Zinfandel (Dry Creek Valley) $18. 89 —*L.W. (9/1/1999)*

Quivira 2004 Zinfandel (Dry Creek Valley) $20. Give credit both to the terroir and Quivira's long experience, for this is a beautiful Zinfandel. A ripe harvest has given it lush blackberry, blueberry, black raspberry, mocha, and spice flavors, but the wine maintains an essential balance and harmony, with a great tannin-acid ratio. **91** —*S.H. (11/1/2006)*

Quivira 2003 Zinfandel (Dry Creek Valley) $20. Shows real Dry Creek character, which is a dry, claret-like balance, modest alcohol, well-ripened fruit, and smooth, grippy tannins, with an herbal undertow. The raspberry, cherry, and blackberry fruit marries well with sweet oak. **90 Editors' Choice** —*S.H. (11/1/2005)*

Quivira 2001 Zinfandel (Dry Creek Valley) $20. Quite tangy and bright. Spicy cherry flavors later reveal themselves, though there are hints of blackberry, cinnamon, and herbs as well. The finish is moderate in length. **87** *(11/1/2003)*

Quivira 2000 Zinfandel (Dry Creek Valley) $20. Defines the appellation with its well-ripened wild berry fruit, dry, dusty tannins, and elegant acids, but marred for me by the taste of raisins. Curiously, the reported alcohol is a modest 13.7%, and the wine doesn't taste hot. But those overripe flavors detract from an otherwise beautiful wine. **85** —*S.H. (11/1/2002)*

Quivira 1999 Zinfandel (Dry Creek Valley) $22. 88 —*D.T. (3/1/2002)*

Quivira 2000 Anderson Ranch Zinfandel (Dry Creek Valley) $35. From the heart of the valley, brilliant Zinfandel that captures the spirit of the appellation in its wild, ripe, juicy fruit flavors, fine tannins, and perfect acidity. The fruit really stars here, suggesting every berry you can think of, but it's not a fruit bomb. The dryness and earthy tartness balance it out. **90** —*S.H. (11/1/2002)*

Quivira 2002 Anderson Road Zinfandel (Dry Creek Valley) $30. This is a darker, richer Zin than Quivira's regular wine. It has a milk chocolate edge to the black currants and cassis, but shares the same claret-like balance and elegance. **91** —*S.H. (11/1/2005)*

Quivira 1997 Reserve Zinfandel (Dry Creek Valley) $25. 91 —*L.W. (2/1/2000)*

Quivira 2002 Wine Creek Ranch Zinfandel (Dry Creek Valley) $30. My favorite of Quivira's Zins. From east-facing slopes, this dense and concentrated wine captures intense berry and cherry flavors and focuses them with laserlike intensity. The fruit sinks down deep into the tastebuds, while rich, dusty tannins provide the proper structure. **92** —*S.H. (11/1/2005)*

QUPÉ

Qupé 1997 Bien Nacido Cuvée Chardonnay (Santa Barbara County) $16. 87 —*S.H. (9/1/1999)*

Qupé 1999 Bien Nacido Reserve Chardonnay (Santa Barbara County) $30. Bob Lindquist's 1999 offering displays a lovely opening of tropical fruit and vanilla custard beneath a smoky veil. The palate's understated nectarine, pear, pineapple flavors are bolstered by firm but not sharp acidity. The mouthfeel is crisp; the wine's fine structure shows through the tangy, nut-pepper finish. Already impressive, but warrants cellaring for two or three years. Top Value. **91** *(7/1/2001)*

Qupé 1998 Bien Nacido Reserve Chardonnay (Santa Barbara County) $25. 89 *(6/1/2000)*

Qupé 1998 Bien Nacido Vineyard Chardonnay (Santa Barbara County) $18. 87 *(6/1/2000)*

Qupé 2001 Bien Nacido Vineyard Block Eleven Reserve Chardonnay (Santa Maria Valley) $25. Dessert in a dry white wine. Tastes like ripe green

apple compote, gingersnap cookies, vanilla ice cream, and smoky maple syrup all mixed together, with bright acidity to make it come alive. How good and rich this cool-coast, southland wine is. **89** —*S.H. (6/1/2004)*

Qupé 1997 Bien Nacido Vineyard Reserve Chardonnay (Santa Barbara County) $25. 92 —*S.H. (7/1/2000)*

Qupé 2002 Bien Nacido Vineyard Y-Block Chardonnay (Santa Maria Valley) $18. Instantly appealing for its well-oaked flavors of ripe tropical fruits, intense spices, and clean, zesty acidity. There's a streak of sweet-and-sour lees throughout. A relative value considering its pedigree. **86** —*S.H. (6/1/2004)*

Qupé 1997 Ibarra-Young Vineyard Marsanne (Santa Barbara County) $14. 90 Best Buy —*S.H. (6/1/1999)*

Qupé 1997 Los Olivos Cuvée Red Blend (Santa Barbara County) $18. 90 —*S.H. (10/1/1999)*

Qupé 2001 Los Olivos Cuvée Rhône Red Blend (Santa Ynez Valley) $20. Syrah dominates this year's fun blend, with Grenache and Mourvèdre. It's quite good and satisfying. The cherry, herb, tobacco, and mocha flavors are restrained by rich, smooth, fully ripened tannins. A delicate, easy wine, but it has deep waters. **90 Editors' Choice** —*S.H. (6/1/2004)*

Qupé 2001 Alban Vineyard Roussanne (Edna Valley) $25. Super-fruity. Peaches, nectarines, limes, wildflowers, and lots of honey, vanilla, and spice all mingle together, brightened with crisp, citrusy acids. It's intricately balanced and totally dry. **88** —*S.H. (6/1/2004)*

Qupé 1997 Alban Vineyard Roussanne (Edna Valley) $25. 91 —*S.H. (10/1/1999)*

Qupé 1996 Alban Vineyard Roussanne (Edna Valley) $25. 91 —*S.H. (6/1/1999)*

Qupé 2003 Syrah (Central Coast) $17. True to winemaker Bob Lindquist's style, this blended Syrah relies more on complexity and spice to wine tasters' hearts than fruit and raw power. Smoky, meaty, and peppery notes rest on a lean structure, finishing with a flourish of bright cherry flavor. **87** *(9/1/2005)*

Qupé 2002 Bien Nacido Hillside Estate Syrah (Santa Maria Valley) $40. Built for the long haul, right now this wine isn't showing its full potential. Instead it's a mass of promise—of dense coffee, spice, and black olive flavors waiting for some day in the future when they will blossom. They're reined in tight right now, but the long finish of this wine plainly identifies its ultimate high quality. Try in 2010. **88** *(9/1/2005)*

Qupé 1997 Bien Nacido Hillside Estate Syrah (Santa Barbara County) $35. 92 —*S.H. (10/1/1999)*

Qupé 1999 Bien Nacido Reserve Syrah (Santa Barbara County) $25. Smoke, cedar, and cherries mark the nose of this Syrah from winemaker Bob Lindquist. The flavors are tart and carry a bit of herbaceousness, finishing mocha-creamy and pruny. Although good, it's a bit below the level of excellence Lindquist has set in the past. **86** *(11/1/2001)*

Qupé 2003 Bien Nacido Vineyard Syrah (Santa Maria Valley) $28. Built more on acid than on tannin, this is a light-bodied, easy-to-drink Syrah that shows all of the requisite varietal characteristics: smoke, meat, and pepper alongside crisp red berry flavors. Nicely complex; an intellectual wine rather than a hedonistic one. **84** *(9/1/2005)*

Qupé 2001 Bien Nacido Vineyard Syrah (Santa Maria Valley) $25. Always a wine that needs a good six years in a good vintage to mature, this release is marked by plummy, blackberry, and chocolate flavors that are framed in stiff tannins. It's not a blockbuster, but should gain complexity by 2007. **87** —*S.H. (6/1/2004)*

Qupé 2000 Bien Nacido Vineyard Hillside Estate Syrah (Santa Maria Valley) $40. This is a reserve selection from an important vineyard. The wine has good plum and berry flavors, with a meaty, coffee edge, but it doesn't really have the concentration or sweet intensity to outlast the significant tannins. If you're a gambler, try cellaring until 2007 or so. **88** —*S.H. (6/1/2004)*

Qupé 1997 Bien Nacido Vineyard Reserve Syrah (Santa Barbara County) $25. 91 —*S.H. (6/1/1999)*

R & B CELLARS

R & B Cellars 1997 Reserve Cabernet Sauvignon (Napa Valley) $74. 90 (11/1/2000)

R. MERLO

R. Merlo 2001 Hyampom Valley Ranch Cabernet Sauvignon (Trinity County) $26. Made from mountain vineyards in the foothills of the Sierra Nevada, this is a tough, chewy Cabernet. It's very dry, and robust tannins surround ripe blackberry fruit flavors. Good now, and should develop for a few years. 85 —S.H. (12/31/2006)

R. Merlo 2002 Hyampom Valley Ranch Merlot (Trinity County) $26. Ripe and fruity, bursting with blackberry and cherry jam flavors balanced with crisp acids and firm tannins, this is a nice, easy wine to enjoy with steaks and chops. 84 —S.H. (12/31/2006)

R. Merlo 2003 Pommard Pinot Noir (Trinity County) $22. Simple and earthy, with semi-sweet, medicinal cherry flavors. Over-priced for what you get. 81 —S.H. (12/31/2006)

R. Merlo 2003 Syrah (Trinity County) $20. Coming from the South Fork of the Trinity River, in the Sierra Foothills, this wine seems to reflect its rugged origins. It has a lusty appeal, with rich, thick tannins and bigtime cherry and pomegranate fruit, finished with chocolate, that leads to a dry, fruity finish. 85 —S.H. (12/31/2006)

R.H. PHILLIPS

R.H. Phillips 2002 Cabernet Sauvignon (Dunnigan Hills) $9. Very dry, rich in sturdy tannins, and pleasant in berry, earth, and coffee flavors, this is an easy-drinking wine at a fair price. 84 —S.H. (6/1/2005)

R.H. Phillips 2000 Cabernet Sauvignon (Dunnigan Hills) $10. A sturdy red wine at a good price, marked by blackberry flavors, some green, minty notes and dry tannins. It's clean and well balanced, with a brisk finish. 85 —S.H. (11/15/2002)

R.H. Phillips 1996 Toasted Head Cabernet Sauvignon (Mendocino) $18. 91 —S.H. (5/1/2002)

R.H. Phillips 2001 Chardonnay (Dunnigan Hills) $10. Fruity and ripe, with apple flavors wrapped in a simple texture. It's a clean, easy-drinking wine, but turns a bit sharp on the finish. 84 —S.H. (12/15/2002)

R.H. Phillips 2000 Chardonnay (Dunnigan Hills) $9. Follows the ripe and sweet, oak and vanilla formula, and does it pretty well. Shades of smoky, caramelly wood highlight peach flavors, with just enough tartness to finish crisp and clean. 84 —S.H. (9/12/2002)

R.H. Phillips 2003 Toasted Head Chardonnay (California) $14. A really good Chard, it satisfies with opulent tropical fruit flavors, buttercream, vanilla, buttered toast, and Asian spice flavors, while the acids keep things crisp and clean. Good price for a wine of this quality. 87 —S.H. (8/1/2005)

R.H. Phillips 2001 Toasted Head Chardonnay (Dunnigan Hills) $16. Pretty lean and citrusy for a Chard, with lemon flavors, although an overlay of oak richens and adds texture and depth. The finish turns tart with acidity. 86 —S.H. (12/15/2002)

R.H. Phillips 2000 Toasted head Chardonnay (Dunnigan Hills) $14. From R.H. Phillips, it's a shade oakier and more refined than their regular bottling. The peach flavors are more concentrated, and sappier, but it comes at the cost of crispness. The wine sags in the mouth, like a Dali melted watch. But it tastes good. 85 —S.H. (9/1/2002)

R.H. Phillips 1999 Toasted Head Chardonnay (Dunnigan Hills) $14. 83 —S.H. (11/15/2000)

R.H. Phillips 1997 Toasted Head Chardonnay (Dunnigan Hills) $12. 82 —J.C. (10/1/1999)

R.H. Phillips 1999 Toasted Head Giguiere Ranch Chardonnay (Dunnigan Hills) $25. A very rich, oaky-toasty wine with oodles of upfront peach and tropical fruit flavors, but not a lot of depth or complexity. The fruit is big and ripely sweet and impressive, and the oak barrels provide layers of vanilla, smoke, and sweet wood-sap nuances. It's all on the surface, but it's a very pretty surface. 87 —S.H. (12/15/2002)

R.H. Phillips 2002 Merlot (Dunnigan Hills) $9. It's no insult to say this is the perfect fast food red wine. It's dry, balanced, and rich in tannins, with pleasant earthy, berry flavors. All this at an everyday price. 84 Best Buy —S.H. (6/1/2005)

R.H. Phillips 1998 Merlot (Dunnigan Hills) $9. 82 —S.H. (11/15/2000)

R.H. Phillips 2002 Toasted Head Merlot (California) $17. Shows real finesse and polish in the smooth, dusty texture and overall balance. The flavors are earthy-fruity, suggesting coffee, blackberries, and plums, with lots of palate-stimulating spices. Easy to find with 48,000 cases produced. 86 —S.H. (8/1/2005)

R.H. Phillips 1997 Toasted Head Merlot (Dunnigan Hills) $17. 86 —M.S. (3/1/2000)

R.H. Phillips 2003 Sauvignon Blanc (Dunnigan Hills) $8. An easy-sipping white wine, with semisweet fruit flavors and soft acids. Finishes clean and honeyed. 84 —S.H. (6/1/2005)

R.H. Phillips 2001 Sauvignon Blanc (Dunnigan Hills) $10. From this interesting appellation in a cool part of the Central Valley, a crisp, very dry white wine brimming with grass and lemon flavors, and a spicy finish. It's a real palate cleanser, and a good value. 86 —S.H. (9/1/2003)

R.H. Phillips 1999 Night Harvest Sauvignon Blanc (Dunnigan Hills) $10. This country-style wine has bright citrus-accented fruit and buttery spice aromas, and drinks pleasant and dry. On the finish, it turns citrusy again. 83 —S.H. (8/1/2001)

R.H. Phillips 1998 Night Harvest Sauvignon Blanc (Dunnigan Hills) $7. 87 Best Buy —M.M. (9/1/1999)

R.H. Phillips 2000 Syrah (Dunnigan Hills) $10. Telltale white pepper aromas, with blackberries and fresh green herbs, mark this dry red wine. It's tannic, with peppery flavors and a rough texture that calls for big, rich foods, but it's well made and clean, with some degree of finesse. 85 —S.H. (12/1/2002)

R.H. Phillips 2002 EXP Syrah (Dunnigan Hills) $14. Slightly marred by a hint of nail polish on the nose, but otherwise notable mostly for its lack of defining features. There's some modest red berry and chocolate fruit and a short finish. 82 (9/1/2005)

R.H. Phillips 1997 EXP Syrah (Dunnigan Hills) $14. 84 —S.H. (10/1/1999)

R.H. Phillips 1999 Toasted Head EXP Syrah (Dunnigan Hills) $25. A rich, dry, somewhat tannic all-purpose red wine, if you're looking for something full-bodied. Doesn't seem particularly true to the variety, with its generic red and black stone-fruit flavors, and could easily be Merlot. But it's clean, well-made, and sturdy enough to stand up to big, rich foods. 85 —S.H. (12/1/2002)

R.H. Phillips 1999 Estate Bottled Viognier (Dunnigan Hills) $14. 87 —M.M. (11/21/2000)

RABBIT RIDGE

Rabbit Ridge 2003 Chardonnay (Paso Robles) $14. Soft in acids, fat, and lush in fruit, and enjoyable. The tropical fruit, vanilla, and smoky oak flavors are explosive but dry, and very spicy. 85 —S.H. (12/15/2004)

Rabbit Ridge 2002 Merlot (California) $8. Good price for a wine this rich in fruit and balanced in alcohol and tannins. Offers lots of pleasure with the berry, cherry, mocha, and oak flavors that are completely dry. 85 Best Buy —S.H. (12/15/2004)

Rabbit Ridge 2001 Avventura Reserve Red Blend (California) $25. This Sangiovese, Cabernet Sauvignon, and Merlot blend is ripe in fruit, with chocolate cherry flavors. It's quite soft in both acidity and tannins. Provides plenty of flavor, and a good cut of meat should make it even sweeter. 85 —S.H. (12/15/2004)

Rabbit Ridge 2003 Rabbit Rosé Blend (Paso Robles) $18. A Provençal-style wine, dark for a blush, and full-bodied. Super-fruity, with great bursts of raspberries, cherries, mocha, and vanilla. There's something fun about this delightfully friendly wine. 86 —S.H. (12/15/2004)

Rabbit Ridge 2001 Brunello Clone Sangiovese (Paso Robles) $14. Tannic and a bit herbal, but saved by decent cherry flavors in the finish. Perfectly dry, and not too hot. Pasta with lots of cheese and hearty short ribs will be good companions. 84 —S.H. (12/31/2004)

Rabbit Ridge 1997 Consiglio Selezione Sangiovese (Sonoma County) $15. 86 —S.H. (11/1/1999)

USA

USA

Rabbit Ridge 2002 Syrah (Paso Robles) $18. A lovely drinking wine, with nicely modulated plummy, chocolate flavors wrapped in rich, sweet tannins. Dry and balanced, with not too much alcohol, it has style and class. **87** —*S.H. (12/15/2004)*

Rabbit Ridge 2002 Russell Family Vineyard Reserve Syrah (Paso Robles) $35. A long name for a simple, but likeable, wine. Fully dry, with easy tannins. The flavors strike a nice balance between berries, stone fruits, coffee, and dried herbs. Turns a bit hot on the finish. Drink now, with rich fare. **86** —*S.H. (12/31/2004)*

Rabbit Ridge 2003 Westside Viognier (Paso Robles) $18. What a treat, with its gobs of juicy fruit, spicy mango, and papaya flavors and the excellent spine of acidity that makes it drink crisp and clean. Exotically flamboyant, but manages to be dry and balanced. **88** —*S.H. (12/15/2004)*

Rabbit Ridge 2001 Westside Zinfandel (Paso Robles) $15. Somewhat smooth-textured and cherry-like, with pleasant spice, toast, and coffee flavors. Mild on the finish. **86** *(11/1/2003)*

RABID RED

Rabid Red 2004 Red Blend (California) $15. Soft and simple, with modest cherry-berry flavors. But it's clean, dry and easy. A blend of too many varieties to mention. Cute label. **83** —*S.H. (12/31/2006)*

RACCHUS

Racchus 2003 Chardonnay (Sonoma County) $10. This screwtopped Chard is perfectly nice for everyday drinking. It's fruity, dry, and clean, with white peach and sweet melon flavors and a smooth, spicy finish. **84** —*S.H. (12/1/2005)*

Racchus 2003 Red Blend (Alexander Valley) $10. My bottle was sulfury, which made evaluating the wine difficult. After a few minutes, the smell blew off, revealing a simple, fruity, soft dry wine. **83** —*S.H. (12/1/2005)*

RADIO-COTEAU

Radio-Coteau 2003 Timbervine Syrah (Russian River Valley) $55. This is a lush, heady, plummy wine, complete with spice, black pepper, and a fair amount of oak. The elements work together as a harmonious, velvety whole, and come to a long close. **91** *(9/1/2005)*

RAFANELLI

Rafanelli 2002 Cabernet Sauvignon (Dry Creek Valley) $40. Starts with side-by-side aromas of cassis and black cherries. Now one stars, then the other. Finally, new oak kicks in. It hasn't begun to come together yet, but when it does, in 4 or 5 years, you'll find a rich, dense wine, soft and smooth, with a wonderful tease of tannins. Drink 2008–2012. **93 Editors' Choice** —*S.H. (11/1/2005)*

Rafanelli 2001 Merlot (Dry Creek Valley) $26. Even for 2001, this is a tremendous Merlot, huge in flavor, and stunning for its volume. Atypically, it has an almost Rhône-like quality of violets and lavender, sweet anise, and cherries, and the woody, charry new oak really stands out. This beautiful wine is very long in the middle and finish, and should improve for several years. **92 Editors' Choice** —*S.H. (11/1/2005)*

Rafanelli 2003 Zinfandel (Dry Creek Valley) $30. Made from scattered vineyards around the appellation, this is a big, hearty Zin, packed with cherries, plums, blackberries, cola, and cassis. This challenging vintage resulted in the highest alcohol level ever measured in a Rafanelli Zin, but it's a balanced wine. **90** —*S.H. (11/1/2005)*

RAINBOW RIDGE

Rainbow Ridge 2003 Chardonnay (California) $13. Earthy, with an herbal, tobaccoey edge to the peach, pineapple, and oaky flavors. Drinks dry and soft, with a finish of almond skin bitterness. **84** —*S.H. (3/1/2005)*

Rainbow Ridge 2002 Chardonnay (California) $13. A big, flavorful Chard from a statewide appellation. It's got lots of coastal influences in the pure, crystalline peach and tropical fruit flavors, and the steely spine of acidity. **86** —*S.H. (6/1/2004)*

Rainbow Ridge 2003 Avid White Chardonnay (California) $10. With no oak, this is a clean, fruity wine, and dry, with peach and apricot flavors and balancing acids. It feels nice and richly spicy in the mouth. **85 Best Buy** —*S.H. (12/31/2005)*

Rainbow Ridge 2001 Alicante Bouschet Red Blend (California) $20. From Lodi grapes, a wine that's dark as midnight, and big. Plums, blackberries, cassis, tobacco, and dried kitchen herb aromas. In the mouth, big, rich, intense, and tannic, and dry as dust. It is just a baby, with plummy flavors, and will improve with cellaring through 2011. Notable for its balance, complexity, and harmony. **91** —*S.H. (12/31/2003)*

Rainbow Ridge 2003 Flaming Red Red Blend (California) $10. This blend of Cabernet, Merlot, Syrah, and Sangiovese is a country-style wine, rustic and a little sweet on the finish. But it's a clean, easy sipper, especially at this price. **83** —*S.H. (12/31/2005)*

Rainbow Ridge 2004 Butch Blush Rosé Blend (California) $10. Here's a big, jammy blush wine. It's certainly full-bodied for a rosé, but has a nice silky feeling. The fruity flavor is powerful in cherries and raspberries, with a semisweet finish. **83** —*S.H. (12/31/2005)*

RAMEY

Ramey 1996 Chardonnay (Carneros) $65. 96 *(11/15/1999)*

Ramey 1998 Hudson Vineyard Chardonnay (Carneros) $55. This big, brawny Chardonnay's potent nose of smoke, hay, orange, banana, and pungent lees is an attention-grabber. Baked apple, buttered popcorn, and vanilla flavors come on strong along with an edge of spicy oak that carries through the finish. The panel rendered a split decision on this wine from veteran winemaker David Ramey. It showed harmony, length, and finesse to some, but appeared edgy, a bit disjointed and obvious to others. **89** *(7/1/2001)*

Ramey 1997 Hudson Vineyard Chardonnay (Carneros) $48. 93 *(5/1/2000)*

Ramey 1998 Hyde Vineyard Chardonnay (Carneros) $55. Opens with a nice nose of roasted nuts, banana, caramel, and a hint of smoke. The palate's pear, baked apple, and apricot flavors wear interesting coconut accents, but all these are unfortunately overrun by a scotch notes peek out from behind an edgy acidity. **85** *(7/1/2001)*

Ramey 1997 Hyde Vineyard Chardonnay (Carneros) $46. 95 *(5/1/2000)*

Ramey 2001 Hyde Vineyards Chardonnay (Carneros) $56. What a great aroma this wine has: refined oak and all the smoky, vanilla trimmings, framing pineapple, orange rind, and lemon custard aromas and flavors. This massive Chard just gives off oodles of fruit. It is balanced with rich, brilliant acidity. **93** —*S.H. (11/15/2004)*

RAMSAY

Ramsay 1996 Reserve Merlot (Carneros) $26. 86 —*J.C. (7/1/2000)*

RAMSPECK

Ramspeck 2002 Cabernet Sauvignon (North Coast) $17. Kind of dry and rough, with a jagged mouthfeel, although there are some decent cherry and blackberry flavors. A good, regional country-style wine. **84** —*S.H. (11/15/2004)*

Ramspeck 2001 Cabernet Sauvignon (North Coast) $18. A nicely flavored Cab, with well-endowed flavors of black currants, herbs, and sweet espresso, and rich, delicate tannins. Feels a bit soft and flabby in the mouth, with the commonness of a regional wine. **85** —*S.H. (12/15/2003)*

Ramspeck 2002 Pinot Noir (North Coast) $18. Correct and clean, with menthol-eucalyptus and sour cherry flavors that turn thin and tannic on the finish. **84** *(11/1/2004)*

Ramspeck 2001 Pinot Noir (North Coast) $18. A thick, pasty wine with considerable tannins and a heavy-handed mouthfeel. Flavors are weedy and generic berry. Not going anywhere. **82** —*S.H. (7/1/2003)*

RANCHO ARROYO GRANDE

Rancho Arroyo Grande 2004 Chardonnay (Arroyo Grande Valley) $15. Grown in the warmest part of the appellation, this Chard is soft and without the acidity you find closer to the ocean. But it's a very tasty wine brimming with tropical fruit, honeysuckle, buttered toast, and vanilla flavors. **85** —*S.H. (12/1/2006)*

Rancho Arroyo Grande 2003 Estate Chardonnay (Arroyo Grande Valley) $15. From one of the state's coolest growing areas comes this acid-filled, streamlined Chard. The flavors are of lime and tropical fruit, with a bracing streak of minerality. This balanced wine will be great with shellfish. **88** —*S.H. (12/1/2005)*

Rancho Arroyo Grande 2002 Private Reserve Chardonnay (Arroyo Grande

Valley) **$15.** Here's an everyday Chard with interesting features. It has citrusy, lime zest flavors and high acidity, and the absolute dryness serves to accentuate the tartness. That makes it very clean, with a razorsharp edge that will be nice with fresh cracked crab. **86** —*S.H. (9/1/2004)*

Rancho Arroyo Grande 2002 Ian Cuvée Red Blend (Arroyo Grande Valley) $20. Dominated now by that meaty, funky Mourvèdre smell you either love or hate, but in the mouth you'll find a tight young wine with plenty of tannins and a core of black cherry. In need of a year or two of aging. Syrah, Mourvèdre, Grenache. **86** —*S.H. (9/1/2004)*

Rancho Arroyo Grande 2003 Ian Cuvée Rhône Red Blend (Arroyo Grande Valley) $20. A Côtes-du-Rhône style wine, this Syrah-based blend has flavors of dessicated fruit, salty leather, and Chinese-style pork. It feels hot and prickly, although the alcohol isn't that high. Definitely a distinct, unique wine from a hot region. **86** —*S.H. (12/1/2006)*

Rancho Arroyo Grande 2002 Thereza Cuvée Rhône Red Blend (Arroyo Grande Valley) $20. With Syrah, Mourvèdre, Grenache, and Counoise, this is a California Provençal-style wine. It's rich in berry, spice, and herb flavors, with finely ground tannins, and is soft, dry, and enjoyable. **85** —*S.H. (12/1/2005)*

Rancho Arroyo Grande 2001 Thereza Cuvée Rhône Red Blend (Arroyo Grande Valley) $28. This Rhône-style blend is very dark and dense in flavor and texture, and not offering a whole lot of taste in its youth. Tannins and acids dominate, making for a firm, unyielding mouthfeel. Seems crafted for aging, although with no history, it's a gamble. A blend of Syrah, Mourvèdre, Grenache, and Counoise. **86** —*S.H. (12/1/2003)*

Rancho Arroyo Grande 2001 Syrah (Arroyo Grande Valley) $28. How dark this wine is, and how youthful in brash tannins and acids. In fact, tannins dominate from entry to firm, tough finish. Way down deep is blackberry that may emerge with age. The winemaker added a small amount of Viognier to add brightness and fruit. **86** —*S.H. (12/15/2003)*

Rancho Arroyo Grande 2002 Private Reserve Syrah (Arroyo Grande Valley) $25. What's so nice about this wine is its balance. All the parts come together, but it is also a big bruiser of a Syrah. Opens with a blast of white pepper, blackberries, coffee, and sweet charred oak, then turns richly fruity in the mouth. But that fruit is accompanied by wonderfully thick tannins and bright acidity. **91** —*S.H. (12/1/2005)*

Rancho Arroyo Grande 2004 Syrah Rosé Syrah (Arroyo Grande Valley) $15. Likable for its delicate mouthfeel, dryness, and complex flavors, this blush wine shows raspberries and vanilla with nuances of apricot skin, thyme, cream-thinned mocha, and sweet pie crust. Easy to drink, and elegant, too. **86** —*S.H. (12/1/2006)*

Rancho Arroyo Grande 2004 Viognier (Arroyo Grande Valley) $20. This is a very fruity wine that's enormously rich in tropical papaya and nectarine flavors. With a smoky, slightly caramelly edge, it finishes in a tremendous fireworks of oriental spices. **87** —*S.H. (12/1/2006)*

Rancho Arroyo Grande 2004 Zinfandel (Arroyo Grande Valley) $15. Soft, full-bodied, and stuffed with baked blackberry, cherry, raspberry, and chocolate flavors, this big, rather hot wine has a bit of superripe sweetness in the finish. Yet it pulls it all off with aplomb and manages to stay balanced. **87** —*S.H. (12/1/2006)*

Rancho Arroyo Grande 2001 Zinfandel (Arroyo Grande Valley) $18. Pretty floral and spice notes are fron and center in this wine, which is also graced by tangy acidity. Velvety texture carries the spice along with raspberry, tea, coffee, and cherry flavors. Zippy on the finish. **87** *(11/1/2003)*

Rancho Arroyo Grande 2002 Dry Farm Zinfandel (Arroyo Grande Valley) $30. From the warmer, eastern part of the valley, but it's still not fully ripe, at least by North Coast standards. You'll find earthy, berry flavors and some firmly astringent tannins. May soften with a few years of age. **85** —*S.H. (9/1/2004)*

Rancho Arroyo Grande 2003 Estate Zinfandel (Arroyo Grande Valley) $15. From a warmer, inland part of this appellation, which probably should have its own AVA, comes this slightly raisined Zin, which is reminiscent of many inland valley reds. It's rather hot, soft, and Porty. **84** —*S.H. (12/1/2005)*

RANCHO NAPA

Rancho Napa 1999 Bordeaux Blend (Napa Valley) $37. 93 Cellar Selection —*S.H. (11/15/2002)*

RANCHO SISQUOC

Rancho Sisquoc 1997 Cabernet Sauvignon (Santa Maria Valley) $22. 81 — *S.H. (9/1/2000)*

Rancho Sisquoc 2001 Flood Family Vineyards Cabernet Sauvignon (Santa Barbara County) $22. A tad under ripe, to judge from the notes of bell pepper and dill that float on top of the cherries. There's also a toughness to the tannins. **84** —*S.H. (3/1/2005)*

Rancho Sisquoc 1998 Chardonnay (Santa Maria Valley) $18. 84 —*S.H. (10/1/2000)*

Rancho Sisquoc 1996 Chardonnay (Santa Maria Valley) $15. 89 —*S.H. (7/1/1999)*

Rancho Sisquoc 2002 Flood Family Vineyards Chardonnay (Santa Barbara County) $18. Oaky and leesy, with a range of fruits from apples through peaches and pineapples, and tingly with dusty spices and acidity. This is a clean, food-friendly Chard, not too sweet **87** —*S.H. (3/1/2005)*

Rancho Sisquoc 2001 Flood Family Vineyards Merlot (Santa Barbara County) $20. Dry, with nice black cherry and cocoa flavors and a hint of oregano. The tannins are soft and sweet, but complex, leading to a firm, fruity finish. **86** —*S.H. (3/1/2005)*

Rancho Sisquoc 1999 Flood Family Vineyard Pinot Noir (Santa Maria Valley) $40. The full brunt of oak is palpable on the nose, where there's toast, vanilla, and even some popcorn. The mouth is ripe and ready, but again the oak is heavy. A buttery mouthfeel and finish fail to work in the wine's favor. There's just too much wood here, masking the fruit. **84** *(10/1/2002)*

Rancho Sisquoc 2002 Flood Family Vineyards Pinot Noir (Santa Barbara County) $30. A nice, Beaune-style Pinot, rich in cherry and spice fruit, with good oak and medium-bodied. It's balanced in acids and tannins, with a smooth mouthfeel, a good food wine. **87** —*S.H. (3/1/2005)*

Rancho Sisquoc 1998 Sauvignon Blanc (Santa Maria Valley) $14. 83 — *S.H. (9/1/2000)*

Rancho Sisquoc 2002 Flood Family Vineyards Syrah (Santa Barbara County) $30. Polished and smooth, with intense blackberry, pepper, grilled meat, and toasty oak flavors. Notable for its balance. The tannins are rich and ripe in this very fine, dry wine. **91** —*S.H. (3/1/2005)*

RANCHO ZABACO

Rancho Zabaco 2002 Pinot Gris (Sonoma Coast) $20. A wonderfully refreshing dry wine, especially notable for the richness of its citrus, guava, and fig flavors. Crisp acidity balances the fruit; finishes pleasant and long. **88** —*S.H. (12/1/2003)*

Rancho Zabaco 2000 Pinot Gris (Sonoma Coast) $16. One of the nicest California Pinot Grigios we've tasted. Pleasing, lively green apple, citrus, almond, and herb notes play from aromatic start to bright, lingering finish. The flavors tend more to the Italian renditions of this grape, yet the fruit expression is all Sonoma. **88 Editors' Choice** *(7/1/2001)*

Rancho Zabaco 2001 Reserve Pinot Gris (Sonoma County) $18. A bit simple, but definitely not shy on flavor, bursting with melon and pear fruit. It's an attempt at an Alsatian style, full and weighty in the mouth, and showing a trace of heat on the finish. **87** *(8/1/2002)*

Rancho Zabaco 2002 Sauvignon Blanc (Russian River Valley) $20. A great evocation of a grassy, gooseberry, limey wine, with a high acidity that cleanses the palate. Subtler notes of fig and cream soften it, but this is still a dry, tart wine. **87** —*S.H. (12/1/2003)*

Rancho Zabaco 2001 Sauvignon Blanc (Russian River Valley) $18. Quite lively, with bright gooseberry, fig, herb, melon, lemon, and grass tones. Viscous yet refreshing on the palate. Moderate on the finish. **89** —*J.M. (9/1/2003)*

Rancho Zabaco 2000 Sauvignon Blanc (Russian River Valley) $16. This smooth wine has good balance, and a fairly full mouthfeel. Even on the palate, it shows a bit of both ends of the Sauvignon Blanc spectrum— the crisp grassy, herb, and grapefruit side and also fig, pear, and melon as foundation. **86** *(7/1/2001)*

Rancho Zabaco 2004 Dancing Bull Sauvignon Blanc (California) $10. This is a good price for this New Zealand-style wine. It's dry and crisp in gooseberry, lime, and fig flavors, and bursts with cinnamon and white pepper spice on the finish. **85 Best Buy** —S.H. (12/15/2005)

Rancho Zabaco 2003 Dancing Bull Sauvignon Blanc (California) $10.
Smells inviting, with grass, gooseberry, pine cone, smoky, and vanilla aromas, and drinks dry and clean, with citrus and fig flavors. There's a tiny hit of honey on the long, spicy finish. Really a nice sipper. **87 Best Buy** —S.H. (6/1/2005)

Rancho Zabaco 2002 Dancing Bull Sauvignon Blanc (California) $10. You'll find some polished flavors of figs, limes, and melon in this simple wine. It has crisp acids, and finishes with a bit of honeyed sweetness. **84** —S.H. (12/31/2003)

Rancho Zabaco 2002 Reserve Sauvignon Blanc (Russian River Valley) $20.
Richly textured, with a strong gooseberry core that fans out to reveal hints of citrus, melon, hay, and herbs. Fairly complex, with a touch of fig on the fresh yet lush finish. **89** —J.M. (9/1/2004)

Rancho Zabaco 2001 Reserve Sauvignon Blanc (Sonoma County) $18. If one word could sum up this wine it would be "safe." It's a Sauvignon Blanc that tastes like Sauvignon Blanc, but avoids any aggressive vegetal notes. Gooseberry and pink grapefruit aromas and flavors, with a slight creaminess to the texture, make it easy to drink. **86** (8/1/2002)

Rancho Zabaco 1999 Syrah (Sonoma County) $18. 84 (6/1/2003)

Rancho Zabaco 2002 Zinfandel (Dry Creek Valley) $18. You'll find a chewiness to this wine from tannins, but sweet fruit, low acidity, and oak soften it to gentility. Has the feel of a fine Cabernet, with Zin's distinctive spicy, feral quality. If it were more intense, it would be an excellent wine. **86** —S.H. (11/15/2005)

Rancho Zabaco 1999 Zinfandel (Dry Creek Valley) $18. Creamy and smooth, with vanilla and milk chocolate aromas and flavors that carry along the bouncy red-berry fruit for a supple ride. Contains 10% Petite Sirah. **87** (8/1/2002)

Rancho Zabaco 1998 Zinfandel (Dry Creek Valley) $17. Blackberry, oak, black olive, and dust on the nose; more of the same, plus some black cherry, on the palate. Medium-weight with a slight mineral-gravel texture, it closes with lots of anise and black licorice, plus a little caramel. Ordinary, but well executed. **87** —D.T. (3/1/2002)

Rancho Zabaco 1997 Zinfandel (Sonoma County) $12. 86 —L.W. (2/1/2000)

Rancho Zabaco 2001 Chiotti Vineyard Zinfandel (Dry Creek Valley) $28.
Plush and richly textured, the wine serves up a broad array of dark, rich coffee, chocolate, black plum, black cherry, mocha, spice, cedar, herb, and toast flavors. It's velvety smooth on the palate and offers an elegant, long finish. **91** (11/1/2003)

Rancho Zabaco 2000 Chiotti Vineyard Zinfandel (Dry Creek Valley) $25. At the top of the Rancho Zabaco hierarchy are the Zinfandels from the company's Chiotti and Stefani vineyards. Unfortunately there will be no Stefani in 2000, but the Chiotti is very good. It's very young, and takes a bit of coaxing to tease out aromas of toast, dried spices, and blackberries before flowing smoothly across the palate in a wave of briary fruit. Finishes with firm acidity and a bit of black pepper. Drink now. **89** (8/1/2002)

Rancho Zabaco 1999 Chiotti Vineyard Zinfandel (Dry Creek Valley) $22. A chewy wine with tremendous extraction and flavor intensity, this has some Port-like qualities, and the flavors are tart-sweet, pruney, with nutty, almost bitter almond notes peeking through. Still young, it will be better in two years. Closes with a big, tooth-staining finish. **88** (7/1/2001)

Rancho Zabaco 2003 Dancing Bull Zinfandel (California) $12. Nearly as good as the '01 and '02, and in the same vein, a dry, balanced Zin that combines an elegant structure with sour cherry, herb, and coffee flavors. Notable for its restraint, in an era when it's all too easy to let Zinfandel ripen to excess. **86** —S.H. (6/1/2006)

Rancho Zabaco 2002 Dancing Bull Zinfandel (California) $10. A lovely Zin for its rich blackberry, cherry, cassis, and chocolate flavors, and the tannins are smooth and velvety. Hits with dusty spices that last through the slightly sweet finish. A solid value from Gallo. **86 Best Buy** —S.H. (6/1/2005)

Rancho Zabaco 2001 Dancing Bull Zinfandel (California) $12. 89 Best Buy —S.H. (11/15/2002)

Rancho Zabaco 2000 Dancing Bull Zinfandel (California) $12. A simple, fruity Zin that blends damp soil and stewed berries with chocolate and toast. Mostly Lodi fruit, with bits and pieces of the blend coming from Mendocino, Sonoma, and Paso Robles; also contains traces of Petite Sirah and Syrah. **84** (8/1/2002)

Rancho Zabaco 2003 Monte Rosso Vineyard Zinfandel (Sonoma Valley) $35. Gallo's Rancho Zabaco has done a fine job with single-vineyard Zins. This one is an excellent wine, dry, balanced, and with the structure of Merlot, with firm tannins encasing berry, earth, coffee, and anise flavors. **90** —S.H. (6/1/2006)

Rancho Zabaco 2003 Monte Rosso Vineyard Toreador Zinfandel (Sonoma Valley) $50. A mere 174 cases of this wine were produced. It shares the essence of the '03 Monte Rosso Zin, reviewed below, but is richer and more concentrated, as well as much higher in alcohol, pushing 16%. Thoroughly dry, with flavors of coffee, dried blackberries, bitter chocolate, and cloves, this is a complex, impressive wine. **92** —S.H. (6/1/2006)

Rancho Zabaco 2000 Reserve Zinfandel (Dry Creek Valley) $20. I love this wine for its Zinny expressiveness, from the flavors of dark, wild berries, herbs, and tobacco to the thick, dry tannins and smooth mouthfeel. It's a big wine and will settle down with age, but then you'd miss the flattering exuberance of youth. **90** —S.H. (9/1/2003)

Rancho Zabaco 2003 Sonoma Heritage Vines Zinfandel (Sonoma County) $18. I really like this wine, which in so many ways is classic Sonoma Zin. It's dry and full-bodied, with sturdy tannins and ripe, forward Zin flavors that finish in a swirl of spicy fruit. It's also high in acidity, which is perfect to cut through meaty fats, butter, olive oil, and cheese. **89** —S.H. (10/1/2006)

Rancho Zabaco 2003 Sonoma Heritage Vines Zinfandel (Sonoma County) $18. Pop a steak on the grill and enjoy this robust wine. A blend of Dry Creek, Russian River, Alexander Valley, and Knights Valley fruit, with a little Paso Robles thrown in for good measure, it's classic Zin, dry, fruity, and peppery. Those cherry-berry flavors will sing against the charbroiled smoky richness of beef. **90** —S.H. (12/15/2005)

Rancho Zabaco 2001 Sonoma Heritage Vines Zinfandel (Sonoma County) $18. Pretty aromas of cherry, raspberry, smoke, vanilla, and citrus. A bit heavy-textured, but with a bright edge that gives balance. Moderate length on the end. **86** (11/1/2003)

Rancho Zabaco 2000 Sonoma Heritage Vines Zinfandel (Sonoma County) $16. The Sonoma County blend is warm and spicy, mixing a trace of alcoholic heat with black pepper. Mixed berries, dried fruits, and a hint of raisins are all underscored by milk chocolate. Finishes tart, cranberry-ish, and oaky. **85** (8/1/2002)

Rancho Zabaco 1999 Stefani Vineyard Zinfandel (Dry Creek Valley) $28.
This Gallo brand excels with Zinfandel, as this brilliant single-vineyard effort demonstrates. It explodes with focused, intense berry fruit, beautifully accented with oak that lends coffee, chocolate and hints of tar. Accents ring through the harmonious finish, with tobacco, cedar and coconut among them. **92 Editors' Choice** —P.G. (3/1/2002)

RANDALL HARRIS

Randall Harris 2001 Merlot (Washington) $10. This one-wine brand was minutes away from folding a year ago, but a drop in price and a series of superb vintages for Washington Merlot made some great juice available. Unlike most Merlots under $20, this one is not just light and fruity. It offers rich, true flavors of ripe cherries, followed by layers of milk chocolate, toast, and spice. Unfortunately, although 2,800 cases were made, distribution is limited to the West Coast. **88** —J.M. (11/15/2003)

RAPHAEL

Raphael 2002 La Fontana Bordeaux Blend (North Fork of Long Island) $20.
Built for aging, this Merlot-dominant wine, with 10% Cabernet Franc and 5% Petit Verdot, has big, smooth tannins that deserve more time to develop. The full, dark mouthfeel delivers flavors of dark berry and green bramble, but the nose offers plummy graham cracker, cassis, and clove. This may be a good wine to lay down for five years. **86** —M.D. (8/1/2006)

Raphael 2004 Cabernet Franc (North Fork of Long Island) $18. Purple colored, with big, dry tannins for a Cabernet Franc from Long Island. Aged in 100% stainless steel, this wine has inviting aromas of grape, blueberry, and graphite, although the flavors lean toward rhubarb and red plum. **84** —*M.D. (8/1/2006)*

Raphael 2001 Cabernet Franc (North Fork of Long Island) $40. Has plenty of dry, extracted tannins alongside dark fruit, tree bark, and vanilla notes. The mouth doesn't deliver as much, with moderate dark fruit flavors matched by green, stemmy notes. Finishes with chalky tannins. **83** —*M.D. (8/1/2006)*

Raphael 1999 Merlot (North Fork of Long Island) $38. This one of New York's full-priced wines, an attempt at the big time. But it's light and herbal, with oregano and tomato aromas and heavy barrel notes of rubber and char. The palate is dry, lean, and leathery, with only a modicum of strawberry fruit. And the finish is bitter and long. **84** —*M.S. (1/1/2004)*

Raphael 2001 Estate Merlot (North Fork of Long Island) $15. Earth, funk, and spice aromas dominate purple fruit, while the palate is extracted and chunky, showing chalky tannins and solid acidity. Generic dark fruit and blueberry flavors are accompanied by ever-present spice, earth, and barnyard. **82** —*M.D. (12/1/2006)*

Raphael 2005 Sauvignon Blanc (North Fork of Long Island) $22. Greenish-yellow in the glass, with aromas of tart tropical fruit, honeydew, and bell pepper. Nice balanced, backed by firm acids. Lemon, lime, and melon appear on the palate, then quickly finish. **83** —*M.D. (8/1/2006)*

Raphael 2003 Sauvignon Blanc (North Fork of Long Island) $20. For the region, this wine is rather stony and firm, with aromas of pineapple and lime. While it fails to reach a high level of expressiveness, what's here is fine. The palate is crisp, with citrus, while the finish is clean and scouring. **85** *(7/1/2005)*

RAPTOR RIDGE

Raptor Ridge 2004 Pinot Noir (Willamette Valley) $20. A fine mix of sweet, young, pretty cherry fruit. Not just a simple fruit basket, it is firm, but yielding, with finishing flavors of earth and wood. **90 Editors' Choice** —*P.G. (5/1/2006)*

Raptor Ridge 2003 Coeur de Terre Vineyard Pinot Noir (Willamette Valley) $29. More of the big, brawny, superripe house style, this one a tad over the top at 15.8% alcohol. Jammy, forward, strawberry/cherry preserves drive this broad, flavorful, drink-now wine. **88** —*P.G. (8/1/2005)*

Raptor Ridge 2003 Harbinger Vineyard Pinot Noir (Willamette Valley) $29. Another high-test (15.5%) fruit-bomb from Raptor Ridge, with well-tamed tomato leaf nuances, spice, sweet, plummy fruit, and a big mid-palate. The long finish sends up toasted cracker scents and flavors, and the thick, sappy fruit drives it home. **90** —*P.G. (8/1/2005)*

Raptor Ridge 2004 Meredith Mitchell Vineyard Pinot Noir (Willamette Valley) $39. There's plenty of toast for the new-oakies, but it's wrapped around lovely raspberry and plum fruit. Light notes of mint and leather add interest; the wine resonates nicely and gently fades rather than falling off a cliff. Not as massively ripe as the 2003, but equally fine. **93 Editors' Choice** —*P.G. (5/1/2006)*

Raptor Ridge 2003 Meredith Mitchell Vineyard Pinot Noir (Willamette Valley) $29. Extremely intense, ripe, almost (yet not) hot at 15.1% alcohol. Juicy and fruit-driven, this full-tilt, jammy wine packs lots of punch with its overflowing bowl of cherries and berries, but keeps itself on track with a zippy spine and dense, concentrated finish. **93 Editors' Choice** —*P.G. (8/1/2005)*

Raptor Ridge 2000 Murto Vineyard Pinot Noir (Willamette Valley) $24. Green and earthy in the nose, with more vegetal aromas than fruity ones. The palate is tangy and also vegetal, while full tannins and some bitterness dominate the finish. Parts of this wine seem to be in shape while others are not. As a whole, it lacks ripeness and overt appeal. **83** —*M.S. (8/1/2003)*

Raptor Ridge 2004 Reserve Pinot Noir (Willamette Valley) $39. Broadly fruity and undeniably delicious, the winery's reserve mixes raspberry and bing cherry preserves, spicy baked apple, and dusty cinnamon. Smooth, young, and ready to go. What's not to like? **90** —*P.G. (5/1/2006)*

Raptor Ridge 2003 Reserve Pinot Noir (Willamette Valley) $29. Big and flat out delicious, this clean, appealing wine sports sweet raspberry and

bing cherry fruit, high-toned aromatics, and a lively, crisp mouthfeel. Well-made and high octane (15.3%). **90** —*P.G. (8/1/2005)*

Raptor Ridge 2004 Shea Vineyard Pinot Noir (Willamette Valley) $39. The Shea is the most dense and concentrated wine among the 2004s. Jammed with blackberry, cherry, plum, licorice, and earthy tannins. Great concentration and a smoky, black tea finish. This is one to tuck away for a few years. **92** —*P.G. (5/1/2006)*

Raptor Ridge 2003 Shea Vineyard Pinot Noir (Willamette Valley) $29. Classic Oregon Pinot, from a premier vineyard. Ripe, round fruit and toasty cracker co-mingle, with some typical leafy, herbal notes as well. **89** —*P.G. (8/1/2005)*

Raptor Ridge 2000 Shea Vineyard Pinot Noir (Willamette Valley) $35. A deep sniff delivers leather, ripe black cherry, marzipan, and some smokiness, but the palate isn't congruent. It's candied, a bit burnt, and it tastes just a tad too much like cherry cough syrup. The texture is fine and the flavors solid, but it falls short in the areas of layering and elegance. It's too one-dimensional and not multifaceted. **86** —*M.S. (7/1/2003)*

Raptor Ridge 2004 Stony Mountain Vineyard Pinot Noir (Willamette Valley) $39. Lovely aromatics here: raspberry jam and fresh-baked brioche. The tart, tangy fruit suggests cranberries and plums; it's a light purple, beautifully clear and brilliant wine, a pleasure to look at as well as to savor. As before, it shows tremendous definition and balance; it's beautifully structured, transparent, and concentrated. **92 Editors' Choice** —*P.G. (5/1/2006)*

Raptor Ridge 2003 Stony Mountain Vineyard Pinot Noir (Willamette Valley) $29. Crisp, stony, and mineral-infused, this wine shows tremendous definition and balance. It is beautifully structured, transparent, and concentrated. Flavors of ripe berries, cranberry, and pomegranate are set up with vivid acids and lead into a very long, satisfying finish. **91 Editors' Choice** —*P.G. (8/1/2005)*

Raptor Ridge 2003 Yamhill County Cuvée Pinot Noir (Willamette Valley) $18. Pretty cherry candy color, with flavors to follow. This is a fruit basket of a wine, friendly, light, and flavorful. A multi-vineyard, barrel-aged blend. **88** —*P.G. (8/1/2005)*

RAVENSWOOD

Ravenswood 2001 Vintner's Blend Cabernet Sauvignon (California) $10. Riper and plusher than you might think at this price, with blackberry flavors that are well oaked. This is a fairly tannic wine, and it leaves the palate with a scour of astringency, but the fruity concentration makes it a value. **85** —*S.H. (4/1/2004)*

Ravenswood 2004 Vintners Blend Cabernet Sauvignon (California) $12. Smells hot, tastes raw and sharp, with blackberry and cherry tea flavors that seem artificially sweetened. This is a pretty clumsy wine. **81** —*S.H. (12/15/2006)*

Ravenswood 2003 Vintners Blend Cabernet Sauvignon (California) $10. A little rough, but this is a pretty good price for a varietally correct wine with some distinction. It shows real Cab character in the blackberry, coffee, and herb flavors that finish dry. **84** —*S.H. (12/1/2005)*

Ravenswood 2002 Vintners Blend Cabernet Sauvignon (California) $10. Here's a value in an everday Cab. It's balanced, dry, and full-bodied, with ripe, dusty tannins, a kiss of toasty oak, and good currant, plum, and blackberry flavors. Earns an extra point for the long finish. **86 Best Buy** —*S.H. (8/1/2005)*

Ravenswood 2003 Vintners Blend Chardonnay (California) $10. Fruity, semi-sweet, and heavily oaked, this bland Chardonnay has too much unnatural wood. **82** —*S.H. (8/1/2005)*

Ravenswood 2002 Vintners Blend Chardonnay (California) $10. One of the best Chards out there in its price range. It has a rich, creamy texture, and flavors of juicy, crisp apples, tangerines, and pineapples. The oak is well integrated, adding spice and smoky vanilla. Buy this beauty by the case. **90 Best Buy** —*S.H. (9/1/2004)*

Ravenswood 1997 Vintner's Blend Merlot (California) $11. **85** *(11/15/1999)*

Ravenswood 2003 Vintners Blend Merlot (California) $10. This is a nice, dry, smooth red wine. It has pleasant flavors of berries and cocoa, and is very soft in tannins. **83** —*S.H. (12/1/2005)*

USA

Ravenswood 2002 Vintners Blend Merlot (California) $10. You get a big bang for your buck here. It's a terrifically fruity wine, packed with black cherry and blackberry flavors that are long and persistent through the finish. Soft in tannins, and so ripely sweet you could pour it over vanilla ice cream, but it's a dry wine. **86** —*S.H. (9/1/2004)*

Ravenswood 2000 Vintners Blend Merlot (California) $10. A good buy in a dry, full-bodied red wine. Clean and balanced, with jammy flavors of plums, earth, and blackberry, it has well-etched and accessible tannins, a rich mouthfeel, and a spicy finish. Value. **86 Best Buy** —*S.H. (8/1/2003)*

Ravenswood 1999 Icon Rhône Red Blend (Sonoma County) $20. Begins with earthy, berry aromas that smell disjointed and sharp. It's a big wine, with sturdy tannins, although it has a soft mouthfeel. There's not much fruit evident, but there is a sharp, dry astringency in the finish. Not offering much pleasure now, and not likely to improve. A Rhône-style blend of Syrah, Mourvèdre, and Grenache. **84** —*S.H. (7/1/2002)*

Ravenswood 2001 Zinfandel (Lodi) $15. Fun and juicy, with bright blackberry, cherry, plum, and spice flavors. They taper off a bit soon, however, leaving a toasty oak edge on the finish. **87** *(11/1/2003)*

Ravenswood 2000 Zinfandel (Napa Valley) $17. Dark and rich, with smoky, black cherry, raspberry, cola, tar, and spice flavors. Tannins are ripe and silky, while the finish is long and bright. Downright fun to drink. **87** *(5/1/2003)*

Ravenswood 2000 Zinfandel (Amador County) $15. Rich and balanced, with well-tamed tannins framing ripe blackberry, cherry, blueberry, and peppery-herb flavors. Very dry, with uplifting acids. Try this in place of Merlot or Cabernet with your next steak. **86** —*S.H. (5/1/2003)*

Ravenswood 2000 Zinfandel (Lodi) $15. A big bruiser with youthful wild berry, sage, and earth flavors and hefty tannins. Has the jamminess and sharp acids of a young wine. Drink with rich meats, tomato sauce, and olive oil. **85** —*S.H. (5/1/2003)*

Ravenswood 1999 Zinfandel (Napa Valley) $15. Earth, herb, and oak stand out on this Zin's nose; taut red plum and caramel flavors are prevalent in the mouth. Medium-bodied, with supple tannins, it finishes with sturdy red fruit and a warming char-toast note. **88** —*D.T. (3/1/2002)*

Ravenswood 1999 Zinfandel (Mendocino) $14. Really funky (that's good funky, not skunky-funky) nose shows plum, nutmeg, burned sugar, chalk, and a slight "fresh-picked garden vegetable" note. Bright palate flavors are mostly more of the same: plum, caramel, oak, and a little smoke. Zingy in the mouth, though slightly minerally, it finishes with burned caramel and oak flavors. Heady, but that's what Zinfandel is for, right? **87** —*D.T. (3/1/2002)*

Ravenswood 1999 Zinfandel (Amador County) $14. Loaded with blackberry, this mid-priced offering has stably, spicy aromas topping the fruit on the nose, and peppery oak additions in the mouth. Medium to full in the mouth, it closes with anise and a tangy metallic-pepper note. On the dark side, and Cab-like in size and texture. **87** —*D.T. (3/1/2002)*

Ravenswood 1999 Zinfandel (Sonoma County) $15. No mistaking this wine, with it's jammy, briary, peppery aromas and jammy wild berry fruit flavors. The sharply dry finish is also classic Sonoma Zin. There's a rough, tart quality to it that begs for olive oil, goat cheese, bbq, anything rich enough to cut through the tannins. **86** —*S.H. (12/15/2001)*

Ravenswood 1999 Zinfandel (Sonoma County) $15. **89** —*D.T. (3/1/2002)*

Ravenswood 1999 Zinfandel (Lodi) $13. **87** —*D.T. (3/1/2002)*

Ravenswood 2002 Barricia Zinfandel (Sonoma Valley) $30. Has the balance, weight, and mouthfeel of a good Cabernet, with soft, fine tannins and black currant, cocoa, and oak flavors. You might think it was a Cab, except for the peppery, briary edge. Shows unusual control for Zin. **90** — *S.H. (3/1/2005)*

Ravenswood 2001 Barricia Zinfandel (Sonoma Valley) $35. Bright and light on the palate. The wine serves up zippy cherry, spice, cedar, and herb flavors. Tannins are firm, while the finish is moderate in length. Toasty at the end. **87** *(11/1/2003)*

Ravenswood 2000 Barricia Zinfandel (Sonoma Valley) $35. The color is a beautiful ruby-garnet, and the scents are of warm blackberry pie, leather, smoke, chocolate, and anise. Deliciously dry and complex, a softly round wine whose gentle mouthfeel disguises power and heft. **87** *(5/1/2003)*

Ravenswood 1999 Barricia Zinfandel (Sonoma Valley) $30. In the mouth, chewy tannins, stewy blueberries, ink, and a ripple of caramel run into dark fruit, char, chalk, and a green-herb twinge on the back end. One whiff of its blackberry, blueberry, and sinus-clearing black peppery bouquet and you'll know what people mean when they call wines "black beauties." It is brooding, chalky, and has loads of tannin; a fellow taster compared it to a young Barolo. With that in mind, consider aging it as you would its Italian counterpart. As it is now, it will be too big for most palates to handle. **89** —*D.T. (3/1/2002)*

Ravenswood 2002 Belloni Zinfandel (Russian River Valley) $30. Fairly closed and tannic, a wine you might want to cellar for a few years to let the blackberry, gingerbread, coffee, grilled meat, and spice emerge. It's a dry and balanced Zin, with great integrity. **91** —*S.H. (3/1/2005)*

Ravenswood 2001 Belloni Zinfandel (Russian River Valley) $35. Tightly wound with firm tannins and a toasty edge, the wine shows hints of raspberry, cherry, cola, and tobacco. It finishes with moderate length and a smoky edge. **88** *(11/1/2003)*

Ravenswood 2000 Belloni Zinfandel (Russian River Valley) $35. A dark, peppery wine that contains just enough Zinfandel to quality for a varietal label, plus Petite Sirah, Carignane, and Alicante Bouschet. In other words, an old-fashioned field blend. It is a well-made wine, and the minor varietals seem to add earth and tannins. **89** *(5/1/2003)*

Ravenswood 2002 Big River Zinfandel (Alexander Valley) $30. Less ripe than Ravenswood's other Sonoma Zins, with an herbal edge to the cherry and cocoa flavors, and not as balanced. The tannins are more pronounced, too. **86** —*S.H. (3/1/2005)*

Ravenswood 2001 Big River Zinfandel (Alexander Valley) $30. A smooth, supple wine that serves up plenty of black cherry, plum, herb, toast, and pepper notes. The finish is long and supple, with a fine-tuned edge that is pleasing and elegant. **89** *(11/1/2003)*

Ravenswood 2000 Big River Zinfandel (Alexander Valley) $35. A big wine whose 15% alcohol sticks out in the prickly mouthfeel and hot, peppery finish. Very dry and tannic, with wild berry, brambly flavors. A bit clumsy now; try again in 2006. **85** —*S.H. (5/1/2003)*

Ravenswood 1999 Big River Zinfandel (Alexander Valley) $30. A smoldering, spicy nose of cedar, raspberry, red plum, and mulling spices makes way for deep flavors, given added texture and depth by sturdy tannins: Juicy blackberry and smoke-ash flavors drift all the way through to the finish, where is punctuated by a light green-herb note. A seamless beauty. **91** —*D.T. (3/1/2002)*

Ravenswood 2002 Cooke Zinfandel (Sonoma County) $50. Compared to Ravenswood's Monte Rossa, a shade less intense and concentrated, but more elegant. Dark and aromatic, with briary herb and tobacco flavors and, under the tannins, blackberries, and coffee. Should develop further by 2006. **89** —*S.H. (3/1/2005)*

Ravenswood 2001 Cooke Zinfandel (Sonoma Valley) $28. Spicy up front, with full-throttle Bing cherry flavors. The wine fans out on the finish to reveal pleasing toast, spice, cola, herb, cedar, and pepper flavors, with a lingering touch of oak. **88** *(11/1/2003)*

Ravenswood 1997 Cooke Zinfandel (Sonoma Valley) $28. **89** —*S.H. (5/1/2000)*

Ravenswood 2002 Dickerson Zinfandel (Napa Valley) $30. Another great success from this famous old vineyard. Rich, dense, and complex, yet dry and balanced, this Zin has a marvelous mélange of flavors. Blackberries, wild blueberries, black cherries, pepper, cocoa, and oak, and a spicy hint of raisins. The finish is amazingly long and vibrant is fresh fruit. **93** —*S.H. (3/1/2005)*

Ravenswood 2001 Dickerson Zinfandel (Napa Valley) $35. Kicks off with some earth and smoke notes. This juicy wine has a distinct cinnamon flavor that neatly frames the racy cherry, blackberry, plum, and other spice notes. The finish is moderate in length. Fun. **88** *(11/1/2003)*

Ravenswood 2000 Dickerson Zinfandel (Napa Valley) $35. Somewhat lean textured, with powdery tannins. The flavors range from blackberry, strawberry, licorice, and herbs. It's got a short finish that leaves heat on the palate. **84** —*J.M. (9/1/2003)*

Ravenswood 1999 Dickerson Zinfandel (Napa Valley) $30. One of Ravenswood's single-vineyard offerings, the Dickerson has explosive blueberry, blackberry, and eucalyptus flavors, spiced up a bit with black pepper. A sweet-spicy, rich blackberry, white pepper, and eucalyptus bouquet starts things off; toasty oak and tannic, blackberry-skin flavors draw the wine to a lingering close. A button-pusher, though perhaps a bit too big for some folks. **90** —*D.T. (3/1/2002)*

Ravenswood 2001 Kunde Zinfandel (Sonoma Valley) $27. Plush plum, black cherry, raspberry, toast, spice, and herb flavors are nicely held together in this full-bodied wine. It's richly textured, with good integration of flavors. The finish is toasty and long. **90** *(11/1/2003)*

Ravenswood 1997 Lodi Zinfandel (Sonoma County) $14.88 —*P.G. (11/15/1999)*

Ravenswood 2002 Monte Rosso Zinfandel (Sonoma Valley) $30. A beautiful example of a mountain Zin, and wears its vineyard designation well. Big-time plum, coffee, chocolate, and herb flavors, powerful but smooth tannins, and a bone-dry finish combine to produce a wine of dramatic heft and complexity. **91** —*S.H. (3/1/2005)*

Ravenswood 2001 Monte Rosso Zinfandel (Sonoma Valley) $35. Somewhat powdery on the palate, with subtle hints of blackberry, raspberry, and toast. The wine is tasty but a bit hollow in the middle, finishing with moderate length and a toasty edge. **86** *(11/1/2003)*

Ravenswood 2000 Monte Rosso Zinfandel (Sonoma Valley) $35. Spicy and bright textured, with jammy black cherry and plum flavors that are framed in powdery tannins. The wine is full bodied but slightly dry on the finish. **92** —*S.H. (9/1/2003)*

Ravenswood 1999 Monte Rosso Zinfandel (Sonoma Valley) $30. Classic aromas of berries, smoke, and spices, with that savage, warm tree bark note that marks the best Zins. Drinks very fruity and big, a fat, jammy wine stuffed with all sorts of berry flavors. The mouthfeel is soft and tannic, and it's really dry. Finishes a bit hot. **89** —*D.T. (3/1/2002)*

Ravenswood 2002 Old Hill Zinfandel (Sonoma Valley) $60. The most marvelous flavors of cherries fill the mouth, enriched with cola and mocha, in this dry, balanced wine. It's fruit-forward, but there's an edge of dusty tannins that provides structure. Really classy, just about a perfect glass of Sonoma Zin. **93** —*S.H. (3/1/2005)*

Ravenswood 2001 Old Hill Zinfandel (Sonoma Valley) $46. Well balanced and integrated, the wine serves up a fine blend of coffee, black cherry, chocolate, plum, toast, and vanilla flavors. Tannins are smooth and the texture is plush. It finishes with a smoky note. **89** *(11/1/2003)*

Ravenswood 2000 Old Hill Zinfandel (Sonoma Valley) $46. A powerful wine marked by huge, aggressive tannins that demand cellaring. Buried deep down inside are flavors of rich, sweet blackberries and tart cranberries. This one will easily last through 2010. **90** *(5/1/2003)*

Ravenswood 1999 Old Hill Zinfandel (Sonoma Valley) $36. Bright blackberries, but enough surprises for it to be anything but run-of-the-mill. Anise and charred oak flavors keep the fruit from being too bright; finishes medium-long with pepper and mineral notes. The nose is a seductive cocoon of mint, eucalyptus, barbecue marinade, brown sugar, and a milky-calcium note that envelops the berry fruit. **92** —*D.T. (3/1/2002)*

Ravenswood 2002 Teldeschi Zinfandel (Dry Creek Valley) $32. Packed with sweet, fruity flavors of cherries, black raspberries, and cocoa, with plenty of spice, this warm-hearted wine is soft but rich in fine, dusty tannins. Picks up more pronounced fruity sweetness on the finish. **89** —*S.H. (3/1/2005)*

Ravenswood 2001 Teldeschi Zinfandel (Dry Creek Valley) $35. Firm and focused, with pretty cherry, toast, herb, and spice flavors. Tannins are ripe. It's a bit tight, but still shows good fruit, finishing with a toasty edge. **87** *(11/1/2003)*

Ravenswood 2000 Teldeschi Zinfandel (Dry Creek Valley) $35. A thick, brawny wine, packed with tannins that numb the palate. Flavors are earthy and veer toward tobacco, dried herbs, and hard spices. Difficult to tell where it's going, but try aging through 2006. **86** *(5/1/2003)*

Ravenswood 1999 Teldeschi Zinfandel (Dry Creek Valley) $30. Deep chalk, forest floor, and stewy red berry aromas morph into homey wheat and burnt sugar notes after a few minutes in the glass. Earthy in the mouth, it has subtle cedar, black cherry, and blackberry notes and a well-bal-

anced but not-so-velvety, gritty-earth mouthfeel. Tannins give the Teldeschi lots of texture on the finish—its charred, even unfiltered-textured finale outlasts even the blackberry flavors. Not huge, and has lots of character. **90** —*D.T. (3/1/2002)*

Ravenswood 1999 Vintners Blend Zinfandel (California) $10. Pretty good varietal character, if a bit rough and ready. It has a berry, woody, green aromas and drinks very dry, with soft acids and furry tannins, and a dry, austere finish. This wine will soften up rich, oily foods. **84** —*S.H. (12/15/2001)*

Ravenswood 2004 Vintners Blend Zinfandel (California) $10. Basic everyday Zin, fruity enough to go with just about anything. Gets the nod for its polished cherry fruit, richly tannic structure, and glyceriney sweetness, although it's really a dry wine. **84** —*S.H. (12/15/2006)*

Ravenswood 2003 Vintners Blend Zinfandel (California) $10. Textbook rural, rustic California Zin, meaning it's dry, peppery, and herbal-fruity, with firm tannins and modest alcohol. Shows Ravenswood's deft hand at blending statewide grapes. **84** —*S.H. (12/1/2005)*

Ravenswood 2000 Vintners Blend Zinfandel (California) $10. Strong, earthy Zin, with basic flavors of wild berries, tobacco, and dried herbs. Dry and pretty tannic. Not much subtlety, and certainly not a wimpy wine. **86** *(5/1/2003)*

RAVINES

Ravines 2003 Pinot Noir (Finger Lakes) $20. Spice, cola, and berry flavors are pleasant and delivered with high but acceptable acidity and moderate tannin. **83** —*M.D. (12/1/2006)*

Ravines 2005 Dry Riesling (Finger Lakes) $16. An Alsatian-style Riesling, this dry, firm wine has aromas of peach and citrus. Minerality backs the mouthfeel, while flavors of orange, melon, spice, and peach pit play on the tongue. Strong acids and a long, minerally finish suggest that this wine will age gracefully over the next five years or more. **90 Editors' Choice** —*M.D. (8/1/2006)*

RAYE'S HILL

Raye's Hill 2003 Red Wine Meritage Bordeaux Blend (Mendocino County) $26. This is the first Raye's Hill Bordeaux wine I've tasted, and it's pretty good. Merlot brings a cherried softness, while Cabernet contributes cassis and a tannic backbone. Drink now through 2008. **86** —*S.H. (7/1/2006)*

Raye's Hill 2000 Merlot (Anderson Valley) $26. Lots of smoky oak has been lavished on this wine, which can't quite overcome a certain leanness. Beneath the wood is a tannic, basic-cherry-flavored Merlot, with an edge of coffee and sage. But it's elegant and clean. **85** —*S.H. (6/1/2004)*

Raye's Hill 2001 Pinot Blanc (Anderson Valley) $22. Some Pinot Blancs are Chard wannabes. This refreshing wine is distinctly itself, with its flavors of freshly picked apples and cold, sweet honeydew melons. It may have a little residual sugar, but the crisp acidity makes it finish clean and dry. **87** —*S.H. (6/1/2004)*

Raye's Hill 2003 Hein Vineyard Pinot Blanc (Anderson Valley) $18. There are lush and ripe peach and mango flavors in this spicy wine, and it's dry, with a thick, heavy texture. Finishes with a massive fruitiness. **84** —*S.H. (12/15/2004)*

Raye's Hill 2003 Pinot Noir (Anderson Valley) $32. Tastes a little full-bodied for a Pinot, with a Grenache-like mouthfeel and cherry flavors, but there's no doubting the goodness and richness of this estate-bottled wine. It has nice acidity to balance the slightly sweet fruit. **86** —*S.H. (7/1/2006)*

Raye's Hill 2002 Pinot Noir (Anderson Valley) $18. In this wine's favor are nice aromatics and a silky, rich texture. Cherries, Oriental spices, oak, cola, and plum flavors mix it up, in a delicate, refined wine that finishes balanced and harmonious. Lots of control here. **89** *(11/1/2004)*

Raye's Hill 2001 Pinot Noir (Anderson Valley) $15. Earthy and simple, with some berry and spice flavors. Dry and tart. **83** —*S.H. (12/15/2004)*

Raye's Hill 1999 Pinot Noir (Anderson Valley) $24. 84 —*S.H. (5/1/2002)*

Raye's Hill 1999 Pinot Noir (Russian River Valley) $20. Caramel and brown sugar abound in this soft, vanilla-tinged wine. Dark cherry fruit and soy accents add interest, but the wine has a sappy feel. With its sweet caramel and chocolate notes, this is decidedly not a lean, racy Pinot. **84** *(10/1/2002)*

USA

Raye's Hill 1999 Pinot Noir (Russian River Valley) $20. A flavor-packed wine that's just beginning to show its age. The pretty cherry, cola, and spice flavors are picking up a fruitcake, candied taste. It's got good acidity, and fine, silky tannins, and is fully dry. **88** —S.H. (6/1/2004)

Raye's Hill 1998 Pinot Noir (Anderson Valley) $24. **88** —S.H. (5/1/2002)

Raye's Hill 2002 Estate Bottled Pinot Noir (Anderson Valley) $26. Cola, tea, black cherries, and some earthy herbs in the nose, turning into straightforward flavors of cherries. There's a nice feminine appeal to this crisp, elegant wine. **88** (11/1/2004)

Raye's Hill 2002 Wightman House Vineyard Pinot Noir (Anderson Valley) $22. Easy drinking, and showing some interest in the cola, dried spice, mocha, hay, and menthol aromas. Turns rather sharp in acidity in the mouth, and lacks the stuffing to age. Drink up. **85** (11/1/2004)

RAYMOND

Raymond 2000 Cabernet Sauvignon (Napa Valley) $18. A fine Cabernet, with everything in common with Napa's best and most expensive, except it's less rich. Drinks very dry, with cassis and oaky flavors and lush, complex but easy tannins. **89** —S.H. (10/1/2003)

Raymond 2001 Amberhill Cabernet Sauvignon (California) $10. Shows real attributes of a fine Cab, with a slightly fierce edge tugging it down a bit. Still, the black currant flavors, oak, and fine tannins are very nice. **84** —S.H. (10/1/2004)

Raymond 2001 Estates Cabernet Sauvignon (California) $15. Displays plenty of fine varietal character, with its currant and blackberry flavors, ripe tannins, and the overall dry, balanced mouthfeel. Ripe and flavorful. **87** —S.H. (10/1/2004)

Raymond 2002 Estates Cabernet Sauvignon (Napa Valley) $20. Marked by strong, drying tannins, this wine has blackberry, herb, and tobacco flavors and citrusy acids. Between the tannins and the acids, it's a tough, astringent Cab. Might benefit from a year or two of aging. **85** —S.H. (11/1/2005)

Raymond 2002 Generations Cabernet Sauvignon (Napa Valley) $75. I can see the intention here, to create a statement, 100% Cab that defines Raymond's historic approach. The grapes got immensely ripe in chocolate and blackberry pie filling flavors, while 100% new French oak adds vanilla and char. But the wine is too soft, almost flat, which accentuates the fruity sweetness and makes the finish sugary. **84** —S.H. (9/1/2006)

Raymond 2001 Generations Cabernet Sauvignon (Napa Valley) $70. This is not one of your big, opulent Napa Cabs. The decision seems to have been made to rein it in, keep it drier and tarter and, in theory, more elegant and ageworthy. It does boast good cherry and cassis fruit and oak, and is thoroughly dry. **88** —S.H. (12/31/2005)

Raymond 1999 Generations Cabernet Sauvignon (Napa Valley) $80. A bright textured Cabernet, loaded with blackberry, licorice, black cherry, tar, herb, and smoky toast flavors. Tannins are a bit powdery, but fine nonetheless, with a long, clean finish. **91** —J.M. (6/1/2002)

Raymond 1999 Generations Cabernet Sauvignon (Napa Valley) $65. One of the final releases of the '99 vintage, this wine is just beginning to show its age. It's quite soft and delicate, although there remains a scour of tough tannin. The flavors were once of blackberries but they're starting to break up into dried herbs and coffee. An interesting wine at an awkward age that will appeal to connoisseurs. **89** —S.H. (8/1/2004)

Raymond 1998 Generations Cabernet Sauvignon (Napa Valley) $80. If you like oak, you'll love this wine. The opening smell is of smoky, charred wood, caramel, and toast. In the mouth, sweet oak and spicy wood-sap dominate. If the fruit were strong enough to carry all these barrels, fine, but it's not. Seems like the vintage was light and the winemaker strove to compensate with wood. **86** —S.H. (6/1/2002)

Raymond 1997 Generations Cabernet Sauvignon (Napa Valley) $65. **91** (11/1/2000)

Raymond 1996 Generations Cabernet Sauvignon (Napa Valley) $50. **92** —S.H. (7/1/2000)

Raymond 2003 R Collection Cabernet Sauvignon (Napa Valley) $19. Shows classy tannins, smooth and rich, and deft oak, but the grapes finish a tad too ripe, with suggestions of rum-soaked raisins. That's not a bad flavor, it's just not quite right for a dry table wine. **84** —S.H. (10/1/2006)

Raymond 2003 Reserve Cabernet Sauvignon (Napa Valley) $35. **88** —S.H. (9/9/1999)

Raymond 2002 Reserve Cabernet Sauvignon (Napa Valley) $34. Depend on Raymond to come out with balanced Cabs. This isn't a soft, gooey, superripe wine. It's got its share of tannins and acids, and there's an earthiness to the blackberry flavors. But it's dry and complex, and should age well for a decade. **90** —S.H. (2/1/2006)

Raymond 2002 Reserve Cabernet Sauvignon (Rutherford) $50. This is a Cab that's drinking well now despite some fairly hefty tannins. There's a forwardness to the red and black cherry fruit and sweet oak that will make it great with a steak now, but it should hold and even improve through the decade. **90** —S.H. (11/1/2005)

Raymond 2002 Reserve Cabernet Sauvignon (St. Helena) $50. From a small estate vineyard comes this lush, complex, and delicious 100% Cabernet. It's concentrated in cassis flavors enhanced with oak, and displays classic Napa tannins that are rich, ripely sweet, and ageworthy. It's a joy to see veteran Raymond continue to produce great Cabernet in Napa Valley. **94 Editors' Choice** —S.H. (7/1/2006)

Raymond 2001 Reserve Cabernet Sauvignon (Rutherford) $50. Opens with a burst of smoky new oak, cherry, and menthol notes, then reveals additional layers of currant and mocha. A little soft, plush in the mouth, almost fat. Certainly an accessible wine. **88** —S.H. (10/1/2004)

Raymond 2001 Reserve Cabernet Sauvignon (St. Helena) $50. Classic Napa in balance, classic Raymond in user-friendliness, and classic '01 in overall quality. This is a well-structured Cab, infused with cassis and oak, and possesses the tannins and acids for the long haul. Drinking well now, and will easily last through 2010. **90** —S.H. (6/1/2005)

Raymond 2000 Reserve Cabernet Sauvignon (Napa Valley) $40. A lovely wine, in the classic Raymond style, soft, voluptuous, balanced, and ripe. Not a blockbuster, just a beautiful sip, with cassis and black currant flavors and gentle, complex tannins. A success for this difficult vintage. **92 Editors' Choice** —S.H. (11/15/2003)

Raymond 1999 Reserve Cabernet Sauvignon (Napa Valley) $40. Kicks off with rich vanilla and spice aromas, which evolve into licorice, black currant, blackberry, herb, chocolate, and toast flavors. Slightly tart at the end, it's nonetheless classy and framed in lush, ripe tannins. **90** —J.M. (6/1/2002)

Raymond 1997 Reserve Cabernet Sauvignon (Napa Valley) $23. **90** —S.H. (3/1/2000)

Raymond 1996 Reserve Cabernet Sauvignon (Napa Valley) $20. **90** (11/15/1999)

Raymond 2003 Chardonnay (Monterey) $13. Here's a super-drinkable Chard. It's rich in jazzy lime custard, mango, peach, and vanilla honey flavors, accompanied by bright acidity, all of it wrapped in a creamy texture. This is a great price for such a good wine. **88 Best Buy** —S.H. (11/1/2005)

Raymond 2002 Amberhill Chardonnay (California) $6. Lots to admire in this inexpensive wine, from the tropical fruit flavors to the generous overlay of oak and the crisp, balanced structure. There's real class and harmony here, and it's a good value. **85** —S.H. (9/1/2004)

Raymond 2002 Estates Chardonnay (Monterey) $10. Three cheers to Raymond for producing a Chard this nice at such a great price. It's rich in tropical fruit, peach, and oak flavors, with opulent spices, and is very dry. What a super value! **87 Best Buy** —S.H. (12/1/2004)

Raymond 2001 Estates Chardonnay (Monterey) $11. Thin going here, with citrusy flavors and big, fresh Monterey acids. Seems to have some oak in it. Finishes dry and tart. **83** —S.H. (8/1/2003)

Raymond 2000 Estates Chardonnay (Monterey) $12. Packs more flavor than any other two wines put together. This fruit bomb explodes on the palate with limes, tangerines, peaches, and the sweetest green apples and papayas, and it's all creamy and spicy. It feels dryish until you swallow, when a peacock's tail of sugar fans out on the way down. **86** —S.H. (9/1/2002)

Raymond 1999 Estates Chardonnay (Monterey) $10. An affordable wine from this Napa veteran, it's made in a tight Chablis style, with mineral, lime peel, and smoke aromas, and a rich fruitiness on the palate. Pretty oak notes add vanilla and sweetness. **87 Best Buy** —S.H. (11/15/2001)

Raymond 1998 Generations Chardonnay (Napa Valley) $30. Offers an attractive nose of white peach, pear, lime, and anise, but fails to come through with much substance on the palate. Simple and buttery-slick in the mouth, it shows some spicy notes but not much else, and turns a bit hot on the finish. **83** *(7/1/2001)*

Raymond 1997 Generations Chardonnay (Napa Valley) $28. 86 *(6/1/2000)*

Raymond 1996 Generations Chardonnay (Napa Valley) $28. 89 *(10/1/1999)*

Raymond 2004 R Collection Chardonnay (Monterey) $13. This is a new line of fairly low-priced varieties from this venerable Napa winery. The Chardonnay, made from very ripe grapes, is good and rich in creamy fruit, with balancing acidity. **84** —*S.H. (10/1/2006)*

Raymond 2004 Reserve Chardonnay (Napa Valley) $20. With crushed pineapple flavors enhanced with a bit of oak, this wine gets the tastebuds watering. It has fine balance, elegance, and varietal character. The winemaker recommends poached salmon, which, with a sprig of dill and a squirt of lemon, seems perfect. **88** —*S.H. (12/1/2006)*

Raymond 2003 Reserve Chardonnay (Napa Valley) $18. Pretty good Chard, rich and creamy, with a vanilla custard thickness balanced by bright acidity. The flavors? Ripe and full, including pineapples, guavas, peaches, and dusty spices. **87** —*S.H. (11/1/2005)*

Raymond 2001 Reserve Chardonnay (Napa Valley) $19. The grapes got really ripe this vintage, and the aromas and flavors are of tropical fruits, like guava and mango. The oak has been lavishly applied, with add smoky vanillins and buttered toast. This is a big, flamboyant wine, but skillfully vinified, and good acidity keeps things bright and crisp. **90** —*S.H. (12/1/2003)*

Raymond 2000 Reserve Chardonnay (Napa Valley) $18. It's all about extract in this kick-in-the-pants Chard. Assaults the palate with oversized fruit and the sting of peppery spice. Words like bright, electric, and bold come to mind. It's also sweet and oaky. **87** —*S.H. (9/1/2002)*

Raymond 1998 Reserve Chardonnay (Napa Valley) $15. 85 *(6/1/2000)*

Raymond 1997 Reserve Chardonnay (Napa Valley) $15. 87 —*S.H. (10/1/1999)*

Raymond 2001 Merlot (California) $10. A serviceable red wine with some nice features for the price. It's dry and balanced, with blackberry and herb flavors. **84** —*S.H. (12/15/2004)*

Raymond 2000 Merlot (California) $11. A nice Merlot at a great everyday price. Drinks very dry, with earthy, blackberry flavors that are pretty rich. The tannins are dry and complex. There are many Merlots out there that cost twice as much and aren't as good. A great value from Raymond. **89 Best Buy** —*S.H. (12/1/2003)*

Raymond 2000 Amberhill Merlot (California) $9. Boasts a lush, opulent texture, reminiscent of Napa, and beautifully ripe black currant flavors. Goes down like velvet on the palate. So tasty, you'll have to double-check the price. **85** —*S.H. (12/1/2003)*

Raymond 2002 Estates Merlot (California) $15. Tough and weedy and slightly green in aroma, although it turns medicinal-sweet in cherries in the mouth. **82** —*S.H. (11/1/2005)*

Raymond 2004 R Collection Merlot (California) $14. This is a new, mid-priced line from venerable Napa producer Raymond. It's okay, maybe a little pricy, but there's some good cherry-berry fruit. Loses a point or two for roughness and sweetness, though. **83** —*S.H. (12/31/2006)*

Raymond 2003 R Collection Merlot (California) $14. Tough in tannins, which added to the extreme dryness and earthiness makes the wine astringent, so you'll want to pair it with something rich. It has an underlying classy elegance that lifts it above the ordinary. **85** —*S.H. (10/1/2006)*

Raymond 2002 Reserve Merlot (Napa Valley) $24. Loads of blackberry, cherry, and chocolate fruit mark this dry, balanced wine, as well as a lot of sweet, vanilla-scented oak. The tannins are rich, but soft and pliant in this charming, delicious Merlot. **86** —*S.H. (3/1/2006)*

Raymond 2000 Reserve Merlot (Napa Valley) $22. A fine Merlot from this venerable Napa winery. The polished flavors of plums and blackberries are joined with earthier ones of dried herbs, green olives, and sweet, smoked meat, all wrapped in softly plush, complex tannins. A tannic edge through the finish calls for rich meats, or a little bit of cellaring. **91** —*S.H. (12/31/2003)*

Raymond 1998 Reserve Merlot (Napa Valley) $22. There's a great burst of plum and blackberry fruit, along with earthy, herbal notes, especially anise; it has a fruity depth of berry flavor that lasts well into the finish. The tannins are very mild, and the acidity is low, resulting in a soft, velvety wine that calls to mind flickering candles and your finest china. **89** —*S.H. (6/1/2001)*

Raymond 1997 Reserve Merlot (Napa Valley) $22. 89 —*S.H. (7/1/2000)*

Raymond 1998 Amberhill Sauvignon Blanc (California) $6. 86 Best Buy —*S.H. (9/1/2000)*

Raymond 2004 Reserve Sauvignon Blanc (Napa Valley) $14. A little on the thin side. Other than that, the wine shows citrus and green melon flavors and a slightly leafy Sauvignon character. **84** —*S.H. (12/1/2006)*

Raymond 2003 Reserve Sauvignon Blanc (Napa Valley) $12. Simple and thin, with slightly sweet peach and lemonade flavors. Finishes with a clean scour of acidity. **83** —*S.H. (11/1/2005)*

Raymond 2002 Reserve Sauvignon Blanc (Napa Valley) $11. A grassy style, with hay, citrus, herb, and mineral flavors at the fore. Bright and crisp, though lacking finish and complexity. A touch bitter at the end. **83** —*J.M. (10/1/2004)*

Raymond 2001 Reserve Sauvignon Blanc (Napa Valley) $11. The grassy, citrusy flavors have an unexpectedly juicy streak of peaches and tropical fruits, courtesy of a little Chardonnay. And there's a lot of oak. A big, flavorful wine, with honey on the finish. **87 Best Buy** —*S.H. (10/1/2003)*

Raymond 2000 Reserve Sauvignon Blanc (Napa Valley) $11. Crisp and fresh, with pretty melon, fig, and citrus overtones. Well balanced, with moderate body, a good finish and a great price! **87** —*J.M. (9/1/2003)*

Raymond 1998 Reserve Sauvignon Blanc (Napa Valley) $11. 86 —*S.H. (9/1/2000)*

Raymond 1999 Reserve Zinfandel (Napa Valley) $22. Bright and tangy, with cedary hints of blueberry, black cherry, vanilla, and spice. Modest tannins and firm acidity keep it clean at the end. **87** —*J.M. (11/1/2002)*

Raymond 1998 Reserve Zinfandel (Napa Valley) $16. Stewy black fruit aromas lead into oak-obscured mixed berry fruit in the mouth. A little thin and tangy, it finishes with more tang plus greenness. **81** —*D.T. (3/1/2002)*

RAYMOND BURR

Raymond Burr 2000 Cabernet Franc (Dry Creek Valley) $38. Here's a simple, one-dimensional wine, with modest berry flavors and soft acids and tannins. Finishes watery and earthy. **82** —*S.H. (11/15/2003)*

Raymond Burr 2000 Cabernet Sauvignon (Dry Creek Valley) $38. Rather light in body and flavor, with strong tannins and a hot finish. Maybe not showing well at this moment. There are some black cherry, plum, and currant flavors that may emerge down the road. **84** —*S.H. (11/15/2003)*

Raymond Burr 1999 Cabernet Sauvignon (Dry Creek Valley) $38. Pretty good, not great, a wine made from obviously ripe, pedigreed grapes. The flavors are of blackberries, with that distinctive earthiness that often marks Dry Creek Cabernets. Has persistence on the palate and length on the finish. A push of tannins suggests midterm ageworthiness. **87** —*S.H. (12/15/2003)*

Raymond Burr 1998 Cabernet Sauvignon (Dry Creek Valley) $38. Smoky, bacon-like notes weave a trail though this viscous, plummy wine. Hints of herb, cherry, and spice add interest. Moderate on the finish. **86** —*J.M. (6/1/2002)*

Raymond Burr 2001 Chardonnay (Dry Creek Valley) $28. Simple, overly soft, and with odd tastes besides the usual array of peach and apple. Very oaky, too. Not much going on, especially at this price. **83** —*S.H. (10/1/2003)*

RDLR

RDLR 2002 Syrah (Mendocino County) $24. Super-dark and extracted, and soft in acids, this is a Syrah that seems to come from a hot climate. The flavors are of blackberries, coffee, and tobacco, with a tarry element, and finish very dry. **86** —*S.H. (9/1/2005)*

USA

RED FLYER

Red Flyer 2003 Red Blend (California) $9. Here's a robust, full-bodied, country-style wine that, at this price, can be a house red for barbecue and that sort of thing. It's totally dry, with plummy-coffee flavors and sturdy tannins. **84** —*S.H. (11/15/2005)*

RED NEWT CELLARS

Red Newt Cellars 2002 Riesling (Finger Lakes) $13. Comes close to a Germanic style, with tight, lean citrusy aromas and flavors balanced by green apples and pears. It's light and refreshing, never heavy or ponderous. Finishes long and tart, full of fresh limes, with just a pinch of sugar for balance. **88 Best Buy** —*J.C. (8/1/2003)*

Red Newt Cellars 2001 Reserve Riesling (Finger Lakes) $20. **85** —*J.C. (8/1/2003)*

RED SKY

Red Sky 2002 Bordeaux Blend (Walla Walla (WA)) $30. A mix of Walla Walla and Yakima grapes yields a rather austere wine with nuances of mineral, gravel, water over stone. It tastes European rather than American; it will reward your attention with a nuanced, lightly peppery, balanced structure that suggests it will open up gracefully over the coming decade. **89** —*P.G. (6/1/2006)*

Red Sky 2003 Cabernet Franc (Walla Walla (WA)) $20. Somewhat in the same tight, austere, guarded mode as the winery's Bordeaux blend, this Cabernet Franc breathes slowly into elegant complexity. Spicy, compact blue and red fruits are lightly accented with sweet spice. **90** —*P.G. (6/1/2006)*

Red Sky 2002 Syrah (Washington) $25. Although at first glance this wine doesn't impress, it seems to get better every time you go back to it, fleshing out with air and slowly revealing more and more nuance. In fact, this rating may seem conservative in a couple of years. Toasty and constructed by oak, gradually showing spice and blackberry flavors that linger delicately on the finish. **87** *(9/1/2005)*

Red Sky 2003 Boushey Vineyard Syrah (Yakima Valley) $30. Though not as ripe or potent as the leading Boushey Vineyard Syrahs, this delicate wine is nicely balanced and reasonably complex, showing light pepper along with tart cherry- and berry-flavored fruit. There's plenty of acid, but the fruit is ripe enough to avoid the sour-candy label. **88** —*P.G. (6/1/2006)*

Red Sky 2003 Boushey Vineyard Syrah (Washington) $30. From what is developing into one of Washington's top Syrah vineyards, this wine features delicious flavors of mixed berries accented by judicious oak aging. The only drawback is its relatively short finish. **86** *(9/1/2005)*

RED TRUCK

Red Truck 2004 Cabernet Sauvignon (California) $13. The California appellation on the label doesn't tell you, but the grapes are from Hames Valley, an interesting little region midway between the cool Salinas Valley and warm Paso Robles. The wine has good acidity and treads a delicate line between cherries and more herbal notes. Light and food-friendly. **85** —*S.H. (11/15/2006)*

Red Truck 2004 Merlot (California) $13. A little too sharp and green. You'll find a minty aroma and flavor somewhat relieved by tart red cherries and a touch of oak. **83** —*S.H. (11/15/2006)*

Red Truck 2004 Red Blend (California) $10. Simple and jammy, filled with fresh cherry and berry flavors, this wine has the acidic youthfulness of a Beaujolais nouveau. It's nothing serious, a nice quaffer at a decent price, meant to wash down pizza, burgers, and similar fare. **84** —*S.H. (5/1/2006)*

RED ZEPPELIN

Red Zeppelin 2003 Syrah (Central Coast) $14. Rustic, edgy, and rather sharp, this Syrah has some dark fruit flavors right next to green, minty ones. It's dry. **83** —*S.H. (12/1/2005)*

REDBUD

Redbud 2002 Viognier (California) $5. Tastes too old, having lost whatever acidity it had and now feels flat. The flavors are thin, veering to vegetal. **81** —*S.H. (12/15/2005)*

REDLINE

Redline 2004 Blue Oaks Vineyard Syrah (Paso Robles) $24. Surprisingly dry and minty for an '04 Paso red wine, this wine, with only 13.8% alcohol, seems early picked. The grapes didn't entirely ripen, nor did the tannins, and the wine feels like it wanted to be lusher than it is. **83** —*S.H. (12/31/2006)*

Redline 2004 Cedar Lane Vineyard Syrah (Arroyo Seco) $30. Arroyo Seco Syrahs always interest for their dry, high-acid profile that also lets the fruit ripen. This is a young, closed wine now, tart and tannic, but it shows promise with a rich core of blackberry and cherry pie filling fruit. Best now with rich fare, or hold through 2010. **89** —*S.H. (12/31/2006)*

Redline 2004 Eaglepoint Ranch Syrah (Mendocino) $32. Classic Eaglepoint red wine: big, high alcohol, dry, and dramatically ripe, with extra layers of complexity. Offers rich blackberry flavors, with a darkly earthy, mulchy undertone of soy-sautéed mushrooms and leather. The tannins are bigtime, but it will lose interest with age. Perfect now with grilled steak. **91** —*S.H. (12/31/2006)*

REDWOOD

Redwood 2004 Select Series Barbera (California) $10. So what do you get in a $10 Barbera? Just what you'd expect: a bone-dry, high-acid wine, with Barbera's furry grapeskin tannins and flavors of black- and purple-skinned fruits. **83** —*S.H. (12/31/2006)*

Redwood 2000 Cabernet Sauvignon (California) $9. Nice and smooth drinking, with some real varietal flavors. This soft, easy wine tastes like blackberries is finishes with a spicy aftertaste. **85 Best Buy** —*S.H. (6/1/2003)*

Redwood 2001 Chardonnay (California) $9. Made in the popular style, with ripe, sunny flavors of peaches and apples, and a rich, honeyed texture. Don't look for layers of complexity, though. **84** —*S.H. (6/1/2003)*

Redwood 2000 Merlot (California) $9. A pleasant sipper at a nice price, this fruity wine has flavors of cherries and plums, and is soft and rich. Has more complexity and depth than you'd think, and is a very good value. **85 Best Buy** —*S.H. (8/1/2003)*

Redwood 2001 Rosé Blend (California) $7. Simple and fruity, a slightly sweet sipper with peach and apricot flavors and tart acids. Inocuous enough, if you like white Zin. **83** —*S.H. (9/1/2003)*

REDWOOD CREEK

Redwood Creek 2004 Cabernet Sauvignon (California) $8. Scores high on the deliciousness factor. It's just loaded with blackberry pudding, cassis, milk chocolate, and licorice flavors, and it finishes soft and dry. Sure, it's not a First Growth, but it offers real Cabernet pleasure at an everyday price. **84 Best Buy** —*S.H. (11/15/2006)*

Redwood Creek 2004 Pinot Grigio (California) $8. With a little Columbard, Viognier, and Chardonnay, plus 2% other unnamed varieties, this sure is fruity. It's a simple, charming glassful of apples, peaches, figs, melons, and grapefruits; dry and well-acidified. **85 Best Buy** —*S.H. (3/1/2006)*

REED

Reed 2000 Fralich Vineyard Syrah (Paso Robles) $29. Rich, soft, and supple, an easy-drinking wine with super-delicious, gooey flavors of violets, chocolate, and raspberries. There's a grace and femininity to the mouthfeel that's really attractive. **89** —*S.H. (12/1/2002)*

REFLECTIONS

Reflections 2001 Meritage (Alexander Valley) $50. Dry, tannic, and ungenerous, not showing the softness and fruitiness you'd expect. Still, it's a well-made wine, with a core of black cherry fruit, and might improve. Try cellaring through 2005. **85** —*S.H. (6/1/2005)*

Reflections 2000 Meritage (Alexander Valley) $55. Opens with herbal, earthy aromas, and drinks tannic and a bit thin in fruit, although oak adds softening and sweetening notes. Drink now. **84** —*S.H. (6/1/2005)*

REGUSCI

Regusci 2002 Cabernet Sauvignon (Stags Leap District) $48. A marvelous Cab that seduces with lush, ripe flavors of black currants, smoked meat, and charry oak. Perfectly balanced, with softly expressive tannins. Displays power and elegance. **92** —*S.H. (10/1/2005)*

Regusci 2002 Merlot (Napa Valley) $40. There's something warm-hearted about this wine. Maybe it's the velvety softness, or the touch of toasted wood, or the flavors that suggest sun-ripened blackberries. Whatever it is, it's easy and delicious, but quite complex. **91** —*S.H.* (10/1/2005)

REININGER

Reininger 2002 Cabernet Sauvignon (Walla Walla (WA)) $32. As with the Merlot this is Ash Hollow fruit (92%), hence young; it seems to represent a significant shift in style from previous Reininger wines. Very nice winemaking brings out interesting herb and grassy notes; the base fruit is quite light, with strawberry, fig, and hints of sour cherry. **89** —*P.G.* (6/1/2006)

Reininger 1999 Cabernet Sauvignon (Walla Walla (WA)) $35. Nice, juicy aromas of black fruits and cassis, with suggestions of licorice and mocha. This is a shade or two tighter and deeper than the excellent Merlot. Inviting and true to varietal, it shows exceptional poise, filling the mouth with subtle, sensual layers of fruit, accented with toasted wood. Elegant effort. **92 Editors' Choice** —*P.G.* (12/31/2001)

Reininger 2002 Carmenère (Walla Walla (WA)) $35. This is 100% Carmenère; a delicious, chewy, tart, racy wine with strong herbal elements and lots of black pepper. Woody and herbal, with powerful tannins, it needs some breathing time; then it opens out and lengthens through a rich, silky finish. **90** —*P.G.* (12/15/2005)

Reininger 2002 Merlot (Walla Walla (WA)) $30. This is mostly young fruit from Ash Hollow, and it shows. Very light through the middle, though cleverly buttressed with a smattering of Cab Franc from Pepper Bridge and Cab Sauv from Spring Valley. It's silky and smooth, with interesting nuances of herb and grass, and a playful lift to the middle which extends rather surprisingly into the finish. The oak is well played, adding butter, toffee, and toast in clever proportions. **90** —*P.G.* (6/1/2006)

Reininger 1999 Merlot (Walla Walla (WA)) $35. A lush scent of fresh Bing cherries greets you from the moment the cork is pulled, afterward, this lovely, textured wine continues to open up beautifully in the glass. Fine grip and body, it's plump, fresh fruit is artfully balanced against acid and oak. Smooth, youthful, and inviting, this isn't a huge wine, just hugely enjoyable. **90** —*P.G.* (12/31/2001)

Reininger 1999 Red Table Wine Red Blend (Walla Walla (WA)) $20. Reininger makes their Red Table Wine from lots not selected for their other wines, but it's a nice effort, and attractively priced. Ripe and plummy, it smells of raisins, spices, and ground coffee. It is open and soft, showing mature fruit and interesting nuances of leaf and toast. **88** —*P.G.* (12/31/2001)

Reininger 2001 Cima Sangiovese (Walla Walla (WA)) $45. This is Reininger's super Tuscan-style blend: half Sangiovese, one quarter Cabernet Sauvignon, 15% Merlot, and 10% Cab Franc. I applaud the innovation, and the care given to its extra aging, but confess puzzlement as to what exactly this wine is intended to be. The extra time in bottle has softened it into a pleasing, mellow condition; it would make a heck of a good spaghetti wine, but the price suggests grander aspirations. **87** —*P.G.* (6/1/2006)

Reininger 2003 Syrah (Walla Walla (WA)) $32. This is pure Syrah, done in a classy, confident style showing the dense, tannic, peppery fruit first and foremost. It hits you upfront with big, youthful, sappy flavors, then follows with barrel notes of toast, light leather, tobacco, and roast beef. Very palate friendly. **91** —*P.G.* (6/1/2006)

Reininger 2002 Syrah (Walla Walla (WA)) $32. Seems a tad overripe, with flavors that veer toward molasses and raisins. Soft and thick, with relatively low acidity. **83** (9/1/2005)

Reininger 1999 Syrah (Walla Walla (WA)) $29. Pretty middle-of-the-road juice, by all panelists' accounts, the Reininger has lots of tart berry fruit and toasted oak flavors and aromas, plus a long, dry, wood-and-peanut shells finish. Has some nice coffee and chocolate notes along the way, but has quite a bit of wood and acid. **86** (11/1/2001)

RENAISSANCE

Renaissance 1998 Cabernet Sauvignon (North Yuba) $17. Modest blackberry aromas start things off, with a funky, cheesy undercurrent. Fruity

in the mouth and dry, with little noticeable oak. This rough, earthy wine will do in a pinch. **82** —*S.H.* (11/15/2001)

Renaissance 1998 Estate Bottled Chardonnay (North Yuba) $17. 82 (6/1/2000)

Renaissance 1997 Première Cuvée Chardonnay (North Yuba) $30. 87 (6/1/2000)

Renaissance 1997 Première Cuvée Chardonnay (North Yuba) $35. The deep gold color here suggests age, as do the soft, vaguely oxidized flavors. Still, it shows some nice vanilla and baked apple notes, as well as slight chalk accents, on its toasty oak frame. Drink now. **85** (7/1/2001)

Renaissance 1995 Vendanges Tardives Chardonnay (North Yuba) $25. 81 —*J.C.* (12/31/1999)

Renaissance 1999 Mediterranean Red Red Blend (North Yuba) $21. Funky and earthy aromas float over fruity-berry ones. Thick and syrupy, with intensely extracted red raspberry and black cherry flavors. Dry and heavy-handed. A blend of 70% Grenache and 30% Syrah. **81** —*S.H.* (12/1/2001)

Renaissance 2000 Viognier (North Yuba) $19. Atypical for a California Viognier, with citrus and honey flavors. You might mistake it for a Sauvignon Blanc, but it's nonetheless tasty and refreshing. Polished, rich, and balanced. Serve it well chilled with a mango salsa. **85** —*S.H.* (11/15/2001)

Renaissance 1999 Zinfandel (North Yuba) $19. Dark and strong stuff here. Smells earthy and plummy, with a cut of green stalkiness and mint; turns heavy and dense in the mouth. Finishes Port-like, with heat and sweetness. **81** —*S.H.* (11/15/2001)

RENARD

Renard 2000 Syrah (Santa Rita Hills) $28. Rich and dense, with the creamy smooth texture of buttery chocolate frosting, and complex flavors of blackberry, mocha, game, vanilla, and dusty brown spices. Structured, with firm but supple tannins. Shows this AVA's potential for well-ripened Syrah, not just Pinot Noir. **91** —*S.H.* (2/1/2004)

Renard 2000 Arroyo Vineyards Syrah (Napa Valley) $28. Nowhere near as lush or complex as the Santa Rita Hills bottling, but still a good wine. Grown in Calistoga, it is ultraripe, brimming with plum pudding and blackberry flavors. The alcohol is high, and the wine finishes soft, with a touch of Porty raisins. **86** —*S.H.* (2/1/2004)

RENWOOD

Renwood 2002 Barbera (Amador County) $20. What a big, dark, rich wine this is. It's classic California Barbera, dense in tannins and loaded with deep, hearty blackberry and plum flavors, with a touch of sweet raisin in the finish. Drink this rustic wine with robust fare, or after dinner with blue cheese and walnuts. **85** —*S.H.* (5/1/2006)

Renwood 2001 Barbera (Amador County) $20. At two-plus years this big, sturdy wine has mellowed and is soft and lush in the mouth, although there are still plenty of sweet, dusty tannins. The fruit is long and rich, suggesting the ripest cherries, with hints of cured leather and olive tapenade. A very well-made wine, perfect for pasta dishes. **90 Editors' Choice** —*S.H.* (6/1/2004)

Renwood 2002 Sierra Series Barbera (Sierra Foothills) $10. Fairly light in color and body for a Barbera, just a little fleshier than a good Pinot Noir, although the flavors are much different. Plums, tobacco, and mocha describe them nicely. A nice sipper for Italian fare. **85** —*S.H.* (6/1/2004)

Renwood 2001 Sierra Series Barbera (Sierra Foothills) $12. Barbera is being discovered as an old-style wine with a sturdy, rich character. This wine is very young, with sharp, jammy wild berry flavors. It will be good now with pasta, but try aging it for a few years to soften the edges. **86 Best Buy** —*S.H.* (12/1/2002)

Renwood 2001 Orange Muscat (Shenandoah Valley (CA)) $12. A nice, clean dessert wine, with tangerine, cinnamon, and vanilla aromas and flavors. It's very fruity, lip-smacking, and sweet, but not that sweet. The creamy smooth mouthfeel is really nice. **87** —*S.H.* (12/1/2002)

Renwood 2005 Orange Muscat (Amador County) $11. Sweet and simple. If you're looking for a nice dessert wine at an everyday price, this is a good choice. It brims with orange juice, tangerine custard, and vanilla cream flavors that are balanced with cleansing acidity. **84** —*S.H.* (12/31/2006)

USA

Renwood 2002 Orange Muscat (Amador County) $12. Quite sweet with orange and tangerine, vanilla, and smoke flavors, but light in alcohol, and the crisp spine of acidity perfectly balances out the sweetness. **90** —S.H. (6/1/2004)

Renwood 2005 Pinot Grigio (Lodi) $10. Dryish and crisp, with a nice balance of green apple and lemon flavors and earthier, green herb notes. Finishes clean and honest. **84** —S.H. (12/31/2006)

Renwood 2004 Select Series Pinot Grigio (California) $10. Lots of puckery acidity in this dry wine, with a metallic, mineral quality to the citrus flavors that could make it a nice match for shellfish. **84** —S.H. (2/1/2006)

Renwood NV Port (Sierra Foothills) $15. Made from traditional Port, this wine is rather like a good tawny. It's very sweet, with compellingly delicious dark chocolate, coffee, cherry pie, and spicy flavors, and a smooth, mellow texture. Not an ager, so enjoy now. **88** —S.H. (6/1/2004)

Renwood 1995 Vintage Port (Shenandoah Valley (CA)) $22. Awkward, opening with vegetal aromas that turn cloyingly sweet in the mouth. It's also a very acidic wine. Not offering much charm now. **83** —S.H. (9/1/2003)

Renwood 2000 Syrah (Amador County) $25. Good varietal character marks this plummy, peppery wine. It's very ripe and fruity, with soft, unctuous tannins and enough acidity to offset the rich flavors. Finishes with a bite of tannin. Should improve in a year or two. **87** —S.H. (2/1/2003)

Renwood 1999 Syrah (Amador County) $25. Black plums, vanilla oak, and enough hickory smoke flavors to make a barbecue chef proud. The finish is long and supple, echoing with sweet smoke flavors. **87** (11/1/2001)

Renwood 2003 Select Series Syrah Rosé (California) $9. Thin in flavor, with watered-down strawberry and raspberry, but dry and clean, and zesty in acidity. Nice for a casual lunch. **83** —S.H. (10/1/2004)

Renwood 2004 Select Series Syrah Rosé (California) $12. Smells jammy and peppery, a fairly inviting aroma that lets you down once the initial strawberry flavors disappear into a watery thin finish. If only there was a little more there. **82** —S.H. (12/31/2006)

Renwood 2002 Sierra Series Syrah (Sierra Foothills) $NA. Quite dark and full-bodied, a big, heavy wine that's also quite tannic and acidic. Consequently it's fairly numbing on the palate. Has plums, tobacco, leather, and a touch of charcoal on the finish. **85** —S.H. (6/1/2004)

Renwood 2001 Sierra Series Syrah (Sierra Foothills) $12. A nice, easy-drinking Syrah, with plum and tobacco flavors and rich, dry tannins. It feels supple and round in the mouth, with a tart, peppery finish. **86** —S.H. (2/1/2003)

Renwood 2000 Sierra Series Syrah (California) $13. A softly fruity and charming wine, with melted tannins and easy acids framing blackberry, plum, tobacco, and spicy flavors. It's a likeable wine that will go well with pizza, pasta, burgers, and similar fare. **85** —S.H. (12/1/2002)

Renwood 1999 Sierra Series Syrah (California) $12. Airy cedar, sunflower, and cherry aromas prepare you for a round mouth full of dark fruit and toast. Finishes with same flavors that mouth offers, plus hints of chalk and lemon. **84** (10/1/2001)

Renwood 2002 Viognier (Amador County) $25. This distinctive wine captures Viognier's juicy, flamboyant flavors of tropical fruits, wildflowers, honey, and spices and keeps them controlled with crisp acidity and balance. It's full bodied and rich, and quite delicious on its own. **88** —S.H. (6/1/2004)

Renwood 2001 Viognier (Shenandoah Valley (CA)) $25. This is why so many people are turning to Viognier. It combines Chardonnay's full-bodied, oaky fruity qualities with Sauvignon Blanc's lemony tartness to create a wine midway between the two. Doesn't go over the top in flowers and eccentric fruit, but keeps things balanced. **88** —S.H. (12/15/2002)

Renwood 2000 Viognier (Shenandoah Valley (CA)) $25. Enticing, with velvety texture but firmness, nonetheless, on the palate. A sleek and subtle blend of apricot, peach, spice, herb, and citrus flavors, all couched elegantly with finesse. **90** —J.M. (12/15/2002)

Renwood 2002 Select Series Viognier (Lodi) $NA. Simple and a little spritzy with effervescence, a pleasant wine with bubblegummy, spicy flavors and good acidity. Easy to drink, with a quick finish. **83** —S.H. (6/1/2004)

Renwood 2001 Select Series Viognier (California) $25. This is very Viognieresque in its ultrafruity, flowery aromas and flavors, which range from apples and peaches to tropical fruits and flowers. The texture is buttercream-rich, but the wine is dry, with good acids. **86** —S.H. (12/15/2002)

Renwood 2001 Sierra Series Viognier (California) $12. Simple and very fruity, with all kinds of peach, apple, flower, and pear flavors. Feels heavy and dense in the mouth, and could use higher acidity to offset the richness. Will appeal to fans of big, explosive flavors. **85** —S.H. (5/1/2003)

Renwood 2000 Sierra Series Viognier (California) $13. 83 —J.M. (12/15/2002)

Renwood 2004 Zinfandel (Sierra Foothills) $10. Rustic, harsh, a little unripe, the wine is thankfully dry and low in alcohol, and is certainly affordable, but that's not enough. It lacks fruit, charm, and drinkability. **81** —S.H. (12/31/2006)

Renwood 2003 Zinfandel (Fiddletown) $25. Such are the tannins here that the wine will benefit from time. It has the balance and above all the fruit to make it through six years. The cherries, blackberries, boysenberries, and cocoa are complex and delicious. **89 Cellar Selection** —S.H. (5/1/2006)

Renwood 2002 Zinfandel (Fiddletown) $25. Right off the bat, there's a Porty aroma to this wine, suggesting overripe, shriveled grapes, and the taste confirms baked fruit. The wine is completely dry, with pleasant blackberry and cherry flavors, but that stewed quality doesn't go away. **84** —S.H. (5/1/2006)

Renwood 2001 Zinfandel (Fiddletown) $25. As big as Zin gets, displaying massive flavors of all sorts of wild forest berries, mocha, coffee, and an array of oriental spices. The lush tannins are the perfect frame for all that flavor. Rather hot with alcohol on the finish. **90** —S.H. (6/1/2004)

Renwood 2000 Amador Ice Zinfandel (Shenandoah Valley (CA)) $35. A pale orange or copper-colored wine, with powerful apricot, orange juice, and honeyed espresso aromas. Attacks the palate with intense sugar, a very sweet wine good on its own with a simple butter cookie. The flavors are apricot-fruity, with soft acids and tannins. **88** —S.H. (12/1/2002)

Renwood 1997 D'Agostini Bros. Zinfandel (Shenandoah Valley (CA)) $30. 87 —P.G. (11/15/1999)

Renwood 2000 D'Agostini Bros. Zinfandel (Shenandoah Valley (CA)) $30. This big, mountain Zin is massively packed with briary berry flavors, wild and sweet with sunshine, and equally upfront alcohol and tannins. It's been vinified bone-dry, so doesn't have any annoying sugar. **88** —S.H. (2/1/2003)

Renwood 1999 D'Agostini Bros. Zinfandel (Amador County) $30. Very masculine, and not for the weak-hearted, this Zin is a roller coaster ride from sweetness to dryness, from big to bigger. Baking spices coat sweet blueberry and red-berry aromas on the nose. The wine's a little hot and dry on the palate thanks to its hefty tannins, but the black plum-mixed berry-molasses profile offers plenty of flavor to get you through the rough spots. Medium-long and dry on the finish, it finishes with more of the above, plus espresso and bitter chocolate. **88** —D.T. (3/1/2002)

Renwood 1999 Fiddletown Zinfandel (Amador County) $25. This old-vine Zin offers black fruit aromas on the palate, though it's a little hot. Medium-full in the mouth, the wine's dark, taut blackberry and black cherry notes are livened up by woodsy spices. Long black cherry finish. A one-trick pony, but its trick is pretty good. **86** —D.T. (3/1/2002)

Renwood 2002 Grandmère Zinfandel (Amador County) $25. Tastes tannically rough and astringent, with coffee and Porty blackberry flavors that seem like they were sweetened with artificial sugar. **82** —S.H. (5/1/2006)

Renwood 2001 Grandmère Zinfandel (Amador County) $25. The tannins are so ripe and sweet, so soft and intricate, in this decadently fruity, feminine wine. It has flavors of ripe blackberries, dusted with cocoa and sprinkled with tangerine zest. This is seriously good stuff, and impossible to resist. **92** —S.H. (6/1/2004)

Renwood 2000 Grandmère Zinfandel (Amador County) $25. Rich and brawny, this Zin could come from no place but the Foothills. The big berry flavors and thick dusty tannins add kicks of alcohol and sweetness on the finish. You'll either like it or you'll find it cloying. **86** —S.H. (2/1/2003)

USA

Renwood 1999 Grandmère Zinfandel (Amador County) $25. White pepper and oak aromas spice up the bouquet; white pepper adds brightness to an otherwise very dark black fruit-and-oak profile on the palate. Naturally recommends itself to steak au poivre. **87** —*D.T. (3/1/2002)*

Renwood 1996 Grandmère Zinfandel (Amador County) $25. 84 —*P.G. (11/15/1999)*

Renwood 2003 Grandmère Zinfandel (Amador County) $25. Here's one mighty fine and interesting Zin. It has the smoothness of a great red wine, with a rich, fruity complexity that lasts through a long finish. The flavors are classic Zin, all wild berries and cocoa, with a dusting of raisins. The alcohol is enormous, but the wine is dry, and doesn't taste hot. With short ribs, it's a marriage made in heaven. **92** —*S.H. (5/1/2006)*

Renwood 1997 Grandmère Zinfandel (Amador County) $25. Full blueberry and blackberry aromas can't overcome the off-putting, solvent-like elements on the nose here. Lots of alcohol, spice-cake, and dark berry flavors, but not much finesse or texture mark this disappointing old-vine offering from this generally solid Zinfandel producer. **81** *(3/1/2001)*

Renwood 2002 Grandpère Zinfandel (Amador County) $35. Tough and mouth-numbing in tannins, this Zin benefits from enormously ripe cherry, berry, and cocoa flavors that emerge through the astringency. It's very dry. Best with barbecue now, because it doesn't have the balance to age. **85** —*S.H. (5/1/2006)*

Renwood 2001 Grandpère Zinfandel (Amador County) $32. This is the biggest, densest, most alcoholic, and most tannic of Redwood's '01 Zins, and while it's a very good wine, it does not possess the opulent hedonism of, say, Grandmère or Jack Rabbit. The cherry, blackberry, and mocha flavors are less intense. A cellar candidate. **89** —*S.H. (6/1/2004)*

Renwood 2000 Grandpère Zinfandel (Shenandoah Valley (CA)) $32. Good example of a big Sierra Foothills Zin. Ripe and rich, with blackberry, raspberry, cherry, and pepper flavors that assault the palate and coat the tongue through the finish. **86** —*S.H. (2/1/2003)*

Renwood 1999 Grandpère Zinfandel (Amador County) $32. I dig the black pepper, cocoa, anise, and stewed fruit bouquet, and the blueberry, blackberry, and unsweetened chocolate palate profile. The mouthfeel is silky smooth, and a bit rich thanks to lots of caramel. The finish is a bit of a conundrum—there's big, sweet ripe berry fruit at first, but it ducks out before you know it and leaves you with a substantial amount of ash and black pepper. Not that pepper's a bad thing, but I do wish that I had some warning. **89** —*D.T. (3/1/2002)*

Renwood 2003 Jack Rabbit Flat Zinfandel (Amador County) $30. The touch of Porty, chocolate-covered raisins doesn't dominate, instead providing an extra layer of flavor to the blackberries and cherries of this dry, substantial wine. It's a rich example of Sierra Foothills Zin, with its high alcohol and sun-ripened fruit. **86** —*S.H. (5/1/2006)*

Renwood 2002 Jack Rabbit Flat Zinfandel (Amador County) $30. Way too tannic for enjoyment, a super-dry, astringent wine. It's not likely to go anywhere, despite a core of ripe berry-cherry fruit, unless you like old Zinfandel. **82** —*S.H. (5/1/2006)*

Renwood 2001 Jack Rabbit Flat Zinfandel (Amador County) $30. The 2000 Jack Rabbit was very good. This one, from a better vintage, is much better. It's the perfect example of a mountain Zin that's big and bold, with its pure flavors of cherry, mocha, raspberry tart, coffee, vanilla, and dusty spices that flood the mouth, and finish with a tannic bite. **91** —*S.H. (6/1/2004)*

Renwood 2000 Jack Rabbit Flat Zinfandel (Amador County) $30. An extraordinarily good Zin that avoids too-high alcohol and residual sugar. The beautiful flavors range from blackberries and blueberries through sage, tobacco, and pepper. The tannins are smooth as velvet, and the mouthfeel is rich and layered. **89** —*S.H. (2/1/2003)*

Renwood 1999 Jack Rabbit Flat Zinfandel (Amador County) $30. Black pepper, dust, and grapey aromas preface a slightly creamy blackberry and blueberry palate. Medium-full, with sturdy tannins, it closes with mixed berries and dashes of green herb and black pepper. **86** —*D.T. (3/1/2002)*

Renwood 2003 Old Vine Zinfandel (Amador County) $20. Has the structure and balance of a fine Cabernet, with a nice balance of tannins, acidity,

and fruit, and an elegantly tailored mouthfeel. Of course, the flavors are pure Zin, ranging from brambly, wild berries and coffee to white pepper and bitter chocolate. **90 Editors' Choice** —*S.H. (5/1/2006)*

Renwood 2002 Old Vine Zinfandel (Amador County) $20. With a touch of raisins in the finish, this is a nice example of a Foothills Zin. It's ripe, alcoholic, dry, and rich, with Zinny flavors wrapped in sturdy but accessible tannins. There's a long finish of black cherries and cocoa. **86** —*S.H. (5/1/2006)*

Renwood 2001 Old Vine Zinfandel (Amador County) $20. A big, galloping Zin, the kind that intense mountain sunshine has ripened to perfection. It's huge in cherry, blackberry, sweet rhubarb, and root beer flavors, and with gutsy tannins. Big in alcohol, too. **88** —*S.H. (6/1/2004)*

Renwood 2000 Old Vine Zinfandel (Amador County) $20. A young, jammy Zin, fresh and sharp as a summer rainfall. Rich and fruity, with brambly blackberry and black raspberry flavors and a jolt of youthful acidity. Soft tannins let it glide down nice and gentle. **87** —*S.H. (12/1/2002)*

Renwood 1999 Old Vine Zinfandel (Amador County) $20. Asian-inspired noes of soy and seaweed emanate from the bouquet—there's deep black fruit underneath, but the other flavors are more interesting, running from bright black and red fruit to peppery, oak-derived notes. Thins out a bit on the end. **85** —*D.T. (3/1/2002)*

Renwood 2003 Sierra Series Zinfandel (Sierra Foothills) $10. Not my favorite kind of Zin because of the sugary fruit and coffee flavors that suggest residual sweetness. On the positive side, the wine has a good structure, with rich tannins and crisp acids. **83** —*S.H. (5/1/2006)*

Renwood 2002 Sierra Series Zinfandel (Sierra Foothills) $10. From a producer that's shown a deft hand at this variety, a good interpretation at an everyday price. It's balanced and even, with earthy, bitter cherry and herb flavors, and completely dry. **85** —*S.H. (12/15/2004)*

Renwood 2001 Sierra Series Zinfandel (Sierra Foothills) $12. A fine example of a brawny Foothills Zin, with wild, brambly berry flavors, rugged but negotiable tannins, and a bite of acidity. The fruit is deep and long and ripe, suggesting cherries. Barbecue with your best sauce is the perfect marriage. **87 Best Buy** —*S.H. (2/1/2003)*

RETRO

Retro 2003 Petite Sirah (Howell Mountain) $40. The vineyard is 1,800 feet up the mountain and the wine was made by Randy Dunn's (Dunn Vineyards) son, Mike. Howell Mountain produces some of California's densest, most ageworthy red wines, and this big, dry, tannic Pet is a sure cellar candidate. Packed with blackberry, coffee, plum, leather, and spice flavors, it should start to open up by 2009 and improve for several years after. **92 Cellar Selection** —*S.H. (11/15/2006)*

RETZLAFF

Retzlaff 2000 Cabernet Sauvignon-Merlot (Livermore Valley) $38. Smells herbal and unripe, with just a trace of cherry-berry to offset the green notes. Pretty thin in the mouth, too, although there's an odd sweetness. Pretty oaky, but the smoky vanilla can't make up for the lack of berry flavor. **83** —*S.H. (11/15/2003)*

Retzlaff 1999 Chardonnay (Livermore Valley) $16. An interesting older wine, still in current release, that is picking up the bouquet and complexity of bottle age. Aromas include ripe pear, mineral, honey, and smoke, while the rich, creamy mouthfeel carries flavors of aging white wine that is still fresh and slightly herbal. **87** —*S.H. (12/31/2003)*

Retzlaff 1998 Estate Bottled Chardonnay (Livermore Valley) $16. 85 *(6/1/2000)*

REVERIE

Reverie 2001 Special Reserve Estate Cabernet Blend (Diamond Mountain) $75. Rather too soft, although the chocolate, black cherry, blueberry, and blackberry flavors are lipsmackingly tasty. But flavor isn't everything. Still, it's a very polished wine. **88** —*S.H. (10/1/2005)*

Reverie 2000 Special Reserve Estate Cabernet Blend (Diamond Mountain) $55. Compelling for its ripeness, balance, harmony, and the way those tannins work to pull it all together. This Cab-based wine has it all, blackberries, cherries, cocoa, great acidity, wonderful oak. Ultimately, it's the soft, intricate tannic structure that makes it complex. **91** —*S.H. (10/1/2005)*

USA

Reverie 2003 Cabernet Franc (Diamond Mountain) $45. This is more tannic and full-bodied than most Cab Francs, more akin to Cabernet Sauvignon, and with darker berry and stone fruit flavors. That must be because of Reverie's steep mountainside vineyard. The black cherry fruit is ripe, but it's elbowed aside by those tough tannins. Still, it doesn't seem like an ager. Best now with a great steak. **90** —*S.H. (9/1/2006)*

Reverie 2001 Estate Cabernet Franc (Diamond Mountain) $42. When Cab Franc succeeds in California, which is rare, it can be very good. When it doesn't, it reminds you why in Bordeaux it's usually a blending wine. This wine is pretty, but light, with earthy, meaty cherry and oak flavors, and is dry. **86** —*S.H. (7/1/2005)*

Reverie 2002 Cabernet Sauvignon (Diamond Mountain) $55. The vineyard is directly across from Diamond Creek's, just a short walk, but with different soils and exposures. The wine is completely different, showing firmer, harder tannins and a youthful stubbornness. This is a tight young wine, but five to seven years should soften and sweeten it. **90** —*S.H. (9/1/2006)*

Reverie 2002 Special Reserve Cabernet Sauvignon (Diamond Mountain) $75. A little sharp and rude for a reserve, thick in tough tannins, and somewhat overripe. This may be a case where the winemaker exaggerated the good qualities of the regular Cab, creating a situation of imbalance. That regular Cab, at $55, is a better wine. **84** —*S.H. (9/1/2006)*

Reverie 2003 Merlot (Diamond Mountain) $45. Reverie's vineyards are on a particularly high, steep slope of the mountain, and they make for wines that are tough in tannins when young, as this one is. It's also very dry, and feels astringently unsatisfying. Most California Merlots are not aging wines, but this one has a solid core of fruit, and might emerge from its coma for a window between 2007 and 2009. **88** —*S.H. (8/1/2006)*

REX HILL

Rex Hill 1993 Champagne Blend (Oregon) $24. **86** —*P.G. (12/1/2000)*

Rex Hill 2002 Chardonnay (Willamette Valley) $12. Mostly neutral oak is used in this budget bottling, but a hint of toast comes through, and adds interest to the soft, ripe, banana flavors. A bit more concentration than the unwooded Chardonnay from Rex Hill. **88** —*P.G. (8/1/2005)*

Rex Hill 1999 Chardonnay (Willamette Valley) $17. You'd never confuse this with a California Chard. Well, Anderson Valley, maybe. It's a cool-climate wine. Aromas of fresh, cold green apples, with what seems like an overlay of buttery oak. Brilliantly dry and crisp in the mouth. It's all about acidity here; flavors are secondary. Clean as a whistle, edgy, a nervously racy wine that practically cries out for shellfish. **88** —*S.H. (8/1/2002)*

Rex Hill 2002 Reserve Chardonnay (Oregon) $24. The wine gleams brightly, pale gold, and the nose entices with rich scents of apples, pears, and peaches. The fruit swells through the mid-palate, firm and supple, and continues with hints of hazelnut and just the right amount of buttery oak. **90** —*P.G. (2/1/2005)*

Rex Hill 2003 Unwooded Chardonnay (Willamette Valley) $16. It's all about the fruit here, with a mix of tropical flavors across a broad, friendly palate. Not a California-style fruit-bomb, but fresh and plenty ripe. **86** —*P.G. (8/1/2005)*

Rex Hill 2002 Unwooded Chardonnay (Willamette Valley) $18. A bit of vitamin pill aroma at first, then light herb, citrus, and spice. It expands into a clean, mouthfilling, green apple-flavored Chardonnay with a hint of fennel, then tails off again in the finish. **88** —*P.G. (2/1/2005)*

Rex Hill 2001 Unwooded Chardonnay (Willamette Valley) $17. Following the Aussie lead, this unwooded wine is straightforward and oak-free. The fruit is simple and dry, like a crisp bite of an apple, and the finish has a little bit of spice to it. **87** —*P.G. (2/1/2004)*

Rex Hill 1998 Pinot Blanc (Willamette Valley) $14. **85** —*L.W. (12/31/1999)*

Rex Hill 2003 Pinot Gris (Willamette Valley) $16. A soft, broad palate makes this wine instantly accessible, and it is fine for near term drinking, though not likely to hold well in the cellar. Compared with many of the winery's other Pinot Gris bottlings, this Willamette Valley blend is a bit fuzzy and unfocused. **85** —*P.G. (8/1/2005)*

Rex Hill 2001 Pinot Gris (Willamette Valley) $14. Clean, varietal, and almost steely in its concentration. Hinting at citrus and mineral, it is subtly persistent. **88 Best Buy** —*P.G. (2/1/2004)*

Rex Hill 2000 Pinot Gris (Willamette Valley) $14. It's hard to get very excited about this wine because it's so average and common. It smells weakly of lemons, and the citrus flavors are watery and thin. It's dry and although there's some good acidity, it feels flat in the mouth. That says it all. **83** —*S.H. (8/1/2002)*

Rex Hill 1999 Pinot Gris (Willamette Valley) $14. **84** —*S.H. (8/1/2002)*

Rex Hill 2003 Carabella Vineyard Pinot Gris (Willamette Valley) $24. This is by far the best Pinot Gris of the vintage for Rex Hill. A proven, top-notch vineyard kicks in with lots of spice, melon, cucumber, hints of grass, and plenty of green apple, ripe to the core. Good effort. **91** —*P.G. (8/1/2005)*

Rex Hill 2002 Carabella Vineyard Pinot Gris (Oregon) $28. This is the best of the new Rex Hill lineup, a perfectly ripened, beautifully balanced wine with an appealing mix of tart fruit, mineral, and spice. **90** —*P.G. (2/1/2004)*

Rex Hill 2001 Carabella Vineyard Pinot Gris (Oregon) $24. It's hard to tell the difference between this single-vineyard release and Rex Hill's reserve. It's spicy and fruity, with apple and fig flavors, with good acidity and a dry finish. It feels nice and smooth in the mouth. Both wines are good, in which case, why pay the extra money? **89** —*S.H. (12/31/2002)*

Rex Hill 2003 Jacob-Hart Vineyard Pinot Gris (Willamette Valley) $24. Medium-bodied with spice, citrus, and melon flavors, this vineyard designate keeps its focus and finishes with a nice lift of savory spice. **88** —*P.G. (8/1/2005)*

Rex Hill 2002 Jacob-Hart Vineyard Pinot Gris (Oregon) $28. Soft and creamy, with vanilla seeping into the core fruit of plums and ripe pears. **89** —*P.G. (2/1/2004)*

Rex Hill 1999 Jacob-Hart Vineyard Reserve Pinot Gris (Oregon) $18. **88** —*S.H. (8/1/2002)*

Rex Hill 2005 Reserve Pinot Gris (Oregon) $24. This is a barrel selection from the best sites at the estate (Jacob Hart) vineyard, planted in 1987. It's done in 3/4 stainless, 1/4 neutral oak, and comes out in a thoroughly delicious, well-balanced, fruit-driven wine. Pear, grapefruit, wet stone, and citrus rind work together to create texture and mouthfeel, with a finish of fresh, lightly bitter pear skin. **90** —*P.G. (12/1/2006)*

Rex Hill 2003 Reserve Pinot Gris (Willamette Valley) $21. Much like the winery's regular Pinot Gris in this hot year, this wine is ripe and fruity, and benefits from a higher percentage of Carabella vineyard fruit, and a higher percentage elevated in oak, albeit neutral. **87** —*P.G. (8/1/2005)*

Rex Hill 2002 Reserve Pinot Gris (Oregon) $21. New label, new winemaker, and new lineup of vineyard-designated Pinot Gris in 2002, beginning with this very ripe, round and flavorful reserve. There is more fleshy fruit than in previous vintages, but the wine retains its balance, elegance, and varietal character. **89** —*P.G. (2/1/2004)*

Rex Hill 2001 Reserve Pinot Gris (Oregon) $18. This smooth, fruity wine is great fun. It offers up a blast of spiced apple, pear, and fig flavors that are fruity-sweet, although the finish is nice and dry. The texture is creamy smooth. Try as an alternative to Chardonnay. **89** —*S.H. (12/31/2002)*

Rex Hill 2000 Reserve Pinot Gris (Oregon) $18. You'll find lots of concentration in this dry, nicely drinkable wine, which opens with citrus and mineral aromas and an inviting waft of white chocolate. It's an earth-driven wine. The citrus flavors are strong but not overpowering. You get the impression of crushed fresh herbs: parsley, mint, cilantro. It's dry and crisp and an excellent white wine. **90** —*S.H. (8/1/2002)*

Rex Hill 1997 Pinot Noir (Willamette Valley) $18. **87** —*P.G. (9/1/2000)*

Rex Hill 2002 Pinot Noir (Willamette Valley) $24. Light and tight, showing some vanilla/cocoa scents and feeble flavors of tea leaf and sour cherry. **84** *(11/1/2004)*

Rex Hill 2001 Pinot Noir (Willamette Valley) $24. Classy and elegant, this artful, value-priced bottle expresses the sweet cherry essence of the grape. Balanced with precise acids, it maintains its feminine style and aromatic purity. **89 Editors' Choice** —*P.G. (2/1/2004)*

USA

Rex Hill 1999 Pinot Noir (Willamette Valley) $24. A perplexing wine that should be better than it is. It's fairly dense and concentrated, with good depth of flavor. Beets, tomatoes, blackberries, sugared espresso, and a myriad of crushed, dusty oriental spices fill the mouth. It's good and dry, with crisp acids and easy tannins. So what's the problem? It just lacks that extra kick. Maybe Rex Hill is diverting the best fruit to their three expensive Pinots. **85** —*S.H. (8/1/2002)*

Rex Hill 2002 Anden Vineyard Pinot Noir (Oregon) $52. Pleasant cherry fruit forms a solid base, but the wine doesn't go much farther than that. Tart and biting, with toasted coconut accents from the new oak. **86** *(11/1/2004)*

Rex Hill 2003 Carabella Vineyard Pinot Noir (Willamette Valley) $49. This outstanding vineyard consistently delivers a complex bouquet of cherry, earth, and citrus rind, leading into sweet red fruits. The citrus peel scent follows through with edgy, lightly bitter flavors that etch the palate. It's a beautifully crafted, slightly exotic, intensely tart, and definitive Pinot, ageworthy and food-ready. **92** —*P.G. (5/1/2006)*

Rex Hill 2002 Carabella Vineyard Pinot Noir (Oregon) $52. A terrific vineyard that expresses itself here with a complex bouquet of floral, citrus, and sweet red fruits. There's a distinct citrus peel scent and follow-through flavors, leading into a ripe, succulent, sweet core of cranberry and cherry. Plenty of snap, shape, and definition in this classy effort. **90** *(11/1/2004)*

Rex Hill 2001 Carabella Vineyard Pinot Noir (Oregon) $52. Very pretty fruit, and what the winemaker calls "sandalwood" spice notes. The flavors are built around a core of solid cherry/berry fruit. Delicious. **89** —*P.G. (2/1/2004)*

Rex Hill 2003 Chehalem Mountains Cuvée Pinot Noir (Willamette Valley) $28. A very nice blend, midway between a reserve and a single vineyard wine. The "Cuvée" series from Rex Hill is designed to express the nuances of several of the newest AVAs and sub-AVAs in the state. This excellent bottle is soft and approachable, with pretty fruit. It lacks a bit of concentration, but what is there is flavorful, with hints of rose petals and raspberries. **87** —*P.G. (5/1/2006)*

Rex Hill 2001 Dundee Hills Cuvée Pinot Noir (Oregon) $30. This is all forward, sweet fruit that tastes like strawberry preserves. Behind it is some milk chocolate and cream, but the flavors have not yet knit together. **86** —*P.G. (2/1/2004)*

Rex Hill 2004 Dundee Hills Cuvée Pinot Noir (Dundee Hills) $32. From the new Dundee Hills AVA in the heart of Yamhill County, this Pinot includes roughly half of its fruit from the excellent Maresh vineyard. It jumps out with bright, fresh red fruits and spice and all in all it's young, vibrant, and bursting with appealing berry and vanilla flavors. This is one to enjoy now, while the bloom of youth is in full force. **90** —*P.G. (12/1/2006)*

Rex Hill 2003 Dundee Hills Cuvée Pinot Noir (Dundee Hills) $28. Classic Oregon Pinot, with penetrating cherry fruit laced with layers of earth and baking spices. Sweet, ripe, very pretty wine with a solid midpalate that resonates through a medium-long finish. Quite a bit of oaky vanilla comes through, but it marries well with the beautiful fruit. **90 Editors' Choice** —*P.G. (5/1/2006)*

Rex Hill 2002 Dundee Hills Cuvée Pinot Noir (Oregon) $29. Rex Hill makes a dizzying selection of wines, but this may be among the most elegant overall. Pure, varietal, and very pretty, with sweet fruit and rose petal accents. Easy drinking, soft, and seductive. **89** *(11/1/2004)*

Rex Hill 2002 Jacob-Hart Vineyard Pinot Noir (Oregon) $52. For whatever reasons, this did not show nearly as well as the rest of the strong lineup from Rex Hill in 2002. Perhaps just a bad bottle, but there were off, sweaty aromas, burnt and sour, and the flavors never came together; it felt awkward and incomplete. **84** *(11/1/2004)*

Rex Hill 2004 Jacob-Hart Vineyard Pinot Noir (Oregon) $49. This vineyard delivers a very smooth, soft, nicely textured Pinot Noir. Very ripe fruit leads into flavors of strawberry preserves dotted with milk chocolate. This is a silky wine, which offers flavor details in the Oregon herb-and-leaf mode. It sails through a very smooth finish. **92** —*P.G. (12/1/2006)*

Rex Hill 2003 Jacob-Hart Vineyard Pinot Noir (Willamette Valley) $49. A substantial, mouthfilling, plump, and seductive wine, offering a chewy

mix of cherry/berry red fruits, mocha, vanilla, and baking spice. It's a solid, ripe, well-crafted wine that delivers a lot of pleasure right up front. A huge improvement over the disappointing 2002. **89** —*P.G. (5/1/2006)*

Rex Hill 2001 Jacob-Hart Vineyard Pinot Noir (Oregon) $52. Nice effort, a chewy mix of tangy red fruits, nicely complemented with spice and chocolatey oak. There is a milk chocolate smoothness in the mouth, which turns a bit flat at the end. **88** —*P.G. (2/1/2005)*

Rex Hill 1999 Jacob-Hart Vineyard Pinot Noir (Oregon) $52. Some Pinots have a distinctly feminine character, and this graceful, elegant wine is a good example. Fine, ripe cherry fruit highlights a silky wine that smoothly rolls across the palate. Seamless and delicious, it concludes with soft tannins in a long finish. **90** —*P.G. (4/1/2002)*

Rex Hill 2001 Kings Ridge Pinot Noir (Oregon) $17. This is simple and plain, but surprisingly sweet and extracted, with a fruity core of pretty cherries. Forward and fruit-driven, it's very well made for its price. **87** —*P.G. (2/1/2005)*

Rex Hill 2004 Maresh Vineyard Pinot Noir (Oregon) $49. Maresh (pronounced 'marsh') is one of the half dozen oldest Pinot vineyards in Oregon, with some blocks dating to 1970. This wine shows a very feminine side of the grape, floral, and elegant, with a soft and lovely nose that floats raspberry, cream, and light perfume scents up from the glass. It concentrates its flavors on the back palate, where things linger nicely with resonant berry and spice. **94** —*P.G. (12/1/2006)*

Rex Hill 2003 Maresh Vineyard Pinot Noir (Dundee Hills) $49. Very soft, smooth, forward, and polished. Clean Pinot flavors are set off with nuances of leaf and light tea tannins. The tart fruit is braced against sharp acids, bringing out flavors of cranberry and wild raspberry. This wine carries itself with a great deal of elegance, and requires some attention to appreciate its neo-Burgundian complexity. But it has an excellent chance of aging into something very special. **91** —*P.G. (5/1/2006)*

Rex Hill 2002 Maresh Vineyard Pinot Noir (Oregon) $52. Nice, forward, varietal fruit, hints of leather, and dried spice. Creamy and soft, with medium length and a polished, easy-drinking style. **85** *(11/1/2004)*

Rex Hill 2001 Maresh Vineyard Pinot Noir (Oregon) $52. This is a great vineyard, that delivers fruit that deserves to be showcased on its own. Precisely defined, tart fruit braced against sharp acids bring out the cranberry wild raspberry flavors; there is a sharp, spicy herbal streak as well, hinting at licorice or anise. Good concentration through a long finish. **91** —*P.G. (2/1/2005)*

Rex Hill 1999 Maresh Vineyard Pinot Noir (Oregon) $52. Maresh (pronounced 'marsh') has been a benchmark Pinot producer for decades, as this lovely wine demonstrates. There is a smoky, almost chipotle-like character laced into the sweet fruit. It's a young wine, still showing tangy acids and slightly chalky tannins, but there is a lot of texture and depth already, and a couple more years in bottle will bring it all together. **91** —*P.G. (4/1/2002)*

Rex Hill 2004 Maresh Vineyard Loie's Block Pinot Noir (Oregon) $75. Loie's Block is the oldest in the Maresh vineyard, and shows the elegance and grace of old vines. The wine is sculpted and feminine, but not bashful. Its sweet cherry core is wrapped in piney tannins—the herbs jut out, as often happens in young Oregon Pinot Noir. The angularity and definition suggest that a bit of time will turn this into a multi-dimensional, Burgundian wine. **94 Cellar Selection** —*P.G. (12/1/2006)*

Rex Hill 2001 Maresh Vineyard Loie's Block Pinot Noir (Oregon) $75. From the winery's oldest block of vines, this punches up the blue and black fruits a notch above the regular Maresh (pronounced 'marsh'). There is a strong (perhaps a bit too strong) vanilla note, along with the vineyard's characteristic herbal/anise flavor. **90** —*P.G. (2/1/2005)*

Rex Hill 2002 Maresh Vineyard Loie's Block Pinot Noir (Oregon) $75. There's plenty of spice up front, anise and clove and vanilla in particular. The wine has a forward, very full, and round mouthfeel; it's sweet and ripe, but not jammy or simple. Concentrated and sappy, it needs breathing time to flesh out and show its best. **90** *(11/1/2004)*

Rex Hill 2001 Melrose Vineyard Pinot Noir (Oregon) $49. A rich, deeply colored wine that shows intense scents of spicy cranberry and cherry. Despite the sharp attack, in the mouth it tastes of young, grapey fruit; pleasant but light. **88** —*P.G. (2/1/2005)*

Rex Hill 2000 Melrose Vineyard Pinot Noir (Oregon) $52. 90 —*S.H. (12/31/2002)*

Rex Hill 2004 Reserve Pinot Noir (Oregon) $39. Complete and fleshy, the reserve is blended from all of the winery's vineyard sites. The fruit is sharp and tangy, spiced with cut leaf tobacco, and the oak treatment is laid back. Tight and angular, it doesn't quite show the finesse and concentration of the single-vineyard wines, but that might also be a simple matter of needing just a little more time in the bottle to pull itself together. **89** —*P.G. (12/1/2006)*

Rex Hill 2003 Reserve Pinot Noir (Oregon) $39. Rex Hill's 2003 reserve is beautifully crafted, soft, smooth, and complete. Flavors of classic Oregon Pinot suggest wild berries, spice, leaf, and herb; the tannins have been subdued and the wine just lolls around in your mouth and delivers the goods. **88** —*P.G. (5/1/2006)*

Rex Hill 2002 Reserve Pinot Noir (Oregon) $45. Tightly wound, it opens slowly into a solid, full-flavored, rather chunky style of Pinot laced with the flavors of cola, root beer, and vanilla. Plump and juicy, it's enjoyable rather than profound. **89** *(11/1/2004)*

Rex Hill 2001 Reserve Pinot Noir (Oregon) $45. Rex Hill's reserve trumps most of its single vineyard efforts; it's simply a more complete wine. Supple and silky smooth, this wine has a real beginning, a solid middle and a lingering, satisfying finish. Mixed and layered berry/cherry fruits are seamlessly married to the oak, and tannins are soft and smooth. **90** —*P.G. (2/1/2005)*

Rex Hill 2000 Reserve Pinot Noir (Oregon) $48. A big wine, with forward, tough, chewy flavors of cherry cola and tea. Pleasant, but very light and simple in the finish. **87** —*P.G. (2/1/2004)*

Rex Hill 1999 Reserve Pinot Noir (Oregon) $48. This winery's top Pinot is a wonder especially in this superb vintage. Lush flavors blend cherry fruit, toasty oak, hints of coconut, chocolate, and cinnamon into a complete and delicious whole. Detailed and supple, it fills the mouth with complex and focused flavors. The long, trailing finish is reminiscent of grand cru Burgundy. **94 Cellar Selection** —*P.G. (4/1/2002)*

Rex Hill 1997 Reserve Pinot Noir (Willamette Valley) $45. 83 *(11/15/1999)*

Rex Hill 2000 Rex Hill Estate Pinot Noir (Oregon) $52. The weakest of Rex Hill's three single-vineyard 2000s, although still a very good wine. Opens with a blast of smoky, well-charred sweet oak, caramel, and white chocolate, with subtle blackberry and cherry scents. Oaky and fruity, with a long, spicy finish. **88** —*S.H. (12/31/2002)*

Rex Hill 2004 Seven Springs Vineyard Pinot Noir (Oregon) $49. This is Eola Hills fruit, though the label simply says "Oregon." It carries some of the region's characteristic youthful aromas of tomato leaf mixed with moist earth. Plenty of acid provides good definition; right now it's got all the right components but they remain angular and separate. The stiff and lean tannins indicate that this will benefit from some cellaring. **92** —*P.G. (12/1/2006)*

Rex Hill 2003 Seven Springs Vineyard Pinot Noir (Willamette Valley) $49. New Dijon clone plantings at this well-established vineyard have cut down the leafy herbaceousness of past vintages. This is delicate, clean, lightly ripe, with hints of fresh tomato and pomegranate. It is the sort of Oregon Pinot that truly emulates cru villages Burgundy; light, appealing, and ready to drink. **88** —*P.G. (5/1/2006)*

Rex Hill 2001 Seven Springs Vineyard Pinot Noir (Oregon) $49. This wine definitely hits the leafy, herbal notes hard. Tomato scents carry through on the palate, with a bit of peppery spice. **87** —*P.G. (2/1/2005)*

Rex Hill 2001 Southern Oregon Cuvée Pinot Noir (Oregon) $30. The grapes were grown in southern Oregon, not the Willamette Valley, and the wine is a much darker and more tannic style of Pinot than what you might think of as coming from Oregon. Earthy and hard, with a rubber tire component. **86** —*P.G. (2/1/2004)*

Rex Hill 2003 Southern Oregon Cuvée Pinot Noir (Southern Oregon) $28. Umpqua and Rogue Valley fruit lends a lush warmth to this fragrant, spicy blend. The sweet cherry and strawberry fruit has a spicy kick, like cinnamon candy, and the tannins have been smoothed over, so the finish is extended and soft. **88** —*P.G. (5/1/2006)*

Rex Hill 2002 Southern Oregon Cuvée Pinot Noir (Oregon) $29. A light but

very lively wine, with plums and herbs. Supple and elegant, it gives a lot of complex pleasure despite its modest weight. **88** *(11/1/2004)*

Rex Hill 2000 Weber Vineyard Pinot Noir (Oregon) $52. Very different in style from Rex Hill's other Pinots. Not fruity, but instead shows earth, sautéed mushroom, leather, mint, and smoke notes and a rich core of cherry. An absolutely delicious and distinctive wine, complex and chewy. Feels very high-char oaky on the finish. **91** —*S.H. (12/31/2002)*

Rex Hill 2001 Weber Vineyards Pinot Noir (Oregon) $49. Supple, light, cherry-scented with some typical tomato leaf notes. The rough tannins are beginning to smooth out as the wine turns the corner from raw youth. Pleasant hints of mushroom in the finish. **88** —*P.G. (2/1/2005)*

Rex Hill 1999 Weber Vineyards Pinot Noir (Oregon) $52. This is a balanced, classy effort, well ripened but not at all raisiny or overextracted. Classic Pinot flavors of sassafras and cherry, with some licorice coming through in the finish. Not a big wine, it nonetheless shows supple texture and enough depth to warrant the single- vineyard bottling. **89** —*P.G. (4/1/2002)*

Rex Hill 2002 Sauvignon Blanc (Oregon) $15. Sauv Blanc has never quite taken hold in Oregon, but wines such as this make you wonder why not. Pretty and packed with honeydew, kiwi, gooseberry, and beeswax, it brings lifted, high acid precision and a hint of minerality to the juicy, tangy bedrock citrus. **89** —*P.G. (2/1/2005)*

Rex Hill 2001 Sauvignon Blanc (Willamette Valley) $14. A very crisp, clean, refreshing style with green apple and lime flavors. Tart and slightly spritzy, it needs food to show its best. **87** —*P.G. (2/1/2004)*

Rex Hill 2000 Sauvignon Blanc (Willamette Valley) $12. The smells and flavors of lemons and grapefruits dominate this wine, and they're very dry and tart. It's almost like sucking on lemon rind. Still, this is a very good wine. Brilliant acids accompany the tastes, and there's a round creaminess that makes for a lush mouthfeel. **88** —*S.H. (12/31/2002)*

REY SOL

Rey Sol 1999 Barbera (South Coast) $15. Once the sulfury fumes blow off, you get aromas of plums and tobacco and peppery spices. This wine shows how good Barbera can be when grown in a warm area like Temecula. It's rich, round, soft, lush, and velvety, and very dry, with exquisite tannins. There are even layers of complexity. **90** —*S.H. (4/1/2002)*

Rey Sol 1999 Syrah (South Coast) $18. From Temecula, a somewhat closed dry red wine, not showing much fruit or vibrancy now. There are modulated berry flavors, yet firm acidity and some hefty tannins dominate the palate. It has a round, supple elegance that's likeable. **86** —*S.H. (4/1/2002)*

REYNOLDS

Reynolds 2002 Estate Cabernet Sauvignon (Napa Valley) $45. This is a fine, posh, if a little immature Cabernet. It seems to reflect its southerly Oak Knoll origins in an acidity and tannic structure not found in Oakville. With its core of cassis and cocoa fruit, it should age well. Try holding until after 2007. **89** —*S.H. (11/15/2005)*

Reynolds 2002 Reserve Cabernet Sauvignon (Stags Leap District) $89. Much better than Reynold's Napa bottling. Maybe it's Stags Leap, maybe block selection, but it's a true reserve, richer, denser, and more concentrated, complex, and rewarding. Deep in cassis and plum fruit, it's quite a tannic wine. Hold until 2007 and beyond. **91 Cellar Selection** —*S.H. (11/15/2005)*

Reynolds 2003 Chardonnay (Carneros) $30. Made in a very dry, early-picked style, this wine shows a firm structure of acids and even some dusty tannins, framing tobacco, apple, and spice flavors. Everything about it, including the oak, has been modulated. **87** —*S.H. (11/15/2005)*

Reynolds 2003 Pinot Noir (Russian River Valley) $45. A year or two might benefit this very dry wine. It's crisply acidic and earthy, with flavors of sweet tobacco, espresso, bitter cherry, and fresh sage. Made in a lighter-bodied style, it's a versatile, elegant food wine. **86** —*S.H. (11/15/2005)*

Reynolds Family Winery 2000 Estate Select Cabernet Sauvignon (Napa Valley) $45. Tempting to think you could blind-taste this and identify it as upscale Napa Cabernet. True, the vintage has limited the richness, but it's still a polished wine, with delicious cassis, olive, and herb flavors and sumptuous, velvety tannins. Turns dry and oaky on the finish, and will hold for several years in your cellar. **90** —*S.H. (11/15/2003)*

Reynolds Family Winery 2001 Reserve Cabernet Sauvignon (Stags Leap District) $85. Beautifully combines layers of silky-smooth fruit—cassis and cherries—with spice notes of cinnamon and vanilla. A creamy texture and a long, richly tannic finish wrap up this impressive package. Drink now–2015. **91** —*J.C. (10/1/2004)*

Reynolds Family Winery 2000 Reserve Cabernet Sauvignon (Stags Leap District) $78. This top-tier release from Reynolds is the hardest of the four new releases. It has a firm streak of metallic acidity and the tannins are somewhat aggressive, limiting the palate's ability to enjoy the underlying blackberry and currant flavors. It is not as immediately enjoyable as the Estate Select, but has greater longterm prospects. **89** —*S.H. (11/15/2003)*

Reynolds Family Winery 2002 Pinot Noir (Russian River Valley) $45. A hard wine to like. Smells like menthol and raisins, and drinks too sweet for a dry table wine. **82** *(11/1/2004)*

Reynolds Family Winery 2002 Pinot Noir (Carneros) $45. Overripe, with stewed fruit, baked cherry pie, and toasted coconut aromas, but you like it for the supple texture and soft mouthfeel. **85** *(11/1/2004)*

Reynolds Family Winery 2002 Persistence Red Blend (Napa Valley) $50. With Syrah blended into Bordeaux varieties, this wine has a dry mouthfeel that carries complexity from entry to finish. It's fruity, but young, and true to its southerly Oak Knoll terroir, which is harder, more tannic and acidic, than further north. Try holding for a year or two to soften and sweeten. **87** —*S.H. (11/15/2005)*

RHR

RHR 2004 Cabernet Sauvignon (Paso Robles) $29. Rich and robust, this soft, full-bodied Cab has a nice array of red and black cherry, blackberry jam, cedar, and coffee flavors. Polished tannins help make it classy. **85** —*S.H. (12/31/2006)*

RHR 2003 Old Bailey Vineyard Cabernet Sauvignon (Paso Robles) $40. Unfiltered, so don't let the heavy sediment bother you—it's harmless. Big, ripe, rich, powerful, and soft, this is Paso Cab near its best, showing unctuous blackberry, cherry, chocolate fudge, old leather, and sweet herb flavors that are generously oaked. It's nicely dry, and finishes in a swirl of cherry, vanilla, and spice. **88** —*S.H. (12/31/2006)*

RHR 2004 Pinot Noir (Paso Robles) $28. Don't dismiss this just because it's a Paso Pinot. It scores well on the deliciousness factor, despite being a bit high in alcohol. Loads of jammy, gooey cherry, cocoa, gingersnap cookie, vanilla wafer, and cinnamon spice flavors lead to a long, dry finish. **87** —*S.H. (12/31/2006)*

RHR 2003 Zinfandel (Paso Robles) $27. Soft as velvet and enormously rich in forward fruit, this Zin shows Paso red wine at its ripe, likeable best. The interplay between the delicate body and the cherry jam, black raspberry pie filling, white chocolate truffle, and vanilla cookie flavors is heightened by crisp acidity, and guess what? The wine is dry. **87** —*S.H. (12/31/2006)*

RIBOLI

Riboli 2001 Cabernet Sauvignon (Rutherford) $40. Sturdy in tannins and young and crisp in mouthfeel, with tart cherry, tobacco, and herb flavors. Not a flamboyant wine but a very balanced one, and ageworthy. **90** —*S.H. (10/1/2004)*

Riboli 1997 Cabernet Sauvignon (Rutherford) $45. Powdery tannins frame this licorice-like wine. Herbal notes offset the anise and add interest, though the wine remains a bit short and simple. **81** —*J.M. (12/1/2001)*

RICHARDSON

Richardson 2000 Sangiacomo Vineyard Pinot Noir (Carneros) $16. 88 Best Buy —*S.H. (11/15/2002)*

RIDEAU

Rideau 2003 Reserve Chardonnay (Santa Barbara County) $48. A combination of intensely ripe fruit and lavish oak has created explosive mango, pineapple custard, and smoky vanilla flavors. This huge, New World

Chard is almost over the top, but good acidity helps balance it. **87** —*S.H. (12/31/2005)*

Rideau 2002 Las Presa Vineyards Petite Sirah (Santa Ynez Valley) $52. I'm not a huge fan of Petite Sirah, but I like this wine for its soft power. It's a big, dark, high alcohol wine, but totally dry, with a nice mélange of blackberry, coffee, root beer, and anise flavors that finish long and spicy. **90** —*S.H. (12/31/2005)*

Rideau 2004 In-Circle Cellar Club Le Fleur de Lis Rose Pinot Noir (Santa Barbara County) $22. One of the fuller-bodied rosés you'll have this year, this copper-colored wine is fat, juicy, and fruity. The tangerine and peach flavors are a little sweet and cloying. **83** —*S.H. (12/31/2005)*

Rideau 2004 Sanford & Benedict Vineyard Pinot Noir (Santa Rita Hills) $52. A thick, young, closed wine with a soft, cloying texture, and jammy fruit and sugared coffee flavors. It's also hot. Might age. **82** —*S.H. (10/1/2006)*

Rideau 2003 Château Duplantier Cuvée Red Wine Rhône Red Blend (California) $39. A southern Rhône-style blend of Syrah, Mourvèdre, Grenache, and Petite Sirah, this effusively fruity wine is chockful of melted chocolate, cherry pie, and cassis flavors. It's soft, dry, and actually quite delicious. **87** —*S.H. (12/31/2005)*

Rideau 2004 Riesling (Santa Barbara County) $22. The winery probably intended this to be a kabinett-style, dryish wine, but it's sweet enough to be considered a dessert wine. It has apple, peach, and wildflower flavors, with good acids. **85** —*S.H. (12/31/2005)*

Rideau 2004 In-Circle Cellar Club Roussanne (Santa Barbara County) $48. Intensity is the name of the game with this superripe, opulent Roussanne, with its flamboyant flavors of ripe white peach, apricot, nectarine, and vanilla spice. The wine is dry and creamy. Try as an alternative to a rich Chardonnay. **88** —*S.H. (12/31/2005)*

Rideau 2003 Sangiovese (Central Coast) $28. With nearly 16% alcohol, this is a heady wine, but it's dry and balanced, and doesn't taste hot. There are very deep and attractive flavors of blackberries, set in a softly tannic, oak-tinged texture. A great barbecue wine. **88** —*S.H. (12/31/2005)*

Rideau 2003 In-Circle Cellar Club Iris' Estate Bon Temps Vineyard Syrah (Santa Ynez Valley) $55. A bit stewed, with rhubarb-tinged fruit alongside cherries and spice. There's a hint of nail polish to the nose, and this volatility is reflected in a pronounced tanginess on the finish. **83** *(9/1/2005)*

Rideau 2003 Iris' Estate Bon Temps Vineyard Syrah (Santa Ynez Valley) $55. Combines an intensely pepery note with dense plum-cake fruit and elevated (16.4%) alcohol, yet remains appealing thanks to a full, rich mouthfeel and supple tannins. The plum, dried spice, and pepper flavors mostly obscure the high alcohol, leading to a long, spicy finish. **87** *(9/1/2005)*

Rideau 2004 Viognier (Santa Barbara County) $35. This is a bit thinner in fruit than Rideau's excellent Iris bottling, but it's still a good wine, thanks mainly to fresh vitality. The flavors are of ripe, tangy citrus fruits. Dry and tart like a Sauvignon Blanc, but richer. **87** —*S.H. (12/31/2005)*

Rideau 2004 Iris Estate Viognier (Santa Ynez Valley) $48. White pepper sprinkled over guava and apricot fruit, drizzled with vanilla and a splash of citrusy lime juice— these are some of the flavors in this crisp, fresh, and tangy wine. It's delicious, elegant, and lush to the point of decadence. **90** —*S.H. (12/31/2005)*

Rideau 2004 Fleur Blanche White Blend (California) $28. Like Rideau's other whites, this one's fresh and clean and vibrant in acidity. It's a little watery, though. A blend of Viognier, Marsanne, Roussanne, and Chardonnay. **84** —*S.H. (12/31/2005)*

RIDGE

Ridge 2001 Home Ranch Cabernet Sauvignon-Merlot (Santa Cruz Mountains) $60. Almost evenly divided between Cabernet Sauvignon and Merlot, this is a big mountain wine, filled with the flavors of ripe blackberries, blueberries, and oak. It's young in tannins and acids. It possesses an extraordinary sense of balance and intensity, but is probably best left to age until 2008. **93 Cellar Selection** —*S.H. (2/1/2005)*

USA

Ridge 1996 Oat Valley Carignan (Sonoma Valley) $18. 88 —*S.H. (10/1/1999)*

Ridge 1997 Chardonnay (Santa Cruz Mountains) $28. 89 *(6/1/2000)*

Ridge 2001 Chardonnay (Santa Cruz Mountains) $30. Amazingly intense and concentrated. Swamps the palate with pear and peach fruit, and a rich acidic structure. Oak plays a role in adding smoke, vanilla, and sweet tannins. Long and penetrating, lush, and vital. Combines power and subtlety in a rare way. **94** —*S.H. (12/15/2004)*

Ridge 1997 Chardonnay (California) $17. 93 —*M.S. (10/1/1999)*

Ridge 2002 Home Ranch Chardonnay (Santa Cruz Mountains) $40. Intensity is the name of the game here. Intensity of fruit, of oak, of creamy lees, of spices, of finish. The lush tropical fruit, vanilla, and buttered toast flavors explode in the mouth, leading to a long and rich finish. **93** —*S.H. (4/1/2005)*

Ridge 1996 York Creek Petite Sirah (Spring Mountain) $20. 88 —*J.C. (11/1/1999)*

Ridge 2002 Geyserville Red Blend (Sonoma County) $30. A big, bold wine, based on an old-fashioned field blend. Predominantly Zinfandel, with smaller amounts of Carignane and Petite Sirah, it shows berry flavors that are ripe to the point of raisins, and the finish turns a little Porty sweet, but not too much. **87** —*S.H. (4/1/2005)*

Ridge 1999 Geyserville Red Blend (Sonoma County) $30. Not a Zin by legal standards (it contains only 68% Zinfandel, plus 16% of both Carignane and Petite Sirah), but synonymous enough with the variety that we had to include it. The Geyserville carries the earthy aromas and flavors that are Ridge's calling card: The bouquet shows light aromas of tree bark, soil, and mixed berry notes, plus some oak-derived spice; tannic deep earth, bark, and tart black fruit flavors on the palate smooth out after a few minutes in the glass. More of the same earthy-blackness, plus chalk and oak, ride out the medium-long finish. **90** —*D.T. (3/1/2002)*

Ridge 1999 Lytton Springs Red Blend (Sonoma County) $30. Dark but not heavy, and livelier than this brooding profile sounds: Black cherry, cocoa, and forest-floor aromas deepen considerably after a few minutes in the glass. Dark black fruit, oak, and fresh green herb flavors smolder on the juicy palate. Finishes really long, with significant doses of blackberry, soil, nut, and mineral (linger over it long enough and you'll also catch traces of unsweetened chocolate). This vintage contains 70% Zin (backed up by Petite Sirah, Carignane, and Mataro). **91** —*D.T. (3/1/2002)*

Ridge 2001 Monte Bello Red Blend (Santa Cruz Mountains) $120. Without doubt this is a wine to cellar. It's massive in flavor, with the purist black currant and cassis fruit you can imagine, and the huge plaster of sweet oak is perfectly balanced. Then there are the tannins. They're fine and complex, but gritty. There's an astringency throughout that a great steak will cut through, but it would be infanticide to open this before, say, 2010. Should improve through 2020 and beyond. **97 Cellar Selection** —*S.H. (4/1/2005)*

Ridge 1999 Lytton Estate Syrah (Dry Creek Valley) $30. Intense, dark, described variously as a "brooding monster" and a "black beauty," this is full-blown Syrah from one of California's most respected wineries. Black currant, leather, espresso, and chocolate evidence the deep fruit and lavish oak. ATP (Advance Tasting Program) was jokingly referred to as "assault the palate" by one taster. No one mistook this for an easy drinker, with its dense color, feel, and hefty alcoholic punch. Not for sipping, and will benefit from three or four years aging. **90 Editors' Choice** *(11/1/2001)*

Ridge 1997 Lytton Estate Syrah (Dry Creek Valley) $28. 89 —*S.H. (10/1/1999)*

Ridge 2003 Lytton West Syrah (Dry Creek Valley) $35. An interesting effort from Ridge, with jammy black cherry-blackberry fruit and a sturdy veneer of cedary oak. There's also a grassy-herbal note to the nose and crisp acids; the overall impression is that the wine is disjointed right now and may or may not come together. Tasted twice, with consistent notes. **85** *(9/1/2005)*

Ridge 2001 Zinfandel (Paso Robles) $25. Somewhat earthy and spicy on the intake. But the flavors are intriguing, showing hints of herbal, plum, cherry, nut, anise, citrus, and spice character. Bright and fresh on the finish. **88** *(11/1/2003)*

Ridge 2001 Dusi Ranch Zinfandel (Paso Robles) $22. Starts off with spicy raspberry aromas. The follow up includes sweet cherry, raspberry, blackberry, cola, spice, chocolate, and high-toned citrus notes. A zippy, nutty edge adds interest to the finish, which is bright. **89** *(11/1/2003)*

Ridge 1997 Dusi Ranch-Late Picked Zinfandel (Paso Robles) $22. 91 —*J.C. (9/1/1999)*

Ridge 2001 Geyserville Zinfandel (Sonoma County) $30. Only 74% Zinfandel, it's not technically Zin. But since it misses the mark by only 1%, we've included it here. It's smooth and rich, yet bright on the palate, showing bing cherry, raspberry, spice, herbs, cocoa, and plum flavors. Fairly long and lush at the end. **89** *(11/1/2003)*

Ridge 1998 Geyserville Zinfandel (Sonoma County) $30. This is the 33rd vintage of this landmark Zinfandel, which, since it's a blend that includes just 74% Zinfandel in it, isn't technically Zinfandel at all. Whatever. It's just plain delicious, old-vine, succulent juice. Jammy, juicy, vibrant, and tight, it has a long life ahead. **90** —*P.G. (3/1/2001)*

Ridge 2002 Late Picked Pagani Ranch Zinfandel (Sonoma Valley) $30. Made in a style you either like or don't. At nearly 16 percent alcohol, it's hot and massive, with flavors of raisins and other dried fruits, but is dry. Difficult to pair with food. **85** —*S.H. (4/1/2005)*

Ridge 2001 Llewelyn Zinfandel (Sonoma County) $22. Fine tuned and elegant, with a spicy cinnamon and ginger edge that highlights the bright plum, blackberry, raspberry, coffee, toast flavors and creamy texture. Supple and smooth on the finish; a classy wine. **90 Editors' Choice** *(11/1/2003)*

Ridge 2001 Lytton Springs Zinfandel (Dry Creek Valley) $30. Firm, focused and concentrated, with a classy array of black plum, black cherry, cola, coffee, chocolate, blackberry, vanilla, spice, and herb flavors. The wine is silky smooth, ripe, and luxuriously long on the finish. **91** *(11/1/2003)*

Ridge 2000 Lytton Springs Zinfandel (California) $30. Balanced, rich, and dramatic, this is another successful vintage for a wine that defines Sonoma Zin at its ripe, spicy best. Succulent in the mouth, brimming with black raspberry, cherry, and black pepper flavors. Finishes dry and with great length, an extraordinary Zin from a great vineyard and producer. **93** —*S.H. (9/1/2002)*

Ridge 1998 Lytton Springs Zinfandel (Dry Creek Valley) $28. A vineyard blend that includes 16% Petite Sirah, 2% Carignane, 4% Mataro, and 1% Alicante Bouschet. Meaty, funky, and ripe, with intense fruit, lots of earthy, barnyardy accents, and a long, tannic finish. This is old style Zin, no holds barred, with full-throttle flavors for aficionados. **92** —*P.G. (3/1/2001)*

Ridge 1997 Lytton Springs Zinfandel (Dry Creek Valley) $28. 93 —*J.C. (9/1/1999)*

Ridge 1997 Pagani Ranch Zinfandel (California) $28. 92 —*S.H. (2/1/2000)*

Ridge 2001 Sonoma Station Zinfandel (Sonoma County) $18. Smooth textured and spicy, with a stewed fruit componant at the center. Coffee, toast, chocolate, spice, plum, raspberry, and herb notes pick up on the palate. The wine finishes nicely with supple tannins. **88** *(11/1/2003)*

Ridge 1997 Sonoma Station Zinfandel (Sonoma) $18. 88 —*J.C. (9/1/1999)*

Ridge 2002 Spring Mountain District Zinfandel (Napa Valley) $24. With a little Petite Sirah, this is a firm, fairly tannic wine. It has a deep core of black cherry and cocoa, with hints of sage. The size suggests aging through 2008, but it will be delicious now with roast tenderloin of pork in a sauce made from the wine. **89** —*S.H. (4/1/2005)*

RIDGEFIELD

Ridgefield 2003 Cinnamon Teal Red Cabernet Blend (Columbia Valley (WA)) $10. This is a competent blend of Cabs—79% Sauvignon, 21% Franc—with a rather broad streak of vanilla being the main flavor note. Decent body and structure. **86 Best Buy** —*P.G. (4/1/2005)*

Ridgefield 2002 Pinot Gris (Red Mountain) $9. This is a distinctive style of Pinot Gris, harder and more herbaceous than either the soft, tropical California bottlings or the fleshy, pear-flavored wines of Oregon. This is closer to a Sémillon, with tart citrus fruit and citrus rind flavors, a spicy middle, and some firm tannins. **88 Best Buy** —*P.G. (9/1/2004)*

USA

RIDGELINE

Ridgeline 2002 Cabernet Sauvignon (Alexander Valley) $40. This is a new producer owned by the Cordorníu winery, in Spain. It's an obvious attempt at the new international style, a very ripe, soft, oaky Cab, and while it's good, it needs more than that to achieve real complexity or age-ability. **85** —*S.H. (12/31/2006)*

RIO DULCE

Rio Dulce NV Sweet Red Wine Red Blend (California) $4. Easy and like-able. Not really sweet at all, but off-dry, with pleasant peach, citrus, vanilla, and spice flavors and refreshing acidity. Great value in this type of wine. **85 Best Buy** —*S.H. (12/31/2004)*

Rio Dulce NV White Red Wine Rosé Blend (California) $4. Not red, but more of a rosé, with intriguing aromas of raspberry sorbet and vanilla. Soda-poppy, with crisp acids, raspberry flavors, and a semi-sweet finish. **84 Best Buy** —*S.H. (12/31/2004)*

RIO SECO

Rio Seco 1999 Rio Seco Cabernet Franc (Paso Robles) $24. Plummy, blackberry flavors taste very dry, with sturdy but accessible tannins and enough acidity to make your tongue tingle. There's a roughness to the wine, an earthiness, that puts it firmly in the country-style category. It's good, but a bit pricey. **85** —*S.H. (12/1/2002)*

Rio Seco 1999 Rio Seco Vineyard Syrah (Paso Robles) $16. Rough, country style, with an aggressive edge that time won't soften. The grapes are fine. They got nice and ripe, and put out berry flavors that are deep and delicious. But somehow, that rustic quality hangs in there. **83** —*S.H. (12/1/2002)*

Rio Seco 2001 Zinfandel (Paso Robles) $24. Bright, zippy acidity high-lights the Bing cherry and raspberry notes here. Tannins are moderate and the finish is a bit short. **84** *(11/1/2003)*

Rio Seco 1999 Rio Seco Vineyard Zinfandel (Paso Robles) $24. There's nothing wrong with superripe grapes as long as they're handled gently. Here, there's nothing stopping the overextracted fruit, including raisins and even prunes. It has high-alcohol (16.2%) heat that burns the palate. Exemplifies everything that can go wrong with Zinfandel, except that it will have its fans. **82** —*S.H. (11/1/2002)*

RIOS-LOVELL ESTATE WINERY

Rios-Lovell Estate Winery 2000 Cabernet Sauvignon (Livermore Valley) $22. A little thin and simple, but has proper varietal notes in the cherry-berry flavors and sturdy tannins. Could use higher acidity. **84** —*S.H. (11/15/2003)*

Rios-Lovell Estate Winery 2000 Petite Sirah (Livermore Valley) $22. Smells funky and herbal, with sweet cough medicine flavors and a gluey texture. **82** —*S.H. (3/1/2004)*

RISTOW ESTATE

Ristow Estate 2002 Quinta de Pedras Vineyard Cabernet Sauvignon (Napa Valley) $64. How a Cab can be completely soft yet filled with power is a wonder, but this is such a wine. It's dry and dustily grippy in tannins, with a finely astringent finish, and will easily hold for a decade. If you must drink it now, a good steak will cut through the density and coax out the sweet cassis and cherry fruit. **93 Cellar Selection** —*S.H. (12/15/2005)*

Ristow Estate 2001 Quinta de Pedras Vineyard Cabernet Sauvignon (Napa Valley) $64. How a Cab can be completely soft yet filled with power is a wonder of modern winemaking technique. This is such a wine. It's dry and dustily grippy in tannins, with a finely astringent finish, and will easily hold for a decade. Now, a good steak will cut through the density and coax out the cassis and cherry fruit. **93** —*S.H. (12/31/2005)*

Ristow Estate 1999 Quinta de Pedras Vineyard Cabernet Sauvignon (Napa Valley) $59. Winemaker Pam Starr is getting the feel for the special ter-roir in this vineyard. The wine's complexity is amazing. There is an underlying minerality that adds to the multifaceted flavors of black cur-rant, plum, and leather. It's solid from start to finish and a relative value in Napa Valley Cabernet. **94** —*C.S. (11/15/2002)*

RITCHIE CREEK

Ritchie Creek 1999 Cabernet Sauvignon (Spring Mountain) $58. Right off the bat, you notice the softness of the tannins. The wine floats like melt-ed butter in the mouth, creating a nice vehicle for the pleasant blackberry flavors to coat the palate. Decent acidity and absolutely no residual sugar provide structure. This is a candy of a wine, but could use more depth. **87** —*S.H. (11/15/2002)*

Ritchie Creek 2000 Chardonnay (Spring Mountain) $28. Simple, ripe fla-vors of peaches and apples have the sweetness of fruit juice, and the acidity is low, making for a soft, cloying wine. There's a rough, common feel to the tannins. **83** —*S.H. (12/15/2002)*

RIVER ROAD VINEYARDS

River Road Vineyards 2004 Hopkins Vineyard Chardonnay (Russian River Valley) $17. Made in a very dry and acidic style, this wine has flavors of limes, honeydew melons, and buttercream. It's tight and minerally, with a tart, high-acid finish, and seems designed to complement food. **86** —*S.H. (5/1/2006)*

River Road Vineyards 2004 Mills Vineyard Chardonnay (Russian River Valley) $20. Made in a very ripe, extracted style, this eccentric wine has flavors of apricots, or more precisely, apricot marmalade on buttered toast, because it's also oaky. It's dry and crisp in acids. A bit unusual, but in its own way, a good wine. **86** —*S.H. (5/1/2006)*

River Road Vineyards 2001 Proprietors Reserve Chardonnay (Russian River Valley) $14. Lip-smackingly tasty, offers a real blast of spicy peach-es, apples, and pears that fills the mouth and lasts through the finish. All that nice taste is accompanied by an overlay of smoky oak and a creamy texture. **85** —*S.H. (6/1/2003)*

River Road Vineyards 2001 Pinot Noir (Russian River Valley) $14. Simple, delicate, and fruity, a jammy style with sweetly ripe flavors of wild rasp-berries and strawberries, as well as espresso, tobacco, and Oriental spices. It's light and silky on the palate. **87** —*S.H. (7/1/2003)*

River Road Vineyards 2004 Stephanie's Vineyard Pinot Noir (Russian River Valley) $21. Good Pinot, showing delicacy and elegance, with fine Russian River character. Cherries, cola, rhubarb pie, and cinnamon spice flavors are wrapped into a crisp, silky structure that finishes dry and complex. **87** —*S.H. (12/1/2006)*

RIVER'S EDGE

River's Edge 2002 Pinot Noir (Umpqua Valley) $16. This earthy, oaky wine carries middle of the road flavors into a short, hot, astringent finish. **85** *(11/1/2004)*

River's Edge 2000 Pinot Noir (Umpqua Valley) $16. Some high toned, nail polish aromas are evident, along with good forward fruit. Still the high tones—nail polish, paint, etc.—are going to be right on the edge for some people's tolerance. **85** —*P.G. (12/31/2002)*

River's Edge 2002 Barrel Select Pinot Noir (Umpqua Valley) $21. There's plenty of barrel all right, and the spicy, vanilla and toasted coconut fla-vors to prove it. The fruit is a bit dilute and slightly baked, with hints of clove. **85** *(11/1/2004)*

River's Edge 2000 Black Oak Vineyard Pinot Noir (Umpqua Valley) $30. **91** —*P.G. (12/31/2002)*

River's Edge 2002 Bradley Vineyard Pinot Noir (Umpqua Valley) $18. Mint and wintergreen notes are evident, and a bit of rubbery Band-Aid. But the wine has better fruit than its siblings, showing more ripeness, a solid midpalate, and good spicy highlights. **86** *(11/1/2004)*

River's Edge 2000 Bradley Vineyard Pinot Noir (Umpqua Valley) $16. Cherry fruit, with some hints of earth. The grapes are grown in the coolest part of the valley. Tannins are tight but well managed, and it is varietally correct and well made for Pinot at this price. **87** —*P.G. (12/31/2002)*

River's Edge 2000 Elkton Vineyard Pinot Noir (Umpqua Valley) $19. The nose is forward and round, with some cheesy Burgundian scents. There is a raisiny edge to this wine, which is very ripe and drinking well right now. The finish is slight hot, and has plenty of tannin. Definitely a wine to drink young. **87** —*P.G. (12/31/2002)*

USA

RIVERBEND

Riverbend 2001 Coquette White Blend (Humboldt County) $NA. Flat, watery, and dry. Almost nothing going on at all. **81** —S.H. (12/31/2004)

RIVERSIDE

Riverside 2002 Cabernet Sauvignon (California) $8. Heavy and gluey, with an odd medicinal flavor and a cherry cough drop finish. **81** —S.H. (12/15/2005)

Riverside 2004 Chardonnay (California) $8. There's plenty of Chard character in this wine, including upfront peach, pear, and pineapple flavors, a creamy texture, and some nice buttered toast from oak. **84 Best Buy** —S.H. (12/15/2005)

Riverside 1997 Syrah (California) $8. Another narrow, cranberry-tomato tartly-fruited red. A hint of sweet, sweaty leather (nicer than it sounds) and the round, smooth mouthfeel add some character here. But this finishes with prickly tannins and a slight metallic note. It needs more and deeper fruit. **83** (10/1/2001)

Riverside NV White Zinfandel (California) $6. Frankly sweet, this simple wine is ripe in strawberry and raspberry flavors, and has decent acidity. **82** —S.H. (12/15/2005)

Riverside NV White Zinfandel (California) $6. Simple, fruity, and sweet, with raspberry syrup and vanilla flavors that finish soft and sweetish. **83** —S.H. (10/1/2004)

Riverside 2004 White Zinfandel (California) $6. Simple, fruity, and pretty sweet, with dessert-type raspberry, vanilla, and spice flavors. The sweetness benefits from excellent acidity. This is a nice beach or picnic-type wine. **84 Best Buy** —S.H. (12/1/2006)

ROAR

Roar 2003 Pinot Noir (Santa Lucia Highlands) $31. Very full-bodied and rich, almost flirting with Rhône-ness, with its big cherry, black raspberry, and plum flavors, and overlay of oak. It's certainly a delicious wine, but is it Pinot Noir? **87** —S.H. (5/1/2005)

Roar 2002 Pinot Noir (Santa Lucia Highlands) $31. Starts off with minty, cherry, and cinnamon aromas, then reveals rich flavors of roasted coffee, cherry, and oak. Creamy and lush on the palate, and dry. **86** (11/1/2004)

Roar 2001 Pinot Noir (Santa Lucia Highlands) $31. Only 94 cases of this first-ever wine from Gary Franscioni, of Garys' Vineyard. Not for fans of delicate Pinot Nor, this is a big, ripe, outsized wine stuffed with flavors ranging from cherries and raspberries to cola, chocolate, Oriental spices, and tobacco. Silky in the mouth, although the acids are young and sharp. **90** —S.H. (7/1/2003)

Roar 2003 Garys Vineyard Pinot Noir (Santa Lucia Highlands) $44. A big, extracted, jammy Santa Lucia Pinot. It oozes cherries, black raspberries, mocha, and smoky char, but is dry and rich in sweet, ripe tannins, with a silky smooth texture. This is an immature wine that needs a couple years to come together. **90** —S.H. (3/1/2006)

Roar 2002 Pisoni Vineyard Pinot Noir (Santa Lucia Highlands) $48. Dark as a Syrah, and with the weight of a big red, this wine shows massively ripe aromas and flavors of meat, blackberries, coffee, and oak, and rich, gentle tannins. It's a very good wine but it doesn't really have the delicacy you expect in a Pinot Noir. **87** —S.H. (11/1/2004)

Roar 2003 Rosella's Vineyard Pinot Noir (Santa Lucia Highlands) $44. Immense—one of those big, ripe Pinots that wows you with the volume of its fruit. Total blackberry, cherry, and cassis, scads of tingly spices, and a dusting of rich but soft tannins. Also, it has that Central Coast acidity, so balancing for fruit like this. Drink now in its fleshy youth, but should improve through 2007. **92** —S.H. (5/1/2005)

Roar 2002 Rosella's Vineyard Pinot Noir (Santa Lucia Highlands) $44. Lots of charm. Once the sulfur blows off, you get ripe red and black cherry, vanilla, oak, and spice notes, wrapped in a silky texture with bright, crisp acids. Notable for its balanced and long finish. **88** (11/1/2004)

Roar 2001 Rosella's Vineyard Pinot Noir (Santa Lucia Highlands) $44. Fantastically sized. Floods the palate with massive flavors of berries, fruits and spices, massive in length and depth. For all this sweet ripeness the wine is dry, while acids and tannins are silky and fine. A stunning Pinot Noir that breaks out into whole new dimensions for the varietal. **93** —S.H. (7/1/2003)

Roar 2003 Syrah (Santa Lucia Highlands) $32. Big and ripe on the nose, with scents of caramel, vanilla, and red berries, but above all, alcohol. If you are less sensitive to high alcohol levels than we are, you may like this flashy Syrah more than we did. **83** (9/1/2005)

ROBERT CRAIG

Robert Craig 1999 Affinity Bordeaux Blend (Napa Valley) $48. The panel agreed that Affinity is an excellent wine, but had very different reads on the wine's flavors and bouquet. Notes on the aromas range from fresh hay and cherry to grapes and watermelon rind; comments on palate flavors run the gamut from cherry liqueur and vanilla to fresh herb and blackberries. One to try for yourself, to be sure. 2,500 cases made; age 5–7 years. **90** (6/1/2002)

Robert Craig 1997 Affinity Bordeaux Blend (Napa Valley) $44. 92 (11/1/2000)

Robert Craig 2002 Affinity Cabernet Blend (Napa Valley) $40. This is a balanced Cabernet that relies on nuance rather than a two-by-four. It has good fruit, tannins, acidity, and oak. It supports, but doesn't compete with, your best food. Finishes dry and cocoa-sweet. **88** —S.H. (10/1/2005)

Robert Craig 1997 Cabernet Sauvignon (Mount Veeder) $44. 91 (11/1/2000)

Robert Craig 2003 Cabernet Sauvignon (Mount Veeder) $70. Riper, softer, and more accessible than Craig's Howell Mountain Cab, this wine, grown at 1,800 feet, shows delicious cherry, currant, and chocolate flavors, with the caramel and toast of new oak. For all the deliciousness, it still has mountain tannins, and should age well for a decade. **91** —S.H. (9/1/2006)

Robert Craig 2003 Cabernet Sauvignon (Howell Mountain) $70. How big this wine got, so juicy and ripe. It's almost over the top, with all that heady black currant, blueberry, Provencal herb, and new oak flavor. With power like this, control is desperately needed. It's not showing its best now, but by 2008, this 98% Cab should begin to reflect the winemaker's vision. **91 Cellar Selection** —S.H. (9/1/2006)

Robert Craig 2002 Cabernet Sauvignon (Howell Mountain) $55. Craig's Howell Mountain Cab is far more tannic than its Mount Veeder version. It's shut down, but has an enormous heart of blackberry fruit that should emerge in time; classically structured. Start drinking it in 2008. **92** —S.H. (12/1/2005)

Robert Craig 2002 Cabernet Sauvignon (Mount Veeder) $55. Drinkable now despite lush, firm tannins, this Cab lets its fruit star. The black currant, black cherry pie, mocha, and vanilla spice flavors are delicious and compelling, and the finish is dry, elegant and upscale. **91** —S.H. (12/1/2005)

Robert Craig 2001 Cabernet Sauvignon (Howell Mountain) $50. Pretty closed down and tannic now, but keep on chewing and you'll hit the cherries and blackberries. That core is pure and rich and fruity sweet, but it will take time to assert itself. Enjoy now with a good steak, or stick in the cellar for a long time. **92** —S.H. (10/1/2004)

Robert Craig 2001 Cabernet Sauvignon (Mount Veeder) $50. Tighter and more tannic than this winery's Howell Mountain bottling, and more concentrated in blackberry and cherry essence. This is an extraordinarily young wine that defines the vintage's potential. It requires patience, but the balance is such that it's a lock for the long haul. Cellar until 2010 and beyond. **93 Cellar Selection** —S.H. (10/1/2004)

Robert Craig 1998 Chardonnay (Carneros) $24. 85 (6/1/2000)

Robert Craig 1997 Chardonnay (Carneros) $24. 93 —M.S. (10/1/1999)

Robert Craig 2002 Chardonnay (Sonoma County) $24. Sweet in caramelized oak and vanilla, with very rich, ripe tropical fruit and pear flavors, this is a decadent Chard. Fortunately, it has good acidity and is clean and firm on the finish. **86** —S.H. (3/1/2005)

Robert Craig 2000 Chardonnay (Russian River Valley) $24. Comes down on the lean, herbal side, despite substantial oak shadings and a solid dose of lees. The underlying fruit veers toward citrus and apples. High acidity makes the middle palate and the finish bitter. **86** —S.H. (2/1/2003)

Robert Craig 2003 Durell Vineyard Chardonnay (Sonoma Valley) $38. Fans of oak will exult over this spicy, Burgundian wine. It's slathered with char, honey, butterscotch, and vanilla. Still, there's some rich pineapple fruit underneath, and good acidity. **89** —*S.H. (10/1/2005)*

Robert Craig 1997 Syrah (Paso Robles) $24. 86 *(3/1/2000)*

Robert Craig 2002 Syrah (Central Coast) $28. On the jammy-gobby side of things, lacking structure but loaded with superripe blueberry-blackberry fruit, vanilla, and caramel. Creamy-textured and shows a bit of heat on the finish. **86** *(9/1/2005)*

Robert Craig 1999 Syrah (Paso Robles) $28. How two reviewers can detect sweet, sugar, cherry, and plum aromas, while others note scents of smoked bacon and menthol, we don't quite know. The palate, though, shows flavors of overripe black cherries and leather. Creamy in the mouth, plus creamy oak on the finish. **86** *(11/1/2001)*

Robert Craig 1998 Zinfandel (Amador County) $24. The blackberry fruit is wrapped in very deeply toasted oak. Aromas and flavors of cassis, vanilla, coffee, and licorice mingle to display a dark flavor profile but positive tart-sweetness. Full and even on the tongue, this black beauty finishes with lingering spice and espresso notes. **88** *(3/1/2001)*

ROBERT FOLEY

Robert Foley 2003 Claret Cabernet Blend (Napa Valley) $110. Nearly 100% Cabernet Sauvignon, this firm young wine showcases Napa Cab at its best. It's powerful in cassis and mocha flavors, with complex spice notes. The considerable new oak fits in fine given the wine's size. Extraordinarily smooth and lush, it's beautiful now, but has the structure to age for a decade. What a beauty. **96** —*S.H. (9/1/2006)*

Robert Foley 2004 Charbono (Napa Valley) $35. Bob Foley has championed this heirloom variety, which so many others long ago abandoned. The wine shows an old-fashioned ruggedness and the kind of in-your-face tannins and grapeskin astringency you don't see much anymore. Yet it's massively fruity and will age well. Six to 10 years should soften and sweeten it, and it will hold for another decade beyond. **91 Cellar Selection** —*S.H. (12/1/2006)*

Robert Foley 2003 Petite Sirah (Napa Valley) $50. Shows true Pet character in the black color, huge tannins, softness, extremely ripe fruit, and obvious ageability. Everything is superrefined, working at its top level. Blackberries, black cherries, blueberries, crème de cassis, coffee, sweet leather, and oak flavors all mingle in a complex wine that loves beef. Drink now through 2020. **92 Cellar Selection** —*S.H. (11/1/2006)*

ROBERT HALL

Robert Hall 2004 Cabernet Sauvignon (Paso Robles) $18. Soft and juicy, with ripe blackberry, chocolate, and coffee flavors that finish somewhat tannic. Ready to drink now, it's an easy Cabernet for steaks and chops. **84** —*S.H. (12/1/2006)*

Robert Hall 2003 Cabernet Sauvignon (Paso Robles) $18. Simple, soft, and intensely fruity, this Cab is bursting with the ripest red cherry, tobacco, cocoa, spice, and smoke flavors. It's easy to imagine sipping this with grilled meats and poultry. **84** —*S.H. (11/1/2005)*

Robert Hall 2000 Cabernet Sauvignon (Paso Robles) $18. From the warm Estrella region, this Cabernet, though not without its charms, can't quite hide raisiny aromas and flavors of blackberry and cassis. Tannins and acids are very soft. **84** —*S.H. (11/15/2002)*

Robert Hall 2005 Chardonnay (Paso Robles) $16. Here's a nice everyday sort of Chard, forward in bright lime, kiwi, and nectarine flavors. Tastes like it comes from a far cooler climate than Paso Robles. A bit more concentration would send the score through the roof. **85** —*S.H. (12/1/2006)*

Robert Hall 2004 Chardonnay (Paso Robles) $16. You'll find good flavors of apples and peaches in this soft, dryish wine, as well as an earthiness. It has some oaky notes, and finishes with a touch of citrus. **84** —*S.H. (11/1/2005)*

Robert Hall 2003 Grenache (Paso Robles) $24. Seems rather muted in all respects, especially for a vibrant variety like Grenache. Yes, there are cherry flavors, but they're earthy, and the wine itself is excessively soft. It's a decent sipper, but overpriced. **84** —*S.H. (11/1/2005)*

Robert Hall 2004 Hall Ranch Grenache (Paso Robles) $24. Smells minty and herbal, and tastes bitterly acidic and underripe. Were the vines overcropped? Either way, this wine lacks the lushness and fruit that a red wine should have, especially a Rhône-style wine from Paso Robles. **82** —*S.H. (12/1/2006)*

Robert Hall 2003 Hall Ranch Meritage (Paso Robles) $34. Here's a wine that's very soft in acids, with melted tannins. It's a little flabby, but nicely dry, with ripe flavors of blackberries, green olives, coffee, and spices. Will go well with a grilled steak. **84** —*S.H. (12/31/2005)*

Robert Hall 2004 Merlot (Paso Robles) $18. Smells great, just like Merlot should, with cherry pie, violet, cocoa, cinnamon, and toasty vanilla aromas. But it turns shockingly sweet in the mouth. It tastes more like ice cream topping than a table wine. **80** —*S.H. (12/1/2006)*

Robert Hall 2003 Merlot (Paso Robles) $18. Heavy, soft, and full. What it lacks in briskness it makes up for in complex flavors of cherries, tobacco, and sweet sage, and rich, intricate tannins. **85** —*S.H. (12/31/2005)*

Robert Hall 2002 Merlot (Paso Robles) $18. A little hot and flabby, but with some lively cherry-berry flavors, this innocuous Merlot will back up most anything that needs a dry red. **84** —*S.H. (11/1/2005)*

Robert Hall 2000 Merlot (Paso Robles) $18. Dark and plummy, a wine grown in a hot region where the grapes got very ripe and the acidity is low. As a result it's got sweet dark berry and stone fruit flavors, but seems a little flat on the palate, with dusty tannins. **85** —*S.H. (11/15/2002)*

Robert Hall 2003 Vintage Port (Paso Robles) $28. Made with Portuguese varieties, this dessert wine is sweet and simple. It has cherry compote, chocolate and sweetened coffee flavors, with a thick texture balanced with good, crisp acidity. **84** —*S.H. (6/1/2006)*

Robert Hall 2004 Rhône de Robles Rhône Red Blend (Central Coast) $18. Kind of sharp and aggressive in the mouth, with medicinal cherry flavors that straddle the border between sweet and dry, with the nod to sweet. It's a Grenache-based Rhône blend. **83** —*S.H. (12/31/2006)*

Robert Hall 2003 Rhône de Robles Rhône Red Blend (Paso Robles) $18. This dark, awkward wine is a little sharp around the edges, with a rough earthiness framing herb and berry flavors. **82** —*S.H. (11/1/2005)*

Robert Hall 2005 Blanc de Robles Rhône White Blend (Paso Robles) $24. Dry and savory, this blend of Grenache Blanc, Roussanne, and Viognier has a tangy spine of minerality that frames lusher notes of papaya, white peach, lemon zest, nectarine, and vanilla. Finishes with a refreshing touch of citrusy acids. **86** —*S.H. (12/1/2006)*

Robert Hall 2004 Rose de Robles Rosé Blend (Paso Robles) $14. Rather thin and watery throughout, but it has such a pretty color, and an invitingly spicy, rose petal and strawberries aroma, that all is forgiven. Bone dry and tart, will pair up with bouillabaisse. **85** —*S.H. (10/1/2005)*

Robert Hall 2005 Sauvignon Blanc (Paso Robles) $14. It's fresh in vibrant acidity, with grapy flavors of citrus and gooseberries. There's a creamy lushness to the texture that softens and attracts. **85** —*S.H. (6/1/2006)*

Robert Hall 2004 Sauvignon Blanc (Paso Robles) $14. Although this dry, Musque-clone wine will go with just about anything, try it with a smoky, honey-baked ham sandwich on a lightly toasted sourdough baguette, slathered with Dijon mustard and garlicky mayo, and layered with sliced fresh tomato, butter lettuce, roasted red pepper, and crumbly chevre. My goodness, pure heaven. **85** —*S.H. (11/1/2005)*

Robert Hall 2004 Syrah (Paso Robles) $18. Opens with aromas and flavors of blackberries, cocoa, and licorice that turn softly fruity and polished in the mouth. There's a scour of acidity that plays point-counterpoint to the ripe fruitiness of this highly drinkable Syrah. **87** —*S.H. (12/1/2006)*

Robert Hall 2003 Syrah (Paso Robles) $18. With a couple of reviewers calling this wine rich and superripe, you might expect a monster in size and weight, but it's not, clocking in at a modest 13.9% alcohol. Bright cherry-berry flavors are accompanied by outsized tannins and what one taster felt was a touch of sweetness. **84** *(9/1/2005)*

Robert Hall 2002 Syrah (Paso Robles) $18. An easy to like Syrah with good character. It's fruity in cherry and chocolate flavors, and very dry, with a pepper and spice aftertaste. **85** —*S.H. (12/1/2004)*

Robert Hall 2000 Syrah (Paso Robles) $18. Dark, young, rough stuff. This is a big jammy wine, filled with fresh juicy berry fruit flavors and pronounced dusty tannins. It's a lusty wine, meant for rip-roaring good times and toasts, to be drunk with barbecued animals. **86** —*S.H. (12/1/2002)*

Robert Hall 2001 Hall Ranch Syrah (Paso Robles) $30. From the east side of the appellation, a polished, supple wine, with easy tannins and the flavors of red and black cherries. Has interesting nuances of coffee, plums, and spices, too. **87** —*S.H. (12/1/2004)*

USA

USA

Robert Hall 2003 Hall Ranch Reserve Syrah (Paso Robles) $34. A bit too soft and simple, although it's a pretty good wine with some nice blackberry jam, black cherry pie, and cocoa-cinnamon flavors. This is a wine in progress, better than the 2002, but not quite as good as the 2001. **85** —S.H. (11/15/2006)

Robert Hall 2002 Hall Ranch Reserve Syrah (Paso Robles) $34. There's a nice blend of cherry or blackberry pie and wintergreen mint on the nose, but the flavors are simple and the mouthfeel a bit clumsy. **84** (9/1/2005)

Robert Hall 1999 Huerhuero Creek Syrah (Paso Robles) $26. Smells curiously inert, with a hint of Port and currants and oak. The flavors are much less fruity than the winery's regular Syrah, veering toward prunes, herbs, and earth. It's very dry. The finish is spartan and scouring. **84** —S.H. (12/1/2002)

Robert Hall 2005 Viognier (Paso Robles) $18. Here's an easy Viognier with a tasty array of peach, pineapple, honeysuckle, green apple, and spice flavors. It's nice and dry, with a bite of acidity and a clean, fruity finish. **84** —S.H. (11/15/2006)

Robert Hall 2001 Zinfandel (Paso Robles) $24. Blackberry, sage, and thyme flavors are at the core of this wine. It's a bit herbal, but well-balanced nonetheless, showing moderate length on the finish. **85** (11/1/2003)

Robert Hall 2000 Zinfandel (Paso Robles) $22. You can smell the hot country sun in the pruny, raisiny aromas and taste them in the mouth. The alcohol is a high 15.1%. Normally all this would be a recipe for disaster, but there's something likeable about this distinctly California, bone dry Zin. Despite the weirdness, it pulls it off. **87** —S.H. (11/1/2002)

ROBERT HUNTER

Robert Hunter 1996 Brut de Noirs Champagne Blend (Sonoma Valley) $38. A flavorful, balanced wine that's dry, creamy, and crisp, with tantalizing hints of lime and red raspberry from its 60% Pinot Noir and 40% Chardonnay. It has a round, full mouthfeel. The finish is dry and tart, but you can taste the charry wood for a long time. **90** —S.H. (12/1/2001)

Robert Hunter 1994 Brut de Noirs Champagne Blend (Sonoma Valley) $30. **88** —S.H. (12/1/2000)

Robert Hunter 2003 Pinot Noir (Sonoma Valley) $35. A little soft for a Pinot, although the cherry, cocoa, and spice flavors are tasty enough, and impress for their long, sweet finish. Drink now for that irresistibly juicy young fruit. **87** —S.H. (11/15/2005)

Robert Hunter 1997 Brut de Noirs Sparkling Blend (Sonoma Valley) $35. This is a sharp, awkward wine, in which the lees stick out. It's fruity and doughy, but lacks elegance. **82** —S.H. (12/31/2005)

ROBERT KARL

Robert Karl 2002 Claret Bordeaux Blend (Columbia Valley (WA)) $17. The blend is 77% Cab, 12% Merlot, 11% Cab Franc, and the alcohol, rather surprisingly, hits 15+%. This is a wonderful claret, with mixed red and blue fruits and berries, plenty of natural acid and no obvious oak. There is a flash of caramel and mocha at the end, but the flavors unwrap luxuriously in a series of gradient layers. Delivers a lot of quality for the dollars. 1,100 cases made. **88** —P.G. (4/1/2006)

Robert Karl 2001 Claret Bordeaux Blend (Columbia Valley (WA)) $17. A balanced, supple young blended red, it includes all five Bordeaux varietals in the blend. The vineyards read like a list of who's who in Washington viticulture—Ciel du Cheval, DuBrul, Pepper Bridge, and more. Pretty berries and cherries set the fruit, and the wine has a classy, confident style all through the finish. **89** —P.G. (12/1/2004)

Robert Karl 2003 Inspiration Reserve Red Bordeaux Blend (Columbia Valley (WA)) $45. All of the best barrels are in here, and it shows. This limited (75 case) Bordeaux blend is wonderfully concentrated with sweet, stiff, sappy fruit. Juicy in the mouth, but tightly wound, it is fleshed out with buttery oak flavors of vanilla, toast, and caramel. Young, hard and a little bit hostile, this needs major decanting; or stick it away and let it blossom for a decade or more. **93** —P.G. (11/15/2006)

Robert Karl 2003 Cabernet Sauvignon (Columbia Valley (WA)) $33. It's not easy to make 100% Cabernet such as this; the fruit must be perfect. Winemaker Joseph Gunselman is up to the challenge. This tight, sappy, clean, wine expresses a marvelous purity of fruit, tightly wrapped, but dense and ripe. Decant, or cellar for 10 years. **91** —P.G. (10/1/2006)

Robert Karl 2002 Cabernet Sauvignon (Columbia Valley (WA)) $26. The blend is 90% Cab, 5% Merlot, 5% Cab Franc. Dense, firm, and muscular, hinting at layers of cassis, berry, cherry, cranberry, and more. A dark, rich, and thick wine, layered with red and black fruits. The tannins are fine-grained and mouthcoating, and the fruit is intense with streaks of smoke, anise, herb, soy, and baking chocolate. Complex and richly, densely layered. Will age beautifully. **93** —P.G. (4/1/2006)

Robert Karl 2000 Cabernet Sauvignon (Columbia Valley (WA)) $20. Good, firm, tart fruit sets the wine up sharply with berry, cherry, and cranberry flavors. It's balanced, not too ripe (13.6% alcohol) and has well-integrated oak in the toasty finish. **87** —P.G. (12/31/2003)

Robert Karl 1999 Cabernet Sauvignon (Columbia Valley (WA)) $29. The blend is 88% Cabernet Sauvignon, 8% Merlot, and 4% Cab Franc. This is a fairly light, well-crafted wine, with strawberry and watermelon fruit, good balance, and surprising length. It stresses elegance over power, but makes a good impression. **87** —P.G. (12/31/2002)

Robert Karl 2002 Reserve Cabernet Sauvignon (Columbia Valley (WA)) $33. All McKinley Springs (Horse Heaven AVA) Vineyard Cab. Tight, austere, and severe in its purity, it shows cassis, plum, and cherry fruit. Herbal, lightly dusty, varietal, and firm; with hard, true tannins. At this stage it is less complete and concentrated than the regular bottling, but with a classy Cabernet feeling. this wine may surprise with its ageworthiness. Just 75 cases made. Now that's a reserve! **92** —P.G. (4/1/2006)

Robert Karl 2003 Claret Meritage (Columbia Valley (WA)) $19. This mini-meritage—53% Cabernet Sauvignon, 17% Merlot, 10% each of Malbec, Cab Franc, and Petit Verdot—is like a lighter version of the winery's reserve. You get meritage style and quality at a mutt wine price. Tight with mixed berries, plums, spice, hints of pepper, and clove. **90 Editors' Choice** —P.G. (10/1/2006)

Robert Karl 2004 Merlot (Columbia Valley (WA)) $24. The 15.5% alcohol does not get in the way of subtlety here. This typically stylish, 100% Merlot is smooth and supple, and it retains the fresh herbal highlights that are usually obliterated in high octane wines. This is substantial Merlot, tight and muscular, with whiffs of smoke and those lovely notes of leaf and herb. **90** —P.G. (10/1/2006)

Robert Karl 2002 Sauvignon Blanc (Columbia Valley (WA)) $10. Some Red Mountain Sémillon fleshes out the Sauv Blanc, with good, tart citrus fruit and graham cracker toastiness on the finish. **86** —P.G. (12/31/2003)

Robert Karl 2004 Syrah (Columbia Valley (WA)) $29. Another pure-blooded varietal from Robert Karl Cellars, this sappy, reductive Syrah needs a lot of airing out. Tart fruit grudgingly shows spicy raspberry/cranberry flavors. Lots of acid, wrapped in vanilla and highlighted with sassafras. Tart, young, and tight. **90** —P.G. (11/15/2006)

ROBERT MONDAVI

Robert Mondavi 1997 Cabernet Sauvignon (Napa Valley) $29. **90** (11/1/2000)

Robert Mondavi 1996 Cabernet Sauvignon (Oakville) $45. **91** —S.H. (11/1/1999)

Robert Mondavi 1996 Cabernet Sauvignon (Napa Valley) $26. **91** —L.W. (10/1/1999)

Robert Mondavi 2003 Cabernet Sauvignon (Napa Valley) $25. Dry, rich, and thick in tannins, and rather soft, this Cabernet is extremely ripe in blackberry, cassis, and coffee flavors. The hot vintage seems to have taken its toll in balance, for the wine is a little heavy, even by Mondavi standards, which are usually leaner than many Napa Cabs. **86** —S.H. (4/1/2006)

Robert Mondavi 2003 Cabernet Sauvignon (Oakville) $40. Ripe, soft, and oaky, this is a voluptuous style of Cab that's complex and ageable but easy to like now. Shows sweet cassis flavors wrapped in finely ground tannins. This is a Cab of great interest. **90** —S.H. (12/1/2006)

Robert Mondavi 2002 Cabernet Sauvignon (Oakville) $45. Soft and oaky, this is a young wine whose parts haven't come together. There's plenty of fruit flavor, with cherries and red currants lasting long and deep, and the tannins are rich and creamy. This is a wine to stash for five to ten years, and allow to mellow and gain bottle complexity. **91 Cellar Selection** —S.H. (3/1/2006)

Robert Mondavi 2001 Cabernet Sauvignon (Napa Valley) $25. Showcases the restraint in fruit that characterizes Mondavi, and so different from many of his neighbors' lavishly ripe Cabs. The hallmark is elegance and drinkability, with its moderated berry flavors, earthiness, and robust tannins. Should age well through the decade. **89**—*S.H. (10/1/2004)*

Robert Mondavi 2001 Cabernet Sauvignon (Oakville) $40. Darker and riper than Mondavi's Napa Cabernet, with the blackberries veering into currants, and newer, smokier tasting oak. Quite dramatic, in the tension of its fruit, oak, acids, and tannins. Young and flashy, and will easily age through 2015. **93 Editors' Choice**—*S.H. (10/1/2004)*

Robert Mondavi 2001 Cabernet Sauvignon (Napa Valley) $25. One of the last released '01 Napa Cabs, this wine exemplifies Mondavi's moderated approach. It's a big wine, but you can sense the pullback in this superripe vintage. Strong in blackberry and cherry fruit, but with a restrained earthiness and good acidity that keeps it from being flabby. Yet it will age with the best of them. **91 Cellar Selection**—*S.H. (11/15/2005)*

Robert Mondavi 2001 Cabernet Sauvignon (Stags Leap District) $40. There's a leathery edge to the blackberry, blueberry, and oak flavors, and a bigger, more full-bodied texture. The tannins also are thicker. This is the least accessible of Mondavi's new Cabs, but such is the concentration that aging should be no problem at all. Drink now through 2015. **92**
—*S.H. (10/1/2004)*

Robert Mondavi 2000 Cabernet Sauvignon (Stags Leap District) $50. It took the utmost talent to succeed in this vintage, when rains hampered so many late-ripening reds. Mondavi did their best to rise above this. Shows master touches of tannin management and the most perfect barrel regimen. It has some modest blackberry flavors, but is obviously a wine of charm rather than longevity. **89**—*S.H. (11/15/2003)*

Robert Mondavi 2000 Cabernet Sauvignon (Napa Valley) $30. Intricately detailed, framed in beautifully scented oak, a rich, ageable wine with a soft delicacy that's almost feminine. Flavors veer toward sweet black currants, green olives, and chocolate-covered cherries, coating the palate with a long-lasting aftertaste. Beautiful, elegant. **92 Editors' Choice**—*S.H. (11/15/2003)*

Robert Mondavi 1999 Cabernet Sauvignon (Oakville) $50. A very nice wine that smells great. Opens with perfumed scents of black currant and oak. Quite soft in the mouth, with thoroughly melted tannins and low acids. Could use a little bit more structure, but it's seductive stuff. **90**—*S.H. (2/1/2003)*

Robert Mondavi 1998 Cabernet Sauvignon (Oakville) $50. From Napa Valley's heart, this Cab shows blackberry, cassis, and new oak aromas, good Cabernet flavors, and the very best barrels make it classy. The light vintage, however, reults in a thin, tart quality. Oils and meaty fats will bring out sweetness. **86**—*S.H. (12/1/2001)*

Robert Mondavi 1998 Cabernet Sauvignon (Napa Valley) $35. Smells sharp and minty, with a green streak of raw oak, and tastes similarly thin and oaky. It stings with tannins from entry through dusty finish. Blackberry and plum flavors deep inside are smothered in tannins. **85**—*S.H. (12/1/2001)*

Robert Mondavi 1998 Cabernet Sauvignon (Stags Leap District) $50. Purists will find it thin and tannic, but it also defines the iron-fist-in-a-velvet-glove quality of Stags Leap. Dry and structured, with intricate tannins, its initial impression is austere. Then you start to think about it, and royal complexities are revealed. **91**—*S.H. (12/1/2001)*

Robert Mondavi 1996 Cabernet Sauvignon (Stags Leap District) $45. 86—*S.H. (9/1/1999)*

Robert Mondavi 1996 30th Anniversary Cabernet Sauvignon (Napa Valley) $150. 95—*S.H. (7/1/2000)*

Robert Mondavi 1996 30th Anniversary To Kalon Cabernet Sauvignon (Napa Valley) $NA. 100 percent To Kalon [including Detert and Horton]. Similar to the '91. Rather stubborn at first. The fruit is there, the balance, acidity, oak, but hasn't knitted together. Disjointed but distinguished. Could really surprise later on. 2010 and beyond. **89 Cellar Selection**—*S.H. (6/1/2005)*

Robert Mondavi 1998 Coastal Cabernet Sauvignon (North Coast) $13. 83—*S.H. (12/15/2000)*

Robert Mondavi 1997 Coastal Cabernet Sauvignon (North Coast) $13. 86—*S.H. (2/1/2000)*

Robert Mondavi 2000 Coastal Private Selection Cabernet Sauvignon (Central Coast) $11. Whatever "Private Selection" means, it's not an indication of quality. This is a weak, simple wine, with thin fruit and more than a bit of the veggies. The dry mouthfeel leads to a cough-syrup finish. **82**—*S.H. (12/31/2002)*

Robert Mondavi 1998 Equilibrium Cabernet Sauvignon (Stags Leap District) $85. One sniff makes you want to taste it. One sip makes you want more. This is international-style red wine at its sleek, soft finest. The fruit is ripe enough to sustain a fair amount of new oak, which contributes smoky, spicy elements. The balance is superb, the tannins slick; meant for early drinking. **92**—*S.H. (12/1/2001)*

Robert Mondavi 2001 M-Bar Ranch Cabernet Sauvignon (Oakville) $100. Tastes flashy and important, a Cab to drink now or cellar for a few years. Ripe black currant and cherry-infused fruit has been well-oaked, adding smoke and sweet vanilla flavors, while the mouthfeel is smooth and velvety. Keeps you reaching back for another glass. **93**—*S.H. (12/31/2004)*

Robert Mondavi 1998 Marjorie's Sunrise Cabernet Sauvignon (Oakville) $85. A limited-production wine (185 cases), it captures the quintessence of central Napa Valley Cabernet, and even in this less than successful vintage, testifies to the great terroir. It's plush, elegant, harmonious, delicate, powerful, graceful, and frankly delicious. **95**—*S.H. (12/1/2001)*

Robert Mondavi 1997 Oakville Cabernet Sauvignon (Oakville) $45. 91 *(11/1/2000)*

Robert Mondavi 2003 Private Selection Cabernet Sauvignon (California) $11. Very soft and a little sweet, this Cab shows forward flavors of black cherries and blackberries, and some sharp, edgy tannins. **83**—*S.H. (12/15/2005)*

Robert Mondavi 2001 Private Selection Cabernet Sauvignon (Central Coast) $13. There's some nice, plush blackberry and cherry fruit in this dry wine. It will match well with foods that spar with its crisp acids and edge of tannins. **85**—*S.H. (10/1/2004)*

Robert Mondavi 2003 Reserve Cabernet Sauvignon (Napa Valley) $125. Shows all the hallmarks of great Mondavi Reserve. Ageworthy and complex, with enormously ripe, rich fruit, classic chocolate, cassis plus cream and spice from new oak. So smoothly voluptuous now, it goes down like velvet, but the tannin-acid balance will easily hold this wine through 2015. **92 Editors' Choice**—*S.H. (12/15/2006)*

Robert Mondavi 2002 Reserve Cabernet Sauvignon (Napa Valley) $125. Mainly from To Kalon grapes, this dark, young wine is not showing its best now. It hasn't pulled the oak, alcohol, acids, tannins, and fruit together into a seamless package. The individual parts stick out, nakedly, yet possess an innate balance. Mondavi Reserves age well; this one should start to open by 2010 and hold for years after. **92 Cellar Selection**—*S.H. (3/1/2006)*

Robert Mondavi 2001 Reserve Cabernet Sauvignon (Napa Valley) $125. Contains 67% To Kalon Vineyard fruit. Still a baby. Closed, brooding, very deep, very dry. Fabulous cassis fruit, a huge wine. Lots of delicious, sweet new oak. Superbly balanced, impressive. Drinkable now, but best 2010–2020. **94 Cellar Selection**—*S.H. (6/1/2005)*

Robert Mondavi 2000 Reserve Cabernet Sauvignon (Napa Valley) $125. Oak dominates in the wine's youth, with scents of wood and smoky earth. In the mouth, rich and dense. The tannins are thick, but soft and melted. Acidity kicks in on the finish. Structurally superb, but curiously lean and herbal in flavor, as thought it were deliberately picked early. No doubt meant for the cellar. **92**—*S.H. (11/15/2003)*

Robert Mondavi 1999 Reserve Cabernet Sauvignon (Napa Valley) $NA. 68% To Kalon. Young. Cigar ash nose, blackberries, oak. A big, firm, assertive wine, fairly tannic. Scads of juicy cherries and blackberries. Very fine, lots of character, and elegance. Drinks well now with rich fare through 2020. **95 Cellar Selection**—*S.H. (6/1/2005)*

Robert Mondavi 1999 Reserve Cabernet Sauvignon (Napa Valley) $125. This flagship wine shows impeccable balance and finesse. It's well put together, as the couture people say, and drips with lavish, minty French oak. Soft tannins add interest as well as ageability. The wine is not lavishly fruity; instead, the flavors are consciously restrained and subtle. Very high quality, and worth holding through 2010. **96 Editors' Choice** —*S.H.* *(11/15/2002)*

Robert Mondavi 1998 Reserve Cabernet Sauvignon (Napa Valley) $125. Soft and succulent blackberry and cassis fruit upfront, framed by squeaky clean tannins and solid oak elements. This is most notable for its voluptuous, velvety texture, which coats the palate with sweet flavors. It's not a big wine but a balanced, harmonious one, and a success for the vintage. **92** —*S.H. (12/1/2001)*

Robert Mondavi 1997 Reserve Cabernet Sauvignon (Napa Valley) $120. 91 *(11/1/2000)*

Robert Mondavi 1991 Reserve Cabernet Sauvignon (Napa Valley) $NA. 54% To Kalon. Showing good varietal character. Fresh, attractive. One of Genevieve Janssen's favorites. To me, on the first pour it was unyielding, tight, closed. After lots of time in the glass, became more forthcoming. Needs lots of decanting. Now-2016. **90 Cellar Selection** — *S.H. (6/1/2005)*

Robert Mondavi 1986 Reserve Cabernet Sauvignon (Napa Valley) $NA. 57% To Kalon. Gorgeously fresh bouquet. Blackcurrants, oak, cocoa, buttery caramel and char. Drinking really young, firm, fresh. Very dry, balanced, not a powerful wine but elegant, harmonious. Light and pretty. Now-2012. **93** —*S.H. (6/1/2005)*

Robert Mondavi 1978 Reserve Cabernet Sauvignon (Napa Valley) $NA. Unknown % of To Kalon; the winemaker thinks "a big chunk, maybe most." Still good color, getting a pretty bouquet of old Cabernet. Delicate, inviting, refined, not at all morbid. Very dry, lots of week cassis. Soft, distinguished, still lots of life ahead. Sweet vanilla, butter. Old claret. Now-2010. **94 Editors' Choice** —*S.H. (6/1/2005)*

Robert Mondavi 1997 SLD Cabernet Sauvignon (Stags Leap District) $45. 89 *(11/1/2000)*

Robert Mondavi 1999 To Kalon Reserve Cabernet Sauvignon (Oakville) $150. Absolutely delicious. Complex flavors of berries, herbs, spices, and tannins mingle together on the palate, always shifting and fascinating. The whole is wrapped in sweetly toasted oak. Feels lush and creamy, like butter. **94 Cellar Selection** —*S.H. (2/1/2003)*

Robert Mondavi 2001 To Kalon Vineyard Reserve Cabernet Sauvignon (Napa Valley) $135. Young and closed, with mint and oak accenting black cherry fruit. Powerful, elegant, smooth. Polished with big time tannins that are sweet and refined. Tremendous fruit. Should have a long, long life. Drink now–2020. **95 Cellar Selection** —*S.H. (6/1/2005)*

Robert Mondavi 1999 To Kalon Vineyard Reserve Cabernet Sauvignon (Napa Valley) $NA. Oaky. A bit backward, closed. Lots of primary fruit varietal character in the aroma. Coffee, smoke, ash, cedar. In the mouth, potent black currants, cassis, massive middle. Wonderful tannins, rich, ripe, sweet. The finish is long and intense. 2006-2020. **97 Editors' Choice** —*S.H. (6/1/2005)*

Robert Mondavi 1998 To Kalon Vineyard Reserve Cabernet Sauvignon (Napa Valley) $NA. Much lighter, more polished, forward than the '97. Delicate mouthfeel, with powerfully sweet crème de cassis flavors. Probably best now-2012. **90** —*S.H. (6/1/2005)*

Robert Mondavi 1997 To Kalon Vineyard Reserve Cabernet Sauvignon (Napa Valley) $NA. Younger, bigger, tighter than the '96. Lots of currants upfront; chocolate layer cake. Fairly tannic. A bit sharp in acids and lacks the elegance of '96. Should develop well after 2010. **92 Cellar Selection** —*S.H. (6/1/2005)*

Robert Mondavi 1996 To Kalon Vineyard Reserve Cabernet Sauvignon (Napa Valley) $NA. I far prefer this to the 30th Anniversary bottling. Complete, wholesome, healthy, very delicious. Smoky, ashy nose, cherry, vanilla, char. Sweet cherry-mocha flavors, soft, velvety mouthfeel. Combines power with delicacy. Very fine. Now-2012 and beyond. **96 Cellar Selection** —*S.H. (6/1/2005)*

Robert Mondavi 1997 Chardonnay (Napa Valley) $20. 87 *(6/1/2000)*

Robert Mondavi 2004 Chardonnay (Carneros) $20. Clean, minerally, and streamlined, with citrus zest, lees, oak flavors, and a very dry finish. This will go well with shellfish. It's made in Mondavi's restrained, elegant style. **85** —*S.H. (12/1/2006)*

Robert Mondavi 2003 Chardonnay (Carneros) $18. Mondavi's Chards

never seem as ripe as most others, instead coming in with higher acids and a tinge of dusty tannins framing the fruit. So it is with this dry wine, with its touch of mineral and rich coating of oak. **87** —*S.H. (3/1/2006)*

Robert Mondavi 2002 Chardonnay (Napa Valley) $18. The softest and least concentrated of Mondavi's current trio of Chards. Peaches and cream, vanilla, and dusty spices. **85** —*S.H. (12/15/2004)*

Robert Mondavi 2002 Chardonnay (Carneros) $25. It's all about ripe apples and oak in this crisp, elegant wine. Like biting into a fresh Granny Smith, that burst of acidic flavor startles, but is quickly softened by sweet oak. **90** —*S.H. (12/15/2004)*

Robert Mondavi 2002 Chardonnay (Carneros) $18. Here's a dry, stylish Chard, the kind that references minerals and steel rather than overt fruit, although you'll find green apples and persimmons, dusted with cinnamon. It has good acids and a firm finish. **89** —*S.H. (11/15/2005)*

Robert Mondavi 2001 Chardonnay (Napa Valley) $18. Comes down firmly on the earthy, leesy side, a wine with modulated fruit. There are suggestions of tahini, spice, and apples, while oak provides the requisite buttered toast and vanilla cream. This wine is the opposite of opulent, and will be an unobtrusive food partner. **87** —*S.H. (6/1/2004)*

Robert Mondavi 2001 Chardonnay (Carneros) $25. Smells young and fresh, with apple and pear flavors given a boost by bright underlying acidity. Not very oaky, so the fruit and acids take center stage. Almost delicate in weight, with persistent flavors on the finish. **87** —*S.H. (12/1/2003)*

Robert Mondavi 1999 Chardonnay (Napa Valley) $22. Tight, lemony, and leesy, this wine strides off in it's own direction, away from pronounced oak superripe fruit, more in the direction of mineral and stone. It's austere, sleek, and steely, softened by lees creaminess, but angular. Call it Chablisian. **86** —*S.H. (12/1/2001)*

Robert Mondavi 1999 Chardonnay (Carneros) $23. Round, silky, and polished, this clean wine is streamline and almost austere in terms of fruit. Beyond the crisp acids and dusty tannins, the main influence is lees, although some figgy, peach flavors develop in the finish. Reflect's the winery's emphasis on lees flash, more structure and longevity. **86** —*S.H. (12/1/2001)*

Robert Mondavi 1997 Carneros District Chardonnay (Carneros) $23. 88 *(6/1/2000)*

Robert Mondavi 2000 Coastal Chardonnay (Central Coast) $11. In this everyday Chard, apple, peach, and even tropical fruits are wrapped in spicy oak. The wine drinks dry and crisp, although the finish picks up a little sugar. **84** —*S.H. (5/1/2002)*

Robert Mondavi 1999 Coastal Chardonnay (Central Coast) $NA. From cool coastal vineyards, this wine shows an unusual degree of richness for this price. The nose offers tropical fruits and spicy oak, and the flavors are boldly fruity. It almost achieves a degree of complexity. All in all, a fine value. **87 Best Buy** —*S.H. (5/1/2001)*

Robert Mondavi 1998 Coastal Chardonnay (Central Coast) $12. 86 —*S.H. (11/15/2000)*

Robert Mondavi 2000 Huichica Hills Chardonnay (Carneros) $50. Currently, its heritage of lees aging and new oak barrels dominates. Beneath is a layer of apple, citrus, and pear and spice. It will probably soften and increase in complexity over the next five years. **92** —*S.H. (10/1/2003)*

Robert Mondavi 2002 Huichica Hills Vineyard Reserve Chardonnay (Carneros) $50. Much brighter in overall profile than Mondavi's regular '02 Carneros Chard, and also considerably oakier, this wine offers more of everything. It has pineapple and custard flavors and very crisp acidity that makes for a clean, polished finish. **91** —*S.H. (11/15/2005)*

Robert Mondavi 2003 Private Selection Chardonnay (Central Coast) $11. There's Monterey fruit in here, to judge by the rich lime zest flavor and crisp acidity. There's also a great deal of oak flavor in this easy, likeable Chardonnay. It finishes dry and clean. **84** —*S.H. (12/15/2005)*

Robert Mondavi 2002 Private Selection Chardonnay (Central Coast) $11. A citrusy Chard, with mineral and sweet lime flavors that just nudge into peach and a kiss of used oak. It's clean and vibrant, and the crisp acidity will nicely complement food. **84** —*S.H. (11/15/2004)*

USA

Robert Mondavi 2001 Private Selection Chardonnay (Central Coast) $11. A thin, uninspiring wine with citrus and apple sauce flavors and lots of acidity. Tastes watered down, but will do in a pinch. **83** —*S.H. (8/1/2003)*

Robert Mondavi 2004 Reserve Chardonnay (Carneros) $35. Made in a less ripe style, with citrusy, herbal flavors that are well-oaked and leesy, this very dry Chard displays both elegance and a long finish. If you're into aging Chardonnays, try cellaring this through 2010. Should be fine. **89** —*S.H. (12/15/2006)*

Robert Mondavi 2003 Reserve Chardonnay (Carneros) $35. Built along the same lines as Mondavi's regular Chard, this is an earthy wine whose fruit is restrained. It's sleek and elegant, very Chablisian in style, with a minerality through the finish. Should hold and improve. **90** —*S.H. (3/1/2006)*

Robert Mondavi 2001 Reserve Chardonnay (Napa Valley) $38. Big in fruit, oak and creamy lees, but expressively balanced. Pear and tropical fruit flavors are enhanced with smoky vanillins and buttered toast, while the acid-tannin structure is sleek and classic. **92** —*S.H. (12/15/2004)*

Robert Mondavi 2000 Reserve Chardonnay (Napa Valley) $38. Smooth and distinguished, a flamboyant wine with enough flavor to last all day. Peaches, pears, and tropical fruits are encased in lush, toasty oak, while lees adds a creamy, mealy texture. This classy wine is rich and balanced. **91** —*S.H. (8/1/2003)*

Robert Mondavi 1998 Reserve Chardonnay (Napa Valley) $36. Another solid effort from Mondavi, the 1998 reserve shows fine structure and an attractive spectrum of citrus, peach, crème brûlée, and nut aromas and flavors that work in lovely harmony. It's full but not heavy, and balances fruit and acidity, sweetness and tartness, and light and full elements. The positive fruit, style and restraint are notable. **90** *(7/1/2001)*

Robert Mondavi 1997 Reserve Chardonnay (Napa Valley) $36. 90 —*S.H. (12/31/1999)*

Robert Mondavi 2004 Fumé Blanc (Napa Valley) $18. Here's the latest Mondavi Fumé in the frosted bottle. As always, it's super-dry and grassy, with kiwi, gooseberry, lemon, and lime flavors. Oak barrels and sur lie aging have added rich textural complexities. What a sophisticated, polished wine. **92 Editors' Choice** —*S.H. (7/1/2006)*

Robert Mondavi 2002 Fumé Blanc (Napa Valley) $18. As always, dry, tart, lemony, and clean. So citrusy and high in acidity, it's almost metallic. Leaves the mouth sandpapery dry; the perfect foil for mussels or clams. **86** —*S.H. (9/1/2004)*

Robert Mondavi 2001 Fumé Blanc (North Coast) $11. This wine's grapefruit and lemon flavors are lean, showing too much tartness and heat. **83** —*S.H. (7/1/2003)*

Robert Mondavi 1999 Fumé Blanc (Napa Valley) $18. Here's a crisp, bone-dry wine of tart acidity with aromas and flavors of lemons and grapefruits. The hard mineral quality is softened by barrel fermentation and lees aging, which contribute round, creamy notes. The lemony theme re-emerges on the finish. **86** —*S.H. (11/15/2001)*

Robert Mondavi 1997 Fumé Blanc (Napa Valley) $13. 83 —*M.S. (6/1/1999)*

Robert Mondavi 2000 Coastal Private Selection Fumé Blanc (North Coast) $11. A nice, easy-drinking wine that takes grassy, lemony flavors and smooths them out with what tastes like a softening dose of oak. The middle has some pretty notes of melons, leading to a fruity, clean, and slightly sweet finish. **85** —*S.H. (9/1/2003)*

Robert Mondavi 2003 Private Selection Fumé Blanc (North Coast) $11. Here's a wine of sophistication for those who like their whites ultra-dry and with some prickly acidity. The flavors are light but pleasant, suggesting grapefruit, melon, and fig. Mondavi's Fumé is especially notable for its balance. **86 Best Buy** —*S.H. (12/15/2005)*

Robert Mondavi 1999 Reserve To Kalon Fumé Blanc (Napa Valley) $NA. Fabulous spice and oak complexity. Ripe lime custard, honeysuckle, vanilla, smoked butter, peach, soapstone. Long, rich, fruity-spicy, bone dry, good acidity. Complex, harmonious, a complete wine. Really showing beautifully now at 4-1/2 years. **94** —*S.H. (6/1/2005)*

Robert Mondavi 1997 Reserve To Kalon Fumé Blanc (Napa Valley) $NA. Breaking down. Somewhat vegetal. Some good citrus and passionflower fruit remains. Interesting, but its prime is past. **84** —*S.H. (6/1/2005)*

Robert Mondavi 1994 Reserve To Kalon Fumé Blanc (Napa Valley) $NA. Fresh and complex. Layers of citrus peel, pineapple, oak, and a fruity compôte. Bone dry, crisp. Lots of minerality, stone. Creamy. Fabulous, long, firm quality. Fresh, smooth, dryish-sweet, long satisfying finish. From old vines. **95 Editors' Choice** —*S.H. (6/1/2005)*

Robert Mondavi 2003 Reserve To Kalon Vineyard Fumé Blanc (Napa Valley) $35. Another fine To Kalon fumé from Mondavi. The wine shows citrus zest, gooseberry, mineral, and slate flavors that are boosted and enriched with acidity, toasty oak, and lees. It's hard to find descriptors except for qualitative adjectives like elegant, streamlined, classic, and pure. This one's an ager. Best now–2013. **92** —*S.H. (12/15/2006)*

Robert Mondavi 2002 To Kalon Vineyard I Block Fumé Blanc (Napa Valley) $65. Explosive. Like the Reserve Fumé on steroids. Tons of tropical fruit, persimmon, passion fruit, lime, and fig, with rich, bright acidity, all seamlessly married to oak. Showy, flashy, and flamboyant. **94 Editors' Choice** —*S.H. (6/1/2005)*

Robert Mondavi 2002 To Kalon Vineyard Reserve Fumé Blanc (Napa Valley) $35. Fairly oaky, but in between the wood grain are aromas of stone-encrusted peach and pungent citrus. A model fumé-style wine that will suit grilled shrimp or lobster like a fine-fitting suit. The flavors of lemon curd, grapefruit, and pineapple are rock solid, while the feel from front to back is ideal. **93 Editors' Choice** *(7/1/2005)*

Robert Mondavi 2001 To Kalon Vineyard Reserve Fumé Blanc (Napa Valley) $35. You have to give Mondavi credit for sticking to the dry, acidic theme in this wine over the years. It's classic in its own way. Tart to the point of lemony astringency, almost raw, with a richer overlay of fine oak and lees. Really gets the juices flowing. **90** —*S.H. (12/15/2004)*

Robert Mondavi 1997 To Kalon Vineyard I Block Fumé Blanc (Napa Valley) $50. 91 —*J.C. (9/1/1999)*

Robert Mondavi 1998 To Kalon Vineyard Reserve Fumé Blanc (Napa Valley) $28. 88 —*S.H. (11/15/2000)*

Robert Mondavi 1997 To Kalon Vineyard Reserve Fumé Blanc (Napa Valley) $28. 90 —*S.H. (2/1/2000)*

Robert Mondavi 2000 Unfiltered Fumé Blanc (Napa Valley) $19. Very funky and confounding at first, but then it opens to reveal smoke, stone fruit, and mineral aromas. The mouth is quite spicy, with green herbs accenting citrus and mineral. The tangy lemon finish has a chalky grip to it, which only adds to the overall complexity of this unique Napa white. **89** *(8/1/2002)*

Robert Mondavi 2000 Coastal Johannisberg Riesling (Monterey County) $9. With a bit of residual sugar, it tastes slightly sweet, with aromas and flavors of honey, citrus fruits, and riper notes of apricot. Stunning acidity makes it tingle on the tongue. This fresh wine will be nice with ripe fruits. **84** —*S.H. (11/15/2001)*

Robert Mondavi 2001 Coastal Private Selection Johannisberg Riesling (Central Coast) $9. Soft, fruity, and simple, with upfront flavors of bubble gum and vanilla. Finishes slightly sweet and clean. **84** —*S.H. (9/1/2003)*

Robert Mondavi 2004 Private Selection Johannisberg Riesling (Monterey County) $11. Sweetish, simple, and flabby, with apricot and peach syrup flavors. **81** —*S.H. (12/15/2005)*

Robert Mondavi 2003 Private Selection Johannisberg Riesling (Central Coast) $11. Slightly sweet, with honeyed flavors of flowers and white peach, this wine gets the job done with crisp acidity. **83** —*S.H. (9/1/2004)*

Robert Mondavi 2002 Private Selection Johannisberg Riesling (Central Coast) $9. Quite fruity and straightforward, with pleasant peach, melon, and citrus flavors. The finish is clean and fresh and the wine well balanced. **84** —*J.M. (8/1/2003)*

Robert Mondavi 1998 Malbec (Stags Leap District) $45. One of the lesser-known grapes of Bordeaux, Malbec is typically dark and aromatic. This one certainly is, with it's inky color and forceful scent. Oak dominates, with intensely smoky, vanilla notes, but in the mouth it's interesting and complex, withthe weight and cassis of a good Cabernet. **89** —*S.H. (12/1/2001)*

Robert Mondavi 2000 Merlot (Napa Valley) $21. Opens with scents of green olives, sweaty leather, currants, and spice, in addition to smoky oak. On the palate, there is plenty of rich, polished blackberry flavor. The tannins poke up and are a bit hard, but they're nothing a good steak can't handle. Drink now. **87** —*S.H. (6/1/2004)*

Robert Mondavi 2000 Merlot (Stags Leap District) $40. Not flashy or flamboyant, but complex, with flavors of green olives and black cherries and dried herbs. Is that smoked meat, bacony note brettanomyces? Who knows, but it adds interest. Completely dry and well oaked, with tannins on the finish that suggest mid-term aging. **89** —*S.H. (12/1/2003)*

Robert Mondavi 1998 Merlot (Napa Valley) $28. Made with the best intentions, but this wine can't get beyond it's vintage. The fruit is light and earthy, and not even lovely oak can change that. Nonetheless, it's a dry, elegant wine filled with harmony and chewey tannins. **87** —*S.H. (12/1/2001)*

Robert Mondavi 1998 Merlot (Stags Leap District) $35. Dominated by oak, with cedar, vanilla, clove, smoke, and mint aromas and flavors, this wine does the best it can with rather sharpley flavored grapes. It's pretty acidic, tart, and tannic, so the question is whether or not it's got the fruit to age. Probably not. **86** —*S.H. (12/1/2001)*

Robert Mondavi 1998 Merlot (Carneros) $35. Disturbingly vegetal aromas, like canned asparagus—evidence of incompletely ripe grapes—that lots of oak can't hide. Structurally, the wine is fine, with silky smooth tannins and crisp acids, yet the flavors are thin and disappointing. **83** —*S.H. (12/1/2001)*

Robert Mondavi 1997 Merlot (Carneros) $35. 87 —*S.H. (11/15/2000)*

Robert Mondavi 2000 Coastal Merlot (Central Coast) $11. An everyday wine with some ripe berry fruit but also powerful green, herbal flavors. Of course, it's very dry, with high acidity and a peppery mouthfeel and finish. Possesses some elegance at an affordable price, and is very clean. **85** —*S.H. (6/1/2002)*

Robert Mondavi 1999 Coastal Merlot (Central Coast) $11. Light and modest; a wine that doesn't pretend to be any more than it is. With some decent berry and spice flavors, a kiss of oak and suitable tannins and acidity, it's an adequate dinner wine. Won't do for your best table, but will get the job done for quick late night meals that need something dry and red to drink. **83** —*S.H. (5/1/2001)*

Robert Mondavi 1998 Coastal Merlot (Central Coast) $13. 86 —*S.H. (12/31/1999)*

Robert Mondavi 2003 Private Selection Merlot (California) $11. Intensely jammy in blueberry and black cherry flavors, and sharp in young, juicy grape acidity, this basically dry wine has a lot of fruity ripeness in the finish, with a touch of cocoa and vanilla. **83** —*S.H. (12/15/2005)*

Robert Mondavi 2001 Private Selection Merlot (Central Coast) $11. Thin and earthy, with notes of blackberries, olives, and tobacco and thick, harsh acids and tannins that show up on the gritty finish. Pretty good for everyday fare at a decent price. **84** —*S.H. (12/1/2003)*

Robert Mondavi 2004 Moscato d'Oro Moscato (Napa Valley) $20. Still with some spritz, this is a sweet, but not too sweet, clean and vibrant wine, with rich flavors of apricots and vanilla. The effervescence should disappear in time. **86** —*S.H. (3/1/2006)*

Robert Mondavi 2001 Moscato d'Oro Moscato (Napa Valley) $18. A very pretty wine with lip-smacking flavors of ripe, sweet oranges, apricots, and cherries, with a luscious edge of smoke, vanilla, and cinnamon. Tastes quite sweet, with a crisp backbone of steely acidity. **88** —*S.H. (12/1/2003)*

Robert Mondavi 2005 Pinot Grigio (California) $11. Gives exuberant flavor and slight sweetness, just what so many American consumers want in an everyday PG. Bursting with green apple, pear, fig, apricot, and honeysuckle flavors, the finish is honeyed and clean. **84** —*S.H. (12/31/2006)*

Robert Mondavi 2003 Pinot Grigio (California) $11. Easy drinking and pleasant for its flavors of juicy ripe green apples, with crisp tree fruit acidity and a dash of vanilla on the finish. Very clean, and will pair well with a wide variety of foods. **85** —*S.H. (11/15/2004)*

Robert Mondavi 2004 Private Selection Pinot Grigio (California) $11. Definitely on the ripely sweet side, but nicely crisp in acids, this cocktail-style wine has rich and juicy flavors of pineapples, pears, figs, apples, and dusty spices. **85** —*S.H. (12/15/2005)*

Robert Mondavi 2003 Private Selection Pinot Grigio (California) $11.

Pleasant and dry, with a swift, vibrant mouthfeel due to high acidity and a lemony-clean flavor. Finishes with notes of figs and white pepper. Shows real complexity throughout. **85 Best Buy** —*S.H. (3/1/2005)*

Robert Mondavi 1996 Pinot Noir (Carneros) $24. 88 —*M.S. (6/1/1999)*

Robert Mondavi 2005 Pinot Noir (Central Coast) $11. Dull, with candied flavors and a medicinal finish. There's funk in there, too. **81** —*S.H. (12/31/2006)*

Robert Mondavi 2004 Pinot Noir (Carneros) $21. All the work that the winery did for so many years with Pinot Noir is brought home with this delicate, elegant wine. It combines lovely Carneros cherry, pomegranate, cola, and spice flavors with cool-climate acidity to produce a dry, silky table wine that's easy to like. It's not an ageable blockbuster, but will be irresistible now with roast duck, pork, or salmon dishes. **91 Editors' Choice** —*S.H. (7/1/2006)*

Robert Mondavi 2003 Pinot Noir (Carneros) $21. Mondavi's basic Carneros Pinot has been dependable for years, and this one continues the tradition. It's dry and balanced, with cherry, cola, coffee, and herb flavors, and has the silky tannins and crisp acids you want in a Pinot. **87** —*S.H. (3/1/2006)*

Robert Mondavi 2002 Pinot Noir (Napa Valley) $22. Pleasant rather than profound, showing weak cola, sassafras, and sugared cherry flavors and soft tannins. Finishes cranberry-skin tart in acids. **84** —*(11/1/2004)*

Robert Mondavi 2002 Pinot Noir (Carneros) $35. Tasters found an off-smell that quickly blew off to reveal oaky, minty, cherry notes. The flavors suggest cherries, root beer, and Hawaiian punch. Very dry, silky, and crisp in acids. **86** —*(11/1/2004)*

Robert Mondavi 2001 Pinot Noir (Napa Valley) $22. Restrained, delicate, and light in body, but there's true complexity in the mélange of cherry, smoked meat, peppery spice, and vanilla flavors. They create a sunburst of sensations across the palate, yet the wine always retains its elegance. **88** —*S.H. (12/1/2004)*

Robert Mondavi 2001 Pinot Noir (Carneros) $40. Jammy and easy, showcasing Carneros's tutti-fruity flavors and crisp acids, with pretty cherry and raspberry flavors. Has a bit of stuffing that pushes it beyond a simple fruit bomb. Very dry, with good, firm tannins. **88** —*S.H. (12/1/2003)*

Robert Mondavi 2000 Pinot Noir (Carneros) $40. From the beginning there is a piercing oakiness to this wine, but not in away that forces aromas and flavors of butter and vanilla. It's more toasted, almost burnt. But under the wood is the full allotment of cherry, tea, structure, and intensity. **89** —*(10/1/2002)*

Robert Mondavi 1998 Pinot Noir (Carneros) $35. 92 —*S.H. (12/15/2000)*

Robert Mondavi 1999 Coastal Pinot Noir (Central Coast) $12. 83 —*S.H. (12/15/2000)*

Robert Mondavi 1998 Coastal Pinot Noir (Central Coast) $11. 82 —*S.H. (10/1/2000)*

Robert Mondavi 2000 Coastal Private Selection Pinot Noir (Central Coast) $13. A nice, light feel and good fruit-acid balance are the best qualities of this dry, tart cherry-flavoreded. Soy, chocolate, and herb accents add interest, but a strong ash-like note pervades throughout. **84** —*(10/1/2002)*

Robert Mondavi 2002 PNX Pinot Noir (Carneros) $35. A big wine that's rather hard and tight now. Has lovely cherry, vanilla, and oriental spice flavors and bright, citrusy acidity that cleans the mouth. Feels delicate and silky, a dry Pinot that needs a year or two to come into its own. **89** —*(11/1/2004)*

Robert Mondavi 1999 PNX Pinot Noir (Carneros) $45. We've come to expect Pinot to be soft, delicate, spicy, and fruity, withan assertiveness that makes it an iron fist in a velvet glove. This wine doesn't disappoint. The red-berry flavors are very spicy, and the tannins are intricate and finely meshed. There's an airiness, but nothing light about this powerful wine. **91** —*S.H. (12/15/2001)*

Robert Mondavi 2004 Private Selection Pinot Noir (Central Coast) $11. Simple but clean, this Pinot shows good varietal character in the light body, dry finish, crisp acids, and flavors of cola, smoked cherries, and peppery spices. **84** —*S.H. (12/15/2005)*

Robert Mondavi 2002 Private Selection Pinot Noir (Central Coast) $11.

Strawberries, cherries, smoke, and coffee flavors in this delicately structured, somewhat lean wine. It has good acidity and a pleasant mouthfeel. **85** *(11/1/2004)*

Robert Mondavi 2001 Private Selection Pinot Noir (Central Coast) $13. It's Pinot-esque in the cherry and raspberry flavors and light, silky tannins, which make for easy drinking. Crisp acidity boosts the flavors and adds zest and life. Certainly a simple wine of little depth, but will suffice for an inexpensive Pinot Noir. **85** —*S.H. (7/1/2003)*

Robert Mondavi 2002 Reserve Pinot Noir (Napa Valley) $50. Everyone agreed on how nice this wine is, without being great. It's delicate and crisp in acids, offering pleasant sour cherry, tea, and charry flavors. Achieves elegance in the silky and racy finish. **87** *(11/1/2004)*

Robert Mondavi 2001 Reserve Pinot Noir (Napa Valley) $50. Certainly a bigger, denser wine than the Carneros Pinot. The plummy-berry flavors are wrapped in sturdy, rich tannins, with extra notes of earth and herbs. Feels weighty on the palate, a wine of importance, not to mention elegance. The density suggests meats on the bone. **91** —*S.H. (8/1/2003)*

Robert Mondavi 1998 Reserve Pinot Noir (Napa Valley) $50. 93 —*S.H. (12/15/2000)*

Robert Mondavi 1999 Boomerang Red Blend (Oakville) $60. Seductively soft and mellow, but with beautiful flavors, this offbeat wine combines powerfully assertive berry and tree fruit flavors with plush tannins. it's very dry and fashionable, a candlelight wine of enormous complexity and charm. A blend of Syrah, Cabernet Sauvignon, and Cabernet Franc, largely from To Kalon. **92** —*S.H. (12/1/2001)*

Robert Mondavi 1997 Sauvignon Blanc (Stags Leap District) $18. 89 —*S.H. (9/1/1999)*

Robert Mondavi 2003 Sauvignon Blanc (Stags Leap District) $23. Pungent and lively, with pineapple, passion fruit, nettle, and citrus aromas. Fairly forward and powerful on the palate; the lime and gooseberry flavors are propelled by jet-like acidity. A full-bore wine with a lot of flavor. **88** *(7/1/2005)*

Robert Mondavi 2002 Sauvignon Blanc (Stags Leap District) $23. If tart acidity and grassy Sauvignons are your thing, you'll love this. It's dry as dust, mouthwatering in acids and the flavors are solidly hay-like and gooseberry. The finish of sweet lemon and lime and sweet oak provide richness. **86** —*S.H. (12/15/2004)*

Robert Mondavi 2001 Sauvignon Blanc (Stags Leap District) $23. A traditionally biting version with bright, persistent citrus flavors that last through the tart finish. Saved from mediocrity by the nuances of fig, spice. **87** —*S.H. (10/1/2003)*

Robert Mondavi 1999 Sauvignon Blanc (Stags Leap District) $23. One of the more austere examples of the vintage, this is a terrifically lemony wine, dry as dust, with high acidity that makes it tart and just this side of sour. It's a very clean wine, one that scours the palate and prepares the taste buds for food: Goat cheese comes immediately to mind. **86** —*S.H. (12/1/2001)*

Robert Mondavi 1998 Sauvignon Blanc (Stags Leap District) $18. 89 —*S.H. (11/15/2000)*

Robert Mondavi 1999 Botrytis Sauvignon Blanc (Napa Valley) $50. A ripe dessert wine, not shockingly sweet but an easy companion for sorbet or a fruit tart. The apricot flavors are wrapped in a honey-thick texture, balanced with firm acids, and the intensity lasts through a long finish. **90** —*S.H. (12/1/2003)*

Robert Mondavi 2000 Coastal Sauvignon Blanc (Central Coast) $9. Aggressively grassy, with hay and grapefruit flavors dominating this bone-dry, somewhat acidic wine. Yet, the tart crispness and scouring mouthfeel are refreshing and palate cleansing. Try it on a summer evening with grilled veggies and goat cheese. **84** —*S.H. (11/15/2001)*

Robert Mondavi 1998 Coastal Sauvignon Blanc (Central Coast) $9. 85 *(3/1/2000)*

Robert Mondavi 2004 Private Selection Sauvignon Blanc (Central Coast) $11. Semisweet and with crisp acidity, this simple, clean wine has pink grapefruit and vanilla flavors with a spicy finish. **83** —*S.H. (12/31/2005)*

Robert Mondavi 2003 Private Selection Sauvignon Blanc (Central Coast) $9. Tastes too sweet for a variety that should be dry and crisp. Almost

dessert with the sugary finish to the apple, pear, and fig flavors. **84** —*S.H. (12/15/2004)*

Robert Mondavi 2002 Private Selection Sauvignon Blanc (Central Coast) $9. Smells pleasant with its perfume of sweet citrus, smoke, and vanilla, but unacceptably thin and watery, even for an inexpensive wine. There's no there there. **82** —*S.H. (9/1/2004)*

Robert Mondavi 2001 Private Selection Sauvignon Blanc (Central Coast) $9. Quite lean and tart, a thin wine with modest grapefruit and melon flavors. Tastes like a shellfish wine, minerally and crisp, with bright acidity, but there is some richness to the finish. **83** —*S.H. (10/1/2003)*

Robert Mondavi 2000 SLD Sauvignon Blanc (Stags Leap District) $23. Very grassy and citrusy, with hints of garden-fresh vegetables and a slight floral note. It's light and almost airy on the tongue, finishing crisp and clean. A refreshing burst of anise caps things off. **88** *(8/1/2002)*

Robert Mondavi 1999 Coastal Syrah (Central Coast) $14. Rhubarb, sour herb, and raisin aromas lead into smoke, ripe plum and Sweet Tart on the palate and on the finish. One reviewer called it "candy wine;" others found it a little thin. **83** *(10/1/2001)*

Robert Mondavi 1998 Coastal Syrah (Monterey County) $15. 81 —*L.W. (2/1/2000)*

Robert Mondavi 2000 Coastal Private Selection Syrah (Central Coast) $11. An awkward, unripe wine, with green stalky notes and harsh tannins. There are some nice fruity flavors, and it's dry and clean, but it feels austere and aggressive in the mouth. **83** —*S.H. (12/1/2002)*

Robert Mondavi 2002 Private Selection Syrah (Central Coast) $11. Rather raw and sharp, a young wine with carbonic tastes of jammy fruit and berries. It's smooth in tannins, and an easy sipper. **84** —*S.H. (2/1/2005)*

Robert Mondavi 2001 Zinfandel (Napa Valley) $21. Smooth and supple textured, with a fine-tuned blend of plum, blackberry, black cherry, spice, and toast flavors. Firm and focused, the wine is made in a subdued but classy style. **88** —*J.M. (11/1/2003)*

Robert Mondavi 1999 Zinfandel (Napa Valley) $21. Mondavi has tried to create a Bordeaux-style Zin, and has largely succeeded. It possesses all the necessary pepper, wildberry, and earth notes, and it's a full-bodied wine, but it's controlled, a stallion in stirrups. It's very dry, dusty, and atypical and, if a Zin can be so called, subtle. **89** —*S.H. (12/15/2001)*

Robert Mondavi 1997 Coastal Zinfandel (North Coast) $12. 84 —*S.H. (2/1/2000)*

Robert Mondavi 2000 Coastal Private Selection Zinfandel (North Coast) $11. There are some blackberry notes alongside less ripe green pepper and stemmy ones. The wine has some sharp, acidic flavors as well. **83** —*S.H. (12/1/2002)*

Robert Mondavi 2003 Private Selection Zinfandel (California) $11. A nice Zin and while it's a little light, this is a decent price for a wine of this character. It's dry and full-bodied, with ripe cherry, blackberry, raisin, and chocolate flavors and a spicy finish. **86 Best Buy** —*S.H. (12/15/2005)*

Robert Mondavi 2002 Private Selection Zinfandel (California) $11. Rough and weedy with hints of cherries, this dry red wine is okay if you're on the run in a fast food restaurant and need something to go with that pizza. Extra cheese will help. **83** —*S.H. (9/1/2004)*

Robert Mondavi 2001 Private Selection Zinfandel (North Coast) $11. Oaky and bright, with a modest core of cherry and spice. Modest on the finish too. **81** *(11/1/2003)*

ROBERT PECOTA

Robert Pecota 1997 Kara's Vineyard Cabernet Sauvignon (Napa Valley) $35. 90 *(11/1/2000)*

Robert Pecota 1997 Steven Andre Vineyard Merlot (Napa Valley) $30. 92 —*S.H. (3/1/2000)*

Robert Pecota 2002 Moscato d'Andrea Muscat Canelli (Napa Valley) $12. Delicious and refreshing, a dessert wine to have at the end of a great meal to revive the tastebuds. Zesty acidity frames mouthwateringly ripe tangerine, apricot honey, nectarine, vanilla, and spice flavors. **92** —*S.H. (11/15/2006)*

Robert Pecota 2005 L'Artiste Sauvignon Blanc (Napa Valley) $15. A crisp, ripe wine, rich in spearmint, lemon and lime, fig, melon, and white peach flavors, with a refreshing streak of grassy tang. Nice for an apéritif on a warm summer day. **85** —*S.H. (8/1/2006)*

Robert Pecota 1997 Syrah (Monterey County) $24.83 —*M.S. (2/1/2000)*

Robert Pecota 1999 Syrah (Monterey County) $24. This wine's tart black fruit core wears smoky, ashy accents. But most of all it sports a tart, heavy green-pea mantle. The mouthfeel is smooth and easy, the finish long, sweet and sour and slightly metallic. But the pervasive vegetal-herbal cloak keeps the fruit at bay. **84** *(11/1/2001)*

ROBERT PEPI

Robert Pepi 1996 Sauvignon Blanc (Napa Valley) $15.90 —*S.H. (6/1/1999)*

ROBERT RUE VINEYARD

Robert Rue Vineyard 2003 Zinfandel (Russian River Valley) $25. Fairly tannic and very dry at the moment, with a cut of acidity, this Zin may reveal more in a few years. The deeply fruity flavors of blackberry preserves are tucked down inside a blanket of astringency. Try after 2006. **86** —*S.H. (2/1/2006)*

Robert Rue Vineyard 2001 Wood Road Century Old Vines Zinfandel (Russian River Valley) $30. Smooth, plush, classy, and elegant. This wine balances upfront, racy fruit—black cherry, blackberry, and plum—with sleek texture, ripe tannins, and good acidity. It's beautifully balanced. The finish is long and sleek, with anise, herb, and chocolate flavors at the end. **90** *(11/1/2003)*

Robert Rue Vineyard 2003 Wood Road Reserve Zinfandel (Russian River Valley) $32. This reserve is considerably bigger than Rue's regular '03 Zin, but shares the same qualities of dryness and astringent tannins. The fruit is enormous, and grows stronger mid-palate, with ripe black cherries and cocoa. Cheese, olive oil, and meaty fats will stand up well. **89** —*S.H. (2/1/2006)*

ROBERT SINSKEY

Robert Sinskey 2001 Cabernet Franc (Carneros) $36. A perfumed style of Cabernet Franc, which benefits from its relatively cool climate location in Carneros. It has a rich, complex style, with bitter cherry flavors of firm, dry tannins. There is just a slight note of bell pepper and the final impression is of a restrained elegant style, never too powerful. **89** —*R.V. (4/1/2005)*

Robert Sinskey 1997 Chardonnay (Carneros) $25.92 —*S.H. (2/1/2000)*

Robert Sinskey 2001 Three Amigos Vineyard Chardonnay (Carneros) $30. A fine, elegant Chardonnay from Robert Sinskey's Carneros vineyards, that shows some pure, crisp, cool climate flavors of pears and green plums to balance the subtle wood flavors. A finely-crafted wine, which is very food friendly. **89** —*R.V. (4/1/2005)*

Robert Sinskey 1995 Reserve Merlot (Carneros) $33.89 —*S.H. (3/1/2000)*

Robert Sinskey 2003 Pinot Blanc (Carneros) $18. A very fresh, crisp style of Pinot Blanc, full of green apple flavors with just a touch of cinnamon. The fruit is pure, concentrated, dry, and floral but also just plain drinkable. It comes in a friendly, just right for two people, 375 ml bottle. **87** —*R.V. (4/1/2005)*

Robert Sinskey 2001 Four Vineyards Pinot Noir (Carneros) $46. A fruit-driven Pinot Noir that still manages to evoke so many of the undergrowth, damp leaf aromas associated with this elusive grape variety. It has elegance, subtlety, mineral flavors, and spicy, smoky, toasty wood. From vines that were first planted in 1982, this is a wine that should evolve well over five to ten years. **91** —*R.V. (4/1/2005)*

Robert Sinskey 2000 RSV Four Vineyards Pinot Noir (Carneros) $46. Lots of oak here, with a burst of vanilla and charry new barrel scents at first. Warm it up and a myriad of fantastic aromas wafts out: red cherries, cola, anise, sautéed mushrooms, and rosehip tea. Firm and well-structured, this wine is full-bodied and sturdy, and fairly tannic. Drink now through 2010 **92** —*S.H. (12/1/2004)*

Robert Sinskey 2001 Three Amigos Vineyard Pinot Noir (Carneros) $46. A soft, seductive style of Pinot Noir, full of ripe, strawberry flavors and very pure fruit tastes. There are firm tannins, but they do not dominate the smoky fruit along with flavors of dark plums, and beautiful acidity. A lovely, understated wine. **89** —*R.V. (4/1/2005)*

Robert Sinskey 2001 Vandal Vineyard Pinot Noir (Carneros) $46. The first impression of this wine is that it is still very young. The fruit is full of primary tastes, raspberries and red currants. There are firm, smoky tannins, and very fresh acidity. But it is going to be a very fine, elegant wine when it comes together. Give it three years and it will have grown up. **90** —*R.V. (4/1/2005)*

ROBERT STEMMLER

Robert Stemmler 2004 Estate Grown Chardonnay (Carneros) $34. Earthy and minerally, an austere Chard by today's standards, with a thyme and tobacco edge to the modest peach fruit. My bias is for either impossibly rich, oaky Chards or sleek, fruity, unoaked ones. This falls between those goal posts. **84** —*S.H. (12/31/2006)*

Robert Stemmler 2003 Estate Grown Chardonnay (Carneros) $34. Co-released with the '04, but the wine is tired. It's already showing old flavors, with an earthy, herbal undertow. **82** —*S.H. (12/31/2006)*

Robert Stemmler 2002 Three Clone Chardonnay (Carneros) $26. Very bright and zingy, with that brilliant shine of citrusy acidity you find in a good Carneros Chard. The apple, peach, and spice flavors finish in a rich, creamy swirl of fruit and oak. **90** —*S.H. (12/15/2005)*

Robert Stemmler 2001 Pinot Noir (Carneros) $32. A little green and toma-toey, but there's enough raspberry, cherry, pepper, vanilla, and smoke to satisfy. The easy tannins and soft, silky texture are underscored by nice Carneros acidity. **87** —*S.H. (6/1/2004)*

Robert Stemmler 2000 Pinot Noir (Carneros) $38. Smoke, burnt toast, and vanilla aromas are all indicative of a full-fledged barrel regimen, but that's O.K., because the raspberry fruit can handle it. This wine has near-perfect structure: The acidity is bracing but stops short of being sharp, while the tannins are firm but friendly. By the time winter rolls around, this should be just about ready. **90** *(10/1/2002)*

Robert Stemmler 2002 Estate Grown Pinot Noir (Carneros) $32. Dry, medium-bodied and crisp, this wine has an earthiness to the cola, rhubarb, coffee, herb, and cherry flavors. It's a stylish wine of elegance and finesse, and will perform its basic Pinot duties dependably. **86** —*S.H. (12/15/2005)*

Robert Stemmler 2003 Ferguson Block Pinot Noir (Carneros) $44. The hope for this wine is that it will age, like certain Burgundies that are deceptively simple when young. Though elegant. it's thin and acidic now, with cola and tea flavors and a skinny texture that doesn't seem to be going anywhere. But who knows? **85** —*S.H. (12/31/2006)*

Robert Stemmler 2002 Ferguson Block Pinot Noir (Carneros) $40. The flavors are rich, spanning cherry pie and raspberry tart, vanilla, and cinnamon-sprinkled cappuccino, and a hint of ripe, sweet Heirloom tomato. For all the richness, the wine is dry, silky, and balanced. **91 Editors' Choice** —*S.H. (12/15/2005)*

Robert Stemmler 2001 Ferguson Block Pinot Noir (Carneros) $40. Not flashy, but there's something really likeable about the balance and complexity. This is a delicate Pinot that combines a mushroomy earthiness with fruitier cherry flavors. It's very dry, with a scour of acidity and dusty tannins, and will be excellent with grilled meats. **89** —*S.H. (6/1/2004)*

Robert Stemmler 2002 Nugent Vineyard Pinot Noir (Russian River Valley) $32. Tasted beside Stemmler's estate Pinot, this one's richer and more concentrated, but very similar, even though it's from a different appellation, suggesting a consistent winemaker approach. It's medium-bodied and silky, with ripe rhubarb, cola, and cherry-pie flavors finished with oak and vanilla. Drink this elegant and complex wine now. **88** —*S.H. (12/15/2005)*

Robert Stemmler 2001 Nugent Vineyard Pinot Noir (Russian River Valley) $32. Provides that extra edge of meaty complexity you find in the better Pinots of this appellation. That's on top of the blackberry, coffee, rhubarb, herb, and cola flavors. Very dry, and marked by rich, sweet tannins and crisp acids, this wine will hold for several years. **90** —*S.H. (6/1/2004)*

ROBERT YOUNG

Robert Young 2000 Scion Bordeaux Blend (Alexander Valley) $60. After a trio of stunning successes, this year's Scion, well made as it is, just can't outrun the vintage.The berry-cherry flavors are less forceful than in the

'99, with a touch of dill. Still, it's a soothing wine, with soft, gentle tannins and powerful oak. **88** —*S.H. (12/1/2004)*

Robert Young 1997 Scion Bordeaux Blend (Alexander Valley) $50. The second wine, and first red, from this famous vineyard-owning family, it's a blend of Cabernet Sauvignon, Merlot, and Cabernet Franc. The wine is, in a word, classic. This great vintage provided super fruit, and the winemaking takes full advantage of it. This is very great Cabernet. It's so delicious you find yourself putting the glass down and thinking about it. A new First Growth enters the California pantheon. **97** —*S.H. (6/1/2003)*

Robert Young 2002 Scion Cabernet Blend (Alexander Valley) $54. The Youngs produce a stunning Cabernet from their vineyard on the eastern benchlands of the valley. This Cab is the polar opposite of Napa, and defines the alternative possibilities. Soft, intricate, and herbal-earthy, it has beautiful black cherry, cocoa, tobacco, and new oak flavors, and it's thoroughly dry. Drink now through 2015. **95 Editors' Choice** —*S.H. (9/1/2006)*

Robert Young 2001 Scion Cabernet Blend (Alexander Valley) $54. Robert Young's Scion has become the quintessential Alexander Valley Cab. The opposite of a big Napa Cab, it has a soft, gentle texture, with good cherry and anise flavors, and a rich gout de terroir earthiness. Not an ager, it's among the best drink-now Cabs of the vintage. **92** *(6/1/2006)*

Robert Young 1999 Scion Cabernet Blend (Alexander Valley) $50. So good, it makes you want to shout. Possesses the beautifully ripe flavors that are expected of a great vintage, such as black currant, cherry, white chocolate, and cassis, with extra edges of smoky caramel and vanilla. The tannins are perfect, soft, and easy, but as rich and complex as a Renoir. Differentiates itself from Napa with its softness and accessibility, but as great as anything from across the Mayacamas. **96 Editors' Choice** —*S.H. (11/15/2003)*

Robert Young 1998 Scion Cabernet Sauvignon (Alexander Valley) $50. The much-anticipated second vintage of this wine struggled with a poor vintage. Ironically, the inability to super-ripen the grapes resulted in a Bordeaux-like wine, rather like a good St.-Emilion, although it's 100% Cabernet Sauvignon. Sweet cassis is offset with sage and tobacco in this early maturing wine of great distinction and charm. **94 Editors' Choice** —*S.H. (11/15/2002)*

Robert Young 2003 Chardonnay (Alexander Valley) $37. What an amazing record Robert Young has with its Chardonnay, which has been famous as a vineyard-designate by Château St. Jean since the 1970s. As ever, the '03 is rich and opulent, soft in acids and instantly addictive for the purity of fruit. Peaches and cream star, with a baked meringue complexity that's simply irresistible. **92** —*S.H. (5/1/2006)*

Robert Young 2002 Chardonnay (Alexander Valley) $37. Another winning Chard, consistent with past vintages. Oozes flamboyant tropical fruit flavors, complex Asian spices, and plenty of buttered toast and caramel char from good oak. All this in a rich, soft, vanilla-custardy texture that fills the mouth with pleasure. Drink now. **93 Editors' Choice** —*S.H. (8/1/2005)*

Robert Young 2001 Chardonnay (Alexander Valley) $35. This wine is finding its style, namely, ripe in tropical fruit, peach, pear, and apple flavors, soft acids, lavish oak, plenty of lees, and a full malolactic fermentation that helps make the texture buttery and creamy smooth. This year's fine effort is not as big as the magnificent '99, but is opulent and delicious. **92** —*S.H. (2/1/2004)*

Robert Young 1999 Chardonnay (Alexander Valley) $35. This long-anticipated wine from a longtime grower-turned-vintner swings for the fences. Begins with fascinating, complex aromas—highlighted by lees, pineapple, cinnamon, smoke, and white chocolate—and dazzles with its sheer opulence. Everything comes together in pinpointed harmony, right down to the mind-bogglingly beautiful finish. **96 Editors' Choice** —*S.H. (12/1/2001)*

Robert Young 2002 Merlot (Alexander Valley) $42. Robert Young is one of Alexander Valley's greatest wineries. After others achieved success with their Merlot grapes, they started making their own wine, and consumers are the beneficiaries. Truly soft and voluptuous, yet richly structured, the wine is totally dry, with a dried herb edge to the cherry flavors. The complexity is enormous, but somehow the wine remains delicate and elegant. **94 Editors' Choice** —*S.H. (6/1/2006)*

ROBIN CREST

Robin Crest 2000 Chardonnay (Sonoma County) $6. Simple, everyday Chard, with ripe apple and peach flavors that drink dry and crisp, with a

touch of oak. Perfectly decent sipper, well made, with a fruity, spicy finish. At this price, you could buy it by the case. **84** —*S.H. (6/1/2003)*

ROBLEDO

Robledo 2000 Pinot Noir (Carneros) $27. Quite cherry-like in the nose. On the palate, it's smooth and fairly silky, packing more bright cherry flavors, tinged with vanilla and spice. A bit peppery on the finish. Not complex, but quite pleasant. **86** —*J.M. (7/1/2003)*

Robledo 2002 The Seven Brothers Sauvignon Blanc (Lake County) $12. A mild-mannered Sauvignon Blanc, with a hint of candied lemon peel at its core. Acidity seems a bit low for this variety, while the simple flavors come up short. **80** —*J.M. (10/1/2004)*

ROCCA

Rocca 2001 Cabernet Sauvignon (Yountville) $50. A fine Cab that shows off its pedigree in the ripe, exuberant cherry and blackberry flavors and the smooth, sweet tannins. Oak plays a large part in this wine's creamy sweetness. Some dusty tannins show up in the finish. Drinkable now. **90** —*S.H. (6/1/2005)*

Rocca 2002 Syrah (Yountville) $38. Starts off a bit herbal and stemmy-smelling, with bright red berry aromas, but turns creamy and soft in the mouth, caressing the palate with ripe red berries and vanilla. Easy to drink. **86** *(9/1/2005)*

Rocca 2001 Syrah (Yountville) $38. Quite firm and tannic in its youth, but shows promise in the overall balance, and the core of rich, ripe cherry and blackberry fruit. There's a meaty, leathery edge that meshes well with oak on the finish. Should develop through 2008. **90** —*S.H. (6/1/2005)*

Rocca 2000 Syrah (Yountville) $38. This pleasant wine, while on the light side, still packs plenty of pleasure and class. The blackberry and herb flavors have a slightly green quality, emphasizing the tannins. Best consumed now. **86** —*S.H. (5/1/2004)*

Rocca 1999 Syrah (Yountville) $38. Decant this puppy; it's young and backward and will improve considerably with airing. Then, pretty aromas open up of blackberries, white pepper, raw meat and smoky oak. In the mouth, the wine is rich and tannic, with a solid core of blackberry fruit. **90** —*S.H. (10/1/2003)*

ROCHE

Roche 2003 Cabernet Sauvignon (Napa Valley) $36. Offers lots to like in a Cab that's drinkable now. Firmly tannic, with some sharp, minty elbows, but enough blackberry and plum fruit to satisfy. **86** —*S.H. (11/15/2006)*

Roche 1997 Chardonnay (Carneros) $19. **90** *(6/1/2000)*

Roche 1998 Barrel Select Reserve Chardonnay (Carneros) $30. **86** *(6/1/2000)*

Roche 2004 Reserve American Oak Chardonnay (Carneros) $31. Super-ripe in tropical papaya, pineapple, and white peach flavors, with a charry, caramel sweetness that seems to come from oak. Sweet clove and anise on the finish. **90** —*S.H. (11/15/2006)*

Roche 2004 Reserve French Oak Chardonnay (Carneros) $33. Outwardly fruity, offering up a wealth of tropical papaya, mango, and nectarine flavors, complete with a baked, buttery, vanilla-tinged base. Give it a little time to breathe or warm up; it seems to balance it. **88** —*S.H. (11/15/2006)*

Roche 2003 Estate Merlot (Carneros) $26. Rough and ready, with mocha, blackberry, and earthy tobacco flavors wrapped in firm, astringent tannins. Doesn't seem like an ager, so drink up. **84** —*S.H. (11/15/2006)*

Roche 2003 Estate Reserve Merlot (Carneros) $33. Picture-perfect Carneros Merlot, with rich cherry, cassis, cola, and spiced coffee flavors as well as a superb structure. You can almost taste the fog in the crisp acids and furry tannins. Finishes dry and long. **91** —*S.H. (11/15/2006)*

Roche 2003 Estate Syrah (Carneros) $26. Earthy and tannic. There's some cherry-berry fruit, but it's thin and buried under harder, tarter coffee, tobacco, dried herb, and alcohol tastes. Needs greater richness. **83** —*S.H. (11/15/2006)*

ROCHIOLI

Rochioli 1999 Estate Chardonnay (Russian River Valley) $30. At 2,523 cases, this is fabled grower Rochioli's largest-production Chardonnay. The bouquet sings with complex roasted nut, pineapple, citrus, toast, and banana aromas. Tart apple and anise flavors play off the sweet caramel and vanillin oak to create an elegant balance on the palate. Persistent fruit and smoky accents on the finish—it's hard to resist. Top Value. **91 Best Buy** (7/1/2001)

Rochioli 1998 Estate Chardonnay (Russian River Valley) $29. 89 (6/1/2000)

Rochioli 1997 Estate Chardonnay (Russian River Valley) $28. 90 (11/15/1999)

Rochioli 2001 Estate Grown Chardonnay (Russian River Valley) $37. Richer, riper, and bigger than in the past, the usual green apple flavors veer into well-ripened pears and even tropical fruits, with spicy oak all over the place. Dry and sleek in texture, the kind of wine that despite its opulence feels ultra-clean through the finish. Good for Rochioli for leaving all these fresh, young acids. **93** —S.H. (7/1/2003)

Rochioli 2000 Estate Grown Chardonnay (Russian River Valley) $37. Defines seamless in its perfect integration of oak and fruit—it's virtually impossible to tell where one leaves off and the other begins. Toasty, nutty notes combine with vibrant apple, pear, and citrus flavors for a winning combination. **90** —J.C. (9/1/2002)

Rochioli 2004 Pinot Noir (Russian River Valley) $47. For many wineries, this would be their top Pinot. For Rochioli, it's their basic bottling. Shows ripe cherry pie, root beer, cola, tea, spice, and what Michael Broadbent used to call beetroot flavors, yet is delicate and silky, almost weightless. Drink this yummy wine now. **93** —S.H. (11/1/2006)

Rochioli 2002 Pinot Noir (Russian River Valley) $40. Simple, dry, and friendly, with modest black cherry and vanilla flavors. Easy to drink, with a soft mouthfeel. **84** (11/1/2004)

Rochioli 2000 Pinot Noir (Russian River Valley) $40. Juicy fruit shines in this winning Pinot, and why not? It's from one of the Russian River Valley's most respected growers. Smoke swirls around cherry and blackberry flavors in a lovely pas-de-deux, enveloping yet never obscuring the fruit. The delicious chalky, smoked meat, and licorice finish is long. Drink now–2007. **90 Editors' Choice** (10/1/2002)

Rochioli 1999 Pinot Noir (Russian River Valley) $37. A stylish wine, and one that still has a few years in it until it peaks. The nose brings charred wood, leather, and smoky meat notes. The juicy, properly acidic palate dances, and overall the wine offers a fine sense of balance. **88** (10/1/2002)

Rochioli 2003 East Block Pinot Noir (Russian River Valley) $90. Lots of oak, vanilla, and char aromas, mingled with cherry jam, cocoa, and dusty spices. Very rich in cherries, oak, and spices. Dry with firm, dusty tannins. Finishes long, rich, and spicy. Full-bodied. Young, sappy, needs time. Best 2007 and beyond. **93 Cellar Selection** —S.H. (6/1/2005)

Rochioli 1999 East Block Pinot Noir (Russian River Valley) $NA. 14.2%. Pretty. Char-toast, allspice, five-spice, cola, tea, cocoa, dried cherry skin, pepper. In the mouth, a blast of sweet oak and cherry, but very dry. Rich, full-bodied, dry, sour cherry. Intricate. Fairly tannic. Sweet, cocoa-ey finish. Now–2010. **93** —S.H. (6/1/2005)

Rochioli 1997 East Block Pinot Noir (Russian River Valley) $NA. Very dry. Fairly tannic. Tea, cola, cherry flavors. Has a heaviness and lack of subtlety. Drink now. **84** —S.H. (6/1/2005)

Rochioli 1994 East Block Reserve Pinot Noir (Russian River Valley) $NA. Only 13 percent alcohol. Smells ripe and oaky. Red cherries, spices, root beer, cola. Touch of sweet beet. Nice balance of cherries and more herbal notes. Beautiful tannins, acids. **90** —S.H. (6/1/2005)

Rochioli 2001 Estate Grown Pinot Noir (Russian River Valley) $42. Even with its standard bottling, Rochioli rises above most other wineries' vineyard designates. It strikes just the right balance between the rich berry and cherry flavors and earthier ones of coffee, herbs, meat, and earth. **91** —S.H. (2/1/2004)

Rochioli 2000 River Block Pinot Noir (Russian River Valley) $55. Shares the same characteristics as West Block, but this one is undeniably thinned down, maybe because the vineyard is closer to the river. Supple tannins and refreshing acidity frame leather, earth, and tart cherry flavors. **89** —S.H. (2/1/2003)

Rochioli 2003 Three Corner Vineyard Pinot Noir (Russian River Valley) $65. Dusty, young, a bit raw. Oozes Chinese five-spice, earth, wood, berry, and oak aromas. Very fruity in the mouth, showing forward cherries and

cocoa: almost candied, but very dry. Sappy, full-bodied, rich, and jammy. Needs time. Drink 2006–2012. **93 Cellar Selection** —S.H. (6/1/2005)

Rochioli 1999 Three Corner Vineyard Pinot Noir (Russian River Valley) $NA. 13.5%. Very dry. Dusty. Tomato, cola, rhubarb, spice rub. Young. Sour cherry. Bone dry. Fairly big, tight, awkward now. Huge, angular. Needs a few years to soften and settle down. **92** —S.H. (6/1/2005)

Rochioli 1997 Three Corner Vineyard Pinot Noir (Russian River Valley) $NA. Smells oaky-beetrooty. Cherries, cocoa, nut, an aggressive, slightly vulgar, raw quality. Dusty. Not a great success. **84** —S.H. (6/1/2005)

Rochioli 1994 Three Corner Vineyard Reserve Pinot Noir (Russian River Valley) $NA. Turning leafy-foresty, very delicate. Subtle tea, clove, cinnamon, cherry, dusty, cedar, cocoa. Fresh. Lots of sweet fruit, cherries, balanced, silky, so supple and clean. Lots of rich dusty tannins. Bone dry. Complex, interesting. Now-2010. **94** —S.H. (6/1/2005)

Rochioli 2003 West Block Pinot Noir (Russian River Valley) $75. Shows aromas of cherries, dust, spices, and oak, with a twiggy, earthy note. Tastes very fruity, sappy, jammy, thick and full-bodied. Bone dry, youthful and tannic. Immature. Should begin to come together after 2006. **92 Cellar Selection** —S.H. (6/1/2005)

Rochioli 2000 West Block Pinot Noir (Russian River Valley) $65. Smells big and meaty, suggesting earth, mutton, tobacco, and anise, but there's also a burst of dark stone fruits, berries, and dark chocolate. In the mouth, it's gigantic yet balanced and harmonious. Massive flavors of perfectly ripened berries are offset by gorgeous acids and luscious tannins. **94 Editors' Choice** —S.H. (2/1/2003)

Rochioli 1999 West Block Pinot Noir (Russian River Valley) $NA. Dusty. Chinese black tea, blackstrap molasses, anise, allspice. Tons of spice rub, Chinese five-spice, a hint of cherry. Mouth: Fruity sweetness that quickly recedes behind a wall of tannins. Spicy. Dried cherry, sour cherry candy. Rich, big, intricate, nuanced. Now–2010. **91** —S.H. (6/1/2005)

Rochioli 1997 West Block Pinot Noir (Russian River Valley) $NA. Fairly tannic, herbal, pale. Very thin, transparent in flavor. Used to be "delicious" (Tom Rochioli) but past its prime. **84** —S.H. (6/1/2005)

Rochioli 1995 West Block Reserve Pinot Noir (Russian River Valley) $NA. Alcohol a modest 13%. Smells "dry," dusty-woody, briary. Bits and pieces of twigs, spices, anise, tomato, cola, rhubarb. Old Pinot, very dry and brittle. Some sweet cherries, sweet oak, vanilla, char. Delicate and refined, though big. Still some dusty tannins. Now–2008. **90** —S.H. (6/1/2005)

Rochioli 1994 West Block Reserve Pinot Noir (Russian River Valley) $NA. More herbal than Three Corner. Tomatoes, rhubarb, cola, not quite ripe. Anise, cocoa powder. Dry, brittle. Showing its age, but interesting and layered. **87** —S.H. (6/1/2005)

Rochioli 1992 West Block Reserve Pinot Noir (Russian River Valley) $NA. Officially 13.0, but probably higher. Clear, vibrant. Cherry, cigar box/cedar, sweet-sour sauce, cola, soy, earth. Very dry, some sweet fruit remains, sour cherry, coffee, spice. Smooth, supple, silky, with a long, fruity finish. Will soften and sweeten through 2010, but an acquired taste. **90** —S.H. (6/1/2005)

Rochioli 1998 Sauvignon Blanc (Russian River Valley) $22. 90 (11/1/1999)

Rochioli 2005 Sauvignon Blanc (Russian River Valley) $30. Most of the grapes are from the winery's original 1959 planting. It's a beautiful, refined Sauvignon Blanc, brimming with lemon and lime, freshly mowed green grass and tangy green apple flavors. Partial barrel fermentation adds a creamy complexity. The wine is totally dry and bright in acidity, but it's really the fruit that stars. **92 Editors' Choice** —S.H. (8/1/2006)

Rochioli 2004 Sauvignon Blanc (Russian River Valley) $29. Starts with rubbery, tar aromas, but they fade with time. But along the way there's a funky, sort of smoked ham note. Flavors of ginger and citrus are full and round, and they carry a honeyed accent. With that said, one reviewer was not a fan and found the wine far outside the parameters of "varietal correctness." **87** (7/1/2005)

Rochioli 2003 Sauvignon Blanc (Russian River Valley) $29. Another wonderful Rochioli Sauvignon, which always seems to have that extra something most other ones don't. You'll find the usual ripe citrus, fig, and melon, but it's extra deep, with the most wonderful balance of acidity. **90** —S.H. (12/1/2004)

Rochioli 2002 Sauvignon Blanc (Russian River Valley) $24. Whether it's the age of the vines, the unique warm-cool vineyard location, or Rochioli's deft touch, this is always one of the best California Sauvignons. Citrusy-grassy, complexed with fig, pear, and vanilla, and just the right touch of oak and cream from barrel fermentation. Rich, luxurious, crisp, and as complete as California Sauvignon Blanc gets. **92 Editors' Choice** —*S.H. (12/1/2003)*

Rochioli 2001 Sauvignon Blanc (Russian River Valley) $24. In this vintage, one of Sonoma's top SBs scores points in all the requisite areas. A tiny bit of talc softens the tropical fruit bouquet. More exotic fruit is on the palate, highlighted by firm edges and some citrus rind. A bit of banana sweetens the long, dry finish, leaving you with the right overall impression. **90 Editors' Choice** *(8/1/2002)*

ROCINANTE

Rocinante 2004 Palindrome Vineyard Syrah (Dry Creek Valley) $35. From a winery new to me comes this aspirational Syrah. It's new oaky, with robust but refined tannins and very ripe flavors of cherries, blackberries, and plums. There's an edge of raisins that testifies to the extreme heat of the vintage. The wine straddles an interesting line between rustic and classic, and is one to watch. **88** —*S.H. (12/31/2006)*

ROCK RABBIT

Rock Rabbit 2004 Sauvignon Blanc (Central Coast) $10. Here's a crisp, refreshing dry white that holds nothing back, despite the everyday price. It's packed with lemon and lime, green grass, ripe honeydew melon, and vanilla flavors that finish long and clean. **86 Best Buy** —*S.H. (12/1/2005)*

Rock Rabbit 2003 Syrah (Central Coast) $10. For ten bucks this is pretty good. Kind of simple and soft, but you'll find plenty of blackberry, blueberry, and cherry flavors, with a creamy, milk chocolatey taste. **84** —*S.H. (12/1/2005)*

Rock Rabbit 2002 Syrah (Central Coast) $10. Rock Rabbit is based in Sonoma County, but they specialize in Central Coast wines. This beautiful wine is definitely one of the greatest Syrah values you'll find. It's just bursting with juicy cherry, chocolate, plum, and peppery spice flavors, and is as lush and extravagant as anything out there. Sourced from Santa Barbara, Monterey, and Paso Robles, this Shiraz-style wine is spectacular. **89 Best Buy** —*S.H. (11/15/2004)*

ROCKBLOCK

Rockblock 2002 Carpenter Hill Vineyard Syrah (Rogue Valley) $40. One of several microproduction wines (50 cases of this bottling) from Rockblock, the Carpenter Hill Syrah offers up a lovely combination of dried spices and fresh blackberries couched in a silky texture. Velvety and extremely supple on the finish, giving a great sense of elegance. **90** *(9/1/2005)*

Rockblock 2001 Del Rio Vineyard Syrah (Rogue Valley) $40. This is Rockblock's big production Syrah, at 1,100 cases, and it's a beauty, boasting understated oak and ripe blackberry and plum flavors. As you might expect from a Pinot Noir maker (Rockblock is Domaine Serene's Rhône brand), the texture is silky and delicate. **89** *(9/1/2005)*

Rockblock 2000 Del Rio Vineyard Syrah (Rogue Valley) $40. Rockblock is a new brand launched by Domaine Serene to showcase Syrah. Full, lush, satiny fruit explodes across the palate, wrapped in stiff, smoky, but well-managed tannins. **90** —*P.G. (2/1/2004)*

Rockblock 2002 Seven Hills Vineyard Syrah (Walla Walla (WA)) $40. Ripe to near the point of overripeness, according to our tasters, with dark plum aromas and flavors that turn chocolatey. Tannins are supremely soft and creamy smooth, while the finish lingers delicately. **87** *(9/1/2005)*

Rockblock 2000 Seven Hills Vineyard Syrah (Walla Walla (OR)) $40. Though technically in Oregon, this well-known vineyard is most closely associated with the many Walla Walla (Washington) wineries that purchase its fruit. This is great juice, ripe and vibrant, with pretty, luscious blackberry and black cherry fruit, sweetly wrapped in cinnamon-spiced oak. **91** —*P.G. (2/1/2004)*

Rockblock 1999 Seven Hills Vineyard Syrah (Walla Walla (WA)) $40. Veers solidly away from most New World Syrahs in its tart berry flavors and lean texture, focusing on meat, smoke, tobacco, and pepper. Very complex, with charms that should unfurl gracefully over the next few years. **90** *(11/1/2001)*

ROCKING HORSE

Rocking Horse 2001 Garvey Family Vineyard Cabernet Sauvignon (Rutherford) $30. An average Cabernet made in an average way, with very ripe blackberry and chocolate flavors, melted tannins, and obvious oak. Finishes like a cup of cocoa. **84** —*S.H. (10/1/2005)*

Rocking Horse 2000 Last Call Cabernet Sauvignon (Napa Valley) $24. Opens with sulfury aromas that disturb the equilibrium, and tastes unbalanced, with sticky tannins and a medicinal finish despite well-ripened blackberry flavors. **82** —*S.H. (10/1/2005)*

Rocking Horse 2000 Merlot (Napa Valley) $20. Soft and simple, with blackberry and cocoa flavors and an oakiness that brings vanilla and char to the aftertaste. Finishes too sweet. **83** —*S.H. (10/1/2005)*

Rocking Horse 1998 Garvey Family Vineyard Merlot (Rutherford) $30. Strong espresso aromas give way to smooth mocha and vanilla cream on the palate. Supple and almost pillowy, this is a drink-me-now wine that doesn't pretend to be anything more than a superficial charmer. A hint of alcohol shows through on the coffee-tinged finish, so drink young. **85** —*J.C. (6/1/2001)*

Rocking Horse 2001 Zinfandel (Napa Valley) $18. Very dry, high enough in acids to create a tart mouthfeel, this is a balanced wine with earthy, berry flavors. It's not a show-stopper, but has subtle sophistication that won't overshadow carefully prepared foods. **87** —*S.H. (10/1/2005)*

Rocking Horse 1999 Zinfandel (Napa Valley) $20. Black fruit and oak run rampant from start to finish; acid's a little high in the mouth, and tart tannins dry out the long finish. A good but ordinary Zin, characterized by one taster as the "IKEA of wine." **86** —*D.T. (3/1/2002)*

Rocking Horse 1998 Zinfandel (Napa Valley) $18. Red berry, rhubarb, herb, and smoke aromas show in this lighter, claret-styled Zin. Good acidity supports its tart cherry flavors, and the herb note in the bouquet reprises on the finish, accompanied by an attractive pepperiness. Balanced and attractive, it will pair well with many foods. **87** *(3/1/2001)*

Rocking Horse 2001 Monte Rosso Vineyard Zinfandel (Sonoma County) $22. Black as night, and with an inviting aroma that suggests a just-baked blackberry tart. Smells sweet, drinks dry, soft, and tannic, with intense blackberry flavors and a peppery finish. **87** —*S.H. (10/1/2005)*

ROCKLAND

Rockland 2000 Petite Sirah (Napa Valley) $30. An exquisite Napa wine, filled with strong, rich flavors of blackberries, raspberries, orange peel, and cherries, as well as funkier notes of leather, soy, and smoke. Flashy and full-bodied but dry, with rich tannins and a long, spicy finish. **90** *(4/1/2003)*

ROCKLEDGE VINEYARDS

Rockledge Vineyards 2003 Cabernet Sauvignon (St. Helena) $25. With the '03, Rockledge returns to form with a ripe, lush, and balanced Cab that contains a drop of Petite Sirah. It's deliciously deep and long in blackberry pie filling, chocolate, green olive, and smoky oak flavors, in a voluptuous texture. **90** —*S.H. (12/31/2006)*

Rockledge Vineyards 2002 Cabernet Sauvignon (St. Helena) $32. Another wine made in the international style. There seems to be terroir here, but this Cab is so soft, fruity-sweet, and vague that it could be from anywhere. Lots of cherries, blackberries, and spicy plums. **84** —*S.H. (11/1/2005)*

Rockledge Vineyards 2001 Cabernet Sauvignon (St. Helena) $45. Quite sleek and elegant, with a fine-tuned core of richly textured flavors, redolent of cassis, blackberry, coffee, tar, herbs, anise, and toast. The tannins are firm but ripe, giving good structure to the wine, which tastes like Bordeaux in a great vintage. Long and lush on the finish. A good price for this kind of quality. **91** —*J.M. (8/1/2004)*

Rockledge Vineyards 1999 Reserve St. Helena Cabernet Sauvignon (Napa Valley) $50. A well-structured Cabernet, with complex layers of blackberry, cassis, chocolate, herb, coffee, and spice flavors. Tannins are firm and ripe with a good long finish and a tangy note at the end. A fine first release from this new winery. **90** —*J.M. (11/15/2002)*

Rockledge Vineyards 2003 The Rocks Cabernet Sauvignon (St. Helena) $45. More tannic than Rockledge's regular '03 Cab, this wine is also more concentrated in black currant fruit, and seems oakier, too. It has that elusive quality of importance, hard to define but so obvious in the mouth. Rich, luscious, and on the soft side, it's a gorgeous wine, drinkable now and with the balance to ride smoothly for ten years or longer. **93 Editors' Choice** —*S.H. (12/31/2006)*

Rockledge Vineyards 2002 The Rocks Cabernet Sauvignon (St. Helena) $49. This first wine of Rockledge has much more integrity than the regular '02. It shows the same forward cherry and blackberry flavors, but firmer tannins, resulting in a greater structure. It's not going anywhere, so drink now. **88** —*S.H. (11/1/2005)*

Rockledge Vineyards 2002 Primitivo (Napa Valley) $25. Interesting to compare this to Rockledge's '02 Zin, with which it has little in common. This is a ruder, more rustic wine in tannins. It's extracted and jammy in red berry fruit, and dry. **83** —*S.H. (11/1/2005)*

Rockledge Vineyards 2001 Primitivo (Napa Valley) $24. Somewhat floral up front, with a sleek, elegant mouthfeel. Silky smooth tannins frame a core of black cherry, coffee, herb, spice, anise, herb, and clove flavors. It's made in a classy style from Zinfandel's alter ego, Primitivo, which is just a clone of the quintessential California variety. **90** —*J.M. (8/1/2004)*

Rockledge Vineyards 2000 Primitivo (Napa Valley) $28. Rich, plush aromas lead off. The wine is smooth-textured and dense, with robust tannins that give good structure and staying power. Spicy black cherry, plum, chocolate and herb flavors are well integrated. Toasty oak frames the ensemble. Related to but different from this winery's Zinfandel. **90** —*J.M. (12/1/2002)*

Rockledge Vineyards 2002 Zinfandel (Napa Valley) $22. My oh my, this Zin is ripe. It's fully dry, but tastes as sweet as a cherry pie, drizzled with cassis and dusted with cocoa. Too soft, though. **84** —*S.H. (11/1/2005)*

Rockledge Vineyards 2001 Zinfandel (Napa Valley) $20. Kicks off with rich, dark black cherry, smoke, and spice notes. On the palate, it's got bright textured, almost brambly raspberry, anise, herb, and earth flavors. Finishes with a bit of a bite, but is fresh and interesting. Powdery tannins give it good structure. **88** —*J.M. (8/1/2004)*

Rockledge Vineyards 2000 Zinfandel (Napa Valley) $22. Plush and velvety, with a core of black cherry and herbs couched in firm, powdery tannins. Anise, chocolate, and coffee flavors finish nicely here. **88** —*J.M. (11/1/2002)*

Rockledge Vineyards 1999 Zinfandel (Napa Valley) $22. A lively wine, with a blend of forward, plush plum, licorice, chocolate, earth, and spice notes. Bright on the finish. **87** —*J.M. (11/1/2002)*

ROCKPILE

Rockpile 2004 Cemetary Vineyard Zinfandel (Rockpile) $35. I wanted to like this Zin, and while there are some good things, there are problems. The wine is very hot, with a chile pepper heat that comes from extremely high alcohol. That makes the underlying wild berry, coffee, and tobacco flavors hard to enjoy. From Mauritson, although it doesn't say so on the front label. **83** —*S.H. (12/15/2006)*

RODNEY STRONG

Rodney Strong 2000 Symmetry Meritage Cabernet Blend (Alexander Valley) $55. Smooth and polished, with a great, velvety mouthfeel, this balanced wine shows intense cassis flavors modulated with sweet herbs and toasty oak. It's really quite elegant now, and should hold through the decade. **91** —*S.H. (10/1/2005)*

Rodney Strong 1996 Cabernet Sauvignon (Sonoma County) $16. 86 —*L.W. (9/1/1999)*

Rodney Strong 2003 Cabernet Sauvignon (Sonoma County) $19. Rodney Strong has vineyards across the county, from cool to warm, and winemaker Rick Sayre is a master blender. This is a terrific wine at this price. It's rich and opulent in blackberry, cassis, cocoa, and sweet oak, with ripe tannins and a beautiful balance. At this enormous production level— nearly a quarter-million cases—this is a tremendous achievement. **90 Editors' Choice** —*S.H. (12/15/2006)*

Rodney Strong 2002 Cabernet Sauvignon (Sonoma County) $19. Juicy, flavorful, and just a bit raw, this dry wine offers up black currants, smoke, and vanilla, the classic recipe for California Cab. It has a wonderfully long, rich finish. **87** —*S.H. (11/1/2005)*

Rodney Strong 2001 Cabernet Sauvignon (Sonoma County) $18. Well-

ripened black currant and cherry fruit shows oaky, vanilla influences, in this dry, softly tannic wine. It has a polish and easy drinkability that make it fine now. **87** —*S.H. (12/31/2004)*

Rodney Strong 2000 Cabernet Sauvignon (Sonoma County) $18. A very nice Cabernet, and in its own way, classic Alexander Valley. Well-ripened black currant fruit is dry, with soft but lithe tannins and gentle acids. Despite the softness, the wine has a good, firm mouthfeel, and quite a bit of richness and depth. **90** —*S.H. (3/1/2003)*

Rodney Strong 1999 Cabernet Sauvignon (Sonoma County) $18. For an astounding 121,000 cases produced, this is surprisingly rich. Consider the vintage. If you couldn't make good Cab in '99, forget it. Ripe and fruity, with plenty of oak, it's a fine expression of Sonoma Cabernet. Just don't look for depth or ageabilty. **87** —*S.H. (11/15/2002)*

Rodney Strong 1998 Cabernet Sauvignon (Sonoma County) $16. Classic Northern California Cabernet at a fair price, which makes it a value these days. It begins with aromas of black currants, anise, and smoky, charry oak, and doesn't disappoint on the palate. There's plenty of polished blackberry and currant fruit, with a nice blast of oak. Very dry and clean. You notice how well it scours the mouth and stays crisp and elegant on the finish. **88** —*S.H. (5/1/2001)*

Rodney Strong 1997 Cabernet Sauvignon (Sonoma County) $16. 88 —*S.H. (12/15/2000)*

Rodney Strong 2001 Alden Vineyards Cabernet Sauvignon (Alexander Valley) $30. From a vineyard way high in the Mayacamas Mountains above Alexander Valley, this Cab has massive, palate-numbing tannins. But it's also humongous in blackberries and cherries, and is balanced. There's no reason it shouldn't do fabulous things in the cellar. Drink after 2008. **91 Cellar Selection** —*S.H. (11/1/2005)*

Rodney Strong 1999 Alden Vineyards Cabernet Sauvignon (Alexander Valley) $30. From vineyards quite high up in the eastern mountains, this wine is from stressed, low-yielding grapes. The blackberry and cassis flavors are concentrated and dense, and the tannins are tough and firm. Oak plays a supporting role. Rich foods, such as lamb or gongonzola cheese, will soften and sweeten it, but you're best off cellaring for a few years. **91** —*S.H. (11/15/2003)*

Rodney Strong 1998 Alden Vineyards Cabernet Sauvignon (Alexander Valley) $30. Simple and dull, a soft, flat wine lacking vibrancy. The flavors are herbal, tending toward tobacco and sage. But there are some tough tannins that kick in on the finish. **84** —*S.H. (11/15/2002)*

Rodney Strong 2001 Alexander's Crown Cabernet Sauvignon (Alexander Valley) $30. Drinkable now for its ripe, sweet tannins, balance, and pretty flavors of black cherries and cocoa. Perfectly dry, and leaves a pleasantly spicy aftertaste. **88** —*S.H. (8/1/2005)*

Rodney Strong 2000 Alexander's Crown Cabernet Sauvignon (Alexander Valley) $28. Rich and thoroughly enjoyable, brimming with black currant and cassis flavors and a balanced overlay of smoky, spicy oak. This pretty wine drinks very dry and smooth, and the tannins are just right. It is elegant from start to finish. Drink now. **90** —*S.H. (11/15/2003)*

Rodney Strong 1999 Alexander's Crown Cabernet Sauvignon (Alexander Valley) $28. From a vineyard at the southern end of the appellation, a soft, fruity and immensely likeable Cabernet. Don't let the accessibility fool you. The upfront berry-cherry flavors and rich texture are instantly likeable, but there's enough complexity and balance for the cellar. **92** —*S.H. (3/1/2003)*

Rodney Strong 1998 Alexander's Crown Vineyard Cabernet Sauvignon (Alexander Valley) $28. Of this winery's two new releases, the less expensive is better, because this usually fine release is from the infamous '98 vintage. It just can't overcome a basic thinness and wateriness, despite an obvious pedigree and plush oak. That said, it's a good wine. The '99 will undoubtedly be much better. **86** —*S.H. (8/1/2003)*

Rodney Strong 1997 Alexander's Crown Vineyard Cabernet Sauvignon (Northern Sonoma) $26. 90 *(9/1/2000)*

Rodney Strong 1996 Alexander's Crown Vineyard Cabernet Sauvignon (Northern Sonoma) $25. 86 *(12/31/1999)*

Rodney Strong 2001 Reserve Cabernet Sauvignon (Sonoma County) $40. A bit piquant, as if the blackberry and currant flavor is just beginning to enter a new phase in which older, dried fruit character emerges. It's an interesting phase, too, intermixed as it is with plenty of toasty, newish oak. This is a wine that could do interesting things over the next five years. **88** —*S.H. (12/1/2006)*

Rodney Strong 2000 Reserve Cabernet Sauvignon (Sonoma County) $40. Considerably more Cabernet-oriented than Rod Strong's 2000 Meritage, this wine shows pronounced cassis and black currant flavors, as well as some pretty powerful tannins. It's also very oaky. Seems best to let it mellow for a good five years. **90** —*S.H. (10/1/2005)*

Rodney Strong 1999 Reserve Cabernet Sauvignon (Sonoma County) $40. If you compare this winery's reserve bottling with its Alden release, the latter, despite its tannins, is more drinkable. This reserve is very closed, with strong, numbing tannins. The flavors are minty and you have to search for any fruit. It's interesting, but aging this wine is a big gamble. **86** —*S.H. (11/15/2003)*

Rodney Strong 1997 Reserve Cabernet Sauvignon (Northern Sonoma) $40. This fabulous vintage offered all sorts of possibilities. The winery chose an austere route. Tightly controlled blackberry and cassis notes are wrapped in oak, and the wine is very dry. It may age. If you drink it now, do so with the richest beef or lamb you can find. **87** —*S.H. (9/1/2002)*

Rodney Strong 1996 Reserve Cabernet Sauvignon (Northern Sonoma) $40. **92** *(9/1/2000)*

Rodney Strong 1995 Reserve Cabernet Sauvignon (Northern Sonoma) $40. **89** *(11/1/1999)*

Rodney Strong 1999 Symmetry Cabernet Sauvignon (Alexander Valley) $55. From Rodney Strong, an oaky, ripe wine made in the international Cabernet style. It's strong and extracted in fruit, and drenched with woody char and vanilla. Some tough tannins lurk throughout. **85** —*S.H. (11/15/2004)*

Rodney Strong 2004 Chardonnay (Sonoma County) $15. Straddles the line between an earthy herbaceousness and riper notes of peaches and apples. Either way, this is a balanced, crisp young wine, with a creamy texture and a very dry finish. **85** —*S.H. (4/1/2006)*

Rodney Strong 2003 Chardonnay (Chalk Hill) $19. A nice, easy Chard with decent fruit, a coating of oak, and good acidity. Turns a little thin toward the end, though. **84** —*S.H. (10/1/2005)*

Rodney Strong 2003 Chardonnay (Sonoma County) $15. Here's a fine, flavorful Chard. It's got jazzy flavors of white peaches, pineapples, vanilla custard, buttered toast, and Asian spices, wrapped in a rich, creamy texture. **89** —*S.H. (11/1/2005)*

Rodney Strong 2002 Chardonnay (Sonoma County) $18. Just what the doctor ordered in a rich Chard. It's lavish in ripe peach, tropical fruit. and vanilla flavors, with the sweetness of a fresh-baked buttery biscuit. The creamy texture carries spice flavors through a long finish. **90 Editors' Choice** —*S.H. (6/1/2004)*

Rodney Strong 2002 Chardonnay (Chalk Hill) $18. Shows some nicely ripened pear and peach flavors that are enriched with sweet vanillins and toasty oak and a hit of yeasty lees. A firm spine of acidity provides cleanliness and balance to this tasty Chard. **88** —*S.H. (11/15/2004)*

Rodney Strong 2001 Chardonnay (Sonoma County) $14. This is a nice, flavorful wine with lots of peach, pear, and apple tastes, and a round, creamy mouthfeel. It's a bit soft, but offers up lots to like at a gentle price. **85** —*S.H. (6/1/2003)*

Rodney Strong 1999 Chardonnay (Sonoma County) $14. **86** —*S.H. (11/15/2000)*

Rodney Strong 1999 Chardonnay (Chalk Hill) $18. Super-ripe grapes put their shoulder to the wheel for a highly extracted wine characterized by masses of peach and pear flavors. Oak contributes added spice, vanilla, and smoke. It's as plush as could be, but it's also soft and a bit flabby. An impression of sweetness lingers in the finish. **87** —*S.H. (5/1/2001)*

Rodney Strong 2004 Chalk Hill Chardonnay (Sonoma County) $19. Immediately likeable for its direct, ripe flavors of candied peaches, kiwis, limes, and pineapples. It has just the right acidity and a creamy texture. **86** —*S.H. (12/1/2006)*

Rodney Strong 2000 Chalk Hill Chardonnay (Sonoma County) $18. The grapes got ripe enough to veer into mangoes and guavas and other tropical fruits, and barrel fermentation adds spicy notes a round, creamy

mouthfeel. It's a classic New World Chard. It's also basically simple, well-made. and clean, but Johnny-one-note, with a touch of citrus acids in the finish. **85** —*S.H. (5/1/2002)*

Rodney Strong 1998 Chalk Hill Chardonnay (Chalk Hill) $16. **87** *(6/1/2000)*

Rodney Strong 1997 Chalk Hill Chardonnay (Sonoma County) $14. **88** *(11/15/1999)*

Rodney Strong 1998 Chalk Hill Vineyard Reserve Chardonnay (Northern Sonoma) $30. This is an impressive bottling with complex caramel, toasted nut, and tropical fruit aromas. It's big bodied and coats the mouth with rich butterscotch, banana, apple, and toasty oak flavors. A touch short on acid, it could use bit more backbone, but it's still big on toasty style. Its long, satisfying finish is an oak lover's paradise. **89** *(7/1/2001)*

Rodney Strong 1999 Chalk Hill Vineyard Reseve Chardonnay (Sonoma County) $30. Extremely well-oaked, this wine has flavors of apples and citrus fruits that veer into peaches. It's a big, fleshy wine, a bit of a bruiser that trades elegance for sheer power. **87** —*S.H. (12/15/2002)*

Rodney Strong 2003 Reserve Chardonnay (Chalk Hill) $30. This very dry wine is earthy, with a dusty, tannic flavor of hazelnut skin and a slight bitterness, but it rewards with deeper tastes of white peach, and a rich overlay of oak. **85** —*S.H. (11/1/2005)*

Rodney Strong 1997 Reserve Chalk Hill Vineyard Chardonnay (Northern Sonoma) $30. **92** —*S.H. (11/1/1999)*

Rodney Strong 1997 Symmetry Meritage (Alexander Valley) $55. This flamboyant wine won't let down fans of expensive, good vintage North Coast Cabs. It has it all, starting with almost aggressive new oak. If you're looking for flavor, you'll find it in the extracted blackberry and cassis fruit. The tannins are considerable. If it has a fault, it's softness. Drink within the next few years. **91** —*S.H. (7/1/2002)*

Rodney Strong 2001 Symmetry Red Wine Meritage (Alexander Valley) $55. A bit sharp in acids, but the wine nonetheless has attractive Cabernet flavor, ripe tannins, and finishes with a dried herb taste. Seems like it was picked early. Try decanting for an hour or so before serving. **85** —*S.H. (12/15/2006)*

Rodney Strong 2002 Merlot (Sonoma County) $19. A fine, ripe Merlot from a dependable producer, this is totally dry, with polished cassis, coffee, green olive, and subtle oak notes. It shows a nice balance of modest alcohol and rich, intricate tannins. **87** —*S.H. (11/15/2006)*

Rodney Strong 2001 Merlot (Sonoma County) $18. Smooth, sophisticated, and fancy tasting with its balance of plummy, blackberry fruit, rich tannins, and alcohol. Drinks fully dry, with good acidity. **87** —*S.H. (5/1/2005)*

Rodney Strong 2000 Merlot (Alexander Valley) $26. A polished, soft Merlot with some lovely flavors and a discrete layer of oak. You'll find cherry, cocoa, and herb flavors and gentle tannins. **87** —*S.H. (12/31/2004)*

Rodney Strong 1999 Merlot (Sonoma County) $18. Winemaker Rick Sayer has found a nice balance between fruity, blackberry notes and elements of green olives. In the mouth, this yin-yang creates complexity and interest. Ultrasmooth tannins and soft acidity make it velvety. **89** —*S.H. (7/1/2002)*

Rodney Strong 1999 Merlot (Alexander Valley) $26. Really lovely in texture, with the plushest, most velvety tannins. They're thick, but sweet and dusty. Decant it for a few hours, to give the cherry and blackberry flavors a chance to develop. **87** —*S.H. (5/1/2004)*

Rodney Strong 1997 Merlot (Sonoma County) $16. **88** —*S.H. (11/15/2000)*

Rodney Strong 1998 Estate Vineyards Merlot (Alexander Valley) $26. At four-plus years, the tannins are resolved, although far from absent. Acidity is also high. Finally the wine is coming around, with spicy plum and cassis flavors, but it is teetering on the verge of old age already, and has an edge of senility. **85** —*S.H. (8/1/2003)*

Rodney Strong 2004 Pinot Noir (Russian River Valley) $19. Lovely, a Pinot that doesn't slap you silly with extract, just flatters with sensuous pleasure. It's a light-colored wine, with a delicately silky texture framing cherry, cranberry, cola, and tea flavors, and is quite dry. Easy to find, with 12,000 cases produced. **88** —*S.H. (11/1/2006)*

Rodney Strong 2002 Pinot Noir (Russian River Valley) $19. There's a dividing line between Pinots that are good and simple and those that are fabulously complex. This delightfully drinkable wine is right in the middle. As easy as it is, it possesses layers of fruit and minerals, and is thoroughly dry and balanced. **89** —*S.H. (8/1/2005)*

Rodney Strong 2000 Pinot Noir (Russian River Valley) $18. Coffee and cinnamon notes show atop vague cherry flavors. But in this light wine, the wood wins. Smoke and cedar prevail from start to close, and it finishes tart with charcoal and black coffee notes. This is oak in excess without a solid fruit presence to support it. **83** *(10/1/2002)*

Rodney Strong 1997 Estate Bottled Pinot Noir (Russian River Valley). **86** *(12/15/1999)*

Rodney Strong 2003 Estate Vineyards Pinot Noir (Russian River Valley) $19. Thin in flavor, tart in acids, this wine struggles to find its fruit, which barely breaks into cola and red cherries. It's dry, with sandpapery tannins. **83** —*S.H. (12/31/2005)*

Rodney Strong 2003 Jane's Vineyard Reserve Pinot Noir (Russian River Valley) $35. Softly fruity, with ripe cherry, raspberry, cola, rhubarb pie, pomegranate, cola, vanilla, and toast flavors all wrapped in a silky texture. This is a Pinot of great charm. Drink now. **88** —*S.H. (12/1/2006)*

Rodney Strong 2002 Jane's Vineyard Reserve Pinot Noir (Russian River Valley) $35. Simple and fruity, with one-dimensional cherry, cola, and coffee flavors that drink dry and silky, with crisp acidity. The finish turns tart in dusty tannins. **84** —*S.H. (12/31/2005)*

Rodney Strong 1999 Reserve Pinot Noir (Russian River Valley) $30. Wears a toasty mantle of smoke, meat, and burnt marshmallow. Yet we found the dark cherry and tart plum fruit core to be strong enough to weather its oak. The wine's polished rusticity has great appeal, with earthy, dusty tannins, pepper, and cola accents. Drink now through 2007. **90 Editors' Choice** *(10/1/2002)*

Rodney Strong 1998 Reserve Pinot Noir (Northern Sonoma) $30. Capture's Pinot's delicate side, with smoky raspberry and vanilla notes and traces of tomato, rhubarb, and tea. The tannins are delicate with soft acidity. A certain earthiness in the aroma and finish suggests mid-term cellaring. **87** —*S.H. (12/15/2001)*

Rodney Strong 1999 Russian River Valley Pinot Noir (Russian River Valley) $18. **81** *(10/1/2002)*

Rodney Strong 2005 Charlotte's Home Sauvignon Blanc (Sonoma County) $14. This wine has been pretty consistent over the years, a dry, crisp sipper, modest in citrus, lemongrass, and spice flavors. It's a good cocktail drink, or for picnics and barbecues. **85** —*S.H. (12/15/2006)*

Rodney Strong 2002 Charlotte's Home Sauvignon Blanc (Sonoma Valley) $12. An awfully nice white wine made even more attractive by its value price. Shows cool-climate notes of grass and citrus, but the blend includes grapes from warmer areas that contribute fig and peach. The result is a complex, dry, and crisp sipper that leaves the palate refreshed. **87** —*S.H. (12/31/2003)*

Rodney Strong 1998 Charlotte's Home Estate Bottle Sauvignon Blanc (Northern Sonoma) $10. Clean and crisp with grapefruit, lime, and slate on the nose. There's apparent oak but it's in balance here with the melon, fig, and almond flavors. Balances sweet and creamy qualities with tanginess. A very nice example. **87** —*M.M. (9/1/2003)*

Rodney Strong 2001 Charlotte's Home Vineyard Sauvignon Blanc (Sonoma County) $12. Tutti-fruity S. Blanc here, with figgy-apple flavors and a dollop of sugar. Very clean and bright, and good acidity balances out the sweetness. This polished wine will be good by itself, or with lamb or salmon with chutney. **86** —*S.H. (9/1/2003)*

Rodney Strong 2003 Charlotte's Home Sauvignon Blanc (Sonoma County) $12. A nice, easy-drinking white wine that appeals for its ripe, fruity flavors and crisp acids. It's a little on the sweet side, and clean in the finish. **84** —*S.H. (12/31/2004)*

Rodney Strong 2004 Charlotte's Home Sauvignon Blanc (Sonoma County) $14. Clean and simple, this is a dry wine with refreshingly tart flavors of lemons, limes, grapefuits, and figs. It's a very pleasant sipper and would work well as a cocktail wine. **85** —*S.H. (3/1/2006)*

Rodney Strong 2003 Knotty Vines Zinfandel (Sonoma County) $19. Balanced and elegant, yet with all the briary, wild character of Zin, this wine, a blend of Russian River and Alexander Valley, captures the spirit

of Sonoma Zin. It's nice and dry and balanced, with polished blackberry, blueberry, mocha, and spice flavors. **90** —*S.H. (11/1/2006)*

Rodney Strong 1999 Knotty Vines Zinfandel (Northern Sonoma) $18. Alexander and Russian River Valley fruit contributed to this dry wine, which is distinctively Zinfandel in its wild briary aromas and flavors. There's a peppery note, and it's bone-dry. It's the perfect wine for the barbecue or the tailgate party. **86** —*S.H. (9/1/2002)*

Rodney Strong 1998 Knotty Vines Zinfandel (Northern Sonoma) $18. This lavishly oaked, opaque Zinfandel sports a dense nose of blackberry with pronounced toasty and menthol shadings. The mouthfeel is full and smooth, there's dark fruit and plenty of espresso, bitter chocolate, and tar on the palate and finish, with tannins to lose on the back end. The wine may open up and the fruit ascend more in a year; lovers of heavy toast can eagerly drink it up now. **85** *(3/1/2001)*

Rodney Strong 1997 Old Vines Zinfandel (Sonoma County) $18. Old vines from Russian River and Alexander valleys go into this spicy, briary, gamy Zin. There's a dark undercurrent of tar, pipe tobacco, and smoke that runs through the finish. The fruit is subsumed to clove and tobacco flavors; best with strongly spiced grilled foods. **87** —*P.G. (3/1/2001)*

ROEDERER ESTATE

Roederer Estate 1999 L'Ermitage Champagne Blend (Anderson Valley) $45. Extraordinarily fine for its smoothness and finesse, and the way the wine glides over the palate with a yeasty creaminess that turns smoky and spicy on the finish. The dosage stands out, yet this bubbly is also very acidic now. It should age well for at least 10 years. **94** —*S.H. (6/1/2005)*

Roederer Estate 1998 L'Ermitage Champagne Blend (Anderson Valley) $45. Among the top sparklers in California, the wine this year is even more smooth and polished. It's positively French in its classic structure and elegance. Feels ultra-refined in the mouth, with subtle flavors of dough, smoke, and fruit. **93** —*S.H. (12/31/2004)*

Roederer Estate 1997 L'Ermitage Champagne Blend (Anderson Valley) $46. This half-and-half blend of Pinot Noir and Chardonnay is often referred to as California's best. This year, it's very dry, with nuanced flavors of citrus, peach, and yeast. But it feels a little rough on the palate. This youthful scour should soften in a few years. **90** —*S.H. (12/1/2002)*

Roederer Estate 1996 L'Ermitage Champagne Blend (Anderson Valley) $42. A great sparkling wine, one of the best from California, it has the classic structure, harmony, and finesse of all but the best Champagnes. Light as a feather, this Brut has delicate flavors and is very dry. Its youthful vigor suggests aging until 2003. **93** —*S.H. (12/15/2001)*

Roederer Estate 1994 L'Ermitage Champagne Blend (Anderson Valley) $43. **88** *(12/31/2000)*

Roederer Estate 1993 L'Ermitage Champagne Blend (Mendocino) $38. **92** —*E.M. (11/15/1999)*

Roederer Estate NV Brut Sparkling Blend (Anderson Valley) $22. A pretty wine, almost flamboyant with ripe flavors of raspberries, strawberries, citrus, brioche, and smoke, but so controlled by its acidity that it's balanced. It's a bit on the sweet side for a Brut, and finishes with a lemony tartness. **87** —*S.H. (12/1/2003)*

Roederer Estate NV Brut Sparkling Blend (Anderson Valley) $23. Shares many of the same qualities as Roederer's vintage Brut, which is one of California's best. It's crisp and elegant and delicately flavored, with a rich yeasty edge, but it's a little too sweet in the dosage. **86** —*S.H. (6/1/2006)*

Roederer Estate NV Brut Rosé Sparkling Blend (Anderson Valley) $27. A lovely, blush-colored bubbly, with strong aromas and flavors and a full, rich body. Citrus, rose petal, strawberry, vanilla, yeast, and toast flavors mingle in a crisp, dry wine that has a very long, fruity finish. **87** —*S.H. (6/1/2006)*

Roederer Estate 1999 L'Ermitage Rosé Sparkling Blend (Anderson Valley) $72. Much more robust and full-bodied than the L'Ermitage Brut, but still elegant and fine. Offers yeast, smoke, and vanilla-tinged strawberry flavors, in a slightly rugged texture. Age through the end of the decade. **93** —*S.H. (6/1/2005)*

ROESSLER

Roessler 2004 Dutton Ranch Pinot Noir (Russian River Valley) $38. Smells herbal and minty, which is strange given the vintage's heat, and tastes earthy, too, with oregano and barely ripe cherry flavors. Turns dry and crisp on the finish. Consider this an elegant style. **85** —*S.H. (10/1/2006)*

RONAN

Ronan 2003 Lakeview Vineyards Reserve Cabernet Franc (Monterey County) $24. Clumsy, with a harsh mouthfeel and a sugary edge to the cherry flavors. **81** —*S.H. (12/31/2005)*

Ronan 2003 Lakeview Vineyards Cabernet Sauvignon (Monterey County) $24. Rough, tannic, and common, with herbal-earthy berry flavors and an astringent finish. **83** —*S.H. (12/31/2005)*

Ronan 2003 Lakeview Vineyards Petite Sirah (Monterey County) $26. Tannic and acidic, this wine tastes like it could have used a couple extra days of hang time in order to develop more fruitiness and sugar. The blackberry and coffee flavors have a green, peppery edge. Drink now. **83** —*S.H. (12/31/2005)*

Ronan 2003 Lakeview Vineyards Zinfandel (Monterey County) $18. Light in color, light in the mouth and softly textured, this Zin has a caramelized sugar taste to the berry fruit flavors. It's an easy drinking, everyday sort of wine. **84** —*S.H. (12/31/2005)*

ROSA D'ORO

Rosa d'Oro 2001 Barbera (Lake County) $17. Still a tough, bitter wine at 4 years, with a slightly sweet finish. Not going anywhere. **82** —*S.H. (5/1/2005)*

Rosa d'Oro 2001 Primitivo (Lake County) $18. Odd and medicinal, with a harsh, burnt taste. **81** —*S.H. (5/1/2005)*

Rosa d'Oro 2002 Syrah (Lake County) $16. A little too sweet, too rustic, and too soft for a higher score. There are also notes of over-ripeness. **82** —*S.H. (5/1/2005)*

ROSENBLUM

Rosenblum 2001 Gallagher Ranch Black Muscat (California) $18. A plummy, semi-sweet dark red wine that could stand a bit of a chill in the fridge. It has a nice chocolatey edge that would be a good partner with dark chocolate desserts. Finishes clean and with good acidity. **85** —*S.H. (8/1/2003)*

Rosenblum 2001 Holbrook Mitchell Trio Bordeaux Blend (Napa Valley) $36. A Bordeaux blend and a very good one, with plush black currant, cherry, and smoky flavors grounded in earthier tobacco and herbs. The tannins are rich and firm. This classy wine exudes pleasure and is best in its youth. **92 Editors' Choice** —*S.H. (10/3/2004)*

Rosenblum 2002 Holbrook Mitchell Trio Red Wine Bordeaux Blend (Napa Valley) $32. A blend of Merlot and Cabernets Sauvignon and Franc, this is a big, exuberantly ripe, hands-on wine. It's like a puppy that jumps all over you with affection. Stuffed with ripe blackberry, blueberry, and red cherry fruit, it's a happy wine, but not a particularly complex or ageable one. **86** —*S.H. (3/1/2006)*

Rosenblum 2000 Holbrook Mitchell Trio Red Wine Cabernet Blend (Napa Valley) $44. A trio of Cabs Sauvignon and Franc and Merlot, from a vineyard near Yountville. Very ripe, and shows classic cassis, black currant, and olive flavors, spiced up with sweet, smoky oak. Rich, refined, and pure. A first-class wine for tonight or for the cellar. **92** —*S.H. (5/1/2003)*

Rosenblum 2003 Kenefick Vineyard Cabernet Franc (Napa Valley) $30. Made in the classic Rosenblum style, which is late-picked and superripe in fruit. Imagine a slice of cherry pie washed down with a chocolate brownie. Yet the wine is dry. The alcohol is very high, with a hot finish, but balanced in its own way. **87** —*S.H. (4/1/2006)*

Rosenblum 2002 Yates Ranch Cabernet Franc (Napa Valley) $28. Super ripe in cassis and chocolate, almost decadently soft and gooey, and fully dry, without too much alcohol. Good but ultimately simple, like a sauce you'd pour over ice cream or cake. **86** —*S.H. (12/31/2004)*

Rosenblum 2001 Yates Ranch Cabernet Franc (Napa Valley) $28. Yummy! This will titillate your taste buds with its rich flavors of cherries, pomegranates, and chocolatey herbs. Has a soft, gentle mouthfeel with just enough acids and tannins to keep it lively. Try with roast chicken, calf's liver, or a smoky ham. **88** —*S.H. (4/1/2004)*

Rosenblum 2000 CRS Yates Ranch Reserve Cabernet Sauvignon (Mount Veeder) $25. This flagship Rosenblum wine does not disappoint, with its expressive black currant and cassis aromas and flavors. The overlay of toasted oak adds a sweet vanilla edge. Softly textured, with a bright spine of acidity that keeps it fresh. **92** —*S.H. (2/1/2004)*

Rosenblum 1997 Holbrook Mitchell Trio Cabernet Sauvignon (Napa Valley) $30. 90 *(11/1/2000)*

Rosenblum 1997 Reserve Cabernet Sauvignon (Napa Valley) $45. Clean and nice upfront, with blackberry aromas and sweet vanilla. A lot of heft to the palate, and plenty of cassis flavor and tobacco nuance on the finish. Oak rears up on the finish. Needs some time. **91** *(11/1/2000)*

Rosenblum 1999 Yates Ranch Reserve Cabernet Sauvignon (Mount Veeder) $59. This is a special wine, clearly mountainous in origin. The fruit is condensed and intense. It could not be riper and still be dry and balanced. Flavors range from blackberries to chocolate. It's drinkable now, if big tannins don't bother you. Best with well-marbled beef, or with chocolatey desserts. **91** —*S.H. (3/1/2003)*

Rosenblum 1998 Chardonnay (Edna Valley) $19. 87 *(6/1/2000)*

Rosenblum 2002 Lone Oak Vineyard Chardonnay (Russian River Valley) $25. So pectin-ripe and oaky it's gooey-sweet, like a creamy dessert. Mango, papaya, pear, vanilla, buttered toast, the works. Needs elegance and flair, though. **86** —*S.H. (12/31/2004)*

Rosenblum 2000 Lone Oak Vineyard Chardonnay (Russian River Valley) $35. Full-bodied and mouthfilling, a big wine with green apple and pear flavors and overtones of citrus. Oak and lees are subtle and balanced. The finish has a rich spiciness. **86** —*S.H. (5/1/2003)*

Rosenblum 2001 Lone Oak Vineyard Reserve Chardonnay (Russian River Valley) $25. Don't look for that deft, delicate touch here. This is a late-picked, extracted wine stuffed with tropical fruit flavors and lots of oak. A bit over the top, in Rosenblum fashion, but definitely with a personality and style all its own. **87** —*S.H. (12/1/2003)*

Rosenblum 1998 Lone Oak Vineyard Reserve Chardonnay (Russian River Valley) $24. 88 *(6/1/2000)*

Rosenblum 2002 Napa Valley Select Chardonnay (Napa Valley) $12. Weak and watery, with oak dominating the slight peach and citrus flavors. **83** —*S.H. (12/31/2004)*

Rosenblum 2001 Napa Valley Select Chardonnay (Napa Valley) $14. Middle of the road stuff. Some nice peach, citrus, and apple flavors, a bit of oak, and dry. Hard to find anything in particular to praise or blame, just good clean Chardonnay. **85** —*S.H. (6/1/2003)*

Rosenblum 2001 RustRidge Chardonnay (Napa Valley) $22. A big, somewhat clumsy wine. Filled with jammystone fruit flavors, such as peaches and pears, and lots of oak, in a thick, soft texture. Lots of bells and whistles that don't quite come together. **84** —*S.H. (12/1/2003)*

Rosenblum 2000 RustRidge Vineyard Chardonnay (Napa Valley) $30. Dark and jammy, a big, youthful wine brimming with blackberry and other thorny berry flavors. Drinks full and rich in the mouth, with sharp acidity that creates some bitterness. Tame this puppy with at least a year or two of cellaring. **87** —*S.H. (9/1/2003)*

Rosenblum 2003 Marsanne (Dry Creek Valley) $18. Golden and extracted. Butter-sautéed bananas, intense tangerine and peach and pineapple custard and vanilla are among the flavors. Good acidity, but so sweet and delicious. **90 Editors' Choice** —*S.H. (10/1/2005)*

Rosenblum 2001 Marsanne (Dry Creek Valley) $15. An unusual and distinctive Rhône white. It has the weight and texture of a good Chardonnay, with flavors that ping-pong between flamboyant mango and guava, and crisper notes of ripe green apples. The creamy texture is rich and unctuous. **89** —*S.H. (2/1/2004)*

Rosenblum 2000 Marsanne (Dry Creek Valley) $28. Strongly fruity, packed with so much tree fruit and wildflower flavor it will swamp many foods. In fact, it's over the top with the relentless flood of peach, apricot, pear, honeysuckle, lemon sherbert, and vanilla flavors. Fortunately, the wine is fully dry. May be best enjoyed on its own as a cocktail wine. **85** —*S.H. (3/1/2003)*

Rosenblum 2002 Lone Oak Vineyard Merlot (Russian River Valley) $30. Ripe, juicy, and balanced, with satisfying blackberry, black cherry, coffee, and oaky vanilla flavors wrapped in smooth tannins. This polished wine is supple and elegant through the finish. **89** —*S.H. (12/31/2004)*

Rosenblum 2001 Lone Oak Vineyard Merlot (Russian River Valley) $21. Made in Kent Rosenblum's inimitable style, late picked until the grapes are high in sugar and flavor. The resulting wine gives an explosion of black raspberry, cherry, tobacco, and spice flavors that are rich in fruity sweetness. Lush tannins and a nice bite of acidity provide structure and balance. Best with big foods, especially barbecue. **90** —*S.H. (5/1/2004)*

Rosenblum 1998 Lone Oak Vineyard Merlot (Russian River Valley) $18. Bright berries are all dressed up in cedary, pencil-like oak and kissed with velvety black tea and creamy chocolate notes that linger through the finish. Closes a bit lean, probably a function of the less-than-stellar vintage, but a solid effort. **87** —*J.C. (6/1/2004)*

Rosenblum 2000 Mountain Selection Merlot (Napa Valley) $30. This is a very big, full-bodied Merlot that's as ripe as grapes got in this vintage. Blackberry and plum flavors are wedded to violets and sweet licorice, wrapped in dry tannins. Acids are on the soft side. **86** —*S.H. (12/2/2003)*

Rosenblum 1997 Oakville Merlot (Napa Valley) $14. 85 *(11/15/1999)*

Rosenblum 2001 Continente Vineyard Mourvèdre (San Francisco Bay) $16. Big, rich, and with a full, chalky mouthfeel, a well-ripened wine stuffed with flavors of cherries, boysenberries, plums, and chocolate, with raisiny notes. Dry, but so fruity, it seems almost sweet. **85** —*S.H. (5/1/2003)*

Rosenblum 2003 Old Vines Mourvèdre (San Francisco Bay) $25. Made in the Rosenblum manner, which is soft and gooey in chocolatey fruit. In this case, the wine is vast in red cherry flavors, with sweet, smoky pie crust and vanilla. It's high in alcohol. Depending on how you look at it, it's either a vinous triumph or an eccentricity. **88** —*S.H. (4/1/2006)*

Rosenblum 2000 Muscat de Glacier Muscat (California) $22. Made from three different Muscat varieties, Alexandria, Canelli, and Blanc, this wine is fantastically sweet, with a residual sugar of nearly 18 percent. It has flavors of apricots and peaches and high enough acidity to balance, and is very clean and good. **90** —*S.H. (9/1/2003)*

Rosenblum 2004 Heritage Clones Petite Sirah (San Francisco Bay) $20. On the off-dry side of the fence, this zaftig wine has gigantic flavors of blackberry jam, cassis-laced cola, raspberry tart, and smoke. It's hot in alcohol, but the heat expresses itself as a white peppery, nutmeggy spice that seasons the fruit. **87** —*S.H. (11/15/2006)*

Rosenblum 2003 Heritage Clones Petite Sirah (San Francisco Bay) $20. High in alcohol, with a hot mouthfeel, this wine has caramel and raisin aromas. It turns dry and tannic in the mouth. **82** —*S.H. (11/15/2005)*

Rosenblum 2004 Pickett Road Petite Sirah (Napa Valley) $35. Here's an industrial strength Petite Sirah, from vineyards in the hotter, northern part of the valley. It's a bold, powerful wine that slams the palate with blackberry marmalade and chocolate flavors that coat the mouth and last for a long time. For all that, this only-in-California wine is fully dry. Be warned, the alcohol is 16%. **90** —*S.H. (11/1/2006)*

Rosenblum 2002 Pickett Road Petite Sirah (Napa Valley) $24. As balanced and impressive as a fine Napa Cabernet, with its sweet tannins, velvety texture, and overall quality. The only difference is in the flavors. Here, you get cassis, cherries, chocolate, and that distinctive brambly pepperiness that Zin owns. **92** —*S.H. (12/15/2004)*

Rosenblum 2001 Pickett Road Petite Sirah (Napa Valley) $22. There are few wines that pour as dark as a young Pet. This massive, extracted wine is filled with flavors of plums, blackberries, herbs, and unsweetened chocolate. The tannins are considerable, but they're supposed to be. Drink it with rich meats. It will also age for a very long time—maybe forever. **90** —*S.H. (12/31/2003)*

Rosenblum 2000 Pickett Road Petite Sirah (Napa Valley) $28. Dark and incredibly rich, a classic California "Pet" brimming with plum and blackberry flavors. Completely dry, with lush, complex tannins and a voluptuous texture. Like a sexy dessert wine, but dry. **90** —*S.H. (9/1/2003)*

Rosenblum 2004 Rockpile Road Vineyard Petite Sirah (Rockpile) $45. Kent Rosenblum's customers can't get enough of this small-production wine, and it's not hard to tell why. It's a high-alcohol, double-whammy punch of a wine. Dark, dry, soft, and glyceriney, with enormously deep blackberry, blueberry, spicy rum, chocolate, and coffee flavors that go on

and on. **93 Editors' Choice** —*S.H. (12/31/2006)*

Rosenblum 2002 Rockpile Road Vineyard Petite Sirah (Dry Creek Valley) $34. Comes as close as Petite Sirah can to elegance and world-class finesse. It's big in alcohol, but the tannins are soft and lush, and you certainly can't complain about the cassis and mocha flavors. Don't bother aging it. The youthful decadence will never be better. **91** —*S.H. (12/15/2004)*

Rosenblum 2001 Rockpile Road Vineyard Petite Sirah (Dry Creek Valley) $34. This is a very rich wine with blackberry, cassis, chocolate, and spice flavors, and this richness is framed in lavishly fine, thick tannins and lots of smoky oak. It's very dry, with a long finish. Easily one of the best of the current crop of Petite Sirahs. It will age, if you can keep your hands off it. **91** —*S.H. (4/1/2004)*

Rosenblum 2000 Rockpile Road Vineyard Petite Sirah (Dry Creek Valley) $35. Although the black stone fruit, chocolate, and currant flavors are a bit light, the wine is polished, with plenty of toasty oak that provides nuances of smoke and vanilla. The tannins are pretty solid; most tasters felt the wine needs time to come around. **87** *(4/1/2003)*

Rosenblum 1999 Rockpile Road Vineyards Petite Sirah (Dry Creek Valley) $25. This dark purple baby has very oaky scents of caramelized char and smoky, sweet vanillins. In the mouth, there's a sudden burst of voluptuous wild berry fruit and pepper, and sumptuous, velvety tannins. This wine, an ager, is so good it's addictive. **89 Cellar Selection** —*S.H. (12/1/2001)*

Rosenblum 2001 Chateau La Paws Cote du Bone Roan Rhône Red Blend (San Francisco Bay) $16. Distinct and eccentric, a powerfully rich and strong wine brimming with aromas and flavors of hung meat, white pepper, wild forest berries, and freshly picked green, savory herbs. Dry in the mouth, but super-fruity and big. Tannins need some time to calm down. Carignane, Syrah, Mourvèdre, and Grenache. **87** —*S.H. (6/1/2003)*

Rosenblum 2002 Chateau La Paws Cote du Bone Blanc Rhône White Blend (California) $13. From Rosenblum, a blend of Viognier and Roussanne, with fruit and honey flavors. But don't expect a dry wine. It tastes almost as sweet as a late harvest dessert wine. **83** —*S.H. (10/1/2005)*

Rosenblum 2005 Appellation Series Rosé Blend (North Coast) $14. This is a Gamay-Grenache blend from Redwood Valley and northern Napa Valley. It's a rustic wine, full-bodied and dry and with unusually high tannins for a blush. It could almost stand in for a red wine. **84** —*S.H. (12/15/2006)*

Rosenblum 2004 Rhodes Vineyard Grenache Rosé Blend (Redwood Valley) $18. What a blast of cherries this wine gives. Black ones, red ones, with peppery spices and a dollop of vanilla. It's dry, light-bodied, elegant, and crisp, and those delicious cherries reprise on the finish. **87** —*S.H. (11/15/2005)*

Rosenblum 2003 Fess Parker Vineyard Roussanne (Santa Barbara County) $18. Honeysuckle, buttercup blossom, sweet buttered biscuit, peach custard, vanilla. Sound sweet? Tastes sweet. A challenging wine to review. Undeniably delicious, but brings the word "dry" into new territory. **87** —*S.H. (10/1/2005)*

Rosenblum 2002 Fess Parker Vineyard Roussanne (Santa Barbara County) $18. Shows the thick, custardy mouthfeel, banana-like flavors and spicy, honeyed finish this varietal often has in California. That makes it sound sweet, but it's dry. A little unelegant, though. **84** —*S.H. (12/1/2004)*

Rosenblum 1997 Syrah (Solano County) $18. 83 —*S.H. (6/1/1999)*

Rosenblum 2004 Abba Vineyard Syrah (Lodi) $18. Dark, soft, and delicious, like drinking a glass of melted chocolate truffles laced with crème de cassis. This is the kind of California wine that freaks the French out. It's unbalanced, eccentric, and unique. You either love it or hate it. **86** —*S.H. (11/15/2006)*

Rosenblum 2003 Abba Vineyard Syrah (Lodi) $24. Called overoaked by one taster and jammy and over the top by another, this style of California Syrah has its fans—and you know who you are. Huge berry and vanilla flavors, a rich, syrupy mouthfeel, and firm tannins make this a love-it-or-hate-it wine. **83** *(9/1/2005)*

Rosenblum 2002 Abba Vineyard Syrah (Lodi) $18. A big, ripe, galumphing Syrah that's almost Port-like in its chocolatey, stewed blackberry flavors, although it is dry. Not for the faint of heart at 15-plus alcohol. **84** —*S.H. (12/1/2004)*

Rosenblum 2001 Abba Vineyard Syrah (Lodi) $18. Lodians always tell you that their city isn't as hot as you think it is, but it really is. This hothouse wine has very forward, fruity-sweet flavors of cassis and chocolate milk, but it's like drinking Coke without the carbonated water. In other words, syrupy. Deliciously sweet, but rather cloying, and not really a table wine. Try it as a dessert wine, or pour it over vanilla ice cream. **84** —*S.H. (12/15/2003)*

Rosenblum 2000 England Shaw Vineyard Syrah (Solano County) $37. An inky dark, young wine, with cassis and berry flavors accented with sweet tobacco, espresso, and white pepper notes. Drinks dry and rich, packed with ripe fruity flavors and a wild, brambly note. High quality Zin, and heady with alcohol. **87** —*S.H. (6/1/2003)*

Rosenblum 2002 England-Shaw Vineyard Syrah (Solano County) $30. Dark, soft, extracted, and chocolatey. The vines give up acidity under relentless heat, but in exchange they offer flavors that are rare to find in this world. Massively fruity yet dry, with lots of alcohol, this is a perfect foil for BBQ. **87** —*S.H. (12/31/2004)*

Rosenblum 2001 England-Shaw Vineyard Syrah (Solano County) $30. Solano is well inland, where it's very hot, and this is a hot climate wine. The cherry-berry flavors are ripely sweet to the point of jam, and the tannins are soft, almost non-existent. Tastes like a syrupy topping for ice cream. **84** —*S.H. (12/15/2003)*

Rosenblum 2003 England-Shaw Vineyards Syrah (Solano County) $33. Rosenblum is sourcing Syrah from select vineyards and making them in a bold, full-throttle style. The England-Shaw bottling is full-bodied and tannic, with intense blackberry and plum fruit so powerful it seems almost like a barrel sample. Hold 1–2 years, and drink it over the next 10. **88** *(9/1/2005)*

Rosenblum 1999 England-Shaw Vineyard Syrah (Solano County) $21. A dark, dense beast that could use a few years to round into form—right now the toasty oak is prominent and the tannins plentiful. Full-bodied, with espresso, tar, and blackberry flavors that fold in smoked bacon and cocoa on the finish. Top Value. **89** *(11/1/2001)*

Rosenblum 2001 Fess Parker Vineyard Syrah (Santa Barbara County) $24. One big wine. Inky black, huge in white pepper, blackberry and baked pecan pie aromas, and massive in black cherry and cassis flavors. At the same time, it's dry, balanced, and complex. Calls for equally big foods, like babyback ribs slathered with BBQ sauce. **91** —*S.H. (4/1/2004)*

Rosenblum 2004 Hillside Vineyards Syrah (Sonoma County) $25. Kent Rosenblum readily concedes some of his reds have residual sugar, and I'm certain this one does. Yet lots of people like these wines, with their chocolatey, blackberry, and blueberry pie filling, toffee, and caramelly oak flavors. This one will please Rosenblum's many fans. **87** —*S.H. (12/15/2006)*

Rosenblum 2003 Hillside Vineyards Syrah (Sonoma County) $28. A blend of fruit from several Sonoma vineyards, this wine features Rosenblum's hallmark lavish oak and concentrated fruit. Caramel, coffee, and vanilla notes complement full, soft notes of blackberry and plum. Long and a bit tannic on the finish, this wine is approachable now, yet promises to be even better in another year or two. **88** *(9/1/2005)*

Rosenblum 2002 Hillside Vineyards Syrah (Sonoma County) $26. True to Rosenblum's style, dark, ripely extracted and dry, with the resulting high alcohol. It's a bit hot and clumsy, but powerful in coffee, chocolate, and cherry flavors that will play off against a ribeye steak. **87** —*S.H. (12/31/2004)*

Rosenblum 2001 Hillside Vineyards Syrah (Sonoma County) $26. Rich and fruity, a hugely flavorful wine stuffed with black currant, cherry, plum, coffee, and herb flavors. It's pretty tannic now, with lots of acidity, but the fruit is big enough to pair with beef or cheese. **86** —*S.H. (4/1/2004)*

Rosenblum 2000 Rodney's Vineyard Syrah (Santa Barbara County) $30. Despite some nice blackberry fruit, this is a tough wine to fall in love with. It feels hot and tannic in the mouth, with a certain tart sourness. Blame it on an unbalanced vintage. When the grapes don't deliver, even the best winemaking can't compensate. **84** —*S.H. (9/1/2003)*

Rosenblum 2003 Rominger Vineyard Syrah (Yolo County) $26. Intense and tannic, yet well-managed and ageworthy. White pepper and plum on the nose, with masses of well-ripened tannins and rich fruit alongside. From a hillside vineyard planted to French clones that yielded only 1.5 tons

per acre, we can only hope wines like this represent the future of California Syrah. **91 Editors' Choice** *(9/1/2005)*

Rosenblum 2003 Kathy's Cuvée Viognier (Santa Barbara County) $14. Packs a whallop with intense flavors of honey, superripe mango, peach, vanilla, and a nutty, caramelly richness as sweet as pecan pie. Fortunately there's good acidity and minerality to balance. **86** —*S.H. (10/1/2005)*

Rosenblum 2005 Kathy's Cuvée Viognier (California) $18. Classic Viognier, with enormously attractive pineapple, mango, peach, and honeysuckle flavors and a rich honeyed finish, and the wine is dry and crisp. There's a voluptuously creamy texture that makes it especially attractive. **90** —*S.H. (11/1/2006)*

Rosenblum 2004 Kathy's Cuvée Viognier (California) $16. If you're going to do California Viognier, might as well let 'er rip with the exotic stuff. This heady wine does just that, offering a mouthful of ripe mango, papaya, nectarine, peach, clove, and vanilla flavors in a richly creamy package. There's nothing subtle about it, just sheer hedonism. **87** —*S.H. (3/1/2006)*

Rosenblum 2002 Kathy's Cuvée Viognier (Lodi) $14. An exotic Viognier, packed with wild flavors, everything from mangoes and papayas through bananas to honeysuckle and ripe white peach. Finishes with a honeyed sweetness, yet it's basically dry. **87** —*S.H. (11/15/2004)*

Rosenblum 2001 Late Harvest Ripken Ranch Viognier (Lodi) $19. Look for Viognier's floral, tropical fruit flavors in this intensely sweet wine. It's almost like injecting pure honey into your tongue, sending it into jolts of diabetic coma. But fundamentally simple despite the sweetness. **85** —*S.H. (12/15/2003)*

Rosenblum 2000 Late Harvest Ripkin Ranch Viognier (Lodi) $22. Sweet going here, with honeyed flavors of peaches and pears that are delicious in themselves. Yet there's a burn to the finish and a certain one dimensionality. Best with a rich, decadent dessert. **86** —*S.H. (5/1/2003)*

Rosenblum 2001 Ripken Vineyard Viognier (Lodi) $19. Quite typical of warm appellation Viognier, with juicy, ripe flavors of peaches, apricots, and tropical fruits, and soft, flaccid acids and tannins. The flavors are very good but the absence of structure makes for a syrupy mouthfeel. Chill this wine very well. **85** —*S.H. (3/1/2003)*

Rosenblum 2000 Ripkin Vineyard Viognier (Lodi) $14. Smells fresh, flowery, and fruity, with lemon flower, night jasmine, honey, smoke, tobacco, and spice aromas. The taste is rich and full, with a blast of ripe peach, honey, and spice. There's some glyceriney sweetness in the finish of this pretty, expressive wine. **88 Best Buy** —*S.H. (11/15/2001)*

Rosenblum 2001 Rodney's Vineyard Viognier (Santa Barbara County) $25. A strong, eccentric wine that will not be to everyone's liking. For starters, it's very smoky and oaky, and also very leesy, which lends sour cream notes to the underlying apricot, peach, and citrus flavors. A creamy texture from barrel fermentation leads to a spicy finish. **86** —*S.H. (3/1/2003)*

Rosenblum 2001 Rodney's Vineyard Viognier (Santa Barbara County) $18. Quite a nice Viognier, in the sense of its huge wildflower and tropical fruit flavors and rich, honeyed texture. The slight sweetness works to emphasize the wine's lushness and flamboyance. So big, it's best drunk on its own. **88** —*S.H. (12/1/2003)*

Rosenblum NV Vintners Cuvée Blanc III Vin Blanc Extraordinaire White Blend (California) $11. Simple, earthy, and dry. If that's your minimum requirement for a white, try this blend of Chardonnay, Symphony, and Viognier from vineyards in Napa, Lodi, and San Luis Obispo. Feels a bit thick and heavy in the mouth, with apple and peach flavors. **84** —*S.H. (7/1/2003)*

Rosenblum 1998 Alegria Zinfandel (Russian River Valley) $26. Big, fruity wine, with layers of fruit, earth, toast, and oak. Spicy cranberry/raspberry fruit leads into toasty, dry tannins. There is a lovely density, buttressed with new oak, but anchored with ripe, firm fruit. Lovely winemaking. **91** —*P.G. (3/1/2001)*

Rosenblum 2002 Alegria Vineyard Zinfandel (Russian River Valley) $22. This pretty wine is light in body, with an unusually silky mouth feel for Zin, but it packs lots of flavor. Oodles of jammy berries, stone fruits, and cocoa, in soft tannins and a fruity, spicy finish. Lip-smackingly easy to down. **87** —*S.H. (12/31/2004)*

Rosenblum 2001 Alegria Vineyard Zinfandel (Russian River Valley) $22. Rich and thick-textured, with up-front hints of bright cherry, plum, anise, blackberry, spice, and herbs. Tannins are a tad rustic; powerful. The finish is quite viscous, almost prune-like. Big stuff. **87** *(11/1/2003)*

Rosenblum 2000 Alegria Vineyard Zinfandel (Russian River Valley) $34. This dark, rich wine is redolent with scents of the earth. Powerful in the mouth, with sweetly ripe flavors of blackberries, cherries, and plums, although the wine is dry. Has soft tannins and a long finish. **88** —*S.H. (5/1/2003)*

Rosenblum 1997 Alegria Vineyard Zinfandel (Russian River Valley) $30. **83** —*J.C. (2/1/2000)*

Rosenblum 2002 Annette's Reserve Zinfandel (Redwood Valley) $28. From this inland Mendocino appellation, a chocolatey Zin, with notes of cassis, coffee, and cinnamon. Soft and luscious in texture, with a slightly sweet finish. Perfect with short ribs. **90** —*S.H. (3/1/2005)*

Rosenblum 1997 Annette's Reserve Rhodes Viney Zinfandel (Redwood Valley) $26. **89** —*P.G. (11/15/1999)*

Rosenblum 1996 Annette's Reserve Rhodes Viney Zinfandel (Redwood Valley) $26. **89** —*S.H. (9/1/1999)*

Rosenblum 2001 Annette's Reserve Rhodes Vineyard Zinfandel (Redwood Valley) $28. Very full-bodied, with big, astringent tannins. The flavors don't quite live up to the body, however, with modest cherry, blackberry, plum, and vanilla notes. A little hollow on the mid-palate. **84** *(11/1/2003)*

Rosenblum 2000 Annette's Reserve Rhodes Vineyard Zinfandel (Redwood Valley) $35. One of the darker wines of the year, and heady to sniff. You'd swear it was Port, with those big plummy aromas. Tastes as rich as it smells, with huge flavors of chocolate, blackberry, and white pepper, yet the wine is dry. This is a high alcohol wine and packs a punch. **88** —*S.H. (5/1/2003)*

Rosenblum 1999 Annette's Reserve Rhodes Vineyard Zinfandel (Redwood Valley) $27. From an inland Mendocino County district well regarded for ripe Zin comes this deeply flavored version. It's stuffed with wild berry and spice notes and drinks sweetly ripe, yet it's balanced and harmonious despite hefty alcohol. The finish is intricately dry and fruity. **91 Editors' Choice** —*S.H. (9/1/2002)*

Rosenblum 2003 Aparicio Vineyard Zinfandel (Amador County) $22. **86** *(2/1/2006)*

Rosenblum 2003 Carla's Vineyards Zinfandel (San Francisco Bay) $29. **89** *(2/1/2006)*

Rosenblum 2001 Carla's Vineyards Zinfandel (San Francisco Bay) $23. Dense and licorice-like at first. The wine then opens up to reveal a complex array of black cherry, black plum, blackberry, spice, chocolate, coffee, camphor, and sweet oak. A beautiful example of an effusive but nonetheless controlled style. Long and lush at the end. **91** *(11/1/2003)*

Rosenblum 2000 Carla's Vineyards Zinfandel (San Francisco Bay) $29. An inky black, thick wine that feels like Port in the mouth, with alcohol and heat carrying dark berry flavors. Acidity is pretty high, which adds to sense of heat and bitterness. **85** —*S.H. (5/1/2003)*

Rosenblum 2002 Carla's Vineyards Zinfandel (San Francisco Bay-Livermore Valley) $24. Here's what made Zin famous to begin with. It's a big, dark, rich wine that's bursting with ripe, juicy berry and spice flavors, and is very dry. Has an instant appeal, with its fine, sweet tannins. **87** —*S.H. (11/15/2004)*

Rosenblum 2001 Castanho Vineyard Zinfandel Port Zinfandel (San Francisco Bay) $17. If sweet Zinfandel is your thing, enjoy. It has cherry and chocolate flavors, unguently soft tannins and acids, and enough sugar to kill a horse. Lacks balance and finesse, however. **83** —*S.H. (12/15/2003)*

Rosenblum 2003 Continente Vineyard Zinfandel (San Francisco Bay) $20. Dark, dry, and a little earthy, this is not my favorite of Kent Rosenblum's current crop. There's a mushroomy tinge to the fruit flavors that detracts. Still, it's textbook Rosenblum. **85** —*S.H. (10/1/2005)*

Rosenblum 2002 Continente Vineyard Zinfandel (San Francisco Bay) $18. From Contra Costa, a thick, rather syrupy Zin, soft in acids, with gooey chocolate and cassis flavors. Seems more like something you'd pour over ice cream than a dinner wine, but lots of people like this style. **85** —*S.H. (12/31/2004)*

Rosenblum 2001 Continente Vineyard Zinfandel (San Francisco Bay) $16. Lush and round textured, with pleasing black cherry, blackberry, plum, blueberry, chocolate, coffee, herb, and spice flavors. It all sits on velvety smooth tannins, finishing long and lush. **90 Editors' Choice** *(11/1/2003)*

Rosenblum 2000 Continente Vineyard Zinfandel (San Francisco Bay) $20. It's very rich and textured, a sumptuous, velvety wine with classic Zin flavors of brambly berries and chocolate and dry, fine tannins. Has that explosively vibrant, jammy character of young Zin. **88** —*S.H. (5/1/2003)*

Rosenblum 1999 Continente Vineyard Zinfandel (San Francisco Bay) $16. Kent Rosenblum, the Zinmeister from Alameda, owns no vineyards but consistently produces some of California's best Zinfandels. He sources grapes from some of the state's oldest vineayrds, including Continente, where vines planted in 1879 by the Continente family are still farmed by them today in what may be the oldest surviving Zinfandel vineyard. The '99 edition opens with plum, cherry, and boysenberry notes that are echoed on the long finish, where they are joined by hints of chocolate and black pepper. With its full body, velvety mouthfeel and excellent balance, this wine will turn even jaded tasters into Zinfanatics **90** —*M.N. (11/15/2001)*

Rosenblum 1997 Continente Vineyard Zinfandel (Contra Costa County) $19. **90** —*J.C. (9/1/1999)*

Rosenblum 1996 Continente Vineyard Old Old Vine Zinfandel (Contra Costa County) $20. **91** —*J.C. (9/1/1999)*

Rosenblum 2001 Cullinane Vineyard Zinfandel (Sonoma County) $45. A menthol and spice edge is quite forward here. The wine is viscous and almost prune-like in its ripeness. Coffee, chocolate, cola, and spice are the hallmarks in this one. Not for everyone. Try it with chocolate or a cigar. **89** *(11/1/2003)*

Rosenblum NV Cuvée XXV Zinfandel (California) $11. Sassy and saucy, with raisin, blueberry, pepper, and earth aromas. Kent Rosenblum has crafted a wine that, within its class, is well above average, and we challenge you to find Zin this authentic for this price. What it lacks in nuance is made up for in girth and guts. It's chewy and rich, and it becomes more complex with each minute spent in the glass. Nothing weedy or green here, and the mouthfeel rocks. **87** —*M.S. (11/15/2004)*

Rosenblum 2002 Eagle Point Vineyard Zinfandel (Mendocino County) $27. A solid effort in a big Zin that could have been unbalanced but isn't. Dark and dry, with lush tannins and a full-bodied mouth feel, and long, rich flavors of berries, spices, and coffee. Has that brawny, briary Zin character that does so well with barbecue. **89** —*S.H. (12/31/2004)*

Rosenblum 2000 Eagle Point Vineyard Zinfandel (Mendocino County) $30. Has flavors of all sorts of wild berries, chocolate, and white pepper, with fine, complex tannins and pretty good acids. The addition of some Petite Sirah adds even more body and substance. **88** —*S.H. (5/1/2003)*

Rosenblum 2004 Harris Kratka Vineyard Zinfandel (Alexander Valley) $35. Huge, big, thick, gooey, and high in alcohol, this only-in-California wine will turn on Zin lovers. It explodes with chocolate, blackberry, vanilla, fudge, and cappuccino flavors, with a suggestion of currants in the soft, honeyed finish. **90** —*S.H. (12/15/2006)*

Rosenblum 2003 Harris Kratka Vineyard Zinfandel (Alexander Valley) $35. **91** *(2/1/2006)*

Rosenblum 2002 Harris Kratka Vineyard Zinfandel (Alexander Valley) $30. An earthy, rustic Zin with the robust wild fruit and robust tannins that often mark the variety. Completely dry and moderate in alcohol, the wine shows blackberry, coffee, and spice flavors, with a streak of orange rind. **85** —*S.H. (11/15/2004)*

Rosenblum 2001 Harris Kratka Vineyard Zinfandel (Alexander Valley) $30. Sleek and supple, with a core of black cherry, blackberry, menthol, coffee, tea, herb, and spice flavors. The tannins are velvety smooth, finishing with an herbal edge. **88** *(11/1/2003)*

Rosenblum 2002 Hendry Vineyard Zinfandel (Napa Valley) $40. A fabulously complex Zin, decadent in the elaboration of ripe cassis and chocolate fruit, lush oak trappings, and texture like a mink coat. Lots of alcohol here, but so dry and balanced, you hardly notice. **92** —*S.H. (3/1/2005)*

Rosenblum 2001 Hendry Vineyard Zinfandel (Napa Valley) $38. Incredibly smooth, plush, and ripe. Beautifully balanced between power and finesse, with a fine-tuned balance of coffee, chocolate, black cherry, plum, blackberry, spice, pepper, tar, licorice, and herbs. Lush tannins add supple focus, with a long, lingering finish. Great winemaking; great vineyard. **93** *(11/1/2003)*

Rosenblum 2003 Hendry Vineyard Reserve Zinfandel (Napa Valley) $44. 92 *(2/1/2006)*

Rosenblum 2000 Hendry Vineyard Reserve Zinfandel (Napa Valley) $47. Beautiful Zin, balanced and elegant despite its native wild and woolly nature. Powerful flavors of blackberries, chocolate, and pepper are wrapped in lush Napa tannins that are one of the wine's nicest features. Dry and luscious, a distinctive achievement in Zinfandel. **92** *—S.H. (3/1/2003)*

Rosenblum 1998 Hendry Vineyard Reserve Zinfandel (Napa Valley) $30. Full bodied and well-oaked, this full-throttle Zin comes on with intense blackberry and vanilla aromas and flavors accented by cinnamon and chocolate notes. Ripe and even on the palate, the handsome fruit plays out on the lengthy finish with tart, dark berry, and pepper notes. **90** *—P.G. (3/1/2001)*

Rosenblum 1997 Hendry Vineyard Reserve Zinfandel (Napa Valley) $30. **86** *—J.C. (2/1/2000)*

Rosenblum 2002 Hillside Vineyards Zinfandel (Sonoma County) $26. As exotic and opulent as an elaborate dessert, but dry. Flavors of blackberries sautéed in butter and brown sugar, sprinkled with cocoa and cinnamon, finished with a drizzle of lemon zest. Smooth and velvety, yet firm in tannins. Just delicious. **91** *—S.H. (3/1/2005)*

Rosenblum 2001 Lyons Vineyard 25th Anniversary Zinfandel (Napa Valley) $38. A ripe, plush style that sports good acidity and plenty of sweet oak. Toasty, smoky flavors frame the plum, black cherry, spice, and herbs that follow. Good length on the finish. **90** *(11/1/2003)*

Rosenblum 2004 Maggie's Reserve Zinfandel (Sonoma Valley) $45. High in alcohol, with some heat throughout, but the wine wears it well, with huge fruit and a dry finish. Tastes almost desserty, with crème de cassis, milk chocolate, blackberry jam, and coffee flavors and a distinct dried thyme and briary nettle edge. Very nice, but wow, that alcohol! **89** *—S.H. (12/15/2006)*

Rosenblum 2003 Maggie's Reserve Zinfandel (Sonoma Valley) $46. 91 *(2/1/2006)*

Rosenblum 2004 Monte Rosso Vineyard Zinfandel (Sonoma Valley) $45. Oh, what a rich Zin this is. It's like biting into a chocolate truffle that melts in your mouth. Then comes the blackberry liqueur, cherry pie, cinnamon roll. The wine is dry, but at the cost of mind-blowing alcohol, 16.5%. Love it or not, there's nothing like it. **93 Editors' Choice** *—S.H. (11/1/2006)*

Rosenblum 2002 Monte Rosso Vineyard Zinfandel (Sonoma Valley) $38. As tasty as this wine is, and it's surely delicious in cassis and chocolate flavors, it's simply too hot. With 16.6% alcohol, it has a hot, red pepper mouthfeel. That was the price of dryness under the hot sun. **87** *—S.H. (12/15/2004)*

Rosenblum 2001 Monte Rosso Vineyard Zinfandel (Sonoma County) $38. Smooth tannins and spicy acidity co-exist nicely here. Jammy raspberry and cherry flavors form the center, while a framework of tangy spice, vanilla and toast adds good structure. **89** *(11/1/2003)*

Rosenblum 2002 Oakley Vineyards Zinfandel (Contra Costa County) $14. This is a great price for such a delicious and balanced red wine. It's classic warm-coastal, with lush wild blackberry, blueberry, pepper, and sage flavors and sweet, rich tannins. Completely dry and moderate in alcohol, it's a lovely Zin. **89** *—S.H. (12/15/2004)*

Rosenblum 2001 Oakley Vineyards Zinfandel (San Francisco Bay) $12. Nowhere near the class and style of Rosenblum's more expensive Zins. Smells tobaccoey and earthy, and drinks rough in texture, with pronounced sweetness. **83** *—S.H. (3/1/2004)*

Rosenblum 2000 Oakley Vineyards Zinfandel (San Francisco Bay) $18. Starts off with an herbal, composty aroma, like decaying organic material, although there are richer notes of berries. This clumsy wine has flavors of sweetened coffee, blackberries, and tobacco. **84** *—S.H. (5/1/2003)*

Rosenblum 2000 Old Vines Zinfandel (Russian River Valley) $18. From vines averaging 72 years of age, a dark and brooding Zin that smells young and earthy. Air it, and it gives up blackberry and chocolate scents.

In the mouth, this is a big, youthful wine, packed with berry jam. Dry and well-balanced, with a tart bite of acid. **89 Editors' Choice** *—S.H. (5/1/2003)*

Rosenblum 2000 Pato Vineyard Zinfandel (San Francisco Bay) $26. From a vineyard east of San Francisco, a wine that tastes like it baked under the heat and produced raisined berries. Although it's fully dry, it's big and hot, sort of like Port without the sugar. **84** *—S.H. (5/1/2003)*

Rosenblum 2003 Planchon Vineyard Zinfandel (San Francisco Bay) $22. From Contra Costa County, a dark, dry wine with very high alcohol (15.6%) that flirts with Portiness but avoids it. Still the blackberry and chocolate flavors have a hint of raisins. Really an only-in-California Zin. **87** *—S.H. (10/1/2005)*

Rosenblum 2002 Planchon Vineyard Zinfandel (San Francisco Bay) $20. Big, rich, bold, and extracted, a thrilling Zin from Contra Costa County. It's gigantic in blackberry, blueberry, cherry, and spice flavors, with a delicious edge of sweet herbs and white pepper. There are substantial tannins but they're sweet. **91** *—S.H. (12/15/2004)*

Rosenblum 2001 Planchon Vineyard Zinfandel (San Francisco Bay) $19. Another smooth, silky wine from this Zinfandel specialist. It's packed with bold flavors: Chocolate, coffee, plum, blackberry, cherry, vanilla, mocha, and toast are all well integrated. The tannins are quite smooth and firm, giving the wine excellent structure and a long finish. **91 Editors' Choice** *(11/1/2003)*

Rosenblum 2000 Planchon Vineyard Zinfandel (San Francisco Bay) $24. The appellation implies cool conditions, but the vineyard is in hot Oakley, which gives the fruit some overripe, Port-like notes. Flavors of raisins are encased in a high-alcohol (15.2%) wine that's fully dry and a little unbalanced. **85** *—S.H. (5/1/2003)*

Rosenblum 2002 Richard Sauret Vineyard Zinfandel (Paso Robles) $18. My favorite Rosenblum Zin of the vintage. Delicious for its rich blackberry, raspberry, chocolate, and toffee flavors, with easy, sweet but complex tannins, and completely dry. The fruit flatters the palate like a fur coat on a bare thigh. Irresistibly good. **90** *—S.H. (12/31/2004)*

Rosenblum 2001 Richard Sauret Vineyard Zinfandel (Paso Robles) $19. Smooth and lush, this pretty wine is filled with bright coffee, chocolate, plum, black cherry, toast, and spice flavors. Elegant, with firm, smooth tannins. Really nice. **91 Editors' Choice** *(11/1/2003)*

Rosenblum 2000 Richard Sauret Vineyard Zinfandel (Paso Robles) $24. Kick-butt Zin that pulls off the elusive quest to balance size with elegance. Warm country aromas of Port, chocolate, and raisins, but goes down smooth despite 15% alcohol and a bit of residual sugar. **87** *—S.H. (2/1/2003)*

Rosenblum 1997 Richard Sauret Vineyard Zinfandel (Paso Robles) $22. 88 *—P.G. (11/15/1999)*

Rosenblum 2004 Richard Sauret Vineyards Zinfandel (Paso Robles) $25. Somehow, Kent Rosenblum has figured out how to craft these big, high-alcohol, hot-country Zins and keep them balanced and dry. This single-vineyard Zin bursts with chocolate-filled raspberry and cherry candy flavors, and the alcoholic heat actually works with the wine, lending it a toasted pepper note. What a California experience. **92 Editors' Choice** *—S.H. (11/1/2006)*

Rosenblum 2003 Richard Sauret Vineyards Zinfandel (Paso Robles) $22. 90 Editors' Choice *(2/1/2006)*

Rosenblum 2001 Rockpile Road Zinfandel (Dry Creek Valley) $26. A brambly blend of spicy oak, blackberry, herbs, menthol, coffee, and toast flavors. Fun, but a bit disjointed, finishing bright. **86** *(11/1/2003)*

Rosenblum 1998 Rockpile Road Zinfandel (Dry Creek Valley) $19. Old vine clone, with brambly, gamy notes throughout. Lifts up the palate with lively, bright flavors. Good concentration, balance, and follow-through. **90 Editors' Choice** *—P.G. (3/1/2001)*

Rosenblum 2004 Rockpile Road Vineyard Zinfandel (Rockpile) $35. Rich as sin, the '04 Rockpile Zin got enormously ripe but has been fermented to dryness, at the cost of very high alcohol. The flavors are a wonder. It's all about chocolate, crème de cassis, anisette, and the most wonderfully rich, spicy buttery, toasty vanilla bean. **92** *—S.H. (12/15/2006)*

Rosenblum 2002 Rockpile Road Vineyard Zinfandel (Dry Creek Valley)

$26. Big in flavor, high in alcohol, this is an only-in-California Zin. The ripe flavors are explosive, delighting the mouth with cassis, cherry, milk chocolate, and vanilla fudge flavors, but as sweet as this sounds, the wine is totally dry. Lip-smackingly good. **92** —*S.H. (12/15/2004)*

Rosenblum 1999 Rockpile Road Vineyard Zinfandel (Dry Creek Valley) $21. Big, luscious aromas of dark chocolate, blackberry, pepper, earth, and smoke erupt from the glass. The flavors are extracted and bold, suggesting masses of wild berries. It's a big hot, with 14.6% alcohol, while aficionados will debate the Port-like notes and raisiny sweetness. **86** —*S.H. (12/15/2001)*

Rosenblum 1997 Rust Ridge Vineyard Zinfandel (Napa Valley) $22. 88 —*P.G. (11/15/1999)*

Rosenblum 2001 Rust Ridge Vineyard Zinfandel (Napa Valley) $25. Bigtime, ripe Zin, with flavors of berries and cherries that are wrapped in sturdy but ripe, sweet tannins, and are fully dry. Somehow this Zin keeps its alcohol level moderate, and despite the size, is elegant and balanced. **91** —*S.H. (5/1/2004)*

Rosenblum 1998 Rust Ridge Vineyard Zinfandel (Napa Valley) $18. Blueberry, spices, fruitcake, even a maple syrup note mark the nose of this fairly sweet Zinfandel. The somewhat candied quality to the berry fruit was not favored by all tasters, but the plush yet structured mouthfeel has significant appeal. Dark sweet-tart fruit and moderate, even tannins work together to provide a positive finish. **87** *(3/1/2001)*

Rosenblum 2002 Samsel Vineyard Maggie's Reserve Zinfandel (Sonoma Valley) $42. This is a high-octane Zin, rich in alcohol, which has more flavor than a glass can hold. Bursting with dark chocolate fudge, blackberry, leather, sweet cherry pie, and spice, in a creamy smooth, velvety texture. Finishes a bit sweet in sugar. **87** —*S.H. (12/31/2004)*

Rosenblum 2001 Samsel Vineyard Maggie's Reserve Zinfandel (Sonoma Valley) $42. 90 *(11/1/2000)*

Rosenblum 1997 Samsel Vineyard Maggie's Reserve Zinfandel (Sonoma Valley) $35. 87 —*J.C. (2/1/2000)*

Rosenblum 1998 St. Peter's Church Vineyard Zinfandel (Sonoma County) $40. Inky, opaque, and tight, this wine offers a bouquet of black fruits and toast. Though the mouthfeel is full and supple, it is presently very closed and yields scant flavor definition beyond the presence of a very good depth of dark fruits and well-charred oak. Finishes dry, with somewhat more discernable blackberry and vanilla notes and moderately puckering tannins. Best for keeping; try in two-plus years. **88** *(3/1/2001)*

Rosenblum 2000 St. Peter's Church Zinfandel (Sonoma County) $50. Packaged in a heavy, fancy bottle, this wine attempts to make a statement. It's darkly colored and thick, offering up youthful, jammy aromas of blackberries, coffee, and dark chocolate. It's a heavy, thick wine, weighing down the palate with the size of the fruit, tannins, and hefty alcohol. **86** —*S.H. (5/1/2003)*

Rosenblum NV Vintners Cuvée XXI Zinfandel (California) $10. Lots of mushrooms in the nose, giving it a lively, gamy, forest floor quality. The fruit is there as well, wild berries and cherries, and the finish lingers through layers of complex, interesting flavors. **88 Best Buy** —*P.G. (3/1/2001)*

Rosenblum NV Vintners Cuvée Millenium Zinfandel (California) $10. 84 —*J.C. (2/1/2000)*

Rosenblum NV Vintners Cuvée XXIV Zinfandel (California) $11. Super-basic Zin, with brambly flavors of assorted wild berries and a strong herbal tobacco note. Bone dry, with pretty fierce tannins that coat the palate. Best with simple, rich fare, like pizza. **84** —*S.H. (3/1/2004)*

Rosenblum 2001 Vintners Cuvée XXV Zinfandel (California) $10. Spicy, bright raspberry and cherry notes are most evident here. Tannins are fairly ripe and firm, while the finish serves up a toasty vanilla edge. **87 Best Buy** *(11/1/2003)*

Rosenblum 2002 Vintners Cuvée XXVI Zinfandel (California) $9. This is a good price for a wine of this caliber. Rich and thick in jammy cherry, mocha, and spice flavors, dry, and with ripe, sweet tannins. It's rather hot in alcohol, but that's what Zin lovers like with ribs slathered in sauce. **86 Best Buy** —*S.H. (12/31/2004)*

ROSENTHAL

Rosenthal 1996 The Malibu Estate Cabernet Sauvignon (Malibu-Newton Canyon) $35. A bright-edged wine with a very tangy wild cherry character. Hints of blackberry, chocolate, earth, tomato, spice, and herbs also are in evidence, finishing long. **88** —*J.M. (6/1/2002)*

Rosenthal 2000 The Malibu Estate Chardonnay (Malibu-Newton Canyon) $22. Peaches, pears, and herbs run the roost in this medium-bodied wine. It's fresh and clean on the finish, and ends on a lemon-lime note. **87** —*J.M. (5/1/2002)*

Rosenthal 1997 The Malibu Estate The Devon Vineyard Merlot (Malibu-Newton Canyon) $35. A fine blend of ripe cherry, berry, spice and herb flavors, all framed in toasty oak and spice nuance. Smooth but bright on the palate, with a zippy finish and subtle earth tones at the end. **92** —*J.M. (6/1/2002)*

ROSENTHAL-MALIBU ESTATE

Rosenthal-Malibu Estate 2001 Cabernet Sauvignon (Malibu-Newton Canyon) $35. Smells like asparagus, tastes sweet and flat, with cherry cough medicine flavors. **81** —*S.H. (12/1/2005)*

Rosenthal-Malibu Estate 1999 Cabernet Sauvignon (Malibu-Newton Canyon) $35. Polished in tannins and firm with acids, but just a little overripe, with a touch of raisins and excessive heat in the finish. Nonetheless there's a wealth of blackberry flavor. **85** —*S.H. (11/15/2004)*

Rosenthal-Malibu Estate 1999 Founder's Reserve Cabernet Sauvignon (Malibu-Newton Canyon) $70. Certainly richer and more balanced in every way than this winery's regular '99 Cabernet. It has well-ripened blackberry and spicy plum flavors that are generously oaked, and is dry. **90** —*S.H. (11/15/2004)*

Rosenthal-Malibu Estate 2003 Chardonnay (Central Coast) $18. Clearly cool-climate, to judge from the tart, citrusy acidity and lemon-and-lime flavors. Would be lean if it weren't for the toasty oak and creamy texture. As it is, it's a great food wine. **87** —*S.H. (12/15/2004)*

Rosenthal-Malibu Estate 2001 The Devon Vineyard Merlot (Malibu-Newton Canyon) $25. A schizophrenic wine. It smells vegetal, like canned asparagus, but tastes better, with berry-cherry flavors and a polished texture. **83** —*S.H. (12/1/2005)*

Rosenthal-Malibu Estate 1999 The Devon Vineyard Merlot (Malibu-Newton Canyon) $35. From suburban L.A., a well-oaked, medium-bodied wine with cherry and herb flavors. It's rich but delicate in tannins, with good acidity. Softer than the typical North Coast Merlot. **87** —*S.H. (12/15/2004)*

ROSHAMBO

Roshambo 2003 Chardonnay (California) $10. Pretty nice for this price, with lots of oak framing tropical fruit and spice flavors and a creamy texture. Bright, crisp acidity helps to maintain balance. **85 Best Buy** —*S.H. (10/1/2005)*

Roshambo 2004 Imago Chardonnay (Sonoma County) $18. Tastes like one of those Aussie Chards, with big, flamboyant mango, papaya, and guava flavors framed in crisp acidity. If there's any oak, it's not much. What you get in this bone-dry Chard is clean, pure, ripe Sonoma Chardonnay fruit. **85** —*S.H. (12/15/2005)*

Roshambo 2003 Rock Paper Scissors Merlot (California) $10. Smooth and ripe, this good value wine is loaded with cherry, blackberry, and chocolate flavors. It's soft, with a nice backbone of tannins. **85 Best Buy** —*S.H. (10/1/2005)*

Roshambo 2003 Sauvignon Blanc (Dry Creek Valley) $12. A bit sweet in spearmint chewing gum and ripe fig flavors, but the crispness keeps it balanced. Turns honeyed on the finish. **84** —*S.H. (5/1/2005)*

Roshambo 2002 Justice Syrah (Dry Creek Valley) $21. Young, fresh, and jammy, this Syrah might benefit from a year or two in the cellar. It's dry and filled with blueberry, blackberry, and cherry flavors, with a cut of dusty tannins. Good now with steak, or hold through 2007. **87** —*S.H. (12/15/2005)*

Roshambo 2003 Rosé Syrah (Dry Creek Valley) $15. Pretty dark and full-bodied, and strong, too, in powerful acids, spicy rose petal, dried herb, and strawberry flavors and even a dusting of tannins. Try this dry wine with substantial foods, like bouillabaise. **86** —*S.H. (12/31/2004)*

Roshambo 2004 Think Rosé of Syrah (Sonoma County) $15. Unusually dark and full-bodied for a rosé, this wine could almost be served at room temperature. It's dry, with ripe, jammy cherry and black raspberry flavors, and a spicy, peppery finish. **86** —*S.H. (12/15/2005)*

Roshambo 2003 Frank Johnson Vineyards Late Harvest Traminer (Dry Creek Valley) $19. Smells distinctively spicy, throwing off a huge bouquet of cinnamon, clove, and nutmeg, along with apricots and honey. In the mouth, it is sweet and simple. **84** —*S.H. (5/1/2005)*

Roshambo 2001 Zinfandel (Dry Creek Valley) $21. Rich in berry and herb flavors, this Zin has the crisp tannins and dry, brambly taste associated with the appellation. There's a peppery edge to the sweet, wild blackberries and blueberries that really perks up the palate. **90** —*S.H. (10/1/2004)*

Roshambo 2001 Zinfandel (Alexander Valley) $18. Its soft, gentle tannins, rich plummy, chocolatey flavors and long, spicy finish could only come from Alexander Valley. Perfect with a nice, juicy steak. **88** —*S.H. (10/1/2004)*

Roshambo 2002 The Reverend Zinfandel (Dry Creek Valley) $21. Clean, balanced, and very drinkable, this Zin shows well-ripened cherry-berry flavors and smooth, rich tannins, and finishes dry. It's an easy, assured wine that shows real Dry Creek character. **86** —*S.H. (12/15/2005)*

ROSS VINEYARDS

Ross Vineyards 2000 Sauvignon Blanc (Napa Valley) $18. Quite lemony, with intriguing mineral, fig, melon, and grass tones that are neatly intertwined. Fresh, clean, and elegant, the wine sleekly shows the fine pedigree of this snappy variety. **90** —*J.M. (9/1/2002)*

ROTH

Roth 2002 Cabernet Sauvignon (Alexander Valley) $40. A very nice and smooth Cab, with a texture like velvet and an elegant overall feeling. It shows cassis, green olive, smoke, and cedar flavors and is bone dry. **88** —*S.H. (5/1/2005)*

Roth 2000 Heritage Red Wine Red Blend (Alexander Valley) $30. A second label from Lancaster Estate, and a very good one. Starts with evocative aromas of cassis and black currants, smoky oak, vanilla, and a hint of sweet green olive. Round and smooth in the mouth, with pronounced but fine tannins that cover blackberry and herb flavors. **89** —*S.H. (12/31/2003)*

ROUND BARN

Round Barn 2003 Cabernet Franc (Lake Michigan Shore) $45. Holiday spice aromas are interesting enough, although heavy cream and brown, stemmy notes are a bit odd. Takes a turn for the better with flavors of dark berry, cherry, and allspice. Sour cherries mark the finish. **84** —*M.D. (8/1/2006)*

Round Barn NV Chardonnay (Lake Michigan Shore) $18. Toasty oak cradles this wine, while flavors of yellow fruits shine through. The wine has a smooth, light body, with nice balance, and finishes crisp, with more oaky nuance. **83** —*M.D. (8/1/2006)*

Round Barn 2003 Pinot Noir (Lake Michigan Shore) $28. A vegetal wine dealing rhubarb flavors along with mint and leather on the nose. It has high acidity but just enough sweetness to hold it. **81** —*M.D. (12/1/2006)*

Round Barn NV Vineyard Tears White Blend (Lake Michigan Shore) $15. A blend of German varietals, thie has nice white fruit aromas touched with vanilla and oak. In the mouth it's simple and a bit oily, with overbearing oak that gives butter and spice flavors, but there is some tropical fruit which is pleasant. **82** —*M.D. (8/1/2006)*

ROUND HILL

Round Hill 2000 Cabernet Sauvignon (California) $8. You get a pretty basic varietal wine here. It has thinned-down flavors of blackberries and herbs, and is firmed up with dry tannins. Not a bad little Cab for the price. **84** —*S.H. (11/15/2003)*

Round Hill 1999 Cabernet Sauvignon (California) $9. Almost shockingly green and weedy for a '99. Hard to taste anything beyond the tart pepper flavors and raspingly dry tannins, that leave the palate numb. **81** —*S.H. (12/31/2002)*

Round Hill 2003 Chardonnay (California) $9. Drinks like what it is, a country-style wine, rustic and clean. Provides enough fruit, cream, and oak to satisfy. **83** —*S.H. (10/1/2005)*

Round Hill 2002 Merlot (California) $9. Stands up to wines that cost much more. Yes, it's a bit sharp, but there's ripe black cherry and oak flavors, smooth tannins, and some real finesse. **86 Best Buy** —*S.H. (10/1/2005)*

Round Hill 2002 White Zinfandel (California) $4. Of course it's possible to make a good white Zin, but this isn't it. It's a thinly flavored, slightly sweet plonk, with a trace of raspberries. You get what you pay for. **82** —*S.H. (3/1/2004)*

Round Hill 2001 White Zinfandel (California) $4. Easy, simple peach and strawberry flavors are watered down, but the wine is clean and zesty. It has just a hint of sweetness in the finish. **83** —*S.H. (9/1/2003)*

ROUND POND

Round Pond 2003 Cabernet Sauvignon (Rutherford) $50. Bold and direct, this wine appeals for its fruity flavors and dry balance. Blackberry pie, olive tapenade, roasted coffee bean, and smoky oak aromas and flavors lead to a tannic midpalate and finish. Will benefit from moderate aging through 2010. **87** —*S.H. (12/15/2006)*

ROW ELEVEN

Row Eleven 2002 Pinot Noir (Santa Maria Valley) $29. This is a big Pinot, dark and full-bodied, Rhône-like. It is not typical Santa Maria, although the acidity is cool-climate. It's very dry and fairly tannic, and calls for a slow-cooked meat dish, like short ribs, to play off its smoky, cherry flavors. **88** —*S.H. (10/1/2005)*

Row Eleven 2002 San Luis Obispo Mendocino Counties Pinot Noir (California) $24. An unusual blend of two widely separated coastal counties. Dry, full-bodied, crisp, and tasty in cherry, cola, and oak, this Pinot also has some pretty firm background tannins that make it a bit tough now. **89** —*S.H. (10/1/2005)*

ROWLAND

Rowland 2001 Mountainside Cabernet Sauvignon (Napa Valley) $27. Seems to possess that mountain character of a tightly wound wine, tannic and firm, with a rich and solid core of black cherry and currant fruit. Those tannins are pretty fierce now, but should develop nicely. Best after 2008. **90** —*S.H. (10/1/2004)*

Rowland 2000 Red Triangle Cabernet Sauvignon (Napa Valley) $28. Good, rich Napa Cabernet. Has a purity of fruit and focus that appeals. Has classic flavors of black currants and spice, fine, soft tannins in the modern style, and an overlay of oak adds smoke but does not overwhelm. **91 Editors' Choice** —*S.H. (12/15/2003)*

Rowland 1999 Red Triangle Cabernet Sauvignon (Napa Valley) $28. 92 —*S.H. (6/1/2002)*

Rowland 1997 Red Triangle Cabernet Sauvignon (Napa Valley) $22. 86 —*M.S. (10/1/1999)*

Rowland 1999 Red Triangle Syrah (Napa Valley) $24. Dark and red berry fruit with anise, mineral, and mint accents marks this full, very even wine. The soft, slightly syrupy palate has eucalyptus, caramel, and burnt-marshmallow flavors, while the tart, dry, peppery finish displays even tannins. Nicely structured, it will hold through mid-decade. **88** —*(11/1/2001)*

Rowland 2001 Red Triangle Mountainside Syrah (Napa Valley) $27. There's a lot of new, smoky oak on this wine, to judge from the burst of smoky caramel and vanilla, but the underlying fruit is big enough to carry it. Ripe blackberries, sweet, spicy plums, raw red meat, dark chocolate, and espresso, white pepper and a hint of leather flood the mouth. The tannins are bigtime, and ageable. **90** —*S.H. (12/1/2004)*

ROY J. MAIER

Roy J. Maier 2003 Sonoma County Mountains Cabernet Sauvignon (Sonoma County) $60. This inaugural vintage from an ambitious winery is ripe and powerful and oaky, as expensive Cabs tend to be. On the deficit side is overripe fruit, with a raisiny finish and a heavy texture, but the wine is fully dry and does possess some elegance. Drink over the next five years. **87** —*S.H. (8/1/2006)*

USA

ROYAL OAKS

Royal Oaks 1999 Aristocrat Bordeaux Blend (Santa Ynez Valley) $18. From the warmer, inland part of the valley, this Bordeaux blend is dominated by Cabernet Franc. Herbs—rosemary, thyme, and oregano—highlight the aroma, with a hint of berries. The flavors are much fruitier, and the acid-tannin balance is fine. **89** —*S.H. (4/1/2002)*

Royal Oaks 1999 Westerly Vineyard Reserve Cabernet Franc (Santa Ynez Valley) $30. One-dimensional, although there are some pretty notes. Berry and earth aromas are light, and the wine has some fine cherry and spice flavors. The texture is light and airy, the mouthfeel soft and silky, with a few dusty tannins showing up in the finish. **86** —*S.H. (4/1/2002)*

Royal Oaks 2000 Chardonnay (Santa Ynez Valley) $16. A lighter style of Chard. It has modest apple and peach flavors, spice and oak influence and refreshing acidity. Not a blockbuster, this Chard won't overwhelm your favorite foods, but will support dishes like salmon in butter sauce. **85** —*S.H. (4/1/2002)*

Royal Oaks 1999 Chardonnay (Santa Barbara County) $18. Crisp and clean; a bit leaner than you'd expect from South Coast grapes, veering into citrus fruits like grapefruit. New oak and lees aging adds complexity, but still, it's an angular, structural wine. Food will wake it up. **86** —*S.H. (5/1/2001)*

Royal Oaks 1999 Los Alamos Vineyard Reserve Chardonnay (Santa Barbara) $20. Rich and packed with spicy tropical fruit. New oak imparts smoke and vanilla notes. The texture is creamy and smooth, kind of custardy, with high acidity that makes it drink whistle-clean. A very nice wine. **88** —*S.H. (5/1/2001)*

Royal Oaks 2000 White Hawk Vineyard Reserve Chardonnay (Santa Barbara County) $86. Simple peach and apple flavors provide surface charm, but the wine is light despite being generously oaked. The dominant feature is spice, from the middle through the short finish. It's also very clean. **86** —*S.H. (4/1/2002)*

Royal Oaks 1998 Whitegate Vineyard Chardonnay (Santa Ynez Valley) $20. **86** *(6/1/2000)*

Royal Oaks 1999 Merlot (Santa Ynez Valley) $20. Honest and workman-like, a well-made wine with juicy blackberry and black cherry flavors that are jammy and ripe. Very soft in the mouth, with a silky texture and light tannins. Turns simple on the fruity, spicy finish. **85** —*S.H. (4/1/2002)*

Royal Oaks 1998 Merlot (Santa Ynez Valley) $20. A pretty wine with aromas of black cherry liqueur and a dash of espresso, or maybe it's the other way around. Round, full, and lushly flavored. The high acidity gives it real bite; in fact, the finish is somewhat bitter because of it. Food will soften it up nicely. **86** —*S.H. (5/1/2001)*

Royal Oaks 1999 Reserve Merlot (Santa Ynez Valley) $25. Rich and concentrated, this South Coast wine has berry and stone fruit flavors and a cut of herbs and olives. It's a little low in acidity, but very silky on the palate, and finishes with an elegant flourish. **89** —*S.H. (4/1/2002)*

Royal Oaks 2000 Westerly Vineyard Merlot (Santa Ynez Valley) $30. From the warmest part of the appellation, this is a well-ripened, juicy wine whose cherry, berry, and tobacco flavors are easy to like. Soft and silky on the palate, a gentle sipper with some spicy complexities. **86** —*S.H. (3/1/2004)*

Royal Oaks 1998 Westerly Vineyard Merlot (Santa Ynez Valley) $25. A little more full-bodied than Royal Oaks's regular bottling, it also has black cherry notes, but it's also earthier—and oakier, too—with currents of vanilla and dark chocolate. Still has a bite of acidity, which stings the palate, and demands food. **87** —*S.H. (6/1/2001)*

Royal Oaks 2000 Pinot Noir (Santa Maria Valley) $22. From a great appellation, this wine displays true Pinot notes of raspberry and tomato, sautéed mushroom and crushed hard spices, smoke, vanilla, and toast. There's a scent of wild honey that carries through the finish, but the wine is fully dry. Light and evanescent, it has lots of charm. **88** —*S.H. (4/1/2002)*

Royal Oaks 2000 Sangiovese (Central Coast) $18. This pale red wine is simple and clean. Cherry cola aromas, in the mouth, raspberry and cherry fruit explodes, sweetly ripe, although the wine is fundamentally dry. A silky texture and adequate acidity completes the picture. **85** —*S.H. (5/1/2002)*

Royal Oaks 2000 Sauvignon Blanc (Santa Barbara County) $15. Lets off a blast of sulfur that eventually reveals oak, smoke, spice, and peach aromas. Spicy, clean, and simple—a refreshing wine with no flaws and no particular complexity. **85** —*S.H. (4/1/2002)*

Royal Oaks 1999 Sauvignon Blanc (Santa Barbara County) $16. A simple wine that straddles the balance between grassy, citrusy flavors and riper, more melony ones. It's crisp and dry and offers pleasure without a great deal of complexity, although there are some oaky, leesy notes. From Santa Ynez and Santa Maria valleys. **86** —*S.H. (5/1/2001)*

Royal Oaks 2000 Reserve Sauvignon Blanc (Santa Ynez Valley) $19. Pretty, grassy aroma, with hay and dried straw and more than a hint of cat pee. But it tastes richer and creamier than it smells. Dry and balanced, it's a nice mouthful, by itself or with food. **86** —*S.H. (4/1/2002)*

Royal Oaks 1999 Valley View Vineyard Reserve Sauvignon Blanc (Santa Ynez Valley) $18. They aged this 100% varietal wine on the lees in French oak to make it layered and complex, but it's still a pretty one-dimensional wine. Some citrus aromas and flavors, but they're thin and watery. Very well made, but needs a bit more concentration. **85** —*S.H. (5/1/2001)*

Royal Oaks 2001 Westerly Vineyard Sauvignon Blanc (Santa Ynez Valley) $22. Doesn't smell fully ripe, with its opening blast of grassy hay and gooseberry only partially relieved by an undercurrent of peach. It's very dry and tart in the mouth, too. Has high acidity and citrusy finish. **85** —*S.H. (12/31/2003)*

Royal Oaks 2000 Syrah (Central Coast) $20. Clean aromas of cola, meat, and wild berries are simple, and so is the wine in the mouth. Big fruit, spicy and sugary ripe, is wrapped in soft acids and tannins and a round, silky texture. Doesn't really drink like a California Syrah; more like a jammy, early drinking Aussie Shiraz. **85** —*S.H. (9/1/2002)*

Royal Oaks 2001 Westerly Vineyard Viognier (Santa Ynez Valley) $28. An exotically opulent wine, filled with flair and zest. The mélange of flavors includes pineapple, breadfruit, white peach, honeysuckle, vanilla, and all sorts of other fruity, flowery things. But it's dry, with a pretty streak of acidity. **87** —*S.H. (12/31/2003)*

ROZA RIDGE

Roza Ridge 2002 Roza Ridge Vineyard Syrah (Yakima Valley) $14. Full-bodied and buttressed by oak, but doesn't seem to have great depth of fruit. Simple berry and vanilla flavors are pleasant enough, but finish with tough-edged tannins. **84** *(9/1/2005)*

ROZAK

Rozak 2003 Pinot Noir (Santa Rita Hills) $30. This ripe Pinot has a roasted aroma of charry oak and cherry pie, with a smooth, silky texture. It's rich in cherry and mocha flavors, with a fairly stiff dose of tannin. A bit brawny now, so decant it, or let it mellow for a few years. **87** —*S.H. (3/1/2006)*

RUBICON ESTATE

Rubicon Estate 2002 Cabernet Blend (Rutherford) $110. Fragrant, showing cascades of violets, caramelized new oak, sweet cherry pie, cocoa, and cassis aromas. In the mouth, it's unctuous, and floods the palate with sweet, savory flavors. Has a youthful jamminess right now, which will melt off and refine as time goes by. Such is the elegance and balance that cellaring it for 20 years will be no problem. This is the best Rubicon ever. **98 Cellar Selection** —*S.H. (9/1/2006)*

Rubicon Estate 2003 Cabernet Franc (Rutherford) $44. This bottling has ripe cherry and toasty oak flavors, wrapped in fine tannins, and is thoroughly dry. It's a light-bodied, pleasant wine, but is a little one-dimensional, especially at this price. **86** —*S.H. (5/1/2006)*

Rubicon Estate 2003 Cask Cabernet Sauvignon (Rutherford) $65. I always think of Francis Coppola's Cask Cabernet as his hommage to the old Inglenook. It's 100% varietal, grown at the Rutherford estate, and a spectacular wine. Enormously oaky now, with an explosion of char and vanilla, it shows an underworld of black currants, and is huge in sweet, youthful tannins. Yet those tannins are so polished, so refined. This is a glamorous wine, tremendous now, and will hold and develop through 2020. **95 Cellar Selection** —*S.H. (12/15/2006)*

Rubicon Estate 2002 Cask Cabernet Cabernet Sauvignon (Rutherford) $65. This is not the same wine as Niebaum-Coppola's Cask Cabernet, although it sells for the same price. It's made in a different style, more tannic and not as apparently oaky. To judge from the depth of flavor, it's extremely cellarworthy. Should unfold by 2008 and develop for years beyond. **90 Cellar Selection** —S.H. (12/15/2005)

Rubicon Estate 2004 Blancaneaux White Wine Rhône White Blend (Rutherford) $40. A blend of Roussanne, Viognier, and Marsanne, this estate-grown wine is voluptuously rich. It presents almost as a dessert, suggesting mango-laced crème caramel, papaya custard, candied apricots, and similar flavors. Almost too much of a good thing. **86** —S.H. (11/15/2006)

RUBISSOW-SARGENT

Rubissow-Sargent 1999 Cabernet Sauvignon (Mount Veeder) $30. Still hard and tough in tannins, but that's Mount Veeder. Tastes like it was just bottled. Bigtime blackberry and cherry fruit is buried deep. Hold until 2008 and try again. **87** —S.H. (5/1/2005)

Rubissow-Sargent 2000 Reserve Cabernet Sauvignon (Mount Veeder) $75. Smells beautiful, with a nuanced perfume of rich cassis, black cherry, and new smoky oak and vanilla. But be warned, the tannins are potent. They grip the palate and fundamentally close it down. Absolutely requires further cellaring. Drink 2010-2020. **89 Cellar Selection** —S.H. (5/1/2005)

RUDD

Rudd 2000 Jericho Canyon Vineyard Red Wine Bordeaux Blend (Napa Valley) $100. Smooth and velvety, with rich aromas and flavors of toast and cassis that glide elegantly across the palate. The tannins are soft and the acids seem low, making it attractive to drink now **91** —J.C. (5/1/2004)

Rudd 2001 Cabernet Sauvignon (Oakville) $75. Classic Oakville, detailed and refined, powerful in fruit and tannins; assertive and authoritative, yet manages to be graceful and elegant. A fulfilling wine, balanced and harmonious. Clearly has the stuffing to enjoy a ripe old age. Drink now through 2015. **94 Cellar Selection** —S.H. (10/1/2004)

Rudd 2004 *Barrel Sample* Cabernet Sauvignon (Oakville) $NA. Very young and tannic, and crisp with acids as well as heavily oaked. Rich, sweet core of black cherry, mocha, and cassis fruit. Thick, huge, should age very well. **93** —S.H. (8/1/2004)

Rudd 2003 Estate Grown Cabernet Sauvignon (Oakville) $125. Made in a very ripe, almost in-your-face style, with flamboyant blackberry pie and cassis flavors veering into rum-soaked raisins and prunes. Defines size and power rather than elegance; a brawny, slightly hot wine that nonetheless is compellingly good to drink. **92** —S.H. (9/1/2006)

Rudd 2002 Oakville Estate Cabernet Sauvignon (Oakville) $90. Wow, what a fantastic wine. Bursts open with scads of fine French oak, cedar, and char, with a rôti quality riding high over the cherries, cassis, and white chocolate. So good, it's scary. Rich, long, powerful in cassis and cherry fruit, yet wonderfully firm and tannic, this wine is fabulous now, but will easily improve through 2015 and possible beyond. **96 Cellar Selection** — S.H. (11/1/2005)

Rudd 1998 Chardonnay (Carneros) $35. The fragrant and flavorful nose's butter, lychee, and banana aromas create an alluring opening. Pink grapefruit and tropical fruit flavors accent a sweetly spicy, baked-apple mouth that has medium weight and a nice texture. The wine finishes dry and nutty, with moderate length. Smoky and lush, it's ready to drink tonight. **90** (7/1/2001)

Rudd 1998 Chardonnay (Russian River Valley) $35. Some very appealing apple, Asian pear, mint, smoke, and toast notes mark the nose of this even, medium-weight wine. It has fine fruit-to-acid balance and offers apple-peach flavors with a mild but evident butterscotch element. The tangy oak that's present from the start shows most prominently on the spicy finish. **87** (7/1/2001)

Rudd 2000 Estate Red Wine Red Blend (Oakville) $100. A notable success for the vintage, Rudd's Estate offering does display slightly herbal characteristics, but amply compensates for that with plenty of lush, rich fruit. Oak-imparted toast and supple tannins frame ripe berry flavors that extend through the finish. Drink now–2010. **92** —J.C. (5/1/2004)

Rudd 2003 Sauvignon Blanc (Napa Valley) $28. An oaky, hearty wine that in many ways wants to be Chardonnay. The nose exudes fresh-cut wood, while the flavor profile is all about buttered toast, apple, and peach. Stylistically, it's California all the way, yet there's enough acid and natural

flavor to help it from being too heavy. **89** (7/1/2005)

RULO WINERY

Rulo Winery 2002 Cabernet Sauvignon (Columbia Valley (WA)) $30. Pure, classic Cabernet. Young, tight, tannic, and tart, yet it is already drinking well and built for aging. Great balance and structure. **92** —P.G. (9/1/2004)

Rulo Winery 2004 Sundance Vineyard Chardonnay (Columbia Valley (WA)) $20. Yet another outstanding effort from Rulo, this appealing Chardonnay marries pretty peach flavors to a mix of spices from 100% French oak barrel fermentation. Cinnamon and other Asian spices, along with barrel toast, provide a nice counterpoint to the ripe fruit. **90** —P.G. (6/1/2006)

Rulo Winery 2001 Sundance Vineyard Chardonnay (Columbia Valley (WA)) $23. An attractive wine that takes clean, precise fruit and carefully showcases it in a very pretty, balanced, concise, elegant style. This is not a blockbuster, but it is a beautifully structured wine which shows a masterful sense of craft. Hints of butter, lemon, citrus, floral, honey are all suggestively layered together. **90** —P.G. (9/1/2003)

Rulo Winery 2003 Vanessa Vineyard Chardonnay (Walla Walla (WA)) $20. From a two acre plot in Walla Walla, this lush, elegant wine shows Kurt Schlicker's deft, complex approach to winemaking. 100% barrel fermented, it clocks in at 14% alcohol and tastes of clean fruit, with light hints of buttered toast and toasted nuts. Elegant and sophisticated, it shows a deft touch with the wood. **91** —P.G. (12/15/2005)

Rulo Winery 2004 Combine Sauvignon Blanc (Columbia Valley (WA)) $15. This is Sauvignon Blanc with a 14% blast of Viognier; the combination is vivid and bracing, like a dash through a cold mountain spring. All stainless, no malolactic. It's cool as ice, clear and leesy, and the tart fruit is edged with citrus rind flavors, a nice mix of orange, lemon and lime. **91 Best Buy** —P.G. (6/1/2006)

Rulo Winery 2004 Syrah (Columbia Valley (WA)) $19. Don't let the nondescript label fool you; this is serious juice. Dark, sappy, spicy, and dense, it comes on with flavors of baking chocolate and smoked meat, scented with violets and citrus, and finishes with bracing green tea tannins. A strong, muscular, substantial effort. **92 Editors' Choice** —P.G. (8/1/2006)

Rulo Winery 2002 Syrah (Columbia Valley (WA)) $18. A gem. Meaty, bacon fat nose, strikingly clear, purple-hued colors, and sweet, seductive fruit. What more can one ask of an $18 Syrah? This is elegant, strong, and supple, with a long life ahead of it. **90** —P.G. (9/1/2004)

Rulo Winery 2001 Syrah (Columbia Valley (WA)) $18. This wine really should cost more. It shows good, sweet, complex fruit flavors mixing red fruits and hints of leaf and spice; it has a bit of oak that doesn't get in the way, and it packs plenty of power without being too alcoholic or obliterating the nuances. **89** —P.G. (9/1/2003)

Rulo Winery 2002 Silo Syrah (Columbia Valley (WA)) $25. This is a single-vineyard Syrah, from a Wahluke Slope vineyard, and it has plenty of grapy, gamy, juicy fruit. Clean and light-footed, with bracing acid and sweet/tangy fruit, this is a high-wire wine made for a big, fat, meaty burger or steak. **90** —P.G. (9/1/2004)

Rulo Winery 2004 Viognier (Columbia Valley (WA)) $18. Here is Viognier picked early enough to feature flavors of citrus rind rather than ripe peach. There is also a powerful herbal note, tasting of juniper and quinine, that lays down a spicy spine in the wine. All stainless, no malolactic; it's crisp, precise, and laser-like in its focus. **90** —P.G. (6/1/2006)

Rulo Winery 2003 Viognier (Walla Walla (WA)) $18. A full, intense wine, with concentrated scents of perfumed citrus. The flavors are big but balanced, and the wine captures the elegance and power of the grape with perfect symmetry. **90** —P.G. (9/1/2004)

Rulo Winery 2001 Viognier (Columbia Valley (WA)) $18. Very fresh and clean, like a drink of fresh air. There is a slight saltiness to it, a pleasing lightly bitter flavor of citrus rind; good presence, persistence, and length, all in a light, food-friendly style that has plenty of crisp, lively yeastiness. **88** —P.G. (9/1/2003)

RUSACK

Rusack 2001 Anacapa Bordeaux Blend (Santa Ynez Valley) $38. The two Cabernets and Merlot combined in this great vintage produce as near a

USA

North Coast red as the valley has yet produced. It is very ripe, with the blackberry flavors nudging into currants and cassis, and the tannins are also nice and sweet. A wine to watch. **90** —*S.H. (10/1/2003)*

Rusack 1997 Anacapa Bordeaux Blend (Santa Ynez Valley) $32. 85 *(11/1/2000)*

Rusack 2002 Anacapa Cabernet Blend (Santa Ynez Valley) $36. This wine is okay, but rather sour and green. It offers little palate pleasure, and is the victim, not of winemaking, but of terroir. Santa Ynez is not Cabernet country! **84** —*S.H. (10/1/2005)*

Rusack 2004 Chardonnay (Santa Barbara County) $20. This junior version of Rusack's reserve is ripe in tropical fruit flavors and well-oaked, and the acids are bright and clean. Shows lots of sophisticated cool-climate Santa Barbara character at a fair price. **88** —*S.H. (8/1/2006)*

Rusack 2003 Chardonnay (Santa Barbara County) $20. This is a very dry, crisp Chard that shows mineral, sweet Meyer lemon, and green apple aromas and flavors. It's polished and elegant, with a long, oaky-spicy finish. **87** —*S.H. (10/1/2005)*

Rusack 2002 Chardonnay (Santa Barbara County) $18. Well-oaked, this likeable wine features perky, citrusy acids that frame an array of peach, pineapple, sweet lime, and other tropical fruits flavors. The texture is really pretty, like buttercream. Finishes with a touch of lees. **90 Editors' Choice** —*S.H. (6/1/2004)*

Rusack 2001 Chardonnay (Santa Barbara County) $18. South Coast fruit is vividly etched, with fresh tropical fruit flavors and crisp acids. Framed in a creamy texture, it leaves behind an aftertaste of ripe mango. Yet the wine is dry and steely, and as good as the reserve. **90 Editors' Choice** —*S.H. (5/1/2003)*

Rusack 2004 Reserve Chardonnay (Santa Maria Valley) $32. Rusack turns to two vineyards, including Bien Nacido, for their reserve Chard, which is richer and finer than their regular county-wide botting. It's a nice Chard, but a bit young and angular now. The parts are there for a rich, creamy, tropical fruit and mineral show stopper to emerge. Give it until late 2006 and into 2007. **91** —*S.H. (8/1/2006)*

Rusack 2003 Reserve Chardonnay (Santa Maria Valley) $32. Very similar in terroir-driven flavors to Rusack's less expensive Chardonnay, with citrus and orange blossom flavors, a steely, minerally note and modest oak. The structure is more angular, with very high acidity leading to a long finish. **91** —*S.H. (10/1/2005)*

Rusack 2001 Reserve Chardonnay (Santa Maria Valley) $32. Richly ripe, with flamboyant green apple and peach flavors, and lots of oak. Nice creamy texture, and dry. Notable for the lush quality of its acids, which make the wine crisp and tart through the finish. **90** —*S.H. (6/1/2003)*

Rusack 1997 Reserve Chardonnay (Santa Maria Valley) $30. 90 *(6/1/2000)*

Rusack 1998 Reserve Lucas Select Chardonnay (Santa Maria Valley) $35. Mint, fresh fruit, and decidedly floral aromas led to yet another split-decision wine you may just have to taste yourself. Some tasters found elegance, white stone fruits, citrus, and good acidity leading to a rich, silky finish with buttery and nutty notes. Others (same bottle!) found it soft, sweet, and a bit cloying in a "your auntie's perfume" manner. Strange, but true…we can't make this stuff up. **88** *(7/1/2001)*

Rusack 1997 Silver Moon Merlot (Santa Ynez Valley) $15. 85 —*J.C. (7/1/2000)*

Rusack 2004 Pinot Noir (Santa Maria Valley) $30. This was a tough vintage, with multiple days above 100° during harvest, but winemaker John Falcone pulled it off. The wine is graceful despite a background of raisins, which add a spicy piquancy to the cherry and crushed spice flavors. Drink now. **90** —*S.H. (8/1/2006)*

Rusack 2002 Pinot Noir (Santa Maria Valley) $25. A very pretty and supple wine, silky and complex in cherry, herb, spice, rhubarb, coffee, and vanilla notes. Has some tannins in the finish that suggest midterm aging. Drink now through 2007. **89** *(11/1/2004)*

Rusack 2001 Pinot Noir (Santa Maria Valley) $25. Not bad with its liltingly soft tannins and brisk acidity, but Santa Barbara's weakness in cool years, tomato flavors, dominate, along with cranberry. It's dry, with high acids. The lean fruit leads to a tart, acidic finish. **85** —*S.H. (7/1/2003)*

Rusack 2001 Pinot Noir (Santa Barbara County) $18. There's a lot of

unripeness going on here, showing up as lean, tobaccoey flavors verging on mint. Drinks acidic and thin, and while there are some black cherry flavors, the wine is basically herbal. Yet it's not without its charms. **85** —*S.H. (7/1/2003)*

Rusack 2000 Pinot Noir (Santa Maria Valley) $28. Bright and light, this Pinot's tart-sweet cherry and herb profile make it a good choice as a cocktail red or to pair with light foods. There was some divergence in the panel: One taster found it syrupy and more sweet than tart, others enjoyed its dusty, smoky notes and mildly lively astringency. Drink this now and over the next year. **84** *(10/1/2002)*

Rusack 2004 Reserve Pinot Noir (Santa Rita Hills) $38. A blend of grapes from three of the appellation's best-known vineyards, this complex, sumptuous wine has it all. Medium-bodied and forward in cherry, pomegranate, cola, bitter cocoa, and spice flavors, it maintains a delicate harmony from the entry through the silky midpalate to the long, deeply satisfying finish. Drink this dry, elegant wine now–2008. **93** —*S.H. (8/1/2006)*

Rusack 2002 Reserve Pinot Noir (Santa Rita Hills) $32. Clean, refreshing, and balanced, this wine's cherry, raspberry, smoke, and vanilla flavors are delicious. It lacks a certain intensity in the middle, but the tannins are rich and sweet. **87** *(11/1/2004)*

Rusack 2001 Reserve Pinot Noir (Santa Rita Hills) $32. Marginally riper and plusher than Rusack's other two Pinots, but not by a lot. This is still a lean, earthy wine, short on flavor and long on acidity and tannins. Sift through the herbal, bay leaf and sage tastes and you'll find a note of cherry. Aging may help. **86** —*S.H. (7/1/2003)*

Rusack 1999 Reserve Lucas Select Pinot Noir (Santa Maria Valley) $35. Powerful aromatics of tomato, coffee, raisins, and drying wood on the nose. The palate is rich enough, if a bit candied. Cola and charcoal mix with raspberry on the finish. The weight is medium, but there's a hollowness to the wine that holds it back. **86** *(10/1/2002)*

Rusack 2005 Sauvignon Blanc (Santa Ynez Valley) $16. Rich in lemon and lime, fig, melon, and apricot flavors and fruity-sweet, but balanced with crisp acidity. Has an upscale creaminess that lifts it above the ordinary. **86** —*S.H. (8/1/2006)*

Rusack 2002 Sauvignon Blanc (Santa Ynez Valley) $15. From a warmer area near Ballard, a delicately structured wine with crisp acidity that is very rich in lemon and lime, fig, and peach flavors. There's a summery feeling to the vibrant fruit, which finishes with a spicy-honeyed aftertaste. **87** —*S.H. (12/31/2003)*

Rusack 2003 Syrah (Santa Barbara County) $25. Smoky and even a bit funky on the nose, then delivers rich, earthy flavors on the palate, veering toward coffee and chocolate and backed by blackberries and plums. Give it one or two years to settle down, then drink it over the next five to six. **89** *(9/1/2005)*

Rusack 2001 Syrah (Santa Ynez Valley) $25. A blend from around the appellation, and a charming wine that lacks a bit of fruity richness, but makes up for it with its intricate tannin-acid structure and overall finesse. Flavors of blackberry, herbs, and black tea are detailed; the wine's exceeding dryness invites contemplation. **90** —*S.H. (3/1/2004)*

Rusack 2003 Ballard Canyon Reserve Syrah (Santa Barbara County) $36. Big and bold, with sturdy blackberry and coffee flavors that pick up a hint of vanilla on the lingering finish. A hint of shoe polish on the nose dampened our enthusiasm, but this is still a fine example of American Syrah. **88** *(9/1/2005)*

Rusack 1999 Estate Vineyard Syrah (Santa Barbara County) $25. A hint of shoe polish on the nose gives way to aromas of toast and blackberries. Flavors are full and soft, big, and black: toast, blackberry, plum, and earth, kissed with chocolate and coffee, on the finish. **88** *(11/1/2001)*

RUSSELL CREEK

Russell Creek 2002 Tributary Red Wine Bordeaux Blend (Washington) $20. The blend is three quarters Cab, one quarter Merlot, and it reflects the winery style, which is smooth-drinking, supple, simple wines that show monochromatic fruit and some chocolate. **86** —*P.G. (4/1/2005)*

Russell Creek 2002 Walla Walla Valley & Columbia Valley Cabernet Sauvignon (Washington) $28. This 100% Cab is thick and chewy, with lots of chocolatey tannin, and a solid core of cherry/berry fruit.

USA

Substantial and tasty, if a bit one-dimensional. **88** —*P.G. (4/1/2005)*

Russell Creek 2002 Winemakers Select Cabernet Sauvignon (Walla Walla (WA)) $38. The rule here seems to be more oak, more tannin, more chocolatey flavors over fruit that is very similar to the regular Cab. Good stuff, solid and very clean, with plump berry flavors. **88** —*P.G. (4/1/2005)*

Russell Creek 2002 Merlot (Walla Walla (WA)) $26. Very smooth, succulent style which marries fresh berry flavor to lots of milk chocolatey oak. It's appealing, broadly accessible, fairly simplistic, but certainly delicious. **87** —*P.G. (4/1/2005)*

Russell Creek 2000 Merlot (Columbia Valley (WA)) $32. This has sharp, cedary oak dominating the fruit right now. The fruit is good, solid black cherry, but it is not quite big enough to tackle all that new oak, though some bottle time will help. Good, ambitious winemaking. **88** —*P.G. (9/1/2002)*

Russell Creek 2002 Winemakers Select Merlot (Walla Walla (WA)) $36. The winemakers select is bigger than the regular bottling, with high-toned fruit, bigger and rougher tannins, and more obvious oak. The extra extraction makes it less, not more accessible for near-term drinking. **87** —*P.G. (4/1/2005)*

Russell Creek 2002 Winemakers Select Syrah (Columbia Valley (WA)) $35. The grapes come from Alder Creek and reflect the less than fully ripe flavors of cranberry, sour cherry, and pepper. Lots of unresolved oak and hints of pickle barrel; this wine needs additional airing and/or bottle age to fully come together. **86** —*P.G. (4/1/2005)*

RUSSIAN HILL

Russian Hill 2004 Gail Ann's Vineyard Chardonnay (Russian River Valley) $30. Acidity saves this wine. It's ripe in pineapple and peach pie filling flavors; the grapes soar to high sugars, compounded by a good amount of custardy oak. But that crispness balances it completely. **88** —*S.H. (12/31/2006)*

Russian Hill 2003 Gail Ann's Vineyard Chardonnay (Russian River Valley) $28. If you like your Chards citrusy, tart, and on the mineral side, this is for you. Some will find it thin, others will call it elegant and food friendly. For me, at this price, it's a disappointment, although it's certainly oaky. **84** —*S.H. (12/15/2005)*

Russian Hill 2002 Gail Ann's Vineyard Chardonnay (Russian River Valley) $30. Crisp in fresh acids, with a leesy flavor and texture. The fruit veers toward tart citrus fruits, candied apples, and metallic minerals. Finishes with a lime-skin bitterness. **87** —*S.H. (3/1/2005)*

Russian Hill 2001 Gail Ann's Vineyard Chardonnay (Russian River Valley) $26. Lots of toasty, vanilliny oak has been sprinkled on the pear, cinnamon apple, and tropical fruit flavors of this rich but dry wine. It has good structure, with crisp acids and sweet tannins. It's lush, but elegant through a very long, fruity finish. **91** —*S.H. (5/1/2004)*

Russian Hill 2003 Pinot Noir (Russian River Valley) $32. Too extracted, flat and candied for my tastes, this Pinot has a medicinal cherry flavor, with a thick, sappy texture. **82** —*S.H. (12/15/2005)*

Russian Hill 2002 Pinot Noir (Sonoma Coast) $42. A fascinating Pinot that showcases the evolution of the varietal in this cool-climate growing region. The fruit isn't quite ripe, with tomato, cola, and rhubarb flavors, although oak does its best to fatten and sweeten. The wine is totally dry and rather tart. It's also dense and full-bodied, with the weight of Merlot. **89** —*S.H. (3/1/2005)*

Russian Hill 2000 Pinot Noir (Russian River Valley) $28. It's hard not to like the healthy fruit offered by this cola and leather-accented wine. Described by tasters as furry and woody but wonderful, it stays poised and keeps all elements in harmony through the long, earthy finish. **89** *(10/1/2002)*

Russian Hill 2000 Pinot Noir (Sonoma Coast) $22. Full—almost pulpy, one taster noted—with aromas of dark ripe cherries, chocolate, spice, and cedar, this weighty, cedary Pinot has a tobacco-tinged, rustic quality. It's big and a bit one-dimensional, and finishing with plenty of oak and just a touch of heat. **84** *(10/1/2002)*

Russian Hill 1999 Pinot Noir (Russian River Valley) $28. Bramble, cedar, and cinnamon aromas are the introduction to this tight, tangy wine that runs a bit hot. It's very racy, indicating high acidity. The finish features some biting raspberry but also some balancing oak. **86** *(10/1/2002)*

Russian Hill 2002 Estate Pinot Noir (Russian River Valley) $33. Rather heavy in texture, with the weight of a Rhône wine, and thick, fruity flavors of plums, heirloom tomatoes, cola, espresso, and oak. Very dry, with smooth tannins. This is a big Pinot, clean and complex, although not particularly delicate. **87** —*S.H. (3/1/2005)*

Russian Hill 2004 Estate Vineyards Pinot Noir (Russian River Valley) $32. A little on the thin, wintergreen side, but the wine has a fresh, young appeal, and enough fanciness to go with lamb, pork, and roast beef. The fruit is all cherry pie filling, with classic Russian River cola, rosehip tea, and rhubarb, and a tasteful overlay of toasty oak. Not an ager. **86** —*S.H. (12/31/2006)*

Russian Hill 2004 Leras Vineyard Pinot Noir (Russian River Valley) $40. I love the elegance of this Pinot. This is so light and delicate, yet so interesting, with rosehip tea, tangerine zest, Asian spice, and cola flavors that are accented by toasty new oak. It just fascinates all along. **91** —*S.H. (12/31/2006)*

Russian Hill 2000 Leras Vineyard Pinot Noir (Russian River Valley) $38. **86** *(10/1/2002)*

Russian Hill 1999 Leras Vineyard Pinot Noir (Russian River Valley) $44. Cherries and chocolate run wild on the nose of this single-vineyard wine. There are more chocolate-covered cherries in the mouth, and the finish is streamlined and very clean. A smooth, chalky mouthfeel amplifies its total presence. **89** *(10/1/2002)*

Russian Hill 2004 Tara Vineyard Pinot Noir (Russian River Valley) $42. Very dry, delicately structured and crisp, with a mushroomy, leathery earthiness that adds extra layers to the cherry and cola flavors. A lovely, silky, complex Pinot that should hold well through 2010. **90** —*S.H. (12/1/2006)*

Russian Hill 2003 Tara Vineyard Pinot Noir (Russian River Valley) $47. Soft to the point of flatness, syrupy but dry, this wine has baked cherry flavors and a gluey finish. **81** —*S.H. (12/15/2005)*

Russian Hill 2002 Syrah (Russian River Valley) $22. Creamy and soft-textured, Russian Hill's blended Syrah is an easy-to-drink Syrah made for immediate appeal. Caramel, coffee, and vanilla notes envelop ripe red berries in a cocoon of accessibility. Drink now. **88** *(9/1/2005)*

Russian Hill 1999 Syrah (Russian River Valley) $22. In this firm, understated Syrah, toast, earth, and leather aromas segue into coffee, blackberry, and vanilla flavors. The plum-maple finish is a little rough—but we have confidence that it'll smooth out with a little age. Top Value. **89** *(11/1/2001)*

Russian Hill 2002 Ellen's Block Syrah (Russian River Valley) $30. All three tasters preferred Russian Hill's blended Syrah, but the Ellen's Block bottling is no slouch. Green herb and peppery notes dominate the nose, but add meat and violet notes with airing. Tart red berries play a supporting role, couched in firm tannins. **86** *(9/1/2005)*

Russian Hill 2001 Ellen's Block Syrah (Russian River Valley) $30. This wine starts with a blast of white pepper that yields to plushly layered flavors of blackberries and cherries. You find yourself savoring the delicious fruity flavors and then the wine's balance and structural harmony shine through. Best now through 2005. **91** *(5/1/2004)*

Russian Hill 2002 Top Block Syrah (Russian River Valley) $30. Thickly textured and low in acidity, this Syrah also boasts plenty of mixed berry fruit and dried spices. A hint of white chocolate gives a rich, fatty note, while pepper and cloves linger on the finish. **85** *(9/1/2005)*

Russian Hill 2001 Top Block Syrah (Russian River Valley) $30. This is a striking Syrah. It's a huge wine that opens with a peppery aroma. One sip and the flavors explode, yielding blackberries, Kahlúa, and sweet cherry marmalade. For all its size, the wine never loses its sense of balance and control. **92 Editors' Choice** *(5/1/2004)*

Russian Hill 2001 Windsor Oaks Summit Syrah (Russian River Valley) $40. Marked by rich oak and massive flavors of blackberry jam, Indian pudding, and cocoa, with a sprinkling of white pepper through the long finish. The tannins are pretty strong now, suggesting midterm aging, but it will be great with roast lamb. **90** *(5/1/2004)*

RUSTON

Ruston 2002 La Maestra Red Wine Cabernet Blend (St. Helena) $50. A Cabernet-based Bordeaux blend, and what a nice wine it is. Rich in cherry, raspberry, cassis, and mocha flavors, but saved from simple fruit

USA

overload by good acidity and finely ground, though sizable, tannins. Has the structure to age though 2015. **93 Editors' Choice** —*S.H. (8/1/2006)*

Ruston 2000 Merlot (St. Helena) $30. A richly textured, luscious Merlot that's loaded with ripe plum, prune, black cherry, coffee, chocolate, toast, licorice, herb, and spice flavors. Smooth, lush, and delicious. A full-bodied wine that's top notch for this varietal. **91** —*J.M. (4/1/2004)*

RUSTRIDGE

RustRidge 1998 Cabernet Sauvignon (Napa Valley) $28. Blackberry, cassis, and oak aromas are accompanied by an unusual caramelized note suggesting marzipan. In the mouth, it's extremely soft, almost flabby, with light fruit. Doesn't seem like it's going anywhere. **83** —*S.H. (12/1/2001)*

RustRidge 1997 Reserve Cabernet Sauvignon (Napa Valley) $30. Light and rustic, with a tart edge, this wine has flavors of semi-ripened berries and a thin, watery finish. The middle palate is very acidic, almost sour. There are no technical faults, but it doesn't offer much pleasure. **81** —*S.H. (12/1/2001)*

RustRidge 1999 Chardonnay (Napa Valley) $22. Rich and textured, this wine brims with peach, tropical fruit, and smoky oak aromas, and drinks fruity and crisp. In fact, the acidity gives it a burn in the middle palate and finish, pushed along by leesy notes. This structured wine demands food. **86** —*S.H. (12/1/2001)*

RustRidge 1998 Estate Bottled Chardonnay (Napa Valley) $25. 83 *(6/1/2000)*

RustRidge 1999 Sauvignon Blanc (Napa Valley) $20. Shows good varietal character in the citrus and apple aromas and flavors, framed by clean, refreshing acidity. The mouth-cleaning quality follows through the lemon-flavored, tart finish. **84** —*S.H. (11/15/2001)*

RustRidge 1999 Zinfandel (Napa Valley) $20. Aromas of brambly, wild berries, peppery spices, tar, and smoke erupt from the glass, leading to a well-ripened wine with pretty flavors of blackberries and black raspberries. One minor quibble is its softness. It lacks backbone. Another is 15.6% alcohol, which makes it finish hot and heady. **85** —*S.H. (11/15/2001)*

RustRidge 1997 Zinfandel (Napa Valley) $18. 87 —*P.G. (11/15/1999)*

RUTHERFORD

Rutherford 2001 Cabernet Sauvignon (Napa Valley) $32. Rich, opulent, and lush, showcasing everything that went right in Napa this vintage. Not as intense as some others, but flavorful in black currants and chocolate, with balancing acidity. **87** —*S.H. (10/1/2004)*

RUTHERFORD GROVE

Rutherford Grove 2001 Cabernet Sauvignon (Napa Valley) $40. Very ripe and forward in cherry and blackberry fruit flavors, while the oak adds toast and vanilla notes. Finishes dry, with sturdy, dusty tannins leading to a sharp finish. **87** —*S.H. (10/1/2005)*

Rutherford Grove 2001 Cabernet Sauvignon (Rutherford) $40. Very dark and very extracted in jammy blackberry and cherry flavors, although dry. A big, flashy wine of great panache that may age, but now it's a bit heavy and ponderous. **87** —*S.H. (10/1/2004)*

Rutherford Grove 2001 Merlot (Napa Valley) $28. Very dry and rather tart, this simple wine has easy flavors of berries, herbs, and oak. It's a little astringent, and at its best now. **84** —*S.H. (10/1/2005)*

Rutherford Grove 2001 Spring Creek Vineyard Petite Sirah (St. Helena) $35. A classically big Pet, dark in color, shy in aroma and overwhelmed by tannins in its youth. Decant for a few hours, and it begins to give off blackberry marmalade. The balance suggests a long and distinguished life. Best after 2010. **90** —*S.H. (10/1/2004)*

Rutherford Grove 2003 Sauvignon Blanc (Rutherford) $14. It's rich in appley, citrus fruit flavors, with spicy fig notes, and the acidity and balance are really good. Has that sweet edge you get in many California Sauvignons. **86** —*S.H. (9/1/2004)*

Rutherford Grove 2005 Estate Sauvignon Blanc (Napa Valley) $16. Here's a nice, cool-climate, long hangtime wine. The warm days coaxed citrusy, figgy, melon-rich flavors, while the cool nights preserved fresh acidity. The winemaker kept wood off, and finished the wine just a tiny bit sweet, but it's fundamentally dry. Very polished. **87** —*S.H. (12/31/2006)*

RUTHERFORD HILL

Rutherford Hill 2003 Cabernet Sauvignon (Napa Valley) $35. Well-structured and dry, this Cab has proper varietal flavors framed in sturdy but fine tannins. It's a velvety smooth wine, but the fruit is on the thin side. **83** —*S.H. (11/1/2006)*

Rutherford Hill 2002 Cabernet Sauvignon (Napa Valley) $35. Tastes sharp and a little unripe, with a green, minty streak that cuts through the cherry fruit. Other than that, the tannins, acids and oak are fine. **83** —*S.H. (11/1/2005)*

Rutherford Hill 1999 25th Anniversary Cabernet Sauvignon (Napa Valley) $30. Rutherford Hill keeps putting out quality juice at affordable prices. The 25th Anniversary Cabernet has aromas of a new cedar closet and blackberries. The flavors are of juicy berries with a touch of Indian spices. Full, rich tannins on the palate are enjoyable now, but will hold up to some bottle age. Drink now until 2010. **90** —*C.S. (11/15/2002)*

Rutherford Hill 2004 Chardonnay (Napa Valley) $18. This wine comes down on the earthy side, with a dried herb note to the apple, peach, and fig flavors. It's very dry, with decent acidity. Finishes with a vanilla flourish. **84** —*S.H. (11/1/2006)*

Rutherford Hill 2002 Chardonnay (Napa Valley) $18. Just pour it, and the aromas of peaches, tropical fruits, and smoky oak waft out of the glass. Dry and easy, with tons of fruit and spice into the finish. **85** —*S.H. (12/15/2004)*

Rutherford Hill 1998 Chardonnay (Napa Valley) $17. Full and smooth, with ripe apple-pineapple aromas and flavors offset by spice accents, this mainstream Napa Chardonnay delivers plenty of pleasure. Oak and buttered popcorn play on the lingering finish. **88** *(11/1/2001)*

Rutherford Hill 2000 26th Anniversary Chardonnay (Napa Valley) $17. Hits all the right notes, from the rich, sweet tropical fruit to the butter and toast accents, but like the third violin in the symphony, lacks that extra flair to really stand out. The oak is well proportioned, and some zesty lime notes that should make it reasonably versatile with food grace the finish. **87** —*J.C. (9/1/2002)*

Rutherford Hill 1997 Reserve Chardonnay (Carneros) $28. Much smokier than the regular Chardonnay, this is a more reserved, smoothly textured style. Pear, apple, and lemon flavors mingle with toasty oak in a package that shows a good deal of finesse. It should last longer than the regular 1998 bottling, but is decidedly different, though not necessarily better. **88** *(11/1/2001)*

Rutherford Hill 2003 Malbec (Napa Valley) $28. If you're looking for fat, opulent Napa fruit, go elsewhere. This wine has an unrelieved austerity. The coffee and soy flavors are super-tannic and searingly dry. Hard to tell what the winemaker was thinking. Maybe it'll go somewhere in the cellar. **84** —*S.H. (11/15/2006)*

Rutherford Hill 2002 Malbec (Napa Valley) $26. Normally used for blending, Malbec on its own can be one-dimensional, as this wine is. It's dark, full-bodied, dry, and tannic, with berry and herb flavors. That about says it all. **84** —*S.H. (11/1/2005)*

Rutherford Hill 2003 Merlot (Napa Valley) $25. Rutherford Hill used to make one of the best Merlots in the valley. Nowadays, the wine is obviously mass-produced (more than 57,000 cases), a simple but varietally correct Merlot with cherry, blackberry, and mocha flavors. **84** —*S.H. (11/1/2006)*

Rutherford Hill 2002 Merlot (Napa Valley) $25. Pretty smooth and supple, this is a very soft, high thread-count wine that glides across the palate. It carries very ripe flavors of cherries and cocoa, with a finish that's almost sweet. **84** —*S.H. (11/1/2005)*

Rutherford Hill 2001 Merlot (Napa Valley) $25. Generous in ripe black currant and cherry fruit, and well oaked. There's an angularity to the mouthfeel and a sharpness to the finish that detract. May soften with a few years of aging. 72,000 cases produced. **85** —*S.H. (12/15/2004)*

Rutherford Hill 1999 Merlot (Napa Valley) $24. Berry and earth aromas open to a palate with a strong herbaceous note and a lean, structured feel. Perhaps more European in style, it shows surprising hardness and a tart quality to the fruit. Should open and soften some with aging, but seems as if it will always be on the lean side. **87** *(11/1/2001)*

Rutherford Hill 1998 Merlot (Napa Valley) $22. Dark cherry fruit and herb flavors with chocolate/cocoa accents mark this mid-weight red. Not as deep or rich as the 1997 and somewhat backward, it has good Merlot character but can use a year or two to smooth and perhaps flesh out a bit. Finishes dry with even tannins and decent length. **88** *(11/1/2001)*

Rutherford Hill 1997 Merlot (Napa Valley) $21. This nicely textured wine shows a stylish nose and good depth, with a bouquet of black cherry, cocoa, and anise. A big wine, with a plush, rich mouthfeel, it pours on classy plum and chocolate flavors in an accessible manner. Full but even tannins show on the tart cherry finish. Enjoyable now, even better in one or two years. **90** *(11/1/2001)*

Rutherford Hill 1996 Merlot (Napa Valley) $21. Full on the palate with cedar, smoke, earth, and plum notes, this solid wine shows good structure and complexity. Features black cherry and mocha flavors, a soft, velvety mouthfeel and a long, softly tannic finish. **88** *(11/1/2001)*

Rutherford Hill 1995 Merlot (Napa Valley) $20. A gamy note and some earthy accents highlight the black cherry fruit in this mid-weight wine. The oak shows, and there are attractive cocoa and black tea accents on the smooth palate. Closes with moderate length, dark berry and earth notes. **86** *(11/1/2001)*

Rutherford Hill 1994 Merlot (Napa Valley) $19. This is a light, pleasant Merlot with cherry, herb, and cedar aromas and flavors and a smooth mouthfeel. Evenly textured, but lacks that extra depth to push it to higher levels of quality. Finishes a little short, with a peppery tang and modest tannins. **85** *(11/1/2001)*

Rutherford Hill 2003 Reserve Merlot (Napa Valley) $90. Rutherford Hill has a great history with this variety, and it seems like they are making a statement here. The wine is very dry, quite tannic, and not showing much flavor now. Doesn't seem like it's a cellar candidate, but may be. **90** —*S.H. (11/15/2006)*

Rutherford Hill 2002 Reserve Merlot (Napa Valley) $76. What a beautiful wine. It has Merlot's fleshy softness, but with a firm structure of finely ground tannins. Flavorwise, it packs cherry, blackberry, plum, coffee, and cocoa flavors, with oak contributing a rich overlay of sweet vanilla and char. Drink now in its exuberant youth. **92 Editors' Choice** —*S.H. (11/1/2005)*

Rutherford Hill 2001 Reserve Merlot (Napa Valley) $86. Back in the '70s, this winery specialized in Merlot and helped put it on the fine wine map. This wine, in a thick, heavy bottle, is elegant, complex, and probably ageable. It's fairly tannic, but possesses a molten core of cherry and mocha fruit and a lilting balance that bode well for the future. Now through 2010. **94** —*S.H. (4/1/2005)*

Rutherford Hill 1999 Reserve Merlot (Napa Valley) $70. Has an inviting nose of dry loam, driftwood, toffee, coffee bean, toasted nuts, marshmallows, and greens. Similar flavors are rounded out with sautéed mushrooms, dried dates, and figs. Offers plenty to explore and savor within a balanced, straightforward package founded on approachable fruit. **90** —*K.F. (4/1/2003)*

Rutherford Hill 1997 Reserve Merlot (Napa Valley) $60. Aromas of dark chocolate, licorice, cedar, and spice open this burly wine. Tart black cherry and ample oak show on the palate, but the wine is rather closed now and will benefit from two to four years of aging. Closes long, with a chocolate note and big tannins that need some time to resolve. **90 Cellar Selection** *(11/1/2001)*

Rutherford Hill 1996 Reserve Merlot (Napa Valley) $50. A nose of spice, earth, and cedar opens this medium-bodied wine that offers more than the 1995 and is a step toward the richer, more impressive 1997. Black cherry and charred oak notes play on the palate. The finish, with its hints of clove and tarragon, displays good length and some nuance. Closes with dusty tannins. Could use another year in the bottle. **88** *(11/1/2001)*

Rutherford Hill 1995 Reserve Merlot (Napa Valley) $47. A complex, inviting bouquet of black cherry, cocoa, herb, toast, and tobacco sets up this medium-bodied wine. The palate doesn't follow through fully on that promise—its flavors lighten up rather than build in intensity, while maintaining the same basic profile. Finishes juicy and spicy with lots of oaky notes. The nose is great, the wine very good. **87** *(11/1/2001)*

Rutherford Hill 2005 Rosé of Merlot (Napa Valley) $19. Simple and dry, but the big problem with this blush is that it has no flavor! If you close your eyes and concentrate, you can conjur up some cherries. But it's basically alcoholized water. **82** —*S.H. (11/15/2006)*

Rutherford Hill 2003 Rosé of Merlot (Napa Valley) $19. Seems pricey for a rather thin, inert wine. A flavorful blush Merlot from Napa would be a good thing, but this one is just too diluted. **83** —*S.H. (12/15/2004)*

Rutherford Hill 2003 Petite Verdot (Napa Valley) $28. Midnight black, super dry, and bitterly tannic, but with structural elegance, this is a wine that calls for imagination with food pairing. Good beef comes to mind, charbroiled and garlicky. Gamblers will cellar it. **85** —*S.H. (11/15/2006)*

Rutherford Hill 2004 Rose of Merlot Rosé Blend (Napa Valley) $19. A little simple and easy, but there's a wealth of raspberry, strawberry, and floral notes in this delicate wine. It's a bit too sweet for my tastes, although it does have good acidity. **84** —*S.H. (11/1/2005)*

Rutherford Hill 1996 22nd Anniversary Sangiovese (Napa Valley) $30. **88** —*M.S. (9/1/2000)*

RUTHERFORD OAKS

Rutherford Oaks 1999 Hozhoni Vineyard Cabernet Sauvignon (Rutherford) $50. Inky-dark, it stains the glass; this is a big wine. It's tannic now, and comes across as earthy and austere, but astute tasters will detect an intense core of fruit that needs time to express itself. **90** —*S.H. (11/15/2002)*

Rutherford Oaks 2000 Hozhoni Vineyard Syrah (Rutherford) $30. Starts off with bell pepper, smoke, spice, and earth on the nose. The follow-up features black chery, plum, coffee, cola, and toast flavors. Tannins are fairly soft, while the finish is bright, with an herbal twist. **88** —*J.M. (6/1/2003)*

Rutherford Oaks 1999 Hozhoni Vineyard Syrah (Rutherford) $38. Reminds me of the young Picasso, before he developed his style. But what promise! Obviously great grapes, yielding intense fruit. Super balance between acids and tannins. This is a single-vineyard wine that will be dependent on the vintage. With some tweaking, in a great year this will be a great wine, one to follow. **90** —*S.H. (12/1/2002)*

RUTHERFORD RANCH

Rutherford Ranch 2002 Cabernet Sauvignon (Napa Valley) $16. As ripe as they come, with lush, mouthfilling flavors of blackberry pie, cherry tart, chocolate, and vanilla cream. Fortunately there's a wealth of dusty tannins and good acidity for balance. Finishes dry, although the fruit is so ripe, it's almost sweet. **86** —*S.H. (5/1/2006)*

Rutherford Ranch 2001 Cabernet Sauvignon (Napa Valley) $15. Okay drinking from a great vintage, but it's a tough, acidic young wine. Satisfies with cherry and oak flavors in the finish. **83** —*S.H. (10/1/2005)*

Rutherford Ranch 1999 Cabernet Sauvignon (Napa Valley) $14. Thin for a '99, with modest black currant, plum, tobacco, and earthy flavors and a little bit of oak. The tannins are pretty puckery, although the acids feel low and soft. **84** —*S.H. (12/31/2002)*

Rutherford Ranch 2002 Reserve Cabernet Sauvignon (Napa Valley) $30. The wine is dry and tannic right out of the bottle, with a firm, hard mouthfeel that combines austerity with elegance. Buried deep is a core of oak-accented cassis and cherry fruit. Best to decant this young wine for up to eight hours to let it breathe and develop. **91** —*S.H. (8/1/2006)*

Rutherford Ranch 1999 Silverado Trail Vineyard Limited Release Reserve Cabernet Sauvignon (Napa Valley) $35. A very good Cab with polished blackberry, plum, and herb flavors, and some gritty tannins that turn astringent on the finish, although they're accompanied by ripe, sweet fruit. It's very dry, with a great structure that calls for fine foods. **89** —*S.H. (5/1/2004)*

Rutherford Ranch 1999 Stagecoach-Krupp Vineyards Limited Release Reserve Cabernet Sauvignon (Napa Valley) $35. There's plenty of concentrated Cabernet fruit to stand up to the smoky oak in this delicious new wine. It has ripe flavors of black currants, cherries, herbs, and chocolate, toned up with ripe, sweet tannins that turn gritty on the finish. Tastes like an ager, but it's awfully nice right now. **91** —*S.H. (5/1/2004)*

Rutherford Ranch 2003 Chardonnay (Napa Valley) $13. Dry, earthy, and a little green and herbal, this wine shows modest apple and peach flavors. It's the kind of Chard you can gulp easily without worrying about the price. **84** —*S.H. (10/1/2005)*

Rutherford Ranch 2001 Chardonnay (Napa Valley) $12. Average in every way, from the decent peach and apple flavors to the okay acidity and the dollop of oak to the quick finish. Doesn't rise above the ordinary, doesn't sink to the abyss. **84** —*S.H. (12/1/2003)*

Rutherford Ranch 2000 Chardonnay (Napa Valley) $12. There are some pretty apple and pear flavors, wrapped in spicy oak, and a fairly rich mouthfeel. Seems a little flat in acidity, with an earthy finish. Pretty good for the money. **84** —*S.H. (6/1/2003)*

Rutherford Ranch 2002 Merlot (Napa Valley) $13. Dry and earthy, with red stone fruit and berry flavors, this wine has complex notes of coffee, grilled meat, and cocoa, as well as oaky nuances. It really impresses all around. **87** —*S.H. (10/1/2005)*

Rutherford Ranch 2000 Merlot (Napa Valley) $12. Despite the Napa appellation, there's not much going on. This is a berryish wine, dry and tart with tannins. Feels tough and resistant on the palate, and stays firm through the finish. **84** —*S.H. (12/31/2002)*

Rutherford Ranch 2001 Sauvignon Blanc (Napa Valley) $10. This wine is so good for the money, it must be because of the grape glut that's pushing prices down. Firmly fruity, with melon, fig, lime zest, and sage flavors that last through the spicy finish. Good acids make the palate feel clean and refreshed. **86** —*S.H. (9/1/2003)*

Rutherford Ranch 2000 Zinfandel (Napa Valley) $14. Good, rich, and ripe, a feisty little Zin with all kinds of tasty flavors. Blackberries, blueberries, pecan pie, sweet dried herbs, orange zest, vanilla, and smoke, to name a few. Completely dry, with soft, easy tannins and a firm mouthfeel. Really fine, although it turns just a bit thin on the finish, but that's nitpicking. **87** —*S.H. (3/1/2004)*

RUTHERFORD VINTNERS

Rutherford Vintners 2003 Cabernet Sauvignon (Napa Valley) $16. Far too sweet to qualify for a higher rating, this Cab has good varietal flavors that taste like a spoonful or two of white sugar has been added. Perhaps that explains the low alcohol, only 12.5 percent. **82** —*S.H. (7/1/2006)*

Rutherford Vintners 2003 Chardonnay (Napa Valley) $12. Simple and syrupy, with canned peach and apricot flavors and enough acidity to cut through the semi-sweetness for balance. **83** —*S.H. (7/1/2006)*

Rutherford Vintners 1997 Barrel Select Fumé Blanc (California) $8. 81 *(3/1/2000)*

Rutherford Vintners 1999 Barrel Select Syrah (Stanislaus County) $9. On the nose, apple and Concord grape aromas take on a stewed quality; add cream and graham cracker to the mix, and you've got a pretty sweet opening. Mouthfeel is soft and even, but perhaps hollow; palate and finish shows blackberry fruit, cocoa, and toasted oak **83** *(10/1/2001)*

RUTZ

Rutz 2000 Chardonnay (Russian River Valley) $18. Bright, crisp, and really likeable, not just another me-too oaky monster. Well-etched fruity flavors of tart green apples, nectarine, and guava are balanced with brilliant acids and just the right amount of smoky oak barrels. The spicy finish goes on for a long time. **90** —*S.H. (12/1/2003)*

Rutz 1998 Chardonnay (Russian River Valley) $20. A rich, complex Chardonnay with apple and peach notes and a strong mineral component. A scent of something like gunmetal or flint follows through in the flavors and helps give the wine a steely backbone. A distinctive wine; very dry and crisp. **87** —*S.H. (5/1/2001)*

Rutz 2001 Dutton Ranch Chardonnay (Russian River Valley) $38. A tight, minerally Chard that's a bit tough now. The acids stick out, and there's an earthy edge to the apple, peach, and pear flavors. Give it a year or so for all the parts to knit together. **89** —*S.H. (8/1/2005)*

Rutz 2000 Dutton Ranch Chardonnay (Russian River Valley) $35. A brilliant evocation of Russian River Chard, beginning with the strong fruit. Flavors veer toward guava, nectarine, and breadfruit, with plenty of Oriental spices. Oak and lees provide creamy complexities, but are in balance. Finally, wonderfully bright acidity undergirds the structure. **92** —*S.H. (12/1/2003)*

Rutz 1999 Dutton Ranch Chardonnay (Russian River Valley) $30. Lush and appealing, the spicy peach, apple, and tropical fruit flavors are nicely highlighted by rich lees and toasted oak. Crisp acids offset the lush flavors perfectly, creating balance and harmony. The wine has an elegant, limpid quality despite its size. **91** —*S.H. (9/1/2002)*

Rutz 2001 Maison Grand Cru Chardonnay (Russian River Valley) $30. This is a high-acid Chardonnay that's not one of those buttery fruit bombs. It hits with a mouthful of minerals and stones, as well as lees and oak, but there is a tantalizing hint of lemon curd and peach yogurt. Will benefit from a little airing. **91** —*S.H. (8/1/2005)*

Rutz 2000 Maison Grand Cru Chardonnay (Russian River Valley) $25. Lovely and inviting, a well-structured wine due to its good acids and sprinkling of dusty tannins. The flavors are a bit tight, suggesting riper, sweeter citrus fruits such as tangerines, and the texture is rich and creamy. **90** —*S.H. (12/1/2003)*

Rutz 1999 Maison Grand Cru Chardonnay (Russian River Valley) $25. A rich, balanced Chard, one that impresses with ripeness, wood, and winemaker bells and whistles without tripping into excess. Perfectly ripened peach and pear fruit is nicely offset by oaky notes and just-right acids. The creamy texture is a pleasure, but it's really balance that defines this wine. **92 Editors' Choice** *(9/1/2002)*

Rutz 2001 Merlot (North Coast) $25. A very good regional wine that tastes ripe and fruity. There are plummy, chocolatey flavors and a rich streak of cherry that really opens up on the long finish. It's dry, with firm but supple tannins, making it an easy sipper tonight. **87** —*S.H. (5/1/2004)*

Rutz 2001 Pinot Noir (Sonoma Coast) $18. An interesting wine that straddles the line between herbal-earthy and richly ripe. Now it suggests black cherries and raspberries, now mushrooms and soy. The balance is perfect, with crisp acidity, silky, lush tannins and a bit of heat from alcohol. Turns spicy on the finish. Seductive, and as good as many Pinots that cost far more. **91 Editors' Choice** —*S.H. (12/1/2003)*

Rutz 2000 Pinot Noir (Sonoma Coast) $20. Candied cherry fruit, smoke, vanilla, and leather accents, plus a light, bright feel—all "good things," as Martha would say—don't add up here. Cola and mocha hints show, but the whole is somehow less than the sum of the parts. In a split panel, this seemed simple and lacking depth to some, but long, dry, and needing one or two years to others. **84** *(10/1/2002)*

Rutz 1998 Pinot Noir (Russian River Valley) $20. Very pale in color, just beyond rosé. Wonderfully fragrant aromas of black cherries, cola, Oriental spices, smoke, and mushroomy earth. It packs a real punch in the mouth, too, with a great depth of rich, fruity, spicy flavor. Dry, with soft tannins but lively acidity. **87** —*S.H. (5/1/2001)*

Rutz 2002 Burnside Vineyard Reserve Pinot Noir (Russian River Valley) $60. There's lots of ripe berry flavor in this Pinot, whose mouthfeel has a certain rustic character. It's a heavy wine, dark, thick, and jammy, with a chocolatey feel to the cherries and rhubarb pie flavors, although it's completely dry. **86** —*S.H. (12/15/2005)*

Rutz 2001 Dutton Ranch Pinot Noir (Russian River Valley) $38. An exquisite jewel of a Pinot, crisp, dry, delicate, and light-bodied, with a satin and silk texture, yet complex in flavor. Layers of raspberry, cherry, mocha, cola, rhubarb, and peppery spice unfold in waves, through a long, richly sweet finish. **91** —*S.H. (8/1/2005)*

Rutz 1999 Dutton Ranch Pinot Noir (Russian River Valley) $30. Fleshy and rich. It's like a bite of filet mignon, tender and soft, juicy and chewy, and completely mouthfilling and delicious. Straddles the border between raspberries and tomatoes, with fresh green herbs and oaky nuances. A very fine Pinot. **91 Editors' Choice** —*S.H. (9/1/2002)*

Rutz 2001 Maison Grand Cru Pinot Noir (Russian River Valley) $30. The fabulous wine showcases the best that Russian River can give Pinot, and wisely avoids the overripe tendency now common in the appellation. Elegant, light-bodied, silky, and crisp, with elaborately complex flavors that range from sweet raspberries, cocoa, cherries, and cola to bitter cranberries and coffee. Simply irresistible, and it doesn't aspire to be an ager. Drink now for its exuberant, flashy beauty. **92 Editors' Choice** —*S.H. (8/1/2005)*

Rutz 2000 Maison Grand Cru Pinot Noir (Russian River Valley) $25. How lush and delicious this wine is! Juicy and rich in the mouth, meaty and full-bodied and quite acidic, yet the texture is light as a feather. The complex flavors range from blackberry and cherry through dried herbs to sautéed mushroom and soy, with a honey-sweet finish. Sheer delight, textbook Russian River Valley Pinot Noir. **93** —*S.H. (12/1/2003)*

Rutz 1999 Maison Grand Cru Pinot Noir (Russian River Valley) $25. This is a blend of Rutz's single-vineyard Pinots. Displays the fleshy, berry, and

USA

tomato flavors of Dutton Ranch and Martinelli, and is very similar to both. Makes the case for blending. It doesn't hit the heights, but is a refined wine, and a versatile one. **87** —*S.H. (9/1/2002)*

Rutz 2000 Martinelli Vineyard Pinot Noir (Russian River Valley) $35. Quite delicious, like drinking pure velvet and silk, so soft and caressing on the palate. Rich in flavor, too, with cherry-blackberry, vanilla, and spice. A shade less complex than Rutz's Maison Grand Cru. **90** —*S.H. (12/1/2003)*

Rutz 1999 Martinelli Vineyard Pinot Noir (Russian River Valley) $30. . Nice drinking wine, dry and silky, with generous berry and herb flavors and a tasteful touch of fine oak. That said, it's fuller-bodied than you'd expect, given the league it plays in. Seems to lack the delicacy and transparency that cool-weather Pinot typically achieves. **87** —*S.H. (9/1/2002)*

Rutz 1999 Weir Vineyard Pinot Noir (Mendocino) $30. This vineyard straddles the cool-hot line between Anderson Valley and Alexander Valley, but in this vintage, warm weather won out. The wine is good, but too full-bodied, and wants the delicacy Pinot Noir demands. The flavors have a heaviness more akin to Syrah. **86** —*S.H. (9/1/2002)*

Rutz 2002 Windsor Gardens Pinot Noir (Russian River Valley) $60. Rather heavy and thick for a Pinot, with cherry, coffee, and cocoa flavors that finish dry. Fans of fuller-bodied Pinots will like this style, but it really could use more delicacy. **85** —*S.H. (12/15/2005)*

RYAN PATRICK

Ryan Patrick 1999 Bordeaux Blend (Columbia Valley (WA)) $29. This bold, vivid wine is 54% Merlot, 39% Cabernet Sauvignon, and 7% Cabernet Franc. The fruit is amazing—layers of red, blue, and blackberries, seamless and compact, lead into accents of mineral and anise. The tannins are proportional and the oak is just a light seasoning. **92** —*P.G. (9/1/2002)*

Ryan Patrick 2003 Rock Island Bordeaux Blend (Columbia Valley (WA)) $14. This Redblend of 61% Merlot, 28% Cabernet Sauvignon, and 11% Cab Franc is always a fine value. This year's version is noticeably softer and more textured, sleek and well-made with highlights of light spice and herb. Through a smooth and lingering finish it adds notes of anise, graphite, and slate. **87** —*P.G. (8/1/2006)*

Ryan Patrick 2002 Rock Island Red Bordeaux Blend (Columbia Valley (WA)) $18. Named not for a railroad line, but the winery's home town, this blend remains essentially the same as 2001—56% Merlot, 39% Cabernet Sauvignon and 5% Cab Franc. Shows a rougher profile, with big flavors of raw meat, plum, grape, and earth. The core of pure, sweet cherry fruit ramps up the quality, which is excellent for the price. **88** —*P.G. (12/1/2004)*

Ryan Patrick 2000 Chardonnay (Columbia Valley (WA)) $15. This is excellent; barrel-fermented and richly textured without being overbearing. Soft fruit, sweet nutty oak and a buttery, sweet cream finish all meld together in a seamless, satisfying whole. **89 Best Buy** —*P.G. (9/1/2002)*

Ryan Patrick 2004 Estate Chardonnay (Columbia Valley (WA)) $14. Bright entry leads to a softer midpalate. A change in style from previous years, more approachable, less acidic, with more obvious flavors of buttered nuts and popcorn. The smooth, soft, slightly soapy style may be a welcome change for some palates, but I miss the old snap and sizzle. **88** —*P.G. (8/1/2006)*

Ryan Patrick 2003 Estate Chardonnay (Columbia Valley (WA)) $18. Consistent with the stylish '02, this young, spicy wine hits the palate with bright, snappy flavors of pineapple, lime, and green berries. Some buttery toast nicely fills in the back end. **89** —*P.G. (12/1/2004)*

Ryan Patrick 2002 Estate Chardonnay (Columbia Valley (WA)) $15. A very stylish effort with crisp, zippy fruit showing pineapple, lime, and star fruit. Great mouthfeel and a very refreshing finish. The wine puts the fruit out in front; if there is any new oak, it is restrained, and not missed. **89 Best Buy** —*P.G. (5/1/2004)*

Ryan Patrick 2001 Red Blend (Columbia Valley (WA)) $29. Tasty, though rough, it comes on with chocolatey fruit, green coffee bean tannins, sweet toast, and ultimately, a very pleasing set of flavors. The cherry fruit, nuanced with tobacco leaf and herb, prevails over the somewhat rustic structure. **89** —*P.G. (12/1/2004)*

Ryan Patrick 2003 Reserve Red Blend (Columbia Valley (WA)) $42. The reserve comes from many of the same vineyard sources as the budget Rock Island Red, and quite honestly, doesn't taste all that different. It got

a bit more barrel time in a bit more new oak, but from a fruit standpoint it's not any bigger or more interesting. Elegant and pleasant, it's well made but not really up to its reserve moniker. **87** —*P.G. (8/1/2006)*

Ryan Patrick 2001 Rock Island Red Red Blend (Columbia Valley (WA)) $15. A blend of 56% Merlot, 42% Cabernet Sauvignon, and 2% Cab Franc, nicely crafted and eminently quaffable. Light spice, hints of pepper and herb, and very pretty fruit tell the story. **87 Best Buy** —*P.G. (5/1/2004)*

Ryan Patrick 2004 Sauvignon Blanc (Columbia Valley (WA)) $14. A full-flavored, spicy bottle showing off tart pineapple and citrus fruit, lightly dusted with cinnamon. The addition of 11% Sémillon punches up the core, and the barrel fermentation (15% new oak) adds lovely, spicy highlights. **89 Best Buy** —*P.G. (8/1/2006)*

Ryan Patrick 2003 Vin d'Été White Blend (Columbia Valley (WA)) $20. This "summer wine" blend is mostly Sauvignon Blanc, with about 16% Sémillon adding lemongrass and lanolin. Soft, lightly nutty, almost Italian in style, it is smooth and rich across the palate, with a pleasing nuttiness to the lingering finish. **88** —*P.G. (12/1/2004)*

S. ANDERSON

S. Anderson 1997 Richard Chambers Vineyard Cabernet Sauvignon (Stags Leap District) $75. 93 *(11/1/2000)*

S. Anderson 1994 Blanc de Blanc Champagne Blend (Napa Valley) $46. 90 —*S.H. (12/1/2000)*

S. Anderson 1997 Blanc de Noirs Champagne Blend (Napa Valley) $28. Peach, melon, and citrus flavors are at the core. The finish is soft and mellow, turning toasty and nutty at the end. **89** —*J.M. (12/1/2002)*

S. Anderson 1996 Blanc de Noirs Champagne Blend (Napa Valley) $28. 90 —*S.H. (12/1/2000)*

USA

S. Anderson 1997 Brut Champagne Blend (Napa Valley) $28. Bright and fresh, with peach and citrus notes. The wine is light on the palate, but offers a long, toasty finish at the end. **88** —*J.M. (12/1/2002)*

S. Anderson 1996 Brut Champagne Blend (Napa Valley) $28. 86 —*S.H. (12/1/2000)*

S. Anderson 1997 Merlot (Stags Leap District) $30. Aromas of cedar and mocha lead into a medium-bodied wine with a creamy, plush mouthfeel and flavors of tart cherries and tobacco. Cedar accents the softly tannic finish. Ready to drink now. **87** —*J.C. (6/1/2001)*

S. P. DRUMMER

S. P. Drummer 1999 Blair Vineyard Cabernet Blend (Napa Valley) $45. Silky smooth and elegant, this initial release from veteran winemaker Scott Peterson is loaded with layers of spice, cherry, blueberry, mocha, and coffee notes. It's got plenty of power, but remains feminine in its charm, with intriguing earth and herb flavors at its core. **93** —*J.M. (11/15/2002)*

S.E. CHASE FAMILY CELLARS

S.E. Chase Family Cellars 2001 Zinfandel (Napa Valley) $36. Another top-notch wine from this relatively new producer. This vintage is packed with complex, ripe black cherry, blackberry, plum, spice, toast, vanilla, coffee, chocolate, and herb flavors, all supported by smooth, supple tannins. It's lush and long to the end. **93** —*J.M. (4/1/2004)*

S.E. Chase Family Cellars 2000 Zinfandel (Napa Valley) $36. This wine struts it power with great elegance. Made from old vines in a famous vineyard, it offers smooth, silky tannins, rich ripe black cherry, plum, chocolate, sandalwood and spice flavors too. Firm, clean, and long at the end. **91** —*J.M. (9/1/2003)*

SABLE RIDGE

Sable Ridge 2000 Petite Sirah (Russian River Valley) $28. Another controversial wine. It received among the highest and lowest scores. Some raved over its rich array of berry and stone fruit flavors, and its lush mouthfeel, while others felt the tannins and acids were out of whack. Everyone agreed it was easy to drink. **86** *(4/1/2003)*

Sable Ridge 1999 Petite Sirah (Russian River Valley) $28. It's a crying shame California doesn't get serious about Petite Sirah because this wine shows just how good it can be. It's got Cabernet's full-bodied character, Zinfandel's spicy fruit, the airy, weightless quality of Pinot Noir, and Syrah's smoky, notes. Add it up and it makes for one tasty if slightly savage wine. **92** —*S.H. (9/1/2002)*

Sable Ridge 1999 Hensley-Lauchland Vineyard Old Vine Zinfandel (Lodi) $20. Opens with the prettiest wildberry and brambly, peppery aromas, and gorgeous, sumptuously fruity flavors. It's round and supple, with some nice weight; a sheer joy to drink. Of course, it's soft, but that's warm country old-vine Zin for you. **89** —*S.H. (12/15/2001)*

Sable Ridge 1998 Old Vine Zinfandel (Lodi) $18. Nice aromas here, of wild berries, smoke, and earth, and strong, ripe berry, fruit and spice flavors. But it's very light in body and substance, almost airy. I longed for some tannins, some flesh. **85** —*S.H. (11/15/2001)*

SACRED STONE

Sacred Stone NV Master's Red Blend Rhône Red Blend (California) $9. Rustic and easy, with cherry and cocoa flavors and soft tannins. Finishes dry and fruity. A good value at this price. Rhône blend. **84** —*S.H. (5/1/2005)*

SADDLEBACK

Saddleback 2003 Cabernet Sauvignon (Napa Valley) $50. Kind of tough and reticent now, very dry and showing lockdown tannins and upfront acidity. It doesn't offer immediate delight, although it's a well-made wine, with a deep core of Cabernet flavor. Decanting will help. Could age out by 2010. **87** —*S.H. (12/31/2006)*

Saddleback 2000 Cabernet Sauvignon (Napa Valley) $48. Quite dark and rich, though still holding back in its youth. The wine offers layers of complex flavors. Blackberry, cassis, chocolate, coffee, herbs, toast, cedar, and smoke blend nicely here. The tannins are quite firm but ripe, while the finish is long and lush. **92** —*J.M. (12/31/2003)*

Saddleback 2001 Chardonnay (Napa Valley) $22. When you measure this against Testarossa's other single-vineyard wines, this release is earthy and lean, with citrus and tobacco flavors. Like all the rest, it's quite oaky. Doesn't share the rich opulence and hedonism of the others, although it's certainly a good wine. **87** —*J.M. (12/15/2003)*

Saddleback 2002 Merlot (Napa Valley) $32. It sure is ripe and rich, in line with the wonderful vintage, with a wealth of cherry, licorice, mocha, and smoky oak flavors. On the other side are a certain roughness and semi-sweet finish that detract from elegance. **85** —*S.H. (12/31/2006)*

Saddleback 2001 Merlot (Napa Valley) $36. Smoky lean, with hints of black cherry, blackberry, herb, spice, and licorice notes. Tannins are powdery, and the wine finishes with moderate length. **87** —*J.M. (12/31/2003)*

Saddleback 2005 Pinot Blanc (Oakville) $18. Here's a fresh young wine with flavors that are really kind of interesting, suggesting citrus fruits, peaches, apricots, and limes. Barrel-fermented, it resembles a creamy Chardonnay, but with a zippy tangerine zest brightness and good, crisp acidity. **86** —*S.H. (12/31/2006)*

Saddleback 2003 Pinot Blanc (Oakville) $18. Extracted and jammy in peach and pineapple fruit, this wine is slightly rustic in body and texture. It's oaky and dry, with plenty of acidity, the kind that makes the tastebuds tingle. **85** —*S.H. (3/1/2006)*

Saddleback 2001 Pinot Blanc (Napa Valley) $18. Lush and richly textured, with upfront vanilla and spice aromas. On the palate, it's loaded with pretty citrus, mineral, and herb notes. Long, clean and bright at the end. **89** —*J.M. (2/1/2004)*

Saddleback 2005 Pinot Grigio (Oakville) $18. One of the rare PGs that comes from this prestigious appellation, which is patently too warm for the variety. The wine is dull and soft, with earthy flavors, and all that oak doesn't help. **82** —*S.H. (12/31/2006)*

Saddleback 2001 Pinot Grigio (Napa Valley) $18. More steely than this winery's Pinot Blanc, the wine is crisp and clean, with citrus and mineral notes leading the way. It finishes zippy clean and fresh. **87** —*J.M. (12/1/2003)*

Saddleback 2005 Viognier (Clarksburg) $19. A bit simple, but dry and clean, this barrel-fermented Viognier has nice tropical fruit and floral flavors. The acidity is very food-friendly, and the wine wisely avoids that over- the-topness that Viognier can have. **84** —*S.H. (12/31/2006)*

Saddleback 2003 Viognier (Clarksburg) $19. Clarksburg is in the Delta, and grows decent whites due to the Bay breezes that reach this far inland. This wine is fruity and floral, with a nice apricot finish that's dry and crisp. **84** —*S.H. (3/1/2006)*

Saddleback 2001 Viognier (Napa Valley) $19. Quite zippy, with bright acidity and lemony overtones. The wine is also blessed with exotic apricot, melon, and honeyed tones as well as pretty floral notes on the finish. Very refreshing. **88** —*J.M. (12/1/2003)*

Saddleback 1997 Zinfandel (Napa Valley) $26. 85 —*S.H. (5/1/2000)*

Saddleback 2004 Old Vines Zinfandel (Napa Valley) $36. Lots to like in this ripe, complex wine. It shows Zin's briary, brambly, wild nature, with that acidic, delightfully sharp fruit taste you get from freshly-picked berries plucked from thorn bushes in the height of summer. Yet it possesses an elegant, Merlot-like softness that's just luscious. That touch of raisins in the finish just adds another layer. **92** —*S.H. (12/31/2006)*

Saddleback 2003 Old Vines Zinfandel (Napa Valley) $32. With sweet and sour flavors of cherries, and a scour of burning acidity, this Zin is harsh and unbalanced. **82** —*S.H. (3/1/2006)*

Saddleback 2001 Old Vines Zinfandel (Napa Valley) $30. A plush, firm style that holds back a bit, yet still reveals plenty of dark black cherry, plum, cassis, licorice, spice, and herb flavors. It's framed in classy oak and ripe tannins, finishing with moderate length on the finish. **90** *(11/1/2003)*

SADDLEBACK CELLARS

Saddleback Cellars 2004 Pinot Grigio (Oakville) $18. Imagine a PG as rich, creamy, and complex as a great Chardonnay, with, of course, a different flavor profile. This wine is ripe in apple, apricot, nectarine, peach, fig, and spice flavors, with a slightly sweet finish. But the acidity works to keep it clean and balanced. **88** —*S.H. (2/1/2006)*

Saddleback Cellars 2003 Sauvignon Blanc (Napa Valley) $20. Fully oaked, thus you get aromas of butter, vanilla, and ultraripe melon. Plenty of smoke and butter carries onto the palate, where green apple and citrus come into the picture. Solidly structured, with more than enough wood to satisfy a hungry beaver. **86** *(7/1/2005)*

SAGELANDS

Sagelands 1999 Cabernet Sauvignon (Columbia Valley (WA)) $18. This is the first vintage made after Chalone purchased the old Staton Hills winery and renamed it Sagelands, and it's clear that improvements are being made. This is spicy and herbal, with ripe but not overripe fruit. The winemaking is straightforward and the flavors clean, with some dill and herb. **86** —*P.G. (12/31/2001)*

Sagelands 2001 Four Corners Cabernet Sauvignon (Columbia Valley (WA)) $12. This is a really nice Cabernet. It's very oaky, but the acidy structure and sappy, fresh young blackberry fruit provide more than enough counterpoint to all that sweet wood. The tannins are just beautiful. An incredible value in New World Cabernet. **88** —*S.H. (1/1/2004)*

Sagelands 2003 Merlot (Columbia Valley (WA)) $13. The fleshy, fruity nose suggests very ripe, mixed berry and cherry fruits, and there is a liberal amount of oak. A good, open, broadly fruity mouthfeel knits the wine together nicely. In fact, its flavors seem woven throughout, mixing the fruit with notes of oak, bacon, smoke, and ham. Surprisingly long. **91 Best Buy** —*P.G. (6/1/2006)*

Sagelands 1999 Merlot (Columbia Valley (WA)) $15. This Chalone-owned property was purchased in 1999, and this represents the first serious red wine made under the new administration. Bright and herbal, it has cherry fruit nuanced with tobacco leaf and brightened with crisp acids. Clean and lively, and attractively priced. **88** —*P.G. (12/31/2001)*

Sagelands 2002 Four Corners Merlot (Washington) $12. A very pretty wine, smooth and supple, with more finesse than ever before. It displays clean plum and strawberry fruit flavors and well-managed tannins. A light touch with the American oak gives it a bit of extra flavor. **87 Best Buy** —*P.G. (4/1/2005)*

Sagelands 2001 Four Corners Merlot (Columbia Valley (WA)) $12. A seriously good wine, and it's hard to believe they're practically giving it away. With its depth of black currant, herb, and coffee flavors that are long and deep, its rich tannins and near perfect balance, it's impressive from start to finish. A very great value from Chalone Wine Group. **90 Best Buy** —*S.H. (12/31/2003)*

Sagelands 2000 Four Corners Merlot (Columbia Valley (WA)) $15. A round, solidly made wine, with Bing cherry flavors. However, the middle seems to disappear and, as a result, the following tannins feel a bit harsh. **86** —*P.G. (9/1/2002)*

Sagelands 2003 Pinot Gris (Oregon) $12. Very dry and tart in acids, a steely wine that cleanses the palate with citrus, almond skin, and white pepper flavors. **85** —*S.H. (12/15/2004)*

SAINT GREGORY

Saint Gregory 1998 Pinot Blanc (Mendocino) $14. Begins with pretty but light aromas of peaches and cream and vanilla, and turns watery and citrusy in the mouth, with high acidity. Whistle-clean, it finishes with lemony notes. **83** —*S.H. (8/1/2001)*

Saint Gregory 1999 Pinot Noir (Mendocino) $19. Quite closed on the nose, this wine showed only faint cherry and leather notes. It opens up on the palate, where plum fruit wears more saddle and also caramel accents. Coffee-and-anise finish. **84** *(10/1/2002)*

SAINT LAURENT

Saint Laurent 2001 Solé Riché Red Bordeaux Blend (Columbia Valley (WA)) $22. This oddly named blend of Merlot, Cabernet and Cab Franc is a well-made effort, with moderately ripe fruit flavors of plum and black cherry, green tea tannins, and spicy oak. Still hard and a showing some stemmy tannins, but should smooth out with a little more bottle time. **86** —*P.G. (4/1/2005)*

Saint Laurent 2001 Cabernet Sauvignon (Columbia Valley (WA)) $18. Red cherry, raspberry, and flavors of fresh-turned earth are all here, with hints of herb and leather. There's an odd finish with a plastic, gluey grip; it seems off. **84** —*P.G. (4/1/2005)*

Saint Laurent 2003 Chardonnay (Columbia Valley (WA)) $15. Soft and smooth, with flavors of peach, banana, and papaya. Broadly fruity and accessible, but lacks focus and definition. **85** —*P.G. (4/1/2005)*

Saint Laurent 2001 Merlot (Columbia Valley (WA)) $15. Light and open, with strawberry and rhubarb flavors, dried herb and sweet cracker. Fairly tart and tangy through the finish. **85** —*P.G. (4/1/2005)*

SAINTSBURY

Saintsbury 2001 Chardonnay (Carneros) $20. A pleasant, citrusy Chardonnay, but one that is well-oaked, with the resulting aromas and flavors of vanilla and buttered toast. Lemon and lime flavors veer into riper peach, and are wrapped in a creamy texture. Acidity is quite high and bursts on the palate with a mouthwatering zest. **88** —*S.H. (8/1/2003)*

Saintsbury 2000 Reserve Chardonnay (Carneros) $35. Interesting to taste Saintsbury's Reserve next to the regular Chardonnay. Both naturally share the same taste and textural characteristics, but this wine is oakier and softer in the mouth, especially in acidity. It lacks the crispness and zest of the regular. Seems a bit heavy and flat, although it's still a nice wine. **85** —*S.H. (8/1/2003)*

Saintsbury 1999 Reserve Chardonnay (Carneros) $35. We enjoyed the vanilla, pear, butter, and toasty flavors on this classy Chard, but the high alcohol it contains almost does it in. The nice acid backbone holds it together though and leaves a good overall impression. Enjoy it with grilled seafood. **87** *(7/1/2001)*

Saintsbury 2002 Pinot Noir (Carneros) $26. Rather simple and thin, and not quite ripe, with stemmy, grassy flavors, but saved by the cherry finish and supple texture. **84** *(11/1/2004)*

Saintsbury 2001 Pinot Noir (Carneros) $26. Fruity and simple, a mélange of thorn bush berry and tree fruit flavors encased in silky tannins and adequate acids. A good candidate for a tutorial on Pinot Noir. **85** —*S.H. (7/1/2003)*

Saintsbury 2000 Pinot Noir (Carneros) $24. 86 *(10/1/2002)*

Saintsbury 2000 Brown Ranch Pinot Noir (Carneros) $75. An amazingly good wine that's very dry and austere now, and rather on the tight side. At first it reveals a tobaccoey mintiness, but as it warms up, the rich scent of cherries and mocha wafts out. For all its initial reserve and tannins, this muscular wine is very good, and should age well for ten years or longer. **92** —*S.H. (12/1/2004)*

Saintsbury 1999 Brown Ranch Estate Bottled Pinot Noir (Carneros) $75. Saintsbury's top-of-the-line '99 offering is a solid wine, with a core of cherry fruit framed by toasty oak. Strawberry, ginger, and chocolate nuances add to the appeal, but this doesn't possess the complexity, depth, or length we might have expected. Solid and attractive now, this should improve over the next year or two. **87** *(10/1/2002)*

Saintsbury 2001 Garnet Pinot Noir (Carneros) $17. Drinks rather earthy and simple, and also short on fruit. There's some cherry and raspberry flavor but it's thin. Instead, oaky flavors are meant to substitute. **84** —*S.H. (7/1/2003)*

Saintsbury 2004 Lee Vineyard Pinot Noir (Carneros) $45. Don't look for the full body one expects of Russian River, but rather a lighter color and body in this first bottling of Lee from Saintsbury. There's an earthy herbalness to the complex rosehip tea, cola, and cherry flavors, yet the wine is silky and elegant, with a lilting quality. Drink now through 2010, before it loses fruit. **90** —*S.H. (12/31/2006)*

Saintsbury 2000 Reserve Pinot Noir (Carneros) $50. From a respected old hand at Pinot Noir comes this impressive wine, full, thick, and mouthcoating, with ripe black cherry fruit adorned by coffee, toasty oak, molasses, and herbs. This flavorful Pinot finishes intensely, with black chocolate and earth notes. Drink now–2007. **90** *(10/1/2002)*

Saintsbury 1999 Reserve Pinot Noir (Carneros) $50. Certainly denser and richer than the regular bottling. Still, it is not a lot to get excited about. Berry-cherry flavors are well-oaked and framed in silky tannins. Feels easy and slippery in the mouth, but lacks the depth you want, especially at this price. **86** —*S.H. (7/1/2003)*

Saintsbury 2004 Stanly Ranch Pinot Noir (Carneros) $45. For me, this is the most successful of Saintsbury's new trio of single vineyard Pinots for its depth of flavor. It's a silky, lightly-textured wine, deceptively drinkable, with very gentle tannins, yet has complex cherry, cola, strawberry, rhubarb, Asian spice, and oak flavors, enriched with toasty new oak, that flatter the palate and last long on the finish. **91** —*S.H. (12/31/2006)*

Saintsbury 2004 Toyon Farm Pinot Noir (Carneros) $45. Reminds me of a good Beaune, a dry, silky, light-bodied, somewhat earthy wine of great charm, without super-complexity. Yet the cherry, raspberry, cola, herb tea, cinnamon, and vanilla flavors are delicious. Could pick up nuance with five years in the cellar. **89** —*S.H. (12/31/2006)*

SAKONNET

Sakonnet 1996 Brut Champagne Blend (Southeastern New England) $30. An immediate air of salinity says "coastal," but who would have guessed Rhode Island? Buttercream, bright citrus, toast, and stone fruit aromas and flavors complete this balanced blend of Pinot Noir and Chardonnay. **87** —*K.F. (12/1/2002)*

Sakonnet 1995 Samson Brut Champagne Blend (Southeastern New England) $25. 90 *(12/15/2000)*

Sakonnet 1999 Chardonnay (Finger Lakes) $15. Firm and focused, with pretty mineral and herb notes at its center. The wine has good body and is a bit racy on the finish, with a zingy citrus edge. Well integrated and refined. **89** —*J.C. (7/1/2002)*

Sakonnet 1999 IceWine Vidal Blanc (Southeastern New England) $25. Pretty and sweet, with citrus and herb notes at the fore. A hint of woodiness shows through, though, followed by apricot and peach flavors. **86** —*J.M. (12/1/2002)*

SALMON CREEK

Salmon Creek 1999 Cabernet Sauvignon (California) $NA. Sometimes you just need an inexpensive, clean red wine to gulp down with that pizza or those burritos, a wine that's dry, soft and filled with ripe berry flavors. This is such a wine. There's nothing wrong with it, because it doesn't pretend to be anything more than an everyday quaff. **85 Best Buy** —*S.H. (7/1/2002)*

Salmon Creek 1997 Bad Dog Ranch Chardonnay (Carneros) $19. 82 *(6/1/2000)*

SALMON HARBOR

Salmon Harbor 2000 Chardonnay (Washington) $8. Here is another pleasant, budget effort, with a smooth, surprisingly rich palate impression, soft and forward. All stainless steel-fermented, though I thought I detected just a wee hint of oak, but it's clearly made for right-now drinking. **85** —*P.G. (2/1/2002)*

Salmon Harbor 1997 Chardonnay (Central Coast) $10. 85 —*L.W. (7/1/1999)*

Salmon Harbor 2000 Merlot (Washington) $9. Dark and plum-scented, with a grapey sweetness as well. The flavors are of sweet cherry and strawberry, plump and forward, with a minty finish. It is a hearty, forward, cleanly made wine that offers a great deal of immediate pleasure. **87** —*P.G. (12/31/2001)*

Salmon Harbor 1999 Merlot (Washington) $9. A young wine that smells and tastes as though it leapt from the fermenter to the glass. It's packed with jammy, ripe fruit and the high acidity that usually accompanies it. Juicy and thick, it's almost rude in its impertinence. But it's fun, and the price is right. **85 Best Buy** —*P.G. (6/1/2001)*

SALMON RUN

Salmon Run 2001 Chardonnay (New York) $10. A dichotomy of flavors that reach from the ultra zippy lemon-like acidity to the somewhat sweet-edged peach and apple notes. So it's lacking in balance, but pleasant, nonetheless. Tastes a bit contrived. **82** —*J.M. (1/1/2003)*

Salmon Run 2000 Johannisberg Riesling (New York) $10. Watery aromas of green apple and lime. But there's nice balance between the sweet and

tart elements, like a good Granny Smith. Soft and fruity, an easy-quaffing second label from Dr. Frank. **83** —*J.C. (3/1/2002)*

SALVESTRIN

Salvestrin 1999 Cabernet Sauvignon (Napa Valley) $45. From the famous class of '99 Cabs, a softly rich, voluptuous wine, brimming with cassis and blackcurrant flavors generously framed in oak. Lacks a bit of stuffing and complexity, but on the surface, tasty stuff. **88** —*S.H. (8/1/2003)*

Salvestrin 1997 Cabernet Sauvignon (Napa Valley) $41. 92 *(11/1/2000)*

Salvestrin 2001 Salvestrin Estate Vineyard Cabernet Sauvignon (Napa Valley) $45. Classic Napa Valley '01 Cab. Ripe, soft, complex, juicy, and delicious, showing upfront black currant, cassis, chocolate, and smoky oak, with a caramel richness from well-charred wood. The tannins are deft, lush, and sweet. Gets more interesting as it warms up on the table. Try decanting for a few hours. **90** —*S.H. (8/1/2005)*

Salvestrin 2001 Sangiovese (Napa Valley) $26. Black cherry flavors dominate, with oak providing smoke and vanilla notes. In the mouth, the flavors also veer toward ripe cherries. Tannins are fairly strong, with a puckery finish, but it's nothing that Parmesan cheese and olive oil can't tame. **86** —*S.H. (3/1/2004)*

SAN JUAN VINEYARDS

San Juan Vineyards 2003 Cabernet Sauvignon-Merlot (Columbia Valley (WA)) $12. Strong new barrel flavors, surprising in a wine at this price, send up a lot of butterscotch and caramel over light cherry and plum flavors. There's chocolate in here also, making it a tongue-pleasing budget bottle with more polish than you would expect. **87 Best Buy** —*P.G. (8/1/2006)*

San Juan Vineyards 2004 Celilo Vineyard Chardonnay (Columbia Gorge) $19. Celilo grows some of the most distinctive and eagerly sought-after Chardonnay in Washington, and this little-known producer does a stand-up job with the fruit. Gorgeously etched with bright lime tones around fresh apple/pear fruit; good concentration, balance and length in a subtle style that shows the minerality to full advantage. **90** —*P.G. (9/1/2006)*

San Juan Vineyards 2001 Reserve Chardonnay (Columbia Valley (WA)) $17. Has a strong core of pear and ripe apple, buttressed with some spicy oak. The wood tannins are now showing a hard, slightly bitter edge, but if the finish smooths out the wine could rate higher. **86** —*P.G. (5/1/2004)*

San Juan Vineyards 2001 Gewürztraminer (Columbia Valley (WA)) $11. Distinctly honeyed, with pretty flavors of pollen and sweet flower. The finish is spicy, stiff, and just slightly bitter, but shows a lot of promise. Could be wonderful in 3–5 years. **87 Best Buy** —*P.G. (5/1/2004)*

San Juan Vineyards 2001 Merlot (Yakima Valley) $23. 100% Merlot, with Yakima Valley black olive/black cherry flavors, nicely ripened, and set against milk chocolatey oak. The barrel flavors of mocha and Bourbon overtake the modest fruit, but it's a very tasty quaff. **86** —*P.G. (5/1/2004)*

San Juan Vineyards 2004 Pinot Gris (Columbia Valley (WA)) $13. Barrel-fermented and put through complete malolactic fermentation, this well-made Gris may have started out quite acidic, but the winemaker has softened things up without sacrificing the crisp definition. Fresh apple flavors with suggestions of honey and lemon to add interest set this up as an archetypical summer seafood wine. **89 Best Buy** —*P.G. (8/1/2006)*

San Juan Vineyards 2004 Pinot Gris (Columbia Gorge) $13. Very nice texture, and snappy fruit led by green apples and pear skin. There is an undercurrent of gravel, from the volcanic soil that is full of shot-sized rock. Sharp, clean, and very flavorful. **88 Best Buy** —*P.G. (2/1/2006)*

San Juan Vineyards 1999 Sémillon-Chardonnay (Washington) $9. This is a 50/50 blend, made in a fruity, forward style. It smells of green berries and pears, and has an edgy crispness that will set up nicely with food. The finish is a bit astringent, dusty, herbaceous, and suggests fresh spices and new-mown hay. The Chardonnay half of the equation adds some tart, green apple fruit. **87** —*P.G. (6/1/2001)*

San Juan Vineyards 2002 Syrah (Columbia Valley (WA)) $23. Almost tropically fruity, this wine's ultraripe berries nevertheless turn tart and balanced on the finish. Pepper and herb notes add complexity. It's not the richest, most textured wine, but it's crisp, clean, and—most of all—delivers pleasure. **86** *(9/1/2005)*

San Juan Vineyards 2001 Syrah (Columbia Valley (WA)) $23. A nice effort, with well-ripened fruit that shows streaky plum and cherry flavors, layers of mineral, licorice, and smoke. It all adds up to a plenty flavorful wine, with a lot of texture and a lively, extended finish. **88** —*P.G. (5/1/2004)*

SAN MARCOS CREEK

San Marcos Creek 2002 Estate Reserve Cabernet Sauvignon (Paso Robles) $27. Smells caramelly and Porty, and tastes dry and astringent. A bitter Cab with little to recommend it. **82** —*S.H. (12/1/2006)*

San Marcos Creek 2002 Estate Merlot (Paso Robles) $17. Very ripe, soft, and chocolatey, in the Paso style, with blackberry and coffee flavors. Despite the softness, there's a good dose of dusty tannins in this dry, balanced wine. It's quite a nice, supple Merlot. **88** —*S.H. (4/1/2006)*

San Marcos Creek 2002 Epiphany Red Blend (Paso Robles) $30. Soft and thick, in the way of big Paso reds, this Syrah, Cabernet, and Petite Sirah blend is dry and robust in blackberry, coffee, cocoa, and spice flavors. It will be nice with grilled meats. **86** —*S.H. (9/1/2006)*

San Marcos Creek 2002 Estate Syrah (Paso Robles) $21. Although the alcohol on this Syrah is mercifully below 14%, there's a country-style coarseness and heat to the texture, with jagged tannins. Yet the wine is dry, with rich coffee, blackberry, and currant flavors. Good now with grilled meats and poultry. **85** —*S.H. (4/1/2006)*

San Marcos Creek 2002 Estate Zinfandel (Paso Robles) $22. Tannic and a little overripe, with raisin and cherry flavors and and some Porty sweetness in the finish, this style of Zin will have its fans. It's definitely a hot climate wine. **83** —*S.H. (4/1/2006)*

SAN SABA

San Saba 1997 Chardonnay (Monterey County) $20. 81 *(6/1/2000)*

San Saba 2004 Chardonnay (Monterey) $18. What a nice wine this is, fruity and wonderfully bright and crisp in citrus acidity. It doesn't taste very oaky, despite barrel fermentation, and that allows those pure Monterey peach, lime, apricot, and papaya flavors to shine. **91 Editors' Choice** —*S.H. (7/1/2006)*

San Saba 2001 Chardonnay (Monterey) $16. Distinctly Chardonnay in the ripe apple, peach, and pear flavors veering all the way into tropical papaya. There is some tremendous, supercharred oak here, lending notes of caramel, vanilla, and meringue. Despite the richness, the wine needs a little more depth and pizzazz **85** —*S.H. (12/15/2002)*

San Saba 1998 Chardonnay (Central Coast) $20. 88 *(6/1/2000)*

San Saba 1996 Merlot (Monterey County) $20. 83 —*J.C. (7/1/2000)*

San Saba 2004 Merlot (Monterey) $22. From the winery's vineyard at the foot of the Santa Lucia Highlands comes this ripe, pleasant wine. It's dry and crisp, even a little sharp, with full-bodied wintergreen mint, cherry, coffee, and herb flavors. Drink now. **85** —*S.H. (12/15/2006)*

San Saba 2003 Merlot (Monterey) $22. Soft and cloying, this wine has medicinal cherry and chocolate flavors. **81** —*S.H. (12/15/2005)*

San Saba 2002 Merlot (Monterey) $22. Here's a good everyday Merlot. It's soft and dry, with good chocolate and blackberry flavors that persist on the finish. **84** —*S.H. (5/1/2005)*

San Saba 1999 Pinot Noir (Central Coast) $19. It's bizarre that they call it a Central Coast wine because it's from a single vineyard in Santa Maria Valley. It does have the valley's profile of crisp acids, framing, in this vintage, ripe blackberry fruit and soft tannins. The flavors are pretty, although it could use more depth. **86** —*S.H. (2/1/2003)*

San Saba 2005 Sauvignon Blanc (Monterey) $15. No oak, nothing but the Musque clone, with its bright acids and gooseberry, grapefruit, lime, and fig flavors. Easy to drink, and as versatile as dry white wines get with an enormous array of food. **85** —*S.H. (12/15/2006)*

SAN SIMEON

San Simeon 2002 Cabernet Sauvignon (Paso Robles) $22. The alcohol is relatively moderate, but seems to be at the expense of residual sugar, to judge by the Lifesaver-sweet cherry and blackberry flavors. Beyond that, this Cab has lush, smooth tannins. **84** —*S.H. (7/1/2006)*

San Simeon 2001 Cabernet Sauvignon (Paso Robles) $22. Here's a dry, somewhat gritty Cab, with pronounced tannins framing coffee and blackberry flavors. Full-bodied, it should be nice with beef dishes. **84** —*S.H. (6/1/2005)*

San Simeon 2003 Chardonnay (Monterey) $19. The aromas and flavors of dill overpower the underlying fruit here, almost masking the citrus, pear, and peach flavors. This may be due to oak or something else, but it's off-putting. Too bad, because somewhere in here is a very fine Chardonnay. **84** —*S.H. (11/1/2006)*

San Simeon 2002 Chardonnay (Monterey) $19. Tight and lemony, with firm acids that make the tastebuds whistle. This is a dry Chard well suited to crab dishes. **85** —*S.H. (6/1/2005)*

San Simeon 2000 Chardonnay (Monterey) $14. A nice mouthful of Chard, one that shares the finer features of the appellation. Well-ripened fruits, ranging from peaches and pears to mangoes, provide delicious flavors, while acids are crisp and bright. The wine is fully dry, with oaky notes. It's not complex or layered. **86** —*S.H. (6/1/2003)*

San Simeon 2002 Merlot (Paso Robles) $22. Drinks very soft, almost collapsed, in the mouth, but the flavors are pretty enough, suggesting a red cherry tart drizzled with vanilla and sprinkled with cocoa. The wine is fully dry, with dusty tannins on the finish. **85** —*S.H. (12/1/2005)*

San Simeon 2001 Merlot (Paso Robles) $22. Very dry and robust in the mouth, a clean wine with earthy-berry flavors that finishes with some sturdy tannins, although it's nice and soft in acidity. **84** —*S.H. (6/1/2005)*

San Simeon 2002 Petite Sirah (Paso Robles) $22. Harsh in texture and cloying, with cherry cough medicine flavors. **81** —*S.H. (12/1/2005)*

San Simeon 2001 Petite Sirah (Paso Robles) $18. This is fairly dense wine, packed with rich black cherry, spice, plum, toast, and licorice flavors. It's got a very non-varietally appropriate bright edge, however, which leads one to believe that it needs to be drunk sooner than later. **82** —*J.M. (9/1/2004)*

San Simeon 2000 100% Petite Sirah Petite Sirah (Paso Robles) $22. Distinctly hot climate "Pet," a black wine with heavy aromas and flavors. Chocolate, jammy plums, and blackberries, pepper and earth encased in soft tannins and acids. Fully dry, and the acids turn a bit harsh on the finish. **85** —*S.H. (9/1/2003)*

San Simeon 2004 Pinot Gris (Monterey) $15. From an estate vineyard in the Arroyo Seco, balanced due to its coolish climate and rocky soils, this is a delicious wine. The bright acids frame juicy flavors of ripe peaches, figs, and citrus fruits, with a long, clean, spicy finish. **89** —*S.H. (2/1/2006)*

San Simeon 2004 Pinot Noir (Monterey) $20. A bit sweet, this Pinot, grown in the Arroyo Seco area, is soft and silky, with very ripe, extracted cherry pie flavors and a spicy finish. **83** —*S.H. (11/1/2006)*

San Simeon 2003 Pinot Noir (Monterey) $20. From the Arroyo Seco AVA, this wine shows tasty, cool-climate Pinot flavors of cola, rhubarb, pie, cherry, cocoa, and oaky vanilla flavors, and plenty of pepper and cinnamon spice. It's silky in texture. The drawback is excessive softness. **85** —*S.H. (12/1/2005)*

San Simeon 2002 Pinot Noir (Monterey County) $18. Fruity and simple, with bright cherry and vanilla flavors. Rather oaky-sweet throughout. **84** *(11/1/2004)*

San Simeon 2000 Pinot Noir (Monterey) $20. There's a definite note of cola, but also burning leaves and earth and game accents on the nose of this Monterey offering. It's light and angular, but the burning leaves element is strong in the mouth, rendering it astringent and edgy. **83** *(10/1/2002)*

San Simeon 1999 Pinot Noir (Monterey) $18. Cherry and spice, plum and anise notes sit well in this plush-textured wine. Soft and sensual, it finishes moderately long with hints of herbs. **87** —*J.M. (11/15/2001)*

San Simeon 2002 Syrah (Paso Robles) $22. Here's a Syrah that impresses for its complexity and depth. It's dark, full-bodied, and fully dry, with a rich tannic structure carrying berry-cherry flavors with a spicy, peppery edge. Sure is an easy wine to drink with roast pork or grilled lamb. **87** —*S.H. (12/31/2005)*

USA

San Simeon 2001 Syrah (Monterey) $20. Rich and smooth, with finely-grained tannins framing ripe plum, blackberry, cocoa, and sweet-coffee flavors. There's a lot going on in this elegant, sophisticated wine. **89** —S.H. (6/1/2005)

San Simeon 2000 Syrah (Monterey) $20. Comes down on the rustic side, with peppery, berry flavors and a thick texture. It's dry, with soft acids and tannins. Provides easy drinking with no major flaws, but way too expensive for the quality. **84** —S.H. (6/1/2003)

San Simeon 1999 Syrah (Arroyo Seco) $16. Dark and rich, with plummy, tomato flavors and quite a bit of tannin. It's very dry, with a real bite of acidity. Doesn't have the stuffing for aging, but it is a big, clean bruiser of a wine, and will drink nicely with rich foods. **85** —S.H. (7/1/2002)

San Simeon 1998 Syrah (Monterey) $15. The inky color is followed by a blast of dark chocolate and licorice, tinged with coconut, smoke, and floral aromas. It's very smooth and supple in the mouth, yet finishes with enough juicy acidity to keep the dark flavors lively and balanced. **87 Editors' Choice** (10/1/2001)

SANCTUARY

Sanctuary 2003 Usibelli Vineyard Cabernet Sauvignon (Rutherford) $32. This Cabernet is instantly likeable for its soft, lush tannins and blackberry and smoky oak flavors that finish with the taste of cocoa-dusted cappuccino. It's a bit on the light side, but tasty. **86** —S.H. (11/15/2006)

Sanctuary 2004 Bien Nacido Vineyards Pinot Noir (Santa Maria Valley) $45. This full-bodied Pinot has classic Santa Maria character. It's fairly tannic, but very dry, with blue and black fruit and berry flavors veering into leather, overtones of violets, and masses of crushed spices, not to mention smoky oak. Few California Pinots are ageable, but this seems like a slam dunk. Best 2008 through 2012. **90 Cellar Selection** —S.H. (11/1/2006)

SANDHILL

Sandhill 2000 Cabernet Sauvignon (Red Mountain) $25. Forward, medium-style Cabernet with clean cassis and cherry flavors, some light herb, and a firm mineral streak in the tight, chalky finish. **85** —P.G. (1/1/2004)

Sandhill 1999 Cabernet Sauvignon (Red Mountain) $25. Classic scents of cassis fruit, laced with leaf and herb, lead into a firm, confident, balanced wine that is elegantly structured for the long haul. A cellar candidate; this could go 15–20 years. **93 Cellar Selection** —P.G. (9/1/2002)

Sandhill 2000 Merlot (Red Mountain) $20. Another excellent Merlot from Sandhill, though not as big as the previous vintage. This is more loose, more open, with flavors of cherry and raspberry out front. Firm acids and the stiff, mineral finish that characterizes Red Mountain grapes. **88** —P.G. (9/1/2004)

Sandhill 1999 Merlot (Red Mountain) $20. A new producer on Red Mountain debuts with a fine Merlot, showing the tight, taut profile of the appellation. Black cherry and cassis, anchored to an iron/mineral foundation, with some bitter chocolate in the balanced, muscular finish. **90** —P.G. (9/1/2002)

SANFORD

Sanford 1998 Chardonnay (Santa Barbara County) $19. 83 (6/1/2000)

Sanford 2004 Chardonnay (Santa Barbara County) $21. Soft, ripe, and oaky, with flamboyant tropical fruit pastry flavors that are almost sugary sweet on the finish. There's good acidity to balance. **84** —S.H. (12/15/2006)

Sanford 2003 Chardonnay (Santa Barbara County) $21. Very forward in ripe tangerine, peaches and cream, Key lime pie, and asian spices, this pretty Chard also has a coat of smoky oak. Those fruity flavors last through a long, rich finish. **88** —S.H. (12/1/2005)

Sanford 2002 Chardonnay (Santa Rita Hills) $21. A lovely Chard, filled with crisp acids and steely, stony minerals. The fruit flavors suggest powerfully ripened tropical fruits, and there's a bracing overlay of oak. Notable for its balance and integrity. **90** —S.H. (4/1/2005)

Sanford 2001 Chardonnay (Santa Rita Hills) $27. This wonderful Chard showcases the quality of its appellation. The smoky oak is pretty, and complements the pineapple and guava fruit, which has a firm streak of

mineral running through it. The creamy smooth texture is balanced by refreshing acidity. **90** —S.H. (5/1/2004)

Sanford 2000 Chardonnay (Santa Barbara) $19. A lemony Chardonnay that serves up snappy mineral, pear, apple, and mango notes with a clean, fresh finish. Well balanced and elegant. **89** —J.M. (5/1/2002)

Sanford 1999 Barrel Select Chardonnay (Santa Barbara County) $30. The green apple and menthol toast bouquet shows some unusual tobacco-like aromas that are usually associated with red wines. A sip reveals mint, apple, and caramel flavors on a full, oaky frame. Nicely balanced and still tight, it ends with slightly subdued but persistent caramel and toast flavors. Previous vintages of this Santa Barbara classic have performed well—often better—after cellaring. Try in two years. **89** (7/1/2001)

Sanford 1998 Barrel Select Chardonnay (Santa Barbara County) $30. 85 (6/1/2000)

Sanford 1997 Sanford & Benedict Vineyard Chardonnay (Santa Ynez Valley) $27. 84 (6/1/2000)

Sanford 1997 Santa Barbara County Chardonnay (Santa Barbara County) $18. 89 —S.H. (7/1/1999)

Sanford 2005 Pinot Grigio (Santa Barbara County) $19. Clean, crisp, and fruity, this refreshing wine offers polished citrus, apple, fig, melon, and clover honey flavors, with high, fizzy acidity. Straddles the line between dry and off-dry. **86** —S.H. (12/31/2006)

Sanford 2004 Pinot Grigio (Santa Barbara County) $18. Delightfully clean, dry, and crisp, this PG has delicate citrus, fig, melon, and spice flavors, with depth and complexity unusual in California Grigios. It finishes long, with stylish elegance. **89** —S.H. (2/1/2006)

Sanford 2004 Pinot Noir (Santa Rita Hills) $28. What a nice glass of Pinot this is. It shows off the terroir of its famous appellation very well, with high acidity perking up cherry, cola, tea, spice, and mineral flavors, and with a wonderful balance. It's not a cheap wine, but is a comparative value. **89** —S.H. (11/1/2006)

Sanford 2002 Pinot Noir (Santa Rita Hills) $27. Shows all the hallmarks of this appellation without being a great, complex wine. The acids are crisp, brightening cherry, rhubarb, and tobacco flavors that are well-oaked. The wine is dry, silky, and elegant, with a good depth of flavor. Drink now. **88** —S.H. (12/31/2005)

Sanford 2001 Pinot Noir (Santa Rita Hills) $30. Silky and fine in the mouth, with cherry, raspberry, vanilla, and oak flavors. Finishes oaky and dry. This is a fun, easy wine that will be good with many different foods. **86** —S.H. (4/1/2005)

Sanford 2001 La Rinconada Pinot Noir (Santa Rita Hills) $50. An interesting Pinot, although it's young, in terms of both vine and bottle age. Seems like a work in progress, with its lush, ripe black cherry flavors and wonderfully crisp acidity. Well oaked, too. But the tannins are tough and astringent. **88** —S.H. (3/1/2004)

Sanford 2000 La Rinconada Pinot Noir (Santa Barbara County) $50. This is big stuff—"Pinot on steroids," wrote one taster, with a dense, smoky, meaty, neo-Syrah nose. Leather and cola notes accent the dark briary, raisiny fruit and the texture is chewy. There was dissent, however—one panelist found the scale and sweet flavors just too much and too un-Pinot-like. But the majority said, bring it on, typical or not. **90** (10/1/2002)

Sanford 2002 La Rinconada Vineyard Pinot Noir (Santa Rita Hills) $46. This superior Pinot Noir gives everything the appellation is famous for. Lively acidity makes the wine bright and clean. The flavors are deep and complex, suggesting black cherries, cola, rhubarb, dried leaves, crushed spices, and smoky oak. There's a dusting of fine tannins, the texture is pure silk and velvet, and the finish is dry. **94 Editors' Choice** —S.H. (12/31/2005)

Sanford 2005 Pinot Noir Vin Gris Pinot Noir (Sta. Rita Hills) $14. Here's a nice rosé with some real complexity, and it's rich enough to stand in for an actual red Pinot Noir. Basically dry, with a silky texture, it has cherry, herb, and vanilla flavors that are complemented with crisp acidity. **87** —S.H. (12/15/2006)

Sanford 2002 Vin Gris Pinot Noir (Santa Rita Hills) $13. Hard to figure why Rick Sanford would take Pinot grapes from this upscale AVA and make an inexpensive blush. Tastes like press wine, thin and watery, with hardly any fruit flavor to be found, and just barely deserves even this modest score. **83**—*S.H. (2/1/2004)*

Sanford 2004 Pinot Noir Vin Gris Rosé Blend (Santa Rita Hills) $14. Light in color, even for a rosé, but there's nothing shy about the flavors. This wine is powerful and complex in red cherries, tobacco, vanilla, and sweet Provençal herbs, and is totally dry, with a fine acidic structure. **87**—*S.H. (12/1/2005)*

Sanford 1998 Sauvignon Blanc (Central Coast) $15. 88—*L.W. (3/1/2000)*

Sanford 1997 Sauvignon Blanc (Central Coast) $14. 88—*S.H. (9/1/1999)*

Sanford 2001 Sauvignon Blanc (Central Coast) $13. Not much happening flavorwise with this little wine, which has thinned-down notes of unsweetened grapefruit juice. It is very dry, with crisp acidity. **83**—*S.H. (12/1/2003)*

SANFORD & BENEDICT

Sanford 2002 Sanford & Benedict Vineyard Pinot Noir (Santa Barbara County) $43. This is a big, ripe, juicy Pinot, with powerful cherry and blueberry flavors accented with nuances of cola, coffee, cocoa, and oak. It's rich and intricately detailed, and very young, even impertinent. Give it a few years to soften and sweeten. Should improve for five years or more. **93 Cellar Selection**—*S.H. (6/1/2005)*

Sanford 2001 Sanford & Benedict Vineyard Pinot Noir (Santa Rita Hills) $42. Tons of ripe, lush cherry, blackberry, and spice flavors here, but the wine overcomes simple fruitiness to achieve real complexity. Fully dry, with no residual sugar and moderate alcohol, and the tannins are rich yet supple and yielding. Of course, those cool climate acids provide a bracing structure. The finish is long, intricate and detailed. **92**—*S.H. (10/1/2003)*

Sanford 2000 Sanford & Benedict Vineyard Pinot Noir (Santa Barbara County) $NA. Spicy, oaky, rhubarb, beet, lots of sweet cherries, and raspberries. Jammier, fruitier than the ABC 2000, though less delicate and elegant, and rather more accessible. Perhaps less acidic; certainly higher alcohol. **91**—*S.H. (6/1/2005)*

Sanford 1999 Sanford & Benedict Vineyard Pinot Noir (Santa Barbara County) $42. The aromas lean toward stewed fruit with a touch of tomato. But cola notes and hints of strawberry keep it vital. The cherry fruit manages to peek through on the palate, where there's also a fair amount of leafy character not unlike bramble or underbrush. **86** *(10/1/2002)*

Sanford 1999 Sanford & Benedict Vineyard Pinot Noir (Santa Barbara County) $NA. Good, rich pure garnet color. Excitingly clean, spicy cherry, beet, oak aromas seamlessly meshing into pure Pinot. Lively in bright, zingy acidity. Long, rich, intense in cherry fruit, rosehip tea, cola, root beer, smoky oak. Vibrant, distinguished, delicious. **94 Editors' Choice**—*S.H. (6/1/2005)*

Sanford 1998 Sanford & Benedict Vineyard Pinot Noir (Santa Barbara County) $NA. Alcohol: 14.0%. Very forward and fresh, with a young aroma. Tons of red cherries, charry oak, with a fresh, clean, forest-floor scene. Pine needles, spice. Intense sour cherry candy, rhubarb, and spice flavors. Very sweet, intense. Clean, long finish, with great racy acids. Beet root. Delicious now-2012. **94 Editors' Choice**—*S.H. (6/1/2005)*

Sanford 1997 Sanford & Benedict Vineyard Pinot Noir (Santa Barbara County) $23. 87 *(12/15/1999)*

Sanford 1997 Sanford & Benedict Vineyard Pinot Noir (Santa Barbara County) $42. 93 *(10/1/1999)*

Sanford 2000 Sanford & Benedict Vineyard Pinot Noir (Santa Barbara County) $43. A poised, well-balanced wine, smooth yet tangy, full yet not heavy. The nose offers complex roasted meat, cardamom, graham cracker, and crème brûlée aromas. Black cherry flavors wear tomato, herb and leather accents. There's fine depth of fruit plus a long, spicy, evenly tannic close. Better in two or three years. **89** *(10/1/2002)*

Sanford & Benedict 1980 Pinot Noir (Santa Ynez Valley) $NA. Pale, browning. Sediment. Potpourri bouquet, cedar, cigar box, raspberry-cherry crème brûlée. Delicate, dry, refined. Rosehip tea, spice flavors. Elegant, silky, still some sweet fruit. Finishes vibrant, crisp, very fine. Alcohol only 12 percent! **92**—*S.H. (6/1/2005)*

SANTA BARBARA WINERY

Santa Barbara Winery 1998 Chardonnay (Santa Barbara County) $16. 89 *(6/1/2000)*

Santa Barbara Winery 1997 Reserve Chardonnay (Santa Ynez Valley) $24. 84 *(6/1/2000)*

Santa Barbara Winery 2000 Pinot Noir (Santa Ynez Valley) $18. 86 *(10/1/2002)*

Santa Barbara Winery 2000 Pinot Noir (Santa Barbara County) $13. 86 Best Buy *(10/1/2002)*

Santa Barbara Winery 2001 Joughin Vineyard Primitivo (Santa Barbara County) $18. Kicks off with dark, rich black cherry and blackberry aromas. Richly textured and intensely flavored, with a plush core of berry, licorice, herb, spice, toast, and vanilla notes. Soft tannins and firm acidity frame it nicely. Great value too. **90 Editors' Choice**—*J.M. (11/1/2003)*

Santa Barbara Winery 2001 ZCS Red Blend (California) $13. Quite fruity, with lots of bright cherry and raspberry flavors. Zippy acidity keeps it fresh on the finish. 59% Zinfandel; 28% Carignane; 17% Sangiovese. **85**—*J.M. (12/31/2003)*

Santa Barbara Winery 2000 ZCS Red Blend (California) $13. This is an old-fashioned field blend of Zinfandel and Carignane, with a newer grape, Sangiovese, added for complexity. It's fruity and vivacious and fun, giving a jolt of ripe plums, blackberries, pepper, and cherries. The mouthfeel is sharp, but the price is right. **85**—*S.H. (9/1/2003)*

Santa Barbara Winery 2005 Lafond Vineyard Riesling (Santa Rita Hills) $15. Most cool-climate Rieslings are made dry. This one pays hommage to Germany. With its acidity and honeysuckle, citrus, and peach flavors, it's off-dry to sweet, with 2.4% residual sugar. **84**—*S.H. (11/1/2006)*

Santa Barbara Winery 2005 Rosé of Syrah Rosé Blend (Santa Rita Hills) $15. This is one of the few rosés from this appellation that I'm aware of. It's a little full-bodied for a blush, but pretty good. Dry and rich, it has deep, long flavors of raspberries and vanilla, with very high acidity that desperately needs food. **85**—*S.H. (11/1/2006)*

Santa Barbara Winery 2001 Lafond Vineyard Late Harvest Sauvignon Blanc (Santa Ynez Valley) $16. Picked at an unbelievable 38 degrees of brix, with residual sugar of 12.5%, this is a very, very sweet wine. It has an unctuous, honeyed texture, but super-high acidity breaks it up. Flavorwise, it's botrytis-infected, apricot-infused crème brûlée. Wow. **95 Editors' Choice**—*S.H. (11/1/2006)*

Santa Barbara Winery 1998 Late Harvest Sauvignon Blanc (Santa Ynez Valley) $30. Viscous and silky, with loads of apricot, mandarin orange, spice, apple, citrus, and herb flavors. Sweet and lush, yet long and bright on the finish. Who needs dessert with a wine like this? **92**—*J.M. (12/1/2002)*

Santa Barbara Winery 1999 Syrah (Santa Ynez Valley) $22. An impressive, deep, and darkly fruited nose shows smoke, leather, cinnamon, coconut, even mushroom notes. On the round, textured palate, earth and coffee accent ripe blackberry, plum, and toast flavors. The finish—tart berry, citrus, and licorice-tinged—shows good length and even tannins. Intense, youthful Syrah that will evolve for 2–4 years, and hold well through 2008. Top Value. **89** *(11/1/2001)*

Santa Barbara Winery 2003 Rosé Syrah (Santa Rita Hills) $14. Fairly dark and full-bodied for a rosé, and you'll find cherry-plummy flavors with a finish of white pepper. **84**—*S.H. (10/1/2004)*

Santa Barbara Winery 2001 Lafond Vineyard Zinfandel (Santa Rita Hills) $18. A rich, plummy, earthy character marks this wine, with a briary center and toasty, oaky overtones. Spicy cherry and herb notes lead the way, ending with a bright finish. **87**—*J.M. (11/1/2003)*

Santa Barbara Winery 2003 Lafond Vineyard Zinfandel Essence Zinfandel (Santa Rita Hills) $34. Super sweet and super-fruity in blackberry purée, apricot nectar, and sweet mocha-espresso flavors, this dessert wine doesn't have the acidity needed for balance. It's like soda syrup. **81**—*S.H. (11/15/2006)*

SANTINO

Santino 2005 Pinot Grigio (Lodi) $10. What a nice PG, at this price and even more expensive. Tremendously likeable for its well-ripened pineapple, apple, peach, fig, pear, honeysuckle, and cinnamon spice flavors. A dash of Viognier certainly helps. Finishes a little sweet, but balanced with crisp acidity. **86 Best Buy** —*S.H. (12/31/2006)*

Santino 2003 Syrah (Sierra Foothills) $10. Young, sharp, dry, and jammy, with freshly picked cherry and blackberry flavors and a burst of peppery green thyme and dill. Turns tannic on the finish. Shows real flair. What a great by the glass restaurant wine. **85 Best Buy** —*S.H. (12/31/2006)*

Santino 2005 Syrah Rosé Syrah (Sierra Foothills) $10. Says Syrah on the label, but it contains a dollop of Nebbiolo and Mourvèdre. Despite the light color, the wine is deeply flavored, although dry, with a complex array of red cherry, strawberry, tea, herb, and spice flavors. Best of all is the refreshing acidity, which makes this wine a natural for food. **86 Best Buy** —*S.H. (12/31/2006)*

Santino 2005 Viognier (Lodi) $10. A few years back, veteran winemaker Dave Crippen decided to pick his Viognier earlier. "I learned from Jed Steele that my wines need acidity to get away from overripeness and flabbiness," he says. That lesson shows in this crisp wine, where the tanginess offsets the slightly sweet Meyer lemon, green apple, peach, and peppery spice flavors. Most of the grapes were grown at the well-regarded Mohr Fry Ranches, in Lodi, with a little Sémillon from Amador. The brand is from Renwood. **86 Best Buy** —*S.H. (11/15/2006)*

Santino 2003 Zinfandel (Sierra Foothills) $10. Beautiful everyday Zin, just picture perfect Foothills. Dry and spicy, with blackberry, cherry, licorice, cola, and wild thyme, but never heavy. The wine has a silky, elegant lightness. This is a fabulous ten dollar bottle of Zin. **86 Best Buy** —*S.H. (12/31/2006)*

Santino 2003 Zinfandel (Fiddletown) $19. Alone of all Santino's wonderful '03 Zins, this is one I can't recommend because it's raisiny. Opens with that telltale baked fruit and caramelized brown sugar aroma of Port, then turns dry and fiercely tannic, with little possibility of improvement. **82** —*S.H. (12/31/2006)*

Santino 2003 Old Vine Zinfandel (Amador County) $15. Wonderful, rewarding Zin that somehow got the fruit enormously ripe, yet maintains an elegantly silky balance and modest alcohol. Floods the palate with spicy blackberry, cherry, licorice, and cola pie filling flavors, soft and luscious, while remaining thoroughly dry. **88** —*S.H. (12/31/2006)*

SANTO STEFANO

Santo Stefano 1997 Cabernet Sauvignon (Sonoma County) $30. **86** *(11/1/2000)*

SAPOLIL CELLARS

Sapolil Cellars 2003 Syrah (Columbia Valley (WA)) $33. On the crisp side, with bright berry flavors that pick up a touch of herbaceousness. Finishes tart and a little short. **84** *(9/1/2005)*

SAPPHIRE HILL

Sapphire Hill 1998 Chardonnay (Russian River Valley) $22. **84** *(6/1/2000)*

Sapphire Hill 1997 Chardonnay (Russian River Valley) $20. **90** —*S.H. (11/1/1999)*

Sapphire Hill 2004 Sapphire Hill Vineyard Pinot Noir (Russian River Valley) $38. Made in a very ripe, forward style, with cherry jam, chocolate pudding, and smoky oak flavorings. This straightforward Pinot flatters with its juicy opulence. **86** —*S.H. (12/1/2006)*

Sapphire Hill 2000 Winberrie Old Vine Zinfandel (Russian River Valley) $30. An herbal, not to say earthy, wine with sage and oregano aromas and flavors. Dry and supple, it's softened by a hint of cherry cola in the finish, and will wake up with rich barbecue. **87** —*S.H. (9/1/2002)*

SARACINA

Saracina 2001 Sauvignon Blanc (Mendocino County) $24. Refreshing and zesty, with peach, grass, juniper berry, and grapefruit flavors that drink a little sweet, although crisp acidity cleanses and soothes the palate. This nice cocktail wine is fun and easy to drink. **84** —*S.H. (7/1/2003)*

SARIAH CELLARS

Sariah Cellars 2000 Syrah (Red Mountain) $25. Add this new winery to the growing list of Walla Walla-based boutiques. The Syrah is plump and

juicy, a round, fruity red wine that is perfectly enjoyable. **87** —*P.G. (9/1/2002)*

SASS

Sass 1998 Dunning Vineyard Chardonnay (Oregon) $12. Opens with a powerful blast of spiced apple, peach, and pear aromas. A lush overlay of oak adds smoke, vanilla, and buttered toast, but the wine remains balanced. Notable for the integration of fruit, lively acidity, and oak, this racy wine is a great value. **88 Best Buy** —*S.H. (4/1/2002)*

SATURDAY RED

Saturday Red NV 1 Liter Red Blend (California) $9. All this wine wants to be is a useful, friendly, everyday red, and it succeeds quite well. Made from Lodi area grapes, it's dry, full-bodied, and fruity, with a good dusting of tannin. **84** —*S.H. (12/15/2005)*

SAUCELITO CANYON

Saucelito Canyon 2004 Cabernet Sauvignon (Arroyo Grande Valley) $20. Grown in the warmest part of the appellation, a region that really needs its own designation, this is a dry, rustic Cab, with herb and cigarette aromas and tart red cherry flavors. Drink now. **83** —*S.H. (11/1/2006)*

Saucelito Canyon 2004 Zinfandel (Arroyo Grande Valley) $20. Rather hot, with Porty aromas and flavors, this warm-climate Zin, with very high alcohol, finishes dry and raisiny-fruity. **83** —*S.H. (11/1/2006)*

Saucelito Canyon 2000 Zinfandel (Arroyo Grande Valley) $20. They did a nice job of keeping the alcohol below 14% without sacrificing the lush fruit. The result is a beautiful wine to drink, dry and clean, with soft tannins. Flavors of berries, cherries, and red tree fruits are delicious. **90 Editors' Choice** —*S.H. (9/1/2003)*

Saucelito Canyon 2004 Dos Ranchos Zinfandel (Arroyo Grande Valley) $30. With alcohol of 16% and a sweet finish, this raspberry- and cherry-flavored Zin defines a hot-climate style. You either like it or you don't, but it flies its flag proudly. **83** —*S.H. (11/1/2006)*

Saucelito Canyon 2003 Estate Zinfandel (Arroyo Grande Valley) $18. This is the sort of Zin that turns me off. It's not only hot in alcohol, it's definitely sweet in residual sugar, with the flavors of rum-soaked raisins. **82** —*S.H. (10/1/2005)*

Saucelito Canyon 2001 Estate Zinfandel (Arroyo Grande Valley) $17. Smooth-textured and plush, with deep, rich black cherry, blackberry, coffee, chocolate, and spice flavors. Firm, ripe tannins frame it, while a spicy rich finish adds more interest. Fine wine from this long-time Zin specialist. **90** —*J.M. (4/1/2004)*

Saucelito Canyon 2001 Late Harvest Zinfandel (Arroyo Grande Valley) $20. Decadance in a glass, a brutally delicious wine with flavors of cassis, sweet cherry pie, kirsch, and melted white chocolate sweetened with sugar. It's all framed in a texture of pure velvet. This heady dessert wine wears its high alcohol well. **91** —*S.H. (3/1/2004)*

Saucelito Canyon 2004 Reserve Zinfandel (Arroyo Grande Valley) $36. Very high in alcohol, but with the benefit of dryness, this Zin has a white-pepper note riding high above the blackberry, red cherry, and raspberry aromas and flavors. It's easily the best of the winery's current Zins, avoiding the pitfalls of such ripe wines and offering rich flavor and mouthfeel. **88** —*S.H. (11/1/2006)*

Saucelito Canyon 2001 Reserve Zinfandel (Arroyo Grande Valley) $28. Similar to the Estate bottling, this reserve shows a bit more power, with a fine array of blackberry, coffee, chocolate, spice, and vanilla notes. Rich and smooth, it's got a little bite at the end, and finishes long. **91** —*J.M. (4/1/2004)*

SAUSAL

Sausal 2002 Cabernet Sauvignon (Alexander Valley) $30. Soft in acids and gentle in tannins, and a little sweet on the finish, this Cab has cherry marmalade and spice flavors. **84** —*S.H. (11/1/2005)*

Sausal 2001 Cabernet Sauvignon (Alexander Valley) $26. The warm vintage ripened the grapes to sugary deliciousness, yielding a wine of irresistible blackberry and currant flavors. It's big, bold, and bright in the mouth, with earthy tannins. Completely dry, with moderate alcohol. **87** —*S.H. (4/1/2004)*

Sausal 2000 Cabernet Sauvignon (Alexander Valley) $26. Richly fruity, with black cherry, green olive, and herb flavors wrapped in soft, gentle tannins. Easy on the mouth, a classically dry red wine that will appeal to a broad range of aficionados. **90** —*S.H. (3/1/2003)*

Sausal 2004 Sangiovese (Alexander Valley) $20. Soft and ripe, with sugared cherry pie and cinnamon spice flavors. This simple wine will appeal to those who like a little sweetness in their reds. **83** —*S.H. (11/15/2006)*

Sausal 1997 Zinfandel (Sonoma County) $12. 86 Best Buy —*J.C. (5/1/2000)*

Sausal 2001 Zinfandel (Alexander Valley) $14. This one's a bit muted. There are hints of plum and cherry, but the flavors are hiding behind the dried-out tannins. A smoky edge adds interest, but it's short on the finish. **81** *(11/1/2003)*

Sausal 1996 Alexander Valley Zinfandel (Sonoma County) $12. 86 *(9/1/1999)*

Sausal 2003 Century Vines Zinfandel (Alexander Valley) $30. Smells like a chocolate brownie, tastes dry and raisiny and strong in cooked cherry pie flavors. This Zin was a victim of excessive heat. **82** —*S.H. (11/1/2006)*

Sausal 2002 Century Vines Zinfandel (Alexander Valley) $28. Wonderful Zin. Showcases just what these old vines are capable of. Intense, focused flavors of cherries, raspberries, and ripe pomegranates, wrapped in a rich, creamy texture that finishes with a scour of spice. Totally dry, and best of all, it's not too high in alcohol. **92 Editors' Choice** —*S.H. (11/1/2005)*

Sausal 2001 Century Vines Zinfandel (Alexander Valley) $26. A blend of bright cherry, plum, and herb notes that start off strong but come to a finish somewhat quickly. Bright and somewhat herbal at the end. **84** *(11/1/2003)*

Sausal 2000 Century Vines Zinfandel (Alexander Valley) $26. Terrific Zinfandel, a big bruiser of a wine that blasts your palate off, but does it tastefully. Filled with ripe, briary berry flavors, and while it's a hot wine, it's dry and balanced. The irresistible flavors are perfect with grilled meats. **89** —*S.H. (9/1/2003)*

Sausal 1997 Century Vines Zinfandel (Sonoma County) $22. Old-vine straw, tobacco, and herb in the nose. The wine is subtle, sensual and complex, with layers of interesting spicy flavor. Nicely balanced and flavorful, with a long, firm finish. **90** —*P.G. (3/1/2001)*

Sausal 2003 Old Vine Zinfandel (Alexander Valley) $18. Sausal's old vines are about 50 years old, which may account for the unusual concentration and balance of this wine. It floods the mouth with blackberry, spice, and mocha flavors, yet is dry and balanced and not at all hot. Drink now. **86** —*S.H. (11/1/2006)*

Sausal 2002 Old Vine Zinfandel (Alexander Valley) $18. Here's an old-timey Zin, dry, fruity, robust, and spicy. Don't be too fussy, just grill the sausages and enjoy. **86** —*S.H. (8/1/2005)*

Sausal 2000 Old Vine Family Zinfandel (Alexander Valley) $15. From vines averaging fifty years, a big, bold Zin, brimming with wild berry flavors. It's a saucy wine, jammy and spicy, but dry. Has quintessentially Alexander Valley tannins and acids, soft and velvety. Easy to drink and to like, and should age well. **89** —*S.H. (3/1/2003)*

Sausal 2002 Private Reserve Zinfandel (Alexander Valley) $22. Here's a big, bold, brawny Zin, rustic and earthy, the kind that will go down easily with barbecue. It's powerful in briary wild blueberries, with a cocoa finish and lots of peppery spice. **88** —*S.H. (11/1/2005)*

Sausal 2001 Private Reserve Zinfandel (Alexander Valley) $20. Quite zingy on the palate. The wine serves up some bright cherry and spice notes, then dissipates somewhat quickly. Smoke and tar bring up the rear. **83** *(11/1/2003)*

Sausal 2000 Private Reserve Zinfandel (Alexander Valley) $20. Dark, rich, and dramatic. There's no doubting the varietal, with its mouthfilling wild berry and tobacco flavors, exuberant tannins and dry, peppery, and alcoholic finish. Best of all is the rich, velvety texture. **88** —*S.H. (9/1/2003)*

Sausal 1997 Private Reserve Zinfandel (Sonoma County) $16. 84 *(9/1/1999)*

Sausal 1996 Sogno della Famiglia Zinfandel (Sonoma County) $25. 90 *(9/1/1999)*

SAUVIGNON REPUBLIC

Sauvignon Republic 2005 Sauvignon Blanc (Russian River Valley) $18. Stimulatingly fresh and clean, this polished Sauvignon benefits from very high acidity that makes those tastebuds whistle. It shows fig, Tequila, grapefruit, and nectarine flavors and a finish of white pepper. Notable for its dry, keen freshness. **86** —*S.H. (10/1/2006)*

Sauvignon Republic 2004 Sauvignon Blanc (Russian River Valley) $18. Very, very extracted, almost overwhelming in spearmint, fig, and white pepper flavors, this wine leaves nothing to the imagination. It's big, but totally dry, and has a nice, clean brisk acidity. **87** —*S.H. (12/1/2005)*

Sauvignon Republic 2003 Sauvignon Blanc (Russian River Valley) $16. This new label isn't off to a good start, to judge by the watery flavors here. Doesn't taste like much of anything, except alcohol and a drop of lime. **82** —*S.H. (5/1/2005)*

SAVANNAH-CHANELLE

Savannah-Chanelle 1998 Estate Bottled Chardonnay (Santa Cruz Mountains) $22. 86 —*S.H. (2/1/2000)*

Savannah-Chanelle 1998 Laetitia Vineyard Pinot Blanc (Arroyo Grande Valley) $16. 88 —*S.H. (3/1/2000)*

Savannah-Chanelle 2002 Pinot Noir (Santa Cruz Mountains) $20. Decent, clean, and correct, with simple orange peel, cherry, herb, and coffee flavors. Smooth and light through the thin, sharp finish. **85** *(11/1/2004)*

Savannah-Chanelle 2002 Pinot Noir (Russian River Valley) $22. Minty, oaky, and herbal, a simple, dry wine with modest black cherry and toast flavors. Clean and decent, if not very complex. **85** *(11/1/2004)*

Savannah-Chanelle 2001 Pinot Noir (Central Coast) $20. Cola-like in flavor, with earthier notes of tobacco and leather. Drinks pretty lean, and the tannins are strong. Finshes with a bitterness of acids and tannins. **84** —*S.H. (7/1/2003)*

Savannah-Chanelle 2000 Pinot Noir (Central Coast) $20. Varietally true, with beetroot, tomato, crushed hard spice, raspberry, and mushroom aromas and flavors. It's also dry, with velvety tannins and good acidity. Not terribly complex, the flash is all on the surface, but it will drink nice with an olive tapenade or halibut in a tomato sauce. **85** —*S.H. (5/1/2002)*

Savannah-Chanelle 2000 Pinot Noir (Santa Lucia Highlands) $28. From this increasingly well-regarded appellation, a Pinot showcasing bright, pure and focused raspberry, mint, and spicy cola flavors in a wonderfully light, silky texture. It really is elegant and creamy on the palate, and high acidity provides a crisp counterpoint. **89** —*S.H. (5/1/2002)*

Savannah-Chanelle 2002 Armagh Vineyard Pinot Noir (Sonoma Coast) $30. Attractive for the aromatics and the pretty flavors of tart cherries, vanilla, and herbs, Crisp, supple, and elegant in the mouth, this polished wine has a long, oaky-sweet finish. **86** *(11/1/2004)*

Savannah-Chanelle 2000 Garys' Vineyard Pinot Noir (Santa Lucia Highlands) $42. The darkest and richest of this winery's trio of Pinots, a big-boned wine with surface flavors ranging from blackberries and cherries to cola, leather, and tobacco. There's a meatiness to the texture that makes it a perfect match for food. Feels smooth and silky in the mouth, but lacks the depth to merit a higher score. **89** —*S.H. (7/1/2003)*

Savannah-Chanelle 2002 Garys' Vineyard Pinot Noir (Santa Lucia Highlands) $35. One of this winery's best single-vineyard offerings, showing plenty of cherry, plum, cola, and vanilla flavors despite a light, delicate structure. Complex, spicy, and dry through the finish. **88** *(11/1/2004)*

Savannah-Chanelle 2002 Laetitia Vineyard Pinot Noir (Arroyo Grande Valley) $25. A meaty, oaky wine with lots of cherry cola, smoke, and sweet herbs. It's quite balanced and dry, with a supple mouthfeel. Not real fruity, but complex and nuanced. **89** *(11/1/2004)*

Savannah-Chanelle 2002 Sleepy Hollow Vineyard Pinot Noir (Santa Lucia Highlands) $25. Very fruity and ripe. Hits strong with forward, jammy cherry, rhubarb, fresh herb, and sweet oak, and tastes racy and savory. Ultimately, though, it's a bit simple in structure. **85** *(11/1/2004)*

USA

Savannah-Chanelle 2000 Sleepy Hollow Vineyard Pinot Noir (Santa Lucia Highlands) $35. Tasty and wonderfully drinkable. The basic flavors are cola and soy, with extra nuances of blackberries, cherries, and quite a bit of smoky, sweet oak. Drinks very dry and spicy. **87** —S.H. (7/1/2003)

Savannah-Chanelle 2002 Coast View Vineyard Syrah (Monterey County) $18. Smoky and tarry on the nose, followed by blueberry, blackberry, coffee, and caramel flavors. Round and velvety in the mouth, lush, with a soft, easygoing finish. **87** (9/1/2005)

Savannah-Chanelle 1999 Zinfandel (Santa Cruz Mountains) $36. Good Zins from this appellation are not common, which is too bad, considering how fine this one is. The fully ripened berry and spice fruit is married to intricate, lacy tannins, and the wine is dry. Despite the big flavors, it has an airy, feathery quality, anchored in crisp acidity. **91** — S.H. (7/1/2002)

Savannah-Chanelle 1998 Zinfandel (Paso Robles) $22. This is bright and smooth, with forward berry fruit and just the right amount of chocolatey oak. Supple and tangy, with a lip-smacking finish. **87** —P.G. (3/1/2001)

Savannah-Chanelle 1997 Estate Zinfandel (Santa Cruz Mountains) $36. 84 —S.H. (5/1/2000)

Savannah-Chanelle 1997 Westside Zinfandel (Paso Robles) $18. 88 —S.H. (5/1/2000)

SAVIAH CELLARS

Saviah Cellars 2003 Big Sky Cuvée Bordeaux Blend (Columbia Valley (WA)) $35. This 46% Merlot, 31% Cabernet Sauvignon, 23% Cab Franc blend has got some real muscle and Cabernet strength, with black cherry, cassis, and plenty of chocolatey oak. It seems to fade a bit in the mid-palate and then regroup, finishing strong and slightly hot, with coffee-flavored tannins. It can certainly benefit from additional bottle age. **89** —P.G. (6/1/2006)

Saviah Cellars 2002 Big Sky Cuvée Red Wine Bordeaux Blend (Columbia Valley (WA)) $35. The blend is 56% Merlot, 22% Cabernet Sauvignon, and 22% Cab Franc, showing lots of new oak at this early stage. Winemaker Richard Funk has a nice touch with this fruit, bringing the flavors out brightly, with clean, crisp edges and just the right amount of oak. **90** —P.G. (9/1/2004)

Saviah Cellars 2000 Uné Vallee Bordeaux Blend (Columbia Valley (WA)) $28. A Bordeaux blend, well balanced, with good blended fruits and plenty of milk chocolate toasty oak. It's soft, forward, and friendly, but it lacks a bit of definition and focus. **86** —P.G. (9/1/2003)

Saviah Cellars 2002 Une Vallée Red Wine Bordeaux Blend (Walla Walla (WA)) $30. A wonderful blend of Pepper Bridge Cabernet Sauvignon and Seven Hills Merlot and Cab Franc. This wine showcases the generous, open style of the wines made from Walla Walla fruit in 2002. Fruit flavors are rich and full, and wrap the palate in luscious layers. Ripe strawberries, cherries, and cassis mingle with judicious amounts of new oak. Plump but not fat, it's a lovely bottle to sip and savor. **90** —P.G. (9/1/2004)

Saviah Cellars 2004 Stillwater Creek Vineyard Chardonnay (Columbia Valley (WA)) $25. This is a thoroughly modern style: 100% French oak, Dijon Clone 75, plenty of lees contact. The yeasty nose introduces a very rich, mouthcoating sensation of butterscotch. Those leesy, creamy, butterscotch flavors surround the palate; the green apple fruit carries a bit of crisp authority and keeps the structure firm. Long, smooth, and very sensual without being too tiring. **90** —P.G. (6/1/2006)

Saviah Cellars 2003 Syrah (Walla Walla (WA)) $28. This fleshy sexpot of a Syrah doesn't show a lot of structure, so drink it up over the next year or two for its lush fudge, spicecake, and dried fruit flavors. **88** (9/1/2005)

Saviah Cellars 2003 Syrah (Red Mountain) $30. Inky in color and full in body, this ultradark, muscular Syrah reveals a trace of alcoholic heat alongside firm acids and tannins. Tight plum, earth, and vanilla flavors need a couple of years to unwind and become more approachable. **85** (9/1/2005)

Saviah Cellars 2002 Syrah (Red Mountain) $26. Young, grapy, and seductively laden with primary red and blue fruits; a big step forward from their 2001. The grapes come from a young vineyard high on the mountain called "The Ranch at the End of the Road" and show why Syrah is

as important to the region's future as Cabernet or Merlot. **90** —P.G. (11/15/2004)

Saviah Cellars 2001 Syrah (Red Mountain) $30. Scents of herb and saddle leather mix it up at the start; the wine hits the palate with a broad swath of chalky tannin. The fruit is tight and leans toward black cherry, and the wine finishes with plenty of smoke and thunder; good but rough. **87** —P.G. (7/1/2004)

Saviah Cellars 2000 Syrah (Red Mountain) $30. Simple, lightly spicy fruit in a pleasant, simple wine. A good quaff. **87** —P.G. (9/1/2003)

Saviah Cellars 2003 Stillwater Creek Vineyard Syrah (Columbia Valley (WA)) $30. Spicy, slightly volatile, with smooth plum and chocolate flavors across the palate. There's some lift from the VA, and then the silky tannins carry it along for a very pleasant ride. It just lacks the extra bit of depth that would ramp it up to the next decile. **89** —P.G. (6/1/2006)

SAVIEZ

Saviez 1998 Zinfandel (Napa Valley) $28. Beaucoup d'oak. Delicious, toasty, roasty, mocha-flavored oak. But the fruit is missing in action. The color suggests that there is some light, plummy fruit underlying all the oak, but it's hiding. **84** —P.G. (3/1/2001)

SAWKAR

Sawkar 2003 Reserve Cabernet Sauvignon (Napa Valley) $42. This is a young, tough wine, with big-time astringent tannins, which begs the question, will it age? There's primary blackberry and cherry fruit, and a streak of juicy acidity. It's not really drinkable now, but should improve through 2010. **88** —S.H. (3/1/2006)

Sawkar 2003 Reserve Merlot (Sonoma Mountain) $28. From a warmer part of this complex appellation comes this lovely Merlot, which despite some gritty tannins has a soft voluptuousness. It has deep flavors of plums and savory fresh herbs, and isn't too oaky. It's a fine wine now with a nice steak and gorgonzola butter sauce, but has the integrity to age for a decade. **90 Cellar Selection** —S.H. (3/1/2006)

Sawkar NV Red Table Wine Red Blend (California) $14. With Sonoma Mountain Syrah and Cabernet and quite soft in acids, and rich in ripe, finely ground tannins. It displays a good mixture of fruit and earthy, herbal, coffee flavors. There's a pleasant subtlety that makes it an unobtrusive accompaniment to food. **87** —S.H. (4/1/2006)

Sawkar 2003 Reserve Syrah (Sonoma Mountain) $25. Right out front, what bothers me about this wine is the taste of excessive heat and overripeness. The challenge for vintners when there are harvest heat waves, as there were in 2003, is to minimize the raisins and porty flavors. This wine partially but not wholly succeeded. **84** —S.H. (4/1/2006)

SAWTOOTH

Sawtooth 1999 Merlot (Idaho) $14. A full, husky set of clean but nondescript red-fruit aromas lead into a firm palate of strawberry and raspberry. The finish is smooth, but light, and throughout it gives off an air of confidence despite some hard tannins. A nice surprise from a state better known for potatoes. **86** —M.S. (4/1/2003)

Sawtooth 2002 Syrah (Idaho) $15. A bit gamy for some, but this blackberry-driven Syrah has a ripe, creamy mouthfeel and a long, softly tannic finish, so if you don't mind a little funk in your Syrah, climb aboard. **86** (9/1/2005)

SAWYER

Sawyer 1999 Bradford Meritage Bordeaux Blend (Napa Valley) $42. 92 — S.H. (11/15/2002)

Sawyer 2002 Bradford Meritage Red Table Wine Cabernet Blend (Rutherford) $42. Seems soft and one-dimensional, a wine that got so ultraripe the acids and tannins left, leaving pure flavor behind. That flavor is good, all blackberries, cherries, and cocoa, but the wine lacks structure and depth. **84** —S.H. (12/31/2006)

Sawyer 2002 Cabernet Sauvignon (Rutherford) $46. Here's a balanced, intricately structured young Cab. It opens with upfront aromas of cherry pie, coffee, cocoa, and vanilla, and while the tannins are firm, they're finely ground and pliant. The flavor is pure cherry, seasoned with oak. Good now, and should hold for some years. **90** —S.H. (12/15/2005)

Sawyer 2001 Cabernet Sauvignon (Rutherford) $46. Here's a Cab without the sweet flamboyance of some, but it possesses a balance and elegance that make it versatile at the table. The blackberry and herb flavors are framed in rich tannins. **89** —*S.H. (10/1/2004)*

Sawyer 1999 Cabernet Sauvignon (Rutherford) $46. This is great Cabernet, and gives you what you expect from a high-end wine in a great vintage. The aroma is all black currants and pretty oak, with brilliantly pure cassis flavors. Bone-dry, with dusty, fine tannins and soft acids, it's long on the finish. **93** —*S.H. (11/15/2002)*

Sawyer 2000 Bradford Meritage (Rutherford) $42. This blend of four varieties, topped by Cabernet Sauvignon and Merlot, shows off its terroir in the richly smooth, soft, complex tannins. There are pleasant flavors of blackberries and cassis, as well as an earthy streak that brings to mind mushrooms sautéed in soy sauce. It will probably age, but is terrific now with a grilled ribeye steak. **91** —*S.H. (6/1/2004)*

Sawyer 2001 Merlot (Rutherford) $37. This polished Merlot has pretty flavors of plums, currants, and herbs, with a sweet dash of mocha. It's dry, and the tannins are soft and lush. Drink now. **87** —*S.H. (12/15/2004)*

Sawyer 1999 Merlot (Rutherford) $34. A rich, opulent wine that stains the glass. Big, ripe flavors of currants, plums, tobacco, and sage are framed in thick but fine tannins. A streak of bright acidity and a deft overlay of oak add brightness and complexity. This young, juicy wine will improve over the next few years. **93** —*S.H. (11/15/2002)*

Sawyer 2003 Estate Merlot (Rutherford) $38. There's a briary, rustic nature to this Merlot, almost like Zinfandel, with its wild berry, white pepper, coffee, and tobacco flavors. It has sandpapery tannins that scour the mouth. **83** —*S.H. (12/31/2006)*

Sawyer 2002 Estate Merlot (Rutherford) $38. Here's a rich, dense Merlot that's very dry, yet packed with fruity flavors suggesting red and black cherries, red plums, cocoa, and green olives. It's smooth, but could use firmer acids. **85** —*S.H. (12/15/2004)*

Sawyer 2002 Sauvignon Blanc (Rutherford) $15. It's rare to find a Sauvignon Blanc from this appellation, and rarer still to get one this good. It's full-bodied, dry, and tart, with a mélange of flavors including citrus fruits, grilled figs, ripe melons, and currants. As it sits on the table, the better and more complex it gets. **91 Best Buy** —*S.H. (12/1/2004)*

Sawyer 2000 Sauvignon Blanc (Rutherford) $18. A high-quality Sauvignon Blanc, maybe one of the better ones of the year. Has a nice balance of grassy, citrus flavors and riper ones of apples and peaches. Especially notable for the lush, distinguished tannins and acids you expect from this appellation. **90** —*S.H. (6/1/2004)*

Sawyer 2004 Estate Sauvignon Blanc (Rutherford) $17. Very soft and gentle in the mouth, this fruity wine seems to lack the vivacity you want in a Sauvignon Blanc. But the flavors of white currants, fig, vanilla, lemon, and lime are very nice. **84** —*S.H. (12/15/2005)*

SAWYER CELLARS

Sawyer Cellars 2000 Cabernet Sauvignon (Rutherford) $46. Pours dark, and opens with aromas of cassis and smoky oak and vanilla, suggesting a very young wine. Enters with smooth, gorgeous tannins and a rich, velvety mouthfeel that carries along flavors of blackberry nectar that explode mid-palate. This crescendo tapers off in the long finish, where the young, ripe tannins show up. Age through 2010. **91** —*S.H. (11/15/2003)*

Sawyer Cellars 2000 Merlot (Rutherford) $34. Delicious and compelling, a huge, juicy wine of concentration and power. Stuffed with flavors of blackberry preserves and plum pudding, with layers of cocoa and spice and a sweet, tropical note of orange rind. Floods the mouth with all this, coating the palate in richly smooth, suave tannins and leading to a long finish. A very great success of the vintage. **93** —*S.H. (12/31/2003)*

Sawyer Cellars 2001 Sauvignon Blanc (Rutherford) $15. Here's a stylish white wine that can be enjoyed by itself or with a wide variety of foods. The spicy, lemon and lime flavors are accented by the taste of figs, and there are even tropical fruit notes. Just a little sweet on the finish, with nice, crisp acidity. **87** —*S.H. (10/1/2003)*

SAXON BROWN

Saxon Brown 1999 Pinot Noir (Russian River Valley) $35. Rich and deeply scented, with cherry, mushroom, tomato, smoke, and vanilla aromas. Shows wonderful depth of flavor, and explodes on the palate with cola, cherry, and herb flavors. Tart, crisp acidity and silky tannins give this vibrant wine great structure. **90** —*S.H. (2/1/2003)*

Saxon Brown 2005 Casa Santinamaria Vineyards Sémillon (Sonoma Valley) $30. A flavorful, full-bodied white with the body of a leesy Chardonnay, but different flavors. Citrus fruits, almond skin, apricots, and an almost Musqué-type floweriness lead to a long, citrusy, crisp finish. **86** —*S.H. (12/1/2006)*

Saxon Brown 2002 Casa Santinamaria Vineyards Old Vine Sémillon (Sonoma Valley) $20. From a 75-year-old white field blend. The winemaker has put no oak at all on this wine in order to preserve its intense flavors. They include melon, fig and a Chinese sweet and sour sauce taste that make this dry, crisp wine distinctive. Try with roast pork with a sweet apricot glaze. **86** —*S.H. (12/1/2003)*

Saxon Brown 2002 Syrah (Napa Valley) $40. The panel's scores for this wine ranged from 80 to 88, so you know it was somewhat controversial. One reviewer found it slightly volatile and raisiny, while at the other extreme, another found it dense, chocolatey and complex. One you'll definitely want to taste for yourself. **84** *(9/1/2005)*

Saxon Brown 2005 Flora Ranch Syrah Rosé Syrah (Chalk Hill) $20. Quite dark for a rosé, and very extracted, with a thick cherry taste that's fine for a red but a bit heavy and dense for a blush. **84** —*S.H. (12/1/2006)*

Saxon Brown 2003 Parmelee Hill Vineyard Syrah (Sonoma County) $30. Melds citrus, herb, pepper, and cranberry hints with riper flavors of blackberries and oak-derived notes of brown sugar and caramel. Firmly structured on the finish, with some troublingly hard tannins. Drink young, with a well marbled steak, or age it several years and hope for the best. **86** *(9/1/2005)*

Saxon Brown 2000 Casa Santinamaria Old Vine Zinfandel (Sonoma Valley) $35. Marches to the beat of good Cabernet with its cassis and chocolate aromas and flavors, lush, complex tannins and overlay of finely smoked French oak. But the persistant undertow of wild, brambly berry and the peppery finish finger it as Zin. **90** —*S.H. (3/1/2004)*

Saxon Brown 2002 Casa Santinamaria Vineyards Zinfandel (Sonoma Valley) $32. From an old-field blended vineyard with all sorts of varieties, the wine has a real sense of style and place. It's not modernly elegant, but it is a true representative of old-time Sonoma red wine. It's like drinking history. **86** —*S.H. (12/1/2006)*

Saxon Brown 1999 Casa Santinamaria Vineyards Zinfandel (Sonoma Valley) $35. A huge Zin, filled with ripe flavors ranging from wild forest berries to stone fruits to pepper and tobacco. The most notable feature is the tannins, which are rugged and fierce. This dry wine makes your tongue stick to the roof of your palate. **86** —*S.H. (2/1/2003)*

Saxon Brown 1999 Fighting Brothers Cuvée Zinfandel (Sonoma Valley) $30. A big Zin that opens with a blast of crushed white pepper aromas and then reveals its blackberry fruit in the mouth. It's got big, rough tannins and prickly acidity; there's nothing shy or subtle about it. **86** —*S.H. (2/1/2003)*

SAXUM

Saxum 2004 Broken Stones Rhône Red Blend (Paso Robles) $38. With enough Syrah to qualify for a varietal label, the wine is certainly high in alcohol and sweet in ripe, jammy fruit. But it works. It's sweet but not cloying, with cassis, cherry liqueur, and chocolate flavors, and a sexy, velvety texture. Combines power with softness. **90** —*S.H. (12/1/2006)*

Saxum 2004 Heart Stone Vineyard Rhône Red Blend (Paso Robles) $45. Almost a dessert wine, it's so sweet and high in alcohol. This Syrah, Mourvèdre, and Grenache blend has tremendous flavors because the vintage heat was freakish. One can only hope Mother Nature will afford drier wines going forward. **85** —*S.H. (12/1/2006)*

Saxum 2004 James Berry Vineyard Rhône Red Blend (Paso Robles) $45. Almost equal parts Syrah, Grenache, and Mourvèdre from the estate vineyard. This is a real step down from Bone Rock, mainly because of overripeness. It shows sugary sweet cherry pie, vanilla, and caramel flavors, and the alcohol weighs in at 16%. What a notoriously hard vintage this was. **84** —*S.H. (12/1/2006)*

Saxum 2004 James Berry Vineyard Bone Rock Rhône Red Blend (Paso Robles) $65. A gorgeous wine, soft as old kid leather, with impressively ripe blackberry pie, chocolate, anise, and coffee flavors. Although it's high in alcohol, the wine isn't hot. Defines West Paso Rhône reds. 85% Syrah, plus Grenache and Mourvèdre. **93** —*S.H. (12/1/2006)*

Saxum 2003 James Berry Vineyard Rocket Block Rhône Red Blend (Paso Robles) $45. First-ever release of this Grenache, Mourvèdre, and Syrah blend from Saxum, and what a pleasant wine it is. It drinks nice and spicy, not as robust as Saxum's other reds, but rich in red and black cherry and pepper aromas and flavors, with a lush, dry mouthfeel. **89** —*S.H. (10/1/2005)*

Saxum 2003 Bone Rock Syrah (Paso Robles) $56. Here's a young wine that opens with a blast of white pepper, then airs slowly to reveal layers of cassis, grilled meat, chocolate, anise, tar, and toasty oak. In the mouth, it's flamboyant and full-bodied, a little soft, but decadent. This wine is so rich in fruit, you could pour it over vanilla ice cream. It will be fabulous with a charbroiled steak. **94 Editors' Choice** —*S.H. (10/1/2005)*

Saxum 2002 Bone Rock Syrah (Paso Robles) $48. Similar to Saxum's Broken Stones Syrah, but more refined and, paradoxically, more intense. The sweet core of cherry, cola, mocha, and oak finishes spicy and very long. This wine is as plush and smooth as they get, one of the best in the state. **93** —*S.H. (12/1/2004)*

Saxum 2002 Bone Rock James Berry Vineyard Syrah (Paso Robles) $52. This is awesome Syrah. It starts with wonderfully rich and inviting aromas of Provencal herbs, such as thyme, bay leaf, and rosemary, and a note of lavender. The fruit is all cherries and blackberries, sweet and pure, seasoned with smoky oak. Fresh in acids, backed with firm but soft and complex tannins, this is a dramatic and beautiful wine. What a long, rich finish. **95** —*S.H. (12/31/2004)*

Saxum 2003 Broken Stones Syrah (Paso Robles) $38. Huge, big, rich, and gobby in blackberry, cassis, and white pepper flavors, this 80% Syrah is blended with Grenache, which adds a vibrant cherry note. The wine has lots of alcohol, but is balanced, complex, and lush. **91** —*S.H. (10/1/2005)*

Saxum 2002 Broken Stones Syrah (Paso Robles) $35. Sweet, refined, and pure, a wine that feels delicate despite massive fruit and a considerable overlay of oak. Cherry, smoke, oriental spice, and hung meat flavors are wrapped in smooth, polished tannins. The finish is clean and long. **91** —*S.H. (12/1/2004)*

Saxum 2000 James Berry Bone Rock Syrah (Paso Robles) $50. No problem at all getting the grapes rich and ripe, with scads of red and blackberry and stone-fruit flavors that go on forever into the finish. Yet the wine manages to keep this tremendous mouthful of fruit balanced and elegant through exquisitely fine tannins and judicious oak. A bit alcoholic and hot in the finish, but wears its size well. **92** —*S.H. (12/1/2002)*

SBRAGIA

Sbragia 2002 Monte Rosso Cabernet Sauvignon (Sonoma Valley) $50. Released with the winery's Howell Mountain Cab, the differences couldn't be clearer. This wine is softer and not as ripe. There's a peppercorn herbaceousness to the blackberry fruit flavors. It's a very young wine, but given the vineyard, it should develop well. Try holding for eight years. **90** —*S.H. (2/1/2006)*

Sbragia 2002 Rancho del Oso Cabernet Sauvignon (Howell Mountain) $75. True to its mountain appellation, this is a big, dark, young tannic wine. It is dramatically lush in black currant and chocolate fruit, seasoned with 100% new French oak. The tannins have been wrestled into soft, lush compliance. This is a fabulous Cabernet, drinkable now but with the structure to age for many years. **95 Cellar Selection** —*S.H. (2/1/2006)*

Sbragia 2001 Rancho Del Oso Cabernet Sauvignon (Howell Mountain) $75. Beringer's longtime executive winemaker Ed Sbragia finally has own brand, and this is his first, eagerly anticipated Cabernet. Like Beringer's Private Reserve, it's a gigantic wine. Concentrated and intense in currant, cherries, and cocoa, solidly oaked, and those Howell Mountain tannins

are sweet and ripe. Delicious now. Soft, so it's hard to predict how long it will age. Through 2010? **94** —*S.H. (5/1/2005)*

Sbragia 2002 Gamble Ranch Chardonnay (Napa Valley) $40. Ed Sbragia's inaugural Chardonnay has much in common with the Reserve he crafts at Beringer, but perhaps not as much finesse. Impressive for the huge tropical fruit and overlay of toasty oak, and pretty acidic. Should hold for a few years. **90** —*S.H. (4/1/2005)*

Sbragia 2003 Gamble Ranch Vineyard Chardonnay (Napa Valley) $40. The wine is Sbragia-esque in stature, in a word, big. Layers of tropical fruit, peaches, pineapples, green apples, spiced pears, smoky oak (100% new French), lees, all that good stuff. Acidity isn't all that high, but enough to balance and refresh. **91** —*S.H. (2/1/2006)*

Scarecrow 2003 Cabernet Sauvignon (Rutherford) $100. This is one of those tiny-production wines that gets tongues buzzing in San Francisco restaurants. The 100% Cab was aged for nearly two years in almost all new French oak. It is rich and flavorful in ripe blackberry and cassis fruit, with tannins co-contributed from the grapes and the barrels that suggest mid-term aging. It's a very fine, New World-style Cab that should be at its best between 2007 and 2010. **91 Cellar Selection** —*S.H. (9/1/2006)*

SCHARFFENBERGER

Scharffenberger NV Brut Sparkling Blend (Mendocino County) $16. Here's a polished, elegant wine, very dry, with delicate flavors of citrus rind, bread dough and yeast, toast and vanilla. It's has a lightness and charm on the palate that make it irresistible. **91** —*S.H. (3/1/2006)*

SCHEID VINEYARDS

Scheid Vineyards 2001 Chardonnay (Monterey) $15. A toasty wine with oaky and vanilla notes that frame apple, pear, and peach flavors. It has a nice, creamy texture and a dry finish. **84** —*S.H. (2/1/2004)*

Scheid Vineyards 2001 Riverview Vineyard Pinot Noir (Monterey) $20. Simple and light, with cola, coffee, and cherry flavors, and a slight dusting of smoky oak. Silky in texture, with good, crisp acids. **84** —*S.H. (12/15/2004)*

SCHERRER

Scherrer 2002 Cabernet Sauvignon (Alexander Valley) $32. An exotic style, but despite some shortcomings it's an interesting Cab. Almost overripe, with raisiny flavors and a slight burn, but it's good raisins, as you'd find in a currant pastry tart. Gets better in the glass. A wine to contemplate. **88** —*S.H. (12/1/2006)*

Scherrer 2001 Cabernet Sauvignon (Alexander Valley) $32. This Cabernet is instantly likeable for its delicious black currant, cocoa, and sweet anise flavors. It's as soft as velvet, with just enough acidity and tannins to make it balanced. **89** —*S.H. (11/15/2005)*

Scherrer 2001 Scherrer Vineyard Cabernet Sauvignon (Alexander Valley) $42. Both of Scherrer's '01 Cabs are quite distinctive, but this vineyard designate is superior both in terms of flavor and structure. It's a big wine that rewards in cassis, black currants, and cocoa, and even though it's very soft, it's layered and complex. **93** —*S.H. (11/15/2005)*

Scherrer 2002 Fort Ross Vineyard Chardonnay (Sonoma Coast) $28. Deliciously firm and complex, this Chard shows well-ripened tropical fruit flavors with a mineral-and-steel tanginess and high acidity. It's well-oaked, but those sappy, charry vanilla flavors really play well against the fruit. **92** —*S.H. (11/15/2005)*

Scherrer 2002 Fort Ross Vineyard Reserve Chardonnay (Sonoma Coast) $28. Released at the same price as Scherrer's regular Chard from this vineyard, this one's more intense and focused in tropical fruit. It may have more oak, too, to judge from the flamboyant spice and vanilla. Either way, it's a darned good wine. **92** —*S.H. (11/15/2005)*

Scherrer 2002 Helfer Vineyard Chardonnay (Russian River Valley) $35. Spicy and rich, this Chard is a bit softer than Scherrer's Fort Ross bottling, and is also leesy and oaky. The flavors are of peaches and apples. It shows a balanced complexity throughout. **91** —*S.H. (11/15/2005)*

Scherrer 2003 Scherrer Vineyard Chardonnay (Sonoma County) $26. Here's a high-acid, minerally Chard, that's clean in citrus zest, pink grapefruit, and richer peach and pear flavors. With a touch of smoky oak, it's balanced elegance. **88** —*S.H. (12/1/2006)*

Scherrer 2002 Scherrer Vineyard Chardonnay (Alexander Valley) $25. By far the softest of Scherrer's Chards, this one's slightly earthy, like sautéed peach slices wrapped in grape leaves. It also shows its oak treatment in the char and vanilla notes, and tons of spice. **88** —*S.H. (11/15/2005)*

Scherrer 2001 Scherrer Vineyard Chardonnay (Alexander Valley) $25. This is an interesting, terroir-driven wine. It's at that fascinating knife's edge where it's losing its peach and apple fruit and picking up a rich, honeyed minerality. Bone dry, it's crisp in acids and complex, a "food wine" to use that overused term. **90** —*S.H. (11/15/2005)*

Scherrer 2003 Pinot Noir (Russian River Valley) $35. Good Russian River Pinot that's very ripe and pretty tannic. Stuffed with lipsmacking cherry, blackberry, cola, and cocoa flavors. Feels thick and a little soft and heavy in the mouth. Not an ager. **87** —*S.H. (12/1/2006)*

Scherrer 2002 Pinot Noir (Russian River Valley) $35. A bit soft in acidity, this is nonetheless a delicious, balanced Pinot Noir. It has the silkiness you want from the variety, with cherry, cola, and cocoa flavors that mix well with the oak, and a long, fruity finish. **88** —*S.H. (11/15/2005)*

Scherrer 2002 Pinot Noir (Sonoma Coast) $30. Shows real coastal character in the bright, crisp acids that tingle the palate, and the cola, rhubarb, and cherry flavors that end with peppery spices. The silky, airy texture is pure Pinot. **87** —*S.H. (11/15/2005)*

Scherrer 2000 Pinot Noir (Russian River Valley) $35. 87 *(10/1/2002)*

Scherrer 2002 Fort Ross Vineyard Pinot Noir (Sonoma Coast) $38. Tasted alongside Scherrer's regular Sonoma Coast Pinot, this one's considerably richer and crisper. It's tart in fresh young acids, with marvelously complex waves of cherries, pomegranates, cola, sweet rhubarb, espresso, and pepper, in a silky-smooth texture. Offers compellingly good drinking. **93** —*S.H. (11/15/2005)*

Scherrer 2003 Fort Ross Vineyard High Slopes Pinot Noir (Sonoma Coast) $45. This is a prototypical Pinot from the most famous neighborhood of the Coast appellation. It's a big, full-bodied, heavy wine that's compelling for its dramatic dark fruit. Almost Syrah-like in weight, it defines an emerging style. Not an elegant Pinot Noir but it may be mid-term ageable. **89** —*S.H. (12/1/2006)*

Scherrer 2000 Helfer Pinot Noir (Russian River Valley) $35. 86 *(10/1/2002)*

Scherrer 2000 Hirsch Pinot Noir (Sonoma Coast) $45. Lively and lovely from the start, this shows a pretty, vibrant, dark cherry, cola, molasses, and spice nose. The red fruit, mint, tobacco, and citrus shadings are supported by bright acidity; still, the wine is smooth and well balanced. Closes strong with tangy plum, cocoa, and brambly underbrush notes. Drink now–2007, and possibly beyond. **90** *(10/1/2002)*

Scherrer 2002 Laguna Pinot Noir (Russian River Valley) $35. I don't know why Scherrer's Laguna bottling costs the same as their regular Russian River Pinot, because it's a better wine. Firmly structured in acids and tannins, it shows waves of cherries, black raspberries, cola, sweet leather, rhubarb, and spices that are endlessly complex and rewarding. **93** —*S.H. (11/15/2005)*

Scherrer 2004 Dry Rosé Wine Rosé Blend (Sonoma County) $14. This pale wine is indeed dry. It's also crisply tart in acids, making for a clean, brisk mouthfeel. Flavorwise, it's subtle, suggesting a delicate, raspberry-infused tea, with a touch of rose petal and cinnamon. **87** —*S.H. (11/15/2005)*

Scherrer 2005 Vin Gris Dry Rosé Wine Rosé Blend (Sonoma County) $14. A fine, copper-colored blush with intricate flavors of raspberries, rosehip tea, peach, and cinnamon spice. Goes beyond simple rosé-ness to achieve complexity. **87** —*S.H. (12/1/2006)*

Scherrer 1999 Old Mature Vines Zinfandel (Alexander Valley) $28. Rich, plush, and loaded with blackberry, cassis, raspberry, tar, and chocolate flavors. Tangy acidity and firm, ripe tannins carry the wine neatly along the palate in an elegant blend that's showing beautifully now and should age nicely, too. **92** —*J.M. (3/1/2002)*

Scherrer 2002 Scherrer Old & Mature Vines Zinfandel (Alexander Valley) $28. Denser, heavier, and more tannic than Scherrer's '01, this is also a less successful Zin. The fruity flavors aren't as bright, and the finish isn't as crisp, although it's still a very nice sipper. **86** —*S.H. (11/15/2005)*

Scherrer 2001 Scherrer Old & Mature Vines Zinfandel (Alexander Valley) $28. Fairly densely structured, with lots of toasty oak up front. Black cherry, blackberry, cassis, plum, cedar, spice, coffee, and chocolate are well integrated into a complex whole. **91** *(11/1/2003)*

Scherrer 2001 Scherrer Shale Terrace Zinfandel (Alexander Valley) $24. Bright, spicy, and opulent on the nose. The wine serves up a fine array of spice, bright cherry, blackberry, toast, and herb flavors. A tad bright on the finish, but quite nice nonetheless. **89** *(11/1/2003)*

Scherrer NV Zinfandoodle Zinfandel (Sonoma County) $16. Fred Scherrer says his grandfather used to call wines like this Zinfandoodle. That's a good word for an easy, uncomplicated wine with plenty of flavor and no particular pretensions. Finishes a little sweet. **83** —*S.H. (12/1/2006)*

SCHNEIDER

Schneider 1998 Cabernet Franc (North Fork of Long Island) $24. This wine is so big, lush, and soft on the palate that you can almost overlook the strong herbal aromas that mark the bouquet. Black cherries and chocolate complete the package. **87** —*J.C. (4/1/2001)*

Schneider 1998 Chardonnay (North Fork of Long Island) $19. Offers ripe fruit—yellow peaches and golden apples—in a medium-bodied package that's virtually guaranteed not to offend. A good, versatile quaffer. **85** —*J.C. (4/1/2001)*

SCHRADER

Schrader 2002 Beckstoffer Tokalon Vineyard Cabernet Sauvignon (Oakville) $75. Smells young, closed, and dusty, with toast accenting cocoa and cherries. Very dry, tannic, and earthy. Finishes astringent in tannins. Needs lots of time but should be a very good bottle by 2008. **89** —*S.H. (6/1/2005)*

Schrader 2001 Beckstoffer Tokalon Vineyard Cabernet Sauvignon (Napa Valley) $75. Smells ripe, balanced, attractive. Rich cohesion of toasted oak, anise, blackberry, dust in the aroma. Rich, smooth, long, very ripe in blackberry fruit. More tannic than Provenance's bottling of the same vintage. Classic structure. 2006-2015. **94 Cellar Selection** —*S.H. (6/1/2005)*

Schrader 2000 Beckstoffer Tokalon Vineyard Cabernet Sauvignon (Napa Valley) $75. Minty, green aroma. Herbal, with oak and modest blackberries. Well-made, elegant, but thin. Drink now. **85** —*S.H. (6/1/2005)*

Schrader 2004 Double Diamond Beckstoffer Cabernet Sauvignon (Red Hills Lake County) $25. This Cab shows potential. It's a big, ripe wine, with great flavors of black currant extract. But the sharp-elbowed, astringent tannins are unlikely to age out, and need refinement in future vintages. **86** —*S.H. (12/31/2006)*

SCHRAMSBERG

Schramsberg 1999 Blanc de Blancs Champagne Blend (Napa Valley) $30. Incredibly good, so rich and complex you'd swear you were drinking vintage Champagne. Flavors of yeast, lees, and baking bread dominate now, with underlying accents of sweet lime. This young, elegant wine will improve with extended cellaring. **91** —*S.H. (12/1/2003)*

Schramsberg 1998 Blanc de Blancs Champagne Blend (California) $30. Angular in the mouth with a slight citrus tanginess, this Blanc de Blancs finishes with more of the same mineral-citrus flavors. McIntosh apple, pear, and fresh cut grass aromas start things off. It's on the tangy side; drinking it with food would help keep the acid in check. **86** —*D.T. (12/1/2001)*

Schramsberg 1997 Blanc de Blancs Champagne Blend (Napa Valley) $29. 84 *(12/1/2000)*

Schramsberg 1999 Blanc de Noirs Champagne Blend (California) $31. Smooth, yet still has crisp acidity and bubbles. The flavors are subtle: not-yet-ripe strawberries, vanilla, a squeeze of lime, smoke, yeasty bread dough. **91** —*S.H. (6/1/2004)*

Schramsberg 1997 Blanc de Noirs Champagne Blend (Napa Valley) $30. This solid effort blends strawberries with fresh herbs and toasty, yeasty aromas. Flavors are earthier and strongly herbal, finishing chalky, with good length. The creamy mouthfeeland dry finish add a sense of elegance. **87** —*J.C. (12/1/2001)*

USA

Schramsberg 1996 Blanc de Noirs Champagne Blend (Napa Valley) $29. 87 —P.G. (12/31/2000)

Schramsberg 1996 Brut Champagne Blend (Napa Valley) $27. 86 —J.C. (12/1/1999)

Schramsberg 1995 Brut Blanc de Noirs Champagne Blend (Napa Valley) $27. 87 —J.C. (12/1/1999)

Schramsberg 1999 Brut Rosé Champagne Blend (California) $33. Flinty rich, with hints of strawberry, citrus, melon, and toast. Fresh, clean, and light on the palate. Clean at the end. **89** —J.M. (12/1/2002)

Schramsberg 1996 Cuvée de Pinot Brut Rosé Champagne Blend (Napa Valley) $27. 86 —J.C. (12/1/1999)

Schramsberg 1998 Cuvée de Pinot Brut Rosé Champagne Blend (Napa County) $30. The pale-copper color adds a level of elegance not usually found in bold, brash California. This sparkler's aromas are deep and meaty, with brine and soy accents. Turns earthier on the palate, but also folds in strawberry and herb flavors, ending with a flourish of anise. **87** —J.C. (12/1/2001)

Schramsberg 1996 J. Schram Champagne Blend (Napa County) $80. Incredibly rich and smooth, with subtle flavors of peaches, vanilla, yeast, and smoke. Very dry, but so rich and creamy—just luscious. Feels light and airy and elegant all the way through the long finish. **93 Editors' Choice** —S.H. (12/1/2002)

Schramsberg 1995 J. Schram Champagne Blend (Napa Valley) $75. A full, bready nose opens this impressive wine from perhaps America's most consistent producer of high-quality bubbly. It shows mature notes and apple fruit, with a faint, liqueur-like sweetness on the full palate. The bead is fine and steady, and class and complexity continue to shine through the long, tangy finish. **92** —M.M. (12/1/2001)

Schramsberg 1993 J. Schram Champagne Blend (Napa Valley) $65. 93 (12/31/2000)

Schramsberg 1996 Reserve Champagne Blend (Napa County) $60. Re-release. What a pretty bouquet on this 7-year-old wine! It is delicate but assertive, with flavors of dried hay, bread dough, vanilla, rich cream, smoke, and peach. The mouthfeel is dry and a bit scoury in acidity, with a biscuity vanilla flavor. Still seems young. Best left in a cool cellar for another seven years. **93 Cellar Selection** —S.H. (9/1/2003)

Schramsberg 1994 Reserve Champagne Blend (Napa Valley) $47. 90 —S.H. (12/31/2000)

Schramsberg 1993 Reserve Brut Champagne Blend (Napa Valley) $43. 87 —J.C. (12/1/1999)

Schramsberg 1998 Blanc de Noirs Pinot Noir (California) $30. Smells rich and complex, offering up a myriad of strawberry, white chocolate, toasted almond, vanilla, and bread dough aromas and flavors. Absolutely delicious bubbly, creamy, and clean. The rich, spicy finish has a taste of yeast. **92 Editors' Choice** —S.H. (12/1/2002)

Schramsberg 1995 Reserve Cuvée Pinot Noir (Napa Valley) $60. Rich and ripe, yet light and elegant, too. A wonderful blend of toasty citrus, melon, floral, honey, and herb flavors, all couched in a classy bubbly base. **92** —J.M. (12/1/2002)

Schramsberg 2002 Blanc de Blancs Sparkling Blend (Napa Valley) $32. Crisp and fruity, with pronounced peach, apple, quince, and vanilla flavors that taste a little sweet, with a full dosage, but nicely offset by very high acidity. Finishes clean and doughy. **87** —S.H. (12/31/2006)

Schramsberg 2000 Blanc de Blancs Sparkling Blend (Napa-Sonoma) $30. This is really a beautiful bubbly. It's dry, balanced, and elegantly structured, with fine acidity and a deft suggestion of bread dough and yeast on top of subtle citrus and smoke notes. Easy to drink, clean as a whistle, a real beauty. **90** —S.H. (12/31/2004)

Schramsberg 2001 Blanc de Blancs Brut Sparkling Blend (North Coast) $32. It's crazy that this is Schramsberg's "regular" Brut because it's really reserve quality. Utterly smooth and elegant, it has a satin texture framing delicate layers of citrus, peach and yeast, with a long finish of toasted almond. **91** —S.H. (12/31/2005)

Schramsberg 1994 Blanc de Blancs Late Disgorged Sparkling Blend (Napa County) $60. This is a highly pedigreed wine. You can judge that by the exceptionally smooth texture, and the fine quality of all the parts. It's elegant and complex, and despite being 11 years old, the wine is still scoury and pert in acids, guaranteeing it a long future. The dosage gives it a honeyed finish. **92** —S.H. (12/31/2005)

Schramsberg 2003 Blanc de Noirs Sparkling Blend (Napa-Mendocino-Sonoma) $34. Exceptionally refined in texture, this is a rich, layered sparkler. Based mostly on Pinot Noir, it has full-bodied nectarine, strawberry, and jasmine tea flavors, complexed with bread dough and smoky char, and finishes very dry. But best of all is that texture, pure silk and satin. **92** —S.H. (12/31/2006)

Schramsberg 2002 Blanc de Noirs Sparkling Blend (North Coast) $32. With a dash of Chardonnay added for brightness, this Pinot Noir-based sparkler sure is rich and complex. It's fierce in fine little bubbles, with long, deep flavors that are just a teensy bit sweet in dosage, but very high acidity balances that right out. The wine has a certain roughness that should melt away with three to five years of bottle age. **90** —S.H. (12/31/2006)

Schramsberg 2000 Blanc de Noirs Sparkling Blend (Napa-Sonoma) $30. Pale in color, with delicate dough, smoke, and vanilla notes, but you'll find the Pinot Noir in the suggestion of cherries in the aroma, and a red-berry weight in the mouth. This is a beautiful wine, elegant and crisp, filled with balance and harmony and length. **91** —S.H. (12/31/2004)

Schramsberg 2001 Blanc de Noirs Brut Sparkling Blend (North Coast) $30. A pale copper color, Schramsberg's Blanc de Noirs is richer than the Blanc de Blancs, with a fuller body. It's also a little more coarse, with pretty flavors of cherry cream and yeast. Try this powerful bubbly with curried lamb. **89** —S.H. (12/31/2005)

Schramsberg 1994 Blanc de Noirs Late Disgorged Sparkling Blend (Napa-Mendocino) $60. LD Blancs de Noirs are rare. The trick is to take the heaviness of all that lees and and Pinot Noir fruit and transmute it into elegance. Schramsberg displays a sure hand. The wine is still leesy and oaky, and certainly acidic, but despite its age, it should coast easily through the next 10 years and beyond, mellowing with each passing year. **92 Cellar Selection** —S.H. (12/31/2005)

Schramsberg 2002 Brut Rosé Sparkling Blend (North Coast) $36. This is the fullest, biggest of Schramsberg's current lineup of Bruts, a powerfully fruity but dry wine that never loses sight of elegance, delicacy, and finesse. There's something joyfully effervescent about the way the cherry, cream, yeast, and spice flavors come together and play on the palate. **92** —S.H. (12/31/2005)

Schramsberg 2001 Brut Rosé Sparkling Blend (California) $34. Smooth and refined, this classic blush offers subtle aromas of raspberries and lime, smoky oak and bread dough, with a floral tone. Although it's bone dry and even a bit tannic, it feels lush, right down to the polished finish. **91** —S.H. (12/31/2004)

Schramsberg 2000 Brut Rosé Sparkling Blend (California) $33. A terrific tri-county bubbly. Coppery in color, with fierce bubbles. Has rich aromas of strawberry, yeast, smoke, vanilla, and cinnamon, and drinks ripe, dry, and clean. Lots of finesse and elegance in this beautiful wine. **92** —S.H. (12/1/2003)

Schramsberg 2003 Brut Rosé Sparkling Blend (North Coast) $39. This polished bubbly hits the palate with a blast of fizzy acidity, then settles down to deliver rich, subtle peach, strawberry, vanilla, and smoky, doughy flavors. It's a dry wine, but you can taste the dosage. All the parts haven't come together yet. Age this copper-colored beauty for four or five years. **90** —S.H. (12/31/2006)

Schramsberg 2001 Crémant Sparkling Blend (Mendocino) $34. Off-dry, this bubbly has a little sugar boosting the peach, bread dough, citrus, and vanilla-smoky flavors. Balancing the semi-sweetness is crisp acidity and a clean finish. **87** —S.H. (12/31/2004)

Schramsberg 2003 Crémant Sparkling Blend (Napa-Mendocino) $34. The numbers tell the story. Residual sugar of nearly 4% makes it overtly sweet. Acidity of 8.6 grams per liter makes it scouringly crisp. The fruit, based on the Flora grape, is tangerine-like, with vanilla bean, honeysuckle and sweet bread crust. If you like California crémants, this is a good one. **87** —S.H. (12/31/2006)

USA

Schramsberg 2002 Crémant Demi-Sec Sparkling Blend (North Coast) $36. If you like your bubbly a little sweet but balanced and elegant, with a high-class touch, this is a good choice. Believe it or not, it's based on the grape Flora, supported by Gewürztraminer. It's fruity, with a honeyed finish and wonderful acidity. **85** —*S.H. (12/31/2005)*

Schramsberg 2000 Crémant Demi-Sec Sparkling Blend (California) $32. A sweetie with a round, smooth taste of lemon custard and vanilla offset by pretty acids, and wrapped in a rich Champagne-like body. Feels clean and lively despite the sugar, and finishes with a creamy flourish. **86** — *S.H. (12/1/2003)*

Schramsberg 1999 J. Schram Sparkling Blend (North Coast) $80. Compared to the winery's '99 Reserve, with which it was co-released, this bubbly is slightly sweeter, softer, and smoother. It's a fancy wine, drinkable now with crabcakes or smoked salmon or on its own, of course. Chardonnay-based, the wine possesses a light elegance and very great finesse. But it should age well over the next ten years. **93 Cellar Selection** —*S.H. (12/31/2005)*

Schramsberg 1998 J. Schram Sparkling Blend (Napa County) $80. Ultra-refined, super-elegant, the superlatives go on and on. Pours clear and bright, with the most subtle and inviting aromas, all dough and smoke and custardy vanilla with that tease of strawberry. So silky and light on the palate, airy, like silk, and perfectly dosed to a smooth dryness. You will find youthful acidity and scour on the finish, suggesting a wine fully capable of aging. Now through 2010. **95** —*S.H. (12/31/2004)*

Schramsberg 1998 J. Schram Sparkling Blend (North Coast) $120. This is a first tête de cuvée rosé from Schramsberg. The North Coast appellation is because the grapes come from four counties. It's 75% Chardonnay, with the rest Pinot Noir, and it's seriously good. The residual sugar is noticeable, but the acidity (8.7 grams) is so high that it balances out, and also ensures a long life. Don't touch until at least 2007, but it's likely to gain interest and complexity through 2015, at least. **94** —*S.H. (12/31/2006)*

Schramsberg 1997 J. Schram Sparkling Blend (California) $80. This French-styled sparkling wine is still far too young to enjoy. It is aggressively acidic, even tannic, and austere. There is a subtle core of cherry and raspberry flavor, however, that demand long-term aging. Drink this wine after 2010, or even later. **93** —*S.H. (12/1/2003)*

Schramsberg NV Mirabelle Sparkling Blend (North Coast) $18. Rather rough in the mouth, with sharp elbows, but dry and clean. **84** —*S.H. (12/31/2004)*

Schramsberg NV Mirabelle Sparkling Blend (California) $17. Serviceable, a clean bubbly that's sweetish, with peach and vanilla flavors that have a smoky edge. It's rough in the mouth, with a hot finish. **84** —*S.H. (12/1/2003)*

Schramsberg NV Mirabelle Brut Sparkling Blend (North Coast) $19. Shares the properties of Schramsberg Bruts with a good balance of fruit, yeast, and acidity, a robust mouthfeel and a long, tart strawberries and cream finish. This is actually a pretty good price for a bubbly of this elegance. **86** —*S.H. (12/31/2005)*

Schramsberg NV Mirabelle Brut Rosé Sparkling Blend (North Coast) $23. Made from Chardonnay and Pinot Noir, this bubbly is a little rough in texture, but it's nicely dry and clean, with pleasant strawberries and cream, yeasty lees and vanilla flavors. **86** —*S.H. (12/31/2006)*

Schramsberg 2000 Reserve Sparkling Blend (Napa-Mendocino-Sonoma-Marin) $80. An astonishingly brilliant bubbly, one of the best ever from Schramsberg or indeed any California winery, this Pinot Noir and Chardonnay blend strikes with sheer beauty. It's so delicate and refined yet so powerful, defining Champagne qualities of finesse and elegance. Rewarding now, but the parts are far from melding. Best 2007–2012. **96 Cellar Selection** —*S.H. (12/31/2006)*

Schramsberg 1999 Reserve Sparkling Blend (North Coast) $70. For starters, this is a very fine wine, architecturally clean, bone dry, and strong in acids. It's too young to fully enjoy now, though, all raw elbows and yeast. If you don't mind that edgy sharpness, try it as an apéritif, but it will benefit from five years or longer in the cellar. **90 Cellar Selection** —*S.H. (12/31/2005)*

Schramsberg 1998 Reserve Sparkling Blend (North Coast) $65. This is a fabulously rich wine, full-bodied and complex in cherry, peach, vanilla, yeast, lychee, roasted almond, and charcoal. It's also exceptionally delicate and fine, with a silk-and-satin mouthfeel that's as light as air. It's showing a bit of age but has yet to come into its own, suggesting a good 5–10 additional years of cellaring. **93 Cellar Selection** —*S.H. (12/31/2005)*

Schramsberg 1997 Reserve Sparkling Blend (California) $65. Very good now, it will eventually become great. It brims with fresh citrusy acids, and is very dry. There's an undertow of lush peach fruit, vanilla, bread dough, and smoke, fading into a long finish. **95** —*S.H. (6/1/2004)*

Schramsberg 1997 Reserve Sparkling Blend (California) $60. If you read the review of Schramsberg's J. Schram, you'll get a sense of this wine. It's nearly identical, but less refined, a bit rougher by comparison. Still, it's a very fine wine, youthful and sharp in acids, but balanced and controlled. Very tight, and clearly needs time. 2006 and beyond. **91** —*S.H. (12/31/2004)*

Schramsberg 1994 Reserve Late Disgorged Sparkling Blend (Napa Valley) $200. This is a gigantic wine, but it's so well structured and refined, so beautiful, you can drink it now and fall in love with it. It's perfectly balanced, enormously complex, and not too sweet; the highest-scoring California sparkler we've ever tasted, blending rich toasty notes with well-ripened fruit. This fabulous wine should come together, mellow and gain complexity for a decade. Only available in magnums or larger bottles. **97 Editors' Choice** *(12/31/2005)*

Schramsberg 1999 Crément Demi Sec White Blend (California) $33. Creamy smooth, yet sparkling with pretty hints of fig, apricot, melon, and spice. Very slightly sweet, it makes a marvelous apéritif. **89** —*J.M. (12/1/2002)*

SCHUG

Schug 2003 Cabernet Sauvignon (Sonoma Valley) $22. In a time when so many Cabernets are hard to drink with food because they're overextracted, this controlled wine is a welcome find. It's dry, with the alcohol a modest 13.5%. The fruit flavors have a nice earthy, herbal component reminiscent of Bordeaux. **90** —*S.H. (7/1/2006)*

Schug 2001 Cabernet Sauvignon (Sonoma Valley) $20. Fairly soft in the mouth with a smooth, chalky texture; the mixed plum fruit on the palate is juicy, yet not jammy or overripe. Aromas are of plums and black soil. A nice Cabernet, at an agreeable price. **88** *(5/1/2004)*

Schug 2000 Cabernet Sauvignon (Sonoma Valley) $20. Classic Sonoma Cab, with black currant, cassis, and herb aromas highlighted by smoky oak and vanilla. Enters soft and plush, with full-bodied berry and cherry flavors. Notable for the fine, velvety texture, although it finishes a bit short. **87** —*S.H. (11/15/2003)*

Schug 1997 Cabernet Sauvignon (Sonoma Valley) $20. 84 —*S.H. (12/15/2000)*

Schug 2002 Heritage Reserve Cabernet Sauvignon (Sonoma Valley) $50. What a great job Schug is doing with Bordeaux varieties. This is an extraordinarily rich Cab, with ripe blackberry flavors folded into thick, fine tannins. There's a cut of acidity that brings balance, and will help the wine age for six years or so. Compared to Napa Cabs, it's more structured and angular, but right up there. **92** —*S.H. (9/1/2006)*

Schug 2001 Heritage Reserve Cabernet Sauvignon (Sonoma Valley) $50. This is a balanced and elegant Cab. It's almost muted in the quiet interplay of cassis fruit, smoky oak, and rich tannins. It's the sort of wine you reach for with real food, as opposed to tasting competitions, and it's likely to age well through the decade. **90** —*S.H. (5/1/2005)*

Schug 2000 Heritage Reserve Cabernet Sauvignon (Sonoma Valley) $50. This Cab's black fruit is sturdy, rather than fleshy and ripe—not surprising, since the fruit comes from a cool part of the valley. In the mouth, tannins are chewy, and fairly soft; finishes with chalk, char, and a little herb. Contains 24% Merlot. **89** *(5/1/2004)*

Schug 1999 Heritage Reserve Cabernet Sauvignon (Sonoma Valley) $50. A stylish Cab, with ripe aromas and flavors of blackberries, licorice, and herbs, wrapped in smoky oak. Drinks dry, polished, and smooth. A bit lean, especially considering the vintage, but balanced and elegant. **89** —S.H. (11/15/2003)

Schug 1997 Heritage Reserve Cabernet Sauvignon (Sonoma Valley) $40. 94 (11/1/2000)

Schug 1996 Heritage Reserve Cabernet Sauvignon (Sonoma Valley) $40. 92 —S.H. (2/1/2000)

Schug 1998 Chardonnay (Sonoma Valley) $14. 87 —S.H. (5/1/2000)

Schug 1997 Chardonnay (Carneros) $18. 88 —S.H. (6/1/1999)

Schug 2004 Chardonnay (Carneros) $20. Ripe enough in fruit, with massive, explosive peach custard, Key lime pie and vanilla flavors and a solid overlay of smoky oak. The finish is quick and somewhat simple. **85** —S.H. (12/31/2005)

Schug 2003 Chardonnay (Carneros) $20. Less rich than the Heritage Reserve, but has much in common with it. It's crisp with toasty oak, pear, and pineapple flavors, a creamy texture and a long finish. **88** —S.H. (5/1/2005)

Schug 2001 Chardonnay (Sonoma Valley) $15. Pretty good Chard, with very ripe, pronounced flavors of white peach and pear all the way into tropical fruits. Fairly oaky, with sweet vanilla and buttered toast. A bit soft in acids, but perfect for a rich salmon dish, perhaps served with a buttery cream sauce. **86** —S.H. (12/1/2003)

Schug 2001 Chardonnay (Carneros) $20. Crisper and brighter than Schug's Sonoma Valley bottling, with more upfront acids, its flavors veer more toward citrus fruits, although there are touches of exotic nectarine and guava. The creamy richness comes from oak and lees. Feels long and rich in the mouth; a wine to savor and enjoy. **88** —S.H. (12/1/2003)

Schug 2000 Chardonnay (Sonoma Valley) $15. This is an earthy Chard. There are hints of green apples with a slight hint of wood, and the wine drinks dry. It's far from opulent, but there is good structure and mouthwatering acidity, and the finish is very clean. **85** —S.H. (5/1/2002)

Schug 2000 Chardonnay (Carneros) $20. Here's a lean, angular wine that drinks surprisingly tart and lemony, despite sur lies aging and 100% barrel fermentation. Airing reveals notes of pippin apples and a wallop of smoky oak, but the palate impression is acidly citric and dry. A Chardonnay for shellfish? **86** —S.H. (5/1/2002)

Schug 1998 Chardonnay (Carneros) $18. 93 —S.H. (11/15/2000)

Schug 2002 Barrel-Fermented Sur Lie Chardonnay (Carneros) $20. Walter Schug likes his "Chards creamy, not buttery," and this one fits the bill. Yellow peach, banana, and toast flavors complement the creamy, fat mouthfeel. Finishes clean and bright. Aged six months sur lie. **88** (5/1/2004)

Schug 1996 Carneros Reserve Chardonnay (Carneros) $25. 91 —S.H. (6/1/1999)

Schug 2004 Heritage Reserve Chardonnay (Carneros) $30. Bright and tart in green apple and pink grapefruit flavors that have high, puckery acidity, this Chard from the Sonoma side of the appellation is softened with the buttercream of oak and lees. Try with lemon chicken. **87** —S.H. (11/1/2006)

Schug 2003 Heritage Reserve Chardonnay (Carneros) $30. Always rich and well structured, Schug's '03 is a dense, weighty Chard, supporting flavors of sweet lime, pear, and pineapple elaborately seasoned with toast and vanilla. Finishes crisp and fruity. **90** —S.H. (5/1/2005)

Schug 2002 Heritage Reserve Chardonnay (Carneros) $30. An elegant Chardonnay, with a smooth mouthfeel. Has a yellow-fruit core that's not at all tropical. Finishes with nuances of nut, ginger, and spice. A good food wine, more complementary than showy. **89** (5/1/2004)

Schug 2001 Heritage Reserve Chardonnay (Carneros) $30. Complex aromas of peaches, pears, and tropical fruits mingle with leesy, oaky notes and Oriental spices. The palate shows ripe, fruity flavors wrapped in a dense, creamy texture. Crisp acidity makes it bright and inviting. **92** —S.H. (12/1/2003)

Schug 2000 Heritage Reserve Chardonnay (Carneros) $30. Richer than this winery's other two current releases, in terms of lavish oak, but still curiously lean in fruit. Lemons and grapefruits form the underlying theme. French oak adds vanilla, smoke, and spicy sweetness, but a lean tartness persists throughout. Yet it's impeccable in its way. **87** —S.H. (5/1/2002)

Schug 1999 Heritage Reserve Chardonnay (Carneros) $30. Attractive pear, citrus, melon, and mild spice aromas open this lean and elegant wine. The mouthfeel is light, but not insubstantial and slightly tense (in a good way), showing good acid spine, crisp citrus flavors, and taut mineral accents. A slight creaminess keeps it from getting too sharp, and it closes with a nice chalky note. Has the stuff to keep and may well merit a higher score with a few years of aging. **88** (7/1/2001)

Schug 1998 Heritage Reserve Chardonnay (Carneros) $25. 88 (6/1/2000)

Schug 2003 Merlot (Sonoma Valley) $22. This is a wine that may get lost in a blind tasting because it's restrained and balanced. Fruit bombs will overwhelm it, but with great food, at the table, its simple, dry elegance and refreshingly crisp acidity will support, not overwhelm, steak, lamb, duck, or other rich fare. **91 Editors' Choice** —S.H. (7/1/2006)

Schug 2001 Merlot (Sonoma Valley) $20. A claylike flavor and texture is the backdrop for black plum and cherry fruit on the palate, and continues on through the finish, where a dark ash or char note takes over. A classy wine. **88** (5/1/2004)

Schug 2000 Merlot (Sonoma Valley) $20. Very soft and fruity, a dense wine with lip-smacking aromas and flavors of plum pudding, blackberry, and black cherry, coffee, herbs, smoky vanilla, and violets. There are some pretty good tannins, and while they're soft, they impact the mouthfeel. **90** —S.H. (12/31/2003)

Schug 1997 Merlot (North Coast) $18. 86 —S.H. (11/15/2000)

Schug 2002 Heritage Reserve Merlot (Carneros) $30. What a terrific Merlot. Cool Carneros is a natural home to the variety, and this wine is so ripe in blackberry, cherry, coffee, and leather flavors, and so dry and balanced. The tannins are pure and supple. All in all, it's just a tremendously rewarding red wine. **92** —S.H. (11/1/2006)

Schug 2001 Heritage Reserve Merlot (Carneros) $30. Soft and gentle, with olive, black cherry, and coffee flavors, this wine also shows heat in the midpalate through the finish. **85** —S.H. (5/1/2005)

Schug 2000 Heritage Reserve Merlot (Carneros) $30. We found very ripe, dark-fruit aromas on the nose, and juicy black plums and cherries on the palate. Has an undercurrent of earth that shows up as tree bark on the juicy finish. Stately and elegant, not overblown or overoaked. **90** (5/1/2004)

Schug 1997 Heritage Reserve Merlot (Carneros) $35. 89 —S.H. (11/15/2000)

Schug 2004 Pinot Noir (Sonoma Coast) $16. Light-bodied and delicately structured, with tight acids and a bone dry mouthfeel, this Pinot features cherry, cola, rhubarb, and spice flavors. Tasted alongside some muscular Pinots, it's a featherweight, but it is elegant and food-friendly. **86** —S.H. (3/1/2006)

Schug 2004 Pinot Noir (Carneros) $22. Schug's estate Carneros bottling represents a less popular style today, one of control and balance. Not for this winery gobs of extract and jam. They like their acidity and modest alcohol, which means a leaner Pinot. But it's an elegant, complex accompaniment to food, and will age for a decade. **90** —S.H. (3/1/2006)

Schug 2003 Pinot Noir (Carneros) $20. Simple, tart, and very dry, with modest cherry and cola flavors that finish with a scour of gritty tannins. Might soften and improve in 3 years. **84** —S.H. (5/1/2005)

Schug 2002 Pinot Noir (Carneros) $20. A good entry-level Pinot, with flavors of seeped tea, earth, and bright cherries. Similar flavors show on the finish, where there's also some dried spice and herb notes. On the lean side in terms of body, but still a very good wine. **87** (5/1/2004)

Schug 2001 Pinot Noir (Sonoma Valley) $15. Pale in color, and drinks dry and crisp, with silky tannins. Tasty and easy, although it makes few pretenses to complexity or depth. **85** —S.H. (12/1/2003)

Schug 2001 Pinot Noir (Carneros) $20. A pretty, polished Pinot, with very nice, ripe flavors of raspberries, strawberries, and spices. This is a lightly textured wine with silky tannins. **88** —S.H. (12/1/2003)

Schug 2000 Pinot Noir (Sonoma Valley) $15. Schug's basic Pinot is a blast of spicy flavor. It's not a big, ageworthy wine—what California Pinot is? But with its full-throttle cherry, raspberry, and pepper notes, it will stand up to rich, spicy foods. The tannins are properly silky, and crisp acids hoist up the sweet fruit. **88 Best Buy** —*S.H. (2/1/2003)*

Schug 2000 Pinot Noir (Carneros) $20. Considerably less ripe than the winery's Sonoma Valley bottling, with tomato, beet, sautéed mushroom, and herb aromas and flavors, although there's a chewy core of black cherry in there. Of course, Carneros is a cold, foggy place. I don't think this wine will age, but this is a solidly made, good wine. It's a question of pairing it with appropriate food. **88** —*S.H. (4/1/2003)*

Schug 1999 Pinot Noir (Sonoma Valley) $15. The workhorse wine from this Pinot master is pretty darned good, especially considering the price. Lovely, deep aromas of black cherry, tobacco, coffee, and nutmeg, with a waft of vanilla-tinged oak introduce a wine that is ripe and sweet in the mouth. The vintage was a good one, and the fruit is really succulent. It's not a keeper, however, and it won't improve in the cellar, but it's so good there's no reason not to drink it all up now. **90** —*S.H. (2/1/2001)*

Schug 1999 Pinot Noir (Carneros) $20. With a chunky, smoky nose to kick it off, this medium-weight Pinot features ample berry fruit, toasty oak notes, vanilla, and cocoa. It's plump and chewy, with caramel and chocolate on the finish. **83** *(10/1/2002)*

Schug 1998 Pinot Noir (Carneros) $18. Cherry-berry fruit, spice, a velvety texture and a long finish make for a lovely wine, soft and limpid, but with underlying power. The tannins are as light as air, but somehow substantial anyway. The framework is exceptional. You'll be smacking your lips over this beauty. **92** —*S.H. (2/1/2001)*

Schug 2003 Heritage Reserve Pinot Noir (Carneros) $30. This veteran winery continues to produce a Pinot Noir that's less mind-blowingly opulent than some, hewing stubbornly to European traditions of balance. Acidity and tannins co-star with oak. Schug's flavors get riper every vintage, this year cornering sweet black cherries and spicy cola. **89** —*S.H. (12/31/2005)*

Schug 2002 Heritage Reserve Pinot Noir (Carneros) $30. This textbook Pinot shows cherry, cola, and rhubarb flavors that finish dry. It has some gritty tannins and good acidity, and calls for something rich, like lamb. Schug's reserve has a history of aging well. Drink now through 2010. **88** —*S.H. (5/1/2005)*

Schug 2001 Heritage Reserve Pinot Noir (Carneros) $30. Classic Schug, a very dry young wine with concentrated black stone fruit flavors, tobacco, and lots of herbs. It is well structured. The tannins are easy and fine, and the acids are firm and crisp. This wine has proven its ability to improve with age. Best after 2007. **91** —*S.H. (4/1/2004)*

Schug 2000 Heritage Reserve Pinot Noir (Carneros) $30. A rich and complex Pinot. Carneros jammy berry-cherry fruit is there, joined with earthier herbal notes and a meaty streak. Feels dense and full bodied in the mouth, with some youthful, dry tannins that suggest midterm cellaring, an impression furthered by the long, spicy-fruity finish. **90** —*S.H. (2/1/2004)*

Schug 1999 Heritage Reserve Pinot Noir (Carneros) $30. This wine, from selected barrel lots, combines the best of riper grapes filled with cherry fruit and leaner ones, with their herbal, cranberry, and tomato flavors. The result is complex. Neither sweet nor dry, it tantalizes the palate, and seems to change with every sip. Oak provides some smoky, spicy accents. **92 Editors' Choice** —*S.H. (2/1/2003)*

Schug 1998 Heritage Reserve Pinot Noir (Carneros) $30. Specially selected lots account for this top-of-the-line bottling. It's really very good. The fruit tends toward raspberries and cherries, and it's smooth as silk in the mouth. The nutmeg, ginger, cinnamon, and peppery notes last for a long time on the finish. The difference between this and the typical Carneros bottling is intensity; the fruit is more focused. It's the difference, say, between a flashlight and a laser. **93** —*S.H. (2/1/2001)*

Schug 1997 Heritage Reserve Pinot Noir (Carneros) $30. 86 *(11/15/1999)*

Schug 1998 Rouge de Noirs Pinot Noir (Carneros) $25. A tasty package of ranier cherry, red plum, caramel, toast, tobacco, basil, and a hint of tomato. Acids and a touch of tannins are well integrated. Light and elegant throughout. **88** —*K.F. (12/1/2002)*

Schug 1998 Sauvignon Blanc (North Coast) $12. 90 Best Buy *(3/1/2000)*

Schug 2005 Sauvignon Blanc (Sonoma County) $15. Just about everybody will like this food-friendly wine, with its bright, happy citrus, green grass, and peach flavors. It's smooth and polished, with crisp acidity and a rich, fruity finish. **86** —*S.H. (11/1/2006)*

Schug 2004 Sauvignon Blanc (Sonoma County) $15. You'll taste some riper fig and peach notes along with tart citrus and white pepper in this stylish Sauv. It's dry and crisp, with a long, fruity finish. **86** —*S.H. (8/1/2005)*

Schug 2003 Sauvignon Blanc (Sonoma County) $15. Sweet in fig, honeydew, apple, and spice flavors, this wine has enough acidity to balance out the richness. Has a creamy mouthfeel that adds to the pleasure. **86** —*S.H. (5/1/2005)*

Schug 2002 Sauvignon Blanc (Sonoma County) $15. Citrus, particularly grapefruit, aromas dominate, along with some chalk dust. The dusty, chalky quality comes back on the palate, where there's light yellow fruit. Mouthfeel is a little viscous; finishes with textural notes akin to peach fuzz. **87** *(5/1/2004)*

Schug 2001 Sauvignon Blanc (Sonoma County) $15. Made in a straightforward, unoaky manner that lets the fruit through. Displays varietal flavors of lemons and grapefruit with tart acidity and a cleansing mouthfeel. Kind of thin, probably because the vines were stretched, but a pleasant enough sip. **84** —*S.H. (9/1/2003)*

Schug 2000 Brut Rouge de Noirs Sparkling Blend (Carneros) $25. Pretty dark for a bubbly, with dough, strawberry, smoke, and vanilla aromas and delicate flavors of strawberries and cream. A bit rough in texture, but clean and dry. Might soften with a few years in the cellar. **86** —*S.H. (12/1/2003)*

Schug 2001 Rouge de Noirs Sparkling Blend (Carneros) $25. From Pinot Noir grapes. It's rare to find a California bubbly this red in color. Opens with bright and expressive cherry, vanilla, and yeast aromas, and turns rich in cherry fruit in the mouth. Unusually full-bodied for a sparkling wine, but very fine. **90** —*S.H. (6/1/2005)*

Schug 2002 Rouge de Noirs Brut Sparkling Blend (Carneros) $25. Made from Pinot Noir, this bubbly is quite dark in color, and those Pinot flavors of cherries, strawberries, cola, and tea really star. As full-bodied as it is, the wine is effervescently delicate, and completely dry. Try with sushi. **88** —*S.H. (6/1/2006)*

SCHWEIGER

Schweiger 2000 Cabernet Sauvignon (Spring Mountain) $45. There's a schizophrenic aroma here, which conjoins ripe blackberry and cassis with green, herbal, minty notes, all in one sniff. That split continues in the mouth, where the black currant flavors are invaded by mint, and tough, astringent tannins numb the palate through the finish. **86** —*S.H. (12/31/2003)*

Schweiger 1999 Cabernet Sauvignon (Spring Mountain) $48. This unblended Cab pours as dark as they come, and the aroma is muted, indicating a baby wine. What reaches the nose is largely the smoky, spicy smell of oak barrels. Oak dominates the taste, too, although it's obvious there's some good, rich blackberry fruit inside. Aging it is a gamble. **86** —*S.H. (12/15/2003)*

Schweiger 2000 Chardonnay (Spring Mountain) $30. A nice, lush wine with a lot of smoky oak and lees framing well-ripened apple and peach flavored fruit. Feels rich and creamy in the mouth, and oriental spices tingle the palate on the long finish. **90** —*S.H. (6/1/2003)*

Schweiger 1999 Merlot (Spring Mountain) $45. Unfined and unfiltered, this is a superextracted wine, almost chunky in the mouth and full of red and black stone fruit and berry flavors. The tannins are sizable and very dry. A few years of age will soften it. **89** —*S.H. (10/1/2003)*

Schweiger NV Port III Port (Spring Mountain) $45. Lush yet bright, with black cherry, black currant, chocolate, cedar, spice, and sweet oak flavors. Tannins are a bit powdery and the finish is moderate in length. A fine treat for after dinner. **88** —*J.M. (3/1/2004)*

Schweiger 2000 Dedication Red Blend (Spring Mountain) $65. Smells and tastes pretty good, with currant notes accented by considerable oak, which brings vanilla, smoke, and sweet wood-sap flavors. Yet the tannins are enormous and problematic, striking midpalate and leaving the

USA

mouth feeling numb, and the depth of flavor just isn't there to counterbalance them. **88** —*S.H. (12/31/2003)*

Schweiger 2001 Uboldi Vineyard Sauvignon Blanc (Sonoma Valley) $22. Bright and fresh on the palate, with zippy citrus and gooseberry aromas up front. They continue along the palate, blending with melon and herb flavors to deliver a pleasing, refreshing quaff. **88** —*J.M. (10/1/2003)*

SCOTT AARON

Scott Aaron 2003 Integrity Cabernet Blend (Paso Robles) $60. If you can open the faux wax capsule on this pompously packaged bottle, you'll find a vin ordinaire Bordeaux blend. It's lifelessly soft, with herb and berry flavors, and a dry finish. **82** —*S.H. (12/15/2005)*

Scott Aaron 2004 Viognier (Paso Robles) $30. Very fruity, with flavors of peaches and nectarines, this simple white wine is soft, and finishes a little sweet. **83** —*S.H. (12/15/2005)*

SCOTT HARVEY

Scott Harvey 2003 Barbera (Amador County) $25. Smells and tastes cooked by heat, with raisiny, pruny, coffee flavors. Yet there's something likeable about this honest, bone-dry country wine. **85** —*S.H. (6/1/2006)*

Scott Harvey 2003 Syrah (Amador County) $25. Rustic and a little sweet on the finish, this Syrah has edgy tannins and powerfully fruity plum, coffee, and blackberry flavors. It needs rich meats and cheeses to break it up and soften it. **84** —*S.H. (4/1/2006)*

Scott Harvey 2003 Mountain Selection Syrah (Amador County) $15. Kind of hot and overripe in raisiny, stewed fruit flavors, but dry, this rustic wine is made for quaffing. It'll be fine with a grilled steak or broiled chicken. **83** —*S.H. (5/1/2006)*

Scott Harvey 2003 Mountain Selection Zinfandel (Amador County) $13. Light in color, but robust and intense in fruit, this Zin has dried fruit, dill, coffee, and leather flavors, wrapped in firm, jagged tannins. There's a rusticity that calls for simple fare, like pizza or pasta. **83** —*S.H. (6/1/2006)*

Scott Harvey 2003 Old Vine Selection Zinfandel (Amador County) $22. A tremendous concentration of cherry, white pepper, coffee, and thyme flavors marks this distinctive, complex Zin. It's very dry and supple, with good heft and fairly thick tannins. Best over the near term. **89** —*S.H. (6/1/2006)*

SCOTT PAUL

Scott Paul 1999 Kent Ritchie Vineyard Chardonnay (Sonoma County) $35. Announces itself with an unusual and pleasant Gewürztraminer-like tangerine, lychee, and ginger nose. Its mild but decidedly unique character is clearer on the melon, butter-cinnamon, and peach palate. Nice acidity and a tangy-spicy finish. **89** *(7/11/2001)*

Scott Paul 2004 Audrey Pinot Noir (Willamette Valley) $50. Much as I love the winery's La Paulée, this tops it. There's more concentration and complex blueberry, mulberry, black cherry, and plum flavors. It shows a whiff or two of mint, sage, and chervil, and as with all Scott Paul wines it is impeccably balanced, non-interventionist and studiously clean. **91** —*P.G. (12/1/2006)*

Scott Paul 2003 Cuvée Martha Pirrie Pinot Noir (Willamette Valley) $20. This is like the younger sibling to the lovely La Paulée—same vineyard sources but younger vines. Round and pleasing, it has young vine flavors of red currant and pomegranate, with a snappy tartness in the finish. **89** —*P.G. (8/1/2005)*

Scott Paul 2002 Cuvée Martha Pirrie Pinot Noir (Willamette Valley) $20. Sour and sweaty to start, this wine never quite opened up. Slightly sweet, moderately spicy, and lacking in charm, it retained a sweaty, horsey undertone through the finish. **84** *(11/1/2004)*

Scott Paul 2004 La Paulée Pinot Noir (Willamette Valley) $35. This is the delightful follow-up to the gorgeous 2003; it's an elegant wine that was not fined, filtered or manipulated with designer yeasts and enzymes. Feminine and truly Pinot-like in its grace and balance, it's a rare—sadly, too rare—instance where Oregon Pinot is much more French than Californian. **90** —*P.G. (12/1/2006)*

Scott Paul 2003 La Paulée Pinot Noir (Willamette Valley) $35. Older vines from the Shea and Stoller vineyards anchor this gorgeous wine. A beauti-

ful, bright cherry-red color, it is packed with sweet cherry fruit, cherry candy, and spice. Hints of mint and citrus peel provide extra interest, and despite the ripe vintage it retains a sense of elegant proportion. **91** —*P.G. (8/1/2005)*

Scott Paul 2002 La Paulée Pinot Noir (Willamette Valley) $30. Pretty black cherry and cranberry fruit, hints of mushroom, and a good, lingering finish that leads into roasted coffee, nutmeg, and other spices. Ageworthy, but delicious now. **88** *(11/1/2004)*

Scott Paul 2000 Pisoni Vineyard Pinot Noir (Santa Lucia Highlands) $40. This rendition of Pisoni is big, but also lush and soft. Dark, earthy, and rich, loaded with plum and dried-spice flavors, the wine finishes long, picking up hints of smoked meat. With a wine this ready to please, why wait? Drink now–2005. **92 Editors' Choice** *(10/1/2002)*

Scott Paul 1999 Pisoni Vineyard Pinot Noir (Santa Lucia Highlands) $38. Very flavorful tart cherry and plum fruit emerges after an unusual, almost completely mute opening. Handsomely balanced, the wine is crisp, yet smooth. Tangy fruit and dusty tannins play on the long finish. The young closed nose was the only thing between this tasty wine and excellence. **89** *(10/1/2002)*

SCREAMING EAGLE

Screaming Eagle 2003 Red Wine Cabernet Blend (Oakville) $500. Ripe and flashy, offering tiers of cassis, chocolate, and charry new oak flavors, wrapped in sweet, smooth tannins. Has an acidic bite midpalate that balances the lushness, and will add to the wine's cellar-worthiness. Defines sheer power, but never loses control. Best now and through 2017, at least. **96 Cellar Selection** —*S.H. (9/1/2006)*

Screaming Eagle 2002 Cabernet Sauvignon (Oakville) $300. Dark, super-extracted in fruit, and with oak detailing, the '02 Eagle is drinkable now, due to its soft, creamy mouthfeel. Floods the palate with black cherry, crème de cassis, and milk chocolate flavors. Has enough rich tannins and acids to balance and hold through 2010. **92** —*S.H. (11/1/2005)*

Screaming Eagle 2001 Cabernet Sauvignon (Oakville) $250. The oak certainly screams out, and it's good oak, freshly hewn and smokily charred. Underneath is superripe fruit, plummy to the point of milk chocolate pudding. This big, heavily extracted Cab is classic Eagle in style. **91** —*S.H. (10/1/2004)*

SCREAMING JACK

Screaming Jack 2003 Syrah (North Coast) $12. The result of a joint venture between Billington Imports and winemaker Tom Larson (formerly of Sonoma Creek), this blended Syrah is actually 60% from the Sonoma side of Carneros. The mouthfeel is very smooth and supple, the flavors easy to enjoy: red berries and cherries and hints of vanilla and pepper. Drink now. **88 Best Buy** *(9/1/2005)*

SCREW KAPPA NAPA

Screw Kappa Napa 2003 Cabernet Sauvignon (Napa Valley) $14. Ripe and juicy, with an assortment of red, blue, and black fruits and a smoky touch of oak. **85** —*S.H. (12/1/2006)*

Screw Kappa Napa 2002 Cabernet Sauvignon (Napa Valley) $12. A soft, supple, user-friendly Cab, with cassis, dried spices, and hints of brown sugar or caramel. Smooth and easy to drink. **85** *(12/1/2004)*

Screw Kappa Napa 2002 Cabernet Sauvignon (Napa Valley) $14. Re-released a year after its debut, this wine has become more subtle and nuanced with bottle age. It's one of the better Cabs you'll find at this price, with polished blackberry, currant, cherry, mocha, and vanilla-oaky flavors, a villages-type wine from California's most distinguished Cabernet region. Don't let the screwtop bother you one bit. **89 Best Buy** —*S.H. (11/15/2005)*

Screw Kappa Napa 2004 Chardonnay (Napa Valley) $14. There's lots of richness in this well-ripened wine, with tropical fruit and peach flavors, a creamy texture, and a notable overlay of spicy, vanilla-tinged charred oak. **84** —*S.H. (12/15/2005)*

Screw Kappa Napa 2003 Chardonnay (Napa Valley) $12. Lots of oak here, with the requisite vanilla, buttered toast, and sweet wood notes on top of modest peach and tropical fruit flavors. **85** —*S.H. (3/1/2005)*

Screw Kappa Napa 2002 Chardonnay (Napa Valley) $12. Lighter and fruitier than the Aquinas Chard, this one features similar toast and nut nuances but also bright pineapple and pear flavors. **84** *(12/1/2004)*

Screw Kappa Napa 2003 Merlot (Napa Valley) $14. Dry, fruity, and smooth, this likeable wine has much in common with more expensive Merlots. Although it's a bit one-dimensional, it shows black cherry, mocha, and herb flavors with a good mouthfeel. **85** —*S.H. (12/15/2005)*

Screw Kappa Napa 2002 Merlot (Napa Valley) $12. Some minty notes add nuance to this wine's black cherry, plum, and spice aromas and flavors. Brown sugar and allspice notes on the finish balance the wine's assertive tannins. **85** *(12/1/2004)*

Screw Kappa Napa 2002 Pinot Noir (Napa Valley) $12. From Don Sebastiani & Sons, a polished, interesting wine, with cherry, leather, dried spice, lavender, and tree bark aromas. Turns lush, long, and rich, with candy-cherry, vanilla flavors, and a silky texture. **87 Best Buy** *(11/1/2004)*

Screw Kappa Napa 2003 Sauvignon Blanc (Napa Valley) $14. Another successful bottling from this brand that nails the style of ripe, slightly sweet fruit, offset by crisp acidity, and delicious flavors of figs, peach custard, and vanilla. Easy to like. **85** —*S.H. (12/15/2005)*

Screw Kappa Napa 2003 Zinfandel (Napa Valley) $14. A wild and woolly, feral wine that screams of underbrush-picked berries foraged under a hot sun. Some of them aren't entirely ripe, but the fun's in the sipping. **84** —*S.H. (12/15/2005)*

SEA SMOKE

Sea Smoke 2002 Botella Pinot Noir (Santa Rita Hills) $25. Another fine wine from this interesting producer. It's dark, ripe, and extracted, with blackberry, chocolate, cherry, and caramel flavors. It is similar to Sea Smoke's Ten bottling in its huge, Rhône-like flavors and texture. Almost guaranteed to age well through 2010. **89** *(11/1/2004)*

Sea Smoke 2001 Botella Pinot Noir (Santa Rita Hills) $25. A nice, easy drinking Pinot with a bit of complexity. The jammy flavors of raspberry, cherry, and mint are encased in soft, supple tannins and crisp acidity. Saved from being a simple fruit bomb by a rich earthiness and a streak of tannin. **87** —*S.H. (3/1/2004)*

Sea Smoke 2002 Southing Pinot Noir (Santa Rita Hills) $45. Everyone found this wine muscular and full-bodied, and noted it's ripe flavors of blackberries that veer into chocolate, and high alcohol. As rich as the flavors are, tasters felt the wine could use more elegance and finesse. **87** *(11/1/2004)*

Sea Smoke 2001 Southing Pinot Noir (Santa Rita Hills) $45. This newish appellation is trying to figure out what it does best, and this wine is a study in progress. It's a bit simple-jammy, with raspberry and cherry flavors and silky tannins. New French oak adds smoke and vanilla and a creamy texture. It's yummy, but needs to develop depth and complexity. **89** —*S.H. (3/1/2004)*

Sea Smoke 2002 Ten Pinot Noir (Santa Rita Hills) $65. Everybody liked the complexity and balance of this big wine. Opens with a blast of blackberry, cherry pie, smoky vanilla, and molasses, leading to a very rich, full-bodied mouthfeel. Superextracted and tannic, but balanced and elegant nonetheless. Now through 2007. **90** *(11/1/2004)*

SEAN THACKREY

Sean Thackrey 2000 Orion Rossi Vineyard Native Red Wine Red Blend (St. Helena) $65. Not labeled as Petite Sirah, but included in the tasting based on Dr. Carole Meredith's analysis of the vineyard. Winemaker Thackrey doesn't necessarily agree. The wine itself is big, bold, and black, with strong eucalyptus elements that will polarize a crowd. Richly textured, with firm tannins and a long finish that bodes well for aging. **89** *(4/1/2003)*

SEASIDE

Seaside 2003 Chardonnay (California) $11. Here's your basic, average Chard, clean and proper. It's got a malted mouthfeel with peach and cream flavors. **83** —*S.H. (12/31/2005)*

Seaside 2003 Merlot (California) $11. Soft, inoffensive, and fruity, this Merlot will play well against almost anything calling for a dry red wine. It has some lush berry and cherry flavors. **83** —*S.H. (12/31/2005)*

SEAVEY

Seavey 1997 Cabernet Sauvignon (Napa Valley) $64. **92** *(11/1/2000)*

Seavey 2000 Cabernet Sauvignon (Napa Valley) $64. The fancy oak hits you first, offering up a blast of vanilla, char, and sweet wood aromas and flavors that also contribute to the overall tannins, which are considerable. Is there fruit downstairs? It's hard to judge now, because the wine is so oaky. Cellaring seems risky. **86** —*S.H. (6/1/2004)*

SEBASTIANI

Sebastiani 2004 Barbera (Sonoma Valley) $24. Sebastiani knows Barbera. At its best, which this one is, the variety produces a very dry, very tannic, and high-acid wine, rich in earthy, coffee, cherry-berry flavors. This bottle, which is robust now, will easily achieve 20 years of age, softening and sweetening all the way. **87 Cellar Selection** —*S.H. (10/1/2006)*

Sebastiani 2000 Appelation Selection Barbera (Sonoma Valley) $18. Winemaker Mark Lyon has bent over backward to enrich his Barberas, using advanced vineyard techniques and more French oak. This is a very good wine, rich and tannic, with plum, black cherry, sage, and tobacco flavors and a very long, juicy finish. It retains the variety's quintessentially rustic character, and will live for decades. **89** —*S.H. (12/1/2002)*

Sebastiani 2003 Appellation Selection Barbera (Sonoma Valley) $15. How dark this wine is, and how young. Primary fruit is blackberries, with strong charry oak aromas. In the mouth it's clean and vibrant, but immature, hung with blackberry and cherry baby fat. Try aging this lovely wine until 2010 and beyond. **88** —*S.H. (10/1/2005)*

Sebastiani 2001 Appellation Selection Barbera (Sonoma Valley) $15. You don't expect much elegance or breed from a Barbera, but this Cabernet-like wine has both. It's rich in plum, blackberry, and chocolate flavors, and has very gentle but complex tannins. Feels smooth on the palate, with a firm finish. Nice now, and will age for a decade or two. **90 Best Buy** —*S.H. (11/15/2004)*

Sebastiani 2003 Secolo Red Wine Bordeaux Blend (Sonoma County) $30. Now in its third vintage, this complex Bordeaux blend, which is mostly Cabernet Sauvignon, performs at the height of Sebastiani's red portfolio. Mainly from great vineyards in Alexander and Sonoma valleys, it's very much in the modern style, soft and ripe. Yet it maintains an elegant dignity, and it passes the threepeat test: You want a second glass, and then a third. **92 Editors' Choice** —*S.H. (4/1/2006)*

Sebastiani 2003 Cabernet Sauvignon (Sonoma County) $17. Shows a nice balance, with ripe black currant and cherry fruit flavors wrapped in smooth, supportive tannins, and a fruity but dry finish. This elegant Cab drinks well now, and should hold for a good 10 years. **87** —*S.H. (10/1/2006)*

Sebastiani 2003 Cabernet Sauvignon (Alexander Valley) $30. Here's a classic Alexander Valley Cab from a winery that knows what it's doing. The wine is very soft but complex and elaborately tailored, with delicious blackberry pie, chocolate, and cherry flavors that just don't stop coming. Fortunately, the tannins and acids are rich enough to stand up to the fruit. **90** —*S.H. (4/1/2006)*

Sebastiani 2002 Cabernet Sauvignon (Sonoma County) $17. Good and correct, if not exciting, a very dry wine with blackberry, coffee, plum, and herb flavors, and an oaky veneer. Full-bodied and balanced. **84** —*S.H. (11/1/2005)*

Sebastiani 2001 Cabernet Sauvignon (Sonoma County) $17. What you get in this pretty wine is the character of a much more expensive Cab, just a little thinned down. Black currant and cherry flavors, a nice veneer of oak, rich, intricate tannins and good acidity combine to make this balanced. **87** —*S.H. (2/1/2005)*

Sebastiani 2000 Cabernet Sauvignon (Sonoma County) $17. What a nice wine, so easy to drink, you might miss the complex nuances. It's very soft and lush, with well-ripened flavors of currants and cherries, and a hefty dose of oak. This lush Cab has a classy depth and elegance. **90 Editors' Choice** —*S.H. (5/1/2004)*

USA

Sebastiani 1998 Cabernet Sauvignon (Sonoma Valley) $24. Richer and more layered than the Sonoma County bottling, presumably due to better, warmer vineyards. Lush, fat, and deeply flavored. For early drinking. The black currant taste lingers on the tongue for a long time. **90** —*S.H. (11/15/2002)*

Sebastiani 1998 Cabernet Sauvignon (Sonoma County) $24. They struggled mightily to find grapes that were ripe enough in this dismal vintage, and Sebastiani had to halve the number of cases produced. But this wine clears enough hurdles to be good. Black currant flavors, some juicy oak, pronounced tannins, and very dry. **86** —*S.H. (11/15/2002)*

Sebastiani 2002 Appellation Selection Cabernet Sauvignon (Alexander Valley) $28. This is a dark, tannic wine that's slightly unbalanced. It seems to have some residual sugar, making any sort of aging iffy. If not, it still seems sweet. **84** —*S.H. (10/1/2005)*

Sebastiani 2001 Appellation Selection Cabernet Sauvignon (Alexander Valley) $28. Absolutely lovely, so gentle and limpid you can't get enough. The flavors of blackberries, black cherries, dark chocolate, and herbs are so sweet and ripe, while the tannins are lush, sweet, and velvety. Combines drinkability with class and elegance. **91** —*S.H. (6/1/2004)*

Sebastiani 1999 Appellation Selection Cabernet Sauvignon (Alexander Valley) $24. This is quintessential Alexander Valley Cab, a soft, immensely likeable wine, packed with perfectly ripened blackberry and cassis fruit. Firm acids and melted tannins underscore and support the rich flavors. **90** —*S.H. (11/15/2002)*

Sebastiani 2001 Cherryblock Cabernet Sauvignon (Sonoma Valley) $70. Aging quietly in 70% new French oak, the 2001 is potentially the winery's finest Cherryblock ever. Crammed with berry fruit and tasting softer and plusher than earlier efforts, if the oak integrates into the wine it may merit an even higher score on release. **90** *(7/1/2003)*

Sebastiani 1999 Cherryblock Cabernet Sauvignon (Sonoma Valley) $70. This winery has been working on this Cabernet for many years, laboring to find the true expression of the vineyard. In a great year like 1999, the grapes ripen beautifully, and the flavors, of blackberries and currants, are very pretty. Alcohol is a modest 13.8%, and the wine is balanced and harmonious. A soft wine of grace and charm. **91** —*S.H. (11/15/2002)*

Sebastiani 1999 Cherryblock Cabernet Sauvignon (Sonoma Valley) $70. Chocolatey and spicy, loaded with cinnamon and anise, and backed by sturdy plum-flavored fruit. The mouthfeel is creamy and rich; the finish, long and oaky. **90** *(7/1/2003)*

Sebastiani 1996 Cherryblock Cabernet Sauvignon (Sonoma Valley) $95. Lean and angular right now, showing hints of mint and chocolate—the oak sticks out a bit over the tart cherry flavors. **87** *(7/1/2003)*

Sebastiani 1994 Cherryblock Cabernet Sauvignon (Sonoma Valley) $150. The 1994 vintage saw the largest production of Cherryblock yet achieved, at 2,500 cases. But could the selection have been more severe? The wine seems mature and ready to drink, with a pleasant blend of toast and cassis, coffee and some herbaceous notes. **88** *(7/1/2003)*

Sebastiani 1992 Cherryblock Cabernet Sauvignon (Sonoma Valley) $120. The Cherryblock Cabs seem to share a common minty characteristic that's particularly noticeable in this vintage. There's also a decent amount of cassis, earth, and tobacco, and the finish remains firmly tannic. Drink or hold. **87** *(7/1/2003)*

Sebastiani 1987 Cherryblock Cabernet Sauvignon (Sonoma Valley) $170. Dark, earthy aromas of soy or fruitcake pick up cherry flavors on the palate. While it's supple and mature, it's also the most alive of the three wines from the '80s, showing a lively, fresh finish. **89** *(7/1/2003)*

Sebastiani 1986 Cherryblock Cabernet Sauvignon (Sonoma Valley) $170. Minty and leafy, with fading fruit. The wine is still firm, the finish a bit sharp, but this wine isn't going to get any better than it is now. **86** *(7/1/2003)*

Sebastiani 1985 Cherryblock Cabernet Sauvignon (Sonoma Valley) $170. Mature and smooth, showing brown sugar and caramel sweetness alongside tobacco and soy. Drink now. **86** *(7/1/2003)*

Sebastiani 1991 Cherryblock Vineyard Cabernet Sauvignon (Sonoma Valley) $160. Mint again, with earth and tobacco; one taster found traces

of bell pepper. Coffee and brown sugar further soften a supple, mature mouthfeel. Drink now. **88** *(7/1/2003)*

Sebastiani 1998 Madrone Ranch Cabernet Sauvignon (Sonoma County) $46. 88 —*S.H. (11/15/2002)*

Sebastiani 1999 Sonoma County Selection Cabernet Sauvignon (Sonoma County) $17. Solidly in the long Sebastiani tradition, a rich, well-crafted Cab. Many wines that cost $25 and more are not as good. Dry and full-bodied, with ripe black currant flavors and complex, easy tannins, this is a first-rate wine and it is delicious. **90 Editors' Choice** —*S.H. (3/1/2003)*

Sebastiani 2001 Secolo Sonoma Red Wine Cabernet Sauvignon-Merlot (Sonoma County) $30. An auspicious start for this new Bordeaux blend from one of Sonoma's oldest winemaking families. Rich in black currant and cassis flavors, and well-oaked, with a melted chocolate finish. Soft and gentle, this pretty wine is drinking perfectly now. **92 Editors' Choice** —*S.H. (10/1/2004)*

Sebastiani 1997 Chardonnay (Sonoma County) $13. 87 —*M.S. (10/1/1999)*

Sebastiani 2001 Chardonnay (Sonoma County) $13. Combines all the essentials of a big California Chard in an affordable package. Ripe tropical fruit, plenty of smoky oak, lees, a creamy texture, and a long, spicy finish combine to make for a nice wine. **86** —*S.H. (5/1/2004)*

Sebastiani 2000 Chardonnay (Sonoma County) $12. Inexpensive, but an odd wine. It has peach flavors, with the vanilla and creamy overlay of barrel fermentation and oak aging. But there's a funky quality that may come from the use, for the first time at this winery, of wild yeast. The aroma and finish both have off notes. **82** —*S.H. (12/15/2002)*

Sebastiani 1999 Appellation Selection Chardonnay (Russian River Valley) $20. Strikes just the right balance between lush, ripe fruit and acidity, creating an exciting wine. Apple and peach flavors, subtly tinged with smoky oak, are crisp and bright, without being over the top. The perfect wine for a toast, or to accompany fine food. **91** —*S.H. (5/1/2002)*

Sebastiani 2004 Dutton Ranch Chardonnay (Russian River Valley) $25. Sebastiani reaches to the Russian River Valley Duttons for this rich, crisp and complex Chardonnay. It displays classic cool-climate acidity that makes the tropical fruit flavors sing, while oak adds intriguing smoke, vanilla and woodspice notes. **89** —*S.H. (7/1/2006)*

Sebastiani 2001 Dutton Ranch Chardonnay (Russian River Valley) $25. Pretty good Chard, with some polished white stone fruit flavors and an overlay of oak and lees. Feels a bit flat and simple; a well-made, decent Chard with no special features. **85** —*S.H. (12/1/2003)*

Sebastiani 1999 Dutton Ranch Chardonnay (Russian River Valley) $35. Extreme lees-aging seems to dominate this wine. Those mealy, yogurty aromas and flavors persist into the finish. The aroma is also marked strongly by mint and sage that may come from the oak. Otherwise, ripe apple, peach fruit, and dense oak are present. But the wine's eccentricity is its most notable feature. **89** —*S.H. (5/1/2002)*

Sebastiani 1998 Dutton Ranch Chardonnay (Russian River Valley) $33. 87 *(10/1/2000)*

Sebastiani 1998 Sonoma Cask Chardonnay (Sonoma County) $13. 87 *(10/1/2000)*

Sebastiani 2004 Sonoma County Selection Chardonnay (Sonoma County) $13. Yummy Chard, complex and delicious. Offers lots of ripe, rich peach and pineapple custard flavors, sweet, toasty oak and a buttery texture. Nice, perky acids keep things lively and clean. **89 Best Buy** —*S.H. (4/1/2006)*

Sebastiani 1996 Merlot (Sonoma County) $16. 90 *(3/1/2000)*

Sebastiani 2002 Merlot (Sonoma County) $17. This is an awfully good wine. It's a great example of a coastal Merlot from a good vintage, lush and sweet cherry, cassis, and cocoa flavors, yet completely dry, and the tannins are rich and smooth. There's a complex velvety softness that caresses the finish. **91 Editors' Choice** —*S.H. (10/1/2006)*

Sebastiani 2001 Merlot (Sonoma County) $17. Has smooth texture and rich tannins, but the cherry, coffee, and chocolate flavors seem a bit too sweet, and they snap to a quick finish. **84** —*S.H. (11/1/2005)*

Sebastiani 2001 Merlot (Alexander Valley) $24. A wine that excites, not only for its deliciously gooey flavors, but for the restraint and subtlety of

USA

its structure. Those flavors are rich and extracted, ranging from black currants, fine coffee, and the ripest black cherries to the sweet vanillins and toast contributed by oak. The tannins are a wonder, sweet and lush, and the finish grows even sweeter. **92 Editors' Choice** —*S.H. (5/1/2004)*

Sebastiani 2000 Merlot (Sonoma County) $17. Here's a soft, gentle wine that's gooey-rich in cherry, cocoa-puff, and ripe, sweet black raspberry flavors. Lightly oaked, it has a cleansing, espresso bitterness on the finish. **87** —*S.H. (2/1/2005)*

Sebastiani 1999 Merlot (Sonoma County) $17. Still dark and young after nearly four years, a big, brooding wine of considerable complexity and interest. Opens with big, lush flavors of blackberries and currants, chocolate, and coffee, very dry and rich in fruity extract. Tannins are thick and intricately detailed. Quite delicious and impressive. **93 Editors' Choice** —*S.H. (12/1/2003)*

Sebastiani 1998 Merlot (Sonoma County) $22. From volcanic red soil, a deeply fruity wine. Even in this vintage they managed to wring some fine blackberry and cassis flavors from the grapes. Wrapped in rich, mellow tannins and backed by soft acidity, the wine spreads across the palate carrying waves of flavors. **88** —*S.H. (7/1/2002)*

Sebastiani 2003 Appellation Selection Merlot (Alexander Valley) $24. Soft and common, with very dry tannins, the fruit in this wine is unbalanced, now showing cherries, now green peppers. There's a sharpness throughout that won't disappear. **83** —*S.H. (12/15/2005)*

Sebastiani 1998 Madrone Ranch Merlot (Sonoma Valley) $40. Only 1,100 cases of this lovely liquid, but you'll swear you're drinking Pomerol. The fruity profile is strong, mellowed by oak influences and designer tannins. A dry limpidity and softness to the structure makes you appreciate it all the more. Twenty-four percent Cabernet Sauvignon adds curranty complexities. **91** —*S.H. (7/1/2002)*

Sebastiani 2003 Pinot Noir (Sonoma Coast) $15. This is a Syrah-like Pinot, rather heavy, but good. It's full-bodied, with good tannins and acids, and is balanced and dry, with a touch of oak. Certainly shows off its California sunshine in the sweet finish, which is a swirl of cherries, blackberries, and raspberries. **87** —*S.H. (10/1/2005)*

Sebastiani 2002 Pinot Noir (Russian River Valley) $25. Big, ripe, and extracted, with black cherry fruit and notes of cocoa, dark-roasted coffee and Kahlúa. Fairly tannic now and very dry. This is a big Pinot that will go well with a juicy steak. **87** *(11/1/2004)*

Sebastiani 2002 Pinot Noir (Sonoma Coast) $15. Rather light in fruit, with sour cherry, tomato, and rhubarb flavors. One taster found the polished texture and spicy finish is pleasing. **85** *(11/1/2004)*

Sebastiani 2000 Pinot Noir (Russian River Valley) $22. **86** *(10/1/2002)*

Sebastiani 2000 Pinot Noir (Sonoma Coast) $15. Very dense up front, with delectable aromas of plum cake, black cherry, and vanilla. The palate is not enormous, but it's big enough to satisfy any lover of modern-style Pinot Noir. If there's a fault here, it's a buttery note to the finish. **89 Best Buy** *(10/1/2002)*

Sebastiani 1999 Pinot Noir (Russian River Valley) $22. The aromas are dense and meaty, bordering on ultra ripe. It's yet another sweet, extracted Russian River wine, one that followers of Burgundy and Oregon might struggle with, but one that fans of big, bulky reds should enjoy. **87** *(10/1/2002)*

Sebastiani 2004 Appellation Selection Pinot Noir (Russian River Valley) $28. A good wine, not a great one. It's a bit heavy for a Pinot, with almost the weight of a Merlot and some firm, dusty tannins. Blackberry, cola, and toast flavors. **85** —*S.H. (11/15/2006)*

Sebastiani 2001 Appellation Selection Pinot Noir (Russian River Valley) $22. A first-rate, deliciously drinkable wine from venerable Sebastiani, and how nice to see this old-line winery run with the big dogs. Textbook RRV Pinot, delicately structured with firm acids and smooth tannins, but with the enormous flavors you expect from this vintage. Raspberry, cherry, vanilla, smoke, and peppery spices finish with a honeyed flourish. **92 Editors' Choice** —*S.H. (12/1/2003)*

Sebastiani 2002 Sonoma County Selection Pinot Noir (Sonoma Coast) $15. Pinots in this price range can be risky, but this one represents a good investment. It's got real Sonoma personality in the silky texture, crisp

coastal acids, and raspberry, cherry, vanilla, and cola flavors. **86** —*S.H. (6/1/2004)*

Sebastiani 2001 Sonoma County Selection Pinot Noir (Sonoma Coast) $15. It's rare to get a wine at this price from this appellation. And what's a winery whose name is synonymous with Sonoma Valley doing out on the cold coast? A Pinot that straddles the two regions, this is a fascinating wine, with sumptuous blackberry fruit and an exciting edge of minty tartness. Fantastic value in Pinot Noir. **91 Best Buy** —*S.H. (7/1/2003)*

Sebastiani 2002 Secolo Red Blend (Sonoma County) $30. This is a blend of Cabernet Sauvignon, Merlot, and Zinfandel. The Bordeaux varieties make for a balanced claret, rich in black currant flavors. The Zin is way in the background, but seems to add spice and a brambly edge. Oak brings cigar box and cedar complexities. Drink now. **92 Editors' Choice** —*S.H. (11/1/2005)*

Sebastiani 2001 Cohen Vineyard Sauvignon Blanc (Russian River Valley) $18. This is Sebastiani's best Sauvignon Blanc in memory. From the very cool Green Valley, it's lean, crisp, and minerally, with bright gooseberry flavors and refreshing acidity. Has great structure, a racy and sleek Bauhaus of a white. **90** —*S.H. (9/1/2003)*

Sebastiani 2000 Cohen Vineyard Sauvignon Blanc (Russian River Valley) $18. Aromas of fresh green straw and citrus set the stage for a mouth full of grass and citrus, which may sound strange, but it's what we found. The finish is tangy and hard-edged, but a touch of sweetness saves it from a worse fate and actually brings the wine to a good finish. About 40% of the cuvée was barrel-fermented, which gives it a softer feel than it might otherwise have. **86** *(7/1/2003)*

Sebastiani 2004 Zinfandel (Sonoma County) $15. The source of this very good Zin was old vine Sonoma Valley and Russian River, but winemaker Mark Lyon reached to Amador and Lodi to spice things up. The result is textbook Zinfandel, dry and balanced, with a rich array of wild berry and spice flavors. **87** —*S.H. (11/15/2006)*

Sebastiani 2003 Zinfandel (Sonoma County) $13. This is a nice Zin with some classy notes. It's bone dry and balanced, with moderate alcohol and good acidity that boosts the blackberry and mocha flavors. There's a raisiny edge that adds some interest to the finish. **86** —*S.H. (4/1/2006)*

Sebastiani 2000 Zinfandel (Sonoma County) $15. A young, jammy Zin whose fresh wild berry flavors drink sharp, almost aggressive. Acidity is high, and the wine has a freshness and vivacity that's best savored in its youth. A blend of Sonoma Valley and Dry Creek Valley grapes. **85** —*S.H. (11/1/2002)*

Sebastiani 1999 Domenici Vineyards Zinfandel (Sonoma Valley) $25. Smells sulfury on opening, and these fumes blow off only with difficulty. Afterward, the wine reveals black cherry aromas veering into chocolate, and drinks rich. There's a blast of fabulously ripe wild berry fruit, and it's dry. But loses points for the opening odor. Tasted twice, with consistent results. **86** —*S.H. (9/1/2002)*

Sebastiani 1997 Domenici Vineyard Old Vines Zinfandel (Sonoma Valley) $24. **89** —*P.G. (11/15/1999)*

Sebastiani 2000 Old Vines Zinfandel (Sonoma Valley) $20. Here's a good, easy-drinking Zin with some pleasant black cherry, tobacco, and spice flavors that are wrapped in firm, dusty tannins. It's very dry and balanced in acidity and wood, and will be versatile with everything from pizza to pork. **86** —*S.H. (9/1/2004)*

Sebastiani 1999 Old Vines Zinfandel (Sonoma Valley) $20. Mainly from 120-year old vines, this wine showcases Zin in one of its aspects. It's bone dry, and modern tannin management makes it softly drinkable. From the middle palate through the finish, sumptuous, spicy fruit takes over. It lacks Cabernet's glamour, but captures Zin's rough and ready personality perfectly. Even at this price, it's a good value. **92** —*S.H. (9/12/2002)*

Sebastiani 1998 Old Vines Zinfandel (Sonoma County) $22. The fruit is on the tart side, cranberries and raspberries, but the wine is fleshed out with plenty of vanilla oak, and fills the mouth with soft, seductive flavors. Well made and approachable, with some added interest from Carignane, Petite Sirah, and Mourvèdre in the blend. **87** —*P.G. (3/1/2001)*

Sebastiani 1997 Old Vines Domenici Vineyard Zinfandel (Sonoma Valley) $24. **89** —P.G. (11/15/1999)

SEBASTOPOL

Sebastopol 2001 Dutton Ranch Chardonnay (Russian River Valley) $24. Shares much in common with the winery's Morelli bottling, except it's a shade less rich. Spicy tropical fruit flavors, smoky oak, a creamy texture and bright acidity make it wonderful to drink now. **90** —S.H. (12/15/2004)

Sebastopol 1999 Dutton Ranch Chardonnay (Green Valley) $24. What a pretty wine, with its spiced green apple flavors and lush, crisp flavors. Fully ripened fruit fills the mouth in a burst of sunshiney sweetness, although it drinks dryish. The finish is chockful of oriental spices. **89** — S.H. (5/1/2002)

Sebastopol 1998 Dutton Ranch Chardonnay (Russian River Valley) $22. **91** —S.H. (11/1/1999)

Sebastopol 2000 Dutton Ranch Dutton Palms Vineyard Chardonnay (Green Valley) $46. A streamlined Chard, with flinty-appley flavors and a rich dose of lees and toasty oak. Comes alive on the long, peppery finish. **87** —S.H. (5/1/2003)

Sebastopol 2001 Dutton Ranch Morelli Lane Vineyard Chardonnay (Russian River Valley) $40. Absolutely delicious, a Chard to ponder, or just to enjoy. Voluptuous flavors of tropical fruits, figs, and spiced plums flood the mouth to the edge of sweetness. This wine is well-oaked, with a rich, creamy texture and an enormously long, spicy finish. **92** —S.H. (12/15/2004)

Sebastopol 2002 Dutton Estate Jewel Block Vineyard Pinot Noir (Russian River Valley) $48. Full, ripe, rich, and delicately structured, this lovely Pinot shows complex flavors of cherries, herbs, mocha, and currant. Feels soft and elegant in the mouth, a finely textured wine with lots of spice in the finish. **89** (11/1/2004)

Sebastopol 2002 Dutton Estate Thomas Road Vineyard Pinot Noir (Russian River Valley) $40. Perfect varietal notes of strawberry and tart cherry fruit wrapped in well-charred oak and vanilla. Cool-climate acidity gives the wine a citrusy bite. The silky mouthfeel continues through the long, spicy finish. Easy to like this one. **87** (11/1/2004)

Sebastopol 2001 Dutton Ranch Pinot Noir (Russian River Valley) $20. Likeable for its gentle, easy texture, silky tannins and ripely pleasant flavors of cola, cherries, coffee, spices, and smoky oak. Almost the perfect restaurant by the glass wine, tasty and versatile. **86** —S.H. (2/1/2005)

Sebastopol 1999 Dutton Ranch Pinot Noir (Green Valley) $30. Combines a delicate body with punchy flavors to create a feminine wine of considerable power and finesse. It avoids jamminess, coming down on the side of less ripe earth and tomato, although there are gorgeous stone fruit notes and a sumptuous overlay of smoky oak. The flavors and texture are absolutely terrific. **93** —S.H. (7/1/2002)

Sebastopol 2000 Dutton Ranch Jewell Block Pinot Noir (Russian River Valley) $52. Though endowed with attractive rhubarb-strawberry fruit and cedary, brown sugar and marinade accents, this wine also shows an astringent edge. This usually comes from high acidity, which makes wines bright and lively, yet paradoxically the wine has a vaguely fatigued feel. The modest close shows white pepper and lemon. **85** (10/1/2002)

Sebastopol 2001 Dutton Ranch Morelli Lane Vineyard Pinot Noir (Russian River Valley) $40. Despite its translucency, this is a big wine in flavor. Fills the mouth with lush cherry, leather, smoke, cola, rhubarb, spicy pepper, and sweet rosehip tea flavors accented with fine smoky oak. What a lovely texture, delicate and silky, yet firm. **91** —S.H. (12/15/2004)

Sebastopol 2000 Dutton Ranch Morelli Lane Vineyard Pinot Noir (Russian River Valley) $46. **87** (10/1/2002)

Sebastopol 2000 Dutton Ranch Morelli Lane Vineyard Pinot Noir (Green Valley) $46. Lovely body and texture in this light and silky wine, with its soft tannins and crisp acidity. The flavors suggest tea, cranberry, and fruits such as black cherry and raspberry. Complex and interesting, this is fun to drink. **90** —S.H. (8/1/2003)

Sebastopol 2002 Syrah (Russian River Valley) $14. Very spicy, with ripe blackberry and cherry flavors tinged with a sweet bacon edge. Smooth in

tannins, and soft, this pretty wine will go with a variety of meats and cheeses. **86** —S.H. (10/1/2004)

Sebastopol 1999 Dutton Estate Gail Ann's Vineyard Syrah (Russian River Valley) $24. A creamy, hazelnut and berry nose opens this smooth wine. On the palate, though, the charred oak runs rampant over the cherry fruit, and the mouthfeel is thinner than we expected. Closes short, with more of the same flavors. Some good elements here, but the wine's ultimately a bit disjointed, and slightly hollow. **84** (11/1/2001)

Sebastopol 2002 Dutton Ranch Syrah (Russian River Valley) $30. Light and herbal. Once a brief funk blows off, there's decent cherry fruit edged in coffee and tobacco, but it lacks heft and length. Reminiscent of berry zinger tea on the finish. **84** (9/1/2005)

Sebastopol 2000 Dutton Ranch Gail Ann's Vineyard Syrah (Russian River Valley) $32. Dynamite Syrah, a joy to drink. It's a rich mélange of blackberry, white pepper, espresso, and tobacco. Near-perfect tannins, complex and accessible, and just the right overlay of toasty oak. Beautiful stuff, a vision of Syrah's future in California. **94 Editors' Choice** —S.H. (6/24/2003)

Sebastopol 2001 Gail Ann's Vineyard Syrah (Russian River Valley) $32. The mouth knows quality when it feels it, and this sensational Syrah is great. Ripeness was no problem, to judge by the blackberry, cherry, mocha, and spice flavors. The quality is in the soft tannins and the way they interplay with fresh acidity. **92** —S.H. (10/1/2004)

Sebastopol 2004 Three Blocks Syrah (Sonoma County) $25. From three Russian River and Green Valley vineyards comes this fruity, appealing Syrah. It has black cherry, cola, and mocha flavors wrapped in a light, silky texture. Enjoyable now. **87** —S.H. (11/1/2006)

SECRET HOUSE

Secret House 1998 Pinot Noir (Willamette Valley) $22. **84** —M.S. (12/1/2000)

Secret House 1998 Doerner Vineyard Pinot Noir (Umpqua Valley) $30. **86** —M.M. (12/1/2000)

SEGHESIO

Seghesio 2000 Arneis (Russian River Valley) $15. A flowery, honeyed wine, framed by moderate toasty oak. Fruity, with apple and peach flavors and riper notes of tropical fruits. High acidity makes it zesty and clean. There's a trace of sugar on the finish. **84** —S.H. (11/15/2001)

Seghesio 2001 Barbera (Sonoma County) $25. This family knows from Barbera, but even they can't overcome its big tannins, which make it bitter and numbing in its youth. That said, it's a very good wine, with excellent plum, blackberry, and espresso flavors and good acids. If you're into aging wines, stick it in your cellar for a decade and enjoy later. **89** — S.H. (12/1/2003)

Seghesio 2001 San Lorenzo Petite Sirah (Alexander Valley) $30. Somewhat astringent, the wine nonetheless harbors a fine blend of black plum, licorice, coffee, chocolate, spice, and herb flavors. It's a big wine that might actually benefit from cellaring. Meanwhile, try it with a big, juicy steak. **89** (3/1/2004)

Seghesio 2000 Pinot Grigio (Russian River Valley) $14. From an increasingly popular varietal, this bottling brims with figgy, lemony, spicy scents. The flavors are bold and electric, with stinging white peach and citrus notes highlighted by high acidity that jolts the palate. It's very dry, and the finish is clean and spicy. Enjoy this with a wide range of foods, or by itself. **88** —S.H. (11/15/2001)

Seghesio 1999 Pinot Noir (Russian River Valley) $25. A fleshy, earthy, yet very dry wine, with cherry, cranberry, and rhubarb aromas and flavors cradled in sweet oak. There's a pretty, layered texture of soft velvet, and a spine of crisp acidity for balance. Not an anger, but made for immediate pleasure. **88** —S.H. (12/15/2001)

Seghesio 2001 Omaggio Red Blend (Sonoma County) $45. This old Sonoma grapegrowing family's hommage to their forebears is a blend of Cabernet Sauvignon and Sangiovese. It is an excellent wine, succulently filled with juicy flavors of cherries and black currants, with sexy tannins that are muscular, but negotiable. It will probably soften in a few years. **91** —S.H. (11/15/2003)

Seghesio 1998 Sangiovese (Sonoma County) $20. 87 —S.H. (12/15/1999)

Seghesio 2001 Sangiovese (Alexander Valley) $20. No one is working harder in California to get Sangiovese right than Ted Seghesio, and this wine shows his progress. It is soft and silky, yet packed with power and authority. The flavors of cherries and spices are affirmed by crisp acids. Tannins are pretty big, but negotiable. 90 —S.H. (12/1/2003)

Seghesio 1999 Chianti Station Sangiovese (Alexander Valley) $32. This delicate wine has flavors of cherries, Chinese tea, and tobacco. It is dry and acidic; the tannins assert themselves immediately, especially on the finish where they turn tough and sticky. It is not an opulent wine but it's a complex, layered one, dry and tart. Will probably be at its best with food such as roast duck with a cherry sauce, or Chinese barbecued pork. 89 —S.H. (4/1/2004)

Seghesio 2001 Rattlesnake Hill Venom Sangiovese (Alexander Valley) $45. Absolutely the best Sangiovese Seghesio can make, from steep, low-yielding hillside vineyards. Dense and concentrated, a wine that impresses the palate with the intensity of its cherry and spice fruit flavors and rich, complex tannins. Yet it has a light, silky mouthfeel. Addictively good, as near perfect and versatile a dinner wine as you could imagine. 93 Editors' Choice —S.H. (12/1/2003)

Seghesio 1998 Zinfandel (Sonoma County) $15. 88 —S.H. (2/1/2000)

Seghesio 2001 Zinfandel (Sonoma County) $19. Firm and ripe in style, with fine-tuned tannins that frame the core of bright blackberry, cocoa, plum, and spice flavors. Moderate length marks the finish, which is fairly elegant. 88 (11/1/2003)

Seghesio 2000 Zinfandel (Sonoma County) $19. Rough-and-ready Zin that captures the grape's wild and woolly side. Briary berry flavors mingle with earthy tobacco notes and soft tannins to produce a fun, everyday wine that seems perfect with barbecue. 85 —S.H. (11/1/2002)

Seghesio 2001 Cortina Zinfandel (Dry Creek Valley) $30. Somewhat oak-driven, with big tannins framing the black cherry, blackberry, tea, and spice flavors. The flavors are pleasing but take a backseat to the toasty oak. 86 (11/1/2003)

Seghesio 2000 Cortina Zinfandel (Dry Creek Valley) $30. 87 —S.H. (11/1/2002)

Seghesio 1998 Cortina Zinfandel (Dry Creek Valley) $26. Cortina refers to the soil type. The wine shows forward, pretty fruit, mixing berries and cherries, and follows up with bright, clean, mouth-friendly flavors. Falls off in the finish, with some dry tannins. 86 —P.G. (3/1/2001)

Seghesio 2001 Home Ranch Zinfandel (Alexander Valley) $30. A fairly full-on wine, with lots of body and rich, ripe tannins. Hints of bright berry, stewed fruit, plum, and spice notes mark the wine, which is fairly bright on the finish, though moderate in length. 87 (11/1/2003)

Seghesio 2000 Home Ranch Zinfandel (Alexander Valley) $30. Smells exciting, with blackberry, tobacco, and chocolate aromas and an elusive, spicy-earthy note, with nuances of vanilla and char from oak. In the mouth, it turns rather hot, although the flavors are delicious. If you don't mind high alcohol, this is a fine Sonoma Zin. 86 —S.H. (11/1/2002)

Seghesio 1998 Home Ranch Zinfandel (Sonoma County) $26. Good, bright, spicy fruit, with fine balance and a silky, extended finish. There's lovely concentration in the back end, suggesting blackberries and loganberries and plenty of toast. 89 —P.G. (3/1/2001)

Seghesio 2001 Old Vine Zinfandel (Sonoma County) $28. Smooth, sleek, and finely tuned, with a core of flavors that includes black cherry, cassis, cocoa, coffee, blackberry, spice, and anise. Tannins are velvety smooth and ripe, offering a classy structure for the ensemble. 91 (11/1/2003)

Seghesio 1998 Old Vine Zinfandel (Sonoma County) $18. Some of Seghesio's plantings are over a century old, and the wine has a classic, briary quality to it. Supple and inviting, it drinks well now but has the balance and structure to age for a few years. 87 —P.G. (3/1/2001)

Seghesio 1997 Old Vine Zinfandel (Sonoma County) $25. 89 —S.H. (2/1/2000)

Seghesio 1998 San Lorenzo Zinfandel (Sonoma County) $28. Young, tight, firm fruit, with nuances of blueberry dominating. Tannic, dry, and tight, it's well made with excellent structure and balance. Tight right now,

high-toned and tart, but with a good, long life ahead. 91 —P.G. (3/1/2001)

SEIA

Seia 2004 Clifton Hill Vineyard Syrah (Wahluke Slope) $23. Sourced from one of the mainstay vineyards in Washington's new Wahluke Slope AVA, this Syrah is fragrant with berry, citrus, and mint. It explodes on the tongue with tart, snappy raspberry and boysenberry fruit; clean and bracing and as fresh as a summer day. Sappy and sharp, bright and powerful; it's supple and bracing. 92 Editors' Choice —P.G. (10/1/2006)

SELBY

Selby 2001 Cabernet Franc (Alexander Valley) $28. Tastes like a very good and properly varietal Cabernet Sauvignon, minus the depth of cassis, leaving ripe red and black cherries and oak. The wine is very soft, which suggests drinking now. 85 —S.H. (12/15/2005)

Selby 1999 Dave Selby Reserve Chardonnay (Sonoma County) $40. Rich and opulent, featuring glorious tropical flavors redolent of mango and papaya. Apricot and citrus notes add complexity, while the ensemble is framed in seductively sweet oak. Plush, long, and lush at the end. Only 360 cases made. 93 —J.M. (12/1/2001)

Selby 1998 David Selby Reserve Chardonnay (Sonoma County) $38. Susie Selby's homage to her late father has some sulfur and earthy notes on the nose, but there's good fruit behind. This full-bodied, nicely textured Chardonnay has nutty, smoky, and spicy flavors melding with tangy tropical fruit to create a tasty, fairly lush wine that's easy to enjoy. Finishes soft, with a faint whiff of petrol—in the Alsace manner—and is drinking well now. 88 (7/1/2001)

Selby 2002 Merlot (Sonoma County) $24. Ripe in cherry and chocolate fruit, with a slightly rustic mouthfeel of edgy tannins and an earthy, mushroomy quality, this Merlot has enough fanciness to accompany a nice leg of lamb or roast pork. 87 —S.H. (12/15/2005)

Selby 1999 Merlot (Sonoma County) $24. Intriguing in the nose, with hints of blackberry, wintergreen, cedar, and cinnamon. Silky smooth tannins support a solid core of black cherry, plum cassis, vanilla, and herb flavors. Juicy but sophisticated. A lovely example of what this variety can do. 91 Editors' Choice —J.M. (12/1/2001)

Selby 1999 Syrah (Sonoma County) $24. Blackberry and tarragon, sour berry, and nougat aromas have promise but are marred by volatile acidity expressed as a strong alcohol-acetone element. In the mouth, it is medium-weight and smooth, but has a somewhat hard feel, with tart cherry and leather flavors. Finishes slightly sharp, with edgy tannins that may smooth out with a year or two of aging. It will always be on the lean side. 84 (11/1/2001)

SELENE

Selene 2005 Hyde Vineyards Sauvignon Blanc (Carneros) $26. What a rich wine this is. It shows ripe varietal character in the tangerine, fig, and cantaloupe flavors, but more than that, a white Bordeaux-inspired interventionist technique brings a leesy, oaky creaminess. Add to that refreshingly crisp Carneros acidity, and the bottom line is great Sauvignon Blanc. 92 Editors' Choice —S.H. (10/1/2006)

Selene 2003 Hyde Vineyards Sauvignon Blanc (Carneros) $22. Plenty going on here. The nose is more oblique than fruity, with herb, anise, vanilla bean, and baked apple. Unexpectedly crisp and stony on the palate, with bright, full-force pineapple, yellow apple, and stone fruits. Not heavy, and finishes clean. A lively, balanced wine. Excellent for the region. 92 Editors' Choice (7/1/2005)

Selene 2000 Hyde Vineyards Sauvignon Blanc (Carneros) $29. From this well-known Carneros vineyard comes this lighter lemon-lime SB with mixed citrus flavors and intense acidity. It's a medium-weight wine with a rather short pineapple finish. It has some creaminess to the mouthfeel, but overall it just doesn't ring the right bells to rate higher. Made by Mia Klein of Etude fame. 86 (8/1/2002)

SEQUEL

Sequel 2003 Syrah (Columbia Valley (WA)) $55. John Duval makes this satiny and very smooth Syrah for the Long Shadows collective. It's got strong coffee-accented flavors, along with fairly astringent tannins.

USA

Young, tight, and a bit hot as it winds through the finish. The blend includes 5% Cabernet Sauvignon, from vineyards scattered across the state. **88** —*P.G. (4/1/2006)*

SEQUOIA GROVE

Sequoia Grove 2002 Cabernet Sauvignon (Napa Valley) $32. Young, elegant, and impeccably structured, this classic Napa Cab is 90% Oakville and Rutherford. It's a dry, fairly oaky wine, with polished black currant flavors, wrapped in thick tannins that finish with rich complexity. **91** — *S.H. (12/31/2005)*

Sequoia Grove 1999 Cabernet Sauvignon (Napa Valley) $29. Gentle and fruity, with pleasant cassis flavors and soft tannins. The oaky overlay adds smoky notes. Not an ager, it's best enjoyed in its precocious youth. **86** —*S.H. (11/15/2002)*

Sequoia Grove 2003 Morisoli Vineyard Cabernet Sauvignon (Rutherford) $85. Displays classic Napa-Rutherford qualities of grace, power, and harmony, with red currant and herb flavors that are complexed with toasty new oak. It's a powerhouse, but never gets over the top, keeping a tight grip on its parts. Drinkable now for its sweet lushness, but has the balance to age effortlessly for at least 15 years. **93** —*S.H. (12/31/2006)*

Sequoia Grove 2002 Reserve Cabernet Sauvignon (Rutherford) $57. Fine and forward now, really pretty in red cherry, licorice, and mocha flavors, this blend of all five Bordeaux varieties has a long, rich finish. The tannins are puckery but sweet and finely ground. Delicious and elegant now, but has the power and balance to age through 2012. **93 Cellar Selection** —*S.H. (12/31/2005)*

Sequoia Grove 2001 Reserve Cabernet Sauvignon (Rutherford) $55. This is one California Cab that hasn't gone over the top, beautifully balancing dried spices and vanilla with bold berry and cassis fruit. It's medium-bodied, its tannins and alcohol in check, finishing long and soft. Drink now–2012. **93 Editors' Choice** *(12/1/2005)*

Sequoia Grove 2000 Reserve Cabernet Sauvignon (Rutherford) $55. A wine so well crafted, with such a fine tannic structure, that all it's missing is the richness of fruit to earn a higher score. Opens with earthy aromas that suggest dried hay, sage, and dust, although if you really swirl, you'll find underlying traces of cherries. Tastes fruitier than it smells. There's a delicate deliciousness, but it's a wine for the near term. **89** —*S.H. (11/15/2003)*

Sequoia Grove 1999 Reserve Cabernet Sauvignon (Rutherford) $55. An extraordinary Napa Cabernet, the essence of everything right from Rutherford in a great vintage. Ripe, intense flavors of black currants persist all the way through the long finish, supported by toasty oak. The tannins are a delight, rich, and plush. Feels a bit soft, in the modern style, but is absolutely delicious. **94 Editors' Choice** —*S.H. (12/31/2002)*

Sequoia Grove 1997 Reserve Cabernet Sauvignon (Napa Valley) $42. 94 *(11/1/2000)*

Sequoia Grove 1997 Chardonnay (Carneros) $16. 84 *(6/1/2000)*

Sequoia Grove 2003 Chardonnay (Carneros) $20. There's lots of flamboyant, ripe fruit here, concentrated and intense in papayas, pineapples, pears, and lime custard. The oak is of equal heft, sweet and spicy in vanilla and woodsap flavors. The wine's a little awkward at this time. It could knit together and turn elegant in a year or so. **87** —*S.H. (12/31/2005)*

Sequoia Grove 2003 Merlot (Atlas Peak) $48. Not known as much for Merlot as for Cabernet, Sequoia Grove's bottling is rich, ripe, and delicious, quite sumptuous in cherry, plum, cassis, and mocha fruit flavors that finish dry. It feels like a wine you can age over the short term, because the tannins and acids are ample and the wine is a little untogether. Try holding until early in '07. **90** —*S.H. (7/1/2006)*

Sequoia Grove 2003 Syrah (Atlas Peak) $32. Extract and weight mark this dry Syrah from Cabernet specialist Sequoia Grove. The wine tastes fresh and unresolved, with a grapy jamminess reminiscent of black-berry purée. Firm tannins and rich oak add complexity, but this wine needs a few years to come together. **88** —*S.H. (7/1/2006)*

SEVEN DEADLY ZINS

Seven Deadly Zins 2001 Zinfandel (Lodi) $16. Pretty smooth and plush, this wine's got a soft, velvety texture that frames layers of black cherry, plum, blackberry, chocolate, herb, and spice flavors. Lush and fairly long on the finish. **89** —*J.M. (11/1/2003)*

Seven Deadly Zins 2004 Old Vine Zinfandel (Lodi) $17. Hot and unbalanced in fruit, with flavors that span the gamut from raisins to mint, this Zin is bone dry. It's a rustic wine, with some rugged tannins and a coarse finish. **82** —*S.H. (10/1/2006)*

SEVEN HILLS

Seven Hills 2003 Pentad Bordeaux Blend (Walla Walla (WA)) $50. Once again the winery's estate-grown, super-premium Bordeaux blend adds Carmenère (8%) to the usual mix of Cabernet Sauvignon (53%), Merlot (13%), Cab Franc (13%), and Malbec (13%). The oak and vanilla flavors dominate, ahead of tart, racy red fruits. But the Cabernet, from the same vineyard, is every bit as good at roughly half the price. **88** —*P.G. (12/31/2006)*

Seven Hills 2002 Cabernet Sauvignon (Walla Walla (WA)) $30. This is from Seven Hills vineyard grapes, soft on entry with spicy, warm, black cherry and blackberry fruit, wrapped nicely in well-integrated barrel flavors. Mocha, chocolate, hints of mulberry, and a soft, fruity midpalate that seems to fall off just a bit at the tail end. **89** —*P.G. (12/15/2005)*

Seven Hills 2002 Cabernet Sauvignon (Columbia Valley (WA)) $30. This Klipsun vineyard/Red Mountain Cab is thickly tannic and showing fairly strong herbal/black olive flavors, along with wild berry. Big and a bit rugged, but great for steaks. **88** —*P.G. (12/15/2005)*

Seven Hills 1999 Cabernet Sauvignon (Columbia Valley (WA)) $22. This is a good, every day sort of wine, which shows some earthy power. An initial whiff of volatile acidity quickly blows off, revealing sweet black cherry fruit and a bit of smoky coffee beneath. **88** —*P.G. (6/1/2002)*

Seven Hills 1998 Cabernet Sauvignon (Columbia Valley (WA)) $20. Though it's the least expensive of Seven Hills' four Cabernets, this wine is just a step behind the others. There is good concentration in the color and in the nose, with cassis fruit pushing through a tight, compact structure. Fine balance with firm acids and some interesting mineral flavors, plus a hint of coffee in the finish. **90 Editors' Choice** —*P.G. (6/1/2001)*

Seven Hills 1999 Klipsun Vineyard Cabernet Sauvignon (Columbia Valley (WA)) $30. Another fine Klipsun-designated wine, medium weight, tightly wound and hinting at depth. It's balanced and inviting, yet shows less of the terroir-driven mineral flavors than the Klipsun Merlot from this producer. **90** —*P.G. (6/1/2002)*

Seven Hills 1998 Klipsun Vineyard Cabernet Sauvignon (Columbia Valley (WA)) $25. The '98 Klipsun, from a premier vineyard on Red Mountain, is even better than the '97. It has a richness and ripeness in the cherry-flavored fruit, but retains the extra dimensions that Red Mountain soil imparts: flavors of iron, mineral, and chalk. It's just a little hot in the finish, but not distractingly so. This is a very cleanly made wine, with no earthiness to it. As with all Seven Hills wines, it's built to age, though fine for near-term enjoyment. **92 Editors' Choice** —*P.G. (6/1/2001)*

Seven Hills 1997 Klipsun Vineyard Cabernet Sauvignon (Columbia Valley (WA)) $25. 90 —*P.G. (11/15/2000)*

Seven Hills 2003 Seven Hills Vineyard Cabernet Sauvignon (Walla Walla (WA)) $30. Tart, citric, and built upon tart berry and cassis fruits, this Cabernet is still quite young and showing primary fruits and plenty of acid. It's a wine that seems destined to open up and soften up with additional bottle time; not that it isn't a good food match right now. It's got the fruit and the grip to age a while. **88** —*P.G. (12/31/2006)*

Seven Hills 1999 Seven Hills Vineyard Cabernet Sauvignon (Walla Walla (WA)) $30. This flagship effort comes from the oldest blocks in this pioneering Walla Walla vineyard, planted some two decades ago. Elegant and layered, there are nice notes of licorice coming through a core of deep, fragrant black cherry fruit. Some nice cocoa accents and a hint of mint add interest as well. **91 Editors' Choice** —*P.G. (6/1/2002)*

Seven Hills 1998 Seven Hills Vineyard Cabernet Sauvignon (Walla Walla (WA)) $25. Tight and still a bit closed down, this is a dark, compact, somewhat mysterious wine that keeps its cards close to its chest. Dig a little deeper than the clear, cassis fruit, and you'll find layers of subtlety, dark flavors of tar and licorice, hints of rock and iron, all wrapped in unyielding tannins. Let it breathe and the fruit begins to open up, and a

USA

softer, more elegant wine begins to emerge from its tough, tannic shell. 91 —*P.G. (6/1/2001)*

Seven Hills 1997 Seven Hills Vineyard Cabernet Sauvignon (Walla Walla (WA)) $25. 89 —*P.G. (11/15/2000)*

Seven Hills 1997 Seven Hills Vineyard Reserve Cabernet Sauvignon (Walla Walla (WA)) $32. 91 —*P.G. (11/15/2000)*

Seven Hills 1998 Walla Walla Valley Reserve Cabernet Sauvignon (Walla Walla (WA)) $32. Were this from a more prestigious winery it would command a considerably higher price, but evaluated on its own merits, it is a stunning success. There is a vivid, broad middle palate of black cherry, cassis, and plum; a fine acid structure, and hard, stiff tannins. But there is also an elegant complexity, highlighted with flavors of earth and iron, that comes from the soil. They speak to the extra care taken in the winemaking process so as not to obliterate the fragile taste of terroir with excess oak or overripe fruit. 93 —*P.G. (6/1/2001)*

Seven Hills 2003 Merlot (Columbia Valley (WA)) $28. Three quarters Merlot, the rest filled out with 15% Cab Franc and 9% Cab Sauvignon. Sweet, plump black cherry fruit is highlighted with scents of violets; the chocolatey tannins make for a forward, plush, appealing wine. It's light enough to drink now, but another year or two will add polish and help to pull it all together. 88 —*P.G. (6/1/2006)*

Seven Hills 1999 Merlot (Columbia Valley (WA)) $35. Seven Hills makes this Merlot from diverse Columbia valley vineyards, and it's a youthful, tart mouthful of cassis cranberry and cherry fruit. "Substantial" (says the winemaker) amounts of Cabernet Franc, Cabernet Sauvignon, and Syrah are included in the blend. Good, solid effort. 88 —*P.G. (6/1/2002)*

Seven Hills 1999 Kilpsun Vineyard Merlot (Columbia Valley (WA)) $28. Fruit from the Klipsun vineyard is among the most sought after in the state, and here's why: Laced with mineral, iron, and coffee accents, this hard, tight, dry and substantial Merlot is built like a rock, for aging. 91 **Cellar Selection** —*P.G. (6/1/2002)*

Seven Hills 2001 Klipsun Vineyard Merlot (Columbia Valley (WA)) $28. Big, chewy, and intense, this dense Merlot, blended with small amounts of Cabernet Sauvignon and Cabernet Franc (as if it needed more tannin) masks its fruit in layers of hard tannin, salty mineral, and scents of sweaty saddle. Hard, tough, and definitely in need of decanting or some serious cellar time. 89 —*P.G. (7/1/2004)*

Seven Hills 1999 Reserve Merlot (Columbia Valley (WA)) $40. The reserve Merlot draws grapes from both the Seven Hills and the DuBrul vineyards, both excellent. It is forward and ripe, with pomegranate, cherry, berry, and plum fruit showing, plenty of acid, and fairly lightweight tannins. Somewhat oddly for a reserve, it seems more appropriate for near-term drinking rather than cellaring. 89 —*P.G. (6/1/2002)*

Seven Hills 2002 Seven Hills Vineyard Merlot (Walla Walla (WA)) $30. A very spicy style, built upon substantial, tart, berry fruit. Tannins taste of tea leaves, and it finishes with a nice, balanced, moderately alcoholic (13.5%) bit of light toast. 89 —*P.G. (12/15/2005)*

Seven Hills 2000 Seven Hills Vineyard Merlot (Walla Walla (WA)) $28. The scents jump from the glass, rich and cloaked in sweet cracker, toast, and mocha. The fruit is delicious and broad, the oak generous and chocolatey, the tannins soft and textured. This is a friendly, flavorful style of winemaking, with plenty of rich flavors in a loose-knit, accessible wine. 89 —*P.G. (9/1/2002)*

Seven Hills 1999 Seven Hills Vineyard Merlot (Walla Walla (WA)) $28. This is the Merlot that Seven Hills (the winery) makes with fruit from Seven Hills (the vineyard). A bit more dark and firmly concentrated than their Columbia Valley bottling, it has some chewy tannins and weight, but is a bit one-dimensional. 88 —*P.G. (6/1/2002)*

Seven Hills 1998 Seven Hills Vineyard Merlot (Columbia Valley (WA)) $25. Right now, the fruit emphasizes cassis; with time, some blueberries and cherries will emerge. It's still a tight young pup, closed and a bit standoffish, but the layers of licorice and fruit, hints of earth and wood, and overall structural balance suggest lovely development ahead. The finish is just a little light. 89 —*P.G. (6/1/2001)*

Seven Hills 1997 Seven Hills Vineyard Merlot (Walla Walla (WA)) $25. 89 —*P.G. (11/15/2000)*

Seven Hills 1998 Seven Hills Vineyard Reserve Merlot (Walla Walla (WA)) $32. Seven Hills' Reserve comes from the oldest vines in the vineyard, which were planted in the early 1980s and are among the oldest bearing Merlot vines in the region. Its soft tannins and ripe black cherry fruit make it accessible even at this young age. It was aged in 100% new French oak, though not so much as to dominate the elegant fruit—just enough to put a nice toasty frame around the picture. 91 —*P.G. (6/1/2001)*

Seven Hills 1998 Helmick Hill Vineyard Pinot Blanc (Willamette Valley) $10. 86 —*P.G. (11/15/2000)*

Seven Hills 2004 Pinot Gris (Oregon) $15. Elegant and spicy, with a lively lift to the mixed citrus and stone fruit flavors. It is a fresh, appealing wine perfectly balanced with tart fruit and crisp acid. 90 **Best Buy** —*P.G. (2/1/2006)*

Seven Hills 1999 Pinot Gris (Willamette Valley) $12. 87 —*P.G. (11/15/2000)*

Seven Hills 1998 Coleman Vineyard Pinot Gris (Willamette Valley) $12. 87 **Best Buy** (8/1/1999)

Seven Hills 2003 Ciel du Cheval Red Blend (Red Mountain) $30. Many wineries work with the spectacular grapes grown at Ciel on Red Mountain, but Seven Hills uses it to craft a deceptively light and airy wine, that promotes elegance and grace over sheer power. Let this wine breathe—decanting would be a good idea—and it fills out into a classic show of tart black cherry, plum, and cranberry fruit, along with gravelly stone. Deceptively concentrated, supple, and tart with finishing whiffs of sandalwood and cinnamon. A fine display of sensitive, detailed winemaking. 91 —*P.G. (12/15/2005)*

Seven Hills 2002 Pentad Red Wine Red Blend (Walla Walla (WA)) $50. An unusual blend of Cab (62%), Merlot (12%), Malbec (12%), Carmenère (10%), and Petit Verdot (4%)—hence the name. The smoky oak aromas and flavors are out in front; at this stage of the game the fruit is polished and silky but seems somewhat insubstantial. 89 —*P.G. (6/1/2006)*

Seven Hills 2001 Planing Mill Red Table Wine Red Blend (Columbia Valley (WA)) $16. A tight, tangy, terrific blend of Syrah, Merlot and Cab Franc, this humble table wine has some real muscle. Great fruit is the key, backed with espresso-smoked tannins. The spice of the Syrah marries the coffee/blueberry fruit of the Franc; everything works together. 89 **Best Buy** —*P.G. (7/1/2004)*

Seven Hills 2001 Riesling (Columbia Valley (WA)) $10. Fragrant, with scents and flavors of pears and orange blossoms. This wine has 1.8% residual sugar, which qualifies it as off-dry, but it is still quite suitable for a wide range of foods, especially spicy Asian dishes. Full, fleshy, and well-made, it delivers plenty of fresh fruit flavor with enough spice and acid to give a lift to the finish. 88 —*P.G. (9/1/2002)*

Seven Hills 2003 Syrah (Walla Walla (WA)) $25. It's been co-fermented with Viognier—instantly apparent in the spicy, citrus aromas that permeate the nose. An invigorating, lifted scent combines lemon and lime and orange peel with raspberry syrup and mocha, and that's before you even taste it. It continues in an elegant style, with lovely, interesting flavors that blend together seamlessly and never overpower the palate. Notes of pine, wild herb, and smoked meat add interest through the finish. 91 —*P.G. (6/1/2006)*

Seven Hills 2002 Syrah (Walla Walla (WA)) $25. Featuring a perfumed, raspberry-herb-spice bouquet, this wine shows off its fine complexity right up front. The flavors are a little more sedate, with raspberry and vanilla melding in a supple, creamy mouthful of Syrah. Firms up on the finish, where it shows more acids and tannins. 89 (9/1/2005)

Seven Hills 1999 Syrah (Walla Walla (WA)) $32. This Washington Syrah's backbone is ripe blackberry—on the nose, the berry is muted slightly by a powdery Sweet Tart-cocoa aroma. On the palate, the fruit is bolstered by earth and oak flavors. Juicy berries come to the fore again on the long finish. A smooth and appealing wine, if not supremely complex. 87 (11/1/2001)

Seven Hills 1999 Syrah (Columbia Valley (WA)) $20. Very black in color and flavor, with a heavy overlay of black oak and cedar, there's good ripe cherry (black, of course) fruit beneath. Medium-full and plush, it has a black gumdrop finish and barely noticeable tannins. A one-dimensional black beauty? Yes, but it's still very likable. **87** *(10/1/2001)*

Seven Hills 1998 Syrah (Walla Walla (WA)) $30. 84 —*P.G. (9/1/2000)*

Seven Hills 2003 Tempranillo (Walla Walla (WA)) $28. Here's a rarity—pure Walla Walla Ttempranillo—dark, gamy, and exotic. It instantly fascinates you from the first sniff. What a truly beguiling blend of roasted meats, vanilla, licorice, clove, and black cherry. The fruit is light and tastes of roses and cherries. **89** —*P.G. (6/1/2006)*

Seven Hills 1999 White Riesling (Columbia Valley (WA)) $8. 88 Best Buy —*P.G. (11/15/2000)*

SEVEN LIONS WINERY

Seven Lions Winery 2000 Blakeman Vineyard Chardonnay (Anderson Valley) $NA. Lean and angular, a wine whose fruity ripeness stops at citrus and apples. Yet the structure is interesting, with high acidity. Lees and oak add a touch of complexity. Finishes slightly bitter. **88** —*S.H. (2/1/2003)*

Seven Lions Winery 2000 Buena Tierra Vineyards Chardonnay (Russian River Valley) $55. Firm and bright, yet smooth and silky, this wine offers a classy mix of subtle herb and mineral tones, backed by rich pear, citrus, melon, and toasty oak flavors. Long at the end. **91** —*J.M. (12/15/2002)*

Seven Lions Winery 2000 Wes Cameron Vineyard 60 Year Old Wente Clone Chardonnay (Russian River Valley) $35. Somewhat earthy and quite complex, with an unusual array of citrus, hazelnut, butterscotch, toast, melon, and mineral flavors. Full-bodied, it's weighty yet clean and fresh at the end. **90** —*J.M. (12/15/2002)*

Seven Lions Winery 2000 Pinot Noir (Russian River Valley) $45. Cherry and tart berry fruit, menthol, and woodsy-spicy accents appeal, but don't harmonize as well as hoped for. Cola, cocoa, and orange nuances also show, but the whole is somehow less than the sum of its admirable parts. Closes with mild tannins and sweet-and-sour notes that some tasters found a touch medicinal. **86** *(10/1/2002)*

Seven Lions Winery 1999 Butch & David's Knoll Pinot Noir (Russian River Valley) $65. This is a big, extracted wine. The 14.9% alcohol is downright intimidating. Flavors of black plum and black cherry are accented by cola and licorice. With better balance it would fare better; as is it's just too darn burly. **84** *(10/1/2002)*

Seven Lions Winery 2000 Hansen Vineyards Pinot Noir (Russian River Valley) $55. Blackberry, black plum, black toasty oak—you get the idea, there's a wealth of very dark notes here, but there's also tart red cherry and currant fruit, plus interesting cigar-box elements. This juicy mid-weight closes dry, with good length, a slightly chalky feel and licorice-espresso flavors. Drink now–2007. **88** *(10/1/2002)*

Seven Lions Winery 1999 Joe and Emily's Vineyard Zinfandel (Russian River Valley) $65. This joint effort from Alyssa Barlow and Fred Williams (son of Williams Selyem's former winemaker-owner, Burt Williams) has some of the most impressive packaging that I've seen all year—though getting through the fancy wax seal takes some doing. Wide, sexy aromas of sweet cocoa and blackberry, plus a little baking flour, lead to anise, oak, and more blackberry on the palate. Medium-bodied and silky-smooth in the mouth; the finish waters out a bit, leaving you with a dose of peppery heat and a little mineral. From 125-year-old vines; one to watch in future vintages. **88** —*D.T. (3/1/2002)*

Seven Lions Winery 1999 Martinelli & Duckhorn Vineyard Zinfandel (Russian River Valley) $60. Made from 125-year-old vines, this Zin's nose offers spicy black cherry aromas coated in sweet cream. On the front palate, there's black fruit and oak, but it's interrupted by a brief yet searing lemony tang on the back palate. The medium-long finish picks up where the black fruit and oak left off, plus adds an interesting, smoldering-char flavor. **84** —*D.T. (3/1/2002)*

Seven Lions Winery 2000 Poor Man's Flat Vineyards 100 Year Old Vines Zinfandel (Russian River Valley) $30. Smells superripe and overly extracted, with jammy, fruit-tart aromas underscored by earthy, herbal notes of tobacco and sage. It's a big wine, and a little awkward, but it might knit together in the cellar. **86** —*S.H. (9/1/2002)*

Seven Lions Winery 2000 Three Amigos Vineyards Zinfandel (Sonoma County) $38. A complex, amazing wine that is one of the best Zins of the

vintage. The perfume is extraordinarily detailed, suggesting black raspberry preserves, white chocolate, black pepper, tobacco, vanilla, and smoke. All these flavors commingle in the mouth. Drinks dry, with dusty tannins. This is a brilliant wine, with a sensationally rich, vital finish. **96** —*S.H. (9/1/2002)*

SEVEN PEAKS

Seven Peaks 2002 Cabernet Sauvignon (Central Coast) $15. This is quite a good Cab for the ripe currant and black cherry flavors, firm tannins and smooth mouthfeel. It has that fancy complexity you want from a good red wine, and is priced fairly for the quality. **87** —*S.H. (11/15/2004)*

Seven Peaks 2003 Chardonnay (Arroyo Seco) $16. This extremely ripe wine goes for big size at every turn. It's oozing with sweet tropical fruit flavors that drip with oaky vanillins and buttered toast, and has a creamy texture and spicy finish. From an up-and-coming appellation in Monterey County. **87** —*S.H. (12/1/2004)*

Seven Peaks 2000 Chardonnay (Central Coast) $12. Rough and earthy, with funky flavors barely nudging into apples, and lots of acidity. Feels jagged and angular in the mouth, and turns bitter on the finish. **82** —*S.H. (6/1/2003)*

Seven Peaks 1997 Reserve Chardonnay (Edna Valley) $21. 85 *(6/1/2000)*

Seven Peaks 2002 Merlot (Paso Robles) $15. Soft, juicy, and easy, this wine has excellently ripe berry-cherry flavors and a nice grip of tannins. It's very dry, and picks up interest with the long, pepper-spice finish. **85** —*S.H. (12/15/2004)*

Seven Peaks 2003 Pinot Noir (Monterey) $16. From an increasingly well-regarded region for crisp coastal Pinots, a fruity, light-bodied wine with plenty of appeal. It has good spice, coffee, and raspberry flavors, and is silky in the mouth. **85** —*S.H. (12/1/2004)*

Seven Peaks 2002 Shiraz (Paso Robles) $17. Here's a nice, easy drinking dry red wine from a region that produces them so easily. It's clean and friendly, with juicy fruit and spice flavors and soft acids and tannins. **84** —*S.H. (12/1/2004)*

Seven Peaks 1999 Shiraz (Paso Robles) $20. The tasting panel agreed that this wine's nose was black, but we all had different ideas of what "black" meant: Some said that black grape and licorice dominated the bouquet; others said the aromas were more earthy and leathery. We had the same debates about the dark palate, too—blackberry, clove, black pepper, and licorice flavors got the most votes, all with a minerally overlay. Finishes with prickly tannins and black pepper. **87** *(10/1/2001)*

SEVENTH MOON

Seventh Moon 2001 Merlot (California) $10. If you can overlook the green, minty aspects of less-than-ripe grapes, you'll find a very dry wine, sharp in acids, with a streak of black cherry. **83** —*S.H. (8/1/2004)*

Seventh Moon 2001 Zinfandel (California) $9. Bright and cherry-like, with firm tannins framing light plum, tea, and berry flavors. Moderate to short on the finish. **83** *(11/1/2003)*

SEXTANT

Sextant 2004 Night Watch Red Blend (Paso Robles) $42. With Zinfandel and Petite Sirah, this is a big, hot, high-alcohol wine with chocolatey, stewed flavors. It's too soft and Porty, and isn't going anywhere. **82** —*S.H. (11/15/2006)*

Sextant 2005 Beachcomber Rhône White Blend (Paso Robles) $19. Simple and soft, with canned apricot and peach flavors. Nothing really wrong, but the price seems a little excessive for what you get. **83** —*S.H. (11/15/2006)*

SHADOW CANYON

Shadow Canyon 2001 Shadow Canyon Vineyard Cabernet Sauvignon (Yorkville Highlands) $30. A dark, ripe wine with blackberry, olive, chocolate, and herb flavors that are enriched by smoky oak. Fully dry, with ripe tannins that turn a bit astringent on the finish. Pretty good for this west-of-Paso Robles appellation, but needs to work on depth and nuance. **87** —*S.H. (2/4/2003)*

Shadow Canyon 2003 Larner Vineyard Grenache (Santa Ynez Valley) $30. Rhône specialist Gary Gibson has crafted an intense Grenache filled with

USA

essence-of-cherry flavors. It's bone dry, with a firm backbone of tannins, and soft in acids. This is a winery and a wine to watch. **89** —*S.H. (4/1/2005)*

Shadow Canyon 2002 Paeonia Bien Nacido Vineyard Late Harvest Pinot Blanc (Santa Maria Valley) $45. This sweetie is totally decadent. It's not only the residual sugar, which is a mind-blowing 28 percent, it's the wealth of apricot jam, vanilla, wild honey, and cinnamon spice flavors that blast the palate to ecstasy. Has a syrupy, liqueur-like texture that would be cloying were it not for the excellent acidity. This is one of the best dessert wines of the year. **94** —*S.H. (12/1/2004)*

Shadow Canyon 2003 Syrah (Santa Barbara County) $25. Not quite in the same league as the winery's estate Syrah off York Mountain, reviewed earlier, but the ripe berry flavors, sturdy tannins and elegant balance come close. Dry and complex, this wine shows the enormous potential of Syrah in Santa Barbara. **89** —*S.H. (4/1/2005)*

Shadow Canyon 2003 Shadow Canyon Vineyard Syrah (York Mountain) $38. From this old appellation west of Paso Robles, a big, rich wine with extremely ripe blackberry, cherry, and blueberry flavors and a long, spicy finish. It's pretty tannic now, but that astringency will cut right through a juicy steak or even Chinese-style duck. **90** —*S.H. (12/1/2004)*

Shadow Canyon 2002 Shadow Canyon Vineyard Syrah (York Mountain) $40. Not a rich blockbuster, but controlled and interesting for its balanced flavors of cherries, Provencal herbs, and tobacco, and lush, soft tannins. Finishes dry. **87** —*S.H. (12/31/2004)*

Shadow Canyon 2001 Shadow Canyon Vineyard Syrah (Yorkville Highlands) $40. From a coolish appellation west of Paso Robles, a very good interpretation of a cool-climate Syrah. It is fruity, with cherry and blackberry flavors that have an edge of leather and white pepper, and the tannins are firm, but they are smooth, ripe, and thoroughly enjoyable. A winery to watch. **92** —*S.H. (3/1/2004)*

Shadow Canyon 2002 Larner Vineyard Viognier (Santa Ynez Valley) $22. This is a lean Viognier without the exuberant floral and tropical notes that can put it over the top, but it's an elegant wine. The flavors veer toward melon and citrus, and crisp acidity provides a zesty mouthfeel. A minor flaw is the exceptionally high alcohol, nearly 16%. It definitely creates a burn. **85** —*S.H. (12/31/2003)*

Shadow Hill 1998 Cabernet Sauvignon (Washington) $11. The Shadow Hill Cabernet is more successful than the Merlot; it carries identifiably Cabernet-like scents of cassis and earth, with some interesting mushroom smells as well. Don't expect the lush, ripe fruit of the high-priced juice; this is thin and hard and quite tannic, but well-made and a fair value. **85** —*P.G. (6/1/2001)*

Shadow Hill 1998 Merlot (Columbia Valley (WA)) $11. Shadow Hill is a budget brand entry from Corus Brands, best known for their flagship Columbia winery. This lightweight Merlot has some simple, tomato-flavored fruit, watery acids, and a quick finish. It's clean and correct, but rather dull. **82** —*P.G. (6/1/2001)*

SHAFER

Shafer 1997 Cabernet Sauvignon (Napa Valley) $45. 89 *(11/1/2000)*

Shafer 2003 Cabernet Sauvignon (Napa Valley) $55. Enormously rich in crème de cassis, cherry pie, and cocoa flavors, which many Cabs have these days. But what's so special is the tannic structure, which is world class, and could only come from a premier Napa vineyard. This is an amazingly delicious wine, a joy to drink, but it's best enjoyed now and for a year or three, to appreciate its youthful opulence. **95 Editors' Choice** —*S.H. (9/1/2006)*

Shafer 2000 Cabernet Sauvignon (Napa Valley) $48. Epitomizes the New World style of a superripe, soft, plush wine, bursting with fruity-berry flavors, and generously oaked. Hard to imagine a wine flattering the palate more, with its graceful tannins and heaps of black currant, sweet roasted pepper, olive, and white chocolate flavors. Instantly appealing, although it may be a difficult match for food. **93** —*S.H. (8/1/2003)*

Shafer 1999 Cabernet Sauvignon (Napa Valley) $48. Continues the Shafer tradition of richly fruity Cabs, with near-perfect tannins and just-right oak, and an elegant suppleness that's delicious and distinctive in youth, but ageworthy. The fine vintage has made the wine extra-complex and balanced. Over the years, many wineries have arisen, but few have a better track record than Shafer. **93** —*S.H. (6/1/2002)*

Shafer 2002 Hillside Select Cabernet Sauvignon (Stags Leap District) $190. The impression is of a young, tannically closed but enormously promising Cabernet. Floods the mouth with dramatic black currant, cherry, and chocolate flavors, masses of toasty, caramelized new oak, and a rich, minerally earthiness. For all the power, there's elegance and refinement. If you must drink it now, decant it; best 2008–2015. **97 Cellar Selection** —*S.H. (9/1/2006)*

Shafer 2001 Hillside Select Cabernet Sauvignon (Stags Leap District) $175. No Cabernet smells better. This is an enormously attractive, well-oaked wine constituted from the best possible fruit. In the mouth, it immediately seduces. Shafer knows it has to rise to expectations with this wine, and the 2001 does not disappoint. The fruit is spectacular, all cassis. The oak is rich, flamboyant, and delicious. Structurally, the wine has the best tannin-acid structure Napa is capable of. Immediately delicious now, this wine should develop over the next 10 years. **98 Cellar Selection** —*S.H. (12/31/2005)*

Shafer 2000 Hillside Select Cabernet Sauvignon (Stags Leap District) $150. Extremely well-oaked, with lovely tannins that are soft and gentle, and subtle flavors of black currants and herbs that finish a little thin. It's a very good wine but certainly not on a par with the magnificent '99. Drink now. **89** —*S.H. (12/31/2004)*

Shafer 1998 Hillside Select Cabernet Sauvignon (Stags Leap District) $150. An absolute joy, and a very great success for this vintage, which produced so many disappointing Cabernets. Unusually dark. Begins closed, but swirling brings out cassis and loads of smoky oak. Dense and lush, it's incredibly long on flavor, with fabulous intensity. The reputation of this collector's wine is undiminished. **95 Cellar Selection** —*S.H. (12/31/2002)*

Shafer 1997 Hillside Select Cabernet Sauvignon (Stags Leap District) $150. Fabulous. Dominated now by oak, from the smoky charry aroma to the sappy, sweet flavor. If you chew on it, you find absolutely brilliant blackberry fruit, ripe and pure. Breathtaking structure, with near perfect creamy tannins and soft but supportive acidity. Gorgeous now in it's flamboyant, fleshy youth, or worth aging—have it your way. **96** —*S.H. (12/31/2001)*

Shafer 1995 Hillside Select Cabernet Sauvignon (Stags Leap District) $110. 94 —*L.W. (12/31/1999)*

Shafer 2001 Napa Valley Cabernet Sauvignon (Napa Valley) $52. Shafer makes it look so easy to produce these lush, massively textured Cabs. This baby has polished flavors of cassis and cherry so rich that they practically overwhelm the powerful tannins. It will certainly be succulent now with a juicy T-bone but is clearly a cellar candidate. However, age will rob it of the robust, juicy fruit of youth. **94** —*S.H. (10/1/2004)*

Shafer 2004 Red Shoulder Ranch Chardonnay (Carneros) $43. Another great RSR. A bit soft, but that's okay, as the pineapple custard, white peach and vanilla-oak flavors are perked up by bright citron and Meyer lemon. The finish is pure honey, rich and long and spicy. Such a complex wine. **94 Editors' Choice** —*S.H. (12/1/2006)*

Shafer 2003 Red Shoulder Ranch Chardonnay (Carneros) $40. No malolactic fermentation makes this wine very acidic in feeling, with a fresh, green apple crispness. The flavors veer towards apples, limes, and Meyer lemons, with complexities of mango and apricot. It's a very intense wine, and a notably good one. One sip is not enough. A bottle may be. **93** —*S.H. (10/1/2005)*

Shafer 2002 Red Shoulder Ranch Chardonnay (Carneros) $38. This Chardonnay has a long life ahead of it. Strikes the palate as extraordinarily rich with steely, mineral notes and underlying tropical fruit flavors. As good as it is now, it would be a shame to consume it too early. Best after 2006. **92** —*S.H. (9/1/2004)*

Shafer 2001 Red Shoulder Ranch Chardonnay (Carneros) $37. Another wonderfully complex wine from this single vineyard on the Napa side of the A.V.A. It's a tight, young wine, showing lime, apricot, and mineral flavors. A sunburst of acidity marks the clean, dry finish. Oak and lees play supporting roles. It's likely this wine will improve over the long haul. **91** —*S.H. (6/1/2003)*

Shafer 2000 Red Shoulder Ranch Chardonnay (Carneros) $37. Lavish and opulent, this 100% barrel-fermented wine is oaky, with an ultra-creamy texture and that sweet-and-sour flavor you get from extensive lees aging. The underlying fruit is very sophisticated, suggesting ripe apples. The finish is long and spicy. This wine has depth and offers plenty of interest. **93 Editors' Choice** —S.H. (12/15/2002)

Shafer 1999 Red Shoulder Ranch Chardonnay (Carneros) $37. A pear, apple-orange, and earth bouquet sets the stage for a palate chockful of pineapple, pear, and lemon flavor. Toast notes offset and vibrant acidity uplifts the fruit nicely. The finish is long and tart-sweet with complex leesy, earthy notes. Medium-bodied and restrained, this complex wine shows depth. Give it six months to a year to unfold. **89** (7/1/2001)

Shafer 1998 Red Shoulder Ranch Chardonnay (Carneros) $35. 91 (10/1/2000)

Shafer 1997 Red Shoulder Ranch Chardonnay (Carneros) $35. 93 —L.W. (6/1/1999)

Shafer 1997 Merlot (Napa Valley) $35. 91 —L.W. (12/31/1999)

Shafer 2003 Merlot (Napa Valley) $44. Here's a Merlot with all the hallmarks of Shafer's approach to Cabernet. It's big, ripe, flamboyant, oaky, complex, and immediately enjoyable. Cherries and blueberries are the flavors, accented by sumptuous sweet vanilla. The tannic structure is sweetly rich. Drink now for its youthful beauty. **92 Editors' Choice** —S.H. (12/31/2005)

Shafer 2002 Merlot (Napa Valley) $41. A Merlot that showcases ripe blackberry, cherry, and cocoa flavors with lush, sweet tannins. A little soft, but who cares. The oaky overlay merges well. Gentle and drinkable, yet complex and layered. **89** —S.H. (12/31/2004)

Shafer 2001 Merlot (Napa Valley) $39. As the 2001s come out, the reds are looking good; this Merlot is evidence of the vintage's quality. It's intense and concentrated, with laserlike blackberry, cherry, and coffee flavors that are so ripe, they're practically sweet. Yet it is a dry, balanced wine, notable for the quality of its tannins. **93** —S.H. (2/1/2004)

Shafer 2000 Merlot (Napa Valley) $39. This is brutally good wine. The dark color promises ripeness, and the stains on the side of the glass guarantee a rich, sweet mouthfeel. Just packed with dark berry and chocolate fruit, with the most gorgeous overlay of smoky oak. Fabulous Merlot, and all the more remarkable for being an assembled wine from six different Napa subappellations. **93** —S.H. (12/31/2002)

Shafer 1999 Merlot (Napa Valley) $38. This is one of the most beautiful Merlot's of the vintage. It's hard to describe the depth of aroma and flavor. Blackberry and cassis, violets and a lush overlay of smoky oak doesn't do it justice. Sumptuous, complex tannins and a brilliant, velvety texture and an unending finish also suggest the real deal. Delicious. **91** —S.H. (12/31/2001)

Shafer 1998 Merlot (Napa Valley) $36. What sets this wine apart from the rest of the pack is its sexy, creamy mouthfeel; it simply caresses your taste buds as it delivers solid black cherry fruit touched with milk chocolate, dried thyme, and cinnamon. Plush and low-acid, this is made to be drunk young with prime, dry-aged beef. **90** —J.C. (6/1/2001)

Shafer 2003 Last Chance Firebreak Red Blend (Napa Valley) $42. The name refers to Shafer discontinuing this wine, which is 92% Sangiovese, with the balance Cabernet. Sangiovese, it seems, doesn't sell. What a pity, because it's one of the best super Tuscan wines in California. The '03 is extraordinarily rich and complex, a fruit-forward wine but no bomb. It's controlled in every respect. Some of us will miss it. **93 Editors' Choice** —S.H. (9/1/2006)

Shafer 2000 Relentless Red Blend (Napa Valley) $55. Shafer's annual contribution to the Rhône gene pool is one incredible Syrah. It is inky black in color, due perhaps to some added Petite Sirah, with, yes, relentless aromas of blackberries, cassis, mocha, toast, and vanilla. Doesn't let you down once you sip, when it floods the mouth with dense berry-cherry flavors that, for all their lusciousness, are bone dry. On the finish, you can taste blackberry nectar for a full minute. **94 Editors' Choice** —S.H. (12/31/2003)

Shafer 2002 Firebreak Sangiovese (Napa Valley) $36. Continues the tradition of ripe, intricate Firebreaks of recent years, although not quite in the same class as the '99, '00 or '01. Still, it shares the intense cherry and cassis fruit, smooth, complex tannins, and delicious veneer of oak. Drink now. **91** —S.H. (10/1/2005)

Shafer 2001 Firebreak Sangiovese (Napa Valley) $35. Massively oaked, but massive in every other respect, too. The fruit is explosive, suggesting the ripest, purest blackberries distilled to sweet crème de cassis, with notes of olives, white chocolate, and oak sap. Cabernet Sauvignon character dominates, although it's only 7 percent of the blend, but the Sangiovese contributes an earthy, tobaccoey pepperiness, and perhaps smooths the tannic grip. Cellar through this decade. **93** —S.H. (9/1/2004)

Shafer 2000 Firebreak Sangiovese (Napa Valley) $33. This is brutally good, as it has been for the past several vintages, although the concentration is off a notch. Only 6% Cabernet Sauvignon from estate vineyards, but it dominates, with massive flavors of black currants. What the 94% Sangiovese brings is notes of cherry, tobacco, and earth, and a streak of clean acidity. Defines style and grace in a gigantic wine. **93 Editors' Choice** —S.H. (9/1/2003)

Shafer 1999 Firebreak Sangiovese (Napa Valley) $32. While others struggle to figure out Sangiovese, Shafer takes the lead to produce one of the most distinctive, noteworthy efforts in California. Tobacco, earth, and cherry flavors, and a light, airy texture, mark the Sangiovese, while 5% Cabernet Sauvignon adds currants and tannic structure. The result is complex, stylish, and compelling. This surely is one of the best super Tuscans in the state, and perhaps anywhere. **93 Cellar Selection** —S.H. (12/1/2002)

Shafer 1996 Firebreak Sangiovese (Stags Leap District) $28. 92 —L.W. (6/1/1999)

Shafer 2002 Relentless Syrah (Napa Valley) $62. Epitomizes the rich, extracted style of Napa Syrah, cramming jammy blackberries onto a large, sturdy structure, framed by considerable toasty oak. Yet despite the concentration, it doesn't lack for complexity; there are hints of coffee, chocolate, meat, and leather to be sniffed out, and these should become even more notable after cellaring. Drink 2008–2015, maybe beyond. **91 Cellar Selection** (9/1/2005)

Shafer 2001 Relentless Syrah (Napa Valley) $60. This spectacular wine is drinkable now for its softness and finesse, and should hold well for a few years. Floods the mouth with cassis, cherry, cocoa, and oaky flavors wrapped in sweetly ripe tannins, and feels sturdy and balanced. Mainly Syrah, with Petite Sirah. **93** —S.H. (12/31/2004)

Shafer 1999 Relentless Syrah (Napa Valley) $46. Incredibly intense, with dense, focused, vivid black cherry, berry, spice, cassis, herb, and licorice flavors. Lush, supple textured, round, and elegant, it's quite peppery, nonetheless, and framed in ripe, meaty tannins. Named for the relentless efforts of winemaker Elias Fernandez, the wine is silky smooth and long at the end. An outstanding first Syrah from this winery, best known for Cabernet. **94 Cellar Selection** —J.M. (5/1/2002)

SHALE RIDGE VINEYARD

Shale Ridge Vineyard 2001 Estate Grown & Bottled Cabernet Sauvignon (Monterey County) $8. Rare to find a California Cab this good at this price, but that's the benefit of the economy. Filled with blackberry jam flavors and rich, ripe tannins, and fully dry. There's even a coating of oak. **85 Best Buy** —S.H. (11/15/2003)

Shale Ridge Vineyard 2001 Estate Grown & Estate Bottled Chardonnay (Monterey) $8. A good and inexpensive Chard. It has plenty of peach, apple, and pear flavors and oaky vanillins, and a creamy texture. Finishes with some apparent sweetness. **84** —S.H. (12/1/2003)

Shale Ridge Vineyard 2002 Lockwood Vineyard Chardonnay (Monterey County) $8. A real value at this price, considering its rich array of tropical fruit and creamy texture. Finishes with a swirl of spicy vanilla. **85 Best Buy** —S.H. (7/1/2005)

Shale Ridge Vineyard 2001 Estate Grown & Bottled Merlot (Monterey County) $8. This is an easy-drinking and affordable Merlot of a kind flooding the market now. It has ripe flavors of blackberries and cherries and is dry, with good weight and some complexity. Finishes with a youthful bite of acid. **84** —S.H. (3/1/2004)

Shale Ridge Vineyard 2001 Estate Grown & Estate Bottled Sauvignon Blanc (Monterey County) $8. A very nice everyday sort of Sauvignon Blanc. It packs a lot of flavor into a low price. Especially nice is the ripe pear, fig, and citrus midpalate. 86 Best Buy —S.H. (10/1/2003)

Shale Ridge Vineyard 2003 Syrah (Monterey) $8. If only all the inexpensive California Syrahs could be this good. Sure, it's a little simple, but it's varietally true, with blackberry fruit, peppery spice, and some herbal overtones. Round and reasonably full in the mouth, with enough tannins on the finish to stand up to fatty burgers. 86 Best Buy (9/1/2005)

Shale Ridge Vineyard 2001 Estate Grown & Bottled Syrah (Monterey County) $8. Pop the cork, and the grapey perfume floods the room: Blackberry preserves, dark chocolate, plum pudding, and smoky vanilla aromas. In the mouth, it's a dense, young and jammy wine, with huge berry flavors, but very dry and balanced. 87 Best Buy —S.H. (12/1/2003)

SHANNON RIDGE

Shannon Ridge 2005 Barbera (High Valley) $19. A young, immature wine; it's all primary blackberry and cherry fruit, chewy tannins, oak and, above all, acids. You could slug it down now, or you can let it mellow for 10–20 years. 86 —S.H. (12/31/2006)

Shannon Ridge 2003 Barbera (Lake County) $20. Impossibly sweet for a dry table wine, with sweetened cherry, blackberry, and coffee flavors that taste like they have measurable residual sugar. 81 —S.H. (5/1/2006)

Shannon Ridge 2003 Cabernet Sauvignon (Lake County) $19. With polished black currant, cherry, coffee, and toasty oak flavors, this Cabernet has lots to like. Its tannins are smooth and thick, but finely-ground, and the overall balance is right up there. This is a winery to watch. Drink now. 89 —S.H. (5/1/2006)

Shannon Ridge 2002 Cabernet Sauvignon (Lake County) $19. There's lots of good stuff in this Cab, which showcases Lake County's potential. It has ripe, fruit-foward flavors of blackberry and cherry jam, with balancing acidity and tannin. Feels a bit rough around the edges, but it's a nice drinking wine. 86 —S.H. (6/1/2005)

Shannon Ridge 2003 Petite Sirah (Lake County) $27. This is a wild, untamed wine. Pours dark and thick, with a young, shut-down aroma of wild blackberries. In the mouth, it explodes, rich in blackberry and cassis flavor packed into huge, astringent tannins. Clearly will live for a very long time. Best now after decanting; will age through 2015 if not longer. 90 Cellar Selection —S.H. (5/1/2006)

Shannon Ridge 2002 Petite Sirah (Lake County) $27. This is a big wine, but it shows considerable finesse. Pours inky black, and explodes in mulberry, cassis, coffee, and herb flavors that are very dry. The tannins are chewy, suggesting either aging through the decade, or something ribsticking, like short ribs. 88 —S.H. (6/1/2005)

Shannon Ridge 2005 Wrangler Red Red Blend (High Valley) $14. This is a Cab Franc, Barbera, and Syrah blend. It's interesting, in a rustic way. Fully dry, it brims with young, jammy black stone fruit flavors backed up with hefty tannins, the kind of wine to toss back with barbecue. 85 —S.H. (12/31/2006)

Shannon Ridge 2005 Sauvignon Blanc (Lake County) $15. This is a wonderfully versatile wine. Great acidity brightens the citrus flavors and makes the finish clean and zesty. No oak, just stainless steel. 86 —S.H. (12/31/2006)

Shannon Ridge 2004 Sauvignon Blanc (Lake County) $15. Made in a slightly sweet, accessibly fruity style, this easy wine features lush fig, lemon and lime, melon, and peach flavors that are offset by crisp acids. It's a refreshing thirst-quencher. 84 —S.H. (5/1/2006)

Shannon Ridge 2003 Sauvignon Blanc (Lake County) $15. Dry, tart in acidity, and whistle-clean, this is a nice apéritif-style wine. It has lemon rind flavors and a brisk finish. 84 —S.H. (6/1/2005)

Shannon Ridge 2005 Syrah (High Valley) $19. Shows its aspirations to the northern Rhône in the 100% varietal that's wrapped in dense young tannins now, but deep down below brims with finely ripe fruit. Black currants, licorice, mu shu pork plum sauce, sweet worn leather, and Asian spice flavors mingle into a long, complex finish. This is a wine to watch. 88 —S.H. (12/31/2006)

Shannon Ridge 2003 Syrah (Lake County) $30. This full-bodied Syrah skirts the boundary of overripe, with some reviewers calling it dense, smooth and supple, while Tasting Director Joe Czerwinski found it thick and Port-like. At nearly 16% alcohol, maybe he has a point. But for lovers of the style, this chocolatey Syrah will hit the mark. 85 (9/1/2005)

Shannon Ridge 2003 Zinfandel (Lake County) $22. This winery does a good job with Petite Sirah and Cabernet, but Zin isn't yet a strong point, although this wine shows promise. It's bone dry and sharp in acids and tannins, with bitter coffee and black cherry flavors that will play well against rich meats and cheeses. 85 —S.H. (5/1/2006)

Shannon Ridge 2002 Zinfandel (Lake County) $22. A little rustic in its country-style tannins and mouthfeel, and offers plenty of berry, cherry, and spice flavors. It's soft, and finishes slightly sweet and syrupy. 84 —S.H. (6/1/2005)

SHARK TRUST

Shark Trust 2001 Sixgill Syrah (Lodi) $11. Shows Lodi's distinctive hot climate softness and a stewed fruitiness, with loads of blackberry and cherry pie flavor. Yet there's complexity in the layers and spices. Some of the proceeds go toward shark conservation, hence the name. 85 —S.H. (12/1/2006)

SHARP CELLARS

Sharp Cellars 2003 Tyla's Point Vineyards Pinot Blanc (Sonoma Valley) $19. For a variety with little identity in California, this one has plenty of personality. It's nutty and creamy, with detailed flavors of citrus rind and peach and a rich, but balancing, overlay of oak. It's also very dry with good acidity. 90 Editors' Choice —S.H. (6/1/2005)

Sharp Cellars 2001 Hailey's Creek Vineyard, Premices Zinfandel (Sonoma Valley) $45. Distinctly cola-like in the nose, this over-the-top jammy style isn't the best advertisement for the varietal. Ultra-bright and zippy, with plummy, blackberry flavors and acidity that shocks. Not for everyone. 81 (11/1/2003)

SHEA

Shea 2000 Shea Vineyard Chardonnay (Willamette Valley) $25. A paradigm for the new, vivacious and fruit-driven Oregon Chardonnays. Rich and fleshy, with ripe, buttery fruit and plenty of stuffing. This moves into a blazing finale of fresh pear and butterscotch. 90 —P.G. (12/31/2002)

Shea 2002 Block 25 Pinot Noir (Willamette Valley) $48. Plump and richly tannic, with cola and plum flavors. Long, layered, and tannic. 88 (11/1/2004)

Shea 2002 Block 32 Pinot Noir (Willamette Valley) $48. Leathery and ripe, with the vineyard's classic blackberry and cassis fruit. Plenty of smoky oak gives it a tannic heaviness that is a bit unbalanced. 86 (11/1/2004)

Shea 2000 Shea Vineyard Pinot Noir (Willamette Valley) $42. We tasted two samples of this wne which is elegant and made in a light, Burgundian style. The fragrant nose offers lavender, bacon, and faint cherry, while the mouth is racy and spicy but not overly aggressive. A feminine wine—one that won't blow you over. 87 (10/1/2002)

Shea 2002 Shea Vineyard Estate Pinot Noir (Willamette Valley) $35. Pungent, austere, and awkward with distracting scents of sulfur and cracker. There's light cherry fruit here, quite tart and tannic, unyielding. 84 (11/1/2004)

Shea 2002 Shea Vineyard Homer Pinot Noir (Willamette Valley) $65. Good, dark color and plenty of pizzazz, with black cherry and cola signaling a ripe, spicy, flavorful wine. Viscous and long, with a dry, dusty, tannic finish. 88 (11/1/2004)

Shea 2002 Shea Vineyard Pommard Clone Pinot Noir (Willamette Valley) $38. This has a funky nose, with barnyard scents of leather and manure. The wine seems to fall off in the mid-palate, then comes back to finish with some thick flavors of blackberry, black cherry, and spicy oak. Somewhat controversial. 87 (11/1/2004)

SHELDON

Sheldon 2004 Unfiltered Chardonnay (Santa Lucia Highlands) $25. This is a new brand for me, and they're off to a promising start with this dry, min-

USA

erally Chardonnay. It packs a punch with upfront lemon and lime, passion fruit, and pineapple flavors that are pushed forward by great acidity, while oak adds a fine appliqué. This wine is notable for its balance, elegance, and sheer deliciousness. **93 Editors' Choice** —*S.H. (4/1/2006)*

Sheldon 2003 Ripken Vineyard Petite Sirah (Lodi) $18. This is quite a rich wine, and although it can't quite overcome Petite Sirah's rustic character, it is a great example of the variety. Fully dry and full-bodied, with thick tannins, it's filled with blackberry, black cherry, and mocha flavors, with a meaty edge. **87** —*S.H. (6/1/2006)*

Sheldon 2003 Vinolocity Red Blend (Santa Barbara County) $28. This Rhône blend is harsh and dry. It has a green, twiggy edge, but also super-ripe flavors, as if the grapes were unevenly ripened. **82** —*S.H. (6/1/2006)*

SHELDRAKE POINT

Sheldrake Point 2002 Cabernet Franc (Finger Lakes) $17. Tomatoey in the nose, with hints of wood, mint, and red berry. Stalky flavors of red berry and earth are wrapped in a nice package of moderate tannin that is smooth, with a hint of sweetness. The acidity picks up on the finish. **84** —*M.D. (8/1/2006)*

Sheldrake Point 2002 Barrel Reserve Cabernet Franc (Finger Lakes) $24. This wine has a stalky quality to the dark berry flavors, while the barrels impart a eucalyptus quality and aromas of spearmint. Hints of rhubarb poke through, but the overall impression is positive, with moderate tannins and acidity. **86** —*M.D. (8/1/2006)*

Sheldrake Point 2005 Riesling (Finger Lakes) $15. Sprightly in the mouth, this wine has lemon verbena and citrus pith aromas that lead to orange and tropical fruits in the mouth, picking up spice on the finish. The evident sweetness will pair well with Asian foods. **87** —*M.D. (8/1/2006)*

Sheldrake Point 2001 Bunch Select Riesling (Finger Lakes) $22. **82** —*J.C. (8/1/2003)*

Sheldrake Point 2005 Dry Riesling (Finger Lakes) $15. Aromas of nail polish blow off to reveal moderate white fruit, but this wine shines in the mouth with mineral, spice, yellow fruits, and citrus. Dry to the point of being austere, nevertheless a touch of sweetness adds roundness. Citrus and spice on the finish. A good value in New York Riesling. **89** —*M.D. (8/1/2006)*

Sheldrake Point 2002 Dry Riesling (Finger Lakes) $13. Another "dry" Riesling that's not quite dry, this one starts off with spiced pears and hints of peaches that seem a bit soft at first, then turn gradually tarter and more focused on the finish. **86** —*J.C. (8/1/2003)*

Sheldrake Point 2003 Reserve Riesling (Finger Lakes) $21. Gold in color, this wine blossoms with aromas of petrol, lychee, spice, and vanilla, followed by flavors of the same. Sheldrake Point, on the west side of Cayuga Lake, has been making a name for itself in New York Riesling, showing with this mostly-dry wine how a couple of years can add complexity and a rich mouthfeel. **89** —*M.D. (8/1/2006)*

Sheldrake Point 2001 Semi-Dry Spring Riesling (Finger Lakes) $13. **83** —*J.C. (8/1/2003)*

SHELTON VINEYARDS

Shelton Vineyards 2002 Riesling (North Carolina) $10. Lean and racy, with limes and tart green apples playing major roles. If not for a dollop of sugar, it might seem a bit sour, but as it is it comes across as pleasantly tart and properly acidic. **86** —*J.C. (8/1/2003)*

SHENANDOAH

Shenandoah 1997 Barbera (Amador County) $15. **81** —*J.C. (10/1/1999)*

Shenandoah 2000 Reserve Barbera (Shenandoah Valley (CA)) $24. Still one of California's most widely planted red grapes, Barbera when taken seriously, as it is here, produces a dry, fruity wine of considerable depth and complexity. The berry flavors have a rough, country edge and enough acidity to warrant long-term aging. In time this wine will achieve grace. **87** —*S.H. (12/1/2002)*

Shenandoah 2003 Rezerve Barbera (Shenandoah Valley (CA)) $24. Dark, bitterly dry, and mouth-puckeringly tannic, this is not a wine for those looking for immediate hedonistic pleasure. Although extensive decanting and big, rich meats and cheeses will help, it's really built for the cellar. Should hold and soften for 20 years. **87** —*S.H. (10/1/2006)*

Shenandoah 2003 Rezerve Barbera (Shenandoah Valley (CA)) $24. Classic California Barbera here. It's probably softer and gentler in tannins than Grandpa ever had, but still offers the same midnight black color, deep flavors of plums, blackberries, coffee, and leather, and overall balance and integrity. Try as a very interesting alternative to a fine Cabernet. **90 Editors' Choice** —*S.H. (12/15/2005)*

Shenandoah 2002 Rezerve Barbera (Shenandoah Valley (CA)) $24. Mountain red wine, big, bold, brawny, hot and packed with ripe red and black stone fruit flavors. Completely dry, with outsized but velvety tannins, this wine defines a long-lived style of Barbera, and is really quite wonderful. **91** —*S.H. (9/1/2004)*

Shenandoah 1999 $13 Black Muscat (Amador County) $7. A simple, sweet wine. It has pretty flavors of red and black cherry liqueur that are sprightly and lip-smacking, and the sugar is high but not overwhelming. Acids are good enough to balance everything out. Fine with vanilla ice cream or some butter cookies. **84** —*S.H. (12/1/2002)*

Shenandoah 2000 Rezerve Cabernet Sauvignon (Shenandoah Valley (CA)) $24. Tries to mimic the modern, Napa-esque style, with very ripe currant fruit, thick but fine tannins, an overlay of oak, and dry. Not a bad wine, but nowhere close to the real thing, and overpriced for the quality. **85** — *S.H. (11/15/2003)*

Shenandoah 2003 Vintage Port (Amador County) $17. Very sweet and high in acidity and tannins, this wine's forward black currant and chocolate flavors are easy to take, but the overall mouthfeel and structure are awkward. **83** —*S.H. (10/1/2006)*

Shenandoah 2002 Vintage Port (Amador County) $18. Made from Portuguese grape varieties, a modest Port-style wine that's sweet, with chocolate, coffee, and blackberry flavors. **85** —*S.H. (12/1/2004)*

Shenandoah 2003 Rezerve Primitivo (Shenandoah Valley (CA)) $24. At 15.8% alcohol and observable sweetness, we really are talking Port here. It's a good wine, rich and clean and loaded with chocolate and cherry fruit, but is clearly not a dry table wine. **84** —*S.H. (10/1/2006)*

Shenandoah 2002 Rezerve Primitivo Red Blend (Shenandoah Valley (CA)) $24. Porty in its inky black color, caramelized aroma, raisiny flavors and burn from high alcohol, although there's no residual sweetness. Has plummy, chocolatey notes all the way through, and is quite tannic. **86** — *S.H. (9/1/2004)*

Shenandoah 2001 Sangiovese (Amador County) $14. Decently drinkable, a wine with slightly baked flavors of cherries and chocolate and tough, gritty tannins. Feels dry and rich in the mouth. Although simple, a good partner to your next lasagna. **85** —*S.H. (9/1/2003)*

Shenandoah 1999 Sangiovese (Amador County) $13. Smells darkly fruity, with plum and earth aromas, but turns watery and thin in the mouth. The middle palate is tannic, and the rough finish is hot. If you must drink it, try with oily, buttery, and meaty-fatty foods to soften it up. **82** —*S.H. (12/1/2002)*

Shenandoah 2000 Rezerve Sangiovese (Shenandoah Valley (CA)) $24. A wine that tastes like cheap Port. Smells caramelly and tastes overtly sweet, with berry flavors framed in tough, rugged tannins. Could be any red varietal under the sun. **82** —*S.H. (9/1/2003)*

Shenandoah 2004 Sauvignon Blanc (Amador County) $11. Opens with a minty, eucalyptus-like aroma, and taste dry and bitter, with herbal, spicy flavors. Unusual, even exotic for Sauvignon Blanc, but not unattractive. **85** —*S.H. (10/1/2005)*

Shenandoah 2003 Sauvignon Blanc (Amador County) $11. Strongly flavored, with apple, lemon and lime, fig, and spice flavors that finish with a smoky, herbal edge. Bright in acidity and completely dry, this wine has some interesting nuances, and will challenge a chef's creativity. Nice value. **86** —*S.H. (10/1/2004)*

Shenandoah 2002 Sauvignon Blanc (Amador County) $10. Apple and citrus flavors drink ripe and full but rather sweet, with decent acidity. Finishes clean. Good everyday drinking, and will be fine for the beach. **84** —*S.H. (7/1/2003)*

Shenandoah 2001 Sauvignon Blanc (Amador County) $NA. Syrupy and fruity, with flavors of peach and apple juice, spearmint, and guava. The full-throttle flavors finish a little sweet, and the acid is low. **82** —*S.H. (9/1/2003)*

Shenandoah 2004 Rezerve White Port White Blend (Amador County) $17. Made from Viognier and Roussanne, this intensely sweet wine has rich flavors of the ripest apricots and white peaches, drizzled with vanilla and cinnamon spice. The texture can only be described as voluptuous. Acidity is good, providing a cleansing balance. The alcohol is a very high 18 percent. This is sheer decadence. **93** —*S.H. (5/1/2006)*

Shenandoah 2002 Rezerve White Port (Shenandoah Valley (CA)) $11. Made from the Viognier grape, this is a very sweet wine that oozes flavors of orange custard, honeysuckle, vanilla, caramel, and white fudge. It's tremendously spicy, with a firm acidity that creates a clean zestiness despite the sugar. **90** —*S.H. (9/1/2004)*

Shenandoah 2001 Paul's Vineyard Rezerve Zinfandel (Shenandoah Valley (CA)) $24. A densely structured wine that sports deep, rich plum, blackberry, cassis, smoke, toast, licorice, coffee, and chocolate flavors. The texture is firm and rich, with a smoky edged note on the finish. **88** *(11/1/2003)*

Shenandoah 2002 Rezerve Zinfandel (Shenandoah Valley (CA)) $24. From Sobon Estate, and certainly richer and meatier than the regular Sobon Zins, yet marked by similar characteristics. It's hot in alcohol, overripe in raisiny flavors, and thick and heavy in the mouth, although it's nicely dry. **86** —*S.H. (9/1/2004)*

Shenandoah 2003 Rezerve Paul's Vineyard Zinfandel (Shenandoah Valley (CA)) $24. Showcases the powerful ripeness of Sierra mountain Zins in the massive blackberry pie, cherry tart, and Kahlúa flavors that are wrapped in thick, finely ground tannins. This is a beautiful Zin that would score higher except for some excessive sweetness, despite 15.2% of alcohol. **87** —*S.H. (5/1/2006)*

Shenandoah 2002 Rezerve Paul's Vineyard Zinfandel (Shenandoah Valley (CA)) $NA. Just what you want a great mountain Zin to be. Marvelously rich and ripe in berry, cherry, chocolate, coffee, and spicy flavors, a wine that just blows you away with fruit, but balanced and even elegant. Fully dry despite the size. Perfect with grilled meat or poultry. **91** —*S.H. (8/1/2005)*

Shenandoah 2004 Special Reserve Zinfandel (Amador County) $10. Here's a big, jammy mountain Zin, ripe in blackberry, cherry, and mocha flavors, with a balance of acids and tannins that makes it clean and gulpable. It finishes a little sweet, and will be perfect with barbecue-sauced meats and poultry. **85 Best Buy** —*S.H. (5/1/2006)*

Shenandoah 2003 Special Reserve Zinfandel (Amador County) $10. Good price for a lusty Zin filled with ripe cherry, blackberry, and chocolate flavors. It has that briary nettle quality that marks the variety, and is soft. **85 Best Buy** —*S.H. (10/1/2005)*

Shenandoah 2002 Special Reserve Zinfandel (Amador County) $10. Here's a great value for a Sierra Foothills Zin, where you get some real mountain character. The sturdy tannins buck up wild berry flavors laced with coffee and herbs, and while the wine is bone dry, it finishes with ripe sweetness. **86** —*S.H. (9/1/2004)*

Shenandoah 2001 Special Reserve Zinfandel (Amador County) $10. Fruity in the nose, with hints of raspberry and spice. On the palate, the wine is somewhat restrained, though it still serves up a pleasing blend of anise, black cherry, herbs, and coffee, finishing nicely. **87 Best Buy** *(11/1/2003)*

Shenandoah 1998 Special Reserve Zinfandel (Amador County) $10. High toned, alcoholic nose, with cherry nail-polish scents. Cherries and plums fill the mouth, along with tongue-lashing tannins. The blend includes 6% Grenache and 4% Mourvèdre, which gives it a nice, peppery edge. Lots of flavor for this price. **87 Best Buy** —*P.G. (3/1/2001)*

Shenandoah 1997 Special Reserve Zinfandel (Amador County) $9. **87 Best Buy** —*L.W. (9/1/1999)*

Shenandoah 2004 White Zinfandel (Amador County) $6. Simple and a little sweet, but real clean, with zesty raspberry flavors that trail off to a spicy finish. **82** —*S.H. (10/1/2005)*

Shenandoah 2003 White Zinfandel (Shenandoah Valley (CA)) $6. There's not much color to this pale wine, and not much flavor either, except for sugar and weak, diluted strawberries. But it's acceptable. **83** —*S.H. (9/1/2004)*

Shenandoah VA 1997 Cabernet Sauvignon (Virginia) $NA. **85** —*J.C. (8/1/1999)*

Shenandoah VA 1997 Founder's Reserve Chambourcin (Shenandoah Valley) $17. **86** —*J.C. (8/1/1999)*

Shenandoah VA 1997 Chardonnay (Virginia) $13. **84** —*J.C. (8/1/1999)*

Shenandoah VA 1997 Founder's Reserve Chardonnay (Virginia) $16. **82** —*J.C. (8/1/1999)*

Shenandoah VA NV Lot 95 Merlot (Virginia) $17. **86** —*J.C. (8/1/1999)*

SHERIDAN VINEYARD

Sheridan Vineyard 2003 Cabernet Franc (Yakima Valley) $33. Slightly murky, with vague aromas hinting at green beans and slightly stewed vegetables. It is certainly not a boring wine—it's got unusual nuances of spicy clove, tart cranberry, sliced orange, and mixed citrus. There is a bit more volatility than some tasters will enjoy, but also lots of chocolatey oak, hints of tobacco leaf, and thick, soft tannins. **87** —*P.G. (6/1/2006)*

Sheridan Vineyard 2003 Cabernet Sauvignon (Yakima Valley) $45. This 100% Cabernet Sauvignon is a more subtle, and more interesting wine than the winery's Cab Franc. Here the ripeness seems more stable and balanced, with just the right hints of leaf and bark, and a subtle suggestion of chocolate. The finish is smooth and textural, and a bit of coffee kicks in right at the end; very nice. **90** —*P.G. (6/1/2006)*

Sheridan Vineyard 2000 Red Blend (Yakima Valley) $30. This has some stuffing, but it's rustic, rough, and stemmy. The flavors show some good fruit went into the mix, but the tannins are really harsh. **86** —*P.G. (9/1/2003)*

Sheridan Vineyard 2003 Kamiakin Red Blend (Yakima Valley) $18. A very nice effort at this price, it's smooth and supple, with surprising chocolatey notes (surprising because the winemaker insists that no new oak was used). It's developing more quickly than Sheridan's higher-priced wines, but drinking very well right now, showing the forward, delicious, mixed fruit flavors of this extremely warm vintage. **88** —*P.G. (6/1/2006)*

Sheridan Vineyard 2002 L'Orage Red Blend (Yakima Valley) $35. "L'Orage" means "the storm," acknowledging a big blow that devastated the vineyard in June 2001. Sheridan is a rising star in the valley, and was first selected by Andrew Will's Chris Camarda for vineyard-designated status some years ago. This is the winery's own top wine, a Cab-heavy Bordeaux blend. Gorgeously smooth and fragrant with sandalwood, cocoa, tobacco, and black fruits, it was made by Charlie Hoppes in his silky, generous and seductive style. There is nothing hard, sharp, bitey or bitter, just big, smooth, voluptuous flavors, a generously broad palate and texture texture texture. **93** —*P.G. (12/15/2005)*

Sheridan Vineyard 2003 L'Orage Red Blend (Yakima Valley) $38. Lovely texture, a smooth but slightly astringent tannic base, good acid and a hint of citrus that lifts and refreshes. It doesn't seem to have the complexity or the sheer power of the 2002 L'Orage, but it's well made and appealing. Flavors of strawberry, raspberry, red cherry, and blueberry carry it. **89** —*P.G. (6/1/2006)*

Sheridan Vineyard 2003 Syrah (Yakima Valley) $38. A smooth, supple, flat-out delicious wine. It strikes a perfect balance, showing ripe but not heavy fruit flavors in a pleasing mix of strawberry, pomegranate, hints of berry, citrus, and plenty of acid. This just hits the nail right on the head; no huge alcohol, no new oak. **91** —*P.G. (6/1/2006)*

Sheridan Vineyard 2002 Syrah (Yakima Valley) $36. Smells just like blackberry preserves at first, but reveals additional complexity with a little time in the glass, developing hints of pepper and herbs. Ultrasmooth in the mouth—almost a little syrupy in consistency—leading elegantly into a full, creamy-textured finish. **88** *(9/1/2005)*

SHERWIN FAMILY

Sherwin Family 1997 Cabernet Sauvignon (Spring Mountain) $65. **94** *(11/1/2000)*

USA

Sherwin Family 1996 Cabernet Sauvignon (Spring Mountain) $52. 92 —J.C. (7/1/2000)

SHERWOOD HOUSE VINEYARDS

Sherwood House Vineyards 2001 Proprietor's Reserve Chardonnay (North Fork of Long Island) $23. 84 —J.C. (10/2/2004)

Sherwood House Vineyards 2002 Merlot (North Fork of Long Island) $24. Notes of barnyard and green bean grace red-fruit aromas, while the palate follows with cherry, green bean, spice flavors, and a hint of char. The mouthfeel is a bit leathery, but overall this is a balanced, medium-bodied wine with good acidity and a cherry finish. **86** —M.D. (12/1/2006)

Sherwood House Vineyards 2001 Merlot (North Fork of Long Island) $27. 83 —J.C. (10/2/2004)

SHINN ESTATE

Shinn Estate 2004 Nine Barrels Reserve Merlot (North Fork of Long Island) $42. Husband-wife team David Paige and Barbara Shinn upped the reserve bottling from six to nine barrels, but they've still managed to increase the quality with help from a good vintage. Cinnamon graham cracker coats cherry and blueberry aromas, leading to a solid core of blueberry and eraser flavors. Secondary flavors of mushroom, normal for North Fork Merlot, and wood segue into a lovely finish of spice, cherry, and mineral. A smooth wine, and easily drinkable now. It will only get better with a little age. **89** —M.D. (12/1/2006)

Shinn Estate 2002 Six Barrels Reserve Merlot (North Fork of Long Island) $34. A soft, easy-drinking Merlot, with black cherry, herb, and vanilla aromas and flavors and earth and carob undercurrents. Nice wine, even if it doesn't show the richness expected of a reserve bottling. **85** —J.C. (3/1/2006)

SHOOTING STAR

Shooting Star 2005 Aligoté (Washington) $12. Sassy and stylish white wine from Burgundy's most obscure white grape. Well-ripened flavors of apple and pear, sliding gracefully toward the peach end of the spectrum, create a full, fleshy wine that retains its crisp definition around the edges. No oak here, none needed; just good, ripe fruit. **88 Best Buy** —P.G. (8/1/2006)

Shooting Star 2001 Aligoté (Washington) $12. Like Burgundian Aligoté, Jed Steele's version is sharp and lean, probably best used in a traditional kir (add crème de cassis and drink). The flavor profile is sharp and tart, offering just some lemon and orange pith. The basic finish is lengthy as it deals flavors of lemon and white peach. Interestingly, this wine has some overt oaky notes. Overall it's kind of strange and hard to pinpoint. **84** —M.S. (6/1/2003)

Shooting Star 2000 Aligoté (Washington) $13. This is not a grape frequently seen in these parts. This is a tart, grassy wine, reminiscent of simple Sauvignon Blanc. Herbaceous and dry, with a quick finish. **85** —P.G. (6/1/2002)

Shooting Star 1997 Chardonnay (California) $14. 86 —L.W. (7/1/1999)

Shooting Star 2004 Blue Franc Lemberger (Washington) $12. Just a hint of horsey leather over dense, cherry liqueur flavors. The wine is earthy but carries it well, and the super-saturated fruit offers substantial flavors that carry the authority and taste of old vines. **88 Best Buy** —P.G. (8/1/2006)

Shooting Star 2001 Blue Franc Lemberger (Washington) $12. Known as Blaufränkisch in Europe and some say a relative to Gamay, this grape does quite well in Washington. The wild berry aromas have a pleasant floral quality, and the blackberry flavors finish juicy and ripe, making for an entertaining wine. **88 Best Buy** —C.S. (12/31/2002)

Shooting Star 1997 Merlot (Lake County) $15. 89 (3/1/2000)

Shooting Star 2000 Pinot Noir (Carneros) $14. 81 (10/1/2002)

Shooting Star 1998 Sauvignon Blanc (Lake County) $11. 84 —M.S. (3/1/2000)

Shooting Star 1999 Syrah (Lake County) $12. Takes a lot of character from the barrels it was aged in, with butterscotch, caramel, and pine notes dominating the juicy grape flavors. Displays a real dichotomy of sweet

oak and tart fruit flavors on the finish. Odd, but pretty good if you like the style. **84** (10/1/2001)

Shooting Star 2002 Zinfandel (Lake County) $12. From veteran Jed Steele, a solid Zin that offers berry, chocolate, and coffee flavors. It's dry and soft, with dusty tannins. Easy to drink, and versatile as a food wine. **86** —S.H. (8/1/2005)

Shooting Star 1998 Zinfandel (Lake County) $12. Full, forward, fleshy nose shows lots of bright, spicy fruit. Unlike a lot of lower cost Zins, this wine has a lot of sweet fruit, and enough body and weight to carry through past the nose into a big, satisfying finish. Nice toast, plenty of acid, a bit hot in the finish. **87** —P.G. (3/1/2001)

SHOWKET

Showket 2003 Cabernet Sauvignon (Oakville) $75. They must have let some of the grapes shrivel, because there's a blast of raisins. They're good raisins, the sweet, curranty kind that taste drizzled with rum and crème de cassis. This is a big, dry, extracted wine with some fairly hefty tannins. It drinks beautifully now and should hold well through 2020. **94 Cellar Selection** —S.H. (9/1/2006)

Showket 2002 Cabernet Sauvignon (Oakville) $69. More tannic than many other Oakville Cabs tasted at the annual Taste of Oakville event, this blackberry and chocolate-flavored tough young wine may do interesting things. Try cellaring until 2007. **88** —S.H. (11/1/2005)

Showket 2001 Cabernet Sauvignon (Oakville) $75. How sweet the fruit got during this ripe vintage. There's a crème de cassis flavor and a liqueury texture, drizzled with a sprinkle of vanilla dust and cinnamon. That makes it sound like a dessert wine, but it's dry. The balanced structure suggests midterm aging. **92** —S.H. (10/1/2004)

Showket 2002 Asante Sana Red Blend (Oakville) $45. This Super-Tuscan blend of Cabernet and Sangiovese seems excessively sweet, which is probably due to high alcohol. It has a tart, brittle mouthfeel, with flavors of chocolate. Tasted twice. **84** —S.H. (11/1/2005)

Showket 1997 Sangiovese (Napa Valley) $35. 88 —S.H. (12/15/1999)

Showket 2002 Sangiovese (Oakville) $30. This wine challenged me. At first it seemed underripe, then a wave of gooey melted chocolate and cherry preserves popped up. It also tastes sweet, which winemaker Heidi Barrett attributes to, not residual sugar, but high alcohol. **85** —S.H. (11/1/2005)

Showket 2001 Sangiovese (Oakville) $30. A dark wine, impressive for its brooding color, oak, and tremendous black currant and cherry fruit. Don't expect anything Tuscan; this is chocolatey and soft, but quite delicious. In the top ranks of current Sangioveses. **89** —S.H. (10/1/2005)

SIDURI

Siduri 2004 Pinot Noir (Russian River Valley) $26. Siduri's basic Russian River bottling is very ripe in fruit, heavy in texture, and soft, with a cherry, coffee, and chocolate syrup flavor. It's as tasty as a candy. Drink now. **84** —S.H. (5/1/2006)

Siduri 2004 Pinot Noir (Santa Rita Hills) $29. Shows true Santa Rita character, although it's slimmed down compared to the appellation's star bottlings. Brilliantly crisp in acidity, with ripe, silky tannins, the flavors veer toward cherries, cola, coffee, and rhubarb. **88** —S.H. (5/1/2006)

Siduri 2002 Pinot Noir (Central Coast) $25. This Pinot, a blend from a large, cool region, shows modest aromas and flavors of cherries, herbs, and tobacco. It's very dry, with some sharp acids and earthy tannins. Try this versatile table wine with barbecued sausages, and pasta with olive oil and herbs. **85** —S.H. (5/1/2004)

Siduri 2002 Pinot Noir (Sonoma County) $25. You'll find lots of ripe cherry, raspberry, and peppery spice flavors in this gentle, silky wine. It has some richness and complexity, and the firm acids and sweet tannins are nicely balanced. **86** (11/1/2004)

Siduri 2002 Pinot Noir (Santa Lucia Highlands) $35. Strong, acidic, and jammy, with youthful cherry-berry flavors. It's very dry, with a coating of oak. Not particularly subtle, but a well-made regional wine. **85** —S.H. (5/1/2004)

Siduri 2001 Pinot Noir (Sonoma Coast) $28. Clearly from a cool climate, dominated by tomato, mushroom, and herb flavors just breaking into black cherry. Dry, with great acidity and complex tannins. This is a subtle Pinot that will appeal to tasters who enjoy thinking about what's in their mouth. **91 Editors' Choice** —*S.H. (7/1/2003)*

Siduri 2001 Pinot Noir (Santa Lucia Highlands) $34. From some of this appellation's best vineyards, an interesting wine that captures your imagination. Has broad flavors of cherry, earth, sautéed mushroom, cola, and toast, and is very dry. Uplifting acids and soft but complex tannins make for terrific structure. A winery to watch. **92 Editors' Choice** —*S.H. (7/1/2003)*

Siduri 1999 Pinot Noir (Santa Lucia Highlands) $34. Another big, dark Pinot from Adam Lee. It opens with a plum, pine, spice, and leather bouquet. The feel is round and full, but the flavors—if tasty—are dark and a bit indistinct. A touch hot, too, this closes deep, long, and spicy. **88** *(10/1/2002)*

Siduri 2000 Cerise Pinot Noir (Anderson Valley) $50. This intensely extracted wine came off more like Port than Pinot to our tasters. Which isn't to say that it lacks appeal. It opens with smoked meat, spice cake, and grilled nut aromas. Fat blackberry-plum flavors, a plush, low-acid mouthfeel and a full tannic finish complete the Port profile. It's tasty if overblown, and not what most people expect. Probably best paired with a cheese course. **86** *(10/1/2002)*

Siduri 1999 Garys' Vineyard Pinot Noir (Santa Lucia Highlands) $49. Like 'em big and deep, with a solid tannic structure? Here, rich black cherry and plum fruit wears smoky oak, herb, and spice accents. But the fruit holds its own against the wood. The mouthfeel is rich and supple; the close long and evenly tannic. And it will be better in one to two years. **90** *(10/1/2002)*

Siduri 2000 Garys' Pinot Noir (Santa Lucia Highlands) $48. The bouquet is big, black, and bordering on syrupy and there's even an uncanny aroma of cinnamon buns. The mouth is equally dark and rich, potentially too much so for fans of leaner, Burgundian Pinots. But if a big wine is up your alley, then you'll love the blackberry fruit, barrel char, sugar beets, and brown sugar that swarm the palate here. Coffee and caramel flavors grace the layered finish. **90** *(10/1/2002)*

Siduri 2001 Garys' Vineyard Pinot Noir (Santa Lucia Highlands) $50. From this well-regarded vineyard, a big, juicy wine that is very ripe and jammy. It offers up an array of blackberry, cherry, boysenberry, espresso, and tobacco flavors, emphasized with Asian spice. Very dry, with silky tannins and crisp acidity. **88** —*S.H. (3/1/2004)*

Siduri 2001 Hirsch Vineyard Pinot Noir (Sonoma Coast) $45. From one of the Coast's most famous vineyards, a big, superripe bruiser of a Pinot. This was a difficult, hot vintage on the Coast, and it shows in the wine, which opens with a Porty scent suggesting raisins and cooked fruit, and turns very dry in the mouth. The cherry fruit flavors turn hot and raisiny on the finish. **86** —*S.H. (3/1/2004)*

Siduri 1999 Hirsch Vineyard Pinot Noir (Sonoma County) $49. Always a complex wine, Adam and Dianna Lee's '99 Hirsch is a bit rusty in color, with smoke, oak, and baking spice aromas. The palate offers a complex conglomeration of spicy red fruit and licorice, while the finish provides length and smoky flavors akin to ham and bacon. Some drying tannins ensure that the structure is maintained throughout. **90** *(10/1/2002)*

Siduri 1998 Hirsch Vineyard Pinot Noir (Sonoma Coast) $46. 88 *(10/1/2000)*

Siduri 1997 Hirsch Vineyard Pinot Noir (Sonoma Coast) $42. 92 *(10/1/1999)*

Siduri 2000 Muirfield Vineyard Pinot Noir (Willamette Valley) $48. Deep aromatics of plum liqueur, black cherry, cinnamon, and clove start it off. Next come flavors of cherry, vanilla, brown sugar, and toast. The finish is a mile long, offering coffee, black pepper, and firm but friendly tannins. Give it a couple years to fully knit together. **90** *(10/1/2002)*

Siduri 2000 Pisoni Pinot Noir (Santa Lucia Highlands) $50. Big, firmly structured and built to last, this Pinot starts off tight. But dark fruit flavors explode on the palate, delivering plums and black cherries by the bushelful. The long, softly tannic finish suggests cellaring until 2005 or beyond. **93 Editors' Choice** *(10/1/2002)*

Siduri 2000 Sapphire Hill Vineyard Pinot Noir (Russian River Valley) $49. Offers beefy, dried spice, and leather hints, followed by a core of deep,

rich blackberry-cherry fruit wearing a toasted-oak mantle. Black pepper, meat, coffee, and plum notes show on the firmly tannic finish, which one panelist found excessively alcoholic. Drink 2005–2010. **93 Editors' Choice** *(10/1/2002)*

Siduri 2000 Van Der Kamp Pinot Noir (Sonoma Mountain) $48. Atypically for Siduri, this wine lacks intensity and body, coming off lean, with dry, ashy flavors that are rather shallow. A surprising disappointment that closes a bit prickly, with cocoa and astringent lemon hints. Tasted twice, with consistent notes. **83** *(10/1/2002)*

Siduri 2001 Van Der Kamp Vineyard Pinot Noir (Sonoma Mountain) $45. Jammy and big, combining fruit-forward flavors of cherries and boysenberries with a streak of smoked meat or game. Acidity is high through the tart finish, and the rich, thick tannins suggest a wine that will improve for a year or two in the cellar. **87** —*S.H. (3/1/2004)*

Siduri 1999 Van Der Kamp Vineyard Pinot Noir (Sonoma Mountain) $49. Starts out with barnyard and forest floor aroma; eventually, some dried currant and raspberry emerge. There's an abundance of depth to the funky, esoteric palate as well as the full allotment of tobacco and herbs. Is it an easy wine? Not at all. But connoisseurs could find it right up their alley. **87** *(10/1/2002)*

Siduri 1997 Van Der Kamp Vineyard Pinot Noir (Sonoma Mountain) $38. 90 *(10/1/1999)*

SIERRA CLUB

Sierra Club 2000 Atira Vineyards Cabernet Sauvignon (Napa Valley) $19. Decently drinkable, with some sweetness to the cherry-berry flavors, and a rough mouthfeel that turns gritty with tannins in the finish. **83** —*S.H. (8/1/2005)*

SIERRA VISTA

Sierra Vista 2005 Unoaked Chardonnay (El Dorado) $13. You'll find some peach and apple flavors in this wine, but they're rather watery, and the wine lacks the acidity to make it bright, like those Australian and New Zealand unoaked Chards. It's not bad, just an underachiever. **83** —*S.H. (11/1/2006)*

Sierra Vista 2002 Unoaked Chardonnay (El Dorado) $12. Tastes strongly of apples, peppermint, and tobacco, making it an earthy Chard, but there's also a rustic, gritty edge to it that's peppery and harsh. **82** —*S.H. (10/1/2003)*

Sierra Vista 2005 Fumé Blanc (Sierra Foothills) $13. Made Sancerre style, with no oak, this beautiful wine bursts with fresh citrus, honeydew, green grass, sweet pea, and peppery spice flavors that stimulate the palate. It's so easy to drink, yet has the complexity to sustain interest. Try with raw shellfish or a salad of bitter greens, chevre, grapefruit, and shrimp. **90 Best Buy** —*S.H. (11/15/2006)*

Sierra Vista 2001 Belle Rose Rhône Red Blend (El Dorado) $9. This Rhône blend of Grenache, Syrah, and Mourvèdre drinks semi-sweet, like a cherry Coke. It also has peppery, earthy flavors and a nice, crisp texture. It's a good value in a beach or picnic sipper. **86** —*S.H. (9/1/2003)*

Sierra Vista 2001 Fleur de Montagne Rhône Red Blend (El Dorado) $21. Smells raw and jammy, offering up sharp aromas of young wild berries along with herbs, earth, and less ripe green notes. This country wine is simple, fruity and dry. A blend of Grenache, Syrah, Mourvèdre, and Cinsault. **84** —*S.H. (6/1/2003)*

Sierra Vista 2000 Fleur de Montagne Rhône Red Blend (El Dorado) $21. Rustic and naïve, a country style wine that will seem simple to some, but has its own charms. Filled with vibrant cherry and spice flavors, and girded with soft tannins and crisp acids, it will be good with pasta, barbecue, and similar everyday fare. **85** —*S.H. (5/1/2003)*

Sierra Vista 2004 Syrah (Sierra Foothills) $12. Soft and likeable for its polished blackberry, blueberry, coffee, and cocoa flavors, this fruity wine is quite dry. It's a nice, easy sipper, soft and silky in the mouth. **84** —*S.H. (5/1/2006)*

Sierra Vista 2000 Syrah (Sierra Foothills) $12. This inky dark wine is mouth-numbingly tannic and earthy. It is heavy on the palate, with a deeply buried core of blackberry fruit, and is extremely dry. Tannins

USA

might soften with a little age. Best consumed with barbecue and similar rich fare. **84** —S.H. (6/1/2003)

Sierra Vista 1997 Five Star Reserve Syrah (El Dorado County) $60. Smoky, with leather and cedar nuances that pick up a briny or seaweed-like note, this smooth blackberry beauty has an almost furry texture, coating the mouth with supple tannins. Finishes long and a bit tart; drink now or age several more years. **90** (11/1/2001)

Sierra Vista 2004 La Grande Syrah (Sierra Foothills) $20. Soft and supple, with ripe cherry, blackberry, mocha, and spice flavors. There's a nice tannic structure to the wine, which finishes dry and satisfying. **87** —S.H. (11/15/2006)

Sierra Vista 2004 Red Rock Ridge Syrah (El Dorado) $25. There's lots of loveliness in this estate wine, with its perfume of lavender and polished flavors of cherries and blackberries. It has a good structure, combining dryness with acidity and fine tannins. Loses a couple points, though, because it turns thin in the middle and doesn't recover. **84** —S.H. (11/15/2006)

Sierra Vista 1999 Red Rock Ridge Syrah (El Dorado) $25. Red, ripe, and juicy, a fun wine to slosh around your mouth and enjoy the berry, cherry, and cola flavors. Dryish, although there's a honeyed core of fruit swimming in a gentle wash of tannins. **87** —S.H. (6/1/2003)

Sierra Vista 1997 Red Rock Ridge Syrah (El Dorado County) $19. 89 —S.H. (10/1/1999)

Sierra Vista 2001 Viognier (El Dorado) $25. On the delicate side for this variety, which can be so explosively fruit. Flavors tend toward citrus fruits and white peach, although there's a richer edge from oak. Has good acids and a bitter, almond-skin finish. **85** —S.H. (5/1/2003)

Sierra Vista 1998 Viognier (El Dorado County) $20. 89 —S.H. (10/1/1999)

Sierra Vista 2000 Zinfandel (El Dorado) $12. Typical of lower-priced Sierra Foothills Zin, with bright and pure wild berry flavors liberally dosed with pepper and herbs. Very dry and nicely balanced, with a rustic edge that feels authentic, almost homemade. **85** —S.H. (9/1/2003)

Sierra Vista 2004 Estate Zinfandel (El Dorado) $12. Gentle, smooth, and flavorful, this Zin has polished berry, cherry, cocoa, and spice flavors that finish long and spicy. It has an elegant, silky texture and isn't very tannic. **86** —S.H. (5/1/2006)

Sierra Vista 1999 Reeves Zinfandel (El Dorado) $16. A blast of oak hits you right off, smacking of vanilla and toast. Then you sip, and the ripe blackberry and pepper flavors kick in. Dry and rich, with substantial tannins, this is a big, rustic wine. There's nothing shy about it. **85** —S.H. (11/1/2002)

SIGNORELLO

Signorello 2000 Padrone Bordeaux Blend (Napa Valley) $75. Massive and brilliant, a distinctly Napa Bordeaux blend made succulent by its deep, rich flavors of black currant, cassis, and sweet black cherry. The tannins are soft and modulated, and crisp acidity gives the mouthfeel a clean feel. This is a wine to ooh and aah over, and is a special success for the vintage. **93** —S.H. (4/1/2004)

Signorello 1997 Padrone Bordeaux Blend (Napa Valley) $125. 92 (11/1/2000)

Signorello 2002 Padrone Cabernet Blend (Napa Valley) $95. Signorello's proprietary Bordeaux blend is largely Cabernet Sauvignon, with Merlot and Cabernet Franc. If you're laying down '02s to cellar, this is a very good bet. It's shut down right now, but offers tantalizing hints of black currants and cassis that quickly disappear into a dry, tannic underworld. But the wine has the balance and authoritative class to age well beyond 2010. **95 Cellar Selection** —S.H. (12/1/2005)

Signorello 1997 Cabernet Sauvignon (Napa Valley) $48. 91 —S.H. (2/1/2000)

Signorello 2001 Cabernet Sauvignon (Napa Valley) $48. Plush and chewy, with smoky, toasty aromas and a core of black plum and red berry fruit. Nicely textured, but also brightly acidic. One dissenting taster found it overly tannic and questioned whether it would evolve positively. **87** (6/1/2005)

Signorello 1999 Cabernet Sauvignon (Napa Valley) $48. Pretty fancy stuff here. The blackberry and cassis aromas are given complexity by oak, lots of it, new and well charred. It drinks fruity, but with a more austere note suggesting olives and green peppers. This dry, herbaceous note makes it food-friendly. It may be an ager, but it will be at its best in a year or two. **91** —S.H. (6/1/2002)

Signorello 2002 Estate Cabernet Sauvignon (Napa Valley) $48. As fine as this Cab is, it's best to leave it alone for some years to develop bottle complexity. It's a big, rich, dry wine, with a huge core of black currant and cassis fruit, but the sticky tannins kick in right away and don't quit. Should be very good after 2008. **92 Cellar Selection** —S.H. (12/1/2005)

Signorello 2000 Estate Unfiltered Cabernet Sauvignon (Napa Valley) $48. Clearly well-made and from pedigreed grapes, with very fine tannins, the sort that are tough and dusty but go down like velvet. It is a bit light on the blackberry and plum, no doubt a problem of the light vintage. Best to drink up soon. **89** —S.H. (6/1/2003)

Signorello 2000 Chardonnay (Napa Valley) $38. A classy Chardonnay, brimming with fine pear, citrus, apple, herb, mineral, and toast flavors. Tangy and sleek, yet smooth and elegant. Long at the end. **91** —J.M. (5/1/2002)

Signorello 1998 Estate Chardonnay (Napa Valley) $38. 89 —S.H. (5/1/2000)

Signorello 1999 Estate Bottled Chardonnay (Napa Valley) $38. This barrel-fermented Chardonnay shows smoky new oak and telltale matchstick leesy aromas. Real spiciness comes through on the palate. The apple fruit wears strong clove, nutmeg, and butterscotch notes. There's a firm acid backbone that's lively, but slightly jarring to some tasters. Give this one four to six months to knit itself together. **88** (7/1/2001)

Signorello 2002 Hope's Cuvée Chardonnay (Napa Valley) $60. The acids are high, the oak is powerful and this densely structured wine is wrapped in a cloak of steel and mineral. It hasn't all come together yet. But the flavors are ripe and pure, straddling the line between tropical fruits and juicy apples, and this is one of those rare Chards that needs age. Best toward 2005, and will hold for several years afterward. **93** —S.H. (8/1/2004)

Signorello 2000 Hope's Cuvée Chardonnay (Napa Valley) $60. Firm and focused, this elegant, full-bodied wine offers a striking mineral core backed by hints of lemon, pear, and apple. A slightly earthy component adds interest. Clean and sleek on the finish. **91** —J.M. (5/1/2002)

Signorello 1999 Hope's Cuvée Chardonnay (Napa Valley) $60. This opens with a muted but very pleasing nose of orange, pineapple, clove, almond, and baked apple aromas. The palate's tropical fruit is complemented by butterscotch, clove, and allspice flavors. Soft but well-constructed, it's a medium-weight wine with balanced fruit and well-utilized oak on the finish. **89** (7/1/2001)

Signorello 2002 Vieilles Vignes Chardonnay (Napa Valley) $38. Heavily oaked, heavy on the lees, one of those wines that sits creamy and thick on the palate. The flavors are ripe and candied, suggesting vanilla ice cream, tangerines, and sweet limes. A real lip-smacker, but has elegance and complexity. **91** —S.H. (8/1/2004)

Signorello 2001 Vieilles Vignes Chardonnay (Napa Valley) $38. A bit on the lean side, with apple and citrus flavors, which are typical of the appellation. Acidity is also sharp and mouth-watering. This is not a big, fat Chardonnay but it is a well-structured, food-worthy wine, with oaky influences. This tight structure is very clean. **90** —S.H. (6/1/2003)

Signorello 2003 Vieilles Vignes Estate Chardonnay (Napa Valley) $38. A controversial wine with our panel. Some loved it for its idiosyncratic aromas and thick, unctuous mouthfeel, while others penalized it for the same characteristics. One reviewer's complex, hard-to-describe aroma was canceled out by another's earthy, mulchy scents. There is a solid core of peach and pineapple fruit, so on balance, our rating is positive. **88** (6/1/2005)

Signorello 1999 Estate Merlot (Napa Valley) $45. A big, rich, thick wine, marked by substantial tannins and smoky, sweet oak. Buried down deep are pretty blackberry and coffee flavors, along with some peppery spice. The stubborn tannins suggest midterm aging. **89** —S.H. (2/1/2003)

USA

Signorello 2004 Las Amigas Vineyard Pinot Noir (Carneros) $38. This is a really good Carneros Pinot, showcasing the terroir in the most delicious way. Complex and dry, it has red cherry, cola, and oak flavors, with a rich streak of dried herbs, Asian spices, and sweet leather. Really first rate, an elegant, silky Pinot from the Napa side of the appellation. **92** — *S.H. (11/1/2006)*

Signorello 2002 Las Amigas Vineyard Pinot Noir (Carneros) $32. Ripe and sweet in polished raspberry, red cherry, mocha, and spun sugar, with zingy spices, this complex wine is also silky and firm. The impression of sweetness is heightened by new oak, but it's fundamentally a dry wine. **90** — *S.H. (11/1/2004)*

Signorello 2001 Las Amigas Vineyard Pinot Noir (Carneros) $32. There's an amazing density to this wine, which has a molten quality to the mouthfeel. It's as if the cherry, raspberry, mocha, and cinnamon flavors were dissolved in mercury. On the other hand, the tannin-acid structure is a wonder. Intricate and dry, this single-vineyard beauty feels easy and silky. **93** — *S.H. (4/1/2004)*

Signorello 2000 Las Amigas Vineyard Pinot Noir (Carneros) $32. Screams Carneros. Fleshy, jammy fruit flavors of cherries, strawberries, and raspberries are highlighted by good acidity and drink very dry, with soft but complex tannins. It's not a simple wine, and has enough stuffing to cellar for a few years. **89** — *S.H. (7/1/2003)*

Signorello 1999 Las Amigas Vineyard Pinot Noir (Carneros) $50. Displays powerful North Coast Pinot notes, with aromas of black raspberry, beetroot, tomato, chocolate, smoke, and spice. In the mouth, there's tremendous extraction, an explosion of superripe, spicy fruit and berry flavors, but they're controlled. Soft acids and tannins create a candied mouthfeel. **89** — *S.H. (9/1/2003)*

Signorello 1998 Las Amigas Vineyard Pinot Noir (Carneros) $50. Released at the same time as the '99, this wine shows a very different profile, beginning with meaty, bacon fat aromas along with tomato, and leaner in the mouth. But it's not austere or earthy. It has some pretty black raspberry and spice flavors, wrapped in silky tannins. In a way, it's a more balanced wine than the riper '99 because it doesn't have that fruit bomb quality. **91** — *S.H. (9/1/2003)*

Signorello 1997 Las Amigas Vineyard Pinot Noir (Carneros) $45. 90 *(10/1/1999)*

Signorello 2001 Padrone Red Blend (Napa Valley) $110. Some of the Napa '01s are instantly drinkable. Not this one. It's power-packed with tannins that numb the palate into submission. Hard to like now, and difficult to tell where it's going. Set it aside for a good six years and hope for the best. **86** — *S.H. (6/1/2005)*

Signorello 1998 Barrel-Fermented Sémillon (Napa Valley) $22. Shows terrific concentration, with aromas and flavors of cashew butter, citrus, and apricot, and some classy French oak notes. Very smooth and oily on the palate, it's low in acidity, keeping it round and plush. Finishes long, dry, and complex. Will probably age, but it's a great Chardonnay alternative tonight. **91 Editors' Choice** — *S.H. (8/1/2001)*

Signorello 2001 Seta Sémillon-Sauvignon Blanc (Napa Valley) $25. A good wine, grape-wise, with sharply etched, pure fruity flavors of citrus, fig, and sweet tobacco. Acidity is fresh and juicy, and the wine is fully dry. Barrel-fermented, it is super-oaky, maybe too much so, from the charry aromas to the woody flavors. **87** — *S.H. (7/1/2003)*

Signorello 2000 Seta Sémillon-Sauvignon Blanc (Napa Valley) $25. This blend of Sauvignon Blanc and Sémillon has seen a lot of smoky oak and lees, and it shows in the rich, creamy texture. The flavors are an absolute delight, fruity and spicy and not too unnaturally sweet. This wine has a limpid elegance and layered complexity that's lip-smackingly good. **90** — *S.H. (9/12/2002)*

Signorello 2004 Seta White Wine Sémillon-Sauvignon Blanc (Napa Valley) $25. Always a sophisticated dry white wine, this year's Sémillon-Sauvignon Blanc blend is rich and complex. It has citrus rind, nectarine, peach, and white pepper flavors, while barrel fermentation and sur lie aging add even richer, creamier notes. **89** — *S.H. (11/1/2006)*

Signorello 2003 Seta White Wine Sémillon-Sauvignon Blanc (Napa Valley) $25. A barrel-fermented blend of Sémillon and Sauvignon Blanc, this is a great wine to drink with almost anything. It's stylishly dry and crisp with acids, with a creamy texture framing subtle flavors of lime, gooseberry, and dried herbs. **90** — *S.H. (6/1/2005)*

Signorello 2002 Seta White Wine Sémillon-Sauvignon Blanc (Napa Valley) $25. This fabulous blend of Sémillon and Sauvignon Blanc approaches a great white Bordeaux in complexity and sheer deliciousness. There's a lushness and intricacy to the texture beyond the ripe peach, lemongrass, fig, and buttercream flavors. The result is balanced, elegant, and harmonious, with great finesse. One of the best wines of its type in recent vintages. **92** — *S.H. (8/1/2004)*

Signorello 2001 Syrah (Napa Valley) $NA. Just beautiful, a wine that's so rich and delicious, and yet so balanced. It oozes gorgeous flavors of cassis and blackberry pie, blueberry, white chocolate truffle, Kahlúa, and smoky spices, and the tannins are amazingly soft, sweet, and complex. All this opulence drinks perfectly dry, with a good backbone of acidity. **94** — *S.H. (5/1/2004)*

Signorello 2004 Estate Syrah (Napa Valley) $36. There's only 4% Viognier in this wine, but it really shows in the fresh burst of acidic citrus and honeysuckle that brightens and elevates the Syrah's deeper plum, blackberry, and coffee notes. The result is a complex wine, dry and stylish. Enjoyable tonight through 2008. **88** — *S.H. (11/1/2006)*

Signorello 2002 Estate Syrah (Napa Valley) $32. Straddles a fine line between ripe, plummy-blackberry flavors and a leathery, peppery side. You'll also like the plush, rich tannic structure. Best now. **91** — *S.H. (6/1/2005)*

Signorello 2000 Estate Bottled Unfiltered Syrah (Napa Valley) $32. What an interesting aroma. Veers from ripe blackberry jam to crackling bacon to freshly ground white pepper and back again, all encased in smoky oak. The flavors are very similar. Pretty tannic at the moment, and bone dry, but distinguished. Very fine now with the richest possible meats, and a likely candidate for 3-5 years of cellaring. **92** — *S.H. (6/1/2003)*

Signorello 2004 Luvisi Vineyard Zinfandel (Napa Valley) $36. Big is the word here. Big in volume and mouthfeel, big in flavor. The fruit is a bit cooked, with blackberry pie filling, rum-soaked raisins, and melted milk chocolate splashed with crème de cassis. Finishes with Zin's distinct white pepper. Perfect with grilled pork loin. **91** — *S.H. (11/15/2006)*

Signorello 2002 Luvisi Vineyard Zinfandel (Napa Valley) $34. Oaky and jammy and a little sweet in cherry flavors, this Zin also finishes hot. It lacks overall finesse, especially at this price. **84** — *S.H. (6/1/2005)*

Signorello 2001 Luvisi Vineyard Zinfandel (Napa Valley) $34. Distinctive and elegant, with black currant, black raspberry, tobacco, and peppery spice flavors that are big but kept in control by smooth, sweet tannins. Brings waves of taste sensations as it rolls over the tongue. This wine captures Zin's spirit with grace and finesse. **91** — *S.H. (4/1/2004)*

Signorello 2000 Luvisi Vineyard Zinfandel (Napa Valley) $34. An inky dark, unfiltered wine brimming with strong zinny flavors and bigtime tannins. The flavors are of dark fruits and berries, but are marred by raisiny, pruny notes from dehydrated berries. The finish is tough and tannic. **85** — *S.H. (3/1/2003)*

Signorello 1999 Luvisi Vineyard Zinfandel (Napa Valley) $34. This is one of those young, jammy Zins that makes you lick your lips and take another sip just for the sheer fun of it. It's a great heap of berries in a glass, light and soft, with silky tannins and a peppery finish, with just a trace of sugar. **88** — *S.H. (9/12/2002)*

SILK OAK

Silk Oak 1999 Chardonnay (Lodi) $16. Smells earthy and funky, with aromas of canned mandarin oranges, crushed hard spices, coffee, and roasted wood. Has flavors of peaches, apples, and earth. Kind of rough around the edges and simple, but drinkable. **80** — *S.H. (11/15/2001)*

SILVAN RIDGE

Silvan Ridge 2000 Cabernet Sauvignon (Rogue Valley) $26. Smooth and round from the start, with aromas of plum, cassis, and cola. In the mouth, there's cherry and more cassis, and as a whole it's downright tasty. On the back side, the finish is firm and chocolatey, with good tannins. After tasting many a mediocre Pinot Noir from this Eugene-based winery, this flavorful if one-dimensional Cabernet is a revelation. Only 150 cases produced. **88** — *M.S. (8/1/2003)*

USA

Silvan Ridge 1999 Cabernet Sauvignon (Rogue Valley) $26. The aromas of coffee and tree bark have a hint of red fruit that comes through more on the palate. The mouthfeel is a little thin and short on the finish, making for a simple, easy-to-drink Cab. **84** —C.S. (12/31/2002)

Silvan Ridge 2001 Chardonnay (Oregon) $14. Heavily oaked, with lemon and coconut aromas. The palate is overwhelmed by wood, and that oak buries any fruit one might be able to dig up. Yes, the texture and feel are fine, but 90% of this wine's character is determined by the essence of the barrel, and that isn't an ideal oak-to-fruit ratio in anyone's book. **81** —M.S. (8/1/2003)

Silvan Ridge 1999 Bing Vineyard Ice Wine Gewürztraminer (Umpqua Valley) $20. Complex and honeyed, with apricot, melon, peach, herb, and spice flavors. Silky-smooth and lush on the palate; sleek and refined. Delicious. **92** —J.M. (12/1/2002)

Silvan Ridge 2003 Merlot (Rogue Valley) $19. Soft and oaky, this Rogue Valley Merlot doesn't have any particular varietal character, but here the oak dominates with sweet vanilla and toasted cracker. It's a smooth and drinkable, all-purpose red. **86** —P.G. (9/1/2006)

Silvan Ridge 1999 Merlot (Rogue Valley) $19. Chocolate and spicy cinnamon aromas accent the wild strawberry and dusty earth flavors. The finish is thin but soft, making for an easy-drinking, well-balanced red wine. **85** —C.S. (12/31/2002)

Silvan Ridge 2002 Early Muscat Semi Sparkling Muscat (Oregon) $14. This Beaver State answer to Moscato d'Asti is sweet, sweet, and more sweet. Who knows what the actual residual sugar reading is? That said, the lemon-lime aromas with notes of basil and tarragon are nice, and the wine is currently quite fresh (although it likely won't last long). Not too bubbly or aggressive, and pretty in the mouth due to fairly snappy acids. Drink now with fruit-based desserts or frosted cake. **85** —M.S. (8/1/2003)

Silvan Ridge 2002 Pinot Gris (Oregon) $15. This nicely showcases the fresh-cut Bartlett pear flavors of Oregon Gris. Balanced and lightly spicy, with a wonderful kiss of cinnamon, it's a lovely effort. **88** —P.G. (10/1/2004)

Silvan Ridge 2001 Pinot Gris (Oregon) $14. Fairly light and innocuous; you really have to make an effort to draw anything from the nose. The palate is sweet and sugary, especially for Pinot Gris, which should be more dry and snappy. And that sweetness carries onto the finish and all the way out the back door. Not offensive, but overly sweet and thick given the grape and origin. **83** —M.S. (8/1/2003)

Silvan Ridge 2004 Pinot Noir (Willamette Valley) $19. This clean, light, fruity wine might be taken for an inexpensive, generic Pinot from California. Sweet, simple candy flavors disappear quickly into a dilute middle palate. The notes say 100% French oak, but I could find no trace of it in the finish. **86** —P.G. (9/1/2006)

Silvan Ridge 2003 Pinot Noir (Willamette Valley) $19. This pleasant effort is light and cherry-flavored. It shows little evidence of any barrel flavors despite aging in 100% French oak. The tannins stiffen up and give it a bit of backbone. **87** —P.G. (5/1/2006)

Silvan Ridge 2002 Pinot Noir (Willamette Valley) $19. Showing orange at the rim, this has a bright, cherry/vanilla core of fruit, silky and crisp. Clean, pure, vibrant, and racy. Not a blockbuster, but balanced, with a long, spicy finish. **85** (11/1/2004)

Silvan Ridge 2000 Pinot Noir (Willamette Valley) $23. The bouquet might seem murky at first, but it gains clarity with time. In the mouth, the cranberry and strawberry fruit is lean and tangy, while the finish is smooth and easy. There's plenty of sweet and candied cherry fruit to this wine, so if you like that flavor of Lifesavers candy, by all means dig in. **86** —M.S. (9/1/2003)

Silvan Ridge 1998 Pinot Noir (Willamette Valley) $22. Starts with penetrating, inviting aromas of cherry cola, blackberry, and hard crushed spices, with a lush dose of smoky oak and vanilla. It drinks a bit dense and closed now, with solid tannins and acids hiding the pretty core of cherry fruit. Age through 2004. **87** —S.H. (8/1/2002)

Silvan Ridge 2002 Bradshaw Vineyard Pinot Noir (Willamette Valley) $35. Tree bark, beet, some musty scents. Simple, cherry Kool-Aid, dry. **84** (11/1/2004)

Silvan Ridge 2002 Reserve Pinot Noir (Willamette Valley) $35. Pungent, leafy, with a sharp, volatile edge. Spice, beets, and a green, tannic, stemmy finish. **84** (11/1/2004)

Silvan Ridge 2003 Syrah (Rogue Valley) $20. Most Rogue Valley Syrahs seem to have oppressively dry, heavy tannins, but here the grainy flavors are well-integrated into the mixed red fruits. There is plenty of lightly roasted, coffee bean flavors, and some baker's chocolate lining the finish. Drinks very well right now. **87** —P.G. (9/1/2006)

Silvan Ridge 2001 Del Rio Vineyard Syrah (Rogue Valley) $20. Southern Oregon is working hard on growing Syrah, and this is a promising effort. Thick, hard tannins are characteristic of this vineyard's fruit, which has a tight, concentrated core of cherry liqueur. It's young, hard, and tart, but promising. Give it time. **87** —P.G. (10/1/2004)

Silvan Ridge 2000 Del Rio Vineyard Syrah (Rogue Valley) $26. This burly, saturated Syrah hails from a five-year-old vineyard, and it shows some size and potential. The initial aromas seem straight from the barnyard, but that's not a bad thing in this case. Because below that rusticity there's dark fruit and the essence of sauvage. The palate is round, chewy, and rich, with blackberry fruit and ample spice. And the finish is tannic and full, to say the least. **87** —M.S. (9/1/2003)

Silvan Ridge 2002 Del Rio Vineyards Viognier (Rogue Valley) $18. Southern Oregon fruit, quite ripe and alcoholic, puts a somewhat bitter edge on this difficult grape. Captures the fruit and tannin, but not the floral elegance. **86** —P.G. (12/1/2003)

Silvan Ridge 2001 Del Rio Vineyards Viognier (Rogue Valley) $18. While not smelling much like typical Viognier, this southern Oregon offering is round, sweet, and ripe, with honey and apple flavors. The finish is sweet and honeyed, and also quite short. A chunky, full-bodied mouthfeel is the most typical characteristic of the wine. **82** —M.S. (8/1/2003)

SILVER

Silver 2000 Cabernet Sauvignon (Santa Barbara County) $30. Starts off with toasty cedar and spice aromas. The wine then fans out to show off cassis, blackberry, black cherry, raspberry, coffee, and herb flavors. Tannins are supple, and the finish is moderate in length. **88** —J.M. (12/31/2003)

Silver 2001 Larner Vineyard Mourvèdre (Santa Barbara County) $20. An inky wine that sports a core of black cherry, cassis, blackberry, spice, herbs, tar, and licorice flavors. Tannins are quite firm yet supple enough. A well-made wine from an unusual variety that should age quite nicely. **90 Editors' Choice** —J.M. (6/1/2004)

Silver 2000 Nebbiolo (Santa Barbara County) $22. Pretty and elegant. Winemaker Benjamin Silver has tamed Nebbiolo's notoriously bright acidity and coarse tannins in the smooth-textured wine. It's redolent of cherry, plum, spice, earth, cedar, and toast flavors, finishing with moderate length and a tangy edge. **88** —J.M. (12/1/2003)

Silver 2000 Julia's Vineyard Pinot Noir (Santa Barbara County) $45. This is a full-bodied Pinot, packed with ripe cherry and strawberry flavors and framed in spicy nuance. A shade hot on the finish, ending with an unusually bright licorice and herbal edge. **87** —J.M. (7/1/2003)

Silver 2001 Lake Marie Vineyard Pinot Noir (Santa Barbara County) $40. A smooth, complex wine brimming with pretty cherry, anise, spice, and herb flavors. A hint of sage and thyme adds finesses to the finish, which is long. Well balanced and fine-crafted. **90** —J.M. (12/31/2004)

Silver 2001 Larner Vineyard Syrah-Mourvèdre Red Blend (Santa Barbara County) $22. Full bodied and richly textured, the wine serves up cassis, blackberry, toast, herb, and licorice flavors. Tannins are fairly ripe, highlighted by bright acidity. Finishes with a hint of bitterness. **89** —J.M. (6/1/2004)

Silver 2002 Syrah & Mourvèdre Rhône Red Blend (Santa Barbara County) $22. Feels heavy, soft, and simple in the mouth, but there's some rich cocoa-infused blackberry fruit. Okay for everyday fare. **84** —S.H. (11/15/2006)

Silver 2000 Sangiovese (Santa Barbara County) $28. Quite bold and fruity, it's more like a Zinfandel. But so what? The wine is delicious, with ripe cherry and plum flavors backed by pretty chocolate and spice notes.

Finishes long, with a subtle vanilla touch. From young Central Coast winemaker Benjamin Silver. **89** —*J.M. (2/1/2003)*

Silver 2003 Vogelzang Vineyard Viognier (Santa Barbara County) $22. What a disappointment, as previous vintages have been better. Starts off a little tanky, and airing doesn't help it. There's some simple fruit in the taste. **83** —*S.H. (11/15/2006)*

Silver 2002 Vogelzang Vineyard Viognier (Santa Barbara County) $22. Smooth and nutty up front, with good acidity holding it together. The wine also shows pretty hints of peach, almond, pear, and apple, and finishes with a touch of spice. **88** —*J.M. (9/1/2004)*

Silver 2001 Vogelzang Vineyard Viognier (Santa Barbara County) $22. Pretty peach, apricot, melon, and spice notes frame a core of refreshing, lemon-like acidity. The finish shows a hint of vanilla and more spice. This wine is fun, fresh, and lively to the end. **89** —*J.M. (6/1/2003)*

SILVER LAKE

Silver Lake 1998 Cabernet Sauvignon (Columbia Valley (WA)) $14. Coffee, mocha, and barbecue-smoke aromas smolder on the nose, and continue on the medium-bodied palate. Tannins are chalky and smooth, but largely obscure the black cherry fruit. Finishes with oak, tobacco, tannin, and a burst of sweet black cherries. Very good, but I'm not convinced that aging it any is going to resolve the chalky, powdery tannins. **87 Best Buy** —*D.T. (12/31/2002)*

Silver Lake 1998 Reserve Cabernet Sauvignon (Columbia Valley (WA)) $25. Root beer and snow pea aromas—no, that was not a typo. The bing-cherry flavors finish with gritty tannins that will need 2–5 years to integrate. **84** —*C.S. (12/31/2002)*

Silver Lake 1999 Cabernet Sauvignon-Merlot (Columbia Valley (WA)) $7. The nose mixes (or tries to mix) disparate scents of herb, bell pepper, and sweet, toasted cracker. The wine has an artificial, manipulated flavor-set, with jarring juxtapositions and a flat finish. **82** —*P.G. (6/1/2002)*

Silver Lake 2000 Chardonnay (Columbia Valley (WA)) $12. The high-pitched, fairly sharp nose isn't oaky, but it's not terribly fruity either. Some citrus and melon flavors work well on the properly textured palate, while the finish is dry and a touch bitter. Starts well but fades quickly. **85** —*M.S. (6/1/2003)*

Silver Lake 1999 Chardonnay (Columbia Valley (WA)) $7. Tart and lemony, without anything to elevate it above the crowd. Some slight butterfat flavors hint at malolactic fermentation, but it falls flat in the finish. **84** —*P.G. (7/1/2002)*

Silver Lake 2000 Reserve Chardonnay (Columbia Valley (WA)) $14. This fairly plump yet sturdy Chard delivers creamy oak aromatics supported by notes of perfume and beeswax. The palate is ample, with clean flavors of pear, lemon, and apricot. Lastly, a buttery but welcome taste appears on the long finish. With more expressive fruit, this could be a star. Even as is it's quite good. **88** —*M.S. (6/1/2003)*

Silver Lake 1998 Reserve Chardonnay (Columbia Valley (WA)) $13. There is modest fruit and creaminess in the mouth that suggests extra time on the lees. It finishes a trifle hot; doesn't really live up to the reserve designation. **85** —*P.G. (7/1/2002)*

Silver Lake 2001 Fumé Blanc (Columbia Valley (WA)) $9. A sharp white with thistle-like aromas as well as notes of white pepper and tarragon. The mouthfeel and weight are good, but the flavor profile struggles. It's dry and forceful, but there isn't much fruit or charm. A bland finish doesn't elevate the wine. **84** —*M.S. (6/1/2003)*

Silver Lake 1998 Merlot (Columbia Valley (WA)) $14. This is competent, simple, and straightforward, with light cherry fruit and enough heft to keep it balanced. **86** —*P.G. (6/1/2002)*

Silver Lake 1999 Reserve Merlot (Columbia Valley (WA)) $25. Dark berry aromas are touched with cedar, char, and a pleasant animal quality. White chocolate and blackberry flavors roll into a juicy, lingering finish. **89** —*C.S. (12/31/2002)*

Silver Lake 2001 Roza Hills Vineyard Late Harvest Riesling (Columbia Valley (WA)) $8. Here's a tasty, semisweet, single-vineyard Riesling that does a good job of emulating the German style. The nose features ripe green melon, white pepper, and petrol, while the palate turns fruity and racy, much like lemon-lime soda with a twist. The finish is light, zippy,

and rewardingly sweet. This wine has a good pulse, although you still wouldn't call it electric. **88** —*M.S. (12/1/2003)*

SILVER MOUNTAIN

Silver Mountain 1997 Chardonnay (Santa Cruz Mountains) $18. **85** *(6/1/2000)*

Silver Mountain 2001 Estate Chardonnay (Santa Cruz Mountains) $20. Made from organic grapes, this Chard has tremendously forward fruit flavors, ranging from ripe white peaches to tropical mangoes and guava. It's also well-oaked and juicy in acids. It's a powerhouse that, despite its age, tastes fresh and lively. **88** —*S.H. (3/1/2006)*

Silver Mountain 2002 Pinot Noir (Monterey) $28. This is a very dry, high-acid Pinot that comes across as a bit lean and angular right now, with coffee and cola flavors that just hint at cherries. But the fruit is there. Give it a year or two to settle down and express its complexity. **88** —*S.H. (3/1/2006)*

SILVER PINES

Silver Pines 2004 Sauvignon Blanc (Sonoma Mountain) $32. Out of the ordinary, with intense aromas of petrol, smoke, roasted corn, and musky citrus. In many ways it does not seem Californian in that it isn't a pure, polished wine. Instead, it offers herbal notes, cured-meat flavors, and funky spice. Finishes a touch stark and acidic. **88** *(7/1/2005)*

Silver Pines 2003 Sauvignon Blanc (Sonoma Mountain) $35. An extraordinary Sauvignon Blanc, and so clean. If you like your Marlboroughs, you'll love the dry gooseberry, hay, and lime zest flavors, with their edges of white pepper and smoke. Possesses real complexity in the penetratingly crisp acids and long finish. **90** —*S.H. (12/31/2004)*

SILVER RIDGE

Silver Ridge 1999 Barrel Select Cabernet Sauvignon (California) $10. Dark and fruity, with blackberry and sage flavors edged with rustic tannins. Very dry, with some richness in the finish. **84** —*S.H. (11/15/2002)*

Silver Ridge 2003 Chardonnay (California) $10. Lots of peach, pear, and pineapple fruit here, with a tasty layer of vanilla and smoke. A good value. **84** —*S.H. (8/1/2005)*

Silver Ridge 2003 Merlot (California) $10. It's easy to imagine enjoying this easy wine over a burger or ribs grilled in the backyard. It's soft, dry, and fruit-filled, with tasty blackberry, cherry, mocha, and peppery-spice flavors. Very nice, rich, and affordable. **85 Best Buy** —*S.H. (12/1/2005)*

Silver Ridge 1999 Barrel Select Syrah (California) $10. The creamy, soft mouthfeel has instant appeal in this well-oaked wine. Cocoa and a slight mint note provide interest, accenting the ultraripe, almost raisiny fruit. Not complex, but pleasing, with full oak showing on the back end. **86** *(10/1/2001)*

SILVER RIDGE VINEYARDS

Silver Ridge Vineyards 2003 Barrel Select Syrah (California) $10. Sweet Tart and leather aromas and flavors segue to pruney, stably flavors. Medium-weight, it closes with tart cranberry and spice flavors. **84** *(9/1/2005)*

Silver Ridge Vineyards 2000 Barrel Select Syrah (California) $10. The aroma is suggestive of plums, blackberries, and white pepper, and a nice overlay of oak. Tastes rich, too, although the tannins are like a stick in the eye. **86 Best Buy** —*S.H. (10/1/2003)*

Silver Ridge Vineyards 2000 Barrel Select Viognier (California) $10. Sweet, syrupy, and simple, like the fluid in canned fruit salad. Flavors range from pineapple juice to peaches and apples, finishes sugary. **83** —*S.H. (12/1/2003)*

SILVER ROSE CELLARS

Silver Rose Cellars 1999 Chardonnay (Napa Valley) $23. A light texture, pleasant Chardonnay that serves up pretty pear, apple, and citrus flavors. Clean on the finish. **86** —*J.M. (12/31/2001)*

Silver Rose Cellars 1999 D'argent Chardonnay (Napa Valley) $30. Tangy, lemony notes annouce a creamy textured wine that serves up plenty of pear, citrus, apple, and vanilla flavors. The finish is smooth yet bright. **88** —*J.M. (12/31/2001)*

USA

USA

SILVER SPUR

Silver Spur 2003 Sangiacomo Vineyards Chardonnay (Carneros) $18. Properly varietal, with peach, pear, and spice flavors and a woody, creamy texture, but can't quite rise above average. **83** —*S.H. (10/1/2005)*

Silver Spur 2002 Casa Carneros Vineyards Pinot Noir (Carneros) $22. This is an easy Pinot Noir, elegantly silky, with pretty flavors of red cherries, cola, and peppery spices. It has a light body, firm acids, and is very dry and balanced. **88** —*S.H. (10/1/2005)*

SILVER STONE WINERY

Silver Stone Winery 2001 Cabernet Sauvignon (California) $9. You'll get real Cab character in this wine, with its black currant and oak flavors. It's dry and balanced and has some real richness. **85 Best Buy** —*S.H. (10/1/2004)*

Silver Stone Winery 2000 Cabernet Sauvignon (California) $9. Mellow and easy in the mouth, with soft tannins and gentle acids. The flavors range from blackberries to espresso, with a cough mediciney edge. Fine for everyday occasions. **84** —*S.H. (5/1/2004)*

Silver Stone Winery 2003 Chardonnay (California) $9. A pretty good everyday Chard, with peach and oak flavors and a creamy texture. Finishes a little syrupy. **83** —*S.H. (10/1/2005)*

Silver Stone Winery 2000 Chardonnay (California) $9. Starts off with an interesting bouquet of honey, tapioca, peach, tropical fruit, and vanilla, but it's disappointingly thin and hollow in the mouth. Leaves behind a faint fruitiness and lots of acidity. **84** —*S.H. (2/1/2004)*

Silver Stone Winery 2003 Bien Nacido Vineyard Chardonnay (Santa Maria Valley) $25. A decent Chardonnay with some interest, although it's a little thin on the finish. Smells of toasty oak, vanilla, butterscotch, and tangerines, and while that sounds good, the intensity isn't so great. **85** —*S.H. (10/1/2005)*

Silver Stone Winery 2001 Merlot (California) $9. Simple and a bit raw, with syrupy flavors of blackberries and cherries. **82** —*S.H. (2/1/2005)*

Silver Stone Winery 1999 Merlot (California) $9. The fruity flavors are beginning to dry out, yet there's still some cherry-berry stuff going on. Tannins turn tough and gritty on the finish. **83** —*S.H. (5/1/2004)*

Silver Stone Winery 2004 Sauvignon Blanc (Arroyo Seco) $15. An okay wine for everyday fare, with slightly sweet citrus flavors and a big burst of acidity. Tastes like it has a little wild honey in it. **83** —*S.H. (10/1/2005)*

Silver Stone Winery 2001 Shiraz (California) $9. A bit sharp in youthful acidity, but the jammy berry and cherry flavors are tasty, and the wine is serviceable. **83** —*S.H. (6/1/2004)*

Silver Stone Winery 2003 Syrah (Paso Robles) $33. Dry and cedary, not your typical Paso Syrah in some ways, but it does have enough jammy cherry fruit to give some sense of place and enjoyment. **83** *(9/1/2005)*

Silver Stone Winery 2002 Hall Ranch Syrah (Paso Robles) $33. Table wines hardly get bigger in fruit than this soft, luscious wine. It's explosive in red cherry, chocolate fudge, pecan pie, and spice flavors, but seems totally dry. It would have scored higher had one taster not been bothered by some nail polish and vinegar notes. **85** *(9/1/2005)*

SILVER THREAD

Silver Thread 1999 Chardonnay (Finger Lakes) $12. 85 —*J.C. (1/1/2004)*

Silver Thread 1999 Reserve Chardonnay (Finger Lakes) $17. A breakthrough Chardonnay from upstate New York. Aromas of toasted nuts and buttered spiced pears are classic, with flavors of cinnamon, pears, and cashews that feel custardy in the mouth. Finishes long, with tangy acids and nutty overtones. **90 Editors' Choice** —*J.C. (1/1/2004)*

Silver Thread 1999 Pinot Noir (Finger Lakes) $15. Sure, it's a light hue of red, but one whiff tells you it's not going to lack for flavor. Strawberries and tart cherries mingle with scents of wet bracken, and a sweet spicy sensation lingers on the finish. Light in body but pretty, with a sense of elegance and harmony. Drink now. **86** —*J.C. (1/1/2004)*

Silver Thread 2002 Riesling (Finger Lakes) $13. Although the aromas are sweet, oozing with pear nectar, stone fruit, dried spices, and apple blossoms, this wine features only 1.5% residual sugar. It's fairly big for a Finger Lakes Riesling, with a slightly oily texture, and comes across as being close to dry thanks to firm acids on the finish. The only problem with this wine is its limited availability. **90 Best Buy** —*J.C. (8/1/2003)*

SILVERADO

Silverado 2003 Cabernet Sauvignon (Napa Valley) $40. Beautiful Cabernet. Has all the big, ripe juicy fruit and lavish oak of most Napa Cabs, plus elegance and harmonious balance, the hallmarks of tasteful, knowledgeable winemaking. Gets better and more interesting as it warms in the glass. Hard to believe it's this good with the high case production. **94 Editors' Choice** —*S.H. (12/15/2006)*

Silverado 2002 Cabernet Sauvignon (Napa Valley) $40. With a little Merlot and Cabernet Franc, this wine is softer and more immediately approachable than Silverado's other current Cabs, although like them, it's fairly tannic. Rich in currant and cassis fruit, it's an elegant powerhouse. **91** —*S.H. (3/1/2006)*

Silverado 2001 Cabernet Sauvignon (Napa Valley) $40. A well behaved Cab that displays forward fruit and softly smooth, gentle tannins, as well as polished oak. The flavors of currants and cassis impress on the finish. **87** —*S.H. (12/31/2004)*

Silverado 2000 Cabernet Sauvignon (Napa Valley) $35. This is a wine of pedigree. It shows in the exquisite acids and tannins and overall balance of its parts, including oak. The flavors are classic black currants and cassis, with a nice edge of dried herbs. Not a blockbuster, it's probably at its best now. **90** —*S.H. (5/1/2004)*

Silverado 1999 Cabernet Sauvignon (Napa Valley) $35. A bright-edged wine with an herbal kick that's followed by blackberry, cassis, and licorice notes. Tannins are firm yet soft. **88** —*J.M. (11/15/2002)*

Silverado 1999 Cabernet Sauvignon (Stags Leap District) $65. No way you can drink just one glass of this magnificent, rich, even decadent wine. It can't be beat for the sheer sumptuousness of its rich cassis flavors and soft intricate tannins. Absolutely delicious now in its youth, yet complex and ageworthy. **95 Editors' Choice** —*S.H. (11/15/2002)*

Silverado 1998 Cabernet Sauvignon (Stags Leap District) $65. Bright cherry, spice, and herb notes lead the way here in this medium bodied wine. An herbal edge frames the finish. **87** —*J.M. (5/1/2002)*

Silverado 2002 Limited Cabernet Sauvignon (Napa Valley) $100. With a preponderance of Stags Leap fruit, this 100% Cabernet is aggressive in tannins. It's not at all ready to drink now, so astringent and dusty is it. But the core is rich in black currant and cherry fruit, and the wine should develop, despite being low in acidity. Best after 2009. **91 Cellar Selection** —*S.H. (3/1/2006)*

Silverado 2001 Limited Reserve Cabernet Sauvignon (Napa Valley) $100. Another fabulous Cab from this supernatural vintage. It stuns for the ripeness of the black currant, cherry, and chocolate fruit, and the richness of the soft, sweet tannins. So easy to drink, yet never loses its sense of balance, harmony, and complexity. **94** —*S.H. (12/31/2004)*

Silverado 1999 Limited Reserve Cabernet Sauvignon (Napa Valley) $95. Well structured, firm, focused, and made in a lean style. Still, the wine is filled with rich, ripe blackberry, cassis, plum, chocolate, and complex herb notes. Tannins are silky and smooth. **91** —*S.H. (11/15/2002)*

Silverado 2000 Single-Vineyard Selection Cabernet Sauvignon (Stags Leap District) $65. A very fine wine that is soft and voluptuous in the mouth. Its power is in the deep core of blackberry fruit and the tightly wound tannins. Not a long-term ager, but should gain complexity through 2008. **90** —*S.H. (11/15/2004)*

Silverado 2002 Solo Cabernet Sauvignon (Stags Leap District) $75. Oh, what a perfect expression of Stags Leap this is. The 100% Cab does have a soft voluptuousness, but it's also strong in tannins, and packed with black currant and cherry flavors. Absolutely delicious now, and should hold and improve through 2015 at least. **93 Cellar Selection** —*S.H. (3/1/2006)*

Silverado 1998 Chardonnay (Napa Valley) $19. 83 *(6/1/2000)*

Silverado 1997 Chardonnay (Napa Valley) $21. 90 —*S.H. (11/15/1999)*

Silverado 2002 Chardonnay (Napa Valley) $20. On the lean, small side, almost tart, with citrusy flavors and robust acids. Try with shellfish, cracked crab. **84** —*S.H. (11/15/2004)*

Silverado 2001 Chardonnay (Napa Valley) $20. Kind of tart and lean, with citrus flavors just nudging into green apples. Oak adds considerable richness and viscosity, and most of the barrels underwent malolactic fermentation, but it's still an angular Chardonnay. The finish is lemony. **87** —*S.H. (6/1/2003)*

Silverado 2000 Chardonnay (Napa Valley) $20. Not-too-ripe fruit is blended with modest oak and a scattering of lees to make a Chablis-style wine of high quality. It's lean by contrast with today's hugely ripe Chards, with flavors of peaches and green apples. But the winemaker additions add richness to this sleek, stylish wine. **91** —*S.H. (12/15/2002)*

Silverado 1999 Chardonnay (Napa Valley) $20. A pretty blend of apple, pear, citrus and herb flavors. Medium-bodied and moderate on the finish. **86** —*J.M. (5/1/2002)*

Silverado 1997 Limited Reserve Chardonnay (Napa Valley) $40. **91** —*S.H. (11/15/1999)*

Silverado 2004 Vineburg Vineyard Chardonnay (Carneros) $35. This sure is an oaky Chard, but it's big enough to handle it. The fruit is extraordinarily ripe and forward, bursting with mango, pear, and sautéed banana flavors. What the wine lacks in subtlety it makes up for in sheer, unadulterated power. **90** —*S.H. (4/1/2006)*

Silverado 2002 Merlot (Napa Valley) $28. Despite a classic Napa structure of fine, smoothly complex tannins and proper acidity, this wine seems to have too much sugar to qualify as dry. The sweetness makes it cloying. **83** —*S.H. (3/1/2006)*

Silverado 2000 Merlot (Napa Valley) $25. Soft and supple in the mouth, with ripe blackberries and spiced plums joined by smoky oak. Firms up on the finish, showing some rough edges, but still an excellent effort from a challenging vintage. **90** *(5/1/2004)*

Silverado 1999 Merlot (Napa Valley) $25. Good, rich, and earthy, a dark, full-bodied wine with olive, earth, tobacco, and plum flavors and dense but accessible tannins. Strikes a balanced note, not a hedonistic blockbuster, but elegantly drinkable tonight. Might soften and improve with a few years in the cellar. **89** —*S.H. (8/1/2003)*

Silverado 1997 Sangiovese (Napa Valley) $20. **88** —*S.H. (12/15/1999)*

Silverado 2000 Sangiovese (Napa Valley) $16. Silverado's done a credible job with Sangiovese for some time now, and this wine continues the tradition. It's light in body, with good natural acidity. The flavors are of cherries and herbs, and gritty tannins hit after you swallow. This is a good food wine. **87** —*S.H. (11/15/2004)*

Silverado 1998 Sangiovese (Napa Valley) $18. Delightful to drink, with its ripe berry flavors, dry light tannins, and soft acidity. There's a sleekness and delicacy that will match all kinds of foods. It's not a big wine or terribly complicated, but it's very drinkable, an all-purpose wine. An American Chianti that won't let you down. **88** —*S.H. (5/1/2002)*

Silverado 1998 Sauvignon Blanc (Napa Valley) $15. **89** —*S.H. (2/1/2000)*

Silverado 2002 Sauvignon Blanc (Napa Valley) $16. My bottle had a stubborn sulfury smell that was slow to blow off, but that may resolve itself with a few more months. In the mouth, it's just fine, with very dry lemongrass, citrus, and mineral flavors and a crisp finish. **85** —*S.H. (12/1/2004)*

Silverado 2002 Sauvignon Blanc (Napa Valley) $16. Quite lovely in the nose, with a vivid passionfruit quality. On the palate, it's fairly lean, though refreshing, with a core of lemon and grapefruit, finishing with a grassy edge. Perfect for shellfish. **88** —*J.M. (9/1/2004)*

Silverado 2001 Sauvignon Blanc (Napa Valley) $14. Comes down firmly on the grassy, lemony side, although these flavors are softened by partial barrel fermentation. The tart acidity has been tempered by partial malolactic fermentation. Still, it's a hard, clean wine with a brisk, citrusy finish. **86** —*S.H. (3/1/2003)*

Silverado 2000 Sauvignon Blanc (Napa Valley) $14. A delicate style, with silky texture, good acidity, and a subtle blend of melon, fig, and grassy notes that are well integrated and pleasing. The finish is clean and fresh, with a bracing mineral-and-citrus edge. **90 Best Buy** —*J.M. (9/1/2002)*

SILVERSMITH

Silversmith 2000 Petite Sirah (Redwood Valley) $30. A difficult wine. The aroma is okay, with lots of ripe cherry, mint, and leather scents, but it turns supertart in the mouth, and stings with unbalanced acidity. **80** *(4/1/2003)*

Silversmith 1998 Zinfandel (Redwood Valley) $25. A rustic, country-style Zin with good structure. Has simple, fruity-berry flavors of cherry cola and red raspberry jam and durable tannins, but is overly sweet—almost sugary—especially in the finish. **84** —*S.H. (5/1/2002)*

SIMI

Simi 2002 Cabernet Sauvignon (Alexander Valley) $25. Tough and raw in texture, with dried herb and coffee flavors. **83** —*S.H. (3/1/2005)*

Simi 1996 Cabernet Sauvignon (Sonoma County) $24. **86** —*L.W. (12/31/1999)*

Simi 1996 Cabernet Sauvignon (Sonoma County) $22. **90** —*S.H. (2/1/2000)*

Simi 2003 Landslide Vineyard Cabernet Sauvignon (Alexander Valley) $33. With its Landslide bottling, Simi brings to the table an important, affordable single-vineyard Cabernet. It typically shows a beautiful balance of sweet, ripe fruit and firm tannins, backed by crisp acidity, and is big enough to handle considerable oak. Young and juicy, it's delicious now, and should develop through 2012. **92 Editors' Choice** —*S.H. (12/15/2006)*

Simi 2001 Landslide Vineyard Cabernet Sauvignon (Alexander Valley) $33. This fabulously complex wine shows how you can merge power and nuance with the most complex and satisfying results. Cherries, dried herbs, vanilla, and toasty oak, with ripe, lush tannins and great balance. Shows an exciting finesse throughout. Hard to exaggerate the quality. A perfect companion at the table. **95** —*S.H. (12/15/2004)*

Simi 2000 Landslide Vineyard Cabernet Sauvignon (Alexander Valley) $40. Dense and tannic, with lots of black currant and cherry flavors and elaborate oak. Acids and tannins help it to achieve a certain complexity. Notable for its smooth structure. It's best consumed soon, with a good steak. **90** —*S.H. (4/1/2004)*

Simi 2001 Reserve Cabernet Sauvignon (Alexander Valley) $60. The softness and herbaceousness, and the light structure, define this as Alexander Valley, albeit a very fine specimen. With a little Cab Franc, the wine defines a feminine elegance, with cherry, herb and oak flavors. Beautiful and complex now, this wine should gain complexity over the next five years. **91** —*S.H. (12/1/2005)*

Simi 1999 Reserve Cabernet Sauvignon (Alexander Valley) $75. This classic Alexander Valley wine is soft and gentle throughout, and in this great vintage it packs so much compelling flavor that it merits the high score. The black currant and cassis fruit is huge and sweetly delicious, easily able to handle tons of new oak. Yet the tannins add a textural dimension. There's a charm and elegance to the wine that belies its considerable complexity and ageability. **94 Cellar Selection** —*S.H. (12/31/2003)*

Simi 1998 Reserve Cabernet Sauvignon (Alexander Valley) $70. Just terrific, a gorgeous mouthful of wine that tastes so good, you don't want to swallow. Defines a feminine approach to Cabernet, filled with elaborate fruit, designer oak and a velvety texture that's beguiling. Fabulous concentration, a little soft, but that's splitting hairs. **93** —*S.H. (11/15/2002)*

Simi 1995 Reserve Cabernet Sauvignon (Sonoma County) $45. **93** —*L.W. (12/31/1999)*

Simi 2005 Chardonnay (Sonoma County) $17. A junior version of the very fine Reserve, the '05 is ripe and forward in tropical fruit and flowery spice flavors, with an overlay of smoky, creamy oak. It's explosive, but balanced and controlled. **86** —*S.H. (12/15/2006)*

Simi 2003 Chardonnay (Sonoma County) $17. Fruity, oaky, creamy, and slightly sweet, this Chard is solidly in the international style. It offers flavors of peaches, pears, vanilla, and buttered toast. **85** —*S.H. (3/1/2005)*

Simi 2000 Chardonnay (Sonoma County) $17. Starts off with a somewhat yeasty aroma that later reveals lemon, pear, and grapefruit on the palate. Squeaky clean on the finish. **83** —*J.M. (5/1/2002)*

Simi 1999 Chardonnay (Sonoma County) $21. Pear and citrus aromas lead the way in this bright, lemony wine. It has good weight on the palate, hints of melon and spice, and finishes clean with a hint of flintiness. **88** —*J.M. (12/1/2001)*

Simi 1998 Chardonnay (Sonoma County) $17. 87 *(6/1/2000)*

Simi 1997 Chardonnay (Sonoma County) $19. 89 —*S.H. (10/1/1999)*

Simi 1998 Goldfields Vineyard Reserve Chardonnay (Russian River Valley) $30. Full and focused, the nose of orange, crème brûlée, and vanilla opens to a handsomely balanced palate of lively citrus, Granny Smith apple and vanilla cream flavors. Moderately plump and pleasing, good underlying acidity here keeps it elegant and maintains fine flavor definition. Butterscotch, lemon, and spicy oak flavors mingle on the long finish. Top Value. **92 Editors' Choice** *(7/1/2001)*

Simi 1999 Goldfields Vineyard Reserve Chardonnay (Russian River Valley) $30. Brims with pronounced peach, oak, and lees notes. Big, full-bodied, and rich, it's marked by scads of new smoky oak and opulently ripe fruit. A shade obvious in all its respects, it could use more subtlety and finesse. **87** —*S.H. (2/1/2003)*

Simi 2004 Reserve Chardonnay (Russian River Valley) $25. Achieves the alchemy of well-toasted oak and perfectly ripe fruit to produce this luscious, creamy Chardonnay. Mangoes, papayas, pineapple custard, caramel, vanilla, it's all there, along with crisp, balancing acidity. **90** —*S.H. (12/15/2006)*

Simi 2003 Reserve Chardonnay (Russian River Valley) $25. Like most Chards these days, this wine is boldly flavored, oaky, and rich. But it goes beyond the tropical fruits, vanilla, and buttercream to achieve real finesse and elegance. The crisp acidity helps make it balanced. **90** —*S.H. (12/1/2005)*

Simi 2002 Reserve Chardonnay (Russian River Valley) $25. Textbook RRV Chard, with its bright, clean acids and savory flavors of ripe apples, pears, and minerals, and dusty spices. All of this is well oaked, but the vanilla and char fit in just fine. The creamy texture adds allure. **90** —*S.H. (3/1/2005)*

Simi 1998 Reserve Chardonnay (Russian River Valley) $35. A flinty wine, with toasty oak nuances. Bright acidity supports a core of citrus and pear flavors that finish quite clean. **88** —*J.M. (12/1/2001)*

Simi 1996 Reserve Chardonnay (Russian River Valley) $29. 89 —*S.H. (10/1/1999)*

Simi 2002 Sonoma County Chardonnay (Sonoma County) $17. There's lot of oak on top of a somewhat thin wine, but it's pleasant enough, with modest pineapple and peach flavors and dusty spices. Finishes quick, with oak flavors. **85** —*S.H. (9/1/2004)*

Simi 2002 Merlot (Sonoma County) $20. A middle of the road Merlot, dry and fairly tannic, with berry and earth flavors. **83** —*S.H. (3/1/2005)*

Simi 2001 Merlot (Alexander Valley) $20. From a venerable producer, a fine Merlot. It's soft and gentle in tannins and acids, but that doesn't detract from complex interest. The flavors veer toward black cherries, with a chocolatey edge. Perfect with a T-bone steak. **90** —*S.H. (4/1/2004)*

Simi 2005 Sauvignon Blanc (Sonoma County) $14. Crisp and grassy-citrusy, with fig and melon overtones and a touch of wildflower honey in the finish, this is textbook Sauvignon Blanc. It has a streamlined elegance that makes it easy to drink, and will be versatile with an enormous range of foods. **85** —*S.H. (12/15/2006)*

Simi 2003 Sauvignon Blanc (Sonoma County) $14. Pleasant and clean, a zesty wine of bright acidity boosting slightly sweet flavors of peaches, figs, spices, and smoky oak. This is a pretty, cocktail-style wine. **85** —*S.H. (12/15/2004)*

Simi 2002 Sauvignon Blanc (Sonoma County) $14. A solid effort, on the grassy side but with richer flavors of spearmint, melon, and white peach. The firm streak of zesty acidity is very cleansing, and the finish turns spicy and ripe. **84** —*S.H. (12/15/2003)*

Simi 2001 Sauvignon Blanc (Sonoma County) $14. Nice, stylish white wine, with plenty of well-ripened citrus and melon fruit, and a rich overlay of toasty oak. Zesty acidity refreshes the palate. Finishes a bit sweet, with a palate-coating honeyed flavor. **86** —*S.H. (3/1/2003)*

Simi 2000 Sauvignon Blanc (Sonoma County) $14. Lemony fresh on the nose. Then it fans out to reveal hints of gooseberry, melon, grapefruit, and mineral tones. Quite delicate and lovely. **88** —*J.M. (12/15/2001)*

Simi 1999 Sauvignon Blanc (Sonoma County) $15. Hints of lemon lime and gooseberries permeate this medium-bodied, refreshing wine. It's clean and crisp on the finish, closing with a citrus-like edge. **87** —*J.M. (11/15/2001)*

Simi 1997 Sauvignon Blanc (Sonoma County) $13. 84 —*S.H. (9/1/1999)*

Simi 1999 Reserve Sendal Sauvignon Blanc (Sonoma County) $20. A blend of 78% Sauvignon Blanc and 22% Sémillon that really defines the white Meritage approach. Sauvignon's lemony, herbal personality meshes perfectly with Sémillon's fig flavors and fatness. New oak—and what seems like lees contact—provide sweetness, vanilla, and a lush, creamy mouthfeel. **91** —*S.H. (9/1/2002)*

Simi 1998 Sendal Sauvignon Blanc (Sonoma County) $20. Full-bodied yet sleek and elegant, this high-end Sauvignon Blanc serves up loads of bright lemon and grapefruit flavors that are balanced by broader melon and fig notes. A mineral component adds complexity, while the finish is long and rich. **90** —*J.M. (11/15/2001)*

Simi 1996 Sendal Sauvignon Blanc (Sonoma County) $20. 89 —*S.H. (9/1/1999)*

Simi 1999 Shiraz (Sonoma County) $20. So many different flavors and aromas surface in the Simi that it's like a day at the market. The bouquet shows appealing raspberry sorbet, root-beer, popcorn, and cigar-box notes. The mouth bursts with rich caramel, semi-sweet chocolate, paprika, and deep black fruit flavors. Well-balanced and nicely integrated, it finishes with pepper-herb-mineral notes and medium tannins. **89** *(10/1/2001)*

Simi 1999 Reserve-Sendal White Blend (Sonoma County) $20. 91 Editors' Choice —*S.H. (9/1/2002)*

Simi 1999 Zinfandel (Dry Creek Valley) $22. Medium-bodied, and not overly brooding or alcoholic, the Simi is oakier and less jammy than what you'd expect of its Dry Creek neighbors. On the palate, earth, oak, and black fruit flavors are dusted with a little chalk. Opens with oak, blueberry, and wheat flour aromas; stewy red-berry and a peppery zing draw this Zin to a close. If you tasted it blind, you might even have guessed that it's a Syrah. **87** —*D.T. (3/1/2002)*

SINE QUA NON

Sine Qua Non 2002 Whisperin' E Rhône White Blend (California) $72. This is a very fine dry white wine. It's intense in ripe fruit, but is hardly a bomb, the flavors reined in by superb acids, judicious oak, and a minerality and earthiness that ground the power. A blend of Roussanne, Viognier, and Chardonnay. **93** —*S.H. (6/1/2005)*

Sine Qua Non 1998 Alban Vineyard Syrah (Central Coast) $NA. Still tastes young and jammy, with cassis, blackberry, and cocoa flavors wrapped in rich, thick tannins, and very dry. It's a pleasant wine without being spectacular, and I suspect it's at its best now. **87** —*S.H. (6/1/2005)*

Sine Qua Non 1998 E-Raised Syrah (California) $75. Starts off closed, showing little but hints of smoke and toast. Like so many great wines, it gets better the longer it sits in the glass, developing deep blackberry scents and herbal, Rhône-like notes. The lush, juicy blackberries on the palate would be simple on their own, but they're accompanied by smoked meat, toast, vanilla, and Provençal herbs. Rich and full-bodied without being overblown, it's understated yet packs subtle flavor nuances into every corner. **93 Editors' Choice** *(11/1/2001)*

Sine Qua Non 1997 Impostor McCoy Syrah (California) $59. 94 *(6/1/2003)*

Sine Qua Non 1999 The Marauder Syrah (California) $75. Though, at present, it isn't quite as powerful as past vintages, the winery's newest Syrah still shows some classic SQN hallmarks, such as malted milk and powdered-cocoa aromas and flavors, a smooth mouthfeel, and dusty tannins. Smoke, ash, and bacon fat notes appear on both the nose and the palate, as does a hint of green herb. Is, as always, an ode to ripe, juicy blackberries. **91** *(7/1/2002)*

SINEANN

Sineann 2004 Champoux Vineyard Cabernet Franc (Columbia Valley (WA)) $42. From a new block of vines, this effusive, dense, and concentrated wine really puts on a show. Rich, ripe, luscious cherry fruit explodes from the glass, deepening into black cherry liqueur and extending into a long, lush finish. **93 Editors' Choice** —P.G. (4/1/2006)

Sineann 2004 Cabernet Sauvignon (Columbia Valley (WA)) $30. Seductive and pungent with a wide array of Asian spices, incense, and fresh earth. There are gentle reminders of umami—soy and balsamic, salt and mushroom—and the fruits are ripe and very slightly cooked. Raisin, spice cake, plum pudding—this is a baker's dream! **92** —P.G. (12/31/2006)

Sineann 2004 Baby Poux Cabernet Sauvignon (Columbia Valley (WA)) $42. Another fine effort, firm and full-bodied, with a mix of cherry, red currant, and berries. Wines this young really need to breathe; decanting is not a bad idea at all. Once this begins to open up it hints at more complex elements of tar and leaf, which will be the rewards of further aging. **92** —P.G. (4/1/2006)

Sineann 2003 Baby Poux Cabernet Sauvignon (Columbia Valley (WA)) $42. Baby Poux is what, you ask? The name of a particular block of grapes in the Champoux (pronounced shampoo) vineyard in Washington's Horse Heaven Hills, just now coming into maturity. Nice cherry and red currant fruit is matched to gorgeous new oak, with flavors of toast and graham cracker, butter cookie, and caramel. This is a wine to put in the cellar and enjoy in 10-15 years. **92 Cellar Selection** —P.G. (4/1/2005)

Sineann 2001 Baby Poux Vineyard Cabernet Sauvignon (Columbia Valley (WA)) $27. This is the new section of Paul Champoux's highly respected Washington vineyard. As such, it is not quite as deeply concentrated as the old-vine stuff, but can be expected to age well, developing Bordeaux-like highlight of cedar, earth and mineral as it does. Just 150 cases were made. **90** —P.G. (12/31/2003)

Sineann 2000 Block One Cabernet Sauvignon (Columbia Valley (WA)) $60. The grapes come from 30-year-old vines in the Champoux vineyard, near Canoe Ridge in southeast Washington. Deeply concentrated and Bordeaux-like, this beautifully made wine layers black fruit, cedar, and streaks of iron ore with sculpted, refined tannins. Just 70 cases made. **93 Cellar Selection** —P.G. (12/31/2002)

Sineann 2001 McDuffee Vineyard Cabernet Sauvignon (Columbia Valley (OR)) $30. Eastern Oregon-grown Cabernet is unique; not quite Washington, not southern Oregon either. This is balanced and elegant, with smooth fruit flavors and sweet, toasty tannins. Not a powerhouse, but well-styled for grilled meats, with the acid to cut through the fat. 170 cases made. **89** —P.G. (12/1/2003)

Sineann 2000 McDuffee Vineyard Cabernet Sauvignon (Columbia Valley (OR)) $27. Dark, sensual, and loaded with spicy, smoky black fruits, this eastern Oregon-grown Cabernet offers thick, perfectly ripe flavors and smooth tannins. Still young and grapey, it finishes with dark expressions of coffee, cedar, and roasted meats. Just 70 cases made. **91** —P.G. (12/31/2002)

Sineann 2002 Celilo Vineyard Gewürztraminer (Columbia Valley (WA)) $18. Great vineyard meets supertalented winemaker, and voilà—a Gewürztraminer good enough to make you rethink the potential for this grape here in the Northwest. Perfectly ripened fruit catches hints of grapefruit, citrus, and stone fruits accented with rind and stone. It's varietal without being too floral or talc-like. Nice, dry, and ready to drink. 90 cases were made. **90** —P.G. (12/31/2003)

Sineann 2001 Celilo Vineyard Gewürztraminer (Columbia Valley (WA)) $18. You may never have tasted domestic Gewürztraminer any better than this. Fresh and elegant, it reaches for extra dimensions, without ever seeming blowsy or fat. A spicy mix of stone fruits is set against crisp citrus and mineral; the effect is hauntingly correct. A paltry 80 cases made. **93 Editors' Choice** —P.G. (12/31/2002)

Sineann 2002 Reed & Reynolds Gewürztraminer (Willamette Valley) $18. This has more intensity and laser-like precision than the Celilo; flavors of lime, rock, anise, and rind cut through the palate. Persistent and balanced, it seems to permeate the palate with flavor. Just 100 cases made. **91 Editors' Choice** —P.G. (12/1/2003)

Sineann 2000 Merlot (Columbia Valley (OR)) $27. 94 Editors' Choice —P.G. (12/31/2002)

Sineann 2003 Hillside Merlot (Columbia Valley (OR)) $30. Very tight, still pulling itself together. Give this one lots of breathing time! There is plenty of concentrated black cherry and plum fruit, and hints of clove and Asian spice. Not your typical Merlot; this has real muscle and concentration. **91** —P.G. (4/1/2005)

Sineann 2004 Hillside Vineyard Merlot (Columbia Valley (WA)) $30. Flavorful and interesting, with citrusy acids elevating the mouthfeel and supporting the plump, round cherry fruit. Beautifully crafted, it's already drinking like a well-integrated wine, though barely a year out of the fermenters. **91** —P.G. (4/1/2006)

Sineann 2001 Hillside Vineyard Merlot (Columbia Valley (OR)) $36. Low-cropped (2.1 tons/acre), well-drained, eastern Oregon fruit gives exceptional structure and intensity to this fine Merlot. The nose is a rich mix of fruit, meat, and smoke. Loaded with black cherry and blackberry fruit, spiced up with toasty oak and hints of herbs. Just 330 cases made. **91** —P.G. (12/1/2003)

Sineann 2002 Pinot Gris (Oregon) $15. This rich, aromatic Pinot Gris is a crisp, spicy expression of green apple, pineapple, and pear, nicely balanced against just-right natural acids and tannins. Alcohol is a sensible 13%, and availability (1,200 cases) is good. **89** —P.G. (12/1/2003)

Sineann 2001 Pinot Gris (Oregon) $15. This precision-crafted pinot Gris is a blend of grapes from three excellent vineyards, all cropped down to about two tons per acre, what the winemaker rightly calls "ridiculously low for Pinot Gris." Flavors are pineapple and pear, proportionately balanced against just-right natural acids and tannins. Hints of honey, caramel, and spice complete the show. **91 Best Buy** —P.G. (12/31/2002)

Sineann 2004 Pinot Noir (Oregon) $30. Lush, fragrant, and ripe with spicy scents of sage, thyme, cocoa, and vanilla, this young Pinot opens up to display sweet cherry fruit. It's solid and persistent up the middle, hanging in with pretty fruit flavors through a long and satisfying finish. **92 Editors' Choice** —P.G. (5/1/2006)

Sineann 2003 Pinot Noir (Oregon) $30. The best Oregon bottling ever from this exceptional producer. Spectacular, ripe, plush aromatics open into plummy, jammy, purely varietal fruit. But there is more, a textural complexity that incorporates light herb, leaf, and vanilla notes. This has it all, and offers every bit as much pleasure as any of the single-vineyard bottlings. **92** —P.G. (12/15/2004)

Sineann 2001 Pinot Noir (Oregon) $30. Lovely aromatics, with soft, cherry fruit, very pretty, round, and rich. No heat, no heavy hand with the oak, but it has the "yum" factor, which Pinot so often lacks. Forward and ready now. **88** —P.G. (12/1/2003)

Sineann 2001 Covey Ridge Pinot Noir (Oregon) $42. Interesting, pretty fruit, sweet and forward, but it seems to have a little bit of a hole in the middle. Very seductive and pleasurable; give it plenty of extra air time. **88** —P.G. (12/1/2003)

Sineann 2003 Covey Ridge Vineyard Pinot Noir (Willamette Valley) $42. This is the best Covey Ridge Pinot to date, a beautiful wine showing gorgeous spice, cranberry/cherry fruit, and penetrating notes of pine resin and new wood. Young and vibrant, it is perfectly framed but needs a bit more time to smooth out the edges and let the glorious flavors knit together. **91** —P.G. (12/15/2004)

Sineann 2004 Lachini Vineyard Pinot Noir (Willamette Valley) $42. This is super-saturated, dense and decadent with sweet, jammy blackberry fruit. Powerful and intense, the ultraripe fruit seems to explode on the palate. **93** —P.G. (5/1/2006)

Sineann 2004 Phelps Creek Vineyard Pinot Noir (Columbia Gorge) $42. This terroir-driven Pinot, from the Oregon side of the Columbia River, shows a dramatically different profile than the Willamette Valley Pinots commonly associated with the state. Kudos to winemaker Peter Rosback for finding great Pinot all over Oregon. This unique vineyard shows classic varietal fruit laced with mineral, kissed with toast, and finished with delicious mocha flavors from new oak barrels. The tart, tangy spine keeps it balanced and extends the fruit flavors well into a long, crisp finish. **93 Editors' Choice** —P.G. (5/1/2006)

USA

Sineann 2003 Phelps Creek Vineyard Pinot Noir (Columbia Gorge) $42. Sporting the brand-new Columbia Gorge AVA designation, this terroir-driven Pinot, from the Oregon side of the Columbia River, is a world apart from the Willamette Valley Pinots commonly associated with the state. Here the purity of sweet Bing cherry fruit is buttressed with clear mineral notes, and wrapped in very pleasing, caramel and cocoa barrel flavors. It shows a tart, tangy spine that keeps it balanced and extends the fruit flavors well into the long, crisp finish. **93 Editors' Choice** —*P.G.* (12/15/2004)

Sineann 2001 Reed & Reynolds Pinot Noir (Willamette Valley) $42. Pungent and ripe, with whiffs of smoke, herbs, roasted meats, and sassafras. Beautifully balanced, with fairly stiff, slightly green tannins. This one needs some time to really show its stuff. Only 350 cases made. **90** —*P.G.* (12/1/2003)

Sineann 2000 Reed & Reynolds Vineyard Pinot Noir (Oregon) $54. Pungent, ripe fruit is perfectly entwined with whiffs of smoke, herbs, roasted meats, and cedar. This powerful, complex wine is already displaying some of the signs of age, a result perhaps of its generously ripe, somewhat alcoholic structure. Only 200 cases made. **88** —*P.G.* (12/31/2002)

Sineann 2004 Resonance Vineyard Pinot Noir (Willamette Valley) $48. This biodynamically farmed vineyard delivers stunning, elegant, textured Pinot. Layer upon layer upon layer develops in the mouth, from the ripe strawberry/cherry fruit, masterfully speckled with toast, espresso, and cola notes. The mouthfeel is silky and supple, and this lovely wine lives up to its name with an innate resonance that lingers gracefully in the mouth. **93** —*P.G.* (5/1/2006)

Sineann 2003 Resonance Vineyard Pinot Noir (Willamette Valley) $42. This elegantly styled, precision Pinot opens with ripe strawberry/cherry fruit, masterfully speckled with toast, espresso, and cola notes. Immaculately clean and focused, it's silky and supple, and lives up to its name with an innate resonance that invites you to luxuriate in the flavor harmonics of each new sip. **93** —*P.G.* (12/15/2004)

Sineann 2004 Schindler Vineyard Pinot Noir (Willamette Valley) $42. The fruit is from the Eola Hills, and it has an interesting bloody character, like raw meat. It's a more Burgundian style than most Sineanns, and riper than most Eola Hills fruit. It hints at earth, leather, and marrow, with pretty, plummy fruit laced with cinnamon. An elegant, yet distinctive wine. **90** —*P.G.* (5/1/2006)

Sineann 2004 Whistling Ridge Pinot Noir (Willamette Valley) $42. Concentrated flavors of Kirschwasser, blackberry, and raspberry. Intense and alcoholic, with some heat in the finish. Plump, round, and full-bodied, with soft tannins and a hit of alcohol in the finish. **89** —*P.G.* (5/1/2006)

Sineann 2003 Whistling Ridge Vineyard Pinot Noir (Columbia Valley (OR)) $36. The cherry flavors are so concentrated here that it is almost like a liqueur, with some pretty raspberry highlights as well. Compact and wrapped in toast and cracker, this is stylish and elegant despite the density and concentration. Firmly tannic, it seems destined to age along classic Burgundian lines. Cellar 8–10 years. **91 Cellar Selection** —*P.G.* (12/15/2004)

Sineann 2004 Wyeast Vineyard Pinot Noir (Columbia Gorge) $42. Tart red fruit, spicy, pine needle notes, more typical Oregon flavors of resin in this Pinot. Classic styling, with stiffer tannins that set it up well for food. **90** —*P.G.* (5/1/2006)

Sineann 2003 Wyeast Vineyard Pinot Noir (Columbia Gorge) $42. Along with the ripe but tart red fruit, there are more of the typical Oregon flavors of pine and resin in this Pinot, along with a more pronounced streak of vanilla from the barrel aging. It's well made, with some stiff tannins that will benefit from further time in the bottle. **90** —*P.G.* (12/15/2004)

Sineann 2003 Red Table Wine Red Blend (Oregon) $12. In case you miss the hard to read Red Table Wine print, there's a cartoon drawing of a red table with wine on it on the label. An unidentified blend, it tastes of strawberries, raspberries, and milk chocolate, in a light (for Sineann) and very pleasant blend. Just a hint of stem in the tannins. **87 Best Buy** —*P.G.* (4/1/2005)

Sineann 2004 Red Wine Red Blend (Columbia Valley (WA)) $24. Somehow through the magic of winemaker Peter Rosback this wine doesn't taste like a barrel sample. It's smooth, round, supple, and packed with ripe fruits. Blend's blend is 42 percent Syrah, 40 percent Cabernet Sauvignon, and 18 percent Merlot; a combination that is becoming increasingly popular among Columbia valley winemakers. Ripe, primary fruit flavors show lots of raspberry and cherry, lightly coated with chocolate, cinnamon, and mocha. **90** —*P.G.* (4/1/2006)

Sineann 2002 Covey Ridge Vineyard Riesling (Willamette Valley) $18. Somehow this very limited (45 cases) Sineann Pinot Gris manages to outshine the excellent Oregon bottling, without adding over-the-top oak and alcohol. It's just riper fruit, nuanced with honeysuckle and lemon tea, and it shows a bit more length while retaining elegance. **91 Editors' Choice** —*P.G.* (12/1/2003)

Sineann 2002 Medici Vineyard Riesling (Willamette Valley) $15. This is the first-ever Sineann Riesling. The vineyard will be familiar to Pinot lovers, as it is one of Oregon's oldest, planted in the mid-'70s. This is juicy, beautifully ripened Riesling, catching all the floral highlights along with concentrated fruit flavors and hints of honey and butterscotch. Just enough residual sugar to sweeten the finish perceptibly. **92 Best Buy** —*P.G.* (12/1/2003)

Sineann 2005 Old Vine Zinfandel (Columbia Valley (WA)) $36. These are century-old vines—unique in the Northwest. The new vintage brings the alcohol down to a welcome 14.8%, and offers complex, soft, plummy fruit with the grace of old vines. The grapes seem to quietly show their mastery of scents and flavors, lightly liquorous, but laden with plums, cherries, dates, and figs. Turley eat your heart out! **93** —*P.G.* (12/31/2006)

Sineann 2004 Old Vine Zinfandel (Columbia Valley (OR)) $36. Peter Rosback's old-vine Zin is always dark and dense and unabashedly alcoholic (15.8%). In this vintage more herbal flavors dominate, along with olives, dates, figs, and a decidedly salty note. Unique and not for everyone, but absolutely exceptional. **93** —*P.G.* (5/1/2006)

Sineann 2003 Old Vine Zinfandel (Columbia Valley (OR)) $36. Peter Rosback's old-vine Zin is always dark and dense and unabashedly alcoholic (here, 15.8%). But it is never any better than this. This is Turley without the heat or Portlike flavors. It tastes like the absolute concentrated essence of Zinfandel, with racy, vivid acids, jammy blackberry fruit, and enough new oak to keep it all together. **93** —*P.G.* (12/15/2004)

Sineann 2000 Old Vine Zinfandel (Columbia Valley (OR)) $36. I know what you're thinking. Zinfandel from Oregon? For $36?! Yes, and from a century-old vineyard to boot. Powerfully scented with dark fruits and roasted espresso, it's ripe but not raisiny, concentrated, and striated with mineral, earth, and wood. 400 cases made. **92** —*P.G.* (12/31/2002)

Sineann 2005 The Pines Zinfandel (Columbia Valley (WA)) $27. The same vineyard that produces the winery's Old Vine Zinfandel makes this thick, concentrated wine, from vines now almost 20 years old. It's packed with black raspberry and black cherry fruit, wafts of smoke and clove and meat. Young, tannic, thick, and quite ripe, it's got more raw power than the O.V., but a tad less complexity. **92** —*P.G.* (12/31/2006)

Sineann 2003 The Pines Zinfandel (Columbia Valley (OR)) $27. Like the winery's Old Vine bottling, which comes from the same vineyard, this is a thick, concentrated Zinfandel, packed with black cherry and boysenberry fruit, smoke and clove, and hints of ham and leather. Young, tannic, fascinating. **90** —*P.G.* (4/1/2005)

SINGLE LEAF

Single Leaf 1999 Cabernet Franc (El Dorado) $16. Curiously lean, given the fine vintage. It's filled with green, stalky aromas and flavors. The palate wants to find some ripe berries and discovers only tart acids and austerity. There's some hidden fruit that would come out with the right foods, but on its own it's one dimensional. **82** —*S.H.* (9/1/2002)

Single Leaf 1999 Zinfandel (El Dorado) $16. Wow. This wine is dry to the point of austerity. And the tannins are powerful, leaving the palate numb. It's also on the alcoholic side. The core of black cherry fruit will wake up, soften and sweeten with rich foods like barbecue. **85** —*S.H.* (11/1/2002)

Single Leaf NV Pammie's Cuvée Zinfandel (El Dorado County) $10. This Zin-based blend is Exhibit A in what can go wrong if you're not careful up under the fierce, thin-air summer sun of the Sierra Foothills. It is filled with the hot, bitter taste of raisins that have been drained of all their sweetness. That leaves tannins and alcohol and not much else. **82** —*S.H. (3/1/2004)*

SIQUEIRA

Siqueira 2002 Cabernet Sauvignon (Stags Leap District) $42. Quite ripe and smooth, showing classic dimensions of soft but complex tannins. There must have been great lot selection, to judge from the concentrated cassis flavors. **92** —*S.H. (5/1/2005)*

SISKIYOU VINEYARDS

Siskiyou Vineyards 2000 La Cave Rouge Bordeaux Blend (Oregon) $15. From a very warm site in pear country comes this Cabernet/Merlot blend. It shows ripe fruit, dense tannin, and some dark, toasted-coffee notes. The forward fruit is appealing, but the wine falls off in the middle and finishes quickly. **86** —*P.G. (8/1/2002)*

Siskiyou Vineyards 1998 Pinot Noir (Willamette Valley) $15. 86 —*M.S. (12/1/2000)*

Siskiyou Vineyards 1999 La Cave Blanche White Blend (Oregon) $10. A mix of Sauvignon Blanc and Sémillon. The two are blended and fermented together in barrels, from a vineyard east of Medford. The wine has pleasant herbal, grassy notes, and some very tart fruit. **86** —*P.G. (8/1/2002)*

SIX PRONG

Six Prong 2001 Red Table Wine Red Blend (Columbia Valley (WA)) $10. Negociant blend of six different grapes, with plenty of bold, spicy flavors. Coffee and toast underpin the red fruits, and it's a fun, lively wine with real personality. **87** —*P.G. (1/1/2004)*

Six Prong 2003 Red Wine Red Blend (Columbia Valley (WA)) $13. Very dark, plum-colored wine with a super ripe nose of raisins and ripe red fruits. The mongrel blend (30% Cabernet Sauvignon, 23% Sangiovese, 13% Merlot, 12% Malbec, 11% Grenache, 11% Syrah) delivers strong scents and flavors of toast and coffee, surprising in a wine at this price. Round, mature flavors give the impression that some older wine has been blended in, though it has not. The soft, fruit-driven center leads into a toasty finish with substantial, medium-grained tannins. **88 Best Buy** —*P.G. (11/15/2005)*

SIX SIGMA

Six Sigma 2005 Sauvignon Blanc (Lake County) $20. Beautiful Sauvignon that shows off Lake County at its best. Bone dry, zesty in acids, with lemon and lime flavors and a hint of tart green gooseberry, the wine has an elegant structure reminiscent of Marlborough. **87** —*S.H. (12/31/2006)*

SJOEBLOM WINERY

Sjoeblom Winery 2001 Chauvignon Reserve Blanc de Noirs Cabernet Sauvignon (Napa Valley) $39. Looks as golden pale as a classic Brut, but the full-bodied, ripe flavors of cherries and cassis-infused cream give it away as Cabernet Sauvignon. It's an unusual bubbly, but delicious, and fruity-rich enough to wash down everything from steak to chocolate cake. **89** —*S.H. (6/1/2006)*

Sjoeblom Winery 2000 Chauvignon Sparkling Rosé Cabernet Sauvignon (Napa Valley) $39. This is a pink-hued Blanc de Noirs made from Cabernet rather than Pinot Noir. It's bright and fresh, with pretty citrus, raspberry, cherry, toast, and herb flavors at the fore. Clean and zippy on the finish, it's full and round. Shows that fine bubbly can be made outside its normal varietal parameters. **90** —*J.M. (12/1/2003)*

SKETCHBOOK

Sketchbook 2000 Mendocino Collection Cabernet Sauvignon (Mendocino) $22. With ripe black currant fruit, lush French oak, and rich tannins, what it lacks in depth and complexity, it makes up for with charm. **87** —*S.H. (10/1/2003)*

Sketchbook 1997 Syrah (Mendocino) $20. Toasted marshmallows, cream cheese, baked apple, and licorice on the nose lead into a mallowy, cardboard-woody palate with a hint of blackberry flavor. Finishes short, with toasty-chalky sweetness. **84** *(10/1/2001)*

Sketchbook 2001 Estate Syrah (Mendocino) $23. Smells a little funky, with a raw meat note floating on top of the blackberry and cherry aromas. Turns extremely dry and tannic in the mouth; it may mellow out in a year or two. **84** —*S.H. (6/1/2004)*

SKEWIS

Skewis 2001 Bush Vineyard Pinot Noir (Russian River Valley) $42. A bit of leathery funk joins the smoky, oak-infused flavors of cherries and sweet rhubarb pie in this enjoyable wine. It's dry and crisp and elegant, with a polished mouthfeel and a long, spicy finish. **89** —*S.H. (12/15/2004)*

Skewis 2001 Demuth Vineyard Pinot Noir (Anderson Valley) $35. Pretty aromas of cherries, cola, tea, smoke, and vanilla, and very delicate in the mouth. Not especially concentrated, but elegant in tea and cola flavors and an overlay of oak. **86** —*S.H. (12/15/2004)*

Skewis 2001 Montgomery Vineyard Pinot Noir (Russian River Valley) $45. Offers lots of pleasure with its flavors of cola, root beer, cherry, rose, and herbs, and despite the dryness, there's a sweet overlay of oak and fruity ripeness. Delicately structured, with silky tannins, this is a wine to enjoy now. **90** —*S.H. (12/15/2004)*

Skewis 2001 Salzgeber Vineyard Pinot Noir (Russian River Valley) $40. Fleshy and opulent, with forward cherry, raspberry, and earthy-rhubarb flavors and a lush mouthfeel. Bone dry, with orange peel acidity and a sprinkling of dusty tannins, this is a great food wine. **90** —*S.H. (12/15/2004)*

SLAUGHTERHOUSE CELLARS

Slaughterhouse Cellars 2003 Cabernet Sauvignon (Rutherford) $60. Beautiful Cab, although it's young and needs time to blossom. It has a chewy mouthfeel, with significant tannins that frame ripe berry-cherry fruit. Polished and refined, this Cab should open gracefully over the next 15 years. **91 Cellar Selection** —*S.H. (12/15/2006)*

Slaughterhouse Cellars 2002 Cabernet Sauvignon (Rutherford) $60. Starts off with a big waft of new oak and mint, then opens to reveal fruitier notes of cherries and sweet herbs. The tannins are pure Rutherford, sweet, firm, complex, and dusty. A little hard now, but should soften and sweeten by 2008. **90** —*S.H. (12/15/2005)*

SLOAN

Sloan 2002 Red Wine Cabernet Blend (Rutherford) $245. Impossibly aromatic. Hard to imagine greater claret perfume. Shows the most refined mingling of smoky oak, cassis, cherries, roasted coconut macaroon, cocoa puff, and spice scents. Absolutely first rate, as good as anything Napa Valley produces. Compellingly, addictively delicious, but so dry and voluptuous. Classic wine, with perfect alignment of fruit, acids, tannins, oak, alcohol, the works. The grapes are from Sloan's portion of the Sacrashe Vineyard, high above the Silverado Trail in the Vaca Mountains. Mostly Cabernet Sauvignon, aged in 100% new French oak. Perfection in a bottle. Drink now–2020. **100** —*S.H. (9/1/2006)*

SMASHED GRAPES

Smashed Grapes 2004 Pinot Grigio (California) $10. Adequate pine and apple aromas on what is otherwise a neutral opening. Citrus and apple flavors feature a touch of mineral, while the finish is dry and crisp, with mouthwatering acidity. **85** *(2/1/2006)*

SMITH & HOOK

Smith & Hook 1996 Baroness Reserve Cabernet Sauvignon (Santa Lucia Highlands) $40. 84 —*L.W. (12/31/1999)*

Smith & Hook 2003 Grand Reserve Cabernet Sauvignon (Santa Lucia Highlands) $25. No winery in this appellation has worked harder on Cabernet, and the results are showing. This wine is soft and rich in black currant and chocolate flavors. It's very dry, with firm, fuzzy tannins, and the finish is rich and complex. **87** —*S.H. (11/1/2006)*

Smith & Hook 2002 Grand Reserve Cabernet Sauvignon (Santa Lucia Highlands) $25. I like this wine a lot for the fruity flavors, rich tannins, subtle oak, crispness, long finish, and overall balance. It's not as ripe as Cabs from warmer climates, and therefore may well be better with complex food. **88** —*S.H. (6/1/2005)*

Smith & Hook 2001 Grande Reserve Cabernet Sauvignon (Santa Lucia Highlands) $20. There will never be a lushly ripe Cab from this cool appellation, but no one has worked harder to craft interesting ones than Smith & Hook. This release is rich in earthy flavors and tannins. It has tantalizing hints of black cherries, and is very dry. It's a fine food wine with considerable finesse. **89** —*S.H. (10/3/2004)*

Smith & Hook 1997 Baroness Reserve Masterpiece E Chardonnay (Monterey County) $25. **85** —*L.H. (12/31/1999)*

SMITH WOOTON

Smith Wooton 1999 Cabernet Franc (Napa Valley) $40. Smells oaky and herbal, with white pepper and mint aromas, and tastes very dry and tannic. There are some berry flavors but they're very sparse. The finish leaves numbing tannins all along the palate. **84** —*S.H. (12/1/2002)*

Smith Wooton 2002 Gallagher's Vineyard Cabernet Franc (Napa Valley) $32. This wine shows the full-body of a Cabernet Sauvignon, but the fruit profile is entirely different. Here, it's all red cherries. Yet the oak, tannins, and acids are those of a fine Cab. It's a little lighter, but no less fine. **91** —*S.H. (11/1/2005)*

Smith Wooton 2001 Gallagher's Vineyard Cabernet Franc (Napa Valley) $32. A bit sharp in acids, with a raw mouthfeel and the fresh taste of just-picked berries, this dry, young wine is best paired with rich fare, like barbecue. **84** —*S.H. (7/1/2005)*

Smith Wooton 2003 Tanner Brothers Vineyard Syrah (Calaveras County) $28. Dark and exuberant, this dry wine packs a punch thanks to elevated alcohol. It has some fine black currant, plum, dark chocolate fudge, tobacco, and leather flavors, and finishes with some dusty tannins and a hint of pepper-cured meat. **88** *(9/1/2005)*

SMITH-MADRONE

Smith-Madrone 2001 Cabernet Sauvignon (Napa Valley) $35. Power is the name of the game here. It starts with the intense currant and oak aromas, then really shows up in the mouth, which is very tannic and closed. But there's a tantalizing hint of blackberries that bodes well for the future. Hold for a few years. **89** —*S.H. (8/1/2005)*

Smith-Madrone 1997 Cabernet Sauvignon (Napa Valley) $35. From a tiny estate vineyard on Spring Mountain, this is a rich and tremendously concentrated Cabernet. Blackberry and cassis flavors are tightly wound around firm but pretty tannins, and the oak is modulated. Polished and elegant, it's ready to drink tonight, but will age for many years. **92 Editors' Choice** —*S.H. (12/1/2001)*

Smith-Madrone 2002 Chardonnay (Napa Valley) $25. Nice and crisp in acids, with a sleek oak coat that adds smoke and vanilla notes, this Chard sure tastes good by itself. But it's balanced and food-friendly, with flavors of perfectly ripened white peaches. **88** —*S.H. (8/1/2005)*

Smith-Madrone 2000 Chardonnay (Napa Valley) $25. Ripe and fancy, and not your usual oak-drenched Chardonnay. Fat, lush flavors of apples, peaches, and pears have smooth accents of smoke and spice from wood, and crisp acidity makes for a bright mouthfeel. Possesses great concentration and intensity. **91** —*S.H. (2/1/2003)*

Smith-Madrone 2001 Riesling (Napa Valley) $17. California's best Riesling grown for 25 years at 1,800 feet above Napa Valley. Crisp and concentrated flavors of apples, lime, and minerals are encased in fine acidity and drink steely and sleek. The residual sugar us 0.7%, which is off-dry, but the acids are so good, the wine feels dry in the mouth. By the way, this wine will age for a long time. **90** —*S.H. (8/1/2003)*

Smith-Madrone 1999 Riesling (Napa Valley) $17. This long-time producer of dryish Rieslings is still one of California's best. Apple, honey, and peach aromas lead to juicy, fruity flavors, and rich acidity spreads spices all over the palate. This stylish wine will be versatile at the table. Adventurous types will age it. **87** —*S.H. (12/1/2001)*

SMOKING LOON

Smoking Loon 2003 Cabernet Sauvignon (California) $9. Richness and depth, at a giveaway price. This dry, full-bodied wine features cherries, blackberries, and good, smoky oak. **85 Best Buy** —*S.H. (7/1/2005)*

Smoking Loon 2002 Cabernet Sauvignon (California) $9. Easy and silky, this Cab features cherry-berry flavors with a hint of raisins. It's a little rough around the edges, but serviceable. **83** —*S.H. (5/1/2005)*

Smoking Loon 2005 Chardonnay (California) $9. Clean and tasty, this crisp, dry Chard has modest peach, apple, and tropical fruit flavors. It's a nice country wine at a fair price. **84** —*S.H. (12/1/2006)*

Smoking Loon 2003 Chardonnay (California) $9. Starts with spicy oak and smoky vanilla flavors, and offers modest peach and tropical fruit flavors suggesting pineapple grilled on a skewer. Clean and tasty. **86 Best Buy** —*S.H. (3/1/2005)*

Smoking Loon 2002 Chardonnay (California) $9. Lots of ripe peach, pear, tropical fruit, and Oriental spice flavors, lots of smoky, toasty oak, a vanilla-cream texture and a honeyed richness that lasts through the finish. That's the formula for popular success in Chard, and you get it all here, at an everyday price. **85** —*S.H. (12/31/2003)*

Smoking Loon 2004 Merlot (California) $9. Shows much the same character as Don Sebastiani's 2004 Pepperwood Grove Merlot, perhaps a touch more tannic, and veering more toward blackberries instead of cherries. Still it's a lovely sipper, fresh and jammy. **86 Best Buy** —*S.H. (5/1/2006)*

Smoking Loon 2002 Merlot (California) $9. Dry and a little tannic, with deep flavors of blue and black stone fruits, such as plums. Turns a bit thin after you swallow. **84** —*S.H. (5/1/2005)*

Smoking Loon 2001 Merlot (California) $10. Has earthy, tobaccoey flavors, with notes of plum and blackberry, wrapped in sturdy tannins. Dry, with a tart finish. **84** —*S.H. (12/1/2003)*

Smoking Loon 2004 Pinot Noir (California) $9. This tastes like it came from premium cool growing areas. It's crisp in acids, light-bodied and dry. The flavors are all on the surface, but totally delicious. They include raspberries, red cherries, cola, cocoa, vanilla, toast, and Asian spices. **86 Best Buy** —*S.H. (12/1/2005)*

Smoking Loon 2003 Pinot Noir (California) $9. A good affordable introduction to Pinot. Soft and silky in texture, with good acidity and pleasant cherry and smoke flavors **84** —*S.H. (12/15/2004)*

Smoking Loon 2002 Pinot Noir (California) $9. Straightforward, with modest cherry and floral aromas and flavors and a delicate structure. Good, clean, and simple. **84 Best Buy** *(11/1/2004)*

Smoking Loon 2001 Pinot Noir (California) $9. From Sebastiani, proof that Pinot Noir has been overplanted in California. This has some pleasant Pinot character in the cherry, spice, and earth flavors and light, silky tannins, but it's a simple, one-dimensional wine. **84** —*S.H. (7/1/2003)*

Smoking Loon 2004 Syrah (California) $9. So ripe and juicy in jammy cherry, currant, and mocha flavors, you just have to take another sip. This winning Syrah is dry and balanced despite the abundance of fruit, with a lush, smooth texture. **85** —*S.H. (5/1/2006)*

Smoking Loon 2003 Syrah (California) $9. This Syrah deals plenty of sweet fruit flavors (blackberry preserves, ripe plums) on the palate, and much the same (plus some herb) on the nose. A simple, easy wine at a good price. **86 Best Buy** *(9/1/2005)*

Smoking Loon 2002 Syrah (California) $9. Too sweet and clumsy in the mouth, but it's okay with simple fare. **83** —*S.H. (6/1/2005)*

Smoking Loon 2005 Viognier (California) $9. Dry and crisp just like a Sauvignon Blanc, but with Viognier's blast of pineapple, nectarine, and honeysuckle flavors. Appealing for the wealth of fruit and bright acidity that makes it so clean. **85 Best Buy** —*S.H. (11/15/2006)*

Smoking Loon 2004 Viognier (California) $9. Provides all the flowery, exotic fruits you expect from a Viognier, in a dry, crisp wine. Has a minerally backbone that adds structure. **84** —*S.H. (10/1/2005)*

Smoking Loon 2003 Viognier (California) $9. This is a great price for a fresh, clean wine with such fruity complexity. Floods the mouth with peach, apple, pineapple, and spice flavors that are ripe and rich. A good value. **86 Best Buy** —*S.H. (10/1/2004)*

Smoking Loon 2000 Viognier (California) $10. A bit cloying at first, but healthy acidity adds balance. Flavors are pleasant, with nice apple and peach notes at the fore. **82** —*J.M. (12/15/2002)*

SNOB HILL WINERY

Snob Hill Winery 2002 Le Snoot Cabernet Sauvignon (North Coast) $11. Easy to drink and likeable for its dry flavors of ripe cherries and blackberries and the smooth, polished tannins. Finishes soft and quick. **84** —S.H. (12/31/2004)

Snob Hill Winery 2002 Le Snoot Chardonnay (North Coast) $11. This is your basic everyday oaky Chard, and if it's not the world's greatest, it gets the job done. Lots of ripe pears and tropical fruits. **84** —S.H. (12/31/2004)

Snob Hill Winery 2002 Merlot (North Coast) $11. A bit herbaceous, with a cut of white pepper that slices across the black cherries, but clean and dry. Turns very juicy in the mouth, with soft, soft tannins. **84** —S.H. (12/31/2004)

SNOQUALMIE

Snoqualmie 2003 Reserve Cabernet Sauvignon (Columbia Valley (WA)) $23. Lightly herbal, tight, and dry, this is pure Cabernet from a warm year. Nonetheless it is austere almost to the point of metallic, and the fruit carries a lot of herbal notes, with a hint of green bean. **87** —P.G. (8/1/2006)

Snoqualmie 2002 Reserve Cabernet Sauvignon (Columbia Valley (WA)) $23. A compact wine, with more than a trace of sweaty saddle, along with red currant, herbs, and spice. Depending upon your liking for barnyard notes, this could warrant a higher score. **87** —P.G. (6/1/2005)

Snoqualmie 2001 Reserve Cabernet Sauvignon (Columbia Valley (WA)) $23. A compact wine, crisply defined with red currant and cherry fruits, and a grainy, roasted coffee finish. Tight, stylish, and ageworthy. **89** —P.G. (5/1/2004)

Snoqualmie 1997 Reserve Cabernet Sauvignon (Columbia Valley (WA)) $21. **86** —P.G. (9/1/2000)

Snoqualmie 2004 Rosebud Vineyard Cabernet Sauvignon (Columbia Valley (WA)) $15. Rosebud vineyard is now in its 25th vintage, and its grapes go into many of Snoqualmie's best efforts. This 100% varietal Cabernet Sauvignon is nicely defined, a mix of spicy berry and citrus. Flavors are set up on firm acids and the alcohol is a sensible 13.2 percent; no insane levels of sugar or extraction here. The oak flavors, a mix of new American barrels, French oak inserts and older, neutral barrels, deliver the goods. The finish is as smooth as coffee gelato, with shavings of bitter chocolate set on top. 3,000 cases produced. **88 Best Buy** —P.G. (11/15/2006)

Snoqualmie 2002 Rosebud Vineyard Cabernet Sauvignon (Columbia Valley (WA)) $15. Soft and sweet, with no solid middle, this is fruity enough but never quite sits right in the mouth. The vineyard, planted in 1981 on the Wahluke Slope, has great creds but this 100% varietal Cab doesn't ever really come together like the previous vintage did. **85** —P.G. (12/15/2005)

Snoqualmie 2001 Rosebud Vineyard Cabernet Sauvignon (Columbia Valley (WA)) $15. Fragrant with pleasant whiffs of barnyard, leather, and spice over firm cassis and pomegranate fruit, this shows lots of penetrating flavor as well. Tart cranberries and clean, nose-tickling scents of fresh roasted coffee suggest a much pricier Cab. There's just a hint of green to the tannins, but overall a very nice effort. **88 Best Buy** —P.G. (12/15/2004)

Snoqualmie 1999 Cabernet Sauvignon-Merlot (Columbia Valley (WA)) $11. The blend is almost equal—53% Cab and 47% Merlot—and the definite dill and bell pepper aromas indicate less- than-stellar fruit. But the wine is well made and budget priced, and enough black cherry fruit is bobbing beneath the surface to make things work. Stiff tannins lead into a roasted coffee finish. **86** —P.G. (9/1/2002)

Snoqualmie 1998 Chardonnay (Columbia Valley (WA)) $11. **85** —P.G. (6/1/2000)

Snoqualmie 2001 Chardonnay (Columbia Valley (WA)) $11. Snoqualmie has lively, varietal wines in the $11 range and a lineup of excellent reserve wines priced a bit higher. This is bracing, stylish, and plain interesting, with layers of green and yellow fruits streaked around tangy acids and a hint of mineral. **88 Best Buy** —P.G. (5/1/2004)

Snoqualmie 2000 Chardonnay (Columbia Valley (WA)) $11. Tasty fresh fruit, leaning toward grapefruit and pineapple, peach, and lemon. Zesty and forward, it refreshes rather than fatigues the palate, and is perfect for sipping on a spring afternoon. **87 Best Buy** —P.G. (7/1/2002)

Snoqualmie 2004 Chenin Blanc (Columbia Valley (WA)) $7. It starts out rough, showing strong burnt match/rubber scents. But swirl it a bit and out come the solid, lightly sweet flavors of melon, peach, and cantaloupe, with substantial weight and length. **86 Best Buy** —P.G. (6/1/2006)

Snoqualmie 2001 Chenin Blanc (Columbia Valley (WA)) $7. Peaches, melon, and the unmistakable scent of fresh cream cheese comprise the nose, which is backed up by a good mix of tangerine, melon, pear, and apple. The mouthfeel is round and satisfying, while the finish is broad and substantive. Not a bad domestic Chenin. **86 Best Buy** —M.S. (6/1/2003)

Snoqualmie 2000 Chenin Blanc (Columbia Valley (WA)) $7. **84** —S.H. (6/1/2002)

Snoqualmie 2003 Merlot (Columbia Valley (WA)) $11. Tight and slim, with crisp black cherry fruit highlighted with clove and earth. There are subtle suggestions of soy and mushroom—umami, if you must—that show this winemaker's exceptional ability to bring detail and nuance even to base level corporate wines. **86** —P.G. (12/31/2006)

Snoqualmie 2002 Reserve Merlot (Columbia Valley (WA)) $23. Starts out with pleasant notes of supple fruit, but there's too much oak showing at the moment, and the fruit quickly gets buried. Some bitter tannins conclude; give this one extra airtime to soften it up. **87** —P.G. (6/1/2005)

Snoqualmie 2001 Reserve Merlot (Columbia Valley (WA)) $23. Smooth and chocolatey, with lots of supple fruit and layers of sweet oak. This is a wine to gulp down by the glass, with foods such as pizza and burgers. There's plenty of creamy vanilla to soften the finish. **89** —P.G. (5/1/2004)

Snoqualmie 2000 Reserve Merlot (Columbia Valley (WA)) $23. Continuing the expansion of this former budget brand into premium territory, this reserve Merlot makes a nice complement to owner Stimson Lane's runaway success with Columbia Crest. If CC is the big, brawny, masculine Merlot, Snoqualmie is more elegant, restrained, and feminine. Ripe fruit suggests strawberry preserves, and the wine is balanced, full, and flavorful. **88** —P.G. (9/1/2004)

Snoqualmie 1999 Reserve Merlot (Columbia Valley (WA)) $23. This Stimson Lane property has recently added a more upscale line of reserve wines, along with classy packaging. The reserve Merlot is a limited selection of the top lots, just 600 cases produced. But it seems to lean heavily on new oak aging to mask ordinary fruit, that can't really stand up to all the barrel time. **86** —P.G. (6/1/2002)

Snoqualmie 1997 Reserve Merlot (Columbia Valley (WA)) $21. **84** —P.G. (9/1/2000)

Snoqualmie 2005 Winemaker's Select Riesling (Columbia Valley (WA)) $11. Sweet and penetrating, with surprisingly deep flavors of spicy pear, dried apricots, and candied citrus. **88** —P.G. (8/1/2006)

Snoqualmie 2004 Winemaker's Select Riesling (Columbia Valley (WA)) $7. Here's another delicious riesling, this one sweet and penetrating, with surprisingly deep and protracted flavors of candied orange peel, lemon peel, and grapefruit. Drink this lovely wine with fruit-driven desserts, or chill it and sip it all by itself. **88 Best Buy** —P.G. (11/15/2005)

Snoqualmie 2004 Sauvignon Blanc (Columbia Valley (WA)) $7. Smooth and creamy, this pure-blooded Sauvignon Blanc is as light and clean as a spring breeze. Nicely ripened to flavors of fig and grapefruit, it adds accent notes of lemon rind and fresh herb. **87 Best Buy** —P.G. (6/1/2006)

Snoqualmie 2001 Sauvignon Blanc (Columbia Valley (WA)) $7. The light and easy nose is misleading. At first some pear and flower aromas stir interest, but the palate disappoints. It's dilute, with just a touch of green apple. The finish has little to it as well, and as a whole the wine is watery. **81** —M.S. (6/1/2003)

Snoqualmie 1998 Blanc Sémillon (Columbia Valley (WA)) $7. **83** —P.G. (6/1/2000)

Snoqualmie 2003 Syrah (Columbia Valley (WA)) $8. Snoqualmie's reserve Syrahs are very good efforts, but the real deals are the winery's Columbia Valley bottlings. This is pure Syrah, from the Wahluke

Slope's Rosebud vineyard, and I would be hard-pressed to find a better Syrah at this price in the country. It's got genuine varietal character, whereas most cheap Syrah/Shiraz is just light red wine—could be Zinfandel, could be anything. Here there are zippy flavors of mixed berries, spicy black pepper, and claret-like tannins. A beautiful sense of proportion and balance invigorates this wine; at less than 14 percent alcohol, it delivers more actual, nuanced flavor than many far more expensive, over-extracted versions. 25,000 cases produced. **88 Best Buy** —*P.G. (11/15/2006)*

Snoqualmie 2001 Syrah (Columbia Valley (WA)) $11. There is no better entry-level Syrah made in Washington than Snoqualmie, which captures the forward, juicy, tart, and mixed berry flavors of the grape without drowning them in new oak. Tannins are soft and lightly toasty, and the sappy tang of the fruit sails through a smooth finish. **88 Best Buy** —*P.G. (7/1/2004)*

Snoqualmie 2000 Syrah (Columbia Valley (WA)) $11. This is a young wine and tastes like a Beaujolais. Spicy, grapey, and showing an almost spritzy lightness; it has good, clean fruit with a lively, tangy, spicy mouthfeel. **88** —*P.G. (9/1/2002)*

Snoqualmie 1999 Syrah (Columbia Valley (WA)) $11. Every winery on the West Coast is scrambling to make at least one Syrah, but bargain bottles are few and far between. This is a gem; richly scented with berries and chocolate, smooth and seamless with sweet, fresh fruit flavors. Balanced and light, it is perfect for a Thanksgiving turkey. **87 Best Buy** —*P.G. (10/1/2001)*

Snoqualmie 2002 Reserve Syrah (Columbia Valley (WA)) $23. The '02 ups it another notch from the juicy, spicy 2001. Here again is are beguiling aromas of plum, cherry, dust, and cocoa; a chewy, ripe fruit core, and a dense finish that runs from citrus to coffee, with everything in between. **91 Editors' Choice** —*P.G. (6/1/2005)*

Snoqualmie 2001 Reserve Syrah (Columbia Valley (WA)) $23. Young and ripe, this has the juicy, spicy red fruits that distinguish Washington Syrah, outlined with tart acids and set against a splashy background of new French and American oak. **90 Editors' Choice** —*P.G. (5/1/2004)*

SNOSRAP

Snosrap 2001 Cyrano Red Table Wine Bordeaux Blend (Carmel Valley) $24. A Merlot-based Bordeaux blend that's rough in tannins, with a combination of sweet cherry flavors and less ripe earthy tobacco. **83** —*S.H. (8/1/2004)*

SNOWDEN

Snowden 2001 Cabernet Sauvignon (Napa Valley) $60. Kicks off with heady aromas of blackberry, tar, licorice, spice, and modest earth tones. On the palate it fans out to reveal complex layers of more black fruit, cinnamon, anise, cardamom, and herbs. It's framed in firm tannins, finishing long. **91** —*J.M. (12/31/2004)*

Snowden 1998 Cabernet Sauvignon (Napa Valley) $60. Lush and ripe, with firm, silky tannins that support a core of blackberry, licorice, black cherry, herb, chocolate, sage, and mineral notes. Complex and brimming with character. **92** —*J.M. (11/15/2002)*

Snowden 2002 Estate Cabernet Sauvignon (Napa Valley) $50. This young wine is hard and tannic now, with a drying mouthfeel. Buried way down deep are blackberries and cherries, which are considerable, and the wine is balanced. It will probably develop bottle complexity over the next five to seven years. **87** —*S.H. (3/1/2006)*

Snowden 2002 Lost Vineyard Cabernet Sauvignon (Napa Valley) $30. This is a fine Napa Cab, rich and ripe in black currant, and well balanced. It's dry, with fairly sturdy tannins, and although it's soft in acids, it will hold and improve for a few years. **87** —*S.H. (3/1/2006)*

Snowden 1997 Lost Vineyard Cabernet Sauvignon (Napa Valley) $30. 88 *(11/1/2000)*

SOBON ESTATE

Sobon Estate 2003 Cabernet Sauvignon (Amador County) $15. There's beautiful blackberry and cassis fruit in this Cab, undergirded by a rich, coffee-infused earthiness. It's completely dry and the tannins are fairly fierce, but nothing a good steak can't negotiate. In fact, it's a great food

wine, classy and understated. The best Sobon Cab ever and a great value. **91 Best Buy** —*S.H. (10/1/2006)*

Sobon Estate 2001 Cabernet Sauvignon (Amador County) $15. Very smooth and suave, a wine soft in tannins and acids that caresses the palate while carrying ripe flavors of blackberries, currants, cinnamon, and smoky oak. Delicious now for its pure primary fruit, and should be perfect with lamb. **89 Best Buy** —*S.H. (11/15/2003)*

Sobon Estate 2003 Rezerve Carignane (Shenandoah Valley (CA)) $24. Tastes soft and thick and simple, with superripe berry flavors veering into sweetened espresso. This wine is going nowhere, so drink up now. **82** —*S.H. (7/1/2006)*

Sobon Estate 2002 Rezerve Carignane (Amador County) $24. It's hard to make an elegant wine from this workhorse variety, but this one tries. Very dry, with earth, coffee, sweet tobacco, and red stone fruit flavors, it has smooth tannins and crisp acidity. Extra credit for the sweetly fruity finish. **86** —*S.H. (10/1/2004)*

Sobon Estate NV Orange Muscat (Shenandoah Valley (CA)) $17. Fulfills the basic requirements of a sweetie with its tangerine flavors and quite sweet sugar, and crisp acids that keep it from being cloying. Try with fresh fruit, sorbet, or butter cookies. **85** —*S.H. (9/1/2004)*

Sobon Estate 2004 Rezerve Orange Muscat (Amador County) $15. Tastes beautifully rich in orange and vanilla flavors, with notes of apricot liqueur and a spicy dusting of white pepper. The heat may be from the 16% alcohol. This is an elegant way to end a meal. **87** —*S.H. (8/1/2006)*

Sobon Estate 1999 Primitivo (Shenandoah Valley (CA)) $16. Tastes like a garden-variety Zin, with exuberantly fruity, wild berry, and pepper flavors, young acids, and easy tannins. The juvenile insouciance drinks best now, and isn't going anywhere. **83** —*S.H. (12/1/2002)*

Sobon Estate 1997 Primitivo (Shenandoah Valley (CA)) $18. 80 —*J.C. (10/1/1999)*

Sobon Estate 1998 Primitivo (Shenandoah Valley (CA)) $19. This tastes sort of like Zin. Starts with wild berry, pepper, and gamy, leathery notes, and turns rich and full-bodied in the mouth, with robust berry and spice flavors. Fairly strong tannins mark this rustic wine. **84** —*S.H. (8/1/2001)*

Sobon Estate 1997 Rhône Red Blend (Shenandoah Valley (CA)) $18. 87 —*L.W. (2/1/2000)*

Sobon Estate 2005 Rezerve Rosé Blend (Amador County) $10. This Grenache-based Rhône blend is dry and simple, with apricot and cherry flavors and some cleansing acidity. This is a pleasantly rustic sipper that finishes clean and brisk. **83** —*S.H. (12/1/2006)*

Sobon Estate 2004 Rezerve Rosé Blend (Amador County) $10. Delicious in cherries, raspberries, and vanilla, with subtle herb flavors, this blush is dry, crisp, and balanced. It's really a lovely rosé that will be versatile at the table. **86 Best Buy** —*S.H. (12/15/2005)*

Sobon Estate 2002 Roussanne (Shenandoah Valley (CA)) $15. This richly fruity, superripe white wine features flavors of tropical fruits and flowers. It's very spicy, with pleasant accents of oak. Drinks fully dry, with a soft, slightly thick texture. **85** —*S.H. (2/1/2004)*

Sobon Estate 2000 Roussanne (Shenandoah Valley (CA)) $15. Softly fruity, clean, and vibrant, this is a pleasant wine that seems made to sip in a garden. It smells like flowers and tastes like fresh tree fruits. The finish is a bit sweet, and very spicy. **86** —*S.H. (12/15/2002)*

Sobon Estate 2002 Sangiovese (Amador County) $15. A nicely drinkable wine reminiscent of Zinfandel for its dark color and earthy, wild berry and pepper flavors. But it has a light texture and silky tannins more like Pinot Noir. **85** —*S.H. (10/1/2004)*

Sobon Estate 1998 Sangiovese (Amador County) $13. 87 —*L.W. (10/1/1999)*

Sobon Estate 2003 Syrah (Amador County) $14. Smells invitingly fine, with a classic rotie Syrah nose, but quickly turns Porty and sweetly hot in the mouth, with the flavor of stewed raisins and a sugary finish. **82** —*S.H. (7/1/2006)*

Sobon Estate 2001 Syrah (Shenandoah Valley (CA)) $15. Plenty of Rhône-style Syrah character, with pretty notes of blackberry, blueberry, and

USA

lavender, in a very dry package. Has a tannic density that is rich, well structured, and finishes dry. **87** —*S.H. (12/1/2003)*

Sobon Estate 1999 Syrah (Shenandoah Valley (CA)) $15. "Herbal, earthy, and woodsy" is this Syrah's calling card, from start to finish. Red berry aromas couple with dried spice notes that show up again on the palate. It's lean and a bit tart—coax the fruit out of this baby with an herb-marinated leg of lamb. **86** *(10/1/2001)*

Sobon Estate 1997 Syrah (Shenandoah Valley (CA)) $15. 87 —*J.C. (11/1/1999)*

Sobon Estate 2001 Rezerve Syrah (Shenandoah Valley (CA)) $24. Rich in jammy currant, blackberry, and cherry flavors, this very dry wine also has a peppery, molasses edge that adds complexity. The tannins are sizable, thick and dusty, so this wine calls for a juicy steak. **86** —*S.H. (12/1/2004)*

Sobon Estate 2002 Viognier (Shenandoah Valley (CA)) $15. Not as over the top as some Viogniers, with a tight, lemony structure and crisp acids. On the finish, some pretty flavors of peaches and tropical fruits turn up. Distinctive and clean. **86** —*S.H. (2/1/2004)*

Sobon Estate 2000 Viognier (Shenandoah Valley (CA)) $15. Some will enjoy the sugary flavors that accompany the flower and ripe tree-fruit flavors, but to me they're off-putting. The flavors are so ripe that the excessively sweet mouthfeel makes them cloying. **83** —*S.H. (12/15/2002)*

Sobon Estate 2003 Zinfandel (Fiddletown) $20. Everything about this Zin, from the voluptous texture to the ripe fruit, is perfect, but the wine is overtly sweet in sugar and technically not at all dry, so be forewarned before you buy. **82** —*S.H. (5/1/2006)*

Sobon Estate 2002 Zinfandel (Fiddletown) $18. Superripe, almost overripe, to judge from the Porty, raisiny, caramelized aroma. Exceptionally full-bodied and long on fruity flavor—blackberries, cassis, plums, chocolate, coffee, it all just floods the mouth, accompanied by rich tannins. **85** — *S.H. (9/1/2004)*

Sobon Estate 2001 Zinfandel (Fiddletown) $20. Right off the bat, starts with a disturbingly Porty note of raisins, pie crust, and chocolate, suggesting overly ripe grapes. The winemaker kept the alcohol under 15 percent, but the wine tastes sweet and hot. Fans of this Sierra style will appreciate it. **84** —*S.H. (3/1/2004)*

Sobon Estate 1998 Zinfandel (Fiddletown) $18. Alcoholic, volatile nose, with some pickley edges to it. The wine is smooth and fruity, with a quick, hot, alcoholic finish and very dry tannins. **85** —*P.G. (3/1/2001)*

Sobon Estate 2003 Cougar Hill Zinfandel (Amador County) $16. Just this side of dry, this is a round, soft, polished Zin, rich in cherry, cassis, coffee, and milk chocolate flavors, with a pleasantly spicy, peppery finish. It's a lush wine with a small percent of Syrah. **89** —*S.H. (5/1/2006)*

Sobon Estate 2002 Cougar Hill Zinfandel (Shenandoah Valley (CA)) $17. Smells sugary and caramelly, like Port, although it's basically dry in the mouth, with flavors of ripe blackberries and cocoa. Nice with barbecue, burgers, sausage. **84** —*S.H. (4/1/2005)*

Sobon Estate 2001 Cougar Hill Zinfandel (Shenandoah Valley (CA)) $17. A plush textured wine, it shows intriguing hints of bacon, vanilla, and caramel, in addition to the primary plum, black cherry, cola, and herb notes. Tea and smoke bring up the rear. **89** *(11/1/2003)*

Sobon Estate 2000 Cougar Hill Zinfandel (Shenandoah Valley (CA)) $17. Appreciate this wine for what it is: magnificently distinct, a wine that stands on its own. Dry and earthy, not too alcoholic, it's quintessential Sierra Zin. It's almost your patriotic duty to respect it. **88** —*S.H. (11/1/2002)*

Sobon Estate 1998 Cougar Hill Zinfandel (Shenandoah Valley (CA)) $16. A very elegant wine, made Cabernet-style, it begins with pretty berry and spice aromas. Round, rich in fruit, and dry. Sturdy but accessible tannins complete the picture. **88 Editors' Choice** —*S.H. (8/1/2001)*

Sobon Estate 2000 Fiddletown Zinfandel (Shenandoah Valley (CA)) $18. From a pioneering Foothills Zin master, a boldly dynamic Zin that does a good job of taming the grape's wild character. Think of dressing a grizzled old mountain man in clothes from the Gap. The varietal's berry flavors are sharp and fresh, and it drinks a little tannic. It's a barbecue wine. **86** —*S.H. (11/1/2002)*

Sobon Estate 2001 Lubenko Vineyard Zinfandel (Fiddletown) $18. Quite racy and floral in the nose. Bright-edged raspberry, cherry, plum, vanilla, toast, spice, and herb flavors are lifted along the palate by zippy acidity. **87** *(11/1/2003)*

Sobon Estate 2004 Old Vines Zinfandel (Amador County) $13. Leon Sobon is an Amador pioneer whose Zinfandels are dependably juicy and showcase a Foothills exuberance. This polished bottling is ripe in jammy cherry and blackberry flavors and a Kahlúa finish. It's delicious and easy to drink. **87** —*S.H. (5/1/2006)*

Sobon Estate 2004 Old Vines Zinfandel (Amador County) $13. Intense in raspberry, cherry, and blackberry flavors that have a chocolatey edge, this wine also has some raisiny tastes suggesting shriveled or superripe berries, but it maintains essential dryness. It's a big, rustic, expressive Zin that calls for similar fare. **85** —*S.H. (10/1/2006)*

Sobon Estate 2002 Old Vines Zinfandel (Shenandoah Valley (CA)) $12. Shows why this part of the Foothills has achieved such a stellar reputation for Zin. It's a big wine, packed with sweet cherry, black raspberry, pepper, and smoky vanilla flavors, but drinks balanced and gentle. **91 Best Buy** —*S.H. (11/15/2004)*

Sobon Estate 2001 Old Vines Zinfandel (Shenandoah Valley (CA)) $13. Fairly lean in style, with a blueberry and blackberry center that's framed in toasty oak and silky tannins. It's complex, with vanilla, spice, licorice, and plum notes as well. Moderate finish. **88** *(11/1/2003)*

Sobon Estate 2000 Reserve Zinfandel (Shenandoah Valley (CA)) $24. Seems to have earned its reserve status by dint of high alcohol and super-ripe fruit, but for me, these are negatives. A strong note of raisins and prunes assaults the nose; hot flavors mar the flavors. The finish is hot, peppery, and awkwardly sweet. **84** —*S.H. (11/1/2002)*

Sobon Estate 2002 Rezerve Zinfandel (Shenandoah Valley (CA)) $24. Big, kick-butt Zin, richly flavored and satisfying. Waves of blackberries, coffee, cocoa, spices, and herbs wash across the palate, with oaky notes. High in alcohol, and dry. **88** —*S.H. (3/1/2005)*

Sobon Estate 2002 Rezerve Zinfandel (Shenandoah Valley (CA)) $24. Well-ripened in black cherry and blueberry flavors, this Zin is also ripe and sweet in tannins. It's softly textured, with highlights of cocoa, dried herbs, coffee, and white pepper. Has the elegant structure of a fine Cabernet Sauvignon. **90** —*S.H. (10/1/2005)*

Sobon Estate 2001 Rezerve Zinfandel (Shenandoah Valley (CA)) $24. Sleek and smooth, this one's couched in firm, ripe tannins that frame a core of plush blackberry, cassis, plum, and toasty oak flavors. The wine is elegant and long on the finish, well balanced and refined. **90** *(11/1/2003)*

Sobon Estate 2004 Rezerve Zin Zinfandel (Amador County) $24. Big and rich in blackberry and cocoa flavors, with a generous dusting of peppery spice, this Zin, which is mainly from a single vineyard, shows the power and heft of Amador. Drink now with game, cheeses, or pasta. **90** —*S.H. (12/1/2006)*

Sobon Estate 2004 Rocky Top Zinfandel (Amador County) $18. Tastes over-ripe and raisiny, with a Porty finish. It's not quite sweet and not quite dry, but falls awkwardly in the middle. **82** —*S.H. (10/1/2006)*

Sobon Estate 2003 Rocky Top Zinfandel (Amador County) $18. A style of Zin not to my liking. Dry and hot, with tobacco and berry flavors and raw elbows of tannin. Turns raisiny and pruny on the finish. **83** —*S.H. (10/1/2005)*

Sobon Estate 2002 Rocky Top Zinfandel (Shenandoah Valley (CA)) $16. With well over 15 percent alcohol, this wine drinks hot, and is astringent in tannins. It's pretty palate-numbing. If you like this over the top style, you'll appreciate the plummy, mocha flavors. **84** —*S.H. (9/1/2004)*

Sobon Estate 2001 Rocky Top Zinfandel (Shenandoah Valley (CA)) $16. Somewhat plush in the nose, with smoky, rich black cherry, chocolate, coffee, spice, and herb notes on the palate. Tannins are big and powdery, keeping the toasty finish in check. **87** *(11/1/2003)*

Sobon Estate 2000 Rocky Top Zinfandel (Shenandoah Valley (CA)) $15. A very distinctive Zin that has that purity of flavor and individuality that tells you it comes from a particular piece of earth. It's dry and earthy-rich, with finely ground tannins reminiscent of espresso. **91 Editors' Choice** —*S.H. (11/1/2002)*

Sobon Estate 1998 Rocky Top Zinfandel (Shenandoah Valley (CA)) $15. Firm, fruity wine, with good clean varietal flavors. Simple and ripe, with a big, tannic finish. **85** —*P.G. (3/1/2001)*

Sobon Estate 1997 Rocky Top Zinfandel (Shenandoah Valley (CA)) $15. 86 —*P.G. (11/15/1999)*

Sobon Estate 1997 Rocky Top Vineyards Zinfandel (Shenandoah Valley (CA)) $15. 90 —*L.W. (11/1/1999)*

Sobon Estate 1997 Vintner's Selection Zinfandel (Amador County) $12. 91 Best Buy —*L.W. (2/1/2000)*

Sobon Estate 2003 Zinfandel Port Zinfandel (Amador County) $15. Put enough sugar in anything and it tastes pretty good! So it is with this simple, fruity Port-style Zin. It's ripe in blackberry, chocolate, and coffee flavors; overall it's very sweet. **86** —*S.H. (12/1/2006)*

SOCKEYE

Sockeye 2002 Cabernet Sauvignon (Washington) $11. This is a firmly fruity, tart, steak-friendly wine with some good 'grip' and a solid core of peppery black cherry fruit. Light notes of licorice and roasted coffee finish up quickly; the blend includes six percent Merlot. 2500 cases were made. **87 Best Buy** —*P.G. (11/15/2005)*

Sockeye 2004 Pinot Gris (California) $12. This is a nice everyday example of why Pinot Gris is catching on. It's a crisp, dry wine, with peach and apricot flavors and a nice streak of minerality that leads to a zesty, clean aftertaste. **84** —*S.H. (2/1/2006)*

Sockeye 2002 Syrah (Columbia Valley (WA)) $12. Shows some decent complexity for a bargain-priced Syrah, blending herbal, grassy notes with cinnamon, vanilla, and blackberries, all wrapped in a light-bodied package. Reveals some tea-like notes on the finish. **84** *(9/1/2005)*

SOFIA

Sofia 2000 Blanc de Blancs Champagne Blend (California) $20. From Francis Coppola, the Sofia's sweet floral aromas, peach, and pear flavors are paired with a very soft mouthfeel. Consider a neo-Muscato but with decidedly lower acidity than the best of those Italian sparklers. It can look rosé in it's lovely cellophane wrap, but it isn't. Will make a great gift, with broad appeal to those who prefer soft and sweet bubbly. **83** *(12/1/2001)*

SOGNO

Sogno 2001 Reserve Cabernet Franc (El Dorado County) $22. This harshly tannic wine tastes dried out and stemmy. It numbs the mouth and the most fruity flavor in it is of blackberries that are still half green. **81** —*S.H. (11/15/2003)*

Sogno 2000 Giocchino Red Blend (El Dorado) $16. A super-Tuscan wannabe from the Sierra Foothills that's a blend of Sangiovese and three Bordeaux varieties, but doesn't quite hit the mark. Has some funky aromas and flavors of cola and Lifesavers candy, with a cough-medicine streak. **82** —*S.H. (5/1/2002)*

Sogno 2000 Syrah (El Dorado) $15. Just barely acceptable as a table wine due to the unnatural cherry cough syrup flavors and insipid mouthfeel. They vinified it dry, but it still feels insipid, with very flat acidity. **81** —*S.H. (9/1/2003)*

Sogno 2001 Zinfandel (El Dorado County) $14. Fairly astringent, with hints of dried cherry, blackberry, herb, and smoke flavors. A rustic style. **81** *(11/1/2003)*

Sogno 2001 Karma Vineyard Zinfandel (Amador County) $17. A light, tea-like style of Zin, sporting hints of cherry and spice, couched in fairly firm tannins. **82** *(11/1/2003)*

SOKOL BLOSSER

Sokol Blosser 2003 Pinot Gris (Willamette Valley) $21. Whole-cluster pressed and slow-fermented in stainless steel, this nonetheless comes on a bit hot, ripe, and "pushed" past the optimal point of freshness. It's lush to a fault, and needs to be drunk up quickly. **86** —*P.G. (11/15/2005)*

Sokol Blosser 2001 Pinot Gris (Willamette Valley) $18. Aromas of white pepper and pear start it off, and it smells snappy and inviting. The palate is all about grapefruit and orange; in a word, it's citrusy. The finish comes in waves, with notes of stone fruit and licorice. As a whole it's

round and satisfying, but it's also a tad bit dilute and dull, which is why it rates where it does. **85** —*M.S. (8/1/2003)*

Sokol Blosser 2000 Pinot Gris (Willamette Valley) $19. The opening of ripe pears and apples seems right on the money, however, the palate is a bit overzealous and spritzy, with sharper than expected orange, grapefruit, and lemon flavors. This wine exemplifies the overt, lively style of Pinot Gris, but it's one-dimensional and lacks subtlety. **85** —*M.S. (12/31/2002)*

Sokol Blosser 2003 Pinot Noir (Dundee Hills) $26. Substantial and soft, this lush Pinot from a hot year displays flavors of buttery vanilla, cherry, and beet. Herbal notes slide into green tea tannins; it's consistent with the winery's past Dundee Hills bottles. **87** —*P.G. (12/1/2006)*

Sokol Blosser 2002 Pinot Noir (Dundee Hills) $26. Substantial and dark, this late-breaking '02 offers cherry and beet flavors, with some of the tomato leaf scents that typify Oregon Pinots. Good structure for near-term drinking. **88** —*P.G. (11/15/2005)*

Sokol Blosser 2000 Pinot Noir (Willamette Valley) $25. Fresh cherry, mint, and cola flavors are underpinned by wood and earth. Compact and youthful, it will reward some serious breathing time. **87** —*P.G. (4/1/2003)*

Sokol Blosser 1999 Pinot Noir (Willamette Valley) $30. A somewhat delicate wine, with orange and tea accents on the chocolate-tinged dark cherry flavors. Medium-weight, it has a full yet angular mouthfeel. Finishes with spice and earth notes, tangy acids, and tannins. Not deeply fruited but nevertheless shows some complexity. Drink now–2006. **85** *(10/1/2002)*

Sokol Blosser 1998 Pinot Noir (Willamette Valley) $28. A pale, pretty Pinot, a year older than most of the current releases, it shows mature scents of red fruits, cola, and root beer. Light, tasty, and cleanly rendered, it has good varietal character and balance, moderate tannins, and plenty of overall charm. **87** —*P.G. (4/1/2002)*

Sokol Blosser 2003 Estate Cuvée Pinot Noir (Dundee Hills) $28. From the hot hot 2003 vintage, this has a bit more sweet ripe fruit than the 2004s. It's showing light cranberry/cherry flavors just trickling into Lifesaver candy, and backed with moderate tannins and a green tea astringency. Light/medium-bodied, well-built, and good for aging for another six or eight years. **88** —*P.G. (9/1/2006)*

Sokol Blosser 2001 Old Vineyard Block Pinot Noir (Willamette Valley) $50. This was the first block of Pinot Noir planted by the Sokol Blossers in the early 1970s, and it benefits from its maturity, its peerless location in the Red Hills of Dundee, and the fact that it is own-rooted and has escaped the ravages of phylloxera. Scents of cherry, baking spice, and cinnamon follow through in the mouth, where the perfect balance of fruit oak and acid support a gentle, expressive yet delicate wine. **90** —*P.G. (2/1/2005)*

Sokol Blosser 1998 Old Vineyard Block Pinot Noir (Willamette Valley) $65. Another limited production (212 case), unfiltered wine from Sokol Blosser's oldest vines. This one shows sweet cherry scents, mint, and tobacco—a very flavorful blend of fruit and leaf. Forward, plump, and sweet, with a lively, spicy finish. **89** —*P.G. (4/1/2002)*

Sokol Blosser 2001 Twelve Row Block Pinot Noir (Willamette Valley) $66. The name refers to a small section of vineyard planted in 1975, in the heart of a mini-banana belt in the area. It's a gorgeous looking wine, that breathes class and elegance. Well-defined cranberry, raspberry, and cherry fruit flavors come to a focused middle; it's a high-wire style, still young and fresh, but certainly ageworthy. Cellar Candidate (6–10 years). **92 Cellar Selection** —*P.G. (2/1/2005)*

Sokol Blosser 1998 Twelve Row Block Pinot Noir (Willamette Valley) $75. From 23-year-old vines, this limited (102 cases) unfiltered Pinot has a thick, murky look. It smells of strawberry/cherry preserves, and carries those sweet preserve flavors throughout. Medium-weight and properly balanced, it mixes its generous fruit with barrel toast and firm tannins. **89** —*P.G. (4/1/2002)*

Sokol Blosser 1999 Twelve Row Block Limited Production Pinot Noir (Willamette Valley) $65. This limited-production Pinot is a puzzler. Right now the wine is hard as a rock and overrun with tough tannins. There are some flavors of sour cherry and red berry poking through, but at this price one wants more. **86** —*P.G. (4/1/2003)*

Sokol Blosser 2001 Watershed Block Pinot Noir (Willamette Valley) $50. Many Oregon wineries aspire to make Burgundian Pinot Noir, but few actually do. This classy, elegant offering truly captures the fragrance, seductive texture, and feminine grace of good Burgundy. Sexy, tart red fruits, hints of flowers, and a light dusting of cocoa and herb keep it interesting through the finish. **90** —P.G. (2/1/2005)

Sokol Blosser 1998 Watershed Block Pinot Noir (Willamette Valley) $65. Sokol Blosser makes three different block-designated Pinots, all unfiltered and quite limited (198 cases of this one). Its full, rich bouquet has an arresting blend of raisins, tea, cherry-tobacco, and Port-like scents. Underneath are nuances of licorice and tobacco, and it smells and tastes like a Chianti riserva. Lovely weight, perfect ripeness, and good persistence. **90** —P.G. (4/1/2002)

Sokol Blosser 1999 Watershed Block Limited Production Pinot Noir (Willamette Valley) $65. For a wine in this price range, this is showing some seriously green fruit. The nose is all beets and fresh earth, and green flavors of stem and soil continue in the mouth. Has good depth, and may soften up over time. **87** —P.G. (4/1/2003)

Sokol Blosser NV Evolution 5th Edition White Blend (Oregon) $15. This oddly packaged, nonvintage wine is a mongrel mix of nine different varietal grapes, and the result is a fragrant, citrus-flavored blend with all the appeal of a friendly new puppy. Juicy, lemony, and bracing, it calls out for oysters, creamy pasta, or anything in butter sauce. **86** —P.G. (4/1/2002)

Sokol Blosser NV Evolution 6th Edition White Blend (Oregon) $15. This funky white blend, now in its 6th rendition, carries no vintage or regional designation, but we know it's a blend of several white grapes grown mostly in Oregon. The nose is ripe and full of melon, while the spunky palate deals orange and lemon, but not in sour-ball fashion. The finish has some thickness and a slight sticky feel, but ample acidity throughout renders it a good, brisk drink. **86** —M.S. (8/1/2003)

SOLARIS

Solaris 2002 Reserve Cabernet Sauvignon (Napa Valley) $25. Soft and luxurious as an aged tapestry, this wine shows intricate layers of blackberries and black currants, cherries, cocoa, anise, and smoky oak. Although it's fully dry, the fruit is so lush, it feels sweet. Drink now and through 2006. **87** —S.H. (12/15/2005)

Solaris 2000 Reserve Cabernet Sauvignon (Napa Valley) $25. Classy Cab here, all cassis and ripe blackberries and oak, wrapped in lush, smooth tannins. It's elegant, and shows how even in a lesser vintage, an excellent wine succeeds. **90** —S.H. (5/1/2005)

Solaris 2002 Special Release Cabernet Sauvignon (Napa Valley) $15. Here's a pretty nice Cab, showing a wealth of finely ripened cherry and blackberry flavors, and that fancy Napa structure. Smooth tannins and fine acids give it good balance. Should hold and improve for three or four years. **85** —S.H. (3/1/2006)

Solaris 2004 Chardonnay (Monterey) $12. Bright and zesty in lemon and lime, kiwi, pineapple, and vanilla flavors, this Chard is very dry and high in acidity. Finishes a little bitter and green, but otherwise shows Monterey character at a decent price. **84** —S.H. (11/15/2006)

Solaris 2003 Chardonnay (North Coast) $13. Fruity and simple, with peach and citrus flavors that weaken on the finish. **83** —S.H. (6/1/2005)

Solaris 2001 Merlot (Napa Valley) $16. Soft and one-dimensional, this wine shows ripe cherry and cocoa flavors that are semisweet. It has enough tannins and acidity to balance out the fruit. **83** —S.H. (6/1/2005)

Solaris 2002 Special Release Merlot (Napa Valley) $15. Dry and tart, this Merlot has some rough edges to the cherry and mocha flavors. It's a good, country-style wine to quaff with simple fare. **84** —S.H. (3/1/2006)

Solaris 2004 Pinot Noir (Carneros) $15. This unfortunate wine is heavy and soft, with the flavor of cooked cherries and coffee. It's bone dry. The main problem is a harsh, burnt feeling. **81** —S.H. (3/1/2006)

Solaris 2003 Pinot Noir (Carneros) $13. Raw and tough, with overly sweet, cherry cough medicine flavors. **81** —S.H. (6/1/2005)

Solaris 2004 Zinfandel (Mendocino County) $14. Varietally pure, this Zin from inland benchland vineyards in the warm Ukiah area features ripe

cherry and cocoa flavors with a balancing earthiness. It's soft in acidity, but firm tannins make up for that. **84** —S.H. (11/15/2006)

SOLEIL & TERROIR

Soleil & Terroir 1997 La Colline-Reserve Chardonnay (Arroyo Grande Valley) $30. 91 —J.C. (3/1/2000)

SOLÉNA

Soléna 2004 Pinot Gris (Oregon) $20. A cut above the competition, this hits on all cylinders. Plenty of texture, rich, round mouthfeel, and nicely ripened but not over-the-top pear and stone fruits. There's a hit of cinnamon spice in the finish, and the flavors seem to resonate through a long and satisfying finish. **92** —P.G. (2/1/2006)

Soléna 2003 Pinot Gris (Oregon) $18. Laurent Montalieu, who made so many memorable Pinot Gris during his years at WillaKenzie, shows a masterful touch here again. The pure expression of pear-flavored Pinot Gris fruit anchors the wine from the core out, enhanced with natural, varietal spice. No malolactic fermentation, no oak. Just a lovely expression of great fruit. **90** —P.G. (8/1/2005)

Soléna 2003 Grand Cuvée Pinot Noir (Willamette Valley) $25. This modestly priced effort is a blend of four Willamette Valley vineyards. Winemaker Laurent Montalieu applies his sophisticated skills to craft a very classy, barrel-fermented, aromatic Pinot Noir. Just the right mix of berries and tart red fruits, with floral nuances and a hint of earthy herb. This delicious, complex wine shows why less expensive vineyard blends often outshine the pricey, single-vineyard Oregon Pinots. **90 Editors' Choice** —P.G. (9/1/2006)

SOLO ROSA

Solo Rosa 2002 Sangiovese (California) $15. Pretty and easy to drink, a dry wine that opens with the scents of raspberries and smoky oak. In the mouth, delicate in structure, with the tangy taste of raspberries and strawberries and herbs. This Sangiovese-Merlot-Syrah blend is from Wine Enthusiast's Editor-at-Large Jeff Morgan and the winemaker at Lynmar Winery, Daniel Moore. **87** —S.H. (3/1/2004)

SONNET

Sonnet 2003 Kruse Vineyard Pinot Noir (York Mountain) $40. From a new winery in this coolish Central Coast appellation, this is a pretty good early effort. It has rich, gooey blackberry and chocolate flavors, but is a little soft in acids, although the silky mouthfeel is a delight. Advice: go for better structure and complexity, less ripeness. **86** —S.H. (8/1/2005)

SONOMA COAST VINEYARDS

Sonoma Coast Vineyards 2003 Pinot Noir (Sonoma Coast) $60. Made from grapes grown close to the chilly Pacific, this is a wine with bright acidity and elegance. It's got some size, too, but unlike many big, rich Pinots from warmer areas this one toes the line of balance like a pro. The cherry cola, raspberry, tea, and gentle spice flavors are satisfying and complex. Best next year and through 2008. **91** (12/1/2006)

SONOMA CREEK

Sonoma Creek 2003 Cabernet Sauvignon (Sonoma County) $13. There's lots of toasty oak in this wine's aroma and flavor, but the cherry-berry fruit quickly catches up to it. It's dry and fairly tannic, with a rustic signature. **84** —S.H. (2/1/2006)

Sonoma Creek 2004 Chardonnay (Sonoma County) $10. This new young wine is quite a treat in an everyday Chard. It has tasty Chardonnay flavors of ripe pineapples and peaches, with spicy, vanilla-tinged oak and a smooth, creamy texture. **84** —S.H. (2/1/2006)

Sonoma Creek 2003 Chardonnay (Sonoma County) $10. Simple and oaky, with woody, high char, and vanilla flavors and one-dimensional fruit. **82** —S.H. (3/1/2006)

Sonoma Creek 2003 Merlot (Sonoma County) $13. Dry and balanced, this Merlot has some real complexity, from the fruity-oaky flavors to the complex, accessible tannins. There's also a pretty coating of toasty oak. **84** —S.H. (2/1/2006)

Sonoma Creek 2005 Pinot Noir (Sonoma County) $13. Soft, simple, and sweetish, this Pinot has cherry pie filling, cola, and rhubarb pie flavors. It

USA

contains a dollop of Petite Sirah, which gives it more body. **83** —*S.H.* *(12/15/2006)*

Sonoma Creek 2004 Pinot Noir (Sonoma County) $13. An everyday Pinot that shows many of the noble characteristics of the variety. It's silky and dry, with pleasant cherry and tobacco flavors and a touch of oak. **85** — *S.H. (2/1/2006)*

Sonoma Creek 2000 Pinot Noir (Sonoma County) $9. Dark cherry fruit is offset by herb, toasty oak and coffee notes. Panelists were divided, some finding it dry and over-wooded, others liking the dark and tangy flavors and creamy feel. **84 Best Buy** *(10/1/2002)*

Sonoma Creek 2000 Pinot Noir (Carneros) $11. Toasty oak adorns tart cherry fruit in this midweight wine. A peaty and toasted marshmallow nose sets the stage, and attractive caramel, sour plum/cherry, and earth flavors follow. Finishes with good length, slightly tangy tannins, charred oak and cocoa accents. **86 Best Buy** *(10/1/2002)*

Sonoma Creek 1998 Pinot Noir (Sonoma County) $15. 82 —*M.S.* *(12/15/2000)*

Sonoma Creek 1998 Duarte Old Vine Zinfandel (Contra Costa County) $15. Fleshy, sweet, ripe, jammy fruit tastes like spicy strawberry preserves. This is a big, briary, vanilla-laced Zin, with firm acids and a fat finish. **89 Best Buy** —*P.G. (3/1/2001)*

SONOMA HILL

Sonoma Hill 2001 Cabernet Sauvignon (Sonoma County) $15. There are some nice things going on here, including the blackberry, espresso, and spicy flavors infused with pleasant herbs. It's also quite dry and the tannins are firm enough to stand up to a big roast. Turns rough and astringent on the finish. **84** —*S.H. (2/1/2004)*

Sonoma Hill 2002 Chardonnay (Sonoma County) $13. Starts with modest aromas of fruits and oak that turn tart and earthy in the mouth, with suggestions of peaches and apples. Finishes short and dry. **83** —*S.H.* *(4/1/2004)*

Sonoma Hill 2001 Merlot (Sonoma County) $15. An easy wine with pleasant aromas and flavors of cherries, plums, and violets. It's quite dry in the mouth, with dusty tannins. Has lots to like, although it could use more fruity concentration. **85** —*S.H. (4/1/2004)*

Sonoma Hill 2002 Pinot Noir (Sonoma County) $12. Oaky and weak in flavor, with modest cherry and spice tastes and a chocolatey finish. Crisp and tart in acids. **84** *(11/1/2004)*

SONOMA-CUTRER

Sonoma-Cutrer 1999 Founders Reserve Chardonnay (Sonoma Valley) $65. This is a connoisseur's wine, and requires understanding to appreciate. If you're a fan of blowsy Chards, the lean, mineral, and citrus flavors will pass by unnoticed. Impressive with its rich, oaky complexities and layers of flavor and texture. **93** —*S.H. (10/1/2003)*

Sonoma-Cutrer 1997 Les Pierres Chardonnay (Sonoma Valley) $30. 86 *(6/1/2000)*

Sonoma-Cutrer 1998 Russian River Ranches Chardonnay (Sonoma Coast) $18. 87 *(6/1/2000)*

Sonoma-Cutrer 1997 The Cutrer Chardonnay (Russian River Valley) $30. 89 *(6/1/2000)*

SONORA

Sonora 1998 Story Vineyard Old Vine Zinfandel (Amador County) $21. A dense purple color, with jammy, grapy fruit. Plenty of extraction, yielding a grapy, fruity wine with a little bit of fizz to it. The wine promises more depth than it delivers; the finish falls off quickly and feels flat. **84** —*P.G. (3/1/2001)*

Sonora 1997 Story Vineyard Zinfandel (Shenandoah Valley (CA)) $19. 86 —*P.G. (11/15/1999)*

Sonora 1998 TC Vineyard Old Vine Zinfandel (Amador County) $21. Dark and deep purple/black, with a Port-like nose. There's a little fizz on the palate, which seems odd in a wine this big, and the flavors are locked in tight. Flat, dry, tannic finish. **84** —*P.G. (3/1/2001)*

Sonora 1997 TC Vineyard Old Vine Zinfandel (Amador County) $19. 86 — *P.G. (11/15/1999)*

SOOS CREEK

Soos Creek 2001 Artist's Series #1 Bordeaux Blend (Columbia Valley (WA)) $27. This Bordeaux blend has some good, firm, juicy red fruits, well-managed tannins, some sweaty scents in the nose, and a tannic, tarry, earthy finish. Needs more time to smooth out the rough edges and tone down the volatile scents. **86** —*P.G. (7/11/2004)*

Soos Creek 2003 Artist's Series #3 Red Wine Bordeaux Blend (Columbia Valley (WA)) $28. A full-on Bordeaux blend, with 61% Cab Sauvignon, 19% Merlot, 11% Cab Franc, and 9% Petit Verdot. Tight and slatey, it's got firm, hard—but certainly ripe—tannins wrapped around concentrated cassis and mulberry fruit. It's very well made but can use some softening up; a few more years will add to its complexity and develop its bouquet. **93** —*P.G. (6/1/2006)*

Soos Creek 1999 Cabernet Sauvignon (Columbia Valley (WA)) $30. Here is an inviting, almost exotic nose-mixing ripe fruit and sexy oak in a rich, textured, seamlessly deep wine. This easily compares with top of the line Washington efforts costing far more. Just 150 cases made. **92** —*P.G. (6/1/2002)*

Soos Creek 2003 Champoux Vineyard Cabernet Sauvignon (Columbia Valley (WA)) $30. You'll find this underrated producer offers wines with wonderful density and concentration, ripely balanced, plummy, mixed red fruits, and elegantly astringent tannins. There is real winemaking craft on display here, every detail beautifully rendered, substantial but not out of whack in any way. The fragrant, evocative results showcase the fruit but also buttress it with properly managed acids, tannins, and new oak. **94** —*P.G. (6/1/2006)*

Soos Creek 1999 Champoux Vineyard Cabernet Sauvignon (Columbia Valley (WA)) $30. Red fruits and toast, pepper, and coffee race to the front of this delicious young wine. It comes right at you, fresh and tangy, and suggests that a bit of time in the cellar might soften up the edges. Excellent winemaking. **91** —*P.G. (6/1/2002)*

Soos Creek 1998 Champoux Vineyard Cabernet Sauvignon (Columbia Valley (WA)) $30. Look closely or you will miss the vineyard designation, hidden in a tiny black banner in the upper left corner of the label. It's important, because Champoux is one of the state's oldest and best Cabernet vineyards. Ripe, satiny black cherry/red berry fruit is on display here, with firm acids, moderate tannins, and just enough oak to add a dash of toast at the end. **89** —*P.G. (10/1/2001)*

Soos Creek 2003 Ciel du Cheval Cabernet Sauvignon (Red Mountain) $33. A bit more austere (for the moment) than the Champoux bottling, this has the vineyard's characteristically tight streak of mineral running through its core. Mixed scents suggest hay and pie cherries. There is plenty of substantial viscosity, but nothing heavy about the mouthfeel. This is sleek, deceptively light, tasting of stones, with soft hints of berry, good acids, and nothing sharp or bitter. **93** —*P.G. (6/1/2006)*

Soos Creek 1999 Reserve Cabernet Sauvignon (Columbia Valley (WA)) $36. This is the first reserve for this unassuming, low-profile winery whose wines clearly belong in the first rank of Washington's boutiques. It shows classic Cabernet fruit from three top vineyards, long, and persistent, yet never over extracted or alcoholic. True Bordeaux style in an elegant, ageworthy wine. **93 Editors' Choice** —*P.G. (6/1/2002)*

Soos Creek 2001 Merlot (Columbia Valley (WA)) $25. The first Merlot in the winery's 15-year history is restrained, aromatic, and lightly leafy, showing hints of tobacco under the pretty, soft, plum, and berry fruit. Just the right amount of smooth, chocolatey tannins follow through; the wine is ripe, yet not too ripe. A pleasing spiciness comes out as it breathes. **91** —*P.G. (6/1/2006)*

Soos Creek NV Sundance Red Blend (Columbia Valley (WA)) $20. Mostly (70%) Merlot, with the rest Cabernet, the grapes for this soft, fragrant red wine come from the Charbonneau and Ciel du Cheval vineyards. It's an open, engaging style, fruity and textured with some nice cocoa and toast to finish. Drinking really well right now. **90** —*P.G. (6/1/2002)*

SORENSON

Sorenson 2000 Cabernet Sauvignon (Napa Valley) $40. Dark and richly textured, with black currant, cassis, chocolate, herb, coffee, and smoky

USA

overtones. The wine is full bodied, and plush, framed in ripe tannins and long on the finish. **90** —*J.M. (9/1/2003)*

SOTER

Soter 2002 Little Creek Cabernet Franc (Napa Valley) $75. I've criticized Napa Cab Franc as too one-dimensional to bottle on its own, but this wine is so fruity, so charming that it borders on the exception to the rule. It's a soft, complex beauty, silky and delicate, brimming with cherry and oak flavors and a lovely, elegant finish. **90** —*S.H. (4/1/2006)*

SPANGLER VINEYARDS

Spangler Vineyards 2004 Sundown Vineyard Cabernet Franc (Southern Oregon) $30. Dark and earthy, with substantial tannins, this includes a small amount of Merlot. But in this part of the world Merlot doesn't offer much in the way of softness. It's a hard, severe wine with black cherry and brambly blackberry fruit. Decanting will help soften it up. **86** —*P.G. (12/1/2006)*

Spangler Vineyards 2004 Doerner Vineyard Pinot Noir (Southern Oregon) $18. Bright and spicy, with cherry and cranberry fruit. It's got Christmas cake spices and a lively, tart core. Vivid and truly Burgundian, it does not overreach nor hide behind too much new oak. A sturdy bottle; well made and food-friendly. **87** —*P.G. (12/1/2006)*

Spangler Vineyards 2005 Viognier (Southern Oregon) $19. Spangler (formerly La Garza) is in the central Oregon region that is beginning to show real potential for unusual grapes not generally associated with the state. This is a fine Viognier, cutting and clear, and fragrant with a mix of peach, grapefruit, and papaya. Flavorful and restrained, with just a hint of residual sugar. **88** —*P.G. (12/1/2006)*

SPANN VINEYARDS

Spann Vineyards 2001 Mayacamas Range Five Barrels Cabernet Sauvignon (Sonoma Valley) $30. Balanced, with good acidity and easy tannins framing a nice mix of cherry-berry flavors and a tobacco, coffee, and herb edge. Aims for elegance and detail rather than power. **87** —*S.H. (12/15/2004)*

Spann Vineyards 2004 Chardonnay-Viognier (Sonoma County) $20. Here's a clean, dry, elegant wine showing quite a bit of creamy, smoky oak and sophisticated peach, kiwi, and apricot flavors. The Chard dominates. Viognier seems to bring acidic lift and a floral note. **85** —*S.H. (12/1/2006)*

Spann Vineyards 2002 Chardonnay-Viognier (Sonoma County) $17. A fruity, toasty blend, full-bodied and lush, with pleasing hints of peach, melon, apricot, herb, citrus, and spice flavors. The finish is moderate in length. **88** —*J.M. (6/1/2004)*

Spann Vineyards 2001 Red Blend (Sonoma County) $18. Balanced, complex, and elegant, a lovely dry wine with cherry, herb, cola, and oak flavors. Has extra qualities of harmony and grace that make it excellent. Zin, Mourvèdre, and Alicante Bouschet. **90** —*S.H. (12/15/2004)*

Spann Vineyards 2001 Mo Jo Red Blend (Russian River Valley) $30. An unusual blend that's rich in berry, cocoa, and spice flavors. Delicious and elegant, with real complexity of sweet tannins and crisp acids. Great, versatile food wine. Sangiovese, Cabernet Sauvignon, Merlot, Syrah, and Petite Sirah. **89** —*S.H. (12/15/2004)*

Spann Vineyards 2002 Mo Jo Ten Barrels Red Blend (Russian River Valley) $40. The old Italian field blends must have been like this. Rustic, hearty, and dry, with good, rich earthy, berry flavors, the wine has the tannic body to wash down almost anything. But roasted meats will be particularly nice, especially a rosemary-scented leg of lamb. **86** —*S.H. (12/31/2006)*

Spann Vineyards 2002 Syrah (Sonoma County) $20. Showing rich, fruity concentration and good balance, this is an appealing Syrah. It's full-bodied and very soft, with cascades of red and black cherry flavors and a mocha mousse finish. **86** *(9/1/2005)*

Spann Vineyards 2003 Chardonnay-Viognier White Blend (Sonoma County) $18. This is a subtle blend with some very nice features. It's fruity in peaches, honeysuckle, and vanilla, yet dry, with a rich, creamy texture and good acidity. Fabulous spice on the finish makes it alluring. **87** —*S.H. (11/1/2005)*

Spann Vineyards 2002 Mo Zin Zinfandel (Sonoma County) $18. This delightful wine allows Zin to express its wild and woolly, feral side, but keeps it balanced. The briary, brambly berry flavors drink bone dry, with firm tannins. **86** —*S.H. (10/1/2005)*

SPARROW LANE

Sparrow Lane 1999 Beatty Ranch Zinfandel (Napa Valley) $35. Quite fragrant, with pretty cherry and vanilla notes up front. The tannins are ripe, though a bit rustic, and support a blend of black cherry, spice, cassis, and earth tones. Moderately long finish. **88** —*J.M. (12/15/2001)*

SPELLETICH CELLARS

Spelletich Cellars 1998 Bodog Red Bordeaux Blend (Napa Valley) $25. A big, dark wine, with deep flavors of red and black stone fruits, and wild blackberries. Despite the size, it's a simple wine, easy to understand—it's a ribs-and-barbecued-chicken wine. A Bordeaux-style blend, but with 36% Howell Mountain Zinfandel. **86** *(8/1/2001)*

Spelletich Cellars 1999 Cabernet Sauvignon (Napa Valley) $44. A blend from all over the valley, it brings to mind blackberries and cassis, and earthier notes of chocolate and tobacco. This is a good wine, but it's seriously overpriced. It lacks the layers of refinement you're entitled to expect. There's a syrupy feeling in the mouth, and the finish is rough and bitter. **84** —*S.H. (11/15/2002)*

Spelletich Cellars 1998 Cabernet Sauvignon (Napa Valley) $80. They must have let the grapes get as ripe as possible, and then macerated the crushed fruit for a long time, as this wine explodes with berry flavors. There's also a good amount of smoky and spicy oak accents. It's a balanced, harmonious Cabernet. **90** —*S.H. (8/1/2001)*

Spelletich Cellars 1999 Heroncroft Vineyard-Keefur Ranch Chardonnay (Russian River Valley) $29. Quite different from Spelletich's Spotted Owl release, this wine has spiced green-apple aromas. While it's as rich in flavor as the other offering, the acidity is lower, so the wine seems softer and creamier. **86** *(8/1/2001)*

Spelletich Cellars 2000 Ochoa Chardonnay (Carneros) $29. Much lighter and brighter that the Rustridge bottling, with pure, focused aromas of tropical fruits, limes, and ripe peaches. In the mouth, it shines with crisp acidity and deep flavors, accented by oak and lees. This is a first-rate Chard and very typical of its region. **89** —*S.H. (12/15/2002)*

Spelletich Cellars 2000 Rustridge Chardonnay (Napa Valley) $24. From Chiles Valley, this wine has vivacious tropical fruit, peach, and pear flavors, but seems a little heavy in the mouth, with dull acids. Oak provides creamy spice and vanilla, and it finishes with earthy heat. **85** —*S.H. (12/15/2002)*

Spelletich Cellars 1999 Spotted Owl Chardonnay (Mount Veeder) $25. From mountain vineyards, the peach fruit is wrapped in a tight, steely wine, with a firm tannic backbone. There are also complex crushed spices and the sweet vanilla of oak. A wine of great structure, it's also rich and delicious. **90** *(8/1/2001)*

Spelletich Cellars 1999 Bodog Red Blend (Napa Valley) $27. This blend of Zinfandel, Cabernet Sauvignon, and Merlot frm various sections of Napa is a rustic wine and pretty tannic too. By "rustic" I mean it's like a Shaker chair, simple and fundamental. That can be just fine in the right place. It has flavors of black and green tea and blackberries and is very dry. **85** —*S.H. (9/1/2003)*

Spelletich Cellars 2001 Alviso Vineyard Zinfandel (Amador County) $24. Lightweight in fruit flavors, the wine banks on toasty oak to give it structure. Somewhat herbal and bright, the fruit flavors lean toward cherry and raspberry. Finish is moderate in length, with a hint of vanilla and toast. **84** *(11/1/2003)*

Spelletich Cellars 2001 Tim and Edie's Vineyard Zinfandel (Shenandoah Valley (CA)) $23. Smoky rich and smooth up front, with a fine array of layered fruit: Black cherry, plum, chocolate, coffee, cinnamon, smoke, and a hint of tar come to mind. The fine tannins give good support; the finish is long and elegant. **90** *(11/1/2003)*

SPENCER ROLOSON

Spencer Roloson 2001 Palaterra Red Blend (California) $16. This big, brawling bruiser of a red wine is a blend of Carignan, Syrah, and

Valdigue. It has outsized tannins, a rugged texture and enormously extracted fruit. Cherries, blackberries, black raspberries, chocolate, and coffee cascade across the palate, and finish dry and spicy. **87** —*S.H.* *(11/15/2004)*

Spencer Roloson 1999 Palaterra Red Blend (California) $16. A Rhône blend that captures the wild exuberance of Châteauneuf. It's got berry and herb flavors and is very dry and a little tannic. It's not a sophisticated wine. It could use some grace, but it may improve in two or three years. A mixture of Carignan, Syrah, Valdiguié, and Grenache. **85** —*S.H.* *(12/1/2002)*

Spencer Roloson 2002 Palaterra Red Wine Red Blend (California) $16. Straddles the line between an innocent little country wine and a pedigreed red. It is dry, and has forward-fruit flavors of cherries, blackberries, and cocoa, and sturdy tannins. Might improve for a year or two. One-third each Carignane, Syrah, Valdiguie. **86** —*S.H. (6/1/2005)*

Spencer Roloson 2000 Vin Gris Rosé Blend (California) $15. Pretty cherry aromas are forward in this simple, bracing wine. Finishes moderately with a slightly tart, tannic, and tangy edge. **82** —*J.M. (9/10/2002)*

Spencer Roloson 2002 Balyeat Vineyard Sauvignon Blanc (Chiles Valley) $24. For a nice, light and delicate Sauvignon Blanc, this one's hard to beat. It's got great fruity flavors of lemon and lime and peach, with refreshing acidity. Smooth and polished, this is a great cocktail wine. **87** —*S.H. (12/1/2004)*

Spencer Roloson 2003 La Herradura Vineyard Syrah (Napa Valley) $38. This wine is almost over the top. If it had any more ripe, jammy fruit, it would be. As it is, it's balanced enough in tannins and acids so that the flood of blackberry pie and mocha flavors go only so far before dryness and structure kick in to check. Those tannins are a modern-day wonder, ripe, sweet, and sturdy. **90** —*S.H. (3/1/2006)*

Spencer Roloson 2002 La Herradura Vineyard Syrah (Napa Valley) $35. The Northern Rhône is the paradigm here, to judge by this wine's dry density, seriousness, and its white-pepper aroma. It's full and rich on the palate, with fine blackberry, cherry, cocoa, and oak flavors. Really quite fabulous in all respects. Best now for its flamboyant youthfulness and intensity. **92** —*S.H. (6/1/2005)*

Spencer Roloson 1999 Sueno Syrah (Lodi) $28. From an emerging northeast corner of Lodi that will probably get its own appellation, this dark, dense wine brings to mind the Syrahs of southern Monterey County. Exceedingly ripe, with sweet blackberry, tobacco, plum, and chocolate notes, it's very dry, and the tannins are soft. Doesn't seem likely to age. Try with grilled steaks and veggies. **89** —*S.H. (12/1/2002)*

Spencer Roloson 2001 Sueno Vineyard Syrah (Lodi) $28. There's a density and chalky texture to this wine that make it very full-bodied. It sinks into the palate, carried by the weight of the tannins and the sweet ripeness of the dark stone fruits. At the same time, it's properly dry. An excellent Syrah, and another testament to how good wines from Lodi can be. **90** —*S.H. (12/1/2004)*

Spencer Roloson 2001 Tempranillo (Clear Lake) $26. You could almost mistake it for a warm-climate Syrah, with its rich but dry blackberry, chocolate, and herb flavors and full-bodied tannins, yet there's a dustiness that makes it unique. **87** —*S.H. (3/1/2006)*

Spencer Roloson 2002 Madder Lake Vineyard Tempranillo (Clear Lake) $25. A very nice example of this experimental variety in California. It's very dry, with an enticing dustiness that carries subtle flavors of cherries. The tannins are soft and easy, yet complex, and turn grippy on the finish. A fine interpretation of this Spanish grape. **87** —*S.H. (6/1/2005)*

Spencer Roloson 2000 Viognier (Rutherford) $19. An interesting wine, grown in Cabernet country, that's as full-bodied as a red wine. The flavors are solidly Viognier, though, with exotic tropical fruits and wild flowers that drink almost off-dry. Plenty of oak and sur lie aging provide textural complexities. **86** —*S.H. (9/1/2002)*

Spencer Roloson 2004 Noble Vineyard Viognier (Knights Valley) $NA. This is an awkward, clumsy wine. It's exotic and fruity, but uncontrolled. It tastes like sweet-and-sour sauce, which is not a bad flavor, but not one you want in a dry table wine. **83** —*S.H. (3/1/2006)*

Spencer Roloson 2001 Skellenger Vineyards Viognier (Rutherford) $24. Shows how far winemakers have come with this variety. All the exotic

flavors you expect are there, from citrus through white peach, apricot, and honeysuckle, but the wine is well balanced. **90** —*S.H. (5/1/2003)*

Spencer Roloson 2003 Sueno Vineyard Viognier (Lodi) $26. Not over the top like so many others, but keeps its lively menagerie of tropical fruit, vanilla, wildflower, and oak flavors controlled by crisp acidity. A pretty lime-and-honeysuckle flavor lasts forever on the finish. **90** —*S.H. (6/1/2005)*

Spencer Roloson 2002 Sueno Vineyard Viognier (Lodi) $26. In Lodi the grapes got enough sun and heat to get nice and ripe. The flavors are explosive with complex tropical fruit, wildflower, sweet fig, wild honey, and vanilla flavors, to name a few. A crisp spine of acidity provides good structure. This classy wine, for all its flavor, is balanced and elegant. **90** —*S.H. (2/1/2004)*

Spencer Roloson 1999 Zinfandel (Chiles Valley) $30. From a little-known appellation in a warmer, eastern part of Napa, a rather hot, rugged, and raisiny wine. Alcohol of 15% backs up overripe berry flavors that verge on prunes, while hefty tannins make your tongue feel sticky and furry. This wine will appeal to some, but lovers of balance will find it excessive. **84** —*S.H. (11/1/2002)*

Spencer Roloson 1999 Zinfandel (Sonoma County) $25. A blend of Dry Creek and Alexander Valley grapes that were picked superripe, resulting in an almost Port-like wine, although thankfully they vinified it dry. The winemaker calls it "brooding and intense." I find it cumbersome and awkward. But this alcoholic, big Zin perfectly illustrates one extreme of a school of thought in California, and you either like it or you don't. **84** —*S.H. (11/1/2002)*

Spencer Roloson 2003 Madder Lake Vineyard Zinfandel (Clear Lake) $30. Great blackberry and mocha flavors in this dry wine, but it's so hot and soft in acids, it's unbalanced. The softness accentuates the tannins, making the wine harsh. **83** —*S.H. (3/1/2006)*

SPIRIT RIDGE

Spirit Ridge 1998 Chardonnay (California) $7. 80 —*J.C. (7/1/2000)*

SPOTTSWOODE

Spottswoode 2002 Estate Cabernet Sauvignon (Napa Valley) $110. The estate is in St. Helena. The wine is dry, tannic, and too young, an obvious cellar candidate. Those tannins mask the underlying core of black cherry, black currant, and cocoa fruit. This is a lovely, fine Cabernet, rich and supple, that should start showing well by 2010. **92 Cellar Selection** —*S.H. (3/1/2006)*

Spottswoode 2001 Estate Cabernet Sauvignon (Napa Valley) $90. Another fabulous '01 Napa Cab. This beauty maintains a pleasing balance between the sheer power of its well-ripened cherry and blackberry fruit flavors, and an earthy quality grounded in firm tannins and good acidity. Totally balanced, dry, and harmonious, this Cab exudes elegance and style. Drink now through 2015. **94** —*S.H. (3/1/2005)*

Spottswoode 1999 Spottswoode Estate Vineyard Cabernet Sauvignon (Napa Valley) $80. Opening aromas range from well-ripened blackberry fruit to leaner, herbal notes of peat, green olive, and dried leaves. Vanilla, caramel, and smoke are contributed by oak. Feels creamy and dense in the mouth, with solid tannins, and finishes long, with a trace of bitterness. **88** —*S.H. (11/15/2002)*

Spottswoode 2004 Sauvignon Blanc (Napa Valley) $32. Not quite as ripe as the '03, this bottling has grass and hay notes alongside melons and figs. It's a dry, polished, elegant wine, easy to drink, and with quite a lot of complexity. **88** —*S.H. (3/1/2006)*

Spottswoode 2003 Sauvignon Blanc (Napa Valley) $32. Terrific Sauv Blanc, rich, dry, and complex. Brims with citrus, fig, and melon flavors, with riper tropical fruit notes and an oaky veneer. Perfect with shrimp in risotto and goat cheese. **90** —*S.H. (3/1/2005)*

Spottswoode 2000 Sauvignon Blanc (Napa Valley) $25. The bouquet is a bit flat at first, offering nothing more than white stone fruits and pear. Green melon is amplified by a dose of white pepper on the palate, while the finish is layered and solid; it's the best part of the wine by far. **87** *(8/1/2002)*

SPRING MOUNTAIN

Spring Mountain 1997 Miravalle-La Perla-Chevalier Bordeaux Blend (Spring Mountain) $50. 89 *(11/1/2000)*

Spring Mountain 1997 Reserve Bordeaux Blend (Spring Mountain) $90. 92 *(11/1/2000)*

Spring Mountain 2002 Elivette Reserve Cabernet Blend (Napa Valley) $90. This is a very fine Cabernet Sauvignon-based wine. It's immense in extracted black currant and chocolate flavors that are framed in soft, luxurious tannins. Acidity is soft, too, but adequate. The overall impression is of high quality. Despite the mountain origin, it doesn't seem like an ager, though, so drink now through 2009. 92 —*S.H. (12/15/2006)*

Spring Mountain 2002 Estate Cabernet Sauvignon (Spring Mountain) $50. The mountain plays its part in the intense tannins and concentrated fruit. You could drink it now against rich fare, but it's also a cellar candidate. It's a tough, dry, masculine wine, with heady currant and blackberry flavors and a lot of new French oak. Drink now and for the next 15 years. 92 —*S.H. (12/31/2005)*

Spring Mountain 2000 Elivette Cabernet Sauvignon-Merlot (Napa Valley) $90. An estate blend from a classic Napa property, and a very fine one. Shows concentrated blackberry, cassis, and blueberry flavors and soft enough acids to let the sweet fruit shine, yet those mountain tannins are firm and astringent. They're tough enough to demand very rich foods or time in the cellar. It's a delightful choice. 91 —*S.H. (4/1/2004)*

Spring Mountain 2000 Estate Cabernet Sauvignon-Merlot (Spring Mountain) $50. Bigtime Napa Cab blend with one-third Merlot. World class in aspiration, with well-ripened cassis flavors and a rich overlay of well-smoked, vanilla-tinged oak. Notable for its tannins, as fine, soft, and complex as they come. 92 —*S.H. (11/15/2003)*

Spring Mountain 2003 Pinot Noir (Spring Mountain) $50. A good wine, filled with cherry, coffee, and oak flavors, with light, silky tannins. But acidity, that most vital component of California Pinot Noir, is lacking. 85 —*S.H. (2/1/2006)*

Spring Mountain 2001 Elivette Red Blend (Spring Mountain) $90. Dark and rich, with a smooth, supple texture that seamlessly delivers flavors of cassis, vanilla, and plum pudding. Tannins are plentiful but remarkably ripe and caressing on the finish. 91 —*J.C. (10/1/2004)*

Spring Mountain 1999 Reserve Red Wine Red Blend (Napa Valley) $50. Gorgeous and lush, another beautiful '99 that impresses with its ripeness and balance. The black currant and cassis flavors are perfectly offset with toasty oak, and the sweet tannins of the vintage are amply in evidence. Made in a feminine style, not a blockbuster, but controlled and elegant. 92 —*S.H. (12/31/2003)*

Spring Mountain 2004 Sauvignon Blanc (Spring Mountain) $28. This fascinating wine is bone dry and tart in acids, with citrus, melon, fig, and gooseberry flavors that finish with a rich spiciness. Be careful not to chill it too much. You might even want to decant it for a while before refrigerating. It gets better as it breathes in the glass. 90 —*S.H. (5/1/2006)*

Spring Mountain 2003 Sauvignon Blanc (Spring Mountain) $28. Very dry, rich and complex, with an array of fig, kiwi, vanilla, lemon and lime flavors that are wrapped in a creamy texture accentuated by good acidity. 90 **Editors' Choice** —*S.H. (12/31/2005)*

Spring Mountain 2001 Sauvignon Blanc (Spring Mountain) $28. Drinks off-dry and simple, with ripe flavors of lemon custard. The acids are clean and vibrant, but the sweetness is jarring. So is the price. 84 —*S.H. (10/1/2003)*

Spring Mountain 1999 Syrah (Napa Valley) $NA. Pours dark as a graveyard, and one whiff tells you it's lavishly oaked in fine, charred barrels. You have to taste it to find what the vineyard brings, namely, black cherry fruit. Then those mountain tannins kick in, and wham! Everything stops. An obvious cellar candidate through 2006, when you try again. 89 —*S.H. (2/1/2004)*

Spring Mountain 2003 Co-Ferment Syrah (Spring Mountain) $50. Co-fermented with Viognier, this is a softer, fruitier, less tannic, and less complex and impressive wine than Spring Mountain's Miravelle bottling. The idea seems to have been to make it more accessible, but the flavors clash and don't fully resolve. 85 —*S.H. (2/1/2006)*

Spring Mountain 2003 Miravelle Syrah (Spring Mountain) $50. This is a big, dark, tannic, dry wine. But the tannins are rich and sweet in the modern Napa style, and the flavors are enormous. Blackberries, black cherries, and new oak unroll in waves through a long finish. Good now, but should have a fine future through 2010 as those tannins fall out. 91 **Cellar Selection** —*S.H. (2/1/2006)*

SPRING MOUNTAIN VINEYARD

Spring Mountain Vineyard 2001 Bordeaux Blend (Napa Valley) $50. This is a big, lushly textured wine that has the intensity of mountain fruit without the hard tannins. Blackberry and vanilla coat the palate, followed by lingering notes of plum, cassis, and sweet oak. 92 *(6/6/2005)*

Spring Mountain Vineyard 2003 Sauvignon Blanc (Napa Valley) $28. Heavily toasted, with buttery aromas of peach, lemon, and pineapple. Very sweet on the palate, with honey, caramel, coconut, and baked-apple flavors. What may be too sweet and sickly for some could trigger happiness for others. Not a unanimous choice among our panel. 86 *(7/1/2005)*

Spring Mountain Vineyard 2001 Estate Syrah (Napa Valley) $50. Chewy and tannic, this densely packed Syrah deserves 2–3 years of cellar time before opening. Dark berry and tobacco notes mark the nose, while the flavors revolve around berries, chocolate fudge, and olive. 88 *(9/1/2005)*

Spring Valley Vineyard 2003 Frederick Red Table Wine Bordeaux Blend (Walla Walla (WA)) $40. This is three quarters Cabernet Sauvignon, the rest a mix of Merlot, Cab Franc, and a drop of Petit Verdot. Dense and extracted, it is almost syrupy, like concentrated raspberry or boysenberry juice. What keeps it from being tiring are the powerful acids; they set up the berry flavors and create a bright, tartly chewy mouthfeel. Very young; this will improve for at least another five years before hitting its peak. 92 —*P.G. (6/1/2006)*

SPRING VALLEY VINEYARD

Spring Valley Vineyard 2004 Uriah Bordeaux Blend (Walla Walla (WA)) $40. The 2004 Uriah blend is 60% Merlot, 31% Cab Franc, and the rest divided between Cabernet Sauvignon and Petit Verdot, all estate grown. Ripe Walla Walla fruit, quite rare in 2004, gives structure and sleek, racy, vibrant flavors of boysenberry, currant, and cherry. The vineyard's characteristic wild hay aromatics are less evident, as the fruit soars. This is a wine that should reward significant cellaring time, up to a decade or more. 93 —*P.G. (12/31/2006)*

Spring Valley Vineyard 2003 Uriah Red Table Wine Bordeaux Blend (Walla Walla (WA)) $40. Roughly three quarters Merlot, the rest Cab Franc with a drop of Petit Verdot, this is the mirror image of the Frederick. More fruit-forward, ripe, and accessible, the spicy red fruits are set into thick, chocolatey tannins. It holds its balance despite the 15% alcohol, but it may be somewhat precarious. I would drink it early for maximum pleasure. 91 —*P.G. (6/1/2006)*

Spring Valley Vineyard 2003 Cabernet Franc (Walla Walla (WA)) $18. All estate-grown, this Cab Franc has 12 percent Petit Verdot added into the blend. Deliciously crisp and bright, with cranberry and pomegranate red fruit flavors. The tannins are stiff and slightly chalky, and the wine finishes with hints of bitter baking chocolate. Give it some good breathing time to soften it up. 90 —*P.G. (6/1/2006)*

Spring Valley Vineyard 2003 Derby Cabernet Sauvignon (Walla Walla (WA)) $42. This is a fascinating effort loaded with unusual grace notes, the sort of hints of herb, grass, leaf, and bark that characterize this unique vineyard. Resonant and complex, it does not show its 14.9% alcohol; the fruit and tannins are in good balance, though not quite integrated. Give it another couple of years to knit together and you'll have a sensational bottle of Walla Walla Cabernet. 91 **Editors' Choice** —*P.G. (10/1/2006)*

Spring Valley Vineyard 2004 Nina Lee Syrah (Walla Walla (WA)) $50. Almost no one got fruit in Walla Walla in 2004—a freeze year—and it's a sure bet no one got Syrah fruit any better than this. A bottle-full of thick, black juice, sappy, and saturated both in color and pure fruit flavor, this massive Syrah matches its brawn with brio—peppery spice, delicate herb, and toasty cracker. Nonetheless, it is the monster fruit that carries the wine through an extravagant middle and soaring into a satiny, juice-bomb of a finish. 92 **Editors' Choice** —*P.G. (12/31/2006)*

Spring Valley Vineyard 2003 Nina Lee Syrah (Walla Walla (WA)) $40. All estate-grown. Sappy, saturated, and deep purple in color, it is vibrantly youthful despite two years of aging. The mixed berry and Bing cherry fruit flavors are highlighted with racy acids, and the aromas carry the characteristic Spring Valley nuances of fresh hay and alfalfa. There seems to be a little CO2 remaining, and the wine needs still more time to knit together. Just 169 cases produced. **89** —*P.G. (6/1/2006)*

Spring Valley Vineyard 2002 Nina Lee Syrah (Walla Walla (WA)) $40. Has an intriguing bouquet of mineral, licorice and flowers, followed by concentrated berry flavors. There's also fairly high acidity and astringent tannins, making this Syrah perhaps a little too structured for its own good. **85** *(9/1/2005)*

ST AMANT

St Amant 1999 Barbera (Lodi) $14. Dark in color, this single-vineyard wine was made from 30-year-old vines. Aromas are deep and plummy, with roasted coffee-bean and caramelized, raisiny notes. Very dry and austere, with high acidity and rich tannins. Try aging this quintessentially Californian wine for a decade. **88** —*S.H. (11/15/2001)*

St Amant 1999 Syrah (California) $12. Bright and fresh, with pretty cherry and plum notes. Finishes moderately with interesting herb essence. A blend of Amador and Lodi fruit. **86** —*S.H. (11/15/2001)*

St Amant 1999 Reserve Syrah (Amador County) $18. Quite spicy, with vibrant black cherry, blackberry, clove, and herb notes, all couched in supple tannins. Long and bright on the finish. **89** —*S.H. (11/15/2001)*

St Amant 1999 Berghold Vineyard Viognier (Lodi) $12. Earth, peach, butter, and smoke aromas lead to rich, fruity, spicy flavors, ripe, and full-bodied, of extracted stone fruits. Balanced, with a creamy texture and a fruity, spicy finish. **86 Best Buy** —*S.H. (11/15/2001)*

ST STALEY THOMAS

St Staley Thomas 1997 Chardonnay (Russian River Valley) $13. 92 Best Buy —*L.W. (7/1/1999)*

ST. AMANT WINERY

St. Amant Winery 2001 Zinfandel (Amador County) $15. Bright and zippy cherry, blackberry, plum, spice, and herb flavors are prevalent here. They fan out to reveal additional hints of licorice and coffee. The finish is moderate in length and the tannins are well structured. **87** *(11/1/2003)*

St. Amant Winery 2001 Marian's Vineyard Zinfandel (Lodi) $20. A ripe, smooth wine, filled with pretty black cherry, plum, strawberry, and herb flavors. Smoky oak frames the ensemble, which finishes with a toasty, woody edge. **87** *(11/1/2003)*

ST. CLEMENT

St. Clement 2001 Oroppas Bordeaux Blend (Napa Valley) $50. Despite ripe flavors of black currants, cocoa, and spice and a sweet veneer of oak, this wine needs more acidity to perk it up. It's soft to the point of melting, and finishes thin. Good, but disappointing. **86** —*S.H. (2/1/2005)*

St. Clement 1999 Oroppas Bordeaux Blend (Napa Valley) $50. What a complex nose on this blend of Cabernet Sauvignon, Merlot, and Cab Franc. The dominant aroma is a leathery, grilled meat scent, alongside charred oak. Blackberry tea and cherry flavors show up in the mouth, where it's dry, with pure, soft tannins. It's a bit disjointed now. A few years may bring things together. **88** —*J.M. (6/1/2002)*

St. Clement 1997 Cabernet Sauvignon (Howell Mountain) $65. 92 *(11/1/2000)*

St. Clement 1997 Cabernet Sauvignon (Napa Valley) $35. 94 *(11/1/2000)*

St. Clement 2001 Cabernet Sauvignon (Napa Valley) $35. Starts with green olive, oak, and blackberry-cherry aromas, and the palate impression is velvety and refined. There are some tannins, especially on the finish, but the flavors are rich and pure. Could improve after 2006. **89** —*S.H. (3/1/2005)*

St. Clement 2000 Cabernet Sauvignon (Napa Valley) $35. Firm and polished, an elegant Cab with pretty flavors of blackberries, currants, dried herbs, and dark chocolate, with hints of menthol and an oaky overlay. The fruit turns a bit thin on the finish, and picks up some astringent tannins. **87** —*S.H. (4/1/2004)*

St. Clement 1999 Cabernet Sauvignon (Napa Valley) $32. What's odd about this wine is how tough and tannic it is for the vintage, when so many wineries made supple, approachable wines. Possibly the grapes were picked too early, in fear of rain. Framed in considerable oak, with a chewy core of blackberries, it's a cellar candidate. Give it a good seven years to soften and sweeten. **87** —*S.H. (11/15/2002)*

St. Clement 1998 Cabernet Sauvignon (Howell Mountain) $35. A very pretty wine, with near-perfect balance and that elusive quality of elegance. Definitely comes down onthe herbal side, with pronounced flavors of green olives. Oak provides some sweetness and spice, but it's a bone-dry wine, with dusty tannins. Demands rich foods. **92** —*S.H. (6/1/2002)*

St. Clement 1998 Cabernet Sauvignon (Napa Valley) $35. Earth, anyone? The aromas suggest mushrooms, warm tree bark, and hummus, although airing reveals black cherry notes. So it's not the ripest wine ever, but it's smooth as silk, with velvety tannins, and lots of pretty spice in the finish. Drink now. **86** —*S.H. (6/1/2002)*

St. Clement 1996 Cabernet Sauvignon (Howell Mountain) $50. 90 —*S.H. (9/1/2000)*

St. Clement 1996 Cabernet Sauvignon (Napa Valley) $30. 92 *(11/15/1999)*

St. Clement 1999 Howell Mountain Cabernet Sauvignon (Napa Valley) $70. Fruit is redder than it is black, with prominent plum, cherry, and even raspberry fruit; one reviewer found an offputting hint of greenness. Smooth and supple in the mouth, it's a solid, well-built Cab that should be drunk sooner than later. **89** *(8/1/2003)*

St. Clement 2003 Oroppas Cabernet Sauvignon (Napa Valley) $50. Wonderful Napa Cabernet, with the opulence of fruit and textural balance you expect. Ripe black currant and cocoa flavors, with a rich, complex raw-beef streak and layers of toasty, spicy oak. The wine is powerful, yet elegant and restrained. Fine now, but best from 2009–2015. **91 Cellar Selection** —*S.H. (12/1/2006)*

St. Clement 2002 Oroppas Cabernet Sauvignon (Napa Valley) $50. There's tremendous flavor in this wine, with its depth charges of blackberries and jammy currants, cherries, and spicy plums and spiced coffee. The tannins are wonderfully smooth and intricate. It could be a little firmer in acids, though, because it's very soft and melted. **88** —*S.H. (12/15/2005)*

St. Clement 2003 Star Vineyard Cabernet Sauvignon (Rutherford) $80. The wine, with a classic Cab profile, is young and needs time to pull it all together. Shows beautifully ripe blue and blackberries and stone fruits, wrapped in dusty tannins and lots of new oak. Really fine, polished, and high-end. Should begin to harmonize by 2008, and hold through 2020. **93 Cellar Selection** —*S.H. (12/15/2006)*

St. Clement 2002 Star Vineyard Cabernet Sauvignon (Rutherford) $80. This wine is very ripe in red cherry and currant fruit, with a mocha edge and a touch of prunes in the finish. It's a little inelegant now, with a sharpness that accentuates the tannins. May calm down in a year or two. **85** —*S.H. (12/31/2005)*

St. Clement 2002 Chardonnay (Carneros) $16. Delicious Chardonnay from the Napa side of the appellation. Filled with ripe tropical fruit, pear, honey, caramel, and smoky vanilla, in a rich and creamy texture that finishes long. **90** —*S.H. (3/1/2005)*

St. Clement 2001 Chardonnay (Napa Valley) $16. Textbook all the way. Well-ripened apples, pears, and peaches, crisp, citrusy acids, and oaky wood are what you get in this clean, well-made wine. The texture is rich and creamy. **87** —*S.H. (6/1/2004)*

St. Clement 1999 Chardonnay (Napa Valley) $16. Another opulent, fat Chard, dripping with oak. Aromas of hazelnut, butterscotch, smoky vanilla, intensely ripe peaches and pears, and even crème brûlée, precede equally rich flavors. The texture is creamy and custardy, and the finish is long, spicy, and honeyed. **88** —*S.H. (11/15/2001)*

St. Clement 1999 Abbotts Vineyard Chardonnay (Carneros) $23. If you like the smell and taste of well-toasted oak barrels you'll flip over this wine. Opens with a blast of char, vanilla, and woody spices. Sweet oak dominates the flavors. Buried under all that wood are peach and apple flavors that straddle the border between dry and off-dry. **86** —*S.H. (5/1/2002)*

St. Clement 1998 Abbotts Vineyard Chardonnay (Carneros) $20. 84 *(6/1/2000)*

St. Clement 1997 Merlot (Napa Valley) $26. 89 —*S.H. (7/1/2000)*

St. Clement 2002 Merlot (Napa Valley) $28. Strikes you as a bit weedy and sharp, a not-quite-ripe wine despite the high alcohol. You'll find dill and fresh asparagus aromas, topped off by oak and just nudging into tart, sour cherry. **82** —*S.H. (11/1/2006)*

St. Clement 2001 Merlot (Napa Valley) $28. Quite rich and sumptuous, though it's still very young and unformed. There are beautiful cherry and olive flavors, fine, intricate tannins and a tasteful overlay of oak, but it hasn't all come together yet. Try it next year, and then enjoy for a few more years. **89** —*S.H. (9/1/2004)*

St. Clement 1999 Merlot (Napa Valley) $28. An astonishingly good Merlot that reeks with distinction and class. Fully ripened blackberry fruit is nuanced with tobacco, sage, and smoke. The mouthfeel is out of this world. It's liquid velvet, full of subtle but powerful flavors, dry and rich, that linger into a long, complex finish. **92** —*S.H. (6/1/2002)*

St. Clement 1998 Merlot (Napa Valley) $26. Here's a fruity wine, with blackberry, white-chocolate, herbaceous, green olive notes. Moderate oak treatment adds the usual woody complexities. The flavors are bold and ripe. Most notable is the ultrarich, creamy texture leading to a clean, ripe finish. **89** —*S.H. (12/1/2001)*

St. Clement 1999 Petite Sirah (Napa Valley) $32. The ripe black raspberry, cherry, tar, chocolate, pepper, and spice flavors are a sheer delight, but won't surprise fans of this overlooked varietal who know how fine it can be. In today's fashion, the wine is very soft and plush, with modulated tannins, and drinks like liquid candy. Probably has a long aging profile. **90** —*S.H. (9/1/2002)*

St. Clement 2000 Oroppas Red Blend (Napa Valley) $50. Another fine vintage for this veteran Napa winery. Shows a classic Napa character, with ripe flavors of cassis and black currants and finely-ground, complex but easy tannins. The oak, which contributes vanilla, smoke, and woody spice, is strong, but not oppressive. Doesn't seem to be an ager, and best enjoyed soon. **90** —*S.H. (11/15/2003)*

St. Clement 1998 Sauvignon Blanc (Napa Valley) $13. 88 —*S.H. (3/1/2000)*

St. Clement 2001 Sauvignon Blanc (Napa Valley) $13. Here's a typical village-style Sauvignon from Napa. The fruity flavors range from lemons to ripe summer peaches, and there's a trace of sweetness to boost the crisp acids. The wine is simple and very easy to drink with fruits or barbecue. **86** —*S.H. (10/1/2003)*

St. Clement 1999 Sauvignon Blanc (Napa Valley) $13. This light delicate wine comes from warmer parts of Napa Valley, including Calistoga and Pope Valley. The aromas suggest lemons, limes, and buttery smoke, and so do the flavors. It's also dry, crisp, and a little tart. Not a whole lot of substance here, but it does have its cocktail-type charms, and a good price. **84** —*S.H. (8/1/2001)*

ST. FRANCIS

St. Francis 2002 Cabernet Sauvignon (Sonoma County) $18. Dry, tart, and fairly one-dimensional, this Cab has mixed flavors of blackberries, cherries, and Kahlúa, with a peppery, minty streak. The tannins are a bit edgy. Might improve with a year or two of cellaring. **85** —*S.H. (6/1/2006)*

St. Francis 2001 Cabernet Sauvignon (Sonoma County) $20. This is a pretty good Cab with some pleasant features. It's dark, very dry, and rich in tannins, with blackberry and earthy-tobacco flavors and a touch of oak. A good example of a decent county-wide blend. **85** —*S.H. (10/1/2004)*

St. Francis 2000 Cabernet Sauvignon (Sonoma County) $16. A blend of the big three Cabernet valleys, Alexander, Sonoma, and Dry Creek. Polished and elegant, with good berry flavors balanced with green olive, dill, unsweetened chocolate, and earth. Feels plush in the mouth, smooth and soft, but complex. Good enough for your best fare. **90 Editors' Choice** —*S.H. (11/15/2003)*

St. Francis 1999 Cabernet Sauvignon (Sonoma County) $16. Winemaker Tom Mackey has a justified reputation for producing rich, concentrated red wines, but this one seems to be an exception. It's austere to the point of being rasping. He's thankfully avoided the modern temptation to sub-

stitute sugar for complexity, but the dryness is unrelieved. Nor is there the hidden depth of fruit to suggest ageworthiness. **85** —*S.H. (6/1/2002)*

St. Francis 1997 Kings Ridge Reserve Cabernet Sauvignon (Sonoma County) $85. 87 —*J.C. (6/1/2003)*

St. Francis 2001 Kings Ridge Vineyard Reserve Cabernet Sauvignon (Sonoma County) $NA. Smoke and dried spice notes define the nose of the Kings Ridge Reserve Cab. Medium- to full-bodied and more firmly structured than the Nuns Canyon bottling, with black cherry and coffee flavors that merge seamlessly with earth and spice notes. Chewy tannins on the finish suggest short-term cellaring; try in 2008. **91** *(11/15/2005)*

St. Francis 2001 Nuns Canyon Reserve Cabernet Sauvignon (Sonoma County) $28. This soft, fully-ripened Cabernet boasts aromas of cocoa, cassis, and chocolate fudge, veering dangerously close to prune and over-ripeness. Still, it maintains a precarious sense of balance and a wonderfully silky mouthfeel that suggest near-term drinking. Drink now–2010. **89** *(11/15/2005)*

St. Francis 1999 Nuns Canyon Reserve Cabernet Sauvignon (Sonoma Valley) $45. This is a very good wine, but a young one. It tastes immature now, with its brash, dusty tannins that hide the underlying plum, currant, and herb flavors. Even with the softness of its acids, it calls for time in the cellar to open up its hidden treasures. Try after 2005. **92** —*S.H. (11/15/2003)*

St. Francis 1997 Reserve Cabernet Sauvignon (Sonoma Valley) $40. 90 *(11/1/2000)*

St. Francis 2004 Chardonnay (Sonoma County) $12. High in acidity, almost sour despite complete malo, this is a very dry wine, and it's thin in fruity flavor. Will do in a pinch, but you can do better for the money. **82** —*S.H. (10/1/2006)*

St. Francis 2003 Chardonnay (Sonoma County) $12. Even the regular St. Francis Chard is all barrel-fermented and frequently stirred, adding layers of texture to the pineapple and citrus fruit. Enough young oak is used to impart smoke, vanilla, and marshmallow notes. **85** *(11/15/2005)*

St. Francis 2001 Chardonnay (Sonoma County) $12. This is a pretty nice wine, well-crafted and rich, sort of a junior version of bigger, more expensive Chards. Fruity flavors range through ripe peaches to tropical fruits, and there's a thick overlay of smoky oak. The texture is creamy and smooth. **87 Best Buy** —*S.H. (9/1/2003)*

St. Francis 2000 Chardonnay (Sonoma County) $6. Sweetish and simple, it has some thin but ripe flavors of peaches, and quite a dose of oak. The wood adds spicy, smoky, and vanilla notes, but they're not integrated. Finishes sappy and sugary. **84** —*S.H. (5/1/2002)*

St. Francis 1999 Chardonnay (Sonoma County) $13. A likable, easy-drinking Chard that won't bust your budget, with plenty of ripe flavors and winemaker bells and whistles. It's got spicy, vanilla-accented peach aromas, and while it drinks a bit thin, it's got some class and style. The finish lasts for a pretty long time, with oaky, spicy flavors. This is a good value, especially from a top winery. **87 Best Buy** —*S.H. (5/1/2001)*

St. Francis 2004 Behler Reserve Chardonnay (Sonoma County) $25. Tart and minerally, this high-acid Chard has green apple pie flavors, sprinkled with cinnamon and nutmeg. It's bone dry, an angular, somewhat lean wine that needs food to show what it can do. Try with grilled salmon. **85** —*S.H. (10/1/2006)*

St. Francis 2003 Behler Reserve Chardonnay (Sonoma Valley) $24. Tough and earthy, with coffee and dried herb flavors, this wine has buried peach and apple fruit that might emerge with decanting or a year or two of aging. It's very dry, with a good cut of acidity. **85** —*S.H. (3/1/2006)*

St. Francis 2002 Behler Reserve Chardonnay (Sonoma County) $24. This full-throttle Chard receives 100% malolactic fermentation and frequent lees-stirrings to build in even more richness. The result is a perfumed, full-bodied wine with flavors reminiscent of pear, melon, and vanilla. There's a custardy texture to the warm, slightly woody finish. **87** *(11/15/2005)*

St. Francis 2001 Behler Reserve Chardonnay (Sonoma Valley) $24. Oaky and tart, a big wine with strong flavors of citrus fruits, green apples, and dusty brown spices. Crisp acidity adds a steeliness that is almost minerally. This sleek wine is not a big, fat opulent blockbuster, but is refined and controlled through the spicy, oaky finish. **88** —*S.H. (12/15/2003)*

St. Francis 2000 Behler Vineyard Reserve Chardonnay (Sonoma Valley) $NA. Has a beautiful bouquet, loaded with smoky oak and vanilla and the lushest, ripest pears. But the flavors aren't quite as rich: It turns citrusy in the mouth, with a creamy texture. Very clean and tart on the finish. **87** —*S.H. (2/1/2003)*

St. Francis 2000 Anthem Meritage (Sonoma Valley) $55. A blend of all five Bordeaux varieties, this wine is soft, and flatters with its polished flavors and fine veneer of oak. The flavors shift from blackberries and cherries to sweet herbs and back again, and finish with a kick of tannin. Very drinkable now, and should improve for a few years. **91** —*S.H. (10/1/2004)*

St. Francis 1999 Anthem Meritage (Sonoma Valley) $65. A big, dark, dense young wine that is flamboyant now, but give it a few years to really stun. As soft as velvet, with huge stuffing of berries, chocolate, herbs, coffee, and oak, but carefully balanced. Winemaker Tom Mackey's first Meritage, an unusual blend dominated by Petit Verdot and Malbec. **93** —*S.H. (10/1/2003)*

St. Francis 1997 Merlot (Sonoma County) $20. 87 —*J.C. (7/1/2000)*

St. Francis 1999 Merlot (Sonoma County) $24. A smoky-hued blend, with hints of plum, black cherry, and herbs. On the finish, it's got a resiny edge. **86** —*J.M. (6/1/2002)*

St. Francis 1998 Merlot (Solano County) $25. Smells sharp and weedy, with aromas of green stems and chlorophyll that are softened by a hint of blackberry. It's also a tannic wine, the kind that makes the tongue stick to the palate. Copious oak attempts to further soften the wine and adds a creamy lushness. **86** —*S.H. (6/1/2001)*

St. Francis 2001 Behler Reserve Merlot (Sonoma County) $28. Shows an herbal or dill-like note on the nose, then plush aromas and flavors of chocolate, coffee, and plum. It's full-bodied and soft-textured, picking up a trace of alcoholic warmth alongside caramel on the finish. **87** (11/15/2005)

St. Francis 1999 Behler Reserve Merlot (Sonoma Valley) $45. Very young and tannic, and not showing its best at the time of tasting. Aromas of spiced plum, dried herbs, and oak, and those powerful tannins numb the palate and plaster over the fruit. Try decanting for a few hours, or better yet, drink after 2008. **90** —*S.H. (12/31/2003)*

St. Francis 1996 Reserve Merlot (Sonoma Valley) $39. 88 (3/1/2000)

St. Francis 2001 Port (Sonoma County) $25. This interesting California version of a Port is rich, balanced, and inviting. It features an array of crème de cassis, chocolate fudge, vanilla, and spice flavors wrapped in a velvety texture. Refreshing acidity cuts through the sweetness. Cab Sauvignon, Merlot, Syrah, Zinfandel, and Alicante Bouschet. **91** —*S.H. (12/1/2004)*

St. Francis 2001 Claret Red Blend (Sonoma County) $17. There's a wealth of black cherry and blackberry fruit inside this wine, which is also tannic and dry. It has good acidity, with some oak, and is balanced. Merlot, Cabernet Sauvignon, and Zinfandel. **85** —*S.H. (11/15/2004)*

St. Francis 2002 Red Blend (Sonoma County) $12. With a little of this and a little of that, this wine gets the job done if you want a dry, ripe, affordable, full-bodied red. It's got cherry-berry flavors, firm tannins, and good acids, and will wash that lasagna down easily. **84** —*S.H. (2/1/2006)*

St. Francis 2002 Red Wine Red Blend (Sonoma County) $12. Pizza, lasagna, cheeseburgers, and similar fare come to mind when tasting this simple country wine. It's rustic in tannins, with ripe cherry-berry and cocoa flavors, and very clean. **84** —*S.H. (11/15/2006)*

St. Francis 2003 Syrah (Sonoma County) $20. Simple, dry, and fruity, with a raw, acidic pungency framing jammy blackberry, boysenberry, and coffee flavors. A bit of oak adds smoke and vanilla notes. **84** —*S.H. (11/1/2006)*

St. Francis 2002 Syrah (Sonoma County) $20. Stewed and pruny, with a dull mouthfeel and syrupy texture. What went wrong here? **82** (9/1/2005)

St. Francis 2001 Nuns Canyon Vineyard Syrah (Sonoma Valley) $35. An interesting wine that flirts with greatness. It's obviously pedigreed, with a very fine balance of strong tannins, acidity, and plummy, blackberry

fruit, and has been well-oaked. It's a bit of a brute now, lurching about the mouth with a tough grittiness, but the finish is spectacularly long and sweet. Now through 2010. **92** —*S.H. (12/1/2004)*

St. Francis 2002 Old Vines Zinfandel (Sonoma County) $18. This is a solid Sonoma Zin, exhibiting a classic profile of full-bodied wild berry flavors, a dry, firmly tannic mouthfeel and a spicy, peppery finish. It could have greater concentration, though. **85** —*S.H. (12/31/2005)*

St. Francis 2002 Old Vines Zinfandel (Sonoma Valley) $18. Briary and medium-weight, with a hint of vinyl on the nose as well. The blackberry and raisin fruit gives the impression of warmth, then thins out and turns a bit tart and cranberryish on the finish. **85** (11/15/2005)

St. Francis 2001 Old Vines Zinfandel (Sonoma County) $22. Smooth and ripe, with plum, cherry, blackberry, cassis, and chocolate flavors at the fore. Tannins are a tad rustic, but the wine is quite pleasurable to drink. **88** (11/1/2003)

St. Francis 2000 Old Vines Zinfandel (Sonoma County) $22. From various vineyards with a minimum age of 50 years, and all the vines are head-trained. This dark wine is built along solid lines, a big, tough Zin with stubborn tannins. It's lean in flavor, most likely due to the vintage, but should soften and sweeten in time. **86** —*S.H. (9/1/2003)*

St. Francis 1999 Old Vines Zinfandel (Sonoma County) $22. In the absence of official regulations regarding the use of the term "old vines," St. Francis insists on 50 or more years of age. These vines run closer to 80. The wine is concentrated and dense, with spicy berry flavors. It's dry and balanced. Acids are soft. **88** —*S.H. (11/1/2002)*

St. Francis 1998 Old Vines Zinfandel (Sonoma County) $25. Intense, alcoholic, and wonderfully complex, with layers of toast, spice, and fruit. The vines range from 50 to 80 years old or more; the wine is robust, balanced, and muscular. St. Francis makes a flat-out wonderful Zin year after year, vintage after vintage, big and bellisimo. **91** —*P.G. (3/1/2001)*

St. Francis 1997 Old Vines Zinfandel (Sonoma County) $24. 90 —*P.G. (11/15/1999)*

St. Francis 1998 Pagani Reserve Zinfandel (Sonoma Valley) $40. Extracted, tannic, dark, and dense, with briary, jammy fruit and thick tannins. Blackberries and chocolate, set off with lots of acid. It's a sensational, balanced, bold, ageworthy Zin. **91** —*P.G. (3/1/2001)*

St. Francis 2002 Pagani Vineyard Reserve Zinfandel (Sonoma County) $46. According to winemaker Tom Mackey, "size counts with Zin," and his Pagani Vineyard Zin has never lacked for size. There's some smoke and vanilla-scented oak, but there's also masses of Zinberry fruit and a juicy, fresh finish, with none of the raisin notes that can sometimes creep into high-octane Zins. **90** (11/15/2005)

St. Francis 2001 Pagani Vineyard Reserve Zinfandel (Sonoma Valley) $45. A bit spicy in the nose. On the palate the wine is marked by a distinct coconut flavor; we suppose from the oak. Tannins are smooth, with fruit flavors redolent of black cherry, blackberry, plum, and cocoa. Long on the finish. **90** (11/1/2003)

St. Francis 1999 Pagani Vineyard Reserve Zinfandel (Sonoma Valley) $44. Gleams with a wickedly purple intensity, and startles by the sheer size. Huge, jammy scents of blackberries, cherries, and blueberries are lifted by charry, smoky oak, while the flavors are enormous and extracted. Balanced, harmonious. **92** —*S.H. (9/1/2002)*

St. Francis 1997 Pagani Vineyard Reserve Zinfandel (Sonoma Valley) $39. **88** —*P.G. (11/15/1999)*

St. Francis 2001 Reserve Pagani Vineyard Zinfandel (Sonoma Valley) $45. Clearly stands above the competition for its exquisite harmony. Completely dry but totally ripe, with well-developed spicy blackberry and dark chocolate flavors, and wonderfully rich, sweet tannins. So balanced, you don't notice the 15.6 percent alcohol. Only in California, and a world class wine. **93** —*S.H. (11/15/2004)*

ST. GEORGE

St. George 2002 Cabernet Sauvignon (Sonoma County) $10. You'll find lots of Cabernet character in this ripe, fruity wine. It has polished cherry-berry, coffee, and herb flavors, with a smattering of oak, and is dry and balanced. **84** —*S.H. (11/1/2005)*

St. George 2002 Barrel Reserve Cabernet Sauvignon (Sonoma County) $11. Sneak this one into a blind tasting of Cabs costing twice as much and it will hold its own. It's smooth and opulent, with oak-kissed blackberry, licorice, tobacco, and mocha flavors and rich tannins, and the finish is dry and balanced. 86 Best Buy —S.H. (9/1/2006)

St. George 2003 Chardonnay (Sonoma County) $10. Common and rustic, this is a Chard that is properly fruity, although it has some vegetal flavors. 82 —S.H. (10/1/2005)

St. George 2002 Chardonnay (California) $8. Earthy and simple, with a taste of canned peach juice. 82 —S.H. (5/1/2005)

St. George 2004 Barrel Reserve Chardonnay (Sonoma County) $11. There may be a little oak on this Chard, but the fruit really stars. The apple, peach, and apricot flavors are perked up by crisp acidity, and the alcohol is a refreshingly low 13%. This is a good price for a wine of this quality. 86 Best Buy —S.H. (9/1/2006)

St. George 2004 Barrel Reserve Chardonnay (Sonoma County) $10. Fans of oak and fruity tropical flavors will appreciate the price on this well-organized, everyday Chard. It shows pineapple custard, vanilla yogurt, and cinnamon spice flavors wrapped into a dry, creamy texture set off by high acidity. 85 Best Buy —S.H. (10/1/2006)

St. George 2001 Barrel Reserve Chardonnay (Sonoma County) $9. Super-oaky, with what smells and tastes like heavy char that gives it a burnt, ashy note, although there are some decent peach flavors. 82 —S.H. (11/1/2005)

St. George 2004 Coastal Chardonnay (California) $8. You'll find plenty of ripe, forward Chardonnay fruit in this dry, affordable wine. It's packed with pineapple, mango, peach, pear, and oakspice flavors, in a creamy-smooth package. 84 Best Buy —S.H. (4/1/2006)

St. George 2004 Barrel Reserve Merlot (Sonoma County) $11. They kept the alcohol moderate, but at the obvious cost of residual sugar. This overtly sweet wine tastes like the old kosher stuff I grew up with. 80 —S.H. (9/1/2006)

St. George Coastal 2003 Chardonnay (California) $6. Pretty light, but a decent value. Flavors are of apples, oak, and spice. 83 Best Buy —S.H. (11/1/2005)

ST. INNOCENT

St. Innocent 1998 Freedom Hill Vineyard Pinot Blanc (Willamette Valley) $14. 81 —L.W. (12/31/1999)

St. Innocent 1997 O'Connor Pinot Gris (Willamette Valley) $12. 86 (8/1/1999)

ST. SUPERY

St. Supery 1998 Bordeaux Blend (Napa Valley) $20. 90 —L.W. (2/1/2000)

St. Supery 2001 Élu Bordeaux Blend (Napa Valley) $60. From a producer that thoroughly understands Napa Bordeaux wines comes this classically proportioned blend, which is dominated by Cabernet Sauvignon. It impresses by its balance, elegance, and richness. The blackberry and cherry flavors are enriched with oak, leading to a long and satisfying finish. Drink now through 2010. 92 —S.H. (3/1/2006)

St. Supery 1996 Cabernet Sauvignon (Napa Valley) $18. 88 —L.W. (12/31/1999)

St. Supery 2002 Cabernet Sauvignon (Napa Valley) $28. Soft, gentle. and beguiling, with smoky oak and sweet vanilla accenting ripe, plush blackberry, cherry, blueberry, and mocha flavors. The structure is superb, led by rich, smooth tannins. This is a good, fancy wine to drink now while you're waiting for your cellar bottles to develop. 88 —S.H. (11/15/2006)

St. Supery 1999 Dollarhide Ranch Cabernet Sauvignon (Napa Valley) $70. Smooth, viscous, and velvety on the palate. This is always St. Supery's best shot at Cabernet, sporting black currant, blackberry, sage, thyme, coffee and anise flavors. They weave their way along the palate to a long finish. 91 —J.M. (6/1/2003)

St. Supery 1997 Dollarhide Ranch Limited Editi Cabernet Sauvignon (Napa Valley) $70. 92 (11/1/2000)

St. Supery 1999 Limited Edition Cabernet Sauvignon-Merlot (Rutherford) $60. The oak in the nose is strong, much like cedar. Beyond that there's sweet mocha and coffee. The mouth is rich, something akin to plum pie. Even the finish is sweet; it's also chewy and loaded with black licorice. This wine carries a massive oak underlay and it's sweet. If these Napa characteristics appeal to you, then by all means go for it. 90 —M.S. (11/15/2002)

St. Supery 1998 Chardonnay (Napa Valley) $16. 90 (6/1/2000)

St. Supery 2004 Chardonnay (Napa Valley) $18. This is St. Supery's other Chardonnay, the oaked one. It's not super-oaky, but it does have butter-cream and vanilla notes in addition to the wine's apricot, peach, and tangerine flavors. It's a very dry, somewhat tart but elegant wine. 87 —S.H. (12/15/2006)

St. Supery 2000 Chardonnay (Napa Valley) $19. Creamy-rich, with melon, peach, toast, and honey flavors. Full on the finish, with a slightly woody aftertaste. 87 —J.M. (2/1/2003)

St. Supery 2005 Estate Oak Free Chardonnay (Napa Valley) $18. There's no oak to give fans their daily dose of buttered toast and vanilla. But there is plenty of pure, unadulterated fruit—apricots and peaches to be exact. It's a rich, spicy wine that advances the argument for no-oak Chard. 87 —S.H. (12/15/2006)

St. Supery 2000 Élu Meritage (Napa Valley) $50. What a wonderful wine. St. Supery continues to show its mastery with Bordeaux varieties. Rich, polished, and refined, with a good balance of ripe fruit and oak, and gentle but complex tannins. Drink now. 91 —S.H. (8/1/2005)

St. Supery 1999 Final Blend Meritage (Napa Valley) $50. 89 (7/1/2002)

St. Supery 1998 Red Meritage (Napa Valley) $50. Juicy blackberry aromas are spiced up by dried herb, black pepper, and vanilla-bean notes. On the palate, dark berries and toast are accented by earth and green tobacco, and chewy, gritty tannins. Taut red fruit rolled in white and black pepper sums it up. 84% Cabernet Sauvignon, 14% Merlot, 1% Cabernet Franc, 1% Petit Verdot. 88 (7/1/2002)

St. Supery 2000 White Meritage (Napa Valley) $22. This Bordeaux blend is partially barrel-fermented and aged in one-year-old oak, which explains why this blend of 56% Sémillon and 44% Sauvignon Blanc has both an oakiness and a steeliness over its pear and citrus fruit. Mouthfeel is subtly creamy; closes with banana and pear. 87 (7/1/2002)

St. Supery 1999 Merlot (Napa Valley) $21. This medium-bodied Merlot shows as much mineral as it does oak over its sturdy mixed-berry fruit. Spice, green herb, and resin notes add interest to the nose; chalky tannins linger on the finish. 30,000 cases produced. 86 (7/1/2002)

St. Supery 2001 Sweet White Moscato (California) $15. On the nose, lively peach and tropical fruit aromas are kept in check by a cottony-chalky note. Not at all cloying, this Moscato is well balanced, with plenty of mango flavors. Finishes with garden-sweet honeysuckle and sunflower notes. Though Beaulac recommends it with spicy food (especially Thai), we think it'd be just as nice to sip on the beach. 89 (7/1/2002)

St. Supery 2004 Sauvignon Blanc (Napa Valley) $20. Pungency and zest is what this wine is all about. The nose is sharp and angular, with cat pee, green melon, and citrus, while the palate is crisp and intense, with peach skin, tangerine, lime, and mineral notes. Deep and rock solid on the finish, with an aftertaste one taster labeled as "like chicken." Maybe he was subliminally referring to the perfect food pairing for this zippy white. 89 (7/1/2005)

St. Supery 2001 Sauvignon Blanc (Napa Valley) $15. Very fresh and light, with just a bit of a resiny mouthfeel, this Sauvignon Blanc sees only stainless steel. White stone fruit, pear, and citrus flavors dominate; flint and steel notes give the fruit substantial backbone. Drink with risotto, or other rich foods—this wine will cut right through it. 88 (7/1/2002)

St. Supery 2004 Dollarhide Limited Edition Sauvignon Blanc (Napa Valley) $32. Pungent and tight smelling, with aromas of pickle, passion fruit, and grass. Runs tangy on the palate, with flavors of grapefruit, passion fruit, peach, and green herbs. Fairly ripe and a little softer than the green-style flavors might suggest. 88 (7/1/2005)

St. Supery 2005 Estate Bottled Sauvignon Blanc (Napa Valley) $19. Who let the cats out? This sure is a feline-scented wine, with cat pee, grapefruit, lime, and melon flavors. Last year, Wine Enthusiast's collective

Tasting Panel liked the very similar '04. I'm less of a fan of this particular style. **85** —*S.H. (11/15/2006)*

St. Supery 2005 Limited Edition Dollarhide Sauvignon Blanc (Napa Valley) $35. Like the '04, the '05 is pungently aromatic and dry, with green grass, lemongrass, nectarine, and cat pee aromas. In the mouth, it turns tart, with citrus, apricot, grass, and spice flavors. Fortunately, the creamy texture neutralizes the acidity, which otherwise would be too sharp. **88** —*S.H. (11/15/2006)*

St. Supery 2002 Syrah (Napa Valley) $35. Soft and voluptuous, if a bit obvious and simple, with sweet-tasting, candied cherry fruit and hints of black pepper. **84** *(9/1/2005)*

St. Supery 2005 Virtu White Blend (Napa Valley) $25. The same pungency that dominates St. Supery's Dollarhide Sauvignon Blanc is here, even though this proprietarily-named wine is mostly Sémillon. But a little bit of strong Sauvignon Blanc goes a long way. Otherwise, this is a rich, barrel-fermented and lees-aged wine of considerable interest and complexity. **88** —*S.H. (12/15/2006)*

St. Supery 2003 Virtu White Blend (Napa Valley) $25. Sémillon has balanced much of the aggressive grassiness of the Sauvignon Blanc, while what seems like oak also brings sweetness. The result is a fruity, nutty, creamy wine, with a long, spicy finish. **88** —*S.H. (10/1/2005)*

St. Supery 2004 Virtu White Blend (Napa Valley) $25. Here's a fancy wine. It's made with full-blown Burgundian techniques, including barrel fermentation and sur lies aging. Every care was taken to preserve the fruity freshness. The peach, apricot, pineapple, and honeysuckle flavors have a rich edge of smoky oak and vanilla, offset by fine acidity, and the finish is very dry. This is one of the best Sauvignon-Sémillon blends out there. **92 Editors' Choice** —*S.H. (3/1/2006)*

STAG HOLLOW

Stag Hollow 1998 Vendange Sélection Pinot Noir (Willamette Valley) $45. **83** —*M.S. (12/1/2000)*

STAG'S LEAP WINE CELLARS

Stag's Leap Wine Cellars 1998 Cask 23 Bordeaux Blend (Napa Valley) $150. What a great success. Oozes with black currant jam and cassis and a dash of black pepper. Flamboyant oak adds a perfume of vanilla and smoke. Fleshy, long, and full, this beautiful wine is not a monster, but it coats the palate with spicy flavors that epitomize class and style. **95** —*J.M. (6/1/2002)*

Stag's Leap Wine Cellars 2000 Cabernet Sauvignon (Napa Valley) $45. A very fine Cabernet. All of the elements are upfront, including the vivacious berry flavors, oak, and soft, smooth tannins. Dry and clean, this is a wine suited to drinking tonight, but it has the balance to age effortlessly. **91** —*S.H. (3/1/2003)*

Stag's Leap Wine Cellars 1999 Cabernet Sauvignon (Napa Valley) $45. The anticipation of opening a Stag's Leap Cabernet is always high, which is perhaps unfair. But there it is. This wine disappoints. Blackberry flavors sit next to leaner, herbal ones, and the tannins are dry and aggressive. But acidity is low and it feels gooey in the mouth. May mellow with some cellaring. **85** —*S.H. (11/15/2002)*

Stag's Leap Wine Cellars 2003 Artemis Cabernet Sauvignon (Napa Valley) $50. Seems overly soft, with a melted feeling that warns against aging, despite the presence of amply tough tannins. Nearly 100% Cab, the wine is rich in cassis and blackberry flavors, and dry. Could surprise after time, but it's a gamble. **84** —*S.H. (9/1/2006)*

Stag's Leap Wine Cellars 2002 Artemis Cabernet Sauvignon (Napa Valley) $48. Elegant and refined, but rather short, this is a wine for near-term consumption. It has earth, herb, and cherry flavors and is dry in tannins. Drink while your big '01s are sleeping. **87** —*S.H. (5/1/2005)*

Stag's Leap Wine Cellars 2001 Artemis Cabernet Sauvignon (Napa Valley) $45. Textbook Napa Cab, blessed with ripe cassis-scented fruit and hints of mint, toast, and dusty earth. It's velvety and rich in the mouth, picking up notes of chocolate and vanilla on the silky-smooth finish. **91** *(2/1/2004)*

Stag's Leap Wine Cellars 2002 Cask 23 Cabernet Sauvignon (Napa Valley) $150. This is a tough wine to evaluate now because it's not showing well.

It's very dry and tannic. There's a fruity, blackberry, and cherry core, with a coffee and dill herbaceousness and plenty of oak. It's soft, but should develop well, and could eventually surprise. Try holding until 2010. **90 Cellar Selection** —*S.H. (4/1/2006)*

Stag's Leap Wine Cellars 2001 Cask 23 Cabernet Sauvignon (Napa Valley) $150. Classic Napa Cab, right up there with the greats. Somehow manages to combine monstrous power with understated elegance. The strength is obviously in the ripe fruit and elaborate oak, while the subtlety lies in the soft tannins and impeccable balance. It's a wine you return to over and over, trying to figure it out, but it's always a step ahead. Drink now, with rich fare, or age through 2020. **96 Cellar Selection** —*S.H. (2/1/2005)*

Stag's Leap Wine Cellars 2000 Cask 23 Cabernet Sauvignon (Napa Valley) $150. Terrific stuff, a blend of fruit from Fay and SLV that's creamy and supple—just what you expect texturally from Stag's Leap District Cabernet. Knockout aromas are slightly floral and cedary, artfully blending tobacco and black currants, while the flavors are pure plum, vanilla, and spice. Chewy and rich on the finish, suggesting that although delicious now, it should hold up in the cellar just fine. **93 Cellar Selection** *(2/1/2004)*

Stag's Leap Wine Cellars 1999 Cask 23 Cabernet Sauvignon (Napa Valley) $150. Restrained for a '99, this wine hides its potential in a youthful cloak of oak and tannin. Cellar this while you're drinking your cult Cabs, and come back to it in 2009. **92** —*S.H. (2/1/2003)*

Stag's Leap Wine Cellars 2002 Fay Cabernet Sauvignon (Napa Valley) $80. The immediate impression is of extreme youth and mandatory cellaring. Bluntly, this is not an easy wine to like now. It has a peppery edge, and the blackberry fruit is buried under tons of dark, brooding tannins. Best to age until at least 2009, but it should be worth the wait. **90 Cellar Selection** —*S.H. (4/1/2006)*

Stag's Leap Wine Cellars 2001 Fay Cabernet Sauvignon (Napa Valley) $75. Classically proportioned, and drinkable now for its sweet oak, luscious black currant fruit, and immediate appeal. But it packs a real punch on the finish, showing the controlled power of an ager. Will easily cellar through this decade. **92** —*S.H. (2/1/2005)*

Stag's Leap Wine Cellars 2000 Fay Cabernet Sauvignon (Napa Valley) $75. A little light, but silky smooth, with a caressing mouthfeel that pushes polished cherry and tobacco flavors softly along. Turns tart and a little peppery on the finish; drink now. **88** *(2/1/2004)*

Stag's Leap Wine Cellars 1999 Fay Vineyard Cabernet Sauvignon (Napa Valley) $75. Entirely from a vineyard in the Stag's Leap District, which is a little cooler than mid-Napa appellations. This gorgeous, sumptuous, fully ripened wine has aromas of black currants, mushrooms, coffee, and sage. In the mouth, it has classic Cabernet flavors and structure. The tannins are a wonder, rich and thick but easy and delicious. A total delight to sip, and it will age, too. **93** —*S.H. (2/1/2003)*

Stag's Leap Wine Cellars 1998 Fay Vineyard Cabernet Sauvignon (Napa Valley) $75. Here's what a great estate does. there's no mistaking the pedigree, from the sumptuous, velvety texture to the exciting balance. It's class all the way from the elegant entry to the long, spicy finish. A hollow center says it won't age, but it's pretty nice stuff. **93** —*S.H. (6/1/2002)*

Stag's Leap Wine Cellars 2002 S.L.V. Cabernet Sauvignon (Napa Valley) $110. Massive and tannic, and dry to the point of astringency, all this Cab needs is a decade or so to come around. The tannins are bigtime, locking the wine down, but there's a solid core of blackberry and cassis fruit. Once the wine has aged, the sweet fruit will emerge. Don't even think about it until 2010. **91 Cellar Selection** —*S.H. (4/1/2006)*

Stag's Leap Wine Cellars 2001 S.L.V. Cabernet Sauvignon (Napa Valley) $100. This is certainly a wine to lay down. It has a marvelous core of black currant and cherry fruit, and the oak is sweet, but the grip hits mid-palate, and the tannins close everything down on the finish. Will marry well with a rich steak, but should age effortlessly for many years. Now through 2015. **93** —*S.H. (2/1/2005)*

Stag's Leap Wine Cellars 1999 S.L.V. Cabernet Sauvignon (Napa Valley) $100. Starts with young, tough aromas of youthful Cabernet—earth, smoky oak, tobacco, and plum. In the mouth, you get dusty tannins and crisp acids, but way down deep are some pretty blackberries. Its structure suggests aging through 2009. **91** —*S.H. (2/1/2003)*

Stag's Leap Wine Cellars 1996 SLD Cabernet Sauvignon (Stags Leap District) $100. 93 *(12/31/1999)*

Stag's Leap Wine Cellars 2000 S.L.V. Cabernet Sauvignon (Napa Valley) $100. Slightly richer and earthier than the Fay this year, with black cherry and tobacco flavors that glide effortlessly across the palate thanks to a wonderfully supple texture. It does thin out a little on the finish, so it might be best consumed over the near term. **90** *(2/1/2004)*

Stag's Leap Wine Cellars 1998 S.L.V. Cabernet Sauvignon (Napa Valley) $100. Certainly one of the successes of the vintage. Packed with cassis, sage, plum, tobacco, earth, and smoky oak, and perfectly dry and balanced. Sheer joy in the mouth, like liquid velvet. It changes every second, offering up tiers of flavors through the spicy finish. **96** —*S.H. (6/1/2002)*

Stag's Leap Wine Cellars 2004 Chardonnay (Napa Valley) $32. Kind of heavy and dull, with earth and mineral flavors breaking into citrus and green apples. Finishes bone dry and tart in acids. Call it Chablisian. **83** —*S.H. (10/1/2006)*

Stag's Leap Wine Cellars 2003 Chardonnay (Napa Valley) $29. This wine is a bit tough and gritty, with an earthy, tobaccoey edge, but it has enough cream, green apple, and peach flavors to satisfy. Finishes fully dry, with spices and apples. **87** —*S.H. (7/1/2005)*

Stag's Leap Wine Cellars 2001 Chardonnay (Napa Valley) $29. Broad, ripe flavors of green apples and pears are wrapped in a creamy texture and offset by the bold use of oak and lees. Solidly displays the pedigree of this fine winery. **90** —*S.H. (5/1/2003)*

Stag's Leap Wine Cellars 1999 Chardonnay (Napa Valley) $30. Best known for their classic Cabernets, this producer has a confident and skilled hand with Chardonnay, too. This is a well-proportioned wine that displays complex apple, lime, vanilla, and earthy mineral notes. There's a crisp tautness to the apple fruit and tart citrus acidity that carries on the long, spicy finish. A powerhouse that promises to open up over the next year. Top Value. **91** *(7/1/2001)*

Stag's Leap Wine Cellars 1998 Chardonnay (Napa Valley) $26. 89 *(6/1/2000)*

Stag's Leap Wine Cellars 2004 Arcadia Vineyard Chardonnay (Napa Valley) $45. Very dry, and on the earthy side, this Chard is marked more by controlled elegance than by opulent fruit. There are flavors of lemons and limes and tart green apples, with additional complexities from barrel fermentation and sur lies aging. The finish is fairly acidic. **87** —*S.H. (10/1/2006)*

Stag's Leap Wine Cellars 2002 Arcadia Vineyard Chardonnay (Napa Valley) $45. This is a tight, lemony Chardonnay for those who lean more toward the old Chablis style. It's a very dry, structural wine whose acids and tannins star as much as the fruit. Great elegance and pizzazz. **90** —*S.H. (12/15/2004)*

Stag's Leap Wine Cellars 2001 Arcadia Vineyard Chardonnay (Napa Valley) $45. A very fine and stylish Chardonnay made crisp and tight with a spine of steely acidity. The flavors are also cool-climatish, ranging from ripe citrus fruits to apples and peaches. There's quite a bit of oak and lees but both are perfectly in balance. **90** —*S.H. (4/1/2004)*

Stag's Leap Wine Cellars 1999 Arcadia Vineyard Chardonnay (Napa Valley) $45. Opens with a lovely bouquet of lemon and tart pineapple fruit with anise, mineral, and tobacco accents. The lemony note resurfaces on the pear, white peach, and green apple palate. A chalk element adds interest and balances the overall zingy, bright tone in this tangy, high-alcohol wine. **88** *(7/1/2001)*

Stag's Leap Wine Cellars 1998 Beckstoffer Ranch Chardonnay (Napa Valley) $40. 89 —*S.H. (11/15/2000)*

Stag's Leap Wine Cellars 1997 Napa Valley Chardonnay (Napa Valley) $26. 90 —*S.H. (7/1/2000)*

Stag's Leap Wine Cellars 1998 Reserve Chardonnay (Napa Valley) $45. 89 —*S.H. (11/15/2000)*

Stag's Leap Wine Cellars 1998 Reserve Chardonnay (Napa Valley) $45. This Napa stalwart is beautifully integrated. Leesy and citrus notes

accent the solid apple and toast profile on both the nose and in the mouth. It's big, but displays impeccable balance and a great mouthfeel. Lime and spice play against richer butterscotch, vanilla, and toasty elements on the long, handsomely textured finish. **92** *(7/1/2001)*

Stag's Leap Wine Cellars 2003 Merlot (Napa Valley) $42. Finely structured with superb tannins and acids, and bone dry, this Merlot, with some Cabernet added, is very fruity, but it seems too young right now. There's a tight, locked-down, rugged quality. The cherries and blackberries are struggling to get out. Best after 2007, and for a couple years after. **88** —*S.H. (10/1/2006)*

Stag's Leap Wine Cellars 2001 Merlot (Napa Valley) $40. As ripe in cherries and blackberries as this great wine is, it's subtle. Just when you're savoring the fruit, you notice the infusion of fresh, sweet herbs, the coffee, the lush vanilla, and toast. What brilliant tannins, so sweet and complex, and what a stunningly long finish. **93** —*S.H. (12/15/2004)*

Stag's Leap Wine Cellars 2000 Merlot (Napa Valley) $40. Shows varietally correct aromas and flavors of black cherries, mocha, and dried herbs, also some smoke and toast. It's good wine, but fairly tart, lacking the expansiveness and lushness that would bring it to the next level. A victim of the vintage? **86** *(2/1/2004)*

Stag's Leap Wine Cellars 1999 Merlot (Napa Valley) $40. Intense, complicated, and challenging. It's an intellectual wine that will appeal to hedonists with its berry, chocolatey, meaty flavors and instant drinkability. Yet aficionados will find plenty to think about. Will it age? Will the fruit outlast the tannins? Is it merely likeable, or serious? The answers are yes, yes, and serious. **92** —*S.H. (11/15/2002)*

Stag's Leap Wine Cellars 1997 Merlot (Napa Valley) $35. Great vineyards, great winery, great vintage: There's lots to like about this big, bold, fruity wine that manages to be complex and elegant at the same time. Masses of blackberry, black currant, and violets, with smoke and vanilla from oak aging. What's hard to convey is the balance, richness, harmony, and depth of flavor, which are really stunning. Age it for a few years if you want, but it's at or near its delicious best now. **93** —*S.H. (2/1/2001)*

Stag's Leap Wine Cellars 2003 Sauvignon Blanc (Napa Valley) $20. Crisp and tight on the nose, with aromas of green pepper, apple, and mineral. Quite juicy and plump on the tongue, with a hint of green alongside stone fruits and grapefruit. Finishes dry and on the edge of resembling cider. **88** *(7/1/2005)*

Stag's Leap Wine Cellars 2001 Sauvignon Blanc (Napa Valley) $20. Ripe and melony, with smoke and fig notes adding complexity. It's a little creamy and pleasantly plump in the midpalate, then turns tart and grapefruity on the finish. **87** —*S.H. (2/1/2004)*

Stag's Leap Wine Cellars 1999 Sauvignon Blanc (Napa Valley) $20. Comes down on the lemony side, but not aggressively so. The citrus is balanced with creamy, oaky, herbal notes that soften and add complexity. Dry, with a great deal of lemon-and-lime extract, slightly soft, but very elegant. This is a stylish wine, exceptionally well balanced, and one of the better Sauvignon Blancs of the vintage. **90** —*S.H. (5/1/2001)*

Stag's Leap Wine Cellars 2000 Rancho Chimiles Sauvignon Blanc (Napa Valley) $28. Starts off with mineral, lemon, and anise aromas that develop on the palate into dried spices, ground flint, and lime. It's light in body, yet finishes strong, with clean citrus flavors and a lasting sensation of powdery talc. **87** *(8/1/2002)*

STAGLIN

Staglin 2002 Cabernet Sauvignon (Rutherford) $125. Starts with an extraordinarily complex, refined aroma, detailed and inviting in cassis, tobacco, anise, cocoa, and smoky oak. In the mouth, there's fantastic depth and complexity. The wine is rich, profound, a star even in its Rutherford stable of thoroughbreds. It has enormous power, with finely ground, sweet tannins. Absolutely gorgeous now, with the stuffing and balance for improvement. Drink now–2017. **97 Cellar Selection** —*S.H. (12/31/2005)*

Staglin 2001 Cabernet Sauvignon (Rutherford) $110. One of the best Rutherford wines of the vintage. Dramatically concentrated, everything's on steroids, but controlled and beautiful. Very ripe and plush, oaky, and young, fabulously expressive. Flavors are of black currants, sweet cherries, vanilla, smoke. A perfect expression of youthful brilliance and ageworthiness. **96** —*S.H. (10/1/2004)*

Staglin 2000 Cabernet Sauvignon (Rutherford) $100. An oaky wine that does its best to achieve depth and complexity, but it doesn't overcome the vintage's shortcomings. The oak contributes smoke, vanilla, char, and sweet tannins, yet below are diluted blackberry flavors that turn herbal. The tannins are astringent. **87** —*S.H. (2/1/2004)*

Staglin 1999 Cabernet Sauvignon (Rutherford) $85. Juicy plum skins and dark earthy flavors are thick and rich in this valley floor Cabernet. The gingersnap and tobacco aromas are very pleasing. The finish is spicy and dry yet supple at the same time. Enjoy now or in 10 years. **92** *(12/15/2002)*

Staglin 1997 Cabernet Sauvignon (Rutherford) $65. 92 *(11/1/2000)*

Staglin 2003 Estate Cabernet Sauvignon (Rutherford) $135. What a wonderfully rewarding wine. So delicious and elegant it dazzles, staying firm throughout, and getting even better through the finish. It's sweetly, opulently ripe, showing a panoply of red and black cherry and mocha flavors wrapped into ripe, dusty, fine tannins. Defines classic Rutherford. Decant if you drink now, or hold through 2020. **94 Cellar Selection** — *S.H. (12/31/2006)*

Staglin 2000 Salus Cabernet Sauvignon (Napa Valley) $50. Lots of briary, currant and blueberry flavors in this soft, appealing wine, with feathery tannins that melt on the finish. It's oaky, too. As tasty as it is, it loses a few points for the simple structure and lack of intensity. **86** —*S.H. (4/1/2004)*

Staglin 1999 Salus Cabernet Sauvignon (Rutherford) $50. Named for the goddess of well being, and a glass of red wine with your meal is said to aid in digestion, among other benefits. This medium-bodied Cab has aromas of coffee, tobacco, and blueberry. Dark fruit and chocolate flavors in a wine that is made to be drunk young. **88** *(12/15/2002)*

Staglin 2000 Chardonnay (Rutherford) $50. A well-made Chardonnay showing a subtle floral nose with an underlying minerality. Tropical fruit flavors are enhanced with butterscotch and vanilla. The balance of bright fruit and viticultural and vinification elements is admirable. **90** *(12/15/2002)*

Staglin 1999 Chardonnay (Rutherford) $53. An anise note adds dimension to an already attractive lime, toast, melon, and buttery bouquet. With beautiful balance, subtle peach, nut, and crème brûlée flavors come together in a very attractive palate. This is as lithe and balanced as a ballerina on pointe. This Rutherford treat has a long, warm, and smoky-caramel flavored finish. **91** *(7/1/2001)*

Staglin 2000 Salus Chardonnay (Rutherford) $35. Only 30% malolactic fermentation gives the wine some creaminess but maintains the freshness of the fruit. With aromas of pear, pineapple and toast, it has smoky, rich, flavors that end in a soft nutty finish. **87** *(12/15/2002)*

Staglin 2000 Stagliano Sangiovese (Rutherford) $65. Sangiovese is a tough grape to grow in California. The Staglins do a creditable job with this difficult variety. The nose is very floral with lavender, roses, and wild berries. Raspberry and vanilla flavors end in a bright juicy finish that is soft and full of fruit. Only 105 cases produded **89** *(12/15/2002)*

STAGS' LEAP WINERY

Stags' Leap Winery 2002 Cabernet Sauvignon (Napa Valley) $45. This is a very good Cab. The wine is balanced, oaky, and tannic, with the elegant power associated with this winery and appellation. Still, it's astringent now and doesn't seem ageable. Drink now. **87** —*S.H. (12/15/2005)*

Stags' Leap Winery 2001 Cabernet Sauvignon (Napa Valley) $42. There's an edge of hung meat or smoked leather in this wine that, from whatever cause, smothers the fruit. Underneath that is a solid wine, firm in smooth tannins, but it's difficult to appreciate due to the aroma. **84** — *S.H. (4/1/2005)*

Stags' Leap Winery 1999 Cabernet Sauvignon (Napa Valley) $40. Exquisite tannins and acids in this Cabernet. Not many places on earth could produce a wine with this impeccable structure. It is very young and not showing its best now—it's a bit austere, and those tannins show. Best to

let the deep cassis and blackberry flavors emerge over the next decade. **92** —*S.H. (3/1/2003)*

Stags' Leap Winery 1998 Cabernet Sauvignon (Napa Valley) $40. It's blackberry, black pepper, and cassis aromas are encased in charred oak. Soft but intricate tannins and brisk acidity; fruit comes out in the mid-palate and the hot finish. It's a decent wine but lacks size and dimension, given its pedigree. Blame it on the vintage. **86** —*S.H. (12/31/2001)*

Stags' Leap Winery 1997 Cabernet Sauvignon (Napa Valley) $35. 94 *(11/1/2000)*

Stags' Leap Winery 1997 Cabernet Sauvignon (Napa Valley) $35. 92 *(11/1/2000)*

Stags' Leap Winery 1996 Cabernet Sauvignon (Napa Valley) $32. 92 *(12/31/1999)*

Stags' Leap Winery 1999 Estate Grown Reserve Cabernet Sauvignon (Napa Valley) $65. This is a very good wine, yet for the pedigree and price it is not without flaws. It's super-extracted, with jammy flavors of berries that are not supported by a firm structure. There is also a weak middle palate, although the wine re-gathers strength on the finish. **88** —*S.H. (11/15/2003)*

Stags' Leap Winery 2000 Estate Reserve Cabernet Sauvignon (Napa Valley) $65. This is a wonderfully drinkable wine now. Even though it's not a big bruiser for the cellar, it shows impeccable pedigree in the smooth, unctuous texture and the subtle interplay of black currants and oak. Possesses undeniable elegance. **90** —*S.H. (5/1/2005)*

Stags' Leap Winery 2000 Napa Valley Cabernet Sauvignon (Napa Valley) $40. Defines Tchelistcheff's iron-fist-in-a-velvet-glove description of Stags' Leap District Cabernets. Seductively soft, a wine that caresses the palate with gentle tannins and sweet, creamy oak, framing ripe black currant fruit and rich spice. The power is in the focus, brilliance, and overall purity. **95 Editors' Choice** —*S.H. (11/15/2004)*

Stags' Leap Winery 2004 Chardonnay (Napa Valley) $24. Applesauce, peach purée, buttercream, vanilla, and cinnamon spice flavors characterize this tasty Napa Chard. It has a scour of refreshing acidity and a long, pleasant, fairly complex finish. **88** —*S.H. (12/15/2005)*

Stags' Leap Winery 2002 Chardonnay (Napa Valley) $22. A fine job; this Chardonnay emphasizes structure and food compatibility rather than fruity extraction. There's good apple and peach flavor, bright acidity, enough oak to season and a sprinkling of dusty tannin. **87** —*S.H. (9/1/2004)*

Stags' Leap Winery 2001 Chardonnay (Napa Valley) $22. Lush and complex. Fruity flavors range from fresh green apples to spicy ripe pears. The oak is fine and smoky, while barrel fermentation and lees aging help craft a creamy texture. The finish is long and rich. **91 Editors' Choice** —*S.H. (5/1/2003)*

Stags' Leap Winery 2000 Chardonnay (Napa Valley) $29. A well-balanced wine that shows off pretty pear, citrus, melon, apple, and vanilla notes, all tempered by a fine, mineral edge. Delicate, elegant, and lovely. **90** *(5/1/2002)*

Stags' Leap Winery 1998 Chardonnay (Napa Valley) $21. 85 *(6/1/2000)*

Stags' Leap Winery 2002 Merlot (Napa Valley) $31. This wine is not showing well now because of the tannins, which shut everything down. Is there enough fruit for the long haul? I don't think so. Give it an "A" for effort, and wait for the '03. **84** —*S.H. (12/15/2005)*

Stags' Leap Winery 2001 Merlot (Napa Valley) $31. This is a seriously good Merlot. They got the fruit gorgeously ripe so that it bursts with sunny cassis and cherry flavor, and then they drenched it with high-end toasted oak. Near-perfect tannins, and just-right acidity provide the finishing touches. Elegant. **93** —*S.H. (12/15/2004)*

Stags' Leap Winery 2000 Merlot (Napa Valley) $40. A stunning success for its wonderfully extracted, complex mélange of blackberry, cassis, sweet anise, plum, and cured tobacco. That's what rigorous selection can accomplish in a so-so vintage. The flavors are wrapped in the rich, sweet tannins and balanced acids you'd expect from this appellation. Might age, but best now through next year. **93** —*S.H. (5/1/2004)*

Stags' Leap Winery 1998 Merlot (Napa Valley) $31. Notes of chocolate, blackberry, and plum, and a waft of French oak that adds vanilla and clove aromas. It's hard to imagine prettier tannins, at once soft and luxurious. Call it a fine example from a light vintage. **86** —*S.H. (6/1/2001)*

Stags' Leap Winery 1997 Merlot (Napa Valley) $30. 91 *(12/31/1999)*

Stags' Leap Winery 2000 Estate Grown Reserve Merlot (Napa Valley) $50. A wonderful Merlot. It's very soft in the mouth; the blackberry, cherry, and plum flavors are not especially dense, probably because of the vintage. But the tannins are as softly blurry as Renoir colors. This is an early drinker of immense charm. **91** —*S.H. (12/31/2003)*

Stags' Leap Winery 2001 Estate Reserve Merlot (Napa Valley) $50. The attractive aromas of cherries, leather, and smoky oak seem weirdly disconnected from the palate, which is quite hard in tannins and light in flavor. There's a suggestion of cherry and blackberry fruit. Drink now. **85** —*S.H. (5/1/2005)*

Stags' Leap Winery 2003 Petite Sirah (Napa Valley) $38. Long before the boom in "Pet," Stags' Leap was committed to it. And few wineries have performed more consistently over the years. The '03, from the winery's old estate vineyard exhibits dark, dry, rich, robust characteristics. It's a flamboyant, plummy-leathery wine that never loses control. **92 Editors' Choice** —*S.H. (12/1/2006)*

Stags' Leap Winery 2002 Petite Sirah (Napa Valley) $35. Well, this is your basic inky dark, tannic Pet wine, from a producer with a long track record. It's a wine meant to be stuck away in a cool cellar for a decade or longer, and there's no reason not to, given the astringency and the fabulously molten core of blackberry and cherry fruit. Should begin to be approachable after 2008; hold for years after. **90 Cellar Selection** —*S.H. (12/15/2005)*

Stags' Leap Winery 2001 Petite Sirah (Napa Valley) $31. This vintage may surprise you. It's not an inky monster that needs decades to be drinkable, like so many Napa bottlings. You can enjoy it now, with its rich core of blackberry and cherry fruit and sweet, melted tannins. But it will also improve at least through this decade. **91** —*S.H. (11/15/2004)*

Stags' Leap Winery 2000 Petite Sirah (Napa Valley) $31. A smooth-textured wine that is complex and redolent of black cherry, anise, cinnamon, herb, cassis, and coffee flavors. Tannins are firm and supple, and the finish is long and generous. **91** —*J.M. (8/1/2004)*

Stags' Leap Winery 1999 Petite Sirah (Napa Valley) $31. And the Oscar for the darkest wine of the year goes to…Stags' Leap! Black as a moonless midnight, and one whiff sends you to heaven. Plums, blackberries, oak, all the right stuff. Sheer lusciousness, big, rich, and unctuous, fruity, rich and dry. Terrific now with game and roasts, but you can age it forever. **93** —*S.H. (12/1/2002)*

Stags' Leap Winery 1998 Petite Sirah (Napa Valley) $32. An enticing blend of black cherry, blackberry, spice, cocoa, and herb flavors. The tannins are supple and the finish luxuriously long. Delicious. **90** —*J.M. (5/1/2002)*

Stags' Leap Winery 1996 Petite Sirah (Napa Valley) $28. 93 —*S.H. (5/1/2000)*

Stags' Leap Winery 2000 Ne Cede Malis Red Blend (Napa Valley) $54. From old vines, this blend of Carignane, Grenache, and Syrah is a rich, nuanced wine. Even non-sophisticates will find this smooth, delicious and enjoyable, although savvy tasters will appreciate the complexity. **92** —*S.H. (5/1/2005)*

Stags' Leap Winery 1999 Ne Cede Malis Red Wine Red Blend (Napa Valley) $50. This is an old Petite Sirah-based field blend on the estate, and it's classic. Pours dark as night, and is immense in flavor, with blackberry, blueberry, caramel, chocolate, coffee, and roasted nut tastes cascading across the palate. The tannins are rich and dense, but utterly soft. Yummy stuff. **92** —*S.H. (12/31/2003)*

Stags' Leap Winery 1997 Ne Cede Malis Rhône Red Blend (Stags Leap District) $50. This blend of Carignane, Grenache, Syrah, Pelourism, and Mourvèdre grapes serves up a rich textured wine, with hints of cherry, strawberry, spice, and toasty oak notes. A tangy edge frames the moderate finish. **89** —*J.M. (12/1/2001)*

Stags' Leap Winery 2001 Syrah (Napa Valley) $29. This Northern Rhône-style Syrah is clearly in need of cellaring. It's rather closed in aroma now, and assaults the mouth with numbing tannins. It might be just another dull wine, but for the massive underlying fruit, which is muscling to get out. It's a bit of a gamble, but I suspect this will be gorgeous by 2010. **90** —*S.H. (12/1/2004)*

Stags' Leap Winery 2000 Syrah (Napa Valley) $29. A somewhat light-textured wine with bright acidity, zippy cherry flavors and an herbal edge redolent of bell pepper and spice. Shows a moderate, fresh finish. **86** —*J.M. (6/1/2003)*

Stags' Leap Winery 1998 Syrah (Napa Valley) $25. The fragrant, attractive nose of this Napa Syrah has everything from kirsch to mint to butterscotch to dried spices to orange peel. Turns leaner on the palate with a dry, almost ashy feel and medium weight. Picks up again on the back end where the smooth, dark finish shows baked-apple and cinnamon notes. **89** *(11/1/2001)*

Stags' Leap Winery 2002 Viognier (Napa Valley) $25. This one's super-dry and tight in acids and displays citrus flavors. You might think it was Sauvignon Blanc, except for the peacock's tail of white peach and mango on the finish. A great food wine. **87** —*S.H. (11/15/2004)*

Stags' Leap Winery 2001 Viognier (Napa Valley) $25. The flamboyant tropical fruit, pear, citrus, and floral flavors are balanced by crisp acidity. Very dry, but so rich and ripe. It's oakier than many Viogniers out there, but easily handles the smoke and toast. **90** —*S.H. (5/1/2003)*

Stags' Leap Winery 1999 Viognier (Napa Valley) $25. Quite fragrant, with hints of toast, honeysuckle, and white peach. The wine is richly textured with velvety nuances and pretty fig, apricot and mineral notes. Finishes long and lemony. **92 Editors' Choice** —*J.M. (12/1/2001)*

STANDING STONE

Standing Stone 1999 Pinnacle Bordeaux Blend (Finger Lakes) $20. This Cabernet-based blend boasts plenty of weedy tobacco and earth flavors that add complexity to cherry-tinged fruit. The finish combines sweet caramel notes with lemony-tart acids. **84** —*J.C. (1/1/2004)*

Standing Stone 1997 Cabernet Franc (Finger Lakes) $16. 86 —*J.C. (12/1/1999)*

Standing Stone 1999 Cabernet Franc (Finger Lakes) $16. Cherry, vanilla, and marshmallow aromas let you know what to expect, and the palate delivers more of the same. The fruit is a little thin, but the wine is soft and easy to drink, with a finish of caramel and tart cranberries. **84** —*J.C. (1/1/2004)*

Standing Stone 2000 Gewürztraminer (Finger Lakes) $NA. Solid varietal Gewürztraminer, brimming with grapefruit, litchee, lemon, melon, fig, spice, and anise flavors. It's bright and fresh, yet full and lush on the palate, finishing with a long, mineral edge. Delicious. **91** —*J.M. (12/11/2002)*

Standing Stone 2002 Estate Merlot (Finger Lakes) $20. An intensely fruit-driven nose of raspberry and blueberry is touched with tobacco and forest floor. Almost a bit sweet-tasting in the mouth, with ripe tannins and candied cherries wrapped in pie crust. **83** —*M.D. (8/1/2006)*

Standing Stone 1999 Pinot Noir (Finger Lakes) $17. Another relatively weakly colored Pinot, but another that shows color is overrated as an indicator of quality. The intense aromas of caramel-cola, black cherries, and wet dog give way to a medium-weight, silky palate that offers dark chocolate and cherry flavors. Delicate tannins on the finish suggest black tea, but this isn't an ager. **84** —*J.C. (3/1/2002)*

Standing Stone 2004 Riesling (Finger Lakes) $13. Bacon, lychee, and bubble gum aromas are unexpected but not wholly unpleasant, while this semi-dry Riesling is full and a bit bulky. Flavors are more normal but not overpowering, offering citrus, petrol, and spice. **84** —*M.D. (8/1/2006)*

Standing Stone 2002 Estate Bottled Riesling (Finger Lakes) $12. Atypically ripe, weighty, and intense for a Finger Lakes wine, with pear and peach notes buttressed by minerally dry extract. The mouthfeel is thick and viscous and the alcohol level a relatively high 13.1%, but it finishes long and elegantly, with tongue-tingling acids. **89 Best Buy** —*J.C. (8/1/2003)*

Standing Stone 2001 Ice Riesling (Finger Lakes) $32. Smells rich and decadent, with aromas of orange marmalade and honey, but still maintains refreshing touches of citrus and pineapple throughout. It's thick and rich in the mouth, and finishes long, with excellent balance. This can easily compete with Canadian ice wines. **90** —*J.C. (8/1/2003)*

STANGELAND

Stangeland 2000 Estate Reserve Pinot Noir (Willamette Valley) $39. Unrelated aromas hit you right off the bat: dill, mint, cinnamon, cedar, vanilla. Together, it's all a bit strange. In the mouth, cherry fruit comes across a little green, with pronounced herbal notes. The finish is dry, with starching tannins. **85** *(10/1/2002)*

Stangeland 1999 Estate Reserve Pinot Noir (Willamette Valley) $32. There's good depth to this ripe, structured wine's solid, cherry fruit core. Woodsy notes, anise, and chocolate accents add to its angular appeal. Finishes long, displaying firm, even tannins, wood, and cocoa notes. Tasty now, but best 2004–2008. **89** *(10/1/2002)*

Stangeland 1999 Martha's Vineyard II Pinot Noir (Willamette Valley) $30. This wine's tart cranberry-cherry-beet fruit displayed some unusual salty, saddley aromatics. It's dense and earthy, with a sweet-and-sour quality. Ends with firm tannins, pepper, and lemon notes. **84** *(10/1/2002)*

Stangeland 1999 Silver Leaf Vineyard Pinot Noir (Willamette Valley) $40. Saddle leather, soy, violet, and cinnamon accents adorn very dark cherry fruit in this handsome red. The smoky oak is strong, and the palate has a peppery, rustic edge, but still the wine has solid appeal. Finishes with juicy fruit, firm tannins, and chocolate accents. Drink 2003–2008. **88** *(10/1/2002)*

Stangeland 2000 Winemaker's Estate Reserve Pinot Noir (Willamette Valley) $59. The panel was unanimous in its ranking of this deep, briary Pinot, one that simply smells great. There's plenty of cherry, cinnamon, spice, and smoke on the bouquet. The flavors are pure and juicy, emphasizing raspberry and cherry below a thin veneer of oak. Cedar, smoke, and chocolate mix on the smooth, layered finish. **90** *(10/1/2002)*

Stangeland 1999 Winemakers Estate Reserve Pinot Noir (Willamette Valley) $40. Opening saddle-leather, vaguely skunky aromas quickly pass. The lavish oak sits a little heavily on the berry-rhubarb fruit here. Still, an unusual mélange of chalk, vanilla, even mushroom accents peek through. On the tongue, the wine has a full, supple, even slightly chalky feel. Interesting, and tasty, though overtly cedary. If that's your style, you'll really enjoy this. Drink now–2008. **87** *(10/1/2002)*

STANTON

Stanton 2002 Cabernet Sauvignon (Oakville) $65. This wine is a bit too sweet, soft, and obvious for me, although some will admire the blackberry, cassis, and chocolate flavors. Seems at its best now, although a few years of cellaring won't hurt. **86** —*S.H. (11/1/2005)*

Stanton 2001 Cabernet Sauvignon (Oakville) $65. Very ripe with cherry and currant fruit, and elaborately oaked, this juicy wine has plenty of character. It's a bit rough and sharp around the edges, although it might soften over the years. **87** —*S.H. (10/1/2004)*

STAR LANE VINEYARD

Star Lane Vineyard 2005 Sauvignon Blanc (Santa Ynez Valley) $25. This is a fancy Sauvignon Blanc. The underlying wine is cool-climate balanced, with ripe, very dry fig, citrus, green melon, and paprika-spice flavors backed up with firm acids. On top of that is a layer of sweet, smoky oak and the creamy smoothness of sur lies aging. **87** —*S.H. (12/15/2006)*

Star Lane Vineyard 2003 Sauvignon Blanc (Santa Ynez Valley) $25. Rather heavy on the nose, with cream of wheat, toasty wood, and white fruit. Quite straightforward with an acidic streak that brings it to attention. Good mouthfeel and elegant, if not exactly the most fruit-forward kid on the block. **87** *(7/1/2005)*

Star Lane Vineyard 2003 Syrah (Santa Ynez Valley) $35. The vineyard is in the inland eastern part of the valley, and this is a warm-climate Syrah, lush and frankly delicious. A dry wine, it fills the mouth with ripe blackberry, cherry, herb, and peppery spice flavors. The tannins are soft but intricate. **87** —*S.H. (12/31/2006)*

Star Lane Vineyard 2003 Syrah (Santa Ynez Valley) $35. Here's a delicious, rewarding Syrah. It brims with wonderfully ripe fruit, yet maintains balance and dryness. Blackberry pie, cherry preserves, cocoa, sweet tobacco, white peppery spice, and vanilla bean flavors lead to a long, complicated finish. **92** —*S.H. (12/15/2006)*

STARRY NIGHT

Starry Night 2002 Chardonnay (Russian River Valley) $17. Ripe in tropical fruit, peach, pear, and spicy flavors, well-oaked, and with a creamy texture and crisp acidity, this pretty Chard offers plenty of pleasure. **87** —*S.H. (12/15/2004)*

Starry Night 2002 Adara Rhône Red Blend (California) $14. This Rhône blend is sharp in acids and a bit green, but has some good cherry fruit. It's a solid country effort. **83** —*S.H. (12/15/2004)*

Starry Night 1999 Syrah (Lodi) $19. Here's a real find: a serious-fun wine with lots going for it. Opens with black cherry, smoke, and vanilla aromas; rich and fine. The flavors are cherry-smoky and bone dry, with a fine texture. There's something distinguished and high quality about the structure and finish. **91** —*S.H. (7/1/2002)*

Starry Night 2003 Zinfandel (Lodi) $16. Smells great, doesn't taste that good. That's the story on this Zin. The aroma's promising in Zinny wild berries, peppery spices, and chocolate, but the wine turns sweet and too soft in the mouth. **83** —*S.H. (12/1/2005)*

Starry Night 2001 Zinfandel (Lodi) $16. Quite herbal and menthol-like. The wine also has plummy, charry, black cherry notes but they take a back seat to the unusually herbal character. Charry tannins act as a framework. Different. **85** *(11/1/2003)*

Starry Night 2001 Old Vine Zinfandel (Russian River Valley) $22. Plummy, jammy, and spicy up front. It bursts forth with a bright-edged cherry component that's followed by toasty oak, pepper, and herb notes. The finish is moderate, with a slight tannic bite. Quite juicy. **88** *(11/1/2003)*

Starry Night 2002 Terre Vermeille Vineyard Zinfandel (Lake County) $18. As ripe and sweet as a Zin can be before turning to Port. Cherries, black raspberries, mocha, vanilla, and peppery spices are encased in soft tannins, but the acidity provides life. **85** —*S.H. (12/15/2004)*

Starry Night 2001 Tom Feeney Ranch, Old Vine Zinfandel (Russian River Valley) $26. Starts off with rich earth, coffee, and spice aromas that lead into a bright-edged, fruit-driven wine redolent of black cherry, blackberry, black pepper, herbs, coffee, and chocolate notes. Zippy acidity keeps it bright on the finish. Complex, yet still fun. **90** —*J.M. (6/1/2004)*

Starry Night 2003 Wildotter Vineyard Zinfandel (Amador County) $18. This wine suffers from the sins that many Zins commit under California's brutal summer sun. It's chili-pepper hot, flat in vital acidity, and tastes like it was artificially sweetened. **81** —*S.H. (12/1/2005)*

STATON HILLS

Staton Hills 1995 Cabernet Sauvignon (Columbia Valley (WA)) $17. **87** —*M.S. (9/1/1999)*

Staton Hills 1997 Chardonnay (Washington) $12. **82** —*P.G. (6/1/2000)*

STE. CHAPELLE

Ste. Chapelle 2000 Winemaker's Series Cabernet Sauvignon (Idaho) $10. Okay, Idaho Cabernet is never going to be an easy sell. But new winemaker Chuck Devlin is a talent, and he gives this wine a distinct core of sweet black cherry fruit; not big, but perfectly ripe. It's set in a slightly earthy framework of root and rock, with a lightly chalky finish. **88** —*P.G. (9/1/2002)*

Ste. Chapelle NV Sparkling Brut Champagne Blend (Idaho) $8. **83** —*S.H. (12/1/2000)*

Ste. Chapelle NV Spumante Champagne Blend (Idaho) $8. This is a sweet, simple sparkling wine made from 60% Chenin Blanc and 40% Chardonnay. It has a lemon/citrus nose, with some soapy scents that carry through in the flavor. The big bubbles and sugary mouthfeel suggest that it was made by the charmat process; in any event, it's a bubbly best suited for mixing with orange juice or something tart like cranberry juice, and served as a Sunday morning spirit-lifter. **81** —*P.G. (6/1/2001)*

Ste. Chapelle 1999 Chardonnay (Idaho) $10. Very dry and slightly musty, the fruit tastes lightly of apple and citrus, but the wine already seems to be heading over a cliff. **84** —*P.G. (9/1/2002)*

Ste. Chapelle 2001 Soft Chenin Blanc (Idaho) $6. By "soft" the winery means sweet. This is a low-acid style, showing flavors of pear, melon, and mango. It's a good sipping wine, but perhaps a bit too soft for most foods. **86** —*P.G. (9/1/2002)*

Ste. Chapelle 2000 Fumé Blanc (Idaho) $10. The winery's penchant for delicate, lightly balanced wines is again evident here. This has some pleasant herb flavors, gentle nuances of grass, and citrus. Cleanly made and finished with a touch of spice. **87** —*P.G. (9/1/2002)*

Ste. Chapelle 1998 Gewürztraminer (Idaho) $7. 81 —*J.C. (9/1/1999)*

Ste. Chapelle 2001 Dry Gewürztraminer (Idaho) $6. This is quite dry, as the label indicates, and nicely scented with light floral notes. Citrus fruit flavors run through an elegant, textured wine that definitely wants food to go with. **88 Best Buy** —*P.G. (9/1/2002)*

Ste. Chapelle 2001 Johannisberg Riesling (Idaho) $6. Off-dry fruit conjures up flavors of grapes, apricots, peaches, and even kumquats! A balanced, sensuous wine, it has no rough acid or over-the-top tropical fruit flavors. Long and silky. **88 Best Buy** —*P.G. (9/1/2002)*

Ste. Chapelle 1998 Dry Johannisberg Riesling (Idaho) $7. 80 —*J.C. (9/1/1999)*

Ste. Chapelle 1997 Sally's Summit Vineyard Dry Johannisberg Riesling (Idaho) $10. 87 —*J.C. (9/1/1999)*

Ste. Chapelle 2001 Special Harvest Johannisberg Riesling (Idaho) $10. From the winery's best lots of Riesling, this special selection definitely acquires an extra dimension of flavor beyond the excellent "regular" bottling. Bursting with ripe, juicy fruit, it balances its intense flavors atop a delicate, graceful frame. **90 Best Buy** —*P.G. (9/1/2002)*

Ste. Chapelle 2000 Value Series Merlot (Idaho) $7. Idaho and Merlot are not thoughts that generally spring together in the mind of the wine consumer, but Ste. Chapelle makes a good run at crafting an attractive, perfectly balanced wine here. The fruit is cherry and lightly herbal, and there are interesting flavors of earth and mocha, too. **87 Best Buy** —*P.G. (9/1/2002)*

Ste. Chapelle 2000 Winemaker's Series Merlot (Idaho) $10. Fairly tannic, this Merlot has some ripe, even sweet, cherry fruit. It's done in a light style, but it feels and tastes ripe, which means the winemaker knew what he was doing. A lovely effort that takes full advantage of the character of the region's fruit. **88** —*P.G. (9/1/2002)*

Ste. Chapelle 1998 Riesling (Idaho) $6. 83 —*J.C. (9/1/1999)*

Ste. Chapelle 2001 Dry Riesling (Idaho) $6. Riesling has always been a strength of this winery, and this wine clearly shows why. It has a lightness and delicacy missing from most other domestic Riesling, yet it is not simple. Its complex, subtle, food-friendly flavors are right on the money. **88 Best Buy** —*P.G. (9/1/2002)*

Ste. Chapelle 1998 Special Harvest Riesling (Idaho) $8. 85 —*J.C. (9/1/1999)*

Ste. Chapelle 1996 Reserve Syrah (Idaho) $15. 90 —*M.G. (11/15/1999)*

Ste. Chapelle 2000 Winemaker's Series Syrah (Idaho) $10. The grapes come from the Chicken Dinner vineyard, which says it all. Pop this tart, tangy wine, with its Zin-like red berry flavors and hints of white pepper, and bring on the fried chicken. **86** —*P.G. (9/1/2002)*

STEELE

Steele 2003 Cabernet Franc (Lake County) $18. Light and fruity in cherry flavors, with a sprinkling of Provençal herbs, this dry wine has thick, dusty tannins that call for a rich steak or lamb. Drink now. **85** —*S.H. (12/15/2005)*

Steele 2002 Cabernet Sauvignon (Red Hills Lake County) $35. Really nice black currants and cherries, and classy tannins, too, the kind that are noticeable but sweet and soft at the same time. All in all it's a study in balance. It's not a great Cab, a bit too angular, but it proves that this new appellation is an area to watch. **87** —*S.H. (12/1/2006)*

Steele 2004 Bien Nacido Vineyard Chardonnay (Santa Barbara County) $28. Plenty of richness here, mangoes, pineapple custard, Key lime pie, not to mention smoky, caramelly, butterscotchy oak, but there's also a streamlined, sleek minerality that leaves a lip-smacking steely feeling behind. Part of that is acidity. Really fine wine. **92** —*S.H. (12/15/2006)*

Steele 1998 Bien Nacido Vineyard Chardonnay (Santa Barbara) $30. One of seven wines we tasted from this renowned vineyard, and one of six from veteran Chard-meister Jed Steele. This one's a beauty—the top scoring wine from both the winemaker and the site. A floral, orange, vanilla custard and almost mustardy-spice nose opens to a full orange, mineral, and vanilla-spice palate. It's rich and creamy yet spicy, and even shows some bright lemony elements. This multidimensional wine finishes long with tangy, toasty oak. Top Value. **92 Best Buy** *(7/1/2001)*

Steele 1997 Bien Nacido Vineyard Chardonnay (Santa Barbara County) $28. 94 —*L.W. (7/1/1999)*

Steele 1998 Cuvée Chardonnay (California) $18. 90 *(6/1/2000)*

Steele 2004 Du Pratt Vineyard Chardonnay (Mendocino Ridge) $28. There aren't a lot of wines coming off this appellation, and most of them are red. But this is a wonderful Chard. Ripe and detailed, it combines tropical fruit, mineral, and oak flavors, and is dry and tart in acids. This is one of the few California Chardonnays I would age for up to ten years. **92** —*S.H. (12/15/2006)*

Steele 1998 Du Pratt Vineyard Chardonnay (Mendocino) $30. A jazzy bouquet of sour pear, toasted nut, and leesy notes opens this North Coast winner. An unusual mix of dry orange, papaya, and cantaloupe flavors follow on the palate. The medium-full mouthfeel is butter-smooth, yet bright and crisp enough to not be mushy. Spice and lemon accents enliven the long, tangy finish. Top Value. **90** *(7/1/2001)*

Steele 1997 Du Pratt Vineyard (Late Harvest) Chardonnay (Mendocino) $30. 87 —*J.M. (6/1/2003)*

Steele 1997 Du Pratt Vineyard Chardonnay (Mendocino County) $27. 91 —*L.W. (7/1/1999)*

Steele 1998 Durell Vineyard Chardonnay (Carneros) $28. 87 *(6/1/2000)*

Steele 1997 Durell Vineyard Chardonnay (Carneros) $26. 92 —*L.W. (6/1/1999)*

Steele 1998 Goodchild Vineyard Chardonnay (Santa Barbara County) $30. Another one of Jed Steele's many single-vineyard offerings this wine from Santa Barbara is big and perfumey. Pineapple, banana, and caramel flavors are cloaked in sweetness that may be a bit heavy for some. **87** *(7/1/2001)*

Steele 1997 Goodchild Vineyard Chardonnay (Santa Barbara County) $24. 93 —*S.H. (2/1/2000)*

Steele 1998 Lolonis Vineyard Chardonnay (Mendocino) $32. Thyme and lavender notes mingle with orange, tangerine, and banana aromas and flavors in this exotic, stylized wine. An ample dose of spicy new oak brings dimension, but also adds a dry, slightly austere note to the long finish. Appealing now; may integrate better with short-term cellaring. **89** *(7/1/2001)*

Steele 1998 Lolonis Vineyard Chardonnay (Mendocino County) $28. 85 *(6/1/2000)*

Steele 1998 Parmalee-Hill Vineyard Chardonnay (Sonoma Valley) $26. 93 —*S.H. (2/1/2000)*

Steele 2001 Parmelee-Hill Vineyard Chardonnay (Sonoma Valley) $28. Getting pretty old for a Chard, this wine has lost much of its primary fruit and is turning earthy and fragile. There's an old-lees taste, for aficionados of slightly mature whites. **83** —*S.H. (12/15/2005)*

Steele 1998 Parmelee-Hill Vineyard Chardonnay (Sonoma Valley) $30. If you like piña coladas and getting caught in the—oh…I mean…coladas and ripe banana, caramel, and pear aromas and flavors, then this wine delivers. There's an undeniable coconut quality here, and nice acid zip that keeps the fruit in the mix. The oak tannins need a bit of time to smooth out—they're a little edgy on the back end. **89** *(7/1/2001)*

Steele 1998 Sangiacomo Vineyard Chardonnay (Carneros) $30. Jed Steele's wines turned in impressive performances in this tasting—as in this full-bodied, well-integrated, and elegant wine from the respected Sangiacomo Vineyard in Carneros. Tropical fruit, butterscotch, lemon, and hops flavors caress the nose and palate, supported nicely by an acid spine. Creamy yet firm, the mouthfeel is admirable. The wine sports a stylish, mildly spicy finish. Top Value. **90** *(7/1/2001)*

Steele 1997 Sangiacomo Vineyard Chardonnay (Carneros) $24. 93 —*L.W. (6/1/1999)*

Steele 2004 Shooting Star Chardonnay (Santa Barbara County) $12. Earthy and simple, with a scour of acidity that lasts into the finish, this wine is

USA

marked by peach, apple, and dried herb flavors. It's bone dry. **83** —*S.H.* (*12/15/2005*)

Steele 1999 Fumé Blanc (Lake County) $16. Buttered toast and baked bread aromas announce that this is a well-oaked SB. Apple, melon, and lemon flavors all get support from powerful oak, while the finish is spicy, toasty, warm, and full. This is a flavorful, full-bodied wine, but it is on the opposite end of the spectrum from lean. **88** (*8/1/2002*)

Steele 1999 Clear Lake Merlot (Lake County) $26. Starts off with Port-like aromas of caramel, pie crust, sweet blackberry purée and smoke. In the mouth, berry-cherry extract hits strong and coats the palate with ripe flavor. Tannins persist through the tough finish. **84** —*S.H.* (*12/1/2003*)

Steele 1997 Clear Lake Merlot (Lake County) $22. 86 —*J.C.* (*7/1/2000*)

Steele 2002 Pinot Blanc (Santa Barbara County) $16. Chard-like, with peach flavors, oak, a creamy texture and good acidity. It's a little broader than Chard, though, with a nutty herbaceousness that makes it earthy. **84** —*S.H.* (*12/1/2004*)

Steele 1998 Bien Nacido Vineyard Pinot Blanc (Santa Barbara County) $16. 84 —*L.W.* (*3/1/2000*)

Steele 2001 Pinot Noir (Anderson Valley) $22. Cola, leather, and cherry aromas and flavors, in that order. There are tough tannins in this dry wine. **83** —*S.H.* (*12/1/2004*)

Steele 1997 Pinot Noir (Carneros) $19. 90 (*10/1/1999*)

Steele 2003 Bien Nacido Vineyard Pinot Noir (Santa Barbara County) $35. Rich and dry, with a wealth of flavor that immediately takes over and doesn't let up. Raspberries, cherries, mocha, vanilla, and crushed hard-spice notes are wrapped in a silky texture leading to a long, refined finish. **90** —*S.H.* (*12/1/2006*)

Steele 2000 Bien Nacido Vineyard Pinot Noir (Santa Barbara County) $30. Getting old, with the fresh fruit fading to leathery, earthy flavors. The tannins are still firm, and so are the acids. Unlikely to develop, so drink now. **84** —*S.H.* (*12/1/2004*)

Steele 1999 Bien Nacido Vineyard Pinot Noir (Santa Barbara County) $36. This wine has toffee, beet, pickle barrel, and even some sea notes to the nose. The palate is more conventional, with strawberry fruit, black pepper, and juicy acidity. That same acidity causes some tartness on the finish, but it also ensures that everything stays nice and lively as it fades away. **87** (*10/1/2002*)

Steele 1999 Durell Vineyard Pinot Noir (Carneros) $28. "Overblown," "full-throttle" and "juice-ball" are three words tasters used to describe this wine. But no one said it wasn't tasty. The black cherry flavors are almost overripe, but they are undeniably deep. Tons of spicy oak complements the fruit, adding to its almost Port-like quality. **88** (*10/1/2002*)

Steele 2002 Goodchild Vineyard Pinot Noir (Santa Barbara County) $26. Pours dark and glyceriney, and opens with vibrant, spicy aromas of roasted coffee, black cherry, smoked meat, and cinnamon. This is a big, tough wine, tannic and meaty-chunky, and lush and creamy on the palate. Calls for extended aging. Try 2008 and beyond. **92** (*11/1/2004*)

Steele 1999 Goodchild Vineyard Pinot Noir (Santa Barbara) $32. This wine offers roasted coffee and deep coconut and chocolate notes on the nose. It shows more blackberry flavors than most; in fact, it shows a lot of black: chocolate, coffee, and cherry, too. Well balanced and flavorful, it closes long with spice, mineral, and pepper accents, plus some chalky tannins. **88** (*10/1/2002*)

Steele 2001 Sangiacomo Vineyard Pinot Noir (Carneros) $30. Earthy and herbal, with weak cherry flavors. The acids and tannins create a firm, hard mouthfeel. Surprisingly lean, given the vintage and vineyard. **84** — *S.H.* (*12/1/2004*)

Steele 1999 Sangiacomo Vineyard Pinot Noir (Carneros) $32. There's delicious fruit behind the copious wood. The lavish, toasty oak yields a pine-and-dill patina that not everyone will like, but the deep, dark cherry fruit is a solid presence. The tart plum and espresso-tinged close is long, with even tannins. Drink now–2005. **88** (*10/1/2002*)

Steele 1997 Syrah (Lake County) $16. 91 —*L.W.* (*5/1/2000*)

Steele 2001 Clear Lake Syrah (Lake County) $16. A split decision from our panel, but all agreed that oak was a dominant feature, with descrip-

tors ranging from lots of sawdust and vanilla to pie crust. On the fruit, opinions were less unanimous, ranging from cherry to raisin, hence the wishy-washy rating. **85** (*9/1/2005*)

Steele 2000 Parmelee-Hill Vineyard Syrah (Sonoma Valley) $22. Rather earthy, with some cherry-berry flavors and a good deal of peppery spice, this Syrah is very dry. It's a good provincial wine. **84** —*S.H.* (*12/1/2004*)

Steele 2001 Parmelee-Hill Vineyard Syrah (Sonoma Valley) $22. Quite different from other bottlings off this vineyard, Jed Steele's version stresses meaty, savory notes and lashings of caramel-drizzled vanilla toast. Finishes with soft tannins and more oak-derived flavors. **84** (*9/1/2005*)

Steele 2002 Stymie Founder's Reserve Syrah (Lake County) $45. Way too sweet for my palate, as if a perfectly good Syrah had a tablespoon of white sugar added. **82** —*S.H.* (*12/1/2006*)

Steele 2004 Viognier (Lake County) $18. Dry, acidic, and citrusy, this Viognier isn't your typical tropical fruit sipper. It's more like a lean, crisp Sauvignon Blanc, except for an undertow of pineapple. **84** —*S.H.* (*12/15/2005*)

Steele 2001 Viognier (Lake County) $18. Pear and crème brûlée cover the nose prior to flavors of pears and citrus. This wine is thick, bordering on viscous, but that richness ensures that there's an ultrarich mouthfeel. Still, it seems short on subtleties and nuance. **85** —*M.S.* (*5/1/2003*)

Steele 2002 Catfish Vineyard Zinfandel (Lake County) $21. Smells great, with complex and inviting aromas that promise great dry Zinfandel, but once in the mouth, the wine turns sweet and cloying. The sweetness exaggerates the tannins, making them rasping. **83** —*S.H.* (*12/31/2005*)

Steele 1998 Catfish Vineyard Zinfandel (Clear Lake) $19. Soft, rich fruit, with layers of plum, cherry, berry, and accents of toast and vanilla. Smooth, seductive style, plenty of acid, good balance, and the fruit is pure, clean, and ripe all the way to the lingering finish. **91** —*P.G.* (*3/1/2001*)

Steele 1998 Pacini Vineyard Zinfandel (Mendocino) $22. Minty raspberries and chocolate light up the nose. Classy winemaking, with the plump fruit leading into a smooth, rich, and extended finish with distinctly minty highlights. **89** —*P.G.* (*3/1/2001*)

Steele 1997 Pacini Vineyard Zinfandel (Mendocino County) $24. 85 —*J.C.* (*9/1/1999*)

Steele 2003 Shooting Star Zinfandel (Lake County) $12. Too rustic and sweet on the finish for my tastes, with Porty raisin flavors. The wine also feels hot, despite official labeling of 13.5% alcohol. **82** —*S.H.* (*12/31/2005*)

STEFAN DANIELS

Stefan Daniels 2001 Sauvignon Blanc (Redwood Valley) $15. This full-bodied and bracing wine has ultraripe flavors of lime, grapefruit, and currants, girded with zesty acidity. The fruit really hits in the midpalate and lasts through the long, lush finish. Try with spicy Thai fish cakes. **86** —*S.H.* (*12/31/2003*)

Stefan Daniels 1999 Terre Vermeille Vineyard Sauvignon Blanc (Lake County) $17. Here's a rich, lively wine marked by grassy, citrus flavors veering into ripe figs, and shaped by barrel fermentation and oak notes. It has a nice, creamy, leesy texture, and is dry and spicy. **88** —*S.H.* (*5/1/2001*)

Stefan Daniels 2000 Lockeford Syrah (Lodi) $15. Not a big wine, but with some nice plum and blackberry flavors, with hints of coffee, dark chocolate, and herbs. Completely dry, and fairly tannic, too, although the fruit leaves behind a rich sweetness on the finish. **87** —*S.H.* (*3/1/2004*)

Stefan Daniels 1999 Lockeford Syrah (California) $20. Although it carries a California label, the Lockeford designation tells you it's from Lodi. The slightly herbal, black pepper aromas and tangy berry fruit give little indication of its hot-climate origins; The meaty, earthy flavors on the midpalate sing through the finish. **89** (*10/1/2001*)

STELLA MARIS

Stella Maris 2003 Red Blend (Columbia Valley (WA)) $29. The second label for Northstar shines in this warm vintage, with a firm line of dark fruits, streaked with earth and mineral. Cherry fruit holds the center, a bit overwhelmed by the tannins at this time, but looking good for another half decade or so of aging. **88** —*P.G. (10/1/2006)*

Stella Maris 2002 Red Blend (Columbia Valley (WA)) $29. The Stella Maris, a Northstar second label, is a standout among a largely undistinguished crop of 2002s. Sweet fruit shows tangy flavors of red currant and berry, which carry the wine into a puckery finish. It's round and pleasing, though without much weight. **87** —*P.G. (12/15/2005)*

STELTZNER

Steltzner 2001 Claret Bordeaux Blend (Napa Valley) $16. It would be nice to report that this affordable Napa Bordeaux blend is as good as wines costing twice as much, but it's not. It's not bad, but quite thin and herbal, with a tannic finish. **84** —*S.H. (4/1/2004)*

Steltzner 2003 Claret Cabernet Blend (Napa Valley) $18. Based on Cabernet Sauvignon, this Bordeaux blend shows a lovely structure, and ripe black currant and fruit, tarted up with toasty oak. It's dry and balanced and complex. This is a great price for a Napa Cab of this quality. **90** —*S.H. (11/1/2006)*

Steltzner 1998 Cabernet Sauvignon (Napa Valley) $28. Pretty tannic now, with plenty of grip and dust, but underneath is luscious blackberry, black cherry, and cassis fruit. The wine is bone-dry, with lovely acidity. Its pedigree shows in its long, rich finish. Best after 2002, but pretty and elegant now. **90** —*S.H. (6/1/2002)*

Steltzner 1999 Merlot (Stags' Leap District) $26. There's lots to admire in this well-ripened, elegant dinner wine. It has aromas of green olives, white chocolate, and plums, with a waft of smoky oak, while the flavors are spicy and fruity. Bone-dry, it's richly tannic and complex, with depth and interest. **92** —*S.H. (6/1/2002)*

STEPHAN RIDGE

Stephan Ridge 2000 L'Adventure Estate Cuvée Red Blend (Paso Robles) $75. An extraordinary wine. From the cooler west side of the appellation, this blend of Cabernet Sauvignon, Petit Verdot, and Syrah offers a little something from each variety. The overall effect is a concerto, vibrant and complex. Huge oak, but the expressive fruit wears it well. Beautiful tannins coat the palate like a mink coat. **92 Editors' Choice** —*S.H. (11/15/2003)*

Stephan Ridge 2000 Syrah-Cabernet (Paso Robles) $25. A difficult wine to fall in love with. Opens with odd notes of canned vegetables, chocolate, white pepper, and gym socks. Drinks a whole lot better, with pretty fruit and a smooth texture, but the disturbing aroma is so off-putting, it's hard to get past it. A Syrah-Cabernet Sauvignon blend in almost equal proportions. **82** —*S.H. (3/1/2004)*

STEPHEN ROSS

Stephen Ross 2004 Chardonnay (Edna Valley) $20. Classic Edna Valley Chard, bright and zippy in acidity, with rich, purely etched flavors of Key lime pie and toasty oak. This sophisticated wine has a long, spicy finish. **89** —*S.H. (3/1/2006)*

Stephen Ross 2004 Bien Nacido Vineyard Chardonnay (Santa Maria Valley) $25. There's a minerality to this wine that makes it angular and steely clean, despite well-ripened peach and pineapple flavors. It has a smooth, creamy texture and good acidity for balance, not to mention a rich coat of oak. **90** —*S.H. (3/1/2006)*

Stephen Ross 2000 Edna Ranch Chardonnay (Edna Valley) $20. Smells oaky and fruity, with peach and apple aromas compounded with vanilla. The flavors are pretty nice, with apples and oaky influences. Fairly bitter and tart. Acidity creates burn through the finish, and lees add a sour component. **85** —*S.H. (6/1/2003)*

Stephen Ross 2003 Thomann Station Petite Sirah (Napa Valley) $32. This is the quintessential Napa Petite Sirah: rich, balanced, and enormously fruity. It's really as good as Pet gets; it's a firm, chunky dry wine, with the variety's distinctively shabby-chic personality. **90** —*S.H. (3/1/2006)*

Stephen Ross 2000 Thomann Station Petite Sirah (Napa Valley) $32. There's plenty of pleasure in this wine, with its bright, focused flavors of cherries and blackberries. Tasters noted a range of herbal, earthy notes, including eucalyptus and mint. The forward flavors drink soft but are

held in place with firm tannins that melt on the long, slightly hot finish. **88** *(4/1/2003)*

Stephen Ross 2004 Pinot Noir (Edna Valley) $28. Has that magical Pinot Noir quality that combines weight and power with an effortless silkiness. The result is a super-drinkable wine. It shows red, blue, and stone fruits with a coating of ripe, sweet tannins. **89** —*S.H. (12/1/2006)*

Stephen Ross 2003 Pinot Noir (Edna Valley) $28. This Pinot is richer and softer than other Edna Valley Pinots. It's a little heavy now, with dry, sticky tannins, and is not showing well, a function no doubt of youth. Two or three years should let the cherry flavors break out. **87** —*S.H. (3/1/2006)*

Stephen Ross 2002 Pinot Noir (Edna Valley) $28. A marvelously plush, complex wine. Earthy aromas, sautéed mushrooms, cola, smoked meat, ripe cherries, and raspberries and Oriental spices combine in a dense, lush mouthfeel. Fabulous length and harmony in the finish. This is seriously fine Pinot Noir. Drink now or through 2006. **91 Editors' Choice** *(11/1/2004)*

Stephen Ross 2000 Pinot Noir (Edna Valley) $28. Slightly overripe-tasting blackberry and cherry fruit shows some earthy, mushroomy accents. The mouth fills out with a sturdy feel and plum and spice cake notes. A mild bitter-almond quality plays on the finish. **86** *(10/1/2002)*

Stephen Ross 2004 Aubaine Vineyards Pinot Noir (San Luis Obispo County) $40. This is a somewhat heavy and enormously concentrated wine. It reminds me of Calera's Mount Harlan wines. It has a lot of extracted cherry jam flavor and tannins you can feel. A little ponderous in youth, it seems likely to improve. **88 Cellar Selection** —*S.H. (12/1/2006)*

Stephen Ross 2004 Bien Nacido Vineyard Pinot Noir (Santa Maria Valley) $35. This is Stephen Ross's best Bien Nacido Pinot in recent years, showing a great marriage of power and refinement. The wine shows primary fruit, dusty spices, and acids. It's a little dry and angular, but will reward some cellaring. So complex, yet you can drink it now, but decant first. **93 Cellar Selection** —*S.H. (12/1/2006)*

Stephen Ross 2003 Bien Nacido Vineyard Pinot Noir (Santa Maria Valley) $35. Extracted and soft, this single-vineyard Pinot has a full-bodied mouthfeel framing cherry, coffee, blackberry, and cassis flavors. It tastes almost like a Cabernet, except for the silky texture. Heavy now, but it might lighten up in a few years. **86** —*S.H. (3/1/2006)*

Stephen Ross 2002 Bien Nacido Vineyard Pinot Noir (Santa Maria Valley) $35. Complex aromatics here, with cherry, cola, root beer, orange peel, and smoky oak among other notes. Drinks crisp in acidity and clean, with a polished, supple texture. Some tannins on the finish provide grip. **87** *(11/1/2004)*

Stephen Ross 2000 Bien Nacido Vineyard Pinot Noir (Santa Maria Valley) $35. Fine balance and a winning tart-cherry profile mark this medium-weight Pinot. Hickory smoke, tea, green herb, and coffee accents handsomely accent the bright fruit. Tasty and seductive, this shows its fine fruit right through the mildly peppery, evenly tannic finish. Drink now–2006. **89** *(10/1/2002)*

Stephen Ross 2000 Chamisal Vineyard Pinot Noir (Edna Valley) $40. It starts off dense and smoky, and then some mushroom, chocolate, and caramel rises up from the glass. The palate is fairly dense and concentrated, with flavors of black cherry, licorice, and herbs. The finish is expansive and well textured, with cola, coffee, and a hint of barrel char. **90 Editors' Choice** *(10/1/2002)*

Stephen Ross 1999 Chamisal Vineyard Pinot Noir (Edna Valley) $24. Classic South Coast Pinot. The aromas and flavors veer towards herbal and vegetative: tomatoes, sage, hard spices, and rich, black earth. It's a smooth wine, with peppery tannins that hide a core of dark stone-fruit. **87** —*S.H. (12/15/2001)*

Stephen Ross 2000 Edna Ranch Pinot Noir (Edna Valley) $40. An intense aroma of charcoal (or is it pencil lead?) is the first impression, but that fades away, revealing rubber and some stewed plum and tomato. Red fruit flavors walk atop a carpet of buttery sweet oak, yet the finish is mildly tart, offering mostly cranberry and rhubarb along with tight tannins. **86** *(10/1/2002)*

Stephen Ross 1999 Edna Ranch Pinot Noir (Edna Valley) $28. A bit riper than this winery's Chamisal bottling, this one has black cherry aromas well framed by earthier, herbal notes that include tomato and beet. Oak adds chocolate and vanilla notes. It's fairly tannic, with rich berry fruit and earthy complexity. Cellar it for a year or two. **89** —*S.H. (12/15/2001)*

Stephen Ross 2004 Stone Corral Vineyard Pinot Noir (Edna Valley) $45. This is a new vineyard, co-owned by Talley. The vines are young but enormously promising, and this wine already shows the fruit purity and crisp acidity of Edna Valley Pinot. The vibrant black cherry, cola, mint, and dusty spice flavors are supported by a silky smooth mouthfeel and a rich, long finish. **92** —*S.H. (12/1/2006)*

Stephen Ross 2003 Stone Corral Vineyard Pinot Noir (Edna Valley) $45. This is certainly the darkest, most tannic of the winery's current Pinot lineup. Like the others, it has a heavy, extraripe thickness that's not especially varietal, but it's a fairly complex wine, with its dry coffee, blackberry, and oak flavors. Give it a few years. **87** —*S.H. (3/1/2006)*

Stephen Ross 2003 Dante Dusi Vineyard Zinfandel (Paso Robles) $24. Soft and voluptuous in texture, with amazingly rich blackberry pie, cherry marmalade, and cocoa flavors, this Zin finishes a little on the sweet side. But it's a friendly charmer. **85** —*S.H. (3/1/2006)*

Stephen Ross 2001 Dante Dusi Vineyard Zinfandel (Paso Robles) $22. Full bodied and firm textured, with layers of black cherry, plum, raspberry, cola, tea, spice, and toast flavors. The wine is muscular, yet sleek, showing the elegance of this grape variety as well as its effusiveness. **90 Editors' Choice** *(11/1/2003)*

Stephen Ross 2000 Dante Dusi Vineyard Zinfandel (Paso Robles) $22. Only a touch of jammy raspberry aromas to the nose, and then a little bit of char on the edges. Beyond that, this is a lighter-framed, more elegant Zin. The palate is round and fresh, with spicy berry flavors. The finish is warm and expands, exposing the wine's depth and balance. Not a stud but a solid performer. **89** —*M.S. (9/1/2003)*

Stephen Ross 1999 Dusi Vineyard/Martini Vineyard Zinfandel (Paso Robles) $20. Very ripe, it display raisiny aromas riding over wild berry and spice. There's heat and tannins in the mouth, and acids, too, resulting in a certain austerity or angularity. It's not a hedonistic Zin, although rich, oily foods will coax out the underlying sweet berry flavors. **85** — *S.H. (12/15/2001)*

Stephen Ross 2001 Monte Rosso Vineyard Zinfandel (Sonoma Valley) $28. Smooth textured and rich, with plush tannins framing a core of pretty black cherry, plum, blackberry, anise, toast, vanilla, and spice flavors. The wine is well integrated and shows plenty of class. Big and rich on the finish. **89** *(11/1/2003)*

Stephen Ross 1999 Monte Rosso Vineyard Zinfandel (Sonoma Valley) $28. This Zin has lots of alcohol, nearly 16%, but you'd never know it because it's so balanced. It's rich, harmonious, fruity, and very dry, with that wild, savage quality that marks this variety. In its own way, it's classic Sonoma Zin, and from a great vineyard. **92 Editors' Choice** —*S.H. (12/15/2001)*

STEPHEN VINCENT

Stephen Vincent 2003 Cabernet Sauvignon (California) $10. This is a pretty good wine for the price. There's a rustic edge, but the cassis flavors are sweet and savory. **84** —*S.H. (12/31/2005)*

Stephen Vincent 2003 Merlot (California) $10. Starts with an inviting, warm aroma of fine Bordeaux, but turns unexpectedly sweet and sharp in the mouth. A letdown. **82** —*S.H. (12/31/2005)*

Stephen Vincent 2002 Crimson Rhône Red Blend (California) $9. This Rhône blend is a California-style Provençal wine, dry and fruity-spicy. It has cherry-berry and herb flavors, with a pretty finish of lavender and vanilla. **84** —*S.H. (12/31/2005)*

Stephen Vincent 2003 Sauvignon Blanc (Lake County) $9. These Lake County Sauvignon Blancs can be really good values, and this one definitely is. With its juicy flavors of citrus, fig, white peach, and vanilla, and bright, crisp acids, it's a fine cocktail wine, and versatile with food. **85 Best Buy** —*S.H. (12/31/2005)*

Stephen Vincent 2002 Maxwell Vineyard Sauvignon Blanc (Lake County) $8. Lake County has made a play to become the inexpensive Sauvignon Blanc capital of California, and this wine shows why. Stephen Vincent is a Sonoma négociant who finds wines that have already been made and

then buys them to bottle under his brand. This wine is filled with jazzy flavors of ripe figs, white peaches, lime zest, and dusty Oriental spices. It's clean and vibrant with refreshing acidity, and is fully dry. **87 Best Buy** —*S.H. (11/15/2004)*

STEPHEN'S

Stephen's 2004 MacBride Vineyard Chardonnay (York Mountain) $24. Earthy and minerally, and very dry, this Chard has a scour of high acidity. It's a lean wine, by the usual fruity standards, but a clean, complex one, rather Chablisian in its way, and might improve with some time in the cellar. **86** —*S.H. (5/1/2006)*

Stephen's 2003 Encell Vineyard Pinot Noir (San Luis Obispo County) $24. Showcases its terroir in the brisk acidity and light but complex body that wraps bitter cherry and coffee flavors. Bone dry, the wine will be a fine accompaniment to salmon or duck, simply prepared. **86** —*S.H. (5/1/2006)*

Stephen's 2003 William Cain Vineyard Pinot Noir (San Luis Obispo County) $18. Although it's less pricey than the winery's Encell Pinot, I slightly prefer this one for its accessibility. It's a tart, silky wine, with coffee, cherry, and spice flavors, and a real drink-me quality, but it is acidic. Drink it with rich fare, such as duck, salmon, and even pork dishes. **87** —*S.H. (5/1/2006)*

STEPHENSON CELLARS

Stephenson Cellars 2003 Syrah (Yakima Valley) $28. This tiny Walla Walla producer made just 220 cases of this Willow Crest Vineyard Syrah. It's a dazzling display of elegant power, offering polished red fruits with overtones of peach, apricot, and candied orange. Finishes with a well-defined tannic edge nuanced with ash and smoke. **94** —*P.G. (11/15/2006)*

STERLING

Sterling 2002 SVR Reserve Bordeaux Blend (Napa Valley) $50. Sweet-smelling berry and plum aromas show a touch of sur-maturité, balanced by a round, supple mouthfeel and a mouthful of chewy, fudge-like fruit. This SVR delivers well-executed modern winemaking, blending clean fruit with new oak. **88** *(7/1/2006)*

Sterling 2003 Cabernet Sauvignon (Napa Valley) $25. Soft and a bit one-dimensional, but pretty tasty, with well-ripened blackberry and mocha flavors that finish with a hint of anise. Feels polished and supple, but not for the cellar. Drink now. **87** —*S.H. (11/1/2006)*

Sterling 2002 Cabernet Sauvignon (Napa Valley) $24. Gentle and rich, this Cab shows smooth, sweet tannins and a nice touch of oak. The underlying fruit flavors are of blackberries and cassis, with a touch of cinnamon-dusted mocha coffee. **85** —*S.H. (12/1/2005)*

Sterling 2000 Cabernet Sauvignon (Napa Valley) $24. There's lots of charm in this classic Napa Cab. It opens with aromas of black currants, espresso, and tobacco, and has a nice edge of toasty oak. Dry and smooth, with attractive berry flavors and soft tannins. **87** —*S.H. (12/31/2002)*

Sterling 1999 Diamond Mountain Ranch Cabernet Sauvignon (Napa Valley) $40. Sterling made 6,000 cases of this wine—you should have at least two of them. Spicy, musky, forest-fire aromas open onto rich, dark flavors (date-nut loaf, black plum, and tar) on the palate. Full and fleshy with dusty tannins, it closes with lingering, chewy tannins and dusty earth notes. **92** *(6/1/2002)*

Sterling 1998 Diamond Mountain Ranch Cabernet Sauvignon (Napa Valley) $38. A complex nose of earth, saddle leather, toast, and cigar-box notes opens this impressive Cabernet. The deep cassis fruit wears tobacco and olive shadings. Beautifully balanced and classically structured, it finishes long with substantial but even tannins and blackberry and chocolate flavors. **92 Editors' Choice** *(9/1/2001)*

Sterling 1997 Diamond Mountain Ranch Vineyard Cabernet Sauvignon (Napa Valley) $40. 93 *(11/1/2000)*

Sterling 2002 Reserve Cabernet Sauvignon (Napa Valley) $75. With its solid cherry and vanilla aromas and flavors and creamy-textured, medium-weight mouthfeel, this is a nice California Cabernet. But where's the stuffing and complexity? **86** *(6/1/2006)*

USA

Sterling 2001 Reserve Cabernet Sauvignon (Napa Valley) $75. Dull, with weak flavors, and overly soft to boot. How Sterling could have avoided making a great Reserve in this vintage is beyond understanding. **84** — *S.H. (2/1/2005)*

Sterling 2000 Reserve Cabernet Sauvignon (Napa Valley) $70. Starts off soft, oaky and sweet in fruit, with cherry-berry flavors that are easy on the palate. Could use more complexity and concentration in the middle, and turns a bit astringent on the finish. **86** —*S.H. (5/1/2004)*

Sterling 1999 Reserve Cabernet Sauvignon (Napa Valley) $70. Seems a bit hard and lean for a '99, especially a reserve. Pretty tannic now, although there's some blackberry fruit at the core. Oak provides additional nuances of smoke and spice. Hard to tell where it's going. **87** —*S.H. (8/1/2003)*

Sterling 1997 Reserve Cabernet Sauvignon (Napa Valley) $60. 90 *(11/1/2000)*

Sterling 2003 Vintner's Collection Cabernet Sauvignon (Central Coast) $15. Here's a workaday Cab that gets the job done without being fussy. It's dry, with some blackberry flavors and a quick finish. **83** —*S.H. (12/1/2005)*

Sterling 2002 Vintner's Collection Cabernet Sauvignon (Central Coast) $15. Good varietal character, with blackberry and earthy flavors, a touch of oak, rich tannins, and dry. It's all slimmed down, though, in this rustic, country-style Cab. **84** —*S.H. (7/1/2005)*

Sterling 2001 Vintner's Collection Cabernet Sauvignon (Central Coast) $13. Drinks a bit weedy and thin, with herbal flavors occasionally enriched by blackberry. Bone-dry, with pronounced tannins and acids, it's a hard, lean wine, although clean and well-made. **84** —*S.H. (11/15/2003)*

Sterling 2000 Vintner's Collection Cabernet Sauvignon (Central Coast) $13. Here's a good mouthful of Cabernet, with true varietal character. Blackberries and currants are generously framed in oak, and the tannins are nice and rich. It lacks a bit of complexity and subtlety, but this could be your house red. **86** —*S.H. (4/1/2003)*

Sterling 1998 Chardonnay (North Coast) $17. 89 *(6/1/2000)*

Sterling 2004 Chardonnay (Napa Valley) $17. Forward in fruit and a little on the sweet side, this Chardonnay is simple and likeable for its wealth of peach and pineapple flavors. It has a creamy texture and enough acidity to balance. **84** —*S.H. (3/1/2006)*

Sterling 2003 Chardonnay (Napa County) $17. Lots of smoky, vanilla-scented and caramelized oak has been put on this wine, but the flavors themselves are thin and watery **84** —*S.H. (3/1/2005)*

Sterling 2002 Chardonnay (North Coast) $17. A nice, round Chardonnay with loads of ripe, fruity flavors. White peach, pineapple, buttered toast, and vanilla are just a few of the tastes that make this fun to drink. Has a good overlay of oak and a creamy, spicy texture that finishes sweet. **86** — *S.H. (12/15/2003)*

Sterling 2001 Chardonnay (North Coast) $17. Here's a proper wine that delivers plenty of varietal character. It has flavors of white peaches veering into tropical fruits, and is framed in plenty of toasty oak. The finish, with so much ripe fruit and caramel, is a little sweet. **86** —*S.H. (12/15/2002)*

Sterling 2002 Reserve Chardonnay (Napa Valley) $40. Surprisingly light in fruit for a reserve wine, although there's certainly a lot of wood. You'll find peach and honeysuckle flavors in a creamy texture. **84** —*S.H. (4/1/2005)*

Sterling 2001 Reserve Chardonnay (Napa Valley) $40. Richer and riper than Sterling's Winery Lake bottling, a wine whose pear flavors veer all the way into mango. Like the latter wine, this one is very well oaked, and the full-throttle leesy character shows up in the sweet-and-sour finish. It is also acidic and quite subtle, and takes some thinking to appreciate. **91** —*S.H. (12/1/2003)*

Sterling 1999 Reserve Chardonnay (Napa Valley) $40. Gingersnap and graham cracker aromas share the field with golden apple, menthol, and lemongrass on the nose. Winemaker Rob Hunter selects the best lots and crafts a tightly-meshed wine with persistence and a strong backbone. Pear, pineapple, vanilla, and toasty oak linger on the palate. Has personality and closes with impressive length. **90** *(7/1/2001)*

Sterling 2004 Vintner's Collection Chardonnay (Central Coast) $14. Nice and sweet in oak and ripe, forward peaches, pears, apricots, and spices, with a touch of tropical fruit, this everyday Chard also pleases for its creamy texture and smooth finish. **84** —*S.H. (12/1/2005)*

Sterling 2001 Vintner's Collection Chardonnay (Central Coast) $13. Decent, simple Chard, with some apple and peach flavors but also less ripe vegetal ones. Has firm acids and a kiss of oak. Gets the job done without elaboration. **84** —*S.H. (6/1/2003)*

Sterling 2003 Vintner's Collection Chardonnay (Central Coast) $11. A workhorse Chard that fulfills the basic requirements, with peach, buttered toast, and vanilla flavors and a creamy texture. The finish is clean and spicy. **84** —*S.H. (10/1/2004)*

Sterling 2002 Winery Lake Chardonnay (Carneros) $28. Here's a Chard with lots of ripe apple, pear, and fig flavors and zesty acidity. Oak adds vanilla and buttered toast notes. This great food wine is subtle and very enjoyable. **88** —*S.H. (12/1/2004)*

Sterling 2000 Winery Lake Chardonnay (Carneros) $25. Opens with citrus and apple flavors backed up with considerable acidity. Not very oaky or big, but dry and balanced, with a steely, minerally finish. **88** —*S.H. (2/1/2003)*

Sterling 2001 Winery Lake Vineyard Chardonnay (Carneros) $25. I like this Chardonnay for its streamlined green apple flavors, which have been tarted up as much as possible by lots of new oak and sur lies aging. These contribute creamy, smoky, and sweet and sour cream nuances to an acidic wine obviously built for food, rather than by-itself hedonism. **90** —*S.H. (12/1/2003)*

Sterling 1999 Winery Lake Vineyard Chardonnay (Carneros) $25. Ripe, tangy pineapple fruit plays nicely against rich butterscotch and maple syrup notes in this attractive white. On the palate, the flavors turn more to green apple and pear, with chalk and lemon providing tension and interest. Lively acidity supports the fruit well; although there's plenty of oak, it's not overbearing. **89** *(9/1/2001)*

Sterling 1998 Winery Lake Vineyard Chardonnay (Carneros) $24. 87 *(6/1/2000)*

Sterling 2003 Merlot (Napa Valley) $22. Showing a lot of polish and finesse, and although it's not a big wine, it's certainly a rich one. With deliciously ripe cherry, blackberry, chocolate, plum, coffee, and spice flavors, it has a voluptuous softness. Should be easy to find with 104,000-case production. **86** —*S.H. (12/1/2006)*

Sterling 2002 Merlot (Napa Valley) $22. Shows all the fine qualities you want in a Merlot, such as ripe, sweet cherry and blackberry fruit, finely ground tannins, balancing acidity and a touch of oak. If only it had concentration, it would be a far better wine. **85** —*S.H. (12/1/2005)*

Sterling 2000 Merlot (Napa Valley) $22. Soft and easy, with berry, plum, tobacco, and sage flavors and supple tannins. Acidity is low. This is a dry, pleasant wine of no special complexity, but fun to drink. **86** —*S.H. (12/31/2002)*

Sterling 1998 Merlot (Napa Valley) $23. Here's a wine that just cannot overcome the limitations of the vintage. They tried for extract and gave it some pretty oak but nonetheless herbal, bell pepper characteristics overshadow its modest berry fruit. **83** —*S.H. (6/1/2001)*

Sterling 1998 Diamond Mountain Ranch Merlot (Napa Valley) $33. With its aromas of smoke, chocolate, vanilla, and black cherries, this wine pairs lush, forward flavors with firm structure. The long, dark cherry and cocoa finish shows solid tannins. Best held two or three years. **90** *(9/1/2001)*

Sterling 1997 Diamond Mountain Ranch Vineyard Merlot (Napa Valley) $30. **86** —*J.C. (7/1/2000)*

Sterling 2002 Reserve Merlot (Napa Valley) $65. Boasting pure scents of black cherries and mocha, this is a nicely ripened Napa Merlot. Creamy in the mouth and generous in body, it'll pair nicely with a porterhouse for two. **87** *(6/1/2006)*

Sterling 2001 Reserve Merlot (Napa Valley) $65. This is a wine powerful in ripe currant, cassis, cherry, and cocoa flavors, with smoky oak seasonings. It's soft and luscious in the mouth, with complex tannins. Delicious on its own, or with a grilled steak. **89** —*S.H. (4/1/2005)*

USA

Sterling 2000 Reserve Merlot (Napa Valley) $65. Soft enough, with a gentle mouthfeel and lots of new oak. The flavors veer toward blackberries and coffee, but there are hollow spots. Turns rough and unsteady on the finish, with unripe tannins. **86** —*S.H. (5/1/2004)*

Sterling 1999 Reserve Merlot (Napa Valley) $70. Here's a big-boned beauty of a Merlot. Impresses with the sheer size of its fruity-berry flavors and lovely, rich tannins. A layer of well-smoked oak overlays everything. This is a flamboyant wine and will reward careful cellaring. **91** —*S.H. (8/1/2003)*

Sterling 1998 Reserve Merlot (Napa Valley) $71. The lavish oak may be a bit much for some tasters, but it's suave and well integrated. Blackberry, plum, cinnamon, clove, and cocoa flavors ride the solid structure. The long, broad-shouldered finish goes on and on, the spice notes lingering. Tempting now, but will be even better in three years. **91 Cellar Selection** *(9/1/2001)*

Sterling 2001 Three Palms Vineyard Merlot (Napa Valley) $55. Fiercely tannic as usual, yet brimming with well-ripened black currant and blackberry fruit, this is a dry, young wine that needs some time to come around. You wonder if the fruit will outlast the tannins for the long haul, but it will be better in 2006. **90** —*S.H. (8/1/2005)*

Sterling 1998 Three Palms Vineyard Merlot (Napa Valley) $56. Though it's plushly textured and even and supple on the tongue, the flavors are woody rather than fruit-driven, with dried-spice nuances. Finishes dry, with cherry and chocolate notes and mouth-coating tannins. **89** *(9/1/2001)*

Sterling 1997 Three Palms Vineyard Merlot (Napa Valley) $50. A **89** —*J.C. (7/1/2000)*

Sterling 2002 Vintner's Colleciton Merlot (Central Coast) $13. Drinks a bit heavy and thick, but there's no denying the juicy flavors. Plums, sweet blackberries, cherries, and herbs flood the mouth, leading to some astringency from tannins. **85** —*S.H. (10/1/2004)*

Sterling 2003 Vintner's Collection Merlot (Central Coast) $15. With a texturally rich mouthfeel that carries flavors ranging from blackberries, plums, and coffee to sage and tobacco, and firm but fine tannins, this Merlot is easy to like. It finishes thin, but displays good balance. **85** —*S.H. (12/1/2005)*

Sterling 2001 Vintner's Collection Merlot (Central Coast) $13. A dark, earthy wine that will surprise you. The rich, deep flavors of spiced plum, blackberry, and mocha last through the lingering finish. Fully dry, it also has some sturdy tannins that will stand up well to roast meats. **85** —*S.H. (12/1/2003)*

Sterling 2000 Vintner's Collection Merlot (Central Coast) $13. A workaday red wine, not bad for the price. Dark in color, with herbal, olive, and mushroom aromas and flavors backed up by blackberry and plum. Smooth and long in the mouth, with some richness. Fairly tannic on the finish. **85** —*S.H. (4/1/2003)*

Sterling 1996 Winery Lake Merlot (Carneros) $35. **89** —*M.S. (3/1/2000)*

Sterling 1998 Winery Lake Vineyard Merlot (Carneros) $33. A lean and classically structured wine, this 100% Merlot offers tart cherry and plum fruit wrapped in a toasty oak cocoon. Licorice and earth accents and an herb-tobacco note add palate dimension. A firm, lengthy finish, good grip, and precise flavor definition mark this elegant offering. **88** *(9/1/2001)*

Sterling 2005 Pinot Grigio (Central Coast) $13. The grapes come from Paso Robles, which got them nice and ripe, and areas of Monterey and Santa Maria Valley, which preserved vital acidity. The result is a really nice wine brimming with juicy citrus and fig flavors. Refreshing acidity is the offset. **85** —*S.H. (12/1/2006)*

Sterling 2003 Pinot Noir (Napa Valley) $19. No obvious faults, but so light, so diluted, there's no there there. Just a trace of cherry flavor. **82** —*S.H. (10/1/2005)*

Sterling 2003 Vintner's Collection Pinot Noir (Central Coast) $13. A bit simple, but with nice raspberry, cherry, cocoa, and oak flavors, and a silky mouthfeel. It's dry and crisp, with a rich, fruity finish. **84** —*S.H. (7/1/2005)*

Sterling 2002 Vintner's Collection Pinot Noir (Central Coast) $13. This is a type of Pinot that's increasingly showing up, providing bargains for consumers. It has real varietal character in the raspberry and cherry flavors, silky tannins, crisp acids, and dollop of smoky oak. It's on the thin side, but satisfies. **84** —*S.H. (4/1/2004)*

Sterling 2002 Winery Lake Pinot Noir (Carneros) $25. Delicate and refined, with candied cherry, cinnamon, and leather aromas and flavors. Drinks delicate and crisp in the mouth, with a silky texture. Finishes rather short. **85** *(11/1/2004)*

Sterling 2000 Winery Lake Pinot Noir (Napa Valley) $25. Someone (we suspect Mother Nature) pumped the wattage into this big-boned Pinot, which is about fruit, fruit, and nothing but the fruit—maybe to a fault. Heavy-duty black cherry aromas lead into a jammy palate chock full of yet more blackberry and cherry. We like the verve but also wonder about complexity, which isn't very high on the meter right now. **88** *(10/1/2002)*

Sterling 1999 Winery Lake Pinot Noir (Carneros) $27. A full-bodied and toasty Pinot whose sour plum and black cherry fruit wear anise and mineral accents. Bright acidity keeps the wine from feeling heavy; the spicy cherry-toasty oak finish is dry, even and long. Big and solid for a Pinot Noir—almost like a tart Shiraz. **88** *(9/1/2001)*

Sterling 2001 Winery Lake Vineyard Pinot Noir (Carneros) $25. A thin, tough Pinot with black cherry flavors that are buried beneath sizable tannins. Doesn't do much on the entry except stun, although if you chew on it, you'll find the fruit. Turns rough and assaultive again on the finish. **85** —*S.H. (2/1/2004)*

Sterling 1997 Winery Lake Vineyard Pinot Noir (Carneros) $21. **90** *(10/1/1999)*

Sterling 2001 SVR Red Blend (Napa Valley) $45. Soft and fruity in black currant and cassis flavors and a candied finish of cocoa and cinnamon, like mocha. The structure is lush, all silk and liquid velvet. Probably best now. **87** —*S.H. (4/1/2005)*

Sterling 2005 Sauvignon Blanc (Napa Valley) $15. Clean and zippy, with good acidity framing pretty lemongrass, pineapple, apricot, and spicy flavors. Has just a touch of creaminess from brief barrel aging. **85** —*S.H. (11/15/2006)*

Sterling 2004 Sauvignon Blanc (Napa Valley) $13. Although this wine is simple and has a quick finish, it's clean and fruity, with slightly sweet lemon, lime, and grapefruit flavors. **83** —*S.H. (11/15/2005)*

Sterling 2003 Sauvignon Blanc (Napa Valley) $14. Decent and crisp, with watered-down citrus flavors. Finishes a little sweet. **83** —*S.H. (2/1/2005)*

Sterling 2002 Sauvignon Blanc (North Coast) $14. This very pale wine packs plenty of flavor. It's filled with peach, fig, citrus, spearmint, and smoky-vanilla flavors that are slightly off-dry, but the acidity is crisp and clean. Very pleasant, and versatile. **86** —*S.H. (12/1/2003)*

Sterling 2005 Vintner's Collection Sauvignon Blanc (Central Coast) $11. The Central Coast has near-perfect warm days and cool nights, and that's where this wine comes from. It's rich in fig, date, pineapple, and honeydew flavors that don't need any oak to show them off. But it's also dry and zesty in acidity. **85** —*S.H. (12/1/2006)*

Sterling 2003 Vintner's Collection Sauvignon Blanc (Central Coast) $10. This wine, which offers lots of pleasure at a good price, has figgy, citrus, and melon flavors that drink dry and crisp. You can taste the California sunshine in the ripe fruitiness and honeyed finish. **84** —*S.H. (10/1/2004)*

Sterling 2003 Vintner's Collection Shiraz (Central Coast) $13. Dry and a bit rustic, this wine features earthy, cherry flavors and some gritty tannins. The cherries really show up on the finish. Try it with rich fare. **84** —*S.H. (7/1/2005)*

Sterling 2002 Vintner's Collection Shiraz (Central Coast) $13. This generously flavored Syrah packs plenty of blueberry and vanilla flavor onto a lush, fruity frame. Soft, oaky and built for mass appeal, it hits all the right notes. **86** *(9/1/2005)*

Sterling 2001 Vintner's Collection Shiraz (Central Coast) $13. You say Syrah, I say Shiraz. Whatever, this is a big, thick, rich wine bursting with blackberry and white pepper aromas and flavors. It's dry and tannic, with a bitter finish. Well-made, and perfect with barbeque. **85** —*S.H. (12/15/2003)*

STEVEN ANDRÉ

Steven André 2003 Merlot (Napa Valley) $19. From Robert Pecota, although it doesn't say so on the bottle, this is a very dry, very tannic Merlot, with bitter espresso and dill flavors. It's not offering much opulence now, but could soften and sweeten in a few years. **83** —*S.H. (10/1/2006)*

STEVEN BANNUS

Steven Bannus 2002 Reserve Pinot Noir (Central Coast) $8. You'll find some pretty flavors of cherries, cola, and spice in this dry wine. Finishes sharp in acidity, with a rugged texture. **84** —*S.H. (11/1/2004)*

STEVEN KENT

Steven Kent 2002 Cabernet Sauvignon (Livermore Valley) $45. With wines like this, Livermore Valley cleans up its act and returns to historic form. This is a very good Cabernet, rich in varietal character, firm in tannic structure, and beautifully dry. It should improve for at least the next seven years. **90** —*S.H. (7/1/2006)*

Steven Kent 2000 Cabernet Sauvignon (Livermore Valley) $45. From a single vineyard, this is a rich and complex wine. Concentrated aromas and flavors of black currants and cassis are pure and compelling, while oak is lavish but not heavy-handed. Great balance of soft, lush tannins, and acidity. **92** —*S.H. (10/1/2003)*

Steven Kent 2001 Livermore Valley Cabernet Sauvignon (Livermore Valley) $45. Quite an interesting wine that marches in a different direction from the typical North Coast fare, which is very ripe, soft, and opulent. This wine is tighter. Performs a palate quartet with firm tannins, good acidity, black currant flavor and toasty new oak, in beautiful harmony. **91** —*S.H. (8/1/2004)*

Steven Kent 2002 McGrail Vineyard Cabernet Sauvignon (Livermore Valley) $55. What a great job Steven Kent is doing in Livermore Valley. This Cab carefully straddles the line between cool coastal and hot inland, and you can detect the winemaker's intelligent choices every step of the way. Dry, soft, and complex, it's enormously satisfying in the balance of fruit, tannins, and oak. **91** —*S.H. (7/1/2006)*

Steven Kent 2001 Vincerre Cabernet Sauvignon-Barbera (Livermore Valley) $40. Not on a par with the 2000 release, due, I think, to the decision to include a majority of Barbera with the Sangiovese and Cabernet Sauvignon. The Barbera completely dominates the other varieties, with a rustic simplicity, heaviness, and leathery chewiness. **85** —*S.H. (8/1/2004)*

Steven Kent 2000 Vincere Cabernet Sauvignon-Sangiovese (Livermore Valley) $40. A delicious, complex, and young wine, to judge from the tannins. Flavors of tobacco, sage, and blackberries are very dry, and the acidity is fine, but then there are those stubborn tannins. Needs age, but should soften by 2006. If you must drink it before then, do it with big, rich, fatty foods. A 60-40 blend of Sangiovese and Cabernet Sauvignon. **91** —*S.H. (5/1/2003)*

Steven Kent 1999 Folkendt Vineyard Merrillie Chardonnay (Livermore Valley) $36. From a newish winery, this stunning Chard opens with lush, opulent aromas of tropical fruits and peach, lime peel, smoke, butterscotch, mineral, and smoky oak. Fabulous depth and complexity in the mouth, with an almost unnatural limpidity and velvety softness. **93** —*S.H. (12/15/2001)*

Steven Kent 2001 Merrillie Chardonnay (Livermore Valley) $23. Very lush, full, and long on the palate, a rich and quite complex wine that mingles ultraripe tropical fruit flavors with creamy lees, sweet butterscotch, and intense vanilla. It's a little soft in acidity, though. **90** —*S.H. (8/1/2004)*

Steven Kent 2000 Merrillie Chardonnay (Livermore Valley) $36. This Chard will go a long way to restoring the renown of this appellation—where Chardonnay was first grown in California. Rich in fruit, oak, and lees, the wine has a distinguished mouthfeel that's steely and firm, and a long, lush finish. **92** —*S.H. (12/15/2002)*

Steven Kent 2001 Song Bird Sangiovese (Livermore Valley) $32. An interesting approach to a difficult variety. It's a softly silky wine, with the elegant body of Pinot Noir, and earthy, tobacco, bay leaf, thyme, and

cherry flavors. Will strike some as light on fruit, but is not without complexity. **87** —*S.H. (9/1/2004)*

Steven Kent 2005 Ghielmetti Vineyard Sauvignon Blanc (Livermore Valley) $24. Green grass, hay, gooseberry, juniper berry, alfalfa, grapefruit, lime, you get the idea. It's a complex wine. Zestily acidic and clean, it will get the tastebuds going. **87** —*S.H. (12/15/2006)*

Steven Kent 2001 Zin-Tonga Zinfandel (Livermore Valley) $32. Quite fragrant, with smoky, rich hints of plum and spice. It's silky smooth on the palate, refined and yet brimming with plush raspberry, black cherry, cola, spice, herb, and cassis flavors. Very elegant and powerful. **91** *(11/1/2003)*

STEVENOT

Stevenot 2001 Cabernet Franc (Calaveras County) $18. The Sierra Foothills have demonstrated a penchant for producing good Cab Francs. This one has sweet cherry, chocolate, and rosehip tea flavors, with a good balance of acidity and silky tannins. Gentle and charming. **85** —*S.H. (9/1/2004)*

Stevenot 2001 Cabernet Sauvignon (Calaveras County) $12. Textbook Cabernet, with pure cassis and black currant flavors, very dry, and the tannins are smooth and polished. Oak adds smoke, toast, and a woody sweetness. A little soft in acids, but it sure is good. **89 Best Buy** —*S.H. (10/1/2005)*

Stevenot 2000 Gabriel Cabernet Sauvignon (Calaveras County) $25. Quite an interesting Cab with lots to like. Rich in currants and blackberries, with a feel that borders on chalky cocoa. Smooth; finishes sweet in fruit and oak. **90 Editors' Choice** —*S.H. (10/1/2005)*

Stevenot 2001 Chardonnay (Calaveras County) $28. Much oakier and more leesy than Stevenot's estate Chard. Unleashes a blast of well-toasted oak and vanilla that frames underlying flavors of pineapples and pears. Finishes soft, with an earthy, tobaccoey edge. **86** —*S.H. (9/1/2004)*

Stevenot 2001 Chardonnay (Sierra Foothills) $14. A very nice Chard, and a fine example of a Sierra one. Has all the peaches and cream you could want, spiced with vanilla, shining acids, and a long, fruity finish. **86** — *S.H. (2/1/2003)*

Stevenot 2002 Calaveras County Chardonnay (Calaveras County) $12. Opens with candied peach and tropical fruit aromas that lead to a full-flavored wine brimming with pineapple, peach, vanilla, buttered toast, and cinnamon. The acidity is fine, the texture creamy in this easy drinking Chard. **84** —*S.H. (9/1/2004)*

Stevenot 1997 Shaw Ranch Chardonnay (Calaveras County) $18. 86 *(6/1/2000)*

Stevenot 2003 Graciano (Calaveras County) $22. Complex aromas of green olives, grilled meat, cherries, cheese, and lightly smoked oak turn light-bodied in the mouth, with pretty cherry and mocha flavors **86** — *S.H. (3/1/2005)*

Stevenot 1997 Merlot (Sierra Foothills) $13. 84 —*J.C. (7/1/2000)*

Stevenot 2001 Merlot (Calaveras County) $12. This is a nice, smooth Merlot that lives up to its reputation as the soft Cabernet. It's fruity in blackberry, cherry, and coffee flavors, and spicy. On the finish, cassis, pure and true. **90 Best Buy** —*S.H. (10/1/2005)*

Stevenot 2002 Broll Mountain Vineyard Petite Sirah (Calaveras County) $22. Young in tannins now, this is a big, dry wine, but quite fruity. Floods the palate with pomegranate, black cherry, and earthy flavors that last into the finish. Will improve for a few years. **86** —*S.H. (10/1/2005)*

Stevenot 2002 Canterbury Vineyard Syrah (Calaveras County) $22. Smells and tastes a bit like herb-marinated grilled beef, with basil and oregano notes along with smoky, toasty scents from barrel-aging. A bit on the lean side, with a tart and cranberryish finish. **85** *(9/1/2005)*

Stevenot 2001 Canterbury Vineyard Syrah (Calaveras County) $22. Rather soft and flat in mouthfeel, and with some baked, pruny aromas and flavors, defects that detract from the wine's charm and good fruit. Finishes dry and astringent. **84** —*S.H. (8/1/2004)*

Stevenot 1999 Canterbury Vineyard Syrah (Calaveras County) $16. Lively, sweet aromas of cherry, chocolate, and bubble gum amounted to (in the opinion of one reviewer) "a whole candy store for the nose." Medium-

USA

weight but somewhat thin, this wine's bright berry fruit is muted by mineral and leather notes. Finishes minerally, with chocolate, vanilla, and charcoal notes. Could be mistaken for a decent Beaujolais. **86** *(10/1/2001)*

Stevenot 2001 Tempranillo (Calaveras County) $22. There's a bit of complexity in this very dry, rather tannic wine from up in the Sierra Foothills. The best thing about it is the cherry and chocolate flavors, which have a thick, fudgy richness. It's also soft in acidity. Try as an alternative to Merlot. **86**—*S.H. (8/1/2004)*

Stevenot 1999 Tempranillo (Calaveras County) $18. Clean, vivid cherry and raspberry notes are framed in somewhat rustic tannins. A pretty core of olive and herb runs through it for added complexity. The wine finishes moderately with a hint of dryness. Made from Spain's classic red variety. **87**—*J.M. (5/1/2002)*

Stevenot 2004 Olivia Tempranillo (California) $12. This is a nice, cheerful blush wine, but you should chill it well to stun the slight sweetness, which makes it a little insipid. Icy cold, it's refreshing, with strawberry, raspberry, and vanilla flavors. **85**—*S.H. (10/1/2005)*

Stevenot 2003 Verdelho (California) $16. You could easily mistake this for a Sauvignon Blanc, with its lemonade-citrus aromas. It has intense lemon and lime flavors that skirt the edge of sweetness, but high acidity provides a tart edge of balance. **86**—*S.H. (9/1/2004)*

Stevenot 2004 Silvaspoons Vineyard Verdelho (California) $16. Not sure if Stevenot meant this to be a dry table wine, but it has so much sugar I'm classifying it as a dessert wine. It's not bad, with apricot, peach, vanilla, and honey flavors, but forewarned is forearmed. **84**—*S.H. (10/1/2005)*

Stevenot 2001 Silverspoons Vineyard Verdelho (California) $16. Very Sauvignon Blanc-y, with bright citrusy acidity framing intense lemon, lime, fig, and honeydew melon flavors. Finishes dry, crisp, and refreshing. **87**—*S.H. (3/1/2005)*

Stevenot 1997 Zinfandel (Sierra Foothills) $13. 86—*P.G. (11/15/1999)*

Stevenot 2001 Costello Vineyard Zinfandel (Sierra Foothills) $32. The wine has ripe fruit flavors and good texture; however, it suffers from hot, spicy aromas that are over the top and a bit distracting. **80** *(11/1/2003)*

Stevenot 2000 Old Vine Zinfandel (Lodi) $17. Rough and briary, a wine with lots of ripe fruity flavors but also outsized tannins and a country-style texture. Cherry, cola, pepper, and herbs are highlighted by sharp acids into the finish. **85**—*S.H. (2/1/2003)*

STEVENS

Stevens 2003 424 Red Wine Bordeaux Blend (Columbia Valley (WA)) $30. This sleek, subtle blend (55% Cabernet Sauvignon, 25% Merlot, and 20% Cab Franc) offers sharp, tangy mixed fruits and loads of sweet spices. Cinnamon, coconut, and baking spices waft up from the glass and hit the palate explosively, finishing with a grand chocolate finale. Interesting and well-defined. **90**—*P.G. (8/1/2006)*

Stevens 2002 Big Easy Cabernet Sauvignon (Columbia Valley (WA)) $27. This is a tart, racy, exciting wine, showing just a hint of brett, but as a viable accent note. Plenty of acid wrapped around concentrated, juicy red fruits; still tight and in need of airing out, but packed with clean fruit flavor. **91**—*P.G. (8/1/2006)*

Stevens 2003 Reserve Cabernet Sauvignon (Columbia Valley (WA)) $NA. An extra level of moss, tar, and licorice is evident here. Thick and tight, it's great Cabernet, packed and dense, complete in all respects, loaded with rich black fruits set against balancing acids and nicely applied new oak. A star. **92**—*P.G. (8/1/2006)*

Stevens 2003 Black Tongue Syrah (Yakima Valley) $29. The name alone draws your attention (heaven help us if "Black Tongue" ever meets Mark Ryan's "Dead Horse"!) but the wine delivers the goods. Tight, tart, compact, and spicy, it's loaded with intriguing spices. Peppery and expressive, this is still quite young and very much needs decanting or additional years in the bottle to open it up. **89**—*P.G. (8/1/2006)*

STEVENSON-BARRIE

Stevenson-Barrie 1999 Shea Vineyard Pinot Noir (Willamette Valley) $35. This new winery is the project of the winemaker for Panther Creek, who also serves as consulting winemaker for Shea Vineyards. Here again the

bright, spicy Pinot fruit, with its lovely mix of red and blackberry flavors, takes front and center stage. There is plenty of lively acid, some well-managed tannins, and a whiff of black pepper. It was aged in all neutral oak, and the only thing missing is just that pleasing finish of mocha toast that would take the wine to the next level. **89**—*P.G. (11/1/2001)*

STEWART

Stewart 2003 Pinot Noir (Russian River Valley) $42. Young and forward, here's a seductive wine that's instantly attractive for its lush flavors and silky mouthfeel. Cherry pie filling, cola, pomegranate, rosehip tea, cocoa, and coffee flavors mark this delicious Pinot, which finishes with crisp acids. It was made by Paul Hobbs. **92**—*S.H. (12/1/2006)*

STG

STG 2002 Cabernet Sauvignon (Dry Creek Valley) $15. Harsh and burnt, with medicinal, slightly sweet cherry flavors, this disagreeable wine also has rough tannins. **80**—*S.H. (12/1/2005)*

STG 2003 Chardonnay (Chalk Hill) $13. If there's any fruit in this massively oaked wine, it's hard to find. Little but char, vanilla, and toast hit you, with a sweet dill finish. **82**—*S.H. (11/1/2005)*

STG 2002 Chardonnay (Chalk Hill) $14. There are disturbing aromas and flavors in this wine. It smells vegetal, and tastes very dry and bitter. **81**—*S.H. (10/1/2005)*

STG 2004 Merlot (Russian River Valley) $14. From Domaine St. George, a polished, ripe wine, from a premier growing region. It's dry and a little rough in texture, with complex flavors of dried cherries and blackberries, and a cleansing espresso bitterness to the finish. **86**—*S.H. (5/1/2006)*

STG 2003 Merlot (Russian River Valley) $14. Rough around the edges, with earthy tobacco and cherry flavors, this is a big, dry, pretty tannic red wine. Best with a barbecued steak if you're a little fussy, but not too demanding. **84**—*S.H. (10/1/2005)*

STG 2002 Zinfandel (Dry Creek Valley) $14. Way too much residual sugar in this wine, to judge by the white-sugary finish. It's clean and fruity wine, but really should be labeled off-dry or even sweet. **81**—*S.H. (6/1/2006)*

STG 2001 Zinfandel (Dry Creek Valley) $15. It took a while for the sulfur to blow off, but when it did, this was a nice Zin. It's soft in tannins, but with good acids framing pretty flavors of raspberries and red cherries, and shows all kinds of dusty spices on the dry finish. **85**—*S.H. (10/1/2005)*

STILL WATERS

Still Waters 2004 Pinot Gris (Paso Robles) $18. There's a taste of cooked or stewed apricots and peaches in this dry wine, which contains some nice acidity. That fruitiness lasts well into the finish. **84**—*S.H. (2/1/2006)*

STOLLER

Stoller 2002 Pinot Noir (Willamette Valley) $42. This is an over-the-top, Zinfandel-style Pinot, with a pungent, roasted, alcoholic nose. Aggressive and hot, it does not achieve any sort of balance, and simply feels overwrought. **85** *(11/1/2004)*

STOLPMAN

Stolpman 2000 Limestone Hill Cuvée Cabernet Blend (Santa Ynez Valley) $20. The vineyard has lots of chalk, hence the name of this Cabernet Sauvignon-based Bordeaux blend. It's pleasant rather than profound, with sweet cherry and raspberry flavors and an easy tannin-acid mouthfeel. Gentle, easy, and silky all the way down. **87**—*S.H. (11/15/2003)*

Stolpman 2001 La Croce Red Blend (Santa Ynez Valley) $19. This Syrah-Sangiovese blend, the only one from the appellation I know of, is an interesting and imaginative wine. It starts with blackberry, mocha, pepper, smoke, and animal aromas and an intriguing suggestion of wild herbs, and the flavors are similar, with cherries and blackberries taking center stage. The wine is very dry, and its tannins are a wonder. Feels soft and lush but complex and stimulating through the finish. VALUE. **91**—*S.H. (10/1/2003)*

Stolpman 2000 Rhône Ridge Cuvée Red Blend (Santa Ynez Valley) $15. Grenache, Syrah, and Mourvèdre. Plenty of lip-smacking cherry and blueberry flavor here, but also some sharp elbows from tannins, and there's a streak of sugary sweetness that makes the wine not quite dry. **85** —S.H. (12/31/2003)

Stolpman 2002 Rosato Rosé Blend (Santa Ynez Valley) $NA. A happy rose wine, fairly deep in color, and the spowerful raspberry and cherry flavors attest to lots of extraction. Fully dry, with a nice bite of acidity, this full-bodied wine finishes with a long, spicy finish. **86** —S.H. (3/1/2004)

Stolpman 2001 Angeli Sangiovese (Santa Ynez Valley) $42. An offbeat Super-Tuscan style wine (Cabernet Sauvignon, Merlot, and Sangiovese) with lots of interesting things going on. It's very dry, with tannins that are pronounced, but not difficult to negotiate. The complex flavors span the gamut from blackberries and cherries to dried fine herbs, rich tobacco, and mocha. A firm spine of acidity suggests midterm ageability. **92** —S.H. (10/1/2003)

Stolpman 2001 Syrah (Santa Ynez Valley) $29. Here's a complete and balanced Syrah. It strikes all the right notes, from its ripely sweet blackberry, chocolate, and herb flavors to the sweet tannins and velvety softness. Feels posh in the mouth, spreading the fruit around the taste buds through the finish, where the tannins show up again. **90** —S.H. (3/1/2004)

Stolpman 2003 Estate Grown Syrah (Santa Ynez Valley) $25. Peppery and youthful on the nose, this Syrah has good grab in the midpalate, and black plum and berry fruit to recommend it. One taster found it a little on the lean side, with a tart finish. **87** (9/1/2005)

Stolpman 2003 Hilltops Syrah (Santa Ynez Valley) $35. Favorable comments across the board for this Syrah, with reviewers lauding its ripe, fruit-sweet berry aromas and flavors, and its creamy mouthfeel. Bold, peppery aromas, and a long, lush finish complete a fine package. **90 Editors' Choice** (9/1/2005)

STONE CREEK

Stone Creek 2000 Special Selection Cabernet Sauvignon (California) $8. Fruity, simple, and technically clean, a perfectly acceptable little Cabernet with an easy price. The cherry and blackberry flavors are swimming in soft, gentle tannins. **83** —S.H. (10/1/2004)

Stone Creek 2004 Chardonnay (Mendocino County) $9. Weak and vegetal, with just the barest note of Chardonnay juice, this is a pretty forgettable wine. **80** —S.H. (12/15/2006)

Stone Creek 1998 Special Selection Chardonnay (California) $7. **80** —J.C. (10/1/1999)

Stone Creek 2003 Merlot (Mendocino County) $9. Hard to find much to like with this sharply acidic, green young wine. Has flavors of wintergreen and fennel, with a touch of cherry juice. **80** —S.H. (12/15/2006)

Stone Creek 2001 California Merlot (California) $8. Kind of rough around the edges, with a bit of residual sweetness and a few unripe notes. But it drinks much fruitier and friendlier than it sounds, and that makes it a pretty good value in a sandwich wine. **84** —S.H. (9/1/2004)

Stone Creek 1998 Special Selection Merlot (California) $8. A drinkable Merlot at this price is noteworthy; this one, with its aromas of berries, toast, and herbs—even tomatoes—will make lots of friends. Tart cherry-berry fruit and earth is smooth on the palate and blends in some tea notes on the abbreviated finish. **84 Best Buy** (6/1/2001)

Stone Creek 1999 Chairman's Reserve Zinfandel (California) $17. Opens with light cream aromas, which turn woody after a few minutes. Oak reigns on the palate, backed by blackberry and a slightly artificial grape note. Creamy in the mouth, but not rich, it closes with green herb and tobacco notes, plus a twinge of plastic. **82** —D.T. (3/1/2002)

Stone Creek 2001 Special Selection Zinfandel (California) $8. Moderate plum and cherry flavors are at the core here, with hints of toast and vanilla on the follow-up. Simple and straightforward. **82** (11/1/2003)

Stone Creek 1998 Special Selection Zinfandel (California) $8. Lithe and nicely balanced, this flavorful wine shows a red berry-herb bouquet and a pleasingly dry, gently spicy palate. The mouthfeel is good, and shows some texture despite the fact that it's light-weight on the palate. An interesting chalk note comes in on the back end of this pleasant, easy-drinking surprise. **85 Best Buy** (3/1/2001)

STONE GARDEN

Stone Garden 2005 White Merlot (California) $8. Pretty dark and full-bodied for a blush, but it sure is tasty, a simple wine with cherry jam and white chocolate flavors that finish a little sweet. Fine acidity balances it all out. **84 Best Buy** —S.H. (12/31/2006)

Stone Garden 2005 Pinot Grigio (California) $8. Sweet and simple, with Lifesaver candy flavors. There's sourness from acidity, but the wine is basically okay. **82** —S.H. (12/31/2006)

STONE WOLF

Stone Wolf 2001 Chardonnay (Willamette Valley) $10. This is all fruit, fresh and lush, with no frills. Nothing fat, tropical or oaky here, no hints of butter. Just generous, ripe fruit at a good price. **85** —P.G. (12/31/2002)

Stone Wolf 2001 Pinot Gris (Oregon) $10. A fresh, clean, and very satisfying effort from this value brand. A pale bronze blush color sets off a pear fruit explosion, ripe and well made. **88 Best Buy** —P.G. (12/31/2002)

STONECROFT

Stonecroft 1998 Reserve Pinot Noir (Willamette Valley) $30. **88** —M.M. (12/1/2000)

STONEGATE

Stonegate 2001 Cabernet Franc (Napa Valley) $22. There's a feral edge to this interesting wine, but that's not to say it's rustic. It's not. It's dry and tannic, and needs big meats and cheeses to tease out its nuances. **87** —S.H. (7/1/2005)

Stonegate 2001 Cabernet Sauvignon (Napa Valley) $25. All four of Stonegate's Bordeaux single-varietal wines, including this one, share the same characteristics of dryness, rich fruitiness, and strong, dry tannins. They march against the prevailing soft, gooey style, and seem to be built for cellaring. Try holding this Cab past 2007. **87** —S.H. (8/1/2005)

Stonegate 1999 Cabernet Sauvignon (Napa Valley) $40. Almost black and smells youthful, with cassis and oak aromas. Then you taste. The first impression is tannins. They're thick and firm and will take years to melt. But the core of blackberry fruit suggests the wait will be worth it. It's also nice to taste a Napa Cabernet that actually has tannins these days. **91** —S.H. (6/1/2002)

Stonegate 1998 Cabernet Sauvignon (Napa Valley) $29. Light on fruit, with blackberry and cassis flavors that are a bit thin in the middle, this wine is nonetheless distinguished. You have those beautiful Napa tannins, acidity, and structure, and fine toasty oak; even though it's not a blockbuster, the finish is full of sweet, limpid fruit. **90** —S.H. (12/1/2001)

Stonegate 1997 Cabernet Sauvignon (Napa Valley) $25. Somehow, this fine winery gets left off a lot of "best of" lists, which makes it a great value, especially from a super vintage like '97. This is serious Napa Cabernet, filled with fancy black currant, cassis, and mocha, and complex with toasty oak. It's very dry and elegant, one of those wines that fills the palate with the most sumptuous flavors and textures. It's so focused, it's delicious now, but there's no doubt it will age and improve for a long time. **92** —S.H. (2/1/2001)

Stonegate 2001 Diamond Mountain Reserve Spaulding Vineyard Cabernet Sauvignon (Napa Valley) $50. It's extraordinarily, mouth-numbingly tannic, and acidic, too, but even that can't stop the cascade of blackberries and black currants from throttling the mouth. This is an ageable wine, well able to stand and improve beyond 2010. **92 Cellar Selection** —S.H. (8/1/2005)

Stonegate 1999 Diamond Mountain Reserve Spaulding Vineyard Cabernet Sauvignon (Diamond Mountain) $60. Rich and well-oaked, this is a fine example of Napa Valley Cab. Well-ripened cassis flavors lead the way, but the mountain grapes have yielded a tight, somewhat tannic wine that will reward extended cellaring. **91** —S.H. (2/1/2003)

Stonegate 1998 Estate Bottled Chardonnay (Napa Valley) $18. **84** (6/1/2000)

Stonegate 2001 Merlot (Napa Valley) $22. Whoever said Merlot was the soft Cabernet hadn't tasted this wine. It's big and sturdy, almost like a Howell Mountain Cab, with dry, thick, chewy tannins. Yet there is a heart of blackberry fruits. You can try holding until after 2006, but it may not make it. **87** —*S.H. (8/1/2005)*

Stonegate 2000 Merlot (Napa Valley) $22. Pours unusually black for a Merlot, suggesting a lot of extraction on the skins to compensate for thin fruit in this difficult vintage for red wine. Tastes herbal, earthy, and alcoholic, and tannins grip and scour the palate. Not offering much pleasure now, and not likely to improve. **84** —*S.H. (12/15/2003)*

Stonegate 1999 Merlot (Napa Valley) $28. Loveliness in a glass, this finely etched Merlot benefits from the vintage's richness and great vineyards. The aromas are a delight, brimming with blackberry, cassis, mocha, and smoke, and leading to deep, satisfying flavors and a velvety texture. Classy and delicious, and sturdy tannins suggest midterm ageability. **91** —*S.H. (12/1/2001)*

Stonegate 1998 Merlot (Napa Valley) $22. Not bad for this vintage, which has ended up thinner than originally thought. The grapes had to struggle to ripen, and you can taste the tension between greenness and sweetness. Quite a bit of oak adds charred, smoky, vanilla notes and a glyceriny sweetness. This is elegant stuff; not a big wine, but it is very well made and its pedigree is obvious. **88** —*S.H. (2/1/2001)*

Stonegate 2001 Petite Verdot (Napa Valley) $25. As part of a blend, this PV would bring darkness, depth of flavor, and tannins to the finished wine. On its own, it's, well, dark, deep, and tannic. The flavors veer toward dark stone fruits and black berries, with a coffee earthiness. **87** — *S.H. (8/1/2005)*

Stonegate 2003 Sauvignon Blanc (Napa Valley) $14. I had this dry white wine with Chinese food and it was perfect. The citrus and peach fruitiness played off the inherent sweetness of soy sauce and ginger, while the wine's acidity cut through the oils. It's also pleasant on its own. **86** —*S.H. (8/1/2005)*

Stonegate 2000 Estate Bottled Sauvignon Blanc (Napa Valley) $16. There's not much oak in this very fruity, crisp wine, with fig, citrus flavors veering into tropical fruits, and a cinnamon and chocolate finish. The texture is lush, supple, and creamy. **87** —*S.H. (11/15/2001)*

STONEHEDGE

Stonehedge 2000 Cabernet Sauvignon (California) $10. There are some true varietal notes in the black currant and blackberry flavors, but unfortunately the wine also drinks rough and hot. Has a coarse earthiness that puts it firmly in the country-style camp. Yet it's dry, clean, and suitable for big parties where guests aren't too picky. **83** —*S.H. (6/1/2002)*

Stonehedge 1999 Cabernet Sauvignon (Napa Valley) $30. This is a flashy wine. It has only the best stuff: black currant and cassis flavors to die for; plush, velvety tannins; and a refined layer of toasty oak. The finish is very long and sweet, and refrains the currant theme. Lacks a bit of depth in favor of pizazz, but still very good. **89** —*S.H. (6/1/2002)*

Stonehedge 2000 Chardonnay (California) $10. 82 —*S.H. (5/1/2002)*

Stonehedge 2000 Reserve Chardonnay (Monterey) $18. Smells like canned peaches and nectarines, with a syrupy note that lasts through the finish. It's very oaky and ripe, with good acidity. But the elements aren't well integrated. The wine seems more like a study than a finished piece. A few months in bottle may help. **84** —*S.H. (12/15/2002)*

Stonehedge 2000 Merlot (California) $10. Generic red wine here. It brings to mind those jug wines from the old days that were dry and clean and fruity and affordable. The world needs more such wines. Who cares if it could be any one of 10 varietals? It's what it is and it's good enough. **85** —*S.H. (6/1/2002)*

Stonehedge 2001 Petite Sirah (California) $10. Dark and earthy, a thick, heavy wine with plummy, chocolatey flavors and big tannins, although the acidity is soft. The main drawback is residual sugar. Once that sugar hits, the palate is discombobulated. **81** —*S.H. (9/1/2003)*

Stonehedge 2000 Reserve Petite Sirah (Mendocino) $35. Inky black. You could fill your pen with this stuff. It smells very refined and young, sending out flashes of blackberries, white pepper, and pecan pie. Once it hits the mouth it comes across as a very fine wine. It is rich, big, and balanced despite the size, and completely dry, with a fruity intensity that lasts through the finish. The thick tannins suggest mid-term aging. **91** — *S.H. (9/1/2003)*

Stonehedge 2000 Pinot Noir (California) $10. Impertinent, saucy, rude— old-fashioned words to describe young, rustic wines, of which this is one. It's very dry and tannic with earthy-berry flavors, and snaps to a weak finish. **82** —*S.H. (2/1/2003)*

Stonehedge 2003 Sauvignon Blanc (California) $10. One of the drier Sauvignons out there, bony and minerally, with tart acids that make it mouthwateringly clean. Picks up lemon and fig flavors in the finish. A nice cocktail-style wine at a good price. **84** —*S.H. (8/1/2005)*

Stonehedge 2001 Sauvignon Blanc (California) $10. Very fruity, a mouthful of lime, grapefruit, apple, and peach flavors, and turns spicy and peppery on the finish. Feels a bit flat and heavy on the palate. Finishes very dry and with bright fruitiness. **84** —*S.H. (3/1/2003)*

Stonehedge 2000 Sauvignon Blanc (California) $10. Here's a simple little wine that makes for pleasant drinking at an affordable price. It's lemony and dry and soft in acids, but it is very clean and is fine for fried chicken, fruit salad, and other picnic-type fare. **84** —*S.H. (9/1/2002)*

Stonehedge 2000 Syrah (California) $10. Earthy, herbal aromas veer into cardboard, and a distinct waft of raw green peppercorn. The grapes didn't fully ripen. But the wine is dry, tart, and clean and there's a certain food friendliness. Try it with stews or barbecue and you might discover hidden charms. **83** —*S.H. (9/1/2002)*

Stonehedge 1999 Syrah (California) $10. Straightforward, solid Syrah with decent flavor intensity that shows light but juicy fruit with cocoa and earth touches. A low-acid profile makes it an easy-drinking, flavorful, plummy quaff. Bought at a discount, it's Best Buy material. **86** *(10/1/2001)*

Stonehedge 2001 Zinfandel (California) $10. Mild-mannered and fairly lightweight, the wine serves up a reasonable array of plum, cherry, toast, and licorice notes. Equally mild on the finish. **82** —*J.M. (11/1/2003)*

Stonehedge 2000 Zinfandel (California) $10. Pretty nice for a statewide appellation, with true Zin characteristics of wild, brambly berries. The alcohol is high and the wine is very dry, a full-throttle assault on the senses, with its maximum load of jammy fruit. Nothing subtle, just a bases-loaded, ripe wine that leaves little to the imagination. **86 Best Buy** —*S.H. (7/1/2002)*

Stonehedge 1999 Zinfandel (Napa Valley) $30. Comes down firmly on Zin's wild and wooly side. The brambly berry and pepper flavors are accompanied by savage tannins, not big and heavy, but jagged and rustic. High alcohol creates a hot aftertaste, and the wine is fermented to dryness. Finishes with a tart bite of acid. **86** —*S.H. (7/1/2002)*

Stonehedge 1997 Reserve Zinfandel (Napa Valley) $25. Ripe, muscular wine, with a full throttle nose rich with jammy black fruits. Firm structure, smooth tannins, and a chocolatey finish make this an appealing, consumer-friendly style. **88** —*P.G. (2/1/2001)*

STONESTREET

Stonestreet 1999 Legacy Bordeaux Blend (Alexander Valley) $67. Like the Christopher's Cab, this wine is firmly structured; it also has higher-toned aromatics consisting of red cherries and mint. Then the flavors come in waves of black cherry, plum, and cassis, finishing long and chocolatey. Drink 2005–2015. **91** *(9/1/2003)*

Stonestreet 1997 Cabernet Sauvignon (Sonoma County) $35. 86 *(11/1/2000)*

Stonestreet 2000 Cabernet Sauvignon (Alexander Valley) $36. Like many 2000 North Coast Cabernets, this shows a touch of green to its cassis base, blending herbs and tobacco into a solidly structured wine. A bit tight now, but not a long-term proposition either, try 2004–2008 **88** *(9/1/2003)*

Stonestreet 2001 Christopher's Cabernet Sauvignon (Alexander Valley) $80. I have watched this wine for some time and know that it is an ager, especially in a great vintage like this one. Made from very high Mayacamas Mountain grapes, it's relentlessly tannic in its youth. But the core of black cherry and cassis is fabulous. Hold until 2010. **93 Cellar Selection** —*S.H. (7/1/2005)*

Stonestreet 1999 Christopher's Cabernet Cabernet Sauvignon (Alexander Valley) $80. Just what you would expect from a long, cool vintage and hillside vineyards—a tightly wrapped, dense wine that needs some time in the cellar to unfurl its flavors of chocolate, cassis, and lead pencil. Has a richly textured mouthful and, despite some drying tannins, finishes with enough juicy fruit to more than compensate. **92 Cellar Selection** *(9/1/2003)*

Stonestreet 1997 Christopher's Vineyard Cabernet Sauvignon (Sonoma County) $70. **90** *(11/1/2000)*

Stonestreet 2001 Chardonnay (Sonoma County) $23. A blend of Russian River and Carneros fruit, with just a pinch of estate fruit for seasoning, this is California as we all expect it: Pear, baked apple, and citrus flavors dressed up in butter and toast. Soft and easy to drink. **86** *(9/1/2003)*

Stonestreet 1999 Block 66 Alexander Mountain Chardonnay (Alexander Valley) $34. Less fruity, more minerally, it's more restrained than the Upper Barn, with melon and citrus playing supporting roles before toasty oak comes on in a rush at the finish. **88** *(9/1/2003)*

Stonestreet 1998 Block Sixty-Six Chardonnay (Sonoma County) $30. This Chardonnay, from a small vineyard block in Jess Jackson's Alexander Mountain estate, is grand yet graceful. Oozing pear, butterscotch, melon, and menthol flavors, it shows good weight and a positive richness that's supported by firm structure. It's balanced, appealing, admirably not overoaked, and finishes long with flavors of melon, spice, and pear offset by toasty accents. Top Value. **90** *(7/1/2001)*

Stonestreet 2001 Upper Barn Chardonnay (Alexander Valley) $40. I get the idea of this wine. It's to craft a mountain Chard that's lean and acidic now, but a cellar candidate. It is indeed tight and austere, not offering a lot of satisfaction beyond oak and a hint of spicy pear on the finish. If you're adventurous, hold until 2006. **89** —*S.H. (7/1/2005)*

Stonestreet 2000 Upper Barn Chardonnay (Green Valley) $45. This is from the vineyard that Helen Turley originally made famous under her Marcassin label, from vines that are slowly succumbing to phylloxera (winemaker Westrick says that 2003 may be the last vintage before replanting). It's the biggest and most explosive Chardonnay from Stonestreet, with smoke and toast backed by oranges, peaches, and hints of hazelnut and a rich, custardy mouthfeel. **90** *(9/1/2003)*

Stonestreet 1998 Upper Barn Chardonnay (Sonoma County) $40. A big nose of toasty oak, vanilla, and butterscotch opens this offering. There are hints of pear and apple fruit, but the palate has a dominating oakiness and a custardy fatness. It's slightly hot, with dominant butterscotch and vanillin oaky flavors. **87** *(7/1/2001)*

Stonestreet 2000 Merlot (Sonoma County) $30. This great example of varietal correctness shows aromas of black cherries, mocha, and herbs, followed by earthier flavors of tobacco and black cherries. It's the kind of Merlot you wish you saw on more restaurant lists—easy to recognize and easy to like. **87** *(9/1/2003)*

Stonestreet 2001 Upper Barn Sauvignon Blanc (Alexander Valley) $20. Ripe and intriguing, and holding onto its form after four years. Delivers some creamy lemon pudding aromas that are backed by flavors of citrus, apple, and egg yolk. Solid on the finish, and appealing. Even offers a bit of cannoli/crème brûlée flavor at the end. **88** *(7/1/2005)*

Stonestreet 2000 Upper Barn Sauvignon Blanc (Alexander Valley) $25. Despite being entirely barrel-fermented, this doesn't come across as anything like the winery's Chardonnays. There's some smoke, but also pungent gooseberries along with melon and grapefruit. Only 10–15% of the oak is new, so it's not overdone. **88** *(9/1/2003)*

Stonestreet 1999 Upper Barn Vineyard Sauvignon Blanc (Alexander Valley) $23. In line with this winery's penchant for oak, this fast-aging wine is buttery and heavily toasted. As a result, snappy apple or citrus fruit is harder to find than many might want it to be. Nevertheless, there's some bold lemon and creamy vanilla on the thick, mouthfilling palate. And for that, it earns points. **87** *(8/1/2002)*

STONY HILL

Stony Hill 1997 Chardonnay (Napa Valley) $24. **93** —*S.H. (2/1/2000)*

Stony Hill 2001 Chardonnay (Napa Valley) $27. Stony Hill Chards are famous for their longevity, but the price of that is hardness in youth. This is a mineral-laden, acidic young wine. The fruit has barely begun clawing its way to the surface. I've had Stony Hill Chards at 20-plus

years of age and they were fabulous. Best after 2010. **92** —*S.H. (5/1/2005)*

Stony Hill 2000 Chardonnay (Napa Valley) $27. Always lean and sharp in youth, this year's vintage is even leaner than usual. It has citrus and herb flavors undercut by searing acidity, and is bitterly dry. Almost Sauvignon Blanc-like in its profile, and not likely to age. **85** —*S.H. (2/1/2004)*

Stony Hill 1999 Chardonnay (Napa Valley) $27. A superb Chard, very much in the Stony Hill tradition. Tight, appley fruit with high (by Napa standards) acidity creates a taut wine made fatter and sweeter by the judicious use of oak. This is a sleek, elegant Chard that, judging by its track record, will age and improve effortlessly over the next decade. **93** —*S.H. (5/1/2002)*

Stony Hill 1998 Chardonnay (Napa Valley) $NA. One of California's longest-lived Chards, this mountain wine always starts out tight and lemon-spicy, with bracing acidity. Sprightly and drinkable now, with dry, citrusy flavors and sweet oaky vanillins, it will improve with many years of cellaring. **90** —*S.H. (12/1/2001)*

Stony Hill 2002 Gewürztraminer (Napa Valley) $15. Tough, light, bone dry, and acidic, with pretty spice and floral notes, but rather thin on the fruit. You'll find diluted citrus flavors just veering into peach. **84** —*S.H. (2/1/2004)*

Stony Hill 2001 Gewürztraminer (Napa Valley) $15. So different from most other Gewürzes, which can be overly sweet and flamboyant. This one's pert in acids, and only hints at flavors of mangoes, peaches, and various wildflowers. Has a fresh-lime minerality that's appealing. **88** —*S.H. (5/1/2005)*

Stony Hill 2000 Gewürztraminer (Napa Valley) $15. Smells like a walk through a candy shop filled with gingerbread cookies, vanilla wafers, and white chocolate fudge. Oh, and there's a flower shop next door, which explains the honeysuckle and gardenia. Yet it's dry and crisp, and the flavors are modestly citrus and apricot. Elegant and foodworthy. **88** —*S.H. (6/1/2002)*

Stony Hill 2000 Sémillon du Soleil Sémillon (Napa Valley) $15. Here's dessert in a glass. Smells apricotty and botrytisy and vanilla-honeyed, and drinks rich in nectar. This makes it sound astoundingly sweet, but it's not. Tastes like sautéed bananas, caramelized in butter, flamed in amaretto, and served on top of vanilla ice cream. **94 Editors' Choice** —*S.H. (5/1/2005)*

Stony Hill 2002 White Riesling (Napa Valley) $15. Disappointingly thin this vintage. The palate expects a rush of fruit, but encounters watery grapefruit and lime flavors and acidity. The rich floral and riper tree fruit notes just aren't there. **84** —*S.H. (2/1/2004)*

Stony Hill 2001 White Riesling (Napa Valley) $15. Here's a firm, crisp Riesling, made Alsatian style. It's basically dry, with lime and peach flavors and flashes of green apple and steel. Try with grilled trout. **86** —*S.H. (2/1/2005)*

Stony Hill 2000 White Riesling (Napa Valley) $15. Made since 1957, always rich, complex, and steely, and one of the state's great agers, this year's release is an extraordinary Riesling. Its flowery, peach, and jasmine aromas and flavors and streak of mineral are delicately perched between dry and off-dry. Zesty acidity provides vital balance. **90** —*S.H. (6/1/2002)*

STONY RIDGE WINERY

Stony Ridge Winery 2001 Reserve Cabernet Sauvignon (Livermore Valley) $21. Smells unacceptably musty, not corked, but like old dust that's approaching cheese. Turns overly sweet and thick in the mouth. **82** —*S.H. (11/15/2003)*

Stony Ridge Winery 2000 Reserve Johannisberg Riesling (Monterey) $10. Pretty, opening with a rich perfume of wildflower, honeysuckle, apricot, tangerine, peach, vanilla, honey, and smoke. Flavorful and savory, with lovely fruity notes accompanied by crisp acidity. Finishes clean and off-dry. **88 Best Buy** —*S.H. (12/31/2003)*

STORRS

Storrs 2004 Christie Vineyard Chardonnay (Santa Cruz Mountains) $26. Bright in acids and pure kiwi, lime, and peach flavors. Oak plays the

USA

perfect foil, lending buttered toast and vanilla to this lovely, complex wine. **89** —*S.H. (3/1/2006)*

Storrs 2003 Christie Vineyard Chardonnay (Santa Cruz Mountains) $26. It's all here in spades, the toasty oak, ripe tropical pineapple, and mango, peppery spices and creamy texture. Good acidity, too. A little obvious, but will satisfy fans of opulent Chards. **86** —*S.H. (8/1/2005)*

Storrs 2002 Viento Vineyard Gewürztraminer (Monterey) $14. I wish this wine were firmer and steelier, because it really has beautiful perfume and taste, but it's soft. It's showcases Gewürz's exotic side, with dusty spices, tropical fruits, and flowers. **85** —*S.H. (5/1/2005)*

Storrs 2001 Merlot (San Ysidro District) $24. No problem getting the grapes ripe. Sweet cherries, sweet oak, sweet cocoa, but this wine has no residual sugar and must be considered dry. Good, mouth-dusting tannins and nice grippy acids. Next step: finesse and depth. **85** —*S.H. (8/1/2005)*

Storrs 2000 Rusty Ridge Petite Sirah (Santa Clara County) $22. Solidly average in quality, with berry-cherry flavors and a rustic feel in the mouth. It's pleasant, and there's a nice streak of spice in the finish, but it's one dimensional. **83** *(4/1/2003)*

Storrs 2001 Pinot Noir (Santa Cruz Mountains) $25. Released at 4-plus years of age, this is still a young, fresh wine. It has complex cherry compote, cola, and crushed hard spice flavors, with a delicate overlay of oak, and is very dry and well acidified. It makes you wish there were far more Pinot planted in this rapidly urbanizing area. **91** —*S.H. (3/1/2006)*

Storrs 2003 Sauvignon Blanc (San Lucas) $16. Southern Monterey is clearly too warm for a variety like Sauvignon. While the wine has pleasant fig and citrus flavors, it lacks crispness and vitality. **83** —*S.H. (5/1/2005)*

Storrs 2002 Riverview Vineyard White Riesling (Monterey) $14. Here's an Alsatian-style wine, with fairly dry but vigorously rich flavors of honeysuckle, peach, slate, and vanilla. If it had crisper acidity, it would be a great wine. **86** —*S.H. (5/1/2005)*

STORY

Story 2002 Picnic Hill Vineyard Old Vines Zinfandel (California) $30. Hot, sweet, and Porty. **81** —*S.H. (3/1/2005)*

STORYBOOK MOUNTAIN

Storybook Mountain 2001 Eastern Exposures Zinfandel (Napa Valley) $30. Starts off with pretty blueberry and spice aromas. Quite cherry-like and bright on the palate, with hints of spice, chocolate, and toast. Tannins are ripe and the finish is moderate in length. **88** *(11/1/2003)*

Storybook Mountain 2000 Eastern Exposures Zinfandel (Napa Valley) $35. From Zin specialists, this fruity wine will appeal to those who like their Zins big and brawny. The wild berry flavors are dry, and the alcohol is a moderate 14.5%, sparing the wine from excessive heat. No raisins mar the balance. A tomatoey streak suggests barbecue sauce. **86** —*S.H. (11/1/2002)*

Storybook Mountain 1997 Eastern Exposures Zinfandel (Napa Valley) $25. **95** —*P.G. (11/15/1999)*

Storybook Mountain 1997 Estate Reserve Zinfandel (Napa Valley) $50. Blackberries are the story here, boatloads of rich, ripe, jammy blackberries. There is just a whiff of volatile acidity, then a wonderful mouthful of fruit with some stony earth underneath. Shows a light touch with the oak, good acids and a deft handling of the tannins. **90** —*P.G. (3/1/2001)*

Storybook Mountain 2001 Mayacamas Range Zinfandel (Napa Valley) $20. Pretty black plum, blackberry, black cherry, toast, spice, and herb flavors sing out here. Cola, coffee, and a bright-edged texture give the wine added interest. On the finish, its bright and clean. **87** *(11/1/2003)*

Storybook Mountain 2000 Mayacamas Range Zinfandel (Napa Valley) $25. **82** —*S.H. (11/1/2002)*

Storybook Mountain 1997 Mayacamas Range Zinfandel (Napa Valley) $20. **88** —*P.G. (11/15/1999)*

Storybook Mountain 1999 Reserve Zinfandel (Napa Valley) $45. This barrel selection is intense and ripe. You can taste the sunshine in the blackberry, boysenberry, and blueberry flavors, and the winemaker has

wisely made the wine dry and balanced. It possesses Zin's ineffably wild and rugged character, but big meats, such as roast lamb or barbecued ribs, will create the ideal marriage. **89** —*S.H. (11/1/2002)*

Storybook Mountain 2000 The First Hurrah Zinfandel (Atlas Peak) $25. The wine is purple in color, the aromas are big and jammy, and the flavors are youthful, suggesting freshly crushed blueberries, blackberries, cherries, black pepper, and tobacco. That tells you what kind of Zin this is: Mountain Zin, brawny and bold. Thankfully, it is dry and has no residual sugar. **88** —*S.H. (11/1/2002)*

Storybook Mountain 1997 The Last Hurrah Zinfandel (Howell Mountain) $35. 92 —*S.H. (5/1/2000)*

STRANGELAND

Strangeland 2002 Pinot Noir (Willamette Valley) $20. Clove stands out, above cherry and vanilla, some earthy, stemmy tannins, and a tough, unripe, tomatoey finish. **83** *(11/1/2004)*

Strangeland 2002 Stand Sure Vineyard Pinot Noir (Willamette Valley) $20. Really herbal and pungent, with grassy, green flavors. Creamy, soft in the middle, quite light, and finishing with hard, green tannins. **84** *(11/1/2004)*

Strangeland 2002 Winemaker's Estate Reserve Pinot Noir (Willamette Valley) $60. Pale, oaky, herbal, with very light, rhubarb fruit and roasted coconut. Way too tannic. **82** *(11/1/2004)*

STRATA

Strata 2001 Merlot (Napa Valley) $34. Pours dark, smells dramatic with its tapestry of blackberries, green olives, grilled meat, smoky oak, and cocoa. This marvelously rich wine goes down smooth and velvety. Turns intense in flavor through a very long finish. **92** —*S.H. (10/1/2005)*

STRATFORD

Stratford 1999 Syrah (California) $18. Plummy, smoky, chocolatey aromas lead to a richly flavored but slightly heavy wine. The soft, gentle tannins are easy to negotiate. There's a big wad of rich, jammy fruit that hits midpalate, while the finish is juicy and fruity. **84** —*S.H. (7/1/2002)*

STRATTON LUMMIS

Stratton Lummis 2002 Cabernet Sauvignon (Napa Valley) $30. Raspingly dry, rather unripe, and tannic, this wine struggles to achieve some cherry flavors. **82** —*S.H. (10/1/2005)*

STRYKER SONOMA

Stryker Sonoma 2001 Syrah (Dry Creek Valley) $22. Floral and spicy on the nose, with hints of berry zinger tea. Picks up hints of cherries and chocolate on the palate, but without adding any weight, then finishes crisp and clean. Pretty, but light. **83** *(9/1/2005)*

Stryker Sonoma 2000 Syrah (Sonoma County) $22. Hebal and tea-like, dominated by green leafy notes and drying tannins, which doesn't bode well for future development. There's just enough cherry flavor to redeem it, but drink up. **83** *(9/1/2005)*

Stryker Sonoma 2002 Estate Syrah (Alexander Valley) $22. Much different in style from Stryker Sonoma's Dry Creek Syrah, this bottling is riper and more intense. Lush plum and blackberry flavors are broad and mouthfilling, picking up hints of vanilla on the abbreviated finish. Drink now. **85** *(9/1/2005)*

Stryker Sonoma 1999 Old Vine Estate Zinfandel (Alexander Valley) $25. Massively proportioned, this is a wine picked at maximum sugary ripeness and then fully fermented, leaving it very dry, but alcoholic, at 16.2%. The plush berry flavors are delicious and complex, and cover the palate with fruity sweetness. This is long-hangtime California Zin all the way, and in its own style, a classic. **90** —*S.H. (9/1/2002)*

STUART CELLARS

Stuart Cellars 2002 Limited Estate Reserve Tatria Meritage Cabernet Blend (Temecula) $36. Very difficult to find much nice to say about this wine, except it's dry. Otherwise, it's sharp and charmless. **80** —*S.H. (4/1/2006)*

Stuart Cellars 2003 Limited Bottling Viognier (California) $21. Bone dry and tart, this wine offers citrus, peach, and fig flavors. It doesn't have the usual flowery opulence of Viognier, but is a clean, refreshing wine. **84** — S.H. (3/1/2006)

Stuart Cellars 2004 Select Reserve Zinfandel (Temecula) $30. The only thing that's not Porty about this wine is the sugar level. It's dry, but at the expense of dreadfully high, 16.1 percent alcohol. Bring a designated driver if you drink it. **80** —S.H. (7/1/2006)

Stuart Cellars 2003 Select Reserve Zinfandel (Temecula) $30. It's hard to know what to make of this wine. With 17.4% alcohol, it's more of a Port, except that it's dry. It's clean, with firm tannins framing deep coffee, blackberry, and leather flavors, and actually possesses some charm and elegance despite the size. **85** —S.H. (4/1/2006)

Stuart Cellars 1998 Vintage Zinfandel (Temecula) $42. Black as ink, with glints of royal purple and gold, it opens with intense, penetrating aromas of dark chocolate, blackberry preserves, and cassis, caramel, and a smoky, peppery note. Decadently rich, with 10% residual sugar, and heady, with 19% alcohol, but so delicious. The silky, velvety texture is pure seduction. This has got to be one of the best California Ports on the market. **95** —S.H. (4/1/2002)

STUBBS VINEYARD

Stubbs Vineyard 2002 Pinot Noir (Marin County) $24. A very good wine, showing cool, coastal influences in the beet, rhubarb, clove, and cherry flavors and firm acids. Supple, light, and silky. **87** (11/1/2004)

Stubbs Vineyard 2004 Estate Grown Pinot Noir (Marin County) $36. Crisp in acidity, ripe in cherry, cola, and coffee flavors, and delicately tannic. Just a bit too sweet for balance. Has a sugary, soda taste that detracts and makes it medicinal. **83** —S.H. (12/1/2006)

STUHLMULLER VINEYARDS

Stuhlmuller Vineyards 2002 Cabernet Sauvignon (Alexander Valley) $35. Too much sugary sweetness in this for a table wine that's supposed to be dry. Those pretty blackberry and cherry flavors taste like they were sprinkled with white sugar, which is a detraction to me. **83** —S.H. (3/1/2006)

Stuhlmuller Vineyards 1999 Cabernet Sauvignon (Alexander Valley) $35. Aromas are muted, with faint scents of smoky oak and blackberry veering into cassis. Flavors are similarly hard to detect, beyond the sweetness of oak. The tannins meanwhile are substantial, and it finishes bitter. It's a gamble if this will improve in the cellar, but it probably won't. **84** —S.H. (12/15/2003)

Stuhlmuller Vineyards 1998 Cabernet Sauvignon (Alexander Valley) $35. A bit lean, with sleek berry and herb flavors and a sharpness softened only partially by sweet oak. It's dry and clean and has the best wood and tannins that money can buy, but ultimately it's thin, especially for this price. **85** —S.H. (9/12/2002)

Stuhlmuller Vineyards 2001 Estate Cabernet Sauvignon (Alexander Valley) $32. This is a young, dynamic wine that's fancy enough to have with your best food. It shows well-ripened fruit flavors, and is very dry, with a good boost of acidity. Also has some pretty good tannins to cut through beef. I think it's at its best now and for the next three years. **90** —S.H. (10/1/2005)

Stuhlmuller Vineyards 2004 Chardonnay (Alexander Valley) $23. Alexander Valley was the source of some great California Chardonnays back in the 70s, and this wine shows how well the appellation can do. It's a soft, opulent wine, with tropical fruit flavors complexed with the cream and spice of oak and lees. **87** —S.H. (3/1/2006)

Stuhlmuller Vineyards 2001 Chardonnay (Alexander Valley) $23. This is a bold, rich Chard with flavors ranging from apples and pears through hints of pineapple. Oak brings nuances of smoke, vanilla, and buttered toast. The crisp mouthfeel leads to a long, spicy finish. **88** —S.H. (2/1/2004)

Stuhlmuller Vineyards 1999 Chardonnay (Alexander Valley) $23. A steely-clean style, with mineral and citrus overtones. This firm, structured wine offers a refreshing, brisk quaff with a moderate finish of lemon, apple, and herbs. **88** —J.M. (5/1/2002)

Stuhlmuller Vineyards 2003 Estate Chardonnay (Alexander Valley) $23. Ripe in tropical fruits and spicy, with lots of oak and a minerally feel, this Chard is a bit astringent around the edges. Give it a year or so to come together. **86** —S.H. (10/1/2005)

Stuhlmuller Vineyards 2000 Estate Bottled Chardonnay (Alexander Valley) $23. Great structure, with crisp, supportive acids and a fine overlay of oak that seasons but doesn't overwhelm. The flavors are quite lean. The winemaker calls them mineral-like, but it's more like grapefruits and lemons. The main problem with this well-made wine is, in fact, this lack of flavor. **84** —S.H. (8/1/2003)

SULA VINEYARDS

Sula Vineyards 2005 Shiraz (Napa-Sonoma) $12. This wine is nearly black, with a purple rim, and smokey aromas of roasted salsa and leather. Despite the lack of fruit on the nose, there is plenty of dark underlying fruit to the palate, but still a roasted flavor, along with Band-Aid. **82** — M.D. (12/15/2006)

SULLIVAN

Sullivan 1997 Cabernet Sauvignon (Rutherford) $45. 86 (11/1/2000)

Sullivan 2000 Cabernet Sauvignon (Rutherford) $50. Tastes better than it smells. The aromas are herbal, stalky, and even raw vegetal, with an overlay of toasty oak. In the mouth, some blackberry flavors show up, but it's a thin wine and not going anywhere. Still, the rich, soft structure saves it. **85** —S.H. (2/1/2004)

Sullivan 2001 Estate Cabernet Sauvignon (Rutherford) $50. Shows a unique wintergreen or menthol note to the ripe blackberry, cherry, and coffee flavors. Could it be from eucalyptus trees? The flavors are framed in dusty, fine tannins. Elegant now, and should soften and sweeten for many years. **93** —S.H. (10/1/2004)

Sullivan 2003 Estate Bottled Cabernet Sauvignon (Rutherford) $55. Seems like it was picked earlier than most '03s, given the dry tannins and peppery, minty flavors. Still, it has a beautiful structure, classic and refined, with cherry and cocoa flavors and upscale oak. Drink now through 2010. **89** —S.H. (12/15/2006)

Sullivan 2002 Estate Reserve Cabernet Sauvignon (Rutherford) $85. Forward and lush, with a beautiful structure, this dry, balanced wine has cherry, cassis, wintergreen, and oak flavors that finish in a swirl of complexity. This fine wine defines the elegance and femininity of a great Rutherford Cab, and should age well through 2012. **93 Editors' Choice** —S.H. (12/15/2005)

SULLIVAN BIRNEY

Sullivan Birney 2001 Chardonnay (Sonoma Mountain) $28. Big, fruity, and ripe, providing a mouthful of apple and pear flavors that are spiced up with cinnamon and oaky vanilla. The flavors sink deep into the palate and last for a long time. Nonetheless, this full-bodied, creamy wine never loses control. **91** —S.H. (2/1/2004)

Sullivan Birney 2002 Sonoma Coast Chardonnay (Sonoma Coast) $30. Nobody ages Chardonnay, but maybe they should, as the profile of these coastal Chards emerges. This wine is high in acidity, metallic, and lemony in fruit. There's a toughness that the softening, sweetening qualities of oak cannot blur. It's a gamble, but try cellaring until 2005 and try again. **88** —S.H. (8/1/2004)

Sullivan Birney 2002 Sonoma Mt. Chardonnay (Sonoma Mountain) $27. Here's a fat wine, plump in juicy citrus, pear, and tropical fruit flavors, a little soft in acid but rich in smoky oak and Asian spice. It's gooey, like lemon meringue pie, and finishes a bit sweet, in the current fashion. **88** —S.H. (8/1/2004)

Sullivan Birney 2002 Pinot Noir (Sonoma Coast) $28. Easy and simple, rather than profound, with candied raspberry and rhubarb aromas. Rather tart in acids. **83** (11/1/2004)

Sullivan Birney 2002 Katherine Vineyard Pinot Noir (Sonoma Mountain) $34. Rather sulfury on opening, with oaky, smoky notes beneath. Average in the mouth, with modest fruit flavors and a rough texture. **84** (11/1/2004)

Sullivan Birney 2001 Katherine Vineyard Pinot Noir (Sonoma Mountain) $30. This is a new winery to me, and this fabulous release displays its great promise. The wine is dark and dense, with an immature aroma of smoky wood, baked cherry tart, and vanilla. In the mouth it has complex cherry, berry, and spice flavors that are folded into rich but soft tannins. Finishes long. **93 Editors' Choice** —S.H. (5/1/2004)

USA

SUMMERLAND

Summerland 2001 Cabernet Sauvignon (Santa Barbara County) $16. Weedy and herbal, with lacquery, acrylic aromas and flavors. This wine stays stubbornly thin throughout. **82** —S.H. (10/1/2004)

Summerland 2002 Chardonnay (Santa Barbara County) $14. A nice enough Chard for everyday purposes, with some nicely ripened tropical fruit flavors. Has an earthiness in the middle, but finishes fruity and spicy. **84** —S.H. (9/1/2004)

Summerland 2002 Bien Nacido Vineyard Chardonnay (Santa Maria Valley) $22. The real deal from this vineyard and appellation, a cool-climate Chard that bursts with bright tropical fruit flavors and crisp acids. That zesty cleanness is softened and smoothed by creamy oak. **91** —S.H. (9/1/2004)

Summerland 2001 Merlot (Santa Barbara County) $16. Thin and rather weedy, with modest cherry flavors and smooth tannins. Fulfills the basics. **83** —S.H. (12/15/2004)

Summerland 2002 Pinot Noir (Central Coast) $18. There are earthy, forest-floor notes here, and also some raisiny ones. The acids are crisp, but tasters felt there was too much heat throughout. **85** (11/1/2004)

Summerland 2002 Bien Nacido Vineyard Block T Pinot Noir (Santa Maria Valley) $30. A Pinot that goes straight down the middle in varietal correctness but isn't very exciting. Black cherry, oak, and spice flavors drink somewhat tannic, and the acidity is quite high. **84** (11/1/2004)

Summerland 2002 Odyssey-Thurlestone Vineyard Pinot Noir (Edna Valley) $28. A nice, easy wine with some special features. Light in body, silky in texture, with cranberry, cherry, coffee, and spice flavors that turn complex on the finish. **86** (11/1/2004)

Summerland 2002 Syrah (Paso Robles) $16. Overripe and too sweet, a Porty wine with raisiny, caramel, and chocolate flavors, a dense texture, and a sugary finish. That's just not right for a varietal that supposed to be a dry table wine. **83** —S.H. (12/1/2004)

Summerland 2002 Highlands Vineyard Syrah (Santa Barbara County) $20. Joins its blackberry, cherry fruit with meaty, leathery notes that approach bacon frying in the pan, while oak adds to the smokiness. The flavors are encased in rich, smooth, ripe tannins. It's very good, but needs some time in the cellar. Try after 2005. **88** —S.H. (9/1/2004)

SUMMERS

Summers 2003 Cabernet Sauvignon (Napa Valley) $20. Showing good balance and harmony of all its parts, this Cab shows ripe cherry and blackberry flavors. It has thick enough tannins to hold it for a while. **87** —S.H. (2/1/2006)

Summers 2002 Cabernet Sauvignon (Napa Valley) $36. The plush blackberry, cassis, and chocolate flavors hit you on the first sip, flooding the palate, and then acids and tannins kick in to balance. There's a roughness that keeps this Cab from the front ranks, but it has charm. Drink now. **87** —S.H. (11/1/2005)

Summers 2001 Cabernet Sauvignon (Napa Valley) $40. Young, dark purple and massive, this big Cabernet stars black currant and cassis flavors that are generously wrapped in sweet oak. It's very dry, and coats the mouth with impressively ripe, sweet fruit. Fine now, but has the acidity and ripe tannins to age effortlessly for a decade. **90** —S.H. (4/1/2004)

Summers 2000 Cabernet Sauvignon (Napa Valley) $38. You could blind-taste this and know it's a fancy Napa Cab from the lush tannins. Any ripe wine can hit the black currant, plum, and cherry notes, but few can achieve this level of smoothness. Coats the palate like a single-malt Scotch, with luxury and smoothness that carry into the long finish. Delectable now. **93 Editors' Choice** —S.H. (11/15/2003)

Summers 2003 Andriana's Cuvée Cabernet Sauvignon (Napa Valley) $20. Soft and velvety in texture, this delicious Cab is rich in cassis and chocolate flavors. It's not just a fruit bomb, though, due to the complex interplay of finely ground tannins, crisp acids, and toasty oak. **91** —S.H. (5/1/2006)

Summers 1999 Chevalier Noir Cabernet Sauvignon-Merlot (North Coast) $32. A smooth-drinking, pleasant wine with a velvety texture, rich tannins, and soft acids characteristic of the region and vintage. The flavors veer toward blackberries and dill. This is not a lavish blockbuster, but an elegant, somewhat light blend of Cabernet Sauvignon and Merlot. **87** —S.H. (11/15/2002)

Summers 2004 Villa Andriana Vineyard Charbono (Napa Valley) $28. As dark in color as any wine in California, this is a wildly rustic wine. Dry, tannic but soft, it has coffee flavors laced with blackberry liqueur. **83** —S.H. (11/15/2006)

Summers 2000 Villa Andriano Charbono (Napa Valley) $24. Very dark and purple in color, a dense wine whose chief palate impression is of numbing tannins. Acidity also makes the wine strong and austere. Judging from past tastings of this varietal, in 15 years the wine will be drinkable. **84** —S.H. (12/1/2002)

Summers 2005 Chardonnay (Alexander Valley) $24. Shows brisk acidity for this warmish appellation, with upfront, pineapple custard, peach tart, and apricot cobbler flavors wrapped in a honeyed mouthfeel. Just when you think it's a simple Chard, it reveals all kinds of layers. **87** —S.H. (12/1/2006)

Summers 1997 Merlot (Knights Valley) $25. 85 —M.S. (7/1/2000)

Summers 1999 Merlot (Knights Valley) $24. There's some blackberry fruit under fairly sturdy tannins, but this dry, austere wine is mainly marked by earth and herbs now. It may soften and fatten up in a few years. **85** —S.H. (11/15/2002)

Summers 2004 Reserve Merlot (Knights Valley) $28. Made in a heavier, full-bodied style, this Merlot is very dry and fairly tannic. It's an earthy wine, with truffle, tobacco, and herb flavors and deeper blue and black fruit. Drink now. **85** —S.H. (12/1/2006)

Summers 2003 Reserve Merlot (Knights Valley) $30. Dry, fruity, tannic and a bit sharp, this Merlot, from a warm, inland appellation in Sonoma County, could improve in a year or two. **84** —S.H. (11/1/2005)

Summers 2000 Viognier (Monterey) $18. A big, rich wine with the body and mouthfeel of quality Chardonnay, although the flavors are different and more exotic, suggesting peaches, tropical fruits, and flowers. Cool Monterey weather has given it the burst of crisp acidity it needs. **90 Editors' Choice** —S.H. (12/15/2002)

Summers 2000 Villa Adriana Zinfandel (Napa Valley) $24. Good, richly dark color, but this isn't a big, fruity Zin. The aromas are white pepper and tobacco, and the wine drinks pretty herbaceous, although there are underlying flavors of blackberries. It's very dry, and needs big foods to wake it up. **86** —S.H. (11/1/2002)

Summers 2003 Villa Adriana Vineyard Zinfandel (Napa Valley) $28. Summers has established a good track record with this single-vineyard Zin, and while it's not quite in the same league as the '01 or '02, it's very good. Ripe and striking in cherry and tobacco flavors, and liberally spiced, it has a fine, claret-like balance. **88** —S.H. (8/1/2005)

Summers 2004 Villa Andriana Vineyard Zinfandel (Napa Valley) $34. Classic Napa Zin, dry, rich, balanced, and almost with the finesse of a great Cab. It's the tannins that turn the trick. They're so ripe, sweet, and fine. Of course, the flavors are totally Zin, all briary berries and peppery spice. Just delicious. **92** —S.H. (11/1/2006)

Summers 2001 Villa Andriana Vineyard Zinfandel (Napa Valley) $24. Plush and sweet on the nose. On the palate, it's got great density (though it doesn't taste sweet). Flavors are integrated, with charry, dark plum, licorice, toast, and blackberry notes, all couched in silky smooth, elegant tannins. **90** (11/1/2003)

Summers 2002 Villa Andriana Vineyard Estate Zinfandel (Napa Valley) $28. This interestingly complex Zin shows lots of forward cherry, blueberry, black raspberry, and cocoa fruit, sprinkled with peppery spices, and is fully dry. Shows lots of classy balance in the way the sweet tannins, acidity, and subtle oak interplay with the fruit. **90** —S.H. (6/1/2005)

SUMMERWOOD

Summerwood 2001 Sentio III Bordeaux Blend (Central Coast) $50. Smells as fine in currant, vanilla, and smoky oak as a good North Coast Cab. It's rich in fruits and herbs, and in astringent tannins. An acidic bitterness, however, suggests limited ageabilty. Cabernet Sauvignon, Cabernet Franc, and Merlot. **87** —S.H. (12/31/2004)

Summerwood 2001 Diosa Red Blend (Paso Robles) $50. Vibrant cherry, chocolate, olive, and woody-smoky aromas lead to a soft and accessible red wine. Feels good and supple, with generous fruit. Finishes with a dusting of fine tannins. Decant, or best after 2005. Syrah-Mourvèdre-Grenache. **89** —*S.H. (12/31/2004)*

Summerwood 2002 SZG Red Blend (Paso Robles) $35. This is a big, brawling wine that needs decanting to open up. It has aromas of hung meat, coffee, plums, blackberries, and chocolate, and is oaky. Tannic and rather show down now, but you can detect the cherry, chocolate, and spice flavors. Air well, or wait until 2006. **89** —*S.H. (12/31/2004)*

Summerwood 2003 Diosa Rhône Red Blend (Paso Robles) $50. The fruit stars in this Rhône red blend. It's all summer-sweet raspberries, cherry compote infused with milk chocolate and a trickle of cassis, drizzled with vanilla and smoked in oak barrels. The wine is very soft, yet with enough acidity to provide balance and freshness. **91** —*S.H. (10/1/2005)*

Summerwood 2003 Diosa Blanc Rhône White Blend (Paso Robles) $40. Summerwood is an up-and-coming winery in western Paso Robles that's doing a good job with Rhône varieties. This Roussanne-Viognier blend is creamy and unctuous, almost honeyed in extremely ripe tropical fruit, buttery oak, and spice flavors. Fortunately, the acidity is good. **90** —*S.H. (10/1/2005)*

Summerwood 2002 Diosa Syrah (Paso Robles) $50. Dark and ripe, with soft acids and tannins and a velvety texture carrying chocolate and blackberry flavors. Fully dry, though, and balanced. Mainly Syrah, with splashes of Grenache and Roussanne. **86** —*S.H. (12/15/2004)*

Summerwood 2001 Lock Vineyard Syrah (Paso Robles) $40. Quite tannic and tough now, and taut and lean-feeling, with good acidity. Rich in meat, blackberry, smoke, and vanilla. Falls off a bit in the mouth, or would score higher, but still a very good wine. **89** —*S.H. (12/31/2004)*

Summerwood 2001 Zinfandel (Paso Robles) $18. An oaky, firm-textured wine that sports prune, plum, chocolate, coffee, toast, and spice at its fore. The tannins are moderate, as is the finish. **84** *(11/1/2003)*

SUMMIT LAKE

Summit Lake 2000 Emily Kestrel Cabernet Sauvignon (Howell Mountain) $40. Flamboyant in cherries, currants, and sweet garden herbs, this wine's tannins are ample, but intricate and soft. Turns a bit thin in the mid-palate, and then reprises the cherries on the finish. **88** —*S.H. (5/1/2005)*

Summit Lake 2001 Zinfandel (Howell Mountain) $20. Fairly rugged in tannins, with an edgy mouthfeel, this wine shows earth, blackberry, and coffee flavors. It's very dry. **85** —*S.H. (5/1/2005)*

Summit Lake 2000 Zinfandel (Howell Mountain) $20. A lean-styled wine, with powdery tannins framing a bright-edged collection of sour cherry, anise, smoke, and toast. An herbal core runs through it, giving it a bright finish. **84** —*J.M. (10/1/2004)*

Summit Lake 1999 Zinfandel (Howell Mountain) $22. Marvelously rich and dense, with well-ripened fruit and sweet, dessert-like flavors suggesting cherry liqueur-filled chocolate candies. But it drinks dry and dustily tannic, a balanced, although heady, wine of great style. **92** —*S.H. (9/1/2002)*

Summit Lake 2001 Clair Rileys Private Reserve Port Zinfandel (Howell Mountain) $85. Sweet in blackberries and chocolate, but rather rough and unbalanced, with a hot finish. **83** —*S.H. (5/1/2005)*

Summit Lake 1996 Howell Mountain Zinfandel (Napa Valley) $23. **85** — *P.G. (11/15/1999)*

SUNCÉ VINEYARD & WINERY

Suncé Vineyard & Winery 2000 Pl. Franicevic Stryker's Vineyard Cabernet Sauvignon (Clear Lake) $32. Here's a modest Cab from an out-of-the-way appellation. It has pleasant blackberry and cherry flavors that are a bit thin, and the wine finishes with a tannic scour. **84** —*S.H. (6/1/2004)*

Suncé Vineyard & Winery 2001 Pl. Franicevic Stryker's Vineyard Meritage Cabernet Sauvignon (Clear Lake) $40. A nice, well-crafted Cab that pleases on several levels. It's got good varietal character, from the blackberry and currant flavors accented with oak to the soft, sweet tannins. The

wine needs more depth and concentration, though, and finishes thin. **86** —*S.H. (6/1/2004)*

Suncé Vineyard & Winery 1999 Pl. Franicevic Pheasant Glen Vineyard Meritage (Dunnigan Hills) $58. Rustic and country-style, from the brambly berry flavors to the scruffy tannins and earthy mouthfeel. Finishes sharp and a little salty. **83** —*S.H. (6/1/2004)*

Suncé Vineyard & Winery 2000 Pl. Franicevic Stryker's Vineyard Meritage (Clear Lake) $65. Awkward, with a mixture of blackberry and stalky flavors. The elaborate oak doesn't really help. **83** —*S.H. (6/1/2004)*

Suncé Vineyard & Winery 2000 Merlot (Monterey) $18. Unusually concentrated and intense for a Monterey Merlot; a big, rich wine that assaults the palate with flavors of black currant, plum, chocolate, dried herbs, and smoked oak. The tannins are as smooth and plush as anything up north. Would score higher if not for a certain thinness in the middle palate, but that's a result of the vintage. **90** —*S.H. (12/31/2003)*

Suncé Vineyard & Winery 2001 La Rochelle Vineyard Pinot Noir (Monterey) $18. Good example of cool Central Coast Pinot, with its polished, jammy flavors of cherry and raspberry and dusty spices, complexed with smoky oak. Bright acidity and gentle tannins make for an easy drink. Light, but a pretty good value. **86** —*S.H. (12/1/2005)*

Suncé Vineyard & Winery 2000 Pl. Franicevic Karah's Hillside Vineyard Pinot Noir (Sonoma Coast) $28. By far the best of Suncé's current roster of Pinots for its ripe black cherry jam, gingersnap, and root beer flavors. The texture is lively with crisp, citrusy acidity and easy tannins. **85** — *S.H. (6/1/2004)*

Suncé Vineyard & Winery 2001 Pl. Franicevic Piner Ranch Vineyard Pinot Noir (Russian River Valley) $32. Simple, with basic varietal identity, namely, the silky smooth tannins and crisp acidity that underlie cola and watered-down raspberry flavors. My sample bottle was a little fizzy. **83** — *S.H. (6/1/2004)*

Suncé Vineyard & Winery 2001 Nova Vineyard Old Vines Zinfandel (Clear Lake) $25. Bizarre, with medicinal, iodine aromas and flavors riding over the berries, and sharp acids. **82** —*S.H. (6/1/2004)*

SUNSET

Sunset 1999 Zinfandel (Dry Creek Valley) $23. Smells funky, with forest floor, hummus, and mushroom aromas mingling with riper scents of wild berries and sweet oak. The fruity flavors are well developed, and drink sweetly ripe, yet the wine has a one-dimensionality and is excessively soft. **85** —*S.H. (9/1/2002)*

SUNSTONE

Sunstone 2003 Eros Bordeaux Blend (Santa Ynez Valley) $50. Scores high on the deliciousness scale, with melted chocolate, blackberry jam, red cherry pie, and vanilla-coffee flavors. What's not to like? This Merlot-based wine is soft and creamy and dry. It's one of the best Bordeaux-style reds to come out of this valley. **90** —*S.H. (9/1/2006)*

Sunstone 1999 Eros Bordeaux Blend (Santa Ynez Valley) $36. If ever there was a vintage to ripen Bordeaux grapes in Santa Barbara, it was this one. This commendable effort is plush and opulent, balancing cassis fruit with earthy tobacco notes. It has style and class, and if it lacks the extra depth of top North Coast clarets, it's at least coming close. **90** —*S.H. (2/1/2003)*

Sunstone 2001 Chardonnay (Santa Barbara County) $18. Oaky, opening with a blast of char and vanilla that only gradually reveals underlying aromas of peaches and tropical fruit. Rich and full-bodied, with a solid grip of acidity. **86** —*S.H. (12/15/2002)*

Sunstone 2000 Chardonnay (Santa Barbara County) $18. Peaches and cream drizzled with cinnamon and brown sugar, with a swirl of vanilla—that's what this wine tastes like. It has the acidity to balance the sweetness, though, and a round and supple mouthfeel. **86** —*S.H. (4/1/2002)*

Sunstone 2000 Merlot (Santa Ynez Valley) $24. Fewer regions are more sensitive to site selection for Merlot than Santa Barbara County. Put it in a cool spot, and it turns vegetal. This wine has some of those notorious asparagus flavors that can plague South Coast Bordeaux varietals. It's extremely well made, but can't overcome this basic shortcoming. **85** — *S.H. (11/15/2002)*

Sunstone 1999 Merlot (Santa Barbara County) $24. Lots of funky bacon grease on the nose, and some sulfur notes, too, ride atop underlying blackberries. Supple in the mouth, with soft tannins and sharp acids; thoroughly dry. Fairly simple, although it has a textural elegance. **86** — *S.H. (4/1/2002)*

Sunstone 2003 Estate Merlot (Santa Ynez Valley) $36. Very aromatic, with scents of violets, ripe cherries, chocolate wintergreen mints, and smoky oak. This wine is polished and dry. It has a rich acid-tannin balance that calls for a nice barbecued steak. **87** —*S.H. (11/15/2006)*

Sunstone 1999 Reserve Merlot (Santa Ynez Valley) $30. This winery's reserve Merlot is richer than the regular release, and from a better vintage. It's marked by blackberry flavors edged with earth, notable oak, and dry, distinguished tannins. It's a young wine, a little rough now. The winemaker suggests aging for 10 years, which may be pushing it. **88** — *S.H. (11/15/2002)*

Sunstone 2005 Syrah Rosé Blend (Santa Ynez Valley) $26. Despite the pale color and delicate texture, this is a rich, full-bodied rosé, with plenty of flavor. Cherries, raspberries, roseship tea, cinnamon, white pepper, and vanilla mingle to a satisfying, dry finish. **88** —*S.H. (11/1/2006)*

Sunstone 2000 Sauvignon Blanc (Santa Ynez Valley) $14. Nice and refreshing, a lemon-flavored wine with a soft, silky mouthfeel. There are secondary apricot and honeysuckle flavors that add interest. The finish is a bit sweet and honeyed. **85** —*S.H. (4/1/2002)*

Sunstone 2003 Syrah (Santa Barbara County) $32. Unbalanced, with a Porty, caramelly nose leading to syrupy sweet cherry-cola flavors. **81** — *S.H. (11/15/2006)*

Sunstone 1999 Syrah (Santa Ynez Valley) $40. A lovely, elegant wine, with good balance and rich fruit. It's dry, with a soft, velvety mouthfeel and easy tannins. Not too fruity, with blackberry, peppery flavors, and earthier, herbal notes. It has quality written all over it, and is a good example of Syrah from warmer Santa Barbara vineyards. **90** —*S.H. (12/1/2002)*

Sunstone 2003 Estate Syrah (Santa Ynez Valley) $32. Has lots to like in the rich, ripe blackberry, cherry, cocoa, licorice, coffee, and spice flavors that are dusted with a touch of toasty oak. The wine finishes nicely dry, with some furry tannins. Drink now. **86** —*S.H. (11/15/2006)*

Sunstone 2003 Reserve Syrah (Santa Ynez Valley) $42. Richly textured, with blackberry, cola, espresso, and spicy oak flavors that are folded into soft, intricately laced tannins. Shows some heat on the finish. Drink now. **88** —*S.H. (12/1/2006)*

Sunstone 2000 Viognier (Santa Ynez Valley) $24. There's a lot of sulfur upon opening and it takes a lot of airing to blow off. Once it does, the wine reveals peach and smoky-spicy aromas and flavors and a clean, zesty spiciness. A little bit of sugar adds a honeyed richness. **85** —*S.H. (4/1/2002)*

SURH LUCHTEL

Surh Luchtel 2002 Cabernet Sauvignon (Napa Valley) $38. I would decant this wine for a few hours, because at first it's tough and herbal. Once it opens, it shows pretty cherry flavors, and the oak, while lavish, is proportional. Dry and youthful in tannins. Drink now through 2010. **88** —*S.H. (10/1/2005)*

Surh Luchtel 2001 Cabernet Sauvignon (Napa Valley) $35. Tighter, better structured, and more refined than the winery's Meritage bottling due to the higher percent of Cabernet. Shows classic notes of black currants and cassis with an intriguing scent of smoked meat. Finishes rich, dry, and balanced. **91** —*S.H. (10/1/2004)*

Surh Luchtel 1999 Cabernet Sauvignon (Napa Valley) $40. Another terrific Napa '99, this one packed with opulent flavors of cassis, green olives and herbs, wrapped generously in fine toasty oak. The wine is very dry and the tannins are fine and complex. The delicious finish goes on and on. **92** —*S.H. (8/1/2003)*

Surh Luchtel 2001 Sacrashe Vineyard Cabernet Sauvignon (Napa Valley) $40. The tightest, most tannic, and best of the winery's three 2001

releases. It's a wonderful example of a mountain Cabernet, with concentrated black currant fruit, crisp acidity, and intricate, sweet tannins. Just oozes class and distinction. Hard to resist drinking now, but should age gracefully for a decade or longer. **93 Editors' Choice** —*S.H. (10/1/2004)*

Surh Luchtel 1999 Mosaic Cabernet Sauvignon-Merlot (North Coast) $23. Opens with light, earthy aromas of berries and oak and a curious waft of autumn leaves, then turns soft and simple in the mouth. It's a pretty wine, dry and with some good structure, but no special depth. Might improve in the cellar, but it's a gamble. A blend of Cabernet Sauvignon and Merlot. **86** —*S.H. (9/1/2002)*

Surh Luchtel 2001 Mosaique Meritage (Napa Valley) $25. Quite a nice Bordeaux blend, rich in sugary blackberry and cherry fruit, with a chocolate-and-vanilla, desserty quality. Yet it's completely dry. The sweetness is balanced by good acidity and an array of dried herbs. **88** —*S.H. (10/1/2004)*

Surh Luchtel 2004 Garys' Vineyard Pinot Noir (Santa Lucia Highlands) $48. Ripe and exuberant, as you would expect from this vineyard, a mouthfilling Pinot strikes with ripe black cherry, raspberry, and mocha-choca flavors. Not a subtle Pinot Noir, but it certainly is flamboyant. **88** —*S.H. (11/15/2006)*

Surh Luchtel 2003 Garys' Vineyard Pinot Noir (Santa Lucia Highlands) $42. Cabernet specialist Surh Luchtel turns its hand to Central Coast Pinot Noir, with some success. The quality of the grapes must be responsible for the succulent, long-finishing black cherry and blueberry fruit, as well as the good acids. **87** —*S.H. (10/1/2005)*

Surh Luchtel 2003 Page Nord Vineyard Syrah (Oak Knoll) $38. A worthy followup to the excellent '02, this bottling seems riper and more chocolatey, with more apparent sweetness. Yet it has a firm tannic structure with good acidity. The basic flavors are of cassis, blackberry jam, cherries, and smoky leather, with sweet vanillins from new oak. **89** —*S.H. (11/15/2006)*

Surh Luchtel 2002 Page Nord Vineyard Syrah (Napa Valley) $35. This wine displays the fine combination of white pepper aromas and flamboyant blackberry fruit that marks a great California Syrah. It's deep and long in flavors that flood the palate, yet has firm tannins and crisp acids that lend structure. There's all sorts of chocolatey stuff going on, too. **90 Editors' Choice** *(9/1/2005)*

Surh Luchtel 1999 Zinfandel (Napa Valley) $27. From Chiles Valley, a heady wine with 15.3% alcohol that will appeal to fans of superripe Zin. The plummy flavors veer into Port-like notes of raisins and sweet chocolate, although the wine is fully fermented to dryness. **85** —*S.H. (9/1/2002)*

SUTTER HOME

Sutter Home 2000 Family Vineyard Selection Cabernet Sauvignon (California) $12. This simple country wine steps up to the plate with jammy berry flavors and sharp acids to cut through cheese. It's very dry. **83** —*S.H. (10/1/2004)*

Sutter Home 2003 White Cabernet Sauvignon (California) $5. Holds onto some real Cabernet character with its red currant and cherry flavors and smooth tannins. Tastes just off dry and clean. **84 Best Buy** —*S.H. (11/15/2004)*

Sutter Home 2000 Chardonnay (California) $6. This wine recalls the glory days of a decade ago, when there were dozens of delicious California Chardonnays available for under $8. Today this sort of forward, fruity, ripe, round wine is more likely to cost you twice that. Yet here is a creamy, cleanly made wine, showing plump, fresh fruit flavors and a lingering finish. Just 1.9 million cases made. **87** —*P.G. (11/15/2001)*

Sutter Home 1999 Chardonnay (California) $6. A blast of clean, ripe citrus, peach and pear fruit greets you from this well-made, if simple, wine. There are vanilla and smoke elements from wood. It's a little soft, and a tad off-dry, but if you need a case of something white to quench the throats of party-goers who aren't real particular, this is the ticket. **84** — *S.H. (2/1/2001)*

Sutter Home 1998 Chardonnay (California) $6. **85 Best Buy** —*S.H. (11/1/1999)*

Sutter Home 2002 Family Vineyard Selection Chardonnay (California) $11. Juicy, ripely fruity, and oaky, with a creamy texture. Finishes with banana cream pie. **84** —S.H. (10/1/2004)

Sutter Home 2000 Gewürztraminer (California) $6. The attractive passion-fruit, honey, fig, and tangerine aromas lead to a pleasantly fruity, soft wine, with a bit of sweetness. The finish is spicy, with the essence of ripe tree fruits lingering. **85** —S.H. (11/15/2001)

Sutter Home 1998 Rose Merlot (California) $7. It has a deep, candy-red color, but the nose is anything but candied, showing aromas of green olives, herbs, and blackberries. Salivatingly tart and only slightly sweet. The flavors are a combination of green olive and iced tea with lemon. It's not subtle, and would probably work with Buffalo wings. **80** —J.F. (8/1/2001)

Sutter Home 2003 White Merlot (California) $5. Soft and fruity, with cherry vanilla flavors and quite a lot of body. A good value in an inexpensive blush wine. **84 Best Buy** —S.H. (12/15/2004)

Sutter Home 2000 Moscato (California) $5. Delightfully fruity, with the freshest scents of peaches, flowers, and smoky honey. It's pretty sweet, but the peach flavors are balanced by crisp acidity and an ultraclean feel. Finishes sweet and spicy. **85 Best Buy** —S.H. (11/15/2001)

Sutter Home 2004 Pinot Grigio (California) $5. Clean and simple, this wine is very dry and crisp. It has pleasant lemon, lime, and grapefruit flavors and refreshing acids. **83** —S.H. (2/1/2006)

Sutter Home 2002 Pinot Grigio (California) $6. Fairly fresh and flowery in the nose, with a hint of banana. The flavor profile is built on apple and melon, while the finish is surprisingly clean and lengthy. The feel, however, is a bit soft and low-acid. **84 Best Buy** —M.S. (12/1/2003)

Sutter Home 1997 Pinot Noir (California) $6. 84 —T.R. (11/15/1999)

Sutter Home 1998 Sauvignon Blanc (California) $5. 87 Best Buy —S.H. (2/1/2000)

Sutter Home 1998 Shiraz (California) $6. 82 —S.H. (2/1/2000)

Sutter Home 2000 Zinfandel (California) $5. Delicately fruity; strawberry and raspberry flavors dominate this soft, off-dry wine. It's clean in the mouth, and has a spicy, honeyed aftertaste. **83** (11/15/2001)

Sutter Home 1999 Zinfandel (California) $6. From the folks who invented white Zinfandel, a freshly fruity, soft, slightly sweet wine with high enough acidity to keep it from palling. The color is pale pink, and the aromas recall red raspberries and peaches. **83** —S.H. (2/1/2001)

Sutter Home 1997 Zinfandel (California) $6. 82 —S.H. (2/1/2000)

Sutter Home 2002 White Zinfandel (California) $7. A pale, very fruity wine that gives white Zinfanatics everything they want at a good price. Raspberries, vanilla, and a sweet finish. **83** —S.H. (9/1/2004)

SWANSON

Swanson 2000 Alexis Bordeaux Blend (Napa Valley) $50. Kind of tough, with gritty tannins and an edge of herbs, but there's enough cherry-berry fruit to save it. More than that, it has a professional texture and balance that testify to its pedigreed origins. But it's still tough. A blend of Bordeaux varieties. **87** —S.H. (12/15/2003)

Swanson 1996 Alexis Bordeaux Blend (Napa Valley) $35. 91 —S.H. (6/1/1999)

Swanson 1997 Cabernet Sauvignon (Napa Valley) $40. 91 (11/1/2000)

Swanson 1999 Alexis Cabernet Sauvignon-Syrah (Napa Valley) $35. 91 —C.S. (11/15/2002)

Swanson 2001 Alexis Red Table Wine Cabernet Sauvignon-Syrah (Oakville) $50. A Cabernet Sauvignon and Syrah blend off the estate. The winemaker says the Syrah brings complexity and backbone, although I don't know that the Cabernet needs much help. But this is an extraordinary wine. It's richly sumptuous in chocolatey, black currant fruit, and soft as velvet, but without being cloying, due to the sweet tannins and bracing structure. **95 Editors' Choice** —S.H. (11/15/2004)

Swanson 1997 Merlot (Napa Valley) $28. 88 —J.C. (7/1/2000)

Swanson 2003 Merlot (Oakville) $32. Overripe, with a raisiny edge and some sharp Port and coffee acidity to the blackberry flavors. Malolactic probably helped, as does new French oak, but it's still a sharp, disappointing wine. **83** —S.H. (12/31/2006)

Swanson 2002 Merlot (Oakville) $30. I like this Merlot a lot. It's in-your-face with potent cherry, chocolate, and violet notes, as well as plenty of oak, and backed up with firm, chewy tannins. It has subtle nuances that keep you coming back for more. **91 Editors' Choice** —S.H. (11/1/2005)

Swanson 2001 Merlot (Oakville) $32. From a winery that seldom stumbles, a lush, sexy Merlot. Its cassis, unsweetened chocolate, and oak flavors are wrapped in chewy tannins that make your tongue stick to the gums. It's a young, dramatic wine. Drink now, with roast duck or pork tenderloin. **91** —S.H. (5/1/2005)

Swanson 2000 Merlot (Napa Valley) $30. This Merlot combines black cherry flavors with leaner ones of herbs and tobacco, and also contains a tough streak of astringency that seems unlikely to age away. It has some fine oak overlays that soften and sweeten, but it's still a young, aggressive wine best consumed early. **85** —S.H. (4/1/2004)

Swanson 1999 Merlot (Napa Valley) $21. Its concentrated flavors and deep, inky color gave one taster the impression that this wine was a Zin (remember, we're tasting blind, here). That hypothesis was understandable, given this Merlot's raspberry, mocha, and oak flavors, which are accented by some herb and white pepper. Begins and ends with similar notes, plus some mineral dustiness. A tasty, internationally styled wine, though not what you'd find in the dictionary under "Merlot." **87** —D.T. (12/31/2002)

Swanson 1996 Merlot (Napa Valley) $21. 93 (11/15/1999)

Swanson 1998 Pinot Grigio (Napa Valley) $18. 86 (8/1/1999)

Swanson 2004 Pinot Grigio (Napa Valley) $20. If you can imagine a Grigio with the class and balance of a good Napa Cab, this is it. To just describe the citrus flavors, dryness, and acidity doesn't do it justice. If you thought PG can only be a simple wine, try this one. **91** —S.H. (2/1/2006)

Swanson 2003 Pinot Grigio (Napa Valley) $20. Ripe and rich in apples, citrus fruits, and spearmint flavors that drink a little sweet, but there's a strong current of tingly acidity to offset the honeyed finish. Enjoy this stylish wine with shellfish. **86** —S.H. (5/1/2005)

Swanson 2002 Alexis Red Blend (Oakville) $55. This unconventional blend of Cabernet, Syrah, and Merlot is a classic Napa red, soft and luxurious and decadent, yet with a firm structure. It's enormously flavorful in sweet cassis and chocolate, with a firm, dry finish. **90** —S.H. (11/1/2005)

Swanson 1997 Alexis Red Table Wine Red Blend (Napa Valley) $45. 92 —M.S. (9/1/2000)

Swanson 1997 Sangiovese (Napa Valley) $24. 92 —S.H. (11/1/1999)

Swanson 1996 Late Harvest Sémillon (Napa Valley) $33. 88 —J.C. (12/31/1999)

Swanson 1998 Syrah (Napa Valley) $45. "Very fragrant" on the nose, wrote one panelist—a sentiment that was echoed by many who praised Swanson's super-ripe berry, plum, and grape fruit; vanillin oak and slight peach aromas. Red berries, cocoa, and oak pop up on the palate. The finish, however long, intrigued us, with its vanilla and orange flavors, and lollipop-candy texture. **89** (11/1/2001)

SWITCHBACK RIDGE

Switchback Ridge 1999 Cabernet Sauvignon (Napa Valley) $65. A beautifully balanced wine, framed in plush, ripe, velvety tannins and backed by lush, black cherry, plum, blackberry, spice, herb, and chocolate flavors. Gloriously complex, seamless in its elegance, the wine is packed with charm and personality; long on the finish. **95** —J.M. (6/1/2002)

Switchback Ridge 2000 Peterson Family Vineyard Merlot (Napa Valley) $48. A thick, dark Merlot, cloaked in smooth, fat tannins and redolent of cherry, licorice, blackberry, plum, spice, coffee, sage, thyme, and hints of orange peel. Long and sleek, with toasty oak on the finish. Just a hint of tartness at the end, but still a terrific wine. **92** —J.M. (8/1/2003)

Switchback Ridge 1999 Peterson Family Vineyard Merlot (Napa Valley) $48. Kicks off with gobs of chocolate and spice aromas, then fans out to reveal layers of black currant, blackberry, coffee, herb, and spice flavors.

USA

A touch of acidity accentuates the tannins, but the wine is richly textured, full bodied, and delightful nonetheless. Full, ripe, and distinctive. **92** —*J.M. (8/1/2003)*

Switchback Ridge 2000 Peterson Family Vineyard Petite Sirah (Napa Valley) $45. This dark, dramatic young wine was a tasters' favorite. Well-extracted, with huge flavors of black cherry, blueberry, coffee, tar, spice, and herbs, its robust tannins suggest ageability. But it's so ripe and sweet in fruit, it's exciting to drink now. **91** *(4/1/2003)*

SYLVESTER

Sylvester 2002 Syrah (Paso Robles) $14. A little heavy and soft, but the ripe cherry, spice, and oak flavors are nice. Finishes with a dusting of tannins. **84** —*S.H. (12/1/2004)*

SYNCLINE

Syncline 2003 Late Harvest Chenin Blanc (Columbia Valley (WA)) $18. From 22-year-old vines, this is 100% barrel-fermented, and retains 20.5% residual sugar. Still, it's not cloying; it's lively with stone fruits, mown hay, and some high-toned esters. It tastes of apples, butterscotch, and candy; finishes long with plenty of acid support. **92** —*P.G. (9/1/2004)*

Syncline 2003 Rosé Grenache (Columbia Valley (WA)) $13. A gorgeous bottle, dry and persistent, showing pretty strawberry/cherry fruit, some bread dough yeastiness, and a long, smooth finish. This is made as a saignée, with the pressed juice going into the winery's Subduction Red. Gorgeous effort. **90** —*P.G. (9/1/2004)*

Syncline 2002 Celilo Vineyard Pinot Noir (Washington) $20. A sturdy style, with thick, not heavy flavors of strawberry and pomegranate and cranberry. An interesting style, neither Oregonian nor Burgundian, but big and broad, with somewhat rustic but flavorful fruit. Perfumed, clean, and lightly spicy. **88** —*P.G. (11/1/2004)*

Syncline 2001 Subduction Red Red Blend (Columbia Valley (WA)) $14. Here's a very popular, fruity, and accessible blend. No focused, varietal character, and none intended. Just a soft, tasty, value red wine. **87** —*P.G. (9/1/2003)*

Syncline 2004 Milbrandt Vineyards Syrah (Columbia Valley (WA)) $22. A superb follow-up to the winery's 2003 Milbrandt, it's the same 40/60 blend from Clifton and Sundance, both located in Washington's new Wahluke Slope AVA. A penetrating nose of cherries, violets, blueberries, and black olives leads into a wine that masks its power with finesse. Licorice, tar, and smoke wrap around the bright raspberry fruit core, with just a whiff of white pepper. Great winemaking, and a price point more wineries should emulate. **93** —*P.G. (6/1/2006)*

Syncline 2002 Milbrandt Vineyards Syrah (Columbia Valley (WA)) $20. Sweet, spicy, almost pungent with meaty, bright berry scents. It shows a beautiful nose, fragrant, and seductive, spiced with white pepper, blueberry, and violets. It's clean and lifted, with everything—alcohol included—in balance. **89** —*P.G. (9/1/2004)*

Syncline 2001 Milbrandt Vineyards Syrah (Columbia Valley (WA)) $20. Rough, tannic, and oaky, this has a lot of power and presence. A resonant, deep, densely fruity wine, with rich, liquorous, tannic flavors, lingering sweetness and a finishing kiss of sweet oak. **90** —*P.G. (9/1/2003)*

Syncline 2002 Reserve Syrah (Columbia Valley (WA)) $30. The blend is 94% Syrah, 5% Grenache, and 1% Viognier. New oak is apparent, displaying roasted coffee, bitter chocolate, and vanilla cream flavors. Very smooth. **90** —*P.G. (9/1/2004)*

Syncline 2003 Reserve McKinley Springs Vineyard Syrah (Columbia Valley (WA)) $30. Ambitiously styled, with a thick, voluptuous mouthfeel and lavish notes of smoke, toast, and chocolate. If it sounds oaky, it is, but it still tastes good, with enough blackberry fruit to stand up to the wood. Finishes with a softly dusty note and ripe tannins. **89** *(9/1/2005)*

Syncline 2004 Viognier (Columbia Valley (WA)) $20. 360 cases were made of this rich and creamy Viognier. Scents of lemon and lime and rose petals lead into flavors of Meyer lemon, with a custardy mouthfeel. The wine retains a pleasing, citrus/tangerine crispness through the finish. **89** —*P.G. (12/15/2005)*

Syncline 2003 Clifton Vineyard Viognier (Columbia Valley (WA)) $20. This is a penetrating, ripe style. It's a nice effort with this difficult grape, big but not blowsy, with nuances of orange peel, citrus, apricot, and honeysuckle. **88** —*P.G. (9/1/2004)*

SYZYGY

Syzygy 2003 Cabernet Sauvignon (Columbia Valley (WA)) $30. Good vineyard sources, as usual, including Conner Lee, Minnick Hills, Sagemoor and Charbonneau, create a firm foundation for this classic, pure-blooded Cabernet. Cassis and berry flavors infuse the fruit, sculpted with spicy, savory oak. Nicely done, stylish winemaking. **89** —*P.G. (10/1/2006)*

Syzygy 2004 Red Blend (Columbia Valley (WA)) $20. This ripe, high-toned mix of Cabernet Sauvignon, Syrah, Merlot, and Malbec shows ripe cherry and plum flavors, balancing acids and a smooth, lightly chocolatey finish. It's pushing 15% alcohol and finishes with a bit of heat. **88** —*P.G. (10/1/2006)*

Syzygy 2003 Red Blend (Columbia Valley (WA)) $20. Half Merlot, one quarter Cab and one quarter Syrah, this is sappy and packed with good fruit. The mix of red and black berries runs right into nicely-nuanced oak flavors of caramel and mocha. **88** —*P.G. (4/1/2006)*

Syzygy 2003 Syrah (Walla Walla (WA)) $28. Don't ask us how to pronounce the name, we just have to spell it. Combines herbal, minty notes with bright red berries borne along a creamy mouthfeel. Shows just a touch of alcoholic heat on the finish. **87** *(9/1/2005)*

Syzygy 2003 Syrah (Walla Walla (WA)) $28. The excellent fruit sources include Morrison Lane, Les Collines, and Seven Hills vineyards. This is a thick, sappy wine that shows the citrus zest character that often comes from Morrison Lane. Lifted, spicy, and grapy. **88** —*P.G. (4/1/2006)*

TABLAS CREEK

Tablas Creek 1999 Reserve Cuvée Bordeaux Blend (Paso Robles) $35. It has the density of body and texture that big, ageable red wines have, but the stuffing, not to mention the acidity, doesn't seem to be there. It's hard to separate out what you know of the ambitions of this winery, which aims to produce Chateâuneuf-style wine in California. This is a fascinating work in progress. A blend of Mourvèdre, Grenache, Syrah, and Counoise. **87** —*S.H. (11/15/2002)*

Tablas Creek 2000 Antithesis Chardonnay (Paso Robles) $35. Viscous, yet bright and mineral-like with a pretty core of lemon, apple, pear and melon notes. Really sleek and clean, but lush and seductive at the same time. Long and lovely at the end. **91** —*J.M. (5/1/2002)*

Tablas Creek 2004 Grenache Blanc Grenache (Paso Robles) $27. Fairly simple and a little sweet, this wine is tart in citrusy acids, with flavors of lemon sorbet, apricot, and kiwi. The acids make the ripe fruit clean and bright on the long finish. **86** —*S.H. (6/1/2006)*

Tablas Creek 2000 Côtes de Tablas Grenache-Syrah (Paso Robles) $25. Even muskier and more leathery than Tablas' Esprit bottling, with aromas bordering on well-hung meat and chocolate. But the flavors are ripe and completely satisfying. Blackberry, blueberry, cherry, and black raspberry only begin to describe them. Meanwhile, the textural tannins are soft and fine, reminiscent of a very good Napa Cabernet. **89** —*S.H. (3/1/2004)*

Tablas Creek 2003 Mourvèdre (Paso Robles) $32. Like others in California, Tablas struggles to find Mourvèdre's soul. This wine shows flavors of blackberries, plums, and chocolate, with an undercurrent of wild herbs and oak. Yet it's thick and soft. The challenge is to find life and structure. **84** —*S.H. (10/1/2005)*

Tablas Creek 2002 Côtes de Tablas Red Blend (Paso Robles) $22. A bit raw and earthy, with berry-cherry and cocoa flavors and soft, gentle tannins. Easy to drink, and there's a nice spicy finish. **85** —*S.H. (2/1/2005)*

Tablas Creek 2002 Esprit de Beaucastel Red Blend (Paso Robles) $40. This Mourvèdre-dominated wine doesn't have the super-hung meat, gamey aroma that plagued previous vintages. Instead, it offers complex aromas of ripe stone fruits and berries, with a suggestion of leather, herbs, and smoky oak. It's soft and creamy, but the tannins kick in on the finish. Drinkable now, and could improve dramatically through the decade. **89** —*S.H. (2/1/2005)*

USA

Tablas Creek 2001 Côtes de Tablas Rhône Red Blend (Paso Robles) $22. This very enjoyable wine is marked by intense aromas and flavors of cherries. They're very pure and ripe, and nuanced with additional notes of sweet, dried herbs, especially rosemary. Has the soft voluptuousness of a Merlot with the silky tannins of a Pinot Noir. **89** —S.H. (5/1/2004)

Tablas Creek 2003 Côtes de Tablas Rhône Red Blend (Paso Robles) $20. A little simple, but the cherry and vanilla flavors are so tasty, you reach for another glass. There are complexities of vanilla, mocha, cinnamon, and white pepper in this blend of Grenache, Syrah, Mourvèdre, and Counoise. **86** —S.H. (10/1/2005)

Tablas Creek 2003 Esprit de Beaucastel Rhône Red Blend (Paso Robles) $40. Tablas has an increasing roster of red wines, but this flagship remains their best. It's rich, balanced, soft, complex, and satisfying, a fine California-Châteauneuf. A blend of Mourvèdre, Syrah, Grenache, and Counoise, it shows cherry and chocolate flavors, with a delicate veneer of oak. **89** —S.H. (10/1/2005)

Tablas Creek 2000 Esprit de Beaucastel Rhône Red Blend (Paso Robles) $35. A musky, animal-scented wine, which may put some sniffers off. If you can get past that, it is superb. Brilliantly fruity, with a mélange of berry and spice flavors, rich tannins, and the good acidity that comes from West Side Paso grapes. **91** —S.H. (12/1/2003)

Tablas Creek 1999 Petite Cuvée: Grenache, Syrah, Mourvèdre Rhône Red Blend (Paso Robles) $25. A big, fleshy blend of Grenache, Syrah, and Mourvèdre that serves up rich, chewy tannins supporting ripe plum, black cherry, herb, and toast flavors. Moderate and elegant on the finish. **88** —J.M. (7/1/2002)

Tablas Creek 2000 Rose Rhône Red Blend (Paso Robles) $27. Pretty expensive for a blush wine. Strives to marry Big Red-like complexity with the silky clean coolness of a dry white wine. The raspberry and sweet tobacco flavor is lovely, and the finish tastes like wild sage honey. A blend of Mourvèdre, Grenache, and Counoise. **90** —S.H. (9/1/2003)

Tablas Creek 2002 Côtes de Tablas Blanc Rhône White Blend (Paso Robles) $22. Polished, complex, delicious, and compelling, and at the top of the heap of California white Rhônes. The white peach and tropical fruit flavors are joined with slaty minerals and dried herbs, ending with a honeyed flourish. A blend of Viognier, Marsanne, Grenache Blanc, and Roussanne. **91 Editors' Choice** —S.H. (2/1/2004)

Tablas Creek 2003 Vin de Paille Rhône White Blend (Paso Robles) $65. One of the few paille-style wines in California, but I must say this method of inducing sweetness doesn't threaten good old-fashioned botrytis. There's a rusticity to the sweet apricot flavors that does not justify the price. **84** —S.H. (10/1/2005)

Tablas Creek 2005 Rosé Blend (Paso Robles) $27. The first of the highly anticipated '05s are starting to appear, and to judge from this wine, west side Paso Rhônes will be winners. The wine benefited from a cool vintage, allowing the Mourvèdre, Grenache, and Counoise long hang time, yet avoiding overly ripe fruit. Dark, fully dry, racy in acidity and full-bodied for a rosé, this complex blush has an almost Pinot Noir-like weight. **90** —S.H. (11/1/2006)

Tablas Creek 2004 Rosé Blend (Paso Robles) $25. The purest, most powerful aromas and flavors of cherries dominate this Rhône blend, but it's not a simple wine. The cherries are joined with red raspberries, vanilla, sweet anise, white pepper, and tangerine zest, boosted by crisp acidity. This is a beautiful, dry, long-finished wine. **90** —S.H. (10/1/2005)

Tablas Creek 2003 Rosé Blend (Paso Robles) $27. A great California rose, this Provencal-like blush is totally fulfilling. It offers a complex array of flavors ranging from rosehip tea, raspberry, and dried herbs to vanilla bean and cocoa. Dry, lush, and creamy, this wine is one more proof that Tablas Creek is absolutely at the top of their game. **91** —S.H. (3/1/2005)

Tablas Creek 2002 Rosé Blend (Paso Robles) $26. One of the darker rosés you'll ever see, rose petal in color. Opens with clean, inviting aromas of cherries and raspberries, and drinks enormously flavorful, with all sorts of wild berries and tree fruits flooding the palate. Beautiful acidity, the kind that tingles the tongue and makes the wine come alive. Finishes dry and balanced. One of the best California rosés in memory. **90** —S.H. (3/1/2004)

Tablas Creek 1999 Rosé Blend (Paso Robles) $27. Clean and crisp, with light berry and herb flavors forming core elements. It tapers off gently on the finish with classy mineral notes. The wine should work well with oysters, sole, and other mild fish, poultry, and vegetarian cuisine. From the California branch of the folks that make Château de Beaucastel, in Southern France, where rosé is de rigeur for summertime. **88** —J.M. (12/1/2001)

Tablas Creek 2004 Roussanne (Paso Robles) $27. Tablas Creek continues to struggle with this difficult varietal in their vineyards on the far west side of Paso Robles. Like the '03, this wine is fruity, with plentiful peach and vanilla flavors, yet it has a simplicity and sugary finish. Must have been the harvest heat. **84** —S.H. (11/1/2006)

Tablas Creek 2003 Roussanne (Paso Robles) $27. With powerful flavors of peaches, papayas, vanilla honey, and spice, this fruit-forward wine is nicely dry and complex, but a little heavy. Would benefit from more acidity. **86** —S.H. (10/1/2005)

Tablas Creek 2002 Roussanne (Paso Robles) $26. Distinctive for its white chocolate flavor and rich, creamy texture. There are also flamboyant notes of guava, nectarine, peach, wildflowers, vanilla, and smoke. This opulent wine is filled with vibrant acidity, and is excellently balanced. It is a sure candidate to improve for at least five years in the cellar. **90** —S.H. (2/1/2004)

Tablas Creek 2003 Syrah (Paso Robles) $32. Tablas continues to work to advance red Rhônes in their western corner of Paso Robles. The wine shows an edge of tangy acidity and tannin that provides relief to the cherry, cocoa, coffee, and peppery spice flavors. Finishes dry and fruity, and probably at its best now. **87** —S.H. (10/1/2005)

Tablas Creek 2000 Clos Blanc White Blend (Paso Robles) $35. A fascinating wine that weaves tight strands of lemon and mineral flavors. Smooth, silky texture and bright richness offer mounds of pleasure and intrigue on the palate. Long and lush at the end. **92** —J.M. (9/1/2002)

Tablas Creek 2003 Côtes de Tablas Blanc White Blend (Paso Robles) $22. A little brother of the Esprit Blanc, and while it's nowhere as rich, it's a noble wine of considerable nuance. Apricot, peach, fig, vanilla, and toast flavors mingle in a creamy texture that finishes long and spicy. **91** —S.H. (2/1/2005)

Tablas Creek 2003 Esprit de Beaucastel Blanc White Blend (Paso Robles) $35. A fabulous white Rhône blend of enormous complexity and charm. Fills the mouth with butterscotch, crème brûlée, pineapple, stony mineral, vanilla, impossibly ripe white peach, and creamy hazelnut flavors, and as sweet as that sounds, the wine is dry and crisp. The greatest Esprit Blanc ever. Roussanne, Grenache Blanc, and Viognier. **95** —S.H. (2/1/2005)

Tablas Creek 2002 Esprit de Beaucastel Blanc White Blend (Paso Robles) $35. Interesting, complex, and different from the usual fare. This Roussanne, Grenache Blanc, and Viognier blend has nutty flavors subtly enhanced with white peach and tropical flowers. There's a hit of smoky oak and vanilla in there, but not too much. Drinks young and fresh, and should improve through 2008. **92** —S.H. (5/1/2004)

Tablas Creek 2001 Esprit de Beaucastel Blanc White Blend (Paso Robles) $35. An enormously complex wine, a real step forward in a California dry white wine. These Rhône grapes blend tropical fruit and peach flavors with tangy minerals and dried herbs. Despite the big flavors, the wine has lively acidity, and is a guaranteed cellar candidate for a decade. A blend of Roussanne, Viognier, Grenache, and Marsanne. **94** —S.H. (12/1/2003)

Tablas Creek 1998 Tablas Blanc White Blend (Paso Robles) $30. 90 —S.H. (10/1/1999)

Tablas Creek 1997 Tablas Blanc White Blend (Paso Robles) $30. 92 —S.H. (10/1/1999)

TABLE ROCK

Table Rock 1999 Merlot (Rogue Valley) $19. Black pepper, meat, and wild game aromas are interesting and distinct. The dark chocolate and herbal flavors have just a touch of raspberry, and are masked by aggressive tannins that should settle with time. **85** —C.S. (12/31/2002)

USA

Table Rock 1999 Pinot Noir (Rogue Valley) $16. This bright, friendly wine from southern Oregon's Rogue Valley shows appealing sour cherry, plum, and beet flavors on a lean frame. Brisk yet even, its chocolate and herb notes accent tart fruit on the finish. Light and tasty, it's best consumed now through 2004. **85** *(10/1/2002)*

TAFT STREET

Taft Street 1998 Chardonnay (Monterey County) $15. 87 *(6/1/2000)*

Taft Street 1998 Chardonnay (Russian River Valley) $15. 88 *(6/1/2000)*

Taft Street 2001 Chardonnay (Monterey County) $7. Monterey grapes star in this juicy wine, with its bright flavors of tropical and citrus fruits, steely acidity, and spicy notes of toasty oak and vanilla. The yummy flavors float in a creamy-smooth texture. Taft Street has long been known as an overlooked find. Its Chardonnays have consistently scored well in our tastings. **87 Best Buy** —*S.H. (11/15/2003)*

Taft Street 2003 Pinot Noir (Sonoma Coast) $15. This is a pretty nice Pinot that straddles the line between complex and simple. It's very dry and tart with acids, with an earthy, mushroomy profile that carries notes of cherries, blackberries, and oak. A good price for a wine of this quality from this appellation. **87** —*S.H. (12/15/2005)*

Taft Street 2004 Poplar Vineyard Sauvignon Blanc (Russian River Valley) $15. There's a lot going on in this dry, tart wine, with its vivid flavors of gooseberry, lime, grapefruit, and passion fruit. From a single vineyard, it possesses an intensity and focus that make it particularly enjoyable. **88** —*S.H. (12/15/2005)*

Taft Street 1997 Zinfandel (Sonoma County) $12. 83 —*P.G. (11/15/1999)*

Taft Street 1998 Zinfandel (Dry Creek Valley) $NA. Cherry-scented, clean, and fruity. Good concentration mid-palate, with no discernible new oak, just a balanced, firm attack and a strong, chewy finish. Only 123 cases made. **87** —*P.G. (3/1/2001)*

Taft Street 2003 Old Vines Zinfandel (Russian River Valley) $20. Rustic and semi-sweet, this Zin is very fruity. It has a briary, peppery edge to the cherries and blackberries. **82** —*S.H. (12/15/2005)*

TAGARIS

Tagaris 1999 Chardonnay (Columbia Valley (WA)) $10. The fruit is simple and lemony-tart, and there is a hint of pepper, which carries through. Generic and light, it finishes with a hint of onion. **83** —*P.G. (7/1/2002)*

Tagaris 2001 Johannisberg Riesling (Columbia Valley (WA)) $7. Here is a beautifully rendered, vividly fruity Washington Riesling. Crisp green apple flavors combine with succulently sweet citrus in a classic, off-dry style. **88** —*P.G. (9/1/2002)*

Tagaris 2001 Reserve Johannisberg Riesling (Columbia Valley (WA)) $8. Tagaris makes two Rieslings, priced just a buck apart. The "Reserve" may be just a stitch tighter, with more creaminess in the mouth, less in-your-face fruit. **88** —*P.G. (9/1/2002)*

TALBOTT

Talbott 2003 Cuvée Cynthia Chardonnay (Monterey County) $60. This is a best barrel selection from Sleepy Hollow Vineyard, in the Santa Lucia Highlands. Only 430 cases were produced. It's a tremendous Chardonnay, just huge in the white Burgundy mode: ripe tropical fruit, new oak, lees, unfined and unfiltered. Right now, it's a little gangly, like an adolescent who's growing too fast. But we know this wine knits together as it ages. Best 2007–2011. **95 Cellar Selection** —*S.H. (12/31/2006)*

Talbott 2002 Cuvée Cynthia Chardonnay (Monterey County) $55. Anyone can get ripe flavors from Chardonnay grapes these days, but this barrel selection, from the famous Sleepy Hollow Vineyard, is bold in kiwi, pear, and nectarine fruit, with toasty oak and lees seasoning. What makes it spectacular is the acidity, which gashes the palate like a bolt of lightning. Endlessly complex, this is a Chardonnay to linger over. Let it warm up in the glass and watch it change. **95 Editors' Choice** —*S.H. (12/31/2005)*

Talbott 1998 Cuvée Cynthia Chardonnay (Monterey) $45. Rich opening aromas of pineapple, pear, and lime plus toast and leesy accents open to a round palate of sweet pear, apple, vanilla, and pineapple flavors. This nicely balanced, medium-weight wine is smooth, but the new wood really dominates the lengthy close. **89** *(7/1/2001)*

Talbott 2002 Diamond T Estate Chardonnay (Monterey) $65. This has typical Talbottian heft, a gigantic Chard enormously rich in oak and munificent in flavor. Light pressing has captured the quintessence of cool-climate Chardonnay, heavenly rich and powerful, a flood of pineapple tart, Key lime pie, crème brûlée, smoky meringue, and vanilla cinnamon toast. **96 Editors' Choice** —*S.H. (12/31/2006)*

Talbott 2001 Diamond T Estate Chardonnay (Monterey) $65. Tasted with Talbott's wickedly decadent 2002 Cuvée Cynthia. This is a more eccentric wine, showing its extra year of age, and that is its strength and its weakness. The fruit is turning autumn leafy, with hints of oregano and dill, but is bone dry and clean. **87** —*S.H. (12/31/2005)*

Talbott 2000 Diamond T Estate Chardonnay (Monterey County) $65. Pours an unusually dark gold for a Chard, and is picking up aged characteristics, with its fruit overshadowed by a trail mix of toasted cashews and apricots and yeasty sherry. Complex and fascinating for aficionados, but drink now, as it's likely to go downhill from here. **91** —*S.H. (12/1/2004)*

Talbott 1998 Diamond T Estate Chardonnay (Monterey) $55. From the orange, creamy buttermilk and earthy notes on the nose to the dry mineral, herb, and Asian pear palate, there's much to savor here—such as the balance, proportion, and long, citrus-mineral finish. This is a complex and reserved wine, not a conventional, in-your-face bottling. It's rather tight now, but if you give it two years (or more!), you'll be well rewarded. **91** *(7/1/2001)*

Talbott 2002 Diamond T Estate Cuvée Audrey Chardonnay (Monterey) $75. This tiny-production, best-of-barrels bottling is incredibly rich, and not unlike grand cru Burgundy. There are similarities in the Baroque structure and complex, layered lemondrop flavors that new oak so flatters. There's a tight, minerally acidity; it's a little leesy-sour right now, and all the parts haven't come together, but for sheer dazzle, you can't beat it. Cellar until the end of 2006 and drink through 2008. **96 Editors' Choice** —*S.H. (7/1/2006)*

Talbott 2003 Kali Hart Chardonnay (Monterey County) $13. Ripe and juicy in mango, pineapple, and pear flavors, with a generous dollop of toasty oak and a vanilla cream texture. Finishes a bit sharp in acidity, but refreshing and tasty. **85** —*S.H. (6/1/2005)*

Talbott 2003 Sleepy Hollow Chardonnay (Santa Lucia Highlands) $42. The winery must have held this back this long to let the acidity soften, but it's still a crisp Chardonnay. A big one, too, packed with tropical fruit, roasted coconut, creamy lees, steely mineral, and new oak flavors. Give it until 2007 to resolve itself. **90** —*S.H. (12/15/2006)*

Talbott 2001 Sleepy Hollow Chardonnay (Monterey County) $42. What a wonderful wine! It's juicy and zesty in fresh acidity, a wine that makes the palate come alive. At the same time, dazzlingly rich in ripe tropical fruit, spice, and oak, with a long, honeyed finish. Oozes decadence, and will hang in there for 3 to 5 years. **93** —*S.H. (12/1/2004)*

Talbott 2002 Sleepy Hollow Vineyard Chardonnay (Monterey County) $39. Cool climate all the way, from the brisk, metallic, acidic mouthfeel to the flavors of citrus zest, with a hint of peach. The winemaker has added notes of lees and delicate oak that enrich the wine and bring it to completion. **90** —*S.H. (12/15/2005)*

Talbott 2000 Sleepy Hollow Vineyard Chardonnay (Monterey County) $42. Talbott's celebrated Chard, now in its 20th vintage, helped make Monterey's reputation. This year it's vigorous and masculine, with strong acids and a streak of mineral. But the tropical fruit flavors are ripe and opulent, and oak adds layers of cream, toast, and vanilla. Compelling, and it has the structure for aging through the decade. **93** —*S.H. (12/1/2003)*

Talbott 1999 Sleepy Hollow Vineyard Chardonnay (Santa Lucia Highlands) $35. Brilliantly crisp, with a palate-shattering blast of acidity boosting the tight lime and lemon flavors. But oak brings vanilla and a rich, creamy texture. Significant lees aging adds milky, yeasty complexities. Best after 2004. **89** —*S.H. (5/1/2003)*

Talbott 1998 Sleepy Hollow Vineyard Chardonnay (Monterey) $35. A touch of mint graces the tropical fruit-laden nose of this respected Monterey bottling. Fruit driven yet taut, the orange, pineapple, apple, and herbal notes here show an earth-and-mineral complexity without the common overt oakiness. If you are fan of less-overtly oaked wines, this is a medium-weight, stylish offering with personality and fine balance. **88** *(7/1/2001)*

Talbott 1999 Case Sleepy Hollow Vineyard Pinot Noir (Monterey County) $42. The flavors range from cola and soy, to ripe raspberries and cherries to sweet plum, and it's all wrapped in lots of smoky oak. The flavors are big but the texture is easy and lilting, with firm acids. Flirts with simplicity, but has enough layers to rise above it. **90** *—S.H. (3/1/2004)*

Talbott 2001 Logan Pinot Noir (Monterey) $18. A pretty dreadful wine from an otherwise esteemed producer. Clearly vegetal, with asparagus aromas and a syrupy texture. **81** *—S.H. (10/1/2005)*

Talbott 2000 Sleepy Hollow Vineyard CASE Pinot Noir (Monterey County) $45. A challenging wine. Rather raw and heavy out of the bottle, but benefits greatly with long decanting. Then, the cherry and cassis fruit opens up. But it's still a young, hard wine. Could develop through 2008 and beyond. Tasted twice. **87** *—S.H. (6/1/2005)*

TALISMAN

Talisman 2001 Pinot Noir (Russian River Valley) $36. A smooth-textured wine, with pretty cherry notes at its core. It fans out to reveal hints of licorice, smoke, and herbs, all framed in elegant tannins. The finish is moderate in length. **89** *—J.M. (10/1/2004)*

Talisman 2001 Kathy's Cuvée Pinot Noir (Carneros) $40. Well-defined and focused, with fine-tuned tannins that support a complex web of black cherry, licorice, herb, raspberry, coffee, and spice flavors. Long and smooth on the finish. The wine's named in honor of Kathy Polucha-Kessler, who died in an avalanche while skiing. A portion of the profits from sales go to the Truckee Donner Land Trust in her name. **91** *—J.M. (10/1/2004)*

Talisman 2002 Truchard Vineyard Pinot Noir (Carneros) $38. This is a delicious and complex wine that expresses the essence of Carneros Pinot Noir: balance, elegance, and harmony. Not a blockbuster in the Santa Lucia sense, it's a silky, feminine wine, with a great depth of cherry, cola, and mocha flavor, and a racy, sensual mouthfeel. **92** *—S.H. (12/15/2005)*

TALLEY

Talley 2000 Chardonnay (Arroyo Grande Valley) $24. Crisp, delicate Chard, shining with acidity that underscores peach and apple flavors. Considerable oak shows up in the form of smoke, vanilla, char, and toast. Fans out over the palate to finish long and spicy. **89** *—S.H. (2/1/2003)*

Talley 1999 Chardonnay (Arroyo Grande Valley) $24. Man, this sure is good wine, featuring plenty of ripe, forward fruit suggesting spicy green apples, succulent peaches, and even tropical fruits, with plush notes of toasty oak and vanilla. In the mouth, it's absolutely delicious, limpid, and refined. A rich, cream texture carries waves of fruit and spice flavors that seem tot change with every second. Thankfully, it's quite dry. This lovely wine doesn't need a dollop of leftover sugar to flatter the palate. **93** *(12/31/2001)*

Talley 1998 Chardonnay (Arroyo Grande Valley) $22. Deep, layered aromas of smoky honey, lees, and the ripest peaches. In the mouth, it's satisfyingly complex: dry, with a huge blast of fruit, honey, spice, and a creamy texture. The finish lasts a long time. **91** *—S.H. (2/1/2001)*

Talley 2004 Estate Chardonnay (Arroyo Grande Valley) $26. The combination of brisk acidity and perfectly ripened kiwi, tangerine, and papaya fruit makes for one beautiful Chardonnay. Oak adds smoky, vanilla, and buttered toast notes. The result is a captivating wine, rich and elegantly tailored. **91** *—S.H. (6/1/2006)*

Talley 2004 Oliver's Vineyard Chardonnay (Edna Valley) $22. So much richer than the '03, and a really nice example of Edna Valley terroir. The wine is brilliant in acidity, giving it an uplifted, bright mouthfeel. The flavors of kiwi, tangerine, and smoky oak are delicious. **87** *—S.H. (6/1/2006)*

Talley 1999 Oliver's Vineyard Chardonnay (Edna Valley) $20. Ripe, tropical fruit aromas mark this spicy, well-made wine. The aromas veer toward breadfruit, mango, and even banana, with Oriental spice notes of ginger and cinnamon. Drinks rich and powerful, with up-front fruit, and finishes long and spicy. **88** *—S.H. (2/1/2001)*

Talley 1998 Oliver's Vineyard Chardonnay (Edna Valley) $20. 86 *(6/1/2000)*

Talley 2002 Oliver's Vineyard Chardonnay (Edna Valley) $20. Oak hits you first, bringing vanilla, buttered toast, and wood spice. Beyond that, the tropical fruit flavors are strong. This is an interesting, rich wine, and while it is not great, it represents the seductive power of well-grown Chards from this area. **89** *—S.H. (6/1/2004)*

Talley 2000 Oliver's Vineyard Chardonnay (Edna Valley) $20. First rate, with all the snappy pizazz you could ask for. The fruit is tremendously extracted and deeply flavored with peaches and tropical fruits, sprinkled with dusty oriental spices. Long on oak, with bright acidity, it's a clean, extremely enjoyable wine. The long complex finish alone is worth the price, which is a good value for its quality. **90** *—S.H. (12/31/2001)*

Talley 2004 Rincon Vineyard Chardonnay (Arroyo Grande Valley) $38. It's a mystery how, in such a hot vintage, Talley produced this dry, minerally, almost austere Chardonnay. When everyone else was getting mangoes, this wine shows flint along with lime zest and kiwi. Yet the mark of Rincon Chard always has been a steely stoniness. The oak regime is big, but the wine handles it with aplomb. Best now through 2008. **92 Editors' Choice** *—S.H. (12/1/2006)*

Talley 2003 Rincon Vineyard Chardonnay (Arroyo Grande Valley) $36. This is a young, tight wine. It stuns with strong acidity and a bitter lime zest, almost gooseberry tartness. But it's nobly structured, and badly in need of a year or two in the cellar, or extended decanting. Oxygen and warming up bring out exciting notes of tropical fruits, buttercream, and oak. **92** *—S.H. (12/1/2005)*

Talley 2000 Rincon Vineyard Chardonnay (Arroyo Grande Valley) $35. Similar to Talley's Rosemary's Vineyard Chard, with a lean, minerally edge to the polished apple flavors. Bright acids burst on the palate, while doses of oak and lees provide softer, creamier notes. **90** *—S.H. (2/1/2003)*

Talley 1997 Rincon Vineyard Chardonnay (Arroyo Grande Valley) $20. 88 *—S.H. (10/1/1999)*

Talley 2004 Rosemary's Vineyard Chardonnay (Arroyo Grande Valley) $45. This year's Rosemary's is dry, crisp in citrusy acids, and wonderfully complex. It shows fresh, sweet pineapple fruit and spicy overtones of cinnamon and nutmeg along with layers of minerals and dried herbs. Easily takes its place in the front ranks of California Chardonnay. **95 Editors' Choice** *—S.H. (12/1/2006)*

Talley 2003 Rosemary's Vineyard Chardonnay (Arroyo Grande Valley) $44. The fruit is massive, succulent in pineapple custard, Key lime pie, and roasted coconut, and the oak is also powerful in new, charred character. There there's the brilliant acidity that makes it all work. **96** *—S.H. (7/1/2006)*

Talley 2000 Rosemary's Vineyard Chardonnay (Arroyo Grande Valley) $40. A fascinating wine that combines power and charm. Not a blockbuster, it leans toward citrus and apple abetted by oak. On the leesy side; almond-skin bitterness creeps in on the finish. **91** *—S.H. (2/1/2003)*

Talley 1999 Rosemary's Vineyard Chardonnay (Arroyo Seco) $40. Heavy clove and cinnamon-spice notes grace the nose of this very limited single-vineyard offering. Honey, stone, and a nuttiness mark the nose. Ripe and lively pineapple, banana, lime, and grapefruit flavors shine nicely in a medium-weight, well-balanced style. Finishes long and tart. A year or two in the bottle will bring out more complexity. **89** *(7/1/2001)*

Talley 1997 Rosemary's Vineyard Chardonnay (Arroyo Grande Valley) $20. 90 *—S.H. (10/1/1999)*

Talley 2004 Pinot Noir (Arroyo Grande Valley) $32. Lovely as usual; from one of California's finest Pinot producers, here's a wine with tons of cherry and cola fruit cruising on a silky, velvety texture. There's a stewed, baked-fruit quality from the horrendous harvest heat, but it has been handled well. **87** *—S.H. (12/1/2006)*

Talley 2003 Pinot Noir (Edna Valley) $28. A crisp, clean Pinot, simple and straightforward, with high acidity and vibrant cherry, coffee, and earth flavors. Sort of a junior version of Talley's vineyard-designated Pinots. **86** *—S.H. (10/1/2006)*

Talley 2002 Pinot Noir (Arroyo Grande Valley) $30. Oaky, with a blast of smoky char and caramel riding over cherry vanilla. Wonderful mouthfeel, rich, full-bodied, and dry, and lush in tannins and acidity. Near-perfect balance. **88** *(11/1/2004)*

Talley 2000 Pinot Noir (Arroyo Grande Valley) $28. Pinot with great bones. Superb acids and accessible tannins frame flavors that range from tomatoes, tobacco, and herbs to riper ones of cherries and blackberries. The wine is gentle on the palate, with layers of texture. **90** —*S.H. (2/1/2003)*

Talley 1998 Pinot Noir (Arroyo Grande Valley) $28. A little earthy, with plummy aromas accompanied by sun-dried tomato, rhubarb, and hard spice notes. The flavors are along the same lines, with cherry tomato, coffee, and spices. It's very dry, and finishes with a slightly dusty, tannic bite. **86** —*S.H. (2/1/2001)*

Talley 2001 Estate Pinot Noir (Arroyo Grande Valley) $28. The fruit has been restrained here in favor of firm acids and tannins, resulting in a wine that is less flamboyant than it is serious. Yet among the coffee, mushroom, and herb flavors and layers of smoky oak are swirls of black cherry and pomegranate that create complexity and real interest. **90** —*S.H. (6/1/2004)*

Talley 1997 Estate Pinot Noir (Arroyo Grande Valley) $28. 91 *(10/1/1999)*

Talley 2003 Rincon Vineyard Pinot Noir (Arroyo Grande Valley) $50. Talley is at the top of its Pinot game. This is a stunning wine, rich and complex, and true to Pinot's typicity, with bold acids and an elegantly silky texture framing nuanced flavors. It straddles that dangerous line of ripe cherry fruit with tomatoes on the other side, but comes out victorious. That is what makes Pinot Noir exciting. **93** —*S.H. (12/31/2005)*

Talley 2002 Rincon Vineyard Pinot Noir (Arroyo Grande Valley) $48. Just beautiful. Smoky oak, chocolate, cherry, vanilla, sweet herbs, lavender, thyme, oriental spice, just goes on and on. Huge, rich, balanced, and so smooth, bursting with ripe, sweet fruit. Gorgeous tannin-acid balance, and such a delicate mouthfeel. **94** *(11/1/2004)*

Talley 2001 Rincon Vineyard Pinot Noir (Arroyo Grande Valley) $45. Riper and fruitier than last year's release, a big, juicy wine that rewards the palate with layers of blackberry and cherry on top of the usual cola, tomato, and rhubarb flavors. Structurally, it's a big wine, with firm tannins. I would cellar this until next year. **92** —*S.H. (6/1/2004)*

Talley 2000 Rincon Vineyard Pinot Noir (Arroyo Grande Valley) $45. This bottling is similar in every respect to Talley's regular Pinot, which costs far less. It shares the flavor range—tobacco, tomatoes, and herbs through fruits like blackberries and cherries—and has polished tannins and lively acidity. What makes it different is concentration. Everything comes together on the palate at a single intense point. **92** —*S.H. (2/1/2003)*

Talley 1999 Rincon Vineyard Pinot Noir (Arroyo Grande Valley) $40. Incredibly complex and young. It's got that sappy feel you get fresh from the fermenter, overlaid with the best smoky oak. The black cherry core of fruit is promising. Dry and tart, it should soften up and gain complexity in the cellar, and become absolutely first rate. Try after 2002. **92** —*S.H. (12/15/2001)*

Talley 2003 Rosemary's Vineyard Pinot Noir (Arroyo Grande Valley) $65. Collectors will be interested to learn how this bottling compares to Talley's Rincon Pinot. The Rincon is the more immediately likeable. Rosemary's shares the same notes of gorgeous Pinot character, but is more tannic. That doesn't mean it's not fabulous now. Dry and tart, with an earthiness to the cherry flavors, it's a big thumbs up. Drink now through 2006. **94 Editors' Choice** —*S.H. (12/31/2005)*

Talley 2003 Rosemary's Vineyard Pinot Noir (Arroyo Grande Valley) $65. Although this wine is drinkable now, it has the stuffing to improve through 2009 or so. It's absolutely delicious in forward, almost jammy red cherry, sweet rhubarb pie, cola, and mocha flavors, but also has high acidity and dusty tannins, all wrapped in the most elegantly silky mouthfeel you can imagine. The minerally tightness suggests mid-term cellaring. **94 Editors' Choice** —*S.H. (11/1/2006)*

Talley 2002 Rosemary's Vineyard Pinot Noir (Arroyo Grande Valley) $62. An amazing Pinot Noir, very serious stuff. Big, bold, dark, and decadently rich. Oozing with cherry pie, mocha, and oak, with gorgeously firm acids and a smooth, complex texture. Just outstanding. A bit high in alcohol, though. **93** *(11/1/2004)*

Talley 2000 Rosemary's Vineyard Pinot Noir (Arroyo Grande Valley) $60. Extraordinarily rich, complex, and delicious, this wine defines a ripe

approach to cool-climate Pinot Noir. In its youthful state, it's plastered over with smoky oak, but below that are abundant ripe red and black cherry flavors. Near-perfect acids and tannins create wonderful balance and harmony in this ageworthy wine. **92 Cellar Selection** —*S.H. (7/1/2003)*

Talley 1999 Rosemary's Vineyard Pinot Noir (Arroyo Grande Valley) $60. Lush and opulent, with South Coast notes of tomato, cola, and beet, crushed hard spices and earth and some pretty black cherry fruit. It drinks very soft, almost disembodied, with scarcely a tannin to be found, and low acidity. It's elegant, but could use some more crispness and structure. **86** —*S.H. (7/1/2002)*

Talley 1997 Rosemary's Vineyard Pinot Noir (Arroyo Grande Valley) $45. Incredible depth of fruit, a bit reined in right now, but still exhibiting dark cherries, tar, leather, and spices. Deep cherry flavors with a touch of anise or licorice. Excellent mouthfeel. Huge, almost overripe notes on the finish, but quite unevolved. **93** *(7/1/2003)*

TALLULAH

Tallulah 2004 Syrah (Sonoma Coast) $28. Smoky, rich, and dramatic. Opens with peppery, new oaky aromas leading to deep, lush flavors of ripe blackberries, blueberries, and chocolate. Almost perilously sweet, but saved by a tannic finish. Drink now and for a few years. **88** —*S.H. (11/15/2006)*

Tallulah 2004 Bald Mountain Ranch Syrah (Mount Veeder) $40. Here's a fresh, young mountain wine that needs time in bottle, or serious decanting. It's muted now, with powerful tannins, but shows great promise in the wealth of blackberry and blueberry fruit and overall refinement. Best after 2007. **90** —*S.H. (11/15/2006)*

TALOMAS

Talomas 2000 Cabernet Sauvignon-Merlot (California) $14. This is the latest Mondavi partnership—are you keeping track?—this time, with Australia's Rosemount Estate. It is a young, jammy wine, like an Aussie Shiraz, with uncomplicated but ripe and tasty berry flavors and rich, thick tannins. Easy drinking in a big, full-bodied wine. **85** —*S.H. (8/1/2003)*

Talomas 2002 Basket Press Reserve Syrah (Central Coast) $30. Another wine that caused great debate on our panel. One panelist thought that the wine had softly oaky touches around a core of berry fruit, but for another, the oak had a pulpy, heavyhanded quality. Feel is creamy; finish is medium-long. **87** *(9/1/2005)*

Talomas 2001 Basket Press Reserve Syrah (Central Coast) $50. This massive Syrah blows your mind with cassis, roasted coffeebean, spiced plum, chocolate, and sweet oak aromas and flavors, and a and lush texture. Every sip explodes with taste sensations. The score would be higher if the wine had a firmer structure. It spreads all over the place, and needs reining in. **91** —*S.H. (12/15/2004)*

TALTY VINEYARDS & WINERY

Talty Vineyards & Winery 2001 Zinfandel (Dry Creek Valley) $32. Good structure and acidity serves up pretty blackberry, cassis, anise, tar, and spice flavors. Tannins are smooth and ripe, with a bright-edged finish that hints of tar and citrus. **88** *(11/1/2003)*

TALUS

Talus 2004 Cabernet Sauvignon (Lodi) $8. Dry and fruity, this country-style wine has thick tannins and some green acidity that calls for very rich, simple fare, such as a cheeseburger or sloppy joe. **83** —*S.H. (5/1/2006)*

Talus 2004 Chardonnay (Lodi) $8. Here's a good, everyday Chardonnay. It has ripe tropical fruit and vanilla flavors, with a creamy mouthfeel and hints of charry oak. It proves that California can produce value wines of quality and interest in huge quantities. **84 Best Buy** —*S.H. (7/1/2006)*

Talus 2003 Chardonnay (California) $8. Thin and simple, but clean. You get modest peach flavors with oak shadings. **83** —*S.H. (2/1/2005)*

Talus 2001 Chardonnay (California) $NA. Plenty of peach and apple flavors and it's pretty dry. On the down side is a roughness and it's also way too oaky, with flavors of wood sap, spice, and vanilla dominating the finish. **84** —*S.H. (6/1/2003)*

Talus 2004 Merlot (California) $8. Dry and soft, with upfront cherry-berry fruit and a smooth finish. Perfect match for lasagna or hamburgers. **83** —*S.H. (12/15/2006)*

Talus 2003 Merlot (Lodi) $8. This affordable Merlot shows lots of upfront fruit. It's packed with ripe cherries and blackberries, with chocolatey notes, but it's dry and balanced. The finish is soft and polished. **85 Best Buy** —*S.H. (11/15/2005)*

Talus 2002 Merlot (Lodi) $8. Soft and fruity, with cherry flavors. Drinks dry and clean, a pleasant wine that will go with just about everything. **83** —*S.H. (2/1/2005)*

Talus 2000 Merlot (California) $9. A pretty nice dinner wine, full-bodied and firm, with plum and blackberry flavors and firm tannins. It's clean and dry, and will do just fine with barbecue and similar rich fare. **84** —*S.H. (9/1/2003)*

Talus 2004 Pinot Grigio (Lodi) $8. Super-fruity, on the sweet side, and simple, with apricot and citrus flavors that turn a little cloying on the finish. **82** —*S.H. (7/1/2005)*

Talus 2003 Pinot Grigio (California) $8. Far too sweet for a Pinot Grigio. Tastes more like a simple Riesling. **83** —*S.H. (3/1/2005)*

Talus 2001 Pinot Grigio (California) $9. What a great wine when you're looking for something inexpensive and tasty. The citrus, apricot, and melon flavors are boosted by crisp acidity, and there's just enough sweetness to lend a rich, round softness. **85** —*S.H. (12/1/2003)*

Talus 2004 Pinot Noir (California) $8. You'll find lots of true Pinot character in this soft, silky wine. It has flavors of cherry pie, raspberries, coffee, and cocoa, and is nice and spicy. **84 Best Buy** —*S.H. (5/1/2006)*

Talus 2002 Pinot Noir (California) $8. Stewed fruits and alcohol, with a dollop of oak. Yet it's dry, clean, and drinkable. **83** —*S.H. (2/1/2005)*

Talus 2000 Pinot Noir (California) $9. Tart raspberry, grape, cola, and caramel aromas. Mocha accents on the tart cherry-sweet tomato fruit add interest, while the palate feel is light and smooth. This solid basic Pinot closes dry, with coffee and spice notes. **84 Best Buy** *(10/1/2002)*

Talus 1997 Red Blend (California) $9. **86** *(11/15/1999)*

Talus 2004 Shiraz (Lodi) $8. A little sweet, kind of simple, but it's a good, full-bodied red at a fair price, and those ripe cherry-berry flavors have an extra oomph that pleases. **84 Best Buy** —*S.H. (6/1/2006)*

Talus 2003 Shiraz (Lodi) $8. This is a soft wine, with candied flavors of chocolate, cherries, and vanilla, but it has a pleasantly smooth mouthfeel and hints of plum and herb. Fine for weeknight dinners or large, casual gatherings. **84 Best Buy** *(9/1/2005)*

Talus 2002 Shiraz (Lodi) $8. Soft, clean, and dry, with simple cherry and berry flavors and peppery spice. Easy to drink with Italian fare, burgers, or a ham sandwich. **84** —*S.H. (2/1/2005)*

Talus 2000 Shiraz (California) $9. What you see is what you get, an inexpensive wine from the Delta. It's dark, dry, and jammy, and as cleanly made as American winemaking allows. Hamburgers or, better still, cheeseburgers come to mind. **83** —*S.H. (12/15/2003)*

Talus 1999 Shiraz (California) $8. The Australian name is employed by this inexpensive, cranberry-rhubarb, tart, light red. It feels trim with some nice mild licorice-anise notes and a slight chalkiness that adds a little texture. It's not bad, but more ripe fruit is needed to get it above simply good. **83** *(10/1/2001)*

Talus 2003 Zinfandel (Lodi) $8. Fulfills Zin's basic requirements, a big, richly fruity wine, filled with blackberry, cherry, raspberry, and spice flavors, and dry and balanced. Turns briary on the finish. **85 Best Buy** —*S.H. (10/1/2005)*

Talus 2002 Zinfandel (Lodi) $8. Lots of ripe berry and spice flavors in this dry, friendly wine. It's very soft, but has good acidity. Try with BBQ salmon or ribs. **84** —*S.H. (2/1/2005)*

Talus 2001 Zinfandel (Lodi) $8. Toasty-rich, with a pleasing blend of coffee, chocolate, black cherry, spice, and vanilla flavors. The tannins are firm and supple and give it good structure. **87 Best Buy** *(11/1/2003)*

Talus 2000 Zinfandel (California) $9. Lean and herbal, with wild berry flavors and an edge of green stalkiness. There's a hint of oak, and it finishes dry. From vineyards in Lodi and Contra Costa County. **83** —*S.H. (3/1/2003)*

Talus 1998 Zinfandel (California) $8. Plenty of herbal, mushroomy notes in the nose. The wine is light, soft, and fruity. The mushroom flavors could be a real asset with the right food. Finishes true to form, with nothing off. **85 Best Buy** —*P.G. (3/1/2001)*

TAMARACK CELLARS

Tamarack Cellars 2004 Cabernet Franc (Columbia Valley (WA) $25. Purple and blue, it tastes of tart cherry and blueberry fruit. The tannins are stiffer than the winery's other reds, thicker and somewhat chalkier, and they seem a bit distanced from the soft, fruity mid-palate. Overall it's another consistent, ripe, fruity, good, solid effort. **87** —*P.G. (6/1/2006)*

Tamarack Cellars 2003 Cabernet Sauvignon (Columbia Valley (WA)) $32. Substantial and authoritative, with the acid, backbone and structure to support the dense fruit. Happily, it is not smothered in chocolate. The wine unfolds in compact layers of blackberry, black cherry, light chocolate, and a hint of tar. **88** —*P.G. (6/1/2006)*

Tamarack Cellars 2001 Cabernet Sauvignon (Columbia Valley (WA)) $32. This is a nice blend of top vineyards from Walla Walla, Red Mountain, and the Columbia Valley. The winery has tamed down the tough tannins and intrusive oak of past vintages, and created a much more approachable, yet still complex and ageworthy wine. **88** —*P.G. (5/1/2004)*

Tamarack Cellars 1999 Cabernet Sauvignon (Columbia Valley (WA)) $34. This is a soft, sensual wine, with a lovely nose mixing cassis and toast, spice, and coffee. There's a lovely mingling of forward, exotic scents and flavors, then some pickle barrel and dill in the finish. Some may like that more than others, but it's very well made, and food-ready. **87** —*P.G. (12/31/2001)*

Tamarack Cellars 2004 Chardonnay (Columbia Valley (WA)) $18. Well made, with a good mix of green apple and butterscotch, but less weight and density than some of the bigger wines. There's a bit of pineapple fruit also, hints of citrus and judicious use of the oak. The juicy fruit opens into light tropical flavors through the finish. **88** —*P.G. (6/1/2006)*

Tamarack Cellars 2002 Chardonnay (Columbia Valley (WA)) $18. This under-sung Walla Walla winery improves with each new vintage. This is seductive, ripe, and buttery, with citrus and tropical fruit flavors and smooth, buttery oak. It's delicious and balanced for consumption with food. **88** —*P.G. (5/1/2004)*

Tamarack Cellars 2004 Merlot (Columbia Valley (WA)) $28. Along with the Merlot there is about 15% Cabernet Sauvignon/Cabernet Franc. Good, grapey and dark; this is a broad, sturdy, and ripe wine, which sails through the palate on a wide swath of black cherry fruit. It's consistent with the rest of the Tamarack lineup; sweet, ripe fruit and plenty of barrel flavors, muscled together nicely. **87** —*P.G. (6/1/2006)*

Tamarack Cellars 2001 Merlot (Columbia Valley (WA)) $28. The blend here includes 17% Cabernet Sauvignon and Cabernet Franc, which toughens up the tannins and adds a dark, mineral note to the finish. Tight, with green olive/cassis flavors and plenty of smoky, peppery barrel toast. **87** —*P.G. (5/1/2004)*

Tamarack Cellars 2000 Merlot (Columbia Valley (WA)) $28. A very well-made Merlot, with sweet fruit and attractive scents of vanilla and cracker. Though still showing a lot of youthful acidity, it wraps the fruit in a big blast of new oak and finishes with a hint of heat. **89** —*P.G. (9/1/2002)*

Tamarack Cellars 1999 Merlot (Columbia Valley (WA)) $28. Tamarack is named for a tree found around Walla Walla. This is a solidly crafted Merlot, with a seductive nose showing sweet fruit, vanilla wafer, and graham cracker. Young, firm, and tart, it opens up slowly, hinting at rich, textured fruit beneath the oak and considerable acid. **88** —*P.G. (12/31/2001)*

Tamarack Cellars 2001 Du Brul Vineyard Reserve Red Blend (Yakima Valley) $NA. Grapes from one of the valley's top vineyards create this Bordeaux blend of 62% Cabernet Sauvignon, 31% Merlot, and 7% Cab Franc. Fragrant with scents of sandalwood, rose petals, toast, and lead pencil, the wine grudgingly opens out into a beautifully balanced, elegant palate of sweet cherry, cranberry, and pomegranate. Modest in size, but complex and delicious. **90** —*P.G. (5/1/2004)*

Tamarack Cellars 2004 Firehouse Red Red Blend (Columbia Valley (WA)) $20. This prototypical Walla Walla mutt red is half Cabernet Sauvignon and the rest a mix of Syrah, Merlot, Cab Franc, Sangiovese, and even a bit of Carmenère. Lush, fruity, and forward, it's got a little bit of everything going for it flavorwise as well: berries, cherries, cassis, coffee, chocolate, vanilla bean, and cinnamon. All good stuff, schmoozed together and thoroughly delicious. **87** —*P.G. (6/1/2006)*

Tamarack Cellars 2004 Sangiovese (Columbia Valley (WA)) $25. Pure Sangiovese, soft and slightly leafy. It clearly shows its varietal character in the way the wine is structured, with relatively high acids and hints of tobacco leaf. Smooth and easy-drinking. **87** —*P.G. (6/1/2006)*

Tamarack Cellars 2003 Syrah (Columbia Valley (WA)) $28. Dark, smoky, and chewy, this young, tannic effort could stand in for any good Walla Walla Syrah from a dozen different producers. It is a testament to the quality of Washington Syrah; but also an example of the sameness that plagues many of them. There is a nice core of juicy boysenberry, and beyond that it's all about roasted coffee, bitter chocolate, and toast. **88** —*P.G. (6/1/2006)*

Tamarack Cellars 2002 Syrah (Columbia Valley (WA)) $28. Shows a little tar or game on the nose, then opens up into a pleasant fruity Syrah with notes of blackberries and vanilla. The soft, supple mouthfeel sets it a notch above the rest of the crowd. **86** *(9/1/2005)*

TAMÁS ESTATES

Tamás Estates 2004 Pinot Grigio (Monterey) $9. Simple and thin, with a scoury, acidic mouthfeel, this wine has modest lemon and grapefruit flavors, and is totally dry. **83** —*S.H. (2/1/2006)*

Tamás Estates 2003 Pinot Grigio (Monterey) $9. Easy and clean, this white has Monterey acidity backing up flavors of lemons, limes, peaches, ripe green apples, and peppery spices. It's dry, but very fruity. **85 Best Buy** —*S.H. (2/1/2006)*

Tamás Estates 1999 Pinot Grigio (Monterey County) $11. A bestseller in California because of its spicy, appley aromas and racy flavors. It finishes tart and spicy—very palate cleansing. **84** —*S.H. (11/15/2001)*

Tamás Estates 1996 Sangiovese (Livermore Valley) $11. **88 Best Buy** —*S.H. (12/15/1999)*

Tamás Estates 2001 Sangiovese (Livermore Valley) $18. A beautiful wine with a delicate, pedigreed quality. It's light in color and body, with elegant flavors of cranberry, red cherry, cola, and coffee, and is very dry, with crisp acids and fine, soft tannins. This connoisseur's wine is versatile at the table. **90 Editors' Choice** —*S.H. (12/1/2003)*

Tamás Estates 1999 AVA's: San Francisco Bay/Livermore Valley Zinfandel (California) $12. Decent everyday sipper, with heaps of sweet berry flavors wrapped in silky bright acids and dusty tannins. It's kind of thin in structure and in the finish, but is a perfectly nice quaff for the price. **85** —*S.H. (9/1/2002)*

TAMBER BEY

Tamber Bey 2003 Cabernet Sauvignon (Oakville) $50. There's an intense cherry-cocoa flavor, accented by the finest spicy, smoky oak, that makes this wine irresistibly seductive right from the get-go. It's distinguished by finely ground, sweet tannins and an oaky-creamy mouthfeel, and finishes dry and long. Defines the Oakville style of grace and power. **93 Editors' Choice** —*S.H. (8/1/2006)*

Tamber Bey 2002 Cabernet Sauvignon (Oakville) $50. Made in a less ripe style than many of its neighbors, which makes it something of an outlier in Oakville, this Cab is a bit herbal and tightly wound in acids and tannins. It could be an ager. Try holding until 2007. **87** —*S.H. (11/1/2005)*

TANDEM

Tandem 2002 Porter Bass Vineyards Chardonnay (Russian River Valley) $48. Shows great mastery in seamlessly yoking the intensely ripe fruit to vibrant acids, oaky glaze, and creamy texture. Important to keep in mind how tangy and tart this wine is. If you're looking for flavor descriptors, try quince just short of perfectly ripe, with that bite of acid. Should do interesting things over the next 5 years. **92** —*S.H. (12/31/2004)*

Tandem 2002 Ritchie Vineyard Chardonnay (Sonoma Coast) $42. Tasted alongside Tandem's Sangiacomo bottling, this wine shares many of the same characteristics, including crisp acidity, minerality, and a seamless integration of oak. However, it's richer and fatter, although far from fat. It's a wine of intense structure and finesse. **90** —*S.H. (12/31/2004)*

Tandem 2002 Sangiacomo Vineyard Chardonnay (Sonoma Coast) $38. Quite distinctive and complex for the intense minerality and herbal, cured tobacco overtones to the underlying citrus, peach fruit, and oak flavors. There's something steely and metallic about the acidy structure that really gets the taste buds going. **90** —*S.H. (12/31/2004)*

Tandem 2002 Auction Block Pinot Noir (Sonoma Coast) $60. Proceeds for this priciest of Tandem's '02s go to charity, but it's not the winery's best. It's dark, extracted, and jammy, and rather heavy and flat. **86** —*S.H. (11/1/2004)*

Tandem 2002 Halleck Vineyard Pinot Noir (Sonoma Coast) $54. What a beauty, complex as heck. Starts off with meaty, beefy aromas floating above red cherries, vanilla, cocoa, and smoke, and turns intensely rich and delicate in the mouth, offering waves of tart cherry, sweet rhubarb, rose hip tea, and spice flavors. So silky and light, yet unstintingly focused. A real accomplishment. **93** —*S.H. (11/1/2004)*

Tandem 2002 Keefer Ranch Pinot Noir (Green Valley) $38. A wine with silky, gentle tannins and cherry-berry, coffee, and herb flavors, touched with smoky oak, that finish dry and smooth. My only quibble is with a certain syrupy thickness and heaviness in the texture. **88** —*S.H. (11/1/2004)*

Tandem 2002 Sangiacomo Pinot Noir (Sonoma Coast) $48. Translucent in color, this beautiful wine captures the essence of North Coast, cool-climate Pinot in the exciting line it straddles between cheerfully ripe cherry fruit and a more somber undertow of rhubarb and cherry tomato. Delicately structured, dry, silky in texture, and with a cool spine of acidity, this beautiful wine is a star of the vintage. **92** —*S.H. (11/1/2004)*

Tandem 2003 Van der Kamp Vineyard Pinot Noir (Sonoma Mountain) $48. This is a very soft, sensuous Pinot, low in tannins, with a smooth, creamy mouthfeel. The flavors are rich and exuberant in smoky red cherries, raspberries, and cola. The softness suggests against extended cellaring, but why wouldn't you want this silky, complex wine now? **91** —*S.H. (11/1/2005)*

Tandem 2002 Van der Kamp Vineyard Pinot Noir (Sonoma Mountain) $48. The flavors suggest ripe cherry compote, Turkish coffee, leathery notes, and good oak. There is a certain heavy fullness to the wine's body, an abundance of tannins and extract that detracts to some extent from delicacy and elegance, but it's a very good wine. Try cellaring for a few years. **88** —*S.H. (11/1/2004)*

Tandem 2001 Gabrielli Vineyard Sangiovese (Redwood Valley) $32. Under the hot sun the grapes got ripe, and the wine offers loads of blackberry, cherry, coffee, and dried herb flavors. Beyond that, it's dry, with gentle tannins and quite a powerful punch of alcohol. Makes you realize what a difficult grape Sangiovese is. **87** —*S.H. (12/31/2004)*

TANGENT

Tangent 2005 Albariño (Edna Valley) $17. This is a new wine from the family that runs Baileyana. The Albariño is stunning in its purity. It's built along the lines of a Sauvignon Blanc or Pinot Grigio with the most wonderfully detailed citrus, fig, and herbed chèvre flavors. Just a beautiful glass of wine. **90 Editors' Choice** —*S.H. (12/1/2006)*

Tangent 2005 Pinot Blanc (Arroyo Grande Valley) $17. Unoaked Pinot Blancs are rare, but this refreshing wine argues the case. It's high in mouth-cleansing acidity, with subtle peach, pineapple, lime zest, and spicy flavors that finish long and rich. **88** —*S.H. (12/1/2006)*

Tangent 2005 Paragon Vineyard Pinot Gris (Edna Valley) $17. That classic Edna Valley acidity kicks in immediately, brightening and cleansing the lime zest, white peach, and honeysuckle flavors. There's so much vanilla spice here you can hardly believe there's no oak. But there isn't. **90** —*S.H. (12/1/2006)*

Tangent 2005 Paragon Vineyard Sauvignon Blanc (Edna Valley) $13. Here's how good unoaked Sauvignon Blanc can be. Pure Meyer lemon, citron zest, and refreshingly crisp acids are all delicious, zingy, and clean. There's even a backbone of steely minerality. 86 —S.H. (12/1/2006)

Tangent 2005 Ecclestone White Blend (San Luis Obispo County) $20. This is a blend of almost every white grape that grows in the county. Riesling brings a floral note to the citrus zest, apricot, tangerine, and sweet herb flavors. The wine is unoaked, but very rich. 87 —S.H. (12/1/2006)

TANTALUS

Tantalus 1998 Cabernet Sauvignon (Sonoma County) $28. Containing 20% Merlot, the aromas are blackberry, black cherry, and a good deal of smoky oak. Drinks dry and tannic, with berry flavors. The middle palate turns thin, in line with the vintage, but picks up some pretty cherry and cedar notes on the finish 86 —S.H. (12/1/2001)

Tantalus 1999 Sémillon (Russian River Valley) $14. Pretty aromas of figs, cashew nuts, white peach, and oaky, sweet vanilla and toast lead to very rich and ripe flavors of peach, custard on the palate. The creamy texture and mouthfeel is mousse-like, yet for all the fruity richness, it's bone dry and crisp. 88 Best Buy —S.H. (11/15/2001)

TANTARA

Tantara 2004 Bien Nacido Vineyard Chardonnay (Santa Maria Valley) $33. There's a rich streak of mineral that undergirds tremendous ripe tropical fruit, along with crisp acidity and a good amount of smoky oak that's perfectly integrated with the rich fruit. Tremendous extract and weight and a long, impressive finish make this wine addictively good. 92 —S.H. (8/1/2006)

Tantara 2000 Bien Nacido Vineyard Chardonnay (Santa Maria Valley) $26. Fatter and rounder than Tantara's Talley bottling, and not quite as focused. Tastes strongly of lees, with plenty of smoky oak riding over underlying apple and peach flavors. This is a dry, angular wine designed for elaborate food. 90 —S.H. (12/15/2002)

Tantara 2000 Talley Vineyard Chardonnay (Arroyo Grande Valley) $30. An astonishingly rich and complex wine. Lush, ripe, primary fruit flavors of peaches, pears, and tropical fruits are spiced with fine toasted oak and accompanying notes of char. Lees provide mealy, creamy tastes and a rich, milky texture. Brilliant and strong now, and will improve through 2003. 92 —S.H. (12/15/2002)

Tantara 2004 Pinot Noir (Santa Maria Valley) $30. At this price, this is a relative value from Tantara, offering much of the complexity of the single-vineyard bottlings. It's a dry, crisp wine, with masses of cherry, cola, cinnamon spice, and vanilla flavors in a silky, elegant body. 90 —S.H. (12/31/2006)

Tantara 2000 Bien Nacido Vineyard Pinot Noir (Santa Maria Valley) $37. One of five single-vineyard releases from this winery, the Bien Nacido offering is a complex wine that encompasses herbaceous, vegetal notes and fleshier, fruity ones. The wine at this point is lean and hard and veering toward beets and tomatoes. Time may bring out a sweeter face. 86 —S.H. (2/1/2003)

Tantara 2004 Bien Nacido Vineyard Adobe Pinot Noir (Santa Maria Valley) $45. This is from Tantara's 3-acre block at Bien Nacido, and it's a very good young wine, fresh in citrusy acidity but ripe in cherry essence and cola flavors. Planted only in 1999, it shows a young vine exuberance that limits complexity, but not interest. 89 —S.H. (12/31/2006)

Tantara 2004 Bien Nacido Vineyard Old Vine Pinot Noir (Santa Maria Valley) $45. This is a brilliant wine that defines Bien Nacido, the coast, and California Pinot Noir. There were worries about the heat, but somehow this has ended up balanced, dry, and classically elegant, maybe because of vine age; they're now 36-years-old. Impresses for the power of its cherry pie filling, mocha, rum, and cola and spicebox flavors that finish dry and complex, with the longest, most wonderfully complex finish. Drink now–2010. 95 —S.H. (12/31/2006)

Tantara 2004 Brosseau Vineyard Pinot Noir (Chalone) $52. Tasted alongside Tantara's other vineyard Pinots, this is one of the more tannic and acidic. At the same time, the hot vintage yielded immensely ripe fruit, giving the wine jammy, pastry flavors of cherries, red, and black raspberries, mocha, cola, and root beer. The forwardness will probably limit ageability. 90 —S.H. (12/31/2006)

Tantara 2004 Dierberg Vineyard Pinot Noir (Santa Maria Valley) $45. A bit tough and gritty in tannins now, although a charbroiled steak will engage it. The wine is powerful in cherry, black raspberry, and mocha flavors that melt into the palate and last for a long time. It's dry, and despite the power, there's a silky elegance. Hold through 2006, then drink within five years. 90 —S.H. (12/31/2006)

Tantara 2000 Dierberg Vineyard Pinot Noir (Santa Maria Valley) $40. A little riper and fruitier than Tantara's Bien Nacido bottling, with a distinct sour cherry flavor. The delicate tannins and acids are in good balance. Most notable for its luscious, velvety mouthfeel, this wine could improve in the short term. 89 —S.H. (2/1/2003)

Tantara 2004 Evelyn Pinot Noir (Santa Maria Valley) $80. Stunning. Just magnificent. This is from Tantara's little Bien Nacido block. It achieves wonderfully ripe fruit flavors with clean, balancing tannins and acids to produce the utmost California cool-climate Pinot Noir. Cherries, raspberries, cola, rich new oak, and Asian spice flavors all flood the palate, wrapped into a dramatic silky, velvety texture. This is great Pinot Noir. 97 Editors' Choice —S.H. (12/31/2006)

Tantara 2004 Garys' Vineyard Pinot Noir (Santa Lucia Highlands) $52. How ripe the grapes got in this hot vintage. There's a sugary edge to the cherry, peppermint, and smoky, new oaky vanilla flavors that makes the wine almost like a dessert pastry. Fortunately, those dependable Santa Lucia acids kick in to keep it from falling over the edge. 87 —S.H. (12/31/2006)

Tantara 2000 Garys' Vineyard Pinot Noir (Santa Lucia Highlands) $42. Softer than the Pisoni, with a limpid mouthfeel that suggests mountain water. The flavors veer toward herbs and sun-sweetened tomatoes, with a suggestion of sour cherry. Shares the house style of elegance, lightness of body, and complexity; it's a wine of intellectual rather than physical charm. 91 —S.H. (2/1/2003)

Tantara 2004 La Colline Vineyard Pinot Noir (Arroyo Grande Valley) $45. The vineyard, owned by Laetitia and one of their block bottlings, has yielded in this warm vintage a soft, concentrated Pinot. Focused in cherry pie and new oaky smoke and vanilla flavors, it has an elegantly silky texture. What a wonderful, upscale Pinot this is, a natural with great food. 92 —S.H. (12/31/2006)

Tantara 2000 La Colline Vineyard Pinot Noir (Arroyo Grande Valley) $40. This wine feels plush and elegant in the mouth, with a light, silky texture. Tart, sour cherry flavors veer toward herbal, tomato, and sage notes. Despite the absence of fruity flavor, the wine is surprisingly interesting and complex, and will come alive with the right foods. 89 —S.H. (2/1/2003)

Tantara 2004 Pisoni Vineyard Pinot Noir (Santa Lucia Highlands) $60. Here's a big, in-your-face Pinot Noir, offering up a blast of superripe fruit, almost Grenache-like in thick, soft red cherry flavors, complexed with sweet licorice, cola, mocha, and spicy, vanilla oak. It's a roller coaster palate experience, a thrill every second, yet somehow maintains a silky, Pinotesque delicacy. Great wine. 94 Editors' Choice —S.H. (12/31/2006)

Tantara 2000 Pisoni Vineyard Pinot Noir (Santa Lucia Highlands) $54. The fruitiest of Tantara's current offerings, although there's considerable herb, earth, and tobacco accompanying the tart black cherry flavors. This is a dry, acidic wine with noble tannins whose most striking feature, as with all Tantara's Pinots, is its smooth mouthfeel. 92 —S.H. (2/1/2003)

Tantara 2004 Rio Vista Vineyard Pinot Noir (Santa Rita Hills) $45. Although this is a very good wine, it's one of the least of Tantara's current single-vineyard Pinots. A victim of excessive sweetness, which may be from high alcohol, everything in it seems thrown off, hot. The flavors, though, are delicious, a mélange of cherry, blueberry, and blackberry pie filling. 87 —S.H. (12/31/2006)

Tantara 2004 Silacci Vineyard Pinot Noir (Santa Lucia Highlands) $52. The vineyard is in the central-north, cooler part of the Highlands, but in this warm vintage, the wine sure did get ripe. It just detonates on the palate with explosive cherry, raspberry, mocha, cola, and vanilla flavors. Saved from being a mere fruit bomb by a gorgeous acid-tannin balance. 92 —S.H. (12/31/2006)

USA

Tantara 2004 Solomon Hills Vineyard Pinot Noir (Santa Maria Valley) $45. I didn't much care for the '03, but a combination of extra vine age (the vines were only planted in 1999) and a really warm vintage has boosted ripeness and the luxury factor. The wine isn't particularly complex or ageable, but is agreeable for its tasty cherry jam, cola, mocha, and spicy licorice flavors. **87** —*S.H. (12/31/2006)*

Tantara 2003 Solomon Hills Vineyard Pinot Noir (Santa Maria Valley) $45. A bit flabby and sweet, not to mention heavy on the oak, this is the sort of Pinot that has many fans for its full-bodied richness. Yet it's over the top, lacking in delicacy and restraint. **83** —*S.H. (8/1/2006)*

TAPTEIL VINEYARD

Tapteil Vineyard 2002 Cabernet Sauvignon (Yakima Valley) $29. In the nose are whiffs of rubber ball and burnt match, along with a lightly herbal fruit character reminiscent of the sort of grassiness you find in old-vine Zinfandels. The wine shows good texture, and the herbal fruit flavors, though tart, are free of vegetal or green bean aromas. **89** —*P.G. (6/1/2006)*

TARA BELLA

Tara Bella 1999 Cabernet Sauvignon (Napa Valley) $60. A distinguished wine, from the opening scents of fine, toasted oak, vanilla, and char through the ripe, classy black currant and herb flavors. Tannins are rich, fine, and supple. A very nice, upscale-tasting Cab. **90** —*S.H. (11/15/2003)*

TARARA

Tarara 1997 Pinot Noir (Virginia) $15. 83 —*J.C. (8/1/1999)*

Tarara 1997 Vidal Blanc (Virginia) $13. 80 —*J.C. (8/1/1999)*

TARIUS

Tarius 1999 Pinot Noir (Santa Lucia Highlands) $36. A smoke, plum, and spice nose opens this tart yet sweet midweight wine. Berry and plum flavors are bright on the palate and the texture is at once rich and tangy. Herb notes, with a slightly sour cast, come up on the dark finish. **86** *(10/1/2002)*

Tarius 1999 Pinot Noir (Russian River Valley) $33. 86 *(10/1/2002)*

Tarius 1997 Pisoni Vineyard Pinot Noir (Santa Lucia Highlands) $39. 88 *(11/15/1999)*

Tarius 1998 Zinfandel (Mendocino) $23. 88 —*M.S. (10/1/2000)*

Tarius 1999 Aldine Vineyard Zinfandel (Mendocino) $29. Lots of chocolate, carob, and nut on the nose, plus raisin, more chocolate, and tart blackberry on the palate—think granola bar, or trail mix, and you're in the right ballpark. This is a profile that generally piques my interest precisely because it is a little odd. Chalky, even pasty in the mouth, it closes with the same flavors until a long and bitter—half-metallic, half-Brussels sprouts—note takes over the back end. **84** —*D.T. (3/1/2002)*

Tarius 1998 Aldine Vineyard Zinfandel (Mendocino) $29. 84 —*S.H. (5/1/2000)*

Tarius 1999 Korte Ranch Zinfandel (Napa Valley) $29. The Tarius manages to be at once creamy and on the lean side; think—as its palate exhibits—cream, vanilla bean, and a smidge of lemon rind over big blackberry flavors. Just-as-dark berry, plus soil, tangy oak, and slight chocolate notes show on the nose; finishes with nice, tart chalkboard-eraser, oak, and blackberry flavors. **88** —*D.T. (3/1/2002)*

TASSAJARA

Tassajara 2002 Syrah (Paso Robles) $24. Starts a bit herbal and spicy, then broadens out to deliver coffee, cherries, and caramel flavors. Medium- to full-bodied, with soft tannins and crisp acidity, finishing with notes of asphalt. Ready to drink now. **87** *(9/1/2005)*

TATE CREEK

Tate Creek 1999 Cabernet Sauvignon (California) $6. Tastes like a generic red wine, with no particular Cabernet flavors but some berry and fruit ones. No particular problems, just overt simplicity at an inexpensive price. **82** —*S.H. (6/1/2002)*

Tate Creek 1999 Merlot (California) $6. Drinks rough and hot, with some berry flavors and an earthy note. The wine is nicely dry, with a good

mouthfeel and fine tannins, but is marred by that rough, coarse note, especially in the aroma. **81** —*S.H. (6/1/2002)*

Tate Creek 1999 Syrah (California) $6. Simple and fruity, this wine has some polished flavors of black cherries and pepper, and drinks very dry, with a creamy mouthfeel and soft tannins and acids. It's an easygoing wine, and fine for everyday occasions. **84** —*S.H. (9/1/2002)*

TAYLOR

Taylor 2002 Chardonnay (Stags Leap District) $22. Sleek and minerally, a taut young Chard with high acidity and a steely spine. But there's a wealth of peach, pear, pineapple, and vanilla flavor that bursts through the acids and spreads deliciously across the tongue. Tasty, rewarding, and balanced. **90** —*S.H. (8/1/2004)*

Taylor 2003 Hillside Chardonnay (Stags Leap District) $34. This is a good wine, but it provides ammunition for those who suggest that Napa Valley isn't the best place for Chardonnay. Dry, with an earthy edge to the fruit, and lots of oak. **85** —*S.H. (2/1/2006)*

Taylor 2002 Hillside Chardonnay (Stags Leap District) $34. You'll find a wine that's tight and shut down right now. It has strong acids and even some tannins, with citrusy flavors that have a hint of pear. Could use more generosity. **88** —*S.H. (8/1/2004)*

TAZ

Taz 2004 Chardonnay (Santa Barbara County) $20. California Chardonnay is easy to get ripe, but it's hard to get proper acids to boost and brighten the fruit. This cool-climate Chard does it effortlessly. It's a succulent sipper, filled with vibrant peach tart and pineapple custard flavors and that bright, tart acidity. **89** —*S.H. (3/1/2006)*

Taz 2003 Chardonnay (Santa Barbara County) $20. You'll find all the toasty oak you want here, and plenty of ripe peach, Bosc pear, and mango flavors too. The texture is creamy and smooth. It's a little sharp in the finish, but it's a nice Chard with some fancy features. **87** —*S.H. (8/1/2005)*

Taz 2001 Merlot (Santa Barbara County) $20. Crisp and herbal, this is Taz's least successful offering, but it's still solid. Toast, sour cherries, mint, and other green herbs mark the palate. Finishes long, but tart. **86** *(12/15/2004)*

Taz 2004 Pinot Gris (Santa Barbara County) $15. Super-fruity in peaches, citrus, and apricots, with a creamy mouthfeel and brisk acidity, this is a fun wine with some real complexity. It's technically dry, but rich in fruity ripeness. **86** —*S.H. (2/1/2006)*

Taz 2003 Pinot Gris (Santa Barbara County) $15. A rich, slightly alcoholic white, loaded with pear and melon flavors. It's mouthfilling and intense, finishing long and a bit warm. **87** *(11/15/2004)*

Taz 2003 Pinot Noir (Santa Barbara County) $25. This countywide blend is properly dry and silky, but the fruit is thin, leaving the alcohol sticking out like a sore thumb. **84** —*S.H. (12/31/2005)*

Taz 2002 Pinot Noir (Santa Barbara County) $25. This well-priced offering boasts intriguing aromas of cinnamon, graham crackers, and black cherries. A hint of Mexican chocolate adds depth to the lengthy finish. **89** *(11/1/2004)*

Taz 2004 Cuyama River Pinot Noir (Santa Maria Valley) $28. Good Pinot, fairly full-bodied, and deep and long in red stone-fruit flavors and dusty spices. But it's also fairly tannic, and a bit sharp in the finish. Drink now. **86** —*S.H. (12/1/2006)*

Taz 2003 Cuyama River Pinot Noir (Santa Maria Valley) $28. You immediately pick up on the cool-climate origins of this wine. It's all rhubarb and cola, an impression confirmed with the first taste. Acidity stars here, but there are riper flavors of black cherries. Rich tannins, too. The wine is totally dry. It hasn't come together yet. Try aging until 2007. **88** —*S.H. (12/1/2005)*

Taz 2004 Fiddlestix Vineyard Pinot Noir (Santa Rita Hills) $35. A mute young wine, so it comes as a shock how good it tastes. Just yummy in cherry jam, milk chocolate, pomegranate, sweet licorice, toasted coconut, and cinnamon spice flavors. That may sound sweet, but the wine is fully dry, albeit a little soft. Drink now, but decant for a few hours. **89** —*S.H. (11/15/2006)*

Taz 2003 Fiddlestix Vineyard Pinot Noir (Santa Rita Hills) $35. This is a challenging Pinot Noir. It's tough, gritty, and dry, with lots of acidity and even some dusty tannins, and flavors ranging from mint to cola, rhubarb and sour cherry, with a tart finish. There's an elegance to the structure, but it's not an especially rewarding wine. **86** —*S.H. (12/15/2005)*

Taz 2002 Fiddlestix Vineyard Pinot Noir (Santa Rita Hills) $35. This rich, full-bodied Pinot is no simple fruit bomb, featuring complex aromas of smoke, mineral, and rockdust that blend seamlessly into flavors of black cherries, anise, and dried spices. Finishes with supple tannins and juicy acidity. **92 Editors' Choice** *(11/1/2004)*

Taz 2003 Syrah (Santa Barbara County) $25. The Northern Rhône is the model for this dry, rich, complex wine. It opens with white pepper, blackberry tart, and toasted oak aromas, and in the mouth turns full-bodied and dense, with ripe blackberry, plum, and coffee flavors. It's soft for a Santa Barbara wine. **87** —*S.H. (3/1/2006)*

Taz 2002 Syrah (Santa Barbara County) $25. From the North Canyon vineyard, this bold, intensely flavored Syrah is richly fruity without being jammy. Blueberry and blackberry fruit, a hint of black pepper and a long, softly chewy finish add up to a winning combination. **92 Editors' Choice** *(11/1/2004)*

Taz 2004 Goat Rock Syrah (Santa Maria Valley) $28. A worthy followup to the '03, this rich, intricately layered Syrah is fresh in jammy fruits and dusty tannins, although it's not a hard, tannic wine. If you think of a great Napa Cabernet and shift the flavor profile toward red cherries, pomegranates, and pepper, that's it. **92** —*S.H. (12/1/2006)*

Taz 2003 Goat Rock Syrah (Santa Maria Valley) $28. This cool-climate Syrah has Hermitage in its sights, and is well worth the price. Bone dry, full-bodied, and distinguished, the wine opens with white pepper and cassis aromas, and turns deliciously complex in the mouth, offering waves of black currants, grilled meat, and oak that finish tannic. Drink now through 2010. **92 Cellar Selection** —*S.H. (12/1/2005)*

TEADERMAN

Teaderman 2001 Cabernet Sauvignon (Oakville) $48. Makes all the right moves, with ripe fruit flavors, rich tannins, and a sweet coat of oak. There's a rich tobacco and earth note that grounds the fruit. A complex wine that should age well for 10 years. **90 Cellar Selection** —*S.H. (11/1/2005)*

TEATOWN CELLARS

Teatown Cellars 2000 Chardonnay (Napa Valley) $30. 83 —*J.M. (5/1/2002)*

Teatown Cellars 2003 Merlot (Napa Valley) $22. There's well-ripened cherry, blackberry, and mocha fruit in this dryish wine, but it's basically a simple sipper, and seems pricey for what you get. **83** —*S.H. (3/1/2006)*

Teatown Cellars 2000 Merlot (Napa Valley) $20. Any easy drinking wine with supple but somewhat tough tannins that spread sappy blackberry and cherry flavors around the mouth. The wine is very dry, with a numbing astringency. Needs to develop complexity and softer tannins. **85** —*S.H. (2/1/2004)*

TEFFT CELLARS

Tefft Cellars 1999 Merlot (Yakima Valley) $15. The style is usually big and bold, but for the moment this wine, though dense and dark, has a hole in the middle. Rich scents of black cherry, blueberry, and earth seem to vanish, leaving only a tannic finish. **86** —*P.G. (9/1/2002)*

Tefft Cellars 1999 Estate Bottled Syrah (Yakima Valley) $20. Bright blackberry fruit flavors (with a slight lemon-oak tinge that one reviewer described as greenness) flesh out this round, even Washington special. Opens with sour berry, damp soil, and menthol notes, and finishes with dry chalk and tart cranberry flavors. **86** *(10/1/2001)*

TEN MILE

Ten Mile 2004 Proprietary Red Wine Red Blend (California) $11. This is a classic old-style field blend, and it's a pretty good wine. Grown in Lodi, Dry Creek, and Napa Valley, it's a blend of Petite Sirah, Zinfandel, Barbera, Malbec, and Carignane. Drinks very dry and full-bodied, with earthy, cherry, and plum flavors. **87** —*S.H. (12/15/2006)*

TENSLEY

Tensley 2001 Colson Canyon Vineyard Syrah (Santa Barbara County) $30. Different in profile from Tensley's other two bottlings. From northern Santa Barbara County, it opens with aromas of jammy currants, grilled meat, anise, and smoke and vanilla from oak. It is rich in juicy fruit flavors, notably blackberries and cherries, and the tannins are not as tough as those in the other offerings. **89** —*S.H. (3/1/2004)*

Tensley 2001 Purimisa Mountain Vineyard Syrah (Santa Barbara County) $30. This wine, from the central Santa Ynez Valley, smells fantastic. It is jammy with blackberry, black cherry, currant, mocha, smoke, vanilla, and pepper, like some kind of incredibly decadent dessert. The flavors are very rich in cherries and blackberries, but the wine is also significantly tannic, numbing the mouth. **87** —*S.H. (3/1/2004)*

Tensley 2001 Thompson Vineyard Syrah (Santa Barbara County) $30. Vibrant and fruity, with blackberry, cherry, black raspberry, leather, smoke, and herb flavors that erupt from the glass. The flavors are deliciously rich and ripe, in a smoothly textured body, but the tannins are tough and astringent, as they are in the Purisima Mountain bottling. **87** —*S.H. (3/1/2004)*

TERLATO

Terlato 2003 Angels' Peak Bordeaux Blend (Napa Valley) $50. The thinking with this Merlot-based Bordeaux blend seems to have been, if ripeness is good, then superripeness is better. And we might as well throw on a ton of new French oak. The result is excess, imbalance. **82** —*S.H. (12/31/2006)*

Terlato 2005 Pinot Grigio (Russian River Valley) $26. There's much to like about this wine, which shows cool-climate high acidity and minerality, in addition to the pink grapefuit, tart green apple, and fig flavors, with their dash of white pepper and nutmeg. It's dry, sleek, and stylish. **87** —*S.H. (12/31/2006)*

Terlato 2004 Pinot Grigio (Russian River Valley) $24. Bone dry and grapefruity, with high acids, this is a rather austere wine, or maybe "delicate" is a better word. It doesn't clobber you over the head with opulence, but strives, successfully, for elegance and finesse. **87** —*S.H. (2/1/2006)*

TERRA BLANCA

Terra Blanca 2001 Syrah (Red Mountain) $20. Tarry, smoky, and reluctant to show its fruit at first, this wine rewards lengthy decanting with dark, substantial flavors of cherry tobacco and plump plum. Plenty of tannin adds welcome heft. **88** —*P.G. (4/1/2005)*

Terra Blanca 1999 Syrah (Red Mountain) $20. This Syrah sports a licorice-black cherry-cedar bouquet. The creamy, full mouthfeel is backed by blackberry, cherry, cedar, and vanilla flavors. Not complex, but very flavorful, and showing nice integration, it finishes with American oak, firm tannins, and slight prickly heat. **87** *(10/1/2001)*

Terra Blanca 2001 Block 8 Syrah (Red Mountain) $35. This special selection of Syrah may have looked better in the fermenting vat, but it can't hold a candle to the winery's other Red Mountain bottling. Mushrooms, nail polish, saddle leather, and other earthy scents overwhelm the varietal fruit. There's a lot going on, and some tasters will surely love it. **85** —*P.G. (4/1/2005)*

Terra Blanca 1999 Block 8 Syrah (Washington) $28. From Washington state's newest AVA, this Syrah's slightly stewed, dark red-berry fruit wears green herb and metallic notes. Medium-weight and soft on the tongue, it shows an almost apple-butter-like quality. Modest tannins and the apple note (perhaps a Washington thing from the old apple orchards?) again appear on the long finish. **85** *(11/1/2001)*

Terra Blanca 2003 Viognier (Yakima Valley) $15. Very pale, almost colorless, with some light scents of orange and citrus rind. Spritzy and aggressively tart, this thin wine is too sour to deliver much pleasure. **83** —*P.G. (4/1/2005)*

TERRA D'ORO

Terra d'Oro 1997 Barbera (Amador County) $22. This grape seems to be making something of a comeback, and why not? With its deep, ripe aromas of red berries, stone fruits, and tobacco, and soft, generous fruity flavors, it's a good drink. **88** —*S.H. (8/1/2001)*

USA

Terra d'Oro 1999 Syrah (Amador County) $18. The closed nose shows subtle toast, cocoa, and unleavened bread-flour aromas; the palate shows jammy berry fruit and sweet maple-syrup flavors. Finishes with chalk and spicy pepper. This Syrah has depth, but needs two years to open up a bit. **88** *(10/1/2001)*

Terra d'Oro 2000 Deaver Vineyard Old Vine Zinfandel (Amador County) $24. Manages to marry Zin's wild, untrammelled character with the finesse and elegance of a fine red wine. Hard to believe it has nearly 16% of alcohol. The berry and tobacco flavors are dry and perfectly balanced. If you're serving any kind of upscale barbecue, consider this wine. **90** —*S.H. (9/1/2003)*

Terra d'Oro 1998 Deaver Vineyard Old Vine Zinfandel (Amador County) $22. Monster aromas leap out of the glass, rich in plum and blackberry fruit, chocolate, spice, and caramel. Tastes almost Port-like, with huge fruit flavors, a syrupy texture, slight sweetness, and a bit of heat from 15.5% alcohol. **86** —*S.H. (8/1/2001)*

Terra d'Oro 2000 Home Vineyard Zinfandel (Amador County) $24. From a tiny, four-acre vineyard, a wine that defines Amador Zin, which is saying a lot. Bright, briary, and brambly fruit, like picking wild berries on a hot summer day in the mountains. The wine is totally dry, which is why the alcohol is so high, nearly 16%, but completely delicious. **90** —*S.H. (9/1/2003)*

Terra d'Oro 1999 Home Vineyard Zinfandel (Amador County) $12. The Home Vineyard bottling mixes milk chocolate scents, ripe cherries, and streaks of licorice in a pleasing, ripe, full-bodied Zin. There's a good, tight, tart backbone to the wine, and it's just a shade less complex than its brother, the SHR Field Blend. **88** —*P.G. (3/1/2002)*

Terra d'Oro 1999 SHR Field Blend Zinfandel (Amador County) $12. This stylish blend from Montevina's Terra d'Oro brand shows smooth, tangy ripe fruit, highlighted with spice and lifted a bit with acids. Seamless attack and a smooth, stylish mouthfeel. **89** —*P.G. (3/1/2002)*

TERRA VALENTINE

Terra Valentine 2002 Cabernet Sauvignon (Spring Mountain) $35. Dramatically structured and flavored, this is a tough, young mountain wine that deserves to be cellared. It's perfectly dry, with distinct flavors of blackberries, green olives, cocoa, and new oak, but those tannins assault with youthful astringency. Give this wine four or five years to soften. **90 Cellar Selection** —*S.H. (4/1/2006)*

Terra Valentine 2000 Cabernet Sauvignon (Spring Mountain) $35. Nice wine, and just misses a higher score for a trace of herbaceousness, which is due to the vintage. Otherwise there's some sweet black currant fruit wrapped in fine, velvety tannins, and the touch of smoky oak is just right. **90** —*S.H. (8/1/2003)*

Terra Valentine 1999 Cabernet Sauvignon (Spring Mountain) $35. Clean, well-made and textbook Cab, with cassis and plum flavors and gritty, fine tannins. Dry and oaky, with ample concentration and focus. **90** —*S.H. (2/1/2003)*

Terra Valentine 2002 Wurtele Vineyard Cabernet Sauvignon (Spring Mountain) $50. This single-vineyard bottling is great. It's a huge, deep wine, brilliant in black currant, green olive, and cocoa flavors, yet packed in big-time mountain tannins that pretty much shut it down on the finish. If you buy a case, begin popping corks in 2008. If you have a single bottle, it should be great in ten years, if cellared properly. **96 Editors' Choice** —*S.H. (4/1/2006)*

Terra Valentine 2000 Wurtele Vineyard Cabernet Sauvignon (Spring Mountain) $50. Bright yet plush, with black cherry, currant, sage, herb, spice, licorice, blackberry, chocolate, toast, and smoke flavors all neatly layered for complexity. Firm, solid, ripe tannins add good structure. Finishes long and lush. **92** —*J.M. (10/1/2003)*

Terra Valentine 1999 Wurtele Vineyard Cabernet Sauvignon (Spring Mountain) $50. Intensely focused and pure, with powerful flavors of cassis and delicious streaks of green olive and chocolate. Oak adds cedar, vanilla, and sweet tannins. **93 Editors' Choice** —*S.H. (2/1/2003)*

Terra Valentine 2004 Wurtele Vineyard *Barrel Sample* Cabernet Sauvignon (Napa Valley) $NA. Rich, powerful, compelling, with a good marriage of toasty oak, black currant fruit, and finely-ground tannins.

Strong, but balanced and elegant. Definitely cellar quality. **93** —*S.H. (8/1/2004)*

Terra Valentine 2001 Wurtele Vineyard Reserve Cabernet Sauvignon (Spring Mountain) $50. Few California Cabernets can match this wine's flavor package, which takes coffee, black olive, cassis, and cherry notes and folds them into a rich, chewy whole. The long finish, supple tannins and remarkable complexity all add up to a winning wine. **93** —*J.C. (10/1/2004)*

TERRE ROUGE

Terre Rouge 1999 Mourvèdre (Amador County) $20. This winery has really figured out how to make fruit flavors that are remarkably delicious, and this wine displays that talent admirably. It just bursts with the tastiest stone fruit flavors, but they're dry, and the wine's balance is impeccable. **90** —*S.H. (7/1/2002)*

Terre Rouge 2000 Tete-a-Tete Red Blend (Sierra Foothills) $13. A softie, but what it lacks in lively acidity it makes up for in ripe fruitiness. In fact, delicious flavor is its strong point. There aren't many tannins, so the structure is sort of flabby. Thankfully, it's dry. **85** —*S.H. (7/1/2002)*

Terre Rouge 1997 Rhône Red Blend (Sierra Foothills) $20. A bit rough and sharp, with earthy-jammy flavors and a peppery finish. It's a lightly structured wine with thin flavors and a bite of acidity, and dry. Calls for simple foods, the heartier the better. A Rhône blend of Grenache, Mourvèdre, and Syrah. **84** —*S.H. (7/1/2002)*

Terre Rouge 2000 Vin Gris d'Amador Rosé Blend (Sierra Foothills) $12. From the coppery-peach color to the delicate peach, vanilla, and smoke aromas, to the luscious fruity flavors, this is one pretty wine. It's dryish, but filled with sunny ripeness. Especially notable for the round, harmonious mouthfeel. A very good value. A blend of Mourvèdre and Grenache. **89** —*S.H. (9/10/2002)*

Terre Rouge 1999 Syrah (Sierra Foothills) $22. What an interesting wine. It drinks like it really comes from someplace, which is to say, it has terroir. It smells earthy and peppery, with a perfume of cassis. It's soft in tannins and acids, but utterly delicious. Hard to exaggerate the lip-smacking quality and fantastic finish. **93** —*S.H. (7/1/2002)*

Terre Rouge 2000 Les Côtes de L'Ouest Syrah (California) $15. Dark and sexy; there's something erotic about this wine, with its seductive jammy flavors, velvety texture, and spicy, long finish. After an initial bite of acidity, it turns soft as a goose-down pillow. In its own way, it's perfect. And the price is unreal. **92 Best Buy** —*S.H. (7/1/2002)*

Terre Rouge 1998 Sentinel Oak Vineyard Pyramid Bloc Syrah (Shenandoah Valley (CA)) $30. Only 1000 cases of this wine were made, from some of the oldest Syrah vines in the Sierra Foothills. Sharp herbal aromas with a hint of green ride over bacony, meaty notes accented by smoky oak. The texture is velvety smooth, and fruity flavors fan out over the palate. It's dry, balanced, and complex. **89** —*S.H. (8/1/2001)*

Terre Rouge 1999 Sentinel Oak Vineyard Pyramid Block Syrah (Shenandoah Valley (CA)) $35. Hang onto your hat; here's a very great Syrah. The aromas are hiding, now suggesting plum and blackberry, now black pepper, now freshly baked rhubarb pie. In the mouth, it knocks out with grace and power. It's soft as silk, but complex and layered, and the richly tannic finish suggests aging potential. Not too long, though. **94** —*S.H. (7/1/2002)*

Terre Rouge 1999 Enigma White Blend (Sierra Foothills) $18. Opens with very attractive and complex aromas of white peach, apricot, and smoke. The tremendous flavors show layers of fruit and spice that just roll off the palate. Still, this Rhône blend of Marsanne, Viognier, and Roussanne is quite dry, with terrific structure and intricate detail. **93 Editors' Choice** —*S.H. (8/1/2001)*

TERRY HOAGE

Terry Hoage 2004 The 46 Grenache and Syrah Rhône Red Blend (Paso Robles) $40. Very ripe and forward in lush cherry and cocoa flavors, with a soft, velvety texture. The tannins are rich and smooth. **88** —*S.H. (12/1/2006)*

Terry Hoage 2004 The Hedge Syrah (Paso Robles) $45. This 100% Syrah is dark and dramatic looking, with a glyceriney sheen to the inky purple color. Feels soft and voluptuous, and very oaky, too. But the oak works well with the oodles of ripe blackberry, blueberry, cocoa, and anise flavors. **89** —*S.H. (12/1/2006)*

TESSERA

Tessera 1997 Chardonnay (California) $10. 83 —*M.S. (10/1/1999)*

TESTAROSSA

Testarossa 1998 Chardonnay (Santa Maria Valley) $26. 88 —*S.H. (10/1/2000)*

Testarossa 2004 Bien Nacido Vineyard Chardonnay (Santa Maria Valley) $39. Forward in tropical pineapple and lime pie flavors, and well-oaked, this Chard has a lush, creamy texture. What gives pause is the very high acidity leading to a tart finish. Strong enough to cut through lobster, but has the firmness of structure to develop over the next five years. **90** —*S.H. (9/1/2006)*

Testarossa 2003 Bien Nacido Vineyard Chardonnay (Santa Maria Valley) $36. Rich and spicy Chardonnay, and while it's a little soft in acidity, there's luxury in the creamy texture. The flavors veer toward pineapples and peaches, with the vanilla and buttered toast of fine oak. An upscale Chard for shellfish. **91** —*S.H. (7/1/2005)*

Testarossa 2001 Bien Nacido Vineyard Chardonnay (Santa Lucia Highlands) $35. When you measure this against Testarossa's other single vineyard wines, this release is earthy and lean, with citrus and tobacco flavors. Like all the rest, it's quite oaky. Doesn't share the rich opulence and hedonism of the others, although it's certainly a good wine. **87** —*S.H. (12/15/2003)*

Testarossa 2000 Bien Nacido Vineyard Chardonnay (Santa Maria Valley) $45. Elegant flourishes of ginger and Asian spices grace this wine's black cherry aromas and flavors. Despite a supremely supple mouthfeel and smooth vanilla and caramel flavors, the finish seems a bit hard. Give this wine a year or two to smooth out. **90** *(10/1/2002)*

Testarossa 1999 Bien Nacido Vineyard Chardonnay (Santa Maria Valley) $32. Restraint and elegance are not what you usually find in a Bien Nacido Vineyard Chardonnay, but this one offers tart apple, citrus, and peach flavors along with a dose of toasty new oak. Clean and understated style. **87** *(7/1/2001)*

Testarossa 2004 Brosseau Vineyard Chardonnay (Chalone) $39. Super-ripe, superoaky, and while these are potential pitfalls, Testarossa handles them with aplomb. The flavors really impress, offering a detonation of creamy, smoky oak and imposingly rich pineapple custard, and crème brûlée. It's all balanced by zesty acidity. Drink this flashy Chardonnay now. **92** —*S.H. (12/15/2006)*

Testarossa 2003 Brosseau Vineyard Chardonnay (Chalone) $36. Not showing well now, but might be an ager. Tart and closed, with youthful acids, lees, and oak crowding out the pear, litchi, and hazelnut flavors. Could well become interesting after 2007. **88** —*S.H. (10/1/2005)*

Testarossa 2004 Castello Chardonnay (Central Coast) $28. A nice blended Chardonnay that displays finely ripe tropical fruit flavors and bright acids, as well as a rich coating of oak. This is the winery's basic Chard and showcases their flamboyant, New World style. **88** —*S.H. (3/1/2006)*

Testarossa 2003 Castello Chardonnay (Central Coast) $26. Crisp acidity marks this cool-climate wine. The acids balance out the sweet vanilla and oak, and the fruity flavors, which veer toward pineapple, mango, and peach. There's a rich swirl of Asian spice throughout. **88** —*S.H. (7/1/2005)*

Testarossa 2002 Castello Chardonnay (Central Coast) $26. Huge and massive are just two of the words that describe this incredibly fruity wine. It's intensely concentrated in pineapple and papaya flavors, and has a heavy layer of toasty oak. Drinks lusciously smooth and creamy, with a long, spicy finish. **90** —*S.H. (6/1/2004)*

Testarossa 2001 Castello Chardonnay (Santa Barbara) $26. The least expensive of Testarossa's offerings, this blended regional wine is also the least interesting. It is thin in flavors and high in acids, with a curiously burnt, ashy taste on the finish. **83** —*S.H. (10/1/2003)*

Testarossa 2000 Castello Chardonnay (Santa Barbara) $26. Testarossa's basic Chard is more sumptuous than many other wineries' best. It's notably oaky, in the house style, with explosive smoke, toast, vanilla, and

char notes. The fruit was allowed to hang for a long time, and developed intensely ripe flavors of tropical fruits. It's a bit flat, especially considering the sweetness, but delicious. **91** —*S.H. (12/15/2002)*

Testarossa 2004 Diana's Reserve Chardonnay (California) $50. Shows the richness and complexity of all Testarossa's Chardonnays, with masses of tropical fruit and oak flavors balanced by zesty acidity. But this wine, with a statewide appellation, has a mouthwatering minerality, a zesty tang of steel, that gives the wine extra layers. What a delicious, exciting Chardonnay. **94 Editors' Choice** —*S.H. (12/15/2006)*

Testarossa 2003 Diana's Reserve Chardonnay (California) $50. Super-rich, oaky, and ripe in the Testarossa style, this flamboyant wine bursts with tropical fruit, spice, buttered toast, and vanilla aromas and flavors. The texture is creamy, and the acidity high in this crowd pleaser. **90** —*S.H. (11/15/2005)*

Testarossa 1997 George Troquato Signature Rese Chardonnay (California) $42. 92 —*S.H. (5/1/2000)*

Testarossa 2003 Michaud Vineyard Chardonnay (Chalone) $36. There are earthy, leesy, and oaky-woody aromas and flavors to this wine. It's surprisingly unfruity, although there are notes of peaches and tropical fruits in the finish. Dry and crisp in acids. **87** —*S.H. (10/1/2005)*

Testarossa 2001 Michaud Vineyard Chardonnay (Chalone) $35. This is a big, rich Chardonnay, another monster lineup in Testarossa's single-vineyard series. Shows tightly knit apple and peach flavors very generously oaked, with the requisite additions of smoke, vanilla, and woody spices. There's something minerally in the middle that seems likely to preserve the wine, if you wish to age it. Very fine quality, and a super-good food wine. **92** —*S.H. (8/1/2003)*

Testarossa 2000 Michaud Vineyard Chardonnay (Chalone) $36. From the rugged, limestone-infused hills east of Monterey, this is an intensely concentrated wine whose peach flavors are made more complex by a mineral streak that's suggestive of flint or gunmetal. The flavors are enormous, and the structure is gorgeous. Crisp acidity and a creamy texture suit the fruit perfectly. Finishes dry and spicy. **93** —*S.H. (12/15/2002)*

Testarossa 1999 Michaud Vineyard Chardonnay (Chalone) $39. Here's an oaky, lemony wine with the acidity and stuffing for aging. Begins with citrus, cream, and smoke aromas, and turns searingly rich, with lemon mousse and smoky honey flavors that last through the long, spicy finish. **92** —*S.H. (12/1/2001)*

Testarossa 2003 Rosella's Vineyard Chardonnay (Santa Lucia Highlands) $36. This is a big, ripe Chard, well-oaked and brimming with spice and tropical fruit flavors. Plays to the popular taste for rich, creamy Chards that flood the mouth and last through a long finish. Try with lobster bisque. **90** —*S.H. (7/1/2005)*

Testarossa 2001 Rosella's Vineyard Chardonnay (Santa Lucia Highlands) $35. From a cool appellation, a wine that smells bright and clean, like the scent you get when slicing into a fresh peach. There's also a lot of young, toasty oak riding on top of the fruit. Long in the mouth and in the finish, this delicious wine has crisp, supporting acids. **91** —*S.H. (8/1/2003)*

Testarossa 2004 Rosellas Vineyard Chardonnay (Santa Lucia Highlands) $39. This is the ripest and fruitiest of the winery's current Chards, and a decadent one, with rich pineapple custard flavors. Oak adds vanilla, meringue, and woodspice notes. Rich, fat, flashy, and flamboyant, this is a distinctly New World Chardonnay. **93** —*S.H. (3/1/2006)*

Testarossa 2004 Sanford & Benedict Vineyard Chardonnay (Santa Barbara County) $39. The fruit isn't superrich, but what's so likeable about this wine is its Chablis-like mineral intensity, although it's also well-oaked. Under the wet stone and flint is a polished layer of white peach. **91** —*S.H. (3/1/2006)*

Testarossa 2002 Signature Reserve Chardonnay (California) $44. A statewide appellation is usually a lesser wine, but this gigantic beauty is the product of the best lots from select vineyards. It's super-intense in pineapple, mango, vanilla, caramel, coconut, and toasted meringue flavors, with a smooth texture. Finishes with a trace of leesy bitterness, which adds complexity. **93** —*S.H. (6/1/2004)*

Testarossa 1999 Signature Reserve Chardonnay (California) $44. My cousin, who lives in France and likes austere, challenging wines, found this impossibly oversized, but American palates will be in awe. Late-picked grapes have an almost botrytized sweetness, and the whole is lavishly oaked. It's Disneyland in your mouth, always something flashy going on. **93 Editors' Choice** —*S.H. (12/15/2002)*

Testarossa 1998 Signature Reserve Chardonnay (California) $42. This is a big, delicious mélange of pineapple, pears, buttered popcorn, and coconut vying with mineral and toasty oak elements. Fat and friendly, it's got the goods to hold the taster's interest. The "California Cuvée" designation means that it's made of fruit from many places—more proof that good bottles are not all vineyard designates or single AVA wines. Enjoy now and over the next two years. **91** *(7/1/2001)*

Testarossa 1999 Sleepy Hollow Chardonnay (Santa Lucia Highlands) $32. Very bright and forward aromas of tropical fruits and lees introduce this complex wine. High acidity sears the palate, riding over peach and tropical fruit flavors. Very dry, it has a rich, creamy texture and a long, distinguished finish. **90** —*S.H. (12/1/2001)*

Testarossa 2004 Sleepy Hollow Vineyard Chardonnay (Santa Lucia Highlands) $39. Not surprisingly, this is similar to the Chards from this vineyard from Rob Talbott, which develop for a long time in the bottle. The wine is bone dry and very high in acidity, with a stony minerality to the peach and pineapple flavors. It's really too young now, but should begin to be ready by 2007. **91 Cellar Selection** —*S.H. (9/1/2006)*

Testarossa 2003 Sleepy Hollow Vineyard Chardonnay (Santa Lucia Highlands) $36. Rather earthy and herbal, despite plenty of sweet oak. As it airs and warms, pear and citrus flavors emerge. Made in a leaner, acidic, perhaps more food-friendly fashion. **86** —*S.H. (10/1/2005)*

Testarossa 2001 Sleepy Hollow Vineyard Chardonnay (Santa Lucia Highlands) $35. Something special from the west side of the Salinas Valley, with its fogs and wind. Drinks very bright in acids and even some tannins that frame a mélange of flavors, including sweet lime, green apple, and the ripest white peach. Tastes leesy and has the texture of sweet cream. This distinctive wine defines Monterey's interpretation of Chardonnay. **93 Editors' Choice** —*S.H. (8/1/2003)*

Testarossa 2000 Sleepy Hollow Vineyard Chardonnay (Santa Lucia Highlands) $34. The tightest and leanest of Testarossa's amazing array of single-vineyard Chards, this wine from downright cold hills in northern Monterey County has underlying flavors of citrus, flint, mineral, and apple, softened by considerable oak. Lees also make a starring appearance. Not flamboyant, but very well-crafted in its own right. **92** —*S.H. (12/15/2002)*

Testarossa 2002 Pinot Noir (Chalone) $49. Light in color, with a soft, creamy texture, this wine appeals for its cedary, leather and vanilla aromas, and black cherry and and cranberry flavors. It's delicate and silky. **87** *(11/1/2004)*

Testarossa 2002 Bien Nacido Vineyard Pinot Noir (Santa Maria Valley) $49. Very attractive aroma, with raspberries, cherries, vanilla, cocoa, pepper, clove, and smoke all screaming, "Drink me!" Silky smooth; seductive on the palate, lush and long. The finish lasts for a good minute. **89** *(11/1/2004)*

Testarossa 2001 Bien Nacido Vineyard Pinot Noir (Santa Maria Valley) $50. Lots of flavor packed into this light-bodied, smoothly textured wine, although it's a bit one-dimensional. Flavors veer toward raspberry cola and lots of dusty, peppery spices, wrapped in silky tannins and boosted by crisp acids. **86** —*S.H. (7/1/2003)*

Testarossa 1999 Bien Nacido Vineyard Pinot Noir (Santa Maria Valley) $40. Dramatic, showy nose of smoky rasberry tart, vanilla, cinnamon, and deeper notes of blackberry preserves lead to wonderfully fruity flavors. Supple, silky, and dry, this complex beauty offers lots of hedonistic pleasure. **91** —*S.H. (12/15/2001)*

Testarossa 2004 Bien Nacido Vineyard Elder Series Pinot Noir (Santa Maria Valley) $54. The ungainly name refers to older vines from this celebrated vineyard, and the wine does possess a distinguished balance. The pure cherry kirsch flavors are perfectly integrated into the oak, acid, and tannic structure, with an elegantly silky texture. The result is pure Pinot pleasure. Should hold well over the next six years. **92** —*S.H. (9/1/2006)*

Testarossa 2004 Brosseau Vineyard Pinot Noir (Chalone) $54. This hasn't been my favorite Testarossa Pinot, although it's a very good one. It's a big, ripe wine, possibly ageworthy, with exuberant cherry, raspberry, and new oak flavors. It has a gritty tannin structure that contributes to a slightly rustic mouthfeel. **87** —*S.H. (12/15/2006)*

Testarossa 2003 Brosseau Vineyard Pinot Noir (Chalone) $54. I think this wine is lighter than the '03 Pisoni, just across the Salinas Valley. It has tobaccoey, coffee flavors around the dry sour cherries, and is softer in tannins. But it's lively, even tart in acidity. Try holding it for a few years to let it knit together. **87** —*S.H. (11/15/2005)*

Testarossa 2004 Cuvée Niclaire Pinot Noir (California) $75. Testarossa is one of the few wineries to make a statewide bottling that's more expensive than their vineyard-designated ones. In this case, the wine is indisputably delicious. It's soft and accessible, with luscious fruit, spice, and oak flavors, and sweetness in the finish. But it's not better than Testarossa's other Pinots. **88** —*S.H. (12/15/2006)*

Testarossa 2003 Cuvée Niclaire Pinot Noir (California) $75. The California appellation is because the wine is made from three Santa Lucia Highlands vineyards and Bien Nacido. It's a really good wine. The cool vineyards give it brisk acidity, while the ripe grapes lend deep flavors of cherries and black raspberries. Oak does its spicy, complexing thing. Shows Pinot's translucent, elegant, silky texture. **93** —*S.H. (11/15/2005)*

Testarossa 2002 Cuvée Niclaire Pinot Noir (California) $72. Classic coastal wine. Fine and elegant in the mouth, light- to medium-bodied and silky, with ripe cherry, vanilla, and spice flavors. Not a powerhouse, but rich, textured, and balanced. **89** *(11/1/2004)*

Testarossa 2000 Cuvée Niclaire Pinot Noir (Santa Lucia Highlands) $68. A fine, complex Pinot, sourced mostly from this well-regarded appellation, but boosted by some Bien Nacido-Santa Barbara fruit. It's rich and opulent, with ripe, fruity flavors. The tannins and acids are silky and softly approachable. **91** —*S.H. (2/1/2003)*

Testarossa 1999 Cuvée Niclaire Pinot Noir (Santa Lucia Highlands) $68. Very dark and rich, showing a black cherry, saddle leather, and toast bouquet. The full, nearly syrupy mouthfeel supports anise, caramel, brown sugar, chocolate, and vanilla flavors. It finishes long with even tannins. This plump, almost creamy Pinot should be at its best from 2003–2007. **89** *(10/1/2002)*

Testarossa 1998 Cuvée Niclaire Reserve Pinot Noir (Santa Lucia Highlands) $60. This hedonistic wine is profoundly satisfying to sniff, with its refined, sappy black raspberry, spice, and smoke aromas. It drinks like a dream. Raspberry nectar, limpid, and mellow, with piquant spices and good acidity give it balance, while melted tannins provide velvety grip. **94 Cellar Selection** —*S.H. (12/15/2001)*

Testarossa 1997 Cuvée Niclaire Reserve Pinot Noir (Santa Lucia Highlands) $50. 91 *(10/1/2000)*

Testarossa 2003 Elder Series Bien Nacido Vineyard Pinot Noir (Santa Lucia Highlands) $54. This well-crafted single-vineyard wine, offers immediate pleasure. We're talking about intense cherry liqueur, raspberry, cola, and root beer flavors that are opulently ripe, although the wine itself is correctly dry. Light and silky, with crisp acidity and a lingering aftertaste. Drink now. **90** —*S.H. (7/1/2005)*

Testarossa 2003 Fritschen Vineyard Pinot Noir (Russian River Valley) $54. There's a lot of well-toasted oak on this wine, but it's easily able to handle it. In fact, the wood meshes seamlessly with the bright, intense cherry, pomegranate, and spice flavors to produce extreme complexity. Still young and vibrant. Best in a year or so. **93** —*S.H. (10/1/2005)*

Testarossa 1999 Garys' Vineyard Pinot Noir (Santa Maria Valley) $40. Smells lush and ripe, with deeply scented raspberry, vanilla, and smoke aromas burnished with toasted oak. Hits the palate with a burst of spicy berry fruit, opulent and sweet, wrapped in lush, smooth tannins. A seductive, silky wine. **91** —*S.H. (12/15/2001)*

Testarossa 2004 Garys' Vineyard Pinot Noir (Santa Lucia Highlands) $54. The youthful acidity really strikes you, and so do the silky texture and enormous flavors, all of which make it textbook Garys'. The raspberry parfait, sweet mint tea, and dusting of white chocolate are delicious, but the wine feels young and unresolved. It needs a little time to come together. Best 2007–2010. **91** —*S.H. (12/15/2006)*

Testarossa 2003 Garys' Vineyard Pinot Noir (Santa Lucia Highlands) $54. Young and a bit aggressive now in acids and tannins, with a raw, jammy quality, but what a good wine it will be in a year or two. Big and warm in red and black cherries, with hints of root beer and cinnamon, it will easily hold for 6 to 8 years. **92** —S.H. (10/1/2005)

Testarossa 2002 Garys' Vineyard Pinot Noir (Santa Lucia Highlands) $55. Ripe, dry, and well made, with complex aromas of cherries, sweet herbs, coffee, menthol, and smoky oak. Full-bodied and big, with a voluptuous mouthfeel. Delicious on its own, and a versatile food wine. **88** (11/1/2004)

Testarossa 2001 Garys' Vineyard Pinot Noir (Santa Lucia Highlands) $50. Lighter in body and substance than the 2000 vintage, with cola, cherry, and spice flavors wrapped in soft, easy tannins and crisp acids. Drinks very dry, with oaky influences. Nice in the mouth, and versatile at the table, but basically simple. **89** —S.H. (7/1/2003)

Testarossa 2000 Garys' Vineyard Pinot Noir (Santa Lucia Highlands) $45. Smoky, brambly raspberry is the dominant aromatic character here, while high-toned cherry and raspberry fruit sings on the racy, spicy palate. While some of the Garys' wines from 2000 are burly and muscled up, this one is a bit more streamlined. The mouth offers more pepper, spice, and heat than sheer opulence. **91** (10/1/2002)

Testarossa 2001 Michaud Vineyard Pinot Noir (Chalone) $50. From up in the Chalone highlands, this is a fruity wine, filled up upfront flavors of cherries, raspberries, cola, and spices. The structure is simple, with silky tannins and decent acids supporting the flavors without establishing any great depth or complexities. **85** —S.H. (7/1/2003)

Testarossa 2004 Palazzio Pinot Noir (Central Coast) $34. From the pale color you might expect a lightweight, but this Monterey-Santa Barbara blend is anything but. It's superripe, with baked cherry pie flavors that flood the palate with sweetness, although the wine is fully dry. Best now. **87** —S.H. (5/1/2006)

Testarossa 2003 Palazzio Pinot Noir (Central Coast) $32. Lots of richness and sophistication here, packed with black cherry, mulberry, cola, coffee, and spice flavors. It's dry, with an elegantly silky texture firmed up by crisp acidity. What you see is what you get. Drink now with a good, charbroiled steak. **88** —S.H. (7/1/2005)

Testarossa 2002 Palazzio Pinot Noir (Central Coast) $32. Although this blend of Monterey and Santa Barbara grapes is Testarossa's least costly Pinot Noir, it's a seriously good wine. You'll enjoy the silky texture and crisp acids that frame the cherry, leather, and herb flavors. The dusty tannins that kick in on the finish will provide a nice counterpoint to rich, marbled meats and cheeses. **90** —S.H. (11/1/2004)

Testarossa 2001 Palazzio Pinot Noir (Monterey) $32. A three-county blend of cool coastal climate Pinots. Shows pretty flavors of cherries and raspberries and peppery spices, in a light, silky package with firm acidity. **85** —S.H. (7/1/2003)

Testarossa 2000 Palazzio Pinot Noir (Monterey) $32. From the cool, wind-sheltered western highlands of Salinas Valley, a wine that combines sumptuous, massive fruit with delicacy of body to produce an outstandingly drinkable Pinot. It has ripe red raspberry and spice flavors in a dry package with silky tannins. Possesses irresistable elegance and finesse. **91** —S.H. (9/1/2003)

Testarossa 2000 Pisoni Pinot Noir (Santa Lucia Highlands) $55. Starts off with deceptively simple aromas of cherries, toast, and vanilla that broaden on the palate to encompass root vegetable and floral notes. The layered mouthfeel makes it go down easily, capped off by hints of coffee and caramel on the finish. **92** (10/1/2002)

Testarossa 1999 Pisoni Pinot Noir (Santa Lucia Highlands) $NA. Dramatically rich and stuffed with black raspberry, spice, tomato, cola, and espresso flavors, it's smooth and silky in the mouth. The fruity ripeness on the palate, not to mention the sweetness of well-toasted oak, lends it a honeyed feel right through the peppery, candied finish. **91** — S.H. (9/1/2003)

Testarossa 2004 Pisoni Vineyard Pinot Noir (Santa Lucia Highlands) $54. Big and mouthfillingly juicy, a humongous Pinot with enormously ripe cherry, raspberry, and vanilla pie filling flavors, and buttery, smoky oak. The amazing thing is how all this power is modified by the acids and delicate structure to yield elegance and finesse. Best now through 2010, depending on how you like older Pinots. **93** —S.H. (12/15/2006)

Testarossa 2003 Pisoni Vineyard Pinot Noir (Santa Lucia Highlands) $54. This is, shall we say, a voluminous Pinot, the kind this vineyard produces regularly. It's dark, full-bodied, and rich in black and red berry fruit, with fresh acidity. We now know that a Pisoni Pinot like this will improve in the cellar. Best to let it be until 2008. **92 Cellar Selection** — S.H. (11/15/2005)

Testarossa 2002 Pisoni Vineyard Pinot Noir (Santa Lucia Highlands) $50. Opens with scads of toasty oak, chocolate, coffee, ripe cherry, blackberry, and menthol aromas that are complex and inviting. Leads to a soothingly lush mouthfeel starring scads of red and black cherry flavors and youthful tannins. Big and full-bodied. Seriously good stuff. **91** (11/1/2004)

Testarossa 2004 Rosella's Vineyard Pinot Noir (Santa Lucia Highlands) $54. Don't be misled by the pale color. This is an immense wine. On the first sip, it explodes in cherry, cola, coffee, cocoa, and rhubarb flavors that take over the palate through the long finish. Fortunately it's totally dry and balanced, not too alcoholic, but rich enough in tannins for short-term aging. Drink now through 2009. **91** —S.H. (9/1/2006)

Testarossa 2003 Rosella's Vineyard Pinot Noir (Santa Lucia Highlands) $54. Luscious. Right now it's youthfully perky in acids, with a slightly thick mouthfeel, but it's a heck of a Pinot that should soften by 2006. Then, those massive cherry flavors will be delicious. **90** —S.H. (10/1/2005)

Testarossa 2002 Rosella's Vineyard Pinot Noir (Santa Lucia Highlands) $49. Good, dark color. Smells ripe and jammy in black cherry and sweet blackberry fruit, with notes of Heirloom tomatoes and vanilla. A little soft in texture, but that makes for a velvety, lush mouthfeel. The long, spicy finish is a bonus. **89** (11/1/2004)

Testarossa 2001 Rosella's Vineyard Pinot Noir (Santa Lucia Highlands) $50. This is a wine that packs a lot of substance, although it has deliciously upfront flavors of cherries and berries. There's a meatiness to the palate that adds depth and interest, while crisp acidity defines the flavors on the palate. Textbook Santa Lucia Highlands Pinot Noir, fruity, complex, and silky. **88** —S.H. (7/1/2003)

Testarossa 2004 Sanford & Benedict Vineyard Pinot Noir (Santa Barbara County) $54. It would be a shame to drink this wine too young. It's tannic, and we know that Pinots from this vineyard need time. It's rich in cherry, cola, coffee, and spice flavors. Should begin to open by '07 and hang in there for another three or four years before it begins to tire. **90 Cellar Selection** —S.H. (5/1/2006)

Testarossa 2004 Schultze Family Vineyard Pinot Noir (Santa Cruz Mountains) $54. This pale-colored wine is light in texture, with a sheer, silk, and satin, airy mouthfeel that reminds you of tea. It's also very acidic, and filled with youthfully immature fruit and spice. Brings to mind certain great Burgundies on release. It should be exciting to age this wine past 2008. **91 Cellar Selection** —S.H. (12/15/2006)

Testarossa 2000 Sleepy Hollow Pinot Noir (Santa Lucia Highlands) $45. Ample vanilla and powdered cinnamon aromas accent earthy beet and forest-floor scents in this lush, creamy-textured wine. While there's plenty of red fruit providing a rich foundation, the surface flavors are vanilla and dried spices; it takes some work to find the strawberry-raspberry flavors hidden within. **90** (10/1/2002)

Testarossa 2004 Sleepy Hollow Vineyard Pinot Noir (Santa Lucia Highlands) $54. I love how translucent in color this Pinot pours, confirmation of the light, elegantly silky texture that is such a varietal pleasure. The flavors are anything but shy. The powerful cherry, cola, rhubarb, cola, and spice flavors battle it out through the long finish, and the wine is commandingly dry. May hold for some years, but it's best now with a lamb chop. **91** —S.H. (9/1/2006)

Testarossa 2003 Sleepy Hollow Vineyard Pinot Noir (Santa Lucia Highlands) $54. A lighter-bodied Pinot, fairly pale in color and delicately structured. The fruit struggled to ripen, and straddles the line between cherries and tomatoes. Finishes rich in smoky oak. **89** —S.H. (10/1/2005)

Testarossa 2002 Sleepy Hollow Vineyard Pinot Noir (Santa Lucia Highlands) $49. Here's a big wine with lots of flair and zest. It has rich aromas of cherries, caramel, mocha, and vanilla, and is quite oaky.

Bursting with ripe cherry and spice flavors wrapped in a smooth, creamy texture with good acidity. **88** *(11/1/2004)*

Testarossa 2001 Sleepy Hollow Vineyard Pinot Noir (Santa Lucia Highlands) $50. A very good wine while somehow failing to rise to expectations. Is it the vintage? All the elements are there, including ripe fruit flavors enriched with herbal and spicy complexities, generous acids and silky smooth tannins. Yet the wine is curiously New World flashy without offering nuance or depth. **89** —*S.H. (7/1/2003)*

Testarossa 1999 Garys' Vineyard Syrah (Santa Lucia Highlands) $42. Taut, with reduced but decidedly complex elements of toast, beef, blackberry, brown sugar, and earth. Full, almost heavy on the tongue, it's chewy, with dense, plummy fruit and solid structure. The back end is big, with large tannins, suppressed fruit, meat, and espresso notes. Needs time— best after 2004, and should last the decade. **89** *(11/1/2001)*

Testarossa 2003 Garys' Vineyard Syrah (Santa Lucia Highlands) $45. Here's a dark, tannic, dry Syrah from a vineyard famous for producing wines of volume and heft. It's dry and full, with rich blackberry, coffee, chocolate, plum, and oaky-spice flavors. Drink now through 2006, with powerfully spiced fare. **90** —*S.H. (3/1/2006)*

Testarossa 2002 Garys' Vineyard Syrah (Santa Lucia Highlands) $42. This is a complex Syrah whose cool-climate origins show in the peppery, leathery profile and crisp acids. It's absolutely dry, and the tannins, while pronounced, are easily negotiated. As good as it is, it could use more fruity concentration. **89** —*S.H. (7/1/2005)*

Testarossa 2000 Garys' Vineyard Syrah (Santa Lucia Highlands) $42. A fabulously rich, generous wine that oozes over the palate like nectar, carrying along black currant, cassis, and herb flavors and substantial flavorings from oak. As good as it is, it feels soft on the palate. A hit of tannin kicks in on the finish. **90** —*S.H. (2/1/2003)*

THE ACADEMY

The Academy 2000 Merlot (Applegate Valley) $20. The color is substantial, and the wine has some spicy tartness. Moderately ripe red fruits, firm acids and balanced tannins tell the story. **85** —*P.G. (8/1/2002)*

The Academy 2000 Pinot Noir (Applegate Valley) $16. Very soft and light, with pale flavors of red fruits and cranberry. **83** —*P.G. (12/31/2002)*

THE EYRIE VINEYARDS

The Eyrie Vineyards 1999 Estate Grown Chardonnay (Willamette Valley) $18. Eyrie's Chardonnays are idiosyncratic, with a distinctive, pungent, tarry note dominating the tight, green apple fruit. The 37-year-old vineyard has unique clones, and winemaker David Lett does a long fermentation sur lie. The result is a tart, citrusy wine with the possibility of aging for quite a long while. **87** —*P.G. (9/1/2003)*

The Eyrie Vineyards 1999 Reserve Chardonnay (Willamette Valley) $25. Chardonnay is not the ace in David Lett's deck, but he does a distinctive style that is built to be tight and ageworthy. Yeasty, creamy and elegant, the reserve spends almost two years on the lees and extra time in the bottle before being released. Green apple and lemon flavors rule; this is a food wine and a wine to lay down for a while longer. **88** —*P.G. (9/1/2003)*

The Eyrie Vineyards 2000 Pinot Gris (Willamette Valley) $15. Eyrie is back in stride with this benchmark Pinot Gris after a sub-par '99 bottling. Fresh flavors of lemon zest and pear highlight a subtle wine whose subtle spice and zesty complexity promise a long, pleasing life ahead. **91 Best Buy** —*P.G. (8/1/2003)*

The Eyrie Vineyards 2000 Estate Grown Pinot Noir (Willamette Valley) $25. Eyrie's Pinots can be quite deceptive when young. This is a sweetly perfumed with ripe fruit, tightly structured, and more Old World than New in its flavors. The emphasis is on high acids, subtle hints of mineral, and a dash of herb. **89** —*P.G. (4/1/2003)*

The Eyrie Vineyards 1999 Reserve Pinot Noir (Willamette Valley) $35. In a great vintage such as 1999, Eyrie's reserve Pinot can be expected to age for as long as any made in America. This is ripely scented with classic Pinot fruit and fertile earth. The Burgundian sweet cherry and plum flavors at the heart of it also carry a bit of barnyard, what the French call gout de terroir. Note: this is not jammy, sweet or unctuous. It is not hedonistic. It is simply excellent. **91** —*P.G. (4/1/2003)*

THE FOUR GRACES

The Four Graces 2003 Pinot Gris (Willamette Valley) $20. This has a flavor of fresh cut Bartlett pear that is almost beyond belief; it's like pear juice without the conversion to wine. It leads into a very floral, fruity, and exceedingly soft finish, with a hint of honey. **87** —*P.G. (2/1/2006)*

THE GREY ROSE

The Grey Rose 2005 Pinot Pinot Rosé Blend (California) $13. This blush, an offbeat blend of Pinot Noir and Pinot Grigio, tastes dry and fine, a silky, light-bodied wine with gentle flavors of raspberries, cinnamon, vanilla, and a squeeze of lime. **86** —*S.H. (11/15/2006)*

THE MAIDEN

The Maiden 2002 Cabernet Blend (Napa Valley) $95. From the home vineyard in the Oakville foothills, this little sister to Harlan Estate is very similar to it. The structure is superb, with a classic elegance of tannins and acids. The flavors are just enormous, all about chocolate fudge, crème de cassis, and cherry cola, yet the wine is dry and crisp. There's something sensual and sexy about this claret, a completely nourishing wine that provides endless pleasure. At this price, it's a value compared to Harlan Estate. **94** —*S.H. (9/1/2006)*

The Maiden 2001 Cabernet Blend (Napa Valley) $95. This companion wine to the famous Harlan Estate comes from the same Oakville vineyard. Decadent and vastly complex, it opens with cassis, grilled meat, cedar, spicebox, cigar box, and cheddar aromas, and then turns medium- to full-bodied in the mouth. Terrific black cherry, blackberry, and cassis fruit, pure and refined. Perfect elaboration of oak, char, tannins, acids, and fruit, like a symphony orchestra working together. Drink now through 2015. **98 Editors' Choice** —*S.H. (6/1/2005)*

THE MATRIARCH

The Matriarch 2002 Cabernet Blend (Napa Valley) $80. This is the second label of Bond, a blend of various vineyards. As such, it's one of the best buys in the Harlan stable, retaining the lyrical balance of all its wines. Super-rich in chocolate and cassis flavors, the wine is distinguished and refined despite its size. Hard to exaggerrate the richness and beauty of this classic claret. **94** —*S.H. (9/1/2006)*

The Matriarch 2001 Cabernet Blend (Napa Valley) $75. This second label of Bond is right up there with the named wines. It is virtually undistinguishable from Vecina, although perhaps a shade less profound and more obvious. A terrific Cabernet-based wine, rich, powerful, and ageable. At less than half the price of Bond, it's a comparative value. **94 Editors' Choice** —*S.H. (6/1/2005)*

THE ORGANIC WINE WORKS

The Organic Wine Works 2001 Proprietor's Reserve Cabernet Sauvignon (Mendocino County) $19. Tastes like a Cab from a hot climate, with rough, dry tannins and a baked flavor, like pie crust that's been a little burnt. The acids are very soft. On the other hand, there are some pretty blackberry and cassis notes, with a streak of blueberry. **85** —*S.H. (11/15/2003)*

The Organic Wine Works 2001 Proprietor's Reserve Merlot (Mendocino County) $19. Drinks a bit hot and harsh. The blackberry, plum, and chocolate flavors veer on the edge of raisins, and the tannins feel rough and jagged. Finishes very dry, with good fruity length and a trace of bitterness. **85** —*S.H. (2/1/2004)*

The Organic Wine Works 2001 Syrah (California) $12. This is a rough hewn bruiser of a wine that is saved by its modest price. It has well-ripened flavors of berries and cherries, but also has rugged tannins, sharp acids, and an overall rustic quality through the swallow. **84** —*S.H. (2/1/2004)*

THE PRISONER

The Prisoner 2000 Red Blend (Napa Valley) $28. Richly textured, but with a seriously tangy edge. The wine is brimming with spicy black cherry, blackberry, cinnamon, blueberry, toast, tar, and herb flavors. The finish is long. An intriguing blend of Zinfandel, Syrah, Charbono, and Petite Sirah. Made by up-and-coming winemaker David Phinney. **90** —*J.M. (4/1/2003)*

THE SEVEN BROTHERS

The Seven Brothers 2001 Sauvignon Blanc (Clear Lake) $12. Melon, citrus, and herb notes are well balanced in this pleasing, refreshing, light wine. Bright and fresh to the end, it's perfect for summer quaffing. **87** —J.M. *(7/1/2003)*

The Seven Brothers 2001 Sauvignon Blanc (Clear Lake) $10. Fairly lightweight, without any of the distinguishing marks of this normally somewhat assertive varietal. It shows hints of melon and citrus, however, and will not offend. **80** —J.M. *(9/1/2004)*

THE TERRACES

The Terraces 1997 Cabernet Sauvignon (Napa Valley) $60. 89 *(11/1/2000)*

The Terraces 1999 Cabernet Sauvignon (Napa Valley) $60. 90 *(8/1/2003)*

The Terraces 2001 Zinfandel (Napa Valley) $25. The wine serves up beguiling black cherry and smoke at its center, then fans out to reveal more toast, blackberry, and anise flavors. The tannins and oak get a little out of balance, however, and overshadow some of these attributes. Still a good wine. **87** *(11/1/2003)*

THE WHITE KNIGHT

The White Knight 2005 Viognier (Clarksburg) $16. A dry, minerally white wine that's crisp and clean in acids. It offers subtle, complex citron, lime, wildflower, vanilla wafer, and spice flavors. Has the weight of Sauvignon Blanc, but with more opulent fruit. **88** —S.H. *(12/1/2006)*

THE WILLIAMSBURG WINERY

The Williamsburg Winery 2004 Acte 12 Chardonnay (Virginia) $16. This wine is clean and well made, with a smooth mouthfeel. Oaky butter and vanilla aromas combine with watery flavors of pear and popcorn. **81** —M.D. *(8/1/2006)*

The Williamsburg Winery 2003 Acte 12 of Sixteen Nineteen Chardonnay (Virginia) $16. A solid effort, this wine, named after a law requiring colonists to plant vineyards, boasts aromas of tropical fruit and grilled nuts, toasty, citrusy flavors and a lemon-pineapple finish. **86** —J.C. *(9/1/2005)*

The Williamsburg Winery 2004 John Adlum Chardonnay (Virginia) $11. Popcorn on the nose leads to citrus in the mouth, with a touch of oak. The wine verges on being tart, giving it a lively mouthfeel. **81** —M.D. *(8/1/2006)*

The Williamsburg Winery 2003 John Adlum Chardonnay (Virginia) $10. Smells oaky at first, with scents of buttered toast, vanilla, and grilled nuts leading the way, then shows more fruit on the palate, blending pear, orange, and melon flavors. Citrus notes linger on the finish. **85 Best Buy** —J.C. *(9/1/2005)*

The Williamsburg Winery 2004 Late Harvest Vidal Blanc (Virginia) $24. Round and full, this wine has moderate acidity that keeps it from cloying and white fruit flavors that are sweet but not up to the richness of most dessert wines. A barnyard note plays a minor role, detracting from the overall sweetness. **84** —M.D. *(8/1/2006)*

The Williamsburg Winery NV James River White White Blend (Virginia) $8. Acidity pokes through the creamy mouth, giving this wine a spiky feel. Starts with foxy aromas that dissipate, revealing generic yellow fruit flavors. **80** —M.D. *(8/1/2006)*

THIRTEEN

Thirteen 2003 Meritage Cabernet Blend (Napa Valley) $115. The wine, which is based on Cab Sauvignon, comes from 13 Napa appellations, hence the name. The wine is distinguished, showing lots of lush, forward cassis, and cocoa flavor. Has the smoothness of a great old Cognac. Drink now–2013. **92** —S.H. *(8/1/2006)*

THOMAS COYNE

Thomas Coyne 1996 Merlot (Sonoma County) $21. 91 *(11/15/1999)*

Thomas Coyne 1996 Contra Costa County Mourvèdre (Contra Costa County) $13. 88 —S.H. *(6/1/1999)*

Thomas Coyne 2000 Petite Sirah (California) $16. Hard to like, with some berry-cherry flavors but otherwise a simple, slightly sweet wine that feels thick and heavy in the mouth. Tannins are hard in the center, leading to a cough mediciney finish. **82** *(4/1/2003)*

Thomas Coyne 1997 La Petite Quest Red Blend (California) $10. 87 Best Buy —S.H. *(10/1/1999)*

Thomas Coyne 1996 Quest Red Blend (California) $10. 86 —S.H. *(6/1/1999)*

Thomas Coyne 1997 Syrah (California) $13. 88 Best Buy —S.H. *(6/1/1999)*

Thomas Coyne 1998 Syrah (California) $12. From Lodi grapes, a jam-scented wine, with pretty raspberry, black cherry, and crushed-pepper aromas. Pleasant, light, and fruity, with dry flavors of berries. No obvious faults or complexities in this soft, almost Beaujolais-like wine. **83** —S.H. *(7/1/2002)*

Thomas Coyne 1997 Viognier (California) $16. 87 —S.H. *(6/1/1999)*

Thomas Coyne 2000 Viognier (California) $15. From Lodi grapes, here's a rich, fruity, powerfully spicy wine, with aromas of fruit cocktail, butter cream, and honey. It drinks very fruity and overtly sweet, saved from flabbiness by crisp acidity. This is a candy of a wine, fruity and tart and frankly delicious. **85** —S.H. *(11/15/2001)*

THOMAS FOGARTY

Thomas Fogarty 2002 Camel Hill Vineyard Cabernet Franc (Santa Cruz Mountains) $48. Fogarty has a great track record with Cabernet, including Cab Franc, and this is an interesting, complex wine. It's dry and tannic. There's a gamey, leathery note to the blackberry and coffee fruit that finishes with great length. Despite the tannins, it doesn't seem like an ager, so drink up. **90** —S.H. *(5/1/2006)*

Thomas Fogarty 2001 Camel Hill Vineyard Cabernet Franc (Santa Cruz Mountains) $45. It takes an incredibly good vineyard to produce a Cab Franc this good. This lovely wine has lush blackberry flavors with nuances of espresso and sweet oregano. It's quite tannic, leaving behind a dusty astringency. **91** —S.H. *(11/15/2004)*

Thomas Fogarty 2001 Cabernet Sauvignon (Santa Cruz Mountains) $55. These mountains seem to give Cab that extra nudge of ripeness and balance that makes the best of them supreme. It's incredibly rich in black currant and sweet cassis, and the smoky edge of oak is perfect. You can hardly keep your hands off it, but try aging until its 10th birthday and beyond. **93** —S.H. *(10/1/2004)*

Thomas Fogarty 2001 Cabernet Sauvignon (Napa Valley) $55. From a Santa Cruz Mountains-based winery that knows how to craft an ageworthy Cab. A young wine, solid in tannins, but dry and well balanced. Oozes beautiful, juicy black currant fruit. Best with a sirloin steak, or age through 2010 and beyond. **90** —S.H. *(10/1/2004)*

Thomas Fogarty 2000 Cabernet Sauvignon (Napa Valley) $50. Quite full-bodied and rich in cassis and black currant fruit, this Cabernet feels weighty in the mouth. Partly that's due to the ripe fruit, and partly to the oak. It has an astringent scour of tannins, suggesting at least a few years of ageability. **88** —S.H. *(11/15/2004)*

Thomas Fogarty 1999 Cabernet Sauvignon (Santa Cruz County) $45. Big, young, kick-butt mountain Cabernet, as concentrated as it gets. Offers an array of berries, tree fruits, and herbs. Tannins are melted and soft, and youthful acids provide a punch to this dense wine. **92** —S.H. *(10/1/2003)*

Thomas Fogarty 2002 Vallerga Vineyard Cabernet Sauvignon (Napa Valley) $59. Drinkable now for its thick but ripely sweet tannins, this Cab has blue and black fruit and berry flavors, like blackberries, plums, black raspberries, and cola, enhanced with spicy, charry oak. What a long, beautiful finish. **90** —S.H. *(9/1/2006)*

Thomas Fogarty 1998 Chardonnay (Monterey County) $19. 88 *(6/1/2000)*

Thomas Fogarty 1997 Chardonnay (Santa Cruz Mountains) $20. 83 *(6/1/2000)*

Thomas Fogarty 2003 Chardonnay (Santa Cruz Mountains) $25. There's a toughness to this Chard, a combination of the acidity and of a taste of dried Italian herbs that accompanies the apple and peach flavors. It's not a lush wine, but it's clean and dry. **84** —S.H. *(2/1/2006)*

Thomas Fogarty 2002 Chardonnay (Santa Cruz Mountains) $24. Comes down firmly on the steely, cool-climate side, with high acidity and fla-

USA

vors of apples and citrus fruits. Sur lies aging adds richer, creamy, and yeasty notes, while oak does its smoky, vanilla thing. An interesting, complex food wine. **88** —*S.H. (2/1/2005)*

Thomas Fogarty 2001 Chardonnay (Santa Cruz Mountains) $23. Small mountain berries have yielded intense pear, peach, and tropical fruit flavors, along with vanilla, butter, Oriental spices, and toasted coconut. It's boldly oaked, too, with the creamy texture of a milkshake. A pure and beautiful expression of its place. **92 Editors' Choice** —*S.H. (6/1/2004)*

Thomas Fogarty 2003 Estate Reserve Chardonnay (Santa Cruz Mountains) $38. Complex, with tiers of tropical fruit, mineral, and oak flavors that unfold in waves. The wine is dry and opulent in spiced papayas and macaroons, leading to a caramel-like finish. **90** —*S.H. (11/15/2006)*

Thomas Fogarty 1997 Estate Reserve Chardonnay (Santa Cruz Mountains) $30. 91 *(6/1/2000)*

Thomas Fogarty 2004 Gewürztraminer (Monterey) $17. Right off the bat, Alsace is the model. The wine is dry and very crisp in tingly acids, and made even more tingly by a wealth of rich, dusty oriental spices. Flavorwise, it's all about nectarines, candied ginger, wildflowers, and kiwi in this well-crafted wine. **87** —*S.H. (2/1/2006)*

Thomas Fogarty 2003 Gewürztraminer (Monterey) $16. A very fine Gewürz with some real depth and concentration. You'll be impressed by the ripe, flashy flavors of exotic fruits, wildflowers, and all sorts of spices, and by the crisp acidity, which is almost sparkling. The wine is bone dry, Alsatian-style. **87** —*S.H. (12/1/2004)*

Thomas Fogarty 2002 Gewürztraminer (Monterey) $15. You'll love the aromatics here. Opens with lush notes of honeysuckle, apricot, wild honey, tangerine, peach, clove, and vanilla, and those flavors flood the palate. It's an opulently fruity, flowery wine, but it's perfectly dry. **86** —*S.H. (12/31/2003)*

Thomas Fogarty 2002 Gewürztraminer (Monterey) $15. Just what you want in a Gewürz, lots of spicy, peppery cinnamon, vanilla, and nutmeg, ripe tropical fruit and wildflower flavors, and a crisp spine of acidity. Finishes with a trace of honeyed sweetness. **85** —*S.H. (2/1/2004)*

Thomas Fogarty 2001 Gewürztraminer (Monterey) $14. This is a good example of California Gewürz near its best, but also why the masses shy away from it. The flavors are overwhelming. They fill the mouth with tree fruits, flowers, and crushed oriental spices that are nuclear in potency. The flavors are balanced by dry acidity, but this special wine requires drinking on its own, or with powerful foods. **87** —*S.H. (9/1/2003)*

Thomas Fogarty 2000 Gewürztraminer (Monterey) $14. If more Gewürzes were like this, the varietal would be more popular. The bouquet shows explosive aromas of wildflowers, honey, jasmine, vanilla, and citrus. Enormously fruity, but nicely dry, in the Alsatian style. Sturdy acidity meanwhile gives the wine life and pizzazz. **88** —*S.H. (11/15/2001)*

Thomas Fogarty 2002 Lexington Meritage (Santa Cruz Mountains) $45. This Bordeaux blend is soft, oaky, and a little sweet, but not excessively so. The fruit is ripe and forward, and there's a slight bite of tannin. The sweet thing reprises on the finish, which is a bit sugary. **84** —*S.H. (7/1/2006)*

Thomas Fogarty 2001 Merlot (Santa Cruz Mountains) $32. Although there is a mountain intensity to the intense blackberry and cherry flavors and rich tannins, this wine is probably at its best now. It's very dry and rich, with evident oak, and a distinguished finish. **91** —*S.H. (10/1/2005)*

Thomas Fogarty 2000 Merlot (Santa Cruz Mountains) $30. Opens with a blast of oak undergirded with distinctive olive, chocolate, cheddar, and cherry aromas. Yet the flavors are dominated by cherries, pure, ripe, and sweet. The wine has a firm tannic structure, and is harmonious and balanced. **91** —*S.H. (12/15/2004)*

Thomas Fogarty 1999 Merlot (Santa Cruz Mountains) $28. At 3 1/2 years of age, this tremendous wine has softened a bit to reveal huge flavors of black currants, spicy plum pudding, and chocolate. It's still a bit awkward, with acids zinging all over the place. Cellar through 2006, at which point you should have a great wine. **91** —*S.H. (10/1/2003)*

Thomas Fogarty 1998 Merlot (Santa Cruz Mountains) $30. The media has dissed this vintage, but here's a wine that makes lemonade from lemons. It's not a blockbuster and the fruit is sparse, but the winemaking is fine.

It tastes elegant and upscale, a sleek, fairly tannic and acidic wine that possesses the ineffable quality of taste. **89** —*S.H. (11/15/2002)*

Thomas Fogarty 2002 Razorback Vineyard Merlot (Santa Cruz Mountains) $35. This is a very ripe Merlot that's brimming with cherry pie filling and vanilla flavors. It's also dry and balanced, and has silky, velvety tannins. There's a veneer of toasty oak that makes you think of a grilled steak that's charred on the outside and juicy within. **86** —*S.H. (12/1/2006)*

Thomas Fogarty 2002 Pinot Noir (Santa Cruz Mountains) $30. What a deliciously drinkable Pinot, with flavors of cherry tart, cola, rhubarb pie, coffee, and spices, boosted by crisp acids. It's a silky, light-bodied sipper. **87** —*S.H. (2/1/2006)*

Thomas Fogarty 2001 Pinot Noir (Santa Cruz Mountains) $25. A very nice Pinot. If it shows no particular complexity, it's has a textbook silky texture, dryness, and flavors of cherries, coffee, and oak. **87** —*S.H. (2/1/2005)*

Thomas Fogarty 2000 Pinot Noir (Santa Cruz Mountains) $23. This wonderful Pinot makes you regret that these mountains south of San Francisco are producing all the wine they can. It's silky and light, with subtle but delicious flavors of cherries, cola, sweet black tea, smoke, and an array of peppery spices. Defines Pinot's elegance and finesse. At its best now. **91 Editors' Choice** —*S.H. (6/1/2004)*

Thomas Fogarty 1999 Pinot Noir (Santa Cruz Mountains) $23. With an abundance of cedar, leather, animal, and earth aromas, you wonder where the fruit is. But one taste delivers plenty of cherry along with menthol and mineral. The round, warm finish confirms that this is a solid wine with ample depth and texture. **88** *(10/1/2002)*

Thomas Fogarty 1998 Pinot Noir (Santa Cruz Mountains) $30. From this veteran producer, a very pretty wine, suitable for early consumption. The berry, tomato, and mushroom aromas are joined to dry, spicy flavors. Drinks light and tart in the middle, but a success for the vintage. **86** —*S.H. (12/15/2001)*

Thomas Fogarty 2003 Estate Pinot Noir (Santa Cruz Mountains) $35. There are rich tannins and a fairly dense mouthfeel to this Pinot, making it a bit ponderous now, although it may improve over the next three to five years. It's a dry wine, with good cherry fruit and significant oak. It feels low in acidity, and lacking zest. **86** —*S.H. (7/1/2006)*

Thomas Fogarty 2001 Estate Reserve Pinot Noir (Santa Cruz Mountains) $45. This very good wine may improve with a few years of cellaring. It's fairly tannic and bright with citrusy acids, and there's a wonderful complex core of flavor that includes black cherry, bitter chocolate, coffee, sweet dried herbs, and pepper. Silky smooth. Now through 2008. **89** —*S.H. (12/1/2004)*

Thomas Fogarty 2002 Rapley Trail Vineyard Block B Pinot Noir (Santa Cruz Mountains) $65. Cherry Jello, vinyl, cola notes. Sharp in acidity, and simple. **83** *(11/1/2004)*

Thomas Fogarty 2002 Rapley Trail Vineyard Block M Pinot Noir (Santa Cruz Mountains) $65. Richer by a hair than the Block B bottling, with black cherry and vanilla flavors leading to a chocolatey finish. Nice supple mouthfeel. **86** *(11/1/2004)*

Thomas Fogarty 2003 Fat Buck Ridge Vineyard Syrah (Santa Cruz Mountains) $55. It's midnight black, thoroughly dry, high in alcohol, and distinctive for the power and authority of its fruity structure. Anyone can achieve ripeness, but this wine's dry balance really makes it special. The tannins ensure a long life. Drink now through 2015. **93 Cellar Selection** —*S.H. (10/1/2006)*

THOMAS MICHAEL

Thomas Michael 2002 Ledgewood Vineyard Syrah (Suisun Valley) $32. Has some hay-like notes that detract slightly from the aromas, which are otherwise just fine, with plenty of jammy blackberries and modest peppery scents. Medium- to full-bodied in the mouth, finishing with supple tannins. **86** *(9/1/2005)*

THORNTON

Thornton 1999 Cabernet Sauvignon-Merlot (South Coast) $13. Smells hot and rubbery, cherry cola-like and syrupy, not a good sign. In the mouth,

USA

it's awkwardly sweet and gluey, with the flavor of sweetened rose hip tea, and fairly hefty tannins. Not going anywhere. **82** —*S.H. (9/1/2002)*

Thornton NV Champagne Blend (California) $11. 85 —*S.H. (12/1/1999)*

Thornton NV Brut Champagne Blend (California) $11. 86 —*S.H. (12/15/2000)*

Thornton 1996 Brut Reserve Champagne Blend (California) $21. This blend of Pinot Noir, Chardonnay, and Pinot Blanc begins with richly attractive scents of dough, straw, vanilla, smoke, and pound cake, and drinks very dry and delicate. Subtle citrus and strawberry flavors lead to a clean, lively finish. **90** —*S.H. (12/1/2002)*

Thornton 1995 Brut Reserve Champagne Blend (California) $21. 90 —*S.H. (12/15/2000)*

Thornton 1992 Brut Reserve Champagne Blend (California) $17. 86 —*S.H. (12/1/1999)*

Thornton NV Brut Reserve Natural Champagne Blend (California) $35. A smooth-drinking, aromatic bubbly that may be a little too dry for some. The initial aromas of raspberries and limes are accented with oak and yeast, and are delicate and inviting. In the mouth, it has an almost Sherry-like tang, but rich texture and clean strength are its nicest features. **89** —*S.H. (12/1/2002)*

Thornton 1995 Brut Reserve Natural Champagne Blend (California) $35. 87 —*S.H. (12/15/2000)*

Thornton NV Cuvée de Frontignan Champagne Blend (California) $22. Made from the Muscat Canelli grape, and delicately scented with hints of peaches, vanilla, smoke, and honey, and a doughy, nutty note. It's off-dry, with pleasant flavors of raspberries and peaches, although it's a bit rough and scoury. **85** —*S.H. (12/1/2002)*

Thornton NV Cuvée Rouge Champagne Blend (California) $11. 88 Best Buy —*S.H. (12/15/2000)*

Thornton NV Limited Release Blanc de Noir Champagne Blend (Temecula) $22. Copper colored. Clean, delicate aromas of cotton candy, strawberry, vanilla, smoke, yeast. In the mouth, subtle flavors suggest strawberries. It's dry, with crisp acids. The mousse is a bit rough, and scours the palate. **86** —*S.H. (12/1/2002)*

Thornton NV Millennium Cuvée Champagne Blend (California) $21. 91 —*S.H. (12/15/2000)*

Thornton 2000 Dos Vinedos Cuvée Coastal Reserve Chardonnay (South Coast) $10. A bit earthy for fans of brightly fruity coastal Chards, but nice enough, and there's plenty of toasted oak to frame the tobacco, dried leaf, and citrus flavors. It's also quite a bit drier than coastal versions, and is versatile enough for a range of foods. **87** —*S.H. (5/1/2002)*

Thornton 2000 Rosé Grenache (Cucamonga Valley) $14. Pretty dark for a blush, and very strongly flavored. The raspberry flavors veer into framboise, it's that extracted and liqueur-like. So there's nothing shy about it. Unusual and eccentric, but a pretty, flavorful wine. **86** —*S.H. (9/1/2002)*

Thornton 2000 Miramonte Vineyards Pinot Blanc (South Coast) $10. It's very dry and tart. Strong flavors of lemon juice are accompanied by biting acids and even some dusty tannins, but it's a clean, zesty drink. **86** —*S.H. (9/1/2002)*

Thornton 1999 Côte Red Rhône Red Blend (South Coast) $NA. Fruity, dusty, and earthy aromas are gentle, clean, and inviting. But the wine turns syrupy and saccharine-sweet, and soft and flabby to boot. You wonder what you could possibly pair this with at the table. A Rhône-style blend of Grenache, Mourvèdre, Syrah, and Cinsault. **82** —*S.H. (9/1/2002)*

Thornton 1999 Temecula Valley Sangiovese (South Coast) $12. After the pretty aromas, of subtle raspberry, gentle tobacco, smoke, and freshly ground coffeebeans, you're ready for a dry, elegant wine. But what you get is bizarrely sweet and unnaturally soft. There's a cherry cough-medicine flavor that makes it hard to get past the first sip. **82** —*S.H. (5/1/2002)*

Thornton 2003 Syrah (Temecula) $22. From a winery that specializes in sparkling wines, this is a surprise—a dry Syrah. Minty on the nose, followed by syrupy flavors of blackberries and menthol. Drink now. **84** *(9/1/2005)*

Thornton 1999 Miramonte Vineyards Limited Bottling Syrah (South Coast) $15. Good elements work hard to stay in harmony here. The jammy berry aromas and flavors have a candied quality, yet also bear fairly strong herb-pine accents. With its soft palate-feel and low acidity, it's a bit sloppy, and ends somewhat greener and more tartly than expected. **84** *(10/1/2001)*

Thornton 2000 Viognier (South Coast) $13. Opens with earthy-honeyed scents, and turns tart, austere, and grapefruity in the mouth, with bright acidity. If you're looking for a lush, exotic Viognier, this isn't it. **84** —*S.H. (9/1/2002)*

Thornton NV Cuvée de Frontigan White Blend (California) $11. 86 —*S.H. (12/15/2000)*

THREE FAMILIES

Three Families 2002 Cabernet Sauvignon (Mendocino County) $16. There's some good, rich cherry and blackberry fruit here, and the wine is fully dry. It's just a tad acidic now, and green tea tannins reinforce the roughness. The wine needs food. Cheddar cheese would do wonders to soften and sweeten it. **84** —*S.H. (5/1/2006)*

Three Families 2005 Chardonnay (Mendocino County) $12. A little sweet, a little rustic, with big, forward pear, apricot, and peaches and cream flavors and a scrubbing of good acidity. **83** —*S.H. (11/1/2006)*

Three Families 2004 Chardonnay (Mendocino County) $12. Dry and acidic, with an unclean finish, this is a Chardonnay to avoid. **80** —*S.H. (12/15/2005)*

Three Families 2003 Merlot (Mendocino County) $14. Very dry and tart with acids, almost sour, the wine is saved by modest cherry flavors. It's pretty rustic. **82** —*S.H. (11/1/2006)*

Three Families 2002 Merlot (Mendocino County) $14. Old-fashioned in its own way, this Merlot tastes like it went straight from barrel to carafe. It's dry and rugged, with good cherry-berry flavors and rich tannins. **84** —*S.H. (5/1/2006)*

THREE RIVERS

Three Rivers 2003 Meritage White Wine Bordeaux White Blend (Columbia Valley (WA)) $19. Great price for this sophisticated white Bordeaux blend, which melds supple fruit with light toast and refreshing acids. Thirty percent Sémillon seems just the perfect counterbalance to the vivid citrus flavors of the Sauvignon Blanc. **92 Editors' Choice** —*P.G. (6/1/2005)*

Three Rivers 2003 Cabernet Sauvignon (Columbia Valley (WA)) $19. This almost pure Cab (just 2% Malbec) is almost midnight black in color. Fragrant with strong barrel scents of toast and char; the fruit has a spicy, citrusy lift to it that keeps the thick tannins from weighing it down. The big tannins and powerful, smoky notes do not overpower the rather delicate fruit; it all works together in a harmonious balance. **89** —*P.G. (6/1/2006)*

Three Rivers 2002 Cabernet Sauvignon (Columbia Valley (WA)) $19. A big improvement over the winery's rather tough and chewy '01 bottling, this shows classic varietal components of black cherry, cassis, light herb, and leafy spice. Wrapped up tightly, but already showing great style and elegance. **89** —*P.G. (6/1/2005)*

Three Rivers 2001 Cabernet Sauvignon (Columbia Valley (WA)) $19. Tough and chewy, this somewhat inaccessible wine consists of hard, tart red fruits, and chalky tannins that are right on the edge of being green and stemmy. Decanting would be a good idea. **85** —*P.G. (12/15/2004)*

Three Rivers 1999 Cabernet Sauvignon (Columbia Valley (WA)) $28. Mostly Cabernet Sauvignon, it includes 14% Cabernet Franc, which gives it some additional flavor interest. A solid, tight nose leads with cassis and new oak, along with some kalamata olive. Soft, tannic, and approachable, it is smooth and coffee-flavored, with a palate-coating, satiny texture. **88** —*P.G. (2/1/2001)*

Three Rivers 2003 Champoux Vineyard Cabernet Sauvignon (Columbia Valley (WA)) $50. Good fruit and a great vineyard count for a lot, but these do not have the same concentration as Cabs from Champoux's old vines. The flavors here have the sweetness and lightness of younger vines, grapy and pleasant, but somewhat insubstantial. It's good, but not discernibly better than the regular Cab at less than half the price. **88** —*P.G.* (6/1/2006)

Three Rivers 2001 Champoux Vineyard Cabernet Sauvignon (Columbia Valley (WA)) $39. This premier vineyard grows some of the state's best Cabernet: naturally dense, dark, licorice, and mineral-infused black cherry fruit. Tannins are stiff, but well-managed within the framework of ripe, tangy fruit. This is a wine that can take plenty of oak without showing it. Very nice effort. **91** —*P.G.* (7/1/2004)

Three Rivers 1999 Champoux Vineyard Cabernet Sauvignon (Columbia Valley (WA)) $40. This is 100% Cabernet Sauvignon, scented with cassis and cherry, the fruit well integrated with leaf, leather, and herb. In the mouth, it's smooth and chocolatey, with a scent of latex underneath. It needs a bit more time to resolve, but it's a rich, powerful, and well-built wine. **89** —*P.G.* (2/1/2002)

Three Rivers 2004 Chardonnay (Columbia Valley (WA)) $17. Spicy and brisk, this is a pleasing mix of crisp pear, melon, and apple. The barrel time adds flavors of butter, toast, and cinnamon, nicely melded. Particularly fine, stylish Chardonnay for the price. **88** —*P.G.* (6/1/2006)

Three Rivers 2003 Chardonnay (Columbia Valley (WA)) $17. Consistent from vintage to vintage, Three Rivers makes their Chardonnay in a soft, buttery, palate-pleasing style, showing round fruit flavors spiced up with citrus highlights. A very good value. **89** —*P.G.* (6/1/2005)

Three Rivers 2002 Chardonnay (Columbia Valley (WA)) $17. Very consistent with the previous vintage, this is a smooth, palate-pleasing wine showing pineapple and banana fruit flavors. Creamy and concentrated, the tropical fruit is set in plenty of vanilla-flavored oak. **88** —*P.G.* (12/15/2004)

Three Rivers 2001 Chardonnay (Columbia Valley (WA)) $17. Nice and smooth, with a palate-pleasing mix of round stone fruits and sweet toasty oak. Nothing overblown or too buttery about this wine, just smooth, supple, flavorful fruit. **88** —*P.G.* (7/1/2004)

Three Rivers 2000 Chardonnay (Columbia Valley (WA)) $24. This wine gets the star treatment: fermentation in small French oak (40% new); hand stirring on the lees, and a lengthy, cool fermentation. It's smooth and sophisticated, with plump, textured fruit and a lightly butterscotchy finish. **90** —*P.G.* (9/1/2002)

Three Rivers 1999 Chardonnay (Columbia Valley (WA)) $22. This is very appealing when first popped, with plenty of forward butter and caramel scents livening up the fresh fruit. Ready to drink right now, it retains enough acid to stand up to food, though the finish is a little bitter from all the new oak. **87** —*P.G.* (7/1/2002)

Three Rivers 2001 Biscuit Ridge Vineyard Late Harvest Gewürztraminer (Walla Walla (WA)) $23. This wine captures much of the fragrant power and floral punch of Alsatian Gewürz, yet despite its late-harvest labeling it's not cloying, heavy, or overly sweet. It is a delight, scented with spices and flowers, tasting of exotic fruits and sweet/dusty spices. **92** —*P.G.* (9/1/2002)

Three Rivers 2003 Meritage (Columbia Valley (WA)) $39. This has some real strength to the fruit, which shows depth, nerve, and muscle. There's a nice high note suggesting citrus, even grapefruit; below that some racy berry fruit flavors; then comes the impact of tannin and espresso. It all adds up to some real excitement in the mouth. A powerful wine that zings the palate and leaves you wanting more. **91** —*P.G.* (6/1/2006)

Three Rivers 1999 Meritage (Columbia Valley (WA)) $45. Here the blend is 53% Cabernet Sauvignon, 27% Merlot, and 20% Cabernet Franc. There's a lot of toasty oak, with layers of chocolate and coffee all through the nose. Oaky but delicious, it's a straightforward wine with good balance, sweet red pomegranate fruit, and a lush, chocolatey finish. **89** —*P.G.* (2/1/2002)

Three Rivers 2004 White Wine Meritage (Columbia Valley (WA)) $19. A classic white Meritage blend—two-thirds Sauvignon Blanc, one third Sémillon, aged sur lie in French oak. Fruity, lively, and fresh, with lime, citrus, apple, and spicy pear. This beautifully crafted wine continues the string of excellent efforts from Three Rivers winemaker Holly Turner; nothing overpowers you, but the flavors take hold and roll along through a lingering, fresh, satisfying finish. **89** —*P.G.* (6/1/2006)

Three Rivers 2003 Merlot (Columbia Valley (WA)) $19. Dark and scented with cocoa, coffee, cherry, and a dash of vanilla, this is a tannic, chewy Merlot. Hints of herb and a big splash of green tea-flavored tannins wrap it up; it's not what you would call a gentle wine. It should really be served with some red meat to cut through the tannins. **88** —*P.G.* (6/1/2006)

Three Rivers 2002 Merlot (Columbia Valley (WA)) $19. A firm and tannic, but young and powerful Merlot. The fruit is arranged vertically, stacked and tight, with the acid and tannin components visible and balanced. It should improve significantly in the bottle over the next five years or more, given its Cabernet-like depth and structure. **90** —*P.G.* (6/1/2005)

Three Rivers 2001 Merlot (Columbia Valley (WA)) $19. A very good representation of mid-priced Washington Merlot, this boasts chunky black cherry fruit wrapped in smoky tannins and some chalky earth. Full, dense and still a bit austere, but built to age well for another 6–8 years. **87** —*P.G.* (7/1/2004)

Three Rivers 2000 Merlot (Columbia Valley (WA)) $26. This rising star winery hits the new millennium with a new label and a very pleasing Merlot that is a big improvement over the '99. This is a gentle, accessible wine with soft cherry fruit, elegant tannins, good length, and a Fred Astaire-like agility. Delicious and evocative, it has more staying power than its weight would suggest. **90** —*P.G.* (9/1/2002)

Three Rivers 1999 Merlot (Columbia Valley (WA)) $28. Not as big or powerful as their Cabernet, this new winery's Merlot is still in a bit of a sulky phase. Tough and reticent, it shows hints of compact, varietal fruit, some tight tannins, and not much else. **86** —*P.G.* (6/1/2002)

Three Rivers 2001 Reserve Merlot (Columbia Valley (WA)) $39. Tart, unyielding, and slightly herbal, this young wine needs some air time. The vineyard sources—Champoux and Conner-Lee—are excellent, but the black cherry fruit seems to be hidden behind a wall of earthy tannins. Tight, with accents of coffee and earth, this could merit a higher score with more bottle age. **88** —*P.G.* (12/15/2004)

Three Rivers 2000 Reserve Merlot (Columbia Valley (WA)) $37. The reserve is soft, powerful, smooth, and chocolatey. Showing a bit more fruit intensity than the regular bottling, but similar in style, it adds light spice, toast, and roasted nuts to the mix of red and black fruits. **91** —*P.G.* (9/1/2002)

Three Rivers 2003 MC2 Red Blend (Columbia Valley (WA)) $10. Half Merlot, half Cab (mostly Franc) this "everyday" wine has lighter fruit but still plenty of the toasty, smoky barrel flavors that the winery's higher-priced reds. In other words, it's a perfect barbeque wine. **87 Best Buy** —*P.G.* (6/1/2006)

Three Rivers 2001 Meritage Red Wine Red Blend (Columbia Valley (WA)) $39. The unusual twist here is 19% Malbec, a grape rarely grown in Washington. It adds some texture and density to the Cab/Merlot blend. This is a dark, juicy, smoky, tarry wine, but still shows forward, tasty fruit that balance out the toasty tannins. **91** —*P.G.* (7/1/2004)

Three Rivers 2003 River's Red Red Blend (Columbia Valley (WA)) $15. Half Cab, one quarter Syrah, the rest split between Merlot and Grenache, this is destined to become a real favorite with steak lovers. It has just the right structure for beef, with layers of ripe red fruits, hints of fresh herb, stiff but not obtrusive tannins, and firm acids. There's a nice spicy pop to the finish from a bit of barrel time. **88** —*P.G.* (6/1/2006)

Three Rivers 2001 River's Red Table Wine Red Blend (Columbia Valley (WA)) $15. A good junkyard blend of Syrah, Cabernet Sauvignon, and Cab Franc, this has plenty of rough tannin but there is also sweet cherry fruit out in front. A great quaffing wine, perfect for swilling with summer grilling. **86** —*P.G.* (7/1/2004)

Three Rivers 1999 Sangiovese (Columbia Valley (WA)) $30. The only place this variety works is in Italy. Napa Valley struggles with it and the Northwest should grow something else. The aromas are very gamey, with barnyard and fresh hay. There is some red raspberry fruit and a touch of oak, also a sharp finish. **84** —*C.S.* (12/31/2002)

Three Rivers 2003 Pepper Bridge Vineyard Sangiovese (Walla Walla (WA)) $39. There isn't much Sangio in Washington, but the Pepper Bridge fruit is the pick of the litter. Ripe and nicely colored, this is 100% Sangiovese and actually shows some hints of pepper, tobacco, and tea leaf. Still, the vineyard is in Walla Walla, not Tuscany, and the wine tastes more like a lightweight Syrah than a Chianti. **87** —*P.G. (6/1/2005)*

Three Rivers 2000 Pepper Bridge Vineyard Sangiovese (Walla Walla (WA)) $35. This is a very young Sangio, with a grapey, bread-dough nose. Caraway and watermelon scents can be found, and it's an interesting, light, and forward wine, with nice balance and some herbal character. The finish is chalky, with charcoal and ash. **87** —*P.G. (2/1/2002)*

Three Rivers 2002 Pepper Bridge Vineyards Sangiovese (Walla Walla (WA)) $39. This is a firm, taut, even steely Sangio, with tart fruit flavors of strawberry and currant. Tannins are firm and slightly green, and there is an earthy, mineral undercurrent. Still quite young and tightly wound. **87** —*P.G. (7/1/2004)*

Three Rivers 2003 Syrah (Columbia Valley (WA)) $24. Very smooth, bright, and juicy, it's got a nice mix of berries and chocolate, cassis and coffee. This has a zippy, tart edge to it, almost racy, but there are plenty of substantial tannins holding up the finish. Big, stylish, and strong. **91** —*P.G. (6/1/2006)*

Three Rivers 2003 Syrah (Columbia Valley (WA)) $24. A solid, well made example of Columbia Valley Syrah, showcasing ripe blackberry and plum fruit tinged with chocolate and coffee. Modest acidity and smooth tannins make it immediately accessible. Drink now. **87** —*9/1/2005)*

Three Rivers 2002 Syrah (Columbia Valley (WA)) $24. Dark, sappy, peppery, and super-saturated, this is not a shy style. There is luscious blueberry/blackberry fruit aplenty, adorned with new oak accents of toast and coffee. The tannins are powerful, firm, and spicy, but well balanced, and the young wine, still battened down tight, has a supple elegance. **89** —*P.G. (6/1/2005)*

Three Rivers 2001 Syrah (Columbia Valley (WA)) $24. The nose jumps right out with new oak scents of toast and coffee, along with some varietal black pepper. The wine is powerful and oaky, showing plenty of roasted, smoky, burnt toast and coffee ground flavors. The fruit is tangy, spicy and tight; the tannins still hard and rough. **88** —*P.G. (12/15/2004)*

Three Rivers 2000 Syrah (Columbia Valley (WA)) $32. This is light, with fresh berry flavors. It's pretty, forward, fruity, and bright; perfect for light grilled foods. **88** —*P.G. (9/1/2002)*

Three Rivers 1999 Syrah (Columbia Valley (WA)) $28. The best red yet from a classy new property on the outskirts of Walla Walla. Forward, grapey young fruit shows inviting scents of shaved chocolate, vanilla, and fresh earth. The wine has a spicy, tart attack, well-balanced, and vivid, with a fruity, refreshing finish that invites a second sip. **89** —*P.G. (6/1/2002)*

Three Rivers 2003 Ahler Vineyard Syrah (Walla Walla (WA)) $39. Seems slightly confected, starting from its aromas of Nilla Wafers and jelly and persisting through the jammy red-berry flavors outlined in vanilla. Turns chewy on the finish. **85** *(9/1/2005)*

Three Rivers 2003 Ahler Vineyard Syrah (Columbia Valley (WA)) $39. A limited-production (183 cases) wine from the estate vineyard. It's a supple, smooth, solid effort, not as substantial as their other Syrah, yet far pricier. You'll find typical Syrah fruit, perhaps a bit too much chalky tannin, and a nicely resolved finish. Overall it's clean, sharp, and true to the varietal. **89** —*P.G. (6/1/2006)*

Three Rivers 2002 Ahler Vineyard Syrah (Walla Walla (WA)) $39. This single-vineyard, single-variety bottling tastes like it was poured right out of the barrel. It sports the sort of firm, nuanced flavors that winemakers look for: clean varietal fruit with highlights of iron filings, gravel, and pepper. But it is not a complete wine unto itself; there's a bit of a hole in the middle. **88** —*P.G. (6/1/2005)*

Three Rivers 2000 Boushey Vineyard Syrah (Yakima Valley) $42. Boushey Vineyard's Syrah is also singled out by Doug McCrea for single-vineyard status; it's ripe, complex, and has pretty fruit with pleasing hints of Provençal herbs and a bit of gaminess. Tart and zingy, with vivid presence and a lipsmacking vitality. **91** —*P.G. (9/1/2002)*

Three Rivers 1999 Boushey Vineyard Syrah (Yakima Valley) $35. A deeply fruited wine with an attractive black fruit, wheat biscuit, meat, and earth nose. The polished, even palate offers layered blueberry, dark-plum, spice, meat, and chocolate flavors. Presently a little closed, it finishes

long with even tannins, licorice, and dry cocoa notes. Drinkable now, it should hold until 2007. **90** Editors' Choice *(11/1/2001)*

Three Rivers 2003 Boushey Vineyards Syrah (Yakima Valley) $39. Made in a big, lush style, this Syrah comes across as a little Port-like, thanks to rich, chocolatey fruit and spicecake notes, but retains a sense of balance and elegance. For fans of soft, mouthfilling wines, not those looking for laser-beam focus. **87** *(9/1/2005)*

Three Rivers 2001 Boushey Vineyards Syrah (Yakima Valley) $39. Boushey is one of the premiere sites for Syrah in Washington, and this dense, almost syrupy wine shows why. Sappy blackberry fruit holds the center, surrounded with dark, tannic flavors of espresso, licorice, and pepper. This is obviously great fruit; a lighter hand at the press would mitigate the rough tannins and up the score. **90** —*P.G. (12/15/2004)*

Three Rivers 2002 Meritage White Wine White Blend (Columbia Valley (WA)) $19. The classic blend is 76% Sauvignon Blanc and 24% Sémillon, a grape that does particularly well in Washington state. Smooth and round, with sweet flavors of ripe peaches and hints of mango. Clean and supple; ready to drink. **89** —*P.G. (7/1/2004)*

<h2 style="text-align:center">THREE SAINTS</h2>

Three Saints 2001 Cabernet Sauvignon (Santa Barbara County) $24. One of the better Cabs from this Southern California county, this displays ripe cherry, blackberry, and cocoa flavors. It's polished in the mouth, with firm but easy tannins and just-right oak shadings. The finish is long and sweet. **90** —*S.H. (10/1/2004)*

Three Saints 2002 Chardonnay (Santa Maria Valley) $20. Earns its stripes with ripe flavors of passion fruit, guava, mango, and other tropical fruits whose sweetness is balanced by crisp acidity. They really jammed the oak on, so there's a ton of toast, spice, and vanilla. **88** —*S.H. (9/1/2004)*

Three Saints 2001 Merlot (Santa Ynez Valley) $24. This is really a terrific Merlot from a valley that's making dramatic strides in Bordeaux reds. It's plump in cherry and blackberry flavors that finish with an edge of mocha. The tannins are ripe, round, and complex, with a sandpapery grip that's perfect for food. **91** —*S.H. (9/1/2004)*

Three Saints 2002 Estate Grown Pinot Noir (Santa Maria Valley) $20. Dark and earthy in its youth, showing tomato and dried spice aromas, and pretty closed and tannic. But there's a big core of cherry and mocha fruit deep down inside, and the wine feels rich and balanced. Decant, or age for a few years. **88** *(11/1/2004)*

<h2 style="text-align:center">THREE THIEVES</h2>

Three Thieves 2002 Bandit 1 Liter Cabernet Sauvignon (California) $7. When you see the price on this wine-in-a-box, you're amazed. How do they make it so ripe, rich, and delectable, at this price? Beats me. But it's just delicious in fruity flavor, and puts to shame many Cabs that cost far more. **86** Best Buy —*S.H. (11/15/2005)*

Three Thieves 2004 Bandit 1 Liter Pinot Grigio (California) $7. Simple and soft, with spearmint and peach flavors that are dry. Comes in an easy-to-use box. **83** Best Buy —*S.H. (2/1/2006)*

Three Thieves 2004 Circle K Ranch Pinot Noir (California) $10. What do you get at this price in a 1-liter jug? Plenty of pleasure. Sure, this isn't a dazzlingly rich Pinot, but it's clean, varietally true, and superdrinkable. **84** Best Buy —*S.H. (12/31/2005)*

Three Thieves 2002 Zinfandel (California) $10. This squat one-liter bottle is not your average jug wine. Au contraire, it's produced by three iconoclastic vintners who like to rock the boat: Charles Bieler, Joel Gott, and Roger Scommegna, the three thieves who call themselves the "liberators of fine wine." This wine, made from a blend of Napa Valley and Lodi grapes, kicks off with pretty cherry and earth tones in the nose. On the palate, it's bright-edged, with tangy acidity to support blackberry, spice, cherry, smoke, and licorice flavors. And with 33% more wine in the jug than in a traditional 750-ml bottle, Three Thieves is a steal. **87** —*J.M. (11/15/2003)*

<h2 style="text-align:center">THUMBPRINT CELLARS</h2>

Thumbprint Cellars 2002 Schneider Vineyard Cabernet Sauvignon (Alexander Valley) $35. Starts off oaky and strong in char and toasty vanilla, and while the wood overpowers the underlying wine, which is quite delicate, it adds a sweet touch to this otherwise earthy, soft, cherry-tinged Cab. **87** —*S.H. (11/1/2005)*

Thumbprint Cellars 2002 Schneider Vineyard Merlot (Dry Creek Valley) $30. Forward and inviting aromas of violets, black cherries, vanilla, and charred oak are complexed with roasted meat and grilled wild mushroom notes, in this smoothly textured, complex Merlot. It's gentle in tannins and well acidified, with a seasoned finish of currants. **90** —*S.H. (11/1/2005)*

Thumbprint Cellars 2002 Schneider Vineyard Pinot Noir (Russian River Valley) $36. Light in color, but robust, this Pinot has pure aromas that invite you right in. Rhubarb, red cherry, cola, tangerine zest, and peppery spice flavors come together in a silky-smooth wine that's rich in sweet, toasty oak. Very fine. **92 Editors' Choice** —*S.H. (11/1/2005)*

Thumbprint Cellars 2002 Threesome Red Blend (Alexander Valley) $35. You'd think this Cab Franc, Cab Sauvignon, and Syrah blend would be full bodied, but it's really quite racy and elegant. It impresses for its airy, transparent quality, and the purity of the plum, coffee, spicebox, cocoa, and grilled meat flavors. The tannins are smooth and subtle. **92 Editors' Choice** —*S.H. (11/1/2005)*

Thumbprint Cellars 2001 C. Teldeschi Vineyard Zinfandel (Dry Creek Valley) $30. Dark-textured, the wine offers a spicy edge that frames a blend of bright cherry, berry, coffee, chocolate, tea, and herb flavors. Tannins are moderate to firm and the finish is a little powdery. **87** *(11/1/2003)*

THUNDER MOUNTAIN

Thunder Mountain 1996 Bates Ranch Star Ruby Bordeaux Blend (Santa Cruz Mountains) $49. **86** —*J.C. (9/1/1999)*

Thunder Mountain 1996 Bate's Ranch Cabernet Sauvignon (Santa Cruz County) $39. **92** —*M.S. (7/1/1999)*

Thunder Mountain 1997 Bate's Ranch Cabernet Sauvignon (Santa Cruz Mountains) $48. **89** *(11/1/2000)*

Thunder Mountain 1997 Miller Vineyards 'Doc's' Cabernet Sauvignon (Cienega Valley) $48. **84** *(11/1/2000)*

Thunder Mountain 1997 Bald Mountain Vineyard Chardonnay (Santa Cruz Mountains) $29. **92** —*M.S. (7/1/1999)*

Thunder Mountain 1999 Beauregard Ranch Chardonnay (Santa Cruz Mountains) $43. High-toned oak and butterscotch flavors lead the way in this richly textured wine. Hints of cinnamon, ginger, clove, melon, fig, and pear weave a dense, heady web of flavor. Not subtle—big and bold. **90** —*J.M. (12/15/2002)*

Thunder Mountain 1999 Ciardella Vineyard Chardonnay (Santa Cruz Mountains) $43. Tight and sulky right now, showing little more than earth and minerals on the nose. Later, it opens up to reveal apple and pear fruit along with some oily flavors. Finishes with citrus and green apple. Hang out the "Do Not Disturb" sign; this crisp, flavorful Chard could use another year or two of cellaring. **87** —*J.C. (9/1/2002)*

Thunder Mountain 1997 Ciardella Vineyard Chardonnay (Santa Cruz Mountains) $29. **92** —*J.C. (7/1/1999)*

Thunder Mountain 1999 DeRose Vineyard Chardonnay (Cienega Valley) $34. Aromas of butter, cream, and popcorn are so prevalent on the nose that you'll swear you're at the movies. Popcorn and butter show again on the palate, but here they're teamed up with ripe golden apple and orange notes. Finishes with pineapple and butter in bold and appealing style. A daring, not gently nuanced, wine. **90** *(7/1/2001)*

Thunder Mountain 1998 DeRose Vineyard Chardonnay (Cienega Valley) $34. **90** *(10/1/2000)*

Thunder Mountain 1998 Merlot (Cienega Valley) $34. **88** —*J.C. (7/1/2000)*

Thunder Mountain 1999 Veranda Vineyards Pinot Noir (Santa Cruz Mountains) $48. **83** *(10/1/2002)*

THURSTON WOLFE

Thurston Wolfe 2002 Destiny Ridge Cabernet Sauvignon (Columbia Valley (WA)) $25. This is a bruiser, tannic, oaky, high in alcohol (15%), and shot full of bold flavors. It's balanced for the moment, chewy and ripe. **88** —*P.G. (6/1/2005)*

Thurston Wolfe 2001 Blue Franc Lemberger (Yakima Valley) $14. Blue Franc Lemberger is redundant; Lemberger is the commonly used name for the Austrian grape Blaufrankisch. It's a rustic, tannic, grapey wine that retains enough tart and tangy acid to match up well with simple grilled meats. **86** —*P.G. (12/31/2003)*

Thurston Wolfe 2003 Horse Heaven Hills Lemberger (Columbia Valley (WA)) $14. Lemberger was one of the first red grapes thought to be sufficiently hardy to survive eastern Washington winters. These days it's a bit of a fan favorite, with thick, roasted tannins over tart fruits, and enough acid to give it a boost in the finish. **88** —*P.G. (6/1/2005)*

Thurston Wolfe 1998 Blue Franc Lemberger-Cabernet (Columbia Valley (WA)) $14. **86** —*P.G. (11/15/2000)*

Thurston Wolfe 2003 Sweet Rebecca Orange Muscat (Yakima Valley) $15. A decadent dessert wine, made with fortified Orange Muscat, it's pungent and spicy with dense aromas of orange, lemon and lime peel, rose petals, and tropical fruits. Big flavors throughout, but never cloying or soft. **93** —*P.G. (6/1/2005)*

Thurston Wolfe 2002 Zephyr Ridge Vineyard Petite Sirah (Columbia Valley (WA)) $18. Very little Petite Sirah is planted in Washington, and this may well be the first 100% varietal bottling ever made. It's a big, brawny wine as you would expect, done in a take-no-prisoners style. Inky and dense, with concentrated black cherry and blackberry flavors, along with some black pepper and bark. **88** —*P.G. (12/15/2004)*

Thurston Wolfe 2000 JTW Port (Columbia Valley (WA)) $17. Thurston Wolfe started out as a dessert wine specialist, and they make the best Port-style wines in the Northwest. In this new vintage, Wade Wolfe has added Touriga, a grape traditionally used in Port, along with Lemberger and Cabernet Sauvignon. Complex, hot, tannic, but very flavorful. Air it out! **87** —*P.G. (12/1/2003)*

Thurston Wolfe 2003 JTW's Port (Washington) $20. This is truly a tour de force; a domestic Port that is not either sticky, too sweet, too hot or unidentifiable as being in any way related to true Port. Credit the use of Touriga Nacional for two thirds of the blend; the rest is Petite Sirah. Intense, extraordinary power in the mixed fruits, enlivened with spicy citrus, clove, orange peel, and pungent blossoms. **94 Editors' Choice** —*P.G. (6/1/2005)*

Thurston Wolfe 2000 Blue Franc Red Blend (Columbia Valley (WA)) $13. Mostly Lemberger, with about 10% Syrah tossed in for spice. Lemberger has rarely tasted so good. The nose features waves of black pepper and brambly red fruits, the flavors are cherry, leaf and earth. It finishes crisply, without any rustic earthiness. **90** —*P.G. (9/1/2002)*

Thurston Wolfe 2002 Sangiovese (Columbia Valley (WA)) $20. Strong scents of tar, funk, meat, leather, and silage jump from the glass. This is a take-no-prisoners wine, rustic, flavorful, and distinctive. Though the tannins are tough and chewy, the fruit has plenty of acid to lift it back off the ground. **86** —*P.G. (12/1/2004)*

Thurston Wolfe 2000 Sangiovese (Columbia Valley (WA)) $20. Walla Walla fruit again shines here, as it is 88% Seven Hills and Pepper Bridge vineyards. Complex and leathery, with intriguing nuances of cherry tobacco showcasing true varietal flavors. A hearty, enjoyable wine with a sweet, fruity core. **91** —*P.G. (9/1/2002)*

Thurston Wolfe 1998 Syrah (Columbia Valley (WA)) $20. **90** —*P.G. (9/1/2000)*

Thurston Wolfe 2001 Syrah (Columbia Valley (WA)) $18. Smoky, dark, tannic, and spicy, this inky-dark Syrah is packed with flavors of sweet cherries and has a big, Port-like structure. It seems built for immediate enjoyment, not cellaring. In the world of pricey Washington Syrah it really stands alone. Big flavor, small price. **89** —*P.G. (12/31/2003)*

Thurston Wolfe 2000 Syrah (Columbia Valley (WA)) $18. An incredibly dark wine, bursting with spicy, cherry, Port-like flavors. The fruit is concentrated, sweetly ripe, and layered with pepper and tobacco. **90** —*P.G. (9/1/2002)*

Thurston Wolfe 2003 PGV White Blend (Columbia Valley (WA)) $12. The blend is about two thirds Pinot Gris, one third Viognier, all showing the heat of the vintage, and giving the wine a solid core of thick, pear-flavored fruit. The alcohol shows in the heat of the finish. **86** —*P.G. (12/1/2004)*

Thurston Wolfe 2002 PGV White Blend (Columbia Valley (WA)) $12.
Mostly (70%) Pinot Gris, which shows itself in very ripe flavors of pear and apple fruit; the Viognier adds hints of light lemon and citrus blossom. A percentage was barrel-fermented in French oak, adding some soft spice to the mix. **87** —*P.G. (12/31/2003)*

Thurston Wolfe 1999 Pinot Gris Viognier White Blend (Columbia Valley (WA)) $11. 87 —*P.G. (11/15/2000)*

Thurston Wolfe 2001 Pinot Gris-Viognier White Blend (Columbia Valley (WA)) $13. The blend is 70% Pinot Gris and 30% Viognier. The Gris provides the fruit base, with pear/apple flavors; the Viognier adds some light lemon and citrus blossom accents. This is a big wine, bone dry. **86** —*P.G. (9/1/2002)*

Thurston Wolfe 2002 Zinfandel (Columbia Valley (WA)) $14. A bit horsey, with barnyard aromas and bold black cherry fruit. Fresh earth and saddle scents are there, and the wine shows plenty of spicy heft. Simple but satisfying, with a tart, chalky finish. **87** —*P.G. (6/1/2005)*

Thurston Wolfe 2001 Zinfandel (Columbia Valley (WA)) $17. Winemaker Wade Wolfe was one of the first to make a Washington Zin; now it's becoming quite common. This is a very nice style, with ripe blue and red fruits, pretty cinnamon spice, tannins in line with the acid, and a pleasing intensity through the finish. **88** —*P.G. (12/31/2003)*

Thurston Wolfe 2000 Burgess Vineyard Zinfandel (Columbia Valley (WA)) $20. There isn't much Zin in Washington, but this makes a good case for more. Thick and tannic, it's a meaty, dark wine that includes 25% Petite Sirah. Seventeen months in new American oak has left an indelible whisky-barrel scent. **87** —*P.G. (9/1/2002)*

Thurston Wolfe 1998 Burgess Vineyard Zinfandel (Columbia Valley (WA)) $20. 87 —*P.G. (11/15/2000)*

TIN BARN

Tin Barn 2004 Sauvignon Blanc (Bennett Valley) $18. Unfortunately thin and watery, with just the barest suggestion of citrus fruit, this wine teases but doesn't follow through. **82** —*S.H. (12/1/2005)*

Tin Barn 2001 Coryelle Fields Syrah (Sonoma Coast) $32. From a region typically thought of as being too cool for the variety, this Syrah possesses that characteristic cracked-pepper scent along with strands of dried herbs that add immense appeal to the solid core of blackberry fruit. Long and tart on the finish, with tannins that are so soft, they glide across the palate. **90** —*J.C. (5/1/2004)*

Tin Barn 2002 Coryelle Fields Vineyard Syrah (Sonoma Coast) $32. Rich, soft, and complex, with intriguing flavors of black cherries, coffee, nutmeg, and chocolate. It tastes like a pie with all those ingredients baked in. Yet it's dry, with a velvety mouthfeel. It's also quite oaky in sweet wood sap. **87** —*S.H. (4/1/2005)*

Tin Barn 2001 Zinfandel (Russian River Valley) $25. Quite bright on the palate, with firm tannins and pretty, zippy cherry, spice, tar, raspberry and herb flavors. The texture is a bit powdery but should calm down nicely with a little more bottle age. **88** —*J.M. (3/1/2004)*

Tin Barn 2000 Jensen Lane Zinfandel (Russian River Valley) $24. A single vineyard wine that's dark and rich and high in alcohol, but manages to hang onto balance and harmony. It brims with black curranty, plummy fruit and a green, minty note that adds an herbal interest. The dryish aftertaste lasts for a long time. **88** —*S.H. (11/1/2002)*

Tin Barn 2001 Jensen Lane Vineyard Zinfandel (Russian River Valley) $27. A bright, tangy style that shows ripe cherry, blackberry, cassis, and smoke flavors up front. Fresh and light on the finish. **87** *(11/1/2003)*

TIN HOUSE

Tin House 2004 Pinot Noir (Edna Valley) $32. Tasted blind, I thought this was Russian River. It has the classic balance, complexity, and flavors of that region, showing cherries, cola, rhubarb pie, pomegranates, and spice, with a full-bodied dryness and long, ageworthy finish. Maybe part of the confusion is the Dijon clones. Whatever, it's a really wonderful Pinot Noir, succulent and compelling. **94 Editors' Choice** —*S.H. (12/15/2006)*

Tin House 2003 Syrah (Edna Valley) $26. I wish this Syrah were just a little drier, but that aside, it's a rewarding wine. Flooded with black cherry

and cassis fruit, as well as smoky oak, it has the beautiful acidity and fine tannins of its terroir. **86** —*S.H. (12/15/2006)*

TIN ROOF

Tin Roof 2003 Chardonnay (California) $9. Lots of fruity essence in this slightly sweet, oaky wine. It has tropical fruit, peach, and apple flavors, and crisp acidity. **84** —*S.H. (3/1/2005)*

Tin Roof 2002 Chardonnay (Sonoma County) $9. Serviceable Chard, with modest apple and peach flavors. Finishes dry and tart. A screwtop wine from Murphy-Goode. **83** —*S.H. (6/1/2004)*

Tin Roof 2003 Rosé Pinot Noir (Russian River Valley) $9. Unusual to find a blush Pinot from this appellation, but this well-crafted one is fine. It has strawberry and mint flavors with nuances of vanilla and gingerbread, and is very dry. **84** —*S.H. (12/15/2004)*

Tin Roof 2003 Sauvignon Blanc (North Coast) $9. As fragrant as fresh-picked lemons, limes, and oranges, sliced and slightly squeezed, with a drizzle of vanilla and honey. Finishes with acidity and stony minerals. Second label from Murphy-Goode. **86 Best Buy** —*S.H. (3/1/2005)*

Tin Roof 2002 Sauvignon Blanc (North Coast) $9. Here's a rough and ready white wine you can serve with appetizers. It's very dry, with lemon and fig flavors, and quite crisp with acids. Finishes clean, with verve. **84** —*S.H. (6/1/2004)*

Tin Roof 2002 Syrah-Cabernet (California) $9. There's an abundance of ripe berry-cherry and spice fruit in this dry, full-bodied wine, which also has silky tannins and a liberal dose of smoky oak. It's robust and satisfying, in a rustic way. **84** —*S.H. (12/15/2004)*

TITUS

Titus 1997 Cabernet Sauvignon (Napa Valley) $32. 91 *(11/1/2000)*

Titus 2003 Cabernet Sauvignon (Napa Valley) $39. Classic Napa Cabernet, rich and sensuous in tannins that are fully approachable now, with ripe black currant and mocha flavors enriched with smoky, spicy oak. The wine is nicely dry. Beautiful now and best in the next few years for its fat, opulently youthful quality. **92** —*S.H. (8/1/2006)*

Titus 2002 Cabernet Sauvignon (Napa Valley) $39. A fine Cab that showcases the ripe fruit and soft, intricate tannins the valley specializes in. It's a little bit soft, but those flavors are just delicious. Lots of oak, too. **87** —*S.H. (10/1/2005)*

Titus 2001 Cabernet Sauvignon (Napa Valley) $39. Shows the classic traits of the appellation and vintage, with well-ripened black currant fruit, elaborate oak, smooth and complex tannins, and good acidity. **91** —*S.H. (10/1/2004)*

Titus 1999 Cabernet Sauvignon (Napa Valley) $36. Sweet roasted red pepper, black plum, black cherry, and delicious apple aromas lead to a palate of simple red to black fruit, toast, and dried herbs. Finishes long with a touch of pepper and grilled meat. The structure provided by balanced tannins and acidity suggest a reward for aging. **88** —*K.F. (8/1/2003)*

Titus 2002 Reserve Cabernet Sauvignon (Napa Valley) $60. Richer and more satisfying than Titus's regular '02, mainly due to more intense blackberry, cherry, and cocoa fruit and a finer structure. For all the ripeness, the acids and tannins keep the palate stimulated for the next sip. But I don't think it's an ager. Drink now. **91** —*S.H. (10/1/2005)*

Titus 2003 Zinfandel (Napa Valley) $24. Has the texture and balance of a good Napa Cab, with rich tannins, but with Zin's distinct briary, wild berry character. The finish is dry and smooth. **87** —*S.H. (3/1/2006)*

Titus 2000 Zinfandel (Mendocino County) $24. Plush and intensely flavored, with deep-edged black cherry, blackberry, tar, cedar, vanilla, anise, and herb notes. It's smooth textured and long on the finish. Delicious. **90** —*J.M. (9/1/2003)*

Titus 2000 Zinfandel (Napa Valley) $24. Firm, focused, and well structured, it offers a solid core of black cherry, plum, anise, and spice flavors with an herbal touch for added interest. Smooth on the palate. **88** —*J.M. (9/1/2003)*

USA

TOAD HALL

Toad Hall 2002 Bodacious Cabernet Blend (Napa Valley) $30. Kind of harsh and raw, this wine shows herbal flavors and dry tannins. It's not going anywhere, so drink up. **82**—*S.H. (10/1/2005)*

Toad Hall 2003 Dijon Clones Pinot Noir (Carneros) $40. Rather tannic and rough, with an earthy, mulchy quality beside the cherries and sweet oak, but there's a nice silkiness to the texture, and a spicy finish. Drink now with steak. **86**—*S.H. (8/1/2005)*

Toad Hall 2002 Lavender Hill Pinot Noir (Carneros) $22. A very nice, easy-drinking Pinot marked by cola, cherry, coffee, and spice flavors that's fancy without being particularly complex. It possesses a silkiness and dryness that make it a versatile companion to a wide range of foods. From Flora Springs. **88**—*S.H. (11/1/2004)*

Toad Hall 2003 Lavender Hill Vineyard Pinot Noir (Carneros) $25. This is a fundamentally good Pinot. It fulfills the requirements of a silky texture and firm acids, and is fully dry. The oak seems outsized compared to the modest fruit, and the wine turns rather rough on the finish. **85**—*S.H. (8/1/2005)*

Toad Hall 2002 Lavender Hill Vineyards Pinot Noir (Carneros) $22. Middle of the road Pinot, dry, silky, and balanced, with cherry, cola, and rhubarb flavors. There's a hit of tannins in the finish. **84**—*S.H. (2/1/2005)*

Toad Hall 2003 Rod's Pride Goldie's Vines Pinot Noir (Russian River Valley) $45. There's lots of rich, ripe Pinot fruit in this wine. The flavors range from black and red cherries to black raspberries and blackberries, with cola and coffee notes and a coating of toasty oak. Has a simple sweetness throughout. **86**—*S.H. (12/31/2005)*

Toad Hall 1999 Bodacious Red Blend (Napa Valley) $30. At 5 years, this wine remains tannic, with modest blackberry and oak flavors. Turns dry and astringent on the finish, and not likely to go anywhere, but it's okay. **84**—*S.H. (2/1/2005)*

TOAD HOLLOW

Toad Hollow 2001 Cacaphony Zinfandel (Paso Robles) $17. Simple and straightforward, with a pleasant blend of cherry, toast, spice, and coffee flavors. Moderate in length at the end; framed in light oak. **84** *(11/1/2003)*

TOASTED HEAD

Toasted Head 1999 Meritage Bordeaux Blend (Dunnigan Hills) $25. This is one of the best Bordeaux-style blends from this area of the state. It's rich and ripe, filled with sumptuous blackberry fruit, and very dry. The oaky overlay is rich and flavorful. On the minus side are some peppery, herbal flavors and fairly aggressive tannins. **87**—*S.H. (11/15/2002)*

Toasted Head 2002 Cabernet Sauvignon (California) $17. A straightforward Cabernet, with good varietal character. Dry and balanced; shows blackberry, cassis, and oak flavors, with a rough, briary finish that turns chocolatey. **84**—*S.H. (8/1/2005)*

Toasted Head 2002 Cabernet Sauvignon (Alexander Valley) $18. Soft, thin, and simple. Just barely gets across a few scrawny berry flavors before it melts into a hot finish. **82**—*S.H. (10/1/2005)*

Toasted Head 2003 Chardonnay (Russian River Valley) $17. A little rough around the edges, but likeable for its good peach and pear flavors. Finishes very dry and crisp, with an aftertaste of lees. This is a good, everyday Chard. **85**—*S.H. (10/1/2005)*

Toasted Head 1999 Merlot (Dunnigan Hills) $18. From this appellation in the Delta region east of San Francisco, a warm-country Bordeaux blend of four varietals dominated by Merlot. It's soft and flavorful, with melted tannins, and glides smoothly across the palate. There's not much structure by coastal standards, but it's a pretty wine. **87**—*S.H. (6/1/2002)*

TOBIN JAMES

Tobin James 1999 Estate Private Reserve Stash Bordeaux Blend (Paso Robles) $38. Assertively fruity, with black cherry, black currant, tobacco, smoke, and sage notes. Drinks dry and flavorful, a nicely balanced wine of harmony and softness. Very low acidity, is the result of a warm climate. A blend of Cabernet Sauvignon, Merlot, and Cabernet Franc. **88**—*S.H. (12/31/2001)*

Tobin James 1997 Notorious Cabernet Franc (Paso Robles) $18. Soft and juicy, with a lot of sweet, ripe, up-front fruit flavors, including blueberries. Deft and supple, with elegant, modulated tannins and low acidity. Creamy and rich, this is a very pleasant, fruit-driven wine that offers solid enjoyment. **90 Editors' Choice**—*S.H. (5/1/2001)*

Tobin James 1999 James Gang Reserve Cabernet Sauvignon (Paso Robles) $28. Has all the correct Cabernet notes of black currants, cassis, green olives, and various herbs and spices, and frames them in very soft tannins, low acidity, and just a kiss of oak. The result is softly elegant if a little flabby, a nice sipping wine with plenty of juicy flavor. **85**—*S.H. (12/31/2001)*

Tobin James 1999 Radiance Chardonnay (Paso Robles) $16. A nice Chardonnay if you like really strong fruit and spice. Mouth-watering flavors of tropical fruits and super-ripe peaches, and a creamy, tangerine note that follows all the way through to the rich, slightly sweet finish. May be too big for some, but that's the style. **84**—*S.H. (5/1/2001)*

Tobin James 1999 James Gang Reserve Merlot (Paso Robles) $45. Soft and lush, with black cherry and blackberry flavors framed in nice but not too noticeable oak. It's most notable for its texture, which is classic warm country, low in tannins, and acids with a caressing mouthfeel. Dry, it finishes with a slight bitterness. Drink with well-marbled beef. **86**—*S.H. (12/31/2001)*

Tobin James 2000 James Gang Reserve Late Harvest Muscat (Paso Robles) $20. Smells incredibly concentrated and sweet, with powerful apricot and honey aromas tinged with vanilla, spice, and smoke. Tastes terrifically sweet, with a gooey, unctuous mouthfeel. There's some brilliant fruity flavor balanced by refreshing acidity, and the finish is long, sweet, and smooth. **90**—*S.H. (12/31/2001)*

Tobin James 2000 Ranchito Canyon Vineyard Petite Sirah (Paso Robles) $NA. Despite some ripe, forward blackberry and cherry fruit, the wine is marred by a one-dimensional structure and a hot mouthfeel, leading to a short finish. Tannins are very dry and dusty. **82** *(4/1/2003)*

Tobin James 1997 Ranchito Canyon Vineyard Petite Sirah (Paso Robles) $18. Dark as you'd expect and chock full of elaborately crafted dark stone fruits. For all its outsized flavors, it's soft in both acidity and tannins; yet, there's something robust and chewy about it, enough so that it could accompany rich meats. It's well-made and nicely balanced. **88**—*S.H. (5/1/2001)*

Tobin James 1999 James Gang Reserve Primitivo (Paso Robles) $38. Maybe it's Zin, maybe it's not. Sure smells and tastes like it, with wild berry and spice notes, full body, and dusty tannins. Somehow, though, it's more rustic than Zin, if that's possible. It's also higher in acidity. There's a real bite on the palate that calls for olive oil and butter. **84**—*S.H. (12/15/2001)*

Tobin James 1999 James Gang Reserve Refosco Red Blend (Paso Robles) $38. A complex, well-made wine whose middle-of-the-road berry flavors can accompany a wide variety of foods. It's got the weight of Cabernet without its authority, the softness of Merlot and the silky tannins of Pinot Noir. It all makes for a very nice drinking wine. **87**—*S.H. (12/15/2001)*

Tobin James 2002 James Gang Reserve Syrah (Paso Robles) $28. Simply fruity, with jammy cherry-berry fruit riding a wave of high alcohol (15.5%) and lavish oak. Vanilla, brown sugar, and caramel notes overtake the fruit by the finish. **85** *(9/1/2005)*

Tobin James 1999 Rock-N-Roll Syrah (Paso Robles) $16. If by rock-n-roll, they mean simple, deep purple, and edgy, Tobin James is going platinum. Deep black, grape, and blackberry aromas smelled overripe and liqueur-ish to a few reviewers; the palate shows similarly deep blackberry, toast, and licorice notes. Rough, tart finish shows a little white pepper. **83** *(10/1/2001)*

Tobin James 1998 James Gang Reserve Viognier (Paso Robles) $20. **87**—*S.H. (10/1/1999)*

Tobin James 2001 Ballistic Zinfandel (Paso Robles) $15. Bright cherry and blackberry flavors are couched in rustic tannins that end in a bright-edge note. A bit astringent, though powerful, on the finish. **85** (11/1/2003)

Tobin James 1999 Blue Moon Reserve Zinfandel (Paso Robles) $38. A very fine example of hot-country Zin, it shows blueberry, blackberry. and black rasberry aromas dusted with spices, and similar punchy flavors. The acidity is low, the tannins soft. Basically dry, but the palate senses the sweetness of huge extract. Nothing shy here, but what it does, it does well. **87**—*S.H. (12/15/2001)*

Tobin James 1997 Blue Moon Reserve Zinfandel (Paso Robles) $35. 90— *S.H. (5/1/2000)*

Tobin James 1997 Commemorative Zinfandel (Paso Robles) $30. 86—*J.C. (5/1/2000)*

Tobin James 2001 Dusi Vineyard Zinfandel (Paso Robles) $28. Soft and plush, with leafy, raspberry notes that are followed up by rich berries and spice. Peppery notes linger on the finish. **88** (11/1/2003)

Tobin James 1999 Dusi Vineyard Zinfandel (Paso Robles) $28. Inky black, and late harvest in style, raisiny aromas and flavors. A big, fat, flamboyant wine, a hot country Zin that's dry and heady, with soft acids and firm tannins. Perfect with greasy BBQ. **87**—*S.H. (12/15/2001)*

Tobin James 2001 James Gang Reserve Zinfandel (Paso Robles) $28. Plush and juicy, the wine has a sweet edge that highlights its bright cherry, berry, cola, coffee, chocolate, and spice flavors. Not quite Port, but a fun wine that would be better after dinner than alongside it. **88** (11/1/2003)

Tobin James 1999 James Gang Reserve Zinfandel (Paso Robles) $28. There are pruny, raisiny notes in the aroma, faintly Port-like, and this impression of super-maturity is confirmed in the mouth. It's a big, hot, dense wine with Porty flavors, but is dry. Not for everyone, but fans out of this style will cheer. **84**—*S.H. (12/15/2001)*

Tobin James 1998 James Gang Reserve Zinfandel (Paso Robles) $26. Even and smooth, this Paso Robles contender comes on strong with round, jammy red berry and rhubarb fruit offset by pepper and dusty rose accents. A green note does show early and persists, but the wine still has very good feel, and the silky finish displays a long pepper and red berry fade. **87** (3/1/2001)

Tobin James 1997 James Gang Reserve Zinfandel (Paso Robles) $22. 86 —*J.C. (5/1/2000)*

TOLOSA

Tolosa 2004 Edna Ranch Chardonnay (Edna Valley) $20. What a great job Tolosa has been doing with Chard, and it's all about that Edna Valley terroir. The fruit develops powerful kiwi and lime flavors, which are generously enriched with caramelly oak. Meanwhile, the climate preserves vital acidity. It's a perfect marriage. **91**—*S.H. (12/1/2006)*

Tolosa 2003 Edna Ranch Chardonnay (Edna Valley) $20. There's something about certain Central Coast Chards that's delicious, bright, pure in tangerine, papaya, and honey, brilliant in acidity, and just so drinkable. This is one. It's quite a wine, and at this price, a comparative value. **92 Editors' Choice**—*S.H. (11/1/2005)*

Tolosa 2001 Edna Ranch Chardonnay (Edna Valley) $20. There's something Aussie about this wine. It's just tremendous in bright, Lifesavery tangerine zest, pear, tropical fruit, and bubblegum flavors, with great acidity that bursts on the palate with a zesty cleanness. Finishes with an oaky, spicy aftertaste. **89**—*S.H. (9/1/2004)*

Tolosa 2004 Edna Ranch No Oak Chardonnay (Edna Valley) $16. If you don't put oak on a Chardonnay, you better have some powerful fruit. It's hard to imagine any Chard being fruitier than this. Absolutely delicious in apples, limes, peaches, and pineapples, with wonderfully bright acidity. **90 Editors' Choice**—*S.H. (11/1/2005)*

Tolosa 2003 Edna Ranch Pinot Noir (Edna Valley) $28. Big, rich, ripe, mouthfilling—there's nothing subtle about this Pinot. It's huge in cherry pie, cola, pomegranate, rhubarb pie, cocoa, and sweet, smoky oak flavors. Backing them up is superb acidity and a dry, racy minerality. This succulent young Pinot should age well for the next five years. **91**—*S.H. (11/1/2006)*

Tolosa 2002 Edna Ranch Pinot Noir (Edna Valley) $25. A nice, plump Pinot that satisfies for the range and depth of its flavors, as well as its

crisp, silky texture and balance. Cherries, black raspberries, cola, and a cinnamon-bun, vanilla frosting sweetness, although it's a dry wine. **88**— *S.H. (11/1/2005)*

Tolosa 2000 Edna Ranch Pinot Noir (Edna Valley) $30. Prominent oak meshes well with dark cherry fruit. Hints of menthol and cola on the nose and the palate's cedar and spice accents keep things lively. Smooth, almost chocolatey on the tongue, the wine tightens up toward the back end, showing firm tannins on the dry, licorice-tinged finish. **88** (10/1/2002)

Tolosa 1998 Edna Ranch Pinot Noir (Edna Valley) $30. 89—*M.S. (12/15/2000)*

Tolosa 2002 Edna Ranch 1772 Pinot Noir (Edna Valley) $52. Showcases its coastal origins with high acids, intense fruit, and purity of varietal character. This isn't one of those dark, alcoholic Pinots, but a silky, elegant one. But there's nothing shy about the powerful cherry, raspberry, coffee, and cinnamon flavors. Has a raisiny overripeness that adds seasoning. **90** —*S.H. (11/1/2005)*

Tolosa 2001 Edna Ranch Reserve 1772 Pinot Noir (Edna Valley) $42. A first-rate Pinot that takes its zesty, jammy flavors and pushes them into real complexity. The cherries, raspberries, and cola have a gingerbready spicy sweetness to them, although the wine is fully dry, backed up with firm acids. Turns meaty and chewy, showing real solidity and finesse. **92** —*S.H. (12/1/2004)*

Tolosa 2004 Heritage Blend Red Wine Rhône Red Blend (Edna Valley) $38. Only 500 cases of this intense, immature wine were produced. Grenache brings bright red cherries, while Syrah contributes weight and tannins and a darker, more brooding streak. The result is a very fine Rhône wine, stylish and complex, but it needs some time. Best 2008 through 2012, or double-decant it now. **92 Editors' Choice**—*S.H. (11/1/2006)*

Tolosa 2003 Edna Ranch Syrah (Edna Valley) $20. A young Syrah, dry and a bit numb in tannins. Cherry pie filling and raspberry purée flavors, with dustings of cinnamon sugar, vanilla, and cocoa. **92**—*S.H. (7/1/2006)*

Tolosa 2002 Edna Ranch Syrah (Edna Valley) $20. They got real ripeness in this superb vintage, resulting in a big wine that's long on jammy cherries, blackberries, and dusty Chinese spices. Drinks dry and full-bodied, with a firm finish. **89**—*S.H. (12/1/2004)*

Tolosa 1999 Edna Ranch Syrah (Edna Valley) $28. This debuts very tight but opens with airing, showing cherry-pepper and in the manner of some Pinots, plus some root-vegetable notes. The mouthfeel is chewy, with plum and beet flavors and a caramel note. Finishes tart, with toasty oak and slight mineral flavors. **87** (11/1/2001)

Tolosa 2003 Edna Ranch 1772 Syrah (Edna Valley) $46. Starts with lovely peppery-spicy notes that include meaty elements and hints of cardamon and cinnamon, all backed up by lush blackberry fruit. Nicely rich and complex, with a hint of warmth showing through on the finish. **90** (9/1/2005)

TOM EDDY

Tom Eddy 1999 Cabernet Sauvignon (Napa Valley) $75. From this veteran winemaker, a wine that, at nearly five years, is beginning to shed its hard tannins. That's not to say its plush now. It's still firm and aloof, but there are some nice currant flavors. Hold for another few years. **88**—*S.H. (11/15/2004)*

TONDRÉ

Tondré 2003 Tondré Grapefield Pinot Noir (Santa Lucia Highlands) $43. Shows that typical enormous Santa Lucia fruit that's so massive that it just stuns. Offers gobs of cherry marmalade, blueberry pie filling, pomegranate, and cola-root beer flavors, yet the wine somehow stays silky-elegant. Who knows where it's going, but it's delicious now. **90**— *S.H. (12/1/2006)*

TOPANGA

Topanga 2003 Celadon Esperanza Vineyard Grenache (Clarksburg) $20. A lovely, fresh, and focused white wine that offers a classy blend of melon, peach, apple, apricot, herb, and mineral flavors. These are layered in a

USA

complex, yet easy-to-drink manner. Smooth yet firm, it's got great balance and a good finish. **90** —*J.M. (10/1/2005)*

TOPEL

Topel 2001 Cabernet Sauvignon (Mendocino) $34. Much work evidently went into crafting this wine. It's intense in black currant flavors, with a beautiful polish of chocolate and green olive. The tannins are softly rich. There's good balancing acidity, and a sweet jacket of spicy oak. This is a Mendocino Cab worth watching. **89** —*S.H. (12/1/2005)*

Topel 1999 Cabernet Sauvignon (Mendocino) $45. Attractive aromas of cedar and blueberries are layered with pine and tar. Flavors of toasted almond, milk chocolate, and juicy blueberries make this full-bodied yet elegant. **90** —*C.S. (5/1/2002)*

Topel 1997 Hidden Vineyard Reserve Cabernet Sauvignon (Mendocino) $45. 89 *(11/1/2000)*

Topel 2002 Cuvée Donnis Syrah (Monterey) $25. Smells a bit green—mint or dill perhaps—as well as fruity. Big, vibrant blackberry and black currant flavors follow up on the palate, finishing crisp and clean. **85** *(9/1/2005)*

TOPOLOS

Topolos 1997 Old Vines Charbono (Napa Valley) $14. 87 —*J.C. (10/1/1999)*

Topolos 1997 Muscat L'Orange Orange Muscat (California) $9. 81 —*J.C. (12/31/1999)*

Topolos 1997 Dulce D'Oro White Blend (Russian River Valley) $18. 80 —*J.C. (12/31/1999)*

Topolos 1997 Pagani Ranch Zinfandel (Sonoma Valley) $30. 88 —*J.C. (5/1/2000)*

Topolos 1997 Piner Heights Zinfandel (Russian River Valley) $17. 82 —*M.S. (9/1/1999)*

Topolos 1997 Rossi Ranch Zinfandel (Sonoma Valley) $25. 86 —*J.C. (5/1/2000)*

TORII MOR

Torii Mor 2000 Olson Vineyard Chardonnay (Yamhill County) $25. This is a full-bodied wine with ripe, round flavors of pineapple and butterscotch. What's not to like? Some nice citrusy acids add lift, and there is plenty of palate-pleasing oak. Big, concentrated, balanced, and full of buttery flavor. **89** —*P.G. (9/1/2003)*

Torii Mor 2000 Pinot Blanc (Rogue Valley) $18. This is a big-flavored wine, aged sur lie, and about 30% was barreled in new French oak. There are pleasant vanilla, lime, and apricot flavors, a creamy mouthfeel and a toasty edge to the finish. **87** —*P.G. (8/1/2002)*

Torii Mor 1998 Pinot Gris (Yamhill County) $15. 90 —*M.S. (11/15/1999)*

Torii Mor 2004 Pinot Gris (Willamette Valley) $16. There is a strong herbal component, almost garlicky, in the back of the throat that doesn't set right. Apart from that, it's standard fruit, rather light, and a simple finish. **85** —*P.G. (2/1/2006)*

Torii Mor 2002 Pinot Gris (Oregon) $13. A pleasing, bone dry style that mixes stone fruits (peach, apricot, pear) with lovely hints of cinnamon candy. Nice balance throughout, and a good, long, clean resolution. **88** —*P.G. (10/1/2004)*

Torii Mor 2000 Pinot Gris (Willamette Valley) $20. The treatment here is fermentation in stainless steel, and the wine shows ripe, tart, tangy fruit. Mostly melon and kiwi flavors, good weight on the palate, and little if any oak. **87** —*P.G. (8/1/2002)*

Torii Mor 2004 Reserve Pinot Gris (Willamette Valley) $21. Textured and full, with a touch of pickle, asparagus, and nuttiness on the nose. Rather full-bodied, with apple, almond, and citrus on a palate that nudges the boundary of cloying but backs off at the last minute. **86** *(2/1/2006)*

Torii Mor 2002 Reserve Pinot Gris (Oregon) $18. It sometimes seems as if winemakers, in pursuit of that something extra, overdo their reserve wines. Here fresh, balanced flavors of the regular bottle have been sacrificed to a wine with more concentration, but less finesse. The fruit seems a bit oxidized, and the mouthfeel flat. **86** —*P.G. (10/1/2004)*

Torii Mor 2004 Pinot Noir (Willamette Valley) $25. Many of the same vineyard sources that supply the winery's reserve are found here as well; this feels like a lighter, less concentrated version of that more expensive bottling. But there is more: nuances of cola, root beer, green tea, grilled meat, and molasses that seem to be missing from the bigger wine. This is not a screamer, but it will make you happy. **89** —*P.G. (9/1/2006)*

Torii Mor 2002 Pinot Noir (Oregon) $17. Light, varietal, slightly musty. **84** *(11/1/2004)*

Torii Mor 2001 Pinot Noir (Oregon) $17. There is definitely an herbal, resiny character here, with upfront scents of pine needles and beetroot. But the wine is balanced, the tannins are restrained, and the flavors nicely melded together. It is structured to improve over the next 4–6 years. **87** —*P.G. (10/1/2004)*

Torii Mor 2000 Pinot Noir (Oregon) $25. There's an ashy, chalky quality to the tart cherry fruit on the front end of this light, slightly astringent Pinot. It shows some complexity —but closes a bit hard with a sharp, lemony finish. **84** *(10/1/2002)*

Torii Mor 1997 Pinot Noir (Oregon) $20. 87 *(11/15/1999)*

Torii Mor 2000 Amelia Rose Pinot Noir (Yamhill County) $42. The peppery nose offers fruity aromas of cranberry and cherry, but also horsehide and a weedy note that grows stronger with airing. The mouth is chunky but fruity enough to remain racy. A spicy, dark finish lasts a while, but it also seems hot. **86** *(10/1/2002)*

Torii Mor 1999 Amelia Rose Cuvée Pinot Noir (Yamhill County) $45. Chocolate and cola predominate at first, then mouth-filling black earth and plum flavors take over. Hints of sweet red cherries emerge on the finish, but the overall impression is of dark, mysterious layers that are best left undisturbed for a few years. **89** —*J.C. (11/1/2001)*

Torii Mor 2004 Anden Vineyard Pinot Noir (Polk County) $60. This shows substantial layers of herb and leaf, precise, persistent, and penetrating. There is an unusual spiciness as well, a minty note. Overall the wine, though the fruit is somewhat muted, seems well-made and authentic; a Pinot lover's Pinot that makes a genuine effort to display its natural terroir-driven flavors. **90** —*P.G. (9/1/2006)*

Torii Mor 1999 Balcombe Vineyard Pinot Noir (Yamhill County) $50. Earthy plum and black cherry aromas are softened by gentle toast and vanilla notes from aging in French oak. Silky and full in the mouth, this wine possesses fine structure that relies more on crisp acidity than firm tannins. In fact, the tannins are almost delicate, yet the wine still gives an impression of quiet power. Should develop some wonderful secondary aromas in a couple of years, then drink well through 2008. Only 258 cases produced. **91** —*J.C. (11/1/2001)*

Torii Mor 1998 Balcombe Vineyard Pinot Noir (Willamette Valley) $38. 89 —*J.C. (12/1/2000)*

Torii Mor 2001 Deux Verres Pinot Noir (Willamette Valley) $40. The name means "two glasses"—the suggestion being that you'll want more than one. Fair enough. It's a substantial, well-managed wine, with some chewy cherry fruit wrapped in herbal flavors of stem and skin. Good fruit in the middle, with the alcohol and oak in check. **88** —*P.G. (10/1/2004)*

Torii Mor 2004 Deux Verres Reserve Pinot Noir (Willamette Valley) $42. Forward and loaded with fruit, this sweet and accessible Pinot will have particular appeal to those who favor a more Californian style. With alcohol pushing 15%, the dominant flavors are sweet fruit rather than herb or earth. **89** —*P.G. (9/1/2006)*

Torii Mor 2002 Hawks View Vineyard Pinot Noir (Washington County) $40. Strawberries, vanilla, and cream. Firms up, long and tannic. **87** *(11/1/2004)*

Torii Mor 2004 Olson Estate Vineyard Pinot Noir (Dundee Hills) $55. Smooth and supple, this well-rounded Pinot tastes of cherries, raspberries, and pomegranate. It's soft and silky in the mouth, with good mid palate depth; very clean and fruity through the finish. **90** —*P.G. (9/1/2006)*

Torii Mor 2002 Olson Vineyard Pinot Noir (Yamhill County) $42. Expressively fruity, bright, polished, and nicely delineated. Pretty, but it lacks concentration. **85** *(11/1/2004)*

Torii Mor 2001 Olson Vineyard Pinot Noir (Yamhill County) $40. This is an odd duck, with plenty of herbal and mineral elements, along with some noticeable barnyard flavors. The fruit seems to be damped down, and there is a hint of secondary fermentation, so that all is not quite right. **85** —P.G. (10/1/2004)

Torii Mor 1999 Olson Vineyard Pinot Noir (Yamhill County) $50. The vines were planted in 1972, making this one of the oldest vineyards in Oregon. Mushrooms and cedar aromas lead into tart cherries and cranberries underpinned by dry bracken and smoke. The silky smooth texture is a treat, and the long finish echoes with hints of cherries and breakfast tea. Production was only 264 cases, so move quickly. **90** —J.C. (11/1/2001)

Torii Mor 2000 Olson Vineyard East Slope Pinot Noir (Willamette Valley) $50. The bouquet is bold yet a bit confounding, what with medicinal aromas mixed with beet greens and pepper. The fruit is dark and deep, but it has a sappy middle. The mouthfeel is soft and velvety; finishes with some green flavors—maybe hay or dill. **87** (10/1/2002)

Torii Mor 2002 Reserve Deux Verres Pinot Noir (Willamette Valley) $35. Firm and authoritative upon entry, with a hard core of spicy cherry fruit. This wine gives the impression that it will expand with more time, but at the moment is tightly wrapped and tannic. **85** (11/1/2004)

Torii Mor 1999 Seven Springs Pinot Noir (Polk County) $50. Cherry, smoke, spice, cola aromas, very complex, and clean, lead to a real bite of tart acidity on the palate. This sting should mellow out with some months of age, allowing the pretty fruit and dry, polished tannins to show through. **91** —S.H. (8/1/2002)

Torii Mor 2002 Seven Springs Vineyard Pinot Noir (Polk County) $40. Some definite off-notes suggesting garlic, skunk cabbage, and unripe, earthy grapes. Something is amiss here. **83** (11/1/2004)

Torii Mor 2000 Seven Springs Vineyard Pinot Noir (Oregon) $48. The vineyard is located in Polk County, and the fruit is round and rich, with soft tannins and a kiss of spice. More approachable than the 1999 vintage, this is a plump, forward style of Pinot that's already drinking well. **90** —P.G. (12/31/2002)

Torii Mor 2004 Shea Vineyard Pinot Noir (Willamette Valley) $75. This outstanding vineyard was extensively re-planted a few years ago due to phylloxera, so these young vines are just in their second or third leaf. Good fruit, to be sure, but simple and light; this is not to be confused with the old-vine Shea, which has extraordinary power and dense, blackberry fruit. Here it's light cherry and berry, nothing more. **87** —P.G. (9/1/2006)

Torii Mor 2002 Temperance Hill Vineyard Pinot Noir (Polk County) $40. Cherries and herbs to start, with a distinctive, spicy edge to the nose. The bright cherry fruit comes open with some breathing time, and this knits beautifully together into a soft, lush, harmonious wine with just the right accents of bark and root to add interest. **90** (11/1/2004)

Torii Mor 1999 Temperance Hill Vineyard Pinot Noir (Polk County) $50. Burly, powerful, and very dark; this is no lightweight wine. There's toasted marshmallow, tree bark, and some road tar in the nose. A palate jammed full of bold black cherry and herbs follows. The acidity is just right—the wine has a nice tang and a fine mouthfeel despite its obvious ripeness and size. **88** (10/1/2002)

Torii Mor 1998 Temperance Hill Vineyard Pinot Noir (Polk County) $40. 87 —M.S. (12/1/2000)

TORTOISE CREEK

Tortoise Creek 2004 Big Smile Pinot Noir (Central Coast) $14. Simple, thin, and tart, this Pinot has some smoky cherry and vanilla flavors, with a medicinal finish. **82** —S.H. (12/31/2005)

TOTT'S

Tott's NV Blanc de Noir Champagne Blend (California) $7. 80 —S.H. (12/15/1999)

Tott's NV Extra Dry Champagne Blend (California) $7. 82 —S.H. (12/15/1999)

Tott's NV Extra Dry Reserve Cuvée Champagne Blend (California) $7. Not bad for an inexpensive bubbly, with its fruity flavors and hint of tangeriney sweetness, and cleansing bubbles. It's a little rough and jagged for a sparkling wine, but well adapted for summertime lawn parties. **84** —S.H. (12/1/2002)

Tott's NV Reserve Cuvée Brut Champagne Blend (California) $11. Starts sulfury, but after that smell blows off, the aromas of apples come through. The wine is properly brisk, crisp, and dry, with the flavor of green apples. It feels rough and jagged, like the bubbles are too big. **84** —S.H. (12/1/2002)

Tott's 2000 Reserve Cuvée Brut Champagne Blend (California) $7. 82 —S.H. (12/15/1999)

Tott's NV Brut Sparkling Blend (California) $7. Clean and robust in fruity flavor, this dry, doughy sparkling wine will fuel thousands of wedding toasts at a fair price. **83** —S.H. (12/31/2005)

Tott's NV Extra Dry Sparkling Blend (California) $7. A little sweet, rough, and sandpapery, but with good fruit and dough, this gets the bubbly job done at a fair price. **83** —S.H. (12/31/2005)

TOWNSHEND

Townshend 2000 Reserve Bordeaux Blend (Columbia Valley (WA)) $35. A classic Bordeaux blend— half Cabernet Sauvignon, 35% Cab Franc, and 15% Merlot—it begins with pretty barrel flavors of butterscotch, vanilla, and toffee, underscoring tart, assertive red fruits. The only quibble? The acids stick out; they seem adjusted rather than natural. **88** —P.G. (4/1/2006)

Townshend 2000 Cabernet Sauvignon (Columbia Valley (WA)) $27. Although the label boasts that the wine received 30 months in American oak, it does not clobber you with wood; rather, it wraps its tight, muscular fruit in soft tannins and tangy acids. Despite its age, it seems young, hard, and unyielding. But what great structure, and potential for aging. **89** —P.G. (4/1/2006)

Townshend 2004 Chenin Blanc (Yakima Valley) $10. Off-dry, with bright acids, this viscous and gloriously peachy Chenin reminds me of why I love this sadly neglected grape. Bursting with stone fruits, lively crisp acids, and softened by the residual fruit sugar and kissed with a streak of honey, it captures so much ripe, autumnal flavor in a single bottle. **90 Best Buy** —P.G. (6/1/2006)

Townshend 2004 Riesling (Yakima Valley) $10. An off-dry style, nicely crisp with good texture and a very lush mouthfeel. This is perfectly balanced, with just enough sweetness to offset the austerity of the skin tannins. Long, penetrating, clean, and persistent, with a lovely texture that goes and goes. Classy stuff. **91 Best Buy** —P.G. (4/1/2006)

Townshend 2002 Syrah (Columbia Valley (WA)) $20. A stylish wine with a light touch, and plenty of tart citrus. Some interesting orange peel flavors slice through the bracing, cranberry/raspberry fruit. This is a high-acid style; don't look for jammy red fruits or obvious oak, though you will find some tastefully layered hints of chocolate and vanilla, along with green tea tannins. Balanced, food-friendly, and a good candidate for the cellar. **90** —P.G. (4/1/2006)

TRAVIESO

Travieso 2003 Watts Vineyard Compañero Ciego Syrah (Lodi) $27. An intensely ripe Syrah with the pure essence of cassis, kirsch, and fudge. Has soft and melted tannins, and so the inclusion of 5% Viognier brings a welcome kick of citrus and acidity. Very delicious now. **87** —S.H. (12/1/2006)

TREANA

Treana 2003 Red Blend (Paso Robles) $52. A blend of Cabernet Sauvignon, Syrah, and Merlot, it's sourced from the western side of Paso, which is the cooler, better side. A great deal of new French oak was put on. The result is promising. It's a full-bodied, dry wine, firm in dusty tannins, and with pronounced blackberry and cola flavors. A wine to watch. **87** —S.H. (12/15/2006)

Treana 2001 Red Blend (Central Coast) $52. You can taste the richness here in the deeply satisfying dark stone fruit and earth complexities of plums, coffee, black cherries, and spices. This is a very dry, full-bodied and balanced wine, with a firm spread of dusty tannins. It's excellent

USA

USA

now, and should develop additional complexities for several years. **90** — *S.H. (7/1/2005)*

Treana 2000 Red Blend (Central Coast) $35. This appealing wine from Paso Robles has well-ripened plum, blackberry, cassis, and herb flavors, and a smoothly elegant texture. It is very dry, and those warm southland tannins are sweet and smooth. Finishes with some astringency. A blend of Cabernet Sauvignon, Merlot, and Syrah. **88** — *S.H. (5/1/2004)*

Treana 1998 Red Blend (Central Coast) $35. You notice this wine's unctuousness from the glycerine that stains the glass. The aromas are closed, suggesting dark stone fruits. In the mouth, tannins mask a core of berry fruit. Acidity is low and makes the wine seem a little flabby. A blend of Syrah, Cabernet Sauvignon, Petite Sirah, Merlot, and Mourvèdre. **85** — *S.H. (8/1/2001)*

Treana 1999 Red Table Wine Red Blend (Central Coast) $35. 89 — *J.M. (9/1/2003)*

Treana 1997 Rhône Red Blend (Central Coast) $35. 88 — *S.H. (11/15/2000)*

Treana 2001 Mer Soleil Vineyard Rhône White Blend (Central Coast) $25. From the northernmost vineyard in the Santa Lucia Highlands, a fantastically interesting wine. Complex and compelling, with brilliant fruit flavors spanning the range from apricots and limes to peaches and guava. All this juicy flavor is boosted by bright and beautiful acidity. Viognier 61%, Marsanne 39%. **93** — *S.H. (7/1/2003)*

Treana 2000 Mer Soleil Vineyard Rhône White Blend (Central Coast) $25. Bright and fruity, with gobs of peach, orange, grapefruit, spice, and vanilla flavors. There's a hint of banana as well. Zingy on the finish, with a riotous grapefruit edge. Not subtle, but lots of fun. **90** — *J.M. (9/1/2002)*

Treana 1999 Mer Soleil Vineyard Rhône White Blend (Central Coast) $25. A brilliantly spicy wine, loaded with mandarin orange, ginger, peach, and mineral notes. Refreshingly different, luscious, and loads of fun. **91** — *J.M. (9/1/2002)*

Treana 2003 Mer Soleil Vineyard Viognier-Marsanne Rhône White Blend (Central Coast) $25. Treana has established this as one of the top Rhône whites in California. The '03 is an amazing wine. It displays the fresh, keen acidity of the vineyard, which grows no reds, and detonates on the palate with tremendous apricot, papaya, mango, pineapple, tangerine, peach, and mineral flavors. It's basically dry, although there's a touch of botrytis honey. **94 Editors' Choice** — *S.H. (12/15/2006)*

Treana 2002 Austin Hope Roussanne (Central Coast) $39. This dark golden wine is extremely rich and full bodied, with a thick, glyceriney texture. It has strong flavors of peaches, apricots, citrus, vanilla, and a caramelly, crème brûlée taste, almost like a late-harvest wine, but it's bone dry. **89** — *S.H. (2/1/2004)*

Treana 2002 Austin Hope Syrah (Paso Robles) $42. The vineyard is in the cooler, western part of the AVA, and the wine opens with a promising blast of white pepper. Turns rich, full-bodied, and complex, with an array of blackberry, plum, coffee, cigar tobacco, spice, and oak notes. The tannins are fairly thick and astringent, suggesting lamb, pork tenderloin, or similar fare. **92** — *S.H. (4/1/2005)*

Treana 2001 Austin Hope Syrah (Paso Robles) $49. Dark, thick, ripe, and juicy, this is a big mouthful of Syrah that calls for roasts or similar fare. It's very dry, with blackberry, plum, and peppery flavors and a tasty overlay of oak. Notable for the smooth ripeness of its rich, sweet tannins, and might even improve for a few years. **91** — *S.H. (12/1/2003)*

Treana 2000 Austin Hope Syrah (Paso Robles) $48. Big, juicy, and interesting. Goes beyond the plummy, meaty flavors to include a complex mélange of dried herb and floral notes. Feels smooth in the mouth, but there are some big, dusty tannins that will provide a good foil for lamb or veal dishes. A new brand from the talented young Rhône-oriented winemaker at Treana. **89** — *S.H. (12/1/2003)*

Treana 2002 Mer Soleil Vineyard White Blend (Central Coast) $25. I have long been a fan of this crisp white Rhône blend. It's zesty and clean in natural acidity due to the cool climate, and generous in fruit, floral, vanilla, and spice flavors, although very dry. Has a full-bodied complexity that is entirely satisfying, and also has a proven ability to age well. Drink now through 2008. **90** — *S.H. (8/1/2005)*

Treana 1997 Mer Soleil Vineyard White Blend (Central Coast) $25. 86 *(10/1/1999)*

TREFETHEN

Trefethen 1997 Cabernet Sauvignon (Napa Valley) $30. 88 *(11/1/2000)*

Trefethen 2002 Estate Grown Cabernet Sauvignon (Oak Knoll) $45. This is a sharp, tannic, astringent Cabernet, loaded with what smells like new oak, and the question is, Will it age? The wine is not nearly as lush or opulent as many, if not most, of its Napa colleagues. My hunch is that it will not reward aging. **83** — *S.H. (11/1/2006)*

Trefethen 2001 Reserve Cabernet Sauvignon (Oak Knoll) $80. This is certainly the best, ripest of Trefethen's current crop of Cabs, but its built along very different lines from more opulent wines further north along Highway 29. It's surprisingly tough, lean, and angular for an '01, loaded with sharp-elbowed tannins, but it does seem to have the fruity stuffing for the cellar. Hold until at least 2008. **86** — *S.H. (9/1/2006)*

Trefethen 1995 Reserve Cabernet Sauvignon (Napa Valley) $60. 90 *(3/1/2000)*

Trefethen 1998 Chardonnay (Napa Valley) $21. 87 *(10/1/2000)*

Trefethen 2004 Chardonnay (Oak Knoll) $30. Grown in the region between Carneros and Yountville, this Chard has good acidity, with juicy lime, peach, mango, and smoky oak flavors. It's a great food Chardonnay, with a round, supple quality that is very high toned. **88** — *S.H. (11/1/2006)*

Trefethen 2000 Chardonnay (Napa Valley) $22. Never big or flashy, Trefethen's Chardonnays are usually good representatives of their vintage. This wine is lean and tight, with citrusy flavors, hefty acids, and an overlay of oak. It's swift, clean, and steely. Try with shellfish, goat cheese, or roast chicken. **87** — *S.H. (2/1/2003)*

Trefethen 1997 Estate Chardonnay (Napa Valley) $21. 86 *(6/1/2000)*

Trefethen 1995 Library Selection Chardonnay (Napa Valley) $37. In good vintages, Trefethen reserves a special portion of their Chardonnay production for late release in their Library Selection series. This latest offering—one of the oldest wines tasted—shows good balance and creamy, yet still crisp, smoothness. The green apple fruit is still holding well, along with a chalky note and a refreshing lime, herb, and flinty tartness reminiscent of Chablis. **89** *(7/1/2001)*

Trefethen 2002 Estate Grown Merlot (Oak Knoll) $30. Trefethen's vineyard is located south of the prime Bordeaux terroir of Napa, toward the Bay, and although Carneros Merlot can be excellent, this one seems unripe. It has a wintergreen aroma, and is dry and sharp in the mouth, with modest blackberry flavors and astringent tannins. **83** — *S.H. (11/1/2006)*

Trefethen 2002 Riesling (Napa Valley) $15. Dry, bright, and light, with simple, modest fruit flavors and a short clean finsih. **82** — *J.M. (8/1/2003)*

Trefethen 2005 Dry Riesling (Oak Knoll) $20. With hefty acidity, this crisp, zesty wine is bone dry, as the label says. Made Alsatian-style, it has tart green apple, peach, floral, and mineral flavors. A wine of great charm and delicacy, and one of the top Rieslings of the vintage. **90 Editors' Choice** — *S.H. (11/1/2006)*

Trefethen 1999 Dry Riesling (Napa Valley) $15. 83 *(9/1/2000)*

Trefethen 1998 Dry Estate Bottled Riesling (Napa Valley) $14. 87 — *M.S. (11/15/1999)*

Trefethen 2001 Late Harvest Riesling (Napa Valley) $40. Lush and creamy on the palate, the wine shows great balance of sweetness and acidity, with rich apricot, peach, melon, and spice flavors that finish with a glorious, lemony edge. Really delightful. **92** — *J.M. (12/31/2003)*

TRELLIS

Trellis 1997 Cabernet Sauvignon (Sonoma County) $15. 83 — *S.H. (9/1/2000)*

Trellis 1999 Cabernet Sauvignon (Sonoma County) $19. A very nice wine, with flavors of blackberries, olives, and herbs wrapped in lush, soft tannins. Doesn't have a great amount of depth, but there's plenty of stuff to like. **86** — *S.H. (6/1/2003)*

Trellis 2000 Alexander Valley Cabernet Sauvignon (Alexander Valley) $19. Soft, velvety, and oaky, a gentle wine with polished flavors of blackberries, cherries, milk chocolate, and cinnamony spices. Not a cellar candidate, but delicious tonight and through 2005. **87** —*S.H.* *(11/15/2004)*

Trellis 1997 Reserve Cabernet Sauvignon (Sonoma County) $39. 88 —*S.H.* *(12/15/2000)*

Trellis 1997 Chardonnay (Sonoma County) $11. 86 —*S.H. (11/1/1999)*

Trellis 2000 Chardonnay (Russian River Valley) $15. Solidly middle of the road, with sturdy flavors of peaches, some toasty oak notes, and a creamy texture. Finishes with some real richness and the tart, sour taste of lees. **85** —*S.H. (6/1/2003)*

Trellis 1998 Chardonnay (Russian River Valley) $11. 85 —*S.H. (10/1/2000)*

Trellis 2001 Clone #15 Chardonnay (Russian River Valley) $25. From a popular clone developed at U.C. Davis, an interesting, complex wine brimming with flavors of tart green apples and a richer streak of fig. Oak adds nuances of smoke, cream, vanilla, and spice. **89** —*S.H. (5/1/2003)*

Trellis 2002 Russian River Valley Chardonnay (Russian River Valley) $15. There's some nice fruity flavor of ripe green apples and white peach, and oak provides additional layers of vanilla, and toast in this modest wine. Turns bitter and rather harsh on the finish, though. **84** —*S.H. (9/1/2004)*

Trellis 2000 Merlot (Alexander Valley) $17. Quite ripe and seductive, with heady aromas of black currant, cassis, and well-charred oak, and soft, lovely tannins. Glides across the tongue like velvet, carrying complex, pretty flavors. Try cellaring for a year to let the flavors knit together. **90** —*S.H. (9/1/2004)*

Trellis 1999 Merlot (Sonoma County) $17. This delightful drink is just what you want a nice Merlot to be. Fruity and rich, with a nice balance between the blackberry flavors and deeper ones of earth and sage, it's marked by soft, dry tannins and a dollop of smoky oak. **90 Editors' Choice** —*S.H. (8/1/2003)*

Trellis 1997 Sauvignon Blanc (Sonoma County) $13. 88 —*S.H. (11/1/1999)*

Trellis 2002 Sauvignon Blanc (Dry Creek Valley) $13. Swift and clean, a bright, zesty wine with high acidity and modest flavors of citrus fruits, figs, and vanilla. There's an appealing creaminess to the texture. Finishes spicy. **85** —*S.H. (9/1/2004)*

Trellis 1998 Special Selection Sauvignon Blanc (Sonoma County) $11. 84 *(9/1/2000)*

TRENTADUE

Trentadue 2003 La Storia Meritage Red Wine Bordeaux Blend (Alexander Valley) $45. Smells distinctly Porty, with caramel and baked brown sugar, and turns meltingly soft and sweetish in blackberry pie filling and sweetened espresso flavors. Drink now. **84** —*S.H. (12/15/2006)*

Trentadue 2001 Cabernet Sauvignon (Sonoma County) $18. From two warm regions, Dry Creek and Alexander Valley, a well-ripened wine with classic flavors of sweet black currants, cassis, cherry pie, and dark chocolate. The tannins are worthy of mention for their velvety texture. There's really a lot of enjoyment here, at a relatively cheap price for good Cab. **89** —*S.H. (6/1/2004)*

Trentadue 2003 Geyservile Estate Cabernet Sauvignon (Alexander Valley) $22. Raw, sweetly medicinal, and acidic, offering little pleasure. Okay in casual circumstances. **81** —*S.H. (12/15/2006)*

TRENTADUE

Trentadue 2000 La Storia Red Meritage (Alexander Valley) $45. A lovely wine, solidly in the classic North Coast style of elaborate fruit and lush, soft tannins. Floods the mouth with delicious blackberry and currant flavors, well-framed with smoky vanillins from oak barrels. Straddles a nice line between sweetness and toughness. Best now. **90** —*S.H. (5/1/2004)*

Trentadue 2003 Merlot (Alexander Valley) $18. Semi-sweet, with a sugary, Porty taste and, paradoxically, green, minty flavors and high acids. Not exactly flawed, but a difficult wine. **82** —*S.H. (12/15/2006)*

Trentadue 2001 Merlot (Alexander Valley) $16. This great red wine vintage has produced a splendidly ripe Merlot from this warm region. Shows sweet blackberry and cherry fruit; it's fully dry, with lush tannins and a subtle overlay of oak. **87** —*S.H. (6/1/2004)*

Trentadue 2004 Petite Sirah (North Coast) $18. Pet fans will like the volume of this wine. It's black as ink and immensely tannic and fruity, more

of a food group than a wine. Chew on it, and you'll discover humongous depths of ripe cherries, blackberries, licorice, cocoa, and sweet oak. Nothing subtle here. **87** —*S.H. (12/31/2006)*

Trentadue 2002 Petite Sirah (Alexander Valley) $28. From a "Pet" pioneer, a big, dark, thick red wine. It's soft but rich in tannins, and very ripe in blackberry, chocolate, and coffee flavors. It's also very oaky. Easy to drink, and earns extra points for nuance. **89** —*S.H. (3/1/2005)*

Trentadue 2000 Petite Sirah (Dry Creek Valley) $20. Goes right down the middle in style, with a little something for everyone. The fruity-berry flavors are rich and ripe, with a nice peppery note. The wine is generously wrapped in oak, and the tannins are firm but supple. **87** *(4/1/2003)*

Trentadue 2003 La Storia Cuvée 32 Red Wine Red Blend (Alexander Valley) $32. This is the best of the winery's current red releases. A blend of Sangiovese, Merlot, and Cabernet Sauvignon, it's ripely sweet in blackberry pie filling and mocha flavors, and while it's soft in acids, the tannins are pretty and polished. Try with grilled steak and a rich, wine-infused mushroom sauce. **88** —*S.H. (12/15/2006)*

Trentadue 2004 Old Patch Red Red Blend (Sonoma County) $14. Tastes like an old field blend wine, with all kinds of wild berry, chocolate, and Asian spice flavors that finish hearty and fulfilling. There's a bit of sweetness in the finish, and plenty of acidity. **85** —*S.H. (12/31/2006)*

Trentadue 2002 Old Patch Red Red Blend (North Coast) $16. Tastes like an old-style red wine, very dry, and rugged in texture, yet able to stand up to tomato sauce and animal fat. The berry flavors are encased in firm tannins and crisp acids. **84** —*S.H. (5/1/2004)*

Trentadue 2001 Sangiovese (Alexander Valley) $16. Marches to a different beat, with a full-bodied mouthfeel and dark berry and chocolate flavors that drink heavy and dense. There's a little residual sugar that shows up in the finish. **83** —*S.H. (5/1/2004)*

Trentadue 2000 La Storia Cuvée 32 Sangiovese (Alexander Valley) $32. Although this wine is mainly Sangiovese, the 18% of Cabernet Sauvignon rules, with its intense black currant and cassis flavors. New French oak also stars, contributing smoky vanillins. It's a lush wine that highlights its appellation's soft but complex tannins. As drinkable as it is, it will probably develop through the decade. **92** —*S.H. (5/1/2004)*

Trentadue 2005 Sauvignon Blanc (Dry Creek Valley) $14. Dry Creek Valley seems to coax a wild, feral quality from Sauvignon Blanc. Gooseberries, nettles, fresh green thyme, and dandelion greens all give a rich earthiness to the usual citrus, fig, and melon flavors. Acidity in this wine is high, too, giving it a crisp, clean mouthfeel. Very nice, at a great price. **87** —*S.H. (12/15/2006)*

Trentadue 2003 Sauvignon Blanc (Dry Creek Valley) $14. Quite a nice Sauvignon, creamy smooth but with good acidity, and flavored with spicy oak. The flavors run toward ripe citrus fruits, figs, and sweet tobacco. **86** —*S.H. (2/1/2005)*

Trentadue 2000 Viognier (Dry Creek Valley) $18. Fairly bursting with mandarin orange and lemon lime flavors, the wine serves up pleasing medley of bright texture and vivid fruit. Long at the end. **89** —*J.M. (12/15/2002)*

Trentadue 2002 Zinfandel (Dry Creek Valley) $18. Dark and intense in spicy blackberry, cherry, cocoa, and earthy flavors with a hint of bitter espresso. The rich but smooth tannins and crisp acidity of this ripe wine cry out for beef or lamb. **87** —*S.H. (3/1/2005)*

Trentadue 2001 Zinfandel (Dry Creek Valley) $14. Fairly sleek and elegant, with pretty black cherry, plum, raspberry, and spice flavors, all smoothly integrated and fashioned in a classy, elegant manner. Smoky oak and a touch of anise add interest. Bright on the finish. **89 Best Buy** *(11/1/2003)*

Trentadue 2004 La Storia Zinfandel (Alexander Valley) $28. Trentadue's La Storia bottlings are their reserves, and the designation is justified for this Zin. Soft and melted in texture, with succulent wild blackberry jam, milk chocolate, and cherry flavors, it's very dry, with gentle tannins. There's a butterscotchy, vanilla richness on the finish that probably comes from charred oak. **91** —*S.H. (12/15/2006)*

TRES SABORES

Tres Sabores 2003 Perspective Cabernet Sauvignon (Rutherford) $48. Very young and pretty tannic now with a mouth-numbing astringency, so you don't want to pop that cork tonight. But give it time. There's a deep, molten core of blackberry fruit, and the wine is dry and balanced. Should soften by 2009 and hold, if not improved, for another ten years. **90 Cellar Selection** —*S.H. (12/15/2006)*

Tres Sabores 2002 Perspective Cabernet Sauvignon (Rutherford) $45. Shows notes of white pepper, wintergreen, and chlorophyll, and drinks a little awkward, with a rather heavy mouthfeel and sweet cherry fruit on the finish. Might improve with time in the bottle. **84** —*S.H. (12/15/2005)*

Tres Sabores 2001 Perspective Cabernet Sauvignon (Rutherford) $45. Oaky, with a meaty, leathery edge to the blackberry and cherry flavors, and very dry. The tannins are rich and firm but sweet and fine, and don't get in the way. Long in the finish, this balanced wine should hold well for 10 years. **89** —*S.H. (10/1/2004)*

Tres Sabores 2000 Karen Culler Zinfandel (Napa Valley) $30. Shows the plush texture of the other Tres Sabores wines, with a little more spice and brightness. Front loaded with chocolate, black cherry, and cedar notes, the wine is rich and smooth on the palate, a wonderful Zin. Full and complex to the end. **92 Editors' Choice** —*J.M. (9/1/2003)*

Tres Sabores 2001 Ken Bernards Zinfandel (Rutherford) $38. Quite smooth, with plush tannins that frame a web of coffee, cocoa, blackberry, raspberry, and herb flavors. Acidity is bright, with an almost citrus-like edge, keeping the flavors moving along the palate nicely. Long, sleek, and supple to the end. **90** *(11/1/2003)*

Tres Sabores 2000 Ken Bernards Zinfandel (Napa Valley) $30. Plush, ripe, rich, and packed with black cherry, chocolate, spice, tar, cinnamon, blackberry, and herb flavors. The wine is silky smooth yet sports the kind of balance and structure of a great wine. Firm and profound. Great Zinfandel. **93 Editors' Choice** —*J.M. (9/1/2003)*

Tres Sabores 2001 Rudy Zuidema Zinfandel (Rutherford) $38. Aromas of menthol and eucalyptus are up front here, followed by ripe, jammy black cherry, spice, chocolate, coffee, plum, and herb flavors. Thick and plush-textured, this is an ultra-ripe style with finesse. **90** *(11/1/2003)*

Tres Sabores 2000 Rudy Zuidema Zinfandel (Napa Valley) $30. Big, bright, ripe fruit here, with blackberry, black cherry, cassis, plum, spice, and cedar notes all intertwined. The texture is plush and full, with round, ripe tannins in place to frame it all and a long, lush finish for staying power. **92 Editors' Choice** —*J.M. (9/1/2003)*

TREY MARIE

Trey Marie 1999 Trutina Cabernet Sauvignon-Merlot (Columbia Valley (WA)) $29. Tree bark, moist earth, and toast aromas segue into meaty black fruit on the palate. A little lean on the midpalate; finishes with smooth oak, chalk, and herb flavors. A blend of Merlot, Cab, and Cab Franc—if it's a Bordeaux style they're after, it's working. **87** —*D.T. (12/31/2002)*

Trey Marie 1998 Trutina Merlot-Cabernet Sauvignon (Columbia Valley (WA)) $30. Trey Marie is another project of the tireless Eric Dunham of Dunham Cellars, a rising star in the Walla Walla Valley. This blended red is 75% Merlot and 25% Cabernet Sauvignon, and most of the fruit comes from the Pepper Bridge vineyard in Walla Walla. It has a fine nose with cassis and dark berry fruit, firm tannins, and a Bordeaux-like mouthfeel. Despite the predominance of Merlot, it is a firm wine with nuances of lead pencil, tobacco, and cedar. **89** —*P.G. (6/1/2001)*

TRIA

Tria 1998 Pinot Noir (Carneros) $21. This big, mouth-filling Pinot starts off with juicy aromas of freshly crushed black raspberries, tomato and earth, and blasts off in the mouth with spicy berry and cola flavors. The tannins are silky and light. Crisp acidity keeps it lively. **86** —*S.H. (12/15/2001)*

Tria 1996 Syrah (Sonoma County) $20. 87 —*S.H. (10/1/1999)*

Tria 1997 Syrah (Monterey) $19. This ripely fruity wine has a lot of charm, from the fruity, peppery aromas with their dash of hung meat, to the intense, extracted berry flavors. It's very soft and velvety. Purists may object to sugar that's a bit high, but it's really a nice mouthful. **86** —*S.H. (11/15/2001)*

Tria 1997 Viognier (Napa Valley) $14. 89 —*S.H. (10/1/1999)*

Tria 1998 Zinfandel (Dry Creek Valley) $18. Here's a soft, juicy wine with plenty of flavor and depth. Starts out with plummy, spicy aromas and a hint of coffee and pepper, and quickly turns ripely sweet and spicy on the palate. Bone dry, with velvety tannins. Drink now. **87** —*S.H. (11/15/2001)*

TRINCHERO

Trinchero 2000 Mario's Reserve Meritage Cabernet Blend (Napa Valley) $45. Interesting to taste beside the winery's 2000 Lewelling Cabernet, with which it shares much in common. But this Meritage is a little more tannic and has a broader and more interesting range of flavors. **92** —*S.H. (5/1/2003)*

Trinchero 2001 Chicken Ranch Reserve Cabernet Sauvignon (Rutherford) $24. Lovely balance and finesse. Shows deft restraint in the blackberry and coffee flavors that finish with an herbal streak of green olive, and in the subtle oak nuances. Good price for the appellation and ageworthiness. **89** —*S.H. (10/1/2004)*

Trinchero 2002 Chicken Ranch Vineyard Cabernet Sauvignon (Rutherford) $25. This lovely Cabernet shows well-defined black currant, olive, and spice flavors, and has a good balance of acidity and grippy tannins. It's rich, dry, and complex. The oak is pronounced, but perfectly balanced with the fruit. Really displays class and pedigree. **92 Editors' Choice** —*S.H. (10/1/2005)*

Trinchero 2003 Family Selection Cabernet Sauvignon (California) $12. A bit light, but still a good wine, with dusty cassis, earth, and tobacco flavors and some brighter cherry and herb notes. Turns tart and grapy on the finish. **85** *(4/1/2006)*

Trinchero 1999 Family Selection Cabernet Sauvignon (California) $12. Blackberry, olive, and herb fruit aromas and flavors, dry soft tannins, and slight kiss of oak. Acidity stings the palate on the tart finish. **85** —*S.H. (2/1/2003)*

Trinchero 1998 Family Selection Cabernet Sauvignon (California) $14. Classic Cab aromas, ranging from blackberry and cassis to an herbal, green olive note. A slight daub of oak adds smoke. Fruity flavors are accompanied by sturdy but approachable tannins and adequate acidity. **84** —*S.H. (11/15/2001)*

Trinchero 2002 Lewelling Vineyard Cabernet Sauvignon (Napa Valley) $40. Smells like graphite and rich, dark fruit—very promising. Soft, plush, and plummy on the palate, just comes up a bit short on the finish. **89** *(4/1/2006)*

Trinchero 2001 Lewelling Vineyard Cabernet Sauvignon (Napa Valley) $45. Here's an easy Cab. It's soft and smooth, and dryish, although the blackberry and coffee flavors are very ripe and sweet, with a chocolatey finish that contains a touch of raisins. **85** —*S.H. (10/1/2005)*

Trinchero 1999 Lewelling Vineyard Cabernet Sauvignon (Napa Valley) $38. This is the kind of honest, clean Cabernet I imagine made Napa Valley famous. It's perfectly varietal, with currant and cassis flavors and impeccable balance. Rich tannins are classy, and the wine finishes dry and spicy. It's not big on oak, and it doesn't have the flamboyance of more famous Napa Cabs, but it will age seamlessly. **91** —*S.H. (6/1/2002)*

Trinchero 2002 Main Street Vineyard Cabernet Sauvignon (Napa Valley) $40. The most structured of Trinchero's single-vineyard Cabernets, with supple tannins to counter the lush chocolate, cassis, and tobacco flavors. Longest on the finish as well. **90** *(4/1/2006)*

Trinchero 2001 Main Street Vineyard Cabernet Sauvignon (St. Helena) $40. Good black currant and coffee flavors, but a little soft in acidity, which makes the sticky tannins more evident than they ought to be. Turns truly tough and astringent on the finish. **84** —*S.H. (10/1/2005)*

Trinchero 1999 Mario's Reserve Cabernet Sauvignon (Napa Valley) $45. This Cabernet is marked by perfectly ripe grapes showing powerful black currant aromas and considerable oak. Technical notes state that all the barrels were new. In the mouth, it's mouth-puckeringly tannic. A dense core of berry-cherry fruit suggests aging possibilities. **91** —*S.H. (12/31/2002)*

Trinchero 1998 Mario's Reserve Cabernet Sauvignon (Napa Valley) $40. Opens with a classic burst of charry oak and well-ripened black currant and cassis fruit. Turns dry and delicious in the mouth, with jammy flavors and a round, velvety texture. The tannins are supportive and don't get in the way of this drinkable, soft wine. **90** —*S.H. (6/1/2002)*

Trinchero 1997 Proprietor's Series Cabernet Sauvignon (Napa Valley) $18. From Sutter Home's upper tier of wines, this is a fully ripened Cabernet brimming with rich black currant fruit, complex with oak. Full-bodied but supple. The finely meshed tannins and soft acidity make it fully approachable now. **88** —*S.H. (5/1/2001)*

Trinchero 2003 Reserve Chicken Ranch Vineyard Cabernet Sauvignon (Rutherford) $30. Seems to have been picked earlier than most Napa Cabs, to judge by the acids, firm tannins, and the fruit that was snapped off before it developed voluptuous flavors. This is not a hedonistic wine nor is it an ager, but a dry red that won't compete with food. **86** —*S.H. (12/31/2005)*

Trinchero 2000 RSVP Lewelling Vineyard Cabernet Sauvignon (Napa Valley) $45. A fine Cabernet from Sutter Home's upscale line, it shows its pedigree with rich, complex flavors of black currant and sweet olive. The oaky shadings are perfect, and the finish is pure and tasty. Delicious drinking. **90** —*S.H. (8/1/2003)*

Trinchero 1999 Family Selection Chardonnay (California) $12. Lime and other citrus fruits predominate in this lean and tangy wine that's a refreshing relief to the multitude of oversugared and overoaked wines in this category. There's a faint spritz on the palate and the citrus profile makes up for slightly low acidity. Finishes mild and even. **85** *(8/1/2001)*

Trinchero 2000 Mario's Reserve Chardonnay (Napa Valley) $30. Lots of charry oak and lees give this wine notes of vanilla, sour cream, and a smooth texture, but the flavors are pretty thin. They veer toward citrus fruits, with a sprinkling of oregano and dill. It's so austere, dry, and tart, it's almost Chablisian. **85** —*S.H. (12/1/2003)*

Trinchero 2000 Trinity Oaks Vineyard Chardonnay (California) $10. Very ripe and extracted, with flavors ranging from white peaches to tropical fruits. Acidity is crisp and refreshing, and there's a lot of oak-induced notes, including smoke, vanilla, toast, and sweet tannins. Yummy, but one-dimensional. **85** —*S.H. (6/1/2003)*

Trinchero 2003 Mario's Reserve Meritage (Napa Valley) $40. Cedar and tobacco on the nose, alongside some lovely floral notes. The most complex of Trinchero's Reserve offerings, this wine combines mint, flowers, cedar, and cherries with a higher level of tannin than found in the winery's Cabernets. **90** *(4/1/2006)*

Trinchero 2002 Mario's Reserve Meritage (Rutherford) $45. Defines a super-extracted style of Cabernet, with cherries and blackberries just flooding the mouth with flavor. Structurally, could use more grip and tannic firmness. **85** —*S.H. (10/1/2005)*

Trinchero 2002 Chicken Ranch Vineyard Merlot (Rutherford) $25. Smooth, oaky, and flavorful in cocoa, black cherry, and cassis flavors, this crowd-pleasing wine is solidly in the international style. It's ripe, extracted, and soft, with a nice edge of tannins. **87** —*S.H. (10/1/2005)*

Trinchero 1999 Chicken Ranch Vineyard Merlot (Rutherford) $25. From the family's (Sutter Home) vineyard, this distinguished red wine is elegant, and worthy of the finest foods. It has deep flavors of blackberries, olives, and black cherries, and is very dry. It's not a big wine, despite the flavors and tannins, but it's chewy and interesting. **89** —*S.H. (6/1/2002)*

Trinchero 2003 Day Break Block Merlot (Napa Valley) $25. From a block of a vineyard near Napa's Chardonnay Golf Club, this is cool-climate (by Napa standards) Merlot, with herbal overtones to the brandied cherry aromas. Plump and soft on the palate, with short but pleasant flavors of black cherries and dried herbs. **87** *(4/1/2006)*

Trinchero 2002 Family Selection Merlot (Monterey County) $10. This is a great value in a dry red dinner wine. Sourced from three counties, it's fairly rich in cherry and black raspberries, with sweet, thick tannins and a dry finish. Balanced and harmonious. **86** —*S.H. (10/1/2004)*

Trinchero 2000 Family Selection Merlot (California) $12. Pretty wine, and pleasant with rich meats or pasta. Straddles the line between plum and blackberry flavors, and leaner herbs and green olives. Soft tannins make it an easy drink, although it's fairly acidic. **86** —*S.H. (4/1/2003)*

Trinchero 1999 Family Selection Merlot (California) $12. Pretty cherry flavors and aromas are backed by herb and cedar notes and smooth tannins. **87 Best Buy** —*J.M. (6/1/2002)*

Trinchero 1998 Family Selection Merlot (California) $12. Ripe berry, subtle herb, and slight earth notes combine to produce an elegant, complex wine with beautiful balance. The palate offers solid flavors and texture and the wine finishes well, with decent length and berry, cocoa, and toast elements. **88 Best Buy** *(8/1/2001)*

Trinchero 1998 Family Selection Merlot (California) $12. Ripe berry, subtle herb, and slight earth notes combine to produce an elegant, complex wine with beautiful balance. The palate offers solid flavors and texture and the wine finishes well, with decent length and berry, cocoa, and toast elements. **88** *(8/1/2001)*

Trinchero 1999 Mee Vineyard Merlot (Rutherford) $28. One sniff, one taste, and it's the '99 vintage all the way. Just packed with superlative berry-cherry-chocolate fruit, and so rich, so balanced. The tannins and acids do a sort of minuet with each other. Dry, stylish, complex, and immediately drinkable, this is a super wine to have with, say, roast pork. **91** —*J.M. (6/1/2002)*

Trinchero 1998 Proprietor's Series Moscato (California) $12. This delightful wine is fruity and easy to drink, and offers real pleasure, especially at this price. Scents of peach blossoms in late spring, honeysuckle, vanilla, and sweet butter. An absolute delight to drink; rich in fruity, floral flavors and ultrarefreshing acidity. Almost a dessert in itself. Try it with something simple: butter cookies, vanilla ice cream, or fresh peaches. **89** —*S.H. (5/1/2001)*

Trinchero 2003 Petite Verdot (St. Helena) $40. From a small vineyard at the winery, a fascinating wine of place. It's black as night, dry as dust, and so tannic, it shuts down the palate. Chew on it, and you'll find deep, ripe black raspberry flavors of great purity. It's worth cellaring this puppy for a good five years and possibly longer. **88 Cellar Selection** *(4/1/2006)*

Trinchero 2002 Pinot Noir (Napa Valley) $12. Pretty and plump, with cherry, root beer, coffee, and creamy, smoky nuances from oak. Feels big, heavy, and full, in a pleasantly rich way, but a bit raw in acids. Needs a few years to settle down. **88** *(11/1/2004)*

Trinchero 2004 Family Selection Pinot Noir (Napa Valley) $12. Fruity, dry, and rustic, this Pinot has a silky texture framing cherry and oak flavors. It's a good introduction to the variety. **84** —*S.H. (3/1/2006)*

Trinchero 2003 Family Selection Pinot Noir (Napa Valley) $10. A good entry-level Pinot. It has all the correct textbook characteristics, including a silky texture, cherry, and spice flavors and a clean finish. **84** —*S.H. (10/1/2004)*

Trinchero 2004 Vista Montone Pinot Noir (Napa Valley) $25. From lower on the same hill as the Merlot—and hence an allegedly cooler site—this Pinot is round, ripe, and low in acid. Chocolate, brown sugar, spice, and black cherry flavors finish a bit short. **87** *(4/1/2006)*

Trinchero 2003 Vista Montone Pinot Noir (Napa Valley) $25. A nice, easy Pinot that has a silky texture and cherry, cola, and oak flavors. It's very dry, with bracing acidity. Turns rather oaky on the finish. **85** —*S.H. (10/1/2005)*

Trinchero 2000 Sauvignon Blanc (California) $12. A grassy style, with hints of fig and melon around the edges. Bright and lemony on the finish. **85** —*J.M. (9/1/2002)*

Trinchero 2005 Family Selection Sauvignon Blanc (Santa Barbara County) $12. Smells of green pea and grapefruit jump from the glass, slowly yielding to flavors of peach, pear, and a bit of grassiness. This is a plump, readily quaffable Sauvignon, not too extreme to provide mass appeal. **85** *(4/1/2006)*

Trinchero 2003 Family Selection Sauvignon Blanc (Napa Valley) $9. Here's a good value in a fruit-forward wine that has some real complexity and depth. You'll find flavors of apples, peaches, melons, and figs. Finish is crisp, ripe, and spicy. **85 Best Buy** —*S.H. (10/1/2004)*

Trinchero 2001 Family Selection Sauvignon Blanc (California) $12. Citrus flavors of lemons, limes, and grapefruits are accompanied by soft acidity and a lush, creamy mouthfeel. This pleasant wine can do double duty as a cocktail, or accompanying shellfish. **84** —*S.H. (3/1/2003)*

Trinchero 1999 Mary's Vineyard Sauvignon Blanc (Napa Valley) $18. This vineyard-designated Sauvignon Blanc is full and round, with lots of oak over the mild grapefruit flavors, and very creamy texture. It tastes like a California version of a white Bordeaux, and finishes with spicy oak notes **87** *(8/1/2001)*

Trinchero 1998 Proprietor's Series Sauvignon Blanc (Monterey County) $14. Ripe, juicy, and extra fruity, this wine is chock full of candied flavors—lemons and limes, peppermint, and vanilla. Slightly sweet; probably too much for, say, mussels or clams, but ideal with fusion foods. Serve it very cold because it's a little soft. **85** *—S.H. (5/1/2001)*

TRINITAS

Trinitas 2003 Old Vine Mataro (Contra Costa County) $25. From Matt Cline, Rhône-minded co-founder of Cline Cellars who has access to some of Contra Costa's oldest vines, comes this dry, stylish Mourvèdre. It has a tough, tannic quality that calls for something substantial, like roast pork with an olive tapenade stuffing. **88** *—S.H. (11/15/2005)*

Trinitas 2003 Petite Sirah (Russian River Valley) $32. Dark, rich, deep, and full-bodied, this is a classic Petite Sirah. It's bone dry, with sturdy tannins and good acids framing impressively ripe flavors of blackberries, coffee, and sweet leather. Drink now through 2015. **90** *—S.H. (3/1/2006)*

Trinitas 2002 Petite Sirah (Russian River Valley) $32. Be prepared to cellar this wine because it's very tannic. It should age well, with its crisp acids and lush core of black cherry, blackberry pie, and milk chocolate flavors. However, it will be great now with a juicy steak. **88** *—S.H. (12/15/2004)*

Trinitas 2003 Old Vine Petite Sirah (Lodi) $22. The vines are over 50 years old, and the wine has good fruity intensity and is very dry and tannic. But a taste of overripe raisins and prunes, as well as alcoholic heat, drags the score down. **83** *—S.H. (3/1/2006)*

Trinitas 2002 Old Vine Petite Sirah (Lodi) $22. Lush and soft, this dry red wine has a velvety mouthfeel that carries very ripe flavors of blackberries, cherries, mocha, and peppery spices. There's nice acidity to balance. **85** *—S.H. (12/15/2004)*

Trinitas 2004 Pinot Blanc (Russian River Valley) $20. If you thought Pinot Blanc was a Chardonnay wannabe, think again. This one's more like a Sauvignon Blanc, with its dry, tart citrus flavors and high acidity, although that touch of peaches and cream on the finish gives it away. **87** *—S.H. (11/15/2005)*

Trinitas 2003 Pinot Blanc (Russian River Valley) $20. This wine is very dry and stimulates the taste buds with its fresh acidity, but it has a fat streak of glyceriney lime, peach, apple, and oak that softens and sweetens. Try with sushi or barbecued salmon. **86** *—S.H. (12/15/2004)*

Trinitas 2003 Old Vine Cuvée Red Blend (Contra Costa County) $18. A field blend from an old vineyard, this food-friendly mixture of who knows how many varieties is dry, rustic, and attractive for its full-bodied richness. It's not a particularly fruity wine, but has earthy flavors, like coffee and tobacco, with a dried cherry finish. **86** *—S.H. (11/15/2005)*

Trinitas 2001 Zinfandel (Russian River Valley) $28. A fairly dense style, with black cherry, blackberry, cocoa, coffee, spice, and anise flavors at the core, surrounded in toasty oak. The tannins are firm but ripe, giving good structure to the blend. **89** *(11/1/2003)*

Trinitas 2002 Bigalow Vineyard Zinfandel (Contra Costa County) $28. Porty, tannic, and high in alcohol, with raisiny flavors. **82** *—S.H. (12/15/2004)*

Trinitas 2002 Old Vine Zinfandel (Contra Costa County) $18. From ancient vines in this warm county, a bruising, brawling Zin whose flavors, tannins and alcohol slug it out in the mouth. Lots of juicy black cherries and blackberries, and the spicy black pepper packs a punch too. **85** *—S.H. (6/1/2004)*

TRINITY OAKS

Trinity Oaks 1998 Cabernet Sauvignon (California) $10. Dark berry fruit, toasty notes, and an attractive herbaceousness mark this mid-weight offering. It has nice balance, and is less sweet than many other inexpensive Cabs. The red berry fruit and herb flavors close with even tannins. **86** *(8/1/2001)*

Trinity Oaks 1999 Chardonnay (California) $10. The pineapple and Golden Delicious aromas are right on target, and are followed by apple and mildly oaky flavors. An easy texture and smooth finish with mild spice notes close this crowd-pleaser. **85 Best Buy** *(8/1/2001)*

Trinity Oaks 1998 Merlot (California) $10. Red-berry and herb flavors are overly enveloped by woody notes. The smooth mouthfeel and dry, even finish are positive, but the berry flavors are deeply buried. **83** *(8/1/2001)*

Trinity Oaks 2004 Pinot Grigio (California) $5. Simple, dry, and citrusy-figgy, with a crisp dose of acids, this easy-drinking wine is a fine everyday sipper. **83 Best Buy** *—S.H. (2/1/2006)*

Trinity Oaks 2002 Pinot Grigio (California) $8. Light aromas of apple and pear are pleasant, probably more so than the flabby palate that carries melon and citrus flavors as well as a dose of sugar. Some lemon-lime on the finish makes it a lot like a liquid lollipop. **82** *—M.S. (12/1/2003)*

Trinity Oaks 1999 Zinfandel (California) $10. Solid varietal character marks this perfect intro Zinfandel. Its classic berry-and-pepper profile is handsomely accented by well-utilized oak. Soft but not unstructured, it shows that peppery back-end tang that true Zinners love. **87 Best Buy** *(8/1/2001)*

TROON VINEYARDS

Troon Vineyards 1999 Cabernet Sauvignon (Applegate Valley) $15. A firm and fruity effort with some nice toasty elements. Precise and tangy, it offers some ripe berries and cranberries, and a pleasantly toasty finish. **85** *—P.G. (8/1/2002)*

Troon Vineyards 1999 Reserve Cabernet Sauvignon (Applegate Valley) $19. Troon's reserve is not all that different from the regular bottling. The color is a bit darker, and the tannins have been boosted. The fruit is compact and tightly wound. **85** *—P.G. (8/1/2002)*

Troon Vineyards 2002 Ltd. Reserve II Cabernet Sauvignon-Syrah (Applegate Valley) $25. Half Cabernet Sauvignon, half Syrah. It has a funky open, with scents of latex and rubber that open into bubblegum. Light and fruity in the mouth, it is surprisingly simple. **85** *—P.G. (9/1/2006)*

Troon Vineyards 2003 Estate Reserve Zinfandel (Applegate Valley) $60. The 2003 version of the estate Zinfandel clocks in at just 15.5% alcohol, but carries a fair amount of volatile nail polish aromas. It is marinated in new oak—French, American, Hungarian—so that whisky barrel scents and flavors cover up any taste of the varietal fruit. **84** *—P.G. (9/1/2006)*

Troon Vineyards 2002 Estate Reserve Zinfandel (Applegate Valley) $100. Yes, that is the correct price. This Applegate Valley Zin might be considered the Turley of Oregon. The bottle alone must weigh several pounds. Concentrated raspberry and boysenberry fruit retains enough acid to keep it from becoming syrupy. The supremely oaky flavors carry streaks of Kahlua and dark chocolate. But the density that might balance the 16.5% percent alcohol just isn't there. **87** *—P.G. (9/1/2006)*

Troon Vineyards 1999 Reserve Zinfandel (Applegate Valley) $19. This lightweight Zin offers an interesting mix of spices, with hints of cocoa adding complexity to the finish. **86** *—P.G. (8/1/2002)*

TROU DE BONDE

Trou de Bonde 2004 Bien Nacido Vineyard Pinot Blanc (Santa Maria Valley) $18. From the head winemaker at Zaca Mesa, a phenomenal wine from this top vineyard. Easily one of the best California Pinot Blancs I've ever tasted. It's rich and honeyed, almost decadent in marzipan flavors, but richly dry, with a wonderful streak of acidity. Try as an alternative to a top Chard. **94 Editors' Choice** *—S.H. (8/1/2006)*

TRUCHARD

Truchard 1997 Cabernet Sauvignon (Carneros) $35. **94** *(11/1/2000)*

Truchard 1996 Cabernet Sauvignon (Carneros) $32. **86** *—L.W. (12/31/1999)*

Truchard 1998 Cabernet Sauvignon (Carneros) $38. A bit tight. The wine harbors dark berry, licorice, and herb flavors. On the finish, it's bright and tangy, smoky, and with a touch of bitterness. **85** *—J.M. (6/1/2002)*

Truchard 1997 Reserve Cabernet Sauvignon (Carneros) $75. Concentrated cassis and blackberry flavors are tinged with tangy herb notes and hints of smoky coffee and chocolate. The wine is focused and still a bit tight, framed in toasty oak, and bright at the end. Should age beautifully. **91** —J.M. (6/1/2002)

Truchard 1995 Reserve Cabernet Sauvignon (Carneros) $55. 88 —L.W. (12/31/1999)

Truchard 2002 Chardonnay (Carneros) $28. Very good Chard, with plenty of upfront pineapple, pear, peach, apple, and toasty oak flavors. Feels brisk and clean in acidity, with a creamy texture. Turns rather sweet on the finish. **87** —S.H. (8/1/2005)

Truchard 2000 Chardonnay (Carneros) $30. A big, buttery Chard, brimming with ripe apple tart, cinnamon, and smoky flavors. Bright and acidic, feels clean in the mouth, packing plenty of flavor. Pleasant apple and spice flavors linger on the finish. **90** —S.H. (5/1/2003)

Truchard 1999 Chardonnay (Carneros) $30. Full and fat with a delightful mix of tropical fruit and new oak spiciness. Both a creamy texture and good acid—a feat in itself—offset nicely the rich pineapple, peach, coconut, clove, and exotic spice flavors. Has style, balance, and length. Drink this Carneros champ now and over the next two years. Top Value. **91** (7/1/2001)

Truchard 1998 Chardonnay (Carneros) $28. 90 (6/1/2000)

Truchard 1996 Merlot (Carneros) $26. 92 —L.W. (12/31/1999)

Truchard 1998 Merlot (Carneros) $32. Chocolate, spice, and blackberry aromas are evident here, backed by tangy-edged tar, black cherry, and earth tones. The finish is bright with an herbal quality; all framed in ripe tannins. **88** —J.M. (6/1/2002)

Truchard 2001 Pinot Noir (Carneros) $28. A decent, everyday Pinot, dry and elegantly light, with okay acidity. The flavors suggest cherries, cola, pepper, and smoky oak. It's giving all it has now, so drink up. **85** —S.H. (8/1/2005)

Truchard 2000 Pinot Noir (Carneros) $32. In recent years, Truchard has been one of the most consistent wineries in the North Coast, and with prices that aren't an affront. This Pinot fits that bill; it offers blackberry, cola, and vanilla aromas, tea, cherry, and chocolate flavors and a smooth, dry, woody finish. All the elements are here, and in the right sequence and quantity. **89** (10/1/2002)

Truchard 1999 Pinot Noir (Carneros) $32. Bright, briary black cherry, raspberry, earth, and herb flavors give this medium bodied wine a refreshing, yet complex, expression of fine Carneros Pinot Noir. Plush, yet clean on the finish. **90** —J.M. (5/1/2002)

Truchard 2002 Roussanne (Carneros) $25. Has a rich, buttery creaminess and very forward tropical fruit flavors that are like a great Chard, but there's a broad, nutty taste and texture, and a distinctly floral note, that make it distinct. Try this soft, flavorful wine as an alternative to Chardonnay. **90** —S.H. (8/1/2005)

Truchard 2000 Roussanne (Carneros) $28. Crisp, lively, and elegant, with peaches, pears, apricots, orange, and spice flavors all beautifully integrated. Long and bright to the very end. **91** —J.M. (12/1/2001)

Truchard 1997 Syrah (Carneros) $30. 89 —S.H. (6/1/1999)

Truchard 2002 Syrah (Carneros) $28. Boasts the ideal combination of fruit and spice—a lively blend of blackberry and black pepper aromas that comes across as brandied spicecake with dried fruit on the palate, yet without any excess alcohol. The full-bodied, lush mouthfeel moves seamlessly into a long, peppery finish. Bravo! **93 Editors' Choice** (9/1/2005)

Truchard 1999 Estate/Carneros Syrah (Carneros) $35. Deep, darkly fruited and funky (in a good way) with a horsey-stabley, earthy Syrah character. The smooth, full palate delivers harmonious black fruit, meat, and smoke flavors. Finishing with a handsome pepper, mineral, and espresso fade, this can be cellared a few years, and may well improve further. Drink now through 2008. **88** (11/1/2001)

Truchard 1997 Zinfandel (Carneros) $20. 91 —L.W. (9/1/1999)

Truchard 2000 AVA's: Carneros/Napa Valley Zinfandel (California) $28. A big wine bursting with the wildest of brambly berry flavors, and a peppery, herbal hint of earth and wood. The tannins are smooth and dusty. It's a nice bit of winemaking, but a little too big and uncontrolled for its britches. **88** —S.H. (9/1/2002)

TSILLAN

Tsillan 2003 Syrah (Columbia Valley (WA)) $23. Starts with scents of candied fruit, and continues in this vein all the way through to the finish. Jammy, mixed-berry flavors possess plenty of intensity and the wine has a supple, syrupy mouthfeel, yet it lacks nuance and complexity. **84** (9/1/2005)

TUALATIN ESTATE

Tualatin Estate 1999 Estate Grown Chardonnay (Willamette Valley) $18. Light and fragrant in the nose, with a hint of lemon and canned pineapple. The palate seems rich and creamy, partially a result of age but also due to relative low acidity. In the mouth, there's banana, papaya, and cinnamon, while the finish is nicely textured and rich (again a result of maturity). All in all, there seems to be more coconut and tropical influences than verve. As a result, it's a bit flat. **86** —M.S. (9/1/2003)

TUALATIN ESTATE

Tualatin Estate 2001 Semi-Sparkling Muscat (Willamette Valley) $16. Smells like Muscat, with pretty apricot and orange-blossom aromas, and as the name suggests, it's just a little bubbly. The sweetness level is high, but not exceptional. This clean wine is fun and perfect for fresh fruits or wedding cake. **86** —S.H. (12/1/2002)

Tualatin Estate 1999 Pinot Blanc (Oregon) $15. A fine Chardonnay alternative, similar in weight—heftier than many—but with its own character. The lively peach, pear, and vanilla nose sets up a round, fullish palate with dry pear fruit and pepper accents. Hefty but not flabby; good underlying acidity holds this together. It finishes long, with more pepper. **88 Best Buy** —M.M. (11/1/2001)

Tualatin Estate 1998 Pinot Blanc (Willamette Valley) $15. 86 —L.W. (12/31/1999)

Tualatin Estate 2001 Estate Grown Pinot Blanc (Willamette Valley) $11. This very ripe wine hits a rich fruit note suspended midway between spicy apple and fresh-cut pear. Alcohol is on the high side (14.5%). It's bigger overall than many Pinot Blancs, but generous and flavorful. Drink up. **87 Best Buy** —P.G. (12/1/2003)

Tualatin Estate 2000 Pinot Noir (Willamette Valley) $29. Tart strawberry-cherry fruit is accented by pine, licorice, and earth notes in this bright, sassy wine. This shows good acidity, but it's also thin and a bit sour to some. Still, most panelists found pretty elements, if not a great deal of depth. Closes dry, with a mildly chalky feel. **85** (10/1/2002)

Tualatin Estate 1999 Pinot Noir (Willamette Valley) $24. Plummy, toasty fruit launches this into a friendly orbit right out of the bottle. It's got nice weight and some depth, and there is plenty of tannin to finish it out. The clean, attractive fruit tastes of beet root and ripe cherries. **88** —P.G. (4/1/2002)

Tualatin Estate 1998 Pinot Noir (Willamette Valley) $24. 88 —M.S. (12/1/2000)

TUCKER

Tucker 2001 Gewürztraminer (Yakima Valley) $7. There are true, varietal scents of apricot, peach, and honeysuckle. Fresh fruit in the mouth shows crisp, citrus, and orange flavors, with some spritzyness on the tongue, and plenty of orange rind in the finish. This is fruity and dry enough to be well suited to spicy foods. **86** —P.G. (9/1/2002)

Tucker 2001 Riesling (Yakima Valley) $8. This wine starts off well, with a pretty nose and fruit that shows nice ripeness. But once in the mouth all the fruit seems to disappear, and the wine falls flat. **83** —P.G. (9/1/2002)

TUDOR WINES

Tudor Wines 2003 Pinot Noir (Santa Lucia Highlands) $35. Size marks this wine. It's huge in flavor, swamping the palate with black and red cherries, pomegranates, sweet rhubarb pie, coffee, and vanilla. At the same time, it's fairly light in color, and certainly light and silky in body, with crisp acids. Shows enough complexity to serve with your finest entrées. **90** —S.H. (12/1/2005)

Tudor Wines 2000 Pinot Noir (Santa Lucia Highlands) $35. Here's a rich and tasty regional Pinot Noir. It is not especially complex, but is well-structured, with lush but soft tannins and crisp coastal acidity. The flavors are in a nice tension between berries and cherries and earthier herbal notes. Goes down like silk, and will pair well with a wide range of foods. **90** —*S.H. (12/1/2003)*

Tudor Wines 2000 Tondre Vineyard Pinot Noir (Santa Lucia Highlands) $25. Very tasty, but simpler in structure and content to Tudor's regular Pinot. Opens with cola, raspberry, and white chocolate aromas that lead to very deliciously ripe candy-jammy flavors of raspberries and spice. Seductive in its way, a silky smooth wine of great charm. **87** —*S.H. (12/1/2003)*

TULAROSA

Tularosa 2003 Shiraz (New Mexico) $12. Almost undrinkable, with strong Port aromas that turn astringently dry and watery. **80** —*S.H. (3/1/2006)*

Tularosa 2004 Viognier (New Mexico) $14. An interesting wine, clean, dry, and well-made, with a rich array of fruity, earthy flavors. There's a tobaccoey edge to the peaches and tropical fruits. Could use more acidity. **84** —*S.H. (3/1/2006)*

TULE BAY

Tule Bay 2002 Chardonnay (Mendocino County) $15. This modestly flavored Chard tips its hat to fresh peach and apple flavors, and has a creamy texture. It's a bit on the thin side, but very clean, with a swift finish. **84** —*S.H. (12/31/2003)*

Tule Bay 2000 Merlot (Mendocino County) $15. A modest red wine with plummy flavors that have a strong edge of herbs. It's fully dry, with some dusty tannins that turn astringent on the finish. **84** —*S.H. (2/1/2004)*

TULIP HILL

Tulip Hill 2000 Cabernet Sauvignon (Napa Valley) $24. There's a big gulp of intensely ripe fruit flavor that fills the mouth with sweet blackberries and mocha. You'll also find hints of overripeness in the slightly raisiny notes and a Porty sweetness on the finish. **84** —*S.H. (6/1/2004)*

Tulip Hill 2001 Mount Oso Vineyard Cabernet Sauvignon (California) $22. Acidity and tannins burn the mouth in this thin, rustic wine, which has faint cherry and berry flavors. **82** —*S.H. (11/15/2004)*

Tulip Hill 2001 Mount Oso Vineyard Cabernet Sauvignon-Syrah (California) $28. Smooth in texture, with a velvety softness that carries blackberry and coffee flavors. This dry wine finishes with a tannic astringency from the Cabernet that's unlikely to age away. **84** —*S.H. (10/1/2004)*

Tulip Hill 2001 Mount Oso Vineyard Chardonnay (California) $22. There's something sharp and vegetal to this wine despite a generous helping of sweet oak. **82** —*S.H. (11/15/2004)*

Tulip Hill 2001 Mt. Oso Vineyard Merlot (California) $18. A fine and delicious Merlot from underrated Lake County, filled with juicy flavors of blackberries, cassis, and cherries. This well-made wine also benefits from smooth, ripe tannins and balanced acidity. Shows the potential of its appellation. **90 Editors' Choice** —*S.H. (5/1/2004)*

Tulip Hill 2002 Mount Oso Vineyard Mirage Merlot-Syrah (California) $24. This unusual Merlot-Syrah blend is fresh and tasty. It has soft tannins, a gentle mouthfeel and ripe flavors of cherries and chocolate cream pie, although it's fully dry. **87** —*S.H. (10/1/2004)*

Tulip Hill 2001 Sauvignon Blanc (Lake County) $12. Starts off with slightly weedy aromas, followed up by mild acidity and herbal, hay-like flavors. **80** —*J.M. (4/1/2004)*

Tulip Hill 2001 Mt. Oso Vineyard Syrah (California) $16. A little heavy in body, with berry-cherry flavors and nice tannins. This dry wine has an earthy, herbal edge to it, but the solid core of fruit is enjoyable. **85** — *S.H. (5/1/2004)*

Tulip Hill 2001 Old Vine Zinfandel (Lake County) $18. A light style of Zin, with pleasant floral and raspberry notes that are framed in moderate tannins and toasty oak. Finishes with a touch of vanilla. **84** —*J.M. (4/1/2004)*

TURLEY

Turley 2000 Estate Petite Sirah (Napa Valley) $60. Opens with a blast of leathery bacon and saddle aromas next to blackberry and cherry, with leaner notes of cranberry and tobacco. The wine is extremely dry, and the tannins are fierce and in your face. The question is, will the wine improve with age, or just fade away? **83** *(4/1/2003)*

Turley 2003 Hayne Vineyard Petite Sirah (Napa Valley) $80. What an aroma. So Côte-Rôtie, so powerful and rich, yet so refined. Masses of white pepper, cassis, freshly ground French roast, cocoa, gingersnap cookie, char, vanilla, cinnamon—and that's just the smell! In the mouth, there's all that and more. Dry, massive, deep, and long. A triumph. 2008–2020. **94 Cellar Selection** —*S.H. (12/1/2006)*

Turley 2001 Old Vines Zinfandel (California) $25. Rich and plush on the nose, with hints of chocolate, plum, and spice. It fans out on the palate to reveal a complex web of spicy black cherry, cola, coffee, blackberry, anise, and chocolate flavors, all couched in supple, smooth tannins and finishing long on the palate. **91** *(11/1/2003)*

Turley 2000 Tofanelli Vineyard Zinfandel (Napa Valley) $32. Zippy bright in texture but also lush and round on the palate, the wine offers a fine multidimensional drinking experience. Smooth tannins support a core of cherry, spice, anise, raspberry, cedar, and spice flavors, all seamlessly integrated. Finishes long and rich. **92** —*J.M. (9/1/2003)*

TURNBULL

Turnbull 2003 Cabernet Sauvignon (Napa Valley) $40. With a fair degree of new French oak, this lovely wine has a toasty, cedary edge that meshes well with the underlying fruit. Small amounts of Syrah, Cab Franc, and Merlot bring a lighter, red cherry note to Cab's deeper, darker blackberries and currants. Very stylish and sophisticated wine. **92** —*S.H. (10/1/2006)*

Turnbull 2002 Cabernet Sauvignon (Oakville) $40. Firm and drily tannic now. There's a green mintiness that suggests against longterm aging, but enough blackberry and oak to be pleasing. **86** —*S.H. (8/1/2005)*

Turnbull 2003 Merlot (Oakville) $30. Opens with a bright, clean burst of red cherry pie, with teases of wintergreen, clove tea and smoky oak. This inviting aroma leads to an elegant, balanced mouthfeel, rich in dusty tannins and complex cherry, coffee, and grilled mushroom flavors. **91** — *S.H. (10/1/2006)*

Turnbull 2001 Petite Sirah (Oakville) $35. This controversial wine attracted a great range of scores among the tasters. Several found it overoaked and astringent, while others liked it for its fruity flavors and firm texture. It is young and backward now, and will probably improve with a few years in the cellar. **87** *(4/1/2003)*

Turnbull 2003 Old Bull Red Wine Red Blend (Napa Valley) $20. Based on Cabernet Sauvignon, with a hodgepodge of seven other varieties, this is a fun wine, but it's also sophisticated and complex. Bone dry, it's smooth in the mouth, with earthy, berry flavors and hints of lavender and anise. **91 Editors' Choice** —*S.H. (10/1/2006)*

Turnbull 1997 Sangiovese (Oakville) $20. 88 —*S.H. (12/15/1999)*

Turnbull 2004 Sauvignon Blanc (Oakville) $16. Oakville is beginning to come out with some pretty interesting Sauvignon Blancs, and this is one of them. Good as it is, I wish it were more concentrated, because it would be fabulous. It's crisp, clean, bone dry, and complex, with a swirl of citrus, peach, green herb, tobacco, mineral and oak flavors leading to a satisfying finish. **88** —*S.H. (12/15/2005)*

Turnbull 2000 Sauvignon Blanc (Oakville) $16. Aromas of glue, bacon fat, and earth make for a confounding bouquet that really doesn't welcome you in. The plump, creamy palate has some bright citrus, but mostly it's about underripe melon. The tart, short finish is clean, but not terribly convincing. **86** *(8/1/2002)*

Turnbull 1998 Syrah (Oakville) $25. There's plenty of dark appeal in this Napa wine with blackberry, smoke, and toasty oak aromas and flavors. Leather and bitter chocolate show on the medium-full, even palate, but the oak comes on terrifically strong there and through the finish, rendering the wine rather narrow. Still, it's not without appeal, and will be well-liked by the many fans of the black, oaky style. **86** *(11/1/2001)*

Turnbull 2000 Estate Grown Viognier (Oakville) $25. Rich and round on the palate, with apricot, lemon, melon, spice, and herb notes at the fore. Long and bright at the end. **88** —*J.M. (12/15/2002)*

TURNER ROAD

Turner Road 2004 Cabernet Sauvignon (Paso Robles) $11. Smells sharp and hot, like Port, indicating high alcohol, although the official reading is only 13.5%. You'll find some ripe blackberry and cherry flavors, and the wine is thoroughly dry. **83** —S.H. (12/15/2006)

Turner Road 2003 Cabernet Sauvignon (Paso Robles) $11. Kind of hot and peppery, and a little overripe, but shows a polished texture and lots of tasty currant, blackberry, and bitter chocolate flavors. **84** —S.H. (6/1/2005)

Turner Road 2002 Cabernet Sauvignon (Paso Robles) $11. Shows true varietal character in the ripe black currant and cured olive flavors, sweetened with a touch of smoky oak. Ultrasoft in texture, and dry. **84** —S.H. (6/1/2005)

Turner Road 2005 Chardonnay (Central Coast) $11. Rough and ready, this is a dry, crisply tart wine with thinned-down citrusy flavors that will do in a pinch. **83** —S.H. (12/1/2006)

Turner Road 2003 Chardonnay (Central Coast) $11. Has real Monterey character in the ripe tropical fruits and zesty acidity, only the flavors are a bit thin. If you can find this wine for a few bucks less, it's a real value. **84** —S.H. (6/1/2005)

Turner Road 2004 Merlot (Central Coast) $11. This is really a nice Merlot. It's a blast of cherry marmalade, blackberry, coffee, and peppery spice flavors with a rich dusting of fine tannins. Sure, it's a little rustic, but with a steak on the barbie, who cares. **85** —S.H. (12/15/2006)

Turner Road 2005 Pinot Grigio (Lodi) $11. Not much going on in this watery wine. It tastes like alcohol with a few drops of grapefruit juice. **81** —S.H. (12/1/2006)

Turner Road 2003 Shiraz (Lodi) $11. Dark, full-bodied, and dry, this wine has bigtime flavors of black cherries and blackberries. It's also rich in dusty tannins. Has balance, and is the kind of red wine that will go well with a wide assortment of foods. **85 Best Buy** —S.H. (6/1/2005)

Turner Road 2002 Shiraz (Lodi) $11. Soft, dry, and easy, with ripe blackberry, cherry and cocoa flavors that finish with a dusting of pepper and spice. **84** —S.H. (6/1/2005)

TURNING LEAF

Turning Leaf 2004 Reserve Cabernet Sauvignon (California) $8. Soft as velvet, this easy wine is rich in blackberry and chocolate flavors that finish dry and are wrapped in ripe, dusty tannins. It's great if you're cooking for lots of people and don't want to break the bank. **84 Best Buy** —S.H. (11/15/2006)

Turning Leaf 2004 Reserve Chardonnay (California) $8. Superripe and oaky, with tropical fruit, vanilla, and buttered toast flavors, this wine leaves little to the imagination. It's sweet on the finish, but fortunately has good acids. **84** —S.H. (4/1/2006)

Turning Leaf 2002 Reserve Chardonnay (California) $12. Not too concentrated, but what there is is pretty. Peach and apple flavors have gentle oak shadings, and the wine is creamy and dry. **84** —S.H. (12/1/2004)

Turning Leaf 2003 Sonoma Reserve Chardonnay (Sonoma County) $12. This is obviously a cool climate Chard, to judge from the brisk acids, citrusy flavors, and hint of minerality that makes the wine bracing and strong. Yet oak and lees lend softening, complexing notes. **87 Best Buy** —S.H. (12/15/2005)

Turning Leaf 1997 Reserve Merlot (Sonoma County) $10. **82** —J.C. (7/1/2000)

Turning Leaf 2004 Reserve Pinot Grigio (California) $8. Crisp in acids, and with the flavor of tart green apples, figs, and white peaches, this is an easy, satisfying wine. It's fully dry and very clean, leaving the palate ready for food. **85 Best Buy** —S.H. (3/1/2006)

Turning Leaf 2002 Coastal Reserve Pinot Noir (North Coast) $10. Smells and tastes a bit herbal and peppery, with plummy flavors. Very dry, with gentle, soft tannins. **83** —S.H. (11/1/2004)

Turning Leaf 1999 Coastal Reserve Pinot Noir (North Coast) $NA. Gallo's ubiquitous Turning Leaf brand occasionally turns up a real winner, as this plummy, fragrant Pinot Noir shows. Though not for purists, qho will be put off by its careless use of the term "Reserve" and the inclusion of Sangiovese (9%), Barbera (4%) Mourvèdre (2%), and "Other" (2%) in the blend, it is a softly delicious wine that adds some sweet chocolate to its classic sassafras and beetroot flavors. **87** —P.G. (11/15/2001)

Turning Leaf 2003 Sonoma Reserve Pinot Noir (Sonoma County) $11. Pretty thin despite the price. You get alcohol and oak, with thinned-down cherry cola flavors. **83** —S.H. (10/1/2005)

Turning Leaf 2001 Reserve Riesling (Monterey) $7. The "Reserve" on the label is hardly appropriate in this banal version of what is normally a racy varietal. This version shows a mild fruit in a somewhat stewed version. **80** —J.M. (8/1/2003)

Turning Leaf 2002 Vineyards Riesling (Monterey County) $9. Here's a refreshing summer quaffer with off-dry flavors of apricots and peaches and good acidity. Enjoy with watermelon, fried chicken, and similar fare. **84** —S.H. (12/1/2004)

Turning Leaf 2003 Sauvignon Blanc (California) $9. Dry and tart, this easy sipper has citrus and spice flavors that finish zesty and clean. Drink with Chinese food. **83** —S.H. (12/1/2004)

Turning Leaf 1999 Shiraz (California) $8. Slight cocoa, smoke, and leather notes don't compensate for the essentially sour quality of the juice. There are blackberry flavors but they're lean; the mouthfeel is light and a bit thin. Closes with tangy, prickly tannins. **83** (10/1/2001)

Turning Leaf 2003 Syrah (California) $8. Descriptors ranged all over the lot for this wine, from berry and cherry to meaty and peppery, yet all reviewers agreed that this was a solid little Syrah. A bit simple and short, but satisfying. **85 Best Buy** (9/1/2005)

TUSK 'N RED

Tusk 'n Red 2003 Red Wine Red Blend (Mendocino County) $15. This old-style field blend leaves little to the imagination. It's full-bodied, dry, and astringently tannic, with fruity, earthy flavors. **83** —S.H. (12/31/2005)

TWIN FIN

Twin Fin 2003 Cabernet Sauvignon (California) $10. What a value we have here. The aroma is inviting, suggesting a rich, complex Cabernet. In the mouth, it's dry, ripe, and smooth, with a long finish. **86 Best Buy** —S.H. (12/31/2005)

Twin Fin 2002 Cabernet Sauvignon (California) $10. This is a gently structured, full-bodied wine with pizazz and flair. It's rich in cherry, currant, and coffee flavors, in a dry, elegant package. **85 Best Buy** —S.H. (10/1/2005)

Twin Fin 2004 Chardonnay (California) $10. Powerfully ripe and expressive in tropical fruit and tangerine flavors, with a lot of brio and zest. High acids brighten the fruit and push it upfront. What a nice value. **86 Best Buy** —S.H. (10/1/2005)

Twin Fin 2003 Merlot (California) $10. This is a good value Merlot because there's a lot going on in the bottle, at a fair price. The wine is fully dry and balanced. Flavorwise, it offers a subtle blend of cherries, herbs, sweet tobacco, and smoky oak. Nothing stands out, but the end result is a gentle wine that you don't get tired of sipping. **85 Best Buy** — S.H. (12/15/2005)

Twin Fin 2002 Merlot (California) $10. Here's a robust, full-bodied wine rich in blackberry flavors, with some oaky overtones, yet the tannins are soft and refined. Easy to drink with anything calling for a dry red. **85 Best Buy** —S.H. (10/1/2005)

Twin Fin 2004 Pinot Grigio (California) $10. This is a crisp, dry wine with citrus and apple flavors, and a pleasing scour of spice. It will go well with a wide variety of food. Finishes with lively acids. **85 Best Buy** —S.H. (7/1/2005)

Twin Fin 2004 Pinot Noir (California) $10. The price is right, but the wine is raw and rustic. The Twin Fin brand gets it right with almost all varieties, but Pinot Noir is tough to make into a value wine. **82** —S.H. (12/31/2005)

Twin Fin 2003 Pinot Noir (California) $10. A nice, rich red wine, dry, and soft, with black cherry flavors veering into chocolate and a silky mouthfeel. Shows real complexity in the balanced interplay of tannins, fruit, and acids. **85 Best Buy** —S.H. (10/1/2005)

Twin Fin 2003 Shiraz (California) $10. If you're into Aussie Shirazes, the kind that stain your teeth and taste like an explosion in a fruit factory, this is your everyday vino. It's dry and tannic, and packed with blackberry, cherry, and blueberry jam flavors, with a white-pepper scour that screams for a good steak off the barbie. **86 Best Buy** —*S.H. (12/15/2005)*

Twin Fin 2002 Shiraz (California) $10. Jammy and sweet-tasting, with the emphasis on cherry and cranberry flavors. The texture is soft, the finish a bit rough, but this is a serviceable sipper. **82** *(9/1/2005)*

TWISTED OAK

Twisted Oak 2004 Grenache (Sierra Foothills) $24. Soft and simple, with cherry, black raspberry, and cocoa flavors wrapped in a somewhat hot mouthfeel. Finishes dry and spicy. **84** —*S.H. (12/1/2006)*

Twisted Oak 2002 Grenache (Sierra Foothills) $20. This is an extremely dry, fairly tannic, earthy wine. It has basic flavors of cherries, with a tobaccoey edge and enough acidity to lend it structure. Picks up points for the sweet finish of ripe cherries. **85** —*S.H. (9/1/2004)*

Twisted Oak 2004 The Spaniard Red Blend (Calaveras County) $45. The softness and rusticity that almost always mark Sierra Foothills wines are here, yet the wine rises to what might be called coastal elegance. A Spanifornia blend of Tempranillo and Cab Sauvignon, it has a complexity that unfolds in waves of blackberry, tobacco, clove, anise, and espresso. Drink now. **91** —*S.H. (12/1/2006)*

Twisted Oak 2002 The Spaniard Red Blend (Calaveras County) $35. Compared to Twisted Oak's *%#&@! Rhône blend, this is more full-bodied and tannic, no doubt due to the Cabernet Sauvignon and Petit Verdot in the blend, which also includes Tempranillo. It's rich in black currants and spices and a touch of smoky oak. Very sophisticated, it represents a tremendous advancement in Calaveras County winemaking. **92** —*S.H. (11/15/2005)*

Twisted Oak 2004 *%#&@! Rhône Red Blend (Sierra Foothills) $32. The '03 was more balanced. The '04 has more stewed, raisiny flavors that must have been the result of the heat. Drink now with steaks and grilled chicken. Mourvèdre, Syrah, and Grenache. **85** —*S.H. (12/1/2006)*

Twisted Oak 2003 *%#&@! Rhône Red Blend (Sierra Foothills) $32. The Twisted Oak guys are determined to raise the level of winemaking in their area. This Rhône blend has the hallmarks of a fine, warm country wine. It blasts off with cherry, cocoa, and blueberry flavors, and then the structure locks in to give it balance and harmony. **90** —*S.H. (11/15/2005)*

Twisted Oak 2002 *%#&@! Rhône Red Blend (Sierra Foothills) $28. A Rhône blend with a really weird name. Extremely dry and tannic, with a rasping bite on the tongue, although there are some pretty flavors of cherries, chocolate, and peppery spices. You can taste the sunny ripeness of the grapes. **86** —*S.H. (12/1/2004)*

Twisted Oak 2003 Syrah (Calaveras County) $24. Lots of rich, ripe cherry jam notes in this softly structured wine, with overtones of kirsch, blueberries, black raspberries, and chocolate. It's a direct hit of fruit, a little bomby, and voluptuously packaged. **86** —*S.H. (12/1/2006)*

Twisted Oak 2001 Syrah (Sierra Foothills) $26. Made under the fierce, thin-air sun of the mountains, this wine has Port-like aromas and flavors of raisins, although it's dry. It's also pretty tannic, leading to an astringent finish. **84** —*S.H. (9/1/2004)*

Twisted Oak 2003 Tanner Syrah (Calaveras County) $28. Rustic, with big, drying tannins on the finish, this wine divided the panel. All enjoyed it for its bold, gutsy dried-fruit flavors and sense of Sierra Foothills individuality, but two reviewers felt the tannins were a bit overpowering in the long run and the wine should be enjoyed young. One felt the wine would age well. Our advice? Buy two, try one, and decide when to drink the other one yourself. **87** *(9/1/2005)*

Twisted Oak 2002 Tanner Vineyard Syrah (Calaveras County) $22. Shows the promise of this area. Jammy and extracted in blackberry, coffee, grilled meat, lavender, and smoky oak, a big wine. Powerful and fairly tannic, yet balanced in acids. Should age well. **90** —*S.H. (2/1/2005)*

Twisted Oak 2004 Tempranillo (Calaveras County) $22. Soft and earthy, with jammy cherry and raspberry liqueur flavors. Notes of crushed, fresh sage, and smoky vanilla lead into a spicy finish. Texturally, this is medium-bodied and silky, rather like Pinot Noir. **86** —*S.H. (12/1/2006)*

Twisted Oak 2002 Tempranillo (Calaveras County) $22. Very Cabernet-like, with its full-bodied flavors of blackberries and cherries and big

tannins. The difference is a subtle floweriness. Finishes dry and oaky. **85** —*S.H. (9/1/2004)*

Twisted Oak 2005 Silvaspoons Vineyard Verdelho (Lodi) $16. Kind of like Pinot Grigio, in that it's a delicate, unoaked (although leesy) wine with citrusy, figgy flavors and bright, citrusy acidity leading to a slightly sweet finish. It's food-versatile and user-friendly. **85** —*S.H. (12/1/2006)*

Twisted Oak 2004 Silvaspoons Vineyard Verdelho (Lodi) $16. Here's a vibrant, assertive wine that's something like a very dry Sauvignon Blanc. It's citrusy and minty-grassy, with an edge of white peach and green apple that makes for complexity. **88** —*S.H. (11/15/2005)*

Twisted Oak 2005 Viognier (Calaveras County) $20. Sure packs a lot of flavor, with everything from lemon-drop candy and pineapple sorbet to butterscotch and creamy vanilla milkshake. There's probably some residual sugar in there, but not too much, and the acidity helps along the balance. **86** —*S.H. (12/1/2006)*

Twisted Oak 2003 Viognier (Calaveras County) $18. Here's a beautiful Viognier, filled with ripe tropical fruit and flavor notes, spices, minerals, and smoky oak. It's crisp in acids, balanced, and elegant, with a fabulously long, spicy finish. Just first rate. **91** —*S.H. (2/1/2005)*

TWO ANGELS

Two Angels 2003 Petite Sirah (Lake County) $24. Stylistically similar to Cabernet in weight, this Pet is dry and full-bodied, with a velvety mouthfeel and big tannins that frame well-ripened blackberry fruit. It's really a lovely wine that drinks well now and should fade very slowly over the next 15 years. **90** —*S.H. (12/1/2005)*

Two Angels 2004 Shannon Ridge Vineyard Petite Sirah (Lake County) $30. From this warmish county, inland from Napa, comes this dark, soft, dry, tannic wine that's saved by its enormous palate of fruit. The blackberries, cherries, mocha, plums, and blueberries are hugely rich and savory. Try with short ribs or barbecued ribs slathered with your most delicious sauce. **90** —*S.H. (3/1/2006)*

Two Angels 2005 Sauvignon Blanc (High Valley) $15. This is from Hook & Ladder, the new project from former DeLoach owner Cecil DeLoach. The grapes come from a new appellation in Lake County, grown at an altitude of more than 2,000 feet. The wine is dense in citrus rind, gooseberry, and honeysuckle flavors, and absolutely dry, with very crisp acids. It shows lots of flair and complexity. **89 Best Buy** —*S.H. (10/1/2006)*

Two Angels 2004 Shannon Ridge Sauvignon Blanc (Lake County) $15. Lake County is making a play as the best place in California for inexpensive Sauvignon Blanc, and this wine shows why. It's dry and very crisp, with pure, intense flavors of figs and pineapples, and is simply irresistible. **86** —*S.H. (10/1/2005)*

Two Angels 2003 Shannon Ridge Syrah (Lake County) $25. If your tolerance for alcohol and volatility is high, you may like this more than we did. One of our tasters found it round, soft, and harmonious, while the other two disapproved of its heat and and volatile acidity. **82** *(9/1/2005)*

TWO MOUNTAIN

Two Mountain 2002 Cabernet Sauvignon (Yakima Valley) $25. Pleasant and light, with fruit that suggests barely ripened, young grapes. Hints of strawberry, melon, and raspberry carry into flavors that seem dilute. The medium-deep color and chewy, green tannins suggest it was pushed a bit hard at fermentation. **85** —*P.G. (6/1/2006)*

Two Mountain 2002 Merlot (Yakima Valley) $20. The color is a slightly murky garnet. The wine sends up sweet fruit scents of strawberry preserves along with toasted cracker. There's enough acid here to stiffen it up, but all around it the fruit is soft, broad, and open. Lightly spicy with a hint of burnt rubber in the finish. **86** —*P.G. (6/1/2006)*

TWO TONE FARM

Two Tone Farm 2002 Chardonnay (Napa Valley) $13. Toasty and ripe in tropical fruit, vanilla, and buttered toast, this is a fancy Chard at an everyday price. Stays clean with fresh acidity. **88 Best Buy** —*S.H. (3/1/2005)*

Two Tone Farm 2001 Merlot (Napa Valley) $16. Lovely wine. Dry and rich in berry, plum, and herb flavors that turn oaky and chocolatey on the finish. Smooth, supple, and complex, with a lingering finish. Don't be put off by the screwtop. **87** —*S.H. (3/1/2005)*

TY CATON

Ty Caton 2001 Cabernet Sauvignon (Sonoma Valley) $24. A soft, easy Cab, with gentle tannins, low acidity, and blackberry fruit that seems just a little baked. Goes down gently, with a fruity finish. **86** —*S.H. (12/31/2004)*

Ty Caton 2003 Merlot (Dry Creek Valley) $29. There's some nice plummy, berry fruit and rich tannins in this wine, but it suffers from Porty, brown sugar aromas and a sweetness to the finish that's inappropriate in a dry table wine. **83** —*S.H. (4/1/2006)*

Ty Caton 2001 Merlot (Sonoma County) $24. This is one of those Merlots that keep you coming back for more. It's lush in black currant, cocoa, coffee, and spicy fruit flavors, wrapped in soft, creamy tannins, and is well oaked. Has just enough acidity to finish clean and vibrant. **89** —*S.H. (12/31/2004)*

Ty Caton 2003 Tytanium Red Blend (Sonoma Valley) $39. A blend of Bordeaux and Rhône varieties, this is a dry, somewhat rugged wine, whose best feature is fruit. Blackberries, cherries, plums, even cranberries and cocoa show up in the complex flavors. There's a tannic, acidic streak that makes it a little tough, though. **86** —*S.H. (5/1/2006)*

Ty Caton 2002 Ty Caton Vineyards Syrah (Sonoma Valley) $19. A well-ripened Syrah with lots of plump fruit. Although it's dry, the plummy coffee and chocolate flavors are sweet in fruity essence. Feels plush and soft in the mouth, with a long, berry-and-spice finish. **88** —*S.H. (12/15/2004)*

Ty Caton 2003 Zinfandel (Sonoma County) $24. Pricy for what you get. It's a country-style Zin, with rustic berry flavors and some dry tannins. **83** —*S.H. (2/1/2006)*

TYEE

Tyee 1996 Pinot Blanc (Willamette Valley) $12. 86 —*L.W. (12/31/1999)*

Tyee 1997 Pinot Blanc (Willamette Valley) $12. This Pinot Blanc is pretty mute from start to finish. Though its nose is very tight, it still shows light fig and peach aromas. Bone-dry in the mouth, its palate flavors are those of lemon pith and green apples. Finish is also dry, with mineral and metallic flavors. **83** —*D.T. (11/1/2001)*

UNITED WE STAND

United We Stand 2003 Reserve Chardonnay (California) $10. Earthy and a little sweet, a common wine that's a little too rustic. **82** —*S.H. (3/1/2005)*

United We Stand 2003 Reserve Merlot (California) $10. Not even the most patriotic American will drink this harsh, vegetal wine. **80** —*S.H. (3/1/2005)*

UNKNOWN BOTTLING

Unknown Bottling 1983 Pinot Noir (Santa Ynez Valley) $NA. Label missing, but probably an early S&B Vineyard from Sanford Winery. Alcohol 13.5%. Brownish-orange color, like cognac. Maderized. Dry, sherry-like flavors. **81** —*S.H. (6/1/2005)*

UNTI

Unti 2003 Barbera (Dry Creek Valley) $24. Drink this dark, chewy wine with full-flavored Italian beef or veal dishes. It's packed with dry, strong tannins and is high in acids. By itself it's austere, but rich meats will coax out the blackberry and roasted coffee flavors. **87** —*S.H. (11/1/2005)*

Unti 2003 Grenache (Dry Creek Valley) $26. With a little Syrah and Mourvèdre, this young, dark purple wine is tight, tannic, and acidic. It desperately needs time. Even as little as six months should soften it, and tease out the sweet cherry and spice flavors. Finishes with fabulous complexity. **92 Editors' Choice** —*S.H. (11/1/2005)*

Unti 2004 Rosé Grenache (Dry Creek Valley) $16. From a warmer part of Dry Creek Valley, Rhône specialist Unti has crafted a pale, but rich, blush wine with such an inviting aroma of raspberry sorbet and vanilla, you can't wait to dive in. It doesn't disappoint, being delicately silky and drily delicious. Try with grilled sausage and raw veggies with a spicy hummus dip. **88** —*S.H. (8/1/2004)*

Unti 2003 Segromigno Red Blend (Dry Creek Valley) $15. This Sangiovese, Barbera, and Dolcetto blend is a fantastic value in a Chianti-style red.

It's bone dry, tart in acids, and dusty, with polished flavors of cherries, backed up by puckery plum-skin tannins. This elegant wine shows real sophistication. **89 Editors' Choice** —*S.H. (11/1/2005)*

Unti 2003 Sangiovese (Dry Creek Valley) $30. Unti has succeeded in overcoming Sangiovese's tendency to dull herbaceousness in favor of a cherried, blackberry richness. Tannins and acids, however, are hefty, suggesting rich cheeses, olive oil, and fatty meats. Drink now through 2011. **89** —*S.H. (11/1/2005)*

Unti 2002 Syrah (Dry Creek Valley) $24. Consistent with our impessions of Unti's Benchland bottling, our tasters' view diverged considerably on Mick Unti's regular Syrah. The drying tannins on the finish gave pause to one of our reviewers, while another found them balanced by the wine's dense blackberry, plum, and coffee flavors. **87** *(9/1/2005)*

Unti 2002 Benchland Syrah (Dry Creek Valley) $30. Hits the palate with the force of a sledgehammer: Very tannic and dry, but with enough blackberry flavor to (mostly) balance things out. West Coast Editor Steve Heimoff was a huge proponent of this wine, calling it likely to age gracefully for a decade, while Tasting Director Joe Czerwinski was less enthusiastic, finding the tannins hard. **88** *(9/1/2005)*

Unti 2002 Zinfandel (Dry Creek Valley) $22. Zin hardly gets better than this dark, deeply flavored wine. The aroma suggests grilled meat, leather, blackberry pie, espresso, cinnamon, and vanilla. Drinks full bodied and tannic, but very dry, combining power and authority with finesse. This wine is beautiful now, and should hold and improve for years. **93 Editors' Choice** —*S.H. (11/1/2005)*

URSA

Ursa 2002 Merlot (Santa Clara Valley) $16. Smells sharp and minty, like toothpaste, with green, stalky overtones. In the mouth, you'll find modest cherry and berry flavors and some sweet oak. **84** —*S.H. (8/1/2004)*

Ursa 2003 Petite Sirah (Paso Robles) $22. This is a very nice Petite Sirah, rich and soft and dry, although it's not quite as complex as Ursa's Sierra Foothills bottling. The cherry, blackberry, cola, leather, and raw red meat flavors are forward and ripe, and definitive of the variety. **88** —*S.H. (10/1/2006)*

Ursa 2003 Petite Sirah (Sierra Foothills) $22. This is one of the best Pets I've had this year. It's dry and compellingly delicious, a subtle wine of great intricacy, from the blackberry and coffee flavors to the smoothly tannic structure to the classic finish, but be forewarned: The alcohol is 15.9%. **93 Editors' Choice** —*S.H. (10/1/2006)*

Ursa 2002 Petite Sirah (Paso Robles) $22. Raises this variety, which can be excessively tannic and ponderous, to a more interesting level with some well-polished fruit. Opens with a very pretty perfume of blackberry jam, chocolate, and cassis, and turns sweetly fruity in the mouth, although it's very dry. The tannins are still there, but they're ripe and sweet. **88** —*S.H. (8/1/2004)*

Ursa 2002 Petite Sirah (Lodi) $16. Full-bodied and dense on the palate, this wine is very dry, carrying plummy, herbal flavors and thick tannins. At first it came across as simple and dull. But then a certain taste of the earth perked it up. Spicy barbecued pork or beef will nicely set it off. **86** —*S.H. (8/1/2004)*

Ursa 2003 Vineyard Blend Petite Sirah (California) $16. This blend is from the Foothills, the Central Coast and Lodi, and the wine is very nice. Polished, dry, tannic, and rich in fruit, it has unrestrained blackberry, cherry, coffee, and chocolate flavors, but maintains balance all the way. What a great short ribs wine. **89** —*S.H. (10/1/2006)*

USED AUTOMOBILE PARTS

Used Automobile Parts 2002 Red Table Wine Bordeaux Blend (Napa Valley) $50. From Don Sebastiani and Sons, known for inexpensive value wines, comes this first release. Don't let the weird name fool you, this is a serious Napa Bordeaux, mostly Merlot but with the other four varieties. There's a smoked leather scent hovering over the blackberry, mocha, root beer, and oak, and once in the mouth, the wine is exceptionally smooth. Drink now through 2010. **92** —*S.H. (9/1/2006)*

UVADA

Uvada 2001 Merlot (Oakville) $28. Flashy and flamboyant, this Merlot seduces with scads of toasty oak in keeping with the size of the blackberry, cherry, and cocoa fruit. The tannins are soft and sweet, the finish elegant. If it was any softer, it would collapse, but the acids and tannins work. **91 Editors' Choice** —*S.H. (10/1/2005)*

V. SATTUI

V. Sattui 2002 Cabernet Sauvignon (Napa Valley) $29. An interesting, enjoyable wine that straddles the line between age-me and drink-me-now. It's ripe and forward in sunny blackberry and cherry fruit, dry and balanced, with a tasteful edge of oak. But it's so balanced, it should hang in there for a decade. **90** —*S.H. (12/1/2005)*

V. Sattui 2000 Cabernet Sauvignon (Napa Valley) $21. Showcases those dependably ripe flavors of black currant and cassis that typify Napa Valley Cabernet. The tannins are tough and gritty, like an old style wine that needed age to come around. On the finish, acidity leaves a bitter feeling. **84** —*S.H. (12/15/2003)*

V. Sattui 2000 Cabernet Sauvignon (Sonoma County) $16. There are flavors of blackberries and cassis in this very dry wine, and they are wrapped in tough, stubborn tannins, the kind that stun the palate. It seems unlikely to be going anywhere, so drink up now. **84** —*S.H. (12/15/2003)*

V. Sattui 1999 Cabernet Sauvignon (Napa Valley) $21. Ripe and fat, marked by classic Napa flavors of sweet cassis and blackberries. It's very soft in tannins and acids. It could have more structure, but then, so could many other California Cabernets. But there's no arguing with the delicious taste. **87** —*S.H. (11/15/2002)*

V. Sattui 1999 Morisoli Cabernet Sauvignon (Napa Valley) $32. Another super-ripe Cab marked by spectacular fruit. Unbelievable concentration and density of flavors, mainly cassis and blackberries, that spread all over the palate. But it's very soft, and needs acidity and tannins to balance all that ripeness. **87** —*S.H. (11/15/2002)*

V. Sattui 2000 Morisoli Vineyard Cabernet Sauvignon (Napa Valley) $35. Delicious, and very different in flavor from the winery's Carsi bottling. There's a distinct note of green olive in addition to the array of blackberry, cherry, and sweet tobacco. Once again, lavish oak provides the final treatment, but the wine wears it well. **92** —*S.H. (12/31/2003)*

V. Sattui 1999 Preston Cabernet Sauvignon (Napa Valley) $32. The cassis flavors just explode in the mouth, coating the palate with rich sweetness, but the palate longs for structure to balance all that flavor out. Here, the acids and tannins are very soft. The result is a bit syrupy and flabby. **87** —*S.H. (11/15/2002)*

V. Sattui 2000 Preston Vineyard Cabernet Sauvignon (Napa Valley) $33. Another fine Cab from this veteran producer. Deep, penetrating flavors of cassis and green olive coat the palate with great persistence. Oak is notable, and the tannins are lush, soft, and dry. Made in the Sattui style, which is immediate accessbility, but will no doubt age. **90** —*S.H. (12/31/2003)*

V. Sattui 1999 Suzanne's Cabernet Sauvignon (Napa Valley) $25. Plush, opulent, and soft as velvet, but lacking in acidity and tannic structure. On the other hand, if you enjoy full-throttle flavor, you'll fall in love with the seductive taste of cassis, blackberries, and rich spice. There's little difference between any of Sattui's single-vineyard wines, so choose this one and save yourself a few bucks. **87** —*S.H. (11/15/2002)*

V. Sattui 2000 Suzanne's Vineyard Cabernet Sauvignon (Napa Valley) $25. Quite a distinguished Cabernet, with well-ripened black currant flavors and a rich overlay of smoky, spicy oak. The tannins are near-perfect, smooth, and velvety but firm and supportive. The long finish leaves the palate with a delicious flavor of currants. **91 Editors' Choice** —*S.H. (12/31/2003)*

V. Sattui 2000 Carsi Chardonnay (Napa Valley) $21. Very ripe and extracted, with an almost late-harvest bouquet of unctuously sweet tropical fruits. Smoky, vanilla-tinged oak is laid on thick. Lacks delicacy, a big, rich wine that smothers with excess. **84** —*S.H. (12/15/2002)*

V. Sattui 1999 Carsi Vineyard Chardonnay (Napa Valley) $20. Toasty oak frames the citrus-like core here. Hints of pear and apple are also in evidence, finishing moderately. **84** —*J.M. (5/1/2002)*

V. Sattui 2001 Carsi Vineyard Old Vine Chardonnay (Napa Valley) $25. An amazing wine, so rich and unctuous it's like a late harvest dessert wine. May even have a little botrytis in the intense pear, banana, and tropical fruit flavors, but it's really very dry. A whole lot of sweet oak pushes the volume even higher. **89** —*S.H. (8/1/2003)*

V. Sattui 2001 Sattui Family Chardonnay (Napa Valley) $15. An unbalanced wine despite some pretty apple and peach flavors, an overlay of oak, and a creamy smooth texture. The parts are nice but somehow they don't knit together and the wine feels disjointed. Turns quite bitter on the finish. **84** —*S.H. (8/1/2003)*

V. Sattui 2001 Rouge Gamay (California) $15. Oversulfured, but once you get past that, there are raspberry flavors that are on the dry side and quite acidic, with silky tannins. The finish picks up some sweet jam. A nice wine, except for the sulfur. **83** —*S.H. (12/1/2002)*

V. Sattui 2001 Dry Johannisberg Riesling (Napa Valley) $15. It really is bone dry, and with very high acidity, almost what the French call petillant, or slightly sparkling. The flavors veer to fresh green apples. Unusual, and not for everyone, but distinctive and clean. **86** —*S.H. (9/1/2003)*

V. Sattui 2001 Off-Dry Johannisberg Riesling (Napa Valley) $15. This isn't sweet enough to be a dessert wine. In fact, this self-described "off-dry" wine is no sweeter than many pop style Chardonnays these days that claim to be dry. It has apple and honeysuckle flavors and almost an effervescence. **85** —*S.H. (9/1/2003)*

V. Sattui 2000 Merlot (Napa Valley) $24. Pretty tannic. Numbs the mouth with a dry, gritty toughness, which lets the acids stand out. There is some blackberry fruit buried down deep but you have to seek it out. **84** —*S.H. (12/1/2003)*

V. Sattui 1999 Merlot (Napa Valley) $24. A well-made wine from this midvalley veteran winery. Juicy and plump, an unctuous red wine packed with mouthwatering flavors of cassis and black raspberry jam. Yet it's dry, with finely ground, dusty tannins. The raspberry theme reprises on the long finish. **90** —*S.H. (11/15/2002)*

V. Sattui 2001 Muscat (California) $16. You'll think of peaches, apples, and nectarines when you sip this wine, and Moscato d'Asti, too, because of the effervescence. That prickly, acidic mouthfeel is pleasant and clean, and carries the semisweet fruit through the long finish. **89** —*S.H. (12/1/2002)*

V. Sattui NV Angelica Muscat (California) $22. Like a good cream Sherry, a whitish-yellow wine with orange muscat, apricot, toffee, and vanilla-custard flavors and a strong, spicy finish. It's very sweet, not shockingly so, but pretty rich. Try with vanilla ice cream. **88** —*S.H. (12/1/2002)*

V. Sattui 2001 Hendry Ranch Pinot Noir (Carneros) $35. Thick and heavy, with flavors of raspberries and cherries. The wine has an earthy texture more reminiscent of a Syrah, and finishes with mouth-numbing tannins. **84** —*S.H. (7/1/2003)*

V. Sattui 2003 Henry Ranch Pinot Noir (Carneros) $NA. This is a Pinot that's too soft, almost flabby in texture. The softness accentuates the ripeness of the raspberry and coffee flavors, making them a little cloying. **82** —*S.H. (12/1/2005)*

V. Sattui 2000 Cuvée Rouge Red Blend (Napa Valley) $20. Dark for a rosé, a deep salmon and garnet color. The aroma is reduced or sulfury, not exactly the most inviting scent. Like Sattui's Brut, this rosé also is sharp in acids and low in flavors, although it does show modest strawberries. Lacks the delicacy and finesse of a fine sparkler, especially at this price. **83** —*S.H. (12/1/2003)*

V. Sattui 1999 Sattui Family Red Red Blend (California) $13. Here's an easy -wine that's old fashioned in its rugged earthiness and solid tannins. It's dry, clean and feels good in the mouth. A blend of Zinfandel, Cabernet Sauvignon, and Merlot, from the Napa and Dry Creek Valleys. **86** —*S.H. (5/1/2002)*

V. Sattui 2000 Beatty Ranch Zinfandel (Howell Mountain) $27. This is mountain fruit all the way, big and impressive. Grapes don't get much riper than this, offering up a huge blast of wild berry, dark stone-fruit and chocolate flavors. The wine is very dry and fairly tannic. Best of all, it has the crisp acidity needed to add focus to all this seductive flavor. **91** —*S.H. (12/1/2002)*

V. Sattui 2000 Duarte Vineyard Ancient Vine Zinfandel (Contra Costa County) $35. These vines are 100 years old, and although this wine stems from the same vineyard as the Old Vine bottling, it has important differences. It's much softer in acidity. It's also much denser and thicker in the mouth, and the flavors suggest dark chocolate, plum preserves, and elderberry wine. To my mind, it lacks the balance and verve of the Old Vine Zin. **86** —*S.H. (12/1/2002)*

V. Sattui 2000 Duarte Vineyard Old Vine Zinfandel (Contra Costa County) $22. From 30-year-old vines, this is excellent Zin, a textbook example of a richly concentrated, dry and balanced red wine. It has wild berry flavors and wonderfully fine tannins, and feels great in the mouth. It's a big, brawny wine, but manages to be elegant and focused. **90** —*S.H. (12/1/2002)*

V. Sattui NV Madeira Zinfandel (California) $29. Needs the right atmosphere to be appreciated, but this is a fine, sweet sip. Starts with aromas of warm pecan pie and dark honey that make the mouth water, and doesn't disappoint with its rich crème brûlée and white chocolate flavors. Sweet, but not shockingly so, the wine has the acids to balance. **90** —*S.H. (12/1/2002)*

V. Sattui 1999 Quaglia Vineyard Zinfandel (Napa Valley) $24. Not big or concentrated. In fact it's on the light side, in alcohol and fruity flavors, with diluted black raspberry fruit. Because the fruit is so light, the tannins come forward, and so does the acidity. **84** —*S.H. (12/1/2002)*

V. Sattui 2000 Suzanne's Vineyard Zinfandel (Napa Valley) $20. Has Zin's full-bodied exuberance and complex flavors of wild berries, tobacco, pepper, and herbs, and also dense but finely ground tannins. Loses a few points for an awkward sweetness on the finish. **86** —*S.H. (9/1/2003)*

V. Sattui 1999 Suzanne's Vineyard Zinfandel (Napa Valley) $20. Very dark, almost inky in color, and smells big, young, and jammy. Intense aromas of cassis and blueberries erupt from the glass, with added nuances of tobacco and rich hummus. The flavors are similar, deeply fruity, but tannins are ultrasoft and acidity is very low, so it seems a little flabby and syrupy. **86** —*S.H. (12/1/2002)*

VA PIANO

Va Piano 2003 Syrah (Columbia & Walla Walla Valleys) $38. Very pretty fruit, mostly from the young estate vineyard, sports flavors of fresh-squeezed grapes, plums, and spicy cranberries. The oak is nicely applied, lending flavors of light cocoa and espresso bean to the well-balanced finish. **88** —*P.G. (6/1/2006)*

VACHE

Vache 2000 Cabernet Sauvignon (Cienega Valley) $37. Dry and smooth, and a bit coarse, this wine shows berry, oak and leather flavors. Short finish. **84** —*S.H. (5/1/2005)*

Vache 2002 Chardonnay (Cienega Valley) $37. This awkward, soft Chard has some forward fruit flavors, but is dominated by a burnt, caramelly note that seems to come from supercharged oak. It feels heavy and harsh in the mouth. **82** —*S.H. (12/1/2005)*

Vache 2001 Chardonnay (Cienega Valley) $37. Smells vegetal and oaky, but tastes a little better. Finishes sweet. **83** —*S.H. (4/1/2005)*

Vache 2002 Pinot Noir (Cienega Valley) $37. Smells burnt, and tastes hot, baked, and gnarly, with coffee and dried cherry flavors. **81** —*S.H. (12/1/2005)*

Vache 2001 Pinot Noir (Cienega Valley) $37. Smells rubbery, and drinks dry and harsh. **82** —*S.H. (4/1/2005)*

VALDEZ

Valdez 2005 Sauvignon Blanc (Sonoma County) $23. I thought this was a Pinot Grigio, so flowery was it in aroma, but no, it's Sauvignon. Those honeysuckles show up in the flavors, too, along with lemons and limes, tangerines, and a touch of vanilla cream. The finish is a little sweet, but the wine has nice, clean acids. **85** —*S.H. (12/31/2006)*

Valdez 2004 Lancel Creek Reserve Zinfandel (Russian River Valley) $35. This is the real deal when it comes to Zin. It's a big, impressive wine,

ripe and opulent in briary berry, cherry, chocolate, coffee, and peppery spice flavors, with a touch of raisiny cassis, and it leaves a powerful impression through the finish. Yet for all that, it somehow maintains elegance and balance, despite the ridiculously high alcohol. **93** —*S.H. (12/31/2006)*

Valdez 2004 Rockpile Road Vineyard Zinfandel (Rockpile) $38. Rockpile Zins have earned a reputation as big, complex, and interesting, and this is a great example. It sure is ripe, with a flood of blackberry and cherry pie-filling fruit, fudgy chocolate, licorice, root beer, and spicy flavors. Yet it's balanced and dry, or at least as dry as a 16.5% Zin can be. Yes, it's a freakish wine, but you can't deny the deliciousness. **92** —*S.H. (12/31/2006)*

VALENTINE

Valentine 1999 Echo Valley Cabernet Sauvignon (Mendocino County) $27. Rough going, with herbal, raisiny aromas and raw tannins in the mouth. There's some good fruit down deep but it's pushed aside. The wine is also soft. Not a promising start for a debut release. **84** —*S.H. (11/15/2002)*

VALLEY OF THE MOON

Valley of the Moon 1999 Cuvée de la Luna Cabernet Blend (Sonoma County) $28. A Bordeaux blend, and a stylish one at that. Excellent flavors of black currants and cherries, with an herbaceous streak of green olives and sage. Feels light and airy on the palate, yet it's a serious red wine that should be consumed with good fare. **91** —*S.H. (5/1/2003)*

Valley of the Moon 2001 Cuvée de la Luna Cabernet Blend (Sonoma County) $30. Combining ripe fruit with substantial oak, this Bordeaux blend is another example of how great the '01 vintage continues to be. The flavors, of cassis, black currants, cocoa, and licorice, are impressively deep and long-lasting. Drink now and over the next few years. **91** —*S.H. (11/15/2005)*

Valley of the Moon 2002 Cabernet Sauvignon (Sonoma County) $20. Good fruit here, rich in black currant, coffee, and spice flavors, with an edge of mint and herbs. The wine is a bit sharp in acids, and bone dry, with good grip. Should soften with a year or two of age. **85** —*S.H. (10/1/2006)*

Valley of the Moon 2001 Cabernet Sauvignon (Sonoma County) $20. At four-plus years, this wine has mellowed to extreme softness, although it retains balancing acidity. It's on the light side, flavor-wise, with suggestions of cola and cherries, and is totally dry. **84** —*S.H. (11/15/2005)*

Valley of the Moon 2000 Cabernet Sauvignon (Sonoma County) $20. A polished Cab with sturdy tannins and a nice overlay of subtle oak. The blackberry flavors have an edge of sweet herbs. **85** —*S.H. (11/15/2004)*

Valley of the Moon 1998 Cabernet Sauvignon (Sonoma Valley) $20. Ripe black cherry, plum, and herb flavors are framed in very toasty oak. The tannins are firm but supple and the finish moderate, ending with a hint of greenness. **86** —*J.M. (6/1/2002)*

Valley of the Moon 1999 Sophomore Sensation Cabernet Sauvignon (Sonoma County) $20. Lots of pretty Cabernet character here, with well-ripened flavors of black currants and herbs and a rich, smooth character. This dry wine has elegance and finesse and will go well with a grilled T-bone steak. **88** —*S.H. (11/15/2002)*

Valley of the Moon 2005 Chardonnay (Sonoma County) $16. Rich and full bodied, this is a tremendously ripe Chardonnay that explodes with peach custard, orange popsicle, pineapple, crème brûlée, and cinnamon spice flavors, leading to a long, fruity finish. **88** —*S.H. (12/15/2006)*

Valley of the Moon 2004 Chardonnay (Sonoma County) $16. This is a full-bodied, heavy Chard, a bit on the soft side, with a balance of apple, dried herb, and peach flavors that taste well-oaked. It's fully dry. **84** —*S.H. (12/31/2005)*

Valley of the Moon 2003 Chardonnay (Sonoma County) $15. Nice and rich in toasty oak, framing mouthfilling flavors of pineapples, papaya, peach, and cinnamon spice. Feels creamy-smooth, with a good tang of acidity. **86** —*S.H. (6/1/2005)*

Valley of the Moon 2002 Chardonnay (Sonoma County) $15. A delicious wine that bodes well for the vintage. Filled with flavors of ripe tropical fruits, peaches, and pears, vanilla, and buttered toast, in a creamy texture perked up with crisp acidity. Finishes with a smoky, spicy aftertaste.**90 Editors' Choice** —*S.H. (12/15/2003)*

Valley of the Moon 2001 Chardonnay (Sonoma County) $15. Another winner from this undervalued winery. Consistent with past vintages, this one is ripely fruity, with tasty flavors of apples and peaches and a rich overlay of vanilla and smoke from oak. Crisp acidity keeps it clean and vibrant on the palate.**87** —*S.H. (12/15/2002)*

Valley of the Moon 2000 Chardonnay (Sonoma County) $14. Toasty oak, citrus, peach, and pear flavors find their stride in this medium-bodied wine. Though not seamless, it serves up plenty of bold character.**87** — *J.M. (5/1/2002)*

Valley of the Moon 1999 Chardonnay (Sonoma County) $18. This Sonoma County Chardonnay is a mainstream success, with ripe, peachy fruit, leesy notes, and not that much oak. It finishes dry, clean, and crisp, with a slight bitter-almond note.**86** —*S.H. (8/1/2001)*

Valley of the Moon 1998 Chardonnay (Sonoma County) $17.86 *(6/1/2000)*

Valley of the Moon 1998 Cuvée de la Luna Meritage (Sonoma County) $25. Spicy vanilla and black cherry aromas are seductive here in this sleek, smooth, medium-bodied red blend, consisting of Caberent, Merlot, and Cabernet Franc. Toasty oak and smoky, firm tannins support the ensemble, which finishes on a bright note.**89** —*J.M. (5/1/2002)*

Valley of the Moon 2000 Cuvée de la Luna Meritage (Sonoma County) $25. This Bordeaux blend is rich, complex, and satisfying. Everything's reined in and in balance. The fruity flavor is quite ripe, the tannins smooth and intricate, the oak shadings just right to accompany fine food without competing with it.**90** —*S.H. (6/1/2004)*

Valley of the Moon 2005 Pinot Blanc (Sonoma County) $16. With its creamy texture and opulent tangerine, lime zest, vanilla custard, and spice flavors, this polished wine finishes with a cashew butter richness. Great acidity makes it bright and zingy. Very nice by itself or with a wide range of foods.**88** —*S.H. (12/15/2006)*

Valley of the Moon 2004 Pinot Blanc (Sonoma County) $16. Lots of tangerine cream, pineapple custard, and other tropical fruit flavors in this dry, very crisp wine. The acidity works so well to brighten and boost the fruity flavors. Try as a delicious alternative to Chard.**87** —*S.H. (12/31/2005)*

Valley of the Moon 2003 Pinot Blanc (Sonoma County) $15. Young, fresh, and jammy in lime, peach, and nectarine flavors, this wine has crisp acids and a clean, fruity finish. Will go well with fruit.**85** —*S.H. (5/1/2005)*

Valley of the Moon 2002 Pinot Blanc (Sonoma Valley) $15. If you like rich, ripe flavors of tropical fruits, apricots, and tangerine vanilla in your white wine, you'll love this one. It is delicately oaked, with a creamy texture that carries the opulent flavors through a long finish.**87** —*S.H. (2/1/2004)*

Valley of the Moon 2001 Pinot Blanc (Sonoma County) $15. Creamy, rich texture, with good mineral notes for balance. Flinty fresh on the palate, focused and firm, with subtle citrus and apple flavors.**87** —*J.M. (12/15/2002)*

Valley of the Moon 2000 Pinot Blanc (Sonoma County) $15. Here's a spicy, fragrant wine that's bursting with citrus, peach, and hazelnut flavors. There's a beautiful creaminess in the texture, and a honeyed sweetness that makes it almost meringue-like. Yet it's dry enough for chicken, veal, salmon.**87** —*S.H. (11/15/2001)*

Valley of the Moon 1999 Pinot Blanc (Sonoma County) $15. Here's a Pinot Blanc that's not a Chardonnay lookalike, with its mélange of wildflower and tropical fruit aromas. There's something almost Rhône-like in the opulence of its flavors, with chocolate, honey, brown-crushed spice, and nectarines in a crisp wine with a long finish. It misses a few points because of a certain lack of complexity, but flavor freaks won't be disappointed by this jolting wine.**88** —*S.H. (2/1/2001)*

Valley of the Moon 1998 Pinot Blanc (Sonoma County) $20.80 —*L.W. (3/1/2000)*

Valley of the Moon 2004 Pinot Noir (Carneros) $20. Simple but satisfying, with classic structure. It's very dry, with a silky-smooth texture and satis-

fying cherry, cola, and vanilla flavors that finish in a swirl of peppery spice.**85** —*S.H. (7/1/2006)*

Valley of the Moon 2003 Pinot Noir (Carneros) $20. A bit earthy, with herb, cherry, and spice flavors, this Pinot is dry, with gentle tannins and crisp acids. The fruity finish is very pretty.**85** —*S.H. (11/15/2005)*

Valley of the Moon 2002 Pinot Noir (Carneros) $20. Bright, clean, spicy, and really tasty, this Pinot offers heaps of cherry, raspberry, clove, cinnamon, vanilla, cola, and toasty flavors. It's light and silky on the palate.**88** —*S.H. (3/1/2005)*

Valley of the Moon 2001 Pinot Noir (Carneros) $20. Quite a rich Pinot, and not a simple fruit bomb. Plenty of ripely sweet berry flavors accompanied by earthier notes of chocolate and herbs. Delicious on its own, but great with everything from BBQ to high-end dishes.**90 Editors' Choice** —*S.H. (12/1/2003)*

Valley of the Moon 2000 Pinot Noir (Sonoma County) $20.87 *(10/1/2002)*

Valley of the Moon 2003 Sangiovese (Sonoma County) $16. Like almost all of this winery's wines, this Sangiovese is clean, varietally true, and polished. It's dry, with a medium-bodied silkiness and cherry, coffee, and spice flavors. It's also fairly tannic, something you'll want to consider.**86** —*S.H. (11/15/2006)*

Valley of the Moon 2002 Sangiovese (Sonoma County) $16. Chianti-like, a dry, acidic wine with pronounced cherry flavors and easy tannins. Of course, it's riper than anything you're likely to get from Tuscany, and those cherries veer into cocoa.**86** —*S.H. (10/1/2005)*

Valley of the Moon 2001 Sangiovese (Sonoma County) $15. This Chianti-like wine is very dry and rich in tannins and acids. A hint of cherries emerges mid-palate, then disappears on the finish. Try with a pesto pasta or a good steak.**85** —*S.H. (10/1/2004)*

Valley of the Moon 2000 Sangiovese (Sonoma County) $15. Delicious. Straddles the line between the soft, silky lightness of Pinot Noir and the full, rich mouthfeel of Merlot. Very dry with its fine, dusty tannins, adequate acidity, and a nice, smooth texture. The flavors? Cherries, tobacco, and peppery spice.**89** —*S.H. (12/1/2003)*

Valley of the Moon 1999 Sangiovese (Sonoma County) $15. Combines greenish, stalky aromas of white pepper and tobacco with fruitier flavors approaching cherries, but it's a lean, tart wine. Feels angular in the mouth, and the tannins are stark. This dry, Chianti-like wine demands the richest fare.**86** —*S.H. (12/1/2002)*

Valley of the Moon 1998 Sangiovese (Sonoma County) $16. Sangiovese still isn't a major varietal in California but wines like this push it a notch in that direction. You'll like the pretty berry flavors, integrity of tannins and acidity and rich, dry finish. It's a terrific food wine. You might find yourself reaching for a third glass of this pretty wine over that luxury Cabernet.**90** —*S.H. (7/1/2002)*

Valley of the Moon 2005 Rosato di Sangiovese (Sonoma County) $16. This is one of those fresh, young rosés that's sharp in juicy acidity, primary fruit, and grapey flavors of cherries and raspberries. It's nice, with nuances of vanilla and cinnamon spice.**84** —*S.H. (12/1/2006)*

Valley of the Moon 2003 Syrah (Sonoma County) $16. Syrah is easy to grow just about anywhere, but that doesn't mean it's always good. This one shows a fancy quality that lifts it above the ordinary. Lush in cherry, blackberry, and cocoa fruit, it has extra layers of wild lavender and anise, with a long, dusty finish. For all the mouth-filling ripeness, the wine is thoroughly dry.**87** —*S.H. (12/31/2006)*

Valley of the Moon 2002 Syrah (Sonoma County) $16. A little raw, but you'll find some pleasantly ripe cherry-berry flavors in this dry, somewhat tannic wine. Finishes with a long, cherry liqueur flourish.**84** —*S.H. (5/1/2006)*

Valley of the Moon 2001 Syrah (Sonoma County) $15. A winning wine. It's polished enough to enjoy with almost anything that calls for a dry red wine, but Syrah aficionados will appreciate the intricate interplay of cherry, leather, pepper, and oak flavors and soft tannins.**88** —*S.H. (12/15/2004)*

Valley of the Moon 2000 Syrah (Sonoma County) $15. Has all the hallmarks of the winery's style, which are good varietal character at a fair price. This time around, however, the wine's plum and berry flavors are thin, and are accompanied by some harsh tannins. **84** —*S.H. (12/1/2003)*

Valley of the Moon 1999 Syrah (Sonoma County) $15. A pleasant Syrah, tangy-textured, and with pretty cherry and herb flavors at the core. **85** — *J.M. (12/1/2002)*

Valley of the Moon 1998 Syrah (Sonoma County) $17. An unusual, almost Christmas-spice note shows on the nose of this mid-weight Sonoma offering. The tart red berry fruit has cedar, herb-garden, and spice qualities that play all the way to the finish. The dry fruit and oak marriage is almost Tempranillo-like. **88 Editors' Choice** *(10/1/2001)*

Valley of the Moon 2003 Zinfandel (Sonoma County) $16. From a blazingly hot harvest comes this wine, with baked fruit flavors and a Porty sweetness to the finish. It shows that not every vintage in California is perfect for every variety. **82** —*S.H. (5/1/2006)*

Valley of the Moon 2002 Zinfandel (Sonoma County) $15. Nowhere near as good as the 2001, with thinner flavors, but it's still a good Zin. Blackberries, coffee, and herbs, in thick but gentle tannins. **85** —*S.H. (5/1/2005)*

Valley of the Moon 2001 Zinfandel (Sonoma County) $15. Fairly smooth, with a hint of astringency however. The flavors range from black currant to raspberry and herbs. On the finish, the wine is moderate in length, with a toasty edge. **87** *(11/1/2003)*

Valley of the Moon 1998 Zinfandel (Sonoma County) $15. This is classic Sonoma Zin, supple and pure, with sweet raspberry and red cherry flavors generously dusted with crushed spices, and bone dry. Soft, melted tannins make it user-friendly. Goes down easy with barbecue, ham, or herbed goat cheese. **88 Best Buy** —*S.H. (11/15/2001)*

Valley of the Moon 1997 Zinfandel (Sonoma Valley) $15. **88 Best Buy** — *S.H. (12/1/2000)*

VALLEY VIEW VINEYARD

Valley View Vineyard 2000 Anna Maria Chardonnay (Oregon) $15. Lots of ripe apple and tropical fruits, lots of butterscotch and caramel flavors, but not too heavy. Good balance, good acids, a very appealing, forward style which isn't too oaky or heavy for food. **87** —*P.G. (8/1/2002)*

Valley View Vineyard 1999 Anna Maria Chardonnay (Rogue Valley) $22. Valley View has made this wine in a consistent style for over a decade: pick the fruit as ripe as possible and give it a generous amount of new oak. Some nice spicy clove and cinnamon scents light up the nose; but the oak is dominant to the point of harshness. **85** —*P.G. (2/1/2002)*

Valley View Vineyard 1999 Meritage (Rogue Valley) $40. Half Merlot, 40% Cabernet Franc, and just 10% Cabernet Sauvignon is the formula for this thick, heavy-set Bordeaux blend. It carries the weight handily, showing plummy, sweet fruit and lots of mocha flavor from aging in 80% new oak. Soft, thick tannins lead into a smooth, flavorful finish. **88** —*P.G. (4/1/2002)*

Valley View Vineyard 1998 Anna Maria Merlot (Oregon) $18. This is a light and leafy effort, whose soft and forward fruit mixes flavors of leaf, beet, tomato, and red fruits. It is balanced but insubstantial. **85** —*P.G. (8/1/2002)*

Valley View Vineyard 1999 Anna Maria Old Stage Vineyard Merlot (Rogue Valley) $22. A pretty nose, plummy and rich, with a nice toasty, roasted finish. Elegant and medium bodied, in a ripe year like this the fruit gets past all unripe flavors and into some nice, slightly leafy, pretty fruit with hints of cherry tobacco. **87** —*P.G. (8/1/2002)*

Valley View Vineyard 1999 Anna Maria Quail Run Merlot (Rogue Valley) $30. A softer, more forward style than the Old Stage, showing more density and soft tannins. Light cherry fruit, good balance, texture, weight. Some hints of wood, earth, and mineral too. **87** —*P.G. (8/1/2002)*

Valley View Vineyard 1999 Anna Maria Pinot Gris (Rogue Valley) $12. The fruit shows pears, some high tones, some bitter rind. The style is fruit forward, with flavors of pears and citrus, leading to a light, toasty finish. **86** —*P.G. (8/1/2002)*

Valley View Vineyard 1999 Anna Maria Syrah (Applegate Valley) $30. Sweet, grapey fruit, plum, and cherry, enhanced with peppery spice. The

tannins are a bit ashy, but well integrated; with not too much oak. Overall, a balanced and elegant approach. **87** —*P.G. (8/1/2002)*

VAN ASPEREN

Van Asperen 1995 Cabernet Sauvignon (Napa Valley) $18. **88** —*L.W. (7/1/1999)*

Van Asperen 1997 Krupp Vineyard Cabernet Sauvignon (Atlas Peak) $50. **89** —*J.C. (6/1/2003)*

Van Asperen 1997 Zinfandel (Napa Valley) $18. **90** *(5/1/2000)*

Van Asperen 1997 Zinfandel (Napa Valley) $18. Raspberries, strawberries, and blackberries, with smooth coffee and cream flavors streaking through the finish. Nicely made in a clean, classic Napa Zin style. **87** — *P.G. (3/1/2001)*

VAN DER HEYDEN

Van Der Heyden 2000 Chardonnay (Napa Valley) $18. A controversial wine. Although the winemaker says it has little oak, it seems super-oaky, with overwhelming vanilla and smoke flavors. Also a lot of flamboyant tropic fruit. The combination is huge, bold, and distinctive. Certainly not for the faint-hearted. **85** —*S.H. (12/1/2003)*

VAN DUZER

Van Duzer 2000 Chardonnay (Willamette Valley) $15. Fresh and refreshing, Van Duzer hits it right with tart, spicy fruit and a nice kick to the finish. A racy, lean style, built for food, but quite appealing all by itself. **88** —*P.G. (2/1/2002)*

Van Duzer 2002 Pinot Gris (Willamette Valley) $13. A pleasant, lightly grapefruity wine, with a lot of pucker to it. Deserves kudos for keeping the alcohol down where it should be (13%), and for making a food-friendly style with a clean, crisp finish. **87** —*P.G. (12/1/2003)*

Van Duzer 2003 Estate Pinot Gris (Willamette Valley) $14. Snappy flavors of fresh, cinnamon-spiced Asian pears are the focus of the firm, tart fruit. Flavors remain light through the mid-palate, then tail off into a simple, lightly lemony finish. **86** —*P.G. (1/1/2004)*

Van Duzer 2001 Pinot Noir (Willamette Valley) $19. Not much is going on here. It's very pale, like a dark rosé, and barely tastes of tart fruits; more like under-ripe cherries. It finishes very citric and acidic. **84** —*P.G. (12/1/2003)*

Van Duzer 2002 Dijon Blocks Pinot Noir (Willamette Valley) $33. Violets, lavender, and sweet cherries rise from the glass, though the wine is less interesting in the mouth. Tart, light, and somewhat routine. **85** *(11/1/2004)*

Van Duzer 2002 Estate Pinot Noir (Willamette Valley) $22. Cherry fruit and plenty of chocolatey, mocha barrel flavors. Mainstream, clean and simple. The twin parts—fruit and oak—are like two halves of a sandwich, separate, equal, but unintegrated. **86** *(11/1/2004)*

Van Duzer 2002 Flagpole Block Pinot Noir (Willamette Valley) $33. Spicy and herbal, like a Châteauneuf-du-Pape, with lots of barrel scents and flavors following. There are baking spices aplenty, coconut, sandalwood, cinnamon, and more. Hard to resist. **87** *(11/1/2004)*

Van Duzer 2002 Homestead Block Pinot Noir (Willamette Valley) $33. Plum, citrus, and some brambly red fruits are mixed together, creating a forward, fruity wine with plenty of toasty oak up front. **86** *(11/1/2004)*

VAN ROEKEL

Van Roekel 2000 Viognier (Temecula) $13. An eccentric style, with aromas of cotton candy, white chocolate, and other sweet candies. Yet it tastes dry, with peach flavors and a thick, honeyed mouthfeel. **84** —*S.H. (4/1/2002)*

VAN RUITEN

Van Ruiten 2002 Cabernet Sauvignon (Lodi) $15. Soft, dry, and earthy, with diluted fruit flavors that have an off-putting medicinal note. This wine is just barely acceptable. **80** —*S.H. (7/1/2006)*

Van Ruiten 2004 Pinot Gris (Lodi) $12. Sweet and insipid, with a heavy, gluey texture and flavors of stewed tree fruits. **81** —*S.H. (2/1/2006)*

Van Ruiten 2003 Cab-Shiraz Red Blend (Lodi) $15. Dry and rustic, with sharply edged coffee and black cherry flavors, this simple wine has a homemade quality. **81** —*S.H. (7/1/2006)*

Van Ruiten 2003 Late Harvest Zinfandel (Lodi) $26. Soft, simple, and not even very sweet, with cherry and mocha flavors that have a harsh, bitter tinge to the finish. **80** —*S.H. (7/1/2006)*

VAN RUITEN-TAYLOR

Van Ruiten-Taylor 1999 Chardonnay (Lodi) $10. This first release from these growers-turned-vintners is a pretty good value. It starts with earthy apple and peach aromas and leads to fresh apple and stone-fruit flavors. A pleasantly fruity, everyday wine with zesty acidity that keeps things lively and fresh. **84** —*S.H. (11/15/2001)*

VARNER

Varner 2001 Amphitheater Block Chardonnay (Santa Cruz Mountains) $30. Here's a rich, round Chard that delivers with its ripe, mouth-filling flavors. White peach, papaya, spicy fig, smoke, buttered toast, vanilla are accompanied by crisp, clean acidity. The intense finish lasts for a long time. **91** —*S.H. (6/1/2003)*

Varner 2001 Bee Block Chardonnay (Santa Cruz Mountains) $32. Similar to Varner's Amphitheater bottling but with added shades of interest and complexity. The peach and tropical fruit flavors are compounded with woody, oaky notes and a rich streak of dusty earth. **92** —*S.H. (5/1/2003)*

Varner 2001 Home Vineyard Chardonnay (Santa Cruz Mountains) $34. Oakier, leesier, and riper than Varner's two other Chards, but not superior, because the wine loses balance. Charry, smoky oak dominates the fruit from entry to finish. **90** —*S.H. (5/1/2003)*

Varner 2000 Spring Ridge Vineyard Amphitheater Block Chardonnay (Santa Cruz County) $30. Aims for the fences with ripe fruit, and certainly with oak. In fact the barrels dominate, giving peppery, spicy, vanilla notes and that unmistakable oaky flavor. It's a pretty wine, and a big one, but you wish they'd let the fruit speak for itself. Still, it will impress a lot of people. **87** —*S.H. (5/1/2002)*

Varner 2000 Spring Ridge Vineyard Bee Block Chardonnay (Santa Cruz County) $32. A vineyard selection that contains a little more concentration, with tropical fruit notes and oriental spices. Generous oak frames everything, but the fruit is big enough to stand up to it. Pulls off that elusive balancing act of tasting honeyed sweet but being basically dry. A fancy Chard, well-made and opulent. **92** —*S.H. (5/1/2002)*

VAROZZA

Varozza 2001 Cabernet Sauvignon (St. Helena) $45. A very ripe style, rich in cherry, plum, and cocoa flavors. A little chunky now, with firm, dry tannins that lead to some astringency on the finish, but it could gain ground after 2007. **89** —*S.H. (8/1/2006)*

VELOCITY

Velocity 2002 Red Wine Red Blend (Rogue Valley) $30. A new project from Gus Janeway, showcasing his careful and detailed touch with Rogue valley grapes. The blend is 30% Malbec, 30% Cabernet Sauvignon, 21% Merlot, 12% Cab Franc and 7% Syrah, but rather than being a smorgasbord it is a focused, complex, and layered wine that all knits together. Most telling, Janeway has successfully tamed to tough, rugged tannins that are the biggest challenge for southern Oregon reds. **88** —*P.G. (2/1/2005)*

VENEZIA

Venezia 1996 Meola Vineyards Cabernet Sauvignon (Sonoma County) $14. **87** —*J.C. (9/1/1999)*

Venezia 1997 Regusci Vineyard Chardonnay (Napa Valley) $20. 83 —*J.C. (10/1/1999)*

Venezia 1996 Regusci Vineyard Chardonnay (Napa Valley) $20. 83 —*M.S. (6/1/1999)*

Venezia 1996 Alegria Vineyard Sangiovese (Russian River Valley) $23. 83 —*J.C. (10/1/1999)*

Venezia 1997 Nuovo Mondo Sangiovese (Sonoma County) $24. 87 —*S.H. (10/1/1999)*

Venezia 1996 Van Noy Vineyard Sangiovese (Russian River Valley) $22. 86 —*J.C. (10/1/1999)*

Venezia 1997 Sonoma Moment Viognier (Sonoma County) $20. 82 —*J.C. (10/1/1999)*

VENGE

Venge 2000 Family Reserve Cabernet Sauvignon (Oakville) $95. This is a young wine marked by intense tannins, intense cassis fruit, and intense oak. All three elements stand out. You'll want to cellar for a good six years to allow it all to mature and come together. **90** —*S.H. (11/1/2005)*

Venge 1999 Merlot (Oakville) $46. Really smooth and silky on the palate. This is some of the best Merlot out of Napa. Plush and ripe, with mounds of complex plum, cassis, blackberry, chocolate, herb and smoke flavors. Beautifully integrated and long on the finish. **93** —*J.M. (4/1/2003)*

Venge 2001 Family Reserve Merlot (Oakville) $46. This wine sure is oaky now, although it's sweet, high-class oak. But there's a broad swath of ripe blackberry and cherry fruit, and enough tannins to hold this pretty wine for at least ten years. **91 Cellar Selection** —*S.H. (11/1/2005)*

Venge 1997 Reserve Merlot (Napa Valley) $35. 94 —*S.H. (3/1/2000)*

Venge 2000 Scout's Honor Red Blend (Napa Valley) $30. Rich, plush aromas of dark plum and blackberry lead the way in this wine made mostly from old-vine Zinfandel and named after winemaker Nils Venge's old dog, Scout. Full-bodied and brash, with smoky toast and jammy fruit (sounds like breakfast, right?) the wine has enough acidity to give it good balance. **89** —*J.M. (11/15/2003)*

Venge 2000 Penny Lane Vineyard Sangiovese (Napa Valley) $30. Ripe and smooth for this varietal. The wine shows pretty, ripe cherry and blackberry flavors at its center. Dried herb and anise notes add complexity. Lush and long on the finish. **90** —*J.M. (2/1/2003)*

Venge 2003 Syrah (Napa Valley) $32. A wood-dominated wine at the moment, this Syrah from Nils Venge showcases modest blackberry fruit buried under an avalanche of oak-derived toast and cinnamon. Drying on the finish, but might improve with short-term cellaring. **84** *(9/1/2005)*

Venge 2002 Family Reserve Syrah (California) $32. A trifle vegetal on the nose, but boasts a supple, medium-weight mouthfeel to help compensate. Sappy cherry fruit and toasty oak define the flavors. **84** *(9/1/2005)*

VENTANA

Ventana 2001 Cabernet Sauvignon (Arroyo Seco) $18. Dark and dense, a full-bodied Cab with herbal, even vegetal aromas and flavors accompanying riper notes of blackberries. The tannins are on the fierce side. **84** —*S.H. (10/1/2004)*

Ventana 2000 Cabernet Sauvignon (Arroyo Seco) $18. From a warm part of Salinas Valley, but not warm enough to completely ripen the grapes this vintage. There are aromas and flavors of bell peppers, sage, and green tomatoes. Tannins are fine, acids are crisp. **85** —*S.H. (4/1/2003)*

Ventana 2000 Due Amici Cabernet Sauvignon-Sangiovese (Arroyo Seco) $18. A 50-50 blend with Cabernet Sauvignon, and a better wine than Ventana's straight Cabernet. Sangiovese has added enough cherry and sweet tobacco to offset the slight unripeness, yielding a wine with richness and subtlety. **87** —*S.H. (2/1/2003)*

Ventana 1997 Chardonnay (Monterey County) $13. 86 —*S.H. (2/1/2000)*

Ventana 1999 Chardonnay (Arroyo Seco) $14. Intensely bright fruit and high acidity characterize this Monterey County wine, with its peach and guava flavors. It's very clean, and scours the palate. The long, fruity finish is a little sweet, with a slightly sour note of lees. **86** —*S.H. (12/31/2001)*

Ventana 2001 Gold Stripe Chardonnay (Arroyo Seco) $16. Minerally and crisp, a sleek, angular wine without the big tropical fruits normally found in this AVA, but very nice nonetheless. Flavors of stone and citrus are accompanied by bracing acids. Nice with shellfish. **86** —*S.H. (12/1/2003)*

Ventana 2000 Gold Stripe Chardonnay (Arroyo Seco) $14. Winemaker Doug Meador says this is not a "California Fats" Chardonnay, by which he means he went light on the oak and allowed the fruit to speak for itself. It's pretty fruit, with the smell and taste of apples. However, that slight touch of oak adds just the right amount of vanilla and cream to the mix. **86** —*S.H. (9/1/2002)*

VENTANA

Ventana 1999 Reserve Chardonnay (Arroyo Seco) $20. Barrel fermentation, malolactic fermentation, and lees aging add buttery, creamy, spicy complexities to this clean, steely wine. The underlying fruity flavors are not intense and veer toward leaner citrus and green apple flavors. It's a focused wine, not overblown. **87** —*S.H. (9/1/2002)*

Ventana 2000 Dry Chenin Blanc (Monterey) $12. Drinks dry and bitter, with lemony, citrus flavors and an almond-skin tart finish. This is an austere, steely wine of integrity and fine structure. It's a nice palate cleanser, and stimulates the appetite. **85** —*S.H. (9/1/2002)*

Ventana 2005 Gewürztraminer (Arroyo Seco) $17. An interesting wine that depends on the right food matching to succeed. It's dryish to honeyed, and enormously ripe and fruity, with apricot, nectarine, pineapple, jasmine, honeysuckle, and all kinds of Asian spice flavors. Calls for complex dishes, such as lake fish or chicken and a savory chutney. **86** —*S.H. (12/15/2006)*

Ventana 2004 Gewürztraminer (Arroyo Seco) $16. Drinks like a taste tapestry, with different flavors unfolding all the time. Lime, passion fruit, white peach, apricot, vanilla, and of course oodles of crushed Asian spices wash across the palate. The wine is totally dry, with high, vibrant acidity. **87** —*S.H. (12/1/2005)*

Ventana 2001 Gewürztraminer (Arroyo Seco) $12. Pretty much as good as California Gewürz gets. Offers up a myriad of orange, honeysuckle, white peach, fig, cinnamon, and vanilla flavors, off-dry. Very nice acidity, bright and shining, preserves balance. **88** —*S.H. (9/1/2003)*

Ventana 2004 The Lady Grenache (Arroyo Seco) $28. Tastes like an Arroyo Seco white wine that's red, meaning the acidity and dryness hit you upfront, and also the purity of the fruit. Cherries all the way, with a spicy undertow. The body is very light, and you find yourself wishing the wine had a little more depth and intensity. **85** —*S.H. (12/15/2006)*

Ventana 2001 Merlot (Arroyo Seco) $18. What a good job Ventana has done in Monterey with improving the ripe fruitiness of red Bordeaux varieties. You'll find cherry-berry flavors here, with spice and coffee nuances that make for a complex drink. It's a bit sharp in acidity. **87** —*S.H. (9/1/2004)*

Ventana 2000 Merlot (Arroyo Seco) $18. Polished tannins and bright acids give it good mouthfeel, and there are some nice flavors of blackberries with overt oaky influences. But there is also some less-than-ripe fruit that shows up as herbs and asparagus. **85** —*S.H. (4/1/2003)*

Ventana 1998 Merlot (Monterey) $16. You don't get sun-ripened Merlot from Monterey the way you do from warmer inland valleys, but this charming wine might surprise you. Yes, it's on the earthy side, with hints of sweeter black cherries and some smoky oak, but it's so well balanced, that it's really delightful. It's also very dry, with manageable tannins. **89** —*S.H. (2/1/2001)*

Ventana 1999 Muscat d'Orange Muscat (Monterey) $12. Super aromatic, with apricot, orange marmalade, and honey aromas. The wine is not as sweet as you expect, with residual sugar of 4%. It's also terrifically acidic. This creates imbalance. It's too tart for the sweetness or, conversely, not sweet enough. **87** —*S.H. (9/1/2002)*

Ventana 2000 Pinot Blanc (Arroyo Seco) $16. From rocky benchlands in a cool area, a brilliantly evocative wine. Exotic, well-etched aromas and flavors of orange blossom, white chocolate, white peach, and pear drink dry, soft, and round, with a fair degree of oak and lees. **87** —*S.H. (9/1/2003)*

Ventana 1999 Pinot Blanc (Monterey) $14. Here's a nice, refreshing wine very close in profile to Chardonnay, with its ripe peach aromas and flavors and generous dose of oak. It has a strong streak of tangerine and vanilla that makes it especially pretty. Finishes a bit sweet. **87** —*S.H. (2/1/2001)*

Ventana 2001 Pinot Noir (Arroyo Seco) $24. A good, rich wine, with black cherry, cola, pomengranate, and rosehip tea flavors that suggest its cool climate origins. Acidity does its part, along with oak, to add complexities. Basically light bodied, generous, and easy. **87** —*S.H. (12/1/2004)*

Ventana 2003 Due Amici Red Blend (Arroyo Seco) $28. The best thing about this wine is the acid-tannin balance. Sure, it's ripe in blackberry and blueberry jam and cocoa flavors, but so are plenty of other red wines. But it has a cool-climate structure that makes it impressive. The Sangiovese in this blend with Cabernet Sauvignon lends a peppery, meaty note. **90** —*S.H. (12/15/2006)*

Ventana 2005 Riesling (Arroyo Seco) $16. From one of the most under-rated white wine appellations in California comes this crisp, fruity wine, resembling a nice German Kabinett. With apple, jasmine, peach, and grapefruit flavors, it straddles the line between dry and off-dry. Good with Asian fare or fusion. **85** —*S.H. (12/15/2006)*

Ventana 2001 Riesling (Arroyo Seco) $12. Easy-drinking and clean, with mineral and acidic crispness from high acidity, and delicate flavors of citrus, apricot, and apple. Has a full degree of residual sugar, but that brilliant acidity makes it drink almost dry. The finish turns tart and almond-skin bitter. **87** —*S.H. (9/1/2003)*

Ventana 2002 Sauvignon Blanc (Arroyo Seco) $14. This very good wine flatters the palate with the most succulent citrus, apple, and tropical fruit flavors, with just a touch of grassiness. One-half was barrel-fermented, adding smoky vanilla notes and a creaminess offset by refreshing tartness. It's a good value considering the quality. **89** —*S.H. (9/1/2004)*

Ventana 1997 Sauvignon Blanc (Monterey County) $9. 88 Best Buy —*S.H. (2/1/2000)*

Ventana 1997 Syrah (Monterey County) $18. 88 —*L.W. (2/1/2000)*

Ventana 2001 Syrah (Arroyo Seco) $18. This junior version of Ventana's Maverick Syrah is quite good, with its polished blackberry, plum, and coffee flavors and stylish tannins. It's dry, with a firm tannic grip that will prove an ample match to a leg of lamb. Finishes long and fruity, suggesting midterm ageability. **90** —*S.H. (9/1/2004)*

Ventana 2000 Syrah (Arroyo Seco) $18. This cool-climate Syrah is firmly structured, and boasts a blast of pepper and herb flavors alongside riper ones of blackberries. This is a young, fresh wine with some complexity. **88** —*S.H. (2/1/2003)*

Ventana 1999 Syrah (Arroyo Seco) $20. You want to like this wine more than you do, because it's from a great vineyard and a great vintage. The problem is thinness. It's got great bones, superb texture and dry tannins, and it's easy to taste the quality of the blackberry, pepper-infused fruit because it flatters the palate. But everything is diluted. **85** —*S.H. (9/1/2002)*

VENUS

Venus 1998 Cervina Zinfandel (Sonoma County) $22. This is the first wine from this new winery. Clean, light berry fruit is the whole show, and it's a forward, fruity Zin with friendly, simple flavors. **85** —*P.G. (3/1/2001)*

Venus 1999 Eve Zinfandel (Sonoma County) $22. Red berry on the nose is jazzed up with spicy, oak-derived aromas. It's bouncy and lighter-weight than you'd expect of a Sonoma Zin, thanks to raspberry and red plum flavors on the palate, and cherry, cranberry, and spicy barbecue flavors on the finish. **87** —*D.T. (3/1/2002)*

VERITÉ

Verité 1998 Cabernet Sauvignon-Merlot (Sonoma-Napa) $150. Lush and delicious, this richly fruited wine roars from glass with a serious, yet still sexy plum, chocolate, spice, and cedar nose. Plush tannins and an even mouthfeel full cherry, plum, and cocoa flavors, and this impressive first release finishes long and dry. Appealing now, but has tannins to lose, should be even better in two years and hold until 2008. **93 Cellar Selection** *(12/1/2001)*

Verité 2000 Le Desir Meritage (Sonoma County) $100. A tough, brittle young wine. It is so tannic, you have to think about what the winemaker intended. There seems to be a core of black cherry fruit that could live long enough to age, but who knows? **86** —*S.H. (11/15/2003)*

Verité 1999 La Muse Merlot-Cabernet Sauvignon (Sonoma County) $100. This is a tough, briary wine, very tannic, with flavors of dried herbs, earth, and blackberries. A Merlot–Cabernet Sauvignon blend, it may blossom into a magnificent wine in a decade, but it's a gamble. **87** —*S.H. (11/15/2003)*

USA

Verité 1999 La Joie Red Blend (Sonoma County) $100. Richer and more complete than the '98 La Joie, with which it was simultaneously released. This wine shows its mountain origins in its tough young tannins and hard edges, but there is enough cherry and blackberry fruit for the long haul. Oak adds vanilla and toast, but this is a wine you need to cellar until 2009. **90** —*S.H. (11/15/2003)*

Verité 1998 La Joie Red Blend (Sonoma County) $100. Firmly tannic and rather mouth-numbing even at five years of age. Enters with a hard edge and finishes tough and gritty. Will it age? There are some black cherry flavors inside, but it's a gamble. **85** —*S.H. (8/29/2003)*

VERSANT VINEYARDS

Versant Vineyards 2001 Cabernet Sauvignon (Napa Valley) $70. Richly textured and plush on the palate, with a broad array of raspberry, black cherry, plum, spice, coffee, herb, and cocoa flavors, all couched in firm, ripe tannins and sweet oak. Only 200 cases made from this relatively new producer high in the hills of Napa. **92** —*J.M. (6/1/2004)*

VERSO

Verso 2003 Cabernet Sauvignon (Grand Valley) $30. Bengay, tomato, and rhubarb waft from the glass before aromas of holiday spice emerge. This wine has dusty, underripe tannins and a medium body. A good try from an emerging growing region, but lack of ripeness still seems to be a factor, leading to rhubarb flavors. **82** —*M.D. (8/1/2006)*

VIA FIRENZE

Via Firenze 1995 Charbono (Napa Valley) $14. 86 —*M.S. (6/1/1999)*

Via Firenze 1995 Dolcetto (Napa Valley) $15. 85 —*M.S. (6/1/1999)*

Via Firenze 1994 Nobella Red Blend (Napa Valley) $18. 87 —*M.S. (6/1/1999)*

VIADER

Viader 2002 Cabernet Blend (Napa Valley) $85. This wine has delicious flavors of cherries, blackberries, and oak, and is complex enough to return to glass after glass. At the same time, it's overly soft and simple in structure, and will not age. **87** —*S.H. (11/1/2005)*

Viader 2002 V Cabernet Blend (Napa Valley) $100. Actually Petit Verdot-based, this wine is darker and deeper than Viader's '02 regular Cabernet blend. It has flavors of plums, boysenberries, cocoa, and blackberries. It's dry, but lush in fruit. One wishes it were firmer in tannins and acids, but there's no denying its lusciousness. **90** —*S.H. (11/1/2005)*

Viader 1999 Red Blend (Napa Valley) $75. 92 —*J.M. (6/1/2002)*

Viader 2002 Syrah (Napa Valley) $65. A decent wine, but a disappointing effort from such a well-respected winery. Coffee and cherry aromas are joined by a hint of green bean, while the mouthfeel is supple but not particularly dense or rich. These are young vines, so perhaps the wine will gain strength in subsequent vintages. **85** *(9/1/2005)*

Viader 2001 Syrah (Napa Valley) $65. Dense and taut in acids and fresh tannins, a young, chewy wine with a good future, to judge from the muscularity. Black cherry, pepper, and herbs are framed in plenty of new oak. Immature, but should age well. Try after 2008. **92** —*S.H. (12/15/2004)*

Viader 2003 DARE Tempranillo (Napa Valley) $41. Not clear what Viader was trying to do. Overly soft and featureless in texture, this wine has earthy, dusty flavors with hints of cherries and oak, and a thick, cloying finish. **83** —*S.H. (11/1/2005)*

VIANO

Viano 2001 Reserve Selection Old Vines Zinfandel Port (Contra Costa County) $11. Simple, soft, and not even that sweet, this is a thin wine with modest chocolate and cherry flavors. The thinness makes the alcohol stand out. **82** —*S.H. (12/15/2005)*

Viano 2000 Reserve Selection Zinfandel (Lodi) $9. Tastes rather old and flat, with cherry-coffee flavors and a hit of residual sugar. **81** —*S.H. (12/15/2005)*

VIANSA

Viansa 2002 Athena Dolcetto (California) $19. Almost a late-harvest wine, with its sweetish flavors of currants and raisins with their edge of chocolatey hazelnut. Dusty tannins kick in on the finish. This is an old-style wine that still has aficionados. **84** —*S.H. (9/1/2004)*

Viansa 2001 Piccolo Sangiovese (Sonoma Valley) $25. Rather heavy and dull, with extracted cherry-berry flavors and soft acids. This dry wine is very full-bodied. **84** —*S.H. (9/1/2004)*

VICTOR HUGO

Victor Hugo 2000 Petite Sirah (Paso Robles) $18. Another soft, easy-drinking wine from warm Paso Robles. Everyone admired the rich, ripe fruity flavors, with hints of mint, tobacco, and pepper. The finish is short and simple, with a spicy cinnamon taste. **86** *(4/1/2003)*

Victor Hugo 2000 Syrah (Paso Robles) $20. From Westside grapes grown near Templeton, this is a nice, easy-to-drink wine packed with pretty black cherry and blueberry flavors. The tannins and acids are soft and gentle. Has real richness and vibrancy, and even some complexity in the finish. **86** —*S.H. (12/1/2002)*

Victor Hugo 2001 Zinfandel (Paso Robles) $16. The bright edge is over the top here, with spicy bright raspberry, cherry, spice, and toast flavors that zip across the palate. **81** *(11/1/2003)*

VIENTO

Viento 1999 Nocturne Muscat Canelli (Columbia Valley (WA)) $25. Made to emulate a decadent Rutherglen Muscat, this sensationally long, buttery, well-aged dessert wine unfolds gracefully with layers of nuts, caramel, candied orange peel, and ginger. At almost 20% alcohol and 16% residual sugar, a little goes a long way. **92** —*P.G. (6/1/2005)*

VIERRA VINEYARDS

Vierra Vineyards 2002 Claret Bordeaux Blend (Walla Walla (WA)) $20. Very nice fruit, polished and bright, with big berry/cherry flavors standing out against firm acids. Nicely made, forward and accessible, with plump, juicy fruit. 50% Cab Sauvignon, 10% Cab Franc, and 40% Merlot. **88** —*P.G. (7/1/2004)*

Vierra Vineyards 2002 Syrah (Walla Walla (WA)) $22. Still quite young, it has very tart fruit flavors of grapes and berries. There are also hints of pepper, and it is cleanly made and varietally correct, without much weight or muscle. Typical of Walla Walla Syrahs from young vines. **87** —*P.G. (7/1/2004)*

VIEUX - OS

Vieux - Os 2002 Ira Carter Vineyard Zinfandel (Napa Valley) $36. A bright, zippy style that still shows depth, with complex layers of black cherry, black currant, ginger, coffee, herb, and cinnamon flavors. The wine is framed in firm tannins that give good structure and finishes long. From Fred Schrader, best known for his Cabernet. **90** —*J.M. (10/1/2004)*

VIGIL

Vigil 1997 Solari Vineyard Cabernet Franc (Napa Valley) $25. 86 —*L.W. (9/1/1999)*

Vigil 1997 Terra Vin Reserve Red Blend (Napa Valley) $22. 92 —*L.W. (11/1/1999)*

Vigil 1998 Zinfandel (Napa Valley) $24. 90 —*S.H. (9/1/2000)*

Vigil 1998 Marissa Vineyard Zinfandel (California) $16. This gets the award for the most confusing label of the month. It says Vigil "Tradicion" and also names the vineyard, then writes Mokelumne River Old Vines, and finishes with Lodi. Talk about information overload! Bottom line: it's a fruity, oaky, simple, and straightforward bottle of Zin. 'Nuff said. **85** —*P.G. (3/1/2001)*

Vigil 1998 Mohr-Fry Ranch Zinfandel (California) $18. 89 —*S.H. (9/1/2000)*

Vigil 1998 Tres Condados Zinfandel (California) $14. Pronounced mint and menthol in the nose, with good, ripe cherry fruit underneath. It's like a mint chocolate covered cherry in the mouth, distinctive and delicious. **87** —*P.G. (3/1/2001)*

Vigil 1997 Tres Condados Zinfandel (California) $14. 88 Best Buy —*S.H. (9/1/2000)*

USA

VILLA CREEK

Villa Creek 2002 James Berry Vineyard Garnacha (Paso Robles) $24. 100 percent Grenache, with lovely French herb, cherry, raspberry, and vanilla-oaky aromas and flavors. Lush, soft, and rich in the mouth, with a good grip of acids and tannins. Easy and delightful, with real complexity. **90** —S.H. (12/31/2004)

Villa Creek 2002 Avenger Red Blend (Paso Robles) $24. Here's a big, emphatic wine with tons of jammy blackberry and mocha flavors and a layering of sweet oak. As bold as it is in fruit, it has balancing tannins and crisp acidity. The ripe fruit reprises on the long, spicy finish. Decant for a few hours, or cellar through 2006. **91** —S.H. (12/31/2004)

Villa Creek 2002 James Berry Vineyard High Road Red Blend (Paso Robles) $40. You'll find tons of bacon, meat, leather, ripe blackberry, and cassis aromas and flavors in this Châteauneuf-style blend of Grenache, Syrah, and Mourvèdre. It's sweet, gently soft, and harmonious, with lively acids and a good, clean mouthfeel. **92** —S.H. (12/31/2004)

Villa Creek 2002 Mas de Maha Red Blend (Central Coast) $24. Good, dry red wine, with earthy-fruity-berry flavors. Has a bite of tannin throughout. A blend of Tempranillo, Mourvèdre and Grenache. **85** —S.H. (12/31/2004)

Villa Creek 2001 Avenger Rhône Red Blend (Paso Robles) $20. The first-ever wine from this West Side property, and a very great wine it is. A beautifully balanced Rhône blend with aromas of raspberry, cherry, sweet wood smoke, and vanilla, it is extracted and jammy, but complex. Layers of oak, chocolate, cherry, cream, and spices cascade across the palate. The finish is long and spicy-sweet. **94** —S.H. (3/1/2004)

VILLA HELENA

Villa Helena 2001 Viognier (Napa Valley) $16. This is a wine that obviously comes from superior grapes, to judge by the excellent flavors and fine tannins. What's disturbing is its excessive sweetness. It's almost a dessert wine. Buy it if you like a sugary-simple white. **84** —S.H. (12/15/2002)

VILLA MT. EDEN

Villa Mt. Eden 1997 Coastal Cabernet Sauvignon (California) $10. 80 —S.H. (7/1/2000)

Villa Mt. Eden 2002 Grand Reserve Cabernet Sauvignon (Napa Valley) $15. Thoroughly disagreeable, from the oaky, Porty smell to the semi-sweet medicinal flavors. **81** —S.H. (12/31/2005)

Villa Mt. Eden 1998 Grand Reserve Cabernet Sauvignon (Napa Valley) $20. Indicative of the vintage, this wine is crafted of light fruit. There's only so much that oak can add to the thin, tart flavors. The result is astringent, with a bitter, almost Chianti-like finish. Rather like a Bordeaux from a poor year. **84** —S.H. (11/15/2001)

Villa Mt. Eden 1996 Grand Reserve Cabernet Sauvignon (Napa Valley) $20. **91** (2/1/2000)

Villa Mt. Eden 2001 Grande Reserve Tall Trees Vineyard Cabernet Sauvignon (Napa Valley) $15. From Yountville, a nice, dry wine, with polished cherry and blackberry flavors and enough oak to satisfy. Medium-bodied, with a soft, easy mouthfeel. **85** —S.H. (10/1/2004)

Villa Mt. Eden 1998 Signature Cabernet Sauvignon (Napa Valley) $54. Could fool you as a Pauillac, with pencil lead and cassis aromas that suggest the best French oak. It's elegantly dry and perfectly structured, with a lacy, intricate feeling in the mouth. It is, however a victim of it's vintage, suffering a paucity of fruity concentration, which makes it a delicate wine for early consumption. **87** —S.H. (12/1/2001)

Villa Mt. Eden 1997 Chardonnay (California) $10. **87 Best Buy** —S.H. (2/1/2000)

Villa Mt. Eden 2002 Chardonnay (California) $10. Smells sour from excessive lees, making it hard to appreciate the underlying peach and pear flavors. Finishes dry, simple, and oaky. **83** —S.H. (10/1/2005)

Villa Mt. Eden 2004 Bien Nacido Vineyard Grand Reserve Chardonnay (Santa Maria Valley) $15. From this famous vineyard comes a pretty good Chardonnay. It's a bit thin in fruit, with a green peppercorn edge to the peaches, but the creamy texture and oaky veneer offer pleasure. **84** —S.H. (12/31/2005)

Villa Mt. Eden 2003 Bien Nacido Vineyard Grand Reserve Chardonnay (Santa Maria Valley) $15. There are some fabulous flavors here. It's all about Key lime, roasted pineapple, butterscotch, buttered toast, caramel, and Asian spices, wrapped in a creamy texture and offset by brisk acidity. **88** —S.H. (5/1/2005)

Villa Mt. Eden 2002 Bien Nacido Vineyard Grand Reserve Chardonnay (Santa Maria Valley) $15. This is not a bad price for such a good wine, from such a pedigreed vineyard. It's classic cool South Coast, with a crisp spine of citrusy acids that brighten the tropical fruit flavors. This is a generous, fat wine that offers lots of pleasure. **90 Best Buy** —S.H. (6/1/2004)

Villa Mt. Eden 1998 Bien Nacido Vineyard Grand Reserve Chardonnay (Santa Maria Valley) $17. **87** —S.H. (11/15/2000)

Villa Mt. Eden 2001 Bien Nacido Vineyard Signature Chardonnay (Santa Maria Valley) $32. Santa Barbara seems to produce these exquisitely layered Chardonnays so effortlessly. The cool coastal climate has preserved vital acids, while a long growing season allowed the most extraordinary tropical fruit flavors to develop. Finally, there are the rich, creamy influences from oak and lees. This four-year-old wine shows no sign at all of age. **92** —S.H. (12/1/2005)

Villa Mt. Eden 1999 Bien Nacido Vineyard Signature Chardonnay (Santa Maria Valley) $32. A real crowd-pleaser, this wine has big, bold aromas of citrus fruits, apples, and peaches, with a streak of smoky oak and complications from sur lies aging. It drinks very rich and fine. Citrus flavors dominate, with a flinty element, and high acidity suggests midterm aging. **90** —S.H. (12/1/2001)

Villa Mt. Eden 1999 Coastal Chardonnay (Monterey County) $10. Extreme leesiness marks this dry, astringent wine. It's light on fruit, with the suggestion of peaches and grapefruit, while those cheesy-leesy notes provide most of the aromas and flavors. Not bad for the price, though. **84** —S.H. (11/15/2001)

Villa Mt. Eden 2000 Grand Reserve Chardonnay (Santa Maria Valley) $14. A big bells-and-whistles wine whose tropical fruit flavors are enhanced by large quantities of smoky oak and lees. Vanilla, buttered toast, and that sour flavor that comes from sur lies aging take front stage at the cost of some subtlety. **87** —S.H. (2/1/2003)

Villa Mt. Eden 1999 Grand Reserve Chardonnay (Santa Maria Valley) $17. Rich and supple, this wine is a junior version of the winery's Bien Nacido bottling. Citrus and peach fruit gain complexity from sweet oak and vanilla and lees-aging adds aromatic and textural notes. **88** —S.H. (11/15/2001)

Villa Mt. Eden 1997 Grand Reserve Bien Nacido Vineyard Chardonnay (Santa Maria Valley) $18. **89** (6/1/2000)

Villa Mt. Eden 1997 Coastal Merlot (California) $10. **88 Best Buy** —J.C. (3/1/2000)

Villa Mt. Eden 1997 Pinot Noir (California) $12. **87 Best Buy** (5/1/2000)

Villa Mt. Eden 1997 Bien Nacido Vineyard Grand Res Pinot Noir (Santa Maria Valley) $20. **86** (10/1/1999)

Villa Mt. Eden 2003 Bien Nacido Vineyard Grand Reserve Pinot Noir (Santa Maria Valley) $22. This is a well-made wine with all the hallmarks of a fine coastal Pinot, although without the richness that would merit a higher score. It has thinned-down flavors of cherries, cola, and mocha, and is dry and elegantly silky. **85** —S.H. (12/31/2005)

Villa Mt. Eden 1998 Bien Nacido Vineyard Grand Reserve Pinot Noir (Santa Maria Valley) $20. **89** —S.H. (12/15/2000)

Villa Mt. Eden 2000 Coastal Pinot Noir (California) $10. A light wine that's lean yet soft, built on a slightly sweet cherry-strawberry fruit platform. Pleasing spice and herb accents add interest, but the palate displays a cola/black cherry quality. Closes drier and spicier, with moderate length. Drink now. **84 Best Buy** (10/1/2002)

Villa Mt. Eden 1999 Coastal Pinot Noir (California) $10. Yes Virginia, there is a Santa Claus, and it is still possible to get a solid Pinot Noir for close to half a sawbuck. Sweet caramel, cherries, and beets are counterbalanced by lemony acidity and an herbal edge that's strikingly similar to green tea. Finishes with cinnamon and chocolate notes, buoyed by bright cranberries. **85** —J.C. (11/15/2001)

Villa Mt. Eden 2002 Grand Reserve Pinot Noir (Russian River Valley) $22. There's plenty of pleasant drinkability in this light-bodied, elegant Pinot. It has cola, rhubarb, and cherry pie flavors wrapped in soft tannins and boosted by bright acids. Great with roast chicken or pork. **87** —*S.H. (11/1/2004)*

Villa Mt. Eden 2000 Grand Reserve Pinot Noir (Sonoma County) $22. A complex nose of ripe cherries, cedar, smoke, root beer, and spice opens this richly textured Pinot. A solid core of bright yet round fruit shines from start to finish, offset by caramel, bacon, and grilled portobello accents. Closes long and flavorfully with full, even tannins. Drink now–2005. **89 Editors' Choice** *(10/1/2002)*

Villa Mt. Eden 1999 Grand Reserve Pinot Noir (Santa Maria Valley) $21. Boy this is good stuff. Starts with those big, rich, sappy Pinot aromas of dark berry marmalade and dark chocolate and turns velvety smooth on the palate. There's a ton of rich, ripe fruit in the middle, and the dry, spicy finish is full of flavor. Yet it's dry, light, and elegant—a candlelight wine. **92 Best Buy** —*S.H. (12/15/2001)*

Villa Mt. Eden 2004 Grand Reserve Bien Nacido Vineyard Pinot Noir (Santa Maria Valley) $19. This is a good price for a wine of this pedigree. Shows classic Santa Maria Pinot notes of dusty, crushed brown spices, cherries, and cola, with cool-climate acidity and a rich coat of tannins. This Pinot should drink well at least through 2010. **89** —*S.H. (12/15/2006)*

Villa Mt. Eden 1999 Coastal Sauvignon Blanc (Central Coast) $10. 85 — *S.H. (11/15/2000)*

Villa Mt. Eden 1998 Syrah (California) $10. 84 *(5/1/2000)*

Villa Mt. Eden 1999 Coastal Syrah (California) $10. There's plenty of blackberry and cream on the nose here, mingled with a bit of cocoa and a distinctly green, herbal note. Tart blueberry, oak, and caramel notes on the palate and a short, sweet-and-sour berry finish mark this simple, jammy Syrah. **84** *(10/1/2001)*

Villa Mt. Eden 1998 Grand Reserve Syrah (California) $21. If, to quote The Smiths, black is what you wear on the outside because black is how you feel on the inside, this wine's for you. Woodsy mushroom-and-earth and roasted fruit aromas segue into a palate rife with equally brooding coffee, leather, pepper, and black fruit flavors (and firm tannins to boot). Winds up with dry-toast flavors. **88** *(11/1/2001)*

Villa Mt. Eden 1999 Fox Creek Vineyard Grand Reserve Zinfandel (Sierra Foothills) $21. Dark and rich; color stains the side of the glass on this highly extracted wine. It's full-bodied with powerful berry and spice flavors, but it's so well structured that it seems as elegant as Bordeaux. Really shows the heights to which Sierra Zin can rise. **91** —*S.H. (12/15/2001)*

Villa Mt. Eden 2003 Grand Reserve Antique Vines Zinfandel (Napa-Amador) $16. Napa brings classic elegance, Amador a lusty exuberance, to this very fine Zinfandel. The fruit is extraordinarily lush, with ripe blackberry jam, cherry pie filling, cassis-laced chocolate candies, and peppery spices, and very little briar or bramble. This is great California Zinfandel. **90** —*S.H. (12/15/2006)*

Villa Mt. Eden 2001 Grand Reserve Fox Creek Vineyard Zinfandel (Sierra Foothills) $22. From Amador County, a dry and tasty Zin with rich berry and tobacco flavors, but oh, how hot it is. In excess of 16% alcohol, it leaves a peppery burn behind on the finish. **85** —*S.H. (12/15/2004)*

Villa Mt. Eden 2002 Grand Reserve Mead Ranch Vineyard Zinfandel (Napa Valley) $22. When they talk about claret-like Zins, they have this one in mind. It has the effortlessly controlled balance, the smooth tannins of a fine Napa Cab, but never loses Zin's peppery, wild, fresh-from-the-forest personality, or zesty acidity. This is Zin at a very high level of expression. **92 Editors' Choice** —*S.H. (12/1/2005)*

Villa Mt. Eden 2001 Grand Reserve Mead Ranch Vineyard Zinfandel (Napa Valley) $22. I like the dryness of this wine. It shows good fruit, but isn't a fruit bomb, and the flavors are balanced by a good acid-tannin equilibrium. Has a harmonic elegance that persists through a satisfying finish. **90 Editors' Choice** —*S.H. (10/1/2005)*

Villa Mt. Eden 1995 Grand Reserve Monte Rosso Vine Zinfandel (Sonoma Valley) $20. 92 —*S.H. (9/1/1999)*

Villa Mt. Eden 2001 Grand Reserve Monte Rosso Vineyard Zinfandel (Sonoma Valley) $24. This high-altitude vineyard, way above Sonoma Valley, is often the source of tannic, ageworthy reds. In this warm vintage, the grapes grew very ripe, almost raisined, and the wine is soft. It's not going to age. But it's tasty now in black currant and chocolate flavors, and will be nice with barbecue. **86** —*S.H. (12/1/2005)*

Villa Mt. Eden 1999 Mead Ranch Vineyard Grand Reserve Zinfandel (Napa Valley) $21. Seldomly flashy, Napa Zins at their best show control and elegance. So it is with beauty, with its blackberry and spice aromas and deep, exquisite flavors. There's a purity and suppleness that are rare in Zin, with deft tannins. At its youthful best now, this is a classic Napa interpretation of California's own grape. **90** —*S.H. (12/15/2001)*

Villa Mt. Eden 1997 Monte Rosso Vineyard Grand Res Zinfandel (Sonoma Valley) $21. 85 —*J.C. (5/1/2000)*

Villa Mt. Eden 1998 Monte Rosso Vineyard Grand Reserve Zinfandel (Sonoma Valley) $21. Ripe, round, toasty wine, with rich, plummy fruit and a full-throttle palate feel. Nicely made and surprisingly evolved; jammy and pleasure-packed. Finishes with a pleasing fruit sweetness. **90 Editors' Choice** —*P.G. (3/1/2001)*

Villa Mt. Eden 1999 Monte Rosso Vineyard Grand Reserve Zinfandel (Sonoma Valley) $21. From a famous mountain vineyard, a huge, concentrated wine of power rather than subtlety. Massive flavors of wild berries explode in the mouth, along with dry tannins. It's outsized at the moment, but not the kind of wine to benefit from age. Enjoy it now in all its Hulkian glory. **88** —*S.H. (12/15/2001)*

Villa Mt. Eden 1999 Old Vines Zinfandel (Napa Valley) $10. This is a good buy in an old vine Zin because of the big, ripe burst of juicy berry flavors, rich texture, and refined, dry finish. Lacks some depth, but makes up for it with all that pretty fruit. **87** —*S.H. (12/9/2002)*

VILLA SPALLA

Villa Spalla 2002 Tuscia Red Blend (Amador County-Oregon) $36. A soft, fruity blend of Sangiovese and Cabernet Sauvignon. A little too sweet on the finish, with a taste of toasted meringue and baked cherry pie. **83** — *S.H. (12/31/2005)*

VILLICANA

Villicana 2000 Cabernet Sauvignon (Paso Robles) $25. Framed in smoky, toasty oak, the wine serves up moderate char, blackberry, and plum flavors. Tannins are a bit rustic, and the finish is somewhat powdery. **84** —*J.M. (4/1/2004)*

Villicana 2001 Merlot (Paso Robles) $30. Fresh and dark hued, with well-balanced though modest black cherry, plum, and toast flavors that are highlighted with bright acidity. Tannins are firm and the finish is moderate in length. **87** —*J.M. (4/1/2004)*

VIN DE MANIES

Vin de Manies 2003 Cabernet Sauvignon (Napa Valley) $45. Shares so much of the quality of the Reserve that, at 30 bucks cheaper, you might as well buy this one. Soft, elegant, and delicious in blackberry pie, cassis, and chocolate flavors, it has wonderfully ripe tannins and finishes totally dry. **89** —*S.H. (12/15/2006)*

Vin de Manies 2003 Reserve Cabernet Sauvignon (Napa Valley) $75. French-born Daniel Manies was the first cellarmaster at Opus One. Now he has his own winery. This inaugural Cab is plush and extremely soft to the point of melted. It's also seriously flavorful. It's like an ambrosiac nectar, all gooey blackberry pie filling and mocha vanilla cream. It's a good start. **90** —*S.H. (12/15/2006)*

VINA ROBLES

Vina Robles 2002 Cabernet Sauvignon (Paso Robles) $19. Despite a roughness around the edges, this Cab appeals with its ripe flavors of cherry jam, blackberries, and espresso coffee. It's very dry, with a soft complexity that makes it easy to drink. **84** —*S.H. (12/31/2005)*

Vina Robles 2001 Estate Cabernet Sauvignon (Paso Robles) $19. A little raisiny, not too much, but that's what the sun does down in Paso Robles, where Cabernets are dependably ripe and soft in acidity. This one is, and it also has firm tannins. It's very dry, and has an intriguing taste of earth. **87** —*S.H. (8/1/2004)*

Vina Robles 2003 Jardine Petite Sirah (Paso Robles) $26. This is Pet in all its full-bodied glory. It's a dark, rich wine, stuffed with enormous plum, black currant, coffee, and bitter chocolate flavors that finish absolutely dry. Despite the size, it achieves balance and harmony. This is one of the best Petite Sirahs I've had this year. Good now, and should hold for at least a decade. **92 Editors' Choice** —*S.H. (7/1/2006)*

Vina Robles 2002 Jardine Petite Sirah (Paso Robles) $26. Dark, tannic, dry, and way too thin. Tastes like it was watered down. **82** —*S.H. (10/1/2005)*

Vina Robles 2001 Jardine Vineyard Petite Sirah (Paso Robles) $22. Pet fans will immediately respond to this wine. It's a big, dark, extracted bruiser, with a hefty dose of tannins that sting the palate. The underlying flavors are of plums, blackberries, coffee, and bitter chocolate. So dry it puckers the mouth. **86** —*S.H. (8/1/2004)*

Vina Robles 2003 Signature Red Blend (Paso Robles) $29. This Petit Verdot, Syrah, and Petite Sirah blend has absolutely delicious flavors, stunning in fact. Blackberry jam, blueberries, cassis, chocolate, coffee, toasty oak, spices, the list goes on and on. Plus, it's dry. The only critique is that it's overly soft, in the manner of Paso Robles. **87** —*S.H. (12/31/2005)*

Vina Robles 2002 Signature Red Blend (Paso Robles) $28. Sweet in plum, blackberry, and coffee flavors, rich in tannins and full-bodied, this dry wine has an edge of rusticity. Try with barbecue with a slightly sweet sauce. Petite Verdot, Syrah, and Petite Sirah. **86** —*S.H. (4/1/2005)*

Vina Robles 2001 Jardine Vineyard Sauvignon Blanc (Paso Robles) $14. Tart and crisp, this pleasant sipper offers lots to like in a dry, stylish white wine. The citrus, peach, and fig flavors are in harmonious balance with the acids, and are not overly sweet. **86** —*S.H. (8/1/2004)*

Vina Robles 2001 Estate Syrah (Paso Robles) $18. A broad, soft expression of Paso Robles Syrah, featuring roasted fruit flavors, chocolate, caramel, leather, and brown sugar. Easy to drink and easy to enjoy. **86** *(9/1/2005)*

Vina Robles 2000 Estate Syrah (Paso Robles) $19. The tannins have sharp elbows in this wine, with its modest cherry and blackberry flavors. It's very dry, and there's quite a hefty dose of citrusy acids. The result is rather angular and austere. **84** —*S.H. (8/1/2004)*

Vina Robles 2001 Huerhuero Vineyard Syrah (Paso Robles) $24. The herbal-fruity aromas are a hypothetical blend of raspberries and roasted tomatoes, while the flavors thankfully favor raspberries. Plump, but a bit candied and slick-feeling, with some drying tannins on the finish. **84** *(9/1/2005)*

Vina Robles 2005 Roseum Syrah (Paso Robles) $13. I like this wine for its pretty color and pleasant flavors of raspberries and cherries, and the acidity works. But it's definitely a sweetie, which detracts. Take away the sweetness and you have a world class rosé. **84** —*S.H. (7/1/2006)*

Vina Robles 2004 Roseum Syrah (Paso Robles) $13. This blush wine has Viognier blended in with Syrah. It's a pretty salmon color, and has flavors of raspberries, peaches, and vanilla. Fully dry, it will be nice with grilled salmon. **84** —*S.H. (11/15/2005)*

Vina Robles 2003 Westside Zinfandel (Paso Robles) $24. Smells classically Zinny, but turns excessively sharp in the mouth, with a hit of raw acidity that won't age out, and makes the wine unpleasant. **82** —*S.H. (12/31/2005)*

Vina Robles 2002 Westside Zinfandel (Paso Robles) $24. So ripe, so sweet, so soft, it's almost like chocolate-infused cherry juice. High alcohol, though, gives it a kick. **87** —*S.H. (10/1/2005)*

Vina Robles 2001 Westside Zinfandel (Paso Robles) $24. Very high in alcohol, with heat that's like a chile pepper, but it works with a wine of this size. The flavors are immense, among them blackberry jam and cassis, cherry-filled chocolate candy, and Indian pudding sweetened with molasses. For all that, this beautiful Zin is balanced and dry. **91** —*S.H. (8/1/2004)*

VINE CLIFF

Vine Cliff 2003 Cabernet Sauvignon (Napa Valley) $49. A blend of Oakville, Rutherford, and Calistoga, this Cab shows a classic Napa profile. The most beautifully ripe cassis and black cherries are the flavors,

with a chocolate edge enriched with classy, smoky oak, and the tannins are wonderfully rich and detailed. It doesn't seem like an ager, but if you're looking for an immaculate Cab tonight, this is the one. **92** —*S.H. (11/1/2006)*

Vine Cliff 2003 Cabernet Sauvignon (Oakville) $65. A beautiful Cabernet that displays classic Oakville character. To begin with, the tannins, which always are the star of Oakville, are so lush, ripe, and richly structured. Then there's the elegant balance and refinement. I wish this well-oaked wine, as good as it is, had a bit more fruity intensity, because that would make me appreciate this even more. **93** —*S.H. (9/1/2006)*

Vine Cliff 2002 Cabernet Sauvignon (Oakville) $75. Here's a young wine not offering much now beyond tons of ripe cherry and blackberry fruit and sharp, immature acids and tannins. It's well made, with a toasty oak edge. You might want to age it for a couple years. **86** —*S.H. (12/15/2005)*

Vine Cliff 2002 Cabernet Sauvignon (Napa Valley) $45. This blend of Oakville and Calistoga is marked by intensely ripe cherry, cassis, cocoa, and oak flavors and fabulous balance. Superbly rich and massive, with rich, smooth tannins, this lovely Cab maintains elegance and structural integrity through the long, polished finish. It's better than most Napa Cabs that cost far more, making it a fantastic value. **95 Editors' Choice** —*S.H. (11/1/2005)*

Vine Cliff 2001 Cabernet Sauvignon (Napa Valley) $45. This complex and distinctive wine is dark and brooding, and reveals itself reluctantly through an elaborate overlay of well-toasted oak. Below all that char and vanilla is polished black currant and cassis fruit. The sweet tannins and weight of the wine are pedigreed, but there's a rawness that demands cellaring. Best beyond 2008. **92** —*S.H. (6/1/2004)*

Vine Cliff 2001 Cabernet Sauvignon (Oakville) $75. This is a difficult wine to drink now, due to its palate-numbing tannins. Yet there's something big and flashy going on. The finish is long in black currant fruit, so stunningly rich it can only survive as the tannins fall out. Try after 2008, but it could go long beyond that. **91** —*S.H. (10/1/2004)*

Vine Cliff 1998 Cabernet Sauvignon (Oakville) $75. Drying tannins make the already quite tart flavors even harder to handle. Metallic notes coat plummy-pruny aromas on the nose, and cranberry notes in the mouth. Finishes with more metal, and some oak. **83** —*D.T. (6/1/2002)*

Vine Cliff 2002 16 Rows Cabernet Sauvignon (Oakville) $125. Made from selected lots, this is a young, sharp, tannic wine not showing its best now. It doesn't have that sumptuously soft, sexy quality a ready-to-drink Cab shows. But it's rich and balanced, with a core of cassis, cherry, and coffee flavors, and should age well. Hold until 2009. **91 Cellar Selection** —*S.H. (12/15/2005)*

Vine Cliff 1996 Oakville Estate Cabernet Sauvignon (Napa Valley) $45. **91** *(3/1/2000)*

Vine Cliff 2001 Private Stock 16 Rows Cabernet Sauvignon (Oakville) $125. Very young and tannic, a wine that's impossible to drink now. The beesting of tannins numbs the palate, leaving a painful astringency. Drink 2010 and beyond. **92 Cellar Selection** —*S.H. (10/1/2004)*

Vine Cliff 1997 Chardonnay (Napa Valley) $34. **87** *(10/1/2000)*

Vine Cliff 2004 Chardonnay (Carneros) $34. Beautiful Chardonnay, ripe, rich, oaky, and complex, the kind you fall in love with from the start. Crisp in acids, it flatters the palate with pineapple custard and crème brûlée flavors that are as deep and long as they are broad. Perhaps a shade less rich than the fabulous '03, but a gorgeous, succulent wine. **93** —*S.H. (11/1/2006)*

Vine Cliff 2003 Chardonnay (Carneros) $34. Hits the jackpot with incredibly intense swirls of pineapple, mango, orange blossom, butterscotch, lemon custard, vanilla, and spice flavors that come together in a rich, creamy drink. Fabulous intensity and length to this completely satisfying Chardonnay. **94 Editors' Choice** —*S.H. (11/1/2005)*

Vine Cliff 2002 Chardonnay (Napa Valley) $25. A fine wine, with enough oaky richness to please Chard lovers. The flavors suggest cool peach custard sprinkled with vanilla and a drizzle of butterscotch sauce, while the acids keep this gooey quality crisp and fresh. **90** —*S.H. (11/15/2004)*

Vine Cliff 1998 Chardonnay (Napa Valley) $34. This is a ripe pear-scented butterscotch-infused Chardonnay. The palate shows more ripe pear and melon flavors, along with lots of toasty new oak, which yields delicious hazelnut shadings. Soft and easy to enjoy, it closes long, and creamy-spicy. **90** *(7/1/2001)*

Vine Cliff 2003 Bien Nacido Vineyard Chardonnay (Santa Maria Valley) $34. From down Santa Maria way comes this high-acid wine, with yummy flavors of pineapple custard, Key lime pie and vanilla spice, all of it pepped up with lots of rich, toasty oak. **90** *—S.H. (12/31/2005)*

Vine Cliff 2002 Bien Nacido Vineyard Chardonnay (Santa Maria Valley) $39. Ripe and tasty in tropical fruit flavors, this creamy wine is quite good, and would be even better with a little more focus and structure. It falls apart a bit, a fault at this price. Still, the smoky oak veneer is fancy. **87** *—S.H. (12/1/2004)*

Vine Cliff 2000 Bien Nacido Vineyard Chardonnay (Santa Maria Valley) $39. Gorgeous, explosive, a real crowd pleaser. Rich tropical fruit flavors, layered with brown spices, are framed in toasty oak. A burst of refreshing acidity makes this massive wine drink bright and firm. Lush and vibrant in the mouth, perfectly balanced, with a long, spicy finish that lasts a full 30 seconds or more. **94 Editors' Choice** *—S.H. (2/1/2003)*

Vine Cliff 2002 Proprietress Reserve Chardonnay (Carneros) $50. From the Napa side, this is one irresistible Chard, the kind you can't get enough of. Makes love to the palate with its rich, creamy texture, sweetly ripe peach, tangerine, and mango flavors, oaky buttery vanilla, and crisp acids. The finish is enormously spicy and long. As big as it is, it's a study in classic harmony. **94** *—S.H. (12/1/2004)*

Vine Cliff 1997 Merlot (Napa Valley) $35. **87** *—J.C. (7/1/2000)*

Vine Cliff 2002 Merlot (Napa Valley) $30. Fully drinkable now, because the tannins are smooth, soft, and approachable, and the flavors are so lush and easy. Cherries, blackberries, milk chocolate, anise, and cola mingle with toasty oak, leaving a long, spicy finish. **89** *—S.H. (11/1/2006)*

Vine Cliff 2001 Merlot (Napa Valley) $30. Displays real mastery at this often difficult variety. Fairly tannic now, but the spiced plum, black currant, and coffee flavors are so rich, they burst through the astringency to dazzle the palate. Completely dry and beautifully balanced, this is a wine that will easily improve over the next five years. **92** *—S.H. (12/15/2004)*

VINEYARD 29

Vineyard 29 1999 Cabernet Sauvignon (Napa Valley) $160. How could you go wrong with the team assembled by owner Chuck McMinn? You have David Abreu as your vineyard manager and Philippe Melka making the wine, from a vineyard less than 100 yards from Grace Family Vineyards. This Cabernet is jam-packed with dark fruit, chocolate, and leather. There is great complexity and richness that carries through from start to finish. **95 Cellar Selection** *—C.S. (12/31/2002)*

VINEYARD 48

Vineyard 48 2004 Cabernet Franc (North Fork of Long Island) $28. An aromatic wine with dark berry, cherry, mushroom, and grass aromas that lead to more of the same in the mouth with a smooth feel. An earthy character develops, meshing well with moderate tannins and a hint of acidity. **87** *—M.D. (8/1/2006)*

VINEYARD 7&8

Vineyard 7&8 2002 Vineyard 7 Reserve Cabernet Sauvignon (Spring Mountain) $85. This 100% mountain Cab is very, very tannic. Ripe blackberry fruit begins to flatter, and then those tannins rush up like linebackers and shut everything down. This suggests aging. Balanced and dry, it should begin to come into its own by 2008 and develop for many years. **92 Cellar Selection** *—S.H. (12/31/2006)*

Vineyard 7&8 2001 Vineyard 7 Reserve Cabernet Sauvignon (Spring Mountain) $75. From the former general manager at Château Lafite, this is a young, tannic wine, with a considerable amount of new oak, yet it shows quite a degree of balance and finesse. Very dry, with a fresh Cabernet nose, this wine is also earthy and a bit astringent. **90** *—S.H. (8/1/2005)*

Vineyard 7&8 2003 Vineyard 8 Reserve Chardonnay (Spring Mountain) $50. This is a wine to age, or at least to decant. Opened young it shows a hard steely character, even a tannic toughness, that only hints at what's

to come. But older examples prove its ageability. This is a Grand Cru Chablis-style Chardonnay of enormous depth and vast potential. Open through 2010, and don't serve it too cold. **93 Cellar Selection** *—S.H. (12/31/2006)*

Vineyard 7&8 2001 Vineyard 8 Reserve Chardonnay (Spring Mountain) $45. Fresh and racy, with big, tight acidity and a stony minerality that brings the Central Coast to mind. There are underlying fruit complexities of lime zest and pineapple, with a buttercream texture and a sweet layering of toasty oak. Distinguished Chardonnay. **92** *—S.H. (8/1/2005)*

VINO CON BRIO

Vino Con Brio 2004 Pinot Grigio (Lodi) $16. Despite never having seen a splinter of wood, this wine is hugely rich and enormous in the most palate-flattering flavors. It's an explosion of jammy peaches, delicious apples, mangoes, and kiwi fruits. The acidity is high and the wine is balanced and clean, but it's the amazing fruit that really stars. **90** *—S.H. (5/1/2006)*

Vino Con Brio 2003 Pinot Grigio (Lodi) $16. Thin and rather raw, with decent citrus flavors. Will do in a pinch. **83** *—S.H. (5/1/2005)*

Vino Con Brio 2001 Pinotage (Lodi) $20. Soft, flat, and dry, with light flavors and a hot finish. **81** *—S.H. (5/1/2005)*

Vino Con Brio 2000 Pinotage (Lodi) $20. Puts out hot country scents of baked cherry pie, pie crust, and tar, and those hot notes continue in the mouth. There's something Port-like in the raisiny flavors and thick texture. Turns semi-sweet on the finish. **82** *—S.H. (8/1/2003)*

Vino Con Brio 2002 Vibrante Red Blend (Lodi) $16. Harsh and disagreeable, with cherry and tobacco flavors that finish sharp in acids. **80** *—S.H. (6/1/2006)*

Vino Con Brio 2002 Goehring Vineyard Sangiovese (Lodi) $16. Light to medium bodied, with a translucent ruby color and only 13.4% alcohol, this is a pleasantly drinkable wine. It's young and firm in acids, with simple cherry flavors and a dry finish. **84** *—S.H. (6/1/2006)*

Vino Con Brio 2001 Goehring Vineyard Sangiovese (Lodi) $16. Smells old, tired, and vegetal, and doesn't taste much better. **81** *—S.H. (5/1/2005)*

Vino Con Brio 2002 McQueen Vineyard Syrah (Lodi) $16. Kind of harsh in dry, astringent tannins, with undeveloped coffee flavors just suggesting blackberries, this is a tough wine to like. **80** *—S.H. (5/1/2006)*

Vino Con Brio 2001 McQueen Vineyard Syrah (Lodi) $16. Ripe and fruity in cherry and plum flavors, with a drying earthiness suggestive of dill and thyme, this wine also shows easy tannins. **84** *—S.H. (5/1/2005)*

Vino Con Brio 2002 Ripken Vineyard Viognier (Lodi) $17. Simple, soft, and clean, with fruit and wildflower flavors and a spot of honey. **83** *—S.H. (3/1/2006)*

Vino Con Brio 2001 Ripken Vineyard Viognier (Lodi) $17. Interesting and unique, with upfront smells of sweet roasted red pepper, lime, white peach, apricot, and wildflower, and similar flavors. The texture is unctuous and syrupy, but is relieved by fresh acids. **85** *—S.H. (6/1/2003)*

Vino Con Brio 2001 Matzin Estate Old Vine Zinfandel (Lodi) $21. Classically full and rich, really extraordinarily extracted in blackberry and cherry jam and that mouthwatering Zin pepperiness, but dry and smooth. Quite a nice Zin, although it's soft. Finishes like melted milk chocolate. **90** *—S.H. (5/1/2005)*

Vino Con Brio 2003 Matzin Old Vine Zinfandel (Lodi) $21. Although it's very dry, with plenty of lush Zinny fruit flavor, the raisiny finish and hot mouthfeel are a little offputting, despite an official alcohol of only 14.5%. On the plus side there's a rich, velvety texture. **83** *—S.H. (6/1/2006)*

Vino Con Brio 1999 Matzin Old Vines Zinfandel (Lodi) $21. Clearly from a hot appellation, with raisiny flavors veering into Swiss chocolate, and a texture so rich and unctuous, it coats the palate like honey. But this wine is dry and has flair and interest. It's California's own, unlike any other in the world. **85** *—S.H. (3/1/2004)*

VINO NOCETO

Vino Noceto 2003 Sangiovese (Shenandoah Valley (CA)) $16. This limpid wine defines one style of Sangiovese and does it well. It's light- to medium-bodied and dry, with long, deep, red cherry flavors finished with oak, spice, and vanilla. **87** —*S.H. (3/1/2006)*

Vino Noceto 2002 Riserva Sangiovese (Shenandoah Valley (CA)) $24. Contrasted with the winery's very good regular Sangiovese, released at the same time, this is far deeper. It's a medium-bodied, delicate wine, packed with delicious cherry and oaky-vanilla flavors wrapped in soft tannins. What's notable is the balance, harmony, and elegance. Try with veal scallopine. **90** —*S.H. (3/1/2006)*

VINOCE

Vinoce 2000 Bordeaux Blend (Mount Veeder) $60. Rich, smooth, and silky, the wine shows good weight on the palate. Plum, fig, chocolate, coffee, spice, and cedar flavors are at the core of this gently muscular, well-integrated wine. The finish is long and lush. **93 Editors' Choice** — *J.M. (10/1/2003)*

Vinoce 1999 Bordeaux Blend (Mount Veeder) $60. Lush and elegant, with intriguing blackberry, plum, spice, vanilla, currant, and herb flavors. The tannins are ripe and smooth, but firm. The finish is long, ending with a fine balance of richness and brightness. The blend is 60% Cabernet Franc, 25% Merlot, and 15% Cabernet Sauvignon. **92** —*J.M. (2/1/2003)*

Vinoce 2001 Sauvignon Blanc (Rutherford) $18. Richly textured, viscous but with good acidity for balance. The wine shows pretty melon, citrus, herb, grass, peach, and spice flavors and features a mineral edge that is fresh and clean at the end. **88** —*J.M. (7/1/2003)*

VINUM CELLARS

Vinum Cellars 2003 The Scrapper Cabernet Franc (El Dorado) $30. Years ago I found out how good these Sierra Foothills Cab Francs can be, and here's another one. It really impresses for its dry finesse, a wine that exhibits true gout de terroir in the earthy, mushroomy flavors with their subtle hint of black cherries and violets. Try as an alternative to Cabernet Sauvignon or Merlot. **93 Editors' Choice** —*S.H. (10/1/2006)*

Vinum Cellars 2005 Rosé It's Okay! Cabernet Sauvignon (Napa Valley) $10. The packaging is amusing, the wine is 100% Cabernet Sauvignon, and it's quite a nice, refreshing sipper. Drinks totally dry and crisp in acids, with rosehip tea and black cherry flavors that finish long and spicy. **85 Best Buy** —*S.H. (10/1/2006)*

Vinum Cellars 2003 Slow Lane Cab Cabernet Sauvignon (Napa Valley) $27. Ripe enough in blackberries and cherries, but there's a raw, sharp, green, stalky note that tastes like stems. Not likely to soften, so drink up. **82** — *S.H. (4/1/2006)*

Vinum Cellars 2005 Chard No Way Chenin Blanc (Clarksburg) $10. Showcases a distinctive approach to Chenin that Clarksburg practically owns, which is to say, very dry, very acidic to the point of sour, with a flavor of grapefruit zest and tamarind seed. It's a simple but wholesome wine, and fills an important niche in California whites. **85 Best Buy** — *S.H. (10/1/2006)*

Vinum Cellars 2000 CNW Wilson Vineyards Chenin Blanc (Clarksburg) $10. "CNW" Stands for "Chard No Way"—these jokers captured my heart from the start. Pear, citrus, and a tiny bit of burned caramel on the nose; pineapple and melon flavors on the palate and on the finish. **86** *(11/15/2001)*

Vinum Cellars 2003 CNW Cuvée-Wilson Vineyards Chenin Blanc (Clarksburg) $10. From one of the few California appellations specializing in this varietal, a dry, crisp wine with citrus flavors that's almost indistinguishable from a very dry Sauvignon Blanc. **85 Best Buy** —*S.H. (7/1/2005)*

Vinum Cellars 2004 Late Harvest Gewürztraminer (San Benito County) $20. Enormously aromatic and very sweet, this rich, thick dessert wine has good acidity, and it needs it to balance out the honey, apricot purée, lemon custard, vanilla, and honeysuckle flavors. A refreshing and delicious wine. **91** —*S.H. (4/1/2006)*

Vinum Cellars 2000 Vista Verde Vineyard Late Harvest Gewürztraminer (San Benito County) $20. A wonderful dessert wine, spicy, rich, and lush, with fig and grapefruit flavors at the fore. Layers of floral qualities are interspersed with herb, citrus, beach plum, and honey notes. Sweet but not cloying thanks to zingy acidity. **91** —*J.M. (12/1/2002)*

Vinum Cellars 2004 Pets Petite Sirah (Clarksburg) $14. Tastes so young and jammy, it's like it just came out of the tank. Huge in black and red cherry, pomegranate, and cocoa flavors, the wine is completely dry, with a slight finish of raisins. It's a big, rustic, hearty wine meant to accompany similar fare. **84** —*S.H. (4/1/2006)*

Vinum Cellars 2000 Pets Wilson Vineyards Petite Sirah (Clarksburg) $13. Funky, tanky aromas and a stewed, vegetal quality that's almost dirty. Tastes like sweet cherry cough medicine, and turns harsh and acidic on the short finish. **80** *(4/1/2003)*

Vinum Cellars 2003 Red Dirt Red Red Blend (El Dorado) $30. With Syrah, Mourvèdre, and Grenache, this Châteauneuf-style wine offers lots of bang. It's huge in red cherry and cocoa fruit flavors, so rich and delicious you want a second and third sip. Never mind there's a rusticity to the tannins, the wine is dry, balanced, and drinkable now. **87** —*S.H. (4/1/2006)*

Vinum Cellars 2004 Red Dirt Red Rhône Red Blend (El Dorado County) $30. Okay Rhône blend of Syrah, Mourvèdre, and Grenache, with a little oak. Can't quite get beyond a rusticity in the coarse mouthfeel, but it's nicely dry, with a good array of herb-infused fruit. **84** —*S.H. (12/31/2006)*

Vinum Cellars 2002 Vista Verde Vineyard Syrah (San Benito County) $22. Reviewers came up with very different reads on this wine, but rated it unanimously: One found aromas of chocolate and herb, with sour plum flavors; another taster commented on the thick, syrupy aromas and flavors. All found it lean in the mouth, with soft tannins. **84** *(9/1/2005)*

Vinum Cellars 1999 Vista Verde Vineyard Syrah (San Benito County) $20. With its smoke and bacon-fat aromas coupled with bright red berries, this wine smells like Syrah should. The fruit is soft and round, even if it does have a slightly vegetal side to it. **85** *(10/1/2001)*

Vinum Cellars 2004 Vista Verde Vineyard Viognier (San Benito County) $25. This vineyard was made famous by a Williams Selyem Pinot Noir bottling, and this wine shares its characteristics. It's soft and full-bodied, with a rich earthiness. It's not the fruitiest Viognier on the block, but shows apple, dill, and spicy oak flavors that finish a little sweet. **85** — *S.H. (4/1/2006)*

Vinum Cellars 2003 Vista Verde Vineyard Viognier (San Benito County) $22. Shows Viognier's exotic side in the wildly lush tropical fruit, white peach, vanilla, and honeysuckle flavors, but stays nicely dry and balanced in acids. Nothing subtle here, just plenty of fruity flavor to set off against slightly sweet Asian-inspired fare. **85** —*S.H. (8/1/2005)*

Vinum Cellars 2000 Vista Verde Vineyard Viognier (San Benito County) $20. Rich, lush, and elegant, with hints of apricot, peach, honey, and violets. The wine is full-bodied and velvety on the finish, with an attractive mineral-vanilla edge. **90** —*J.M. (9/1/2002)*

Vinum Cellars 2005 Vista Verde Vineyard Vio Viognier (San Benito County) $25. The vineyard is best known for a Williams Selyem Pinot Noir. It's a cool climate that ripens grapes well, but preserves plenty of acidity. This dry, barrel-fermented wine is complex and delicious, packed with Meyer lemon, pear, peach, tart green apple. and spice flavors. **90** —*S.H. (12/31/2006)*

Vinum Cellars 2002 Elephantus Blanc White Blend (California) $15. Rustic and dry, this wine has tart acids and an earthy, herbal taste with highlights of lemons. Based on Chenin Blanc, it has a touch of Viognier that adds a peach note to the finish. **84** —*S.H. (8/1/2005)*

Vinum Cellars 1998 Pointe Blanc White Blend (California) $15. **86** —*J.C. (9/1/2000)*

Vinum Cellars 2004 White Elephant White Blend (California) $15. This offbeat blend of Clarksburg-grown Chenin Blanc, Stolpman Vineyard Roussanne from Santa Ynez Valley, and Central Coast Viognier is remarkable. As you might expect, it's floral and fruity, but dry, with very high acidity and a modest 13.5% alcohol. It's a clean, food-friendly wine with a great degree of complexity. **90 Best Buy** —*S.H. (4/1/2006)*

VIRGIN

Virgin 2001 Sauvignon Blanc (Central Coast) $11. A charmer, with bright and clean citrus flavors enriched with riper notes of melon, fig, and

USA

Granny Smith apples. Really fun in the mouth, and just a tiny bit sweet. From Lucas & Lewellen. **85** —*S.H. (12/31/2003)*

VISION CELLARS

Vision Cellars 2000 Pinot Noir (Sonoma County) $39. This is textbook Sonoma Pinot, with its aromas of cherries, cola, coffee, and smoke, rich flavors and silky tannins. Drinks long and deep, with masses of berry and spice flavors and firm acidity. A perfect accompaniment to a wide range of foods, and thoroughly enjoyable. **90** —*S.H. (5/1/2004)*

VITA LUCE

Vita Luce 2002 Syrah (Paso Robles) $36. Full and intense, packed with all of the sun-warmed flavors Paso Robles can offer, ranging from savory, meaty flavors to jammy raspberry fruit. Firmly tannic on the finish; a bit rustic but flavorful and bold. **87** *(9/1/2005)*

VIVIANO

Viviano 1997 Noble Cepage Bordeaux Blend (Texas) $32. Basically a Bordeaux blend with a little Sangiovese added, this wine offers up aromas of oak and vanilla, blackberry, and cassis, spiced plums, and a chocolate malt note. Drinks rich and dense, with tremendous extract of blackberry liqueur. It's an ager, with sizable tannins. From Llano Estacado. **90** —*S.H. (5/1/2001)*

VIXEN

Vixen 2004 The Villain Red Blend (Santa Barbara County) $29. Mainly Syrah, with Cabernet Sauvignon, this is a southern Rhône-type wine, fruity and dry in cherries, with a pleasantly light body. It's very clean, a nice wine for sandwiches, especially ham. **85** —*S.H. (12/31/2006)*

Vixen 2005 V Cuvée Rhône White Blend (Santa Barbara County) $32. Definitely cool climate wine, to judge from the acidity and minerality. Underneath are subtly engaging fruit pastry filling flavors of mangoes, guavas, peaches, and nectarines, spiced with cinnamon and nutmeg and enriched with vanilla and brown sugar. Yet this wine is totally dry. It's a classy, complex food wine. **91** —*S.H. (12/31/2006)*

Vixen 2005 Vivant Rose Rosé Blend (Santa Ynez Valley) $22. It's so easy to imagine drinking this at a sidewalk café in Los Olivos, over a perfectly grilled entrecote with pommes frites. Though it's really a simple country wine, this Grenache Noir, blended with a little Syrah, offers lots of charm. **85** —*S.H. (12/31/2006)*

Vixen 2004 Harmony Syrah (Santa Barbara County) $45. Drinkable now for its richness, smooth texture, and exuberant fruit, although there's a firm tannic structure to play off a smoky grilled steak or chop. Blackberries, black cherries, mocha, toasty oak, and a hint of worn leather make this Syrah complex. **90** —*S.H. (12/31/2006)*

Vixen 2005 Viognier (Santa Barbara County) $29. Shows Viognier's exotic character in the intense floral and tropical fruit and Asian spice notes, a complex mélange of flavors wrapped into a rich texture. Balanced with fine acidity and dryness, this racy white wine doesn't have much oak, which makes the fruit deliciously transparent. **90** —*S.H. (12/31/2006)*

VJB

VJB 2004 Barbera (Mendocino County) $34. Dark, dry, tannic, and a little hot, with enormously ripe plum, blackberry, and coffee flavors, this Barbera combines old-time ruggedness with modern purity. Nice now with rich beef dishes, yet it will hang in there for 20 years, gradually softening and sweetening. **90** —*S.H. (12/1/2006)*

VJB 2003 Barbera (Mendocino) $30. Rustic and slightly sweet, this inky-black wine is thick in tannins that frame plummy, coffee flavors. It's also soft in acids, which will probably limit its ageability. **83** —*S.H. (3/1/2006)*

VJB 2003 Dante Cabernet Sauvignon (Sonoma Valley) $40. Nice and ripe in blackberry, currant, cherry, coffee, tobacco, and herb flavors, this Cab has fairly aggressive tannins that may soften with a year or two of bottle age. The fruity flavors finish very dry and balanced, with some complexity. **85** —*S.H. (9/1/2006)*

VJB 2002 Dante Cabernet Sauvignon (Sonoma County) $36. With a bit of Sangiovese blended in, this wine is earthier, drier, and tarter than VJB's "V" Cabernet, with which it was released. It has flavors of herbs and cherries, and is very dry. The extra acidity and firmer structure make it a more interesting wine, perfect for a barbecued steak. **91** —*S.H. (11/15/2005)*

VJB 2000 Dante Cabernet Sauvignon (Sonoma County) $24. This very oaky wine offers a veneer of smoky vanillins and char atop underlying flavors of cherries and other ripe red fruits. It is very dry, with some dusty tannins in the finish, and rather soft in structure. **86** —*S.H. (11/15/2003)*

VJB 1999 Dante Cabernet Sauvignon (Sonoma County) $23. Has distinctly varietal flavors, with cassis flavors, and those pretty Napa tannins are fine. There's a note in the aroma that's out of place, suggesting tobacco. It's due to 15% Sangiovese, which also lends a cherry-sweet element to the finish. **89** —*S.H. (11/15/2002)*

VJB 2000 V Cabernet Sauvignon (Sonoma County) $35. Tastes like sweet wild blackberries and black cherries drizzled with crème de cassis and a sprinkling of brown sugar, with the usual smoke and vanilla from oak. For all the flavor, structurally, the wine falls apart. It's too soft, and doesn't offer up the acidity and tannins to achieve true complexity. **87** —*S.H. (11/15/2003)*

VJB 2001 V Private Reserve Cabernet Sauvignon (Sonoma County) $40. This smooth, dry wine shows all the hallmarks of this warm, balanced vintage. It has upfront black currant, cherry marmalade, chocolate, and spicy flavors, with very soft, gentle tannins, balancing acids, and a deft touch of smoky oak. **89** —*S.H. (11/15/2005)*

VJB NV Baci di Famiglia Chardonnay Port 375mL Chardonnay (Sonoma Valley) $28. If you can get past the hard, faux-wax plastic seal, you'll find a sweetish wine, with peaches and cream flavors, and a spicy, honeyed finish. **84** —*S.H. (10/1/2006)*

VJB 2000 Gabriella Ranch Chardonnay (Sonoma Valley) $11. Pretty thin, with watery flavors barely suggesting the apples and peaches of Chardonnay. That leaves a dominant mouthfeel of alcohol and acidity. It's almost Muscadet-like in its leanness. Try it with crab or oysters. **84** — *S.H. (12/15/2002)*

VJB 2003 Syrah (Dry Creek Valley) $28. Two things you should know about this wine: it's very dry and very tannic. It is not a soft, mushy, fruity Syrah. The intention seems to have been ageability. But cellaring this is for the brave of heart, because the wine's future is totally unknown. **85** —*S.H. (2/1/2006)*

VJB 2002 Syrah (Alexander Valley) $28. Huge jammy fruit is the hallmark of this wine, with blackberries cascading over the palate in a mouthfilling rush. Some coffee, meaty, and hay-like notes add complexity. Tastes almost sweet, yet clamps down on the finish with drying tannins. **87** *(9/1/2005)*

VJB 2003 Zinfandel (El Dorado County) $26. This Foothills Zin will have its fans, with its chunky, raisiny, dry tannins, but by standards of balance and finesse, it's lacking, although it's easy to imagine drinking copious amounts of it at a carefree barbecue where you don't really care. **84** — *S.H. (2/1/2006)*

VJB 2000 Zinfandel (Sonoma County) $23. An awkward wine, the victim of bad winemaking decisions. The grapes obviously were left so long on the vine, the sugar levels soared. In order to keep alcohol levels down to reasonable levels, residual sugar had to be kept. The result is cloyingly sweet, filled with dark berry flavors saturated in brown sugar. **82** —*S.H. (12/1/2002)*

VOLKER EISELE

Volker Eisele 2002 Terzetto Bordeaux Blend (Napa Valley) $75. With one-third each of Cabernet Sauvignon, Cab Franc, and Merlot, this wine hits many high notes, including the delicate, elegant fruity-oaky balance, soft, rich tannins and just-right oak. On the minus side, it's too soft. It lacks that vivacity and structure that a great wine requires. **87** —*S.H. (12/1/2005)*

Volker Eisele 2001 Terzetto Bordeaux Blend (Napa Valley) $75. There's a tannic sturdiness here that suggests ageability, but it's really delicious now. Black currant, chocolate, cherry, and sweet herb flavors are perfectly meshed with fine, toasty oak. Brims with class and distinction. One-third each Cabernet Sauvignon, Cab Franc, and Merlot. **94** —*S.H. (10/1/2004)*

USA

Volker Eisele 2003 Terzetto Red Wine Cabernet Blend (Napa Valley) $75. Grown in the Chiles Valley part of Napa, this contains one third Sauvignon, Cab Franc, and Merlot. It's rich in chocolatey, blackberry, cola, and fruit flavors, dry and tannic, with a rustic touch of raisins. But it suggests a good future. Drink 2009 through 2015. **88** —*S.H. (12/31/2006)*

Volker Eisele 2002 Cabernet Sauvignon (Napa Valley) $38. From highlands vineyards in Napa's Chiles Valley, this is a young, tough Cab. It has some dry, numbing tannins. Still, there's a heart of blackberry and currant fruit, and good acidity. Try cellaring for a couple years to soften. **88** —*S.H. (12/1/2005)*

Volker Eisele 2001 Cabernet Sauvignon (Napa Valley) $38. This is a big wine clearly designed for the cellar. Not that it's not drinkable now—you could enjoy the sweet chocolatey, blackberry, cherry, and spicy oak flavors tonight, especially with a great cut of meat. If you do, decant it for a few hours. But the tannins are rich and finely ground, and this wine should improve through the decade. **92** —*S.H. (10/1/2004)*

Volker Eisele 1999 Cabernet Sauvignon (Napa Valley) $40. Smoothly textured, with subtle berry, earth, herb, and spice aromas. The wine fans out on the palate to reveal a focused, sleek, and refined style, brimming with blackberry, cassis, anise, coffee, chocolate, and herb flavors. Tannins are firm but ripe. It's all framed in sweet, toasty oak. Long at the end. **92** —*J.M. (2/1/2003)*

Volker Eisele 1998 Cabernet Sauvignon (Napa Valley) $35. A smooth-textured, sleek, and complex Cabernet. Packed with bright blackberry, anise, coffee, and herb flavors, the wine is framed in supple tannins that will allow it to age beautifully. Drinking well now, it is an excellent result from a challenging vintage **91** —*J.M. (12/1/2001)*

Volker Eisele 2003 Estate Cabernet Sauvignon (Napa Valley) $40. Shows pure Napa Cabernet flavors with a classic Napa structure. Brilliantly focused in black currant, blackberry, mu shu plum, and chocolate flavors, with a rich overlay of charry oak, it's soft and dry. The tannins are dusty and thick, but very fine now. **92 Editors' Choice** —*S.H. (12/31/2006)*

Volker Eisele 2005 Gemini White Blend (Napa Valley) $25. Sémillon brings a fat, oily richness, suggesting peaches, buttercups, and cashews, while Sauvignon Blanc adds a refreshingly tart touch of lemongrass. The overall impression is of a rich, creamy, upscale, softly dry white wine. **87** —*S.H. (12/31/2006)*

Volker Eisele 2004 Gemini White Blend (Napa Valley) $25. The winery seems to have put more Sémillon in this year, possibly to ameliorate the feline aspects of the Sauvignon Blanc. The result is a richer, more complex wine which barrel fermentation in partially new French oak helps. The flavors include honeydew melon, figs, and pink grapefruit. **90** —*S.H. (12/1/2005)*

Volker Eisele 2003 Gemini White Blend (Napa Valley) $25. This blend of Sauvignon Blanc and Sémillon starts with those telltale cat-pee aromas that tell you what to expect. It's bone dry and high in acidity, with flavors of citrus fruits and a touch of oak. Nice as a cocktail, and versatile at the table. **86** —*S.H. (2/1/2005)*

VON STRASSER

Von Strasser 2001 Sori Bricco Vineyard Bordeaux Blend (Diamond Mountain) $60. A luscious wine that merges Cabernet's tough, mountain personality with softer, more chocolatey notes to produce a smooth, polished wine. Complex in flavor, young in acids and tannins, it should age well through this decade, but is nice now with sturdy fare. **91** —*S.H. (2/1/2005)*

Von Strasser 1997 Cabernet Sauvignon (Diamond Mountain) $50. 92 *(11/1/2000)*

Von Strasser 2001 Cabernet Sauvignon (Diamond Mountain) $50. Fine and complex. The streamlined texture hits you first, with its balance and harmony. There's a subtle interplay of ripe black currant and cassis fruit with herbs. Dry and elegant. **88** —*S.H. (2/1/2005)*

Von Strasser 2000 Cabernet Sauvignon (Diamond Mountain) $45. 89 *(8/1/2003)*

Von Strasser 1999 Diamond Mountain Cabernet Sauvignon (Napa Valley) $50. Smooth and supple texture frames this sleek and complex wine that is both elegant and powerful. It offers a fine blend of blackberry, cassis, anise, spice, herb, and toasty oak flavors that fan out on the long finish. **91** —*J.M. (6/1/2002)*

Von Strasser 2001 Estate Vineyards Cabernet Sauvignon (Diamond Mountain) $60. Well-oaked, with sweetly ripe, smooth tannins, this wine features a smooth texture and polished flavors of black currants. It's a trifle soft in acidity, and probably not a cellar candidate. **87** —*S.H. (2/1/2005)*

Von Strasser 2002 Estate Vineyards Cabernet Sauvignon (Diamond Mountain) $70. Diamond Mountain Cabs are notorious for their tannins, and this is no exception. It's tough and tight now, a dry wine that ends in total astringency. Then there's the fruit, rich in blackberry and cherry flavors. Should begin to open by 2008 and hold and improve for many years after. **90 Cellar Selection** —*S.H. (8/1/2006)*

Von Strasser 2000 Estate Vineyards Cabernet Sauvignon (Diamond Mountain) $70. 91 *(8/1/2003)*

Von Strasser 2002 Post Vineyard Cabernet Sauvignon (Diamond Mountain) $75. Straddles an interesting line between drinkability and a wine that needs cellaring. This is lush with opulently ripe cherry and cassis fruit alongside tannins that, while fine, are strong. This distinguished wine should hit its stride in 2008, and hold for many years after. **92 Cellar Selection** —*S.H. (9/1/2006)*

Von Strasser 2001 Post Vineyard Cabernet Sauvignon (Diamond Mountain) $60. Fairly tannic now, with a tart, dusty bite of grape skin, and also hefty in acidity. Underneath all that are ripe currant and cassis flavors. This is an age worthy wine that should develop great complexity after 2010. **91** —*S.H. (2/1/2005)*

Von Strasser 1997 Chardonnay (Diamond Mountain) $36. 89 —*M.S. (10/1/1999)*

Von Strasser 2000 Aurora Vineyard Chardonnay (Diamond Mountain) $40. The underlying fruit is tight and lean, with apple and citrus flavors, although it's fattened up with winemaker bells and whistles. Oak adds a creamy texture and smoky vanilla, while lees contribute more cream. The finish turns acidic and tart. **87** —*S.H. (2/1/2003)*

Von Strasser 2000 Rainin Vineyard Chardonnay (Diamond Mountain) $40. Almost as tight as the Aurora bottling, maybe a shade richer in pear fruit flavors. Still, it's a lean wine, a structural drink dominated by acids, alcohol, and dusty tannins. Oak provides vanilla. The finish turns tart and earthy. **87** —*S.H. (2/1/2004)*

Von Strasser 1999 Rainin Vineyard Chardonnay (Diamond Mountain) $45. Crisp yet smooth and velvety on the palate, this complex, elegant wine is loaded with layers of pear, apple, mineral, vanilla, coconut, spice, apricot, and lemon notes. Really gorgeous, with a finish that is clean and luxurious. **94** —*J.M. (5/1/2002)*

Von Strasser 2002 Reserve Red Blend (Diamond Mountain) $100. Some great Cabs are drinkable when young, while others require patience. This is the latter sort. It's a tough, young wine, dominated by dusty tannins leading to an astringent finish. But it's incredibly fine, showing a balance and grace rare even in Napa Valley. As it warms up and breathes in the glass, it gets even better, giving tantalizing hints of ripe cassis and cherries that now are buried. You could open it now, after decanting, but it should begin to blossom in 2008, and will improve for many years. **97 Cellar Selection** —*S.H. (9/1/2006)*

Von Strasser 2001 Reserve Red Blend (Diamond Mountain) $100. This is a big wine for folks who like to age their Cabs. It's huge in mountain tannins now, but the underlying structure is so fine, and the cassis and cherry fruit so pure, that it's guaranteed to improve through this decade and beyond. **93** —*S.H. (2/1/2005)*

Von Strasser 2002 Sori Bricco Vineyard Red Blend (Diamond Mountain) $70. Compared this to the winery's Cabernet Sauvignon, it's softer, richer, and more accessible despite the big tannins that will enable the wine to age. Flavorwise, you'll find a delicious mélange of blackberry, cherry, plum, coffee, and herb flavors that are intricate and complexed by flashy new oak. Drink now through 2014. **92 Cellar Selection** —*S.H. (8/1/2006)*

USA

Von Strasser 2000 Sori Bricco Vineyard Red Blend (Diamond Mountain) $65. 90 *(8/1/2003)*

Von Strasser 1999 Sori Bricco Vineyards Red Blend (Diamond Mountain) $60. A young, dramatic wine, with lots of plushly ripe plum, berry, licorice, coffee, chocolate, and cherry flavors and a rich overlay of well-smoked oak. The tannins are thick and chewy, and should age well. **90** —*S.H. (11/15/2002)*

Von Strasser 2001 Monhoff Vineyard Zinfandel (Diamond Mountain) $40. A rich, dense wine that sports plenty of black cherry, cola, coffee, tar, tea, blackberry, and herb flavors. Toasty oak frames it all, giving it good structure. Firm and plush on the finish. **90** *(11/1/2003)*

Von Strasser 2000 Monhoff Vineyard Zinfandel (Diamond Mountain) $40. 88 *(8/1/2003)*

VOSS

Voss 1997 Merlot (Rutherford) $20. 84 —*J.C. (3/1/2000)*

Voss 1998 Sauvignon Blanc (Napa Valley) $15. 86 *(3/1/2000)*

Voss 2005 Sauvignon Blanc (Rutherford) $19. I drank this at the end of a long, hot summer day, which is when a cold, crisp white is at its best. What a delicious wine. Bold citrus and apricot flavors, acids so strong they almost fizz and a rich creaminess even though there's no oak. **89** —*S.H. (12/15/2006)*

Voss 2003 Sauvignon Blanc (Napa Valley) $19. Has a smart, snappy Sauvignon aroma of lemons and limes, apricots, figs, and lusher notes of white apricots and peaches. Drinks very ripe and fruity, but fairly dry, with good minerality and acidity. **90** —*S.H. (10/1/2005)*

Voss 2001 Sauvignon Blanc (Napa Valley) $18. From a winery that has studied this varietal for a long time, and it shows in the deftly managed fruit. Straddles the line between riper peach and melon flavors and tarter, leaner gooseberry and lime. There's a spicy, honeyed richness throughout. Clean and refreshing on the finish. Nice stuff. **88** —*S.H. (9/1/2003)*

Voss 2000 Sauvignon Blanc (Napa Valley) $18. Grapefruit mixed with honey and some green veggies welcome you in, while the intriguing palate provides citrus, more honey, apricots, and even some scallions. Simple and straightforward it's not; but it is fairly easy to drink. Served chilled on the front porch during the summer. **88** *(8/1/2002)*

Voss 1997 Botrytis Sauvignon Blanc (Napa Valley) $NA. 86 —*J.C. (12/31/1999)*

Voss 1996 Shiraz (Oakville) $24. 92 —*M.S. (3/1/2000)*

Voss 1999 Shiraz (Napa Valley) $25. This Shiraz is peppered with such intriguing spices (hickory smoke and cinnamon on the nose, and some Moroccan spices on the palate) that we'll overlook the fact that they're wood-derived. The bouquet also offers lush berry fruit and a little coffee; fruit on the bouquet is a little more tart—blueberry and sour blackberry prevail. Mouthfeel is low in acid, with chewy tannins. Finish is long, with lots of toasty oak and spice. Top Value. **90** *(11/1/2001)*

Voss 2001 Syrah (Napa Valley) $20. Smooth and enjoyable. It starts with white-pepper flavors, then bursts on the palate with cherries, mixed berries, and lavish oak. Nicely textured, finishing with lingering notes of vanilla and caramel. **87** *(9/1/2005)*

Voss 2001 Ocala Syrah (Napa Valley) $45. Compared to Voss's regular Syrah, this one is more concentrated and packed with fruit, blending mixed berries with shadings of cinnamon and black pepper. Lingers elegantly on the finish. **88** *(9/1/2005)*

Voss 2003 Viognier (Carneros) $25. Smells almost like a dessert wine, with aromas of papayas, kiwis, peach custard, Key lime pie, and honey, and similar flavors. Certainly delicious, but it's not really a dry table wine. **85** —*S.H. (10/1/2005)*

Voss 2000 Botrytis White Blend (Napa Valley) $25. Extraordinarily sweet and concentrated, coating the mouth with sugar and honey and the distinctive apricot flavor of botrytis. The underlying fruit flavors veer toward mangoes and papaya, although high acidity makes for a citrusy undercurrent. It's not just rich, it's elegant. **95** —*S.H. (12/1/2002)*

W.H. SMITH

W.H. Smith 2004 Pinot Noir (Sonoma Coast) $28. Showcases the terroir and potential of this extreme appellation, but if you're a fan of rich, opulently fruity Pinots, go elsewhere. This is a minimalist wine, dry, and acidic, with a firm minerality undergirding cherry and cola flavors. Burgundy-oriented Pinotphiles will appreciate the complexity. **91** —*S.H. (10/1/2006)*

W.H. Smith 2002 Pinot Noir (Sonoma Coast) $24. Beautiful and gentle, yet quite complex. It hits the palate with pure silk and satin, so airy and lilting you first think it's a lightweight. Then the flavors hit. Waves of raspberries and cherries, spices and herbs, cola and soy, and vanilla unroll across the palate. Compellingly tasty, and a great expression of the far Sonoma Coast. **91 Editors' Choice** —*S.H. (11/1/2004)*

W.H. Smith 2002 Maritime Ridge Pinot Noir (Sonoma Coast) $45. I would have held this wine back for at least an additional year to let the grapey, cherry, raspberry, and chocolate flavors and sweet oak knit together, but cellaring it will do that. It is a very fine wine, silky and potentially complex. All the parts are there. Hold until 2005. **92** —*S.H. (11/1/2004)*

WAGNER

Wagner 2000 Estate Bottled Ice Wine Riesling (Finger Lakes) $30. 84 —*J.C. (8/1/2003)*

Wagner 2002 Fermented Dry Riesling (Finger Lakes) $10. 84 —*J.C. (8/1/2003)*

Wagner 1998 Ice Wine Riesling (Finger Lakes) $18. Orange, apricot, and pineapple aromas ride over a deep bass note of earth and spice. The earth nearly takes over on the palate, providing a rich, complex counterpoint to the fruit-driven sweetness. Could use a touch more acidity to really make the flavors sing. **89** —*J.C. (3/1/2001)*

Wagner 1998 Ice Wine Vidal Blanc (Finger Lakes) $18. The more I taste Vidal, the more I find it an acquired taste—a taste I've yet to acquire. This one has intense aromas of canned creamed corn, with a few other vegetal hints thrown in for good measure. Yes, it's sweet, with balancing acidity and a rich, lush mouthfeel, but the flavors—well, let's just say they're unique. **81** —*J.C. (3/1/2001)*

Wagner 1998 Ice Wine Vignoles (Finger Lakes) $18. Shows off the exotic musky-spicy side of this grape in its peppery, leathery aromas. Turns tropical in the mouth: papaya and mango are joined by zippy citrus-tinged acidity. Finishes long, with some of the peppery notes returning. **87** —*J.C. (3/1/2001)*

Wagner 1999 Late Harvest Vignoles (Finger Lakes) $15. Honeyed mango and papaya flavors are accented by a citrus streak that provides much-needed verve, while the aromas are more along the lines of pear and lemon. A solid effort, with only a hint of the musky or foxy quality that can sometimes dominate wines from hybrid grapes. **86** —*J.C. (3/1/2001)*

WALLA WALLA

Walla Walla 2003 Sagemoor Vineyard Cuvée Bordeaux Blend (Columbia Valley (WA)) $40. A Bordeaux blend, smooth and ultra-chocolatey in the house style. The cherry fruit is coated in flavors of hazelnut, cocoa, espresso, and chocolate. Good indeed, but somewhat difficult to find the flavors of the vineyard under all that creamy barrel. **89** —*P.G. (6/1/2006)*

Walla Walla 2002 Cabernet Franc (Walla Walla (WA)) $25. Bright berry and cassis, with smoke and licorice woven through. This is firm and chewy, with the tannins showing smoke and herbs. The roasted coffee character of the Cab Franc comes through beautifully at the end. **89** —*P.G. (12/15/2005)*

Walla Walla 2003 Cabernet Sauvignon (Walla Walla (WA)) $35. Scents and flavors of cranberry and raspberry are followed with layers of caramel, brown sugar, espresso, and dark chocolate. Very smooth, very seductive, very creamy, it leads into a long, smooth finish. **89** —*P.G. (6/1/2006)*

Walla Walla 2002 Cabernet Sauvignon (Columbia Valley (WA)) $35. Classy from the get-go, with an appealing mix of strawberry preserves, anise, licorice candy, smoke, and cedar. The fruit and oak are beautifully matched and laced together, and the flavors unfold with a slightly salty, mineral edge. Long, persistent, and consistently interesting, right through the finishing notes of dried herb and toasted nuts. **92** —*P.G. (12/15/2005)*

Walla Walla 1999 Cabernet Sauvignon (Columbia Valley (WA)) $35. Fans of the Leonetti style are sure to find this fragrant, plummy wine a winner. Loaded with ripe fruit, the wine smells of cedarbox and roasted coffee, layer upon layer of smoky oak adding dimensions of flavor and texture. Very good right now. **92 Editors' Choice** —*P.G. (6/1/2002)*

Walla Walla 2003 Vineyard Select Cabernet Sauvignon (Walla Walla (WA)) $45. Clearly a cut above the winery's regular Cab, this is just the second time in 10 years the winery has made a vineyard select. Loaded with sweet/tart berries, this concentrated, pure Cabernet turns up flavors of coffee liqueur and chocolate-covered espresso beans. Good structure and concentration keep it from being top-heavy with oak. **92** —*P.G. (6/1/2006)*

Walla Walla 1997 Windrow Vineyard Cabernet Sauvignon (Washington) $32. 90 —*M.S. (4/1/2000)*

Walla Walla 2003 Merlot (Walla Walla (WA)) $28. Firm and spicy, with a lovely spine of tight flavors running right through the middle of the palate. Light fruits—strawberry, rhubarb, melon, and red plum—lead through a long, elegant finish. **88** —*P.G. (12/15/2005)*

Walla Walla 2000 Merlot (Walla Walla (WA)) $25. Like this cult winery's Cabernet, the Merlot is loaded with layer upon layer of rich, textured, chocolatey oak. The flavors are right out of Ben and Jerry— caramel, cocoa, roasted nuts, vanilla, and sweet milk chocolate. But there is plenty of fruit there too, and the combo is beguiling, instant gratification. **91** —*P.G. (9/1/2002)*

Walla Walla 2003 Cordon Grove Vineyard Cuvée Red Blend (Yakima Valley) $28. Smooth, buffed, and toned, with luscious toffee, coffee, and chocolate-covered cherry flavors. Buttery, polished, and just plain sexy, it also shows off some interesting, slightly grassy, sweet herb scents. **90** —*P.G. (12/15/2005)*

WALTER DACON

Walter Dacon 2003 C'est Beaux Syrah (Columbia Valley (WA)) $35. Aged in American oak, with mostly similar vineyard sources. The American oak, with more spice to the fruit, and less smoothness overall than the C'est Belle Bottling. Cherry and berry flavors abound; it's sturdy, solid, and well-made. Just 170 cases produced. **88** —*P.G. (6/1/2006)*

Walter Dacon 2003 C'est Belle Syrah (Columbia Valley (WA)) $28. Just 370 cases produced. This pure Syrah is soaked in sweet, cedary oak. The cedar and whiskey barrel scents hit first, but the fruit is substantial and goes deep, with rich cherry, plums, and spice. The tannins, smooth and soft, lead into a creamy caramel, layered finish. Balanced and big; it's a style that many consumers will love for its rich, plush flavors. **89** —*P.G. (6/1/2006)*

Walter Dacon 2003 C'est Magnifique Syrah (Columbia Valley (WA)) $38. Walter Dacon's three Syrahs are well made, but so very much alike it is hard to understand why they warrant three separate bottlings, at three different prices. The Magnifique takes us back to the French oak treatment, again pure Syrah, from a mix of Red Mountain, Horse Heaven Hills, and Yakima Valley vineyards. Just 160 cases produced. **88** —*P.G. (6/1/2006)*

Walter Dacon 2003 C'est Syrah Beaux Syrah (Columbia Valley (WA)) $35. Spicy, smoky, toasty notes, courtesy of American oak aging, accent this wine, nose to close. It's supple and soft on the palate, with mixed berry flavors. Grows tart toward the finish, when lively acids emerge. **88** *(9/1/2005)*

Walter Dacon 2003 C'est Syrah Belle Syrah (Columbia Valley (WA)) $28. A bit simple and grapey, with bold fruit aromas right upfront. You get the flavors of sun-warmed fruit, a squirt of lemon juice and a hint of alcoholic warmth in this medium-bodied wine. **85** *(9/1/2005)*

Walter Dacon 2003 C'est Syrah Magnifique Syrah (Yakima Valley) $38. Spicy on the nose. The smooth, supple palate offers baked blackberry flavors that fade into a medium-long finish. One reviewer found the finish a little hard and metallic, and another lauded it for its meaty, brown-sugary flavors. **87** *(9/1/2005)*

Walter Dacon 2004 C'est Beaux Syrah (Columbia Valley (WA)) $35. The Beaux is the winery's American-oaked Syrah, with mostly similar vineyard sources to the Belle. The two wines are quite similar, though the Beaux has a bit more spice to the fruit and a bit less suppleness. Sturdy, solid, and well made. **89** —*P.G. (11/15/2006)*

Walter Dacon 2004 C'est Belle Syrah (Columbia Valley (WA)) $28. This is the winery's French-oaked Syrah. It's smoky, focused, and powerful, with sweet, cedary oak melded to dark, substantial fruit. The tannins are smooth and soft and lead into a creamy, caramel, layered finish. Full throttle, balanced and big. **90** —*P.G. (11/15/2006)*

Walter Dacon 2004 C'est Syrah Magnifique Syrah (Columbia Valley (WA)) $38. The Magnifique is Dacon's top Syrah, a barrel selection from the French oak-aged side of the winery. It's 98% Syrah, with a splash of Viognier, and indeed it shows a bit more fruit-driven power than the Belle. Blackberry, black cherry, and a good lift from streaks of citrus mitigate the overpowering barrel flavors; there's also plenty of fresh acid to provide extra thrust on lift-off. Firm and tannic, with a hint of minerality; this is the winery's best effort to date. **91** —*P.G. (11/15/2006)*

WALTZING BEAR

Waltzing Bear 2003 Cargasacchi Jalama Vineyard Pinot Noir (Santa Barbara County) $42. Medium-ruby in color, with an inviting aroma of dried cherry, cinnamon, cola, and smoky oak, this Pinot shows classic varietal structure and elegance. It's very, very dry, with a silky texture and penetrating acidity. Rather austere and angular now, the wine needs decanting or short-term aging. **90** —*S.H. (8/1/2006)*

Waltzing Bear 2003 Garys' Vineyard Pinot Noir (Santa Lucia Highlands) $45. Typical Garys' Pinot, a big, dry, high-alcohol wine ripe in cherry-berry fruit character, fairly hefty in tannins for a Pinot and crisp in coastal acidity. You wouldn't call this wine elegant, but it's admirable for its Santa Lucia-esque muscularity. Should benefit from three to five years' aging. **89** —*S.H. (8/1/2006)*

Waltzing Bear 2003 Rancho Ontiveros Vineyard Pinot Noir (Santa Maria Valley) $42. The vineyard is near Bien Nacido and owned by one of its senior executives. The wine is extremely dry, with high acidity and soft, silky tannins. Qualitatively, it feels austere in the mouth, with dried fruit character and a firmness that borders on minerality, but there's a complexity that makes it interesting to drink. **91** —*S.H. (8/1/2006)*

Waltzing Bear 2003 Solomon Hills Vineyard Pinot Noir (Santa Maria Valley) $45. This particular wine is rather heavy and thick in malted cherry, mocha, and cassis flavors, with a syrupy mouthfeel. What it needs is refinement and elegance. **85** —*S.H. (8/1/2006)*

WASHINGTON HILLS

Washington Hills 1999 Cabernet Sauvignon (Columbia Valley (WA)) $10. Granted, this is a budget bottle, but it is almost indistinguishable from the winery's Merlot. Tannic and woody, it mixes bell pepper and earthy flavors of bark and root. **84** —*P.G. (6/1/2002)*

Washington Hills 2000 Fumé Blanc (Yakima Valley) $7. This is a straightforward, fruity style of Sauvignon Blanc, with juicy, citrus flavors dominant. Tart and refreshing, simple and clean. **86 Best Buy** —*P.G. (6/1/2002)*

Washington Hills 1999 Merlot (Columbia Valley (WA)) $10. Dry, somewhat bitter tannins dominate, with stemmy, earthy undertones. There is bell pepper, the barest hint of cherry, and some interesting coffee/spice in the finish. **84** —*P.G. (6/1/2002)*

Washington Hills 2001 Dry Riesling (Columbia Valley (WA)) $7. This is just the second vintage for this value producer's "dry" Riesling. Though labeled dry, this wine definitely lights up the fruity side of the street, with detectable (0.7%) residual sugar. Exceptionally fragrant, with candied honeysuckle scents, and sweetly alluring. 705 cases produced. **88 Best Buy** —*P.G. (12/31/2002)*

Washington Hills 2000 Sémillon-Chardonnay (Columbia Valley (WA)) $7. A roughly even (55/45) blend, this is a tasty, herbal style, with fresh gooseberry and lemon fruit. There's a nice kick to the mouthfeel and a vibrant, food-friendly finish. **87 Best Buy** —*P.G. (6/1/2002)*

Washington Hills 2002 Shiraz (Columbia Valley (WA)) $9. Another well-priced offering out of Washington's Columbia Valley, this one offering pretty caramel and coffee scents and raspberry and herb flavors. It's light in body, but creamy-textured, with a decent finish that echoes with coffee, vanilla, and ground pepper. **85 Best Buy** *(9/1/2005)*

Washington Hills 2000 Syrah (Yakima Valley) $17. The color is right, but the flavors are thin and acidic. In the mouth it feels like a Beaujolais nouveau from a not-so-good year; earthy, yeasty, and tannic. **83** —*P.G. (6/1/2002)*

Washington Hills 1999 Syrah (Columbia Valley (WA)) $14. Even on the palate, yet overly tart with sour herb, green olive, and leather accents marking the black fruit. Has a mineral-citrus tang, and the high acidity that shows in so many Washington Syrahs. **83** *(10/1/2001)*

WATERBROOK

Waterbrook 1998 Red Mountain Meritage Bordeaux Blend (Columbia Valley (WA)) $36. The nose could pass for Médoc; it has the depth and complexity, the tight cassis fruit, the hints of cedar and lead pencil. In the mouth it is firm, tannic, and refined, with elegant flavors of leather and earth. Not a huge wine, but stylish, and a fine example of how Washington can emulate the flavors of Bordeaux. **89** —*P.G. (6/1/2001)*

Waterbrook 1997 Cabernet Sauvignon (Columbia Valley (WA)) $22. 90 *(6/1/2000)*

Waterbrook 2003 Cabernet Sauvignon (Columbia Valley (WA)) $21. Firm, hard, tannic, and smoky with black cherry, red currant, light earth, and pepper. French, American, and Hungarian oak adds some toasted cracker flavors around the cherry fruit. Well crafted and quite interesting. **90** —*P.G. (4/1/2006)*

Waterbrook 2002 Cabernet Sauvignon (Columbia Valley (WA)) $24. This is clean, straight-ahead, and disarmingly simple. The fruit is pretty rather than powerful, and it's lightly dusted with cocoa and toast, making a very agreeable, but not very impactful, Cabernet. **86** —*P.G. (11/15/2004)*

Waterbrook 1998 Chardonnay (Columbia Valley (WA)) $9. 85 —*P.G. (6/1/2000)*

Waterbrook 2004 Chardonnay (Columbia Valley (WA)) $12. Oaky, supple, and structured, this features fresh green apple fruit and plenty of toasty new oak. It's just well made, mostly barrel-fermented (one-third was new French oak) and captures the broad, fruit-driven, barrel-enhanced flavors that make Chardonnay so popular. **88 Best Buy** —*P.G. (4/1/2006)*

Waterbrook 2001 Chardonnay (Columbia Valley (WA)) $10. Waterbrook consistently delivers crisply rendered, varietally true white wines at attractive prices. This has a palate of melon, light citrus, and peach, with a long, lively, fresh, and textured mouthfeel. **89** —*P.G. (9/1/2002)*

Waterbrook 1997 Merlot (Columbia Valley (WA)) $20. 89 —*P.G. (6/1/2000)*

Waterbrook 2003 Merlot (Columbia Valley (WA)) $19. Plump, soft, and appealing with cherry tobacco scents and fruit flavors mixing berry, black cherry, plum, and fig. Smoke, hints of herb, and green tea-flavored tannins lead into a substantial finish with buttery cocoa, coffee, and spice. **88** —*P.G. (4/1/2006)*

Waterbrook 2002 Merlot (Columbia Valley (WA)) $20. This reliable producer makes a pleasant, lightweight but solid, mainstream Merlot. The fruit is on the strawberry/red currant end of the spectrum, light but flavorful. It's dusted with cocoa/baking chocolate barrel flavors. **87** —*P.G. (11/15/2004)*

Waterbrook 2004 Mélange Red Blend (Columbia Valley (WA)) $14. Released quite young, this grapey red blend is a perennial favorite, for it mixes well-sourced grapes and substantial flavors of Washington-grown fruit at a modest cost. 40% Merlot, 32% Cab, 11% Cab Franc, 9% Sangiovese, and 8% Syrah in this vintage, an interesting blend that brings dark tar and licorice along with plum and black tea. Just the slightest taste of oak and chocolate. **87** —*P.G. (4/1/2006)*

Waterbrook 1999 Mélange Red Blend (Columbia Valley (WA)) $15. Mélange is Waterbrook's blend of Cabernet Sauvignon (41%), Merlot (32%), Sangiovese (14%), and Cabernet Franc (13%), and it's a lot of wine for the price. There's plenty of rich cassis/berry fruit, lots of toasty oak, and a beefy, firm weight to the wine that speaks of power. On the downside, there is some stemminess, tough tannins, and a green flavor to the finish. **86** —*P.G. (6/1/2001)*

Waterbrook 2000 Ciel du Cheval Vineyard Sangiovese (Red Mountain) $28. This lush, fruity wine absolutely explodes from the glass with a bright burst of red currant and ripe raspberry fruit. The oak barrels add a smooth splash of milk chocolate; who can resist? **90** —*P.G. (9/1/2002)*

Waterbrook 2004 Sauvignon Blanc (Columbia Valley (WA)) $12. This always seems to be a strength of the winery, and 2004 is one of the best yet. Tasty, toasty, and thick, with layers of fig, melon, pear, and sweet cracker. **89** —*P.G. (4/1/2006)*

Waterbrook 2001 Sauvignon Blanc (Columbia Valley (WA)) $14. Waterbrook makes a lovely, lighthearted, citrus- and melon-flavored Sauv Blanc. Crisp and elegant, it manages to be flavorful without being overpowering; it's a delightful summer sipping wine that will add zip to almost anything you serve it with. **88** —*P.G. (9/1/2002)*

Waterbrook 1998 Sauvignon Blanc (Columbia Valley (WA)) $8. 89 Best Buy *(6/1/2000)*

Waterbrook 2000 Klipsun Vineyard Sauvignon Blanc (Red Mountain) $9. This is the last vintage that Waterbrook will bottle a Sauvignon Blanc, because the fruit from this Washington vineyard is in such demand that a budget-priced bottling is no longer possible. So grab this fresh, succulentvivid and bracing wine by the case and enjoy each every sip. you may not see its like for another millenium. **88** —*P.G. (11/15/2001)*

Waterbrook 1999 Klipsun Vineyard Sauvignon Blanc (Columbia Valley (WA)) $8. Future vintages of this wine will bear the new Red Mountain appellation, for that is where Klipsun is located. Waterbrook does the grapes proud: This is a juicy, ripe white wine bursting with scents and flavors of fresh fruits, cut grass, light spice and even some toasted coconut in the extended finish. **90 Best Buy** —*P.G. (6/1/2001)*

Waterbrook 2004 Syrah (Columbia Valley (WA)) $21. The blend includes 4% Grenache and 2% Viognier, which bring some lovely nuances to this spicy effort. Bright citrusy aromas lead into spicy wild red fruits. Whiffs of smoke, toffee, and a bit of caramel add intrigue. Fairly light, but nicely rendered and persistent through a clean, refreshing finish. **88** —*P.G. (4/1/2006)*

Waterbrook 2002 Syrah (Columbia Valley (WA)) $20. There's plenty of color here, and scents of citrus and toast, but the fruit is quite tart and light, lacking any of the flesh that makes Syrah such a crowd-pleaser. This hits the palate with a crisp, clean, thin seam of flavor, balanced but quite light. **86** —*P.G. (11/15/2004)*

Waterbrook 2004 Viognier (Columbia Valley (WA)) $17. Easily one of the best Viogniers of the vintage, this juicy, leesy wine is ripe with crisp, fragrant tangerine, guava, and tropical fruits. Luscious, tart, and snappy, it is plenty ripe without excessive alcohol or any hint of bitterness. **91** —*P.G. (4/1/2006)*

Waterbrook 2001 Viognier (Columbia Valley (WA)) $20. Sweetly perfumed with citrus blossoms, this is a juicy, mouthfilling wine with ripe citrus, melon, and light tropical flavors. The wine fills the palate and lingers, adding hints of anise and mineral to the delicious fruit as it winds through a long, sinuous finish. **90** —*P.G. (9/1/2002)*

WATERS

Waters 2004 Interlude Red Bordeaux Blend (Columbia Valley (WA)) $25. Roughly half Cab, half Merlot with a splash of Cab Franc, this excellent Bordeaux blend comes on with well-ripened fruit, pretty cherry flavors accented with barrel notes of kahlùa, espresso, and smoke. Concentrated and smooth throughout, it is the star of this new winery's first lineup of wines. **91** —*P.G. (6/1/2006)*

Waters 2003 Cabernet Sauvignon (Walla Walla (WA)) $38. Borderline funky with somewhat quirky, but interesting scents of tea, cola, licorice, plums, vanilla, and spice. It flattens out in the mouth; the interesting suggestions of nuanced flavors don't translate from nose to tongue, but still it is a flavorful, intriguing first effort. **88** —*P.G. (6/1/2006)*

WATERS CREST

Waters Crest 2004 Chardonnay (North Fork of Long Island) $16. Smells of yellow Runts, with a brambly edge. Like the '04 Private Reserve Chardonnay, this wine doesn't lack in body, but the flavors are diminished. Salted yellow fruits die out quickly, leaving nothing behind. **80** —*M.D. (8/1/2006)*

Waters Crest 2004 Private Reserve Chardonnay (North Fork of Long Island) $25. An interesting wine, in that it doesn't lack for body (it's weighty enough), just flavor. Aromas of toast, marshmallow, and apple seem to fade on the palate, finishing soft and short. **81** —*J.C. (3/1/2006)*

Waters Crest 2004 Private Reserve Merlot (North Fork of Long Island) $35. Despite struggling with some white wines, Jim Waters has hit a home run with this reserve Merlot. A light grapey color hides a complex array of blueberry, pie crust, mushroom, rubber, mint, and even sausage aromas. Young and vibrant, with ripe tannins and good acidic backing, there is plenty of wood which needs another year to integrate. Underneath is grapey fruit and mushroom, finishing solidly with graham cracker. **89** —*M.D. (12/1/2006)*

WATERSTONE

Waterstone 2003 Cabernet Sauvignon (Napa Valley) $24. Tastes overripe and hot, with a raisiny, stewed prune edge to the otherwise pleasant black currant and cherry flavors. Too bad, because the tannic structure is very nice. That cooked taste is not going to age out. **82** —*S.H. (5/1/2006)*

Waterstone 2002 Cabernet Sauvignon (Napa Valley) $20. Shows an herbaceous, earthy element that dilutes the fruity flavors, and this is compounded by tough tannins that lock in on the finish. Beef, lamb, or similar fare will coax out the underlying sweetness. **85** —*S.H. (6/1/2005)*

Waterstone 2001 Cabernet Sauvignon (Napa Valley) $20. There's a ton of ripe black currant, cassis, and cherry fruit in this well-ripened wine. It also possesses smooth, complex tannins and a good mouthfeel. Really sweet and tasty sipping. **87** —*S.H. (10/1/2004)*

Waterstone 2004 Chardonnay (Carneros) $18. Distinct for its powerfully intense lemondrop and lime pie flavors, this Chard also is rich and zesty in citrusy acids. Oak plays a supporting role, bringing toast and vanilla accents. Perfect with shellfish, especially cracked crab. **89** —*S.H. (5/1/2006)*

Waterstone 2002 Chardonnay (Carneros) $18. Citrusy, oaky, and leesy, with high acidity. This is a sleek, streamlined Chard whose lemon and green apple flavors are enriched with smoke and vanilla. **86** —*S.H. (12/31/2004)*

Waterstone 2003 Pinot Noir (Carneros) $20. Here's a nice, easy Pinot for everyday drinking. It's dry and elegant, with an earthiness to the cherry, rhubarb, and cola flavors. Drink this spicy wine now. **85** —*S.H. (7/1/2006)*

Waterstone 2002 Pinot Noir (Carneros) $18. This dry wine has cherry and tobacco flavors and a solid dose of sweet oak. It has a silky mouthfeel and adequate acidity. A good by-the-glass restaurant wine, it will be versatile at the table. **84** —*S.H. (10/1/2005)*

Waterstone 2001 Pinot Noir (Carneros) $18. Marked by the cherry, cola, and peppery spice flavors and silky tannins that characterize the Carneros, this light-bodied wine is also a good value. It's not a blockbuster, but has plenty of charm and some complexity. **86** —*S.H. (10/1/2004)*

Waterstone 2002 Sauvignon Blanc (Napa Valley) $12. Clean and tart with acidity, but it's basically flavored water, with just a trace of squeezed lime. **83** —*S.H. (10/1/2004)*

WATTLE CREEK

Wattle Creek 2002 Cabernet Sauvignon (Alexander Valley) $50. Good Cab from a hot vintage in a hot valley. The wine sure is ripe, with cassis and plum flavors dusted with cocoa, and dry, with enough tannins to leave the palate puckery. It straddles the line between drink-me-now and a more complex age-me, without resolving the issue. **88** —*S.H. (9/1/2006)*

Wattle Creek 1997 Cabernet Sauvignon (Sonoma County) $50. 90 *(11/1/2000)*

Wattle Creek 1995 Cabernet Sauvignon (Sonoma County) $50. Solid black currant and cedar aromas and flavors predominate in this dry, well-structured red. Toasty oak complements dark, dusty Alexander Valley fruit. The wine finishes elegantly, with spicy notes and ripe, even tannins. Ready to drink now. **90** *(6/1/2001)*

Wattle Creek 2000 Alexander Valley Cabernet Sauvignon (Alexander Valley) $47. Notable for the soft, velvety texture that glides over the

palate and leaves behind a pleasant scour of tannin. The flavors are restrained but elegant, suggesting black currant, cherry, and sage. This balanced wine is feminine in its charm. **89** —*S.H. (8/1/2004)*

Wattle Creek 2004 Chardonnay (Mendocino County) $26. Opens with a burst of charry, toasty oak, then settles down to show ripe white peach, pineapple, caramel, and tapioca flavors. The grapes are from the Yorkville Highlands. **85** —*S.H. (11/15/2006)*

Wattle Creek 2000 Chardonnay (Alexander Valley) $25. Creamy smooth, with hints of cinnamon and spice, vanilla, peaches, pear, and citrus flavors. Quite viscous, with a lush, fat finish. **88** —*J.M. (12/15/2002)*

Wattle Creek 1999 Chardonnay (Sonoma County) $30. Smooth apple-pear and buttery, toasty aromas open to like flavors. That fruit core is offset by mild mango accents and lots of spicy oak, which continue through the long finish. For fans of rich, oaky full-bodied Chardonnay. **87** *(6/1/2001)*

Wattle Creek 2001 Alexander Valley Chardonnay (Alexander Valley) $24. Very oaky and leesy, with crisp acidity and a good structure, this wine would benefit from more fruity concentration. The peaches and cream flavors disappear quickly on the watery finish. **84** —*S.H. (8/1/2004)*

Wattle Creek 2003 The Triple Play Red Wine Blend Rhône Red Blend (Yorkville Highlands) $28. I never much cared for Bordeaux wines from this coolish appellation. Now, with this new blend of Syrah, Petite Sirah, and Viognier, Wattle Creek is trying the Northern Rhône, with success. The wine shows some rustic toughness, but there's a gorgeous core of cherry and blackberry fruit. A wine to watch. **87** —*S.H. (12/31/2006)*

Wattle Creek 2005 Sauvignon Blanc (Mendocino) $17. Too grassy and feline for me, an acidic, dry wine that reeks of hay and nettles. They put some new French oak on, but it doesn't really make things any richer. **82** —*S.H. (12/31/2006)*

Wattle Creek 2004 Sauvignon Blanc (Mendocino) $15. Strong, distinctive, and powerful, this Sauvignon Blanc explodes with gooseberry, lime zest, grapefruit, vanilla, and wildflower flavors. It's light-bodied and very dry, with super acidity that makes it clean and vibrant. **86** —*S.H. (12/1/2005)*

Wattle Creek 2003 Sauvignon Blanc (Mendocino) $18. This is really a beautiful Sauvignon Blanc. The fruit is exceptionally expressive, filling the mouth with sweet citrus, fig, cantaloupe, and spice, wrapped in a honeyed texture. The acidity is perfect, all bright and zesty, and provides needed dryness and balance. **88** —*S.H. (8/1/2004)*

Wattle Creek 2001 Sauvignon Blanc (Mendocino County) $18. Pretty scents of grapefruit, green apple, and wild flowers rise up from the glass, followed by tasty citrus in the form of orange, lemon, and grapefruit. Some oak adds texture and character to the mix, while chalkiness provides grip to the finish. **89** *(8/1/2002)*

Wattle Creek 1999 Sauvignon Blanc (Sonoma County) $20. A fig, herb, and grapefruit bouquet sets the stage. The fig element becomes a more nut-like flavor on the palate and the wine has a round, slightly viscous texture, in the full style of the other Wattle Creek whites. Finishes dry, with just a hint of tartness. **87** *(6/1/2001)*

Wattle Creek 2001 Shiraz (Alexander Valley) $25. Has some pretty dried spice notes, particularly on the finish, but also a whole lot of drying, oaky flavors backed by tart berries. Rather lean and ungenerous. **84** *(9/1/2005)*

Wattle Creek 1998 Shiraz (Sonoma County) $39. Both Old and New World elements are evident in this Shiraz. The round, easy mouthfeel and nose of berry, chocolate, and cumin say "New World." The palate has more Old World notes of leather, game, and dry licorice surrounding the fruit core. Dark oak, licorice, and tart berry flavors play out on the complex finish. **89** *(6/1/2001)*

Wattle Creek 2000 Alexander Valley Shiraz (Alexander Valley) $35. They called it Shiraz instead of Syrah, I guess, because it's a young, jammy wine with lots of forward fruit. Those blackberry and plum flavors are accompanied by some pretty fierce tannins, although the acids are soft and low. At this price, you expect more breed and finesse. **85** —*S.H. (8/1/2004)*

Wattle Creek 2005 Viognier (Alexander Valley) $31. The grapes come from the northern part of the valley, the warmest spot, but the first thing

USA

you notice is the acidity. It's citrusy-juicy, and makes those flowery citrus and apple flavors taste almost like minerally Pinot Grigio. It's an elegant Viognier, crafted for food. 87 —*S.H. (12/31/2006)*

Wattle Creek 2000 Viognier (Alexander Valley) $25. Hardly a cookie-cutter wine; this one features sharp aromatics of white grapefruit and pineapple as well as some thistle. The mouthfeel is heavy, as are the flavors of orange, tangerine, and banana. When all is said and done it tastes much like a Tropicana juice blend, maybe more so than it should. 85 —*M.S. (3/1/2003)*

Wattle Creek 1999 Viognier (Sonoma County) $24. Light floral, orange blossom, and peach aromas open this large-scaled white. The weighty palate shows mild orange and spice flavors. Has plenty of zip for its relative heft, and finishes long, with tangy pepper notes. 88 *(6/1/2001)*

Wattle Creek 2002 Alexander Valley Viognier (Alexander Valley) $24. Soft, luscious and creamy smooth, with a caressing texture that conveys exotic flavors of tropical fruits, wildflowers, butter, sweet tree nut, vanilla, and orange zest. This dry wine has complexity and versatility at the table. 89 —*S.H. (8/1/2004)*

WATTS

Watts 1999 Old Vine Zinfandel (Lodi) $14. From vines planted in 1937, this grower-turned-vintner family has crafted a first-rate Zin that perfectly reflects its terroir. It's dry, bold, and peppery, with brambly fruit that has a wild edge, and lots of alcohol. This value wine will benefit from mid-term aging. 90 **Best Buy** —*S.H. (9/1/2002)*

WAUGH CELLARS

Waugh Cellars 2002 Cabernet Sauvignon (Napa Valley) $45. Ripe and juicy, with upfront blackberry, cherry, cocoa, and cassis flavors that finish thoroughly dry, with a trace of raisins. This nice Cab has some gritty tannins to cut through meats and cheeses. 85 —*S.H. (4/1/2006)*

Waugh Cellars 2005 Indindoli Vineyard Chardonnay (Russian River Valley) $30. Classic RRV Chard, bright in minerally acids, with a spectrum of flavors including pineapples, green apples, peaches, and papayas. Lots of spicy, toasty oak, too. 88 —*S.H. (12/31/2006)*

Waugh Cellars 2004 Indindoli Vineyard Chardonnay (Russian River Valley) $30. Not quite as rich or complex as the Reserve, but close on its heels, with well-ripened tropical fruit flavors accented by spicy, toasty oak. This is a classic California cool-climate Chard, with bright, zesty acidity. 89 —*S.H. (7/1/2006)*

Waugh Cellars 2003 Indindoli Vineyard Chardonnay (Russian River Valley) $28. Not much going on. Clean and dry, with watery flavors of apples and oak. 83 —*S.H. (2/1/2005)*

Waugh Cellars 2002 Indindoli Vineyard Chardonnay (Russian River Valley) $28. A rather lean, citrusy Chard, and with high acidity. There was no malolactic fermentation. Flavors of limes, honeydew, and apples drink clean and bright, and there is little oak influence beyond the creamy texture. 86 —*S.H. (12/1/2003)*

Waugh Cellars 2004 Indindoli Vineyard Reserve Chardonnay (Russian River Valley) $40. Impressive for the enormous depth and range of the fruit, which is a blast of pineapple custard, kiwi, Key lime pie, and the ripest, sweetest white peach, all of it coated in fine, toasty oak. This is a big Chardonnay that calls for rich fare, like lobster. 91 —*S.H. (7/1/2006)*

Waugh Cellars 2003 Susy's Cuvée Sauvignon Blanc (Napa Valley) $20. A pleasant sipper, with good acids and forward flavors of passion fruit, grapefruit, and figs. It has a creamy texture and a long finish. 85 —*S.H. (2/1/2005)*

Waugh Cellars 2002 Susy's Cuvée Sauvignon Blanc (Napa Valley) $24. Pleasant and easy, with no special complexity, but offering a nice mélange of dry lemon and lime flavors. There's a creamy texture from barrel fermentation, and a good spicy mouthfeel. 86 —*S.H. (12/15/2003)*

Waugh Cellars 2001 Susy's Cuvée Sauvignon Blanc (Napa Valley) $18. So ripe and soft, it's hard to believe this is Sauvignon Blanc. Anise-tinged guava, pear, and other ripe tree fruits mingle on the palate, finishing gently. Its delicate and low-acid nature argues for drinking soon, probably on its own. 86 *(8/1/2002)*

Waugh Cellars 2004 Zinfandel (Dry Creek Valley) $38. Wild, briary, brambly, and semi-sweet from this hot vintage, this is a Zin made for easy drinking with roasts and cheeses. It's a big, hot wine, with some raisiny flavors mixed in with the cherries and spices. 83 —*S.H. (12/31/2006)*

Waugh Cellars 2003 Zinfandel (Dry Creek Valley) $38. You'll find exotic flavors in this ripe wine, from the usual blackberries and cherries to espresso, anise, and baked pie crust. It's soft and voluptuous, but quite sweet, almost off-dry, which lowers the score. 85 —*S.H. (5/1/2006)*

Waugh Cellars 2002 Zinfandel (Dry Creek Valley) $35. Overtly sweet, with Porty flavors, but clean. If this is your style, enjoy. 82 —*S.H. (2/1/2005)*

Waugh Cellars 2001 Zinfandel (Sonoma) $28. Pretty racy acidity starts this one off, with earthy, bright, brambly blackberry, cherry, and spice notes at the fore. Zippy on the finish, too. 83 *(11/1/2003)*

WEDELL CELLARS

Wedell Cellars 1999 Chardonnay (Edna Valley) $24. This is a lean and young wine, whose flavors tend toward grapefruits and limes. There's also a streak of mineral and slate, and the finish is very dry and acid tart. Clearly from a cool climate, it may gain additional complexities in the cellar. 86 —*S.H. (6/1/2003)*

Wedell Cellars 2002 Hillside Vineyard Chardonnay (Edna Valley) $45. Richly creamy, the flavors suggest dried peaches and mangoes and a buttery, vanilla-rich pineapple crème brûlée, with a complex spicebox finish. 95 —*S.H. (7/1/2006)*

Wedell Cellars 2003 Pinot Noir (Arroyo Grande Valley) $60. Here's a Pinot that stands out even among its appellative peers. The usual cherry and cola fruit is there, but there's a thyme-and-lavender edge that calls to mind certain southern French wines, and a savage, sweet leather and animal character that practically cries out for duck or game. The wine is very dry, fairly oaky, and young in raw, juicy acidity. Give it until 2007 to soften. 94 **Editors' Choice** —*S.H. (11/1/2006)*

Wedell Cellars 2000 Pinot Noir (Edna Valley) $30. Tastes strong and distinctive, with well-etched white pepper, black raspberry, tobacco, and herb flavors. This earthy wine feels silky smooth on the palate, with crisp acids, but is a little one-dimensional for the price. 85 —*S.H. (7/1/2003)*

Wedell Cellars 2002 Hillside Vineyard Pinot Noir (Edna Valley) $95. Made from the Dijon clones so popular in the mid-'90s, this is a tremendous wine. It's dark and vigorous, with massive cherry pie, raspberry tart, white chocolate fudge, and coffee flavors, properly dry and rich in fine tannins. I have given it a point less than Wedell's outstanding '03 Pinot simply because this wine is so rich, so dense that it's lost a bit of varietal character. But there's no denying its deliciousness. 93 —*S.H. (11/1/2006)*

Wedell Cellars 2000 Hillside Vineyard Pinot Noir (Edna Valley) $90. One of the best Central Coast Pinots in memory. Incredibly rich and full bodied, filled with juicy flavors of blackberry, cherry, raspberry, tobacco, smoke, vanilla, and earth. Yet the body is delicate and light as air on the palate. The spicy aftertaste lasts for a full minute. 92 —*S.H. (7/1/2003)*

Wedell Cellars 2001 Viognier (Edna Valley) $21. California whites don't get much fruitier or more fragrant. Just packed with juicy flavors of white peach, nectarine, fig, and vanilla. Despite its size, it never loses sight of balance and elegance. 90 —*S.H. (5/1/2003)*

WEDGE MOUNTAIN

Wedge Mountain 2003 Dry White Riesling (Columbia Valley (WA)) $14. Nice effort in a bone-dry style; it's immaculate, crisply fruity, with spice and citrus peel lingering through the extended finish. 88 —*P.G. (12/15/2004)*

WEINSTOCK CELLARS

Weinstock Cellars 2001 Cellar Select Cabernet Sauvignon (Napa Valley) $20. Rather raw, with stemmy, woody flavors next to the riper cherries and blackberries, and a bitter finish. Not going anywhere, so drink now. 83 —*S.H. (8/1/2005)*

Weinstock Cellars 1997 Chardonnay (California) $11. This medium-weight offering shows caramel and butterscotch aromas, slightly sweet apple-pear flavors, and a soft, generous mouthfeel. Smooth vanilla and a touch of toast show on the finish. 86 *(4/1/2001)*

USA

Weinstock Cellars 2003 Cellar Select Chardonnay (Sonoma County) $14. If you're looking for a kosher Chard, try this one. It's a fine wine, rich in fruit, well-oaked, and balanced, with the creamy, full-bodied mouthfeel you want in this varietal. The peach custard, pineapple, and kiwi flavors are simply delicious. **88**—*S.H. (5/1/2006)*

Weinstock Cellars 2001 Cellar Select Chardonnay (Sonoma County) $15. Oaky and fruity, with a pleasant peaches-and-cream texture to the peach, pear, and pineapple flavors. This is a nice everyday Chard with some fancy edges. **85**—*S.H. (8/1/2005)*

Weinstock Cellars 2004 Cellar Select Sauvignon Blanc (Central Coast) $14. Everything about this wine is good except for the thinness. It's dry and tart, with crisp acids framing lemon and lime, fig, and melon flavors, and a fine, clean finish. You find yourself liking it so much, you wish it had a little more depth and length. **84**—*S.H. (5/1/2006)*

Weinstock Cellars 2002 Cellar Select Zinfandel (Lodi) $18. Distinctly Zinny in the wild blackberry and raspberry flavors and that briary, brambly mouthfeel, with its overtones of pepper. This is a medium-bodied wine with very soft tannins. It's dry, but there's a creamy cocoa taste on the finish. **85**—*S.H. (8/1/2005)*

WEISINGER'S OF ASHLAND

Weisinger's of Ashland 2000 Petite Pompadour Bordeaux Blend (Rogue Valley) $27. This Bordeaux blend features charred, barrel-driven aromas along with leather and black fruit aromas. The palate is snappy and acidic, with plum and raspberry flavors poking through a heavy coating of concrete tannins. The finish is equally tight and grippy, and here the tannins are even more pronounced. Very tight and hard; time in the cellar could be the prescription. **85**—*M.S. (8/1/2003)*

Weisinger's of Ashland 1999 Petite Pompadour Bordeaux Blend (Rogue Valley) $25. Weisinger's Bordeaux blend red is named after its Pompadour Vineyard. The '99 is a step up from the previous vintage; riper grapes and none of the veggie scents. An earthy nose of black fruits and ash leads into a tart, tannic wine that equally mixes flavors of grape and soil. **85**—*P.G. (4/1/2002)*

Weisinger's of Ashland 1999 Pompadour Vineyard Cabernet Franc (Rogue Valley) $25. This is exceptionally dark, with a sappy, vinous nose showing black cherry, smoke, sweet chocolate, some stem, and a hint of dill. There is more than a hint of pickle barrel, and lots of acid, chalky tannins **84**—*P.G. (8/1/2002)*

Weisinger's of Ashland 1999 Chardonnay (Rogue Valley) $15. There is an attractive, fresh scent of herbs and clean, crisp apples, which leads into a firm-structured palate impression, like biting into a ripe fresh piece of fruit. Ten percent was barrel-fermented, adding just the right touch of oak. **87**—*P.G. (2/1/2002)*

Weisinger's of Ashland 1999 Gewürztraminer (Rogue Valley) $15. Tart, apricot/white peach flavors offer no real hint of varietal perfume, though classic Gewürz flavors can be found in the lightly floral finish. High acid wine. **85**—*P.G. (8/1/2002)*

Weisinger's of Ashland 1997 Merlot (Rogue Valley) $19. **83**—*P.G. (6/1/2000)*

Weisinger's of Ashland 1999 Pompadour Vineyard Merlot (Rogue Valley) $20. From the winery's premiere vineyard comes this inky, earthy wine with woodsy aromas. Flavors of plum and pie cherry dominate the fruit, along with a definite smoky, charred flavor, perhaps from overroasted barrels. **85**—*P.G. (8/1/2002)*

Weisinger's of Ashland NV Mescolare Lot 12 Red Blend (Rogue Valley) $19. Spicy and green at first, with an aromatic resemblance to salsa and bell peppers. In the mouth, that bell pepper character never goes away, but with time it becomes more subdued as powerful berry fruit and chocolate come on strong. The finish, however, is hard as nails, courtesy of fierce tannins, thus an affinity for tannin is required to get much from this unusual wine. **83**—*M.S. (8/1/2003)*

Weisinger's of Ashland NV Mescolare Red Wine Red Blend (Oregon) $18. A proprietary Cab/Pinot/Nebbiolo blend. Flavors are light and the tannins are tough: a grapey, cherry-candy start that finishes with serious toast and tannin. The mid-palate simply isn't there, and can't support the thick, tannic finish. **84**—*P.G. (8/1/2002)*

Weisinger's of Ashland 1999 50% CH / 50% SEM Sémillon-Chardonnay (Rogue Valley) $15. Some nice toasty flavors underscore generic fruit. When all is said and done, it is a neutral, crisp white wine enlivened with a bit of spice and toast from the barrel aging. Still, a bit of veggie/canned pea flavor dampens the finish. **84**—*P.G. (8/1/2002)*

WELLINGTON

Wellington 2004 Noir de Noirs Alicante Bouschet (Sonoma Valley) $25. For well over a century, this rugged old French variety has produced a clean, full-bodied, and dry red wine in California. It can't quite overcome its country-style character, but has tons of personality, and should age well for 15 years. **87**—*S.H. (3/1/2006)*

Wellington 2003 Old Vines Noir de Noirs Alicante Bouschet (Sonoma Valley) $25. These old vines have yielded an extraordinarily dark, dense wine, the quintessence of black cherry flavors, but weighty with currants. It's extremely dry and pretty tannic, with a puckery grapeskin finish, and should age well. Try this interesting wine as an alternative to Zinfandel. **92**—*S.H. (6/1/2005)*

Wellington 2001 Cabernet Sauvignon (Sonoma Valley) $20. A good wine, with honest varietal flavors and easy tannins. Turns dry and rich, with upfront black currant fruit flavors lightly seasoned with oak. **85**—*S.H. (5/1/2005)*

Wellington 2000 Cabernet Sauvignon (Sonoma Valley) $25. Aromas of black currants and smoky oak, with an attractive note of cured French olives. In the mouth, there's ripe blackberry fruit. The tannins are strong, and acidity is soft and low. It's not an ager. **86**—*S.H. (12/15/2003)*

Wellington 2001 Hulen Vineyard Cabernet Sauvignon (Dry Creek Valley) $28. A very nice, well-structured Cab. It has blackberry flavors with a rich earthiness, and a unique note of blueberries; the oak is light and subtle. Finishes with a scour of rustic tannins. At its best now. **88**—*S.H. (6/1/2005)*

Wellington 2000 Hulen Vineyard Cabernet Sauvignon (Dry Creek Valley) $28. Has those gritty but fine Dry Creek tannins, and a slightly wild and woolly edge to the currant and blackberry flavors, which suggests midterm aging. Very gentle in the mouth, with a good, rich finish. Crisp acids stimulate the palate throughout. **86**—*S.H. (12/15/2003)*

Wellington 2001 Mohrhardt Ridge Cabernet Sauvignon (Sonoma County) $22. Here's a plush, well-ripened Cab with forward flavors of black currants, cocoa, and oak. It has velvety tannins and finishes with an overall impression of sweetness. Best in its youth. **90**—*S.H. (5/1/2005)*

Wellington 1999 Mohrhardt Ridge Cabernet Sauvignon (Sonoma County) $22. What rich flavors there are here. With this fabulous vintage that ripened the grapes perfectly, it would be hard not to find plush blackberry, cassis, and other herb and spice flavors. The tannins are just a bit brash and bold, suggesting a year or so of aging to calm things down. **87**—*S.H. (8/1/2003)*

Wellington 1997 Mohrhardt Ridge Vineyard Cabernet Sauvignon (Sonoma County) $18. **88** *(9/1/2000)*

Wellington 2000 Mohrhardt Vineyard Cabernet Sauvignon (Sonoma County) $22. Odd that this wine costs less than Wellington's Sonoma Valley bottling, because while it shares the same qualities of cassis, smoke, and a smooth texture, it's a shade richer and more concentrated. Feels absolutely beautiful as it slides across the palate, all the way through the pleasing aftertaste. **92 Editors' Choice**—*S.H. (11/15/2003)*

Wellington 2003 Chardonnay (Sonoma Valley) $16. A little heavy in the mouth, this earthy Chardonnay also features peach flavors and a dollop of toasty oak. It's totally dry and modest in alcohol, and might improve over the next year. **84**—*S.H. (3/1/2006)*

Wellington 2002 Chardonnay (Sonoma County) $16. A good, common wine, with fruity flavors and an earthiness to it. Finishes sweet and soft. **84**—*S.H. (5/1/2005)*

Wellington 2001 Chardonnay (Sonoma County) $16. Intensely oaky and ripe, almost dessert-like with its crème brûlée, sweet pineapple tart, and vanilla custard flavors and rich, creamy texture. **87**—*S.H. (6/1/2004)*

Wellington 2000 Chardonnay (Sonoma Valley) $17. Strikes a middle of the road note, offering solid varietal notes of apples, peaches, and pears

USA

wrapped in toasty oak, with crisp acids. Feels round and smooth in the mouth, and finishes with a slight bitterness. **86** —*S.H. (6/1/2003)*

Wellington 2001 Reserve Chardonnay (Russian River Valley) $26. Not big and super-oaky, not a blockbuster, but offers a little something for everyone. Polished, pretty apple, pear, and tropical fruit flavors, crisp, fresh acidity and a nice smoky layering of sweet oak make for smooth drinking. **89** —*S.H. (6/1/2004)*

Wellington 2000 Estate Grown Marsanne (Sonoma County) $20. Odd, opening with guava, guacamole, and banana-like aromas that verge into soft, runny cheese, and turning bitter on the palate. Almost Sauvignon Blanc-like with its tart, grapefruity flavors and acidic bite. **83** —*S.H. (6/1/2003)*

Wellington 1997 Merlot (Sonoma County) $18. 88 —*L.W. (12/31/1999)*

Wellington 2002 Merlot (Sonoma Valley) $18. Young and fairly tannic now, although quite soft in acids, this is a lush Syrah, with powerful cherry-berry flavors that have a complex edge of coffee and leather. It turns a little sweet on the finish. **85** —*S.H. (3/1/2006)*

Wellington 2001 Estate Merlot (Sonoma Valley) $18. Lots to like here, with a chocolatey, creamy smooth mouthfeel that carries rich, ripe flavors of black cherries and cocoa. **86** —*S.H. (5/1/2005)*

Wellington 2001 Old Vines Port (Sonoma Valley) $14. Drinks gluey, with a flavor like artificially sweetened coffee and cocoa. Carignan and Syrah. **82** —*S.H. (6/1/2005)*

Wellington 1997 Côtes de Sonoma Old Vines Red Blend (Sonoma Valley) $18. 88 —*S.H. (6/1/1999)*

Wellington 2001 Reserve Victory Red Blend (Sonoma County) $32. Quite rich and extracted in cassis and chocolate flavors, with ultra-smooth tannins. Too soft to age for any length of time, and it's a little sweet and gooey, like a liquid candy bar. **86** —*S.H. (5/1/2005)*

Wellington 2002 Roussanne (Sonoma County) $18. As white wines go, this is tasty enough, with semi-sweet fruity flavors and a good balance of cream and acidity. **84** —*S.H. (5/1/2005)*

Wellington 2001 Roussanne (Russian River Valley) $20. Another bizarre wine from this producer, similarly marked by cheesy aromas only partially relieved by peaches. Has a buttery texture and hint of melon but the tart acidity and dryness are more like a Fume Blanc. Is there a bacterial problem in this winery? **83** —*S.H. (6/1/2003)*

Wellington 1998 Sauvignon Blanc (Sonoma Mountain) $14. 87 —*L.W. (3/1/2000)*

Wellington 2003 Sauvignon Blanc (Sonoma Valley) $14. Slightly sweet in spearmint gum and lemonade flavors, this wine has decent acidity. It leaves the mouth clean and refreshed. **84** —*S.H. (6/1/2005)*

Wellington 2001 Sauvignon Blanc (Sonoma Mountain) $14. Decent everyday fare, a grassy wine with extremely dry flavors of grapefruit and a bit of complexity. It's well made and has some elegance. Turns tart and bitter on the finish, with the taste of citrus rind. **84** —*S.H. (7/1/2003)*

Wellington 1997 Syrah (Russian River Valley) $17. 86 —*S.H. (6/1/1999)*

Wellington 2002 Syrah (Sonoma Valley) $18. Young and fairly tannic now, although quite soft in acids, this is a lush Syrah, with powerful cherry-berry flavors that have a complexing edge of coffee and leather. It turns a little sweet on the finish. **85** —*S.H. (3/1/2006)*

Wellington 2000 Syrah (Sonoma County) $20. Dark and thick, opening with aromas of freshly crushed white pepper and blackberries. Not bad in the mouth, with some pretty flavors of blackberry and tobacco, but lean. Given the tannins and the velvety texture, it longs for depth and concentration that aren't there. **85** —*S.H. (12/15/2003)*

Wellington 2002 Reserve Syrah (Sonoma Valley) $28. This is a wine that really merits its Reserve status. It's big and rich in dark stone fruit and coffee-mocha flavors, with a velvety texture and thick but refined tannins. Bone dry and soft, which probably limits its ageability, but this is one you want to drink young, anyway. **90** —*S.H. (3/1/2006)*

Wellington 1997 Viognier (Sonoma County) $18. 87 —*S.H. (6/1/1999)*

Wellington 2001 Timbervine Ranch Viognier (Russian River Valley) $20. A featureless, almost barren wine, with such lean, watered down citrus fruit flavors that the main palate impression is of acids and alcohol. Bears

nothing in common with Viognier, and it's amazing how they could have missed out on all the fruit. **82** —*S.H. (6/1/2003)*

Wellington 1998 Zinfandel (Russian River Valley) $16. 88 —*S.H. (5/1/2000)*

Wellington 1997 Zinfandel (Russian River Valley) $16. 87 —*L.W. (2/1/2000)*

Wellington 2001 Zinfandel (Sonoma County) $18. Full and rich on the palate, the wine shows plenty of sweet oak up front, backed by ripe plum, raspberry, and cherry flavors. Toast, spice, chocolate, and coffee flavors carry through the bright finish. **89** *(11/1/2003)*

Wellington 2000 Zinfandel (Sonoma Valley) $22. Decent, everyday Zin, with wild berry and earthy flavors wrapped in thick but easy tannins. Thankfully, it's fully dry, although the alcohol is on the high side, and the wine feels hot in the mouth. There's a sharp tartness in the finish. **84** —*S.H. (9/1/2003)*

Wellington 2003 100 Year Old Vines Zinfandel (Sonoma Valley) $30. Fully dry, at the cost of 15.8% alcohol, this enormous Zin wears its size well. There's a Port-like, raisiny note, but it's more of a subtle seasoning than a takeover, and the wine is balanced in its own distinctively Zinny way. **89** —*S.H. (3/1/2006)*

WENTE

Wente 2004 Cabernet Sauvignon (Livermore Valley) $12. Grown in Wente's home territory east of San Francisco, this wine shows ripe blackberry, plum, coffee, and herb flavors, with thick, dusty tannins. It's very dry, with real elegance. Good value from this venerable winery. **86** —*S.H. (12/31/2006)*

Wente 2001 Cabernet Sauvignon (Livermore Valley) $14. Dry and earthy, with a likeable core of ripe currant and oak. The tannins are sweet and smooth. The more this wine sits in the glass, the better it gets. **87** —*S.H. (12/31/2004)*

Wente 2000 Cabernet Sauvignon (Livermore Valley) $13. Modest in its aspirations, with proper aromas of berries, currants, and herbs, and flavors that are similar, but thin. Feels dry and clean in the mouth, and finishes with some astringency. **83** —*S.H. (12/31/2003)*

Wente 1997 Cabernet Sauvignon (Livermore Valley) $11. 88 Best Buy —*S.H. (12/15/2000)*

Wente 2000 Charles Wetmore Reserve Cabernet Sauvignon (Livermore Valley) $27. Wente's top offering is rather thin and herbal, and the oak overlay does little to help. There are some modest blackberry and cherry flavors, but the absence of fruit leaves the astringent tannins and alcohol front and center. **84** —*S.H. (3/1/2004)*

Wente 1999 Charles Wetmore Reserve Cabernet Sauvignon (Livermore Valley) $24. At three-plus years, this is still a young, tannic wine, filled with tart youthful acidity. It's not especially drinkable now, but there is a core of blackberry fruit that suggests aging. Try after 2007. **86** —*S.H. (3/1/2003)*

Wente 1998 Charles Wetmore Reserve Cabernet Sauvignon (Livermore Valley) $24. Another successful vintage for this very fine wine. Rich and jammy-candied, it's got lavish aromas of blackberry, tobacco, and spice, with smoke and vanilla from medium-charred oak. Balanced with extracted blackberry and cassis flavors and an opulent, smooth texture. Complex and satisfying. **91 Editors' Choice** —*S.H. (12/1/2001)*

Wente 1997 Charles Wetmore Reserve Cabernet Sauvignon (Livermore Valley) $25. 92 —*S.H. (12/15/2000)*

Wente 1996 Charles Wetmore Reserve Cabernet Sauvignon (Livermore Valley) $20. 89 *(1/1/2000)*

Wente 2002 The Nth Degree Cabernet Sauvignon (Livermore Valley) $50. Wente is trying to reinvigorate itself, and this is a step in the right direction. It's solid in varietal character, with black currant and cassis flavors and a rich full-bodiedness that's spiced up with oak. Good now, but its firm tannins suggest mid-term ageability. **88** —*S.H. (11/1/2005)*

Wente 2001 Wetmore Reserve Cabernet Sauvignon (Livermore Valley) $25. Wente's Reserve got real ripe and sweet under its hot sun. The grapes fattened and oozed black currants and chocolate, and the winemaker put on sweet, spicy oak. This is a good, generous wine with sweetly smooth tannins, and it's soft. Drink now. **89** —*S.H. (12/31/2004)*

Wente 1997 Chardonnay (Central Coast) $10. 88 Best Buy *(1/1/2000)*

Wente 2004 Chardonnay (Livermore Valley) $12. I like everything about this wine. Peaches, pineapples, vanilla custard, and buttered toast flavors, crisp acids, a creamy, oaky veneer, a nice, long dry finish—it's all there. It doesn't have the concentrated intensity of greater wines, but it's very nice. **86** —*S.H. (12/31/2006)*

Wente 2001 Chardonnay (San Francisco Bay) $8. A nice Chard from a winery that pioneered it in the Livermore Valley. Has delicate flavors of apples, peaches, apricots, and herbs and is fully dry, with a rich overlay of smoky oak. There's a density and weight in the mouth that are especially impressive at this price. **86** —*S.H. (12/15/2003)*

Wente 2004 Riva Ranch Reserve Chardonnay (Arroyo Seco) $16. Wente, which has sourced this region for years, again has produced a clean, crisp, minerally Chard, with a delicious core of peaches and apricots refreshed by brisk acidity. **89 Editors' Choice** —*S.H. (12/31/2006)*

Wente 2001 Riva Ranch Reserve Chardonnay (Arroyo Seco) $17. This year the wine displays a tight structure of high acidity framing flavors of minerals, stones, and lime. On the finish a rich vein of tropical fruit and spice shows up. This young, steely wine possesses great authority and style, and may be an ager. **88** —*S.H. (8/1/2003)*

Wente 2000 Riva Ranch Reserve Chardonnay (Arroyo Seco) $15. Massively huge flavors of tropical fruits are balanced by crisp acidity, high enough to make the pineapple, guava, and mango flavors shine. New, smoky oak adds the depth to make this wine truly complex and delicious. Big and unctuous, this is a flashy wine meant to complement rich, showy foods. **92 Best Buy** —*S.H. (12/15/2002)*

Wente 1999 Riva Ranch Reserve Chardonnay (Arroyo Seco) $15. From a true Chardonnay pioneer in California, and always a great value, this crisply wine is rich and balanced. The fruit is not weighed down by too much oak, leaving the bright apple and peach flavors to shine through. The finish is long and fruity. **89 Best Buy** —*S.H. (12/31/2001)*

Wente 1998 Riva Ranch Reserve Chardonnay (Arroyo Seco) $15. 85 *(6/1/2000)*

Wente 1997 Riva Ranch Reserve Chardonnay (Arroyo Seco) $14. 88 *(1/1/2000)*

Wente 2003 The Nth Degree Chardonnay (Livermore Valley) $35. Despite the best efforts of a new generation of Wentes to make Chardonnay succeed in Livermore, they can't subdue Mother Nature. It's just too hot out there. This is a decent wine, with good fruit and lots of attention to detail, but it lacks freshness and acidity. **86** —*S.H. (11/1/2005)*

Wente 1997 Merlot (Central Coast) $10. 83 *(1/1/2000)*

Wente 2004 Merlot (Arroyo Seco) $12. This appellation, on the west side of Salinas Valley just below Santa Lucia Highlands, is great for whites. Reds fare less well, especially when the vines are overcropped, as they seem to have been with this thin, acidic Merlot. It shows candied flavors of cherries and mint. **82** —*S.H. (12/31/2006)*

Wente 2001 Merlot (Central Coast) $12. There are plenty of plummy, blackberry and black cherry flavors and it's quite dry, with soft, east tannins and a pinch of tight acidity. Turns a bit thin on the finish. A nice quaffer. **85** —*S.H. (2/1/2004)*

Wente 1999 Crane Ridge Merlot (San Francisco Bay-Livermore Valley) $15. A luscious wine brimming with black cherry, chocolate, plum, licorice, and smoky oak aromas. Wonderfully rich and lush in the mouth, it also has lots of berry fruit flavors in a dry, harmonious package. **91 Best Buy** —*S.H. (11/15/2001)*

Wente 2003 Crane Ridge Reserve Merlot (Livermore Valley) $18. Definitely on the rustic side, showing some overripe, raisiny flavors alongside greener, minty ones, and a sugary sweet finish. A clumsy wine. **80** —*S.H. (12/31/2006)*

Wente 1997 Crane Ridge Reserve Merlot (Livermore Valley) $16. 87 *(1/1/2000)*

Wente 2001 Crane Ridge Vineyard Reserve Merlot (Livermore Valley) $18. Entirely too thin in flavor, as though the vines were stretched to the max.

Despite the dark color the aroma is herbal, and the dill and earth flavors just manage to suggest cherry. These vines await optimal winemaking. 22,200 cases produced. **85** —*S.H. (2/1/2004)*

Wente 2000 Reliz Creek Reserve Pinot Noir (Arroyo Seco) $17. Good, rich Pinot, with flavors and a mouthfeel fans will instantly respond to. Soft, silky tannins drink easy, and slide over the tongue with raspberry, pepper, and tobacco flavors. Acids are just fine, with a bit of tingle on the palate. **88** —*S.H. (2/1/2003)*

Wente 1996 Reliz Creek Reseve Pinot Noir (Arroyo Seco) $15. 85 *(1/1/2000)*

Wente 2005 Riesling (Monterey) $9. There's a place in the market for simple, off-dry wines like this. It has candied peach and pineapple flavors and finishes in a sugary swirl. **82** —*S.H. (12/31/2006)*

Wente 2004 Sauvignon Blanc (Livermore Valley) $9. Fruity and slightly sweet to the point of off-dry, this simple wine has pleasant fig, citrus, and vanilla flavors. Fortunately, it also has good, crisp acidity. **83** —*S.H. (12/31/2006)*

Wente 1999 Sauvignon Blanc (Central Coast) $8. Nice and rich, with plenty of chewy, upfront lemon and lime fruit, and more full-bodied notes from Sémillon. Finishes fruity, spicy, and clean. This is a super food wine. **86 Best Buy** —*S.H. (11/15/2001)*

Wente 2003 Vineyard Selection Sauvignon Blanc (Livermore Valley) $9. Released together with the '02, and a shade more concentrated in grapefruits, with richer notes of figs and honeydew melon. It's a totally dry, clean wine with a zesty finish. **86 Best Buy** —*S.H. (10/1/2005)*

Wente 2002 Vineyard Selection Sauvignon Blanc (Livermore Valley) $9. One of the drier whites recently, as tart as biting into a fresh grapefruit. Cleanses the palate and is refreshing in its own right. **85 Best Buy** —*S.H. (10/1/2005)*

Wente 2002 The Nth Degree Shiraz (Livermore Valley) $45. I like the fruit in this new label from Wente. It's powerfully ripe and forward in cherries, blackberries, and raspberries that finish fruity sweet, although the wine is balanced and dry. Defines the modern style in international red wines. **87** —*S.H. (9/1/2005)*

Wente 2004 Syrah (Livermore Valley) $12. A little sharp and green minty in the mouth, this Syrah is very dry. As far as fruit goes, it has modest cherry-berry flavors, but it's really a pretty thin wine. **82** —*S.H. (12/31/2006)*

Wente 2002 Syrah (Livermore Valley) $12. Seemed a bit confected to our tasters, with watermelon and strawberry flavors that lacked varietal typicity yet didn't lack some charm. A rather simple, fruity wine that maintains a certain appeal. **84** *(9/1/2005)*

WESTERLY VINEYARDS

Westerly Vineyards 2002 Sauvignon Blanc (Santa Ynez Valley) $20. Generally clean and correct, with a touch of bitter greens and tropical fruit to the bouquet. Seems a bit heavy and clumsy on the palate, but the flavors are largely nice as they veer first to mango and then nectarine. Finishes with a shot of citrus peel and funky sweat. **86** *(7/1/2005)*

WESTOVER VINEYARDS

Westover Vineyards 2002 Palomares Vineyards Reserve Chardonnay (San Francisco Bay) $15. Dominated by char and the dilly, sharp scent of new American oak, although beneath that is some rich apple and pear fruit. The texture is creamy, acidity high in this otherwise nice wine, except for that opening aroma. **84** —*S.H. (3/1/2004)*

Westover Vineyards 2000 Beyer's Ranch Vineyard Zinfandel (Livermore Valley) $15. Smells Porty and raisiny, with an underlying fruity note of cherry-raspberry jam. Despite the sweet smell the wine is fully dry, but also very hot, at 15.3 percent alcohol. A bit thin in flavor, and the high acidity feels unnatural. **83** —*S.H. (3/1/2004)*

WESTPORT RIVERS

Westport Rivers 1999 Estate Classic Chardonnay (Southeastern New England) $18. Connecticut does Chardonnay, combining buttered popcorn aromas with anise and toast. Lithe and lean on the palate, loaded with green apple and lemon flavors that finish tart. Another good shellfish Chard. **86** —*J.C. (1/1/2004)*

USA

USA

WESTREY

Westrey 2002 Pinot Noir (Willamette Valley) $19. Lots of almost tropical fruit flavors here, forward and braced with citrusy acidity. Very drinkable, but definitely a lightweight. **86** *(11/1/2004)*

Westrey 2002 Abbey Ridge Vineyard Pinot Noir (Willamette Valley) $32. Fresh, spicy, and bright, marked with tart cranberry, light cherry, and just a hint of chocolate. If it were Burgundy, it would be Volnay. **89** *(11/1/2004)*

Westrey 1999 Croft-Bailey Pinot Noir (Willamette Valley) $22. Very different from this winery's Temperance bottling. Starts with sour cherry aromas along with sumptuous smoke, vanilla, and spice notes. Drinks very soft and gentle, with melted tannins framing generous cherry-berry fruit. This is a supple, easy-drinking wine for early consumption. **86** — *S.H. (8/1/2002)*

Westrey 2002 Reserve Pinot Noir (Willamette Valley) $29. Big, broad, ripe flavors of strawberries and raspberries are on the verge of jamminess, but the wine lacks power and concentration. Forward, fruity, middle-of-the-road style. **86** *(11/1/2004)*

Westrey 2002 Shea Vineyard Pinot Noir (Willamette Valley) $32. Pretty opening scents of pure Pinot fruit, rose petals, and some acetone. The fruit touches on grape, plum, and cherry; there is some pretty cinnamon, too. But in the mouth the wine comes across as a bit awkward and simple. Bottle shocked? **85** *(11/1/2004)*

Westrey 1999 Temperance Hill Pinot Noir (Willamette Valley) $22. A bit shy on the nose now, showing herbal, vegetal notes, including tomato and beetroot, accompanied by flamboyant oak. It's unyielding on the palate, too, with some solid tannins to shed. Could blossom after 2003, so give it time in the cellar. **87** —*S.H. (8/1/2002)*

WHALER

Whaler 1999 Flagship Shiraz (Mendocino) $28. Dark and brooding-looking, with an inky-purple robe that's almost black. The aromas begin with earthy, truffle-and-mushroom notes and slowly open up to reveal plums and other dark stone fruits. Drinks thick, tannic, and dry, with a core of plummy-berry fruit. This sturdy, big-boned wine will stand up to rich game, and also will age. **87** —*S.H. (12/1/2002)*

Whaler 1999 Flagship Zinfandel (Mendocino) $NA. Dark as the grave, and pretty closed in the aroma right now, offering up hints of blackberry, pepper, earth, chocolate, and bacon. Tastes late-picked, with pruny flavors and lots of mouth-numbing tannins, although the alcohol is a modest 13.7%. What it lacks in depth and nuance it makes up for with sheer chutzpah. **84** —*S.H. (11/1/2002)*

WHETSTONE

Whetstone 2002 Hirsch Vineyard Pinot Noir (Sonoma Coast) $38. Those coastal acids really shine in this tart, crisp wine. Flavors veer toward cranberries, tobacco, herbs, and cherries, and the wine is full-bodied and very dry. It has a high-toned quality that makes it attractive. **89** *(11/1/2004)*

Whetstone 2002 Savoy Vineyard Pinot Noir (Anderson Valley) $46. Simple and enjoyable for its supple texture, tangy spices, and cherry and herb flavors that finish a little sweet. Decant to let some sulfur blow off. **84** *(11/1/2004)*

WHIDBEY ISLAND WINERY

Whidbey Island Winery 2003 Madeleine Angevine (Puget Sound) $12. From the estate vineyard, this bone-dry white wine shows very tart citrus flavors, with a lightly bitter pear skin edge. The alcohol clocks in at just 11%; it's almost Germanically austere, but what a match for crab cakes. **87 Best Buy** —*P.G. (6/1/2006)*

Whidbey Island Winery 2000 Madeleine Angevine (Puget Sound) $11. This unusual grape grows well in the Puget Sound appellation of western Washington. It shows a gunpowder nose, spicy, herbal, and very dusty/dry; with tart, grassy flavors. **84** —*P.G. (2/1/2002)*

Whidbey Island Winery 2002 Composition Red Wine Bordeaux Blend (Yakima Valley) $19. A Yakima Valley Médoc, this Bordeaux-style blend is quite dry, just barely hinting at Cabernet's inherent earthiness. It fin- ishes with the sort of drying tannins one expects to find in a well-made cru classé. **87** —*P.G. (6/1/2006)*

Whidbey Island Winery 2004 Cabernet Franc (Yakima Valley) $18. Fragrant and ripe, this brightly colored Cab Franc mixes flavors of pomegranate, red currant, spicy cherry, and red apple. Forward and nicely fruity, it leaves out the new oak and finishes clean and crisp. **88** —*P.G. (6/1/2006)*

Whidbey Island Winery 1999 Merlot (Yakima Valley) $15. Here is a firm, tart wine, still quite young and showing some hard, green tannins. The winemaking is solid, and there is a core of tart, sour cherry fruit, but these were not the ripest of grapes. **85** —*P.G. (2/1/2002)*

Whidbey Island Winery 2003 Pinot Grigio (Yakima Valley) $13. Pink grapefruit and peach flavors dominate, with creamy, leesy textures and a clean, lime-infused snap to the finish. **87** —*P.G. (2/1/2006)*

Whidbey Island Winery 2000 Pinot Gris (Columbia Valley (WA)) $13. There are scents of fresh pears in the nose, along with a Riesling-like whiff of kerosene. The color suggests that this is maturing rapidly, and should be consumed quickly. The finish shows plenty of heat, and a somewhat chemical taste. **84** —*P.G. (2/1/2002)*

Whidbey Island Winery 2004 Sangiovese (Yakima Valley) $17. Scents of cherry, crackers, and milk chocolate lead pleasantly into a light, bright strawberry and cherry candy-flavored Sangiovese. Just a touch of spice adds life to the tannins, but it's the balance overall that makes this a standout. **88** —*P.G. (6/1/2006)*

Whidbey Island Winery 2004 Siegerrebe (Puget Sound) $12. Puget Sound is the smallest and least-well-known appellation in Washington State, but among the dozen or so wineries that actually grow grapes here, Whidbey is the standout. Their Siegerrebe (a relative of Gewürztraminer) is an off-dry white wine, rich with citrus, spice, honey, pear, apricot, and pine tar. The overriding impression is one of fresh-squeezed grapefruit, and the alcohol is just 11.5%. **88 Best Buy** —*P.G. (6/1/2006)*

Whidbey Island Winery 2002 Syrah (Yakima Valley) $19. Worth buying by the case if you can find it (only 270 cases were produced), as this wine is underpriced relative to its quality. Blackberry fruit is accented by hints of dried spices, pepper, licorice, mineral, and smoke. Picks up vanilla notes on the lush, captivating palate, then finishes long. **90 Editors' Choice** *(9/1/2005)*

Whidbey Island Winery 1999 Syrah (Yakima Valley) $20. Blackberry and cream, coffee and cola, but also an overt tartness to the fruit, was noted by tasters in this offering. The moderate, even mouthfeel opens to a tangy, anise-leather-tinged finish. A bit of a split decision. How you'll feel about this will depend on your palate for tart or sweet fruit. **84** *(10/1/2001)*

Whidbey Island Winery 2003 Viognier (Yakima Valley) $15. The color seems off—an unusually deep gold—and the honeyed nose has a sweaty component. Viognier can go bitter in the finish, and this one does. Two bottles tasted, both exactly the same. **82** —*P.G. (6/1/2006)*

WHITCRAFT

Whitcraft 2004 Bien Nacido Vineyard Barrel Select Chardonnay (Santa Maria Valley) $NA. This is a bizarre wine. The alcohol is extremely high, and the fruit is enormously ripe, to the point of bananas. The wine will have its fans, but to me it's Chardonnay-Port, over-manipulated and over-stylized. Tasted twice. **81** —*S.H. (8/1/2006)*

Whitcraft 2000 French Camp Vineyard Lagrein (San Luis Obispo County) $20. Wins the darkest wine of the decade award. Absolutely black, except for a gleam of purple at the edge. Smells big, deep, and oaky, with berry and chocolate scents. In the mouth, similar to Cabernet, with blackberry flavors and rich, thick tannins. Interesting as an alternative-type wine, and an ager. An ancient grape from the north of Italy and Austria **89 Editors' Choice** —*S.H. (8/1/2003)*

WHITE BARN

White Barn 1992 La Romanee Pisoni Pinot Noir (Santa Lucia Highlands) $NA. Pretty bouquet, clean and pure, showing cherries, spice, but beginning to crack up. Very dry, with lots of sweet-sour cherry flavors on the finish. **88** —*S.H. (6/1/2005)*

WHITE CRANE WINERY

White Crane Winery 2001 Folkendt Vineyard Cabernet Sauvignon (Livermore Valley) $48. Begins with sugary, caramelized aromas and then turns heavy and syrupy in the mouth. You sense that the grapes are fine, with polished blackberry flavors and rich tannins, that simply have been allowed to get out of hand. **83** —S.H. (11/15/2003)

WHITE HAWK

White Hawk 2001 Syrah (Santa Maria Valley) $20. Peppery and meaty, yet backed by a full complement of blackberry fruit, this wine contains all of the balanced attributes we're looking for in California Syrah. Ripe fruit, peppery spice, and meaty complexity are together in a harmonious whole. Picks up a hint of anise on the long finish. **92 Editors' Choice** (9/1/2005)

White Hawk 2000 Syrah (Santa Maria Valley) $30. A dark-hued wine, brimming with black cherry, cola, and spice aromas. On the palate, it's richly textured, with bitter herb and charry smoke tones followed by chocolate, blackberry, and sage flavors. Tannins are a little rustic, but on the whole, this wine serves up plenty of hedonistic pleasure. A first release. **90** —J.M. (4/1/2004)

White Hawk 2001 Estate Syrah (Santa Maria Valley) $25. Here's a big, tough, gritty wine in its youth. There's a cherry and blackberry sweetness poking through the tannins, and the wine is fully dry. Should age well. Try after 2005. **87** —S.H. (12/1/2004)

WHITE HERON

White Heron 2003 Piper Frenchman Hill Vineyard Chardonnay (Columbia Valley (WA)) $10. A sharp, edgy wine, lifted with a bit of volatility, then smoothed over with a honeyed sweetness. Very ripe, soft, peachy, and definitely ready to drink. **87 Best Buy** —P.G. (10/1/2006)

White Heron 2002 Roussanne (Columbia Valley (WA)) $15. Bigger and more robust than Viognier, Roussanne is the "other" white Rhône grape. A fragrant, flavorful, lush, plush, soft, and seductive wine that's ready to rock right now. **88** —P.G. (11/15/2004)

White Heron 2004 Mariposa Vineyard Roussanne (Columbia Valley (WA)) $15. Opens with scents of honey, pear, cracker, and spice, leading into warm, round fruit flavors. The deep gold color and the soft, open palate indicate a bit of oxidation, and the wine goes flat in the midpalate, though for near-term drinking it offers unusual pleasures. Serve this one slightly chilled. **86** —P.G. (10/1/2006)

WHITE OAK

White Oak 2003 Cabernet Sauvignon (Napa Valley) $26. Nice and dry, with a pretty acid-tannin balance and enough Cabernet character to satisfy. Shows blackberry, coffee, spice, and herb flavors that are elegant and balanced in the mouth. **86** —S.H. (12/1/2006)

White Oak 2002 Cabernet Sauvignon (Napa Valley) $26. The aroma alone suggests a well-ripened, classically structured Cabernet, and the wine doesn't let you down. It's dry and delicious, with cassis and fine oak flavors, and lush, smooth tannins. **91 Editors' Choice** —S.H. (3/1/2006)

White Oak 2000 Cabernet Sauvignon (Napa Valley) $18. Dark and concentrated, a young wine filled with tannins and sharp acids. There's a solid overlay of smoky oak, but the fruity core you want isn't there. Instead, the heat of alcohol is the dominant mouthfeel, and the wine is not likely to improve with age. **84** —S.H. (6/1/2003)

White Oak 1999 Maripose Cabernet Sauvignon (Napa Valley) $22. Actually from the Chiles Valley section of Napa, this wine begins with vegetal aromas and turns rough in the mouth. You'll find some berry flavors swathed in tannins. The overall impression is rustic and ordinary. It's just not good enough for the price. **83** —S.H. (9/12/2002)

White Oak 2004 Chardonnay (Russian River Valley) $20. White Oak has done a good job with Chard over the years, and this fruit-forward bottling offers lots of pleasure. Apples, peaches, kiwis, and limes star in this crisply tart, dry wine, which is only lightly oaked. **88** —S.H. (7/1/2006)

White Oak 2002 Chardonnay (Russian River Valley) $20. Deep, lush, and opulent, this complex wine has plenty of interest for its complexity. The fruity flavors are very ripe and veer into pineapple and mango, with a generous dose of smoky oak. The creamy texture and crisp acidity provide balance. **90 Editors' Choice** —S.H. (6/1/2004)

White Oak 2001 Chardonnay (Russian River Valley) $20. A nice example of a middleweight Chard from this region. It shows all the proper characteristics while remaining solidly in the middle of the pack. Flavors range from apples and peaches through riper tropical fruits, with good acidity, while oak frames it all in smoky vanillins. **86** —S.H. (12/31/2003)

White Oak 2000 Chardonnay (Russian River Valley) $16. Extraordinarily rich and fragrant with the suggestion of spicy green apples, this wine also brims with aromas of brown honey, crushed spices, and the vanilla and smoke that come from charred oak barrels. It's dry, with a creamy, custardy feeling. Fun to drink, and as good as other Chards costing a lot more. **90** —S.H. (12/15/2002)

White Oak 1999 Chardonnay (Russian River Valley) $17. Unusually ripe and forward even for this vintage, this massive wine explodes with tropical fruit, spice, and vanilla aromas and flavors, generously framed in oak. It has the usual slight residual sugar that's in fashion now, but retains balance and finesse through the long finish. **90** —S.H. (5/1/2002)

White Oak 2000 Myers Limited Reserve Chardonnay (Russian River Valley) $22. Here's a tight, lemon-and-lime flavored wine with crisp acidity, for those who like their Chards on the steely, minerally side. It's very clean, refreshing, and sleek, and the winemaker did not slather a ton of oak on the fresh, pretty fruit. **88** —S.H. (6/1/2003)

White Oak 2002 Merlot (Napa Valley) $24. The fruit sure got ripe. This wine is powerful in cherry pie and milk chocolate flavors, and is soft in acids, with ripe, sweet tannins. It's one-dimensional, but that dimension is a deliciously gooey one. **86** —S.H. (3/1/2006)

White Oak 2001 Merlot (Napa Valley) $24. Balanced, soft, and feminine, with generous black currant, cassis, and olive flavors. Feels plush on the palate, with an easy but complex structure. Tannins kick in on the finish. Best now through 2006. **90** —S.H. (6/1/2004)

White Oak 2000 Merlot (Napa Valley) $24. One sniff warns you there's a great deal of unripe fruit here. Smells like broken green twigs and celery, and tasting confirms this impression of mint and green tea, although if you try, you can find some blackberries. It's increasingly evident the vintage was vegetal for some reds. This was one of them. **82** —S.H. (11/15/2002)

White Oak 2000 Merlot (Alexander Valley) $28. From a small estate vineyard, a dark purple wine that stains the glass. This visual clue suggests the density of the extract, but can't convey the soft, hedonistic tannins. It's austere now, the farthest thing from a fruit bomb, suggesting earth, tart berry skins, and herbs. Doesn't have the stuffing for the long haul, but is so well structured, it would be perfect with a rack of lamb. **91** — S.H. (11/15/2002)

White Oak 1999 Merlot (Sonoma County) $25. Marries Merlot's dark stone fruit character with an earthier one redolent of mushrooms, violets and an intriguing meaty note. A portion of Cabernet Sauvignon adds blackcurrant aromas. In the mouth, it's really nice, round, supple and lush, with good balance. Dry, tart acids and dusty tannins make it drinkable now. **90** —S.H. (9/1/2002)

White Oak 2005 Sauvignon Blanc (Russian River Valley) $15. Stimulatingly fresh and clean, this polished SB benefits from crisp acidity provoked by its cool growing region. The flavors are of figs, citrus fruits, and nectarines, but they could be a bit more focused. **85** —S.H. (10/1/2006)

White Oak 2004 Sauvignon Blanc (Russian River Valley) $15. This Sauvignon is very New Zealandy in gooseberry, green grass, alfalfa, and citrus fruit. It's also totally dry, with good, crisp acids. It has a complex, layered creaminess that lifts it above the ordinary. **88** —S.H. (12/1/2005)

White Oak 2003 Sauvignon Blanc (Russian River Valley) $14. A wine of considerable finesse and charm. It has Sauvignon's racy, citrusy side, but much more in the way of fresh sweet herbs and smoky oak. Finishes with minerals and honey. **87** —S.H. (12/31/2004)

White Oak 2002 Sauvignon Blanc (Napa Valley) $13. Great acid structure in this clean, pleasant wine, with its savory flavors of grapefruit, lime, peach, and guava, and creamy texture. Wonderfully balanced and rich;

could use a tad more concentration, but at this price, it's a good value. **87** —*S.H. (12/1/2003)*

White Oak 2001 Sauvignon Blanc (Napa Valley) $18. A bit thin and earthy, with lemony flavors that are diluted in the middle palate. It's also soft. Turns slightly sweet in the finish. **84** —*S.H. (9/1/2003)*

White Oak 2001 20th Vintage Sauvignon Blanc Sauvignon Blanc (North Coast) $12. Tries to mimic Marlborough Sauvignon with its intensely grassy, lime, and grapefruit flavors and nervy acidity, and comes pretty close. It's a clean, scouring wine, and while it's pretty good, it's just too thin and watery to merit a higher score. **83** —*S.H. (9/1/2003)*

White Oak 2001 Pantianna Ranch Sauvignon Musqué (Mendocino) $25. From the Sanel Valley, a wine that smells better than it tastes. The aroma is evocative and inviting, with gooseberry, lime zest sweetened with honey, and vanilla notes. But it's strangely inert in the mouth. The citrusy flavors are watery and thin. **84** —*S.H. (9/1/2003)*

White Oak 2002 Syrah (Napa Valley) $25. A lovely wine that reveals everything in the first sip. Black currants, smoked meat, milk chocolate, and vanilla mingle together in soft tannins and easy acids. Finishes long and sweet. **87** —*S.H. (12/31/2004)*

White Oak 2001 Syrah (Napa Valley) $24. This first-ever Syrah from White Oak starts off with peppery, woodsy aromas that suggest forest twigs and wild blackberries. It's very soft and easy on the palate. Blackberry and coffee flavors lead to a quick finish. **86** —*S.H. (2/1/2004)*

White Oak 2000 Zinfandel (Alexander Valley) $24. Just what I think of in Sonoma Zin, a ripely fruity wine with bright blackberry, black cherry, and pepper flavors. It's very dry, with a slightly rough edge of country tannins. Alexander Valley provides the soft acidity and velvety mouthfeel. This easy-drinking wine will support everything from roast salmon to baby-back ribs. **88** —*S.H. (11/1/2002)*

White Oak 1999 Pourroy Zinfandel (Alexander Valley) $25. A fine example of its appellation, with its melted tannins, soft acids, and plush, fat fruit. It's also classically Zinfandel, with briary, spicy red and black raspberry flavors offering hints of tobacco and clove. The flavors are strong, but there's a gentle elegance to the mouthfeel that's addictive. **89** —*S.H. (11/1/2002)*

WHITE ROSE

White Rose 2002 Pinot Noir (Yamhill County) $65. This is bright and clear in the glass, it shines like a ruby. Light, with sweet/tart candy cherry fruit flavors, it tastes of cherry Lifesavers and tart cranberry. Fun, pretty, and solidly fruity, it is very appealing. But it seems a bit insubstantial for the price. **87** —*P.G. (2/1/2005)*

WHITE ROSE ESTATE

White Rose Estate 2002 White Rose Vineyard Pinot Noir (Yamhill County) $65. Complex and dark, with mixed red and blue fruits, earthy/leathery notes, and a wild bouquet of lavender and mint. Young and tight, but well crafted. **89** *(11/1/2004)*

WHITE TRUCK

White Truck 2005 Chardonnay (California) $13. The winemaker says the grapes come from Santa Barbara, although it doesn't say that on the label, but the wine certainly is bright, clean, and crisp in cool-climate acidity. Flavors of limes, green apples, and spice finish a bit thin. **85** —*S.H. (11/15/2006)*

White Truck 2004 White Blend (California) $9. Here's an easy-drinking, dry, fruity white wine made from Sauvignon Blanc, Pinot Grigio, Viognier, and Chardonnay. From Cline Cellars. **85 Best Buy** —*S.H. (12/31/2005)*

White Truck 2005 White Wine (California) $11. A little of this, a little of that, but it's a boringly soft, simple wine, and sweet as well. **81** —*S.H. (12/31/2006)*

WHITEHALL LANE

Whitehall Lane 2003 Cabernet Sauvignon (Napa Valley) $40. Polished and complex, this Cab, from Rutherford and St. Helena, shows ripe blackberry, red and black cherry, chocolate, and blueberry flavors with rich oak seasoning. The wine is very dry and the tannins are soft but intri-

cate. This is a lovely restaurant wine if the mark-up isn't too great. Drink now. **88** —*S.H. (11/15/2006)*

Whitehall Lane 2001 Cabernet Sauvignon (Napa Valley) $21. A special lot of half-bottles closed with screwtops, this is a soft, supple wine, a bit light, with pleasant flavors of blackberries and herbs. A scour of tannins shows up in the dry finish. **85** —*S.H. (10/1/2004)*

Whitehall Lane 2001 Cabernet Sauvignon (Napa Valley) $40. So ripe in black currant and mocha fruit, so rich in sweet tannins, so well structured. It's an impeccable Cabernet that's beautiful now, but should hold through the decade. **93 Editors' Choice** —*S.H. (10/1/2004)*

Whitehall Lane 1997 Cabernet Sauvignon (Napa Valley) $28. 87 —*L.W. (12/31/1999)*

Whitehall Lane 2003 Leonardini Vineyard Cabernet Sauvignon (Napa Valley) $100. A very good Cab, a little young and in need of cellaring, but such is the fruit that you can drink it now. It's plush in black currant, crème de cassis, and new oaky flavors wrapped in soft, velvety tannins, with a chocolatey, licorice finish. Should hold for a good ten years. **90** —*S.H. (12/15/2006)*

Whitehall Lane 1997 Leonardini Vineyard Cabernet Sauvignon (Napa Valley) $75. 90 *(11/1/2000)*

Whitehall Lane 2003 Reserve Cabernet Sauvignon (Napa Valley) $75. Nice Cab, a Rutherford-St. Helena blend that's tannic enough to warrant time in the cellar. Too young to really show its stuff now, but there's a chunk of flashy blackberry and cherry fruit, and enough balancing acids, to let it develop well through 2012. **89** —*S.H. (12/15/2006)*

Whitehall Lane 2002 Reserve Cabernet Sauvignon (Napa Valley) $75. Soft, gentle, and beguiling in its texture, this Cab has a silk-and-velvet mouthfeel. The flavors are very ripe, all cherries and blackberries and milk chocolate. In fact, the wine seems a little too soft for ageability, so drink up now. **87** —*S.H. (12/1/2005)*

Whitehall Lane 2001 Reserve Cabernet Sauvignon (Napa Valley) $70. A sensational Cab that exhibits power and opulence in the ripe black currant, cherry, cocoa, and new oak flavors, yet is subtlety balanced and harmonious. Showcases preternaturally gorgeous tannins, soft and sweet. The more you sip, the greater the impression. **95 Cellar Selection** —*S.H. (4/1/2005)*

Whitehall Lane 1997 Reserve Cabernet Sauvignon (Napa Valley) $60. 90 *(11/1/2000)*

Whitehall Lane 1998 Chardonnay (Carneros) $20. 89 *(6/1/2000)*

Whitehall Lane 1997 Chardonnay (Napa Valley) $16. 91 —*S.H. (2/1/2000)*

Whitehall Lane 1997 Merlot (Napa Valley) $24. 87 —*L.W. (12/31/1999)*

Whitehall Lane 2003 Merlot (Napa Valley) $26. A lush, ripe wine packed with appealing black currant, cherry, cocoa, and wintergeen flavors. Grip is provided by sweet, dusty tannins and fine acidity. Drink this stylish, dry wine now. **88** —*S.H. (11/15/2006)*

Whitehall Lane 2001 Merlot (Napa Valley) $26. Soft, gentle and seductive, with its cherry-chocolate, sweet green olive, vanilla, and pecan pie flavors wowing the palate. Best of all are the tannins, which are rich and fine. They provide structure, while being sweet themselves. What a sensational Merlot. It deserves the best food you can rustle up. **93** —*S.H. (12/15/2004)*

Whitehall Lane 1998 Sauvignon Blanc (Rutherford) $15. 90 —*S.H. (2/1/2000)*

Whitehall Lane 2005 Sauvignon Blanc (Napa Valley) $15. A nice, clean wine with citrus, fig, melon, and spice flavors, and a creamy texture and zesty acidity. A touch of Sémillon gives it extra richness. Finishes dry and balanced. **85** —*S.H. (11/15/2006)*

Whitehall Lane 2004 Sauvignon Blanc (Napa Valley) $15. Made New Zealand style, this Sauvignon Blanc is strong in gooseberry, juniper, lime, and white pepper flavors. It's absolutely dry, with crisp acidity. **86** —*S.H. (12/1/2005)*

Whitehall Lane 2003 Sauvignon Blanc (Napa Valley) $15. Displays intensity in the citrus, melon, and fig flavors that are so rich and concentrated, they're almost sweet. This is a crisp, dry wine, with a spicy finish. **87** —*S.H. (12/15/2004)*

Whitehall Lane 2000 Sauvignon Blanc (Napa Valley) $15. A touch of the veggies, particularly asparagus and bell pepper, mix with citrus in this fuller-bodied white. While it isn't exactly a heavyweight, the ample body is weighed down by lower than average acidity. On the back end, the long, persistent finish is adequate, but the green element that's so present up front comes back in force. **87** (8/1/2002)

WHITFORD

Whitford 2003 Haynes Vineyard Chardonnay (Napa Valley) $20. From the cooler, southeast part of the valley, but the wine still has that heavy softness that so many Napa Chards have, with the flavor of pears and oak. Tasty enough, but lacks the vital spark you get from cooler climates. **86** —S.H. (11/1/2006)

Whitford 2002 Haynes Vineyard Chardonnay (Napa Valley) $20. Clean and sleek, a rather austere Chard whose flavors veer toward green apples and figs, with good acidity. Finishes with some earthiness. **85** —S.H. (10/1/2005)

Whitford 2001 Haynes Vineyard Chardonnay (Napa Valley) $19. Gloriously rich to the point of decadence, a flamboyant wine that oozes pear, melon, nectarine, tangerine, honey, vanilla, and smoke flavors. All this is encased in a creamy, leesy texture leading to a long, spicy finish. The finish turns dry and a little peppery. **91 Editors' Choice** —S.H. (12/1/2003)

Whitford 2000 Haynes Vineyard Old Vines Chardonnay (Napa Valley) $25. From a well-known Napa vineyard, massive amounts of oak and lees result in a creamy, soft, buttery wine. The underlying flavors range from pears through tropical fruits and vanilla. Rather soft in acids, this wine is all about flavor and texture. **92** —S.H. (12/1/2003)

Whitford 2002 Haynes Vineyard Pinot Noir (Napa Valley) $23. Hard in acids now, this Pinot should reward time in the cellar, to judge from the well of sweet cherry and currant fruit and sturdy tannins that now make it rather tough. Hold until 2007. **88** —S.H. (10/1/2005)

Whitford 2001 Pinot Noir (Napa Valley) $22. From the theoretically cooler southern part of the valley, but still a region too warm to preserve Pinot's delicacy. Not a bad wine at all, with its pretty flavors of cherry pie, rich overlay of oak, and silky mouthfeel. But from a varietal point of view, rather hot and baked, with a stewed note throughout. **85** —S.H. (2/1/2004)

Whitford 2003 Haynes Vineyard Syrah (Napa Valley) $25. Coming from a cool vineyard, but a hot vintage, this polished Syrah has intensely ripe fruit, balancing acidity. The tannins are soft and melted, making the wine instantly drinkable. Blackberries, red plums, coffee, sweet leather, and spice flavors mingle into a long, rich finish. **89** —S.H. (11/15/2006)

Whitford 2002 Haynes Vineyard Syrah (Napa Valley) $25. A bit of funk on the nose had some reviewers throwing the brettanomyces flag, but there's also some pleasant blackberry and pepper notes and a smooth texture. Turns a bit tannic on the finish, so hold for a couple of years. **85** (9/1/2005)

WHITMAN CELLARS

Whitman Cellars 2002 Cabernet Sauvignon (Walla Walla (WA)) $36. It's not always easy making a pure varietal, as this is. Without the addition of Merlot and Cab Franc, as in Whitman's other 2002 reds, this has a tighter, sleeker profile, with tart flavors of plum, rhubarb, and sour cherry. **85** —P.G. (12/15/2005)

Whitman Cellars 2001 Cabernet Sauvignon (Walla Walla (WA)) $36. From Pepper Bridge, Seven Hills, and other top vineyards, this shows the strawberry preserves and forward, spicy fruit that characterizes Walla Walla. Nicely balanced, it uses new oak well, adding notes of cocoa, licorice, and hints of tobacco. **88** —P.G. (5/1/2004)

Whitman Cellars 1999 Seven Hills Cabernet Sauvignon (Walla Walla (WA)) $40. The Cabernet from this new producer has considerably more color and concentration than their Merlot. You have to work to get past the tough, chalky tannins, but the fruit has a pleasant, cherry Lifesaver sweetness, and there is a hint of cocoa in the finish. **86** —P.G. (6/1/2002)

Whitman Cellars 2002 Merlot (Walla Walla (WA)) $32. The nose perks your interest with unusual scents of fresh cut herb, cherry, anise, and watermelon. A modest wine, not especially ripe-tasting despite its relatively high brix (26.2). **85** —P.G. (12/15/2005)

Whitman Cellars 2001 Merlot (Walla Walla (WA)) $32. Scents of new oak jump out, with pretty, plummy fruit behind. Right now the wine seems a bit oaky, but time may smooth it out. The finish is tight and chewy. **86** —P.G. (5/1/2004)

Whitman Cellars 1999 Seven Hills Merlot (Walla Walla (WA)) $32. Maybe it's just a case of a very young wine, but despite the pedigree (Seven Hills is one of Walla Walla's premiere vineyards), this wine seems a bit green. It shows light, tight, sour cherry fruit, with a bit of spice and some hard, stemmy tannins. **85** —P.G. (6/1/2002)

Whitman Cellars 2002 Narcissa Red Blend (Walla Walla (WA)) $24. There's plenty of toast for lovers of new oak, with cinnamon and mocha giving it an assertive come-on like a vinous Frappucino. The core fruit is soft and round, mixing cherries and plums in with all that toast and chocolate. Pleasant and smooth; best for near-term drinking. **86** —P.G. (12/15/2005)

Whitman Cellars 2001 Narcissa Red Red Blend (Walla Walla (WA)) $24. Flavorful, with black currants and cassis, along with hefty accents of leather, saddle, and barnyard. Smooth and balanced, with dry, astringent tannins, this predominantly Cabernet (68%) blend is enjoyable now and over the next few years. **87** —P.G. (5/1/2004)

Whitman Cellars 2002 Syrah (Walla Walla (WA)) $28. Tight and slightly rubbery when first opened, but soon the spicy notes of chocolate, coffee, and cinnamon come through over tasty cherry fruit. Styled more like a Merlot than a Syrah, it's a smooth, nicely balanced, and really tasty effort. **88** —P.G. (12/15/2004)

Whitman Cellars 2003 Viognier (Walla Walla (WA)) $19. Pretty and round, showing characteristic orange peel scents without the volatility that marks so many Washington Viogniers. The fruit is sweet and ripe, with a hint of baby aspirin on the slightly candied finish. **87** —P.G. (12/15/2004)

WIDGEON HILLS

Widgeon Hills 2002 HRP Ranch Area 51 Syrah (Yakima Valley) $22. Despite the name, there's nothing alien about this wine—it just delivers briary, herbal notes layered over more classic blackberry and plum flavors. Broad and soft, so drink now. **86** (9/1/2005)

WIENS CELLARS

Wiens Cellars 2001 Zinfandel (Lodi) $14. Somewhat earthy in the nose, the wine follows through with bright cherry and spice flavors. It remains zippy on the palate right through the finish, ending with a charry, smoky edge. **86** (11/1/2003)

WILD BUNCH

Wild Bunch 2003 Red Wine Red Blend (California) $10. An inexpensive house wine to buy by the case. A blend of Zin, Syrah, and Barbera, it showcases the richness of each variety, and is dry and interesting. A great vin ordinaire from Montevina, which is owned by the Trinchero family. **86 Best Buy** —S.H. (12/31/2005)

Wild Bunch 2004 White Wine White Blend (California) $10. There's a user-friendliness to this wine, with its flamboyant flavors of peaches, nectarines, pineapples, and half a dozen or so other fruits. A blend of five major varieties, it possesses the crispness and cleanness for balance. **85 Best Buy** —S.H. (12/31/2005)

WILD COYOTE

Wild Coyote 2001 Lisenshes Zinfandel (Paso Robles) $14. A modestly constructed wine, with lots of upfront oak, hints of black cherry, plum, and spice, and a somewhat woody finish. Pleasant enough. **84** (11/1/2003)

WILD HORSE

Wild Horse 2000 Blaufränkisch (Paso Robles) $NA. I never heard of it either, but it's very dry and austere. Flavors are lean and earthy, veering toward tobacco and sage. Acids are soft and so are the tannins. Not very flattering by itself, but could reward oily foods, like pizza. **85** —S.H. (9/1/2003)

Wild Horse 1997 Cabernet Sauvignon (Paso Robles) $19. **85** —S.H. (2/1/2000)

Wild Horse 2002 Cabernet Sauvignon (Paso Robles) $20. A bit herbal and minty, but also loaded with cassis scents. This medium- to full-bodied Cab is big without seeming overdone. Blackberries, baking spices, and coffee notes harmonize on the palate. Good steakhouse wine. **88** *(10/1/2005)*

Wild Horse 1999 Cabernet Sauvignon (Paso Robles) $20. Rough and earthy, it's Cabernet-ish in the black currant aromas, but exceedingly tannic on the palate. This gum-numbing harshness is unrelieved by fruit or ripe sweetness of any kind. It's surprisingly unfriendly for a Paso Robles red wine. **83** —*S.H. (11/15/2002)*

Wild Horse 1998 Chardonnay (Central Coast) $16. 87 —*S.H. (11/15/1999)*

Wild Horse 2004 Chardonnay (Central Coast) $18. Ripe, user-friendly Chardonnay. Vanilla, toast, and pear aromas and flavors delivered with a plump, easy to swallow mouthfeel enlivened by just a touch of citrusy zip on the finish. **86** *(10/1/2005)*

Wild Horse 2004 Chardonnay (Central Coast) $20. Awfully weak in flavor, especially at this price, like a pretty decent Chard that was watered down. You'll find trace elements of peaches, pineapples, and oak. **82** —*S.H. (11/15/2006)*

Wild Horse 2003 Chardonnay (Central Coast) $16. This is an easy, soft Chard, with suggestions of peaches and tropical fruits. There's quite a bit of oak, which adds vanilla and buttered toast. **84** —*S.H. (5/1/2005)*

Wild Horse 2002 Chardonnay (Central Coast) $16. A bit on the thin side, but you'll find some decent peach and apple flavors, and the requisite dollop of smoky oak. Turns watery on the finish. Seems pricy for what you get. **84** —*S.H. (4/1/2004)*

Wild Horse 2000 Chardonnay (Central Coast) $16. Another good value from this winery. The apple and peach flavors have something dusty about them, like dry, red California dirt on a hot summer day. Just a little oak spices up this dry and crisp wine. **87** —*S.H. (12/15/2002)*

Wild Horse 1997 Merlot (Paso Robles) $18. 83 —*S.H. (12/31/1999)*

Wild Horse 2003 Merlot (Paso Robles) $20. The sort of Merlot that gained the grape a following—medium-weight, supple, and easy to drink. Black cherry, mocha, and dried-spice flavors show very little herbaceousness, finishing on a bright note. **87** *(10/1/2005)*

Wild Horse 2002 Merlot (Paso Robles) $20. Soft in acidity and light in color, with briary, coffee and plum flavors. Gritty tannins on the finish. **83** —*S.H. (5/1/2005)*

Wild Horse 2001 Merlot (Paso Robles) $18. There's real complexity in this dark, dry red wine. It has flavors of blackberries and plums, but they're rolled into interesting herb and tobacco notes, with a spicy finish of tangerine peel and espresso. The tannins are rich and thick. Best now. **89** —*S.H. (4/1/2004)*

Wild Horse 1999 Merlot (Paso Robles) $18. Limpid and soft, with luscious black cherry and anise flavors that are refined and high class. Dry, dusty tannins are fairly pronounced, and will help to cut through fats and oils. This is a wine that's fun but still has enough complexity for those white-tablecloth dinners. **87** —*S.H. (9/1/2003)*

Wild Horse 1998 Pinot Blanc (Monterey County) $14. 90 Best Buy —*S.H. (3/1/2000)*

Wild Horse 1997 Pinot Noir (Central Coast) $20. 87 —*J.C. (5/1/2000)*

Wild Horse 2003 Pinot Noir (Central Coast) $23. An eight-vineyard blend of 20,000 cases or so, Wild Horse's Central coast Pinot is an admirable effort, blending forward fruit (black cherries) with darker, earthier notes of cola and spice. Light-bodied and silky-textured, drink it over the next year or so. **85** *(10/1/2005)*

Wild Horse 2000 Pinot Noir (Central Coast) $20. A pretty wine in a lighter style, with earth and mocha accents adorning its lean cherry and plum fruit. It's bright and even, and though the fruit is lively, the mouthfeel is supple. It finishes dry, with pleasant herb notes. **86** *(10/1/2002)*

Wild Horse 2004 Unbridled Solomon Hills Vineyard Pinot Noir (Santa Maria Valley) $45. Achieves a wonderfully dry, silky, delicate quality without losing complexity and depth. It's so different from the big, juicy, lip-smacking Pinots that usually come from Dijon clones. **92** —*S.H. (8/1/2006)*

Wild Horse 1998 Roussanne (Paso Robles) $18. 90 —*S.H. (10/1/1999)*

Wild Horse 2002 Syrah (Paso Robles) $18. Smells like good Syrah should, with complex scents of espresso, meat, and even a gamey edge layered over fresh blackberries. It's medium-bodied, crisper than the Cabernet, with just a hint of black pepper on the finish. Drink now. **88** *(10/1/2005)*

Wild Horse 2001 Syrah (Paso Robles) $18. Really a first-rate wine, packed with juicy blackberry, cherry, and herb flavors, but it's no mere fruit bomb. There's a firm backbone of gritty tannins and a nice slash of acidity and oak to provide nuance and balance. Will be versatile at the table. **87** —*S.H. (12/1/2004)*

Wild Horse 2002 James Berry Vineyard Syrah (Paso Robles) $38. Big and firmly structured, this inky Syrah comes from a series of terraces at this justly renowned vineyard. Cinnamon, toast, and coffee notes from new oak complement bold blackberry fruit. Hold 3–5 years. **90** *(10/1/2005)*

Wild Horse 1998 Viognier (Central Coast) $24. 87 —*S.H. (10/1/1999)*

Wild Horse 2004 Viognier (Central Coast) $18. This plump, medium-bodied wine is made in a fruit-forward, easily accessible style. On the nose you get hints of sweet corn, white pepper, and nasturtium blossoms, while the palate rounds out with flavors of pear, apricot, and a bit of dusty minerality. **87** *(10/1/2005)*

Wild Horse 2003 Viognier (Central Coast) $18. Simple, dry, and actually a little bitter, with grapefruit-rind flavors and high acidity. Tastes almost like a Muscadet; might go well with oysters. **84** —*S.H. (5/1/2005)*

Wild Horse 2002 Viognier (Central Coast) $16. Easy drinking and tasty with flavors of peaches, oranges, and vanilla. Balances the richness out with crisp acidity and a light touch of oak. This is a nice cocktail-style wine. **85** —*S.H. (11/15/2004)*

Wild Horse 1997 Zinfandel (Paso Robles) $14. 85 —*J.C. (2/1/2000)*

Wild Horse 2001 Zinfandel (Paso Robles) $16. Leads off with spice, toast, and vanilla notes. Cherry and berry flavors are also in evidence, though they are tempered by the tannins. **85** *(11/1/2003)*

WILDHURST

Wildhurst 2002 Reserve Cabernet Sauvignon (Lake County) $16. From this county north of Napa, a well-ripened Cab with lots of excitingly rich flavor. Big in blackberry, cherry, and mocha, and dry, with soft, gentle tannins, it's a real crowd-pleaser. **87** —*S.H. (11/15/2004)*

Wildhurst 1997 Chardonnay (Clear Lake) $11. 85 —*M.S. (10/1/1999)*

Wildhurst 1999 Chardonnay (Lake County) $14. Opens with aromas of peaches, butter cream, vanilla, and caramel, then turns fruity and rich in the mouth. It's a bit awkward, as there's a blast of herbs or veggies in the middle palate that doesn't seem to belong. **83** —*S.H. (8/1/2001)*

Wildhurst 1997 Private Reserve Chardonnay (Sonoma County) $18. 80 *(6/1/2000)*

Wildhurst 2003 Reserve Chardonnay (Lake County) $14. Bright in fruit and rather tart, this pretty wine is enriched by smoky oak and a creamy texture. It's spicy through the finish. **86** —*S.H. (12/15/2004)*

Wildhurst 2002 Reserve Merlot (Lake County) $16. Here's a Merlot that lives up to the moniker of the soft Cab. It's gentle in the mouth, with polished flavors of cherries and chocolate. Easy to drink, with some real complexity. **87** —*S.H. (12/15/2004)*

Wildhurst 2004 Sauvignon Blanc (Lake County) $11. This is a great price for a delicious, complex wine. It's quite dry, but so filled with rich, fruity lemon, fig, and vanilla flavors. Refreshes with big, clean acidity. **88 Best Buy** —*S.H. (10/1/2005)*

Wildhurst 2001 Sauvignon Blanc (Clear Lake) $11. A very clean, tasty wine, with pronounced flavors of grass, citrus fruits, sweet figs, and peppery spices. Has a ripely honeyed edge, but a crisp streak of acidity keeps it fresh and balanced. **86** —*S.H. (7/1/2003)*

Wildhurst 2000 Sauvignon Blanc (Clear Lake) $11. Here's an herbaceous, lemony wine with those telltale cat aromas and flavors. In the mouth, it's clean and citrusy, with just enough acid to balance. Finishes dry and smooth. **84** —*S.H. (11/15/2001)*

Wildhurst 2004 Reserve Sauvignon Blanc (Lake County) $11. I love the aroma on this wine, all figgy-citrusy and so clean. It leads you to expect a bone-dry, intense wine, and that's pretty much what you get. Clean and acidic, with focused lemon and lime flavors. **86 Best Buy** —*S.H.* *(10/1/2005)*

Wildhurst 2002 Reserve Syrah (Lake County) $16. A little hot and sharp, but you'll find nice black cherry, plum, and cocoa flavors, and an overlay of oak. The fruit's the star here. **84** —*S.H. (12/15/2004)*

Wildhurst 1998 Catfish Vineyard Zinfandel (Clear Lake) $14. Spicy, ripe fruit, with an edge to it. Well-defined wine, which shows briar, toast, berry, and coffee flavors sprinkled throughout. Well-built, sturdy, a little hot, but balanced and long. **88** —*P.G. (3/1/2001)*

WILDWOOD

Wildwood 2002 Jackson's Vineyard Cabernet Sauvignon (San Luis Obispo County) $35. Coming from such a cool climate, this Cab isn't as opulent or ripe as, say, Napa. There's a wintergreen mint note alongside the sweet red cherry and black raspberry flavors, and a lightly elegant weight. It's a different kind of Cab, but a dry, good one, and very friendly with food. **87** —*S.H. (11/1/2006)*

Wildwood 2001 Syrah (San Luis Obispo) $35. Pretty tannic and tough now, this cool-climate wine nonetheless has well-developed black cherry flavors, with earthier overtones of white pepper, coffee, and herbs. It's likeable for the full-bodied fruit and balance. Decant for a few hours. **86** —*S.H. (12/1/2004)*

Wildwood 2002 Gina's Vineyard Syrah (San Luis Obispo County) $28. Fragrant in raspberry, cherry, and sweet lavender, this gentle Syrah finishes with a dusty cocoa note. It's an easy but sophisticated wine, dry and well-structured. **85** —*S.H. (11/1/2006)*

Wildwood 2002 Sheri's Vineyard Syrah (San Luis Obispo County) $28. Distinctly ripe, with plum, blackberry, dark chocolate, and coffee flavors, this Syrah is firm in rich, thick tannins, totally dry, and a bit rustic. The vineyard is located just north of the Edna Valley, in a warmer location. **85** —*S.H. (11/1/2006)*

WILLAKENZIE

WillaKenzie 1999 Estelle Chardonnay (Willamette Valley) $25. This limited (250 case) production, Dijon-clone wine shows the ripe, bright flavor profile of the "new" Oregon Chardonnays. Oily and slightly hot, with opulent, assertive, high-toned aromas, it is a big wine that finishes with a burst of sweet vanilla. **89** —*P.G. (8/1/2002)*

WillaKenzie 1998 Gamay (Oregon) $16. 87 —*P.G. (9/1/2000)*

WillaKenzie 2005 Pinot Blanc (Willamette Valley) $19. The Pinot Blanc from this property puts many Oregon Pinot Gris to shame; it's got more polish, more detail, and more class overall. Compared to its estate-grown cousin, the Blanc is a bit more delicate, with lovely stone fruit, Asian pear, and pink grapefruit highlights. Whole-cluster pressing and cold fermentation enhance aromas and bring out nuances of citrus rind. **90** —*P.G. (12/1/2006)*

WillaKenzie 2004 Pinot Blanc (Willamette Valley) $18. The Pinot Blanc from this property is one of the best in Oregon, though not as big and brawny overall as their Pinot Gris. Stone fruits and green apple flavors mix nicely in a tart but not sour wine that shows a bit of cinnamon/baking spice also. **87** —*P.G. (11/15/2005)*

WillaKenzie 1998 Pinot Blanc (Willamette Valley) $16. 90 —*P.G. (9/1/2000)*

WillaKenzie 1997 Pinot Grigio (Willamette Valley) $15. 87 *(8/1/1999)*

WillaKenzie 2005 Pinot Gris (Willamette Valley) $19. WillaKenzie's oldest Pinot Gris vines are almost 15 years of age, and their estate bottling seems to gain in weight and power with each passing year. Chewy and substantial, layered and meaty, it's a succulent fruit salad; hints of pear and peach, mango, and papaya, grapefruit, and pineapple. The wine is beautifully proportioned and its richness is never heavy or fat. **91 Editors' Choice** —*P.G. (12/1/2006)*

WillaKenzie 2004 Pinot Gris (Willamette Valley) $18. WillaKenzie pulls off a powerhouse Gris in this hot, ripe vintage. A chewy core of ripe pear is substantial, layered, and texturally satisfying. Hints of vanilla custard are laced throughout, and the finishing kiss of lime and citrus zest is just about perfect. **90** —*P.G. (11/15/2005)*

WillaKenzie 2001 Pinot Gris (Oregon) $20. I don't know anyone making better Pinot Gris in Oregon than this premiere property. Rich, ripe, round, and sensuous, this lush and textured wine unwraps its ripe fruit in layers of pear/apricot flavor, enhanced with bright spice and finished with flavors of vanilla cream. **92 Editors' Choice** —*P.G. (8/1/2002)*

WillaKenzie 2000 Pinot Gris (Oregon) $18. This excellent property has been a leader in Oregon Pinot Gris and Pinot Blanc since its inception. The new Gris is a delicious and spicy bottling, with tart, vivid fruit that leaves a clean, racy impression in the mouth. Lean and inviting. **90** — *P.G. (2/1/2002)*

WillaKenzie 1999 Pinot Gris (Oregon) $16. 90 —*P.G. (9/1/2000)*

WillaKenzie 1997 Pinot Gris (Willamette Valley) $15. 87 *(8/1/1999)*

WillaKenzie 1998 Pinot Meunier (Oregon) $20. 88 *(9/1/2000)*

WillaKenzie 2004 Pinot Noir (Willamette Valley) $23. Good fruit, with plenty of soft cranberry/cherry flavor, and very light milk chocolate in the finish. **87** —*P.G. (9/1/2006)*

WillaKenzie 1998 Pinot Noir (Oregon) $22. 87 —*P.G. (9/1/2000)*

WillaKenzie 2003 Aliette Pinot Noir (Willamette Valley) $36. Lush and extracted, spicy, and full-bodied, this is a wonderful effort that showcases the ripeness of the 2003s. Spicy, tannic, and laden with grace notes of mineral, iodine, and licorice. **90** —*P.G. (9/1/2006)*

WillaKenzie 2002 Aliette Pinot Noir (Willamette Valley) $36. This is very fruity, with a sweet, grapy, Kool-Aid character. Candied and sweet up front, it shows substantial, dry, tea-like tannins as it resolves. **86** *(11/1/2004)*

WillaKenzie 2003 Emery Pinot Noir (Willamette Valley) $45. Soft and approachable, this has mixed red fruits kissed with a strong piney accent. Comes on somewhat tannic, tough, and stemmy, but opens up nicely with some breathing time. **89** —*P.G. (9/1/2006)*

WillaKenzie 2003 Kiana Pinot Noir (Willamette Valley) $45. Good concentrated, almost jammy fruit and strawberry preserves streaked with coffee. This is showing a lot of tannin also, mixed flavors of black tea, silage, soy, and balsamic. It's a very interesting wine that needs more time to completely knit together. **90** —*P.G. (9/1/2006)*

WillaKenzie 2002 Kiana Pinot Noir (Willamette Valley) $45. Tangy citrus and light berry fruit flavors make for a straightforward, seemingly simple wine. **85** *(11/1/2004)*

WillaKenzie 2000 Kiana Pinot Noir (Willamette Valley) $35. Red fruit, vanilla, and brambly spice aromas. Clean black cherry and plum flavors carry the lively palate, which leads into a dry but potent finish of coffee, mocha and vanilla. **88** *(10/1/2002)*

WillaKenzie 1999 Pierre Leon Pinot Noir (Willamette Valley) $35. Complex but rather closed, this plummy Pinot wears lots of well-toasted oak. Some funky, charred-oak aromas show early but recede. The rich fruit, with its bramble and smoke accents rides a full mouthfeel. Very dark, closing with big but soft tannins, this will always be a fairly black beauty. Drink now–2008. **88** *(10/1/2002)*

WillaKenzie 2003 Pierre Léon Pinot Noir (Willamette Valley) $36. Tight, herbal, and showing lots of green tea flavors, this complex wine offers some of the soy and silage notes that often seem to show up with organically farmed fruit. **89** —*P.G. (9/1/2006)*

WillaKenzie 2002 Pierre Leon Vineyard Pinot Noir (Willamette Valley) $36. Though we found a hint of soapiness in the nose, the wine quickly showed prettier floral and citrus notes, then continued to reveal a concentrated, flavorful, distinctly floral center. The powerful citrus notes are unusual, but interesting. **88** *(11/1/2004)*

WillaKenzie 2003 Terres Basses Pinot Noir (Willamette Valley) $55. The most depth and weight of the lineup; black cherry and blackberry fruit holds down a solid, sweet center. The tannins are ripe and full, and the wine has an appealing roundness. **91** —*P.G. (9/1/2006)*

WillaKenzie 2003 Triple Black Slopes Pinot Noir (Willamette Valley) $55. Here the fruit is pure blackberry, the tannins ripe and redolent of black tea, the wine smooth and rich. This pulls it all together; and puts it on a solid foundation of mineral and graphite. **91** —*P.G. (9/1/2006)*

WILLAMETTE VALLEY VINEYARDS

Willamette Valley Vineyards 2000 Chardonnay (Willamette Valley) $10. Time was, Oregon Chardonnay was a sad creature, overpriced and underripe, but those days are long gone. Even in this budget bottling, almost half of the juice is estate grown from the Dijon clone. Another 20% is 30-year-old Draper clone from the old Tualatin vineyard. Barrel fermented sur lie; this is one heckuva good bottle of Chardonnay for 10 bucks! **88 Best Buy** —*P.G. (12/1/2003)*

Willamette Valley Vineyards 1999 Estate Vineyard Chardonnay (Willamette Valley) $22. Bright gold in color, with creamy custard and caramel aromas. The palate is soft, with banana, baked apple, and corn-like flavors, while the finish is heavy and rather mute. Very thick and heavy given the level of balance, acidity, and fruit pedigree. **83** —*M.S. (8/1/2003)*

Willamette Valley Vineyards 2000 Late Harvest Ehrenfelser (Willamette Valley) $20. Honeyed notes mingle sweetly with spice, apricot, peach, and pear flavors. Lush and lingering on the finish. **88** —*J.M. (12/1/2002)*

Willamette Valley Vineyards 2002 Gewürztraminer (Willamette Valley) $12. No one gives Gewürz much respect, but it is really lovely when done well, as it is here. Fragrant, complex, and rich with lush fruits and interesting accents, this is quite dry, hence food-friendly, and has a resonant, persistent finish. **88 Best Buy** —*P.G. (12/1/2003)*

Willamette Valley Vineyards 2005 Pinot Gris (Oregon) $16. Small amounts of Pinot Blanc, Muscat, and Auxerrois are blended in, adding some interesting herbal highlights. But the wine tastes mostly of green apples and lightly spiced pears. The fruit is neither deep nor especially ripe, but it's a perfectly serviceable everyday white. **85** —*P.G. (9/1/2006)*

Willamette Valley Vineyards 2004 Pinot Gris (Oregon) $15. Pinot Gris has never been more popular, and this user-friendly, soft, and spicy style is bursting with varietal flavors of fresh cut pears. The splash of acid keeps the flavors on their toes (and dancing on your tongue) through a smooth, lingering finish. Great with sandwiches, salmon, salads, and savory dips. **89** —*P.G. (8/1/2005)*

Willamette Valley Vineyards 2002 Pinot Gris (Oregon) $13. This is a textbook example of Oregon Pinot Gris. It shows characteristic pear-flavored fruit, balanced against firm acids, with good midpalate richness and a full, clean, satisfying finish. **89 Best Buy** —*P.G. (12/1/2003)*

Willamette Valley Vineyards 2001 Pinot Gris (Willamette Valley) $13. Flat but clean, with very light and distant apricot and celery aromas. The flavors veer toward green apple and lemon, while the finish is bland. From a texture standpoint, it's watery, with only modest fruit quality. **82** — *M.S. (8/1/2003)*

Willamette Valley Vineyards 2000 Pinot Gris (Willamette Valley) $14. Here is a straightforward rendering of Pinot Gris, with tart, tangy citrus fruit leading to a clean, crisp finish. Solid and flavorful, though completely one dimensional. **86** —*P.G. (4/1/2002)*

Willamette Valley Vineyards 2000 Founder's Reserve Pinot Gris (Willamette Valley) $18. There is an attractive, creamy mouthfeel to this Pinot Gris, which showcases fresh citrus fruit with spicy vanilla flavors coming from the barrel aging. It's a beautifully balanced, precision-tooled effort that is big but avoids palate fatigue by staying light on its feet. **88** —*P.G. (4/1/2002)*

Willamette Valley Vineyards 2001 Founders' Reserve Pinot Gris (Willamette Valley) $18. The wine's pale translucence is a fair indicator of what's coming next, which is not much. Light citrus and canned-fruit aromas portend a dilute palate. The finish is mildly bitter, with little more than white pepper. Oregon has proven itself capable of producing Pinot Gris with more guts than this. **81** —*M.S. (12/31/2002)*

Willamette Valley Vineyards 2004 Pinot Noir (Oregon) $19. Spicy cranberry and rhubarb flavors hold down the center, and the rest is fleshed out with herb, leaf, beet root and earth. Not as ripe as the 2003, it comes across as fairly austere and tannic, and some breathing time and/or decanting would be a good idea. **86** —*P.G. (9/1/2006)*

Willamette Valley Vineyards 2003 Pinot Noir (Willamette Valley) $19. This is a good effort for the price, showing spicy cherry and raspberry fruit, light hints of herb, beet root, and moist earth. It seems to get a bit earth-ier as it weaves into the finish, but it's well balanced and certainly well matched to salmon, swordfish, or poultry dishes. **87** —*P.G. (9/1/2006)*

Willamette Valley Vineyards 1999 Pinot Noir (Oregon) $17. The oaky mantle on this wine's dark cherry and cranberry fruit was too weighty to our panel. Even, but not soft on the palate, the wine displays a vaguely chalky feel. Citrus accents adorn its tart, cedary profile. Drink now–2004; best with food. **84** *(10/1/2002)*

Willamette Valley Vineyards 2000 Barrel Select Pinot Noir (Willamette Valley) $15. Light and appealing aromas of cherry, leather, rose petals, and rubber kick it off, followed by some tea-like dried cherry and raspberry flavors. The wine is very clean and svelte, with a layered finish and an overall ripe, healthy freshness. It's no blockbuster, but for a lightweight domestic Pinot it has almost all of what it should have. **87** —*M.S. (9/1/2003)*

Willamette Valley Vineyards 2004 Estate Pinot Noir (Oregon) $28. Stiff and hard, with green, leafy flavors and tough, tight tannins. It shows a bit more concentration than the regular bottling, but it comes in the form of tannin and earthy, herbal flavors that may need quite a lot of time to show what's really in there. **87** —*P.G. (9/1/2006)*

Willamette Valley Vineyards 2003 Estate Pinot Noir (Willamette Valley) $28. Stiff and hard, it has green, leafy flavors and tough, tight tannins. This is the type of Oregon Pinot that needs breathing time, decanting, and perhaps a few years in the cellar. **87** —*P.G. (9/1/2006)*

Willamette Valley Vineyards 2002 Estate Pinot Noir (Willamette Valley) $30. More than a hint of green bean in the nose. This wine has a vegetal streak, but recovers long enough to show some pleasant flavors of pomegranate and light red cherry. **84** *(11/1/2004)*

Willamette Valley Vineyards 2000 Estate Vineyard Pinot Noir (Willamette Valley) $31. Lean, green-ish aromas mixed with an artificial sweetness akin to bubble gum or marzipan. The black cherry fruit is mildly tart, bordering on thin. And while it finishes warm and airy, with coffee nuances, it just doesn't sing a harmonious song. **84** *(10/1/2002)*

Willamette Valley Vineyards 1999 Estate Vineyard Pinot Noir (Willamette Valley) $45. The fruit smells of earth and root, suggesting less than optimal ripeness, but there are also clean light cherry flavors and nuances of beet and tomato. It's a midweight effort, but not up to the quality of the other single-vineyard Pinots from this producer. **85** —*P.G. (4/1/2002)*

Willamette Valley Vineyards 1999 Founders' Reserve Pinot Noir (Oregon) $27. Black cherry, vanilla, and chocolate aromas open this full-scaled Pinot. The palate is tangy, with pepper- and raisin-accented berry fruit, but doesn't show the fleshiness the rich nose promises. Closes quite dry and dark, with coffee and bitter chocolate notes. Drink now–2006. **85** *(10/1/2002)*

Willamette Valley Vineyards 2002 Freedom Hill Vineyard Pinot Noir (Willamette Valley) $45. Controversial, some tasters found it elegant and classical; others thought it was reductive and bitter. The fruit is clean and varietal, and the wine is crisp and acidic, though the finish is tough and tannic. **85** *(11/1/2004)*

Willamette Valley Vineyards 1999 Freedom Hill Vineyard Pinot Noir (Oregon) $45. Ripe and tangy, there are rich, jammy flavors of berries up front, backed with ample tannins and tasty toast. It all leads to a thick, chocolatey finish. Definitely a consumer-pleasing style. **87** —*P.G. (4/1/2002)*

Willamette Valley Vineyards 1998 Freedom Hill Vineyard Pinot Noir (Willamette Valley) $44. Character and flavor abound in this lovely, even wine. The cherry fruit core wears interesting and complex chalk, sage, and mineral accents. The mouthfeel is nicely textured—smooth, with a subtle graininess. The long, refined finish shows very even tannic structure and good grip. They come deeper, but not much more polished than this. **91** —*M.M. (11/1/2001)*

Willamette Valley Vineyards 2000 Hoodview Vineyard Pinot Noir (Willamette Valley) $31. Tree bark, briar patch, and smoke are three potent aromas you'll get on the nose of this middleweight that runs fast with tart cherry fruit, an herbal streak and a clean, tannic finish. Because it's leaner than it is chunky, it would pair well with baked salmon. **88** *(10/1/2002)*

Willamette Valley Vineyards 1999 Hoodview Vineyard Pinot Noir (Oregon) $45. This is a fine, sweet-scented wine, with clean, crisp fruit and a pleasing balance. Here the fruit takes center stage, with no obvious new oak, just vivid acids to set it off. What's here is delicious, but regarding balance it is a simple, one-dimensional wine. **86** —*P.G. (4/1/2002)*

Willamette Valley Vineyards 2002 Joe Dobbes Signature Cuvée Pinot Noir (Willamette Valley) $50. Opens with pretty floral scents—violets and rose petals—that lead into sweet, cranberry fruit. Tart and tangy, with a somewhat sharp, acidic mouthfeel, this is a wine that will improve with food. **84** *(11/1/2004)*

Willamette Valley Vineyards 2000 Joe Dobbes Signature Cuvée Pinot Noir (Willamette Valley) $42. Bright red berry and cola aromas open WVV's top-shelf Pinot. The flavors are pure red fruit—like a bowl of berries, plums, and cherries. The finish has some fruit skin to it (tannins) as well as a coffee-like flavor and some underlying vanilla. **88** *(10/1/2002)*

Willamette Valley Vineyards 1999 Joe Dobbes Signature Cuvée Pinot Noir (Willamette Valley) $60. This bottling is the winery's top cuvée, a blend of the best lots of the other single vineyard Pinots. Tight and steely, its tart, cranberry fruit plays hard against a background of mineral, herb, and light coffee. Clearly ageworthy, it has the complexity and structure to merit the score. **91 Cellar Selection** —*P.G. (4/1/2002)*

Willamette Valley Vineyards 2000 Karina Vineyard Pinot Noir (Willamette Valley) $31. Tree bark, cherries, cigar ash, and green vegetables are the detectable aromas. There are some generic red-fruit flavors that follow, but they're on the thin side. Oak, black pepper, and earth comprise the finish. Overall, we found this wine to be somewhat rough and lean. **83** *(10/1/2002)*

Willamette Valley Vineyards 1999 Karina Vineyard Pinot Noir (Willamette Valley) $45. This lovely wine appeals instantly with its racy, tannic fruit, balanced weight, and textured layers of flavor. There's plenty of acid backbone and distinct flavors of mineral and soil, adding welcome dimension and depth of flavor. **90** —*P.G. (4/1/2002)*

Willamette Valley Vineyards 2002 Mt. Hood Pinot Noir (Willamette Valley) $45. Vinous and alcoholic, this mixes sweet fruit with toast and graham cracker flavors from the barrel. Flashy and high-toned, it doesn't quite hang together. **83** *(11/1/2004)*

Willamette Valley Vineyards 1998 O'Connor Vineyard Pinot Noir (Willamette Valley) $39. This may not be the current vintage, but it's a mature wine that's ready to drink. It starts with cherry aromas along with mint and licorice. The mouth is not too heavy, and the red cherry fruit on the palate is expressive and pure. The finish is a tad short, but what's there is fine, and as a whole this wine is likable and easygoing. **88** —*M.S. (9/1/2003)*

Willamette Valley Vineyards 2001 Whole Cluster Pinot Noir (Oregon) $17. Just a step away from Beaujolais, this is fresh, fruity, forward, and lightly spicy, with the distinctive flavors of whole-cluster fermentation. Some pretty cinnamon highlights accompany the juicy red berry fruit flavors. Tasty. **87 Best Buy** —*P.G. (4/1/2003)*

Willamette Valley Vineyards 2000 Whole Cluster Pinot Noir (Oregon) $12. This wine has bubble gum, banana, and plum cake aromas similar to Beaujolais. It's a bit awkward and bulky, but for most people it's a good quaffer, one with an abundance of black fruit flavor and no oak. But some might find the carbonic aromas odd and the mouthfeel overly chunky. **86 Best Buy** *(10/1/2002)*

Willamette Valley Vineyards 2005 Whole Cluster Fermented Pinot Noir (Oregon) $18. Young, grapey and tannic, with loads of tomato leaf flavors. It's definitely on the herbal side of Pinot Noir, but a nice streak of vanilla and boysenberry comes across in the finish. **86** —*P.G. (9/1/2006)*

Willamette Valley Vineyards 2004 Whole Cluster Fermented Pinot Noir (Oregon) $18. This might be likened to a Beaujolais-style Oregon Pinot, with bright, snappy fruit flavors and plenty of the penetrating herbal stemminess common to Oregon Pinots. Light, fruity, and well made, this might be the perfect hot dog wine. **85** —*P.G. (8/1/2005)*

Willamette Valley Vineyards 2001 Riesling (Oregon) $8. 88 —*P.G. (8/1/2003)*

Willamette Valley Vineyards 2002 Founders' Reserve Sauvignon Blanc (Oregon) $16. There's not much Sauv Blanc being made in Oregon these days, which is unfortunate, if this intense, spicy, focused wine is representative of what can be achieved. It captures some of the herbaceousness of Sancerre, some of the lime-driven fruit of New Zealand, and all of the ripe, juicy, crispness of the best Oregon white wines. **90** —*P.G. (12/1/2003)*

Willamette Valley Vineyards 2001 Viognier (Rogue Valley) $28. A step forward from previous hot, overripe efforts. This is better balanced, though still quite ripe (14.5% alcohol), and the flavors run through stone fruits and citrus, with hints of lovely floral highlights. Nice wine, but it's hard to believe that consumers will be seduced by Viognier at this price point. **87** —*P.G. (12/1/2003)*

WILLIAM HARRISON

William Harrison 2002 Estate Cabernet Sauvignon (Rutherford) $45. Here's an oaky wine, sending out powerful waves of vanilla, toast, and woodspice. The oak carries through in the mouth, where it joins ripe, sweet cherry and mocha flavors. Drink now. **86** —*S.H. (12/15/2005)*

WILLIAM HILL ESTATE

William Hill Estate 1997 Cabernet Sauvignon (Napa Valley) $20. 86 *(3/1/2000)*

William Hill Estate 1996 Cabernet Sauvignon (Napa Valley) $16. 88 *(11/1/1999)*

William Hill Estate 1996 Cabernet Sauvignon (Napa Valley) $16. 88 *(11/1/1999)*

William Hill Estate 1995 Cabernet Sauvignon (Napa Valley) $16. 90 Best Buy —*S.H. (6/1/1999)*

William Hill Estate 2003 Cabernet Sauvignon (Napa Valley) $20. From the winery's estate vineyard, in a cooler part of the valley south of Stags Leap, comes this dry, tannic, full-bodied wine. Far from a jammy monster, it has a bell pepper earthiness in addition to cherries and blackberries, and could develop some bottle complexities in a few years. **85** —*S.H. (10/1/2006)*

William Hill Estate 2001 Cabernet Sauvignon (Napa Valley) $22. This lovely Cab is soft and lush in blackberry and cherry fruit, with a pretty veneer of smoky oak. It has enough structure and finesse to accompany good food. Really satisfies for its sheer drinkability. **89** —*S.H. (10/1/2004)*

William Hill Estate 2000 Cabernet Sauvignon (Napa Valley) $22. Always reliable, and often a value, this vintage William Hill hits paydirt with well-etched black currant flavors wrapped in a shroud of toasty oak. The dry tannins are dusty and complex, and the wine feels velvety on the palate. **90** —*S.H. (8/1/2003)*

William Hill Estate 1999 Cabernet Sauvignon (Napa Valley) $22. Ripely fruity, as you'd expect from the vintage, it brims with black currant and sage flavors and some pretty oak. There's a refreshing cut of acidity, and it's nicely dry, with dusty tannins. No depth, and it's not going anywhere, but good for tonight. **86** —*S.H. (9/12/2002)*

William Hill Estate 1998 Cabernet Sauvignon (Napa Valley) $22. Still dependable despite changes in ownership, this winery again delivers an elegant, well-made wine. With this vintage, it veers more toward herbaceous notes than fruity ones. The dominant flavors are of green olives and sweet bell pepper. Don't think, however, that it's lean. Oak provides fatness, and the right foods, like grilled red meat, will coax out the berry sweetness. **87** —*S.H. (2/1/2001)*

William Hill Estate 2003 Reserve Cabernet Sauvignon (Napa Valley) $36. Way too young to enjoy now, to judge by the awkward way the parts jostle against each other. Sharp-elbowed tannins and citrusy acids battle with jammy blackberry tart flavors and fresh, spicy oak that is unintegrated. But this seems like a very fine cellar candidate. Start drinking in 2007, and should improve for a decade. **91 Cellar Selection** —*S.H. (9/1/2006)*

William Hill Estate 2002 Reserve Cabernet Sauvignon (Napa Valley) $36. It must be the coolness of the estate, because even in this hot vintage, this wine is dry, tannic, and relatively moderate in alcohol. It's an old-fashioned Napa Cab, in the best sense, made in a balanced, ageworthy style that impressed before the modern era of superripe opulence. Fine

USA

now, and should hold and improve for a good ten years. **91** —*S.H. (8/3/2006)*

William Hill Estate 2001 Reserve Cabernet Sauvignon (Napa Valley) $36. Released about a year later than the regular '01, this is still a pretty tannic Cab. But it's rich enough now to have with a good steak, and in fact a beef dish with a wine reduction sauce could be perfect. The oak is smoky-sweet and filled with vanilla, the overall impression high-class. **92** —*S.H. (11/15/2005)*

William Hill Estate 1999 Reserve Cabernet Sauvignon (Napa Valley) $38. Quite a distinguished '99, with its flamboyant aromas of spicy black currants and cassis, with an oaky overlay of smoke and vanilla. Feels good as soon as it hits the palate, with blackberry flavors that last through the finish. The jolt of dry tannins that makes the palate puckery suggests midterm aging. **90** —*S.H. (11/15/2003)*

William Hill Estate 1998 Reserve Cabernet Sauvignon (Napa Valley) $38. This winery, in official notes on this wine, calls the vintage "erratic," and indeed it was. With every new release of a '98 Cab, the judgment is confirmed. This wine is sharp, tannic and herbaceous, dominated by green olive aromas and flavors that well-toasted oak can't fatten. Drink early. **85** —*S.H. (11/15/2002)*

William Hill Estate 1996 Reserve Cabernet Sauvignon (Napa Valley) $35. **88** —*S.H. (7/1/2000)*

William Hill Estate 1995 Reserve Cabernet Sauvignon (Napa Valley) $27. **91** *(11/1/1999)*

William Hill Estate 1995 Reserve Cabernet Sauvignon (Napa Valley) $27. **91** *(11/1/1999)*

William Hill Estate 1998 Chardonnay (Napa Valley) $15. **86** *(6/1/2000)*

William Hill Estate 1997 Chardonnay (Napa Valley) $14. **88 Best Buy** *(11/1/1999)*

William Hill Estate 2004 Chardonnay (Napa Valley) $20. Here's a nice, clean Chardonnay whose best features are dryness and a rich coating of oak. The flavors veer toward peaches, apples, and pineapples, along with a distinct spiciness and a bracing streak of minerality. **85** —*S.H. (10/1/2006)*

William Hill Estate 2003 Chardonnay (Napa Valley) $13. Everybody likes ripe tropical fruit, toasty oak, Asian spices, a buttercreamy texture and a long, fruity finish in their Chards, and this one gives it all, in an everyday, friendly sort of way. **85** —*S.H. (11/15/2005)*

William Hill Estate 2002 Chardonnay (Napa Valley) $15. What a perfect cocktail wine. It's so refreshing in tropical fruit, buttercream, and sweet oak. But the spicy complexity also calls for very rich fare, such as broiled lobster. **89** —*S.H. (10/1/2004)*

William Hill Estate 2001 Chardonnay (Napa Valley) $15. Plump and juicy, packed with well-ripened flavors of peaches and pears. The texture is creamy, with a smoky, spicy edge to the finish. A bit flat, but tasty. **85** —*S.H. (6/1/2003)*

William Hill Estate 2000 Chardonnay (Napa Valley) $15. Quite fragrant, with loads of citrus, apricot, melon, and apple notes up front. On the palate, toasty oak, lemon, and herb flavors leave a bright, refreshing, and clean feel to the end. **88** —*J.M. (5/1/2002)*

William Hill Estate 2004 Reserve Chardonnay (Napa Valley) $26. From the winery's Carneros vineyard, a true reserve-style, low-production wine. It's built along the same lines as the regular Chard, with a mineral tang to the fruit flavors and a finish that combines spices and oak. Notable for its elegance and balance. **89** —*S.H. (10/1/2006)*

William Hill Estate 2003 Reserve Chardonnay (Napa Valley) $20. The regular Chard was released last spring. The Reserve, out now, is quite a better wine. It's rich, oaky, and creamy, with a great big burst of tropical fruit and peach flavors and scads of sweet cinnamon and vanilla on the finish. **88** —*S.H. (12/31/2005)*

William Hill Estate 2001 Reserve Chardonnay (Napa Valley) $21. Lean, with leesy, oaky flavors but not much in the way of fruit. Finishes with modest pear and spice. **84** —*S.H. (12/31/2004)*

William Hill Estate 2000 Reserve Chardonnay (Napa Valley) $23. Shares with many other Chards the aromas and flavors of ripe peaches, apples,

and tropical fruits, with an overlay of spicy, smoky oak and a creamy texture. But this pretty wine earns extra points for its balance, harmony, and sheer yummy deliciousness. **90** —*S.H. (12/15/2002)*

William Hill Estate 1998 Reserve Chardonnay (Napa Valley) $22. **88** *(6/1/2000)*

William Hill Estate 1997 Reserve Chardonnay (Napa Valley) $20. **90** *(11/1/1999)*

William Hill Estate 1996 Merlot (Napa Valley) $18. **89** *(11/1/1999)*

William Hill Estate 2003 Merlot (Napa Valley) $23. Ripe and classy, this wine, with a little Cabernet, captures the rich power of a fine Bordeaux blend. It's very dry, and has intricate, dusty tannins that frame blackberry, cherry, mocha, dried herb, and oaky spice flavors. Easy to find, with 15,300 cases produced. **88** —*S.H. (12/15/2006)*

William Hill Estate 2001 Merlot (Napa Valley) $22. Wow, is this a good wine. It's filled with succulent blackberry and cherry flavors, and the oak is just right. It's dry, balanced, and harmonious, with exquisitely soft, sweet tannins. It would earn an even higher score with greater fruit concentration. **91** —*S.H. (10/1/2005)*

William Hill Estate 2000 Merlot (Napa Valley) $21. Rich and balanced, an easy-drinking Merlot that packs in plenty of plum, blackberry, and dried herb flavors. Goes down smooth due to the soft tannins, but there's decent structure and a spicy finish. **87** —*S.H. (2/1/2004)*

William Hill Estate 1999 Merlot (Napa Valley) $21. Usually a trusted producer of red wines, but this wine seems weak and diluted, even unripe. There are sharp green, minty aromas and flavors that are almost vegetal, and wipe out the blackberries. The wine is also thin on the palate and into the finish. From a good vintage, but with 24,000 cases, maybe they overcropped the vines. **84** —*S.H. (6/1/2002)*

William Hill Estate 1998 Merlot (Napa Valley) $22. A little less than ripe, it's got hints of blackberries but really veers toward an earthy herbaceousness. There's a cut of greenness in the aroma, and in the flavors, too. Finishes a bit rough and thin. **83** —*S.H. (8/1/2001)*

William Hill Estate 1999 Chardonnay (Napa Valley) $15. With a hefty case production, the wine is light and thin, but there are pleasant enough flavors. It's average Chardonnay, with just enough appley fruit, oak, and sweetness to satisfy. It's clean and well-made, and there's not much more you can say about it. **84** —*S.H. (2/1/2001)*

WILLIAM ROAN

William Roan 2002 Shiraz (North Coast) $12. Simple, fruity, and rough, with a flavor of Chinese sweet-and-sour sauce. **83** —*S.H. (6/1/2005)*

WILLIAMS SELYEM

Williams Selyem 2004 Chardonnay (Russian River Valley) $35. Bob Cabral has crafted a wine that combines purity of fruit with power and silky elegance. The wine explodes with baked apricot, nectarine, and guava flavors, the kind of fruit filling that oozes out of a buttery tart fresh from the oven. Yet bright acidity balances it out. Oak adds the perfect touch of vanilla and marzipan. **93 Editors' Choice** —*S.H. (11/1/2006)*

Williams Selyem 2001 Allen Vineyard Chardonnay (Russian River Valley) $48. The aroma changes with every sniff, ranging from ripe apple to sweet pear, smoky, clove-accented oak, butterscotch, Asian spice, Juicy Fruit gum, the works. It's enormous, a long hangtime wine of high alcohol and massive extraction. Hard to describe the nuance and complexity. **94** —*S.H. (2/1/2004)*

Williams Selyem 2003 Hawk Hill Vineyard Chardonnay (Russian River Valley) $46. It's hard to describe this as Chablisian, given the 15-percent-plus alcohol, but that word captures its minerality. There's a flintiness underlying the oak, citrus, and peach flavors of this bone-dry wine. Similar to grand cru Chablis—it's tough in its youth. Hard to tell where it's going. **87** —*S.H. (3/1/2006)*

Williams Selyem 2001 Hawk Hill Vineyard Chardonnay (Russian River Valley) $44. Stunning, a hugely aromatic wine bursting with lemondrop, lemon meringue pie, and smoky oak aromas. It detonates in the mouth with sweet lemon custard, vanilla, and pear flavors that are enormously rich, accompanied by bright acids that penetrate the nerve endings. Lasts for a long time on the finish. **95 Editors' Choice** —*S.H. (2/1/2004)*

Williams Selyem 2000 Hawk Hill Vineyard Chardonnay (Russian River Valley) $44. Kicks off with a hint of citrus and butterscotch on the nose. It's a densely structured wine, framed in toasty oak and showing tightly wound hints of lemon, melon, pear, and peach flavors. Bright on the finish, this is a powerful wine that should unfold nicely with time. **92** —*J.M. (2/1/2003)*

Williams Selyem 2003 Heintz Vineyard Chardonnay (Russian River Valley) $44. High in alcohol, bone dry, and even a little tannic, this wine has citrus and mineral flavors with an edge of candied peach and sweet cured tobacco. Oak and sur lies aging add richness, but this is still an earthy wine. Could soften and improve in a couple years. **87** —*S.H. (3/1/2006)*

Williams Selyem 2001 Heintz Vineyard Chardonnay (Russian River Valley) $40. From a cool area near the Sonoma Coast, very similar to the winery's Hawk Hill bottling, with lemondrop, custard, and butterscotch flavors, although it's less sharp in acids. You'll love the softly creamy texture, which accentuates the fat, opulent fruit. **94** —*S.H. (2/1/2004)*

Williams Selyem 2000 Heintz Vineyard Chardonnay (Russian River Valley) $40. On the nose, it starts off with racy tangerine, spice, and earth aromas. Beautifully balanced on the palate, with good body, moderate acidity, and just the right amount of toasty oak—all framing a complex web of pear, apple, mango, papaya, melon, citrus, and herb flavors. Long at the end. **93** —*J.M. (2/1/2003)*

Williams Selyem 2000 Hirsch Vineyard Chardonnay (Sonoma Coast) $42. Creamy smooth but balanced by firm, tangy acidity, and toasty oak and hazelnut flavors. This complex, elegant, and sensual wine coats the palate with ripe melon, pear, fig, and apple flavors, all highlighted by fresh lemon, orange, and herb notes. Clean and long on the finish, this is top-notch Chardonnay. **95 Editors' Choice** —*J.M. (2/1/2003)*

Williams Selyem 2003 Vista Verde Vineyard Late Harvest Gewürztraminer (San Benito County) $35. Winemaster Bob Cabral has crafted a dessert wine that's sweet, balanced, and refined, in no small part due to excellent acidity, which keeps you coming back. The flavors of apricots, honey, and spices are delicious, and finish long and clean. **91** —*S.H. (11/1/2005)*

Williams Selyem 2001 Vista Verde Vineyard Late Harvest Gewürztraminer (San Benito County) $32. Exceptionally sweet, with 16% residual sugar, and balanced with a hefty dose of citrusy acids. The apricot, orange honey, and toffee flavors, however, need to be more concentrated to earn a higher score. **86** —*S.H. (5/1/2004)*

Williams Selyem 2000 Vista Verde Vineyard Late Harvest Gewürztraminer (San Benito County) $32. Honey, spice, apricot, fig, citrus, cinnamon, clove, litchee, and apple flavors are all couched in a silky, viscous, and vivacious blend. Sweet and rich, but bright and fresh on the finish. Really a fine dessert wine. **93** —*J.M. (9/1/2003)*

Williams Selyem 2000 Windsor Oaks Vineyard Late Harvest Muscat Canelli (Russian River Valley) $32. A zippy blend of bright lemon and herb flavors that presage a powerful mix of Mandarin orange, grapefruit, peach, melon, spice, clove, apricot, and honeyed notes. Ultra-long on the finish **93** —*J.M. (7/1/2003)*

Williams Selyem 2003 Weir Vineyard Pinot Nero (Yorkville Highlands) $49. This single-vineyard bottling has never been one of my favorites. It's a big, dry wine, with plenty of cherry, black raspberry and chocolate flavors that are well-oaked, but always seems a little soft and heavy, not to mention one-dimensional. **86** —*S.H. (3/1/2006)*

Williams Selyem 2004 Pinot Noir (Central Coast) $39. Tart but super-tasty, this wine has cola, red cherry pie, pomegranate, and cinnamon spice flavors wrapped into a silky, crisp mouthfeel. It's totally dry and modest in alcohol, showing real elegance and finesse. Drink now. **89** —*S.H. (11/15/2006)*

Williams Selyem 2004 Pinot Noir (Sonoma Coast) $39. Right off the bat you can taste the acidity in this wine, which is brighter and crisper than, say, the winery's Russian River Pinot. The tartness lifts the black cherry, cherry, and raspberry flavors, heightening their impact through the long, spicy finish. Still, it's a wine for early drinking. **90** —*S.H. (11/1/2006)*

Williams Selyem 2004 Pinot Noir (Sonoma County) $32. This is a gentle, easy Pinot for drinking tonight, yet it has something of the power and complexity of the winery's top bottlings. Which makes sense, given Williams Selyem's access to top grapes. Silky and dry, the wine has flat-

tering flavors of cherry compote, cola, and Provençal herbs. **88** —*S.H. (11/1/2006)*

Williams Selyem 2004 Pinot Noir (Russian River Valley) $35. Darker and meatier than the winery's basic Sonoma County bottling, this Pinot has a fleshy fullness and tannins that suggest midterm aging. It's very dry and a bit soft, with powerful black cherry, cola, rhubarb, coffee, and leather flavors. **89** —*S.H. (11/1/2006)*

Williams Selyem 2003 Pinot Noir (Central Coast) $29. This textbook regional Pinot Noir displays a deft touch in the delicacy and silky finesse of the body, while holding nothing back in the way of flavor. Cherries, cola, sweet leather, and dusty spices come together in a dry, smooth finish. **88** —*S.H. (11/1/2005)*

Williams Selyem 2003 Pinot Noir (Russian River Valley) $42. This Pinot is so addictively delicious. It's a big wine, in color and even some tannins, with juicy cherry, plum, and cola flavors, but somehow manages to maintain elegance and delicacy. What a finish. It goes on for a full minute. **92** —*S.H. (11/1/2005)*

Williams Selyem 2003 Pinot Noir (Sonoma Coast) $38. You can taste the acids in this crisp wine, and the tannins also are sizable. Without offering the immediate pleasure of Bob Cabral's other Pinots, this one might benefit from short-term cellaring. **87** —*S.H. (11/1/2005)*

Williams Selyem 2003 Pinot Noir (Sonoma County) $32. Although the immediate impact of this wine is obvious in the soft silk and satin mouthfeel and cherry, cola, mocha, and spice flavors, it's not a simple wine. The palate understands the complexity, and wants more . . . and more . . . and more. **90** —*S.H. (11/1/2005)*

Williams Selyem 2002 Pinot Noir (Central Coast) $29. A bit harsh around the edges, but likeable for its rustic elegance. Shows tea, sour cherry, cola, and oaky flavors, wrapped in sturdy tannins that provide good grip. Very dry. **87** *(11/1/2004)*

Williams Selyem 2002 Pinot Noir (Russian River Valley) $39. Smoky, cedary oak stars here, and the wine is closed at first. After airing, it shows chocolate, leather, and raisiny notes, with some complexity. Needs short-term cellaring to show its best. **87** *(11/1/2004)*

Williams Selyem 2002 Pinot Noir (Sonoma Coast) $35. Fruity and simple aromas of orange popsicle, cherry Lifesaver, and mocha lead to a thick, rather soft wine, with ripe, heavy flavors. Might turn into something more interesting in a few years. **86** *(11/1/2004)*

Williams Selyem 2002 Pinot Noir (Sonoma County) $29. Starts off cedary and oaky, and as it warms reveals rich cherry, vanilla, and spice notes. Has a good fruity intensity in the mouth, and feels supple, with a tannic finish. **88** *(11/1/2004)*

Williams Selyem 2000 Pinot Noir (Central Coast) $27. Quite spicy, with cinnamon and peppery cherry, raspberry, black currant, anise, tea, and plum notes. Smooth, silky tannins frame it all, with a mellow finish. Quite nice. **91 Editors' Choice** —*J.M. (7/1/2003)*

Williams Selyem 2000 Pinot Noir (Sonoma Coast) $34. Somewhat light-bodied, with tangy acidity that supports a core of raspberry, plum, earth, and spice flavors. Smooth tannins and moderate length on the finish. **88** —*J.M. (2/1/2003)*

Williams Selyem 2000 Pinot Noir (Russian River Valley) $39. Substantially more open and fruitier than the Sonoma Coast bottling, this is a junior version of the fabulous 1999. This wine is rich and tannic, with fleshy earth and berry flavors. **87** —*S.H. (2/1/2003)*

Williams Selyem 2003 Allen Vineyard Pinot Noir (Russian River Valley) $75. After a dropoff in the quality of the '02, this wine marks a welcome return. Ripe and fruity in cherry and blueberry fruit, it's easy to enjoy now for its silky, oaky drinkability and classic structure. There are some superripe, raisiny flavors that add a piquant note, but I think this limits ageability. **92** —*S.H. (6/1/2005)*

Williams Selyem 2003 Allen Vineyard Pinot Noir (Russian River Valley) $75. If you're into aging Pinot Noir, here's one to lay down with a reasonable certainty. It's young, with a silky texture, and the oak, acids, alcohol, and fruit haven't knit together yet. But it's massive in dark cherry, pomegranate, and blackberry flavors. If you must drink it now, decant it. Even overnight isn't too long. **91** —*S.H. (3/1/2006)*

Williams Selyem 2002 Allen Vineyard Pinot Noir (Russian River Valley)
$72. Somewhat of a disappointment for all tasters. Opens with smoky, new oak aromas and a young, grapy mélange of blackberries and chocolate. Rich in tannins, with a chunky mouthfeel. Hard to really find nuance in it now, but try aging and see what develops. **85** *(11/1/2004)*

Williams Selyem 2001 Allen Vineyard Pinot Noir (Russian River Valley)
$69. Nearly as good as the Flax bottling, opening with a gorgeous aroma of mushroom, tobacco, coffee, Asian spice, cherry, blackberry, and oaky vanillins. Like all the current releases, it's very dry, but rich in sweetly ripe fruit and sweet oak. A little sharp now in acids, which should enable this beauty to age effortlessly through the decade. **93** — *S.H. (5/1/2004)*

Williams Selyem 2000 Allen Vineyard Pinot Noir (Russian River Valley)
$NA. Alcohol 14.2%. Still pretty tannic and youthful, with perky acids, and not showing at all its age. Big in fruit, with cherries and blueberries. Oak adds its thing, and there's a cocoa finish. No sign at all of raisins or overripeness. Beautiful now, and should hold throughout the decade. **92** — *S.H. (6/1/2005)*

Williams Selyem 2000 Allen Vineyard Pinot Noir (Russian River Valley)
$68. The vibrant, tangy black cherry aromas and flavors have real depth, accented stem to stern by cola, clove, cedar, chocolate, and exotic Bourbon-like notes. Yet it remains elegant, with fine fruit-to-acid balance and exceptional harmony. **92** *(10/1/2002)*

Williams Selyem 1995 Allen Vineyard Pinot Noir (Russian River Valley)
$NA. 13.7% alcohol. Really past its prime. Showing its age in the dull, cherry, vanilla, and oak aromas and flat, tart mouthfeel. Lovers of old Pinot will find it exciting. **84** — *S.H. (6/1/2005)*

Williams Selyem 2003 Bucher Vineyard Pinot Noir (Russian River Valley)
$49. Lots of bright cherry fruit marks this dry, young wine. It's fairly tannic, with good acidity. If you play with it in the mouth, the flavors really explode, coating the palate with sweet cherry essence complexed with fine oak. This is a big, young, exuberant wine that requires ample decanting. **91** — *S.H. (3/1/2006)*

Williams Selyem 2003 Coastlands Vineyard Pinot Noir (Sonoma Coast)
$62. There's more acidity in this wine than most Williams Selyem Pinots. Take a sip, and the flavor of cherries explodes on the palate, along with oak. Compared to the winery's '03s, it seems sweet, almost cloying, on the finish. **87** — *S.H. (3/1/2006)*

Williams Selyem 2002 Coastlands Vineyard Pinot Noir (Sonoma Coast)
$59. Very dark, almost inky in color, and powerful in extract, showing high-char oak, cherry candy, raspberry, and dark chocolate flavors. Certainly a big, robust wine, with good acidity. A little clumsy now, but should develop complexities. Drink now through 2008. **88** *(11/1/2004)*

Williams Selyem 2001 Coastlands Vineyard Pinot Noir (Sonoma Coast)
$59. From a chillier part of the appellation, a wine that struggled to get ripe. Smells of mint and menthol, with cedar, Asian spice, and coffee nuances. In the mouth, it's bone dry. Not a fruit-driven Pinot, but interesting for the interplay of acids and tannins. **87** — *S.H. (5/1/2004)*

Williams Selyem 1999 Coastlands Vineyard Pinot Noir (Sonoma Coast)
$52. From this memorable vintage, a huge, tannic wine, dark almost to the point of blackness, and dense and rich in blackberry and pepper fruit. You could easily mistake it for Syrah, it's that full-bodied. Amazingly, the grapes were not picked until November. **86** — *S.H. (2/1/2003)*

Williams Selyem 2003 Ferrington Vineyard Pinot Noir (Anderson Valley)
$59. Whoa—this is a tough, acidic baby on opening. No way you want to drink it immediately. Give it time, either by decanting or cellaring. It's big, dry, and tart, stuffed with black cherry, cola, coffee, and Asian spice flavors. Best after 2007. **89** — *S.H. (3/1/2006)*

Williams Selyem 2002 Ferrington Vineyard Pinot Noir (Anderson Valley)
$59. Tasters found consensus that this wine, while ripe, failed to inspire, beyond offering pleasant cherry, mocha, spice, and oak flavors. It's heavy, alcoholic, and tannic, but might soften with a few years of age. **84** *(11/1/2004)*

Williams Selyem 2001 Ferrington Vineyard Pinot Noir (Anderson Valley)
$57. Seems like a textbook Pinot from this appellation, with its jammy, forward cherry and raspberry scent enriched with mocha and hints of

dried herbs and dust. It's very big in the mouth, a sunburst of cherry flavors wrapped in fairly heavy tannins. Should improve through 2007. **89** —*S.H. (5/1/2004)*

Williams Selyem 2003 Flax Vineyard Pinot Noir (Russian River Valley)
$54. This is a big, full-bodied wine, huge in fruit, yet it has the silky elegance that Pinot needs. It's bone dry, with adequate acidity and a young, unresolved mouthfeel. There's a tremendous core of baked cherry pie fruit, drizzled with cinnamon and vanilla. Cellar this puppy for a couple years, or decant for up to 24 hours now. **92** —*S.H. (3/1/2006)*

Williams Selyem 2002 Flax Vineyard Pinot Noir (Russian River Valley)
$49. Another Williams Selyem wine that tasters had differing opinions about. Several liked its rich array of black cherry, spicy plum, and smoky oak, and overall balance and lushness. But one reviewer found it flabby and soft, with some residual sugar. You decide. **90** *(11/1/2004)*

Williams Selyem 2001 Flax Vineyard Pinot Noir (Russian River Valley)
$46. The Real McCoy of the Middle Reach, a fabulous wine. The aroma is a joy, with intricate fruit, herb, meat, spice, coffee, and oak scents mingled in harmony. Turns lush and soft in the mouth, very fat, amazingly complex, with near-perfect acidity and tannins. Bone dry, and intricately layered, it's a taste treat through the fantastically long finish. Drink now through 2010. **94 Editors' Choice** —*S.H. (5/1/2004)*

Williams Selyem 2001 Hirsch Vineyard Pinot Noir (Sonoma Coast) $59.
From a very warm vintage, an enormously ripe, fruity wine. The dramatic aromas include smoky oak, dried autumn leaves, and herbs, cherry, cranberry, and dried porcini, with similar flavors. Fabulously interesting and complex, a rich, sweetly earthy wine whose tannins and weight promise even better things to come. **92** —*S.H. (5/1/2004)*

Williams Selyem 2000 Hirsch Vineyard Pinot Noir (Sonoma Coast) $57.
Promising black plum, caramel, coffee, and spice aromas open to high-toned black cherry fruit, cola, licorice, and herbs. The feel is rich, slightly chalky, mouthfilling and velvety. Long and intense, the finish is packed with sweet and sour fruit. **93 Editors' Choice** *(10/1/2002)*

Williams Selyem 1997 Olivet Lane Pinot Noir (Russian River Valley) $45.
90 *(10/1/1999)*

Williams Selyem 2003 Peay Vineyard Pinot Noir (Sonoma Coast) $49.
Here's a dark, dense Pinot, brooding under its cloak of tannins and acids. It's absolutely dry, with intense cherry pie, cola, root beer, and oak flavors. If you drink it now without decanting, you'll find a tough, hard wine. Let it breathe for a day, and it will begin to suggest its charms. Or let it develop naturally in the cellar for six years. **92** —*S.H. (3/1/2006)*

Williams Selyem 1999 Precious Mountain Pinot Noir (Sonoma Coast) $80.
The aromas are elusive, with cinnamon, clove, and orange peel hints. There is an oaky element to the lighter-style strawberry fruit, and the finish is spicy, yielding heat at first before performing a smoother fade. Very pretty and not terribly big-boned or extracted. **89** *(10/1/2002)*

Williams Selyem 2003 Precious Mountain Vineyard Pinot Noir (Sonoma Coast) $85. Williams Selyem's priciest Pinot is an acidic, tannic wine in extreme youth. It's fruity and dry, showing great depth, balance, and complexity. There's a wealth of deep, unexpressed cherry, cranberry, cola, tobacco, cocoa, and sweet oak flavors. Something rich, like duck or a fine steak, will finesse the tannins, but you can also lay this wine down for a good five years, if not longer. **93** —*S.H. (3/1/2006)*

Williams Selyem 2002 Precious Mountain Vineyard Pinot Noir (Sonoma Coast) $80. A controversial wine among the tasters. Some found it seriously rich and deep in fruit, while others called it simple and hot in alcohol. It's certainly dark and brooding now. Berry-cherry flavors and lots of oak, with a lush, soft mouthfeel. Aging is a gamble. **87** *(11/1/2004)*

Williams Selyem 2001 Precious Mountain Vineyard Pinot Noir (Sonoma Coast) $80. Fruitier than the winery's Hirsch bottling, with a blast of raspberry, loganberry, mulberry, and other wild berries, and crushed Asian brown spices. Completely satisfying and complex, a wine that changes with every sip but is delicate and charming despite its size. **93** — *S.H. (5/1/2004)*

Williams Selyem 1999 Rochioli Riverblock Pinot Noir (Russian River Valley) $60. This dark and earthy Pinot pleased but did not wow tasters. Panelists applauded the forward raspberry fruit, but not all thought it was up to the ultratoasty oak veneer. Some found it a touch grainy and overly earthy; others thought it very tasty and not at all heavy. Only time will tell if the deep, sweet fruit will prevail **88** *(10/1/2002)*

Williams Selyem 2003 Rochioli Riverblock Vineyard Pinot Noir (Russian River Valley) $72. This is the most forward and varietally representative of the winery's current Sonoma releases. It's a Russian River Valley classic, showing ripe cherry, cola, rhubarb, and coffee flavors, with a mealy chewiness. The texture is silky, the acidity fine. It's big and bone dry, and should benefit from a few years in the cellar. **92** —*S.H. (3/1/2006)*

Williams Selyem 2002 Rochioli Riverblock Vineyard Pinot Noir (Russian River Valley) $69. Most tasters loved the huge complexities of this ripe, dense young wine. They praised its massive cherry and cocoa flavors that flirt with overripeness, and the smooth, silky texture. Another taster, however, found it super-oaky and clumsy. Likely to soften and knit together with a few hours of decanting, or aging through 2007. **93** *(11/1/2004)*

Williams Selyem 2001 Rochioli Riverblock Vineyard Pinot Noir (Russian River Valley) $64. The '99 was a joy and so is this stunning wine. It has a perfume of violets, blackberries, dried autumn leaves, succulent raspberry tart, licorice, coffee, and all sorts of other wholesome scents. The flavors, which are similar, drink complete and complex, at once subtle and compelling. Absolutely addictive in its interesting complexities, and undoubtedly will improve with a few years in the bottle. **93** —*S.H. (5/1/2004)*

Williams Selyem 2000 Rochioli Riverblock Vineyard Pinot Noir (Russian River Valley) $64. Smooth, rich, round, and packed with lush black cherry, raspberry, cedar, spice, and cinnamon flavors. The tannins are silky, and the acidity is firm and bright. Slightly warm at the end. **92** —*J.M. (7/1/2003)*

Williams Selyem 2003 Vista Verde Vineyard Pinot Noir (San Benito County) $49. This is the most rustic of the winery's current offerings. It's dry and soft, with syrupy flavors of cherries, with silky tannins. Not going anywhere, so drink now. **85** —*S.H. (3/1/2006)*

Williams Selyem 2002 Vista Verde Vineyard Pinot Noir (San Benito County) $49. A big, fruity wine, bursting with chocolate fudge, black cherry, and vanilla flavors, and made vibrant with keen acidity. Feels plush and warming in the mouth, and could develop for a few more years. **90** *(11/1/2004)*

Williams Selyem 2001 Vista Verde Vineyard Pinot Noir (San Benito County) $46. From a cool area, a lovely, intricately detailed wine. It has lots of cherry, cola, herb, and coffee notes, and is very dry. Complex and elegant, this wine turns tannic on the finish, and should age well through the decade. **88** —*S.H. (5/1/2004)*

Williams Selyem 2000 Vista Verde Vineyard Pinot Noir (San Benito County) $32. Quite ripe but a bit chewy on the palate. Pretty cherry, strawberry, tea, spice, and herb flavors are at the core. Tannins are slightly robust, but still ripe. The wine finishes long, clean, and elegant. **90** —*J.M. (7/1/2003)*

Williams Selyem 2002 Weir Vineyard Pinot Noir (Yorkville Highlands) $49. Dark and strong, with lots of heft and weight, this full-bodied Pinot shows oodles of ripe cherries, wintergreen, vanilla, and toast. Feels intense and creamy, with tons of cherry fruit flavor. For all the size, we wish it had greater finesse. **86** *(11/1/2004)*

Williams Selyem 2001 Weir Vineyard Pinot Noir (Yorkville Highlands) $48. Some will like the distinctive coffee, cola, menthol, cherry candy, and mineral flavors, and the rather heavy, thick mouthfeel of this tannic wine. It should soften up with a few years in the bottle. **86** —*S.H. (5/1/2004)*

Williams Selyem 2000 Weir Vineyard Pinot Noir (Yorkville Highlands) $48. This is the softest and fruitiest Pinot that Williams Selyem produces; it's filled with black raspberry and cherry flavors. This obscure Mendocino region is a cool area but not as cool as Russian River Valley, so this is a fatter, more accessible wine. **87** —*S.H. (2/1/2003)*

Williams Selyem 2004 Westside Road Neighbors Pinot Noir (Russian River Valley) $62. This is a blend of vineyards from which the winery sources its fruit. It's a very good wine, dry and crisp, with ripe flavors of cherries,

raspberries, root beer, and herbs. The texture is silky, the balance impeccable, but it's a tad thin in the midpalate. **88** —*S.H. (11/1/2006)*

Williams Selyem 2003 Westside Road Neighbors Pinot Noir (Russian River Valley) $62. Compared to the winery's regular Russian River bottling, this is considerably more tannic. Yet it doesn't take long for the spiced plum pudding, cherry compote, black raspberry, cola, and smoky oak flavors to kick in. Fantastic now, and should hold for the remainder of this decade. **93** —*S.H. (11/1/2005)*

Williams Selyem 2002 Westside Road Neighbors Pinot Noir (Russian River Valley) $59. Dark as midnight, and youthful with thick tannins and fresh acids. The fruity flavors are jammy and thick, almost like molasses. It's a big, ripe wine that lacks delicacy and charm, but it sure does pack a punch. **87** *(11/1/2004)*

Williams Selyem 2001 Mistral Vineyard Port (Central Coast) $35. Like a nice LBV Port, this is a not too sweet, richly fruited wine balanced by crisp acids. The flavors veer toward dark chocolate, with crème de cassis and roasted coffeebean accents and an orange peel or marmalade flourish. It's a marvelous, delicious sipper on a late, cold night. **93 Editors' Choice** —*S.H. (3/1/2006)*

Williams Selyem 2001 Zinfandel (Russian River Valley) $25. A fine-tuned blend of pretty plum, blackberry, black cherry, coffee, cola, toast, and herb flavors, all couched in silky tannins. The wine shows both restraint and opulence, finishing with a velvety edge. **90** *(11/1/2003)*

Williams Selyem 2000 Zinfandel (Russian River Valley) $25. Quite plush. Redolent of black cherry and plum in the nose. This is classic, deep, lush Zin, packed with sweet fruit, spice, pepper, and chocolate flavors. Zippy acidity lends freshness to the finish. Downright hedonistic. At this price, you might call it a cheap thrill. **92 Editors' Choice** —*J.M. (2/1/2003)*

Williams Selyem 2004 Bacigalupi Vineyard Zinfandel (Russian River Valley) $45. The vineyard, in a warmer part of the valley, is old, but the wine has intense, youthfully jammy flavors of raspberries, cherries, and blueberries, with Zin's great edge of peppery spice. It's a big, audacious wine, but never loses poise despite very high alcohol. **91** —*S.H. (11/1/2006)*

Williams Selyem 2003 Bacigalupi Vineyard Zinfandel (Russian River Valley) $42. I criticized Williams Selyem's Feeney Vineyard Zin for overly high alcohol, at 15.8 percent. This one is an inexcusable 16.3 percent. I wish someone would explain to me why it's necessary to harvest at these levels, unless you're making Port. **80** —*S.H. (11/1/2005)*

Williams Selyem 2004 Feeney Vineyard Zinfandel (Russian River Valley) $45. While this Zin is clinically dry, it's so explosive in cherry, rhubarb, pomegranate, and cola flavors that it's almost sweet, like pie filling. The acids and tannins rush in at the last minute, balancing it with a dusty dryness. It's a classically ripe coastal Zin, and savvy sommeliers will have fun figuring out what to pair it with. **90** —*S.H. (11/1/2006)*

Williams Selyem 2003 Feeney Vineyard Zinfandel (Russian River Valley) $42. This wine has too much alcohol, namely 15.8%, and finishes hot and raisiny. Awkward exaggerations of what Zin should be. **83** —*S.H. (11/1/2005)*

Williams Selyem 2002 Feeney Vineyard Zinfandel (Russian River Valley) $38. The downside of this wine is its enormous alcohol, nearly 16 percent. That's the price you pay for a dry wine with gargantuan flavors. Black currants, cherry pie, tobacco, pepper, bitter chocolate, and dill only begin to describe the palate. Yet the wine is balanced and even elegant. Truly an only-in-California experience. **91** —*S.H. (10/1/2004)*

Williams Selyem 2003 Forchini Vineyard Zinfandel (Russian River Valley) $42. True to form, winemaker Bob Cabral has crafted a humungous Zin, with 16.2% alcohol and the ripest flavors imaginable. Dry, with tremendous blackberry and cherry marmalade flavors that finish in a swirl of vanilla, spice, and chocolate. **92** —*S.H. (3/1/2006)*

Williams Selyem 2001 Forchini Vineyard North Flats Zinfandel (Russian River Valley) $32. Fairly bright, with tangy cherry and plum flavors. Tannins are silky, despite the brightness, with tea, coffee, spice, and peppery notes on the finish. Long, lush, and exciting to the end. **90** *(11/1/2003)*

WILLIAMSON

Williamson 2003 Amourette Chardonnay (Dry Creek Valley) $28. A touch of dust, dried sage, clover, and dried tobacco accompanies the peach and apricot flavors in this wine. The finish is semisweet, and a bit soft. **84** — *S.H. (12/1/2005)*

Williamson 2002 Amour Merlot (Dry Creek Valley) $38. Pretty and polished, this Merlot has well-ripened cherry, cocoa, and blackberry flavors, with a nice swoosh of wintergreen. It's dry, with decent acids, and is quite balanced. Will make a good, versatile food wine. **87** — *S.H. (12/1/2005)*

WILLIS HALL

Willis Hall 2003 Stone Tree Reserve Syrah (Columbia Valley (WA)) $35. Divergent opinions on this wine, but it's mostly academic, as only 25 cases were produced. One taster found it smooth and creamy in the mouth, with building layers of berry and spice flavors; the other found it weedy, stewy, and watery. If you try a bottle, let us know what you think. **86** *(9/1/2005)*

WILLOW CREST

Willow Crest 2001 Black Muscat (Yakima Valley) $8. Ripe, forward scents of plums and apricots. This is concentrated but not syrupy, fleshy and ripe but not cloying or too sweet. Delicious sipping wine. **88** — *P.G. (9/1/2002)*

Willow Crest 1999 Cabernet Franc (Yakima Valley) $15. It takes a moment or two for this tight, herbal wine to unwind in the glass. Once it unwraps a bit it's a delight, with pleasing flavors of green olive, leaf, and herb along with ripe, plummy fruit, coffee, and chocolate. There's lots of acid, balanced and smooth tannins, and a long, persistent finish. **88** — *P.G. (6/1/2002)*

Willow Crest 2005 Chenin Blanc (Yakima Valley) $10. Off dry, with flesh and fresh fruit sweetness. Fruit mixes pear, honeydew, and sweet citrus. **87** — *P.G. (12/31/2006)*

Willow Crest 2003 Merlot (Yakima Valley) $16. This is Willow Crest's first bottling of Merlot; it's quite good and substantial. Full-flavored and fleshy, it retains the grip of cooler-climate Merlot, without turning vegetal. There is a clear scent of mint, and after the tart red fruits, the wine finishes with a chocolate mint wafer kiss. **88** — *P.G. (12/31/2006)*

Willow Crest 2000 Mourvèdre (Yakima Valley) $20. The winery says this is the first time anyone has bottled this varietal in Washington; they get no argument from me. It's young, grapey, effusive, and loose-knit, and not for everyone. But if you like gregarious, slightly rustic, spicy/tangy red wines, with plenty of fresh fruit, give it a try. **87** — *P.G. (6/1/2002)*

Willow Crest 2005 Pinot Gris (Yakima Valley) $10. This is the winery's best white, and a standout Pinot Gris for Washington. You'll find more pear than apple flavor here, with light melon also. The wine feels and tastes of lees, and plenty of crisp skin tannins that put a clean edge on it. Nothing fancy, just well-ripened fruit and clean winemaking. **88** — *P.G. (12/31/2006)*

Willow Crest 2000 Pinot Gris (Yakima Valley) $8. A tawny-blush color, a prettily-scented wine redolent of apples and pears, this is a tasty, no-frills bottle of slightly spicy, tart white wine perfect for the deck or porch. **87** **Best Buy** — *P.G. (6/1/2002)*

Willow Crest 2003 Collina Bella Red Blend (Yakima Valley) $24. A Sangiovese-Cabernet blend that captures the firmness of Yakima Valley Cabernet, without the veggies. The Sangio really smoothes it out, giving it a much softer mouthfeel, with traces of leaf, coffee grounds, and fresh, moist earth. **87** — *P.G. (12/31/2006)*

Willow Crest 2003 Syrah (Yakima Valley) $16. The best of the winery's reds, this outstanding value carries rich scents of boysenberry and blueberry pie. It's plenty ripe but not unctuous, and remains below 14% alcohol, good for Syrah. There's a nice spine of fresh acid, and lightly earthy tannins, tasting of black tea. **89** — *P.G. (12/31/2006)*

Willow Crest 1999 Syrah (Yakima Valley) $18. Willow Crest is a Yakima Valley grower, bottling a few cases of wine under their own label. Syrah is clearly a strength. This is a dark, spicy bottle showing classic varietal fruit and coffee scents. Mocha, cocoa, and some pleasant herbal elements

add interest, but the star is the fruit, which is dense and powerful. **88** — *P.G. (6/1/2002)*

Willow Crest 1998 Sparkling Syrah Syrah (Yakima Valley) $15. Muted aromas of cherry candy and earth open this medium-weight sparkler from Washington State. Dry and tangy with tart, dark-but-not-rich berry flavors, it is interesting but a touch hard on the palate. Finishes earthy and tart, as one would expect of a simple Syrah, but this one has bubbles to boot. **84** — *M.M. (12/1/2001)*

Willow Crest 2005 Viognier (Yakima Valley) $12. This is very tart, no frills, for acid lovers. Bracing, tooth-cleaning lime and grapefruit. Viognier can get hot and overripe; this is much more on the lean, cool, green side. **86** — *P.G. (12/31/2006)*

WILLOWBROOK CELLARS

WillowBrook Cellars 2002 Owl Ridge Vineyard Chardonnay (Russian River Valley) $28. Smells oaky and spicy, but it's almost shockingly lean in fruit. Tastes like oak-flavored alcohol, acids and tannins. **82** — *S.H. (12/1/2004)*

WillowBrook Cellars 2001 Owl Ridge Vineyards Chardonnay (Russian River Valley) $28. The underlying fruit has flavors that veer toward green apple tart, with the baked, sweet taste of pie crust. Acids are crisp and uplifting. A generous overlay of oak and lees adds the final touches of buttercream and a rich texture to this nice, foodworthy wine. **88** — *S.H. (7/1/2003)*

WillowBrook Cellars 2004 Dutton Morelli Vineyard Pinot Noir (Russian River Valley) $42. Simple and sweet, with cola and cherry cough medicine flavors. The sugary taste reprises on the finish. **82** — *S.H. (12/1/2006)*

WillowBrook Cellars 2002 Owl Ridge Vineyard Pinot Noir (Russian River Valley) $34. Herbal and earthy, with mint, dill, clove, and rhubarb notes that drink dry and a little unripe. **84** *(11/1/2004)*

WILRIDGE

Wilridge 2002 Cabernet Sauvignon (Red Mountain) $29. Despite its excellent Klipsun vineyard pedigree, this wine has a funky nose, sweaty and sour, with mousy flavors. The fruit is buried under severe tannins and off-notes vaguely reminiscent of fur. **81** — *P.G. (12/31/2006)*

Wilridge 1998 Klipsun Vineyards Cabernet Sauvignon (Yakima Valley) $29. Klipsun fruit is known for its firm tannins, iron, and mineral elements, dark fruit and sturdy ageworthiness. Here a touch of the barnyard in the bouquet brings it ever closer to Bordeaux. It's a complex wine, which, despite its youth, shows a wonderful range of flavors, from black cherry to coffee to steel and smoke. The iron and acids and tannin are there to age, but it drinks beautifully right now, so why wait? Just 138 cases made. **90** — *P.G. (6/1/2001)*

Wilridge 2003 Merlot (Columbia Valley (WA)) $19. Tight and substantial, this is powered by black cherry fruit laced with smoke, charcoal, and coffee liqueur. There is some light volatile aromas, and the fruit is somewhat generic, but hey, that's Merlot. **87** — *P.G. (12/31/2006)*

Wilridge 2002 Merlot (Red Mountain) $29. This seems like an old release and shows just how much this winery has improved since the disappointing vintages of the early 2000s. Scents show a lot of volatility and nail polish, while the flavors are an odd mix of tired fruit with burnt rubber and more nail polish. **82** — *P.G. (12/31/2006)*

Wilridge 1998 Klipsun Vineyard Merlot (Yakima Valley) $29. Here is a classic Klipsun nose, scented with dark streaks of metal and earth. The dark, mineral notes are not yet integrated with the fruit, which is high-toned and earthy, with some barnyard flavors. The tannins are rough and rustic, and give the impression that the wine needs more time to smooth out. **86** — *P.G. (6/1/2001)*

Wilridge 2000 Klipsun Vineyards Merlot (Red Mountain) $NA. Hard and tough, this wine shows a core of black cherry with streaks of mineral and metal, but the tannins are in the way. Some additional bottle time will be a big help. **86** — *P.G. (9/1/2004)*

Wilridge 1997 Klipsun Vineyards Merlot (Yakima Valley) $29. **91** — *M.S. (4/1/2000)*

Wilridge 1998 Spring Valley Vineyards Merlot (Walla Walla (WA)) $29. This is a soft, sensual Merlot, with lovely strawberry/cherry fruit and

USA

hints of herb. Complex, layered, elegant, and subtle, it is a delightful showcase for the cherry-pie pleasures of Walla Walla fruit. **90** —*P.G.* *(6/1/2002)*

Wilridge NV Di Klipsun Nebbiolo (Red Mountain) $19. Nebbiolo has not distinguished itself in Washington, but here is the wine that could change all that. From the esteemed Klipsun vineyard, it is a pretty, Pinot-colored wine scented with tea, tobacco, pie cherry, and hints of leather. Clean and aromatic, with sweet fruit and an amazingly long, spicy finish, it is a light wine, but quite serious and flavorful. Alas just 226 cases made. **91** —*P.G. (6/1/2002)*

Wilridge 2004 Klipsun Nebbiolo (Red Mountain) $24. This shows good color for Nebbiolo, with a soft attack and round, warm flavors of light cherry and tobacco. A well-made wine, smooth and balanced, with refreshing, varietal tartness and detail that keeps it distinctive and closer to Italian in style. **87** —*P.G. (12/31/2006)*

Wilridge 2004 Sangiovese (Yakima Valley) $19. A pretty rosé color sets up a wine with pleasant mixed red fruits, some spicy highlights and a warm, soft mouthfeel. There is nothing here that shouts "Sangiovese," but that is rare in Washington. It's a good, all-purpose pizza red. **85** —*P.G. (12/31/2006)*

Wilridge 2004 Rattlesnake Hills Syrah (Washington) $29. Spicy and peppery, this comes on with a lot of youthful pizzazz. I like the way it hits the palate full force, with a blast of raspberry fruit, a streak of leather and a dusting of black pepper. There's the typical citrusy lift of Washington Syrah, and a sense that this wine is meant to be appreciated right now, in the full bloom of youth. **88** —*P.G. (12/31/2006)*

WILSON

Wilson 1999 Sydney Vineyard Cabernet Sauvignon (Dry Creek Valley) $28. The blackberry and plum flavors ride next to earthier ones of tobacco and dried herbs, with strong, gritty but balanced tannins. Very dry and a bit rugged, but showing integrity. Drink with roasted meats. **87** —*S.H. (11/15/2003)*

Wilson 2000 Chenin Blanc (Clarksburg) $11. A strongly flavored wine from an appellation almost exclusively known for Chenin Blanc. Has tart, peppery flavors of grapefruit, with powerful acids that sting the palate and call for food. Try with mussels or oysters. **85** —*S.H. (5/1/2003)*

Wilson 2001 Isabella Late Harvest Chenin Blanc (Clarksburg) $16. Fragrant with peach and floral notes, the wine offers a light texture with hints of honey, herb, and apricot on the finish. **86** —*J.M. (12/1/2002)*

Wilson 1999 Sydney Vineyard Merlot (Dry Creek Valley) $24. Opens with a strong aroma of smoked meat and bacon, not bad, but indicative of brettanomyces in the winery. In the mouth are flavors of red and black cherries, with a spicy edge of clove. **84** —*S.H. (12/1/2003)*

Wilson 2001 Petite Sirah (Clarksburg) $10. Seems very overripe, with an aroma of raisins and cooked honey that's almost like Port. There are sweet berry-cherry flavors on the palate, wrapped in notable but negotiable tannins, and the sweetness continues into the finish. **82** *(4/1/2003)*

Wilson 1999 Petite Sirah (California) $10. Most tasters faulted this wine for various flaws, including funky aromas, medicinal flavors, and a tart, sour mouthfeel, but it's not bad for the price. Gets better with aeration. **84** *(4/1/2003)*

Wilson 2000 Carl's Vineyard Zinfandel (Dry Creek Valley) $25. Rather underripe, with herbal aromas and flavors beside riper notes of blackberries, and dry, green tannins. There are some pretty flavors, but they drink semi-sweet, and finish short and simple. **84** —*S.H. (9/1/2003)*

Wilson 2001 Reserve Zinfandel (Dry Creek Valley) $38. A nice mouthful of Zin. Bursts on the palate with ripe, jammy berry and fruit flavors, spiced with cinnamon, clove, nutmeg, white pepper, and mocha. The tannins are lush and rich. Could be drier, though, with a finish that tastes like fruit compote. **86** —*S.H. (3/1/2004)*

WINCHESTER

Winchester 2000 Syrah (Paso Robles) $30. An intense perfume of raspberries, lavender, sage, and smoke wafts from the glass, alongside a good dose of lightly charred oak. This pretty aroma leads to a very dry, supple mouthfeel, soft in acidity and light in tannins, which makes the wine

deliciously gentle and silky. From the appellation's west side. **91** —*S.H. (12/1/2002)*

WINDEMERE

Windemere 2003 Chardonnay (Edna Valley) $12. Shows many of the qualities of Chardonnay from this appellation, with high acidity and pure citrus fruit flavors. There's also a lot of new-oaky extract. **84** —*S.H. (10/1/2006)*

Windemere 1997 Cathy MacGregor Vineyard Signature Chardonnay (Edna Valley) $32. 87 *(6/1/2000)*

Windemere 2002 MacGregor Vineyard Pinot Noir (Edna Valley) $18. Simple, with cola and candied cherry flavors with a touch of raisins. Finishes hot. **83** —*S.H. (10/1/2006)*

WINDMILL

Windmill 2003 Syrah (Lodi) $12. Jammy and soft, with cherry and vanilla flavors that hang just this side of flabby. Picks up attractive brown sugar and caramel notes on the tangy finish. **84** *(9/1/2005)*

Windmill 2005 Old Vine Zinfandel (Lodi) $12. Decent everyday Zin, dry and spicy, with rich tannins and ripe dark berry, coffee, and tobacco flavors veering into bitter dark chocolate. Nice with pasta in a tomato sauce. **85** —*S.H. (12/15/2006)*

Windmill 2001 Old Vine Zinfandel (Lodi) $10. From the land of old-vine Zinfandel, this one pours out more concentration than its price would suggest. It's rich on the palate and offers ripe black cherry at the core. Smoke, vanilla, and licorice flavors follow suit, though it's somewhat bitter on the end. Still, at this price, Windmill Zin shines brightly. **86** —*J.M. (11/15/2003)*

Windsor 1999 Private Reserve Cabernet Sauvignon (Mendocino) $17. A clean, well-made wine, with gentle but flashy new oak and good balance, and a modest 13.7% alcohol. However, the fruit is a bit thin in relation to the tannins, which coat the palate with numbing dust. It doesn't have the stuffing to age. **86** —*S.H. (11/15/2002)*

Windsor 2000 Chardonnay (Sonoma County) $17. 88 —*S.H. (6/1/2003)*

WINDSOR

Windsor 1997 Barrel-Fermented Private Reserve Chardonnay (Russian River Valley) $17. 83 *(6/1/2000)*

Windsor 1997 Preston Ranch Private Reserve Chardonnay (Russian River Valley) $15. 88 *(6/1/2000)*

Windsor 2000 Middle Ridge Vineyard Private Reserve Fumé Blanc (Mendocino County) $13. It's a bit shy in the nose, but the flavors are full enough, with spearmint, citrus, and apple-fruit. It's dryish, crisp, round, bright, and tart. A nice mouthful at a fair price. **86** —*S.H. (12/15/2001)*

Windsor 1997 Toni Stockhausen Signature Series Meritage (Sonoma County) $23. Ripe and smoky, this quintessentially Californian wine is softly fruity, with big, effusive berry and stone fruit flavors and melted tannins. It's dry and rich, with a long delicious finish. **89** —*S.H. (12/1/2001)*

Windsor 1999 40th Anniversary Reserve Merlot (Dry Creek Valley) $40. This venerable private label winery pulls out all the stops with what may be their most expensive wine ever. It's dry, with plush, stylish tannins, but marred by excessive softness and, worse, overripe flavors of raisins. It's primarily from Dry Creek Valley, natural home to Zinfandel, but not the greatest source of Merlot, which needs cool weather for balance. **84** *(11/15/2002)*

Windsor 1996 Shelton Signature Series Merlot (Sonoma County) $25. 83 —*J.C. (7/1/2000)*

Windsor 1998 Signature Series Merlot (Sonoma County) $25. Pretty aromas of cherries, chocolate, and vanilla open into berry flavors that are balanced, rich, and very dry, with some dusty tannins. Has a round elegance that's tableworthy. **86** —*S.H. (6/1/2001)*

Windsor 1997 Stockhausen Signature Series Merlot (Sonoma County) $25. Smells warm, with well-ripened plummy, blackberry aromas. The flavors are deeply fruity and full bodied, with masses of berry fruit in a dry, soft package. This is an easy-drinking fun wine. **87** —*S.H. (12/1/2001)*

Windsor 1998 Toni Stockhausen Signature Series Merlot (Sonoma County) $25. Ripe and smoky, this quintessentially Californian wine is softly fruity, with big, effusive berry and stone fruit flavors and melted tannins. It's dry and rich, with a long delicious finish. **87** —*S.H. (12/1/2001)*

Windsor 2000 Murphy Ranch Late Harvest Muscat Canelli (Alexander Valley) $15. Very sweet and caramelly, with apricot liqueur and vanilla aromas and a thick, viscous mouthfeel. It's a little rough around the edges, a direct wine rather than a nuanced one. Best consumed with sweet desserts like vanilla ice cream or butter cookies. **86** —*S.H. (12/31/2001)*

Windsor 1999 Petite Sirah (Mendocino County) $13. The panel was divided on this wine, with some liking the full, rich blackberry and cherry flavors and smooth tannins, while others knocked it for being common and uninteresting. **83** *(4/1/2003)*

Windsor 2000 Pinot Noir (Sonoma County) $19. A cherry-cola nose displays some menthol, toast, and burnt matchstick accents. In the mouth it's thick, with dark cherry fruit fighting against the heavy oak overlay. Black plum and coffee on the finish complete this very woody package. **84** *(10/1/2002)*

Windsor 1999 Private Reserve Pinot Noir (Sonoma County) $17. Think of a cedar-paneled sauna, and you have pegged the major component of this wine's nose. Brambly berry flavors also carry a heavy oak note, which hangs in there through the dry, spicy finish. **85** *(10/1/2002)*

Windsor 1999 Signature Series Pinot Noir (Sonoma County) $19. Dry cedar aromas with notes of sweaty leather announce this as a rustic wine, but one balanced by cherry and plum scents and similar fruity flavors. There's plenty of dry wood accenting the smoky, tangy qualities in the wine, and that wood turns starching on the finish. **86** *(10/1/2002)*

Windsor 2000 Private Reserve Sémillon (Mendocino) $15. Nice, with buttery, nutty aromas and deep flavors suggesting Key lime and other citrus fruits and spices. It's a dry wine, polished and bright, with a creamy texture and a long, ripe fruit finish. **86** —*S.H. (12/15/2001)*

Windsor 1998 Private Reserve Syrah (Sonoma County) $16. The initial aromas from this wine can only be described as funky, combining some tarry, sulfurous qualities with heavy-toast oak barrels—thankfully they burn off after a few minutes in the glass. There's nice fruit underneath all of that: Dark chocolate and plum flavors accompany a rich, chewy mouthfeel. Some brighter notes emerge on the softly tannic finish. **87** *(10/1/2001)*

Windsor 1997 Zinfandel (Sonoma County) $18. Firm, fruity, with tropical flavors and lots of alcohol. The flavors are tight and contained, the fruit tends to strawberry, and the finish is tannic. **86** —*P.G. (3/1/2001)*

Windsor 1997 Old Vines Wild Thing Zinfandel (Mendocino County) $16. **89** —*P.G. (11/15/1999)*

Windsor 1997 Private Reserve Zinfandel (Mendocino) $15. A very oaky nose leads into a tough, tannic wine. There's good fruit under all the wood and tannin, and the tight, rugged finish should smooth out in time. **85** —*P.G. (3/1/2001)*

Windsor 2001 Signature Series Zinfandel (Mendocino County) $15. Bright, brambly raspberry and herb flavors start this one off. The tannins are quite robust and somewhat astringent, though, and the wine finishes with a large dose of toasty oak. **86** *(11/1/2003)*

Windsor 1999 Toni Stockhausen Signature Series Zinfandel (Mendocino County) $17. Good, interesting wine from this specialty winery. It starts with clean, complex Zinny aromas of briary, brambly berries, and turns rich and complex on the palate. It's bone dry, with the structure of a fine red wine, and Zin's particular exuberance. The long finish suggests midterm aging potential. **90 Best Buy** —*S.H. (12/15/2001)*

WINDWALKER

Windwalker 1999 Reserve Chardonnay (El Dorado) $18. From mountain vineyards, and you can taste an iron-y concentration, bordering on iodine, that frames the peach and apple flavors. The flavors are long and ripe and spicy, yet there's a spine of acidic steel that makes it drink bright and fresh. **85** —*S.H. (5/1/2002)*

WINDWARD VINEYARD

Windward Vineyard 2000 Monopole Pinot Noir (Paso Robles) $30. This dark, medium-weight wine wears black chocolate, prune, tar, and earth accents on dark fruit. Slightly low acidity makes it seem a little heavy. Closes with more dark flavors and hints of tobacco. **85** *(10/1/2002)*

Windward Vineyard 1999 Monopole Pinot Noir (Paso Robles) $30. Smooth and fairly standard in the nose, with aromas of mint, caramel, and wood-driven spice. The full wood treatment obscures the cherry fruit a little, but enough berry and cola emerges to salvage the palate. **85** *(10/1/2002)*

WINDY OAKS

Windy Oaks 1999 Pinot Noir (Santa Cruz County) $39. Easy to drink, with soft, melted tannins and appealing flavors of raspberries, cherries, and chocolate. Acidity is also rather low. Could use a lot more structure. **86** —*S.H. (12/1/2003)*

Windy Oaks 2002 Schultze Family Vineyard Estate Blend Pinot Noir (Santa Cruz Mountains) $18. Light in color, light and silky in texture, this elegant wine shows pure cherry, cola, coffee, oak, and vanilla flavors. It goes down easy, with enough seriousness to stand up to fine fare. **87** —*S.H. (11/1/2005)*

Windy Oaks 2001 Schultze Family Vineyard Estate Reserve Pinot Noir (Santa Cruz Mountains) $36. A deft and suave Pinot, racy and elegant, all silk and satin on the palate. Yet there's nothing shy about the assertive flavors. Cherries and black raspberries flood the mouth, encased in rich acids and a vivid coat of oak. **91 Editors' Choice** —*S.H. (11/1/2005)*

WINDY POINT

Windy Point 2003 Estate Cabernet Franc (Yakima Valley) $18. Firm, young fruit with coffee, cassis, and blackberry. Still tight and compact, showing good structure and aging potential. Just 155 cases made. **88** —*P.G. (4/1/2006)*

Windy Point 2002 Merlot (Yakima Valley) $15. This handsome new winery makes a worthy estate Syrah and a pleasant Cab Franc, but I was most utterly charmed with the Merlot, which includes Portteus grapes as well. Sweet cherry pie never tasted so good. **87** —*P.G. (11/15/2005)*

Windy Point 2003 !Exclamation Point! Red Blend (Yakima Valley) $15. Sixty percent Cab Franc and 40% Merlot, it's firm and deep, with flavors of coffee, blackberry, light herb, and damp earth. Just 209 cases produced. **88** —*P.G. (4/1/2006)*

WINE BLOCK

Wine Block 2002 Cabernet Sauvignon (California) $10. At the equivalent of five bucks a bottle, this is a super value in Cabernet. You'll find real richness in the ripe black currant, chocolate, and sweet oak flavors, and in the smooth texture. It's also wonderfully dry and balanced. **86 Best Buy** —*S.H. (12/1/2005)*

Wine Block 2004 Chardonnay (California) $10. This wine in a box, the equivalent of two regular bottles, has plenty of fruity flavor and a dollop of oak, with a creamy texture. A country-style wine. **84 Best Buy** —*S.H. (12/1/2005)*

Wine Block 2002 Merlot (California) $10. I like this wine a lot for the great fruit. It's just jam-packed with ripe cherries, black raspberries, sweet blackberries, coffee, and cocoa flavors that are rich in fruity essence, yet dry, soft, and balanced. This is a good value in a red table wine. **86 Best Buy** —*S.H. (12/1/2005)*

WINE BY JOE

Wine by Joe 2004 Pinot Gris (Oregon) $13. A fair effort, light and tasting of green apples and pears, with good acidity. Perfectly pleasant, but nothing special. **85** —*P.G. (2/1/2006)*

WINEGLASS CELLARS

Wineglass Cellars 1998 Rich Harvest Red Wine Bordeaux Blend (Yakima Valley) $50. This is the winery's first Bordeaux blend— it's 40/40 Cabernet Sauvignon/Merlot. The rest is Cabernet Franc. There is amazing depth and concentration to this wine, not from new oak barrels, which have intentionally been minimized, but simply from ripe, dark fruit. Smoke, ash, leather, and toast add layer after layer of depth: The wine, young and tight as it is, seems to go on forever. **91** —*P.G.* (*6/1/2001*)

Wineglass Cellars 2000 Cabernet Sauvignon (Yakima Valley) $20. Tangy and pleasantly herbal, this has light red berry and tomato leaf scents, set against firm Washington fruit. Good feel to the midpalate; it's made in a drink-now style, but strong enough to hang tough with grilled meats. **87** —*P.G.* (*9/1/2004*)

Wineglass Cellars 1999 Cabernet Sauvignon (Yakima Valley) $21. A late release '99, this displays the tough, chewy tannins of that excellent vintage, and has the dry, tight, concentrated flavors of a good unclassified Bordeaux. Air it out and some nice spice starts to emerge. This is a fine effort in a good year. **88** —*P.G.* (*9/1/2004*)

Wineglass Cellars 1999 Cabernet Sauvignon (Yakima Valley) $21. A late release '99, this displays the tough, chewy tannins of that excellent vintage, and has the dry, tight, concentrated flavors of a good unclassified Bordeaux. Air it out and some nice spice starts to emerge. This is a fine effort in a good year. **88** —*P.G.* (*9/1/2004*)

Wineglass Cellars 1998 Cabernet Sauvignon (Yakima Valley) $25. Deeply colored, almost black, with plummy edges, this wine sends out layers of scents: black fruits, coffee, smoke, pencil shavings, and ash. I like the confident way it sets up in the mouth, firm but not closed, tannic but not chalky, dark but not bitter. Everything is in balance, and the flavors mingle seamlessly. A wonderful example of the Bordeaux-like qualities that many of the best Washington Cabernets possess. **90** —*P.G.* (*6/1/2001*)

Wineglass Cellars 2000 Elerding Vineyard Cabernet Sauvignon (Yakima Valley) $45. This superb vineyard delivers, once again, an elegant, textured, subtle wine that will reward cellaring. Not as powerful as the '99, yet it shows the same smoky, dusty black cherry and cassis scents, ripe cassis fruit, and hints of earth and mineral. Tannins are quite tough and chewy. **89** —*P.G.* (*9/1/2004*)

Wineglass Cellars 2000 Elerding Vineyard Cabernet Sauvignon (Yakima Valley) $45. This wine shows thinnish flavors of pomegranate, cranberry, and rhubarb, despite the hefty 14.5% alcohol. The fruit has not quite met the oak on an even playing field, and the whole seems less than the sum of its parts. **87** —*P.G.* (*9/1/2004*)

Wineglass Cellars 1999 Elerding Vineyard Cabernet Sauvignon (Yakima Valley) $45. This is an elegant, textured, subtle wine that will reward cellaring. Very fragrant and stylish, it shows smoky, dusty black cherry and cassis scents, ripe but not raisiny fruit, tightly wound, and revealing hints of earth and mineral. Some sweet cocoa adds interest to the finish. Cellar candidate 6-10 years. **92** —*P.G.* (*6/1/2002*)

Wineglass Cellars 1998 Elerding Vineyard Cabernet Sauvignon (Yakima Valley) $40. Here winemaker David Lowe expresses the purity of this single vineyard fruit with admirable focus. Dark plum, scented with strawberry preserves, cassis, and raspberries, the flavors are clean and true. Pure fruit, dark tannins, fine focus; interesting iron and mineral streaks add depth to the finish. **92** —*P.G.* (*6/1/2001*)

Wineglass Cellars 2000 Reserve Cabernet Sauvignon (Yakima Valley) $28. This is a very well-made, sleekly styled wine, with classy mixed red fruits leading into a sweet, sculpted midpalate. The fruit is perfectly ripe, and the oak is a seasoning, not a lumber yard. A textbook example of Washington Cabernet. **90** —*P.G.* (*9/1/2004*)

Wineglass Cellars 1999 Reserve Cabernet Sauvignon (Yakima Valley) $35. Still youthful and firm, the fruit seems slightly "green" with bell pepper flavors showing through. Tannins are hard and earthy, and the wine is so tightly wound that it seems ungenerous. More bottle time could certainly help. **86** —*P.G.* (*6/1/2002*)

Wineglass Cellars 2003 Chardonnay (Yakima Valley) $13. Macintosh apple, whiskey barrel, and some volatile high notes set this wine in motion. The midpalate fruit is crisp and tangy, with a citrusy snap to the finish. **85** —*P.G.* (*9/1/2004*)

Wineglass Cellars 2001 Chardonnay (Yakima Valley) $13. A clean, spritzy style that mixes crisp green apple/malic acid flavors with heavier, fleshier pear and tropical fruits. There's a spicy bite to the finish; nice effort. **87** —*P.G.* (*9/1/2004*)

Wineglass Cellars 1999 Chardonnay (Yakima Valley) $13. Wineglass Cellars is a boutique producer whose focus has been on red wines; this, notes winemaker David Lowe, is their first Chardonnay that's "serious." It takes the crisp structure of Washington fruit and adds a healthy dose of new oak, giving it plenty of toast, spice, and vanilla. It's a winning combination, and sure to please. Just 277 cases made. **88 Best Buy** —*P.G.* (*6/1/2001*)

Wineglass Cellars 2005 In The Buff Chardonnay (Columbia Valley (WA)) $13. "In the buff," as you might suppose, means no oak, no malolactic. It is nonetheless quite stacked with flavor, thick currents of pear, peach, and other stone fruits, and plenty of natural acid to keep it lively in the mouth. This is the sort of honest, no-nonsense wine that Chardonnay rarely can be—more like a sturdy red in the way it coats the tongue and lingers. **89 Best Buy** —*P.G.* (*10/1/2006*)

Wineglass Cellars 2001 Reserve Chardonnay (Yakima Valley) $16. Unlike the regular bottling, this sees some new oak and goes through complete malolactic. It's a softer, nuttier style with plenty of sweet vanilla toast over light pineapple fruit. **87** —*P.G.* (*9/1/2004*)

Wineglass Cellars 2001 Merlot (Yakima Valley) $22. Dark, ripe, and vinous, this is a flavorful wine with plump, pruney fruit above oak-driven flavors of roasted nuts and milk chocolate. Tasty, near-term drinking. **88** —*P.G.* (*9/1/2004*)

Wineglass Cellars 2000 Merlot (Yakima Valley) $22. Black cherry mixes with black olive and bell pepper, with a hard, earthy edge to the substantial tannins. A couple more years of bottle age will help smooth out the rough edges. **86** —*P.G.* (*9/1/2004*)

Wineglass Cellars 1999 Merlot (Yakima Valley) $22. The lush, satiny nose mixes ripe fruit and pleasing herbal, dusty scents. There's even a little bit of jalapeño (from young tannins) in the finish, along with some red licorice. On balance, a distinctive style, with all kinds of interesting, subtle notes, yet still classic, varietal Washington-style Merlot. **90** —*P.G.* (*2/1/2002*)

Wineglass Cellars 1998 Merlot (Yakima Valley) $20. This 3,500-case boutique specializes in Merlot. The Yakima Valley bottling has a fine dark cast to it, and the fruit tends toward black cherry with extra dimensions of coffee, tobacco, and smoke. There's a slight hint of earth here, too. The wine has dimension, depth, and power, all in a precisely wound, tightly coiled style that says, "Age me!" Don't let the cheesy label fool you; this is seriously good Merlot. **92 Editors' Choice** —*P.G.* (*6/1/2001*)

Wineglass Cellars 1998 DuBrul Vineyard Merlot (Yakima Valley) $30. This single-vineyard selection shows bright fruit, with raspberry, cherry, and vanilla in equal measure, and it opens up broadly on the palate, with lush, ripe flavors. It's significantly different in style from the Yakima Valley bottling (which also includes some DuBrul fruit), and it shows a careful hand at the tiller. This is a winery to watch. **91** —*P.G.* (*6/1/2001*)

Wineglass Cellars 2000 Reserve Merlot (Yakima Valley) $35. Wineglass makes its Merlot 100%, and it's fun to taste the grape straight up like this. Light, with pretty cherry/rhubarb flavors, it has a nice tart, acidic edge, and balanced tannins, with some herbal notes through the finish. **87** —*P.G.* (*9/1/2004*)

Wineglass Cellars 1999 Reserve Merlot (Yakima Valley) $35. Over half of the barrels were new, giving the wine a rich, bacon fat aroma. The fruit is ripe and fleshy, showing sweet cherries and finishing with nuances of coffee, tar, and pepper. Just 150 cases were made. **88** —*P.G.* (*6/1/2002*)

Wineglass Cellars NV Capizimo Red Red Blend (America) $15. The name is a compound of Cab, Pinot, Zin, and Merlot, though there is no Pinot in the wine. It's a blocky, tannic, pleasant "mutt" of a red wine, ready for near term drinking. **84** —*P.G.* (*2/1/2004*)

Wineglass Cellars 2000 Rich Harvest Red Blend (Yakima Valley) $50. Tannic and firm, this has some pretty cherry fruit lurking behind the stiff tannins. It's still tight, despite the bottle time, but it's well made. Nice oak flavors of hazelnut, spice, and sandalwood liven up the finish. **89** —*P.G.* (*9/1/2004*)

Wineglass Cellars 1999 Rich Harvest Red Blend (Yakima Valley) $50. A Meritage blend of 50% Cabernet Sauvignon, 33% Merlot, and the rest Cabernet Franc. The nose is intense, smoky, and appealing, leading into a palate of forward, sweet red fruits. There are whiffs of bell pepper as well, and the finishing tannins are a bit earthy and rough. **88** —*P.G. (6/1/2002)*

Wineglass Cellars 2003 Sangiovese (Yakima Valley) $18. The fruit comes from two great Yakima Valley vineyards, Boushey and Elerding, and although the alcohol pins the meter at 15.3% it holds together with pretty cherry fruit, plenty of acid and tannin to provide the backbone. 266 cases produced. **88** —*P.G. (6/1/2006)*

Wineglass Cellars 2002 Boushey Vineyard Syrah (Yakima Valley) $23. Great mouth presence, built upon stylish, racy fruit. It's tangy and spicy and handles the 100% new French oak with ease. Sappy and loaded with bright, tart red fruit flavors, this is a really pleasurable wine. Unfortunately, just 25 cases were made. **91** —*P.G. (6/1/2006)*

Wineglass Cellars NV Batch OO Zinfandel (America) $19. From Lodi grapes, this hi-test (15.5% alcohol) Zin has plenty of sweet grapey, cherry fruit. There's a liquorous flavor from the alcohol and possibly the barrels, and some green tannins. This one will appeal to those who like Amador Zins; it's built to drink now rather than later. **86** —*P.G. (1/1/2004)*

WINES OF CARMEL

Wines of Carmel 2001 Carmel Chardonnay (Monterey County) $23. From the warmer Carmel Valley, a wine with flavors of fruit pie, especially apples and peaches, including the sweet, buttery crust. Creamy, with an almond-skin bitterness on the finish. **85** —*S.H. (2/1/2004)*

WINESMITH

WineSmith 2002 Student Vineyard Faux Chablis Chardonnay (Napa Valley) $30. What they seem to mean by "faux Chablis" is searingly high acidity, little or no oak, rasping dryness, and early-picked, green fruit that's supposed to be minerally. Not a generous wine. **84** —*S.H. (11/1/2005)*

WING CANYON

Wing Canyon 2000 Cabernet Sauvignon (Mount Veeder) $25. Shows good intensity and focus, and while it's not very fruity, it displays a range of plum, leather, herb, cedar, and earthy flavors. Tannic now, but doesn't seem like an ager. **87** —*S.H. (5/1/2005)*

WINGS

Wings 2003 Cabernet Sauvignon (Napa Valley) $60. This is the kind of fleshy, oaky Cabernet that Napa produces so effortlessly. The fruit got really ripe in blackberries and cocoa, the tannins are sweet and intricate, if a bit sandpapery, and the balance is impeccable. It's an upscale wine that is very good now, and should develop well for many years. **91** —*S.H. (12/31/2006)*

WINTER'S HILL

Winter's Hill 2000 Pinot Gris (Willamette Valley) $12. A huge improvement over their previous vintage, this Pinot Gris feels good and fleshy in the mouth, smells of citrus rind and herbs. It has plenty of lively fruit, and a pleasant hint of sweetness in the finish. **87** —*P.G. (2/1/2002)*

Winter's Hill 2002 Pinot Noir (Willamette Valley) $20. Baked fruit, with a flat, oxidized mouthfeel. Flavors are pruney and stewed, and lead into a somewhat sugary, tough, tannic finish. **82** *(11/1/2004)*

Winter's Hill 2000 Pinot Noir (Willamette Valley) $25. Crisp and varietal, with nicely ripened fruit that delivers nuanced flavors. Fruits, cola, spice, and a nice cherry finish highlight this well-balanced effort. **88** —*P.G. (12/1/2003)*

Winter's Hill 1999 Pinot Noir (Willamette Valley) $25. Light, pretty cherry fruit, overcome with smoky oak. Earthy and smelling of wet wood, it has good, straight-ahead fruit flavors. Given the prices of Oregon Pinot these days, this is a relative bargain. **85** —*P.G. (12/31/2001)*

Winter's Hill 2002 Reserve Pinot Noir (Willamette Valley) $29. Tight and resiny, it hints at pine needles and mint, along with plenty of vanilla-laced oak. The toasted, oaky component seems over-matched to the thin fruit. **85** *(11/1/2004)*

WITNESS TREE

Witness Tree 2000 Estate Pinot Noir (Willamette Valley) $20. This estate wine features a nose of forest floor and dry leaves along with some tobac-

co and smoke. The earthy, raspberry palate carries with it a strong underlay of oak, and that woodiness is even stronger on the finish; essentially obscuring what fruit there is. **83** *(10/1/2002)*

Witness Tree 1997 Estate Pinot Noir (Willamette Valley) $34. **85** *(11/15/1999)*

Witness Tree 2000 Vintage Select Pinot Noir (Willamette Valley) $40. Big, burly aromas of smoke, matchstick, and barnyard join flavors of black plum and cherry mixed with soy and earth. The chewy finish seals the deal in favor of this plump but balanced smoothie. **89** *(10/1/2002)*

Witness Tree 1997 Vintage Select Pinot Noir (Willamette Valley) $18. **90** **Best Buy** *(11/15/1999)*

WOLFF

Wolff 2004 Old Vines Chardonnay (Edna Valley) $19. Fans of acidity will like this wine for its bright crispness that really gets the tastebuds whistling. It's a very dry, streamlined wine, with citrus zest and vanilla flavors that will play well off a nice cracked crab and sourdough baguette. **88** —*S.H. (7/1/2006)*

Wolff 2003 Old Vines Chardonnay (Edna Valley) $19. I'm always struck by Edna Valley acids, and so it is with this tart, tightly wound Chardonnay. It's got pretty peach and apple flavors, with a stoniness that must come from the terroir. It's also very dry. **87** —*S.H. (11/15/2005)*

Wolff 2002 Old Vines Chardonnay (Edna Valley) $19. Balanced and harmonious, and has extra clarity due to its lovely acidity. There's an array of fruity flavor ranging from ripe green apples to candied grapefruit and mango, while oak adds vanilla and toast. Finishes long and spicy. **90** —*S.H. (9/1/2004)*

Wolff 2001 Old Vines Chardonnay (Edna Valley) $19. Lots of big, ripe fruity flavors in this dense wine, including peaches, pears, and tropical fruits. Lees and oak are poured on lavishly, adding style and flair. **90** **Editors' Choice** —*S.H. (5/1/2003)*

Wolff 2004 Estate Grown Petite Sirah (Edna Valley) $19. Petite Sirah seems a curious choice to grow in one of the coolest AVAs in California. This wine is bone dry and tannically acidic, with a deeply attractive, ripe juiciness that's like the essence of black currants and chocolate-coated cherries. The wine is very young, but so beautifully balanced. Good now with big rich meats, but should hold and improve through this decade and longer. **92** **Cellar Selection** —*S.H. (7/1/2006)*

Wolff 2001 Dijon Clones Selection Pinot Noir (Edna Valley) $25. The new clone on the block finally makes it onto the front label. Soft and silky, this wine has cherry-berry flavors with an earthy streak of tobacco and sage. There are some firm tannins that kick in on the finish, which suggest six months of aging. **87** —*S.H. (7/1/2003)*

Wolff 2003 Estate Dijon Clones Selection Pinot Noir (Edna Valley) $25. Edna Valley makes coastal California's most delicate and crisp Pinot Noirs. They tend to be food-friendly, as is this wine. Dry and elegantly silky, with high acidity and modest but complex cherry and cola flavors that will enhance, rather than dominate, your best entrées. **88** —*S.H. (8/1/2006)*

Wolff 2002 Syrah (Edna Valley) $19. This cool-climate Syrah features pepper, smoked meat, soy, and sautéed mushroom aromas and flavors, with a streak of tart cherry. It's very dry and balanced with crisp acidity. Drinks austere now, with a firm edge of tannins. **87** —*S.H. (9/1/2004)*

Wolff 2001 Syrah (Edna Valley) $18. A wine that takes the Northern Rhône as a model, it does share that peppery, plum, and blackberry flavors, rich tannins, and full-bodied character. Has a certain one-dimensionality, but not without interest. A wine and winery to watch. **88** —*S.H. (6/1/2003)*

Wolff 2003 Wolff Vineyards Syrah (Edna Valley) $20. I had the feeling there is seriousness of purpose behind this wine, and there's a lot to like about it. Namely, the firm structure, including crisp acids, and plummy, spicy flavors. But there's an awkward sweetness that detracts. **84** —*S.H. (11/15/2005)*

WÖLFFER

Wölffer 2003 Cabernet Franc (The Hamptons, Long Island) $40. Mushroom and tomato are coated with spicy oak, while the palate deals out carob, plum, and tomato. A bit on the unripe side, the wine nevertheless has good dark tannins, although the finish is a bit tart. **84** —M.D. (8/1/2006)

Wölffer 1998 Cabernet Franc (The Hamptons, Long Island) $25. Aromas of tobacco, dried flowers, and earth segue into fairly rich dark fruit flavors of black cherry and plum. Very velvety on the palate, with cedar notes on the finish. Drink now. **88** —J.C. (4/1/2001)

Wölffer 1997 Brut Champagne Blend (The Hamptons, Long Island) $27. Crisp, firm, and packed with intensity. The wine serves up lots of hazelnut, toast, spice, citrus, apple, melon, pear, honeysuckle, and herb flavors. Creamy and rich on the finish, with a bright, refreshing edge. **90 Editors' Choice** —J.M. (12/1/2002)

Wölffer 1995 Brut Champagne Blend (The Hamptons, Long Island) $30. Very young and crisp, this is an example of New World sparkling wine that should prove ageable, if purchasers are so inclined. Shows some yeasty complexity to go with clove and tart green apple flavors. **87** —J.C. (4/1/2001)

Wölffer 2000 Cuvée Christian Brut Champagne Blend (The Hamptons, Long Island) $29. Has some yeasty, apple-y notes on the nose, but this is blander than some other vintages have been, offering modest apple and citrus flavor. Perhaps it just needs more time in the cellar. **84** —J.C. (12/31/2004)

Wölffer 2001 Estate Selection Chardonnay (The Hamptons, Long Island) $27. Modest apple and citrus aromas and flavors are accented by hints of charred sweet corn and vanilla. Medium-bodied, with a lemony finish. **84** —J.C. (3/1/2006)

Wölffer 2000 Estate Selection Chardonnay (The Hamptons, Long Island) $27. 84 —J.C. (10/2/2004)

Wölffer 1998 Estate Selection Chardonnay (The Hamptons, Long Island) $27. Nutty aromas reminiscent of cashews lead the way, followed up on the palate by more roasted nuts, white peaches, and nectarines. Picks up some elegant citrus notes on the long finish. Based on a recent tasting of the 1997 Estate Selection (rated 90), this should improve over the next six months to a year. **89** —J.C. (4/1/2001)

Wölffer 2003 Late Harvest Chardonnay (Long Island) $35. 87 —J.C. (10/2/2004)

Wölffer 2000 Late Harvest Chardonnay (The Hamptons, Long Island) $35. A syrupy sweet dessert wine that serves up gobs of apricot and peach flavors. But searingly bright lemon-like acidity, reminiscent of eiswein, balances the richness and leaves the palate fresh. **88** —J.M. (7/1/2002)

Wölffer 2002 Reserve Chardonnay (The Hamptons, Long Island) $20. Still young-looking, with a touch of green to the pale yellow color, this wine offers white fruit aromas in addition to burnt popcorn. The oak is more subdued in the mouth, where toasty flavors play a secondary role to white fruits and citrus. **84** —M.D. (8/1/2006)

Wölffer 1999 Reserve Chardonnay (The Hamptons, Long Island) $19. A disappointing effort from this normally reliable producer. The tropical fruit is dominated by buttered popcorn, caramel, and charred oak. Feels almost oily in the mouth but without the substance to sustain it. **83** —J.C. (1/1/2004)

Wölffer 1998 Reserve Chardonnay (The Hamptons, Long Island) $18. This is the middle tier of Wölffer's Chardonnay offerings, squarely between the top-of-the-line Estate Selection and the entry-level La Ferme Martin label. The Reserve exhibits plenty of buttered-pear flavors, complemented by faint nutty aromas and some toasty oak notes that gain steam on the finish. **87** —J.C. (4/1/2001)

Wölffer 1998 Merlot (The Hamptons, Long Island) $20. Dark, with dense spice-cake aromas on the nose that turn earthy and plummy on the palate. Some dried-herb nuances come through as well. Shows uncommon length. **87** —J.C. (4/1/2001)

Wölffer 2002 Estate Selection Merlot (The Hamptons, Long Island) $35. Wölffer Merlots are similar in style: high acidity and mild tannins on a light- to medium-bodied frame. This vintage has aromas of red berry, earth, spice, and dill, while the palate is similar, but with a burnt character and dill playing a leading role. **84** —M.D. (12/1/2006)

Wölffer 2001 Estate Selection Merlot (The Hamptons, Long Island) $35. Starts off with cassis, tobacco, and mint on the nose, then delivers bright cherry-berry fruit marked by spicy oak. It's a bit lean and sculpted in style, ending on a crisp note, but the tannins are soft and rounded, making it easy to drink. **85** —J.C. (3/1/2006)

Wölffer 2000 Estate Selection Merlot (The Hamptons, Long Island) $35. 85 —J.C. (10/2/2004)

Wölffer 1999 Estate Selection Merlot (The Hamptons, Long Island) $33. Smooth textured, with soft but firm tannins and moderate acidity. The wine serves up black currant, tea, cola, sage, toast, and citrus flavors. The feel turns a bit powdery on the end, finishing clean and fresh. **88** —J.M. (1/1/2003)

Wölffer 1998 Estate Selection Merlot (The Hamptons, Long Island) $30. Elegant nose of sandalwood and cedar. Black cherries come on strong and carry through to the finish. A very smooth and polished wine; finishes on an expansive note with fine tannins. **89** —J.C. (4/1/2001)

Wölffer 2000 La Ferme Martin Merlot (The Hamptons, Long Island) $14. 83 —J.C. (10/2/2004)

Wölffer 2003 Reserve Merlot (The Hamptons, Long Island) $22. A bit disappointing on the nose; pickle barrel and onion are supported by moderate spice. This is a dark, extracted wine with dusty tannins and a lean feel. Cherry/berry fruit flavors are shy as they compete with tomato, spice, and onion before finishing metallic. **83** —M.D. (12/1/2006)

Wölffer 2002 Reserve Merlot (The Hamptons, Long Island) $22. Lovely aromas of kirsch and bacon are wrapped in toasty oak, which also lends graham cracker flavors to blueberry and tobacco. Tightly structured, with firm, dry tannins and an earthy-oaky finish, this wine will be enjoyable over the next five years. **87** —M.D. (8/1/2006)

Wölffer 2001 Reserve Merlot (Long Island) $22. 86 —J.C. (10/2/2004)

Wölffer 2004 Pinot Gris (Long Island) $22. Green pea, herb, and corn aromas are followed by a lean, lemony wine with an herbal finish. **81** —J.C. (2/1/2006)

Wölffer 2004 Pinot Noir (The Hamptons, Long Island) $50. Red fruit and celery aromas have a nice touch of oak, while the palate, which is light and lacking zest, deals red cherry, rhubarb, and spice. **82** —M.D. (12/1/2006)

Wölffer 2002 Pinot Noir (The Hamptons, Long Island) $50. Light in color, and turning orange at the rim, this soft, gentle wine has pretty flavors of cherries, mocha, and cola. It's very delicate, with a good balance of tannins to acids. **88** (11/1/2004)

Wölffer 2002 Rosé Blend (The Hamptons, Long Island) $NA. 83 —J.C. (7/1/2003)

Wölffer 1999 Rosé Blend (Long Island) $11. Tart green apple flavors are joined on the palate by a touch of fresh berries. Clean and crisp; a good summertime wine that's the local version of a Provençal rosé (but made from a blend of Chardonnay and Merlot). **84** —J.C. (4/1/2001)

Wölffer 2001 Estate Bottled Rosé Blend (The Hamptons, Long Island) $11. Quite bright and lemony, the wine has the refreshing characteristics desired in dry rose, but it's lacking in fruit. An herbal core runs through it. **81** —J.M. (1/1/2003)

Wölffer 1998 Cuvée Christian Brut Sparkling Blend (The Hamptons, Long Island) $27. The nose bears an uncanny similarity to applesauce, yet it's certainly not unpleasant. The palate features an expressive blend of apples and citrus, while the finish is smooth and of moderate length. If there's anything to fault here it's that the wine feels sharp on the tongue, and at the center it seems a touch candied. **86** —M.S. (6/1/2003)

WOOD FAMILY VINEYARDS

Wood Family Vineyards 2001 Quail Creek Cabernet Sauvignon (Livermore Valley) $24. A nice Cab that's likeable for its polished currant, cherry, and herb flavors and delicate but rich tannins. There's something softly feminine about the way it coats the palate and remains easy and flavorful through the long finish. **87** —S.H. (11/15/2003)

WOODBRIDGE

Woodbridge 1997 Barbera (Lodi) $12. Opens with complex, inviting aromas of blackberry jam, sweet oak, smoke, vanilla, and mint. In the mouth, it's pretty austere now, with tart acidity and rich tannins masking underlying plum and blackberry flavors. This is a young, big wine with aging potential, but balanced enough for early drinking. **88 Best Buy** —*S.H. (11/15/2001)*

Woodbridge 1997 Cabernet Sauvignon (California) $8. 83 —*S.H. (2/1/2000)*

Woodbridge 2002 Cabernet Sauvignon (California) $8. Lean, although clean, with earthy flavors and dry, smooth tannins. Fine for those big block parties where value counts. **83** —*S.H. (7/1/2005)*

Woodbridge 2000 Cabernet Sauvignon (California) $8. Thin and weedy, with sage and chlorophyll aromas. Tastes a little fruitier than it smells, with some dry berry flavors, but it's pretty rough going. **82** —*S.H. (12/31/2002)*

Woodbridge 1998 Cabernet Sauvignon (California) $8. Inexpensive Cabernet can often be slightly weedy, even rubbery, with a hot feeling to it. So it is with this wine. The Mondavi folks managed to pack in as much blackberry and cassis fruit as they could, but there's really just a hint of it. The tannins are light, the acidity soft, and that's about it. **82** —*S.H. (5/1/2001)*

Woodbridge 2001 California Cabernet Sauvignon (California) $8. Sharp, jammy, and pungent with acids, this wine shares its berry flavors with earthy, green notes. Tannins and acids kick in on the finish. **82** —*S.H. (10/1/2004)*

Woodbridge 2001 Red Dirt Ridge Cabernet Sauvignon (Lodi) $11. Clean, country-style, and not bad for a Cabernet of this price. Marked by good flavors of blackberries and herbs and dry tannins. This full-bodied wine has real quality and is a very good value. **84** —*S.H. (10/1/2004)*

Woodbridge 2000 Red Dirt Ridge (PT) Cabernet Sauvignon (Lodi) $11. A bit shy on the nose, but fills the mouth with medium-weight flavors of earth and cassis. Finishes clean, with a hint of blackberry tea. **84** *(11/15/2003)*

Woodbridge 1999 Twin Oaks Cabernet Sauvignon (California) $12. The Twin Oaks is definitely a step up from the regular Woodbridge bottling. It has real Cabernet richness and character. Suggestions of black currants and plums turn toasty on the dry finish. **85** —*S.H. (12/31/2002)*

Woodbridge 1998 Chardonnay (California) $8. **85 Best Buy** —*S.H. (11/15/1999)*

Woodbridge 2003 Chardonnay (California) $8. A workhorse Chard, fruity and simple, with an artificially oaky, slightly sweet taste. **83** —*S.H. (7/1/2005)*

Woodbridge 2000 Chardonnay (California) $9. There are some Chard elements in this rustic, countrified wine. The apple and peach flavors, with oaky vanilla overtones, are familiar. But it's a rough wine, with some odd, vegetal qualities. Satisfactory, if you're not very fussy. **83** —*S.H. (9/1/2002)*

Woodbridge 1999 Chardonnay (California) $9. Pleasant enough and Chard-like, with aromas of tangerine, peach, and a kiss of honeyed oak. It's got enough residual sugar to almost fall into the off-dry category. Well-made and certainly affordable. **83** —*S.H. (5/1/2001)*

Woodbridge 2001 Barrel-Aged Chardonnay (California) $8. Like a photocopy of a good Chardonnay, this wine is indistinct. There are some decent peach and apple flavors and what tastes like a dose of oak, but it's really thin and watery. **83** —*S.H. (8/1/2003)*

Woodbridge 2002 California Chardonnay (California) $8. You'll find modest apple and peach flavors in this easy-drinking wine. It has a nice creamy texture, although it's a bit watery on the finish. **83** —*S.H. (9/1/2004)*

Woodbridge 2002 Ghost Oak Chardonnay (California) $11. They did a nice job with this affordable wine. It's creamy, with well-focused peach, pear, and mango flavors and lots of vanilla and smoke. Even the finish is fruity and spicy. **85** —*S.H. (11/15/2004)*

Woodbridge 2001 Select Vineyard Series Ghost Oak (PT) Chardonnay (California) $11. Only a small proportion of this wine went through malolactic fermentation, but it still comes across as quite low acid, with a heavy mouthfeel. Hints of toast, pear, and tangerine provide an accessible flavor package. **84** *(11/15/2003)*

Woodbridge 2002 Select Vineyard Series Ghost Oak Chardonnay (California) $11. Gentle in fruit, with modest peach, apple, and vanilla-oaky flavors and a creamy texture. Best for the clean, citrusy finish. **84** —*S.H. (12/15/2004)*

Woodbridge 2003 Johannisberg Riesling (California) $7. Fruity and clean, with flowery, peach, and apple flavors and good acidity. This is a wine that will appeal to people seeking something white that's comfortable and affordable. **84 Best Buy** —*S.H. (12/1/2004)*

Woodbridge 2002 Johannisberg Riesling (California) $7. Sweet and simple, with pleasant peach, apple, and spice notes. Fresh and clean on the finish. **83** —*J.M. (8/1/2003)*

Woodbridge 1997 Merlot (California) $8. 80 —*L.W. (12/31/1999)*

Woodbridge 2002 Merlot (California) $8. Cherry fruity, rough and ready, and dry, with good tannins. This is a country-style wine for picnics and informal barbecues. **83** —*S.H. (7/1/2005)*

Woodbridge 2000 Merlot (California) $9. Unripe and weedy, with minty, vegetal flavors only slightly softened by berries. Feels dry and thin on the palate, with a thick, unnatually oaky taste. **83** —*S.H. (12/31/2002)*

Woodbridge 1999 Merlot (California) $8. Sharp, earthy aromas of blackberries and licorice usher in this young, jammy wine. The flavors are forceful, with tons of extracted berry fruit—ripe and rich—but it tastes very dry, with scoury tannins. **84 Best Buy** —*S.H. (11/15/2001)*

Woodbridge 1998 Merlot (California) $8. It's red, it has some ripe blackberry and plum fruit, and it's dry, with enough acidity and tannins to make it balanced. Beyond that, there's not much to say about this clean, proper wine that might even improve with a year or two in the cellar. **83** —*S.H. (9/1/2003)*

Woodbridge 2001 California Merlot (California) $8. Sharp and angular, with rather green flavors and only a hint of riper cherry, and a tart bite of acidity. Will do in a pinch, and the price is right. **83** —*S.H. (9/1/2004)*

Woodbridge 2000 Clay Hollow (PT) Merlot (California) $11. Features cinnamon, herb, and chocolate notes alongside modest black cherry fruit. It's medium in body, with bright fruit showing more prominently on the finish. **84** *(11/15/2003)*

Woodbridge 2001 Select Vineyard Series Clay Hollow Merlot (Lodi) $11. Plenty of richness here, with cherry and blackberry flavors finished with an edge of sweet herbs and roasted coffee. Totally dry, and the tannins are ripe and fine. Great value. **86 Best Buy** —*S.H. (12/15/2004)*

Woodbridge 1998 Winemaker's Selection Muscat (California) $12. Unctuous and sweet, a smooth-drinking wine with the aroma and flavors of apricots, honey, oranges, smoke, and vanilla. Delicious and assertive, with the bright acidity to boost the flavors and make the finish clean and sharp. Perfect with ripe fruit or an apricot tart. **89 Best Buy** —*S.H. (12/1/2003)*

Woodbridge 2003 Pinot Grigio (California) $8. Nice for your next block party, an affordable wine with crisp apple, citrus, and wildflower flavors that's dry and clean. **83** —*S.H. (12/15/2004)*

Woodbridge 2002 Pinot Grigio (California) $8. Opens with a blast of sulfur, which blows off to reveal earth and peach aromas. In the mouth, it's fruity and dry, with correct acidity. Gets the job done. **83** —*S.H. (12/1/2003)*

Woodbridge 2000 Pinot Grigio (California) $8. Appley, with citrus and peach flavors, and very dry. The clean fruit flavors are highlighted by refreshing acidity. It finishes on a sweet-spicy, green-apple note. **84** —*S.H. (11/15/2001)*

Woodbridge 1997 Portacinco Port (Lodi) $20. Made from traditional Port varieties, Woodbridge's Portacinco is always a rich, sweet dessert wine, satisfying in fruit and body. You'll find dark chocolate, white chocolate, cassis and cherry flavors, with good balancing acidity. **88 Editors' Choice** —*S.H. (7/1/2005)*

Woodbridge 1995 Portacinco Port (Lodi) $20. Quite a luscious vintage-style Port wine. It's very sweet, with opulent flavors of all sorts of decadent dessert treats, such as pecan pie, chocolate brownies, caramel candy, and Kahlúa truffles. Yet the firm acids hold it all together. The spicy flavors last forever. **91** —*S.H. (8/1/2004)*

Woodbridge 1994 Portacinco Port (California) $20. 90 —*S.H. (12/31/2000)*

Woodbridge 2002 Sauvignon Blanc (California) $6. A good value for its concentrated flavors of slightly sweet peach nectar, citrus, and apricot. There's good acidity and the wine is clean and balanced. 84 —*S.H. (9/1/2004)*

Woodbridge 2001 Sauvignon Blanc (California) $6. Shows plenty of varietal character. Spearmint, lemon and lime flavors, with a crisp, tart texture and a rich, spicy finish. Pleasant to drink and a good value. 84 Best Buy —*S.H. (7/1/2003)*

Woodbridge 2000 Sauvignon Blanc (California) $7. There's something vegetal and unripe about this wine, although it is cleanly made and crisp. Smells like asparagus, and tastes very austere, with diluted tastes of lemon and grapefruit. 83 —*S.H. (10/1/2003)*

Woodbridge 1999 Sauvignon Blanc (California) $7. 83 —*S.H. (11/15/2000)*

Woodbridge 2001 Syrah (California) $9. Young, fresh, and jammy, with blueberry, black cherry, and milk chocolate flavors, dry tannins, and citrusy acids. 83 —*S.H. (12/15/2004)*

Woodbridge 2000 Syrah (California) $9. You can put this next to Syrahs costing four times as much and smell them both, and this Robert Mondavi wine will win out. It's all about white pepper, blackberries, and oak. Tastes fine and yummy, with rich berry flavors and soft, creamy tannins. Could use a bit more depth, but at this price, you can't have everything. 88 Best Buy —*S.H. (12/1/2002)*

Woodbridge 1999 Syrah (California) $8. Leather, damp soil and burned rubber aromas pointed tasters in the direction that the palate flavors would take: equally dark blackberry, burned toast, and sour cherry. Finishes tart, with faint black tea flavors. 83 *(10/1/2001)*

Woodbridge 1997 Zinfandel (California) $7. 82 —*S.H. (2/1/2000)*

Woodbridge 2002 Zinfandel (California) $8. A bit raw in acid and unripe fruit, mingling green tastes side by side with riper blackberries and cherries. 83 —*S.H. (12/15/2004)*

Woodbridge 2001 Zinfandel (California) $7. Fairly mild-mannered, with modest cherry, plum, and spice notes. Toasty at the end. 82 *(11/1/2003)*

Woodbridge 2000 Zinfandel (California) $7. Decent and likeable Zin, a friendly wine you can pull out for barbecue. Fruity and dry, with soft tannins and a clean, spicy finish. The perfect house red for everyday dining. 85 Best Buy —*S.H. (12/1/2002)*

Woodbridge 1999 Zinfandel (California) $6. Unmistakably Zin, with its brambly, wild berry character. There's not a whole lot of depth, but the fruity, earthy flavors are pleasant, and it's nicely dry, with soft tannins and acids. At this price, it's a bargain for picnics and outdoor barbecues. 84 —*S.H. (9/12/2002)*

Woodbridge 2001 Select Vineyard Series Fish Net Creek Zinfandel (Lodi) $11. A nice Zin that's provides some real richness and authenticity. The flavors of wild berries and bitter cherries are dry and balanced, with rich tannins and acidity. 85 —*S.H. (9/1/2004)*

Woodbridge 2000 Select Vineyard Series-Old Vine-Fish Net Creek Zinfandel (Lodi) $11. The best of the new lineup, this old-vine Zin offers a big but not particularly lush mouthful of fruit, along with earthy notes and a hint of licorice on the finish. 86 *(11/15/2003)*

Woodbridge 2003 White Zinfandel (California) $5. Easy and a bit sweet, with raspberry-strawberry flavors and a nice spiciness. 83 Best Buy — *S.H. (12/15/2004)*

Woodbridge 2002 White Zinfandel Zinfandel (California) $5. Simple and crisp, with decent flavors of raspberries and a peppery tinge. Fundamentally a dry wine, but there's a honeyed richness that will make it ideal for a hot summer day at the beach. Stock up the cooler! 84 — *S.H. (3/1/2004)*

WOODBRIDGE BY ROBERT MONDAVI

Woodbridge by Robert Mondavi 2004 Pinot Grigio (California) $8. Understated but fresh and easy. Nothing complicated, but presents clean melon and pear notes. Finishes light and largely dry. 85 Best Buy *(2/1/2006)*

Woodbridge by Robert Mondavi 2003 Sauvignon Blanc (California) $6. Hard to find much to like here. It's thin and tart, with a sulfury smell that blows off to reveal . . . nothing. 82 —*S.H. (8/1/2005)*

WOODEN VALLEY

Wooden Valley 1999 Suisun Valley Cabernet Sauvignon (Solano County) $12. Pretty nice drinking at a fair price. Opens with fat, appealing aromas of currant, green olive, chocolate, and oak. Drinks rich, round, supple, and polished, with huge, ripe fruity flavors. Could use more complexity and depth, but it's a good value. 86 —*S.H. (11/15/2003)*

Wooden Valley 2002 Pinot Noir (Suisun Valley) $10. Very pale, very delicate and silky, but light and thin in melon and peach flavors, with a cheesy smell. 83 *(11/1/2004)*

WOODENHEAD

Woodenhead 2000 Elk Prairie Pinot Noir (California) $42. Displays ample toasty oak over caramel and cherries. Vanilla and dried-spice accents and a chewy mouthfeel round out this full-bodied candidate. Substantial tannins show on the long, smoky finish. May well improve over the next year or two. 85 *(10/1/2002)*

Woodenhead 2001 Braccialini Vineyards Zinfandel (Alexander Valley) $30. Smells almost like cola up front. The theme carries through, adding hints of coffee, black cherry, prune, plum, and toast. Tannins are fairly ripe. The finish is moderate in length, toasty at the end. 86 *(11/1/2003)*

Woodenhead 2001 Martinelli Road Vineyard Old Vine Zinfandel (Russian River Valley) $30. Cola and cassis lead off here. There is a strong cherry cola center that's backed by menthol, toast, coffee, spice, plum and black cherry too. This is a fairly powerful wine-spicy and rich. A bit warm on the finish. 87 *(11/1/2003)*

WOODINVILLE WINE CELLARS

Woodinville Wine Cellars 2003 Ausonius Bordeaux Blend (Columbia Valley (WA)) $35. The Bordeaux blend is 83% Cab Sauvignon, 17% Cab Franc. Very clean and bright, with spicy cranberry and plum, boysenberry, and cherry. There are hints of spice and pretty herb beginning to show. It's a fruit-forward style, with good midpalate concentration and some extra tannin and espresso highlights from the Cab Franc. 415 cases made. 89 —*P.G. (4/1/2006)*

Woodinville Wine Cellars 2003 Merlot (Yakima Valley) $25. Pure Merlot, dark and sappy, with juicy, perfectly ripe boysenberry, blackberry, and black cherry fruit. It offers plenty of spice, along with the ripe fruit flavors. Starts out big and bold but fades out in the middle. 210 cases made. 88 —*P.G. (4/1/2006)*

Woodinville Wine Cellars 2005 Artz Vineyard Sauvignon Blanc (Red Mountain) $17. Very fresh and crisp, with mixed flavors of melon, grapefruit, pineapple, and a glimmer of celery. It finished with a suggestion of sweetness—residual sugar or just very ripe Red Mountain fruit? Either way, it's a well-crafted, tasty effort. 87 —*P.G. (8/1/2006)*

Woodinville Wine Cellars 2003 Syrah (Washington) $28. Good effort in the dark, syrupy vein of Washington Syrah. The scents are ripe and somewhat raisiny, almost Port-like, but the oak has been reined in and the wine reflects the character of the vintage, which was quite warm. The flavors are dense with mincemeat pie, rum raisin, prune, soy, and chocolate, a veritable baker's box of spices. Notes of cherry tobacco lead into dry, herbal tannins; hot and assertive, yet packed with flavor. 89 —*P.G. (4/1/2006)*

WOODINVILLE WINE COMPANY

Woodinville Wine Company 2001 Red Wine Bordeaux Blend (Washington) $32. A Cab-dominated Bordeaux blend that is still quite tight and austere. Once open awhile, cassis and red currant flavors come into focus, with firm tannins that show some green tea character. There's a whiff of barnyard here also; moist earth, some stem. 88 —*P.G. (11/15/2004)*

Woodinville Wine Company 2002 Syrah (Washington) $28. Very juicy, fruity, and showing a lot of tangy citrus flavors. This is a fruit-loaded wine, pleasing and forward, but lacking much stuffing or follow-through. 87 —*P.G. (11/15/2004)*

USA

WOODWARD CANYON

Woodward Canyon 2003 Estate Red Bordeaux Blend (Walla Walla (WA)) **$55.** The wine is 44% Cab Franc, 41% Merlot, and 14% Cab, with a splash of Petit Verdot. Complex and fragrant, it suggests a varied mix of fruit and leaf, from dried cranberry, cherry, and raisin to tobacco, soy, and spice. The feel seems a bit chalky, and it is difficult to assess the potential lifespan of the wine at this point in time. **89** —*P.G. (11/15/2006)*

Woodward Canyon 2001 Estate Red Bordeaux Blend (Walla Walla (WA)) **$55.** A lovely estate wine, from Walla Walla fruit, that is a blend of 50% Cab Sauvignon, 28% Merlot, and the rest Cab Franc. Wild yeasts add some gamey complexity, and every effort is made to ripen the grapes at sensible alcohol levels. This is a vin de garde, with subtle textures, grip and very well-managed tannins that set up a lingering, resonant finish. **93** —*P.G. (9/1/2004)*

Woodward Canyon 2000 Estate Red Bordeaux Blend (Walla Walla (WA)) **$55.** A new bottling for the winery, this blend is 43% Cab Franc, 43% Merlot, and the rest Cab Sauvignon. Wild yeasts were used, and the aromas show some gamey complexity. Good grip, with blueberry/coffee highlights from the Cab Franc, and very well-managed tannins set up an "age me" finish. **91** —*P.G. (9/1/2003)*

Woodward Canyon 1998 Cabernet Sauvignon (Walla Walla (WA)) $45. Although this winery has been a leading producer in the Walla Walla Valley for over two decades, this is only their second Walla Walla-designated Cabernet. Half of the grapes are estate-grown, half are from the Pepper Bridge vineyard. The smooth, chocolatey nose is a Woodward trademark and, despite its youth, the wine has a satiny mouthfeel. Polished, saturated fruit is set off with restrained new oak, and leads to a silky, seamless, satisfying finish. Just 247 cases made. **93** —*P.G. (6/1/2001)*

Woodward Canyon 2001 Artist Series Cabernet Sauvignon (Columbia Valley (WA)) $42. A big, tannic Cabernet that flexes its cassis and blackberry muscles and cloaks itself in layers of tar and smoky oak. Hints of leaf and earth emerge with time, but this is very young and compact. A serious wine that needs substantial decanting and/or cellar time. **91** —*P.G. (7/1/2004)*

Woodward Canyon 2000 Artist Series Cabernet Sauvignon (Washington) $42. Comes on like the big dog it is, with powerful scents of brash berries, cassis, and smoky oak. Meaty, big, and bouncy (apologies to The Who) this is a flavor-laden explosion of power and grace. Still young and relatively tight, this is a polished, textured wine with immense potential over the next decade. **92** —*P.G. (9/1/2003)*

Woodward Canyon 2003 Artist Series #12 Cabernet Sauvignon (Columbia Valley (WA)) $44. Stylish and tight, with compact flavors of cassis, black cherry, and berry in a wrap of baby fat. This muscular Cab has the toasty joie de vivre of a new Bordeaux, without all the herbal stuff. New (as of 2003) winemaker Kevin Mott seems to have solved the issues that were creating severely reduced, hard-as-nails wines in recent vintages. **91** —*P.G. (11/15/2006)*

Woodward Canyon 1998 Artist Series #7 Cabernet Sauvignon (Washington) $37. 93 —*P.G. (11/15/2000)*

Woodward Canyon 1999 Artist Series #8 Cabernet Sauvignon (Washington) $43. Earthy aromas are intertwined with dried meat. Rich, chewy flavors are of blackberries and caramel. The balance of fruit, acid, and tannins is exceptional, and the finish is extremely complex. With 3,100 cases produced, it should be readily available. **92 Editors' Choice** —*C.S. (12/31/2002)*

Woodward Canyon 1999 Klipsun Vineyard Cabernet Sauvignon (Columbia Valley (WA)) $45. This is the first vineyard-designated Klipsun Cabernet for Woodward Canyon, though the vineyard has its name on dozens of wines from as many producers. This wine is quite tightly bound, and very tannic, with a strong medicinal streak of bitter anise running through it. Earth and iron are also there, knowing the vineyard and winemaker, it has plenty of aging potential. But right now its fruit is buried in tannin. **89** —*P.G. (6/1/2002)*

Woodward Canyon 2001 Old Vines Cabernet Sauvignon (Columbia Valley (WA)) $67. Old vines from two classic Washington vineyards (Champoux and Sagemoor) give this a wonderful plushness; its dark fruit is set against a background of herb and mineral. Dig and you'll find berries, cherries, plums, and cassis, lovely hints of rosemary and thyme, sturdy tannins and a lingering, grainy finish. **93 Cellar Selection** —*P.G. (9/1/2004)*

Woodward Canyon 2000 Old Vines Cabernet Sauvignon (Columbia Valley (WA)) $67. Ah, those old vines! Smooth, svelte even, they don't shout, they seduce with soft, sweet vibrant flavors that mingle effortlessly. Dancing among berries, cherries, plums, and cassis, the oak handled responsibly, the tannins sturdy but substantial. Beautiful effort. **92** —*P.G. (9/1/2003)*

Woodward Canyon 1999 Old Vines Cabernet Sauvignon (Columbia Valley (WA)) $60. The old vines bottling blends grapes from the Champoux and Sagemoor vineyards, from vines dating to the mid-1970s. This is a showstopper, thick, chocolatey, and densely packed with red and black berries, smoke, cedar, anise, and chocolate. It's a full-throttle wine that will require extra breathing time. Delicious now, or cellar it for another decade. **91 Editors' Choice** —*P.G. (6/1/2002)*

Woodward Canyon 1998 Old Vines Cabernet Sauvignon (Columbia Valley (WA)) $60. The old vines in question hail from what used to be the Mercer Ranch Vineyard (now Champoux), and date back to the 1970s, making them ancient for Washington state. Purple black, spicy, and deep, this is a sensational wine that manages to be both elegant and powerful at the same time. Dense, ripe fruit, detailed spices, balanced oak, and perfect tannins make this a textbook Washington Cabernet. **94 Cellar Selection** —*P.G. (6/1/2001)*

Woodward Canyon 2000 Charbonneau Red Cabernet Sauvignon-Merlot (Walla Walla (WA)) $50. A 51%/49% Cab/Merlot blend. The nose is open and inviting, with scents of chocolate and berries, cherries, and tobacco. Still young, but approachable, it has broad, friendly flavors and some complexity, though not the depth and muscle of the top Woodward Cabs. There's a clear, ringing licorice note in the finish. **89** —*P.G. (9/1/2003)*

Woodward Canyon 2004 Chardonnay (Columbia Valley (WA)) $36. In this freeze-plagued year the estate vineyard was shut out, but any Chardonnay that is made of 100% Celilo Vineyard fruit has nothing to apologize about. Lots of toasty oak jumps out from this still-tight, acidic wine, but as it opens the crisp mix of pear, pineapple, and citrus, along with a hint of rock, creates a firm and balanced, very pleasing wine. **88** —*P.G. (10/1/2006)*

Woodward Canyon 2002 Chardonnay (Columbia Valley (WA)) $33. Mixed, roasted nuts set up the layered aromas. Following are layers of stone fruits, spicy and textured, and fresh, ballpark roasted peanut flavors. Good penetration and a nice balance that captures the flavors of oak without making the wine oaky. **91** —*P.G. (7/1/2004)*

Woodward Canyon 2001 Chardonnay (Columbia Valley (WA)) $32. It was his rich, brilliant Chardonnays that really put Rick Small on the map, though his red wines have been the stars of the show recently. This is a return to form, plush and oily, with roasted nuts and tropical fruit. The acids are high enough to keep it all in focus. **89** —*P.G. (9/1/2003)*

Woodward Canyon 2000 Chardonnay (Columbia Valley (WA)) $33. There is an unfortunately strong scent of burnt match to this wine, so much so that it can be tasted as well. Oversulfured though it may be, it's a delicious bottle, with ripe, round fruit, made in a big, balanced style and enhanced with generous new oak. Air it out! **88** —*P.G. (7/1/2002)*

Woodward Canyon 1999 Chardonnay (Columbia Valley (WA)) $28. 90 —*P.G. (11/15/2000)*

Woodward Canyon 1998 Unfined/Unfiltered Estate Chardonnay (Walla Walla (WA)) $40. Comprised of 100% estate-grown grapes and barrel-fermented in new French oak, this is Woodward Canyon's premier Chardonnay. The richness of the oak almost overpowers the nose, but when one thinks of premier cru Burgundy it's hard to tell the difference. In the mouth, the fruit more than holds its own, with firm acids and plenty of ripe peach and apricot flavors. Additional time in bottle is needed to soften the hard edges. Just 143 cases made. **93** —*P.G. (6/1/2001)*

Woodward Canyon 2003 Merlot (Columbia Valley (WA)) $39. An excellent lineup of vineyards, including estate, Red Mountain, and Champoux fruit, contribute to this firm, meaty Merlot. It is chewy and substantial, with a core of black cherry and plenty of new oak. It resolves into flavors of mushroom, earth, coffee grounds, and grainy baking chocolate. A return to form after the disappointing '02. **89** —*P.G. (10/1/2006)*

Woodward Canyon 2000 Merlot (Walla Walla (WA)) $45. Here is a sumptuous, earthy, tight, and terrific example of Walla Walla Merlot. Still quite young and compact, but well-structured and layered with mineral and earth; the tannins are hard and muscular, the flavors a powerful mix of black cherry, cassis, and red currant. Give it six more months to integrate the luscious new oak. **92 Editors' Choice** —*P.G. (9/1/2002)*

Woodward Canyon 2000 Merlot (Columbia Valley (WA)) $38. Flavorful, forward, and tasting of a pleasing mix of light, toasty oak and pretty cherry fruit, this is a solid, immediately enjoyable wine. It doesn't have the muscle to go long term, but it offers a lot of pure Merlot pleasure in the near term. **88** —*P.G. (9/1/2002)*

Woodward Canyon 1999 Merlot (Columbia Valley (WA)) $38. This luscious Merlot jumps out with a big, bold nose and mouth-filling flavors of ripe cherry fruit. Forward, luscious, and chocolatey, it's a wide-open style of Merlot with lots of instant appeal. There isn't a great deal of depth to the finish, but it's well-built and can certainly be cellared for the next 5-6 years. **89** —*P.G. (6/1/2001)*

Woodward Canyon 1999 Charbonneau Merlot-Cabernet Sauvignon (Walla Walla (WA)) $50. Though it's mostly Merlot (95%), the 1999 Charbonneau is a bit tight and ungenerous at this stage of the game. The flavors are a mix of red fruits and berries, along with some leafy, herbal elements, that suggest that perhaps the grapes did not ripen as fully as in hotter years such as 1998. No doubt it's a pleasing, well-made wine, but not quite as exciting as in the past. **87** —*P.G. (6/1/2002)*

Woodward Canyon 1998 Charbonneau Red Blend (Walla Walla (WA)) $50. Woodward Canyon makes both a Charbonneau white and red; this is a 60/40 Merlot/Cabernet blend from a vineyard in northwest Walla Walla county. Seductive and concentrated, it starts with layers of ripe fruit, rich spice, and dense scents of coffee, toast, tobacco, and chocolate. It broadens out in the mouth, with lots of delicious, chocolatey cherry fruit, smooth tannins, and a sweet, lingering finish **92** —*P.G. (6/1/2001)*

Woodward Canyon 2003 Old Vines Dedication Series #23 Red Blend (Columbia Valley (WA)) $75. This wine is immediately fascinating. A rich mix of fruits, ripened to compote intensity, offers both power and detail. Subtle streaks of herb, leaf, and wet hay suggest old-vine complexity, and the acids are naturally firm and supportive. Everything is nicely knit together, full-bodied and deep. **93** —*P.G. (10/1/2006)*

Woodward Canyon 2002 Dry White Riesling (Columbia Valley (WA)) $22. This limited-production Riesling is a tasting room favorite, with ripe but not heavy flavors of fresh-cut pear and apple extending into a long, textured and thoroughly delicious finish. Clearly one of the top Rieslings in a state known for them. **89** —*P.G. (5/1/2004)*

Woodward Canyon 2001 Dry White Riesling (Columbia Valley (WA)) $22. A limited-production wine, made in a bone-dry style. It is at once searingly tart and loaded with fresh, tangy lemon and citrus and green apple fruit. It shows terrific concentration and focus, and lingers in the back palate, begging for some spicy food to wash down. **88** —*P.G. (9/1/2002)*

Woodward Canyon 2005 Sauvignon Blanc (Walla Walla (WA)) $24. From the estate vineyard, a windblown hilltop in the western end of the valley, this lean, yet creamy SB rewards your attention with subtle, clean, nicely crafted flavors. Pineapple, pink grapefruit, and sliced almond can be found, with plenty of natural acid (no malolactic) and some cracker flavors that come from the land, not from barrels (none were used). **87** —*P.G. (10/1/2006)*

Woodward Canyon 2003 Estate Sauvignon Blanc (Walla Walla (WA)) $24. Edgeless and hard to quantify. The nose smells like peach juice and aged cheese, while the palate offers very little heft or zest. A flat wine without much pulse. **81** *(7/1/2005)*

Woodward Canyon 2001 Charbonneau Blanc Sémillon-Sauvignon Blanc (Walla Walla (WA)) $28. This is 77% Sémillon and 23% Sauvignon Blanc; a rich, oaky, barrel-fermented style with plenty of palate weight.

The alcohol remains below 14%, so the wine is balanced and refreshing despite its size. Offers herbs, figs, and melons, with a hint of clover. **90** —*P.G. (9/1/2003)*

Woodward Canyon 2002 Syrah (Columbia Valley (WA)) $34. Lusciously creamy and supple for Syrah—although it could be criticized on precisely those grounds. Caramel and toffee from oak, but there's also plenty of meaty, blackberry fruit and a long finish. **86** *(9/1/2005)*

Woodward Canyon 2000 Charbonneau White Blend (Walla Walla (WA)) $28. Named for the vineyard that sources the grapes, Woodward Canyon's Meritage white wine is 83% Sémillon and 17% Sauvignon Blanc. Intensely aromatic, it smells of grass and herbs, tastes of citrus, apple, pineapple, and apricot, and picks up texture and oak from barrel fermentation. Big, spicy, ripe, and slightly hot, it's a no-holds-barred style for those who believe size counts. **90** —*P.G. (6/1/2002)*

Woodward Canyon 1999 Charbonneau Blanc White Blend (Walla Walla (WA)) $28. Charbonneau is Woodward Canyon's proprietary name for its white and red blended wines. The blanc is predominantly Sémillon, with 10% Sauvignon Blanc added to round it out. The nose is scented with freshly mown hay, spice, and herbs. It has plenty of crisp fruit in the mouth, and a distinctive spiciness that begs to be paired with Thai food, crabcakes, or something with cilantro. Great food wine. **90** —*P.G. (6/1/2001)*

<h3>WOOLDRIDGE CREEK</h3>

Wooldridge Creek 1998 Cabernet Sauvignon (Applegate Valley) $18. This wine carries fairly broad fruit flavors of mixed red fruits, along with leaf and earth. Tannins are well-managed; the finish light and fruity. **84** —*P.G. (8/1/2002)*

Wooldridge Creek 1999 Merlot (Applegate Valley) $16. A tart, tight, and tannic Merlot, that shows simple flavors of young red fruits. It is still quite hard and compact, and seems likely to remain so. **85** —*P.G. (8/1/2002)*

Wooldridge Creek 1999 IL Carrino Rosso Red Wine Red Blend (Applegate Valley) $15. This is a blend of 50% Cabernet Sauvignon, 30% Sangiovese, and 20% Zinfandel. Spicy, light, and fruity, it sports plenty of acid beneath tart red fruits. The addition of Sangiovese gives it a little bit of leather and toast for added interest. **85** —*P.G. (8/1/2002)*

Wooldridge Creek 1999 Syrah (Applegate Valley) $16. Hints of spicy cranberry and white pepper suggest Syrah, but lack all of the grape's power. There is a fair amount of unripe leafiness as well. **84** —*P.G. (8/1/2002)*

Wooldridge Creek 2000 Viognier (Rogue Valley) $16. This is made in a very rich style, with lots of forward fruit, flavors of pears, citrus, and citrus rind. Somehow the floral elegance of the variety is lost in all the ripe fruit. **85** —*P.G. (8/1/2002)*

Wooldridge Creek 1999 Viognier (Rogue Valley) $20. A distinctly musky scent carries aromas of mushrooms mixed with toast and grapefruit, if you can follow that trail. Tart and fruity, it shows green fruit flavors with more of that musty, sweaty saddle undertone, carrying into a high-acid finish. **83** —*P.G. (4/1/2002)*

<h3>WORK</h3>

Work 2003 Sauvignon Blanc (Napa Valley) $23. As bright and rich in sweet lime, fig, and tropical fruit flavors as last year's release, and as crisp, with a lush, creamy texture. The creamy texture leads to a very long, spicy finish. **89** —*S.H. (12/15/2004)*

Work 2002 Sauvignon Blanc (Napa Valley) $23. Another fine release from Work. This wine shows bright, rich flavors of sweet lime, fig, and even a smattering of tropical fruits. Yet it is crisp and dry, with a steely mouthfeel that cleanses the palate. The creamy texture leads to a very long, spicy finish. **89** —*S.H. (12/1/2003)*

Work 2001 Sauvignon Blanc (Napa Valley) $23. Shares more than a little in common with New Zealand Sauvignons in the intense gooseberry, juniper, and lemon rind flavors. The wine is crisp and nervy, with a streak of acidity that penetrates the palate. The finish is very long and spicy. One of the more interesting Sauvignons of the current crop, and a wine to watch. **91** —*S.H. (9/1/2003)*

Work 2005 Work Vineyard Sauvignon Blanc (Napa Valley) $25. The vineyard is in the warmer, northern valley. The cool, dry harvest permitted the grapes to achieve maximum ripeness, and this is a superfruity wine. No oak touched it, but it was stirred on the lees, which gives the citrus and tropical fruit flavors a rich, creamy texture. This is a polished, sophisticated Sauvignon Blanc. **90** —*S.H. (11/1/2006)*

WORKHORSE

Workhorse 2000 Syrah (Dry Creek Valley) $15. A rather earthy and closed wine, and pretty tannic, too. There are some blackberry flavors but the mouthfeel is tough, and the finish turns astringent. May benefit from five years of aging. **82** —*S.H. (3/1/2004)*

Workhorse 2002 Zinfandel (Dry Creek Valley) $15. Take last night's Syrah, pour some water into it, and bottle. That's what this wine tastes like. There are echoes of blackberries and plums, in a stale, tannic package. **83** —*S.H. (3/1/2004)*

WORTHY

Worthy 2002 Sophia's Cuvée Red Blend (Napa Valley) $29. This Bordeaux blend, made with all five red grapes, is fruity in cherry, cocoa, blackberry, and oak flavors, with smooth, sophisticated tannins. Made solidly in the new style of softness, ultraripeness, and highish alcohol. **88** —*S.H. (10/1/2005)*

WRITER'S BLOCK

Writer's Block 2002 Syrah (Lake County) $14. Reduced and sulfury on the nose to one reviewer, while the others, who liked it more, found stewed fruit and a bristly, tart mouthfeel. **81** *(9/1/2005)*

WYNELAND ESTATES

Wyneland Estates 2002 Proprietor's Reserve Alicante Bouschet (Lodi) $26. Rich, dry, full-bodied, and tannic like a Cabernet, this wine has a feral quality of garrigue, that wild herb Provençal quality that is so food friendly. With its soft acids and smooth tannins, it's a natural for calf's liver. **87** —*S.H. (12/31/2005)*

WYVERN

Wyvern 1998 Cabernet Sauvignon (Yakima Valley) $25. This delicious wine was so light, so airy on the palate that I checked the alcohol: 12.5%. You won't find this in California, but you will in Bordeaux. The blackberry flavors, infused with smoky oak, are pure and elegant with subtle tannins. There's a depth and complexity that make for added interest. **90** —*S.H. (6/1/2002)*

Wyvern 2000 Syrah (Columbia Valley (WA)) $25. From an area that is constantly pursuing excellence with this grape, a deeply fruity wine of enormous charm. On one level it seems simple, with blackberry flavors and rich, dry tannins that are well-oaked and delicious. Then you sip again and discover all sorts of interesting tidbits. It's drinkable now, especially with braised beef or duck with plum sauce, but has the inherent balance to age gracefully. **90** —*S.H. (6/1/2002)*

X

X 2002 Cabernet Sauvignon (Napa Valley) $22. A perfectly fine Napa Cab that makes all the right moves, without necessarily inspiring. It's dry and ripe in currant fruit, with firm, sweet tannins and good oak. **85** —*S.H. (10/1/2005)*

X 2001 Cabernet Sauvignon (California) $15. A pretty good Cab with some ripe flavors of blackberries, cherries, and blueberries. It has a soft, melted mouthfeel, and the fruit penetrates deep into the taste buds. **84** —*S.H. (2/1/2004)*

X 2000 Cabernet Sauvignon (Napa Valley) $20. A new winery from a trio with long years in the industry, but this is not a good start. Tastes like Port, with flavors of raisins. Someone thought shriveled berries would give consumers the superripe flavors they clamor for. Huge mistake, this is a clumsy wine. **81** —*S.H. (11/15/2002)*

X 2002 Napa-Sonoma-San Luis Obispo Cabernet Sauvignon (Napa-Sonoma) $19. Dry, rich, and balanced, with dusty tannins and balanced currant, blackberry, and oak flavors. A nice, versatile Cabernet with plenty of fanciness that won't break the bank. **87** —*S.H. (3/1/2005)*

X 2002 Chardonnay (Carneros) $19. Full-bodied and a little heavy. Showing apple, peach, and pear flavors, generously oaked, with a slightly sweet finish. **84** —*S.H. (3/1/2005)*

X 2002 Chardonnay (Carneros) $19. This oaky wine has vanilla and buttered toast aromas, but it's pretty watery in the mouth. There are some peach and apple flavors. **84** —*S.H. (10/1/2004)*

X 2000 Chardonnay (Russian River Valley) $15. What a juicy, tasty Chard this is. It's classic Russian River, with its flavors of tart green apples veering into ripe peach and pear, and that sleek backbone of minerality. Well-oaked with smoky, spicy wood, adding to the complexity. The texture is rich and smooth. **90 Best Buy** —*S.H. (12/31/2003)*

X 2004 Truchard Vineyard Chardonnay (Carneros) $20. Fruity and oaky, yet a little one-dimensional, this dry wine is sharply tart in acids, with an herbal, earthy note to the green apple and grapefruit juice flavors. **84** —*S.H. (8/1/2006)*

X 2003 Two Rivers Vineyard Chardonnay (Yountville) $17. Earthy and dull, a very dry wine that's as thin as water. A trace of sweetened lemonade is about it. **82** —*S.H. (10/1/2005)*

X 2002 Merlot (Napa Valley) $25. Oaky and full-bodied, with earthy-cherry flavors, this is a dry wine that has lots of hard-edged tannins. It's rustic in its impact, and could soften and sweeten with a few years of age. **86** —*S.H. (8/1/2005)*

X 2003 Petite Sirah (Paso Robles) $22. Here's what Paso does so well with full-bodied red wines. It's an inky, voluptuously rich wine, almost decadent in chocolate and cassis flavors, yet dry and balanced. This big, burly, tannic wine will be great now with short ribs. **87** —*S.H. (3/1/2006)*

X 2000 Petite Sirah (Paso Robles) $19. An odd wine that opens with Port-like aromas of caramelized sugar, honey, and pepper, but seems bone dry, without much fruity flavor at all. What fills the mouth is the heat of alcohol and the bite of tannins. May improve, but it's a gamble. **83** —*S.H. (12/1/2002)*

X 2004 Truchard Vineyard Pinot Noir (Carneros) $25. Dry, silky, and crisp in acidity, this single-vineyard Pinot shows delicacy of structure along with finely ground tannins and some nice fruit. The cherry, cola, and pomegranate flavors turn earthy on the finish. **87** —*S.H. (12/1/2006)*

X 2003 Truchard Vineyard Pinot Noir (Carneros) $22. Dark, full-bodied and rich in black currants and oak, this is more like a Syrah than Pinot, except for the silky tannins. Exemplifies the ripe, high-alcohol style so prevalent in the North Coast. It's a good wine, but atypical for a Pinot. **88** —*S.H. (10/1/2005)*

X 2003 Red X Red Blend (California) $13. Rustic, with a sharp edge and a semi-sweet fruity finish of cherries and cocoa, this blend of five varieties is okay by the glass with a midweek dinner. **82** —*S.H. (12/1/2005)*

X 2002 Red X Red Blend (California) $13. Rustic and country-style, with rugged tannins and a harsh mouthfeel, but saved by rich berry flavors. Fine with pizza, burgers. Syrah, Merlot, Cab Franc, Cab Sauvignon. **84** —*S.H. (4/1/2005)*

X 2003 Syrahtica Red Blend (California) $14. Very ripe and juicy in blackberry, mocha, cola, toasty oak, and spice flavors, this dry wine is also soft in acids and tannins, making it instantly drinkable, if a little one-dimensional. **84** —*S.H. (5/1/2006)*

X 2002 Syrahtica Red Blend (California) $14. Decent, with cherry, cocoa, cassis, and tobacco flavors and rich, easy tannins. Stays fruity through the finish. Syrah, Merlot, Cab Sauvignon, Cab Franc. **84** —*S.H. (5/1/2005)*

X 2002 Sauvignon Blanc (Lake County) $15. Further advances this county's case for Sauvignon, with an exciting balance of lush, ripe fig, peach and apricot flavors, crisp acids and a long, spicy finish. Feels creamy and tart in the mouth, like a rich sorbet, and is very complex. Will be fabulous with a goat cheese and endive salad and a roasted chicken. **89** —*S.H. (12/15/2003)*

X 2005 ES Vineyard Sauvignon Blanc (Lake County) $17. Lots of cat's pee and gooseberry in this crisp wine, with richer notes of ripe figs and pineapple. The finish is dryish and peppery-spicy. **84** —*S.H. (12/15/2006)*

X 2004 ES Vineyard Sauvignon Blanc (Lake County) $17. Citrusy and figgy, backed up by brightening acidity. It finishes sweet in candied pineapple and lemon Lifesaver, although it's probably technically dry. **85** —*S.H. (12/1/2005)*

X 2003 Eutenier Sylar Vineyard Sauvignon Blanc (Lake County) $17. There are some good lime, fig, and melon flavors here, but they're really watered down. Definitely needs more concentration, especially at this price. **84** —*S.H. (3/1/2005)*

X 2003 Nova Vineyard Zinfandel (Lake County) $20. Almost everything about this is nice, from the smooth, rich tannins to the clean acidity and the ripe, forward berry, coffee, and spice flavors. The only gripe is the sugary sweet finish that makes it almost a dessert wine. **82** —*S.H. (10/1/2006)*

XYZIN

XYZin 2002 Sandy Lane Vineyard Zinfandel (Contra Costa County) $29. You sure can taste the sunny, fruity extract in this wine. It's massive in black cherry liqueur, cassis, and mocha-choca flavors. It's also very soft, with a long, almost sweet finish. **85** —*S.H. (11/1/2005)*

YAKIMA CELLARS

Yakima Cellars 2002 Elephant Mountain Vineyard Syrah (Yakima Valley) $20. This wine caused a big rift among our panelists. One appreciated the wine's meaty, blackberry, coffee-like flavors. A dissenter, however, found roasted-fruit aromas and charred flavors that were detractions. Could age 3–5 years. **87** *(9/1/2005)*

YAMHILL COUNTY VINEYARDS

Yamhill County Vineyards 1999 Pinot Noir (Willamette Valley) $20. **80** *(10/1/2002)*

YAMHILL VALLEY

Yamhill Valley 1998 Pinot Blanc (Oregon) $14. **85** —*L.W. (12/31/1999)*

Yamhill Valley 1998 Pinot Noir (Willamette Valley) $28. **87** —*P.G. (9/1/2000)*

Yamhill Valley 1999 Reserve Pinot Noir (Willamette Valley) $30. A smoky, nutty, grilled-meat quality is strong in this dryly fruited wine. Though not at all plush, there is a definite appeal to its tart, structured style. Closes with firm tannins, and should reward cellaring for one or two years. Best from 2004–2008. **87** *(10/1/2002)*

Yamhill Valley 1998 Reserve Pinot Noir (Willamette Valley) $48. Smells young, fresh, and oaky, with flamboyant black cherry fruit as well as roasted coffeebean and oriental spices. Very rich and extracted, with dry cherry fruit and a creamy texture. It's a bit hard now with tannins, so give it a few years, or drink it sooner with duck or lamb. **89** —*S.H. (8/1/2002)*

YELLOW HAWK CELLAR

Yellow Hawk Cellar 2004 Barbera (Columbia Valley (WA)) $17. The wine has a very soft entry, with sweet, almost candied strawberry fruit flavors. Then it seems to hit a reductive wall, with flavors of burnt rubber sending a bitter streak through the midpalate and continuing through the finish. **84** —*P.G. (6/1/2006)*

Yellow Hawk Cellar 2001 Muscat Canelli (Columbia Valley (WA)) $12. A wine designed for summer, if ever there was one. Bone-dry and fragrant, with lemon, jasmine, and fresh pear scents evolving into complex layers of pear, grapefruit, and honey. **89** —*P.G. (9/1/2002)*

Yellow Hawk Cellar 2003 Sangiovese (Walla Walla (WA)) $19. Aromas of cracker, rubber, and oatmeal swirl around the light, pretty strawberry fruit. It gets leathery in the mouth, and finishes sour. **82** —*P.G. (6/1/2006)*

YN

YN 2000 White Blend (California) $4. **83** —*S.H. (6/1/2002)*

YOAKIM BRIDGE

Yoakim Bridge 2002 Syrah (Dry Creek Valley) $34. From central Dry Creek Valley, this single-vineyard wine got a lot of afternoon sun, and you can taste the warm, wild blackberry flavors. Complexed with coffee and sweet smoky oak, and very dry, this wine will be perfect with roast pork. **91** —*S.H. (11/1/2005)*

Yoakim Bridge 2002 Zinfandel (Dry Creek Valley) $30. This richly textured Zin comes from old vines off the estate, in the warmer, upper part of the valley. It's ripe, with suggestions of raisins, but it's not overripe or hot. In fact, it's a chewy wine long in cherries and pepper. **88** —*S.H. (11/1/2005)*

Yoakim Bridge 2001 Zinfandel (Dry Creek Valley) $26. Toasty rich aromas sally forth here, while the bright raspberry, plum, vanilla, toast, and spice flavors follow nicely. It's a little short on the finish, but the wine is quite pleasing nonetheless. **87** *(11/1/2003)*

Yoakim Bridge 1999 Zinfandel (Dry Creek Valley) $25. Pretty aromas of rose petal, dust, and vanilla cover deeper ones of wild berries, clove, and allspice. Drinks very briary and luscious, with blackberry and black-rasberry flavors and rich, earthy tannins. This dry, supple wine is classic Zin. **90** —*S.H. (12/15/2001)*

YORK MOUNTAIN WINERY

York Mountain Winery 2003 Albariño (Edna Valley) $17. Grown in this cool appellation, this Spanish variety is crisp in acidity and bone dry, a refreshing sipper that shows flavors of citrus zest not unlike a Sauvignon Blanc, but fuller-bodied. **87** —*S.H. (7/1/2006)*

York Mountain Winery 2003 Unfiltered Chardonnay (Edna Valley) $25. Like all Edna Valley Chards, this bottling is bone dry, with high acidity. The flavors are very citrusy, with richer notes of honeydew melon and sweet, oaky vanilla. This is a polished, elegant wine. **88** —*S.H. (7/1/2006)*

York Mountain Winery 2001 Merlot (Napa Valley) $26. The red cherry, olive, smoked meat, tobacco, and coffee flavors drink a little astringent in acids and tannins, but this is a good wine, dry and balanced. **85** —*S.H. (10/1/2004)*

York Mountain Winery 2003 Pinot Noir (Edna Valley) $25. Compared to the winery's county-wide bottling, this Pinot is remarkably similar in the high acidity, light, silky texture and pleasant cherry, cola, and subtle oak flavors. Yet it possesses an extra depth and complexity. Drink this polished wine now. **88** —*S.H. (7/1/2006)*

York Mountain Winery 2003 Pinot Noir (San Luis Obispo County) $15. Shows true Central Coast Pinot character in the high acidity, lightly silky texture, and polished flavors of red cherries, cola, vanilla, and spicy white pepper. **86** —*S.H. (7/1/2006)*

York Mountain Winery 2002 Pinot Noir (Paso Robles) $25. Here's a nice, easy Pinot made in an accessible style. It's soft and fruity, with cherry and herb flavors that finish with a touch of oak. **84** —*S.H. (2/1/2005)*

York Mountain Winery 2001 Pinot Noir (San Luis Obispo County) $15. Pale in color and tart with acids, this user-friendly wine has flavors of cola, rhubarb, and cherries and a dollop of oak. It's dry and silky in the mouth. **84** —*S.H. (2/1/2005)*

York Mountain Winery 2001 Pinot Noir (Edna Valley) $25. Quite tart in acids, and dry. This wine is austere and well-structured, with flavors of cola, tea, and tart cherries. **84** —*S.H. (2/1/2005)*

York Mountain Winery 2003 Jack Ranch Pinot Noir (Edna Valley) $25. The winery's regular Edna Valley Pinot was quite good, but this single-vineyard bottling, which shares many of its qualities, suffers from an apparent sweetness that makes it cloying. It's hard to figure out how this got past the winemaker. **82** —*S.H. (7/1/2006)*

York Mountain Winery 2000 Stephen's Pinot Noir (San Luis Obispo County) $28. From a little-used San Luis Obispo County appellation, a simple wine with little to recommend it beyond cleanliness and some berry flavors. Fully dry, it has silky tannins and some firm acids. **83** —*S.H. (7/1/2003)*

York Mountain Winery 2003 Jack Ranch Syrah (Edna Valley) $22. This is a blend of the three clones that the winery has bottled separately. Strangely, it seems sweeter in sugar than any one of them, a defect given the beautiful dryness of the clones. It's hard to account for this, as the wine, in theory, should be superior to any one of them. Instead, it's not. **85** —*S.H. (4/1/2006)*

York Mountain Winery 2003 Jack Ranch Clone 174 Syrah (Edna Valley) $18. This is an excellent Syrah, and it's right up there with the winery's Clone 877 bottling. It's nearly identical, with rich, sweet tannins, crisp acids, and complex, intricate flavors of blackberries, plums, coffee, white pepper, sweet leather, and smoky oak. The finish is dry and satisfying. **90** —*S.H. (4/1/2006)*

USA

York Mountain Winery 2003 Jack Ranch Clone 383 Syrah (Edna Valley) $18. Shares many of the qualities of the wonderful Clone 877 bottling, except for acidity. This wine is too soft to be fully balanced. Still, the flavors, of blackberries, plums, coffee, sweet leather, and spices, are complex and ever-changing, and the finish is rich and dry. **88** —S.H. (4/1/2006)

York Mountain Winery 2003 Jack Ranch Clone 877 Syrah (Edna Valley) $18. Opens with a blast of white pepper, blackberries, and cigar box, and quickly turns rich, dense and fruity in the mouth. Backed up by substantial but fine tannins, this Syrah is dry, with blackberry, plum, coffee, and spice flavors. It's as good as Syrahs costing two and even three times as much. **90** —S.H. (4/1/2006)

York Mountain Winery 2004 Viognier (Paso Robles) $25. The alcohol is high, yet it doesn't feel hot in the mouth. Dry, crisp, and elegant, the wine has citrus flavors with subtle hints of peaches and honey. **88** —S.H. (8/1/2006)

YORKVILLE CELLARS

Yorkville Cellars 1997 Richard the Lion-Heart Bordeaux Blend (Mendocino County) $25. A Mendocino wine with all five major Bordeaux varietals. Nonetheless Cabernet Sauvignon dominates, with black currant and cassis notes and elaborate but not excessive wood. Very dry, this wine has higher acids than you get in Napa, meaning it's not as plush. But it's more food-friendly. **90** —S.H. (6/1/2002)

Yorkville Cellars 2001 Cabernet Franc (Yorkville Highlands) $19. A bit raw in tannins, and rather unripe, with herbaceous flavors next to the blackberries. Finishes dry, with a scour of acidity and tannin. **83** —S.H. (3/1/2005)

Yorkville Cellars 1998 Cabernet Franc (Mendocino) $17. There's a note on the nose that suggests dried hay or cardboard, although airing reveals better aromas of berries and chocolate. The flavors are thin and a little weedy, with suggestions of black cherries. Give the benefit of the doubt to the winemaker. He struggled with a poor vintage. **84** —S.H. (5/1/2002)

Yorkville Cellars 1997 Cabernet Franc (Yorkville Highlands) $17. This Bordeaux variety more often than not produces a light, fruity wine of charm and early drinkability. Here, the sour cherry fruit is framed in dry, dusty tannins and soft acids. There's an elegance and spicy aftertaste that are very nice. **87** —S.H. (9/1/2002)

Yorkville Cellars 1999 Cabernet Sauvignon (Yorkville Highlands) $19. Good blackberry flavors, smooth tannins, and very dry, although there is a sharp bite of acidity. Might soften with a year of cellaring. **85** —S.H. (5/1/2003)

Yorkville Cellars 1997 Cabernet Sauvignon (Mendocino) $19. An interesting wine that combines cassis and black currant notes with a rich earthiness suggesting sage and tobacco. This limpid, soft wine is easy to drink. It's filled with summery berry flavors and mild, complex tannins and is nicely dry. Yet it has an elusive elegance that makes it special. **91** —S.H. (6/1/2002)

Yorkville Cellars 2001 Rennie Vineyard Cabernet Sauvignon (Yorkville Highlands) $22. From a Mendocino winery that makes steady but sure progress in Bordeaux varieties, a rich, ripe wine, with big flavors of blackberries and chocolate. **88** —S.H. (10/1/2004)

Yorkville Cellars 1998 Malbec (Mendocino) $17. Inky-purple in color, with deep aromas of plums, violets, earth, and a touch of smoked meat. Tastes very extracted and jammy, with dark stone fruit flavors, although it's quite dry. Tannins are evident but not a problem. A well-made example of this variety, which is usually lost into blends. **87** —S.H. (5/1/2002)

Yorkville Cellars 1997 Malbec (Yorkville Highlands) $17. Inky dark, this is a big wine in every way. Rich, sweet aromas of blackberry cobbler drizzled with cassis suggest enormous fruit. The flavors follow up, big and jammy, filled with berries of every kind. But it drinks dry and mellow, with soft tannins and acids. This is an interesting but not great wine from a variety normally used for blending. **89** —S.H. (9/1/2002)

Yorkville Cellars 2003 Rennie Vineyard Malbec (Yorkville Highlands) $20. Sharp and sweet-sour, like Chinese moo shu pork sauce, this Malbec has plum and cherry flavors and very high acidity. **82** —S.H. (10/1/2006)

Yorkville Cellars 1999 Merlot (Yorkville Highlands) $18. From a Mendocino producer who defends this appellation as Bordeaux country, a rather rough wine, compared to its southerly neighbors from Napa and Sonoma. Blackberry fruit barely ripened, and there are green, stalky flavors in this dry, fairly tannic wine. **85** —S.H. (8/1/2003)

Yorkville Cellars 1997 Merlot (Mendocino) $18. How good this dark young wine smells! Cassis and blackberry aromas have subtle hints of butter, smoke, and vanilla, with broader notes of olives and chocolate. In the mouth the subtlety and delicacy fall apart, with the palate assaulted by oversized fruit and rude acidity. I wish it were more balanced. **85** —S.H. (6/1/2002)

Yorkville Cellars 2002 Rennie Vineyard Merlot (Yorkville Highlands) $20. Dry and fruity and a little rugged, this wine from Mendocino County has ripe cherry-berry flavors that are tinged with some sharp tannins, and a tart, astringent finish. Drink now. **84** —S.H. (8/1/2006)

Yorkville Cellars 2001 Rennie Vineyard Merlot (Yorkville Highlands) $22. This wine is so ripe, it tastes like chocolate milk with a dollop of crème de cassis. Fortunately, it's dry, with balancing acidity. Yet it does have a thick, malted mouthfeel and a slightly cloying finish. **85** —S.H. (12/15/2004)

Yorkville Cellars 1998 Petite Verdot (Mendocino County) $17. An eccentric wine, bordering on the bizarre, although it has some nice elements. Starts with aromas of cotton candy and raspberry fruit tart, and drinks extracted and jammy, with raspberry-red cherry flavors. High acids and dusty tannins make for a rough mouthfeel. **84** —S.H. (5/1/2002)

Yorkville Cellars 1997 Petite Verdot (Yorkville Highlands) $17. This variety, not usually used on its own, has produced an inky dark wine of considerable power and ample tannins. The blackberry and rhubarb fruit has great depth, and is very dry. It's not a bad wine, but seems better suited as a blender to Cabernet Sauvignon. It just might be interesting in 6–8 years. **86** —S.H. (9/1/2002)

Yorkville Cellars 2001 Sauvignon Blanc (Yorkville Highlands) $13. This cool region, above Anderson Valley, has produced a very acidic Sauvignon Blanc, so tart it makes your mouth water. Flavors are of wild grasses and lemons and limes, and the wine is dry. It's very delicious, and the acidity makes it perfect for the table. **88** —S.H. (9/1/2003)

Yorkville Cellars 1999 Sauvignon Blanc (Mendocino) $12. You'll notice the acids are among the highest in California. They scour and tingle the palate and nicely balance the lean citrus flavors of this bone-dry wine, from a Mendocino appellation. It's a simple wine but refreshing and clean. **85** —S.H. (5/1/2002)

Yorkville Cellars 1999 Eleanor of Aquitaine Sauvignon Blanc (Mendocino) $17. Opens with earthy aromas of crushed spices and herbs, and a streak of peaches and citrus. In the mouth, it's overtly sweet, with lemonade flavors although crisp acidity makes it drink bright and lively. **84** —S.H. (5/1/2002)

Yorkville Cellars 1999 Sémillon (Mendocino) $13. From a Mendocino appellation just east of Anderson Valley, an easy-drinking white. It has pretty flavors of peaches, pears, and nectarines, and is clean, with a swift, slightly sweet finish. **84** —S.H. (5/1/2002)

Yorkville Cellars 2004 Randle Hill Vineyard Sémillon (Yorkville Highlands) $18. This is an interesting wine that marches to its own beat. What gets to you is the dry, acidic structure and fruity, earthy flavors that are quite complex. Try this wine with roasted pork loin. If you like aging your California whites, this should fare well over the next five years. **90 Editors' Choice** —S.H. (7/1/2006)

Z-52

Z-52 2002 Agnes' Vineyard Old Vines Zinfandel (Lodi) $16. Drink this country-style Zin with grilled meats or poultry. It's dry and fruity, with blackberry and spice flavors. Finishes a bit sweet, which suggests a rich, tomato-based BBQ sauce with a little brown sugar or molasses. **84** —S.H. (12/1/2005)

Z-52 2001 Agnes' Vineyard Old Vines Zinfandel (Lodi) $16. No problem getting the grapes ripe, to judge from the explosion of berry and chocolate flavors. You'll find some smooth tannins backing it all up. Feels just a bit rustic. **84** —S.H. (12/15/2004)

Z-52 2003 Clockspring Vineyard Old Vines Zinfandel (Amador County) $20. This single-vineyard wine showcases the ripeness and smoothness of Amador Zin at its best. It has briary, wild berry flavors, with a roasted coffee and chocolate finish. It's a rustic wine, which is a huge part of its appeal. **88** —S.H. (12/1/2005)

Z-52 2001 Clockspring Vineyard Old Vines Zinfandel (Lodi) $20. A bit hot and peppery, for those sensitive to that sort of thing, but if you're big on warm-country Zin, you'll like the way this one takes over your mouth. Black currants, herbs, coffee, tobacco, and spices, and totally dry. **86** —S.H. (12/15/2004)

Zaca Mesa 1998 Chardonnay (Santa Barbara County) $15. 88 (6/1/2000)

ZACA MESA

Zaca Mesa 2000 Zaca Vineyards Chardonnay (Santa Barbara) $15. Lots of herbal and leafy notes in this cool vintage wine, with flavors ranging from mint and oregano to riper apples and white peach. A dash of Viognier plumps it up with floral fruit. Dry and crisp. **87** —S.H. (5/1/2003)

Zaca Mesa 1997 Zaca Vineyards Chardonnay (Santa Barbara County) $13. 85 —S.H. (7/1/1999)

Zaca Mesa 1999 Chapel Vineyard Mourvèdre (Santa Barbara County) $15. Quite fruity, with an intriguing blueberry quality that dominates. However, the wine is dry and focused, with layers of black currant, herb, toasty oak, and spice flavors. Moderate and bright on the finish. **88** —J.M. (7/1/2002)

Zaca Mesa 2001 Z-Gris Red Blend (Santa Ynez Valley) $9. A "saignee" wine, where a portion of juice is bled off to produce a light, fruity wine that has little, if any oak. Apricot, peach, and rose flavors drink dry and simple. The mouthfeel is light and airy, like silk on the palate. **85** —S.H. (9/1/2003)

Zaca Mesa 2003 Z Cuvée Rhône Red Blend (Santa Ynez Valley) $18. Not as good as the '02, because it finishes a bit sweet and Porty. The coffee, blackberry tea, and cola flavors taste rather sugared. **83** —S.H. (11/15/2006)

Zaca Mesa 2002 Z Cuvée Rhône Red Blend (Santa Ynez Valley) $15. I think of this as a softer Rhône equivalent of the Zinfandel-based field blend. With Grenache, Mourvèdre, Syrah, and Cinsault, there's a spicy, herbal garrigue flavor to the cherry and red raspberry fruit. Crisp acidity and fine, rich tannins make it balanced and appealing and even complex. **88** —S.H. (12/1/2005)

Zaca Mesa 2000 Z Cuvée Rhône Red Blend (Santa Barbara County) $16. Could double as a good Châteauneuf. It's pleasantly fruity, with sweet blackberry and black raspberry flavors and a peppery undercurrent. It's also nicely dry, with fine tannins that support the structure but don't overwhelm. Not very deep or complex, but lovely. A blend of Grenache, Mourvèdre, Counoise, Syrah, and Cinsault. **87** —S.H. (11/15/2002)

Zaca Mesa 1997 Z Cuvée Rhône Red Blend (Santa Barbara County) $17. 90 —S.H. (10/1/1999)

Zaca Mesa 2000 Z Gris Rhône Red Blend (Santa Barbara County) $9. It says "dry" on the label, but when sampled in a flight of dry rosés it tasted distinctly off-dry. Cotton candy and strawberry aromas combine with a unique herbal note. The flavors are strawberry, bell-pepper, and lemongrass, with citrusy acidity and an herbal, green apple finish. **82** —J.F. (8/1/2001)

Zaca Mesa 2003 Z Three Red Wine Rhône Red Blend (Santa Ynez Valley) $40. What a beautiful, balanced, succulent wine. It's mostly Syrah and Mourvèdre, with a dash of Grenache for spicy cherries. As delicious as it is right now, it has a good, medium-range shelf life ahead. With a texture of silk and velvet, it's one of those wines that just feels important in your mouth. **92 Editors' Choice** —S.H. (12/1/2006)

Zaca Mesa 1998 Z-Gris Rhône Red Blend (Santa Barbara County) $8. 89 Best Buy —S.H. (10/1/1999)

Zaca Mesa 1998 Roussanne (Santa Barbara County) $16. 87 —M.S. (8/1/2000)

Zaca Mesa 2004 Estate Roussanne (Santa Ynez Valley) $25. Zaca Mesa has been exploring the outer limits of Roussanne for years, and the 2003 was not a very good wine. This is far better. Dry, medium-bodied, and fruity, with crisp acidity framing citrus, peach, apricot, and buttercream flavors, it's an intriguing alternative to Chardonnay. **87** —S.H. (5/1/2006)

Zaca Mesa 2003 Estate Roussanne (Santa Ynez Valley) $25. There were some unripe, even vegetal notes in the bottle I opened, and the wine smacked mainly of oak, although the taste of canned peaches turned up on the finish. **82** —S.H. (10/1/2005)

Zaca Mesa 1997 Zaca Vineyards Roussanne (Santa Barbara County) $16. 86 —S.H. (6/1/1999)

Zaca Mesa 2002 Syrah (Santa Ynez Valley) $20. A bit lean and constricted on the midpalate, but there is some lovely blackberry fruit, so maybe it just needs a little time to blossom. Hints of black pepper and coffee add complexity, while the finish turns tart. **86** (9/1/2005)

Zaca Mesa 2000 Syrah (Santa Ynez Valley) $20. A nice mouthful of Syrah, rich and full-bodied. Drinks dry and rather tannic, with plummy, blackberry, peppery flavors. But it's very complex. If you use your imagination, you can find anise, white chocolate, bacon, and all sorts of other things. Dry, rich, and long in the finish, a distinctive wine that pushes the reputation of this valley for Syrah. **90 Editors' Choice** —S.H. (6/1/2003)

Zaca Mesa 2003 Black Bear Block Syrah (Santa Ynez Valley) $50. This block selection has been terrific in recent years, and the '03 is right up there in wicked deliciousness. It's softly tannic, cushioning the mouth with blackberry, blueberry, coffee, cola, chocolate, and pepper flavors that last for a long time on the finish. Drink now–2009. **91** —S.H. (12/15/2006)

Zaca Mesa 2002 Black Bear Block Syrah (Santa Ynez Valley) $50. Densely packed and tightly wound, this richly tannic and thickly textured Syrah needs plenty of time to come around. Scents of flavors of blackberry, hickory smoke, and cured meats are enticing, but hard to get at right now. See if cellaring this bear several years will tame it. **87** (9/1/2005)

Zaca Mesa 2001 Black Bear Block Syrah (Santa Ynez Valley) $50. Whart a splendid job Zaca Mesa is doing lately. This is a huge wine, distinctly Californian, explosive in black cherry, chocolate, black currant, leather, coffee, and spiced rum flavors, yet richly balanced in fine tannins and acids, and dry. It's mind-blowingly good now, and probably best in its flashy, fleshy youth. **92** —S.H. (8/1/2005)

Zaca Mesa 1999 Black Bear Block Syrah (Santa Ynez Valley) $45. Intensely concentrated, this wine is almost black. The aroma is all about pepper, but there's also plenty of blackberry, dark chocolate, and oak. Rich, fat, and full-bodied, with considerable tannins. **92** —S.H. (2/1/2003)

Zaca Mesa 1996 Black Bear Block Syrah (Santa Barbara County) $20. 88 —M.S. (2/1/2000)

Zaca Mesa 2002 Eight Barrel Syrah (Santa Ynez Valley) $35. Mint-garnished raspberries and blackberries mingle with dusty earth on the nose of this attractive Syrah. Delivers more red fruit on the palate, where it feels smooth and silky. A lighter style, but pretty. **85** (9/1/2005)

Zaca Mesa 2002 Estate Syrah (Santa Ynez Valley) $20. What a good job Zaca Mesa has done over the years with Syrah. Their block and barrel selections are typically the best, but this is their best estate bottling yet, a rich, dense, complex wine brimming with blackberry, cherry, coffee, dry chocolate, and wild herb flavors and a distinguished mouthfeel. **91 Editors' Choice** —S.H. (10/1/2006)

Zaca Mesa 2001 Estate Bottled Syrah (Santa Ynez Valley) $20. Nice and smooth, like a good cognac, with velvety tannins and firm, supportive acids. Showing young, fleshy flavors of blackberries, black cherries, and coffee, with an overlay of smoky oak. Finishes a bit earthy and raw. **86** —S.H. (8/1/2005)

Zaca Mesa 2001 The Mesa O & N Syrah (Santa Ynez Valley) $40. It's fascinating to taste this side by side with Zaca Mesa's Black Bear Block bottling. This one is certainly drier and a lot more tannic, and requires more patience. From entry to finish it's a bit numbing, but those cassis, blackberry, cherry, and coffee flavors, plus the overall balance, bode well. Hold until 2007. **92** —S.H. (8/1/2005)

Zaca Mesa 1999 Zaca Vineyards Syrah (Santa Barbara County) $20. Dark, dry fruit, earth-herb notes, and prominent oak characterize this vintage of this well-known Santa Barbara Syrah. Light to medium weight, it has a fairly dry, tart profile compared to the best years. It's good, and the fruit isn't stifled by the wood and tangy acids. **85** *(10/1/2001)*

Zaca Mesa 2004 Viognier (Santa Ynez Valley) $15. There's not much oak on this wine, but there is quite a bit of lees, which gives it a rich, creamy mouthfeel. The flavors are ripe and juicy, suggesting pineapples and lime zest, peaches, and tangy tangerines. The wine is nicely dry. **87** —*S.H. (12/31/2005)*

Zaca Mesa 2001 Viognier (Santa Ynez Valley) $14. Pretty sweet, like the juice from canned peaches and grapefruit. Decent acidity makes it lively, and the finish is fruity and rich. **84** —*S.H. (12/15/2002)*

Zaca Mesa 2005 Estate Viognier (Santa Ynez Valley) $17. Just delicious. Packed with superrich and refined Viognier flavors of pineapple and mango chutney, apricot honey, vanilla, and spices, the wine is dry and creamy, with brisk, refreshing acidity. Perfect for a cocktail sipper. **90** —*S.H. (11/15/2006)*

Zaca Mesa 2003 Estate Viognier (Santa Ynez Valley) $15. Very dry, and a little tart in acids, with spice, peach, and pear flavors. There's a creamy texture that makes it a pleasant sipper. **85** —*S.H. (10/1/2005)*

Zaca Mesa 2000 Zaca Vineyards Viognier (Santa Barbara) $15. A pleasing blend of spice, apricot, apple, and floral notes. Lush yet bright, the wine serves up plenty of fun with its flavors. Lemony on the finish. **89** —*J.M. (12/15/2002)*

ZAHTILA

Zahtila 2003 Cabernet Sauvignon (Napa Valley) $33. This certainly is a ripe wine. Such power and mass, with huge black currant and beef flavors. Liberally oaked, with brooding tannins. Best left alone until 2008. **88** —*S.H. (12/1/2006)*

Zahtila 2002 Cabernet Sauvignon (Napa Valley) $33. There's an orchard of fruit in this dry, smooth wine. The flavors range from blackberries and plums to cherries, with slightly bitter coffee notes. The tannins and acids stick out a bit now. Try holding until mid-2006. **86** —*S.H. (12/1/2005)*

Zahtila 2001 Cabernet Sauvignon (Napa Valley) $27. Perfectly ripe and balanced, smooth in the mouth, and long on flavor. Fills the mouth with black currants, minty chocolate, oak, and sweet green olives, and very dry. Drink now, or hold for a couple of years. **90** —*S.H. (10/1/2004)*

Zahtila 2000 Beckstoffer Georges III Cabernet Sauvignon (Rutherford) $40. The blackberry, currant, and sweet plum flavors are saturated with an overlay of oak that adds vanilla and smoke to an already overweight wine. Tannins are soft, and the wine feels like velvet gliding across the palate. Hold until 2006. **86** —*S.H. (2/1/2004)*

Zahtila 2003 Beckstoffer Vineyard Georges III Cabernet Sauvignon (Rutherford) $48. Ripe, rich, and classic, this Cab strikes you with the flashy opulence of its cassis and new-oak flavors and balance of acids and tannins. It's so rich, and delicious, with a chocolate fudge finish that lasts and lasts. Just beautiful now, and should age for ten years. **93** —*S.H. (12/1/2006)*

Zahtila 2002 Beckstoffer Vineyard Georges III Cabernet Sauvignon (Rutherford) $48. The pedigree of this wine shows in the flavors, posh in cassis, sweet black currant, bitter chocolate, and finely ground hard brown spices, and in the smooth, rich tannins. The winemaker has added a coating of smoky oak. There's a sharp elbow of acidity that suggests cellaring through 2006, but this isn't a long term wine. **90** —*S.H. (12/1/2005)*

Zahtila 2001 Beckstoffer Vineyard Georges III Cabernet Sauvignon (Rutherford) $48. Too young now, but there's every indication of longterm potential, from the balance and harmony to the dense, chewy nucleus of potent cherry, cassis, and mocha flavors. This brilliant young wine should begin to be drinkable in a few years, and will age through 2020. **93** —*S.H. (10/1/2004)*

Zahtila 2005 Chardonnay (Napa Valley) $18. Ripe and oaky, with powerful tropical fruit, candied pear, peach, apricot jam, and pineapple custard flavors. Nice acidity balances the earthiness and makes the finish clean and lively. **87** —*S.H. (12/1/2006)*

ZD

ZD 1996 Cabernet Sauvignon (Napa Valley) $38. **87** —*M.S. (7/1/2000)*

ZD 2002 Cabernet Sauvignon (Napa Valley) $42. Shows good varietal character in the full-bodied mouthfeel and well-ripened cherry and blackberry fruit. The oak is subtle, even a little rustic. Thoroughly dry, with some gritty tannins to negotiate. Drink now. **86** —*S.H. (8/1/2005)*

ZD 2001 Cabernet Sauvignon (Napa Valley) $40. What a lovely wine. You'll miss its subtle charms if you're just into power. It's a delicately structured, feminine Cab, with currant, olive, herb, and oaky flavors, and soft, gentle tannins. The kind of wine that lets the food star, while playing a supporting role. **91** —*S.H. (10/1/2004)*

ZD 1999 Cabernet Sauvignon (Napa Valley) $42. Multifaceted on the nose, including eucalyptus, arugula, rose stems, dark chocolate, toast, and a wisp of cherry. In the mouth, there are neat cocoa, earth, and red berry flavors that finish a little lean. **88** *(3/1/2003)*

ZD 2001 Reserve Cabernet Sauvignon (Napa Valley) $115. Ripe and smooth, soft and chocolatey as a candy bar, with currant and blackberry flavors, this is an easy drinking, instantly likeable wine. It's meant to be consumed early and will not age. **85** —*S.H. (8/1/2005)*

ZD 1999 Reserve Cabernet Sauvignon (Napa Valley) $100. Cinnamon, cassis, currant, mint, and cherry aromas provide a strong display of varietal character that continues to the palate with milk chocolate, plums, and barrel char. A meaty mouthful of rich, full tannins leaves a lingering complex sensation on the finish. **91** *(3/1/2003)*

ZD 2001 Chardonnay (California) $30. A pleasing nose of toast, honey, and wheat blends well with the same on the palate, with pear and citrus notes throughout. The fruit and acidity are balanced and lightweight. Finishes clean, with a tinge of minerality. **87** *(3/1/2003)*

ZD 2002 Reserve Chardonnay (Napa Valley) $48. This is quite a dry Chard, rustic and earthy and even a bit austere, although the dryness is relieved both by pronounced oak and an underlying current of pear and peach fruit that shows up in the finish. **87** —*S.H. (8/1/2005)*

ZD 2000 Reserve Chardonnay (Napa Valley) $48. Toast, caramel, and anise aromas are accented by a twist of lemon peel. In the mouth, this is slightly viscous, with a blend of cream and toasted marshmallow. Overall, it's full and rich, with a lean, crisp citrus finish. **89** *(3/1/2003)*

ZD 1998 Reserve Chardonnay (Napa Valley) $48. There's plenty of ripe fruit in this 1998. An intense nose of coconut, jasmine, sweet pineapple, toasted marshmallow, and cloves opens this lush beauty. A lovely, positive tension prevails in the mouth between tropical fruit flavors, pear, apple, and citrus elements, all accented by intriguing spice notes. Finishes long, again relying on a fine tension between sweet and tart notes to create a harmonious and sensuous close. **92** *(7/1/2001)*

ZD 2002 Pinot Noir (Carneros) $30. Ripe cherry, chocolate, vanilla, and herb flavors swarm out of the glass, leading to a medium-bodied mouthfeel with cherry and herb flavors. Feels soft and gentle in the mouth, balanced and smooth. **88** *(11/1/2004)*

ZD 2000 Pinot Noir (Carneros) $34. With a rustic nose of soft cheese, herbs, and cedary wood shadings, this wine will come across as either complex and Burgundian or lean and woody, depending on where you're coming from. We liked the spicy red berry palate, which gives some orange tea and underbrush for nuance. A clean finish with soft tannins and healthy acidity make it easy to drink now. **88** *(10/1/2002)*

ZD 2002 Reserve Pinot Noir (Carneros) $48. Smoke, herb, cherry, and tomato notes intermingle in the aroma of this tasty wine. It's a bit one-dimensional, but creamy and ripe in fruit, with firm tannins on the finish. **87** *(11/1/2004)*

ZD 2001 Reserve Pinot Noir (Carneros) $48. Shows the Carneros quality in the delicate but racy structure, silky tannins, and purity of red cherry and spice flavors. There is also a cherry tomato, beetroot herbaceousness that the winemaker says is a signature of the estate vineyard. **87** —*S.H. (12/1/2004)*

ZD NV Abacus IV Red Blend (Napa Valley) $300. This solera-style wine blends the 1992–2001 Reserve Cabernets in a rich presentation. Leather, cedar, mint, and a menagerie of ripe fruits tempt the nose, while the palate delivers with pepper encrusted meat, caramel, strawberries and cherries. This only hints at the elaborate sensory parade found in the

USA

glass, and the enduring impression this will surely leave. Only 250 cases produced. **93** *(3/1/2003)*

ZEALEAR

Zealear 2001 Reprise Cabernet Sauvignon (Napa Valley) $40. Well-made, and dry, with good tannins and berry-oak balance. Has a rustic quality that makes it an everyday sort of quaffer. **85** —*S.H. (5/1/2005)*

Zealear 2002 Bolero Syrah (California) $20. This is a black, velvety soft, dense wine. It is dry, with interesting plum, blackberry, leather, and cocoa flavors. It's not very concentrated, but offers pleasure. **85** —*S.H. (5/1/2005)*

Zealear 2001 Fusion Zinfandel (Sonoma County) $25. Decent, dry Zin, with firm tannins and an earthy edge to the blackberry flavors. **83** —*S.H. (5/1/2005)*

ZEFINA

Zefina 2001 Serience Red Wine Red Blend (Columbia Valley (WA)) $35. Unusual mix includes Grenache, Syrah, Mourvèdre, and Counoise. Forward, ripe aromas of berries, cherries, and plums atop layers of tobacco and malted chocolate. Soft and accessible, but somewhat shapeless. **87** —*P.G. (1/1/2004)*

Zefina 2002 Serience White Wine White Blend (Columbia Valley (WA)) $20. Not what you'd expect; this is a 55% Viognier/45% Roussanne blend, robust and balanced. It crisply mixes the honey/floral and citrus/tropical characters of the two grapes, while walking the stylistic tightrope between stainless steel and barrel fermentation. **88** —*P.G. (1/1/2004)*

Zefina 2001 Zinfandel (Columbia Valley (WA)) $25. Homegrown Zin is catching on in Washington, and this captures the style nicely. Claret-like, with bright berries and juniper spice highlight a taut, fresh, tangy wine. **88** —*P.G. (1/1/2004)*

ZENAIDA CELLARS

Zenaida Cellars 2000 Pinot Noir (Paso Robles) $20. It's too hot for Pinot Noir in Paso Robles, right? This wine shows why. It's not bad, but clumsy, with heavy, earthy flavors. It lacks delicacy and subtlety, which is what Pinot Noir is all about. **83** —*S.H. (7/1/2003)*

Zenaida Cellars 2001 Sangiovese (Paso Robles) $21. Earthy, smoky aromas with a hint of bacon turn gluey and artificaly sweet in the mouth, with the taste of cherry cough syrup. An acceptable wine. **81** —*S.H. (9/1/2003)*

Zenaida Cellars 2000 Syrah (Paso Robles) $24. There are some nice plum and spice flavors in this dry wine, with its smooth texture and long finish. It's marred by an overly hot mouthfeel and a peppery burn in the finish, though. **84** —*S.H. (12/15/2003)*

Zenaida Cellars 1999 Syrah (Paso Robles) $20. From cooler hillside vineyards on the Westside, this lovely wine has cherry aromas with a touch of smoky bacon fat and sautéed mushrooms. The cherry-kirsch flavors continue in the mouth, fine and sweet, with supple tannins and soft but lively acidity. A lush, velvety mouthfeel adds to the pleasure. **91** —*S.H. (11/15/2001)*

Zenaida Cellars 2001 Estate Zinfandel (Paso Robles) $24. Ripe tannins give good structure, but the fruit isn't as ripe as one would think. Plum and cherry flavors are there, but so is a slightly vegetal streak. Pleasant nonetheless. **85** *(11/1/2003)*

ZINGARO

Zingaro 2000 Zinfandel (Mendocino) $13. Another strong, high-alcohol (15%) North Coast Zin. Kind of flat and featureless, beyond the plum and herb flavors and dry tannins. Try with roasts, barbecue, burgers. **84** —*S.H. (9/1/2003)*

Zingaro 1999 Reserve Zinfandel (Mendocino) $18. Dark, saturated, and dense, from warm vineyards in the county's inland, this field blend contains Syrah and Petite Sirah. It's very good, as far as brash, young, big wines go. Powerful, wild brambly fruit is fully dry, and the wine is fairly tannic. From Parducci. **87** —*S.H. (5/1/2002)*

ZUCCA

Zucca 2003 Tesoro Red Wine Red Blend (Sierra Foothills) $15. This Zin-Syrah blend is a bit raisiny and Porty. Finishes sweet. **83** —*S.H. (2/1/2005)*

Zucca 2002 Syrah (Calaveras County) $20. Funky, barnyardy, sweet. **82** —*S.H. (2/1/2005)*

USA

Glossary

Acidity: A naturally occurring component of every wine; the level of perceived sharpness; a key element to a wine's longevity; a leading determinant of balance.

Ageworthy: Wines whose general characteristics make it likely that they will improve with age.

Alcohol: The end product of fermentation; technically ethyl alcohol resulting from the interaction of natural grape sugars and yeast; generally above 12.5 percent in dry table wines.

Alsace: A highly regarded wine region in eastern France renowned for dry and sweet wines made from Riesling, Gewürztraminer, Pinot Blanc, Pinot Gris, and others.

Amarone: A succulent higher-alcohol red wine hailing from the Veneto region in northern Italy; made primarily from Corvina grapes dried on racks before pressing.

AOC: *Appellation d'Origine Contrôlée*, a French term for a denominated, governed wine region, such as Margaux or Nuits-St.-Georges.

Aroma: A scent that's a component of the bouquet or nose; i.e. cherry is an aromatic component of a fruity bouquet.

AVA: American Viticultural Area; a denominated American wine region approved by the Bureau of Alcohol, Tobacco, and Firearms.

Bacchus: The Roman god of wine, known as Dionysus in ancient Greece; a hybrid white grape from Germany.

Balance: The level of harmony between acidity, tannins, fruit, oak, and other elements in a wine; a perceived quality that is more individual than scientific.

Barrel Fermented: A process by which wine (usually white) is fermented in oak barrels rather than in stainless steel tanks; a richer, creamier, oakier style of wine.

Barrique: French for "barrel," generally a barrel of 225 liters.

Beaujolais: A juicy, flavorful red wine made from Gamay grapes grown in the region of the same name.

Beaujolais Nouveau: The first Beaujolais wine of the harvest; its annual release date is the third Thursday in November.

Blanc de Blancs: The name for Champagne made entirely from Chardonnay grapes.

Blanc de Noirs: The name for Champagne made entirely from red grapes, either Pinot Noir or Pinot Meunier, or both.

Blend: The process whereby two or more grape varieties are combined after separate fermentation; common blends include Côtes de Rhône and red and white Bordeaux.

Blush: A wine made from red grapes but which appears pink or salmon in color because the grape skins were removed from the fermenting juice before more color could be imparted; more commonly referred to as Rosé.

Bodega: Spanish for winery; literally "room where barrels are stored."

Body: The impression of weight on one's palate; "light," "medium," and "full" are common body qualifiers.

Bordeaux: A city on the Garonne River in southwest France; a large wine-producing region with more than a dozen subregions; a red wine made mostly from Cabernet Sauvignon, Merlot, and Cabernet Franc; a white wine made from Sauvignon Blanc and Sémillon.

Botrytis Cinerea: (also Noble Rot) A beneficial mold that causes grapes to shrivel and sugars to concentrate, resulting in sweet, unctuous wines; common botrytis wines include Sauternes, Tokay, and German Beerenauslese.

Bouquet: The sum of a wine's aromas; how a wine smells as a whole; a key determinant of quality.

Breathe: The process of letting a wine open up via the introduction of air.

Brettanomyces: An undesirable yeast that reeks of sweaty saddle scents.

Brix: A scale used to measure the level of sugar in unfermented grapes. Multiplying brix by 0.55 will yield a wine's future alcohol level.

Brut: A French term used to describe the driest Champagnes.

Burgundy: A prominent French wine region stretching from Chablis in the north to Lyons in the south; Pinot Noir is the grape for red Burgundy, Chardonnay for white.

Cabernet Franc: A red grape common to Bordeaux; characteristics include an herbal, leafy flavor and a soft, fleshy texture.

Cabernet Sauvignon: A powerful, tannic red grape of noble heritage; the base grape for many red Bordeaux and most of the best red wines from California, Washington, Chile, and South Africa; capable of aging for decades.

Cap: Grape solids like pits, skins, and stems that rise to the top of a tank during fermentation; what gives red wines color, tannins, and weight.

Carbonic Maceration: A wine-making process in which whole grapes are sealed in a fermenter with carbon dioxide and left to ferment without yeast and grape crushing.

Cava: Spanish for "cellar," but also a Spanish sparkling wine made in the traditional Champagne style from Xarello, Macabeo, and Parellada grapes.

Chablis: A town and wine region east of Paris known for steely, minerally Chardonnay.

Champagne: A denominated region northeast of Paris in which Chardonnay, Pinot Noir, and Pinot Meunier grapes are made into sparkling wine.

Chaptalization: The process of adding sugar to fermenting grapes in order to increase alcohol.

Chardonnay: Arguably the best and most widely planted white wine grape in the world.

Château: French for "castle;" an estate with its own vineyards.

Chenin Blanc: A white grape common in the Loire Valley of France.

Chianti: A scenic, hilly section of Tuscany known for fruity red wines made mostly from Sangiovese grapes.

Claret: An English name for red Bordeaux.

Clos: Pronounced "Cloh," this French word once applied only to vineyards surrounded by walls.

Color: A key determinant of a wine's age and quality; white wines grow darker in color as they age while red wines turn brownish orange.

Cooperative: A winery owned jointly by multiple grape growers.

Corked: A wine with musty, mushroomy aromas and flavors resulting from a cork tainted by TCA (trichloroanisol).

Crianza: A Spanish term for a red wine that has been aged in oak barrels for at least one year.

Cru: A French term for ranking a wine's inherent quality, i.e. Cru Bourgeois, Cru Classé, Premier Cru, and Grand Cru.

Decant: The process of transferring wine from a bottle to another holding vessel. The purpose is generally to aerate a young wine or to separate an older wine from any sediment.

Denominación de Origen: Spanish for appellation of origin; like the French AOC or Italian DOC.

Denominazione di Origine Controllata: Italian for a controlled wine region; similar to the French AOC or Spanish DO.

Disgorge: The process by which final sediments are removed from traditionally made sparkling wines prior to the adding of the dosage.

Dosage: A sweetened spirit added at the very end to Champagne and other traditionally made sparkling wines. It determines whether a wine is brut, extra dry, dry, or semisweet.

Douro: A river in Portugal as well as the wine region famous for producing Port wines.

Dry: A wine containing no more than 0.2 percent unfermented sugar.

Earthy: A term used to describe aromas and flavors that have a certain soil-like quality.

Enology: The science of wine production; an enologist is a professional winemaker; an enophile is someone who enjoys wine.

Fermentation: The process by which sugar is transformed into alcohol; how grape juice interacts with yeast to become wine.

Filtration: The process by which wine is clarified before bottling.

Fining: Part of the clarification process whereby elements are added to the wine, i.e. egg whites, in order to capture solids prior to filtration.

Fortified Wine: A wine in which brandy is introduced during fermentation; sugars and sweetness are high due to the suspended fermentation.

Fumé Blanc: A name created by Robert Mondavi to describe dry Sauvignon Blanc.

Gamay: A red grape exceedingly popular in the Beaujolais region of France.

Gewürztraminer: A sweet and spicy white grape popular in eastern France, Germany, Austria, northern Italy, and California.

Graft: A vineyard technique in which the bud-producing part of a grapevine is attached to an existing root.

Gran Reserva: A Spanish term used for wines that are aged in wood and bottles for at least five years prior to release.

Grand Cru: French for "great growth;" the very best vineyards.

Green: A term used to describe underripe, vegetal flavors in a wine.

Grenache: A hearty, productive red grape popular in southern France as well as in Spain, where it is called Garnacha.

Grüner Veltliner: A white grape popular in Austria that makes lean, fruity, racy wines.

Haut: A French word meaning "high." It applies to quality as well as altitude.

Hectare: A metric measure equal to 10,000 square meters or 2.47 acres.

Hectoliter: A metric measure equal to 100 liters or 26.4 gallons.

Herbaceous: An aroma or flavor similar to green; often an indication of underripe grapes or fruit grown in a cool climate.

Hollow: A term used to describe a wine that doesn't have depth or body.

Hybrid: The genetic crossing of two or more grape types; common hybrids include Müller-Thurgau and Bacchus.

Ice Wine: From the German *eiswein*, this is a wine made from frozen grapes; Germany, Austria, and Canada are leading ice wine producers.

Jeroboam: An oversized bottle equal to six regular 750 ml bottles.

Kabinett: A German term for a wine of quality; usually the driest of Germany's best Rieslings.

Kosher: A wine made according to strict Jewish rules under rabbinical supervision.

Labrusca: Grape types native to North America, such as Concord and Catawba.

Late Harvest: A term used to describe dessert wines made from grapes left on the vines for an extra long period, often until botrytis has set in.

Lees: Heavy sediment left in the barrel by fermenting wines; a combination of spent yeast cells and grape solids.

Legs: A term used to describe how wine sticks to the inside of a wineglass after drinking or swirling.

Library Wines: Wines kept by the bottler as a reference of previous wines bottled.

Loire: A river in central France as well as a wine region famous for Chenin Blanc, Sauvignon Blanc, and Cabernet Franc.

Maceration: The process of allowing grape juice and skins to ferment together, thereby imparting color, tannins, and aromas.

Madeira: A fortified wine that has been made on a Portuguese island off the coast of Morocco since the fifteenth century.

Maderized: Stemming from the word Madeira, this term means oxidization in a hot environment.

Magnum: A bottle equal to two regular 750 ml bottles.

Malbec: A hearty red grape of French origin now exceedingly popular in Argentina.

Malolactic Fermentation: A secondary fermentation, often occurring in barrels, whereby harsher malic acid is converted into creamier lactic acid.

Médoc: A section of Bordeaux on the west bank of the Gironde Estuary known for great red wines; Margaux, St. Estèphe, and Pauillac are three leading AOCs in the Médoc.

Merlot: A lauded red grape popular in Bordeaux and throughout the world; large amounts of Merlot exist in Italy, the United States, South America, and elsewhere.

Must: Crushed grapes about to go or going through fermentation.

Nebbiolo: A red grape popular in the Piedmont region of northwest Italy; the grape that yields both Barolo and Barbaresco.

Négociant: A French term for a person or company that buys wines from others and then labels it under his or her own name; stems from the French word for "shipper."

Noble Rot: *see* Botrytis Cinerea.

Nose: Synonymous with "bouquet;" the sum of a wine's aromas.

Oaky: A term used to describe woody aromas and flavors; butter, popcorn, and toast notes are found in "oaky" wines.

Organic: Grapes grown without the aid of chemical-based fertilizers, pesticides, or herbicides.

Oxidized: A wine that is no longer fresh because it was exposed to too much air.

pH: An indication of a wine's acidity expressed by how much hydrogen is in it.

Phylloxera: A voracious vine louse that over time has destroyed vineyards in Europe and California.

Piedmont: An area in northwest Italy known for Barolo, Barbaresco, Barbera, Dolcetto, and Moscato.

Pinot Blanc: A white grape popular in Alsace, Germany, and elsewhere.

Pinot Gris: Also called Pinot Grigio, this is a grayish-purple grape that yields a white wine with a refreshing character.

Pinot Noir: The prime red grape of Burgundy, Champagne, and Oregon.

Pinotage: A hybrid between Pinot Noir and Cinsault that's grown almost exclusively in South Africa.

Plonk: A derogatory name for cheap, poor-tasting wine.

Pomace: The mass of skins, pits, and stems left over after fermentation; used to make grappa in Italy and marc in France.

Port: A sweet, fortified wine made in the Douro Valley of Portugal and aged in the coastal town of Vila Nova de Gaia; variations include Vintage, Tawny, Late Bottled Vintage, Ruby, White, and others.

Premier Cru: French for "first growth;" a high-quality vineyard but one not as good as Grand Cru.

Press: The process by which grape juice is extracted prior to fermentation; a machine that extracts juice from grapes.

Primeur (en): A French term for wine sold while it is sill in the barrels; known as "futures" in English-speaking countries.

Pruning: The annual vineyard chore of trimming back plants from the previous harvest.

Racking: The process of moving wine from barrel to barrel, while leaving sediment behind.

Reserva: A Spanish term for a red wine that has spent at least three years in barrels and bottles before release.

Reserve: A largely American term indicating a wine of higher quality; it has no legal meaning.

Rhône: A river in southwest France surrounded by villages producing wines mostly from Syrah; the name of the wine-producing valley in France.

Riddling: The process of rotating Champagne bottles in order to shift sediment toward the cork.

Riesling: Along with Chardonnay, one of the top white grapes in the world; most popular in Germany, Alsace, and Austria.

Rioja: A well-known region in Spain known for traditional red wines made from the Tempranillo grape.

Rosé: French for "pink," used to describe a category of refreshing wines that are pink in color but are made from red grapes.

Sancerre: An area in the Loire Valley known mostly for wines made from Sauvignon Blanc.

Sangiovese: A red grape native to Tuscany; the base grape for Chianti, Brunello di Montalcino, Morellino di Scansano, and others.

Sauternes: A sweet Bordeaux white wine made from botrytized Sémillon and Sauvignon Blanc.

Sauvignon Blanc: A white grape planted throughout the world; increasingly the signature wine of New Zealand.

Sémillon: A plump white grape popular in Bordeaux and Australia; the base for Sauternes.

Sherry: A fortified wine from a denominated region in southwest Spain; styles include fino, manzanilla, oloroso, and amontillado.

Shiraz: The Australian name for Syrah; also used in South Africa and sparingly in the United States.

Silky: A term used to describe a wine with an especially smooth mouthfeel.

Solera: The Spanish system of blending wines of different ages to create a harmonious end product; a stack of barrels holding wines of various ages.

Sommelier: Technically a wine steward, but one potentially with a great degree of wine knowledge as well as a diploma of sorts in wine studies.

Spicy: A term used to describe certain aromas and flavors that may be sharp, woody, or sweet.

Split: A quarter-bottle of wine; a single-serving bottle equal to 175 milliliters.

Steely: A term used to describe an extremely crisp, acidic wine that was not aged in barrels.

Stemmy: A term used to describe harsh, green characteristics in a wine.

Super Tuscan: A red wine from Tuscany that is not made in accordance with established DOC rules; often a blended wine of superior quality containing Cabernet Sauvignon and/or Merlot.

Supple: A term used to describe smooth, balanced wines.

Syrah: A red grape planted extensively in the Rhône Valley of France, Australia, and elsewhere; a spicy, full, and tannic wine that usually requires aging before it can be enjoyed.

Table Wine: A term used to describe wines of between 10 and 14 percent alcohol; in Europe, table wines are those that are made outside of regulated regions or by unapproved methods.

Tannins: Phenolic compounds that exist in most plants; in grapes, tannins are found primarily in the skins and pits; tannins are astringent and provide structure to a wine; over time, tannins die off, making wines less harsh.

Tempranillo: The most popular red grape in Spain; common in Rioja and Ribera del Duero.

Terroir: A French term for the combination of soil, climate, and all other factors that influence the ultimate character of a wine.

Tokay: A dessert wine made in Hungary from dried Furmint grapes.

Trichloroanisole (TCA): A natural compound that at higher levels can impart "musty" flavors and aromas to wines, other beverages and foods. Wines that contain TCA at a detectable level are described as either being "corked" or having "corkiness," a damp, musty smell from a tainted cork.

Trocken: German for "dry."

Varietal: A wine made from just one grape type and named after that grape; the opposite of a blend.

Varietal Character: The distinct flavors, aromas, and other characteristics of each type of grape used to make wine.

Veneto: A large wine-producing region in northern Italy.

Vin Santo: Sweet wine from Tuscany made from late-harvest Trebbiano and Malvasia grapes.

Viticulture: The science and business of growing wine grapes.

Vintage: A particular year in the wine business; a specific harvest.

Viognier: A fragrant, powerful white grape grown in the Rhône Valley of France and elsewhere.

Volatile Acidity (VA): The development or presence of naturally occurring organic acids (acetic acid) in wine.

Yeast: Organisms that issue enzymes that trigger the fermentation process; yeasts can be natural or commercial.

Yield: The amount of grapes harvested in a particular year.

Zinfandel: A popular grape in California of disputed origin; scientists say it is related to grapes in Croatia and southern Italy.

We invite you to try Wine Enthusiast Magazine at no risk!*

- Each month read over 600 expert ratings & reviews of wines and spirits from around the world in each and every issue, so you can choose what to drink, why and when.

- One-of-a-kind cocktail and food recipes and inventive wine and food pairings, ideal for a party or a romantic dinner à deux.

- Exclusive interviews, tips, trends and profiles of leading winemakers, chefs and other trend-setters—found nowhere else.

- Savvy travel features, so you can plan your next food-and-wine related trip in style.

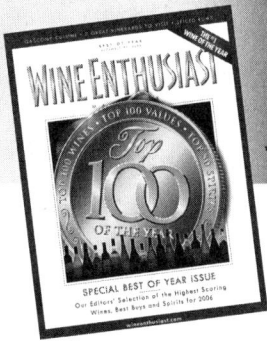

*Visit wineenthusiast.com/magazine to sign up for a FREE issue.

WINE ENTHUSIAST

MAGAZINE • CATALOG • ONLINE • EVENTS

800.356.8466   WINEENTHUSIAST.COM

From stemware to storage, pairings to parties, tastings to ratings, Wine Enthusiast is the number one resource for anyone with a passion for wine and all the joy, romance and fun that comes with it.

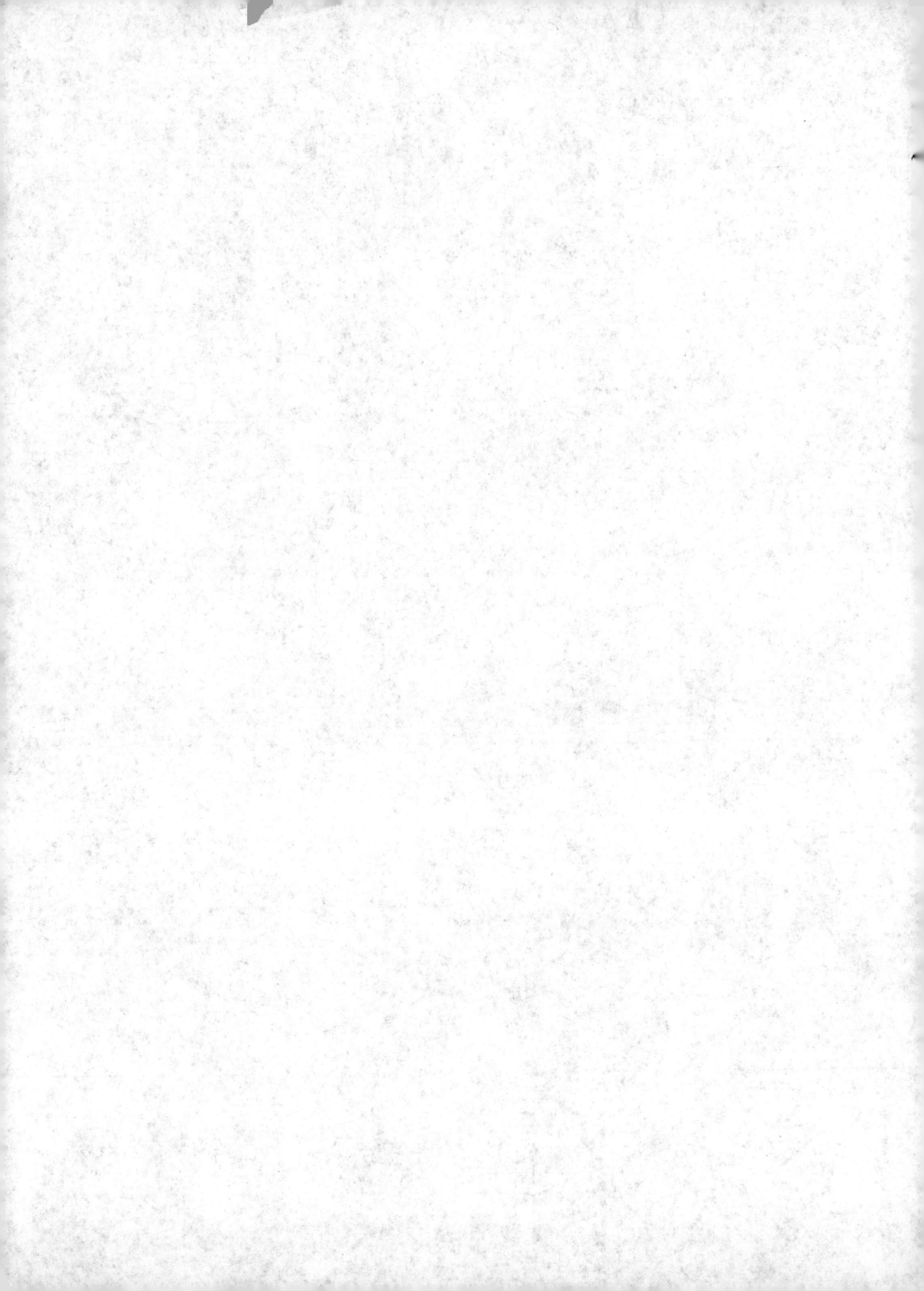